THE CATHOLIC BIBLE

PERSONAL STUDY EDITION

The Catholic Bible

Personal Study Edition

Jean Marie Hiesberger

EDITOR

The New American Bible

Including the Revised New Testament and Psalms

Translated from the Original Languages with

Critical Use of All the Ancient Sources

OXFORD
UNIVERSITY PRESS

OXFORD
UNIVERSITY PRESS

Oxford University Press, Inc., publishes works that further Oxford University's objective of excellence in research, scholarship, and education.

Oxford New York
Auckland   Cape Town   Dar es Salaam   Hong Kong   Karachi
Kuala Lumpur   Madrid   Melbourne   Mexico City   Nairobi
New Delhi   Shanghai   Taipei   Toronto

With offices in
Argentina   Austria   Brazil   Chile   Czech Republic   France   Greece
Guatemala   Hungary   Italy   Japan   Poland   Portugal   Singapore
South Korea   Switzerland   Thailand   Turkey   Ukraine   Vietnam

Copyright © 2007 by Oxford University Press

Published by Oxford University Press, Inc.
198 Madison Avenue, New York, New York 10016
www.oup.com

Oxford is a registered trademark of Oxford University Press

Oxford Introductions, Reading Guides, General and Reference Articles, copyright © 2007 by Oxford University Press, Inc.

Nihil Obstat
Reverend John G. Lodge, S.S.L., S.T.D.
Censor Deputatis
Reverend Robert L. Schoenstene, M.A., S.S.L.
Censor Deputatis
October 2, 2006

Imprimatur
Reverend John F. Canary, S.T.L., D.Min.
Vicar General
Archdiocese of Chicago
October 4, 2006

The *Nihil Obstat* and *Imprimatur* are official declarations that a book is free of doctrinal and moral error. No implication is contained therein that those who have granted the *Nihil Obstat* and *Imprimatur* agree with the content, opinions, or statements expressed. Nor do they assume any legal responsibility associated with publication.

Old Testament
Nihil Obstat
Stephen J. Hartdegen, O.F.M., S.S.L. and Christian P. Ceroke, O. Carm., S.T.D.
Imprimatur
† Patrick Cardinal O'Boyle, D.D., Archbishop of Washington
July 27, 1970

New Testament
Nihil Obstat
Stephen J. Hartdegen, O.F.M., S.S.L., Censor Deputatis
Imprimatur
† James A. Hickey, S.T.D., J.C.D., Archbishop of Washington
August 27, 1986

Psalms
Imprimatur
Most Rev. Daniel E. Pilarczyk, President,
National Conference of Catholic Bishops
October 10, 1991

"The Biblical Texts and their Backgrounds," "The Bible in Catholic Life," and "The Bible in the Lectionary" taken from The Catholic Study
Bible, second edition, © 2006 Oxford University Press
"Reading the Bible" adapted from The Oxford Study Bible, © 1992, Oxford University Press

Biblical Fundamentalism: What Every Catholic Should Know, Copyright © 2001 by The Order of St. Benedict, Inc., Published by
The Liturgical Press, Collegeville, Minnesota. Reprinted with permission.

Printed in Korea
9 8 7 6 5 4 3

CONTENTS

New Testament Reading Guides

The Old Testament of the *New American Bible*

The New Testament of the *New American Bible*

LIST OF ESSAYS,
CHARTS, AND DIAGRAMS

LIST OF MAPS

ALPHABETICAL LISTING OF THE
BOOKS OF THE BIBLE

Acts	1508	Job	681	Obadiah	1259
Amos	1248	Joel	1243	1 Peter	1710
Baruch	1138	John	1467	2 Peter	1717
1 Chronicles	457	1 John	1722	Philemon	1681
2 Chronicles	493	2 John	1728	Philippians	1644
Colossians	1652	3 John	1729	Proverbs	827
1 Corinthians	1582	Jonah	1261	Psalms	719
2 Corinthians	1606	Joshua	254	Revelation	1733
Daniel	1205	Jude	1731	Romans	1559
Deuteronomy	209	Judges	283	Ruth	313
Ecclesiastes	867	Judith	581	1 Samuel	320
Ephesians	1636	1 Kings	388	2 Samuel	358
Esther	598	2 Kings	423	Sirach (Ecclesiasticus)	911
Exodus	75	Lamentations	1129	Song of Songs	877
Ezekiel	1147	Leviticus	125	1 Thessalonians	1658
Ezra	533	Luke	1414	2 Thessalonians	1662
Galatians	1625	1 Maccabees	612	1 Timothy	1666
Genesis	6	2 Maccabees	651	2 Timothy	1673
Habakkuk	1276	Malachi	1298	Titus	1678
Haggai	1284	Mark	1380	Tobit	564
Hebrews	1682	Matthew	1312	Wisdom	885
Hosea	1230	Micah	1264	Zechariah	1287
Isaiah	975	Nahum	1273	Zephaniah	1280
James	1703	Nehemiah	547		
Jeremiah	1054	Numbers	160		

ALPHABETICAL LISTING OF THE
BOOKS OF THE BIBLE

ACKNOWLEDGMENTS

Any project of this scope requires the combined efforts of many people, and I will not be able to thank them all here. But I would like to thank, first of all, my editors at Oxford University Press, Donald Kraus and Elisabeth Nelson, who brought all of this material together and made sure that it was both accurate and readable. I also thank Peachtree Editorial and Proofreading Service for carefully checking all of the typeset pages.

This work builds on the earlier edition of this Bible, and I am grateful to all those who contributed to its development. This edition also has the benefit of treasures from other writers in *The Catholic Study Bible, The New Oxford Annotated Bible, The Jewish Study Bible, The Access Bible,* and *The Oxford Study Bible.*

Finally, for invaluable help in researching information and gathering the most relevant comments on the biblical text, I thank my husband, Robert Heyer. Any remaining errors in the text must remain my responsibility.

Jean Marie Hiesberger

October 4, 2006
The Feast of St. Francis of Assisi

ABBREVIATIONS OF THE BOOKS
OF THE BIBLE

Old Testament

Gn	Genesis	Neh	Nehemiah	Lam	Lamentations
Ex	Exodus	Tb	Tobit	Bar	Baruch
Lv	Leviticus	Jdt	Judith	Ez	Ezekiel
Nm	Numbers	Est	Esther	Dn	Daniel
Dt	Deuteronomy	1 Mc	1 Maccabees	Hos	Hosea
Jos	Joshua	2 Mc	2 Maccabees	Jl	Joel
Jgs	Judges	Jb	Job	Am	Amos
Ru	Ruth	Ps(s)	Psalms	Ob	Obadiah
1 Sm	1 Samuel	Prv	Proverbs	Jon	Jonah
2 Sm	2 Samuel	Eccl	Ecclesiastes	Mi	Micah
1 Kgs	1 Kings	Song (or Sg)	Song of Songs	Na	Nahum
2 Kgs	2 Kings	Wis	Wisdom	Hb	Habakkuk
1 Chr	1 Chronicles	Sir	Sirach (Ecclesiasticus)	Zep	Zephaniah
2 Chr	2 Chronicles	Is	Isaiah	Hg	Haggai
Ezr	Ezra	Jer	Jeremiah	Zec	Zechariah
				Mal	Malachi

New Testament

Mt	Matthew	Eph	Ephesians	Heb	Hebrews
Mk	Mark	Phil	Philippians	Jas	James
Lk	Luke	Col	Colossians	1 Pt	1 Peter
Jn	John	1 Thes	1 Thessalonians	2 Pt	2 Peter
Acts	Acts of the Apostles	2 Thes	2 Thessalonians	1 Jn	1 John
Rom	Romans	1 Tm	1 Timothy	2 Jn	2 John
1 Cor	1 Corinthians	2 Tm	2 Timothy	3 Jn	3 John
2 Cor	2 Corinthians	Ti	Titus	Jude	Jude
Gal	Galatians	Phlm	Philemon	Rv	Revelation

KEY TO REFERENCES

For greater clarity and convenience, the footnotes and cross references are printed at the bottom of each page and cross-indexed in the text itself. An *asterisk* (*) in the text indicates that there is a footnote to the text in question. Each footnote is in turn clearly marked with the number of the chapter and the verse to which it pertains. Similarly a *superior letter* (ᵃ) in the text indicates that there is a cross-reference to a particular verse. The reference itself is also clearly marked with the same letter. Hence, the reader is always aware of a footnote or a cross-reference simply by *reading the text.*

Key to Scripture References

Gn 1, 1	refers to Genesis, chapter one, verse one.
Gn 1, 1a	refers to Genesis, chapter one, first part of verse one.
Gn 1, 1f(f)	refers to Genesis, chapter one, verse one and the following verse (verses).
Gn 1, 1–10	refers to Genesis, chapter one, verses one through ten.
Gn 1, 1–10.24	refers to Genesis, chapter one, verses one through ten and verse twenty-four.
Gn 1–5	refers to Genesis, chapters one through five inclusive.
Gn 1, 1—2, 3	refers to Genesis, chapter one, verse one through chapter two, verse three inclusive.
Gn 1, 1; 2, 3	refers to Genesis, chapter one, verse one and chapter two, verse three.

READING GUIDE

GENERAL INTRODUCTION

The book you hold in your hand contains one of humanity's greatest treasures. No one can deny that the Bible has had a profound impact on world civilization. Its epic stories, its powerful language, and its compelling images have left their imprint on human history, especially in cultures touched by Judaism and Christianity.

For the Christian, the Bible has an importance far more profound than its impact on culture. The Christian believes that through the turbulent and wonderful chapters of biblical history, God speaks to us. Although expressed in genuinely human terms and through very human authors, the Bible is, at the same time, the Word of God for us. Therefore, as Christians we revere and love the Scriptures. Because of that love, we seek to understand them as deeply as we can.

The purpose of *The Catholic Bible: Personal Study Edition* is to enable the reader to read the Scriptures with new understanding and depth. In writing and editing the study materials contained here, our primary aim has been to serve an audience of Roman Catholics. Some of the comments in the notes to the text, the Reference Articles, and the Reading Guides deliberately reflect Catholic experience and Catholic interests. However, the editors do not wish to exclude other Christian readers from the focus of this book. In most instances, the materials included here will be useful for all Christians who want to enter deeply into the mysteries and marvels of the Bible.

Introducing the Bible

Although it is bound under one cover and bears a single title, the Bible is not a single, unified book. It is, in fact, a collection of some 73 different works by different authors, using very different styles and perspectives, composed over a span of many centuries, and in three different languages (Hebrew, Aramaic, and Greek). Most of the Old Testament (46 books) was written in Hebrew, but parts of the books of Daniel (2, 4—7, 28), Ezra (4, 6—6, 18; 7, 12–26), and one verse from Jeremiah (10, 11) were originally composed in Aramaic, a Middle Eastern language related to but different from Hebrew. Other Old Testament books, such as Tobit and the Wisdom of Solomon, were written in Greek. And all 27 of the New Testament books were composed in Greek.

The rich diversity of the Bible is one of its glories because it allows the story of God's people to be told from various perspectives. It also presents a challenge to the reader who should be aware of the different cultural, historical, and literary contexts of each biblical book. But there is a deeper unity to the Bible that binds together these individual pieces of literature. Through the many biblical books flows the continuing saga of God's love for Israel and for the Church. Each of the biblical authors, no matter how much separated in time, culture, and literary style, shares a conviction that God's presence is felt in human history and that God invites the human family to respond with faith and integrity.

The Writing of the Bible

As its diverse makeup implies, the Bible was not written at a single point in history. The events covered in the Old Testament span nearly 2,000 years of history, from the time of Abraham and the patriarchs (around 1800 B.C.) to the period of the Maccabean wars (140 B.C.). If one includes the epic accounts of the creation and prepatriarchal stories such as Noah and the flood, then the reach of the biblical saga goes back to the beginning of time. But the actual formulation of the biblical accounts, although making use of earlier stories and traditions, is confined to a narrower period of time, probably beginning with the monarchy (around 1000 B.C.) and concluding in the century before the birth of Christ.

The New Testament books were all written during the latter half of the first century A.D. The letters of Paul were probably the earliest New Testament works to be put in writing, dating mainly from the decade of the fifties. The sayings of Jesus and the many stories about his ministry circulated in the Christian community all during these early decades of the Church but were probably not put in writing until shortly after A.D. 70, with Mark the first Gospel to be written. Matthew, Luke (and his second volume, the Acts of the Apostles), and John follow, with the compositions of their Gospels taking place sometime during the last quarter of the first century. The other non-Pauline letters and writings, including the book of Revelation or the Apocalypse, also date from this period.

Forming a "Bible" from Diverse Books: The Story of the Canon

The gathering of these diverse writings into a single collection or "book" (the literal meaning of the word "Bible") was itself a long-term and laborious process. The technical term for the authoritative list of books belonging in the Bible is "canon" (which means "measuring rod"). Both Judaism and Christianity had to make choices about which books to include and which books to exclude from their respective "Bibles." Judaism would not make any official decision about which books belonged to its "Bible" until the end of the first century A.D. But that does not mean it was without a Bible for so much of its history. There was little or no dispute about the major books of the Old Testament, books which were constantly used in Jewish liturgy and teaching. But there was debate about the inclusion of later and less central works such as Esther or Ecclesiasticus (the Wisdom of Jesus ben Sirach).

The Jewish or Hebrew canon ultimately recognizes 39 books, divided into three major categories:

1. The Law (sometimes referred to as the Pentateuch, or first five books of the Bible): Genesis, Exodus, Leviticus, Numbers, Deuteronomy.

2. The Prophets: Subdivided into the Former Prophets: Joshua, Judges, 1 and 2 Samuel, 1 and 2 Kings; and the Latter Prophets: Isaiah, Jeremiah, Ezekiel, and the Twelve (Hosea, Joel, Amos, Obadiah, Jonah, Micah, Nahum, Habakkuk, Zephaniah, Haggai, Zechariah, Malachi).

3. The Writings: Psalms, Proverbs, Job, Song of Songs, Ruth, Lamentations, Ecclesiastes, Esther, Daniel, Ezra-Nehemiah, 1 and 2 Chronicles.

As we shall explain below, not included in the official Jewish or Hebrew canon are seven other books that Roman Catholics (and Orthodox Christians) consider part of their Scriptures. Judaism reveres these books and considers them sacred, but they are not part of their canon or official list. These books are: Tobit, Judith, 1 and 2 Maccabees, Wisdom, Ecclesiasticus, and Baruch. There are also some additional passages in the books of Daniel and Esther.

The formation of the Christian canon also took place over a considerable period of time. In fact, the official Roman Catholic decision about the canon did not come until the Council of Trent in the sixteenth century, but by that time the choice of which writings were to be included in the Bible was well established. There were many sacred writings in the early decades of the Church that presumably could have been included in the Bible. We cannot always tell what criteria or decision-making processes were used to establish the canon. Some "gospels" evidently portrayed Jesus in a way unacceptable to the vast majority of Christians and so were not included. Other early writings, however, such as the Didache (Greek, "teaching")—a short handbook of moral behavior and church practice—seem perfectly acceptable in content and tone but nevertheless were not included. Probably the early Church considered a work's content, its authorship, and the frequency of its usage in the liturgy and teaching of the Churches as important criteria for judging if a sacred writing was inspired by God and worthy of inclusion in its official canon or Scriptures.

All Christians agree on the 27 books to be included in the New Testament. But there is a dispute about some of the books in the Old Testament. As noted above, Roman Catholics and Orthodox Christians agree on the 46 books that make up the Old Testament (the Orthodox include additional books in their canon: 1 and 2 Esdras; the prayer of Manasseh; Psalm 151; 3 Maccabees). Judaism and Protestant Christians hold for the shorter list of 39 books sketched above; the remaining seven or more are designated as the apocryphal books.

The reason for this divergence is that earliest Christianity used an ancient Greek translation of the Old Testament (called the Septuagint) as its Bible. This Greek version of the Bible included 46 books. Since most of the early Christians were Greek-speaking, this is the Bible they preferred. But when Judaism officially set out to determine its canon at the end of the first century, it drew up a shorter list of 39 books: those written in Hebrew. In the Reformation period, Protestants went back to this shorter Hebrew canon, considering it more authentic.

Today, many of the doctrinal tensions that separated Catholics and Protestants have eased. Some Protestant editions of the Bible include the "aprocryphal" (what Roman Catholics call "deuterocanonical") books in an appendix of their Bibles or in a special section between the Old and New Testaments. Following usual Catholic practice, the *New American Bible* integrates the deuterocanonical books into the order of the Old Testament canon. A table showing the different canons for each group—Jews, Protestant Christians, Catholic Christians, and Orthodox Christians—is on p. 1789.

The Diverse Literary Forms and Historical Value of the Bible

The broad span of biblical history, and the fact that the Bible is a collection of various books, help to form its rich diversity. The reader of the Bible needs to be attentive not only to the historical context of a particular passage but to the varieties of literary forms and the specific style and intent of each biblical author. The prophetic oracles of Isaiah or Jeremiah are very different in literary style from the legal codes of Leviticus or the narratives of Exodus. The long lists of wise sayings in Proverbs are dramatically different in tone, style, and theology from the sweeping liturgical poetry of the Psalms. So, too, do the parables of the Gospels differ greatly from the letters of Paul or the dramatic apocalyptic scenes in the book of Revelation. The notes and Reading Guides found in this Study Bible help the reader to understand more about these various literary forms and their implications for interpreting the meaning of a particular biblical passage.

The presence of various literary forms or means of expression in the Bible also complicates the issue of the historical value of the Bible. Some Christians, particularly fundamentalist Christians, fear that admitting the Bible contains poetry, stories, and other literary forms is somehow an attack on the veracity of the Bible and dilutes its witness to history. They prefer to regard the story of creation in Genesis, or the episode of Jonah's sojourn in the belly of a great fish, as literally true.

Roman Catholic teaching—and that of many other Christian denominations—sees no incompatibility between recognizing the truth of the biblical witness and the fact that it is expressed in many forms of literature characteristic of human communication. Credible witness to the truth of history is not confined to an objective reporting of the facts in the manner of a police report or a mere factual description of what happened. All reporting of history involves a degree of interpretation. And such means as poetry, hymns, stories, myths, and other literary forms can also communicate historical truth about past events and the perspectives of our ancestors.

Undoubtedly, both the Old and New Testaments contain many accurate historical facts and descriptions reflecting the times and events of biblical history. But the biblical writers also wanted to interpret the *meaning* of that history and present it unabashedly from their perspectives. Previous traditions are given new interpretations and adapted to the circumstances of a different generation. In most instances their intent was not to provide a historical archive for subsequent generations but to see in the events of this history the presence of God's grace, and to communicate that conviction to their readers. The Bible is a witness to the vitality of the people who lived its events and pondered their meaning in a spirit of faith.

Each biblical passage, therefore, must be evaluated on its own terms in attempting to distinguish between factual historical data and the theological and historical interpretation provided by the biblical writer.

The Transmission of the Biblical Text and its Modern Translations

Each modern reader of the Bible is in debt to countless numbers of people—Jewish and Christian—who faithfully handed on to the next generations the treasures of the Bible. For much of biblical history, such transmission of the biblical tradition was done orally, not in written form. Stories, sayings of great teachers and leaders, hymns and poetry were lovingly memorized and handed down from parents to children, teacher to disciple, from leader of prayer to congregation and, thereby, formed the growing body of the biblical heritage.

In ancient (and some modern) cultures, oral transmission of important literature was not a casual, haphazard affair. For our modern culture, so dependent on written means of communicating information, it is hard to realize that in oral cultures subtle and often unspoken rules govern how information is shaped, retained, and transmitted from one person and one generation to another.

But as styles of writing and writing materials became more sophisticated in Israel, and when it had the social organization under the monarchy to have archives and develop an educated class of scribes, then undoubtedly some parts of the Bible were preserved in written form as well.

In the New Testament, much of the Gospel materials were first preserved in oral form. Sayings of Jesus, his parables, the stories about his healings, his conflicts with opponents, and the narrative of his Passion would have been preserved and transmitted in a variety of settings such as the liturgy, instruction within the home or small Christian communities, or, perhaps even more formally, in some early centers of Christian learning. But eventually these oral materials were gathered and put in written form by the evangelists. It is likely that the oral transmission of the biblical materials, both Old and New

Testaments, continued to exist and be employed even after the biblical text had been put into writing.

Paul's letters and other New Testament texts such as the catholic epistles and the book of Revelation were composed or dictated into written form immediately, although, as the study materials will show, some of these letters may be composites of several different writings. Nevertheless, it is important to recognize that some writings in the Bible—the book of Ezekiel, the Letter to the Romans, and others—were written by one author in the form in which we have them. Many other books, however—Genesis or Isaiah, for example—were put together from various separate writings created over a lengthy period.

Regardless of whether a biblical book was written at one time by one author or over a period of time by several writers, no original manuscript of any biblical book exists. Copyists from one generation to the next transcribed the biblical materials and enabled them to be available for subsequent generations. The earliest written manuscripts we have of some Old Testament biblical materials date from the first century B.C. These were part of the wealth of written materials discovered in 1948 on the northwest shore of the Dead Sea and thereafter named the "Dead Sea Scrolls." Most of the other surviving early written materials for both the Old and the New Testaments are papyrus fragments of biblical passages dating from the early second century A.D. and more complete manuscripts of the Bible on parchment from the third and fourth centuries A.D.

The hands of many copyists, with different personal interests and levels of skill, inevitably introduced some variations and errors into the numerous editions of the biblical text. Ancient translations (or versions) of manuscripts into other languages, such as Latin or Syriac or Coptic, could also introduce errors or varying interpretations not found in the original biblical language.

The science of textual criticism attempts to trace the relationships of ancient manuscripts to each other and to reestablish the most reliable form of the biblical text. The discovery of biblical texts among the Dead Sea Scrolls rolled back the age of extant biblical manuscripts several centuries. Surprisingly, although some variants exist, there is still remarkable correspondence between the state of the biblical text in the first century B.C. and the third or fourth century A.D.—testimony to the accuracy and care with which ancient peoples handed on the biblical tradition.

Besides recognizing that we do not have original manuscripts of the books of the Bible, we should also note that the biblical texts of the ancient Church did not have the neat format of our modern Bible. Division into the present system of chapters and verses was introduced only in the Middle Ages. Prior to that, demarcations between individual sentences and sections of a particular biblical book were much more casual and fluid.

The New American Bible Translation

Most modern translations, including that found in the *New American Bible (NAB)*, are based on the most reliable texts of the Bible we have and are translated from the original biblical languages rather than using any intervening translations. Many previous Catholic translations had been based on the Vulgate, or Latin version of the Bible, first prepared by Jerome in the fifth century.

The translation of the *NAB* was a collaborative achievement of some 50 Catholic biblical scholars, determined to use the best of modern scholarship to bring a fresh and accurate translation of the Bible to the American Catholic community.

The first full edition of the Old and New Testaments appeared in 1970. A revision of the New Testament appeared in 1986, and a revision of the Psalms in 1991. It is this fully revised edition that is used in *The Catholic Bible: Personal Study Edition*. Every translation, no matter how accurate and faithful, falls short in attempting to communicate the subtlety and meaning of another language. All translators have to make decisions about the purpose and audience of their translation and the consequent principles they will use in translating the Bible from its original languages to a modern language such as American English. And, to some degree, every translation is a subtle interpretation of the biblical text.

The translators of the *New American Bible* wanted as much as possible to accurately reflect the nuance and form of biblical Hebrew and Greek, while recasting the language to make it compatible with the rules and style of modern English and in harmony with traditional Catholic interpretations of Scripture. The translators, however, wanted to avoid making the *NAB* a paraphrase or quasi-interpretation of the biblical text. Some modern translations attempt this. While such paraphrases perhaps make the biblical texts more palatable to a modern audience, they also risk a high degree of subjectivity in recasting the contents of the Bible. The *NAB* translation is faithful to the biblical text and takes its place alongside rigorously literal translations such as the Revised Standard Version. This makes it particularly suitable for deeper study of the biblical message, as well as its use in prayer and liturgy.

Accuracy of translation from one language to another also involves issues that are more than linguistic. For instance, the editors of the revised New Testament translation had to struggle with the question of inclusive language. This is a sensitive issue in modern American culture and in the Catholic Church in particular. The translators adopted a compromise stance here. Where the original biblical language clearly intended a generic reference to human beings, the translation is careful to use inclusive language. Where the original text uses a gender-specific reference, however, such as many references to God through male pronouns, the translation does not attempt to use inclusive language.

Modern political issues can also cause difficulties for the translator. Such geographical terms as Israel or Palestine have highly charged meanings in the political arena of today's Middle East. But their appearance in the biblical translation of the *New American Bible* implies no endorsement of any modern political stance on these difficult issues. So, too, can modern religious sensitivities come into play. Judaism in all its modern forms, out of reverence, avoids the use of the name Yahweh for God. Readers in the synagogue, for example, will substitute Adonai (My Lord) wherever the divine name appears in the biblical text. The modern translator and commentator have to make a decision on whether to try to respect this understandable religious sensitivity.

It should be noted that the Reading Guides and major Reference Articles included in the *Personal Study Edition* attempt throughout to use inclusive language, and, wherever possible, to avoid offense to modern religious, cultural, or political sensitivities. The editors believed that such a spirit is in accord with both the biblical witness and sound Catholic tradition. Some use of the geographical terms Israel and Palestine was unavoidable in some of the Reading Guides, but no reference to modern geopolitical realities is intended.

Reading, Studying, and Praying the Scriptures

From the beginning of its existence, the Bible has been the object of intense study, prayerful reading, and even heated debate. The Bible is not meant to be a coffee-table book.

One could say that the Bible was formed in a context of prayer and reflection. The various biblical authors reflected on significant events in the life of Israel, of Jesus, and of the early Church. Their discovery of God's presence working within history gives the Bible its force. For all Christians the Bible has unique authority as writings inspired by God's Spirit working within the communities of Israel and the Church, and impelling the biblical writers to give expression in human words to their faith perspective. (For a Catholic view of biblical inspiration, see "The Bible in Catholic Life," RG 13.)

Judaism has always maintained a rich tradition of reflection on its Scriptures. The rabbis lovingly studied every detail of the biblical text and saw an infinite possibility of applications to everyday life. The Scriptures were reverenced as God's Word and took a central place within the prayer life of the synagogue. Christian tradition has had the same character. Until the late Middle Ages, almost all of the Church's theology and teaching was little more than an elaboration of the biblical text.

Some of this biblical focus was lost in the Catholic Church when philosophical analysis—always important—became over-dominant, and theological reflection could often be far distant in focus and spirit from our biblical foundations. While biblical symbols remained dominant in Catholic liturgical life and architecture, in popular preaching and much popular piety, the Bible was a more distant echo. In the past 50 years, that trend has been radically reversed. The Second Vatican Council gave a strong impetus to a biblical renewal in every dimension of Catholicism (see "The Bible in Catholic Life," RG 13).

One can approach reading and study of the Bible from several vantage points.

The Historical Approach

One purpose in reading the Bible is to comb through the biblical books, seeking leads to the historical context of a given period or culture. While this is a legitimate historical enterprise, it does not correspond to the fundamentally religious character of the Bible. The Bible does have strong historical value; but its purpose is not simply to inform the reader about history but to probe the meaning of past history for the life of faith.

The Theological Approach

Another way of entering the biblical world is to seek what the Bible, or a particular biblical book, has to say on a specific doctrinal or moral issue. What, for example, does the Bible say about violence? Or what is the biblical perspective on justice? Because the Bible is such a rich and diverse body of literature, we soon discover that the Bible will yield many perspectives on such important issues. There is seldom a single biblical viewpoint on any specific theological or moral issue. Only by first understanding the context of each biblical period and biblical book, and then interrelating the Bible's varied approaches to profound questions of faith, can one weave together a biblical theology.

The Inspirational Approach

For most Christians, reading the Bible has a more modest, yet still important goal. They turn to the Scriptures for inspiration in living out their life of faith. Such inspiration can be gained in many different ways.

For some, the Scriptures are an important stimulant for prayer. The words of the Psalms, the challenge of the prophets, the compassionate mission of Jesus, the soaring words of Paul—all of these give form and expression to the longing of our own hearts as we seek the face of God.

Very often the biblical words are able to express the feelings and fears and hopes we could not put into words ourselves. And in reaching out to the Bible we unite ourselves with the faith of countless generations of Christians who found the same solace and strength in the Scriptures.

For others, probing the Scriptures either in private or with a group of Christians helps guide and illumine their daily lives. Study of the biblical text and discussion of its meaning with other thoughtful Christians can help us understand our own experience of faith and expand our perspective on what it means to be a believer in the modern world. This approach works best when the participant is not afraid to reflect on his or her own experience, and then relate that reflection to the ideas and images of the Bible. Very often the Bible opens its treasures when we bring to it questions and hopes that spring from our life of faith. Then, in turn, the biblical message can give new insight and nourishment to our faith experience.

A profound sense of grief or loss, for example, might lead a Christian to read with new understanding the lament psalms of the Old Testament or the passion of Jesus. And these biblical passages, in turn, can bring new strength to the one who suffers.

Whatever approach one takes to reading and praying the Bible, it is important from a Catholic perspective that it not be done in isolation. The Bible is the Church's book, not a private library. Only in the context of the Church's faith and tradition as a whole can the full meaning of the Bible be discovered. Some Christians who isolate themselves from common sense and from the sound wisdom of the Church community can interpret the Scriptures in a bizarre and even destructive manner. That is why the effort to understand the biblical text in its context, to sound out its possible meaning with other thoughtful Christians, and to be open to the guidance of the Church and its teaching forms the best context for full integration of the Bible into our lives (on this see the 1993 statement of the Pontifical Biblical Commission, *The Interpretation of the Bible in the Church*, which fully endorses the use of modern biblical methods).

The Personal Study Edition is designed to open the beauty and power of the Bible to the reader. The editors and the Oxford University Press hope that the guides, articles, and other resources provided in this unique volume will serve you well as you step into the marvelous world of the Bible.

Donald Senior, C.P., Editor,
The Catholic Study Bible
(from which this essay is adapted)

Jean Marie Hiesberger, Editor,
The Catholic Bible:
Personal Study Edition

HOW TO USE *THE CATHOLIC BIBLE: PERSONAL STUDY EDITION*

We have included much information and many study aids in the *Catholic Bible: Personal Study Edition*. These aids will help you to use this study Bible in a great variety of ways and settings. This outline suggests some ways of starting your studies and reflections, using the features contained in this book. As you read further, we hope you will discover other approaches for yourself.

If your goal is to read and reflect on a single biblical book or major passage of the Bible, the two key sections of the Study Bible to use are the biblical text itself and the Reading Guides. These work together to help you grasp the overall character of a biblical book, its main themes, and specific issues that arise in a particular passage. In turning to the Gospel of Luke, for example, you can work through the Reading Guide for Luke, including the Discussion/Reflection questions, and then turn to the Bible section on p. 1414 and read the Introduction given there. Now when you go through the gospel itself, your reading will be much richer and more meaningful. You will not only have a better understanding of what you read, but with the Discussion/Reflection questions in mind, you will be reading it while attuned to their challenges. Of course, footnotes and sidebars, where they exist, will help "unpack" the text as you go.

For Individual and Group Reading or Study

Whether you are using the Study Bible alone or in a group, learning about our "family history" in the biblical story can be a rich and, in some cases, life-changing experience. And, of course, we believe that Christ is among us where two or three gather in his name. A group can be the instrument of powerful insights helping us to make connections with our own story or applications to our life that we might miss otherwise. The Reading Guide is designed to walk us through the particular book of the Bible with a little background to "plow the ground" so that the seed of the scripture can take root in us more deeply and fruitfully.

The Reading Guide for each book follows a set pattern of three basic parts:

A section called "At a Glance" begins each guide with a kind of snapshot of the book to be read. It briefly addresses:

Who are the main players?

What should I look for?

When did this take place?

Where did these events occur?

Why was this book written?

What is the story?

Next comes a brief "walk through" the book, which gives important and helpful background information. This makes reading the actual biblical text much more understandable as well as meaningful.

Finally, the Reading Guide for each book ends with a set of discussion/reflection questions. These are meant for you to use after you have read and studied both the Reading Guide and the Bible text. These questions always follow the same three-part format, a format typically used with Catechumens and Candidates in the R.C.I.A. process:

• The first set of questions is *Group Sharing/Discussion*. This set explores the Bible text itself, allowing for reviewing, digesting, and thinking about the story or the setting itself. Taking time for this step helps to synthesize and clarify what was read so that the next step will be easier and richer.

• The second set is *In Our Lives*. Here the questions push us to think about what might be called the "So what?" of reading the text. What is the lesson? What does it teach us? How does it apply to me or to us as a church community? As the first questions are about using our head, this set is for the heart also.

• The final set of questions is *Individual/Personal Reflection/Action*. Whether using the Study Guide alone or in a group, this is where we take time to decide on what we will do as a result of the lessons contained in this part of the Bible. This takes the scriptures one step beyond head and heart and helps us put them into our lives. And this, of course, is the whole point of scripture study.

Because scripture study is not learning an abstract or academic subject, but is about sharing faith and sharing personal insights and experience, the human dimension of our relationship with the others in Bible study groups needs attention. In addition to preparing for a group session by studying the Reading Guide and the Bible text, it is important for parish groups, R.C.I.A. sessions, or informal groups of any age to begin each session by welcoming everyone. When members are allowed to connect on the human level, catch up a bit on what has happened in their lives since the last meeting, perhaps share a cup of coffee and some refreshments, the relationships deepen and so does the ability to comfortably share insights and ideas. This "hospitality dimension" is the responsibility of everyone in the group, whether or not there is a designated leader. Most groups find that beyond 90 minutes there is little capacity for listening and learning, so it is important to respect the time frame agreed upon in advance. Some groups take a break in the middle of the session, others at the beginning or end.

The *Personal Study Edition* is also useful for the college or religious education classroom. It provides virtually a one-volume textbook and reference library on the Bible. Experienced and imaginative teachers will find their own way to best utilize a book like this. Here are some suggestions to get you started.

The Study Bible can certainly serve as a textbook for a course on the Bible as a whole or for introductions to the Old or New Testaments. Here again interplay between pertinent sections of the Reading Guides and the biblical text and notes is very important.

Teachers in a Catholic setting may want to give special attention to the Reference Article on "The Bible in Catholic Life" as an important summary of Catholic teaching on the role of the Bible in the Church's life and thought. The Reference Article on "The Bible in the Lectionary" will help Catholics (and Christians from other mainline denominations) understand how the liturgy is a major source of biblical inspiration for Roman Catholic tradition.

Other Helpful Features of this Study Bible

Within this study Bible, you will find a full range of aids to help you discover the meaning of the Bible. The following description of its contents, and suggestions for using the book, might help you take full advantage of its unique resources.

The *New American Bible*

Beginning on page 1, following the Reading Guides, you will find the full text and notes of the *New American Bible*. Each major section of the Bible and each biblical book has a brief introduction. Extensive notes explaining words or individual verses are found at the bottom of the page. An asterisk (*) alongside a particular word or verse signals to you that an explanatory note is provided for that biblical text. These notes provide a wealth of information for the studious reader.

The *New American Bible* also provides cross-references to other related biblical passages. These cross-references are signaled by a small italic letter printed at the end of specific verses. The cross-reference is found at the bottom of the page.

There are sidebars set off within the text of the Bible. These contain information to make the text more understandable and meaningful as you read.

Finally, along the side margins there is another set of cross-references, directing you to the

Reading Guide for that particular biblical book. These cross-references are indicated by page numbers enclosed within a shaded box. Page numbers for the Reading Guides are preceded by the letters RG.

General and Reference Articles

Another helpful feature of the *Catholic Bible: Personal Study Edition* is that it provides extensive and detailed studies of key issues for understanding and using the Bible. In addition to this introduction, the reader will find the following Reference Articles:

• The Bible in Catholic Life
• Catholics and Fundamentalism
• How to Read the Bible
• Understanding the Historical Background to the Biblical Texts

• The Catechism of the Catholic Church
• Catholic Beliefs in Scripture
• The Bible in the Lectionary
• Lectionary, Historical, and Canon Tables

Glossary

The glossary provides clear explanations of the less familiar or more technical terms used in the Bible or in the Reading Guides and Reference Articles.

Maps

Aside from maps dealing with specific matters in various points of the biblical text, there are full-color maps and a map index at the very end of the Bible. These will provide you with the entire geographical canvas on which the biblical drama is portrayed.

THE BIBLE IN CATHOLIC LIFE
DANIEL J. HARRINGTON

Church Life Today

One of the great achievements of the Second Vatican Council (1962–1965) has been the renewal of interest in the Bible among Catholics. How dramatic this renewal has been can be grasped by comparing Catholic practice around 1950 and the situation in the early years of the twenty-first century.

At mid-twentieth century the Scriptures were read at Mass in Latin. There were few selections from the Old Testament, and a rather small number of New Testament passages dominated the one-year cycle. In response to the mandate of the Second Vatican Council we now have a three-year cycle of Sunday readings and a two-year weekday cycle. (See "The Bible in the Lectionary," p. 1769.) The Old Testament is very prominent, and almost the entire New Testament (Gospels and Epistles) is represented. The passages, of course, are read in the vernacular (English, Spanish, or whatever is the dominant local language).

In the 1950s study of Bible texts was not an integral part of the primary- or secondary-school curriculum in Catholic schools. At best Bible content was conveyed through summaries of the texts. Catholic college students might work through parts of the Bible with the aid of cautious and approved textbooks as guides. But now the texts of the Bible form a primary resource for Catholic religious education at all levels. And Bible courses and Bible-study groups have become especially popular forums for adult education.

At the mid-twentieth century, Catholic seminarians took most of their Scripture courses toward the end of their theology programs. In comparison with dogma and moral theology, Scripture study was considered a minor course. Now biblical studies are a major component of the seminary curriculum at all stages. And such courses are very popular. Students in Catholic seminaries assume that much of their preaching and teaching in the future will be devoted to the Bible, and so they study it with eagerness. There is also a lively dialogue and interdisciplinary cooperation between professors of Scripture and their theological colleagues.

Since Vatican II the Bible has become prominent not only in Catholic liturgy and education but also in popular piety. The revised prayers for the sacraments and other liturgical actions use biblical language almost entirely. Charismatic groups and base communities have found biblical reflection and prayer to be the source of great spiritual energy. Even traditional Catholic observances like the Rosary are (and always have been) thoroughly biblical. The language of Catholic prayer in almost every instance derives from the Bible.

The Scriptures have also been a major element in the ecumenical movement since the council. The serious historical and theological differences between the Christian churches remain. But the most progress has been made where the different Church groups have focused on the Bible as their common heritage and have reexamined their differences in light of the Bible's language and thought patterns. When this has occurred, the usual result has been the recognition that what unites the Christian churches is more important and fundamental than what divides them. In the new and more positive relationship that has emerged between Christians and Jews in recent years, Bible study has been a vital force toward greater mutual understanding and respect.

Catholic theology since the council gives far more attention to biblical sources and is likely to express itself more in biblical than in philosophical language. Official church documents on theological matters or current problems almost always begin from Scripture and try to ground their arguments in biblical texts. The Catholic Church today is far more "biblical" than it was in the mid-1950s.

Bible Study in History

In order to understand the Bible's place in Catholic thinking today, it can be helpful to see how Christians in other times and places thought about and interpreted the Bible. The Bible has not always been studied according to the principles of modern historical criticism. Nor should scientific study of the Bible be understood as superseding, and thus making obsolete, all earlier approaches. A brief history of biblical interpretation will reveal important insights that remain valid today.

The Old Testament constituted the Bible for Jesus and the early Christians. According to the Gospels, Jesus sometimes quoted or alluded to Old Testament texts in order to establish a theological point or to suggest a way of acting. He clearly accorded these texts a certain degree of authority. Nevertheless, Jesus emerges from the New Testament as displaying flexibility toward the Old Testament and even asserting his authority over it. He distinguishes what comes from God and what comes from Moses (see Mk 10, 1–12), goes beyond certain scriptural teachings (Mt 5, 21–48), and rates love of God and neighbor (Mk 12, 28–31) over strict observance of the Sabbath.

New Testament writers such as Paul and Matthew looked upon the Old Testament Scriptures as fulfilled in Jesus Christ. Basing themselves on what apparently was a widespread early Christian understanding, they interpreted the Old Testament Scriptures in the light of the life, death, and resurrection of Jesus. Like other Jews of the time, they understood the Old Testa-

ment to be a mystery—that is, something that could not be understood without guidance or explanation. Whereas the Qumran community (the Jewish group that gave us the Dead Sea Scrolls) found the key to the Scriptures in their own sect's history and life, the early Christians discovered Jesus to be the key that opened up the mystery of the Hebrew Bible.

By the time of the Fathers of the Church (the patristic period), the Christian Bible contained two Testaments—Old and New. These Fathers, or early theologians, generally adopted one or the other of two basic approaches to the reading and interpretation of Scripture: the allegorical and the literal methods.

The allegorical method, favored particularly by those theologians who lived in Alexandria in Egypt, emphasized uncovering the spiritual truths beneath the surface of the biblical stories. This method had been developed by Greek thinkers who interpreted the stories in Homer's *Iliad* and *Odyssey* as symbolizing emotional or spiritual struggles within the individual. It had also been adopted by Jewish interpreters, like Philo of Alexandria, who used the method on the Hebrew Bible in order to appeal to non-Jews and especially to Jews who had come under the influence of Greek philosophy and culture. Christian theologians who used this method included Origen and Clement of Alexandria.

In contrast to this method was the more literal reading of the Bible, favored by those Christian thinkers who lived in Antioch, the capital of Syria in Roman times. The literal approach focused more on the historical realities described in Scripture and insisted that any higher or deeper sense should be based firmly on the literal sense of the text. John Chrysostom and Theodore of Mopsuestia were among those who favored this approach.

It is important to recognize that these different emphases were not completely opposed to each other. Thus, the allegorical method did not deny the historical truth of events in Scripture, nor did the literal method deny the spiritual meaning of those events. Later theologians tended to blend the two approaches, although favoring one tendency or the other. Augustine, for instance, tended toward the allegorical and Jerome toward the literal.

Medieval interpreters, building on both these approaches, distinguished four senses in a scriptural text: literal (what took place), allegorical (the hidden theological meaning), anagogical (the heavenly sense), and moral or tropological (the significance for the individual's behavior). The classic example was the term "Jerusalem" (see Gal 4, 22–31), which can refer to a city in Palestine (literal), the Church (allegorical), the heavenly home of us all (anagogical), and the human soul (moral). Since this wide-ranging approach to Scripture could easily degenerate into subjectivity, careful interpreters like Thomas Aquinas insisted that "nothing necessary to faith is contained under the spiritual sense that is not elsewhere put forward by Scripture in its literal sense." Thomas Aquinas also used human reason as a tool in explaining the Scriptures and tried to bring together philosophical truth (especially as proposed by Aristotle) and biblical truth.

With the Renaissance and the rise of Humanism came a new interest in studying the Scriptures in their original languages and their historical settings. Erasmus produced a new edition of the Greek New Testament to go along with his revision of the Latin Vulgate translation. He also used the Greek and Roman classics of paganism along with the writings of the Church Fathers to interpret the biblical texts. Catholic enthusiasm for the study of the Scriptures cooled, however, in response to the claims for the Bible (*sola scriptura* or Scripture alone) made by Martin Luther and other Protestant Reformers, especially their statements about the clarity of Scripture (so that there is no need for the Church as the final interpreter) and its sufficiency (so that there is no need for Church tradition).

The rationalist claims of the European Enlightenment made matters even more complicated for Catholic interpreters of the Bible. For example, the philosopher Baruch Spinoza maintained that when Scripture and philosophy come into conflict (as in the case of miracles), then Scripture is to be rejected in favor of reason. Thus the Catholic Church was backed into being the defender of biblical "truth," sometimes with unfortunate consequences.

This survey reveals some abiding principles of Catholic biblical interpretation: the central significance of Christ, the struggle to be faithful to the literal meaning while searching for spiritual meaning, the conviction that faith and reason are not opposed, the insistence that the Bible should be interpreted in the Church, and the emphasis on biblical truth against the attacks of rationalism.

Modern Developments

The gradual Catholic acceptance of scientific biblical criticism (or the historical-critical method), while remaining true to the Church's heritage, can be traced with reference to a series of official Roman documents issued during the late nineteenth and the twentieth century. For a full collection of official Roman Catholic documents pertaining to the study of the Bible, see Dean R. Bechard (ed.), *The Scripture Documents: An Anthology of Official Catholic Teachings* (Collegeville, MN: Liturgical Press, 2002).

A cautious beginning was made with the papal encyclical *Providentissimus Deus* by Pope Leo XIII in 1893, only to be blunted by fears of Modernism under Pius X and by Benedict XV's encyclical *Spiritus Paraclitus,* issued in 1920. A new age dawned with the encyclical entitled *Divino Afflante Spiritu,* which was promulgated by Pius XII in 1943, in which the historical study of the Bible was given official approbation. The approach outlined by Pius XII was put into practice by the Pontifical Biblical Commission in its 1964 *Instruction Concerning the Historical Truth of the Gospels.*

The culmination of official Catholic pronouncements on biblical studies was the Second Vatican Council's *Dogmatic Constitution on Divine Revelation.* The nature of these documents is cumulative; that is, the latest document generally restates the teachings contained in previous documents and clarifies matters not discussed earlier in detail. However, the document of an ecumenical council has far more official weight than a papal encyclical or an instruction from the Pontifical Biblical Commission. Moreover, the council's document on Scripture was a "dogmatic constitution," the most authoritative kind issued by Vatican II. Thus Vatican II's *Dogmatic Constitution on Divine Revelation* can be taken as the authoritative climax of a long series of developments in the Church's attitude toward the Bible.

Vatican II was a "pastoral" council. It sought to address the needs of the Church and the world in the twentieth century and beyond. Its constitution on divine revelation (also known by its Latin title, *Dei verbum*) was addressed not so much to scholars or theologians as to the Church at large. In effect, the bishops were saying, "This is what the Catholic Church thinks and believes about the Bible and related matters." The document had a rocky history from its first draft in 1962 to its final form in 1965. Pope John XXIII's rejection of the initial draft, which favored a propositional understanding of revelation (revelation consists of statements of abstract truths) and a theory of two sources of revelation (Scripture and tradition), set the Second Vatican Council on its path of *aggiornamento* (Italian for "bringing up to date"). (All quotations are from the translation by Liam Walsh and Wilfrid Harrington in Austin Flannery [ed.], *Vatican Council II: The Conciliar and Post-Conciliar Documents* [Northport, NY: Costello, 1975] 750–65.)

The six chapters in *Dei verbum* treat divine revelation itself, the transmission of divine revelation, sacred Scripture—its divine inspiration and its interpretation, the Old Testament, the New Testament, and sacred Scripture in the life of the Church. What the constitution teaches on these topics will be taken up in the remaining parts of this essay. Here only what it teaches about scientific biblical criticism will concern us.

The conciliar statement about biblical criticism appears in paragraph 12, which is part of the chapter on the inspiration and interpretation of Scripture. It is prefaced by an acknowledgment that since God speaks in Scripture through human beings, and so in human fashion, interpreters should give careful attention to the ways in which the sacred writers thought and expressed themselves:

In determining the intention of the sacred writers, attention must be paid, *inter alia,* to literary forms for the fact is that truth is differently presented and expressed in the various types of historical writing, in prophetical and poetical texts, and in other forms of literary expression. Hence the exegete must look for that meaning which the sacred writer, in a determined situation and given the circumstances of his time and culture, intended to express and did in fact express, through the medium of a contemporary literary form.

Rightly to understand what the sacred author wanted to affirm in his work, due attention must be paid both to the customary and characteristic patterns of perception, speech and narrative which prevailed at the age of the sacred writer, and to the conventions which the people of his time followed in their dealings with one another.

The statement, which is really a condensation of Pius XII's 1943 encyclical *Divine Afflante Spiritu,* makes three points. First, it insists that we take into account the various literary forms in which the Bible is written, and it warns us against confusing historical, prophetic, and poetic texts. Next, it urges us to pay attention to the historical setting in which the sacred author wrote, suggesting that such historical awareness is necessary for grasping what the author intended. Finally, it recommends that we learn about the literary conventions and cultural assumptions that people accepted at the time when the biblical books were composed. Thus the conciliar document encourages the literary, historical, and sociological study of biblical texts.

The acceptance of biblical criticism, of course, does not reduce the Sacred Scriptures to the status of other, strictly human books. In fact, the very next sentence in the document affirms the divine authorship of the biblical texts and urges biblical interpreters to take that into consideration:

But since sacred Scripture must be read and interpreted with its divine authorship in mind, no less attention must be devoted to the content and unity of the whole of Scripture, taking into account the Tradition of the entire Church and the analogy of faith, if we are to derive their true meaning from the sacred texts.

In this way the conciliar document achieves a balance between the human and the divine contributions to Scripture. Interpreters are thereby encouraged to apply all the tools of biblical criticism, while bearing in mind the Church's long-standing conviction that the Bible contains "the Word of God in the words of men."

In 1993, to mark the 100th anniversary of *Providentissimus Deus* and the 50th anniversary of *Divino Afflante Spiritu,* the Pontifical Biblical Commission, with the full approval of Pope John Paul II, issued a document entitled "The Interpretation of the Bible in the Church." Prepared by an international team of distinguished Catholic biblical scholars, this document describes various methods of and approaches to biblical interpretation, examines certain questions of a hermeneutical nature, reflects on the characteristic features of a Catholic interpretation of the Bible, and considers the place that biblical interpretation has in the life of the Church. This document spells out in some detail many of the directions recommended in the papal encyclicals and in Vatican II's *Dei verbum*.

The Pontifical Biblical Commission's document describes the historical-critical method as "the indispensable method for the scientific study of the meaning of ancient texts." While giving attention to the many possible contributions from certain "new" literary and social-scientific approaches, it criticizes fundamentalism as "dangerous" and even as inviting people to "a kind of intellectual suicide." And it insists on the pastoral significance of the whole exegetical enterprise when it states: "Exegesis produces its best results when it is carried out in the context of the living faith of the Christian community, which is directed toward the salvation of the entire world."

Methods of Biblical Interpretation

The term *biblical criticism* refers to various methods of scientific biblical study that have as their goal establishing the text, understanding the content and the literary style of biblical books, and determining their origin and authenticity. This undertaking is sometimes called the historical-critical method—historical because it focuses on the original historical settings of the biblical texts and the historical processes that gave rise to them, and critical because it applies reason to the texts and makes judgments about them in the effort to be as objective as possible. Biblical criticism aims to understand what a text was saying to its original audience and to make clear its significance then (and now).

Textual criticism (sometimes called lower criticism) seeks to establish the wording of the biblical text as the biblical authors wrote it. Since we no longer have direct access to the manuscripts written by the biblical authors (autographs), textual critics try to come as close as possible to the original form of the texts by gathering all the pertinent manuscript evidence (Hebrew and Aramaic

for the Old Testament, Greek for the New Testament, ancient translations for both Testaments). When the evidence has been assembled, textual critics determine where the ancient manuscripts differ and proceed to decide which reading is original and to explain how the other readings arose. The rejected readings may have been unconscious mistakes (for example, confusing similar letters of the alphabet, omitting words or phrases, inserting marginal comments into the main text) or deliberate modifications (for example, harmonizing with parallel texts, "correcting" grammar or style, removing "offensive" material). The accepted readings should be consistent with the content and style of the document and follow the rules of grammar and good sense.

Literary criticism attends to the words and images, the characters and their relationships, the structure and progress of thought, the literary form, and the meaning. These processes are used today in studying all kinds of literature; they are by no means confined to biblical study. Bible concordances, dictionaries, and encyclopedias make it possible to trace the development of a word (for example, faith) or a theme (for example, covenant) and to locate a particular occurrence within such a framework. Careful inspection of a text enables one to chart out the interactions among the characters or to outline the progress of the argument. The biblical writers used many different literary forms. The Old Testament consists of law codes, narratives, psalms, prophecies, proverbs, visions, and even love poetry. The New Testament contains stories of Jesus' words and deeds (Gospels), the actions of some apostles (Acts), letters (Epistles), and visions (Revelation). Rather than stating theological truths in the form of theses or propositions, the biblical authors conveyed their message in artistic and memorable ways. Literary criticism helps us to read the biblical books on their own terms and thus to appreciate their artistry and their truth.

Historical criticism concerns the world behind the biblical texts; that is, the origin and growth of the biblical documents. Scholars assume that sometimes a complicated process of composition lies behind a finished book of the Bible. Smaller literary units—for example, a saying from Jesus, or a hymn—were told and retold, or used orally in worship. Later, perhaps, a collection of sayings or hymns was made. Still later, a writer created a longer narrative into which various sayings were fitted, or which quoted a hymn in order to make a point. At each stage, the original small unit was being used in a slightly different context, and it may have been changed in small ways in order to fit its new use better.

Scholars have various names for this sort of investigation of a biblical text, depending on what level they are examining. *Source criticism* attempts to establish where previously existing material (for example, a hymn, a saying, or a vision account) has been used by a later author in a longer work, either by accepting what is stated in the work itself or by noticing differences in content, vocabulary, and literary style. *Form criticism* seeks to classify literary genres or forms, and to isolate the historical settings in which the forms developed and functioned before they became part of the main text. A sermon, for instance, will have characteristics that are different from those of a letter or a story. *Redaction criticism* deals with the ways in which a biblical author or editor (redactor means editor) used sources, and sometimes changed them, to address problems and concerns facing his readers. So biblical criticism takes account of historical settings at three levels: the sources, the small units, and the finished document.

Archaeological excavations and textual discoveries such as the Ugaritic texts and the Dead Sea Scrolls can shed light on the material world and culture in which the biblical books were written. For example, ancient epics outside the Bible have helped us to appreciate the creation stories in the book of Genesis. And the Dead Sea Scrolls, besides providing the earliest extant manuscripts of the Hebrew Bible, have illumined the thought and organization of the early Church.

The interpretive process can also be enriched by the application of concepts and methods used in the *social sciences* such as sociology, cultural anthropology, and psychology. These approaches help in exposing the cultural assumptions about the human condition and the world that people in biblical times took for granted, and in explaining the development of ancient Israel into a nation and the early Christian communities into what we call the Church.

Historical criticism is sometimes defined narrowly to refer to the reality of the event behind the text, to determining what actually occurred at

(for example) the first Passover or the first Easter. What really happened in detail is sometimes hard to discern, since the biblical authors were often more interested in the meaning of the events than in their precise details. Some historical critics (in the narrow sense) rule out the miraculous and divine intervention on philosophical grounds and make negative judgments about the communities that handed on the biblical texts. But this is not true of all historical critics, nor is it at all consistent with the Catholic approach to Scripture, which assumes that the biblical texts tell the "honest truth" about the events described in the texts.

While the classic historical-critical method is oriented mainly to illuminating the history of the text and the world behind the text, certain "new" methods of literary analysis focus more on the text as it now stands (the world of the text) and on its effects on the reader today (the world before or in front of the text). *Rhetorical analysis* explores the capacity of a biblical text to persuade and convince the reader, while *narrative analysis* investigates how a text works in the sense of its success in telling a story involving plot, characters, and point of view. *Structuralist analysis* and *semiotic analysis* are modern linguistic methods that examine the various temporal and spatial relationships in a text, with an eye toward revealing the deeper patterns of meaning underlying the text.

Another set of approaches to biblical interpretation privileges the interpreter and the social location of the interpreter. *Liberation theology* takes as its starting point the lived experience of poor people today and enters into conversation with biblical texts (e.g., Israel's Exodus from Egypt, or Mary's Magnificat in Lk 1, 46–55) as a way of illumining both the biblical text and the present situation of the poor. *Feminist interpretation* calls attention to the prominence of certain women in the Bible, exposes the patriarchal or male-centered assumptions of the cultures in which the Bible was originally produced, and challenges interpreters to recognize the liberating contributions of women to the biblical story of salvation.

Other reader-oriented resources in biblical interpretation include the *history of interpretation* (how a text has been understood by Jewish and Christian readers throughout the centuries) and the *history of effects* (the impact or influence that a text has exercised in the course of history). Canonical criticism focuses on the final canonical form of a biblical text, explores its place within the biblical canon as a whole, and considers its significance for the Church's faith and way of life. *Hermeneutics* is concerned with discerning the present significance of a biblical text. While this is what preachers have always done, the hermeneutical phase of the interpretive task is open to and incumbent upon all Bible readers. It involves the fusion of horizons between the ancient text and the reader in the present and envisions a process by which the reader is changed intellectually and spiritually by encounter with the biblical text.

Two terms that have recently become prominent with regard to Catholic biblical interpretation and its practical impact in church life are *actualization* and *inculturation*. The Christian Scriptures are ancient texts, and so they need to be presented in ways in which they can speak to peoples of different times (actualization) and places or cultures (inculturation). The Scriptures are made "actual" whenever their spiritual insights are presented in such a way that they can address the problems and possibilities of the present day. Likewise, the Scriptures are "inculturated" whenever they are translated, interpreted, and applied in terms that peoples from outside the ancient Mediterranean world can understand and so live out their challenges and opportunities.

One traditional way of bringing together all these different methods in a simple and coherent framework is through the traditional Catholic approach developed in monastic circles and known as *lectio divina* (divine [or, spiritual] reading). There are four steps. The first step is *lectio* (reading); that is, a careful reading of the text from various critical perspectives (literary, historical, and theological) and the assimilation or appropriation of the text on both intellectual and emotional levels. The second step is *meditatio,* which explores what this text may be saying to me (or us) now. One can open up the text by focusing on a theme or a few phrases, by applying the senses (sight, hearing, smell, taste, touch) to the biblical scene, and by trying to make connections between the text and one's present situation. The third step is *oratio* (prayer) in which

on the basis of reading and meditating one may speak words of praise, petition, adoration, and/or thanksgiving to God. The fourth step may take the form of *contemplatio* (relishing the religious experience generated by the encounter with the text and resting in the mystery of God) and/or *actio* (coming to a decision about one's life, or finding new ways to express what one has learned— through dance, drama, artwork, group sharing, homily, etc.).

Scripture as Tradition

The official Catholic emphasis on attention to the literary forms, historical settings, and cultural assumptions of the biblical writings flows from the nature of the books themselves. Far from being individual creations generated in solitude, the biblical books include many ideas, traditions, and even small pieces that already existed before being integrated into the texts in which they now stand. Biblical literature is thoroughly and deliberately traditional.

The traditional character of the Old Testament has long been acknowledged. The first five books, which are customarily called the Pentateuch or Torah, are generally recognized to incorporate material from at least four different sources (Yahwist, Elohist, Deuteronomist, Priestly). See "Introduction to the Pentateuch," pp. 5–6. The historical books (Joshua to 2 Kings, Chronicles, Ezra, and Nehemiah) include earlier accounts, memoirs, genealogies, and so forth. The prophetic books are anthologies of short pieces of poetry and prose, and the wisdom books contain ideas and even sayings that circulated in the ancient Near East for centuries before. The Psalms are a collection of varied kinds of songs used mainly in the Jerusalem Temple; in the Psalms there may even be remnants of non-Jewish hymns (see Psalm 29). So complicated and so rich is the process of transmission that it is difficult in most cases to speak of *the* author of a biblical book as one may speak of an author today. The situation is further complicated by the fact that in biblical times personal creativity and originality were not important values. One displayed real creativity by using traditional ideas and expressions in new settings and in new combinations.

Given the nature of the Old Testament and the ancient concept of creativity, one would expect the New Testament to be thoroughly traditional also. And it is. The earliest complete documents in the New Testament are Paul's letters. Even these highly "original" and occasional pieces rely at key points on preexisting material (for example, Rom 1, 3–4; 1 Cor 13, 1–13; 15, 3–5; Phil 2, 6–11). Those epistles whose direct Pauline composition is doubtful (for example, the Pastorals, Ephesians, Colossians, 2 Thessalonians) are best understood as later attempts to bring the figure and teaching of Paul to bear on situations facing the churches in the late first century. We often regard Paul as a creative genius. However, not only did he use some traditional material, but also almost all his undisputed letters contain some indication of joint authorship (see 1 Thess 1, 1; 1 Cor 1, 1; Rom 16, 22; etc.). Moreover, throughout his letters Paul gives credit to his "co-workers" and encourages the collection for the Jerusalem community as a sign of solidarity with the "mother church" there.

The complicated process of tradition and composition applies to the Gospels too. Most scholars today place the final composition of the four canonical Gospels in the late first century: Mark around A.D. 70, Matthew and Luke around A.D. 80–90, and John around A.D. 90–100. Yet all scholars acknowledge that the evangelists used already-existing material in their Gospels. For example, Matthew and Luke each seem to have read both Mark's Gospel and a collection of Jesus' sayings that modern scholars call "Q" (from the German word *Quelle,* which means "source"). John utilized a collection of miracle stories (signs) and perhaps also some "revelation discourses." The Markan and Johannine passion narratives surely contain much traditional information, accounts that had been passed from one person to another.

The Gospels and the traditions incorporated in them tell the story of Jesus of Nazareth, who was crucified around A.D. 30. Like other Jewish teachers of his time, Jesus taught by word (parables, proverbs, debates, other sayings) and deed (example, healings, symbolic gestures). His disciples remembered and retold his words and deeds, thus providing the basic materials for what became the Gospel tradition. Jesus did not write books. What we know of Jesus comes to us through the process of tradition from Jesus to the early Church and finally to the evangelists.

The nature of the Gospels demands that interpreters attend to three stages in their development. The *Dogmatic Constitution on Divine Revelation* (*Dei verbum* 19) captures that development in this marvelously concise statement:

> The sacred authors, in writing the four Gospels, selected certain of the many elements which had been handed on, either orally or already in written form, others they synthesized or explained with an eye to the situation of the churches, the while sustaining the form of preaching, but always in such a fashion that they have told us the honest truth about Jesus.

The council's document affirms that the Gospels tell us the "honest truth" about Jesus. It recognizes that there was an intermediary stage in which traditions about Jesus circulated in oral and written forms as "preaching" about the significance of Jesus. It acknowledges that the evangelists give us only a selection (see Lk 1, 1–4; Jn 20, 30–31; 21, 25) of the traditions about Jesus. It also recognizes that the evangelists used the traditions about Jesus to address the situations of their own day. Therefore, Catholics must read the Gospels as traditional documents (because they are such) and attend to three stages in their development: Jesus, the early Church, and the evangelists.

Although in the past there has been some Catholic resistance to accepting the "traditional" character of the biblical books, this emphasis is perfectly compatible with the principles of Catholicism. There is no obligation for Catholics to be conservative historians of early Christianity (nor is there any obligation for them to be reckless or indifferent). As long as Catholic scholars make clear the link from Jesus through the early Church to the evangelists, they remain faithful to their theological heritage.

In fact, an emphasis on the traditional nature of the biblical writings is fully consistent with certain distinctively Catholic principles. The Catholic stress on the communal character of our way to God and God's way to us sensitizes Catholics to the complexity of early Christian tradition and to the role of the Church in shaping it and being formed by it. The Catholic emphasis that encounter with God is rooted in history and is a mediated experience helps us to see the continuity between Jesus and the early reflections on him, as well as the significance and correctness of those reflections. The Catholic sacramental approach, which sees God in and through all things, leads us to view the very human process of tradition as a vehicle for expressing, safeguarding, and adapting divine revelation.

Scripture and Tradition

The Catholic Church does not restrict divine revelation to the biblical text. Against the Protestant Reformation's slogan of "Scripture alone," Catholic theologians insisted on "Scripture and tradition." The term "tradition" recognizes the fact that the living reality of the Church has the task of preserving the gospel as well as interpreting and applying it in new situations. Catholic Christianity is not simply a "religion of the Book."

While acknowledging the twofold reality of Scripture and tradition, Catholic theologians have long debated the precise relation between the two. One way of approaching the problem was to assume that Scripture and tradition constitute two separate sources of divine revelation. The Second Vatican Council rejected this view in the second chapter of its *Dogmatic Constitution on Divine Revelation* (*Dei verbum* 10): "Sacred Tradition and sacred Scripture make up a single sacred deposit of the Word of God, which is entrusted to the Church." In other words, the Word of God (or divine revelation) is the source of both tradition and Scripture.

How exactly Scripture and tradition are related remains a problem. The conciliar document uses the analogy of a wellspring or fountain to insist on their unity while preserving their diversity in *Dei verbum* 9:

Sacred Tradition and sacred Scripture then, are bound closely together, and communicate one with the other. For both of them, flowing out from the same divine well-spring, come together in some fashion to form one thing, and move towards the same goal. Sacred Scripture is the speech of God as it is put down in writing under the breath of the Holy Spirit. And Tradition transmits in its entirety the Word of God which has been entrusted to the apostles by Christ the Lord and the Holy Spirit.

The same paragraph rejects the "Scripture alone" principle of the Reformation and preserves the Catholic approach of "Scripture and tradition" by insisting that the Church does not draw certainty about all revealed truths from the holy Scriptures alone. Hence, both Scripture and tradition must be accepted and honored with equal feelings of devotion and reverence. Thus the Second Vatican Council insisted that Scripture and tradition flow from the same divine wellspring and that both must be accepted and honored. Without endorsing any one theological approach to their relation, the council rejected the opinion of those who wished to keep the two separate.

The same tension appears when the *Dogmatic Constitution* addresses the issue of authoritative interpretation of the Scriptures in *Dei verbum* 10:

... the task of giving an authentic interpretation of the Word of God, whether in its written form or in the form of Tradition, has been entrusted to the living teaching office of the Church alone. Its authority in this matter is exercised in the name of Jesus Christ. Yet this Magisterium is not superior to the Word of God, but is its servant. It teaches only what has been handed on to it. At the divine command and with the help of the Holy Spirit, it listens to this devotedly, guards it with dedication and expounds it faithfully. All that it proposes for belief as being divinely revealed is drawn from this single deposit of faith.

On the one hand, this statement entrusts authentic interpretation to the magisterium (the bishops with the pope). On the other hand, it insists that the magisterium is the servant of divine revelation and can only teach what is drawn from the single deposit of faith constituted by divine revelation.

The precise relation between Scripture and tradition also remains a problem. As a "pastoral" council, Vatican II avoided becoming an arbiter of theological disputes. Its insistence on the oneness of Scripture and tradition, however, did have a pastoral dimension. While not conceding to the "Scripture alone" position, it insisted that the Bible take again its rightful place in the center of Catholic life and that appeals to tradition be judged according to their consistency with Scripture.

The Nature of the Bible

What is this book that it should be studied so intensely and guarded so carefully? The

Dogmatic Constitution on Divine Revelation made a theological formula that had become prominent before Vatican II: "the words of God, expressed in the words of men" (*Dei verbum* 13). That formula derives from the classical theological definitions of the divine and human natures in the person of Jesus Christ. In speaking about the Bible in this way, the Second Vatican Council sought to hold together the transcendent nature of Scripture and its human form. Although the Bible may look like other books and may be studied profitably as other books are studied (that is, with the techniques of biblical criticism), the Bible is different with regard to its origin and its nature. The "different" character of the Bible is expressed by means of some rather complicated terms: revelation, inspiration, inerrancy, and canon. As with "Scripture and tradition," the Second Vatican Council used these terms without adjudicating the theological disputes surrounding them. As a pastoral council it sought to express the significance of the words for the way in which the Bible is read within the Church.

Revelation is fundamentally God's self-revelation; it is the communication of the mystery of God to the world: "It pleased God, in his goodness and wisdom, to reveal himself and to make known the mystery of his will" (*Dei verbum* 2). The Christian theological tradition affirms that God's self-revelation comes to us through creation, history, persons, society, and reason. It is also customary to refer to the Bible as a privileged revealer of God—that is, a place where the divine revelation is particularly clear. This tradition appears prominently in *Dei verbum* 6:

> By divine Revelation God wished to manifest and communicate both himself and the eternal decrees of his will concerning the salvation of mankind.

The order adopted in this statement ("both himself and the eternal decrees") is significant, for it gives pride of place to the "personal" character of divine revelation without denying the content and the consequences. Although this point may seem obvious today, the council's emphasis on the personal dimension of revelation was correctly taken as a major step in clarifying Catholic attitudes toward Scripture. Through the

Bible we encounter the mystery of God, not simply lists of commandments or interesting stories. The personal God makes those commandments and stories meaningful.

Two other theological terms for talking about the difference of the Bible from other books are "inspiration" and "inerrancy." Again the *Dogmatic Constitution on Divine Revelation* asserts the basic point expressed by these terms without arbitrating the very complicated theological debates surrounding them. On inspiration *Dei verbum* 11 states:

> The divinely revealed realities which are contained and presented in the text of sacred Scripture have been written down under the inspiration of the Holy Spirit. For Holy Mother Church relying on the faith of the apostolic age, accepts as sacred and canonical the books of the Old and the New Testaments, whole and entire, with all their parts, on the grounds that, written under the inspiration of the Holy Spirit (cf. Jn 20, 31; 2 Tm 3, 16; 2 Pt 1, 19–21; 3, 15–16), they have God as their author, and have been handed on as such to the Church herself. To compose the sacred books, God chose certain men who, all the while he employed them in this task, made full use of their powers and faculties so that, though he acted in them and by them, it was as true authors that they consigned to writing whatever he wanted written, and no more.

The same paragraph treats inerrancy:

> Since, therefore, all that the inspired authors, or sacred writers, affirm should be regarded as affirmed by the Holy Spirit, we must acknowledge that the books of Scripture firmly, faithfully and without error teach that truth which God, for the sake of our salvation, wished to see confided to the sacred Scriptures. Thus "all Scripture is inspired by God, and profitable for teaching, for reproof, for correction and for training in righteousness, so that the man of God may be complete, equipped for every good work" (2 Tm 3, 16–17, Gk. text).

The key expression in this statement is "that truth which God, for the sake of our salvation, wished to see confided to the sacred Scriptures." Without explicitly embracing the theory of only limited inerrancy, that statement suggests that the Bible's inerrancy consists primarily in its being a trustworthy guide on the road to salvation. Thus it expresses "inerrancy" in a positive way, and avoids conceiving it as a defensive program of protecting the Bible against accusations of scientific or historical error.

The council's statement on inspiration refers to the books of the Bible as "sacred and canonical." The word "canon" (whose root meaning is "reed" or "measuring stick") originally meant the rule or characteristics that decided whether a particular book was judged to be part of Sacred Scripture. It now usually refers to the collection of books that are acknowledged to be authoritative in the Church and by which the Church's faith can be measured. The canon of Old Testament books traditional in Catholicism contains all the books of the Hebrew Bible (which is the same as the Protestant Old Testament canon) together with seven others that were part of the Greek and Latin Bible tradition (Judith, Tobit, Baruch, 1 and 2 Maccabees, Sirach/Ecclesiasticus, Wisdom). All Christians today share the same canon of 27 New Testament books. The history of the canon's development is quite complex. The final definitive list of biblical books (including the seven additional Old Testament books) for the Catholic Church was drawn up only at the Council of Trent in 1546, although there was little disagreement about the substance of the canon from the early centuries of the Christian era.

The Bible is different. How it is different has been expressed with the help of some traditional words: revelation, inspiration, inerrancy, and canon. The Second Vatican Council in its authoritative declaration on Scripture (*Dei verbum*) took over those hallowed terms. In interpreting the council's use of these words we must take account of the pastoral orientation of the council as a whole. Rather than working out theological subtleties or choosing among theological schools, the *Dogmatic Constitution on Divine Revelation* used those words to convey basic attitudes about how the Bible differs from other books. It affirmed that God's self-revelation comes to us through the Bible, that in some mysterious way God entered into the composition of these writings and inspired them, that the biblical books provide reliable guidance (inerrancy) for those who walk the way toward salvation with God, and that these books constitute the norm or rule (canon) by which the life of the Church is to be guided and measured in all ages. These are the basic "pastoral" meanings of revelation, inspiration, inerrancy, and canon.

The Authority of the Bible

The terms by which Christians express the "difference" of the Bible indicate that it possesses great authority for them. The Bible is the "words of God, expressed in the words of men." It is revealed, inspired, inerrant, and canonical. The *Dogmatic Constitution on Divine Revelation* goes beyond the general assertions conveyed by the traditional theological vocabulary and speaks about the authority of various parts of the Bible.

The Old Testament (see *Dei verbum* 15) prepares for and declares in prophecy the coming of Christ. It conveys our basic understanding of God and the human situation: "how a just and merciful God deals with mankind." It provides "sound wisdom" and "a wonderful treasury of prayers." The document also mentions "matters imperfect and provisional" in the Old Testament, without specifying precisely what these are (presumably legislation about sacrifices and ritual purity, "vengeful" psalms, and other such material). The unity of the two Testaments is traced back to God who "in his wisdom has so brought it about that the New should be hidden in the Old and that the Old should be made manifest in the New" (*Dei verbum* 16).

The council accorded the Gospels a special place within the Bible "because they are our principal source for the life and teaching of the Incarnate Word, our Saviour" (*Dei verbum* 18). It insisted on the historicity and apostolicity of the Gospels, while recognizing the complex process of their composition from Jesus through the early Church to the Gospel texts. Catholics find a basic continuity between Jesus and the Gospel tradition under the guidance of the Spirit working in the Church. Their tendency is to insist that the tradition is basically historical. They assume that the modifications and reinterpretations made necessary by changing circumstances do not do violence to the original teaching or event. The "apostolic" character of the Gospels refers not so much to their direct composition by apostles as it does to the faithful transmission of the material in them by those who had experienced the risen Lord and bore witness to his resurrection. The term "apostolic" describes the generation between Jesus' death (about A.D. 30) and the composition of the New Testament books. The claim implied by the term is that those witnesses have told us the "honest truth" about Jesus.

The New Testament also contains Paul's letters and other writings (Hebrews, the catholic epistles, Revelation). After affirming their composition under the inspiration of the Holy Spirit, *Dei verbum* 20 describes the contributions that these writings make in the following way:

> In accordance with the wise design of God these writings firmly establish those matters which concern Christ the Lord, formulate more and more precisely his authentic teaching, preach the saving power of Christ's divine work and foretell its glorious consummation.

It would be a mistake, however, to conclude from this description that the epistles have a secondary status as supplements to the Gospels. In fact, Paul's authentic letters (1 Thessalonians, Galatians, 1 and 2 Corinthians, Philippians, Philemon, Romans) are the earliest complete documents in the New Testament from the standpoint of their dates of composition. Thus they give us precious information about how Paul and other early Christians in the fifties of the first century A.D. (some 25 years after the death of Jesus) understood the significance of Jesus' life, death, and resurrection. They show us how early Christians struggled to articulate their new faith in an environment that was often hostile and foreign to them. They reveal the kinds of problems that early Christians faced within their own communities (see especially 1 Corinthians) and so warn us against too easily viewing the apostolic period as a trouble-free and conflictless "golden age."

Enough has been said about the Bible in general (revelation, inspiration, inerrancy, and canon) and about its major parts (Old Testament, Gospels, Epistles) to indicate that it possesses great authority. But what kind of authority does the Bible have? It is surely not the coercive authority of a parent or the state or the police, which have the power to enforce a law or decision and to punish the uncooperative. It is not even the persuasive authority of the lawyer or the mathematician who convinces another by logic, arguments, proofs, and so forth. At some points in his epistles (for example, in 1 Corinthians 15)

Paul does labor to make a convincing case on the basis of logic. But that is not his usual mode of presentation, nor is it the customary idiom of other biblical writers.

The authority that the Bible possesses can perhaps be best described as compelling. Compelling authority is the authority of the witness, the expert, the participant. Much of the Bible concerns what God's people say about God's action on their behalf. Without narrowing the testimony of the Bible to the concept of an eyewitness, it is possible to describe the Scriptures as a collection of testimonies to God. The biblical descriptions of creation, exodus, monarchy, exile, and return from exile all stress God's relatedness to Israel and Israel's responses of praise, confession, thanksgiving, and so forth. The New Testament writers portray Jesus as the revelation of God's power (and weakness). The proper response is faith, hope, and love. Thus the biblical documents contain the proclamation and articulation of people's faith about God and God's ways with creation.

God is the real basis of the Bible's authority. Insofar as the biblical books bear witness to God and thus enable us to understand better who God is and how God acts, and to grow in love for and trust in the God of the Scriptures, the Bible can be aptly called the "Word of God." And so Vatican II's *Dogmatic Constitution on Divine Revelation,* which so emphasizes God's self-communication, is appropriately titled from its initial two words *Dei verbum* (Latin for "Word of God").

Scripture in Church Life

This essay began with a comparison regarding the Bible's place in church life of the 1950s and today. A look at Catholic liturgy, education, piety, and theology led to the conclusion that the Catholic Church today is far more "biblical" than it was in the 1950s. This development mirrors some powerful statements made in the final chapter of Vatican II's *Dogmatic Constitution on Divine Revelation.*

The centrality of Scripture in Catholic liturgy involves both preaching and sacramental practice. *Dei verbum* 21 insists that "all the preaching of the Church, as indeed the entire Christian religion, should be nourished and ruled by sacred Scripture." The same paragraph directly confronts and dissolves the opposition between word and sacrament that had been prominent since the Protestant Reformation. It does so with reference to the celebration of the Eucharist:

> The Church has always venerated the divine Scriptures as she venerated the Body of the Lord, in so far as she never ceases, particularly in the sacred liturgy, to partake of the bread of life and to offer it to the faithful from the one table of the Word of God and the Body of Christ.

The council document insists that Word and sacrament belong together in the Eucharist, to the point of asserting that they form "one table."

The popularity of Scripture in Catholic education and piety responds to a very strong statement in *Dei verbum* 22: "Access to sacred Scripture ought to be wide open to the Christian faithful." The document goes on to urge the production of modern-language translations made from the ancient biblical texts. It also encourages biblical exegetes to examine and explain the sacred texts so that preachers, teachers, and catechists "may be able to distribute fruitfully the nourishment of the Scriptures to the People of God" (*Dei verbum* 23).

The importance of Scripture for Catholic theology is stated in no uncertain terms: "The 'study of the sacred page' should be the very soul of sacred theology" (*Dei verbum* 24). The document mandates that all those officially engaged in the ministry of the Word should "immerse themselves in the Scriptures by constant sacred reading and diligent study" (*Dei verbum* 25). The same paragraph recommends the preparation of volumes such as the present one: "translations of the sacred texts which are equipped with necessary and really adequate explanations." There is overwhelming evidence that in response to the Second Vatican Council the Catholic Church has become much more "biblical." One of its most important documents was the *Dogmatic Constitution on Divine Revelation,* which has served as our principal guide in this article. At nearly every point the post-Vatican II Church has fulfilled the mandates of that council document and thus become more biblical.

The challenge facing the Catholic Church today is to look upon *Dei verbum* not only as the end of a long development (which it was) but also as the beginning of a process that has taken us into the twenty-first century and beyond. A still more biblical Church will paradoxically be better able to adjust to the rapid changes that the new millennium is already bringing upon us. A still more biblical Church will be better prepared to make common cause with other Christians, with Jews and Muslims, and with all truly religious people. A still more biblical Church will preserve its spiritual heritage and open its riches to others. An obvious step in the process toward a more biblical Church is an increase in knowledge and love of the Scriptures.

BIBLIOGRAPHY

Bechard, Dean R. (ed.). *The Scripture Documents: An Anthology of Official Catholic Teachings.* Collegeville, MN: Liturgical Press, 2002.

Brown, Raymond E. *Biblical Exegesis and Church Doctrine.* New York/Mahwah, NJ: Paulist, 1985.

———. *Responses to 101 Questions on the Bible.* New York/Mahwah, NJ: Paulist, 1990.

Brown, Raymond E., Joseph A. Fitzmyer, and Roland E. Murphy (eds.). *The New Jerome Biblical Commentary.* Englewood Cliffs, NJ: Prentice-Hall, 1990.

Fitzmyer, Joseph A. The Biblical Commission's Document "The Interpretation of the Bible in the Church": Text and Commentary. Rome: Editrice Pontificio Istituto Biblico, 1995.

———. *Scripture, the Soul of Theology.* New York/Mahwah, NJ: Paulist, 1994.

Hagen, Kenneth, et al. *The Bible in the Churches: How Various Christians Interpret the Scriptures.* 3rd ed. Milwaukee, WI: Marquette University Press, 1998.

Harrington, Daniel J. *Interpreting the New Testament,* rev. ed. Collegeville, MN: Liturgical Press, 1988.

———. *Interpreting the Old Testament.* Collegeville, MN: Liturgical Press, 1981.

Lienhard, Joseph T. *The Bible, the Church, and Authority.* Collegeville, MN: Liturgical Press, 1995.

Schneiders, Sandra M. *The Revelatory Text. Interpreting the New Testament as Sacred Scripture,* rev. ed. Collegeville, MN: Liturgical Press, 1999.

Williamson, Peter S. *Catholic Principles for Interpreting Scripture: A Study of the Pontifical Biblical Commission's* The Interpretation of the Bible in the Church. Rome: Editrice Pontificio Istituto Biblico, 2001.

CATHOLICS AND FUNDAMENTALISM

In the years prior to the Second Vatican Council one often heard the difference between Protestants and Catholics described this way: "Protestants have the Bible and Catholics have the Sacraments." As with all such humorous generalizations, it contained a grain of truth. Catholics generally opened their Bibles only to record family milestones: baptisms, marriages, and deaths. In the renewal that the Church leaders brought about at Vatican Council II, one significant change was the direct encouragement of Catholics to rediscover the Bible. Among the strong statements in this regard is that the Scriptures are food for the soul (*Dei Verbum* 21) and that access to the scriptures ought to be open wide for the Christian faithful (*Dei Verbum* 22) since ignorance of the scriptures is ignorance of Christ (*Dei Verbum* 25). With this opening of the windows to the Scriptures and opening our eyes to the treasures of our faith therein, Catholics' relationship to the Scriptures has changed dramatically. In parishes all over the world there are Bible study groups; in living rooms and classrooms Catholics are unlocking these treasures and enriching their understanding and often changing how they live their faith. At the same time that the council sent us to our Bibles, it updated the source and summit of our faith, the liturgy, so that the Scriptures are now presented in an organized and more complete manner. Now, Catholics hear a wide variety of readings from both the Old Testament and the New Testament at Mass over the three-year liturgical cycle.

Since most Catholics have little experience and kground in Bible study, responsible church leaders do well when they lead us in a Scripture learning process that is in tune with our Catholic tradition rather than one from a fundamentalist Protestant perspective. Many Catholics, who have no access to Scripture study groups in their own church, join such Bible study groups in other churches, many of whom have a fundamentalist rather than a Catholic perspective. While all who value the Bible share some beliefs, there are differences between Catholics and fundamentalists about some serious and basic views of scripture, about its interpretation and about how we use it for our lives. It is important to note that there are also vast differences between mainstream Protestants and many evangelical Protestants, on the one hand, and fundamentalist Protestants, on the other. It is the fundamentalist perspective that Catholics are cautioned about. It is also important to note that Catholic biblical scholarship has been indebted to the work of (non-fundamentalist) Protestant scholars over the years.

Both the Pontifical Biblical Commission and Pope Benedict VI, when he was head of the Vatican department that oversaw the Doctrine of the Faith, explained the Church's views:

The fundamentalist approach is dangerous, for it is attractive to people who look to the Bible for ready answers to the problems of life. It can deceive these people, offering them interpretations that are pious but illusory, instead of telling them that the Bible does not contain an immediate answer to each and every problem. Without saying as much in so many words, fundamentalism actually invites people to an intellectual suicide. It injects into life a false certitude, for it unwittingly confuses the divine substance of the

Catholics and Fundamentalism

Bible message with what are in fact its human limitations. (The Interpretation of the Bible in the Church [Rome: Pontifical Biblical Commission, 1993] # I.F.)

Fundamentalism is a danger. That is clear. It is absolutely incompatible with Catholic faith, because the Catholic faith supposes that I read the Bible in context of the community of faith and the community of all the centuries of faith. Thus I read the Bible with the Church and with the faith of all times. And I read it reasonably, in a reasonable manner. So we must strive to avoid fundamentalism. (Quoted in Richard John Neuhaus, Biblical Interpretation in Crisis [Grand Rapids, Mich.: Eerdmans, 1989] 140.)

Fundamentalist Perspective on the Bible	Catholic Perspective on the Bible
The Bible is the Word of God	The Bible is God's Word in human words
Scripture *alone*	Scripture *and* Tradition
Emphasis on literalist reading of Bible	Emphasis on literal (not literalist) reading as well as deeper (and spiritual) meanings
Tendency to view inspiration narrowly	Tendency to take a broad view of inspiration
Inerrancy of the Bible in all matters	No errors in the Bible only on matters of faith and morals
Lack of historical perspective in interpretation	Historical perspective is essential for interpretation
Frequent interpretations out of context	Necessity of the interpretations in context, especially the context of the sacred canon
Direct and immediate applicability of most Biblical passages	Mostly indirect applicability of biblical passages
Denial of role of church in canonization of scripture	Recognition of role of Church in Canonization process
Tendency to ignore history of interpretation	History of interpretation essential
Narrow and precise prophetic eschatology often linked to a time line	Broad and imprecise eschatology not linked to any specific time line
Rejection of scientific historical-critical methods of interpretation	Acceptance of scientific historical-critical methods of interpretation (among others)

The Order of St. Benedict, Inc. *Biblical Fundamentalism: What Every Catholic Should Know*, (Collegeville, MN: Liturgical Press 2002). Reprinted with permission.

HOW TO READ THE BIBLE

The various books of the Bible, as most people know, were not written in English, but in languages now "dead": biblical Hebrew, Aramaic, and Koine Greek. To make these texts accessible today, translators have produced the *New American Bible* and other modern language translations. While we can be grateful for the benefits of such translations, we should also be aware that they share certain important limitations. All languages are deeply embedded in the cultural systems out of which they come. Therefore, if we wish to understand a text written in another language, we must understand that other culture as well, and simply reading an English translation does not provide that vital cultural information.

Therefore, although people taught to read English can easily read the *New American Bible,* if they were to do so as though it were a modern English text coming out of contemporary social experience, they would be seriously *mis-*reading the ancient stories, laws, letters, and poetry produced by the ancient authors and editors and understood by the first audiences of the Bible. A modern reader must *learn* something of the alien and long-dead cultures standing behind these texts; that is why publications such as this study Bible contain so much historical, religious, and literary background. If you sometimes think that explaining Isaiah's prophetic books or St. Paul's letters is complicated, imagine how much explanation St. Paul or Isaiah would need if they wanted to read one of *our* books!

"Readers" Yesterday and Today

To speak of people *reading* the Bible in itself points to one of the most striking, yet often least recognized, differences between the modern reader and the ancient one. In the ancient world of the Hebrew people and even the later world of the Greeks, very few men—and almost no women—could read or write. Consequently, the authors of the biblical documents belonged to a tiny literate elite within largely illiterate societies. In addition, because the audience was illiterate, most of the biblical texts were written primarily to be heard with the ear rather than read with the eye. Those who could read would read aloud to a larger group. Hearing a text, rather than seeing it, affected the way ancient material was fashioned; repetition, puns, prologues, and summaries are all devices in biblical material because of the requirements of the ear.

Modern readers use chapter titles, tables of contents, paragraphing, and internal headings as ways of orienting themselves in books or articles. But such "eye helps" did not exist in ancient writings. The verse numbers in the Bible, for instance, were not added until the sixteenth century A.D. by the famous Parisian printer Stephanus. Where to stop and where to start, how to grasp the way the author organized the material, and what type of writing the author had chosen to use, had to be signaled in ways accessible to the ear for an ancient audience. Thus, repeated opening and closing patterns, proverbs, hymns, oracles, laws, letters, and straightforward, reliable narration are all important aspects of biblical literature. Such qualities are not so prevalent in modern writing.

But we must look deeper. It is not only the case that the writings of the Bible, in their final form, were meant to be read aloud. It is also the case that much of the material in those writings—the sayings of the prophets, the stories of Genesis, the accounts of events in the life of Jesus—circulated for years, perhaps centuries, as *oral* tradition before ever being written down. The stories were passed orally from one generation to the next, adapted to new occasions and altered to fit changing social and political circumstances. After a time, collections of these oral stories were made and written. Thus, the absence of widespread literacy in antiquity meant that *oral* communication was the medium of critical importance. Therefore, in order to understand the Bible as its first audiences did, modern readers must learn to *hear* its texts as well as read them.

Even referring to *the* Bible may encourage contemporary readers to *mis*-read, for *the* Bible is not one book but a collection of many books coming from many different countries and several quite distinct cultures. The Hebrew Bible contains books written from the tenth century B.C. to the second century B.C., almost a millennium of human history. The present shape of many of these books evolved over centuries of editing and reworking, from the early legends about the origins of the Hebrew people, most of which originally circulated as oral tradition, to the later apocalyptic visions of the end of the world in the book of Daniel. Because of this complex process of composition, these documents often reflect not only the evolving religious ideas of the Hebrew people but also their changing social and political fortunes. Yet, since the first audiences were themselves living that political and social history, it is in many places assumed that the reader or hearer will understand the context, and therefore that context is not explained. We can get an inkling of the need for explanation if we think about how *we* would explain, to an ancient Israelite or an early Christian, a contemporary news article that begins, "The White House announced today . . . ." And once we have thought about that—about what "the White House" means in contemporary America—we can also think about what we might expect if we are given various dates for this news article. Suppose the dateline were "Washington, D.C., October 1962. The White House announced today . . . ." Suppose it were 1982? Or 2002? What difference does it make if John F.

Kennedy, Ronald Reagan, or George W. Bush is in the White House?

Although the New Testament books were written over a much shorter period—perhaps 60 or so years, from the mid-40s A.D. for Paul's earliest letters to as late as A.D. 100–110 for some of the later letters or the book of Revelation—the political history of that century, containing the war between Rome and the Jews, the subsequent fall of Jerusalem and Qumran, and the destruction of the Jerusalem Temple, as well as—probably—the destruction of the Christian community in Jerusalem, plays a crucial role in the outward growth of the Christian movement. Actually, the 27 separate letters and books that now compose the official New Testament canon are only a small selection from a much larger body of writings by Christians during the first several centuries B.C.

The Hebrew Bible and the New Testament, the two major divisions of the Bible, clearly display certain similarities in form and content: They both draw upon oral traditions; they are both made up of various types of literature, written at different times, directed to separate groups of people for a variety of reasons; and they both relate the continuing story of God's involvement with the Jewish people and the surrounding Gentile world. But we must also acknowledge that, because their audiences, aims, and backgrounds are so different, they often present moral and theological positions aimed at very different concerns. Therefore, to view the similarities as establishing a uniformity of perspective for *the* Bible would be a serious *mis*-reading of the material, for the cultural situation is fundamentally different. To grasp just how different, we can consider the differences in the various conceptions of the universe that are reflected in different parts of the Bible.

The View of the Universe

In the ancient Near Eastern world of the Sumerians, Babylonians, and Hebrew people, the universe was an intimate and fairly compact affair, which might be visualized as three stories, separated by the solid firmament of the earth below and the heavens above. The top story, formed by the heavens, was the abode of the gods and was surrounded at its outermost limits by water, which the gods could allow to fall upon the earth by opening windows in the heavens—a fact that could cause considerable anxiety among the human population for fear that the gods might forget or decide not to close the windows and thus flood the earth. The second story, the space between earth and the heavens, was the location of humanity, while the bottom story with its limits also defined by water, which would rise to the earth above through rivers and oceans, belonged to the spirits of the underworld. All three stories were closely connected to each other. In such a small universe, encounters between the divine and the human worlds were expected and regular. Only when one element or another was out of place or not performing its assigned task (e.g., the gods were asleep or on a journey when they were needed [see 1 Kgs 18, 27] or the king refused to rebuild the city walls or the farmer neglected the time of harvest) was the harmony of an entire system put at risk by an eruption of chaos. Order and a strong sense of place created a very secure world, and religion provided the map or contract set of rules needed to maintain the established order.

By the beginnings of Christianity, that secure, compact universe had exploded. Only a few other periods in the history of Western civilizations can rival the extensive change in perspective that occurred during the Greco-Roman era. The exact causes of that ancient transformation remain unclear, but it was surely influenced by the increasingly sophisticated developments in astronomy, science, and mathematics in Greek circles as well as the growth of large, multinational urban centers around the Mediterranean basin, where cultural, economic, and religious exchange could flourish. These intellectual and social innovations, along with the new mobility permitted by the widespread use of Koine Greek as a general language of commerce and the relative stability of Greek and then of Roman rule, extended the limits of the universe far beyond anything imaginable by earlier peoples.

The view of the universe in the Greco-Roman period, formally codified by Claudius Ptolemy in the second century A.D., might best be visualized as an expanding series of concentric spheres, all in eternal motion around a tiny, stationary earth. The first seven spheres contained the moon and the planets (including the sun), each moving in its appointed round and in the process, rubbing against the other spheres to produce musical notes. The outermost sphere contained the fixed stars. The planets were not the only inhabitants of each sphere, however, for the Greco-Roman people also believed that each sphere housed an order of angels or demons, constantly watching the activities of the human world below, and the closer the sphere to earth, the nastier were its tenants, with the demons responsible for illness, birth defects, and pains of all kinds lodging in the space between the moon and the earth. The intimate, secure universe of the earlier age had disappeared into the vast, threatening reaches of the cosmos, and God no longer dwelt a short distance away but instead resided out beyond the farthest sphere. Religion in such an age existed to help people escape the fears of daily life and to assure them of God's continued care in this world and the next across the outstretched spaces of the stars.

Today we neither live in the ancient three-story universe of the Hebrew people nor even in the Ptolemaic universe of the early Christians. In reading about worries over sleeping deities or threatening demonic powers, modern people probably think of metaphorical language or symbolic meanings, for in modern writings those images would surely function in that fashion. The Bible, however, is not a modern book or collection of modern books. The people who told, wrote, and heard these stories faced uncertain and dangerous worlds, which they attempted to understand as God's creation in ways their societies and theories pictured it. In order to read the Bible in a manner similar to the way they might have heard it, we must learn to appreciate the world in which they lived.

UNDERSTANDING THE HISTORICAL BACKGROUND TO THE BIBLICAL TEXTS

DONALD SENIOR

The biblical writings were created over a lengthy period of time. That broad historical and cultural canvas is one important cause for the Bible's rich diversity. In this Study Bible, the Reading Guides (see RG 47) provided for each biblical book, and the introductions provided in the notes to the biblical text itself, offer specific information about the historical background of the individual books of the Bible. The following paragraphs sketch the relationship of the biblical books to the history out of which they grew.

The accounts of creation and the stories about the first ancestors of the human family, such as the tragic rivalry between Cain and Abel and the story of Noah and the flood, obviously do not have the same historical grounding that later traditions could. These stories answer the question about the origin of humanity and its plight in history. Firm historical traditions begin only with the forging of Israel into an identifiable people, an event that did not begin until probably around 1250 B.C. Traditions about the earlier patriarchal period starting around 1850 B.C. are much less certain historically, and even events from the time of Israel's sojourn in Egypt and during the period of the Exodus and early settlement in the land are sketchy, because there were few means of preserving historical archives.

The Major Periods of Biblical History

The Time of the Patriarchs (1850–1250 B.C.)

The period from Abraham to Joseph is recounted in Genesis 12–50. Historically, this was a period of vast migrations in the Middle East, with clans of herders moving freely from Mesopotamia down through the Fertile Crescent into present-day Israel. Egypt had been a dominant power in the Middle East for more than 2,000 years prior to that time. Egypt's might was counterbalanced by a succession of powerful dynasties at the eastern end of the Fertile Crescent, including the Persians, Assyrians, and Babylonians. Israel, located geographically between those two areas, would often be the battleground for those opposing forces.

Few firm historical traditions exist from this period but the general picture provided in the biblical traditions about the patriarchs does reflect something of the nomadic lifestyle and familial religion typical of the period.

The Exodus, Wilderness Wandering, and Settlement in the Land (1250–1130 B.C.)

This period is covered in Exodus, Deuteronomy, Numbers, and Joshua. The story of Israel as a unified people begins in Egypt with the stories about Moses and the miraculous Exodus from Egypt. During a period of wandering in the desert, the covenant was formed with the LORD, the God of Israel. Under the leadership of Joshua, Israel finally breaks through into the Promised Land, driving the native Canaanites before them.

There is considerable debate about the historical background to this period. Some scholars, particularly conservative ones, are willing to accept the biblical portrayal at face value: namely that there was a mass migration of Hebrews from Egypt and that they invaded the regions of Israel with military force and thereby gained possession of the land.

The lack of clear archaeological evidence supporting such a vast military conquest and some ambiguity in the biblical traditions themselves have led other historians to surmise that both the migration from Egypt and the possession of the land took place over a longer period of time. Some Hebrew tribes may have already settled in Israel prior to the Exodus, and joined with the incoming tribes at a later period. While some Canaanite cities may have been taken by force, some of the land was probably settled in a peaceful fashion.

In any event, the Bible sees this process as a dramatic act of deliverance by God and as the historic beginning of the story of Israel.

The Period of the Judges (1130–1020 B.C.)

This early period of Israelite history is narrated in the book of Judges. It is clear that the Israelites at first resisted the idea of a strong central government. They preferred a loosely organized federation of clans or tribes ruled by charismatic leaders called judges. Only the LORD could claim the right to be called "King." This independent spirit and aversion to the monarchy goes deep into the consciousness of Israel.

The Monarchy (1020–587 B.C.)

This long, but in fact highly diverse, period of Israel's history is taken up in the books of 1 and 2 Samuel; 1 and 2 Kings; and a parallel account in 1 and 2 Chronicles.

The transition from the more informal and charismatic leadership under the judges to the more institutional form of the monarchy begins with Saul (about 1020–1000 B.C.) but reaches its zenith with David (1000–960 B.C.) and Solomon (960–930 B.C.). Threats from surrounding peoples and the need for more complex social organization gradually led Israel to adopt a monarchical form of government. David eventually unified diverse groups of people under a single government system, ruled from his new centrally located capital of Jerusalem. Under David and his son Solomon, Israel's territories greatly expanded.

The united kingdom forged by David did not last very long. Solomon strained it by increasing taxation and by lack of sensitivity to the old tribal loyalties. When Solomon's son Rehoboam ascended to the throne, the seams between north and south split and the separate kingdoms of Judah in the south and Israel in the north began. This divided monarchy would last until 724 B.C., when the Assyrian empire would crush the northern kingdom. Judah would survive until the Babylonian invasion of 587 B.C.

The biblical account has little respect for the northern rulers and takes a critical view of most of the kings of Judah as well, considering them unfaithful to the covenant. During this period the great prophetic movement would ignite in Israel. Elijah, Elisha, Amos, and Hosea were prophets in the northern kingdom. Isaiah served as court prophet to the kings of Judah.

Exile and Return (587–332 B.C.)

This crucial period of Israelite history is narrated in 2 Kings 24–25 and in the books of Ezra and Nehemiah. In the 590s B.C. the Babylonians took over Judah and installed a puppet king; when, in 587, that king attempted a rebellion, the Babylonians moved in with great force. They destroyed most of Jerusalem, pulled down the Temple, and forced all but the lowest members of society into exile.

The Babylonian captivity would last almost 50 years. Systematic deportation as a way of subduing conquered peoples had been used first by the Assyrians and then by the Babylonians. Only a small remnant of Israelites was left behind under the firm control of Babylonian officials. When the exiled Jews eventually returned, they considered the people who had stayed behind as somehow corrupt and would not allow them to take part in the reconstruction of Israel, a source of bitterness that would lead to the sharp divisions between Jews and Samaritans so obvious in the New Testament period.

Under the leadership of Ezra and Nehemiah, Jerusalem and its Temple were rebuilt. But Israel was now only a small and fragile nation, clustered around Jerusalem and very concerned with preserving its identity.

The Greek Conquest and the Rise of the Hasmoneans (332–39 B.C.)

This is a turbulent part of Israelite history, reflected in 1 and 2 Maccabees and Daniel.

Alexander conquered Palestine in 332 B.C., beginning a period in which Greek culture would have a strong impact on the life of Israel. After his death, the Middle Eastern portion of Alexander's empire was divided between the Seleucid dynasty, which ruled from Syria, and the Ptolemies, ruling from Egypt. The Ptolemaic dynasty controlled Israel from approximately 332 to 199 B.C. Their generally benign rule gave way to the Seleucids, who attempted to impose Greek culture and taxation in a more rigorous fashion. Seleucid ruthlessness eventually triggered the Maccabean revolt, which by 160 B.C. had thrown off the yoke of the Seleucids against incredible odds.

The Jewish dynasty of the Hasmonean family now began a 100-year reign. The Hasmonean kings proved to be as corrupt and ruthless as the foreigners who had preceded them. Reactions by pious Jews to the compromises of the Hasmoneans and their Jerusalem aristocracy would give rise to protest groups such as the Essenes and Pharisees. By 60 B.C. Roman influence was growing in the Middle East and brought pressure on Israel itself. The Hasmonean period came to an end with the emergence of Herod the Great, a vassal of the Romans, who would unify the country and hold it in his grip.

The Roman Period (39 B.C.–A.D. 100)

The New Testament writings emerge during this period of biblical history. With the death of Herod in 4 B.C., the Romans divided Israel among his three sons. Eventually the Romans removed the cruel and incompetent Archaelaus, taking over direct rule of Judah and Samaria.

Herod Philip and Herod Antipas would continue to govern in the regions of Upper Galilee, Lower Galilee, and the Transjordan (see Map 12).

Roman rule and its heavy taxation proved intolerable to the Jewish people. Tensions mounted all during the first half of the first century, exploding into revolution in A.D. 66. That revolt would be violently suppressed by the Romans, climaxing with the destruction of Jerusalem and its great Temple in A.D. 70. That event would change the complexion of Judaism forever. Another short-lived revolt would break out in A.D. 132. The Romans would continue to occupy Palestine until the time of the Byzantine empire. All of these events have left a profound impression on the writings of the New Testament.

THE PENTATEUCH

What Is the Pentateuch?

In the United States, the Declaration of Independence, the Constitution, and the Bill of Rights stand as the foundational documents on which the democratic system of government is based. No matter what new laws are written or policies are made, every piece of legislation, every judicial decision is ultimately judged in light of those original documents.

The foundation documents for the people of Israel are the books we now commonly refer to as the Pentateuch, the first five books of the Bible. These books do more than introduce the rest of the Bible: they are the very foundation on which the rest of the Scriptures stand. The Pentateuch serves as the blueprint or constitution by which all other Scripture is interpreted. By understanding the special nature and special role of these first five books of the Old Testament, we will have a better understanding of the entire Bible.

"Pentateuch" means "five scrolls." Rather than five distinct books, however, what we are really dealing with is one book in five volumes. Even in biblical times the Pentateuch was considered a single work. Jewish tradition calls it "Torah," which is often translated as "law" but really means "teaching" or "instruction." In the Torah we find the basic teachings of the Jewish faith. The chart below gives an overview of the Pentateuch.

Partly because the book of Deuteronomy leads into the books of Joshua and Judges, the Table of Contents of the New American Bible lists eight books under the heading "Pentateuch" and groups the books of the Old Testament into four categories: The Pentateuch, The Historical Books, The Wisdom Books, and the Prophetic Books. The Jewish Bible, which has its own

The Pentateuch

Genesis	Origins: Creation and stories of primeval times. Abraham, Isaac, Jacob, Joseph: The great ancestors of the Jewish people.
Exodus	God chooses Moses to deliver Israelites from slavery in Egypt. The giving of the Law at Mt. Sinai. Many laws regarding daily life and religious practice.
Leviticus	Laws for the people of God relating to sacrifice, priesthood, and religious feasts. Recurring call to be "holy" as God is holy.
Numbers	More laws. Desert wanderings and military exploits on the way to the Promised Land. Repeated acts of unfaithfulness to God and Moses extend the wandering to 40 years.
Deuteronomy	A "second law" that sums up the significance of the Exodus. Moses' farewell speech delivered at the borders of the Promised Land, in which Moses warns people they must obey the covenant or risk losing the land.

order, groups the biblical books differently, under three headings:

The Law (Torah)

**Genesis; Exodus; Leviticus;
Numbers; Deuteronomy**

The Prophets	*The Writings*
Former Prophets:	Ruth; Song of Songs;
Joshua; Judges;	Ecclesiastes;
1 and 2 Samuel	Lamentations;
(regarded as one	Esther; Daniel;
book); Psalms;	Ezra-Nehemiah;
Job; Proverbs;	1 and 2 Chronicles
1 and 2 Kings	(regarded as one book).
(regarded as one	
book).	
Latter Prophets: Isaiah;	
Jeremiah; Ezekiel;	
The Book of the	
Twelve (minor	
prophets).	

This arrangement helps us see that the Pentateuch is the source from which all the other books of the Old Testament flow. It may be surprising to find books of history together with those of prophetic writing in the "Prophets" column. But there is an important message in that fact: both the teaching of the prophets and Israel's life-experience call the people back to fidelity to the teachings of the Pentateuch. In our own lives, we often have to face unpleasant consequences of our own actions. Often, these experiences remind us of the differences between right and wrong that we learned when we were younger. In the same way, Israel had both the words of the prophets and their own history to help them determine how well or how poorly they had lived out the message of the Pentateuch in their life as a nation. Even when they were deaf to the prophets' words, the messes they frequently found themselves in were sufficient to remind them that they had indeed been unfaithful to God and the Law.

The Writings are a group of books that also flow out of the Pentateuch. Primarily they contain reflections and explanations intended to help us live the message of the Torah. In short, all the other books of the Old Testament are the result of Israel's reflection on the Torah.

TaNaK Modern Hebrew uses the acronym TNK (pronounced "Tenak") to refer to the Bible. The acronym consists of the first letters of the Hebrew words for the Law (Torah), the Prophets (Nebi'im), and the Writings (Ketubim).

The Pentateuch and the Canon of Scripture

None of the books in the Bible got there by accident. Every decision about whether to include a certain book was carefully thought out, discussed, and probably hotly debated. The final decisions make a difference. When we read the books of the Bible we read them as part of a collection of books, and how we interpret the message of a book is determined, at least in part, by where that book stands in relation to other books. So as we begin to study the Old Testament we will want to determine why Genesis, Exodus, Leviticus, Numbers, and Deuteronomy appear in that order.

How do we do that? By asking questions about the books themselves, about the times during which they were written, and about their meaning for us today. For example:

1. Literary Shape: What kind of literature is this? Is it poetry, story, history, prophecy, myth, or some other form of writing?

2. Historical Development: How did separate pieces of writing composed by different authors come to be put together to make the present book?

3. Actual History: What was happening in Israel during the period this book describes?

Canon is the term used to refer to the list of officially approved books contained in the Bible. It comes from a Greek word meaning "reed, straight stick," that came to mean "ruler, measuring stick." Different groups—Jews, Catholics, Orthodox Christians, and Protestants—have different canons for their Bibles, but in each case there is an official "measure" for what is to be included.

4. Religious Significance: What is the religious message of the book for a modern reader?

Story and Law

We said above that one of the first questions we put to a scripture text is "What kind of literature is it?" It is easy to see from just looking at the pages of the New American Bible that the bulk of the Pentateuch is prose rather than poetry. If you examine the five books carefully, you will soon find that two kinds of prose dominate: laws and stories (narratives). Generally, each book contains some of each, although either stories or laws might predominate. Sections of stories regularly alternate with sections of laws, but within every story segment you will find scattered laws and commands, and in every listing of laws you will find a healthy episode or two of story. The breakdown of laws and narratives is illustrated in the table below.

The stories of the Pentateuch are part of a larger story that continues into the books listed under the Former Prophets (Joshua, Judges, Samuel, Kings). The Pentateuch wraps its many laws in a package of stories that trace the "history" of the world from the moment of creation down to the time of the total collapse of the nation of Israel, just before the Babylonian Exile.

The Larger Picture

The Pentateuch ends with the chosen people standing on the borders of the Promised Land. But the story continues. The books of Joshua and Judges tell the story of the people's entry into the land: stories of conquest and the gradual settling of the land and stories of great military leaders called judges. The books of 1 and 2 Samuel recount how the people abandoned tribal rule and accepted kingship. The two books of Kings present stories of the life of Israel under the kings up to the time of the exile. All of them use the foundation of the Pentateuch to show how Israel's faithfulness to the laws affected its story.

The rich blending of laws and story in the Pentateuch was intentional. Its purpose was to help readers see the many laws as part of their unfolding story. They were not merely regulations tacked on to their life here and there; they were the very stuff of which their life as a nation was made. Without the Law, Israel would have had no story to tell.

A modern reader might be puzzled to find lists of the laws the Congress passed in a given period as part of a history of the United States. But in order to understand the history and culture of the country, we would have to know about the laws. Likewise, in biblical times awareness of the Law brought with it an awareness of how the lives of the ancestors were guided by the same laws. It made the Israelites aware of their continuity with

Book	Content
Genesis	Nearly all stories (Gn 1–50)
Exodus	Half stories (Ex 1–10; 24; 31–34); half laws (Ex 20–23; 25–30; 35–40)
Leviticus	Nearly all laws (Lv 1–27)
Numbers	Half stories (Nm 1–19; 20–26; 31–33); half laws (Nm 1–10; 18–19; 27–30; 34–36)
Deuteronomy	Nearly all laws (Dt 1–34)

	Stories	Laws
Genesis	From Creation to the days of the Patriarchs.	
Exodus	Leaving slavery in Egypt.	Laws delivered to Moses on
Leviticus	Meeting God at Mt. Sinai.	Mt. Sinai that are to become the
Numbers	Desert wanderings and reaching the borders of the Promised Land.	basis of the covenant between God and Israel, and many more laws Moses "receives" from God that govern every aspect of daily life.
Deuteronomy		Moses sums up the Law and applies it to life in the land.

those who went before them. They might think, "Our ancestors obeyed these laws, and we obey these laws, and as a result we are one people."

This sense of continuity helped the Hebrews see the Law as a gift from God. It not only taught them how to live, but, more importantly, it helped assure that they would live. By being faithful to the Law the people were maintaining their end of their relationship with God: "If you keep my commandments, I will be your God and you will be my people." Fidelity meant protection, and protection meant existence.

The Structure of the Pentateuch

Try thinking about the structure of the Pentateuch as a plan within a plan. The plan begins in Genesis with God creating a good world so humanity can come to know and share in God's goodness. When humanity fails to live up to God's hopes (Gn 1–11), God chooses a family, Abraham's, that will be God's special means of revealing the divine goodness to all nations (Gn 12–50). This people will discover God's goodness through hardship (slavery) and deliverance (Exodus) and learn to be an obedient and holy people (Lv and Nm 1–10). Then God will lead them to a promised land (Nm 10–36), which they will keep only if they remain obedient and loyal (Deuteronomy). The diagram below illustrates this plan-within-a-plan structure.

History in the Bible

Anywhere something of importance happens today newspaper and television reporters, photographers, and video cameras record every moment. We live in a world of instant replays where you don't have to wonder what someone said or did; you can even play it back in slow motion. In the ancient world, such technology, of course, was not available.

In a culture like ours, so dominated by science, we value exact observation and documentation for its own sake. We expect historians to prove the claims they make in their books with clear documentation. And we expect them to be unbiased reporters, not propaganda peddlers. That's a lot to ask in any age; even trained historians are never totally free of bias and have their own point of view that colors what they write. If modern historians are never entirely objective even when it's expected of them, then we certainly cannot hope for that kind of objectivity from ancient writers who never made it their goal.

Even if they had wanted that kind of accuracy, ancient writers had no way to get much of the historical information. The reason that little or no information was preserved for its own sake was that history was seen not as a record of "what happened," but as a lesson people were to learn from. History was written to teach that one kind of behavior or attitude was more appropriate than another. It was written more like newspaper editorials, which take sides and argue for their favorite causes.

The bottom line is that ancient "history" was more interested in explaining why something happened than in what happened. It was more concerned with the meaning of events than in an accurate record of those events.

God's Plan: Create Humanity to Praise and Share God's Goodness		
First Plan	**New Plan:** Choose family-nation to teach all nations to praise and share God's goodness.	
Creation. Adam and Eve Gn 1–2 and all creation are created good.		
	Promise to Patriarchs: Abraham, Isaac, Jacob, Joseph.	Gn 12–50
Sin. Human sin and Gn 3–11 alienation grow.	Escape from Egypt to Mt. Sinai.	Ex 1–15
	Laws given to teach Israel to be a holy people.	Ex 19–40 Lv 1–27 Nm 1–10
	Journey to the Promised Land.	Nm 10–36
	Summary of law. Ready to enter Land.	Dt 1–34

History or Theology?

While the Pentateuch is a complete story, it is in no way a complete history. It picks and chooses the events and themes it wants to talk about. And it only talks about those things that will teach a religious lesson. What we have here is a handbook or rule book for right living, a theology book much more than any real history of the people. That is why laws are so generously sprinkled in among the stories. They were part of the lesson the stories were meant to teach.

Clearly, many of the stories in the Pentateuch are not at all about ordinary time in history. Genesis 1–11, for example, does not fit the category of history because it treats the creation of the world and the first events of human existence in a way that does not give them any definite context of place or time. By trying to answer universal questions—questions like: Why did God make humans this way? Why do we sin? Why do we die? Why is it hard to obey God? Why are men and women different?—the stories of Genesis 1–11 fall into the literary genre of myth. Even the stories of the patriarchs and matriarchs in Genesis 12–50 are not like modern history. Although based on real history, they resemble folktale hero stories, and it is hard to pin them down to exact locations and events.

Keep these insights in mind when you run into problems of logic in one of the books. For example, in Genesis 4 Cain and Abel are the only two children of Adam and Eve. Yet, after killing Abel, Cain is banished and, we are told, has "relations with his wife." If this were a real history, we would have to ask how Cain could have a wife when Adam and Eve were the only other living human beings at the time.

The author's intent obviously centers not on literal facts, but on a religious lesson, here concerning how the world came to be populated. Whether or not that lesson is consistent with what has previously been said does not concern the author.

But while it is important not to make the mistake of thinking that the Pentateuch is a record of history, it is also important not to think of it as just a clever story pulled from someone's imagination. It is a masterwork, a work of genius that makes God known to us. In beautiful language and powerful imagery it speaks of humanity's tendency toward sin, about the failure of most of the world to know God, and of God's choice of Israel to demonstrate to the world God's loving concern for humanity. The marvelous storytelling of the Pentateuch reveals God by focusing on a number of central events: the choice of the patriarchs, the giving of the Law, the making of a covenant, and the guidance through the wilderness to a promised land.

Myth "Myth" has many different meanings. Often it is used to refer to something that is false or unreliable: "The story of George Washington chopping down the cherry tree is a myth." But that familiar use of the word is misleading. Narrowly defined, the term refers to traditional stories about heroes, gods, or demi-gods. Defined very broadly, a myth is a story, factual or not, that people live by and that gives meaning to their lives. For instance, Americans have a national ideal of people from various parts of the world coming to this country and being able to participate in "the American dream" of a better life for themselves and their children. It is a powerful motivator in our country regardless of its "truth."

Scholars generally understand myths as attempts by ancient peoples to understand the mysteries of their existence, usually by explaining things as being the result of the actions of divine beings. Myths narrate a "sacred history" and are therefore special, sacred stories. But rather than providing answers, myths offer insights. They get at the core meaning of life and reality. For ancient peoples "myth" meant a "true story." What distinguishes myths is that they are stories that, although they may not be factual, convey a deeper truth about ultimate questions. Myths, therefore, do not contradict scientific knowledge, but rather answer a different question: not, "How did this happen?" but "What does this mean?"

Patriarchs The forefathers of the Israelites, that is, Abraham, Isaac, and Jacob. Because he figures so prominently in the Genesis patriarchal stories, Joseph is often designated a patriarch as well. The New Testament also refers to David and the twelve sons of Jacob as patriarchs. The term overlooks the significance of the wives of these men without whom God's plan would not have moved forward. These matriarchs, Sarah, Rebekah, Rachel, and Leah, can be included by the use of expressions like "forebears," "ancestors," or "patriarchs and matriarchs."

Good storytelling can give us pleasure, teach us about history, and give us philosophical and theological insights. As a great work of storytelling the Pentateuch is multilayered. It tells history, but it does not allow us to question it too closely about exact descriptions. It presents religious and theological lessons but warns us not to treat it like a catechism filled with lists of truths. Most of all it tells a story. The story teaches us by letting us compare our experience with that of the Hebrew people. As we read we begin to discover that their story and our story are intertwined, that the God who was at work in the lives of the Hebrew people works in similar ways in our own lives.

Historical Dating of Pentateuch Traditions

Despite many difficulties, we are not completely in the dark when it comes to dating some of the events of the Pentateuch. Archaeological digs in ancient sites have produced tablets and other records that offer a good idea of what each different period in the second millennium B.C. was like, so we can date the major events of the Pentateuch with a fair degree of confidence.

The patriarchal narratives fall somewhere between 2000 and 1500 B.C., the Exodus event between 1450 and 1250 B.C., and the invasion of the land of Palestine around 1250 to 1200 B.C. Nonbiblical historical information makes some dates more likely than others: Since Egypt was governed by foreign rulers between 1750 B.C. and 1550 B.C., the story of how Joseph, a foreigner,

Did Moses Write the Pentateuch?

For more than 2,000 years Moses was considered the author of the Pentateuch even though no book of the Bible specifically names him as the author. The Pentateuch was often called "the Book of Moses," and throughout the Bible there are frequent references to the "Law of Moses." Jesus, like most of his contemporaries, took for granted that Moses authored the Pentateuch (see, for instance, Lk 16, 29.31; 20, 37).

But even in the ancient world some questioned whether Moses could really have written the entire Pentateuch. How, for example could Moses have written about his own death as in Deuteronomy 34, 5–12? Many of the laws supposedly written by Moses deal with situations that occurred much later than the time when Moses led the people through the desert. Other evidence in the Bible leads scholars to believe the Pentateuch did not exist in its present state until approximately 450 B.C.—nearly 800 years after Moses' death.

No one can say for certain who did write the Pentateuch, but there is no question that Moses played a unique and important role in the events recorded in these books. Modern scholars do not try to prove that Moses directly authored the written books of the Pentateuch. As Catholics, our belief that the Bible is divinely inspired makes the identity of its human author an issue of limited importance. Whatever else we may say, Moses may be regarded as the founder of the Israelite faith.

rises to power best fits this time period. Exodus 1, 11 says the enslaved Israelites built the cities of Pithom and Rameses, pointing to the reign of Seti I as the period of enslavement and the reign of Rameses II as the time of the Exodus.

How Scholars Study the Pentateuch: The Art of Interpretation

Studying the Bible is not easy. Because it was written over many centuries by people living in cultures very different from our own, we cannot simply expect to pick up a Bible and be able to grasp its meaning in its entirety. On the other hand, we must not be intimidated by the amount of scholarly knowledge it takes to understand the Bible properly, so that we start to feel it belongs only to some special caste. The reality lies somewhere in the middle. With some scholarly help, like that provided by this study guide and the excellent footnotes of the New American Bible, a layperson should be able to read the Bible intelligently and find in it religious meaning for his or her life.

When we read the Bible we are looking for two things: what the text meant to its original author and audience, and what it means now to us, its modern readers. (See "How to Read the Bible RG 28–30.) We must be careful, however, not to let one meaning cancel out the other. When we seek the original meaning of a text, we do not rule out the possibility that over the centuries a particular text may have taken on more meaning than even the author intended. So what it meant then and what it means now are not necessarily the same thing.

Some modern churchgoers have rejected scholarly theories and methods of study because they feel these have robbed the Bible of its status as God's inspired Word and have turned it into an ordinary literary document. Why so negative a reaction? Maybe because some scholars approach the Bible with the assumption that they may not use God as the explanation for anything. While they would not deny the possibility of miracles, they believe that what is called the "critical method" requires them to propose natural explanations whenever such explanations are plausible. Even discussions of inspiration are considered off-limits by some scholars. If you read the Bible only on this level, you might think it would tell you little of religious value.

But here is the heart of the matter: The critical method helps us to unlock and clarify what is going on in a text. How? First, by connecting the text to historical events that we may have learned about through nonbiblical sources; second, by helping us understand unusual cultural customs; and third, by helping us understand special literary styles of expression that are no longer in use today.

Without scientific study we would not comprehend those things that are not part of our culture. When archaeologists dig up clay tablets that contain long-lost information, biblical scholars become the bridge that connects that information with the Bible. They study how language works, how people hand down traditions, and how they record events and tell folk tales. All this helps us understand how biblical stories and laws were put together.

All writing is interpretation. The ancient authors interpreted what they thought God was communicating; the churches and synagogues interpret what these words of revelation mean for their congregations. Modern scholars and believing readers must also interpret and decide what relevance these long-ago stories and events have for their lives. Everyone who reads the Bible asks "What does it mean?" But we can find a full answer only if our reading is illuminated by the twin lights of faith and scientific knowledge of the past. And nowhere in the Bible is this more crucial than in reading the Pentateuch.

The study of the Pentateuch has a long history that can be traced back even to the time of Jesus as illustrated in the chart on the next page.

Exegesis The critical or scholarly explanation of a Bible passage. (The term means "to bring out" and refers to the process of explaining meaning.)

Hermeneutics is a term often used interchangeably with exegesis. While exegesis tries to discover what a passage meant in its original context (time and place of composition), hermeneutics uses exegesis to ask what the text means for us now. (The term comes from Hermes, the Greek messenger god, and means "interpretation.")

How the Bible Has Been Read in History

New Testament Times (Jesus and writers of New Testament books)	Scripture viewed as prophecy of Jesus, and used to show connection between Jesus and what went before him.
Early Church (the time after the Apostles to the sixth century)	Scripture read allegorically. Literal meaning rejected because Bible contains deeper meanings put there (inspired) by God. Therefore Bible always says more than the author intended to say.
Medieval Period (from the seventh century through the Renaissance and Reformation)	Allegorical reading still predominates. Growing respect for literal meaning of text. But much of Old Testament still viewed as prediction of Jesus.
Modern Study (from the seventeenth century to the twentieth century)	Critical study of texts. Four-sources theory and source criticism developed. Development of form criticism—the search for literary genres and the earliest and smallest literary units of tradition—and transmission history—the account of how the current texts came to be.

New Testament Times

In New Testament times, Jesus and the authors of various New Testament books referred to texts from the Bible, which at that time was simply the Hebrew Scriptures, what Christians now call the Old Testament. Usually they were referring to stories that were cited as proofs for something Jesus or one of the apostles was teaching. Some stories from the Pentateuch were treated as what has been called a *type,* in which an Old Testament figure is seen as a foreshadowing of a later character—like Abraham, who was seen as a forerunner of the Christian believer, or Isaac, who was seen as a foreshadowing of Jesus. The New Testament treats many passages from the Pentateuch, the Prophets, and the Psalms as a type of prophecy that predicts Jesus and helps explain his suffering, death, and resurrection. It would be fair to say that the New Testament uses the Bible primarily to show the deep connection between Jesus and what went before him.

Early Church

The early Church (the community of believers from about A.D. 100 to 300) saw the Bible operating on three levels of meaning. First, there was the literal or historical meaning of the text. Then there was the *spiritual* or *allegorical* sense: a deep, often hidden, layer that went beyond the literal. The third level expressed the *moral* lesson the text meant to teach.

Level two, the spiritual level, was considered most important. Since Scripture is inspired writing, pious believers thought it therefore must contain layers of meaning of which the author was not even aware. God, after all, was using the ancient author to point the way to Jesus. The meaning of a passage, then, could not be limited to what the author intended to say. The full meaning was much deeper, more spiritual, and not immediately obvious.

This attitude led to an almost total disregard for the literal meaning of the text. All the focus was on the so-called spiritual meaning intended by God. Because of the conviction that every word of Scripture contained a prophecy about Jesus, and thus always said more than it seemed to say, the allegorical method flourished in the early Church.

The Medieval Period

The medieval world was largely a period in love with the allegorical approach, and students of the Bible relied heavily on the opinions of the early Church writers regarding each passage of Scripture. But the rise of scholasticism in the twelfth and thirteenth centuries shifted the focus toward a clear and literal interpretation of Bible texts. Medieval thinkers, however, lacked a knowledge of Hebrew and Greek with which to study the original words, and they still viewed the Bible as prophecy rather than as a history of a people's experience of God working in their lives. So they, too, read the Bible more as a book about Christ and the Church than about Israel.

Modern Study

Truly modern study of the Bible began with a French priest named Richard Simon (1678) who detected different literary styles within the book of Genesis. He concluded that Moses did not write the Pentateuch from scratch, but probably was quoting sources that existed before him. This insight earned him Church condemnation, but it also opened the door for further critical study.

In the next century scholars began investigating the biblical passages that regularly call God by the proper name "Yahweh" (the *New American Bible* renders it as "LORD"), and those that generally call God by the more generic term, "Elohim" (which the *NAB* renders as "God"). Even though the passages that use the two names are intermixed, they run through the entire Pentateuch (up to the book of Numbers) as two parallel stories.

New questions arose. Were these two separate written works that told the same history of Israel, or was one original story embellished and eventually turned into two different versions? The debate was intense. Then scholars began to notice that the so called "Elohist" passages really contained two separate accounts themselves. The one that was more narrative and interested in God's great interventions in history was called the Elohist strand, while the other, which was more concerned with priestly and ritual actions, was called the Priestly strand.

By the mid-1800s scholars generally agreed that there were in fact three independent versions of the Pentateuch's basic story, which could be labeled with the initials J (for "Jahvist," from the German spelling of Yahweh), E (for Elohist), and P (for Priestly). The book of Deuteronomy was considered a fourth and totally separate source of its own, and received the label D. These traditions have often been called "documents," but that name can be misleading if it leads us to think of fully written-out manuscripts containing the different traditions. Rather, these traditions were probably much more fragmentary, consisting of numerous materials, some written, some oral, that were combined into our current books over a lengthy period of time.

The reason that scholars think the first five books of the Bible were put together in this way is that it accounts for certain oddities in the text better than any other explanation that has been proposed.

J and E are generally seen as having been combined at an early stage (and some scholars doubt the existence of a fully-formed E source at all). As a separate source, J presumably dates from the time of David (approximately 1000–960 B.C.) or shortly thereafter, and the E material could have been added after the destruction of the northern kingdom in 722/721. P was assembled later, perhaps during the exile in Babylon (when the First Temple had been destroyed in 587/586), although it reflects materials that were known at least to the priests involved in Temple worship during the time from Solomon (960–920) to the exile. D dates from the reign of King Josiah (640–609) and seems to have been the basis for the Temple reform that was undertaken at the time of his reign.

The J source is marked by the use of the Hebrew word translated LORD in the *NAB:* YHWH or "Yahweh" (German spelling "Jahveh"). The E source, on the other hand, generally uses the word "God" ('Elohim). The Priestly source contains most of the rules for Temple worship, genealogical lists, and legal materials. D designates primarily the separate writer responsible for Deuteronomy. J, E, and P were combined into the first four books at some time during or after the exile in Babylon.

None of these sources have been discovered as separate documents or manuscripts. But scholars have concluded that the first five books, as they now exist, contain variations within particular sections that can best be accounted for by assuming that someone was trying to combine two or more versions of an event into one account.

For example, in the story of the flood (Genesis chapters 6–8), there seem to be two different timelines: one of 40 days plus a few weeks (Gn 7, 17; 8, 6.8.10.12), and one of 150 days plus 150 days plus a few months (Gn 7, 24; 8, 3.5) for a total of a year and 10 days (7, 11; 8, 13–14). There also seems to be a difference regarding the numbers of animals to be brought into the ark: one pair of each creature (6, 19–20) or one pair of the unclean and seven pairs of the clean creatures (7, 2–3). These differences can be

Four Sources Theory

Source and Characteristics	Why Written
J: Yahwist	
Written in tenth or ninth century B.C. Literary artist. Loves stories. Focus on the heart. Earthy, frank language. Emphasis on God's closeness with humanity. Uses name Yahweh for God (in German, spelled "Jahveh," hence the J). Favors strong leaders like David. Southern tradition.	Written in Jerusalem to show that promises to Abraham were fulfilled in the empire of David.
E: Elohist	
Written after 900 B.C. Uses Elohim for God's name. Stresses role of the prophet. Contains strong tone of challenge and stress on morality. Emphasizes role of Jacob and the significance of northern kingdom ideas and places. Northern tradition reflecting anti-Jerusalem view. Like D it stresses that the covenant with Moses is more important than kingship.	After the division of the kingdom, this version gathered up traditions to support the legitimacy of northern kings and institutions.
P: Priestly	
Much of the material dates to eight and seventh centuries B.C., but some materials probably written in sixth century B.C. Very strong interest in ritual and priesthood. Less focus on story and more on religious symbols. Style is more formal. God is more distant, less intimately involved with human beings. Stresses obedience to Law and permanence of God's blessing. The dominant tradition in Pentateuch. Reflects southern point of view. The P editors arranged the four sources into our present Pentateuch around 500 B.C.	Some of the P material reflects and responds to the needs of the exiles in the sixth century B.C.
D: Deuteronomist	
Written in eighth and seventh centuries B.C. Emphasizes role of family (parents) for instruction and fidelity to covenant. Moralistic: stresses preaching and exhortation. Style is eloquent; many often-repeated verbal formulas. Emphasizes Jerusalem as sole place of worship. Northern tradition, which stresses covenant over kingship.	Reassess J and E traditions in light of pagan inroads and unfaithful kings.

explained by the hypothesis that there were two accounts of the flood, and that a later compiler brought them both together. Instead of ironing out the differences, however, the compiler regarded at least some of them as important, so kept them in, even though they were contradictory.

Eventually a German scholar, Julius Wellhausen, proposed dates for the writing of each version and speculated on the historical situation that created the need for each different telling of the history. All this came to be known as the "four source theory," and the method of study is called *source criticism*. Each strand responds to

The Four Sources and the Four Characteristics ("P's")

Who	What	How
Yahwist	Emphasizes role of **Poet**	Storytelling
Elohist	Emphasizes role of **Prophet**	Challenging
Priestly	Emphasizes role of **Priest**	Legislating
Deuteronomist	Emphasizes role of **Parents**	Exhorting

a particular situation or need in the life of the nation, incorporates the particular worldview of its author-editor, and has a distinctive style. This theory is outlined in the table on RG 43.

J and E existed side by side while the two kingdoms lasted from 930 to 722 B.C. (See the guide to the historical books.) When the northern kingdom fell, its E story was carried down to Judah by refugees, and there it was eventually combined (around 700 B.C.) with J into a single account. Still later, when Judah itself fell in 587 B.C. and during its exile, D and P were combined with JE to make our final JEPD. Editors from the Priestly circles applied the final touches. Each of the sources has a distinctive style and emphasis, as described in the table above.

All this speculation on sources led to even more research into the original units that made up each source. Where did the individual incidents, poems, stories, and laws come from? This search for the earliest and smallest units of the tradition gave birth to a new way of studying the Bible called *form criticism*. By identifying the special form of a poem or hymn or law or narrative, scholars thought they could probably determine the cultural-historical situation from which it came.

Some scholars have focused on the *transmission history* of a text, looking at how traditions get passed on and grow or change. Before reaching the final form they have today, original statements, stories, and laws went through a process of being combined with other units, and then combined again in still larger works. Study of how collections grew and how stories were sometimes arranged into a new order helps us understand how they were used and the meaning they were given by different generations. For example, the story of Exodus was the story of escaping from an oppressive situation. However, later on, in the context of the Law and the land, the story of Exodus became a story about the celebration of a feast year

after year: the Passover. The bread, the lamb, and the bitter herbs all became parts of the yearly ritual Passover celebration.

Reflecting on the Message of the Pentateuch

Like navigating a vast ocean, finding our way through the vast array of materials in the Pentateuch can be challenging. A lighthouse now and then can make the going easier. The Pentateuch provides these in the form of themes and topics that recur over and over again. The demand for obedience to God's will, which is seen as a sign of faith, and God's giving of the covenant, which is seen as a sign of God's love, are examples of such lighthouses. Whether it is Adam and Eve's failure to obey, or Moses' own failure when striking the rock for water in Numbers 20, it is clear that obedience is a major issue. Many other examples could be given. In fact, it is difficult trying to limit the themes to a specific number. Every time we read, new themes may capture our imagination or move our hearts.

We will have an easier time understanding the major theological themes of the Pentateuch if we remember that more than being a book *of* or *by* God, the Bible is a book *about* God. Through its many themes and stories, the Pentateuch reveals a God whom Israel has come to know as the one God, who acts in human history, and who has chosen Israel in a special way. All the themes of the Pentateuch reveal God's intimate relationship with people, emphasizing the need for humanity to respond to God's initiative.

Ten Central Themes

God Created a Good World

When Genesis tells us God spoke the world into being, it means that creation was no accident, but part of a divine plan causing all things to work together in harmony. God judged all creation as "very good" (Gn 1, 31). Thus, no matter how bad things get, we must remember that the original blessing is never fully lost and that, ultimately, goodness will prevail.

God Has Blessed Human Life

Twice Genesis tells us that God blessed the human race (Gn 1, 28; 9, 1). If the world is good, so is all life within it.

Humanity Has a Tendency to Sin

Much of the biblical story presents human beings as disobedient and sinful, ignoring God's will. Many of the laws, therefore, center on atonement (particularly in Leviticus) and on the need to repent and turn back to God (Deuteronomy particularly).

God Is a God of Mercy

If humanity tends toward rebellion, God tends toward forgiveness and mercy. God spares Adam and Eve, Cain and Noah, and others in order to give the human race a new start each time after it sins. In the Exodus event, God is revealed above all else as a liberating God.

God Keeps Promises

God promised Noah, Abraham, Isaac, Jacob, and Moses that they would become a great people, and repeatedly the Pentateuch stresses the fulfillment of that promise. Israel's God is a God of the future, not one patterned on the recurring cycles of nature. God inspires hope. Believers can expect that God can act in new and decisive ways.

The Covenant Binds God to Israel

All people believe their god relates to them somehow, but only in Israel do we find a relationship based on love, permanent loyalty, and respect for the human partner. The covenant is the heart of biblical faith because it expresses a unique bond between God and people.

The Law Expresses Israel's Bond to God

The covenant establishes a relationship, but the laws of the Pentateuch show how that relationship can be lived out by the people. Laws are not restrictive rules; they are a joyful way of living that expresses faith in actions as well as words.

Worship Is Praise Is Thanksgiving

An odd way to express a simple but important idea: To pray is to praise, and to praise is to thank God. The Pentateuch constantly reminds Israel of what God has done for them, and the laws express the need to rejoice and give thanks to God in everything.

Religious Life Is Life in Community

God chose a people, not a lot of all-star individuals. Single hearts and voices can't know and praise God properly. Only human minds and voices joined together can do that. God's many faces can be seen only if we share our memories and relate to one another in love.

God Directs All of History

The central conviction of Israel—that there is one, and only one, God—leads to recognition of God's lordship over all peoples and all events. God blesses and punishes, sets obstacles and shows the way through them. All things are in God's hands, so the only thing that makes sense is to walk in the ways of the LORD.

Ten Themes of Biblical Spirituality for Today

The theological themes of the Pentateuch offer rich implications for our own spiritual life as disciples of the one God we find there. Following are some of the important personal demands the message of the Pentateuch places on our lives.

All Things in Our Life Must Flow From Faith

The stories of the Pentateuch reveal that no part of life is outside of God's plan. We must live believing that God's will can be known and followed in all of life's situations.

Our Prayer and Our Daily Life Must Be One

We must not pray on Sunday and go to hell for what we do on Monday. Nothing is so secular that God cannot be a part of it. Our worship and prayer should relate to the real problems and decisions we face in daily life. There is not a single area of life where God is not present.

We Must Respect God's Holiness

The Bible often speaks of God with beautiful human imagery, but it never allows us to forget that God is also the all-powerful creator of the universe who cannot be represented by idols or treated like just another human being. The Pentateuch balances notions of God's closeness to the world with the clear recognition that our job is to do God's will—not try to make God do our will.

We Must Imitate God's Holiness

Since we are made in God's image and likeness, we have a responsibility to act like God. God cares for the poor, the widow, the alien, and the orphan—and so must we. (See how Leviticus 19 outlines our duties to our neighbor.)

Holiness Must Be Translated into Compassion

Forgiveness is the hallmark of God's holiness. God claims to be a God who bestows "mercy down to the thousandth generation, on the children of those who love me" (Ex 20, 6) and who forgives "wickedness and crime and sin" (Ex 34, 7). Holiness is best expressed not in private prayer, but in our forgiving and merciful behavior toward each other.

Life Is a Journey

Among the oldest of metaphors for human existence, this image is deeply rooted in the Pentateuch itself. Abraham is called to a new land; Jacob must find God far from home. Joseph must go to Egypt, and Israel must cross the desert to find a Promised Land. The journey motif not only stresses the future to which we go; even more, it emphasizes the value of the journey itself, for the God toward whom we move is already with us on the road.

Life's Journey Requires Trust in God

What is needed on a risk-filled journey with God? Trust! The Pentateuch asserts that God's guidance never fails even when the people turn from God's way. Keeping God's commandments builds our courage and confidence; we learn to trust in God's promises and find peace.

We Are People of the Land

The Promised Land dominates the stories of the Pentateuch. Israel was in love with her land and never lost her infatuation with it even when it was taken from her. Israel never wanted to be divorced from the concrete realities of everyday life and never embraced asceticism as an ideal. Its spirituality was hardheaded and included wrestling with the proper use of the land and its resources, working for justice in social settings, and molding politics and economics to the demands of God's Law. Genesis says that we are from the earth and to the earth we shall return (Gn 3, 10). Then we must take the earth seriously!

Faith Is a Family Affair

Much of Israel's religious practice was centered in the home: Sabbath observance, Passover, prayer, teaching children the Law. The home-centered religious practices narrated in the Pentateuch can teach us much about how our own families can celebrate together, teach one another about God, and give concrete witness to what we believe.

Prayer Must Fill Our Lives

The Pentateuch provides numerous examples both of public prayer and of the private prayers of individuals responding to every experience of God's presence in their lives. Israel's need and ability to pray in all situations eventually gave birth to the Psalms, a collection of prayers and hymns that express the whole range of human feelings before God. Their boldness and yet humility provide modern believers with an example of how we can live our lives as prayer.

Questions for Discussion and Reflection

Group Sharing/Discussion

1. Much of the Pentateuch is about the laws of the Israelites. What do we learn about the people from these laws? What would someone from another planet learn about us from our laws?

2. Explain the meaning of two words you will meet often in Bible study: exegesis and hermeneutics.

3. Have four people each explain how the Bible was read in one of the four periods of history: New Testament times, Early Church, Medieval Period, Modern Study. What was the same and what was different from age to age?

4. What do you understand "myth" to mean? Is it an appropriate term to use in reference to some of the stories of Genesis? Why or why not?

In Our Lives

1. Depending on the size of your study group, divide up the *Ten Themes for Biblical Spirituality Today,* explaining each one and giving suggestions of how we can put it into practice in our daily lives.

2. One of the 10 central themes in the Pentateuch is that our religious life is in community. What is our individual role in building up our own community? How do certain individuals in your own parish build up the community?

Individual/Personal Reflection/Action

1. See how many of the new words you encountered in this essay are in the glossary.

2. Read over the last two of the *Ten Themes of Biblical Spirituality for Today.* Decide on one thing you will do to more consciously live those themes.

FOR FURTHER STUDY

Lawrence Boadt, C.S.P. *Reading the Old Testament: An Introduction.* Mahway, NJ: Paulist Press, 1985. A readable overview of all the critical and theological issues of Old Testament study.

The New Jerome Biblical Commentary. Englewood Cliffs, NJ: Prentice-Hall, 1990. A superb one-volume commentary on all of Scripture with fine background articles for study of the Pentateuch.

Margaret Nutting Ralph. *"And God Said What?"* Mahway, NJ: Paulist Press, 1986. A very understandable introduction to literary forms in the Bible.

GENESIS READING GUIDE

At a Glance

Who are the main players?	Adam and Eve Cain and Abel Noah Abraham and Sarah Isaac and Rebekah Jacob and Rachel Joseph
What should I look for?	Creation of the world Human rebellion and sin The beginning of the nation of Israel God's Promises: Covenants with Noah and Abraham
When did this take place?	Prehistory and c. 1800 B.C. to 1300 B.C.
Where did these events occur?	The area now called the Middle East: Egypt, Jordan, Lebanon, Israel, Syria, Turkey, Iraq, Saudi Arabia
Why was this book written?	To make the point that God created all things and created them good; that human beings broke faith with God and are responsible for evil in the world; that God never stops loving humanity and, through Abraham, formed a people to whom and through whom God has been revealed.
What is the story?	God creates a good world. Man and woman sin. Noah and family survive the flood. Abraham receives God's promises and trusts God even to the point of being willing to sacrifice his own son. Through Isaac and Jacob, Abraham's clan begins to grow. In Egypt, Joseph provides a safe-haven for the fledgling nation and it begins to prosper and multiply.

When you first approach the book of Genesis, a helpful way to start is by quickly reading all 50 chapters to grasp the "plot" and the style of the book. Then, a second, more careful reading will reveal much more.

The date and setting for the creation of the final form of Genesis is probably the time when the people of Judah were in exile in Babylon (sixth century B.C.) or when the Babylonian exiles returned home to Judah under the Persian empire (fifth century B.C.). The time of exile and the return home forced Israel to think hard about its identity as a people and its mission as the people of God among the nations of the world. By remembering the Genesis stories about the beginnings of the world and Israel's earliest ancestors, they could return to their roots and think about who they were as an exiled people who were returning home to Judah. They could identify with their ancestors in Genesis, who were also a family on the move. Just as the family of Abraham and Sarah migrated back and forth from Mesopotamia to Canaan (see map p. 24) so the exiles would migrate from Babylon back to Judah. The key promise in the midst of this wandering and yearning to return home was the promise God made to Jacob: "Know that I am with you and will keep you wherever you go, and will bring you back to this land" (28, 15).

Structure of Genesis

The book of Genesis received its English name from the Greek translation of the Hebrew word *toledot* (generations, genealogy, account of origins, derived from a verb meaning "give birth" or "beget"), which is used 13 times in Genesis and is translated as "story" (2, 4) or "descendants" (10, 1). In Hebrew, Genesis is known, like many books in the Bible, by its first word, *bereishit,* which means, "In the beginning." Genesis is indeed a book about beginnings—the beginning of the natural world, the beginning of human culture, and the beginning of the people of Israel, whose story occupies most of this book and will dominate the rest of the Bible.

The book of Genesis is thus, in more senses than one, a primary source for Jewish theology. It presents its ideas on the relationship of God to nature, to the human race in general, and to the people of

Israel in ways that are foreign to the expectations of most modern readers. It is therefore all too easy to miss the seriousness of its messages. For Genesis conveys its worldview neither as a theological tract nor a rigorous philosophical proof nor a confession of faith. Instead, it uses narrative or story.

Most often scholars divide Genesis into two parts: chapters 1–11 and 12–50. While the parts seem to constitute a single, continuous story, there are actually significant differences between them in both subject matter and in the kind of literature they contain. The first 11 chapters, often referred to as the "primeval history," discuss the creation of the world and the first human beings—the ancestors of all humanity. The second part, on the other hand, describes the very ancestors of Israel itself. Genesis 1–11 falls into the literary category of "myth" (see box, RG 38) in which every story seems to model the proper (or improper, in some cases) relationship between God and humans. The stories of the latter part of Genesis, however, relate specific events in the life of what came to be a particular nation, Israel.

The characters and worlds of the two sections are very different. The world of the primeval history bears little resemblance to the world we live in. In that world people lived incredibly long lives and spoke directly with God. In contrast, Abraham, Isaac, Jacob, and the other people described in chapters 12–50, seem to live out their joys and struggles in a world like ours, making decisions that affect the whole history of the nation.

Differences between the Two Major Divisions of Genesis

Topic	Genesis 1–11	Genesis 12–50
Time	Set in time before human history	Set in historical times well known to ancient records
Place	Locations vague: somewhere to the East of Israel	Locations exact: Palestine and Egypt and Northern Mesopotamia
Persons	Characters seem like symbols; little is known of their lives	Characters behave like typical people of the second millennium B.C.
Stories	Many stories can be classified as myths; they resemble those known from Mesopotamia	Saga-like stories and epic history narratives similar to oral lore of tribal groups
Events	Most events seem to have supernatural quality	Major events resemble normal human experience
Purpose	Describes the origins of humanity long before Israel's time	Traces the direct tribal ancestors of Israel itself

Genesis 1–11	Genesis 12–50
Primeval History	**Folk History**
Genesis 1–3	Genesis 12–25
The story of God's creation and the first human sin	Abraham is chosen to receive God's special blessing.
Genesis 4–5	Genesis 21–27
The evil sin grows and spreads through the world.	The son, Isaac, inherits the promise and passes it on.
Genesis 6–10	Genesis 27–36; 48–50
Evil overwhelms the world; God must begin again with a new blessing.	Jacob in turn receives the promise; he is blessed with the 12 sons who will become Israel.
Genesis 10–11	Genesis 37–50
People again multiply across the earth but sin persists.	Joseph brings the promise to Egypt and remains completely faithful to God.

The chart on the previous page illustrates some of the significant differences between the two parts.

Subdivisions of Genesis 1–50

By breaking down the two-part division of the book of Genesis into smaller units, we can get a clearer picture of the relationship between the two parts.

Note in the chart above how the four major sections of the primeval history match the four sections of the folk history of Israel's founders. Each column reveals growth, for better or worse: In the primeval history, sin grows; in the folk history, Israel. The Genesis editors' effort to show that there are stages in the history of humanity, and of Israel in particular, clearly succeeds. Each period of history has major impact on those that follow; therefore, as we read Genesis, we should keep our eyes open for signs of growth and development.

Another way to organize Genesis is to break it down into four blocks of material that focus on major characters. When we do this, as the chart below illustrates, we see that the "plot" of Genesis centers on major decisions made by key individuals.

The reader may be surprised to find that Genesis ends with Abraham's descendants living in Egypt instead of in the land of promise. But the book's ending reminds us that the story will continue: God's promise is not forgotten and Israel's future lies elsewhere.

Division by the Special *Toledoth* Lists

The *New American Bible* points out that Genesis contains internal markers that help divide and organize the material. These markers are the genealogical lists, *toledoth,* that always begin "these are the descendants of. . . ." (Note: the *NAB* sometimes varies the translation of that phrase, but in Hebrew it is always the same.) These lists help make the point that while generations come and go, God's plan moves ahead no matter what. Sometimes appearing at the beginning and sometimes at the end of a section, the lists group together all the members of a family line or tribe to signal a break with the events that have just been recounted. The chart on the next page illustrates where these lists appear and the purpose they serve.

Division of Genesis into Four Blocks of Material

A. The Prologue: primeval history of humankind's original blessing and failure through sin	Gn 1–11
B. The story of Abraham: his call and response; his blessing and promise	Gn 12–25
C. The stories of Abraham's son Isaac and grandson Jacob and how they carry on the blessing	Gn 26–36
D. The story of Joseph in Egypt: preparation for God's great self-revelation in the Exodus	Gn 37–50

The Toledoth Lists

Gn 2, 4a	Begins the second story of creation
Gn 5, 1	Introduces the long break between the first family and the days of Noah
Gn 6, 9	Introduces the story of the flood
Gn 10, 1	Marks the great expansion of people all over the world
Gn 11, 10	Marks the addition of a new list of the nations of the world by the P source
Gn 11, 27	Begins the story of Abraham
Gn 25, 12	Closes off the life of Abraham's "other" family through Hagar and Ishmael
Gn 25, 19	Opens the story of Jacob's birth and destiny
Gn 36, 1	Ends the role of Jacob's twin, Esau, and directs us to Jacob's children, especially Joseph
Gn 36, 9	A repetition within the Esau list that marks its conclusion
Gn 37, 2	The phrase "family history" marks the opening of the story of Joseph and his brothers that continues to the end of Genesis

The way a writer organizes material, and the choices made regarding the overall shape of the writing, reveal much about the purpose of the writing. Our purpose in identifying the major outline of Genesis and of naming its various subdivisions is to show that what we have here is a continuous story that runs not only from the beginning to the end of Genesis, but through the entire Pentateuch as well. Once we grasp the overall outline, we can begin to see how individual incidents fit into it.

The Primeval History of Genesis 1–11

In studying these chapters, several aspects should be noted.

1. They are generally described by *form criticism* as a combination of myths and genealogical tables.

2. They are described by the source critics as a combination of the materials from the Yahwist (J) and the Priestly (P) sources. (See the explanation of the source hypothesis in the introductory essay on the Pentateuch, RG 42.)

3. Many of the individual stories have parallels in the literatures of other ancient Near Eastern peoples. These are often much older than the biblical versions. While this means that they are possible sources for the versions of these stories in the Bible, the J and P accounts have a distinctive character that is very different from these ancient sources (see box, "Are Some Genesis Stories Just Rewrites of Ancient Myths?" RG 53).

J and P Sources

If we remember that the J stories are much older (probably) than the P stories, and at first probably stood alone as the basic proclamation of the beginnings of the world, we can first glance at each group separately.

It might be noted that there are several duplications in these lists: both J and P have a list of great ancestors between Adam and Noah (4, 17–26 versus 5, 1–32); both have a flood story that is now hopelessly intermixed as a single account; and both have a Table of Nations that spread over the earth in Genesis 10–11, that is also interwoven as a single narrative list.

The Theology of the Yahwist Source

The incidents chosen by the J author to tell the story of creation focus on the tension between God's goodness and human beings' disobedience. Adam and Eve, Cain and Abel, the wicked generation of the flood, the sons of Noah, and the builders of the tower of Babel all received plenty of evidence of God's love. Yet each generation chose to disobey by embracing one of the deadly vices: greed, envy, lust, pride.

Look at the pattern the Yahwist author uses to structure each story:

This repeated pattern conveys an overarching message: Because humanity repeatedly failed to respond to God's offering of intimate love, sin spread and contaminated all people. Now God must find a new way to demonstrate control over the earth and all of history, and to show love for humanity. As with Adam and Eve and Noah and his family, God begins this

J (Tenth Century B.C.)	**P** (Seventh to Sixth Centuries B.C.)
	Gn 1, 1—2, 4a The creation of the world
Gn 2, 4b—3, 24 The human condition at creation, and sin	
Gn 4, 1–26 Cain and Abel: even the children sin but God continues to care	
	Gn 5, 1–32 The list of long-lived ancestors from Adam to Noah
Gn 6, 1–4 More evil caused by the sin of angels and humans	
Gn 6, 5—9, 29 The flood story with 40 days and 7 pairs of clean animals, etc.	**Gn 6, 5—9, 29** The flood story based on 365 days and one pair of each animal only, etc.
Gn 10, 8–19. 25–30 Table of Nations from a different source	**Gn 10, 1–7.20–24** Table of all the nations
Gn 11, 1–9 The story of the tower of Babel	
	Gn 11, 10–32 The continuation of the Table of Nations down to Abraham

new round by again choosing a single family, Abraham's, and giving them a special revelation of divine goodness to share with the world.

The Theology of the Priestly Source

If later Israelites had only the version of their history given in the J Source—sin, punishment, mercy, and the promise of being formed into a chosen people—they might have misunderstood it as promising absolute control over the land and great power for Abraham's descendants. But by the time the Priestly writers were gathering their own accounts, Israel had already experienced military defeats and the loss of 10 of the 12 tribes. Israel was wondering if God really was in control and would stand by them in hard times.

God . . .

1. . . . acts lovingly toward humanity

3. . . . announces punishment

5. . . . shows mercy and gives a new blessing

People . . .

2. . . . disobey God and sin

4. . . . are punished

The Priestly writers apparently wanted to make sure the promises spoken in the creation stories would suggest two things: first, that God's control over world events was greater than any human power; and second, that it would be shown in ways besides Israel's political fortunes. In other words, Israel's misfortunes did not mean that God had lost control. P clearly states that humans are made in the image of God (Gn 1, 27 and 9, 6) to govern the earth and fill it, but P's stress is not on humanity's independent power; rather, an important element of being made in the image of God is humanity's responsibility to act as God would act.

The genealogies of chapters 5 and 10–11 are also part of P's insistence that God has a plan that cannot be derailed by human whims, nor even upset by human sin. God is always in charge— even when we are experiencing just punishment. God's blessing *can* be relied on. We must learn trust! By stressing the goodness of creation and God's blessing of humanity, P's larger vision brought hope to Israel at a time when circumstances could have led it to despair.

The Overall Message of Genesis 1–11

The combining of J and P reveals the full range of Hebrew thought regarding the origins of humanity:

God is good and all God created is good.

Human beings are morally obligated to obey God's plan.

God alone is worthy of worship.

By the way they used and reshaped Canaanite myths and subtly attacked pagan religious practices, the J and P authors and editors made the point that Canaanite worship and beliefs pervert God's plan. The Israelites did use elements from beliefs of other Near Eastern peoples—for example, creation being a fight between God and Chaos. However, they always modified these in a way that made clear their belief in God's sovereignty over creation. In the same way they took over planting and harvesting celebrations but distanced themselves from the fertility cults they were rejecting.

Two Different Creation Stories

The Bible begins with two different versions of the story of the beginning of the world. These two versions arose at different periods in Israel's history. Most scholars would date the story in Gn 2, 4–25 earlier than the story in 1, 1—2, 3. The former, from the J tradition, was probably written during the time Israel had kings reigning in Jerusalem and before the exile to Babylon in 587 B.C. The usual scholarly designation for this earlier tradition, which extends intermittently throughout the Pentateuch (Genesis—Deuteronomy), is the Yahwist or J tradition. Most scholars would date the later creation story in Genesis 1 to a time after 587 B.C. during the Persian period. This later tradition is the P or Priestly tradition. Allowing two different versions of the creation story to stand side by side suggests that the ancient writers were not interested in defining precisely how the world began in a scientific sense. Rather, they were interested in exploring larger questions of meaning and purpose through multiple perspectives on the same events of creation.

Notes on Individual Creation Passages

Genesis 1, 1—2, 4a

The Priestly creation story contains patterns that structure the individual days and the entire week.

Pattern One: Each day contains a five-point framework:

Opening: "And God said. . . ."

Command: "Let there be. . . ."

Fulfillment: "And so it was. . . ."

Judgment: "And God saw that it was good. . . ."

Naming: "Evening came, and morning followed . . . "

Pattern Two: The six days of creation are divided into two matched sets of three days each as shown in the chart on RG 54. During the first three days of creation we see God building a vast stage of heavens, water, and land by separating one from the other. During the second three days God populates the stage with its primary actors, and the creation becomes one integrated whole. The goodness of the creation is celebrated on the climactic seventh day. This day becomes the model of rest and celebration of God's goodness that humans are to follow each week.

Are Some Genesis Stories Just Rewrites of Ancient Myths?

Sometimes readers point to the similarities between the biblical creation stories and myths of ancient Near Eastern people as a way of discrediting the Bible texts. Since they are derived from pagan myths, they argue, the Bible stories have no more than literary value. But the fact that a biblical writer may have borrowed legends from neighboring cultures in no way diminishes the theological value of the writing.

It is the biblical author's final product, not the original myth, that the Church believes is inspired and has canonized into the body of Scripture. And this final form differs significantly in purpose and theology from the myths the inspired writer not only may have borrowed, but perhaps was also trying to debunk.

To take just two examples: The story of the creation of humanity and the story of the flood both have parallels among ancient Mesopotamian myths. Many of the similarities are even quite striking. But their overall messages are clearly different, especially in their presentation and understanding of God.

The Babylonian creation story called *Enuma Elish* presumes the existence of many gods who haphazardly created the world while fighting among themselves. Their creation is therefore partly good and partly evil, and human beings are nothing more than their slaves. Against this view of creation the biblical writer presents a theology that asserts one, and only one, God who creates consciously and out of love. God's creation is all good and human beings are not slaves, but are made in God's own image and are given dominion over the earth.

The Noah flood story has a close parallel in the *Epic of Gilgamesh,* possibly the oldest of recorded human stories. In the tale, Gilgamesh sets out to find an ancestor who has achieved immortality. The ancestor tells of having survived a great flood and of how he helped save humanity. In details, this flood account is surprisingly similar to the Genesis story. But the two versions present very different images of God.

The Babylonians believed there was an ongoing struggle between gods and humans. Their unpredictable gods found humans annoying and often erupted in hostility toward them. Human beings could never be sure of how to please their gods, nor of what would anger them. Genesis, on the other hand, presents a God who never changes. God is eternally just, yet loving and faithful. Israel's God punishes only when human beings have committed real wrong. And their God is always eager to forgive.

It is important to remember that being related to and derived from similar stories of the ancient Near East in no way compromises the religious truth or value of the stories we find in Genesis.

The pattern of creation was not invented by the P authors. The same order is followed in the ancient creation myth from Babylon called the *Enuma Elish,* in which Marduk, the chief god of Babylon, and at the same time young king of all gods, fashions the world from the body of Tiamat, the mother goddess whom he had slain in battle. The *Enuma* *Elish* describes Marduk's creative actions in a sequence parallel to the account in Genesis 1:

• It begins with a conquest of chaos by order = The opening statement of Gn 1, 1–2

• Heavens created and separated from water = Day 2, the creation of heavens and separation of the waters.

Prologue: Introductory Statement Asserting God's Control of Chaos			
Three Days of Separation		**Three Days of Integration**	
Day 1	God creates heavens and separates light from darkness	Day 4	Sun, moon, and stars join the sky
Day 2	God separates waters above (rain) from waters below (oceans)	Day 5	Birds and fish are added to sky and waters
Day 3	God separates land from waters and adds vegetation to land	Day 6	Animals populate the land and, finally, humans

Day 7   Epilogue: God rests, fully in control of all creation

• The earth is set over the waters = Day 3, the land appears from the waters
• Creation of sun and moon = Day 4, sun and moon are set in heaven
• (No mention of plants or animals) = (Days 5–6, the creation of fish, birds, and animals)
• Creation of human beings = Day 6, the creation of humans
• The gods rest and celebrate = Day 7, God rests

Genesis 2, 4b—3, 24

This is the Yahwist account of creation, a much older story than the Priestly version of chapter 1. Although we can detect here some story themes borrowed from Mesopotamia, the biblical account is unique as a whole and more sophisticated in its vision than anything else found in the ancient world. In the ancient Near East the king was often said to be the "image" of the God and thus to act with divine authority. So here the creation of humanity in God's *image* and *likeness* carries with it a commission to rule over the animal kingdom (1, 26).

Some have seen in that commission a license for ecological irresponsibility. The fact is, however, that the Bible presents humanity not as the owner of nature but as its steward, strictly accountable to its true Owner (see Lv 25, 23–24). The garden of Eden is not a paradise of luxury but a place for human work. Humans will *till* the garden and keep it.

Whereas 1, 1—2, 3 presented a majestic God-centered scenario of creation, 2, 4–25

presents a different but equally profound story of origins. This second account of creation is centered more on human beings and familiar experiences, and even its deity is conceived in more anthropomorphic terms. Here humans' ambition to be like God or like divine beings is the root of their expulsion from Eden. The command not to eat from the tree of knowledge of good and evil carries a grave consequence, which in Hebrew reads literally: "you shall surely die."

This account of creation and sin presents some key biblical insights: Man is created first, at the beginning of creation, and all other creatures are made for his companionship. He participates in shaping the character of the animals by giving them names. God tries a second strategy to satisfy the human's loneliness. God fashions a woman from the rib of the sleeping man. Woman alone, among God's other creatures, is equal to the man and is a suitable helper for him. The term *helper* does not imply an inferior assistant but a genuine partner who comes to the aid of another. God is often called a "helper" for those in need (Ps 10, 14; 54, 4). Unlike the animals, the woman instantly evokes a joyous response from the man. Humans are more than just another creature—they were created to "cultivate and care for" the rest of creation (2, 15). Intimacy is the chief characteristic of the relationship between God and human beings. Sin is a pervasive reality, but it is the result of human choice, not God's.

Genesis 4, 1–16

The story of Cain and Abel tells a moral about how evil flourishes and leads even to fratricide. But it also builds on an age-old theme of the conflict between the farmer and the herder. The musical *Oklahoma* sings how the farmer and the cowman should be friends, but their interests conflict—the farmer wants to fence in and protect his plot of land, the cowman requires wide-open spaces over which the cattle or sheep can move to new pastures. This was a conflict well known to the early Israelites, who as nomadic shepherds came up against the protected and settled lands of the Canaanite farmers. It is no accident that the evil that is displeasing to the LORD just happens to come from the (Canaanite) farmer Cain!

Genesis 4, 17–22; 5, 1–32

The genealogies of Genesis 4–5 with the enormous ages of the patriarchs are not intended to be taken literally. A Sumerian list of kings who lived before the flood ascribes even more astounding ages to its monarchs, some of them living 28,000 years and more. Such genealogy lists are typical of many people who keep largely oral traditions.

Genesis 6, 1—9, 27

Two observations should be remembered during your study of the flood account. First, it must have been very important to the biblical writers, because both the Yahwist and Priestly traditions had their own version of the flood, and they considered each important enough to save. Second, the biblical story bears strong resemblance to other ancient flood stories told in Babylon and Syria. What makes the biblical account unique and religiously important is what it teaches us about God. In the pagan versions God's motives for destroying humanity are either left out or trivialized (human noisiness kept the gods awake). But the Genesis story insists that God acted out of justice and in response to people's moral evil. The relationship between God and people is not characterized by the constant tension of the pagan versions, but by intimate love that continues despite the flood. The story's final image of the rainbow promises hope and blessing.

Genesis 9, 28—10, 32

By being placed after the flood story, this second set of genealogies links the prehistoric flood with the call of Abraham in the very real towns of Ur and Haran in Mesopotamia. Like the genealogy of Genesis 4, 17—5, 32 it connects major moments in the history of God's interventions in human life and tells how, after the flood, people spread out to fill the far corners of the earth. The genealogy is a composite of two separate lists, one from the P school and the other from J. Look at the text and see how easy it is to pick out the more colorful J list with its bits of stories (10, 8–30) from the much drier P list which gives names and nothing more (9, 29—10, 7 and 10, 21–24).

Genesis 11, 1–9

The J writer has crafted an ironic and even humorous story. Having ignored God's earlier command to "fill the earth" (Gn 1, 29; 9, 1), people are united and speak one language. In addition, they want to "make a name for themselves," that is, achieve greatness without any help from God. God attacks this arrogance and forces the people both to disperse and to populate the earth by confusing their language. Note that the great temple they were building to glorify themselves is so small by divine standards that God has to "come down" to see it. Several wordplays add to the humor and irony of this story that makes the point that the growth of sin even turns a people against itself.

Genesis 11, 10–32

In this genealogy the ages of the patriarchs are greatly reduced (compare with Gn 5, 1–32), although still exaggerated. This device shows that growing sin has brought the "golden age" to an end. More sin means less life. Besides illustrating the disintegrating effects of sin, the genealogies show continuity in human history from the dawn of time to Abraham. The periods recorded in the genealogies were times of blessing sandwiched in between times of sin and punishment, as illustrated in the chart on RG 56.

Church Use of the Genesis Story of Human Creation

It is well to note that the account of making humanity in the divine image figures significantly in a number of official Catholic Church documents.

Key Moments of Sin and Punishment
(and Giving the Blessing)

Genealogy Lists
(Living the Blessing)

Genesis 1, 2—4, 16
The story of creation. The blessings and
sins of the first generations.

Genesis 4, 17—5, 32
The long age of blessing of the 10
great patriarchs before Noah's time.

Genesis 6, 1—9, 27
Sin. Flood as punishment. Blessing on
Noah, followed by further sin by his sons.

Genesis 9, 28—10, 32
The lists of all the nations known to
ancient Israel. Shows the blessing of
fertility and having dominion over
the earth.

Genesis 11, 1–9
After blessing, sin again rises up out of
human pride.

Genesis 11, 10–32
God's blessing continues, now focusing on
one family, that of Terah and Abraham.

Genesis 12, 1ff
The story of Abraham and the new
direction of God's blessing.

For example, Pope Paul VI looked to Genesis 1, 28 as a significant reference in his development of the responsibility to subdue the earth and its resources intelligently (*Populorum Progressio #22*). And along the same vein, John Paul II went to Genesis 1, 26–30 for a reference to the "goodness" of creation in the Creator's eyes, and therefore grounding the claim that redemption is possible. (*Redemptor hominis*). Likewise, the United States bishops in their pastoral letter *Economic Justice for All* used Genesis 1, 26f to show that all human relations must be based on the acknowledgement of the dignity of those created in God's image. This helps form the economic reflections of the letter.

Questions for Discussion and Reflection
Group Sharing/Discussion

1. Explain how you would summarize the main ideas in this first section of Genesis to someone who is not familiar with them.

2. What is something helpful or something new you learned from reading the Reading Guide Notes on this section of Genesis?

3. Which part of these chapters is most significant to you? Explain what lesson could be learned from that part of scripture.

4. In this story of the beginning of the human race, God blesses his creatures and they then fail. What are some examples of how this pattern is repeated throughout our human history—God blesses humanity and humanity fails in some way?

In Our Lives

1. All of creation is good, God said, and God created humans in his image and likeness, saying that this was "very good." Share an example of when and how you see God's image in other people in your life.

2. Tell about an individual or organization working to keep the world of God's creation beautiful and good as it was created and intended to be.

3. In contrast to the story of Cain and Abel, what is an example of a person being their "brother's keeper?"

Individual/Personal Reflection/Action

1. Take time to be aware of the beauty of the created world around you, one of God's gifts.

2. Cain and Abel's story is an extreme example of jealousy and interpersonal conflict. Examine where you experience conflict in your life and reflect on what you might do to improve the situation.

The Great Ancestor Narratives of Genesis 12–50

Since humanity as a whole proves stubbornly unresponsive to God's love, God shifts gears and chooses a single people who will respond to God's self-revelation and will testify about God's goodness to all nations. This second major part of Genesis tells the story of God's new plan by focusing on the lives of four patriarchal figures: Abraham, Isaac, Jacob, and Joseph. Through each character, God's plan moves a step further toward fulfillment. The blueprint for this new plan is contained in the story of Abraham's call at the beginning of chapter 12. The first three verses not only describe his call but also present the other major themes that will dominate Genesis and much of Israel's history:

Verse 1   The promise of a land for his family

Verse 2   The promise of blessing through empire and fame, and probably children ("a great nation")

Verse 3   The promise to rule other nations and to mediate God's blessing to them

The promises of a son to carry on the name and a land of their own echo especially loudly in the stories that follow. But Israel did not read these promises as guarantees that life would be rosy. These stories record Israel's failures as well as successes, disobedience as well as obedience,

lessons of deep faith and of sinful lack of trust. Because the Bible is the product of a faith-seeking community, Israel consistently found in its history evidence of God working even through their mistakes, guiding this people through all their troubles, helping them overcome obstacles, and bringing them blessing even in the land of their enemy, Egypt.

The Literary Issues of Genesis 12–50

We can better appreciate what a masterpiece of storytelling Genesis is when we realize that whoever edited the book pulled together three different sources into one continuous story (see RG 42–44). Scholars have been able to identify many passages that came from J, and others that came from P. A third source, the Elohist, which is close to J in spirit but does not yet use the name Yahweh for God, has also been detected in these chapters. The three sources can be easily identified when they each tell their own version of the same story. The following chart shows how the three sources intertwine to tell the Abraham and Sarah story. In telling the story, each source stresses a different aspect of Abraham's personality. J extols his trust in the promise of land and a son, while E marvels at his obedience even to sacrificing his son. P stresses his fidelity to religious regulations, especially circumcision.

The stories of the great patriarchs and matriarchs existed in oral form long before J, E, or P ever wrote a word. The three literary sources did more than simply write down the stories, however. They carefully composed them in a way that revealed their religious value and more clearly pointed to the lessons in the stories. As you read, be aware that the writing contains two kinds of information: the original description of what happened, and Israel's later reflection on

J, E, P Sources in the Abraham and Sarah Story

What Happened	J Version	E Version	P Version
Abraham receives promise of land and/or a son.	Gn 12, 1–3	Gn 15, 1–6	Gn 12, 4–9
God makes a covenant with Abraham.	Gn 15, 7–12	Gn 15, 13–16	Gn 17, 1–14
A son is born and the line of the promise is secured.	Gn 16, 1–16; 18, 1–19	Gn 21, 1–21	Gn 17, 15–27
Abraham's life ends.	Gn 25, 1–6	Gn 22, 1–13	Gn 23, 1–20
Places stress on Abraham's . . .	Faith	Obedience	Fidelity

what happened. As a people of faith, Israel saw many events as clear experiences of God's hand guiding them through history.

The Historical Setting of the Patriarchal Stories

Scholars generally agree that the customs and events described in Genesis 12–50 best fit the period from 1900 to 1500 B.C. From what we know of the ancient world through nonbiblical sources, we can say that items like the names of the patriarchs, customs like the adoption of an heir (Gn 15, 1–3) and marrying a sister (12, 10–20), and Abraham's and Isaac's seminomadic lifestyle accurately reflect this period of history. The story of Joseph rising to the position of prime minister in Egypt is also most plausible in this period; Egypt was ruled by foreign invaders, the Hyksos, who may have been more likely to allow a fellow foreigner to assume power than the strong Egyptian leaders who took control around 1500 B.C.

These examples make the dating of the Genesis stories likely, but not certain. Archaeological finds, however, continue to present a picture of this part of the world that matches well with the descriptions found in Genesis.

Abraham and Sarah, Genesis 12–25

There are several ways to get more out of the Abraham narrative. One way is to read it as the story of a man who is a homeless alien in chapter 12 and has become a wealthy landowner by the time he and Sarah are buried on their own land in chapters 23 and 25. Another way is to follow the series of promises made to Abraham and Sarah as they are slowly but surely fulfilled. Two sets of promises (see below) run parallel throughout these chapters.

A third and perhaps the most religiously fruitful way of reading Genesis 12–25 is to see it as a story of Abraham and Sarah's struggle to continue believing in and trusting God. They struggle because, like most believers, Abraham and Sarah create almost as many obstacles to God's plan as they do faith-filled responses (see next page). Remember, the Bible presents its lead characters honestly, warts and all.

God's Promise to Abraham

God provides another version of the covenant promise, similar to the one made in Genesis 15. For the first time, however, God clearly names both Abraham and Sarah as the parents of the promised child. God also adds an element of assurance involving time: the covenant and God's relationship with the nation that will become Israel is everlasting, and Abraham's family will possess the land of Canaan perpetually. The names of Abram and Sarai are changed to mark the importance of this new promise. "Abraham" means "ancestor of a multitude," so the new name is another sign of the covenant. By also changing Sarai's name to Sarah, God indicates that she is now clearly part of the promise. God also introduces the ritual of circumcision as a physical sign of belonging to the covenant people of God. Circumcision involves cutting off the foreskin of the penis. The ritual was practiced by neighboring cultures around Israel as well as Israel itself and continues to be practiced by Jews, Muslims, and many Christians today.

Abraham laughs at the thought that he and Sarah will have a child at their ages of 100 and 90 years old. He pleads to God to keep Ishmael, who is now 13 years old, as the promised son rather than wait for yet another son (v. 18). But God

Promise of a Son		Promise of Land	
Gn 12, 2	I make you a great nation	Gn 12, 1	"Go to a land I indicate"
Gn 15, 5	At the night covenant	Gn 12, 7	At the terebinth of Moreh
Gn 17, 4	The P covenant	Gn 13, 14	At the departure of Lot
Gn 17, 16	The promise of Isaac	Gn 15, 18	At the night covenant
Gn 18, 10	The three angels	Gn 17, 8	The P covenant
Gn 18, 18	Recap of 12, 2f	Gn 24, 7	The messenger for Isaac
Gn 21, 12	A promise to Isaac	Gn 26, 4	Repeated promise to Isaac
Gn 22, 17	At the sacrifice of Isaac		
Gn 26, 4	Promise repeated to Isaac		

insists that Sarah will have a son, whose name will be Isaac, which means, "he laughs." The theme of laughter and Isaac will come up again (18, 12–15; 21, 5–6). God also responds to Abraham's concern for Ishmael. God promises to bless him, make him exceedingly numerous, and make him a great nation. These are the same promises that Abraham originally receives (12, 1–3) and that now extend to Isaac as the child of promise.

The story of Abraham and Sarah climaxes in the great moment of the test in chapter 22. After Abraham proves himself fully obedient to God's will at that awful moment when he nearly sacrifices his son, the story comes to a rapid conclusion. The promise of a son is secured, Abraham's purchase of a tomb and a small piece of land foreshadows the eventual possession of the entire land God had promised, and so Abraham's role now passes on to Isaac.

Isaac and Rebekah, Genesis 24–27

We may be surprised to find so little space given to the life of Isaac, one of the three great patriarchs of Israel. Although he plays an important role in the life of Abraham as the promised son, his role is primarily passive, even in the scene where he is nearly sacrificed. In Isaac, continuity with Abraham is clearly established, for God appears twice to Isaac, repeating to him the promises made to Abraham. But Isaac himself seems to do little to advance God's plan.

It would be easy to think of Isaac simply as a transitional character between Abraham and Jacob except for the presence in his life of his remarkable wife, Rebekah. The story of the messenger persuading Rebekah and her brother Laban to permit her to marry Isaac is a masterpiece of ancient writing (Gn 24). A total of 67 verses is given to describing this one event. Rebekah will become the key player in the next step of God's plan, the selection of her son Jacob over his older brother, Esau.

Jacob, Genesis 27–36

The theme of promise that dominates the patriarchal stories continues here, but to it is added the theme of rivalry between brothers. When we see how that rivalry is played out, and the other forms of trickery and dishonesty that color Jacob's career, we might be surprised, even horrified that Jacob is God's choice to carry on the covenant. We will better appreciate the value and religious message of this part of the patriarchal history if we keep a few points in mind.

1. The overall purpose of Genesis 12–50 is to show God's promise being carried out despite all obstacles. We should not be surprised then that Jacob, like Abraham, is himself one of those obstacles.

2. These chapters consist of many hero-type folktales that had been told for generations. When these were gathered into written form and their religious meaning highlighted, even the less edifying details were kept and cherished.

3. We are dealing here with a world very different from our own, which did not share our refined sense of ethics. Craftiness and the ability to outfox an opponent were not incompatible with ancient people's standards of honesty and fair

Trusting Responses		Obstacles	
Gn 12, 1–9	Abraham leaves home	Gn 12, 10–20	Abraham pretends Sarah is his
Gn 14, 1–24	War and blessing of		sister
	Melchizedek	Gn 13, 1–8	Lot allowed to choose the land
Gn 15, 1–21	The covenant with God	Gn 16, 1–14	Abraham has a son by his
Gn 17, 1–27	Abraham's covenant		slave wife
	renewed	Gn 18, 1–15	Sarah doubts the promise of a son
Gn 18, 16–33	Abraham intercedes	Gn 20, 1–18	Abraham nearly repeats his
	for Sodom		denial of Sarah
Gn 21, 1–20	The birth of Isaac		
Gn 21, 21–33	Abraham establishes		
	rights to water		
Gn 22, 1–14	Abraham passes test of		
	sacrificing Isaac		
Gn 23, 1–20	Abraham buys land		

play. And we do not have to agree with or like all of what we find in these stories.

4. Israel is recounting its own history here, not the pious biography of a saint, and the central theme of this history is God's relationship with real people, not idealized characters.

Israel saw God working in the events of these stories. In them it recognized a God who had chosen to work through a people that was as imperfect as its leaders. And this very fact built their faith, for it proved that everything works for the good in God's plan. Israel realized God writes straight with crooked lines—including the choice of a younger son (Jacob) over the rightful leader, the older son (Esau), and following the advice of a mother (Rebekah) rather than the good judgment of a father of the promise, Isaac himself. These stories are reminders that despite their faults, the patriarchs never completely turned away from God, and that despite its faults, neither did Israel.

Jacob stands as a model for Israel in addition to being its founding father. Three times God appears to him. God passes on to Jacob the promise made to Abraham and Isaac, wrestles with him and changes his name, and assures him he will father a great nation. In turn, Jacob acknowledges God as the only god of Israel. But those encounters changed more than wily Jacob's name, for he emerged from them as a principled and decent human being. Israel found in Jacob's life a mirror of its own struggle to live out the covenant with God.

Joseph, Genesis 37–50

Like those that precede it, Joseph's story can be read in two ways: to find the traditions and themes that reach far back into Israel's history, and to learn the theological purpose of the story as part of the overall religious message of Genesis. Scholars see the Yahwist and Elohist sources woven together to form this one unified story. The slight differences and inconsistencies found in the text are sure giveaways that two sources were blended into one. An obvious example occurs in chapter 37 where, in alternating sets of verses, J names Joseph's father *Israel*, states that his long *coat* caused his brothers' jealousy, that his brother *Judah* interceded for him,

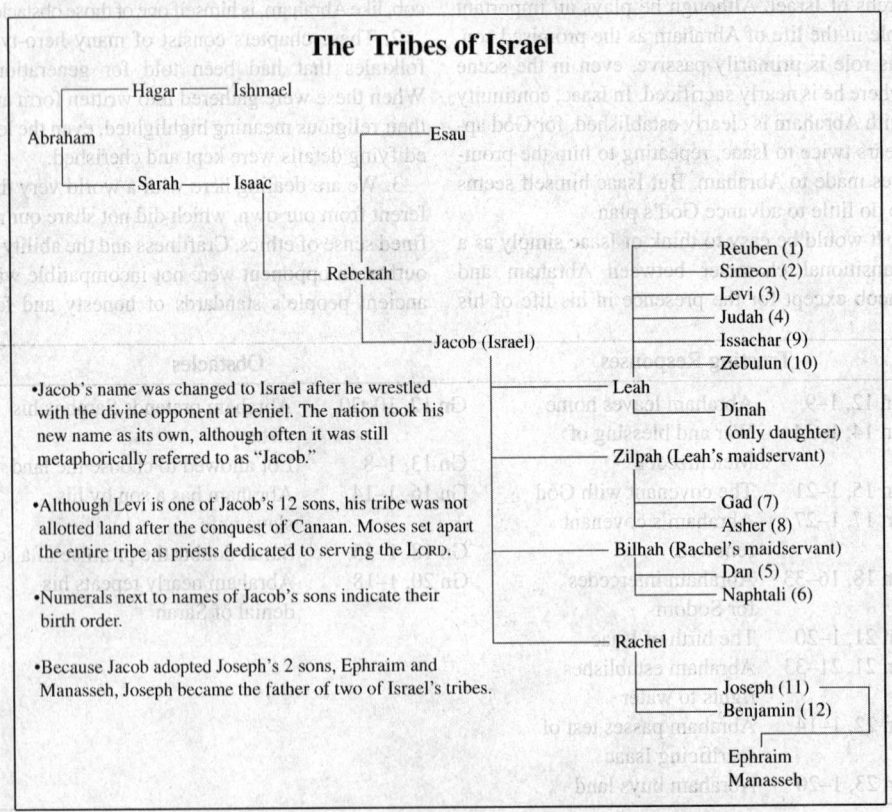

The Tribes of Israel

Hagar — Ishmael

Abraham

Sarah — Isaac

Esau

Rebekah

Jacob (Israel)

Leah
- Reuben (1)
- Simeon (2)
- Levi (3)
- Judah (4)
- Issachar (9)
- Zebulun (10)
- Dinah (only daughter)

Zilpah (Leah's maidservant)
- Gad (7)
- Asher (8)

Bilhah (Rachel's maidservant)
- Dan (5)
- Naphtali (6)

Rachel
- Joseph (11)
- Benjamin (12)

Ephraim
Manasseh

•Jacob's name was changed to Israel after he wrestled with the divine opponent at Peniel. The nation took his new name as its own, although often it was still metaphorically referred to as "Jacob."

•Although Levi is one of Jacob's 12 sons, his tribe was not allotted land after the conquest of Canaan. Moses set apart the entire tribe as priests dedicated to serving the LORD.

•Numerals next to names of Jacob's sons indicate their birth order.

•Because Jacob adopted Joseph's 2 sons, Ephraim and Manasseh, Joseph became the father of two of Israel's tribes.

and that *Ishmaelite* merchants bought him; while the E writer names the father *Jacob,* blames Joseph's *dreams* for causing the jealousy, credits *Reuben* with interceding for Joseph, and says 12 *Midianite* merchants carried him off to Egypt.

Scholars also agree that the Joseph story contains many elements of the Wisdom tradition of Israel. Joseph, once he is on his own in Egypt, fits the image of the ideal man offered by the book of Proverbs (for example, in chapter 4): He says only what is appropriate, keeps his own counsel, accepts misunderstandings, is hard-working and disciplined, is a fine administrator, interprets dreams, plays political games well, and avoids getting involved with foreign women. Most of all, Joseph is a devout, God-fearing man who knows God's ways are different from ours.

The Joseph story is more like a short novel than the string of saga-like stories that make up the previous chapters. There is a wonderful dramatic unity to the narrative: From start to finish, each part of the story fits into the whole like the pieces of a puzzle. If any piece were missing, the story simply wouldn't work. Some genius took all the old themes and separate traditions and created a literary work of art, the earliest such masterpiece that we know anywhere.

Again God has written straight with crooked lines. Joseph, one of the youngest of Jacob's 12 sons, is the instrument God uses to fulfill the promise to the patriarchs. The older and supposedly more deserving brothers are bypassed. What Joseph does is done entirely through divine guidance. Although his vanity caused him initial troubles, God's grace overcomes it and brings this lowly Palestinian shepherd to a position of power in Egypt second only to Pharaoh.

In the story of Joseph, as in all of Genesis, we see God working through flawed human beings, loving them despite their weaknesses, and bringing good even out of their mistakes and sins. At the end of Genesis Jacob's family is living off the fat of the land in Egypt. But this fact poses a question: What has happened to the promise to Israel that it would be a great people in possession of Canaan? Genesis ends with the message that for Israel, as in our own lives, God's work is far from finished.

Questions for Discussion and Reflection
Group Sharing/Discussion

1. The J, E, and P writers each wrote their version of the stories as they heard them passed down orally. Although they write about the same events, individually they stress either faith, obedience, or fidelity. Find examples of each of these virtues in the Genesis stories.

2. Abraham and Sarah continually struggled to believe and trust in God. (See the chart on RG 59.) Sometimes it was difficult because they could not see ahead and trust and other times it was difficult because of their own failures. Choose a particular time when they failed to believe or trust and tell what advice you would have given them to help them in that struggle.

3. The story of Joseph covers many chapters (37–50) and is a rich tale of youthful pride, sibling jealousy, making the best of an unexpected turn in life, brotherly forgiveness, and carrying out God's life-plan without understanding where it was leading. What is one part of Joseph's life with which you can identify?

4. Let different people in your group take on the part of one of Joseph's brothers and tell his side of the story, what he was thinking and feeling early on as well as when they meet again in Egypt. Do the same with Joseph.

5. In what ways is the book of Genesis helpful in understanding where we are today as the People of God?

In Our Lives

1. Jews, Christians, and Muslims (through Ishmael) all consider Abraham their father. Explaining this shared lineage to someone you know who has religious prejudices might help them be more open to their religious "relatives" in other traditions.

2. As you look over the entire book of Genesis, what is the most important lesson for your own life?

3. God is calling and leading us as a people today. Like the people in Genesis, we too sometimes miss the point, fail to trust, stubbornly go our own way, or just do not listen well. What are some ways we as a people can listen well and follow God's call?

Individual/Personal Reflection/Action

1. Have a conversation with someone you trust in which you tell them about how you are like one of the persons in Genesis at their time of failure. Ask for their advice and their support in prayer for you in this matter.

2. Choose a particular significant part of this family story and read it over by yourself slowly. Sit quietly and listen to your own thoughts and insights about it.

EXODUS READING GUIDE

At a Glance

Who are the main players?	Moses Miriam Aaron Zipporah Jethro Pharaoh Pharaoh's daughter Joshua Bezalel Oholiab
What should I look for?	Slavery Deliverance The Passover God's Guidance The Ten Commandments The covenant at Sinai Importance of laws and public worship
When did this take place?	Probably around 1270 B.C. Another possible date is 1440 B.C.
Where did these events occur?	Egypt, Midian (Modern Saudi Arabia), The Sinai Peninsula: The Sinai Desert and Mt. Sinai (also called Mt. Horeb)
Why was this book written?	To make sure Israel never forgot God's saving act of delivering them from slavery in Egypt; that it was God who made Israel a nation and swore, at Sinai, to be their God forever; that the Law is a sign of God's love and presence among them
What is the story?	Joseph's family settles and prospers in Egypt, but after his death the Israelites become so numerous that the Egyptians fear them and force them into slavery. God chooses Moses to lead the people from slavery to freedom in the Promised Land. It takes 10 plagues to convince Pharaoh to let the Israelites go. Finally, they escape across the Red Sea. After long wanderings in the desert, the Israelites make a covenant with God at Mt. Sinai and receive the Law to guide their life as a nation.

Structure of the Book of Exodus

Exodus begins where Genesis leaves off. It carries the story line from security in the land of Egypt through enslavement, deliverance, and escape through a desolate wilderness to a meeting with God at Mount Sinai. But this journey takes the reader only halfway through the book, to chapter 19. The second half dwells at length on two key activities that take place at the mountain. The first is the making of a covenant between God and the people, and the second is the description of the key elements of divine worship: the building of a sanctuary tent and an ark (a wooden chest) to serve as God's throne, and the establishment of priestly ministers. So the book is really an intricate mixture of narratives and legal regulations for the community. This did not happen by accident. The story of God's act of merciful liberation from slavery lays the foundation for his merciful guarantee to be with the people for all times, and that promise of presence is reflected in the laws and institutions for public worship.

Overview

The book of Exodus, like the book of Genesis, is structured quite artistically and purposefully. It be-

gins with a dramatic change—from success to terrible slavery. Is God's promise in doubt? It seems so; yet God is already setting a new plan in motion with the birth of Moses. Will Moses respond to God's plan as Joseph did? Will God overcome the power of Pharaoh? Will the people believe enough to leave Egypt? Will they follow Moses? During the trial in the desert, will they remain faithful? The following diagram illustrates how this story plays out.

Chapters 1–18 create an exciting action story that can keep the reader wondering whether the people will really reach their goal of freedom and a new security. This is achieved by returning to each theme again and again so that they are never quite resolved, and the tension remains—will God be successful? will the people continue to follow Moses?—right up to the moment they arrive at the mountain of God.

The second half of the book maintains this tension, as observed in the people's idolatry in chapter 32. More than in the first half, however, it establishes order and a state of security. God's Law is proclaimed and the people swear that they will keep the covenant. The detailed description of the sanctuary and its elements follows, balancing

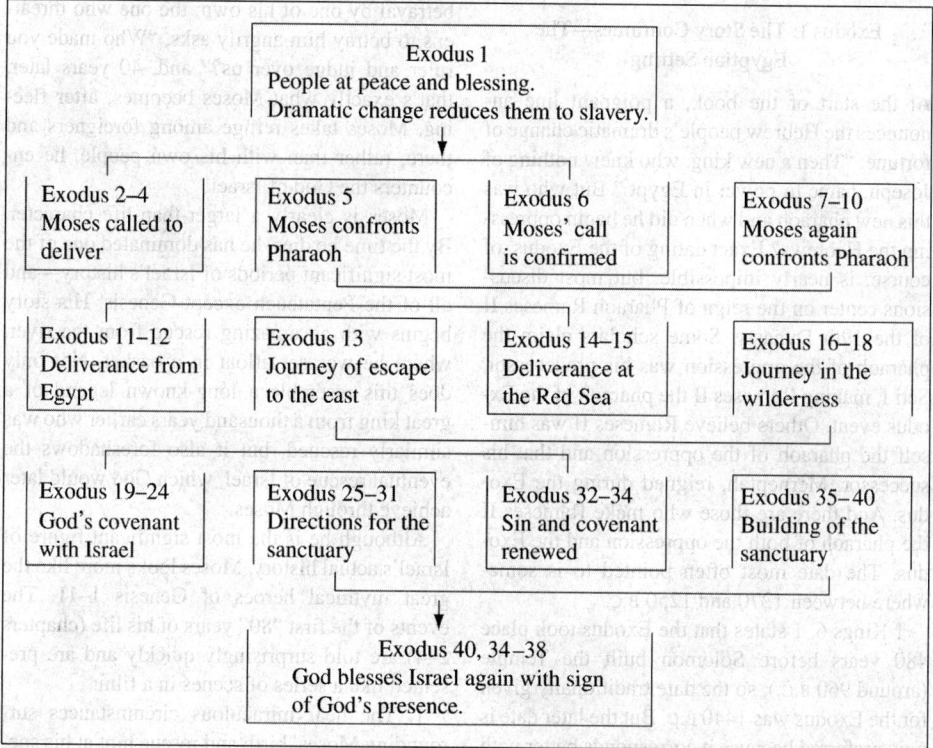

Exodus 1
People at peace and blessing.
Dramatic change reduces them to slavery.

| Exodus 2–4 Moses called to deliver | Exodus 5 Moses confronts Pharaoh | Exodus 6 Moses' call is confirmed | Exodus 7–10 Moses again confronts Pharaoh |

| Exodus 11–12 Deliverance from Egypt | Exodus 13 Journey of escape to the east | Exodus 14–15 Deliverance at the Red Sea | Exodus 16–18 Journey in the wilderness |

| Exodus 19–24 God's covenant with Israel | Exodus 25–31 Directions for the sanctuary | Exodus 32–34 Sin and covenant renewed | Exodus 35–40 Building of the sanctuary |

Exodus 40, 34–38
God blesses Israel again with sign
of God's presence.

legal and liturgical matters. Finally, the descent of the glory of God into the sanctuary in 40, 34–38 concludes this book, with the people now united to the divine presence in harmony just as they were at the beginning of chapter 1. Now, however, they are far from what their condition was there.

The three geographical regions in which God meets Israel, and that track the people's journey from slavery to freedom, provide another way of dividing the book, as illustrated below.

Throughout the book, we see God clearly in control of events. Moses is the leading character, but this is a story of God's power and authority exercised over every land and king. The book's novel-like structure surfaces in the many sudden and unexpected plot twists. Hopeless situations and near-defeats are suddenly transformed into

hope and triumph. The book's structure follows that of the Psalms of Lament: A time of desperate need spurs the people to cry for help; God responds with mercy, and the people sing their thanks and praise (compare Pss 7, 10, and 53).

Notes on Individual Passages

Because the final editor combined into one story the individual retelling of these events by each of the three major sources who recorded them (J, E, and P), you may notice some inconsistencies as well as some duplications in the book. But since this work was done so carefully and smoothly, you are not likely to notice them without careful examination. Where necessary, historical information that sheds light on particular passages will be provided.

Egypt	Exodus 1–12	In Egypt God works wonders to free the people from slavery.
Wilderness	Exodus 13–18	God guides the people safely through the wilderness to personal encounter with God.
Mount Sinai	Exodus 19–40	At Mt. Sinai God establishes a community based on covenant, law, and worship.

Exodus 1: The Story Continues—The Egyptian Setting

At the start of the book, a poignant line announces the Hebrew people's dramatic change of fortune: "Then a new king, who knew nothing of Joseph, came to power in Egypt." But who was this new pharaoh and when did he begin oppressing the Hebrews? Exact dating of the Exodus, of course, is nearly impossible, but most discussions center on the reign of Pharaoh Rameses II of the 19th Dynasty. Some scholars claim the pharaoh of the oppression was his predecessor, Seti I, making Rameses II the pharaoh of the Exodus event. Others believe Rameses II was himself the pharaoh of the oppression and that his successor, Merneptah, reigned during the Exodus. And there are those who make Rameses II the pharaoh of both the oppression and the Exodus. The date most often pointed to is somewhere between 1270 and 1250 B.C.

1 Kings 6, 1 states that the Exodus took place 480 years before Solomon built the Temple (around 960 B.C.), so the date traditionally given for the Exodus was 1440 B.C. But the later date is now preferred because it corresponds better with Exodus 12, 40, which states that the Israelites had been in Egypt 430 years before Moses led them out. If Joseph and his family arrived in Egypt during the reign of the foreign invaders, the Hyksos (around 1700 B.C.—which is quite plausible), then the 1270 B.C. Exodus date is the most likely. In any case, biblical estimates of time cannot always be relied on, because they often use ideal numbers, such as 12 and 40, to arrive at a particular figure. Thus, "480 years" is 12 generations of 40 years each, representing a full (12) number of human lives from birth to death or to becoming a grandparent.

Exodus 2–4: The Choice of Moses

The story of Moses presents some striking contrasts and fascinating ironies: He is an Israelite, but his name and upbringing are Egyptian; the pharaoh orders the killing of all male Israelite babies, but by doing so he sets in motion the very circumstances that bring Moses into the royal family; his mother abandons Moses in order to save him but later is hired to be his wet-nurse; Moses kills an Egyptian to protect one of his own people but soon is forced to flee because he fears betrayal by one of his own; the one who threatens to betray him angrily asks, "Who made you ruler and judge over us?" and, 40 years later, that's exactly what Moses becomes; after fleeing, Moses takes refuge among foreigners and there, rather than with his own people, he encounters the God of Israel.

Moses is clearly a larger-than-life character. By the time he dies, he has dominated one of the most significant periods of Israel's history—and all of the Pentateuch except Genesis. His story begins with an amazing rescue from the river, where he was set afloat in a basket. Not only does this resemble a long-known legend of a great king from a thousand years earlier who was similarly rescued, but it also foreshadows the eventual rescue of Israel, which God would later achieve through Moses.

Although he is the most significant figure of Israel's actual history, Moses looks more like the great mythical heroes of Genesis 1–11. The events of the first "80" years of his life (chapters 2–4) are told surprisingly quickly and are presented like a series of scenes in a film:

1. The near miraculous circumstances surrounding Moses' birth and rescue hint at his special mission.

2. The situation worsens—Moses is not respected by his own people and is forced to flee.

3. While Moses is living among foreigners, God asks him to do the near-impossible; very reluctantly, Moses accepts (Ex 3, 1–12).

4. God communicates more intimately with Moses than with anyone else and even reveals to him the divine name, "I am who am" (Ex 3, 12–22).

5. God reassures the insecure Moses and, grudgingly, assigns his brother, Aaron, as his spokesperson (Ex 4, 1–22).

6. Persuaded by the miraculous signs he performed, the people believe Moses and accept his mission.

God Calls Leaders

The call of Moses is the first instance of an oft-repeated biblical call-pattern that shows up in the call of other great prophets and leaders. This pattern is illustrated in the table below. Note the elements as they occur in the Moses story and see how they parallel the sequence of events in the other stories.

Biblical Call-Patterns

Apparition	God appears and speaks to Moses.	Ex 3, 1–4
Motive	God gives reason for issuing a call.	Ex 3, 4–9
Commission	God commissions Moses for his task.	Ex 3, 10
Objection	Moses protests he is unworthy and unqualified.	Ex 3, 11
Reassurance	God reassures Moses and insists he serve.	Ex 3, 12
Sign	God gives a sign or prediction.	Ex 3, 12; 4, 1–5

Listed below are places you can find the elements of this same pattern in the call of other prophets and leaders

	Gideon	Isaiah	Jeremiah	Ezekiel
Apparition	Jgs 6, 11f	Is 6, 1f	Jer 1, 4	Ez 1, 1–28a
Motive	Jgs 6, 12f	Is 6, 3–7	Jer 1, 5	Ez 1, 28b—2, 2
Commission	Jgs 6, 14	Is 6, 8–10	Jer 1, 5	Ez 2, 3–5
Objection	Jgs 6, 15	Is 6, 11	Jer 1, 6	Ez 2, 6–8
Reassurance	Jgs 6, 16	Is 6, 11f	Jer 1, 7f	Ez 2, 6f
Sign	Jgs 6, 17	—	Jer 1, 9f	Ez 2, 8—3, 11

The revelation of the divine name is an especially important moment in the story. God prepares Moses by first announcing, "I am the God of Abraham, the God of Isaac, and the God of Jacob," and by insisting that love and compassion are God's motives for coming to Moses and intervening in the lives of the Israelites. God then responds to Moses' question: If they ask me your name, what shall I say? God's answer is both surprising and mysterious, for God's is no ordinary name. Several versions of the divine name occur in the text: "I am who I am," "I AM," and "He who is" (or better, "He who causes to be"). Names, especially in the Bible, are handles one can use to control another (note that in C.B. radio jargon a person's broadcast nickname is called his or her "handle"). God's response makes it clear the Israelites will be given no handle on God. God's true identity is beyond their understanding, for God is pure power and being. But the name also suggests that God's existence has a purpose; here it is closely connected with the survival of Israel. By claiming to be the God of Abraham, Isaac, and Jacob, God is assuring Israel that "I am with you totally."

Exodus 5–12: Confrontation with the Pharaoh

The biblical plagues dominate these chapters and contribute to the dramatic, even cinematic feel of this part of the story. There is no shortage of excitement and suspense. First Moses pleads with Pharaoh to allow the Israelites to go and worship the LORD (5, 1–13). Pharaoh not only refuses, he increases the work of the slave laborers, prompting the Israelite foremen to grumble that Moses is making matters worse for them (5, 14–21). An apparent repeat of the call of Moses opens chapter 6 in what is probably a retelling of the story by the P source. But instead of feeling redundant, the retelling serves to emphasize that Moses can rely on God to do exactly what God promised.

The fight for freedom shifts into high gear when God starts sending plagues upon Egypt. The following chart gives details regarding the plagues that should help us keep in mind two important points:

1. Each of the first nine plagues can be seen as an intensification of naturally occurring phenomena (e.g., small organisms still turn the Nile

YHWH (YAHWEH) In Hebrew only the consonants of words were originally written down; "points" (small marks surrounding the consonants) were later added to the word to indicate vowels. Hence the divine name is sometimes referred to as the *Tetragrammaton* (Greek for "four letters"). Much debate surrounds the meaning of the name, but most agree it is a form of the verb "to become."

As a sign of reverence, Jews from the time of the exile onward have refrained from speaking the name aloud (some of the Dead Sea Scrolls substitute four dots for the letters, refraining even from *writing* the name). In the Hebrew text, the letters *YHWH* were surrounded by vowel points for the word *Adonai* ("my Lord"), to indicate that when the text was read aloud, the reader should substitute *Adonai* for *Yahweh*. Misunderstanding of the significance of the vowel points used with the consonants for the divine name resulted, in the sixteenth century, in the word Yehowah, or the modern spelling "Jehovah." Today, pious Jews will frequently substitute the term *ha-shem,* or *has-sem* "the Name." The divine name occurs 6,823 times in the Old Testament. Only in Exodus 3, 14 do we find the unique first person form "I am who I am." Everywhere else the divine name appears in the third person form, *Yahweh*.

Following the Jewish custom, Christians do not normally speak the name in prayer, but replace it with the title "LORD." Whenever you see the word in the *New American* Bible, printed with large and small capitals, it is replacing the Hebrew word *Yahweh*.

red during flood times; ancient Egyptian documents describe the calamity of being overrun by frogs; flies and gnats are a chronic nuisance in that area even today; sandstorms and desert dust are known to block out the sun's light [*see NAB* footnote at Ex 7, 14]).

2. The Israelites saw the hand of God in the timing of these events and in the obvious control God exerted over them. In other words, the miracle was found not in the fact that the plagues happened (they could happen any time), but in when they happened. Such timing could only be explained as God's intervention.

The pharaoh is in a battle of wills with the LORD, and we might wonder if God's power can overcome Pharaoh's hardheartedness. The unfolding action is a little like the story of the Greek hero Sisyphus, who must push a boulder up a mountain only to have it roll down every time he reaches the summit. Each time Pharaoh starts to relent, he reneges at the last moment, and the hard work of pushing events in God's direction starts all over again.

The tenth and last plague, however, is decisive. Terrifying and chilling in our eyes, it was for Israel a clear sign of God's favor and protection. The firstborn males of the Egyptians perish while those of the Israelites are spared. In Israel's eyes this event marked God's clear choice of Israel as his favored nation, the firstborn of all the peoples of the earth. The Passover feast was developed as a celebration of the miracle of the "passing over" of the angel of death and the liberation of Israel from slavery.

So important was this ritual in the life of Israel that it is written into the account of the actual event. Instead of describing a fear-filled meal eaten in haste—as it probably occurred—the text describes the full liturgical ritual as it was *later* celebrated in memory of the original events. The theology of the book of Exodus (and Christian theology as well) stresses the oneness of later rituals and original events. The Hebrew concept of remembrance (*zakir*) emphasizes that remembering makes the past present again. What Israel's ancestors experienced in Egypt and the desert is relived and celebrated again in feasts and rituals. The Catholic Mass is a perfect example of the notion that ritual

The Ten Plagues

Plague What Happened	Duplicated by Egyptians	Naturally Occurring Phenomenon	Pharaoh Starts to Relent
Blood River Nile metaphorically "turned to blood" making most of Egypt's water undrinkable.*†	Yes	Yes	No
Frogs Frogs came up out of the Nile and "covered the land."*	No	Yes	Yes
Gnats The "dust of Egypt" turned into huge swarms of gnats.*†	No	Yes	No
Flies Swarms of flies invaded every home in Egypt.*	No	Yes	Yes
Disease Fatal disease afflicted all Egyptian livestock but none of the Israelites' animals.†	No	Yes	No
Boils Festering boils broke out on all Egyptian people and animals.*†	No	Yes	No
Hail Worst hail storm ever destroyed livestock and crops.*†‡	No	Yes	Yes
Locusts Countless locusts devoured what few crops were left.*‡	No	Yes	Yes
Darkness Total darkness covered Egypt for three days.*	No	Yes	Yes
Death of Firstborn Firstborn son of every Egyptian family died also firstborn among livestock.* †	No	No	Yes

*Plague affected humans; †Plague affected livestock; ‡Plague affected crops.

remembering makes past events present now, for we believe that when we remember what Jesus did, he becomes uniquely present among the assembly.

Exodus 13–15: Escape through the Sea

In addition to two tellings of the escape through the sea, these chapters list two additional practices the Israelites are to observe to remember how God delivered them from death and slavery: refraining from any food containing yeast, and consecration to God of all first-born males (13, 1–16). These practices, in fact, may have existed among the Israelites and their pagan neighbors for generations before the time of the Exodus. But Israel's history persuaded them to give these practices a whole new meaning: They became reminders that Israel's life as a nation depended on the love and mercy of the God who delivered them from death.

The first telling of the flight through the sea (13, 17—14, 31) is a dramatic and detailed prose description. The second (15, 1–21) is a poetic rendition, which probably derived from a feast-day hymn. It is also considered by many to be the oldest written text in the Bible, probably written during the 200-year period when Israel was ruled by judges, before the establishment of the monarchy. It presents God as a fierce warrior fighting on behalf of the people.

The first and older half of the song (vv. 1–12) recounts the actual battle God wages against Egypt, while the second half tells how God led Israel through the desert to the Promised Land. Verses 13–18 in the second half refer to events that have not yet happened at this point in the story (the eventual conquest and settlement of Canaan), leading scholars to conclude that the second half was probably composed later than the first part of the song.

Exodus 16–18: Hardships in the Desert of Sinai

The next stage of the journey takes the Israelites from the location of the sea to the foot of the mount of Sinai in two months. The itinerary of that two-month trek is listed for us, but unfortunately few of the places can be identified with any certainty: Even the place where the Israelites crossed the "Red Sea" and the location of Mt. Sinai are open to discussion. The Hebrew name for "Red Sea" has two other meanings: "reed sea" or the "sea of chaos." If the correct meaning is "Reed" Sea, then any of a number of marshy lakes might be the actual crossing site (although it is possible today's Red Sea was once called the "Sea of Reeds"). If "sea of chaos" is the correct reading, then anyone's guess might do since the name is symbolic, representing the place where God would destroy Pharaoh's army, the servants of chaotic evil.

While no definitive answer can be given about the route of the Exodus, scholars offer three possible options, which are shown on color Map 3 in the back of this book. Least likely is the northern and shortest route that would have led them through the so-called "Way to the Land of the Philistines" (13, 17 notes God's decision to avoid the Philistines for fear that the possibility of conflict with them would turn the Israelites back toward Egypt). The second route would have traversed the Sinai peninsula, also in the northern area moving eastward. This was a major caravan route that passes near Kadesh-Barnea, where according to

Deuteronomy 2, 14 Israel camped for 38 years, and it went through territory known to be hospitable to nomadic groups. The map lists it as "The Way to Shur." Most favored and most probable, however, is the circular route along and around the southern part of the Sinai. What recommends this longest route is the fact that because Egyptians mined gems here, it is quite possible that Moses could have known it. Also, several of the mountain peaks found here are among the most impressive in Sinai and thus are likely candidates for being the mount of the covenant. The length of the route also makes plausible the Israelites' frequent moves as recorded in Exodus and Numbers.

But the book of Exodus is not as concerned with geography as modern scholars are. The reasons it gives for the route taken have little to do with the advantages of one route over another. Instead, the route serves the dual purpose of exposing the tension between Moses and the people and revealing God's protective presence among them throughout their long journey. Despite the people's habit of complaining about their hardships rather than giving thanks for their freedom, God remains present as *healer* (15, 25f: at Marah God restores the water's sweetness), *provider* (16, 16–36: God provides daily manna to feed them), and *reminder* (17, 1–7: at Rephidim God turns the people's anger over lack of water into a reminder of the Red Sea crossing by making water miraculously issue from a rock). In addition, God is again experienced as protector (17, 8–13) when the Israelites successfully fend off the attack of the Amalekites. Finally, Moses' father-in-law Jethro, a Midianite, helps organize judges and leaders to assist Moses, thus establishing a lasting bond between Israel and the Midianites (18, 1–26).

Questions for Discussion and Reflection
Group Sharing/Discussion

1. Look back over the life of Moses. Which do you think are the three most significant moments or events in his life. Explain your choices.

2. Moses was not eager to be a leader. In fact he tried to argue his way out of it. Role-play each of Moses' excuses and the LORD's response each time. Different people could take the roles for each argument.

3. The night on which the Israelites finally were able to leave Egypt was so significant that

it is remembered to this day by the Passover ritual meal. It was this ritual meal that Jesus was celebrating at the Last Supper. During this meal the youngest person at the table asks, "Why is this night different from all other nights?" How would you answer that question?

4. Invite someone from the Jewish community to explain or even demonstrate the Passover Ritual. Or, look up "Passover" on the Web and choose one article to describe to your group.

In Our Lives

1. The Egyptians became afraid of the Israelites living in "their" country because the Israelites began to outnumber them. Eventually the Egyptians became ruthless. Where are there parallels today with regard to fear of other cultures in our own society or other lands?

2. When the daughter of Pharaoh rescued the baby Moses she had no idea what the long-term results of that act would be. She just did the right thing for someone in need. What are some specific ways our community can have an effect on the future by doing the right thing for someone in need?

3. Why is it important to continue the tradition of remembering our history in ritual celebrations as the Jews do in the Passover? What are ways we can make our community celebration of the Eucharist more effective in our lives?

4. Moses' father-in-law, Jethro, gave him the advice of looking among the community for trustworthy people to help lead them. How do we do this in our community? What can we do to encourage ourselves and others to be involved in community leadership?

Individual/Personal Reflection/Action

1. How might Moses as a "reluctant leader" be an inspiration and model for you?

2. The Israelites, under God's protection (*pesach*, which we usually translate "Passover," probably means "protect"), were safe from the death brought by the final plague, and the Jewish people remember that protection and rescue in

their ritual meal to this day. How is Christ our Passover from death to life? What is similar to the Passover in our celebration of the Eucharist?

3. The Israelites sang and danced to praise and thank God for all he had done for them. At the end of each day, remember to look back and praise and thank God.

Exodus 19–24: The Covenant with God

To visualize how these five chapters constitute the high point of the entire Pentateuch, imagine a road starting at the Garden of Creation in Genesis 1, 1 and ending at the borders of the Promised Land in Deuteronomy 34. The road, of course, climbs up and down hills and mountains, so imagine a sudden and steady climb through all of Genesis and Exodus 1–18 to the very top of Mt. Sinai. There the road levels out temporarily while God establishes a covenant with the people (Ex 19–24), and gives them laws that will enable them to live out the covenant (Ex 25—Nm 10). Then (at Nm 11) the road begins a sudden descent that sends it to the edge of the Jordan River (at the end of Deuteronomy). When the Israelites looked back at human history, that's the God-directed route they saw history following, with Israel playing a central role in the history.

Chapters 19 to 24 describe the high point of the Pentateuch. The events recounted here are divided into four stages:

1. Israel prepares to meet God and receive the Law (Ex 10, 1–25).

2. God gives general laws (the Ten Commandments) (Ex 20, 1–21).

3. God gives specific laws (Ex 21, 22—23, 33).

4. Israel accepts God's laws and seals the covenant with God (Ex 24, 1–18).

Note the difference between the commandments and the more specific laws that follow. The commandments present the basic demands of a healthy relationship with God: loving God and neighbor. Limited to 10 (for easy memorizing

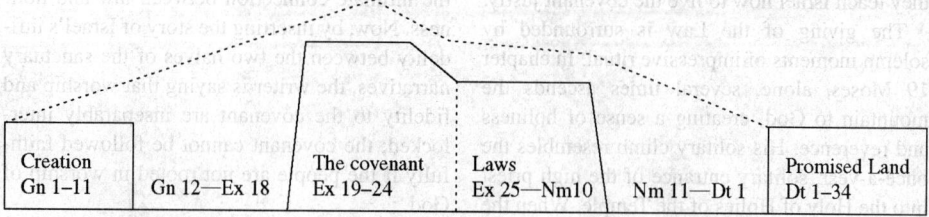

Creation		The covenant	Laws		Promised Land
Gn 1–11	Gn 12—Ex 18	Ex 19–24	Ex 25—Nm10	Nm 11—Dt 1	Dt 1–34

Slavery in the Bible

It may be shocking to find in the Bible a reference to human beings as "property" (21, 21). Remembering that all biblical literature arose out of the culture in which it was written may soften the blow a bit, but it may still be jarring to see apparent approval of slavery in the pages of scripture. Recalling that God's ways are gradually revealed to Israel throughout its history (e.g., the concept of life after death is a late development in their theology) may help put things in perspective. Christians believe that only in Jesus was God's self-revelation complete, yet even the New Testament made accommodation for slavery. God's people were still on the path of discovering God's ways and will.

It should be mentioned that the laws listed in Exodus represented an enlightened view of slavery. Other nations treated slaves as objects rather than as persons, according them no formal rights. Israel, aware of its own enslavement in Egypt, made laws to ensure humane treatment of slaves, provided for their rights, limited the time of enslavement (for Israelite slaves), and allowed slaves to assume positions of responsibility and prestige.

God's Self-Description Chapter 34, 6–7—the most quoted and alluded to passage in the Old Testament—provides a sublime understanding of who God is: "The LORD, the LORD, a merciful and gracious God, slow to anger and rich in kindness and fidelity, continuing his kindness for a thousand generations, and forgiving wickedness and crime and sin; yet not declaring the guilty guiltless."

and counting on the fingers), they state simple demands but do not say what will happen if one disobeys them, while the laws of chapters 21–23 list the consequences of breaking each specific law. These laws are called "The Covenant Code" because, by looking at practical situations and stipulating the proper way to settle each case, they teach Israel how to live the covenant justly.

The giving of the Law is surrounded by solemn moments of impressive ritual. In chapter 19 Moses, alone, several times ascends the mountain to God, creating a sense of holiness and reverence. His solitary climb resembles the once-a-year, solitary entrance of the high priest into the Holy of Holies of the Temple. When the people embrace the covenant in chapter 24, they seal the pact with two rituals: a sprinkling with blood (24, 3–8), and a meal in which Moses, Aaron, and the 70 elders feast with God. Lawgiving and ritual thus combine in a setting of divine holiness and human sanctification to impress on the reader that the Law is the God-given means to becoming holy as God is holy.

Exodus 25–40: Establishing God's Home in Israel

It may well be that there is more material describing the Tabernacle than there is about any other single topic in the Bible. This material helps emphasize one of the themes of Exodus: God is not only a transcendent and mighty warrior God, but also a gracious God who has chosen to live in the midst of the people.

Chapters 25–31 and 35–40 essentially repeat each other by giving directions for building and furnishing the Tabernacle and by describing in detail how the directions were carried out. In between, however, are stories of Israel's first failure to keep the covenant—the worship of the golden calf. This placement is probably no accident. Here, as in the previous section, structure reveals the writer's purpose: In the preceding section two ritual events were wrapped around the giving of the Law to make a statement about the intimate connection between law and holiness. Now, by inserting the story of Israel's infidelity between the two halves of the sanctuary narratives, the writer is saying that worship and fidelity to the covenant are inseparably interlocked; the covenant cannot be followed faithfully if the people are not rooted in worship of God.

| Exodus 19–24 covenant given | Exodus 25–31 sanctuary directions | Exodus 32–34 covenant renewed | Exodus 35–40 sanctuary built |

The Theology of the Covenant

Because the giving of the covenant is the central moment of the entire Pentateuch, reflection on the meaning of the term "covenant" (the Hebrew word is *berit*) will yield a better understanding of Israel's faith. But first, some general points:

1. A covenant, like a contract, is a solemn agreement, legally binding on both parties, but made with a religious ritual.

2. Covenants can be made between individuals, between nations, between a superior and an inferior (king and vassal), or between a god and people.

3. Several types of royal covenants or treaties are known from the ancient Near East. A royal grant was an unconditional covenant between a king and a loyal servant. A parity treaty was made by equals who agreed to respect each other's rights and interests and accepted mutual responsibility. A Suzerain-vassal treaty was a covenant between a great king and the lesser kings of nations conquered or threatened by him. Vassal treaties were not an equal proposition; the vassal agreed to faithfully execute a long list of demands, while the king promised nothing more specific than kindness and protection.

4. Once solemnly made, these treaties were considered binding for all time.

5. The most common form of vassal treaty known from ancient times contains six parts, which, in a general way, can also be found in the Sinai covenant (Ex 19–24).

The similarities as outlined in the chart below are of interest, but they must not be pushed too far. Later in the tradition, legal treaty language

Ancient Treaties and the Sinai Covenant

Typical Thirteenth-Century B.C. Hittite Vassal-Type Treaty	Elements of Typical Vassal-Type Treaty Found in the Sinai Covenant
A preamble stating names of the parties	Ex 20, 2: "I am the LORD your God who brought you out of Egypt, out of the land of slavery."
Historical listing of the good things the king has done	Ex 20, 2 (19, 4): "You yourselves have seen what I did in Egypt, and how I carried you on eagles' wings and brought you to myself."
Duties the vassal must perform	Ex 20, 3–17; 20, 23—23, 17: The commandments and the laws governing daily life.
An order to save the document and read it publicly	Ex 24, 3–8; 24, 12: Blood-sprinkling ceremony and giving of the tablets of the Law to be kept among the people.
List of gods who witness the treaty	There are no divine witnesses because there is no other god who can testify to what the LORD does.
Lists of curses the gods will inflict on those who break the treaty and blessings for those who keep it	Ex 20, 5f; 23, 25: "I the LORD your God am a jealous God, inflicting punishment for their fathers' wickedness on the children of those who hate me . . . but bestowing mercy to the thousandth generation, on the children of those who love me and keep my commandments."

Literary Forms of the Bible

What is the Bible? From a literary point of view it is a collection of many types of literature. Broadly speaking we may classify the books of the Bible into five kinds of literature: (1) Narrative books (e.g. Genesis, Samuel, Kings, Maccabees, the Gospels, the Acts of the Apostles); (2) Poetry (e.g. Psalms, Song of Songs, Proverbs); (3) Prophetic books; (4) Epistles (e.g., the Letters of Paul); and (5) Apocalypses (Daniel, 2 Esdras [4 Ezra]; Revelation).

Of course, there are many types of literature that do not appear in the Bible, for example drama, satire, or autobiography. And none of the types of literature in the Bible are exclusively biblical. They are shared with nonbiblical literature as well. When we pay attention as we read it becomes clear that some books of the Bible contain more than one literary form. For example, Exodus contains narrative, laws, and poetry; Jeremiah contains narrative, poetry, and letters. Some of the Epistles contain poetic passages, such as 1 Corinthians, chapter 13. So, rather than just reading the text in a "flat" way, simply for plot or content, paying attention to the type of literature can deepen our appreciation and understanding of the particular part of the Bible we are reading.

---

became commonplace, such as in the covenant summary statement often found in the prophets, "You shall be my people and I will be your God" (Ex 11, 20; 14, 11; Jer 7, 23; 11, 4; 24, 7; Hos 2, 25, etc.). But Exodus is first of all a record of Israel's momentous encounter with God, and of her promise to worship the LORD, who was the savior and loving benefactor of this small and insignificant group of refugees.

The notion of covenant confirmed in Israel's mind the special and unique relationship they enjoyed with God. God had shown Israel special favor by revealing the divine name to them, saving them from slavery, choosing to live among them in the Tabernacle, and giving them laws to govern their life and ensure a just society among them. Initially the covenant was celebrated in worship with a sense of unalterable national destiny, a kind of "We can't lose because God is on our side" attitude. The later prophets like Jeremiah and Ezekiel, however, emphasized that while even disasters did not mean God had abandoned them, the people's faithlessness could bring punishment upon the nation.

Questions for Discussion and Reflection
Group Sharing/Discussion

1. Imagine you are Moses and you come down from your mountain retreat and discover the people worshiping the golden calf. What would you say to them? Allow time in your group for each person to think about this, then take turns responding.

2. With which of the characters of Exodus can you most easily identify? Is it because of their strengths or their weaknesses? How does it feel to know you have some of the same strengths and weaknesses as these great characters of Exodus?

3. The Ten Commandments are very brief, but that does not mean they do not reach far into our daily living. Take each commandment, perhaps working in small groups, and write out as many "rules" contained in it as possible or ways that we live out the meaning of that commandment.

4. Why would God want the Sabbath to be honored? What is the wisdom in this?

In Our Lives

1. Which of the Ten Commandments do we as a society most need to pay serious attention to today? How can our parish community encourage that?

2. What does it say about Moses that, when the LORD was going to destroy the people and save only Moses, Moses begged God to save the people also? Who is someone in our day who is that selfless and puts the common good above individual wants?

3. The LORD had made a covenant, protected the people, and led them to safety. They seemed to forget all that and made a golden calf to worship. Sometimes people only turn to God when they are in need of help. What can help us to remember God in the good times as well as when things are difficult?

4. Some say the heart of the Old Testament is found in God's command to Moses when Pharaoh pursues the fleeing Israelites: "Go forward," God says. God tells them to move and pursue freedom; to yield to the call to greatness; to stop complaining, take action, and follow their dream. Has God ever given you that same command? When? Why? Can one be afraid of freedom? Why is slavery or dependence sometimes more attractive than freedom?

Individual/Personal Reflection/Action

1. God renewed the covenant after the Israelites failed. God's forgiveness is there for us too, when we fail or even when we just forget and betray our values. Sometimes we need to be forgiven. Sometimes we need to forgive. Where is forgiveness needed in your own life?

2. The Israelites were tempted to disobey the first commandment and failed. What temptations do you face against keeping God first over pursuing the "good life" by giving into the consumerism of our culture? Who or what helps you keep your priorities straight?

3. What are the ways you will "Remember the Sabbath day" this week?

LEVITICUS READING GUIDE

At a Glance

Who are the main players?	Moses Aaron Aaron's sons: Abihu, Nadab, Eleazar, Ithamar
What should I look for?	Holiness of God and nation; relationship of Law and people's holiness Significance of physical perfection Religious ritual and worship Sacrificial offerings Levites and priesthood
When did this take place?	It is presented as perhaps two years after the Exodus from Egypt, during the Israelites' year-long stay camped at Mt. Sinai. (Possible date: around 1272 B.C. or 1442 B.C.) The laws were actually completed over a long period of time, perhaps 1000 B.C. to 600 B.C.
Where did these events occur?	In the Sinai peninsula, at the foot of Mt. Sinai (also called Mt. Horeb).
Why was this book written?	To answer the question: How can a sinful people serve a perfect and holy God? To teach the ways of holiness: observance of Law and religious ritual. To serve as a guidebook: teaching priests and people how to worship the LORD and live holy lives.
What is the story?	Leviticus contains few characters and almost no story line. The book is a very detailed compilation of rules and regulations governing worship and daily life.

If you were working your way through the Bible one book at a time, your reading might come to a grinding halt at Leviticus. All the elements you might normally expect are missing here: plot, poetry, stories of suspense or deep emotion—even the characters are few. Yet the book holds a venerated place in Jewish tradition. That is because the book is rich with laws that define Jewish life and practice. Of the 613 binding commandments found in the Pentateuch, 247 are right here in Leviticus. Despite the fact that a major portion of the laws, those pertaining to temple sacrifice, became impossible to observe when the Jerusalem Temple was destroyed in A.D. 70, Leviticus remains the most important statement of Torah for Judaism. Its laws are much studied and debated, because Judaism has always found in their rich diversity the "teaching" or "way" it needed to follow to be faithful and beloved sons and daughters of God.

In Judaism Torah carries a positive and joyful connotation, not the narrow and restrictive meaning

"Law" often conjures among modern people. Because it means "teaching" or "guide," Torah is celebrated in Judaism as a gift from God that leads to God's favor and salvation. The best expression of this attitude can be found in Psalm 119, the longest Psalm in the Psalter, which, for 176 verses, exults in praise and gratitude for the Law.

Differing Views of Law

Christians come to Leviticus with a very different attitude. Whether horrified by the details of animal sacrifice, or disgusted by the discussions of bodily emissions, or turned off by the many restrictive rules governing what can and cannot be eaten, Christians find little to celebrate here, preferring to emphasize instead the concept of "freedom from the law" that St. Paul stresses in his letters. What Christians who approach the book with these biases miss are the profound insights into the mystery of God that are woven into the fabric of Leviticus. Like golden thread, the insights into the holiness, majesty, power, and love of God shine through regularly and reveal the enduring value of the book. By keeping our eyes on the "big picture" rather than on individual laws, we can focus on the most important question the book raises: How would following these laws make Israel different from other nations?

To tap its fullest meaning, we must approach the book from two angles: First, we can ask what religious insights and meaning the ancient Israelites found in its various laws and practices. Second, we can explore how its major themes reveal the enduring character and purpose of God. Israel relied on these themes for their understanding of God, and Christianity has made them central in its own teaching. Take, for example, the concept of sacrifice. Knowing the importance of sacrifice in Leviticus as a means of relating to God can help Christians articulate the meaning of Jesus' death and an understanding of Eucharist.

Structure of Leviticus

The style in Leviticus is of the Priestly (P) source, whose work is found throughout the Pentateuch—and who is always concerned with classifying and listing things in their proper place (see the P creation story in Genesis 1 and

the list of nations in Genesis 11, 10–32). Another major concern of the P writer is defining the difference between the world of the sacred and that of everyday life. Like wise parents teaching a child how to relate to fire, the P source knows God is not to be dealt with lightly. One must respect fire and understand its power if one is to deal with it and live. P deals directly with the life-and-death question of what is appropriate and inappropriate when relating to God.

Leviticus has two major divisions that are quite different in spirit. Chapters 1–16 live up to the name of the book, which basically means "That which pertains to the levitical priests." (The Hebrew title is the opening word of the text, *wayyiqra,* meaning "And he [the LORD] called"). Chapters 17–27, however, deal with larger areas of community behavior and public worship that express the unique identity of Israel and the call to holiness inherent in the covenant. A simple outline of the book is shown here.

Outline of Leviticus

Part I

A. Laws governing the five types of sacrifice (Lv 1–7)

B. The ceremony of ordination of Aaron and his sons (Lv 8–10)

C. Laws governing legal purity regarding animals, childbirth, leprosy, and sexuality (Lv 11–15)

D. The observance of the Day of Atonement (Lv 16)

Part II

A. Moral and ethical laws of holiness (Lv 17–20)

B. Ritual (liturgical) requirements for holiness (Lv 21–25)

C. Blessings and curses for following and breaking the covenant (Lv 26) (Serves as a conclusion to chapters 17–25 and to entire book)

D. Regulations for redeeming offerings vowed to God (Lv 27) (Added later to the book as an appendix)

In Part I of the outline we find a twice-repeated pattern of *laws* followed by *actions.* After the many regulations on sacrifice in chapters 1–7, there follows a narrative explanation of the

Holiness and Purity

The twin emphases on holiness and ritual purity found in Leviticus reflect attitudes that on the surface might seem contradictory but, in actuality, are complementary.

The stress on holiness expressed the Israelites' belief that God lived among them. Holiness, in fact, might be defined as awareness of and respect for the divine presence that surrounds people everywhere. For Israel the implications were obvious: If a just and merciful God had chosen to "tabernacle" (make a home) among them, then they must be a just and merciful people. Over and over again in Leviticus we hear the refrain: "Be holy because I, the LORD your God, am holy." The expectation was that by living among them, God would rub off on the people.

A doubly opposite expectation is reflected in the stress on ritual purity: The people must not rub off on God. Yes, God was willing to live among them, but God's ways were still light-years away from human ways. People were not to approach God carelessly or take God for granted. Instead, the people were to foster an attitude of carefulness toward God, approaching God as worthily as possible. Keep in mind that ritual uncleanness in itself was not considered harmful or even sinful. Daily life, after all, made uncleanness impossible to avoid. God is the holy one; human beings of necessity fall short of God's holiness. The point, then, was not that one always had to be ritually clean, but that one could not approach God unless he or she was clean. Coming into the presence of God in an unclean state was truly dangerous, for God's holiness could not abide it. While Exodus taught the people how to make holy objects, Leviticus teaches them how to be holy people.

So all the laws regarding holiness and ritual purity point to the same reality: a holy, just, and loving God dwells among us calling us to be a holy, compassionate people; because our God is everywhere, even in ordinary day-to-day life, we must take care to keep our lives pure so that in every aspect of our lives we can stand worthily before the LORD, whose greatness so transcends our ordinary existence.

role of priests and a description of Aaron's first major sacrifice. Chapter 11 begins a new set of regulations, this time relating to proper use of food and respect for bodily functions. What follows in chapter 16 is an elaborate description of the annual Day of Atonement, the ritual that cleansed the people of guilt from all their sins. The message in this pattern of laws followed by actions is simple: Worship and daily life are closely connected—what we celebrate in worship flows out of how we live our lives.

Like Part I, Part II of Leviticus, often referred to as "The Law of Holiness," is dominated by the theme of holiness. This section of laws has a moralistic and preachy tone, which merely lists laws one after another. These later laws are of two types: Chapters 17–20 focus on moral laws that govern the way we relate as social beings

living in community, while chapters 21–25 deal with regulations for priests and liturgical worship. Chapter 26 is an impressive chapter that caps the collection of laws and serves as a conclusion of the whole book.

All commentators agree that the viewpoint that dominates and unites Leviticus is Priestly. Those editors gathered together all the laws that governed the various activities that the priests were expected to monitor—everything from public worship to private matters like food and clothing, skin diseases, and sexual activity, as well as truly ethical questions about just and loving relationships among the people.

The laws of Leviticus were not written all at once. Groups of laws written at different times were joined by the Priestly editors into an ever-growing collection. Although three different

Sacrifices of the Old Testament

Type of Sacrifice What (elements)	Why (function)	Where (citation)
Holocaust or Whole Burnt Offering		
Male and unblemished cattle, sheep and goats, birds (pigeons for the poor)	Because wholly consumed, it acknowledges God as Lord of life: atones for sins; joyful worship	Lv 1, 1–17; 6, 8–13; 8, 18–21; 22, 17
The Grain (or Cereal) Offering		
Grain, flour, frankincense, oil, bread; only a symbolic portion burned, the rest eaten by priests	Substitute for expensive animal offering; thanksgiving for good crops; joyful worship	Lv 2, 1–16; 6, 14–23
The Peace Offering		
Any unblemished animal—male or female (cattle or sheep and goats, but not birds since too small for group to eat)	A "well-being sacrifice"; not burned up, but eaten by offerers and families. Only fat parts (considered choicest) were burned to God	Lv 3, 1–17; 7, 11–34
Sin Offering or "Purgation Offering"		
If offender were whole people or a priest: bull; ordinary person: goat; poor: bird or some fine flour. Blood sprinkled on altar in outer courtyard if lay offender; in holy interior if priest or whole people offended	To atone for usually unintentional sin (violating something sacred); atone for loss of holiness; cleansing from impurity	Lv 4, 1—5, 13; 6, 4–30
The Guilt or Reparation Offering		
A ram sheep (its blood sprinkled on altar). The original wrong must be undone, then additional compensation must be offered to God.	While sin offering cleansed the defiled object or person, guilt offering is a "pay-back" to God for something we should have given or done—atonement to remove guilt	Lv 5, 14–26; 7, 1–6

sets of sacrifice laws, detected by their unique stylistic features, have been identified in chapters 1–7, and although the style of the first 16 chapters differs noticeably from that of the rest of the book, the editors, nevertheless, have blended these elements into a book that, after Deuteronomy, is the most unified of the five in the Pentateuch.

Because so much of the material in Leviticus is not a part of modern Christian religious practice, a look at each section of the outline on RG 74 should increase our understanding.

Leviticus 1–7: The Topic of Sacrifice

The five types of sacrifice that are named in these chapters are described in the following

---

Theology of Sacrifice

Expiation = dedication = fellowship

OR

Being forgiven = being committed = communion with God

---

table. When more than one was presented, the sequence of offerings was as follows: first, the guilt or sin offering, which gave people a way of dealing with their sinfulness. The burnt offering followed, demonstrating the people's total dedication to God. Finally came the peace or fellowship offering, which established communion with God and others in the community. This sequence of expiation to dedication to fellowship reveals both the importance and the theology of Israel's system of sacrifice: To achieve communion with God one first had to be forgiven and totally committed to the LORD.

Leviticus 8–10: The Anointing and Service of Aaron and His Sons

Chapters 25–31 of Exodus gave instructions about religious ritual that are finally put into practice in these chapters of Leviticus. (The instructions for the building of the tent and ark had already been followed by the end of Exodus, but those regarding sacrifice and the consecration of priests are not implemented until now.) Chapter 8 details the installation of Aaron and his descendants as priests of Israel. Chapter 9 narrates the first sacrifice, and chapter 10 deals with infractions of the sacrificial rules.

All three chapters reinforce the message that sacrifices must be approached with deadly seriousness. Close attention to the details of ritual is absolutely necessary, for ritual improperly done will not bring the glory of the LORD into their midst. So serious is this requirement that two of Aaron's sons are struck dead for failing to follow ceremonial rules and approaching God's presence carelessly.

Priests are reminded always to distinguish between the sacred and profane, the clean and unclean. Among other ways, they are to do this by refraining from customs that show disrespect for God's holiness such as improper dress, stepping

outside the Tent of Meeting, and drinking alcoholic beverages. Even excess zeal that violates sacrificial regulations is dangerous. Aaron's sons Eleazar and Ithamar, for example, had refused to eat the portion of the sacrifice to which they, as priests, had been entitled. They allowed it to be burnt as an offering to God instead. They were permitted to get away with this transgression only because they had given up to God what was rightfully theirs. Had it been the other way around, however, they might well have been struck dead.

These chapters reinforce the belief that idolatry is very alluring and the holiness of God easily transgressed. The role of the priests, then, becomes extremely important, for by their careful observance of religious ritual they help preserve the people's relationship with God.

Leviticus 11–15: The Laws of Purity

While the discussion of holiness and purity on RG 75 deals with this topic, some additional comments may aid our understanding of this area that is so foreign to modern Christian experience.

These chapters deal with four types of uncleanness:

1. Animals, Lv 11, 1–47
2. Childbirth, Lv 12, 1–8
3. Contagious disease, Lv 13, 1—14, 57
4. Genital discharges, Lv 15, 1–33

The many regulations that fill these chapters govern (1) which animals are and are not fit for eating, (2) when quarantine is necessary to deal with contagious diseases or infected homes, and (3) how purification is achieved by both men and women following sexual emissions. Although other purity regulations controlled the nation's life (see Ex 12–13 and Dt 20), those listed here deal with matters that come under the direct supervision of the priests.

Reading through all the rules, you might begin to wonder why one animal is deemed clean and edible while another is not. Scholars vary in their opinions. Some say there is sound primitive science underlying the regulations reflected in such rules as the mandatory quarantine of persons with infectious diseases or the ban on pork— long recognized as a carrier of parasites. Others argue that the reason is religious. Some in this group insist certain animals are forbidden because they seem imperfect—freaks of nature perhaps, but certainly not what was intended in

Clean and Unclean

Various reasons are proposed for certain animals being designated clean and others unclean:

1. Medical: reducing exposure to infectious diseases and animals known to carry disease and parasites.

2. Religious: some animals are "defective" and fail to reflect God's original plan of creation.

3. Arbitrary: simply a means of setting Israel apart from its neighbors.

Note that chapter 10 of Acts of the Apostles indicates there is nothing inherently wrong with the animals Leviticus labels unclean.

the creation. Fish that swim, birds that fly, and animals that graze are fully in God's plan, but flightless birds like ostriches, sea creatures that walk like animals, and animals that crawl close to the ground like insects seem to be aberrations and must be shunned. Some scholars who hold for a religious basis for the division between clean and unclean think the divisions are mostly arbitrary—simply a way of making the Israelites different from other people. Canaanites used pigs in their worship, so for the Israelites they were forbidden. Sharing a meal was a very important part of Middle Eastern hospitality, but their strict dietary laws prevented the Israelites from being able to mix socially with their pagan neighbors. The best guess, perhaps, is that a blend of all these motivations influenced those who drew up the lists of clean and unclean foods.

The basis for all these laws is the belief that many areas of human life touch and express the mystery of God. Birth and death and sexuality are such holy areas because they are at the very heart of the divine mystery that controls our lives. As such, those areas cannot be defiled by anything impure or unworthy. Humans penetrate the set-apart world of the sacred not only on holy days, or when they enter a holy place or participate in ritu-

als performed by a consecrated (and thus "holy") person, but also through common everyday moments that involve life and death—like eating to sustain life ("you are what you eat"), the awesome experience of sexual activity, and the sometimes dangerous loss of blood or other bodily fluids.

Leviticus 16: The Day of Atonement

The feast of the Day of Atonement described in chapter 16 was seen as a way of making up for all the instances of impurity that had defiled the land throughout the year. The description of this important ritual is the climax to all the preceding material from chapter 1 onward regarding sacrifice, priestly service, and purity. At one level or other, all those issues deal with the need for atonement. Note how atonement was at the center of most religious practice: The sacrifices always included some atoning function; ritual mistakes requiring atonement were a constant danger in priestly service; and, of course, daily life presented innumerable opportunities for intentional and especially unintentional impurity that required atoning. With this constant need for atonement, it was certainly reassuring that once a year the wickedness and rebellion of all the people could be laid onto a goat that would carry the sins off into the wilderness. Chapter 16 carefully describes each step. It lists first the proper procedures and clothing for Aaron and any future high priest to enter the presence of God in the holy of holies; then it outlines each step of the ritual, including the prayer and hand gestures over the goat; and finally it closes with a command to do this forever. Yom Kippur still occurs on the ninth day after Rosh Hashanah (New Year) each fall.

Scapegoat The term scapegoat is derived from the word Azazel (Lv 16, 8), which may have been a name of Satan and is used nowhere but in this book and chapter. Ancient editions translated the word as "the escaping goat," which eventually became the English word "scapegoat." Today it means anyone who is blamed for wrongs committed by others.

Leviticus 17–25: The Holiness Code

Chapters 1–16 dealt with ritual purity—all the behaviors and regulations that help overcome the natural barrier between God and humanity. Chapters 17–25 have a different focus: Rather than emphasizing what must be avoided in order to remain holy, they stress those positive things that must be done in order to grow in holiness.

While the long lists of laws in chapters 1–16 dealt mainly with liturgical requirements, the sermon-like verses of chapters 17–25 deal with the moral obligations of living in community. From how to worship a holy God, the focus has shifted to how to live a holy life. Because the Holiness Code of chapters 17–25 resembles the homiletic style of the book of Deuteronomy and the fiery oratory of the prophet Ezekiel, scholars think it may have been composed at the same time as these other writings, possibly during the Babylonian Exile (587–538 B.C.)

The Code itself can be divided into two parts: Chapters 17–20 cover laws for living a just and holy life binding on all members of the community, and chapters 21–25 deal mostly with priestly matters of public worship.

Although these lists might seem endless as you read them, remember that these (and the laws listed in Exodus, Numbers, and Deuteronomy) are the nation's entire collection of laws. Compared to modern law books, these are remarkably short and easy to understand. Read the laws and you will note they are not grouped in any systematic way—an inspiring law like the command to love your neighbor as yourself (Lv 19, 18) stands beside one that tells you not to plant your field with two kinds of seed (Lv 19, 19). A law forbidding turning your daughter into a prostitute is followed by one ordering observance of the Sabbath, which is followed by one about consulting mediums, and by another that says you should stand when an elderly person enters the room (Lv 19, 30–32).

These laws comprise an *ideal* code, and it is likely that some of the laws were never really put into practice. For example, the Jubilee Year—which mandated that every 50 years debts were forgiven, Israelite slaves were set free, and all property leased or bought reverted to its original owners—may never actually have been practiced. But it does point to some remarkable characteristics of Israelite law.

These laws established Israel as a nation apart, different from all their neighbors. Israel protected the rights of the weak and the poor. Punishment was not allowed to be excessive, but had to be proportionate to the crime ("An eye for an eye"). Sexuality was to be treated as sacred and not allowed to degenerate into immorality. What went on inside a person was as important as what went on outside—that is, your heart had to be pure as well as your actions. The poor could get justice just as readily as the rich, and even foreigners were assured fair treatment. Property rights never took precedence over human rights. Encoded in this system of laws was the belief that the followers of a compassionate God who "led them out of Egypt" must be known, in turn, for their own compassion and justice.

Leviticus 26–27: The Conclusion of the Holiness Code

This chapter ends both the Holiness Code and the entire book. The regulations regarding how to worship God and how to live as God's holy people have been spelled out. Blessings are promised for those who will obey the covenant, curses for those who will defy it.

The chapter reflects the post-exilic attitude of the Priestly editors and shows signs of having been written with the benefits of hindsight: It predicts blessings but also the eventual curse of exile for disobedience. It also adds a promise of renewed blessing and assurance that God will not forget the covenant completely (Lv 26, 45). The reference to "uncircumcised hearts" (Lv 26, 41) also anticipates the spirit of the exilic prophets Jeremiah (see Jer 9, 26) and Ezekiel, who announced that God was about to establish a new covenant that would be written on people's hearts. This covenant would be obeyed not out of fear of the Law, but out of love of the LORD.

The upbeat and hopeful final verses of chapter 26 were the original ending of Leviticus. Chapter 27 was added later to deal with the question of how to handle vows, sometimes rashly made, of dedicating certain people, animals, or objects to the LORD. When it was inappropriate to actually offer the vowed item, like a family member or an animal that was unclean, monetary value could be assigned to the item and the money, rather than the person or object itself, could be given over to the LORD.

Circumcision In Israel, the medical ritual practice of circumcision initiated a male into the covenant and nation and allowed him to participate in public worship. By speaking of "uncircumcised hearts," Leviticus is pointing out that more than a surgical procedure is needed to be a true follower of God. One's inner attitude is also critical. Moses (Dt 10, 16) also calls the people to circumcise "the foreskin of their hearts" by loving the LORD and ending their disobedience. In essence, following the Law is a call to a deeper relationship with God.

Questions for Discussion and Reflection
Group Sharing/Discussion

1. What is an example of an important law in Leviticus? Which one(s) would you choose to leave out if you were making their laws?

2. The Hebrew people were putting themselves together as a nation, organizing how they would function. These numerous laws were a way to do that. At the founding of the United States as a country, much time and care were put into drawing up the Constitution to help organize us as a people. How would you compare and contrast those approaches?

3. Has your attitude toward Leviticus changed at all as a result of your reading? In what ways? What value, if any, do you find in reading through such long lists of laws?

In Our Lives

1. The laws of Leviticus are to help people be holy, to live and act as God's people. What in the Catholic tradition and liturgy is helpful to people today with regard to helping them live and act as God's people?

2. Why is it important to have laws? When might you decide not to follow a law?

3. The Day of Atonement was and is an important time for the ancient Israelites and modern Jews to reflect on their sins and failings and ask for pardon. When and how do we do this in our own tradition? What can help us do better at reflecting on our failings? Try to end each day by looking at how you've failed and succeeded.

Individual/Personal Reflection/Action

1. Name for yourself five "rules" or ways of living or worshiping in the Catholic tradition that are important to you. In the coming days think about what would help you pay attention to living them more fully.

2. Following the rules is not as important as understanding why we have the rule and choosing to honor that. What rules do you not understand in our Catholic tradition? Ask someone such as a parish staff person to help you understand their purpose.

NUMBERS READING GUIDE

At a Glance

Who are the main players?	Moses, Aaron, and Miriam Joshua and Caleb Balaam, Korah, Eleazar
What should I look for?	Grumbling and rebellion of the people Characterizations of God's wrath God's faithfulness despite people's sin Importance of priests and Levites in developing fidelity through proper ritual and holiness God's use of foreign prophet/magician Balaam
When did this take place?	During the 38 years of Israel's wanderings in the desert following the sealing of the covenant at Sinai.
Where did these events occur?	Three main sites: Mt. Sinai—preparing to set out for the Promised Land; Kadesh—rebellion causes long delay, followed by eventual journey to Moab; the plains of Moab—readying to enter and conquer the Promised Land.

Why was this book written?

To show the consequences of Israel's murmuring and rebellion against the LORD; that God's wrath is to be taken seriously, but God's grace and mercy always prevail, and God will be faithful to the promises made to the Patriarchs; that God's plan for Israel and all peoples will not be thwarted; that the call to holiness and purity cannot be ignored, and that trust in God is a requirement for God's people.

What is the story?

No sooner is the covenant at Sinai sealed, than the people start grumbling against the LORD. God punishes some, but Moses' prayers persuade God to spare the nation. Spies sent into the land of Canaan return with reports of giants and argue against invasion. Joshua and Caleb disagree, but the people refuse to move. Because of their lack of trust, God decides none of the generation that left Egypt will be allowed to enter the Promised Land. The "wandering" period begins and lasts until all adults who left Egypt have died in the desert (except Joshua and Caleb). God uses the pagan prophet Balaam to speak blessings on Israel as they prepare to enter the beautiful land of God's promise.

Overview

The fourth book of the Pentateuch, Numbers, recounts memorable events of the Israelite wanderings from Sinai, God's mountain, to the plains of Moab, just opposite the Promised Land. Thus, Numbers continues the story begun in Exodus and continued in Leviticus of the escape from Egyptian servitude, the desert journey to Mount Sinai, the revelation at Sinai and giving of the Law, and the building of the Tabernacle with instruction on its operation.

Numbers is a complex collection of texts containing an assortment of interwoven kinds of literature: historical narratives, legal texts, ritual prescriptions, and poetic folk traditions. Its final form reflects a long and intricate literary history. Modern critical scholarship identifies separate sources underlying the final version of the book. Primarily, the texts derive from various layers of the Priestly school (P), with additional texts from the two older narrative sources, the Yahwist (J) and the Elohist (E). The predominant Priestly material often functions to expand, supplement, or recast the earlier (J and E) texts to fit the agenda of Priestly circles. The lengthy Balaam section (chs 22–24) in its entirety stands untouched by the Priestly writer.

The book of Numbers has three main sections.

1. Preparations for travel in the wilderness (chs 1–10)

This section is mainly prescriptive, telling how things are to be done. Its focus is the census and the arrangement of the camp of the Israelites (chs 1–2; 5, 1–4); and the arrangement of the tribes and sanctuary when they are on the march (9, 15—10, 36). Interspersed in this are various instructions or descriptions concerning the guilt offering, suspected adultery, the Nazirite vow, the priestly blessing (5, 5—6, 27), and the delayed Passover (9, 1–4). It is not always clear why these laws are placed where they are now found. The section is almost entirely Priestly in origin.

2. Travels in the wilderness (chs 11–25)

This part is mostly narrative, and combines Priestly and non-Priestly material. It tells of rebellions and complaints by Israelites, Miriam and Aaron, and the scouts (chs 11–14); the rebellion of Korah, Dathan, and Abiram (chs 16–17); Israel's encounters with various enemies; Balaam's blessing; and the Baal-Peor incident (chs 20–25). Sections of prescription interspersed among these chapters include rules on offerings, Sabbath violation, wearing fringes (ch 15); priesthood and Levitical duties (ch 18); and corpse contamination (ch 19).

3. The end of the wilderness travels and preparations for entering the land of Canaan (chs 26–36).

This section is mostly prescriptive, containing laws and rules. Portions that are closely connected with the story itself or the topic of acquiring the land of Canaan include the second census (ch 26); laws on female inheritance (27, 1–11); the transfer of civil leadership to Joshua (27, 12–23); revenge against the Midianites (ch 31); the distribution of the Transjordan land (ch 31); a summary of wilderness travels (ch 33); the boundaries of the land of Canaan (ch 34); Levitical cities and homicide laws (ch 35); and a supplement to laws of female inheritance (ch 36). Portions less visibly connected with the narrative context are the ritual calendar (chs 28–29) and the rules about women's vows (ch 30). This section is almost entirely Priestly in origin.

Reading the Book of Numbers

A first reading of the book might begin with the main narrative, chs 1; 10–14; 16–17; 20–27; 31–33. The legal sections are more difficult to understand and may best be read according to different topics: the Levites (chs 3–4; 7–8; 18; 35); priestly and Levitical duties (chs 3–4; 16–17; 18; 35); the arrangement of camp (chs 2–3; 10); laws pertaining to women (ch 5; 27, 1–11; chs 30–36); holy days (9, 1–14; 15, 32–36; chs 28–29); impurity and holiness (chs 6, 1–4; 6, 16–17; 19; 35); sacrifices and offerings (chs 7; 15; 28–29); and distribution of the land (chs 27, 1–11; 32; 34–36). Numbers also contains a few poetic passages. Some of these are especially difficult and might be studied together in connection with the style of the Psalms.

There are few parallels to this type of writing in modern literature. We can learn to value and even enjoy this intense combining of laws and past lessons if we can forget our world a bit and imagine ourselves as one of those Israelites whose unique and passionate faith in a single God set them apart from other peoples. How do they preserve the ties back to the days of salvation and guidance in the desert without losing them in the culture of the people they conquer? They remember the ways in the desert and observe them!

Major Religious Topics of Numbers

While keeping the journey story moving forward, the Priestly editors of Numbers emphasize certain themes over others. Ritual and worship matters are very important, as are questions regarding the duties of priests and Levites. Laws governing conflicts over land also receive attention. But the themes that dominate are theological, that is, issues that center on God's power to fulfill the promise made to Abraham and the other patriarchs. Of these topics four require more detailed attention:

1. The authority of Moses, Aaron, and the elders
2. The people's murmuring and lack of trust
3. God's use of the prophet Balaam
4. The use of war to advance God's plan for Israel

Moses and Aaron

The leadership and importance of Moses in the Pentateuch can hardly be questioned. And yet that is exactly what the people often did during their journeys. Even his sister and brother questioned his right to sole authority. Moses says little in his own defense. He leaves that to God, and God does not disappoint. More than 150 times in Numbers we are told God spoke to Moses directly, and through him to Israel. Those who questioned Moses' role were reminded that God's relationship with Moses was unique.

Yet God did allow Moses to share the burden of leadership with Aaron and some elders of the community. Moses and Aaron were from the tribe of Levi, a tribe that was considered violent renegades in Genesis. Exodus, however, points out that the Levites were the only tribe that did not worship the golden calf, and Deuteronomy adds that the Levites alone were faithful at Massah and Meribah where Moses struck water from the rock.

Priests and Levites

Levites and priests are distinct roles: Aaron is a Levite (Ex 4, 14), but priests are supposedly limited to descendants of Aaron, a subgroup within the larger group of Levites. Levites assist in various Temple activities, and in Numbers their role (and its limits) are spelled out. They alone may carry the Ark and other sacred objects (1, 49–53); they are the consecrated substitutes for each firstborn male from all other tribes (8, 15–19); and they administer the cities of refuge, places where people suspected of crimes may go to avoid revenge-slayings until their cases could be heard (35, 2–8). On the other hand, they may not be priests (chapters 16–17).

Instances of Grumbling and Rebellion

Nm 11, 1	At Taberah, the people grumble against Moses; God sends consuming fire, but the people are spared through Moses' prayer.
Nm 11, 4	At Kibroth-Hattaavah, people grumble over lack of meat; first God sends a plague, but then miraculous quail for food.
Nm 12, 1–16	Miriam and Aaron rebel against Moses' sole authority; Miriam is punished with leprosy, but later is healed by God.
Nm 14, 1-38	At the very edge of the Promised Land, the people cringe in fear, refusing to attack and take possession of the land; they accuse Moses of leading them to their deaths. God decides none of them will ever enter the Promised Land.
Nm 16, 1–36	Korah, Dathan, and Abiram lead 250 council members in open rebellion against Moses; they are destroyed by fire from heaven.
Nm 17, 6–15	The people grumble against Moses and Aaron; God's threatened punishment is averted by Aaron's ritual action.
Nm 17, 27–28	The Israelites express panic and despair.
Nm 20, 2–13	People grumble about lack of water; Moses strikes the rock and God sends water, but Moses won't be allowed to enter the Promised Land.
Nm 21, 4–9	More grumbling about food, so God sends poisonous snakes. Those who are bitten are saved by looking at a bronze serpent made by Moses.

The Murmuring Tradition

In the desert, the people repeatedly grumbled and rebelled against God. (See a few examples above.) But all the instances of grumbling reflect the Priestly interest in showing how God punished the people and then allowed the leaders, Moses or Aaron, to intercede and save them. Through all these grumbling incidents, the Priestly editors emphasize that the community must atone for sin and seek purification through liturgy. Even the bronze serpent episode is an example of healing through ritual action.

The Balaam Oracles

Balaam, a person as mysterious as he is fascinating, takes the stage in chapters 22 through 24. Balaam is no typical biblical prophet. He is more a magician-for-hire, a foreigner belonging to a nomadic clan who is well known and well regarded even by the kings of his day. One king, Balak, tries to hire him to prophesy *against* Israel, but Balaam is able to utter only words of blessing for God's people: "How can I curse whom God has not cursed? It is a blessing I have been given to pronounce" (Nm 23, 8–20) and curses their enemies.

Because the stories in Numbers seem to be a compilation of material from the J and E sources as well as the Priestly, we get two rather contradictory views of Balaam. Chapters 22–24 present him favorably as a true prophet to whom God speaks directly and who is willing to do what the LORD asks of him. Although even here there is a vague indication that Balaam was willing to be led more by greed than God's will, after being rebuked by his own donkey, he delivers four moving oracles about the destiny of Israel. God uses even this foreign prophet of questionable character to do the divine will.

In chapter 31, however, we learn Balaam was slaughtered by the Israelites because he had led the people into sexual immorality and the worship of false gods. Even New Testament books seem to pick up on a tradition that Balaam was a false teacher motivated by greed. In all, nine biblical books refer to Balaam, a sign of the importance given him and the events he dominates. His prophecies confirm Israel's eventual victory in its battle for the Promised Land.

Holy War

In Numbers 31 God tells Moses to take vengeance on the Midianites. Our ears may hear that order differently than did the writers and ancient readers of the Bible. To us it might sound like a random decision to punish innocent people for the sake of God's "chosen people," Israel. But the Israelites heard something different. In their view, the Canaanites were a wicked and sinful people who deserved punishment. What they heard was an expression of the life and death struggle between the LORD and the Canaanite gods. They were reminded that *in their founding days* God was a warrior who fought for them against their enemies. In Deuteronomy Moses bluntly tells the Israelites that "it is not because of your merits or the integrity of your heart that you are going in to take possession of their land; but the LORD, your God, is driving these nations out before you on account of their wickedness" (Dt 9, 5). In thrusting aside the native people of Canaan, Israel also saw God fulfilling the promise of land made to the patriarchs.

But God did not victimize some innocent, unsuspecting nation. When, in Numbers 31, God ordered the destruction of all the Midianites, including the women, it was because they had been the ones who followed Balaam's advice and seduced the Israelites into fornication and idolatry of Baal at Peor. One of the primary purposes of Israel's dietary and purity regulations was ensuring that the nation would be different from all its neighbors. To be different, Israel had to be pure, and to be pure Israel had to avoid idolatry and sexual excess. The best way to prevent contamination was to remove all possible sources of these evils. Those are fierce standards. But Israel saw God inflicting equally brutal punishment on itself for its own unfaithfulness.

Justifying Their War

We must also recognize that the authors of these texts were trying to justify their conquests. It was therefore in their interest to emphasize that the war had God's command behind it, and that the inhabitants who were driven out deserved their fate. Some of the descriptions must be read bearing in mind that they were written by the winning side.

Deuteronomy 20 specifies restrictions for holy war that make it less than total massacre. Numbers, too, embodies some elements of this later attitude. Now, purity and obedience are to be the hallmarks of God's army, not vengeance. It

seems as if the editors of Numbers were trying to soften the old stories of total war and call instead for a total commitment of life to God. The stories of old were plenty exciting, but they were not to be models for present behavior! Over the centuries Israel's theology of war developed, as reflected in the teachings of several prophets who said that war was not the way to do God's will (see Is 7, 1–14; Hos 10, 13f; Jer 21, 3–10; Jer 34, 1–5). In Numbers we find the earlier and later viewpoints on war mixed together.

The Theology of the Priestly Writers

The end of the book of Exodus already presented the Priestly writers' primary theology: God's presence in Israel will be found in the sanctuary (a tent during the desert years, a temple later). Israel's proper response to God's presence among them is observance of the laws of holiness and sacrifice. However, in Numbers, the P authors add important specifications about how this holiness is to be lived out: (1) through national institutions and (2) through relations among the tribes. Moreover, Israel must never neglect its system of religious worship no matter the circumstances. God will surely punish disobedience, but the intercession of priests and leaders can deter God's wrath and bring blessing; inevitably, God follows punishment with mercy. Most important, nothing can prevent God's will from being fulfilled and no one leader, not even Moses, is indispensable.

The end of Numbers finds the people still without a home, but equipped with all the tools of worship and obedience to enable them to hold on until God's promises are fulfilled. Now Moses can depart and the conquest can begin.

Questions for Discussion and Reflection
Group Sharing/Discussion

1. Choose various people who had a role in this part of the story. In your group, take turns telling their part (or highlights of it) from their point of view, explaining their role, defending what they did, and so on.

2. Describe the contradictory role of Balaam and tell how you would explain those contradictions to someone who asked you about them.

3. Compare/contrast the laws about women in the book of Numbers with those of our society in the past and today.

In Our Lives

1. Ritual and worship in the community are a central concern in Numbers. How do we mirror the importance of the community in worship in our own most important liturgical celebration, the Eucharist?

2. Could you use the words *holy* and *war* in the same sentence? How did Israel grow in their understanding of God's use of war? What insights does Christianity bring to that conversation?

3. Grumbling in the community did not stop with the Israelites. What ways do we have to bring our concerns to our religious and political leaders today, rather than grumble to each other?

Individual/Personal Reflection/Action

1. As you ponder the 40-year journey of the Israelites through the desert, what insights do you get about your own journey: the ebb and flow of your relationship with God, the ups and downs in your own commitment? Who or what helps you find your way when you need help?

2. Leaders cannot lead without followers. What are qualities that you look for in a leader you are willing to follow?

3. We can worship better as a community when we know and relate to those with whom we worship. What are some ways you can get to know members in your parish community better?

DEUTERONOMY READING GUIDE

At a Glance

Who are the main players?	Moses and Joshua
What should I look for?	Review of Israel's history and God's saving activity Warm, personal tone of the writing Stress on God's love for the people Emphasis on laws and teaching of laws to children
When did this take place?	At the end of the 40 years of wandering, as Israel prepared to enter the Promised Land
Where did these events occur?	The river Jordan's east bank, in the territory of Moab where the Jordan meets the Dead Sea.
Why was this book written?	To remind the Israelites of God's great love for them, of the mighty saving deeds God had performed for them, and that they must choose fidelity to the covenant in order to reap its benefits.
What is the story?	Poised to enter the land of promise, the Israelites hear three major speeches from Moses, who takes a final opportunity to admonish and instruct the people before his death. The book is a lengthy sermon in which Moses, like an elderly parent, tells his children what really matters and encourages them to choose carefully and well. Having done so, he blesses the tribes and goes off to die.

Reading the Book of Deuteronomy

We can start our examination of this last book of the Pentateuch by naming some of its special characteristics. First, the book is structured like one of the treaties typical of the ancient Near East. Second, the theology of Deuteronomy also runs through the historical books of Joshua, Judges, Samuel, and Kings, making Deuteronomy a kind of preface to these books. Third, Deuteronomy has a distinctive style that sets it apart from all the other writing in the Pentateuch: It reads like a sermon, spoken entirely by Moses, full of urgent pleas for obedience and thundering warnings about what will happen if the people don't obey the Law. Fourth, scholars believe Deuteronomy was written about the seventh century B.C., long after the time of Moses, so it is really looking backward at Israel's history even though it is written as if it were looking ahead to Israel's movement into the land.

Some commentators divide the book very simply into three major addresses of Moses:

1. First Address: Review of Israel's History (1, 1—4, 43)

2. Second Address: God's Covenant and Elaboration of the Law (4, 44—26, 19)

3. Third Address: Moses' Summary and Farewell (27, 1—33, 29); Death and Burial of Moses (34, 1–10)

This simple outline makes clear that the core of the book is in fact a new presentation of the Law that restates many of the laws presented earlier in Exodus through Numbers (*Deuteronomos* is Greek for "second Law" or "repetition of the Law").

The Unique Style of the Book

From beginning to end, Deuteronomy has the feel of a first-person speech. Unlike the other books of the Pentateuch, which show evidence of being patchwork quilts of material drawn together from the J, E, and P sources, Deuteronomy stands alone as having an independent source. Even its vocabulary differs from that of the other books. Certain phrases that are repeated often throughout the book help establish Deuteronomy's special character. Note the following examples:

1. These are the ordinances, statutes, and decrees that the LORD, your God, has enjoined on you (cf. 4, 45; 5, 1; 6, 20; etc.); take care to observe them (4, 5; 5, 1; 6, 3; 7, 12; 8, 1; etc.)

2. You must learn them, or teach them in the land (5, 1; 5, 31; 11, 19; etc.) and teach them to your children (4, 9; 4, 10; 11, 19; etc.)

3. In the land you are about to enter to possess (5, 31; 6, 1; 6, 10; 6, 18; 9, 5; etc.)

4. So that you might live long and prosper (4, 40; 5, 33; 6, 2f; 6, 24; 11, 9; etc.)

5. You will love the LORD your God with all your heart and soul (6, 5; 10, 12; 11, 13; etc.)

6. Do not turn aside after other gods to serve them (6, 14; 7, 4; 8, 19; 11, 16; etc.)

7. Do not forget the LORD (8, 11; 6, 12; etc.)

8. I set before you today a blessing and a curse (11, 26; cf. 30, 19)

9. The land, which the LORD swore to our fathers (6, 10; 6, 18; 6, 23; 7, 13; 10, 11; etc.); a land

flowing with milk and honey (6, 3; 11, 9; etc.)

10. Do what is right and good (6, 18; cf. 12, 28; 13, 19; etc.)

The repeated use of these phrases sounds like a preacher working hard to get a message across. The goal is to make its audience choose and change. By referring constantly to the land as "flowing with milk and honey . . . a good land . . . a land that God swore to your ancestors," it also recalls God's good deeds toward Israel, especially God's help against foreign opposition. Deuteronomy's intense and repetitive language helps make the book's main point: The people must be obedient when they take possession of the land.

The Historical Perspective of the Book

Some people may assume that Israel was always run like a theocracy where knowledge and observance of the Law could be taken for granted. They may also assume that the Bible, as we know it today, was always available to guide the people of ancient Israel. The reality, of course, was much different. The books we now call the Pentateuch did not exist, as we now know them, until late in Israel's history; probably the J and E sources were not pulled together to form Genesis, Exodus, Leviticus, and Numbers until the reign of King Hezekiah (715–687 B.C.). What existed before the books were formalized and finalized were stories, traditions, laws, and legends that were mostly passed on orally and, if they were written at all, were available to very few people.

The Story Continues

The reign of the idolatrous King Manasseh was longer than any other king (687–642 B.C.). The king who followed him after a brief period, Josiah (640–609 B.C.), initiated a reform. He rejected the idolatry of Manasseh and called for renewed obedience of the Law. It was during his reign that the book of Deuteronomy first appeared. The story goes that during the rebuilding of the Temple a "Book of the Law" was found that greatly moved the young king: Upon hearing it read aloud, he tore his garments and wept. Immediately he consulted a well-known prophetess, Huldah, who declared the book's message authentic. Convinced more than ever, the king fully embraced the book's program of reform

Obedience = Reward: Is it That Simple?

Deuteronomy seems to offer a very simple formula for life: obey and you'll be rewarded; disobey and you'll be punished. The national history of Israel as presented by the biblical writers, although often with the benefit of hindsight, would indicate that the formula basically worked. It is hard to say whether the people of Israel would have received constant blessing if they had remained consistently faithful, rather than forgetful and unfaithful as they were. But what is clear is that Israel saw moments and enjoyed periods of great blessing only to watch them dissolve into times of tragic misfortune (a pattern that especially dominates the book of Judges).

Moses clearly says God had established a special relationship with Israel, and Israel's part of the bargain was to live by the covenant made at Sinai. In fact, even the understanding in Deuteronomy—that God will act on behalf of Israel only if the people keep their part of the treaty—is a positive development from earlier theologies that saw God as a warrior who would fight for Israel no matter what. In their infancy as God's people, Israel perhaps needed a mighty, warrior God who would destroy their enemies, solve their problems, and reward their every good deed. But, as time passed, they learned to view God differently.

Christians believe that Jesus continued God's self-revelation. From Jesus we learn that while peace is promised—a peace the world does not understand—it is also a peace that we can, indeed must, find even in the midst of trial, suffering, and possibly persecution. One of the important truths of the Christian tradition is that pain and suffering are an inevitable part of the journey to union with God.

and called the nation to repentance (2 Kings 22, 1—23, 25). Scholars theorize that this "Book of the Law" was in fact Deuteronomy, and that it was written shortly before this time in order to guide a reform of Israelite religion. Therefore, its concerns are those of the seventh century, and not those of five centuries or more earlier, when Moses lived.

Interestingly, a reform similar to Josiah's had been started in Judah nearly 100 years earlier by King Hezekiah, around 715 B.C. But did Hezekiah know about the teachings of Deuteronomy back then? It is just possible that the refugees who had fled the destruction of the northern kingdom only seven years earlier brought with them these same fundamental teachings, traditions, and laws, and that these influenced Hezekiah's reform.

The Importance of the Covenant

While Deuteronomy has the shape of a vassal treaty between two people, it is also written like a speech of Moses, which reminds the people of God's miraculous care for them in the desert. It describes God in the role of a loving father caring for his son, and as a mother giving life to her child. This parent-child language is typical of covenant treaties of the times, which used love as the motivation for loyalty between the parties. In Deuteronomy, love and faithfulness are everything!

The Law Is Not Simply Laws, but Total Commitment

In contrast with Exodus, Deuteronomy talks frequently about *why* laws need to be obeyed. And the reason is love. Before Deuteronomy, the Pentateuch seldom mentions that word as a motive for following the covenant, but this book repeatedly speaks of God's love for the people and their need to respond in kind. In Exodus obedience was a duty, in Deuteronomy it is an act of love. God gave the Law for the people's good, much the way a parent would lay out rules for a child out of concern for his or her welfare. The emphasis on knowing, teaching, reading, and writing the Law is not a sign of legalism, but a reflection of the deeper and more permanent commitment to the LORD that lies beneath.

The Land and God's Blessing Are Conditional

Blessing and curse follow obedience and disobedience. The people of Israel learned that lesson from the events of their lives. Another lesson they had to learn was that even God's gift of the land could be taken away if they misused it or failed to create a just and honest society. By writing Deuteronomy as a farewell speech given by Moses in the desert, the authors make his warnings come from a period *before* the people took possession of Canaan. The writers are saying: Remember what it was like to have no land? Well, that could be the case again if you don't heed Moses' warnings. The book may have been most influential once the exile began (about 587 B.C.), since then readers could see that this tragedy resulted from their failure to obey the LORD as Moses had warned. It spoke to their misery and to their repentant hearts.

There Is to Be One Sanctuary

One of the objectives of Deuteronomy is to focus the people's attention on Jerusalem as the central place of worship, so that they would not be distracted by local shrines and cult centers that often had pagan connections. But since, at the time that Moses is supposedly speaking, the choice of Jerusalem as the nation's capital by King David is still hundreds of years off, the city is never mentioned by name, only alluded to with such references as "the place which the LORD, your God, chooses as the dwelling place for his name" (12, 11) and "the place which the LORD chooses from among your tribes" (12, 14).

Deuteronomy Updates the Covenant Law

We've already mentioned that many of the laws listed in Deuteronomy are a restatement of the laws found in Israel's earliest law code, the "Covenant Code" found in Exodus 20, 22—23, 33. But there is also a difference. In Deuteronomy the laws are stated in a way that addresses the town and city life that had developed in Israel during the centuries since the Exodus. These laws have been fine-tuned to meet the needs of people living under conditions very different from those of the times when the laws were originally written. They accent the obligations of people to each other and especially to the weak and dispossessed, a need that became more visible and pressing once city life developed.

Conclusion

By the time Deuteronomy was written, Israel was no longer a loose-knit alliance of desert tribes. It had become a kingdom. In this new life situation, Israel needed a reinterpretation and summary of the meaning of the events told in the other books of the Pentateuch. Deuteronomy provides this summary in the form of a "repetition of the Law." But Deuteronomy does more than look back at its history, it also anticipates its future in the land, which will be narrated in the historical books that follow. Thus Deuteronomy links those books written by historians from its own school of thought with the earlier Pentateuch traditions. The diagram below illustrates this relationship.

Strong Words

The influence of Deuteronomy is seen in the life of Jesus and the writings of the New Testament authors. Jesus' responses to Satan's three temptations all come from Deuteronomy (6, 13; 6, 16; 8, 3). In the desert preparing for his mission, Jesus draws on the lessons Israel learned

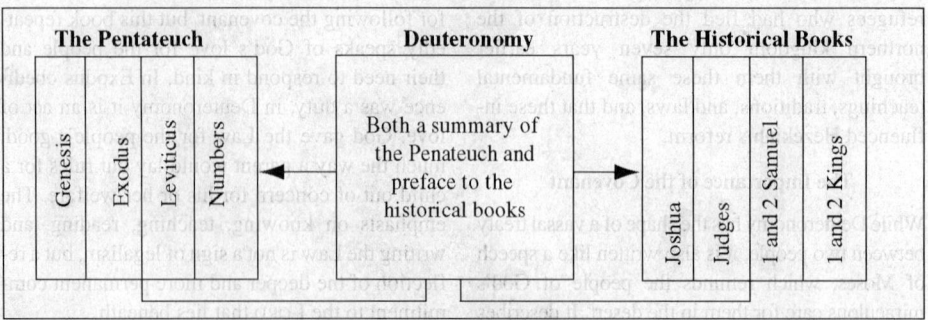

The Pentateuch	Deuteronomy	The Historical Books
Genesis Exodus Leviticus Numbers	Both a summary of the Penateuch and preface to the historical books	Joshua Judges 1 and 2 Samuel 1 and 2 Kings

during its own desert experience to set the course of his journey. Jesus also quoted Deuteronomy when asked what was the greatest commandment.

Twenty-one New Testament books quote Deuteronomy almost 100 times in all, a testimony to its great influence. But that influence is found more in the basic themes of the New Testament than in any specific quotes. Jesus' whole ministry is an embodiment of the attitude in Deuteronomy of total dedication to God, God's love and fatherhood, doing more than the minimum the Law requires, and letting faith guide us to choose obedience over disobedience. The New Testament authors learned from Deuteronomy to see all of life as an integrated whole.

Questions for Discussion and Reflection

Group Sharing/Discussion

1. Have each person name the five most important "teachings" of Moses in these three sermons at the end of his life.

2. What are some of the examples in Deuteronomy of the Law being very important? What are some examples of believing in God's love being very important?

3. What are three things about Jewish law or ritual that you learned from reading this book?

In Our Lives

1. Deuteronomy presents the motivation for obeying similar laws found in Exodus. That motivation is for obedience out of love rather than obedience out of duty. Which motivation is at the core of your own observance of our religious laws?

2. Moses reminds the people that God chose them not because of their merit, but out of pure love (see 7, 7; 9, 5; and 9, 24). How would you explain this to someone who believes they can "earn" God's love?

3. Deuteronomy contains some strong messages about the importance of justice for the health of society. Concern for the poor and the weak is incorporated into the laws of the land. What contemporary laws have this same concern? Is it appropriate for civil laws to demand concern for the needy?

4. In chapter 4 Moses expresses concern for making sure the children learn the story so that their experiences are not forgotten. What are some ways Catholic Christians can help their children not forget the message of Christ?

Individual/Personal Reflection/Action

1. Imagine that like Moses, you were coming to the end of your life. Write what would be the most important messages you would want to leave for your family and friends?

2. In your own words, tell God how you know you are loved by God, and put your thanks for that love into your own words.

3. Name for yourself any important practices of our faith that you want to pay more attention to in your own life.

THE HISTORICAL BOOKS

The story of the Israelite people is told in three major units of the Bible: the Pentateuch, the deuteronomistic history, and the chronicler's history. You will not find these designations used in the Bible itself, however, because they were originally defined by scholars who saw a unity among certain groups of books. By studying the writing style, subject matter, and major themes of each book, scholars are able to conclude that a collection of books was put together by one person or a small group working together.

Since each major section of the Bible covers centuries of history, no section can be a single person's eyewitness account. The ancient authors of the Bible usually began by collecting and organizing stories and oral traditions that already existed. The ancient writers turned those preexisting materials into the final form that became the Bible. Sometimes they did this by simply taking over the old stories with little or no change; other times they rewrote the original story. Scholars often can tell the difference between the older material the writer started with and its final form. Both are important. The *older* material tells us what had been valued by the ancient tradition. The *final form* tells us what the author thought was important and worth emphasizing at the time the collection was being shaped.

The reading guides up to this point have dealt with the Bible's first five books, the Pentateuch. The next section of the reading guide will deal with seven books (Joshua, Judges, 1 and 2 Samuel, 1 and 2 Kings, and Ruth, a later addition), which are called the *deuteronomistic history,* because the book of Deuteronomy serves as

a kind of preface to the whole collection. The last group of historical books (1 and 2 Chronicles, Ezra, and Nehemiah) begins with the books of Chronicles, and therefore is called the *chronicler's history.* By telling the same story from different perspectives, the Bible gives us a clue that we have much to learn not just from the story itself, but also from its unique point of view.

The Deuteronomistic History

Joshua, Judges, 1 and 2 Samuel, and 1 and 2 Kings

The books we commonly refer to by these titles and treat as independent works are actually part of a continuous story that starts in Genesis and ends in 2 Kings. However, these six historical books existed as an independent unit, with the book of Deuteronomy as its preface, long before the Genesis-to-Kings collection was pulled together into its present form. But even before they became a unit, the individual works of this deuteronomistic history also existed independently as stories and traditions (also referred to as "sources"), which sometimes were written and sometimes were known only in oral form.

It is clear that the deuteronomistic writers who wrote the history of Israel used such sources. They even mention some of their sources (none of which have survived) in the history itself: "The Book of Jashar" (Jos 10, 13), "The book of the chronicles of Solomon" (1 Kgs 11, 41), "The book of the chronicles of the kings of Judah" (1 Kgs 14, 29), and "The book of the chronicles of the kings of Israel" (1 Kgs 14, 19).

Deuteronomistic Vision of the Pattern of Israel's History

1. God's offer of love
2. Israel's faithlessness and sin
3. God's just punishment
4. Israel's repentance and cry for help
5. God's forgiveness and mercy
6. Israel's renewed sinfulness

The deuteronomistic writers did not force their original sources to blend into one completely consistent story. They did not even try to blot out the contradictions, inconsistencies, or duplications that resulted from combining several sources. While they did impress an overall unity or perspective on the material they brought together, they also respected their sources and allowed them to speak for themselves, even if that meant letting them disagree with each other. For example, 1 Samuel chapter 8 shows God's displeasure at the request of the people for a king; chapter 9 presents the choice of Saul as God's idea. In 1 Samuel 17, 48–51, David kills the Philistine warrior Goliath; in 2 Samuel 21, 19, it is Elhanan who kills Goliath.

Date and Purpose of the Deuteronomistic History

The final edition of the deuteronomistic books was most likely put together during and after the exile that followed the destruction of Jerusalem in 586 B.C. Much of it, however, may already have been written down during the reign of Josiah, the reformer King of Judah (d. 609 B.C.). This dating helps us to understand, in part, the overall purpose of the history, which was to explain why the nation collapsed and why the people were led into exile.

Typical Deuteronomistic Phrases

"to follow other gods"

"you will know that the LORD alone is God"

"to serve other gods"

"to walk in the ways of the LORD"

"the city that the LORD has chosen"

"to keep all the commandments"

"to sacrifice and burn incense at high places"

"to provoke the LORD to anger"

exile. God did not abandon the covenant, says this history, the people did. Israel deserved destruction because of its sin. By refusing to heed God's constant warnings and shows of mercy, Israel sealed its fate. God was not obligated to stand by one particular country or king. Without the people's voluntary fidelity to the covenant, all bets were off.

The history, however, is not basically a pessimistic work. Signs of hope can be detected in the repeated calls for repentance and in the high value the authors place on God's promise to David of an everlasting dynasty. The recurring pattern in Israel's history—sin, punishment, cry for help, and deliverance—told the people that despite their sin and God's punishment, deliverance was possible again, if they returned to the LORD and asked for help.

The Literary Character of the Deuteronomistic History

The characteristic phrases and repetitions used by the writers of Deuteronomy make their style easy to recognize. These writers pulled together the sometimes detailed and well-written and sometimes sketchy stories of Israel's kings; then they added long speeches that would help readers understand the theological significance of each of the stages of Israel's history. The speeches (Jos 1, 11–15; Jos 23; 1 Sm 12; 2 Sm 7; 1 Kgs 8, 14–61), which usually are put into the mouths of main characters at critical moments of Israel's past, impose a religious interpretation on the events of Israel's history. They express the vision that God's initial offer of love was followed by Israel's sin, which was followed by God's mercy, only to be followed by more sin.

Besides *looking back* and explaining why things happened as they did, these speeches also *look forward* to Israel's future and urge the people to live differently. Past and future are viewed through the same glasses: If Israel obeys the Law, all goes well; if it does not, it is punished.

Theological Concerns of the Deuteronomistic History

It is important to recognize the theological concerns from which the writers of these books operate. Those concerns determine what they choose from their sources and how they use those sources. We do not have a complete history of Israel. We have Israel's history told from the theological perspective of these deuteronomistic writers: when Israel worshiped the LORD, and the LORD alone, all went well for the nation. However, because Israel chose to abandon the LORD and worship the gods of its neighbors, the LORD punished them with defeat and exile.

The book of Deuteronomy provides the key to understanding the deuteronomistic history. It sets forth the requirements of the Law (Dt 4, 44—26, 19), which will become the criteria by which the writers organize and evaluate Israel's history. According to the book of Deuteronomy, obedience to the laws of Moses brings covenant blessing (28, 1–14), and disobedience brings curse (28, 15–68). The deuteronomistic writers see in the events of Israel's history the realization of blessing or curse depending on Israel's obedience or disobedience to the laws of Moses.

The most important law for the writers is the first of the Ten Commandments: "I, the LORD, am your God . . . you shall not have other gods besides me" (Dt 5, 6–7). Exclusive worship of the LORD is so crucial that virtually the entire history of Israel is told in terms of Israel's obedience to this one law. Although they frequently speak of obedience to the laws, statutes, and commandments, in reality all of these are reduced to one law: worship the LORD and the LORD alone. Even the writers' interest in centralized worship in the Jerusalem Temple is a reflection of their concern for obedience to this one law (see, for instance, 1 Kgs 12, 26–30).

It is the word of the LORD that defines and determines the history of Israel. That word is expressed in the deuteronomic Law and repeated by the prophets. A true prophet is one who speaks the LORD's Law and warns the people of the consequences of disobedience (Dt 18, 15–20).

How to Read the Deuteronomistic History

Before beginning, see the "Understanding the Historical Background to the Biblical Texts" section on RG 31 and review the various levels of meaning that are found in the Bible, particularly in the histories.

In referring to this work as a history we must be clear about what we mean by that designation (see also RG 37). All history writing is a process of selection, organization, and interpretation. No history simply tells what happened. Every history tells some of the things that happened, while leaving out other things. That very selection process imposes an interpretation on the events. History is never objective in a strict sense because the facts it presents cannot exist in isolation from the way a historian uses them.

The deuteronomistic writers have taken many stories and combined them to form one story that communicates a fairly simple message to its audience: Learn from the past. Therefore, the focus of our study will not be on what actually happened, but on what the writers were trying to teach through the events they recounted.

Questions for Discussion and Reflection
Group Sharing/Discussion

1. The seven books called the *deuteronomistic history* tell the story in a different way than does the final group of historical books (1 and 2 Chronicles, Ezra, and Nehemiah), called the *chronicler's history.* What is the value of repeating the same story in these different ways?

2. Have your group brainstorm about different perspectives you can use to understand the Bible. Talk about how these apply to studying the deuteronomistic history.

In Our Lives

1. It is the word of the LORD that defines and determines the history of Israel. The Word of the LORD in our Sunday Scriptures is an important way the LORD is present to us. How might we better prepare for, listen to, and live by the Word we hear in the Sunday liturgy readings?

2. The deuteronomistic writers were teaching their people to learn from the past. Specifically, what are some of the lessons we can learn from our past as Catholic Christians?

Individual/Personal Reflection/Action

1. Joshua had a chance to tell people what he believed were the most important things in life. Write down for yourself what message you would pass on to those you love about the most important things to you.

2. Share with another person in your life the parts of your family history that are most significant to you.

JOSHUA READING GUIDE
At a Glance

Who are the main players?	Joshua Rahab, the prostitute Achan Caleb Eleazar, son of Aaron Phineas, the high priest
What should I look for?	The superiority of faith over military might Punishment of evil Reward of good Joshua's leadership Israel's God-given success The people's fidelity and careful observance of the Law The book's pervasive sense of hope
When did this take place?	During the period following the wandering in the desert, beginning around 1250 B.C. or 1406 B.C.
Where did these events occur?	In the land of Canaan, the land promised to Abraham, which is modern Israel
Why was this book written?	To record Israel's conquest of Canaan and the fulfillment of God's promise to give Israel the Promised Land
What is the story?	Still camped east of the Jordan River, the Israelites spy on Jericho, then prepare to march across the river. Joshua leads many successful campaigns of conquest in northern, southern, and central Canaan. Finally conquered, the land is allotted to the tribes. Joshua makes a farewell speech during which the covenant is renewed. Joshua dies and is buried.

Before Beginning

The book of Joshua is the sixth book of the Bible and carries on the story that begins in Genesis and continues through Deuteronomy. Abraham's descendants, who had been slaves in Egypt, are ready to take possession of the land promised to their ancestors. The land was not simply a gift of God to Israel—it was the gift that made God's power and presence in Israel's life something real and tangible. It was an act of grace like no other, for the gift of the land made it possible for the people of Israel to survive. The land provided Israel with its food, clothing, and shelter. Without it, Israel could not be a people. The land as God's gift to Israel was a central theme to the Israelites' faith. It was at the core of ancient Israel's stories, poetry, and prophecy. Refer to color Map 4 for an overview of the land.

Joshua is both the conclusion of one story and the beginning of another. It concludes the story of the liberation of the Hebrew slaves and their guidance through the wilderness to the Promised Land. It is also the first part of the story of Israel in that Promised Land. The books of Judges, Samuel, and Kings continue this story. The story begins with Joshua and the Israelite tribes taking

control of the land, continues with stories about the judges who lead Israel in maintaining their presence in the land, and concludes with the stories of Israel's kings, who eventually lose control of that land. The story ends the same way it begins—with the Israelites outside the land. At the beginning they are ready to cross the Jordan and take control of the land; at the end they are in exile from the land, wondering about their future. It is a tragic story that begins with much promise and ends with great disappointment.

The ancient rabbis called the books that made up the story of Israel in its land "the Former Prophets" because they ascribed these books to prophetic authorship. Scholars have called these books the "Deuteronomistic History of Israel." But that name can be misleading, because these books are not histories—at least not in the modern sense. In the form we now have, the books date to about the middle of the sixth century while Israel was in exile. This story of Israel in the Promised Land turns Israel's past into a sermon in order to provide the exiles some basis for hope by affirming that Israel can have a future, despite the terrible losses it experienced when Jerusalem fell. The book of Deuteronomy provided the theological principles that guided the telling of the story of Israel in its land. The books of Joshua to 2 Kings show what happens when Israel is obedient and what happens when it is not. The story of Israel in its land, then, asserts that Israel can have a future if it chooses— because God has set before Israel the choice of life and death (Dt 30, 15).

The book of Joshua answers two questions that were on the minds of its first readers, Israelites living in exile (see "The Historical Books" Reading Guide):

1. Is God able to restore Israel?
2. Is God willing to do so?

The answer that the book gives to the first question is a resounding yes. The book will tell the story of how Israel acquired its land ostensibly under Joshua's leadership. But as the story unfolds, it will become clear that it was God who was leading Israel all the while. The answer to the second question is a qualified yes. God has promised blessings to those who obey the Torah: if Israel chooses the path of obedience, it can expect to have a future in the land promised to its ancestors. If, however, Israel chooses the way of disobedience, there can be no hope.

Reading Through the Book of Joshua

About 20 percent of the book's text describes the elaborate preparations for the entrance of the Israelite tribes into Canaan. Before the crossing of the Jordan begins, the book makes it clear that the land is a gift God is giving Israel (1, 1–5). The way to ensure that Israel will be in a position to receive that gift is obedience to the Torah (1, 6–9). The rest of the book simply illustrates these two assertions. First, under Joshua's leadership, the tribes will take the land with relative ease because God is handing the land to them. Second, because Israel was obedient, it easily succeeds in taking possession of the land, which is then distributed equitably among the tribes.

Israel Enters the Promised Land (Jos 1, 1—5, 12)

The book's first chapter consists of four speeches: the LORD to Joshua (1, 1–9); Joshua to the Israelite leadership (1, 10–11); Joshua to the

tribes from east of the Jordan (1, 12–15); and the eastern tribes to Joshua (1, 16–18). These speeches are the means of conveying the central religious affirmations of the book: the presence of God with Joshua and the Israelites, the importance of obedience to the Torah, the land as a gift from God, and Joshua as the successor of Moses. These affirmations provide a framework for understanding the stories that will follow. No military preparations are mentioned and none are necessary as long as Israel observes the Torah.

The episode with the two Israelite spies and Rahab, the prostitute from Jericho (2, 1–21), betrays the book's purpose. Rahab's conversation with the two spies makes it seem as if she had been reading the book of Deuteronomy. Because she helps the Israelite spies, she is fulfilling the divine will and will escape the fate that the rest of Jericho's citizens will suffer (6, 22–25). If Israel had followed her example, the fate of Jerusalem and its exiles would have been much different. If, like Rahab, Israel now chooses the way of obedience, it will return to its land to live in peace.

The scene depicting the crossing of the Jordan (3, 1—4, 24) underscores the book's intent to present the taking of the Promised Land as a wonder performed by God to fulfill the commitment made to Israel's ancestors. The book purposely describes the crossing of the Jordan River as a miracle like the crossing of the Red Sea (4, 23), even though the Jordan is, in fact, easily fordable at several places. The miraculous crossing of the Jordan demoralizes the people of Canaan, robbing them of the will to resist (5, 1). Again, it is clear that Israel's possession of the land was God's doing.

At God's instructions, the preparations to enter the land and face its inhabitants involve nothing of a military nature. In fact, these preparations actually render Israel's army quite vulnerable to attack because all the males have to be circumcised, making them temporarily ineffective as a fighting force. But the mass circumcision does, however, make the community fit to celebrate the Passover (5, 2–12). Both these observances became important markers of Jewish identity during and after the exile. Certainly the book of Joshua intends to promote these practices.

Violence in Joshua and the Bible

For many contemporary readers, the most difficult aspect of the book of Joshua and its stories of conquest will not be understanding what happened, but rather accepting the level of violence and the apparent exaltation of annihilation that the book takes for granted. What is there to say about this aspect for those in our world, where many people think that military actions should be a "last resort" and others think we should not engage in such tactics at all? How do we regard the commands, attributed to God, that the people must eliminate everyone who lived in the land? (See, for instance, 6, 21.)

First, we must acknowledge the great difference between our attitudes toward military action and the attitudes of those in the ancient world. To some extent, the book of Joshua is simply reflecting its own world. Those unwilling to fight and conquer in the ancient world ran the probable risk of being conquered themselves, and consequently of being oppressed by some outside invader.

Second, as with other issues, such as slavery, we have moved beyond where the Bible is. Just as all Christians now agree that slavery is wrong, even though the Bible condones it, we can agree that ruthless conquest and the extermination of native peoples is wrong, even though the book of Joshua presents such actions as being commanded by God.

Third, and finally, we must recognize that, whatever the book says about what happened, the conquest of Canaan was nowhere near so complete. In fact, even within the Bible itself there are indications that the inhabitants of the land continued to live there and were not wiped out by the invading Israelites. For instance, it took until King David's time—200 years or so later—for Jerusalem to be conquered (see 2 Sm 5, 7). Since we know this, we can look at the picture of the conquest of Canaan in a different way: not as God's command to the people to conquer and kill all of the inhabitants of the land, but as the people's way of grasping that it was God, and only God, who "owned" the land and who ruled over it. It was God's to give or withhold. This was symbolized by accounts that suggested that all of the inhabitants were driven out or killed; this did not happen, but its meaning was what mattered.

The Battle for the Promised Land
(Jos 5, 13—11, 23)

Although the book of Joshua is often thought of as a chronicle of a massive invasion of Canaan by a united Israelite army under the leadership of Joshua, only one quarter of the book actually deals with the battles for the Promised Land. At the end of this section, the author comments that "Joshua captured the whole country" (11, 23). But the account of the battles fought by the Israelite tribes focuses almost entirely on the central region of Canaan (6, 1—10, 27). Battles in the south (10, 28–43) and the north (11, 1–14) are treated in summary fashion. The two places that receive the most attention are Jericho (6, 1–27) and Ai (7, 2—8, 29). But before Joshua begins the attack on Jericho, the mysterious

"captain of the host of the LORD" arrives (5, 14). Notice the similarity to the story of Moses' encounter with God at the burning bush (Ex 3, 1–6). The true leader of Israel is someone other than Joshua.

Jericho was a town that had been abandoned for centuries before the time of Joshua, probably because its water source had become severely polluted, making its waters no longer drinkable. Ai had flourished in the Early Bronze Age—more than a thousand years before the Israelite tribes emerged in Canaan. It too had been abandoned for centuries before the Israelites made their appearance. The stories of the capture of Jericho and Ai in Joshua (6–8), then, are not historical records. But apparently, the people of Israel celebrated the gift of the land that they received from God at shrines near Jericho. Certainly, the story of Jericho's fall reads more like an account of a liturgical ceremony than that of a military adventure.

The book tells the tale of Jericho and Ai as object lessons for its readers. Neither Joshua's military leadership nor the bravery of the Israelite army was responsible for the fall of Jericho. The town was taken because Israel followed God's directions. The city's walls collapsed after an elaborate procession with the Ark—not because of any military operation. This led to a complete victory, but Israel was told not to enjoy the fruits of the victory: no one was to loot the city nor was there to be any Israelite settlement there. While Israel had no difficulty taking Jericho, Ai was another story (7, 1—8, 30). Because Joshua's spies misjudged the enemy's strength, Israel attacked Ai without sufficient force and suffered a grave defeat. The book accounts for this stunning setback by describing how Achan kept some of the booty from Jericho for himself, contrary to Joshua's instructions (6, 17–21). After Joshua prayed and Achan was punished, God provided Joshua with tactical instructions for the defeat of Ai's army.

Joshua's detour to the north to build an altar on Mount Ebal, which flanks the valley in which Shechem is located (8, 30–35), reminds readers of the significance of the Torah for the people's past and future. (For these locations and others mentioned in Joshua see Map 4 in the back of the book and "The Conquest of Canaan" on p. 262.) On the stones used to make the altar, Joshua wrote the Torah. He then read the Torah—complete with the blessings and curses contained in it—to the people, reminding them that they will shape their future by the choices they make.

The Battle for Canaan

When the book returns to the story of the battle for Canaan, Joshua and his army are at Gilgal. Their victories led kings of the city-states in Canaan to form an alliance to stop the Israelite advance, while the people of Gibeon sought an alliance with the Israelites by falsely claiming to be, like the Israelites, newly arrived in Canaan (9, 1–27). When the Israelites discovered that they were tricked by the Gibeonites, they suggested that the Gibeonites accept a low social status in the Israelite community as laborers in the temple.

Like Jericho and Ai, Gibeon was not inhabited in the thirteenth century B.C. This story serves as a warning to consult with the LORD in difficult circumstances, which the Israelites did not do in this situation—much to their regret (Jos 9, 14). There will be several occasions in the monarchic period when Israel and Judah got into great difficulties because of the treaties they made with other nations, for example, Ahaz's alliance with Assyria (2 Kgs 16, 7–9).

The theme of God making a gift of the land to the people continues when God enlists the sun and moon to seal Israel's victory (10, 1–14). In the ancient Near East, the sun and the moon were gods in their own right, but here they are simply weapons in the LORD's arsenal, demonstrating God's dominion.

Following Joshua's defeat and execution of the kings allied against him, he moved against the south and brought that region under Israelite control (10, 25–43). The story of Joshua's final victory, over a coalition led by Jabin of Hazor (11, 1–23), is meant to account for the taking of the entire northern third of Canaan: the Jezreel Valley and the Sea of Galilee. The second section of Joshua ends with summary statements (11, 15–23), the most important of which is that Joshua carried out the orders that God gave to Moses. The story of the battle for the Promised Land, then, is a story of the success that obedience brings.

The gift of the land is a motif that is woven throughout the Old Testament, but the references to how that land was acquired by Israel are not very specific. For example, although the story of Jericho's miraculous fall is an important part of Joshua, it is not mentioned elsewhere in the Old Testament. Precisely what experiences generated the first stories about Israel's acquisition of its land are unknown. But before they came to have their present form, they were shaped and reshaped by almost 600 years of life in that land. Ancient Israel's storytellers witnessed the rise and fall of the two Israelite national states. These experiences certainly left their mark on the story of Joshua and the emergence of the Israelite tribes in Canaan.

The story of the battle for the Promised Land effectively turned the past into a sermon whose purpose was to stimulate the faith and hope of those who first heard or read it. They learned that there could be a future for the people of Israel if they, like Joshua's generation, were obedient to the Torah. The character of this story makes its use in reconstructing the early history of Israel problematic. Archaeological excavation supports the conclusion that the stories of conquest found in Joshua were not based on memories of actual battles that took place at Jericho, Ai, or in the environs of Gibeon. But archaeology has shown that people living in Canaan in the thirteenth century B.C. experienced serious disruptions. Towns and villages were destroyed and abandoned. The Israelite tribes emerged in the central highlands of Canaan precisely during this difficult period, so it is likely that Israel acquired the land that was to be the scene of its subsequent history, in part, by violence. It is difficult, from the evidence offered by the book of Joshua, to say much more. What the book does affirm unequivocally is that Israel came to possess the land because of God's power, and Israel was able to receive that land as God's gift because of its obedience. These affirmations, however, were meant to give Israel a vision of the future rather than information about the past.

Israel's Inheritance (Jos 12, 1—19, 51)

After listing the territories brought under Israelite control during the battle for the Promised Land (12, 1–24), the book of Joshua has an extensive section dealing with the distribution of the land among the Israelite tribes (13, 8—19, 51). Working through this section is difficult for modern readers since it is full of geographical detail that is meaningless to many. While the precise borders of the various tribal allotments may have been very important to the people of ancient Israel, their significance today is exclusively historical. Still, there are some details in this part of the story that even contemporary readers should attend to.

It is important to remember that ancient Israel's economy was based on agriculture. Ownership of land was crucial to survival in such an economy. Possession of a plot of land enabled an Israelite to produce enough food for his family and livestock with a surplus to be used for replanting and for sacrificial offerings. Without land, a person had no access to the means of production. Such a person was dependent for survival on the charity of his fellow Israelites. Of course, there were some people who supported themselves as merchants and artisans, but they too ultimately depended on Israel's peasant farmers for their prosperity.

The account of the land distribution among the tribes begins with a reminder of the areas of Canaan that the Israelites did not control (13, 1–6). This was a necessary correction to the exaggerations in the previous section of the book, which claimed that Joshua and the Israelites subdued "the entire land," and "the whole country" (Jos 9, 24; 11, 23). Then follows a review of the territories previously allotted by Moses to those Israelites who were going to live east of the Jordan River (13, 7–33). Israel's control over this region was neither firm nor constant, but its inclusion among the tribal allotments expresses Israel's claim on that territory, even though Israel was not always able to support that claim. When Ezekiel described his vision of an Israel restored after the exile, he did not have any of the tribes living east of the Jordan (Ez 48, 1–29).

When the account of the distribution of the land west of the Jordan begins in chapter 14, both Eleazar the priest and Joshua preside over the distribution (14, 1; see also Nm 34, 17). The preceding sections of the book did not emphasize the role of the priest except for liturgical actions (e.g., 3, 6; 6, 1–9). The priority given to Eleazar here may reflect the more significant role that the priests played in the leadership of the community after the state collapsed and the dynasty ended, as is evident from Haggai, Zechariah, and Ezra. Eleazar's presence may also be a consequence of having the land distributed by lot (14, 2). Although Deuteronomy explicitly forbids attempts to determine the divine will through the techniques of divination (Dt 18, 9–12), the casting of lots seems to have been widely practiced and accepted as legitimate. In this method of choosing something, the choice was limited to that between two things: two contending persons, two groups, an individual versus a group, or a "yes-or-no" question. Then a two-sided object was thrown to the ground. Depending on which side fell uppermost, the answer was "yes" or "no" or one of the two choices. It is the same as our "heads-or-tails" coin-toss method. The lot oracle was committed to the priests (Ex 28, 30; Lv 8, 5–9). To show that the distribution of the land was done according to God's will, it was accomplished by the use of lots in a procedure presided over by a priest. The New Testament gives evidence of the continuing popularity and acceptance of using lots to determine the divine will (Acts 1, 26).

Special Towns (Jos 20, 1—21, 45)

Two of ancient Israel's social institutions are the subject of the fourth section of the book of Joshua. The first is the city of refuge. There were six of these cities, three on each side of the Jordan. According to Numbers 35, 9–34, it was Moses who announced God's plan to have such cities where a person who accidentally caused another's death could be safe from the victim's relatives, who might seek vengeance. Moses had already named the three cities east of the Jordan, and now Joshua designated three more west of the Jordan. The books of Samuel, Kings, and Chronicles never mention this institution since they were not needed following the centralization of authority by the monarchy. The book of Judges mentions two examples of private vengeance: 8, 13–21 and 20, 1–11. It is clear from these examples that the biblical tradition does not approve of such acts. A second set of 48 towns was set aside for the Levites. The tribe of Levi received no territory of its own because the men of that tribe served as priests, who were to teach the Torah to Israel and offer sacrifice to the LORD (see Dt 33, 8–11). To fulfill these functions the priests needed to be available to the people; therefore the cities where the Levites had residential and grazing rights were scattered throughout the country.

A Threat of Civil War (Jos 22, 1–34)

The Israelites whose territory was east of the Jordan River had joined in the battle to take control of the area west of the river. Since that battle was successful, Joshua allowed them to return to their homes (vv. 1–9). This is a prelude to a conflict between the Israelites east of the river and those on the west (vv. 10–34). The tribes from the east side of the river built an altar near the Jordan, and this offended the Israelites from the west. War

was averted because Phineas, Eleazar's son, succeeded in negotiating peace between the two groups of Israelites. The precise nature of the offense is not obvious, though it may reflect the deuteronomic belief that there was to be only one place where sacrifices were to be offered. Apparently, the book of Joshua assumed that this place was Shiloh. When the easterners explained that they did not intend to offer sacrifices, this defused the problem.

An Era Ends (Jos 23, 1—24, 33)

The final testament of such an important person as Joshua was highly significant. The storyteller creates a speech for his hero that could have come right out of the book of Deuteronomy. Israel's continued presence in the land depends on its obedience to "all that is written in the book of the Law of Moses. . . ." (23, 6). Joshua reminds Israel to love God (23, 11), the Torah's greatest command. But then Joshua issues a warning that any failure on Israel's part to remain completely and exclusively loyal to God will have the gravest of consequences (23, 15–16). While the land is a gift from God to Israel, the gift can be revoked. Of course, this is a theological conclusion that came from Israel's experience. By the time the book of Joshua took the form that it now has, Israel did "perish from the good land" that it had received from God (23, 16). Israel's faith in God's fidelity, however, led to the hope that a new dedication to the Torah and a renewed commitment to the covenant would bring a reversal of the misfortune that Israel brought on itself. The book then describes an elaborate ceremony in which Israel of Joshua's day renews its commitment to God and the Torah. (24, 1–28.) Like the ancestors in the days of Joshua, Israel must again commit itself to serve and obey God alone.

The burial notices with which the book ends (24, 29–30.32–33) are significant because of the prominence given to Eleazar, the priest. This is very likely another indication of the leadership role assumed by priests after the fall of the Israelite monarchy. Verse 31 is the verdict on the era of Joshua: it was an era marked by obedience and loyalty. That is the reason Israel came to possess the land: obedience brings God's blessing.

The Continuing Significance of the Book of Joshua

The great irony of the book of Joshua was that its stories about the Israelite army conquering great cities and annihilating their populace were written at a time when ancient Israel was at its lowest ebb politically and militarily. The two Israelite national states no longer existed. Their territory was absorbed into the Babylonian provincial system. The leading citizens of Judah were taken to Babylon to prevent them from fomenting any resistance to the new order in the region. Those Judahites who remained in the land were subsistence farmers and not in a position to challenge Babylonian rule. Certainly the stories about the mighty Israelite army winning victory after victory under Joshua was a parody of the military and political impotence of Judah in the sixth century B.C. Unfortunately, the stories of the book of Joshua have served to provide support for the wars of conquest waged by Christians over the centuries. The Crusades, the wars against the Native Americans, and the Boer conquest of South Africa are just three examples of the lethal mixture of war and religion.

The book of Joshua was written not to stir a martial spirit in its readers but instead a spirit of obedience and commitment to the Torah. The book assumes that the exile of Israel from the land that God gave it was not due to any military disadvantages. Israel lost its land because of its failure to keep the Torah that God revealed to Moses. The only hope for restoration was for Judah to join their ancestors in recommitting themselves to their God: "Far be it from us to forsake the LORD for the service of other gods. For it was the LORD, our God, who brought us and our fathers up out of the land of Egypt, out of a state of slavery. He performed those great miracles before our very eyes and protected us along our entire journey and among all the peoples through whom we passed. At our approach the LORD drove out [all the peoples, including] the Amorites who dwelt in the land. Therefore we also will serve the LORD, for he is our God" (Jos 24, 16–18).

Questions for Discussion and Reflection
Group Sharing/Discussion
1. Why is it important for Joshua to be the successor of Moses? What was unusual about the beginning of his leadership?

2. Where did the Israelites live when Joshua was written? How far was this from the Promised Land? Locate as many places as you can on the map.

3. Why does Rahab, the prostitute, escape the fate that the rest of Jericho's citizens suffer?

4. How does Joshua show that the distribution of the land was done according to God's will?

5. If you are in a group, have someone role-play Joshua's final message (ch 23), putting his most important messages into their own words. Then have another person take the same role for ch 24 with the rest of the group taking the role of the responses the people made to Joshua.

In Our Lives
1. God's gift of this Promised Land to Israel was a sign of God's presence in Israelite life. How are we today aware of God's presence in our lives?

2. What does it mean to be "obedient to the Torah?" What are the basic beliefs that we are to be "obedient to" or by which we are to try to live?

3. What do the rituals of circumcision and Passover symbolize? What are the most important rituals in our Catholic faith life? How might we improve our celebration of these key religious events?

4. Lots were cast to see what tribes would get which land. Describe an experience you have had or you know about when someone was trying to divide things fairly. What was similar and different to the casting of lots in Joshua?

Individual/Personal Reflection/Action
1. Joshua was a significant religious leader for his people. Who would you name as a significant religious leader today? Who in your own life helps you follow the pathway of your faith?

2. Rahab made a courageous decision to go against her own culture and follow what she believed in. Recalling your own hard decisions, who or what helps you have the courage of your convictions?

3. In their response to Joshua's challenges in his farewell address the people responded, "We will serve the LORD!" What challenges would you give yourself to show that your life, too, serves the LORD?

JUDGES READING GUIDE

At a Glance

Who are the main players?	Othniel Ehud Deborah and Jael Gideon and his son Abimelech Jephthah and his daughter Samson and Delilah
What should I look for?	The issue of God's lordship over Israel Israel's repeated abandonment of the Lord The fourfold pattern of disobedience/oppression/cries for help/deliverance God's faithfulness despite the people's infidelity God's use of charismatic leaders to rescue Israel The imperfection of God's chosen leaders and lack of real heroes Sad, tragic, often ugly stories that seem out of place in the Bible
When did this take place?	During the period after the conquest of Canaan and before the establishment of the monarchy: probably the years between 1220 and 1000 B.C.
Where did these events occur?	Various locations in the land of Canaan
Why was this book written?	To document Israel's moral downfall and its inevitable consequences; to reiterate the deuteronomic theme that fidelity leads to blessing, but infidelity to certain and tragic punishment (including possible loss of land); and to help explain why God permitted Israel to change its system of government to monarchy.
What is the story?	The Israelites continue their conquest of the Promised Land. But the Canaanite natives who had not been driven out by the Israelites regroup and counterattack. In addition, the Israelites begin to adopt the customs and idolatrous worship of their pagan neighbors. A series of 12 leaders, each in a time of grave national crisis, arises to rouse the people and lead them against the threatening enemy. And every time, in response to the people's repentance, the LORD has mercy and rescues Israel.

The book of Judges can be easily divided into three sections, as outlined on the following page.

Before Beginning

The book of Judges is the second book in the collection the early rabbis called the "Former Prophets" and modern interpreters call the "Deuteronomistic History of Israel." It is a collection of stories about several Israelite heroes, set in the time between the settlement in Canaan under Joshua and the establishment of the Israelite monarchy. The title of the book comes from the designation of its principal characters. The judges were charismatic leaders of the Israelite community, especially in times of fierce competition over the land of Canaan. Their authority came from the LORD, and their duty was to enable Israel to live in faithful obedience. The judges had to deal with two problems:

1. The failure of Israel to serve the LORD alone
2. The competition for control of the land from

other peoples.

The book presents these two problems as interrelated. When Israel failed to maintain its commitment to serve the LORD exclusively, then God allowed Israel's neighbors to make its life very difficult. The competition for control over the land of Canaan in the thirteenth century B.C. was stiff. In the course of that competition, individuals emerged who proved very capable of managing that competition to the benefit of the Israelite tribes. Stories about these individuals and their feats circulated among the Israelites and eventually found their way into the collection we know as the book of Judges. This collection, however, served a purpose beyond simply preserving the exploits of ancient heroes. The Israelites faced a practical and theological problem: the absence of the kind of leadership provided by Moses and Joshua. How should

I. Introduction 1, 1—3, 6	1. Israel's failure to fully conquer the land 2. Israel's disobedience as cause of their failure	
II. Exploits of the judges 3, 7—16, 31	Major Judges	Minor Judges

	1 Othniel (3, 7—11)
	2 Ehud (3, 12—30)
	3
	4 Deborah (4, 1—5, 31)
	5 Gideon (6, 1—8, 35)
	  Abimelech, the illegitimate
	  judge (9, 1—57)
	6
	7
	8 Jephthah (10, 6—12, 7)
	9
	10
	11
	12 Samson (13, 1—16, 31)
		Shamgar (3, 31)
		
		Tola (10, 1—2)
		Jair (10, 3—5)
		
		Ibzon (12, 8—10)
		Elon (12, 11—12)
		Abdon (12, 13—15)

III. Appendices 17, 1—21, 25	1. Idol worship in the tribe of Dan 2. Outrage at the assault of a concubine and Israel's first civil war	

Israel be governed? Who would insure that Israel would live according to the Torah in the land it had received from the LORD? Without a strong leader, the people abandoned their vow to serve the LORD (Jos 24, 21–24). The book of Judges illustrates the consequences of Israel's failure.

Three Significant Parts

The book of Judges has three parts. The first (1, 1—3, 6) gives a framework for understanding the significance of the stories about these ancient heroes. The second part (3, 7—15, 20) describes the exploits of the judges. The book concludes with a few supplementary stories (16, 1—21, 25) that show how the Israelite tribes were on a path of self-destruction. Originally the stories about the individual judges served to excite a certain measure of pride in the achievements of the tribes in maintaining control over the land of

Canaan. But once these stories were put into their present context in the book of Judges, the effect was to show that there was something terribly wrong about the way the Israelite tribes were living their lives in the land that God had given them. Readers are led to conclude that matters could not go on like this—something had to be done, for the life of the Israelite tribes was degenerating into anarchy.

Reading Through the Book of Judges

Understanding the Time of the Judges (1, 1—3, 6)

The book begins by raising the question of leadership: "Who shall be first among us to attack the Canaanites and to do battle with them?" (1, 1). The initial answer is Judah, the tribe that eventually became the nucleus of the southern kingdom.

After some initial success, the tribes' progress bogged down. The first chapter concludes, then, with a list of areas over which the Israelites were not able to assert their control (1, 27–35). The picture here is just the opposite of that given in the book of Joshua when Joshua "captured the whole country, just as the LORD had foretold to Moses. Joshua gave it to Israel as their heritage, apportioning it among the tribes" (Jos 11, 23). The process by which the Israelites achieved control over Canaan was clearly long and complicated.

The second chapter describes the price Israel had to pay for its style of leadership: the Israelite tribes found themselves in danger of being overcome by the other groups competing for the limited territory of Canaan. The reason for the tribes' inability to repeat Joshua's victories was their failure to keep their covenant with the LORD. Israel would have to deal with other contenders for the land by themselves. God's help would not be forthcoming. The contrast between the period of Joshua and that of the Judges could not be more absolute. Under Joshua's leadership, "the people served the LORD" (Jgs 2, 7), and they had experienced victory after victory and came to possess "all the land." Without Joshua's leadership, the Israelite tribes were on the verge of annihilation because of their failure to obey the LORD. The Israelite response was lamentation at a place named Bochim (weepers) (Jgs 2, 5).

Religious Interpretation

The next section (2, 6–3, 6) elaborates on the religious interpretation of the problems the Israelite tribes had in maintaining a foothold in the land promised to their ancestors. The explanation given for Israel's difficulties is simple enough: "the Israelites offended the LORD by serving the Baals" (2, 11). The Israelite worship of Baal, the title ("Lord" or "Owner") by which Hadad, the Canaanite god of the storm and fertility, was known, was incompatible with the exclusive service that Israel owed to its God.

One of the principal sources of anxiety for the Israelites was having enough food to eat. The problem was not the soil—it was fertile enough. The problem was water. The region had no river system as did Egypt and Mesopotamia. Israel was dependent on rain and worshiped the Canaanite deities Baal and Ashtaroth because rain and fertil-

ity were their specialties. Probably most Israelites did not consider their worship of Baal and Ashtaroth as incompatible with loyalty to the LORD, but certainly the author of Judges did. It took centuries for the people of Israel to be convinced of how critically important it was for them to serve the LORD alone. The book of Judges was an important contribution to this process.

Pattern of Judges

The pattern for the way the stories of the judges will be told is set in 2, 11–23. The book introduces the narrative of each of the judges with the formula found first in 2, 11: "Israelites offended the LORD." The consequence of this infidelity was domination over the Israelite tribes by their rivals. But the period of the judges was marked not only by divine judgment but by divine mercy. The LORD always heard the sounds of Israel's pleading and responded by raising up a leader who rescued Israel from the oppression they were experiencing. Unfortunately, at the death of the judge who rescued them, the Israelites returned to their evil ways.

God determined, then, that Israel would have to continue facing the threat of extinction as long as it continued to serve the Baals (2, 16–23). The introduction to the book ends with 3, 1–6, which explains that Israel's competitors will remain in the land to test the loyalty of future generations. But one consequence of this intermingling will be that some Israelites will marry Canaanite spouses, which will often mean that the Israelite partners in such unions will abandon their ancestral religion.

Two final observations need to be made about the introduction. First, in the stories that follow, the threat and resistance are usually local. But Judges transforms the stories of local heroes into stories that have significance for all Israel. Second, as readers work their way though the stories of the judges, the question arises about how long God will continue to put up with Israel's infidelity. Is there some limit to God's patience?

The Stories of the Judges
(Jgs 3, 7—15, 20)

Othniel (Jgs 3, 7–11)

The book of Judges begins with a divine oracle that names the tribe of Judah as the leader of the

Israelites in the attempt to take control over Canaan (1, 1–2), and the first of the judges, Othniel, is from Judah. He has already made an appearance in the book as the conqueror of Debir, a city in the southern hill country of Judah (1, 11–13). Here Othniel's story is told with a minimum of detail, but it clearly follows the basic pattern of Judges: disobedience, oppression, repentance, and mercy. The spirit of the LORD empowered Othniel to accomplish extraordinary deeds.

Ehud (Jgs 3, 12–30)

Ehud came from the tribe of Benjamin, whose territory was immediately north of Judah. The first detail given about Ehud is that he was left-handed. While the people of the ancient world considered left-handedness abnormal, it was a distinct advantage in hand-to-hand combat because it provided an element of surprise and allowed the one who was left-handed to strike with a knife or sword behind his foe's shield. Although the name Benjamin means "the son of my right hand," the tradition behind the book associates this tribe with a high incidence of left-handedness. Judges 20, 16 asserts that Benjamin could boast of 700 highly skilled left-handers.

Once again, Israel's sin was responsible for the oppression, which took the form of raids for 18 years, by Eglon, the king of Moab. Moab was a kingdom located directly across the river from Benjaminite territory, and "the City of Palms" was probably Jericho. Not only did the Moabites occupy Israelite territory, but they required the payment of tribute, a payment that signified the Israelites' submission to and dependence on Moab. Ehud, who was supposed to bring Benjamin's tribute to Eglon, instead assassinated him. After making his escape, Ehud was able to convince men from the tribe of Ephraim to join him in expelling the Moabites from Israelite territory. So total was Ehud's victory that Israel had peace for 80 years.

The story of Ehud's assassination of Eglon ridicules the Moabites. Certainly one can picture the Israelite audience having a good laugh at the expense of the Moabites. The book takes this entertaining story and makes it part of a comprehensive theological presentation about the importance of serving the LORD alone.

Shamgar (Jgs 3, 31)

There is some doubt whether Shamgar ought to be understood as a judge like the others in the book. His name is not Semitic nor does the text claim that God raised him up in response to Israel's cries. The Song of Deborah (Jgs 5) notes that the caravan trade was interrupted "in the days of Shamgar" (v. 6). Perhaps he was responsible for this disruption. While his service on Israel's behalf may have been indirect, he did make life easier for some Israelites by defeating the Philistines.

Deborah and Barak (Jgs 4, 1—5, 31)

With the story of Deborah and Barak, the scene shifts northward to the vitally important Jezreel Valley. Once under Israelite control, communication between the tribes in Galilee and those in the highlands to the south became possible. Also significant was the agricultural and trade potential of the Jezreel Valley. Israel had to control this important piece of real estate. But standing in its way was Jabin, the king of Hazor, who wanted to keep the Jezreel Valley for himself. The story and poem about Deborah and Barak testify to the significance that the Jezreel Valley held. It is the celebration of a great and unexpected victory: that of an army of peasants over professional soldiers with the best of equipment. The book of Judges presents Deborah as the hero of the conflict with Sisera's army. Barak made his contributions with great reluctance.

The story labels Deborah as a prophetess and a judge (4, 4) without further explanation. Because judges and prophets were charismatic leaders, these roles were open to women. The patriarchal structures of ancient Israelite society did not obstruct the "spirit of the LORD," and clearly people understood this. Deborah shamed Barak into raising a force from Naphtali and Zebulon to oppose Jabin's general Sisera and his chariots. Naphtali and Zebulon were Galilean tribes, and their territory was located just to the north of the Jezreel Valley. As the reader expects, God gave victory to the Israelites. Sisera escaped the rout only to be killed by the Kenite Jael while assuming she was protecting him from the pursuing Israelites. This event fulfilled, in an unforeseen way, Deborah's prophecy, which was intended to goad Barak into action (4, 9).

The book of Judges preserves what many consider to be one of the oldest texts found in the Bible: the Song of Deborah (5). This hymn celebrates the victory of Israel over Sisera's army. Here readers find out how the victory was achieved—as in Joshua's victory over Gibeon (Jos 10, 11–13), nature played a role in the battle. Verses 4 and 21 in particular suggest that sudden rain caused a flash flood in the valley and rendered the chariot force immobile, eliminating Sisera's advantage.

The poem contrasts two mothers: Deborah, mother of Israel, and Sisera's unnamed mother. Deborah was responsible for a great victory, while Sisera's mother came to realize that Sisera's failure to return promptly from the battle meant that she would never see her son again.

Gideon (Jgs 6, 1—8, 35)

No judge receives more attention from the book of Judges than Gideon. His story begins with Israel being harassed by the Midianites, who enjoyed a great advantage over Israel. The Midianites were mounted on camels when they raided Israelite territory at harvest time. These mounted attacks made them unstoppable. They simply confiscated the harvest that the Israelites produced, making life impossible for the Israelite peasants (6, 1–6). To the angel sent to recruit Gideon to deliver Israel, the reluctant general pointed out his lack of suitability—a motif also found in the call of Moses (Ex 3, 10), Isaiah (Is 6, 5), and Jeremiah (Jer 1, 6).

In Gideon's story, he is frequently called Jerubbaal, a name that seemingly honors Baal, the LORD's rival for Israel's loyalty. The meaning of that name (let Baal sue or take action), and the story of how Gideon earned it proves otherwise. Gideon's dismantling of an altar for sacrifices to Baal aroused the anger of the local people, and they were ready to kill Gideon for his sacrilege. Gideon's father suggested that they should leave the matter up to Baal—let Baal sue "since he destroyed his altar" (Jgs 6, 25–32).

The rest of Gideon's story describes his efforts to deal with the Midianites and others that were threatening the Israelite tribes in the central highlands. He rallied not only members of his own tribe (Manasseh) but the militia of three others (Asher, Zebulon, and Naphtali). But Gideon refused to proceed without receiving another sign

that his mission was from God (6, 36–40). Next came orders from God to dismiss most of Gideon's militia, including those who knelt to drink, leaving only 300 soldiers out of the original 32,000. This reduction in numbers ensured that the militia could not ascribe the coming victory to their military skills but to God. (7, 1–8). The 300 vanquished the Midianites by a surprise nighttime attack without doing any actual fighting—again underscoring the divine origin of Israel's victory.

After the Midianites were subdued, Gideon's story takes a new twist as the Israelites asked Gideon to rule as king and establish a dynasty to provide ongoing protection from groups like the Midianites. Gideon refused, citing the Israelite notion that the LORD is king of Israel. Gideon then used part of the valuables confiscated from the Midianites to construct an ephod, a priestly vestment. The book does not consider this a positive development but notes that, nonetheless, Israel enjoyed peace for 40 years (8, 22–28).

Gideon's story ends with a transition to what follows by introducing his many wives who bore him 70 children. The one child mentioned by name is Abimelech, who will be the principal character in the next story. After Gideon died, the people of Israel reverted to the worship of Baal and forgot both the LORD and Gideon's achievements (8, 29–35).

Abimelech (Jgs 9, 1–36)

Although it is in the middle of the book of Judges, the story of Abimelech is an oddity because Abimelech is not a judge. He did not free Israel from any oppression. Abimelech convinced the people of Shechem to accept him as the sole ruler of their city and its environs, replacing the more diffuse pattern of leadership as exercised by Jerubbaal's 70 sons. To solidify his one-man rule Abimelech murdered all his brothers except Jotham, who survived, cursed his brother, and then fled the Shechem area—never to be heard from again.

The book places on Jotham's lips a bitter diatribe against his brother (9, 7–15). Jotham addresses Shechem's leadership in a fable about trees who were looking for a king but could persuade only a worthless thorn bush to accept the position. Is this a criticism of the monarchy as an institution or merely a criticism of Abimelech?

The book can barely hide its animosity toward Abimelech. It is important to remember that the book of Judges—in the form in which it now exists—was the product of someone who witnessed the fall of the Davidic dynasty and the end of the national state. Certainly the failure of the monarchy to prevent the disaster that came upon Jerusalem had to weigh heavily on the writer's mind. The role of the monarchy in Israelite life, then, was not simply a theoretical question. It is important to note that the setting of this story is Shechem, where earlier Israel had reaffirmed its covenant with the LORD (Jos 24). In Abimelech, Shechem accepts a human being as its lord. Such a choice will be disastrous. Ironically, Abimelech's very name contrasts with his ambitions: it means "my father [God] is king," a way of affirming the idea that God is the king of Israel. Abimelech wishes to establish himself, not God, as the ruler.

Jephthah (Jgs 10, 6—12, 7)

Because Jephthah, as the son of a prostitute, had an even lower social standing than Gideon or Deborah, he too was at first an unlikely candidate for the leadership of the Israelite militia. He did, however, possess one advantage. As the leader of a group of raiders, Jephthah had military experience and was just the kind of man that the elders of Gilead were looking for when the Ammonites were trying to push their border northward into Gilead's territory. Gilead was an Israelite territory, which lay east of the Jordan; Ammon was a kingdom to the south of Gilead.

There are several unique features to Jephthah's story. First, before resorting to armed conflict, Jephthah tried to negotiate a settlement with the Ammonites (11, 12–28). When the negotiations failed, the spirit of the LORD came upon Jephthah, empowering him. But then there is a second unusual detail in the story. Jephthah makes a hasty and carelessly worded vow before the battle. This promise to God might indicate that the judge was less than confident in the outcome of the approaching battle. When Jephthah handily defeated the Ammonites, it was time to act on the vow he made. Jephthah thought that he was trapped by the imprecise wording of his vow, and so he had to sacrifice the daughter, who ran out to meet him on his return from the battle with the Ammonites (11, 34–35). The religious and cultural significance of the practice of lamenting for Jephthah's daughter (11, 37–40) is not clear.

Although Jephthah did neutralize the Ammonite threat and judged Israel for six years, the impression left by the book is that Jephthah's career was marked by failure and tragedy. He was not able to successfully negotiate with either the Ammonites or the Ephraimites. He lost his daughter because of a carelessly spoken vow, and his victories ignited an intertribal war. The picture of Israel during the time of the judges is getting darker.

Samson (Jgs 13, 1—15, 20)

Although Judges 15, 20 states that Samson was a judge in Israel for 20 years, his career was different from that of the judges whose stories the book has told so far. Samson never led the Israelite tribal army. His was more of a solo act. The setting of Samson's story is the long conflict between the Israelites and the Philistines for control of Canaan. The Bible calls these people *pelishtim* (i.e., "inhabitants of Pelesheth," Philistines), that is, the people who live in the coastal plains. The Philistines organized themselves politically into a confederation of city-states: Gaza, Ashkelon, Ashdod, Ekron, and Gath. As the Philistines expanded to the north, they threatened the tribe of Dan, which was located on in the central part of the coastal plain. Samson was a Danite.

Samson's mother was told that the son she would conceive was to be a Nazirite. The word Nazirite comes from a Hebrew root that means "to separate, consecrate, abstain." Numbers 6 describes the lifestyle of the Nazirite. They were not to drink fermented beverages, wine, or vinegar. They were not even to drink grape juice or eat grapes or raisins. This prohibition probably was meant to insure that Nazirites would not lose the spirit of the LORD because of intoxication. Second, Nazirites were not to cut their hair. This prohibition likely reflects a belief that a person's hair was especially significant as a place where spirits dwelt. Finally, Nazirites were not to touch any corpse because they were to remain ritually pure, and contact with a corpse rendered a person impure. A person could take the vows of a Nazirite for a set time, or a person could become a permanent Nazirite.

Samson's conflicts with the Philistines appear to be private in nature. The first came as a result of a lost wager that Samson made with the Philistines during the celebration of his marriage to a Philistine woman (14, 1–20). The second was a reaction to his wife being given to another man (15, 1–7). The third involved an attempt by some Judahites to turn Samson over to the Philistines (15, 8–20). The story affirms three separate times that the spirit of the LORD came upon Samson.

Each time the spirit gave Samson strength in situations when his life was in danger. The book implies that while Samson's struggles with the Philistines were personal, he caused the Philistines the type of setbacks that eased pressure on Dan for 20 years.

Israel's Self-Destruction (Jgs 16, 1—21, 25)

The book of Judges concludes with a series of stories that show Israel clearly on the path of self-destruction. What God would not allow the Moabites, the Midianites, the Ammonites, or the Philistines to do, Israel seemed bent on doing to itself. The final chapters make it appear that the Israelites became addicted to chaos—chaos that threatened their continued existence as a people.

As the previous section ends with the stories of Samson's private vendettas easing the pressure that the Philistines were bringing to bear on Israel, so this final section begins with Samson's descent into self-destruction. What is even worse is that Samson nearly took Israel with him. In Judges 16, 1–3, Samson's visit to a prostitute nearly cost him his life. Apparently, he learned nothing from that brush with death, and his affair with Delilah did end with his death. Delilah was from the Valley of Sorek, where the land was better for agriculture. Its one disadvantage was that it abutted Philistine territory; there was a constant threat of harassment hanging over the Israelite farmers in the Sorek because the Philistines too had moved into that valley. Delilah is never actually called a Philistine, but the implication is there.

The cutting of a Nazirite's hair was a public statement that he was released from his vows (see Acts 18, 18). In Samson's case, it meant that he no longer had the LORD's support to defend Israel from the Philistine threat. His hair grew back, and Samson had one more opportunity to

avenge himself, but at the cost of his life (Jgs 16, 23–30). Samson's flaws proved fatal.

Micah (Jgs 17, 1–13)

The scene shifts from the fate of Samson to that of Israel as a whole. The story about Micah is a symptom of the disease that afflicted Israel—the failure to serve the LORD alone. Micah built himself a shrine and, with his mother's help, outfitted it with images. Micah had one of his sons serve as the priest of the shrine until a Levite happened to come by. Micah believed that as a result of his installing a Levite as a private priest, he would enjoy blessings from the LORD (Jgs 17, 13). The only comment that the author of Judges makes on what he considers to be a warped notion of Israelite religious traditions is found in Judges 17, 6: "In those days there was no king in Israel; everyone did what he thought best." Without some central authority, religious anarchy reigned in Israel.

Chapter 18 describes the migration of the tribe of Dan from the central part of the coastal plain to the far north of Galilee. The story begins by repeating the refrain, "At that time there was no king in Israel" (Jgs 18, 1). The story continues to describe the religious anarchy among the tribes. The Danites stole the liturgical accessories from Micah's shrine and abducted his priest. After they took the city of Laish, they installed the Levite and the shrine in their new home, which they renamed Dan. Finally, the identity of the Levite is revealed. His name was Jonathan, and he was a grandson of Moses. The book of Judges regards this shrine as illegitimate because the "house of God" was located at Shiloh (Jgs 18, 31). That Moses' grandson was associated with an illegal shrine so scandalized later scribes that they introduced another letter into the name of Moses in 18, 30, changing it to Manasseh, which was also the name of the most notorious apostate of all Judah's kings (see 2 Kgs 21).

This story of the corrupting of a young Levite from Bethlehem is followed by the story of a well-established Levite from Ephraim (Jgs 19). This story, too, begins with the refrain: "At that time . . . there was no king in Israel" (v. 1)—a warning that what follows is another example of the religious anarchy that plagued Israel in the time of the judges. On his way home from reclaiming his secondary wife (concubine), who had returned to her father in a fit of anger, the Levite and his concubine spent the night in Gibeah, a town in the territory of Benjamin. The town was not a model of hospitality, and it was finally a non-native who offered the Levite shelter for the night. In what has been characterized as a "text of terror," the Levite's wife was gang-raped and murdered (vv. 11–30; compare this story to that in Genesis 19, 1–11). Despite his own guilt in facilitating this crime, the Levite summoned the Israelite militia for vengeance.

While the militia reassembled at Bethel, the people realized what they had done: virtually wiped out an entire Israelite tribe. When they sought an oracle from God to determine why one tribe had been virtually wiped out, none was forthcoming. Another rash vow—to not provide daughters in marriage to the remnants of Benjamin—led to yet more war and degeneracy, this time in the form of kidnapping. (The plot device of getting around the vow by acquiescing in this kidnapping scheme is probably meant to have comical overtones, although to us it seems simply cruel. We must remember that marriage in the ancient world was not primarily a matter of love between the married couple but of making sure that there were offspring.)

The author of Judges has painted a very bleak picture of the Israelite tribes. He leaves his readers with the by-now-familiar comment on the religious and civil anarchy that gripped the life of Israel in its land: "In those days there was no king in Israel; everyone did what he thought best" (Jgs 21, 25). What follows is the story of Israel's experience with the monarchy, which ultimately proved just as incapable of forestalling disaster for the people of Israel. This ambivalence about the monarchy is reflected in Judges itself, which both bemoans the lack of a king and (in passages such as Jotham's parable, 9, 7–21) warns against the dangers of kingship.

The book of Judges reflects the disordered state of life in Canaan at the end of the Late Bronze Age. It was a very unsettled time in the region, and certainly the book of Judges gives some idea of the chaos that affected the Israelite tribes who were trying to gain a foothold in the region. This is not to suggest that the book of Judges is a historical account of events as they happened. To some extent the narratives in Judges present an idealization of the early years of Israel's existence in Canaan: the stories of local heroes are arranged in what appears to be chronological order. What these stories show is that loyalty and commitment to the LORD are what stand between Israel's well-being and its destruction.

Continuing Significance of the Book of Judges

If the modern religious reader of Judges is repulsed by its stories, the ancient author has been successful. The picture of Israel—especially at the end of the book—is far from attractive or edifying. But it does show what happens to a nation that ignores traditional ethical and moral values. Disaster inevitably follows. If the people of Judah would restore their community's life in the land promised to their ancestors, they needed to remember the centrality of the covenant that God made with those ancestors. The stipulations of that covenant require fidelity, commitment, and absolute loyalty to the LORD.

Questions for Discussion and Reflection
Group Sharing/Discussion

1. In the book of Judges the meaning of "judge" is a tribal, charismatic leader. Would you add anything to that? What good or bad qualities of leadership did you recognize in their stories?

2. Scholars say the Song of Deborah (5, 1–31) is the oldest part of the Bible. What does it celebrate?

3. What did Samson's Nazirite vow require of him? Did he live up to his vow?

In Our Lives

1. The purpose of the book of Judges is to illustrate Israel's failure to live in faithful obedience to the LORD. What might be described as similar signs of failure today?

2. A typical pattern in the book of Judges—sin, punishment, crying out to the LORD, deliverance—plays out both in communities and personally. Where do you recognize this pattern today?

3. Israel strayed in worshiping Baal, the Canaanite god of storm and fertility. What are false gods that are worshiped in our culture?

Individual/Personal Reflection/Action

1. The book of Judges shows what happens to a people that ignores ethical and moral values.

What message is here for the modern world? In your mind, what are some values we need to pay attention to today? In your life, who or what helps you stop and look at your own values from time to time?

2. Judges describes ongoing "holy war." Do you believe war can ever be "holy"? How would you describe your position to another person?

RUTH READING GUIDE

At a Glance

Who are the main players?	Naomi Ruth, her daughter-in-law Boaz
What should I look for?	The loyalty of Ruth The felt but unseen presence of God The notion of redemption that runs throughout God's use of a non-Israelite to advance the divine plan.
When did this take place?	During the days of the judges, before the establishment of the monarchy (c 1200–1000 B.C.). The book, however, was probably written sometime during the period of the monarchy.
Where did these events occur?	In the land of Moab, east of the Dead Sea, and in Bethlehem.
Why was this book written?	To show that fidelity and integrity are possible even when faithlessness abounds; to illustrate God's faithfulness and protection; to demonstrate that kindness, piety, and loyalty bear good fruit.
What is the story?	Because of famine Naomi's family migrates to Moab where her sons marry Moabite women. Later, Naomi's husband and sons die, so she prepares to return home. One daughter-in-law, Ruth, insists on going back to Canaan with her. There she meets and marries Boaz, a kinsman. They bear a child, Obed, who will become the grandfather of King David.

Ruth and the Rest of the Bible

• The book of Ruth is one of only three books in the Bible that bears the name of a woman (the others are Esther and Judith).

• Ruth is one of the four women mentioned in Matthew's genealogy of Jesus.

Before Beginning

The book of Ruth is a delightful story that continues to captivate its audience no matter how often it is read. Few can forget the loyalty of Ruth, the devastation of Naomi, the forthrightness of Boaz. The story has been of special interest to Christians because Matthew lists Ruth among the ancestors of Jesus (Mt 1, 5).

Ruth as Story

The book of Ruth is a short story, similar to the Joseph story in Genesis 37–50. It is an artistically told tale with a simple plot. While the story of Joseph is set at the court of Pharaoh and deals with important personages and events, Ruth's characters are ordinary people; its events, mundane. Its closeness to life enables us to identify with its characters, to sympathize with their situation, and to rejoice when their problems are solved. The plot of the book is controlled by the problems that Ruth and Naomi encounter as they adjust to their new status as widows—Ruth as a new widow, Naomi as a widowed mother who has lost both her sons. These problems are resolved through the interaction of the book's main characters: Ruth, Naomi, and Boaz, relieving the tension created by the uncertain future that the two women faced. The principal characters are people whose goodness is rewarded in the end, reinforcing the belief that human events are in some sense under the control of a power that insures that good triumphs. As a story, its purpose is to entertain and delight, and this it does; but at the same time it also instructs. Although God never directly speaks or acts in the story, nevertheless it is clear that the story has something to teach us of the way that God is present in life.

An important element in the story is Ruth's Moabite ancestry. It is especially significant because the book presents her as the great-grandmother of David. Although Deuteronomy 23, 3 forbids a Moabite from becoming part of the Israelite community, Ruth not only does so but is a forebear of the great King David. Perhaps the author of the book made a connection between David and the Moabites because the story of David's rise to kingship has him place his parents in the safekeeping of the king of Moab while David is trying to elude capture by Saul (1 Sm 22, 3). There is, of course, no possibility of verifying the details of Ruth's story.

Place in the Canon

While there is universal agreement about Ruth's status in the canon of the books of the Bible, there is some disagreement about the book's placement within the canon. In Christian Bibles, including the *New American Bible,* the book of Ruth occupies a place after Judges and before 1 Samuel, following the order of books in the Septuagint, which was the version of the Old Testament read in the early Church. No doubt the Septuagint placed Ruth after Judges because the story is set "in the time of the judges" (Ru 1, 1). It is important to note that despite its placement, the book of Ruth is not a part of the deuteronomistic history, the story of Israel from conquest to exile found in the books of Joshua, Judges, 1 and 2 Samuel, and 1 and 2 Kings. It does not reflect the thought or style of the deuteronomistic history; it does not have deuteronomistic theological overtones. In Jewish Bibles, the book of Ruth is placed in the third division of the Jewish Canon: the Writings, a collection of miscellaneous works. In the Jewish synagogue lectionary, Ruth is read on the Feast of Weeks (*Shavuoth*), the celebration of the spring harvest; *Shavuoth* occurs 50 days after Passover and is the basis of the Feast of Pentecost, since it was at *Shavuoth* after Jesus' resurrection that the apostles received the gift of the Holy Spirit.

Theology in the Book of Ruth

In an age when the Torah was on the way to becoming the central religious symbol of early Judaism, the book of Ruth presents three characters, Ruth, Boaz, and Naomi, whose actions go beyond what is required of them. Ruth makes a commitment to her mother-in-law Naomi that ignores the claims of religious traditions and national origins. Naomi shows her loving concern for Ruth by devising a scheme to induce Boaz to marry Ruth, even though that scheme could have backfired on her. In spite of the fact that marrying Ruth means that her first child will be regarded not as Boaz's, but as Ruth's deceased husband Mahlon's, and that Naomi will be his responsibility as well (as she would have been her son's), Boaz ignores his self-interest to marry Ruth and redeem the property of Naomi's husband. The story shows how people who think of others' needs before their own find their truest happiness. God approves the conduct of these people by giving a son to Ruth and Boaz—a son who removes the emptiness and uncertainty that faced the widow Naomi. The author of Ruth is certainly saying to the book's readers: "Go you and do likewise."

How to Proceed

Because a story conveys its meaning in terms of what is said of its actors and their actions, it is important to pay close attention to the characterization of Ruth, Naomi, and Boaz, and what they do. Pay particular attention to the subtle presence of God in the story. Notice, too, recurring motifs and patterns that will function as clues to meaning.

The Book of Ruth in Outline

The story is worked out in scenes set between an introduction that presents the problem, and an epilogue that follows the resolution of the problem.

A. 1, 1–5   Prologue: A Family Dies
B. 1, 6–22   Naomi and Ruth in Bethlehem: Emptiness and Uncertainty
C. 2, 1–23   Naomi, Ruth and Boaz (I): A Meeting with Possibilities
D. 3, 1–18   Naomi, Ruth and Boaz (II): A Husband for Ruth

Reading Through the Book of Ruth

The Prologue: A Family Dies (Ru 1, 1–5)

A family from Bethlehem that had been driven by hunger to Moab is now left without any hope of progeny, because the men of the family have recently died. This is a principal problem of the story: Naomi is left without husband or sons (1, 5). The author makes a special note of identifying the family's origin in Bethlehem of Judah (1, 1), noting more specifically that they were "Ephrathites from Bethlehem of Judah" (1, 2). This detail, emphasized as it was, certainly led those who first read the story of Ruth to think of the most famous of all Ephrathites: David, the son of Jesse (see 1 Sm 17, 12). Thus, the opening verses of the story hint at its eventual resolution.

The Geographical and Cultural Setting

The events recounted in these opening verses reflect conditions typical of life in Canaan. Because the region did not have a river system that made large-scale irrigation possible, agriculture was completely dependent on rain. When the rainfall was inadequate, famine was the inevitable result. One way to cope was to move to areas unaffected by the famine—usually this meant Egypt (see Gn 12, 10; 26, 1). Moab was an unusual choice. It was located east of the Dead Sea and like the lands to the west, it too was entirely dependent on rain for agricultural produce. Presumably a drought that affected Bethlehem would have affected Moab as well. Also unusual is that no negative comments are made regarding the marriage of Naomi's sons to Moabite women. But these details, too, serve to prepare the reader for an even greater difference coming at the end of the story.

Childless widows were particularly vulnerable in the social and economic system of the societies of the ancient Near East. A husband and sons provided a woman with security. Naomi found herself without such protection in a foreign land. She bitterly lamented her fate (Ru 1, 13), but in an unusual move, one of her daughters-in-law chose to ignore her own welfare and care for Naomi. Instead of attaching herself to a man to provide for her welfare, Ruth attaches herself to Naomi, who can offer her nothing.

The Motif of Emptiness

Naomi's "emptiness" is the principal problem of the story. With great artistry the author of Ruth weaves into the story a motif of emptiness that sets the action of the story in motion and will be reversed by the end of the story. The emptiness of the land (famine) causes Naomi's family to leave the land. The emptiness of the land gives way to the emptiness of Naomi as she loses her husband and her sons. Naomi dismisses her daughters-in-law because her emptiness cannot be cured. She is too old to give birth again. Naomi's emptiness is accentuated when she contrasts her previous abundance with her present destitution (1, 21). The story ends with Naomi no longer empty. She takes Ruth's child to her breast and cares for him. The neighboring women congratulate her: "A son has been born to Naomi" (Ru 4, 17).

God's Presence in the Story

It is important to note that in the story of Ruth, God is most often referred to in the blessings and oaths that are spoken by the main characters. Naomi blesses her two daughters-in-law (1, 8f); Boaz blesses Ruth for her loyalty to Naomi (2, 12) and her good character (3, 10); Naomi blesses Boaz for his kindness to Ruth (2, 20); the blessing of fertility is bestowed upon Ruth by the citizens at the city gate (4, 11–12). All of these blessings are issued in God's name, but it is through the actions of the main characters that the blessings are fulfilled.

Other references to God in the story imply that God is the cause of all that happens. God is the one who has ended the famine in the land of Israel and filled it with food (1, 6). God is blamed for Naomi's destitution (1, 20f); God is also responsible for Naomi's abundance at the end of the story (4, 14), by enabling Ruth to conceive and bear a child (4, 13). The hand of God is to be found in all that happens in the lives of Naomi, Ruth, and Boaz. But there are no miracles, no appearances of God, no signs and wonders to illuminate Ruth's way. It is through the ordinary lives of ordinary people, who demonstrate extraordinary care for each other, that the divine is manifest.

Naomi and Ruth in Bethlehem: Emptiness and Uncertainty (Ru 1, 6–22)

The length of this scene indicates its importance for the author of Ruth. Naomi decides to return home because the famine is over in the land of Israel. Also motivating her decision must be the realization that she will have a better chance of survival among her own people than as an Israelite widow living among Moabites. Naomi's words to her daughters-in-law accentuate the tragedy of her situation. She is too old to marry and can no longer bear children. She can hope for nothing. Her daughters-in-law share Naomi's desperate situation, but she advises them to return to their people. Among their own people they may be able to find husbands and thus secure their future. With Naomi there can be no future. Ruth's loyalty is shown in her refusal to abandon her mother-in-law in spite of the hopelessness of Naomi's future; she will stay with Naomi despite the prospect of poverty.

The Character of Ruth

By drawing out the hopelessness of Naomi's situation coupled with Ruth's refusal to leave her mother-in-law, the author highlights Ruth's character: she is faithful. While there is nothing wrong with Orpah's returning home, Ruth's virtue is shown in sharp relief by the contrasting actions of these two women. Ruth is willing to share the plight of Naomi. Ruth's character is spotlighted even more in its biblical context. She is not called by God. She receives no promises. No reward awaits her. She acts solely for the good of Naomi. Her loyalty will draw the attention of Boaz, which eventually will lead to the resolution of the problem facing Ruth and Naomi, and thus all in the story depends on this young widow.

Ruth, Boaz, and Naomi (I): A Meeting with Possibilities (Ru 2, 1–23)

Ruth takes the initiative in this scene, requesting permission from her mother-in-law to glean in the fields. Picking the few stalks of grain left by the harvesters was one way that people without land were able to feed themselves. Both Leviticus

and Deuteronomy require that harvesters not be so thorough as to leave nothing for the poor (Lv 19, 9f; 23, 22; Dt 24, 19–21). Ruth, seemingly by chance, enters the fields of Boaz, a prominent relative of Naomi. Boaz has heard of Ruth's kindness to her mother-in-law and sees to it that she is protected and allowed to gather a considerable amount of barley.

The Character of Boaz

The story depicts Boaz as generous and noble. He insists that Ruth glean only in his fields, he extends his protection to her, he provides her with food and water, and he sees to it that she will prosper in her gleaning. The motive for his behavior toward Ruth is her kindness and loyalty to Naomi. We see in his gracious response to Ruth's faithfulness that Boaz is a person of integrity and honor.

Naomi, Ruth, and Boaz (II): A Husband for Ruth (Ru 3, 1–18)

Naomi does not want Ruth to remain a widow, so she decides to take advantage of the positive encounter between Ruth and Boaz. She suggests a plan to Ruth that could lead to marriage with Boaz. Even though the writer uses euphemisms that reflect his culture's reticence about private matters, the sexual overtones of Ruth's actions are clear. Although her encounter with Boaz on the threshing floor could have turned out differently, Boaz's integrity and generosity leads in the direction Naomi hoped: Ruth will have a husband.

The Climax: Boaz Acts (Ru 4, 1–12)

The storyteller introduces a new wrinkle into his tale to complicate matters just before the denouement. For the first time in the story, Naomi's husband Elimelech's land becomes an issue. Probably the story's first readers would have wondered when the storyteller was going to get around to dealing with this most important matter. Boaz assembles 10 of the town's elders to witness how the matter of the land was going to be settled among Elimelech's relatives. The presence of the elders ensured that the details of settlement became "public record." An unnamed relative who had a prior claim on the land was willing to buy it back, thus insuring that Elimelech's land would stay in the family. Of course, doing so would have benefited that man economically. But then Boaz adds that with the land came Ruth, Mahlon's widow. Any child born of Ruth and the relative in question would inherit the land; rights to it could not be controlled by the relative himself. It is at this point that he demurs and cedes his rights to Boaz. The storyteller implies that the unnamed relative was concerned solely about his own interests, unlike Naomi, Ruth, and Boaz, who, throughout the story, are concerned less about themselves and more about the welfare of others. With the tension brought on by this last complication resolved, the storyteller can proceed to the happy ending, which has Ruth acquire a husband, Boaz acquire both a wife and Elimelech's land, and Naomi acquire a son who will fill her emptiness.

Levirate Marriage and Land Redemption

Some interpreters suggest that the marriage of Boaz and Ruth represents a variation of the levirate marriage. A levirate marriage was the marriage of a woman with the brother of her deceased husband ("Levir" is the Latin word for "brother-in-law"). Such a union was mandated if the marriage was childless (Dt 25, 5–10). The practice developed to ensure that the line of the deceased man would continue, in spite of the fact that he died before his wife bore him a child. Although Boaz claims Ruth as wife to raise up a family for her late husband, he is not her brother-in-law and thus the law of levirate marriage did not apply. The storyteller presents Boaz as going beyond his obligations in order to help two widows in need.

Land redemption was a strategy that developed to insure that circumstances that forced a man to sell his land would not lead his family into a permanent state of poverty. According to Leviticus 25, 23–38, it was the responsibility of a relative to buy the land before it was sold outside the family or to buy it back if it already had been sold. The land remained the property of the relative who bought it back until the year of jubilee, when its ownership reverted to the descendants of the man who was forced to sell it.

A Son for Naomi (Ru 4, 13–17)

Ruth's marriage to Boaz is blessed with a child. Naomi's loss is replaced by Ruth's gain; the tragedy of death, with which the story opened, is balanced by the joy of new life. Notice the

women of the village congratulate Naomi as if she were the mother: "A son has been born to Naomi" (Ru 4, 17). The storyteller thus solves the problem of Naomi's emptiness. The *NAB* translation obscures this point by calling the child Naomi's "grandson." While the child indeed was Naomi's grandson, the text nonetheless shows Naomi acting as if she were the mother (Ru 4, 16) and being recognized as such by the women of her village (Ru 4, 17).

The Epilogue: A Family's Genealogy (Ru 4, 18–22)

The story's epilogue takes the reader back to the prologue, which identified Naomi's family as "Ephrathites from Bethlehem" (Ru 1, 2), and informs the reader of the wider significance of this charming story of one family's problems. The most famous Ephrathite from Bethlehem was David, who, it turns out, was a descendant of Boaz and Ruth. Usually a genealogy serves to legitimate the status of the last person named. Here David, the last person named, serves to show the significance for all Israel of what happened to three people from the village of Bethlehem.

Continuing Significance of the Story of Ruth

While Early Judaism came to regard careful observance of the Torah as the key to its future, the book of Ruth shows three people whose relationships with each other are based not on obligations but on love and concern for another in need. Such relationships have significance far beyond the lives of the three people involved directly. Jesus develops these insights in his Sermon on the Mount, in which he calls his followers to go beyond the commandments, as irreplaceable as they are. The charming story of Naomi, Ruth, and Boaz shows that an ethical system fulfills its purpose if those who accept it learn to go beyond its requirements. The Torah asserts that no Moabite is to be admitted into the Israelite community (Dt 23, 3). But the book of Ruth presents a Moabite woman whose actions on behalf of her Israelite mother-in-law proceeded from love that ignored religious and ethnic boundaries. These boundaries keep people from responding to each other in love. The book of Ruth, then, presents this young Moabite woman to its readers and suggests that they follow her example. The ending of the book wishes readers to recognize that when people give of themselves for the sake of others they find their truest happiness. This paradox lies at the heart of the book of Ruth and makes it the charming and admirable story that it is.

Questions for Discussion and Reflection
Group Sharing/Discussion

1. It is important to be attentive to the characterization of Ruth, Naomi, and Boaz and to what they do. Have various people in the group focus on one of these characters and retell who they are and what they did. Explain what their actions say about their character. Besides loyalty, what other qualities do you see in each of them?

2. In ancient Palestine, a woman without a man in her life was destined for hardship. How does this shed light on the character of Ruth?

3. In the book of Ruth, what was the levirate law that Boaz chooses to follow?

4. Ruth, a Moabite; in *Joshua,* Rahab, a woman of Jericho; and Jael, a Kenite woman in *Judges,* are given important roles. Why do you think the writers of the Old Testament give critical roles to non-Israelites and women?

In Our Lives

1. The hand of God is found in all that happens in the ordinary lives of Naomi, Ruth, and Boaz.

No signs and wonders! How do you look for the hand of God in your life? What does Ruth's story teach us concerning the way God is present in our own life?

2. During the exile many Jewish leaders were trying to restrict marriages and contact with foreigners. The story of Ruth challenges these racial and religious purity laws. Why is it significant that Ruth, the great-grandmother of King David, is a foreigner?

3. According to the Israelite Law the poor had the right to glean the fields and the farmers were required to leave part of the harvest for gleaning. Ruth gleans the fields of Boaz. Do we have any similar laws that protect the rights of the poor?

4. Life was difficult for widows such as Ruth. What are the challenges for widows and widowers in our midst? How can we better help with those challenges?

Individual/Personal Reflection/Action

1. Ruth is a woman of service. How much is service a part of your life? Your parish, your diocese, local hospitals, or service centers would be happy to help you with a plan for yourself.

2. So much of what we organize in our churches is couples- or family-centered. Reach out to include someone in the community who does not fit those categories.

1 AND 2 SAMUEL READING GUIDE

At a Glance

Who are the main players?	Eli Hannah Samuel Saul Jonathan David Goliath Bathsheba Joab, David's general Absalom, David's son
What should I look for?	The transition in Israel from theocracy to monarchy The system of checks and balances: the king's power is checked by God's Law and the voice of the prophet How Saul's and David's sins have both personal and national consequences The theme of obedience to God: "Obedience is better than sacrifice" (1 Sm 15, 22)
When did this take place?	From the end of the age of the judges through the monarchy and death of David: approximately 1083 B.C. to 960 B.C.
Where did these events occur?	The land of Israel, especially Ramah, birthplace of Samuel; Shiloh, Israel's center of worship; the desert where David fled; Moab, where David moved his family; Ziklag, the city from which David conducted numerous raids; Mount Gilboa, site of Saul's final battle and death.

Why was this book written?

To depict Israel's transition from theocracy to democracy by narrating the life of Samuel and the reigns of Israel's first two kings, Saul and David.

What is the story?

Samuel, the last judge, anoints Saul as first king of Israel. Saul begins well but ends badly, becoming obsessed with jealousy and hatred of David. Saul turns to occult practices and eventually commits suicide. David succeeds him on the throne and unites Israel into a powerful kingdom. Although he never abandons the LORD, David's own sins bring strife to his family and nation.

The books of Samuel were not written from start to finish by a single author or even a group of authors. Individual stories and blocks of material about the fascinating characters in these books had existed long before anyone pulled them together and gave them their present form. Although it is not as evident here as in the book of Judges, the same deuteronomistic editors who shaped that book shaped these.

As Israel changed, so did its literature. During the tribal era, it produced heroic sagas filled with astounding events. But when Israel became a state, *historical* writing developed. The books of Samuel combine sagas, like the story of David and Goliath, with historical writing, like the report in 2 Samuel 8 of David's conquest of the Moabites and Edomites. Yet, Samuel is not so much teaching history, as preaching the consequences of how Israel lives.

The books of Samuel offer a theological interpretation of how the monarchy was established in Israel. Their basic theological presupposition is this: David, who conquered Jerusalem and made it Israel's religious center, must have been God's chosen leader.

Reading the Books of Samuel

The theological perspective of the editors colors their presentation of the lives of Samuel, Saul, and David (see the discussion of Understanding the Historical Background to the Biblical Texts on RG 31).

Their viewpoint is this: Total obedience to God's Law brings success; disobedience brings failure. Since the deuteronomists see David succeed despite his sins, they conclude that he must have been loyal to the LORD. Saul, on the other hand, fails, so they conclude he must have been disloyal.

Outline of 1 and 2 Samuel

1 Sm 1, 1—3, 21	Birth and youth of Samuel
1 Sm 4, 1–7	Loss and return of the Ark of the Covenant
1 Sm 7, 2–17	Samuel as judge
1 Sm 8, 1—12, 25	Establishment of the monarchy
1 Sm 13, 1—15, 35	Reign and rejection of Saul
1 Sm 16, 1—2 Sm 5, 5	David becomes king of Judah and Israel
2 Sm 5, 6—24, 25	Reign of King David
2 Sm 21, 1—24, 25	Appendices

Samuel's Birth and Youth (1 Sm 1, 1—3, 21)

In Scripture, the circumstances of a child's birth often provide hints about the child's destiny. Samuel's destiny as one chosen by God for special service is foreshadowed by his mother Hannah's barrenness. Harassed by her husband's other wife who has borne numerous children, Hannah prays that God remove her misery by

---

Deuteronomistic: This term is used to refer to both the editors and the style of the history comprised in the books of Joshua, Judges, Samuel, and Kings, as prefaced by the book of Deuteronomy. These books reflect concern for such matters as obedience to the laws given in Deuteronomy, centralized worship in Jerusalem, and support for the Davidic dynasty.

Barren Women Besides Hannah, there are four other seemingly barren Old Testament women who were divinely blessed with a son: Sarah (Gn 11, 30); Rebekah (Gn 25, 21); Rachel (Gn 29, 31); and Samson's mother (Jgs 13, 3). In the New Testament, there is Mary's cousin Elizabeth (Lk 1, 7).

The Ark of the Covenant

The most sacred of Israel's possessions, the Ark was a box of acacia wood measuring approximately 4' x 2½' x 2½'. Kept in the Holy of Holies of the moveable Tabernacle and later the Temple, it contained the Tablets of the Law (and possibly a jar of desert manna and Aaron's rod). It was considered God's throne and signified God's presence among people (at times it was virtually identified with God). Anyone who desecrated it was instantly struck down.

granting her a son. When her prayer for a son is answered, she fulfills her promise to dedicate the boy to God and raise him as a Nazirite (1, 22) and leaves him in the care of Eli the priest at the shrine in Shiloh. Samuel is clearly a gift from God, special and destined for greatness.

After consecrating Samuel to God, Hannah prays a beautifully poetic prayer. Hannah praises God for reversing fortunes by bringing down the mighty and raising up the lowly, for making the barren fertile, and for defending the weak and lowly. Mary's Magnificat (Lk 1, 46–55) resembles this prayer.

Hannah leaves Samuel in the care of Eli the priest at the shrine in Shiloh. While Samuel grew in stature and favor before God and people, the sons of Eli committed grave sins of greed and desecration, making them clearly unworthy for their service as priests of the LORD.

Samuel's special role in God's plan is highlighted by the story of his call (3, 1–21). He is God's chosen servant: Reared as a priest, he is later given a prophetic ministry as well. He will also function as a military leader or judge, Israel's last and finest. Thus, the major institutions of ancient Israel—priest, prophet, and judge—are all manifested in this one man who also anointed Israel's first two kings.

Loss and Return of the Ark (1 Sm 4, 1—7, 1)

In this story the Ark's primary significance is military. Its capture by the Philistines is a devastating blow. In Israel the Ark's presence in the battlefield signified God's presence fighting for the people. Is God's presence now lost? Ancient people believed that capturing an enemy's god and setting it up in your own temple indicated your gods were much more powerful than your enemy's. But this story shows that Israel's God works differently. Despite the Ark's capture, the LORD is still very much in control. This is pointedly (even humorously) demonstrated by the idol of the god Dagon twice falling down in worship before the Ark. Wherever it is held captive, the Ark causes disease and devastation. Every town to which it is sent experiences turmoil.

The Philistines soon learn whose god is most powerful and quickly resolve to return the Ark to Israel. But more than lampooning the god Dagon, the deuteronomistic writers use this story to illustrate that the prophecy God spoke through Samuel (that Eli's family would be punished for their wrongdoing [2, 27–36]) is beginning to be fulfilled.

Samuel as Judge (1 Sm 7, 2–17)

When Samuel reappears in chapter 7, he is a military leader or judge leading the fight against the Philistines. The degree of his success is overstated (7, 13), for the Philistines are not completely overcome until the reign of David. But by stressing Samuel's military victories—all of which were achieved not by Samuel but by God (7, 10.13)—the deuteronomistic writers make a point regarding kingship: Israel does not really need a king to lead its battles, for God can use

Saul and David—First Impressions

We meet Saul chasing after donkeys—animals as stubborn as he turns out to be and possibly symbols of those who demanded a king despite God's displeasure. They were also a sign of his family's wealth. David, on the other hand, is introduced as a simple shepherd tending to his father's flock. Later he will shepherd Israel.

anyone at any time to bring the chosen people victory.

Establishment of the Monarchy
(1 Sm 8, 1—12, 25)

Throughout most of its history, Israel remained ambivalent about monarchy. One of the distinguishing characteristics of its literature is the fact that it preserves both strands of thinking: pro-monarchy and anti-monarchy. By mingling negative with positive overtones, the writers prepare the reader for the negative assessment of the whole institution of the monarchy presented in the books of Kings, and for the more immediate downfall of Israel's first king, Saul.

Request for a King and Samuel's Opposition
(1 Sm 8, 1–22)

Because the Philistine military threat would not go away, Israel was in constant need of strong leadership. Other nations relied on kings, who would be succeeded by their sons when the king got old. Israel had no such assurance of continuity when a leader like Samuel died. So they asked for a king because they wanted to be "like all other nations" (8, 20). But Israel was not supposed to be like other nations. Samuel resisted—perhaps because he was unhappy that his own sons were being rejected as potential future leaders. God instructed Samuel to warn the people that a king would bring higher taxes, forced labor, and a military draft.

Israel's king was the LORD; therefore the request for a human king was theologically repugnant. But in the end God relented. Since theological theory and historical practice seem to conflict, the text, accordingly, reflects ambivalence about God's decision. The editors, unable to deny the historical reality that monarchy existed for centuries in Israel, assume the theological position that therefore, God must have accepted it. The abandonment of God as king of

Israel foreshadows the eventual collapse of Israel as a nation.

Saul Anointed King by Samuel
(1 Sm 10, 1—11, 15)

The story presents Saul in a positive light: His good looks and stature are signs of God's favor. Before his anointing, Saul had never heard of Samuel nor ever dreamed of kingship. Many folk stories depict their hero as someone on a mission to find something that is lost who instead finds something unexpected and better. Saul seeks out Samuel for help finding his asses but ends up with a crown. He is treated with honor at a feast, anointed as ruler, and sent away with three signs that will confirm his selection by God: Two men will tell him that the asses have been found (10, 2); he will be offered bread intended for sacrifice (10, 4); and most importantly, the Spirit of the LORD will come upon him as it had upon the judges (10, 6). Note the existence of parallel accounts of how Saul became king: by Samuel's anointing him (10, 1) and by lot (10, 17–24). The ancient writers often preserved differing accounts of the same event from the sources available to them.

The ambivalence toward monarchy demonstrated in chapter 8 continues here: While the LORD accepts kingship and designates Saul the first king, nevertheless, by wanting a king the people have proven their lack of faith.

Saul seems to have returned to private life at the start of chapter 11. Led by the Spirit and acting more like a warrior judge than a king, he leads a victorious battle against the Ammonites.

Samuel's Address and Acceptance of
the Kingship (1 Sm 12, 1–25)

Chapter 12 confirms the LORD's acceptance of kingship. After publicly asserting his own honesty, Samuel sets out to demonstrate how irrational is Israel's request for a king by telling how God always saved Israel in her times of need. The people have done evil in asking for a king, yet God permits it. However, the LORD is still the ultimate authority in Israel and failure to follow God's Law will bring just punishment.

The deuteronomistic writers present Samuel as the bridge between the eras of judges and kings. Samuel's speech brings the era of judges to an end and sets the stage for prophets to take on greater importance. The people will not have to depend solely on the king, for the prophet (whose power is here demonstrated by the thunderstorm [11, 18]) will act on their behalf in four ways:

1. interceding and praying for them;
2. teaching them what is right;
3. exhorting them to worship the LORD alone;
4. warning them of punishment when they disobey. The prophet checks and balances the king's power and mediates the LORD's judgment.

The Reign and Rejection of Saul (1 Sm 13, 1—15, 35)

In this section, the writers' main interest is in demonstrating why Saul failed as Israel's king.

Saul Is Rebuked for Disobeying Samuel (1 Sm 13, 1–22)

Although eventually successful, primarily because of Saul's son Jonathan's heroics, Saul's campaign against the Philistines begins with Saul's disobedience. The crime seems trivial, but the consequences are serious. While waiting to attack the Philistines, Saul's soldiers begin to desert because Samuel does not arrive at the expected time. Overanxious, Saul disregards Samuel's order to wait for him and offers the sacrifice himself. Disobedience to the LORD's prophet is disobedience to the LORD; consequently Saul's kingdom will not endure.

Jonathan and the Defeat of the Philistines at Michmash (1 Sm 13, 23—14, 46)

Because of the Philistine monopoly on iron, the Israelites have no iron weapons, we are told, but the Philistines are armed with swords and spears. In light of this disparity of weapons, an Israelite victory can only be the LORD's doing.

The deuteronomistic editors continually reinforce the idea of the LORD as the giver of victory. Demonstrating amazing bravado, Jonathan,

aided only by his armor-bearer, takes on and kills some 20 Philistines. At every stage, Jonathan reminds the reader that the LORD is responsible for his victory. It is Jonathan's victory that inspires Saul to attack. Saul leads a successful battle, but a rashly made decision threatens the safety of the army and demonstrates Saul's unfitness to reign as king. Saul had impulsively ordered his army to fast until nightfall on the day of battle, putting them at an unnecessary disadvantage. Knowing nothing of his father's order, Jonathan unwittingly breaks the fast.

Later, Saul is willing to kill his son for the inadvertent violation despite the fact that Jonathan had made the greatest contribution to the day's victory. Increasingly Saul seems ill-suited to lead God's people. Some commentators believe the story is also meant to indicate that Jonathan, too, is unacceptable as Saul's successor because, despite being uninformed, Jonathan did violate the oath and thus is guilty. Though Jonathan's life is spared (an animal is sacrificed in his place), a sense of doom remains.

War with the Amalekites and Rejection of Saul (1 Sm 14, 47—15, 35)

War continues, and Saul wins more victories and continues to have God's support, until he disobeys a command from God, delivered by Samuel. In violation of God's direct order, Saul refuses to enforce the ban against Israel's old enemies the Amalekites. He spares their king and refuses to slaughter the best of the herds of sheep and oxen. Instead he only destroys what is worthless. Because of Saul's disobedience—and subsequent lying about his disobedience, then passing the blame on to his soldiers—and greed, the LORD rejects Saul as king over Israel. He is still king for now, but the end is near. In fact, God sends Samuel to Bethlehem, where he will find and anoint David.

Jealousy of David becomes Saul's final downfall—although he was fond of David the harper and made him his armor-bearer, he resented David's military successes and the honors given him by the Israelites, as well as the LORD's favor. When Saul fails to kill David himself, he begins to plot against him, hoping that one of the many campaigns and tasks he gives David will result in his death. Saul both loves and hates David. He promises to make his daughter, Merob, David's wife, but then marries her to another man. He offers another daughter, Michal, but only on the condition that first David do the impossible: deliver to Saul the foreskins of a hundred Philistines. David not only meets the demand, he doubles it and wins a great military victory in the process. Instead of getting killed, David marries Michal, and Saul watches another plot to undermine his rival fail. Recognizing that the LORD's hand is upon David, Saul hates and fears him all the more.

Saul's Pursuit of David and David's Escapes
(1 Sm 19, 1—28, 2)

Saul is obsessed with David. He fears him and suspects disloyalty. These nine chapters chronicle both Saul's efforts to capture David and David's numerous escapes. Saul wants to kill David, although he allows his son Jonathan to persuade him to let David return to court. But soon his anger boils over again, and now it is Saul's daughter Michal who helps David escape. Even Samuel conspires to obstruct Saul's efforts against David. Throughout, David's innocence and loyalty are reaffirmed. David flees not because of any real crime, but because of Saul's obsessive attempts to destroy him.

David flees with his men and comes to the town of Nob, where the Tabernacle had been relocated after Shiloh's destruction. He lies to the priests in order to get food for himself and his men, an action that receives no comment from the narrator. The priests seek out God's will for David (22, 10. 15) and allow him to take the sword of Goliath, indicating their approval of David as future king. By acting like a madman, David narrowly escapes capture by the king of Gath, then delivers his parents to the safety of the land of Moab (the home of his great-grandmother Ruth) to protect them from Saul's vengeance.

No negative judgment is made on any of David's actions (not even his lies to the priests). But Saul is depicted as becoming increasingly irrational. Although he had been unwilling to enforce the ban against his enemies, Saul now carries it out against his own people. He butchers the residents of Nob, including the priests David had tricked into helping him, and even the "children and infants." This tragic massacre fulfills the prophecy that Eli's family would be cut off from Israel's priesthood (2, 31–36). Although one priest survives and gives his support to David, he, too, is later removed from the priesthood when Solomon sends him into exile, thus leaving no descendant of Eli serving as priest.

Saul keeps David on the run, but David does nothing without first consulting the LORD. God grants David much success in battle and in evading Saul. Even his fleeing reveals David's noble character: Twice he has an opportunity to secretly kill Saul but, despite the encouragement of his men, he refuses to harm the LORD's anointed. Chapters 24–26 emphasize David's innocence— even Saul recognizes it— and his selection as Israel's next king (24, 21f).

In chapter 27 David makes a desperate and startling decision: Driven by Saul's incessant harassment, he joins forces with Israel's hated enemies, the Philistines. While working as a paid mercenary for the Philistines, David takes care never to attack Israel itself, but only her enemies, although he convinces the Philistines that he is attacking his own people.

The Final Days of Saul's Reign
(1 Sm 28, 3—2 Sm 1, 27)

Saul's last days are desperate and sad. When he receives no answers from God to his questions about how to handle a Philistine invasion, he panics and seeks out a sorceress to help him consult the ghost of Samuel. The dead prophet offers no comfort, but instead reminds Saul that God

---

The Philistines The fighting between Israel and her archenemies was constant. The books of 1 and 2 Samuel record at least 13 military encounters between Israel and the Philistines. Israel's success always depended on the degree of her faith in the LORD. Of the 13 battles, Israel was victorious 11 times and one battle was a draw.

has rejected him as king and that he and his sons will lose both the upcoming battle and their lives.

When David reappears, we find him in a serious predicament: He has sworn loyalty to the Philistine king, Achish, yet now that king wants to send David into battle against his own people. What will David do? Because of circumstances, David betrays neither side: The Philistine generals do not trust him, and they force him to leave. So David battles another of Israel's chief enemies, the Amalekites, and distinguishes himself in every way.

While David is enjoying every success, Saul has become a total failure. Rather than die at the hands of the Philistines like his three sons, Saul takes his own life. The once great and beloved leader is dead. As testimony to his former greatness, his soldiers march all night to retrieve and bury Saul's body. The first book of Samuel ends with the death of Israel's first king, who by his disobedience to the LORD doomed himself to failure as a ruler.

Interestingly, the start of the second book of Samuel presents a different version of Saul's death: An Amalekite youth, probably lying to win favor with David, claims that he killed Saul at the king's own request. The boy wins nothing from David but a death sentence.

One might expect David to rejoice, but instead Saul's death brings him great grief. The reader should remember that although Saul wanted David dead, David passed up opportunities to kill Saul and even desired genuine reconciliation. David expresses his sorrow in a mournful poem he chants for Saul and Jonathan (2 Sm 1, 17–27).

David Becomes King of Judah and Israel (2 Sm 2, 1—5, 5)

After consulting the LORD, David travels to Hebron, where he is anointed king of Judah. But the northern territory is under the rule of Saul's son Ishbaal, who has been placed on the throne by Saul's general, Abner, the real power in Israel. A fight between representative warriors of each side—Joab's warriors representing David and Abner's representing Ishbaal—soon escalates into an all-out civil war between Israel and Judah. A series of murders and assassinations follows that results in the deaths of Abner and Ishbaal. The deuteronomistic writers make it

very clear that David is innocent of the killings; he even punishes those who assassinated his rival, Ishbaal. But the result is that David benefits and becomes Israel's king (2 Sm 5, 1–15).

The Reign of King David (2 Sm 5, 6—24, 25)

In this section the deuteronomistic writers advance their basic theological theme: because he is God's chosen, David found success in all his efforts, but he also suffered the consequences of all his sins. Interwoven with this dominant theme are concerns about who will rule after David dies, the activities of his children, and David's affection for Meribbaal, Jonathan's son.

The LORD is with David. Everything points to this fact: his choice as king of Israel, his military victories, the continued blessing of children in his life. David's first achievement as king of Judah and Israel is to take the city of Jerusalem, an act of the greatest political and theological significance. The city not only becomes the political capital of the empire, but, in the view of the deuteronomistic writers, the only legitimate place to worship the LORD.

David Defeats the Philistines and Brings the Ark to Jerusalem (2 Sm 5, 17—6, 23)

When they hear David has become king of both Israel and Judah, the Philistines immediately attack. But the LORD gives David the victory. This triumph, coupled with the previous conquest of Jerusalem, makes it possible for David to bring the Ark from the house of Abinadab, to the capital city, Jerusalem. A man named Uzzah tries to keep the Ark from falling during transport and is struck dead—harsh punishment for apparently well-intentioned behavior. But since the Ark represented God's very presence, only those who were consecrated could touch it. Uzzah's death emphasized the Ark's unparalleled holiness.

David dances naked before the Ark, and his wife, Michal (Saul's daughter), rebukes him for such undignified behavior. But David insists he will be even more enthusiastic (and undignified) in honoring the LORD, who chose him over Saul as Israel's king. Michal faces not only David's censure but the LORD's as well.

God's Promise to David (2 Sm 7, 1–29)

2 Samuel 7 is an enormously significant text. God's promise to David of an eternal dynasty

The Promise to David

*"*Your house and your kingdom shall endure forever before me; your throne shall stand firm forever." Like the covenants with Noah (Gn 9) and Abraham (Gn 15), the promise to David is unconditional, whereas the covenant with Moses at Sinai (Ex 19–24) contained a major condition (*"If* you obey my laws . . . ").

becomes the basis for Israel's expectation of a Messiah after the Davidic dynasty abruptly comes to an end with the destruction of Jerusalem in 586 B.C. The New Testament sees the prophecy fulfilled in Jesus, the Son of David and eternal king. This text climaxes the story of David's rise to power and prepares the way for the future that will be shaped largely by David's dynasty.

Ancient Near Eastern literature sees a connection between building a temple and establishing a dynasty. Nathan's prophecy contains an interesting play on words that may be inferring this connection. The Hebrew word for "house" can also mean both temple and dynasty. David wants to build God a house (temple); but the LORD insists on building a house (dynasty) for David.

David's Exploits (2 Sm 8, 1—10, 19)

These episodes reveal David's noble character. He wins battles (8, 1–18) and rules justly over all; he is the ideal king who shows mercy even to the family of his enemies. In ancient times new kings routinely killed all the relatives of the former king to eliminate any potential rival for the throne. But, because his love of Saul's family never wanes, David keeps his promise to Jonathan not to harm his relatives.

David and Bathsheba (2 Sm 11, 1—12, 25)

One day David sees Bathsheba bathing and immediately decides he must have her. David is king, so what he wants he gets. We are told nothing of Bathsheba's feelings, but we know she is the wife of Uriah, one of David's generals who is away battling the Ammonites. After his lust conceives a child, David conceives a cover-up. He calls Uriah home from battle in the hope that he will have sexual relations with his wife and then think the child she carries is his. But Uriah spoils the plan: In keeping with the rules of holy war, he refuses to sleep with Bathsheba. David's plot turns drastic

and cold-blooded. Uriah's murder, carried out by Joab, costs the lives of other men as well. Now David can marry Bathsheba and hide his double sin from all—but not from the LORD.

Enter Nathan with a heartrending story of abusive power. David does not hesitate in pronouncing judgment on the antagonist of Nathan's tale: "The man merits death!" But Nathan shocks him with the words, "You are the man!" David's uniqueness and true greatness is revealed in his sincere and humble repentance. God forgives him, but his sin will have consequences. The child born of his lust will die and he will live out his life in the shadow of a sword. The stories that follow (the rape of Tamar, the murder of Amnon, and the rebellions of Absalom and Sheba) embody the violence that now will never leave David's house. The second child of David and Bathsheba, however, will be a bright light that comes from their union. He will be Israel's next king, favored by the LORD.

The Rape of Tamar and Absalom's Revenge (2 Sm 13, 1—14, 33)

Prior to David's sin with Bathsheba we heard nothing of problems in his reign. Now, as if set in motion by David's offense, problems multiply.

Like father, like son. Amnon lusts for his half-sister Tamar and will not rest until he has her. Although the customs of the times would have permitted a marriage between a half-brother and -sister, Amnon yields to lust rather than custom and rapes his sister. At times David's dealings with his sons were overindulgent, but taking no action against Amnon reveals a serious weakness, even blindness in David.

It falls to Absalom to avenge his sister. He waits two years, but eventually he slays his brother and in the process becomes next in line for the throne. Absalom goes into exile and David mourns the loss of both sons until Joab persuades him to bring Absalom back.

Rebellions of Absalom and Sheba
(2 Sm 15, 1—20, 26)

Absalom now consolidates his rebellious efforts, suggesting David is a poor enforcer of justice and claiming that if he were king, justice would reign. When he hears of Absalom's rebellion, David flees Jerusalem, barefoot and weeping, in a procession that resembles a penitential rite.

Absalom marches out in pursuit of his father and David is ready to meet him. But the soldiers will not let the king risk his life, so David asks them to deal gently with Absalom. The king's forces quickly rout the rebels, and Joab, in direct disobedience of David's orders, kills Absalom. David's reaction to his son's death (19, 1) is one of Scripture's most moving passages. But the troops are shaken by David's bitter mourning. Joab warns the king he must set the example for the troops and let them rejoice in their victory. David listens and soon regains the support of his forces.

With the rebellion crushed, David returns triumphant to Jerusalem. But tension exists between the peoples of Judah and Israel, a fact that sets the stage for the next rebellion led by Sheba of the tribe of Benjamin. Joab pursues Sheba and quickly brings his rebellion to an end.

Appendices (2 Sm 21, 1—24, 25)

Except that they all speak about David's reign, these final chapters seem to have no common thread.

The Gibeonites Are Avenged; Battles with the Philistines (2 Sm 21, 1–22)

Behind this story are ancient religious beliefs that national disasters are the result of sin. The famine here resulted from Saul's illegal slaughter of the Gibeonites, and such sins must be atoned in order to restore balance to nature. Seven sons and grandsons of Saul are executed to make atonement for his sin. Saul's concubine, Rizpah, protects their decaying bodies, moving David to provide belated proper burial for Saul, Jonathan, and the recently executed men.

What can we make of the claim in verse 19 that it was the warrior Elhanan who slew Goliath? Possible explanations include the following: perhaps the name Goliath became mistakenly associated with David's victim, who was actually a different Philistine; a later period may have romanticized Goliath's slaying as David's own doing; 1 Chronicles 20, 5 credits Elhanan with the killing of Goliath's brother, which would mean David and Elhanan are both giant-killers.

David's Song and Last Words (2 Sm 22–23)

David's hymn (which, with some variations, reappears as Psalm 18) gives thanks to the LORD for military victories. The song reasserts God's faithfulness, the need for obedience, and God's promise to David of an everlasting dynasty.

David's last words review his career and acknowledge him as God's favorite, the recipient of an eternal covenant.

David Takes a Census (2 Sm 24, 1–25)

Ancient writers sometimes confused primary and secondary causes. They believed that since God is all-powerful, God ultimately causes everything, no matter what the immediate causes might seem to be. Eventually they came to see that their all-loving God might permit but never "cause" evil. While this passage claims that God incited David to take the census, the same story retold in 1 Chronicles 21 blames it all on "Satan." The census is viewed as evil because it reflects arrogant pride, a willingness on David's part to put his trust in the size of his army rather than in the protection of the LORD. Even Joab feared angering the LORD by counting Israel's fighting forces.

Continuing Significance of the Books of Samuel

As one reads the books of Samuel and their tales of jealousy, rape, murder, and revolution, one can almost hear their authors saying: "If you want a monarchy, this is what you get." The contemporary reader ought to recognize the folly of making any human institution absolute. The story of David's family shows what can happen when one is unable to keep in check the tendency to make absolute the institution of the monarchy. Second Samuel describes how Judah's royal family began to consume itself. Although monarchies are, for the most part, relics of another age, nations still succumb to the temptation of

making their political, social, and economic institutions into absolutes. The story of Israel in its
land shows what happens when a nation and its
leader ignore the fundamental moral values.

Questions for Discussion and Reflection
Group Sharing/Discussion

1. In David's covenant with the LORD (2 Sm 7)
what promises does the LORD make to David?

2. Why was David interested in having
Michal, Saul's daughter, as his wife? For her
part, why was Michal originally interested in
David? What does this say about their culture
and how does this compare to our culture?

3. Let different members of your group choose
one of the main players in David's story—Saul,
Jonathan, Samuel, Nathan, Michal, Abigail, Absalom, and so on—and explain why they were
important and what lesson/s you learned from
their relations with David.

4. In your view, what do you find admirable in
David's life? How could this be imitated today?

In Our Lives

1. Dressed only in an ephod, David dances
"with all his might" the whole night to celebrate
the Ark of the Covenant's coming to Jerusalem.
David sings, dances, and feasts with the people.
Where and how does joy come into your life, into
your religious experience? How do you plant
seeds of joy?

2. Michal does not join the celebration. She is
critical and uninvolved. She accuses David of
fraternizing with the lowest element of society.
How do you feel about Michal's reaction? In
your life is it easy or difficult to fraternize with
people from other lifestyles, economic classes?
What is the message there?

Individual/Personal Reflection/Action

1. Reread the story of David and Bathsheba (2
Sm 11 and 12). David lusts after and kills for
Bathsheba. His actions affect him, his family and
friends, as well as the people. "Lead us not into
temptation" becomes our daily prayer. Reflect
upon how temptation of all different kinds
touches your life.

2. By his story, Nathan, the wise prophet, reveals David to himself. David confesses he has
sinned against the LORD. We all need wise
prophets to help us see the way. Who are the persons you allow to nourish you on your way? Who
is someone you would choose for that role?

3. In his Song of Thanksgiving (2 Sm 22,
1–51) David prays to the LORD: "You are my
rock, my fortress, and my deliverer." David built
his life on the rock and foundation of the LORD.
Who are people you know who clearly have the
LORD as their rock and foundation, the main influence in how they live their lives? If you are
comfortable doing so, let them know how you
see them in this way.

1 AND 2 KINGS READING GUIDE

At a Glance

Who are the main players?

David Solomon Bathsheba Adonijah, half-brother of
Solomon Rehoboam, son of Solomon and first king of Judah after the split Jeroboam, first king of Israel after the
split Elijah, the prophet Elisha, his assistant and successor
Ahab, a king of Israel Jezebel, his wife the Shunammite
woman Naaman, general cured of leprosy Jehu, a king of
Israel Hezekiah, a king of Judah Sennacherib, Assyrian
king Isaiah, prophet in Judah Manasseh, worst king of Judah Josiah, reformer king of Judah Jehoiakim, a king of
Judah Zedekiah, last king of Judah Nebuchadnezzar, king
of Babylon

What should I look for?

How all kings are judged according to their faithfulness to
the covenant, not by political, social, or economic standards
How the authors pay most attention to the very faithful and

very unfaithful kings or those who most interacted with one of God's prophets How the behavior of the king powerfully impacts the life of the nation, especially as regards idolatry The importance of the Temple in the nation's life How David's reign is used as a standard to measure the reigns of all later kings The importance given to the role of prophets The frequency with which events are seen as the fulfillment of prophecy

When did this take place? During a period of 400 years, from approximately 960 B.C. to 586 B.C., that is, from the end of the reign of David to the Babylonian Exile.

Where did these events occur? In the land of Israel, which becomes divided into two parts: Israel in the north and Judah in the south.

Why was this book written? To help explain the exile; to tell the people that their infidelity to the covenant brought about the collapse of the nation, and to narrate the complete history of the monarchy.

What is the story? David's reign comes to an end, and he is succeeded by his son Solomon, whose reign is described in great detail. After Solomon's reign the kingdom is divided in two: Israel in the north, with its own centers of worship to rival Jerusalem, and Judah in the south. Twenty kings, all judged unfaithful, rule the northern kingdom over a period of approximately 200 years until the north collapses in 722–721 B.C. and its population is led into exile. In the south David's descendants (20 in all, although one was a usurper) rule for a period of about 360 years, until the time of the Babylonian exile in 586 B.C. Several of the southern kings attempt reform but ultimately their efforts are too little, too late.

In summarizing the character of the books of Kings, three distinct but interrelated features stand out. First, these books tell a story; they are narrative literature. Second, the story in Kings is about the past. We are dealing with the effort to write history, known as historiography. For all the artistry of the storytelling, there is a concern to write about a real past that is shared with other peoples in the Near East. Third, it is literature that teaches something about the God of Israel and his ways. There are three prominent theological themes in the story:

1. The LORD is indeed God and must not be confused with the various gods worshiped within Israel and outside, which are simply human creations (1 Kgs 12, 25–30; 2 Kgs 19, 14–19).

2. As the only God there is, the LORD demands exclusive worship. Much of Kings is therefore concerned to describe what is illegitimate in

terms of worship. The main interest is the *content* of this worship (1 Kgs 11, 12, 13); there is also accompanying concern about the *place* of worship, which is ideally the Jerusalem Temple and not the "high places."

3. As giver of the Law that defines true worship, right thinking, and overall behavior, the LORD is also the one who executes judgment upon wrongdoers. The world of Kings is a moral world, in which wrongdoing is punished whether the sinner be king (11, 19–13), prophet (13, 7–25), or ordinary Israelite (2 Kgs 7, 17–20).

Before Beginning

First and Second Kings continue the story of Israel in its land. They are the final two components of the deuteronomistic history of Israel, which turns that story into a sermon that takes its theological principles from the book of

Chronological Tables of Rulers

Problems of chronology of the kings of Israel and Judah permit no easy solution. The following tables are based upon two widely accepted systems of chronology, one developed by W. F. Albright, and the other by E. R. Thiele. The dates of Thiele's system (3rd ed.), which are enclosed within parentheses, are presented in simplified form apart from co-regencies and simultaneous claims to the throne. The two columns show the chronological relationships of the kings of the two kingdoms. The date shown is the year that ruler took the throne.

The United Monarchy

The length of Saul's reign is not known; David and Solomon are each said to have ruled for 40 years, which is often used as a general and somewhat indefinite number. Their reigns must have fallen between about 1020 and 922 (931) B.C., perhaps as follows:

Saul   1020–1000 B.C.

David   1000–961 (or 1000–965) B.C.

Solomon   961–922 (or 965–931) B.C.

The Divided Monarchy, Judah and Israel

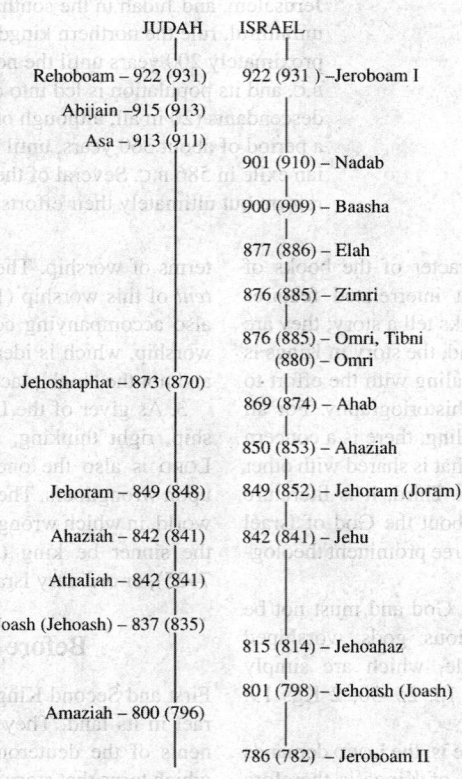

JUDAH	ISRAEL
Rehoboam – 922 (931)	922 (931) –Jeroboam I
Abijain –915 (913)	
Asa – 913 (911)	
	901 (910) – Nadab
	900 (909) – Baasha
	877 (886) – Elah
	876 (885) – Zimri
	876 (885) – Omri, Tibni
	(880) – Omri
Jehoshaphat – 873 (870)	
	869 (874) – Ahab
	850 (853) – Ahaziah
Jehoram – 849 (848)	849 (852) – Jehoram (Joram)
Ahaziah – 842 (841)	842 (841) – Jehu
Athaliah – 842 (841)	
Joash (Jehoash) – 837 (835)	
	815 (814) – Jehoahaz
	801 (798) – Jehoash (Joash)
Amaziah – 800 (796)	
	786 (782) – Jeroboam II

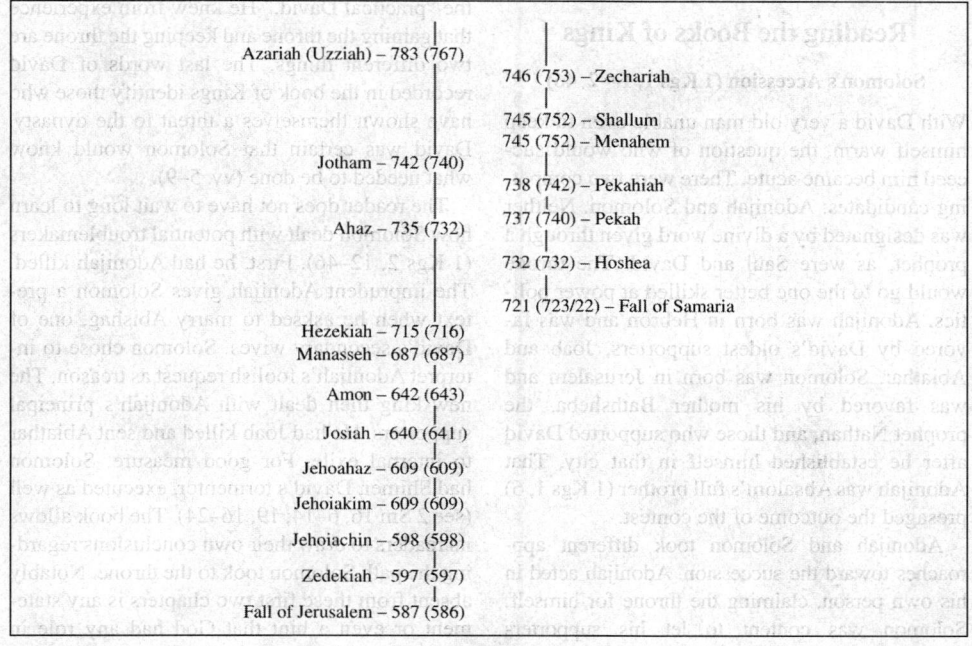

Azariah (Uzziah) – 783 (767)

Jotham – 742 (740)

Ahaz – 735 (732)

Hezekiah – 715 (716)
Manasseh – 687 (687)
Amon – 642 (643)
Josiah – 640 (641)
Jehoahaz – 609 (609)
Jehoiakim – 609 (609)
Jehoiachin – 598 (598)
Zedekiah – 597 (597)
Fall of Jerusalem – 587 (586)

746 (753) – Zechariah
745 (752) – Shallum
745 (752) – Menahem
738 (742) – Pekahiah
737 (740) – Pekah
732 (732) – Hoshea
721 (723/22) – Fall of Samaria

Deuteronomy. First Kings takes up where 2 Samuel 20 ended. It describes how the problem of the succession to David was resolved. The book then goes on to tell the story of the two Israelite kingdoms that arose following Solomon's death. The division between 1 and 2 Kings is artificial, because it is made in the middle of telling the story of King Ahaziah of Israel. Second Kings ends rather abruptly after telling of the parole of King Jehoiachin of Judah from prison in Babylon. The book allows readers to draw their own conclusions regarding the significance of this event. There is, then, no "happy ending" to the story of Israel in its land. What began with so much promise ends with great tragedy.

Certainly, the author of Kings used a variety of sources—from royal archives to prophetic legends—in composing his story. But in the form in which we read the book of Kings, it is probably the work of a single individual, writing during or shortly after the exile when the shape of Judah's future was unclear. The institutions that gave meaning to Israel's national and religious life were dead. The Temple of Jerusalem was in ruins and its priesthood scattered. The likelihood of a restoration of the Davidic dynasty seemed remote. The Israelite nation-states

no longer existed. Their territory was simply incorporated into the conquering Mesopotamian empires. Imbued with the religious perspectives of the book of Deuteronomy, Kings clearly states that the downfall of Israel and Judah was a consequence of their disobedience; but it implies that Judah may still have a future—if it learns obedience.

The books of Kings are anything but objective. First, they reflect a clear bias in favor of Judah and so they write off the northern kingdom as a complete loss. Not a single monarch from the northern kingdom receives a positive evaluation. Second, Kings does praise a few kings of Judah although most are condemned. In the author's eyes, most kings promoted or at least allowed worship that did not reflect the uniqueness of Israel's God and the absolute loyalty that Israel owed to its divine patron. Third, the author was absolutely convinced of the centrality of the Torah in Israel's life with God. Every other religious institution is secondary to it. To make its theological points, the book uses speeches, prayers, and sometimes even editorial comments. Attention to these forms will help the reader become acquainted with the spin the book puts on the events it narrates.

Reading the Books of Kings

Solomon's Accession (1 Kgs 1, 1—2, 46)

With David a very old man unable even to keep himself warm, the question of who would succeed him became acute. There were two competing candidates: Adonijah and Solomon. Neither was designated by a divine word given through a prophet, as were Saul and David. The throne would go to the one better skilled at power politics. Adonijah was born in Hebron and was favored by David's oldest supporters, Joab and Abiathar. Solomon was born in Jerusalem and was favored by his mother Bathsheba, the prophet Nathan, and those who supported David after he established himself in that city. That Adonijah was Absalom's full brother (1 Kgs 1, 6) presaged the outcome of the contest.

Adonijah and Solomon took different approaches toward the succession. Adonijah acted in his own person, claiming the throne for himself. Solomon was content to let his supporters manipulate his father into designating him as the successor to the throne. The book describes two simultaneous ceremonies, each of which was to inaugurate David's successor. The ceremonies took place near Jerusalem at two sites within shouting distance of each other. Adonijah chooses En-Rogel, a spring located at the juncture of the Hinnom and Kidron Valleys just south of Jerusalem, while Solomon had his ceremony at the Gihon Spring, Jerusalem's main water source, at the base of the eastern slope of David's city. Solomon was able to bring more people to his ceremony; after all, he was the candidate of the Jerusalem party. When Adonijah and his supporters heard the crowd acclaim Solomon as their king, they lost heart and fled. Adonijah submitted to Solomon's authority and begged for his life, which Solomon chose to spare.

With the succession settled, David makes his exit. Of course, a person as important as David must have some significant last words to say. The book provides David with a dual personality (1 Kgs 2, 1–9). The first to speak is the "pious David" who charges his successor to be obedient to the written authoritative Torah, that is, the book of Deuteronomy. It will be through his obedience that Solomon will secure the throne for himself and his successors (vv. 2–4). Then it is the turn of

the "practical David." He knew from experience that gaining the throne and keeping the throne are two different things. The last words of David recorded in the book of Kings identify those who have shown themselves a threat to the dynasty. David was certain that Solomon would know what needed to be done (vv. 5–9).

The reader does not have to wait long to learn how Solomon dealt with potential troublemakers (1 Kgs 2, 12–46). First, he had Adonijah killed. The imprudent Adonijah gives Solomon a pretext when he asksed to marry Abishag, one of David's secondary wives. Solomon chose to interpret Adonijah's foolish request as treason. The new king then dealt with Adonijah's principal supporters. He had Joab killed and sent Abiathar to internal exile. For good measure, Solomon had Shimei, David's tormentor, executed as well (see 2 Sm 16, 6–14; 19, 16–24). The book allows its readers to draw their own conclusions regarding the path Solomon took to the throne. Notably absent from these first two chapters is any statement or even a hint that God had any role in Solomon's succession.

It is important to note the role that Bathsheba, Solomon's mother, played in his rise to the throne. After he became king, she enjoyed access to him and was seated near his throne at official functions (1 Kgs 2, 19–20). The books of Kings name the mothers of 17 other kings: all but two kings of Judah (Jehoram and Ahaz) and two kings of Israel. This had led to the conclusion that the "queen mother" had an official position and exercised political and religious power. Unfortunately, the book does not provide the type of information that would permit firm conclusions to be drawn. That the author made it a point to mention the mother of 18 kings by name, however, makes it obvious that the "queen mother" enjoyed a specific rank and exercised some power—especially over domestic matters.

Solomon's Reign (1 Kgs 3, 1—11, 43)

The account of Solomon's reign begins with an introductory statement that summarizes the book's ambivalence toward David's son (1 Kgs 3, 1–3). On the one hand, the reader is told that Solomon "loved the LORD" (v. 3), fulfilling the great commandment of Deuteronomy (see Dt 6, 5). But, on the other hand, he married a foreign princess and worshiped on the "high places."

The deuteronomic tradition takes a dim view of both patterns of behavior (see Dt 7, 1–4; 1 Kgs 3, 2–3, and 28 more times). Like Israel's life in the land, Solomon's reign will begin well enough but it will soon founder because of an unwillingness to be faithful to the most basic of the Torah's commands: absolute fidelity to Israel's God.

The book finally gets around to providing divine approval for Solomon's accession (1 Kgs 3, 4–15). It does so by having God approve of Solomon's status as king through an appearance in a dream, which the Bible considers as one way that God communicates with human beings. The story reflects an ancient Near Eastern practice (called "incubation") of seeking an oracle by sleeping in a sanctuary after offering the prescribed sacrifices. Any dream experienced during this sleep was considered a revelation from the god honored at the sanctuary. The dream concerned Solomon's request for God's help in ruling Israel wisely. The request was granted. The book follows up the account of the dream with a tale illustrating Solomon's wisdom (1 Kgs 3, 16–28). Solomon was able to settle a dispute between two women over an infant, because he knew that the true mother would sacrifice anything to ensure the welfare of her child.

The book pauses in its telling about Solomon's reign to include information about Solomon's administration, wealth, and wisdom (1 Kgs 4, 1—5, 14). In the past the people asked Samuel for a king to rule over them "like the nations." The book implies that the taxation, nepotism, and cronyism assure them that they have such a king. Deuteronomy requires that the king study the Torah so that he not "become estranged from his countrymen" (Dt 17, 20). The list of the king's daily provisions (1 Kgs 5, 1–5) certainly sounded more than extravagant to Judah's poor farmers. The divide between the royal establishment and the general population was becoming more pronounced. Still, 1 Kings 4, 20 and 5, 5 describe Solomon's reign as a time of peace and prosperity.

Just as Moses was associated with Torah and David with the Psalms, Solomon was remembered as a sage (see Prv 1, 1; Sir 47, 12). To conclude its initial portrait of Solomon, the book asserts that Solomon's wisdom was unsurpassed. His wisdom attracted admirers from all over the world (5, 9–14). The reader recognizes that Solomon's court is far different from that of Saul—and even David.

Building the Temple

Next the book describes a project with which Solomon's name is always associated: the building of the Temple (1 Kgs 5, 15–32). While the account implies that God ordained the project, building a temple was a royal prerogative in the ancient Near East. By erecting a temple to Israel's patron deity in Jerusalem, his capital, Solomon was asserting, in most dramatic form, his claim to Israel's throne. The book has Solomon explain that David did not build a temple because he was almost continuously at war (1 Kgs 5, 17). Solomon also used good deuteronomic language as he said that he was going to build a temple "for the name of God" (v. 19). The deuteronomic tradition usually avoided describing the Temple as God's dwelling place, preferring to speak of the Temple as the place for God's name (see Dt 12, 11).

The book goes into some detail in describing the building of the Temple. It gives the date for both the beginning and the completion of the project (2 Kgs 6, 1.37) and describes the dimensions of the building and its three-part structure. The Temple was to have a porch, a nave, and a "holy of holies." The latter was a windowless room that was to contain the Ark of the Covenant, the symbol of the divine presence. In the holy of holies, there were to be two cherubim (1 Kgs 6, 23–28). A cherub was a mythical, composite creature that had the face of a human being, the forequarters of a lion, the hindquarters of an ox, and wings of an eagle. (It is similar to the griffin or gryphon that is depicted in Western sculpture, including carvings on cathedrals.) The Ark of the Covenant would be placed between the two cherubim.

The Temple is presented as a most impressive building. Solomon spared no expense in its construction and ornamentation. He overlaid the entire structure with gold (1 Kgs 6, 22). At the same time, however, the book offers an explanation for the eventual destruction of this structure. It presents God as warning Solomon that God will never forsake Israel, the dynasty, or the Temple if he keeps the commandments (1 Kgs 6, 12). Kings will describe how Solomon and most of Israel's kings failed, leading God to abandon the Temple that Solomon built.

Dedication of the Temple

With the Temple and its furnishings completed, all is ready for the building's dedication. The book provides an explanation (1 Kgs 8, 1–9. 62–66) for a lengthy prayer that Solomon offers at the dedication. The framework describes the transfer of the Ark to the newly built Temple and the sacrifices offered there for the first time. The prayer, however, seems to prepare the reader for a world without a temple. The words of the prayer are, at times, in conflict with each other. Verses 10–13 speak about God's presence in the Temple, while verse 27 asserts that God cannot be contained in the building that Solomon has just built. The prayer also appears to transform the Temple from a place of sacrificial offerings (vv. 5 and 66) into a place of prayer where Israelite and non-Israelite alike can ask for forgiveness (vv. 42–43). Indeed, one does not even need to be present in the Temple to be heard by God. All that is necessary is that one prays in the direction of Jerusalem and its Temple (vv. 38, 48; see Dn 6, 11). The author of Kings composed this prayer to help his readers cope with the loss of the Temple.

The book uses another speech to reiterate its explanation for the disastrous end of the Davidic dynasty and the destruction of the Temple (1 Kgs 9, 1–9). After all, the prayer of Solomon had just praised God for fulfilling the promise to David (1 Kgs 8, 14–29) and celebrated the dedication of the Temple. God appears to Solomon and warns him that the future of the dynasty and the Temple depends on the fidelity of Israel's kings to the commandments and on Israel's exclusive loyalty to its ancestral God. The conclusion is obvious: the destruction of the Temple and the end of the dynasty did not occur because of any lack of fidelity on God's part. The people of Israel and their kings bear full responsibility for the fall of the two Israelite states and the exile of their people. Of course, the book wants its readers to recognize that the converse is true as well: obedience will bring God's blessing to the people and their land.

Queen of Sheba

Next, the book describes the splendor of Solomon's reign by focusing on his wealth, wisdom, and chariot forces (1 Kgs 9, 26—10, 29).

Eleven times the text mentions the gold that the king amassed. It also notes that the Queen of Sheba came to Jerusalem because of Solomon's renown as a sage. Sheba was located at the southwestern corner of the Arabian Peninsula and was likely one of Judah's trading partners. Goods passed between these two countries through the Red Sea port at Ezion Geber. According to an Ethiopian tradition, their country was Sheba and the results of the queen's visit to Solomon included her conversion to his religion and a son fathered by Solomon. This son visited his father and returned to Ethiopia with the Ark of the Covenant. While there is no biblical support for this tradition, it does explain the reason some people claim that the Ark of the Covenant is in Ethiopia.

Judgment Against Solomon

From the book's perspective, the luster of all Solomon's achievements was tarnished by his failure to support the worship of the LORD alone. The reason offered for Solomon's infidelity was his marriage to non-Israelite women. Of course, the book is trying to promote marriage within the Judahite community as one way to maintain Judahite identity. To show the seriousness of Solomon's failure, the text has God speak to Solomon for a third and final time, announcing the end of the united Davidic-Solomonic kingdom and the rise of another Israelite national state, which will occur after Solomon's death (1 Kgs 11, 1–13).

Kings concludes its story of Solomon's reign by mentioning three of Solomon's rivals (1 Kgs 11, 14–40). The first is Hadad, king of Edom. Judah and Edom were perennial rivals for control of the southern part of the Levant, the eastern Mediterranean coast. The second was Rezon who was "king of Damascus," the capital of Aram (now in Syria). Israel and Aram struggled for many years for hegemony in the northern part of the Levant. The most serious threat, however, was an internal one. Jeroboam, one of Solomon's administrators, was supported in a bid for kingship by Egypt and with prophetic designation, threatening the rule of the Davidic dynasty. Although the rebellion was not successful at first, the book explains the origins of the two Israelite national states, Israel and Judah, as a

Kingship In the ancient Near East a king was viewed either as an "adopted" son of god (as in Mesopotamia) or as a god himself (as in Egypt). With absolute authority, kings maintained order, defended the nation from enemies, and dispensed justice. Kings also had important religious roles, so much so that kingship and priesthood were essentially flip sides of the same coin.

In many ways, Israel's kings resembled those of their neighbors: They led the military, upheld justice, maintained order, functioned as priests by offering sacrifice, and were considered the LORD's "adopted" sons. But in the area of absolute authority there was significant difference: Israel's kings were *not* absolute, for they too were under the law. In fact, the deuteronomistic writers define kingship as fearing the LORD and keeping the commandments. Israel's was more like a constitutional monarchy, in which the Law of Moses was the constitution that made demands even on the king.

Prophecy According to the book of Deuteronomy (18, 9–22) prophets speak on God's behalf to both king and people. Primarily prophets *indict* and *warn*: they indict the king, and by extension the people, for not obeying God's commandments, and they warn the king and people of impending punishment in the hope of getting them to repent. The surest test of a true prophet, of course, is seeing whether or not the prophecy comes true (Dt 18, 20–22). Consequently, the books of Kings repeatedly point out the fulfillment of specific prophecies. But while prophets may do miracles, their most important task is to motivate the people to worship only the one, true LORD (Dt 13).

consequence of Jeroboam's attempt to replace Solomon, who simply failed to observe the commandments and to worship the LORD alone. It is important to note that the book asserts that, despite Jeroboam, the Davidic dynasty continued in existence not only for the sake of David but also for the sake of Jerusalem. That city was destined to take on paramount importance for Judaism. The Temple, however, is not mentioned specifically. Also significant is the role played by the prophet Ahijah, who, like Samuel, pronounced words of judgment on the king. The book again was suggesting that Israel listen to the prophets sent to it.

The Two Kingdoms
(1 Kgs 12, 1—2 Kgs 17, 41)

The two Israelite national states arose in the Levant sometime in the ninth century B.C. Historians still have not arrived at a consensus as to the developments that led to their establishment. First Kings, however, describes the origins of the two Israelite states as the result of divine judgment on Solomon's rule, communicated by the prophet Ahijah. What Ahijah foretold was fulfilled almost immediately after Solomon's death and

the accession of his son Rehoboam. But as it did with the origins of the monarchy, the book will describe the origins of the two Israelite national states in economic as well as religious terms (1 Kgs 12, 1–25). Rehoboam refused to lighten the economic burdens that Solomon imposed on his subjects, and before Rehoboam was able to consolidate his hold on his father's realm, there was a revolution, which led to the establishment of the kingdom of Israel separate from the kingdom of Judah. When Rehoboam attempted to use military force against the rebellion, he was dissuaded by another prophetic word given through Shemiah.

While Kings implies that the Israelites had legitimate grievances, it does not approve of religious practices that it characterizes as obscuring the unity of Israel's ancestral deity, as violating the prohibition of images, and as ignoring the place that God chose. The book presents Jeroboam as fearing that the Jerusalem Temple would be a magnet, drawing the people to Jerusalem and to the Davidic dynasty. To counter this, Jeroboam built cultic centers at Dan at the extreme north of his kingdom and at Bethel in the extreme south (1 Kgs 12, 26–33). The book makes its attitude toward these cultic centers absolutely clear when it depicts an unnamed "man of God" from Judah condemning the shrine at Bethel (1 Kgs 13, 1–10). As the story of the northern kingdom unfolds, every king of Israel will be condemned for maintaining these shrines and continuing "the sin of Jeroboam."

First Kings concludes its treatment of Jeroboam by revisiting the theme of succession (1 Kgs 14, 1–20). Abijah, Jeroboam's heir, fell ill and Jeroboam had his wife visit the prophet Ahijah in order to elicit a favorable oracle on behalf of the child. The prophet, however, predicted not only that the child was to die but also that Jeroboam's dynasty would end violently. Ahijah's speech is an intense and sometimes vulgar invective. While the prophet was not specific about Jeroboam's failures, he was quite specific about the king's future and that of the nation. He even blamed the exile on Jeroboam (v. 16).

The book intertwines narratives about the kings of the two Israelite national states until it tells of the fall of the northern kingdom to the Assyrians in 2 Kings 17. The two Israelite kingdoms were rivals at first. Disputes over their shared border were ongoing. The book notes that Israel and Judah fought continuously during the reigns of Jeroboam and Rehoboam (1 Kgs 14, 30). Rehoboam also had to deal with a raid by Pharaoh Shishak, who had given asylum to Jeroboam during the reign of Solomon (1 Kgs 11, 40). While the Egyptians were not in a position to reestablish their hegemony over the region, they raided 154 towns in the two kingdoms. Jerusalem was spared only because Rehoboam paid a large indemnity to Shishak (1 Kgs 14, 26). The book characterizes Rehoboam's reign as a time of unfaithfulness (1 Kgs 14, 21–24).

The book next turns its attention to the northern kingdom for most of the rest of 1 Kings (15, 25—22, 40).

Elijah and Ahab

Ahab succeeded his father Omri as king in the northern kingdom. It was the first successful dynastic succession in the kingdom of Israel. From a military, economic, and political perspective, Ahab's reign was remarkably successful. His only defeat was the loss of Moab toward the end of his 22-year reign. Excavations at several cities in the north show that Ahab's reign was one of economic growth and military strength. His greatest military achievement took place at the battle of Qarqar, which the book ignores. Ahab led a coalition of small states that successfully engaged the Assyrians and prevented them from taking control of the region. Ahab led the largest force in the coalition. The book chooses to focus on Ahab's serious internal problems by introducing several stories about the prophets Elijah and Elisha. Both prophets were highly critical of the religious and social policies of Ahab and his successors.

Kings implies that his Phoenician wife Jezebel, who promoted the worship of Baal, caused Ahab's problems. The prophet Elijah forcefully opposed her. The conflict between Elijah and Ahab over Jezebel's activity dominates the portrait of Ahab in the Bible and makes it appear as if he were a weak and ineffective ruler, when in reality the opposite was true. The worship of Baal was attractive because this god was thought to provide the rain that made Israel's survival on its land possible. To show that Baal was unable to provide rain, Elijah announced a drought (1 Kgs 17, 1). God's power to provide was obvious when a dry riverbed yielded water for the prophet and ravens brought him food. When the stream dried up again, the prophet went to beg in a Sidonian town. A poor widow from that town who took pity on the prophet never ran out of food despite the famine induced by the drought (1 Kgs 17, 2–16). An even more remarkable demonstration of God's power occurred when the prophet brought the widow's deceased son back to life (1 Kgs 17, 17–24).

Elijah finally met Ahab, who blamed the prophet for the drought. Of course, the reader knows that the fault lies with Ahab. While the confrontation with the prophets of Baal on Mt. Carmel was another indication of the power of Israel's God (1 Kgs 18, 20–40), it was the prophet's prayer for rain that brought relief to the suffering people (1 Kgs 18, 41–46). The rain that came on the land does not end the tension in the story, because Jezebel was determined to avenge Elijah's victory at Mt. Carmel. The prophet fled to the south, stopping at Beersheba, a town that abuts the Negev desert. After a brief pause, Elijah continued his journey until he reached Horeb, which is the name by which the deuteronomic tradition knows Mt. Sinai. At the place where the

Israelites experienced God's presence in a most dramatic way, the prophet experienced only God's absence until he realized God was present in a "whispering sound" (1 Kgs 19, 12). God then commissioned the prophet to take specific steps to deal with the apostasy fomented by Israel's royal family. One of these steps was the anointing of a prophet to succeed him. Elijah found Elisha, whom the LORD had designated, and called him to his prophetic ministry (1 Kgs 19, 13–21).

The book returns to the conflict between king and prophet as it tells the tale of Naboth's vineyard (1 Kgs 21, 1–29). Again, it is Jezebel, Ahab's non-Israelite wife, who was responsible for the trouble. Ahab recognized that Naboth was within his rights in refusing to sell the king his vineyard. Jezebel, however, co-opted the elders of Naboth's city into convicting him on trumped up charges of blasphemy and treason. Naboth was executed and his property forfeited to the crown so Jezebel was able to present her husband with Naboth's vineyard. Of course, Elijah condemned this blatant injustice in God's name. Surprisingly, Ahab repented upon hearing the prophet's words of judgment and so God spared his life. Again, the book's message is obvious: if Israel listens to the prophets God sends to it, Israel's life will be spared as well.

But just as the book finished commending the prophetic word to Israel, it shows that discerning that word is not a simple matter. To do so the book describes preparations for a second war between Israel and Aram during the waning years of Ahab's reign (1 Kgs 22, 1–28). This time Ahab sought help from Jehoshaphat, the king of Judah. Relations between the two Israelite states had steadily improved since the time of Ahab's father Omri. Indeed, Ahab offered his daughter in marriage to Jehoram, Jehoshaphat's son (2 Kgs 8, 18). The king of Judah, however, suggested seeking a word from God before embarking on any campaign against the powerful Arameans. Ahab assembled 400 prophets to impress Jehoshaphat. After the 400 encouraged an attack, Jehoshaphat, apparently reluctant to fight the Arameans, asked if there were any more prophets who might be consulted. Ahab summoned Micaiah ben Imlah, who predicted an Aramean victory. Micaiah asserted that God put a "lying spirit" in the 400 prophets to insure that

Ahab would be defeated. How then could prophecy be a reliable guide if God can inspire prophets to lie? The book assumes that the one reliable and unimpeachable guide to Israel's life is the written, authoritative Torah, the book of Deuteronomy. The attitude of Kings toward Ahab is evident from the description of what happened when Ahab's chariot was cleansed of the fallen king's blood (1 Kgs 22, 38).

Elisha

After describing the failures of Ahab and his son Ahaziah, at the very end of 1 Kings and the first chapter of 2 Kings, the author turns his attention back to Elijah and Elisha and the transition from the prophetic ministry of the former to that of the latter (2 Kgs 2, 1–18). The book sees the succession of Elisha to the prophetic ministry as a genuine act of God. Perhaps a story with such spectacular details served to show that Elisha was a true witness to the God of Israel—as was Elijah—in contrast to the prophets that supported the house of Ahab (see 2 Kgs 3, 13). Fifty "guild prophets" witnessed the passing of the prophetic mantle to Elisha (2 Kgs 2, 15). Except for 1 Kings 20, 35, these "guild prophets" are always mentioned in connection with Elisha and may have been his supporters against the king and his prophets. The book concludes its introduction to the cycle of stories about Elisha with two tales that encourage Israel to obey the prophets sent to it (2 Kgs 2, 19–25).

The book shifts the focus of its story away from kings and international political conflicts to ordinary folk in need—people whose names are never given (2 Kgs 4, 1–44). Elisha, whom this chapter refers to as a "man of God," responds to those needs with compassion. While the effect on the reader is to wonder at the miracle-working power of Elisha, the stories do not even hint that the man of God worked these miracles to establish his reputation. The book implies that Elisha did what the kings were supposed to do: respond to the needs of the lowly and poor. In fact, the reason ordinary people were in need was the economic and political policies of the monarchy. God redresses this injustice through Elisha. The prophetic task is not simply to speak words of judgment on injustice but to undo the effects of the greed that creates poverty.

Story of Naaman

With the story of Naaman, Elisha moved back into the arena of international politics (2 Kgs 5, 1–19). This is the second time the book has told a tale of someone searching for healing in a foreign country. In 2 Kings 1, it was King Ahaziah of Israel looking for healing in Ekron from Baal-Zebub. In 2 Kings 5, it is Naaman from Aram who looked for healing in Israel. Whereas the healings in 2 Kings 4 took place because of Elisha's compassion for those in need, here there is an overt apologetic purpose: The Aramean general Naaman was to learn that there was a prophet in Israel who could heal in the name of Israel's God. There is also a homiletic point to the story. Naaman is a model for Israel. Although reluctant at first, the Aramean general obeyed the prophet and was healed. Israel surely should obey the prophets sent to it. Two more stories with a clear homiletic thrust follow (2 Kgs 5, 20—6, 7). Both stories concern the prophet's followers. In the first, Gehazi seeks to reap a monetary profit from his association with Elisha and is duly punished for his avarice. In the second, Elisha's supporters find themselves in an embarrassing situation, which the prophet resolves. The book warns against corruption.

Siege of Samaria

The circumstances change abruptly in the story of Ben-Hadad's siege of Samaria (2 Kgs 6, 24–33). A siege sought to force surrender by cutting off the supply of food. Ben-Hadad's siege of the Israelite capital was working, as is evident from the horrific details that the book gives (vv. 28–29). The king, of course, did not accept responsibility for Samaria's troubles; he blamed the prophet whom the book describes as cowering behind a closed door in fear of the king's anger. The Aramean threat was a sign of things to come. Aram here is an instrument of divine judgment on Israel's abandonment of their faith, or apostasy—apostasy that continued ceaselessly. But Israel's time had not yet come, so 2 Kings 7, 1–20 tells of the lifting of the Aramean siege of Samaria. The book makes it clear that the lifting of the siege and the relief of Samaria were not the work of Israel's military. God's power lifted the siege and four lepers by sheer happenstance

opened the way to the city's relief from the famine. The book shows readers that Israel's God shapes human events through the prophetic word. Just as easily as God made Aram a threat to Israel, God removed that threat. This is another hint to the book's first readers that God could end their exile.

The epilogue to the story of Elisha and the woman of Shunem (2 Kgs 8, 1–6; see 2 Kgs 5, 8–37) is unusual on two counts. First, the prophet did not directly solve her problem. In fact, she was suffering economic privation precisely because she followed the prophet's instructions to relocate from Israel. Upon returning, she found her property had been confiscated. Still, just the power of the prophet's fame was enough to solve her problem. Second, it was the king who restored the woman's property. For once, an Israelite king did act for the benefit of those in need. The book illustrates the power of God to extricate people from difficult situations. That power is such that it can lead people to act contrary to their normal patterns to bring about the fulfillment of the divine will. In a sense, the woman of Shunem is Israel in microcosm. She experienced exile, loss, and eventually restoration. What happened to her, the book implies, can happen to Israel as well. It too can experience restoration after exile.

Jehu's Revolution

To illustrate the disintegration of the kingdom of Israel, the book describes a revolution that brought an end to the house of Omri (2 Kgs 9, 1—10, 22)—a revolution so bloody that it was still remembered with horror a century later (see Hos 1, 4–5). According to Kings, Jehu's revolution was set in motion by the apostasy and injustice practiced by Israel's kings, and the terrible end of these kings reflects the prophetic judgment on their actions (1 Kgs 14, 11; 16, 4; 21, 19–24). The book then presents Jehu's revolution not in political but theological terms, so it begins with the prophet Elisha's naming of Jehu, an officer in Jehoram's army, as the one to replace the king. After Jehu assassinated Jehoram of Israel and Ahaziah of Judah, he turned to Jezebel, who taunted him as no better than Zimri, the assassin who was king of Israel for just seven days (see 1 Kgs 16, 15–19). Jezebel shared the fate of her son Jehoram at Jehu's hand (1 Kgs 9, 1–27).

Jehu had to eliminate claimants to the throne with better credentials. His revolutionary goals were to take Jehoram's place on the throne and end the Phoenician influence over the kingdom of Israel. To secure his throne, Jehu purged the entire royal family (10, 1–11.15–17) and to eliminate Phoenician influence, he killed the prophets of Baal and destroyed their temple (10, 18–27). Because he also killed Ahaziah of Judah, Jehu had to deal with a force from the southern kingdom seeking to avenge Ahaziah. But the book does not tell the story of Jehu's action to give an accurate picture of the progress of his revolution. The book wishes to describe the religious significance of that revolution. From this perspective, for all his brutal thoroughness, Jehu was a failure. He did not follow the LORD when he was king but followed the pattern of apostasy as set by Jeroboam. Because of this sin, Jehu did not stop Israel's slide to oblivion. Like his predecessors, Jehu witnessed Israel's power diminishing. More territory was lost—probably to Aram. Israel's destruction was just a matter of time (2 Kgs 10, 28–36).

Kingdom of Israel

The downward spiral of the Kingdom of Israel continued during the 17-year reign of Jehoahaz (2 Kgs 13, 1–9). Almost constant warfare between Israel and Aram led to the severe depletion of Israel's army (v. 7). Total disaster was averted by an unidentified "savior" (v. 5). It is likely that this savior came in the form of the Assyrian army that invaded Aram at the end of the ninth century, easing the pressure on Israel. With this account of Israel's deteriorating military power, the book begins its description of the fall of the house of Jehu. The end of Jehu's dynasty is inevitable because of the continuing apostasy of Israel's kings (v. 2).

Israel enjoyed a temporary respite from military reverses at the hand of the Arameans during the reign of Jehoash (2 Kgs 13, 10–35). Before Elisha died, he predicted a revival of Israel's military fortunes. The short note about the revival of a corpse that touched the bones of the dead prophet illustrates how the prophetic word can bring life to the sick body of Israel, because God's saving will did not wish to bring the full force of judgment upon God's people. Tangible proofs of that were the victories of Jehoash and his recovery of Israelite territory lost to Aram.

Reign of Jeroboam II

Although the book dismisses the 4-year reign of Jeroboam II in a few verses, it cannot ignore it completely (2 Kgs 14, 23–29). Jeroboam had notable success in expanding the boundaries of his kingdom, which the book usually considers a sign of God's blessing. Here it asserts that Jeroboam's success was the fulfillment of a prophetic word given by Jonah. Although there is a book ascribed to Jonah in the collection of the prophets, the oracle given to Jeroboam is not preserved in that book or anywhere in the Bible. Kings goes on to explain the success of Jeroboam by claiming that it was the result of God's compassion on Israel (vv. 26–27). Although Jeroboam's reign is often described as a time of peace and prosperity, it was not. The expansion of Israel's territory had to come by way of war. His building projects put a strain on the country's resources that eventually led to the severe economic problems that Israel faced following Jeroboam's death. The chasm between rich and poor grew during Jeroboam's time.

Like Jeroboam II, Azariah of Judah enjoyed a very long reign, although it was marred by a skin disease that rendered him unable to perform rituals that were reserved to the king (2 Kgs 15, 1–7). His son Jotham assumed many of Azariah's duties. Although the book praises Azariah, this praise is tempered by the comment that he did nothing about the high places, which the author of the book considered illegitimate. Under Azariah, the kingdom of Judah enjoyed a resurgence, which the book chooses to ignore because it does not reflect its notion of the direction in which Judah is heading.

Following the long reign of Jeroboam II, the northern kingdom began a rush to its total collapse. The text gives little more than the basic outline of a nation devolving into political chaos in the final years of its existence. The book provides few details about the reigns of these five kings, because it is more interested in the fate of Israel as a nation, whose doom it is describing. The five kings each receive the usual condemnation that is given to all the kings of the north, and their individual fates presage the disaster that the northern kingdom would experience.

The Apostasy of Ahaz

The book has no regard for Ahaz, condemning him without reservation (2 Kgs 16, 1–20). Ahaz's desperation in the face of the invasion by the combined forces of Aram and Israel is evident from his resorting to child sacrifice as a way to gain divine favor. Ahaz's situation was grievous, because he had to face hostilities on two fronts since the Edomites were moving in the south (v. 6) and Aram and Israel were coming from the north. This military pressure led Ahaz to align himself with Tiglath-Pileser, to whom he paid a large indemnity. The Assyrian king quickly put an end to the coalition seeking to depose Ahaz. Kings then describes in great detail changes that Ahaz made to the Temple and its altar, modeling the Temple after the Assyrians' altar in Damascus. These are regarded as acts of apostasy (vv. 10–20).

With the account of Ahaz's reign completed, the book returns to Israel, which was on the brink of total collapse. After narrating the events that led to the end of Israel's political existence (2 Kgs 17, 1–6), the book launches into a long editorial comment to explain the fall of the northern kingdom as a consequence of its failure to shape its national life on the basis of the Torah (2 Kgs 17, 7–23).

The Final Years of the Kingdom of Judah (2 Kgs 18, 1—25, 30)

After describing the fall of the northern kingdom, the book details the last years of the southern kingdom. The account begins with the story of Hezekiah, a king that it greatly admired because of his obedience to the Torah and his destruction of the high places. Hezekiah was able to augment Judah's territories at the expense of the Philistines. In contrast to Israel, Judah and its king appeared to be prospering (2 Kgs 18, 1–12). However, the Assyrians ended Hezekiah's peace by invading Judah and besieging Jerusalem. Although Hezekiah offered an indemnity to Sennacherib, the Assyrian king, the siege continued. Sennacherib demanded the surrender of Jerusalem, claiming that Judah's own patron deity had ordered him to conquer the country (2 Kgs 18, 1–37, esp. v. 25).

In his despair, Hezekiah turned to the prophet Isaiah, who assured him that Sennacherib would lift the siege and return to his country (v. 7). For reasons that are not clear to historians, the Assyrian army did retreat and Sennacherib was assassinated later—just as the prophet predicted (2 Kgs 19, 1–37). Of course, Kings sees the lifting of the siege as an act of God. The final episode in Hezekiah's story puts the king's reputation under a cloud. Although God healed him and promised him a longer reign, Hezekiah wanted proof that the promises made to him by Isaiah would be fulfilled. The arrival of an ambassador from Babylon gave Isaiah the opportunity to announce Judah's approaching defeat and exile. Instead of this announcement moving Hezekiah to repentance, the king expressed relief that the disaster would come after he was gone. It is as if Hezekiah learned nothing from the near disaster brought about by the Assyrians (2 Kgs 20, 1–21).

His son Manasseh succeeded Hezekiah. From the point of view of Kings, Judah never fell so low as it did during the 55-year reign of this king. It accuses Manasseh of apostasy, idolatry, and murder, and explicitly identifies him as the Judahite Ahab, leading the southern kingdom to disaster as Ahab had in the northern kingdom. Unnamed prophets pronounced divine judgment on Manasseh's actions. There is no doubt that Manasseh kept his throne by demonstrating his loyalty to the Assyrians, in part by introducing Assyrian religious rituals to the Jerusalem Temple.

Manasseh was succeeded by his son Amon, who continued his father's policies. This led to his assassination by his own courtiers. Evidently the assassination of yet another king provoked the ordinary folk, who supported the Davidic dynasty. They likely believed that another round of assassinations would be the end of Judah, so they killed the conspirators and installed Amon's young son, Josiah, as king (2 Kgs 21, 19–26). It was during Josiah's reign that Judah made one last attempt at reform, although it proved to be too late to avert divine judgment.

Josiah's reign was a short pause as Judah moved to the inevitable (2 Kgs 22, 1—23, 30). Kings describes Josiah as a monarch who "pleased the LORD" (2 Kgs 22, 2). A critical event in Josiah's reign was the discovery of a book in the course of renovations that were being made on the Temple. The author of Kings wants readers to assume that the "book of the Law" was what we know as the book of Deuteronomy. Josiah responded to hearing the words of the book with a gesture of repentance. He had the book authenticated by a prophet. Although Jeremiah was active at this time, the prophet consulted was an otherwise unknown woman named Huldah. She authenticated the book but announced that the curses on the unfaithful found in the book would fall on Judah and Jerusalem, although not in Josiah's time.

Fortunately for Josiah, he came into power about the time Assyria's control over the Levant was waning, so he moved quickly to reclaim Judah's sovereignty in matters of religion and politics. The book concentrates on Josiah's actions in the sphere of religious practice. The king took action against all types of non-Yahwistic religious activity and promoted traditional practices such as the Passover. His move into the north was likely prompted by a determination to take advantage of Assyria's weakness to extend the territory under his control. Josiah's attempts to reassert and expand Judahite sovereignty ended when he died during an ill-advised attempt to involve himself in international politics. He endeavored to stop the Egyptian army as it was advancing into Mesopotamia and was killed in battle. Josiah's reform died with him, because Judah once again came under foreign domination. The Egyptians asserted their control over Judah by deposing Josiah's successor Jehoahaz and exiling him to Egypt. They placed another of Josiah's sons, Eliakim, on the throne, changing his name to Jehoiakim. (2 Kgs 23, 31–35). Judah had to pay an indemnity to the Egyptians. This, of course, burdened Judah's economy, which had been already made fragile by Josiah's military adventures.

Jehoiachin succeeded his father just as the Babylonian siege of Jerusalem was about to end with the city's surrender and the sacking of the Temple. While Judah was able to maintain the appearance of sovereignty, it was more firmly under Babylon's control than ever. Jehoiachin was deposed and exiled along with many of Judah's leading citizens. The Babylonians placed Mattaniah, another of Josiah's sons, on the throne, changing his name to Zedekiah. The book lets the events speak for themselves, as Judah's final collapse appears to be imminent.

Zedekiah was to be the last king of the Davidic line. He managed to keep his throne for 11 years. No longer able to resist calls to rebel against Babylonian domination, Zedekiah sealed the fate of the dynasty and the kingdom. The Babylonians responded to his rebellion by taking Jerusalem a second time, killing Zedekiah's sons, blinding the king, and leading him into exile. Zedekiah was never heard from again (2 Kgs 24, 18—25, 7).

Jerusalem too paid for Zedekiah's folly in revolting against Nebuchadnezzar. The city was put to the torch and its Temple was left in ruins. Many of Jerusalem's leading citizens were executed and the rest were deported to Babylon. And so ends the story of Israel in its land.

As an epilogue, Kings mentions the parole of Jehoiachin from prison in Babylon (2 Kgs 25, 27–30). Unfortunately, the book does not reflect on the significance of the exiled king's new status for Judah's future. At the most critical moment in his story, the author of Kings is inexplicably reticent, leaving the reader to wonder what will become of Judah and Jerusalem. Is the divine judgment brought on by Judah's failure to be loyal to the LORD and shape its life according to Torah final? Perhaps Jehoiachin's parole is a harbinger of Judah's rehabilitation. Unfortunately, the book does not give an explicit answer to these questions. The books of Kings end on a most ambiguous note, requiring readers to make sense out of a tragic tale.

Continuing Significance of the Books of Kings

Like the other books that make up the deuteronomistic history of Israel, the books of Kings put in sharp focus the consequences of failing to remain absolutely committed to the LORD and to the pattern of life given to Israel in the book of Deuteronomy. The book illustrates a continuing pattern of failure to live responsibly. Although Kings focuses almost exclusively on the actions of the ruling class, its message was certainly intended for a wider audience. These books remind believers today that they bear a responsibility to act on the Word. Election offers no guarantees; rather, it calls believers to greater commitment. The books of Joshua to 2 Kings tell a sad and tragic story. What began with so much hope ends in disaster. It is not a pleasant story—especially in 2 Kings when it becomes clear that the two Israelite kingdoms are headed toward self-destruction. But the reader today knows that Jerusalem's fall, the end of the national state, and the collapse of all Judahite religious and political institutions were not the end of the story. God's mercy triumphed over God's justice and a renewed Judah emerged from the exile. The story of Israel in its land makes it absolutely clear that God's moral demands must be taken seriously. Failing to do so brings disaster. But despite this, believers recognize that God is still love.

Questions for Discussion and Reflection

Group Sharing/Discussion

1. Newly anointed King Solomon prayed, "Give your servant an understanding heart to judge your people and to distinguish right from wrong." (1 Kgs 3, 9) What are some signs of Solomon acting wisely in governing his people? When a leader today exercises power, what would be signs of wisdom in his leadership?

2. Despite his wisdom, Solomon slipped when he turned to false worship of foreign gods. (1 Kgs 11, 1–2) What were the personal (internal) and social (external, cultural) reasons for his sin?

3. What parts of Kings do you find most interesting? Which are most lesson-filled for you? Explain.

In Our Lives

1. After Elijah walked 40 days and nights to the mountain of God, Horeb, the LORD said to him, "Go outside and stand on the mountain before the LORD; the LORD will be passing by" (1 Kgs 19, 11ff). God could have come in the fire, or the wind, or the earthquake. But for Elijah God's presence came in the stillness of silence. In our lives, too, God is present. Reflect on when and how you recognize God's presence. How do such things as silence, retreat, and fasting help in this regard? How can our parish

encourage such times of stillness for its busy community members?

2. Elijah and Elisha were passionate prophets proclaiming to the leaders and people of Israel that Yahweh is their God and keeping his covenant means not worshiping false gods. Who are the prophets in your world reminding you of God's love and commands? Remember, also, that at baptism you are called to become a prophet. How do you live this call in your world?

3. Israel's and Judah's kings and people were fascinated with worshiping false gods. What were the attractions of the pagan religions for God's chosen people? Why were they easily led astray? Where, in today's society, do you see signs of idolatry?

Individual/Personal Reflection/Action

1. Elijah, faithful to the LORD's covenant, lived in solidarity with the poor people. He denounced Queen Jezebel and Kings Ahab and Ahaziah for worshiping false gods. These powerful leaders wanted to kill and silence him for speaking out against them. Look at your world through the justice lenses of Elijah. What do you see? Whom would you support and whom would you denounce or challenge? What do you do to promote a just society? Talk with your parish staff about ways you could be more effective in this regard.

2. The story of Elisha feeding a hundred hungry men (2 Kgs 4, 42–44) reminds us of the stories of Jesus feeding the hungry crowd (Mt 14, 13ff; 15, 32ff; Mk 6, 30ff; Lk 9, 10ff; Jn 6, 1ff). It is important to feed the body. It is just as important to feed our soul, our spirit, with hope, with love, with faith. What are your times, the opportunities, and the resources for this spiritual feeding? How can you pay more attention to this care and feeding of yourself?

3. Were the LORD's expectations of the chosen people higher than the expectations of the other nations? Are God's expectations of you different from those of others in your life? What about the expectations of your country?

THE CHRONICLER'S HISTORY AND THE LATER HISTORIES

1 AND 2 CHRONICLES READING GUIDE

At a Glance

Who are the main players?   David Solomon Hezekiah Josiah the chronicler

What should I look for?   Although the chronicler tells the story of Israel's past, the real purpose is to sketch out the prospects of Israel's future. The legitimacy of restored Judah's cultic institutions and continuity with the past are what count.

When did this take place?   From Adam to the fifth century B.C. following the restoration of the Jerusalem Temple after the Babylonian Exile, which lasted from 587 to 539 B.C.

Where did these events occur?   In the land of Israel, but mainly in Judah and Jerusalem.

Why was this book written?   Judah's religious institutions and their continuity with the past are critical for its future. The one aim of the work is to defend the legitimacy of the Temple of Jerusalem and the significance of its worship for Israel's life.

What is the story?   Although beginning with Adam, Chronicles' first nine chapters are genealogical lists without narrative material. The narrative begins with David, which is the chronicler's way of saying Israel's story really begins with David. His selected use and analysis of Israel's history reveals the chronicler's religious message: Israel will secure its future only by worshiping God according to the pattern set by David at God's direction.

The first book of Chronicles is part of a larger work that includes the second book of Chronicles, Ezra, and Nehemiah. This "chronicler's history"—which was assembled after the return from exile, and which was probably not written by one person or one small group—begins with Adam (1 Chr 1, 1) and concludes with the writer's own day, the fifth century, following the restoration of the Jerusalem Temple after the Babylonian Exile (587 to 539 B.C.).

Like Genesis 1, the chronicler's history begins with Adam, but it repeats none of the stories found in the priestly history. Chapters 1–9 are little more than genealogical lists taken from Bible texts and other sources available to the author. The narrative material begins with the story of Saul's death and burial (10, 1–14). This, perhaps,

Cult The ritual and religious practices at a temple or other place of worship.

is the chronicler's way of stating that Israel's story really begins with David, Saul's successor as king.

Like the deuteronomistic history of Israel (Joshua, Judges, Samuel, and Kings, with Deuteronomy as its preface), the chronicler's history tells the story of the Israelite kingdoms and their fall. This second history tries to explain why they fell. Even though the chronicler tells the story of Israel's past, the author's real purpose is to sketch out the prospects for Israel's future.

For the chronicler, what really counts is the validity of Judah's cultic institutions and their continuity with the past. The author wanted to defend David's dynasty and the Temple of Jerusalem. By presenting the Judah of the chronicler's day as a worshiping community that was a direct extension of the community that God had established centuries before, the author aimed to show that Israel could secure its future by continuing to worship God according to the pattern set by David. Israel's hope, then, resided not in the revelation that a messiah could guarantee its future, but in the belief that careful observance of the cultic institutions, handed down by Judah's priests, would be its security. These cultic institutions were kept alive by the remnant that survived the exile and returned to Jerusalem. For the chronicler, the exile was just an unfortunate interruption in the otherwise unbroken history of the worshiping community of Judah.

The Septuagint (the ancient Greek translation of the Hebrew Bible) entitled the books of Chronicles "Paraleipomenon" ("that which was left out"). This was also the name used in the Douay-Rheims version and some other Roman Catholic versions. Those responsible for the Septuagint considered Chronicles a sort of supplement to the books of Samuel and Kings. The placement of these books differs in Bibles used by Jews. In Christian Bibles, the Old Testament ends with the prophets. The final text is Malachi's prophecy of the return of Elijah, who will announce the "day of the LORD" (Mal 3, 23f). The Church reads a messianic meaning in this text and identifies John the Baptist, the pre-

cursor of Jesus, as the returning Elijah (Mt 1, 1–14; 17, 11–13). But in the Hebrew Bible arranged by the rabbis, the prophetic books follow the books of Moses (the Torah or the Pentateuch), because the early rabbis viewed the prophets as explainers of the Torah. The Hebrew Bible has a third part called the "Writings," a collection of books that belong to neither the Torah nor the Prophets. The last books of this collection are 1 and 2 Chronicles. Thus the Hebrew Bible ends with the decree of Cyrus (2 Chr 36, 23) that calls for the people of Judah to return to Jerusalem and rebuild the Temple there.

Reading the First Book of Chronicles

The first book of Chronicles has a very simple arrangement: Chapters 1—9, 34 are extensive genealogy lists; chapters 9, 35—29, 30 tell the story of David.

The Genealogies

The genealogies of Chronicles extend from Adam to the return from the Babylonian Exile. The author uses the genealogies from the book of Genesis in his own tables that begin with the descent from Adam to Abraham. From there the focus is on the 12 sons of Jacob. The chronicler arrives at the centerpiece of his presentation, the family of Judah, one of Jacob's 12 sons. The author traces Judah's descendants down to David and his relatives. Chapter 3 lists David's descendants, all the kings of the Davidic dynasty and their descendants, into the period after the Babylonian Exile. The genealogies of the other tribes follow but are not as extensive as the one for Judah, except for the tribe of Levi. The chronicler had a special interest in the priestly tribe of Levi and the cult that they administered. Finally, the genealogies of Saul's descendants frame a list of those who returned from the Babylonian Exile. From this reading one is left with the impression that the true beginning of Israel was not at Sinai with the giving of the Torah, as the priestly history would have it, but with the rise of David.

The History of David's Reign

This section begins with a report on Saul's death and burial (10, 1–12), along with a short editorial comment on the dangers Saul's reign posed for

Israel because Saul was not faithful to God. Saul is little more than a figure of contrast for David, whose portrait the chronicler painted with strokes of piety and fidelity.

The chronicler wanted to make David's rise to power more impressive than the version found in the deuteronomic history (2 Sm 1–20), one of the sources he used. For example, 2 Samuel states that only "the men of Judah" anointed David as king of their tribe following Saul's death; David ruled over Judah seven years before the elders of Israel chose him as king over the rest of the tribes (2 Sm 5, 1–5). The chronicler, however, states that "all Israel" made David king immediately following Saul's death (1 Chr 11, 1–3). And while the deuteronomic historian paints David's decision to bring the Ark into Jerusalem as a decision made by David alone, the chronicler portrays the same event as an act approved by all the people. The Ark's entrance into Jerusalem highlights the role of the Levites as David appoints them to carry it into the city. And since the king also commissions them to be singers in the Temple, they sing a psalm. The deuteronomic history does not contain these details. The rest of David's story is devoted to the plans for the building of the Temple, which Solomon, David's son, would eventually carry out. This makes Solomon a central figure in the chronicler's story.

The negative features of the story of David and Solomon that are recorded by the deuteronomic historian are omitted in the chronicler's version. Nothing is said about how Solomon succeeded David as king (2 Sm 12, 1–12; 1 Kgs 1–2). Nothing is said about David's adultery with Bathsheba and the prophet Nathan's condemnation of David (2 Sm 12, 1–12). Nor does the chronicler make mention of the two revolts against David (2 Sm 15–18; 20, 1–22).

Solomon's role is to complete the work David began. This seems to be a deliberate effort by the chronicler to imitate the transition from Moses to Joshua (Dt 21 and Jos 1). The author considered Solomon's succession to David as important as Joshua's succession to Moses.

The Establishment of the Temple

The chronicler paints the portraits of David and Solomon so as to underscore their respective roles in the establishment of the Temple and its liturgy. Worship then is one of the chronicler's principal concerns. The God who is present in Judah's experience evokes a response in worship from the people whose destiny this God guides. The chronicler tries to show that Judah's future is dependent upon its faithfulness to the proper forms of worship that God has revealed through David. There is a reciprocal relationship between God and Judah: God blesses Judah and Judah worships God.

For the chronicler, the Temple and its liturgy were symbols of God's continuing presence among the people of Judah. As long as the priests offered the correct sacrifices at the appropriate times in the presence of a grateful people, the LORD would dwell in Judah's midst. For the chronicler, the history of Israel was not a series of unrelated actions by kings and prophets. Its heart was the worship led by the priests appointed by Moses and David. The chronicler recognized that there were times when Judah's sin led to serious failures to offer proper worship, but Judah's sin was never fatal. Judah was always able to recover, resume proper liturgical services, and be certain of God's abiding presence. The fall of Jerusalem and the exile to Babylon formed an unfortunate interruption in an otherwise unbroken history of Judah as a community that offered legitimate worship to its ancestral deity. The only way to avoid a similar disaster in the future was to worship God in the Jerusalem Temple according to rituals that went back to those developed by David.

The Importance of the Temple

For proper worship of the LORD, a Temple was indispensable. Like the books of Kings, Chronicles recognizes the legitimacy of only one temple—the Temple at Jerusalem. At the time of

---

Shalom The Hebrew word for peace. It is reflected in the name Solomon, in Hebrew, *Shelomo*. A contrast is drawn between Solomon, the peaceful man, and David, who waged great wars. David was prevented from building the Temple not only because all his time was taken up in battle but also because he shed much blood, which made him ritually unfit for the task.

The Priests (chief religious officials)
Duties: blow the trumpets, minister in inner sanctuary, offer sacrifice on the altar, burn incense

The Levites ("lower clergy")
Duties: carry the Ark, singers, gatekeepers, judges, prophets, fund raisers

Temple Slaves
Duty: to help the Levites

the composition of the chronicler's history, the worshipers of Israel's ancestral god were not unanimous in recognizing Jerusalem's Temple as the only legitimate place of worship. There was a temple dedicated to the LORD in Samaria, and at Elephantine (a Jewish military colony located on an island near the modern city of Aswan in Egypt). In telling the story of the northern kingdom, the chronicler does not even mention the sanctuaries at Dan or Bethel that Jeroboam I built (see 1 Kgs 12, 26–29). For the chronicler there could be only one Temple. David planned and Solomon built this Temple under the same kind of divine guidance that led Moses to build the Tabernacle in the wilderness. The LORD gave David the plans for the Temple in Jerusalem (1 Chr 28, 19). No other sanctuary could be a legitimate place to worship the God of Israel.

The Temple Personnel

Chapters 23–27 are important for the chronicler's general purpose; proper worship and proper personnel to conduct the liturgy are described in detail. The division of duties among the priests, the Levites, and the Temple slaves is shown here.

First Chronicles concludes with David passing both the kingship and the responsibility for constructing the Temple on to Solomon. According to the chronicler, Solomon was anointed king even before David's death.

Roman Catholic Priesthood

The sacrament of Orders in the Roman Catholic Church is largely a part of our heritage from ancient Israel. The rituals of ordination recognize this heritage. The division of orders in the Roman Catholic Church into the episcopacy, presbyterate, and diaconate mirrors to some extent the chronicler's division of Temple personnel into priests, Levites, and Temple slaves. Of course the status, role, and interrelationships of the orders in the Church are different from those of the Old Testament's cultic personnel, since they descend from the leaders of the early church—bishops or overseers (*episcopos*), priests or elders (*presbyteres*), and deacons (*diakonos*). The church also sees a sacramental connection between the priesthood of Jesus and the ordained priesthood. The concern in the Church for a hierarchy among the people directly concerned with worship is similar to that of the chronicler.

There is not a single instance in the New Testament of anyone called a "priest" presiding at Christian worship. It is the chronicler (and even more the Priestly strand of the Pentateuch, especially Leviticus and Numbers) who tries to make the reader sensitive to the presence of God in the act of sacrificial worship led by "official" ministers. For the chronicler the priests and Levites were those through whom God's abiding presence among the people was evident. The rituals they conducted were a source of blessing for the people and an act of devotion to their God. The chronicler's God was not a hidden God. The people experienced God in worship more than anywhere else. It should be clear that the value that the Church places on the liturgy and priesthood finds a strong support in the chronicler's history.

Reading the Second Book of Chronicles

Chronicles and the Israelite Kingdoms

The second book of Chronicles continues the story of Israel with the accession of Solomon to the throne of David. Comparing the way Chronicles tells this story with the books of Kings helps to see the purpose of the chronicler. For example, after Solomon's death and the breakup of the Davidic-Solomonic empire into the two national states of Israel and Judah, the chronicler all but ignores the northern kingdom (Israel) and its kings. He focuses his attention on the southern kingdom (Judah). The chronicler mentions Israel only when the story of Judah makes it necessary to do so. The chronicler wishes to focus on the Davidic dynasty and its finest achievement: the Temple in Jerusalem. Also, the chronicler's treatment of Judah's kings focuses almost entirely on the promotion of legitimate worship and the performance of the proper ritual.

Solomon

The story of Solomon (2 Chr 1–9) deals exclusively with the building of the Temple as envisioned by David. Again the chronicler does not repeat the negative aspects of Solomon's story that 1 Kings recounts. For example, the chronicler omits the details about how Solomon secured his throne by executing potential opponents, including his half brother Adonijah (1 Kgs 2). Also unmentioned is Solomon's marriage to the daughter of Pharaoh (1 Kgs 3, 1) and other non-Israelite women (1 Kgs 11, 1–13). Throughout the description of Solomon's achievement in building and dedicating the Temple, the chronicler reminds his readers of David's preparations (2, 6.13.16; 3, 1; 5, 1; 6, 3–11). In the eyes of the chronicler, the Temple was the combined enterprise of David and Solomon, who each made his own contribution to the completion of this great work.

The Kingdom of Judah

The remaining chapters of the book (10–36) retell the history of Judah to the Babylonian Exile from the singular perspective of the chronicler. (Remember that after Solomon's death, the Davidic-Solomonic empire broke up into two national states of Israel in the north and Judah in the south.)

Chapters 29–31 describe a thoroughgoing reform of Judah's liturgy under Hezekiah. This reform included a confession of past neglect of proper worship (2 Chr 29, 5–11), the cleansing of the Temple (29, 16f) and the celebration of the Passover. Hezekiah invited the northerners who survived the Assyrian conquest to join the people of Judah in the renewal of the covenant (30, 1–9). The account of Hezekiah's reign in 2 Kings 18–20 says little about Hezekiah's reform because 2 Kings wished to portray Josiah as a second David who restored the covenant (2 Kgs 22–23). Another striking contrast to 2 Kings is the chronicler's portrait of Manasseh, whom 2 Kings presents as the most evil of all Judah's kings. His sins were responsible for the fall of the southern kingdom (2 Kgs 21, 1–18). The chronicler rehabilitates Manasseh by describing his conversion, which led to a reform of Judah's worship (2 Chr 33, 11–17).

The Purpose of the Chronicler

Why did the chronicler bother to retell the story of Judah's monarchy? After all, 2 Samuel to 2 Kings already told that story. Indeed, the chronicler derived much of his story from these books. Still, when we look more closely we can see that the basic purpose of this new version of the story of David and his dynasty was to guide the Jerusalem community as it was reestablishing itself following the exile. In the eyes of the chronicler, the one lasting contribution of the Davidic monarchy was the Temple, its rituals, and its priesthood. The Jewish community as a whole functioned as the successor of that dynasty. Once the people rebuilt the Temple and restored the proper form of its liturgy, the essential elements of Jewish life were in place. According to the chronicler, David and Solomon combined forces to establish a divinely ordained liturgy in Jerusalem. The people, led by Ezra and Nehemiah, resumed the service of God according to the pattern set by David. In the chronicler's scheme, the restoration of the national state and the Davidic dynasty was not as crucial as the reestablishment of the proper worship of the LORD in Jerusalem. The people who supported the Temple and resumed the authentic worship there fulfilled all the really important tasks of monarchy.

Jews and Samaritans

The books of Chronicles reflect one stage in the division that arose between the Jews and the Samaritans, who lived in the northern kingdom. Historical reconstruction has not been able to identify any sudden and dramatic act that divided the two groups irrevocably. According to Samaritan sources, the division took place at the end of the period of the judges (eleventh century B.C.) when Eli left Shechem and established a high-priestly line at Shiloh. According to the biblical tradition (2 Kgs 17), the separation took place in the eighth century B.C. when the people of the former northern kingdom intermarried with foreign peoples whom the Assyrians introduced into their territory. Although it is not possible to treat either of these two accounts as straight history, they do point to important concerns. In the chronicler's perspective, the Samaritans did not have the true priesthood (2 Chr 13, 9) and therefore their sacrificial worship was worthless.

The Samaritans were one example of the rich diversity in early Judaism. Their religious traditions developed independently of the leadership of the community that arose around the priests of Jerusalem. Other examples of the variety of religious perspectives in early Judaism include the Hasidim, the Essenes, and the Pharisees. An important moment in this development was the building of the Samaritan temple on Mt. Gerizim (near Shechem) sometime in the early Hellenistic period (late fourth century B.C.). It was the building of this temple by the Samaritans and its later destruction by the Jewish king John Hyrcanus in 128 B.C. that led to the definitive break between the Jews and the Samaritans.

It is within this context that one should read John 4, in which Jesus meets the Samaritan woman at the well in Shechem. Her comments reflect the religious and historical conflicts between her people and the Jews. Jesus, of course, says that there will come a day when true worship of God will transcend the conflict between Jew and Samaritan (Jn 4, 21). The chronicler's attitude toward those outside the Jerusalem-centered worship community offers a striking example of an unwillingness to accept too great a diversity among those who considered themselves to be worshipers of the LORD. The reasons for the chronicler's attitude are complex. In part they were political and economic. Apparently the province of Samaria wanted to control Jerusalem, while the leadership of the Jerusalem community wished to remain independent of such control. In part the reasons were religious and liturgical. Although the people in the north wished to help with the rebuilding of the Jerusalem Temple (Ezr 4, 2), the Judahites refused their help. Perhaps they did not believe that the northerners were sincere because of their continued use of the sanctuaries at Dan and Bethel. The Judahites considered the cult at these sanctuaries to be illegitimate. In part the reasons for the rift were historical. The Israelite tribes in the north and the south developed somewhat independently of one another, and the northerners cherished this independence fiercely. Whatever the reasons for the chronicler's attitude toward the northerners who considered themselves to be authentic worshipers of the LORD, it was decidedly negative. It contributed to the tension between Jews and Samaritans that has lasted into the present.

The chronicler's approach to the problem of religious diversity was understandable given the political and religious realities of the fourth century B.C. The rigid application of the directives of Ezra and Nehemiah and the intensity of the chronicler's rhetoric (see 2 Chr 13, 4–12) made it difficult for succeeding generations to overcome the division between Jew and Samaritan. Indeed, further divisions occurred within the Jewish community. The Essenes opposed the Hasmoneans. The Pharisees disputed with the Sadducees. The Herodians fought with the Zealots. In the middle of all this, Christianity emerged. Eventually, because of historical circumstances, the Pharisaic party survived the fall of Jerusalem in A.D. 70 and was the precursor of rabbinic Judaism. The Kairites of Babylon refused to accept the authority of the rabbis. Even within Judaism today, some Orthodox rabbis do not accept the legitimacy of Conservative and Reform Judaism. The chronicler did not succeed in eliminating religious diversity among those who considered themselves worshipers of the LORD.

Relationships among Christian Churches

Until the Second Vatican Council, the attitude of Catholics toward other Christians was similar to the lack of tolerance that the chronicler showed toward religious diversity. One of the principal concerns of the council was promoting the restoration of unity among all Christians (*Decree on Ecumenism,* 1). Like the chronicler, who was in part responsible for the rift between Jew and Samaritan, the Catholic Church, according to the council, shares in responsibility for the divisions among Christian churches (*Decree on Ecumenism,* 3). One way to overcome these divisions is through dialogue that leads to a knowledge and appreciation of the doctrine and religious life of the many Christian churches.

Of the two main kinds of division within the Christian community, that which separates the East from the West resembles the separation between Jew and Samaritan that developed in the last four centuries before Christ. Although there were tensions between East and West for a long time, these came to a head in A.D. 1054 with the excommunication of the Patriarch of Constantinople by the papal legate and the patriarch's consequent excommunication of the pope's delegate. Four centuries later, other divisions arose in Western Christianity as a result of the Reformation. The differences between Christian churches are not simply theological but are also historical, political, sociological, cultural, and even psychological.

To help overcome these divisions within Christianity, the council suggested that dialogue among Christian churches focus first on elements which the various Christian churches share: the Scriptures, belief in Christ, baptism, and the Eucharist. The diversity of customs and doctrines will not then necessarily be obstacles to unity. We recognize them as contributing to the Church's beauty, helpful adaptations to differences of culture, necessary for the good of the faithful.

To the Christian churches that today are struggling with the project of restoring the Church's unity, the chronicler presents a lesson regarding what can happen when concern for the survival of one religious community leads to a type of narrow exclusivity that ignores the values of other people's approach to God. The tasks of Ezra and Nehemiah and the duty of the chronicler were clear: to ensure the survival of the small community of the LORD surrounding Jerusalem, whose continued existence was in doubt. They fulfilled their responsibilities. The responsibility of Christian churches is somewhat different today: to restore Christian unity. To make unity a possibility, Christians will need to be more willing to live with religious diversity than they have been. The chronicler's hesitancy regarding religious diversity is understandable. Judaism was struggling for its very survival. Christianity today is not as beleaguered as was Judaism in the chronicler's day. Achieving unity while respecting diversity should be easier for us.

Questions for Discussion and Reflection
Group Sharing/Discussion

1. Give some examples of the chronicler's reinterpretation of the materials from his sources in Samuel and Kings. Why did the chronicler make these adaptations?

2. The chronicler claimed that the Samaritans did not have true priesthood, and therefore their cult was worthless. Why do you think the author had this unwillingness to accept diversity among those committed to the LORD? What do you think of this attitude?

3. The chronicler describes in detail the roles of priests, Levites, and Temple "slaves" for proper worship. The division of the Roman Catholic Sacrament of Holy Orders (bishops, priests, deacons) mirrors to a certain extent the chronicler's division of Temple personnel. What are some of these similarities and some significant differences?

In Our Lives

1. Shalom, the Hebrew word for peace, is reflected in the name Solomon, in Hebrew *Shelomo.* In contrast to David, Solomon was a man of peace. What practices in living make a person a "person of peace"? How was Jesus a "man of peace"? What nourishes a peacemaker? Who are some examples of peacemakers in your parish, your town or city? How can you support them?

2. The Second Vatican Council emphasized that the *Church* is the entire people of God. For centuries the term Church tended to mean the clergy. In chapter five of Vatican II's *Constitution on the Church,* the council spoke of "the universal call of holiness."

How does this reverse the age-old idea that only "the ordained" have a vocation to holiness?

3. Since Vatican II lay ministers have become an accepted part of the liturgical life of the Roman Catholic Church. Today there are more lay ministers than ordained ministers in the United States. What does this lay ecclesial ministry mean for today's Church? What impact has this development had on the formation of church community?

Individual/Personal Reflection/Action

1. Take time to reflect upon your community worship experience. Recall the priests, the lay ministers, the ritual context, the customs and culture of your experience. What contributes to your full participation in community worship?

2. Until Vatican II the attitude of Catholics was similar to the lack of tolerance that the chronicler showed toward religious diversity. Restoration of Christian unity was one of the principle concerns of the Council's Decree on Ecumenism. The council suggested that the dialogue focus first on what we share: the Scriptures, Christ, baptism, and the Eucharist. Reflect on how you would share your Catholic beliefs on these parts of our faith.

EZRA AND NEHEMIAH READING GUIDE

At a Glance

Who are the main players?	Ezra Nehemiah Cyrus the Great Artaxerxes I and II Zerubbabel Jeshua Sheshbazzar
What should I look for?	Restoring of the community and building of Jerusalem. Ezra, the Zadokite priest, was commissioned to reestablish Judahite society based on the Torah. Nehemiah's task was to rebuild the city and Temple.
When did this take place?	Between about 538 and 398 B.C.
Where did these events occur?	Jerusalem Judah Babylon Egypt Persia
Why was this book written?	The books of Ezra and Nehemiah are the only narrative accounts of the period after the Babylonian Exile (587–539 B.C.) that survived in the Hebrew Bible. Ezra provided the community with a source of stability and continuity—the Torah—which Jews came to see as encompassing the eternal order given to Moses by God.
What is the story?	The books of Ezra and Nehemiah deal with the restoration of Judah following years of exile in Babylonia. These books deal with the two phases of restoration: the first is rebuilding the Temple and the second is the reordering of Jewish life. Ezra speaks to a weak religious community on the brink of extinction. Assimilation is one of its main threats. He preaches the Torah as a source of identity and fosters an attitude of separation and exclusion.

The book of Ezra deals with several episodes of the return to Jerusalem by Judeans after the Babylonian captivity; these episodes took place both in the sixth and fifth centuries.

The books of Ezra and Nehemiah are the only narrative accounts of the period after the Babylonian Exile (587–539 B.C.) that have survived in the Hebrew Bible. Originally Ezra and Nehemiah were a single work. In fact, Nehemiah does not even have its own title in Jewish Bibles.

The books of Ezra and Nehemiah do not give a reliable chronology of the restoration of Judah. They are more interested in presenting the religious dimension of the renewed life of Judah.

The Kings of Persia

Cyrus	538–529 B.C.	Darius II	423–404 B.C.
Cambyses	529–521 B.C.	Artaxerxes II	404–358 B.C.
Darius I	521–485 B.C.	Artaxerxes III	358–337 B.C.
Xerxes	485–464 B.C.	(Defeat of Darius III)	336–330 B.C.
Artaxerxes I	464–423 B.C.	End of the Persian Empire	331 B.C.

There are important political reasons why the Persian rulers were concerned about conditions in Judah. The beginning of both Nehemiah's and Ezra's missions coincided with Egyptian revolts against Persia's imperialism. It was important to have a sympathetic Judah at their back as they moved against rebellious Egypt. The above list of the Kings of Persia will be useful for dating the events mentioned in Ezra and Nehemiah.

Reading the Book of Ezra

Outline of the Book of Ezra

Ezr 1, 1—6, 22 The Return from Exile
Ezr 7, 1—10, 44 The Deeds of Ezra

The Return from Exile and Rebuilding of the Temple

The most striking feature of this section is not apparent to those who read it in translation. While the rest of the book of Ezra is in Hebrew, 4, 7—6, 18 are in Aramaic. This is because of the author's citing of a few official Persian documents relating to the restoration of Judah.

Chapters 1–3 cover the return from exile. Cyrus, the king of Persia, proclaimed that every exile from Judah who was ready to return to Jerusalem to rebuild its Temple should do so. The following verses describe the return itself. Chapter 2 gives a list of names of the returnees. At the top of the list is Zerubbabel, a member of the Davidic family, and Jeshua, a member of a prominent priestly family. These two play an important role in chapter 3 in the revival of worship in Jerusalem.

Although the rebuilding of the Temple begins immediately upon the return of the exiles, there were problems. Opposition came from "the enemies of Judah and Benjamin" and from "the people of the land." Both tried to convince the Persians that restoration of Jerusalem was an act of political disloyalty. In the end all opposition failed and the people of Judah completed their project with full support of Persian imperial authorities. The story of the rebuilding of the Temple concludes with a joyful account of the celebration of the Passover (6, 19–22), a sure sign of the return from exile and echo of the Israelites deliverance from slavery in Egypt.

Ezra's Mission

The genealogy in 7, 1–5 shows that Ezra was a Zadokite priest. (The Zadokite priests were those associated with the Jerusalem Temple before the Babylonian Exile. Zadok was a priest who served David and Solomon.) Ezra was an expert in the Torah, which the priests who were in exile developed

---

The Four Stages of Return from Exile

1. Return under Cyrus (538 B.C.) led by Sheshbazzar, who began rebuilding the Temple but left t unfinished because of local opposition.

2. Return under Darius I (521–485 B.C.) led by Zerubbabel and Jeshua, who completed the Temple.

3. A group led by Ezra, who brought a copy of the Mosaic Law, in either 458 or 398 B.C.

4. Another group in 445 B.C. under Artaxerxes I (464–423 B.C.) led by Nehemiah to build the walls of Jerusalem and attempt to establish purity of community and worship. Nehemiah came as governor with his own retinue. He did not, strictly speaking, lead a group of returning exiles.

Timeline: Postexilic Literature

OT Sources	Events in Jerusalem	Persian Rulers
	586 B.C. to 500 B.C.	
	586: Fall of Jerusalem to Babylon; second and final deportation; diaspora Jews in Babylon	550–530: Cyrus II (the Great) 539: Fall of Babylonian Empire to Cyrus the Great
Ezra 1–6	538: First wave of the return to Jerusalem begins (groups continue to drift back over the next century); Zerubbabel begins rebuilding the Temple in Jerusalem; Samaritans thwart their efforts; rebuilding project halts.	538: Cyrus the Great issues Edict of Toleration, allowing Jews to return home 530–522: Cambyses II
Haggai and Zechariah 1–8	520: The prophets Haggai and Zechariah call for the rebuilding of the Temple to continue; work begins. 515: In March, the second Temple is finished.	522–486: Darius I
	500 B.C. to 400 B.C.	
[Esther?] Nehemiah's Memoirs: Neh 1–7 and Neh 11–13 [Jonah and Ruth?] Malachi	444–432: Nehemiah hears of the plight of Jerusalem while in Persia. He is appointed governor of Judah; the walls around Jerusalem are rebuilt.	486–465: Xerxes I ("Ahasuerus" in the book of Esther) 465–423: Artaxerxes I (Age of Pericles in Athens) 423: Xerxes II 423–404: Darius II 404–358: Artaxerxes II
	400 B.C. to 331 B.C.	
The "I" narrative: Ezr 7, 11—9, 15 The "he" narrative: Ezr 10 and Neh 8–10 The king's letter: Ezr 7, 12–26 The lists: Ezr 8, 1–14; Ezr 10, 18–44; Neh 10, 1–27	398(?): Ezra, priest and scribe, institutes reforms of worship. End of OT history, c. 400	331: Alexander the Great conquers the Persian Empire (defeat of Darius III); age of Socrates, Plato, Aristotle; rise of Hellenism

Aramaic is a Semitic language that is related to Hebrew. It was a common language of the diverse people that made up the Persian empire and was the official language of the administration. The use of Hebrew and Aramaic shows that the people were bilingual. Originally Aramaic was the language of the Arameans. Because Arameans were active in commercial affairs in the Near East, the language became widely known. By the sixth century B.C., it became the most commonly used Semitic language and was generally used in Palestine until Greek became the official language after the conquest of Alexander the Great in the fourth century B.C. Aramaic remained the language of the common people until the seventh century A.D., when Arabic replaced it. Aramaic was the language of Jesus, although he may have known Greek as well.

while in Babylon. An imperial commission given to Ezra from Artaxerxes II includes information about contributions to the Temple in Jerusalem and the order to reestablish Judahite society based on the "Law of God." By acceptance or rejection of the Torah, Judahites define themselves as belonging to or rejecting membership in the Jewish community. This means that in the view of the Persian government, the priestly version of ancient Israel's ancestral faith was the "official" religion of Judah. The author's account of Ezra's journey seems to have been modeled on the Exodus from Egypt, the crossing of the Jordan, and the occupation of the land.

Ezra's description of the journey to Jerusalem contains repeated descriptions of how the hand of the LORD was upon them, keeping the travelers safe on their journey. The amount of gold, silver, and other valuables they were carrying would have made them a tempting target for bandits and others. The protection of the LORD—not military might—was their safeguard.

The Problem of Mixed Marriages

The final two chapters deal with Jews who have married outside their religious community. Ezra

finds their behavior unacceptable and recites a long penitential prayer on their behalf. The people ask Ezra for help to set matters straight. The Hebrew text is unclear about the action taken in this matter, but some Jewish men probably divorced their non-Jewish wives in response to Ezra's urging.

Exclusivism in Ezra

In denouncing mixed marriages, Ezra speaks of the Jews as a "holy race." He accuses the people of desecrating themselves with "the people of the land" (Canaanites, Hittites, Perizzites, Jebusites, Ammonites, Moabites, Egyptians, and Amorites). The Jewish community faced the same threats to its existence as did the Israelite tribes centuries before the establishment of the Israelite national state (thirteenth to eleventh centuries B.C.). At that time Israel faced hostile neighbors and was unable to defend herself adequately. There was little unity or even cooperation among the tribes in the eleventh century. As was shown in the books of Samuel, the response to these problems was to establish the monarchy. The king provided order and stability to the foundering Israelite tribes. The Davidic dynasty lasted from the eleventh to the fifth centuries B.C. and furnished a sense of continuity. But in the fifth century B.C. Persian imperialism made the reestablishment of Judah's native dynasty impossible. Ezra provided the community with another source of stability and continuity—the Torah, which the Jews came to see as encompassing an eternal order given to Moses by God. This notion made the Jewish community exclusive and led to the idea of a "holy race," which was to remain unsullied by contact with the nations. To counteract the danger of Jews being absorbed by the non-Jewish culture that surrounded them, Ezra taught that there was a very specific criterion for membership in the Jewish community—heredity. Mixed marriages were no longer permissible and, under Ezra, the community was not open to outsiders.

Elevating heredity to the position of defining the people of God is understandable, yet it separated Israel from other nations. The Samaritans whom Ezra's decrees excluded from the people of God considered him their archenemy. In contrast, the Talmud (the code of rabbinical teaching on the manner of observing the Law) considers Ezra to be a second Moses because he restored observance of the Torah when the people had forgotten about it. Early Christianity also had to deal with Ezra's legacy as it faced the consequences of its highly successful mission to the Gentiles (Acts 10, 1—15, 35). The early Church abandoned the views of Ezra on membership in the people of God.

We need to see Ezra's notion of a "holy race" against the backdrop of the cultural assumptions of ancient Near Eastern people. The key word here is *holy*. According to Ezra, part of observance of the Torah revolved around separation from all that was not *ritually* pure. Holy is a cultic term, not a moral one implying that the Jews were ethically superior to other nations. Books such as Jonah and Ruth reminded their readers among the Jews that Gentiles, too, could please God, showing that the Hebrew Bible affirms inclusive views as well as exclusive ones.

Here and Now: The Call to Inclusion

The book of Ezra speaks to a beleaguered religious community on the brink of extinction. The circumstances faced by Ezra's community are not those faced by the human community today. In our time, the threat to human existence comes from ignorance, prejudice, and hatred that keeps the peoples of the world apart. The Second Vatican Council recognized this when it decided to issue a separate document dealing with non-Christian religions. The council declared that all peoples comprise a single community with a single final goal: God. All the religions of the world have come about from the universal attempt to probe the mystery of the divine. Catholics are encouraged to speak and work with followers of other religions. They are to acknowledge, preserve, and promote the spiritual and moral values found in these non-Christian religions. Judaism and Islam (the other two monotheistic faiths) are singled out by the council for special attention. Any form of persecution and hatred that existed between Christians and Jews at any time is condemned. The Church has rejected any type of discrimination directed at people because of their religion and calls upon all Catholics to maintain "good fellowship" with all peoples by living with them in peace.

Reading the Book of Nehemiah

It is important to see the work of both Nehemiah and Ezra against the deplorable conditions that the prophet Malachi describes (see Mal 1–2). Without the strong communal structures that Ezra and Nehemiah provided for Judah, the people would have found it impossible to live according to the high ideals of their ancestral religion, because they lacked a healthy social and religious life. Nehemiah was a man of good practical sense, combined with deep faith in God. He was a layman, and his generous dedication of talents to the service of God and God's people remains an example for lay people today.

Outline of the Book of Nehemiah
Neh 1, 1—7, 22 The Deeds of Nehemiah
Neh 8, 1—13, 31 Promulgation of the Law

The Rebuilding of Jerusalem

Because of bad reports that came to the Persian imperial court from Jerusalem, the emperor Artaxerxes I agreed to send Nehemiah, his cupbearer, to rebuild the city. There was great opposition from the governors of neighboring provinces, who even proposed military action against Jerusalem when they saw the wall being rebuilt. When their criticism and threats failed to dissuade Nehemiah, they began to plot against his life. Some within the Judahite community associated themselves with these plots against Nehemiah. This internal opposition came from the upper classes, who had a stake in maintaining the status quo. But despite all this opposition, Nehemiah completed the project of rebuilding the walls of the city in just 52 days.

From the time of David, Jerusalem was the central city of ancient Israel—at least for those devoted to the Davidic monarchy. David and Solomon wanted their Temple to solidify their capital's importance in the hearts of their people. But in spite of its great splendor, the Babylonians leveled the Temple and the city around it in 587 B.C. Although the Temple was rebuilt and Nehemiah refortified the city, the second Temple was never as elaborate as the one built by Solomon. Jerusalem was no longer a symbol of unity of north and south. It was, now, the center for preserving the particular worship of the Jewish community.

The Promulgation of the Torah

At this point the Nehemiah memoirs break off and chapters 8–10 describe a ritual that Ezra conducted. This ceremony brought closure to the rebuilding of the city and the restoration of its religious life. The community heard the words of the Torah and responded by celebrating the Feast of Booths according to its prescriptions. Two weeks later they began a fast, and then Ezra made a great confession of sin in the name of the people.

The Confession

Nehemiah 9, 6–37 is one of the important creedal statements in the Old Testament. It recounts Israel's experience of God from the time of Abraham to the period of restoration. This remarkable act of faith acknowledges God's goodness and fidelity despite Israel's failure to keep the commandments. The similar prayer of confession in Ezra 9, 7–15 suggests that these two confessions were originally parts of the same prayer.

The Agreement of the People

Chapter 10 contains a written pledge made by those listed in verses 1b–27 to observe the Torah of Moses. Among the specific points made in this pledge are the prohibition of marriage with Gentiles and the observance of the Sabbath. Those who made the pledge promised to provide firewood for the altar, first fruits for sacrifice, and tithes for the support of the Levites. Chapter 11 begins with a lottery used to resettle Jerusalem. Nehemiah 12 lists returning priests and Levites, followed by a description of the dedication of the walls. The book concludes with a list of the various reform measures that the people pledged themselves to observe.

Ritual Purity

At first glance, the books of Ezra and Nehemiah may seem to be concerned with racial or ethnic discrimination. Although this issue could have been at work here, it is important to note that the emphasis on purity primarily involves cult and ritual. Mixing two peoples in marriage or in worship offends the Near Eastern notion of order. Exclusion of Gentiles from worship did not come from a belief in ethnic superiority but was associated with the rebuilding of the Temple and

the restoration program led by both Ezra and Nehemiah. In order for the Jewish religion to continue and the worship of the LORD to be revived in Jerusalem, it was crucial that the practices and rituals not be watered down by those of other groups. Religion and ethnicity tended to parallel each other.

According to the Gospel of John in the New Testament, Christians worship in "Spirit and in truth" (Jn 4, 23), transcending these ethnic patterns. Paul makes it clear that in Jesus there is "no Jew or Greek" (Gal 3, 28). And Matthew writes that Jesus' final command was to "make disciples of all nations" (Mt 28, 10). This did not occur to the first Christians automatically. The Acts of the Apostles shows that the inclusion of the Gentiles into the Christian community was a matter of spirited debate among Jewish Christians (Acts 15, 1–35).

The synagogue also struggled with the question of inclusion or exclusion of the Gentiles. Some rabbis favored the more exclusive strain as found in Deuteronomy, Ezra, and Nehemiah. Others endorsed the more inclusive tendencies in texts such as Isaiah 56, which states that the Temple was to be "a house of prayer for all peoples."

Questions for Discussion and Reflection
Group Sharing/Discussion

1. Ezra provided the community with a source of stability and continuity. He offered the Jewish community the Torah, which the Jews came to see as encompassing an eternal order given by God to Israel alone. This notion of Torah had some profound effects in the social order. What do you think were some signs of this in the community?

2. Ezra found "mixed marriages" unacceptable (chs 9–10) and elevated heredity to a position of defining the people of God. What are the effects of limiting Jewish identity to physical heredity?

In Our Lives

1. The teachings of the Torah are not considered a burden but as principles or a moral code given by a loving parent to the children. Tell about what teachings you view in this manner.

2. Ezra created an *exclusive* community. Explain the kind of exclusions you see or experience in your community, our country, the world.

The Torah

An important theme in both Ezra and Nehemiah is the Torah as a written official guide for the life of the Jewish community. In Nehemiah 8–10, Ezra reads the Law, the people confess their failure to observe it, and then they agree to live according to its precepts. Unfortunately, too many Christians have very distorted notions of the Torah. These may have arisen because of the tense atmosphere in the Gospels, which recount Jesus' debates with the Pharisees regarding the interpretation of the Torah, and the bitter exchanges between Paul and some early Christians who thought that the Torah should be observed by everyone. But both Jesus and Paul often gave praise to the Torah: "Do you think that I have come to abolish the law or the prophets. . . . Whoever breaks one of the least of these commandments and teaches others to do so will be called the least in the kingdom of heaven. . . ." (Mt 5, 17–19) and "So then the law is holy, and the commandment is holy and righteous and good" (Rom 7, 12). Still the word "law" has a negative ring to it in the ears of most Christians.

The key to understanding and appreciating the Torah is to discover where it came from. Like most important words in the Hebrew Bible, *Torah* is used in several different ways. *Torah* could have come from the Hebrew word *yarah*, which means to cast lots, to point the way, or to instruct. Torah may have derived from the instructions priests gave to the people.

In the Bible, *Torah* usually refers to God's instructions to Moses at Sinai that he handed on to ancient Israel. In the book of Deuteronomy, *Torah* takes on a more extensive sense and becomes that which determines Israel's cultural, religious, and national identity. The prophets use Torah in several ways: cultic regulations, God's moral commands and ethical norms, and even the divine teachings given through the prophets. The Psalms praise both the Torah and those who live by it.

The early rabbis believed that they were responsible for transmitting not only the written Torah but also an oral Torah, which contained the teachings of revered sages who furthered the obligations of the Law beyond the words of the written Torah and made it much more difficult to violate the written Torah. Around A.D. 200, Rabbi Judah the Prince committed this oral Law to writing in a work called the Mishnah. This was the beginning of the Talmud (the code of rabbinical teaching on the manner of observing the Law). In Judaism today, *Torah* refers not only to the books of Moses but to the Talmud and the entire Jewish ethical tradition.

The Bible often speaks of Israel as God's children. Some people understood the Torah as the teaching given by the loving parent, God, to the child, Israel. In this light, the giving of Torah is an act of highest love. Jews of ancient Israel or modern times do not experience Torah as a burden, but as a way to life and as a source of joy. This devotion to ethical principles—the attitude of self-examination and self-correction that comes from loving observance and the preservation of identity through a specific moral code—are values that Christians could learn from Judaism, ancient and modern.

3. Ezra responded to the severe problems of his day with passionate commitment. To what do you have a passionate commitment? What calls Christians today to this kind of passionate commitment?

Individual/Personal Reflection/Action

1. In *Nostra Aetate* the Vatican Council encouraged Catholics to speak and work with followers of other religions. They are to acknowledge, preserve, and promote the spiritual and moral values found in non-Christian religions. Take some time to reflect on what this Church directive invites you to do.

2. In the *Declaration on the Relationship of the Church to Non-Christian Religions* the Church rejects any type of discrimination directed at people because of their religion. The bishops called upon all Catholics to maintain "good fellowship" with all peoples by living with them in peace. Examine your experience to recognize discrimination and to form attitudes of good fellowship. What can be done today to help people overcome prejudice against other people or religions?

3. The call for ritual purity and separation is pervasive in Ezra and Nehemiah. The New Testament affirms that the Christian worship transcends these patterns. According to John, Christians worship in "spirit and truth" (Jn 4, 23). Paul makes it clear that in Jesus there is "no Jew or Greek" (Gal 3, 28). Matthew writes that Jesus' final command was to "make disciples of all nations" (Mt 28, 19). This insight did not occur to the first Christians automatically. The Acts of the Apostles shows that the inclusion of the Gentiles into the Christian community was a matter of spirited debate among the Jewish Christians (Acts 25, 1–35). Meditate on this contrast: exclusive/inclusive, in spirit and truth/ritually pure. Rejoice in Jesus' inclusiveness and Christian worship.

TOBIT READING GUIDE

At a Glance

Who are the main players?	Tobit Sarah Tobiah
What should I look for?	This book is not history but a religious story. The purpose of this engaging tale is to show that God controls events and manages circumstances to ensure that God's purposes come to fruition. Reflect upon how God answers the prayers of the innocent Tobit and Sarah.
When did this take place?	Probably written in the early second century B.C. The author is unknown.
Where did these events occur?	Purportedly, in Nineveh, capital of Assyria, and Ecbatana, in Media. This book is a kind of religious novel. The historical and geographical details are there simply to provide setting for the story.
Why was this book written?	The book of Tobit reflects the importance that the book of Deuteronomy came to have in early Judaism. It maintains that the exile is not God's final judgment on Israel; rather there is hope for mercy, and the Temple in Jerusalem is the only legitimate place for worship.
What is the story?	This is the story of a pious Jew in exile who, after many misfortunes and trying events, finally sees the victory of God's providence in a happy family reunion and a peaceful end. Apart from the fascination of the tale itself, the book reflects aspects of Jewish piety during the Hellenistic period. The account is presented as history and as having taken place in Nineveh in the eighth century B.C.

The book of Tobit is a complex literary work with a very simple moral. The book tells the tragedies and triumphs in the lives of three people: Tobit, Sarah, and Tobiah. The author, by weaving the stories together in three different but related plots, has a theological purpose: to show that God can manage the circumstances of people's lives to bring God's plans to fulfillment. The primary message is simple: God rewards those who are faithful.

Approaching the Book: The Literary Form of Tobit

This book is a kind of religious novel. The historical and geographical details are there simply to provide a setting for the story. The author confuses the kings of Assyria, shows ignorance of the topography of Mesopotamia, and dates Tobit's exile earlier than it could have been. There is little to suggest that the author meant this work to be historical.

The book is the work of a single author and not the product of tradition. What is especially important to notice is how the author tells the stories of Tobit and his relative Sarah, both of whom suffer undeservedly. This cleverly told story is short enough to read in a single sitting. One key to understanding the purpose of the story is the unfolding of how God answers the prayers of the innocent Tobit and Sarah in a way they hardly expected. The story assumes God's determination to reward the just. When they suffer, there is a limit to that suffering. Once the limit is reached, God will intervene, sometimes miraculously.

The Judaism of the Book

The book of Tobit was probably written in the second century B.C.; it is not known where. It reveals a form of Judaism that accepts magic and sees angels and demons as having important roles to play in the drama between God and human beings. This differs sharply from the books such as Judith and Esther, where human beings are in control of their own destiny without any intervention from angels or demons. The author of Tobit considers angels to be more than God's messengers: They mediate prayers in God's throne room; they oppose demons; and they authorize the writing of books. While angels expend efforts on behalf of good people, demons are malicious powers.

The book of Tobit reflects the importance that the book of Deuteronomy came to have in early Judaism. This is especially clear in Tobit 14, 4–7, which claims that the exile happened because of Israel's infidelity. But it maintains that the exile is not God's final judgment on Israel; rather there is hope for mercy, and the Temple in Jerusalem is the only legitimate place for worship. Fidelity to God is measured in terms of fulfillment of the Torah, just as Deuteronomy preaches.

Finally, Tobit seems to reflect the circumstances of Jews in the diaspora (Jewish settlements outside Palestine). The book depicts Gentiles as unsympathetic to Tobit's activities and as persecutors. The book presents marriage within Judaism as a duty. It teaches that God is supreme over all people and is present to those in exile in the midst of their suffering. It emphasizes the need to preserve Jewish identity in the diaspora.

Reading the Book of Tobit

The only way to savor the book's literary artistry and to appreciate its religious perspectives is to follow the way the author unfolds the events of Tobit's, Sarah's, and their families' lives. Notice how the stories of Tobit and Sarah parallel one another:

Tobit's piety (2, 1–7)	Sarah's innocence (3, 14)
Tobit's blindness (2, 9–10)	Sarah's demon (3, 8)
Tobit's reproach (2, 14)	Sarah's reproach (3, 7–10)
Tobit's prayer (3, 1–6)	Sarah's prayer (3, 10–15)

God hears these prayers but responds to them in a totally unexpected manner. Although Tobit and Sarah felt abandoned by God, God was, nonetheless, with them in the midst of their suffering. The reader should notice the movement in the book from despair to thanksgiving and praise.

Questions for Discussion and Reflection
Group Sharing/Discussion

1. All the biblical short stories are told from the third-person point of view; that is, the

About Angels and Demons

The book of Tobit reflects the belief of early Judaism in angels and demons as supernatural beings. The first form of this belief seems to be "the messenger of the LORD," which belongs to the earliest narratives in the Hebrew Bible. In some of these stories the messenger is not different from the LORD (see Gn 16, 13; 21, 18; 31, 13). Because God confronts people directly in many early stories, the appearance of angels is somewhat rare. As people begin to think of God as far beyond the human sphere, angels appear more regularly in the stories. Ideas develop about good angels and bad angels (demons), a hierarchy of angels, and the various duties of angels. It is possible to see popular imagination at work in the description of angels. They wear white garments and have wings. Around the time Tobit was written, there seems to be the belief in a few Jewish texts that it was permissible to portray figures from Israel's past, especially Adam and Jacob, as angels. Some Jews must have held that it was possible for a select few to transcend humanity and become angels. However, not all Jews believed in angels. The Acts of the Apostles asserts that the Pharisees, who represented more liberal, popular belief, acknowledged the existence of angels while the Sadducees rejected the existence of angels as well as belief in spirits and the resurrection from the dead.

narrator tells us about the characters by describing their actions through dialogue and speech. How would the story of the book of Tobit be affected if it were told by the characters themselves? (Note that Tobit begins in the first person [1, 1—3, 6]. Does this affect how you read it?) Choose a character who interests you and pick a particular scene or episode from the story. Allow that person to tell the story from his or her own point of view. Give lots of details, emotional reactions, and insights *based* on the story.

2. This story assumes God's control in people's lives and God's determination to reward the just. It says that when the just suffer, there is a limit to that suffering. Once that limit occurs, God will intervene and sometimes that intervention is miraculous. Share what you believe about suffering and God's relationship to it.

In Our Lives

The purpose of the book is to move its readers from despair to prayer. The most important message in this story is that God is with Tobit and Sarah even when they do not experience the divine presence. Mention how you perceive God's fidelity to you in time of suffering. Pray together Tobit's Song of Praise (13, 1–18).

Individual/Personal Reflection/Action

1. Tobit is about how God answers the prayers of innocent Tobit and Sarah in an unexpected way. What experience have you had similar to Tobit's in your own life?

2. Tobit presents marriage within Judaism as a duty, for Jewish identity is important. It teaches God is sovereign over all people and is present to those in exile. Reflect on what you learned concerning marriage, God's sovereignty, and God's presence that is relatable to your own life.

JUDITH READING GUIDE

At a Glance

Who are the main players?	Judith Holofernes
What should I look for?	Do not read this as history. It is a faith-filled meditation on God's providential care for Israel. The book attempts to show how the invisible hand of God rescues Israel through Judith. It also sets up a confrontation between the false

belief that kings were the equivalent of gods on Earth, and faith in the one true God of Israel.

When did this take place?   May have been written as late as first century B.C., but in some ways it reflects the Maccabean revolt of the second century B.C.

Where did these events occur?   Although set in earlier times, the narrative reflects conditions prevalent during the turmoil of the Hellenistic period described in 1 and 2 Maccabees.

Why was this book written?   The name Judith is not a proper name; it means "Jewish woman." By rescuing her people from destruction at the hands of the Gentiles, Judith is a model for the Jewish woman as the preserver of tradition. Judith is a paradigm for the Jewish woman who protects her family from intrusions from the outside that threaten to dilute their loyalty to their ancestral religion.

What is the story?   Judith is a good story—a well-paced combination of description and action with purposeful realism. The heroine represents Israel's faith and spirit, strong and resourceful despite a weak appearance, which emerges triumphant in the confrontation with the great powers of the Near East.

The Book's Literary Form

There have been several attempts to classify the book of Judith according to its literary type. Clearly it is not history. It is useless to try to read it against the backdrop of Jewish history or that of other nations in the ancient world. There are just too many historical errors. Is it then a historical novel, *midrash,* or a fictional drama? None of these is completely satisfactory. The book is the result of a conscious, faith-filled meditation on God's providential care for Israel. The story shows how the invisible hand of God rescues Israel through the hand of Judith.

Over the centuries this story has attracted remarkable attention from writers, artists, and composers. Mozart chose Judith as the subject of his oratorio "La Betulia Liberata" ("The Liberation of Bethulia"). Painters, including Artemisia Gentileschi, have represented her story on canvas, and sculptors—Donatello is probably the

most famous—have represented the story in bronze. Anonymous stonemasons even carved her story on the great cathedral of Chartres in France. The reason for all this attention is that Judith's story is such a good one. It is a heroic tale in which an unlikely character overcomes the cowardice of her own people in the face of the enemy.

The book of Judith is a piece of literature for difficult times. It was hoped that the reader would take to heart the lesson that God was still the master of history who could save Israel from her enemies. There is a parallel with the time of the Exodus: As God had delivered the people by the hand of Moses, so God could deliver them by the hand of the pious widow Judith.

The heroine's name is probably not a proper name. It simply means "Jewish woman." Judith is more than an individual: She is a composite of all the women who have saved Israel in the past by their piety, wisdom, and action. These heroines saved the people of ancient Israel when the more usual channels of leadership (the king, priests, and other notables) were not able to meet the challenges of faith. Some examples include Rahab (Joshua), Deborah (Judges), and Esther.

The first people to hear the story of Judith lived in a traditional society in which roles

---

Midrash is the expansion, probing and exposition of biblical texts to bring out their full new meaning for changed circumstances.

The Image of Women in the Church

A type of tension similar to that in Judith is visible in the U.S. Bishops' Pastoral Response to Women's Concerns for Church and Society, *Partners in the Mystery of Redemption* (1988). The first draft attempted to integrate the responses the bishops received from Catholic women through conversations that were part of the formulation of this first draft. Reading these responses makes it clear that there is great diversity among Catholic women. "The typical Catholic woman" does not exist. Like Judith, Catholic women see themselves as preservers of what is best in the tradition, although some are ready to cross what they perceive as artificial barriers set up by that tradition. The book of Judith offers a model for the process of contemporary theological reflection on the role and status of women in the Church. The book itself is a product of early Judaism's reflection on the role of women in its social and religious system. At the very least, the book sees women as, at times, better fit to be instruments of salvation than men—a conclusion that was most unexpected in the cultural milieu in which it arose.

assigned to men and women were clearly distinct. Change, if it took place at all, occurred very slowly. This story offers a surprising contradiction to what the culture assumed the role and status of women should be. In this story the men proved to be utter failures in the face of the threats of the king Nebuchadnezzar and Holofernes, the commander of his armies. The impact that this story made on a traditional society such as early Judaism is difficult for us to appreciate because we live in a society where change occurs much more quickly.

On the other hand, the book of Judith is quite conservative in its outlook. By rescuing her people from destruction at the hands of Gentiles, Judith is a model for the Jewish woman as the preserver of tradition. Judith is a paradigm for the Jewish woman who protects her family from intrusions from the outside that threaten to dilute their loyalty to their ancestral religion. The heroine of the book carries out the role assigned her by her culture but also surpasses that role.

The Irony of the Book

The story of Judith is full of unexpected turns. The most obvious, especially to those who first heard or read the story, is that a woman—not a man—saved Judah in time of severe distress. Judith is more faithful and resourceful than any of the men of Bethulia. She is more eloquent than the king and more courageous than the leading

citizens of the city. Yet Judith is a very unlikely heroine. As a childless widow, she occupied a very low place in the social hierarchy. While the king, priests, and leaders show themselves incapable of dealing with the crisis, Judith stands up to the threat posed by Holofernes and takes decisive action to end that threat.

The means she uses to accomplish her end may offend some. She uses her beauty to gain access to the enemy camp and to beguile Holofernes. Judith, though, is using the one weapon she has available to her. This leads to the second irony. Judith destroys the enemy not with military might but with her charm and disarming beauty.

Finally, Judith is a childless widow, yet the book portrays her as the mother of faith. That is why the high priests praise her so highly. The Latin hymn, *Tota pulchra es,* applies these words in praise of Mary. The story of Judith provides the liturgy with an appropriate image for the Virgin Mary as the Mother of the Church.

The Judaism of the Book

The book of Judith affirms that the deliverance of the Jews of Bethulia depends not on power and might but on fidelity to the Law and guidance from the LORD. The author portrays Judith as living according to the Law as Jews interpreted it at the time. As a widow, she lives in a state of mourning marked by fasting. She prays daily at the hour of the incense offering in the

Temple. She observes Jewish dietary laws. She purifies herself by bathing in running water at the appropriate time. Judith criticizes the people for violating the law of first fruits and tithes. But while the book presents Judith's obedience to the Torah as the key to Israel's deliverance, it shows a type of flexibility that is able to respond to a person such as Achior the Ammonite, who wishes to join the Israelites in the service of God. According to Deuteronomy, Israel was never to admit an Ammonite into their community. The issue of inclusion and exclusion was a perplexing one for Judaism, as it was also for the first Christians (see Acts 10, 1–49; 11, 1–8; 15, 1–12).

Questions for Discussion and Reflection
Group Sharing/Discussion
1. Judith is a model Jewish woman. What religious qualities show in her actions?
2. What are the role expectations out of which

you live your life? Who have been your heroes or heroines? How does society's expectations influence the kind of man or woman you want to be?
3. Imagine a modern story of a religious Judith for a TV drama. Role-play the parts.
In Our Lives
1. How have experiences of women's faith nourished your life?
2. What are some ways that women's faith sustains the Church?
Individual/Personal Reflection/Action
1. Scripture uses both masculine and feminine images as revelatory of God. See how many of each you can name. Reflect on how thinking and speaking of God through masculine and feminine images make a difference in our sense of the divine.
2. Consider ways that you could bring to the attention of your parish the need and practice for both feminine and masculine images of God in nourishing spirituality.

ESTHER READING GUIDE

At a Glance

Who are the main players?	Ahasuerus (Xerxes I) Vashti Esther Haman Mordecai.
What should I look for?	Esther is a novella on the theme of the persecuted righteous and their deliverance. The central concern of the book of Esther is the survival of the Jewish minority in the midst of a world that is growing hostile to it. The book makes it clear that God will act to preserve the Jewish community.
When did this take place?	At the end of the Persian empire toward the close of the fourth century B.C.
Where did these events occur?	The story describes the plot of Haman to destroy all Jews as happening in the Persian empire about 485 B.C.
Why was this book written?	The book was intended to console Israel and remind them that God's providence continually cares for them, never abandoning them when they serve God faithfully or turn to God, asking for forgiveness. God does not intervene directly to resolve the problem, but even though the divine action may be hidden, it is nonetheless real.
What is the story?	Set in the royal court of Persia, the book of Esther recounts how, through a series of dramatic events, a Jewish woman becomes queen and uses her influence to win for her people the right to fight off a threat of genocide. The Jewish holiday of Purim, described at the end of the book, celebrates this victory.

The central concern of the book of Esther is the survival of the Jewish minority in the midst of a world that is growing more hostile to it. This book tells the story of Mordecai, a Jewish courtier in the service of the Persian emperors, and his beautiful and courageous niece, Esther, and how they averted one threat to Jewish survival. The book was intended to console Israel and remind them that God's providence continually cares for them, never abandoning them when they serve God faithfully or turn to God, asking for forgiveness. God does not intervene directly to resolve the problem, but even though the divine action may be hidden, it is nonetheless real.

Structure of the Book

A confusing aspect to the arrangement of this book in the New American Bible is the order and numbering of its chapters and verses. Besides the familiar numbering common to the rest of the Bible, there are six chapters that have letter identifications scattered in the midst of chapters that have the usual number identifications. This is the result of the way the book of Esther has come down to us.

This book has survived in two forms: a shorter Hebrew text and a longer version preserved in the Septuagint (the ancient Greek version of the Hebrew Bible). The Greek has about 107 verses more than the Hebrew. When St. Jerome revised the Old Latin translation and compared these two ancient versions, he concluded that the extra verses in Greek were not inspired. Jerome took these verses out of their proper context and put them in an appendix at the end of the book. The Greek additions also did not become part of the Jewish canon, and their place in the canon of the Roman Catholic Church was not settled until the Council of Trent in the sixteenth century. Protestant churches do not accept the additions to Esther as canonical. The arrangement in this New American Bible attempts to follow the order of the Greek version without losing the arrangement of numbering of chapters and verses that is universally followed. The table below compares the two versions.

The purpose of the Greek additions to the Hebrew version of Esther is clear. They introduce a religious element into a secular story. The Hebrew version is a tale about how the Jews were able to outsmart their enemies and does not make a single reference to God (although the phrase in 4, 14, "from another source," is interpreted by both Jewish and Christian writers as referring to God). The additions also lend an air of authenticity by introducing "documents" (B, 107; E, 1–24) that make the book read as if it were a historical work. This is important to encourage the celebration of the Feast of Purim with which the story became associated.

> **P**urim The holiday named for the pur (lot) Haman cast to determine when the Jews would be destroyed. Purim is the feast celebrated on the 14th and 15th of Adar (around the first of March) commemorating the deliverance of the Jews from Haman's pogrom (an officially organized massacre).

Hebrew Bible	Greek Septuagint
1, 1 – 3, 13	A. Mordecai's dream; the conspiracy against the king
3, 14 – 4, 17	B. The royal edict of Haman
	C. The prayers of Mordecai and Esther
5, 1–2 (omitted in Septuagint)	D. Expansion of the account of Esther's audience with the king
5, 3 – 8, 12	E. The royal edict of Mordecai
8, 13 – 10, 3	F. Explanation of Mordecai's dream, conclusion, and postscript

From *Women's Bible Commentary* edited by Carol Newsom and Sharon H. Ringe. ©1992 Westminster John Knox Press. Used by permission of Westminster John Knox Press.

The Story and Its Personalities

The story takes place in the diaspora (the Jewish settlements outside of the land of Israel) and makes no reference to the homeland of the Jews. Two royal officials, Mordecai the Jew and Haman the Agagite, vie for power and position in the court of the Persian emperor. The rivalry between them soon sweeps up the entire Jewish community because of their particular customs and patterns of behavior. When Esther joins her relative, Mordecai, in a plan to frustrate Haman's murderous plots, the tension is resolved. What was to have been an officially organized massacre of the Jews becomes a celebration of the Jews because Haman and his conspiracy fail.

The story begins with the dethronement of Vashti, the queen of Persia. Vashti refused to obey the command of her drunken husband, Ahasuerus, king of Persia, when during a banquet he ordered her to "display her beauty" before his male courtiers. Because she refused to submit to this indignity, the king's officials advised him to remove her as queen. They feared that their own wives might imitate and refuse to obey their orders. The king issued a decree deposing Vashti and declaring that "every man should be lord of his own home."

Unlike Judith, Esther is hardly a model for feminists. She participates in the process to replace Vashti, who is the real heroine according to a feminist reading of this text. Vashti lost her crown but preserved her dignity. Esther betrayed the queen by seeking to replace her. While this story shows that the author was familiar with the royal court and the administrative system of Persia, the story of Esther is fictional and was not intended to report an actual event. It is an early Jewish novella on the theme of the persecuted righteous and their deliverance.

The Book of Esther and the Feast of Purim

According to F, 10, God wished the Jews to celebrate the feast on the 14th and 15th of Adar to

> **Novella** A novella is a fictional piece of prose and is not meant to be historically accurate. A novella is shorter than a novel. It is written by a single author and meant to be read, not recited. The plot moves from tension to complication to resolution, concentrating on the development of characters and situations.

celebrate their deliverance. The Bible mentions this feast nowhere else except a possible allusion in 2 Maccabees 15, 36 that mentions Mordecai's day. Did the feast come first and the story of Esther later or did the feast come from the book? It may be that the Jews in the Persian diaspora adopted a local spring festival and attached a story of deliverance to it. Passover, the principal Jewish spring festival, shows a similar origin. Passover was a festival celebrated by nomads as they changed grazing areas for their flocks in spring. The Israelites attached the story of the deliverance from Egypt to this celebration. Since the Torah did not mandate the observance of Purim, the story of Esther serves to promote a religious celebration commemorating the story of a frustrated massacre and the secular triumph of the Jews over their enemies. Although a minor fast precedes Purim, the festival itself is a joyous one and includes a boisterous reading of the story of Esther, plenty of food and drink, and much merriment. Jews are also to give gifts of food and to support charity. These prescriptions symbolize the turning from sorrow to joy and give a religious dimension to what was a purely secular story. The Jews are to understand their survival not just in nationalistic terms but as a religious obligation.

The story of Esther describes intrigues and plots, power plays and schemes for murder. The Bible text does not approve the actions of either Esther or Mordecai but only the results. What God intended was the survival of the Jewish community. God did not dictate the means for that survival: The human personalities in the story controlled these. Perhaps the Hebrew version's refusal to speak about God directly in the story was an attempt to emphasize the importance of the Jews taking the matter of their survival into their

> **The name Esther** The name Esther was a Mesopotamian name. Her Jewish name was Hadassah, which means "myrtle."

Additions to the Book of Esther

Additions A and F	Mordecai's dream makes it clear that God controls the destiny of Israel.
Addition B	The decree of the Persian king against the Jews emphasizes the peculiarity of Jewish customs and alleges that they are not loyal to him.
Addition C	The deliverance of the Jews is in response to the prayers of Mordecai and Esther.
Addition D	The king's change of opinion regarding the Jews resulted from God's answer to Esther's prayer.
Addition E	God condemns the enemy of Israel. The Jews are innocent. The king acclaims the God of the Jews sovereign over all.

own hands. The additions to the Greek version, however, show that some people saw this reticence as something that needed correction. The list above summarizes these additions.

How do Christians read a book so highly saturated with Jewish nationalism? The message of the book of Esther has an important role in the Christian canon. It offers an opportunity to check the tendency to spiritualize the people of ancient Israel and their descendants today. Where Vatican Council II declared that there is a spiritual bond between Jews and Christians, the book of Esther asserts that the preservation of the Jewish people is a *religious obligation*. The presence of the book of Esther in the Christian canon is a statement of the religious importance of the Jewish people as an ethnic group. It makes the sin of anti-Semitism even more shameful than the irrational injustice that most Christians understand it to be today.

Questions for Discussion and Reflection
Group Sharing/Discussion

1. This story begins with Queen Vashti's refusal to submit to indignity before the king's courtiers. Compare and contrast her response to the king with the courtiers' request.

2. The book of Esther makes it clear that God will act to preserve the Jewish community. What meaning does this story of Esther have for you and the Christian community?

In Our Lives

1. The central character in both Esther and Judith is a beautiful Jewish woman whose bravery and wiles save her people from certain destruction. Recall some stories of heroes or heroines throughout history and in your life today.

2. In the book of Esther, Haman practices anti-Semitism. Do you recognize this evil of anti-Semitism in your world? In Christian history?

3. Because they were living outside their land and faith community, the Jews in this story were "aliens." How does it feel to be aliens or alienated? Does the story of Esther speak to you about these experiences? What can you as an individual or your parish as a community do to help everyone feel welcome in your parish and your community?

Individual/Personal Reflection/Action

1. Vatican Council II declared there is a spiritual bond between Jews and Christians. Take time to reflect on how this is true both in the origin of Christianity and in our life today.

2. Both Esther and Judith are novellas in form, that is, they are fictional prose and not historical narratives. But they do have a spiritual message. How important is awareness of the literary form of a book in the Bible in receiving its message? Research some of the other forms of writing contained in the Bible.

1 MACCABEES READING GUIDE

At a Glance

Who are the main players?   Mattathias Judas and his brothers Antiochus Epiphanes

What should I look for?   Observance of the Torah Saving Jews from persecution

When did these events take place?   The first book of Maccabees is a historical narrative of events in the life of the Jewish community in and around Jerusalem from the reign of the Greek Antiochus IV (175–164 B.C.) to the accession of the Jewish ruler, John Hyrcanus (134–104 B.C.).

Why was this book written?   The first book of Maccabees is one of the main sources for reconstructing the history of the Jews in Palestine during the middle of the second century B.C. The purpose of the work was to assert the legitimacy of the Hasmonean high-priestly dynasty. The book implies that the right of the Hasmoneans to rule is clear from the achievements of their ancestors: (1) the Maccabees saved the Jews from persecution; (2) they restored observance of the Torah; and (3) they inaugurated an era of peace and prosperity. The author of this book believed that God willed that the Hasmoneans assume the mantle of leadership over the Jews of Palestine.

What is the story?   The story told in this book is a small part of a much larger story: Hellenization, the shifting of cultural orientation from East to West, in the eastern Mediterranean region. The Greek ruler and general Alexander the Great conquered this area in the fourth century B.C. It was his dream to take the culture of Greece and wed it to the cultures of the ancient Near East so that people could benefit from the best of each. Although Alexander's premature death in 323 B.C. prevented him from fulfilling that dream, the process of Hellenization proceeded in the cultural, political, and economic spheres. The response of the Jewish community to Hellenism was equivocal: some Jews resisted Hellenization; others eagerly accepted the new wave that was sweeping the world.

By 326 B.C., Alexander the Great had conquered the lands surrounding the eastern end of the Mediterranean. At his sudden death in 323 B.C., however, his empire fell apart into three separate sections. One, which included Egypt and parts of present-day Israel, Jordan, and Lebanon, was ruled by Ptolemy, one of Alexander's generals. Another general, Seleucus, ruled a territory including what is now Syria, Iran, and Iraq, and extending eastward at one point as far as India. The portion of the empire centered on Greece was ruled (and fought over) by various members of Alexander's family and court.

The word "Maccabee" derives from the Hebrew word for hammer and was the nickname for Judas, a leader in the Jewish revolt against the Seleucid ruler Antiochus Epiphanes (165–161 B.C.). The nickname later became a designation for other members of Judas's family who succeeded him in the revolt. Judas and his brothers became known as "the Maccabees" and "Maccabean" came to designate the period of Jewish history that witnessed the successful revolt against the Seleucid Empire.

After the revolt, the descendants of the Maccabees took over religious and later political leadership of the Jewish community in Palestine. They ruled an independent Judah from about 164 B.C. (beginning with Judas Maccabee) until Pompey conquered Palestine for Rome in 63 B.C. This dynasty was called the "Hasmonean" dynasty. That name comes from the ancestor Asamonaeus whom Josephus (a first-century A.D. Jewish historian) identifies as the father of Mattathias and grandfather of Judas and his brothers. Mattathias started the revolt against Antiochus.

What Is the Maccabean Literature?

There are four books of the Maccabees that have survived from early Judaism. None are in the Hebrew Bible and so are not included in Jewish or Protestant Bibles. An overview of the contents of these books can be found below.

History and Theology in First Maccabees

Unlike the books of Tobit, Judith, and Esther, which use historical events and persons as a backdrop for fictional tales, the first book of Maccabees is a historical story. The author tries to show the significance of the events in the middle of second century B.C. Palestine. But the book is more than a catalogue of events. Its purpose was to affirm the legitimacy of the Hasmonean high-priestly dynasty, whose right to rule was based on the achievements of their ancestors:

1. The Maccabees saved the Jews from persecution.

2. They restored observance of the Torah.

3. They set up an era of peace and prosperity.

The author believed that it was God's will that the Hasmoneans assumed leadership over the Jews of Palestine. The members of this dynasty were not without their opponents. After all, they ruled as kings when many Jews believed that the only legitimate political leaders ought to be descendants of David. As a priestly family the Hasmoneans were not of David's tribe (Judah), let alone part of his family. In addition, the Hasmoneans functioned as high priests even though they were not descendants of Aaron, as required by tradition. The chief opponents of the Hasmoneans were the Hasidim, who were the spiritual ancestors of the Essenes and the Pharisees.

The first book of Maccabees reflects a type of pragmatism that was incompatible with the religious zeal of the Hasidim. 1 Maccabees 8 is lavish in its praise of the Romans. This shows that the Hasmoneans were willing to compromise with foreigners when circumstances made it necessary. Later the Pharisees adopted the same

---

First Book of Maccabees Historical narrative of events in life of Jewish community in and around Jerusalem from 175 B.C. to 104 B.C. (Included by Jerome in Vulgate; became part of the Catholic canon.)

Second Book of Maccabees Abridgement of a five-volume history of the Maccabees that no longer exists. Covers period in Palestine from 180 B.C. to 161 B.C. (Became part of Catholic canon.)

Third Book of Maccabees A misnamed work that has nothing to do with the exploits of the Maccabees. It is a first-century B.C. work that describes the persecution of the Jews in Egypt under Ptolemy IV (221–203 B.C.). (Included in the canon of Eastern Christianity.)

Fourth Book of Maccabees A first-century A.D. tract on religious reason as exemplified by Jewish martyrs during the Maccabean revolt. (No Christian tradition accepts this book as divinely inspired, although some Eastern churches include it as an appendix to the Bible, and it has had some influence in their spirituality.)

Hasidim were the "pious ones" who saw themselves as the careful observers of the Law. They were sometimes not very prudent in their self-styled devotion to the Torah (see 1 Mc 7, 8–18).

position, and so did the early church (see Rom 13, 1–7 and 1 Pt 2, 13–17).

First Maccabees also shows that both Spartans and Romans, the major political powers of the day, recognized the Hasmoneans as the political leaders of the Jewish people.

Reading the Book

The story told in this book is part of a much larger story: the Hellenization in the eastern Mediterranean. It was the dream of Alexander the Great, who conquered this area in the fourth century B.C., to take the culture of Greece and wed it to the cultures of the ancient Near East so that people could benefit from the best of each. But his premature death in 323 B.C. prevented him from fulfilling that dream. Alexander's generals divided his empire among themselves. The area of the former Israelite kingdoms came under the control of Ptolemy, who ruled from Egypt. Ptolemy permitted the Jews to practice their religion without much interference. The process of Hellenization grew in the other areas of Jewish cultural, political, and economic life. Some Jews resisted Hellenization while others eagerly accepted the new wave that was sweeping the world.

The region of the ancient Mesopotamian Empire fell to another of Alexander's generals: Seleucus. He thought that the territory of the old Judahite and Israelite kingdoms rightfully belonged to him. The Ptolemies and Seleucids fought over this region until it passed into the hands of the Seleucids in 200 B.C. At first the Jews were permitted to practice their religion. But circumstances changed in 168 B.C. when the Seleucid king Antiochus IV Epiphanes ("Epiphanes" means "[god] manifest," and indicates that Antiochus was supposed to be regarded in his own culture as a divine, or at least deified, being) seized upon the opportunity provided by divisions within the Jewish community. He favored the Jewish Hellenizers for reasons that were partly economic but also in some part cultural. To ensure the victory of the Jewish Hellenizers, Antiochus forbade the practice of the Jewish religion. Without anyone to resist his policies, the future of Judaism looked bleak.

Mattathias (1 Mc 1, 1—2, 70)

The first chapter sets the scene for the bloody confrontation between the Jews and the Seleucids. It describes the Hellenization of Jerusalem, the military attacks on the city by two Seleucid armies, and the prohibition of Jewish religious practices. The king's efforts at destroying the Jewish religion culminated in the "horrible abomination," which was the setting up of an altar to Zeus Olympus upon the altar of holocausts, the holy place in the Temple where burnt offerings were made (Dn 11, 31; 12, 11).

The second chapter importantly describes the specific type of opposition that the Maccabees and their followers mounted against the Hellenization of Antiochus and his Jewish collaborators. Not all Jews who opposed Antiochus responded in the same way. While some reacted with a type of passive resistance, the Maccabees, in the person of Mattathias, opposed these policies militantly. A key text is 2, 23–46, which describes Mattathias's fury at the prospect of Jewish apostasy. By comparing Mattathias's response with that of Phinehas (see Nm 25, 6–14), the author implies that Mattathias's action prevented God's anger from consuming the Jews because of their apostasy. This merited the high-priestly office for the Hasmoneans. Mattathias became the leader of a large guerilla force whose aim was to end the Seleucid military domination of the Jews and the banning of their religion.

The Militancy of First Maccabees

The United States Bishops' Pastoral, *The Challenge of Peace,* asserts "the sacred scriptures provide the foundation for confronting war and peace today" (27). In trying to formulate a Christian response to these issues, one has to face the armed resistance of 1 Maccabees to the Seleucid persecution. Theologically, they were responding from the religious traditions of ancient Israel.

It is important to remember that the response of the Maccabees was not the only response among religious Jews in Palestine. Although

> **S**eleucid was the name of the Greek dynasty that ruled in Syria following the death of Alexander the Great. The name derived from Seleucus, one of Alexander's generals.

there was an agreement that they ought to oppose Antiochus, there was a variety of viewpoints on how they ought to resist. While the Maccabees insisted on violent resistance, there were others who opted for martyrdom, nonviolent resistance, and even pacificism in the face of the threat of anti-Jewish laws.

While 2 Maccabees shares the militancy of 1 Maccabees, it expands the meaning of the revolution by adding martyrdom as another way the faithful may contribute to the final victory over their enemies. The blood of martyrs who died rather than violate the Torah cries to God for vengeance and thereby seals the victory for the Jews.

Mattathias's Farewell

Chapter 2 ends with Mattathias's statement in which he turns over his military authority to his sons, commending to them the example of Israelite heroes of the past to support his militant ideology.

Hanukkah, or the Feast of Dedication is a Jewish feast celebrating the purification and rededication of the second Temple during the Maccabean revolt. Judas Maccabee mandated the observance of this festival. Three years to the day after Antiochus's "horrible abomination" of the Temple, the Maccabees gained control of the area, purified the Temple, and rebuilt the altar. Josephus calls this festival "the feast of lights": The rededication involved rekindling the Temple's menorah (a lamp stand with seven branches). Jews observe this festival at home by lighting one candle on a special Hanukkah menorah each night. According to a legend in the Talmud, the family is reminded of how one day's supply of oil lasted for the full eight days of the original festival until the priests could obtain more oil for the menorah in the Temple. This festival is glorification of the deeds of those who refused to give up their faith.

Judas (1 Mc 3, 1—9, 22)

About 40 percent of the story centers on the exploits of Judas, who succeeded his father as leader of the Jewish guerilla forces. Although the text acclaims his exploits and praises his bravery, the author is careful to imply that Judas's victories came because of divine help. Judas prayed before every battle. He reminded his army of how God helped their ancestors in the face of overwhelming odds. Judas dismissed those that Deuteronomy exempts from war (3, 56, see Dt 20, 5–8). That, and the way he dealt with the defeated enemy and the spoils of war, shows a man who was certain that he was fighting in accord with a divine command. Finally, Judas praised God when he celebrated his victories.

Jonathan (1 Mc 9, 23—12, 54)

Judas dies in battle and his brother Jonathan succeeds him. While the text hails Jonathan's military exploits, of particular importance is his acceptance of the appointment as high priest from the Seleucid king Alexander who succeeded Antiochus.

Simon (1 Mc 13, 1—16, 24)

When the followers of Trypho, the pretender to the Syrian throne, assassinate Jonathan, the succession passes to his brother Simon. The first book of Maccabees reaches its climax with the succession of Simon as leader and high priest. Remember, the purpose of the book is the establishment of the Hasmonean house as the legitimate political and religious dynasty for the Jews in Palestine.

A poem in 14, 4–15 is a combination of biblical themes suggesting that with Simon has come to the Jews a state of peace and prosperity not seen since the days of David and Solomon. A beleaguered minority stood up to a powerful empire for the sake of their religion. The author of 1 Maccabees believed that God was working through the Hasmonean family.

However, the book closes on a tragic note. Simon is murdered by a political rival who is captured and executed by John, Simon's son. The succession is safe and another Hasmonean, John Hyrcanus, continues the line of those "men to whom it was granted to achieve Israel's salvation" (5, 62).

> ### The Story of the Maccabees in Music
>
> George Frederick Handel's oratorio *Judas Maccabeus* tells the story of the Maccabean revolt. It includes the famous chorus "Hallelujah, Amen."

First Maccabees in Catholic Tradition

This book is not part of the Hebrew Bible. There is no evidence that it formed part of the Qumran library, and Josephus did not include it on the list of his sacred books. Reverence for the book by the early church's theologians was perhaps the reason that the Councils of Florence and Trent affirmed it canonically. But it has never had a real impact on Christian theology, and its use in the liturgy is minimal.

2 MACCABEES READING GUIDE

At a Glance

Who are the main players?	Onias Jason Menelaus Judas Maccabee Antiochus Greeks
What should I look for?	How God dealt with those who disregarded the divine will. Also, martyrs who would accept death rather than be disobedient
When did this take place?	The second book of Maccabees is an abridgement of a five-volume history of the Maccabees that no longer exists. It covers the period of Jewish history in Palestine from the time of the high priest Onias III (180 B.C.) to the victory of Judas Maccabee over the Greeks in 161 B.C.
Where did these events occur?	Palestine
Why was this book written?	Second Maccabees is intensely devoted to the Torah. Death, even suicide (2 Mc 14, 37–46), is preferable to violating the Torah. The reward for such loyalty for the individual is resurrection, and for the community it is the possession of Jerusalem. Despite this opposition to Hellenization, it is impossible to escape the influence of Hellenistic culture. Second Maccabees itself uses rhetorical forms that come from Greek literature.
What is the story?	The story of 2 Maccabees overlaps with that of 1 Maccabees. While 2 Maccabees does not cover as much of the history of the Maccabees as does 1 Maccabees, it is a more polished literary work. Also 2 Maccabees is less of an apology for the Hasmonean dynasty and more of an attempt to illustrate an important theological theme: God's justice in rewarding the faithful and punishing the impious. The book provides an inventory of how God dealt with both Jews and Greeks who disregarded the divine will. Its focus, however, is on those Jews who accepted death rather than be guilty of an act of disobedience. Second Maccabees highlights the death of Jewish martyrs to affect the emotions of its readers so that they may recommit themselves to faithful observance.

The Relationship between 1 and 2 Maccabees

The second book of Maccabees does not continue the history of the Jewish revolt against the Seleucid Empire but is an abridgement of a five-volume work on the Maccabees by one Jason of Cyrene (2 Mc 2, 23). This longer work has not come down to us. The unknown editor who is responsible for the present form of 2 Maccabees wished to simplify Jason's work so that readers could remember its most important features (2 Mc 2, 25). The book is not simply a digest of a much longer work. There are portions of the book that do not come from Jason but were written by the person who made the abridgement.

Second Maccabees begins its story of the Jews in Palestine with the reign of the Syrian king Seleucus IV when Onias III was the high priest and ends with the defeat of the Syrian army by Judas Maccabee. The period extends from approximately 180 to 160 B.C. The story overlaps with that in 1 Maccabees 1, 10—7, 5, with great similarity between 2 Maccabees 8–15 and 1 Maccabees 3–7.

Second Maccabees is less defensive of the Hasmonean dynasty and gives more emphasis to God's justice in rewarding the faithful and punishing both Jews and Greeks who disregard the divine will. The book focuses on those Jews who accepted death rather than be guilty of an act of disobedience.

Reading the Book

Second Maccabees begins with two letters directed to the Jewish community in Egypt, calling them to celebrate a festival in honor of the rededication of the Temple following the victory of the Maccabees over the Seleucids. Since the Torah could not mandate the celebration of the feast of Hanukkah, the leadership of the Jewish community had to take this special step to encourage its observance.

The Jewish community in Egypt built its own temple under the direction of Onias IV, the last legitimate high priest. Perhaps these letters were directed to the Jews in Egypt to keep them from forgetting their ties with Palestine. But it could be that the person responsible for the present form of 2 Maccabees added these letters to the story of the Maccabees in order to make the book into a festal scroll for Hanukkah as the book of Esther is for the Feast of Purim.

The Story of the Maccabees (2 Mc 3, 1—15, 36)

The author has a theological purpose in the way the story of the Maccabees is presented. The events of Jewish history from the time of Onias the high priest to the time of Judas Maccabee show a God who cares for the Jewish people by rewarding the faithful and punishing evildoers. The author uses a scheme first devised by the authors of the deuteronomic history of Israel, who told how Israel came to own the land under Joshua and then how Israel lost the land under its kings. Infidelity transformed a blessing into a curse.

Blessing—Sin—Punishment

1. Period of *blessing* (3, 1–40): during the time of Onias III when people observed the Torah
2. Period of *sin* (4, 1—5, 10): during the time of the high priests Jason and Menelaus when the

---

Looking at the Past

Legend, chronicle, and history are all ways of narrating the past. A *legend* is a popular story, often with a fantastic character. It may be based on an actual historical event, or it may be entirely fictitious. In the context of religious literature, legends are meant to edify rather than to convey factual information. A *chronicle* is a factual account of events in the order in which they occurred. It usually reads as a simple sequence of events, without interpretive comments. *History* or *historiography,* like a chronicle, attempts to give an accurate account of the past but includes discussions of causes and consequences. Historical writing normally involves the use of sources and the critical evaluation of evidence. Chronicles and legends, then, might serve as the source for the historian.

Hellenization is a term that describes Greek culture, ideals, and institutions that reached their peak in fifth-century B.C. when Athens came to have huge influence throughout the eastern Mediterranean. Until the time of Alexander the Great, the region was oriented culturally to the East: Assyria, Babylon, and Persia. Alexander effected a genuine cultural reorientation that lasted until the Muslim conquest in the seventh century A.D.

The city or "polis" with its marketplace *(agora)*, colonnaded streets, temples, theaters, and gymnasium was the instrument of economic prosperity, and of the spread of Hellenism as well. Throughout Palestine the Greeks remade ancient cities. Even Jerusalem was made over (1 Mc 1, 11–14).

It is not surprising that there was resistance among some Jews to Hellenization. After all, the Jews had a very traditional culture in which change occurred only gradually. There were people—especially among the upper class of Jewish society—who embraced the new cultural wave. At first the Hellenism the Jews faced was a mild type. Matters changed dramatically under the Seleucid king Antiochus IV, who imposed Hellenism upon the Jews. His policies sparked the Maccabean revolt.

Similar to 1 Maccabees, 2 Maccabees is opposed to the forced Hellenization program of Antiochus. It is intensely devoted to the Torah. Despite this opposition to Hellenism, it works in favor of the author when 2 Maccabees appeals to the emotions of its readers. The work does not hesitate to describe the death of Jewish martyrs in vivid detail. This approach is typical of Hellenistic history writing. It is impossible to escape the influence of Hellenistic culture. The miraculous episodes in 2 Maccabees are also comparable to episodes in Greek histories.

As opposed to the Greeks as 2 Maccabees is, it is not simplistic in the way it deals with Jews and Greeks. It presents some Greeks as sympathetic to the Jews. Antiochus even converts on his deathbed. The Jews do not object to the rule of the Greeks as such. The Jews can be good citizens. What they do object to are the abuses that came with Antiochus.

There comes a point when the pious must choose. With Hellenism there came a whole collection of gods and goddesses. There were even deified kings. But more subtle were the novelties in philosophy and ethics. For the pious Jew, Hellenism represented a religious ideology and practice that was completely foreign. But there was no escaping the influence of Greek culture at this time and on into the future. For example, almost 700 years later during the Byzantine period (fourth to sixth centuries A.D.) there were a few synagogues in Palestine that had decorative motifs that included a zodiac complete with the god Helios in the center of the mosaic floor.

Second Maccabees represents an earlier view that rejected any compromise with Hellenism. There are absolute values that do not allow any compromise. Even in the face of death, the righteous will choose fidelity to the Torah and be confident that such a choice is not in vain because of their belief in the resurrection.

people and the leaders violated the Torah and followed the customs of the Greeks

3. Period of *punishment* (5, 11—6, 17): Antiochus is the agent of God's judgment.

Turning Point—Blessing

1. The prayers of the people and the heroic death of the Jewish martyrs bring a change in circumstances. Although the book is aware of the victories of Judas Maccabee that ended the domination of Antiochus, it assumes that the death of the martyrs turned God's anger to mercy and made the victories possible.

2. The cycle is complete: *blessing* has returned to the Jewish community.

Another story runs parallel to this story of salvation: retribution. The enemies of the Jews come to a terrible end:

• Antiochus dies in agony (9, 8).

• The Greek who murdered Onias is himself killed (4, 38).

• The general who commanded the siege against Jerusalem is dead and his head hangs from the citadel of the city (15, 35).

• The wicked among the Jews suffer under divine judgment.

• The high priests Jason and Menelaus both come to miserable ends (5, 1–10 and 13, 7f).

The Book's Influence in Christian Theology

This section of the book has influenced the development of the notion in Christian theology that suffering can have a positive value. Suffering can be a form of divine education. God did not send suffering to destroy the Jewish people but to discipline them. God's people are never abandoned. The suffering of the innocent leads the author to affirm his belief in the resurrection of the dead (7, 9; 7, 11; 7, 14; 7, 23; 14, 46). This enables the Jewish martyrs to accept their suffering, for God will deliver the faithful despite their death at the hands of the wicked.

One of the most important texts in this book for Roman Catholic theology is 12, 42–46. The author tries to show that Judas Maccabee believed in the resurrection of the dead, because he ordered prayers and sacrifices for those who had fallen in battle. Such prayers would be useless unless Judas believed that they would rise again (12, 44). This text is sometimes used as support for the Roman Catholic belief in purgatory and the power of prayers for the living and the dead. Another important text for Roman Catholics is 2 Maccabees 15, 12–16. Here Judas Maccabee sees the prophet Jeremiah in a dream praying for the Jews and Jerusalem. Catholic tradition accepts this text as one support for the belief in the power of the intercession of the saints.

Questions for Discussion and Reflection

Group Sharing/Discussion

1. Hanukkah is a Jewish feast celebrating the rededication of the second Temple during the Maccabean revolt. Josephus calls this festival the "feast of lights." Why did Judas Maccabee mandate this celebration? Why was it called the "feast of lights"? What is the significance of Hanukkah for a pious Jew? Talk with Jews about how they celebrate Hanukkah or invite them to come to your group.

In Our Lives

1. The principle opponents of the priestly family of Hasmoneans were the Hasidim (the pious ones) who were the spiritual ancestors of the Essenes and the Pharisees. The Hasidim saw themselves as careful observers of the Law; they saw the Hasmonean high priests as illegitimate. Do you see any of their traits in the New Testament? How do they appear in modern Jewish life? What qualities are religiously attractive?

Individual/Personal Reflection/Action

1. One of the most significant texts in this book for Roman Catholic theology is 12, 42–46. Here the author wished to show that Judas Maccabee believed in the resurrection of the dead since he ordered prayers and sacrifices for those who had fallen in battle. The author concludes that such prayers would be futile unless Judas believed that they would rise again (12, 44). Take some time to meditate on the resurrection of the dead and praying for the departed.

2. Reflect upon the story of the Seven Brothers' (7, 1–42) motives for going to martyrdom. What would you say to them about their decisions?

THE WISDOM BOOKS

At a Glance

Job	A dramatic poem that treats the problem of suffering of the innocent, and of retribution.
Psalms	A collection of religious songs under the major headings of hymns, laments, and songs of thanksgiving.
Proverbs	An anthology of mostly short sayings in poetical form whose purpose is to teach wisdom for successful living.
Ecclesiastes	A treatise on the vanity, or emptiness, of all things. The book is concerned with the purpose and value of human life.
The Song of Songs	A collection of love poems full of sensuous imagery. It could be seen as a portrayal of ideal human love.
Wisdom	Oratory from the Jewish community of Alexandria about 100 years before the coming of Christ, explaining traditions and themes familiar to Judaism but reinterpreting them from the experience of living in a Greek or Hellenistic culture.
Sirach	A collection of proverbs dealing with moral instruction, written to show that real wisdom was to be found in the traditions of Israel and not in the godless philosophy of the day.

Beginning around the time of the Davidic-Solomonic monarchy (tenth century B.C.) and continuing for centuries after that, writers and thinkers in ancient Israel developed the "wisdom" tradition in their literature. This literature shows how Israel encountered God *through* human experience, not *in addition* to it. A new question was being asked: What kind of role does God play in everyday life? The answers to that question form a "guide for successful living." Since every person in every culture must struggle with the questions of life, this literature has universal appeal. This might explain why, even today, people of other religious cultures can more easily identify with the teaching of the wisdom books than with the other books found in the Bible.

Wisdom is the ability to perceive the order of the universe and to live in harmony with it. The Israelites believed that their God was the great Creator-God, the one responsible for the world and everything in it. By observing the regularity in creation, they concluded that there was some kind of order in nature itself. If they could understand how this order operated and then attune their lives with it, they would be successful and at peace.

The writers of wisdom literature used various teaching techniques such as storytelling, exhortation, warning, and questioning. They also used proverbs, riddles, parables, and metaphors to instruct, advise, and persuade. Usually there were very definite lessons they wanted to teach, so it should not surprise us to come across what appears to be "the moral of the story."

The sages were humanists; that is, they were concerned with the study of human beings and attentive to human welfare, values, and dignity. They taught that whatever benefited humanity was a good to be pursued; and whatever was harmful should be avoided. The gauge for judging the value of any undertaking was the degree of success or happiness that it brought. Success was a concrete sign of the wisdom of the person who succeeded.

Although the wise woman or man believed that there was a right way of behaving, there was no insistence on a rigid standard that would fit everybody. Each case was unique. The wise person was the one who had a store of wisdom gained from experience and who knew which way of behaving was appropriate for each

situation. The idea that the good shall be rewarded and the evil shall be punished undergirds most of the wisdom literature.

The wisdom tradition, unlike the Pentateuch, Historical books, and Prophetic books, does not refer to central aspects of the religious history of Israel, such as the Exodus; to religious practice as centered in the Temple; or to central concepts, such as covenant. It is more concerned with the human ability to discern pattern and stability in ordinary life, and to develop a religious understanding on that basis.

Israel's wisdom tradition did not develop in a vacuum. It was part of a much broader movement within the Near Eastern world. There is a remarkable similarity between the biblical wisdom material and some Egyptian, Mesopotamian, and Canaanite texts. The non-Israelite texts are significantly older, and more likely than not, Israel borrowed from its neighbors and adapted and reinterpreted when necessary.

JOB READING GUIDE

At a Glance

Who are the main players?	Eliphaz Bildad Zophar Job Elihu the LORD
What should I look for?	Job's struggle with suffering is a universal and perennial problem. The universal appeal stems from the nature of the questions posed by the tormented Job.
When did this take place?	Evidence from the book itself is often given in support of a pre-exilic dating (seventh century B.C.), but there is no agreement regarding when it was written. Job is not a record of actual events, but a dramatic, philosophical dialogue.
Where did these events occur?	No location is given. Job's complaints are reminiscent of the laments of Jeremiah, and some consider the book an outcry against the destruction of Jerusalem and deportation.
Why was this written?	Job as wisdom literature asks the question: What kind of role does God play in everyday life, specifically in the sufferings of life? The innocent, good Job's sufferings will shed light on the meaning of suffering and the integrity of God.
What is the story?	Job, a good and upright man, loses his considerable wealth, health and family. Although he questions the cause of his suffering, and his supposed friends insist that he must have brought it on himself, he remains righteous and refuses to curse God.

About the Book of Job

Job's struggle with suffering is a universal problem. There are older Near Eastern accounts of innocent sufferers that may have influenced the author of Job. The names and places of origin of Job's three visitors suggest foreign influence. Still, whatever may have originated elsewhere has been used here with Israelite theology in mind. Israel's wisdom tradition is clearly in accord with its Yahwistic faith. It may not focus on specifics of religion, but it is highly ethical, fundamentally monotheistic, and, at times, equates wisdom with fidelity to the Law of Israel.

When it Was Written

There is no agreement about the book's date, its place of origin, or the source of some of its parts. There is not even total agreement as to its principal theme. Evidence from the book itself is often given in support of a date before the Babylonian Exile (seventh century B.C.). Job's complaints are reminiscent of the lamentations of Jeremiah, and some consider the book an outcry of impending destruction of Jerusalem and deportation into exile. However, similarities with the theology and style of Deutero-Isaiah (the portion of Isaiah beginning with chapter 40) seem to tip the scale in favor of it being after the exile (sixth to fifth century B.C.). It certainly appeared before the third century B.C. when "Satan" appears as a proper name (1 Chr 21, 1) instead of the designated role of an adversary in a court of justice, as is found in the book of Job.

Like most pieces of ancient literature, Job is a composite rather than the work of a single author. It appears to be a prose folktale (1, 1—2, 13; 42, 7–17) into which extensive poetic speeches (3, 1—42, 6) have been inserted. Even within the speeches, we can detect units believed to have originated from someone other than the principal author. But regardless of when or from whom these different sections originated, they all belong to the final form, and it is this final form that has been handed down to us as sacred Scripture. Therefore we read it as a unified literary work.

The universal appeal of the book of Job stems from the nature of the questions by this innocent man. Who has not struggled with the dilemma of bewildering suffering? Who has not cried out to God, or at least wondered, "Why?"

As the drama unfolds, each section of the book of Job has its own dynamic. From the beginning, Job's innocence is established beyond any doubt and we see who is responsible for Job's misfortune. God permits this righteous man to suffer in order to test the quality of his integrity. Job never knows this, nor do his visitors. It is important that the reader know what took place in heaven as we listen to the theological debate that follows. By the many arguments of the poetic speeches adding layer upon layer of accusation and rebuttal, the author brings us into the very midst of the impasse of this pointless debate. Only God can resolve this.

The Literary Style

The simple understanding of the story about the innocent man stricken and rewarded in the end for his faithfulness does not accurately represent the story of Job. It is merely the plot of the folktale that frames the poetic dialogues that compose the principal part of the book. The more we understand how the form of the book works, the more we will discover the message within it.

In the following ways, the literary style of the author contributes to the development of the book's message.

1. *The dialogues:* Speeches in Hebrew poetic form. Each time Job cries out about his sorry state, either Eliphaz, Bildad, or Zophar offer counsel or attempt to convince him of his error. The cycles of speech proceed in orderly fashion.

2. *The use of nature as means of instruction:* This is characteristic of the wisdom tradition. While it occurs throughout the entire book, nowhere else does it have the effect it does in God's speeches. By not directly addressing Job's question, God does not ignore Job's concerns. This is the way the author uses nature as a teaching tool.

3. *Poetry:* The kind found within the book is unlike classical or contemporary poetry. There is no rhyme and the rhythm follows tonal patterns that are lost when the original Hebrew is translated.

4. *Lawsuit:* Again and again Job demands that God meet him in court where his case will be tried and he will be found innocent (23, 2–4).

5. *Lament:* Job cries out to God in complaint and laments the day of his birth (3, 1–10) and life

itself (10, 1–7), and he pleads for help (13, 20–27).

The Message

While the book of Job is a poetic narrative, it is also a theological statement made up of several themes. The way we understand this theology will influence the way we perceive the arguments in this book. The themes here are presented not in any order of importance but as they appear in the book.

Reward and Punishment

The belief that goodness should be rewarded and evil punished undergirds most of the wisdom literature. This theory probably arose out of life experience itself. When in the natural course of events it does not happen, someone in authority steps in to see that justice is done. We need this in order to live with a certain degree of security.

Job's real agony, however, lies in the incomprehensibility of his situation. Because he is suffering, it is assumed that he must have sinned. Because his suffering is so intense, his sin must be great. Job's visitors argue this point and try to persuade him to repent because they assume he is guilty. This same kind of thinking prompted the apostles to ask Jesus whether it was the sin of the blind man or of his parents that resulted in the man's blindness (see Jn 9, 2).

Job holds to this theory as well, but from a different point of view. Since he has done nothing to deserve such misfortune, he blames God. He believes that it is God who usually decides who will be rewarded and who will be punished and accomplishes this through the laws set at creation. When these laws fail, the tradition of Israel claims that God intervenes to enforce justice. So from Job's point of view, God has failed to do this in his case.

Since the speeches argue in defense of or in opposition to Job's innocence, one would think that when God finally does thunder from the whirlwind, everything would become clear. But the question of justice is not addressed. Instead, the issue is the creative wisdom and power of God. This is not an avoidance of the question. Remember that God is cast in the role of a wisdom teacher who asks rhetorical questions and makes reference to the natural world in order to

Theodicy, from the Greek for "justifying God," is the name given to our attempt to explain the problem of evil, while at the same time maintaining the belief that God is a moral creator who is in control and who loves those who suffer. For the wisdom tradition, theodicy was of particular importance because the standard view of wisdom was that right behavior in life generally led to prosperity. The book of Job argues against this standard view.

make a point. God leads Job to see that just as there is much in nature he cannot understand, so there is much in human experience that is beyond him. In this way God reveals the inadequacy of the theory of retribution. Happiness and success are not rewards for righteous living, nor are grief and failure punishment for unfaithfulness. Suffering is not a sure sign of alienation from God.

Once we are convinced that certain suffering is undeserved, we are faced with a very troubling question: Why does God seem to allow injustice to occur? If Job did not believe God is a moral God, the question of evil would take a totally different turn. If God is not righteous then Job's suffering might be just as difficult to bear but would not be the puzzle it is. He would know that he could not depend on God. Such a view was foreign to Israel's faith. Job's counselors never question God's integrity, and Job does so only reluctantly and at the risk of falsely accusing God.

Another view holds that God could be moral but not able to control evil completely. This is the theory held by some thinkers concerning the Holocaust when they cannot explain why God allowed so many millions of innocent people to be exterminated during World War II. This thinking is not found in the Bible. Israel believed its God was the undisputed creator (see Is 45, 7; Am 3, 6).

Some may think God is both moral and omnipotent but unconcerned about simple people. Surely the Almighty has more important things to do than worry about the fortunes or misfortunes of one person. The traditions of Israel contradict this notion as well. From the stories of their ancestors we see God portrayed as attentive to the most personal needs of the individual (see Genesis). This memory causes Job to lament his present situation. How could God, who cared for him in earlier years, turn against him now?

While theodicy is not an issue for Job or for his visitors, it is of major importance for the author of the book, who depicts God as all-powerful and provident and a God of unchallenged goodness. At the end, the question of suffering may be left unanswered but the integrity of God is no longer questioned.

Reward or Vindication

In a very real sense, the drama of the book stems from Satan's challenge found in 1, 9: "Is it for nothing that Job is God-fearing?" It is easy to be loyal to God when things are going right and he is happy with life. Take away these good things, and Job will not only give up his way of integrity, he will actually curse God. God takes the dare.

Twice Job is assaulted and he neither curses God nor veers from his attachment to God. His confidence has not been shaken and he actually praises God. It is probable that he did expect to be blessed for being faithful. So the question remains: Was Job faithful for the sake of reward or was his piety really disinterested?

Job's laments and pleading show that he does not look for reward; he wants vindication. He is not concerned about possessions; he insists that his integrity be acknowledged. When he finally understands the lesson God set out to teach him, he is silent and seems content with his new insights. Now we know that the depth of Job's piety is based on his relationship with God, not on some promise of reward.

We must remember that at that time Israelites did not have a clear idea of reward or punishment in an afterlife, as Christian theology teaches. If justice was not received in this life, they had no hope at all for retribution.

Suffering

Although the customary way of understanding suffering was a punishment for sin, the book of Job does provide other explanations for it. The prologue itself tells us that God allowed Job's misfortunes to befall him so that Job's integrity might be tested (1, 11; 2, 3–5). In the book of Genesis "God put Abraham to the test" (Gn 22, 1) and told him to sacrifice his son Isaac. The difference, however, is that in the end Abraham was told that he had been tested while Job never knows about God's dealings with Satan.

Suffering is sometimes seen as a source of moral discipline, a warning against sin and a defense against pride and self-satisfaction.

Other interpretations include suffering endured for others (the Suffering Servant: Is 52, 13—53, 12); undergoing purification (Ps 66, 10); a necessary way of accomplishing the will of God (Joseph in Egypt: Gn 50, 20). Only the first two explanations are found in the book of Job.

The ancient Near East offered another explanation referred to as the "curse of the evil deed." It claimed that those who engage in evil infect themselves in the process: "He who digs a pit falls into it" (Prv 26, 27). God does not intervene to punish.

The writers appear to be more interested in the reason and purpose of suffering than in its origin. They offer temporary explanations to strengthen people in their struggle. Circumstances change and the advice might cease to be appropriate, which is precisely the case in Job. No one seems able to offer him an adequate explanation for his suffering.

God in the Life of Humans

Up to this point the themes have focused our attention on Job. Now we turn our gaze toward God. In his complaints, Job characterizes God as powerful and oppressive when near and unconcerned when at a distance. Job's companions describe God as a prosecuting judge. But the image unveiled in the speeches of the LORD is quite different.

God is indeed powerful, but it is a wondrous, awe-inspiring power. It is true that God is transcendent, but this does not prevent God from being attentive to the mountain goat about to kid (see 39, 1). Finally, God does not assume the role of divine judge to find Job guilty. Instead, God as the divine teacher leads Job to new horizons of understanding. Now Job understands that he has been treading on mystery—"things too wonderful for me" (42, 3). This provident yet mysterious God of creation is the same God who works in the life of each of us yet remains a mystery.

The enigma of the suffering of good people and the good fortune of the wicked was one addressed by Israelite literature, both in the Psalms and in other wisdom texts. Distinctive to the book of Job is the way it situates these issues. The book is neither a treatise on innocent suffering, as often supposed, nor an apology for God's justice in the face of inexplicable human suffering. Rather, the principal theological issue that the book raises is, ironically, the question posed by the adversary in the divine council (see 1, 9): Will mortals be religious apart from rewards and punishment or do they act as they should simply because God will reward or punish them accordingly? As the dialogue develops, however, the questions of divine justice that torture Job's mind are not satisfactorily met by the arguments of his friends. Yet when God answers Job, it is neither as the friends have imagined God would speak nor as Job had hoped God would answer him.

The meaning and significance of the divine speeches continue to be among the most debated issues in the book. Some interpret the speeches as a repudiation of a human's right to question God. Others understand them as a necessary correction to Job's too-limited understanding of the world as a place where all suffering can be reduced to legal categories of guilt and innocence. All agree that the extraordinary beauty of the poetry is part of its meaning. Perhaps the very elusiveness of the divine speeches implies that no answer from God to Job's questions can satisfy the human intellect. Yet the ending suggests that there is a resolution to be found in the depth of a pious life lived before a mysterious God.

Questions for Discussion and Reflection
Group Sharing/Discussion

1. What are the most important lessons you can find in this book of the Bible?

2. In this literary tradition of the wisdom writings, Israel claimed that it encountered God *through* human experience, not *in addition* to it. Explain how Job is an example of this. How do you believe you encounter God in your human experience?

3. Israel's wisdom tradition is clearly in accord with its Yahwistic faith. It may not focus on specifics of religion, but it is highly ethical and

fundamentally monotheistic, or believes in only one God. How is the faith of Christians today similar or different?

In Our Lives

1. Job remained faithful to God but did not hesitate to complain to God. He certainly can be a model to us of having the courage to remain faithful, but also a model of staying in conversation with God. Prayer is described as talking with God. We tell our joys and our troubles to our best friend, even lamenting, although not blaming them. How is Job's relationship with God similar or different to your relationship with God?

2. Some of Job's "friends" were hardly helpful when they came to visit him. There are people in pain of different kinds today who do not have anyone to even come visit them. How does our community look out for those who suffer alone? Sometimes, as in chapter 2, 11–13 they just need someone to sit with them. How does our parish reach out to families at times of loss? What more might we consider doing?

3. Job's visitors accused him unjustly. They assumed he had sinned and was being punished. It can be hard to put aside our prejudices and assumptions about people or things we feel strongly about—issues in politics or Church or among our family members. Some people suggest checking yourself out by "arguing with yourself" from the opposite point of view as yours. When would it be helpful to you to put aside your prejudices and be more open? What will help you to do this?

Individual/Personal Reflection/Action

1. A young, talented priest with cancer was asked by a friend why was this happening to him of all people; his immediate response was, "Why not me?" Job's question was the opposite, "Why me?" How would you respond to each of those questions?

2. If you are suffering, have the courage and humility to ask for help, from God and from your friends. If you see people who are suffering, be the friend to them that Job could have used.

3. Spend a few minutes each morning or evening this week just talking with God, telling God what is on your mind and in your heart in a familiar way, such as Job did.

PSALMS READING GUIDE

At a Glance

Who are the main players?	David Korah Asaph
What should I look for?	Psalms are prayerful responses to life experiences. Types of psalms are mainly classified as lament, hymns, and thanksgiving, also wisdom poems and royal psalms. The fact that the psalmist cries out to God demonstrates Israel's belief that God has the power and will to deliver the nation in present distress.
When did this take place?	Different times. Depending upon the dating of a particular psalm, the events could have been the fall of the northern kingdom (c. 722 B.C.), the Babylonian Exile (c. 586 B.C.), or the Maccabean conflict (107 B.C.).
Where did these events occur?	In general in Israel. Our present book of Psalms was composed from earlier collections. Some are attributed to David in Jerusalem. Several in the second and third books are ascribed to Korah and Asaph, two guilds of Temple singers during the period of the second Temple.
Why was this book written?	The expressions of rich piety found in the book of Psalms give us an insight into the theology in ancient Israel. The portrait of God found in the Psalms draws together all the divine faces found in the rest of Israel's tradition. For Jews and Christians the Psalms are much more than profoundly moving poetry. They are voices of our respective faiths.
What is the story?	The Psalms reveal Israel's understanding of and relationship with God. For the early Christians the Psalms were not only prayer but contained statements of faith, statements that found fulfillment in the person and mission of Jesus.

The book of Psalms, also known as the Psalter, is a collection of poetical prayers. Its title in Hebrew, "tehillim," means "praises," and the English title comes from the Greek word "psalmos," meaning a song that is accompanied by a stringed instrument. The Psalter is divided into books, each of which ends with a short hymn of praise called a doxology:

The First Book:
  Psalms 1–41 end with a doxology in 41, 14
The Second Book:
  Psalms 42–72 end with 72, 18f
The Third Book:
  Psalms 73–89 end with 89, 53
The Fourth Book: Psalms 90–106 end with
  106, 48
The Fifth Book:
  Psalms 107–150 end with an entire
  psalm of praise (Ps 150)

Who Wrote the Psalms?

Evidence within the book of Psalms itself indicates that it is made up of earlier collections. Several psalms, found principally in the first book, are attributed to David. (This may account for the popular but probably not historically accurate tradition that David himself wrote most of the psalms.) Several psalms in the second and third books are ascribed to Korah and Asaph, the two great guilds of Temple singers during the period of the second Temple (see 1 Chr 6, 33f; 25, 1f), a period that began around 400 B.C., six centuries after David's time. The fourth book also has possible references to the destruction of Jerusalem (587 or 586 B.C.); for instance, Psalm 102, 13–22 fits with the time when Jerusalem lay in ruins and was about to be restored. Finally, the fifth book is made up of a number of Songs of Ascent—probably songs sung by those on pilgrimage to Jerusalem—and psalms of praise known as the Hallel ("praise") or Hallelujah collection. These groupings may have been the original collections around which other psalms clustered.

Types of Psalms

The three major categories are: lament, hymn, and thanksgiving. There are also royal psalms, wisdom psalms, and some that might fit into more than one category.

Laments

The most common type of psalm is the lament. Nearly a third of the psalms belong to this category. Depending on who the speaker is, they are further classified as either community or individual laments.

Community Laments (Pss 12, 14, 44, 53, 58, 60, 74, 79, 80, 83, 85, 90, 94, 106, 123, 126, 137)

• Apparently part of Israel's Temple liturgies
• Used when people were gathered to fast and pray because of national humiliation or distress
• Israel's rivals were viewed as opposed to the LORD
• A recital of the former deeds that God accomplished in the history of the nation
• Purpose: to remind God of past favors and encourage God to grant new ones
• Used to remind people of God's earlier blessings and to instill confidence in their hearts

Individual Laments (Pss 3–7, 13, 17, 22, 25–28, 31, 35, 36, 38–40, 42, 43, 51, 52, 54–57, 59, 61, 63, 64, 67–71, 77, 86, 88, 102, 109, 120, 130, 140–143)

• Prayerful responses to personal misfortunes such as illness or persecution
• An integral part of personal liturgical devotion
• Frequently suffering people went to the Temple or a shrine to request help or deliverance

The usual structure of the lament is an introduction, a plea for deliverance from misfortune, praise of God or an expression of confidence that God will come to the rescue, and a vow to perform an act of worship in gratitude for God's help. Some laments include an acknowledgment of guilt or a claim of innocence. Often the psalmist hurls a curse at those responsible for the situation that brought about the lament.

Hymns

The hymn is a song praising God and can be either an individual's prayer or for the whole community to use in the liturgies of Israel's major festivals.

Hymns of Praise (Pss 8, 19, 29, 33, 100, 103, 104, 111, 113, 114, 117, 135, 136, 145–150)

The structure of a hymn is quite simple. It begins with a call to praise, which suggests that this type of psalm originated in a community setting, followed by an account of the wondrous acts of God, and ends with a repetition of the initial call to praise, some expression of exaltation of God, and a plea for God's blessing.

Hymns of the Lord's Kingship (Pss 47, 93, 96–99)

This is a distinct group among the psalms. Their focus is the LORD, the universal king. They were a way that perhaps helped the Israelites deal with the fact that creation is not always friendly and life does not always favor us. Nonetheless, the LORD was truly in charge.

The Songs of Zion (Pss 46, 48, 76, 84, 87, 122)

These psalms extol Zion as God's holy mountain and Jerusalem as the city God chose to inhabit. We are not certain about the setting at which the songs of Zion were sung.

Thanksgiving

Thanksgiving psalms are similar to hymns in that they praise the marvelous works of God. Like the laments, they were probably part of the liturgy or personal prayer life of the people and were used when thanksgiving was in order. It is difficult to classify these psalms because expressions of confidence and gratitude are also often found within the laments. There are some psalms that might be considered explicit psalms of thanksgiving:
• Communal Psalms: Pss 115, 125, 129
• Individual Psalms: Pss 11, 16, 23, 62, 91, 121, 131
• Psalms of General Thanksgiving: Pss 9, 10, 30, 32, 41, 116, 138

Royal Psalms

Israel was a nation that perceived its king as the representative of the whole people before God and as God's special envoy for the people. This assured the king of the special place he enjoyed. Various occasions in the king's life form the settings for these psalms: coronation hymns (Pss 2, 72, 101, 110), an anniversary hymn (Ps 132), a royal wedding song (Ps 45), petitions on behalf of the warrior-king (Pss 20, 144), and prayers of thanksgiving for his success (Pss 18, 21). These psalms are often referred to as "messianic psalms," since "messiah" means "anointed one" and that is what a king was. They take on new meaning in the Christian tradition when they are applied to Jesus, the supreme "anointed one" of God.

Wisdom Poems

These psalms (1, 37, 49, 73, 112, 119, 127, 128) call people to listen and learn, rather than to pray. They are, in general, concerned with the problem of evil, the suffering of the righteous, and the justice of God. These psalms use the language and imagery of the wisdom tradition.

The sages of ancient Israel used several techniques that helped people learn. Some of these appear in the wisdom psalms. One of the most popular was the acrostic arrangement. In this form the letters of the alphabet in order determine the beginning letter of the first word of each successive line (Ps 37, 111, and 119). Because they follow this pattern, some commentators include them as wisdom poems rather than hymns (Ps 145), laments (Ps 125), or thanksgiving psalms (Pss 9, 10, 34).

Various Psalms

These are other psalms, like Songs of Ascent (going up to the Temple) used during pilgrimage (Pss 120–134) or those for processions around Jerusalem (Pss 15, 24, 95). Since people frequently came to the Temple or to a shrine in search of some word from the LORD, some psalms trace their origin to a style of prophetic speech.

A few psalms do not fit into any of the categories we have mentioned. They are either stories about the feats of the LORD (Pss 78, 105), combinations of other psalm forms (Pss 108, 133, 139), or general liturgical songs (Ps 134).

The Theology in the Psalms

The expressions of piety found within the book of Psalms give us insight into the theology of ancient Israel.

The God of Israel

The portrait of God sketched in the Psalms draws together all of the divine traits found in the rest of the Israelite tradition. This God is

• the creator of the universe (Ps 8, 4)
• the source of all life (Ps 36, 10)
• enthroned in heaven (Ps 47, 6)
• yet dwelling in Jerusalem (Ps 76, 3)
• Israel's exclusive liberator (Ps 66, 6)
• yet gradually seen as concerned for all people (Ps 117)

This majestic God inspires both fear (Ps 89, 8) and confidence (Ps 23) and is demanding (Ps 75, 83) as well as forgiving (Ps 85, 3). Above everything God is "merciful and gracious . . . slow to anger and abounding in kindness" (Ps 103, 8; see Ps 86, 5). The LORD is the "covenant partner." Everything that is important to Israel flows from this perception of God.

The Image of God

The human person is held in high regard in the Psalms. Honored as the culmination of creation, humanity is given responsibility for the other living creatures of the earth (Ps 8; see Gn 1). The psalmist marvels at this singular work of divine artistry.

Why should God be personally committed to such an insignificant being (Pss 8, 5; 144, 3f)? As extraordinary as they are, humans live a fleeting life (Ps 39, 5f) and then perish like flowers in the field (Ps 103, 15f). At the time the Psalms were written, Israelite religion did not include any clear notion of life after death. Human dignity was related to life in this world. In the Psalms

• God fully knows what human beings are, and they are totally dependent on God (Ps 139)
• God provides for their basic needs (Ps 65, 10–14) and protects them from harm (Ps 121)
• God is the guardian of the poor and the afflicted (Ps 40, 18), defenseless widows and orphans (Ps 68, 6), and the *anawim* or lowly (Ps 147, 6)

The Piety of the Psalmist

The psalms generally speak *to* God rather than *about* God, but it is a particular kind of God that the psalms address. We can learn much about God by seeing how God is spoken to, and what the psalms expect of God. It will be helpful to return to the classifications (hymns, laments, thanksgiving, etc.) to look at the piety of Israel contained in the Psalms.

Praise

Praise is the primary nature of psalms, and hymns of praise are the most common type of psalm in the Psalter. Most psalms are, in one way or another, aimed at praising God—for his power and assistance, for his creation of the world, and for his past acts of deliverance to Israel. Often the praise comes after the psalmist has prayed for help from sickness or enemies (the typical subject of complaints) and that prayer has been answered. As part of such a complaint, the psalmist promises to praise God when God has delivered from trouble one who prays. Thanksgiving for God's help is another form of praise. According to the outlook of Psalms, the main religious function of human beings is to offer praise to God, to proclaim God's greatness throughout the world. Thus, the Psalms encourage others to praise God, and they envision a world in which everyone and everything will praise God. This implies a relationship between God and humans, another important dimension of Psalms. God's character is one that hears prayers and responds. Worst of all is when he "hides his face" and refuses to pay attention to the psalmist, because this puts into question the power of prayer, one primary underlying assumption in the book of Psalms.

The Songs of Zion

"Zion" seems originally to have meant the fortified hill that was the basis of the city of Jerusalem, originally a Canaanite settlement. It came to mean both Jerusalem as the religious center of Israelite life and the people who lived there. These songs contain some of the same images as the psalms in honor of the LORD King. In ancient Canaanite mythology, after the forces of evil have been conquered, a palace is built for the victor on the summit of the highest mountain, as was done by Solomon, David's son, after David conquered Jerusalem and made it his capital city.

From this summit the hero holds sway over the entire universe.

Israel revered Zion as this sacred mountain and revered the Temple as the palace of the victorious creator God. God's creative power is now associated with the nation and, because of the close connection between Zion and David, specifically with the monarchy.

In these psalms God is praised as totally committed to the welfare of Israel. God is not distant from the people but lives in their midst, allowing them to approach the divine presence mysteriously dwelling in the Temple. Other nations were also allowed to worship the LORD in this holy place.

Grief, Fear, Repentance, and Confidence

The conviction of God's special love and care led Israel to hope for security in a hostile world and a life of serenity and prosperity. This state of affairs is what the Bible refers to as *shalom,* or peace. Psalms of lament grew out of the absence of such peace.

Community laments apply to some national disaster that has already taken place. Depending on the date of the particular psalm, this calamity could have been:

• the fall of the northern kingdom of Israel (about 722 B.C.)

• the destruction of Jerusalem and the Babylonian Exile (about 586 B.C.)

• the desecration of the second Temple and the Maccabean revolt (about 167–164 B.C.)

The fact that the psalmist cries out to God indicates that Israel's belief in God's saving power is based on former saving events in the history of the people (Pss 44, 2–4; 74, 2; 83, 10). Even as the people cried out in complaint, they were proclaiming God's all-encompassing power and declaring God's continued concern for them based on covenantal promises.

Gratitude

Gratitude is obvious in the Psalms. The structure and content of thanksgiving psalms resemble those of the hymn. First the worshiper praises God's goodness and only then offers thanks.

National Loyalty

Since the king was perceived as the representative of the whole people before God and as God's special envoy, loyalty to the king and to the nation was considered an act of devotion to God.

An Understanding Heart

The wisdom psalms generally do not address God but are usually directed toward the community. The piety of the psalmist is shown in the way themes are presented.

The problem of evil, the suffering of the innocent, and the justice of God are all facets of the same issue: the right order of the universe. Evil that is clearly not a punishment for wrongdoing can challenge the sovereignty of God over creation. God either cannot repress evil or is unwilling to do so. While Job and Ecclesiastes live with the unanswered question of innocent suffering, the wisdom psalms do not challenge the prevailing situation. They presume that the suffering of the righteous is due to some legitimate purpose, which God will reveal at the appropriate time (see 1 Kgs 3, 10–12).

Enthusiasm, Humility, and Faithfulness

We can see these characteristics in the processional psalms, which invite the observant Israelite to participate with heart and soul in various liturgical celebrations. During the three "pilgrim feasts"—Passover or Unleavened Bread, Pentecost or Feast of Weeks, and Sukkoth or the Feast of Tabernacles—people traveled to Jerusalem, singing psalms as they approached the city. There were shouts of profound joy as well as humble acknowledgments of the need for pure hearts when approaching the holy city and the Temple of the LORD.

Natural Creation

The Psalms reveal a special regard for creation as the handiwork of God (Ps 104). This view

> **S**heol The Psalms say very little about life beyond the grave, but they frequently mention a shadowy existence known as *Sheol* (Ps 49, 141). This was a place of neither reward nor punishment, but merely of darkness and dust, the abode of the dead. While Israel did not have a clear idea of a life after death, it entertained the possibility that the dead did not cease to exist.

does not see nature itself as divine, or its mysterious powers as manifestations of many different gods, but rather shows nature to be a fellow creature along with humankind. God is revealed in the thunderstorm (Ps 29) and in the design of the natural world (Ps 65, 7), where creation is no longer seen as a rival for the homage of the people but as a partner in the praise of God (Ps 148).

The Future

Ancient Israel was interested in both the future of the nation and the fate of the individual. The positive view it takes on this issue of *eschatology* stems from its faith in the goodness of God. Despite the struggles of attempting to live in a quarrelsome world, Israel believed that the final victory would be the LORD's. Individuals, too, clung to the conviction that God would right all wrongs and that they would enjoy the happiness that was their due.

An earlier theology taught that reward and punishment would be worked out in the community or down through the generations. But this theory was challenged when the wicked prospered, and even more when Jerusalem and the Temple were destroyed, leaving future generations without a place in which God could vindicate their trust. In response, the psalmist claimed that such prosperity would not last and the upright should not envy sinners (Ps 37, 2). Still, the apparently peaceful death of the prosperous wicked and the suffering of the righteous remained an unresolved problem.

The Psalms and the New Testament

It is clear that the early Christian community did not tend to distinguish between explicit theological statements on one hand and prayer on the other. For them, the Psalms were not only prayer but also contained important statements of faith, statements that found their fulfillment in the person and mission of Jesus (see Lk 24, 44). The New Testament cites various psalms. Five seem to be referred to more than the rest:

• The messianic psalms 2 and 110: cited in discussions of Jesus' Messianic preeminence (Acts 13, 33 and Heb 1, 5)

• The individual laments 22 and 69: used in descriptions of Jesus' passion and death, suggesting that the psalmist was foretelling Jesus' suffering

• The communal thanksgiving Psalm 118: speaks of the rejected stone that becomes the cornerstone (v. 22; see Mt 21, 42) and the blessedness of the one who comes in the name of the LORD (v. 26; see Mk 11, 9)

The Psalms Today

Most people are acquainted with the Psalms as they are used in the liturgy and the prayer life of the Church. Others may be more familiar through personal prayer and private devotion.

The Psalms are some of the most beautiful poetry that the human spirit has created. One need not be familiar with the historical situations from which the Psalms originated in order to appreciate them. Like all classic poetry they speak to every culture and every age. We may not come to the Psalms with hearts filled with praise, thanksgiving, or grief, but the world mirrored there relates to our own. We know that world, or at least we sense that we should know it, and we cry out with praise, thanksgiving, or grief. This poetic imagery can become a starting point of meditation on the Psalms.

For Jews and Christians the Psalms are the voice of their respective faith. Liturgy is not merely a celebration of some past event. It is an enactment through which promises and claims that were made in the past become present realities. Now these are *our* sentiments; this is *our* prayer.

Questions for Discussion and Reflection

Group Sharing/Discussion

1. Allow time for each person in your group to choose a favorite psalm. Take turns reading them aloud and tell why you chose what you did.

2. Sheol is mentioned many times in the Psalms, such as Psalms 49 and 141, as the shadowy place where all the dead are. How does this compare with your own idea of heaven?

3. Lament, hymn and thanksgiving. Divide into three subgroups and have each choose a lament, a hymn, or a thanksgiving psalm. Before sharing it with the entire group, explain its meaning or significance to your group.

4. How would you describe this book of the Bible to someone who has never been exposed to it?

In Our Lives

1. Right after the first scripture reading at every Mass, we pray a psalm in community, so we hear many psalms over the three-year liturgical cycle. How will this study of the Psalms help you pray them better at Mass?

2. As we praise God for the splendor of creation and acknowledge it is God's gift to us, we are moved to profound respect for the world of which we are a part. The hymns of praise can instill in us a sense of responsibility to care for God's creation. What are ways in our own town or community that we can better care for the treasure of God's gift of the environment?

3. The songs of Zion honor the mountain as the dwelling place of God to which all nations are invited. The LORD is not in some distant, remote place, inaccessible to people, but in the midst of people, approachable, even inviting. Think of times you are aware of the LORD's presence. What would help you feel that God is inviting and approachable?

Individual/Personal Reflection/Action

1. Jesus prayed the Psalms at the last supper, and on the cross he prayed Psalm 22. The apostles and early Christians also used the Psalms as prayers. Commit yourself to spending a few minutes each day reading or praying one of the psalms.

2. Psalms of thanksgiving help us remember that whatever we enjoy has come to us from the hand of a gracious God and we would do well to be as generous with these gifts toward others as God has been toward us. Choose one concrete way you can put your generosity into action.

3. Solidarity with those who suffer is one way to enter into the world of the laments. As we share their suffering, their prayer becomes our own. Laments can strengthen us in our commitments to justice and peace. Learn about the peace efforts of our church and other religious organizations.

PROVERBS READING GUIDE

At a Glance

Who are the main players?	Solomon Hezekiah
What should I look for?	The Hebrew word translated as "proverb" embraces a broad category of literary forms: oracle (Nm 23, 7); discourse (Jb 29, 1); parable (Ps 78, 2); taunt-song (Is 14, 4). In each case there is a lesson to be learned. Proverbs describe how things work. Their purpose is not to indoctrinate, but to educate. They are not precepts that call for obedience, but adages that invite prudent response. The book of Proverbs clearly insists on the importance of living an ethical life. The ethics it promotes, however, issue from reflection on life rather than from conformity to Law.
When did this take place?	Although there is not enough information to reconstruct accurately its historical period, the Proverbs attests to both Hezekiah's influence and Solomon's reputation.
Where did these events occur?	Israel
Why was this book written?	Proverbs is probably the biblical book that best characterizes the wisdom tradition. It appears to be the "guide for successful living" referred to in the introduction. Its primary purpose is to teach wisdom.
What is the story?	It makes its appeal to various groups of people in different walks of life. It exhorts children (not necessarily or only young children) to heed the teaching of their parents (1, 8), and it directs citizens to act with respect toward the king (16, 10–15). It warns young men of the dangers of undisciplined living (5, 1–14; 23, 29–35), and it offers a portrait of the model wife for women to emulate (31, 10–31).

Introduction

The book of Proverbs is an anthology—a collection of instructions plus speeches of wisdom (chs 1–9), two large collections of two-line sayings (chs 10–22 and 25–29), a booklet of counsels (22, 17—24, 34), and some poems (chs 30–31). The two chief literary types represented in the book are the instruction or lecture and the proverb or pithy saying. The instructional passages are examples of the instruction used in Mesopotamia, but especially favored in Egypt. In a typical instruction, a king, high official, or father instructs his son (or disciple or successor) how to live so as to enjoy the blessings of life and avoid unnecessary trouble. Despite their practical and common-sense approach, instructions were thoroughly religious, for they were written in the assumption that the world yields its blessings to those who respect the gods and direct their lives in accord with the order and

rhythms of the divinely fashioned universe. The second type, the saying or proverb, was also very common in the ancient Near East. The two-line proverbs of Proverbs are broader than the modern proverb, which in one definition is "a concise statement of an apparent truth." Some verses in Proverbs are proverbs in this sense, but there are also witty sayings, paradoxes, and riddles. The sayings are hard to translate. In their original language, however, the sayings are incisive and witty, provoking readers to take a fresh look at life.

The universal truths of Proverbs remain relevant today. Proverbs proclaims that God's world is good, yielding its full blessings only to those who seek wisdom, do justice, and revere God. To those, however, who do not listen to the wisdom God has placed in the world and who are hostile to their neighbor, the world will prove a dangerous place: Evil comes back upon the wicked. The virtues of wisdom, justice, and piety are acquired through discipline, a process requiring sincerity, persistence, and openness to those more experienced. The book declares that right, wise, and reverent conduct is the only way to happiness, which God is invited to grant as a gift.

The book is difficult for some modern readers to enjoy. Some find the instructions without content and the sayings trite. It must be remembered that the instructions of chs 1–9 are concerned with forming character—developing an open-hearted person who is faithful to the basic relationships of life (God, spouse, household, and neighbors) and who rejects easy compromises. They contain traditional insights that help us to grow in wisdom as we decode and ponder them.

Outline of the Book of Proverbs

1–9	Collection of wisdom speeches and instructions
10, 1—22, 16	Proverbs of Solomon
22, 17—24, 22	The words of the wise
24, 23–34	Appendix to words of the wise
25–29	Proverbs of Solomon edited by Hezekiah's scribes
30, 10–14	The words of Agur
30, 15–33	Numerical sayings
31, 1–9	The words of Lemuel king of Massa
31, 10–31	Praise of the capable wife

Who Wrote Proverbs?

That question is vigorously debated. Some believe the sayings and instructions originated with scribes in the royal court (or a scribal school), whereas others believe the materials originated with tribal elders instructing the young in ancestral traditions and customs, the material being written down later by scribes. Much material may be ultimately of folk origin, although the uniform and sophisticated style of the sayings and the foreign influence on the instructions suggests the book was essentially the work of palace scribes.

The first verse of the book states that Solomon is the author of the proverbs. There was a tradition that this king was not only versed in human wisdom (see 1 Kgs 3, 16–18) but had encyclopedic knowledge as well (see 1 Kgs 3, 4–14). Ancient people believed that wisdom belonged by

right to the god, and since the king was the human representative of the god, it was the special possession of the king. Since Solomon ruled during a time of splendor and enlightenment, he became known in popular devotion as the wise man par excellence. His reputation gave credibility to wisdom writing and, as more wisdom writing was attributed to him, his reputation grew. Ascribing Solomonic authorship to Proverbs gives the book the status of official teaching and credits the king with comprehensive wisdom.

There is a possibility that the *real* royal authority behind the Proverbs is Hezekiah. Collections of proverbs could well have been compiled during the time of his religious reform and *he* could have ascribed them to Solomon. We do not have enough information to accurately reconstruct this historical period. The book of Proverbs, itself, however, attests to both Hezekiah's influence (25, 1) and Solomon's reputation (1, 1; 10, 1; 25, 1).

About the Book

Proverbs is probably the biblical book that best characterizes the wisdom tradition. It appears to be the "guide for successful living" referred to in the Introduction. Its primary purpose is to teach wisdom. It makes an appeal to various groups of people in different walks of life. It teaches children (not necessarily or only young children) to heed the teaching of their parents (1, 8), and it directs citizens to act with respect toward the king (16, 10–15). It warns young men of the dangers of undisciplined living (5, 1–14; 23, 29–35), and it offers a portrait of the model wife for women to emulate (31, 10–31).

The book itself is composed of eight collections of teaching. These are quite distinct sections. Several of them are identified within the biblical text itself. Others can be distinguished by their particular literary forms.

The first section consists of a general introduction to the entire book (1, 1–7) and a collection of instruction (1, 8—9, 18). It is in this section that we find the student addressed again and again as "my son" and exhorted to listen to the teaching that is advanced. Fifteen of the 23 instances of this address appear in the first seven chapters of the book. The form clearly marks this section as instruction.

The second section (10, 1—22, 16) is explicitly identified as "the Proverbs of Solomon" (10, 1).

Each verse in this section is a saying in its own right. Its meaning does not depend on what precedes it nor what follows it.

It is possible that the third section of the book (22, 17—24, 22), instructions entitled "The sayings of the wise," is patterned after a collection of an Egyptian scribe, Amen-em-Ope (22, 19). If this is the case, it is probably the most obvious example in the wisdom tradition of Israel's literary borrowing from other ancient Near Eastern cultures.

The fourth section (24, 23–34), a group of sentences designated "also . . . sayings of the wise" (24, 23) is quite short. It is followed by a much longer collection of sentence literature (25, 1—29, 27) titled "the Proverbs of Solomon" (25, 1). This collection is further linked with the sages of the court of Hezekiah, the Judean king who ruled around the turn of the seventh century B.C. It appears that he inaugurated a period of religious reform and literary activity. The mention of his name in a collection of proverbs may be evidence of this movement.

The sixth section, called "The words of Agur" (30, 1), is the shortest (30, 1–6). It is followed by a collection of proverbs that are distinguished by their literary form (30, 7–33). The numerical proverbs, so named because of their use of numbers, have much in common with the riddle. The latter is a form mentioned in one of the introductory verses (1, 6) and in other places of the Bible (see the riddle of Samson, Jgs 14, 12, and the test of the queen of Sheba, 1 Kgs 10, 1), but found nowhere in the book of Proverbs itself. The eighth and last section can be divided into two parts: instruction (31, 1–9), entitled "The words of Lemuel" (31, 1); and a poem describing the ideal wife (31, 10–31).

The Role of Wisdom Today

Proverbs may not be popular reading today because it seems to describe a world that does not exist—a world that has a proper order and in which events follow a cause-and-effect sequence. We know that life is very unpredictable and the events of life cannot be foreseen.

• Proverbs does not claim to describe everything, but each proverb does depict a snippet of life. Together they offer a collage, not a blueprint.

• The process that produces proverbs may be more important than the content of the proverbs themselves. It teaches us the importance of serious reflection on experience and the need to adjust our behavior as circumstances change.

Proverbs offers us an appreciation of life and encouragement to live it well.

Questions for Discussion and Reflection
Group Sharing

1. Divide into two or more small groups. Let one "make the case" for each of the following proverbs. Do not criticize the other proverb but just explain why "yours" is good to follow.

The beginning of wisdom is: get wisdom (4, 7)

The beginning of wisdom is the fear of the LORD (9, 10).

2. Discuss how women are perceived or described in Proverbs. Compare that with today's views of women. Talk about the characterization of wisdom as a woman.

In Our Lives

1. Reflecting upon your ordinary experiences of this past week, think of an event that could be the basis for a contemporary proverb. Jot it down. Test out the wisdom of your proverb with the group. Does it resonate with others' experience?

2. Many people struggle with parenting today. Look through the book of Proverbs. Which ones offer valuable guidance for the training of children and youth in our contemporary world? If you are a parent, how might you apply them today? If you are a young person, how would you want them applied to you?

3. If you were writing your own book of Proverbs, what are some things you would absolutely want to include?

4. How can/does our parish share the wisdom of people within the community? How can we do this better rather than ignore these treasures in our midst?

Individual/Personal Reflection/Action

1. Remember a wise person you have encountered in your lifetime (a grandparent, parent, teacher, etc.). What bit of wisdom did they offer you or others? Think about how you can thank them for this.

2. Choose one or two of your favorite proverbs and copy them down. Put them on your desk or bathroom mirror or refrigerator door for a week or two.

ECCLESIASTES READING GUIDE

At a Glance

Who are the main players?	Qoheleth
What should I look for?	Qoheleth is a wise teacher who searches for the meaning of all life. He sets out to discover everything of value in human experience. He is also troubled by the inevitability of death and the futility it imparts.
When did this take place?	The inclusion of several Aramaic words has led scholars to date the book around the third century B.C.
Where did these events occur?	The place of origin is more difficult to determine. Some say it was Phoenicia, others suggest Egypt.
Why was this book written?	Ecclesiastes manifests some of the characteristics of a Royal Testament, a common literature of the Near East intended for the education of the king's successor.
What is the story?	Qoheleth accomplished all he set out to do. He acquired wisdom and wealth; he enjoyed pleasure and prosperity. He achieved all his goals and yet he declares "All is vanity!" To suppose that the attainment of goals, even noble goals, can fulfill human longings, according to Qoheleth, is vanity. The wisdom of Qoheleth consists not only in a critical examination of everything that is supposed to bring happiness, but also in providing positive counsel.

You may not be as familiar with the book of Ecclesiastes as you are with other writings from the wisdom tradition. But you are probably not unfamiliar with some of its expressions: "There's nothing new under the sun!" and "You can't take it with you!"

About the Book

Ecclesiastes demonstrates some of the literary characteristics of a Royal Testament, a common type of literature in the ancient Near East intended for the instruction of the king's successor. It was written in the third person and claimed to be advice gleaned from the experience of life. Although the book begins and ends in the third person (12, 9–14), everything else suggests but one speaker and, despite some conflicting statements, one point of view.

The language of the book resembles the kind of Hebrew that appeared during a very late biblical period and was used almost exclusively for literary purposes. The inclusion of several Aramaic words has led scholars to date the book around

the 3rd century B.C. Some say it originated in Phoenicia; others suggest Egypt. Because the wisdom tradition was common to the ancient Near East, precise identification of origin is difficult.

Ecclesiastes is one of the five books that make up the *Megilloth* (see sidebar RG 184). It was read during the harvest celebration of Sukkoth, also known as the Feast of Tabernacles or Booths. This major pilgrim feast was so named because the harvesters lived in booths as they gathered their crops. It is not clear how this practice began or why Ecclesiastes was chosen. Perhaps the somber tone of the book fit the dreariness of autumn. Although reading the book was not always a consistent synagogue practice, Ecclesiastes continues to be considered part of the *Megilloth*.

A Note About the Ending

The book clearly begins with the distinctive, "Vanity of vanities, says Qoheleth, vanity of vanities! All things are vanity!" (1, 2) and ends on the same tone: "Vanity of vanities, says

Who Was Qoheleth?

The very first verse identifies the speaker as "David's son, Qoheleth, king of Jerusalem." There is no biblical mention of a Davidic son by this name, so some other meaning must be intended. The exact meaning of Qoheleth is debated. It probably comes from the Hebrew word *qahal,* assembly, and refers to someone who calls forth or presides over a meeting, perhaps for the purpose of teaching. The form of the word *Qoheleth* suggests that it is not a name, but rather a participle that designates someone who does something. The Greek word used to translate *qahal* is *ekklesia,* a citizens' assembly in Greece. The one who presides over this particular assembly is called Ecclesiastes or Preacher.

The man is further designated as king of Israel. This is an obvious reference to Solomon, the one revered in popular devotion as the wise king. The author claims that Solomon is the speaker, and therefore his teaching has the authority of Solomon's wisdom. From the outset it has authority even though it may prove to be unorthodox. Because the author uses instruction, proverbial quotations, contrasting proverbs, rhetorical questions, parables, the words of the wise, and riddles, the characterization of Qoheleth is of a respected teacher of wisdom.

Qoheleth, all things are vanity!" (12, 8). What some consider a kind of prologue (1, 1–11) might well come from the original author. The epilogue (12, 9–14) is different: At least one, possibly two people besides the main author have added something. Whoever added verses 9–11 plainly agreed with Qoheleth's conclusions. The tone changes with verse 12. This might be a second epilogue. The student is warned about too much speculation and is advised to trust in the punishing justice of God, a theme that Qoheleth, in contrast, consistently challenged.

Megilloth or "Scrolls" This is a special collection in the Hebrew Bible that also includes Song of Songs, Ruth, Lamentations, and Esther. These books were read during various liturgical festivals and were gathered together for the sake of convenience.

It appears that the author created a literary character, Qoheleth, and attributed Solomon-like authority to him to give his own instruction credibility. A later editor further authenticated this teaching by explicitly assuring the reader of Qoheleth's wisdom. However, with two short verses, a second editor tried to temper Qoheleth's statements. There are two possible explanations for this inconsistent ending:

1. The book was already well enough accepted so that the critics could not dismiss it. Still, someone added a caution to what might be considered questionable teaching.

2. If only one editor agreed with Qoheleth's teaching, that person realized that without some kind of tempering it would not be preserved. The last verses restate the traditional view of punishment and seem to return the entire teaching to the circle of orthodoxy.

A Critical Point of View

There is a wide range of scholarly opinion regarding the meaning of the book. Qoheleth has been described as a skeptic, a cynic, or more positively, a pragmatist. His view of life has been called everything from pessimistic and fatalistic to realistic. Some judge his religious outlook as pleasure-seeking, while others think it is faithful to Israelite values. It is clear that he is disillusioned with certain parts of his society, yet he lacks the enthusiasm of a reformer or the vision of a mystic. Because of this some critics label him a frustrated man who is resigned to the

---

Retribution This theory claims that there is a direct relationship between the uprightness of one's behavior and the good fortune that one enjoys.

injustice and meaninglessness of life and has decided to make the most of fleeting pleasures.
Careful reading of Qoheleth will show that he
does not really despair of life but of the unrealis-
tic expectations regarding it. His real struggle is
with the meaning of life.

A Chase after the Wind

Qoheleth sets out to discover everything within
human experience (1, 13). Since he is a king, he
has both wealth and the leisure to embark on this
quest. As one with extraordinary wisdom (1, 16),
he of all people is equipped to experience life to
the fullest. But what he really sought was always
beyond his grasp, "a chase after the wind"
(1, 17). It is clear that in his search for wisdom,
he was looking for something else as well. Qoheleth next turned to the search for self-
gratification. In many ways he was successful,
but still he was not satisfied (2, 1–11). He accomplished everything he set his mind to in his
search to answer the fundamental question:

> What profit has man from all the labor
> which he toils at under the sun? (1, 3)

He constantly arrived at the same conclusion:
There is no lasting gain, no tangible dividend,
"with nothing gained under the sun" (2, 11).

According to the theory of retribution, Qoheleth's wisdom and wealth would be perceived
as a concrete proof of his goodness and the
guarantee of his future prosperity. But Qoheleth
really does not enjoy his good fortune, so he
questions its value. Since death comes to everyone, he wonders, "Why then should I be wise?
Where is the profit for me?" (2, 15). It is not
life, nor the search for fulfillment in life, that
frustrates him. What he loathes is the unprof-
itability of human striving. It is not fulfilling.

Qoheleth's term for the futility of
life—"vanity"—is the Hebrew word
"hevel," which literally means a puff of air
or vapor. In Jeremiah 10, 15 the prophet
calls idols *"hevel,"* translated "nothingness"in the NAB. In Psalm 39, 6.12, "mortals" (human beings) are compared to a
"hevel"—a "breath."

He is asking more of life than success and
prosperity.

Since death comes to all, any advantage one
might have because of righteousness, wisdom, or
wealth is only temporary, and therefore questionable. Maybe the fool who disregards the rules of
society may actually have an edge over the one
who conforms to them at the cost of enjoyment.
So he wonders if perhaps life itself is "a chase after the wind."

Nothing is New under the Sun

We have already seen how the wisdom teachers
appealed to the obvious order within the natural
world as they urged people to live in obedience
to the acceptable social custom. The author of
Job used the same technique with a slightly different twist. Job was overwhelmed by the wonders of nature and led to acknowledge the incomprehensible dimension of life. The author of
Ecclesiastes also directs our attention to the regularity in nature (1, 2–11) but does so in order to
highlight its monotony. The sun rises and sets
day after day. Although the wind appears to be
irregular, upon observation its paths can be predicted. Although the sea is constantly fed, it is
never full. The regularity of the earth appears to
be lacking any progress. There is nothing new
under the sun.

What advantage does the earth have in being so
constant? The sage urges us to learn another lesson from nature. Human striving for gain is nothing but wearisome labor that must be repeated and
repeated with no promise of conclusion and no assurance of satisfaction. Human life is basically the
same regardless of the society or the generation
into which one is born. Life itself follows the same
cycles, and experiences are quite similar. As nature repeats itself, so does human history. Nothing
seems to have lasting significance.

An Appointed Time

"There is an appointed time for everything . . .
under the heavens." In what may be the most familiar section of the entire book, Qoheleth declares that each event of human life has its own
appointed time. Each event is linked in poetic
construction with its opposite. There are two
ways of understanding the pattern:

1. Juxtaposing opposites is a way of expressing totality. It encompasses both poles and

everything in between. For examples, "knowledge of good and evil" (Gn 2, 9–17) means comprehensive knowledge; "bone and flesh" (Gn 2, 23) refers to the entire body.

2. A second poetic form is an expression of relativity. The circumstances of life determine what is fitting and what is not. What is appropriate at one time can be out of place when circumstances change. This may be the author's way of insisting that there are no absolutes; everything is relative to everything else. There is a time to die as well as a time to be born. Neither seems to have an advantage over the other. Still, we do not know the rules that govern these appointed times, so we are helpless and may feel that we are at their mercy.

The task of living is not easy. Qoheleth explains why in 3, 11. This verse may be the most difficult one in the book because of the questions surrounding the translation and interpretation of the Hebrew word *olam*. Although some versions translate the word as "world," or "future," or even "ignorance," the *New American Bible* translates it as "the timeless." God has put *olam* in the human heart, and we want to know and understand, even to control everything in the world. It seems that while human beings are finite, their desires transcend the limits of time.

> You have made us for yourself, O Lord,
> and our hearts are restless
> until they rest in you. (St. Augustine)

All Is Vanity

Qoheleth accomplished all his goals and yet he declares, "All is vanity!" All the energy he put into his projects was pointless. We might expect him to advise others against ever trying to be happy but he does not. On the contrary, he urges people to enjoy what they have. Then what is it about life that he regards as vanity?

Qoheleth observed in the lives of others what Job experienced, that is, the inadequacy of the theory of retribution. The righteous do not always enjoy the good things of life, nor are the wicked always deprived of them (4, 1; 8, 10f). While Qoheleth shares this insight with Job, his dissatisfaction in the face of his own prosperity and success has led him a step further in challenging the theory. It is not only that a righteous

person sometimes does not prosper; it is also that, even when one does realize some desired goal, there is no guarantee of fulfillment. To suppose that the attainment of goals, even noble ones, can fulfill human longings is, to Qoheleth, vanity.

The Wisdom of the Sage

The wisdom of Qoheleth consists not only in a critical examination of everything that is supposed to bring happiness, but also in positive advice. Although he finds fault with some aspects of human striving, he encourages something that is often overlooked in busy lives. The key to true fulfillment may be to relish the simple pleasures of life that are at hand (2, 24; 3, 13–22; 5, 19; 8, 15; 9, 9). These pleasures can be experienced in the very act of living: in eating, in drinking, in the work itself rather than in the wealth that one may hope to produce by it. The pleasure, like everything, has come from the hand of God and should be enjoyed.

Life is not a business transaction with a strict *quid pro quo* (this for that) return. Such a rigid interpretation of retribution will only end in disappointment. To wait in anticipation of something more is foolish, because the future is uncertain. Rather, people should value the present satisfaction that accompanies human activity.

Qoheleth objects to making human accomplishment the primary goal in life. He calls upon all to find pleasure in what they are doing and, if they are fortunate enough to become successful in the process, to see this as a gift from God as well.

Questions for Discussion and Reflection
Group Sharing/Discussion

1. A strict interpretation of retribution often expects God to respond to our actions with proper reward or punishment. Looking at the scripture itself, find passages where Qoheleth reminds us that God is not bound by these expectations that people may have.

2. Reread together the section above entitled: "A Critical Point of View." Let group members choose one of the words that describe Qoheleth and tell why they think it is an accurate description. Then let each person say how he or she would describe Qoheleth, having read Ecclesiastes.

3. What are some things in Ecclesiastes that you disagree with and things that you agree with?

In Our Lives

1. Our economic system feeds into the materialism that Qoheleth criticizes. What are ways you and your family protect yourselves against acquiring more and more things? What are some ways parents teach their children to resist the pressure of wanting more and "the latest" and "bigger and better" in such an atmosphere?

2. How does your parish community provide opportunities to follow Qoheleth and experience the joy and satisfaction of doing the right thing by sharing with those in need? How could it do more to preach and practice this?

3. Describe someone who does not have a lot of material possessions but is a happy and fulfilled person. What lessons does their life contain for us?

4. Many people spend a lifetime climbing the ladder of power. How would Qoheleth challenge the struggle for "upward mobility"?

Individual/Personal Reflection/Action

1. What are some pieces of advice you would want to take from Ecclesiastes? Write down three things to help you put them into effect in your life. Put them on the bathroom mirror or your desk or someplace you will see them each day.

2. Spend five or ten minutes each day this week writing down what advice and values you would pass along if you were today's Qoheleth.

THE SONG OF SONGS READING GUIDE

At a Glance

Who are the main players?	The voices belong to a young woman, her lover, and the daughters of Jerusalem. The way one understands the meaning and function of this book will influence the way one identifies these characters.
What should I look for?	What is the book's theological value? What does it teach us? Think about this poetry as showing a figurative way of understanding our relationship with God, the conviction that death does not have final victory, and an example of faithful love. The literal understanding affirms sexuality as one of God's gifts.
When did this take place?	The appearance of the Persian word for orchard or park suggests a post-exilic date (after 589 B.C.).
Where did these events occur?	The geographic references mentioned northern locations, places in Transjordan, and Judah.
Why was this book written?	This relatively short book is a collection of poems on the meaning of love. Song of Songs is read on the last day of the celebration of Passover.
What is the story?	A maiden takes the initiative in this romantic pursuit. This wisdom book teaches that human passion is both noble and ennobling. Furthermore, its attraction and vitality are natural to both women and men. As with the characters and theology, the interpretation of the romance depicted here depends greatly on how the reader approaches the book.

Language and Authorship

This short book has an unusually large number of uncommon words. Its 117 verses contain 49 words that appear nowhere else in the Old Testament. This adds to the difficulty of understanding the book, for we are prevented from comparing the meaning of a word in one context with its meaning in another. This unfamiliar vocabulary opens the poem to many interpretations, but it also allows for rich differences of understanding and meanings.

Like Proverbs and Ecclesiastes, the Song is associated with Solomon. Attribution to the famous king occurs only in the editorial introduction (1, 1) and is preceded by a preposition that can be translated in various ways: "by" Solomon; "to" Solomon; "for" Solomon; "of" Solomon; "concerning" Solomon. This does not mean Solomon was the author. Connecting the king's name to the Song probably gave it credibility and linked it to the other wisdom traditions. Since the book includes other references to Solomon (3, 7–11; 8, 11f) some interpreters identify Solomon as the amorous shepherd. But because the king never speaks in these passages, the references could be merely figurative allusions to fabulous wealth.

The Song of Songs presents many barriers to interpretation. It is clearly a collection of love poems full of sensuous imagery. It does not offer any apparent theological or moral values, and it never even mentions God. It is no wonder that both Jewish and Christian writers at various times have questioned its acceptance into the canon of inspired writings. The very character of the book has led to many distinct interpretations.

About the Book

The Song of Songs is a collection of poems of various lengths, but scholars differ about how to arrange these poems into sections. Some see a pattern of separation, longing, and union. Others maintain that while these elements are present, they do not follow a particular pattern. Others see unity in verbal echoes, for instance the repetitions in 2, 6–7; 3, 5; 8, 3–4. Since there is no narrative plot and the speakers are neither identified nor introduced, one can only speculate about the original intention of the compiler.

The geographic references are wide-reaching. Northern locations are mentioned (2, 1; 3, 9; 4, 8; 6, 4; 7, 5–6), as are places to the east (4, 1) and in Judah (1, 14; 3, 5). This variety may reflect the early northern Israelite source of some of the original poems and a later southern (perhaps Jerusalem) setting for the final edition. The appearance of the Persian word for orchard or park (4, 13) suggests a date after the exile in Babylon (after 539 B.C.).

The Song of Songs is also found in the *Megilloth,* or the collection of five festal scrolls (the others are Ruth, Lamentations,

Voices in the Song of Songs

Daughters of Jerusalem	A Chorus of Voices
Bride	Meaning is not clear. Hebrew text refers to a young woman betrothed but not yet married to a man. While the text alludes to the sexual union of the lovers, it never describes a marriage. The male partner is not necessarily a "groom."
Lover	There seem to be two distinct lovers, one a royal figure from Jerusalem (1, 12–17; 3, 6–11) and the other a rustic youth from the north (1, 7f; 2, 8–17). Nowhere is there a combination of the two.

Interpretation When we talk about interpretation, it is important to distinguish between what the book meant in the past and what it means for the present. Those interpreters who use a strict historical-critical approach insist that the original sense must be the focus of our explanation. Discovering the earliest form and meaning of the book is crucial. It is this original meaning, they would argue, that continues to be revelatory for us today. Other commentators do not categorize methods as "right" or "wrong" but as "helpful" or "not helpful." They would be more open to various interpretations of the Song of Songs.

Ecclesiastes, and Esther), and is read on the last day of the celebration of Passover. Perhaps the announcement of the end of winter (2, 11) made the poem suitable for a spring festival. Reference to horses and chariots of Pharaoh (1, 9) is an allusion to Exodus, the event commemorated at Passover.

Several different voices are heard in the Song of Songs, as outlined in the table at the bottom of RG 188.

Who are these mysterious lovers? The way one understands the meaning and function of the book will influence the way one identifies the characters within it. If these are ancient wedding songs, then the lovers are bride and groom. The New American Bible takes this approach,

labeling the "Lover's" words as those of a bridegroom. If it is love poetry, then the "bride" is understood in a figurative sense; her partner the man with whom she is intimately involved. He is called "lover," not "husband."

Form and Meaning

For more than 2,000 years, the Song of Songs has been not only a source of fascination but also something of a riddle. Its very uniqueness has made understanding it a challenge. There are four ways of interpreting it: allegorical, cultic, dramatic, and literal. Each of these approaches reveals different possibilities for our religious enrichment. All of them have gained acceptance within Roman Catholic tradition. It is interesting to note that while the first and preferred method of interpreting the Bible has been the literal approach, the opposite has been true with this book. It seems that the suggestive sexual imagery offends the sensitivities of many of the faithful. Therefore commentators have presumed that the poems were not intended to be taken literally but must have some concealed religious meaning.

Allegorical Interpretations

An allegorical method presumes that the surface meaning of a figure of speech, character, or image signifies some deeper spiritual truth. This approach was quite popular in Jewish circles around the time of Christ (Philo, 20 B.C.–A.D. 54) as well as among early Christian writers (Origen, A.D. 185–254). Jewish commentators who allegorize the Song interpret it as symbolizing God's

What Is Allegory?

An allegory is a comparison between two areas of human experience, usually a concrete or everyday area and an abstract one more removed from ordinary experience. For example, justice in our courts is often represented as a beautiful woman wearing a blindfold and holding balancing scales. The woman's beauty symbolizes the attractions of justice: Just as we are drawn to beauty, so we should be drawn to justice. Her blindfold symbolizes the impartiality of justice. No matter how important or unimportant the person who appears before her, she is concerned only with the merits of the case. The balancing scales symbolize the idea that decisions are made according to public standards and anyone can observe how they are made. By using everyday images, the allegorical figure helps us understand our ideals of justice.

relationship with Israel, tracing it from the time of the Exodus to the coming of the Messiah. They believe it celebrates God's steadfast love bestowed on Israel and describes the fickleness that characterized Israel's attitude toward its divine lover.

As Christians began to read the Hebrew traditions in light of their faith in Christ, this allegorical method produced new meanings. They identified the lovers as Christ and the Church. Some read it as a description of the mystical union of God and the individual soul.

The bride has even been explained as the Virgin Mary. Although not easily accommodated to the poem, this interpretation has been quite prominent within the Roman Catholic tradition. One reason for this is the belief that Mary is the model of the individual soul in union with God. A stronger reason for this interpretation is the fact that sections of the Song are read during the liturgy on several Marian feasts. Thus by association this interpretation has become common in popular devotion to Mary.

Cultic Interpretation

A second way of understanding the Song of Songs assumes that it was originally a liturgical reenactment of a drama that takes place in nature each spring. In a well-known fertility myth of the ancient Near Eastern world, the great god (the Canaanite Baal or the Babylonian Tammuz) dies after the harvest and is mourned by the fertility goddess (Anath or Ishtar respectively). She searches frantically for him during the barrenness of winter. Her efforts are successful and they are finally united. Nature is revived with the coming of spring and the cycle of life continues. The fact that this book was read during the springtime festival of Passover seems to support the theory that Israel was influenced by the agricultural celebrations of the era.

There is ample evidence in the Bible of Israel's use and reinterpretation of Canaanite cultic practices. A Canaanite nomadic festival took on historical meaning when it was used to commemorate God's deliverance of the people from Egyptian bondage. It was associated with the Feast of Unleavened Bread after the people had settled in Canaan and had moved from a nomadic to an agricultural form of life. These two festivals merged into one celebration, and elements of both became details of the standard story of the first Passover celebration. *Passover* is probably a combination of two festivals: an early nomadic celebration intended to ensure the fertility of the flock, and an agricultural one, the Feast of Unleavened Bread, intended to ensure the growth of the crop.

Dramatic Interpretation

This third approach has had a long history in the Church's tradition. As early as the second century of the Christian era, Origen claimed that the Song was a wedding poem written in dramatic form by Solomon himself. Some interpreters today divide the book into a drama of five movements:

1. The anticipation and meeting of the lovers (1, 1—2, 17)
2. The separation (3, 1–11)
3. Reunion (4, 1—5, 1)
4. A second separation (5, 2—6, 3)
5. Final union (6, 4—8, 14)

The commentators assign the speeches to the characters, as indicated in the New American Bible, and identify the various scenes by means of subtitles within the text.

The two major characters are the royal shepherd and the Shulammite maiden. A two-character interpretation has serious deficiencies. There is no dramatic development, and the book lacks ethical purpose. A three-character approach was developed to address these weaknesses. It distinguishes two male individuals, the king and the shepherd. The king tries to win the love of the maiden, but she remains faithful to her shepherd lover. In the first interpretation the royal shepherd is worthy of the faithful love of the Shulammite. This personage might well represent Solomon. In the second interpretation, the king is a villain who tries to seduce the maiden with the promise of luxury and comfort. One wonders how this disapproving portrait of Solomon could survive as part of the wisdom tradition, which ascribed wisdom to the very king who is depicted in this manner.

The weaknesses of this approach are obvious. Since the biblical text does not supply names for the speeches, the decisions about their identification are influenced by the biases of the interpreter. Stage directions are imposed from without rather than discovered within the poems themselves. Finally, there is neither story line nor character development, essential traits of good drama.

Literal Interpretation

It may be that the original meaning of the Song is found in its literal interpretation. The Song of Songs is most likely a collection of love poems that neither symbolize divine love nor were developed from fertility rites. It teaches no lesson; it tells no story. It simply celebrates the passion of human love. While some believe that the poems are secular, others doubt that purely secular love songs would ever be admitted to the canon. These latter commentators believe that the poems are examples of Judean wedding songs. They also discover traces of a poetic form called *wasf*: an Arabic word meaning description. These are poems that use images from nature to describe parts of the male or female body. The *wasf* form uses one point of comparison between the image and the object being described (the whiteness of the woman's teeth compared to that of freshly washed sheep, for example), and often results in an extravagant or amusing combination. This may explain some of the strange imagery found in the Song (see 4, 1–5; 7, 2–6).

The Song's claim of Solomon as its author may be the main reason this book is part of the Bible. Each of the three books attributed to Solomon addresses a central issue of life basic to the wisdom thinking of the ancient Near East, Israel included.

• Proverbs provides directions on how to achieve peace and prosperity by coming to an understanding of order and stability in the world.

• In Ecclesiastes, Qoheleth addresses the search for meaning in life.

• The Song of Songs celebrates a fundamental human emotion—erotic love.

None of these books fits into the category of "salvation history," but each one is an example of the "way of wisdom."

Once the writings were associated with Solomon and the wisdom attributed to him, it was not long before they possessed their own authoritative significance. This seems to have been enough to ensure inclusion in the canon. Although the three books are quite distinct, they have come to represent different moments in the life of the same man.

The Song of Songs reveals a young, passionate, unguarded Solomon.

Proverbs shows a moderate but optimistic man who has learned from his experience of life.

The musings of Qoheleth in Ecclesiastes come from someone who comes to the end of life challenging the enduring value of human accomplishment.

The quality of these human, but nonetheless theological, concerns is evidence of their religious value. Ascribing them to Solomon provided them with canonical status.

Questions for Discussion and Reflection
Group Sharing/Discussion

1. From each of the interpretive approaches described above, what does the Song of Songs teach us? What is its theological value? We have

---

An Independent Woman in a Patriarchal Society

The portrait of the maiden is exceptional for literature from a patriarchal and male-dominated society. This is not the image of a sexually naive and passive woman, dependent upon a man for protection and sustenance. It is the woman who takes the initiative in this romantic pursuit. She utters almost twice as much of the erotic poetry as does the man. Her language is quite explicit, and she shatters any stereotypes that suggest that women may be romantic but not sexually inclined. The Song of Songs does not portray male dominance and female subordination. The maiden is an independent person. She tends vineyards (1, 6) and shepherds flocks (1, 8), occupations normally assigned to men. This wisdom book teaches that human passion can be both noble and ennobling, and its attraction and vitality are natural to both men and women.

considered four different methods of interpretation, so there are four distinct approaches to these questions. Read through these summaries and discuss what can be valued or learned from each of them.

A. The Allegorical Approach

A symbolic approach provides us with a figurative way of understanding the nature of our relationship with God, which is dynamic, energizing, and mutually loving. Contrary to an image of God as an impassive creator or avenging judge, the Song of Songs offers us a portrait of a passionate lover, one who desires union with us. Some may find this notion scandalous, but the wisdom tradition (especially Job and Ecclesiastes) repeatedly teaches something about God or human nature that has been unconventional.

B. The Cultic Interpretation

At the heart of the dying/rising ritual is the conviction that death does not have the final victory. The love of the grieving goddess is strong enough to bring her lover back to her and revitalize the lifeless earth.

C. The Dramatic Interpretation

Understanding the poem as a dialogue or interaction among various characters provides an example of faithful love. The fidelity of the bride is held up for all to admire and

imitate. This image of a faithful woman conforms to the one found in other places in the wisdom tradition (see Prv 31, 10–31).

D. The Literal Interpretation

Seeing the work as lyrical poetry makes no apology for its erotic interpretation. It affirms that sexuality is one of the gifts that God gave for our enjoyment (see Prv 5, 15–21; Eccl 9, 9). The sexual pleasure is not sought promiscuously but pursued only within the context of a faithful and exclusive commitment.

In Our Lives

1. What do you think is the message or lesson we can take from Song of Songs? If the most basic way of experiencing God's love and saving presence is through human friendship, what does this tell us about who God is?

2. What is our culture's attitude toward the human body? What is the different message proclaimed in the Song of Songs?

Individual/Personal Reflection/Action

1. Who are people you have known who are models of healthy love? Examine your own attitudes towards friendship/love/commitment and see how you want to deepen and mature them.

2. Pray each day this week for ways to spread a healthy and holy understanding of how God wants us to love each other as human beings.

THE BOOK OF WISDOM READING GUIDE

At a Glance

Who are the main players?	The author, a Hellenized Jew
What should I look for?	The dimensions and facets of divine wisdom. Many passages of the first section are used in our liturgy (e.g., 3, 1–8). The way that the Exodus is presented (11, 2ff.) shows the special providence of God.
When did this take place?	About a hundred years before the coming of Christ.
Where did these events occur?	In the ancient Jewish community in Alexandria, Egypt.
Why was this book written?	Even during persecution the author attempts to exhort and inspire his readers to embrace wisdom through his flair with words and the way he uses biblical history in his preaching.
What is the story?	The book of Wisdom is divided into three parts: (a) chapters 1–6, rewards of living justly; (b) 7, 1—11, 1, reflections on wisdom by "Solomon"; (c) 11, 2—19, 22, the religious meaning of the Exodus.

Background for Understanding the Book of Wisdom

The last half of the fourth century saw rapid and sweeping changes in the ancient world. Alexander the Great had brought the entire eastern world under the influence of Greek culture, thereby unifying a diverse, disorganized world. This, however, threatened the integrity of other cultures and religious perspectives. With his death in 323 B.C., the empire was divided among his followers, and three independent kingdoms were formed. These kingdoms were hostile to each other. Two of these kingdoms played an important role in the affairs of the Jewish nation. Ptolemy gained control of Egypt and established himself in Alexandria; Seleucus triumphed over Babylon and made Antioch his center. Each kingdom contributed to the shaping of the biblical tradition.

Hellenization was forced upon the Jewish community by the ruler Antiochus Epiphanes. A large colony of Jews lived in Alexandria and adapted itself to Greek language and culture. This was the group that translated its religious traditions from Hebrew into Greek, producing what has come to be known as the Septuagint.

This Greek version was probably the one in popular use during the first century of the Christian era. During the same time, the Jewish community adopted the older Palestinian or Hebrew version of the Bible as its official text. The

Christian practice of adding their own writings to the collection may have contributed to this decision.

Christians continued to revere the Alexandrian (Greek) tradition of the Septuagint. Scholars comparing Old Testament citations used by New Testament writers conclude that a good number, if not all of them, came from the Alexandrian rather than from the earlier Palestinian version.

At the time of the Reformation, the official version of the Old Testament became a point of disagreement among Christian denominations. Protestant churches kept the shorter, more ancient Hebrew canon, while the Roman Church accepted the wider Greek canon, preserving an early Church tradition. This explains why some Bibles include such books as Wisdom and Sirach, while others do not.

About the Book

Over the centuries this book has been called "The Book of Wisdom" (from the Latin translations), "The Wisdom of Solomon" (from the Septuagint), or variations of either title. Although the author does not explicitly identify himself as Solomon, speaking in the first person, he does describe himself as such (7, 5; 8, 21; 9, 7f; see I Kgs 3, 5–15). The author may have presumed that the unconventional character of the book's ideas might need the authority of Solomon to be accepted as orthodox teaching.

The book suggests an origin from within the Jewish community of Alexandria. It is clear that the author was steeped in the history of the Exodus (11, 2–16; 12, 23–27; 16, 2—19, 22), was acquainted with the religious practices of Egypt

---

Septuagint The Latin for "seventy," frequently designated LXX, Septuagint is the name for the main ancient Greek translation of the Hebrew Bible with additions. Tradition claimed that 70 scribes, working independently of each other, labored over the translation of the Bible for 70 days in 70 different locations and produced identical versions. This was seen as evidence of the inspired nature of the translation. In reality, the translation probably took decades, but this did not detract from the reverence accorded the Septuagint over the years.

Deuterocanonical ("second listing"). Those books accepted as Scripture by Catholics but not found in the Hebrew canon.

Apocryphal (originally meaning "hidden"). Understood as inspirational but not in the canon of official scripture.

(15, 14—16, 1), and was well versed in Hellenistic philosophy and science (6, 22—11, 1). The author reinterpreted his own heritage and critiqued the traditions, practices, and insights of the other two cultures. He did this to support those Jews who were questioning the relevance of their ancient faith in the face of radical cultural changes they were undergoing.

Date of the Book

Most scholars date it somewhere during the first century B.C. The primary threat at this time did not arise from the Hellenizing Greeks but from the Hellenized Jews themselves. The outside oppression at the time of the Maccabean Revolt had given way to a subtle undermining of traditional teaching and values. Even religious leaders were not immune to this kind of worldliness. The author appears to have been concerned that:

1. The pious not be led astray
2. Those enthralled by Greek culture be convinced of the value of the work of their own religious heritage
3. Those already carried away by the currents of change be brought back.

Literary Features of the Book

Wisdom was originally written in Greek. The style is natural and free-flowing, not awkward, as might be the case if this were a translation from Hebrew.

1. The vocabulary reveals an author who possessed an extensive comprehension of Hellenistic (Greek) learning.
2. References to earlier religious tradition correspond to the style of the Alexandrian rather than the Palestinian version.
3. The thought is similar to what is found in Jewish-Alexandrian works of this period.
4. The author frequently used a form of expression that resembles the diatribe. The diatribe is a method of argument that creates imaginary opponents who raise questions that the philosopher then refutes.

Despite these Greek characteristics, this is basically a Jewish work. The description of God's care during the Exodus is a kind of midrash homily. Midrash is an interpretation that the Jewish community devised in order to apply the Bible to new situations. Thus a law (*halakah*) was restated or a narrative (*haggadah*) retold in such a way as to give new direction to a new generation. The Greeks, especially Philo, developed allegory as a principal method of interpreting traditions. It is significant that the author of Wisdom employed midrash rather than allegory. This further verifies the Jewish, rather than Greek, origin of the book.

Wisdom Teaching

The unifying theme of this biblical book is "the praise of wisdom." Each of the three major sections addresses this theme from its own distinctive point of view. Each section will highlight the significant theological elements found there.

Immortality of the Soul

The soul's immortality is a central issue in the first half of the book of Wisdom. Virtually all the books contained in Hebrew Scripture assume that human life ends at death. During the Hellenistic period, many Jews came to believe in life after death. Generally speaking, there were two ways of thinking about life after death: resurrection of the body and immortality of the soul. New Testament texts assert belief in resurrection (for example, 1 Cor 15, 12–58). Other Jewish texts outside the scriptural canon (such as the writings of Philo) reflect belief in the immortality of the soul, much like Wisdom. There was no agreement on the issue. The author of Sirach states repeatedly and with absolute certainty that life ends at death (38, 21–23; 41, 1–4). Sirach may be two centuries earlier than Wisdom, but even in the first century A.D., the Sadducees denied there was life after death (Mt 22, 23–33; Acts 23, 8). The debate is closely tied to the problem of theodicy, as is evident in the text of Wisdom. How does one believe in the goodness of God if there is evil and suffering in the world? If righteous people can be unjustly accused and wrongly condemned to death, where is justice? Belief in life after death allows for the possibility that wrongs may be set right, which is exactly what is described in 3, 1–9.

The Reward of Justice (1, 1—6, 21)

The first section is often called "The Book of Eschatology." (Eschatology traditionally refers to the last or final things: the end of the age, death, judgment, reward, and punishment.) In this section we find the destinies of the righteous and of the wicked described in vivid contrast. The righteous, regardless of their obvious suffering, "are in the hand of God" (3, 1), while the wicked "shall receive a punishment to match their thoughts" (3, 10). This entire section serves as a call to be faithful to the religious traditions of Israel, a fidelity that will guarantee these rewards of wisdom.

This is a radical departure from the traditional understanding. Indeed, the author of Wisdom diverges from tradition on several topics.

1. The author insisted that childlessness, a condition that brought reproach in ancient society (see Gn 16, 4; 1 Sm 1, 7) is not a mark of divine displeasure (3, 13f; 4, 1). Moral goodness, not physical fruitfulness, is emphasized.

2. The author denied that suffering itself presumes that the person has sinned. In fact, an untimely death may be a righteous person's rescue from the wickedness of life (4, 14). We are reminded of the popular saying: "The good die young." The author agreed with Job and Qoheleth that virtue is not always rewarded in this life, nor is evil punished. Whoever thinks that death of the righteous is an affliction or destruction is foolish (3, 2f). It is rather a trial they must endure.

3. The author brought two earlier creation narratives together and reinterpreted them. The statement about being made in God's image (2, 23), an allusion to Genesis 1, 16.28, is followed by the claim that the devil's envy brought death into the world 12, 24), a reinterpretation of Genesis. Some think that the latter refers to Cain's envy, which resulted in the death of Abel (Gn 4, 1–6). Another writer of this time says that Satan led Eve astray (Enoch 60, 6). The author of Wisdom was the first biblical writer to identify the serpent of the Genesis account with the devil.

What about Life after Death?

In the book of Wisdom, the reader is introduced for the first time to the Greek concept of *psyche* (soul, 1, 11; 3, 1). The Greeks held that human nature was a combination of a perishable material (body) and an eternal spiritual (soul). This combination was dissolved at death. We must be careful, however, not to take this Greek thought further than the author did. Nowhere does this book speak of an immortal soul. Rather, the author argues that God intended human life to continue without death (2, 23); what survives is the full human being.

Life after death is quite different from the earlier perception of *Sheol*, the abode of the dead. There is just enough lack of clarity in the words "immortality" (3, 4; 4, 1; 8, 13.17; 15, 3) and "incorruptibility" (2, 23; 6, 18f) to prevent us from making definite statements about the author's view. One thing seems clear. Immortality is not an automatic quality of human nature; it is the result of union with wisdom (8, 13.17; 15, 3). Although 2, 23 claims that God made humans to be imperishable, 6, 18 suggests that it is possible only when one is faithful to wisdom.

We are not sure if the author was speaking of physical death, of physical death followed by spiritual death, or of spiritual death alone. The thought does seem to be directed to spiritual death. St. Paul will have to face the same question when dealing with the unexpected deaths of Christians (1 Thes 4, 13–18). Unlike the author of Wisdom, his answer is quite specific.

Praise of Wisdom by Solomon (6, 22—11, 1)

The second major section of the book is an address acclaiming the glories of wisdom. It is from this section that the book receives its name, and it is from here that we find a representation of personified Wisdom. This representation of Wisdom is quite different from that found in earlier tradition. The author may have realized that he needed to claim the authority of Solomon to gain acceptance for this reinterpretation. This section begins with an account of his humble origin, his own prayer for wisdom, and God's immeasurable gift in answering his plea (7, 1–7; also see 9, 1–18). This is an allusion to the prayer of Solomon (1 Kgs 3, 5–15), and it characterizes the author as the wise king.

The description of Wisdom is composed of elements from:

• Israelite tradition (7, 22a; see Prv 8, 30).
• The cult of the Egyptian deity Isis (goddess

of wisdom and patron of culture whose praises were in the form of listings similar to those found in 7, 22—8, 1).

• Hellenistic philosophy and science (see 8, 7 for mention of the cardinal virtues of Plato). This may be the way the author argues for the superiority of the religion of Israel. The author confers on the figure of Wisdom the characteristics of Isis already found in the Israelite tradition and draws upon Hellenistic religious and scientific concepts to praise her as he argues that real wisdom is a gift from God bestowed on the faithful.

Christianity and the Book of Wisdom

In this book wisdom is referred to as "the Spirit of the LORD" (1, 7). The theology of this verse functions significantly in the liturgy of Pentecost. Although spirit played a major role in Stoic philosophy, it was clearly a theme in Jewish tradition as well. The author ascribed to Wisdom what earlier writers attributed to the Spirit of the LORD:

• The creative power of the world (7, 22a; see Jdt 16, 14)

• The source of Joseph's honor in Egypt (10, 13; see Gn 41, 38)

• The inspiration that prepared Moses for the Exodus and led the people through the wilderness (10, 16f; see Is 63, 11.14).

What is the influence of the figure of Wisdom on New Testament writings? Some scholars believe that the influence is direct. Others hold that there was a treasury of thought, imagery, and language that served as a common source. Whichever the case may be, early Christian theologians reinterpreted the figure of Wisdom as they struggled to understand Jesus the Christ.

Paul explicitly referred to Christ as the wisdom of God (1 Cor 1, 24.30). The most obvious example of this is found in the Gospel according to John. There we find Jesus described in ways that Wisdom had been depicted earlier: as being with God in the beginning before the world existed (Jn 1, 1; 17, 5; see Wis 2, 22) and as sent from heaven to accomplish the will of God (Jn 6, 38; see Wis 9, 10). Current scholarship is only

beginning to seek the implications of this imagery for Christology.

This section ends with a summary of the way Wisdom guided the ancestors of Israel by bringing them out of Egypt through the agency of Moses (see Hos 12, 14); and by enabling them to prosper (Wis 10, 1—11, 1). It is clear that Wisdom, once thought to be the possession of the king, was now to be understood as the constant companion of true Israelites, those faithful ones of the past as well as committed Jews of the present.

Special Providence of God during the Exodus (11, 2—19, 22)

At this point there is an observable shift in focus. The poem in praise of Wisdom gives way to midrash that praises the God of Israel. This version of the experience of the Exodus and the time in the wilderness illustrates two points:

1. The sufferings that befell the Egyptians were the direct result of their sinfulness (11, 16).

2. The very elements that afflicted the Egyptians benefited the Israelites (11, 51).

This reading of the past is done through creative selection of biblical data as well as addition of material not found anywhere else.

The author did not set out to recount historical facts but seemed intent on addressing the challenge raised by Hellenism. His goal was to remind the Alexandrian Jews that once before they had suffered at the hands of the Egyptians and, in the face of impossible odds, they had been rescued. This provides a "historical" basis for continued trust in the God of Israel.

There are two digressions within this third division of the book. Both of them are found in the second example of God's providence:

1. A testimony to God's mercy (11, 17—12, 22). Although it breaks the midrash style of thought, it may have been prompted by the mention of punishment in the preceding verses.

2. A condemnation of idolatry (13, 1—15, 17). It follows the claim that the Egyptians "saw and recognized the true God whom before they had refused to know" (12, 27) but continued in their idolatry. The language used in the condemnation of nature worship (13, 1–9) may be the best example of the author's broad grasp of scientific knowledge.

Theology in a New Context

The author of Wisdom did not set out in search of new theological insights. Since he was committed to proving the lasting value of the religion of Israel, he explained traditions and themes that were familiar to the Jews of his day. What made his contribution unique was the method that he employed as he went about his task.

Throughout its history, Israel had been forced by circumstances to deal with religious and cultural tensions of other societies. The Bible itself shows that these encounters were sometimes peaceful and at other times violent and destructive. Whatever the situation may have been, elements from those cultures found their way into the traditions of Israel. It was the religion of Israel that reinterpreted features of other cultures and then took these new ideas into their own perspective. Israel seldom took seriously the religious worldview of the other culture.

This attitude changed with the Hellenization of the world. It was precisely the attraction of Greek civilization itself that threatened Jewish faith. The community wrestled with an agonizing dilemma: Could one accept the Greek culture and remain faithful to the traditions of the ancestors? The author of Wisdom undertook the task of answering this question in the affirmative. He did not try to reconcile Judaism with Hellenism but used the ideas, the language, and the literary style of Greek culture to demonstrate the excellence of the Jewish faith.

In taking Greek culture seriously, this theologian did what theologians after him would have to do, which was not so different from the task facing us: that is, adapt and transfer a religious heritage that started in one cultural context into another. His purpose was to defend the ancestral faith. Ours is to proclaim the Word of God. We have much to learn from this wisdom teacher and his method of theological reinterpretation.

Questions for Discussion and Reflection
Group Sharing/Discussion

1. Why was the author concerned about the Hellenized Jews being influenced by the Greek culture?

2. What are some of the differences described in store for the righteous and the unrighteous?

3. Read aloud 11, 17–26. Describe in your own words the kind of God described in this section.

In Our Lives

1. The first half of the book of Wisdom has as a central issue the immortality of the soul. What is your own description of life after death? What would change in the way you live if you did not believe in life after death?

2. Chapters 1, 1—6, 21 deal primarily with the differences between the treatment of the good and the wicked. What there do you agree with or disagree with?

3. The author describes himself as a seeker of wisdom in 7, 1–22a. What are ways you seek wisdom? Describe someone you know who could be called a wisdom figure.

Individual/Person Reflection/Action

1. Write down five words that describe your own image of God. How do these compare with the description you had of God when you were a child? How has your image of God matured as you have aged?

2. Some parts of Wisdom explain why bad things happen to good people. How would you explain them? How does your faith help you deal with bad things in you life?

3. Name for yourself someone who has helped you by sharing their wisdom. Perhaps you have just observed how they handle life or you may even have had conversations with them about your life. Let them know what this has meant to you.

SIRACH (ECCLESIASTICUS) READING GUIDE

At a Glance

Who are the main players?	Jesus, son of Eleazar, son of Sirach
What should I look for?	The careful maxims of a sage who loves and lives the Torah and wants to share his experience to maintain religious faith and integrity.
When did this take place?	Written in Hebrew around 180 B.C., the text was translated into Greek c. 132 B.C. by the author's grandson.
Where did these events occur?	A respected Jerusalem scribe wrote the Hebrew; the Greek was written in the Diaspora.
Why was this book written?	Both editions were written for those who wished to gain learning and were disposed to live according to the Law.
What is the story?	The book contains reflections grouped according to various subjects such as individual, family, and community relations. It treats of friendship, education, poverty and wealth, worship, and many religious and social customs.

About the Book

Over the years the book of Sirach has been known by different names: "The Wisdom of Jesus Ben Sira" (of which Sirach is the Greek form); "The Book of Sirach" (a shortened title); and "Ecclesiasticus" (from the Latin for book of the Church, a designation that probably stems from its frequent use as a catechetical aid in the early centuries of the Western Church).

The book appears to be a collection of proverbs organized in such a way as to resemble short essays. While there is no explicit arrangement in the book itself, one can divide the material into themes and according to literary form.

Sirach is the only biblical book that:
• Identifies its author (50, 27)
• Refers to its translator (a grandson of Ben Sirach)
• Dates its translation ("the 38th year of the reign of King Euergetes," sometime after 132 B.C. (see the foreword preceding chapter 1).

Although the prophetic books claim to originate from the prophets and do locate their ministry during the reign of specific kings (for example, Hos 1, 1; Is 1, 1; Jer 1, 2f; etc.), the references there are to the activity of the prophets, not to the books that bear the prophets' names. Here we have a clear reference to when the book was written.

The foreword also provides us with some interesting information about the composition of the biblical canon (the official list of inspired books). Three times the grandson of Ben Sirach speaks of "the Law, the Prophets, and the later authors" (or "the rest of the books"). This tells us that by the second century B.C. the Jewish community already had what came to be known as a tripartite (three-part) Bible. Scholars believe that the first two parts (the Law and the Prophets) most likely include the books as we have them today. The third part (the Writings) was probably quite fluid well into the Christian era.

Like the book of Wisdom, Sirach belongs to the collection called Deuterocanonical by Roman Catholics or Apocryphal by Protestants (see Glossary). The foreword, which is considered historical introduction and not inspired instruction, recounts the translator's arrival in Egypt, where he discovered that the Jews' "valuable teaching" had been rendered from Hebrew into Greek, the language of the day. This inspired him to undertake the translation of his grandfather's teachings. The Hebrew version from which he worked seems to have dropped out of sight until copies of it were found in 1806. Its absence from the Jewish list explains why it is missing from the Protestant canon.

The way the high priest Simon is described (50, 1–21) leads one to conclude he had recently died. This would locate the writing of the original Hebrew version of Sirach sometime during the first quarter of the second century (200–175) B.C. The description of Simon's priestly performance suggests that the author was quite familiar with the Jerusalem ritual and perhaps was even a resident of the city and wrote there.

The Reason for Writing

The Hellenization of the Near East had already taken hold among the educated upper classes by the time Ben Sirach (meaning son of Sirach) put his teachings into writing. Many Jews must have wondered whether their ancient traditions could match the breadth and depth of Greek thought. Being a well-traveled man (34, 11) and an observant Jew, Ben Sirach would have witnessed the decline in fervor that overtook his fellow Jews, and it would have troubled him. His object in writing was to show the Jews of his day that real wisdom was to be found in the traditions of Israel and not in the godless philosophy of the Greeks. He intended his work to be a guide to every circumstance of life:

• Ben Sirach encouraged his readers to study the ancient traditions to find direction needed to cope with their new, challenging situation (2, 10).

• He warned against trying to live according to the standards of both Judaism and Hellenism (2, 12).

• He condemned those who chose Hellenism over Judaism (2, 13f).

• He identified the wise ("those who fear the LORD") as those who were faithful to the religion of Israel (2, 15–17).

Although most of Ben Sirach's wisdom teaching is quite conventional, the way he blended it with Israel's history and legal and cultic traditions is distinctive. Earlier wisdom writing showed little interest in Israelite matters. Ben Sirach's way of arguing in favor of faithfulness to Judaism was:

• To claim that true wisdom resided in Israel (24, 1–21)

• To use history to support this claim (44, 1—49, 16)

• To identify Wisdom with the Law of Moses (24, 22), giving this a place of honor above the traditions of other cultures

• To demonstrate a profound concern for the cult and role of the priesthood (46, 6–20; 47, 12f; 50, 1–21).

Wisdom Teaching

Like the book of Proverbs, the primary focus of Ben Sirach's teaching is moral guidance. The book is like an instruction manual containing maxims, many of which are grouped according to topic. A series of short essays addresses topics such as duties toward God, toward one's parents, and toward rulers. There are instructions on how to train children, how to choose friends, and how to guard one's speech. There are warnings against excess, laziness, and foolishness. Whatever one needs to succeed in life, while at the same time remaining faithful to the traditions of the elders, is addressed in the instruction.

Like Proverbs, Sirach celebrates the glories of personified Wisdom (chapters 1 and 24). But it takes the characterization a step further than the earlier work. Here we see Wisdom searching for a place to dwell and finally pitching her tent in Jerusalem. Traces of this poetic characterization can be found in the Gospel of John where the Word, present with God from the beginning and involved in the creation of all things, "made his dwelling [literally "lived in a tent"] among us" (Jn 1, 1–14).

Ben Sirach's poems describing the role of divine wisdom in creation (16, 22—17, 18; 39, 12–35; 42, 15—43, 35) are really commentaries on the opening chapters of Genesis. The rather technical way he develops his thought shows us the extent to which Ben Sirach was influenced by the scientific knowledge of his day.

The book contains some of the harshest statements about women found in the Bible. Proverbs may have warned the naive youth to beware of wily and seductive women, but this author seems to speak disparagingly against women in general. Ben Sirach is the one who blames woman for sin and death (25, 23). He expected wives to be subservient to their husbands, for he seems to be in favor of punishment, even including divorce, if they refuse to obey (25, 24f). Perhaps the worst example of this is found in the description of the unwed daughter (42, 9–14). The author considers her a liability, and his concern is exclusively with the reputation of the father. As with biblical passages about slavery and other practices of ancient society, we need to use care in present-day interpretation.

The author holds a traditional view of retribution (4, 11–19; 7, 1–3; 16, 1–21; 21, 1–10). Reward or punishment after death does not seem to be the concern of this wisdom teacher (14, 15–19). He counsels mourning at the death of another but cautions his reader to moderation in the expression of grief. The reason the display should be temperate is that the dead are dead and nothing can be changed by uncontrolled sorrow (38, 1–23).

While this view of death may be similar to earlier notions of retribution, it was not universally held in Israel at this time. Hope of reward after death for fidelity during persecution is found in other writings of this period (for example Dn 12, 1–3; 2 Mc 7, 9–29). Although Ben Sirach probably lived before the Maccabean Revolt (events surrounding this period are recorded in other books), his grandson-translator certainly lived after the rebellion, and he upheld his ancestor's traditional view.

The Influence of Sirach on Jewish and Christian Communities

The New Testament writers primarily used the ancient Greek version of the Hebrew Bible called the Septuagint, which contained additional works such as Sirach. It is not surprising that the influence of Sirach can be detected in some of their writings. The Letter of James is a clear example of this. Both books address questions of pride (Sir 10, 7; Jas 4, 6) and humility (Sir 3, 18; Jas 1, 9), of rich and poor (Sir 10, 19–24; Jas 2, 1–6), and of true wisdom (Sir 19, 17–21; Jas 3, 13–17), to name but a few.

There are also parallels between directives found in Sirach and those in the Gospels. This includes teaching on magnanimity (Sir 29, 12; Mt 6, 19) and forgiveness (Sir 28, 2; Mk 11, 25) and

against placing false hope in possessions (Sir 11, 18f; Lk 12, 16–21).

From the time of its appearance Sirach has been very influential in both the Jewish and Christian communities. Over the years it has served as a kind of handbook of practical ethics, and its teachings can be found in the liturgical texts of both groups.

Although the canonical status of Sirach was and remains a question for debate in the larger Judeo-Christian community, for Catholics, Sirach is a canonical book. It continues to exercise its influence even today. Passages from Sirach are used as lectionary readings and, for many Catholics, the liturgical celebration is their primary exposure to the Bible.

Questions for Discussion and Reflection
Group Sharing/Discussion

1. Choose several maxims from Sirach that especially appeal to you. Why do you think they are appropriate for life today?

2. Give examples from Sirach that are inappropriate for the way we live today.

3. If you were Ben Sirach, what 10 teachings would you leave for your children and their children?

In Our Lives

1. Where do most people today find the principles by which they live?

2. How does our parish leadership take responsibility for helping our people follow the teachings of Christ in their daily lives?

3. Share ideas on passing along to children the principles by which a Christian lives.

Individual/Personal Reflection/Action

1. When you hear a particularly helpful homily, remember to tell the preacher you appreciate it.

2. Make a list for yourself of the 10 most important principles by which you live. After each one write down how you learned it, and who and what helped form in you that belief.

3. Ask helpful people to recommend a book you might use in your own life to stay encouraged and challenged to live by your principles.

THE PROPHETS

If you are studying this in a group, it would be helpful to read this essay and the following one, "The Prophetic Books," together before beginning Isaiah and the other prophets.

Prophetic Themes

Before getting into the individual characteristics and message of each of the prophetic books, it will be important to know a little about prophets and prophecies. For most people, the common understanding of a prophet is that a prophet is a person who predicts the future. This is not, however, what the Bible means.

A biblical prophet is a person deeply concerned and called by God to address the present-day events that affect the moral and spiritual lives of people. Having experienced God's presence and love in a profound way, the prophet becomes attuned to the wishes of God for individual lives and in the life of the community. Taking on the perspective of God awakens the prophet to concerns of faith and justice— especially concern for the poor, the afflicted, the alienated, and the marginalized. The prophet, having become a very intimate friend of God, consults with God on various matters, who then compels the prophet to share those insights and discussions with the rest of the community. The prophet uses all possible techniques to communicate with the people: symbols, stories, word plays, and speech forms and patterns common to that day.

How Does a Prophet Come to Be?

Most biblical prophets are instructed by God in what to say, how to act, and whom to address. For some, such as Isaiah and Ezekiel, the initial call comes in the form of a dramatic vision; for others, all readers are told is that "The word of the LORD came" to the prophet. The prophet, through that personal relationship with God, takes on the role of God's messenger and sees the world around him in terms of how it relates to God. The prophet assesses people and events not on the basis of wealth, status, or possessions, but rather on the basis of the value and dignity of every single person created in the image and likeness of God. This viewpoint is so much the prophet's own that the prophet dares to speak for God, often using the phrase, "Thus says the LORD . . ." This conviction comes to the surface most clearly when the prophet perceives the lack of justice, faithfulness, or compassion in individual lives and especially in the life and actions of the community. These experiences of injustice call the prophet forth to speak, no matter what the cost. The prophet's challenge is hard to listen to, because the prophet speaks of matters that go counter to the accepted actions within the community, whether in religion, culture, or politics. Usually, the prophet's message concerns a movement away from being preoccupied with our own selfish concerns, to a movement toward being concerned for others—especially those who have no power: the poor, the widows, the afflicted, the outcasts, the alienated, the marginalized, the stranger.

As an integral member of this community, the prophet's own challenge is to renounce self-righteousness and to speak as one also in continual need of healing and conversion. Self-righteousness is not the true stance of the prophet, although that danger is ever present. Rather, the prophet speaks as a member of this sinful community. Despite this stance, the messenger is often clearly unpopular, because the message is difficult, even painful. Think about it for yourself: Would you want to live with someone who constantly pointed out your injustices or social evils, as if God were constantly watching you?

Demands of the Prophet

Although the prophets differ from one another in what they emphasize and in the particular themes and applications of their prophetic words, one or more of three main subjects preoccupy almost all of the prophetic books. The prophets maintain that the social life of Israel or Judah is unjust; that the worship life of the people is corrupt; and that the relations between Israel or Judah and other countries are evidence of the lack of faith in God on the part of the people and their leaders. Social injustice is manifested in the treatment of the poor and marginalized, such as orphans and widows. Corruption in worship appears in the introduction of practices from other religions into Temple worship and in the belief that carrying out the form of sacrifice, while maintaining unjust or unfair social policies, is sufficient to satisfy God's demands. Faithlessness in foreign policy is shown when the leaders rely on treaties with the great powers of the day, and payment of tribute to emperors, rather than on following the commandments of God.

In speaking from the perspective of God, the prophet always laments over the injustices and points out and accuses the wrongdoers, hoping for repentance and reform. Usually, a warning is included, in which the prophet, in a general manner, tells of possible dire consequences if matters are not corrected, or if attitudes are not changed. The prophet's message always demands a change of heart, mind, and attitudes—aligning them to the mind, heart, and attitudes of God. Only in this manner can justice once again prevail and God be intimately present to the community.

However, the prophet's message is not always one of doom and gloom. Rather, the prophet continually reminds the people of God's faithful love and concern for them. In this context, the prophet offers the opportunity and the guidance for the community to realign itself with God's love, reconciliation, and peace. But the challenge is that this will only occur if the people continue to do the LORD's work, the work of justice. Just as God is faithful, the prophet spurs the people on to be faithful also. God's love and peace will be manifest if the people attend to the concerns of the poor and to the works of justice. Reform of self in order to be of service to others is the key message of all the prophets. In order for the reform to take place, the prophet continually reminds the people of God's loving arms and faithful care. If the people continue to remember God's love and fidelity toward them, then justice will indeed flourish in the land.

THE PROPHETIC BOOKS

Many of the books of the Bible were written much later than the time period and the events they recount. This is true for the collection of the prophetic books. The prophetic books follow a pattern somewhat like this. First the prophet experiences life within a believing faith community. This community nourishes and sustains the prophet's relationship with God and enables the prophet to grow in intimacy with God and others. Sometime during the prophet's life, he experiences God intimately and profoundly, and the prophet feels called to help bridge the gap between God and the community. The prophet develops an acute sensitivity to violations of justice, especially toward the poor and rejected. The prophet has an inherent need to call these incidents to the attention of the community. Often, warnings of dire consequences accompany the prophet's words, challenging the community to action on behalf of those who are experiencing injustice.

Some in the community reject the prophet's message and try to out-shout, silence, imprison, exile, or even kill the prophet. Others see the wisdom in the prophet's words and begin to live and act accordingly. This segment of the community preserves the message and memory of the prophet by acting on the challenge and by passing the words and story on to anyone who will listen. Prophets were origi-

nally speakers rather than writers, but once their words were written down, the writings were brought together and edited so their lasting message could be kept alive and understood. In this process of handing on the stories, the words of the prophet are shaped and reshaped, so that they speak not only to the prophet's original audience but also to those presently in the community.

There is, nevertheless, a viewpoint for these prophetic collections. This viewpoint, the theology of the book, reflects the human relationship with God and tries to be faithful to the living memory of the original prophet. At the same time, it also continues to be relevant to changing times and experiences of the believing community. Thus, the words of the prophet still challenge our generation and times in the same way that they challenged the prophet's own generation and times.

Questions for Discussion and Reflection
Group Sharing/Discussion

1. In your own words, tell what a prophet is.
2. How is the role of the prophet helpful and important to the community?
3. Why would the prophet take such personal risk and share bad news?
4. Share something you learned or thought about as a result of these essays.

ISAIAH READING GUIDE

At a Glance

Scholars conclude three different authors at three different times were edited into this one book:
I: chapters 1–39; II: chapters 40–55; III: chapters 56–66.

Who are the main players?

I. Isaiah; super-power Assyria is dominant foreign power threatening Israel.
II. Written in Babylon for the exiled Hebrews, the poets/theologians were key authors; Cyprus, king of Persia
III. Israelites are back in Zion, intent upon rebuilding; the prophet's criticisms and promises center on Zion.

What should I look for?

In general the three-fold pattern (a) appearance of the LORD in power (b) requiring a response by the people or their representative, followed by (c) a divine intervention that implements justice. Look for the linkage of salvation and justice.
I. Denunciations of Zion and Judah; promises of blessings; announcements of God's judgments; oracles about foreign nations and narratives of the prophet.
II. No narratives, denunciations, or prophetic biography; rather carefully fashioned speeches announcing forgiveness to exiles in Babylon and inviting them to Zion; Servant Songs that note consolation and hope amid internal tensions.
III. Exclusively on internal affairs of the community—on deep religious, social, and economic divisions within the Judean community; also attention is projected to a future intervention of God in judgment and salvation; an apocalyptic vision of a purified people and Jerusalem as religious capital of the world.

When did it take place?

I. Preserves the preaching and deeds of Isaiah of Jerusalem of the late eighth century B.C.
II. Second Isaiah written in the mid-sixth century, about a century and a half after First Isaiah.
III. Third Isaiah written several decades later.

Where did these events occur?

I. In Palestine during occupation of Assyria
II. In Babylon while in exile
III. In Jerusalem after the Babylonian Exile

Why was this book written?

I. The prophet indicts the people and King Ahaz for refusing to trust in God's promises, tells of God's choosing Assyria as the punisher and gives promise of a better king.
II. The authors of Second Isaiah were poet-theologians who developed their ideas in new ways to persuade the people to certain modes of action.
III. The prophet announces that the LORD will rebuild the community in Zion, and Israel, to be authentic, needs to adhere to God's commands in worship and social justice.

What is the story?

I. Isaiah tries to lead the people to trust in God's promises and to be faithful and just.

II. In Babylonia the prophet reminds the people of their religious identity in their teachings.

III. The prophet reveals the internal problems of the Israelite community. He urges them to follow the commands of worshiping God and doing justice. He nourishes the community with a vision of God's salvation.

The chapters of Isaiah comprise a "collection of collections." This complex structure might bewilder the reader unless you realize there are essentially three themes dominating Isaiah.

First is the unity and destiny of Israel as the people of the LORD God as they face the military threat of Mesopotamia (Assyria, Babylonia, and Persia).

Second, Jerusalem is the spiritual center and symbol of Israel's role among the nations of the world.

Third, the dynasty of David bears a special significance. David, the founder, had first established a united kingdom of Israel, with a capital in Jerusalem. The fate of this royal house plays a dominant role in the prophecies of chapters 6–12, but less so in later chapters. However, this link with the language and themes of the kingship of these Davidic leaders has made Isaiah the "messianic" prophet of the Old Testament.

Three in One: The Book of Isaiah

Since the Bible presents us with a single work, under one title, it is natural to assume that the entire book of Isaiah was written by one person called Isaiah. Scholarly research, however, has shown that one person could not have written the entire book. Close analysis reveals that the people, places, and events in this book span several centuries. This is important to realize as you attempt to read this well-known and beloved book of the Bible. It is a book that has had a significant influence on both the Old and New Testaments, with Isaiah being one of the books most often quoted in the New Testament.

At least three different authors or communities, spanning three centuries, wrote and edited materials that were actually compiled into the one book we now know as Isaiah. Biblical schol-

ars have assigned names to each of the three collections of materials in the book of Isaiah: First Isaiah, or *Isaiah of Jerusalem,* chapters 1–39; Second or *Deutero-Isaiah,* chapters 40–55; and Third or *Trito-Isaiah,* chapters 56–66. They are briefly described here and more detail follows.

Isaiah of Jerusalem

First Isaiah, or Isaiah of Jerusalem (chs 1–39) is usually dated to a very turbulent period in the history of Israel, 740–687 B.C. First Isaiah witnessed the events that led Assyria to annihilate and exile the northern kingdom of Israel, in 721, as well as to place Judah itself under their control. Isaiah of Jerusalem was still ministering in 701 when Hezekiah, king of Judah, grew tired of being subject to Assyria and asked Egypt for help in rebelling against Assyria. In response to this rebellious league against him, Sennacherib, the king of Assyria, came back and captured all the key Judean towns, ultimately surrounding Jerusalem. In the biblical version of the story, a plague sent by God broke out, and Sennacherib retreated with the war spoils from the other cities. The Assyrian version of the story, found recorded in a recent archaeological discovery known as Taylor's prism (an inscribed stone, called a prism because of its shape), is that Hezekiah knew he was defeated, so he called a truce and agreed to pay a very large sum of money if Sennacherib would leave and not destroy the city. Sennacherib agreed, and the battle ended.

Isaiah in Babylonia

Second or Deutero- (from the Greek word meaning second) Isaiah, chapters 40–55, covers the years 540–537 B.C., in Babylonia. Babylonia, roughly modern-day Iraq, had defeated the previous superpower, Assyria, in 612, when

---

Steps of Transforming Life Experience into a Text and Beyond

1. An experience—immediate or of long duration

2. Reflecting on that experience over time

3. Verbal articulation of that experience—storytelling and reshaping of story over a period of time

4. Written texts—collections of stories, sayings, rituals, insights, wisdom, proverbs, poetry, narration

5. Editing of the written material into a coherent whole with an overarching point of view or theology

This entire process is repeated every time an individual or a community reads or hears and experiences the text as speaking directly to them. Applying the text to one's own personal experience starts this process over and over. In this context, the text becomes a living document able to speak to those willing to listen and take it to heart.

At some point, certain texts were accepted as *final* or *canonical,* and no more changes could be made to the text. But up to that point, the text was still in a process of shaping and reshaping.

Babylonia captured Assyria's capital city, Nineveh. Nebuchadnezzar, the king of Babylonia, went on a campaign to capture as much territory as he could handle. In 587, he captured the southern kingdom of Judah, destroyed Jerusalem and its Temple, and exiled or deported the people of Judah to Babylonia. From 587 to 538, the people of Judah were in Babylonia, without land, temple, or roots. In 538, Cyrus, the king of the Persians, defeated the Babylonian empire and restored the people to their homeland. It was during the last few years of the Babylonian Exile, and the beginning of the return under Cyrus, that Second Isaiah spoke to the people in Babylonia.

Isaiah of the Return from Exile

Third Isaiah, also known as Trito-Isaiah ("trito" is the Greek word meaning third), chapters 56–66, is dated to the period after the return of the people from Babylon, 537–500 B.C. There was great joy in returning, but soon worry, depression, and defeat set in because of the vast amount of work that needed to be done to rebuild the land, the city walls and structures, and the Temple. These preoccupations were further complicated by the attitude of some of those who returned to the land.

Even though they had come to see their exile as a consequence of their faithlessness, and their liberation as God's new mighty act that renewed the covenant relationship, people still sinned, acted from motives of greed, and showed injustice toward the poor and oppressed. These chap-

ters presume the Temple had been rebuilt, dating them after 515 B.C. Judah had become a province of Persia, and the people were caught up in the frustrating process of rebuilding the land and their Jewish identities. It is in this context that Third Isaiah speaks to the people.

Editors, who gave them final shape, pulled these three blocks of material, each with its unique message, together. The description above helps us set a context for reading and understanding Isaiah. Unless we are familiar with the historical background, the prophet's words will not be clear, because we will not understand the specific references. God speaks and acts in and through human events and through people. To know what God is saying, therefore, we must be aware of the events, practices, and culture of the times. Only those who see matters from God's perspective will be true guides in reading the signs of the times.

First Isaiah

Overview of Chapters 1–39

First Isaiah, or Isaiah of Jerusalem, speaks from the very turbulent events of 742–700 B.C. In its final form, the work begins with a particular message to Jerusalem in chapters 1–12. It then addresses the nations as a whole in chapters 13–23, and finally speaks about the fate of the whole world in chapters 24–27, which probably do not go back to Isaiah of Jerusalem. Chapters 28–39 will be discussed later.

Biblical Vocation Call Pattern

1. God significantly enters a human life.

2. God gives the person a mandate or a mission.

3. The person being called usually objects.

4. God makes creative use of this objection.

5. God reassures the person.

Some Biblical Texts Indicative of this Pattern:

- Exodus 3, 1–12
- Jeremiah 1, 4–10
- Isaiah 6, 1–8
- Isaiah 40, 1–9
- Luke 1, 28–38
- Acts 9, 10–19

The account of the prophet's call usually provides significant clues to the prophet's perspective. (See the explanation above.) Chapter 6 of Isaiah recounts First Isaiah's call.

Isaiah experiences the LORD as king and glorious majesty during Temple worship and prayer. This majestic, overwhelming, holy presence is suffused in and through "all the earth." The prophet's experience of this presence leads to his understanding of himself as a person, like everyone else, full of imperfections, infidelities, and weaknesses. Yet, when the LORD touches and cleanses the mouth of the prophet with a fiery ember, the prophet is empowered to speak in spite of his weak and sinful human condition. The prophet sees the need for someone to speak to the people, feels called to respond to this need, and volunteers as the spokesperson for the LORD. Isaiah will speak the LORD's message but the people will not listen or understand. When Isaiah asks how long this will continue, he receives the answer: until all is destroyed, laid waste, and made desolate.

Thus, the message that Isaiah brings, the people will not listen to, and therefore destruction will come upon both the people and the land. Yet, throughout there is the ultimate hope for peace, harmony, and messianic salvation. No matter how stubborn the people are in their refusal to listen and repent, God will still work peace and future salvation in and through that very stubbornness and refusal. Suffering and punishment will prove to be a purifying, refining fire that will bring the community closer to God and that will make them more concerned with each other, especially the poor, the oppressed, and the alienated.

Remember, however, that the original prophetic material has been shaped and reshaped as it has been handed down and further modified by the final editors into a message that will be pertinent to their own particular community. These ancient editors even added material to stress a particular aspect of the original message. Therefore, while Isaiah's call is located in chapter 6, the editors have provided a summary section, chapters 1–6, showing what Isaiah's message was to be, and how the people would respond, along with how God would eventually work out the loving plan of salvation.

Isaiah, Chapters 1–6

Chapter 1 of Isaiah boldly states that unless the community repents its injustices and cares for the poor and defenseless in their midst, God will bring severe punishment upon the people. God punishes them (for instance, by the Assyrian conquest) not to destroy them, but rather to purify them, so that they will become a more just and loving community.

Isaiah 2, 1–5 speaks of a vision of future peace in a passage that is one of the most quoted and best-known passages of all Scripture. It speaks of that ideal time when instruments of war are turned into tools of peace—tools that can be used for meeting the hungers of the human family. This is the ideal to which God has called Israel and the entire community, the vision that is integral to Isaiah's message as prophet. Yet chapter 2, 6 to chapter 5 continue what must have been Isaiah's enduring, poorly received, and unheard message. In this section the prophet calls to mind the selfishness of the people, their lack of justice, their lack of concern for others, and their utter disregard for the loving relationship into which

God and Suffering

A theological perspective in Isaiah focuses on God as an impatient parent who is fed up with the sinful actions of the children. Punishment is seen by the parent as a means of redirecting or redefining the focus of the child. Isaiah seems to be saying that God punishes in order to purify the sinful actions and inclinations of the people. Other nations are used by God as instruments to accomplish this punishing and purifying process.

A question that needs to be asked is whether this is an image of God that makes sense to us today. Does this image of God speak to our experience and consciousness of what we have come to understand as God? Just as corporal punishment of children is no longer considered an appropriate form of punishment for misbehavior, so this image of God as child-punisher has to be also reevaluated. We have come to realize that suffering is not something that God causes to happen in order to help us learn a lesson. Rather, suffering is part and parcel of what it means to be human.

God is experienced as one who is always life-giving, life-enhancing, life-producing. All the experiences of our lives are means by which we can enter into a greater personal and loving relationship with God. Suffering and pain are key moments in our experience that help us to realize that we are not the center of the universe. It is at these particular moments that God invites us to an ever deeper relationship, challenging us to believe very firmly that new life will come out of this seemingly life-denying experience. God is always on the side of life, on our side, in the sense of a loved one who is faithful no matter what the sorrow or pain. It is this faithfulness of God toward the people that is truly Isaiah's message.

God brings about redemption in and through those very experiences of pain and sorrow that bring us to our knees. God does not cause the pain and suffering, but rather, God uses it to bring new life out of death. This is what we mean when we speak of the Christian life as one deeply imbedded in the Paschal Mystery, the mystery of death and resurrection that Jesus experienced and in which we participate. God does not cause the pain; neither does God free us from this very human experience. Rather, God transforms our very pain and sorrow into an occasion of greater understanding of self as human, of deeper sympathy with others in pain, and of greater depth in our personal, loving relationship with God and all of creation.

God called Israel. Chapter 6 relates Isaiah's vocation call experience, a willingness to devote himself to the work of the LORD despite the frustration, futility, and hardships that the work and message will bring.

The Book of Immanuel

Chapters 7–12, usually referred to as the "Book of Immanuel" because it contains the famous verses of the Immanuel prophecy (Is 7, 12), deal with salvation that comes only with reliance on God, and not on one's own strength or alliances for security. Isaiah 7, 9 clearly expresses the intent of this whole section, as well as all of the book of Isaiah, when it states that "unless your faith is firm, you shall not be firm." Faith in God is the root that will maintain us no matter what comes along. Yet even if we are overwhelmed by what comes along, God will continue to be with us bringing new life, birth, and creation out of death, destruction, and pain. Although the material in these chapters comes from different times in Isaiah's ministry, it has been carefully arranged to stress the themes of reliance on God and God's fidelity to the promises made to the people.

Oracles against the Nations

Chapters 13–23 make up a collection of oracles against the nations. The prophet uses these to show that God will not allow Israel to be unjust indefinitely. Just because the Israelites have an established relationship with God does not mean that they can do whatever they want. God will draw the line at some point, and Isaiah's message is exactly that: You cannot go on being unjust and expect to get away with it.

Usually, God's plan for punishment of the people was understood by the prophets to be the key reason that other nations were successful in defeating Israel. God uses other nations to accomplish his purifying purposes upon the community of Israel. However, God does not allow the other nations to overstep their bounds either. God makes sure that other nations merely accomplish the purifying punishment desired, and no more. The key to these oracles in Isaiah is that the final editors have inserted another revolutionary concept, that of universal salvation. They saw God's saving hand operative even in these foreign nations. Like Israel, they will not be completely destroyed. Rather, there is hope that they, too, after experiencing their own purification through suffering, will ultimately place their reliance on God, and God alone. They too, like Israel, will be saved.

The Apocalypse of Isaiah

Chapters 24–27 are referred to as the "Apocalypse of Isaiah." Apocalypse, a style of writing, is a term meaning to reveal or to draw aside the veil of the mysteries of life, and discern God's plan at work, especially those experiences that are the most puzzling or opaque to such insights, like pain and suffering. Often such writings were intended primarily to offer encouragement and support to those suffering and oppressed. Highly symbolic language was used to reveal how God would ultimately accomplish the plan of salvation, especially how salvation would be brought out of the pain, suffering, and evil in the midst of the community.

These chapters of Isaiah provide a future vision, a peek into the end times, when all the ruin, destruction, and suffering will be put into perspective, and new life will come out of it.

Those who have continually trusted in the LORD will be fully rewarded and recompensed with new life and the defeat of death (25, 7f.19). Full intimacy with God, explored here in the image of an eternal divine banquet on God's holy mountain (25, 6ff), will be reestablished.

The defeat of death and the universal salvation of all nations are two of the most revolutionary concepts found in the book of Isaiah, if not in the entire Old Testament. Up to this time, future survival was seen exclusively in terms of the memory of an individual living on in the family, in the children, and in the survival of the nation of Israel.

Later Addition to First Isaiah

Chapters 28–33 and 34–35 are later additions made by a second editor or group who were inspired by the words and tradition of Isaiah of Jerusalem. It is important to remember that inspiration applies to the entire process that resulted in the biblical text, not just to one author but also to those who collected and edited the material, as well as those who reflected upon and reshaped the original words or message of Isaiah. In other words, the final book that we know as Isaiah is the result of a whole tradition, begun by Isaiah and ending when the final editing touches were placed on the entire book. Chapters 28–33 and 34–35, although they are the work of a different group of editors, are consistent with the previous 27 chapters.

They stress once again the need to put away all injustice and to trust in God. Since the people will refuse to listen, God will punish the people, yet this punishment will lead to recognition of the need to place faith and trust completely in God. The vision of 35, 5–6 focuses on the lame, deaf, and blind placing their trust in God, and establishing their home in the new Jerusalem that God has prepared for the faithful. After the pain and anguish caused by the purifying punishment, God will gather all the scattered and bring them back home to a new Jerusalem that will be faithful to the loving relationship God has initiated.

Historical Appendix to First Isaiah

Chapters 36–39 are a historical appendix provided by the editors and based primarily on 2 Kings 18, 13—20, 19, giving a quick summary of the historical events surrounding the oracles of First Isaiah of Jerusalem. This quick summary is intended to provide a link back to the message of Isaiah and the actual historical events surrounding Hezekiah and Sennacharib. Also, this summary provides a link forward to the Babylonian attack and the destruction of Jerusalem, as well as the exile of the people to Babylon. The time that has elapsed between chapter 39 and chapter 40 is approximately 150 years. Second Isaiah, chapters 40–55, picks up the themes of First Isaiah, especially God's plan for universal salvation, and expands them significantly.

Second Isaiah

Second Isaiah speaks to a community that has indeed experienced the terrifying, purifying punishment of God and still continues to do so. The Babylonians defeated Assyria, and in 583 B.C. they captured and destroyed Jerusalem and exiled its entire people. Second Isaiah speaks in the very midst of this exile, observing how it is about to end, with Cyrus, king of the Persians, referred to as God's anointed, coming to defeat the Babylonians and setting God's people free. The tone of Second Isaiah is one of comfort, hope, restoration, and of God's loving arms reaching out to comfort and console the people.

Overture to Second Isaiah's Symphony

Like an overture to a good piece of music, chapter 40 summarizes, in beautiful poetry, all the key themes of chapters 40–55. At the time when Israel is most discouraged and ready to despair, Isaiah speaks God's word of comfort and love to the people. The setting for Second Isaiah's message is the entire world, for God's saving action on behalf of the people will be so evident that all will see and experience God's saving plan, love, and power. Greed, corruption, and reliance on false gods are again condemned, making their elimination the key condition upon which God's loving and saving activity will become realized.

The Suffering Servant and God's Faithfulness

Chapters 41–48 take up several themes that are beautifully and poetically developed by Second Isaiah. The "servant" theme is one that has great

meaning, both in its application to Israel as the suffering servant of God, and to Jesus, the ultimate model of the suffering servant of God. There are at least four servant passages in all of Second Isaiah: 42, 1–4; 49, 1–7; 50, 4–11; 52, 13—53, 12.

Another rich theme that Second Isaiah explores concerns the comparison that is made between God's saving action on behalf of the people now in Babylon, and God's foundational saving action on behalf of the people in their Exodus from Egypt. Second Isaiah exhorts the people to be faithful to God, for God is about to unleash a new salvation experience for the people, just like the one their ancestors experienced in the desert. Second Isaiah uses the image of God as the master engineer who will design and build a wonderful road right through the desert so that Israel will be able to take a direct route back to its home. What God did for the people in the beginning of their relationship he will do again, to show his great love and fidelity toward the people. Second Isaiah emphasizes the fact that God is still faithful now, as God was in the infancy stages of Israel's growth. God continues to work those great and mighty deeds that were worked in the midst of their ancestors. Faith and reliance on God are the only key requirements for God's mighty deeds to take place.

Salvation Involves Suffering

Chapters 49–55 have a less exalted, less hopeful tone, with more of a tragic sense of what is needed to bring about God's plan. One aspect of this deeper view is the prophet's identification of himself as the suffering servant. Another is in the recognition of the importance of suffering.

Salvation will come about, but often through one who suffers with and for the people, as an ultimate example and model of what suffering is all about. These passages about the suffering servant were identified with Second Isaiah and with the whole people of God. Most of all, however, they are identified with Jesus. In chapters 49–55 the hopeful message of joy and comfort is still there, but it is deepened through the realization that the very messenger of the good news must endure pain and suffering for the good news to take root in the minds and hearts of the community.

Third Isaiah

Isaiah of the Return

With these ideas in mind, we now move to Third Isaiah, whose melancholy tone is much more pronounced than that in Second Isaiah. Third Isaiah presumes a time when the people have returned from exile and have rebuilt the Temple. From a variety of sources, the date can be set any time after 515 B.C. The people are home; they are changed and purified by their experience of suffering, yet authentic worship and a concern for justice are not central to the lives of the restored people of God.

The author of Third Isaiah, whether one person or a community of persons, experiences this lack in the community and is moved to use the vision of the Isaiah tradition to address the current situation. The author reinterprets the message of Isaiah of Jerusalem and Isaiah of the exile to address the needs of the community of that time, resulting in the Isaiah of the return.

Chapters 56–59 pick up themes of the previous chapters, especially themes of salvation in and through suffering. Suffering has the potential to make the worshiping community more sensitive to the needs of others who suffer in their midst, especially the foreigner, the outcast, and the marginalized. These people are welcomed into the house of God—a radical proposal—because of the key insight developed in 56, 7 that the house of God is a house of prayer for all peoples. Yet worship can also result in self-righteousness and complacency that says: We have done our part in worship, God. When are you going to do yours?

Ritual and Life Are Related

Third Isaiah challenges this notion by connecting worship with actions that flow from worship. If worship does not lead to a greater concern for those who are in need, if it does not lead to justice for the oppressed and outcasts, then worship is indeed meaningless. Chapter 57, 1–2 continues a theme central to the whole of Isaiah (see chapters 24–27, especially 25, 7f. 19), a belief in the continuation of life after death, especially for the just, for those who have tried to rely on God, and who are concerned for the poor, the needy, and the alienated.

Suffering as Purifying Fire

Chapters 60–62 form the heart of Third Isaiah's message. By using a variety of images that echo Second Isaiah, Third Isaiah speaks of the salvation that has come upon the community once the purifying punishment has ended. Because the community remained faithful to God during this time of testing and trial, God will more than reward the people. Not only will God restore the people to their former glory, but God will make them a light to all other nations. All the nations will see what God has done for the people, and they will stream toward Israel, and begin their own relationship with God.

Third Isaiah emphasizes that the clear sign of this salvation will be that of the Jubilee experience. The Jubilee (every 50 years) celebration, like the sabbatical experience (every 7 years), was a time of celebration and joy that spilled out into every facet of the community's life. During this time, the community is to remind itself forcibly that everything belongs to God. Thus, the land is to lie fallow, and what grows on it belongs to all people. Debts are to be wiped out, offenses are to be forgiven, the needy are to be taken care of, and all are to be at peace. Salvation is to spill into every facet of life and make itself visible to all people and nations. Jesus himself understood his mission and ministry in terms of the insights communicated here by Third Isaiah, even quoting them, and applying them to his own vocation as God's salvation to the people.

Reliance on God Brings Eternal Rewards

Chapters 63–66 are parallel to the key themes in chapters 56–59. Sorrow is expressed over the sins of the community and the need of the community to be punished because of its sinfulness and injustice. This punishment is seen as the only way that God could curb the excesses, greed, and selfishness of this sinful people. Yet, once the punishment is accomplished, God reaches out with double the effort to restore the people and make them even better and greater than before. A universality is evident in the salvation theme, where Jew and Gentile will live as one and worship God together. Those who refuse to rely on God will be severely punished, but those who trust in God will be abundantly rewarded.

Conclusion

Thus ends the book of Isaiah, a book that spans about 200 years. Throughout that period of turmoil, tension, and suffering, Isaiah focuses on one key theme: reliance, trust, faith, and confidence in God. This trust in God will lead to the recognition that God and others are the center of the universe, and not any individual person. Faith in God leads to reaching out to those in need, even when this might lead to conflict, frustration, and rejection. The book can probably be summed up by a phrase St. Paul uses in his letter to the Romans: "We know that all things work for good for those who love God. . . ." and another Pauline text that states that "What eye has not seen, and ear has not heard, and what has not entered the human heart, what God has prepared for those who love him."

Questions for Discussion and Reflection
Group Sharing/Discussion

1. Isaiah uses many strong images to speak to the people of God, of their role, of the relationship between God and the people, and so on. These images include violence and war, a vineyard, brothers and sisters, wild and tame animals together, and tears being wiped away. Choose one image in Isaiah and tell why it was an appropriate image for the prophet to use at the time.

2. Chapter Six describes how a reluctant Isaiah was eventually able to agree to speak for the LORD. How would you explain the significance of the symbol of the live coal on his lips?

3. Throughout this book there are many threats and many promises. Choose a threat and a promise that strike you as most significant.

4. What is the significance of this book being edited over the course of many generations? What effect do you think that had on the message?

In Our Lives

1. First Isaiah's message was very hard on people's ears. They did not like the sound of its challenges to their life, such as caring for the poor, living a life that was fair and just, and worshiping God. If you were today's Isaiah, what challenges would you give to our society, our culture, and our religious groups?

2. How do you understand the role of the suffering servant as portrayed by Second Isaiah? How was this image applied to Jesus? What role does it play in the life of a Christian?

3. One message in this book is about being faithful and trusting in God even during difficulties, unfairness, and painful happenings in life. This can be a difficult message to hear when undergoing trials and suffering. How can our community "be Isaiah" to those undergoing hardship? What will help us do this better?

4. Recall an experience in which someone offered hope, comfort, and consolation to you while you were taken up with your pain and suffering. How did this make you feel? How did you respond to the person?

5. What in the message of Isaiah is especially relevant for our own life and times?

Individual/Personal Reflection/Action

1. Isaiah was at first reluctant to speak out but overcame his hesitation. What opportunities do you have to speak and offer Christ's message of hope or the message of the challenges that being a Christian brings with it? Who or what will help you have the courage to speak of these things?

2. Who is someone you might call a prophet today—someone who has the courage to challenge us, to question the way we live?

3. Our society today tempts us with many false gods such as power, money, materialism, self-centeredness. What is the hardest temptation for you to resist? What can you do to become stronger in recognizing and resisting it?

4. In the book of Isaiah, God's constant and tender love reaches out continually toward goodness, especially those who suffer. Try to remember to thank God each evening for this constant and tender love for you.

JEREMIAH READING GUIDE

At a Glance

Who are the main players?	Jeremiah Josiah Jehoiakim Nebuchadnezzar Jehoiachin Zedekiah Gedaliah
What should I look for?	Three views: 1. Jeremiah's poetry-sermons, focused on Exodus and covenant, very personal, agonizing, interacting with the community and God (chs 1–25; 30–33). 2. The "Confessions" of Jeremiah where he argues with God over his vocation and message (12, 1–5; 15, 10–21; 17, 12–18; 18, 18–23; 20, 7–18). 3. Narrative sections regarding the theology of Jeremiah collected by Baruch, his secretary (chs 26–29; 34–35).
When did this take place?	Jeremiah began his prophetic ministry in 627 B.C. during the reform of Josiah and was last heard from as an unwilling exile in Egypt about 570 B.C.
Where did these events occur?	Jeremiah was born in Anathoth, just three miles from Jerusalem. He preached in Jerusalem and Israel. He was left behind when all were deported to Babylon, and he was dragged off to Egypt where he died.
Why was this book written?	Jeremiah's life spanned a tumultuous age in religion, politics, and war. During these times Jeremiah's message is the attitude of compassion and prayer. This is intimately linked to fidelity to a new covenant inscribed upon the heart. More than any other prophet Jeremiah made his own life the message.
What is the story?	Although his ministry began in a period of bright promise and reform, his recorded preaching focused on the disintegration of Judah from 609 B.C. forward, after King Josiah was killed and Babylon's assaults began. Especially noteworthy is his preaching during the grim period leading up to the destruction of Jerusalem and the Temple in 586. Four central themes are the new covenant, sin and atonement, faith and prayer, and true and false prophecy.

Jeremiah: The Person, the Message

Jeremiah's life speaks as loudly as his message. Both his life and his message thus need to be examined in order for the book to have its full impact.

Jeremiah hails from the town of Anathoth, 3.6 miles northeast of Jerusalem. His father, Hilkiah, may have been the one by that name who found the book of the Law of Moses (the book of Deuteronomy) during the repair of the Temple by King Josiah in 622 B.C. (2 Kgs 22, 8). This fact partially explains the influence of Deuteronomy on Jeremiah.

Politics helped to form the message of Jeremiah. The words and actions of Jeremiah were intimately caught up with the political happenings of the day, particularly the demise of the Assyrian Empire and the rise of Babylon as the world power.

Jeremiah's ministry began in 627 B.C. With the collapse of the Assyrian Empire, he joyfully announced the return of the northern tribes. This is the context for chapters 30–31. Jeremiah also condemned idolatry at Jerusalem but was strangely silent during the deuteronomic reform under King Josiah. In 609 B.C. Josiah was killed in battle against the Egyptians. His son Jehoiakim succeeded him and revolted against the new world power, the Babylonians. They responded by capturing Jerusalem in 597 B.C., sacking the city and deporting many of its leading citizens.

King Zedekiah was warned by Jeremiah not to join with the Egyptians in another rebellion against the Babylonians. Zedekiah gave in to the rebellion temptation and the Babylonians once again stormed the city in July, 587 B.C. They burned Jerusalem and the Temple to the ground. The king and the people were all deported to Babylonia. Jeremiah was left behind, choosing to remain in the land as a sign of hope for the future (Jer 40, 1–6). When the remaining few in Jerusalem rejected his advice to stay on the land and fled to Egypt, they dragged Jeremiah with them (Jer 42, 1—43, 7). There Jeremiah died, leaving behind a tradition and a book.

The character of Jeremiah shines brightly from any page of the book. Jeremiah manifests:
- Joyful optimism (ch 31)
- Honest, painful struggling with God (12, 1–5; 15, 10–21; 20, 7–18)
- Courage in confronting kings (ch 37)
- Agony over the tragic fate of Jerusalem (8, 18—9, 10)
- Perseverance amid continuous rejection (20, 9)
- Irritability and, at times, a desire for revenge, showing itself especially in his Confessions (12, 1–5; 15, 10–21; 17, 12–18; 18, 18–23; 20, 7–18)
- Sensitivity to the beauties and wonder of nature (1, 11; 2, 13; 4, 25)
- Celibacy, a hard choice from which he suffered much (16, 1–4); yet at the same time it kept him in tune with the suffering of the people and their need to trust and have faith in God, leading to peace.

Jeremiah gave a solid focus to the piety of Israel. This focus centered on the laments against pain and evil, as well as the bold questioning of God and God's motives. Examples of laments and questioning existed before Jeremiah, but not to the extent or degree exemplified by him. Jeremiah's Confessions were such deep questionings of God that they became seared in the community's consciousness, never to be forgotten. They have the same effect on modern readers.

Jeremiah's name, in Hebrew, means, "The LORD raises up." It is the LORD who raises Jeremiah up to be a prophet and to communicate with God's people through his life and words. Yet Jeremiah sometimes struggled with his role. In Jeremiah's struggle to determine what God wanted and how God wanted it, we also see our own struggle in trying to live in a loving, faithful relationship to God. With Jeremiah, we realize that this is not easy. God's word comes to us not in clearly defined terms and directions, but rather in the messiness of life, with all its ambiguities and fuzziness.

Like Jeremiah, our struggle in relating to God is to be continually asking and discovering where God is in all of this. Where is God in the good times? Where is God in the bad times? Where is God at those times when I am in need? Why doesn't God leave me alone? It is not that Jeremiah wants to live without God. Jeremiah cannot live without God. Jeremiah cannot ignore God, either in his life or in the life of the community, and sometimes God's message to Jeremiah is unwelcome.

Jeremiah's life and message is continually intermixed with all these questions and concerns. While desiring to be faithful and obedient to God's message at work in his life, Jeremiah is continually overwhelmed by it. This feeling causes him to question God, to get angry with God, to doubt, to feel abandoned by God.

All of Jeremiah's reactions to God are most clearly expressed in passages scattered throughout his book, known as the Confessions of Jeremiah (12, 1–5; 15, 10–21; 17, 12–18; 18, 18–23; 20, 7–18). In these passages Jeremiah vents his anger and frustration, yet he continually works through the anger by placing his reliance on God, who, no matter what the situation, is always faithful. Through the venting, Jeremiah arrives at a sense of peace and renewed commitment to that loving relationship with God, along with all that the relationship demands.

If Jeremiah the person is the message as much as his words are, then we need to look at the very human change and adaptation that Jeremiah endures in order to work out God's purpose in his life and in the life of the community. This discernment is as much our own journey with God

Historical Background

Chapters 1–6	Reign of King Josiah (640–609 B.C.). Collapse of the Assyrian Empire. Independence of many vassal states like Babylonia and Judah. Deuteronomic reform at Jerusalem (2 Chr 34f). Reunification of all Israel (2 Kgs 23). Violent death of Josiah while attempting to block the Egyptian army at the pass of Megiddo (2 Chr 35, 20–25). Josiah's son, Jehoahaz, taken captive to Egypt; another son, Jehoiakim, installed as king (2 Chr 36, 1–8).
Chapters 7–20	Reign of Jehoiakim (609–597 B.C.), a ruthless tyrant despised by Jeremiah. Nebuchadnezzar defeats Egypt at Carchemesh in Syria (605 B.C.), takes Jerusalem in 603 B.C. for the Babylonians and confirms Jehoiakim in office 601 B.C. Jehoiakim revolts. Babylonians return to Jerusalem in 597 B.C. Jehoiakim is dead; his son Jehoiachin is taken captive to Babylon and Zedekiah is installed as king (2 Chr 36, 9f).
Chapters 21–29	Reign of Zedekiah (597–587 B.C.); chapters 30–33 come from an earlier period, probably after the fall of Nineveh (612 B.C.).
Chapters 34–45	Fall and last days of Jerusalem (587–583 B.C.). City and Temple destroyed, August, 587 B.C. Most of the people deported. Gedaliah governor; Jeremiah remains at Jerusalem. Gedaliah assassinated; people flee to Egypt, dragging Jeremiah with them, 583 B.C. Third Babylonian deportation, 582 B.C. Jeremiah dies in Egypt.
Chapters 46–51	Oracles against the Nations.
Chapter 52	Historical appendix.

as it is Jeremiah's. Jeremiah's journey with God has often been compared with Jesus' journey with God. Jesus, like Jeremiah, had to struggle with faith, doubt, and feelings of abandonment to determine what the will of God was for him in his own life and community. Every person who tries to live in relationship with God and attempts to be continually faithful to God, no matter what the results, shares this process.

Jeremiah, the Book

The table above gives the historical background to Jeremiah. However, the development of the book as a story, and as a collection of the words and actions of Jeremiah, follows a different format. This can be sketched out in the table of literary background, which follows.

The book of Jeremiah is clearly a tradition, begun by the prophet and also continued by disciples who composed a major part of what is entitled in 1, 1 "the words of Jeremiah." "Words" mean actions as well as statements, disciples' response, as well as the master's leadership.

Sources of the Book of Jeremiah

The organization of the book indicates a long, complex development. The sources of this development are the sermons of the prophet himself, often in poetic form. Jeremiah is usually associated with traditions that developed in the northern kingdom, especially the focus on the Exodus and the covenant. While working out of these traditions, Jeremiah is not a slave to them but rather stamps his words with his own uniqueness and individuality. Chapters 2–25 and 30–33 are uniquely Jeremiah: very personal, agonizing, and continually interacting with the community and God.

Literary Background

Chapter 1	The prologue, or Jeremiah's prophetic call from God.
Chapters 2–25	The preaching of the prophet. The ordering of the material in this section remains close to the chronology of Jeremiah's life.
Chapters 26–45	A disciple's justification of the prophet, with a message of hope from Jeremiah in chapters 30–33. Chapters 30–33 probably represent Jeremiah's earliest preaching. By placing it in the middle of the book, Jeremiah's followers showed that they never gave up on the hopeful message of the prophet, despite the tragic events of chapters 2–29.
Chapters 46–51	The Oracles against the Nations. These balance well with Jeremiah's call to be "a prophet to the nations" at the beginning of the book (1, 4f).
Chapter 52	A fulfillment of Jeremiah's threats, concluding hopefully with the release from prison of King Jehoiachin.

The ultimate example of Jeremiah's struggle with his vocation and mission from God is located in sections of the book called the "Confessions" of Jeremiah. In these Confessions Jeremiah argues with God and anguishes over his vocation and the message God has given him to proclaim to the community: 12, 1–5; 15, 10–21; 17, 12–18; 18, 18–23; 20, 7–18. These Confessions might have originally been a diary of Jeremiah that was possibly split up and inserted into the text by an editor. The insertion of these Confessions at particular places in the text is confirmed by the fact that wherever they appear, the sequence of the verses is disturbed.

There are two long prose sections about Jeremiah (chs 26–29 and 34–45), which are generally considered to have been collected and edited by Jeremiah's secretary, Baruch. Even though they tell of Jeremiah, the key purpose of these sections is theological and not necessarily biographical.

The book of Jeremiah also contains sermons based on phrases from a number of discourses from the book of Deuteronomy. These sermons are evident in 7, 1—8, 3; 11, 1–17; 16, 1–13; 21, 1–10. It is possible that these sermons were originally discourses preached by disciples of Jeremiah, reflecting upon the prophet's words or actions.

The Editing of Jeremiah's Preaching

The development of the text of the book of Jeremiah has an extensive and complex history. Scholars have arrived at several conclusions regarding this complex history of the text:

1. The prophet's words were originally preserved in separate booklets.

2. Several editions of the book were made during the prophet's lifetime; several more editions were made after his death.

3. The book contains not only the preaching of the prophet, but also extended accounts about him, as well as sermons based on his words.

4. Jeremiah might not have intended all of his words, most especially his confessions, to be made public.

We should not focus simply on Jeremiah as being inspired by God. Rather, we need to focus on an inspired Jeremiah tradition, in which inspiration was shared among prophet, disciples, editors, and community.

Introduction and Call to Prophecy (ch 1)

This chapter represents more than God's call to the prophet. Either Jeremiah or one of his disciples wrote his call into the accepted form for a prophet. (See other examples of this form in Ex 3; Is 6 and 40; Lk 1, 5–38.) In doing this, the editors affirmed in the very beginning of the book what God wanted for the prophet and for the community. Two separate visions (vv. 11–16) anticipate the fulfillment of Jeremiah's prophecy about the destruction of Jerusalem.

Oracles from the Reign of Josiah (chs 2–6)

Jeremiah's preaching centered on the tender love of God as manifested in the covenant during the days of Moses (2, 2f). Sin brings its own punishment, but this punishment can be purifying and transforming (2, 19.30; 4, 14). Jeremiah 3, 12—4, 4 repeats one of Jeremiah's key themes: Return to the LORD. In these chapters Jeremiah makes several very radical observations. In 3, 14–18 a whole new series of religious and civic leaders is called for, along with the removal of the necessity of the Ark of the Covenant, and the call to welcome foreigners to the new Temple.

Oracles from the Reign of Jehoiakim (chs 7–20)

In this section we meet the first of the famous sermons in the style and theological content of the book of Deuteronomy. These sermons were probably composed by disciples of Jeremiah, reflecting on earlier texts of Jeremiah. Chapter 7 is the most important of these sermons. When Jeremiah threatened the destruction of the Temple, the people shouted, "Blasphemy." Yet Jeremiah reminded them of such an occurrence at an earlier time, at Shiloh, done by an act of God. The preservation of the Temple did not depend blindly upon divine promises, nor upon more and better ceremonies. Rather, it depended on the following: "If you thoroughly reform your ways . . . if each of you deals justly with his neighbor; if you no longer oppress the resident alien, the orphan, and the widow, . . . will I remain with you" (7, 5–7).

The first of Jeremiah's Confessions occurs at 12, 1–5. Jeremiah's complaint against God is courageous, tender, impatient, and obedient. God never answers Jeremiah's initial question but addresses his faith, basically encouraging him to continue his task even though things are going to get worse.

Many symbols and parables are used to communicate God's messages to the people of Israel: Jeremiah's celibacy (ch 16), the potter (chs 18–20), and the purchase of a field (ch 32). Visions and symbolic actions were key vehicles used by prophets to get people's attention and to communicate their message in a way that would make an impression and be remembered by the community.

Oracles from the Last Years of Jerusalem (chs 21–25)

Most of chapter 21, like chapter 7, is a sermon along the lines of the book of Deuteronomy, de-

veloped by Jeremiah's disciples as they reflected on his words to the community. In chapter 22, Jeremiah explodes in anger against the greedy, cruel, and devious King Jehoiakim, wishing for him "the burial of an ass" (vv. 13–19). Along with this outburst, there is an elegy to Jehoiakim's successor, King Jehoiachin, a young man lost to the Babylonian Exile.

In chapter 23 Jeremiah reaffirms his loyalty to the dynasty of David, but only on the condition that the entire family tree be cut to the roots. From these roots, God will raise a new shoot to shepherd the people rightly. This chapter also severely denounces false prophets, individuals who claim insights into God's ways but only end up fostering their own greed and immorality. They condone sin in others to excuse their own sin.

Chapter 25 announces the "70 years" of exile (v. 11). "Seventy years" is used several times in Jeremiah and in other parts of the Old Testament. This number, like seven, should be taken as a symbolic number indicating completion and fulfillment. In other words, it announces that the exile will run its full course, but it will also be completed and come to an end.

Biographical Accounts about Jeremiah (chs 26–29 and 34–45)

Baruch, Jeremiah's secretary, shows how true the prophecies of Jeremiah were, especially about the destruction of Jerusalem and its Temple. By showing us the eventual reality of the exile and its destruction, Baruch contrasts the truth of Jeremiah's message from God with the falsity of those prophets who chose to believe themselves and not God. In this fashion, Jeremiah is shown to be the prophet faithful to God, involved in the agony of the community, and yet already preparing for the restoration of the people, the land, and the coming of the messianic age.

The Book of Consolation (chs 30–33)

An editor gathered this material from various moments in the life of Jeremiah, especially from his earliest preaching. That editor placed it here between chapter 29, a letter of encouragement to those in exile since 597 B.C., and chapters 34–45, detailing in a gruesome fashion the end of Jerusalem and the second deportation to Babylonia in 587 B.C. As a result of this editing, words intended for a different context were reinterpreted to apply to this particular context. This process occurs often in Scripture, especially when a new context shows a new way of looking at the text and of applying that text to this new situation.

Oracles against the Nations (chs 46–51; Appendix, ch 52)

These oracles are intended to show that God is in control and that God will overcome all hostile powers. By doing this, God will ensure that the covenant and the divine plans will be fulfilled. Israel's exile into foreign lands does not mean the end of Israel. The appendix, chapter 52, ends with a ray of hope for all exiles: King Jehoiachin is released from prison. It is significant that a prophet of doom like Jeremiah ends on a hopeful note.

The Message of Jeremiah

Central to Jeremiah's message is the attitude of compassion and prayer. This is intimately linked to faithfulness to a covenant inscribed upon the heart. Four crucial themes central to Jeremiah are the new covenant, sin and atonement, faith and prayer, and true and false prophecy.

The New Covenant

The key passage for this theme of the new covenant is Jeremiah 30–33, the Book of Consolation. These passages of hope were reinterpreted to apply to the context of restoration after exile. There are frequent references to "the days are coming" or "the coming days." Before Jeremiah, the Israelites thought mostly in terms of a future fulfillment of God's promises in a single great day of the LORD. Under Jeremiah's influence this future "day" began to appear in stages: first suffering; then "the coming days" or the in-between period; and finally, the definite completion of all the hopes and promises.

Jeremiah's "new" covenant written on the heart is closely tied with the Mosaic covenant of Mount Sinai. This covenant of Exodus 34, 6f had already bonded Israel with a compassionate, forgiving God. Jeremiah's covenant was "new" in that it reminded people of the covenant terms they had forgotten or neglected. This idea of the new covenant, one which was taken into the

personality or character of each person, greatly influenced Jesus and the early Church and continues to influence our current understanding of what it means to be a member of the people of God.

Sin and Atonement

Jeremiah rightly declares that sin brings its own sorrow. People are transformed, for good or bad, into those very things that they seek or desire. Yet the punishment resulting from sin can be a source of purification of our desires and a strengthening of our resolve to change our lives. All this is linked to God's compassion, leading us to hope in being forgiven and restored. This sequence of sin—suffering—repentance—forgiveness—new life undergirds the theology of the books of Joshua, Judges, 1 and 2 Samuel, and 1 and 2 Kings. By recovering this existing tradition and applying it to the present, Jeremiah makes this tradition new again, bringing it to life with new meaning and vigor.

Faith and Prayer

Jeremiah continually bares his heart and soul as he struggles in his relationship to God and to the community. This wrestling with God is most evident in his Confessions (12, 1–5; 15, 10–21; 17, 12–18; 18, 18–23; 20, 7–18). In these prayer experiences, Jeremiah confronts God with defiant and bold questions. Yet, throughout the questioning and the doubts, Jeremiah never wavers from his reliance on God's faithfulness and God's concern for him and for the community. God never resolves Jeremiah's questions or concerns, yet this venting out to God seems to help Jeremiah in coming to grips with his own pain, anguish, and struggle.

Jeremiah arrives at the conviction that his relationship with God is the only one he can depend upon, and once again he finds peace and reassurance in that reality. The recounting of this human experience of Jeremiah proved to be very powerful and very attractive to the community, for it modeled for them a realistic relationship to God and to one another.

True and False Prophecy

Throughout his ministry Jeremiah had to struggle with the charge of being a false prophet, because the message that he proclaimed was neither acceptable nor popular. The criteria for determining a true prophet just did not fit the personality, mission, prayer life, or credentials that Jeremiah exhibited. Jeremiah is the classic example of the rejected prophet. Despite continuous rejection and persecution, Jeremiah eventually became one of the most popular and accepted prophets. His genuine expressions of piety made an impact on the community for generations to come. His spontaneous and continuous interaction with God, openly and honestly, authenticated the genuineness of his mission and message.

True prophecy is usually judged by the lasting impact that the prophet and the message have on the community. This long-term community acceptance of the prophet also determined which prophet's words and works were to be preserved in the collection of books that came to be known as the Bible. Jeremiah has proven to be a true prophet indeed.

Questions for Discussion and Reflection
Group Sharing/Discussion

1. Jeremiah experienced many emotions in the course of his message. Name as many as you can. Find examples of each of them in the text.

2. When the LORD called him, what excuse did Jeremiah give? How did God answer it?

3. Was Jeremiah a prophet of good news, bad news, or both? Explain your conclusion.

In Our Lives

1. Certainly Jeremiah's influence was greater after his death. Think of other people whose influence grew after they were no longer alive—persons in your own life, in our country's history. Why do you think this often happens?

2. Chapter 7, 5–6 tells how God wants the people to reform. Read those verses slowly several times. How do those conditions apply today in our country and throughout the world? What might we do as a religious community to help, even in a small way, with such needed reforms?

3. When, like Jeremiah, have you been misjudged, ignored or falsely accused? How did you handle the situation?

Individual/Personal Reflection/Action

1. Jeremiah has a mission in life. The same can be said of each one of us. Ours is not necessarily to be a prophet but it is to use our gifts and talents to the best of our ability and in service of others. Discovering our mission gives purpose to our life, for it helps us answer the question, "Why was I born?" much as Jeremiah had that question answered for him. Spend time in reflection and prayer or talking with someone who knows you well to identify your life's mission for yourself.

2. Despite many setbacks and disappointments, Jeremiah maintained a hopeful stance in life. What are the things in life that give you hope? How do they do this? What role does your relationship to God play in the things that give you hope in life?

LAMENTATIONS READING GUIDE

At a Glance

Who are the main players?	It is important to understand that Lamentations are prayers asking God to do something for Israel. They are not merely expressions of personal or communal misery.
What should I look for?	Attentive readers will see subtle dramatic movement within each poem and between the poems; a range of emotions is fully expressed—grief, anger, near despair, glimmers of hope and joy, and the will to carry on.
When did this take place?	The early sixth century when the Temple and Jerusalem were destroyed.
Where did these events occur?	In Jerusalem.

Why was this book written?

In the two centuries before Lamentations were composed, Israel was in political decline and its religious and national traditions in crisis. Although the immediate cause of the composition was the destruction of the city and Temple in 586 B.C. the poems actually mourn a much longer period of divine absence and national humiliation.

What is the story?

Destruction of the Temple dealt a terrible blow to the ordinary way in which public prayer was carried out. For the people of Israel, the LORD dwelled on Zion (Jerusalem) and there received the praise and petitions of the people of Israel. Zion was the privileged place of encounter between Yahweh and the holy people. But with the Temple and city lying in ruins, Israelite worship changed profoundly. Lamentations is a reaction to that loss.

The Human Reality

Imagine your feelings if you experienced the loss of someone who had been of great significance in your life. It could be the death of a loved one, a mentor or guide, or a person who was supportive and kind when you needed it the most. Now imagine that, at the same time that this loss occurs, your home, your means of income, all your personal possessions, as well as all that was of material value to you, were also gone or destroyed. Add to this the fact that your church, your priests, and your community were no longer there to lend a helping hand in this time of sorrow.

Imagine the feelings that would stir in you. Imagine the anger, frustration, despair, and hopelessness that would overwhelm you. Imagine the questions that you might be asking of God. Imagine also the possible feelings of guilt. Was there something that you could have done to prevent or minimize this pain, suffering, or destruction? If you can imagine this overwhelming human experience of pain, suffering, and privation, then you can at least begin to understand the human context out of which the book of Lamentations was written.

Prayer Poems

The book of Lamentations consists of five prayers of complaint and mourning about the destruction of Jerusalem and the Temple. Because Jerusalem and the Temple were destroyed by the Babylonians in 586 B.C. and a new Temple was constructed sometime after 515, the prayers must

have been composed in the 70-year period when the Temple lay in ruins.

These poems have an interesting acrostic form. That is, the initial word of each verse or each stanza begins with a successive letter of the 22-letter Hebrew alphabet. Each poem, therefore, has either 22 stanzas or 22 verses. Although the fifth poem does not use initial letters of the alphabet, it also has 22 verses and so, in a broad sense, is influenced by the acrostic pattern.

First-time readers may find the five poems dreary, repetitive, and far too comfortable with the role of victim. Closer study reveals subtle dramatic movement within each poem and between the poems; they skillfully explore and express a range of emotions—grief, anger, something near despair, acceptance, glimmers of hope and joy, and an indomitable will to carry on.

Historical Background

It is helpful to situate these poems in Israel's history. In the two centuries before the Lamentations were composed, Israel was in political decline, and its religious and national traditions in crisis. For most of those two centuries, the people lived under the control of two great empires, Assyria and then Babylon. The early sixth century, when Lamentations was written, was particularly difficult. That period witnessed Babylonian pressure, uncertain Judean leadership, the destruction of Jerusalem and the Temple, and large deportations to Babylon. The countryside was devastated, and the economy destroyed. Such dismal conditions called into question the national traditions that had provided earlier generations with meaning and helped them make sense of everyday life. The traditions proclaimed that Israel's God was supreme over all gods and nations and had liberated Israel from the Egyptians and given them the land of Canaan; the LORD made the land fertile and protected the people from their enemies. Now, the people were not liberated; their land belonged to others; many of them had been shipped off to servitude in Babylon. Where was the LORD in all this? What could the people hope for? Although the immediate cause of the composition of Lamentations was the destruction of the city and Temple in 586, the poems actually mourn a much longer period of divine absence and national humiliation.

Destruction of the Temple dealt a terrible blow to the ordinary way in which public prayer was carried out. Public prayer texts such as the psalms presupposed that the LORD chose to dwell on Zion (Jerusalem) and there receive the praise and petitions of Israel. Zion was the privileged place of encounter between Yahweh and the holy people. Modern people might assume that the LORD can appear equally at any time and any place, but ancients thought otherwise. Although the LORD, the God of Israel, might appear and act in other places, Zion was his preeminent place of disclosure and encounter with Israel; only here was Israel fully "before the LORD." Here the LORD was enthroned upon the cherubim (Pss 80, 1; 99, 1) and "judged," that is, governed Israel and the nations. Zion was the goal of the three annual feasts of pilgrimage. Although the universe might totter, Zion, it was believed, would remain unshaken and secure (Pss 46, 2–3; 48, 4–8; 76, 3). With the Temple lying in ruins, Israelite worship changed profoundly. Lamentations attempted to find new modes of prayer in time of destruction.

Genre of the Book

Two traditional genres (or types) of prayer influenced the book of Lamentations. One was the communal lament found in the Psalms, and the other was the city lament, common in Mesopotamian religious literature and found here and there in the Bible. A major difference between the Psalms and Lamentations is that the lament psalms *remember*, that is, tell in words (and perhaps in ritual actions) the divine act of God that installed the king, gave the land, or built the Temple in order that the LORD would renew the original act. With confidence in God's great acts of the past, they pray to God to renew those powerful acts now. Lamentations, on the other hand, does not remember or review in that sense; the poems do not work from the same confidence in the national traditions. Lamentations' poems explore the human emotions evoked by the catastrophe—the sorrow, guilt, anger, and hope—and bring them before the LORD. Just as the Psalms made it possible for every Israelite, even those far from Jerusalem, to participate in the worship carried out in the Temple, so Lamentations made it possible for all Israelites during the exile to explore and express their grief, anger, and hope concerning the Temple and the God who once dwelt there. Today, the book makes it possible for all Christians and Jews to explore and express their own sorrows and forms of exile.

It is important to underline that Lamentations are prayers asking God to *do* something for Israel. They are not merely expressions of personal and communal misery. Although their tone is disappointed and often bitter, they believe that the LORD is behind the present distress of the community and has the power to turn and bring healing and prosperity. The strategy of the prayers is to remind God of his failure to carry out his promises to protect the people and make them prosperous. Thus, they proclaim that they are miserable and abandoned in the hope (however dim) that God will finally come to their rescue. The prayers ask the LORD to turn from his callous ways.

Poetic Style of the Book

Lamentations blends the fixed forms of Hebrew poetry with exceptionally free movement. The first four poems follow the alphabetic or acrostic arrangement: the first letters in the stanza follow the order of the letters of the alphabet. In the third Lamentation all three lines of a stanza start with the same letter.

An exceptional variety of attitudes are included: national and individual laments of misery (1, 12–16; 3, 43–45); prayer for help (1. 9c);

confidence in the LORD (3, 22–25); faith in the wisdom of God to assure that all receive what they deserve (3, 26–42); and a hymn of praise (5, 19). Jerusalem is described by the congregation (1, 1) and also speaks for herself (1, 12–16).

While lamenting how chaos erupts everywhere, the poetry implies that God is still in control; all is not lost. Good order must return and Israel's theology must absorb and teach the lessons of Jerusalem's destruction and exile. Lamentations asks that this process not be hurried. Israel needs space for mourning. Theology too, cannot be hurried in unraveling an explanation of this redemptive suffering.

Authorship and Place in the Bible

Despite later tradition, quite a few signs point to someone other than Jeremiah as the author. Lamentations speaks favorably of the Davidic kings (4, 20, "The anointed one of the LORD, our breath of life, was caught in their snares, he in whose shadow we thought we could live on among the nations"), whereas Jeremiah suffered severely from them (Jer 22, 13–19; 37) and did not put his hopes for the future on them. The vocabulary and religious perspective of the two books are quite different. The most ancient manuscripts of Lamentations do not mention Jeremiah as the author. Moreover, the two books are found in different parts of the Hebrew Bible (the Jewish arrangement of the Old Testament), Jeremiah among the Prophets, and Lamentations among the Writings. Ascribing the book to Jeremiah came much later, an example of the ancient practice of ascribing originally anonymous works to a famous hero. The statement in 2 Chronicles 35, 25 that Jeremiah composed a lamentation over King Josiah, "which can be found written in the Lamentations," does not refer to the present book of Lamentations. In the Septuagint, the second-century B.C. Greek translation, this book and that of Baruch (see Jer 36) are found immediately after the prophecy of Jeremiah, and Christian Bibles have maintained that order (sometimes excluding Baruch, which does not exist in the Hebrew Bible, completely).

A Christian tradition points to a hillside cave north of the walled city of Jerusalem as the place where Jeremiah wept over the city and composed these laments. So common was the ascription to Jeremiah that the Council of Trent's enumeration of the inspired books of the Old Testament does not name Lamentations, but only "Jeremiah with Baruch" (Session IV, 8 April 1546). Lamentations became a part of the tradition of Jeremiah in reflecting upon suffering as a way of expiating sin.

Was there a single author of Lamentations? Even though the five poems of Lamentations have much in common, it is difficult to decide upon a single author. They are better explained by traditions of prayer amid Israelites struggling to survive in the rubble of Jerusalem.

Praying with the Book

These five chapters are not intended to solve the problem of suffering; rather, they let us sorrow in God's presence. Prayer, like friendship, is not meant to accomplish something, only to be aware of the one we love. Nonetheless, we may find help in a few markers along the way.

The first lamentation begins with the sorrow of the author at the sight of the ruined city (vv. 1–11a). Then Jerusalem herself confesses her sins, her hopes, and her anger against the enemy (vv. 11b–22).

The second lamentation lays the devastated city before God (vv. 1–10). Technically this is the style of a lament: simply to present the situation as it is in its pain and horror. After revealing personal sorrow (vv. 11f), the poet addresses the city from the depths of compassion (vv. 13–22), beginning: "To what can I liken or compare you, O daughter Jerusalem?"

The third lamentation turns into an *individual* cry of sorrow. It begins with an assertiveness that startles us at a time when people's spirits, like their homes, are broken apart:

I am a man who knows affliction
from the rod of his [God's] anger.
One whom he has led and forced to walk
in darkness, not in the light.

While the poet speaks during most of the poem, in verses 25–47 other voices speak from a group of sages or wise persons and other friends, baffled by the tragedy (vv. 40–47). Despite the torture and misery of verses 1–24, the poem ultimately expresses deep faith in God's grace and power. This poem is the most complex of all.

The fourth lamentation returns to the style and mood of the first two. The opening verses tell the end of nobles and children (vv. 1–10), followed by a meditation on Jerusalem (vv. 11f). After the responsibility is placed upon the religious leaders (vv. 13–20), the poem ends with a curse upon the enemy (vv. 21f). The fifth and last lamentation was entitled by the Latin Vulgate "The Prayer of Jeremiah." This liturgical prayer sustains its beauty and serenity despite its topic of rejection and tragedy. It asks very little, only that the LORD remember.

Lamentations and Christianity

The Christian Church has used Lamentations in reference to Christ's passion. In the Roman Catholic Church, Lamentations played an important and memorable role in the Holy Week services prior to the reforms of Vatican II. They were sung during the ceremony of Tenebrae (darkness), probably named from the custom of extinguishing one candle after each psalm until the church was left in darkness. Several of the Tenebrae texts (although not Lamentations) have survived in the revised morning offices for Good Friday and Holy Saturday. In general, the Lamentations are used sparingly in the Roman Catholic lectionary; there are only three selections among the many Old Testament readings for masses for the dead and only one in the readings for masses "for any need." It remains a challenge for the Church to learn how to incorporate laments into its public prayer so that the pains and difficulties of Christian discipleship are represented as fully as the peace and joy of faith.

Questions for Discussion and Reflection
Group Sharing/Discussion

1. In small groups or individually, list the various things being lamented in these poems. Share and discuss your lists with each other.

2. Give examples of the many attitudes toward God represented in this book.

3. How would you describe what it is the people want from God?

4. Find the poem or part of the poem with which you can most identify and explain why.

In Our Lives

1. Our Catholic tradition uses sign, gesture, music, ritual action, and words in our community prayer. Name something in our liturgies that helps people deal with grief in the face of loss or suffering.

2. What is the role of the community toward the person undergoing pain and suffering? How might we respond better in our parish?

3. When the whole community is suffering greatly from loss or disappointment, what are some appropriate ways for the community to respond to the crisis?

4. What is our role to those outside our community, even outside our country who are in pain? How are we "response-able" to them?

Individual/Personal Reflection/Action

1. Recall an experience of your own pain and sorrow. How did you respond to the experience? What supports were there to sustain you? What challenges did you need to address or confront?

2. When people blame God for their suffering, what kind of God does that say they believe in? How would you answer them?

3. Think about how you can be more responsive to others suffering pain or loss. Talk with someone who can help you do this.

BARUCH READING GUIDE

At a Glance

Who are the main players? "Baruch" Jeremiah

What should I look for? Baruch is a guide for people who are separated or lost, physically and emotionally, from their normal environment. It shows that hope is in the LORD and in the scriptures. It provides a long prayer of lament and exalts wisdom, found in the Torah.

When did this take place?	The date of composition was some time in the late second or early first century B.C.
Where did these events occur?	Only a few books admit the possibility of an Israelite living permanently outside the Promised Land. Baruch is one. It does not refer to place.
Why was this book written?	With the disappearance of the old institutions of religion and government in Judea, questions arose about the divine presence and religious authority, as well as related questions about wisdom and authoritative teaching or *torah*. These concerns are addressed in the book of Baruch.
What is the story?	The postexilic period was a time of literary creativity. Some of these late books looked back at the preexilic period with awe and reverence, regarding its literature as a timeless standard. Baruch gives lessons on how to live in exile. Jeremiah attacks the worship of more than one God, ridiculing idols.

Baruch is in the Orthodox and Roman Catholic canon of sacred scripture. However, since it is only in the ancient Greek version of the Bible, the Septuagint, and not in the Hebrew Bible, in the Protestant canon it is classed among the Apocrypha (this word means "hidden" in Greek). Catholic Bibles add the Epistle of Jeremiah to Baruch as its sixth chapter.

Outline of the Book of Baruch

1, 1–14	Introduction recalling the Feast of Tabernacles and the renewal of the covenant
1, 15—3, 8	Offers to God a humble confession of sin
3, 9—4, 4	A reflection in the style of wisdom literature, acting as a bridge to conversion and renewed loyalty to God's Law
4, 5—5, 9	A response of consolation, forgiveness, and renewed hope to the humble confession of sin in 1, 15—3, 8
6, 1–72	In a letter format, idolatry is ridiculed with irony and sarcasm. There is a question concerning this chapter: Was it part of the original editing of the book, or was it added later on by another editor?

Reading the Book of Baruch

As the essay introducing the book of Baruch on page 1138 reminds us, Baruch was secretary to the great prophet, Jeremiah. He shared Jeremiah's fate as an exile in Egypt. Eventually, the Jewish exiles were allowed to return to Jerusalem. However, most of them did not return but, instead, stayed where they were living.

Introduction (1, 1–14)

The purpose of this section is not to provide details but to set a mood of exile and separation. Many of the details in this section are out of place both in time and situation, in fact. The exile provides a framework for those who are displaced or estranged, either physically or emotionally, to understand their situation. Displaced people need solidarity, religious assemblies, outreach in helping others, and a point of contact for unity. The wrath of God has not yet turned away from the exiles (1, 13), and Baruch advises fervent prayer as well as teaching them how to seek wisdom in this less than perfect situation of exile.

A Long Confession of Sin (1, 15—3, 8)

This is a style of prayer common in the Bible (Ezr 9, 6–15; Neh 1, 5–11; 9, 5–37; Dn 9, 4–19). These prayers were probably derived from a common collection of prayers for exiles. The prayer does not encourage violence to regain freedom but rather counsels acceptance of the government in control. Yet moral ideals and practices are not to be abandoned, even in such conditions. The prayer recalls God's fidelity to the people during their miseries in Egypt, and how God was compassionate and faithful during their sufferings and their desert journey. It acknowledges that the people have sinned and all their ills are deserved.

In Praise of Divine Wisdom (3, 9—4, 5)

It is significant that this poem praising wisdom and urging Israel to "walk in the way of God" (v. 13) comes immediately after the community has confessed their helplessness and blindness. This section is parallel to Job 28 and Sirach 24, both books within the wisdom tradition of the Jewish people. Because of these parallels, and Baruch's influence on later works in Judaism, Baruch provides a key link between the earlier and the later development of the wisdom tradition in Judaism.

Where is wisdom to be found, especially when they are in exile? Human beings cannot lay hold of wisdom by their own means. It must be given by God, who has in fact given wisdom to Israel in the Torah or their Law: "[Wisdom] is the book of the precepts of God, the law that endures forever; All who cling to her will live, but those will die who forsake her. Turn, O Jacob, and receive her: walk by her light toward splendor" (4, 1–2).

A Poem of Encouragement (4, 5—5, 9)

In this section voices that provide needed hope for a desolate people surface slowly and repetitively. Meditating on the promises expressed in Isaiah 40–66, the people renew their hopes and are reminded once again of God's love and fidelity. In 4, 5–8, the prophet talks encouragingly to the people Israel. In 4, 9–16, Jerusalem addresses to her neighbors a lament about her lost children. In 4, 17–29, Jerusalem turns and speaks to the children, her people in exile. In 4, 30—5, 9, the prophet addresses Jerusalem in words of hope and consolation based on Isaiah. God will manifest power and glory in and through Jerusalem, and she will rejoice greatly as God rescues the people once again and returns them to their land and their holy city.

Letter of Jeremiah (6, 1–72)

The author of this section is different from the author of the rest of the book. Often, this chapter is not included as part of the book of Baruch, but rather as a separate book altogether, referred to as the Letter of Jeremiah. However, for our purposes, this chapter is treated as an integral part of the final editing of the book of Baruch.

Drawing upon a tradition about Jeremiah as a letter writer (Jer 29) and a holder of divine secrets (2 Mc 2, 2), the author, most probably a synagogue preacher, attacks idolatry with great irony and sarcasm. This attack seems to be modeled on earlier prophets (Jer 10, 1–16 and Is 44, 9–20). The gist of the attack focuses on the inability of these carved idols to do anything for themselves or for their human creators. Why fear or be threatened by such silliness? The sermon gathers momentum with its frequent refrain, which the gathered community would quickly learn and repeat: verses 14, 22, 28, 39, 44, 50, 56, 64, and the grand finale, 71f. Here, idolatry seems more foolish than threatening.

Religious Teaching of Baruch

Because of the dangers of living in exile, several key themes are meant to reinforce the people's identity, as well as their core beliefs, values, and traditions. These themes are summarized in the table that follows.

Questions for Discussion and Reflection
Group Sharing/Discussion

1. Read aloud chapter 3, 24 to 4, 4, letting different people in the group each read a few lines. What is the impression you get about who God is and who Wisdom (she/her) is from this part of the prayer?

2. In chapter 6 on idolatry, what are some of the negative things the author has to say about idols that are worshiped?

In Our Lives

1. Baruch insists that one must place all one's hope in the LORD; that one can find the LORD in the inspired scriptures. What are some ways you see us doing these things as a Church, especially since Roman Catholics' study of the scriptures is much more recent than many other denominations? What are particular places in scripture that have helped you "find" the LORD?

2. The prayer in Baruch was to be prayed not as an individual's prayer but as the prayer of the community. What is the value in your life of community prayer?

Key Themes in Baruch's Religious Teaching

Monotheism	All other gods are to be scorned (ch 6). Israel's God created all of creation (3, 32–35) and is enthroned in the highest heaven (3, 3). God is the supreme source of wisdom (3, 12–32), justice (1, 15; 2, 6–10), and mercy (2, 27; 3, 1; 5, 9).
Sin	Sin is an act of rebellion (1, 22; 4, 7), which disrupts and repudiates God's wisdom for the universe (2, 12). Sin is seen in terms of communal sin, not personal, individual sin (1, 16–20; 2, 1–6). Sin always brings suffering in its wake (1, 13–15; 2, 1–5).
Repentance	This is the principal reason for putting together the book of Baruch. Israel needs to be honest in confessing her faults (2, 14; 3, 2). She needs to return to the sole fount of goodness (2, 8; 4, 28).
Hope	Hope in the LORD is the dominant attitude in this book. Further, the LORD can be found in the inspired scriptures. God lives eternally (3, 3) and establishes an eternal covenant with Israel (2, 35). Salvation is from this eternal God (4, 8). Eternity pervades God's consolation to Israel (4, 10.21–24.35; 5, 2–5) as well as announcements of eternal joy (4, 23–29; 5, 1–4).

3. If you, like the exiles, were living in a foreign country, what kinds of support and encouragement would you need? Who are similar persons in your own area today? Why do you think more people do not reach out to them? What are some things you can do to support and encourage them?

Individual/Personal Reflection/Action

1. Each morning this week, spend a few minutes recalling someone who has been a sign of hope to you or encouraged you when you needed support. Send an email or note to one of them in thanks.

2. Think about the "idols" in our society that some people worship. Make a list of the top 10 things many people spend their time, energy and money working/hoping for. Make a list of your own potential idols and compare the two.

EZEKIEL READING GUIDE

At a Glance

Who are the main players?	Ezekiel Leaders and the People the Temple
What should I look for?	Notice that Ezekiel, priest and prophet, demands both exactness in rituals and compassion toward one's neighbor. As a priest, his categories are purity and impurity. As a prophet, his purview included social justice and fidelity required by the covenant. Holiness implied social justice and social justice implied right worship.
When did this take place?	Ezekiel's prophetic ministry began with his call in July 593 B.C. near Nippur, a few miles south of the city of Babylon. The last dated formula in his book is 571.
Where did these events occur?	Babylon; Jerusalem; Israel
Why was this book written?	Ezekiel had a twofold task: to interpret the national traditions in the light of the ever-changing course of history and

to persuade people to act in accord with the required changes. His message emphasizes the centrality of the Temple and the LORD's presence, the awesome wonder of God, and individual responsibility.

What is the story?

His public career was spent completely in dismal circumstances of the destruction of Jerusalem and the Temple and the exile in Babylon. Yet it is a tribute to his faith and imagination that the prophet's message is ultimately about the bright future God has in store for his people. With other exiles he settled in Nippur and occupied a prominent place in the transplanted community and was often consulted by them. To judge by his opposition to the community and his vigorous criticism of their opinions, he had a very different understanding of the exile than they did. He saw the exile as a long process of judgment that required faith. The people, however, saw themselves as hapless victims.

Ezekiel, the Person

The book opens in 593/2 B.C. with Ezekiel already in exile at a village called Tel Abib (1, 1; 3, 15). It is not clear when Ezekiel made the journey northward from Israel, eastward across Syria, then southward down the Euphrates River into modern-day Iraq. The Babylonians may have deported him in 597 B.C., the year of their first attack on Jerusalem. Or he may have gone freely to join the exiles sometime before 593/2 B.C. The latest date in the book is 571 B.C. (29, 17). Ezekiel was born into a priestly family (1, 3), and was married (24, 16–18).

Although the written text is the starting point, writing seems to have been of secondary importance to Ezekiel. The focus throughout the book is on symbolic actions, gestures, public demonstrations of faith, confrontations with others, and a total focus on God. Ezekiel is continually being ordered to: hear the word (6, 2–3; 13, 2; 34, 2); prophesy and speak that word to his countrymen (14, 4; 20, 3); or raise a lament (19, 1–3; 27, 2f). This focus on action and speaking make Ezekiel truly a public person in the community. This may explain how he could be objective and distant, and yet intensely present with his audience.

Ezekiel continually speaks in the first person singular, yet it is not he who speaks but the LORD speaking through him. Ezekiel remains obedient to God, like clay in the hands of the potter, never questioning God's complete control over all things. Ezekiel's prophetic career was very colorful, even puzzling, with all kinds of strange symbolic actions. Gifted as well with visions and mystical insights, Ezekiel is an interesting and intriguing character.

No matter how we regard the prophet's unusual behavior and miraculous gifts, Ezekiel remained a strong, influential person in his community. Elders gathered round him (8, 1; 14, 1; 20, 1); the messenger from Jerusalem came first to Ezekiel (32, 21f), as did other people (33, 30–33). Also, Ezekiel had an extraordinary influence on later prophecy and the history of Judaism.

Theological Background

Ezekiel combined and spoke out of various theological traditions, like Hosea, Jeremiah, and other prophets usually associated with the northern part of Israel. Jeremiah and Ezekiel both speak of a new covenant written within each person (Jer 31, 31–34; Ez 30, 26f), leading to a more personal responsibility for the covenant itself (Jer 31, 27–30; Ez 18). As Isaiah, Micah, and traditions associated with the south and Jerusalem did, Ezekiel emphasizes the importance of the holy city and its Temple.

The rituals and the traditions of the Temple greatly affected Ezekiel. This may explain his tendency to include many details in his account of events. It also may explain why he frequently expresses himself in symbolic actions and stories.

Ezekiel, the Message

Ezekiel's message can be summarized under five topics:

1. The central importance of the Temple and the LORD's presence
2. The awesome wonder of God
3. Individual responsibility
4. Prophecy and beyond
5. The influence of Ezekiel on the New Testament

The Centrality of the Temple and the LORD's Presence

Ezekiel's book of prophecy opens with a vision of the LORD enthroned as in the Temple. The book closes with the sacred stream flowing from the Temple altar (47, 1–12) and with the proclamation of Jerusalem's new name, Yahweh Shamah, "the LORD is here" (48, 35). In Ezekiel, God is portrayed either in the Temple, or in a style that is associated with the Temple.

Ezekiel's vision of God that begins the book also dominates the whole book. Significant events including God anointing Ezekiel as prophet (ch 1); God departing from the Temple and the city, setting it up for destruction (ch 10); God preparing for the resurrection of the people (37, 1); and God reconsecrating the new Temple and city (43, 1–9). These events are told with language involving priestly details and symbols. But Ezekiel the priest is also Ezekiel the prophet. Thus prophecy is evident throughout these priestly descriptions.

Ezekiel the prophet insists that the Temple is not holy of itself, but only because the LORD is present there. And significantly, the LORD's presence requires that the people practice justice. The LORD can therefore choose to depart from the Temple and reappear in foreign lands, areas that priests considered unclean. The announcement in chapter 34 of the destruction of Jerusalem and its Temple led to the second major period in Ezekiel's preaching, which focused on the new purified Israel.

The Awesome Wonder of God

Ezekiel's God is overpowering and awesome, reaching beyond human relationships (24, 15–24) and human explanations (20, 25f). God is neither someone to be argued with, as in Jeremiah; nor someone agonizing over the fate of the people, as in Hosea. Ezekiel does not portray the LORD as parent or family member. For Ezekiel, God is close, yet also very distant.

A phrase constantly used by Ezekiel to portray God's majestic and overpowering presence is "the glory of the LORD" (1, 28; 3, 12–23; 8, 4; 10, 4). This phrase usually accompanies the vision of the cherubim or the four living creatures. Still another word is "holiness." The name of the LORD is usually qualified as holy. These two descriptions are usually associated with events that take us beyond normal human existence. Although the LORD is continually communicating through the prophet, the character of the prophet is lost within the overpowering message of the LORD.

Individual Responsibility

Ezekiel is generally referred to in any discussions on the topic of individual responsibility. Like Jeremiah he quotes a well-known proverb, only to prove how wrong it really is: "Fathers have eaten sour grapes, thus their children's teeth are on edge" (Ez 18, 2; Jer 31, 29). Both prophets insist that this proverb is a denial of the actual reality of a situation, along with a refusal to take responsibility for one's actions. Ultimately, this proverb blames others for one's present condition. In a long chapter Ezekiel insists "only the one who sins shall die" (18, 4).

For Ezekiel, the entire nation is God's chosen people. Thus each individual Israelite is personally responsible for living out the covenant. Each person lives or dies according to his or her virtuous or wicked way of life. Ezekiel focuses not only on exterior behavior, but also on interior change of heart (11, 19; 18, 31; 36, 26f). Here, as well as with Ezekiel 18, 2, we see important points of comparison with Jeremiah (see Jer 31, 31–34). Both prophets speak of a new heart.

Prophecy and Beyond

While remaining within the prophetic tradition of Israel that he inherited, Ezekiel also went beyond it. He changed the tradition in many ways; prophecy after him would never be the same. After the return from exile, prophets like Haggai, Zechariah, Joel, and Malachi seem as much priest as prophet. Their words and preaching seem to be more concerned with liturgical action in the Temple, or the Temple itself, than with social justice and compassion.

Apocalyptic means "drawing aside the veil" so as to perceive mysteries hidden in God. Ezekiel had turned the style of prophecy in the direction of the apocalyptic movement. Apocalyptic prophets are often called "seers" rather than prophets because of the awesome mysteries they foresee about Israel's future. To communicate these mysteries, they resort to symbols rather than plain speech. At times, these symbols are so beyond human understanding that angels are needed to interpret the vision or the symbol. Apocalyptic prophets actually speak of present realities and situations in the context of the ultimate end of all things, using visions, dreams, and all sorts of symbols.

Influence on the New Testament

Ezekiel's influence on the New Testament shows up in the Gospels whenever Jesus refers to himself as the "Son of Man" or "ben-Adam" in Hebrew. This title reflects someone absorbed within humanity (Adam) and overwhelmed before God's mighty presence (Ez 2, 2f). Ezekiel's notion of the "son of man" seems to have been more influential on Jesus than the more exalted "son of man" in Daniel (Dn 7, 13f, although Daniel's vision clearly

influenced Jesus' statement to the high priest during his trial; see Mk 14, 62). Ezekiel's image of the shepherd, in chapter 34, influenced Jesus' use of the image of the good shepherd (Jn 10).

It is in the book of Revelation that the influence of Ezekiel shows up consistently: the four living creatures (Ez 1; Rv 4, 6–9); a voice like the sound of many waters (Ez 1, 24; Rv 1, 15); Gog from the land of Magog (Ez 38–39; Rv 20, 8); the seer being carried to a high mountain (Ez 40, 2; Rv 21, 10). The book of Revelation tends to change or simplify the stranger features of Ezekiel's prophecy, but the connection between the two books is clear.

Ezekiel, the Book

The overall plan of the book can be clearly seen from the way it is structured. There are two major sections to the book: one condemning Jerusalem to total destruction (chs 1–24) and the other announcing the resurrection of a new people and a new Jerusalem (chs 25–48). A second organizing structure, overlapping the first, can also be seen as dividing the book: Ezekiel the prophet (chs 1–39) and Ezekiel the priest (chs 40–48).

Major Historical Developments

The format of the book follows national and world events as these affected Israel:

Chapters 4–24	The nations are God's instruments for punishing a sinful people. After the exile, the prophet prepares for the rebirth of his people.
Chapters 25–32	The prophet gives oracles that proclaim the destruction of those foreign nations responsible for Israel's suffering and exile, especially Egypt and Tyre.
Chapters 33–37	He also gives speeches and visions that announce Israel's religious renewal beyond anyone's expectations.
Chapters 38–39	Because the restoration of the people was not final, Ezekiel foresees another victory for the LORD, against the most powerful of the world's forces.
Chapters 40–48	Description of the LORD finally achieving the total peace of Jerusalem and the transformation of the Promised Land into paradise.

- Chapters 1–39, Ezekiel the Prophet

Chapters 1–3	The call to prophesy
Chapters 4–24	The condemnation of Jerusalem
Chapters 25–32	The oracles against the nations
Chapters 33–37	Israel's revival and transformation
Chapters 38–39	The final defeat of world forces

- Chapters 40–48, Ezekiel the Priest

Chapters 40–43	The new Temple
Chapters 44–46	The new way of life
Chapters 47–48	The new promised land

Literary Themes

In its final form, Ezekiel contains several key themes and repetitions that run throughout, giving it a sense of unity. Identical words and phrases appear at different places throughout the book, as illustrated by these examples:

• "the hand of the LORD came upon me" 1, 3; 3, 14–22; 8, 1; 33, 22; 37, 1; 40, 1
• "know that I the LORD" 6, 7.10.13.14; 7, 4.9.27; 11, 10.12; 32, 15; 33, 29; 38, 23
• "I, the LORD, have spoken" 5, 13.15.17; 12, 25; 17, 24; 21, 22; 22, 14; 34, 24; 36, 36
• "glory of the LORD," "glory of the God of Israel" 1, 28; 3, 12.23; 8, 4; 9, 3; 10, 4–19; 11, 22.23; 43, 2.4.5; 44, 4
• "rebellious house" 2, 5–8; 3, 9.26.27; 12, 2.3.9.15; 17, 12; 24, 3; 44, 6
• "abominations" 5, 9.11; 6, 9.11; 7, 3.4.8.9; 8, 6.9.13.15.17; 9, 4; 11, 18.21; 12, 16; 14, 6; 16, 2.22.43.47.51.58; 20, 4; 33, 26.29; 43, 8; 44, 6.7.13

Visions

The book is bound together by a series of visions, starting with that of the four living creatures in chapter 1. Visions introduce key sections of Ezekiel's prophecy:

• The four living creatures (1, 4—3, 15): Vision of the witnesses to Ezekiel's call to be a prophet
• Idolatry in the Temple (chs 8–11): Vision of the activity that seals the ultimate destruction of Jerusalem
• The dry bones (ch 37): Vision that prepares for the resurrection of exiled Israel to new life
• New Jerusalem (chs 40 and 43): Vision that prepares for the resurrection of Jerusalem and the Temple to new splendor and glory
• Stream of water flowing from the altar (47, 1–12): Vision of new life restored once more at the very heart of Israel, and also the vision that brings Ezekiel's prophecy to a close

Major Sections of the Book of Ezekiel

The Four Living Creatures (chs 1–3)

This opening vision sets the tone and scene for the entire book. The editors have united the entire prophecy of Ezekiel around the cherubim, the four living creatures who once upheld the throne of the LORD in the Holy of Holies of the Jerusalem Temple (Ex 25, 17–22). The four living creatures appear first in 1, 4–28. They reappear in 8, 1–4; 10; 11, 22f, providing the setting for the eventual destruction of the Temple.

Symbolic Actions (chs 4–12)

Not only the visions but also many symbolic actions surround Ezekiel. Each symbolic action follows a precise pattern:

1. A command from the LORD
2. The carrying out of that command by Ezekiel, with all the care and attention required in response to God's command
3. The meaning that this action has for Israel

Because of this pattern, Ezekiel sometimes seems to be almost like a robot, acting blindly on divine orders. This strong preference for patterns may be Ezekiel's answer to the chaos that resulted from Israel's lack of faithfulness.

The first set of four symbolic actions occurs in 4, 1—5, 17. In these verses, the fiery destruction of Jerusalem and the people's long journey into exile are symbolically acted out by Ezekiel. This sequence of events is shown below. Symbols, words, and actions all combine to tell the community the reality of their fate, because of their infidelity and idolatry.

Symbolic Actions of the Destruction and Exile of Israel

4, 1–3	Siege of Jerusalem is acted out with a ramp, battering rams, and other actions of siege.
4, 4–8	The long siege is symbolized by the prophet lying for 390 days on his left side, and 40 days on his right side, while bound with cords.
4, 9–17	The hunger and thirst of the siege are acted out by the prophet in eating and drinking very little while lying on his side.
5, 1–17	The shaving of his hair and beard (a very demeaning action for an Israelite male— 2 Sm 10, 4), and the burning of some of the hair, as well as the striking with the sword and the scattering of the hair, are all symbolic of the burning of Jerusalem and the dispersal of the survivors.

Editors reinterpreted Ezekiel's symbolic actions and visions. Additions are inserted at different places. One example is in 5, 3f, where a small amount of hair is preserved in the hem of the garment, to show that not all will be lost in the destruction and the exile. The symbolic action with the hair in 5, 1–4 is given four related but separate interpretations: 5, 7–10; 5, 11–13; 5, 14f; 5, 16f.

There are other symbolic actions in the book that portray further the destruction of the city and the exile. Further symbols of exile are:

12, 1–16	Packing one's baggage and crawling through a hole in the city wall
12, 17–20	Eating and drinking with trembling and horror
21, 11f	Groaning bitterly
21, 19–22	Clapping hands and waving a sword
24, 15–17	Ezekiel not mourning the death of his wife, just as the people are not to mourn the death of Jerusalem

Symbolic actions also extend to hopeful prophecies for the future as in 37, 15–28. Here the symbolic tying of two sticks together shows that the people from both the northern and southern kingdoms who survive the destruction will be united peacefully under a Davidic prince around the sanctuary.

Other Literary Forms (chs 13–24)

The book of Ezekiel displays many literary forms as it tries in creative ways to get the message of destruction and exile across to the community. The following table shows some examples of the various literary forms used.

This ends the first major part of Ezekiel's prophecy, which emphasized the fact that God is determined to destroy Jerusalem, which is too wicked to be purified any further. Ezekiel will now await the news of the city's destruction in chapter 33 and then begin to reconstruct a new people. First, however, the editor records the oracles against the nations, chapters 25–32.

Oracles against the Nations (chs 25–32)

Making prophetic speeches condemning foreign nations and singing mocking laments over their death are consistent biblical patterns (see Am 1, 2—2, 16; Is 13–23; Jer 46–51). This pattern

Variety of Literary Forms in Chapters 13–24

13, 1–23	Two prophecies of woe against false prophets, both male and female
14, 1–23	A legal case against idol-worshipers
15, 1–8	A scornful disputation with the inhabitants of Jerusalem
16, 1–63	An allegory about Jerusalem
17, 1–24	A fable, featuring an eagle, a cedar, and a vine
18, 1–32	A long disputation on personal responsibility
19, 1–14	A funeral dirge, ridiculing Jerusalem, speaking to her as if already dead
20, 1–44	A prophetic speech, about God's interventions to save Israel, with a litany of the people's infidelities
21, 1–37	Three prophecies of doom linked by the image of a sword
22, 1–31	Prophecy and allegory decreeing the punishment of Jerusalem, a city of blood and guilt
23, 1–49	A long allegory about two immoral sisters
24, 1–14	An allegory
24, 15–27	A symbolic action

probably has its source in Temple prayers for victory, as well as in ritual curses against the enemy.

Ezekiel concentrates his speeches against the nations of Egypt and Tyre, both of which represent forces that caused harm and division within Israel. There are seven oracles against the nations. Seven is a symbolic number representing perfection. Thus seven oracles represent the complete defeat of the enemy forces, as well as the seven nations of Palestine that Joshua was told to defeat so that Israel could gain the land (Dt 7, 1–4).

Message of Consolation (chs 33–37)

Chapter 33 recalls earlier passages and moves into a new age for Israel. The prophet as watchman (vv. 1–9) links with 3, 16–21 and Ezekiel's initial call. The passage on individual responsibility for one's actions (vv. 10–20) links with chapter 18, a key passage in understanding

Ezekiel's notion of sin, guilt, and punishment. The arrival of the fugitive from Jerusalem and the end of Ezekiel's muteness (vv. 21f) links well with 3, 22–27 and 24, 25–27. The final verses 23–33 insist that salvation is reserved for those exiles who have been internally transformed, anticipating 36, 16–38.

Chapter 34 comes from a long tradition of referring to kings as shepherds (2 Sm 5, 2; Mi 5, 4; Jer 2, 8; 3, 15; 23, 1–6). Ezekiel's passage in turn influenced Zechariah 11, 4–17, and together they helped to form New Testament readings like Mark 6, 34 and John 10.

Chapter 36, 16–38 makes an interesting study with Jeremiah 31, 31–37. Both speak of an internal renewal, with Ezekiel introducing many external details or rituals to accompany the internal transformation.

Chapter 37, 1–14 tells of Israel's revival. In verses 1–11, the dry bones in the valley come together to form living people. In verses 12–14, God explains how the similarly lifeless bones of Israel will rise out of their graves. Ezekiel's prophecy over the dead bones enables him to summon the spirit that brings them back to life.

The LORD's World Victory (chs 38–39)

After the purifying renewal of Israel during the exile and the return to the Promised Land, why did Israel not experience the final glorious fulfillment of God's promises? The crisis behind chapters 38–39 may be the long, dreary, frustrating stretch of existence after the return from exile. This is the in-between period of time, between the initial renewal of Israel and the definitive, everlasting victory of peace that was still to come.

In this literary form the forces of good are always at war with the forces of evil. God's mighty intervention on behalf of the forces of good is the only way that the forces of evil will ever be finally defeated. During severe crises, preachers and writers turn to the final day of the LORD as a means of offering hope and consolation to those enduring pain or suffering.

For Ezekiel, the forces of Gog (the land of Magog) represent the forces of evil that have to be defeated before final and lasting peace can be experienced by Israel. The final verses of this section (39, 21–29) may once have concluded the book of Ezekiel. They summarize well the goals of Ezekiel's preaching.

Vision of the New Temple, Land, and Community (chs 40–48)

Visions surround this final section (40, 1—44, 3; 47, 1–12). Between these visions and after 47, 12, Ezekiel provides rules or instructions for the community and its leadership. Some of the outstanding passages are summarized below. The book of Ezekiel ends fittingly with the new name for Jerusalem, "The LORD is here" (48, 35).

Important Passages from Chapters 40–48

43, 1–9	The glory of the LORD reverses the journey of chapter 10 and returns to its place above the Ark of the Covenant, between the wings of the cherubim. This return promises the Temple a place in the final age.
44, 4–31	Ezekiel takes a strong stand against the more open positions of Deuteronomy and Third Isaiah (56–66). In verses 5–9 Ezekiel forbids all foreigners from entering the Temple. Also, Ezekiel favors the priestly family of the Zadokites over all the other Levite families. The Zadokites are "the only Levites who may come near to minister to the LORD" (40, 46; 43, 19).
45, 18–23	This section includes a calendar of feasts.
46, 2	This verse drops the title of king and reduces the heir of the Davidic royalty to the rank of a "prince." Royal privileges and power are being transferred to the high priest. The eternal promises made to David are no longer applied to his heirs but are understood as promises for the future Messiah.
47, 1–12	This passage offers a vision of fresh water, flowing from the altar, down the Kidron Valley, into the Dead Sea. This is part of the biblical tradition that declares symbolically that all life flows from God, enthroned at the Temple. The Temple becomes a symbol of the messianic era and mirrors God's true and everlasting home in heaven.

Questions for Discussion and Reflection

Group Sharing/Discussion

1. Ezekiel emphasized that God was acting in the life and history of the people. Give examples of positive and negative actions of God that Ezekiel describes.

2. Chapter 34 is the Parable of the Shepherds. How do(es) the message(s) here compare with the Parable of the Good Shepherd?

3. In your own words, describe the significance of Ezekiel and his main message.

In Our Lives

1. Is there a person or a group today who reminds you of Ezekiel? Explain why.

2. As a Jewish priest, Ezekiel spoke much about the Temple and his vision of it. How well do we honor our church buildings as the house of the Lord?

3. Chapter 18 describes the reflection of an individual's good works or sins upon family members. How does our society react to the family of those who do good or do evil? How does this compare with Ezekiel's description?

Individual/Personal Reflection/Action

1. In chapter 2, Ezekiel eats the scroll and is empowered and changed. How does "chewing on the scriptures" affect what you do and say? When has it especially made a difference for you in how you think or how you act?

2. The closing verse says that the name of the city is to be "The LORD is here." In what ways is that true of your city or town? In what ways is it not a description of where you live?

3. What is one quality of this prophet that you would like to imitate? How can you grow in that quality?

DANIEL READING GUIDE

At a Glance

Who are the main players?	Daniel Hananiah Mishael Azariah
What should I look for?	Daniel is an example of apocalyptic writing. This type of literature is usually written in a time of distress and persecution; it points ahead to the day of the LORD, who is Lord of history. The stories of trials and triumphs of Daniel and his companions show how men of faith can resist temptation and conquer adversity.
When was this written?	This was written during the persecution of Antiochus IV Epiphanes in 167–165 B.C.
Where did these events occur?	The stories of Daniel are rooted in the history and myths of Judah and take place in Babylonia.
Why was this book written?	Written during persecution, these stories of its popular traditions strengthened and comforted the Jewish people in their ordeal.
What is the story?	Chapters 1–6 present Daniel and his companions in the Diaspora as wise, observant, and faithful Jews who adhere to their Jewish identity even in exile, thus demonstrating that God supports Jewish practice outside the land of Israel. The four visions, chapters 7–12, show the divine control over events and that the kingdom of God will ultimately triumph.

As the NAB introduction says, the book of Daniel falls into three sections. The first (chs 1–6) consists of stories in which Daniel and his three companions are the heroes. The second (chs 7–12) is made up of revelations told by Daniel in the first person. The third (chs 13–14) contains short stories that are not found in the Hebrew/Aramaic text of Daniel, but only in the Greek and Latin versions. Jews and Protestant Christians do not accept these stories as canonical, but the

Protestants include them in the Apocrypha, a collection of ancient Jewish writings that they consider edifying even if not inspired. The different kinds of material in the three divisions of Daniel reflect the gradual growth of the book. The stories in 1–6 are the oldest part and may originally have been independent stories. We know that the revelations were composed during the persecution of the Jews by Antiochus IV Epiphanes of Syria in 168–164 B.C. The "appendix" was added some time later, probably before the beginning of the Christian era.

The Authorship and Date of Daniel

The book of Daniel was written by an unknown author probably in the middle of the second century B.C., but it presents itself as the composition of a wise Israelite, Daniel, during the fifth century B.C. This false attribution of authorship was a common practice in the ancient world, when a composition needed the extra authority of a prominent author or of having been written a long time before.

Daniel therefore predicts a future that is already known to the author. This means that, in reading the book, we must concentrate on the lessons that the author thought were important for contemporary readers. If we do not pay attention to this, we will be misled into concentrating on Daniel as a predictor of the future.

Outline of the Book of Daniel

Dn 1–6   Stories of Daniel and his companions. These may have once been independent stories.

Dn 7–12   Revelations as told by Daniel and composed during the persecution of the Jews by Antiochus IV Epiphanes of Syria (168–164 B.C.).

Dn 13–14   This "appendix" was added sometime later, probably before the Christian era.

The Tales (chs 1–6)

These stories are similar to historical novels: They mention historical names and places, but they are fictional. They are not concerned with historical accuracy but, instead, carry a religious message, like the parables of Jesus. Daniel, like Noah and Job, may never have existed, but that does not take away from the religious value of the stories.

The stories paint an ideal picture of the life of Jewish exiles in Babylon. The situation is idealized in order to express hope and define acceptable behavior. The modern situation of religious people living in the secular world is not so far removed from ancient Jews living in the pagan world of Babylon. The message has two facets: It affirms the possibility of living in a Gentile environment, and it insists on the importance of fidelity to the essentials of the Jewish tradition.

Affirmation of the Gentile Environment

This affirmation is demonstrated in the story in chapter 1 when Daniel and his companions are trained and even excel in "the language and literature of the Chaldeans." They express no reservations about this training. In chapter 2, Daniel, with God's assistance, is able to interpret the king's dream when the Babylonian wise men fail. There are more instances of Daniel's ability to interpret mysteries in chapters 4 and 5.

Several instances in these chapters reveal Daniel's attitude toward Gentile kingship. One dream foretells that all Gentile kingdoms will eventually be destroyed, but there is no urgency about this prophecy. God has willed a long Gentile rule and Jews can find fulfillment in the service of a pagan king. The stories about King Nebuchadnezzar and King Belshazzar make it clear that Gentile kings must be subject to God and not become too proud or arrogant. They must act with restraint. If they do this, Daniel has no objection to their rule. Only when the kings exceed their limits do they incur the judgment of God.

The Importance of Fidelity

This second facet of the message is presented in the actions of Daniel and his companions. They remain faithful to their Jewish religion even as they enjoy their success at the pagan court. They refuse to eat the king's food, because it is not kosher (ch 1). The three youths refuse to worship the king's statue, at the risk of death (ch 3). Daniel refuses to depart from his custom of daily prayer even at the cost of being thrown into the lions' den. Each time the Jews ultimately win the respect of their rulers and become more successful.

The stories of the fiery furnace and the lions' den, like all miracle stories, are meant to arouse a sense of wonder. They are not realistic stories. The essential point in Daniel's stories is that God has the power to save, or to do what is for the best. Daniel and his companions trust in God, and this liberates them to do whatever they ought to do regardless of the immediate circumstances. This attitude is expressed in the words of the three youths: "If our God, whom we serve, can save us from the white-hot furnace and from your hands, O king, may he save us! But even if he will not, know, O king, that we will not serve your god or worship the golden statue which you set up." Their fidelity is not conditional.

Daniel 1–6 conveys a sense that God is in control and that all will work out for the best. The will of God can be exercised through the rule of pagan kings. True religion does not require any particular political system.

Apocalyptic Literature

Daniel's visions (chs 7–12) belong to a kind of literature called apocalyptic (see Glossary, apocalypse). This word is from the Greek for "revelation" and has come to be associated with a particular kind of revelation, with certain recurring characteristics. The table below lists some of those characteristics, some examples from Daniel, and a few of the ways the characteristics function.

These characteristics create numerous difficulties for the modern reader and call for some caution in interpreting books like Daniel.

1. *Heavy Use of Symbolism.* Apocalyptic authors do not speak directly but use symbols or images instead. For example, all scholars agree that King Antiochus is a major figure in Daniel, but his name is never mentioned. He appears as the eleventh horn on a beast. Sometimes this veiled language might be used to save the community from persecution from the king. It also strengthens the impression of supernatural origin and allows later generations to make their own interpretations. This characteristic can easily lead to misinterpretation and misapplications. Two hundred years later the eleventh horn might have been interpreted as the Roman emperor instead of Antiochus. In our own time the beasts rising out of the sea might be interpreted as meaning the outbreak of the Second World War. It is important to remember that the author of Daniel was speaking of persecution in the second century B.C. and not predicting any later event. The book of Daniel can help us understand our modern situation because it describes patterns that recur throughout history, but it cannot be used to predict specific events or persons in our world. The same can be said for the New Testament book of Revelation.

2. *Angels and Demons.* The first thing to remember when trying to interpret the meaning of

Characteristics	Function
Heavy use of symbolism Example: beasts = kingdoms; sea = chaos	Veils meaning; lack of specificity adds mystery, allows long-term interpretation
Angels and Demons Example: Interpreting angel; Archangel Michael	Angels emphasize supernatural, add to sense of mystery, and dramatize divine control.
Pseudonymity Example:second-century author writes as if living during exile	Antiquity adds to prestige of writings. Allows accurate "predictions" that foster hope and inspire right conduct.
Determinism Example: History has fixed ratio (70 weeks of years or 490 years)	Divine control. Course of history is set with fate of righteous and wicked. Human decisions not predetermined.
Predictions of the End Example: End of persecution (Daniel) or end of the world	During persecution, easier to keep going if the specific day of relief is known.

the heavenly beings in Daniel is that, like other apocalypses, this is a work of imagination. The author is trying to build up hope in the people by saying that earthly war is not entirely under earthly control. To understand an apocalypse, we should ask, not, "Do these angels exist?" but, "What do they stand for?"

3. *Pseudonymity.* Many readers today consider the practice of claiming ancient authorship and, therefore, accurate predictions as deceptive and unethical. It was widely accepted in the ancient world, however, and helped the people believe in the real predictions of what was to come. The question is not whether Daniel really predicted all these things in advance, but whether his stance in the face of religious persecutions is a valid one.

4. *Determinism.* In dealing with the notion of fixed periods of history, the modern reader needs to remember that human decisions are not predetermined. On the contrary, the book of Daniel is basically a call for decision in a time of crisis. The fact that God has control over history strengthens the people's hope and their ability to make decisions.

5. *Predictions of the End.* Whether the end predicted was of persecution or of the world, the point of the specific predictions was, again, to encourage people to stand firm in their faith in the midst of suffering.

The problems of interpreting apocalyptic literature can be minimized if the believer reads for inspiration or exhortation rather than information. It has ethical value and relevance for modern times if the focus is placed on the attitudes and actions it was designed to support.

A Symbolic Vision (ch 7)

This vision of four human kingdoms that will be followed by a kingdom set up by God is one of the most famous and influential of all apocalyptic visions. In biblical poetry the sea is often a symbol of chaos, of all that is opposed to God; that is the point Daniel makes when he represents the pagan kingdoms as beasts from the sea. This is much more negative than the view of pagan kingdoms in Daniel 1–6. The experience of persecution colored the author's perception of all Gentile kingdoms.

After the vision of the four beasts, Daniel sees a judgment scene in which the "Ancient One" sits on a throne, the fourth beast is con-demned to the fire, and "one like a son of man" appears on the clouds of heaven. There have been a variety of interpretations of this "son of man" figure. Early Christian tradition, beginning with the Gospels, identified this figure with Jesus Christ, but that could not have been the case in the second century B.C. Jewish tradition identified the "son of man" as the Messiah. Modern scholarship is divided between two interpretations: a symbol for Israel, or Michael the archangel. Either interpretation, however, can be understood as representing the triumph of the Jewish people over their persecutors under their heavenly patron.

The message of the vision is one of hope. Even when the opposing forces seem overwhelming, the power of God will eventually defeat them. The symbolism of the vision (beasts, fire, figure riding on the cloud) expresses the message with exceptional power and vividness. The image has been used over and over again in new situations. It provides language to express the power of evil that erupts from time to time in human affairs (for example, the Holocaust), and it can also express a hope that does not depend on human power. A similar symbolic vision is found in chapter 8 and, again, the message is one of hope.

Prophecy Reinterpreted (ch 9)

A prophecy of Jeremiah provides the basis for a different kind of revelation in this chapter. Jeremiah prophesied in the seventh century that the land would be subject to Babylon for 70 years. The second book of Chronicles credits Cyrus of Persia with fulfilling the prophecy (after 50 years had passed). Zechariah related it to the rebuilding of the Temple (after 66 years). The author of Daniel obviously does not think the prophecy has been fulfilled, but rather than discard it as a failure, he reinterprets it. Seventy years, he says, really means 70 weeks of years or 490 years. Like the dreams and visions of earlier chapters, Jeremiah's number is treated as a symbol. It is not meant to stand for an exact number of years. Rather, it reminds the readers that they can depend on God's promises even when the time of fulfillment is completely unknown.

Daniel's prayer in chapter 9 contains another important reminder: We should not expect our prayers to alter the course of events. Daniel receives a revelation in response to his prayer, but his prayer does not result in a shortening of the time of trial.

Daniel's Apocalyptic View of History (chs 10–12)

This long vision explains to Daniel that the ongoing war between Judah and her enemies is not the whole picture. The earthly battle is only a reflection of the more important heavenly battle between the archangels Michael and Gabriel opposing the angelic princes of Persia and Greece. The vision shows that Michael will eventually be victorious (12, 1) and the resurrection will follow. It is important to notice some key points about history in the vision.

1. The vision presumes that the outcome of warfare between human kingdoms depends on God's power, not human power (illustrated by the battle between the angelic powers).

2. The vision gives the impression that what happens in history is fixed in advance. It is written as if Daniel is writing during the exile, some 400 years before the actual events of persecution under Antiochus Epiphanes. This is done not to deceive, but to build up confidence in the prediction about the death of the king (11, 40–55) and the resurrection (12, 1–3).

3. The vision clearly affirms the resurrection of individuals (the only book of the Hebrew Bible to do so). Other books use the language of resurrection to refer to the restoration of the Jewish nation but not of individuals. This new emphasis was probably influenced by the experience of martyrdom in the time of persecution (see 2 Mc 7).

Belief in the resurrection made an enormous difference to Judaism and was essential to the beginnings of Christianity. Before this, Jewish religion taught that the reward for a just life was to see one's children's children to the fourth generation and the welfare of the nation as a whole. Now, however, pious Jews were being put to death for obeying the Law and were being cut off from the traditional reward. Just as the 70-year prediction of Jeremiah was reinterpreted in a new situation, so too, the reward of a just life had to be reinterpreted. Belief in life beyond the grave put martyrdom in a new perspective.

For Daniel, the Jews who remained faithful in the time of persecution were the wise persons (11, 33–35). These put their trust in Michael and the heavenly world and apparently did not join in the fighting. The faithful stance of these wise teachers illustrates the ethical stance of the book of Daniel, which is the most enduring message of the book.

The apocalyptic message of chapters 10–12 has some basic beliefs in common with the older stories found in chapters 1–6, although the stories are more optimistic. Both affirm the belief that God rules all kingdoms and has the power to save, and that the individual must act with integrity even at the cost of life itself. This last is helped by the belief in the resurrection.

It is important to remember when reading Daniel that apocalyptic writing comes out of difficult, troubled times, and therefore the writer's position may be presented as the only right way of seeing things. Daniel presents one possible way in which a faithful person might respond to a situation of oppression and persecution. It would be a mistake to think that it is the only appropriate response. The Bible presents many different responses in a variety of situations.

The Additions or Appendix (chs 13–14)

These are independent stories added here probably because Daniel happens to be one of the characters.

Susanna

This story may be described as a parable because it reverses our expectations. Daniel appears as a young but wise judge, as suggested by his name (Dan comes from the Hebrew verb "to judge"). Usually elders who have been appointed judges are the righteous ones, and the word of a young woman would carry little weight against theirs. However, it is characteristic of biblical narrative that the underdog prevails or is justified.

The story of Susanna is similar to the rest of Daniel in her response when she is trapped: "Yet it is better for me to fall into your power without guilt than to sin before the Lord."

Bel and the Dragon

Daniel 14 contains two stories that make fun of pagan idolatry and are not meant to be taken as accurate descriptions of Babylonian religion. The Babylonians are portrayed as excessively stupid, and the stories are more fantastic than Daniel 6. Although the fantastic elements give the tale a lighthearted quality, the background here is more tense than Daniel 1–6. Bel and the Dragon allows for no ecumenical relations with pagan religion and reflects a more serious situation than indicated in Daniel 1–6. The present-day reader must remember that biblical stories are shaped by historical circumstances, and this affects how we read them.

Questions for Discussion and Reflection
Group Sharing/Discussion

1. Retell how Daniel and his companions remain faithful to their Jewish religion, in relation to food, worship, and prayer.

2. Give examples from the stories of the five characteristics of apocalyptic literature, that is, use of symbolism, angels and demons, pseudonymity, determinism, prediction of the end. Can you identify any apocalyptic characteristics in the way you express your faith?

In Our Lives

1. Daniel's stories affirm that God rules all kingdoms, that God has the power to save, and that the individual must act with integrity at the cost of life. What do your stories of God affirm?

How is your integrity linked to these stories?

2. Daniel reminds us that God controls history even though human decisions are not predetermined. In times of crisis this inspiration strengthens people's hope and ability to decide. Reflect on your strengths, your hopes, your decisions. What are the convictions that strengthen your hope and enable you to make ethical decisions?

3. Daniel's vision of history (chs 11–12) affirms resurrection of the individual. This reflects also the beliefs of the New Testament. What does individual resurrection mean to you?

Individual/Personal Reflection/Action

1. Daniel's prayer (ch 9) teaches us not to expect our prayers to alter the course of events. Think about your patterns of prayer. Do you usually pray to change God, to change events or conditions, or to change yourself and strengthen your fidelity?

2. Take time to meditate on the situations that might affect your fidelity to God (e.g., your financial goals, government policies, job requirements, personal decisions, etc.).

THE TWELVE MINOR PROPHETS

The authors of this collection of books (referred to as the Book of the Twelve) are called minor prophets because their writings are short compared to the four major prophets, Isaiah, Jeremiah, Ezekiel, and Daniel. Like the others, however, they were "here and now" kinds of people dealing with specific situations; so it is important to know as much as possible about the time and place of their activity (see the timeline on RG 146):

1. This collection covers a period of about 300 years of prophetic activity.

2. Amos, Hosea, and Micah were active in the eighth century B.C. at the same time Isaiah was beginning his career. Recall that there were two kingdoms at this time. Hosea was in the north and Micah in the south. Amos was from the southern kingdom but prophesied in the north.

3. Zephaniah, Nahum, and Habakkuk were active toward the end of the seventh century B.C. during the Babylonian period.

4. Haggai and Zechariah (chs 1–8) were involved in the rebuilding of the Temple in Jerusalem in 520 B.C.

5. Joel, Jonah, Obadiah, and Malachi are from the time after the exile (called the post-exilic period) but are difficult to date more precisely.

Most of these books are made up of short poetic oracles or messages from God delivered through the prophets. The book of Jonah, a short story, is an exception.

We can discover a pattern in the content of these books: sin followed by judgment followed by salvation or the promise of restoration. Not all of the prophets get to the end of the pattern (Amos), while others focus primarily on restoration (Haggai and Zechariah). Within this overall pattern there is diversity, as well as some dominant themes:

1. Most of these prophets focus on the sins of their own people. There are a few exceptions, but generally you could say that these prophets are critical of those around them.

2. They concentrate on two kinds of sin. Social sin, the mistreatment of the poor, the weak, and the unprotected, is clearly denounced in Amos and Micah but is found throughout the collection. Cultic sin, the worship of false gods and abuses within their own religious rituals, is also condemned. We would expect the prophets to be hard on the people of Israel when they worship gods other than the LORD. They are even stronger when it comes to the worship of the LORD that is only empty ritual. Amos and Micah draw social and cultic sin together. They condemn the cult of their people because it makes them too comfortable and distracts them from the injustices of their society.

3. These prophets expand the common biblical belief that God acts in history. They teach that whatever actually happens is the work of God. They understood the destruction of the northern kingdom in 721 B.C. and the southern kingdom of Judah in 587/586 B.C. as acts of divine judgment.

Salvation and restoration become more prominent after the exile, but they are also evident in earlier prophets, most notably Hosea. It is appropriate to talk of restoration after a time of destruction. Very often the prophets imagine a situation that is very different from the present. This is the case especially with the post-exilic prophets when they are trying to encourage the people in the rebuilding of the Temple. The phrase "on that day" often introduces prophecies of transformation. The reader needs to be aware that some of these messages of hope may have been added at a later date by the editors of the prophetic books.

Taken as a whole, the Book of the Twelve is both a reflection on the past and a lesson for the future. The editors of the prophetic books were heavily influenced by the theology of Deuteronomy: Sin does not go unpunished, but God is ultimately merciful and wants only the repentance and restoration of Israel. This call to repentance can be heard throughout this collection.

HOSEA READING GUIDE
At a Glance

Who are the main players?	Hosea Gomer
What should I look for?	Recognize the variety of ways in which the images of marital infidelity are employed to picture Israel's disloyalty. It is important also to notice how much of Hosea's message of faithlessness is directed against abuses in Israelite religion: its priesthood, rites, and sacred sites and altars.
When did this take place?	In the later part of the eighth century B.C.
Where did these events occur?	In the northern kingdom
Why was this book written?	Hosea began the tradition of describing the relationship between Yahweh and Israel in terms of marriage. His description of God's love for his people in chapter 11 is one of the high points in the Old Testament.
What is the story?	Hosea's primary image of Israel's disloyalty to God is the wife who is unfaithful to the husband and has become a prostitute. This image of the unfaithful wife gave him a strong image with which to criticize the abuses of Israel's elite.

Introduction

Hosea's central concern is Israel's loyalty to its God. He denounces Israel for worshiping other gods, in particular the Canaanite god Baal, and pleads with Israel to return to the faithful worship of its God alone. To gain his audience's attention and to make his message vivid, Hosea used the metaphor of marriage to describe Israel's relationship to God. God is pictured as a husband and Israel as his faithless and promiscuous wife. Israel, the disloyal wife, is urged to repent and return to her husband. The marriage metaphor is enacted by Hosea himself in chapters 1–3, when Hosea marries Gomer, described as a prostitute (2, 2) and an adulteress (3, 1). And Hosea uses the marriage metaphor repeatedly in the speeches in chapters 1–14, which make up the bulk of the book. A prophet fond of metaphors, Hosea also compares Israel's disloyalty to a barren tree (9,

13–17), a stubborn heifer (4, 16; 10, 11–15), and a rebellious son (11, 1–7).

Hosea's prophecy can be divided into two parts, the first a collection of narratives in chapters 1–3 that describes Israel's disloyalty in terms of Hosea's faithless wife. Narratives about prophets, such as these, typically take up less space in a prophetic book than the prophet's speeches themselves, and they frequently describe prophets acting out the message they wish to deliver. The second and larger part of Hosea is a collection of prophetic speeches (chs 4–14) that condemn Israel's deceit, predict God's punishment, and express hope for Israel's renewal. It is difficult to know where one speech ends and the next begins, but a dominant pattern can be detected in which indictments of sin are followed by sentences of judgment. In the brief speech that begins this collection, for example, an indictment listing Israel's crimes (4, 1–2) is followed by a sentence describing God's punishment (4, 3). Much less common are speeches predicting Israel's restoration (11, 8–11). Hosea's own speeches may have been supplemented at points by later editors who wished to relate Hosea's message to the southern kingdom of Judah or to the Judeans in exile (11, 10–11).

Hosea lived and prophesied in the northern kingdom of Israel, also called Ephraim, at the time of the divided monarchy when Israel and Judah were separate kingdoms. Hosea was the only native northerner among the prophets, the rest of whom all lived in or came from Judah. His career covered the last 30 years of the kingdom of Israel (750–721 B.C.), when Israel was under the constant threat of Assyrian imperialism and was wracked by a series of violent coups in its own capital, Samaria. Hosea deplores the internal political violence of this period (7, 5–7) and Israel's attempt to protect itself by international alliances (7, 11), and he believes Israel's impending doom in the face of Assyrian expansion to be God's punishment for its social and religious corruption.

Hosea is especially critical of the religious scene in Israelite society during this period. His frequent references to Baal (2, 8; 13; 16), indicate that many Israelites had turned from their own God to worship this Canaanite deity. This attraction to Baal-worship among the Israelites was an old and continual problem, as the contest between Elijah and the prophets of Baal a century earlier shows (2 Kgs 17–19). The Israelites believed that Baal, like Israel's own God, could deliver the rains and agricultural productivity on which their economy and survival depended. The calves that Hosea criticizes (8, 5–6), although possibly pedestals or throne images for Israel's God, are also associated with Baal in this period, and Hosea regards them as idols of Baal.

Hosea's work appears first in the collection of minor prophets, sometimes called The Book of the Twelve. Although not chronologically first, Hosea provides a good introduction to these prophets. He is unrivaled for the beauty of his poetry and the emotional power of his oracles.

Hosea lived at a time of great difficulty and instability for the northern kingdom of Israel, caused by the westward expansion of the mighty Assyrian empire. During Hosea's time, Assyria moved from merely being a threat to actually

bringing about the end of the northern kingdom in 722 B.C. Even before this tragic date, there was unrest in the kingdom. In the 14 years between the death of Jeroboam II and 722, five kings ruled.

We get an insight into the personal life of Hosea from his use of the metaphor of marriage. Like some of the other prophets, he uses metaphor not just as a matter of spoken or written words; his life itself conveys his message. This speaks clearly of his total involvement in his prophecy. Even his children are given symbolic names, "not pitied" (Lo-ruhama, 1, 6) and "not my people" (Lo-ammi, 1, 8). The prophet and his family are living signs of God's concern for the welfare of his people.

Outline of the Book of Hosea

Hosea is usually divided into two parts:

Hos 1–3	The metaphor of marriage
Hos 4–14	Oracles of Israel's destruction. Two exceptions: Prophecy of restoration 11, 8–11; Invitation to repentance 14, 2–9

The Metaphor of Hosea's Marriage (chs 1–3)

The LORD's first recorded words to Hosea capture the power of this metaphor, "Go take a harlot wife. . . . " It may be that Gomer was not a harlot at the time of her marriage to Hosea. However, many scholars see the choice of a harlot wife as a deliberate symbolic act on the part of the prophet. And if, as some think, Gomer was not only a prostitute, but a cult prostitute serving the pagan god Baal (see below), then Hosea's action is even more dramatic. In any case, the prophet's message is clear: Israel's behavior toward God is like that of an unfaithful spouse. This metaphor illustrates several significant insights:

Covenant

Hosea believes that God and Israel are bound together by the covenant given to Moses, symbolized here by the marriage covenant, an agreement that forms the basis of a relationship. Hosea's words, "you are my people" and "My God" (2, 25), recall not only the standard marriage formula, but the covenant language of Exodus as well.

Metaphor as a Second Language

The study of any type of literature would be enhanced by a good course on metaphor. This is especially true for the study of the Bible. This need for the language of metaphor, image, or symbol comes from the Bible itself. To respond to the thinking of the biblical writers, to get to their message, one must be able to use this language because it was their language. The need also arises from our modern pragmatic, conceptual approach. As one participant in an adult Bible study class said, "Can't you skip the flowery stuff and cut to the bottom line? Tell us what it means."

Metaphor is especially appropriate to convey meaning in the Bible because it reminds us that we are dealing with the divine, with a reality that can never be fully understood. This is one way of describing mystery. A mystery is not something that our reason cannot grasp; it does not put an end to our efforts to comprehend it. Rather, it is a never-ending process of coming to new understanding. The love of God for us is a mystery, not because we cannot understand what love is, but because we cannot comprehend the fullness of God's love, no matter how hard we try. When Israel tried to put into words how God had entered into relationship with them or how God acted in their history, they were at a loss for words. The language of metaphor at least allowed them to point to the reality that was beyond what was tangible or measurable.

In Hosea we have a prime example of the beauty of metaphorical language and its power to convey meaning that is almost beyond our power to communicate. Perhaps his most famous is the "lived metaphor" of his marriage to Gomer, which portrays Israel as the unfaithful spouse. In other places he compares Israel to a "cake unturned" (7, 8), a "wild ass" (8, 9), or a "luxuriant vine" (10, 1). These examples have an emotional effect that evokes a response in the reader because of the many associations they carry.

Another striking example is in chapter 11, which begins, "When Israel was a child I loved him." The reference is to the Exodus event, but the effect is very different from our response to the Pentateuch. By portraying Israel as a child, Hosea paints a vivid picture of God as the loving parent, teaching the infant to walk and lifting it up. The comparison strongly implies that Israel should have the same kind of bond with the Lord that a toddler has with its parents.

The metaphorical language of the Bible points the reader to something beyond our ability to completely understand, to the mystery of God.

Idolatry and Infidelity

A major problem addressed by Hosea was idolatry, specifically the cult of the Canaanite god Baal. Baal was a real temptation for the people because he was a fertility god who was supposed to guarantee the productivity of the land, animals, and people. Think about how much farmers and ranchers depend on good weather for their livelihood, and you will understand the strength of this temptation.

The worship of Baal may have included sexual acts with prostitutes. If Gomer was such a prostitute, then Hosea's comparison was all the more pronounced: Israel's covenant with the Lord, understood as marriage, contrasted with the worship of Baal, understood as prostitution. Gomer exemplified the behavior of Israel by straying from the marital relationship.

Hosea was not concerned just with Israel's participation in the Baal fertility rites. Her infidelity was more pervasive, as he says in 4, 1–3:

There is no fidelity, no mercy,
  no knowledge of God in the land.
False swearing, lying, murder, stealing and
    adultery!
  in their lawlessness, bloodshed follows
    bloodshed.
Therefore, the land mourns . . .

According to Hosea, one cannot pick and choose when it comes to the LORD. As we say of some things today, "It's a package deal." When the Israelites acknowledge the LORD as LORD, they have to accept the covenant code of ethics as well.

Understanding of God

Hosea understands God as the best in human nature, only more so. And, for him, a faithful marriage is the culmination of love between a man and a woman. Therefore, the love between the LORD and Israel is best understood as a faithful marriage.

Concentric Circle Thinking and Writing

Sometimes reading the Bible can be confusing. For example, you might be reading along focusing on one idea and a new image is introduced, and even another. Or, you are reading a text and you think, "Haven't I read this before?" What at first seems confusing can really be helpful to understanding the biblical message.

This could be called concentric circle thinking or writing. It is a way of organizing information that many of the biblical writers felt at home with, although it may seem strange to us. The way we've been taught to think or reason is more linear; you go through certain steps in a particular order to reach a conclusion. The people who produced the Bible generally thought in a more circular fashion. It doesn't mean that they weren't logical; it's a different kind of logic.

Picture someone throwing a rock into a pond or lake. When the rock hits the water, there is a splash—that's the main point of the writer. Then a circle appears and begins to expand—the development of the main point. Another circle appears and moves out—a related idea is added and developed. Soon there are several concentric circles all visible and moving at the same time.

Hosea is a good example of this; his images sometimes seem to be tumbling over one another. In chapter 2, Hosea is in the process of developing the marriage metaphor, comparing Israel to his own unfaithful wife. Then he brings in the image of the desert, then back to his harlot wife. Several lines later he is talking about laying waste her vines and fig trees, building a wall against her, then leading her into the desert to allure her. Later on there's talk of the covenant and more marriage talk and several more images in between. Finally the chapter ends with, "You are my people," and the response, "My God!"

By going around and around and bringing in many familiar words and images, Hosea is pleading with his people to be faithful once again to the LORD who is faithful to them. He has already said that God is like a faithful spouse; he brings up the desert to remind them of God's saving action on their behalf and of the covenant relationship. He warns them about how destructive unfaithfulness can be to a relationship. Even though he knows that they won't really listen and will suffer the consequences, he sows the seeds of hope.

When you are reading this circular kind of structuring, it is important to remember not to get caught up in trying to figure out what is first, second, or third. Let the images circle around. Through the use of a commentary, try to find out what the people of Hosea's time would have heard when these words were spoken or read to them. Let the message just sink in.

Land and Desert

While Hosea is developing the marriage metaphor, he weaves in the familiar Exodus images of the promised land and the desert with all their rich associations. He recalls the foundational experience of Exodus/Covenant that gave Israel its identity as a people. This reminds the people of what is really important, their covenant with God.

The prophet focuses on the gift of the land "flowing with milk and honey," the primary symbol of salvation from ancient times. This is where the prophet delivers the threat with full force: The land will be reduced to a desert. Because there is no belief in an afterlife at this time, to lose the land is to undo the Exodus. The expression, "to have the rug pulled out from under you," is apt. For Israel it was that and more.

Hosea transforms the desert image; it is not only a place of wandering and death, but a place where a man might court a young woman in privacy. He is suggesting that away from the cult of Baal and other abuses, after being stripped down by the Assyrians, something new is possible, a new Exodus.

So, hope is introduced. It may not be full-fledged, flag-waving hope, but it is there. After all, Hosea is a realist. Second Isaiah (Is 40–55) will develop this new Exodus theme after the Exile, and it reappears in the Dead Sea Scrolls and in the New Testament.

Questions for Discussion and Reflection

Group Sharing/Discussion

1. An important lesson we can learn from Hosea has to do with theological method, that is, that one way to knowledge of God is through observing human experience. How is God like a faithful spouse, a loving parent, a friend seeking a lasting relationship?

In Our Lives

1. What does infidelity do to human relationships? Would the same things apply to our relationship with God?

Individual/Personal Reflection/Action

1. Meditate on this passage from Hosea. How does this relate to "burning incense to idols" in modern life? Does this Old Testament depiction of God as healer shed light on your own image of God? (from Hos 11, 1–4)

When Israel was a child, I loved him,
out of Egypt I called my son.
The more I called them,
the farther they went from me,
Sacrificing to the Baals
and burning incense to idols.
Yet it was I who taught Ephraim to walk,
who took them in my arms;
I drew them with human cords,
with bands of love;
I fostered them like one
who raises an infant to his cheeks;
Yet, though I stooped to feed my child,
they did not know that I was their healer.

JOEL READING GUIDE

At a Glance

Who are the main players? Joel

What should I look for? Joel is unique among the prophets in his focus on a natural catastrophe, a locust plague. To appreciate the danger of the crisis Joel faced, one must recover a sense of the terrible destructiveness of a locust infestation for a preindustrial agricultural society. This prophecy is rich in apocalyptic imagery and is eschatological in tone.

When did this take place? It was composed about 400 B.C.

Where did these events occur? Judah

Why was this book written? Joel's unique focus on the locust plague as an image of divine judgment offers some religious vision for the not-uncommon plagues, both natural and symbolic, that Israel experienced.

What is the story?
A plague of locusts ravages Judah. Joel sees this as a symbol of the coming of the LORD. He summons the people to repent and turn to the LORD with fasting. They convene a solemn assembly of prayer for deliverance. The LORD answers their prayer and promises to drive away the locusts and bless them with peace and prosperity.

Outline of the Book of Joel

The book moves from specific concern with the plague of locusts to a more general prophecy of universal judgment:

Joel 1, 1—2, 17	The plague of locusts and prayer for deliverance
Joel 2, 18–27	Reply and reassurance from God
Joel 3	Future time when God will intercede
Joel 4	Final judgment of the nations and salvation for the elect

The Day of the LORD

The theme of the Day of the LORD runs through the book as a unifying thread. This theme with its two related aspects, the vision of plenty and the desire for vengeance, is important for understanding Joel's message.

In Amos (eighth century B.C.), the meaning of the Day of the LORD shifts from the original festive day to one of a day of darkness, not light. By the time the book of Joel was written, any great disaster might be called a "Day of the LORD."

In developing this theme, Joel starts with something specific, the plague of locusts. He takes something that was surely terrible and uses it to teach the people what the real disaster, the Day of the LORD, will be like. The locust plague is a rehearsal, an image of the end of the world, the day of judgment of the nations.

The locusts transform the land from being like the "garden of Eden" to a "desert waste" (2, 3). Joel also uses the similarity of the locust plague to an invasion to describe them as an invading army, with the LORD at their head (2, 11), affirming the conviction that whatever happens is the work of God. The people respond to the plague in a way typical of the ancient world, by bringing offerings and libations. Joel also responds typically, like other Hebrew prophets, by turning the crisis into an occasion for reform and repentance. In 2, 13 we find a classic expression of the prophetic view of proper ritual: "Rend your hearts, not your garments."

In our day we do not usually regard natural disasters as visitations from God, or seek relief primarily through rituals. But in Joel's time, the situation was beyond human control. The ritual was the only thing they could do. It was a way of expressing their desperation and their hope that God would give them relief. And the prophet, by urging reform, was trying to bring some good out of a bad situation. This is a good example of the "here and now" attitude of the prophets. For them, salvation is primarily concerned with the welfare of the people on earth.

In chapter 3, the Day of the LORD takes on a different meaning. It now refers to the Day of Judgment, and the passage suggests the end of the world: "The sun will be turned to darkness, and the moon to blood, . . . " (3, 4). We are dealing here with the language of metaphor. The darkening of the sun and moon is a way of expressing a time of tumult and confusion; the world as we have known it will be turned upside down. Unlike later apocalyptic writers, who took the image of the end of the world literally, Joel looks for a transformation of this world rather than a new creation.

Vision of Plenty

Joel's hope for the transformation of the earth is captured in his prediction of a time of plenty. It is a natural reaction to the locust plague and also appeals to the universal hope for freedom from hunger. In a time of scarcity, Joel comforts his people with the promise that they will eat and be filled (2, 26). This is very common in the prophets and serves two functions: It gives hope to the poor, and it gives a goal for people to work toward.

Vengeance on the Nations

The occasional desire for vengeance in the Hebrew scriptures can be distasteful to Christians, although not unknown to their experience. Joel's presentation of Judah's desire for vengeance recalls the "eye for an eye" attitude. It is not enough that Judah flow with wine and milk; the hated neighbor Edom must be a desert waste (4, 10). If their enemy sold Jews into slavery, then the enemy's children must be sold. Some prophets called for peace, calling the people to beat their swords into plowshares (Is 2, 4; Mi 4, 3); Joel calls for a showdown.

Vengeance is not noble, but it is understandable in some situations. We must not overlook the fact that the prophet's call for vengeance is a call for justice. In Joel it is a protest of the powerless who had seen their children sold into slavery.

Questions for Discussion and Reflection
Group Sharing/Discussion

1. The plague of locusts transformed the land into "desert waste." The Israelites' rituals express their desperate concern and hope that God will bring relief. Joel comforts his people with the promise that they will eat and have their fill.

Share your insights on how the plague affected the people; on their views of what caused it; on the role of the prophet for his people; and on their views of their neighbors.

In Our Lives

1. It is not enough that Judah flow with milk and wine; their hated neighbor Edom must be a desert waste (4, 19). Joel's presentation of Judah's desire for vengeance recalls the "eye for an eye" attitude.

Try this as an examination of conscience about vengeance. For one week be aware of all the people who might feel like "turning the tables" on you, or you might feel that way toward them. See how you can improve one of these situations.

Individual/Personal Reflection/Action

1. "Rend your hearts, not your garments." Think about what attitudes of your heart need to be changed to return to the LORD.

AMOS READING GUIDE

At a Glance

Who are the main players?	Amos, Priest of Bethel
What should I look for?	Note that this is an anthology of Amos' oracles. Keep in mind the typical two-part form: indictment of sins followed by announcement of punishment.
When did this take place?	Amos was a shepherd of Tekoa in Judah, who exercised his ministry during the prosperous reign of Jeroboam II (786–746 B.C.).
Where did these events occur?	He prophesied in Israel at the great cult center of Bethel.
Why was this book written?	Amos proclaims that true religion requires not just ritual observances, but a moral life.
What is the story?	Amos preached against the northern kingdom and is the first of Israel's prophets to have his speeches preserved in a collection. He is a prophet of divine judgment during a time of political and economic stability and growth.
	Amos' harsh criticism of Israelite society and the expectation that its injustice would bring divine judgment seemed exaggerated and outlandish to his audience. A mere 25 years later, his predictions came true when Samaria fell to Assyrian armies.

Introduction

Amos is Israel's prophet of social justice, proclaiming that true religion consists not just of ritual observances, but in a moral life based on fair and equitable treatment of all members of society, powerful and powerless alike. This concern for justice lies at the heart of Israel's prophetic involvement, but no other prophet expresses it with more passion and substance. Amos demands justice in all areas of society: political (6, 10), judicial (5, 10.12), and economic (8, 4–6), and he mercilessly attacks Israel's elite for their abuse of power (4, 1; 6, 1). He believes Israel's religious assemblies, sacred music, and elaborate sacrifices are pointless without principled and ethical behavior in daily affairs (5, 21–24). And he regards the demise of Israelite society as the inevitable outcome of its internal corruption and injustices (5, 6–7). The power of social justice in the imagination of Western society derives in large part from Israel's prophets and from Amos' passionate appeals in particular.

Amos, the Book

The book of Amos contains one brief narrative about an event in his career (7, 10–17) and several reports of his visions (7, 1–9; 8, 1–3; 9, 1–4), but the book is primarily made up of short judgment speeches with a simple two-part structure: an indictment listing Israel's sins and a sentence of judgment prescribing God's punishment for these sins. This structure is clearly visible, for example, in Amos' speech to the priest Amaziah at Bethel, in which Amos indicts Amaziah for restricting prophetic speech (7, 16) and announces the divine sentence punishing Amaziah and his family (7, 17). While judgment speeches against Israel predominate, the book of Amos actually begins with a series of judgment speeches, with this same two-part structure, directed against Israel's neighbors (1, 3—2, 5).

Amos must be read as an anthology of short, independent speeches rather than as a book with a single thesis developed from beginning to end. The reader must also be aware that Amos (and other prophets) composed speeches in a poetic form based on verse units of two parallel lines: "then let justice surge like water,/ and goodness like an unfailing stream" (5, 24). Keeping these two features of Amos' work in mind can help make sense of a book that might otherwise appear disorganized and repetitious.

Amos, the Prophet

Only one episode of Amos' career is recounted in this book. Although he came from the southern kingdom of Judah, Amos proclaimed his oracles in the northern kingdom, especially around the temple of Bethel. (After the northern tribes split off from Judah to form their own kingdom, King Jeroboam set up two official sanctuaries at Dan and Bethel to discourage people from worshiping at the Jerusalem Temple.) Amaziah, the priest at Bethel, was worried because Amos was prophesying against the king in the temple precincts. The priest could not afford to offend the king, so he told Amos to go back to Judah. The reply of Amos (7, 14) about not being a prophet, nor belonging to a company of prophets, until the LORD called him, points to his independence. He did not have to rely for support on the priest or the king. He could take care of himself working as a shepherd or a dresser of sycamores (a kind of fig tree).

This independence, added to his obvious personal conviction, gave rise to a style that is blunt and sometimes offensive. He calls the women of Samaria "cows of Bashan" (4, 1) and tells the priest that his wife will be a harlot in the city (7, 17). He had nothing to gain by soft pedaling his message. He was not a trusted adviser to the king, as the prophet Nathan was to David; and as an outsider, he had no hope of influencing the upper classes. He simply proclaims the doom that is coming.

Amos and the Covenant

Amos consistently treats Israel the same as the other nations in the sight of God. Did the prophet consider Israel as a chosen nation and, therefore, special in any sense? Certainly Amos considered the Exodus as fundamental to Israel's identity, but this did not give the Israelites any guarantees, nor put them into a position of privilege. Rather, it gave them more responsibility.

Two passages make this very clear. Chapter 3, verse 2 says, "You alone have I favored, more than all the families of the earth." The modern-day reader is probably surprised to read the verse that follows: "Therefore I will punish you for all your crimes." Amos' audience was no doubt shocked and maybe even angered. This was not what they wanted to hear. Similarly and even more bluntly, we read in 9, 7: "Did I not bring the Israelites from the land of Egypt as I brought the Philistines from Caphtor and the Arameans from Kir?" Israel is special but so is every other nation.

Organization of the Book

Outline of the Book of Amos

Amos 1–2	Oracles against the nations ending with a denunciation of Israel
Amos 3, 1—5, 9	"Words"—three long oracles (strings of short utterances). Note that 5, 7–9 has been reordered by the NAB editors.
Amos 5, 7—6, 14	Three "woes" against Israel and Judah
Amos 7, 1—9, 8b	Visions of destruction
Amos 9, 8c–15	An epilogue, probably added later

Oracles against the Nations (chs 1–2)

The book begins with oracles of judgment against Israel's immediate neighbors (present-day Lebanon, Syria, Jordan, and part of the occu-pied territory of Palestine). It is not unusual for a prophet to denounce other nations, but what is unusual is that Amos goes on to pronounce a similar judgment on Israel. He insists that Israel is no different from other nations in the eyes of God. According to Amos, any nation that sins against humanity deserves punishment. Moab is condemned for burning to lime the bones of the King of Edom (2, 1); Israel is condemned for selling the just man for silver and the poor man for a pair of sandals (2, 6).

The oracle in 2, 6–16 is in the form of a speech in which a "lawsuit" is brought against Israel for failing to keep the Sinai covenant. This style of writing follows a pattern: recalling God's action on behalf of Israel in the Exodus; pointing out Israel's unfaithfulness in not keeping the commandments; usually issuing a threat. Many scholars think that this recollection of the Exodus may have been added by an editor of the prophetic books who wanted to put the prophetic preaching in the context of the theology of Deuteronomy as found in the Books of Joshua, Judges, Samuel, and Kings. This opinion seems reasonable because Amos' own focus was broader. He believed that people of any nation are bound by the requirements of justice, whether or not they know the law of Moses. In other words, Amos affirms the natural law as it was understood in the ancient Near East. Paul makes the same point in the first chapter of Romans when he says that pagan idolaters have no excuse, "for what can be known about God is evident to them."

Words and Woes (3, 1—6, 14)

The three "words" of Amos are really a string of shorter oracles, mainly concerned with Israel's sins. There is a short section in 3, 3–8, however, that is important because it focuses for the reader part of what Amos believes about God. This kind of insight helps the reader understand the rest of the prophet's work.

For Amos, everything that happens is God's doing. The order in nature is God's design. Nothing happens by chance. The acts of God in history are not confined to special events but take in everything, good as well as bad. (There was no devil in Israel's religion at this time to blame for the evil in the world.) This basic conviction about God accounts for Amos' interpretation of political events. For example, if Assyria is more powerful than Israel, this is not by chance; it is God's will. All this is another way of saying that Amos is a radical monotheist; he not only ignores other gods, but he attributes everything that happens to the God of Israel.

In both the "words" and the "woes," Amos criticizes the cult of Israel, its religious rituals and practices. In 4, 4, he uses a play on words to make his point. The words for "sin offering" and "sin" in Hebrew are so similar that the people would, no doubt, understand Amos' implication, that they come to the sanctuary at Bethel to sin, rather than to make an offering for sin.

The prophet's sharpest critique of the cult is the "woe" against those who yearn for the Day of the LORD (5, 18–25). This yearning was expressed in a major harvest festival in the fall, an occasion celebrating the victory of the God of Israel and the defeat of God's enemies. Amos turns a celebration into its opposite, a day of judgment. He was the first prophet to speak of the Day of the LORD as a day of judgment on Israel.

Amos goes on to issue a broadside against all the festivals of Israel. His point is not that all ritual is necessarily bad, but that ritual is not the essence of religion. The essence of religion is social justice. If ritual furthers justice, well and good, but too often it does not. Amos thought that ritual made the upper classes complacent, so much so that they thought that God would protect them no matter what and that they need not be concerned about the plight of the poor. They could leave the festival and go back to cheating in the marketplace (8, 5). Amos labels all this as self-delusion.

In the final "woe" in chapter 6, Amos predicts that the upper classes of both kingdoms, "the complacent in Zion [and] the overconfident on the mount of Samaria," would be the first to go into exile. They had sold the poor into slavery while they lived in luxury. Amos knew what he was talking about; he knew that the practice of the Assyrians was to take the upper classes into exile so there would be no one left to organize a revolt. In his view, it was a fate they richly deserved.

Visions of Destruction (7, 1—9, 8b)

Amos is so moved by the enormity of the destruction he envisions that, at first, he intercedes and God relents. Once again, using a play on words, he makes the point that the time for forgiveness has run out. The vision is of a basket of

---

"They Sell the Just Man for Silver"

With this phrase, Amos strikes at the heart of Israel's guilt (2, 6; 8, 6). He criticizes not just an abuse here and an injustice there, but an economic system that condones the accumulation of great wealth in the hands of a few (6, 1–6) and the growth in the gap between rich and poor (5, 11). In Israel's traditional economy, families supported themselves by farming their ancestral lands, as Amos himself may have done (1, 1; 7, 14–15). But as the wealthy imposed heavy taxes (2, 8; 5, 11), took collateral for themselves (2, 8), and cheated customers in the marketplace (8, 5), the poor were eventually forced off their lands and reduced to debt-slavery, where they were bought and sold by the rich. Such an economic system was intolerable, according to Amos, for a society that had itself been once freed from slavery (2, 10; 3, 1).

ripe fruit. The Hebrew for "ripe fruit" is similar to the word for "end," so "the time is ripe" (8, 2) can be translated "the end has come."

This was the first time that the idea of the "end" was proclaimed in ancient Israel. For Amos, the end was the end of Israel as an independent nation that had existed for 200 years. It was primarily the Israel of the upper classes that would end. The peasants would continue to suffer under Assyria, but, for them, it probably didn't make much difference whether they paid taxes to a foreign power or to oppressive Israelite landlords. For Amos and for the peasants, what mattered was not political identity, but the living conditions of the poor within society.

Epilogue (9, 8c–15)

Another example of the work of an editor is found in the epilogue. The force of Amos' prophecy was in its finality, as we read in the last line before the epilogue (9, 8a and b), "The eyes of the LORD God are on this sinful kingdom: I will destroy it from off the face of the earth." In the very next line, a later editor adds, "But I will not destroy the house of Jacob completely, says the LORD."

The editor puts the prophecy of Amos in a broader historical perspective, that of the whole of Israel. The message of the prophets of Israel, in general, was not of destruction, but of hope. Death and destruction have their place and time,

but hope remains. Ultimate optimism is an essential ingredient of biblical faith.

Questions for Discussion and Reflection
Group Sharing/Discussion

1. Although Israel was special, why did Amos treat Israel the same as other nations?

In Our Lives

1. In the ancient world it was the role of the prophet to be the conscience of the nation and to speak up for the powerless.
   a. Who are the powerless of our day?
   b. Who speaks for them? Religious leaders? Social workers?
   c. Do you ever feel motivated to speak for the powerless? Who or what will help you act on this?

Individual/Personal Reflection/Action

1. Reflect on Amos' words on justice and worship (Am 5, 23–24).

Away with your noisy songs!
I will not listen to the melodies of your harps.
But if you would offer me holocausts,
then let justice surge like water,
and goodness like an unfailing stream.

2. How is acting justly linked to prayer and worship in your life? In your parish? Who can you speak with to help make your parish worship more linked to acting justly?

OBADIAH READING GUIDE

At a Glance

Who are the main players?	Obadiah
What should I look for?	The 21 verses of this book contain the strongest and sternest prophecy in the Old Testament.
When did this take place?	Sometime in the fifth century B.C.
Where did these events occur?	Judah
Why was this book written?	This book is unique because it contains only a single speech and that is directed against Edom, a neighboring nation, and not Israel. The Edomites entered Jerusalem when the Babylonians had invaded it, looting it and mistreating the people. See Psalm 137, 7–8.
What is the story?	God's judgment of Edom is viewed as a fair punishment for the Edomites' disloyalty to their Israelite neighbors. Though their relations were often marked by conflict, Israel believed they were closely related as descendants of the two brothers, Jacob and Esau.

Outline of the Book of Obadiah

Obadiah is the shortest of the prophetic books with only 21 verses:

Verses 1–14   Short oracles against Edom
Verses 15–16   An oracle against all the nations
Verses 17–21   Prediction of restoration for Judah

Oracles against Edom and the Nations (1–16)

Oracles of vengeance against Edom were common in the time after the Exile (compare Jer 49, 7–22; Jl 4, 19). Obadiah then extends this vengeance to all the nations. The basic message of these oracles is stated clearly in verse 15, "As you have done, so it shall be done to you."

Once more the reader is challenged to deal with the notion of vengeance. The prophet says that if you do violence to your neighbors and gloat over their distress, you deserve the same treatment. When the prophet extends the attack beyond Edom to all the nations, he uses the familiar motif of the Day of the LORD. Here it refers to the day of judgment, not the end of the world. The judgment is based on the law of retribution: As you have done, so it will be done to you.

The Restoration of Judah (17–21)

Modest hope is expressed at the end of Obadiah. Judah will rule over its neighbors, and this kingdom will be the LORD's. There is a slight notion of vengeance in this image of the kingdom, but the hope for the survival of the people is far more significant.

Questions for Discussion and Reflection
Individual/Personal Reflection/Action

The Edomites incurred the lasting hatred cf the Jews by exploiting the weaknesses of Judah and pillaging its territory after the Babylonian invasion. Obadiah's oracle of vengeance is stated clearly: "As you have done, so shall it be done to you, your deed shall come back upon your own head."

1. Does this vengeance, which is similar to Amos', express the natural law of the punishment fits the crime?

2. How would you contrast this attitude with modern "hatred" of one country against another?

3. Does Jesus' teaching of "love your enemy, do good to those who hurt you" contrast with this attitude? Are they compatible? Is Jesus' teaching on love of neighbor limited to personal relations or does it also apply to groups and nations?

JONAH READING GUIDE

At a Glance

Who are the main players?	Jonah People of Nineveh
What should I look for?	Look for the message of God's action through the disobedient prophet Jonah. Also notice the universality of God's mercy.
When did this take place?	Written in the post-exilic era, probably in the fifth century B.C., this book is an instructive story with an important message.
Where did these events occur?	Nineveh, a great Assyrian city feared and hated by the Israelites
Why was this book written?	This prophecy strikes directly at the intolerant nationalism, which limited God's mercy to the chosen people of Israel. It is a parable of mercy, showing God's threatened punishments are but the expressions of a merciful will that moves all people to repent and seek forgiveness.
What is the story?	The book of Jonah is full of humor and irony. The author repeatedly undercuts expectations. Jonah is commanded to go in one direction and goes in the other; the sailors are more devout than the prophet; Jonah is disappointed when his mission succeeds; he is more concerned about a plant than about a populous city. God withheld his punishment and Jonah complained. From this humorous story a sublime lesson may be drawn.

Jonah the Book

Jonah is unique among the prophetic books. It is a story rather than a series of oracles. Jonah is himself a sort of anti-prophet: His actions are the opposite of what we expect of prophets. The story is more a fable, because of the role of the fish (like the animals in Aesop's fables). It's also a parable, a short story that goes against the expected. It is clearly meant to be humorous. It was written sometime in the post-exilic period but has a different outlook from other writings of that period.

The chapter headings reveal the outline of the book. The long psalm in chapter 2 was probably added by a later editor, who focused on the miracle of Jonah's survival.

To appreciate Jonah, we need to consider that:

1. the book is deliberately humorous;
2. it is about the proper attitude to foreign nations, not about Jonah's miraculous escape from drowning;
3. the story is mildly critical of the religious zeal usually connected with prophecy.

The Story's Humor

The humor is apparent from verse one: A prophet shamelessly disobeys a divine command; pagan sailors fear the LORD of Israel; a fish swallows a man and then spits him up on the shore; wicked Assyrians and even animals repent.

The author is not interested in historical plausibility; he uses this fantastic tale to teach a theological lesson. Ironically, in this "prophetic book," the prophet is not given the dignity usually associated with the office, nor are his convictions taken seriously. The reader is asked to reconsider the stereotype of both pagan and prophet.

The Attitude to Foreign Nations

The wickedness of Assyria is the premise of this story, and Jonah is upset at being sent to preach to those who seem not to deserve God's mercy. Incredibly, the Assyrians repent, and Jonah questions whether they deserve divine forgiveness. One might react thus if the leaders of some dictatorial regime made a show of repentance for their crimes and were pardoned. It is not that

Jonah is exceptionally narrow-minded but, rather, that his God is exceptionally tolerant. To God the Creator, Assyrians are as important as Israelites (or, in our terms, no racial or ethnic group is beyond redemption).

The last verse of the book recognizes that ordinary Assyrians are no more guilty of the crimes of their nation than are the cattle. In any case, guilt or innocence is not the point; the astonishing magnanimity of God is the message. The book of Jonah sees God in the same terms as the much later book of Wisdom 11, 24: "For you love all things that are and loathe nothing that you have made; for what you hated, you would not have fashioned." The penitent Assyrian is as great a contradiction as the "good Samaritan" of the Gospel, and as hard to accept, given the situation of the Jews of the post-exilic period in which the book was written.

The Perspective on Prophetic Zeal

Jonah reacts to God's mercy by sulking and praying for death (4, 8). He is a prophet in the same mold as Elijah who, with great zeal for destroying sinners, had done the same in 1 Kings 10, 4f. But the book of Jonah sees the limitations of prophetic zeal. Jonah is well-intentioned and acts out of a long tradition, but God rebukes him mildly. Earlier, Hosea had broadened the tradition by recognizing that it is more fitting for God to have mercy than to punish. This book goes further and extends that mercy to foreign nations. Even prophets must learn that reconciliation is a higher value than strict retribution. Not all the prophetic books reflect this insight, but it is the view affirmed for Christianity in the Gospels.

The Sign of Jonah

The episode in the belly of the fish, a minor humorous motif in the story, acquires greater meaning in later tradition. It is taken to prefigure (Mt 12, 39f) Jesus' time in the tomb. Jonah is a frequent symbol of the Resurrection in early Christian art. In chapter 2 the belly of the fish is equated with the netherworld, and Jonah's regret about being there is that he is separated from God's presence. Jonah asks to be restored to that presence, which is the fullness of life for most Old Testament writers.

The Relevance of Jonah

Jonah's message is as urgent in today's world as it was in his time. It teaches us not only tolerance and understanding for those who are different from us, but also forgiveness for those who have truly behaved wickedly, if they are willing to accept it.

The sign of Jonah is a sign of hope that we can afford to forgive the injustices of life. The wicked deeds of the oppressor are not as final as they seem. Belief in resurrection is often associated with a hope for the damnation of the wicked. The book of Jonah, read in the light of the New Testament and Christian tradition, suggests that resurrection can also give a larger perspective on life, one that has room for tolerance and forgiveness.

Questions for Discussion and Reflection

Group Sharing/Discussion

1. The prophet Jonah is often described as an anti-prophet. Retell some incidents when Jonah acts in the opposite manner of a prophet.

In Our Lives

1. The story is deliberately humorous: a disobedient prophet, sailing to a remote place to get away from the LORD; pagan sailors exhibiting more fear of the LORD than Jonah; fantastic Assyrian repentance, including the animals; the big fish saving and delivering Jonah to Nineveh. The ironic humor of the story invites us to reconsider our stereotypes of prophet and pagans.

Jonah's message of tolerance and forgiveness prompts us to recognize, practice, and pray for the grace to be tolerant and to forgive. Decide on ways to make this message part of your life.

2. Humor enriches life. How do you recognize it, nourish it in your life, and share it?

Individual/Personal Reflection/Action

1. For later generations and for us who have the New Testament, the sign of Jonah is the sign of hope. The book of Jonah suggests resurrection and hope, which teaches the message of tolerance and forgiveness. Reread the story of Jonah consciously in the light of the resurrection. Pray for the grace and light of hope that gives tolerance and forgiveness.

MICAH READING GUIDE

At a Glance

Who are the main players?	Micah
What should I look for?	Micah must be read as an anthology of short speeches rather than as a unified narrative. It is especially important to distinguish the judgment speeches from the salvation speeches and to keep the historical context in mind.
When did this take place?	Micah's prophetic career spanned the latter part of the eighth century B.C.
Where did these events occur?	Micah's home was the small village of Moresheth, southwest of Jerusalem, but his speeches are directed to Samaria and Jerusalem, capital cities of the north and the south.
Why was this book written?	Micah, a contemporary of Amos, Hosea, and Isaiah, was largely preoccupied with the same issues of social justice and the coming Assyrian invasion. He accuses the ruling elite of corruption and misleading the people. He has little patience for false prophets.
What is the story?	His judgment speeches (chs 1–3; 6 and 7, 1–7) focus on Samaria and Jerusalem and their ruling elite who were both corrupt and complacent. Rulers, judges, and prophets are accused of corruption and mistreating and misleading the people. His salvation speeches (chs 4–5, and 7, 8–20) describe the misfortune their listeners have experienced and predict a period of renewal and restoration for them. He ends with a note of hope and promise.

Micah, in his role as prophet, resembles Jeremiah. He spoke out against prophets who wanted to be popular. They said what people wanted to hear and were more concerned about their own well-being than that of the nation. Micah saw the role of the true prophet "to declare to Jacob his crimes and to Israel his sins" (3, 8). Because of this position, Micah stands as a lonely figure. Like Jeremiah, he was not successful in reaching the people, but trusted that God would vindicate him (7, 7–10).

Outline of the Book of Micah

Mi 1–3	Impending judgment
Mi 4–5	(Added later) Restoration
Mi 6	Indictment of Israel
Mi 7	The prophet's reflection

The Impending Judgment (chs 1–3)

Micah begins with a description of an apparition of God. In Israel's tradition, such appearances of God were associated with God's saving action, as on Sinai. But in Micah, God is not coming to save, but to judge. Eighth-century Israel experiences God's presence in the invasion of the Assyrian army rather than in Sinai's fire and earthquake. According to Micah, the destruction would center on Jerusalem and Samaria, home to royalty and the ruling classes.

In chapter 2, the prophet gives the reason for the coming destruction: The rich force the small property owners into debt and eventually seize their property. It is only right, says Micah, that the Assyrians will seize the land from the rich.

In chapter 3, Micah attacks the complacency and illusion of some religious teaching and practice. It is not enough to say that no evil can come upon Israel because the LORD is in its midst. Such faith is not virtue for Micah. Virtue is in the practice of justice and in facing reality honestly. Faith cannot be based on any religious institution, no matter how sacred. Micah's prophecy that Zion would be plowed like a field was not what people wanted to hear. The prophecy was not fulfilled in Micah's time, but his words were justified later.

The Prophecies of Restoration (chs 4–5)

As indicated above, these prophecies of restoration were probably added to Micah after the Babylonian exile. Two of them in particular show us the work of the post-exilic editor. The prophecy of the restoration of the house of the LORD in 4, 1–3 is also found in Isaiah 2, 24. The idea of nations streaming to Jerusalem is not new, but it speaks of the time after the exile when Jews who lived in other lands came to Jerusalem on pilgrimage. The placement of this prophecy immediately after the prediction that Zion would become a plowed field is typical of the editors of the prophetic books. They often spoke of hope after destruction or judgment. In the same way, the Temple and its rituals had taken on too much importance in the eighth century; now, after the exile, the Temple has a potential for uniting the people and strengthening faith.

The prophecy about Bethlehem in Micah 5, 1–4 is familiar to Christians for obvious reasons. The post-exilic editor had at least two reasons for inserting it here: first, to build up hope, suggesting that David's kingly line would be restored, and second, by mentioning Bethlehem rather than Jerusalem, the editor is pointing to a humbler, simpler monarchy free of big city corruption.

The Indictment of Israel (ch 6)

Micah recalls the covenant, God's faithfulness, and Israel's failure in a speech that sounds like a courtroom scene (compare Am 2). The prophet returns to the themes of justice and honesty in his indictment of Israel's false religion, which included performing rituals to further their own interests.

Micah's solutions sound simple on the surface. Although offerings of thousands of animals, vats of expensive oil, and even first-born children sound impressive, God rejects these showy attempts at faithfulness. True religion is not based on certain rituals or beliefs, only this, "to do the right and to love goodness, and to walk humbly with your God" (6, 8). Notice the emphasis on action and humility.

The Concluding Indictment and Prayer (ch 7)

The first six verses of this chapter describe a society where corruption and lawlessness are prevalent. The only solution, according to Micah, is repentance and renewed reliance on the LORD. The confession and hope for ultimate victory in verses 8–10, spoken probably by a personified Jerusalem to the enemy, Assyria, is followed by the vision of a return from exile (vv. 12–13) and hope for the restoration of prosperity (vv. 14–15) and the downfall of enemies (vv. 16–17). Finally, Micah ends with the hope in a God who will forgive the sins of the people and restore them to divine favor.

Questions for Discussion and Reflection
Group Sharing/Discussion

1. In the eight century B.C., Israel experienced God through the invading and destroying Assyrian army. In chapter 2 Micah gives the reasons for this coming destruction. What does he say are the reasons that God destroys Zion?

In Our Lives

1. The rich devised ways of forcing smaller landowners into debt and then seized their land. Their greed would be in vain because of the Assyrian army. What parallels do you see in modern life? What makes greed so wrong?

2. A true prophet who points out the ills of a society is often not popular. What true prophets today are unpopular? How might we respond to them as individuals, as a church, as a nation?

3. Micah had little respect for the professional prophets who told people what they wanted to hear and led them astray. Who are the modern professional prophets who lack integrity and mislead us?

Individual/Personal Reflection/Action

1. An oracle of hope immediately follows Micah's prediction that Zion would become a plowed field. In 5, 1–4 he speaks of a ruler who will come from Bethlehem, David's birthplace. Christians have treasured this prophecy. What did this mean for the early Christians? Does the fact that Jesus comes from Bethlehem have any significance for you?

NAHUM READING GUIDE

At a Glance

Who are the main players?	Nahum City of Nineveh
What should I look for?	The oracles of Nahum are concerned with a single event, the fall of Nineveh in 612 B.C. Because Assyria long dominated Israel with taxes and colonial acquisitions, the euphoria of the prophet is understandable. Yet behind these emotions lies a belief in God's just government of world affairs.
When did this take place?	Shortly before the fall of Nineveh in 612 B.C.
Where did these events occur?	In Nineveh, the capital of the Assyrian empire for one hundred years
What is the story?	Nineveh, an ancient and powerful Assyrian city, became the capital and symbol of the entire empire itself, until it fell to the armies of the Medes and the Babylonians in 612 B.C. These speeches predicting Nineveh's end were written by the prophet Nahum shortly before that fall.

Nahum's Message

Nahum's sole concern is the fall of the Assyrian capital city of Nineveh. The prophet is euphoric:

> See, upon the mountains there advances the bearer of good news, announcing peace! Celebrate. . . . For nevermore shall you be invaded by the scoundrel . . . (2, 1)

It is characteristic of biblical prophecy that the fall of one Gentile nation at the hands of another is assumed to be the work of the LORD.

Outline of the Book of Nahum

Na 1, 2—2, 1.3 The LORD's coming in judgment

Na 2, 2—3, 19 The fall of Nineveh

A Jealous God

The opening verse of Nahum's prophecy is somewhat shocking to modern ears: "A jealous and avenging God is the LORD" (1, 2). However, this image of God is neither new nor incompatible with a God of mercy and love. In the book of

Exodus, the LORD is called a "warrior" (15, 3) and described as jealous on Sinai (20, 50). Even Nahum, in the very next verse after "jealous and avenging," says that "The LORD is slow to anger . . ." (1, 3).

The modern reader could, no doubt, benefit by taking on the ancient Hebrew's ability to deal with ambiguity when it comes to God. This means letting diverse or seemingly contradictory statements about God stand side by side. It is an acknowledgment that God is beyond our ability to completely explain. It also allows God's wrath to be seen as an expression of justice.

The Fall of Nineveh

Nahum's description of Nineveh's destruction is a series of vibrant images showing the once-formidable city brought to its knees. The city once full of loot is now plundered and laid waste (2, 10–11; 3, 1); the strongest walls crumble at a mere shake (3, 12); and those who are supposed to protect the city have fallen asleep on the job (3, 18). Nineveh will suffer the same fate it brought to the cities conquered by Assyria.

Is it any wonder that "All who hear this news of you clap their hands over you; For who has not been overwhelmed . . . by your malice?" (3, 19).

A Short-Sighted Prophecy

Judah's freedom, proclaimed by Nahum, was short-lived. It was only 15 years before another oppressor would lay siege to Jerusalem. Nahum's short prophecy is a lesson in realistic hope; no power lasts forever, but neither is complete freedom attained in this life.

Nahum's influence can be seen in the book of Revelation. John uses the image of the harlot from Nahum (3, 4) in anticipating the fall of Rome.

Questions for Discussion and Reflection
Group Sharing/Discussion
1. What event in history does the prophecy of Nahum deal with? How did Assyria treat the countries it conquered?

In Our Lives
1. What do you think of the opening verse of Nahum's prophecy, "A jealous and avenging God is the LORD"? This aspect of divinity was never thought to be incompatible with mercy and love. What do you think is the image of God in the minds of Nahum's listeners? Our image of God both personally and socially grows with experience and learning. Take time to reflect upon your personal image of God.

Individual/Personal Reflection/Action
1. The lesson of Nahum is two edged: The fall of Nineveh reminds us all tyrants fall sooner or later, which is cause for hope. But the fall of a particular tyrant is not the end of all tyrants. Nahum's exaltation over the fall of Nineveh is echoed in the New Testament in John's anticipation of the fall of Rome (Rv 17–19). Meditate on the rhythm of God's hope in the history of nations and peoples.

2. Words worth pondering and remembering from Nahum 1, 2a.3a.7.

A jealous and avenging God is the LORD,
an avenger is the LORD, and angry; . . . (Na 1, 2a)
The LORD is slow to anger, yet great in power,
and the LORD never leaves the guilty
   unpunished. . . . (Na 1, 3a)
The LORD is good, a refuge on the day of
   distress;
He takes care of those who have recourse to
   him, . . . (Na 1, 7)

Try the "both/and" approach when thinking about God. See how many times you can fill in the blanks: God is both _____ and _____.

HABAKKUK READING GUIDE

At a Glance

Who are the main players?	Habakkuk
What should I look for?	Note how the prophet calls God to account for his government of the world. Also, be enriched by the religious faith of the prophet, especially in chapter 3, Habakkuk's prayer that his vision be fulfilled.
When did this take place?	This prophecy dates from the years 605–597 B.C.

Where did these events occur?

In Judah where the situation was desperate at this time, with political intrigue and religious idolatry widespread in the small kingdom

Why was this book written?

The prophet Habakkuk is primarily concerned about believing in God's just rule over the world, which appears to be overwhelmingly unjust.

What is the story?

The prophecy of Habakkuk is considerably more reflective than that of Nahum. He prophesied a few years later. Habakkuk prophesied when the Babylonian threat had become obvious. He ponders not only that danger, but also the underlying problem of injustice and questions why God allows such a situation to prevail.

Outline of the Book of Habakkuk

Habakkuk 1–2	A dialogue between the prophet and the LORD
Habakkuk 3	A hymn of faith

The Dialogue (chs 1–2)

Habakkuk's prophecy comes shortly after that of Nahum (see timeline for Nahum), when the Babylonian threat was even more obvious, but Habakkuk is more reflective than Nahum. He reacts to the immediate danger, but he also seeks to understand the problem. He asks the age-old questions: Why do the wicked prevail over the just? How can God allow such a situation to exist? Is God just? These types of questions, called theodicy, or the effort to explain the existence of evil, are more typical of wisdom literature (particularly Job) and apocalyptic (see Apocalypse in the glossary) literature than of prophecy.

Habakkuk was concerned first of all with the injustice within Jewish society. He applies the woes in chapter 2 to the arrogant and wealthy. This section is similar to chapter 22 of Jeremiah, written at about the same time (609–598 B.C.), accusing King Jehoiakim of oppression and exploitation. Habakkuk's woes could be directed to the king as well.

Habakkuk's answer to the questions of God's justice is not an explanation, but a promise that the situation will be set aright in the future. At first the solution seems worse than the problem: God will raise up the Babylonians (1, 6–11) to conquer Israel. Just as Isaiah (ch 10) had spoken of Assyria as the rod of the LORD's anger, Babylon will bring about the downfall of King Jehoiakim. The com-

parison to Isaiah continues in the implied hope of Habakkuk; like the rod that would eventually be destroyed, so too will Babylon. It is unclear in the prophecy whether Habakkuk is referring to Babylon or the wicked in Judah because their behavior is similar (the wicked devouring the just). The lesson, however, is clear. Even though justice is not apparent in the world, one should trust in the LORD and be patient.

Righteousness and Faith (ch 3)

Faith according to Habakkuk might be closer to the traditional Christian understanding of hope. For the prophet, faith is simply the trust in God that enables one to wait for the future. The person who only looks at the present and sees no justice in the world and, therefore, judges that God is not in control lacks faith. The righteous or faithful one takes a longer view, trusts that justice will prevail, and is content to wait for it.

This hope in the future is expressed poetically in the hymn in chapter 3. The image of God coming in triumph as a warrior stands in a long tradition of such hymns (see Dt 33; Jgs 5; Mi 1). The early hymns of this kind referred to God's past activity on behalf of Israel. Habakkuk expects this victory in the future. It will be directed against "the people who attack us" (3, 16), presumably the Babylonians but maybe the Jewish oppressors as well. The prophet pictures a decisive intervention of God to wipe out all wickedness and oppression. This whole description of the future is close to what we find later in the apocalyptic literature and explains why Habakkuk was popular in apocalyptic circles; for example, the Dead Sea Scrolls include a commentary on Habakkuk.

Questions for Discussion and Reflection
Group Sharing/Discussion

1. The message of Habakkuk is clear. Even though justice is not apparent in the world, one should trust in the LORD and be patient. After some reflection share your view on this. Why are the wicked successful? Why does God allow the wicked to devour the righteous? Why should we be patient? What helps with being patient?

In Our Lives

1. The contrast in Habakkuk is between the rash man and one who is able to take the long view. His famous saying reads, "the just man, because of his faith, shall live." St. Paul builds on this in his reflections on faith (e.g., see Rom 1, 17 and Gal 3, 11.) Take time to compare Habakkuk's vision with Paul's development.

Individual/Personal Reflection/Action

1. The faith of Habakkuk is a faith against appearances (3, 17ff). It is based on the conviction that God is just and so justice will ultimately prevail. The value of this faith does not depend upon its fulfillment, but on its power to transform the lives of the faithful. It is a faith that encourages us to trust in God's activity in our midst. It is a faith that also encourages us to work against oppression and exploitation. Reflect on your faith. What is its source and foundation? Its strength? Its expressions?

ZEPHANIAH READING GUIDE

At a Glance

Who are the main players?	Zephaniah
What should I look for?	In a time of religious decline, notice the worshiping of false gods in rites that are false to the monotheism of Moses. Yet, the LORD in His mercy will spare a holy remnant.
When did this take place?	During the reign of Josiah, who governed the southern kingdom of Judah during 640–609 B.C.
Where did these events occur?	In the kingdom of Judah
Why was this book written?	The emphasis of Zephaniah is not on the sins of Judah, but on the destructiveness of the Day of the LORD, the result of idolatry by the people. It is portrayed in cosmic terms: God will make an end of all who live on earth. The day of judgment is seen as the vindication of the majesty of God against the unworthiness of the people.
What is the story?	Zephaniah's prophecy has three sections: A Day of Judgment for Judah, A Day of Judgment on the Nations, and Reproach and Promise for Jerusalem.

Zephaniah prophesied a little earlier than Nahum and Habakkuk and at the same time that Jeremiah was getting started, during the reign of Josiah who instituted the deuteronomic reform (2 Kgs 22–23). Idolatry is one of Zephaniah's themes because purifying Temple worship was the focus of the reform, but almost everything is expressed in terms of the Day of the LORD.

A Day of Judgment for Judah (ch 1)

The first oracle on the Day of the LORD is directed against Judah for idolatry and lack of faith in the LORD (1, 12). Zephaniah emphasizes not the sins of Judah, but the destructiveness of the Day of the LORD. It is portrayed in cosmic terms: God will make an end of all who live on earth. The day of judgment is a vindication of the majesty of God against the unworthiness of the people.

A Day of Judgment on the Nations (ch 2)

Judah is not the only object of the LORD's wrath. Chapter 2 lists the surrounding nations and seems to build up to Assyria, the most arrogant of all. The prophet quotes Nineveh's boast: "There is no other than I" (2, 15), the same as that of Babylon (Is 47, 10). The most fundamental human sin is self-divinization, and it is seen again and again throughout the Bible. Zephaniah's prophecies of the Day of the LORD dramatize the gulf between God and humanity and are basically a put-down of human pride.

Reproach and Promise for Jerusalem (ch 3)

Chapter 3 does not use the phrase "Day of the LORD" but deals with related themes. The phrase "on that day" (3, 11) refers to the Day of the LORD and is often used to introduce additions to the prophetic books in this period after the exile.

Jerusalem is denounced as the tyrannical city that accepts no correction (3, 1–8), which may refer to the failure of the reform or the rejection of the prophet. Finally, the last oracle (3, 11–20) promises restoration for Jerusalem, when God "will leave as a remnant in your midst a people humble and lowly." This reference to the remnant, familiar from the preaching of Isaiah, could be a sign of Isaiah's influence on Zepha-

niah, but it is more likely that it is another example of an optimistic oracle added on by an editor.

Whether or not these last words come from Zephaniah, they have their own validity. Just as the judgments on Assyria and Babylon were not God's last words to Israel, hope is still possible even after the destructive Day of the LORD.

Questions for Discussion and Reflection
Group Sharing/Discussion

1. One of Zephaniah's themes concerns idolatry (1, 4–8). The prophet speaks against the king's sons for adopting foreign customs. Why is this considered idolatry?

In Our Lives

1. What idolatries does Zephaniah refer to in his first oracle?

Individual/Personal Reflection/Action

1. Self-divinization is a charge often made by the prophets. Meditate on the many forms of self-divinization in the world. What does it look like? How is it expressed?

2. Remember that God will send as a remnant in your midst a people humble and lowly. Who do you know who might fit the description in 3, 12–13? What can you do to emulate them?

HAGGAI READING GUIDE

At a Glance

Who are the main players?	Haggai Zerubbabel
What should I look for?	Haggai preached to a people who returned from exile to a ruined land and are no longer in control of their own affairs. He encourages reconstructing the Temple.
When did this take place?	In the second year of Darius, 520 B.C.
Where did these events occur?	In Judah
Why was this book written?	At a time of defeatism, Haggai exhorted and encouraged the people to complete the great task of rebuilding the Temple.
What is the story?	His prophecy is divided into five oracles: (1) the call to rebuild the Temple; (2) the glory of the Temple; (3) an instruction on offering sacrifice; (4) the blessings of rebuilding the Temple; and (5) a pledge to Zerubbabel.

There are two main emphases of Haggai's prophetic work, and they both have to do with the Temple and the difficult situation of the returned exiles (the "remnant of the people"). Along with Zechariah, Haggai encourages the people to complete the Temple (Ezr 5, 1), and then he must help them deal with their disappointment after its completion.

Exhortation to Rebuild (ch 1)

The reasons for delaying the completion of the Temple all make sense, whether in ancient or modern times. The returned exiles were poverty-stricken; in addition, they were suffering under drought and crop failure. It was obvious that they needed houses for shelter and God did not. Haggai's interpretation of this situation was that their difficulties were due to the fact that they had not rebuilt the Temple but had concentrated instead on rebuilding their own homes.

There is wisdom in the prophet's exhortation to rebuild the Temple. The morale of the community would also be built by working on a common project, especially one that would focus the people's attention on God. Recall the experience of the poor European immigrant communities in the United States in the late nineteenth and early twentieth centuries. They built impressive churches and schools at great sacrifice to themselves. Their value to these communities was enormous, not just economically, but as a sign of their faith in God and what they could accomplish by working together.

The Reaction to the Finished Temple (ch 2)

The completion of the Temple was a disappointment. Those who could remember Solomon's Temple lamented because this new Temple was so puny by comparison (2, 3). Not only that, the completion did not bring about the reversal of fortunes that Haggai had predicted. His reaction is typical of prophets whose predictions don't come to pass. He says it is delayed, and the reason for the delay is that the people are not observing the purity laws, and their offerings are unclean. He ends by reaffirming that God will shake the heavens and the earth when conditions are right.

This situation points out the problem with prophecies that make specific predictions. The hopes raised are good for the morale of the community, but only for a time. When they are not fulfilled, it leads to disillusionment. The same problem will tend to discredit apocalyptic and messianic expectations of later times.

The Lessons of Haggai

There are two lessons to be learned from Haggai. One is that hope should not be focused on specific predictions, and the other is the value of religious symbols and ritual for bringing people together. The Temple may not have satisfied immediate expectations, but it contributed to Jewish life for the next 500 years and far outweighed the initial disappointments.

Questions for Discussion and Reflection
Group Sharing/Discussion

1. The completion of the Temple did not bring dramatic reversal of their fortunes for the people that Haggai had predicted. He learned that hope should not be focused on a specific prediction. Give an example of how you have learned a similar lesson.

In Our Lives

1. The people had put building their own homes before the building of the Temple. Building the Temple helped their morale by focusing on the community project rather than their own problems. Why was this helpful? What were the values of religious symbols, for example, the Temple and rituals, for the people? Were there any long-term values? What role do religious symbols play in our life?

2. Describe a situation when you have experienced the value of people working together on a common project for the community. Is there a community project we should initiate for ourselves?

Individual/Personal Reflection/Action

1. Reflect upon and remember these words of Haggai (2, 4c–5).

> For I am with you says the LORD of Hosts
> This is the pact I made with you
> when you came out of Egypt,
> And my spirit continues in your midst;
> do not fear!

Spend time reflecting on those expressions of your faith that sustain you through the difficulties and disappointments of life. Try writing them in your journal.

ZECHARIAH READING GUIDE

At a Glance

Who are the main players?

Zechariah Joshua Zerubbabel

What should I look for?

Zechariah should be read as a book in two parts: the visions of Zechariah (chs 1–8) and the speeches of an anonymous prophetic figure of a later time (chs 9–12). The eight visions are meant to promote the rebuilding of the Temple and to encourage exiles to return. In the second section the messianic vision of the coming of the Prince of Peace begins with chapter 9, verse 9. These verses are used by the Evangelists to describe the entry of Christ into Jerusalem.

When did this take place?

Zechariah's initial prophecy is dated to 520 B.C., the same year that Haggai received the prophetic call.

Where did these events occur?

In Judah

Why was this book written?

The prophet encouraged the people to complete the Temple after their return from exile.

What is the story?

The original oracles of Zechariah are characterized by a series of visions, which disclose the prophet's view of what is really going on in the post-exilic period. In all eight of these visions, the hidden, heavenly activity is assuring and a source of confidence for the fledgling Jewish community. In the second section the messianic coming is envisioned, and the oracle proclaiming the final victory of God's people over the heathens is proclaimed.

The book of Zechariah contains the work of more than one prophet. It is named for the prophet who, along with Haggai, encouraged the people to complete the Temple after their return from the exile. His work is found in chapters 1–8. The prophet of chapters 9–14 comes from a much later time. Some scholars point to a third prophet as the author of chapters 12–14.

The Original Zechariah (chs 1–8)

These oracles are a series of visions that are explained to the prophet by an angel. This is the first time that the interpreting angel appears in biblical literature; it becomes common in later apocalyptic writings. The visions show the prophet's view of what is really going on in these times after the exile, revealing something that is hidden from the ordinary person. It is God's activity that is hidden. The prophet wants to assure the returned exiles that God is active among them. For example, the first vision shows four

horsemen sent by God to patrol the earth to indicate that God is in control, although not visible. Similarly, in chapter 2, four heavenly blacksmiths come to beat down the nations and an angelic "man" makes preparations for the restoration of Jerusalem. All this is aimed at building up the confidence of the struggling community.

High Priest and Governor

When Zechariah prophesied to the returned exiles, the monarchy had been destroyed, and there was no king. The Persians ruled the area. Zerubbabel, a descendant of David, was governor, and Joshua was the High Priest. In the absence of a king, the High Priest had additional power and authority.

Up until the time of the Babylonian exile, the prophets had been sharply critical of the king and usually the priests as well. Prophets like Amos condemned the monarchy and its religious practices for making the people complacent and, therefore, unfaithful. In this new situation, Zechariah takes a different stance and comes to the defense of the leaders, in opposition to their critics.

In the vision in chapter 3, the High Priest, Joshua, stands before the angel of the LORD and is accused by Satan. This is one of the earliest appearances of Satan in the Old Testament (see Jb 1–2 and 1 Chr 21, 1). Satan is not yet portrayed as the Devil; rather, he is an angel in the service of God, serving as a prosecuting attorney. In Zechariah's vision, Satan represents the people in the community who are criticizing Joshua and receives a stinging rebuke from the angel of the LORD. Zechariah's point is not that Joshua is without fault, but that criticism is not appropriate when the community is struggling.

The prophet is equally positive about Zerubbabel, the governor. In chapter 4, the two leaders are pictured as olive trees, because both priest and king were anointed with oil. This type of anointing, incidentally, which goes back to the earliest days of kingship (see 1 Sm 10) is the source of the title "messiah" or "anointed one." In chapter 6, the prophet goes further and says that he has been commanded to make a crown for Zerubbabel. To make a king of a Davidic prince would have been extremely dangerous because the Persian rulers would, no doubt, have seen this as an act of rebellion. We don't know whether Zechariah ever carried it out, but we do know that the understanding of the monarchy became more and more idealized in the minds of the people in this period after the exile. The people hoped for a future messiah-king, the anointed one who would make Jerusalem again a holy city (8, 3). Zechariah's visions helped keep alive this dream of justice and freedom.

The Appreciation of Ritual

A positive view of ritual is another contrast to earlier prophets that we see in Zechariah. He shows that ritual is powerful in expressing human desires because it engages the emotions and motivations of the people performing it. In 5, 5–11, he relates a vision of wickedness, pictured as a woman, placed in a bushel container and shipped off to Babylon (similar to the Scapegoat ritual in Lv 16). The ritual action of getting rid of wickedness is meant to strengthen the people's resolve to rid society of evil and to move them to action.

Zechariah also appreciates the limits of ritual. After the experience of the exile and the destruc-

tion of the Temple, Zechariah knew the importance of sacrifice but still leaned more toward the position of Hosea; "It is love that I desire, not sacrifice" (Hos 6, 6).

Messianic Oracle and Allegory of the Shepherds (chs 9–11)

The messianic oracle in chapter 9 is famous because of its association with the Palm Sunday passages in Matthew 21, 5 and John 12, 15. The ass was not as humble an animal in the ancient world as in modern times and was used by the nobility in Genesis and Judges. Here, however, the image is used to recall an earlier, simpler time to express the hope for a ruler to restore Solomon's empire without the arrogance of the monarchy, symbolized by the horses and chariots. Although the messianic age is usually described as a time of universal disarmament, the messianic oracle in chapter 9 sounds very war-like. The point here, similar to what is found in later apocalyptic writing, is that the LORD will fight for Judah. The human role is to maintain purity and be obedient to the law. This role of the LORD as warrior is in accord with much of Israelite tradition (see Ex 15, 3).

The allegory of the shepherds in chapter 11 must be read against the background of two passages in Ezekiel, because Zechariah 11 reverses this earlier prophet's predictions of salvation. Ezekiel 34 speaks against the shepherds of Israel who exploited their flock. The mood changes, however, from judgment to salvation as the LORD takes over as shepherd. In chapter 37, Ezekiel takes two sticks, representing the two kingdoms of Israel and Judah, and joins them together, signifying that they would be one nation under David their king. In Zechariah 11 there are also exploitive shepherds but no movement to salvation, only slaughter. Also in Zechariah there are two staffs symbolizing two covenants, one with the nations and one between Judah and Israel. Both are broken in the course of the prophecy.

It is not clear when this prophecy was written or what context it addressed, but it is clearly an expression of extreme dissatisfaction and disillusionment with the situation after the exile. There is not a hint of the support for the institutional leaders found in chapters 1–8 or of the dream of justice and freedom. This anonymous prophet (sometimes called Deutero-Zechariah or "Second" Zechariah) can only proclaim judgment and try to make the people see reality for what it is.

Chapters 12–14

The last three chapters of Zechariah are even more confusing than chapters 9–11. There is persistent criticism of the rulers, especially in chapter 13: a "song of the sword" against the shepherd with a prediction that only a third of the people will be spared; and a surprising prediction of the end of prophecy. A motif of a final battle in Jerusalem runs through these chapters, especially 12 and 14, with the prophet expressing hope for reconciliation (between the leaders in Jerusalem and the people they oppressed) and a remarkable universalism (wanting to include the Egyptians in the worship of the true God).

After Haggai and Zechariah, prophets seemed to have lost status. This was partly due to the failure of predictions, the conflict between prophets themselves, and the willingness of some to mislead the people for their own gain. Although some of this could be said of some earlier times, these late post-exilic prophets do not command the same respect as their predecessors; their real names are not even used (e.g., Deutero-Zechariah).

Questions for Discussion and Reflection
Group Sharing/Discussion

1. Zechariah's first vision shows four horsemen whom the LORD has sent to patrol the earth.

What do you see as the meaning or implication of this vision?

2. In chapter 2 the visions show four heavenly blacksmiths coming to beat down the "horns" of the nations. What understanding do you find in this vision?

In Our Lives

1. In chapter 7 Zechariah is asked about the proper number of fast days. He answers that motivation is more important than number. What do you think? Should there be specific fasting days? What motivates you to fast?

2. Zechariah's attitude toward the institutions and their leadership differed from the earlier prophets. He was more supportive because the community was struggling. Pick an institution to which you belong, such as your local church or local government, and list some ways in which you can be both supportive and yet constructively critical.

3. What values govern whether or not you give support to designated leaders?

Individual/Personal Reflection/Action

1. Zechariah thought that what is most important is "to render true judgment, and show kindness and compassion toward each other" (7, 9). He echoes Hosea's "it is love that I desire, not sacrifice." Take some time to reflect and evaluate your life in respect to these qualities: living truthfully and showing kindness and compassion.

MALACHI READING GUIDE

At a Glance

Who are the main players?	Malachi Priests People
What should I look for?	Malachi preached to a disillusioned people and a failed leadership. This challenge he faced must be kept in mind as you read his speeches. He is primarily concerned about a lack of devotion and seriousness in Temple worship and about a lack of fidelity in Judah's social relationships.
When did this take place?	This work was composed by an anonymous writer shortly before Nehemiah's arrival in Jerusalem (455 B.C.).
Where did these events occur?	Judah
Why was this book written?	The prophecy gives a picture of life in the Jewish community returned from Babylon; his criticism of the abuses and religious indifference prepare the way for reforms.

What is the story?

The prophet addresses these issues in a series of disputations: He blames the Temple Priesthood for its impure offerings and improper teachings and Judah's people for the meager contributions. Further, he blames the people for the lack of faithfulness in family relationships and in obligations to the poor. He replies to the question, "Where is the God of justice?" that the Day of the LORD is coming. But first the forerunner must clear the way for repentance and true worship.

We do not know who wrote these three chapters that make up the last prophetic book. "Malachi" is probably not a proper name but simply a characterization: "my messenger." The word is taken from 3, 1, "Lo, I am sending my messenger," to designate the one through whom this word of the LORD is given. The book is made up of six oracles; all except the first are critical of Judah, the priesthood, and the people.

The Priesthood (1, 6—2, 9)

Malachi, like many prophets before him, is critical of the priesthood. However, the prophet is not opposed to the priesthood as a whole; in fact, he has the greatest respect for the ideal of the priesthood. His problem with the priests is that they have been offering cheap sacrifices, sick and lame animals. His point is that an offering represents the person bringing it. No one would offer a sick animal to the governor, so why would the priests offer one to God?

A familiar and somewhat surprising line is found in 1, 11, "from the rising of the sun, even to its setting, my name is great among the nations." It is not certain what the prophet had in mind, because the Gentiles did not worship the LORD explicitly. It could refer to those Jews who were spread out among all the nations (the Diaspora) or to the Persian kings who were generous in supporting the Temple. A third possibility would point to a decidedly broad-minded and liberal attitude. Because the LORD is called the God of Heaven (Ezr 6, 10), then the High God of the Persians and other deities could also be acknowledged as "the God of Heaven." This would mean that the Gentiles worshiped the same God as the Jews!

Breaches of Faith (2, 10–17)

Another surprising phrase is found in the third oracle (2, 10–17). The prophet begins with the question: "Have we not all the one Father?" Then he denounces two breaches of faith: Judah's marriage to "an idolatrous woman" (2, 11) and the divorce of "the wife of your youth" (2, 14).

The usual explanation for this passage is that Jewish men were divorcing the Jewish wives of their youth and marrying Gentile women, possibly for social reasons. This led to their involvement in the cult of pagan deities. So the question "Have we not all one Father?" is addressed only to Jews and does not reflect as universal an attitude as it seems.

Another interpretation is based on the fact that there is no other evidence that Jews in the postexilic period divorced their Jewish wives. Once a marriage had been entered into, it was sacred. The Jewish men should have seen to it that their offspring were "godly" (2, 15). Conversion of the spouses, rather than divorce, was the solution. The "one Father," then, is the creator of all, Jews and Gentiles. Ethnic distinctions do not matter if one is willing to recognize the one God.

If this interpretation is correct, Malachi exhibits some of the spirit of St. Paul in his openness to the Gentiles. It also points to the diversity of opinion in Judaism at this time. Ezekiel (44, 7) insisted that no "foreigners, uncircumcised in heart and flesh" be admitted to the Temple.

The Day of the LORD (ch 3)

The final chapter of the book is dominated by the expectation that God will come in judgment, an adaptation of the traditional Day of the LORD. It is from this chapter that Handel borrowed the image of the refiner's fire for his *Messiah*. Malachi is also the source of the motif of the messenger who prepares the way and is first identified as Elijah the prophet. In the New Testament, John the Baptist is cast in this role (Mt 11, 14; 17, 12f). It is likely that the prophet we call Malachi saw himself in this role.

The final oracle of Malachi is also the conclusion of all the prophetic books. The editors refer to Moses as a way of reinforcing the laws of the Pentateuch. They also underline the theme of the coming judgment. The prophetic books not only remind us of the past, but motivate us in the present by making us look into the future.

Questions for Discussion and Reflection
Group Sharing/Discussion

1. The most startling statement in Malachi is the declaration that "from the rising of the sun, even to its setting, my name is great among the nations" (1, 11). The Gentile nations did not worship the LORD explicitly, but what do you think the prophet had in mind?

2. Malachi stands in a long line of prophets who are critical of the priesthood who were offering "cheap sacrifices." What did this "cheap sacrifice" consist of? What did such a cheap sacrifice imply regarding the relationship with God?

In Our Lives

1. Malachi has the greatest respect for the ideal of priesthood. He mentions a covenant with Levi (2, 4), which is never mentioned in the Pentateuch or historical books. What is your vision of the ideal priest? After reflecting on your own vision, compare this with what the Church

teaches, for instance, in the Vatican II document, *Decree on the Ministry and Life of Priests*.

2. "For I hate divorce says the LORD" (2, 16). Malachi states this categorically. This view contrasts with Ezra's strong policy for Jews to divorce their foreign wives. Malachi, despite his disapproval of those mixed marriages, thought once a marriage was entered into, it was sacred. How do you feel about Malachi's view of marriage and divorce?

Individual/Personal Reflection/Action

1. Malachi says that "one Father" is creator for all, Jews and Gentiles. He believes if foreigners were willing to convert to Judaism, he would welcome them into the Temple. Ethnic distinctions don't matter. Ezekiel (44, 7) believes that no foreigners were allowed into the Temple. In contrast, Isaiah had a more open attitude to foreigners, similar to Malachi's. The prophets in Israel had different religious views, for example, concerning foreigners in the Temple and the one God of all.

Do you see any modern parallels to the prophets' diversity? How can you ensure that all ethnic groups feel welcome in your church? In your workplace? In your home? What might you do to encourage such diversity in your church?

THE GOSPELS

The Synoptic Gospels

Because of their striking similarities, the three Gospels of Matthew, Mark, and Luke have traditionally been called the "synoptic" Gospels, from the Greek meaning to "view together." The observer of these three Gospels would, in fact, notice many parallels among these stories of Jesus if they were laid side by side. (See the "Harmony of the Gospels" that follows.)

At the same time, the synoptic Gospels are different from John's Gospel. For example, in each of the synoptic Gospels, Jesus begins his public ministry of teaching and healing in Galilee, travels with his disciples on a single purposeful journey to Jerusalem, and there experiences final rejection, death and, ultimately, resurrection. Jesus' sayings in these Gospels are generally either succinct and pointed or in the story form of the parable; his actions are characterized by marvelous healings and exorcisms; a major theme of his preaching is the advent of the "Rule of God." In John, on the other hand, Jesus moves back and forth between Galilee and Judea, and his teaching is often expressed in long, meditative discourses. There are no parables in John, no exorcisms, and fewer healing stories; the Rule of God motif plays a very minor role.

But the three synoptic Gospels develop their own distinct view of Jesus and his mission. Mark, for instance, begins his story of Jesus with his baptism at the Jordan, whereas Matthew, by means of the Infancy Narrative at the beginning of the Gospel, traces Jesus' origin back into the history of Israel. Luke, too, begins with an infancy narrative, but gives much more positive emphasis to Jerusalem than either Mark or Matthew. In Luke's Gospel the young Jesus goes to Jerusalem to listen to the teachers in the Temple courtyard, and the disciples of Jesus will gather to pray after his resurrection in the Jerusalem Temple. Luke also adds a second volume to his Gospel; the Acts of the Apostles picks up the story of Jesus and his apostles where the Gospel left off and shows its continuing force as the community of the Risen Christ moves out into the world.

Both the similarities and the differences among the synoptic Gospels have led to ongoing debate about their interrelationship. Analyses of the style and content of Mark led scholars to conclude that Mark was the first Gospel written, with Matthew and Luke directly dependent on Mark. The presence of other material in Matthew and Luke that was not found in Mark, such as the sayings of Jesus in the Sermon on the Mount, led to the hypothesis of an additional source for Matthew and Luke. This hypothetical source of material—which scholars call "Q" (from the German word *Quelle* or "source")— was probably a collection of sayings and parables of Jesus that circulated in the earliest Christian community. Independently of each other, if this hypothesis is correct, Matthew and Luke blended this source with their new renditions of Mark and perhaps with some other materials or traditions specific to their own communities.

Scholars assume, therefore, that Mark was the first Gospel to be written and that Mark, in fact, set the basic format for the story of Jesus, a format that both Matthew and Luke used as the starting point for their own narratives. This relationship accounts for the similarities among the Gospels. Each Gospel writer's particular interpretation of Mark, the use of other sources, and the unique pastoral and theological perspectives of the writers and their local churches lead to the distinctiveness of each of the synoptics.

The issue of the relationship of John's Gospel to the synoptics is more problematic. Until the midpoint of this century, most modern biblical scholars assumed that John knew of the synoptic Gospels and that his own Gospel was a very distinctive variation on the synoptic tradition. But more recently, a significant number of scholars speculate that John may represent an independent stream of tradition that had little, if any, contact with the synoptic Gospels.

The Four Gospels at a Glance

Matthew	Mark	Luke	John
DATE OF WRITING			
A.D. 70–90	A.D. 65–70	A.D. 70–90	A.D. 90–100
PLACE OF WRITING			
Antioch in Syria	Rome	Greece	Syria or Palestine
TARGET AUDIENCE			
Jewish Christians	Gentiles	Greeks	All Christians
PURPOSE FOR WRITING			
To assert that Jesus is the long-awaited Messiah who fulfills Israel's hopes and the words of the prophets	To present the person of Jesus through his actions and miracles	To give an orderly account of the ministry of Jesus, so readers will rely on the gospel to build their faith	To lead to faith in Jesus as God's son, so those who believe will gain eternal life
PORTRAIT OF JESUS			
Promised Messiah	Suffering servant, hidden Messiah	Son of Man	Son of God/Word of God
CHARACTER OF THE AUTHOR			
Teacher/Catechist	Storyteller	Historian	Theologian
MAJOR EMPHASIS			
Jesus' teachings	Jesus' actions	Jesus' humanity	Jesus' teachings
THEMES			
Jesus fulfilled Old Testament prophecy	The identity of Jesus	Salvation is a joyous surprise	The role of "signs" in building faith
Jesus identifies with the lowly	The importance of the cross	Salvation is offered to everyone	Dualistic struggle between forces of light and darkness
Jesus is the world's savior, not just Israel's	Discipleship	Jesus identifies with the lowly and respects and defends the dignity of all	Faith in Jesus is necessary for eternal life
		Mary is the first disciple	Jesus is the divine son of God

Harmony of the Gospels

	Matthew	Mark	Luke	John
The Divinity of Jesus				1, 1–5
Announcement of the Birth of John the Baptist			1, 5–25	
The Betrothal of the Virgin Mary	1, 18		1, 27	
The Announcement of the Birth of Jesus			1, 26–38	
Mary Visits Elizabeth			1, 39–56	
Joseph's Dream	1, 20–25			
The Birth of John the Baptist			1, 57–80	
The Birth of Jesus			2, 1–7	
The Visit by the Shepherds			2, 8–20	
The Circumcision and Naming of Jesus			2, 21	
The Presentation in the Temple			2, 22–29	
The Genealogy of Jesus	1, 1–17		3, 23–38	
The Visit of the Magi	2, 1–12			
The Flight to Egypt	2, 13–15			
The Massacre of the Infants	2, 16–18			
The Return from Egypt	2, 19–23		2, 39	
The Boy Jesus in the Temple			2, 41	
With the Teachers in the Temple			2, 46–50	
Youth of Jesus			2, 51	
The Preaching of John the Baptist	3, 1–4	1, 1–8	3, 1–18	1, 6–15
Baptism by John	3, 6	1, 5	3, 21	
The First Testimony of the Baptist to Christ	3, 11–12	1, 7–8		1, 29–34
The Baptism of Jesus	3, 13–17	1, 9–11	3, 21–22	
The Temptation of Jesus	4, 1–11	1, 12–13	4, 1–13	
John the Baptist's Testimony to Himself				1, 19–35
The Call of the First Disciples	4, 18–22	1, 16–20	5, 1–11	1, 37–51
First Miracle at Cana				2, 1–11
Visit to Capernaum				2, 12
Cleansing of the Temple	21, 12–13	11, 15–17	19, 45–46	2, 13–23
Nicodemus				3, 1–21
The Final Witness of the Baptist				3, 22–36
The Samaritan Woman				4, 1–42
The Return to Galilee				4, 43–45
The Second Sign at Cana				4, 46–54
The Cure on a Sabbath				5, 1–47
Imprisonment of John the Baptist	4, 12; 14, 3	1, 14–15		3, 24
The Beginning of the Galilean Ministry	4, 12–17	1, 14–15, 4	14–15	
The Rejection at Nazareth	13, 54–58	6, 1–4	4, 16–27	
Jesus Preaches at Capernaum	4, 13–17			
The Cure of a Demoniac		1, 23–27	4, 33–36	
The Cure of Peter's Mother-in-law	8, 14–15	1, 29–31	4, 38–39	
Other Healings	8, 16–17	1, 32–34	4, 40–41	
Circuit through Galilee		1, 38–39	4, 42–44	
The Cleansing of a Leper	8, 1–4	1, 40–45	5, 12–18	
Retirement for Solitary Prayer		1, 45	5, 16	
The Healing of a Paralytic	9, 1–8	2, 1–12	5, 18–25	

	Matthew	Mark	Luke	John
Call of Matthew	9, 9–17	2, 13–22	5, 27–39	
Ministering to a Great Multitude	4, 23–25		6, 17–19	
Picking Grain on the Sabbath	12, 1–8	2, 23–28	6, 1–5	
The Man with the Withered Hand	12, 9–14	3, 1–6	6, 6–11	
Retirement for Solitary Prayer			6, 12	
The Mission of the Twelve	10, 1–4	3, 13–19	6, 13–16	
		6, 7–13	9, 1–6	
The Sermon on the Mount	5, 1–12		6, 20–26	
The Healing of the Centurion's Servant	8, 5–13		7, 1–10	
The Raising of the Widow's Son			7, 11–17	
The Messengers from John the Baptist	11, 2–19		7, 18–35	
The Pardon of the Sinful Woman			7, 36–50	
The Beatitudes	5, 2–12		6, 20–26	
Galilean Women Follow Jesus			8, 1–3	
Jesus and Beelzebul	12, 22–28	3, 23–30	11, 14–23	
Blasphemy against the Holy Spirit	12, 31–32			
The Return of the Unclean Spirit	12, 43–45		11, 24–26	
The True Family of Jesus	12, 46–50	3, 31–35	8, 19–21	
The Parable of the Sower	13, 1–9	4, 1–9	8, 6–8	
		4, 14–20	8, 11–15	
The Parable of the Weeds among the Wheat	13, 24–30			
The Parable of the Mustard Seed	13, 31–32	4, 30–32	13, 18–19	
The Parable of the Yeast	13, 33		13, 20–21	
The Parable of the Lamp	5, 15	4, 21	8, 16; 11, 33	
The Parable of the Buried Treasure	13, 44			
The Parable of the Fine Pearl	13, 45–46			
The Parable of the Thrown Net	13, 47–48			
The Calming of the Storm at Sea	8, 24–27	4, 3 7–41	8, 23–25	
The Healing of the Gergesene Demoniacs	8, 28–34	5, 1–20	8, 26–39	
The Parable of the Bridegroom	9, 15			
The Parable of the New Cloth	9, 16	2, 21	5, 36	
The Parable of the New Wine in Old Bottles	9, 17	2, 22	5, 37–38	
Miracles: Jairus' Daughter and the Woman with a Hemorrhage	9, 18–26	5, 22–43	8, 41–56	
The Healing of Two Blind Men	9, 27–31			
The Healing of a Mute Person	9, 32–34			
The Mission of the Twelve	10, 1–4	6, 7–12	9, 1–6	
Herod's Opinion of Jesus	14, 1–12	6, 14–29	9, 7–9	
The Return of the Twelve and the Feeding of the Five Thousand	14, 13–21	6, 31–44	9, 10–17	6, 1–14
The Walking on the Water	14, 22–33	6, 47–52		6, 16–21
The Bread of Life Discourse				6, 22–65
Retirement for Solitary Prayer	14, 23	6, 46		
The Tradition of the Elders	15, 1–20	7, 1–23		
The Canaanite Woman's Faith	15, 24–29	7, 24–30		
The Healing of Many People	15, 29–31			
The Feeding of the Four Thousand	15, 32–39	8, 1–9		

	Matthew	Mark	Luke	John
The Parable of the Lost Coin			15, 8–10	
The Parable of the Prodigal Son			15, 11–32	
The Parable of the Dishonest Steward			16, 1–8	
The Parable of the Rich Man and Lazarus			16, 19–31	
The Raising of Lazarus				11, 38–44
The Return of Jesus from				
Peraea to Bethany				11, 11–16
The Resurrection of Lazarus				11, 38–44
The Session of the Sanhedrin				11, 45–54
The Last Passover				11, 55
The Last Journey in Jerusalem	19, 1	10, 1	17, 11	
The Cleansing of the Ten Lepers			17, 11–19	
The Parable of the Persistent Widow			18, 1–8	
The Parable of the Pharisee and				
the Tax Collector			18, 9–14	
Marriage and Divorce	10, 1–12	10, 1–12		
Blessing of the Children	19, 13–15	10, 13–16	18, 15–17	
The Rich Young Man	10, 16–30	10, 17–22	18, 18–23	
The Workers in the Vineyard	20, 1–16			
The Third Prediction of the Passion	20, 17–19	10, 32–34	18, 31–34	
The Request of James and John	20, 20–28	10, 35–45		
The Healing of Two Blind Men	20, 29–34	10, 46–52	18, 35–43	
Zacchaeus the Tax Collector			19, 1–10	
The Parable of the Talents	25, 14–30		10, 11–27	
The Supper in Simon's House	26, 6–13	14, 3–9		12, 1–9
Mary Anoints Jesus	26, 7–13	14, 3–9	12, 3–8	
The Entry into Jerusalem	21, 1–11	11, 1–10	19, 29–44	12, 12–19
The Survey of the Temple		11, 11		
The Cursing of the Fig Tree	21, 18–19	11, 12–14		
The Cleansing of the Temple	21, 12–17	11, 15–18		
The Lesson of the Fig Tree	21, 20–22	11, 20–25		
The Authority of Jesus Questioned	21, 23–27	11, 27–33	20, 1–8	
The Parable of the Two Sons	21, 28–32			
The Parable of the Tenants	21, 33–46	12, 1–12	20, 9–19	
The Wedding Feast	22, 1–14		14, 15–24	
Paying Taxes to the Emperor	22, 15–22	12, 13–17	20, 20–26	
The Question about the Resurrection	22, 23–33	12, 18–27	20, 27–39	
The Greatest Commandment	22, 34–40	12, 28–34	11, 25–28	
The Question about David's Son	22, 41–46	12, 35–37	20, 41–44	
Denunciation of the Scribes and Pharisees	23, 1–33	12, 38–40	11, 37–54	
The Poor Widow's Contribution		12, 41–44	21, 1–4	
The Coming of Jesus' Hour				12, 20–23
The Destruction of the Temple Foretold	24, 1–2	13, 1–3		
The Parable of the Ten Virgins	25, 1–13		10, 11–27	
The Judgment of Nations	25, 31–46			
The Conspiracy Against Jesus	26, 3–5	14, 1–2	22, 1–2	
The Betrayal by Judas	26, 14–16	14, 10–11	22, 3–6	18, 2–5
Preparation of the Passover	26, 17–19	14, 12–16	22, 7–13	
The Washing of the Disciples' Feet				13, 1–17

	Matthew	Mark	Luke	John
The Lord's Supper	26, 26	14, 22	22, 14	
The Betrayal Foretold	26, 21	14, 18	22, 21	13, 21
The Giving of the Morsel				13, 26–27
The Departure of Judas				13, 30
Peter's Denial Predicted	26, 31–35	14, 27–31	22, 21–23	13, 36
Blessing the Cup	26, 27–28	14, 23–24	22, 17	
Last Supper Discourses				14, 1–14
The Prayer of Jesus				17, 1
The Hymn	26, 30	14, 26		
The Agony in the Garden	26, 36	14, 32–42	22, 39–46	18, 1
	26, 44			
Jesus is Comforted by the Angel			22, 43–44	
The Sleep of the Apostles	26, 40–45	14, 37–41	22, 45–46	
The Betrayal and Arrest of Jesus	26, 47–50	14, 43–46	22, 47–54a	18, 1–13a
Peter Smites Malchus	26, 51	14, 47	22, 50	18, 10
Jesus Heals the Ear of Malchus			22, 51	
Jesus Forsaken by His Disciples	26, 56	14, 50		
Jesus Led to Annas				18, 12–13
Jesus Before the Sanhedrin	26, 57	14, 53	22, 66	
Peter Follows Jesus	26, 58	14, 54	22, 55	18, 15
The High Priest's Adjuration	26, 63	14, 61	22, 66	
Jesus Condemned	26, 66–67	14, 64–65	22, 70–71	
Peter's Denial of Jesus	26, 69–75	14, 66–72	22, 54–62	18, 17–27
Jesus before Pilate	27, 1	15, 1	23, 1	18, 28
The Death of Judas	27, 3			
Pilate Comes out to the People				18, 29
Pilate Speaks to Jesus Privately				18, 33
Mockery by the Soldiers	27, 27	15, 15	22, 63–65	19, 1
Jesus Crowned with Thorns	27, 29	15, 17		19, 2
Jesus Exhibited by Pilate				19, 5
Jesus Questioned by Pilate	27, 11	15, 2	23, 2	
Jesus Sent by Pilate to Herod			23, 6–11	
The Sentence of Death	27, 15	15, 6	23, 17	19, 12–16
Pilate Receives a Message from his Wife	27, 19			
Pilate Washes his Hands	27, 24			
Pilate Releases Barabbas	27, 26	15, 15	23, 25	
Pilate Delivers Jesus to Be Crucified	27, 26	15, 15	23, 25	19, 16
The Way of the Cross	27, 32	15, 21	23, 26	
The Crucifixion	27, 33–44	15, 22–32	23, 33–43	19, 17–30
The Death of Jesus	27, 45–56	5, 33–41	23, 44–49	
The Burial of Jesus	27, 57–61	15, 42–47	23, 50–56	19, 38–42
The Guard at the Tomb	27, 62–66			
The Resurrection of Jesus	28, 1–10	16, 1–8	24, 1–12	20, 1–10
The Report of the Guards	28, 11–15			
The Appearance to Mary Magdalene		16, 9		20, 14
The Appearance to the Women				
Returning Home	28, 9			
The Appearance to Two Disciples				
Going to Emmaus		16, 12	24, 13	

	Matthew	Mark	Luke	John
The Appearance to Peter			24, 34	
The Appearance to the Disciples in Jerusalem			24, 36	20, 10
The Appearance to the Eleven Apostles		16, 14		
The Appearance to Thomas				20, 27
The Appearance to the Seven Disciples				21, 1–22
Jesus and Peter				21, 15–19
The Commissioning of the Disciples	28, 16–20	16, 14		
The Ascension of Jesus		16, 19–20	24, 50–43	

Parables

The word *parable* comes from a Greek word that means "to throw alongside" or "compare." A parable is a story about a situation, usually one that would be very familiar to the hearers. The story is told to make a point about another reality, moral or spiritual, that is not as easy to speak of in down-to-earth terms.

Jesus' parables are *similes* (statements comparing one thing with another by using *like* or *as*, such as, "The kingdom of heaven is like a mustard seed . . . " in Mt 13, 31) or *metaphors* (statements identifying one thing with another, for instance, "Beware of false prophets, who come to you in sheep's clothing, but underneath are ravenous wolves" in Mt 7, 15). Sometimes these comparisons grow into stories. They make their points by using everyday objects and characters drawn from real-life situations in families, farms, the marketplace, and the courts of kings. Jesus used parables as a main part of his teaching, and their primary purpose was to reveal some dimension of God's Kingdom.

As you read through the parables, keep in mind this combination of day-to-day reality and great spiritual insight. The parables are famous, rightly so, for their ability to take the most ordinary situations—cleaning house, growing grapes, the rivalry between two brothers, the preparations for a wedding, the story of a mugging in a bad part of town—and find in them an endless source of spiritual meaning.

The parables can be grouped into three categories according to their length and complexity.

1. Similes and metaphors that have minimal elaboration and are basically "one-liners." Some examples are the lamp under the basket (Mt 5, 14–16); the mustard seed (Mt 13, 31–32); and the two debtors (Lk 7, 41–43).

2. Comparisons that are more extended; these are more elaborate than the simple metaphors above, but are not yet full-blown stories like those in category 3. Some examples are the two sons (Mt 21, 28–32); the growing seed (Mk 4, 26–29); the rich fool (Lk 12, 16–21); and the un-profitable servants (Lk 17, 7–10).

3. Stories that contain characters, dialogue, plot, and setting; these stories have a clear beginning, middle, and end. Some examples are the good Samaritan (Lk 10, 30–37); the prodigal son (Lk 15, 11–32); the wicked vinedressers (Mt 21, 33–41); and the wise and foolish virgins (Mt 25, 1–13).

Parables were used by Jesus to reveal the Kingdom he came to initiate through his life and ministry. But, ironically, Jesus also used them to obscure his teaching (Mk 4, 11–12). Knowledge of the Kingdom is available to all who sincerely seek it, but this knowledge requires some effort. Parables make their points indirectly, so people will only discover their truths if their ears and eyes are open, and if they have the hearts of seekers. Even the disciples of Jesus did not always understand the significance of his parables. However, because they were committed to Jesus, they sought, and the doors of understanding were opened to them. Those who stand on the "outside" at a safe distance from Jesus, unwilling to make a commitment, are locked into misunderstanding. They are unable to "hear" the truth expressed in the parables because they are unwilling to open their ears and eyes and hearts.

For many centuries parables were viewed primarily as allegories in which every element carried some kind of symbolic significance or hidden meaning. For example, St. Augustine allegorized the parable of the Good Samaritan. He saw the victim as Adam, the robbers as Satan and his angels, the priest and Levite who walked by as representative of the Torah and the prophets, the Samaritan as Jesus, and the inn as the church, etc. But scholars would say Augustine went way beyond what Jesus intended. The point the parable

Parables in the Synoptic Gospels

Parable	Matthew	Mark	Luke
The Weeds among the Wheat	13, 24–30		
The Buried Treasure	13, 44		
The Fine Pearl	13, 45–46		
The Thrown Net	13, 47–48		
The Unforgiving Servant	18, 21		
The Workers in the Vineyard	20, 1–16		
The Two Sons	21, 28–30		
The Wedding Feast	22, 2–14		
The Talents	25, 14–30		
The Judgment of Nations	25, 31–46		
Seed Grows of Itself		4, 26–29	
Need for Watchfulness		13, 32–37	
The Two Debtors			7, 41–42
The Good Samaritan			10, 30–35
The Persistent Friend			11, 5–8
The Rich Fool			12, 16–20
The Vigilant and Faithful Servants			12, 35–40
The Faithful and Prudent Steward			12, 42–48
The Barren Fig Tree			13, 6–9
The Great Feast			14, 15–24
The Tower			14, 28–30
The King Marching into Battle			14, 31–33
The Lost Coin			15, 8–10
The Prodigal Son			15, 11–32
The Dishonest Steward			16, 1–8
The Rich Man and Lazarus			16, 19–31
Attitude of a Servant			17, 7–10
The Persistent Widow			18, 2–5
The Pharisee and the Tax Collector			18, 9–14
The Ten Gold Coins			19, 11–27
The Two Foundations	7, 24–29		6, 46–49
The Yeast	13, 33		13, 20–21
The Lost Sheep	18, 10–14		15, 1–7
The Lamp	5, 15	4, 21	8, 16
			11, 33
The New Cloth	9, 16	2, 21	5, 36
The New Wine in Old Wineskins	9, 17	2, 22	5, 37–38
The Sower	13, 1–9	4, 1–9	8, 4–8
The Mustard Seed	13, 31–32	4, 30–34	13, 18–19
The Tenants	21, 33–46	12, 1–12	20, 9–19
The Lesson of the Fig Tree	24, 32–35	13, 28–31	21, 29

was meant to make (that God's love is extravagant and unconditional) almost gets lost in the elaborate analogy. Modern scholarship has therefore turned away from that kind of interpretation, insisting that parables make only a single point. The details of the story have just one point

of contact with the spiritual teaching the story is trying to convey.

Although modern readers have moved away from an overly allegorical reading of parables, avoiding allegorical interpretations entirely is not an absolute rule. Some parables, in fact, do have more than one point of contact with the teaching they convey. The parable of the sower is one of them. One must be careful, of course, to make sure that the points of contact they discover are coming *from* the text, not being read *into* the text. Besides the parable of the sower (Mk 4, 14–20), see the parable of the wheat among the weeds (Mt 13, 37–40) as another example of a parable that does have more than one point of contact with the teaching it presents. However, the general approach is that interpretation is derived from the story as a whole, rather than from its individual details.

The parables are designed to make us see differently. They don't just present moral teaching; they offer a whole new way of perceiving how God rules over and is present in our lives. They also help us understand how we are converted by this presence and thus how we enter God's Kingdom. Certain truths just cannot be explained directly. So we resort to imagination. Because they appeal to the imagination, parables can touch us in ways that an abstract explanation cannot. They supply jolts to the imagination, as for example Mt 13, 33: "The kingdom of heaven is like yeast that a woman took and mixed with three measures of wheat flour until the whole batch was leavened." They penetrate deeper and plant their truths inside us.

But they do much more than provide folksy examples that make a point. They shake us up, make us ask questions. They challenge our categories and make us think our way through to a conclusion. Often they do this by reversing our expectations: A host who is stood up by the guests invites the poor, the lame, and the blind to his banquet (Lk 14, 21); the owner of a vineyard pays those hired *last* the same amount as those hired *first* (Mt 20, 8); a man acquires a treasure not because of his hard work, but out of dumb luck (Mt 13, 44).

Most of us approach life with certain expectations or a particular worldview: The good are rewarded, and the bad are punished; those who work harder and longer get paid more than those who work fewer hours, and so on. Then we read a parable, and it shakes us up; it turns our world upside down: The *prodigal* got the party, not the good older brother; the workers hired last were paid as much as those hired first! We become disoriented by such a perspective. But if we do the work the parable calls for, we will be rewarded; if we seek, we will discover the profound truth the parable wants to teach us. For example, the parable of the good Samaritan is not a pious story about being compassionate, but a radical challenge to consider as "neighbor" those we had previously viewed as "enemy." Out of this seeking and struggle, a sense of reorientation emerges.

The parables invite us into a process of questioning. Within that process, we become an essential part of their meaning. They are incomplete in themselves. They invite and await a response. Our response completes the process that they initiate. Their truth does not stand alone. It combines with our efforts and springs to life in our hearts as a revelation of God's mysterious Kingdom.

MATTHEW READING GUIDE

At a Glance

Who are the main players?	John the Baptist Mary Joseph Herod Jesus the disciples Mary Magdalene the religious leaders Caiaphas the high priest Pilate
What should I look for?	Matthew's Gospel is a dynamic story. Follow the story of Jesus' life and ministry. Notice how Matthew has organized the sayings of Jesus into discourses that contain the major themes of his Gospel.
When did this take place?	Jesus' life spanned the first three decades of the first century A.D. The probable date for Matthew's writing is between A.D. 70 and 90. His theology, his command of Greek,

and rabbinic training indicate Matthew the evangelist was probably a second generation Jewish Christian.

Where did these events occur? In Palestine

Why was this book written? Matthew wrote to show the essential dependence of Jesus and the early church on Judaism. At the same time he is concerned with how the Jewish Jesus is the messiah for the whole world.

What is the story? Matthew's work is a narrative of Jesus' life. It begins with the roots of Jesus' family tree, describes the circumstances of his birth, then turns to the events of his ministry, culminating in his death, resurrection and final appearances to his disciples.

Healings in Matthew	Cleansing a leper 8, 2–4 (Mk, Lk)
	The centurion's servant 8, 5–13 (Lk)
	Peter's mother-in-law 8, 14–15 (Mk, Lk)
	Evening time healing of the sick 8, 16–17 (Mk, Lk)
	The paralytic 9, 2–8 (Mk, Lk)
	The woman with a hemorrhage 9, 20–22 (Mk, Lk)
	Two blind men 9, 27–31
	The mute demoniac 9, 32–34
	The man with a withered hand 12, 10–13 (Mk, Lk)
	The blind and mute demoniac 12, 22–32 (Lk)
	The Canaanite woman's daughter 15, 21–28 (Mk)
	The boy with a demon 17, 14–20 (Mk, Lk)
	Two blind men 20, 30–34 (Mk, Lk)
	(Mk and Lk indicate the healing miracle is recounted in Mark and Luke as well.)
Other miracles found in Matthew	Calming the storm at sea 8, 23–27 (Mk, Lk)
	The Gadarene demoniacs cured 8, 28–34 (Mk, Lk)
	Raising the official's daughter 9, 18.23–26 (Mk, Lk)
	Feeding the five thousand 14, 13–21 (Mk, Lk, Jn)
	Walking on the water 14, 22–33 (Mk, Jn)
	Feeding the four thousand 15, 32–38 (Mk)
	Finding tax payment in fish's mouth 17, 24–27
	Cursing the fig tree 21, 18 (Mk)
	(Mk; Lk and Jn indicate the miracle story also occurs in Mark, Luke, or John)
Parables found only in Matthew	Weeds and wheat 13, 24–30
	The hidden treasure 13, 44
	The pearl of great price 13, 45–46
	The dragnet 13, 47–50
	The lost sheep 18, 12–14
	The unforgiving servant 18, 23–35
	The workers in the vineyard 20, 1–16
	The two sons 21, 28–32

The wedding feast 22, 2–14
The wise and foolish virgins 25, 1–13

Stories told only in Matthew

Joseph's dream 1, 20–24
The visit of the Magi 2, 1–12
The flight to Egypt 2, 13–15
The massacre of the infants 2, 16–18
The death of Judas 27, 3–10
The dream of Pilate's wife 27, 19
The dead rise after Jesus' resurrection 27, 52
Guards are posted at Jesus' tomb 27, 62–66
The resurrection earthquake 28, 2–4

When Jesus prays in Matthew

The Lord's Prayer 6, 9–15
Praising the Father 11, 25
Blessing the children 19, 13
When multiplying leaves and fishes 14, 9; 15, 36
At the Last Supper 26, 26–27
In the garden of Gethsemane 26, 36–44
On the cross 27, 46

Matthew's portrait of Jesus

Paints Jesus as a lawgiver and Messiah, the great teacher of Israel

Matthew's unique perspective

A convert to Christianity, Matthew traces Jesus' origins back into the history of Israel. He has great interest in showing that Jesus is the promised Messiah who fulfills Old Testament prophecy ("Son of David" and other messianic language is utilized throughout). His Jesus is a kind of catechist, teaching the law and preaching the kingdom of God.

While all share common elements, each of the Gospels is unique. Matthew has traditionally held a place of honor among the four Gospels because it had long been considered the first written. Though that thinking has changed, it still contains elements that set it apart: Matthew contains more of Jesus' sayings than any of the other Gospels; more forcefully than the other Gospels, it connects the story of Jesus with the story of the people of Israel; and it does all this in the form of a powerful story.

A Story

Matthew's Gospel contains an unfolding plot, fascinating characters, and various settings. In

other words, it has all the elements of a good story. The plot traces Jesus' life from his birth, through his ministry of some success and much rejection, to his death and the final triumph of his resurrection. The characters are sometimes flat and one-dimensional (the Pharisees), and sometimes well developed (Jesus, Peter). And the settings, even though briefly described, help establish the drama and reality of the various scenes. These are characteristics of all good stories.

In describing Matthew's Gospel as a story, we are not implying that it has no historical basis. There is no doubt that Matthew uses materials rooted in history (most of which he draws from the Gospel of Mark, one of his principal

Why Matthew Isn't Matthew Anymore

Scholars no longer believe Matthew the apostle is Matthew the evangelist (Gospel writer). Why?

1. Because he uses 90 percent of Mark's Gospel: Why, ask the scholars, would one of the Twelve who was an eyewitness to the life of Jesus depend so heavily on the account of a non-eyewitness?

2. His theological perspective, his command of the Greek language, and his apparent rabbinic training all indicate Matthew the evangelist was probably a *second generation* Jewish Christian.

sources). But the evangelist, or Gospel writer, casts these traditions about Jesus into the form of a running story. A story or narrative helps catch up the reader into the dynamism and feeling of the events being recounted. This feature of the Gospel can engage us when we come to study or read it in more depth.

A Source of Teaching

While Matthew's Gospel remains a dynamic story, it is also enriched—more than any of the other Gospels—with the sayings of Jesus. This feature has led commentators over the centuries to consider Matthew a kind of "catechism" or teacher's manual. In addition to the basic story of Jesus' life and ministry, which Matthew drew mainly from the Gospel of Mark, he also had a supply of the important sayings of Jesus (many of which he shares in common with the Gospel of Luke). The evangelist has organized many of these sayings into discourses or speeches of Jesus. These are not transcripts of actual talks given by Jesus because there is little logical progression found in the discourses as a whole. Rather, the evangelist has clustered the sayings of Jesus around basic themes. These discourses bring the reader of Matthew's Gospel into vital contact with the power of Jesus' teaching.

The Jewish Heritage of Jesus and the Early Church

While all of the New Testament writings illustrate the essential dependence of Jesus and the early church on Judaism, none does it more forcefully than Matthew's Gospel. In fact, one of the primary purposes of this Gospel may have

been the attempt to link the story of Jesus with the history of Israel. Any reader of Matthew who wants to go deeply into this Gospel must be alert to its Jewish background.

This feature of Matthew springs to our attention from the opening lines of the Gospel, which begin with a genealogy or family tree, tying Jesus into the history of Israel. The frequent use of Old Testament quotations, the concern with the Jewish law and customs of purity and prayer, the sharp critique of the Jewish leaders for their rejection of Jesus and for their failure to lead a life of holiness—all of these show that Matthew was absorbed with Jesus' Jewish heritage.

Strange as it may seem, Matthew's Jewish roots may also explain another difficult feature of his Gospel: his strong critique of the Jewish leaders. The Jesus of Matthew's Gospel blisters his opponents for their hypocrisy and lack of faith. They are held up to the reader of the Gospel as negative examples of what an authentic disciple should avoid becoming. The sharp edge to Matthew's critique may stem from the tragic division and hostility that grew between Judaism and Jewish Christianity in the early decades of the church. For Matthew, the fact that most of Israel did not accept Jesus or the Gospel—while many Gentiles did accept it—was a baffling and unexpected turn in salvation history, and his telling of the story of Jesus reflects this. Unfortunately, Matthew's characterization of the Jewish leaders also provided an opportunity for later anti-Semitism to develop (itself a violation of the Gospel's teaching).

Messiah for the Whole World

But it is also apparent that Matthew is concerned with how this Jewish Jesus is messiah for the whole world. As we will indicate below, the universal mission of the church is also a prime motif of this Gospel. In fact, Matthew seems to be telling the story of Jesus so that it can help both the Jewish Christians and the Gentile converts of his community. After reading the Gospel they would be able to understand that Jesus fulfills the hopes and dreams God planted in the people of Israel, and He now extends the offer of God's salvation to all the world.

Reading through Matthew's Gospel

The outline or major segments of Matthew's Gospel can be determined only by paying attention to his story.

• The Origin of Jesus (1, 1—2, 23). Here Matthew presents the events surrounding Jesus' birth and infancy.

• Preparation for the Ministry of Jesus (3, 1—4, 7). The test in the desert and the ministry of John the Baptist help prepare for the formal beginning of Jesus' mission.

• The Galilean Ministry of Jesus (4, 7—16, 12). This major section spans the ministry of Jesus from his entrance into Galilee until his announcement of the Passion and his intent to go to Jerusalem. It can be subdivided into other important segments:

    1. The Sermon on the Mount (4, 17—7, 29)
    2. Jesus the Healer (8, 1—9, 35)
    3. The Mission Discourse (9, 36—11, 1)
    4. Mounting Hostility to Jesus (11, 2—12, 50)
    5. The Parable Discourse (13, 1–53)
    6. The Kingdom and the Disciples (13, 54—16, 12) This section includes the ongoing activity of Jesus and reaction to it, but with special emphasis on Jesus' relationship with Peter and the rest of the disciples.

• The Way to Jerusalem (16, 13—20, 34). Jesus' fateful journey to Jerusalem with his disciples dominates this section. Three times during this journey Jesus predicts his Passion and Resurrection (16, 21; 17, 22f; 20, 17–19) and instructs his disciples on the cost of following him. There is also the important discourse on community life (18, 1–35).

• Final Teaching in Jerusalem (21, 1—25, 46). This section of the Gospel takes place in Jerusalem. It concentrates on Jesus' final exchanges with his opponents (esp. 21, 12—22, 46),

his condemnation of the scribes and Pharisees (23, 1–39), and the long discourse on the final age and judgment (24, 1—25, 46).

• Death and Resurrection (26, 1—28, 20). The concluding segment of the narrative contains the Passion narrative and the account of Jesus' burial (26, 1—27, 66), the events surrounding the discovery of the empty tomb (28, 1–15), and Jesus' final appearance to the eleven disciples on a Galilean mountaintop (28, 16–20).

The Origin of Jesus (1, 1—2, 23)

Right from the start Matthew underlines Jesus' Jewish heritage. He is "son of David, son of Abraham" (1, 1). From this beginning to the end of the Gospel, Matthew announces repeatedly and loudly that Jesus is the promised Messiah through whom God's longed-for salvation would be realized.

A Messiah Close to His People

The experiences of Jesus and his family evoke another theme important to this Gospel, namely Jesus' identification with the "least." Matthew's Christmas story has a sober mood to it. Jesus and his family are threatened with death by a tyrant. Innocent people are killed because they are identified with Jesus. The holy family is forced into exile (just as Israel had been in its tortured history). Even when they return from Egypt (a new exodus), they are unable to go home to Bethlehem but must become displaced persons, living in Nazareth (2, 22f).

This identification with Israel's struggle to be free may help explain one of the names given Jesus in Matthew's story. He is to be called Emmanuel, that is, "God is with us" (1, 23). As subsequent events of the Gospel will show, the Matthean Jesus has extraordinary compassion for the suffering (e.g., see the healings in chs 8 and 9), explicitly identifies himself with the "least" (see Mt 25, 31–46; 10, 42), and promises to remain with his church as it continues its mission in the world (28, 20; 18, 20).

Messiah of Israel and Savior of the World

As Herod and the leaders of Jerusalem plot to destroy Jesus, the magi, Gentile wise men, come seeking to pay homage to him (2, 1–12). The account of this visit may well be influenced by Isaiah

60, 3: "Nations [i.e., non-Jews] shall walk by your light, and kings by your shining radiance." Even in the family tree of Jesus, Matthew may be hinting at the wider horizons of Jesus' mission. While most of the genealogy traces the male line of Jesus' ancestry, there are several women mentioned—Tamar, Rahab, Ruth, Bathsheba—all of whom were foreigners whose entry into Jewish history was under unusual, sometimes even scandalous, circumstances. Even Mary, the mother of Jesus, seems to be put in this category because her association with the royal Davidic line is not by natural means, but only through the initiative of the Holy Spirit—something that causes consternation to Joseph (1, 18–19).

Thus, from the beginning outsiders were part of Jesus' history. This is a major theme of Matthew's Gospel. He will emphasize the rejection Jesus experiences from the Jewish leaders and at the same time provide scattered examples of Gentiles groping toward faith (e.g., the centurion in 8, 5–13; the Gadarene demoniacs in 8, 28–34; the Canaanite woman in 15, 21–28). Matthew carefully notes that Jesus' historical ministry focused on Israel (10, 5), but with the new age of resurrection, that mission of salvation would now extend to all nations (28, 19).

Who Jesus Is

The infancy narrative also hints at the kind of salvation Jesus will bring. Of all the Gospels, Matthew alone stresses the significance of the name "Jesus." The angel gives the divine instruction that the child is to be named Jesus (Hebrew Yehoshuah, "the LORD saves"—the name of Joshua, the leader of the Israelites after Moses) "because he will save his people from their sins." Jesus is depicted as savior throughout the Gospel as he delivers people from their burdens of sickness, oppression, and sin. This is a Jesus who thirsts for justice or righteousness (3, 15) and blesses those who, like the prophets before them, suffer in the pursuit of justice (5, 10). Jesus exercises divine power in forgiving sins (see 9, 1–8) and urges his disciples to reflect this same sense of reconciliation in dealing with each other (see especially 5, 43–48; 18, 21–35).

The Christmas Story

The overall mood of Matthew's Christmas story is quite different from that of Luke's. There are no triumphant angels, no picturesque gathering of shepherds, little focus on a tender vision of mother and child. Instead there are ominous plots against the child, outbreaks of violence, displacement, and exile. But throughout there is also the promise of God's abiding presence, bringing salvation in spite of sin and rejection. Perhaps we can think of Matthew's infancy Gospel as an "adult" Christmas story, one that has a special truth for the many people experiencing violence and persecution today. It tells a story that begins in the strength and beauty of a particular history and culture but will ultimately reach across boundaries to touch all peoples. In any case, these two chapters prepare us for the story that will follow, a story that will trace Jesus' mission of salvation through bitter rejection to ultimate triumph.

Preparation for the Ministry of Jesus (3, 1—4, 17)

This brief section serves as a transition between the infancy narrative and the beginning of Jesus' ministry in Galilee. John the Baptist's preaching in the desert opens the section, and Jesus' entry into Galilee ends it. In between we find two of Matthew's major themes.

The Dawn of the New Age

Israel had long awaited the return of the prophet Elijah whose coming would signal the end of the world and the appearance of the kingdom of God. Matthew sees the promise of Elijah's return fulfilled in the person of John the Baptist. John declares the nearness of God's kingdom and prepares the way for Jesus who, being greater than John, is the one who ushers in the kingdom. Matthew's awareness that the coming of Jesus represents the culmination of God's plan for salvation runs throughout the Gospel. Jesus, the "beloved son" (3, 17) of God has come to dispel darkness and offer hope to all people who stumble in the dark of sin and death.

Repentance and Good Deeds

In Matthew's Gospel repentance means a change in one's way of thinking and acting. Real change is evident in the good deeds that flow from it. When John and Jesus call for repentance, they are challenging their listeners not to rely on their status as children of Abraham (3, 15), but to respond concretely to God's love offered in Jesus.

Jesus' temptations in the desert illustrate this same point. As he did in the details of his birth, Jesus here relives the experience of Israel in the desert. Only his story ends differently. Similarly tempted, Jesus does not yield to temptation and sin as Israel did in the desert. Jesus practices what he preaches. He demands fidelity to God and teaches how by being fiercely faithful himself.

The Galilean Ministry of Jesus (4, 17—16, 12)

This major section of the Gospel begins with Jesus' entry into Galilee and the inauguration of his ministry of teaching and healing.

The Sermon on the Mount (4, 17–7, 29)

The Sermon on the Mount, the first of Jesus' five great discourses in this Gospel, is perhaps the best-known passage of Matthew's Gospel. The sermon itself spans chapters 5 through 7, but preparation for this great discourse begins in chapter 4. After sounding the theme of the Kingdom of God (4, 17), Jesus calls his first disciples to follow him and to share in his mission (4, 18–22). Jesus is committed to teaching, proclaiming the Kingdom of God, and healing (4, 23). That liberating mission draws a response from every point of the compass as throngs of broken and needy people surge toward Jesus and his message of God's mercy (4, 24f). Jesus' teaching, Matthew implies, is not mere abstract truth. Jesus' words and his healing touch have the power to transform lives.

The Sermon on the Mount does not have a neat progressive structure; rather, sayings of Jesus are clustered around basic themes.

A New Teaching for a New Age.

Matthew's conviction that Jesus is the Messiah, and therefore the authoritative teacher of God's will, runs throughout the Sermon. With Jesus the final age of salvation dawns and with it, new insight into God's will. Matthew's Jesus sees the will of God as being in continuity with the revelation that came through the Law of Moses in the Old Testament, but now bringing that law to its

fullest and most compelling expression. In the opening verses of the Sermon, Jesus states: "Do not think that I have come to abolish the law or the prophets. I have come not to abolish but to fulfill" (5, 17).

The conviction that the end of the world will be a triumph of God's grace—a conviction based on belief in the life, death, and resurrection of Jesus—runs throughout the Sermon and gives it special force. The false values assumed by the world are crumbling. This is the message of the beatitudes (5, 3–12): those who are "poor in spirit" or who "hunger and thirst for righteousness" or are "peacemakers" are blessed because God will vindicate their hopes. Similarly, because it is a new age with new possibilities, the old wisdom is no longer adequate. A series of six contrast statements mark off the difference between former interpretation of the Jewish law and Jesus' own radical teaching (see 5, 21–48).

The Supreme Law of Love Expressed in Committed Action

Matthew's emphasis on good deeds, cited above (see comments on Preparation for the Ministry of Jesus), is clearly in evidence here. The words of Jesus at the conclusion of the Sermon are unequivocal: "Not everyone who says to me, 'Lord, Lord,' will enter the kingdom of heaven, but only the one who does the will of my Father in heaven" (7, 21). But the Sermon demonstrates that Matthew's Jesus is not simply talking about frenetic action. The heart and soul of Jesus' teaching is the command to love. That comes to its fullest expression in the last of the contrast statements where Jesus tells his disciples they are to love even the enemy (5, 44) because God's own love is lavish and indiscriminate, bathing both just and unjust in its light and refreshment (5, 45). Matthew is consistent on this point throughout the Gospel (see 7, 12; 22, 34–40). Asking his disciples to strive for love of enemies—the most challenging demand that can be made on the human heart—expresses the ultimate spirit of all of Jesus' teaching on human relationships. For this reason, the disciple is to strive for complete honesty (5, 33–37), avoid retaliation for injury (5, 38–39), and not violate another through lust or manipulation (5, 27–30).

Jesus' teaching roots all of this in God's relationship to us. The teaching on love of enemy

and no retaliation is, therefore, not a minor part
of the Gospel nor is it an abstract ideal. This fundamental teaching of Jesus remains a challenge
for Christians who live in a violent world where
the use of force is commonplace.

Revelation of a Close and Compassionate God

Jesus' teaching in this part of the Gospel also
gives a profound insight into the Gospel's image
of God. God's boundary-breaking love is not
based on merit but reaches out even to the unjust
and the "enemy" (5, 45–48). God cares for us
more than for birds of the air or the wild flowers,
whose freedom and beauty are signs of God's
provident love (6, 25–32). Therefore, the disciple is to have complete trust in God and to pray
with confidence and without pretense (7, 7–11).
Jesus' model prayer (6, 9–15) catches up much of
the spirit of the entire sermon. There is a wonderful simplicity and honesty about the instructions
on piety in the sermon (6, 1–18); God's relationship to us is direct and close. There is no place
for pretending before such a loving God.

The Authority of the Sermon

How to live with the Sermon on the Mount has
been a constant point of discussion in the church.
Are these demanding words to be taken as impossible ideals, meant only for a perfect world or
for perfect people? Or do they make sense only
in the setting of Jesus' own times, when people
thought the end of the world was near and so
might be capable of responding heroically in
such an emergency situation?

None of these solutions are adequate. The instructions of Jesus are not a system of clear-cut
laws spelling out exactly how we are to act in
every circumstance, nor are they abstract or impossible ideals. These teachings give us practical guidance as we seek to live a life faithful to
the Gospel. They illustrate the core spirit of
Jesus' teaching, a spirit we must embody in our
own circumstances. The possibility of living in
accord with the teaching of Jesus is based on
God's grace; the Sermon illustrates the difference grace can make in a person's life and relationships. Within the array of moral choices that
confront us, the *examples* Jesus gives in the
Sermon—such as the call for integrity in our
relationships, for nonretaliation, and for a

commitment to reconciliation—help direct us in
the right way.

Jesus the Healer (8, 1—9, 35)

In this powerful section, Matthew presents Jesus
the healer. Though he draws most of his material
here from Mark's Gospel, Matthew significantly
edits the material he borrows. He wants to concentrate on Jesus' most essential actions and
words, so he shortens Mark's stories and eliminates some of Mark's most colorful details.
Matthew arranges the stories of this section into
three groups, each with its own dominant motif:

Group 1: 8, 1–17 Emphasizes Jesus' healing
power (the leper, centurion's servant, Peter's
mother-in-law).

Group 2: 8, 18—9, 17 Emphasizes the demands
of discipleship (calming the storm, healing the
demoniacs, the paralytic).

Group 3: 8, 18–34 Emphasizes the indispensable role of faith in the healing stories (the official's daughter, the woman with a hemorrhage,
two blind men, the mute demoniac).

Christology

By narrowing the spotlight on Jesus in the first
three stories, Matthew emphasizes the divine
power that works through the Messiah. Jesus
cleanses the leper, heals the servant of a Gentile
soldier, and dispels the fever of Simon's mother-
in-law. Except in the case of the centurion, there
is little attention to the plight or disposition of the
sick person in these stories. The concluding
verse of the section (8, 17) makes Matthew's intended point; by his healing touch Jesus fulfills
the prophetic promise of Isaiah 53, 4: "He took
away our infirmities and bore our diseases."

By their very nature the healing stories serve
Matthew's purpose. All of us experience sickness
or disability at one time or another in our life. We
all experience our limitations and realize too well
that death looms before us. Jesus is moved with
compassion (9, 36) and does not hesitate to stand
in solidarity with those whose condition makes
them "outsiders" (see his association with the
leper, the Gentile, the tax collectors).

The Conditions of Discipleship

In the second set of stories Matthew illustrates
some of the demands of discipleship. Only those
fully committed to proclaiming the Kingdom of

God and following Jesus are able to go with him across the sea (see 8, 18–23). But even for those who remain, following Jesus can mean the threatening experience of the storm at sea (8, 24–27) and strange encounters with the power of evil (8, 28–34). The true disciple is one who learns that mercy and compassion drive Jesus, a lesson the Pharisees (whom Matthew consistently portrays in negative tones) seem unable to grasp (9, 9–13).

Faith

The healing stories often serve to illustrate the meaning of faith. Faith is, first of all, trust in Jesus' power to heal and transform us. Such faith is evident in the leper who approaches Jesus (even though the law forbade him to do so), in the centurion who pleads on behalf of his servant (see 8, 10), in the friends who bring the paralytic to Jesus (9, 2), in the woman with the hemorrhage who touches the tassel of his cloak (9, 22), and in the two blind men who trust that Jesus can do what no one else can (9, 28f).

Note, too, that the faith illustrated in these stories often takes a very active form. The leper boldly comes up to Jesus; the woman dares to touch him; the Gentile swallows his pride and pleads with a Jewish healer; the friends of the paralytic gain him access to Jesus. For the characters in this story, trusting in God does not mean mere passivity, waiting for a bolt from heaven. Transformation comes when they exercise their trust in God, and commit their own resources to seeking a new life.

The Mission Discourse (9, 35—11, 1)

Now that Matthew has completed his portrait of Jesus as teacher and healer, he moves to a new segment of the Gospel. Using his own mission as a model, Jesus gathers his twelve apostles and commissions them to proclaim the Kingdom of God, and to heal. The motivation for their mission is the same that animated Jesus' own energetic healing in the previous two chapters: the crowds are "troubled and abandoned, like sheep without a shepherd" (see Mt 9, 36–38).

This forms the second of the five great discourses of Matthew's Gospel. The evangelist draws some of the material in this discourse from chapter 13 of Mark's Gospel.

Note that the discourse can be read from two different perspectives: (1) as part of the unfolding story of Jesus' ministry and his relationship with his disciples; and (2) as an instruction for the post-Easter church. In the former time frame, Jesus tells his apostles to restrict their mission to Israel, the chosen people of God (10, 5f); in the new age, when the gospel must be proclaimed to all the world (see 28, 16–20), Jesus' words apply to the universal mission of the church.

Typical themes for Matthew run through the discourse. The Twelve (including Matthew the tax collector, 10, 3) share in Jesus' own mission of proclaiming the Kingdom and healing those in need (10, 7f). Note that the apostles are not yet commissioned to "teach"—that comes only after the Resurrection (see 28, 20) when they have a deeper grasp of Jesus' mission. Any disciple who follows Jesus can expect to meet indifference, hostility, or rejection (e.g., see 10, 16–25.34–39). Jesus clearly warns the apostles about the cost of proclaiming the gospel in an authentic way.

But there is also strong affirmation of the power of the gospel and of the sense of confidence that should go with those on mission. They are not to be afraid of those who threaten their lives (10, 26–28) or flinch before the divisions that may come. The loving God who has an eye for the sparrows and counts the hairs on our heads will not abandon those who follow the way of Jesus. Christians who live in circumstances of persecution and violence understand well these words of Jesus. Those who live in more comfortable circumstances need to ask themselves if the gospel values they reverence are not sometimes co-opted by the seductions of the dominant culture.

Matthew's concern with the mission of the church will reemerge in the final scene of the Gospel when the mission of Jesus, confined to Israel during his lifetime, bursts out into the world through the mission of the church (28, 16–20).

Mounting Hostility to Jesus and His Mission (11, 2—12, 50)

Jesus warned that his message would be opposed. Now opposition hits him (and the Baptist) square in the face.

John is in prison awaiting death. He sends his

disciples to Jesus with the poignant question: "Are you the one who is to come, or should we look for another?" We can hear 2000 years of longing in that question. Jesus uses the inquiry to summarize his great deeds and to comment on John's ministry and his own. No one else in all the Gospels receives praise like Jesus gives John here.

One of the Gospel's most beautiful passages, which sheds light on the nature of the relationship between Jesus and his Father ("No one knows the Father except the son," 11, 25–27), is juxtaposed against scenes of opposition from enemies who are unable to recognize Jesus for who he is and who attack him for violating the Sabbath.

Another of Matthew's themes now emerges: judgment. Opposition to Jesus will not go unnoticed. Those who reject him (like the unrepentant towns of 11, 20–24) will bear responsibility. Matthew makes it very clear that good intentions alone are never enough. To avoid judgment, a tree must bear good fruit (12, 33). And blood kinship alone does not make one a family member with Jesus, but doing God's will does (12, 50).

The Parable Discourse (13, 1–50)

Parables were the trademarks of Jesus' teaching style. These pointed stories both reveal and veil the mystery of the Kingdom. Unless the listener is willing to probe beneath the surface of the parables, the true meaning of Jesus' words will escape them (13, 14f).

Typical themes of Matthew's Gospel emerge again in this discourse. The certain triumph of the Kingdom, which was a strong theme of the Sermon on the Mount, dominates the parable of the sower (13, 1–9) as well as the parables of the mustard seed (13, 31f) and the yeast (13, 33f). Discipleship motifs stand out in the parables of the treasure and the pearl (13, 44–46): true followers of Jesus are to put aside everything and be fully committed to the compelling beauty of God's reign.

The Scribe who is instructed (literally: "discipled") in the kingdom of heaven (13, 52) is like the householder who can bring from the storehouse "both the new and the old." Preserving the best of the past and yet making it come alive for a new generation seems to be one of the main purposes of Matthew's Gospel. Matthew was convinced that Jesus did not destroy the beautiful traditions of Judaism but gave them new meaning. Bridging past and present in an open and respectful manner is one of the greatest challenges of religious leadership in any age.

The Kingdom and the Disciples (13, 51—16, 12)

It is difficult to characterize this long section of Matthew's story under any single heading. Jesus' ministry of teaching and healing continues but now begins to burst beyond the confines of Galilee into Gentile territory. Clashes with his opponents, mainly the Pharisees, also continue to erupt. But the haunting story of Jesus' walking on the water and Peter's awkward attempts to trust his master (14, 22–33) may give us a clue to the special character of this section. With new intensity Jesus begins to instruct his disciples on the mystery of the Kingdom, and they begin to realize the awesome identity of the Messiah. Several motifs run through these chapters.

The Inclusive Mission of Jesus

Following the lead of Mark's Gospel, Matthew begins to trace the boundary-breaking nature of Jesus' ministry After another conflict with the Pharisees (15, 1–20), Jesus ventures near the Gentile region of Tyre and Sidon and there encounters a "Canaanite" woman (15, 21–28). This is one of the most intriguing stories in the Gospel. At first Jesus resists the woman's entreaties on behalf of her daughter. The Matthean Jesus remains committed only to the people of Israel (see 10, 5f). But the woman's insistence, an expression of her active faith, breaks down Jesus' resistance and seems to open the horizons of his own vision. Matthew uses this story to instruct his own church: they, too, may have had too narrow a concept of their mission, thinking that only Jews could become Christians. But the needs and genuine faith of the Gentiles showed the early church that God intended to extend the boundaries of the Kingdom to include all people.

The two stories of the miraculous feedings (14, 13–21; 15, 32–39) give a similar impression of expansiveness. Jesus will not let the vast crowds go hungry and uses the occasion to instruct his disciples. Another epic scene takes place on the mountaintop, a favorite place of revelation in Matthew's Gospel (15, 29–31).

Similar to the vista at the beginning of the Sermon on the Mount (see 4, 23–25), vast crowds of the sick and disabled surge toward Jesus, and he cures them. Once again the disciples can observe the boundless compassion that drives Jesus.

Opposition and Rejection

Despite the mercy of Jesus, his opponents continue to resist and misunderstand his message. The Parable discourse had warned that some would prefer not to "see" and not to "hear" what Jesus preached. That prediction comes true in Nazareth (13, 54–58) where Jesus' own people rebuff him and take offense at his "wisdom and mighty deeds." The story of Herod and the death of John the Baptist (14, 1–12) are early warning signs about Jesus' own fate. His enemies were so immersed in their opposition that they would carry it to the point of trying to destroy Jesus.

In the conflict about the tradition of washing hands before eating (15, 1–20), the Gospel offers one explanation of the stubbornness of Jesus' opponents. They have allowed their own traditions to "nullify the word of God" (15, 6). In other words, they had lost a sense of priority, placing good but not essential values ahead of those that were most fundamental. Matthew continues to stress that Jesus was not opposed or indifferent to the Law, but he wanted to inject new life into its observance by insisting that the love command was the basis of all fidelity.

The Disciples

The story of Peter walking on the water contains material unique to Matthew's Gospel and illustrates both the importance of traditions about Peter in this Gospel and the evangelist's view of discipleship. Peter begins to sink in the waves because he "doubted" or "hesitated" and because he has "little faith" (14, 31). The latter phrase is particularly characteristic of Matthew's Gospel. Matthew's portrayal is sympathetic and realistic: The disciples believe, but their faith is weak. Deeper trust in Jesus is needed.

At the same time, the disciples are quite different from the opponents of Jesus. While the opponents reject Jesus and align him with Satan (12, 24), the disciples acclaim Jesus as "the Son of God" (14, 33). The enemies of Jesus cannot understand his teaching, but the disciples, although hesitantly, do "understand" (16, 12; see also 13, 16.51).

The Way to Jerusalem
(16, 13—20, 34)

A dramatic shift in the setting of the gospel story is about to take place. Jesus goes with his disciples to the northernmost reaches of Israel, Caesarea Philippi (16, 13). There he will ask the fundamental question of the gospel: "Who do you say that I am?" (16, 15). Jesus' question and Peter's response represent a turning point in the story. "From now on" (16, 21) Jesus will begin to speak openly about his approaching death, and the action of the gospel will point toward Jerusalem and the events of the Passion and Resurrection.

The announcement of Jesus' journey to Jerusalem (16, 21) thus introduces the motif of a "journey," a theme already present in Mark's Gospel and one greatly expanded in the Gospel of Luke. The threefold prediction of the Passion (in Mt, see 16, 21; 17, 22f; 20, 17–19) punctuates the journey and keeps the reader's attention directed to Jerusalem and Jesus' death and resurrection. That great climax to the gospel, already alluded to as early as the infancy narrative, dominates and gives urgency to Jesus' teaching. The transfiguration reflects this: Immediately after Jesus predicts his death for the first time, the light of resurrection glory seems to emanate from his person in a mountaintop scene reminiscent of the revelation given to Moses on Sinai.

During the journey narrative, the spotlight seems to fall with new intensity on Jesus' relationship with his disciples. Although some conflicts with the Pharisees take place (e.g., see the dispute about divorce, 19, 1–12), most of Jesus' words are directed to his disciples, revealing to them what it means to follow a Crucified Messiah. Special traditions about Peter are present in this section, too, including his confession at Caesarea Philippi and Jesus' blessing upon him, his mediating role in paying the Temple tax on behalf of Jesus and himself (17, 24–27), and his lead question about forgiveness in the discourse on community life (18, 21).

The Ministry of Leadership

In the scene at Caesarea Philippi (16, 16), Peter does what the disciples had done before him: confess his faith in Jesus. Then, as he does

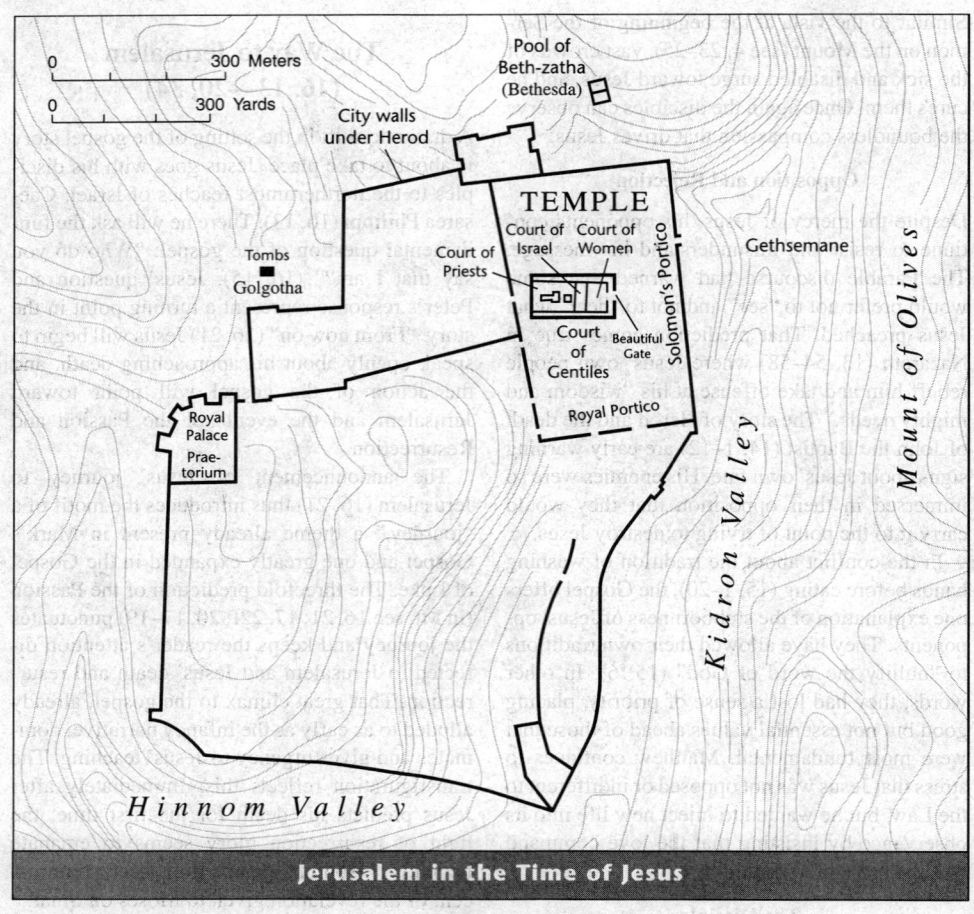

Jerusalem in the Time of Jesus

elsewhere in the Gospel, Matthew immediately zeroes in on Peter. Jesus blesses Peter for his faith, changes his name to "Peter" or "Rock" because he will be the foundation of the church, and gives him the "keys of the kingdom" and the power to "bind" and "loose" (giving the "keys" is a sign of the unique leadership role given to Peter).

Matthew will balance out this focus on Peter by also asserting the authority of the community in chapter 18, but at this point in the Gospel he is showing the important role entrusted to the leader of the community. Undoubtedly, this reflects a ministry of leadership already present in Matthew's church. The Gospel uses Peter as a model for leadership. Historically, Peter had been an important leader in the church. In the Acts of the Apostles, we are told that he helped

mediate between the Jewish Christian church of Jerusalem and the emerging Gentile churches (see Acts 10–15).

While it would be going too far to impose on this Gospel scene the full-blown institution of the papal office, Roman Catholic tradition can legitimately see in the figure of Peter the founding model for the later emergence of this office in the church. Peter is blessed because of his strong faith in Jesus and because he served a key role in maintaining the unity of the church. Equally important to remember, however, is that the Gospel refuses to idealize Peter or to place him above the demands of the gospel. The same Peter that Jesus blesses lavishly here is also called "Satan" and "obstacle" (16, 23), will underestimate the need for reconciliation (18, 21), and will deny his discipleship in the face of the

Passion (26, 69–75). Leaders within the community must remain disciples (see 23, 10).

Life in the Community

The Discourse on Community, the fourth of Matthew's major discourses, occurs here. It is built around two parables, the Lost Sheep (18, 10–14) and the Unforgiving Servant (18, 21–35), that communicate the two major themes of this discourse.

The Lost Sheep parable reveals God's great interest in the weak or alienated members of the community. Community members are to be humble and should never "scandalize" or shun those who are weak or living on the margins of the church (18, 6–10).

The second half of the discourse concludes with another key saying: "So will my heavenly Father do to you, unless each of you forgives his brother (or sister) from the heart" (18, 35). The need for reconciliation dominates the latter half of the discourse. Disputes are to be settled in a fair and practical manner (18, 15–17), and even if strong discipline must be taken toward a recalcitrant member, he or she is to be treated "like a Gentile or a tax collector"—a poignant note in a Gospel where Jesus seeks out just such people (e.g., see 9, 9–13). Those who have experienced limitless forgiveness from God should not put limits on reconciliation within the community. That is the radical message of Jesus' reply to Peter, and the concluding parable of the story. Its message is similar in content to Jesus' teaching on love of enemies in the Sermon on the Mount (see 5, 43–48).

Final Teaching in Jerusalem (21, 1—25, 46)

The Gospel drama now enters Jerusalem, the capital city, where Jesus will experience death and resurrection. The great temple of Herod dominated this city in the time of Jesus, and its shadow falls across the scenes Matthew narrates in these chapters.

Jesus the Messiah enters his city in triumph, but he is seated on a donkey's colt, which Matthew interprets as a sign of Jesus' humility. As a fearless prophet, Jesus cleanses the house of God, another sign of his God-given mission to call Israel to repentance. The next day Jesus returns to the Temple compound and begins to teach the crowds (21, 13). There follows a number of key texts that reveal the heart of Jesus' message. But the Jewish authorities (the Pharisees now joined by the "chief priests and elders of the people," all members of the Sanhedrin, an informal ruling body whose base would, in fact, have been Jerusalem) remain hostile to Jesus and his message. This section of the Gospel is filled with sharp clashes between Jesus and his opponents.

Two important clusters of sayings and parables are found here. In the first, 23, 1–39, Jesus excoriates the scribes and the Pharisees, portraying them in purely negative tones for their hypocrisy and lack of fidelity. This is Matthew's most intense assault on the Jewish leaders. The second collection of sayings and parables forms the fifth and final discourse of the Gospel, the so-called Eschatological Discourse or discourse on the end of the world. While gazing at the stunning Temple from the Mount of Olives, Jesus reflects on the fate of the Temple and the end of human history. This leads to a series of parables, some of them unique to Matthew, urging the disciples to remain faithful and to exemplify that fidelity through good deeds (see 24, 36—25, 46).

The Authority of Jesus

Like a fine conductor, Matthew orchestrates the elements of this section to trumpet a grand Messiah chorus. Jesus' triumphant entry into Jerusalem shakes the entire city (21, 10). Strength and authority accompany him wherever he goes. On his own authority this "Lord of the Sabbath" (12, 8) drives the money changers from the Temple and reasserts the Temple's proper role as a house of prayer (21, 12–27). And he backs down from none of the religious authorities who challenge him—not the scribes or the chief priests, not the elders of the people, nor the Sadducees. Matthew leaves no room for doubt about Jesus' status as Messiah and true Teacher of Israel.

And what is the source of Jesus' authority? He is the Son of God. For Matthew the evidence is clear and irresistible. Even the parable of the tenants affirms it (21, 33–46). In that allegory Jesus describes himself as the vineyard owner's son and "heir." And later he asserts his preeminence even over King David who called the future Messiah his "Lord" (22, 41–46).

When Jesus is questioned about the Law, his reaction is typical of Matthew's Gospel: He reinterprets, never rejects, the Law. Though surrounded by hostile opponents, Jesus fields their questions with the poise and ease of a master teacher, reminding them that the "whole law and the prophets" (22, 40) depend on the command to love God and neighbor.

Jesus and His Opponents

Suddenly the tone changes. The poised Jesus shifts into an offensive mode, hammering the scribes and Pharisees for their hypocrisy and infidelity. Jesus points to them as negative role models, the opposite of what disciples should be, Through the series of seven "woes" ("Woe to" was a phrase used by the prophets to express horror over sin and the punishment it will bring), Matthew reveals the values that really matter to Jesus:

- Practicing what you preach (23, 3)
- Showing compassion rather than burdening others (23, 4)
- Not using religion for self-glorification (23, 5f)
- Letting mercy and justice guide interpretation of the law (23, 23–38)
- Expecting religious leaders to show respect rather than arrogance toward the community (23, 8–12)

This strong indictment of the failings of the leaders is not intended solely to pummel the opponents of Jesus. Rather, it is meant as a sober instruction for the Christian readers of the Gospel. Nevertheless, the negative stereotyping of the Jewish leaders, especially when it is read apart from its historical context in the Gospel, can have destructive effects. We who live in the horrible shadow of the Holocaust must be responsible readers of this Gospel and, while taking to heart the important lessons of this discourse, must not allow its negative image of the Jewish leaders to influence our attitude to Jews today. Every modern pope and the teaching of the Second Vatican Council has attacked anti-Semitism and reminded Catholics of their spiritual and historical roots in the living faith of Judaism (see particularly the 2002 statement of the Pontifical Biblical Commission, The Jewish People and their Sacred Scriptures in the Christian Bible).

The Death and Resurrection of God's Son (26, 1—28, 20)

The Passion (26, 1—27, 66)

The Passion story moves quickly from Jesus' prediction of the plot against him (26, 1–5), through the last supper with his disciples (26, 20–30), his anguished prayer and arrest in Gethsemane (26, 36–56), the interrogation and trial before the Sanhedrin or Jewish Council (26, 57–75), the Roman trial before Pilate (27, 1–31), and the final scene of crucifixion, mockery, and death (27, 32–56). The burial in Joseph of Arimathea's tomb and the Pharisees' demand that Pilate post a guard (27, 57–66) prepare the reader for the explosive events of the resurrection.

The peculiar emphases Matthew gives the Passion story can be summarized under three major themes:

The Majesty of Jesus

Even in the Passion story, Jesus remains the majestic Messiah of Israel. This is already true in Mark's account, but it is given particular emphasis by Matthew. Jesus is imbued with prophetic knowledge of the events about to take place: He predicts the plot of the leaders (26, 1f), is fully aware of his impending death (26, 12.18), knows the identity of his betrayer (26, 25), and sees the certainty of Peter's denials (26, 34). His captors cannot seize him until Jesus confronts Judas with his treachery (26, 50). And when the high priest commands with an oath that Jesus reveal his identity, Jesus predicts with calm majesty his eventual triumph as the Son of Man who will be exalted at the right hand of God (26, 64). Death cannot destroy or defeat God's Son—that is the heart of Matthew's message in the Passion story. The parade of mockers who file past the cross jeer Jesus and ridicule his claim to be God's Son (27, 39–44). But as death comes, Jesus is acclaimed as the true Son of God, and nature itself erupts in testimony to Jesus' victory.

The Dawn of the New Age

The death of Jesus is the center point of sacred history in Matthew's perspective. Matthew, along with all of the New Testament, considered Jesus as the coming of the final and decisive age of salvation promised by God to Israel. The death of Jesus was the climactic act of his entire mission: Here all of his love and commitment were compressed into one intense act of faithfulness to the will of his Father. Thus, the death of Jesus becomes in a special way the turning point between the old and the new age. With the death and resurrection of Jesus, the final age of human history had begun and, therefore, humanity must respond to God's grace in a new way.

Several features of Matthew's Passion story proclaim this theology of history. At the moment of death (27, 51–57), signs of the new age break out: nature convulses, the tombs are split open, and the dead are liberated—just as the dream of the prophet Ezekiel had envisioned, with the dead bones of Israel's hopes taking flesh and escaping the tomb (see Ez 37). The age of death is over; the age of resurrection begins.

The attention Matthew gives to the response of the leaders and people of Israel to Jesus is another part of his theology of history (e.g., see 27, 24f). Paradoxically, because Israel rejects Jesus, the way will now be open for the gospel to be proclaimed to the Gentiles. This does not mean that Matthew despairs of having the Jews accept the message of Jesus (he seems to offer some hope of this in 23, 39), but he does believe that the mission to the Gentiles is now possible in the new and final age of salvation. One of the catalysts for that mission was the fact that the mission to Israel had failed. Paul, too, has a similar theology in Romans 9–11, where he reminds his readers that in the mystery of God's providence, the failure of Israel becomes a moment of grace for the Gentiles. For Paul, Israel remains special because God is faithful and will never forget the promises made to the chosen people. This biblical teaching is echoed in the theology of Vatican II where it is insisted that the Jewish people have a special place in the history of salvation (see decree on non-Christian religions), and therefore Christians should not impose conversion on the Jewish people.

Examples and Counterexamples

The Passion story also serves Matthew's teaching about discipleship. In the crucible of suffering and death, one's true character is revealed. The Passion is filled with examples, both positive and negative, of how people respond to the gospel in crisis. The leaders remain implacably hostile to Jesus and demand his death. Peter and the rest of the disciples prove their "little faith," with Peter denying he knows Jesus and the others fleeing in panic. Judas betrays his master and gives in to despair rather than seeking repentance (27, 3–10).

There are also bright moments: the woman of Bethany who performs a last kindness for Jesus, anointing him for burial despite the protests of the disciples (26, 6–13); Pilate's wife who pleads on behalf of "that righteous man" (27, 19); the centurion and his companions who acclaim the crucified Jesus as the "Son of God" (27, 54); the women who stand by Jesus at the cross and see to his burial (27, 56); and Joseph of Arimathea, the rich disciple, who risks his reputation by burying a publicly executed man in his own new tomb (27, 57–61). And, of course, Jesus himself is the prime example of fidelity—seeking God's will despite the threat of death, refusing violence at the moment of his arrest, and trusting in God even as his life's breath is taken from him.

There is no doubt that Matthew intended the readers of the Passion to place themselves in the story and to ask the troubled question posed by the disciples: "Is it I, Lord?" (26, 22).

The Resurrection (28, 1–20)

The Gospel concludes with the events surrounding the empty tomb and Jesus' appearances to his disciples. None of the Gospels attempts to describe the resurrection itself, but Matthew comes closest to that in mentioning an "earthquake" and an "angel of the Lord" who comes from heaven to roll back the stone from the tomb (28, 2). Marvelous events such as these and the opening of the tombs at the moment of Jesus' death (see 27, 51–53) continue to signal the final and glorious age when God's presence would be felt in a vivid way.

Mark's original ending does not include the report of any appearances of the Risen Christ; the discovery of the empty tomb, and the words of the heavenly messenger about Jesus' triumph over death are enough to proclaim the message (see Mk 16, 1–8). But in Matthew's Gospel, Jesus appears first to the women as they leave the empty tomb (28, 9f), and then to the eleven remaining disciples in Galilee (28, 16–20). Matthew's denunciation of the Jewish leaders continues right to the end of the Gospel: when the chief priests and elders learn from the soldiers about the astounding events at the tomb, instead of believing in Christ's triumph, they concoct a false story about the disciples stealing the body of Jesus (28, 11–15).

The final scene of the Gospel (28, 16–20) is on a mountaintop, the favored site of special revelation throughout the Gospel (e.g., see the temptation, the Sermon on the Mount, the transfiguration, the healing of the crowds, 15, 29–31). The Risen Christ comes in triumph, as he had predicted during his Passion, and commissions his disciples to go to "all nations," making disciples, baptizing them into the community, and teaching them to observe all that Jesus had commanded.

Major themes of the Gospel are compressed into this scene: Matthew's concern with the universal mission of the church; his emphasis on Jesus as teacher; his realistic portrayal of the disciples (who even now "hesitate" as they encounter the Risen Christ, see 28, 17); his interest in the church. This scene has inspired countless Christian missionaries throughout the centuries to leave their homeland to bring the gospel to others. Above all, the gospel's majestic portrayal of Jesus as the church's firm foundation and abiding hope is reaffirmed. No matter how turbulent the church's future will be, the Risen Jesus will not abandon it. Matthew concludes his Gospel with the final promise of one who was named Emmanuel, "God is with us" (see 1, 23): "I am with you always, until the end of the age" (28, 20).

Judgment

Here we find a theme we've seen before in Matthew: The true disciple is a doer of good deeds. Look at the many examples that state and restate that point:

• The "faithful and prudent servant" is the one caring for the house and doing good for the needy (24, 45–51).

• The "wise virgins" are those who have their oil ready (25, 1–13).

• The servant who is rewarded when the master returns is the one who used his or her talents (25, 14–30).

• Those who inherit the Kingdom are those who live the law of love by feeding, clothing, visiting, and welcoming the needy (25, 31–46).

There is no better lesson on the value of good deeds than the climactic parable of the sheep and goats. The "sheep" are blessed because in life they showed compassion even though they did not realize it was the risen Lord who was present in the needy they served. The good do good. Hypocrites just talk about it. Matthew's Jesus has little tolerance for that.

Questions for Discussion and Reflection
Group Sharing/Discussion

1. Take time for members of the discussion group to re-read Jesus' sayings. Have each person choose their favorite two or three sayings and explain why those were chosen. Each person should take a turn with the first saying on his or her list before repeating.

2. Read as many references as you can find that connect Jesus' message with his Jewish heritage. Why is this an important message then and now?

3. What events in the story of the birth of Jesus have their echo in the history of the Jewish people or parallel later events in Jesus' life?

4. Imagine you are sitting on a hillside listening to the Sermon on the Mount for the very first time. Read aloud chapter 5, 1–12. What would/did you find surprising? Explain why.

5. Look again at 15, 21–28. Having read the Gospel of Matthew, how would you explain to someone what Jesus taught and who he cured?

In Our Lives

1. Read the familiar 6, 9–13. How could we apply verse 11 today? How could we apply verse 12?

2. In 7, 21, Jesus explains that Heaven is for those who do the Father's will. In the course of Matthew's Gospel, Jesus gives many lessons on how to do the Father's will. After the resurrection he told them to teach people "to observe all that I have commanded . . ." (28, 20). Describe how you interpret this today.

3. Review The Last Supper (26, 26–30). Discuss at least five ways our celebration of the Eucharist is the same as this event.

4. Read together The Greatest Commandment: 22, 34–40. Give examples of someone who has followed the second part. Name one way you will try to more fully live that part of the commandment in the future.

Mark in the Liturgy

Until Vatican II revised the lectionary, the Gospel of Mark was rarely heard in Roman Catholic liturgy. Mark had been largely ignored because the Gospel was considered a poor condensation of Matthew's Gospel. His literary style is unsophisticated and at times blunt. Today, Mark's Gospel is used for an entire year (Year B) in the three-year cycle of the Sunday lectionary.

The Messianic Secret

It may seem curious that throughout Mark's Gospel (seven times in all) Jesus tries to keep his true identity a secret: He instructs those he heals, his disciples, and even demons not to talk about his miracles or reveal who he is. Jesus knows the kind of Messiah the people want and expect. He is not prepared to be that kind of Messiah— a military leader overthrowing Roman rule, or an easy Messiah who fills empty stomachs and relieves every burden. Jesus has come to be a suffering Messiah, not a king of glory and triumph. Jesus' consistent effort in Mark's Gospel to conceal his identity as Messiah is called the "Messianic Secret."

responding to the message and mission of Jesus. Mark's story is packed with conflicts between Jesus and his religious opponents and between Jesus and demonic forces. Mark wants to let his readers know that to follow Jesus demands radical changes that inevitably will put them, too, in conflict with the forces of this world.

Christology

Jesus himself poses the central question of Mark's Gospel: "Who do you say that I am?" (8, 20). Yet, ironically, in this Gospel Jesus works very hard to keep his identity as the Messiah a secret. But the secret keeps "leaking" out through everything Jesus says and does: He heals, expels demons, argues with opponents, teaches his disciples, shares parables, and, most importantly, he dies and rises from the dead. All this proclaims Jesus' unmistakable identity as the Son of God and the Messiah.

Jesus' healings and exorcisms were evidence that God was breaking into human history, offering liberation and salvation. But for Mark the most convincing sign of that fact was the cross. Real faith in Jesus means embracing his cross. The liberation and salvation Jesus came to bring were only made possible by his death. Yes, he was "Messiah," "healer," and "Son of Man," but those titles can only be understood in the context of Jesus' redemptive death.

Discipleship

Mark is very intent on teaching what it means to be a disciple of Jesus. And yet the disciples, Jesus' inner circle, do no better than anyone else at understanding who Jesus is and what he came

to do. First, they openly misunderstand Jesus, and then they totally abandon him.

In Mark the disciples are both historical figures and the subject of lessons. Mark wanted his readers to see themselves in the disciples, who failed Jesus but received his love and forgiveness nonetheless. The Gospel ends with hope and promise of renewal: The "young man" at the tomb asks the women to tell the disciples to go to Galilee where they will see Jesus again. The same hope is offered to the reader who, like the disciples, may have been slow to understand Jesus, and may even have failed him, but who now can hope for the same forgiveness and renewal Jesus offered the disciples.

Reading through Mark's Gospel

It is very helpful to read all of Mark at one sitting; the compact story makes for compelling reading. Then you can begin to focus on individual passages.

Mark uses geography to organize his story of Jesus into four main parts:

1. The *Judean desert,* where Jesus is baptized by John;

2. *Galilee,* the locus of most of Jesus' ministry;

3. The *journey to Jerusalem,* as Jesus prepares to embrace his fate; and

4. *Jerusalem* itself, where the story climaxes in death and resurrection.

Thus, the basic outline of Mark's Gospel can be sketched simply in four parts:

I. Overture in the Desert (1, 1–13). In the Judean desert John preaches a baptism of repentance. Jesus accepts John's baptism and, at that very moment, his identity as God's son is revealed. Jesus then goes off alone and is tempted by Satan.

II. The Galilean Ministry of Jesus (1, 14—8, 21). In Galilee, the northern region of Israel, Jesus embarks on his public ministry. The central events are:
   A. Announcing the Kingdom of God (1, 14–15)
   B. Calling his first disciples (1, 16–45)
   C. Tangling with the religious leaders (2, 1—3, 6)
   D. Experiencing continued opposition and misunderstanding (3, 7—4, 34)
   E. Expanding his mission to include Gentile territory (4, 35—8, 21)

III. The Journey from Galilee to Jerusalem (8, 22—10, 52). Starting in Caesarea Philippi, where Peter acknowledges Jesus as the Christ, Jesus and the disciples travel down to Jerusalem for Jesus' upcoming Passion. Much teaching on discipleship is found in this section.

IV. Death and Resurrection in Jerusalem (11, 1—16, 8). The story climaxes in Jerusalem where Jesus:
   A. Enters triumphantly into the city and then drives the money changers from the Temple (11, 1—12, 44)
   B. Predicts the destruction of the Temple (13, 1–37)
   C. Is arrested, tried, flogged, and crucified (14, 1—15, 47)
   D. Achieves victory over death and the grave (16, 1–8)

The Gospel of Mark originally ended at chapter 16, 8. Writers other than the evangelist added additional endings they felt made for a smoother, more suitable conclusion.

Overture (1, 1–13)

A desert can be many things. It can be a place of new beginnings—Israel, after all, was led into the desert, and there it was forged into a people covenanted to God. But it can also be a place of testing; it was in the desert that the Israelites first rebelled against the Lord and discovered their true character. In Mark's Gospel Jesus comes to the desert to inaugurate his mission, and in the desert, Satan puts him to the test. Like the overture of an orchestral piece, Mark's brief introduction announces the major themes that will surface again throughout the Gospel:

1. *A new age is beginning.* John, dressed like the long-awaited Elijah who was to return at the end of the world, comes as the herald of a new age. By casting John in this light, Mark indicates that God is doing something new. People must reform their lives to be ready for God's new dawn.

2. *Jesus is the Son of God.* At his baptism, God's voice announces Jesus' true identity; then God's Spirit descends on Jesus to fill him with power for his messianic mission. Christology (understanding the nature of Jesus) will remain a major concern of the Gospel.

3. *Jesus' ministry will be marked by conflict with the forces of darkness.* What Jesus experienced in the desert is but a preview of what is to come: In carrying out his mission, Jesus will often confront opponents and cast out demons. Struggle is a constant in any effort for true liberation.

The Galilean Ministry of Jesus (1, 14—8, 21)

This major section, which constitutes half the Gospel, can be divided into five distinctive segments.

The Keynote of Jesus' Mission (1, 14–15)

A single verse, 1, 15, announces three major themes of Mark's Gospel:

"This is the time of fulfillment." What Israel had longed for is finally here: the new and final age of salvation. And Jesus is the one who ushers it in. In this new age, old ways will have to yield to new responses, just like new wine must be poured into new wineskins (2, 18–22).

"The Kingdom of God is at hand." The "Kingdom of God" is a biblical symbol that expresses Israel's hope for a time when God would rule the earth with justice and peace. Jesus not only announces the rule of God, he actually inaugurates

it by healing, working for justice, and freely giving his life for others.

"Repent and believe in the gospel." The gospel of Jesus demands a response, a turning around: repentance. Jesus asks his disciples to see, hear, and think differently, to view reality with eyes of faith and to change their lives accordingly.

The Call of the Disciples and Jesus' First Day of Ministry (1, 16–45)

In Mark's account, Jesus gets busy immediately. Set in the small fishing village of Capernaum where Mark situates most of Jesus' ministry, this section is typical of Mark's portrayal of Jesus: As soon as he's chosen his disciples, Jesus tackles sickness and pain and casts out demons wherever he meets them.

The Call of the Disciples (1, 16–20)

The importance of discipleship is reinforced by the fact that Jesus' first act is the calling of his disciples to join him in his ministry. A theology of discipleship is compressed into this brief episode:

• Discipleship is a gift: Jesus calls them; the disciples don't volunteer.

• Disciples follow Jesus: that's the essence of the call; nothing is more important.

• Discipleship is a privilege, and it is defined here as "fishing" for people.

Exorcism and Healing (1, 20–45)

Again the beginning is typical of the rest of Jesus' ministry. Jesus enters a synagogue and liberates a man tormented by an "unclean spirit" (called "unclean" because they separated their victim from the worship of God). The demons, unlike most of the humans in Mark's story, recognize Jesus and even announce his identity. That Jesus can expel the demon with words alone causes the crowd to marvel at his "authority." The exorcisms, which occur frequently in Mark, are an important part of his overall design. They demonstrate in the most dramatic terms the ultimate purpose of Jesus' mission: to free humanity from the power of death in all its forms.

Immediately Mark's succinct and simple style makes frequent use of a Greek word that can be translated as "at once," "quickly," "just then," and "immediately." The word is used more than 40 times in the short 16 chapters of the Gospel, adding to the urgency and immediacy of Mark's account and giving the impression that Jesus was constantly active.

Conflict (2, 1—3, 6)

The more Jesus continues to heal, the greater the opposition builds against him. Five stories of conflict between Jesus and the scribes and Pharisees crowd this section. They culminate in the leaders' plot to kill Jesus. Though it is still far off, Mark has already set our sights on the Passion.

Note that Jesus and the leaders disagree on precisely the issues that are at the heart of Jesus' mission: healing and forgiveness of sins. The very things that make Jesus distinctive are what anger the Pharisees: Jesus associates with sinners and outcasts and refuses to allow the law to override compassion. For Jesus, healing on the Sabbath is simply putting the spirit of the law ahead of the letter of the Law, but for the Pharisees, it is the final straw.

In the discussion on fasting (2, 18–22), Mark reiterates his message that Jesus has ushered in a new age that will operate by new standards. The images here are of newness and change. The arrival of the "bridegroom" calls for new ways of seeing and responding. When he describes faith in this new age, Mark uses images of perception—"hearing," "seeing," and "understanding"—and stresses the need to perceive differently.

The call of Levi reminds us that the call to discipleship is a gift that God can give to anyone—the sinner as well as the just. This point is lost on the Pharisees who criticize Jesus for eating with "tax collectors and sinners." But Jesus responds that it was precisely for sinners (the "sick") that he came (2, 17).

Like Jesus, those who take the Gospel seriously had best be prepared for opposition and conflict, for those who live by the ways of the world will bitterly resent the Gospel's insistence

The Company They Keep

If it is true that a person can be known by the company he or she keeps, then here are some hints regarding the kind of person Jesus was. In Mark, he spent time with, healed and/or touched the following:

- A paralyzed man 2, 1–12
- A demon-possessed man 5, 1–15
- A leader of the synagogue 5, 22
- A woman with a chronic bleeding problem 5, 22
- A young girl 5, 41
- A Gentile mother of a possessed child 7, 25–30
- A boy with an evil spirit 9, 17–27
- A group of little children 10, 13–16
- A rich young man 10, 17–23
- A blind beggar 10, 46
- The Jewish religious authorities 12, 13–37

on justice and compassion. And even the church needs the reminder of Jesus' example so that it does not neglect to care for the sick, disabled, and society's outcasts.

The Mystery of the Kingdom (3, 7—4, 34)

Several elements—the portrayal of Jesus' family, the portrayal of the disciples, and the series of parables—all work together in this section to amplify Mark's message that the Kingdom is a mysterious reality that is beyond human control. God grants it to those who are called to be Jesus' disciples.

The disciples present a great irony: Though they are the privileged few called to be followers of Jesus, they are always out of step, unable to understand what Jesus is really all about (4, 13).

One might expect that Jesus' family would be the first to express faith in him, yet two scenes here demonstrate the opposite. In 3, 21 his "relatives" want to take Jesus home because they think "he is out of his mind." In a later scene of the same incident, Jesus' "mother and his brothers" also come to take him back home (3, 31–35). Jesus responds by shunning his uncomprehending family and, pointing to the disciples gathered around him, announces "whoever does the will of God" is his brother and sister and mother (3, 35).

The reason for all this misunderstanding is provided by the parable discourse (4, 1–34). Jesus, like his parables, is a mysterious revelation of God's Kingdom. Understanding does not come

easily. It is a gift given by God, not earned solely through our own effort. While Mark respects human freedom, his point is that God is always in control—even a person's rejection of Jesus is somehow part of God's overall will and plan.

The "seed" parables teach another important point. All three—the sower casting seed onto fertile and infertile ground (4, 3–9), the tiny mustard seed (4, 30–32), and the seed growing while the farmer sleeps (4, 26–29)—make the point that the Kingdom has a life of its own. It grows unnoticed, even into our own lives. Because of this hidden but sure growth, the Kingdom's ultimate triumph is assured. No opposition can prevent the final harvest from being lavishly abundant, "thirty, sixty, and a hundredfold."

The Universal Mission of Jesus (4, 35—8, 21)

In this section, which begins to bring to an end the Galilean ministry of Jesus, the Sea of Galilee takes on prominence as a symbolic boundary between Jew and Gentile (the western shore was mostly Jewish, while the eastern shore was mainly Gentile).

Crossing the Sea several times, Jesus and the disciples make excursions into Gentile territory. Among the Gerasenes (5, 1) Jesus frees a man from a horrifying demon. Later, on another missionary journey that takes him through the Decapolis (on the eastern side of the Sea of Galilee), Jesus encounters the Syrophoenician woman whose daughter he heals (7, 24–30).

Decapolis A loosely knit federation of Gentile cities north of the Dead Sea and east of the Sea of Galilee. Though the word is Greek for "ten cities," the actual number was greater and varied from time to time.

Mark's Gentile Audience

One indication that Mark's Gospel is addressed to a Gentile audience is the fact that he often defines Aramaic words and explains Jewish customs to his readers. For examples, look up the following: "*Talitha koum*" 5, 41; handwashing regulations 7, 3; "*qorban*" 7, 11; and "*Eloi, Eloi, lema sabachtani?*" 15, 35.

Several blocks of material give a missionary flavor to this section: Jesus sends the twelve disciples out to preach and expel unclean spirits, giving them full participation in his own ministry (6, 7–13). Herod's murder of John the Baptist and Jesus' continuing disputes with his enemies are stark reminders that discipleship comes at a high cost (6, 14–29). And the two miraculous feedings of the huge and hungry crowds, one on the Jewish side and one on the Gentile side of the lake, give insight into the universal nature of Jesus' mission.

Following are some of this section's major themes:

The Universality of the Gospel

Human beings tend to exclude outsiders. Mark's Gospel gives evidence of both the need to overcome these tendencies and the courage it takes to do so.

Jesus heals the Gerasene demoniac (5, 1–20), the Greek woman's daughter (7, 24–30), and the deaf-mute from the Decapolis (7, 31–37), but to do so he and the disciples must endure the terror of the storm to get to the Gentile side of the lake. The sea and the storm can be seen as metaphors for the difficulty of crossing religious and cultural boundaries.

Nourishing God's People

The two feeding stories reveal the nature of Jesus' mission. He must feed God's hungry people (a lesson the disciples who want to send the crowd away hungry apparently need to learn). The feeding stories both recall the miraculous feeding of Israel with manna during the Exodus, and anticipate the Eucharistic meal (notice how Jesus takes, blesses, breaks, and gives the bread exactly as he does at the last supper, 14, 22).

The Struggle of the Disciples

Jesus' ministry in Galilee draws to a close. The disciples have seen many wonders (calming the storm, 4, 38–41; walking on water, 6, 45–51) and have heard Jesus' parables and words of instruction. Yet they are still stumbling in the dark of misunderstanding about who Jesus is. After so much evidence, Jesus' question echoes with judgment and pathos: "Do you still not understand?" (8, 21).

The Journey from Galilee to Jerusalem (8, 22—10, 52)

Significantly, Mark begins and ends this section with a healing of a blind man, symbols of the disciples' inability to see Jesus for who he is. From the northernmost section of Galilee, Caesarea Philippi, Jesus and the disciples journey to Jerusalem. But first Jesus asks the central question of the Gospel: "Who do you say that I am?" (8, 29). Of course, the answer has been consistently given by the eloquent words and powerful healings that have accompanied Jesus' ministry. But those signs are not enough for either Jesus' opponents or his disciples to fully comprehend that Jesus is the Messiah.

Now Jesus begins to speak openly (8, 31; 9, 31; 10, 33–34) about his impending death and resurrection. Understanding the cross becomes the key to understanding who Jesus is and what discipleship means. The journey toward Jerusalem becomes part of the instruction on the meaning of the cross. Jesus' trip to the holy city is very deliberate: He knows what awaits him there, and he willingly accepts the Father's call to this act of selfless love for others. All who would follow Jesus, Mark suggests, must be willing to travel the same road he walks. Because Jerusalem with its great Temple is the place where Jesus will be rejected and die, the

Jerusalem Temple will be replaced by a new temple, Jesus himself.

The disciples become incredibly thick-headed. To each of Jesus' Passion predictions, they make inappropriate responses: Peter by scolding Jesus (8, 32); the disciples by arguing over who is the greatest (9, 33ff; and James and John by requesting places of special honor in the Kingdom (10, 35–37). In addition, they misjudge Jesus' willingness to spend time with children (10, 13) and can't even perform an exorcism on a sick boy (9, 18)—despite having been given the power to do so (see 6, 7).

Jesus intensifies his instruction on discipleship after each of the Passion predictions:

• Disciples must be as humble as their master, putting aside self-interest and becoming the "servant of all" (10, 35f).

• The cross is an indispensable part of the formula for discipleship. It in no way represents failure.

• Rather than being concerned with their own importance or preoccupied with fears, disciples must be as willing as Jesus to give up their lives for others.

But the only way the disciples will overcome their stubborn, deep-seated spiritual blindness will be to imitate the physically blind Bartimaeus, who begs Jesus to make him see (10, 51). Unless they ask Jesus for the light of faith, they will remain in a darkness far more disabling then Bartimaeus' lack of sight.

Death and Resurrection in Jerusalem (11, 1—16, 8)

The final phase of Jesus' story can be subdivided into four sections. The first two focus on the Temple, the latter two on the Passion and the empty tomb.

Jesus and the Temple (11, 1—12, 44)

For a glowing moment Jesus' true identity shines out clearly. But the exultant crowd that greets him will soon become the menacing mob that calls for his execution. The peculiar story of the fig tree (11, 12—14, 20f) introduces a somber note into this section. Mark wraps the fig tree story around the story of the cleansing of the Temple. Just like the tree that failed to produce fruit, the Temple has failed to produce just and contrite hearts and authentic worship of the

Lord. Jesus not only cleanses the Temple, he declares the temple invalid. It will be replaced by a temple "not made by hands" (14, 58) that will be Jesus himself and his future community of disciples. In that new temple, love of God and neighbor will replace burnt offerings and sacrifice as forms of worship. The hypocritical leaders who delight in the trappings of religion while "devouring the houses of widows" will have no place there; but the humble, like the poor widow who gives all she has to God, will be assured a place (12, 38–44).

Towards the End-time (13, 1–37)

Set in the context of Jesus' prediction that the great Temple of Herod would be leveled (and it was, in A.D. 70), this final discourse of Jesus is one of the Gospel's most puzzling, but important, passages. It focuses on the future of the Christian community and how it will carry out its mission in history after Jesus' death and resurrection. From the sayings of Jesus and Old Testament quotations that Mark has woven together in this discourse, three main themes can be identified:

Warnings of persecutions and divisions as the community carries out its mission. The world cannot end until the gospel has been proclaimed throughout the world (13, 10). But that evangelization effort will be met with opposition, persecution (13, 9–11), and internal divisions (13, 12f).

The Christian must "stay awake." Without becoming doomsayers endlessly speculating about the end of the world, Christians must be sober and alert, aware of God's presence breaking into human history. False prophets will say, "I am he," and, "There he is" (13, 6.21), but true disciples will faithfully proclaim the Gospel while anticipating God's soon-to-be-revealed presence in history.

God's triumph in history. Without denial or sugar-coating, Mark acknowledges that the Christian community will suffer and face crises, but ultimately grace will triumph and human history will be full of hope.

The Passion (14, 1—15, 47)

In keeping with the important role that the Passion plays in Mark's understanding of Jesus, these chapters constitute the longest single narrative of the Gospel; yet the story moves quickly to its climax at the cross.

The opening scenes (14, 1–11) set contrasting moods: While Judas and the leaders plot, a faithful woman anoints Jesus' body for death. The next section is dominated by the last supper, where the broken bread and shared cup become signs of Jesus' impending death for others. Gethsemane is a scene of profound pain and sorrow (14, 32–52). As darkness closes in around Jesus, the disciples take a nap—disappointing Jesus' hope that they would keep watch with him (13, 36). Then Jesus is arrested by an armed band led by one of his own disciples. The rest of the disciples flee, leaving Jesus alone to face his trials before the Sanhedrin (14, 53–72) and Pilate (15, 1–20), and deserting him at his crucifixion and death.

Two motifs dominate the Passion story: the crisis of discipleship and the revelation of Jesus as the Son of God.

The Crisis of Discipleship

Throughout the Gospel the disciples have come off rather badly, and now their behavior is even scandalous. They professed loyalty at the last supper (14, 31), but in the midst of crisis they run like frightened rabbits. Peter, the leader of the lot, denies even knowing the man he so recently confessed as the Messiah. While suffering and persecution make a hero of Jesus, it makes cowards of his friends.

The only people who come off looking good are those one would least expect: the woman who anoints Jesus despite the objections of his disciples (14, 3–9); a Roman centurion who proclaims his faith in Jesus (15, 39); and Joseph of Arimathea who courageously recovers and buries the body of Jesus (15, 42–47).

The Revelation of Jesus Christ, the Son of God

In the Passion story we learn the answer to this Gospel's chief question: Who is Jesus? Jesus himself makes the bold announcement before the Sanhedrin: he is the Christ, the Son of God (14, 61f). This Messiah stands as a prisoner soon to be condemned to death. He came to liberate Israel, but he has no army or weapons. He liberates not with power and might, but by freely surrendering his life. Jesus is the son of a God who is revealed in the "weakness" of selfless giving.

For Mark, it is in the shadow of the cross that Jesus is seen most clearly.

The Empty Tomb (16, 1–8)

This brief but important passage is probably the original ending of Mark's Gospel. Someone writing later than Mark added the longer ending.

Jesus' Victory over Death

The crucified Jesus has conquered death: The empty tomb proclaims the fact and so does the mysterious "young man" who greets the women there. It is the truth of the young man's announcement that "Jesus of Nazareth, the crucified, has been raised" that makes Mark's story "gospel"—good news.

Reconciliation with the Disciples

Jesus does not wait for the disciples to come seeking him. The women are told to "go tell his disciples and Peter, 'He is going before you to Galilee; there you will see him.'" As he had promised at the last supper (14, 24), Jesus will be reunited with his disciples despite the fact that they deserted him. Significantly, the messenger at the tomb instructs the women to tell the disciples and Peter. Peter, who had not only abandoned Jesus but denied him, is singled out.

Back to Galilee: The Mission Begins

In Galilee, where Jesus began his ministry and first called the disciples to share it with him, is where the reunion of master and disciples will occur. But it is not clear what kind of reunion Mark has in mind. It may be a resurrection appearance, a final end-of-the-world meeting with the disciples, or perhaps a reunion in spirit—Jesus promising to be with the disciples as they go forth to spread the gospel. Mark doesn't say.

Mark's Abrupt Ending

Why does Mark's Gospel end so suddenly? Some speculate that he may have been prevented from finishing the Gospel. More likely, the original ending has been lost, or perhaps Mark thought that after the empty tomb nothing more need be said. The vocabulary, literary style, and theological content of the longer ending differ enough from Mark to convince scholars it came from another's pen.

The Longer Ending (16, 9–20)

A later writer added the longer ending that re-counts Jesus' appearance to Mary Magdalene, who brings the message of Jesus' resurrection to the disciples. The report of Jesus' appearance to the eleven begins with rebukes for their lack of faith in his resurrection. It concludes with a com-missioning of the disciples and with promises that signs and wonders will accompany their min-istry. Finally, without mention of a mountaintop, Jesus is taken up into heaven. The disciples go forth to preach, and the risen Lord is with them.

Questions for Discussion and Reflection
Group Sharing/Discussion

1. Discuss how the beginning and end of this Gospel are different than those in the other Gospels.

2. In this Gospel Jesus teaches more by his ac-tions than by his words. Give examples of what/how he was teaching.

3. In your group, let different people represent different disciples from the Gospel. Have them tell who they are, what they did according to this Gospel, and how that person might explain their actions.

4. What are examples of the fact that Mark was writing, not for Jews, but for non-Jews?

In Our Lives

1. Discuss which disciple with whom you can most identify.

2. Jesus' family publicly rejected him. Why do you imagine they did that? Is there an example of that behavior towards you or someone you know? How do you think Jesus would want peo-ple to handle it today?

3. What can we learn for our own lives from the kind of company Jesus kept: for example, a paralyzed man (2, 1–12); a demon-possessed man (5, 1–15); a leader of the synagogue (5, 22); a young girl (5, 41); a Gentile mother of a possessed child (7, 25–30); a rich young man (10, 17–23); and a blind beggar (10, 46). How does our church imi-tate Jesus in this regard? What might we do better?

4. Name the qualities of a disciple of Christ as portrayed by Mark. Choose one that you want to develop further for yourself. Talk about how you might "grow" that quality.

Individual/Personal Reflection/Action

1. The central question of Mark's Gospel is "Who do you say I am?" (8, 20). After reading the Gospel, how would you answer that question?

2. The cross looms large in Mark's Gospel. Why is it so central to his understanding of who Jesus was? Paul said the cross was a scandal and a stumbling block. Yet Christianity has clung to the cross as a mark of faith and a sign of hope. What is the message of the cross? What meaning does it hold for you and your faith?

3. In your own words in your heart, thank Mark for what you appreciate in this presentation of Christ's life.

LUKE READING GUIDE

At a Glance

Who are the main players?	Elizabeth an Angel of the Lord Zechariah John the Baptist Mary Joseph the disciples Zacchaeus Herod the Great Pilate Mary Magdalene
What should I look for?	Luke provides an account of Jesus' life and teaching for the universal mission. He was engaged in intercultural dialogue when he told the story of Jesus for Greek-speaking, non-Jewish converts. Also note his addition of Jesus praying at the major moments of his mission.
When was this book written?	Proposed dates vary between A.D. 63 and 90. Some evi-dence suggests a date between A.D. 80–85.
Who wrote this book?	The unanimous tradition of the church has held that Luke, "the beloved physician" of Colossians (4, 14), is the author of the Gospel. Probably a well-educated member of a

wealthy urban family, and very likely from Antioch of Syria, Luke was writing for a Hellenistic audience. The only Gentile among the four evangelists, he was a companion of Paul who accompanied him in his travels.

Why was this book written?

The introduction suggests Luke is a second or third generation Christian looking back on the founding years of the movement. Luke provides an account of the life and mission of Jesus for the universal mission of the gospel. Luke's Gospel shows that the preaching of the church is rooted in the life of Jesus.

What is the story?

Luke is interested in showing us how God's plan of salvation is fulfilled in the Christian movement. The infancy stories or narratives review the hopes of the faithful people of Israel. Later, as Jesus begins his journey up to Jerusalem, he knows he is going to be taken up from there in death. This journey is a time to prepare the disciples for the events in Jerusalem and for their future role as witnesses to Jesus' teaching. In the telling of Jesus' death and resurrection, Luke emphasizes the necessity for the Messiah to suffer and die in Jerusalem. The episode with the repentant criminal shows that the death of Jesus extends salvation and forgiveness to others.

Healings in Luke

A leper 5, 12 (Mk, Mt)
The centurion's servant 7, 1 (Mt)
Peter's mother-in-law 4, 38 (Mk, Mt)
Evening healings of the sick 4, 40 (Mk, Mt)
A paralytic 5, 18 (Mk, Mt)
A man with a withered hand 6, 6 (Mk, Mt)
The woman with a hemorrhage 8, 42 (Mk, Mt)
A mute demoniac 11, 14 (Mt)
An epileptic boy 9, 38 (Mk, Mt)
Two blind men 18, 35 (Mk, Mt)
The crippled woman 13, 11
The man with dropsy 14, 1
The ten lepers 17, 11
Restoring the ear of the servant Malchus 22, 50
(Mt and Mk indicate the healing miracle is reported in Matthew and Mark as well.)

Other Miracles Reported in Luke

Casting out an unclean spirit 4, 33 (Mk)
Calming the storm at sea 8, 22 (Mk, Mt)
Curing the Gerasene demoniacs 8, 26 (Mk, Mt)
Raising of Jairus's daughter 8, 40 (Mk, Mt)
Feeding the five thousand 9, 10 (Mk, Mt)
Escape from hostile Nazareth crowd 4, 30
The catch of fish 5, 1
Raising of son of the widow of Nain 7, 11–17
Luke is the only Gospel that does not report the miracle of walking on the sea.
(Mk, Mt, and Jn indicate the miracle story also occurs in Mark, Matthew, or John.)

Parables Found Only in Luke

The two debtors 7, 41–43
The good Samaritan 10, 29–37
A friend at midnight 11, 5–13
The rich fool 12, 16–21
Faithful servants 12, 35–40
The vigilant steward 12, 42–48
The barren fig tree 13, 6–9
The great feast 14, 16–24
Constructing a tower and a king preparing
 for war 14, 25–35
The lost coin 15, 8–10
The lost (prodigal) son 15, 11–32
The dishonest steward 16, 1–13
The rich man and Lazarus 16, 19–31
The master and servants 17, 7–10
The persistent widow 18, 1–8
The Pharisee and the tax collector 18, 9–14
The ten gold coins 19, 11–27

When Jesus Prays in Luke

At the Jordan River 3, 21
In desert places 5, 16
On a mountain 6, 12
In solitude 9, 18
On the Mountain of Transfiguration 9, 28
In a "certain place" and teaching the "Our
 Father" 11, 1–4
The upper room 22, 32
In the garden 22, 39–46
From the cross 23, 34.46
With the Emmaus disciples 24, 30
At the ascension 24, 50
(Luke records more instances of Jesus at prayer
than any other evangelist.)

Luke's Portrait of Jesus

Luke's Jesus is a man of mercy and compassion
with a particular concern for the poor and outcast.
His Jesus prays often, especially before important
events. Though he is the son of God, Luke's Jesus
is also fully human and his concern for all people
makes him the universal Messiah.

Luke's Unique Perspective

Luke aims at a clear, orderly, and faith-
affirming presentation of the words and deeds
of Jesus. Wanting his readers to know the truth
and reliability of the gospel, he pays attention
to historical detail. He stresses Christian
prayer and the value of renunciation. He sees
the fulfillment of prophecy in Jesus and thus
stresses the fidelity of the God of Jesus. His
Jesus shows a special interest in sinners,
women, and family

Luke's Unique Perspective *(cont.)*

life. His Gospel expresses joy at the announce-ment of the "good news," makes frequent use of the title "Son of Man," and reveals the active participation of the Spirit in the ministry of Jesus.

Some Accounts Found Only in Luke

- Announcements of the birth of John (1, 5–25) and Jesus (1, 26–38)
- Canticles of Mary (1, 46–55) and Zechariah (1, 67–79)
- Birth in Bethlehem, visit of the shepherds, and presentation in the Temple (2, 1–40)
- Twelve-year-old Jesus in the Temple (2, 41–52)
- Imprisonment of John (3, 19.20)
- Jesus is rejected at Nazareth (4, 16–30)
- A sinful woman washes Jesus' feet (7, 36–50)
- Galilean women follow Jesus (8, 1–3)
- The meeting with Zacchaeus (19, 1–10)
- The trial before Herod (23, 6–12)

Before Beginning

Luke tells us that he was not an eyewitness to the events of Jesus' ministry. He is dependent upon others who did witness and have already given their testimony in writing (1, 2). Scholars have identified three of the sources that Luke used: Mark's Gospel; a collection of Jesus' sayings that was also used by Matthew, called "Q"; and a source for additional material about Jesus, which scholars designate "L" (see the NAB introduc-tion to Luke, p. 1415). The introduction suggests that Luke is a second- or third-generation Christian looking back on the founding years of the movement. Luke's ability to write in different styles—including that of the Septuagint (the Greek translation of the Hebrew Scriptures, which was the Bible for most of the early Chris-tian communities)—and to use conventions of Greek literature, such as the opening dedication to a prominent patron, suggest a well-educated author. To have received a literary education of this sort, Luke probably came from a prosperous urban family. Unlike the other Gospel writers, Luke's account did not end with the Gospel. He wrote a second volume, Acts of the Apostles, which showed that God's salvation, begun in Jesus, moved beyond Jerusalem and the pious of Israel into the whole world.

Luke's Gospel provides an account of Jesus'

life and teaching for that universal mission. To-day, people sometimes think that Christianity and its Gospels belong to North American and European culture. But the story of Jesus origi-nated in a Semitic culture. Luke and other early Christians were already engaged in intercultural dialogue when they retold the story of Jesus for the Greek-speaking, non-Jewish converts who inhabited cities in the eastern part of the Roman empire. Their example shows that the gospel message is not limited to any one culture.

An Assured Teaching

Luke's desire to establish Christianity within the larger world of the Roman Empire is evident in references to Roman emperors and events. For example, he links the birth of Jesus to Caesar Augustus (2, 1). People have sometimes thought that Luke was attempting to write what we would call a history of Jesus and the earliest disciples. Most of the "historical" references, however, are not accurate even by ancient standards. Luke calls his work a *diegesis*, meaning a "narrative account," not a history. He claims that it is thor-ough, accurate, and orderly. He has traced the events that have occurred among "us" (i.e., the Christian community) from the beginning (1, 1–4). The purpose of his writing is to provide "assurance" for the instruction that Christians

Luke's "History"

Luke is sometimes characterized as the "historian" among the evangelists. While he does make historical references to Roman emperors and Jewish kings (2, 1–3; 3, 1–2), his details are vague and not always accurate. He also shows faulty knowledge of Palestine, for example, in describing its climate and the way homes were built. Clearly, he is not a historian by modern standards. His chief interest is theological.

give. In other words, Luke's book will show that what the church preaches is rooted in the ministry of Jesus and the preaching of the first apostles.

Luke takes patterns for his story from biblical history. We see this, for example, in the infancy narratives, which show God's promises of salvation being fulfilled in Jesus. When Luke claims that his narrative is "orderly," he refers to the literary order, which sets out the periods of salvation. In the second volume, Acts of the Apostles, he shows the same Spirit at work in the developments in the early community. Civic authorities were suspicious of new religious movements. Luke's work addresses those fears by highlighting the high moral standards and social value of Christianity.

An Ordered Narrative

Luke has told us that he is dependent upon earlier accounts but that he has reworked his material to provide a more accurate and orderly account. This refers to Luke's desire to set forth the way in which God's plan of salvation is fulfilled in the Christian movement. Scholars have made detailed studies of additions, deletions, and changes that Luke has made in the order of material taken over from Mark. There are three major additions that even the beginning Gospel reader can spot. Mark begins abruptly with the appearance of John the Baptist. Luke (as does Matthew) begins with an account of Jesus' birth (1, 5—2, 40). He adds a tale about the child Jesus (2, 41–52). Then, between the Baptism and

Temptation stories, Luke reintroduces Jesus by giving his genealogy (3, 23–38).

A long section in which Jesus is journeying toward Jerusalem with the disciples (9, 51—19, 27) contains much of the teaching of Jesus. It includes parables that Luke has taken from "Q" (and from his special tradition) and retold in a way that serves as instruction for the church. By contrast, Mark's Gospel has only a short section of instruction to the disciples on the trip to Jerusalem.

Finally, there are several differences in the Passion and the Resurrection section. Mark ends with the women running from the empty tomb. Luke 24, on the other hand, has accounts of appearances by the Risen Lord, as well as instructions to the disciples. Luke's Passion narrative differs from Mark (and Matthew) as well. Jesus is never formally tried by the Jewish court. There is an unusual episode in which Pilate sends Jesus to be investigated by Herod (23, 6–12). Pilate persists in declaring that Jesus is innocent of the charges against him (23, 4.14f.22). The dying Jesus prays for forgiveness for his enemies (23, 34) and enacts the message of the gospel by promising salvation to a repentant criminal who dies with him (23, 39–43). Each of the above contributes to our sense that God's plan of salvation is being carried out.

The Tragedy of Israel

The infancy stories awaken the joyful expectation that Israel's messianic king has arrived to bring salvation. Through him, God's peace and blessings will come to both Jews and Gentiles (2, 29–32). Yet, as the story unfolds, this promise will not be fulfilled. Persistent rejection, first of Jesus and then of the disciples' mission, leaves Israel excluded. Luke points out the tragedy of this situation in a series of prophetic laments that Jesus utters over Jerusalem and her inhabitants. The first is a "Q" tradition (13, 34f; Mt 23, 37–39), which Luke has attached to an episode from his special tradition (13, 31–33). The episode contained a warning that Herod was seeking Jesus' life. Jesus connects the divine necessity that he die in Jerusalem (13, 33) with a lament for the city. The second, from Luke's special tradition, occurs as Jesus is looking out over the city where he is to die (19, 41–44). Jesus weeps at the thought of the peace that will elude the city and the terrible devastations of war that it is to suffer. The final lament, also from "L," occurs as Jesus is on the way to his death. He looks out at the weeping women of Jerusalem and warns them to weep for themselves instead (23, 27–31).

The church has constantly reminded Catholics that, even though the ancestors of today's Jews chose not to accept Jesus as Messiah, Christians cannot reject or persecute Jews. The church has also insisted that Christians share a common heritage with the Jewish people that is rooted in the Hebrew Scriptures. Luke insists that the heritage of the Christian movement lies in the faithful and just persons of Israel. Jesus' own family are among the righteous ones who trust in God for salvation. Though Luke's Passion holds certain Jewish leaders responsible for some of the events, Jesus does not condemn them but asks God's forgiveness. Luke also presents us with a Jesus who is able to weep as he foresees the terrible fate of Jerusalem. The prosperous and beautiful city of his day will be reduced to the rubble of war. Jerusalem will not enjoy the peace that God so longs to give the people.

Reading through Luke

Before you begin to study Luke, read through the whole Gospel. Many of the stories will be familiar, because Luke contains some of the best-loved stories in the Gospels. Luke is a gifted storyteller. Even in the parables of Jesus, he creates short episodes and switches from the third-person report into dialogue between the characters. Young children often enjoy the stories in Luke more than those in the other Gospels. As you are reading, you might note passages that particularly appeal to you. Do you find any common themes in those stories? Here are some of the themes that you will find running through the Gospel.

Salvation Is a Joyous Surprise

Luke has many images of celebration and rejoicing. From the very beginning to the very last verse, people are praising and thanking God for the salvation that they experience in Jesus. Salvation is a "surprise" or gift because those who receive it could never have anticipated that it would come. Mary's Magnificat (1, 46–55) sets the tone. God has come and rescued the humble, poor, oppressed, and lowly people of the land. Jesus begins his ministry (4, 18) by quoting a promise from Isaiah: a threefold release from poverty, from sickness, and from sin. Luke drives home this point about salvation by showing that Jesus has the power to forgive sins and to heal people (see 5, 17–26). Even the rich tax collector Zacchaeus hears the message, demonstrates his repentance by making restitution to those he had cheated, and shares his joy by throwing a banquet (19, 1–10).

God's mercy is the source of this salvation. Christians are to show mercy in the same way that God is merciful (6, 36). When Jesus gives examples of what God's mercy and forgiveness are like, he uses very active images. God is not waiting for people to come crawling back, begging forgiveness. God is out looking for people to help like the shepherd and the lost sheep, the woman and the lost coin, or the wayward son's father, who goes running out of the house and immediately orders a large celebration.

Salvation Includes Everyone

In Acts, Luke will show us that God directed the disciples to take the gospel to all the peoples of the earth. The Gospel demonstrates the universality of God's love and salvation in a different way. It stresses the fact that Jesus reached out to all sorts of people, even to those who seemed to have no chance at salvation. Zacchaeus, the tax collector, was a sinner who had defrauded people to enrich himself (19, 1–10). The Samaritans, traditional enemies of the Jews, turn out to be examples of Jesus' teaching. The mercy shown by the Good Samaritan (10, 37) is so well known that we can speak of anyone who shows mercy or unmerited assistance to another as a "Samaritan." Less well known is the Samaritan leper (17, 11–19) who is the only one of the group healed by Jesus to return and give him thanks. Women—often excluded from education, public leadership, and cultural events in those days—are constantly included in Jesus' ministry. A sinful woman provides a better demonstration of love and hospitality than the Pharisee. Her sins are forgiven (7, 31–50). Mary is permitted to sit and listen to Jesus as a disciple. She does not have to busy herself with the business of serving the male guests that has her sister so distracted (10, 38–42). When Jesus defended Mary's listening to his teaching, he was not condemning Martha's devotion to serving her guests or the traditional tasks of women in the home. Jesus was really issuing an invitation to her to join her sister. Martha was so busy that she was missing the one necessary thing, to hear Jesus' message about the Kingdom (10, 41f).

Special Concern for Those in Need

Salvation has very concrete aspects in Luke. Those who are poor, helpless, in prison, sick, and the like are promised release. Jesus and the apostles are able to relieve the suffering of the sick by healing. Acts contains many stories in which God intervenes to free the apostles from prison. To achieve this goal, however, miraculous events are not required. The story of the Good Samaritan (10, 29–37) shows how this salvation can come about through concrete actions. The Samaritan uses his own resources to see that the man beaten up by robbers is restored to health, even though, as a Jew, the victim is his enemy. The parable of the Great Supper, in which the host replaces the friends who refused to come with the poor, and the sayings about showing aid to those who cannot repay (14, 12–24) are other examples of how salvation can come to those in need.

Luke often returns to the theme of rich and poor. The rich often fail to receive salvation because they are trapped by their own desires for money or pleasure (see 12, 13–21; 16, 19–30). Even those who are good people like the Rich Ruler (18, 18–24) are so locked in by possessions that they cannot achieve the eternal life they desire. That does not mean that Luke thinks all rich people are excluded from the Kingdom. The Samaritan, Zacchaeus, and anyone else who is willing to share his possessions generously with those who are in need can become a disciple of Jesus. Acts will return to this theme in its picture of sharing possessions in the early community. Luke also retains the sayings of Jesus that call upon followers to renounce material goods to become disciples (6, 35; 9, 3; 10, 4; 12, 33; 14, 33; 16, 13). By doing so, Jesus, and later

the apostles, demonstrate that they are completely dedicated to God. But Luke knows that such discipleship is possible only if the basic needs of the group are met through the generosity of others. He reports that a group of women followers provided the necessary support (8, 1–3). In Acts, he reports that Paul achieved the same end by laboring at his trade (Acts 20, 33–35).

Mary Is the First Disciple

Catholic Christians have always paid special honor to Mary, the mother of Jesus. Luke's Gospel provides the basis for the devotion to Mary. Her assent to God's work of salvation initiates the whole story. Her Magnificat is a strong statement of God's faithfulness and mercy. It is not just because of the miracle of Jesus' birth that Mary is honored. That is not Luke's picture. For Luke she is both the epitome of the faithful people of Israel who wait confidently for God's salvation and the beginning of the new life of those who will be disciples of Jesus. Jesus defines her role in 8, 21. She is one who hears and does the word of God. He repeats this affirmation in 11, 27f. The crowd praises Jesus' biological mother. Jesus corrects them by insisting that hearing and keeping the word of God constitutes the true source of blessing.

Discipleship Luke's formula for discipleship is clear: Don't just hear the word of God; live it. Luke uses parables, more than the other evangelists, to teach about discipleship. Look at the following parables for what they teach about the way a disciple should behave:

- The good Samaritan (10, 29–37)

- The rich fool (12, 16–21)

- The lost sheep; lost coin; lost son (15, 1–32)

- The dishonest steward (16, 1–13)

- The rich man and Lazarus (16, 19–31)

- The Pharisee and publican (18, 9–14)

The infancy narrative demonstrates that Mary has this quality of true discipleship. She has accepted God's will in the Annunciation scene. Later she keeps in her heart words spoken to her about Jesus, as well as the extraordinary events she witnesses (2, 19.51). Simeon includes her in his prayer about the impact of Jesus' ministry in Israel (2, 34f). Mary remains among the faithful disciples of Jesus. She was present among those disciples gathered in Jerusalem after Easter (Acts 1, 14).

An Outline of Luke

Luke's Gospel falls into a neat pattern that moves from the infancy narrative, through the ministry in Galilee, back to the Jerusalem Temple, and finally to Jesus' death and resurrection. The Gospel ends with the disciples in Jerusalem awaiting the coming of the Spirit. Acts will take the Gospel from Jerusalem out into the world. Jerusalem forms a symbolic center to the Gospel, as much of the narrative takes place either in or on the way to the holy city. The major divisions in the story are clearly marked transitions in the unfolding of the plot:

Prologue (1, 1–4)
Infancy Narrative (1, 5—2, 52)
Preparation for the Public Ministry (3, 1—4, 13)
The Ministry in Galilee (4, 14—9, 50)
The Journey to Jerusalem (9, 51—19, 27)
Teaching Ministry in Jerusalem (19, 28—21, 38)
The Passion Narrative (22, 1—23, 56)
The Resurrection Narrative (24, 1–53)

In reading through the Gospel of Luke in detail, notice how Luke develops a picture of Jesus, salvation, and Christian discipleship. Because Luke preserves important blocks of the teaching of Jesus, note also how Luke presents the teaching of Jesus for Christians in his time. Discipleship requires living the word of God as well as hearing it.

The Infancy Narrative (1, 5—2, 52)

This section is built on an elaborate similarity between Jesus and John the Baptist. In each case, Jesus is greater than the Baptist, who is only the forerunner of the Messiah. The most detailed parallels occur between the two angelic birth announcements (John: 1, 5–25; Jesus: 1, 26–38):

1. Neither parent is expecting a child;
2. An angel appears, the parent is troubled and told not to fear;
3. A child is announced, his name given, and a statement is made about his future greatness;
4. The parent raises a question about how this can happen;
5. The angel gives an assertion that it will happen, and a sign;
6. Zechariah is forced to be silent; Mary's spontaneous answer affirms God's will.

The birth announcements are followed by an episode that brings the two together and confirms the angel's statement to Mary, the Visitation (1, 39–56). In this episode the Baptist testifies to the presence of Jesus as savior by moving in the womb.

The next cycle recounts the births (John: 1, 57f; Jesus: 2, 1–20) and circumcision/naming of the two children (John: 1, 57–80; Jesus: 2, 21–40). Each birth section includes mention of the joy at the birth. Each naming section concludes with an affirmation that the child grew. This cycle is followed by an episode that prefigures Jesus' last days, the Finding in the Temple (2, 41–52). Jesus will return to the Temple to teach before his death (see the outline of the Gospel).

It is made clear that God is responsible for the origins of both children. For the Baptist, God has overcome the barrenness of his parents, just as other barren women in the Hebrew Bible, like Sarah and Hannah, had been given children For Jesus, God has done something even greater by bringing the child into existence in the womb of his virgin mother.

Songs of Salvation: The Canticles

These episodes contain several canticles, which have become a treasured part of Christian worship: Mary's Magnificat (1, 46–55); Zechariah's Benedictus (1, 68–79); the canticle of the angels (2, 13f); and Simeon's Nunc Dimittis (2, 29–32). Many scholars think that Luke has taken the Magnificat, the Benedictus, and perhaps the Nunc Dimittis from a Jewish Christian source. They use expressions taken from the Hebrew Bible and other Jewish psalms and hymns from the time of Jesus.

Mary's Magnificat is an individual song of praise, which seems to be modeled on the Song of Hannah (1 Sm 2, 1–10). After celebrating God's greatness toward the lowly handmaid (vv. 51–53), in a series of strong, active verbs, the song refers to God's past deeds of salvation. The final verses (54f) relate the career of Jesus to the covenant God had made with Abraham. Scholars think that this hymn originated among Jewish Christians who identified themselves with the "poor ones," the "anawim," of Israel. That term designated those who were unfortunate, lowly, sick, or downtrodden. The rich and powerful, those who feel no need of God, are opposed to the anawim (see Ps 149, 4; Is 49, 13; 66, 2). The poor ones are the righteous remnant in Israel who know that they must look to God for salvation.

The Benedictus begins as a song of thanksgiving (vv. 71–75) recalling the dynasty expectation of the house of David (see 2 Sm 7, 12f). The hymn affirms that Jesus will fulfill this messianic role. It then shifts to the form of an oracle concerning the destiny of the newborn (76–79). The Baptist will prepare God's people for the coming Messiah. We are reminded that God comes to save the people out of merciful compassion. Luke will make the theme of mercy a central theme in the ministry of Jesus.

The Nunc Dimittis draws upon two passages of Isaiah (Is 40, 5; 49, 6). Simeon has now seen the salvation that these two passages promised. The image of an elderly patriarch blessed with a glimpse of God's promise is rooted in the Hebrew Bible (see Joseph, Gn 46, 30; Moses, Dt 32, 49–50; 34, 1–5; Anna and Tobit, Tb 11, 9.14). Verses 31–32 point to another important theme in Luke: God's salvation is given for all peoples. The aged prophet Simeon not only recognizes the dawning of salvation; he also warns that Jesus' coming will bring about divisions. God's plan includes the rejection of the Messiah by his own people (see 4, 29; 13, 33–35; 19, 44.47f; 20, 14.17).

Virgin Birth and Christology in the Infancy Narrative

As mentioned, the canticles celebrate Jesus' coming as the fulfillment of all God's promises to the faithful people of Israel. The Benedictus pointed to Jesus as the anticipated Messiah of the Davidic house. The announcement of Jesus' birth by the angels is made in two stages. Verses 32f parallel 2 Samuel 7, 9.13.14.16. Jesus will inherit the throne of David and rule over Jacob's house forever as "son" of God. The second stage in the announcement moves beyond these promises of a messiah to the special sense in which Jesus is Son of God: Jesus is begotten through God's intervention. Some scholars suggest that Luke created this two-step process from older statements of Christ such as Romans 1, 3f. There, Jesus is "Son of David" during his earthly life and is designated "Son of God" through the power of the Holy Spirit when he is exalted to God's right hand at the Resurrection. The announcement to Mary speaks of God's Spirit overshadowing her and bringing into being a child who is Son of God from the time he is conceived. For Luke, Jesus is fully human but is never just another ordinary human being.

Mary's virginity serves to sharpen the Christological focus: the child to be born is God's Son. Mary is not like the barren woman, someone whose womb could unexpectedly open and produce a child. As virgin, there is no human way for her to have a child without God's unique presence in that process. Ancient Greek biology taught that the spirit in a father's sperm gave shape to the material in a mother's womb. The more active the spirit, the more closely a child resembled its father. Thus, Mary's virginity indicates a relationship between Jesus and God unlike that of any other human being. The honor that Mary enjoys is not due to the fact of her virginity, but to her willingness to accept a role in God's plan for the salvation of humanity.

A second angelic announcement, that of the angels to the shepherds, accompanies the story of Jesus' birth (2, 1–20). Luke introduces this section with a reference to Caesar Augustus and the expansion of Roman rule indicated by the census. Historically, there was no worldwide census under Quirinius. When the Romans took over administration of Judaea in A.D. 6–7, they took a census of that province. Residents of Galilee, which was still ruled by one of Herod's sons, would not have been obligated to return to their ancestors' village in Judaea. The tradition in the Gospel of Matthew claims that Jesus was born toward the end of the rule of Herod the Great, who died in 4 B.C. Though Luke lacks precise historical information in this scene, its Roman associations permit a symbolic contrast. The Roman emperor Augustus emphasized the fact that his rule had brought peace in the world. The doors to the temple of war, pictured on coins, were shown closed. Luke uses the announcement by the angels (2, 10–14) to show that the true source of peace lies elsewhere: in the Messiah who has been born in David's town, Bethlehem.

Preparation for the Public Ministry (3, 1—4, 13)

Before Luke begins to recount the public ministry, he introduces three additional blocks of material: (1) John the Baptist's mission in preparing the way for Jesus and Jesus' baptism; (2) a genealogy; and (3) the Temptation of Jesus.

The Baptist's Ministry (3, 1–22)

Luke has gathered together traditions about John the Baptist from different sources. John the Baptist is fulfilling the mission given him to serve as forerunner for God's Messiah. Luke has arranged his account so that the fiery preacher of repentance also serves as precursor to Jesus in what the message says about: (1) repentance and forgiveness, two of the effects of salvation in Luke, and (2) the requirements for dealing with material possessions. The ethical section of John's preaching (vv. 10–14) illustrates the "good fruit," which must come from repentance (v. 9).

As the episode comes to a conclusion, the Baptist separates himself clearly from the Messiah. John belongs to the age of prophets. Jesus will inaugurate the messianic age. Luke then completes the story by reporting the fact that John was imprisoned by Herod Antipas before Jesus appears on the scene. This order creates some chaos in the account of Jesus' baptism, which follows it (vv. 21f). For Luke, the baptism of Jesus can never suggest that Jesus was dependent upon the Baptist. Rather, the episode permits a divine affirmation that Jesus is son of God and provides the occasion for the Spirit to descend on Jesus and inaugurate his ministry.

Genealogy of Jesus (3, 23–38)

This unusual genealogy corrects a misapprehension about Jesus. People may think he is the son of Joseph. The Christian community knows better. It traces Jesus' ancestry back to the first "son of God," Adam, and thus links Jesus to the entire human race, not just to the house of David.

Temptation of Jesus (4, 1–13)

Jesus goes to the desert under the impulse of the Spirit. The temptations Satan poses are challenges to Jesus' identity as Son of God, which has been the central title in Luke's narrative to this point. Temptation, in this sense, is not toward some sinful act. Rather, as in the testing of Abraham by the demand that he sacrifice Isaac, temptation puts the person before a crisis that will demonstrate whether their faith in God can be destroyed. Jesus refuses to use his status as Son for personal gain. Though Satan is silenced,

---

The Evangelists Symbolized

Since ancient times, artists have used the four living creatures of the book of Revelation (Rv 4, 7) to symbolize the four evangelists.

Mark is linked with the desert lion because his Gospel opens with John, the voice of one "crying out in the desert."

Luke is linked with the calf, a sacrificial animal, because his Gospel opens with Zechariah offering sacrifice in the Temple.

Matthew is associated with the human figure because his Gospel begins with a record of Jesus' human ancestors.

John is linked with the eagle because his Gospel starts with a hymn of praise to Jesus who uniquely can look on the face of God just as the eagle uniquely looks upon the sun.

the story ends on an ominous note; though Jesus' ministry will undermine Satan's power (10, 18; 13, 16), Satan may yet return. In Luke 22, 31f Jesus speaks of a confrontation with Satan on behalf of his disciples; though they will be seriously tested by the events of the Passion, Jesus has prayed that their faith will not fail. When the temptations are finished, Jesus has demonstrated that he is the obedient Son of God who will carry out God's plan of salvation—whatever the cost.

The Ministry in Galilee (4, 14—9, 50)

The introduction to this section (4, 14f) highlights the power of the Spirit active in the ministry of Jesus (1, 35; 3, 22; 4, 1.14.18).

In Nazareth and Capernaum (4, 16–44)

Luke's sources had Jesus' ministry begin in Capernaum (see Mk 1, 21–35). Luke has reordered events (v. 23 refers to the Capernaum tradition) to open with a sermon in Nazareth that depicts Jesus as the one who fulfills what the Hebrew prophets foretold (vv. 17–21). Throughout Luke and Acts, announcements occur in synagogues and at the Temple. Jesus announces the joyous freedom of the Year of Jubilee (combining Is 61, 1–11 and Is 58, 6). Once again, Luke previews the story yet to come. Jesus points to Hebrew prophets Elijah and Elisha, who were directed to assist persons who were not Israelites. These words provoke a deadly hostility in the hearers (vv. 25–30).

The rest of the chapter consists of healing stories that illustrate the liberation Jesus has just announced. The demons acknowledge that Jesus is "from God." However, the popular acclaim, which results from the miracles, makes it so difficult for Jesus even to move about that he leaves for synagogues in Judea (vv. 42–44).

Jesus Gathers Disciples (5, 1–39)

Jesus' activities in Nazareth and Capernaum come before he has any disciples. This arrangement provides those who are called with a reason for following Jesus. By the time he gathers his first disciples, Jesus already has a reputation as healer and teacher. Simon Peter's call to follow Jesus is linked with a story of a miraculous catch of fish. Peter, viewing the catch of fish, announces that he is unworthy to be in the presence

of the divine (v. 8). Peter's acknowledgment that he is a "sinner" is also similar to the "fear" exhibited at the appearance of the angels in the birth announcement stories. Like the angel, Jesus first tells Peter not to be afraid. Then he states what Peter's future destiny is to be: "from now on you will be catching men" (v. 10). The Christian reader knows of Peter's role as missionary apostle in Acts. Peter and the sons of Zebedee, James and John, respond as exemplary disciples. They will leave everything to follow Jesus.

Jesus continues to establish his authority through healings, first of a leper (vv. 12–16), then of a paralyzed man (vv. 17–26). When Luke took over the account of the healing of the paralyzed man, it was already a controversy story—that is, an account of a controversy or conflict between Jesus and the religious authorities—over Jesus' authority to forgive sins (see Mk 2, 1–12). The reader already knows that Jesus has the power to heal anyone he wishes. In this case, the miracle becomes both an occasion to free the man from sin through forgiveness and a demonstration of the authority by which Jesus can claim that the man's sins have been forgiven. The crowd goes home praising God, but the Pharisees and scribes become suspicious of Jesus. His offer of forgiveness appears to be a blasphemous attempt by a human being to claim power that belongs to God (v. 21). Luke's reader knows that Jesus is not just any human being, but the obedient Son of God. Jesus would never seize any power that rightly belongs to God (see 4, 5–8).

As Jesus calls his next disciple, the toll collector Levi, the Pharisees and scribes complain further. They go to Jesus' disciples to ask why he eats with persons who are considered sinners. Jesus first cites a proverb in defense of his actions and then insists that the goal of his mission is to call sinners. He is not out to preach to the righteous.

Jesus is accused of not instructing his disciples in piety as a true teacher would do. The disciples of both the Baptist and the Pharisees fast. Jesus' disciples do not. Jesus' defense consists of a brief parable and a string of proverbs (5, 33–39). The first uses a human analogy: It is impossible to fast at a wedding. The abundance of the wedding feast was also a common metaphor for the time of salvation. When Jesus is no longer present, Christians will fast (v. 35). The proverbs demonstrate the absurdity of trying to mix the old ways

The Beatitudes In contrast with Matthew, Luke lists only four beatitudes or "blessed" statements, which he contrasts with four "woes." *Blessed* refers to those who receive God's favor. The woes threaten God's wrath against those who value material wealth over the things of the Kingdom. Note that the future will see the hungry and weeping satisfied and laughing, while those who are filled and laughing will hunger and weep. It is especially noteworthy that while Matthew spiritualizes the beatitudes—blessed are the poor *in spirit* (Mt 5, 5), those who hunger and thirst *for righteousness* (Mt 5, 6)—Luke refers to very real economic and social circumstances.

of life with the new time of salvation. Persons used to the old way may find it difficult to accept the new (v. 39).

Jesus then defends his disciples against charges of breaking the Sabbath (6, 1–5), first by appeal to Scripture (1 Sm 21, 1–6), then by insisting on his authority as Son of Man (cf 5, 24), and finally on humanitarian grounds: It is always right to preserve rather than destroy life (vv. 6–11). The section concludes with the choice of the Twelve from the larger group of disciples who will share Jesus' mission and serve as witnesses to what Jesus has done and said.

Sermon on the Plain (6, 17–49)

In Jesus' first major sermon (4, 18), the Kingdom is good news for the poor and oppressed, and divine judgment is against the wealthy and prosperous. As the stories of Christian missionaries in Acts will demonstrate, Christians must expect rejection and persecution for preaching about Jesus (see Acts 7, 52). The love command (vv. 27–30) covers all forms of mercy because it is to be modeled on the mercy of God. Examples point to general ethical precepts: give to one who asks; lend to those who cannot repay; treat others as you would be treated. Judgment sayings add strength to this ethical teaching: We are judged by the judgments we make about others (vv. 37–42).

Jesus is the Promised Savior (7, 1—9, 18)

Jesus' ministry in Galilee continues with a series of traditional miracle stories told so that they testify to Jesus' identity: cure of the centurion's slave indicates that there is greater faith among the Gentiles than in Israel (7, 9); the widow's son evokes the allusions to Elijah and Elisha in the opening sermon (4, 25f); awestruck, the people acknowledge that a great prophet has arisen (7, 16). Further miracles demonstrate the truth of Jesus' reply to the Baptist's disciples: he is indeed the one to come (vv. 18–23). Luke edits his sources to make a distinction between those who received John's baptism and also receive Jesus with praise, and those who reject the plan of God—the lawyers and Pharisees (vv. 28–30). The call of Levi (5, 27–32) illustrated the conversion of tax collectors. This contrast prepares the reader for the sharp contrast between the Pharisee Simon, who failed to show Jesus the hospitality due an honored guest, and the sinful woman, who anoints Jesus and whose sins are forgiven (7, 36–50). The parable of the Pharisee and the tax collector makes a similar point (18, 9–14).

Examples of women who followed Jesus (8, 1–3) and Jesus' mother as a model disciple, one who hears and keeps the word of God (8, 19–21), frame the instruction about discipleship given in the parable of the sower (8, 4–15), the lamp (8, 16–17), and a general warning to be careful how one hears the word (v. 18). The interpretation of the sower parable indicates the threats to discipleship: some will not believe the initial preaching; some will be turned from discipleship by temptation, cares, riches, and pleasure; and still others will lack the patient endurance necessary to bring forth the harvest.

Other Miracles

Another series of miracles emphasizes Jesus' power to save. The disciples are rescued from the storm (8, 22–25); the Gerasene is saved from the multitude of demons that made it impossible for any human bonds to restrain him (vv. 26–37). The concluding instructions are pointed toward Christians as well: go and declare what God has done for you (vv. 38f). The healing of Jairus's daughter and the woman with the hemorrhage focus on the faith of the recipients (vv. 40–56). This section concludes with the feeding of the five thousand (9, 13–17). As Luke shapes the story, this miracle represents food for the hungry (6, 21), as well as a response to Satan's challenge to turn stones into bread (4, 3f). Jesus does live by the word of God alone.

The Messiah Who Must Suffer (9, 18–50)

None of the opinions about Jesus' identity capture the truth that Jesus is the Messiah who must suffer. Luke applies this insight to the followers of Jesus by insisting that the disciple must be ready to take up the cross "daily" (9, 23). Not only does God affirm Jesus' sonship at the Transfiguration (as in Mk 9, 7), but Moses and Elijah also talk with Jesus about his coming departure from the world at Jerusalem (9, 30f). Luke has omitted Mark's material that is critical of the disciples from the Passion prediction (Mk 8, 33), the Transfiguration (Mk 9, 6), and the healing of an epileptic boy (Mk 9, 28–29). In doing so, Luke brings the dramatic Transfiguration closer to the predictions of the Passion. God prevents the disciples from understanding what Jesus has said to them. Their arguments over greatness and jealousy of a outsider who uses Jesus' name (9, 46–50) show that they are not yet ready to follow Jesus in suffering.

The Journey to Jerusalem (9, 51—19, 27)

The journey to Jerusalem is the time of preparation for the disciples. Teachings of Jesus dominate this section of the Gospel. Miracles underline Jesus' conflict with the Pharisee teachers over the merciful application of the Law (13, 10–17; 14, 1–6); they point to the virtues of faith and gratitude (shown by a Samaritan leper, 17, 11–19), and they anticipate Jesus' triumphal entry into Jerusalem (18, 35–43).

Criticism of the Pharisee Opponents of Jesus

The shape of the Pharisees' criticism was anticipated by the story of the sinful woman in the house of a Pharisee (7, 36–50). Luke sharpens the charges and also generalizes them to apply to Christians as well: it is hypocritical to use the Law to condemn in one case what one's actions in another approve; applications of purity regulations demonstrate this principle (11, 37–44);

and lack of love of God leads to self-aggrandizement and even persecution of those sent by God (11, 45–52). The Pharisees are persistently pictured as driven by love of money, desire for honor, and self-justification that stems from their application of the Law. The first two characteristics (16, 14f) reappear in Acts as typical of magicians and false prophets in paganism (see Acts 8, 9–25).

Warnings about Judgment

Luke does not anticipate the return of Jesus in judgment in the immediate future. Therefore, warnings to be watchful apply to both Jesus' opponents and Luke's Christian readers. Demands for a sign only prove that there was more wisdom among Gentiles in the past than among God's people in the present (11, 29–32). Hypocrisy can never be hidden from God's judgment (12, 1–3). The stories of faithful and unfaithful servants warn against presuming that the delay in Jesus' return means that all restraints are removed (12, 35–48). Although they can read the signs of the weather, Jesus' contemporaries are unable to see what is before them in Jesus (12, 54–56). People must not fall into false confidence because of the tragedies that happen to others. The fact that we have not suffered the disasters that happen to others does not mean that those who suffer are worse than we are, or that God is more pleased with us (13, 1–5). The parable of the barren fig tree provides a different understanding of the situation. It could be that we are like the tree being given its one last chance (13, 6–9). The narrow door and shut door warn that Jesus' audience could be excluded and replaced with foreigners in the Kingdom (13, 22–30). Framing the parable of the servants entrusted with the master's wealth with the parable of the ruler who had gone into a distant country emphasizes the problem of discipleship in a time of delay (19, 11–27). Delay doesn't necessarily mean the kingdom is absent. Luke preserves sayings that point out the presence of the Kingdom for Jesus' disciples as well as its sudden arrival (17, 20–37). Luke expands the traditional saying about the coming of the Son of Man in judgment with another affirmation that the Son of Man must first suffer and be rejected by his own generation (17, 25).

Discipleship: Renunciation, Devotion, and Suffering

The journey to Jerusalem opens with sayings that warn would-be disciples that they must be completely devoted to the Kingdom (9, 57–62). Such disciples renounce normal human ties to family. They are the ones sent to heal and to preach the approach of the Kingdom (10, 9). Their words are equivalent to the words of Jesus (10, 16). Luke 10, 17–20 acknowledges the potential dangers that the disciples face. However, Satan's fall from heaven indicates that the mission is weakening evil's power over humanity. Stories of the apostles in Acts will illustrate the certainty of divine protection. Sayings against anxiety require the disciple to have confidence in the generosity of others (12, 22–34). Luke's addition to the traditional saying—sell possessions, give alms, and so provide yourself with heavenly treasure (v. 22)—points to one way in which the material needs were met. The good news for the poor depends upon consistent efforts by Christians to help those in need. This should not make people feel looked down upon or rejected. Jesus and the early church welcomed such people into the community in addition to providing food and clothing for them.

The Martha and Mary story (10, 38–42) also illustrates a discipleship that abandons the cares of this world, even the obligations of hospitality, for the one thing necessary to salvation—hearing and keeping the word of Jesus (also see 11, 27–28).

Disciples must also expect division. Jesus' ministry brings division even within families (12, 49–53; see also 2, 34f). Jesus challenges disciples to recognize the full cost of being a disciple: both suffering and patient endurance to follow Jesus to the end are required (14, 25–33). The slave can never tell the master, "I quit" (17, 7–10).

Discipleship and Material Possessions

Riches can be a major hurdle to becoming or remaining a disciple of Jesus (8, 14; 18, 18–25). Disciples have left everything to follow Jesus (18, 26–30). Luke's parables demonstrate the folly of being possessed by wealth: The rich farmer dies before he can build his barns (12, 13–21), and the rich man who cannot see the poor Lazarus at his door is so blind to his own sinful behavior that he thinks he can bargain even with Abraham from hell (16, 19–31). Alongside the call for renouncing everything, Luke presents another way in which Christians can use material possessions: They can share them with the unfortunate as the Good Samaritan does (10, 29–37). Instead of feasting friends, they can provide for those who have no resources (14, 12–24). Luke presents the parable of the dishonest steward as a warning not to mix service to God with the pursuit of wealth (16, 1–13). The final episode in the travel narrative, the parable of the ten gold coins (19, 11–27), draws on a common experience in a world without instant communications, uncertainty about the fate or return of those on a journey. Luke recognizes that Jesus may not return in judgment for a long time. Disciples must remain faithful stewards of what God has given them.

Prayer in the Life of Disciples

Jesus frequently turns to prayer (3, 21; 6, 12; 9, 18.28; 11, 2; 22, 32.41; 23, 46). Two times the disciples are instructed about prayer. The first is as a response to their request to be taught as the Baptist had taught his disciples (11, 1; see also 5, 33). Luke follows the Lord's Prayer (11, 2–4) with the parable of the persistent friend (vv. 5–8) and instruction on the efficacy of prayer (vv. 9–13). In the parable of the importunate widow (18, 1–6), if an unjust judge with no moral conscience can be badgered into hearing the widow, how much the more quickly will God respond to the pleas of the suffering lowly ones? After all, God is not withdrawn, waiting for humans to come begging, but is actively seeking those who are lost (see ch 15).

Jesus' Teaching Ministry in Jerusalem (19, 28—21, 38)

Jesus' arrival in Jerusalem brings the narrative back to its beginning.

The Messiah Comes to City and Temple (19, 28–48)

The Messiah who should have brought peace to Jerusalem will not be able to do so (19, 41–44). Luke has revised the story of Jesus' entry into Jerusalem (Mk 11, 1–10) so that the crowd consists of followers testifying to the works Jesus has done in Galilee (v. 37). Jesus goes directly to the Temple so that his entry reflects the Greek version of Malachi 3, 1, "the LORD whom you seek shall suddenly come to his own temple." But Jesus has not come to set up the kingdom of David (19, 11; Acts 1, 4). The city is the object of a prophetic lament—peace comes in the heavens, not on earth (v. 38). Allusion to Habakkuk 2, 11, the stones crying out from the walls against a nation that plunders the people (19, 39f), heightens the sense of a city about to meet its divine destiny. Jesus purges the Temple so that it can be a place of prayer as well as the location for Jesus' teaching in Jerusalem (19, 45–48).

Jesus Teaches Daily in the Temple (20, 1—21, 4)

A traditional series of pronouncement stories (Mk 11, 27—12, 44) provides the content of Jesus' teaching now that he has returned to "his Father's house" (2, 49).

The Authority for Jesus' Actions

One day Jesus was teaching the people in the temple, and the Pharisees came and asked him, "Tell us by what authority are you doing these things?"(20, 1–2). Jesus answers with a counter question hinting that those who reject him do not believe the Baptist either. Compare Jesus' answer (20, 8) with his response to the Council when they demand to know whether Jesus is Messiah (22, 67). If Jesus speaks, they do not believe; if Jesus asks a question, they do not answer.

Wicked Tenants

Christians have traditionally read this parable as an allegory for the replacement of Israel as God's covenant people. Today we recognize that neither Jesus nor Luke think that a faithful God would give up on the Jewish people. Jesus directs this tale at his opponents.

Tribute Due God and Caesar

Luke's addition of verse 20 intensifies the hostility implied in the question. Jesus' opponents are seeking evidence for charges of stirring up political rebellion to bring against Jesus at trial (see 23, 2–5). The spies pose their malicious question under the guise of pious flattery. Jesus, they say, teaches the truth and exhibits a godlike impar-

tiality toward persons. Again, Jesus responds with a question. He forces the opponents to acknowledge that they are carrying coins with Caesar's image, and they utter Caesar's name. Jesus' reply serves as a judgment against their failure to pay God the honor due God. Readers know that Jesus' disciples have left coins and human positions of honor behind. They recognize that only God claims our loyalty. Thus, this passage does not teach the doctrine of separate powers of church and state that has traditionally been attached to it.

Resurrection of the Dead

The final challenge receives a double answer. The absurd case that a man must marry his dead brother's wife if she had not yet borne children (see Dt 25, 5; Gn 38, 8) probably came from the debates between the Sadducees and Pharisees over resurrection. Jesus' first answer affirms that the "children of God" (note the contrast with the woman who dies childless) are resurrected to an angelic existence. His second answer (20, 37f) points to the revelation of God to Moses. If God is God of the patriarchs, they must be living.

Jesus Challenges the Opposition

Having silenced those who came to question him, Jesus poses challenges of his own. The question about how David's Son can be greater than his ancestor draws upon Psalm 110, 1, a text frequently used in early Christianity to speak of Jesus' exaltation. The warning about the scribes (20, 45–47) invokes the contrast in Luke between the wealthy and the oppressed poor. Jesus emerges as advocate for the poor. Finally, the comment on the widow's offering (21, 1–4) repeats the contrast between a poor person and the wealthy. The radical gift of the widow condemns

---

Apocalyptic The term refers to the revelation of mysterious truth that was previously hidden regarding future events that deal with the end of human history and final judgment. Both "revelation" (from Latin *revelatio*) and "apocalypse" (from Greek *apokalypsis*) mean "take away the veil."

the abundance that stands behind the gifts of the rich. Jesus is not approving the poverty in which the widow lives, but he is asserting that her acts demonstrate a piety greater than that of the rich.

Fate of the Temple and the Coming End-time (21, 5–38)

The Jerusalem teaching ends with Luke's version of the apocalyptic sayings in Mark 13. He has recast the traditional material to support the view that the end-time is not about to come. He does this by separating the destruction of the Temple (21, 5–7) from events that signal the end-time.

Even traditional signs of the end, false messiahs and rebellions, do not point to an immediate second coming (vv. 8–11). They are part of a time of persecution. God protects the Christian who must face hostility or even death from Jews, Gentiles, and even family (21, 12–19). The fall of Jerusalem does not lead to the end-time. Instead, it begins a new stage in salvation history. Jerusalem will be overrun until the age of the pagans reaches its conclusion (21, 20–24). After all these events the Son of Man will return in glory (21, 25–28). The Christian who lives in the world between Jesus' ascent to heaven and the second coming can remain confident that Jesus' words will never pass away (21, 29–33). Christians remain watchful and pray for strength to endure and appear before the Son of Man (21, 24–36).

The Passion Narrative (22, 1—23, 56a)

The Passion narrative is not a court record of what happened, but a telling of what happened that is shaped by the belief that Jesus is the suffering Messiah, the obedient Son who has been raised by God. Political charges (23, 2.5.18f) are false and recognized as such by Pilate, who declares Jesus innocent three times (vv. 4.14f.22). Pilate yields to pressure from Jewish leaders, to whom he hands over Jesus for crucifixion (23, 23–26). In the conspiracy to kill Jesus (22, 1–6), Luke blames only certain Jewish leaders for the plot that costs Jesus his life (22, 1–2).

The Last Supper (22, 7–38)

Jesus is aware of the suffering he is about to undergo. A new covenant will be made in the death of Jesus as symbolized by the interpretation of the cups of wine and the bread at the Passover meal. As the Jews had been told to remember the Exodus during Passover, Jesus tells his disciples to remember his death as the new focal point of salvation history.

The second element in the Last Supper scene is the farewell speech. Such speeches were delivered by dying patriarchs to their children, encouraging them to remember the ancestor's example by remaining faithful to the Law and then predicting their failures to do so. Luke creates Jesus' speech out of four independent sayings:

1. oracle against the betrayer (22, 21–23);
2. the disciples' place in the Kingdom (vv. 24–30);
3. prophecy of Peter's denial and eventual restoration (vv. 31–34); and
4. a saying about two swords (vv. 35–38).

Jesus sets the disciples an example in his death. The worst sin committed by a disciple is Judas's betrayal, which is rendered even worse by the echoes of covenant sacrifice associated with the meal. Luke puts the disagreement about greatness (see Mk 10, 42–45) here at the Supper, where it forms a contrast with Jesus' example as "one who serves" (22, 27). Jesus' earlier instructions to invite persons to your banquet who cannot repay you rather than invite those, like you, who can afford to give banquets, and Jesus' own appearance as slave or servant rather than master, provide additional illustrations of the Lucan theme of reversal in the Kingdom.

Beyond the ominous events of Jesus' death, Judas's betrayal, and Peter's denial, there are images of fulfillment. The Twelve who stand by Jesus will occupy the twelve thrones of the tribes of Israel. (Judas will be replaced; see Acts 1, 15–26.) The meal anticipates a future celebration with Jesus in glory—a communal celebration with Jesus, not the ranked banquets of those whose idea of greatness Jesus rejects. Before this banquet can occur, Jesus must suffer to enter glory. Satan makes the threatened return (4, 13) in Judas (22, 3) and in testing Peter.

Arrest of Jesus (22, 39–53)

Jesus demonstrates his faithfulness as God's obedient Son in his prayer before his Passion. Luke deflects criticism of the disciples for failing to stay awake by alluding to their grief. They are warned that they must pray to avoid being tested.

Jesus exhibits his freedom from fear over his fate in his words to those who come to seize him. He is no robber in hiding. They could have taken him publicly in the Temple, but the present hour of darkness is permitted by God's plan (v. 53).

Trial of Jesus (22, 54—23, 25)

Jesus' predictions are fulfilled, and this gives further evidence that God's will, not the plan of his enemies, controls the events around Jesus' death. Luke puts the story of Peter's denial before the trial of Jesus begins. Jesus reminds Peter of the earlier prediction by looking at him; Peter breaks down in tears. When Jesus' captors challenge him to prophesy as a form of mockery (22, 64), readers have evidence from the Peter episode to shows that Jesus is a true prophet. Luke does not report a legal trial by Jewish authorities. The false accusations and the verdict have been fixed before the Passion even begins. Jesus responds to the question about his messiahship with a judgment saying about the Son of Man. The Sanhedrin concludes that Jesus claims to be "Son of God" (22, 66–71).

Luke's version of the trial before Pilate insists that Jesus was innocent of the charges of stirring up political rebellion, which was used as a reason to put him to death. Luke adds the geographical note, "from Galilee where he began even to here" (23, 5), and then clears Jesus from guilt in Galilee by having him appear before Herod (vv. 6–12). That scene represents the climax of the earlier accounts of Herod's reaction to Jesus, which shifted from fascination to opposition (9, 9; 13, 31–33). Herod desires a miracle, but all he sees is the silent prisoner who is the object of violent accusations and mockery. Ironically, the incident creates peace between the old enemies, Herod and Pilate (v. 12). Even though Pilate persists in affirming Jesus' innocence, he is manipulated by the angry crowd into handing Jesus over for crucifixion. The leaders who orchestrated Jesus' death are really the ones fostering rebellion. They ask for the release of a known murderer and rebel (23, 25).

Crucifixion and Burial of Jesus (23, 26–56a)

As he is led to his death, Jesus prophesies the terrible fate awaiting Jerusalem once more (23, 26–32; 19, 41–44). Scorned and considered a criminal, Jesus is able to offer salvation to the repentant sinner (23, 39–43). The crowd challenges Jesus to save himself from his fate, which, as it turns out, is the entry into paradise both for him and for those who repent and are forgiven (see 22, 28–30; the disciples who feast with Jesus in the Kingdom are those who have endured with him in his trials). This shows that God's mercy can be experienced even in the midst of brutal hostility. Apocalyptic signs accompany Jesus' death, which is witnessed by the women and other followers from Galilee. The centurion proclaims Jesus' innocence while the crowd laments (23, 44–48).

Joseph, a member of the Council, buries Jesus as an act of piety. He represents the righteous of Israel who sought the Kingdom of God (v. 51). The women prepare to anoint the body, but they are interrupted by the Sabbath. The burial scene shows that Jesus was buried with honor, not like a criminal, and that the place was known to his followers. Luke is telling us that when the women return to complete the anointing, there can be no possibility that they have mistaken the place of burial.

Resurrection of Jesus (23, 56b—24, 53)

Jesus' departure takes place in Jerusalem on the third day after the crucifixion (24, 21.51). Luke has rewritten traditional stories about the empty tomb and about mealtime appearances of the Risen Lord to create a sequence of three scenes. He arranges these scenes so that the Resurrection faith is more and more explicitly spelled out. The Gospel concludes with the disciples offering prayer and praise in Jerusalem while waiting for the Holy Spirit to initiate the next stage in the drama of salvation, the spread of the Gospel from Jerusalem to the whole world.

The Women at the Tomb (23, 56b—24, 12)

The first of the three scenes opens when the women return to the tomb. Angels chide them for seeking the living among the dead (cf 20, 38). Instead of a simple proclamation of the Easter faith as one finds in Mark 16, 6b, Luke's angels remind the women of Jesus' predictions of the Passion and Resurrection. The women report that the angels said Jesus was alive (24, 22f).

Women in Luke

Luke was especially sensitive to outcasts and outsiders. Women in his day could claim few of the rights men enjoyed. But Jesus often crossed social, religious, and political barriers; he treated all people with compassion and respect. Luke reflects this by introducing thirteen women who are mentioned in no other Gospel. He also includes five incidents involving women that are not reported by any of the other evangelists:

• Raising the widow's son (7, 11–17)

• Pardon of a sinful woman (7, 36–50)

• Galilean women follow Jesus (8, 1–3)

• Visit to Martha and Mary (10, 38–42)

• Cure of a crippled woman (13, 10–17)

Jesus Appears on the Road to Emmaus (24, 13–35)

In the second scene, Luke uses a folktale motif: the appearance of a divine being disguised as a stranger who must be shown hospitality. Jesus expands on what the angels at the tomb said, and he interprets Moses and the prophets to demonstrate that the suffering of the Messiah was God's plan.

Then a new theme comes in: the manifestation of Jesus in the breaking of bread. (John 21, 1–14 contains a variation of the manifestation of Jesus in the guise of a stranger at a meal.) The Messiah has suffered, entered into glory, and now renews his presence to the disciples in the meal.

Jesus Appears to the Disciples in Jerusalem (24, 36–49)

Luke knows the tradition that Jesus had appeared to Peter (24, 34; 1 Cor 15, 5) but recounts only the appearance to the disciples at a meal. The third appearance confirms the fact that the Jesus who appears is the crucified one, raised up by God, not some ghost or other psychic phenomenon. The body that was missing from the tomb has been taken up by the risen Jesus.

Jesus Commissions the Disciples (24, 44–49)

In this third scene, as in the previous two episodes, Luke reminds us that the Messiah had to suffer and die to fulfill Scripture (vv. 44–46). The story then takes up the central element in all resurrection appearance stories: commissioning the recipients. These stories all point to the future mission of the disciples and founding of Christian communities in which Jesus continues to be present. The commission in verses 47–49 is a prelude to the story of the first apostles, which Luke will tell in Acts. The disciples' mission to preach repentance and baptism to all nations in Jesus' name, beginning from Jerusalem, continues the

Jesus' Resurrection

Christian belief in the resurrection of Jesus cannot be supported by near-death experiences—well-intentioned as such efforts might be. Christians do not believe Jesus was *resuscitated* in the sense that his dead body came back to life in the same way as a near-death survivor's. Nor was his resurrection merely a spiritual phenomenon, that is, he rose in the minds and hearts of his followers who experienced his presence through his teachings and his "spirit" among them. Both attitudes miss the mark. Christian belief says God transformed Jesus, body and spirit. Lazarus was resuscitated or revivified, meaning he returned to the same state of life he had enjoyed previous to his death. But Jesus was truly and fully transformed. He experienced a bodily resurrection, which meant his body was now different from anything we know or understand. His body was freed from the limitations of time and space. Disciples who had known him in life now could not recognize him. Luke shows him needing to convince the apostles that he is Jesus and to prove he is no ghost by eating. The transformation of Jesus gives hope to all Christians that the ultimate fate of all creation is a like transformation in the fullness of the Kingdom.

preaching that occurred during Jesus' ministry and reflects a new stage in salvation history.

Jesus Departs (24, 50–53)

The ending of the Gospel reflects the departure that Jesus discussed with Moses and Elijah (9, 31), as well as showing the Son of Man in glory at the right hand of God (22, 69). Jesus' resurrection appearances are understood to be from his place of glory with God (24, 26). The stories have introduced ways in which Jesus will now be present to the church, through the Spirit promised by the Father (v. 49) and in the breaking of the bread (v. 35). The church's mission will be to take Jesus' teaching throughout the world.

Things We Have Learned from Luke

Jesus Is Savior for All Peoples

From the very beginning, Luke shows that the hopes that poor, weak, suffering, righteous persons have are fulfilled in the coming of Jesus. The Gospel shows that women as well as men; foreigners and Gentiles as well as Israelites; sick, weak, sinful, and despised persons as well as the well-off and respected people can come to Jesus. God seeks to reverse the situation of the poor and suffering. Consequently, Jesus comes as a suffering, servant Messiah, not as a liberator or king, who will take his place with the powerful of this world. Jesus' parables reveal that the love and mercy of God prompts this gift of salvation.

Disciples Participate in the Mission of Jesus

The disciples do not simply preach about Jesus or the Kingdom of God; they also participate in the reversal of roles, status, and concerns that the coming of salvation brings. Some disciples renounce everything that ties them to the social structures of the world. Others use their material resources in ways quite different from those around them. They do not seek exchanges between friends, which would create obligations. They do not try to pile up wealth or to indulge themselves and their friends in consuming luxurious goods. Their lives are not dominated by concern for acquiring and preserving material things. Instead, they aid people who will never be able to repay them. They give away wealth to meet the needs of other people.

Their only "anxiety" is acquiring heavenly treasure. All disciples are willing to follow Jesus' example of suffering service rather than demanding that others honor and serve them.

Prayer and Worship are the Center of Christian Life

Even acts of mercy and compassion would not establish a relationship with God if people did not praise God in worship and ask God's assistance in meeting the challenges that the life of discipleship poses. Throughout the Gospel, Jesus sets the example. He worships with others in the synagogue and withdraws for prayer at critical moments. The disciples turn to prayer and praise after the Resurrection. Luke also contains examples of prayer in the Lord's Prayer and the canticles of the infancy narrative. Jesus warned the disciples in the garden that they would have to pray to be spared testing, a reminder of the last petition of the Lord's Prayer.

Questions for Discussion and Reflection
Group Sharing/Discussion

1. What are the three sources that Luke depended upon in writing his Gospel?

2. What is the main purpose of Luke's Gospel (1, 1–4)?

3. Let each person select a story from Luke—for example, infancy narrative (1, 4—2, 52), Zacchaeus (19, 1–10), Good Samaritan (10, 29–37), Mary and Martha (10, 35–42), Sinful Woman (7, 31–50), and so on—and retell it in their own words, being sure to include how you think Luke was using the story.

4. Luke retains Jesus' call to renounce material goods to be a disciple (6, 35; 9, 3; 10, 4; 12, 33; 14, 33; 16, 13). Read each aloud and explain Jesus' teaching.

5. What role does John the Baptist play in Jesus' mission? What message does the Baptist preach?

6. Role-play the story of the Good Samaritan (10, 29–37). Afterwards, let each person explain his or her actions and reactions afterwards.

In Our Lives

1. The parable of the sower (8, 4–15) is an instruction for discipleship. Explain the meaning of the seeds and discipleship.

2. The meeting of Mary and Martha with Jesus (10, 38–42) illustrates the demands of disci-

pleship—hearing the word and keeping the word of Jesus. Have individuals role-play the story, then discuss the meaning of this incident and lesson.

3. In Luke, riches are obstacles to becoming a disciple (8, 14; 18, 18–25). His parables show the folly of being possessed by wealth (12, 13–21; 16, 19–31). Read these sections aloud, give time for silent reflection, and then let each person tell how they interpret these teachings on wealth and discipleship and how they apply them to their lives.

4. Luke writes the traditional resurrection stories into three stories. What are these? Retell these aloud: 24, 13–35.36–43.44–49. What do you discover as you hear this retelling?

5. In Luke Jesus is the advocate of the poor. He challenges the leaders about their wealth and oppression of the poor (20, 25–47). Luke often focuses attention on the theme of the rich and the poor. Because the rich are trapped by their desires for money and pleasure, they often fail to receive salvation—for example, 12, 13–21 and 16, 19–30. However, this does not mean all rich people are excluded from the Kingdom. The Good Samaritan, Zacchaeus, and others who share their wealth with those in need can become disciples of Jesus. Where do you stand in regard to your wealth and your faith? How does your belief affect your attitude toward the poor? What actions for the poor should you take?

Individual/Personal Reflection/Action

1. Prayer and worship are center to Christian life. Jesus sets the example. Luke regularly presents Jesus at prayer during major moments in his ministry:

At his baptism (3, 21)
At the choice of the Twelve (6, 12)
Before Peter's confession (9, 18)
At the Transfiguration (9, 28)
When he teaches his disciples to pray (11, 1)
At the Last Supper (22, 32)
On the Mount of Olives (22, 41)
On the cross (23, 46)

Disciples must also ground their life of seeking justice in prayer and worship. At his disciples' request, Jesus instructs his disciples about praying, about persistence in prayer, and about its efficacy (11, 1–13; 18, 1–6). Prayer is essential to becoming a Christian disciple. Review your own habits of prayer and worship. What is positive in these habits? Decide what changes you might want to make.

2. Luke's beatitudes (Lk 6, 20–26) differ in style as well as content from Matthew's (Mt 5, 3–12). What significance do you find in Matthew's spiritualized beatitudes in contrast to Luke's more economically oriented beatitudes? Which do you find more challenging, which more comforting? Luke's version includes four "woes." How do these very real social and economic conditions impact your life and challenge your beliefs?

3. Women play an important role in Luke's Gospel. In a patriarchal culture, what did you find surprising or noteworthy about the roles that women play in this Gospel? Why do you think Luke includes this strong emphasis on women? What can you do and what can the church do to nourish women more effectively?

4. Mary is the first disciple because she is one who hears and does the word of God (8, 21). Because Mary became the Mother of God, this is the ultimate foundation of all Marian devotions. Take some time to reflect on this by meditating on the Magnificat (1, 46–55).

JOHN READING GUIDE

At a Glance

Who are the main players?	Jesus John the Baptist the twelve disciples the beloved disciple Lazarus Martha Mary, Mother of Jesus Pilate Mary Magdalene Peter
What should I look for?	The Fourth Gospel uses symbols, signs, and metaphors to help present its message that Jesus is the unique Son of God. No one who reads Jesus' words solely on the literal level will understand the truth Jesus reveals. As you read

the Gospel, you will see that Jesus often identifies with the great symbols like light, life, water, bread, shepherd, and vine. The author assumes that the reader will recognize these symbols have roots in Jewish scripture. The Fourth Gospel also often uses the expression "the Jews" as a symbol of all those who oppose Jesus.

When was this book written and by whom?

Most likely between A.D. 90 and 100. The author may have been a disciple of the Apostle John but almost certainly was not the Apostle himself, though that had been the belief from the second century on. Several things are clear: The Gospel shows the hand of more than one writer (several sources may have been combined into one Gospel); the Gospel contains many accurate details that argue for its being based on eyewitness testimony; the Beloved Disciple may be the source of that testimony, but the story was likely told and retold within the community before being written down.

Where was this book written?

Though the place of composition traditionally was considered to be Ephesus, some scholars today propose a location in Syria or Palestine.

Why was this book written?

The Fourth Gospel has a double conclusion (20, 30ff and 21, 24ff). Both conclusions remind the readers that the Gospel has been written to inspire and confirm their faith in Jesus. Also the readers faced being forced out of the Jewish communities, as well as conflict between the Petrine and Johanine communities. These tensions are answered in the Gospel.

What is the story?

Like the other Gospels, John tells the story of Jesus' life. However, John is very different from the other Gospels. The story is a theological narrative. Jesus speaks in long symbolic discourses, not in short sayings or episodes that end in short sayings. The only piece of ethical teaching is the love command. There are two major differences in order of events: Jesus' ministry extends for three Passovers, and the cleansing of the Temple comes at the beginning, not the end of Jesus' ministry, giving a context to the entire Gospel. Jesus' death is attributed to the followers coming after his raising of Lazarus. Many miracles are presented as claims about Jesus' relationship with God.

Before Beginning

The Fourth Gospel has a double conclusion. After the Resurrection stories in Jerusalem, we are told that Jesus did many other signs, but those in this book seek to lead people to belief in Jesus as Son of God (20, 30f). After the Resurrection stories in Galilee, we learn that the Beloved Disciple was the source of the Johannine tradition and that all the things Jesus did could not be written down (21, 24f). Expanded or revised editions of a book were not uncommon in those times. This is to remind the people who read it that this Gospel has been written to inspire and confirm their faith in Jesus.

Composition of the Fourth Gospel

The double ending of this Gospel indicates that there was an earlier version. Other additions to the story and some of the awkward transitions

Differences between John's Gospel and the Synoptics

Synoptics	John
Jesus' teaching focuses on the Kingdom of God.	The Kingdom is not a focus of John's Gospel. He stresses instead Jesus' relationship with the Father.
Writing style makes use of proverbs, maxims, and parables. Sayings of Jesus are probably closer to their original form in these Gospels. Numerous ethical teachings are given.	Retells no parables and avoids use of proverbs. Instead, uses metaphor to describe Jesus' role ("I am the way," "I am the bread of life," etc.) Freely shapes and phrases the teachings of Jesus in his own style and imagery. The only ethical teaching here is the command to love one another.
Focuses on Jesus' human origins by recounting his conception, birth, and childhood.	Focuses on Jesus as the preexistent, divine Word who was with God from the beginning.
Jesus' ministry centers on Galilee, and scant time is spent in Judea. He makes only one trip to Jerusalem where he cleanses the Temple at the end of his ministry.	Jesus' ministry spans several years and includes three trips to Jerusalem in Judea. The Temple cleansing occurs at the beginning of his ministry.
The Last Supper is a Passover meal, which would take place on the evening of the first day of Passover.	The Last Supper takes place the evening of the day before Passover. Jesus dies on the cross at the time the lambs for the Passover meal are being killed.
The disciples only gradually realize the meaning of messiahship.	The disciples profess Jesus as Messiah from the start.
Miracles are recounted in rapid succession and tend to speak for themselves.	Miracles are related within extended narratives followed by discourses that explain their meaning and provide insight into the identity of Jesus.
Jesus starts his ministry just as John the Baptist comes to the end of his. No mention of Jesus baptizing.	John's and Jesus' ministries overlap. Jesus has a baptizing ministry at the same time as John.

between sections also lead to this conclusion. For example, John 14, 31 brings the discourse to an end. Yet the Gospel as we have it contains three more chapters of discourse material. In addition, John 12, 44–50 appears to be tacked on at the end of chapter 12. Some of the additional material may have been added to the Gospel by later disciples of the author. As you read the Gospel, you will also see that Jesus often identifies with great religious symbols such as light, life, water, bread, shepherd, and vine. The author of the Gospel assumes that its readers will recognize that these symbols have roots in the Hebrew Scriptures. This symbolic way of speaking about Jesus was probably developed within a commu-

nity of Christians, which included the Beloved Disciple, followers who compiled the final edition of the Gospel, and another teacher who wrote the Johannine letters.

The Fourth Gospel and the Other Gospels

John's Gospel is very different from the other gospels. You will immediately notice that Jesus speaks in long symbolic discourses, not in short sayings or episodes that end in sayings. The only piece of ethical teaching in this Fourth Gospel is the love command. There are also major differences in the order of events. John pictures Jesus' ministry extending over three Passovers. The cleansing of the Temple comes at the beginning (2, 13–22), not at the end of Jesus' ministry. Jesus' death is attributed to the reports to the Sanhedrin after he restored Lazarus to life. John attaches symbolic discourses to many of the miracles so that the miracle becomes a claim about Jesus' relationship to God. Most scholars think that John draws on traditions about Jesus that were independent of those preserved in the synoptic (Matthew, Mark, Luke) Gospels.

Symbols, Irony, and Misunderstanding

The Fourth Gospel uses symbols to present its message that Jesus is the unique Son of God. No one who persists in taking Jesus' words literally can understand the truth that Jesus reveals (see the rejection of literal understandings of Jesus' words and deeds in 3, 4–10; 4, 10–15; 6, 26–33). The reader knows the true meaning of Jesus' words when the characters in the story do not.

The Fourth Gospel and the Jews

Though some Jews, like Nicodemus, are sympathetic to Jesus (3, 1–11; 7, 50–52; 12, 42), the Gospel often uses the expression "the Jews" as a symbol for all those who oppose Jesus. They display a murderous desire to kill God's envoy and will be condemned by the founders of their own tradition, who testify to Jesus (Moses, 5, 41–47; Abraham, 8, 48–59). The hostility in the Johannine account may have had its roots in the expulsion of Christian Jews from the synagogues, referred to in John 9, 27 and 16, 1–4a.

If you read carefully, you will notice that John often does not bother to distinguish the various groups within Judaism at the time of Jesus, such as Sadducees, Herodians, scribes, lawyers, and Pharisees. He often speaks of "the Jews" as though summarizing a story in which Jesus is facing "the bad guys." This habit creates a tension between the fact that Jesus and his followers were also Jews and the way in which the Gospel is using "Jews" as a term for a role in the story. John 18, 35f illustrates this tension. Pilate treats Jesus with scorn because Jesus is a Jew, handed over by

fellow Jews. Jesus' answer distinguishes himself and his followers from "the Jews," that is, the group opposed to him. John is not making a statement about the Jewish people when he uses "the Jews" to fill the role of "bad guys." The Vatican has reminded Catholics that anti-Semitism is one of the worst forms of racism. We must acknowledge that in the past people have not distinguished between John's use of "the Jews" as characters and the Jewish people as a whole. Today, we must be very careful not to continue that misreading. In some contexts, it might be appropriate to substitute another phrase like "Jesus' enemies" or a more literal rendering of the term used for "the Jews," "the Judeans," when retelling the Johannine story to avoid confusion. Such substitutions are particularly important when working with young children who cannot make the distinction easily between "the Jews" as characters in a story and their Jewish classmates and neighbors.

Reading through John

In reading John, we must be sensitive to the use of symbols, irony, and misunderstanding. The characters who interact with Jesus in the story are at different levels of understanding as to who Jesus is. The disciples begin with faith that Jesus fulfills the promise of a messiah given to Israel, but this faith is not yet knowledge of Jesus as this revelation of God. Their faith must be completed by the post-Easter process of coming to understand Jesus, the perspective that the evangelist shares with readers (16, 25). Jewish sympathizers and the crowds have a vague idea that Jesus might be "from God" or even the Messiah. John often divides the opinions of the crowd in two. One opinion is wrong or literal-minded; the other is partially correct (12, 27–29). Unlike the Jewish crowds, who sometimes accept Jesus, John also uses the expression "the Jews" to represent religious authorities hostile to Jesus. They reject all testimony to the truth that Jesus comes from God, and they are the ones responsible for his death.

Signs and Faith in the Fourth Gospel

The symbolic perspective influences John's account of miracles (see the NAB introduction to John, p. 1467). Taken literally, they cannot lead a

Miracles are sometimes seen as events that transcend the ordinary laws of nature or even all the laws of nature. The Bible presents the marvelous or wonderful elements of miracles for a reason. God is active throughout our lives and history, but a miracle is an event in which God's participation is made clear to everyone.

Some modern scholars have dismissed the Gospel miracles as later additions to the original Gospel preaching. Their premise is that miracles just don't happen in the real world, so the miracles of Jesus must be made up. This position ignores Jesus as the unique manifestation of God. Though using miracles as a way of proving Jesus' identity misses the main point of the Gospel miracle stories, those stories must, nonetheless, be seen as authentic memories of the extraordinary presence of God in the ministry of Jesus.

person to faith (2, 23–25), but seen as signs pointing to Jesus' identity with God, his "glory" (2, 11), they may serve as the beginning point for faith. John embeds four of the miracles in discourses, which interpret their symbolic meaning. The symbols of life, light, and bread point to Jesus as the source of eternal life for all who believe.

Dualism in the Fourth Gospel

The Gospel uses a number of dualistic or opposite expressions, such as light/dark, life/death, from above (heavenly)/from below (earthly), not judged/condemned. They show a process of division that occurs within the story. Persons confronted with Jesus' word either believe and become children of God who will inherit eternal life, or they reject Jesus and are condemned by God. This dualism gives John a certain harshness. There is no middle ground between belief and unbelief (12, 44–50). Believers are united with Jesus and the Father. They may even experience the larger world as hostile (15, 1–27). Dualistic imagery and a negative picture of the nonbelieving world often appear in sectarian groups.

Belief and Eternal Life

Christians usually think of salvation or eternal life as a reward that comes in the future when they join Jesus in heaven (14, 2f; 17, 24) or when Jesus returns to judge the world (5, 27–29). John retains this traditional language but introduces a new perspective on salvation. Belief brings persons into unity with Jesus. Therefore, they can be spoken of as already having passed through death to life

(5, 24–26; 3, 16–21). Those who reject Jesus are already condemned. Judgment really occurs when Jesus, who has come into the world as light, is accepted or rejected. Though various sources provide testimony—John the Baptist, Scripture, and the deeds which Jesus does—the believer must accept Jesus' word about God. Only Jesus comes from heaven to reveal God (3, 31–36).

Jesus as God in the Fourth Gospel

The Gospel presents Jesus as "from above" by identifying him with the Word, which is always present to God and through which God created the world (1, 1–5). John defends the claim that Jesus is equal to God in functional terms: (1) Jesus makes God known; (2) Jesus exercises functions attributed to God, giving life and judging; and (3) humans ought to respond to Jesus with the honor appropriate to God. John also emphasizes the special Father/Son relationship between Jesus and God. Jesus is obedient to the mission the Father has given him. Jesus' death will be a sign of God's love for humanity. The disputes between Jesus and "the Jews" (ch 5–12) turn on the issue of Jesus' relationship to God. This section ends with the ironic fact that Jesus' opponents seek to kill the source of life.

An Outline of John

The plot of the Fourth Gospel follows a pattern of descent into the world and ascent to glory. Jesus comes into the world from the Father seeking "his own," those who will believe.

Then, Jesus confronts the world. His ministry divides believers from unbelievers. The hostility of unbelief leads to the "hour" of his crucifixion, which John treats as an exaltation. Jesus then returns to the glory that he had enjoyed with the Father from the beginning. The Gospel is clearly divided into two parts: first, the account of Jesus' confrontation with the world, which many scholars refer to as the book of Signs (ch 1 through 12); and second, the account of Jesus' return to the Father when the destined hour arrives, referred to as the book of Glory (ch 13 through 20).

• Prologue (1, 1–18). A hymnic section introduces us to Jesus as God's Word, which has come into the world.

• The book of Signs (1, 19—12, 50). Jesus' confrontation with the world represents God's judgment against unbelief. This section falls into two parts:

Gathering witnesses to Jesus (1, 19—4, 54).

Jesus demonstrates his glory to disciples and others who will believe in him before the confrontation with unbelief begins.

Confrontation with the world (5, 1—12, 50). The light (Jesus) comes into the world for judgment. He confronts those who refuse to believe with testimony to his divine origin.

• The book of Glory (13, 1—20, 31).

Jesus' whole life has been moving toward the hour of his glorification and return to the Father. This section falls into two parts:

Preparing the disciples for the hour (13, 1—17, 26). At the Last Supper, Jesus delivers lengthy discourses about his return to the Father and its meaning for the disciples.

Jesus' arrest, crucifixion, and resurrection (18, 1—20, 31). John understands the crucifixion as the moment of Jesus' life-giving exaltation and return to the Father.

• Epilogue: Resurrection Appearance in Galilee (21, 1–25). The second conclusion reports further appearances of Jesus and points toward the destiny of two leading disciples, Peter and the Beloved Disciple.

The Prologue (1, 1–18)

A Hymn to the Divine Word

The introduction to John is different from all of the other Gospels. It begins even before creation. John might even be following the opening words of Genesis 1, in which God creates the world out of formless chaos by speaking. Because of Jesus, John has a new insight about the divine Word. The Word is not simply speech or some abstract power that God can use to create. The Word actually became known to us in a person, Jesus. This is the Incarnation—God becoming human. This idea of God is the special revelation of Christianity. It differs from the monotheism of Judaism and Islam, which insists that the unity of God cannot be shared. The Christian claim that Jesus can be spoken of as God is at the core of the controversies in the Fourth Gospel. John makes it clear right at the beginning that we can speak about God under two distinct aspects: God as the ultimate source of all things (i.e., the Father) and as the Word, through whom God creates and sustains the world and guides humans (i.e., the Son). Later in the Gospel we will also learn that the Spirit comes from God to those who believe. Christians believe that the Father, Son, and Spirit are three distinct persons that make up the one God.

Notice that many of the verses in this section have a poetic quality made up of short parallel lines that use the symbols of life, light, darkness, and glory. Also notice that other verses speak of the role of John the Baptist as witness to the light (1, 6–8.15). Still other verses speak in the first person plural of what "we" have received from the coming of the light (vv. 12.14b.16). "We" clearly means the Christian community that believes in Jesus. They have received the power to become children of God thanks to Jesus (v. 12). Many scholars think that the poetic verses belonged to an early hymn, which John has used for the introduction. The NAB prints these verses in a poetic form so that you can distinguish them from the prose comments that the author inserted to create the introduction.

Salvation, a Gift from the Word

This section makes it clear that only those people who receive Jesus as the incarnate Word can attain salvation. The Word actually existed before anything was created, but people may still fail to receive the Word when it comes to them. The Prologue contains several hints about the fate of the light when it comes into our world. People who should receive Jesus, do not. But those who do, receive the grace of becoming children of God and coming to know God as revealed by Jesus. The contrast between the Law that came through Moses and the "grace and truth" that comes through Jesus, probably meaning the Hebrew expression for God's love and fidelity to the covenant, anticipates the conflict between Jesus and the Jewish leaders. Jesus will establish a new covenant between God and those people who come to believe in him.

The Book of Signs (1, 19—12, 50)

John uses the word "signs" to emphasize the symbolic role of Jesus' miracles in pointing to Jesus' true, divine origin. To understand the truth revealed by the signs, a person must think of their symbolism, not of the literal words or events. "The Jews" will be portrayed as persons who are unable to see the symbolic truth of Jesus' words.

Gathering Witnesses to Jesus (1, 19—4, 54)

The Prologue told us that the Baptist was sent to testify to Jesus. He opens this section with that testimony (1, 19–34). Although there are hints of hostility to come, the first four chapters are generally positive. Jesus gathers followers who believe in his divine mission.

John Testifies to Jesus (1, 19–34)

The Baptist testifies on different occasions to two different groups of officials that he himself is not the Messiah. He is simply preparing the way for the one who is coming (1, 19–28). The Synoptic Gospels contain a scene in which Jesus is baptized and hears God announce that he is God's beloved Son (see Mk 1, 9–11). Jesus has no need of such a revelation in the Fourth Gospel. The evangelist transforms the traditional scene into another example of testimony about Jesus. The Baptist sees the Spirit descend from heaven like a dove and remain on Jesus. God has given him that sign to identify the Messiah, who will baptize with the Spirit and will take away the sin of the world (1, 29–34).

Titles of Jesus

Besides the titles used in this section, Jesus gives himself other names in this Gospel that reveal his identity and mission:

Bread of life 6, 35

Light of the world 8, 12

Gate for the sheep 10, 7

Good shepherd 10, 11

The vine 15, 1

    He also calls himself "the resurrection and life" (11, 25) and "the way and the truth and the life" (14, 6).

Jesus Gathers Disciples (1, 35–51)

A series of brief scenes shows us how Jesus gathered the rest of his disciples. They follow a set pattern. Persons who come to Jesus through the testimony of others have their own experience with Jesus, which makes them true disciples. The Baptist sends Jesus the first disciples (vv. 35–37). Notice that this chapter contains many of the titles that early Christians used to speak of Jesus: Lamb of God (v. 36); Messiah (v. 41); the one predicted by Moses and the prophets (v. 45); Son of God (v. 49); King of Israel (v. 49); and Son of Man (v. 51). The final verse is very enigmatic. It hints at the story of the ladder, which Jacob saw in a dream vision (Gn 28, 12). But Jesus as the heavenly figure, the Son of Man, has replaced the ladder. According to John, no one sees God except through Jesus (see 1, 18).

Cana Miracle Manifests his Glory (2, 1–12)

Now that he has gathered the disciples, Jesus' first miracle reveals his divine glory to them. The real revelation of Jesus' glory, however, cannot come until the crucifixion. Therefore, Jesus first appears to reject his mother's request (vv. 4f). A wedding feast was often used as a symbol for the time of rejoicing that would follow God's judgment. Jesus has provided the wine for such a feast. We will see that Jesus replaces some of the most important Jewish feasts and customs.

Christians no longer follow traditional patterns of worship. Here, Jesus replaces the water, which was to be used for ritual purification.

Cleansing of the Temple (2, 13–25)

Unlike the Synoptic Gospels, which include only one visit to Jerusalem in Jesus' ministry, John has three different Passover visits as well as episodes during other feasts. The other Gospels link the cleansing of the Temple with the Passover of Jesus' death. John puts that episode much earlier. It enables him to tell the Christian reader that Jesus will also replace the Temple. The evangelist reminds readers that Jesus' disciples could not have understood the saying until after the resurrection (2, 22). The end of the chapter warns against faith that is based simply on miracles (vv. 23–25). Many attracted by Jesus' miracles will not remain faithful.

Dialogue with Nicodemus (3, 1–21)

The next two dialogues, with Nicodemus and with the Samaritan woman, both use the technique of misunderstanding in which the person to whom Jesus speaks takes Jesus' words literally and thus provokes further comment from him. Jesus always responds with an even more difficult statement than the one that provoked the original misunderstanding. In this case, Jesus' words appear to leave Nicodemus behind, but he will reappear as someone sympathetic to Jesus (7, 50–52). Since Jewish writings of the period also speak of a cleansing of the righteous by the Holy Spirit, Nicodemus might have been expected to understand that Jesus was speaking about a rebirth "from above," that is, through the Spirit rather than "again" (see note to 3, 3). John's Christian readers probably saw a reference to baptism in the insistence that people had to be reborn to enter the Kingdom. The episode marks a clear distinction between the teacher of Israel who cannot understand the idea of spiritual rebirth, and Jesus who is, in fact, the very source of life.

A sudden shift to the plural "we" and "you people" echoes the confrontation between Christians and their synagogue opponents in the evangelist's time (v. 11). Verses 12–15 follow a pattern similar to 1, 50f. Belief on the grounds of some "earthly" sign is challenged by the heavenly reality, which is to be revealed in Jesus. In both cases a saying about the Son of Man represents the higher truth. Drawing upon the story of Moses lifting up a bronze serpent in the wilderness (Nm 21, 9), the evangelist asserts that Jesus will have to be lifted up (on the cross) to become a source of eternal life for all believers. Verses 16–21 speak to the Christian reader about the coming of Jesus. Elsewhere in the Gospel, "world" is a negative symbol for those who are hostile to the Word. Here the world refers to all humans as the object of God's love. The passage offers one explanation for the tragic fact that people will prefer darkness to light; they would rather hide their evil ways than "live the truth," a Semitic expression for following the will of God revealed in the Law.

Jesus and John the Baptist (3, 22—4, 3)

John once again testifies to Jesus as the one to come. The saying about the Bridegroom appears in the Synoptic Gospels as part of an exchange over fasting. John's disciples fast while Jesus' do not (see Mk 2, 18–19). In John's Gospel the emphasis lies on the identity of the two men. The Baptist's role ends once he has given witness to Jesus. Verse 27 points to the importance of grace

---

Samaritans The animosity between Jews and Samaritans was long-standing. The books of Kings pass a consistently negative judgment on the northern kingdom of Israel for its infidelity to the Jerusalem Temple and the true worship of the LORD. Those who lived in the territory of the northern kingdom after the fall of the North at the hands of Assyria were non-Israelites settled there by the Assyrian overlords. These foreigners intermarried with the few Jews not carried into exile and adopted Jewish religion but mixed it with their own polytheism. Even after the Hebrew nation was restored under Ezra and Nehemiah, the Samaritans were considered outsiders and never assimilated. The mutual hatred was so great that when Jews traveled, they would take routes that bypassed Samaria even though that meant many extra miles of travel.

in the Gospel: no one can have anything that God has not given to that person. Verses 31–36 seem to be the evangelist's summary of the entire chapter. The contrast between the "one from heaven," who testifies to the truth and speaks the words of God, and those who belong to earth, who reject the Son, once again demonstrates that the coming of the Son also brings judgment (v. 36b).

The Samaritan Woman (4, 4–42)

John has divided this story into a series of scenes that gradually reveal the truth about Jesus and his mission. Jesus comes to be known as greater than the patriarch Jacob, who met his future wife at a well. Jesus is more than a messiah figure who would vindicate the Jews by exalting Jerusalem. Jesus is more than the prophet whom the Samaritans expected to establish their version of the Law and place of worship against the claims of their Judean neighbors. We know that when Jesus speaks of a gift of living (i.e., flowing) water, he speaks symbolically of the gift of the Spirit (3, 8). The woman persists in treating Jesus' words literally until Jesus' reference to her marital status persuades her that Jesus is a prophet. When Jesus responds to her challenge to settle the old dispute between Jews and Samaritans over where to worship God by speaking of worship in "spirit and truth," Jesus is alluding to himself as the replacement of the Temple (see 2, 13–22). The woman finally accepts Jesus as Messiah. Like the disciples in chapter 1, she puts that insight into action by bringing others to Jesus (v. 29).

Jesus' dialogue with his disciples about mission and harvest (4, 31–38) indicates that, like the woman, they too are sent to preach to others. Along with the previous episode, in which Jesus was said to be baptizing more people than John the Baptist, this story makes it clear that Jesus was able to convert people with his preaching. The hostile controversies of the next section might otherwise give the impression that Jesus' mission was largely a failure. The large numbers of Samaritans who come to Jesus indicate the truth of Jesus' words to the disciples about the rich harvest. The story concludes with the ringing affirmation that Jesus is "Savior of the world."

Healing the Royal Official's Son (4, 43–54)

The section on gathering followers concludes with a second miracle in Cana. Jesus' word spoken at a distance is enough to heal the official's son (4, 53).

Now that Jesus' identity as the Son sent from God to save the world has been established, we are ready for the confrontation between Jesus and those who do not believe.

Confrontation with the World (5, 1—12, 50)

The sharp confrontation with unbelief that makes up this section of the Gospel does not represent failure, because it leads to the hour of Jesus' exaltation and return to the Father. Jesus succeeds in gathering those persons who believe his words despite all the obstacles that others put in their way.

Healing on the Sabbath: Jesus Gives Life and Judges (5, 1–47)

The tradition that Jesus provoked hostility among religious leaders by healing a paralyzed man on the Sabbath and associating that healing with the forgiveness of sins is well known (see Mk 2, 1–12). John uses the discourse that follows the miracle story to draw out the real issue: Jesus' claim to equality with God (5, 16–18). Opposing teachers could appeal to the Law of Moses to argue that no human being can claim to do things which are God's alone, to give life to the dead and to judge (see notes to 5, 21.22). Jesus defends his right to give life and to judge by appealing to the special relationship he enjoys with God. As Son, Jesus does what the Father has given him to do. He does not act on his own authority (v. 30). Furthermore, those who question his behavior should look to the witnesses he can bring forward: the Baptist (vv. 31–35), the deeds that God has enabled him to do (v. 36), and the witness that God has given through Scripture (vv. 37–39). Jesus accuses his opponents of failing to recognize that he is from God because they are not really concerned with the glory that belongs to God. They are only interested in the human glory they receive from other people. He warns them that their confidence in Moses is misplaced. Moses witnesses to Jesus and will condemn anyone who rejects that testimony (vv. 40–47).

Jesus Is the Bread from Heaven (6, 1–71)

Chapter 6 is based upon a traditional cycle of material that included the feeding of the multitude, calming the storm at sea, a demand that Jesus give people a sign, a challenge to Jesus based on his human origins, and Peter's confession of faith in Jesus as Messiah. John reshapes this material by including a lengthy discourse on Jesus as the bread of life, which has come down from heaven (vv. 22–59). Those who fail to see the symbolism of the feeding miracle or who focus on earthly facts about Jesus will not receive Jesus as the bread of life. Just as Jesus had promised the Samaritan woman a gift of water that would lead to eternal life, he promises bread that will give life to the believer. But "the Jews" are going to copy the behavior of their ancestors, who murmured against Moses. John explains that those who do come to believe in Jesus have been brought to him by God (vv. 37–39.44f). The comment that Jesus will not cast out those who come to him (v. 37) probably refers to the members of John's church who had been expelled from the Jewish community by officials. That experience is prefigured in the story of the blind man (9, 22).

Jesus' words are the source of eternal life in the first part of the discourse. Christian tradition associates the manna and the "bread of life" with the Eucharist. This tradition appears in 6, 51–59. It is necessary to eat the life-giving bread and wine, the flesh and blood of Jesus. This meal establishes a special relationship between Jesus and the believer: They "abide in" one another. Just as the Father is the source of Jesus' life, so Jesus becomes the source of life for the Christian. According to John, receiving eternal life is not the result simply of thinking that Jesus is God's Son. It really involves an entirely new relationship with God that is possible in Jesus. John 6, 51–58 places the Eucharist at the center of that relationship. If Jesus' words about eating his flesh and blood were taken in too literal a fashion by his audience, they would consider it to be a blasphemous participation in a human sacrifice. The flesh and blood are real means of participating in the life that Jesus shares with God. Even if Jesus' audience understood that Jesus was speaking symbolically, they might be horrified at the idea that Jesus could identify himself with God so closely. Indeed, these words were too difficult for many to accept.

Conflict and Division at the Feast of Tabernacles (7, 1—8, 59)

The episodes in this section occur at the Feast of Tabernacles and at an unnamed feast that follows it. The symbolism of light and water were part of the Tabernacles ritual, and Jesus uses them to express his identity (7, 37–39; 8, 12). Throughout the section we are reminded that officials are seeking Jesus' death even when they deny that fact (7, 1.19f.25; 8, 39f). Jesus is accused of "leading the people astray." He is also accused of being possessed by a demon. Several scenes picture the divided opinion among the crowd. These scenes may also provide answers to Jewish objections against Jesus:

1. Jesus did not keep the Law in healing on the Sabbath, but the Law permits activities like circumcision on the Sabbath (7, 19–24);

2. Jesus' origins make it impossible for him to be the Messiah, yet Jesus' real origins are "from heaven," and the signs he has done testify to that fact (7, 25–31.40–44);

3. Jesus is not an established teacher of the Law, yet Jesus has received his words and teaching from God so that he does not seek personal glory as human teachers do (7, 15–18).

Jesus begins to prepare the reader for his departure. He speaks of it in a symbolic way, which the crowd cannot fully understand. Jesus will go to a place where they cannot follow him (7, 32–36). The crowd thinks that Jesus will go to the Jewish communities outside Palestine. There is a symbolic truth in that statement: Christianity will spread in those communities. Or, perhaps, Jesus intends to commit the blasphemous act of killing himself (8, 21f). The ironic truth of that statement is that Jesus will give up his life on behalf of others. He predicts that when his enemies have executed him, they will find that Jesus is the one who comes from the Father. Jesus even bears the divine name *I AM* (8, 28). The bitter conflict between Jesus and the Jewish leaders in chapter 8 repeats this

God's Mercy Revealed

In this story Jesus discredits the commonly held belief that physical suffering was the result of sin. Neither the man nor his parents sinned, Jesus says. His blindness was an opportunity for God's power and mercy to be revealed.

identification of Jesus with God's *I AM* in a dispute over his descent from Abraham. Those who seek to kill Jesus cannot be descendants of Abraham, because what Abraham saw and rejoiced in was Jesus. Therefore, they are branded children of Satan (8, 39–59). The story acknowledges the difficulty of Jesus' words. He is asking us to identify a human being with the God revealed to Abraham and to Moses.

The Blind Man Believes in Jesus (9, 1–41)

This story shows that it was possible for the blind man to move from the miracle by which Jesus restored his sight to true faith in Jesus. He does so as the religious authorities pressure him to condemn Jesus. He comes to recognize more and more clearly that Jesus cannot be a sinner and therefore Jesus must have come from God. The fear that "Jews" (authorities) will drive them out of the synagogue keeps the man's parents from testifying (9, 22f). This story may represent the experience of members of the Johannine community. Jesus returns at the end of the story to show the man his identity and condemn the blindness of the Jewish leaders (vv. 39–41).

True Shepherd Gives his Life (10, 1–42)

We already know that Jesus' death is an expression of God's love for the world (3, 16). Religious authorities have said that Jesus deserves death for leading people astray (7, 45–52). Here, parables of the shepherd and his sheep demonstrate that Jesus is the true leader of the people, at least for those whom God has enabled to respond to his call (10, 1–30). Jesus will even give his life for the sheep, something that none of the hired hands who claim to lead the people will do.

Shepherds In first-century Palestine shepherds tended their flocks without dogs. The sheep knew the voice of the shepherd and responded only to that voice. Sheep were often herded together into a common pen with other flocks, but when a shepherd called his flock, only those sheep that belonged to him would come out.

Offended by his claim to identity with the Father (vv. 30–39), the crowd again tries to stone Jesus. We are reminded that Jesus' death is a free offering on his part, not a victory for those allied against him (vv. 17f).

Raising Lazarus: Gift of Life Means Death (11, 1–57)

John has used the raising of Lazarus to bring out the irony of what the religious leaders are seeking to do. Jesus is the source of life (vv. 24–26), yet they think that they can silence Jesus by killing him. The Lazarus episode also serves to remind Christians that if they truly believe that Jesus is resurrection and life, then they should not mourn physical death as others do. Jesus often seems remote from others, but here Jesus displays his love for Lazarus and his sisters. Ironically, the following that Jesus gained from his greatest sign led to the formal decision of the Jewish Council to arrange his death (11, 45–57). Although the high priest does not know the truth of his words, it will turn out to be a good thing that one person dies for the people, and, as the evangelist points out, for all the peoples of the world (vv. 50–52).

The Light is Departing (12, 1–50)

John locates the traditional story of Jesus' anointing at Bethany (Mk 14, 3–9) in the home of Lazarus and identifies the anonymous woman as his sister, Mary. She recognizes the approach of Jesus' death. Hints of the future Christian mission are evident in the Pharisees' response to the entry "the whole world has gone after him" (v. 19) and the coming of some Greeks to seek Jesus. Their arrival marks the hour of Jesus' death. He prophesies that when he is lifted up on the cross, he will draw all people to himself (vv. 20–32). The book of Signs concludes with reflections on the tragedy of disbelief (vv. 39–43 and 44–50).

The Book of Glory (13, 1—20, 31)

We already know that Jesus offers his life out of love; that Jesus' crucifixion is the moment of his exaltation and return to the Father; and that this death is the source of eternal life for all who believe and the manifestation of a new relationship between believers and God. The truth about Jesus' death lies in the revelation that occurs on the cross, not in the plots of Jesus' enemies.

The Supper Discourses (13, 1—17, 26)

Jesus prepares the disciples for the events to come, as well as their future life as a community of believers. The foot-washing not only reflects the service Jesus is about to perform in his death, it also sets a pattern for relationships among disciples. They are going to be the ones sent to represent Jesus and must follow the model given by their teacher (13, 1–20), being a servant as Jesus is to them. John has never let us forget that one of Jesus' disciples, Judas, does not really belong to Jesus. He is the agent of God's purpose even though he is in the grip of Satan (6, 70f; 12, 4–6; 13, 2.11.21–30; 17, 12). Throughout this section, the evangelist reminds us that the disciples understood the significance of what Jesus said and did only after he had been glorified (13, 7; 14, 29; 16, 4.25). As Judas is about to depart, a new character, the Beloved Disciple, appears in the narrative. He is closer to Jesus than any other disciple (13, 23) and will show special insight into events of the Passion and resurrection. The Johannine community revered the Beloved Disciple as the source of its tradition.

The discourses in 13, 31—17, 26 may have been composed as independent units. John 13, 36–14, 31 treats the disciples' grief, Jesus' departure and return, and the coming of the Advocate. Jesus also promises to return to the disciples to dwell within them along with the Father (14, 20). John 16, 4b–33 also deals with the disciples' grief, Jesus' departure and return, and the coming of the Advocate. It lacks the development of the return theme, however, as the mutual indwelling of Father and Son. John 15, 1—16, 4a encourages the disciples to remain united with Jesus the true vine and to love one another. This unity may be severely tested, because the disciples must also expect hatred, persecution, and even death from the world (15, 18—16, 4a). Finally, John 17, 1–26 contains a prayer in which Jesus speaks to the Father about the disciples he is leaving behind. They are the evidence that Jesus has completed the task he was sent into the world to accomplish (17, 6–11a). Left in the world, the disciples are no more "of the world" than Jesus, but without Jesus they require God's protection (17, 13–19). As the Father sent him,

so Jesus is sending the disciples into the world. The prayer looks beyond the immediate community of disciples to the community that will be the result of their preaching. Jesus expresses a vision of Christian community that runs throughout these discourses. The community is to express the love and unity, which has its source in the love and unity that exists between the Father and the Son (17, 20–26).

Mutual love and unity grounded in their vision of God are the focal points of the discourses. You may have noticed that the only explicit commandment given in the Fourth Gospel is the command to love one another (13, 34f). This love expresses the love of God (14, 21.23f; 17, 23) and of Jesus for "his own" (13, 1; 14, 21b; 15, 11–15). These discourses also suggest that mutual love and unity will be severely tested. The disciples do not yet fully understand what Jesus has revealed to them. The Advocate, who comes from God, must continue the process of bringing understanding to the community (14, 25f; 16, 13–15). Hatred and persecution from outsiders may also take their toll, as the synagogue exclusion apparently did. The Advocate will help the disciples who have to stand trial (15, 26f) and convict the world of its unrighteousness and sin (16, 8–11). The community may not remain in

---

The Trial of Jesus

There are differences in the four evangelists' descriptions of Jesus' trial.

- Only John records a hearing before Annas (18, 13–23).

- All four mention the hearing before Caiaphas (Mt 26; Mk 14; Lk 22; Jn 18).

- Only the synoptics record the hearing before the Sanhedrin (Mt 27; Mk 15; Lk 22).

- All recount the trial before Pilate (Mt 27; Mk 15; Lk 23; Jn 23).

- Only in Luke is the Pilate trial interrupted by an appearance before Herod (Lk 23), after which the Pilate trial resumes.

the "name of God," which Jesus has revealed (17, 11). If you read 1 John, you will see that the Johannine churches suffered serious internal divisions. These discourses remind us that Jesus' revelation of God's love is the foundation of Christian unity.

Jesus' Arrest, Crucifixion, and Resurrection (18, 1—20, 31)

Throughout his Passion, Jesus remains in complete control of his destiny. Jesus himself lays down his life; others do not take it from him. When Jesus identifies himself with the name *I AM*, used of God in the Old Testament, all those who came to seize him fall to the ground (18, 1–14). Jesus confronts his accusers with the evidence of his public teaching. He demands that they bring evidence against him, which they are unable to do (18, 19–24). Jewish officials try to hand Jesus over to Pilate without a formal charge (18, 28–32). Consequently, the inquiry that Pilate conducts picks up the theme of kingship. John's use of double meanings throughout the Gospel has prepared us for the dialogue that follows. Jesus both denies any earthly kingship and assents to the title "King of the Jews" (18, 33–38). Nor are we surprised to find the soldiers' mockery turns Jesus into a king symbolically and then to see Pilate present the "king" to the Jewish people (19, 1–5).

When Jesus is presented as "king," the trial scene breaks out into vicious hostility. Pilate knows Jesus is innocent but can only speak to the Jewish officials and to Jesus with bitterness and sarcasm. He knows nothing about truth (18, 38). Jesus does not accept Pilate's claim to authority (19, 10f). Pilate is the one who fears the political power of others. He will give in to the threats of being denounced to Caesar and execute an innocent man. At the same time, he retaliates against those responsible by insisting that the charge read "King of the Jews." The chief priests demonstrate how far away from God they are by proclaiming that they have no king but Caesar (19, 12–22). The violent cruelty and bitterness of this scene show what brute force and political power are like when those in power have no awareness of their responsibilities toward God.

Pilate is interested only in asserting Roman control over the conquered Jews. The death of this obscure Galilean is of no concern to him.

His Bones Were Not Broken

The leg bones of crucified men were broken to speed up their death: Because they could no longer support their weight with their legs, they slumped and suffocated. The urgency reported here was due to the need to remove the bodies before sundown and the start of the Passover feast. Because Jesus was already dead, his bones did not need to be broken, though his side was pierced— fulfilling Scripture (Ex 12, 46; Zec 12, 10).

Details in the crucifixion scene, which fulfill passages of Scripture, demonstrate that everything is happening according to God's plan (19, 23f.28.33–37). Jesus provides for those faithful to him by entrusting his mother to the Beloved Disciple as "son" (19, 25–27).

Jesus' crucifixion and death are witnessed by friends and enemies alike. When Pilate releases the body to Joseph of Arimathea and Nicodemus for burial, we know that Jesus has really died and been buried according to accepted customs (19, 38–42). Consequently, Mary's reaction to discovering the tomb open is to conclude that "they" (possibly hostile authorities) have taken the body (20, 1f). Though the Beloved Disciple arrives at the tomb and is said to believe, all he and Peter discover are the grave wrappings in one pile and the face cloth rolled up in another place. The evangelist comments that they could not understand what had happened because they did not know the Scripture about Jesus' Resurrection (20, 9).

Mary of Magdala's encounter with the Risen Lord combines the old tradition of an angelic appearance to the women at the tomb, announcing the Resurrection, with the tradition that Jesus himself appeared to the women in the vicinity of the tomb (20, 11–18; see Mt 28, 1–10). As in the other tomb stories, Mary receives a message for the disciples. She is not to cling to the Lord but to announce Jesus' return to God. John's account puts the occurrence of all the events—Resurrection, ascent to the Father, and bestowing the Spirit on the disciples—on Easter. When Jesus appears among the disciples, the marks on his body prove that the Risen Lord is the one who had been crucified. The disciples are now officially sent to the world as Jesus had been, and they receive the promised gift of the Spirit, a sign that Jesus' mission has been completed (7, 39; 3, 34). Forgiveness of sins as an activity of the Spirit within the Christian community (21, 23) appears only here in John's Gospel, but it is familiar from the Synoptics (see Lk 24, 47; Mt 18, 18). First John presupposes some form of "forgiveness" available within the community (see 1 Jn 1, 8—2, 2; 5, 16f).

John creates a second episode from the tradition of Thomas's doubt. The demand for physical evidence is a sign of unbelief. Christians who have not seen and yet believed are the ones who are really blessed (20, 28f).

Epilogue (21, 1–25)

This chapter seems to have been added to the Gospel sometime after its completion (see NAB introduction to John). It elaborates on a tradition of Resurrection appearances in Galilee. The miraculous catch of fish has a parallel in the miracle associated with the calling of Peter in Luke 5, 1–11. This chapter focuses upon the two heroes: Peter, who inherited Jesus' role as shepherd, and the Beloved Disciple, who established the Johannine tradition. Peter had died a martyr's death. The Beloved Disciple lived a long time but has also died. Johannine Christians can look back upon that generation of disciples as faithful witnesses to Jesus.

Things We Have Learned
from John

John has presented a unique story of Jesus. Instead of collecting sayings and parables in which Jesus spoke about the Kingdom of God, the evangelist focuses attention on the special relationship between Jesus and God. We need to remember this special relationship between Jesus and God, because we can slip into thinking of Jesus as though he were just another human religious leader. If we think that way, then Jesus becomes something of a hero, someone could just as easily be replaced by another person whose life and message seemed more inspiring at another time in our lives. We need to

remember that Jesus is more than a great human being. Jesus is our revelation of God.

Jesus Is the Unique Son of God

No one can come away from this Fourth Gospel without recognizing that Jesus is identified with God. The Prologue described that relationship as the *Word,* which is always with God and through which God acts in the world. In the narrative, Jesus appears as the unique Son of the Father. The Son is the only one who can reveal the Father. Father and Son are united by a common love and the Son's obedience to everything the Father requires.

Salvation Comes through Belief in the Son

Salvation, which John usually describes as eternal life, requires belief in Jesus as God's Son. It cannot be delivered by human institutions such as those the Jewish leaders think will provide security. Salvation consists in a new relationship to God through Jesus. This relationship is open to anyone to whom God has given the grace to believe in Jesus. Sometimes we meet evangelical Christians who tell us that unless we accept Jesus Christ as our personal Lord and savior, we cannot be saved. They try to suggest that there is something wrong with the belief in Jesus that we have unless we go through the type of conversion experience typical of members of that church.

Reading the Gospel of John makes it clear that anyone who believes that his or her salvation has come through the revelation that Jesus brought has already accepted Jesus as Lord and Savior. That special relationship is what we mean when we talk about faith.

Jesus' Death Expresses God's
Love for Humanity

Jesus is not the victim of human injustice. Jesus chose to offer his life for others so that they could see God's love revealed on the cross. When we see God's love on the cross, we are reminded that God identifies with the lowly, suffering people of the world by joining with them. God does not approve of the injustice that creates such suffering. Jesus reminded Pilate that Jesus' death was an "offering" and not the triumph of Pilate's power. Christians must look for ways of identifying with and helping the suffering, rather than expecting God to act through the powers of the world.

Mutual Love and Unity in the Church Express the Love of God

The love shown by Christians is not simply an expression of a moral virtue. Christians always have the example of Jesus' love to follow. They also have the experience of the Father and Son dwelling in the community to inspire their efforts to achieve unity.

Questions for Discussion and Reflection
Group Sharing/Discussion

1. Name some of the differences between John and the synoptic Gospels (Matthew, Mark and Luke). What is the significance of these differences?

2. Jesus defines himself more than thirty times in John's Gospel as "I am . . . ."—I am bread, light, gate, the good shepherd, the resurrection, the way, the truth, the life, the vine, etc. Explore his meaning of "I am." Let different group members take one of these metaphors and describe what they think it signifies.

3. Discuss the meaning of "world," which occurs quite frequently in John, for example, John 2, 16–21, where it is use as a symbol.

4. John 3, 16, is famous on TV as a hanging banner in many sports events and may be the best-known verse in John. "For God so loved the world that he gave his only Son, so that everyone who believes in him may not perish, but may have eternal life." What does this mean?

5. Each person should tell what his or her favorite story in John is (e.g., Nicodemus, Woman at the Well, Cana, Man Born Blind, Lazarus, Feeding of the Multitude, etc.). Remember that John wrote to encourage faith in Jesus as the Son of God. Retell the story in your words accenting what happens to the faith of the person in the story.

6. Jesus places Eucharist in the center of the new relationship with God (6, 51–58). Jesus' words about eating his flesh and drinking his blood caused some of his followers to leave. What would his words mean if taken literally? If taken symbolically?

7. Why does John see the crucifixion as the hour of glory?

In Our Lives

1. In John the word "Jews" is symbolic. It is not an ethnic group. But it sounds like it is when you hear John's Passion read in the Good Friday liturgy. As a symbol both in Scripture and liturgy, it means all those who oppose Jesus, the powers of darkness. If you read John carefully, you meet many good Jews; also you realize that the term "Jews" has different meanings, but generally it refers to those who oppose Jesus. The Vatican has reminded Catholics that this error of taking "Jews" as an ethnic group is wrong and the cause of anti-Semitism over the centuries, and this is evil racism. Recount the many good Jews you meet in John and in life. What are some ways you can live out and be a witness against anti-semitism?

2. "Washing feet" was a most demeaning task for anyone in that society. Only Gentile slaves were called to perform this work. If there was no Gentile slave, then each washed their own feet. Take time to prepare a role-play of the drama of the washing of the feet (Jn 13, 1–38). After this, talk about Jesus' intentions in washing their feet and Peter's reluctance to let him. Notice that in John, Jesus washes feet but doesn't share the bread and wine as in the other Gospels. This gives serious significance to the washing of the feet as the way to be a disciple. How do we symbolically wash each other's feet in our own daily lives?

3. "Unless I wash you, you have no inheritance with me" (13, 8b) is the fifth time John has Jesus make an "unless" statement. Together they spell out John's vision of Christian identity (3, 3; 3, 5; 6, 53; 8, 24; 13, 8). Review these statements, having different people read them and explain their significance.

4. Reread 2, 13–25. The Temple, the place of worship, had become a marketplace, and Jesus exorcized this. How did Jesus' purging of the Temple become a threat to the people and the authorities? What message could this have today?

5. In John's Gospel, Mary requested the first miracle at Cana; the Samaritan woman was the first convert and disciple; Mary of Magdala, a follower from the beginning, was the first witness of the risen Lord. In a patriarchal culture does John have a message here? What might this remind us of?

6. What is the only commandment in John's Gospel (13, 34f)? Discuss whether this is the only commandment you need.

Individual/Personal Reflection/Action

1. The Samaritan Woman's "Come and see" (4, 1–43) echoes Jesus' words to his first disciples. Why does John put Jesus' words on the lips of the Samaritan woman? Carefully, reread the story and note the stages of conversion you see in the dialogue. Compare this to the stages of conversion of the man born blind (9, 1–41). This takes time, but it will nourish your understanding of your own stages of faith.

2. When you see the cross, are you reminded that God chose to identify with the lonely, suffering people of the world? Meditate on what you see in the cross. What does this say to you?

3. The supper discourses of Jesus (13, 1–17.26) are to prepare the disciples for their mission. They suggest also that their mutual love will be tested. But they remind us that Jesus' revelation of God's love is the foundation of Christian unity. Reflect on these passages. How can they nourish your own mission in life? Let them deepen your conviction that Jesus is God's revelation of love and the foundation of the mission.

ACTS READING GUIDE

At a Glance

Who are the main players?	Peter Stephen Philip Paul Cornelius James Timothy Barnabus Lydia Titus Apollos Felix Festus King Agrippa Luke
What should I look for?	How the Spirit-led church spreads from Jerusalem to Rome, the center of the empire.
	How the church thrived even during times of opposition, demonstrating its divine guidance.
	The defense of Christianity that runs through the book.
	The internal struggles present in and survived by the early church.
	The continuing presence of Lukan themes first seen in his Gospel: the work of the Spirit; the importance of prayer; the pervasive presence of joy; the significance of women, including Mary, the mother of Jesus
When did this take place?	Sometime after the destruction of Jerusalem and the Temple (A.D. 70), probably between A.D. 80 and 90. From the late second century onward, church tradition has held that Luke, the sometime companion of Paul and the author of the Gospel, is also the author of the book of Acts. He was a well-educated Syrian from Antioch who was himself a Gentile convert to Christianity. Luke addresses the book of Acts to Theophilus, the same individual to whom he addressed the Gospel and whose name means "one who loves God." But the book is also intended for all who love and fear God.
Where did these events occur?	In Jerusalem and various cities of what we now call the Middle East: Joppa, Antioch, Derbe, Lystra, Ephesus, Iconium, the island of Cyprus, Philippi, Thessalonica, Berea, Corinth, Athens, the island of Malta, Rome
Why was this book written?	To continue Luke's record of biblical or salvation history and to provide a historical account of the founding of the church.

To explain that the salvation brought by Jesus has been extended to Gentiles.

To demonstrate the working of the Holy Spirit in the life of the early church.

To assert that the spread of the gospel was accomplished through the apostles who were chosen by God and commissioned by Jesus.

What is the story?

The book centers on the preaching and ministry of Peter and Paul. After the Ascension, Peter begins to preach boldly and to work many miracles. Though initially he resists preaching the gospel to Gentiles, he eventually realizes that God wants all people to come to know Jesus. Paul, a devout and zealous Jew, at first persecutes the followers of Jesus until a miraculous encounter with the risen Jesus changes his life. He becomes a missionary preaching about Jesus throughout much of the Roman Empire. After the church is established in Jerusalem, conflicts arise with Jewish authorities that climax in the martyrdom of Stephen and the imprisonment of Peter. The gospel spreads throughout the Gentile world largely due to the efforts of Paul, Barnabas, and others. Internal conflicts arise but are resolved. The book ends with Paul imprisoned in Rome where he has witnessed to the gospel in the very heart of the empire.

Before Beginning

The Acts of the Apostles continues the story that began with Luke's Gospel. What began with Jesus' life did not end on Easter. God's plan requires another act: the gospel must spread beyond Jerusalem to all the peoples of the earth (Lk 24, 47; Acts 1, 8). Luke recounts the deeds of the first generation of apostles by which God took the movement out of the Galilean and Judean environment of its birth. He has not provided a detailed chronicle of everything that occurred during the period between the resurrection of Jesus and Paul's arrival in Rome (ca. A.D. 30–62). Peter disappears from the story once Paul's mission to the Gentiles is established as God's plan. Acts ends with Paul under benign house arrest in Rome, able to preach to visitors (28, 17–31). We hear nothing of the martyrdom of Peter and Paul there under Nero, although allusions show that Luke's readers are expected to know of Paul's death (20, 25; 21, 13).

A Story of God's Salvation

Acts has an unusual ending. One of its heroes is under arrest in Rome, and we never find out what

happens to him. As soon as you read Paul's letter to the Romans, you find out that he was not the first missionary to reach Rome. There was an established Christian community before he arrived (1, 8–15). Paul mentions a number of people associated with that church at the end of the letter (16, 1–16). Luke knew about these people. He mentions the fact that two famous missionaries, Aquila and Priscilla (Acts 18, 2; see Rom 16, 3f), had to leave Italy when the Emperor Claudius expelled Jews from Rome. Roman sources tell us that the cause was riots over the name of "Chrestus" (Suetonius, Life of Claudius 25). This event may have taken place as early as A.D. 40 (see note to Acts 18, 2). While Luke has not included all of the events in early Christian history that were known to his readers, he has adopted a literary style close to what the ancients would consider an "historical monograph." Unlike secular histories of great wars, lives of emperors, the founding of states, and the like, Luke has models for history writing in the Jewish Scriptures. Biblical history wants to show how God's plan of salvation worked out through special people and events. We use the expression "salvation history" for this type of writing.

Understanding Salvation History

How do we even know what God's plan is? You will see as you read the stories in Acts that even the disciples did not know what God intended. They had certain guideposts. The most important was what they knew about Jesus. Jesus had also told them in very general terms that a new stage in God's plan was about to unfold and that they would be an essential part of carrying it out. They also knew passages from the Old Testament that helped them understand how Jesus' life and death fit into God's plan. Luke makes it very clear, however, that even with these resources the disciples would not have been able to figure out God's plan in advance. God intervenes through the Holy Spirit at the critical turning points in the story.

Though God's intervention is crucial to salvation history, human beings are not manipulated like puppets. You will notice that the disciples in the story have to figure out the significance of the unusual experiences that happen to them during their mission. They pray to God for further assistance. They also discuss the events that have occurred as they prepare to take new steps in preaching the gospel. Their ability to look back on past examples of God's action helps them understand what God is doing in the present. Sometimes they might even have taken the wrong step if God had not intervened. Acts 16, 6–10 reports that the Spirit of Jesus actually caused Paul to change his travel plans in Asia Minor and then to go over to Greece. It was time for Paul to spread the word farther to the west.

Preaching in Acts of the Apostles

A large part of Acts, about one-fourth of the book, consists of sermons, 18 in all. These are Luke's reconstructions of sermons given by Peter, Paul, and other leaders of the early church. They are not verbatim reports, but they do communicate a good sense of the flavor and the content of the teachings of the early church.

The Plan of Salvation History in Acts

The book uses a geographical plan for the spread of the gospel. It begins where the ministry of Jesus had ended, in Jerusalem. Moving west, it comes to the center of the empire that embraced the whole circle of the Mediterranean: Rome. By the end of the book, Christianity is no longer confined to the band of followers in Jerusalem. Christian churches dot the empire. The map of Paul's missionary journeys in Acts shows that Paul touches the major cities along the roads and sea routes of his time (see Map 14).

As you read through Acts, you will also notice another feature of the early mission. The disciples preach first to Jews and then to Gentiles. Apollos is active in the synagogues (Acts 18, 26–28). Some of Luke's summaries refer to converts among both Jews and "Greeks," an expression used for non-Jews, or Gentiles, rather than purely for persons of Greek descent (see Acts 18, 10). But often the mission to non-Jews begins only when influential people in the synagogue turn the audience against the missionaries (see Acts 13, 44–52). Israel has first place in the plan of salvation. It receives another chance after the rejection of Jesus when the disciples begin to preach the gospel (see 3, 11–26). The pattern of rejection by Jews followed by enthusiastic reception on the part of Gentiles, makes us aware of a turning point in the story of salvation. The Hebrew Scriptures and the public ministry of Jesus told of God's dealings with Israel. From now on, the story of salvation would involve all the peoples of the world. Luke's pattern of Jews first, then Gentiles, also reminds us that Christianity is indebted to Judaism. That link is not a trivial cultural accident but part of the divine plan of salvation.

Reading through Acts

Before studying about Acts, read through the whole book. You will notice that there are some types of stories that occur again and again. The apostles are put in jail. They must make speeches before various courts and officials. Sometimes God rescues them from jail or another hostile action. Besides the legal speeches, Luke adds the drama of speeches that announce the gospel.

Often the apostles gain attention through miracles, which they are able to work in Jesus' name. Other times the apostles challenge the religious beliefs, superstitions, and magical practices of the Gentiles. As the gospel moves out from Jerusalem, these dramatic episodes fit into a pattern of journeys.

Acts as Entertainment

As Luke tells the story of God's plan of salvation, he provides the reader with a number of entertaining incidents (e.g., confusing Paul and Barnabas with pagan gods in Acts 14, 8–18). Persecutions, trials, imprisonments, journeys, and dramatic shipwrecks all had their counterparts in novels that were popular during this period. The novels usually had a romantic theme rather than a religious one, but the use of comparable tales reminds us that Acts provided readers with pleasure as well as instruction.

Acts and the Early Community

There appears to be great harmony among Christians in the early communities. We know from Paul's letters that the early churches were sometimes torn by dissent and often needed encouragement by the apostle to demonstrate in their actions the love that Christians were to show one another.

Luke knows that the early communities were not always perfect. Acts shows us how the churches *ought* to live together. It even shows us how Christians should work out difficulties that they face. They are never to forget that their purpose is to thank God for the salvation they have received and to preach the same message to others. There is no place for the love of money, for the jealousy, maliciousness, and deceitful behavior that those who persecute the apostles.

An Outline of Acts

• Preparation for the Christian Mission (1, 1—2, 13). This section includes all of the events between Easter and the first missionary sermon that Peter preaches on Pentecost.
    Waiting in Jerusalem (1, 1–14)
    Replacing Judas (1, 15–26)
    Pentecost, the Coming of the Spirit (2, 1–13)

• The Mission in Jerusalem (2, 14—8, 3)
    Two Sermons by Peter (2, 14—3, 26)
    Peter and John before the Sanhedrin (4, 1–31)
    Sharing Possessions in the Community (4, 31—5, 16)
    Trial before the Sanhedrin (5, 17–42)
    Deacons for the Hellenists (6, 1–7)
    Trial and Death of Stephen (6, 8—8, 3)
• Mission in Judea and Samaria (8, 4—9, 43). The gospel begins to spread into areas around Jerusalem.
    Philip Preaches Outside Jerusalem (8, 4–40)
    Conversion of Paul (9, 1–30)
    The Church Continues to Grow (9, 31–43)
• Inauguration of the Gentile Mission (10, 1—15, 35). These chapters set the stage for the mission of Paul by showing that the Gentile mission began from Jerusalem itself.
    Conversion of Cornelius (10, 1—11, 26)
    Paul's First Missionary Journey (11, 27—14, 28)
    Gentile Mission Confirmed in Jerusalem (15, 1–35)
• Paul's Mission to the Ends of the Earth (15, 36—28, 31). Paul now fulfills the mission that God gave him by carrying the gospel throughout the Roman Empire from Jerusalem to Rome itself.
    Second Missionary Journey (15, 36—18, 23)
    Third Missionary Journey (18, 24—21, 14)
    Paul's Arrest and Imprisonment at Jerusalem (21, 17—26, 32)
    Paul's Journey to Rome (27, 1—28, 31)

Read through each section of Acts in detail, looking to see how Luke describes the development of the early church. Even though the apostles do not always know where God is leading, they remain open to the Spirit. The apostles experience hostility and some deaths, but they never cease to tell people about Jesus. God has shown them that Jesus came to be the savior for all the nations of the world.

The Preparation for the Christian Mission (1, 1—2, 13)

Waiting in Jerusalem (1, 1–14)

Acts continues the story that Luke's Gospel had ended with Easter (Lk 24, 50–53). The New Testament refers to a number of different ap-

> **Casting Lots** This (1, 23–26) is the last time casting of lots is mentioned in the Bible. From Pentecost on, the disciples seek the guidance of the Holy Spirit for important decisions.

pearances by the Risen Lord (see 1 Cor 15, 3–7). Jesus did not continue to appear to his disciples indefinitely. Nor did he remain with them continuously as he had during his lifetime (see Jn 20, 19–29). Luke has used the biblical number of 40 to set a time frame for the appearance of the Lord (see note to Acts 1, 3). He insists that the risen Jesus is identical with the person who had died on the cross. Jesus' teaching during this interim period repeats the Kingdom theme of the gospel.

The disciples must wait in Jerusalem until the Holy Spirit comes on them as it had come on Jesus at the beginning of his mission (see Lk 3, 22). This event will mark the transition to a new phase of the salvation story—the age of the church. The Ascension (vv. 6–12) also marks a change in the idea of how God will bring salvation. Jesus has not gone to heaven so that he can return with divine power and set up God's kingdom in Jerusalem as some people thought (1, 6–7). After receiving the Holy Spirit, Jesus' disciples will become witnesses to Jesus throughout the world.

The apostles and other followers of Jesus, including his mother, Mary, and some other women, form the first community. Luke emphasizes the importance of prayer in the life of the church. Gathering for prayer and celebration of the meal together is one pillar of the church. We will see that the other is charity toward the poor.

Replacing Judas (1, 15–26)

The number of apostles has to be restored to Twelve. The Twelve represented the twelve tribes of Israel (see Lk 22, 30). The church was to become the new Israel (see note to 1, 26). By using lots to determine which of two candidates would take Judas's place, the early Christians are permitting God to have the final say in this decision. The qualifications for the candidates—that they followed Jesus from the beginning to

the end of his ministry—reflect Luke's understanding of the apostles as the "witnesses" who guarantee the validity of the gospel that is being preached in the churches (see Lk 24, 48; Acts 1, 8). Luke also takes this occasion to repeat a legend about the death of Judas (vv. 17–20; a different legend about Judas's death appears in Mt 27, 3–10). Peter uses Scripture to show that Judas's betrayal did not destroy God's plan. Judas's death reflects divine punishment for a person who has committed a blasphemous act against God.

Pentecost, the Coming of the Spirit (2, 1–13)

Fire and strong winds are typical elements in appearances of God (see notes to 2, 2f). The Greek translation of Isaiah 66, 15.18 says of God's coming: "For behold the LORD will come as a fire, with a flame of fire . . . I am coming to gather all the nations and tongues." The new turn in salvation history, represented by Acts, shows us that God is gathering the "nations and tongues" into one church through the Christian mission. Luke makes Pentecost a double miracle. Not only does the Spirit inspire the disciples' speech, but persons from different nations are able to understand their message. Pentecost anticipates the goal of the missionary effort that the Spirit will inspire in the Church.

The Mission in Jerusalem (2, 14—8, 3)

Two Sermons by Peter (2, 14—3, 26)

Luke follows a similar pattern in all of Peter's sermons. His Pentecost Sermon is the most famous (2, 14–36). It begins with the theme of prophetic fulfillment. The prophets anticipated a powerful outpouring of God's Spirit in the last days. Though the world is not ending, God has given that Spirit to the disciples. Peter uses several Old Testament quotations to demonstrate that the risen Jesus is the Messiah whom God had promised. God has established the crucified Jesus as Lord and Christ in heaven (v. 36).

Peter's speech has a profound impact on the crowd. The universality of the Christian mission is represented by these converts from the distant corners of the earth. Baptism is the rite though which the new converts receive forgiveness of sins and the gift of the Holy Spirit (2, 37–41). Acts 2, 42–47 describe the unity of the growing community. The fundamental elements of Christian community are presented: teaching, fellowship, breaking bread, and prayer.

Luke frequently uses miracles to provide evidence for the faith that people should have in Jesus. The healing of a crippled man (3, 1–10) provides the occasion for Peter's second speech (3, 11–26). Once again the speech is a brief telling of the salvation history, which has been fulfilled in Jesus. God's promise to Abraham has been realized in Jesus (3, 25f).

Peter and John before the Sanhedrin (4, 1–31)

This scene is the first of a number of trial scenes in Acts. A pattern is developed:

1. the miracle attracts attention;
2. the apostles teach those who have been attracted by the miracle;
3. arrest of the missionary by jealous (Jewish) officials;
4. trial of the missionary;
5. miraculous escape or vindication of the missionary.

At first, the trials are orderly. The judges take a moderate approach and only warn the disciples, but opposition to the Christian mission will increase until Stephen is murdered by an enraged mob. The apostles never claim any miraculous powers for themselves. Miracles are done in the name of Jesus (v. 10). All of the miracles have some connection with the mission to spread the gospel. Acts 4, 12 expresses the belief that motivates preaching the gospel throughout the world: "There is no salvation through anyone else, nor is there any other name under heaven given to the human race by which we are to be saved."

The communal prayer that follows the apostles' release (4, 23–31) shows that Christians never lost their confidence in God's power to rescue them from danger. What happened to Jesus, and will shortly happen to martyrs like Stephen, is not a defeat for Christians. God's plan for salvation can make use of such events. God responds to this prayer with a second Pentecost: The Holy Spirit comes to all who are present.

Sharing Possessions in the Community (4, 32—5, 16)

Christians demonstrate their care for one another by giving to the poor. The early church did not force members to renounce everything, as Peter and the others had done. Many would continue to own property and practice their trade. In this the church was different from groups like the Jewish sect called the Essenes, which expected members to turn over property to the sect as a condition of joining monastic-like groups. Essenes who lived in villages were required to turn over a set number of day's wages to the group's overseer. Ancient philosophers described the ideal relationship between friends as sharing all things in common. Acts depicts a Christian community that spontaneously fulfills such ideals.

Luke presents striking examples of generosity by persons who were willing to follow the sayings of Jesus, which encouraged people to sell all and become disciples (see Lk 12, 33; 16, 9.11.13). The story of Ananias and Sapphira provides an illustration—perhaps deliberately harsh to get the reader's attention—of what might happen to persons who attempt to pretend that they have the generosity of disciples while hiding money for their own use (compare the Rich Fool, Lk 12, 16–21). Once again, death is viewed as God's judgment against persons who have done something blasphemous. They were not required to sell the property to be part of the community. Their sin was in the attempt to deceive the Holy Spirit. Human beings can be taken in by fraud, but God will always know what is in a person's heart. No one can cheat God. We may refuse to follow these examples of Christians helping those in need. We may even devise a scheme to appear to help the poor while keeping more for ourselves, but if we do, we will have to answer to God.

Trial before the Sanhedrin (5, 17–42)

The miracles of the previous passage lead to jealousy and another imprisonment. This time we learn that no one could keep the apostles in jail if God wished them to continue preaching elsewhere. An angel takes them from prison to preach in the Temple area. This miraculous sign further enrages the opposition. The apostles are released thanks to Gamaliel, a Pharisee who demonstrates respect for God's plan (v. 39), but some people are now angry enough to kill the apostles (v. 33).

Deacons for the Hellenists (6, 1–7)

This passage presents several difficulties, because it does not fit with what follows. The distinction between Hebrews and Hellenists seems to be based on an individual's mother tongue. The Hellenists would be Jewish converts to Christianity who spoke Greek. The description of the Seven as persons who would take care of the distribution of food, so that the apostles could devote themselves to prayer and preaching, suggests that the Seven were to be like deacons in the church at a later date. They must oversee the material arrangements and aid to the poor. Verse 6 describes the process, prayer and laying on of hands, by which persons were installed in offices in the church during Luke's time. In the next episode (v. 8) the most famous of the persons chosen engages in ministry of preaching like Peter and the other apostles.

Trial and Death of Stephen (6, 8—8, 3)

This trial scene is the longest in Acts. Stephen emphasizes Israel's past failures. His speech prepares the reader for the mission to the Gentiles as it develops in the plot of Acts. Luke creates a link between Stephen and the hero of that mission, Paul, by picturing Paul—who tells us that he had persecuted the church out of zeal for ancestral tradition (see Gal 1, 13; 1 Cor 15, 9b; Phil 3, 6)—as a witness to Stephen's death (8, 1). Luke uses the Stephen episode to tie the beginning of a non-Jewish Christianity to the ministry of Jesus. The charges against Stephen (6, 13f) are similar to those brought against Jesus. False witnesses testify that Stephen attacks the Temple and the Law, and they predict that Jesus will destroy the Temple. The tradition that Jesus' predictions about the destruction of the Temple were brought into his Jewish trial is established in the Synoptic Gospels (see Mk 14, 58; Mt 26, 61; Mk 15, 29; Mt 27, 40). Luke omits this detail from the appearance of Jesus before the Council in his Gospel and places it here.

Predictions that God will destroy a corrupt Temple to establish one that is a holy place appear in the prophets (see Jer 7, 11; Zec 14, 21; Mal 3, 1; Is 56, 7). One Jewish sect (known as the Essenes) was severely critical of the corrupt priesthood and calendar used in the Temple. Their criticism stemmed from a concern for more exact observance of the Law. By contrast, the Stephen episode ties criticism of the Temple to an attack on the Law.

Later in Acts, similar suspicions will be voiced against Paul (see 22, 20f). Like Stephen, he will be seized on the grounds that he is attacking the Temple (sometimes referred to as "this place") and the Law. Two further charges are made against Paul. He speaks against the Jewish people, and he has committed a sacrilegious act by bringing a Gentile into the area reserved for Jews (22, 28). Luke's narrative shows that Stephen and Paul were not attacking the Law. Luke has shown that the Jerusalem Christians were constantly in the Temple praying. There is no basis for the accusations brought against either Stephen or Paul, just as there had been no basis for the charges against Jesus (see Lk 23, 4f.13–15.22).

Many interpreters have suggested that Luke is using the trial scenes here to defend Christianity against the suspicions of outsiders (see NAB introduction to Acts). Political insurrection, disregard for ancestral traditions, and acts of impiety like defiling a temple were terrible deeds, all of which could stir local as well as Roman officials to punish those guilty. The Roman authorities were particularly suspicious of groups that they thought might lead rebellion among the people of the empire. At the same time, the Romans protected sacred places and traditional religious practices. Special edicts from the emperor prohibited local officials from taking advantage of their Jewish population by taking money collected for the Temple in Jerusalem, forcing Jews to appear in court on the Sabbath, and such things. Christians were particularly suspect, because their religious practices were not the traditions of an ancient people. Luke may be attempting to answer this objection by demonstrating that Christianity is the true heir of the Jewish tradition. Stephen's speech (7, 2–53) recites salvation history to indict Israel for failure to obey God's commands. Such a speech would not be out of place in a Jewish context. One of the rule books of the Essene sect, The Damascus Document, begins in a similar way. It concludes that because Israel had been unfaithful, even though she had suffered punishment for various misdeeds, God had taken the promises away from the nation as a whole. They thought that only the small remnant of righteous Jews who made up the Essene sect would experience the blessings of salvation when the Messiah comes.

By implying that the audience shares hostility to God's prophets (vv. 51–53), Stephen fuels a rage that not only kills him, but also spawns persecution against other Christians. Because it scatters Christians outside Jerusalem (8, 1), this hostility indirectly furthers God's plan. Stephen's vision of the risen Lord exalted in heaven recalls a saying that Mark reports Jesus using before the high priest (Mk 14, 62). Visions of the heavenly Son of Man usually carry overtones of divine judgment in the New Testament (cf Rv 1, 7–18). Another similarity between the death of Stephen and that of Jesus is that Stephen dies peacefully with words of forgiveness on his lips (cf Lk 23, 34.46). There is one important difference. Jesus had prayed to God, the Father; Stephen addresses his prayer to Jesus whom he has seen standing at God's right hand.

Mission in Judea and Samaria (8, 4—9, 43)

Philip Preaches outside Jerusalem (8, 4–40)

The gospel begins to be spread outside Jerusalem to those who have some contact with Judaism: the Samaritans, who had their own version of the Law of Moses, and an Ethiopian, who was already interested in the traditions of the Jewish people. Several Lucan themes appear in this section. Philip's instruction about Isaiah (8, 30–35) shows that Jesus is the fulfillment of what is written in the prophets. Unlike the Jerusalem crowd who had turned a deaf ear to such arguments, the Ethiopian demonstrates the proper response: He becomes a disciple of Jesus by being baptized. This story also introduces a minor theme: Prominent people become Christians, listen to the apostles' preaching with sympathy, and often ask them to return or provide some other form of assistance.

The conversion of the Samaritans and the conflict with Simon the magician introduce two more themes: the continuity of the new Christian mission with the apostles in Jerusalem and the superiority of Christianity to all forms of pagan superstition and religion. The gift of the Holy Spirit defines Christian baptism for Luke (Acts 2, 38; 10, 48), who contrasts it with the water baptism of John the Baptist (Lk 3, 16; Acts 1, 5; 11, 16; 18, 25; 19, 3f). Christians are baptized in the name of Jesus. Baptism involves forgiveness of the past sins of a life without God, as well as receiving the Spirit. Acts 8, 16 departs from the normal pattern, because Philip has baptized in the name of the Lord, but his converts did not receive the Spirit until Peter and John came from Jerusalem to lay hands on them (8, 14–17).

This text has often been used as evidence to support the need for a second sacrament, confirmation, to confer the Spirit. Pentecostal Christians claim that persons who have not experienced the Spirit coming over them are not yet fully Christian. Neither development represents the view presented in Acts. Episodes in which the Spirit is separated from water baptism reflect unusual occurrences and not the norm. In the conversion of Cornelius (ch 10), the Spirit will indicate that God has accepted the new converts even before water baptism. Here, the separation between water baptism and receiving the Spirit allows Luke to show that the new mission takes place under the sponsorship of Jerusalem. Luke indicates that the Spirit always operates in and through the church.

The encounter with Simon the magician (sometimes called Simon Magus) allows Luke to address another possible objection to Christianity. Luke frequently uses miracle stories or references to miracle working to initiate interest in the Christian preaching. In the past, healings and other extraordinary events that occurred through assistance from a god or goddess might be called miracles, but a hostile bystander might accuse the miracle worker of being nothing more than a magician. The contest between Moses and the magicians at Pharaoh's court (Ex 7, 8f.12) provides a biblical pattern for evaluating magic. Even though they may duplicate some of Moses' miracles, no magician can duplicate or withstand the power that comes from the Lord. The conversion of Simon demonstrates the power of Christianity to destroy such superstitions. Luke mentions another common charge against religious charlatans: greed. The Christian mission is not driven by desire for money (3, 1–10). Christians sell property and share their possessions.

Conversion of Paul (9, 1–30)

Paul's conversion demonstrates God's power to use everything, even the hostile persecutor, to achieve the divine purpose. Paul himself tells us little about the call from God that transformed him from being an enemy of the Jesus movement to being its advocate (see Gal 1, 11–24). Luke presents the story of Paul's conversion three times (Acts 9, 1–19; 22, 4–16.17–21; 26, 12–18), with some differences. Each of the four accounts serves a purpose. Paul's own account in Galatians 1 belongs to an impassioned defense of his preaching to the Gentiles. He must show that, in telling them they could be saved through belief in Jesus without also taking on obligations of the Jewish Law, he is not distorting the gospel or breaking agreements made with Jerusalem. Acts 9 must vindicate Paul as the representative of God's offer of salvation to the Gentiles. The next two accounts (Acts 22 and 26) of Paul's conversion occur in speeches that Paul gives while imprisoned in Jerusalem.

Luke's accounts share a core of details: (a) letters from the high priest; (b) Saul is approaching Damascus; (c) light from heaven shines around Paul (and in #3, Acts 26, around those with him); (d) he (#3: we) falls to the ground; (e) hears a voice speaking to him (#3: in Hebrew); (f) "Saul, Saul, why are you persecuting me?" (#3: "hard for you to kick against the goad"); (f) Saul asks identity of speaker; and (g) "Jesus, whom you are persecuting." This core suggests a common story about Paul's conversion. After this point the three accounts diverge. Acts 9, 12–16 expands on the theme of Paul's blindness. Ananias comes to Paul as "healer" (note the emphasis on the cure in v. 18). Acts 22, 11a.12f gives a more abbreviated account, and Acts 26 omits these details altogether as it does the details about the actions of Paul's companions after the appearance, the visit of Ananias, and Paul's baptism. In Acts 9, 16, the Lord tells Ananias of Paul's commission. In Acts 22, 14f, Ananias gives the commission to Paul, but in 26, 16b–18, Paul receives the commission directly from the Lord.

The blinding/healing sequence in Acts 9, 12–19 suggests that the blinding of Paul is an act of God's displeasure similar to the temporary blindness God inflicts on the magician Elymas (Acts 13, 9–11). Paul's own version and the later stories in Acts emphasize Paul's commission, but this plays no role in the narrative about Paul. God uses it as an argument to persuade Ananias to go to Paul. Acts 9, 15 has been phrased so that it reflects the commission given the disciples in 1, 8. The ensuing versions of the story will relate the commission to Paul's vision of Christ and to the

details of his specific role in the Gentile mission as it has unfolded in Acts. Here, Luke uses the story of the miraculous conversion of the persecutor of Christianity to initiate the preparation for that global mission, which is the subject of this section of the book.

The Church Continues to Grow (9, 32–43)

Luke concludes the section with two stories from Peter's mission. The healing of Tabitha follows the same pattern as Jesus' own healing of the little girl, (see Mk 5, 41). Tabitha indicates the important roles that women believers play in the growth of Christianity. Not only is she an example of piety and charity, but she also has a group of poor widows who assemble in her home. This period of peace and growth shows that the community has successfully weathered the storm of persecution that began with Stephen's martyrdom.

Inauguration of the Gentile Mission (10, 1—15, 35)

Conversion of Cornelius (10, 1—11, 26)

Before Paul can fulfill his role as one who carries the gospel from Jerusalem to Rome, the leaders of the church must formally accept Gentiles into the Christian fellowship. The common meal was the basic expression of Christian unity. Paul reports an episode in which Jewish Christians from Jerusalem were unwilling to eat with the Gentile members of the Antioch church, presumably because they felt that such behavior would have violated the food laws that set Jews apart from other peoples. Paul says that before these people came, Peter himself was willing to share the meal with Gentile Christians, but that when the stricter Jewish Christians arrived, Peter, Barnabas, and other Jewish Christians began to celebrate a separate meal (see Gal 2, 11–14). Peter may have been attempting to preserve harmony in the church by not offending Jewish Christians who could not bring themselves to change a whole lifetime of kosher food laws. The story of how Peter came to accept Gentile converts, which Luke repeats here, bears traces of that old dispute. God directs Peter in a vision to renounce his former understanding of what represented clean and unclean food.

Christians The followers of Jesus were not always known as Christians. The name originated in Antioch (Acts 11,26) where Jews and Gentiles worshiped together in a single Christian fellowship for the first time. Before that believers were known variously as "the Way" (9, 2); "the sect of the Nazoreans" (24, 5), and other improvised names. The name "Christians" was probably given by outsiders and may have carried a derogatory connotation (see 26, 28).

Peter takes others with him to Cornelius's house so that he has witnesses to what has happened. His sermon acknowledges the fact that God is impartial. Anyone can receive salvation through Jesus if that person honors God and acts justly. The Spirit even demonstrates to Peter and the others that Gentiles are to be accepted into the church by granting Cornelius and his household a mini Pentecost before they are baptized (10, 44–48). Upon his return to Jerusalem, Peter gains official approval for his actions from the other leaders there. He reports everything that had happened in connection with the Cornelius episode so that those in Jerusalem agree, "God has then granted life-giving repentance to the Gentiles too" (11, 18).

The first church to include Jews and Gentiles in a single fellowship is founded by anonymous Christians in Antioch. Quickly, however, they obtain the services of two famous apostles, Barnabas and Paul. Barnabas is sent by the authorities in Jerusalem. He provides the link between Antioch and the church in Jerusalem (11, 19–26). Acts 11, 26 notes that the name "Christians" originated in Antioch. It appears that this name was first given to followers of Jesus by outsiders. It may have implied some scorn for the leader whom Christians worshiped, as appears to be the case when Agrippa uses it in Acts 26, 28.

Paul's First Missionary Journey (11, 27—14, 28)

The missionary efforts of Barnabas and Paul illustrate one of the principles of Luke's account of salvation history. *Jewish rejection* of the gospel leads the apostles to turn to the Gentiles, who receive God's salvation with joy. Paul's first missionary journey establishes the pattern of first preaching in Jewish synagogues and then turning to the Gentiles. Paul makes this principle explicit in his sermon at Pisidian Antioch (13, 44–47).

Persecution. The Jerusalem church suffers yet another round of persecution. We are told that James, the son of Zebedee, was martyred by the Jewish king and that Peter was imprisoned. He would have been executed if God had not intervened to rescue him from jail (Acts 12, 1–19).

Death of Herod. Herod Agrippa suffers a tortured death as divine punishment for his impiety (12, 20–24). In ancient stories, being eaten by worms was a typical punishment for tyrants who scorned the gods. The historian Josephus has preserved a Jewish account of Herod's death. His version agrees with Luke that Herod had accepted divine honors from his subjects and so had been struck down.

Superiority of Christian Faith. Luke wishes to show that Christianity is superior to pagan superstition. Paul overcomes a Jewish magician who had influence with the Roman proconsul on Cyprus (13, 4–12), and in keeping with Luke's interest in the conversion of prominent persons, the proconsul becomes a believer. Throughout this journey the apostles are plagued by hostility from Jews at the same time that they receive warm receptions from the Gentiles.

Gentile Mission Confirmed in Jerusalem (15, 1–35)

All of these events prove to the leaders of the church that God does want them to accept Gentiles into the church. They must face the objections of Jewish Christians, however, who feel that to admit Gentiles without requiring them to observe the Law contradicts the whole story of God's covenant with Israel. They insisted that Jesus was the Messiah for those who sought to be faithful children of Abraham and followers of Moses. In addition to Acts, we have Paul's report of the council in Jerusalem (Gal 2, 1–10). The two versions of the meeting in Jerusalem do not agree in many of their details. Some scholars think that Paul is referring to an earlier meeting.

The Council of Jerusalem

The growing number of Gentile converts posed challenges to the church that had started within Judaism and whose early members were all Jewish. It was approximately ten years since Peter had the vision that persuaded him to accept Cornelius into the church. By then there are probably more Gentile believers in the church than Jewish. But some of the Jewish disciples (called "Judaizers" by scholars) thought that non-Jewish Christians should be required to accept certain aspects of the Mosaic law (including circumcision) to be baptized. The Council of Jerusalem represents the first gathering of church elders to resolve a matter of faith or discipline. Their Spirit-led solution was a compromise of the two extreme positions.

When the agreement to divide missionary efforts, with Peter going to Jews and Paul to Gentiles, failed to resolve the difficulties that arose in mixed churches like Antioch, another meeting was held. At that meeting some restrictions were laid on the Gentiles. They had to avoid idolatry, avoid meat that Jewish law would have considered impure, and not enter into marriages that Jewish law considered incestuous. The decree is mentioned again in Acts 21, 25. The list of prohibitions is based on rules in Leviticus 17–18 that regulate the behavior of non-Jews who live among Jews. Adopting these rules would make it possible for Jewish and Gentile Christians to enjoy table fellowship.

Luke knew of a letter sent by James to Antioch that stated these rules. He presumed that they came from the same meeting at which Paul and Barnabas received authorization for a mission to the Gentiles that would not require the Gentiles to observe Jewish practices. Paul insists that there were no rules imposed on the Gentiles (Gal 2, 6). By Luke's time most churches were predominantly Gentile. The significance of the Jerusalem Council lies in the way in which church leaders were able to recognize and officially affirm the new direction in salvation history. The gospel could expand beyond the nation and culture in which it was born to all peoples of the earth.

The Mission of Paul to the Ends of the Earth (15, 36—28, 31)

Second Missionary Journey (15, 36—18, 23)

Paul now begins the journeys that will take the gospel throughout the rest of the empire. On this journey, he will take the decisive step of crossing from Asia Minor into Greece, where some of the most important Pauline churches would be founded. The New Testament contains Paul's own letters to churches in Thessalonica, Philippi, and Corinth. When Paul arrives in Europe, the narrative style suddenly changes from the third person to the first person "we." Sections in the "we" style appear throughout the rest of Acts (16, 6–12 [beginning of the European mission]; 20, 1–7.13–16; 21, 1–9.15–17 [last journey to Jerusalem]; 27, 1—28, 16 [voyage to Rome]). Some scholars attribute the "we" sections to a travel diary kept by a companion of Paul. The content of these sections matches that of the journeys that Luke has already used to describe the Pauline mission. A shift into the first-person plural was often used by ancient authors for its literary effect. The change in style may represent Luke's way of telling us that we have now arrived at the mission for which the rest of the narrative has prepared us. The gospel is to be taken completely beyond Judaism. In time these Gentile Christians will be the sole keepers of a tradition, which God has been preparing since Abraham. It will be their responsibility to see to it that the gospel continues to be preached in all the nations of the earth.

Philippi

A dream vision takes Paul into Macedonia (16, 6–16). Dream visions were frequently cited as the source of divine guidance in the ancient world. Paul's first major foundation is at Philippi, a Roman colony that enjoyed the rights of an Italian city. Paul's letter to the Philippians indicates that he enjoyed close relationships with this church. They sent assistance to Paul when he was imprisoned or working in other areas, and both men and women from the Philippian church worked as missionaries (see Phil 1, 14; 4, 2f). Acts does not contain much information about the extensive periods of time that Paul lived in communities like Philippi, Thessalonica, and Corinth, nor does Luke refer to persons and issues mentioned in Paul's letters to those churches. There is no evidence in Acts that Luke was familiar with any of Paul's letters. If he had accompanied Paul on some part of his missionary work (see Phlm 24; Col 4, 14), Luke cannot have been involved in the major events of Paul's mission in the way that Timothy, Titus, and Silvanus were.

Luke appears to have drawn upon anecdotal material for the major events in each of the cities. He then shapes that material to illustrate his understanding of the growth of the early church. The Philippi episode repeats themes that we have already encountered. Christian preaching is well received by wealthy, respectable citizens, in this case Lydia, a woman who trades in purple cloth (16, 12–15). Christianity triumphs over pagan superstition and exploitation of the supernatural for personal gain when Paul exorcises the demon from a slave girl (16, 16–18). Like the demons in the Gospel stories (see Lk 4, 31–37), this demon recognizes the purpose for which the apostles have come.

Thessalonica, Beroea

The episodes at Thessalonica (17, 1–9) and Beroea (17, 10–15) repeat the patterns. Initial success, including prominent converts, leads to jealousy and charges that the apostles are destroying public order and encouraging revolt against Rome. Luke's readers already know that such accusations are false and that hostility will not impede the apostles' mission.

Athens

Paul tells us nothing of his stay in Athens except that he remained there alone after sending Timothy to strengthen the faith of the recent converts in Thessalonica (1 Thes 3, 1f). Paul may not have succeeded in establishing a church there. Luke, however, uses the occasion to advance his case for the religious superiority of Christianity by showing it to be equal to the philosophical understanding of the divine principle governing the universe, and not simply another form of religious cult, magic, or supersti-

tion that sought to sway the masses for the financial gain of its preachers. Its reputation was built on its philosophic schools. Luke refers to the two most popular types of philosophy among the Romans, Epicurean and Stoic (17, 18–21). The speech that Paul delivers at their request (17, 22–34) touches on common themes in the philosophical account of religion, which was opposed to the superstitious beliefs about the gods found among the masses. God, the invisible, omnipresent creator and sustainer of the universe, is not swayed by rituals or is partial to one group of people over another. Hellenistic Jews had also taken over the language of philosophical monotheism to advocate the superiority of their religious tradition.

Those in Athens were well known for their piety and their curiosity. Following the practice of ancient rhetoric, the speech opens by seeking to render the audience friendly to the speaker. Paul praises them for these traits. In composing the speech, Luke has apparently modified a common type of altar inscription," . . . altars of the gods, names unknown, and heroes . . . " to the singular (v. 23). Paul then develops three claims about God that were philosophic commonplaces among both pagan and Jewish authors:

1. God is the creator of the entire universe and consequently has no need of human service or temples (vv. 24f);

2. God has allotted certain zones of the earth for the nations of human beings, who should be grateful for God's ordering of the universe and seek to serve God, who sustains and is present to all created things (vv. 26–28);

3. true worship of God will reject all superstitious practices, such as identifying the creator with the products of human artistry and imagination (v. 29).

The conclusion shifts from the common ground between the Christian preacher and philosophical enlightenment to an appeal for conversion (vv. 30f). It recalls the "unknown" taken from the altar inscriptions, which had served as an example of piety in Athens in verse 24. Inscriptions to unknown gods are a feature of those who believe in many gods, because they point to an anxiety to honor deities who might influence events but who are not "named" in the local traditions. Now is the time for a true monotheism. There is only one God, and God is not an abstract principle. God is the one who calls on Paul's listeners to repent (abandon even their philosophical paganism) and accept the message about Jesus as the one in whom all the nations of the earth are to receive salvation. As was the case in earlier missionary speeches, the Resurrection appears as evidence that Jesus is judge of all. This draws skepticism or, at best, a puzzled willingness to hear more.

Corinth

Luke's account of Paul's extensive work in Corinth (18, 1–17) refers to the fact that Paul worked at his trade while preaching there, as he did in all of his churches (see 1 Thes 2, 9; 1 Cor 4, 12; 9) and supplies the additional information that his trade was that of tentmaker, probably someone who made tents of leather and rough cloth, as well as making other items such as harnesses. It mentions two of Paul's close associates from that mission, Priscilla and Aquila (1 Cor 16, 19; Rom 16, 3). After success in attracting influential persons, hostility from the Jews forces the apostle to turn to the Gentiles. They bring Paul before the Roman proconsul Gallio, who refuses to hear a charge involving Jewish religious law. Gallio's response (v. 14f) reflects what Luke considers to be the ideal response when Christians accused of disturbances, which are internal Jewish affairs, are brought before officials. His reference to Priscilla and Aquila's being exiled from Rome (18, 2) shows that he knows that Romans often responded differently to disputes that Christian preaching caused within the Jewish community.

Third Missionary Journey (18, 24—21, 14)

Ephesus

This section of Acts builds on episodes about the mission in Ephesus, which was the residence of the governor of the province of Asia and the fourth largest city in the empire. Ephesus was also the location of a famous temple of the goddess Artemis, which was one of the wonders of the Hellenistic world. Silver coins from the city depict the temple with the statue of the goddess inside. Paul's confrontation with that cult occupies most of the account of his mission there (19, 8–41). Later Paul delivers his farewell speech to leaders of the church in Ephesus (20, 17–38).

Luke's emphasis on Ephesus may have led him to locate two episodes there that seem to come from separate traditions: (1) the instruction of Apollos, who had received only the baptism of John (18, 24–28) and (2) the conferring of the Spirit on persons who had received only the baptism of John (19, 1–7). Luke's account assumes that Priscilla and Aquila have moved to Ephesus from Corinth and that Ephesian Christians urged Apollos to go to Corinth. Luke seems to assume that Apollos and Paul had not met (19, 1), although Paul writes 1 Corinthians from Ephesus or its environs and says that Apollos was unwilling to return to Corinth (1 Cor 16, 8.12). And although Apollos had only received John's baptism, he is not rebaptized. Priscilla and Aquila are able to bring persons into full Christian discipleship. Yet, the disciples of 19, 1–7 have not even heard of the Holy Spirit! Scholars have suggested that this episode would be more appropriate in the area of Syro-Palestine, where Jewish baptismal sects would continue to exist well into the third century.

The episode is similar to one in which Peter and John confer the Spirit on Samaritan converts (8, 14–25). It serves two functions in Luke's schema for the expanding mission: (1) it shows that Paul is able to win over Jewish sectarians, and (2) it demonstrates the continuity between the Pauline mission and the activity of the Jerusalem church. He brings persons into the community that the Holy Spirit has been creating through the apostles since Pentecost.

Paul's mission in Ephesus is the last story of Paul's activity that is not shadowed by his impending arrest at Jerusalem. Luke's summary continues the pattern of synagogue preaching followed by withdrawal to a Gentile environment. Miracles draw attention to the new movement. They also demonstrate the power of Christianity to destroy superstition and magical practices among the people (19, 8–20). The success of Christian preaching, however, awakens hostility from persons who exploit the presence of the temple of Artemis.

Demetrius's speech (see v. 26) to his fellow silversmiths alludes to the speech of Acts 17, 24f. Christian preaching teaches people that human temples and artifacts do not represent God. As had been the case in earlier conflicts with magicians, fears for the economic loss that would

The famous saying of Jesus, "It is more blessed to give than to receive," quoted everywhere from greeting cards to Hollywood movies, is never mentioned in any of the four Gospels. Only Paul quotes it (Acts 20, 35) to encourage hard work for the sake of the weak and needy.

result from accepting the Christian gospel spark the hostility. As in the Gallio case, the local town clerk refuses to become involved. The Christians have not committed any impious acts such as robbing the temple or dishonoring the goddess. Demetrius is the one who is endangering public order by inciting the crowds.

This conclusion seems to represent an ideal rather than reality. As Luke fills out the rest of the journey with brief notices of stops and miracles performed by the apostle (20, 1–16), he makes it appear that Paul left Ephesus of his own volition and that he avoided returning there to save time needed to reach Jerusalem by Pentecost (20, 16). Yet the summons to the officials of the church in Ephesus for a farewell meeting at Miletus (20, 17f) suggests that in fact Paul may have been banished from Ephesus. Paul's obscure reference to conflict in Ephesus (see 1 Cor 15, 32a) implies that at one time he suffered imprisonment or punishment there.

Paul's farewell to the Ephesians (20, 17–35) provides the occasion for Luke to reflect on the transition from the generation of the apostles to the church of his own day. The farewell speech of the dying patriarch was an established custom. The Old Testament contains a farewell speech from Moses to Israel (Dt 29–32). In such speeches, the dying patriarch advises his offspring to follow the Law, anticipates their future disobedience (in most cases), and sets before them the example of his own life. Moses also provides for the future leadership of the people by appointing Joshua as his successor. Luke has incorporated many of these elements in this speech. The Spirit has been warning Paul that he faces imprisonment and hardship in Jerusalem. He holds up his own life as an example of complete devotion to bearing witness to the gospel no

matter what. Unlike the pagans, who sought to enrich themselves from the superstitions of the people, Paul has never sought money from his converts. He commends his own example of working at a trade, not only because it frees the apostle and his associates from suspicion of greed, but also because it provides the opportunity to give aid to the weak (v. 35). Thus, we find Paul's final word of advice returning to the example that the earliest Jerusalem community had set. Christians donate their property for support of the poor.

The farewell speech is also the time to look from the ideal of the past into the dangers of the future. Paul warns of divisions even within the ranks of the community's leaders. He admonishes the presbyters (v. 17; the Greek word means "elders") and "overseers" (v. 28; Greek *episkopoi;* see Phil 1, 1), who have charge of the community left behind by the apostles, to watch over themselves as well as the church. They must continue proclaiming the gospel and exhorting others to faith and repentance. In Luke's writing we have now seen the completion of the apostolic period. Officials from local churches must take over the community. These persons have been appointed by apostles and commissioned by the laying on of hands (14, 23). In that sense, they appear as successors to the apostles. But just as Joshua could not be another Moses, so they are not replacement apostles. The Spirit that has guided the church throughout the developments of the apostolic period must continue to direct her course.

James

The James often referred to in the book of Acts is not James, the brother of John, the son of Zebedee. He is, instead, James, "the brother of the Lord" (Mt 13, 55; Mk 6, 3; Acts 12, 17), that is, one of four half-brothers or cousins of Jesus mentioned in the Gospels. James became the first leader or bishop of the Jerusalem community. He was killed at the instigation of the high priest and the Sanhedrin soon after the death of the Roman procurator, Festus.

Paul's dedication to his mission, even in the face of suffering, leads him to continue the journey (21, 4). Even the Christian prophet Agabus, whom we know to be reliable because he predicted the famine under Claudius (see 11, 28), warns Paul that in Jerusalem the Jews will bind him and hand him over to the Romans. See what Paul himself wrote to the Romans just before he left for Jerusalem (Rom 15, 31). He was concerned about what he might suffer from unbelievers as well as the fact that the Jewish Christian church might reject the offering that he brings.

Paul's Arrest and Imprisonment at Jerusalem (21, 15—26, 32)

As soon as Paul arrives in Jerusalem, James warns him that devout Jewish Christians suspect Paul of leading Christians who are Jewish away from the traditions of their ancestors. James proposes that Paul demonstrate his own piety by paying the expenses for some persons who had taken a private vow. Ironically, Paul's participation in these rites leads to his arrest. Luke uses Paul's imprisonment in Jerusalem to provide speeches in which Paul defends and explains his mission. His first speech to the Jerusalem crowd (22, 1–21) points to the extreme piety of his early life. Only the direct intervention of God could change Paul's behavior. Paul refers to his conversion as evidence for God's direction of his life and ministry. This theme is underlined by a second vision of Christ as Paul is praying in the Temple (22, 17–21).

During his imprisonment at Philippi, Paul said nothing about his Roman citizenship until after he had been flogged (16, 37). Here he stops the Roman commander as he is about to interrogate Paul under torture (22, 25–29). Though Paul is able to stall the Sanhedrin by pitting the Pharisees against the Sadducees, the Romans must intervene by moving Paul to Caesarea under heavy guard (Acts 23). With the transfer to Caesarea, Paul is now in Roman hands. However sympathetically they listen to Paul's preaching, the Roman authorities take no steps to have him released. Paul's first speech before Felix, the Roman procurator of Judea, defends the Jewish character of his own personal conduct (24, 10–21). He remains in prison through a change in the Roman administration. The Jews hope that the

new procurator will turn Paul over to them. Faced with the possibility that he might be tried in Jerusalem, Paul invokes the ultimate privilege of a Roman citizen, the right to be heard by a court in Rome itself (25, 1–12). The Roman procurator repeats the details of Paul's situation to the visiting Jewish king, Herod Agrippa II. Festus, the procurator, clearly understands that Paul has not been charged with any crime under Roman law. At best, the squabble concerns points of Jewish law. Felix arranges for a final speech by the apostle (26, 1–23). Paul defends himself by repeating the circumstances of his life as a devout Jew who was converted by a divine vision, which no one could ignore. In this account of Paul's conversion, Luke focuses upon the divine commission to be a missionary to the Gentiles (26, 16–18). After the hearing, both Festus and Agrippa agree that Paul is innocent. Luke may be following the pattern set out in Jesus' trial. Pilate and Herod both agree that Jesus is innocent. But Paul cannot be released, because he has demanded a hearing in the imperial court (26, 30–32).

Paul's Journey to Rome (27, 1—28, 31)

The conclusion of Acts, in which Paul is preaching the gospel at Rome, though under house arrest (28, 17–31), brings Luke's plot to a climax. The gospel has reached the capital of the civilized world. Luke's account of how Paul came to Rome makes use of another type of ancient adventure story, the sea voyage. Such voyages frequently included descriptions of how the hero escaped from shipwreck, pirates, and other such dangers. The story of Paul's journey is told with all the high drama of such tales. During the vicious storm that destroys the ship and has the survivors washed up on the beach at Malta, Paul demonstrates his own confidence in God and superiority to the fears of the ship's crew. Paul is even able to celebrate a meal of bread, which he has blessed (27, 35f). The wording reminds Christians of the Eucharist (note to 27, 35). It is impossible to sail across the Mediterranean in winter, so the group is forced to stay on Malta. The episode associated with that stay includes the drama of native peoples watching the shipwrecked party. When Paul is unharmed by a poisonous snake, they conclude that he must be a god (28, 3–6). Paul wins more friends on the island by healing the sick, and they are provided with everything needed to continue the journey (vv. 7–10). Although clearly told with an eye toward entertaining the reader, the Malta story also points out that God will provide whatever is necessary for the apostle to fulfill his mission. The superstitious pagans had ignored Paul's prophetic warning that attempting to sail so close to winter would destroy both ship and cargo. The island natives thought that the snake was divine punishment for some evil Paul had committed until they saw that he escaped unharmed. In each case, the apostle comes through the threat to his life because he places all of his trust in the Lord.

Things Learned from Acts

Luke has made striking use of traditions he inherited about the apostles—a plan of salvation history and the art of storytelling to instruct us about the development of God's plan of salvation in the apostolic age.

Judaism Is the Inherited Tradition of the Church

The church developed according to a divine plan of salvation, which remains rooted in the experiences of Israel. When God led the church to turn toward the Gentiles, this heritage was not forgotten, although it was no longer necessary for a person to be culturally and legally a Jew to experience salvation.

God Seeks the Salvation of All the Peoples on Earth

Acts shows us that the apostles had to venture beyond their own Jewish culture to take the gospel to the ends of the earth. Though they found this task difficult, because it often resulted in hostility from fellow Jews, all the apostles accepted this growth toward becoming a truly universal church as an expression of God's will. The task is not over. The church still must venture into other lands and cultures to fulfill the mission that is hers until the end of time: to bear witness to the gospel everywhere.

The Church Is a Spirit-guided Institution

In Acts, the Spirit works in and through the official leaders and structures of the community. Developments like the admission of Gentiles were clearly difficult adjustments, but the leaders of the community in Jerusalem eventually came to express what is the will of God. Furthermore, as the apostle Paul leaves the scene, he has established "elders" or "overseers" in his churches. It is necessary that persons be designated as leaders now that the apostolic age has passed. Although many people think that an institution can never be the vehicle for the Spirit, Acts insists that the church is such a vehicle.

Christians Must Be Willing to Suffer for the Gospel

Because the apostles overcome the sufferings and imprisonments they face, we may forget how relentless the onset of hostility is. No form of suffering causes any of the apostles to stray from the mission given by God and cease to proclaim the gospel. There is no instance in which preaching the gospel does not awaken some form of resistance.

The Christian Fellowship Has Special Marks of Its Identity

Luke has presented us with ideal pictures of what the church should be. We see the harmonious gathering of diverse peoples for prayer, preaching by the apostles, and community meals. We also see a community in which concern for the weak and needy is one of the most important parts of its communal life.

The Church Calls People to Religious Conversion

Because the church preaches religious conversion, it comes into conflict with all forms of pseudo-religion and superstition. Magical practices have no place in Christian life, nor do movements that use the religious sentiments of the masses to collect money from those who are taken in by the propaganda of such false cults. Christians give their resources to help those in need. They speak out against any false idea of God that would require buildings and other material goods for God or God's servants. Christians remain loyal to the basic institutions of their society, even when those institutions seem to be used against them by persons who do not like the criticism of false beliefs and behavior that comes from the gospel.

Questions for Discussion and Reflection
Group Sharing/Discussion

1. What role does Peter play in Luke's Acts of the Apostles?

2. Prepare and role-play the meeting of Philip and the Ethiopian (8, 26–40). Afterwards consider what each person in the Scripture story learned and what he taught.

3. Luke did not intend to include all events of early Christian history. He wrote Salvation history. What does this mean?

4. What is the link between Christianity and Judaism?

5. Why did the apostles use "drawing of lots" to determine the replacement for Judas?

6. How is Stephen's death similar to Jesus' trial and death?

7. Luke is clear about the differences between the water baptism of John the Baptist and Christian baptism. What is this difference?

8. Where did the name "Christians" originate (11, 26)?

9. In their first missionary journey to Antioch Paul and Barnabas first visited the synagogues and then preached to the Gentiles. What were the results?

10. Demetrius of Ephesus spoke out against the Christians there. Why? (19, 26)

11. Why did Paul evoke his privilege as a Roman citizen? What resulted from his exercising this right?

In Our Lives

1. Discuss the significance of the Jerusalem Council. Name some questions that they discussed: What was recognized in the early growth and affirmed as Salvation history? Why was the incorporation of the Gentiles into the new Christian community such a controversial issue? What problems and issues did it raise with the Jewish believers? What do you think of the solution that was offered by the Jerusalem leaders?

2. Read aloud the first sermon of Peter (2, 14–3, 6). Share the message concerning the fundamental elements of the Christian community.

How do these look in the modern Church?

3. Were you surprised to learn there were struggles and disagreements in the apostolic church? What insights and inspiration can you draw from the knowledge of that experience? What is our role when disagreements arise in our church today?

4. Luke is clear and strong concerning riches and the mission of the Church. Read aloud 2, 42–47 concerning how Christians sell their property and share their possessions. Reflect on how this basic element of charity to the poor is lived out in the Christian community today. What steps can our parish community take to come closer to this teaching? What can you personally do better?

Individual/Personal Reflection/Action

1. Recall how Luke presented the development of the early Church. Consider how even though the apostles did not know where God is leading, they remain open to the Spirit. Reflect on the gift of the Spirit and the need to be open to the Spirit's inspiration personally and as a community.

2. Through his storytelling Luke instructs us about the development of God's plan of salvation. We learn the following:

A. Judaism is the inherited tradition of the church.

B. God seeks the salvation of all peoples.

C. The Church is a Spirit-guided institution.

D. Christians must be willing to suffer for the gospel.

E. Catholic identity includes: prayer, preaching of the apostles, community meals and special concern for the poor and needy.

F. The Church calls the people to religious conversions from all sorts of forms of false religion and superstition.

Think about each of these learnings from reading and studying Acts. Make your own list of the three most important things you learned from the Acts of the Apostles. What difference will these make in your life?

THE WRITINGS OF PAUL

According to the Acts of the Apostles, Paul was born in Tarsus, a city on the eastern end of the Mediterranean Sea, in what is now Turkey, around A.D. 10. He was a Roman citizen from birth, a status that carried certain privileges. He was also, according to Acts, a student of Gamaliel, a renowned rabbi. Paul was a Pharisee, that is, a member of a strictly observant Jewish party. His own writings indicate that he was well-educated in the Greek language and in methods of biblical interpretation used by the Pharisees. Both Paul and Acts of the Apostles tell that he was so zealous for the Jewish Law before his conversion that he persecuted those who, he believed, had strayed from the Law because they believed that Jesus was the Christ. During this earlier part of the sketch of Paul's life in Acts, he is called by his Jewish name, Saul. When in the narrative story, he begins to encounter the Roman world (13, 9), Luke calls him by his Roman name, Paul.

After experiencing a revelation of the Risen Christ from God, however, Paul himself joined these followers of "the Way" as a young adult, about A.D. 34. He firmly believed that his conversion included a call to preach the Christian message of salvation to all people, including the Gentiles. Paul spent the rest of his life, about 30 years, in carrying out this mission. After 3 years in Arabia and a brief visit to Jerusalem, he embarked on his missionary career. After some years working in the Eastern Mediterranean area as far west as Greece, Paul visited Jerusalem to deliver relief funds collected in Asia Minor and Greece. He then intended to visit Rome and Spain, but in Jerusalem he met with increasing opposition from some Jewish leaders and was arrested and brought to Rome around A.D. 60. Between A.D. 48 and his death around A.D. 62, Paul wrote letters to communities with which he had worked, answering their questions, and preaching the gospel as he understood it to have been revealed to him.

Sources

We learn about Paul's life from his own letters and from Luke's account in the Acts of the Apostles (cf. Acts 9, 1–30; 11, 1—28, 31). There are some differences between what Paul says and what Luke records about certain incidents of Paul's career. For example, Luke and Paul do not agree about whether the Council of Jerusalem, around A.D. 50, decided that the Gentiles should keep some aspects of the Jewish Law (see Acts 15 and Gal 2, 1–10). We must remember that when Luke writes about Paul's life, his account is a secondary source. It was written about A.D. 85, more than a generation after Paul lived. This was a time when the major issue of non-Jewish converts was no longer as pressing. Luke minimizes the tensions involved in integrating the Gentiles into the church.

The Epistles of Paul

There are thirteen letters or epistles ascribed to Paul, but most commentators recognize only seven of these as definitely written by the apostle; the others are attributed to disciples of Paul. The seven letters certainly written by Paul himself are:

Romans
1 and 2 Corinthians
Galatians
Philippians
1 Thessalonians
Philemon

The remaining six letters (Ephesians, Colossians, 2 Thessalonians, 1 and 2 Timothy, and Titus) are often called "Deutero-Pauline." Among this latter group Paul's authorship of 2 Thessalonians and Colossians is most disputed.

For various reasons commentators believe that these six letters were not actually written by Paul but instead were written by later Christians familiar with his teachings. Disciples could have claimed to be writing in Paul's name to gain authority for their own adaptations of his teaching, an accepted practice among the ancients. In the New Testament, the Pauline writings are arranged in two groups: first, letters to communities; second, letters to individuals. Within each group they run roughly from the longest to the shortest. Thus, the letters are not arranged in the order in which they were written.

Letters and Epistles

Paul's letters follow the fairly simple structure of a usual letter in Greek or Roman culture. Letters were not placed in envelopes, so the address is given right at the start. Then comes the body of the letter; finally, the conclusion which contains personal greetings and instructions. Some scholars have suggested a distinction between more formal, systematic "epistles" and informal "letters." In this way of thinking, Romans would be an example of a formal epistle, whereas Philemon or Titus would be examples of an informal letter. Even some of those letters supposedly written to individuals may really be formal "epistles" intended for wider circulation. Many interpreters have also noted that a fundamental structure can be seen in many of Paul's writings, but most clearly in Romans. Paul first outlines his most basic teachings in a section sometimes called the doctrinal or "indicative" part. This is followed by an application of these teachings in Paul's exhortations to the community, a section called the "imperative."

The Apostle and His Gospel

Much of the Christian vocabulary we have become so familiar with and associate with the ministry of Jesus actually originated with Paul.

For example, Paul was, as far as we know, the first to coin a Christian meaning for the words apostle, gospel, charism, ministry, and many doctrinal phrases such as "justification by faith." As the first Christian writer, Paul began to develop specifically Christian terminology, even though many of the terms he uses will have roots in Judaism, or other meanings in secular Greek.

Paul's writings predate any of our written gospels. Paul is the first to speak about preaching the gospel, although he does not conceive this as a story about the life and ministry of Jesus. The idea of the gospel, which appears even in the Old Testament (e.g., see Is 61, 1–2, "glad tidings"), means the "good news." For Paul this is the message of salvation now accessible to all through faith in Jesus Christ. In Romans, Paul describes the gospel as the "power of God" to save all who believe (Rom 1, 16). Thus, Paul does not think of the gospel as a story of the events in Jesus' life, nor even as a set of beliefs about Jesus. Rather, the gospel is the "good news" that all who believe in Jesus are already saved.

Paul rarely speaks of any actions or words of Jesus during his lifetime. Rather, he focuses on God's power, working through the death and resurrection of Jesus, to save Jews and Greeks (i.e., all people) alike. Keep in mind that for Paul, the term "gospel" means the proclamation of faith in God's forgiveness or realizing the "good news" that Jesus Christ has come to bring salvation to all people.

In his writings, Paul usually identifies himself as an apostle (Rom 1, 1; 11, 13; 1 Cor 1, 1; 4, 9; 9, lf.5; 15, 9; 2 Cor 1, 1; 11, 5.13; 12, 11.12; etc.). The term apostle literally means "one sent," who represents the sender and is entrusted with the sender's authority and message. God is the source of Paul's apostleship.

The Letters in Circulation

The apostle's authority was in his words and in his example. It became real when the community as a whole discerned Paul's meaning and decided on what actions they as believers should take as a result of Paul's words. In his letters, Paul teaches, exhorts, encourages, and corrects. The communities revered his instructions. They read them and preserved them. They also circulated his letters, sharing them with other communities. In this way the letters eventually gained the authority of Christian scriptures as the communities were increasingly strengthened, formed, and informed by a common tradition. Most people in Pauline communities probably could not read, so a reader would read Paul's letter aloud to the assembly of believers. There they reflected together on its contents. From Paul's writings we can get a picture how the early church operated, how it worshiped, how it governed itself, and how it grew.

When we read Paul's letters, we need to keep in mind that we are, in effect, reading one side of a conversation. Paul frequently seems to be responding to particular questions or concerns that Christians in various local churches have asked him about. Sometimes they have raised these questions with him on a visit, and sometimes they have written to him, and he is answering their letters. But we do not have any of this correspondence, so in many cases we have to deduce what they were asking from how Paul answers them.

ROMANS READING GUIDE

At a Glance

Who are the main players?	Paul Roman church
What should I look for?	In Romans, Paul describes the gospel as the "power of God" to save all who believe, not as the life and ministry of Jesus. Much of the Christian vocabulary we are familiar with originated with Paul. For example, Paul coined the Christian meaning of the words *apostle, gospel, charism, ministry* and many doctrinal phrases such as *"justification by faith."*
When did this take place?	Paul's writings predate any of our written gospels. He joined the "followers of the way" about A.D. 34. Between 48 and his death in 62, Paul wrote letters to communities. Romans was written between A.D. 56–58, most likely from Corinth.
Where did these events occur?	Paul was about to go to Jerusalem with money for the poor. After this he hopes to visit Rome. Meanwhile he writes this letter to the Romans to share the good news of Jesus Christ.
Why was this book written?	Romans is the longest of Paul's letters, but also it is the most important. More than any other Pauline writings, Romans is like a formal treatise, a summary of Paul's theology that serves as an introduction to Paul as well as a summary of the message Paul preached.
What is the story?	In no other authentic Pauline letter besides Romans does Paul write in his name alone. In the first section (chs 1–11), he describes his view of Christian life. He develops his teaching that justification by faith is already given in Christ and describes the life of freedom from sin, death, and the law. In the second section (chs 12–15) Paul derives some ethical conclusions from these teachings.

Before Beginning

Placing Paul's letter to the Romans at the beginning of the New Testament letters is appropriate not only because it is the longest of Paul's letters, but also because it may very well be his most important work. Romans has always held a special place among Paul's writings. Especially since the time of the Protestant Reformation in the sixteenth century, the importance of the doctrine of "justification by faith," which Paul develops in Romans (and, in a more succinct version, in Galatians), has been recognized by Catholics and Protestants alike as one of the most significant teachings of Paul and, in fact, of Christianity.

Paul and the Roman Christians

The Roman Christian community must have been fairly large by the time Paul arrived there. It is estimated that the Jewish community of Rome in the early first century numbered 50,000. Among Christians, it seems from Paul's letter that there were both Jews and Gentiles.

Some of the information given in chapter 16 indicates quite a few house churches existed. Of course, Paul did not intend to arrive in Rome as a prisoner, as told in Acts, but as a free missionary.

Several unique characteristics of Romans distinguish this letter from the other writings of Paul. In this letter, Paul addresses a church he has not founded. He writes to introduce himself and his gospel and to seek the Roman community's acceptance and help. Before fulfilling his desire to come to Rome on the way to Spain (cf. Rom 15, 22–33), Paul must first deliver the collection of money from the Gentile churches for the "poor saints of Jerusalem" (15, 26), who have been suffering from a famine. When these funds are delivered, his sights will be set for Rome.

So it is that both the Jewish mission field represented by the church in Jerusalem and the open-ended Gentile mission represented by Rome and Spain are on Paul's mind as he writes this letter. Paul is concerned about unity among Christians. Although he has not founded the Roman church, he refers to the common faith he shares with believers there. He stresses the common fund of teaching from which both he and they draw. The issues of reconciliation and of being a community in faith go through all of Romans and contribute to its appeal to believers of every age.

Except for chapter 16, which may have been added later (cf. below), Romans lacks the personal tone of most of Paul's letters. Some manuscripts omit the words "in Rome" in 1, 7 and 15. Without this designation and the greetings of chapter 16, Romans might be considered as a circular letter, a general development of Paul's most basic theological ideas. In Romans, Paul teaches about universal salvation, the notion of justification by faith, and on the relationship between Israel and the church as transformed by Christ. These are some of the most important and generally applicable aspects of all of Paul's theology. The general nature and universal applicability of Romans contribute to its wide appeal as an introduction to Paul.

Romans as a "Diatribe"

More than any other Pauline writing, Romans is like a formal treatise, a summary of Paul's theology. It serves two purposes: as a self-introduction to a community not yet personally acquainted with Paul and as a summary for the message Paul preaches. Even though Romans has the formal features of an epistle, it can also be understood as a *diatribe* or a written exposé that tries to anticipate real or supposed objections or rebuttal. The diatribe, which was used by some ancient philosophers in teaching and writing, often interjected traces of dialogue to answer questions that opponents might offer. For example, Paul brings his arguments forward by sprinkling through Romans such imagined questions as "What advantage is there then in being a Jew?" (3, 1) or "Well, then, are we better off?" (3, 9) or "What then can we say that Abraham found, our ancestor according to the flesh?" (4, 1). Thus, in comparison to Paul's other works, Romans is structured more as a philosophical treatise. Most of the other letters reflect more the give and take of real dialogue among people actually working and interacting together.

Working through Romans

The typical Greco-Roman letter form applied to Romans yields the following divisions:

the address, consisting of a greeting and a thanksgiving, is contained in Rom 1, 1–15; the body of the letter comprises 1, 16—15, 13. It contains the essential message of Paul, basically following what has helpfully been called the "indicative imperative" structure (see "Letters and Epistles"). The conclusion in 15, 14—16, 27 contains Paul's travelogue, his personal greetings, and a final doxology.

A working outline of Romans follows:

I. The Address (Rom 1, 1–15)
II. The Body of the Letter (1, 16—15, 13)
  A. The Theme; the "Indicative" (1, 16–17)
  B. The Common Predicament of Gentiles and Jews (1, 18—3, 20)
  C. Central Declaration of Justification by Faith (3, 21–31)
  D. Abraham, Model of Faith (4, 1–25)
  E. The Two Adams (5, 1–21)
  F. A Preliminary "Imperative" (6, 1–23)
  G. Life without the Spirit (7, 1–25)
  H. Life in the Spirit (8, 1–39)
  I. But what of Israel? (9, 1—11, 36)
  J. The Final "Imperative" (12, 1—15, 13)
III. Conclusion (15, 14—16, 27)

The Address (1, 1–15)

The address typically includes greetings and a thanksgiving, which is how Greco-Roman letters usually began. Here and in some other letters, notably Philippians, Paul has woven this brief feature into an extended prayer. In no other authentic Pauline letter besides Romans does Paul write in his name alone. He usually has with him some co-worker known to the letter's recipients. In chapter 16, this is certainly the case. But even in Romans, Paul is not entirely independent. He needs the Romans' acceptance. He is grateful for their perse-

verance, and he looks forward to being strengthened by them through their common faith (1, 11). Paul says that although he is personally unknown to the Romans, the gospel or Christian message he preaches is the same as that which they have received from other Christian missionaries.

Although Paul usually refers to his addressees as "the church in _____," he does not use the term "church" in the address of Romans. But he does remind the Roman Christians of their vocation to holiness. In developing a Christian terminology in the Greek language, Paul will consistently draw upon images and phrases that appear in the Hebrew Scriptures. An example is Paul's description of the believing community as holy, as saints, called and sanctified by God (e.g., 1 Cor 1, 2). Israel is a "kingdom of priests, a holy nation," according to Exodus 19, 6. The Law sets Israel apart, making it distinct from its neighbors because it has a covenant relationship with God. This holiness has nothing to do with the virtue of the members but arises from the fact of God's call. Their personal holiness is then a response to that call.

The Body of the Letter (1, 16—15, 13)

The Theme (1, 16–17)

Romans 1, 16–17 states the theme. In the chapters that follow, the gospel is described as the power of God for universal salvation. This theme is developed in both its positive and negative implications. Positively, Paul insists that faith is accessible to all through Christ. But Paul also realizes some negative implications, even of his belief that all are saved in Christ. For example, it is clear that all have sinned and are in need of salvation. The emphasis on universal sinfulness deserving of God's wrath is the negative pole of the

Paul's Fundamental Doctrine: Justification by Faith

Universal Sinfulness	Universal Salvation
Sinfulness of all is manifested in	We are already justified by faith
• both Jews and Gentiles (1, 18—3, 31)?	• Exemplified by Abraham (4, 1–25)
• Sin of all since sin of Adam (5, 12 –21)	• Fulfilled in Christ (5, 1–11; 6, 1–23; 8, 1–39)
• The human dilemma—knowing what is right (the Law) does not enable us to do what is right (7, 13–25)	

In Romans these two poles are in constant dynamic tension.

theme of Romans. There is no human means of achieving salvation; it must be given to us.

It is important to note that for Paul the starting point is not that all have sinned but, rather, that all have been saved. This is the conviction of faith. Paul considers sin to be an illustration of the universal need for salvation. This explains why Paul's hope, eloquently expressed especially in chapters 5, 8, and 15, is so deep and certain. No human sin is sufficient to separate us from the love of God that saves us.

Paul's Fundamental Conviction

The Greek words that we translate "just," "justice," "justify," and "righteousness" are all derived from the same root word, *dikaios* (just), *dikaiosyne* (justice, righteousness, or justification). Even more important, for Paul the concepts are closely linked. He connects the justice of God with God's power and will to "justify" all people, that is, to regard them as just.

The Scriptures show that God's justice is revealed, that is, it cannot be completely comprehended through human effort or study. Isaiah reminds us that God's thoughts are not human thoughts, and God's ways not our ways (see Is 55, 7–8). Yet the Scriptures also tell us that we are to be just, that we must act in imitation of God, that we are to walk blamelessly before God and be perfect (see Gn 17, 1; Hos 6, 6). Thus, justice is not completely foreign to us. The God-fearing Israelite seeks to act justly, act in ways that are acceptable to God and in accord with God's covenant. These ways are also revealed through the Jewish Torah ("instruction") or Law. The Torah was handed down from Moses and interpreted throughout the history of the Jewish people, who reverenced it as the revealed will of God. So, for example, Abraham in Genesis (Gn 15, 6) and Joseph in the infancy narrative (Mt 1, 19) are described as "righteous" (*dikaios*) men. It is not that acting justly or keeping the Law earns salvation or God's approval but, rather, the opposite. The covenant is God's gift to Israel. Israel's response is to keep the Law. The Jewish person seeking justice is enjoined to study and to follow the Torah or the instruction of God. In the covenant is the hope of being justified, that is, "made just" in God's sight. Thus, for the Old Testament as for Paul, the related terms "justice," "just," and "justified" all originate in God, who reveals how we are to act and judges us accordingly. Although all people are sinners, Jewish theology teaches that we may expect to learn the way of justice through a faithful following of the Law in all things. This is the background for Paul's understanding of justification through Jesus Christ.

Justification or Salvation

There are two main ideas that we must understand if we are to grasp the argument about justification that Paul puts forth in Romans and in some of his other writings. The first is the meaning for him of trying to attain justification or salvation by obeying the Law. (This is dealt with particularly in chapter 3 of his Letter to the Galatians; see the Reading Guide to Galatians.) The second main idea pertains to Paul's explanation of how the Gentiles, or those who do not have the Law, are justified.

First, for Paul, justification through the works of the Law is a false hope for several reasons. The idea that the Law held the key to justification was the position of the Jews who did not become Christians, as well as of the Christian-Jewish group led by Peter and James. This was the majority of the church when Paul began his mission. The theological challenge Paul faces is that his experience of the Risen Christ and his mission to preach that justification is available to all, both Jews who have the Law and the Gentiles who do not, convinced Paul that justification is an act of God, given freely to all who believe. Like his Jewish contemporaries, Paul himself was zealous for the Law (cf. Rom 10, 1–3; Phil 3, 3–7; Gal 1, 11–14), but now his experience has taught him that this is not the way to go. Now in his zeal to win people over to the way he is convinced is right, Paul argues that the Law is impossible to keep and can only lead to frustration and self-righteousness. This caricature of the Law must be understood as rhetorical attempts to persuade Gentiles attracted by Law observance to his point of view.

Second, justification through the Jewish Law is insufficient because it excludes the Gentiles, who, as Paul has described the situation in Romans 1, 18—3, 31, are in the same sinful predicament as are the Jews. But both Abraham and Christ show that the Gentiles, no less than the Jews, are now justified through faith. According to the Law, Jesus was condemned to death. But God overturned the Law's verdict in raising Jesus to life (see Gal 3, 10–14). Thus, for Paul, the death and resurrection of Jesus has taken the place of the Law. As a result, the Gentiles are now included among the justified. By accepting Jesus' gift of justification, and consequently living in accord with God's will, Jews and Gentiles both are saved. Following the just requirements of the Law or the precepts of the church is not a prerequisite for but a result of being justified.

Paul thus understands justification as already having taken place through the death and resurrection of Christ. Salvation is in the future, promised to those who believe in Christ and live according to this belief. As Paul himself says it, "Indeed, if, while we were enemies, we were reconciled to God through the death of his Son, how much more, once reconciled, will we be saved by his life" (Rom 5, 10).

Faith and Salvation

We must also understand Paul's idea of faith to understand the argument of Romans. It may seem that he is simply replacing one human action, obedience to the Law, with another human action, faith in Jesus Christ. But for Paul faith is trust: the belief that it is God's power, not our own, and our reliance on God, not on our own abilities, that saves us. Paul saw the obvious danger for sinful people: the danger that they would continue in their wrong behavior and close themselves off from God forever. But Paul also saw the danger for those people who seemed moral and upright: the danger that they would believe God was forced to save them because they had earned their way into God's love.

For Paul, this thinking is a fatal mistake. It assumes that we can manipulate God by our actions. Paul explains away this misunderstanding by the necessity of faith. Faith is our acknowledgment that it is God's power that saves us, not our own efforts. We are helpless, in that we are all sinners; and in spite of that, we can trust in God to save us.

Notice that Paul begins with the affirmation of faith in God's work of salvation to which everyone has access in Christ. He does not start with the premise of defeat nor emphasize that each person must individually become convicted of sin. Rather, Paul stresses first the goodness and

power of God to save, and then tries to demonstrate the universal need for salvation to be given.

Paul uses terms such as "redeem" and "justify" and "reconcile" in relationship to one another and sometimes almost interchangeably (see Rom 5, 9–11 and discussion on that passage below). These terms originally belonged to the world of finance; for Paul they appropriately illustrate the economy of salvation. The "debit" columns of sin and guilt and punishment are converted by God into the "credit" columns of forgiveness, redemption, and reconciliation. Through faith we are reconciled to God and to one another. We are redeemed by the blood of Christ, and our sins are forgiven.

Paul came to believe that the revelation of the Law was fulfilled by the death and resurrection of Christ. In Romans, Paul will develop a dichotomy between what was "formerly" and what is "now." For Paul, God's justice is only fully revealed in Jesus. The emphasis on "now" also implies an emphasis on the accessibility of God's justice to all through faith. The Law (or Torah) formerly divided humanity into "Jews and Gentiles," the latter not sharing in the promise represented by the Law. This division is overcome, and all now have equal access to God's revelation of justice expressed in Christ.

The Common Predicament of Gentiles and Jews (1, 18—3, 20)

Having stated his conviction that the gospel is God's power to save all people through faith (1, 1–16f), Paul proceeds to demonstrate the need of all people for salvation. Universal sin illustrates this need. Paul shows that "all," both Gentiles and Jews, have sinned and incurred the wrath of God. The "wrath of God" is being revealed in that the Gentiles are experiencing disastrous consequences of their own behavior (Rom 1, 18–32). The wrath of God is an image borrowed from the Old Testament prophets (see Is 9, 8–12; 10, 5; Jer 50, 11–17; Ez 5, 13; 36, 5–6). It depicts God's rejection or "abandonment" (Rom 1, 24.26.28) of people to their own sin. The story of Saul's disobedience to God in 1 Samuel 15 dramatizes this dynamic: From the moment when God no longer accepts Saul's kingship, Saul's downfall is certain.

Although the Gentiles could know God through creation, the evidence of their godless lives means that they have rejected knowledge of God. Belief in God is no mere intellectual affair but involves a conversion to "the living and true God" (see 1 Thes 1, 9) expressed in a virtuous life. Paul adopts the Old Testament notion of the relationship between idolatry and immorality evident among the pagans. (But see the New American Bible [NAB] note on 1, 18–32 that cautions that the lives of many in the Greco-Roman culture could serve as models for Christians today.) Paul speaks in generalities here, trying first to indict the Gentiles (1, 18–31) and later (in 2, 1—3, 9) the Jews, in an effort to show the effects of universal sin and the need of all humanity for God's salvation.

Central Declaration of Justification by Faith (3, 21–31)

Paul summarizes his previous demonstration of universal sinfulness (3, 23) but prefaces it with the way out, accomplished by God through Christ, then makes the central assertion: we are justified by faith apart from the works of the Law (3, 28). He emphasizes that God's just judgment comes upon all people, for God shows no partiality (2, 11; see also Dt 10, 17; 2 Chr 19, 7; Sir 35, 12f; Acts 10, 34; Gal 2, 6; Eph 6, 9; Col 3, 2.5; 1 Pt 1, 17). Having indicated that the Gentiles are sinners, Paul turns to concentrate throughout Romans 2, 1—3, 20 on the Jews. Here Paul adopts the language of the prophets, who not only charged sinfulness to the pagans, but also accused the Jews of having "a stubborn and impenitent heart."

Abraham, Model of Faith (4, 1–25)

For Paul, Abraham is a type of Christ; that is, Abraham follows the pattern of Christ. Adam and Moses, on the other hand, are antitypes or reverse patterns. For Jews, circumcision, the ritual removal of the foreskin of the penis of infant boys, symbolizes the individual's membership in the people of God and, therefore, the individual's acceptance of God's law and teaching. Because Abraham was justified before his circumcision, he was justified independently of the Law. Therefore, Abraham is the ancestor of both Jews and Gentiles. Abraham's example illustrates the theme of Romans: All have access now to salvation through faith. (For further discussion of the image of Abraham for Paul, see the Reading Guide to Galatians.)

The Two Adams (5, 1—6, 23)

In chapter 5 Paul contrasts Christ's saving actions (i.e., his death and resurrection) with the devastating consequences of the sin of the first Adam. By the time of Paul, it was generally understood that the first human beings were created immortal (Wis 2, 23f) but that their sin brought death into the world. Subsequent generations continue the sentence of death by continuing to sin (Rom 5, 12). Adam represents all people under sin with its curse of death. But Adam is also a figure drawing out God's promise of redemption. The writer of Genesis portrays the situation of Adam as obviously in need of some divine action: even before the curse for sin is pronounced in Genesis 3, 16–19, God promises to save the human family in the end (Gn 3, 15). The early church fathers, above all St. Augustine, used these passages, especially Romans 5, 12, as a basis for describing the devastating effects of original sin, although Paul does not use this term. Instead, he argues that if the first sin had such widespread effects that all people since Adam have been under its influence, how much more effective and powerful is the gift of salvation won through Jesus Christ. That gift is called "grace," which brings eternal life (5, 21). The mode of argument here is a familiar pattern of argument: from lesser to greater. If so much damage was caused by the first human being, Adam, how much greater is the grace and redemption won by the ultimate human being, Christ. Paul's thinking is at the basis of the church's ecstatic thanksgiving, "O happy fault that has merited so great a redeemer!" The Roman liturgy recalls this prayer during the Easter Vigil each year in the singing of the Exsultet, which tells this story.

Salvation is a reality that Paul describes here and elsewhere (see 1 Cor 6, 11; 2 Cor 5, 10–15; 10, 5–10), using words like "reconciliation," "redemption," "justification," and "sanctification." The verb "to save" refers to God's intervening action when human beings are in need. It connotes actual, sometimes physical, rescue as well as deliverance from spiritual distress. The Old Testament often refers to God as "Savior." Reference to God's saving action is one of the Bible's most frequent ways of referring to God, appearing literally hundreds of times. In the New Testament this term is often used in connection with Jesus. The disciples, for example, prayed "Lord, save us" (e.g., Mt 8, 25). Paul assumes we are familiar with the long Old Testament tradition of God's saving actions on behalf of people. But Paul, in

Paul's "Justification by Faith" Argument in 5, 1—8, 39
5, 1–21 Justification already given in Christ
6, 1—7, 25 Baptism has freed us from sin and the Law now plays a different role
8, 1–39 The effects of the Spirit's work in us, giving us hope

relating God's action to the death and resurrection of Christ, gives a new emphasis in the theology of salvation or "soteriology." Many scholars point out that all of Paul's christology (or thinking about Christ) is really a soteriology or doctrine of how God saves through Christ.

Paul's view of humankind (i.e., his theological anthropology) is evident in this chapter. He considers all people to be under some dominant influence, living either for God under grace or living for sin. This is a different perspective from our contemporary one that considers human freedom as an autonomous, absolute ideal. For Paul, freedom is related to life for God (6, 10) in contrast with slavery to sin (6, 6). By means of the opposites of death and life, Paul contrasts the former condition of sin and death to the new life of freedom won by Christ and obtained by the believer through baptism.

The term baptism means "immersion," and Paul plays on this original sense even as he has the initiatory rite in view. He coins several expressions in chapter 6 that signify believers' solidarity with Christ. We have "died with" him and are "buried with" him; therefore we will be "raised with" him and now "live with" him. This incorporation into the death-resurrection of Christ by means of baptism necessarily has implications for the moral life. As a result of this incorporation, we "walk" (a term designating moral living) in the newness of life (6, 4). Paul will postpone a fuller discussion of the implications of this "newness of life" until chapters 12 through 15.

Life without the Spirit (7, 1–25)

The major part of chapter 7 follows the style of a diatribe (see the NAB introduction and notes on ch 7). Paul anticipates the objections of real or imaginary opponents in a kind of dialogue designed to present his own ideas in an orderly fashion. The most important aspects of Paul's argument are three.

1. The Christian views the Law differently now, having been freed from its service (Paul says "bondage") by participation in the death of Christ.

2. The purpose of the Law is to name what is sinful. Thus, the Law did not encourage grace or freedom but only identified sin.

3. Anticipating an objection that the Law is therefore sin, Paul responds emphatically, "No!" Yet knowledge of what is good does not enable us to do what is good. The Law is one more factor, then, in the judgment against humanity, convicting all of sin. The Law concurs with human conscience, judging us as sinners. This is the meaning of the expression, "the good that I want to do I avoid and the evil I wish to avoid I do" (see 7, 19–21).

But it is important to realize that his statements about this unhappy predicament are not expressions about him personally but of the situation of humanity without God.

Life in the Spirit (8, 1–39)

Chapter 8 celebrates the message of salvation. "There is no condemnation for those who are in Christ Jesus" (8, 1). Nothing will "be able to separate us from the love of God in Christ Jesus our Lord" (8, 38f). Nowhere is Paul's understanding of the role of the Spirit more eloquently expressed than here. Paul begins chapter 8 with a consideration of the opposition between the flesh and the spirit. He often tries to illustrate his meaning by opposing two poles of thought. This is a way of showing the mutually exclusive categories of sin and death versus grace and life. Paul adapts the Greek notion of the flesh to express the sinful condition of humanity before grace. In the Greek philosophical tradition, flesh, like spirit, had several connotations. "The flesh" means, of course, that which pertains to the body. But it can also mean the inferior aspect of human existence, whatever in human life is weak or limited. For the

Greeks, the flesh referred to what they regarded as baser desires, which for them included sensual and sexual instincts. The flesh is mortal and must be controlled by the spirit (i.e., the mind and will), which in Greek thought is immortal. Paul adapts this notion to sometimes speak of the flesh as the moral equivalent of sin. For Paul, however, sins of the flesh include not just bodily sins, such as gluttony, but also spiritual sins, such as pride. Drawing on the same tradition, Paul uses the term "spirit" to refer to the new life accessible to all through Christ. In stressing the life of the spirit, Paul contrasts the present salvation with the past that was characterized by sin, death, and slavery to the dictates of the flesh.

The Holy Spirit is an advocate, coming to our aid and strengthening us. Like the Israelites in Egypt, we formerly could only groan in the suffering and weakness caused by sin. The Spirit converts our cries into a prayer that recognizes God as Father and ourselves as children of God. Thus, through the Spirit we are liberated from slavery to sin and enabled to pray as the children of God, saying "Abba" (8, 15). From Paul's use of this prayer, we can assume that he is indirectly referring to the Gospel tradition that tells us that Jesus himself addressed God as "Abba, Father" (Mk 14, 36). We are confident, too, that the suffering we experience and witness is as nothing compared to the glory that is to come. All creation shared in the sin of Adam and groans with humanity in its suffering. Now all creation awaits the revelation of the children of God (8, 20–25).

At the end of chapter 8, Paul exclaims that nothing can separate us from the love of God. But he goes on to acknowledge in chapters 9 through 11 that the Jewish rejection of the Christian message is a challenge to this belief. Some may say that now God has run out of patience with Israel. But if Israel's rejection of Christ could limit God's fidelity to the covenant and God's justice, what does that mean not only for Israel but for the Christian church, which is adopting the prerogatives of Israel? Has God had a change of mind? These are some of the questions Paul puzzles out in these chapters in a remarkable review of the history of salvation.

But what of Israel? (9, 1—11, 36)

The form of this three-chapter unit is a philosophical diatribe. Paul responds to anticipated questions or challenges in the form of an artificial dialogue. In the course of developing his views, he makes abundant use of the Old Testament. Before dealing with some ethical conclusions to the doctrines in chapters 12 through 15, Paul senses the necessity of taking up this personally painful question about God's fidelity to the Jews. Israel's rejection of Christ was clearly a problem not only for Paul, but also for the early church. Paul's consideration of this question properly belongs with the doctrinal development of Romans.

Paul's summary of the privileges of Israel in Romans 9, 1–5 prompts him to redefine the term Israel in chapters 9 through 11. Israel is not a mere ethnic or historical reality, but one that always had theological connotations. The Jewish scriptures show, Paul argued, that "not all of Israel are Israel" (9, 6). The element of divine choice was operating throughout Jewish history, illustrating that God is free to show mercy as God wishes. Not all are children of Abraham simply because they descended from him, as the preference for Isaac over Ishmael shows (see 9, 7–9; Gal 4, 22–31). God chose Jacob over Esau (Rom 9, 10–13). God hardens some, as in the case of Pharaoh; but divine mercy is shown to Moses and the Hebrews in Egypt (9, 15–17). Paul also cites examples from the prophets, especially Jeremiah, Hosea, and Isaiah to support God's freedom to choose. For Paul, God's mercy is God's justice. Paul carefully builds his arguments to show how God is now including the Gentiles among the new "Israel of God" (Gal 6, 16).

Paul begins chapter 10, as he had chapter 9, with a defense of his kinspeople. He testifies to Jewish zeal in conforming to the Law, as he himself was zealous for the Law prior to his faith in Christ (see Gal 1, 14). But as the "end of the law" (Rom 10, 4), Christ brings justification for all who believe. Thus, Christ renders the Law useless and eliminates the differences between Jew and Gentile. To support his assertion that Christ is the end of the Law, Paul develops an explanation of scripture in the style of a Jewish Midrash or "running commentary." Paul applies the Old Testament to Christ and so gives an example of how the "law and the prophets testify" to the righteousness given by God in Christ (cf. Rom 3, 2ff). Paul argued that there is only one God of Jews and Gentiles in Romans 3, 21–31. Similarly, here in chapter 10, Paul says that there is only one Lord over all and accessible to all who call upon him. That Lord is Christ. Near the end of the chapter, in 10, 14–21, Paul echoes the traditional prophetic denunciation of Israel who alone is responsible for her infidelity. But God continues to reach out to a "disobedient people"(10, 21).

God's fidelity, proven in the past and present (chs 9 and 10) will ultimately be for the salvation of "all Israel" in the future (Rom 11). God has not finally abandoned Israel because a remnant remains faithful to God as a sign of the ultimate salvation of "all Israel" (Rom 11, 26). Paul cautions the Gentiles, included by the action of Christ into "all Israel," to remember that it is only by grace that they are saved. This is a mystery revealing God's infinite mercy. The power of God is the divine compassion by which all are enfolded into the salvation of "all Israel."

The Heart of Paul's Ethics (12, 1—15, 13)

Paul's ethical conclusions apply his teaching, and form the "imperative" part of the letter. This can be subdivided into consideration of the church and the world (12, 1—13, 14) and a call for reconciliation and unity (14, 1—15, 13). Romans 12, 1–2 has been called the heart of Pauline ethics. Here Christians, who do not yet have a sacrificial ritual like most of their neighbors in their temples or the Jews in Jerusalem, learn that their lives are their living sacrifice, purifying them to be able to live not in conformity to the world (seen as being in opposition to God), but with transformed understanding. In describing the Christian community, Paul adapts the image of the "body" (12, 4–8), a popular image used by Stoic philosophers to illustrate the interdependence of members in a state. Older Catholics may be familiar with this image for the church and probably relate it to ideas developed by Pope Pius XII in an encyclical titled "The Mystical Body" (*Mystici Corporis*). This encyclical stressed the various ways members of the Christian community, both now and in past ages, are related to one another. We can also note that Paul develops the image to stress the very real mutual dependency of Christians who "ought not to think of themselves more highly than others" (12, 3) but as "one body" (12, 4) having many parts. The image of the body provides the transition between the liturgical language that describes Christians'

behavior as "spiritual worship" (12, 1), and the obligations of the mutual love that is to be characteristic of Christians.

Christians and Government

Romans 13, 1–7 takes up the question of the Christian community's relation to civil government. We must remember that Paul is speaking to a minority community within an alien state. At first glance his advice appears simplistic. Paul says that all authority is ordained by God and has its origin in God. Christians in Paul's time were trying simply to survive. Society expected citizens to follow the religion of the state. Paul instructs Christians to be good citizens while not being conformed to the standards of the world around them. Then, having spoken about giving society its due, Paul considers the question of the debt believers owe one another: Love is the fulfillment of the law. Apparently, Paul is acquainted with the love command of Jesus (see Rom 13, 8–10). He reviews the commandments from adultery to covetousness, repeating finally in verse 10 what he stated in verse 8: "Love is the fulfillment of the law."

Divisions over Observances and the Call to Unity (14, 1—15, 13)

Paul frequently says that Christians should be of one and the same mind (e.g., Phil 2, 1–4). However, disagreements over ethical issues threaten the unity that should characterize the Christian church. The Roman Christians disagree over dietary matters and the observance of certain feast days. In a mixed community of Jewish and Gentile Christians, such questions could not help but arise.

Referring to the different sides of this debate, Paul speaks of those with "weak" and those with "strong" faith. His emphasis is not so much on the opinions or positions of individual believers but on the common attitudes to be cultivated among believers. He refers to the faith of the community and of members' responsibility to be united with the faith of the whole body. Paul exhorts the Christians to a fundamental harmony that is expressed in mutual respect and concern for one another. Paul reminds the Roman Christians, many of whom are Jewish, that the Scriptures are written for our instruction and encouragement. The term "encouragement" is linked to the hope that abounds in the community "by the power of the Holy Spirit" (15, 13). Hope, joy, and peace are linked to belief. Faith is a confession about the meaning of Jesus' death and resurrection (see Rom 10, 9). But it is also, according to 15, 7–13, acceptance of other members of the Christian community.

Conclusion (15, 14—16, 27)

Paul reminds the Romans again, as he did at the beginning of his letter, about their common faith as well as his confidence in them. In 15, 14–33 the apostle speaks of his need for their hospitality soon; he requests prayers as he embarks on his mission to Jerusalem to take the collection there. Although Paul is not personally acquainted with the Romans, he has written "boldly" because he is a "minister" of Jesus Christ. He describes his ministry in liturgical language, as a "priestly" (*leitourgos*) duty (15, 16). Paul is of course not referring to a sacramental priesthood, because Christians have not yet developed a theology of sacrificial cult, but to his mission to preach the Christian message to the Gentiles. He uses language common to the Jerusalem Temple priesthood and to other religious worship of the day.

Paul reports that his immediate plans include a visit to Rome in passing on the way to Spain, after taking the collection to Jerusalem. He understands the collection as a symbol linking Jews and Gentiles, the fulfillment of a responsibility he accepted at the Jerusalem council (Gal 2, 10). The term *debt* occurred in Romans 13, 8–10 where Paul described love as the only legitimate debt a believer can incur. Because spiritual blessings are much greater than material things, the Gentiles owe these lesser goods to the Jews as a consequence of their inheriting Israel's spiritual blessings now through Jesus Christ. Common faith makes kin of Jews and Gentiles and links both in mutual responsibility. Paul's strategy, then, is twofold: to ensure that the offering is sizable and that it is accepted as symbolic of the true faith and equal status of the Gentile Christians. If the Jewish Christians accept the gift, they are thereby accepting the mission to the Gentiles.

Chapter 16 consists mostly of greetings to and from various people known to Paul. It is possible that it was originally part of a letter intended for Ephesus and was for some reason later added to the preceding 15 chapters of Romans. This chapter seems almost like an afterthought, and further examination suggests it even contains some discrepancies to material stated or implied in the first 15 chapters. Paul commends Phoebe, bearer of the letter to the Romans, speaking of her as *diakonos* (the only named person in the New Testament who is a "deacon" of a particular church) and *prostatis,* that is, his patron and benefactor. Then he greets numerous people as if he is well known to them and as if he and the Romans have a number of mutual acquaintances. Until now the apostle has maintained a certain distance from the Roman Christians, insinuating that his introduction to himself and to his gospel could serve in place of the personal contact he usually has with communities he has founded. But if Paul knows as many Romans as this chapter indicates, the uncharacteristically general and impersonal tone of chapters 1 through 15 of the letter is strange. The note on 16, 1–23 draws attention to the mixture of Jewish and Gentile names, representative of the mixed background of the Roman community. Much valuable social information about acquaintances and collaborators of Paul, both male and female, whether in Ephesus or Rome, is contained in these verses.

The placement and authorship of the final doxology or blessing is debated. But its appropriateness at the end of this epistle is not. The doxology echoes several themes developed in the letter. Paul speaks of "my gospel" (see 1, 16–17), the mystery kept secret for long ages (11, 25–32), manifested through prophetic writings (numerous allusions to the Old Testament throughout this epistle), and to the obedience of faith (see 1, 5; 15, 28). Paul has pronounced a blessing at various points (7, 24; 8, 35–39; 11, 33–36), as if carried away by the abundance of God's wisdom and mercy. This reflects the Jewish custom of celebrating the wonders of God with praise. Nowhere is the doxology more fitting than after Paul has reviewed the fundamentals of his gospel, with emphasis on the universality of redemption and the imminence of God's victory over all evil in the triumph of Jesus Christ.

Concluding Remarks

Thus important themes are: justification by faith, the emphasis on the present reality of justification contrasted with the former life of sin, and most importantly, the inclusion of all—Jews and Gentiles—in a new Israel of God, the church. The ethical section of Romans may be seen as a description of the church living in but not of the world. It would be hard to overestimate the influence of Romans in the development of Christian doctrine and morality throughout history.

Questions for Discussion and Reflection
Group Sharing/Discussion

1. The issues of community in faith and of reconciliation permeate the book of Romans. Discuss what these mean and why they were important for Paul.

2. Romans contains Paul's basic theological ideas. Some are: universal salvation, justification by faith, the relationship of Israel and the church as transformed by Christ. Let each person choose a theme to review and explain to the group.

3. According to Exodus 19, 6 Israel is "a holy nation." Explain how the Law and God's covenant related to its holiness.

4. Jews and many Jewish Christians, including James and Peter, thought that following the Law held the key to justification. What convinced Paul that justification is an act of God given freely to all?

5. The God-fearing Israelite acted justly by living according to God's covenant. This way of living was revealed in the Torah. The covenant is God's gift to Israel and Israel's response is to keep the Law. Explain Paul's two reasons why this was an inadequate view of justification.

6. Paul shows all, both Gentiles and Jews, have sinned and incurred the "wrath of God" (Rm 1, 18–32). What does this "wrath of God" mean and what does it refer to?

7. In light of time and experience, Paul redefines "Israel" (chs 9–11). For Paul, Israel is not a mere ethnic or historical reality but a reality that always had theological meaning. Explain what Paul is teaching regarding "Israel."

In Our Lives

1. "Following the just requirements of the Law or the precepts of the Church is not a prerequisite for but a result of being justified." Have some people explain what this means for Paul and

others explain what it means and implies for Catholic doctrine.

2. Paul says that justification has already taken place through the death and resurrection of Christ. Salvation is in the future, promised to those who believe in Christ and live according to that belief. For Paul it is God's power, not our own, and our reliance on God, not on our own abilities that saves us. Explain this belief of Paul's in your own words. Reflect on this to make it your own.

3. In chapter 13 Paul instructs Christians to be good citizens while not being conformed to the standards of the world around them. Name the standards of the world around you. Spell out what it means to be Christian working for the common good in this world. How do you communicate this vision? How can you do it more effectively?

4. This is an important letter because it explains Paul's theology and views. What, if anything, was surprising to you? What is especially appealing or important for you? Was anything surprising to you?

5. Paul explains baptism (6, 1–23) by a common preposition: "with," that is, we have "died with, are buried with, we are raised with and now live with" him. As a result, we walk in newness of life. Share what this all means in living your baptism.

Individual/Personal Reflection/Action

1. Look through Romans 8 again and choose part of it to re-read and reflect on. Think about the role of the Spirit in your life and in the life of the Christian community. The power of the Spirit enables us to work toward unity and a loving relationship with one another. How does this affect the way you relate to the Christian community? To people of other faiths? To the people of the world?

2. Paul's doctrine of "justification by faith" is central to his whole relationship with Jesus. What does "justification by faith" mean in Romans? Reflect on this essential Pauline doctrine. Then consider what it means in your life. Does it help you to grow in your relationship with Christ? What role does concern and care of others play in relationship to "justification by faith"?

THE LETTERS TO THE CORINTHIANS

Introduction

The letters to the Corinthians reveal Paul the pastoral theologian in ways that his other letters do not. The sheer number of pastoral problems posed and answered, especially in 1 Corinthians, leads us to think that here Paul was most challenged to apply the principles he knew to the lives of his community. The Corinthians could never be accused of lack of initiative. Rather, they seem to have taken (perhaps more seriously than Paul would have liked) his encouragement to find new freedom in Christ, so that his relationship with them was complex and tumultuous.

Corinth was the capital and central city of the Roman Province of Achaia, which comprised southern Greece. Its location near the isthmus dividing the Peloponnesus from mainland Greece made it a major seaport and trading center. It was also a Roman freedmen's colony, and therefore its population was made up of people of various groups, but with a heavy concentration of Roman citizens and Roman interests. With its mixture of national and religious groups, rich and poor, Jews, pagans, and Christians, and moral and immoral people, it was an exciting but difficult environment for the small Christian community, which was predominantly Gentile, but probably had a small Jewish minority.

The letters we call 1 and 2 Corinthians formed part of a larger collection that originally consisted of several letters Paul wrote to the community. He speaks in 1 Corinthians 5, 9 of a previous letter written to the Corinthians instructing them to avoid immoral people. Such a letter no longer exists, and nowhere do we have this instruction from Paul, unless, as has been suggested, a piece of it survives as 2 Corinthians 6, 14—7, 1. Similarly, the reference to a letter written in "much affliction and anguish of heart" (2 Cor 2, 4) hardly fits the tone of 1 Corinthians. Furthermore, 2 Corinthians is characterized by discontinuity, suggesting that it is actually composed of several letters put together (see NAB, introduction to 2 Cor).

We learn that the Corinthians also wrote to Paul (see 1 Cor 7, 1), and that the Corinthian church, difficult as it was for Paul, preserved and honored his advice, undoubtedly reading his letters at liturgical gatherings as Paul had instructed them. We are left with the impression that the existing letters reflect an editing and combining of writings, compiled as the community processed and integrated the words of the apostle.

1 CORINTHIANS READING GUIDE

At a Glance

Who are the main players?	Paul Christian Community at Corinth Chloe Apollos Sosthenes
What should I look for?	1 Corinthians is a particularly fruitful source of reflection because it raises many issues that are still relevant: divisions based on different world views, marriage and celibacy, theology of women and the participation of women in church, the Eucharist, charismatic gifts, and belief in the Resurrection.
When did this take place?	In writing this around A.D. 56, Paul was responding to disquieting reports he had received while he was in Ephesus.
Where did these events occur?	Corinth was a Roman freedmen's colony and therefore its population was made up of various peoples but with a heavy concentration of Roman citizens. With its mixture of national and religious groups, rich and poor, Jews, pagans, and Christians, it was an exciting but difficult environment for the small Christian community.

Why was this book written?

The Corinthians were not a single large community. Several small communities gathered at different houses. These communities represented different competitive factions and developed divergent expressions of Christian life and worship. Paul addresses these real situations.

What is the story?

The Corinthians disagreed about Christian life after baptism. Paul responds to these issues. Although our problems and divisions may be expressed somewhat differently, Paul's admonitions to the Corinthians on the importance of charity, unity, and mutual respect based upon a common faith provide us with a model of approaching our own problems.

Before Beginning

In writing 1 Corinthians around A.D. 56, Paul was responding to some disquieting reports he had received about the community. First Corinthians addresses real, not theoretical, situations. Paul's knowledge of what was going on was based on verbal accounts from reliable sources, letters from members of the community, and Paul's own 18-month experience of living in this community (Acts 18, 11).

First Corinthians is a particularly fruitful source of reflection for our contemporary church because it raises so many issues that are still relevant: divisions based on ideologies or different world views, incest, lawsuits among Christians, scandal, marriage and celibacy, theology of woman and the participation of women in the church, the proper way to celebrate Eucharist, charismatic gifts, and belief in the Resurrection. We, like the Corinthians, are challenged to find the right role and qualifications of leadership in a pluralistic society. Like the Corinthians we need to recognize that how we live and behave is a sign of what we believe.

In a sense, the singular "community" might misrepresent the Corinthians. We may tend to think of the community as a specific group that met at the house of a particular individual in a city. But the Corinthians were not a single large community. It is likely that in that particular city there were several Christian communities that congregated at different houses. Apparently, these communities represented different competitive factions. Each community was developing divergent expressions of Christian life and worship. Some groups were homogeneous,

preferring to worship with like-minded people from similar social and religious backgrounds, who followed certain diets and enjoyed certain prestigious spiritual gifts.

A variety of liturgical celebrations developed. The Corinthians disagreed about whether Christians ought to marry or, if married, should remain married after baptism. Paul responds to these issues among the Christians at Corinth. Although our problems and divisions may be expressed somewhat differently, Paul's admonitions to the Corinthians on the importance of unity, charity, and mutual respect based on a common faith provide us with a model for approaching our own problems. First Corinthians discloses to us the pastor, Paul, who encourages the Corinthians to imitate him as he imitates Christ (11, 1).

Working through 1 Corinthians

Our comments on the major themes and relevance of this epistle will follow the structure suggested in the NAB introduction to the book. with some rather minor adjustments. First Corinthians contains the usual letter format: an address in 1, 1–9, the body of the letter in 1, 10—15, 58, and a conclusion in 16, 1–24.

Because this letter is a response to the concerns of the Corinthians, there is not the same kind of objective, formal structure as in Romans. Yet in 1 Corinthians there is a structural pattern that helps shed some light on the emphasis and meaning of Paul's message. Paul's general approach to issues follows an A-B-A' pattern by which Paul introduces and begins to develop a topic (A), disrupts his reflections by bringing up a second issue (B), and then returns to the original topic (A). Often he uses this pattern to emphasize the middle, or B, statement. One illustration is Paul's discussion of abuses in the celebration of the Eucharist.

1. 11, 17–22. Paul describes the abuses in 1 Corinthians (A).

2. 11, 23–25 Paul interjects into the middle of this description his account of Jesus' Last Supper the night before he died (B).

3. 11, 26–34. Paul's discussion of abuses continues (A).

In this way Paul tries to remedy the abuses at Corinth by recalling what Jesus did and reminding the Corinthians that they are to act "in memory of" Jesus. Further examples of Paul's use of the A-B-A′ pattern will be discussed as they appear in this letter. For the moment simply note that the pattern has the effect of emphasizing the B section as a corrective for the situations described in A and A′.

A working outline of 1 Corinthians is the following:

I. Address (1, 1–9)
II. The Body of the Letter (1, 10—15, 58)
  A. Reported Divisions and Abuses (1, 10—6, 20)
    1. Factions (1, 10—4, 21)
    2. Immoral Behavior (5, 1—6, 20)
  B. Answers to the Corinthians' Questions (7, 1—11, 1)
    1. Marriage and Virginity (7, 1–40)
    2. Food Offered to Idols (8, 1—11, 1)
      a. Exercising Knowledge and Love (8, 1–13; 10, 1—11, 1)
      b. The Example of Paul (9, 1–27)
  C. Problems in Liturgical Assemblies (11, 2—14, 40)
    1. Dress and Decorum in the Assembly (11, 2–16)
    2. Celebration of the Eucharist (11, 17–34)
    3. The Spiritual Gifts (12, 1—14, 40)
  D. The Resurrection (15, 1–58)
III. Conclusion (16, 1–24)

Reading through 1 Corinthians

The Address (1, 1–9)

The address contains a greeting (1, 1–3) and thanksgiving (1, 4–9). In the greeting, Paul refers to himself as an "apostle of Jesus Christ" and identifies a "brother," Sosthenes, as co-author who, however, does not reappear in the letter. He is perhaps to be identified with the synagogue official of the same name in Acts 18, 17. Paul addresses the community as a "church" (*ekklesia*), which has been "sanctified in Jesus Christ" and "called to be holy." Paul thus reminds the Corinthians that they have a common vocation (*ekklesia* literally means "called out of"). This is Paul's usual word for the assembly of believers, taken from the civic word for the assembly of citizens in a free city-state. It may also be a conscious translation of the Hebrew *qahal*, the biblical assembly of Israel. The Corinthians have a new identity, rooted in God, that distinguishes them from the world around them.

Paul's adaptation of the thanksgiving usually found in Hellenistic letters focuses on the blessings received by his addressees. The thanksgiving also announces themes Paul will develop in the letter. The Corinthians lack no spiritual gift (1, 7). The factions among them that so concerned Paul are rooted precisely in their envy of and competition for extraordinary gifts.

The Body of the Letter (1, 10—15, 58)

All of 1 Corinthians addresses specific issues that caused dissension and strained the fabric of the Corinthian community. In the first section of the body or main part of the letter, Paul discusses the divisions he has heard about among the Corinthians (1, 10—6, 20). He then turns to address matters that the Corinthians had themselves directed to him (see 7, 1—11, 1). Finally, Paul will consider other issues relevant to the Corinthian community; namely, appropriate ways of celebrating the Eucharist (11, 2—14, 40) and the meaning of the Resurrection (15, 1–58).

Reported Divisions and Abuses (1, 10—6, 20)

Reports from Chloe's people (see 1, 11) identified some problems at Corinth stemming from two matters: (a) factions (1, 10—4, 21) and (b) immoral behavior (5, 1—6, 20).

Factions in Corinth (1, 10—4, 21). The variety of backgrounds of its members caused many problems in the community of Corinth. Various members of the community turned to different leaders, and groups began to vie with one another for superiority and recognition. Paul first takes up the slogans adopted by groups who profess allegiance to the various leaders. He names group leaders, specifically Cephas (i.e., Peter), Apollos, and himself. He shows the absurdity of divisions based on leadership, which is superficial compared to the common baptism by which all Christians are sanctified and saved.

The Corinthians disagreed among themselves about which leaders were the most important and which group of Christians was the most prestigious. They may have taken their lead from disagreements among the great figures themselves. James disagreed with Paul, for example, about whether any aspects of the Jewish Law were required of Gentile Christians (Gal 2). Peter favored at least minimal requirements, while Paul advocated complete freedom from the Jewish Law for Gentile converts. First Corinthians suggests that the leaders' disagreement affected the Corinthians and caused many to side with one leader against another. But the Corinthians also had their own divisions.

Another leader was Apollos who, for very different reasons, had a following that competed for the Corinthians' loyalty. Apollos attracted many Corinthians because of his eloquence in speaking (see Acts 18, 24–28). Meanwhile, some of the Corinthians cited Paul's unimpressive physical presence and speaking abilities as reason to reject him (1 Cor 2, 1–5; 2 Cor 1, 10). Paul chided the Corinthians for judging by human standards, not by God's as revealed in the cross of Christ. Paul reminded them that neither he nor Peter nor Apollos were crucified for them. The Corinthians were baptized in Christ's name and belonged to Christ. The formation of competitive groups within the Christian community is absurd. Paul admonishes the Corinthians to remember who they are—that by worldly standards few among them have any reason to boast (1, 26–31)—but that "in the Lord" they can boast that they are saved and form a "new creation" (2 Cor 5, 17). They do not have wealth or nobility or education, but they are rich in the blessings of the Spirit of God. The "not many of you" in verse 26 has been read both ways: Paul is stressing the humble origins and status of most, but in saying this he suggests that some really were of higher social status and wealth.

The first part of this letter (1, 10—4, 21) may be summarized as the gospel paradox, the teaching that God's wisdom is greater than human wisdom, that the power of the cross outweighs all human power. The Corinthians portrayed themselves as sophisticated, mature, and truly wise. Paul describes them as rather immature, of the "flesh" rather than spiritual (3, 1), deceiving themselves and therefore lacking in the most fundamental knowledge. They erroneously judged according to standards that are transitory rather than eternal. The riches and wisdom of God surpass all understanding and may be perceived only through wisdom that is revealed by the Spirit (2, 10).

Immoral Behavior (5, 1—6, 20). In chapters 5 and 6, Paul gives examples of when judgments on the appropriate behavior for believers would be necessary. The Christian message of salvation has many implications—doctrinal, liturgical, ethical. Certain behavior is inconsistent with belonging to the Christian community. Chapters 5 and 6 specifically mention incest, bringing lawsuits against other members of the community, and sexual promiscuity, as up to the community's judgment.

The Corinthians were complacent about keeping in their community someone who violated Jewish incest laws by living with his stepmother.

Paul uses a traditional image of "yeast" to help describe the impact of the presence of such a one in their midst. The proverb "a little yeast leavens all the dough" illustrates the extent to which the sinner's action corrupts the whole community. Jesus uses this same image to warn about the influence of the Pharisees on the disciples (Mt 16, 6; Mk 8, 15; Lk 12, 1). Paul was concerned about the impact of the sinner on the community and the "contagion" of sinful actions. Throughout this letter, a fundamental point of Christian theology is emphasized: Namely, as Christians we cannot act alone without regard for one another. Our actions affect others, for good or evil. Paul sees conversion as a "turning from idols to worship of the one living and true God." (1 Thes 1, 9). This conversion requires a readiness to change not only our hearts, but also our actions so that we may live in accordance with our baptism. Continuing the yeast image, Paul cites the formula of the Paschal Lamb and unleavened bread, pure and free from yeast. Yeast, as it is here, is usually a negative symbol. The connection is especially relevant at the time of the year in which Paul writes, the season of Passover (16, 8).

It troubles Paul to hear that some in the community are bringing lawsuits against one another, when what they should be doing is suffering wrongs in imitation of Christ. At best, they should settle such disputes among themselves. He reminds them of the scenario in which God's holy ones will judge the earth. They therefore have no business submitting their grievances to unbelieving judges now. Nor do they know what they are doing by participating in prostitution. "All things are lawful" to the one who is free in Christ, but this does not mean all things are acceptable. The body of every believer is a temple of the Holy Spirit that cannot be profaned.

Answers to the Corinthians' Questions (7, 1—11, 1)

Paul then takes up the Corinthians' own questions about how daily life is an expression of their faith. The Corinthians themselves identified certain issues within their community that were disturbing their unity. They wrote to Paul about these two types of questions: those about marriage and virginity (see 7, 1–40) and those pertaining to the eating of idol meats and participation at pagan meals (8, 1—11, 1).

Marriage and Virginity (7, 1–40). In chapter 7 Paul specifically discusses three life choices that many Christians believed were affected by baptism with an advantage on one side: marriage or virginity (7, 1–7.16), fidelity to Judaism signified by circumcision versus noncircumcision (vv. 18–20), and slavery versus freedom (vv. 21–24). According to 1 Corinthians 7, a specific question arose concerning whether married Christians ought to remain married. An understanding of baptism as initiation into the eschatological community seemed to imply that the baptized should renounce the constraints and responsibilities of marriage. Jesus' opposition to divorce is first attested here (7, 10.11). Some asked whether a Christian married to an unbeliever could or should remain in the marriage. Some men wondered if there was an advantage to circumcision. Some slaves thought, and perhaps expected, that they would be better off freed.

Paul's general advice is to "remain in the state in which you were called" (see 7, 17.20.24). His reasoning is that the time is short (7, 29.31), too short for unnecessary social entanglements. It is debatable whether Paul believed literally that the end was imminent or whether this was his way of seeing all of life as dependent on the absolute power and will of God. Although Christians are "in" the world, they are not "of" it as John says (Jn 17, 14–16). The particular circumstances of believers do not interfere with or lessen the effect of the new status of their identity in Christ. Christians have always sensed the need to express the implications of their new identity as baptized persons with an appropriate way of life.

Paul agreed with a position held by some in Corinth, that "it is a good thing . . . not to touch a woman" (1 Cor 7, 1). Paul acknowledged his own preference for celibacy that leaves one "free of anxieties" (7, 32). The Gospels record Jesus' saying that "in heaven there is neither giving nor taking in marriage" (see Mk 12, 25 and parallel passages). Sexuality, circumcision, even slavery do not have significance in the new age. Indeed, the hope for a new society of equals was one of the reasons Christianity was so appealing to many "minority" groups, including women, slaves, and others who lacked status in the Greco-Roman world.

Paul's response is to advocate no change in social status because it is unimportant in the Christian context. Responding to those who challenge the right of Christians to marry, Paul drew on the word of Jesus regarding the indissolubility of marriage (7, 10–11). Yet Paul added an exception that considerably weakens the effect of Jesus' statement. In the case of unwillingness of the unbelieving spouse to remain married to a baptized person, they may separate. Furthermore, Paul applied the exception to both men and women, giving women the same rights as men.

We should note Paul's remarkable freedom in relating Jesus' words to the pastoral situation of Corinth. In all of the questions with which he has to deal, Paul demonstrates a surprising creativity and flexibility.

Food Offered to Idols (8, 1—11, 1). Here Paul responds to three very practical situations about which the Corinthians must make everyday decisions: whether they should (a) eat meat bought in the marketplace that was probably originally offered in sacrifice at a pagan temple; (b) accept dinner invitations in rented banquet rooms in pagan temples, during which there was a sacrificial libation to the god in whose temple they were; (c) accept dinner invitations to the homes of unbelievers. He asserts a basic theological position that these gods are not really gods at all, supports it with reference to Israel's history as recorded in the Scriptures (10, 1–13) and with the example of his own experience. But the bottom line is the unity of the community. If anyone of weaker conscience will be scandalized, then it is not to be done.

Exercising Knowledge and Love (8, 1–7 and 10, 23—11, 1). Paul quotes a Corinthian slogan, acknowledging the truth that "all of us have knowledge" (8, 1). The Corinthians apparently assumed that such knowledge made some of them superior to others. So, for example, it was their "knowledge" that allowed them to overlook incest in one of their members (see ch 5). It was the competition for the gifts considered superior that was disrupting their assemblies (14, 20–33) and even the LORD's Supper (11, 17–18). Paul proposes charity as a remedy for the rivalry of the various kinds of "knowledge" that inflate the ego and that were causing factions in the Corinthian church. Whereas knowledge divides, love unites, enabling the Corinthians' many gifts to supply various needs in the community, helping them to "build up" (see the description of the role of prophecy in 1 Cor 14, 3), rather than destroy (1 Cor 11, 17–34).

In discussing the factions between the "weak and the strong," Paul speaks of "conscience," a term that appears almost exclusively in Pauline writings with little impact on other New Testament authors (e.g., Rom 2, 15; 9, 1; 13, 5; 1 Cor 8, 7.10.12; 10, 25.27.28.29; 2 Cor 1, 12; 1 Tm 1, 5; 2 Tm 1, 3; Ti 1, 15; see also Acts 23, 1; Heb 9, 9.14; 1 Pt 2, 19; 3, 16.21). In biblical thinking, conscience never involves only the individual. It always has to do with how one sees oneself in relation to one's community. Paul gives a communal meaning to conscience and places it in a new Christian context. In this context, the personal consciences of both the "weak" and the "strong" are subordinate to the obligations of mutual charity. The weak must not judge the strong and the strong not scandalize the weak. For Paul, conscience is not autonomous. It cannot be the last court of appeal among Christians. It is subject to charity and concern for one "for whom Christ has died" (8, 11).

In 1 Corinthians 10, 23—11, 1, Paul summarizes his discussion of knowledge of the specific issues regarding pagan meals and customs, and of imitation of his own example. Quoting another Corinthian slogan (as he did in 8, 1 where he said "all of us have knowledge"), Paul agrees "Everything is lawful" (10, 23). Yet, he continues, not everything is beneficial. The merit of an action is related to its effects on the community. Concrete questions about whether to eat or not should be resolved in view of their effect on the other members of the community. For Paul, the morality of a decision depends upon its impact on the conscience of other brothers and sisters. Paul's attempt to win others over rather than to alienate them keeps their salvation in view. Thus, he concludes that Corinthian Christians ought to imitate him as he does Christ (11, 1).

The Example of Paul (9, 1–27). To support his argument about mutual love and avoidance of scandal, Paul inserts between the two parts of the argument the example of his own conduct (ch 9 represents B in the A-B-A' pattern discussed in the introduction.) Though he could demand material support, though he could exercise a great deal more freedom and authority, he instead tries to become all things to everyone by being as much like them as possible. The hint is clear: You too do not need to exercise all the freedom to which you have a right, but you can subordinate some of it for the good of the whole. The Corinthians' problems reflect their mixed makeup of predominantly Gentile but also partly Jewish members, as well as a certain level of education and intellectual refinement. Greek intellectual life valued gifts of mind and spirit, such as knowledge and eloquent reasoning. Such gifts contributed to the status of the individuals who possessed them, sometimes to the detriment of charity.

In many of his letters, Paul refers to the fact that he works with his hands and thus gives an example for his addressees to follow (1 Thes 2, 9; 2 Thes 3, 7–10). Paul freely forfeited the privilege of support "not to place an obstacle to the gospel of Christ" (1 Cor 9, 12). He served all—Jews, Gentiles, the "strong and the weak"—so that through this service the gospel message would be available to them. No one should be denied the gospel because of inability to pay. This forfeiting of privilege makes Paul freer to serve.

Yet, as he will argue in 2 Corinthians 8, 1—9, 15, after receiving the gospel message, Christians have a responsibility to contribute to the support of other Christians in need. Here he ends this digression about his own example with an athletic image. Just like a professional athlete, he disciplines himself, training not for a perishable crown of laurel or celery, as did the athletes of the day, but for an imperishable one.

Asceticism has played an important role in Christian spirituality throughout the history of the church. Paul legitimizes asceticism or self-denial for apostolic reasons. Today we live in a world that encourages individual freedom without constraints and the pursuit of happiness almost to any length. Such a mentality is not so distant from the sophisticated world of the Corinthians. Paul's corrective view suggests another approach altogether. The community's pursuit of charity should be the focus of the individual's energies and form the individual's conscience. Freedom is for the service of the gospel message. A person's rights are subject to God's call to preach the gospel. The charity of God compels us, training us in the school of self-denial and the pursuit of God's will in our lives.

Problems in Liturgical Assemblies (11, 2—14, 40)

Paul now turns to issues affecting the ways that the Corinthians are worshiping together. They fall into three categories: decorum at assemblies (11, 2–16), celebration of the Lord's Supper (11, 17–34), and the unity and variety of spiritual gifts (12, 1—14, 40).

Dress and Decorum in the Assembly (11, 2–16). This is a problematic passage that has received much attention. Throughout the ancient Mediterranean world, among Jews, Greeks, and Romans alike, the subordination of women to men was a common part of the thinking, even though by this time women of sufficient wealth and status exercised a great deal of social and economic autonomy. It was common custom that respectable adult women veiled themselves in public, even though that custom was changing in social circles that were more sensitive to Roman customs. In more traditional circles, as is still the case in some cultures, the unveiled female head was a sign of sexual availability. It appears that some female members of the Corinthian church,

however, were combining their knowledge of newer social customs with Paul's own preaching about freedom in the Spirit and concluded that the veil was no longer necessary in some circumstances, particularly the church assembly, where others, including Paul, judged that it was. While never questioning women's right to pray and prophesy publicly (11, 5), he simply judged that it must be done with traditional dress. In his attempt to provide a theological explanation, Paul draws on traditional images of headship and subordination, using as illustration three parallel examples.

Christ and man, man and woman, God and Christ. He then goes on to appeal to "nature," which really means "common sense," that is, what people were used to. Finally, he realizes that he has not proved his case and simply withdraws to the position of authority: We just don't do it that way (11, 16)! While affirming women's full position in the church, he capitulates on the question of dress in favor of something that will not cause scandal among conservative outsiders (and perhaps some insiders, too) who are undoubtedly watching this new movement.

Celebration of the Eucharist (11, 17–34). There were divisions among the Corinthians on social and economic grounds. Wealthy Christians apparently boasted great meals at which the poor were either not welcomed or were treated badly. Some people became drunk while others went away hungry (11, 20–22.33–34). Paul says that this is not the Lord's Supper and that the Corinthians are eating and drinking their own condemnation (see 11, 27–29). Within the context of the discussion of abuses in the community's liturgical celebrations, Paul inserts his account of the institution of the Last Supper to put the troubles in the proper context. This is the earliest written account of the institution of the Lord's Supper in the New Testament (see the note on 11, 23–25). Paul's version, also reflected in Luke 22, 14–20, contains at least three significant differences from the version given in Mark 14, 22–25 and in Matthew 26, 26–29. These variants are in the additions of the words "for you," the command "Do this in remembrance of me" (v. 24), and the qualifier "new" before "covenant" in 11, 25. These variants witness to several early versions of the eucharistic sayings.

By emphasizing that Jesus' body was given "for you," Paul reminds the Corinthians of Jesus' self-giving act in which they participate by receiving the bread and the cup. They are then warned that an "unworthy" reception would not bring salvation but rather condemnation. The command to do this in memory of Jesus calls the Christians to offer a fitting memorial, including calling to mind Jesus' self-offering and imitating him in this. The insertion of "new" before "covenant" reminds the Corinthians that Jeremiah's prophecy of a "new covenant" is fulfilled in Christ (see Jer 31, 31; 2 Cor 3, 3.6). This is an inclusive covenant, one that is already proclaimed in ancient Israel and that will be extended to all, one that provides the basis for a new society and a new relationship with God. It is important to realize that Paul's critique of the Corinthian Eucharist is not primarily concerned with proper reverence toward the sacrament, but with proper reverence toward the poor and proper respect for all members of the community who participate in the celebration of the Eucharist.

The Spiritual Gifts (12, 1—14, 40). The divisions among the Corinthians based on competition for the higher gifts continues to occupy Paul. He reminds the Corinthians that when they were pagans they were "attracted and led away" by idols (12, 2). Idolatry attributes the honor and devotion that belongs to God to false gods. Paul advises the Corinthians that in true conversion to Jesus Christ, there is unity with others who also worship the same God.

The hymn of love in 1 Corinthians 13, inserted within the context of chapters 12 and 14 on the variety of gifts, may not be a Pauline composition but something borrowed from Stoic sources, which he found helpful to illustrate the unity that should characterize the Corinthians (see note on 13, 1–13). In chapter 11, Paul alluded to the divisions between the wealthy and the poor at the common table. In chapters 12 and 14, it is not so much the social distinctions as striving for spiritual gifts that threatens the Corinthians' unity. As remedy, Paul offers reflections on the community as the body of Christ (12, 12–27), a new adaptation of an old image of social unity. A very high estimation is placed on prophecy, the action of the Spirit through members of the community. But the new context Paul provides emphasizes that love is the highest spiritual gift, one to which all believers must aspire to achieve (13, 13). Love remains the most important of all the spiritual gifts in the church. This is not to diminish faith and hope and the other spiritual gifts such as teaching and administration. Love is an expression of God's own love, enabling us to act mercifully and kindly toward one another. Love in action, at the service of others, is the essential message of the gospel.

The Resurrection (15, 1–58)

For Paul, the death, burial, and resurrection of Christ make up the central mystery of the Christian life—but not in isolation. If we are to experience death and burial, we are also to experience resurrection. Paul claims to have met the Risen Christ directly, and we can assume that some of his assertions about the Resurrection are derived from that experience (Gal 1, 12.15–16). Others perhaps came from his meeting with Cephas (Gal 1, 18), who had participated in the post-Easter appearances. Paul implies that if the Corinthians really grasped and accepted the Resurrection and its implications, many of the problems he has addressed throughout the letter would have been resolved. In the first part of this chapter (15, 1–11), he states the fundamental teaching on the resurrection of Christ and recites the earliest surviving creed and list of appearances. He stresses the appearances of the Risen Christ that were the foundational experiences, beginning with Peter's and ending with his own.

A second section (11, 12–28) states emphatically, "If Christ is not risen, our faith is in vain" (15, 14.17). The resurrection of Christ forms the basis of faith and causes believers to reassess all of life and death. By his resurrection, Christ is revealed as the "first fruits of those who have fallen asleep" (15, 20). Christ is our hope, our assurance that we too will have the same experience. Without it, perseverance in faith, including the sacrifices involved in suffering persecution, is pointless.

In a third section (11, 29–34), Paul is trying to shame the Corinthians by showing them the absurdities of some Christian practices and beliefs without faith in the Resurrection as the fate of all the faithful. The slogan quoted by Paul, "Let us eat and drink for tomorrow we die" (15, 32) is the wisdom of those without hope in the life to come.

In the next section (11, 35–50), he takes up those who speculate on the nature of resurrection and the risen body. He uses the example of dissimilar creatures, such as birds and fish, the sun and the moon, to show the qualitative difference between bodies as a way of stressing, without going into detail, the differences in our bodies before and after the resurrection. The seed sown in the ground is not the same as the green shoot that springs from it, yet the shoot is continuous with the life of the seed that must die to produce it. Paul draws a contrast between the first Adam, the earthly, corruptible one whose image we now bear, and the last Adam, Christ, the incorruptible and eternal one, whose image we will bear in the resurrection.

The last section of 1 Corinthians 15 (vv. 51–58) incorporates a hymn celebration of God's victory through Christ over sin and death, compiled from verses of Isaiah and Hosea. Conquered by Christ, sin and death have lost their sting. By the resurrection of Christ, God has shown us that sin and death are not the last word, but only lead to life. Therefore, Paul sings God's praises for the hope that the Resurrection gives. He reminds the Corinthians that their "labor is not in vain in the Lord" (1 Cor 15, 58). The rousing message of the chapter is: hang on! The best is yet to come!

Conclusion (16, 1–24)

Finally, Paul speaks of the collection of money and how it is to alleviate the suffering of the saints (16, 1–4). Paul then reports his travel plans, sends greetings to his friends, and concludes with a blessing. Comparison of the persons named with those mentioned in 1 Corinthians 1 and Acts 18 renders an interesting profile of the Corinthian community with its mixture of notable men and women, rich and poor, powerful and ordinary citizens. Paul greets representatives of all categories, personally demonstrating the acceptance and unity he has been advocating.

Concluding Remarks

Some readers may find it surprising to realize that Paul deals in 1 Corinthians with some of the same questions that continue to challenge the church today. Christians still struggle with whether there are more limits on the freedom allowed to women than to men. The rights and responsibilities of ministers in the church are at the heart of the renewal of the priesthood initiated by Vatican II and continued in various important pastoral and ecclesial efforts locally and in the universal church. Issues such as the requirements for a sacramental marriage and qualifications for the ordained ministry, the possibilities for lay ministries, or the role of the sacraments (especially baptism and the Eucharist) in Christian life were not answered by Paul, or even by Vatican II, once and for all. But the church continues to use Paul's pastoral approach to guide and to respond to the needs of its members.

The Corinthians were a church like ours— real people with real problems. They struggled for charity in the midst of disagreements, for respect for leaders without exaggerating these leaders' roles. Paul stressed the role of ministers as servants of God and Jesus Christ. Paul recognizes the authority of the church to discipline its members, including the immoral, those in dispute, the strong as well as the weak. Paul tried to help remedy their problems by advising them to seek spiritual gifts, especially charity. Paul advocated a healthy respect for the body without failing to see the value of asceticism. Paul recognized roles for both women and men in the liturgy. He gave some concrete examples of practical implications of living the gospel message as a community of equals. He protests discrimination against the poor or those considered inferior because they possess lesser gifts. Further, Paul stresses already in 1 Corinthians, and more so in 2 Corinthians, the necessity of aiding the less fortunate. The first epistle to the Corinthians is truly an interpretation of the gospel message that continues to challenge us with its many implications.

Questions for Discussion and Reflection
Group Sharing/Discussion

1. Where is Corinth? What was the make-up of the population of Corinth in Paul's time?

2. What was the occasion of Paul's writing 1 Corinthians?

3. Present a role-play dialogue between the following:

  a. Peter and Paul;

  b. Paul and Apollos. Have the players present the disputes that cause the frictions among the Corinthians, cf. 1, 10—4, 22. At the end have Paul present his solutions to these frictions.

4. In the United States today, describe a mature, sophisticated, wise person. In Paul's day Corinthians thought they were so! Paul considered them immature. Why?

5. Paul names incest, lawsuits against Christians, and sexual promiscuity as behavior inconsistent with belonging to the Christian community. Do you agree with this? Would you add or qualify this list?

6. Jesus' word on indissolubility of marriage and his opposition to divorce are attested to here (7, 10–11). But Paul also allows for making exceptions to this. What are these?

7. Paul proposes charity as a cure for various kinds of "knowledge" (8, 1–7; 10, 23—11, 1. 17–18; 14, 20–33). Give some concrete examples of this principle that knowledge divides, charity unites.

8. Here are several principles of the Christian life as Paul taught in Corinthians. Have a person or team explain each in context of Corinthians and of today.

  a. Conscience is never a merely individual function.

  b. The morality of a decision depends upon its impact on others (11, 1).

  c. Forfeiting of privilege make one freer to serve (9, 12).

  d. Asceticism plays an important role in Christian spirituality.

  e. Freedom is for the service of the gospel.

9. Paul emphasizes that love is the highest spiritual gift, one which all believers must aspire to achieve (13, 13). Read aloud the hymn of love (1 Cor 13), each taking a part. Afterwards, spell out examples of these verses.

In Our Lives

1. For Paul, the death, burial, and resurrection of Christ make up the central mystery of the Christian life. "If Christ has not been raised, your faith is in vain" (15, 14–17). Share what you understand by this central mystery. How does this impact your beliefs and behavior?

2. Paul emphasizes the importance of unity, charity, and mutual respect in solving problems. How can these provide a model for personal and community problem solving? When have you seen this in your life?

3. In Paul's account of the institution of the Last Supper (the earliest in writing), he notes three significant differences from versions in Matthew and Mark. These additions are: (a) "for you"; (b) "Do this in remembrance of me"; and (c) "new" before covenant. What do each mean? What do they mean to you?

4. Like the Corinthians we need to appreciate that our behavior is an indicator of what we believe. How does this express itself in your life and community?

Individual/Personal Reflection/Action

1. Remember that "in the Lord" we can boast that we are saved (1, 26–31) and form a "new creation" (2 Cor 5, 17). Reflect and pray that this may be your own expression of faith.

2. As Christians, we cannot act alone without regard for one another. This is a fundamental Christian belief according to Paul. Count the ways that you are called to show regard for others and the community. What can you do to become closer to your own parish community? Pray to nourish this commitment in your life.

3. Return to chapter 13. Take a few minutes a day for the next month and use this as food for mediation.

The Influence of Apocalyptic Thinking on Paul

Apocalyptic literature (Greek *apokalypsis* "unveiling"; Latin *revelatio*) contains mysterious revelations, usually veiled in symbolic language and delivered by a heavenly guide such as an angel. It intends to show the true meaning of history, current events, and the future, especially the final judgment. The book of Revelation and Daniel 7–12 are examples within the Bible. It was intended to encourage the people to remain faithful during times of suffering, oppression, and disappointment.

The list below shows some of the ways that apocalyptic thinking influenced Paul. It is based on four elements of Jewish apocalyptic thought that had significant impact on Paul and other New Testament writers. (For more about apocalyptic literature, see the Reading Guides to Daniel, RG 233, and Revelation, RG 455.)

Four Elements of Jewish Apocalyptic Thought Found in Paul

1. Salvation is available to all. For the Jews all of history, good and bad, was tied to the divine plan for Israel's salvation. Paul extends this concern to all of humanity, saved in Christ.
   - God shows no partiality (Rom 1, 16; 3, 22 and 29; 10, 12; Eph 2, 14)
   - "neither Jew nor Greek . . . all one in Christ" (Gal 3, 28)
   - The new Israel of God is inclusive of the Gentiles (Rom 9, 6; Gal 6, 15)
   - Christ eliminated the barrier between Jew and Gentile, establishing peace (Col 1, 20; Eph 2, 15–16)

2. Salvation of the Faithful and Punishment of the Wicked. This pattern is typical of apocalyptic writers. The basis for the judgment for Paul is acceptance or rejection of the gospel.
   - The "saved" and the perishing (1 Cor 1, 18; 2 Thes 2, 10)
   - Judgment according to "good and evil" (2 Cor 5, 10)
   - The faithful delivered from the wrath (1 Thes 1, 10) but not the "enemies of the cross" (Phil 3, 18; 1 Thes 2, 16)

3. Dualism—Two Powers (conflict between good and evil). This is a way of explaining the tension and even hostility between how things are now and the time of fulfillment to come. In apocalyptic writings, good will eventually triumph.
   - Christ is in the process of returning all things to God (1 Cor 15, 28)
   - Dangers threaten the Christian community: factions (1 Cor 1, 10–25; Gal 5, 13–15; Phil 2, 1–4); idleness 1 Thes 4, 11f; 5, 14; 2 Thes 3, 6–15); persecution from outside (Phil 1, 28–30)
   - All creation is involved in the conflict (Rom 8, 20–25; Phil 3, 21)

4. The End Will Be Soon. Apocalyptic writers used this as a way of encouraging people to "hold on."
   - This influenced Paul's views on marital and social status (1 Cor 7); prayerful vigilance (1 Thes 5, 1–11); enduring suffering or oppression while striving to build up the community (Phil 2, 12–18)

Paul adapts these elements, avoiding the extremes of some apocalyptic thinkers. His adaptations are due to his experience as an apostle to the Gentiles and his conviction that the end times have already begun in Christ.

2 CORINTHIANS READING GUIDE

At a Glance

Who are the main players?	Paul Timothy Titus Christian Community at Corinth.
What should I look for?	Note the problem relations Paul has with the Corinthians. Note also the qualities of his ministries to them; that is, his ministries are based upon Scripture and the new covenant in Christ. A paradox of appreciating God's mysterious ways as well as being "earthen vessels." A ministry of reconciliation and concern for the poor.
When did this take place?	In writing this around A.D. 57, Paul was responding to disquieting reports of dissension and distrust he had received.
Where did these events occur?	Corinth was a Roman freedmen's colony and therefore its population was made up of various peoples but with a heavy concentration of Roman citizens. With its mixture of national and religious groups, rich and poor, Jews, pagans, and Christians, and moral and immoral people, it was an exciting but difficult environment for the small Christian community. The Christian communities shared this diversity and the consequent conflicts.
Why was this book written?	Despite the many troubles and misunderstandings between Paul and them, the Corinthians seem to have respected Paul's authority enough to preserve his words, reflect upon them, and circulate them to other churches. In 2 Corinthians Paul reaffirms his love and concern for them and reviews his past relationship and the roots of his ministry with them.
What is the story?	The message of 2 Corinthians develops in three main dimensions: A. Paul reviews his past relationship with the Corinthians (1, 8—7, 16); B. Paul develops a theology of giving, specifically speaking of the generosity of the Corinthians as a symbol of the fruitfulness of the Gentile mission; C. Paul revisits topics he raised in the first part and returns to the theme of his credentials as an apostle, accenting his weakness and the call of God. It is here that Paul develops a theology of suffering, speaking candidly and with great feeling about his own experience of the grace of God.

Before Beginning

Second Corinthians features some of the most profound moments of Paul's theology, but in a puzzling arrangement. If 1 Corinthians has a structure that is clear and easy to follow, his second letter to the same church is characterized by the opposite, to such a degree that many scholars think it is actu-

ally a composite of several letters Paul sent to the same church. The tone tends to be more defensive than most of his letters, and the flow of thought is choppy. Some fragments (e.g., 6, 14—7, 1) appear completely out of context. The transition from 2, 13 to 2, 14 is very rough, while 7, 5 seems to pick up exactly where 2, 13 left off. Further, chapters 8 and 9 seem to have been originally two separate letters, each dealing with the collection, but neither assuming the other nor influenced by chapters 1 through 7 and 10 through 13. Finally, chapters 10 through 13 could stand alone as an "apologia," an explanation in defense of Paul's own spiritual experience, his vocation, and apostolic credentials. Certainly, 2 Corinthians exhibits traces of an ongoing conversation.

Yet the lack of cohesion in Paul's thought may be only apparent. It is also possible that there is an order to the letter that demonstrates Paul's typical A-B-A´ pattern, which also influenced 1 Corinthians. So, for example, Paul begins and ends 2 Corinthians with personal testimony about the painful difficulties both he and the Corinthians have experienced in the course of their relationship (see 1, 12—7, 16 as A, and 10, 1—13, 10 as A´). Within this frame, the two middle chapters, 8 and 9, dealing with the collection for the poor in Jerusalem (B section) illustrate that for Paul, the generosity of the Corinthians symbolizes the success of the Gentile mission.

Older scholarship, with its emphasis on literary sources and redactions, tends to see the letter as composed of several fragments. In this view, a later editor combined the pieces into the whole that we now have, but the parts sometimes do not fit together well. Why not? Why did the editor do such a poor job? Newer scholarship tries to look at the letter as a unified whole. In this case, the disruptions in the flow of the text are due to Paul's deliberate digressions for effect.

Whichever may be the true situation, we need to work through 2 Corinthians in this final form, even if it also represents originally separate letters or letter fragments. We approach 2 Corinthians as part of the New Testament canon, a letter preserved by the early church and read at liturgical gatherings in spite of its criticisms of the Corinthians and the many challenges it raised for the church there. Lest we think that ours is the only age in which deep divisions appear in the church, this letter reveals that Christian community in the first years was no idyllic experience. The Corinthian letters will serve as a corrective to such mistaken idealism.

Working through 2 Corinthians

Some initial observations about connection of parts of the text will help us read 2 Corinthians

with better understanding. As already indicated, 2 Corinthians follows a rather disrupted and choppy sequence. Following the usual Greco-Roman letter structure, 2 Corinthians has the three main parts:
- the *address* in 1, 1–7,
- the *body* of the letter in 1, 8—13, 10,
- and the *conclusion* in 13, 11–13.

A working outline of 2 Corinthians is as follows:
I.   The Address (1, 1–7)
II. The Body of the Letter (1, 8—13, 10)
   A. Crisis between Paul and the Corinthians (1, 8—7, 16)
     1. Past Difficulties and Relationships (1, 9—2, 13)
     2. Paul's Ministry (2, 14—7, 4)
     3. Resolution of the Crisis (7, 5–16)
   B. The Collection for Jerusalem (8, 1—9, 15)
   C. Paul's Defense of his Ministry (10, 1—13, 10)
III. Conclusion (13, 11–13)

The Address (1, 1–7)

In the address Paul names Timothy as co-author. The Corinthians apparently trusted Timothy and Titus (2, 13; 7, 6; 8, 16.23; see also Gal 2, 1) more than they trusted Paul. Timothy is not named again in 2 Corinthians, although some suppose he is the unnamed "brother" who accompanies Titus with the collection. Luke tells us that Timothy was a faithful companion of Paul, especially on the second and third missionary journeys (see discussion on The Pastoral Letters).

The greeting includes a doxology or prayer glorifying and praising God whose "encouragement" is strength in affliction (see 2 Cor 1, 3–4).

This word encouragement (*paraklesis*, a Greek word that also is the basis for "Paraclete," the "Advocate" or Holy Spirit in Jn 16, 7ff) in noun or verbal form occurs ten times in five verses, 3 through 7. This addition gives us a hint as to the overriding mood of 2 Corinthians. Paul and the Corinthians have experienced much misunderstanding, but Paul wants to move it on to great consolation. Transcending all the pain is the certainty of God's presence with them and Paul's confidence that God is at work in their lives.

The Body of the Letter (1, 8—13, 10)

The message of 2 Corinthians is developed in three main parts:

1. In the first part (1, 8—7, 16), Paul reviews his past relationship with the Corinthians;

2. Chapters 8 and 9 form a second part in which Paul develops a theology of giving, speaking of the collection among the Gentiles and specifically of the generosity of the Corinthians as a symbol of the fruitfulness of the Gentile mission (A');

3. In the third part, 10, 1—13, 10, Paul revisits topics he raised in the first part and returns to the theme of his credentials as an apostle, accenting his own weakness and the call of God. It is here that Paul develops a theology of suffering, speaking candidly and with great feeling about his own experience of the grace of God. Many in the history of Christianity have seen in these chapters a spiritual reality by which they are helped to interpret their own personal experience of God: "My grace is sufficient for you, for power is made perfect in weakness" (12, 9).

We can read through these three parts of the body of 2 Corinthians, reflecting on the relevance of this composite letter for our own experience as Christians.

The Crisis between Paul and the Corinthians (1, 8—7, 16)

The relationship between Paul and the Corinthians seems to have been marked by crisis. This is evident in both 1 and 2 Corinthians. We shall focus now on the problems Paul mentions in the first part of 2 Corinthians. He first reviews his past relationship with the Corinthians and then his ministry with them. Paul mentions several instances of mistrust and tension between himself and the Corinthians in his review of their past relationship.

Past Difficulties and Relationships (1, 9—2, 13). First, Paul reviews the difficulties he had in "Asia," meaning the Roman province that covered the western part of Asia Minor. He probably alludes to Ephesus, where because of this and 1 Corinthians 15, 32, many scholars think he endured an imprisonment not recorded in Acts.

Paul then focuses on several areas—a change of plans and the Corinthians' subsequently accusing him of inconstancy and lack of sincerity; his confrontation with an offending member of the community and his plea for leniency in the punishment of this person whom he has forgiven; and Paul's anxiety about the lack of information

about the Corinthians from Titus. Paul appears frustrated at the apparent lack of communication, sympathy, and confidence. The factions that were mentioned in 1 Corinthians could have made a simple change of mind such as this a source of strife. Paul's detractors accused him of being unreliable.

Paul appeals to God's own fidelity as part of his response (1, 18), showing that his word is sincere and his care constant. Yet he decided to change his plans in view of the recent painful letter (2, 4) that he had found it necessary to write to the Corinthians. He postponed a promised visit only to give time for healing (2, 1–4). With sufficient reflection Paul is confident that the Corinthians would realize the abundant love he has for them (2, 4).

Apparently someone in the community publicly offended Paul (2, 5–11), though the nature of the offense remains obscure. As in 1 Corinthians 5, Paul advocates a judgment not by outsiders but within the church. The action by the majority was acceptable and judged sufficient by Paul. In the case of the incestuous man of 1 Corinthians, he recommended expulsion from the church (see 1 Cor 5, 2.4–5). But in 2 Corinthians 2, 5–11 Paul says that the time has come for forgiveness and reintegration lest Satan be granted a victory in the offender. Like many other biblical writers, Paul sees the world as an arena where the conflict between good and evil forces is ongoing, each vying for human allegiance. The church is entrusted with the "ministry of reconciliation" as Paul describes it in 2 Corinthians 5, 11–16. The forgiveness of the one who offended Paul is a specific example of that ministry in practice.

In 2, 12–13 Paul mentions the anguish he felt at his inability to find Titus and receive news about the Corinthians. This anxiety is a further indication of Paul's sincere affection for the Corinthians. In 1, 12–24 he defends his change of plans and insistence on his anxious concern for the Corinthians. It would seem that this was written before Paul received the happy news from Titus described in 7, 5–16.

Paul's Ministry (2, 14—7, 4). Paul interrupts his review of the events that troubled his relationship to the Corinthians in order to describe in more general theological terms his apostolic ministry. Within the overall A-B-A' structure of 2 Corinthians, we see subsections like 1, 12—7, 16 also exhibiting this same pattern. In this instance, 2, 14—7, 4 (B), describing Paul's ministry, is framed by, and grounds theologically, the practical and painful experience of Paul's relationship with the community described in 1, 12—2, 13 (A) and 7, 5–16 (A´). Paul's description of his ministry develops several important themes:

1. The New Covenant enacted by Christ (3, 1–18)
2. The paradox of the ministry: strength in weakness (4, 1–21)
3. The ministry of reconciliation entrusted to them (5, 1–21)

This description begins (2, 14–17) and ends (7, 2–4) with expressions of confidence in God and in the Corinthians. We will briefly discuss each of the three Pauline themes.

The New Covenant Enacted by Christ (3, 1–18)

Here, Paul's reasoning is based on the Old Testament passages and on one of his favorite contrasts, between spirit and flesh (see Rom 8, 1–10; Gal 2, 3; 5, 17–23). It exemplifies the method taught him in his biblical training, taking several passages from different sources and combining them to produce a new conclusion. Jeremiah's promise of a "new covenant" (31, 31–34) is combined with Ezekiel's prophecy of God's promise to replace human hearts of stone with hearts of flesh and to give a covenant in the Spirit (Ez 36, 26–36). Exodus 34 described the relationship between God and Moses as so glorious that Moses had to come down from Mount Sinai with a veil covering his head lest the Israelites die at the sight of his glowing face (Ex 34, 33–35). These passages from the prophets and the Law provide the scriptural basis for Paul's argument that the ministry (*diakonia*) of the new covenant, to which Paul is devoted, is superior to that of Moses. Using the familiar rhetorical method from lesser to greater, Paul argues that if Moses' covenant was so spectacular yet was still written on stone, how much greater is Christ's covenant, which is the fulfillment of the prophetic promise of the Spirit!

Paul contrasts the Mosaic covenant written "in ink" or "on stone" with the "new covenant" written by the "spirit" on "hearts of flesh." In the process he uses the phrase "old covenant" (2 Cor 3, 14), the only instance of this expression in the Scriptures. This "old" covenant was enacted by God with Moses. Jeremiah and Ezekiel had spoken of a new enactment of the covenant reality, in which intimate access to God would be realized. Paul picks up this theme to write that this promise of a "new covenant" is realized in the work of Jesus. The difference between the two covenants illustrates the contrast between Moses and Christ and indicates the superiority of the covenant in Christ. Paul and the Corinthians are ministers or agents (*diakonoi*) of the new covenant that brings life and the Spirit. In the last part of the passage, he switches the image of the veil to apply it not as a protection on Moses' face to prevent injury to the people, but as an obstacle to clear vision, now upon the faces of those who are unable to see the glory of the new covenant in Jesus (3, 14–18). Christian readers today should remember that Paul was working within the Jewish context of biblical interpretation to work in a new way with familiar texts and images. While his message was definitely that a new thing had been done in Christ that would fully include the Gentiles, he was not drawing a contrast between an old Jewish covenant, now obsolete, and a new Christian covenant that would replace it. Rather, he wanted new Gentile members of the church to realize their debt to our Jewish brothers and sisters for the spiritual heritage they preserved and which we share with them. The Old Testament Scriptures continue to provide a fertile field for mutual reflection and understanding between Christians and Jews.

The Paradox of the Ministry: Strength in Weakness (4, 1–21)

Even though Paul is a minister of this great new covenant, he knows that the glory is God's, not his, and that the mystery of reception in faith is not within his control. He expresses the weakness and fragility of this ministry by the familiar image: "We hold this treasure in earthen vessels" (4, 7), a poetic translation of meaning that could be said more prosaically: "We hold these treasures in clay pots," as a reminder that the power is from God, not from humans. Paul recalls the price to be paid: "We are afflicted in every way . . . perplexed . . . persecuted . . . constantly being given up to death for the sake of

Jesus" (4, 8–11). But Paul continuously alludes to God as the source of his own hope, confidence, and power.

Grace is given in greater and greater abundance through the mystery of Christ for the glory of God. Even while they experience diminishment of their "outer self," the "inner self" grows stronger. The afflictions they experience are passing, but the invisible power of God is what lasts forever.

The Ministry of Reconciliation (5, 1–21)

Throughout 2 Corinthians 2, 14—7, 4 Paul wrestles with the redemptive aspects of suffering for the sake of the Christian message. This aspect has several implications: first, the negative is not overwhelming; rather, there is always some experience of rescue or salvation. Second, the experience of suffering ends not with the apostle but redounds to the good of the community and, beyond the community, relates to the will of God. Third, for Paul, redemption effects a radical change in believers, taking them out of a particular sinful mode of existence and introducing them into another mode of reality that is in Christ. Fourth and finally, Paul and the Corinthians, like all ministers of the gospel, are involved in the ministry of reconciliation of the whole world to God.

Earthly existence is fraught with difficulties. In Paul's words, we "groan and are weighed down" (5, 4) by the difficulties of human existence and of fidelity to the work entrusted to us. We are longing to be covered not with a "tent" but with a heavenly dwelling not made with human hands. We walk by faith (5, 7), trying to please the Lord by whom, in the end, we will be judged (5, 10) not only on our own deeds, but also on the effect of those deeds on others' actions. Catholic interpretation has always emphasized the communal responsibility or the obligations believers have toward others. Paul goes on to explain in the remainder of chapter 5 (vv. 11–21) that Christ's work is a ministry of reconciling the world to God. But that work is not finished once and for all. Through Christ we have been given the astounding mission and responsibility of carrying on that work of reconciliation (5, 17–20). In this context, Paul pleads with the Corinthians to be reconciled with God and thus, implicitly, with him.

Resolution of the Crisis (7, 5–16)

Paul returns to the concrete situation in Corinth, alluding to his anguished wait until he encountered Titus. Paul's representative, Titus, had now furnished good news about the Corinthians' reception of Paul's difficult letter (2, 4 and 7, 8), which some argue is actually chapters 10 through 12 of the present letter. Now the conflict between Paul and the Corinthians was apparently resolved. Paul's exuberant gratitude overshadows all of the former sadness and anxiety. It appears as though all is completely restored, and there is no more reason for concern.

If we have been reading along with Paul, we have noted that some of the problems that afflict our church were present in the experience of the earliest Christians. Paul was an itinerant preacher who normally traveled from community to community preaching the gospel. But Paul lived among the Corinthians longer than with any other community—18 months (Acts 18, 11). He invested enormous energy in this community and could not be indifferent to their problems and questions and mistakes. No one can doubt that this is a problematic relationship, yet it was not severed. The deliberate rhetorical contrast in this letter is between the apparently conflicting data of 2 Corinthians 1, 12—7, 16: the lofty statements about the ministry of the new covenant as well as the insinuations of distrust, discouragement, and anxiety between apostle and community. Paul describes the Christian ministry as a ministry of reconciliation, but he also reminds us of the fragility of the human agents, as earthen vessels holding the treasure. All the hardships are apparently forgotten in Paul's exuberant conclusion: "I rejoice, because I have confidence in you in every respect" (7, 16).

The Collection for Jerusalem (8, 1—9, 15)

Chapters 8 and 9 appear originally to have been two independent "fund-raising letters" on the importance of a generous and substantial offering to the Jerusalem church. This collection for Jerusalem presumably was the condition for acceptance there of Paul's mission to the Gentiles in Galatians 2, 10. Jerusalem may have been a collection center for distribution of relief to other churches of Palestine and Syria. This collection is important because it represents the full participation of the Gentile Christians in the community of the new Israel, the church. On the one hand Paul encourages the Corinthians to give generously, seeing this request as a "test [of] the genuineness of your love by your concern for others" (8, 8). On the other hand Paul will see acceptance of the Gentiles' offering as evidence of the Jewish Christians', and specifically of the Jerusalem church's, willingness to accept the Gentile mission (Rom 15, 22–33).

Paul uses the tactic of creating competition among the Gentile churches. He encourages the Corinthians to give as generously as the Macedonians (Philippi and Thessalonica), who were generous even when they themselves were "tested by affliction" (8, 2). But in 9, 2 Paul claims that he has boasted of the Corinthians' generosity to the Macedonians. In Romans he says that both the Achaians (the Corinthians) and the Macedonians were only too happy to contribute because they understood it as their obligation (Rom 15, 27). The Gentiles were "indebted" to the mother church in Jerusalem and to the other Jewish Christian churches whose spiritual heritage they shared. The language of wealth and poverty in these passages is rhetorical and should not be taken as economic indicators. At the end of the chapter, Paul speaks of envoys or messengers from and to the churches, among whom is Titus. The others are unnamed but probably known to the recipients of the letter. They are in fact called "apostles" of the churches (8, 23). Along with this title applied to Epaphroditus in Philemon 2, 25 and to Andronicus and Junia in Romans 16, 7, it shows that the title of "apostle" was held by many people in the Pauline churches.

Paul begins chapter 9 as if he has not written chapter 8. Although he has just encouraged generosity in the collection, he says in 9, 1, "It is superfluous for me to write to you" about the collection. There are many other ideas repeated in chapter 9 that were raised in chapter 8. It would be very strange for Paul to say the difficult things he says to the Corinthians before and after these chapters and even deal with their accusations against him (ch 10), while here in the middle asking them for money! These arguments, and the apparent independence of these chapters not only from each other but also from the context of the rest of the letter, prompt many interpreters to

consider them as originally separate letters or letter fragments. For us, however, they represent a crucial example of the importance of Paul's role as apostle to the Corinthians. This is the role he reviewed in chapters 1 through 7 and ardently defends in chapters 10 through 13, to which we now turn.

Paul's Defense of his Ministry (10, 1—13, 10)

In the course of defending his ministry again, Paul can be seen following the A-B-A´ pattern, by which he introduced arguments in 10, 1–18 (A), which he will continue in a concluding section in 12, 19—13, 10 (A´). Between these he interjects 11, 1—12, 18 (B), his own experience with the Corinthians and his own sufferings as an apostle. Thus Paul's development includes responses to accusations that continue among the Corinthians: His is weak (10, 1–2), not an eloquent speaker (10, 10), and he is not supported by the community (11, 7–10). Paul reminds the Corinthians at the beginning (10, 2.11) and end (12, 20—13, 2.10) that he intends to visit them soon and deal with such issues in person. In the midst of his responses to charges, Paul develops in a famous and memorable passage (11, 1—12, 18) his own lived theology of the cross.

Paul's Response (10, 1–18; 12, 19—13, 10)

Paul's impatient tone in chapters 10 through 13 suggests that he has already dealt with their accusations against him, and they ought to have been laid to rest. The Corinthians appear to be elitists, perceiving themselves to be superior in knowledge and moving toward those whom they think possess superior gifts. These gifts include eloquence and an impressive appearance. Some of the Corinthians apparently favored Apollos' eloquence over the "contemptible speech" of Paul (see 1 Cor 3, 4–5; 4, 6–7). They noted Peter's freedom, his authority, and the fact that he accepts support from the community (see 1 Cor 9, 6), and they challenged Paul's reasons for refusing community support. Apparently, the Corinthians are offended by Paul's refusal to accept their patronage and continue to see this as an admission that Paul is not of the same stature as Peter.

The Corinthians' complaint that Paul is an impressive writer but that his presence and speech are disappointing (10, 1.10), is arrogant but perhaps speaks a truth that led him to rely so strongly on the written word. Oratory was highly prized; perhaps Paul did not measure up to expectations in that regard. In response, Paul warned that he was empowered by Christ to "act boldly." He would use spiritual weapons to subdue in the end every enemy and disobedient thought in all to make all things subject to Christ (10, 2–6). Paul warned the Corinthians against false pride and conceits and jealousies. He had earlier told the Corinthians to decide whether he came peacefully or "with a rod" (1 Cor 4, 21). Now he promises to visit again soon and warns that he shall not be lenient with them (13, 1–10). The Corinthians should examine themselves and see whether Christ is in them. For his part Paul is confident that Christ is with him. This warning tone is difficult to imagine in the same letter with and following the reconciling tone of 7, 5–10.

Paul Boasts of His Labors and His Weakness (11, 1—12, 18)

Because the Corinthians are attracted by knowledge, Paul proposes to speak of "foolishness" and asks their indulgence. Remember that in 1 Corinthians 1–3 Paul described the wisdom of God as folly for humans and added that God confounds the wise with the wisdom of the cross. In this section of 2 Corinthians, Paul talks about the role of the cross in his own life.

Again, it is Paul's opponents who draw out this vehement testimony about the source of his authority. There are those Paul sarcastically calls the "superapostles" (11, 5); a few verses later, they are labeled for what Paul really thinks of them, as "false apostles" (11, 13; see the "false brothers" of Gal 2, 4). In any case, others are leading the Corinthians astray; Paul fears that the Corinthians are like Eve (11, 3), deceived by the serpent's cunning. This little aside indicated Paul's acceptance of the prevailing male wisdom of his time, since Sirach 25, 23, that Eve represented the more easily seduced segment of humankind. The comparison with Eve, so regarded, would be insulting to the lofty Corinthians, a strategy Paul uses to bring them back to humility.

Continuing his paradoxical development of knowledge and foolishness, Paul describes the wisdom he has learned through suffering. His beautiful testimony can hardly be adequately paraphrased. It must be read and reflected upon. The

experiences that the Corinthians construe as "failures"—the beatings, humiliations, imprisonments, and dangers—are Paul's apostolic credentials. He has experienced visions and revelations and ecstasies. He might have been tempted to pride in these (as he suggests the Corinthians would be). But Paul also experienced a "thorn in the flesh . . . an angel of Satan to beat me" (2 Cor 12, 7). The wisdom Paul learned from this suffering, so beautifully expressed, is that God's power is made perfect in his human weakness. In the end we can understand why Paul says, "I boast most gladly of my weaknesses, in order that the power of Christ may dwell with me" (12, 9).

Conclusion (13, 11–13)

The conclusion is brief and encouraging and could be the conclusion to any Pauline letter. It does not reveal the depth of pain involved in some of its earlier content. By following Paul's apparently circuitous arguments, we are enriched far beyond the effort of understanding the specific situation Paul addressed in Corinth centuries ago. An outcome of studying 2 Corinthians is the realization that all the suffering involved in creating the church among limited human beings bears fruit in fidelity and hope. From 2 Corinthians we are brought to a whole new appreciation of the role of the cross in the Christian vocation to holiness.

Questions for Discussion and Reflection
Group Sharing/Discussion

1. Who are the co-authors with Paul of Second Corinthians?

2. Paul's teaching uses a good deal of Old Testament scripture to communicate the Christian message to the Gentiles. Give an example. Why do you think Paul did this?

3. "We hold this treasure in earthen vessels" (4, 7) Paul writes. To what paradox was Paul referring?

4. Suffering for the sake of the Christian message is important in Paul's life and teaching. Discuss the dimensions of this reality. Have four members of your group each present one implication of suffering for the sake of the Christian gospel (cf 5, 1–21).

5. We "groan and are weighed down" (5, 4) by the difficulties of human existence and of fidelity to the work entrusted to us. Paul states these clearly. What are these difficulties?

6. Why is the collection for the poor of Jerusalem so important to Paul?

7. Both Paul and Apollos were preachers in Corinth. Role-play their presentations to the community of Corinth on who has the qualities of a better leader (10, 1–18; 12, 19—13, 10).

8. Name and describe what wisdom Paul learned through his suffering (11, 1—12, 18).

In Our Lives

1. In Second Corinthians Paul recalls the suffering he endured. "We are afflicted in every way ... perplexed ... persecuted ... constantly being given up to death for the sake of Jesus" (4, 8–11). Today people have their own trials and sufferings. How would you encourage someone to view and understand them as a Christian?

2. Paul inserted "new" before covenant in the words of consecration. This reference is to Jeremiah's promise (31, 31–34) and Ezekiel's prophecy (Ez 36, 26–36) of a new covenant. Reread Jeremiah and Ezekiel on this "new" covenant. How do you describe this new covenant? How does it affect the way you live?

3. Paul teaches that the ministry of reconciliation is essential for Christian living. How do you or how could you put this ministry into practice—in your own life; within your family; within your parish community; within the world?

Individual/Personal Reflection/Action

1. According to Paul, to be Christian means having real concern for the common good. Chapters 8 and 9 emphasize the financial responsibility of a Christian community for another Christian community that is in need. Reflect on the scripture that reinforces this responsibility. Consider how you may show concern for and affect the common good, not just for what is good for me and mine. How does your church community show regard for the common good of the local community and city?

2. For Paul, to experience the cross of Christ is the true beginning of wisdom needed to carry out the ministry of reconciliation. Name for yourself times when you experienced the cross of Christ in your life. What wisdom have you learned from these experiences? How has this wisdom helped you to relate to and understand others? Share this with others who might be helped or encouraged by your experience.

GALATIANS READING GUIDE

At a Glance

Who are the main players?	Paul the Galatians the "Judaizers"
What should I look for?	The issues of freedom and faith, diversity of teachings and different understandings of the gospel message, and the relationship between Christianity and Judaism. These are as important today as in Paul's day. Also, it is essential to realize that this letter in which Paul talks the most about freedom is also the letter in which he most identifies with the cross of Christ. Freedom is for the sake of service.
When did this take place?	In writing this around A.D. 48–55, Paul was responding to the "Judaizers" who were undermining his authority.
Where did these events occur?	Galatia comprised central and northern Asia Minor, including Iconium, Lystra, and Derbe in which Paul had worked.
Why was this book written?	Paul sees the problem in Galatian communities as a threat to both his reputation and his mission. Other missionaries, the "Judaizers," claimed that Gentiles must follow some aspects of the Jewish law, including circumcision, to be fully Christian. They were undermining Paul's authority and the sufficiency of faith in Christ that Paul preached.

What is the story?

We cannot adequately comprehend Galatians without recognition of an important historical issue that was at the basis of Paul's missionary perspective. That issue involves the relationship between Judaism and the infant church that struggled to integrate the non-Jews or Gentiles into a new "Israel of God" and between Jews and Gentiles in that church. The question "who shall belong?" had to be resolved differently than it was in Judaism, where circumcision was the sign of initiation. The "Judaizers" claimed the Gentiles should fulfill some basic requirements of the Jewish law, particularly circumcision and dietary restrictions, to demonstrate that they were actually converted from their pagan ways. But from the beginning of Christian preaching, faith in Jesus crucified and raised from the dead by God had been the only requirement for baptism.

Before Beginning

Galatians is the only Pauline letter written as a circular letter to various churches of a geographical region rather than an urban center. The old territory of Galatia comprised a large central and northern area of Asia Minor. The Roman province of Galatia included some of the cities, such as Iconium, Lystra, and Derbe, in which Paul worked, according to Acts.

Paul's tone in the opening lines of Galatians is defensive and emotional, shown by the absence of the usual prayer of thanksgiving following the address, which is a common characteristic of Paul's letters. Paul sees the problem in the Galatian communities as a great threat, not only to his own reputation and mission, but to the gospel itself. Other missionaries, whom scholars commonly call "Judaizers," came into Galatia after Paul and claimed that Gentiles must follow some aspects of the Jewish law, including circumcision, to be fully Christian. They were undermining Paul's authority and the sufficiency of faith in Christ that Paul preached. Consequently, he writes heatedly to convince the recipients that he has the full truth. From the emotional tone of chapters 1 and 2, he passes to the complex biblical demonstrations of chapters 3 and 4, finally into the ethical teaching of chapters 5 and 6.

Today's reader of Galatians must see past the combative tone of this letter, the circumstances of its writing, and the historical context in which Paul first developed his dichotomy between faith and works. These tasks are well worth the effort

if we are to understand this important epistle of Paul. It is also essential to realize that this letter in which Paul talks the most about freedom is also the letter in which he most identifies with the cross of Christ. Freedom is for the sake of service.

Jews and Gentiles in the Pauline Churches

We cannot adequately comprehend Galatians without recognition of an important historical issue that was at the basis of Paul's missionary perspective. That issue was the relationship between Judaism and the infant church that struggled to integrate the non-Jews or Gentiles into a new "Israel of God" (Gal 6, 16) and between Jews and Gentiles in that church. Although this may seem like a remote issue unrelated to the problems the church faces today, it is actually quite relevant for us with our increasing ethnic diversity and ecumenical concerns. The question of "Who shall belong?" had to be resolved differently than it was in Judaism, where circumcision was the sign of initiation, and obedience to the Mosaic Law signified membership.

Those Christians who were already ethnically and religiously Jewish saw the message of Jesus largely within the context of Judaism. Indeed, Christianity might have remained as a sect within Judaism had it revolved only around belief that Jesus was the Messiah. Early Christianity, however, was almost immediately open to the conversion of the Gentiles (sometimes called the "nations" or the "pagans" in translations). We must also re-member that before his conversion to Christ, Paul the Pharisee was so zealous for the observance of the Law that he persecuted the church (Gal 1, 13). According to Acts, Paul obtained authorization to hunt down and bring to trial in Jerusalem those fellow Jews who had become convinced that Jesus was the Messiah (Acts 9, 1–2). As a strict Jew, Paul had perceived along with many others that the message of Christ was a threat to Jewish claims to a unique access to the one true God through the covenant.

The Pharisees to which Paul belonged were al-ready open to Gentile membership, based on the universal vision of the later prophets, especially Second and Third Isaiah, but with the require-ment that they convert to Judaism. After Paul had accepted the messianic identity of Jesus through revelation and had begun, as a missionary, to proclaim it (1, 15–16), he held the conviction that this new movement must be able to absorb both Jews and Gentiles, but in a new way. His own special call, based on a personal revelation, was to preach the gospel to Gentiles, a call that he says the leaders in Jerusalem accepted (2, 7–9). Importantly, through his pastoral experi-ence, he had come to the conclusion that the only way to integrate Jews and Gentiles fully into the churches was to eliminate the need for conver-sion to Judaism on the part of the Gentiles.

In other words, Paul reassessed the role of the Jewish Law to which he had always been de-voted. In light of his God-given vocation to preach the message of Christ to non-Jews, Paul began to see the Law as superseded. According to the Law as it was then understood, the Gen-tiles had been excluded from salvation. Through Christ, Paul taught, they are included—and on their own terms, not as converts to Judaism. As a result of a revelation from God, Paul identified himself as an apostle to the Gentiles. Conse-quently, Paul felt as committed to the Gentile mission as he ever had felt formerly with regard to the Jewish Law.

The Gentile mission, however, did not begin with Paul. Stephen (see Acts 6) and others, in-cluding Peter (Acts 10), had preached to Gentiles and baptized them before Paul. Nevertheless, not all of the early Christian leaders felt the same de-gree of freedom from the Jewish Law as Paul did. Nor did everyone agree that Gentiles who were becoming part of the church should neglect the requirements of the Jewish Law. Peter and James, for example, who were recognized Chris-tian leaders, both felt that some observance of Jewish Law should be required of the Gentiles. James was a very significant figure in the Jerusalem mother church. Peter, of course, was one of the Twelve and a leader of the Jerusalem community, as well as a known authority in the predominantly Jewish Christian community at Antioch. Representatives from James apparently were preaching at least a minimal observance of Jewish law and gaining a significant hearing among the Gentile converts (see Acts 11, 1–26; Gal 2, 1–10).

The matter was confusing for several reasons. Christianity incorporated the belief in one God and the high ethical principles of Judaism, which were very attractive to many Gentiles. The appeal of these basics of Judaism made more reasonable the position of those who "Judaized" (a verb Paul uses only in Gal 2, 14, where it is translated "live like Jews"). The "Judaizers" claimed that Gentiles should fulfill some basic requirements of the Jew-ish law, particularly circumcision and some dietary restrictions, to demonstrate that they had actually converted from pagan ways. But from the begin-ning the only requirement for baptism was faith in Jesus crucified and raised from death by God.

Even Peter testified that the Gentiles, like the Jews, were saved through faith and that "God shows no partiality" (Acts 15, 9; Gal 2, 6). Paul vehemently opposed any additional require-ments for the Gentiles. He believed that these ad-ditions would, in fact, constitute deviation from the firm conviction that salvation is a work of God accomplished through grace that is accepted by faith in Jesus as the Christ.

Working through Galatians

Galatians represents Paul's effort to defend his preaching against alternative interpretations and to correct some misrepresentations about the message he preaches. Galatians exhibits the three main parts of a letter: the *address* (1, 1–5), the *body* (1, 6—6, 10), which contains teaching (1, 6—4, 31) and ethical applications (5, 1—6, 10), and a conclusion (6, 11–18).

I. Address (1, 1–5)

II. The Body of the Letter (1, 6—6, 10)

Reading through Galatians

The Address (1, 1–5)

This address, in which Paul greets the recipients, is abbreviated and assertive. It lacks the usual thanksgiving characteristic of the opening of a Pauline letter. Perhaps Paul's eagerness to get to the heart of his message explains this omission. Perhaps, too, he is so distressed at what he has heard about the events in Galatia that he cannot feel thankful. He asserts from the beginning that his credentials are not from any human source, but from God and Jesus Christ.

The Body of the Letter (1, 6—6, 10)

In Galatians we see Paul on the defensive, strongly insisting on his loyalty to the gospel. This defense is occasioned by accusations that he seeks only to please other human beings. He develops several themes as part of his defense of the message he preached and of the divine source of his authority. Key themes in this defense are Paul's vocation, the agreement of his message with that of Jerusalem, and the biblical proofs of the truth of his preaching.

Defense of Paul's Preaching and Authority (1, 6—2, 21)

Paul expresses amazement that the Galatians have so quickly deserted him who called them and who remains faithfully rooted in Christ, while they have deserted to "another gospel" (1, 6). He is about to prove to them that they and those who have taught them this way are wrong.

Paul's Vocation (1, 6–24)

Apparently, there were those who accused Paul of lying. They claimed that Paul neglected to inform the Gentiles that their baptism involved following prescriptions of the Jewish Law. According to these opponents, Paul did not fully explain the gospel to his converts. But Paul countered that it was the opponents, rather than he, who were perverting the message of Christ. There cannot be two versions of the true gospel message. Paul understood the challenge to his authority as also a threat to the message he preached. His appeal to the divine origin of his call serves to emphasize that there only be one true gospel. Even if he himself or any other church leader or an "angel from heaven" (1, 8) should teach otherwise, the one true gospel is the one the Galatians heard from Paul. It does not need to be augmented with certain prescriptions from the Jewish Law.

Although we often speak about his conversion, Paul himself describes what happened as a "vocation." This was not merely a personal call as we might think of vocation today. Paul's call from God involves also a mission specifically to the Gentiles. Paul insists that this call came from God and underlines its divine origin by contrasting it with the role played by human beings, including his own initial unwillingness to accept Christ. It is precisely because he was in conflict with many others, including leaders of the church, that Paul begins Galatians by emphasizing that his call is from God. Paul has received an "apocalypse" or "revelation." He did not even go to Jerusalem nor meet any other apostle until three years after his call (which most scholars date around A.D. 34–35).

Paul uses language from the great prophets to describe his call, suggesting that he stands in their line. He claims that he was called from his "mother's womb," echoing the description of Jeremiah's call (Jer 1, 4; see also Is 49, 1). Paul reviews his own efforts to destroy the church, insisting that it was zeal for the Jewish Law that caused him to seek the authority to bring to trial in Jerusalem his fellow Jews who believed in Christ. Paul insists that he did not consult nor compromise with "flesh and blood," referring to the church authorities such as Peter, whom he did not even meet until later.

Paul and the Jerusalem Authorities (2, 1–21)

According to the authentic gospel preaching, faith in Jesus as the Christ is sufficient for salvation, without any other obligations to the Jewish Law. The single gospel message, Paul argues in Galatians 2, 1–10, was confirmed by a meeting in Jerusalem with all the leaders of the church. Scholars place this meeting around A.D. 50 (see Acts 11 and 15). The only stipulation the leaders expressed was that Paul and the Gentiles be mindful of the poor, which probably refers to the collection of money from the Gentile churches for a common fund in Jerusalem. Paul insists that he was eager to do this. Nevertheless, the Gentiles probably needed to learn that concern for the poor was a priority of Christian life (see 2 Cor 8, 1—9, 15). The Gentiles would not have benefited from the long Jewish ethical tradition that mandated taking care of the poor. Although this just concern was part of Jewish Law, the Law is not the reason Paul gives for accepting this stipulation. Rather, he insists that there was neither discussion nor agreement about the Gentiles following any prescriptions of the Law. This account from Paul is quite at odds with the account of presumably the same Jerusalem meeting in Acts 15, 20.29, where observance of Jewish marital and sexual customs and basic dietary laws are enjoined on the Gentiles. Scholars have always had difficulty with the two versions, some assuming that Luke invented the cultic observances that the Gentiles were expected to observe, others assuming that Paul ignored them. Here Paul insists that no restrictions were part of the accord but were only added after the Jerusalem meeting and only because of pressure from the Jerusalem church headed by James. In Galatians 5, 3 Paul will remind the Galatians that those who are circumcised must observe the whole Law, not just selected precepts.

The issue of imposing at least a minimal observance of the Jewish Law, including circumcision, on the Gentiles was introduced, Paul asserts, by "representatives from James," only after the Jerusalem Conference. Paul accuses them of bad faith, saying that they had come to "spy on our freedom in Christ Jesus" (2, 4). The notion of Christian freedom will be more developed in Galatians 5. Here it is introduced as characteristic of Christians in the Pauline churches. Paul confronted Peter later in Antioch because Peter caved in to the pressure of the "Judaizing" delegation from James in Jerusalem. The picture Paul paints is of a change of mind on the part of James and Peter after the Jerusalem agreement, which had the impact of undermining Paul's authority in Galatia and elsewhere. The "Judaizers" of Galatia may have been witnesses to this discrepancy and thus felt authorized to challenge Paul's authority there. Paul had accused Peter of influencing the Gentiles to "live like Jews" in the observance of some basics of the Law, including circumcision. Peter, who had also baptized Gentiles (Acts 10), was beginning to compromise the Gentiles' freedom after the Jerusalem meeting.

Historical Misinterpretation

This historical conflict provides the context for Paul's important concept of "justification by faith." Within the framework of his conflict with Peter and James, Paul reminds Peter as a fellow Jew that "we who are Jews . . . know that a person is not justified by works of the [Jewish] law but through faith in Jesus Christ" (2, 15–16). Paul appeals to the faith he has in common with Peter and with other Jewish Christians. All Christians of Jewish descent share the belief that Jesus is the Christ. It is Jesus rather than the Jewish Law that justifies all. Generations later in the church, when the preponderance of believers were of Gentile rather than Jewish origin, the historical context of this dispute was forgotten.

Since then, Christians have sometimes mistakenly interpreted Paul's message as somehow considering faith as opposed to works. Furthermore, the word "alone" was added to the formula "justification by faith," and the phrase was understood in an absolute sense. So, for example, Luther portrayed the gospel as "law-free" in his famous objection to indulgences, which were undoubtedly carried to extremes in his day. The Reformers used Paul's doctrine of justification by faith to oppose any notion of salvation as dependent on good works, such as they alleged the Catholic doctrine of salvation taught. They distorted the Catholic teaching of works as a response to faith. For their part, Catholics have sometimes exaggerated the role of good deeds to gain grace. Both Protestants and Catholics have based their arguments on Paul, especially on Galatians and Romans, and both have distorted the Jewish understanding of Law observance as the response of the faithful to the gift of the covenant. As a result, some Christians erroneously read into Paul's message a dichotomy between faith and works that does not accurately interpret Paul's original meaning, and a theological anti-Judaism that characterizes the Jewish way of life as oppressively bound in Law as contrasted to liberating Christian freedom.

We see in all of Paul's letters that his doctrine is consistently followed by ethical applications. Thus Paul teaches that faith is expressed in the moral life. Good works are a response to faith.

Even in passages where Paul speaks of freedom (e.g., in Gal 5), he advocates at the same time the practice of good works. Paul's understanding of Christianity includes a highly developed ethic or lifestyle. He would see no opposition between faith and freedom on one side and good works and obedience on the other, as he will show in the next major section of Galatians.

Faith, Freedom, and the Scriptures (3, 1—4, 31)

Here Paul begins his theological and biblical explanation of his gospel. He appeals first to the experience of the Galatians, then to the biblical exposition of several texts, then to several human examples.

Paul insists that his converts in Galatia have heard the true and complete gospel message from him and that, as a result of their conversion to Christ, they have received the Spirit of God. He asks them a question to which they all know the answer, to shame them into attention: Did you receive the Spirit through Law or through faith (3, 2)? They know it was through his preaching of faith without Law. To emphasize the importance of continuing to live the life of faith, Paul employs a contrast between the "flesh" and the "spirit" designed to show that these are mutually exclusive. Today's reader will find such a contrast problematic unless we understand the Greek philosophical mindset of Paul's audience and the special meanings he attaches to the words.

Today we tend to equate "flesh" with body or material existence, and to affirm the body as a positive and even essential expression of self-fulfillment and human happiness. But the Greeks stressed the tension between the flesh and the spirit, which presupposed the superiority of the spirit and the inferiority of the flesh. For them, the spirit represented the immortal, life-giving aspect of human experience, whereas the body or flesh signified the weaker, sensual, mortal aspect that had to be subordinated to the spirit to find happiness. Though the Hebrews did not generally share this mindset, still earlier biblical language will sometimes use "flesh" or "flesh and blood" to mean the weakness and vulnerability of human existence without the assistance of God (see even 1 Cor 15, 50).

This is usually Paul's meaning for "flesh": human arrogance that tries to live independently of God's grace. To further complicate our task of interpreting Paul's meaning, we note that Paul sometimes refers to the Spirit of God or Holy Spirit (at times simply called the "Spirit") and at other times he designates the human spirit. Often it is hard for the reader to distinguish the two. In English translations God's Spirit is usually capitalized, but that is the choice of the translator, and sometimes the difference is not clear. Paul asserts that the Spirit of God was conferred upon the Galatians by faith, not by "works of the flesh" such as circumcision. Paul therefore concludes that it would be an absurd regression to "end in the flesh" what had begun in the spirit. Faith had moved the Galatians and all believers from the domain of the flesh to that of the spirit. The Spirit of God enables us to share fully in the inheritance of the promise made to Abraham and fulfilled now in Christ. Thus Paul moves from a review of the Galatian experience of the gospel to an illustration of the validity of that experience taken from the Scriptures.

Abraham, Father of Faith (3, 6—16)

Paul reinforces his teaching on justification by faith by giving examples from the Scriptures showing that faith in Christ is sufficient for salvation. Using the exegetical methods in which he was trained, he draws out several biblical passages from different places and puts them together into a new argument to show that Abraham received the promise and was considered to have been justified in God's sight before he was given the precept of circumcision (Gen 12, 3; 15, 6). Then the crucified Christ took upon himself the curse of the

Law by hanging on a tree (Dt 27, 26; Hb 2, 4; Lv 18, 5; Dt 21, 23). Paul relates the experience of Abraham and his sons to the experience of the Galatians. Through faith the Galatians (a predominantly Gentile community) became the "children of Abraham" (3, 7). "Abraham believed God, and it was credited to him as righteousness" (3, 6). God gave a promise to Abraham because of his faith. This promise included the "nations" or Gentiles who are blessed through Abraham. Now, Paul says, the Gentiles have received the blessing of Abraham. The promise has been fulfilled in Christ.

Example of the Human Will (3, 17–23)

Paul then uses the example of a last will or testament (in Greek, the words, "will, testament, covenant" are all the same, *diatheke*, which helps make the analogy in a way that is lost in English). Once made and ratified, it cannot be changed by something that comes along later. In like manner, the covenant with Abraham could not be altered by the Mosaic Law that came later. The original covenant through faith is the prior one that cannot be annulled, and this is the one in which all persons of faith belong.

Example of the Child-minder (3, 24—4, 11)

The next human analogy that Paul uses would have been perfectly comprehensible to his contemporaries, but it needs some explanation today. The "custodian" was a slave in a wealthy family who had authority over the minor son and was responsible for his discipline and education. Once the son came of age and became the heir, the roles were reversed. Paul uses this example to argue that the Law was a temporary custodian until Christ came, which is the time set by the father for our spiritual coming of age. At that point, the Law has no more power over us.

As an example of this maturity in Christ that we now have, Paul uses one of his most famous sayings, probably a baptismal formula that he quotes for effect. "All who have been baptized in Christ have a new identity, so that there is no longer Jew or Greek, slave or free, male and female, but all are one in Christ Jesus (3, 27–28)." We would like to know how seriously this proclamation was taken in Paul's day. The tension between Jew and Greek (i.e., Gentile) continued, but it was precisely to this that Paul was

devoting much of his effort. Nevertheless, Christian persecution of Jews increased rather than decreased in following centuries. Slavery certainly continued for centuries in Christian households and states. Problems between men and women in the church have not yet subsided. Disparities in treatment based on ethnicity, social status, and gender are perennial. This prophetic text remains a challenge for the church in every age.

Assurance of Paul's Affection (4, 12–20)

In spite of the harsh things Paul had to say to the Galatians in the beginning of the letter, he now softens a bit to express his continued affection for them and his remembrance of how well they treated him when he was there. Verse 15 leads some commentators to suppose that Paul had some kind of eye disease that made him less impressive in person (see 2 Cor 10, 10), but this is speculation. He hopes to come again to be with them and to be able to speak more affectionately than he has been able to do in this letter.

Allegory of the Two Wives of Abraham (4, 21–31)

Paul goes on to illustrate his teaching with yet another scriptural example, namely that of Abraham's two sons by two women. The first, Ishmael, is the son of a slave woman, Hagar, whose name never actually occurs here (but see Gn 21). Isaac is Sarah's son, born free. Ishmael and his mother were expelled from Abraham's sight and did not inherit the promise. Paul develops his commentary as an allegory, understanding Ishmael and Hagar to represent slavery to the covenant on Mount Sinai. Isaac represents the promise fulfilled in the freedom of faith without the restrictions of the Law. The words originally spoken to Sarah, who had been barren, are fulfilled in the believers who inherit the promise (4, 27). Paul says of the Galatians that they, like Isaac, are children of the promise, that is, the promise of grace and with it, freedom from the Law. Thus Paul's reading of the Scriptures reinforces his insistence that the Galatians are justified without the Law and freed from the Law. Therefore, to return to the Law's restrictions would be a great foolishness (see 3, 1).

Exhortations for Christian Living (5, 1—6, 10)

Paul draws implications for Christian living from his teaching. While insisting on freedom, he shows how faith has its consequences in Christian life. Chapters 5 and 6 exhort believers to exercise their faith in their relationships with one another. These exhortations focus on the responsibilities Christians share for developing the community. We are struck by Paul's emphasis on social responsibility. Note that Paul does not dwell on a believer's personal, interior life so much as on the relationships that should characterize the Christian community, which is living the blessings of the Spirit of God (see 5, 21–23).

The term "freedom" recurs here (5, 1.13). For Paul freedom is not lawlessness but the liberty to live for God (see Rom 6, 4) and to serve one another through love (Gal 5, 13). The choice between slavery and freedom is the choice between the works of the Law and the works of the Spirit. For Paul, all humans are under some power— either of "sin" and the "flesh" or of the Spirit of God and faith.

In 5, 2–12 Paul refers again to the specific problem that occasioned this urgent letter. The Judaizers are agitating the Galatians, trying to convince them to be circumcised and follow some of the elements of the Jewish Law. Paul reminds the Galatians of a principle certainly upheld by Jews, that circumcision of itself is nothing if not a sign of commitment to follow the whole Law (5, 3). The problem Paul confronts is the imposition of circumcision on the Gentiles. Galatians 5, 11 implies that Paul, even as a Christian, did "preach circumcision" for Jews; perhaps he did at one time earlier in his career, and the Galatians have heard of it. Paul does not dispute the role of the Law in Jewish life. Although some accused Paul of undermining the Law for Jews, he considers himself innocent of that charge (see Rom 9, 1–5; 1 Cor 9, 20; Acts 21, 20–26). The list of "works of the flesh" in 5, 20–21 show that Paul does not equate flesh with the body; many of them are perversions of mind.

In Galatians 6, 1–10 Paul continues to reflect on community life, advocating the virtues of charity, service, and humility. Christians are obliged to "bear one another's burdens." Although they are also called to "do good to all," even those outside

the church, special priority is given to those in the family of faith (6, 10).

Conclusion (6, 11–18)

Paul adds a final note for emphasis and concludes with a short prayer. He probably dictated this letter to a scribe. He adds his own closing remarks, beginning at verse 11. Here he adds a new dimension to the arguments against the agitators: They are insincere, because they themselves do not follow the Law. They are only trying to escape persecution by other Jews, or possibly the Romans (see note on 6, 12–15). Paul contrasts their cowardice and insincerity with his own boldness and consistency, referring to the "marks of Jesus" on his body. All that matters, Paul says, is that we are created anew (6, 15). He concludes with a prayer for peace and mercy, calling down a blessing on his brothers and sisters in Christ.

Concluding Remarks

The letter to the Galatians may be one of the most difficult for us to approach without prior knowledge of the historical circumstances in which it was written, yet no one knows very much about those circumstances. Paul's message here is nevertheless especially appropriate today. Despite painful differences with other leaders, Paul focuses on a single gospel message that all authentic Christian missionaries preach. This message emphasizes the role of faith and the significance of community. Paul's use of Scripture illustrates that this is the same message that has been repeated and refined throughout the Old Testament. Faith is the expression of the bond between God and us, a bond lived out in relationships with others. Paul's exhortation to Christians is to "be free" and therefore responsible for one another. There is no conflict between faith and works, according to Paul. Faith is necessarily expressed in the everyday life of believers. Paul does, however, stress that the works of faith are a result of the gift of the Spirit and a response to it, not a requirement for receiving the Spirit or for meriting salvation.

Questions for Discussion and Reflection
Group Sharing/Discussion

1. Paul's tone in the opening chapter of Galatians is defensive. How is this shown? Why is Paul defensive?

2. Paul sees the problem in Galatia as a threat to his mission and to the gospel. The "Judaizers" are the cause of this. Who are they? What are they doing in Galatia?

3. Role play a scene in Galatia about A.D. 50 where a group in the market are talking about faith and freedom. The speakers are:

    a. a Jewish-Christian convert of Paul

    b. a Gentile-Christian convert of Paul

    c. a disciple of James from Jerusalem

    d. a Gentile convert of Peter.

4. Paul teaches: Freedom is for the sake of service. Give examples of his meaning.

5. For Jews in Galatia, circumcision was the sign of initiation into the people of God, obedience to the Torah signified membership. What was the sign and commitment required to be a Christian?

6. What did the Mosaic Law at the time of Galatians teach concerning salvation? What did Paul teach the Galatians concerning the source of salvation?

7. What did Paul mean by "flesh" (5, 20–21)?

8. According to Paul, when he went to Jerusalem council, what was the only stipulation that the Church leaders expressed about his teaching (2, 1–10)?

In Our Lives

1. The representatives of James from Jerusalem preached to the Galatians that they needed to follow the basics of Jewish Law—circumcision and cultic food observations. Explain why you think they sent disciples to do this? (Read Acts 15, 20.29 for an account of the Jerusalem council that is at odds with Paul's account.) Describe what you imagine might be Jewish/Christian differences today if Peter and James' rule had continued.

2. Paul's meaning for "flesh" is this: human arrogance that tries to live independently of God's grace. Where in our lives today do we see this kind of arrogance?

3. Catholics believe that good works are a response to faith—that, because we believe, we act. This means that good works are not something we store up to earn grace for a better place in heaven. Explain why we don't believe in this image of God who would "keep a list" of our good deeds like Santa Claus does for a child.

4. Invite someone from the Jewish community to explain their belief in good works and the requirements for being an active Jew.

Individual/Personal Reflection/Action

1. Paul teaches that all who have been baptized into Christ have a new identity, so that there is no longer Jew or Greek, slave or free, male or female, but all are one in Christ Jesus (3, 27–28). Reflect upon the new identity you have been graced with and what it means in your daily actions.

2. The Judaizers were so attached to their approach and understanding of what was involved in being a follower of Christ that they lost sight of the authentic gospel message. How open are you to learning new ways of following Christ? What signs would you check out to see if this new way was authentic? What virtues and graces are required for one to be faithful to the gospel?

EPHESIANS READING GUIDE

At a Glance

Who are the main players?	Paul Tychicus
What should I look for?	The Pauline vision of the universal church, Jews and Gentiles united under the headship of Christ with a mission to make God's plan of salvation known throughout the world. This saving plan is anchored in God's love.
When did this take place?	Probably written around A.D. 80, after Paul's death (A.D. 64–65). Some of the language is Paul's, but the theology is more developed.
Where did these events occur?	Probably written from Rome as a "circular" letter to the churches of Asia Minor

Why was this book written?   The resolution of the tensions between Jews and Gentiles called for an adaptation of Paul's theology to new times and circumstances. The mystery of the church, its unity and mission, was the focus of the answer.

What is the story?   The body of the letter concerns the teaching on the Church, its unity and world mission. Then it considers some ethical applications of this teaching.

Before Beginning

Ephesians displays a well-developed theology of the church. The four major epistles of Paul (Romans, 1 and 2 Corinthians, and Galatians) are all addressed to specific congregations or communities in various important locations in the Greco-Roman world. Ephesians envisions not a single congregation but the universal church seen as a spiritual reality entrusted with the worldwide mission of Christ. Here the word "church" (*ekklesia*) acquires that new meaning of universal reality.

There are significant parallels between Ephesians and Colossians. The well-developed theology of Christ (Christology) and of the church (ecclesiology), the apparent absence of Jewish-Gentile tensions, and, finally, the unusual vocabulary unique to these two epistles among the Pauline letters prompt many interpreters to assert that Ephesians and Colossians were written in an era after the death of Paul. If that is the case, the disciple who wrote these letters was familiar with Pauline theology and style and adapted Paul's message to new times and circumstances. In our comments we will follow the usual practice of referring to the author of Ephesians as "Paul," all the while keeping in mind that nearly all Pauline scholars think of Ephesians as not from Paul himself, and a majority think the same of Colossians.

Working through Ephesians

Ephesians follows the pattern of a Greco-Roman letter, beginning with an *address* (1, 1–14) and ending with a *conclusion* (6, 21–24). Moreover, it follows the pattern of a Pauline letter, with initial blessing or prayer in the address and conclusion adapted to a liturgical assembly. These stylized elements enclose the *body* of the letter (1, 15—6, 20), which presents a teaching or doctrine on the church and then applies this teaching to the daily life of believers. The outline is as follows:

I.   The Address (1, 1–14)
II. The Body of the Letter (1, 15—6, 20)
   A. The Teaching on the Church (1, 15—4, 24)
     1. Unity of the Church (1, 15—2, 22)
     2. World Mission of the Church (3, 1—4, 24)
   B. Ethical Applications (4, 25—6, 20)
III. Conclusion (6, 21–24)

The Address (1, 1–14)

Ephesians identifies the sender as "Paul, an apostle of Christ Jesus by the will of God." The absence from some manuscripts of the designation "in Ephesus" (1, 1) is one reason why Ephesians is considered by some to be a circular letter—intended for a wider audience rather than for the specific community at Ephesus alone. No particularities regarding the Ephesian community are mentioned as is customary when Paul writes to a community he knows as well as he should have known the Ephesians (see Acts 19, 10). The lack of a personalized greeting further supports the view that this is a letter to *all* the churches and written by a disciple of Paul.

A doxology or blessing of God replaces the usual personal thanksgiving characteristic of Paul's letters (Eph 1, 3–6). As if conscious of the great mystery of the church he is about to describe, the author begins by proclaiming the blessedness of God. The recurrence of the term "blessed" and the many liturgical references suggest that this prayer of praise is inspired by the Jewish liturgies in which believers, mindful of the wondrous works of God, cannot but bless the Creator. The focus is on God's blessing in Christ in whom the divine plan for the salvation of all people is achieved. The Holy Spirit is described as the "first installment" (1, 14) of our inheritance toward redemption.

The Body of the Letter (1, 15—6, 20)

The message of Ephesians has two parts. The first or doctrinal section (1, 15—4, 24) unfolds the church as the fulfillment of God's plan for salvation, inaugurated in Christ. A second section (4, 25—6, 20) contains ethical "imperatives" concerning the daily conduct of believers, providing practical applications of Paul's teaching.

The Teaching on the Church (1, 15—4, 24)

Ephesians develops the New Testament teaching about the unity of the church and the church's worldwide mission. Integral to this mission is the significant role of the apostle in its promotion. We shall briefly consider each of these teachings.

Unity of the Church (1, 15—2, 22)

The ecclesiology, or theology of the church, in Ephesians is integrally linked to its Christology. That is to say that its view of the church follows from its view of Christ and Christ's saving work. Therefore, to understand the emphasis on the unity of the church that occurs in Ephesians, we must see the perspective on Christ developed there. The Christology and ecclesiology in Ephesians and Colossians is developed beyond that in Paul's major letters to the Corinthians and the Romans. Yet this development has its roots in Paul, for whom the image of the church as the body of Christ helps to express the unity of Christians and the salvific work of Christ's death and resurrection.

The description of the church as the Body of Christ appears first in 1 Corinthians 12, 12–27 and Romans 12, 4–8. Paul urged the Christians in Corinth and Rome to express their unity in mutual love as members of the same body, Christ. But in Ephesians and Colossians, there is a major change in the image. Here Christ is referred to as the "head of the body, the church" (Eph 1, 22–23; Col 1, 18). This shift in the image leads away from the mutual participation and responsibility of all the members to centralized authority in the person of Christ, who is portrayed as above every principality, authority, and dominion (cf. Eph 1, 21–22). Nevertheless, the recipients are still reminded that in the body of Christ, we are members of one another (4, 15) and of Christ (5, 30).

By his resurrection, Paul asserts, Jesus became Lord of all, Jews and Gentiles and every creature (see 1 Cor 12, 3). This is so because in Christ's resurrection God has conquered sin and death; it is the beginning of a new era. Paul's writings speak of the humiliation (death) and exaltation (resurrection) of Christ by which God vindicated Jesus because of his obedience. Jesus now sits at God's right hand. At Jesus' name, every knee bends and every tongue proclaims that Jesus is Lord (Phil 2, 6–11). This is one of the oldest Christological proclamations (Rom 10, 9). Jesus' lordship is an expression of his sovereignty over all created things and his word reconciling the whole of creation to God. Yet even now the universal recognition of Jesus' lordship has not been completed. The mission of preaching Christ's lordship and bringing all creation under God's reign is entrusted to the church.

Some time after A.D. 50, when Paul was writing Galatians and Romans, it is clear that one of the major problems facing the church was the reconciliation of Jews and Gentiles under one God and one Lord. Distinctions between Jews and Gentiles were symbolized by such practices as circumcision, dietary laws, and restrictions regarding table fellowship, intermarriage, and other forms of social interaction. These, Paul insisted, were erased by Christ's death. Yet the apostle himself had to struggle to resolve the tensions between Israel and the Gentiles (e.g., see Rom 9–11). The teaching about the church in Ephesians seems to reflect a time or place in which these tensions are resolved. The Gentiles are portrayed as those who were once "far off . . . strangers to the covenants of promise." Now they have "become near by the blood of Christ" (2, 13). The images of the church as the body of Christ and Christ as the head of the church serve to illustrate the intrinsic unity of the church of Jews and Gentiles, that is, of all people in Christ.

World Mission of the Church (3, 1—4, 24)

The author of Ephesians identifies himself as "Paul, a prisoner of Christ [Jesus] for you Gentiles" (3, 1). He then abruptly interrupts this self-introduction to elaborate on his role in the mystery of God's plan for the salvation of the world. Now imprisoned, Paul continues the work of intercession. Through prayer Paul brings the Gentiles to God. The church—the body of Christ and the family of God—is entrusted with the work of salvation that is to fill all things "with the fullness of God" (3, 19). Paul understands his work to be essential in God's plan, and yet he is unperturbed either by his own imprisonment or by the failure of some to accept the message of Christ. Salvation as well as creation is in God's hands, and God's plan is being fulfilled in inscrutable mystery.

Again the language reflects that introduced by Paul in his earlier writings. But the conception of the divine plan of salvation is more developed. The church, under the impetus of the Spirit, is bringing all to the "one God and Father of all, who is over all and through all and in all" (4, 6). Paul's prayer is that "you may be filled with the fullness of God" (3, 19). The mystery of God who ordained that "all Israel will be saved" (Rom 11, 26) now prescribes that we "no longer live as the Gentiles do" (Eph 4, 17), but "put on the new self, created in God's way in righteousness and holiness of truth" (4, 24). Having described this mystery, Paul goes on to exhort the Ephesians to express their common call to holiness and unity in their daily life.

Ethical Applications (4, 25—6, 20)

Ephesians 5 illustrates how its teaching on the church has practical consequences in the daily lives of believers. Ephesians 5, 1 says, "So be imitators of God, as beloved children, and live in love." This could be the summary of the whole of Christian life. The author of Ephesians draws out some implications of imitating God by living in love. Much of this section consists of general moral exhortation, description of what the ideal Christian life with one another should look like.

Christians relate to one another in ways already established and governed, at least to some extent, by outward society. So, for example, wives and husbands, children and parents, slaves and masters all follow Greco-Roman social norms, which give some direction about the rights and duties of people who are in these kinds of relationships. The author adopts and adapts the traditional philosophical approach to household life that is at least as old as Aristotle, which we call "household rules." In ordinary Greco-Roman society, the lines of authority and of subservience were clearly drawn. Husbands, parents, and masters all have great power over wives, children, and slaves in a rigid social hierarchy.

For Paul these rules or principles become practical applications of faith for members of the "household of God" (2, 19), giving directives for various segments of society in their relationships to one another. Paul does not offer a radical critique of certain social contracts, such as slavery or male dominance. Yet for him, relationships among Christians must reflect a new perspective. Christians are motivated to a new way of thinking, determined by their common baptism. Christians share the conviction that all are one in Christ and saved by Christ. This leads to innovations in the usual treatment of household rules: Here both parties in a relationship are addressed, whereas in the traditional form, only the male authority would be addressed, and here the inferior party is even addressed first. The Ephesians are urged to "live in a manner worthy of the call you have received . . . bearing with one another through love" (Eph 4, 1f). They are exhorted to "be subordinate to one another" (5, 21), to "nourish and cherish" one another because they are members of one body (5, 29–30). The extra verses spent on the analogy of husband to Christ and wife to the church are the springboard for much later mysticism, even as they also have been justification for continued subordinate positions for women. Such a passage as this, along with the exhortations to slave obedience, are contradictions of beauty, grace, and what today can only be seen as social oppression in the name of faith. They require careful interpretation in the context both of the author's world and of ours.

If we do not let these thorny problems be major obstacles, reading Ephesians today can inspire us to a powerful vision of the church. It leads us to reassess the ordinary way of approaching one another as colleagues, family, clients, and the like. We, like the Ephesians, are urged to remember our real identity and to respect others by relating to everyone in a way worthy of members of the "household of God." The ordinary hierarchical system that obtains in the world is superseded by a new way of relating to one another in Christ.

Paul finally urges the Ephesians to "pray at every opportunity in the Spirit" (6, 18). He again asks for prayers for himself, that he may speak "the mystery of the gospel" with boldness and courage even though he is in chains (6, 19–20).

Conclusion (6, 21–24)

Ephesians does not exhibit the usual personal tone and greetings of Paul's authentic letters. In the conclusion, however, the author indicates that he sends the letter with Tychicus (6, 21), the name of Paul's messenger of Colossians as well (Col 4, 7). The final prayers are for peace and love and grace.

Concluding Remarks

Ephesians strikes a balance between reflection on the church as a universal, spiritual reality and application in the daily lives of Christians of their new identity as members of this spiritual creation. The letter also emphasizes the congruence between Christians' personal spirituality and their responsibilities in relationships with one another. Through baptism we are renewed. We have put off the "old humanity," symbolized by Adam; we have been transformed into a "new humanity," in Christ. We are called to be imitators of God and to reflect God's love and compassion in our daily lives.

As part of our Christian Scriptures, Ephesians stands as a continual challenge calling us beyond the present to a deeper reality where all things are in the care of God. The present with its trials, temptations, failures, and limitations can indeed discourage us. The problems of resolving tensions and enduring suffering are temporary. Ephesians is a letter from prison, addressing a church afflicted with oppression from the outside, confusion and dissension from within. Ephesians testifies to the author's faith and by the hope of God's plan for the salvation of the entire world—a plan that will be fulfilled despite, and even by means of, apparent obstacles. When we are confronted by the limitations of our present circumstances or hampered by fear, Ephesians provides encouragement. For us as Christians, the liturgy celebrates a communion with God. Faith is conviction of things unseen, especially about the triumph of God in Christ.

Ephesians is one of the most hope-filled and confident of all the Pauline letters. It may lack the usual personal tone expected of communities Paul knew well. But Ephesians expresses fundamental Christian beliefs that continue to characterize the church today. For example, despite suffering and failures, the church celebrates the reality of salvation already experienced in the daily life of Christians. In our world, where many families are in crisis, we read Paul's advice about mutual relationships with members of God's household and take courage in the advice to serve one another in love. Like the writer of Ephesians, the church at Vatican II complemented reflection on the nature of the church with reconciling the whole of the church in the modern world. Each of us, as members of the Christ's body, no matter what its limitations, is church and has a role in this mission.

Questions for Discussion and Reflection
Group Sharing/Discussion

1. Why do you think Ephesians is called a "catholic" letter, that is, a letter to the whole church and not just to Ephesus?

2. The focus of Ephesians is on God's blessings in Christ in whom the divine plan for salvation of all people is achieved. Share your views on how this focus is expressed in the letter.

3. In Corinthians (1 Cor 12, 12–27) and Romans (12, 4–8) Paul expressed the unity of members in Christ by the image of the body. In Ephesians there is a major change (Eph 1, 22–23; also in Col 1, 18) in this body image. What is this change and what do you feel is its meaning?

4. We are reminded that in the body of Christ we are members of one another (4, 15) and of Christ (5, 30). How would you explain the meaning of this? What is the relationship of this meaning and our behavior?

In Our Lives

1. Paul works passionately for the world mission of the church. Yet he knows that salvation as well as creation is in God's hands and that God's plan is being fulfilled in mystery. Take time to reflect and translate this into your own experience and your own mission.

2. Ephesians 5, 1 says, "So be imitators of God, as beloved children, and live in love." Paint a picture of our life that shows the meaning of this in how you live. Share this with one other person in the group.

3. Paul applies these central religious beliefs to practical applications of living faith in your personal life. He failed to apply his critique and teaching to social evils such as slavery and male dominance. How would you take his principles and apply them to these social evils?

Individual/Personal Reflection/Action

1. Ephesians reminds us that we are called—called to reflect the love and compassion of God in our lives. Pray to see more clearly how this touches your personal home life, your social life, your work life and your commitments to bring compassion to the world beyond yours. Take some action from your prayer.

2. Accepting the challenge of faith helps us to remember a deeper reality where all things are in the care of God. Life always presents problems, failures, temptations, limitations, and suffering. Name your trials and pray for faith and hope. These are always temporary. Ephesians challenges us to live by faith and hope even when it is dark.

3. Faith is conviction of things unseen, especially the triumph of God in Christ. Pray with Paul that "you may be filled with all the fullness of God" (3, 19).

PHILIPPIANS READING GUIDE

At a Glance

Who are the main players?
Paul Euodia Syntyche Clement Epaphroditus Community at Philippi

What should I look for?
The theme of joy. In Philippians Paul shows his human sensitivity and tenderness, his enthusiasm for Christ as the key to death and life, and his deep feeling for the community of Philippi.

When did this take place?
Probably, about A.D. 55 while Paul was in prison in Ephesus

Where did these events occur?
Philippi, in northeastern Greece, was a city of some importance in the Roman province of Macedonia.

Why was this book written?
Philippi was the first church Paul established in his mission to the Gentiles of ancient Macedonia. The relationship between Paul and this church was long and dear, for Paul mentions how often the community shared in a partnership with him. Lydia was his first convert at Philippi. But it is not clear where or why he wrote or whether it is a combination of several letters.

What is the story?
All the themes are related to the mission of the community to proclaim the gospel. Paul accents their partnership for the gospel and his confident joy in spite of suffering. He shows concern for external pressures (Judaizers) and internal divisions.

Before Beginning

Philippians is one of the most appealing of Paul's letters. Along with Ephesians, Colossians, and Philemon, Philippians is traditionally called a "captivity letter" because in all four the author refers to his imprisonment. The authentic Pauline authorship of Philippians and Philemon is never doubted, although there is disagreement regarding the authorship of Ephesians and Colossians.

There are several theories about the location and occasion of the imprisonment from which Paul writes. The oldest and traditional view is that he writes from Rome in his final imprisonment there; this would date the letter to the late 50s or early 60s of the first century. Some have questioned the feasibility of this location, given the apparent frequent exchanges implied in the letter and the great distance from Rome to Philippi. So a second location has been suggested, Caesarea Maritima on the Palestinian coast, during the two years of confinement recorded in Acts 24–26. Still, that is a great distance requiring a month or more of travel. A third suggestion is that Paul was imprisoned earlier in his life in Ephesus, and that Philippians and Philemon date from that time, perhaps in the middle years of the 50s. The mysterious references to trouble in Asia (Ephesus was the principal city of the Roman province of Asia) in 1 Corinthians 15, 32 and 2 Corinthians 1, 8–10 support this idea, as does Paul's avoidance of Ephesus on his journey to Jerusalem (Acts 20, 16). In that case, travel back and forth from Paul's prison to Philippi would have been much easier and faster.

If the Pauline authorship of Philippians is unquestioned, the unity of the letter poses some challenges. The choppy nature of this letter has led many interpreters to suggest that Philippians was originally at least three letters. A later editor (according to this theory), adapting the initial and final greeting, combined the originally separate messages into one edited "letter" for the purpose of later circulation. On the other hand, many more recent interpreters, using methods derived from the principles of ancient rhetoric, argue for the unity of the letter in spite of the rough edges here and there. Whichever is the case, the end result, the "canonical letter," provides the rich spiritual legacy called Philippians so beloved in the Christian tradition.

Themes of Philippians

Important Pauline themes are developed in Philippians, particularly that of unity. We see in the letter the deep love Paul feels for this community. Disregarding the dangers facing him, Paul focuses on the sufferings of the community caused by external persecution and internal divisions. We hear of Paul's gratitude for the material support he has received from the community. We witness his fears about the problems within the community and the pressure from outside, but he subordinates those concerns to expressions of joy for the strength of the Philippians' church. In a surprisingly vehement outburst against those who advocate a return to the Jewish Law, he reminds us that this issue, so central to Galatians and Romans, is not forgotten elsewhere.

Working through Philippians

The basic letter contains the usual *address* (1, 1–11), *body* (1, 12—3, 1), and *conclusion* (4, 21–23). The main themes of Philippians are the following:

I. Address and Thanksgiving (1, 1–11)
II. The Body of the Letter (1, 12—3, 1)
  A. Paul's situation and the progress of the gospel (1, 12–26)
  B. Exhortations for community unity; example of Jesus (1, 27—2, 18)
  C. Travel of Paul and assistants (2, 19—3, 1)
  D. Digression and warning (3, 1–4a)
  E. Example of Paul (3, 4b–21)
  F. Specific appeal to unity (4, 1–9)
  G. A thank-you note (4, 10–20)
III. Conclusion (4, 21–23)

The Address (1, 1–11)

The opening line names Paul and Timothy as senders of the letter, but the speaker quickly changes to "I" in verse 3, for Paul is really the author. Timothy will be mentioned as an ideal companion in 2, 19–24. The address is unique among Pauline letters in its acknowledgment of local leaders by title, "overseers and ministers," which by using later meanings of the words could also mean "bishops and deacons," but there is no evidence that the connotations later brought to those words are active here. Nevertheless, the address shows the beginnings of official titles and functions in the church.

A thanksgiving (1, 3–8) and a prayer (1, 9–11) complete the address. This is one of the longest and most beautifully developed of the Pauline thanksgivings. It introduces the themes of joy and community, themes that recur throughout Philippians. The paradox expressed in this letter is that the intense suffering experienced by Paul and the Philippians pales in comparison to the confident joy they share. Although separated because of Paul's imprisonment, and threatened on all sides, Paul and the Philippians are "partners," participating together in the spread of the gospel message. Paul draws strength from the Philippians' affection and display of concern for him. He prays (1, 9–11) that they will be strengthened and that their love will grow even amid hardships. Together they all await the "day of Christ," which Paul longs for and strains forward to obtain.

The Body of the Letter (1, 12—3, 1)

Paul's Situation and the Progress of the Gospel (1, 12–26)

Paul links faith in suffering and the spread of the gospel. Nowhere is this link more eloquently expressed than in Philippians 1, 12–26 where he refers to the effect his own imprisonment has had on the progress of the gospel message. Paul rejoices that even his enemies are using the opportunity represented by his present circumstances to energetically pursue the spread of the Christian message. For him, the priority is that "in every way . . . Christ is being proclaimed" (1, 18). This position stands in some contrast to his insistence elsewhere, even in 3, 2–3 of this letter, that only he has the right gospel. Paul speaks of joy even though he is in prison and the outcome is uncertain. He could be facing death. As a committed and passionate apostle, Paul worked tirelessly to promote acceptance of the gospel message by Gentiles everywhere. Now, in prison, Paul is equally peaceful, knowing that even should he die, the preaching will be continued.

If 1 Corinthians, especially chapters 1 and 2, represents a theoretical development of Paul's theology of the cross, Philippians represents Paul's own faith as he lives this theology. The wisdom of the cross is that God's power is made perfect in weakness. By this transforming power of the cross, Paul's brothers and sisters take encouragement from his imprisonment and preach the gospel all the more fearlessly. By the wisdom of the cross, Paul considers death to be "gain," and what he formerly considered "gain" to be "rubbish" (see 3, 7–8). Imprisoned, Paul draws strength from the community. He speaks with confidence and joy, expressing hope that is firmly rooted in God.

Exhortations for Community Unity and the Example of Jesus (1, 27—2, 18)

As he does in several other letters, Paul expresses concern that the opposition the Philippians experience will threaten their faith. He knows of internal divisions among these Christians. By appealing to them to "have a common mind and heart," Paul alludes first to his own suffering and imprisonment and then to the example of Christ.

The beautiful hymn about the abasement of Christ of 2, 6–11 is probably taken from an already existing piece of early Christian poetry with which the Philippians are familiar. It recalls their source of encouragement and is a cherished expression of faith in the redemptive aspects of Christ's suffering and death. The example of Christ's death must, above all else, influence the believing community in its own practical acceptance of and obedience to God's will. Thus, Christ who "emptied himself" is the example of behavior for the Philippians who are having trouble preserving unity in the congregation. Further, Christ by his death became "Lord" so that all who profess his Lordship are subject to him. In homage they recognize that they are brothers and sisters, members with one another of one believing community. So Christ is the example and the empowerment of selfless, mutual service in the church. Following the hymn, Paul draws out some implications: The Philippians are to remain blameless and innocent in the midst of adversity and wickedness, waiting for the Day of Christ (2, 16). Conceiving of the Christian life as a liturgical sacrifice, Paul says that even though he is "poured out as a libation" (wine that is offered in sacrifice), he rejoices. He asks only that the Philippians share his joy.

Travel of Paul and Assistants (2, 19—3, 1)

The travel account given here and other indications suggest relatively free and frequent exchanges between the prisoner, Paul, and the Philippians. This would be more easily understood with an imprisonment closer to Philippi than to Rome; thus, there is the Ephesian theory. The news about Epaphroditus's illness and recovery seems to indicate different visits. He probably came from Philippi and was not able to continue his apostolic work because of illness. Timothy is extolled as an ideal assistant, a second example of unity after Jesus. The trust among Paul, Timothy, and Epaphroditus stands in contrast to the squabbling between Euodia and Syntyche and other members of the Philippian community (4, 2–3).

Digression and Warning (3, 2–4a)

The abrupt change of tone and content between the first two chapters of Philippians and the strong warning in 3, 2–4 is one of the strongest arguments that these were originally separate communications. Even so, a skilled rhetorician could also just as abruptly switch topic and tone to get his audience's attention. This sudden theme of resistance to those who agitate for the Gentiles to be circumcised, presented in an insulting tone, is brief and does not reappear in this letter.

Example of Paul (3, 4b–21)

After presenting the example of Jesus and then in a lesser way of Timothy, Paul now proposes himself as example of one who knows how to give up privilege and status for the good of others. He gives us some of our best biographical information about himself and then reflects on the consequences of his encounter with Christ. Using athletic imagery, Paul encourages the Philippians to strain toward the goal of a "perfect maturity." He urges them not to regress into the past, seeking glory in shame (possible allusions to circumcision) or in other practices of the "flesh," such as observances of certain dietary rules. These, Paul says, are earthly things. Paul himself used to glory in his religious accomplishments, but since his conversion, he no longer regards these as significant. Indeed, his former system of valuing is "rubbish" compared with his new way of seeing things in Christ. This is the wisdom of the cross. Those who do not accept this wisdom are "enemies of the cross" (3, 18).

Specific Appeal to Unity (4, 1–9)

Paul turns to an internal crisis that is just as destructive and threatening to the community. He begins chapter 4 by urging the Philippians to live in harmony, a theme he had already developed in chapters 1 and 2. But now he is specific in his appeal to unity, and all the previous rhetoric on the subject may be leading to this climax. There is a conflict between some leading women of the community, Euodia and Syntyche, and Paul solemnly begs them to stop. What position these women occupy we do not know, but their division is obviously central to the community's problems, so they may be significant leaders. Paul addresses a comrade and enlists the help of an otherwise unknown man named Clement to aid in the reconciliation of these women for the betterment of the whole community.

A Thank-you Note (4, 10–20)

Paul expresses thanks for the help received from the Philippians and sent with Epaphroditus. He adds, however, that his gratitude is not so much that he was personally aided as that the Philippians'

generosity is "profit that accrues to your account" (4, 17). Paul testifies to his own indifference and ability to do without. Yet he humbly accepted aid not only to alleviate his own need, but as a symbol of the affection that linked him to the Philippians. Paul speaks of this aid in liturgical terms, referring to it as "a fragrant aroma . . . a sacrifice, pleasing to God" (4, 18–19; see also 2 Cor 2, 14–16). This is the ancient language of liturgical offering and sacrifice. The idea of an offering of mutual love and aid by Christians to one another as a "liturgy" appears also in Romans 12, 1–2 and 15, 17–20.

Conclusion (4, 21–23)

The conclusion of the letter sends greetings to everyone there from everyone here. The reference to "Caesar's household" is to the vast imperial network of civil servants that were present in every major city. We know from this reference that there were Christians among them.

Concluding Remarks

Since the writing of Philippians, the Christian community has been inspired not only by the words of the apostle, but by the example of the imprisoned leader who speaks with such affection, hope, and faith. One of the most beautiful and well known of Paul's letters, Philippians represents a reflection on the meaning of fidelity in the midst of trial. Paul's confidence that in all things "Christ is . . . proclaimed" (1, 18) transcends the threat of others' jealousy and rivalry.

The Christological hymn of Philippians 2 not only inspired the Philippians to greater unity, but also continues to invite believers of every age to imitate Christ. Paul's prayer for his fellow Christians is that they always be happy (Phil 4, 4–9). This serves as a model for our prayers for one another. Paul puts his own life before the Philippians, encouraging them to follow him in everything that he does and says. Paul then promises that the "God of peace will be with you" (4, 9). Such should be our prayer in attracting others to live the Christian life.

Questions for Discussion and Reflection
Group Sharing/Discussion

1. Paul writes this epistle from prison. Let each one in the group choose a theme of Paul's and explain it to the group.

2. Philippians is unique in Pauline letters in that it acknowledges local leaders by title, "overseers and ministers." What were their roles in this early church?

3. Paul links faith and suffering with the spread of the gospel (1, 12–26). Read this aloud and share what you think Paul feels regarding his imprisonment. How does this relate to your experience?

4. The wisdom of the cross is that God's power is made perfect in weakness. Paul's imprisonment gives encouragement to the Philippians. Let each person share their reaction to this.

In Our Lives

1. For Paul the priority is that "in everything ... Christ is being proclaimed" (1, 18). Share how this faith priority speaks to you and your Christian vision.

2. Christ is the model and empowerment of selfless, mutual service in the Church (2, 6–11). Where and in whom do you see this in your life, your parish community?

3. The trust among Paul, Timothy, and Epaphroditus contrasts with the squabbling between Euodia and Syntyche and the Philippians' community. Talk about the necessity of trust in building the Christian community; give examples. Explain what are the needs of increasing trust in your community and suggestions for doing that.

4. Paul proposes himself as an example of one who knows how to give up status and privilege for the good of others. Name this reality and need in your community.

5. Paul used to glory in his religious accomplishments but since his conversion no longer does. He grew in a new way of seeing things in Christ. What would be similar experiences in Christian history (e.g., St. Augustine, St. Ignatius Loyola) and in your life of experiencing of a new way of seeing things in Christ?

Individual/Personal Reflection/Action

1. Set aside time and meditate on the sufferings of Christ (2, 6–11). Recall this is a source of encouragement and an expression of faith. Christ who "emptied himself" is still an example for our Christian life.

2. Philippians presents a reflection on the meaning of Christian faithfulness in the midst of trial. What is your experience of this? To whom can you look for encouragement in this?

3. Make Paul's prayer (4, 4–9) your prayer. It is a treasure. "God of peace be with you" (4, 9).

COLOSSIANS READING GUIDE

At a Glance

Who are the main players?	Paul Epaphras Timothy Christians of Colossae
What should I look for?	Paul encourages fidelity to foundational beliefs in Christ's person and redemptive work, while warning against false teachings concerning spirits and ascetical practices.
When did this take place?	If Paul wrote it, he was imprisoned several times during the decade of the A.D. 50s; if written by a disciple, it could be around A.D. 60–62.
Where did these events occur?	This is addressed to a Gentile congregation at Colossae in the Lycus Valley in Asia Minor.
Why was this book written?	The letter is a response to Epaphras, founder of the community, concerning false doctrines that are disrupting the congregation.
What is the story?	Without debating about angelic spirits, Paul affirms that Christ possesses full redemptive power and that spiritual renewal occurs through contact in baptism with Christ who died and rose again. It is unnecessary to placate spirits. True Christian asceticism consists in avoiding sin and practicing love of neighbor as Christ teaches.

Before Beginning

It is customary to refer to the author of Colossians as Paul, even though many interpreters question whether Paul himself wrote this brief letter. Many characteristics of the letter seem to suggest Paul's presence behind it. The lively style and personal greetings are typical of Paul. Most of the personal names mentioned here also appear in Philemon, a letter that has always been attributed to Paul himself. Yet there are strange expressions, new terms, and a new understanding of the church so that many scholars think it indicates a different author here, writing in Paul's name with the hope of using Paul's authority. A compromise position is that Paul entrusted the message to a secretary who composed it in his own terms and with his own style.

Paul himself did not establish the church at Colossae. Possibly Epaphras, a disciple of Paul, was the founding missionary there. The context is that erroneous teachers implied that Christ's work of redemption was incomplete and therefore that certain other religious practices were required to supplement Christ's saving death and resurrection. These suggested practices were drawn from Jewish as well as non-Jewish or pagan religions.

They amounted to ascetical and superstitious additions to the message Paul and Epaphras had taught. As in Galatians, but less emotionally, Paul adamantly insists in Colossians that adding to the gospel message is really subtracting from grace. Only as a member of Christ's body and under his headship can we fill up "what is lacking in the afflictions of Christ" (1, 24), that is, continuing Christ's redemptive suffering in the world.

At issue in the discussion at Colossae is the primary role of Christ in the salvation of the world. The power and authority of Christ and his relation to the rest of creation are challenged. False teachings at Colossae suggested that other spiritual beings were rivals to Christ's role and that certain ascetical practices were a means of becoming more spiritual while also helping to appease these spiritual beings. Using categories and labels present in these false teachings, Paul insists on the primacy of Christ and that Christ's saving action on our behalf is sufficient. Ethical demands follow from this fundamental faith. It is not a matter of satisfying some angelic spirits or following some ascetical ideals.

Working through Colossians

The *address and thanksgiving* (1, 1–14) and *conclusion* (4, 7–18) enclose the *body* of this letter in 1, 15—4, 6. The body of Colossians follows the basic indicative-imperative pattern characteristic of Paul. The structure of Colossians then is the following:

I. Address and Thanksgiving (1, 1–14)
II. The Body of the Letter (1, 15—4, 6)
   A. Instruction about Christ and false teaching (1, 15—2, 23)
   B. Ethics characterizing the true Christian (3, 1—4, 6)
III. Conclusion (4, 7–18)

The Address (1, 1–14)

The *address* includes not only the usual greeting (1, 1–2) and thanksgiving (1, 3–8), but also a prayer for the continued progress of the Colossians (1, 9–14). Both the *address* and *conclusion* (4, 7–18) contain greetings and personal references that are typical of Paul.

The Body of the Letter (1, 15—4, 6)

Colossians' main message is correct teaching and warnings against false teachings (1, 15—2, 23). This is followed by exhortations to exercise fundamental beliefs in daily Christian living (3, 1—4, 6).

Instruction about Christ and False Teaching (1, 15—2, 23)

Paul is confident that Epaphras has given the community a solid foundation. He reminds the Colossians that by Christ's saving death, "[God] delivered us from the power of darkness and transferred us to the kingdom of his beloved Son" (1, 13). This transference from the realm of sin and error into that of grace and truth is effected in baptism and must be lived out in the daily lives of Christians. The doctrinal presentation of the first major part of Colossians falls into three sections: the Christological hymn and its implications (1, 15–23), Paul's own ministry and example (1, 24—2, 3), and warnings against false teachers and their teaching (2, 4–23).

The Christological Hymn (1, 15–23)

To teach a correct Christology and clarify errors, Paul quotes a liturgical hymn apparently familiar to the Colossians (1, 15–20; see also Phil 2, 6–11). Many interpreters believe that this hymn predates Paul and was already in use by the early Christian communities. The poetic rhythm and language suggest that it was a hymn and that it was at home in the liturgy. Because Paul generally writes in prose, the insertion of a hymn here is easily discerned in the Greek. In this hymn Christians profess and celebrate the authority of Christ in whom all "fullness was pleased to dwell, and through him to reconcile all things for him." Paul stresses the redemption and peace won for us through Christ. He does not badger or scold the Colossians for their errors, but presents Christ's role of reconciling the world to God as the basis of common faith among all believers. The text adapts a variety of traditions about the figure of Wisdom and a cosmic savior to the person of Christ, who begins, as in the prologue of John's Gospel, in the heavenly realm. But he is also the head of the church and first-born from the dead, so that his saving action works in our history.

Paul's Ministry and Example (1, 24—2, 3)

Emphasis on his own example is a remarkable trait of Paul's letters, one expected of a great teacher in his day (see further 1 Thes 1, 6; 2 Cor 11–12). It is also significant that upon reviewing Christ's work of redemption, Paul immediately attaches his own example as a model for the Colossians to emulate. At first this advice may strike us as surprising and almost shocking. How can Paul claim to be a model for all to imitate (see 1 Cor 11, 1; Phil 4, 8)? It springs from the apostle's humility and transparent confidence. Paul is so firmly rooted in God that he dares to advise his addressees to follow his example. By studying Paul's life, others may know the power of God and be converted. Paul always reveals the source of his confidence, which is not self-reliance but hope in God. This hope is best expressed in Christ's gift of salvation evidenced in the life of the apostle. The apostle glories in his vocation and fidelity while also accentuating his sufferings in the service of the gospel.

In describing his own ministry, Paul adapts categories important to the Colossians and to the false teachers who are disturbing them. They are emphasizing "wisdom" and "perfection," so Paul speaks about the "knowledge of the mystery of God, Christ, in whom are hidden all the treasures of wisdom and knowledge" (2, 2–3). Paul

identifies the goal of his mission to "present everyone perfect in Christ" (1, 28). For this he labors and struggles in accord with "God's power working within me" (1, 29).

Warnings against False Teachings (2, 4–23)

Paul encourages the Colossians in their faith, reminding them of their identity in Christ. He observes the "good order and the firmness of your faith in Christ." He celebrates this fidelity and encourages the Colossians to be grateful, with a thanksgiving rooted in faith. Finally, he warns against the seduction of false teaching that is according to mere human tradition and not grounded in Christ. The false teaching was probably a combination of Jewish and pagan philosophies and pagan ideals. Paul denounces the "circumcision administered by human hands" and the ascetical practices regarding "food and drink" alleged to be required at certain times and days (2, 16). Some teachers flaunted their visions and self-abasement and were involved in complicated devotions to angelic beings. Paul labeled all these as passing fads, "shadows of things to come" and "things destined to perish." By contrast, in Christ dwells the fullness of God. All are members of Christ, who is the head of the body, the church. Here and in Ephesians, this specific role of Christ within the church is introduced. Christians are united in one church under one Lord who is Christ. Their common task is the reconciliation of the world to God under Christ.

Ethics Characterizing the True Christian (3, 1—4, 6)

Paul does not really present a new, uniquely Christian ethical system but draws from several existing systems. Often Paul lists vices or virtues similar to lists found in Stoic or other Greek philosophers. The "household rules" found in Colossians (see Eph 5, 21—6, 9; Ti 2, 1—3, 8; 1 Pt 2, 11—3, 7) have parallels in contemporary Greco-Roman literature where elements of household management are discussed. The submission of wives, children, and slaves to the male household head was an expected part of the social order. A fundamental difference for Paul is the motivation and the empowerment to fulfill these ethical principles. The church as the body of Christ distinguishes itself from the outside world in that the love command operates to create a new way for Christians to relate to one another. Paul says that the Colossians once conducted themselves as pagans who practiced immorality, greed, and passion (see 3, 5–7). Now they have "put on the new self, which is being renewed . . . in the image of its creator" (3, 10). In Christ the usual sexual, social, and ethnic distinctions do not exist, "but Christ is all and in all" (3, 11).

Conclusion (4, 7–18)

Tychicus is the messenger entrusted with the letter to the Colossians. Many think that the Onesimus mentioned as his companion (4, 9) is the former slave who returned to Colossae with the letter from Paul to Philemon (see Reading Guide to Philemon). The other companions mentioned at the end of Colossians are well-known Christians named in other Pauline letters except for Nympha (4, 15), a woman who hosts a house church. This list of personal references reminds us about the common Christian teaching upon which Paul depends and to which he urges the Colossians to hold firm.

Concluding Remarks

Today no less than in the times of the Colossians, Christians are pulled in various directions, and people are still searching for spiritual guides and nourishment. The exotic, speculative language in Colossians does not seem so strange to us when we consider the attractions of undemanding spirituality, the ease with which we can adopt superstitious practices, or the popularity of "self-help" books that tell us we can accomplish anything if we "image" it correctly. The epistle to the Colossians stresses the reconciliation of all things in Christ as the fundamental faith assertion with enormous ethical repercussions. As the firstborn of all creation, Christ is a symbol of the value of all creation and a promise of the ultimate salvation of all. That truth translates into the church's responsibility for stewardship in the world, assuming that in preaching reconciliation the rights of all are respected. In carrying out its mission, the church must be a symbol of peace, because Christ is the head of the church, and Christ made peace by the blood of the cross.

Questions for Discussion and Reflection
Group Sharing/Discussion

1. The context of Colossians was false teaching in the community that Christ's work of

redemption was incomplete. How were the false teachings expressed in Colossians?

2. What does Paul say about continuing Christ's redemptive sufferings in the world (1, 24)?

3. Paul speaks and acts with a great deal of confidence. What is the source of this confidence?

4. The central issue in Colossians is the primary role of Christ in the salvation of the world. This involves the power and authority of Christ as well as his relation to all creation. Let each person share with the group what you believe is Christ's primary role and how this relates to the world and all creation. Also, what ethical issues follow from Christ's role?

5. Basically, the lists of virtues and vices that Paul presents are not new; they are found earlier in the Greek philosophers. What Paul did present that was different is the motivation for acting ethically. Explain this significant difference.

In Our Lives

1. Paul includes a liturgical hymn (1, 15–23) that celebrates Christ in whom "all the fullness was pleased to dwell, and through him to reconcile all things for him." Paul stresses redemption and peace won for us by Christ. This is the foundation of his response to the false teachings and ethical problems. Share what this meant to the Colossians in their context. Share what this means today to you and with your friends or community.

2. Paul identifies the goal of his mission to "present everyone perfect in Christ" (1, 28). Reflect and clarify what your mission is as a follower of Christ. Paul labored and struggled for his mission in accord with God's power "working within me" (1, 19). Do you grow aware of God's power working within to face the struggles of being Christ in the world today?

3. In his letters Paul celebrates the faithful by thanksgiving. He gives thanks always. He celebrates their faith and encourages the Colossians to be grateful. Reflect upon your rhythm of living. How do you rise and give thanks each day? How often do you give thanks to God and to persons? Are you conscious at the liturgy that thanksgiving is central to your worship? Share ideas with each other on how to grow in giving thanks.

Individual/Personal Reflection/Action

1. Paul's trait of giving his own life as an example for the Colossians to follow is remarkable

and is common to his letters. Paul followed Christ and taught Christ. He calls his readers to follow Christ and teach Christ by their life. Who are your teachers? Who are your models or mentors? How and to whom are you a teacher or model? What values do you see and follow?

2. All are members of Christ, who is the head of the body, the church. Paul introduces this role of Christ within the church. Christians are united as members with Christ as the head. Their common task is the reconciliation of the world to God under Christ. Christ is head of the body, the Church. All are united in church under one head who is Christ. How are these part of your consciousness? Our common task: Reconcile the world to God under Christ. How do you keep this growing and maturing in your life?

1 THESSALONIANS READING GUIDE

At a Glance

Who are the main players?	Paul Timothy Silvanus
What should I look for?	Be aware of Paul's affectionate thanksgiving. Note the relationship between faith and charity as well as the teaching on the second coming of Christ.
When did this take place?	About A.D. 51, probably written from Corinth
Where did these events occur?	In Thessalonica, the capital of the Roman province of Macedonia. The Christian community there was one of the very first Paul established.
Why was this book written?	Paul sent Timothy back to Thessalonica to strengthen that community in its trials. Timothy's return with a report on the conditions there served as the occasion of Paul's first letter.
What is the story?	Paul experienced a great deal of persecution from the Jews and Gentiles because of his preaching. In this letter he expresses his gratitude to the community for their faith and defends his ministry. In addition he gives specific instructions on sexual conduct, death, and church order.

Before Beginning

Thessalonica was the capital and major city of the Roman province of Macedonia, about one hundred miles southwest of Philippi along a major Roman road. The communities at Thessalonica and Philippi were among Paul's first converts in Greece. This letter indicates that he encountered many troubles there from both Jews and Greeks. The beginning of Paul's ministry in Thessalonica was characterized by suffering and humiliation. He was "insolently treated at Philippi," an incident to which he does not allude in his letter there (see 2, 2; see also Acts 20, 34; 1 Cor 4, 12; 9, 3–18; 2 Thes 3, 7–9). The Thessalonians, too, shared in some of that perse-

cution (2, 14–16). Persecution, illness, misunderstanding, and other forms of suffering plague Paul's ministry. Yet he constantly has hope of being found worthy by God to be entrusted with the preaching of the gospel (2, 4).

Working through 1 Thessalonians

Following the usual letter format, 1 Thessalonians has an address and thanksgiving (1, 1–10) and conclusion (5, 26–28), which envelop the body of Paul's message (2, 1—5, 25). This message falls into two parts: the indicative (2, 1— 3, 13) followed by the ethical exhortations (4, 1—5, 25).

The structure of 1 Thessalonians can be outlined as follows:

I. The Address (1, 1–10)
II. The Body of the Letter (2, 1—5, 25)
   A. Paul's Account and Defense of his Ministry (2, 1—3, 13)
   B. Specific Exhortations and Instructions (4, 1—5, 22)
III. Conclusion (5, 23–28)

The Address and Thanksgiving (1, 1–10)

The address contains a short greeting (1, 1) and an extended thanksgiving (1, 2–10). A distinctive feature of Paul's letters is that the thanksgiving focuses on what God has done for Paul's addressees. In other correspondence of the time, the thanksgiving normally centers on the health and benefits enjoyed by the sender and a wish for the prosperity of the recipient. Paul's co-authors are Silvanus and Timothy. Following his custom, Paul writes not only in his own name, but as a member of a team of Christian missionaries. Unlike many others of his letters that begin with several names, here the second person plural is maintained throughout the letter, Paul's "I" breaking through only at 2, 18 and 5, 27. In what we believe is the first extant letter from Paul, there is a greeting that will become Paul's trademark: "To the church of _____, grace and peace to you in (or from) God the Father and the Lord Jesus." This greeting is seen in its simplest form here; in later letters Paul will elaborate on this basic form.

A function of the thanksgiving in the address is often to anticipate the themes of a letter. In the case of 1 Thessalonians, thanksgiving itself is a major theme. Paul is grateful for the reception of the word of God by the Thessalonians and for the impact that their faith has had on other communities. Paul claims that he himself does not even have to testify to the fruitfulness of the Thessalonian mission because word of it has spread throughout the Greek world (Macedonia and Achaia include the whole of Greece, 1, 8). Besides the initial thanksgiving of 1, 2–10 that properly belongs to the address, two other thanksgivings appear in 2, 13–16; 3, 9–13. In all three places, Paul speaks of the relationship between faith and charity and of the expectation of the Parousia or second coming of Jesus Christ. These are the major themes of 1 Thessalonians.

The Body of the Letter (2, 1—5, 25)

The body contains Paul's main message in two parts; Paul's account and defense (2, 1—3, 13) followed by teachings and exhortation (4, 1—5, 25).

Paul's Account and Defense of his Ministry (2, 1—3, 13)

Paul states clearly that his motives are pure in his work with the Thessalonians. If we can read between the lines, we can surmise the accusations of unworthy motives on his part against which he defends himself. He stresses his gratitude to God for the success of this community and presents a defense of his ministry.

Thanksgiving is a persistent thread that runs throughout 1 Thessalonians. Yet Paul is not a naive optimist. He is aware that this community is experiencing several problems. Although he will return to the theme of gratitude, he launches into a defense of his own ministry with the Thessalonians, thereby implying that some have questioned his authority or actions. Throughout Paul's ministry career, he insists that he is an apostle, called by God to preach the gospel message. Paul's defense of himself and his authority are linked to the call he has from God. He is under a divine compulsion to preach the gospel, and his confidence derives from this vocation. His defense of his ministry is also prompted by some of the dangers represented by false teachers agitating the Thessalonians in Paul's absence. Although this is a painful and threatening problem, Paul interrupts this defense with thanksgivings, as if to say that he is confident in the Thessalonians' perseverance despite the interference of the agitators.

One of the most difficult yet persistent problems that faced the early church was that of false prophets or false teachers. In the ancient world, where travel was difficult and communications took time, often philosophers or religious teachers joined others who traveled for business or personal reasons. News was gathered and disseminated by such traveling groups; new converts were often made along the way. First Thessalonians reflects this kind of mobility where Paul speaks about his own past visits with the Thessalonians as well as his thwarted plans to return. He promises to visit again soon. He warns the Thessalonians about other types of ministers—those who are greedy or who flatter (2, 5) or who rely on the community for support (2, 9). Paul's own example stands out in contrast to these, for he has been "gentle as a nursing mother" among them (2, 7).

Despite his grateful recognition of the sturdy faith of the Thessalonians, Paul found it necessary to remind them of the sacrifices and dedication they saw in him and his companions. Among his characteristic practices, Paul repeatedly notes that he is self-supporting. He "toiled day and night" among them and in so doing, he gave them an example that they ought to imitate. This practice of working with his hands and supporting himself was unusual. The Corinthians misinterpreted it, and he did accept gifts of support from the Philippians (Phil 4, 10–20).

Specific Exhortations and Instructions (4, 1—5, 22)

Concrete ethical applications or "imperatives" follow from Paul's grateful description of the Christian community at Thessalonica. This exhortatory section may be considered a specific example of Paul's concern that faith be exercised in practical living, particularly as expressed in charity.

Sexual Conduct (4, 3–8)

These verses refer to sexual morality, but it is not clear how. The text may refer to a man being faithful to his wife (the usual translation), or to the need for his own sexual control, with no wife mentioned, and verse 6 may refer again to marital fidelity against adultery, or to cheating in business matters. In any case, the text raises a variety of ethical concerns including sexual conduct and business ethics.

For their part, the Jews considered the obligations of marriage and the family to be linked to the covenant relationship with God. This link was an important one Paul wished to adopt for the Gentile Christians. Paul therefore stresses the obligation of believers to develop relationships worthy of them, reflecting respect for one another and for their call to holiness. Charity among believers, in turn, has an effect even on those outside the community who will be impressed with the example of high moral conduct of the Christians.

Death and the Need for Vigilance (4, 13—5, 11)

Paul and other early Christians seem to have believed that the Parousia or return of Jesus was very near. Now members of the Thessalonian community are dying before this event, which was a problem for their faith that Jesus would truly return. They wondered how the dead would participate in the triumphant day of Christ's return. Paul encourages the Thessalonians to persevere in faith and joins to this a warning about continued vigilance. Enthusiastic faith can often wane at the onslaught of opposition, suffering, and frustrated expectations. Paul fears that the death of fellow Christians will so shake the Thessalonians' faith that their grief will give way to doubt, discouragement, and even apostasy.

Paul's view of the second coming is influenced by perception that God is living in heaven, which is "above," beyond the clouds. An archangel and trumpets are standard images accompanying the end of the world and a call to judgment. The second coming of Christ, unlike the first, will be a show of power. It will be cosmic in effect, changing the entire order of creation, not only human existence.

Paul promises that the Christian dead have not been lost or forgotten. They, like us, will be gathered by Christ and judged. The righteous will be restored to God. Paul's emphasis is on the certainty of this event, not on times or manner. The exact manner of the resurrection and of judgment, Paul finally admits in 1 Corinthians 15, is unknown to us (see 1 Thes 5, 1; 1 Cor 15, 35–57).

The death of loved ones may pose painful faith questions for believers in any age. The death of beloved members of the community seems to have challenged the faith of the Christians at Thessalonica. Because the death of fellow Christians was so threatening, Paul admonished: "console one another with these words" (4, 18; 5, 11). He reinforced his warning to persevere by speaking again about the certainty of Christ's coming. The images of the pregnant woman and of the thief in the night are ones that appear in Jesus' own preaching, according to the Gospel accounts (see Mt 24, 43; Lk 21, 23). They stress at once the need for preparedness and vigilance, the certainty of the occurrence, and the threatening aspect of suffering. Continuing his use of stock apocalyptic imagery, Paul envisions a cosmic struggle that differentiates between those who are the children of light and those who remain in darkness.

Spirit and Order (5, 12–22)

Paul teaches respect for those who minister among the faithful, an unusual reference to local leaders (see also Phil 1, 1). But the more important points are about the way in which believers are to exercise mutual love, not returning evil for evil but consistently seeking the good of all. Joy, prayer, and gratitude characterize their lives as they live according to the Spirit, discerning between good and evil.

Conclusion (5, 23–28)

The concluding prayer (5, 23–25) and final greetings (5, 26–28) suggest that this letter was intended for reading in a liturgical setting. Paul says that the Thessalonians will be kept holy and spotless as they wait for the LORD's return. The "holy kiss" with which they are to greet one another was probably the ritual exchange of peace done during the liturgical assembly.

Concluding Remarks

Actions are an expression of faith. Behavior is a key to the way people think and what they believe. Therefore, if there is carelessness about others, or promiscuity, or indifference to one's role in creating a livable society and universe, we have to examine the underlying faith presuppositions to these actions or omissions. Charity, chastity, and an honest, humble bearing in this life are signs for Paul of conversion to the "living and true God." Paul exhorts Christians to live according to the gospel he preaches. It is not hard to see how the message of 1 Thessalonians is appropriate for today.

Questions for Discussion and Reflection
Group Sharing/Discussion

1. What are the main themes in 1 Thessalonians (1, 2–10; 2, 13–16; 3, 9–13)?

2. What is Paul's view of the second coming of Jesus?

3. Paul repeatedly notes that he is self-supporting. Why? Share your views of the results and

how this may or may not apply to the church today.

4. Paul notes that his vocation and his authority came from his call by God. Why does Paul feel he must defend his ministry?

5. In 4, 3–8 Paul talks about sexual conduct. Read this aloud and each comment on how his teaching relates to modern life.

In Our Lives

1. Paul and the early Christians believed that the return of Jesus was very near. When members of the community died before this event, it became a problem of faith and of belief that Jesus would truly return. Remember what Paul said to help them. Reflect on how the second coming of Jesus relates to you and your faith. How would you help someone whose faith was weakened by the death of a dear one?

2. In 1 Thessalonians Paul advises, "do not quench the Spirit" (5, 19). Share what this may mean in today's church. Share how you try to nourish the Spirit in your parish.

3. Paul asks for respect for the ministers and reminds us that there must be mutual care and trust. How do you contribute to this in your parish? How would you teach a group to respect ministers and vice versa?

Individual/Personal Reflection/Action

1. Pray and reflect carefully on 5, 14–22. Make this a frequent examination of conscience. Who are the idle? The fainthearted? The weak? How do I do the following: Admonish? Cheer a person? Support those around us? Pray without ceasing? Give thanks? Recall that this is the will of God for you.

2. Like the Thessalonians, we may find the death of a loved one brings painful questions. Any death leaves a hole in the fabric of a community. How can the community work together to respond helpfully when someone dies? How does your faith respond? Does God seem closer or more remote? How do you nourish your faith and love so as to be helpful?

3. Charity among the community, in turn, has an effect on the outside community. Count the many ways you see this charity in your parish community. Reflect and plan on new ways of increasing this.

2 THESSALONIANS READING GUIDE

At a Glance

Who are the main players?	Paul Silvanus Timothy Community of Thessalonians
What should I look for?	The apocalyptic message of consolation and hope, which does not cause fear but is a message of encouragement in the face of confusion and suffering.
When did this take place?	Probably written around A.D. 70 by a Pauline disciple
Where did these events occur?	In Thessalonica, the capital of the Roman province of Macedonia
Why was this book written?	This is a response to a letter allegedly sent by Paul containing false teaching that the day of the Lord is at hand.
What is the story?	The heart of the letter has to do with the message supposedly sent by Paul that the second coming of Christ is at hand. Thanksgiving, prayers, and teachings add encouragement at a time of fear and suffering.

Before Beginning

The apocalyptic, end of the world, perspective of 2 Thessalonians (see introduction to 1 Thes and the notes on apocalyptic elements in Paul preceding the Reading Guide to 2 Cor) is more pronounced here than in any other Pauline letter. The Pauline authorship of 2 Thessalonians is widely disputed. This letter may be written in Paul's name by someone other than Paul, probably a disciple or admirer. There is a studied attempt on the part of this disciple of Paul to copy Paul's style. For example, the greeting differs only slightly from the greeting of 1 Thessalonians, and the final greeting insists that the letter is based on Paul's authority. There is a rejection of other supposedly Pauline letters circulating (2, 1). One could also say that these are signs of Paul's true authorship, but perhaps the insistence on Paul's authority seems more than a little defensive. Writing in Paul's name assured that a letter would be taken seriously. This practice of Paul's disciples was also an attempt to give continuity to the apostle's message, explicitly interpreting the Pauline traditions in a new context. Despite the reservations of interpreters about Paul's authorship, it is customary to refer to the writer of 2 Thessalonians as "Paul."

There is good reason to believe that 2 Thessalonians was written a decade or more after Paul's death. It is addressed to the same community as 1 Thessalonians but a community that is troubled by the mistaken preaching that the Day of the Lord had now arrived. The preoccupation of early Christians with the times and circumstances accompanying the return of Christ is a problem addressed by many of the New Testament writers, including the Gospels of Matthew, Mark, and Luke, and the book of Revelation. The "apocalyptic" message of 2 Thessalonians is not a frightening one that heightens with fear the anticipation of Christ's return, but is instead a message of consolation and hope for the Christians suffering persecution and confusion. The term "apocalyptic" has come into vogue again today when the future seems uncertain. We need to understand biblical apocalyptic as emphasizing hope for all those who persevere.

Working through 2 Thessalonians

Second Thessalonians exhibits the usual letter characteristics of an address and thanksgiving (1, 1–12) and conclusion (3, 15–18) enclosing the message or body of the letter in 2, 1—3, 16.

I. The Address (1, 1–12)
II. The Body of the Letter (2, 1—3, 15)
III. Conclusion (3, 16–18)

The Address and Thanksgiving (1, 1–12)

The address includes a greeting (1, 1–2), a thanksgiving (1, 3–10), and a prayer (1, 11–12). The greeting is an almost slavish imitation of the greeting of 1 Thessalonians. Paul joins himself with Silvanus and Timothy, fellow missionaries to the Thessalonians (see 1 Thes 1, 1). Also similar to 1 Thessalonians is the fact that thanksgiving is not only a part of the initial address as a formal characteristic of a letter; gratitude is also a central theme in the development of Paul's teaching (see 2, 13–17).

The Body of the Letter (2, 1—3, 15)

Paul's message to the Thessalonians can be subdivided into instruction on right thinking (2, 1–17) and right conduct in the daily life of the Christians who lived in Thessalonica (3, 1–16).

Paul's Teaching on Right Thinking (2, 1–17)

The early Christians' expectation of an imminent return of Christ needed to be adjusted and corrected as the community developed. Unforeseen crises arose, and answers had to be sought in the basics of Christian preaching. Time passed, and the danger was that Christians would become disenchanted and would lose faith, especially in the midst of adversity. First Thessalonians had warned the community about maintaining faith, hope, and love even amid trials such as the death of fellow Christians. There Paul focused on the day of the Lord, which, he assured them, was coming soon. This reminder served as a warning that behavior would be judged, and the faithful would be rewarded, whereas the unfaithful would be punished.

By the time of the writing of 2 Thessalonians, it seems the expectation was being taken too seriously, and this caused new problems. As time passed, the early Christians were wondering about the accuracy of their hope that Christ would return soon. They became alarmed by prophecies and by a letter that they thought came from Paul; it seems to have said that the expected "day of the Lord" had arrived (2, 2). The author denies this and lists a number of events that must come first. This change in 2 Thessalonians 2, 1–10 from the expectation of the near return of Christ seen in 1 Thessalonians is one of the main reasons interpreters suspect that 2 Thessalonians is from a later, second generation Pauline Christian. The early Christians had experienced persecution. History had already shown that any expectation that Christ would speedily return with power, to punish the oppressors of the Christians, was wrong.

The message underlying the apocalyptic references in 2 Thessalonians is "do not be alarmed." The writer avoids any kind of futile speculation concerning times and circumstances of the coming of Christ. He uses standard apocalyptic images portraying the conflict between good and evil, and the ultimate victory of God over evil. Yet he studiously avoids any specific description. It is enough that his readers focus on the hope of God's victory and that they remain vigilant against deception or alarm.

Paul's Teaching on Right Conduct (3, 1–15)

The admonition in 3, 10 not to feed anyone who will not work and the general exhortation against idleness is probably connected to the apocalyptic expectation discussed earlier. Some thought that there was no further point to building the human community if it would all end soon. But Paul warns that idlers only disrupt the peace of the community. Thus he connects idleness and a lack of charity. The apostle presents himself as a model to the contrary to be imitated. His work with his hands is apparently a topic of discussion among his converts. Perhaps, like the Corinthians, the Thessalonians despise labor and prefer the leisure that is considered more conducive to the development of the mind and spirit. Paul gives both social and theological reasons showing that he was not constrained to work but does so freely. Part of the legacy he left with the community was his example of working. This may have been a form of self-abasement Paul practiced to "be all things to all people" (see 1 Cor 9, 21–22). Paul stresses that his aim is to make the gospel accessible to all.

Conclusion (3, 16–18)

The author adds a greeting "in his own hand," apparently to show that this is from Paul. Yet it is such characteristics that make Pauline authorship of 2 Thessalonians suspect. There are no personal greetings and no originality to the abrupt closing of this letter. The author seems to be copying Paul's style rather than adding a more personalized signature as Paul would have done.

Concluding Remarks

Christians today can understand the need for restraint on the belief that the return of Christ was imminent. Perhaps more than ever before, we can appreciate the important balance introduced by 2 Thessalonians between faith that indeed the return of Christ would come and emphasis on the need to work diligently to create a better society. Second Thessalonians offers us a message of hope and encouragement. The events that must come to pass before the end of the world are opportunities inviting us to a change of heart, expressed in careful stewardship of our lives, of the church, and of the world.

Questions for Discussion and Reflection
Group Sharing/Discussion
1. What was the occasion for the writing of this letter?

2. What would you say is the main lesson here?
In Our Lives
1. The writer avoids useless guessing or speculation concerning the time and circumstances of the second coming of Christ. His message expresses the certainty of the coming and the victory of God. How do you focus your hope? Is it in the confidence of Christ's coming?

2. Events that that must come to pass before the end of the world are opportunities inviting us to a change of heart. What are the problem areas in your life, your parish, your city, or the world that require the balance of intense prayer and energetic action? Have you given up on praying or working for solutions of these problems?

Individual/Personal Reflection/Action
1. Second Thessalonians offers us a message of hope and encouragement. Hope and encouragement are necessary for Christian living To have hope and to act with encouragement require prayer and reflection. Take the time: be hopeful and share your hope; be encouraged by Christ and your many gifts and share this encouragement with those in need.

THE PASTORAL LETTERS

Introduction

The two letters to Timothy and the single letter to Titus have been called the "Pastoral Letters" because they deal largely with issues regarding pastoral care in Pauline communities. Most scholars consider them not to have been written by Paul, but by a later writer, because they reflect a degree of church organization not present in Paul's day. We are indebted to these communities for preserving this distinctive correspondence that describes the initial development of church offices and organization. The Pastorals might be read as reflections on Christian ministry. In keeping with the tradition of authorship by Paul, we will refer to the writer as "Paul," although most interpreters would agree that these letters are written at least a generation after Paul's death. In form they are personal letters written to one disciple, but in reality, they are open letters to communities covering church policy on various issues.

Paul himself traveled far and wide preaching the message of Christ, founding churches, and writing letters back to communities he had established. Throughout his missionary career, Paul was joined by others and worked with others. He depended upon others. He kept in touch with local leadership. His letters request prayers and sometimes aid for himself and for his mission. In writing letters, Paul often names coworkers as coauthors. He sends emissaries to communities, sometimes for diplomatic reasons and sometimes because he is prohibited from coming at the time and needs to send a messenger. Among his most trusted and reliable partners in the spread of Christianity were Timothy and Titus.

Both Timothy and Titus served Christian congregations in ancient Greece. The traditional understanding reflected in these letters is that Timothy later became a church leader in Ephesus (1 Tm 1, 3) and Titus in Crete (Ti 1, 5). Both were struggling with the challenge of those who offered alternatives to the teachings of Paul. Paul writes to reinforce the faith of these pastors and to encourage them, reminding them of their own Christian vocation.

1 TIMOTHY READING GUIDE

At a Glance

Who are the main players?   Paul Timothy community of Ephesus

What should I look for?   The ongoing problem of false teaching and practical challenges of the developing communities, for example, relationship of members, authority, money are the two foci of this letter. Also notice what Paul calls the essentials of the Christian message.

When was this written?	Probably written by a disciple of Paul around the beginning of the second century
Where did these events occur?	The letter is addressed to Timothy, who administered the church of Ephesus.
Why was this book written?	To reinforce the faith of the pastors and community as well as to encourage them to guard the tradition of Pauline churches
What is the story?	The central message is to preserve authentic church doctrine from false teaching. It presents principles for relationships with older members, with presbyters, with widows, for charitable ministrations, for liturgical celebrations, for selections of deacons and bishops. This letter is addressed to Timothy, who administered the church at Ephesus. It speaks to the ongoing problem of false teaching that always threatened the church and the practical challenges of the developing communities and their ministries. As with other letters written in Paul's name, the author is referred to as "Paul" in this guide.

Before Beginning

Both of the letters addressed to Timothy struggle with the nagging threat of false teaching. This is a problem that afflicted the church from the beginning.

Working through 1 Timothy

The content of this letter is diverse, and any particular outline seems arbitrary and artificial. Our discussion of 1 Timothy is based on the following structure:

I. The Address and Thanksgiving (1, 1–2.12–17)
II. The Body of the Letter (1, 3–11; 1, 18—6, 19)
  A. Paul's Message to Timothy (1, 3–11; 1, 18—4, 16)
  B. Duties Toward Others (5, 1—6, 19)
III. Conclusion (6, 20–21)

The Address and Thanksgiving (l, 1–2.12–17)

The address consists of a brief greeting in Pauline form (1, 1–2) with the thanksgiving delayed until 1, 12–17. A warning against false doctrines (1, 3–11) appears between these two parts of the address. This intrusion breaks the usual structure of a letter but manifests the gravity of the author's concern. The thanksgiving (1, 12–17) recalls Paul's former blasphemy and persecution of the church, evidence that his

call was unmerited and unsolicited (1, 12–17). Paul's example is a primary instance of the transforming power of grace. Because he sinned grievously (though in ignorance), the grace bestowed upon Paul had to be abundant. Notice that the author does not dwell on guilt or remorse. His allusion to Paul's sinful past only serves to illustrate the greatness of God's mercy. These reflections prompt him to praise God in a short doxology or blessing (1, 17).

The Body of the Letter (1, 3–11; 1, 18—6, 19)

The message of 1 Timothy is primarily a warning against the dangers of false teaching. The writer reminds Timothy about the qualities he should look for in assistants who are true ministers of the gospel, and he discusses Christians' duties toward others.

Paul's Message to Timothy (1, 3–11; 1, 18—4, 16)

The Warning Against False Teaching (1, 3–11.18–20). The teaching attacked in 1 Timothy is a form of gnosis (knowledge) that involved "myths and . . . genealogies [and . . . speculations" (1, 4). All three Pastorals, but especially 1 Timothy, are aimed at secure knowledge of the truth and secure ways of acting it out. These are reflections on the genuine applications of a teaching or knowledge that Timothy knows well.

Gnosis is the Greek word for knowledge and is the root for the word Gnosticism (see the Glossary). Gnosticism was a kind of religion that claimed secret knowledge for its members. It developed during the second, third, and fourth centuries.

It is possible that the so-called knowledge attacked in 1 Timothy is a sign of the beginnings of gnostic influences during New Testament times. (See the note on 1 Tm 6, 20f in the NAB text.)

The threat Paul combats in 1 Timothy is the pursuit of gnosis without any ethical or practical applications for living (1 Tm 1, 4; see 2 Tm 2, 14; 3, 7; Ti 3, 9). Thus, the practicalities of Christian living and church life together are emphasized, along with a pastorally oriented theology. This letter attacks those who would reduce Christianity to a mere doctrine or intellectual exercise, to the neglect of the ethical implications. The letter presumes a common fund of knowledge and emphasizes that authentic Christianity should work itself out in everyday life.

Life and Leadership in the Community (2, 1—4, 16)

The primary example of authentic Christian living is the minister of the gospel message. Timothy has a great responsibility entrusted to him by God and verified in the church (1, 3.18–20; 4, 6–16; 6, 11–16.20–21). The writer impresses on Timothy the importance of his role as example for the church.

The advice to Timothy in this letter proceeds from the admonition to draw strength from the "prophetic words once spoken about you" (1, 18) and the suggestion to "attend to yourself and to your teaching" (4, 16). Timothy should concentrate on "righteousness, devotion, faith, love, patience, and gentleness" (6, 11). He should ignore the seduction of "profane babbling and the absurdities of so-called knowledge" (6, 20). Constancy and perseverance in the faith are required to attract and encourage other believers. Timothy is urged to demonstrate to all his reliance on God.

The discussion of how each group of persons should act toward others is an adaptation of the "household codes" used in Ephesians 5, 21—6, 9 and Colossians 3, 18—4, 1. Here men and women, young and old, male and female should treat each other with the respect due them in traditional society (also 5, 1–2; 6, 1–2). The duties of bishop and deacons (3, 1–13) are drawn from typical descriptions of virtue. The text speaks of a single bishop and a number of deacons, both male and female (or, possibly, of male deacons and their wives, 3, 11). We know from Philippians 1, 1 that these titles were used very early on. Presbyters are not mentioned in this passage (3, 1–7), but only in 5, 17–19. It does not seem, therefore, that there is as yet a triple-tiered ministry of bishop, presbyters, and deacons, which will come in the next years.

In one way, 1 Timothy may be read as a list of rules for people in various offices and positions within the community. There is, however, a common theme in all of Paul's advice. Members of the Christian community should distinguish themselves by their love for and service to one another. Even the dress and decorum of men and women at the liturgy, for example, should contribute to the building up of the community (2, 8–10).

Advice Concerning Women

The particular advice to women, which has been controversial throughout Christian history, should be understood in the context of charity and the importance of good example. False teachers advocating asceticism, especially in the form of renunciation of marriage or restrictions on certain foods (4, 1–3), were particularly successful with women whom the author of 1 Timothy perceives as especially susceptible. The prevailing male wisdom taught that women were gullible and subject to error, as symbolized in the story of Eve who was seduced by the serpent. Contrary to the false teachers, Paul supports marriage and sees the family as conducive to holiness. He therefore advocates the "submission" of women, which was part of traditional views about the well-run family. This, he insists, is not a lifestyle unworthy of Christian women, but a way in which women may, like Timothy, "persevere in faith and love and holiness" (2, 15).

The same thinking drives the advice to slaves in a later passage to honor and respect their owners (6, 1–2), with the warning that believing slaves are not to think of themselves as equal to their owners but are to be even more respectful. This kind of thinking, as can be imagined, has caused difficulty in later centuries when those who resist social change appeal to the authority of the Bible. In his own context, however, Paul is simply trying to uphold human dignity within a social structure that he cannot change.

Duties toward Others (5, 1—6, 19)

This is really a rather artificial division, because the whole letter is preoccupied with community relationships. There is ambiguity in the discussion about widows (5, 3–16), perhaps indicative of uneven editing. First, widows who have no other means of support are to be supported by the church (5, 3–8.16). Then, there is some kind of enrollment of widows who are at least 60 years old, distinguished for practicing virtue and resolved to remain unmarried—hardly issues to consider if a widow is starving. Some kind of service organization is envisioned in 5, 9–15, returning again in verse 16 to the assistance of needy widows. Given lower life expectancy, few women would live beyond 60, and younger widows are to remarry, so they could not hope to qualify later to be enrolled as those married only once (5, 9).

The concrete advice regarding bishops and deacons and other ministers to the community stresses the power of example. This is especially important in those offices that have visibility in the community and represent a community trust. Many interpreters assume that the degree of development of the offices mentioned suggests a late composition of 1 Timothy. It would seem to have taken some years for the church to develop such a variety of roles and recognized ministries. On the other hand, we know that these ministries were beginning to develop already in Paul's day. They pertain to basic needs that arose as the church struggled to respond to its mission in the world. The office of bishop or overseer developed out of the custom of holding all things in common so that the surplus of the rich would supply for the needs of the poor in the Christian community (see 2 Cor 8 and 9). The ministry of deacons reflected the priority of preaching the

word, while not neglecting the physical and material needs of the church's members (Rom 16, 2; Acts 6, 1–6). The earliest writings of Paul, and in fact all of the New Testament, stress the social dimension of the Christian message. Therefore, the stewardships that would assure this dimension were created as soon as the priority was recognized.

Conclusion (6, 20–21)

The conclusion (6, 20–21) is in the form of a final recommendation and warning. First Timothy ends by restating the main message of the letter: "Guard the trust" (see 1, 3–10; 4, 7; 6, 3–5). Authority is stewardship. Many have been deceived by gnosis or false knowledge. Timothy is urged to hold firm to what he knows and to live it quietly.

Concluding Remarks

First Timothy represents several challenges for the modern interpreter. The author's view that women are more susceptible to error than men, for example, betrays the bias of a male dominated culture. Changing attitudes throughout history facilitated the education of women, and consequently the underlying premise of their greater gullibility has been proven false. First Timothy stresses the responsibility of leaders to interpret the essentials of the Christian message and to insure charity as a visible quality of the Christian community. Interpreters today distinguish between the culturally based bias against women and the essential message that included all in the life of charity to be lived by the community. This is a life in which all may grow and mature, women as well as men. The responsibility of leaders and pastors is to nurture that life, providing in their own lives a model of charity for other Christians to emulate.

Questions for Discussion and Reflection
Group Sharing/Discussion

1. What advice did Paul give to Timothy? (6, 11; 4, 16)

2. In the time of Timothy what were the roles of deacon and bishop?

3. *Gnosis* means knowledge in Greek. It is the root of gnosticism, the heresy that says special knowledge gives salvation, and that what you do

doesn't matter. Some roots of this heresy appear in Timothy. What are some examples of this false teaching that Paul talks about?

4. Paul encourages Timothy to focus on the basic teaching of Catholicism. How does Paul describe this in the letter to Timothy?

5. Paul advises slaves to honor and respect their owners (6, 1–2). Does he mean that slavery, as an institution, is morally acceptable? How were his words used in Christian history to validate slavery?

In Our Lives

1. To understand clearly Paul's message to Timothy, you need to know his social context. What is the social context of his teaching on women? Concerning the community? Concerning slavery? Have each individual or team prepare an explanation of the social context of one of these issues. Contrast with your social culture.

2. Contrary to the false teaching, Paul supports marriage and sees family as conducive to holiness (2, 15). Share your views on how to support marriage in our culture; on how to recognize and nourish holiness in today's family.

3. A common theme of Paul's advice to the community and leaders is to distinguish themselves by their love for one another and service. Allow for time to reflect and perhaps take some notes. Then let each person share how he or she has experienced this in the church. Answer the more difficult question: how can you increase this love and service in your life?

Individual/Personal Reflection/Action

1. Paul's teaching that women were more susceptible to error than men betrays the bias of the male-dominated culture. Over time attitudes are changing due to education and political changes. A symbol of this growth of tradition in the Church is that the majority of those receiving Catholic doctorates and graduate degrees in theology and scripture are women. Change has occurred. How do you see this change affecting you and affecting the church?

2. First Timothy stresses the responsibility of leaders to interpret the essentials of the Christian message and to ensure charity is distinctive of the Christian community. As a way of connecting this message to our lives, consider and reflect upon: What upsets me concerning the church? How is this related to spreading the gospel and building the community? What should I do about this?

2 TIMOTHY READING GUIDE

At a Glance

Who are the main players?	"Paul" Timothy community at Ephesus
What should I look for?	Like 1 Timothy, there is concern for false teaching and ministry. Here the tone of the reflections on ministry is more personal and focuses on Timothy.
When was this written?	Possibly at the beginning of the second century, probably written by a disciple of Paul
Where did these events occur?	Probably in Ephesus
Why was this book written?	The author, in Paul's name, seems to be giving the young pastor the benefit of his experience. The elder apostle speaks of his own life, his loneliness, his lack of confidence. Yet he is not discouraged because God is the source of his strength as he is for Timothy.
What is the story?	This letter addresses Timothy in vivid terms and depicts Paul's courage and hope in the face of discouragements; Paul is portrayed as a prisoner; it recalls the mission days with Timothy; it suggests Timothy prepare others to replace him; Paul urges him to persevere in preaching the Christian message with the resurrection of Jesus and his messianic role as the heart of the gospel.

Before Beginning

The same preoccupations appear here as in 1 Timothy: warnings about false teachings, and Paul's exhortation to Timothy as a minister of the gospel like himself. Second Timothy is written in a warmer, more personal tone than 1 Timothy, and therefore its lack of formal structure is understandable. It is really a testament in the form of a letter. Like Moses in Deuteronomy 29–30 or Jesus in John 14–16, the elder Paul, imprisoned in Rome (1, 16–17), looks back on his life with the knowledge of his imminent death (4, 6–8) and gives the younger man the benefit of his experience. He begins and ends the letter with references to his own experiences and the vocation of Timothy, thus linking the two. Their ties of affection and of common vocation are deep and very significant for Paul. The elder apostle speaks of his own life, his loneliness, his lack of confidence in other human beings. Yet he is not discouraged. God is the source of strength for both Paul and Timothy. The deeply personal tone of this letter has led some recent commentators to reevaluate the question of Pauline authorship and to suggest that while 1 Timothy and Titus are of a later era, perhaps 2 Timothy is not.

Working through 2 Timothy

The address and thanksgiving (1, 1–4) and conclusion (4, 19–22) envelop the body of the letter in 1, 5—4, 18. The main themes of 2 Timothy are the minister's experience of God and warnings against false teaching.

I. The Address and Thanksgiving (1, 1–5)
II. The Body of the Letter (1, 6—4, 18)
  A. Instructions to Timothy (1, 6—2, 13)
  B. Warnings about False Teaching
    (2, 14—3, 9)
  C. Final Advice (3, 10—4, 18)
III. Conclusion (4, 19–22)

The Address and Thanksgiving (1, 1–5)

The address (1, 1–5) consists of a greeting (1, 1–2) and a thanksgiving (1, 3–5), following the authentic Pauline style.

The Body of the Letter (1, 6—4, 8)

We have noted previously that Paul generally follows a basic pattern of first presenting his fundamental teaching on various issues and then drawing ethical conclusions from this teaching, though these two parts do not always follow one another in neat order. First Timothy does not follow this pattern very well, and Second Timothy even less so, primarily because it is more of a personal communication that combines reminders about teaching with advice in an informal way. The informal structure of this letter focuses on two main themes that are developed here: the minister's experience of God and warnings against false teaching.

Instructions to Timothy (1, 6—2, 13)

Timothy is not to be ashamed of the gospel or his commission to testify to the truth at all times. He also has the responsibility to guard that truth intact as he has received it. The apostle often uses himself as example, as a source of inspiration and motivation. Paul lives with such integrity that he urges Christians to imitate him in everything (see Phil 4, 8–10). Timothy is reminded that those who follow Christ will suffer persecution. This echoes Jesus' warning to his disciples (Mt 24, 9–14; Mk 13, 9–13; Lk 21, 12–19; Jn 15, 11–27). In the face of such pressure, Timothy is to remain constant.

False Teaching (2, 14—3, 9)

Like the other Pastorals, 2 Timothy is aimed at false teachings that promote a certain gnosis or knowledge and a consequent asceticism or strict discipline. The false teachings Paul attacks attach superior value to those who are "enlightened" with such knowledge and practice stringent customs regarding sexuality and diet. These practices set them apart from others, contributing to their sense of superiority. In all three letters, Paul was assuming that his addressees held the right beliefs so that it was not necessary to review the correct teaching or doctrine that the writer and recipient hold in common. Therefore, Paul spoke in vague and abstract terms about the false teaching, concentrating instead on the appropriate ethical applications that follow from true gospel preaching. Paul urges Timothy not to become embroiled in debates: "Charge [people] . . . to stop disputing about words . . . avoid profane [and] idle talk" (2, 14.16). One of the false teachings actually identified is that baptized Christians are already risen with Christ and that there is no future bodily resurrection (see note on 2, 14–19). Paul understands Christians as living in the last days when there are many dangers and threats to faith.

Warnings about False Teaching (3, 1–9)

While such warnings are also present in other parts of the letter, here they are concentrated and seem aimed at a specific group of people, although they could also be intended more generally. The disparagement of women's intellectual ability that we have seen surface in 1 Timothy is again present (3, 6–7), with perhaps the opposite effect: In fact, the author is telling us that missions among women were very successful, which means that the women were intellectually alert and responsive.

Final Advice (3, 19—4, 18)

Paul describes his life and impending death as a liturgical sacrifice; he is being poured out like a libation, an offering of wine (4, 6). He has run and finished the course (4, 7). He awaits with longing the reward of God (4, 6–8). Such confidence is based in God and meant to serve as encouragement to Timothy who still runs the course. Like other biblical heroes (including Moses and Jesus), Paul is represented in 2 Timothy as giving a kind of farewell address near the end of his life (4, 6–8). In this speech the hero warns his followers about impending dangers and threats to fidelity. They are commissioned with authority and reminded about the source of their confidence. They are promised that God will remain with them and that they will endure. Paul reminds Timothy to hold to the essentials of sound doctrine: scripture and the example of Christ and of other Christians. He reminds Timothy that those who live the gospel message will be persecuted. Paul urges Timothy to be faithful in waiting for the appearance of Jesus Christ.

Conclusion (4, 19–22)

The personal tone and greetings of 2 Timothy mark this as the closest Pastoral Letter to Paul's own style. Paul often experienced failure in his relationships with others. The author of 2 Timothy experiences similar problems. Like Paul, he says that such difficulties are the occasion for more converts to the gospel message. The letter ends with a prayer for God's spirit to be with

Timothy (singular). The plural in the last line may indicate the letter's being read and reflected upon in the assembly.

Concluding Remarks

The church is not a perfect society, nor are its ministers without human faults and failings. Conflicts over a variety of issues have plagued believers from the beginning, making it sometimes difficult to discern right from false teaching and practice. The church has experienced crises of leadership and problems with authority and obedience. Relationships among Christians have often been strained. Paul and other New Testament authors are not strangers to such tensions and problems. The author of 2 Timothy manifests a remarkable vulnerability to the strains in his own relationships with others, but this does not in any way detract from his visions or hopes for the church. In fact, with amazing confidence and humility, the author of 2 Timothy shows that even his failures are opportunities for the spread of the Christian message.

Questions for Discussion and Reflection
Group Sharing/Discussion

1. What are some of the indications in 2 Timothy that it is a more personal communication than the usual letter of Paul?

2. What are Paul's main instructions to Timothy in this letter? How did Paul encourage Timothy?

In Our Lives

1. The church is not a perfect society. What failings do you see in it ? What response or solutions would you offer?

2. Throughout its history the church has experienced crises of leadership or authority in its history. Can you name some? Councils and new religious communities (e.g., Benedict, St. Francis of Assisi, St. Ignatius Loyola, St. Theresa of Avila, etc.) often provided solutions and renewal. Each member of your group should read and share the story of a founder or a council to appreciate how the church grows and faces challenges.

Individual/Personal Reflection/Action

1. Paul urges Timothy not to become embroiled in debate (2, 14–16). The warning in this letter against engaging in useless disputes may strike a cord. Recall some examples of situations where

arguing over words was a way of dodging the real issues. Reflect how debating or arguing sometimes is fruitful and sometimes a waste. What advice would you give others and yourself in such a situation?

2. Timothy often experienced problems in his relationships with others. This book suggests that such difficulties are the occasion to add more converts to the gospel. Good relations are

the life and food of community. Take some time to make a list and examine your own relationships. Are they healthy? Plan how you can heal or grow them.

3. The author of 2 Timothy shows that even his failures are opportunities for spreading the Christian message. Take time to imagine how your failures could also be opportunities for spreading the Christian message.

TITUS READING GUIDE

At a Glance

Who are the main players?	"Paul" Titus Christian community of Crete
What should I look for?	Along with 1 and 2 Timothy, these letters are called "Pastoral" because they deal with the ongoing care of the Pauline communities. All are concerned with choosing and forming Church leaders, virtuous practices of the community, and protecting against false teaching.
When did this take place?	Possibly around the beginning of the second century. Most interpreters agree these pastoral letters were written at least a generation after Paul's death.
Where did these events occur?	Probably sent to Titus, the administrator of the Christian community on the large Mediterranean island of Crete
Why was this book written?	The letter is very similar to 1 Timothy and shows the same concern for those entrusted to care for the local communities. Titus should be careful in appointing ministers who will present sound church teaching.
What is the story?	The first teaching concerns the appointment of reliable ministers to protect against false teachers. The main section concerns the content and motivation of the teaching and authority.

Before Beginning

The third Pastoral Letter is addressed to Titus, who is charged with the administration of the church in the large area of Crete (1, 5). The letter to Titus has many parallels with 1 Timothy and manifests the same concerns for the maintenance duties of those entrusted with the care of the local communities. They are to give particular care to the appointment of reliable assistants and to the presentation of sound church teaching, protecting it from the many threats and dangers of false teaching.

Working through Titus

The address in 1, 1–4 is not followed by the usual thanksgiving, but the text goes directly into the body of the letter in 1, 5—3, 11. This message presents the pastoral charge or responsibilities, especially that of working with others in the preaching of the Christian message. The entire letter may be seen as an encouragement from one pastor to another. A short conclusion (3, 12–15), giving personal information, brings the letter to a close. The simple structure is as follows:

The Address (1, 1–4)

The address follows the usual Pauline pattern, but here it consists of a greeting only. It is slightly more elaborate than Paul's usual greetings but exhibits many of the features of Paul's thinking. As in the other Pastorals, the author emphasizes the apostle's role in the spread of the worldwide mission of Christ. This mission is now entrusted to Paul's "child," Titus, a fellow worker encouraged through this letter to insure the continuing line of good pastors and to preserve the faithful teaching of Christian life. The great dangers that face Titus and the church of Crete are the false teachers and those who would corrupt the Christian message.

The Body of the Letter (1, 5—3, 11)

Pastoral Charge (1, 5–16)

Verses 5 through 9 are parallel to the instruction of 1 Timothy 3, 1–7. Paul is an itinerant preacher who, nevertheless, is keenly aware of the need for stabilized leadership, especially to protect the church against heretical or false teaching. Therefore, the instructions given to Titus concerning the administration of the church at Crete are related first to the appointment of trustworthy and reliable pastors for the various duties required for the growth and development of the church there.

One of the important offices was that of presbyter (elder, v. 5), a term that in meaning is quite close in this letter to *episkopos* (overseer or bishop, v. 7). The two statements seem to be about the same people, as they could also be in 1 Timothy 3, 1–7; 5, 17–20. The main function of the bishop was apparently the overseeing of the financial or material matters in the church. Again, as in Philemon 1, 1, it is difficult to translate *episkopos* accurately, because the title "bishop" has such different connotations today. This bishop is God's "steward," entrusted with the distribution of goods and accountable to the members of the community. Therefore his own

life ought to be exemplary. He must not only avoid excesses, but also represent a model Christian life in his own family. As in 1 Timothy 3, 2–13, the description of the virtues of officeholders is taken from typical descriptions in Greek literature on the virtues necessary for leadership.

Leaders of the church are to offer an alternative example to that of the false teachers who preach for personal gain, living off the community and seeking personal recognition and recompense. These kinds of accusations against one's opponents are also part of traditional rhetoric and should not be taken at face value. The conduct of the presbyters or bishops should, however, be above reproach. Primary among the false teachers are the Judaizers who continue to advocate observance of some aspects of the Jewish Law, a custom that was attractive to some Christians for many centuries. The writer stoops to an ethnic slur by quoting an earlier author to the effect that Cretans are by their very nature prone to deceit, dishonesty, and laziness, thus making them all the more susceptible to falsehoods (1, 12).

Teaching the Christian Life (2, 1—3, 11)

Titus is encouraged to hold on to sound faith in teaching, while resisting pressures from all sides. Because the imagery of moral preaching often depicted the church as the new family, its members are here taught to relate to one another as older and younger people would in a well-ordered family in which respect dominates. Groups singled out include older men and younger men, older and younger women, slaves, and those in authority. Christians must not act in accordance with the world around them. Yet they must survive in an alien world. Paul's instructions focus on how to survive in this world while offering an alternative lifestyle and developing integrity as Christians. The domestic role for women is reinforced. The author reminds them of their duties to be examples within the marital context. Likewise slaves are directed not to rebel against the control of their masters (2, 9–10). The author urges them to fidelity and kindness within the context of slavery. Citizens were also inclined to see Christianity as an alternative to obedience to a corrupt state. The author of Titus advocates exemplary citizenship based on the status of Christians as already justified and relying on the mercy of God. Paul summarizes his advice to Titus, reminding him to avoid controversies and to maintain his integrity in the true faith. The false teachers disturb the community and its ministers. Paul exhorts to vigilance and constancy.

Conclusion (3, 12–15)

The final lines include very specific travel directives and recommendations for travelers passing through Crete. Titus is told to come with an assistant whom he will send, to join Paul at Nicopolis, a common city name; probably the one in western Greece is intended. Mediterranean sea travel shut down from November 10 to March 10, and a traveler thus had to "winter" somewhere waiting out the passage of those

---

Pastoral Letters for Today

Christians continue to wrestle with questions relating practice or behavior to belief. Christianity, like Judaism, has always emphasized the importance of deeds rather than mere knowledge or doctrine alone. Ministers of the gospel are entrusted with the responsibility to preserve teaching while also presenting exemplary lives. The letter to Titus reminds us of the difficulties, yet the importance, of working with others for the advance of the gospel message.

The challenge of the Pastoral Letters for today's church can hardly be overestimated. The Catholic view of Paul has long been unduly influenced by his portrait in these letters. Catholic Christians in particular have inherited a long tradition stressing the communal dimensions of Christian teaching. We do not receive the Christian message individually, nor can we live it in isolation from each other. This emphasis on communal responsibility is part of the legacy of the Pastoral Letters.

---

months. Paul closes with personal greetings. The final greeting "grace be with you all" is the simplest of closing forms. Some manuscripts add "of the Lord" or "of God" and "Amen," which are closer to the usual elaborations of Paul himself.

Questions for Discussion and Reflection
Group Sharing/Discussion
1. Where was Titus administrator of the Church?
2. What is the purpose of Paul's letter to Titus?
3. What were the dangers facing Titus in his church?
4. What was the main function of the elder or overseer in the church at that time?

In Our Lives
1. The writer expresses an ethnic slur (1, 12) that Cretans are deceitful, dishonest, and lazy and therefore more receptive to false teaching. Where do you recognize ethnic slurs in your world? In your church? How do you deal with this in your own reactions and those individuals and institutions in your life?
2. Christians must not act in accordance with the world around them, Paul teaches. How would this teaching apply in your life? Each person should name at least one way of acting in the world that Catholic Christians should *not* imitate.

Individual/Personal Reflection/Action
1. Survive in the world while offering an alternative lifestyle and continue to develop integrity as Christians. This teaching of Paul to Titus applies to living in the world today. Reflect or what it takes to survive while offering an alternative lifestyle. What does/would your alternative lifestyle look like? Name the elements in your life needed to survive and the dimensions of your Christian lifestyle. Where are the difficulties and conflicts between these? How do leaders in the Church offer an example of an alternative lifestyle?
2. Paul's advice to Titus is to avoid controversies and maintain integrity in the faith. Is this good advice for your life? Consider the ways of nourishing your integrity in the faith and how to react to controversies. This requires prayer and reflection concerning your journey of faith in the community.

PHILEMON READING GUIDE

At a Glance

Who are the main players?	Paul Onesimus Philemon
What should I look for?	In a society that accepted slavery as an institution Paul presents a new way of relating to others, including slaves, based on baptism in Christ.
When did this take place?	Between A.D. 61 and 63
Where did these events occur?	Maybe in Rome
Why was this book written?	This short letter to three individuals was written by Paul during imprisonment. It was sent as a plea for welcoming Onesimus, a slave from Colossae.
What is the story?	Onesimus, a slave, was converted to Christ by Paul who sends him back to his master, Philemon, with this letter asking that he be welcomed back not just as a slave but as a brother in Christ.

Before Beginning

Paul's letter to Philemon is a gem of early Christian communication and the only true personal letter that we have from Paul. No one seriously challenges Philemon as an authentic Pauline letter and an integral part of the New Testament. Philemon appears to be a letter between individuals, dealing with a very concrete matter rather than with generalized, abstract theological principles. Neither Paul nor the early Christian community intended to attack slavery directly, so we may well wonder why this letter was preserved at all and why it might be significant for us.

Despite being a brief letter, it is full of interpretive problems and has been intensively studied in recent years. The traditional understanding of it since the fourth century has been that Onesimus, a slave, had run away from his master, Philemon, and had come to Paul for protection. Paul had converted Onesimus to Christianity and now sent him back to Philemon, carrying this letter. But more recently, this interpretation has been questioned and several other possible scenarios proposed. One is that, according to Roman law, a slave who goes to a third party to mediate a dispute with his or her owner is not to be considered a fugitive. If one reads the letter from this perspective, it also fits. A third argument is that Onesimus is not a slave at all, but Philemon's brother, whom Philemon is

treating like a slave (Phlm 16). Paul asks him to reconcile and treat him as he deserves. The interpretation that Onesimus is indeed a slave is the majority one, but why he went to Paul remains an open question, as does what Paul really wants Philemon to do. But it is clear that the relationship between Philemon and Onesimus is not good, and Paul is trying to patch it up.

The informal conversational tone does not detract from the letter's impressive significance within the Christian context. Each part of this letter underscores its community context and gives us a glimpse into the structure of relationship and exchange in the early Christian church. Because nearly all the names mentioned in the letter also occur in Colossians, the usual supposition is that Philemon's house church is located in Colossae.

Working through Philemon

The letter to Philemon has the usual features of letters of Paul:

I. Address and Thanksgiving (1–6)
II. The Body of the Letter (7–22)
III. Conclusion (23–25)

The Address and Thanksgiving (1–6)

It is not Philemon alone who is addressed, but Apphia, perhaps Philemon's wife, Archippus, another member of the household, and the whole "church [that meets] at your house" (1–2). The thanksgiving (4–6) notes the renowned love and faith Philemon has always shown the "holy ones," a reference to his fellow Christians. Paul also names Philemon a "partner" in faith, emphasizing the common life in Christ that they share, which is the basis for the new society that Paul envisions.

The Body of the Letter (7–22)

The varied expressions of Paul's complex relationship with Philemon serve as a model for the new relationships Philemon now has with Onesimus. Their common baptism provides a basis for Philemon and Onesimus (as well as for the whole church) to create an entirely new way of relating to one another and to resolve the tensions between them. In no other Pauline letter is the relationship between the statement of Christian reality (signified by a common baptism) so bound up with the implications or exhortations that flow from this reality.

In 1 Corinthians 7, 21–23, Paul says that slavery or freedom is indifferent in the Christian life. It is not clear in this letter whether Paul appeals to Philemon to free Onesimus from slavery. He may expect that the two of them now continue in a good relationship of master and slave. But if Onesimus is a runaway, the normal punishment against an errant slave (who perhaps also stole from his master, 18–19) is prohibited by Paul. Master and slave are fellow Christians. The community context should help them work out a new way of relating to one another as "brothers." Because of whatever way Onesimus has wronged Philemon, Philemon is in a delicate position. If he does not punish Onesimus, he is lacking in necessary discipline, and his social peers will think him weak. If he does insist on punishment, he will violate his Christian obligation to forgiveness and Paul's express desires. The whole house church is watching to see what he will do! Unfortunately, we do not know the answer.

Paul describes himself as a prisoner (9), as Philemon's brother (7.20), and as father of Onesimus (10). Paul says he is an old man (9), an anticipated guest of Philemon (22) and one to whom Philemon is indebted (19). These descriptions illustrate the various ways in which the patronage system of the culture interacted with Christian expressions of interdependence and ultimately equality in Christ. They are a way of redefining Paul's relationship to Philemon and to the church in Colossae. They also serve as a model for Philemon to develop a new relationship between himself and Onesimus. The letter is a masterpiece of rhetorical strategy. Paul does not mandate any specific set of actions, but rather appeals to Philemon and to the whole community to read and reflect on this letter in light of their common baptism, and to discern a course of action toward Onesimus that will reflect the Christian faith they share.

Conclusion (23–25)

The final greetings mention names of Paul's co-workers also found in Colossians (1, 7; 2, 1; 4, 12–13) and 2 Timothy (4, 9–13). Together with the liturgical blessing (Phlm 25), these greetings underscore once again the communal context in which this letter was written and in which it ought to be reflected and acted upon. Philemon draws out some implications of the baptismal formula quoted in Galatians 3. 28: "There is neither Jew nor Greek, there is neither slave nor free person, there is not male and female; for you are all one in Christ Jesus" (see also Col 3, 11).

Concluding Remarks

The letter to Philemon raises interesting challenges for its original recipients and for us. Apparently, Onesimus himself is bearer of this letter from Paul to his master. The letter is to be read at the liturgy when the Christian community will help Philemon reintegrate Onesimus back into his household as a fellow Christian. The very fact that the community preserved this letter—and that it comes down to us included in the canon of the New Testament—testifies to the spirit of openness, humility, and generosity of Philemon and his congregation that must have successfully resolved this matter. Today the church as a whole and local churches are faced with perplexing social problems, especially with regard to social expectations and their clash with faith values. We can take hope that what was written long ago was written for our instruction. We can well afford to contemplate the role of such a Pastoral Letter and of the community's reflection on its contents.

Questions for Discussion and Reflection
Group Sharing/Discussion

1. Tell the story of the letter. Imagine Philemon as the content for a play, at the house church of Philemon and Apphia, with the community. Assign persons to take the roles of Paul, Onesimus, Philemon, Apphia (Philemon's wife), Archippus (a visitor from Galatia). Scenes:

a. Paul and Onesimus talking about their relations and matters in the letter.

b. Philemon and his wife talking about Onesimus' returning and the community.

c. Onesimus and Philemon when he arrives with the letter.

d. Archippus tells the community how they are identified in Galatia: "There is neither Jew nor Greek, there is neither slave nor free person, there is not male nor female; for you are all one in Christ Jesus" (Gal 3, 28).

2. The letter to Philemon has the usual features of a Pauline letter: (1) Address and Thanksgiving; (2) The Body of the Letter; and (3) the Conclusion. Assign a person to read aloud each of these parts of the letter.

In Our Lives

1. Were Paul and the Christian community concerned with or attacking the institution of slavery? Where does slavery still exist in its different forms? When did American Catholics actively teach that slavery was wrong?

2. "The whole church that meets at your house," Paul writes to Philemon and his wife. Take some time to discover and read about the first communities in Paul. Our roots are in "house churches" (cf C. Osiek "Who Did What in the Church in the New Testament?" in *Lay Ministry in the Catholic Church*, Liguori, MO: Liguori Press, 2005).

3. Paul emphasizes the common life they share in Christ through baptism. This is the basis of the new society that Paul envisions. What are the essential qualities of this new community? Where do you see or experience these same qualities?

Individual/Personal Reflection/Action

1. What are the most pressing social problems facing your local church? What can you do to contribute energy in helping to solve some of these problems?

2. Meditate on being baptized in Christ. How do relationships created by baptism cause you to look at social problems in a different way?

HEBREWS READING GUIDE

At a Glance

Who are the main players?	Author as preacher Christ
What should I look for?	This is not a letter, it is a written sermon. It is best approached by reading it from beginning to end aloud. Study its symbols carefully, because they are difficult to understand. The interpretation of Jesus as priest is unique in the New Testament.
When did this take place?	Some view the date as before A.D. 70, others as early second century, written by a person familiar with Greek philosophy, the scriptures, and allegorical logic.
Where did these events occur?	The exact audience, author, and place of composition have long been disputed. The audience is assumed to be Jewish Christians because of the use of scripture as argument and the Temple and its cult.
Why was this book written?	The author saw the audience in danger of losing their Christian faith due to weariness with the demands of Christian life.

What is the story?

The six movements are: (1) God's revelation in Jesus is superior to the covenant; (2) the Son is higher than the angels; (3) Jesus as faithful and compassionate high priest; (4) Jesus' eternal priesthood and sacrifice; (5) heroes and heroines of the past as examples to imitate; (6) Christians live in the world but are not defined by it or its values.

Before Beginning

Hebrews is not a real letter but a sermon. The best way to experience Hebrews is by reading it out loud from beginning to end. Oral recitation helps to catch the sermonic rhythms of Hebrews, its use of "we" and "you" (so natural to the sermon), and its alternating pattern of exposition and exhortation. Reading straight through also enables the reader to grasp the powerful argument that is the outstanding characteristic of this early Christian writing.

Toward Understanding Hebrews

Hebrews has significantly shaped the liturgy, doctrine, and spirituality of the church. Although other New Testament writings speak of Jesus' death as a sacrifice, Hebrews' unique reflection on Melchizedek (ch 7) and on Jesus as the Great High Priest have influenced the development of Catholic liturgy. Hebrews' insistence on Jesus' full divinity and equally full participation in human nature contributed to the understanding of Jesus' identity as God's Son (chs 1–2). And Hebrews' vision of faith as a pilgrimage toward God (chs 11–12) created a symbolic framework for the Christian understanding of discipleship as a "journey." For all its riches, Hebrews resists easy understanding for two reasons: first, it presents a sustained argument from beginning to end; second, its symbols are hard to understand.

Dealing with these difficulties clears the way to more intelligent and satisfactory reading.

The Argument

Some parts of the New Testament, like the Gospel parables, can be read out of their original context and still make sense. But each part of Hebrews plays a role in a complicated interplay of argument and explanation concerning Jesus and Christian life. Hebrews resists being excerpted or taken out of context. It uses a form of argument, found both in Greek philosophy and rabbinic Judaism, called "from the lesser to the greater." The argument goes, "If something is true in a smaller matter, it is even more true in an analogous greater matter." In Hebrews, the contrast is between the partial revelation of God in the past through angels, law, and priesthood, and the perfect revelation "in the last of these days" through God's Son, Jesus, between that former "lesser" salvation and the present "greater" salvation.

The argument in Hebrews is not theoretical but practical. The real point is the contrast between the response to God's word by the people of the past and the response demanded of the people today. A greater blessing and hope require a greater degree of obedience and loyalty, just as disobedience carries a greater penalty. The stakes are higher all around.

The Symbols

The symbols of Hebrews are sufficiently strange to shake any assumption that the New Testament world was "just like ours." Hebrews demands of its readers, for example, a more sophisticated grasp of Scripture than most Christians possess today. Much of its argument, in fact, is based on complex modes of scriptural interpretation. These are strange to us but were common in the first century. The version of Scripture used by Hebrews (as by other New Testament writings) was not Hebrew but Greek. Its citations and allusions are from the Septuagint. This study edition gives some assistance by providing complete Scripture references. Citations in the text are flagged with small letters; passages are identified at the bottom of each page. To fully appreciate Hebrews' virtuosity, study the citations in their original context as well as how Hebrews can turn them to fit its argument (as in 10, 5–7).

Hebrews' view of the world is strikingly different from that of present-day Christians in an even more fundamental sense. Hebrews works within a philosophical tradition called

Platonism, which saw a great gulf between the spiritual realm and the material world. Spiritual things are eternal, unchanging; material things are transitory. As a result, spiritual things are both more real and better than the material. For Platonic Jews and Christians, the "spiritual" and "material" realms were understood in terms of "heaven" and "earth."

This is the framework for grasping Hebrews' point about the superiority of Jesus' priesthood. By his resurrection, Jesus entered heaven, where he is a "priest forever" (5, 6), in contrast to the Jewish priesthood, which could only be temporary. Likewise the "heavenly sanctuary" is superior to the physical tent of worship described in Scripture (chs. 8–9). The symbolism at times becomes dense and requires patience to disentangle, but the basic point is clear. The human Messiah Jesus now shares God's life in heaven. His priesthood is therefore both the ultimate and eternal "cause of salvation" to others (5, 9).

The Readers

The original hearers of this sermon had experienced the loss of property and friends (10, 32–34). They were tempted to lose hope and seek a more stable framework than that offered by a crucified messiah. Hebrews addresses their longing for stability by offering the hope for "a better homeland, a heavenly one" (11, 16). Their experience can be translated into that of every age: all of us in various ways experience loss, alienation, and despair. Hebrews' message to us is as sharp as it was to them: "Today if you hear his voice, harden not your hearts" (4, 7). We also are called to go on pilgrimage through our troubled circumstances, looking to Jesus, who is still and always the "leader and perfecter of faith" (12, 1).

The Prologue (1, 1–4)

The opening sentence is elegantly constructed and introduces Hebrews' central themes. First is the contrast between God's partial revelation in the past ("to our fathers") and the perfect revelation now ("to us") made through God's Son, which establishes the basic thesis: Jesus is superior to the old dispensation, or Covenant (see 8, 13). Second, Jesus' divine status is clearly expressed by calling him the "image of God." The exalted identity attributed to the Son is similar

to that in John and Paul (e.g., see Jn 1, 1–4 and 1 Cor 8, 6). Third, the prologue states that the way God "spoke" in Jesus was through his death for others (the purification of sins) and his resurrection.

Note the image of enthronement: Jesus "takes his place at the right hand." This alludes to Psalm 110, 1, the favorite resurrection psalm of early Christians: "The LORD said to my Lord, sit at my right hand till I make your enemies a footstool for your feet" (see also 1, 13). Hebrews will also exploit the fourth verse of this psalm when the author develops the comparison between Jesus and Melchizedek in chapter 7. The image of enthronement runs throughout the sermon. Jesus is both priest and king. Finally, we notice that Jesus "inherits" a name better than that of the angels. Jesus is here portrayed as a forerunner. If they follow him, Christians also will enter into an inheritance (1, 14; 6, 12). The mention of angels, in turn, provides a transition to Hebrews' argument.

The Son is Higher than the Angels (1, 5—2, 18)

A series of Scripture citations proves that the Son is superior to angels. The pertinent question for us is, why do angels require putting in place, anyway? Our contemporary view of the world has small room for angels! But in the world of the New Testament, especially in the writings of Judaism, angels were regarded as the most powerful intermediaries between God and humans. The tendency to exalt their role is attested in Galatians 4, 9 and Colossians 2, 18. What concern does the author address? Jesus in his humanity did not appear so impressive as these "spiritual" beings. He was not only human; he suffered and died. Hebrews must overcome the scandal of a "lowly" Messiah.

Citations from Scripture do not by themselves demonstrate the point. As in other New Testament writings (e.g., Gal 3, 1–5), Hebrews argues "the greater" from the fact of the readers' own experience. The work of God's Spirit among them is itself powerful "witness" to the salvation accomplished through Jesus (2, 3f). And never content with the speculative, Hebrews drives home the exhortation. This "greater salvation" demands of the readers a greater response of alertness (2, 1f).

From the perspective of the power of the Risen Lord, Hebrews takes up the issue of Jesus' "lowliness." On the basis of Psalm 8, the author asserts that Jesus was "lower than the angels" only temporarily. And the reason was so that he could "taste death for everyone," that is, act as priest. On the basis of a messianic reading of Isaiah 8, 18f, Hebrews next affirms God's (and the Messiah's) solidarity with humanity. Then, Hebrews turns the tables, and makes Jesus' humanity a positive criterion for authentic priesthood. Because Jesus is one with those he represents before God—he shares the way they are "tested" and the way they "fear death"—he can be a compassionate and merciful priest. It is significant that Hebrews defines priesthood in terms of his personal identity and experience rather than in terms of religious ceremony. Hebrews thereby anticipates an important principle of later doctrine: "what is not assumed [by God] cannot be saved." Precisely because he is human, Jesus can save humanity.

Jesus, Faithful and Compassionate High Priest (3, 1—5, 10)

Moses was so central a figure for Jews that he became a natural point of contrast for Christian claims about Jesus (e.g., see Jn 1, 17). Hebrews now contrasts Moses as "the servant of [God's] House," and Jesus as "Son over the house" (3, 4f). The real contrast in this section, however, is between the people that Moses led and the Christians the author of Hebrews addresses in terms of disobedience and obedient faith (3, 7–13).

The argument here uses complex ancient rules for interpreting Scripture. Much is made, for example, of the occurrence of specific words, such as "rest" and "today," without regard for their original contexts. Hebrews asserts that the "rest" to which Moses led the people (the land) was not the "rest of God," namely, God's own life. For that matter, neither did people of old even succeed in entering that earthly rest because of their disobedience. Christians in contrast have hope for the real rest—of God's own life—won by Jesus' resurrection. The point? They are to obey the call of God and not fall away (4, 6).

Hebrews has identified obedient faith as the fundamental response demanded by God. The comparison to the wandering Israelites also establishes Hebrews' basic image of the church as the people of God on pilgrimage. The image suggests that the church is not simply an institution

like other institutions. It is never fully "at home" in the world. The church exists with reference to a higher goal—the "heavenly city"—toward which it must steadily move like a pilgrim, although this side of death the goal is never reached. Pilgrims need the sort of attentiveness, patience, obedience, and endurance demanded by Hebrews. Above all, they need hope (see 6, 19). They can move lightly through this worldly existence only if convinced that their destination is truly "greater" than their present abode.

Hebrews points the reader again to the leader of the pilgrimage, the "apostle and high priest of our confession" (3, 1). In the description of Jesus as priest (4, 14—5, 9), Hebrews combines what has come to be called both "high" and "low" Christologies (understandings of Jesus). Jesus is definitely "from above"; he is God's Son in the fullest sense, but he is also fully human, "from below." It is his human existence that defines the path "all the children" are to follow. As priest, he is exemplar. Jesus is not only "faithful" (3, 1f) as all are called to be; he "learned obedience from what he suffered" (5, 8). The full implications of this statement will become clear only later (see 12, 1–11), but we already understand that Jesus' suffering deepened his faith, and his obedience

---

Pilgrimage of the Church

Vatican Council II, using this image of pilgrimage, suggested that the church is not simply an institution like other institutions. It is never fully "at home" in the world. The church is steadily moving toward the "heavenly city" like a pilgrim, although on this side of death the goal is never reached.

"High" and "Low" Christologies

High: Jesus is "from above," God's son in the fullest sense. The emphasis is on the divinity of Jesus.

Low: Jesus is also fully human, "from below." The emphasis is on Jesus' humanity.

was itself a form of suffering. Jesus progressively became, in his humanity, perfect Son of God, and therefore the "leader" of all who follow him.

Jesus' Eternal Priesthood and Sacrifice (5, 11—10, 39)

The long middle section of the sermon argues for the superiority of Jesus' priesthood. It begins with an extended exhortation (5, 11—6, 20), and then focuses on Jesus' priestly identity and

activity (7–10). Hebrews presupposes the readers' grasp of the basic teaching about Christ (6, 1), but, in a rebuke as much as an exhortation, he urges them beyond the milk fit for babes to the meat meant for the mature (compare Paul's use of this imagery in 1 Cor 3, 1–3). This "mature teaching" is by no means a matter of moving beyond Jesus or abandoning Jesus. Such apostasy from Christ Hebrews calls "recrucifying the Son of God" (6, 5). Indeed, God's promise based

---

Jesus and Melchizedek (7, 1–28)

Both appearances of Melchizedek in Scripture point toward Christ:

Gn 14, 17–20: Melchizedek was named a priest of God (although he was a Gentile), whom even Abraham acknowledged. A priest descended from Melchizedek would be superior to one descended from Abraham.

Psalm 110, 4: Melchizedek's being without beginning or end (Scripture records neither his birth nor his death) is an anticipation of the Son of God whose priesthood is eternally valid.

In his resurrection, Jesus became priest, "by the power of a life that cannot be destroyed" (7, 16). He remains "forever" (7, 24). His sacrifice is "once for all" (7, 27). "He lives forever to make intercession" (7, 25). The Jewish priesthood descended from Abraham cannot compete.

The Old and New Covenants (8, 1–13)

God's revelation in Jesus does not merely continue the former story, it raises it to a new plane. Jesus' death and resurrection mark an absolute beginning. Platonism is evident in 8, 1–6: Moses' desert sanctuary is "the copy and shadow of the heavenly sanctuary" (8, 5). Heaven is greater than earth. Hebrews turns this Platonism into an interpretation of history: The old covenant is a "shadow" of the new, pointing to but replaced by the work of Jesus. Hebrews exploits Jeremiah's promise of a new covenant "in the heart" to affirm that the old order has in fact passed.

The Priestly Act of Jesus (9, 1–10.18)

The contrast is between the ancient cult and Jesus' death and resurrection. The complicated imagery is daunting. It would be helpful to read through Exodus 25–27 (the Dwelling in the Wilderness) and Leviticus 16 (ritual for the Day of Atonement). Hebrews stresses two points: First, Jewish sacrifices had to be repeated, so they were not effective; Jesus entered "real" life, so his sacrifice is eternally valid. Second, the old cult sacrifices animals. Jesus gave his own life in obedience to God. Now all can enter the sanctuary.

Exhortation to Fidelity (10, 19–39)

In the light of this "greater salvation," Hebrews warns again of the consequences of apostasy (10, 26–31). Despite their losses and trials, Christians are called to a still deeper loyalty (10, 32–30). By mentioning endurance and faith as requisites for receiving the promise (10, 36–38), Hebrews prepares for its final stirring exhortation.

---

on Jesus' resurrection is utterly reliable; Jesus is the "anchor of the soul" (6, 19), to whose priesthood God has bound himself by oath (6, 13). The nature and implications of Jesus' priesthood, however, are precisely what require explication. By it the Christian hope is made secure. By it Christians are able to become "imitators of those who, through faith and patience, are inheriting the promises" (6, 12).

The consideration of Jesus as priest is the climax of the "lesser to the greater" argument. But because the procedures and symbols of Jewish cult are foreign to us today, this section makes for some of the hardest reading in the New Testament. It is important to remember from the start that Hebrews' argument is based on the Christian experience of the Spirit and conviction the life of God (2, 3–4). Only this premise makes Hebrews' reinterpretation of Scripture reasonable. Once that premise is granted, then the major turning points of the exposition make sense.

Examples, Discipline, Disobedience (11, 1—12, 29)

The sermon's long argument reaches its climax in this exhortation to faith, understood as loyalty, endurance, and hope. The recital of heroes and heroines of the past serves to provide examples for the readers to imitate. Why? Just as the listeners had lost property and had been persecuted, so also had the believers who preceded them. Yet the ancestors persevered in the search for a better homeland (11, 14). The repetition of the phrase "by faith" summons the readers to join ranks with those on pilgrimage to God's presence. Unlike the desert generation that fell by the way because of disobedience, they continued faithful, even though they themselves did not receive the full promise (11, 29)! It was left to Jesus, the "leader and perfecter of faith" (12, 2) to provide complete access to God through his death and resurrection. Because Christians can now look to him (12, 2), there is solid reason to hope while still on the journey.

By summoning such a "cloud of witnesses" (12, 1) to support the commitment of the readers, Hebrews states a conviction that eventually became an article of the Christian creed, "the communion of saints." Those struggling for God on earth are not alone. They are joined in a larger fellowship of faith with those who have died and who now support them with their prayers. The people of faith have solidarity in hope. This is not blind optimism: the alienation, suffering, and persecution experienced by the ancients is not trivialized. And Jesus, before he could sit on the throne, had to "endure the cross, despising its shame" (12, 2). Jesus' human response to God is the perfect example for the faith of Christians. Faith is always "evidence of things not seen" (11, 1), which means that it is always a risk taken in the face of a pain more palpably present than the promise. Thus, also, the Christian experience of prayer has as an essential component the "dark night" of the soul when God seems more absent than present.

The connection between Sonship and suffering continues in 12, 5–13. The remarks about fathers disciplining their children at first seem banal if not regressive. But when we remember that Jesus, "although Son, learned obedience from what he suffered" (5, 8), we come to appreciate the profound correspondence between Christology and Christian existence. What we suffer in our lives, if we can perceive and accept such suffering in faith, enables God to shape Jesus' own "sonship" in us. Being educated as children of God requires a painful transformation, for the goal is the holy God (12, 10).

Final Exhortation, Blessing, Greetings (13, 1–25)

Although the final chapter is made up mainly of practical instructions, it is closely joined to the theological argument of chapters 1–12. Notice, for example, the plea to "imitate the faith" of leaders, the motivation of that faith being the eternal priesthood of Jesus who is "the same yesterday, today, and forever" (13, 7–8).

The mix of advice about hospitality, marriage, and possessions, with the command to "go to Jesus outside the camp . . . for we have here no lasting city but seek the one that is to come" is typical of this sermon and of early Christianity's understanding of existence generally:

• Christians live in the world like other people and participate in its structures. But they are not defined by this world or its values, even its religious values (13, 9–11).

• No institutional cult or sacrificial priesthood is made lawful by this severe writing; everything necessary has been accomplished already by Jesus.

• Christians are defined not by their liturgy, but by their following the one who suffered "outside the gate, to consecrate the people by his own blood" (13, 12).

• Christians are never entirely at ease in this world or even in the church. They are pilgrims, struggling toward the "God of peace" into whose care the final blessing (13, 20–21) entrusts the readers of this profound and powerful sermon.

Questions for Discussion and Reflection
Group Sharing/Discussion

1. Why does the author address the issues of the difference between Jesus and the angels?

2. Hebrews describes the Church as the people of God on pilgrimage. Describe what this means in Hebrews.

3. Priesthood is described in Hebrews as identity and experience of Jesus, not ritually as in Jewish tradition. Why does Hebrews so define Jesus' priesthood?

4. Hebrews tells us that "our God is a consuming fire" (12, 29). What might this mean?

5. Hebrews' approach to Jesus is considered containing both "low" and "high" Christology. Give an example of the "high" and "low" approach of studying Christ.

In Our Lives

1. Read Hebrews out loud from the beginning to the end. If you are in a group, share parts according to sections of the sermon.

2. Hebrews' view of the world is Platonic—there is a gulf between the spiritual realm and the material world. The spiritual things are more real and better than the material. How does this view influence the author's understanding of Jesus' priesthood? Do you see any effects of the Platonic influence in your world?

3. How is the Church as institution different from other institutions?

4. In that "cloud of witnesses" spoken of in Hebrews, who are some of these ancient witnesses who pray for the community on pilgrimage? Name some who support you in your pilgrimage.

5. Hebrews' original hearers of this sermon had suffered loss of friends and property. They were tempted to lose hope and look for new hope in a framework other than a crucified messiah. All of us may experience loss, alienation, and despair. How is your Christian faith a source of hope?

Individual/Personal Reflection/Action

1. Jesus "learned obedience from what he suffered." Reflect upon how suffering in faith opens us to God's action of shaping Jesus' own sonship in us.

2. Take some time to reflect on the difference between "being in the world but not of the world" and "enduring this life with an eye on heaven." What pilgrim steps could you take on this journey?

THE CATHOLIC LETTERS AND THE BOOK OF REVELATION

JAMES READING GUIDE

At a Glance

Who is the main player?	James, a relative of Jesus
What should I look for?	This is an exhortation concerned with ethical conduct in the tradition of Jewish wisdom literature such as in Proverbs or Sirach. James emphasized sound teaching and responsible moral behavior based on ethical norms derived from conversion, baptism, forgiveness and judgment.
When was this written?	This is a very Jewish work, written in excellent Greek style. Some attribute it to James of Jerusalem via a secretary, which would date it before A.D. 70; others think it is more like a pseudonymous work of a later period, around A.D. 90–100.
Where did these events occur?	Jerusalem (if James is author) or in the Greek Diaspora if later.
Why was this book written?	This is a "catholic," that is, universal letter. Unlike Paul's letters to specific churches, this is addressed more generally to the universal church. It is concerned with traditional values.
What is the story?	Six movements of this exhortation are: (1) worldly values, where competition reigns without God, versus wholeness of faith and works; (2) discrimination and the law of love; (3) faith without works is dead; (4) speech should conform to faith; (5) friendship with the world and friendship with God are opposing ways of life; and (6) three forms of arrogance and the proper uses of speech in the church.

Before Beginning

James as Moral Exhortation

Letter writing was so popular in antiquity that the epistolary form became a package capable of holding many materials. In the case of James (as noted in the NAB introduction to James), the letter format is the frame for a moral exhortation intended for a general readership.

Before turning to an analysis of the text, it is helpful to consider some of its literary features and major themes. James is not terribly difficult to understand; its style is lucid, its message is straightforward.

The Writing

The form of Greco-Roman moral exhortation called *parenesis* was concerned with reminding readers of traditional values rather than with constructing theory. Such reminders often took the form of short maxims. James's first chapter in particular has such maxims, which are less connected to each other than to other sections of the composition. Chapters 2 through 5 take the form of short essays. The maxims in chapter 1 set themes that are developed in those essays. Note how the "control of the tongue" in 1, 26 is elaborated by 3, 1–12. Moral exhortation also presented models of virtue for readers to imitate. In James, the figures of Abraham, Rahab, Job, and Elijah provide examples from Scripture of the practical virtue James encourages.

James, however, is more than a moral treatise. It is a religious writing that uses the symbols of Scripture. James resembles the Wisdom tradition in its use of maxims and in advocating a "wisdom from above" as the measure of life (3, 13–18). James uses the language and perspective of the prophets in its attack on rich oppressors (5, 1–6). James also uses the Law. For James, both the Decalogue (Ten Commandments) and the Law of Love are binding for Christians. They are to be understood, however, in light of the teachings of Jesus. James has many allusions to the words of Jesus (e.g., see 1, 12; 2, 5; 3, 12; 5, 12).

The Message

James advocates living faith and practical love. His concern is behavior. Like other moralists of his age, he is impatient with fine words that go nowhere (e.g., see 1, 22–25). Above all, faith that is not expressed in love is a charade.

James's target is the Christian who is "of two minds" (1, 8; 4, 8). This person wants to live by two standards at once: that of God, and that of the world. James demands a choice. Not only speech but also the use of possessions and the practice of fairness within the community lie within the range of his concern. He especially attacks envy, which perfectly illustrates the morals of "the world" opposed to God (see esp. 3, 13—4, 10).

But James does not lack theology. He bases his exhortations on the one God who creates and judges all humanity. James centers attention on God rather than on Christ.

The Two Measures (1, 1–27)

Although chapter 1 is made up of separate aphorisms with only loose internal connections, the chapter does more than simply provide a table of contents for the essays to follow. The opening statements also make clear that humans must live by either one sort of measure or another.

The first verses have some word-linkages, but they don't form an easily followed argument. The aphorisms are not, however, simply a random collection of wise sayings. The maxims in chapter 1 provide something of an index to the contents of chapters 2 through 5. The theme of enduring trials (1, 2–4.12–15) is developed in 5, 7–11; the opposition between rich and poor (1, 9–11) recurs in 4, 13—5, 6. Control of the tongue (1, 19–21) is expanded in 3, 1–12. Carrying out words in speech (1, 22–26) is enlarged by 2, 14–26. The theme of true wisdom (1, 5–8.16–18) is argued by 3, 13—4, 10. The prayer of faith (1, 6f) is amplified by 5, 12–18.

The aphorisms also introduce the basic pattern that structures the whole of James: the contrast between the measure of the world and the measure of God. The measure of the world is expressed by envy: "desire conceives and brings forth sin, and when sin reaches maturity, it gives birth to death" (1, 15). The values of the world are self-deceptive (1, 16.27) and are expressed in wrathful behavior (1, 19) and every sort of excess (1, 21), especially the pursuit of illusory wealth (1, 11). These values are based on the perception of life as a closed system; God has no part. Therefore all humans are in competition: one person's gain is another's loss.

The measure of faith is the opposite. All creation—life itself—is a gift: "all good giving and every perfect gift is from above, coming down from the Father of lights" (1, 17). Because God has created humans by "the word of truth" (1, 18), humans are able to receive the implanted word from him (1, 21) and live in the way God does, giving "generously and ungrudgingly" (1, 5). In the Greek, these words suggest the opposite of envy, which always grasps for more. Life by God's measure is expressed by "care for orphans and widows in their affliction" (1, 27). One is thereby "unstained by the world" by living according to a different value system (1, 27).

As in Hebrews and 1 Peter, Christians are regarded as pilgrims and sojourners. They are not hostile to the world but neither are they defined by it. James's whole effort is to persuade those "of

Shared Faith

Paul and James each interpret the same verse from the Old Testament—"Abram put his faith in the LORD, who credited it to him as an act of righteousness" (Gn 15, 6)—to support his own view (Paul in Gal 3, 6–14, James in Jas 2, 21–24). For Paul, the believer's justification comes through faith, not works (Rom 4, 16—5, 2); for James, "faith of itself, if it does not have works, is dead" (2, 17). The conflict, however, is more apparent than real. For Paul, faith is primarily trust in God (Rom 4, 5), a sense of the word that James also shares (1, 5); but, in his critique of faith, James means by it essentially the assent to ideas about God without any personal relationship or commitment to inform them: "Even the demons believe" (2, 19). James sees works as acts springing from the believer's love for God (2, 14), whereas for Paul works are the external observances of ritual, like circumcision, regarded in isolation from any connection to one's relationship to God. For both, the key is understanding where the center is: one's relationship to God.

two minds" (1, 8) to live by God's measure, which is the perfect "wisdom from above" (see 3, 15).

Discrimination and the Law of Love (2, 1–13)

The first essay reveals a voice that resembles that of Paul in Galatians. James uses the same oral, dialogical style known as the diatribe. Vivid and lively, it is filled with rhetorical questions, exclamations, and abrupt transitions. The effect is a direct challenge to every reader—then and now. The challenge is even more clearly heard when the text is read aloud.

Christians, James says, must live consistently with their convictions. "Faith in our . . . Lord Jesus Christ" (2, 1) is incompatible with any form of discrimination within the community. James sketches a lively scene that probably reflects a general situation rather than a local incident. The context is judgment within the community, like that carried out in the Diaspora synagogue to settle disputes. In the background is the injunction of Leviticus 19, 15 that forbids partiality in judgment. How plausible and true to life is his portrayal of a community pandering to rich members and slighting their poor!

That James intends us to see discrimination as an offense against love as well as faith in his allusion to Leviticus 19, 15 is shown immediately by his explicit citation of Leviticus 19, 18 in 2, 8. The "law of love" is also identified by Jesus as the summation of Scripture. James calls it the "royal" law, by which he means the standard regulating relations in the community. It is the "law of the kingdom." James spells out

this commandment by alluding to the Ten Commandments (2, 11) and also to the specific commandments found in the original context of Leviticus 19 that accompany the original exhortation "love your neighbor as yourself" (see Jas 4, 11; 5, 4.9.12.20). James says that breaking any commandment means breaking the whole law, because sin is not against a law but against a lawgiver. In other words, committing a specific wrong is more than simply disobeying a rule; it is a break in a personal relationship. Faith in the one God excludes picking and choosing between commandments, just as it excludes picking and choosing between fellow Christians.

Active Faith (2, 14–26)

The following section is often misunderstood. Because James speaks of "faith" and "works" (terms often used by Paul), people think James is responding to Paul's teaching. In fact, his perspective is entirely different. James speaks not of the commandments of the law, but of active faith. He is a moralist and is concerned with the way speech gets converted to action. Like all moralists, his concern is efficacy: "Of what use is it?" The examples of Abraham and Rahab illustrate James's point. Their faith expressed itself in effective action. Abraham was willing to sacrifice his son; Rahab showed hospitality to God's scouts. James is not debating with Paul over the question of how people are saved. His exhortation is intensely practical and arises from the situation pictured in 2, 14–16: Pious talk does not feed or clothe the needy. Such faith is as "dead" as a corpse; such religion is fraudulent (see l, 26f).

We discover here two distinctive aspects of James. His teaching is not based on what is specifically Christian, but on faith in the one God shared by other monotheistic traditions. For James, the "faith of Christ" and teachings of Jesus do not oppose but refine Torah. James therefore also contains the beginning of a genuine social ethic. His moral teaching is not confined to the Christian community; it can be extended to the world. If there is no partiality in the community, based in the law of God, then forms of discrimination in the wider world can be combated on the same basis. If sister and brother in the community are to be fed, then the community as such should also feed the needy of the world in every changing circumstance.

James also warns us that this can cut both ways. If the Christian community does not live up to its own calling and is unjust, then it bears no witness to the world and is itself subject to condemnation (2, 5–7).

The Power of the Tongue (3, 1–12)

James's concern for the proper use of speech (see 1, 19.26) now becomes thematic. Preoccupation with speech is typical of ancient moralists. Taciturnity as a sign of wisdom was proverbial (e.g., see Prv 10, 19; 11, 12). That such "control of the tongue" was almost insurmountably difficult to achieve was also well known. James therefore considers control of speech to be a mark of perfection (3, 2).

James makes two related points using conventional imagery from Greek philosophy. The first compares the tongue to a horse's bit or a ship's rudder, showing not only how a small organ can direct a large body, but also how much that organ itself, with its disproportionate power, needs to be controlled by someone with a sense of direction and good judgment. James's second point concerns the potential for harm in uncontrolled speech. It is like a flame "setting the entire course of our lives on fire" (3, 6).

The capacity of speech to do evil is more impressive than its power for good: "No human being can tame the tongue. It is a restless evil, full of deadly poison" (3, 8). Sadly, the story of human discourse from the Garden of Eden to the latest garden party only confirms James's harsh

The Value of Silence

The dangers inherent in speech also undergird the value of silence in the monastic/contemplative tradition of both the East and the West. Silence is the necessary precondition to "welcome the word that . . . is able to save your souls" (1, 21).

judgment. No wonder the ancients valued taciturnity: Better no speech than destructive speech.

The theological implications of speech are central to James's exhortation. In 3, 9–12, he contrasts the speech that "blesses God" with that which "curses human beings" who are made in God's image. Once again James combats the "two-minded" person, who thinks that it is possible to have a relationship with God that disregards human obligations. As in 2, 14–17, James insists that religious language and practical human care must go together. The same source cannot yield two kinds of water, and a Christian should not speak with two tongues. Action should follow conviction; speech should conform to faith.

Friendship with God or the World (3, 13—4, 10)

Although the paragraph division of modern translations hides what is clearer in Greek, 3, 13—4, 10 is a self-contained essay stating the central theological framework for understanding James as a whole.

Formally, it is a call of conversion. In 3, 13—4, 6, James presents an indictment. In 4, 7–10, he exhorts his readers to repentance. A powerful spatial metaphor governs both parts, a contrast between what comes "from above" (true wisdom, God's Gift), and that which originates "from below" (false wisdom, human arrogance). Correspondingly, the readers are told to "humble" themselves, so that God can "exalt" them (4, 10). The spatial metaphor points to differing measures of reality. That "from below" James calls "the world." It treats life as though God had no claim; success is measured by human accomplishment and acquisition. But God's measure says that everything comes as a gift from "the Father of lights" (1, 17), and that

Envy

Envy comes from the "wisdom from below." The point clearly is that God's spirit has nothing to do with envy. James associates with envy all the vices commonly attributed to it in Greek moral discourse, especially social unrest, murder, and war.

Why is envy so singled out? Because its underlying assumption is that your gain is my loss. This is the opposite of the Spirit of community, where all gain by anyone's growth, and all rejoice in anyone's good fortune. Envy causes me to sorrow when another has something that I lack. And when life is measured simply in terms of what I possess—"I am what I have"—then for another to have and me to lack is intolerable. Envy drives the acquisitive instinct: "you covet" (4, 2). It is a short step to conflict, war, and murder, between individuals and among nations. Like other Greek moralists, James assigns the cause of war to envy (4, 1–3). It is remarkable that this passage, which alone in the New Testament analyzes the causes of human conflict, should play so little role in moral discussions of war and peace.

arrogance is empty pretense. James, as always, has as his main target the "two-minded" person (4, 8) who wants to live by both measures at once. Within this call to conversion, James develops the theme of envy as exemplifying the measure of the world.

At the climax of the indictment (4, 4), James accuses his readers of being "adulterers" because they have broken covenant both with God and with their fellow humans. The covenant is about loyalty and love. There is no connection between those attitudes and the self-seeking of envy. James also uses the language of Greek philosophy concerning "friendship." He contrasts "friendship with the world" and "friendship with God" as opposing ways of life. James is not condemning the world understood as the place of human activity or God's creation. Rather, it is a system of values that excludes consideration of God. To be "friends with the world" therefore means to live by a measure that leaves God's claim aside.

To this closed system James opposes the measure of faith: God is the source of "every good and perfect gift" (1, 17). God "gives more grace" to the humble even while resisting the arrogant (4, 6). God is not envious of humans but gives to all generously and without grudging (see 1, 5). Those who submit to God are therefore also lifted up by God (4, 10). Their tears of repentance will rapidly turn to joy, because—a remarkable statement—when humans draw near to God, God also draws near to them (4, 8).

Against Arrogance (4, 11—5, 6)

James now turns to three forms of arrogance, which exemplify life according to the measure of the world. The first is the practice of slandering a neighbor (4, 1f). Such critical speech naturally involves both a condemnation of the other and an implied assertion of one's own superiority: "I am in a position to judge." James insists that such judgment breaks the law of love (see Lv 19. 16) and reminds his readers that the lawgiver is also the judge. God alone can both save and destroy life (see 1, 21).

A second form of arrogance is demonstrated by those who make great business plans without ever considering the fragile nature of their own existence (4, 13–17). Once more, their speech gives them away; they assume control over the present and the future. James comments: "You are boasting in your arrogance. All such boasting is evil" (4, 16). The speech of one living by God's measure is also revealing: "If the LORD wills . . ." This is more than pious talk; it refers all of life and all of life's projects to the one who gives and can alone sustain life. (Compare Jesus' parable of the Rich Fool, Lk 12, 16–21.)

Finally, with a prophetic rage like that of Amos, James attacks the insolence of the rich who withhold wages from their laborers. The security gained by such fraud is illusory; the rich fatten themselves for the day of judgment (5, 5). They "know the right thing to do but do not do it" (4, 17), which James defines as sin. How do they know? Because the scriptural context for the law of love in Leviticus 19, 18 states plainly, "you shall not withhold overnight the wages of your day laborer" (Lv 19, 13).

Patience, Plain Speech, Prayer (5, 7–20)

Having called the double-minded to conversion and excoriated the arrogant, James turns to the community's inner life. Speech is again the underlying theme, this time with reference to the proper uses of speech in the church.

Christians should speak plainly. In 5, 12 James repeats the commandment of Jesus (Mt 5, 33–37) that speech should be unadorned and straightforward, without oaths. And in his last exhortation, James encourages the sort of mutual correction that can build up the identity of the church (5, 20).

Because the church is constituted by the word of truth (1, 18), it should above all express that truth in its communal life of prayer. James enumerates the sorts of prayer that are appropriate to the community's diverse circumstances (5, 13f) and then elaborates the prayer with anointing for a sick member. This ritual is the basis for the sacrament of anointing for the sick and has roots in the healing ministry of Jesus (see 5, 15). James's last example from Torah is the prophet Elijah, whose prayer demonstrates the power of faith for those who live by God's measure (5, 17f; cf. 1, 6–8). These final exhortations, down to earth and humane, summarize beautifully the character of James, who from beginning to end finds wisdom in practical faith and active love.

Questions for Discussion and Reflection
Group Sharing/Discussion

1. James's epistle is a moral exhortation reminding readers of traditional values. What are some of the qualities of this form as seen in James?

2. James speaks to Christians who are of "two minds" (1, 8; 4, 8). Explain these two standards, the measure of the world and the measure of God. What are some examples of these?

3. James's first essay (2, 1–13) is a diatribe.

What are some qualities in James of this form of rhetoric?

4. For James breaking any commandment means breaking the whole law. What does he mean by this?

5. Why is proper control of speech a mark of perfection?

In Our Lives

1. James assigns the cause of war to envy (4, 1–3). It is remarkable that this passage, which alone in the New Testament analyzes the causes of human conflict, should play so small a role in discussions of war and peace. Why is envy such a driving force for conflict among nations, family members, and ethnic groups?

2. "Faith in our . . . Lord Jesus Christ" is incompatible with any form of discrimination within the community says James. Who does our society judge should be kept on the fringes? What does our own community do about that? What else can our faith community do?

3. Read James's passage on control of the tongue (3, 1–12). Recall experiences in your life or the life of others that confirm this strong message.

4. James contrasts "friendship with the world" and "friendship with God" (3, 13—4, 10). How would you describe these opposing ways of life in modern terms?

Individual/Personal Reflection/Action

1. James describes three forms of arrogance (4, 11—5, 6), that is, slandering your neighbor, "planning," and stealing from the wages of the poor. Take some time to reflect on these forms of arrogance as they touch your life.

2. James teaches, "Do not complain about one another that you may not be judged." Take time in the coming day to pray about this instruction and how it may fit into your life.

3. Those who submit to God are lifted up by God (4, 10). Recall a time when you turned to God and reflect on the experience of listening for God in your heart. Whisper a prayer of thanks that God is with us always. Ask God to help you remember to listen often.

1 PETER READING GUIDE
At a Glance

Who are the main players?	"Peter" Christian communities of Asia Minor
What should I look for?	Note the difference between social order and virtue. This letter is not an inspired blueprint of an ideal social order or family structure. What we find is the best moral teaching applied to the real world of that age. Social structures and related relationships of the past cannot be transferred to the present. But, then and now, virtues of good order, mutual respect, obedience and authority are very much needed.
When was this written?	Tradition regarded Peter as the author; therefore, the letter was dated prior to A.D. 67. Modern scholars, however, for good reasons would date this at the end of the first century or the beginning of the second.
Where did these events occur?	The letter was addressed to the Christian communities in the five provinces of Asia Minor, which is modern Turkey.
Why was this book written?	This is a letter of exhortation and encouragement to Gentile Christians who were recently converted from paganism. They find themselves still living among pagan symbols and social structures and are experiencing suffering and persecution.
What is the story?	Peter tries to inspire the "chosen sojourners" to live as God's people, remembering Christ's resurrection and future hope. He appeals to their experience of baptism as new birth and to the suffering and death of Christ as a source of salvation and example. He warns them to keep their distance from the values of the world, yet give witness to their neighbors. Be watchful, for the time for serious decision is now. Those who suffer will share Christ's glory.

Before Beginning

First Peter bears all the marks of a real letter. It was written to Christians scattered throughout the provinces of Asia Minor. Although written in clear and even elegant Greek, and although containing an exhortation and witness (5, 12) at once simple and profound, 1 Peter is given far less attention than it deserves. Partly this is because many contemporary scholars think that the letter is pseudonymous and a product of second generation rather than primitive Christianity. There are, however, excellent reasons for considering Peter the apostle to have been the author of 1 Peter. In any case, the authority of New Testament writings does not derive from the identity of the author. Whether it was the apostle or someone writing in his name, this letter speaks

powerfully to a situation of early believers and retains enduring value for readers in every age.

A Letter to the Gentile Christians

The Situation of the Readers

Because the letter is addressed to Christians spread over a large geographical area (1, 1), we do not expect the detailed treatment of local problems. By reading between the lines, however, we are able to learn something about their shared characteristics.

Who Were They?

1. They seem to have been recently converted. Peter reminds them repeatedly of their former

life of vice (1, 18–20; 4, 3–4), as well as their initiation into the messianic community through baptism (1, 3; 1, 22—2, 3).

2. They seem, furthermore, to be direct converts from paganism rather than from Judaism.

3. They continued to live among the symbols and social structures of the Empire. They inevitably felt pulled between an allegiance to their new calling and an attraction to the values of the world they had left.

4. They were, finally, converts who were experiencing suffering. On the basis of 4, 12, some have considered this to be a state-sponsored persecution such as was later the lot of Christians. But Peter's positive view of the state (2, 12–17) does not fit that reconstruction. It is more likely that Peter's readers were experiencing the sort of verbal abuse and social ostracism that Christians experienced from the beginning. The suffering was no less serious. Martyrdom is painful but swift. The corrosion of confidence is slower but terribly effective.

Christian Apologetic

First Peter can best be understood as a form of apologetic literature. This form of writing originated among Diaspora Jews and was taken over by Christians. Ostensibly it explains one's distinctive beliefs to the wider world in terms outsiders can understand. Indirectly, it supports community identity. First Peter has many of the characteristics of this genre. It is positive and open to the dominant culture. Christians are not to flee the world or its structures. They are to be good citizens within those social structures. And they are to be ready to demonstrate by their behavior and their speech that they pose no threat to others (3, 15–16).

At the same time, Peter works to build up the identity of the community.

1. He reminds his readers that they are called to holiness and a standard of behavior higher than that of their neighbors (2, 11–12; 4, 1–2).

2. He reminds them of the fundamental transformation they had undergone in their baptism.

3. He assures them that although they are "strangers" in the world (2, 11), they are part of the "household of God" (2, 4–5; 4, 17).

In doing so, Peter appropriates for these new Gentile believers all the scriptural titles and symbols used of Israel, to give them a sense of continuity with God's people, even though once they were "no people." In 1 Peter we observe a thoroughly Gentile Christianity regarding itself as the "New Israel," taking up a place in the Diaspora not against the world but as a witness to the world.

The Greeting (1, 1–2)

The greeting of this circular letter establishes more than the simple identification of author and addressees. No need to elaborate the simple designation, "Peter, apostle of Jesus Christ," for Peter's authority is unquestioned (see, in contrast, 2 Pt). But the "dispersion" of Asia Minor has religious as well as geographical connotations. We see here a theme found also in James and Hebrews and in the Christian literature of the second century: Christians are in exile from their true homeland in heaven so long as they are on earth. They are, in fact, "sojourners" precisely because they have been "chosen" by God and have an identity distinct from that of their neighbors. They should therefore cultivate attitudes appropriate to exiles and pilgrims (e.g., see 2, 11). The greeting also reminds the readers of the rich complexity of their experience of God: The Father has chosen them; the Son saved them by his obedient sacrifice; and the Spirit has sanctified them.

The Gift and Call of God (1, 3–21)

The opening prayer (1, 3–9) is based on the blessing formula of Jewish worship: God is blessed for his gifts to humans. In this case, Peter gives thanks for the new life his readers have been granted through the resurrection of Jesus. Their new life is real, yet not complete. Their inheritance is one that is kept for them in heaven (1, 4f). They, of course, still remain on earth. This tension establishes them as pilgrims and sojourners. As their salvation "waits for them," so also must they "wait for it." In the meantime, they must experience the trials and sufferings inherent to the life of faith (1, 6f). Peter places his readers between the "already" of God's grace and the "not yet" of salvation fully achieved (1, 9), in a manner typical of New Testament writings. But what they hope for is secure, a "living hope" (1, 3), because it is based not simply on human longing, but in the "power of God" at work among them (1, 4).

Where Is the Place of the Historical Jewish People?

It must be confessed that 1 Peter simply does not take them into account. He appropriates the symbols of Torah for the exclusive use of Gentile believers. Readers today cannot expect to find in this text an answer to the many questions concerning the relations of Christians to Jews, for 1 Peter does not address them.

Despite the fact that his readers have converted from paganism, Peter inserts them into the story of Israel. In speaking of an "inheritance in heaven," Peter implies a contrast to the "inheritance of the land," which was the hope of Israel. Likewise, 1, 10–12 develops a contrast between stages in the story. Peter asserts that the prophets of old did not speak of their own times (1, 12), but spoke of the "sufferings destined for Christ and the glories to follow them" (1, 11). Three aspects of this striking statement deserve notice.

1. The superiority of the Christians' present experience is clearly asserted; as in Hebrews, the claims of the earlier covenant are made secondary. What the Christians have received in the gospel transcends even what angels can know (1, 12).

2. Scripture is taken over completely as messianic prophecy. Everything in Scripture points to Jesus.

3. As in Luke-Acts, the pattern of the Messiah is spelled out in terms of "suffering, then glory." That his readers must follow after this same pattern becomes explicit later in the letter.

Having asserted the reality of God's gift, Peter now sketches the demands it places on those who receive it (1, 13–21). They are to direct their lives by the new form of existence given to them. This means a radical obedience to the giver of the gift, an obedience spelled out in terms of holiness (1, 15f). As their lives have changed, so must their behavior. They must not act as they formerly did but are to become "different." They are to shape themselves in a manner in harmony with the one who "ransomed" them with the gift of the "precious blood of Christ" (1, 18f). Peter again calls his readers "sojourners" (1, 17). Jews of the Diaspora were to be different from pagans; Christians are to be "different" (holy) in the world as they wait for the fulfillment of their salvation (see 1, 9). They are not defined by the norms of others (1, 14.18), but by their allegiance to God so that "your faith and hope are in God" (1, 21).

A Gospel People (1, 22—2, 10)

To strengthen their grasp on their special identity, Peter reminds his readers of the basis of their new life in "the living and abiding word of God" (1, 23). By this, Peter explicitly means the good news (1, 25). This is the message of a crucified Messiah who was raised to new life. By the obedient acceptance of that strange proclamation, they were given "new birth" (1, 23). Immediately, however, Peter asserts the need for them to grow. The "spiritual milk" they now imbibe is appropriate to new converts who have just "tasted and seen that the Lord is good" (see also 1 Cor 3, 1–3; Heb 6, 13); they are to mature "in Christ" by patterning their life according to a new standard of moral behavior. They must leave aside deceit in favor of truth, envy for love.

Peter is not only concerned with the transformation of individuals, but as much as Paul with the identity of the community also. In 2, 4–10, therefore, he reminds them of their communal identity as God's house and people. This section interweaves scriptural passages and allusions. The cross-references provided in the NAE provide valuable assistance. The choice of passages is strikingly similar to that in Romans 9, 25–33. While it's possible that Peter used Romans, it is more likely that both Paul and Peter used community traditions of scriptural interpretation developed from the first days of the church.

The first set of quotations (2, 6–8) portrays the paradox of Christian faith. The stone that God intended to be the basis for his people Israel was rejected by them; yet the rejected one became the basis of a new people, a "spiritual house" made up of living persons (2, 4). The reference here is clearly to the crucified Jesus who was a scandal (a stone that caused stumbling) to his fellow Jews, who expected a messiah with more obvious and impressive credentials than suffering for others (see 1 Cor 1, 18–23).

For the Christian community, however, the rejected Messiah is the basis for a new life and shared identity. In the second set of texts, Peter strings together the most precious epithets applied to Israel as God's people in Torah. Now they apply to these Gentiles "once no people, but now God's people." In the messianic community, these aliens have a home (see also Eph 2, 19–22).

Life within the World's Structures (2, 11—3, 7)

Christians are to maintain distance from the values of this world as "aliens and sojourners" (2, 11). At the same time, they must live within the social structures of the world. Peter is convinced that if they are good citizens, they will turn away slander and persecution. The practice of "good works" is the community's basic witness (2, 12).

Peter uses the traditional form of "household ethics" to sketch the Christians' social obligations. Greek philosophy had elaborated the mutual duties of people who lived in a stratified social order. Over the empire as a whole, the emperor was considered head of the household. In individual families, husbands ruled wives, parents ruled children, and masters ruled slaves. This was simply the conventional arrangement of that time. Neither Paul (see Col 3, 18—4, 1) nor Peter thought that the Christian message demanded the dismantling of society's structures.

In 2, 13–17, Peter portrays the empire and its agents in positive terms. Submission to legitimate authority is both right and expedient, because the state punishes only the wicked: Such an outlook is inconceivable if Christians were in fact being harassed by the state as such. Yet, even here, the relationship with God is primary. Social obligations, if they conflict with that relationship, must give way to it: "Be free, yet without using freedom as a pretext for evil, but as slaves of God" (2, 16). Obedience to God comes before all; and before God, all are slaves.

We might expect in the next section exhortations to both masters and slaves (cf Col 3, 22—4, 1). Perhaps the absence of masters says something about the Christians' social status. But because Peter thinks of all Christians as slaves (2, 16), this exhortation to servants becomes a general teaching to the community at large. The most striking aspect of this teaching is the

What Is Peter Getting At?

The exhortation to wives (3, 1–6) is much more extensive than that to husbands (3, 7). Traditional Jewish and Greek motifs, which stress the value of internal virtue over external adornment, are used to support the command to be submissive. Women are to be subordinate, we notice, not to all men, but to their husbands (3, 1.5). In return, men are to regard women as fully equal in their relationship before the Lord. Women are "joint heirs of the gift of life" (3, 7).

In these instructions, we do not find a divinely inspired blueprint for the ideal social order or Christian family structure. What we find is the best available moral teaching applied to the real world of that age. Just as the social structures of the past cannot be transferred directly to the present, neither can the relationships appropriate to those structures be directly imitated. Yet for families both ancient and modern, for societies then and now, good order, mutual respect, obedience, and authority are very much required. The style of those structures, happily, is left to human creativity.

invocation of Jesus as an explicit example to be imitated, for all who suffer unjustly (2, 21–23). Jesus not only won salvation for others by his death on the cross. In his very manner of suffering, he provided the model for how Christians were to act. Not only what Jesus did but also how he did it becomes a source of life to the community.

Witness in a Hostile World (3, 8—4, 6)

The Christians of Asia Minor were not suffering persecution, torture, and death. Their suffering was nevertheless real and painful. Social ostracism works a slow and insidious poison into a community's sense of identity. They were being "insulted" (3, 9), maligned and defamed (3, 16), and "vilified" (4, 4). Why? Probably they were abused because they no longer followed the ways of their neighbors (4, 3f). They have become different (holy), and people who insist on being different generate resentment.

Peter's response to the community's experience of suffering is remarkable. He does not advocate withdrawal from society or hostility toward outsiders. Instead, Christians are to remain in the world (see 2, 13—3, 7) and are to engage outsiders in dialogue. They are to be ready to "give an explanation to anyone who asks you for a reason for your hope" (3, 15). The expectation that such explanation would be helpful pays a high compliment to the basic reasonableness and goodwill of outsiders. Christians are also to follow the exhortation of Jesus to return a blessing for a curse (see Mt 5, 44). To act in this way toward outsiders, they must cultivate the same qualities of sympathy and love toward each other in the community (3, 8). Within their own hearts, furthermore, they are to "sanctify Christ as Lord" (3, 15), which, Peter asserts, will free them from fear of outsiders (3, 14). How will this happen?

1. They are to remember how Jesus not only "suffered for sins once" (3, 18) but also how he was raised from the dead in power.

2. Using traditions found in apocalyptic literature (such as 1 Enoch), Peter symbolically expresses the conviction that the resurrection was not simply an event concerning the person Jesus but had cosmic extension.

3. "In the spirit," Jesus went to the spirits in prison to preach the good news (3, 19–22). This dramatic announcement is the basis for the statement in the Apostles' Creed that says Jesus "descended into hell." It means that God's power to save reaches everywhere, even to the farthest reaches of human sin and alienation.

Peter's immediate point, however, is that by baptism (3, 21), the Christians of Asia Minor have been given the same power. They need not fear human slander, for the power of God is at work among them. They are like those to whom Jesus preached after his resurrection, "though condemned in the flesh in human estimation . . . alive in the spirit in the estimation of God" (4, 6).

Community Attitudes (4, 7—5, 14)

First Peter does not portray the Christians' moral situation in stark black-and-white tones, but like most New Testament writings, it has a keen sense that the time for decision is now. The final exhor-

tations are colored by the conviction that "the end of all things is at hand" (4, 7). The time of judgment is soon (4, 17). Therefore, Christian life means "resisting the devil" who through affliction such as they are experiencing "seeks to devour them" (5, 8f). Such circumstances call for a "serious, sober" attitude and one that is "vigilant" (4, 7; 5, 8). Those who experience affliction are to regard their sufferings as a share in Christ's own (5, 13f), knowing that they will share in his glory (4, 13; 5, 10). Within the community, attitudes of mutual service are to prevail (4, 9–11), demonstrated by good order and humility (5, 1–16).

When exhorting the community's leaders, Peter forbids lording it over the flock. Leaders are rather to provide a positive example (5, 3). The image of the shepherd recalls the portrayal of Jesus as the "shepherd and guardian of your souls" (2, 25). The connection is made explicit in 5, 4: with characteristic optimism, Peter promises such good leaders that "when the chief Shepherd is revealed, you will receive the unfading crown of glory."

The New Testament contains no writing more positive in its evaluation of the world yet more compelling in its call to holiness than 1 Peter. As Martin Luther correctly noted, it is one of the New Testament compositions that truly "show thee Christ."

Questions for Discussion and Reflection
Group Sharing/Discussion

1. Describe the original audience of 1 Peter.

2. What was Peter's response to the community's experience of suffering?

3. Peter taught that what readers hope for is security, a "living hope" because it is based not simply in human longing, but in the "power of God" at work among them. Describe the hope of human longing and the "living hope" based on God's power.

4. Peter's exhortation was colored by his conviction that "the end of all things is at hand" (4, 7). In this context Peter wrote this letter to urge Christians to live their faith. What virtues and attitudes for the communities did he suggest? If he were writing today what would he be asking Christians to do?

In Our Lives

1. Peter works to build the identity of the community by reminding them of their call to holiness, their transformation in baptism, and that

they are part of the "household of God." What do these three qualities mean in your world today? How would you nourish these in your life? In your community?

2. In his letter Peter teaches that Christians are to remain in the world and to engage outsiders in dialogue (2, 13—3, 7). He teaches: Be ready to give an explanation to anyone who asks you for the reason for your hope (3, 15). How would you give a clear reason for your hope?

Individual/Personal Reflection/Action

1. Sometimes it is easier to love "outsiders" than those within "the household of faith." What are ways Catholics take one another for granted or fail to show appreciation? Choose one concrete action you can take this week to show your care, concern, and gratitude towards someone who shares your faith in Christ.

2. Newborns (the newly baptized) need "spiritual milk." But now you are mature in Christ. Read 1 Peter 2, 1–3. Why is it easier to hold on to the spiritual sweetness of childhood faith than to accept the "solid food" that mature baptismal commitment requires? Describe how your image of God, of Christ, of the church and of Scriptures has changed since your childhood. Discuss the difficulty of letting go of secure religious images. Why do you think we are called to do this?

3. In this letter, Peter encourages civil obligations. Today, as in his day, families and society at large require good order. Read 1 Peter 2, 13. Cite examples of breakdown in modern society where this is lacking. What are some creative ways of rebuilding the human spirit that will affect the quality of life for families, civil institutions, and international relationships?

2 PETER READING GUIDE

At a Glance

Who are the main players?	"Peter" the opponents
What should I look for?	This book is a general exhortation cast in the form of a letter. Notice Peter's response concerning the delay of the second coming of Christ. Also reflect upon the debate between living faith and practical atheism.
When was this writen?	2 Peter is a pseudonymous work, written about the second quarter of the second century, forming a bridge between the apostolic period and the church of subsequent ages.
Where did these events occur?	The author is a Jewish Christian and the audience may be the churches of Asia Minor.
Why was this book written?	The principle problem of the author is the "scoffers" who deny the second coming of the Lord.
What is the story?	His message has three points: (1) he establishes the authority of the writer and of the Scripture that will be used as the source of his proof; (2) he attacks the opponents' "destructive teaching"; (3) he presents the proper understanding of the tradition concerning God's judgment.

Before Beginning

An appreciative understanding of 2 Peter demands more than the normal effort. Hard work is necessary to uncover the situation addressed by the letter. Perhaps even more difficult is the hurdle presented by the letter's sustained argumentative tone. Such effort finds its rewards, however, in the surprising

discovery that the writing, which at first appears to be the New Testament's most irrelevant, can emerge as having perennial pertinence.

A Defense of God's Judgment

The circumstances of 2 Peter's composition are obscure (see the NAB introduction to 2 Peter).

The same author did not write both 1 and 2 Peter. The style, outlook, and concerns of the two letters are too disparate for a common authorship. The main thing they have in common is the mention of Noah and the flood. Second Peter has far more in common with Jude (with which it shares the polemical material of chapter 2) than with 1 Peter. In all likelihood, 2 Peter is a pseudonymous composition. Despite the self-presentation of chapter 1, it is not "Symeon Peter" who writes, but someone who invokes his authority as a support for shared traditions being threatened by deviance. This sermon in the form of a letter may have been addressed to a single church, but it may also have been intended for a larger audience, all "those who have received a faith of equal value to ours" (1, 1). It is thus considered a "general" epistle. The title "Catholic Epistles" was applied to 1 and 2 Peter; James; 1, 2, and 3 John; and Jude because they were written for a broader audience than a local church (in Greek, "catholic" = "pertaining to the whole"). Some readers also consider 2 Peter "catholic" in another sense: Its concern for tradition anticipates the emergence of the Catholic Church in the second century.

At first reading, 2 Peter seems to be a loose collection of observations within which talk about Jesus' second coming plays a particularly significant part. Some scholars have therefore thought that the "delay of the Parousia" was the crisis that stimulated composition. Closer analysis, however, shows that "Peter" and his opponents are debating a deeper and more perennial problem: Does God judge the world? Underlying that issue, in turn, is a still more fundamental one concerning the reality of God and God's relationship to the world. The debate, in short, is between living faith and practical atheism. It is a debate still in progress. The contribution of 2 Peter is worth hearing.

Far from a random collection of statements, the letter as a whole presents a coherent argu-

ment. Chapter 1 establishes the authority of the writer and of the Scripture that will be used as the source of proof. Chapter 2 attacks the opponents' "destructive teachings" on the basis of Scripture. Chapter 3 presents the proper understanding of the tradition concerning God's judgment.

The Common Tradition (1, 1–21)

The first section of the letter establishes the authority of the writer and of the shared tradition (1, 1) that the author represents. Extraordinary emphasis is put on the person of Peter and on the fact that he will soon die (1, 13f). These touches recall the literary genre popular in early Christianity called the "Farewell Discourse." In this sort of composition, a figure from the past, speaking shortly before his death, predicts catastrophes to come and enjoins fidelity on his followers. We notice in this case, however, an equally strong emphasis on memory (1, 9.12.13.15). The opponents "forget" the proper knowledge, and Peter seeks to "remind" his readers of it. The emphasis on memory makes the letter resemble as well the form of moral exhortation called *parenesis*. The connection to parenesis is most obvious in 2 Peter 1, 5–8. Parenesis spelled out moral obligations in terms of maxims. Here, Peter lists the sort of qualities that should follow upon the readers' faith. More important even than the specific items is the overall point made by the list: More than knowledge or faith is involved in being Christian. A whole way of life is demanded. Those who have "forgotten" this lead lives that are "idle and unfruitful" (1, 8f). There is a sharp polemical edge to this comment. In chapter 2, Peter will show that the opponents' "destructive heresies" bring about destructive behavior, which in turn brings down God's judgment

A complex statement provides the basis for Peter's overall argument and a transition to his attack on his opponents (1, 16–21). In a passage that clearly corresponds to the Synoptic Gospels' story of Jesus' transfiguration (see Mt 17, 1–8), he asserts the reality of the Christian experience of God. The tradition out of which Peter writes is not speculation ("cleverly devised myths," 1, 16), but is a power he and others experience personally; "we" saw and heard on the mountain (1, 16–18). The community's tradition is based not in fancy, but in fact. The experience,

Pseudonymous A *pseudonymous* work is one written by a later author who attributed it to an important person according to the literary convention popular at the time.

moreover, was of "the power and coming" of the Lord Jesus Christ. As we will learn, the promise concerning Jesus' return is the bone of contention in chapter 3. Peter claims that the expectation of his return is based on the reality of his already having come.

The disciples' experience of Jesus also grounds the "prophetic message" about Jesus' return for judgment. Peter places this prophecy of Jesus (see Mt 24, 29–31) among the prophecies of Scripture. As with scriptural prophecies, interpretation is not to be personal or idiosyncratic but a decision of the community that is guided by the same Spirit that gave utterance in the first place. With this alignment, Peter has provided the basis for arguing the whole issue of God's judgment (and therefore of Jesus' return) on the truthfulness of Scripture as properly interpreted by the tradition.

Condemnation of False Teachers (2, 1–22)

The claim to a true "prophetic message" in 1, 19 provides a transition to the attack on "false teachers" (2, 1) who are placed in the line of "false prophets." As we will learn more fully in chapter 3, the opponents are denying the power of God to judge, that is, to intervene in the affairs of the world (3, 4). By denying God's ability to judge, they bring judgment on themselves. Their "destructive heresies" bring on them "destruction" (2, 1). But their teaching has proven successful, convincing many (2, 2); Peter's response must therefore be vigorous and pointed.

We saw in 1, 5–8 that Peter was concerned with the moral consequences of faith. The ancient world knew what our world sometimes ignores, that people act on their ideas, and that bad ideas can lead to bad behavior. A real misconception of what life is about leads to a distorted existence. Showing how certain teachings lead to immoral behavior is a way of proving that the ideas are false. Peter therefore pays particular attention to the way of life generated by these doctrines. He attacks the "licentious ways" of the opponents (2, 2), their "greed" and "lies" (2, 3). They are people of "depraved desires" (2, 10), are "irrational" (2, 12) and "adulterous" (2, 14). The catalogue of vices reaches a rhetorical climax in 2, 17f, then takes a sharp turn: "They promise them freedom, though they themselves are slaves of

corruption, for a person is a slave of whatever overcomes him" (2, 19).

What sort of "freedom" did the opponents promise? Apparently, it was freedom from the fear of punishment. If God does not intervene in human affairs to punish the wicked and reward the good, then (they said) one can live immorally, looking out only for oneself, indulging in antisocial behavior.

Peter's first rebuttal is based on the nature of vice. They are slaves of their dominating appetite, which controls their behavior. They are not sophisticated or liberated. They are as compulsive as dogs returning to their vomit, these Christians who once knew righteousness but have now turned back to a novel version of an old atheism: "The fool says in his heart, 'There is no God' " (Ps 14, 1).

The second part of Peter's rebuttal is based on the conviction that the Bible stories relate the facts of history. When Scripture says therefore that God did punish and reward, that is proof of God's ability still to do so. Peter relates the cases of the wicked angels (2, 4), of Noah (2, 5), of Sodom and Gomorrah (2, 6–10) and of Balaam (2, 15f) as evidence of God's intervention. In contrast to the letter of Jude (with which much of this material is shared), Peter does not just emphasize punishment; God also rewards those who are faithful. Here, the issue is whether God acts in human history at all. Peter's recitation from Scripture asserts that in fact God does.

The Coming of the Lord (3, 1–18)

The specific nature of the debate emerges for the first time in this final section. Here, not simply a question of fact but a matter of principle is at stake.

The question of fact is not really in dispute. Jesus clearly had not yet returned to judge the world as all Christians had been expecting. But quite different conclusions were being drawn from that undisputed fact. The "scoffers" challenge the very promise of his coming (3, 4). They base their denial on the immutability of the world "from the beginning." They hold the position of the skeptics of the time, who denied divine providence. (See the box "Where Is Your God?" for more detailed discussion on both sides of this debate and how it continues today.) Because Jesus

Where Is Your God?

What opposition were the early Christians facing? Their neighbors in society ridiculed them for their faith in God's care for the world. The position held by the ancient skeptics such as the Epicureans and (among the Jews) Sadducees was a denial of divine providence. If there was a god, they said, he did not meddle with the world, which was a closed system of natural forces and human desires. God was not a factor to be considered, never had been, never would be. The failure of Jesus to return was only one more piece of evidence that all such prophecies were empty.

Though the debate about divine providence can obviously never be resolved—it has continued down to the present day—the side of those who believe in God is still strongly represented. Ultimately, believers can point to their own experience—the experience of prayer, of worship, of service—and identify that as one basis of their faith. Another basis is community—the sense of a fellowship of believers. A third basis is tradition—really a way of being in community with those who precede us. The debate will continue, but believers will also continue to have reason to maintain their position.

In this argument, both sides base their position on a claim of experience, which then interprets reality as a whole:

The Skeptics
Experience shows no evidence for God's activity: "Nothing has changed." How can you believe that God intervenes if he is so apparently absent?

Peter
Scripture proves that God does intervene, and the apostles experienced such an intervention in Jesus.

Trying to measure God's time on a human scale is impossible. God does not delay, but is waiting to ensure that people are prepared for the day of the Lord.

had yet to return, apparently supporting the scoffers' stance, theirs is a real threat to the whole structure of faith. They challenge not only the reality of the *Parousia,* but the very reality of a living God. Is God, then, merely a figment of the imagination, a projection of human longing? The whole concept of revelation is obviously challenged as well. There can be no real "promise" if there is no living God to speak, or to act.

In this argument, both sides base their position on a claim of experience, which then interprets reality as a whole. The skeptics say that experience shows no evidence for God's activity: "nothing has changed." Peter argues that Scripture (which is after all the record of human history) proves that God does intervene (see all of chapter 2). God created by a word and can destroy by a word (3, 5f). Furthermore—and this is the significance of

1, 16–19—Peter and his companions themselves experienced such an intervention in the transfiguration of Jesus. Thus, their tradition is based on the prophets, on the Lord Jesus, and on the apostles (3, 2).

If God does intervene, how is his apparent absence to be interpreted? Peter invokes the arguments used by other defenders of divine providence. God's time cannot be measured by human time: There is an infinite distance between God and humans (3, 7). God's apparent delay is to bring people to repentance (3, 8f).

Ultimately, those whose experience is different are not likely to be convinced. Peter appeals not to the opponents, but to those attracted to their position. He reasserts the conviction that Jesus will come "like a thief in the night" (see Mt 24, 43; 1 Thes 5, 2; Rv 3, 3) and that his coming will inaugurate "new heavens and a new earth in which righteousness dwells" (3, 13; see Rv 21, 1). His concern throughout this letter, however, has been most of all with the behavior of his readers, and he reasserts "what sort of persons they are to be" during this time of waiting (3, 11). After all debate is over, only the truth of human existence validates doctrine.

The letter concludes with a reference to Paul's letters that the opponents are distorting (3, 15f). The fact that the author refers to "all" of Paul's letters, that he makes them equivalent to "Scripture," and that there is already a history of interpreting (or misinterpreting) them are strong indications that this "Peter" is a writer of the second generation who defends a tradition common to the historical Peter and Paul against the threat of doctrinal and behavioral deviance.

Questions for Discussion and Reflection
Group Sharing/Discussion

1. Second Peter is known as a "Catholic Epistle." What does this title mean?

2. In all likelihood 2 Peter is a "pseudonymous" composition. What does that mean?

3. Second Peter resembles a form of moral exhortation called *parenesis* (cf. 2 Pt 1, 5–8). What qualities of this form of moral exhortation are in 2 Peter?

4. In chapter 2, Peter shows that his opponents' "destructive heresies" bring destructive behavior. What was he talking about?

5. The promise concerning Jesus' return is the bone of contention in chapter 3. What does Peter argue regarding Jesus' return?

In Our Lives

1. Peter writes about the false teachers and skeptics who deny God's ability to judge or intervene in the affairs of this world (2, 1–22). What happened as a result of this false teaching? Reflect upon what you believe concerning God's judgment and actions in the world today. Have you had experience in your religious world with false teachers or skeptics? What is their message? How can you respond?

2. "They promise them freedom, though they themselves are slaves of corruption, for a person is a slave of whatever overcomes him" (2, 19). Give some examples of the truth of this statement in contemporary life. What does "freedom" feel like and mean to you? How do internal and external freedom differ?

Individual/Personal Reflection/Action

1. Peter shows concern about the relations of beliefs and behavior. Read and reflect on how he presents this in chapter 2.

2. In some Christian circles, a great emphasis is placed on "the Lord's second coming." What is the Catholic understanding of the *parousia*? How does this affect your understanding of divine providence?

3. This letter addresses the debate between living faith and practical atheism, a very contemporary subject. What is meant by "living faith" and "practical atheism"? Recall some examples of "practical atheism" at work in our society. Why is this culture so attractive and easy to be caught up in?

1 JOHN READING GUIDE

At a Glance

Who are the main players?	John Johannine community
What should I look for?	Two important values: the declaration of the humanity and divinity of Christ as an apostolic teaching and the development of the intrinsic connection between Christian moral conduct and Christian doctrine.
When was this written?	Early tradition identified this with John the apostle. It is agreed it resembles the Fourth Gospel, and both works are from the same Johannine Christianity. It may be dated toward the end of the first century.
Where did these events occur?	It is not tied to a particular place, but there is a tradition that locates the Johannine literature in and around Ephesus.

Why was this book written? The community is divided by conflict. The purpose of the letter is to combat certain false ideas about Jesus and to deepen the spiritual and social awareness of the Christian community.

What is the story? This is more a theological treatise than a letter. Some former members of the community refuse to acknowledge Jesus as the Christ and thus deny that he was a true man. These theological errors are rejected by the author's declaring that authentic Christian love, ethics, and faith take place only within the historical revelation and sacrifice of Jesus Christ.

Before Beginning

Exhortation to a Divided Church

The New Testament contains three letters attributed to John. How these letters connect to the Gospel according to John and the book of Revelation is not easy to determine. Scholars agree that all came from a community of "Johannine Christianity" in the late first century, but neither their precise authorship nor sequence has been established. We are not even sure of the location of this "Johannine Christianity," although Asia Minor seems most likely. In such a state of uncertainty hypotheses abound. The introductions to each of these letters in the NAB give some sense of the options.

What we can learn of "Johannine Christianity" derives from the writings themselves. Apart from the connection to John, what common characteristics marked this version of messianism?

1. The figure of Jesus played a central role in the identity of the community.

2. These churches had experienced tragic division. In the Gospel and Revelation, there is conflict between these messianists and the Jews. In the letters and Revelation, there is also evidence of divisions within the churches.

3. This experience of division sharpened the community's symbols into a stark dualism: light and darkness, life and death, truth and falsehood, flesh and spirit.

The Three Letters

In the three letters, we see conflict happening within the churches. Disputes involve the proper understanding of Jesus. These letters provide a window on this early Christian conflict, revealing at once both its multiple dimensions and its

seriousness. It is impossible to say at this distance exactly how the letters relate to each other or to the situation. Second and Third John are real letters and claim to come from "the Elder." First John is anonymous and not really a letter so much as a sermon.

Some think that the three letters show three stages of the community's conflict. This hypothesis is possible, but a better one is that the three documents were written at the same time by the same author and sent to a single church. Each letter fulfills a specific function:

• 3 John recommends the mailman, Demetrius, to the church leader, Gaius.

• 2 John is a cover letter to be read publicly to the church.

• 1 John is the centerpiece, an exhortation to a community divided by conflict.

The Reading Guides for 2 and 3 John will describe how they fulfill their functions.

The Character of 1 John

Because it is not so closely tied to the particulars of a specific community's life, 1 John lends itself more readily to every time and place. For a document generated by bitter conflict, it is amazingly positive and loving in tone. Christians through the ages have rightly considered it one of the great spiritual witnesses of the New Testament.

The structure of this writing is not obvious. Certainly it is not a genuine letter. Even as a sermon, it tends to wander a bit, repeating the same points. First John at times has the appearance of an argument but without giving the substance. Readers are sometimes shocked at the lack of consistency. What is stated positively is sometimes denied only a short time later. The reason for this alternation of ideal and real lies in the circumstances being addressed.

The Johannine Christians saw their lives defined by a choice. Their first and basic choice was to follow Jesus. They considered that truth, life, and light characterized them; while falsehood, darkness, and death characterized those who did not follow Jesus. The Christians were the community of true prophecy. But now, the community finds itself divided into two hostile camps, and the cause of division is precisely what should have been the centerpiece of this unity: the proper understanding of the nature and role of Jesus.

First John's apparent indecisiveness reflects the chastened perspective caused by the trauma of division. The symbols of unity and perfection need reshaping. The author urges his readers away from a smug sense of their own perfection, to an awareness of their need to repent. Not only "those who went out from us" have sinned; all have sinned and need the expiation offered by Jesus.

Opening Exhortation (1, 1—2, 17)

First John opens with a poetic prologue (1, 1–4) that resembles the prologue to the Fourth Gospel (Jn 1, 1–8) in its deliberate allusion to Genesis 1, 1 ("in the beginning") and its emphasis on the "word of life." In the epistle's prologue, however, the stress is placed on the community's experience of the Word in Jesus. The writer testifies to what he has "seen and heard and touched" (cf Jn 19, 35). The experience, furthermore, is one shared by the readers. The language of fellowship dominates 1, 3f. The believers have fellowship with God the Father through Jesus. They are also, by that same agency, to have fellowship among themselves. A textual variant in 1, 4 illustrates the dense interweaving: manuscripts differ on reading "your" joy, or "our" joy. For this writer, both meanings coincide.

The section closes with another deliberately rhetorical statement of purpose: "I am writing to you because" (2, 12–14). Different groups in the community are addressed, but the message is basically one message and is more clearly spelled out by 2, 15–17: The church is to live by the "will of God" and not by the standards of the

"world." John's talk about "love of the world" here is very close to that in the letter of James about those who seek "friendship with the world" (Jas 4, 4) and means much the same thing. The writer does not forbid love for humanity; he denounces the "worldliness" that denies God's claim on his creation and bases existence on "sensual lust, enticement for the eyes, and a pretentious life" (2, 16).

Within the framework provided by the prologue and the statement of purpose, the rest of the opening section of this sermon serves to remind the readers of the need to live by the "message we have heard from him and proclaim to you" (1, 5).

The community has, to be sure, already heard that "God is light and there is no darkness in him at all" (1, 5). But now, because of the division in this community, a new sense of reality is required. Behavior must match their ideals. They can no longer simply assume that "we are the light" without hesitation. In fact, sin does occur among them, and they need to repent of it. They cannot claim to be "in the light" while their behavior shows that they "walk in darkness" (1, 6). That is a lie. Likewise, they cannot claim to "know God" while not keeping God's commandments (2, 4).

With a different vocabulary than James, but with a quite similar concern, John seeks to make his readers' actions conform to their convictions. And the great commandment of God that is to govern the life of the community is also, as in James, the law of love for neighbor, the test whether one is "in the light" or "in the darkness." For 1 John, it is not simply doctrinal correctness that spells true fellowship in the community, but ethical consistency.

First John places special emphasis on the role of Jesus as expiation for sin (1, 7; 2, 2) and advocate for believers (2, 1). The community's failure, demonstrated in its division into hostile parties, makes the need for intercession clear. They cannot do it alone. It also makes clear that "love" is not simply a state of mind, but something to be performed. In an atmosphere of hurt and separation, such performance is difficult.

The Divided Community (2, 18—3, 24)

The severity of the community's crisis is indicated by the fact that the writer thinks the end of all things is at hand. The author calls those who have left the community "antichrists." In apocalyptic literature, the presence of antichrist is a sign of the final tribulation (see Mt 24, 24). The theme of Jesus' return occurs again in 2, 28 and 3, 2. Typical of apocalyptic writing also is the exhortation to stand fast ("remain in him," 2, 24.27.28; 3, 6) and to avoid being deceived (2, 26).

The threat to the community is the greater because former members make it: "They went out from us." It is impossible for this writer to acknowledge fully that they had ever been of one spirit with the community: "They were not really of our number." What proof does he have? "If they had been, they would have remained" (2, 19). This is desperate logic. It indicates the shock given to a church devoted to unity and opposition to a world "out there" when it experiences conflict and division from within. The very identity of the community is called into question.

We cannot be sure exactly what the bone of contention was between those who left and those who stayed, only that it involved the proper understanding of Jesus. The author uses the language of "denial" and "confession" (2, 22f), and it seems clear that a formal doctrinal issue is at stake (see also 2 Jn 7). The briefest description of the deviance is that they deny "Jesus is the Christ." This obviously qualifies them to be "anti-Christs" in the narrow sense, but it is hard to imagine how such people could ever have been part of the messianic community. Such a denial is more appropriate to those who rejected Jesus as Messiah and remained Jews. To complicate matters, the author adds other features in 3, 23; 4, 2f; 5, 1.10. These make it appear that outsiders deny either the full divine origin of Jesus (that he is "God's son") or his full humanity (that he "came in the flesh"). In short, John is convinced his party has the full understanding of Jesus and his opponents do not; beyond that general statement we cannot advance.

Characteristic of this writing, however, is its ability to combine a claim to possession of "the truth" (2, 21), with a demand at the same time for transformation. The community is not yet perfect. They are indeed, to use one of their favorite expressions "children of God" (see Jn 1, 12), but they still need to mature. Only when he appears will they become "like him, for we shall see him as he is" (3, 2). Having the truth means living the

Docetism From a Greek word meaning "to seem," docetism is a heresy that claims Christ only seemed to be a human being, but was actually purely God.

Gnosticism From a Greek word meaning "to know," gnosticism is a heresy that claims knowledge, particularly secret knowledge, is the key to salvation, and that actions are of little or no importance.

truth, which demands strict ethical norms. In 3, 4–18, John develops the strongest possible contrast between the way of the world governed by the devil (4, 8; 5, 19) and the way revealed by God through the Messiah, Jesus. The way of the world is driven by the envy that leads to murder (the example of Cain, 3, 12; cf Jas 4, 1–5). The way Jesus reveals is exactly the opposite. This way does not take away life but gives it and in the giving of life reveals love: "The way we came to know love was that he laid down his life for us." The moral correlative follows at once: "so we ought to lay down our lives for our brothers" (3, 16). The New Testament contains no more direct connection between the work of the Messiah and the pattern of Christian existence. And lest anyone think the giving of life can be accomplished in attitude only or once for all, John spells it out in terms of the sharing of material possessions with the needy and concludes in a manner familiar to us from Paul and James: "Let us love not in word or speech but in deed and truth" (3, 18).

Finally, the claim to be in possession of the truth must be qualified by the deeper statement of humility in 3, 19–21. It is because they are in the hands of the one who is "greater than our hearts and knows everything" that they know they belong to the truth. It is not their accomplishment but his gift; their adequate response is to act as he did, in love (3, 23f).

The Remnant Community (4, 1—5, 21)

Because the community is divided, shared symbols are now being interpreted by opposing parties to the dispute. More careful judgment is therefore required. John reminds his readers of the need to "test the spirits to see whether they belong to God" (4, 1). As earlier he had spoken

Discernment

Within this remnant community it-self, discernment was also required. How could the church be sure it was living by the Spirit of God? Discernment, or "testing the spirits," has had a long tradition within Christianity. This is the process by which an individual or a community examines, in the light of the whole value structure of faith, what leads to God and a more perfect service of God and others and what detracts from this goal. Sometimes this is very difficult to distinguish.

That the Johannine community had the right confession of Jesus was taken for granted by its members. But John added the ethical dimension: Keeping the commandment of God showed their love for God (5, 2f). What is that commandment? That they love one another. John joined love for God and love for neighbor in such a way that they could not be separated; doing one was doing the other. "If anyone says, 'I love God,' but hates his brother, he is a liar" (4, 20).

There is a certain parallel to the beginning of Genesis in the Gospel of John when Christ breathes on the apostles and gives them the Holy Spirit (Jn 20, 22). It is the Spirit that secures the unity of the body (1 Cor 12, 13; Eph 2, 16.18; 4, 4). The Spirit holds the body together. Divisions, factions, hurt, and separation are always suspect. However, even these can masquerade as truth. The only way a community can judge itself as being "in the truth" is to measure its members' love for one another. Because human beings do not have direct access to God (4, 12; see Jn 1, 18), their relationship to God is always mediated by their relationship with each other (4, 12.20–21).

of the opponents as antichrists, now he applies to them the epithet "false prophets," another favorite designation in apocalyptic writing (see Mt 24, 11). In this case, the proper confession of Jesus is the criterion for true and false prophecy, certifying whether the speaker belongs to God or to "the world" (4, 2–4.13–16).

Within the remnant community itself, discernment is also required. How can the church be sure that it lives by the Spirit of God? That it has the right confession of Jesus is taken for granted. But John adds the ethical dimension; keeping the commandment of God shows their love for God (5, 2f). What is that commandment? It is that they are to love each other. John indissolubly joins love of God and neighbor; doing one is doing the other: "If anyone says 'I love God' but hates his brother, he is a liar" (4, 20). As earlier in 3, 15f, John grounds such love in the way God has revealed himself to be for humans in the sending of his son and Jesus' expiatory death: "In this is love, not that we have loved God, but that he loved us and sent his Son as expiation for our sins" (4, 10). Because humans do not have direct access to God (4, 12; see Jn 1, 18), their relationship to God is mediated by their relationships with each other (4, 12.20f).

The last section of this sermon is filled with a mixture of confidence and caution. The community living by God's love and faith is sure of victory "over the world" (5, 4f), even though "the whole world is under the power of the evil one" (5, 19). This is because the community's testimony is not isolated. It is supported by the testimony of Father, Son, and Spirit, each working in and through the church (5, 6–9). The community is confident of its gift of "eternal life" (2, 25; 5, 11.13). But the victory over sin and death (see 3, 7–14) is not yet complete.

• Idolatry is a temptation that needs to be avoided (5, 21);

• Perfect love has not yet driven out fear (4, 18);

• Mutual correction is required (5, 16f).

For this divided community, nothing can any longer be taken for granted; division has given new urgency to discernment (5, 20).

Questions for Discussion and Reflection
Group Sharing/Discussion

1. What are the characteristics of Johannine Christianity?

2. What is the context in the community for this letter of John?

3. Johannine Christians saw their life defined by a choice. What was this basic choice?

4. What was the cause of the division of the community into hostile camps?

5. What is the difference between their understanding of "anti-Christ" and the common "modern" understanding?

6. According to John, how do you express your love for your neighbor?

In Our Lives

1. According to 1 John, "the whole world is under the power of the evil one" (5, 19). Have you experienced this evil of the world? How has the Christian community, living by love and faith, nourished you to deal with this evil?

2. John reminds his readers of the need to "test the spirits to see whether they belong to God" (4, 1). How do you test the "spirits" in living your life?

3. Our relation with God is not direct; it is mediated (4, 12.20f) by relationships with each other. Name some specific relationships where this is true for you, that is, some specific

relationships where you meet God through other people."

Individual/Personal Reflection/Action

1. "The way we came to know love was that he laid down his life for us . . . so we ought to lay down our lives for" one another (3, 16). The work of Jesus connects to the pattern of our Christian life. Have you come to know love by knowing "he laid down his life" for you? How do you nourish this love? How do you lay down your life for your neighbor?

2. For many Catholics, examination of conscience has been measured by a list of faults. What is the difference between awareness of sinfulness and simply making a "grocery list" of faults? How can a parish community discern whether it is "walking in the light"?

3. The Christian Churches of the East have a tradition of praying the "Jesus Prayer" below as a kind of mantra. It is said quietly over and over while leaving one's heart open to the action of the Holy Spirit. Try this prayer style each morning when you wake up:

"Lord, Jesus Christ, Son of the Living God, have mercy on me, a sinner."

2 JOHN READING GUIDE

At a Glance

Who is the main player?	John the Presbyter
What should I look for?	Note the concern for mutual love, truth, and integrity. These are the dimensions of establishing and maintaining the community.
When was this written?	At the end of the first century, probably written by a disciple of the apostle John
Where did these events occur?	Probably in Ephesus
Why was this book written?	Second John is a letter of introduction to the community to be read before the sermon is delivered.
What is the story?	The function of this letter is to identify the author, to emphasize its main teaching, and to suggest some practical actions to be taken by the community.

Before Beginning

A Cover Letter to the Church

Unless 2 John and 3 John are connected to the same moment of crisis that generated 1 John, it is hard to explain their preservation by a local church, their exchange between churches, and their eventual inclusion in the New Testament canon. In the Reading Guide to 1 John (RG 444), the suggestion is made that all three letters were sent in a single packet by the emissary Demetrius to the local leader Gaius (see 3 Jn), who was still loyal to "the Elder" in the dispute dividing Johannine Christianity into hostile factions.

Whereas 1 John lacks all qualities of a letter or epistle and appears as a sermon to be delivered aloud to an assembly (or even a number of assemblies), 2 John bears the marks of a genuine letter. It has the formal elements of greeting (1–3), body (4–12), and farewell (13). It mentions the desire of the writer to visit the addressees (12). Unlike 3 John, however, which is addressed to an individual, 2 John is written to the "chosen Lady" and her children (1). The designation is almost certainly an honorary title for the church itself. The argument that it refers to a specific woman leader is doubtful, if the rest of the reconstruction here being suggested makes sense. The "children," of course, are the ones really being addressed; the second-person verbs are predominantly in the plural.

The symbols of Johannine Christianity are very much in evidence. Notice the emphasis on "truth" (1.2.3) and on "walking in the truth" (4); on "keeping the commandment," which is not new but from the beginning (5); on love for one another as the fulfillment of that commandment (6); on the creation of mutual joy as the mark of fellowship (12). Surely, such a cluster of distinctive themes makes best sense when read together with 1 John.

What distinguishes 2 John is its function. In 3 John 9, the Elder says that he "is writing" (or "wrote") something to the church. In all likelihood, this refers to 1 John, the exhortation to a remnant community. Second John, then, is undoubtedly a letter of introduction to the community, to be read before the sermon is delivered, to identify its author, to emphasize its main teaching, and to suggest some practical actions to be taken by the community. These may or may not be fully in accord with the spirit of 1 John, but they are certainly recognizable as a response to the crisis signaled by 3 John.

Strategies for Survival

Again we meet the split between those who "walk in truth" and the "many deceivers who have gone out into the world" (7). As in 1 John, these are designated antichrists because they "do not acknowledge Jesus Christ as coming in the flesh." In the Reading Guide to 1 John, we suggest how difficult it is to determine precisely what this denial implies. For the Elder, however, the opponents appear as "progressives" who have gone too far in their interpretation and no longer "remain in the teaching of the Christ" (or "about" the Christ). The Elder's community is therefore portrayed as defending the traditional understanding of Jesus. The importance of right doctrine is underscored by the equation: having Christ is having God (see 1 Jn 4, 3). For Johannine Christianity, the unique mediation of salvation by Jesus is axiomatic. He alone is the "way and the truth and the life" (Jn 14, 6). The lesson is clear: Misconstruing the mediator means missing the good news entirely. If the Elder's readers do not hold to the proper understanding, they will "lose what they worked for."

The community crisis is so severe that the Elder calls for the extraordinary practice of excommunication. They are neither to offer heretics hospitality nor even to greet them as brothers (10). Notice the connection, everywhere assumed in the New Testament, between message and messenger. Physical fellowship implies spiritual unanimity. Thus, "whoever greets him shares in his evil works" (11). Only those who deliver the proper doctrine are to be welcomed. Here the Elder advocates the same practice of shunning and exclusion of which he accuses Diotrephes in 3 John. The battle is obviously a very bitter one.

It is difficult to know what positive instruction one should draw from these ancient fragments of hostile conflicts. Perhaps it is important for the church to remember that in every age it has never been easy to establish or to secure its identity; deviance and dispute are part of community life. Perhaps also, however, it is important for the church in every age to reflect whether proper doctrine is more important than the fellowship of love. Even in an age of ecumenism, that issue remains unresolved.

Questions for Discussion and Reflection
Group Sharing/Discussion
1. The crisis is so severe that the Elder calls for excommunication of the dissidents. How would you describe excommunication?
In Our Lives
1. Only those who deliver the proper doctrine are to be welcomed into the Community. But

those who greet "heretics" share in their evil works (11). They are not even to be offered hospitality (10). What do you think are the reasons for these community rules? Do you agree with them? Would they be proper for the Church community today? Do they conflict with the message Jesus preaches? How?

Individual/Personal Reflection/Action

1. The task of establishing and maintaining the community identity is difficult for any age. In the epistles of John, the community faced critical difficulties from within the community in the

form of two philosophies:

a. Docetism–the heresy that claims that Jesus only seemed to be human, but was actually purely God; and

b. Gnosticism–a heresy claiming that knowledge is the key to salvation and that actions are really not important.

Do you feel these heresies still infect the Catholic community? Reflect on your own image of Jesus and your understanding of salvation. Recall how these truths are talked about and taught in your parish.

3 JOHN READING GUIDE

At a Glance

Who are the main players?	John the Presbyter Demetrius Gaius
What should I look for?	Notice the hospitality and autonomy of the local church.
When was this written?	At the end of the first century
Where did these events occur?	Probably Ephesus
Why was this book written?	The author's purpose is to secure hospitality and material support for his missionaries. He is writing to another member of the church who welcomed them in the past.
What is the story?	The ancient world had protocol for letters such as these. It was natural for a missionary movement to certify its apostles with such letters to ensure their safety and the hospitality due such "co-workers in the truth."

Before Beginning

A Letter of Recommendation

The New Testament contains two letters written explicitly to individuals: Paul's letter to Philemon, and the Elder's letter to Gaius, which we know as 3 John. Both Paul and John take up matters of community concern, while having the same specific function, that of recommending the bearer of the letter to the addressee. In 3 John, the Elder recommends to the local church leader his emissary Demetrius. He has a good reputation from all, and "we give our testimonial as well, and you know our testimony is true" (12).

The ancient world had conventions for these letters. They were widely used in early Christianity, as we learn elsewhere in Paul's correspondence (see 2 Cor 3, 1; Rom 16). It was natural for a missionary movement to certify its agents (apostles) with such letters to ensure them a safe

reception and the hospitality due such "co-workers in the truth" (8). Receiving such messengers, as we see also in 2 John, meant accepting their message as well, an understanding widespread in Judaism. This principle became problematic when the movement itself divided into hostile parties. Third John points us directly to such a situation.

Third John provides the key to the historical circumstances presupposed by 1 and 2 John (see the relevant reading guides for more). Without it, their religious emphasis would be less intelligible. And without 3 John, an appreciation for the travails of early Christianity would be appreciably diminished.

The Politics of Ecclesial Power

Third John reveals clearly that the struggle for the soul of Johannine Christianity involved structure as much as symbol, power as much as piety. Indeed, the two levels of conflict were intimately connected. On one side we see the Elder writing to his loyal colleague Gaius. On the other side is Diotrephes, who "loves to dominate." Diotrephes not only asserts authority over Gaius at the local level, but he also refuses to acknowledge the authority of the Elder over the regional church. The author says that when he comes, he will "draw attention to what he is doing" (10), but this is a small threat to a rebellious local chieftain. The position of the Elder is threatened. He needs the personal loyalty of Gaius, and his financial assistance as well.

We are thereby brought to the political maneuvering at the heart of this battle. Diotrephes is not content to "spread evil nonsense" about the Elder. He takes positive action to suppress the Elder's authority. He refuses himself to receive the Elder's delegates, and, even more, Diotrephes expels from the church those who want to receive them (10). We can understand why the Elder appreciates Gaius's reception of Demetrius, and we can grasp the significance of verses 5–8. The Elder needs to provide an alternative source of hospitality and missionary outfitting, because Diotrephes has taken up a position among those who "went out from us" (1 Jn 2, 19) and no longer supports the Elder's teaching.

Gaius is being asked to receive Demetrius (and his companions) as well as equip them for their next stage of travel. Perhaps by implication the Elder's future emissaries are also included in the request. Because the Johannine missionaries accept nothing from the "pagans" ("the world"), the need for a network of hospitality and financial support is obvious (7). As in 2 John, financial sharing is tantamount to spiritual fellowship. Helping such missionaries is being "co-workers in the truth" (8). It is clear as well that both parties to the dispute are using the same tactics. Here, Diotrephes is the one shunning and excommunicating. But in 2 John we find the Elder advocating the same actions among his followers.

The hurtful struggles of early Christianity are not terribly edifying, but they are instructive. Christians who long for a golden age of harmony should be reminded that there never was one. Among history's benefits is liberation from myth. And edifying or not, these letters testify to another truth. The struggle for identity is never simply a matter of ideas or even symbols. It inevitably involves the messy realities of money and political power.

Questions for Discussion and Reflection

Group Sharing/Discussion

1. Who was this letter written to?
2. Why was it written?
3. Explain the relations of the Elder, Gaius, and Diotrephes

In Our Lives

1. Third John reveals clearly that the struggle in the Johannine community was not limited to ideas but that politics and money were involved also. How does this letter show this complexity? How does this show its face in the church today? What can your parish do in the face of it today?

Individual/Personal Reflection/Action

1. St. Augustine said that Christians should manifest unity in essentials, diversity in all other things, and charity in everything. How can the Church experience diversity and still profess unity? What are the core essentials in your vision of your faith? How do you nourish this vision?

2. What has been your experience of diversity in the Catholic Church?

JUDE READING GUIDE

At a Glance

Who is the main player?	"Jude"
What should I look for?	Take time to reflect on the Doxology, verse 24 of the letter; the letter is famous for this. Consider how behavior affects the unity of the Eucharistic community.
When was it written?	We do not know the author or his circumstance nor do we have a secure intellectual context. Many scholars consider

Jude a pseudonym and date the work from the end of the first century or later. Some think that the author is Jude, named in the Gospels among the relatives of Jesus.

Where did these events occur?

The content of the letter, including the discussion of ideas from Gnosticism, points to the Gentile world.

Why was this book written?

Jude is an argument against false teachers and an exhortation to his readers to remain steadfast.

What is the story?

Jude accuses his opponents of immoral behavior during the Eucharistic meals and also of being selfish and divisive. He charges them with sexual immorality, greed, slander, and living for themselves. In short they live on a worldly plane, devoid of the Spirit.

Before Beginning

The Obscurity of Jude

Although Jude is among the shortest writings in the New Testament, it bristles with difficulties. Some of these difficulties have to do with placing the composition in the historical development of early Christianity. Others involve grasping its language, which has a number of obscure allusions. The two sorts of problems are related. Our ignorance of the author and his circumstances prevents us from having a secure context for reading the letter. But because Jude so obviously was responding to some kind of specific crisis, every attempt must be made to construct such a context if the letter is to yield any sense at all.

The NAB introduction to Jude states the majority scholarly opinion on most of the questions concerning authorship and occasion. Jude is considered a general epistle of relatively late date. It is an attack on false teachers, probably representing some form of Gnosticism (an early deviant form of Christianity stressing "self-fulfillment"). Another reading of the evidence suggests that Jude could have been written at virtually any period and was concerned less with false teaching than with bad behavior. This minority view will be developed in the paragraphs to follow. The main point, of course, is to make as good sense as possible out of the letter.

Literary Connections

Far more puzzling than the identity of Jude is the placement of his letter among other early Christian literature. The author mentions an earlier draft he had begun, when the crisis among his readers demanded his turning attention to the polemic now being read by them (3). What was that earlier version? A connected issue is the relation of Jude to 2 Peter. Everyone recognizes that the material in 2 Peter 2 is similar to that in Jude 5–13. Less clear is whether one author depended on the other, or both relied on a shared earlier tradition. Neither should the resemblance be overstated. Jude is not simply a source for 2 Peter or vice versa. Each author takes the same material and uses it in a way that is different from the other one.

Further puzzles are provided by Jude's literary allusions. He cites examples of sinners being punished. Some are readily apparent from the Bible, although a few (like Balaam) may derive as well from Jewish biblical interpretation. Jude also cites the apocryphal writing known as 1 Enoch as though it were Scripture (14). And his version of the dispute between Michael and Satan over the body of Moses appears to derive from another apocryphal writing, "The Assumption of Moses" (9). His reference to the "words spoken by the apostles" (17) is no clearer, because it is more an amalgam of early Christian statements on the end-time (e.g., see Mk 13, 22; 1 Tm 4, 1–3) than a specific citation.

That an author could assume familiarity with such sources among his readers seems to presuppose either a Jewish-Christian readership, or a Gentile one familiar with Jewish apocrypha. What the ancient readers presumably understood, we do not, and the lack of literary context continues to make this letter obscure to present-day readers.

Historical Setting

Writings like 2 Peter and Jude remind us how little we know about early Christianity apart from the chronology provided by Acts and Paul's letters. We cannot fit these books into any development we know about and must rely on guesswork. Every hypothesis, furthermore, is based solely on the text itself. Precision concerning what the text does and does not say is obviously critical to the value of any reconstruction.

Jude clearly takes a polemical stand against opponents and exhorts its readers to remain steadfast. Contrary to the usual opinion, however, the text contains no clear indication that Jude was opposing "false teachers" or that they were teaching any "heresy." Their "scorning of Lordship" (vv. 4.8) seems to have been practical rather than theoretical. Jude attacks immoral behavior rather than false teaching. So thorough is his disparagement that it is hard to know even what they were doing. He specifically accuses them of disrupting the community love feasts. The term is usually taken to mean eucharistic meals. They are also accused of carousing and of looking after only themselves (literally: "shepherding themselves," 12). He also calls their behavior divisive (19). Otherwise, Jude uses all the standardized charges common to the polemic of the ancient world: They are sexually immoral (7), greedy (11.16), slanderous (15), and living for their own desires (16). In short, they "live on the natural plane, devoid of the Spirit" (19). They "pervert the grace of our God into licentiousness" (4).

Living by God's Grace

Letters of Paul such as 1 Corinthians attest how difficult it was for the early Christians to translate the gift of God (grace) into consistent patterns of moral behavior. Legitimate disagreement could exist on matters of diet, work, use of possessions, and the like. It was not immediately obvious in all cases what "Life in the Spirit" meant behaviorally. In the case of Jude, however, it appears that disagreement has overstepped the boundary into true moral deviance, hence, the outrage of the author. The opponents are "perverting the gift."

Jude's first line of defense is an attack on the immoral people. He tries to demonstrate from Scripture how there have always been such troublemakers, and they have always been punished. These will be punished as well. In contrast to 2 Peter 2, in which the emphasis is on the power of God to judge the righteous and unrighteous, in Jude the stress is entirely on the punishment of the rebellious.

The polemic is not random but carefully argued, with some rhetorical polish. Notice the repetition of "these people" in verses 8, 10, 12, 16, and 19, which brings the examples of old to bear on the present circumstances. Jude also plays on the Greek words for "keep" in verses 1, 6, 13, 21, and 24. His opponents fail to "keep their place," but Jude's readers are to "keep themselves in the love of God" who is, in turn, able to "keep them from stumbling."

Jude's second line of defense is to edify ("build up") his readers in their "most holy faith" (20). He reminds them that God dealt with troubles like these from of old, and in fact the apostles of Jesus had foretold the emergence of such rebellious "scoffers" (17f). He reassures them that they are being "kept safe for Jesus Christ" despite this turmoil (1). Jude does not suggest that it is the believers' role to punish the reprobate. He exhorts them to avoid such immoral behavior (23) and to build up their own faith. If the opponents are "devoid of spirit," the believers are to "pray in the Spirit" (20). But their love for God is to be demonstrated in an attitude of mercy and care for those who waver and even for those who appear to be lost (22f).

Jude's witness is a limited one. But the use of moral outrage is not entirely exhausted by the circumstances of the first century. The tendency to turn grace into libertinism is a perennial one. Combining justifiable outrage at license with mercy for the licentious is a delicate and difficult art. Few writings have carried it off as well as Jude.

Questions for Discussion and Reflection
Group Sharing/Discussion
1. Why is Jude obscure to present-day readers?
2. What does Jude teach concerning the attitude

of his community toward those who waver in their faith (22f)?

3. In the light of your reading of Jude, what is the difference between legitimate differences and moral deviances in a Christian community?

4. In an argumentative tone Jude accuses his opponents: They "live on the natural plane, devoid of the Spirit" (19). Name the specific actions that Jude condemns.

In Our Lives

1. Jude reminds his readers that "shepherding oneself" is a "division" (19) in the Eucharistic meal of the community (12). Discuss the meaning and importance of this statement both in his text and in today's world.

2. Share the experience of how the Eucharist is the sign and source of unity. Describe how individualism looks in our life and culture. Explain how this helps or weakens the unity of the Eucharistic community.

Individual/Personal Reflection/Action

1. Read verses 20–23. Take time to meditate on their personal meaning. Consider how these words of Jude are heard by present-day Catholics.

2. Pray and reflect upon Jude's ending doxology:
"To the one who is able to keep you from stumbling and to present you unblemished and exultant, in the presence of his glory, to the only God, our savior, through Jesus Christ our Lord be glory, majesty, power, and authority from ages past, now, and for ages to come."

REVELATION READING GUIDE

At a Glance

Who are the main players?	God Jesus Christ John People of the seven churches of Asia
What should I look for?	Do not read this literally, nor as a prediction of coming events. Understanding the literary form is very important in reaching the religious message of Revelation. This is apocalyptic literature, which contains an account of visions in symbolic and allegorical language borrowed extensively from the Old Testament. Look for the use of symbolic colors, metals, garments, and numbers (e.g., *four* signifies the world or wholeness [as in four directions], *six* imperfections, *seven* totality, *twelve* Israel's tribes or the apostles. *one thousand* immensity).
When was this written?	This is an exhortation to Christians to stand firm in their faith despite the threat of adversity and martyrdom. The date is probably near the end of Domitian's reign as Roman emperor, A.D. 81–96.
Who wrote this book?	Probably a disciple of John the apostle writing to the churches in Asia Minor
Why was this book written?	The book of Revelation can only adequately be understood against the historical background that occasioned its writing. It is composed as resistance literature to meet a crisis. The book suggests the crisis was ruthless persecution of the early church by Roman authorities.
What is the story?	John has been exiled to the rocky island of Patmos, a Roman penal colony, because of his Christian faith. The voice of his prophecy is directed to the seven Christian churches of Asia Minor. The author's message is that the

What is the story? *(cont.)*

victory of God over evil has been accomplished through the death and resurrection of Jesus, and the faithful who have been killed already share his victory in heaven. The religious message is simple: to the faithful, it says, "hold on"; to the wavering, it declares, "stand fast." It is a message of hope and consolation and challenge for all who dare to believe.

Before Beginning

A Book of Christian Prophecy

The book of Revelation makes for difficult reading. Many interpretations of it over the centuries have led to disastrous consequences both for individuals and communities. The fundamental error is to take Revelation as a literal set of predictions from the past about current events. Reading Revelation that way has been popular for a long time, but it has become an obsession for many contemporaries. Such readings have successively been disconfirmed by facts; the "end-time" has been awaited many times without occurring. Such readings have caused the distortion of lives. Many have abandoned livelihoods and loved ones to meet the New Jerusalem, only to have their dreams destroyed. Such readings also miss the real religious message of Revelation. They reduce its value to that of an astrological chart.

Although the text itself virtually calls out for such an interpretation, with its promise to reveal "what must happen soon" (22, 18–19), it is critical to recognize that just such statements are standard features of a specific literary genre of the ancient world, called apocalyptic. Two convictions should guide faithful study of Revelation.

1. First, as with all the biblical writings, the Word of God was addressed first to the original audience; a text's "fuller" meaning for successive ages is secondary and never to be divorced from that first, historical, meaning.

2. Second, as in all literature, religious or otherwise, literary genre dictates the way meaning is conveyed.

Newspapers and poetry do not communicate their respective "truths" in identical ways. Knowing the conventions of a literary form is necessary to intelligent reading.

Revelation as Apocalyptic

What is Apocalyptic?

"Apocalypse" is derived from a Greek word, *apokalypsis,* that means "taking away the veil" (the Latin word for this is *revelatio*). The "veil" is the confusing flow of events in the reader's present-day environment, which the particular apocalyptic writing intends to interpret, so that the reader can learn the "true meaning" of history leading to the events of the present. In addition, because apocalyptic writings are often produced in conditions of political oppression, the message is delivered in a coded manner that will not be apparent to the outside reader, particularly one who is a member or agent of the oppressing group.

Beginning at least with the book of Daniel in the Old Testament, the apocalyptic style was widely used in Judaism during the New Testament period. Generated by persecution from without and the threat of apostasy from within, this "literature of the oppressed" quickly gained certain standard features:

1. Revelations about the future are experienced in dreams or visions.

2. The insights are communicated through a complex symbolism involving numbers, animals, and cosmic phenomena.

3. The element of prediction is actually a fiction.

4. The seer interprets events of his own age, using a figure of the past (such as Enoch) or an angelic being as a spokesperson.

These literary features serve to express an interpretation of history. Apocalyptic writing defends God's justice. Events appear to be under the control of evil people or even satanic powers, because those devoted to God are being persecuted. Such is the "present age." But apocalyptic literature places God's blessing in a future time, "the age to come." Just when things become humanly impossible on earth, God will intervene (as through a Messiah) to save his own, and thus inaugurate the "kingdom of God."

Apocalyptic literature reconciles the conviction that God controls history with the experience that suggests God does not. The religious message is simple. To the faithful, it says, "hold on"; to the wavering, "stand fast." It offers the hope of eventual vindication to those now oppressed but remaining loyal to the one God.

Revelation as Prophecy

Revelation fits the apocalyptic genre well. It has visions, animals, numbers, and cosmic catastrophes. It has a two-age interpretation of history. And its basic religious message is a call for the "endurance of the holy ones" (13, 10; 14, 12). In other ways, however, Revelation transcends the genre. The author is not a fictional sage from the past but a leader well known to his readers. The voice of prophecy is directed explicitly (and not in coded fashion) to the seven churches of Asia Minor in chapters 2 and 3. Most importantly, the turn of the ages has already begun. The victory of God over evil has in principle been accomplished through the death and resurrection of Jesus; even more impressively, the faithful who have been killed already share in that victory in heaven.

The self-understanding of the church in this writing is thoroughly prophetic. Those who follow Jesus are "servants and prophets and saints" (11, 18). Their witness is the "spirit of prophecy" (19, 10). Jesus is the first and "faithful witness" (1, 5) whose mission they continue. The nature of their prophecy is to bear witness to the reality of God in the world. In the letters of chapters 2 and 3, this is expressed as fidelity in face of corruption or apostasy. In the visions of chapters 4 through 21, it is expressed as loyalty in face of the idolatrous claims of the state and even of possible death.

The Opening Vision (1, 1–20)

The prologue (1, 1–3) and the epilogue (22, 6–21) provide an explicit prophetic framework for the entire work and reveal a self-conscious literary awareness as well (cf. 1, 3; 22, 18). The understanding of prophecy as witness, which becomes the major theme of the book, is sounded at once (1, 2).

The popularity of letter writing in early Christianity is shown by the fact that this apocalyptic writing contains letters to the seven churches of Asia Minor (Rv 2–3), and even has an epistolary greeting to introduce the work (1, 4–8). The author identifies himself as one known to his readers and recounts the vision that provides the basis for the rest of the book. The phrasing of 1, 9 suggests that John is on the Greek island of Patmos as a punishment for his witness to Jesus. The vision that now comforts him becomes an exhortation to all who are likewise oppressed.

The Risen Jesus is encountered as the Son of Man (the central figure in much apocalyptic writing), described in the most transcendent terms available. The reader is now in the realm of visions, which means the realm of symbols. The terms are obviously not meant literally, any more than are the later fantastic descriptions of heaven. The terms used here and elsewhere are not fresh-minted but are the coinage of biblical

Historical Dates to Assist Understanding of the Book of Revelation

1. The death and resurrection of Jesus: the beginning of the 30s.

2. The martyrdom of Peter and Paul and Nero's persecution of the Christians: the 60s.

3. The capture of Jerusalem and the destruction of the Temple: 70–73.

4. After the destruction of the Temple, conflicts between Jews and Christians increased, resulting in a complete break around the year 90.

5. The Roman emperor Domitian (81–90) imposed the practice of emperor worship. Christians were often suspect and objects of persecution because of their refusal to participate in this ritual.

symbolism. Of all apocalyptic writings, Revelation most artfully weaves together the themes of classical prophecy, especially of the prophet Ezekiel. The footnotes and cross-references in the NAB will repay the effort required. One should quickly realize that Revelation is a self-conscious and complex literary construction.

The Son of Man appears with the stars in his hands, standing amid seven lampstands. Revelation makes clear from the start:

1. It is the risen and powerful Lord (in cosmic control) who reveals, and

2. That he is present to the churches (1, 20), the concerns of which are taken up in the letters that follow.

Letters to the Seven Churches (2, 1—3, 22)

In what are literally "spirit letters" (see chs 2, 7)

What is the Spirit Saying to the Churches? Read the Letters aloud and fill the spaces:					
	Addressed to whom?	Christ described as . . .	Judgment?	Conversion?	What is promised?
Ephesus 2, 1–7					
Smyrna 2, 8–11					
Pergamum 2, 12–17					
Thyatira 2, 18–29					
Sardis 3, 1–6					
Philadelphia 3, 7–13					
Laodicea 3, 14–22					

This activity is based on a chart in Jean-Pierre Prevost's book, *How to Read the Apocalypse* (New York: Crossroad, 1993), p. 70.

from the Risen Jesus, seven churches of well known cities in Asia Minor receive individualized prophecies. Revelation understands "prophecy" not as predictions of the future but as exhortations to remain faithful to the integrity of their calling. The trials and lapses of the Christians in these communities are here put on remarkable display. We also hear fragments of sayings (such as in 2, 3) that occur elsewhere in the New Testament literature (see 1 Thes 5, 2 and Mk 13, 33).

The letters all follow the same format. There is a greeting, followed by an elaborate designation of Jesus. The Risen Lord analyzes each community's spiritual condition and concludes with words of warning or of promise. The description of the church's struggles show how they faced opposition from without (as from the Jews), but even more, division within (as with the Nicolaitans). Corruption, too, appears as a vivid possibility. Typical for Johannine literature, the opposition is pictured in terms of false prophecy (2, 20). The focus of praise and of persuasion in these letters is endurance.

The imagery of the letters is lush. Who can resist the almost fairy-tale quality of this statement: "I shall also give a white amulet upon which is inscribed a new name, which no one knows except the one who receives it" (2, 17)? Beneath the poetry, however, lies grim reality. The difficulty in these letters of maintaining loyalty in the face of social exclusion and human laxity is raised, in the visions that follow, to the level of a cosmic conflict between the Lord and the forces of evil.

God and the Lamb in Heaven (4, 1—5, 14)

John is "caught up in Spirit" (4, 2), and the rest of Revelation consists in the visions he experienced in his ecstatic state. The vision is a staple of apocalyptic writing. It is found with equal frequency in early Jewish mysticism, called Merkabah, or "throne-chariot" mysticism (*merkabhah,* the Hebrew word for "chariot," comes from Ezekiel's vision of the heavenly chariot in Ez 1, 4–28). In prayer, the adept ascended through the heavens to the throne of God's presence. Much of the celestial furniture here resembles that of the Merkabah writings: the jewel-encrusted throne room (4, 3f); the sea of

glass (4, 6); the angelic creatures (4, 6–9); and the numinous hymns sung in praise of God (5, 9–13).

A dramatic departure from standard symbolism is the appearance of "the lamb that seemed to have been slain" (5, 6). Jesus is also called "Lamb of God" in John's Gospel (1, 29; see also Jn 19, 36, a reference to the Passover lamb). It is a bold stroke to picture Jesus in such paradoxical animal terms, but this verse is in a sense the key to understanding Revelation. The salient aspect of the lamb is its sacrificial function: Jesus was slain. But this lamb is also "the lion of the tribe of Judah," who has triumphed over death (5, 5). The ruling power of the universe is identified with self-sacrificing love. In a powerful assertion of Jesus' status after his resurrection, the lamb is at "the right hand of the one who sat on the throne" (5, 7; see Ps 110, 1). Both figures receive the praise of the heavenly creatures (5, 9–11) and indeed of all creation (5, 13f).

The special character of the visions of Revelation is shown by the problem of "the scroll" (5, 1). It contains the secrets to be revealed, and because of its use in Ezekiel, it is immediately recognizable as a symbol for prophecy (10, 8–11, and Ez 2, 9–3, 4). Because of his resurrection, Jesus is empowered to open the scroll (5, 5). What follows, therefore, is both a revelation of and from Jesus Christ (see 1, 1). The visions will show "what must happen afterwards" (4, 1), but the reader is not frightened, knowing from this first vision that the fundamental victory has already been accomplished.

Visions of Cosmic Conflict (6, 1—16, 21)

The next section of Revelation is the most difficult to make sense of, and, not surprisingly, the most worked over for signs of the end. The candidates selected to fit the profile of the "Beast" with the number 666 (13, 18) have ranged from Nero to Hitler.

The visions are so structured as to give the illusion of temporal sequence, linked together as they are by the phrase "and then I saw . . . " It is indeed tempting to translate a series of visions into a sequence of historical events, so readers have tried to compute the overlapping series of

The Cosmic Conflict

On one side we see all the "beasts" who oppose the faithful: the dragon (12, 1–8), the first beast (13, 1–10), and the second beast (13, 11–17). These are not separate enemies but successive masks of the one force of evil. As in modern horror films, the destruction of one gives rise to another more horrifying still. Beneath the different manifestations, one visible enemy is most prevalent: the idolatrous state that persecutes the saints, enslaves them, and seeks to kill them (13, 7–18).

On the other side are those loyal to God, the "servants, prophets, and saints" (11, 18; 19, 9f). They continue Jesus' own faithful witness to God by witnessing to Jesus. By so doing, they reject the idolatrous claims of the state on their obeisance. They suffer the consequences, some of them by shedding blood. Revelation establishes the connection between "witness" and "martyr" by the disciples' imitation of Jesus' death.

sevens: seals (6, 1–17; 8, 1), trumpets (8, 1—9, 21; 11, 15), plagues (15, 1–8), and bowls (16, 1–20). But neither the events reported by headlines nor elaborate literary analyses have ever satisfactorily unlocked this dense poetry. It is in fact more likely that all the visions repeat the same basic message. The saints on earth, locked in conflict with hostile forces, find a cosmic counterpart in the struggle between God and Satan.

The prophetic self-consciousness of this church is most clearly stated in the account of the two witnesses (11, 1–13). This earthly interlude shows two people, who both "witness" and "testify" (the terms are interchangeable). They are killed in imitation of Jesus (11, 7). They are also called into heaven (11, 12). The vignette describes the conviction of Revelation that those who share Jesus' death also share his triumph in heaven. Thus, alternating with scenes of suffer-

ing on earth below are serene descriptions of the saints in heaven celebrating the anticipated and certain victory of the Lamb (5, 9f; 6, 9–11; 7, 4–7; 14, 1–5; 15, 2–4). In standard apocalyptic literature, history moves downward to ever more dismal circumstances, until God finally intervenes. In Revelation, however, the final outcome is not in doubt. Not only Jesus but also those "defeated" with him by evil already share in the resurrection triumph. The earthly conquest is just a matter of tidying up.

It is useless to tease such poetry into a train schedule for current events. The vision here is not one of history unfolding like clockwork; it is a religious vision of God's ultimate conquest despite current appearances. Once the reader lets go of the obsessive "need to know" that twists beauty into charts and tables, it is possible to wonder at the powerful poetic and religious imagination at work in these glorious images.

Punishment of Babylon
(17, 1—20, 15)

The masks fall away, revealing as the real enemy of God's people the Roman Empire, "the great harlot who lives near the many waters" (17, 1). Rome is called Babylon (17, 5) because in the biblical tradition it was Babylon above all that symbolized the desecration of the Temple and the exile of the people. In typical apocalyptic fashion, the sequence of events is laid out: God has given temporary rule to this evil empire to accomplish his ends. It does battle against the lamb and the people.

The persecution and suffering were undoubtedly real. These Christians were faced with the choices of all who suffer oppression. Were they to resist violently and seek the overthrow of Rome? That was futile as well as contrary to their ethos. Were they simply to cooperate? That would be to lose their identity. They chose the path of passive resistance. They did not fight the beast, but neither would they do its bidding. The path of martyrdom, however slow or fast, is not easy. For those who survive, the psychic toll is considerable. Anger at the enemy can easily turn inward; patient endurance is hard. They were convinced that "the lamb will conquer" (17, 14), but in their earthly condition they had not yet seen it happen. Rome's fall is therefore described in delicious detail. The pent-up fury of the oppressed is released in glee over the degradation of the oppressor. Much of this is obviously and literally wish fulfillment, the stuff of fantasy. The anger of a downtrodden people is deflected to a punishing God.

The end-time reveals how "the words of God are accomplished" (17, 17). The "Word of God" himself (19, 13) leads the climactic battle and inaugurates the messianic age, when the saints "will reign with Christ for a thousand years" (20, 4–6). But this is not yet the end. There is another outbreak of demonic destruction (20, 7–10) and the tossing of the Devil into the fire, then the resurrection of the dead for final judgment (20, 11–15). These stages lack poetry, but the final vision overcomes this deficiency.

The New Creation
(21, 1—22, 21)

The conclusion to Revelation is a fitting conclusion to the Bible as a whole. The vision of a new creation (21, 1) is central to the New Testament (e.g., see 2 Cor 5, 17). The Christian experience of Christ was an absolute beginning, rooted in the ever-new life of God himself. God can say, "Behold, I make all things new" (21, 5) because God is "the Alpha and the Omega, the beginning and the end" of all things (21, 6; 22, 13). As Genesis began with the creation by a word, so the vision of the end-time recapitulates that beginning: Creation is renewed.

The hope expressed by Revelation is not simply that souls should be saved after death, or that evil should be conquered, or even that saints should reign for a thousand years over a burnt-out terrain. The hope is that creation itself will be transformed. So the sight of a "New Jerusalem coming down out of heaven from God" is the vision of a civilized order, one that is intrinsically holy in the proper sense. Human society is based on the recognition of God's power and presence. There is no place for those, now, who refuse the "dwelling place of God with the human race" (21, 3.7f).

In this city, there is not even need for "religion" as a separate compartment of life. The temple of the city is "the Lord God almighty and the Lamb" (21, 22). And all the city's people will be priests of [the Lord] God (20, 6), showing at last

that the fundamental human vocation is praise of God (22, 9). There need be no division between peoples. Nothing is here accursed (22, 3). The nations will walk by the light of the Lamb (21, 24), and the trees of the city "serve as medicine for the nations" (22, 2). And what medicine! There will be "no more death or mourning, wailing or pain, [for] the old order has passed away" (21, 4).

Great harm has come to those who have tried by force to make this vision a reality, and establish a thousand-year reign of the saints on earth. Great despair has come to the utopians who have tried on the basis of goodwill to construct a society like the New Jerusalem.

The vision has its value precisely as challenge, as ever-receding prophecy to all human effort for renewal. This renewal does not come about by human cunning but by God's gift. So compelling is the vision that no one who hears it can help joining in the plaintive cry of the epilogue, "Amen! Come, Lord Jesus!" The epilogue also reminds us that we are still in the in-between time when the world is not re-created. There is still need for the witness of prophecy and for endurance of the saints, for "the wicked still act wickedly, and the filthy still [are] filthy. The righteous must still do right, and the holy still be holy" (22, 11).

Questions for Discussion and Reflection
Group Sharing/Discussion
1. Why was John on the Isle of Patmos?
2. In Revelation Rome is called "Babylon." Why?
3. What are the qualities of the "New Jerusalem coming down out of heaven from God" (21, 2–9f)?
4. Throughout Revelation Christ is given many new titles. Example: Jesus, Christ, the firstborn of the dead, who holds the key of David, and so on. Let each person choose one of these titles and explain its meaning.
5. Literary form dictates the meaning of Scripture. What are some qualities of apocalyptic literature as seen in Revelation?
In Our Lives
1. The persecution and suffering from Rome were undoubtedly real. The choices these Christians faced were also real. Should they simply cooperate? Resist Rome violently? Choose

Number	Meaning	References
One or first	Primacy, excellence	1, 17; 2, 8; 22, 13
Three or third	Limited	8, 1; 12, 14; 11, 9; 4, 7; 6, 5; 8, 7–12
Four	Whole, universality	4, 6–8; 5, 6–8, 14; 6, 1.6; 7, 11; 14, 3; 15, 7; 19, 4
Six	Imperfection	13, 18
Seven	Fullness, perfection	1, 4; 1, 12; 1, 16; 4, 5; 5, 1
Twelve	Continuity with the chosen people	12, 1; 21, 12.14.20.21
Thousand	Superlative, very many	Chapters 7; 14; 20

passive resistance? What did they choose? Why? (17, 14)

2. According to Revelation, the Christian experiences Christ as the "Alpha and Omega" (21, 6) who came to make all things new (21, 5). How do you experience Christ in your family, your work, your friends, people in your community? How do you see Christ as the Alpha and Omega who comes to make all things new?

3. The Word of God is addressed to the original audience in their historical context. The fuller meaning for later ages is secondary and never divorced from the original meaning. Select a letter or vision in Revelation and explain this truth about God's revelation.

4. The religious message of Revelation is simple: Apocalyptic literature reconciles the conviction that God controls history with the experience that suggests that God does not. Reflect on how this applies to your experience and your community's experience.

5. The nature of prophecy is to bear witness to the reality of God in the world. Describe prophecy in Revelation (11, 18; 19, 10). Share with someone how this prophecy applies to your world.

Individual/Personal Reflection/Action

1. Take time to read carefully and pray the beautiful acclamations of Christ in the book of Revelation: 1, 2–7; 5, 1; 7, 10; 19, 6–7; 5, 9–10; 5, 13; and 11, 15.

2. Pray the Seven Beatitudes of the book of Revelation: 1, 3; 14, 13; 16, 15; 19, 9; 20, 6; 22, 7; and 22, 14.

3. Ancient peoples gave symbolism to special numbers. Look at the meaning of the numbers listed in the table below, then turn to the book of Revelation and reread the indicated passages. You may come to a better understanding of the poetic imagery.

THE OLD TESTAMENT

NEW AMERICAN BIBLE

PREFACE TO THE *NEW AMERICAN BIBLE*

Old Testament

On September 30, 1943, His Holiness Pope Pius XII issued his now famous encyclical on scripture studies, *Divino Afflante Spiritu.* He wrote: "We ought to explain the original text which was written by the inspired author himself and has more authority and greater weight than any, even the very best, translation whether ancient or modern. This can be done all the more easily and fruitfully if to the knowledge of languages be joined a real skill in literary criticism of the same text."

Early in 1944, in conformity with the spirit of the encyclical, and with the encouragement of Archbishop Cicognani, Apostolic Delegate to the United States, the Bishops' Committee of the Confraternity of Christian Doctrine requested members of The Catholic Biblical Association of America to translate the sacred scriptures from the original languages or from the oldest extant form of the text, and to present the sense of the biblical text in as correct a form as possible.

The first English Catholic version of the Bible, the Douay-Rheims (1582–1609/10), and its revision by Bishop Challoner (1750) were based on the Latin Vulgate. In view of the relative certainties more recently attained by textual and higher criticism, it has become increasingly desirable that contemporary translations of the sacred books into English be prepared in which due reverence for the text and strict observance of the rules of criticism would be combined.

The New American Bible has accomplished this in response to the need of the church in America today. It is the achievement of some fifty biblical scholars, the greater number of whom, though not all, are Catholics. In particular, the editors-in-chief have devoted twenty-five years to this work. The collaboration of scholars who are not Catholic fulfills the directive of the Second Vatican Council, not only that "correct translations be made into different languages especially from the original texts of the sacred books," but that, "with the approval of the church authority, these translations be produced in cooperation with separated brothers" so that "all Christians may be able to use them."

The text of the books contained in *The New American Bible* is a completely new translation throughout. From the original and the oldest available texts of the sacred books, it aims to convey as directly as possible the thought and individual style of the inspired writers. The better understanding of Hebrew and Greek, and the steady development of the science of textual criticism, the fruit of patient study since the time of St. Jerome, have allowed the translators and editors in their use of all available materials to approach more closely than ever before the sense of what the sacred authors actually wrote.

Where the translation supposes the received text—Hebrew, Aramaic, or Greek, as the case may be—ordinarily contained in the best-known editions, as the original or the oldest extant form, no additional remarks are necessary. But for those who are happily able to study the original text of the scriptures at firsthand, a supplementary series of textual notes pertaining to the Old Testament was added originally in an appendix to the typical edition. (It is now obtainable in a separate booklet from The Catholic Biblical Association of America, The Catholic University of America, Washington, DC 20064.) These notes furnish a guide in those cases in which the editorial board judges that the manuscripts in the original languages, or the evidence of the ancient versions, or some similar source, furnish the correct reading of a passage, or at least a reading more true to the original than that customarily printed in the available editions.

The Massoretic text of 1 and 2 Samuel has in numerous instances been corrected by the more ancient manuscripts Samuel a, b, and c from Cave 4 of Qumran, with the aid of important evidence from the Septuagint in both its oldest form and its Lucianic recension. Fragments of the lost Book of Tobit in Aramaic and in Hebrew, recovered from Cave 4 of Qumran, are in substantial agreement with the Sinaiticus Greek recension used for the translation of this book. The lost original Hebrew text of 1 Maccabees is replaced by its oldest extant form in Greek. Judith, 2 Maccabees, and parts of Esther are also translated from the Greek.

3

Preface

The basic text for the Psalms is not the Massoretic but one which the editors considered closer to the original inspired form, namely the Hebrew text underlying the new Latin Psalter of the Church, the *Liber Psalmorum* (1944[1], 1945[2]). Nevertheless they retained full liberty to establish the reading of the original text on sound critical principles.

The translation of Sirach, based on the original Hebrew as far as it is preserved and corrected from the ancient versions, is often interpreted in the light of the traditional Greek text. In the Book of Baruch the basic text is the Greek of the Septuagint, with some readings derived from an underlying Hebrew form no longer extant. In the deuterocanonical sections of Daniel (3, 24—90; 13, 1—14, 42), the basic text is the Greek text of Theodotion, occasionally revised according to the Greek text of the Septuagint.

In some instances in the Book of Job, in Proverbs, Sirach, Isaiah, Jeremiah, Ezekiel, Hosea, Amos, Micah, Nahum, Habakkuk, and Zechariah there is good reason to believe that the original order of lines was accidentally disturbed in the transmission of the text. The verse numbers given in such cases are always those of the current Hebrew text, though the arrangement differs. In these instances the textual notes advise the reader of the difficulty. Cases of exceptional dislocation are called to the reader's attention by footnotes.

The Books of *Genesis to Ruth* were first published in 1952; the Wisdom Books, *Job to Sirach,* in 1955; the Prophetic Books, *Isaiah to Malachi,* in 1961; and the Historical Books, *Samuel to Maccabees,* in 1969. In the present edition of *Genesis to Ruth* there are certain new features: a general introduction to the Pentateuch, a retranslation of the text of Genesis with an introduction, cross-references, and revised textual notes, besides new and expanded exegetical notes which take into consideration the various sources or literary traditions.

The revision of *Job to Sirach* includes changes in strophe division in Job and Proverbs and in titles of principal parts and sections of Wisdom and Ecclesiastes. Corrections in the text of Sirach are made in 39, 27—44, 17 on the basis of the Masada text, and in 51, 13–30 on the basis of the occurrence of this canticle in the Psalms scroll from Qumran Cave 11. In this typical edition, new corrections are reflected in the textual notes of Job, Proverbs, Wisdom, and Sirach. In the Psalms, the enumeration found in the Hebrew text is followed instead of the double enumeration, according to both the Hebrew and the Latin Vulgate texts, contained in the previous edition of this book.

In the Prophetic Books *Isaiah to Malachi,* only minor revisions have been made in the structure and wording of the texts, and in the textual notes.

The spelling of proper names in *The New American Bible* follows the customary forms found in most English Bibles since the Authorized Version.

The work of translating the Bible has been characterized as "the sacred and apostolic work of interpreting the word of God and of presenting it to the laity in translations as clear as the difficulty of the matter and the limitations of human knowledge permit" (A. G. Cicognani, Apostolic Delegate, in *The Catholic Biblical Quarterly,* 6, [1944], 389–90). In the appraisal of the present work, it is hoped that the words of the encyclical *Divino afflante Spiritu* will serve as a guide: "Let all the sons of the church bear in mind that the efforts of these resolute laborers in the vineyard of the Lord should be judged not only with equity and justice but also with the greatest charity; all moreover should abhor that intemperate zeal which imagines that whatever is new should for that very reason be opposed or suspected."

Conscious of their personal limitations for the task thus defined, those who have prepared this text cannot expect that it will be considered perfect; but they can hope that it may deepen in its readers "the right understanding of the divinely given Scriptures," and awaken in them "that piety by which it behooves us to be grateful to the God of all providence, who from the throne of his majesty has sent these books as so many personal letters to his own children" *(Divino afflante Spiritu).*

4

THE PENTATEUCH

See RG 34–47

The Pentateuch, which consists of the first five books of the Bible (Genesis, Exodus, Leviticus, Numbers, Deuteronomy), enjoys particular prestige among the Jews as the "Law," or "Torah," the concrete expression of God's will in their regard. It is more than a body of legal doctrine, even though such material occupies many chapters, for it contains the story of the formation of the People of God: Abraham and the patriarchs, Moses and the oppressed Hebrews in Egypt, the birth of Israel in the Sinai covenant, the journey to the threshold of the Promised Land, and the "discourses" of Moses.

The grandeur of this historic sweep is the result of a careful and complex joining of several historic traditions, or sources. These are primarily four: the so-called Yahwist, Elohist, Priestly and Deuteronomic strands that run through the Pentateuch. (They are conveniently abbreviated as J, E, P and D.) Each brings to the Torah its own characteristics, its own theological viewpoint—a rich variety of interpretation that the sensitive reader will take pains to appreciate. A superficial difference between two of these sources is responsible for their names: the Yahwist prefers the name *Yahweh* (represented in translation as LORD) by which God revealed himself to Israel; the Elohist prefers the generic name for God, *Elohim.* The Yahwist is concrete, imaginative, using many anthropomorphisms in its theological approach, as seen, e.g., in the narrative of creation in Gn 2, compared with the Priestly version in Gn 1. The Elohist is more sober, moralistic. The Priestly strand, which emphasizes genealogies, is more severely theological in tone. The Deuteronomic approach is characterized by the intense hortatory style of Dt 5—11, and by certain principles from which it works, such as the centralization of worship in the Jerusalem temple.

However, even this analysis of the Pentateuch is an over-simplification, for it is not always possible to distinguish with certainty among the various sources. The fact is that each of these individual traditions incorporates much older material. The Yahwist was himself a collector and adapter. His narrative is made up of many disparate stories that have been reoriented, and given a meaning within the context in which they now stand; e.g., the story of Abraham and Isaac in Gn 22. Within the J and P traditions one has to reckon with many individual units; these had their own history and life-setting before they were brought together into the present more or less connected narrative.

This is not to deny the role of Moses in the development of the Pentateuch. It is true we do not conceive of him as the author of the books in the modern sense. But there is no reason to doubt that, in the events described in these traditions, he had a uniquely important role, especially as lawgiver. Even the later laws which have been added in P and D are presented as a Mosaic heritage. Moses is the lawgiver *par excellence,* and all later legislation is conceived in his spirit and therefore attributed to him. Hence, the reader is not held to undeviating literalness in interpreting the words, "the LORD said to Moses." One must keep in mind that the Pentateuch is the crystallization of Israel's age-old relationship with God.

In presenting the story of the birth of the People of God, the Pentateuch looks back to the promises made to the patriarchs, and forward to

5

the continuing fulfillment of these promises in later books of the Bible. The promises find their classic expression in Gn 12, 1ff. The "God of the Fathers" challenges Abraham to believe: the patriarch is to receive a people, a land, and through him the nations will somehow be blessed.

The mysterious and tortuous way in which this people is brought into being is described: Despite Sarah's sterility, Isaac is finally born—to be offered in sacrifice! The promises are renewed to him eventually, and also to the devious Jacob, as if to show that the divine design will be effected, with or without human cunning. The magnificent story of Joseph is highlighted by the theme of Providence; the promise of a people is taking shape.

Israel is not formed in a vacuum, but amid the age-old civilization of Mesopotamia and the Nile. Oppression in Egypt provokes a striking intervention of God.

Yahweh reveals himself to Moses as a savior, and the epic story of deliverance is told in Exodus. This book also tells of the Sinai covenant, which is rightfully regarded as the key to the Old Testament. Through the covenant Israel becomes Yahweh's people, and Yahweh becomes Israel's God. This act of grace marks the fulfillment of the first promise; that Abraham will be the father of a great nation, God's special possession. The laws in Exodus and Leviticus (P tradition) are both early and late. They spell out the proper relationship of the federation of the Twelve tribes with the LORD. He is a jealous God, demanding exclusive allegiance; he cannot be imaged; he takes vengeance upon the wicked, and shows mercy to the good. Slowly the LORD reveals himself to his people; with remarkable honesty, Israel records the unsteady response—the murmurings and rebellions and infidelities through the desert wanderings up to the plain of Moab.

This sacred history was formed within the bosom of early Israel, guided by the spirit of God. It was sung beside the desert campfires; it was commemorated in the liturgical feasts, such as Passover; it was transmitted by word of mouth from generation to generation—until all was brought together in writing, about the sixth century B.C., when the literary formation of the Pentateuch came to an end.

The Book of Deuteronomy has a history quite peculiar to itself. Its old traditions and law code (12—26) are put forth in the form of "discourses" of Moses before his death. The extraordinarily intense and hortatory tone fits the mood of a discourse. The book contains possibly the preaching of the Levites in the northern kingdom of Israel before its fall in 721 B.C. If this book is situated in its proper historical perspective, its true impact is more vividly appreciated. It is the blueprint of the great "Deuteronomic" reform under King Josiah (640–609 B.C.). This was an attempt to galvanize the people into a wholehearted commitment to the covenant ideals, into an obedience motivated by the great commandment of love (Dt 6, 4ff). Israel has yet another chance, if it obeys. The people are poised between life and death; and they are exhorted to choose life—today (Dt 26, 16-19; 30, 15-20).

See RG
47–61

The Book of Genesis

Genesis, the first book of the Bible, opens with the Hebrew word bereshit, which means "in the beginning." The title "Genesis" was given to the Septuagint (Greek) translation of the book because of its concern with the origin of the world (Gn 1, 1; 2, 4), of the human race, and, in particular, of the Hebrew people.

Eleven structural units (toledoth), of unequal length and importance, present the unity and purpose of the book in terms of God's universal sovereignty, his dealings with men, and his choice and formation of a special people to be the instrument of his plan of salvation.

The tracing of the direct descendance from Adam to Jacob constitutes the major part of the book, while the genealogical tables of lateral branches are not so developed nor of such interest as those that pertain to the story of the Israelite people. In fact, these lateral branches gradually disappear from the narrative. And with the introduction of Abraham and his covenant with God, the history of humanity as such becomes contracted to the story of the descendants of Abraham through Isaac and Jacob—the chosen people.

Despite its unity of plan and purpose, the book is a complex work, not to be attributed to a single original author. Several sources, or literary traditions, that the final redactor used in his composition are discernable. These are the Yahwist (J), Elohist (E) and Priestly (P) sources, which in turn reflect older oral traditions (see Introduction to the Pentateuch).

In Genesis, the Yahwist source is the most important by reason of its teaching, its antiquity, and the continuity it gives the book. It constitutes a sacred history, continually drawing attention to the working out of God's design through his interventions in the affairs of men. The Elohist source, less well preserved, is found in fragmentary form only, depicting God's manifestations through visions and dreams rather than theophanies. Angels are God's intermediaries with men. Moreover, there is a solicitude for the divine transcendence and greater sensitivity toward the moral order. The Priestly source contains those elements—chronological data, lists, genealogies—that construct the framework of Genesis and bind its contents together. To the J and E sources it adds such legal institutions as the sabbath rest, circumcision and the alliances between God and Noah and God and Abraham.

The interpreter of Genesis will recognize at once the distinct object that sets chapters 1—11 apart: the recounting of the origin of the world and of man (primeval history). To make the truths contained in these chapters intelligible to the Israelite people destined to preserve them, they needed to be expressed through elements prevailing among that people at that time. For this reason, the truths themselves must therefore be clearly distinguished from their literary garb.

With the story of the patriarchs Abraham, Isaac and Jacob (Gn 11, 27—50, 26), the character of the narrative changes. While we do not view the account of the patriarchs as history in the strict sense, nevertheless certain of the matters recounted from the time of Abraham onward can be placed in the actual historical and social framework of the Near East in the early part of the second millennium B.C. (2000–1500), and documented by non-biblical sources.

Genesis contains many religious teachings of basic importance: the preexistence and transcendence of God, his wisdom and goodness, his power through which all things are made and on which they all depend; the special creation of man in God's image and likeness, and of woman from the substance of man; the institution of marriage as the union of one man with one woman; man's original state of innocence; man's sin of pride and disobedience, its consequences for the protoparents and their posterity. Despite the severity of their punishment, hope of reconciliation is offered by God through the first as well as the subsequent promises of salvation and blessing. Abraham is blessed for his faith and obedience, and he is to be a blessing for all nations through his offspring, Isaac, Jacob, and Jacob's sons (Gn 12, 3; 18, 18; 22, 18), of whom the Messiah, mankind's greatest blessing, will eventually be born (Gal 3, 8).

Frequent references to Genesis are found in the New Testament. Christ becomes the antithesis of Adam: sin and death come to mankind through Adam, justification and life through Jesus Christ (Rom 5, 12. 17ff). Noah's ark becomes the symbol of the church, by which men are saved from destruction through the waters of baptism (1 Pt 3, 20ff); Abraham's faith is the model for all believers; the sacrifice of his son Isaac typifies the sacrifice of Christ, Son of the Father. The liturgy, too, relates the persons of Abel, Abraham and Melchizedek to Christ in his act of sacrifice.

The Book of Genesis is divided as follows:
I: The Primeval History (1, 1—11, 26).
II: The Patriarch Abraham (11, 27—25, 18).
III: The Patriarchs Isaac and Jacob (25, 19—36, 43).
IV: Joseph and His Brothers (37, 1—50, 26).

I: The Primeval History

CHAPTER 1

First Story of Creation.* [1]In the beginning, when God created the heavens and the earth,[a] [2]the earth was a formless wasteland, and darkness covered the abyss,* while a mighty wind swept over the waters.[b]

See RG 52–54

1, 1—2, 4a: This section introduces the whole Pentateuch. It shows how God brought an orderly universe out of primordial chaos.
1, 2: The abyss: the primordial ocean according to the ancient Semitic cosmogony. After God's creative activity, part of this

---

a: Gn 2, 1.4; Pss 8, 4; 38—39; 90, 2; Wis 11, 17; Sir 16, 24; Jer 10, 12; 2 Mc 7, 28; Acts 14, 15; Col 1, 16f; Heb 1, 2f; 3, 4; 11, 3; Rv 4, 11. *b:* Jer 4, 23.

Days of Creation	
LIGHT	LIGHTS *(i.e., sun, moon, and stars)*
day 1 (1, 1–5)	day 4 (1, 14–19)
SKY *(separating waters above from waters below)*	FISH/BIRDS
day 2 (1, 6–8)	day 5 (1, 20–23)
LAND AND PLANTS	LAND ANIMALS AND HUMANS
day 3 (1, 9–13)	day 6 (1, 24–31)
SABBATH	
day 7 (2, 1–3)	

³Then God said, "Let there be light," and there was light.ᶜ ⁴God saw how good the light was. God then separated the light from the darkness. ⁵God called the light "day," and the darkness he called "night." Thus evening came, and morning followed—the first day.*

⁶Then God said, "Let there be a dome in the middle of the waters, to separate one body of water from the other." And so it happened: ⁷God made the dome, and it separated the water above the dome from the water below it.ᵈ ⁸God called the dome "the sky." Evening came, and morning followed—the second day.

⁹Then God said, "Let the water under the sky be gathered into a single basin, so that the dry land may appear." And so it happened: the water under the sky was gathered into its basin, and the dry land appeared.ᵉ ¹⁰God called the dry land "the earth," and the basin of the water he called "the sea." God saw how good it was. ¹¹ᶠThen God said, "Let the earth bring forth vegetation: every kind of plant that bears seed and every kind of fruit tree on earth that bears fruit with its seed in it." And so it happened: ¹²the earth brought forth every kind of plant that bears seed and every kind of fruit tree on earth that bears fruit with its seed in it. God saw how good it was. ¹³Evening came, and morning followed—the third day.

¹⁴Then God said: "Let there be lights in the dome of the sky, to separate day from night. Let them mark the fixed times, the days and the years,ᵍ ¹⁵and serve as luminaries in the dome of the sky, to shed light upon the earth." And so it happened: ¹⁶God made the two great lights, the greater one to govern the day, and the lesser one to govern the night; and he made the stars.ʰ ¹⁷God set them in the dome of the sky, to shed light upon the earth, ¹⁸to govern the day and the night, and to separate the light from the darkness. God saw how good it was. ¹⁹Evening came, and morning followed—the fourth day.

²⁰ⁱThen God said, "Let the water teem with an abundance of living creatures, and on the earth let birds fly beneath the dome of the sky." And so it happened: ²¹God created the great sea monsters and all kinds of swimming creatures with which the water teems, and all kinds of winged birds. God saw how good it was, ²²and God blessed them, saying, "Be fertile, multiply, and fill the water of the seas; and let the birds multiply on the earth."ʲ ²³Evening came, and morning followed—the fifth day.

vast body forms the salt-water seas (vv 9f); part of it is the fresh water under the earth (Ps 33, 7; Ez 31, 4), which wells forth on the earth as springs and fountains (Gn 7, 11; 8, 2; Prv 3, 20). Part of it, "the upper water" (Ps 148, 4; Dn 3, 60), is held up by the dome of the sky (Gn 1, 6f) from which rain descends on the earth (Gn 7, 11; 2 Kgs 7, 2. 19; Ps 104, 13). A mighty wind: literally, "a wind of God," or "a spirit of God"; cf Gn 8, 1.

1, 5: In ancient Israel a day was considered to begin at sunset. According to the highly artificial literary structure of Gn 1, 1—2, 4a, God's creative activity is divided into six days to teach the sacredness of the sabbath rest on the seventh day in the Israelite religion (Gn 2, 2f).

c: 2 Cor 4, 6. *d:* Prv 8, 27f; 2 Pt 3, 5. *e:* Jb 38, 8; Ps 33, 7; Jer 5, 22. *f:* Ps 104, 14. *g:* Jer 26, 10; Ps 19, 1f; Bar 3, 33. *h:* Dt 4, 19; Ps 136, 7ff; Wis 13, 2ff; Jer 31, 35. *i:* Jb 12, 7-10. *j:* Gn 8, 17.

It Is Good

Six times in the first creation story, God observes the same thing about each part of creation: It is good. The seventh time these words are even stronger. When he surveys everything in creation, the sun and moon, the water and earth, the plants and creatures, and, finally, humans, God saw everything he had made and found it "very good." For this reason, according to the *Catechism of the Catholic Church*, the seventh commandment teaches that our dominion over inanimate creation and other living beings is not absolute but, rather, limited. In our use of natural resources, we are to consider the well being of others on our planet today and those who will be here in generations to come (CCC#2415). How do you conserve natural resources as an individual? How might we do better at this as a people?

[24k]Then God said, "Let the earth bring forth all kinds of living creatures: cattle, creeping things, and wild animals of all kinds." And so it happened: [25]God made all kinds of wild animals, all kinds of cattle, and all kinds of creeping things of the earth. God saw how good it was. [26l]Then God said: "Let us make man in our image, after our likeness. Let them have dominion over the fish of the sea, the birds of the air, and the cattle, and over all the wild animals and all the creatures that crawl on the ground."*

[27] God created man in his image;
in the divine image he created him;
male and female he created them.

[28]God blessed them, saying to them: "Be fertile and multiply; fill the earth and subdue it. Have dominion over the fish of the sea, the birds of the air, and all the living things that move on the earth."[m] [29n]God also said: "See, I give you every seed-bearing plant all over the earth and every tree that has seed-bearing fruit on it to be your food; [30]and to all the animals of the land, all the birds of the air, and all the living creatures that crawl on the ground, I give all the green plants for food."

And so it happened. [31]God looked at everything he had made, and he found it very good. Evening came, and morning followed—the sixth day.[o]

CHAPTER 2

See RG 52-54

[1]Thus the heavens and the earth and all their array were completed.[p] [2]Since on the seventh day God was finished with the work he had been doing, he rested on the seventh day from all the work he had undertaken.[q] [3]So God blessed the seventh day and made it holy, because on it he rested from all the work he had done in creation.[r]

[4]Such is the story of the heavens and the earth at their creation.

Second Story of Creation.* At the time when the LORD God made the earth and the heavens— [5]while as yet there was no field shrub on earth and no grass of the field had sprouted, for the LORD God had sent no rain upon the earth and there was no man to till the soil, [6]but a stream was welling up out of the earth and was watering all the surface of the ground— [7]the LORD God formed man out of the clay of the ground* and blew into his nostrils the breath of life, and so man became a living being.[s]

1, 26: Man is here presented as the climax of God's creative activity; he resembles God primarily because of the dominion God gives him over the rest of creation.

2, 4b-25: This section is chiefly concerned with the creation of man. It is much older than the narrative of Gn 1, 1—2, 4a. Here God is depicted as creating man before the rest of his creatures, which are made for man's sake.

2, 7: God is portrayed as a potter molding man's body out of clay. There is a play on words in Hebrew between adam

("man") and adama ("ground"). Being: literally, "soul."

k: Sir 16, 27f; Bar 3, 32. l: 26f: Gn 5, 1. 3; 9, 6; Ps 8, 5f; Wis 2, 23; 10, 2; Sir 17, 1. 3f; Jas 3, 7; 1 Cor 11, 7; Eph 4, 24; Col 3, 10; Mt 19, 4; Mk 10, 6. m: Gn 8, 17; 9, 1; Pss 8, 6-9; 115, 16; Wis 9, 2. r: 29f: Gn 9, 3; Ps 104, 14f. o: 1 Tm 4, 4. p: Is 45, 12; Jn 1, 3. q: Ex 20, 9ff; 31, 17; Heb 4, 4. 10. r: Ex 20, 11; Dt 5, 14; Neh 9, 14. s: Gn 3, 19; 18, 27; Tb 8, 6; Jb 34, 15; Pss 103, 14; 104, 29; Eccl 3, 20; 12, 7; Wis 7, 1; Sir 33, 10; 1 Cor 15, 45

The Major Divisions of Genesis	
First section: 1, 1 to 11, 9	Primeval history, the origins of humankind, and failure through sin.
Second section: 11, 10 to 25, 34	Abraham, his call and response, his blessing and promise, his son Isaac and Isaac's sons Jacob (Israel) and Esau
Third section: 26, 1 to 36, 43	Isaac, Jacob, and the sons of Jacob (Israel)
Fourth section: 37, 1 to 50, 26	The sons of Israel, and Jacob and the Israelites in Egypt

[8]Then the LORD God planted a garden in Eden,* in the east, and he placed there the man whom he had formed.[t] [9]Out of the ground the LORD God made various trees grow that were delightful to look at and good for food, with the tree of life in the middle of the garden and the tree of the knowledge of good and bad.[u]

[10]A river rises* in Eden to water the garden; beyond there it divides and becomes four branches. [11]The name of the first is the Pishon; it is the one that winds through the whole land of Havilah, where there is gold. [12]The gold of that land is excellent; bdellium and lapis lazuli are also there. [13]The name of the second river is the Gihon; it is the one that winds all through the land of Cush.[v] [14]The name of the third river is the Tigris; it is the one that flows east of Asshur. The fourth river is the Euphrates.

[15]The LORD God then took the man and settled him in the garden of Eden, to cultivate and care for it.[w] [16]The LORD God gave man this order: "You are free to eat from any of the trees of the garden[x] [17]except the tree of knowledge of good and bad. From that tree you shall not eat; the moment you eat from it you are surely doomed to die."[y]

[18]The LORD God said: "It is not good for the man to be alone. I will make a suitable partner for him."[z] [19]So the LORD God formed out of the ground various wild animals and various birds of the air, and he brought them to the man to see what he would call them; whatever the man called each of them would be its name. [20]The man gave names to all the cattle, all the birds of the air, and all the wild animals; but none proved to be the suitable partner for the man.

[21]So the LORD God cast a deep sleep on the man, and while he was asleep, he took out one of his ribs and closed up its place with flesh.[a] [22]The LORD God then built up into a woman the rib that he had taken from the man. When he brought her to the man, [23]the man said:

"This one, at last, is bone of my bones
    and flesh of my flesh;
This one shall be called 'woman,'
    for out of 'her man' this one has been
        taken."*

[24b]That is why a man leaves his father and

2, 8: Eden: used here as the name of a region in southern Mesopotamia; the term is derived from the Sumerian word eden, "fertile plain." A similar-sounding Hebrew word means "delight"; the garden in Eden could therefore be understood as the "garden of delight," so that, through the Greek version, it is now known also as "paradise," literally, a "pleasure park."

2, 10-14: Rises: in flood to overflow its banks. Beyond there: as one travels upstream. Branches: literally, "heads," i.e., upper courses. Eden is near the head of the Persian Gulf, where the Tigris and the Euphrates join with two other streams to form a single river. The land of Cush here and in Gn 10, 8, is not Ethiopia (Nubia) as elsewhere, but the region of the Kassites east of

Mesopotamia.

2, 23: There is a play on the similar-sounding Hebrew words ishsha ("woman") and ishah ("her man, her husband").

2, 24: One body: literally "one flesh"; classical Hebrew has no specific word for "body." The sacred writer stresses the fact that conjugal union is willed by God.

t: Is 51, 3; Ez 31, 9.   u: Gn 3, 22; Prv 3, 18; Rv 2, 7; 22, 2. 14.   v: Sir 24, 25.   w: Sir 7, 15.   x: Ps 104, 14.   y: Gn 3, 2f; Rom 6, 23.   z: Tb 8, 6; Sir 36, 24; 1 Cor 11, 9; 1 Tm 2, 13.   a: Sir 17, 1; 1 Cor 11, 8f; 1 Tm 2, 13.   b: Mt 19, 5; Mk 10, 7; 1 Cor 7, 10f; Eph 5, 31.

A Second Creation Story—the Garden of Eden

Genesis 2 begins not with chaotic waters of the deep as in 1, 1–2, but with a dry desert. Like the watery deep, the dry wilderness is a biblical image of evil and chaos (Is 21, 1–3; 43, 15–21). God's creative power turns the wilderness into a fertile garden with the trees of life and "knowledge of good and bad," that is to say, "all knowledge," at its center. Eating from the tree of life would give immortality, and eating from the tree of knowledge would provide wisdom, moral discernment, and the experience of pleasure and pain. The image of Eden is that of a lush garden at the center of the known world from which four major rivers flow to water the earth. We know the location of only two of the rivers, the Tigris and the Euphrates. They are in Mesopotamia. Havilah (v. 11) may be associated with Africa.

The garden of Eden is not a paradise of luxury, but a place for human work. The man is to cultivate the garden and care for it on God's behalf. God soon recognizes that the man needs a partner for this labor. Other translations use the word "helper," but it is important to remember that God's motivation in creating the woman is to provide a companion and someone who will come to his aid, not to provide a subservient assistant. The man's brief poetic response to the woman plays on Hebrew words *ish* (Man) and *ishshah* (Woman). They "become one body" (2, 24) suggests not only sexual union, but also a unity through a common household and the raising of children. This story lays the foundation for marriage.

mother and clings to his wife, and the two of them become one body.* ²⁵The man and his wife were both naked, yet they felt no shame.

CHAPTER 3

See RG 54

The Fall of Man. ¹Now the serpent was the most cunning of all the animals that the LORD God had made. The serpent asked the woman, "Did God really tell you not to eat from any of the trees in the garden?" ²The woman answered the serpent: "We may eat of the fruit of the trees in the garden; ³ᶜit is only about the fruit of the tree in the middle of the garden that God said, 'You shall not eat it or even touch it, lest you die.' " ⁴But the serpent said to the woman: "You certainly will not die!ᵈ ⁵No, God knows well that the moment you eat of it your eyes will be opened and you will be like gods who know* what is good and what is bad." ⁶The woman saw that the tree was

good for food, pleasing to the eyes, and desirable for gaining wisdom. So she took some of its fruit and ate it; and she also gave some to her husband, who was with her, and he ate it.ᵉ ⁷Then the eyes of both of them were opened, and they realized that they were naked; so they sewed fig leaves together and made loincloths for themselves.

⁸When they heard the sound of the LORD God moving about in the garden at the breezy time of the day,* the man and his wife hid themselves from the LORD God among the trees of the garden.ᶠ ⁹The LORD God then called to the man and asked him, "Where are you?" ¹⁰He answered, "I heard you in the garden; but I was afraid, because I was naked, so I hid myself." ¹¹Then he asked, "Who told you that you were naked? You have eaten, then, from the tree of which I had forbidden you to eat!" ¹²The man replied, "The woman whom you put here with me—she gave me fruit from the tree, so

3, 5: Like gods who know: or "like God who knows."
3, 8: The breezy time of the day: literally "the wind of the day." On most days in Palestine a cooling breeze blows from the sea shortly before sunset.

c: Gn 2, 17; Rom 6, 23.   d: 4f: Wis 2, 24; Sir 25, 14; Is 14, 14; Jn 8, 44; 2 Cor 11, 3.   e: Gn 3, 22; 1 Tm 2, 14.   f: Jer 23, 24

How to Read the Account of the Fall

The *Catechism of the Catholic Church* (CCC#390) reminds us that this account of the fall in Genesis 3 uses figurative language, by which it affirms that a choice at the beginning of human history marked the whole of that history, and that the choice was freely made.

I ate it." [13]The LORD God then asked the woman, "Why did you do such a thing?" The woman answered, "The serpent tricked me into it, and so I ate it."[g]

[14]Then the LORD God said to the serpent:

"Because you have done this, you shall
        be banned
    from all the animals
    and from all the wild creatures;
On your belly shall you crawl,
    and dirt shall you eat
    all the days of your life.[h]
[15] I will put enmity between you and the
        woman,
    and between your offspring and hers;
He will strike at his head,
    while you strike at his heel."*[i]

[16]To the woman he said:

"I will intensify the pangs of your
        childbearing;
    in pain shall you bring forth children.
Yet your urge shall be for your husband,
    and he shall be your master."[j]

[17]To the man he said: "Because you listened to your wife and ate from the tree of which I had forbidden you to eat,

"Cursed be the ground because of
        you!

In toil shall you eat its yield
    all the days of your life.[k]
[18] Thorns and thistles shall it bring forth to
        you,
    as you eat of the plants of the field.
[19] By the sweat of your face
    shall you get bread to eat,
Until you return to the ground,
    from which you were taken;
For you are dirt,
    and to dirt you shall return."[l]

[20]The man called his wife Eve, because she became the mother of all the living.*

[21]For the man and his wife the LORD God made leather garments, with which he clothed them. [22]Then the LORD God said: "See! The man has become like one of us, knowing what is good and what is bad! Therefore, he must not be allowed to put out his hand to take fruit from the tree of life also, and thus eat of it and live forever."[m] [23]The LORD God therefore banished him from the garden of Eden, to till the ground from which he had been taken. [24]When he expelled the man, he settled him east of the garden of Eden; and he stationed the cherubim and the fiery revolving sword, to guard the way to the tree of life.*

CHAPTER 4

Cain and Abel. [1]The man had relations with his wife Eve, and she conceived

---

3, 15: He will strike . . . at his heel: since the antecedent for he and his is the collective noun offspring, i.e., all the descendants of the woman, a more exact rendering of the sacred writer's words would be, "They will strike . . . at their heels." However, later theology saw in this passage more than unending hostility between snakes and men. The serpent was regarded as the devil (Wis 2, 24; Jn 8, 44; Rv 12, 9; 20, 2), whose eventual defeat seems implied in the contrast between head and heel. Because "the Son of God appeared that he might destroy the works of the devil" (1 Jn 3, 8), the passage can be understood as the first promise of a Redeemer for fallen mankind. The woman's offspring then is primarily Jesus Christ.

3, 20: This verse seems to be out of place; it would fit better after v 24. The Hebrew name hawwa ("Eve") is related to the Hebrew word hay ("living").

3, 24: The above rendering is based on the ancient Greek version; that of the current Hebrew is, When he expelled the man, he settled him east of the garden of Eden, the cherubim.

4, 1: The Hebrew name qayin ("Cain") and the term qaniti ("I have produced") present another play on words.

---

g: 2 Cor 11, 3. *h:* Is 65, 25; Mi 7, 17; Rv 12, 9. *i:* Is 7, 14; 9, 5; Rom 16, 20; 1 Jn 3, 8; Rv 12, 17. *j:* 1 Cor 11, 3; Eph 5, 22f; 1 Tm 2, 12. *k:* Gn 5, 29; Rom 5, 12; 8, 20; Heb 6, 8. *l:* Gn 2, 7; Jb 10, 9; 34, 15; Pss 90, 3; 103, 14; Eccl 3, 20; 12, 7; Wis 15, 8; Sir 10, 9; 17, 2; Rom 5, 12; 1 Cor 15, 21; Heb 9, 27. *m:* Gn 2, 9; Rv 22, 2. 14.

See RG 55

The *Catechism of the Catholic Church* (CCC#289) underlines the importance of the first three chapters of Genesis. Although these texts have different sources, we read them as a unit in the light of what we know about Christ, as well as the overall unity of the Bible and our living tradition. These chapters thus are our principal source for catechesis on the basic issues of creation, fall, and the promise of salvation—salvation that has come about through the death and resurrection of Christ. In addition, we learn here about the significance of the Sabbath—rest from labor is not just a convenience but a divine mandate—that all creation is good, and that human beings are created in God's image.

Genesis in its final form probably dates to the time when the people of Judah were in exile in Babylon (sixth century B.C.) or when the Babylonian exiles returned home to Judah under the Persian empire (fifth century B.C.). The time of exile and the return home forced Israel to think hard about its identity as a people and its mission as the people of God among the nations of the world. Remembering the Genesis stories about the beginnings of the world and Israel's earliest ancestors was a way to return to their roots and think about who they were as an exiled people returning home to Judah. They could identify with their ancestors, who were also a family on the move. Just as the family of Abraham and Sarah migrated back and forth from Mesopotamia to Canaan, so the exiles would migrate from Babylon back to Judah. The key promise in the midst of this wandering and yearning to return home was God's promise to Jacob: "Know that I am with you; I will protect you wherever you go, and bring you back to this land" (28, 15).

and bore Cain, saying, "I have produced a man with the help of the LORD."* ²Next she bore his brother Abel. Abel became a keeper of flocks, and Cain a tiller of the soil. ³In the course of time Cain brought an offering to the LORD from the fruit of the soil, ⁴while Abel, for his part, brought one of the best firstlings of his flock.ⁿ The LORD looked with favor on Abel and his offering, ⁵but on Cain and his offering he did not. Cain greatly resented this and was crestfallen. ⁶So the LORD said to Cain: "Why are you so resentful and crestfallen? ⁷If you do well, you can hold up your head; but if not, sin is a demon lurking* at the door: his urge is toward you, yet you can be his master."ᵒ

⁸Cain said to his brother Abel, "Let us go out in the field." When they were in the field, Cain attacked his brother Abel and killed him.ᵖ ⁹Then the LORD asked Cain, "Where is your brother Abel?" He answered, "I do not know. Am I my brother's keeper?" ¹⁰The LORD then said: "What have you done! Listen: Your brother's blood cries out to me from the soil! ¹¹Therefore you shall be banned from the soil that opened its mouth to receive your brother's blood from your hand.�q ¹²If you till the soil, it shall no longer give you its produce. You shall become a restless wanderer on the earth." ¹³Cain said to the LORD: "My punishment is too great to bear. ¹⁴Since you have now banished me from the soil, and I must avoid your presence and become a restless wanderer on the earth, anyone may kill me at sight." ¹⁵"Not so!" the LORD said to him. "If anyone kills Cain, Cain shall be avenged sevenfold." So the LORD put a mark* on Cain, lest anyone should kill him at sight. ¹⁶Cain then left the LORD's presence and settled in the land of Nod,* east of Eden.

4, 7: Demon lurking: in Hebrew, robes, literally "croucher," is used here, like the similar Akkadian term rabisu, to designate a certain kind of evil spirit.

4, 15: A mark: probably a tattoo. The use of tattooing for tribal marks has always been common among the nomads of the Near Eastern deserts.

4, 16: The land of Nod: not a definite geographic region. The term merely means "the land of nomads."

n: Ex 34, 19; Heb 11, 4.   o: Sir 7, 1; Jude 11.   p: Wis 10, 3; Mt 23, 35; Lk 11, 51; 1 Jn 3, 12; Jude 11.   q: Dt 27, 24.

Descendants of Cain and Seth. [17]*Cain had relations with his wife, and she conceived and bore Enoch. Cain also became the founder of a city, which he named after his son Enoch. [18]To Enoch was born Irad, and Irad became the father of Mehujael; Mehujael became the father of Methusael, and Methusael became the father of Lamech. [19]Lamech took two wives; the name of the first was Adah, and the name of the second Zillah. [20]Adah gave birth to Jabal, the ancestor of all who dwell in tents and keep cattle. [21]His brother's name was Jubal; he was the ancestor of all who play the lyre and the pipe. [22]Zillah, on her part, gave birth to Tubalcain, the ancestor of all who forge instruments of bronze and iron. The sister of Tubalcain was Naamah. [23]Lamech said to his wives:

"Adah and Zillah, hear my voice;
    wives of Lamech, listen to my
        utterance:
I have killed a man for wounding me,
    a boy for bruising me.
[24] If Cain is avenged sevenfold,
    then Lamech seventy-sevenfold."

[25]Adam again had relations with his wife, and she gave birth to a son whom she called Seth. "God has granted* me more offspring in place of Abel," she said, "because Cain slew him." [26]To Seth, in turn, a son was born, and he named him Enosh.

At that time men began to invoke the LORD by name.[r]

CHAPTER 5

See RG
55

*Generations: Adam to Noah.** [1]This is the record of the descendants of Adam. When God created man, he made him in the likeness of God; [2]he created them male and female. When they were created, he blessed them and named them "man."

[3]Adam was one hundred and thirty years old when he begot a son in his likeness, after his image; and he named him Seth.[u] [4]Adam lived eight hundred years after the birth of Seth, and he had other sons and daughters. [5]The whole lifetime of Adam was nine hundred and thirty years; then he died.

[6]When Seth was one hundred and five years old, he became the father of Enosh. [7]Seth lived eight hundred and seven years after the birth of Enosh, and he had other sons and daughters. [8]The whole lifetime of Seth was nine hundred and twelve years; then he died.

[9]When Enosh was ninety years old, he became the father of Kenan. [10]Enosh lived eight hundred and fifteen years after the birth of Kenan, and he had other sons and daughters. [11]The whole lifetime of Enosh was nine hundred and five years; then he died.

[12]When Kenan was seventy years old, he became the father of Mahalalel. [13]Kenan lived eight hundred and forty years after the birth of Mahalalel, and he had other sons and daughters. [14]The whole lifetime of Kenan was nine hundred and ten years; then he died.

[15]When Mahalalel was sixty-five years old, he became the father of Jared. [16]Maha-

---

4, 17-22: In vv 12-16 Cain was presented as the archetype of nomadic peoples. The sacred author in this section follows another ancient tradition that makes Cain the prototype of sedentary peoples with higher material culture.

4, 25f: Has granted: Hebrew shat, a wordplay on the name shet ("Seth"). Enosh: in Hebrew, a synonym of adam ("man"). At that time . . . name: men began to call God by his personal name, Yahweh, rendered as "the Lord" in this version of the Bible. The ancient, so-called Yahwist source used here employs the name Yahweh long before the time of Moses. Another ancient source, the Elohist (from its use of the term Elohim, "God," instead of Yahweh, "Lord," for the pre-Mosaic period), makes Moses the first to use Yahweh as the proper name of Israel's God, previously known by other names as well; cf Ex 3, 13ff.

5, 1-32: Although this chapter, with its highly

schematic form, belongs to the relatively late "Priestly document," it is based on very ancient traditions. Together with Gn 11, 10-26, its primary purpose is to bridge the genealogical gap between Adam and Abraham. Adam's line is traced through Seth, but several names in the series are the same as, or similar to, certain names in Cain's line (Gn 4, 17ff). The long lifespans attributed to these ten antediluvian patriarchs have a symbolic rather than a historical value. Babylonian tradition also recorded ten kings with fantastically high ages who reigned successively before the flood.

r: 1 Chr 1, 1; Lk 3, 38.   *s:* Gn 1, 27; Wis 2, 23; Sir 17, 1; 1 Cor 11, 7; Jas 3, 9.   *t:* Gn 4, 25.   *u:* 3-32: 1 Chr 1, 1-4; Lk 3, 36ff.

The *Toledoth* ("Generations") Lists

In the text of Genesis, the Hebrew word *toledoth* (pronounced "tole-uh-DOTE" and meaning "generations" or "descendants") serves as a marker for the end of one section of the narrative and the beginning of the next. Here are the places where the word occurs:

2, 4a	The second creation story
5, 1	Introduces the section between the first human family and the days of Noah
6, 9	Introduces the story of the flood
10, 1	The expansion of people over the earth
11, 10	A new list of the nations of the earth
11, 27	The beginning of Abraham's story
25, 12	The end of the story of Hagar and Ishmael, Abraham's other family
25, 19	Introduces Jacob's story
36, 1	The end of Esau's story and the beginning of the story of Jacob's children
36, 9	The conclusion of the list
37, 2	The beginning of the story of Joseph and his brothers

lalel lived eight hundred and thirty years after the birth of Jared, and he had other sons and daughters. *17*The whole lifetime of Mahalalel was eight hundred and ninety-five years; then he died.

*18*When Jared was one hundred and sixty-two years old, he became the father of Enoch. *19*Jared lived eight hundred years after the birth of Enoch, and he had other sons and daughters. *20*The whole lifetime of Jared was nine hundred and sixty-two years; then he died.

*21*When Enoch was sixty-five years old, he became the father of Methuselah. *22*Enoch lived three hundred years after the birth of Methuselah, and he had other sons and daughters. *23*The whole lifetime of Enoch was three hundred and sixty-five years. *24*Then Enoch walked with God,* and he was no longer here, for God took him.*v*

*25*When Methuselah was one hundred and eighty-seven years old, he became the father of Lamech. *26*Methuselah lived seven hun-

dred and eighty-two years after the birth of Lamech, and he had other sons and daughters. *27*The whole lifetime of Methuselah was nine hundred and sixty-nine years; then he died.

*28*When Lamech was one hundred and eighty-two years old, he begot a son *29w*and named him Noah, saying, "Out of the very ground that the LORD has put under a curse, this one shall bring us relief from our work and the toil of our hands."* *30*Lamech lived five hundred and ninety-five years after the birth of Noah, and he had other sons and daughters. *31*The whole lifetime of Lamech was seven hundred and seventy-seven years; then he died.

*32*When Noah was five hundred years old, he became the father of Shem, Ham and Japheth.*x*

CHAPTER 6

See RG 55

*Origin of the Nephilim.** *1*When men began to multiply on earth and daughters were born to them, *2*the sons of heaven* saw

---

5, 24: In place of the usual formula, Then he died, the change to Enoch walked with God clearly implies that he did not die, but like Elijah (2 Kgs 2, 11f) was taken alive to God's abode.

5, 29: There is a similarity in sound between the Hebrew word noah, "Noah," and the verbal phrase yenahamenu, "he will bring us relief"; this latter refers both to the curse put on the soil because of the fall of man (Gn 3, 17ff) and to Noah's success in agriculture, especially in raising grapes for wine (Gn 9, 20f).

6, 1-4: This is apparently a fragment of an old legend that

had borrowed much from ancient mythology. The sacred author incorporates it here, not only in order to account for the prehistoric giants of Palestine, whom the Israelites called the Nephilim, but also to introduce the story of the flood with a moral orientation—the constantly increasing wickedness of mankind.

6, 2: The sons of heaven: literally "the sons of the gods" or "the sons of God," i.e., the celestial beings of mythology.

v: Wis 4, 10f; Sir 44, 16; 49, 14; Heb 11, 5. *w:* Gn 3, 17ff. *x:* Gn 6, 10; 10, 1.

how beautiful the daughters of man were, and so they took for their wives as many of them as they chose.*y* [3]Then the LORD said: "My spirit* shall not remain in man forever, since he is but flesh. His days shall comprise one hundred and twenty years."

[4]At that time the Nephilim appeared on earth (as well as later*), after the sons of heaven had intercourse with the daughters of man, who bore them sons. They were the heroes of old, the men of renown.*z*

Warning of the Flood. [5]*When the LORD saw how great was man's wickedness on earth, and how no desire that his heart conceived was ever anything but evil,*a* [6]he regretted that he had made man on the earth, and his heart was grieved.

[7]So the LORD said: "I will wipe out from the earth the men whom I have created, and not only the men, but also the beasts and the creeping things and the birds of the air, for I am sorry that I made them." [8]But Noah found favor with the LORD.

[9]These are the descendants of Noah. Noah, a good man and blameless in that age,*b* [10]for he walked with God, begot three sons: Shem, Ham and Japheth.

[11]In the eyes of God the earth was corrupt and full of lawlessness.*c* [12]When God saw how corrupt the earth had become, since all mortals led depraved lives on earth,*d* [13]he said to Noah: "I have decided to put an end to all mortals on earth; the earth is full of lawlessness because of them. So I will destroy them and all life on earth.*e*

Preparation for the Flood. [14]"Make yourself an ark of gopherwood,* put various compartments in it, and cover it inside and out with pitch. [15]This is how you shall build it: the length of the ark shall be three hundred cubits, its width fifty cubits, and its height thirty cubits.* [16]Make an opening for daylight* in the ark, and finish the ark a cubit above it. Put an entrance in the side of the ark, which you shall make with bottom, second and third decks. [17]I, on my part, am about to bring the flood [waters] on the earth, to destroy everywhere all creatures in which there is the breath of life; everything on earth shall perish.*f* [18]But with you I will establish my covenant; you and your sons, your wife and your sons' wives, shall go into the ark.*g* [19]Of all other living creatures you shall bring two into the ark, one male and one female, that you may keep them alive with you. [20]Of all kinds of birds, of all kinds of beasts, and of all kinds of creeping things, two of each shall come into the ark with you, to stay alive. [21]Moreover, you are to provide yourself with all the food that is to be eaten,

---

6, 3: My spirit: the breath of life referred to in Gn 2, 7. His days . . . years: probably the time God would still let men live on earth before destroying them with the flood, rather than the maximum span of life God would allot to individual men in the future.

6, 4: As well as later: According to Nm 13, 33, when the Israelites invaded Palestine and found there the tall aboriginal Anakim, they likened them to the Nephilim; cf Dt 2, 10f. Perhaps the huge megalithic structures in Palestine were thought to have been built by a race of giants, whose superhuman strength was attributed to semi-divine origin. The heroes of old: the legendary worthies of ancient mythology.

6, 5—8, 22: The story of the great flood here recorded is a composite narrative based on two separate sources interwoven into an intricate patchwork. To the Yahwist source, with some later editorial additions, are usually assigned 6, 5-8; 7, 1-5. 7-10. 12. 16b. 17b. 22-23; 8, 2b-3a. 6-12. 13b. 20-22. The other sections come from the "Priestly document." The combination of the two sources produced certain duplications (e.g., 6, 13-22 of the Yahwist source, beside 7, 1-5 of the Priestly source); also certain inconsistencies, such as the number of the various animals taken into the ark (6, 19f; 7, 14f of the Priestly source, beside 7,

2f of the Yahwist source), and the timetable of the flood (8, 3-5. 13f of the Priestly source, beside 7, 4. 10. 12. 17b; 8, 6. 10. 12 of the Yahwist source). Both biblical sources go back ultimately to an ancient Mesopotamian story of a great flood, preserved in the eleventh tablet of the Gilgamesh Epic. The latter account, in some respects remarkably similar to the biblical account, is in others very different from it.

6, 14: Gopherwood: an unidentified wood not mentioned elsewhere; gopher is merely the Hebrew word for it.

6, 15: The dimensions of Noah's ark were approximately 440 x 73 x 44 feet, a foot and a half to the cubit. The ark of the Babylonian flood story was an exact cube, 120 cubits in length, width, and height.

6, 16: Opening for daylight: a conjectural rendering of the Hebrew word sohar, occurring only here. The reference is probably to an open space on all sides near the top of the ark to admit light and air. The ark also had a window or hatch, which could be opened and closed (Gn 8, 6).

---

y: Mt 24, 38; Lk 17, 26f.   *z:* Wis 14, 6; Bar 3, 26.   *a:* Ps 14, 2f. *b:* Wis 10, 4; Sir 44, 17.   *c:* Jb 22, 15ff.   *d:* Ps 14, 2.   *e:* Sir 40, 9f; 44, 17; Mt 24, 37ff.   *f:* Gn 7, 4. 21; 2 Pt 2, 5.   *g:* Gn 9, 9; Wis 14, 6; Heb 11, 7; 1 Pt 3, 20.

Clean and Unclean Animals

The differences between clean animals (7, 2) and animals that are not clean (7, 8) involve a whole system of dividing animals and other parts of life into the categories of clean and unclean. Any animals that have two or more characteristics that usually go together are considered clean. For example, animals that live in the sea typically have fins and scales. Therefore, all fish are clean because they have the fins and scales that sea creatures usually have. However, other sea creatures such as clams or oysters are unclean because they live in the sea but do not have fins or scales. They are unclean because they are thought to cross created boundaries or mix characteristics that do not normally belong together (see Lv 11, 1–47 and Dt 14, 3–21). This system of dividing between clean and unclean underlies the Jewish dietary laws of kosher eating.

and store it away, that it may serve as provisions for you and for them." ²²This Noah did; he carried out all the commands that God gave him.

See RG
55

CHAPTER 7

¹Then the LORD said to Noah: "Go into the ark, you and all your household, for you alone in this age have I found to be truly just.ʰ ²Of every clean animal, take with you seven pairs, a male and its mate; and of the unclean animals, one pair, a male and its mate; ³likewise, of every clean bird of the air, seven pairs, a male and a female, and of all the unclean birds, one pair, a male and a female. Thus you will keep their issue alive over all the earth. ⁴Seven days from now I will bring rain down on the earth for forty days and forty nights, and so I will wipe out from the surface of the earth every moving creature that I have made."ⁱ ⁵Noah did just as the LORD had commanded him.

The Great Flood. ⁶Noah was six hundred years old when the flood waters came upon the earth. ⁷Together with his sons, his wife, and his sons' wives, Noah went into the ark because of the waters of the flood.ʲ ⁸Of the clean animals and the unclean, of the birds, and of everything that creeps on the ground, ⁹[two by two] male and female entered the ark with Noah, just as the LORD had commanded him.ᵏ ¹⁰As soon as the seven days

were over, the waters of the flood came upon the earth.

¹¹In the six hundredth year of Noah's life, in the second month, on the seventeenth day of the month: it was on that day that

All the fountains of the great abyss* burst forth,
and the floodgates of the sky were opened.

¹²For forty days and forty nights heavy rain poured down on the earth.

¹³On the precise day named, Noah and his sons Shem, Ham and Japheth, and Noah's wife, and the three wives of Noah's sons had entered the ark, ¹⁴together with every kind of wild beast, every kind of domestic animal, every kind of creeping thing of the earth, and every kind of bird. ¹⁵Pairs of all creatures in which there was the breath of life entered the ark with Noah. ¹⁶Those that entered were male and female, and of all species they came, as God had commanded Noah. Then the LORD shut him in.

¹⁷The flood continued upon the earth for forty days. As the waters increased, they lifted the ark, so that it rose above the earth. ¹⁸The swelling waters increased greatly but the ark floated on the surface of the waters. ¹⁹Higher and higher above the earth rose the waters, until all the highest mountains everywhere were submerged, ²⁰the crest ris-

7, 11: Abyss: the subterranean ocean; see note on Gn 1, 2.

h: Wis 10, 4; Sir 44, 17; 2 Pt 2, 5.   i: Gn 6, 17; 2 Pt 2, 5.   j: Wis 14, 6; 1 Pt 3, 20; 2 Pt 2, 5.   k: Gn 6, 19.

ing fifteen cubits higher than the submerged mountains. *21*All creatures that stirred on earth perished: birds, cattle, wild animals, and all that swarmed on the earth, as well as all mankind.*l* *22*Everything on dry land with the faintest breath of life in its nostrils died out. *23*The LORD wiped out every living thing on earth: man and cattle, the creeping things and the birds of the air; all were wiped out from the earth. Only Noah and those with him in the ark were left.

CHAPTER 8

See RG 55 *7, 24**The waters maintained their crest over the earth for one hundred and fifty days, *1*and then God remembered Noah and all the animals, wild and tame, that were with him in the ark. So God made a wind sweep over the earth, and the waters began to subside. *2*The fountains of the abyss and the floodgates of the sky were closed, and the downpour from the sky was held back. *3*Gradually the waters receded from the earth. At the end of one hundred and fifty days, the waters had so diminished *4*that, in the seventh month, on the seventeenth day of the month, the ark came to rest on the mountains of Ararat.* *5*The waters continued to diminish until the tenth month, and on the first day of the tenth month the tops of the mountains appeared.

*6*At the end of forty days Noah opened the hatch he had made in the ark,* *7*and he sent out a raven, to see if the waters had lessened on the earth. It flew back and forth until the waters dried off from the earth. *8*Then he sent out a dove, to see if the waters had lessened on the earth. *9*But the dove could find no place to alight and perch, and it returned to him in the ark, for there was water all over the earth. Putting out his hand, he caught the dove and drew it back to him inside the ark. *10*He waited seven days more and again sent the dove out from the ark. *11*In the evening the dove came back to him, and there in its bill was a plucked-off olive leaf! So Noah knew that the waters had lessened on the earth. *12*He waited still another seven days and then released the dove once more; and this time it did not come back.

*13*In the six hundred and first year of Noah's life, in the first month, on the first day of the month, the water began to dry up on the earth. Noah then removed the covering of the ark and saw that the surface of the ground was drying up. *14*In the second month, on the twenty-seventh day of the month, the earth was dry.

*15*Then God said to Noah: *16*"Go out of the ark, together with your wife and your sons and your sons' wives. *17*Bring out with you every living thing that is with you—all bodily creatures, be they birds or animals or creeping things of the earth—and let them abound on the earth, breeding and multiplying on it."*m* *18*So Noah came out, together with his wife and his sons and his sons' wives; *19*and all the animals, wild and tame, all the birds, and all the creeping creatures of the earth left the ark, one kind after another.

*20*Then Noah built an altar to the LORD, and choosing from every clean animal and every clean bird, he offered holocausts on the altar. *21*When the LORD smelled the sweet odor, he said to himself: "Never again will I doom the earth because of man, since the desires of man's heart are evil from the start;* nor will I ever again strike down all living beings, as I have done.*n*

22 As long as the earth lasts,
    seedtime and harvest,
    cold and heat,
    Summer and winter,
    and day and night
    shall not cease."*o*

7, 24: This verse belongs to chapter 8 but its contents properly introduce chapter 8.

8, 4: Ararat: ancient Urartu, north of the Mesopotamian plain, part of modern Armenia.

8, 6: In the original Yahwist source, from which this verse is taken, the forty days refer to the full period of the flood itself (cf Gn 7, 4. 17); in the present context, however, they seem to refer to a period following the date just given in v 5

from the Priestly source.

8, 21: From the start: literally "from his youth." It is uncertain whether this means from the beginning of the human race or from the early years of the individual.

l: 21ff; Jb 22, 16; Mt 24, 39; Lk 17, 27; 2 Pt 3, 6.   *m:* Gn 1, 22. 28.   *n:* Sir 44, 18; Is 54, 9; Rom 7, 18.   *o:* Jer 33, 20. 25.

This covenant with Noah was made with all of humankind while other covenants were with individuals or the Hebrew people.

CHAPTER 9

See RG 55

Covenant with Noah. [1]God blessed Noah and his sons and said to them: "Be fertile and multiply and fill the earth.[p] [2]Dread fear of you shall come upon all the animals of the earth and all the birds of the air, upon all the creatures that move about on the ground and all the fishes of the sea; into your power they are delivered. [3q]Every creature that is alive shall be yours to eat; I give them all to you as I did the green plants.* [4r]Only flesh with its lifeblood still in it you shall not eat.* [5]For your own lifeblood, too, I will demand an accounting: from every animal I will demand it, and from man in regard to his fellow man I will demand an accounting for human life.[s]

[6] If anyone sheds the blood of man,
   by man shall his blood be shed;
For in the image of God
   has man been made.[t]

[7]Be fertile, then, and multiply; abound on earth and subdue it."[u]

[8]God said to Noah and to his sons with him: [9]"See, I am now establishing my covenant with you and your descendants after you[v] [10]and with every living creature that was with you: all the birds, and the various tame and wild animals that were with you and came out of the ark. [11]I will establish my covenant with you, that never again shall all bodily creatures be destroyed by the waters of a flood; there shall not be another flood to devastate the earth."[w] [12]God added: "This is the sign that I am giving for all ages to come, of the covenant between me and you and every living creature with you: [13x]I set my bow in the clouds to serve as a sign of the covenant between me and the earth. [14]When I bring clouds over the earth, and the bow appears in the clouds, [15]I will recall the covenant I have made between me and you and all living beings, so that the waters shall never again become a flood to destroy all mortal beings.[y] [16]As the bow appears in the clouds, I will see it and recall the everlasting covenant that I have established between God and all living beings—all mortal creatures that are on earth." [17]God told Noah: "This is the sign of the covenant I have established between me and all mortal creatures that are on earth."

Noah and His Sons. [18]*The sons of Noah who came out of the ark were Shem, Ham and Japheth. (Ham was the father of Canaan.)[z] [19]These three were the sons of Noah, and from them the whole earth was peopled. [20]Now Noah, a man of the soil, was the first to plant a vineyard. [21]When he drank some of the wine, he became drunk and lay naked inside his tent.[a] [22]Ham, the father of Canaan, saw his father's nakedness, and he told his two brothers outside about it. [23]Shem and Japheth, however, took a robe, and holding it on their backs, they walked backward and covered their father's nakedness; since their faces were turned the other way, they did not see their father's naked-

---

9, 3: Antediluvian creatures, including man, are depicted as vegetarians (Gn 1, 29f), becoming carnivorous only after the flood.

9, 4: Because a living being dies when it loses most of its blood, the ancients regarded blood as the seat of life, and therefore as sacred. Although in itself the prohibition against eating meat with blood in it is comparable to the ritual laws of the Mosaic code, the Jews considered it binding on all men, because it was given by God to Noah, the new ancestor of all mankind; therefore the early Christian Church retained it for a time (Acts 15, 20. 29).

9, 18-27: This story seems to be a composite of two earlier accounts; in the one, Ham was guilty, whereas in the other, it was Canaan. One purpose of the story is to justify the Israelites' enslavement of the Canaanites because of certain indecent sexual practices in the Canaanite religion. Obviously the story offers no justification for enslaving African Negroes, even though Canaan is presented as a "son" of Ham because the land of Canaan belonged to Hamitic Egypt at the time of the Israelite invasion.

p: Gn 1, 22, 28; 8, 17; Jas 3, 7.   *q:* Gn 1, 29f; Dt 12, 15.   *r:* Lv 7. 26f; 17, 4; Dt 12, 16. 23; 1 Sm 14, 33; Acts 15, 20.   *s:* Gn 4, 10f; Ex 21, 12.   *t:* Gn 1, 26f; Lv 24, 17; Nm 35, 33; Jas 3, 9.   *u:* Gn 1, 28; 8, 17; 9, 2.   *v:* Gn 6, 18.   *w:* Sir 44, 18; Is 54, 9.   *x:* Sir 43, 12.   *y:* Is 54, 9.   *z:* Gn 5, 32; 10, 1.   *a:* Lam 4, 21; Heb 2, 15.

ness. ²⁴When Noah woke up from his drunkenness and learned what his youngest son had done to him, ²⁵he said:

"Cursed be Canaan!
   The lowest of slaves
   shall he be to his brothers."ᵇ

²⁶He also said:

"Blessed be the LORD, the God of Shem!*
   Let Canaan be his slave.
²⁷ May God expand Japheth,*
   so that he dwells among the tents of
      Shem;
   and let Canaan be his slave."

²⁸Noah lived three hundred and fifty years after the flood. ²⁹The whole lifetime of Noah was nine hundred and fifty years; then he died.

CHAPTER 10

See RG
55

*Table of the Nations.** ¹These are the descendants of Noah's sons, Shem, Ham and Japheth, to whom sons were born after the flood.

² ᶜThe descendants of Japheth:
   Gomer,* Magog, Madai, Javan, Tubal,
      Meshech and Tiras.ᵈ
³ The descendants of Gomer:

Ashkenaz,* Riphath and Togarmah.
⁴ The descendants of Javan:
   Elishah,* Tarshish, the Kittim and the
      Rodanim.

⁵These are the descendants of Japheth, and from them sprang the maritime nations, in their respective lands—each with its own language—by their clans within their nations.

⁶ The descendants of Ham:
   Cush,* Mizraim, Put and Canaan.
⁷ The descendants of Cush:
   Seba, Havilah, Sabtah, Raamah and
      Sabteca.
The descendants of Raamah:
   Sheba and Dedan.

⁸Cush* became the father of Nimrod, who was the first potentate on earth. ⁹He was a mighty hunter by the grace of the LORD; hence the saying, "Like Nimrod, a mighty hunter by the grace of the LORD." ¹⁰The chief cities of his kingdom were Babylon, Erech and Accad, all of them in the land of Shinar.* ¹¹From that land he went forth to Asshur,* where he built Nineveh, Rehoboth-Ir and Calah, ¹²as well as Resen, between Nineveh and Calah,* the latter being the principal city.

¹³ᵉMizraim became the father of the

9, 26: Blessed . . . Shem: perhaps the text read originally, "Blessed of the Lord be Shem," which would be expected in the context.

9, 27: In the Hebrew text there is a play on the words yapt ("expand") and yepet ("Japheth").

10, 1-32: This chapter presents a remarkably good classification of the various peoples known to the ancient Israelites; it is theologically important as stressing the basic family unity of all men on earth. The relationship between the various peoples is based partly on linguistic, partly on geographic, and partly on political grounds according to their . . . languages, . . . lands and nations: (v 31). In general, the descendants of Japheth (vv 2-5) are the peoples of the Indo-European languages to the north and west of Mesopotamia and Syria; the descendants of Ham (vv 6-20) are the Hamitic-speaking peoples of northern Africa; and the descendants of Shem (vv 21-31) are the Semitic-speaking peoples of Mesopotamia, Syria and Arabia. But there are many exceptions to this rule; the Semitic-speaking peoples of Canaan, for instance, are considered descendants of Ham, because at the time they were subject to Hamitic Egypt (vv 6. 15-19). This chapter is a composite from the Yahwist source (vv 8-19. 21. 24-30) of about the ninth century B.C., and the Priestly source (vv 1-7. 20. 22f. 31f) of a few centuries later. That is

why certain tribes of Arabia are listed under both Ham (v 7) and Shem (vv 26ff).

10, 2: Gomer: the Cimmerians; Madai: the Medes; Javan: the Greeks.

10, 3: Ashkenaz: the Scythians.

10, 4: Elishah: Cyprus; the Kittim: certain inhabitants of Cyprus; the Rodanim: the inhabitants of Rhodes.

10, 6: Cush: Biblical Ethiopia, modern Nubia. Mizraim: Egypt; Put: either Punt in East Africa or Libya.

10, 8: Cush: here, the Kassites; see note on Gn 2, 10-14. Nimrod: probably Tukulti-Ninurta I (thirteenth century B.C.), the first Assyrian conqueror of Babylonia and a famous city-builder at home.

10, 10: Shinar: ancient Sumer in southern Mesopotamia, mentioned also in Gn 11, 2; 14, 1.

10, 11: Asshur: Assyria. Rehoboth-Ir: literally "wide-streets city," was probably not the name of another city, but an epithet of Nineveh; cf Jon 3, 3.

10, 12: Calah: Assyrian Kalhu, the capital of Assyria in the ninth century B.C.

---

b: Dt 27, 16; Wis 12, 11.   c: 2-8: 1 Chr 1, 5-10.   d: Ez 38, 2.
e: 13-18: 1 Chr 1, 11-16.

ASHKENAZ (Scythians)

Black Sea

Caspian Sea

JAPHETH

Gomer

Meshech

LUD
(Lydia)

Tubal

Togarmah •

JAVAN

ASSHUR (Assyria)

Nineveh

Calah •

Asshur •

MADAI
(Medes)

Rodanim
(Rhodes)

Caphtorim
(Crete)

Hamath
Arvad

Elishah
(Cyprus)

Aram

Sidon

River Euphrates

River Tigris

Accad

Babylon (Babel)

Shinar

ELAM

Mediterranean Sea

Erech •

Put
(Lehabim?)
(Libya)

Gaza • Canaan
• Gerar

EGYPT

MIDIAN

Persian Gulf

DEDAN
• Dedan

SHEM

River Nile

OPHIR

HAM

CUSH (Ethiopia)

Red Sea

0   100   200 Miles

0   100   200 Kilometers

SEBA

HAZARMAVETH

SHEBA

Havilah

Sabtah

Table of Nations

21

Ludim, the Anamim, the Lehabim, the Naphtuhim, [14]the Pathrusim,* the Casluhim, and the Caphtorim from whom the Philistines sprang. [15]Canaan became the father of Sidon, his first-born, and of Heth;* [16]also of the Jebusites, the Amorites, the Girgashites, [17]the Hivites, the Arkites, the Sinites, [18]the Arvadites, the Zemarites and the Hamathites. Afterward, the clans of the Canaanites spread out, [19]so that the Canaanite borders extended from Sidon all the way to Gerar, near Gaza, and all the way to Sodom, Gomorrah, Admah and Zeboiim, near Lasha.*

[20]These are the descendants of Ham, according to their clans and languages, by their lands and nations.

[21]To Shem also, Japheth's oldest brother and the ancestor of all the children of Eber, sons were born.

[22] *f*The descendants of Shem:
    Elam, Asshur, Arpachshad, Lud and
    Aram.
[23] The descendants of Aram:
    Uz, Hul, Gether and Mash.

[24]Arpachshad became the father of Shelah, and Shelah became the father of Eber. [25]To Eber two sons were born: the name of the first was Peleg, for in his time the world was divided;* and the name of his brother was Joktan.

[26]Joktan became the father of Almodad, Sheleph, Hazarmaveth, Jerah, [27]Hadoram, Uzal, Diklah, [28]Obal, Abimael, Sheba [29]Ophir, Havilah and Jobab. All these were descendants of Joktan. [30]Their settlements extended all the way to Sephar, the eastern hill country.

[31]These are the descendants of Shem, according to their clans and languages, by their lands and nations.

[32]These are the groupings of Noah's sons, according to their origins and by their nations. From these the other nations of the earth branched out after the flood.

CHAPTER 11

See RG 55

*The Tower of Babel.** [1]The whole world spoke the same language, using the same words. [2]While men were migrating in the east, they came upon a valley in the land of Shinar* and settled there. [3]They said to one another, "Come, let us mold bricks and harden them with fire." They used bricks for stone, and bitumen for mortar. [4]Then they said, "Come, let us build ourselves a city and a tower with its top in the sky,* and so make a name for ourselves; otherwise we shall be scattered all over the earth."

[5]The LORD came down to see the city and the tower that the men had built. [6]Then the LORD said: "If now, while they are one people, all speaking the same language, they have started to do this, nothing will later stop them from doing whatever they presume to do. [7]Let us then go down and there confuse their language, so that one will not understand what another says." [8]Thus the LORD scattered them from there all over the earth, and they stopped building the city. [9]That is why it was called Babel,* because there the LORD confused the speech of all the world. It was from that place that he scattered them all over the earth.

10, 14: The Pathrusim: the people of upper (southern) Egypt; cf Is 11, 11; Jer 44, 1; Ez 29, 14; 30, 14. Caphtorim: Crete; for Caphtor as the place of origin of the Philistines, cf Dt 2, 23; Am 9, 7; Jer 47, 4.

10, 15: Heth: the biblical Hittites; see note on Gn 23, 3.

10, 19: Lasha: the reading of this name is uncertain; perhaps it should be "Bela"; cf Gn 14, 2.

10, 25: In the Hebrew text there is a play on the name Peleg and the word niplega, "was divided."

11, 1-9: This story, based on traditions about the temple towers or ziggurats of Babylonia, is used by the sacred writer primarily to illustrate man's increasing wickedness, shown here in his presumptuous effort to create an urban culture apart from God. The secondary motive in the story is to present an imaginative origin of the diversity of the languages among the various peoples inhabiting the earth, as well as an artificial explanation of the name "Babylon."

11, 2: Shinar: see note on Gn 10, 10.

11, 4: Tower with its top in the sky: a direct reference to the chief ziggurat of Babylon, the E-sag-ila, signifying "the house that raises high its head." Babylonian ziggurats were the earliest skyscrapers.

11, 9: Babel: the Hebrew form of the name "Babylon"; the native name, Bab-ili, means "gate of the gods." The Hebrew word balil, "he confused," has a similar sound. Apparently the name referred originally only to a certain part of the city, the district near the gate that led to the temple area.

---

f: 22-29: 1 Chr 1, 17-23.

The Line from Shem to Abraham.*
[10g]This is the record of the descendants of Shem. When Shem was one hundred years old, he became the father of Arpachshad, two years after the flood. [11]Shem lived five hundred years after the birth of Arpachshad, and he had other sons and daughters.

[12]When Arpachshad was thirty-five years old, he became the father of Shelah.* [13]Arpachshad lived four hundred and three years after the birth of Shelah, and he had other sons and daughters.

[14]When Shelah was thirty years old, he became the father of Eber. [15]Shelah lived four hundred and three years after the birth of Eber, and he had other sons and daughters.

[16]When Eber* was thirty-four years old, he became the father of Peleg. [17]Eber lived four hundred and thirty years after the birth of Peleg, and he had other sons and daughters.

[18]When Peleg was thirty years old, he became the father of Reu. [19]Peleg lived two hundred and nine years after the birth of Reu, and he had other sons and daughters.

[20]When Reu was thirty-two years old, he became the father of Serug. [21]Reu lived two hundred and seven years after the birth of Serug, and he had other sons and daughters.

[22]When Serug was thirty years old, he became the father of Nahor. [23]Serug lived two hundred years after the birth of Nahor, and he had other sons and daughters.

[24]When Nahor was twenty-nine years old, he became the father of Terah. [25]Nahor lived one hundred and nineteen years after the birth of Terah, and he had other sons and daughters.

[26]When Terah was seventy years old, he became the father of Abram, Nahor and Haran.[h]

II: The Patriarch Abraham

Terah. [27]This is the record of the descendants of Terah. Terah became the father of Abram, Nahor and Haran, and Haran became the father of Lot. [28]Haran died before his father Terah, in his native land, in Ur of the Chaldeans.* [29]Abram and Nahor took wives; the name of Abram's wife was Sarai, and the name of Nahor's wife was Milcah, daughter of Haran, the father of Milcah and Iscah.[i] [30]Sarai was barren; she had no child.

[31]Terah took his son Abram, his grandson Lot, son of Haran, and his daughter-in-law Sarai, the wife of his son Abram, and brought them out of Ur of the Chaldeans, to go to the land of Canaan.* But when they reached Haran, they settled there.[j] [32]The lifetime of Terah was two hundred and five years; then Terah died in Haran.*

CHAPTER 12

See RG 58-59

Abram's Call and Migration. [1]The LORD said to Abram: "Go forth from the land of your kinsfolk and from your father's house to a land that I will show you.[k]

[2] "I will make of you a great nation,
  and I will bless you;
  I will make your name great,

11, 10-26: This section is a continuation of the genealogical record given in Gn 5, 1-32; see note there. Although the ages of the patriarchs in this list are much lower than those of the antediluvian patriarchs, they are still artificial and devoid of historical value. The ages given here are from the current Hebrew text; the Samaritan and Greek texts have divergent sets of numbers in most cases.

11, 12: The Greek text has a certain Kenan (cf Gn 5, 9f) between Arpachshad and Shelah. The text is followed in Lk 3, 36.

11, 16: Eber: the eponymous ancestor of the Hebrews, "descendants of Eber" (Gn 10, 21. 24-30); see note on Gn 14, 13.

11, 28: Ur of the Chaldeans: Ur was an extremely ancient city of the Sumerians (later, of the Babylonians) in southern Mesopotamia. The Greek text has "the land of the Chaldeans." In either case, the term Chaldeans is an anachronism, because the Chaldeans were not known to history until approximately a thousand years after Abraham's time.

11, 31: The Samaritan and Greek texts include Nahor and his wife in Terah's migration to Haran. Although this is probably due to scribal harmonization, Nahor's family actually did migrate to Haran; cf Gn 24, 10; 27, 43.

11, 32: Since Terah was seventy years old when his son Abraham was born (v 26), and Abraham was seventy-five when he left Haran (Gn 12, 4), Terah lived in Haran for sixty years after Abraham's departure. According to the tradition in the Samaritan text, Terah died when he was one hundred and forty-five years old, therefore, in the same year in which Abraham left Haran. This is the tradition followed in St. Stephen's speech: Abraham left Haran "after his father's death" (Acts 7, 4).

---

g: 10-26: 1 Chr 1, 24-27; Lk 3, 34ff. h: Jos 24, 2; 1 Chr 1, 27.
i: Gn 17, 15; 20, 12. j: Jos 24, 3; Neh 9, 7; Jdt 5, 6-9; Acts 7, 4.
k: Acts 7, 3; Heb 11, 8.

so that you will be a blessing.[l]
[3] [m]I will bless those who bless you
and curse those who curse you.
All the communities of the earth
shall find blessing in you."[*]

[4] [n]Abram went as the LORD directed him, and Lot went with him. Abram was seventy-five years old when he left Haran. [5]Abram took his wife Sarai, his brother's son Lot, all the possessions that they had accumulated, and the persons[*] they had acquired in Haran, and they set out for the land of Canaan. When they came to the land of Canaan, [6]Abram passed through the land as far as the sacred place at Shechem, by the terebinth of Moreh. (The Canaanites were then in the land.)

[7]The LORD appeared to Abram and said, "To your descendants I will give this land." So Abram built an altar there to the LORD who had appeared to him.[o] [8]From there he moved on to the hill country east of Bethel, pitching his tent with Bethel to the west and Ai to the east. He built an altar there to the LORD and invoked the LORD by name. [9]Then Abram journeyed on by stages to the Negeb.[*]

Abram and Sarai in Egypt. [10]There was famine in the land; so Abram went down to Egypt to sojourn there, since the famine in the land was severe.[p] [11]When he was about to enter Egypt, he said to his wife Sarai: "I know well how beautiful a woman you are. [12]When the Egyptians see you, they will say, 'She is his wife'; then they will kill me, but let you live. [13]Please say, therefore, that you are my sister,[*] so that it may go well with me on your account and my life may be spared for your sake."[q] [14]When Abram came to

Egypt, the Egyptians saw how beautiful the woman was; [15]and when Pharaoh's courtiers saw her, they praised her to Pharaoh. So she was taken into Pharaoh's palace. [16]On her account it went very well with Abram, and he received flocks and herds, male and female slaves, male and female asses, and camels.[*]

[17]But the LORD struck Pharaoh and his household with severe plagues because of Abram's wife Sarai.[r] [18]Then Pharaoh summoned Abram and said to him: "How could you do this to me! Why didn't you tell me she was your wife? [19]Why did you say, 'She is my sister,' so that I took her for my wife? Here, then, is your wife. Take her and be gone!" [20]Then Pharaoh gave men orders concerning him, and they sent him on his way, with his wife and all that belonged to him.

CHAPTER 13

See RG 58-59

Abram and Lot Part. [1]From Egypt Abram went up to the Negeb with his wife and all that belonged to him, and Lot accompanied him.[s] [2]Now Abram was very rich in livestock, silver and gold.[t] [3]From the Negeb he traveled by stages toward Bethel, to the place between Bethel and Ai where his tent had formerly stood, [4]the site where he had first built the altar; and there he invoked the LORD by name.[u]

[5]Lot, who went with Abram, also had flocks and herds and tents, [6]so that the land could not support them if they stayed together; their possessions were so great that they could not dwell together. [7]There were quarrels between the herdsmen of Abram's livestock and those of Lot's. (At this time the

12, 3: Shall find blessing in you: the sense of the Hebrew expression is probably reflexive, "shall bless themselves through you" (i.e., in giving a blessing they shall say, "May you be as blessed as Abraham"), rather than passive, "shall be blessed in you." Since the term is understood in a passive sense in the New Testament (Acts 3, 25; Gal 3, 8), it is rendered here by a neutral expression that admits of both meanings. So also in the blessings given by God to Isaac (Gn 26, 4) and Jacob (Gn 28, 14).

12, 5: Persons: slaves and retainers that formed the social aggregate under the leadership of Abraham; cf Gn 14, 14.

12, 9: The Negeb: the semidesert land of southern Palestine.

12, 13: You are my sister: although Abraham's deceit may not be fully defensible, his statement was at least a half-truth; Sarah was indeed his relative, called "a sister" in Hebrew; cf Gn 20, 12. Moreover, the ancient traditions on which this

story and the parallel ones in Gn 20, 1-18 and 26, 6-11 are based, probably come from the Hurrian custom of wife-sister marriage. Among the Hurrians, with whom Abraham's clan lived in close contact at Haran, a man could adopt his wife as his sister and thus give her higher status.

12, 16: Camels: domesticated camels probably did not come into common use in the ancient Near East until the end of the 2nd millennium B.C. Thus the mention of camels at the time of the patriarchs (Gn 24, 11-64; 30, 43; 31, 17. 34; 32, 8. 16; 37, 25) is seemingly an anachronism.

l: Gn 17, 6; Sir 44, 20; Rom 4, 17-22.   *m:* Gn 18, 18; 22, 18; Acts 3, 25; Gal 3, 8.   *n:* 4f: Gn 11, 31; Jos 24, 3; Acts 7, 4.   *o:* Ex 33, 1; Dt 34, 4; Acts 7, 5.   *p:* Gn 26, 1.   *q:* Gn 20, 12f; 26, 7.   *r:* Ps 105, 14.   *s:* Gn 12, 9.   *t:* Ps 112, 1ff; Prv 10, 22.   *u:* Gn 12, 8.

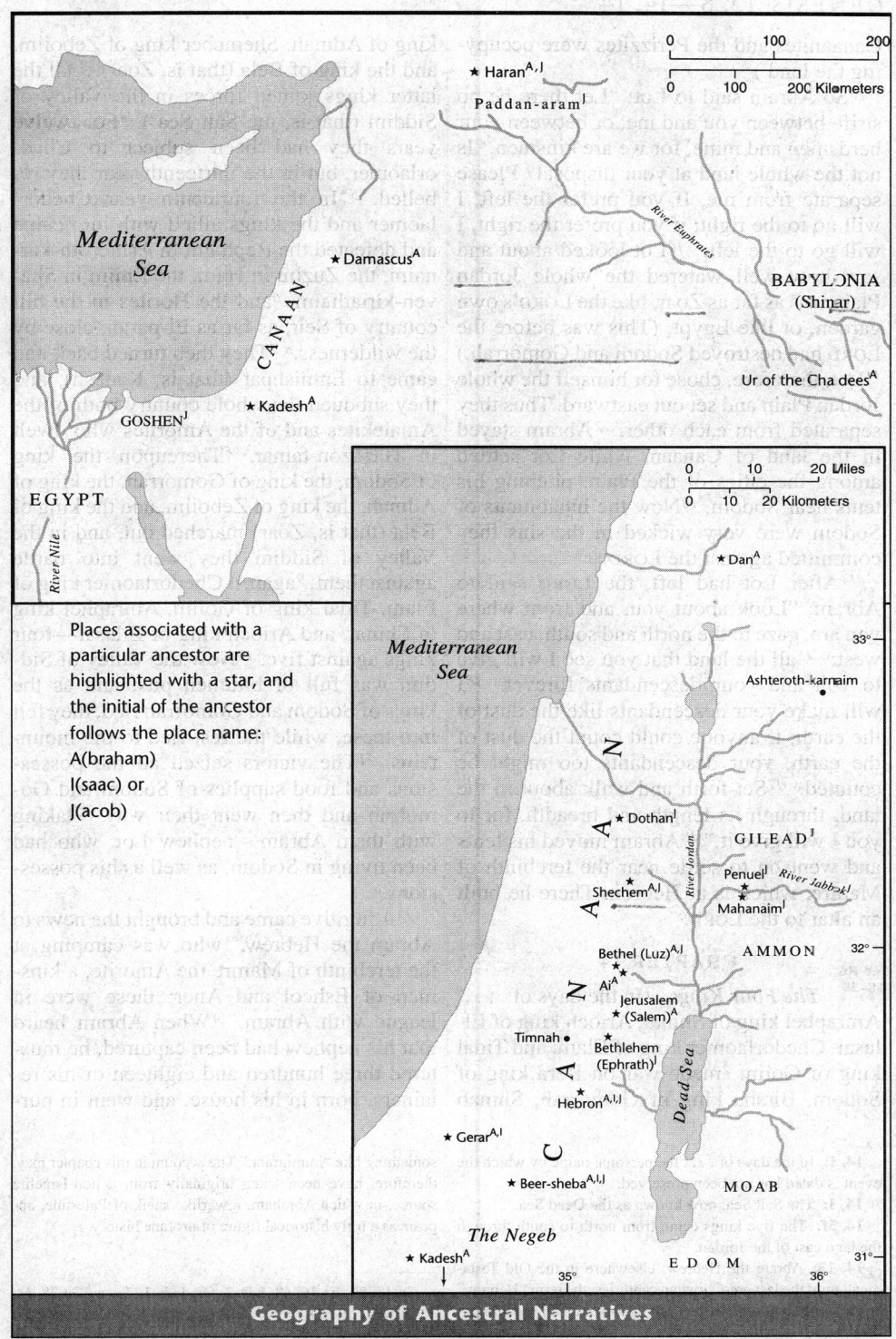

Places associated with a particular ancestor are highlighted with a star, and the initial of the ancestor follows the place name:
A(braham)
I(saac) or
J(acob)

Geography of Ancestral Narratives

Canaanites and the Perizzites were occupying the land.)

⁸So Abram said to Lot: "Let there be no strife between you and me, or between your herdsmen and mine, for we are kinsmen. ⁹Is not the whole land at your disposal? Please separate from me. If you prefer the left, I will go to the right; if you prefer the right, I will go to the left." ¹⁰Lot looked about and saw how well watered the whole Jordan Plain was as far as Zoar, like the LORD's own garden, or like Egypt. (This was before the LORD had destroyed Sodom and Gomorrah.) ¹¹Lot, therefore, chose for himself the whole Jordan Plain and set out eastward. Thus they separated from each other; ¹²Abram stayed in the land of Canaan, while Lot settled among the cities of the Plain, pitching his tents near Sodom. ¹³Now the inhabitants of Sodom were very wicked in the sins they committed against the LORD.ᵛ

¹⁴After Lot had left, the LORD said to Abram: "Look about you, and from where you are, gaze to the north and south, east and west;ʷ ¹⁵all the land that you see I will give to you and your descendants forever.ˣ ¹⁶I will make your descendants like the dust of the earth; if anyone could count the dust of the earth, your descendants too might be counted.ʸ ¹⁷Set forth and walk about in the land, through its length and breadth, for to you I will give it." ¹⁸Abram moved his tents and went on to settle near the terebinth of Mamre, which is at Hebron. There he built an altar to the LORD.ᶻ

See RG 58–59

CHAPTER 14

The Four Kings. ¹In the days of . . . ,* Amraphel king of Shinar, Arioch king of Ellasar, Chedorlaomer king of Elam, and Tidal king of Goiim ²made war on Bera king of Sodom, Birsha king of Gomorrah, Shinab king of Admah, Shemeber king of Zeboiim, and the king of Bela (that is, Zoar). ³All the latter kings joined forces in the Valley of Siddim (that is, the Salt Sea*). ⁴For twelve years they had been subject to Chedorlaomer, but in the thirteenth year they rebelled. ⁵*In the fourteenth year Chedorlaomer and the kings allied with him came and defeated the Rephaim in Ashteroth-karnaim, the Zuzim in Ham, the Emim in Shaveh-kiriathaim, ⁶and the Horites in the hill country of Seir, as far as El-paran, close by the wilderness.ᵃ ⁷They then turned back and came to Enmishpat (that is, Kadesh), and they subdued the whole country both of the Amalekites and of the Amorites who dwelt in Hazazon-tamar. ⁸Thereupon the king of Sodom, the king of Gomorrah, the king of Admah, the king of Zeboiim, and the king of Bela (that is, Zoar) marched out, and in the Valley of Siddim they went into battle against them: ⁹against Chedorlaomer king of Elam, Tidal king of Goiim, Amraphel king of Shinar, and Arioch king of Ellasar—four kings against five. ¹⁰Now the Valley of Siddim was full of bitumen pits; and as the kings of Sodom and Gomorrah fled, they fell into these, while the rest fled to the mountains. ¹¹The victors seized all the possessions and food supplies of Sodom and Gomorrah and then went their way, ¹²taking with them Abram's nephew Lot, who had been living in Sodom, as well as his possessions.ᵇ

¹³A fugitive came and brought the news to Abram the Hebrew,* who was camping at the terebinth of Mamre the Amorite, a kinsman of Eshcol and Aner; these were in league with Abram. ¹⁴When Abram heard that his nephew had been captured, he mustered three hundred and eighteen of his retainers, born in his house, and went in pur-

---

14, 1: In the days of . . . : the personal name by which the event is dated has not been preserved.

14, 3: The Salt Sea: now known as the Dead Sea.

14, 5f: The five kings came from north to south through the land east of the Jordan.

14, 13: Abram the Hebrew: elsewhere in the Old Testament, until the last pre-Christian centuries, the term "Hebrew" is used only by non-Israelites, or by Israelites in speaking to foreigners, since it evidently had a disparaging connotation—

something like "immigrant." The account in this chapter may, therefore, have been taken originally from a non-Israelite source, in which Abraham, a warlike sheik of Palestine, appears as a truly historical figure of profane history.

ᵛ: Gn 18, 20; Ez 16, 49; 2 Pt 2, 6ff; Jude 1, 7.   ʷ: Gn 28, 14.   ˣ: Gn 12, 7; Mt 5, 4; Lk 1, 55; Acts 7, 5; Gal 3, 16.   ʸ: Gn 22, 17; Nm 23, 10.   ᶻ: Gn 14, 13.   ᵃ: Dt 2, 12.   ᵇ: Gn 13, 10ff.

suit as far as Dan. [15]He and his party deployed against them at night, defeated them, and pursued them as far as Hobah, which is north of Damascus. [16]He recovered all the possessions, besides bringing back his kinsman Lot and his possessions, along with the women and the other captives.

[17]When Abram returned from his victory over Chedorlaomer and the kings who were allied with him, the king of Sodom went out to greet him in the Valley of Shaveh (that is, the King's Valley).

[18]Melchizedek, king of Salem,* brought out bread and wine, and being a priest of God Most High,* he blessed Abram with these words:[c]

[19] "Blessed be Abram by God Most High,*
the creator of heaven and earth;
[20] And blessed be God Most High,
who delivered your foes into your
hand."

Then Abram gave him* a tenth of everything. [21]The king of Sodom said to Abram, "Give me the people; the goods you may keep." [22]But Abram replied to the king of Sodom: "I have sworn to the LORD, God Most High,* the creator of heaven and earth, [23]that I would not take so much as a thread or a sandal strap from anything that is yours, lest you should say, 'I made Abram rich.' [24]Nothing for me except what my servants have used up and the share that is due to the men who joined me—Aner, Eshcol and Mamre; let them take their share."

CHAPTER 15

The Covenant with Abram. [1]Some time after these events, this word of the LORD came to Abram in a vision:

See RG 58-59

"Fear not, Abram!
I am your shield;
I will make your reward very great."

[2]But Abram said, "O Lord GOD, what good will your gifts be, if I keep on being childless and have as my heir the steward of my house, Eliezer?" [3]Abram continued, "See, you have given me no offspring, and so one of my servants will be my heir." [4]Then the word of the LORD came to him: "No, that one shall not be your heir; your own issue shall be your heir."[d] [5]He took him outside and said, "Look up at the sky and count the stars, if you can. Just so," he added, "shall your descendants be."[e] [6f]Abram put his faith in the LORD, who credited it to him as an act of righteousness.*

[7]He then said to him, "I am the LORD who brought you from Ur of the Chaldeans to give you this land as a possession."[g] [8]"O Lord GOD," he asked, "how am I to know that I shall possess it?" [9]He answered him, "Bring me a three-year-old heifer, a three-year-old she-goat, a three-year-old* ram, a turtledove, and a young pigeon."[h] [10]He brought him all these, split them in two, and placed each half opposite the other; but the birds he did not cut up. [11]Birds of prey swooped down on the carcasses, but Abram stayed with them. [12]As the sun was about to

---

14, 18: Salem: traditionally identified with Jerusalem (Ps 76, 3), but the Hebrew text is not certain; instead of the present melek shalem ("king of Salem") the original may have been melek shelomo ("a king allied to him"). In Heb 7, 2, "king of Salem" is interpreted as "king of peace" (shalom).

14, 19: God Most High: in Hebrew, el-elyon. In Canaanite texts, each element may occur separately as the name of a specific deity, or they may be applied together to a single deity, as is done here by the Canaanite priest Melchizedek. For the Israelites, el became a poetic synonym for elohim ("God"); elyon ("Most High") became one of the titles of their God Yahweh.

14, 20: Abram gave him: literally "he gave him"; but Abram is to be understood as the subject of the sentence, for the tithes were the tenth part assigned to priests; cf Heb 7, 4-10.

14, 22: Abraham uses the name of the Canaanite god el-elyon ("God, the Most High") in apposition to the name of his God, Yahweh ("the LORD").

15, 6: Abraham's faith in God's promises was regarded as an act of righteousness, i.e., as expressing the "right" attitude of man toward God. In turn, God credited this to Abraham, i.e., gave him title to the fulfillment of God's promises. St. Paul (Rom 4, 1-25; Gal 3, 6-9) makes Abraham's faith a model for that of Christians.

15, 9: Three-year-old: ritually mature.

c: Ps 110, 4; Heb 5, 6. 10; 7, 1. d: Gn 17, 16. e: Gn 22, 17; 28, 14; Ex 32, 13; Dt 1, 10; Sir 44, 21; Rom 4. 18; Heb 11, 12. f: 1 Mc 2, 52; Rom 4, 3. 9. 22; Gal 3, 6f; Jas 2, 23. g: Gn 11, 31; 12, 1; Ex 32, 13; Neh 9, 7f; Acts 7, 2f. h: Lv 1, 14.

Hagar, Sarai, and the Birth of Ishmael

Because Sarai could have no children on her own, ancient custom allowed her to have a child through one of her women servants. Hagar receives a promise (16, 10) that is virtually identical to the promise the Lord made to Abram (15, 5).

set, a trance fell upon Abram, and a deep, terrifying darkness enveloped him.

[13]Then the Lord said to Abram: "Know for certain that your descendants shall be aliens in a land not their own, where they shall be enslaved and oppressed for four hundred years.[i] [14]But I will bring judgment on the nation they must serve, and in the end they will depart with great wealth.[j] [15]You, however, shall join your forefathers in peace; you shall be buried at a contented old age. [16]In the fourth time-span* the others shall come back here; the wickedness of the Amorites will not have reached its full measure until then."[k]

[17]When the sun had set and it was dark, there appeared a smoking brazier* and a flaming torch, which passed between those pieces. [18]It was on that occasion that the Lord made a covenant* with Abram, saying: "To your descendants I give this land, from the Wadi of Egypt to the Great River [the Euphrates],[l] [19m]the land of the Kenites, the Kenizzites, the Kadmonites, [20]the Hittites, the Perizzites, the Rephaim, [21]the Amorites, the Canaanites, the Girgashites, and the Jebusites."

CHAPTER 16

See RG 58-59

Birth of Ishmael. [1]*Abram's wife Sarai had borne him no children. She had, however, an Egyptian maidservant named Hagar.[n] [2]Sarai said to Abram: "The Lord has kept me from bearing children. Have intercourse, then, with my maid; perhaps I shall have sons through her." Abram heeded Sarai's request.[o] [3]Thus, after Abram had lived ten years in the land of Canaan, his wife Sarai took her maid, Hagar the Egyptian, and gave her to her husband Abram to be his concubine. [4]He had intercourse with her, and she became pregnant. When she became aware of her pregnancy, she looked on her mistress with disdain.[p] [5q]So Sarai said to Abram: "You are responsible for this outrage against me. I myself gave my maid to your embrace; but ever since she became aware of her pregnancy, she has been looking on me with disdain. May the Lord decide between you and me!" [6]Abram told Sarai: "Your maid is in your power. Do to her whatever you please." Sarai then abused her so much that Hagar ran away from her.

[7]The Lord's messenger* found her by a spring in the wilderness, the spring on the road to Shur,[r] [8]and he asked, "Hagar, maid of Sarai, where have you come from and where are you going?" She answered, "I am running away from my mistress, Sarai." [9]But the Lord's messenger told her: "Go back to your mistress and submit to her abusive treatment. [10]I will make your descendants so numerous," added the Lord's messenger, "that they will be too many to count.[s] [11]Besides," the Lord's messenger said to her:

15, 16: Time-span: the Hebrew term dor is commonly rendered as "generation," but it may signify a period of varying length. Neither this passage nor the statement about the four hundred years has any value for determining how long the Israelites were in Egypt.

15, 17: Brazier: literally "oven"; a portable one is meant here. The smoke and fire represent God's presence. Although the text does not mention it, Abraham no doubt also walked between the split carcasses. For the meaning of this strange ceremony, see note on Jer 34, 18ff.

15, 18: Made a covenant: literally "cut a covenant"; the expression derives from the ceremony of cutting the animals in two.

16, 1-6: Sarah's actions are all in keeping with the laws of the time, as known from ancient extra-biblical sources.

16, 7: The Lord's messenger: a manifestation of God in human form; therefore in v 13 the messenger is identified with the Lord himself.

i: Ex 12, 40; Nm 20, 15; Jdt 5, 9f; Is 52, 4; Acts 13, 20; Gal 3, 17. j: Ex 3, 8. 21f. k: 1 Kgs 21, 26. l: Ex 32, 13; Neh 9, 8; Ps 105, 11; Sir 44, 21. m: 19f: Dt 7, 1. n: Gn 11, 30. o: Gn 21, 8f; Gal 4, 22. p: 1 Sm 1, 6; Prv 30, 23. q: 5-16: Gn 21, 10-19. r: Ex 15, 22. s: Gn 17, 20; 21, 13. 18; 25, 12-18.

"You are now pregnant and shall bear a
    son;
  you shall name him Ishmael,*
for the LORD has heard you,
  God has answered you.

[12] He shall be a wild ass of a man,
    his hand against everyone,
    and everyone's hand against him;
  in opposition to all his kin
    shall he encamp."[t]

[13] To the LORD who spoke to her she gave
a name, saying, "You are the God of Vision";* she meant, "Have I really seen God
and remained alive after my vision?"[u] [14] That
is why the well is called Beer-lahai-roi.* It is
between Kadesh and Bered.

[15] Hagar bore Abram a son, and Abram
named the son whom Hagar bore him Ishmael.[v] [16] Abram was eighty-six years old
when Hagar bore him Ishmael.

CHAPTER 17

See RG 58-59
Covenant of Circumcision. [1] When
Abram was ninety-nine years old, the LORD
appeared to him and said: "I am God the
Almighty.* Walk in my presence and be
blameless.[w] [2] Between you and me I will establish my covenant, and I will multiply you
exceedingly."[x]

[3] When Abram prostrated himself, God
continued to speak to him: [4] "My covenant
with you is this: you are to become the father
of a host of nations.[y] [5] No longer shall you be
called Abram; your name shall be Abraham,*
for I am making you the father of a host of
nations.[z] [6] I will render you exceedingly fertile; I will make nations of you; kings shall
stem from you. [7] I will maintain my covenant

with you and your descendants after you
throughout the ages as an everlasting pact, to
be your God and the God of your descendants after you.[a] [8] I will give to you and to
your descendants after you the land in which
you are now staying, the whole land of Canaan, as a permanent possession; and I will
be their God."[b]

[9] God also said to Abraham: "On your
part, you and your descendants after you
must keep my covenant throughout the ages.
[10] This is my covenant with you and your descendants after you that you must keep:
every male among you shall be circumcised.[c] [11] Circumcise the flesh of your foreskin, and that shall be the mark of the covenant between you and me.[d] [12] Throughout
the ages, every male among you, when he is
eight days old, shall be circumcised, including houseborn slaves and those acquired
with money from any foreigner who is not of
your blood.[e] [13] Yes, both the houseborn
slaves and those acquired with money must
be circumcised. Thus my covenant shall be
in your flesh as an everlasting pact. [14] If a
male is uncircumcised, that is, if the flesh of
his foreskin has not been cut away, such a
one shall be cut off from his people; he has
broken my covenant."

[15] God further said to Abraham: "As for
your wife Sarai, do not call her Sarai; her
name shall be Sarah.* [16] I will bless her, and
I will give you a son by her. Him also will I
bless; he shall give rise to nations, and rulers
of peoples shall issue from him."[f] [17] Abraham prostrated himself and laughed* as he
said to himself, "Can a child be born to a
man who is a hundred years old? Or can
Sarah give birth at ninety?"[g] [18] Then Abra-

16, 11: Ishmael: in Hebrew the name means "God has heard."

16, 13: The God of Vision: in Hebrew, el-roi; hence the name of the spring. Remained alive: for the ancient notion that a person died on seeing God, cf Gn 32, 31; Ex 20, 19; Dt 4, 33; Jgs 13, 22.

16, 14: Beer-lahai-roi: probably "the well of living sight," i.e., the well where one can see (God) and yet live.

17, 1: The Almighty: traditional but incorrect rendering of the divine title shaddai, of uncertain meaning.

17, 5: Abram and Abraham are merely two forms of the same name, both meaning, "the father is exalted"; another vari-ant form is Abiram (Nm 16, 1; 1 Kgs 16, 34). The additional -ha- in the form Abraham is explained by folk etymology as

coming from ab-hamon goyim, "father of a host of nations."

17, 15: Sarai and Sarah are variant forms of the same name, both meaning "princess."

17, 17: Laughed: yishaq, which is the Hebrew form of the name "Isaac"; other similar explanations of the name are given in Gn 18, 12 and 21, 6.

t: Gn 21, 20; 25, 18. *u:* Gn 24, 62. *v:* Gn 16, 2; Gal 4, 22.
w: Gn 35, 11; Ex 6, 3. *x:* Gn 12, 2; 13, 16; Ex 32, 13. *y:* Sir 44,
21; Rom 4, 17. *z:* Neh 9, 7. *a:* Ps 105, 42; Lk 1, 72f; Gal 3, 16.
b: Ex 32, 13; Dt 1, 8; 14, 2; Lk 1, 55; Acts 7, 5. *c:* Jn 7, 22; Acts
7, 8; Rom 4, 11. *d:* Sir 44, 21. *e:* Lv 12, 3; Lk 1, 59; 2, 21.
f: Gn 18, 10; Gal 4, 23. *g:* Rom 4, 19; Heb 11, 11f.

ham said to God, "Let but Ishmael live on by your favor!" [19]God replied: "Nevertheless, your wife Sarah is to bear you a son, and you shall call him Isaac. I will maintain my covenant with him as an everlasting pact, to be his God and the God of his descendants after him.[h] [20]As for Ishmael, I am heeding you: I hereby bless him. I will make him fertile and will multiply him exceedingly. He shall become the father of twelve chieftains, and I will make of him a great nation.[i] [21]But my covenant I will maintain with Isaac, whom Sarah shall bear to you by this time next year."[j] [22]When he had finished speaking with him, God departed from Abraham.

[23]Then Abraham took his son Ishmael and all his slaves, whether born in his house or acquired with his money—every male among the members of Abraham's household—and he circumcised the flesh of their foreskins on that same day, as God had told him to do. [24]Abraham was ninety-nine years old when the flesh of his foreskin was circumcised,[k] [25]and his son Ishmael was thirteen years old when the flesh of his foreskin was circumcised. [26]Thus, on that same day Abraham and his son Ishmael were circumcised; [27]and all the male members of his household, including the slaves born in his house or acquired with his money from foreigners, were circumcised with him.

CHAPTER 18

See RG 58–59

Abraham's Visitors. [1]The LORD appeared to Abraham by the terebinth of Mamre, as he sat in the entrance of his tent, while the day was growing hot. [2]Looking up, he saw three men standing nearby. When he saw them, he ran from the entrance of the tent to greet them; and bowing to the ground,[l] [3]he said: "Sir,* if I may ask you this favor, please do not go on past your servant. [4]Let some water be brought, that you may bathe your feet, and then rest yourselves under the tree. [5]Now that you have come this close to your servant, let me bring you a little food, that you may refresh yourselves; and afterward you may go on your way." "Very well," they replied, "do as you have said."

[6]Abraham hastened into the tent and told Sarah, "Quick, three seahs* of fine flour! Knead it and make rolls." [7]He ran to the herd, picked out a tender, choice steer, and gave it to a servant, who quickly prepared it. [8]Then he got some curds* and milk, as well as the steer that had been prepared, and set these before them; and he waited on them under the tree while they ate.

[9]"Where is your wife Sarah?" they asked him. "There in the tent," he replied. [10]One of them* said, "I will surely return to you about this time next year, and Sarah will then have a son." Sarah was listening at the entrance of the tent, just behind him.[m] [11]Now Abraham and Sarah were old, advanced in years, and Sarah had stopped having her womanly periods.[n] [12]So Sarah laughed* to herself and said, "Now that I am so withered and my husband is so old, am I still to have sexual pleasure?" [13]But the LORD said to Abraham: "Why did Sarah laugh and say, 'Shall I really bear a child, old as I am?' [14]Is anything too marvelous for the LORD to do? At the appointed time, about this time next year, I will return to you, and Sarah will have a son."[o] [15]Because she was afraid, Sarah dissembled, saying, "I didn't laugh." But he said, "Yes you did."

Abraham Intercedes for Sodom. [16]The men set out from there and looked down toward Sodom; Abraham was walking with them, to see them on their way. [17]The LORD reflected: "Shall I hide from Abraham what I am about to do, [18]now that he is to become a great and populous nation, and all the na-

---

18, 3: Abraham addresses the leader of the group, whom he does not yet recognize as Yahweh; in the next two verses he speaks to all three men. The other two are later (Gn 19, 1) identified as messengers.

18, 6: Three seahs: one ephah, about half a bushel.

18, 8: Curds: a type of soft cheese or yoghurt.

18, 10: One of them: i.e., the Lord. Abraham now realizes this for the first time when he hears the prediction of a miraculous birth. About this time next year: literally "when the time becomes alive," i.e., at the time when birth is due after the period of gestation; the conception is understood as taking place soon after the prediction.

18, 12: Sarah laughed: see note on Gn 17, 17.

h: Gn 11, 30; 21, 2; Ex 32, 13; Sir 44, 22. *i:* Gn 16, 10; 21, 13. 18; 25, 12-16. *j:* Gn 18, 14; 21, 2; 26, 2-5; Rom 9, 7. *k:* Gn 17, 10; Rom 4, 11. *l:* Heb 13, 1f. *m:* Gn 17, 19; 21, 1; 2 Kgs 4, 16; Rom 9, 9. *n:* Gn 17, 17; Rom 4, 19; Heb 11, 11f. *o:* Mt 19, 26; Mk 10, 27; Lk 1, 37; 18, 27; Rom 4, 21.

tions of the earth are to find blessing in him?*p* *19*Indeed, I have singled him out that he may direct his sons and his posterity to keep the way of the LORD by doing what is right and just, so that the LORD may carry into effect for Abraham the promises he made about him." *20q*Then the LORD said: "The outcry against Sodom and Gomorrah is so great, and their sin so grave,* *21*that I must go down and see whether or not their actions fully correspond to the cry against them that comes to me. I mean to find out."

*22*While the two men walked on farther toward Sodom, the LORD remained standing before Abraham. *23*Then Abraham drew nearer to him and said: "Will you sweep away the innocent with the guilty? *24*Suppose there were fifty innocent people in the city; would you wipe out the place, rather than spare it for the sake of the fifty innocent people within it? *25*Far be it from you to do such a thing, to make the innocent die with the guilty, so that the innocent and the guilty would be treated alike! Should not the judge of all the world act with justice?"*r* *26*The LORD replied, "If I find fifty innocent people in the city of Sodom, I will spare the whole place for their sake." *27*Abraham spoke up again: "See how I am presuming to speak to my Lord, though I am but dust and ashes!*s* *28*What if there are five less than fifty innocent people? Will you destroy the whole city because of those five?" "I will not destroy it," he answered, "if I find forty-five there." *29*But Abraham persisted, saying, "What if only forty are found there?" He replied, "I will forbear doing it for the sake of the forty." *30*Then he said, "Let not my Lord grow impatient if I go on. What if only thirty are found there?" He replied, "I will forbear doing it if I can find but thirty there." *31*Still he went on, "Since I have thus dared to speak to my Lord, what if there are no more than

twenty?" "I will not destroy it," he answered, "for the sake of the twenty." *32*But he still persisted, "Please, let not my Lord grow angry if I speak up this last time. What if there are at least ten there?" "For the sake of those ten," he replied, "I will not destroy it."*t*

*33*The LORD departed as soon as he had finished speaking with Abraham, and Abraham returned home.

CHAPTER 19

Destruction of Sodom and Gomorrah.

See RG 58–59

*1*The two angels reached Sodom in the evening, as Lot was sitting at the gate of Sodom. When Lot saw them, he got up to greet them; and bowing down with his face to the ground, *2*he said, "Please, gentlemen,* come aside into your servant's house for the night, and bathe your feet; you can get up early to continue your journey." But they replied, "No, we shall pass the night in the town square."*u* *3*He urged them so strongly, however, that they turned aside to his place and entered his house. He prepared a meal for them, baking cakes without leaven, and they dined.

*4v*Before they went to bed, all the townsmen of Sodom, both young and old—all the people to the last man—closed in on the house. *5*They called to Lot and said to him, "Where are the men who came to your house tonight? Bring them out to us that we may have intimacies with them." *6*Lot went out to meet them at the entrance. When he had shut the door behind him, *7*he said, "I beg you, my brothers, not to do this wicked thing. *8*I have two daughters who have never had intercourse with men. Let me bring them out to you, and you may do to them as you please. But don't do anything to these men, for you know they have come under the shelter of my roof." *9*They replied, "Stand back! This fellow," they sneered, "came here

---

18, 20: Israelite tradition was unanimous in ascribing the destruction of Sodom and Gomorrah to the wickedness of these cities, but tradition varied in regard to the nature of this wickedness. According to the present account of the Yahwist, the sin of Sodom was homosexuality (Gn 19, 4f), which is therefore also known as sodomy; but according to Isaiah (1, 9f; 3, 9), it was a lack of social justice; Ezekiel (16, 46-51) described it as a disregard for the poor, whereas Jeremiah (23,

14) saw it as general immorality.

19, 2: Gentlemen: Lot does not yet know that the distinguished-looking men are God's messengers; cf Gn 18, 3.

p: Lk 1, 55. *q:* Gn 19, 13; Is 3, 9; Lk 17, 28; Jude 1, 7. *r:* Dt 32, 4; Jb 8, 3. 20; Wis 12, 15. *s:* Sir 10, 9; 17, 27. *t:* Jer 5, 1; Ez 22, 30. *u:* Wis 10, 6; Sir 16, 8; Ez 16, 50; Heb 13, 1f. *v:* 4-9; Jgs 19, 22-25; Jude 1, 7.

as an immigrant, and now he dares to give orders! We'll treat you worse than them!" With that, they pressed hard against Lot, moving in closer to break down the door.[w] [10]But his guests put out their hands, pulled Lot inside with them, and closed the door; [11]at the same time they struck the men at the entrance of the house, one and all, with such a blinding light[*] that they were utterly unable to reach the doorway.

[12]Then the angels said to Lot: "Who else belongs to you here? Your sons [sons-in-law][*] and your daughters and all who belong to you in the city—take them away from it![x] [13]We are about to destroy this place, for the outcry reaching the LORD against those in the city is so great that he has sent us to destroy it."[y] [14]So Lot went out and spoke to his sons-in-law, who had contracted marriage with his daughters.[*] "Get up and leave this place," he told them; "the LORD is about to destroy the city." But his sons-in-law thought he was joking.

[15]As dawn was breaking, the angels urged Lot on, saying, "On your way! Take with you your wife and your two daughters who are here, or you will be swept away in the punishment of the city." [16]When he hesitated, the men, by the LORD's mercy, seized his hand and the hands of his wife and his two daughters and led them to safety outside the city. [17]As soon as they had been brought outside, he was told: "Flee for your life! Don't look back or stop anywhere on the Plain. Get off to the hills at once, or you will be swept away."[z] [18]"Oh, no, my lord!"

replied Lot. [19]"You have already thought enough of your servant to do me the great kindness of intervening to save my life. But I cannot flee to the hills to keep the disaster from overtaking me, and so I shall die. [20]Look, this town ahead is near enough to escape to. It's only a small place.[*] Let me flee there—it's a small place, isn't it?—that my life may be saved." [21]"Well, then," he replied, "I will also grant you the favor you now ask. I will not overthrow the town you speak of. [22]Hurry, escape there! I cannot do anything until you arrive there." That is why the town is called Zoar.[a]

[23]The sun was just rising over the earth as Lot arrived in Zoar;[b] [24]at the same time the LORD rained down sulphurous fire upon Sodom and Gomorrah [from the LORD out of heaven].[c] [25]He overthrew[*] those cities and the whole Plain, together with the inhabitants of the cities and the produce of the soil.[d] [26]But Lot's wife looked back, and she was turned into a pillar of salt.[e]

[27]Early the next morning Abraham went to the place where he had stood in the LORD's presence. [28]As he looked down toward Sodom and Gomorrah and the whole region of the Plain,[*] he saw dense smoke over the land rising like fumes from a furnace.[f]

[29]Thus it came to pass: when God destroyed the Cities of the Plain, he was mindful of Abraham by sending Lot away from the upheaval by which God overthrew the cities where Lot had been living.

Moabites and Ammonites.[*] [30]Since Lot was afraid to stay in Zoar, he and his two

19, 11: Blinding light: a preternatural flash that temporarily dazed the wicked men and revealed to Lot the true nature of his guests.

19, 12: Since Lot apparently had no sons, a glossator interpreted the term to mean sons-in-law.

19, 14: It is uncertain whether Lot's sons-in-law were fully married to his daughters or only "engaged" to them (Israelite "engagement" was the first part of the marriage ceremony), or even whether the daughters involved were the same as, or different from, the two daughters who were still in their father's house.

19, 20: A small place: the Hebrew word misar, literally "a little thing," has the same root consonants as the name of the town Zoar in v 22.

19, 25: Overthrew: the consistent use of this term, literally "turned upside down," to describe the destruction of the Cities of the Plain seems to imply that their upheaval (v 29) was

caused primarily by an earthquake; this would naturally be accompanied by a disastrous fire, especially in a region containing bitumen (Gn 14, 10) and its accompanying gases.

19, 28f: From the height east of Hebron, Abraham could easily see the region at the southern end of the Dead Sea, where the Cities of the Plain were probably located.

19, 30-38: This Israelite tale about the origin of Israel's neighbors east of the Jordan and the Dead Sea was told partly to ridicule these racially related but rival nations and partly to give folk etymologies for their names.

w: Gn 13, 12; 2 Pt 2, 7f. *x:* 2 Pt 7, 9. *y:* Is 1, 7. 9; Zep 2, 9; Lk 17, 29. *z:* Wis 10, 6. *a:* Wis 10, 6. *b:* Pss 9, 6; 11, 6; 107, 34. *c:* Wis 10, 7; Is 1, 9; 13, 19; Lam 4, 6; 17, 29; 2 Pt 2, 6. *d:* Dt 29, 22; Jer 50, 40; Am 4, 11. *e:* Wis 10, 7; Lk 17, 32. *f:* Rv 9, 2; 14, 10f.

daughters went up from Zoar and settled in the hill country, where he lived with his two daughters in a cave. ³¹The older one said to the younger: "Our father is getting old, and there is not a man on earth to unite with us as was the custom everywhere. ³²Come, let us ply our father with wine and then lie with him, that we may have offspring by our father." ³³So that night they plied their father with wine, and the older one went in and lay with her father; but he was not aware of her lying down or her getting up. ³⁴Next day the older one said to the younger: "Last night it was I who lay with my father. Let us ply him with wine again tonight, and then you go in and lie with him, that we may both have offspring by our father." ³⁵So that night, too, they plied their father with wine, and then the younger one went in and lay with him; but again he was not aware of her lying down or her getting up.

³⁶Thus both of Lot's daughters became pregnant by their father. ³⁷The older one gave birth to a son whom she named Moab, saying, "From my father."* He is the ancestor of the Moabites of today.ᵍ ³⁸The younger one, too, gave birth to a son, and she named him Ammon, saying, "The son of my kin."* He is the ancestor of the Ammonites of today.ʰ

CHAPTER 20

See RG 58-59

Abraham at Gerar.* ¹Abraham journeyed on to the region of the Negeb, where he settled between Kadesh and Shur. While he stayed in Gerar, ²he said of his wife Sarah, "She is my sister." So Abimelech, king of Gerar, sent and took Sarah. ³But God came to Abimelech in a dream one night and said to him, "You are about to die because of the woman you have taken, for she has a husband." ⁴Abimelech, who had not approached her, said: "O Lord, would you slay a man even though he is innocent? ⁵He himself told me, 'She is my sister,' and she herself also stated, 'He is my brother.' I did it in good faith and with clean hands." ⁶God answered him in the dream: "Yes, I know you did it in good faith. In fact, it was I who kept you from sinning against me; that is why I did not let you touch her. ⁷Therefore, return the man's wife—as a spokesman* he will intercede for you—that your life may be saved. If you do not return her, you can be sure that you and all who are yours will certainly die."

⁸Early the next morning Abimelech called all his court officials and informed them of everything that had happened, and the men were horrified. ⁹Then Abimelech summoned Abraham and said to him: "How could you do this to us! What wrong did I do to you that you should have brought such monstrous guilt on me and my kingdom? You have treated me in an intolerable way. ¹⁰What were you afraid of," he asked him, "that you should have done such a thing?" ¹¹"I was afraid," answered Abraham, "because I thought there would surely be no fear of God in this place, and so they would kill me on account of my wife. ¹²Besides, she is in truth my sister, but only my father's daughter, not my mother's; and so she became my wife.ⁱ ¹³When God sent me wandering from my father's house, I asked her: 'Would you do me this favor? In whatever place we come to, say that I am your brother.' "

¹⁴Then Abimelech took flocks and herds and male and female slaves and gave them to Abraham; and after he restored his wife Sarah to him, ¹⁵he said, "Here, my land lies at your disposal; settle wherever you please." ¹⁶To Sarah he said: "See, I have given your brother a thousand shekels of silver.* Let that serve you as a vindication be-

---

19, 37: From my father: in Hebrew, meabi, similar in sound to the name "Moab."

19, 38: The son of my kin: in Hebrew, ben-ammi, similar in sound to the name "Ammonites."

20, 1-18: This story from the Elohist source (see note on Gn 4, 25) combines elements found in the two very similar but distinct stories of the Yahwist source in Gn 12, 10-20 and 26, 6-11.

20, 7: Spokesman: the Hebrew term nabi used here is reg-

ularly translated as "prophet," but it simply means "one who speaks on behalf of another," whether the latter is God, as in almost all cases, or another man, as in Ex 4, 16.

20, 16: A thousand shekels of silver: not a gift distinct from that of the animals and the slaves (v 14), but the monetary value of these.

g: Dt 2, 9.   h: Dt 2, 19.   i: Gn 12, 13.

Hagar and Ishmael Are Sent Away

The episode in 21, 8–21 contains elements similar to the earlier story of Hagar and Ishmael (16, 1–16): conflict between Sarah and Hagar, journey into the desert, encounter with a divine angel, a well of water, and promises that Ishmael too would have a great future.

fore all who are with you; your honor has been preserved with everyone." [17] Abraham then interceded with God, and God restored health to Abimelech, that is, to his wife and his maidservants, so that they could bear children; [18] for God had tightly closed every womb in Abimelech's household on account of Abraham's wife Sarah.

CHAPTER 21

See RG 58–59

Birth of Isaac. [1] The LORD took note of Sarah as he had said he would; he did for her as he had promised.[j] [2] Sarah became pregnant and bore Abraham a son in his old age, at the set time that God had stated.[k] [3] Abraham gave the name Isaac to this son of his whom Sarah bore him.[l] [4] When his son Isaac was eight days old, Abraham circumcised him, as God had commanded.[m] [5] Abraham was a hundred years old when his son Isaac was born to him. [6] Sarah then said, "God has given me cause to laugh, and all who hear of it will laugh with me.[n] [7] Who would have told Abraham," she added, "that Sarah would nurse children! Yet I have borne him a son in his old age." [8] Isaac grew, and on the day of the child's weaning Abraham held a great feast.

[9] *Sarah noticed the son whom Hagar the Egyptian had borne to Abraham playing with her son Isaac; [10] so she demanded of Abraham: "Drive out that slave and her son! No son of that slave is going to share the inheritance with my son Isaac!"[o] [11] Abraham was greatly distressed, especially on account of his son Ishmael. [12] But God said to Abraham: "Do not be distressed about the boy or about your slave woman. Heed the demands of Sarah, no matter what she is asking of you; for it is through Isaac that descendants shall bear your name.[p] [13] As for the son of the slave woman, I will make a great nation of him also, since he too is your offspring."

[14] Early the next morning Abraham got some bread and a skin of water and gave them to Hagar. Then, placing the child on her back,* he sent her away. As she roamed aimlessly in the wilderness of Beer-sheba, [15] the water in the skin was used up. So she put the child down under a shrub, [16] and then went and sat down opposite him, about a bowshot away; for she said to herself, "Let me not watch to see the child die." As she sat opposite him, he began to cry. [17] God heard the boy's cry, and God's messenger called to Hagar from heaven: "What is the matter, Hagar? Don't be afraid; God has heard the boy's cry in this plight of his.[q] [18] Arise, lift up the boy and hold him by the hand; for I will make of him a great nation." [19] Then God opened her eyes, and she saw a well of water. She went and filled the skin with water, and then let the boy drink.

[20] God was with the boy as he grew up. He lived in the wilderness and became an expert bowman, [21] with his home in the wilderness of Paran. His mother got a wife for him from the land of Egypt.

The Pact at Beer-sheba. [22] About that time Abimelech, accompanied by Phicol, the

---

21, 9-19: This story of Hagar's expulsion, in the Elohist source, is in general a duplicate of the one from the Yahwist source in Gn 16, 5-14; but the two stories differ greatly in detail.

21, 14: Placing the child on her back: the phrase is translated from an emended form of the Hebrew text. In the current faulty Hebrew text, Abraham put the bread and the waterskin on Hagar's back, while her son apparently walked beside her. This reading seems to be a scribal attempt at harmonizing the present passage with the data of the Priestly

source, in which Ishmael would have been at least fourteen years old when Isaac was born; compare Gn 16, 16 with 21, 5; cf 17, 25. But in the present Elohist story Ishmael is obviously a little boy, not much older than Isaac; cf vv 15, 18.

21, 22: Here and in v 32 the Greek text has ". . . Abimelech, accompanied by Ahuzzath, his councilor, and Phicol . . .";

---

j: Gn 17, 19; 18, 10.   k: Gal 4, 23; Heb 11, 11.   l: Mt 1, 2; Lk 3, 34.   m: Gn 17, 10ff; Acts 7, 8.   n: Gn 17, 17.   o: Jgs 11, 2; Gal 4, 30.   p: Rom 9, 7; Heb 11, 18.   q: Gn 16, 7.

"Ready!"

God called Abraham, and he responded, "Ready!" (22, 1). There are other times in the Bible when we read of someone responding to God's call: for example, Samuel (1 Sm 3) and Isaiah (Is 43, 1). This pattern continues in our own time: God calls each person. We listen, with our hearts and minds, to hear that call. The response is up to each one of us.

---

commander of his army,* said to Abraham: "God is with you in everything you do. *23*Therefore, swear to me by God at this place* that you will not deal falsely with me or with my progeny and posterity, but will act as loyally toward me and the land in which you stay as I have acted toward you." *24*To this Abraham replied, "I so swear."

*25*Abraham, however, reproached Abimelech about a well that Abimelech's men had seized by force. *26*"I have no idea who did that," Abimelech replied. "In fact, you never told me about it, nor did I ever hear of it until now."

*27*Then Abraham took sheep and cattle and gave them to Abimelech and the two made a pact. *28*Abraham also set apart seven ewe lambs of the flock, *29*and Abimelech asked him, "What is the purpose of these seven ewe lambs that you have set apart?" *30*Abraham answered, "The seven ewe lambs you shall accept from me that thus I may have your acknowledgment that the well was dug by me." *31*This is why the place is called Beer-sheba;* the two of them took an oath there. *32*When they had thus made the pact in Beer-sheba, Abimelech, along with Phicol, the commander of his army, left and returned to the land of the Philistines.

*33*Abraham planted a tamarisk at Beer-sheba, and there he invoked by name the

LORD, God the Eternal.* *34*Abraham resided in the land of the Philistines for many years.

CHAPTER 22

See RG 58-59

The Testing of Abraham. *1*Some time after these events, God put Abraham to the test.* He called to him, "Abraham!" "Ready!" he replied.[r] *2*Then God said: "Take your son Isaac, your only one,* whom you love, and go to the land of Moriah. There you shall offer him up as a holocaust on a height that I will point out to you."[s] *3*Early the next morning Abraham saddled his donkey, took with him his son Isaac, and two of his servants as well, and with the wood that he had cut for the holocaust, set out for the place of which God had told him.

*4*On the third day Abraham got sight of the place from afar. *5*Then he said to his servants: "Both of you stay here with the donkey, while the boy and I go on over yonder. We will worship and then come back to you." *6*Thereupon Abraham took the wood for the holocaust and laid it on his son Isaac's shoulders, while he himself carried the fire and the knife. *7*As the two walked on together, Isaac spoke to his father Abraham: "Father!" he said. "Yes, son," he replied. Isaac continued, "Here are the fire and the wood, but where is the sheep for the holocaust?" *8*"Son," Abraham answered, "God himself will provide

---

but this is probably a secondary harmonization with Gn 26, 26. Abimelech took Phicol with him in order to intimidate Abraham by a show of strength.

21, 23: This place: Beer-sheba (v 31). Abimelech had come from Gerar (Gn 20, 2), about thirty miles west of Beer-sheba.

21, 31: Beer-sheba: the Hebrew name really means "the well of the seven," i.e., the place where there are seven wells, alluded to in the episode of the seven ewe lambs, vv 28ff; but it can also be interpreted to mean "the well of the oath."

21, 33: God the Eternal: in Hebrew, el olam, perhaps the

name of the deity of the pre-Israelite sanctuary at Beer-sheba, but used by Abraham merely as a title of Yahweh; cf Is 40, 28.

22, 1: God put Abraham to the test: to prove the firmness of Abraham's faith in God's promise that through Isaac all the nations of the earth would find blessing; cf Gn 18, 10. 18; 21, 12.

22, 2: Only one: uniquely precious, especially loved; therefore the same term is rendered in vv 12. 16 as "beloved."

r: Sir 44, 20. *s:* 2 Chr 3, 1; 1 Mc 2, 52; Heb 11, 17.

the sheep for the holocaust." Then the two continued going forward.

⁹When they came to the place of which God had told him, Abraham built an altar there and arranged the wood on it. Next he tied up his son Isaac, and put him on top of the wood on the altar.ᵗ ¹⁰Then he reached out and took the knife to slaughter his son.ᵘ ¹¹But the LORD's messenger called to him from heaven, "Abraham, Abraham!" "Yes, Lord," he answered. ¹²"Do not lay your hand on the boy," said the messenger. "Do not do the least thing to him. I know now how devoted you are to God, since you did not withhold from me your own beloved son."ᵛ ¹³As Abraham looked about, he spied a ram caught by its horns in the thicket. So he went and took the ram and offered it up as a holocaust in place of his son. ¹⁴Abraham named the site Yahweh-yireh;* hence people now say, "On the mountain the LORD will see."

¹⁵Again the LORD's messenger called to Abraham from heaven ¹⁶ʷand said: "I swear by myself, declares the LORD, that because you acted as you did in not withholding from me your beloved son, ¹⁷I will bless you abundantly and make your descendants as countless as the stars of the sky and the sands of the seashore; your descendants shall take possession of the gates of their enemies,ˣ ¹⁸and in your descendants all the nations of the earth shall find blessing—all this because you obeyed my command."ʸ

¹⁹Abraham then returned to his servants, and they set out together for Beer-sheba, where Abraham made his home.

Nahor's Descendants.* ²⁰Some time afterward, the news came to Abraham:

"Milcah too has borne sons, to your brother Nahor: ²¹Uz, his first-born, his brother Buz, Kemuel (the father of Aram), ²²Chesed, Hazo, Pildash, Jidlaph and Bethuel." ²³Bethuel became the father of Rebekah. These eight Milcah bore to Abraham's brother Nahor. ²⁴His concubine, whose name was Reumah, also bore children: Tebah, Gaham, Tahash and Maacah.

CHAPTER 23

See RG 58–59

Purchase of a Burial Place. ¹The span of Sarah's life was one hundred and twenty-seven years. ²She died in Kiriath-arba (that is, Hebron) in the land of Canaan, and Abraham performed the customary mourning rites for her. ³Then he left the side of his dead one and addressed the Hittites:* ⁴"Although I am a resident alien* among you, sell me from your holdings a piece of property for a burial ground, that I may bury my dead wife."ᶻ ⁵The Hittites answered Abraham: "Please, sir, ⁶listen to us! You are an elect of God among us. Bury your dead in the choicest of our burial sites. None of us would deny you his burial ground for the burial of your dead." ⁷Abraham, however, began to bow low before the local citizens, the Hittites, ⁸while he appealed to them: "If you will allow me room for burial of my dead, listen to me! Intercede for me with Ephron, son of Zohar, asking him ⁹to sell me the cave of Machpelah that he owns; it is at the edge of his field. Let him sell it to me in your presence, at its full price, for a burial place."

¹⁰Now Ephron was present with the Hittites. So Ephron the Hittite replied to Abraham in the hearing of the Hittites who sat on his town council:* ¹¹"Please, sir, listen to me! I

22, 14: Yahweh-yireh: a Hebrew expression meaning "the Lord will see"; the reference is to the words in v 8, "God himself will see to it."

22, 20-24: A list of Aramean tribes who lived to the east and northeast of Israel, twelve in number, like the twelve tribes of Israel (Gn 35, 23) and the twelve tribes of Ishmael (Gn 25, 12-16).

23, 3: The Hittites: a non-Semitic people in Canaan; their relationship to the well-known Hittites of Asia Minor is uncertain.

23, 4: A resident alien: literally "a sojourner and a settler," i.e., a long-term resident alien. Such a one would normally not have the right to own property. The importance of Abraham's purchase of the field in Machpelah, which is

worded in technical legal terms, lies in the fact that it gave his descendants their first, though small, land rights in the country that God had promised the patriarch they would one day inherit as their own. Abraham therefore insists on purchasing the field and not receiving it as a gift.

23, 10: Who sat on his town council: probable meaning of the literal translation, "who came in at the gate of his city"; so also in v 18.

t: Jas 2, 21.   *u:* Wis 10, 5.   *v:* Rom 8, 32; 1 Jn 4, 9.   *w:* 16f: Gn 15, 5; Ex 32, 13; Lk 1, 73; Rom 4, 13; Heb 6, 13f; 11, 12.   *x:* Gn 24, 60.   *y:* Gn 12, 3; 18, 18; 26, 4; Sir 44, 21; Acts 3, 25; Gal 3, 16.   *z:* Gn 33, 19; Acts 7, 16; Heb 11, 9.

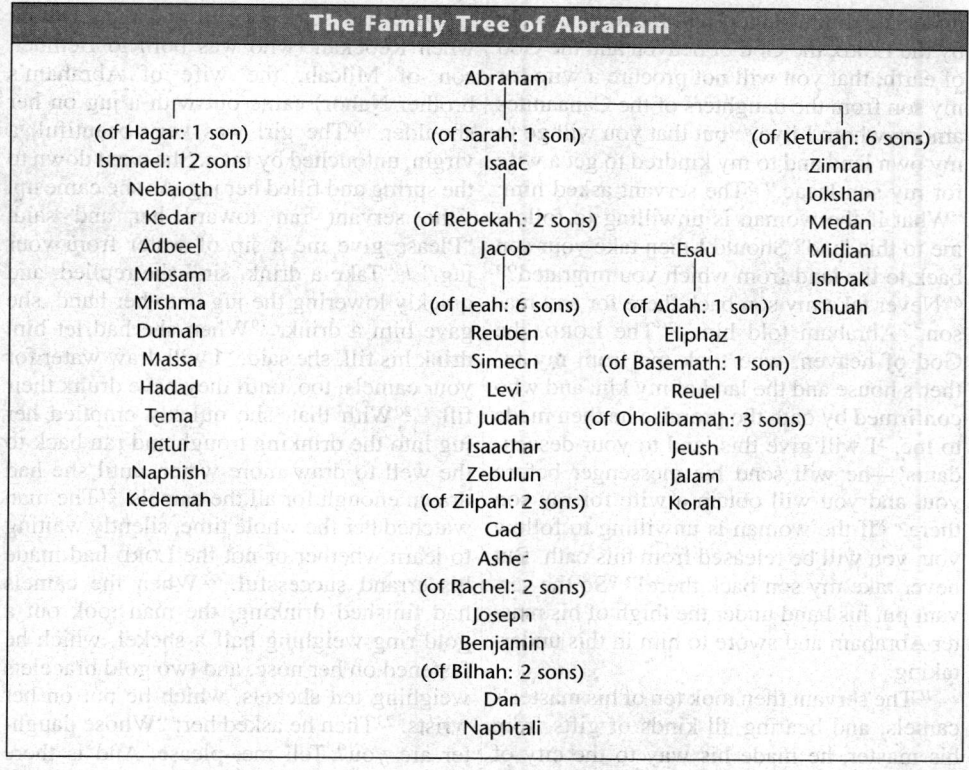

The Family Tree of Abraham

Abraham

(of Hagar: 1 son)	(of Sarah: 1 son)	(of Keturah: 6 sons)
Ishmael: 12 sons	Isaac	Zimran
Nebaioth		Jokshan
Kedar	(of Rebekah: 2 sons)	Medan
Adbeel	Jacob——————Esau	Midian
Mibsam		Ishbak
Mishma	(of Leah: 6 sons) (of Adah: 1 son)	Shuah
Dumah	Reuben Eliphaz	
Massa	Simeon (of Basemath: 1 son)	
Hadad	Levi Reuel	
Tema	Judah (of Oholibamah: 3 sons)	
Jetur	Isaachar Jeush	
Naphish	Zebulun Jalam	
Kedemah	(of Zilpah: 2 sons) Korah	
	Gad	
	Asher	
	(of Rachel: 2 sons)	
	Joseph	
	Benjamin	
	(of Bilhah: 2 sons)	
	Dan	
	Naphtali	

give you both the field and the cave in it; in the presence of my kinsmen I make this gift. Bury your dead!" [12]But Abraham, after bowing low before the local citizens, addressed Ephron in the hearing of these men: [13]"Ah, if only you would please listen to me! I will pay you the price of the field. Accept it from me, that I may bury my dead there." [14]Ephron replied to Abraham, "Please, [15]sir, listen to me! A piece of land worth four hundred shekels* of silver—what is that between you and me, as long as you can bury your dead?" [16a]Abraham accepted Ephron's terms; he weighed out to him the silver that Ephron had stipulated in the hearing of the Hittites, four hundred shekels of silver at the current market value.*

[17b]Thus Ephron's field in Machpelah, fac-ing Mamre, together with its cave and all the trees anywhere within its limits, was con-veyed [18]to Abraham by purchase in the pres-ence of all the Hittites who sat on Ephron's town council. [19]After this transaction, Abra-ham buried his wife Sarah in the cave of the field of Machpelah, facing Mamre (that is, Hebron) in the land of Canaan. [20]Thus the field with its cave was transferred from the Hittites to Abraham as a burial place.

CHAPTER 24

Isaac and Rebekah. [1]Abraham had now reached a ripe old age, and the LORD had blessed him in every way. [2c]Abraham said to the senior servant of his household, who had charge of all his possessions: "Put your hand

See RG 59

23, 15: Four hundred shekels: probably an exorbitant sum; Jeremiah (32, 9) paid only seventeen shekels for his field in Anathoth, though the Babylonian invasion no doubt helped to reduce the price.

23, 16: The current market value: the standard weight

called a shekel varied according to time and place.

24, 2: Put your hand under my thigh: the symbolism of this act was apparently connected with the Hebrew concept of

_a:_ Acts 7, 16.   _b:_ 17f: Gn 49, 29f.   _c:_ 2f: Gn 47, 29.

under my thigh,* *3*and I will make you swear by the LORD, the God of heaven and the God of earth, that you will not procure a wife for my son from the daughters of the Canaanites among whom I live,*d* *4*but that you will go to my own land and to my kindred to get a wife for my son Isaac." *5*The servant asked him: "What if the woman is unwilling to follow me to this land? Should I then take your son back to the land from which you migrated?" *6*"Never take my son back there for any reason," Abraham told him. *7*"The LORD, the God of heaven, who took me from my father's house and the land of my kin, and who confirmed by oath the promise he then made to me, 'I will give this land to your descendants'—he will send his messenger before you, and you will obtain a wife for my son there.*e* *8*If the woman is unwilling to follow you, you will be released from this oath. But never take my son back there!" *9*So the servant put his hand under the thigh of his master Abraham and swore to him in this undertaking.

*10*The servant then took ten of his master's camels, and bearing all kinds of gifts from his master, he made his way to the city of Nahor* in Aram Naharaim. *11*Near evening, at the time when women go out to draw water, he made the camels kneel by the well outside the city. *12*Then he prayed: "LORD, God of my master Abraham, let it turn out favorably for me* today and thus deal graciously with my master Abraham. *13*While I stand here at the spring and the daughters of the townsmen are coming out to draw water, *14*if I say to a girl, 'Please lower your jug, that I may drink,' and she answers, 'Take a drink, and let me give water to your camels, too,' let her be the one whom you have decided upon for your servant Isaac. In this way I shall know that you have dealt graciously with my master."

*15f*He had scarcely finished these words when Rebekah (who was born to Bethuel, son of Milcah, the wife of Abraham's brother Nahor) came out with a jug on her shoulder. *16*The girl was very beautiful, a virgin, untouched by man. She went down to the spring and filled her jug. As she came up, *17*the servant ran toward her and said, "Please give me a sip of water from your jug." *18*"Take a drink, sir," she replied, and quickly lowering the jug onto her hand, she gave him a drink. *19*When she had let him drink his fill, she said, "I will draw water for your camels, too, until they have drunk their fill." *20*With that, she quickly emptied her jug into the drinking trough and ran back to the well to draw more water, until she had drawn enough for all the camels. *21*The man watched her the whole time, silently waiting to learn whether or not the LORD had made his errand successful. *22*When the camels had finished drinking, the man took out a gold ring weighing half a shekel, which he fastened on her nose, and two gold bracelets weighing ten shekels, which he put on her wrists. *23*Then he asked her: "Whose daughter are you? Tell me, please. And is there room in your father's house for us to spend the night?" *24*She answered: "I am the daughter of Bethuel the son of Milcah, whom she bore to Nahor. *25*There is plenty of straw and fodder at our place," she added, "and room to spend the night." *26*The man then bowed down in worship to the LORD, *27*saying: "Blessed be the LORD, the God of my master Abraham, who has not let his constant kindness toward my master fail. As for myself also, the LORD has led me straight to the house of my master's brother."

*28*Then the girl ran off and told her mother's household about it. *29g*Now Rebekah had a brother named Laban. *30*As soon as he saw the ring and the bracelets on his sis-

children issuing from their father's "thigh" (Gn 46, 26; Ex 1, 5). Perhaps the man who took such an oath was thought to bring the curse of sterility on himself if he did not fulfill his sworn promise. Jacob made Joseph swear in the same way (Gn 47, 29). In both these instances, the oath was taken to carry out the last request of a man upon his death.

24, 10: Nahor: it is uncertain whether this is to be understood as the name of Abraham's brother (Gn 11, 27), Re-

bekah's grandfather (Gn 24, 15), or the city of the same name (as known from the Mari documents); Aram Naharaim, situated near Haran (Gn 11, 31) in northern Mesopotamia.

24, 12: Let it turn out favorably for me: let me have a favorable omen; cf end of v 14.

d: Gn 24, 37; 28, 1f; Jgs 14, 3; Tb 4, 12.   *e:* Gn 12, 7; Ex 6, 8; Tb 5, 17; Gal 3, 16.   *f:* Gn 22, 23.   *g:* Gn 27, 43.

ter Rebekah and heard her words about what the man had said to her, Laban rushed outside to the man at the spring. When he reached him, he was still standing by the camels at the spring. ³¹So he said to him: "Come, blessed of the LORD! Why are you staying outside when I have made the house ready for you, as well as a place for the camels?" ³²The man then went inside; and while the camels were being unloaded and provided with straw and fodder, water was brought to bathe his feet and the feet of the men who were with him. ³³But when the table was set for him, he said, "I will not eat until I have told my tale." "Do so," they replied.

³⁴"I am Abraham's servant," he began. ³⁵"The LORD has blessed my master so abundantly that he has become a wealthy man; he has given him flocks and herds, silver and gold, male and female slaves, and camels and asses. ³⁶My master's wife Sarah bore a son to my master in her old age, and he has given him everything he owns. ³⁷My master put me under oath, saying: 'You shall not procure a wife for my son among the daughters of the Canaanites in whose land I live; ³⁸instead, you shall go to my father's house, to my own relatives, to get a wife for my son.' ³⁹When I asked my master, 'What if the woman will not follow me?' ⁴⁰he replied: 'The LORD, in whose presence I have always walked, will send his messenger with you and make your errand successful, and so you will get a wife for my son from my own kindred of my father's house.ʰ ⁴¹Then you shall be released from my ban. If you visit my kindred and they refuse you, then, too, you shall be released from my ban.'

⁴²"When I came to the spring today, I prayed: 'LORD, God of my master Abraham, may it be your will to make successful the errand I am engaged on! ⁴³While I stand here at the spring, if I say to a young woman who comes out to draw water, Please give me a little water from your jug, ⁴⁴and she answers, Not only may you have a drink, but I will give water to your camels, too—let her be the woman whom the LORD has decided upon for my master's son.'

⁴⁵"I had scarcely finished saying this prayer to myself when Rebekah came out with a jug on her shoulder. After she went down to the spring and drew water, I said to her, 'Please let me have a drink.' ⁴⁶She quickly lowered the jug she was carrying and said, 'Take a drink, and let me bring water for your camels, too.' So I drank, and she watered the camels also. ⁴⁷When I asked her, 'Whose daughter are you?' she answered, 'The daughter of Bethuel, son of Nahor, born to Nahor by Milcah.' So I put the ring on her nose and the bracelets on her wrists. ⁴⁸Then I bowed down in worship to the LORD, blessing the LORD, the God of my master Abraham, who had led me on the right road to obtain the daughter of my master's kinsman for his son. ⁴⁹If, therefore, you have in mind to show true loyalty to my master, let me know; but if not, let me know that, too. I can then proceed accordingly."

⁵⁰ⁱLaban and his household said in reply: "This thing comes from the LORD; we can say nothing to you either for or against it. ⁵¹Here is Rebekah, ready for you; take her with you, that she may become the wife of your master's son, as the LORD has said." ⁵²When Abraham's servant heard their answer, he bowed to the ground before the LORD. ⁵³Then he brought out objects of silver and gold and articles of clothing and presented them to Rebekah; he also gave costly presents to her brother and mother. ⁵⁴After he and the men with him had eaten and drunk, they spent the night there.

When they were up the next morning, he said, "Give me leave to return to my master."ʲ ⁵⁵Her brother and mother replied, "Let the girl stay with us a short while, say ten days; after that she may go." ⁵⁶But he said to them, "Do not detain me, now that the LORD has made my errand successful; let me go back to my master." ⁵⁷They answered, "Let us call the girl and see what she herself has to say about it." ⁵⁸So they called Rebekah and asked her, "Do you wish to go with this man?" She answered, "I do." ⁵⁹At this they allowed their sister Rebekah and her nurse to

h: Tb 5, 17; 10, 13.   i: 50f: Tb 7, 12.   j: Tb 7, 14; 8, 20.

take leave, along with Abraham's servant and his men. [60]Invoking a blessing on Rebekah, they said:

> "Sister, may you grow
> into thousands of myriads;
> And may your descendants gain
> possession
> of the gates of their enemies!"[k]

[61]Then Rebekah and her maids started out; they mounted their camels and followed the man. So the servant took Rebekah and went on his way.

[62]Meanwhile Isaac had gone from Beer-lahai-roi and was living in the region of the Negeb.[l] [63]One day toward evening he went out . . .[*] in the field, and as he looked around, he noticed that camels were approaching. [64]Rebekah, too, was looking about, and when she saw him, she alighted from her camel [65]and asked the servant, "Who is the man out there, walking through the fields toward us?" "That is my master," replied the servant. Then she covered herself with her veil.

[66]The servant recounted to Isaac all the things he had done. [67]Then Isaac took Rebekah into his tent; he married her, and thus she became his wife. In his love for her Isaac found solace after the death of his mother Sarah.

CHAPTER 25

See RG 59

Abraham's Sons by Keturah. [1m][*]Abraham married another wife, whose name was Keturah. [2]She bore him Zimran, Jokshan, Medan, Midian, Ishbak and Shuah. [3]Jokshan became the father of Sheba and Dedan. The descendants of Dedan were the Asshurim, the Letushim, and the Leummim.[n] [4]The descendants of Midian were Ephah, Epher, Ha-

noch, Abida and Eldaah. All of these were descendants of Keturah.

[5]Abraham deeded everything that he owned to his son Isaac. [6]To his sons by concubinage, however, he made grants while he was still living, as he sent them away eastward, to the land of Kedem,[*] away from his son Isaac.

Death of Abraham. [7]The whole span of Abraham's life was one hundred and seventy-five years. [8]Then he breathed his last, dying at a ripe old age, grown old after a full life; and he was taken to his kinsmen. [9o]His sons Isaac and Ishmael buried him in the cave of Machpelah, in the field of Ephron, son of Zohar the Hittite, which faces Mamre, [10]the field that Abraham had bought from the Hittites; there he was buried next to his wife Sarah. [11]After the death of Abraham, God blessed his son Isaac, who made his home near Beer-lahai-roi.

Descendants of Ishmael. [12]These are the descendants of Abraham's son Ishmael, whom Hagar the Egyptian, Sarah's slave, bore to Abraham. [13p]These are the names of Ismael's sons, listed in the order of their birth: Nebaioth (Ishmael's first-born), Kedar, Adbeel, Mibsam,[q] [14]Mishma, Dumah, Massa, [15]Hadad, Tema, Jetur, Naphish and Kedemah. [16]These are the sons of Ishmael, their names by their villages and encampments; twelve chieftains of as many tribal groups.[r]

[17]The span of Ishmael's life was one hundred and thirty-seven years. After he had breathed his last and died, he was taken to his kinsmen. [18]The Ishmaelites ranged from Havilah-by-Shur, which is on the border of Egypt, all the way to Asshur; and each of them pitched camp[*] in opposition to his various kinsmen.[s]

24, 63: He went out: the meaning of the Hebrew term that follows this is obscure.

25, 1-11: Though mentioned here, Abraham's marriage to a "concubine," or wife of secondary rank, and his death are not to be understood as happening chronologically after the events narrated in the preceding chapter.

25, 6: The land of Kedem: or "the country of the East," the region inhabited by the Kedemites or Easterners (Gn 29, 1; Jgs 6, 3. 33; Jb 1, 3; Is 11, 14). The names mentioned in vv 2ff, as far as they can be identified, are those of tribes in the

Arabian desert.

25, 18: Pitched camp: literally "fell"; the same Hebrew verb is used in Jgs 7, 12 in regard to the hostile encampment of Bedouin tribes. The present passage shows the fulfillment of the prediction contained in Gn 16, 12.

---

k: Gn 22, 17. l: Gn 16, 13f; 25, 11. m: 1-4: 1 Chr 1, 32f.
n: Is 21, 13. o: 9f: Gn 23, 3-20. p: 13-16: 1 Chr 1, 29ff.
q: Is 60, 7. r: Gn 17, 20. s: Gn 16, 12.

III: The Patriarchs Isaac and Jacob

Birth of Esau and Jacob. [19]This is the family history of Isaac, son of Abraham; Abraham had begotten Isaac. [20]Isaac was forty years old when he married Rebekah, the daughter of Bethuel the Aramean of Paddanaram and the sister of Laban the Aramean.[t] [21]Isaac entreated the LORD on behalf of his wife, since she was sterile. The LORD heard his entreaty, and Rebekah became pregnant. [22]But the children in her womb jostled each other so much that she exclaimed, "If this is to be so, what good will it do me!" She went to consult the LORD, [23]and he answered her:

"Two nations are in your womb,
two peoples are quarreling while still within you;
But one shall surpass the other,
and the older shall serve the younger."[u]

[24]When the time of her delivery came, there were twins in her womb.[v] [25]The first to emerge was reddish,[*] and his whole body was like a hairy mantle; so they named him Esau. [26]His brother came out next, gripping Esau's heel;[*] so they named him Jacob. Isaac was sixty years old when they were born.[w]

[27]As the boys grew up, Esau became a skillful hunter, a man who lived in the open; whereas Jacob was a simple man, who kept to his tents.[x] [28]Isaac preferred Esau, because he was fond of game; but Rebekah preferred Jacob. [29]Once, when Jacob was cooking a stew, Esau came in from the open, famished. [30]He said to Jacob, "Let me gulp down some of that red stuff;[*] I'm starving." (That is why he was called Edom.) [31]But Jacob replied, "First give me your birthright[*] in exchange for it."[y] [32]"Look," said Esau, "I'm on the point of dying. What good will any birthright do me?" [33]But Jacob insisted, "Swear to me first!" So he sold Jacob his birthright under oath.[z] [34]Jacob then gave him some bread and the lentil stew; and Esau ate, drank, got up, and went his way. Esau cared little for his birthright.

CHAPTER 26

Isaac and Abimelech. [1a]There was a famine in the land (distinct from the earlier one that had occurred in the days of Abraham), and Isaac went down to Abimelech, king of the Philistines in Gerar.[b] [2]The LORD appeared to him and said: "Do not go down to Egypt, but continue to camp wherever in this land I tell you. [3]Stay in this land, and I will be with you and bless you; for to you and your descendants I will give all these lands, in fulfillment of the oath that I swore to your father Abraham.[c] [4]I will make your descendants as numerous as the stars in the sky and give them all these lands, and in your descendants all the nations of the earth shall find blessing—[d] [5]this because Abraham obeyed me, keeping my mandate (my commandments, my ordinances and my instructions)."

[6][*]So Isaac settled in Gerar. [7]When the men of the place asked questions about his wife, he answered, "She is my sister." He was afraid, if he called her his wife, the men of the place would kill him on account of Rebekah, since she was very beautiful. [8]But when he had been there for a long time,

---

25, 25: Reddish: in Hebrew, admoni, a reference to Edom, another name for Esau (v 30; 36, 1). Edom, however, was really the name of the country south of Moab where the descendants of Esau lived. It was called the "red" country because of its reddish sandstone. Hairy: in Hebrew, sear, a reference to Seir, another name for Edom (Gn 36, 8). One might expect the text to say, "So they named him Seir"; but Esau (esaw) also means "hairy."
25, 26: Esau's heel: the Hebrew is baaqeb esaw, a reference to the name Jacob; cf Gn 27, 36. Probably, however, the name Jacob has no true etymological connection with the Hebrew word for "heel" (aqeb), but is instead a shortened form of some such name as yaaqob-el ("may God protect").
25, 30: Red stuff: in Hebrew, adom; another play on the word Edom, the "red" land.
25, 31: Birthright: the privilege that entitled the first-born son to a position of honor in the family and to a double share in the possessions inherited from the father.
26, 6-11: The Yahwist's version of the wife-sister episode at Gerar; the Elohist's version (Gn 20, 1-18) is connected with Abraham and Sarah.

---

t: Gn 24, 66.   *u*: Gn 27, 29; Nm 24, 18; Mal 1, 2-5; Rom 9, 11f.   *v*: Hos 12, 3.   *w*: Mt 1, 2   *x*: Gn 27, 6f.   *y*: Dt 21, 17.   *z*: Heb 12, 16.   *a*: 1-14: Gn 12, 10-20.   *b*: Gn 12, 1.   *c*: Gn 12, 7; 15, 18; Ex 32, 13; Ps 105, 9; Sir 44, 22; Heb 11, 9.   *d*: Gn 12, 3; 22, 17f; 28, 14; Ex 32, 13.

Abimelech, king of the Philistines, happened to look out of a window and was surprised to see Isaac fondling his wife Rebekah. [9]He called for Isaac and said: "She must certainly be your wife! How could you have said, 'She is my sister'?" Isaac replied, "I thought I might lose my life on her account." [10]"How could you do this to us!" exclaimed Abimelech. "It would have taken very little for one of the men to lie with your wife, and you would have thus brought guilt upon us!" [11]Abimelech therefore gave this warning to all his men: "Anyone who molests this man or his wife shall forthwith be put to death."

[12]*Isaac sowed a crop in that region and reaped a hundredfold the same year. Since the LORD blessed him, [13e]he became richer and richer all the time, until he was very wealthy indeed. [14]He acquired such flocks and herds, and so many work animals, that the Philistines became envious of him. ([15f] The Philistines had stopped up and filled with dirt all the wells that his father's servants had dug back in the days of his father Abraham.) [16]So Abimelech said to Isaac, "Go away from us; you have become far too numerous for us." [17]Isaac left there and made the Wadi Gerar his regular campsite. ([18]Isaac reopened the wells which his father's servants had dug back in the days of his father Abraham and which the Philistines had stopped up after Abraham's death; he gave them the same names that his father had given them.) [19]But when Isaac's servants dug in the wadi and reached spring water in their well, [20]the shepherds of Gerar quarreled with Isaac's servants, saying, "The water belongs to us!" So the well was called Esek,* because they had challenged him there. [21]Then they dug another well, and they quarreled over that one too; so it was called Sitnah.* [22]When he had moved on from there, he dug still another well; but over this one they did not quarrel. It was called Rehoboth, because he said, "The LORD has now given us ample room, and we shall flourish in the land."

[23]From there Isaac went up to Beer-sheba. [24]The same night the LORD appeared to him and said: "I am the God of your father Abraham. You have no need to fear, since I am with you. I will bless you and multiply your descendants for the sake of my servant Abraham."[g] [25]So he built an altar there and invoked the LORD by name. After he had pitched his tent there, his servants began to dig a well nearby.

[26h]Abimelech had meanwhile come to him from Gerar, accompanied by Ahuzzath, his councilor, and Phicol, the general of his army. [27]Isaac asked them, "Why have you come to me, seeing that you hate me and have driven me away from you?" [28]They answered: "We are convinced that the LORD is with you, so we propose that there be a sworn agreement between our two sides—between you and us. Let us make a pact with you: [29]you shall not act unkindly toward us, just as we have not molested you, but have always acted kindly toward you and have let you depart in peace. Henceforth, 'The LORD's blessing be upon you!'" [30]Isaac then made a feast for them, and they ate and drank. [31]Early the next morning they exchanged oaths. Then Isaac bade them farewell, and they departed from him in peace.

[32]That same day Isaac's servants came and brought him news about the well they had been digging; they told him, "We have reached water!" [33]He called it Shibah;* hence the name of the city, Beer-sheba, to this day.

[34]*When Esau was forty years old, he married Judith, daughter of Beeri the Hittite,

---

26, 12-33: The Yahwist's version of the story about the wells at Beer-sheba; again, the Elohist's version (Gn 21, 22f) is connected with Abraham. A redactor joined the two accounts by means of the parenthetical verses 15 and 18.

26, 20: Esek: "challenge."

26, 21: Sitnah: "opposition"; one might expect the text to be continued by some such words as "because they were in opposition there."

26, 33: Shibah: "seven," for the sake of a closer assonance with Beer-sheba; but the present version of the story says

nothing about there being seven wells there as implied in Gn 21, 28-31. The Greek version understood the Hebrew text more logically as shebua, "oath," in keeping with the present story.

26, 34f: These verses from the Priestly source, which have no logical connection with the preceding stories, serve as an introduction to the following section on Esau's loss of his

e: 13f: Jb 1, 3. *f:* 15-24: Gn 21, 25-31. *g:* Gn 46, 3. *h:* 26-33: Gn 21, 22-31; Prv 16, 7.

Jacob Steals Esau's Blessing

Jacob deceives his old and blind father Isaac by pretending to be his older brother Esau. In this way, he receives the blessing and inheritance that belongs to the first-born son. The grief and anger of Isaac and Esau presuppose that the words and power of a blessing cannot be taken back once they have been spoken. Esau can only receive the opposite of what Jacob already received. Jacob will receive of (the Hebrew preposition *min*) the fertility of the earth (27, 28) while Esau will live far from (the same preposition *min*) the fertile earth (v. 39). The land of Edom was not an agriculturally rich area. The last words we hear from Esau concerning Jacob until they meet many years later (ch 33) are "I will kill my brother Jacob" (v. 41). Rebekah's excuse to Isaac for sending Jacob away is to avoid Jacob's marrying one of the Hittite or Canaanite women of the land as Esau had done (26, 34–35), but her real reason is to stop Esau from murdering his brother Jacob (27, 42–45). Isaac instructs Jacob to return to the original homeland of Abram and of his mother Rebekah in Mesopotamia to obtain a wife as Isaac had done (ch 24).

and Basemath, daughter of Elon the Hivite.[i] [35]But they became a source of embitterment to Isaac and Rebekah.

See RG 59–60

CHAPTER 27

*Jacob's Deception.** [1]When Isaac was so old that his eyesight had failed him, he called his older son Esau and said to him, "Son!" "Yes, father!" he replied. [2]Isaac then said, "As you can see, I am so old that I may now die at any time. [3]Take your gear, therefore—your quiver and bow—and go out into the country to hunt some game for me. [4]With your catch prepare an appetizing dish for me, such as I like, and bring it to me to eat, so that I may give you my special blessing* before I die."

[5]Rebekah had been listening while Isaac was speaking to his son Esau. So when Esau went out into the country to hunt some game for his father,[j] [6]Rebekah said to her son Jacob, "Listen! I overheard your father tell your brother Esau, [7]'Bring me some game and with it prepare an appetizing dish for me to eat, that I may give you my blessing with the LORD's

approval before I die.' [8]Now, son, listen carefully to what I tell you. [9]Go to the flock and get me two choice kids. With these I will prepare an appetizing dish for your father, such as he likes. [10]Then bring it to your father to eat, that he may bless you before he dies." [11]"But my brother Esau is a hairy man," said Jacob to his mother Rebekah, "and I am smooth-skinned![k] [12]Suppose my father feels me? He will think I am making sport of him, and I shall bring on myself a curse instead of a blessing." [13]His mother, however, replied: "Let any curse against you, son, fall on me! Just do as I say. Go and get me the kids."

[14]So Jacob went and got them and brought them to his mother; and with them she prepared an appetizing dish, such as his father liked. [15]Rebekah then took the best clothes of her older son Esau that she had in the house, and gave them to her younger son Jacob to wear; [16]and with the skins of the kids she covered up his hands and the hairless parts of his neck. [17]Then she handed her son Jacob the appetizing dish and the bread she had prepared.

birthright by suggesting a motivation for this in Isaac's and Rebekah's dislike for Esau's Canaanite wives.

27, 1-45: What Jacob did in deceiving his father and thereby cheating Esau out of Isaac's deathbed blessing is condemned as blameworthy, not only by Hosea (12, 4) and Jeremiah (9, 3), but also, indirectly, by the Yahwist narrator of the present story, who makes the reader sympathize with Esau as the innocent victim of a cruel plot, and shows that Jacob and his mother, the instigator of the plot, paid for it by a lifelong separation from each other. The story was told be-

cause it was part of the mystery of God's ways in salvation history—his use of weak, sinful men to achieve his own ultimate purpose.

27, 4: My special blessing: "the blessing of my soul." The same expression is used also in vv 19, 25, 31. In the context it must mean something like a solemn deathbed blessing, believed to be especially efficacious.

i: 34f: Gn 27, 46.   *j*: Gn 25, 28.   *k*: Gn 25, 25.

[18]Bringing them to his father, Jacob said, "Father!" "Yes?" replied Isaac. "Which of my sons are you?" [19]Jacob answered his father: "I am Esau, your first-born. I did as you told me. Please sit up and eat some of my game, so that you may give me your special blessing." [20]But Isaac asked, "How did you succeed so quickly, son?" He answered, "The LORD, your God, let things turn out well with me." [21]Isaac then said to Jacob, "Come closer, son, that I may feel you, to learn whether you really are my son Esau or not." [22]So Jacob moved up closer to his father. When Isaac felt him, he said, "Although the voice is Jacob's, the hands are Esau's." [23](He failed to identify him because his hands were hairy, like those of his brother Esau; so in the end he gave him his blessing.) [24]Again he asked him, "Are you really my son Esau?" "Certainly," he replied. [25]Then Isaac said, "Serve me your game, son, that I may eat of it and then give you my blessing." Jacob served it to him, and Isaac ate; he brought him wine, and he drank. [26]Finally his father Isaac said to him, "Come closer, son, and kiss me." [27]As Jacob went up and kissed him, Isaac smelled the fragrance of his clothes. With that, he blessed him, saying,

"Ah, the fragrance of my son
   is like the fragrance of a field
   that the LORD has blessed![l]

[28] "May God give to you
   of the dew of the heavens
And of the fertility of the earth
   abundance of grain and wine.

[29] [m]"Let peoples serve you,
   and nations pay you homage;
Be master of your brothers,
   and may your mother's sons bow
      down to you.

"Cursed be those who curse you,
   and blessed be those who bless you."

[30]Jacob had scarcely left his father, just after Isaac had finished blessing him, when his brother Esau came back from his hunt. [31]Then he too prepared an appetizing dish with his game, and bringing it to his father, he said, "Please, father, eat some of your son's game, that you may then give me your special blessing." [32]"Who are you?" his father Isaac asked him. "I am Esau," he replied, "your first-born son." [33]With that, Isaac was seized with a fit of uncontrollable trembling. "Who was it, then," he asked, "that hunted game and brought it to me? I finished eating it just before you came, and I blessed him. Now he must remain blessed!" [34]On hearing his father's words, Esau burst into loud, bitter sobbing. "Father, bless me too!" he begged. [35]When Isaac explained, "Your brother came here by a ruse and carried off your blessing," [36]Esau exclaimed, "He has been well named Jacob! He has now supplanted me* twice! First he took away my birthright, and now he has taken away my blessing." Then he pleaded, "Haven't you saved a blessing for me?"[n] [37]Isaac replied: "I have already appointed him your master, and I have assigned to him all his kinsmen as his slaves; besides, I have enriched him with grain and wine. What then can I do for you, son?" [38]But Esau urged his father, "Have you only that one blessing, father? Bless me too!" Isaac, however, made no reply; and Esau wept aloud.[o] [39]Finally Isaac spoke again and said to him:

"Ah, far from the fertile earth
   shall be your dwelling;
   far from the dew of the heavens
      above![p]

[40] "By your sword you shall live,
   and your brother you shall serve;
But when you become restive,
   you shall throw off his yoke from your
      neck."[q]

[41]Esau bore Jacob a grudge because of the blessing his father had given him. He said to

---

27, 36: He has now supplanted me: in Hebrew, wayyaqebeni, a wordplay on the name Jacob, yaaqob; see Jer 9, 3 and note, as well as Gn 25, 26. There is also a play between the Hebrew words bekora ("birthright") and beraka ("blessing").

l: Gn 22, 17f; Heb 11, 20.   *m:* Gn 25, 23; 49, 8; Nm 24, 9.   *n:* Gn 25, 26. 29-34; Hos 12, 4.   *o:* Heb 12, 17.   *p:* Heb 11, 20.
q: 2 Kgs 8, 20. 22; 2 Chr 21, 8.

himself, "When the time of mourning for my father comes, I will kill my brother Jacob."[r] [42]When Rebekah got news of what her older son Esau had in mind, she called her younger son Jacob and said to him: "Listen! Your brother Esau intends to settle accounts with you by killing you. [43]Therefore, son, do what I tell you: flee at once to my brother Laban in Haran, [44]and stay with him a while until your brother's fury subsides [45][until your brother's anger against you subsides] and he forgets what you did to him. Then I will send for you and bring you back. Must I lose both of you in a single day?"[s]

Jacob Sent to Laban. [46]*Rebekah said to Isaac: "I am disgusted with life because of the Hittite women. If Jacob also should marry a Hittite woman, a native of the land, like these women, what good would life be to me?"[s]

See RG 59-60

CHAPTER 28

[1]Isaac therefore called Jacob, greeted him with a blessing, and charged him: "You shall not marry a Canaanite woman![t] [2]Go now to Paddan-aram, to the home of your mother's father Bethuel, and there choose a wife for yourself from among the daughters of your uncle Laban.[u] [3]May God Almighty bless you and make you fertile, multiply you that you may become an assembly of peoples. [4]May he extend to you and your descendants the blessing he gave to Abraham, so that you may gain possession of the land where you are staying, which he assigned to Abraham."[v] [5]Then Isaac sent Jacob on his way; he went to Paddan-aram, to Laban, son of Bethuel, the Aramean, and

brother of Rebekah, the mother of Jacob and Esau.[w]

[6]Esau noted that Isaac had blessed Jacob when he sent him to Paddan-aram to get himself a wife there, charging him, as he gave him his blessing, not to marry a Canaanite woman, [7]and that Jacob had obeyed his father and mother and gone to Paddan-aram. [8]Esau realized how displeasing the Canaanite women were to his father Isaac, [9]so he went to Ishmael, and in addition to the wives he had, married Mahalath, the daughter of Abraham's son Ishmael and sister of Nebaioth.[x]

Jacob's Dream at Bethel. [10]Jacob departed from Beer-sheba and proceeded toward Haran. [11]When he came upon a certain shrine,* as the sun had already set, he stopped there for the night. Taking one of the stones at the shrine, he put it under his head and lay down to sleep at that spot. [12]Then he had a dream: a stairway* rested on the ground, with its top reaching to the heavens; and God's messengers were going up and down on it.[y] [13]And there was the LORD standing beside him and saying: "I, the LORD, am the God of your forefather Abraham and the God of Isaac; the land on which you are lying I will give to you and your descendants.[z] [14]These shall be as plentiful as the dust of the earth, and through them you shall spread out east and west, north and south. In you and your descendants all the nations of the earth shall find blessing.[a] [15]Know that I am with you; I will protect you wherever you go, and bring you back to this land. I will never leave you until I have done what I promised you."[b]

27, 46—28, 9: This section, which is from the Priestly source and a direct sequel of Gn 26, 34f, presents a different, though not contradictory, reason for Jacob's going to Paddan-aram: namely, to preserve racial purity among the chosen people. The account of Esau's marriages is given for the purpose of explaining the racial mixture of the Edomites, who were descended in part from tribes related to Israel, in part from older peoples in Edom called Hittites, Horites or Hivites, and in part from the Ishmaelite (Arabian) tribes who later invaded the region.

28, 11: Shrine: literally "place," often used specifically of a sacred site. Here the place was Bethel (v 19), a sacred site as early as the time of Abraham (Gn 12, 8).

28, 12: Stairway: in Hebrew, sullam, traditionally but inaccurately, translated as "ladder." The corresponding verb, salal, means "to heap up" something, such as dirt for a highway or ramp. The imagery in Jacob's dream is derived from the Babylonian ziggurat or temple tower, "with its top in the sky" (Gn 11, 4), and with brick steps leading up to a small temple at the top.

r: Wis 10, 10; Ob 1, 10. s: Gn 26, 34f. t: Gn 24, 3f; 26, 35. u: Gn 22, 22; 17, 1f. 4f. v: Ex 32, 13. w: Jdt 8, 26. x: Gn 36, 2f. y: Jn 1, 51. z: Dt 1, 8; Mi 7, 28. a: Gn 12, 3; 13, 14f; 15, 5f; 18, 18; 22, 17f; 26, 4; Dt 19, 8; Sir 44, 21. b: Gn 31, 3.

¹⁶When Jacob awoke from his sleep, he exclaimed, "Truly, the LORD is in this spot, although I did not know it!" ¹⁷In solemn wonder he cried out: "How awesome is this shrine! This* is nothing else but an abode of God, and that is the gateway to heaven!" ¹⁸Early the next morning Jacob took the stone that he had put under his head, set it up as a memorial stone,* and poured oil on top if it.ᶜ ¹⁹He called that site Bethel,* whereas the former name of the town had been Luz.ᵈ

²⁰Jacob then made this vow: "If God remains with me, to protect me on this journey I am making and to give me enough bread to eat and clothing to wear, ²¹and I come back safe to my father's house, the LORD shall be my God. ²²This stone that I have set up as a memorial stone shall be God's abode. Of everything you give me, I will faithfully return a tenth part to you."

CHAPTER 29

See RG 59-60

Arrival in Haran. ¹ᵉAfter Jacob resumed his journey, he came to the land of the Easterners.* ²Looking about, he saw a well in the open country, with three droves of sheep huddled near it, for droves were watered from that well. A large stone covered the mouth of the well.ᶠ ³Only when all the shepherds were assembled there could they roll the stone away from the mouth of the well and water the flocks. Then they would put the stone back again over the mouth of the well.

⁴Jacob said to them, "Friends, where are you from?" "We are from Haran," they replied. ⁵Then he asked them, "Do you know Laban, son of Nahor?" "We do," they answered.ᵍ ⁶He inquired further, "Is he well?"

"He is," they answered; "and here comes his daughter Rachel with his flock." ⁷Then he said: "There is still much daylight left; it is hardly the time to bring the animals home. Why don't you water the flocks now, and then continue pasturing them?" ⁸"We cannot," they replied, "until all the shepherds are here to roll the stone away from the mouth of the well; only then can we water the flocks."

⁹While he was still talking with them, Rachel arrived with her father's sheep; she was the one who tended them. ¹⁰As soon as Jacob saw Rachel, the daughter of his uncle Laban, with the sheep of his uncle Laban, he went up, rolled the stone away from mouth of the well, and watered his uncle's sheep. ¹¹Then Jacob kissed Rachel and burst into tears.* ¹²He told her that he was her father's relative, Rebekah's son, and she ran to tell her father. ¹³When Laban heard the news about his sister's son Jacob, he hurried out to meet him. After embracing and kissing him, he brought him to his house. Jacob then recounted to Laban all that had happened, ¹⁴and Laban said to him, "You are indeed my flesh and blood."*

Marriage to Leah and Rachel. After Jacob had stayed with him a full month, ¹⁵Laban said to him: "Should you serve me for nothing just because you are a relative of mine? Tell me what your wages should be." ¹⁶Now Laban had two daughters; the older was called Leah, the younger Rachel. ¹⁷Leah had lovely eyes,* but Rachel was well formed and beautiful. ¹⁸Since Jacob had fallen in love with Rachel, he answered Laban, "I will serve you seven years for your younger daughter Rachel."* ¹⁹Laban replied, "I prefer to give her to you rather than to an outsider.

28, 17: This: the stone Jacob used as a headrest; cf v 22. That: the stairway Jacob saw in his dream.

28, 18: Memorial stone: in Hebrew, *masseba*, a stone which might vary in shape and size, set upright and usually intended for some religious purpose. Since the custom of erecting such "sacred pillars" in Palestine went back to its pre-Israelite period, their pagan associations were often retained; therefore, later Israelite religion forbade their erection (Lv 26, 1; Dt 16, 22) and ordered the destruction of those that were associated with paganism (Ex 34, 31; Dt 12, 3).

28, 19: Bethel: i.e., "house of God"; the reference is to the abode of God in v 17.

29, 1: Easterners: see note on Gn 25, 6.

29, 11: Burst into tears: literally "raised his voice and wept," i.e., for joy.

29, 14: Flesh and blood: literally "bone and flesh," i.e., a close relative; on the Hebrew idiom, see Gn 2, 23.

29, 17: Lovely eyes: The adjective modifying eyes is often translated as "weak," but "lovely" is the more probable word.

29, 18: Jacob offers to render service (Jos 15, 16f; 1 Sm 17, 25; 18, 17) in lieu of the customary bridal price (Ex 22, 16f; Dt 22, 29).

c: Gn 31, 13; 35, 14f. *d:* Gn 35, 6; 48, 3; Jos 18, 13; Jgs 1, 23; Hos 12, 4. *e:* Wis 10, 10. *f:* Gn 24, 11f. *g:* Tb 7, 4.

Stay with me." [20]So Jacob served seven years for Rachel, yet they seemed to him but a few days because of his love for her.[h]

[21]Then Jacob said to Laban, "Give me my wife, that I may consummate my marriage with her, for my term is now completed." [22]So Laban invited all the local inhabitants and gave a feast. [23]At the nightfall he took his daughter Leah and brought her to Jacob, and Jacob consummated the marriage with her. [24](Laban assigned his slave girl Zilpah to his daughter Leah as her maidservant.) [25]In the morning Jacob was amazed:[*] it was Leah! So he cried out to Laban: "How could you do this to me! Was it not for Rachel that I served you? Why did you dupe me?" [26]"It is not the custom in our country," Laban replied, "to marry off a younger daughter before an older one. [27]Finish the bridal week[*] for this one, and then I will give you the other too, in return for another seven years of service with me."[i]

[28]Jacob agreed. He finished the bridal week for Leah, and then Laban gave him his daughter Rachel in marriage. [29](Laban assigned his slave girl Bilhah to his daughter Rachel as her maidservant.) [30]Jacob then consummated his marriage with Rachel also, and he loved her more than Leah. Thus he remained in Laban's service another seven years.[j]

Jacob's Children. [31]When the LORD saw that Leah was unloved, he made her fruitful, while Rachel remained barren. [32]Leah conceived and bore a son, and she named him Reuben;[*] for she said, "It means, 'The LORD saw my misery; now my husband will love me.' "[k] [33]She conceived again and bore a son, and said, "It means, 'The LORD heard that I was unloved,' and therefore he has given me this one also"; so she named him Simeon.[*] [34]Again she conceived and bore a son, and she said, "Now at last my husband will become attached to me, since I have now borne him three sons"; that is why she named him Levi.[*] [35]Once more she conceived and bore a son, and she said, "This time I will give grateful praise to the LORD"; therefore she named him Judah.[*] Then she stopped bearing children.[l]

CHAPTER 30

See RG 59-60

[1]When Rachel saw that she failed to bear children to Jacob, she became envious of her sister. She said to Jacob, "Give me children or I shall die!"[m] [2]In anger Jacob retorted, "Can I take the place of God, who has denied you the fruit of the womb?"[n] [3]She replied, "Here is my maidservant Bilhah. Have intercourse with her, and let her give birth on my knees,[*] so that I too may have offspring, at least through her."[o] [4]So she gave him her maidservant Bilhah as a consort,[*] and Jacob had intercourse with her. [5]When Bilhah conceived and bore a son, [6]Rachel said, "God has vindicated me; indeed he has heeded my plea and given me a son." Therefore she named him Dan.[*] [7]Rachel's maidservant Bilhah conceived again and bore a second son, [8]and Rachel said, "I engaged in a fateful struggle with my sister, and I prevailed." So she named him Naphtali.[*]

29, 25: Jacob was amazed: he had not recognized Leah because a bride was veiled when she was brought to her bridegroom; cf Gn 24, 65.

29, 27: The bridal week: an ancient wedding lasted for seven days of festivities; cf Jgs 14, 12.

29, 32: Reuben: The literal meaning of the Hebrew name is "look, a son!" But in this case, as also with the names of all the other sons of Jacob, a symbolic rather than an etymological interpretation of the name is given, because the name and the persons were regarded as closely interrelated. The symbolic interpretation of Reuben's name, according to the Yahwist source, is based on the similar-sounding, raa beonyi, "he saw my misery." In the Elohist source, the name is explained by the similar-sounding yeehabani, "he will love me."

29, 33: Simeon: in popular etymology, related to shama, "he heard."

29, 34: Levi: related to yillaweh, "he will become attached."

29, 35: Judah: related to odeh, "I will give grateful praise."

30, 3: On my knees: in the ancient Near East, a father would take a newborn child in his lap to signify that he acknowledged it as his own; Rachel uses the ceremony in order to adopt the child and establish her legal rights to it.

30, 4: Consort: the Hebrew word normally means "wife," but here it refers to a wife of secondary rank, who did not have the full legal rights of an ordinary wife.

30, 6: Dan: explained by the term dannanni, "he has vindicated me."

30, 8: Naphtali: explained by the phrase naptule elohim niptalti, literally, "in a divine wrestling match I have wrestled," perhaps implying the concept of an ordeal; hence the above rendering, I engaged in a fateful struggle.

---

h: Hos 12, 13.   i: Hos 12, 13.   j: Dt 21, 15ff.   k: Gn 49, 3. l: Mt 1, 2; Lk 3, 33.   m: Prv 30, 16.   n: 2 Kgs 5, 7.   o: Gn 16, 2ff.

⁹When Leah saw that she had ceased to bear children, she gave her maidservant Zilpah to Jacob as a consort. ¹⁰So Jacob had intercourse with Zilpah, and she conceived and bore a son. ¹¹Leah then said, "What good luck!" So she named him Gad.* ¹²Then Leah's maidservant Zilpah bore a second son to Jacob; ¹³and Leah said, "What good fortune!"—meaning, "Women call me fortunate." So she named him Asher.*

¹⁴One day, during the wheat harvest, when Reuben was out in the field, he came upon some mandrakes* which he brought home to his mother Leah. Rachel asked Leah, "Please let me have some of your son's mandrakes." ¹⁵Leah replied, "Was it not enough for you to take away my husband, that you must now take my son's mandrakes too?" "Very well, then!" Rachel answered. "In exchange for your son's mandrakes, Jacob may lie with you tonight." ¹⁶That evening, when Jacob came home from the fields, Leah went out to meet him. "You are now to come in with me," she told him, "because I have paid for you with my son's mandrakes." So that night he slept with her, ¹⁷and God heard her prayer; she conceived and bore a fifth son to Jacob. ¹⁸Leah then said, "God has given me my reward for having let my husband have my maidservant"; so she named him Issachar.* ¹⁹Leah conceived again and bore a sixth son to Jacob; ²⁰and she said, "God has brought me a precious gift. This time my husband will offer me presents, now that I have borne him six sons"; so she named him Zebulun.* ²¹Finally, she gave birth to a daughter, and she named her Dinah.

²²Then God remembered Rachel; he heard her prayer and made her fruitful. ²³She conceived and bore a son, and she said, "God has removed my disgrace."ᵖ ²⁴So she named him Joseph,* meaning, "May the LORD add another son to this one for me!"

Jacob Outwits Laban. ²⁵After Rachel gave birth to Joseph, Jacob said to Laban: "Give me leave to go to my homeland. ²⁶Let me have my wives, for whom I served you, and my children, too, that I may depart. You know very well the service that I have rendered you." ²⁷Laban answered him: "If you will please. . . .

"I have learned through divination that it is because of you that God has blessed me. ²⁸So," he continued, "state what wages you want from me, and I will pay them." ²⁹Jacob replied: "You know what work I did for you and how well your livestock fared under my care; ³⁰the little you had before I came has grown into very much, since the LORD's blessings came upon you in my company. Therefore I should now do something for my own household as well." ³¹"What should I pay you?" Laban asked. Jacob answered: "You do not have to pay me anything outright. I will again pasture and tend your flock, if you do this one thing for me: ³²go through your whole flock today and remove from it every dark animal among the sheep and every spotted or speckled one among the goats.* Only such animals shall be my wages. ³³In the future, whenever you check on these wages of mine, let my honesty testify against me: any animal in my possession that is not a speckled or spotted goat, or a dark sheep, got there by theft!" ³⁴"Very well," agreed Laban. "Let it be as you say."

³⁵That same day Laban removed the

30, 11: Gad: explained by the Hebrew term begad, literally "in luck," i.e., what good luck!

30, 13: Asher: explained by the term beoshri, literally "in my good fortune," i.e., what good fortune, and by the term ishsheruni, "they call me fortunate."

30, 14: Mandrakes: an herb whose root was anciently thought to promote conception. The Hebrew word for mandrakes, dudaim, has erotic connotations, since it sounds like the words daddayim ("breasts") and dodim ("sexual pleasure").

30, 18: Issachar: explained by the terms, sekari, "my reward," and in v 16, sakor sekartika, literally "I have hired you," i.e., I have paid for you.

30, 20: Zebulun: related to the Akkadian word zubullum, "bridegroom's gift," is explained by the terms, zebadani . . . zebed tob, "he has brought me a precious gift," and yizbeleni, "he will offer me presents."

30, 24: Joseph: explained by the words yosep, "may he add," and in v 23, asap, "he has removed."

30, 32: Dark . . . sheep . . . spotted or speckled . . . goats: In the Near East the normal color of sheep is light gray, whereas that of goats is uniform dark brown or black. Ordinarily, therefore, Jacob would have received but few animals.

p: Lk 1, 25.

streaked and spotted he-goats and all the speckled and spotted she-goats, all those with some white on them, as well as the fully dark-colored sheep; these he left . . . in charge of his sons.* *36*Then he put a three days' journey between himself and Jacob, while Jacob continued to pasture the rest of Laban's flock.

*37*Jacob, however, got some fresh shoots of poplar, almond and plane trees, and he made white stripes in them by peeling off the bark down to the white core of the shoots. *38*The rods that he had thus peeled he then set upright in the watering troughs, so that they would be in front of the animals that drank from the troughs. When the animals were in heat as they came to drink, *39**the goats mated by the rods, and so they brought forth streaked, speckled and spotted kids. *40*The sheep, on the other hand, Jacob kept apart, and he set these animals to face the streaked or fully dark-colored animals of Laban. Thus he produced special flocks of his own, which he did not put with Laban's flock. *41*Moreover, whenever the hardier animals were in heat, Jacob would set the rods in the troughs in full view of these animals, so that they mated by the rods; *42*but with the weaker animals he would not put the rods there. So the feeble animals would go to Laban, but the sturdy ones to Jacob. *43*Thus the man grew increasingly prosperous, and he came to own not only large flocks but also male and female servants and camels and asses.

CHAPTER 31

See RG 59-60 *Flight from Laban.* *1*Jacob learned that Laban's sons were saying, "Jacob has taken everything that belonged to our father,

and he has accumulated all this wealth of his by using our father's property." *2*Jacob perceived, too, that Laban's attitude toward him was not what it had previously been. *3*Then the LORD said to Jacob, "Return to the land of your fathers, where you were born, and I will be with you."*q*

*4*So Jacob sent for Rachel and Leah to meet him where he was in the field with his flock. *5*There he said to them: "I have noticed that your father's attitude toward me is not as it was in the past; but the God of my father has been with me. *6*You well know what effort I put into serving your father; *7*yet your father cheated me and changed my wages time after time. God, however, did not let him do me any harm.*r* *8**Whenever your father said, 'The speckled animals shall be your wages,' the entire flock would bear speckled young; whenever he said, 'The streaked animals shall be your wages,' the entire flock would bear streaked young. *9*Thus God reclaimed your father's livestock and gave it to me. *10*Once, in the breeding season, I had a dream in which I saw mating he-goats that were streaked, speckled and mottled. *11*In the dream God's messenger called to me, 'Jacob!' 'Here!' I replied. *12*Then he said, 'Note well. All the he-goats in the flock, as they mate, are streaked, speckled and mottled, for I have seen all the things that Laban has been doing to you. *13*I am the God who appeared to you in Bethel, where you anointed a memorial stone and made a vow to me. Up, then! Leave this land and return to the land of your birth.' "*s*

*14*Rachel and Leah answered him: "Have we still an heir's portion in our father's house? *15*Are we not regarded by him as outsiders?* He not only sold us; he has even

---

30, 35: By giving the abnormally colored animals to his sons, Laban not only deprived Jacob of his first small wages, but he also designed to prevent in this way the future breeding of such animals in the part of his flock entrusted to Jacob.

30, 39-42: Jacob's stratagem was based on the widespread notion among simple people that visual stimuli can have prenatal effects on the offspring of breeding animals. Thus, the rods on which Jacob had whittled stripes or bands or chevron marks were thought to cause the female goats that looked at them to bear kids with lighter-colored marks on their dark hair, while the gray ewes were thought to bear lambs with dark marks on them simply by visual cross-

breeding with the dark goats.

31, 8-12: This Elohist account of the miraculous increase in Jacob's flock differs somewhat from the Yahwist account given in Gn 30, 32-42.

31, 15: Outsiders: literally "foreign women"; they lacked the favored legal status of native women. Used up: literally "eaten, consumed"; the bridal price that a man received for giving his daughter in marriage was legally reserved as her inalienable dowry.

q: Gn 26, 3; 28, 15; 32, 10.   *r:* Jdt 8, 26.   *s:* Gn 28, 18.

used up the money that he got for us! ¹⁶All the wealth that God reclaimed from our father really belongs to us and our children. Therefore, do just as God has told you."ᵗ ¹⁷Jacob proceeded to put his children and wives on camels, ¹⁸and he drove off with all his livestock and all the property he had acquired in Paddan-aram, to go to his father Isaac in the land of Canaan.

¹⁹Now Laban had gone away to shear his sheep, and Rachel had meanwhile appropriated her father's household idols.ᵘ * ²⁰Jacob had hoodwinked* Laban the Aramean by not telling him of his intended flight. ²¹Thus he made his escape with all that he had. Once he was across the Euphrates, he headed for the highlands of Gilead.

²²On the third day, word came to Laban that Jacob had fled. ²³Taking his kinsmen with him, he pursued him for seven days* until he caught up with him in the hill country of Gilead. ²⁴But that night God appeared to Laban the Aramean in a dream and warned him, "Take care not to threaten Jacob with any harm."ᵛ

Jacob and Laban in Gilead. ²⁵When Laban overtook Jacob, Jacob's tents were pitched in the highlands; Laban also pitched his tents there, on Mount Gilead. ²⁶"What do you mean," Laban demanded of Jacob, "by hoodwinking me and carrying off my daughters like war captives?* ²⁷Why did you dupe me by stealing away secretly? You should have told me, and I would have sent you off with merry singing to the sound of tambourines and harps. ²⁸You did not even allow me a parting kiss to my daughters and grandchildren! What you have now done is a senseless thing. ²⁹I have it in my power to harm all of you; but last night the God of

your father said to me, 'Take care not to threaten Jacob with any harm!' ³⁰Granted that you had to leave because you were desperately homesick for your father's house, why did you steal my gods?" ³¹"I was frightened," Jacob replied to Laban, "at the thought that you might take your daughters away from me by force. ³²But as for your gods, the one you find them with shall not remain alive! If, with my kinsmen looking on, you identify anything here as belonging to you, take it." Jacob, of course, had no idea that Rachel had stolen the idols.

³³Laban then went in and searched Jacob's tent and Leah's tent, as well as the tents of the two maidservants; but he did not find the idols. Leaving Leah's tent, he went into Rachel's. ³⁴Now Rachel had taken the idols, put them inside a camel cushion, and seated herself upon them. When Laban had rummaged through the rest of her tent without finding them,ʷ ³⁵Rachel said to her father, "Let not my lord feel offended that I cannot rise in your presence; a woman's period is upon me." So, despite his search, he did not find his idols.

³⁶Jacob, now enraged, upbraided Laban. "What crime or offense have I committed," he demanded, "that you should hound me so fiercely? ³⁷Now that you have ransacked all my things, have you found a single object taken from your belongings? If so, produce it here before your kinsmen and mine, and let them decide between us two.

³⁸"In the twenty years that I was under you, no ewe or she-goat of yours ever miscarried, and I have never feasted on a ram of your flock. ³⁹ˣI never brought you an animal torn by wild beasts; I made good the loss myself. You held me responsible for any-

---

31, 19: Household idols: in Hebrew, teraphim, figurines used in divination (Ez 21, 26; Zec 10, 2). Laban calls them his "gods" (v 30).

31, 20: Hoodwinked: literally "stolen the heart of," i.e., lulled the mind of. Aramean: The earliest extra-biblical references to the Arameans date from several centuries after the time of Jacob; to call Laban an Aramean and to have him speak Aramaic (v 47) would seem to be an anachronism.

31, 23: For seven days: literally "a way of seven days," a general term to designate a long distance; it would have taken a camel caravan many more days to travel from Haran to Gilead, the region east of the northern half of the Jordan.

31, 26: War captives: literally "women captured by the sword"; the women of a conquered people were treated as part of the victor's booty; cf 1 Sm 30, 2; 2 Kgs 5, 2.

31, 39: Laban's actions were contrary to the customs of the ancient Near East, as recorded in the Code of Hammurabi: "If in a sheepfold an act of god has occurred, or a lion has made a kill, the shepherd shall clear himself before the deity, and the owner of the fold must accept the loss" (par. 266); cf Ex 22, 12.

---

t: Wis 10, 10f.   *u:* Gn 19, 34; 1 Sm 19, 13.   *v:* Wis 10, 12.   *w:* Gn 31, 19.   *x:* Ex 22, 12.

thing stolen by day or night.* ⁴⁰How often the scorching heat ravaged me by day, and the frost by night, while sleep fled from my eyes! ⁴¹Of the twenty years that I have now spent in your household, I slaved fourteen years for your two daughters and six years for your flock, while you changed my wages time after time. ⁴²If my ancestral God, the God of Abraham and the Awesome One of Isaac, had not been on my side, you would now have sent me away empty-handed. But God saw my plight and the fruits of my toil, and last night he gave judgment."ʸ

⁴³*Laban replied to Jacob: "The women are mine, their children are mine, and the flocks are mine; everything you see belongs to me. But since these women are my daughters, I will now do something for them and for the children they have borne. ⁴⁴Come, then, we will make a pact, you and I; the LORD shall be a witness between us."

⁴⁵Then Jacob took a stone and set it up as a memorial stone.ᶻ ⁴⁶Jacob said to his kinsmen, "Gather some stones." So they got some stones and made a mound; and they had a meal there at the mound. ⁴⁷Laban called it Jegar-sahadutha,* but Jacob named it Galeed. ⁴⁸"This mound," said Laban, "shall be a witness from now on between you and me." That is why it was named Galeed— ⁴⁹and also Mizpah,* for he said: "May the LORD keep watch between you and me when we are out of each other's sight. ⁵⁰If you mistreat my daughters, or take other wives besides my daughters, remember that even though no one else is about, God will be witness between you and me."

⁵¹Laban said further to Jacob: "Here is this mound, and here is the memorial stone that I have set up between you and me. ⁵²This mound shall be witness, and this memorial stone shall be witness, that, with hostile intent, neither may I pass beyond this mound into your territory nor may you pass beyond it into mine. ⁵³May the God of Abraham and the god of Nahor [their ancestral deities] maintain justice between us!" Jacob took the oath by the Awesome One of Isaac. ⁵⁴He then offered a sacrifice on the mountain and invited his kinsmen to share in the meal. When they had eaten, they passed the night on the mountain.

CHAPTER 32

¹Early the next morning, Laban kissed his grandchildren and his daughters goodbye; then he set out on his journey back home, ²while Jacob continued on his own way. Then God's messengers encountered Jacob. ³When he saw them he said, "This is God's encampment." So he named that place Mahanaim.*

Embassy to Esau. ⁴Jacob sent messengers ahead to his brother Esau in the land of Seir, the country of Edom,ᵃ ⁵with this message: "Thus shall you say to my lord Esau: 'Your servant Jacob speaks as follows: I have been staying with Laban and have been detained there until now. ⁶I own cattle, asses and sheep, as well as male and female servants. I am sending my lord this information in the hope of gaining your favor.' " ⁷When the messengers returned to Jacob, they said, "We reached your brother Esau. He is now coming to meet you, accompanied by four hundred men."

⁸Jacob was very much frightened. In his anxiety, he divided the people who were with him, as well as his flocks, herds, and camels, into two camps. ⁹"If Esau should attack and overwhelm one camp," he reasoned, "the remaining camp may still survive." ¹⁰Then he prayed, "O God of my father Abraham and God of my father Isaac! You told me, O LORD, 'Go back to the land of your birth, and I will be good to you.'ᵇ ¹¹I am unworthy

See RG 59-60

31, 43-54: In this account of the treaty between Laban and Jacob, the Yahwist and Elohist sources are closely interwoven. The mound or cairn of stones comes from the Yahwist source, the memorial stone or stele comes from the Elohist one.

31, 47: Jegar-sahadutha: an Aramaic term meaning "mound of witness." Galeed: in Hebrew, galed, with the same meaning; also offers an explanation of the regional name Gilead.

31, 49: Mizpah: a town in Gilead; cf Jgs 10, 17; 11, 11. 34; Hos 5, 1. The Hebrew name mispa ("lookout") is allied to

yisep yhwh ("may the Lord keep watch"), and also echoes the word masseba ("memorial pillar").

32, 3: Mahanaim: a town in Gilead (Jos 13, 26. 30; 21, 38; 2 Sm 2, 8; etc.). The Hebrew name means "two camps." There are other allusions to the name in vv 8. 11.

y: Gn 19, 24. 29. z: Gn 28, 18; 35, 14. a: Gn 36, 6. b: Gn 31, 3.

Jacob Prepares to Meet His Brother Esau

Recall that the last words we heard from Esau twenty years before were, "I will kill my brother Jacob" (27, 41). Jacob's preparations to meet Esau exhibit great anxiety about whether Esau still carries this threat with him (32, 11). Forgiveness can be one of life's major challenges. It is also one of the most powerful and life changing acts, whether between individuals, among groups, or between nations.

of all the acts of kindness that you have loyally performed for your servant: although I crossed the Jordan here with nothing but my staff, I have now grown into two companies. [12]Save me, I pray, from the hand of my brother Esau! Otherwise I fear that when he comes he will strike me down and slay the mothers and children.[c] [13]You yourself said, 'I will be very good to you, and I will make your descendants like the sands of the sea, which are too numerous to count.' "

[14]After passing the night there, Jacob selected from what he had with him the following presents for his brother Esau: [15]two hundred she-goats and twenty he-goats; two hundred ewes and twenty rams; [16]thirty milch camels and their young; forty cows and ten bulls; twenty she-asses and ten he-asses. [17]He put these animals in charge of his servants, in separate droves, and he told the servants, "Go on ahead of me, but keep a space between one drove and the next." [18]To the servant in the lead he gave this instruction: "When my brother Esau meets you, he may ask you, 'Whose man are you? Where are you going? To whom do these animals ahead of you belong?' [19]Then you shall answer, 'They belong to your brother Jacob, but they have been sent as a gift to my lord Esau; and Jacob himself is right behind us.' " [20]He gave similar instructions to the second servant and the third and to all the others who followed behind the droves, namely: "Thus and thus shall you say to Esau, when you reach him; [21]and be sure to add, 'Your servant Jacob is right behind us.' " For Jacob reasoned, "If I first appease him with gifts that precede me, then later, when I face him, perhaps he will forgive me." [22]So the gifts went on ahead of him, while he stayed that night in the camp.

Struggle with the Angel. [23]In the course of that night, however, Jacob arose, took his two wives, with the two maidservants and his eleven children, and crossed the ford of the Jabbok. [24]After he had taken them across the stream and had brought over all his possessions, [25]Jacob was left there alone. Then some man[*] wrestled with him until the break of dawn. [26]When the man saw that he could not prevail over him, he struck Jacob's hip at its socket, so that the hip socket was wrenched as they wrestled.[d] [27]The man then said, "Let me go, for it is daybreak." But Jacob said, "I will not let you go until you bless me." [28]"What is your name?" the man asked. He answered, "Jacob."[e] [29]Then the man said, "You shall no longer be spoken of as Jacob, but as Israel,[*] because you have contended with divine and human beings and have prevailed." [30]Jacob then asked him, "Do tell me your name, please." He answered, "Why should you want to know my name?" With that, he bade him farewell. [31]Jacob named the place Peniel,[*] "Because I have seen God face to face," he said, "yet my life has been spared."[f]

[32]At sunrise, as he left Penuel, Jacob

32, 25: Some man: a messenger of the Lord in human form, as is clear from vv 29ff.

32, 29: Israel: the first part of the Hebrew name Yisrael is given a popular explanation in the word sarita, "you contended"; the second part is the first syllable of elohim, "divine beings." The present incident, with a similar allusion to the name Israel, is referred to in Hos 12, 5, where the mysterious wrestler is explicitly called an angel.

32, 31: Peniel: a variant of the word Penuel (v 32), the name of a town on the north bank of the Jabbok in Gilead (Jgs 8, 8f. 17; 1 Kgs 12, 25). The name is explained as meaning "the face of God," peni-el. Yet my life has been spared: see note on Gn 16, 13.

c: Gn 28, 14; 48, 16; Ex 32, 13; Heb 11, 12. d: Hos 12, 4. e: Gn 35, 10; 1 Kgs 18, 31; 2 Kgs 17, 34. f: Jgs 13, 22.

limped along because of his hip. *33*That is why, to this day, the Israelites do not eat the sciatic muscle that is on the hip socket, inasmuch as Jacob's hip socket was struck at the sciatic muscle.

See RG
59-60

CHAPTER 33

Jacob and Esau Meet. *1*Jacob looked up and saw Esau coming, accompanied by four hundred men. So he divided his children among Leah, Rachel and the two maidservants, *2*putting the maids and their children first, Leah and her children next, and Rachel and Joseph last. *3*He himself went on ahead of them, bowing to the ground seven times, until he reached his brother. *4*Esau ran to meet him, embraced him, and flinging himself on his neck, kissed him as he wept.

*5*When Esau looked about, he saw the women and children. "Who are these with you?" he asked. Jacob answered, "They are the children whom God has graciously bestowed on your servant." *6*Then the maidservants and their children came forward and bowed low; *7*next, Leah and her children came forward and bowed low; lastly, Rachel and her children came forward and bowed low. *8*Then Esau asked, "What did you intend with all those droves that I encountered?" Jacob answered, "It was to gain my lord's favor." *9*"I have plenty," replied Esau; "you should keep what is yours, brother." *10*"No, I beg you!" said Jacob. "If you will do me the favor, please accept this gift from me, since to come into your presence is for me like coming into the presence of God, now that you have received me so kindly. *11*Do accept the present I have brought you; God has been generous toward me, and I have an abundance." Since he so urged him, Esau accepted.

*12*Then Esau said, "Let us break camp and be on our way; I will travel alongside you." *13*But Jacob replied: "As my lord can see, the children are frail. Besides, I am encumbered with the flocks and herds, which now have sucklings; if overdriven for a single day, the whole flock will die. *14*Let my lord, then, go on ahead of me, while I proceed more slowly at the pace of the livestock before me and at the pace of my children, until I join my lord in Seir." *15*Esau replied, "Let me at least put at your disposal some of the men who are with me." But Jacob said, "For what reason? Please indulge me in this, my lord." *16*So on the same day that Esau began his journey back to Seir, *17*Jacob journeyed to Succoth.* There he built a home for himself and made booths for his livestock. That is why the place was called Succoth.

*18*Having thus come from Paddan-aram, Jacob arrived safely at the city of Shechem, which is in the land of Canaan, and he encamped in sight of the city.*g* *19*The plot of ground on which he had pitched his tent he bought for a hundred pieces of bullion* from the descendants of Hamor, the founder of Shechem.*h* *20*He set up a memorial stone there and invoked "El, the God of Israel."*i*

CHAPTER 34

See RG 59-60

The Rape of Dinah. *1*Dinah, the daughter whom Leah had borne to Jacob, went out to visit some of the women of the land. *2*When Shechem, son of Hamor the Hivite,* who was chief of the region, saw her, he seized her and lay with her by force. *3*Since he was strongly attracted to Dinah, daughter of Jacob, indeed was really in love with the girl, he endeavored to win her affection. *4*Shechem also asked his father Hamor, "Get me this girl for a wife."

33, 17: Succoth: an important town near the confluence of the Jabbok and the Jordan (Jos 13, 27; Jgs 8, 5-16; 1 Kgs 7, 46). Booths: in Hebrew, sukkot, of the same sound as the name of the town.

33, 19: Pieces of bullion: in Hebrew, kesita, a monetary unit of which the value is now unknown. Descendants of Hamor: Hamorites, "the men of Hamor"; cf Jgs 9, 28. Hamor was regarded as the eponymous ancestor of the pre-Israelite inhabitants of Shechem.

34, 1-31: Behind the story of the rape of Dinah and the revenge of Jacob's sons on the men of the city of Shechem there probably lies a dimly recollected historical event connected with an armed conflict between the earliest Israelite tribes invading central Canaan and the Hurrian inhabitants of the Shechem region.

34, 2: Hivite: The Greek text has "Horite"; the terms were apparently used indiscriminately to designate the Hurrian or other non-Semitic elements in Palestine.

g: Gn 12, 6; Jn 4, 6. *h:* Jos 24, 32; Jn 4, 5; Acts 7, 16. *i.* Jgs 6, 24.

⁵Meanwhile, Jacob heard that Shechem had defiled his daughter Dinah; but since his sons were out in the fields with his livestock, he held his peace until they came home. ⁶Now Hamor, the father of Shechem, went out to discuss the matter with Jacob, ⁷just as Jacob's sons were coming in from the fields. When they heard the news, the men were shocked and seethed with indignation. What Shechem had done was an outrage in Israel; such a thing could not be tolerated.ʲ

⁸Hamor appealed to them, saying, "My son Shechem has his heart set on your daughter. Please give her to him in marriage. ⁹Intermarry with us; give your daughters to us, and take our daughters for yourselves. ¹⁰Thus you can live among us. The land is open before you; you can settle and move about freely in it, and acquire landed property here." ¹¹Then Shechem, too, appealed to Dinah's father and brothers: "Do me this favor, and I will pay whatever you demand of me. ¹²No matter how high you set the bridal price, I will pay you whatever you ask; only give me the maiden in marriage."

Revenge of Jacob's Sons. ¹³Jacob's sons replied to Shechem and his father Hamor with guile, speaking as they did because their sister Dinah had been defiled. ¹⁴"We could not do such a thing," they said, "as to give our sister to an uncircumcised man; that would be a disgrace for us. ¹⁵We will agree with you only on this condition, that you become like us by having every male among you circumcised. ¹⁶Then we will give you our daughters and take yours in marriage; we will settle among you and become one kindred people with you. ¹⁷But if you do not comply with our terms regarding circumcision, we will take our daughter and go away."

¹⁸Their proposal seemed fair to Hamor and his son Shechem. ¹⁹The young man lost no time in acting in the matter, since he was deeply in love with Jacob's daughter. Moreover, he was more highly respected than anyone else in his clan. ²⁰So Hamor and his son Shechem went to their town council and thus presented the matter to their fellow townsmen: ²¹"These men are friendly toward us. Let them settle in the land and move about in it freely; there is ample room in the country for them. We can marry their daughters and give our daughters to them in marriage. ²²But the men will agree to live with us and form one kindred people with us only on this condition, that every male among us be circumcised as they themselves are. ²³Would not the livestock they have acquired—all their animals—then be ours? Let us, therefore, give in to them, so that they may settle among us."

²⁴All the able-bodied men of the town agreed with Hamor and his son Shechem, and all the males, including every able-bodied man in the community,* were circumcised. ²⁵On the third day, while they were still in pain, Dinah's full brothers Simeon and Levi, two of Jacob's sons, took their swords, advanced against the city without any trouble, and massacred all the males.ᵏ ²⁶After they had put Hamor and his son Shechem to the sword, they took Dinah from Shechem's house and left.ˡ ²⁷Then the other sons of Jacob followed up the slaughter and sacked the city in reprisal for their sister Dinah's defilement. ²⁸They seized their flocks, herds and asses, whatever was in the city and in the country around. ²⁹They carried off all their wealth, their women, and their children, and took for loot whatever was in the houses.ᵐ

³⁰Jacob said to Simeon and Levi: "You have brought trouble upon me by making me loathsome to the inhabitants of the land, the Canaanites and the Perizzites. I have so few men that, if these people unite against me and attack me, I and my family will be wiped out." ³¹But they retorted, "Should our sister have been treated like a harlot?"

CHAPTER 35

See RG 59–60

Bethel Revisited. ¹God said to Jacob: "Go up now to Bethel. Settle there and build

---

34, 24: Every able-bodied man in the community: literally "all those who go out at the gate of the city," apparently meaning the men who go out to war. By temporarily crippling them through circumcision, Jacob's sons deprived the city of its defenders.

j: 2 Sm 13, 12.   k: Gn 49, 6.   l: Jdt 9, 2.   m: Jdt 9, 3f.

an altar there to the God who appeared to you while you were fleeing from your brother Esau."ⁿ ²So Jacob told his family and all the others who were with him: "Get rid of the foreign gods* that you have among you; then purify yourselves and put on fresh clothes. ³We are now to go up to Bethel, and I will build an altar there to the God who answered me in my hour of distress and who has been with me wherever I have gone." ⁴They therefore handed over to Jacob all the foreign gods in their possession and also the rings* they had in their ears. ⁵Then, as they set out, a terror from God fell upon the towns round about, so that no one pursued the sons of Jacob.

⁶Thus Jacob and all the people who were with him arrived in Luz [that is, Bethel] in the land of Canaan.ᵒ ⁷There he built an altar and named the place Bethel, for it was there that God had revealed himself to him when he was fleeing from his brother.ᵖ

⁸Death came to Rebekah's nurse Deborah; she was buried under the oak below Bethel, and so it was called Allon-bacuth.*

⁹On Jacob's arrival from Paddan-aram, God appeared to him again and blessed him. ¹⁰God said to him:

"You whose name is Jacob
    shall no longer be called Jacob,
    but Israel shall be your name."�q

Thus he was named Israel. ¹¹God also said to him:

"I am God Almighty;
    be fruitful and multiply.

A nation, indeed an assembly of nations,
    shall stem from you,
    and kings shall issue from your loins.
¹² The land I once gave
    to Abraham and Isaac
    I now give to you;
And to your descendants after you
    will I give this land."ʳ

¹³Then God departed from him. ¹⁴On the site where God had spoken with him, Jacob set up a memorial stone, and upon it he made a libation and poured out oil.ˢ ¹⁵Jacob named the site Bethel, because God had spoken with him there.

Jacob's Family. ¹⁶Then they departed from Bethel: but while they still had some distance to go on the way to Ephrath, Rachel began to be in labor and to suffer great distress. ¹⁷When her pangs were most severe, her midwife said to her, "Have no fear! This time, too, you have a son." ¹⁸With her last breath—for she was at the point of death—she called him Ben-oni;* his father, however, named him Benjamin. ¹⁹ᵗThus Rachel died; and she was buried on the road to Ephrath [that is, Bethlehem].* ²⁰Jacob set up a memorial stone on her grave, and the same monument marks Rachel's grave to this day.

²¹Israel moved on and pitched his tent beyond Migdal-eder. ²²While Israel was encamped in that region, Reuben went and lay with Bilhah, his father's concubine. When Israel heard of it, he was greatly offended.ᵘ

The sons of Jacob were now twelve. ²³The sons of Leah: Reuben, Jacob's first-born, Simeon, Levi, Judah, Issachar, and Zebulun; ²⁴*the sons of Rachel: Joseph and Benjamin;

35, 2: Foreign gods: pagan images, including household idols (see note on Gn 31, 19), that Jacob's people brought with them from Paddan-aram.

35, 4: Rings: Earrings were often worn as amulets connected with pagan magic.

35, 8: This verse may have stood originally in some other context. Rebekah's nurse is spoken of without a name, in Gn 24, 59. Allon-bacuth: the Hebrew name means "oak of weeping."

35, 18: Ben-oni: means either "son of my vigor" or, more likely in the context, "son of affliction." Benjamin: "son of the right hand." This may be interpreted to signify a son who is his father's help and support, but more likely its original meaning was "southerner." In the Hebrew idiom, the south lies to one's right hand, and Benjamin was the southernmost

of the Rachel tribes.

35, 19: Bethlehem: the gloss comes from a later tradition that identified the site with Bethlehem, also called Ephrath or Ephratha (Jos 15, 59; Ru 4, 11; Mi 5, 1). But Rachel's grave was actually near Ramah (Jer 31, 15), a few miles north of Jerusalem, in the territory of Benjamin (1 Sm 20, 2).

35, 24ff: Benjamin is here said to have been born in Paddan-aram, either because all twelve sons of Jacob are considered as a unit, or because the Priestly source, from which vv 23-29 are taken, follows a tradition different from that of the

n: Gn 28, 12f. o: Gn 28, 19; Jos 18, 13; Jgs 1, 22f. p. Gn 28, 12f. q: 1 Kgs 18, 31; 2 Kgs 17, 34. r: Ex 32, 13; Heb 11, 9. s: Gn 28, 18; 31, 45. t: Gn 48, 7; 1 Sm 10, 2; Mi 5, 2. u: Gn 49, 4; 1 Chr 5, 1.

25the sons of Rachel's maid Bilhah: Dan and Naphtali; 26the sons of Leah's maid Zilpah: Gad and Asher. These are the sons of Jacob who were born to him in Paddan-aram.

27Jacob went home to his father Isaac at Mamre, in Kiriath-arba [that is, Hebron], where Abraham and Isaac had stayed. 28The lifetime of Isaac was one hundred and eighty years; 29then he breathed his last. After a full life, he died as an old man and was taken to his kinsmen. His sons Esau and Jacob buried him.

CHAPTER 36

See RG
59–60

Edomite Lists. 1These are the descendants of Esau [that is, Edom]. 2*Esau took his wives from among the Canaanite women: Adah, daughter of Elon the Hittite; Oholibamah, granddaughter through Anah of Zibeon the Hivite;y 3and Basemath, daughter of Ishmael and sister of Nebaioth. 4Adah bore Eliphaz to Esau; Basemath bore Reuel;w 5and Oholibamah bore Jeush, Jalam and Korah. These are the sons of Esau who were born to him in the land of Canaan.x

6Esau took his wives, his sons, his daughters, and all the members of his household, as well as his livestock comprising various animals and all the property he had acquired in the land of Canaan, and went to the land of Seir, out of the way of his brother Jacob.y 7Their possessions had become too great for them to dwell together, and the land in which they were staying could not support them because of their livestock. 8So Esau settled in the highlands of Seir. [Esau is Edom.]z 9These are the descendants of Esau, ancestor of the Edomites, in the highlands of Seir.

10These are the names of Esau's sons: Eliphaz, son of Esau's wife Adah; and Reuel, son of Esau's wife Basemath. 11aThe sons of Eliphaz were Teman, Omar, Zepho, Gatam and Kenaz. 12(Esau's son Eliphaz had a concubine Timna, and she bore Amalek to Eli-phaz.) These are the descendants of Esau's wife Adah. 13The sons of Reuel were Nahath, Zerah, Shammah and Mizzah. These are the descendants of Esau's wife Basemath.b 14The descendants of Esau's wife Oholibamah—granddaughter through Anah of Zibeon—whom she bore to Esau were Jeush, Jalam and Korah.c

15The following are the clans of Esau's descendants. The descendants of Eliphaz, Esau's first-born: the clans of Teman, Omar, Zepho, Kenaz, 16Korah, Gatam and Amalek. These are the clans of Eliphaz in the land of Edom; they are descended from Adah. 17The descendants of Esau's son Reuel: the clans of Nahath, Zerah, Shammah and Mizzah. These are the clans of Reuel in the land of Edom; they are descended from Esau's wife Basemath. 18The descendants of Esau's wife Oholibamah: the clans of Jeush, Jalam and Korah. These are the clans of Esau's wife Oholibamah, daughter of Anah. 19Such are the descendants of Esau [that is, Edom] according to their clans.

20The following are the descendants of Seir the Horite,* the original settlers in the land: Lotan, Shobal, Zibeon, Anah,d 21Dishon, Ezer and Dishan; they are the Horite clans descended from Seir, in the land of Edom. 22eLotan's descendants were Hori and Hemam, and Lotan's sister was Timna. 23Shobal's descendants were Alvan, Mahanath, Ebal, Shepho and Onam. 24Zibeon's descendants were Aiah and Anah. (He is the Anah who found water in the desert while he was pasturing the asses of his father Zibeon.) 25The descendants of Anah were Dishon and Oholibamah, daughter of Anah. 26The descendants of Dishon were Hemdan, Eshban, Ithran and Cheran. 27The descendants of Ezer were Bilhan, Zaavan and Akan. 28The descendants of Dishan were Uz and Aran. 29These are the Horite clans: the clans of Lotan, Shobal, Zibeon, Anah, 30Dishon, Ezer and

Elohistic source found in vv 16-20.

36, 2-14: The names of Esau's wives and of their fathers given here differ considerably from their names cited from other old sources in Gn 26, 34 and 28, 9. Zibeon the Hivite: In v 20 he is called a "Horite"; see note on Gn 34, 2.

36, 20: Seir the Horite: According to Dt 2, 12, the high-

lands of Seir were inhabited by Horites before they were occupied by the Edomites.

v: Gn 26, 34.   w: 1 Chr 1, 35.   x: 1 Chr 1, 35.   y: Gn 32, 4.
z: Dt 2, 4f; Jos 24, 4.   a: 11f: 1 Chr 1, 36.   b: 1 Chr 1, 37.
c: 1 Chr 1, 35.   d: 20f: 1 Chr 1, 38.   e: 22-28: 1 Chr 1, 39-42.

Dishan; they were the clans of the Horites, clan by clan, in the land of Seir.

[f]The following are the kings who reigned in the land of Edom before any king reigned over the Israelites.* [32]Bela, son of Beor, became king in Edom; the name of his city was Dinhabah. [33]When Bela died, Jobab, son of Zerah, from Bozrah, succeeded him as king. [34]When Jobab died, Husham, from the land of the Temanites, succeeded him as king. He defeated the Midianites in the country of Moab; the name of his city was Avith. [35]When Husham died, Hadad, son of Bedad, succeeded him as king. [36]When Hadad died, Samlah, from Masrekah, succeeded him as king. [37]When Samlah died, Shaul, from Rehoboth-on-the-River, succeeded him as king. [38]When Shaul died, Baal-hanan, son of Achbor, succeeded him as king. [39]When Baal-hanan died, Hadar succeeded him as king; the name of his city was Pau. (His wife's name was Mehetabel; she was the daughter of Matred, son of Mezahab.)

[40]The following are the names of the clans of Esau individually according to their subdivisions and localities: the clans of Timna, Alvah, Jetheth, [41]Oholibamah, Elah, Pinon, [42]Kenaz, Teman, Mibzar, [43]Magdiel and Iram. These are the clans of the Edomites, according to their settlements in their territorial holdings. [Esau was the father of the Edomites.]

IV: Joseph and His Brothers

CHAPTER 37

See RG
60-61

Joseph Sold into Egypt. [1]Jacob settled in the land where his father had stayed, the land of Canaan. [2]This is his family history. When Joseph was seventeen years old, he was tending the flocks with his brothers; he was an assistant to the sons of his father's wives Bilhah and Zilpah, and he brought his father bad reports about them.

[3]Israel loved Joseph best of all his sons, for he was the child of his old age; and he had made him a long tunic. [4]When his broth-

ers saw that their father loved him best of all his sons, they hated him so much that they would not even greet him.

[5]Once Joseph had a dream, which he told to his brothers:[g] [6]"Listen to this dream I had. [7]There we were, binding sheaves in the field, when suddenly my sheaf rose to an upright position, and your sheaves formed a ring around my sheaf and bowed down to it." [8]"Are you really going to make yourself king over us?" his brothers asked him. "Or impose your rule on us?" So they hated him all the more because of his talk about his dreams.[h]

[9]Then he had another dream, and this one, too, he told to his brothers. "I had another dream," he said; "this time, the sun and the moon and eleven stars were bowing down to me." [10]When he also told it to his father, his father reproved him. "What is the meaning of this dream of yours?" he asked. "Can it be that I and your mother and your brothers are to come and bow to the ground before you?" [11]So his brothers were wrought up against him but his father pondered the matter.

[12]One day, when his brothers had gone to pasture their father's flocks at Shechem, [13]Israel said to Joseph, "Your brothers, you know, are tending our flocks at Shechem. Get ready; I will send you to them." "I am ready," Joseph answered. [14]"Go then," he replied; "see if all is well with your brothers and the flocks, and bring back word." So he sent him off from the valley of Hebron. When Joseph reached Shechem, [15]a man met him as he was wandering about in the fields. "What are you looking for?" the man asked him. [16]"I am looking for my brothers," he answered. "Could you please tell me where they are tending the flocks?" [17]The man told him, "They have moved on from here; in fact, I heard them say, 'Let us go on to Dothan.' " So Joseph went after his brothers and caught up with them in Dothan. [18]They noticed him from a distance, and before he came up to them, they plotted to kill him. [19]They said to one another: "Here comes that master

36, 31: Before any king reigned over the Israelites: obviously this statement was written after the time of Saul, Israel's first king.

f: 31-43: 1 Chr 1, 45-54.   *g:* Gn 42, 9.   *h:* Gn 50, 17.

dreamer! [20]Come on, let us kill him and throw him into one of the cisterns here; we could say that a wild beast devoured him. We shall then see what comes of his dreams."[i]

[21]*When Reuben heard this, he tried to save him from their hands, saying, "We must not take his life. [22]Instead of shedding blood," he continued, "just throw him into that cistern there in the desert; but don't kill him outright." His purpose was to rescue him from their hands and restore him to his father.[j] [23]So when Joseph came up to them, they stripped him of the long tunic he had on; [24]then they took him and threw him into the cistern, which was empty and dry.

[25]They then sat down to their meal. Looking up, they saw a caravan of Ishmaelites coming from Gilead, their camels laden with gum, balm and resin to be taken down to Egypt.[k] [26]Judah said to his brothers: "What is to be gained by killing our brother and concealing his blood?[l] [27]Rather, let us sell him to these Ishmaelites, instead of doing away with him ourselves. After all, he is our brother, our own flesh." His brothers agreed. [28]They sold Joseph to the Ishmaelites for twenty pieces of silver.*

Some Midianite traders passed by, and they pulled Joseph up out of the cistern and took him to Egypt.[m] [29]When Reuben went back to the cistern and saw that Joseph was not in it, he tore his clothes, [30]and returning to his brothers, he exclaimed: "The boy is gone! And I—where can I turn?" [31]They took Joseph's tunic, and after slaughtering a goat, dipped the tunic in its blood. [32]They then sent someone to bring the long tunic to their father, with the message: "We found this. See whether it is your son's tunic or not." [33]He recognized it and exclaimed: "My son's tunic! A wild beast has devoured him! Joseph has been torn to pieces!"[n] [34]Then Jacob rent his clothes, put sackcloth on his loins, and mourned his son many days. [35]Though his sons and daughters tried to console him, he refused all consolation, saying, "No, I will go down mourning to my son in the nether world." Thus did his father lament him.[o]

[36]The Midianites, meanwhile, sold Joseph in Egypt to Potiphar, a courtier of Pharaoh and his chief steward.[p]

CHAPTER 38*

See RG 60-61

Judah and Tamar. [1]About that time Judah parted from his brothers and pitched his tent near a certain Adullamite named Hirah. [2]There he met the daughter of a Canaanite named Shua, married her, and had relations with her.[q] [3]She conceived and bore a son, whom she named Er. [4]Again she conceived and bore a son, whom she named Onan. [5]Then she bore still another son, whom she named Shelah. They were in Chezib* when he was born.[r]

[6]Judah got a wife named Tamar for his first-born, Er. [7]But Er, Judah's first-born, greatly offended the LORD; so the LORD took his life.[s] [8]Then Judah said to Onan, "Unite with your brother's widow, in fulfillment of your duty as brother-in-law, and thus pre-

---

37, 21-36: The chapter thus far is from the Yahwist source, as are also vv 25-28a. But vv 21-24 and 28b-36 are from the Elohist source. In the latter, Reuben tries to rescue Joseph, who is taken in Reuben's absence by certain Midianites; in the Yahwist source, it is Judah who saves Joseph's life by having him sold to certain Ishmaelites. Although the two variant forms in which the story was handed down in early oral tradition differ in these minor points, they agree on the essential fact that Joseph was brought as a slave into Egypt because of the jealousy of his brothers.

37, 28: They sold Joseph . . . silver: in the Hebrew text, these words occur between out of the cistern and (they) took him to Egypt at the end of the verse.

38, 1-30: This chapter, from the Yahwist source, has nothing to do with the Joseph story in which Judah is still living with his father and brothers. The sacred author inserted this independent account from the life of Judah at this place to mark the long lapse of time during which Joseph's family knew nothing of his life in Egypt. This is apparently a personalized history of the early days of the tribe of Judah, which interbred with several Canaanite clans, though some of these soon became extinct.

38, 5: Chezib: a variant form of Achzib (Jos 15, 44; Mi 1, 14), a town in the Judean Shephelah.

38, 8: Preserve your brother's line: literally, "raise up seed for your brother." The ancient Israelites regarded as very important their law of levirate, or "brother-in-law" marriage; see notes on Dt 25, 5; Ru 2, 20. In the present story, it is primarily Onan's violation of this law, rather than the means he used to circumvent it, that brought on him God's displeasure (vv 9f).

---

i: Gn 44, 28. *j:* Gn 42, 22. *k:* Gn 43, 11. *l:* Jb 16, 18. *m:* Ps 105, 17; Wis 10, 13; Acts 7, 9. *n:* Gn 44, 28. *o:* Gn 42, 38. *p:* Ps 105, 17. *q:* 1 Chr 2, 3. *r:* 1 Chr 4, 21. *s:* 1 Chr 2, 3. *t:* Dt 25, 5; Mt 22, 24; Mk 12, 19; Lk 20, 28.

serve your brother's line."* [9]Onan, however, knew that the descendants would not be counted as his; so whenever he had relations with his brother's widow, he wasted his seed on the ground, to avoid contributing offspring for his brother. [10]What he did greatly offended the LORD, and the LORD took his life too. [11]Thereupon Judah said to his daughter-in-law Tamar, "Stay as a widow in your father's house until my son Shelah grows up"—for he feared that Shelah also might die like his brothers. So Tamar went to live in her father's house.

[12]Years passed, and Judah's wife, the daughter of Shua, died. After Judah completed the period of mourning, he went up to Timnah for the shearing of his sheep, in company with his friend Hirah the Adullamite. [13]When Tamar was told that her father-in-law was on his way up to Timnah to shear his sheep, [14]she took off her widow's garb, veiled her face by covering herself with a shawl, and sat down at the entrance to Enaim, which is on the way to Timnah; for she was aware that, although Shelah was now grown up, she had not been given to him in marriage.[u] [15]When Judah saw her, he mistook her for a harlot, since she had covered her face. [16]So he went over to her at the roadside, and not realizing that she was his daughter-in-law, he said, "Come, let me have intercourse with you." She replied, "What will you pay me for letting you have intercourse with me?" [17]He answered, "I will send you a kid from the flock." "Very well," she said, "provided you leave a pledge until you send it." [18]Judah asked, "What pledge am I to give you?" She answered, "Your seal and cord,* and the staff you carry." So he gave them to her and had intercourse with her, and she conceived by him. [19]When she went away, she took off her shawl and put on her widow's garb again.

[20]Judah sent the kid by his friend the Adullamite to recover the pledge from the woman; but he could not find her. [21]So he asked the men of the place, "Where is the temple prostitute,* the one by the roadside in Enaim?" But they answered, "There has never been a temple prostitute here." [22]He went back to Judah and told him, "I could not find her; and besides, the men of the place said there was no temple prostitute there." [23]"Let her keep the things," Judah replied; "otherwise we shall become a laughingstock. After all, I did send her the kid, even though you were unable to find her."

[24]About three months later, Judah was told that his daughter-in-law Tamar had played the harlot and was then with child from her harlotry. "Bring her out," cried Judah; "she shall be burned." [25]But as they were bringing her out, she sent word to her father-in-law, "It is by the man to whom these things belong that I am with child. Please verify," she added, "whose seal and cord and whose staff these are." [26]Judah recognized them and said, "She is more in the right than I am, since I did not give her to my son Shelah." But he had no further relations with her.

[27]When the time of her delivery came, she was found to have twins in her womb.[v] [28]While she was giving birth, one infant put out his hand; and the midwife, taking a crimson thread, tied it on his hand, to note that this one came out first. [29w]But as he withdrew his hand, his brother came out; and she said, "What a breach you have made for yourself!" So he was called Perez.* [30]Afterward his brother came out; he was called Zerah.[x] *

38, 18: Seal and cord: the cylinder seal, through which a hole was bored lengthwise so that it could be worn from the neck by a cord, was a distinctive means of identification. Apparently a man's staff was also marked with his name (Nm 17, 16f) or other sign of identification.

38, 21: Temple prostitute: the Hebrew term qedesha, literally "consecrated woman," designates a woman who had ritual intercourse with men in pagan fertility rites; cf Dt 23, 18; Hos 4, 14, where the same Hebrew word is used. Hirah the Adullamite uses a word that refers to a higher social class than that designated by the term zona, common "harlot," used in vv 15. 24.

38, 29: He was called Perez: the Hebrew word means "breach."

38, 30: He was called Zerah: a name connected here by popular etymology with a Hebrew verb for the red light of dawn, alluding apparently to the crimson thread.

u: Prv 7, 10.   v: 1 Chr 2, 4.   w: Rv 4, 12; Mt 1, 3; Lk 3, 33.
x: Nm 26, 20; 1 Chr 2, 4; Mt 1, 3.

See RG
60-61

CHAPTER 39

Joseph's Temptation. [1]When Joseph was taken down to Egypt, a certain Egyptian (Potiphar, a courtier of Pharoah and his chief steward*) bought him from the Ishmaelites who had brought him there. [2y]But since the LORD was with him, Joseph got on very well and was assigned to the household of his Egyptian master. [3]When his master saw that the LORD was with him and brought him success in whatever he did, [4]he took a liking to Joseph and made him his personal attendant; he put him in charge of his household and entrusted to him all his possessions.[z] [5]From the moment that he put him in charge of his household and all his possessions, the LORD blessed the Egyptian's house for Joseph's sake; in fact, the LORD's blessing was on everything he owned, both inside the house and out. [6]Having left everything he owned in Joseph's charge, he gave no thought, with Joseph there, to anything but the food he ate.

Now Joseph was strikingly handsome in countenance and body. [7]After a time, his master's wife began to look fondly at him and said, "Lie with me." [8]But he refused. "As long as I am here," he told her, "my master does not concern himself with anything in the house, but has entrusted to me all he owns. [9]He wields no more authority in this house than I do, and he has withheld from me nothing but yourself, since you are his wife. How, then, could I commit so great a wrong and thus stand condemned before God?" [10]Although she tried to entice him day after day, he would not agree to lie beside her, or even stay near her.[a]

[11]One such day, when Joseph came into the house to do his work, and none of the household servants were then in the house, [12]she laid hold of him by his cloak, saying, "Lie with me!" But leaving the cloak in her hand, he got away from her and ran outside.

[13]When she saw that he had left his cloak in her hand as he fled outside, [14]she screamed for her household servants and told them, "Look! My husband has brought in a Hebrew slave to make sport of us! He came in here to lie with me, but I cried out as loud as I could. [15]When he heard me scream for help, he left his cloak beside me and ran away outside."

[16]She kept the cloak with her until his master came home. [17]Then she told him the same story: "The Hebrew slave whom you brought here broke in on me, to make sport of me. [18]But when I screamed for help, he left his cloak beside me and fled outside." [19]As soon as the master heard his wife's story about how his slave had treated her, he became enraged. [20]He seized Joseph and threw him into the jail where the royal prisoners were confined.[b]

But even while he was in prison, [21]the LORD remained with Joseph; he showed him kindness by making the chief jailer well-disposed toward him.[c] [22]The chief jailer put Joseph in charge of all the prisoners in the jail, and everything that had to be done there was done under his management. [23]The chief jailer did not concern himself with anything at all that was in Joseph's charge, since the LORD was with him and brought success to all he did.

CHAPTER 40

See RG
60-61

The Dreams Interpreted. [1]Some time afterward, the royal cupbearer and baker gave offense to their lord, the king of Egypt. [2]Pharaoh was angry with his two courtiers, the chief cupbearer and the chief baker, [3]and he put them in custody in the house of the chief steward (the same jail where Joseph was confined). [4]The chief steward assigned Joseph to them, and he became their attendant.

After they had been in custody for some time, [5]the cupbearer and the baker of the king of Egypt who were confined in the jail

---

39, 1: (Potiphar . . . chief steward): These words in the text serve to harmonize ch 39 from the Yahwist source, with Gn 37, 36, and 40, 1-23, from the Elohist. In the former, the Ishmaelites who bought Joseph from his brothers (Gn 37, 28) sold him to the unnamed "Egyptian master" of ch 39. In the latter, the Midianites who kidnaped Joseph (Gn 37, 28; 40,

15) sold him to Potiphar, Pharaoh's chief steward (Gn 37, 36), whose house was used as a royal prison (Gn 40, 2f).

y: 1 Sm 3, 19; 10, 7; 18, 14; 2 Sm 5, 10; 2 Kgs 18, 7; Acts 7, 9. *z:* Dn 1, 9. *a:* 1 Mc 2, 53. *b:* Ps 105, 18. *c:* Acts 7, 9f.

both had dreams on the same night, each dream with its own meaning. [6]When Joseph came to them in the morning, he noticed that they looked disturbed. [7]So he asked Pharaoh's courtiers who were with him in custody in his master's house, "Why do you look so sad today?" [8]They answered him, "We have had dreams, but there is no one to interpret them for us." Joseph said to them, "Surely, interpretations come from God. Please tell the dreams to me."[d]

[9]Then the chief cupbearer told Joseph his dream. "In my dream," he said, "I saw a vine in front of me, [10]and on the vine were three branches. It had barely budded when its blossoms came out, and its clusters ripened into grapes. [11]Pharaoh's cup was in my hand; so I took the grapes, pressed them out into his cup, and put it in Pharaoh's hand." [12]Joseph said to him: "This is what it means. The three branches are three days; [13]within three days Pharaoh will lift up your head* and restore you to your post. You will be handing Pharaoh his cup as you formerly used to do when you were his cupbearer. [14]So if you will still remember, when all is well with you, that I was here with you, please do me the favor of mentioning me to Pharaoh, to get me out of this place. [15]The truth is that I was kidnaped from the land of the Hebrews, and here I have not done anything for which I should have been put into a dungeon."

[16]When the chief baker saw that Joseph had given this favorable interpretation, he said to him: "I too had a dream. In it I had three wicker baskets on my head; [17]in the top one were all kinds of bakery products for Pharaoh, but the birds were pecking at them out of the basket on my head." [18]Joseph said to him in reply: "This is what it means. The three baskets are three days; [19]within three days Pharaoh will lift up your head and have you impaled on a stake, and the birds will be pecking the flesh from your body."

[20]And in fact, on the third day, which was Pharaoh's birthday, when he gave a banquet to all his staff, with his courtiers around him, he lifted up the heads of the chief cupbearer and chief baker. [21]He restored the chief cupbearer to his office, so that he again handed the cup to Pharaoh; [22]but the chief baker he impaled—just as Joseph had told them in his interpretation. [23]Yet the chief cupbearer gave no thought to Joseph; he had forgotten him.

CHAPTER 41

Pharaoh's Dream. [1]After a lapse of two years, Pharaoh had a dream. He saw himself standing by the Nile, [2]when up out of the Nile came seven cows, handsome and fat; they grazed in the reed grass. [3]Behind them seven other cows, ugly and gaunt, came up out of the Nile; and standing on the bank of the Nile beside the others, [4]the ugly, gaunt cows ate up the seven handsome, fat cows. Then Pharaoh woke up.

[5]He fell asleep again and had another dream. He saw seven ears of grain, fat and healthy, growing on a single stalk. [6]Behind them sprouted seven ears of grain, thin and blasted by the east wind; [7]and the seven thin ears swallowed up the seven fat, healthy ears. Then Pharaoh woke up, to find it was only a dream.

[8]Next morning his spirit was agitated. So he summoned all the magicians and sages of Egypt and recounted his dreams to them; but no one could interpret his dreams for him. [9]Then the chief cupbearer spoke up and said to Pharaoh: "On this occasion I am reminded of my negligence. [10]Once, when Pharaoh was angry, he put me and the chief baker in custody in the house of the chief steward. [11]Later, we both had dreams on the same night, and each of our dreams had its own meaning. [12]There with us was a Hebrew youth, a slave of the chief steward; and when we told him our dreams, he interpreted them for us and explained for each of us the meaning of his dream.[e] [13]And it turned out just as he had told us: I was restored to my post, but the other man was impaled."

[14]Pharaoh therefore had Joseph sum-

See RG 60–61

40, 13: Lift up your head: signifying "pardon you." In v 19 "to lift up the head" means "to behead"; and finally, in v 20, the same expression means "to review the case (of someone)." Joseph couches his interpretation of the dreams in equivocal terms.

d: Gn 41, 16.   *e:* Dn 1, 17.

moned, and they hurriedly brought him from the dungeon. After he shaved and changed his clothes, he came into Pharaoh's presence.[f] [15]Pharaoh then said to him: "I had certain dreams that no one can interpret. But I hear it said of you that the moment you are told a dream you can interpret it." [16]"It is not I," Joseph replied to Pharaoh, "but God who will give Pharaoh the right answer."[g]

[17]Then Pharaoh said to Joseph: "In my dream, I was standing on the bank of the Nile, [18]when up from the Nile came seven cows, fat and well-formed; they grazed in the reed grass. [19]Behind them came seven other cows, scrawny, most ill-formed and gaunt. Never have I seen such ugly specimens as these in all the land of Egypt! [20]The gaunt, ugly cows ate up the first seven fat cows. [21]But when they had consumed them, no one could tell that they had done so, because they looked as ugly as before. Then I woke up. [22]In another dream, I saw seven ears of grain, fat and healthy, growing on a single stalk. [23]Behind them sprouted seven ears of grain, shriveled and thin and blasted by the east wind; [24]and the seven thin ears swallowed up the seven healthy ears. I have spoken to the magicians, but none of them can give me an explanation."

[25]Joseph said to Pharaoh: "Both of Pharaoh's dreams have the same meaning. God has thus foretold to Pharaoh what he is about to do. [26]The seven healthy cows are seven years, and the seven healthy ears are seven years—the same in each dream. [27]So also, the seven thin, ugly cows that came up after them are seven years, as are the seven thin, wind-blasted ears; they are seven years of famine. [28]It is just as I told Pharaoh: God has revealed to Pharaoh what he is about to do. [29]Seven years of great abundance are now coming throughout the land of Egypt; [30]but these will be followed by seven years of famine, when all the abundance in the land of Egypt will be forgotten. When the famine has ravaged the land, [31]no trace of the abundance will be found in the land because of the famine that follows it—so utterly severe will that famine be. [32]That Pharaoh had the same dream twice means that the matter has been reaffirmed by God and that God will soon bring it about.

[33]"Therefore, let Pharaoh seek out a wise and discerning man and put him in charge of the land of Egypt. [34]Pharaoh should also take action to appoint overseers, so as to regiment the land during the seven years of abundance. [35]They should husband all the food of the coming good years, collecting the grain under Pharaoh's authority, to be stored in the towns for food. [36]This food will serve as a reserve for the country against the seven years of famine that are to follow in the land of Egypt, so that the land may not perish in the famine."

[37]This advice pleased Pharaoh and all his officials.[h] [38]"Could we find another like him," Pharaoh asked his officials, "a man so endowed with the spirit of God?" [39]So Pharaoh said to Joseph: "Since God has made all this known to you, no one can be as wise and discerning as you are. [40]You shall be in charge of my palace, and all my people shall dart at your command. Only in respect to the throne shall I outrank you.[i] [41]Herewith," Pharaoh told Joseph, "I place you in charge of the whole land of Egypt." [42]With that, Pharaoh took off his signet ring* and put it on Joseph's finger. He had him dressed in robes of fine linen and put a gold chain about his neck. [43]He then had him ride in the chariot of his vizier, and they shouted "Abrek!"* before him.

Thus was Joseph installed over the whole land of Egypt. [44]"I, Pharaoh, proclaim," he told Joseph, "that without your approval no one shall move hand or foot in all the land of Egypt." [45]Pharaoh also bestowed the name

---

41, 42: Signet ring: a finger ring in which was set a stamp seal, different from the cylinder seal such as Judah wore; see note on Gn 38, 18. This is an authentic detail. By receiving Pharaoh's signet ring, Joseph was made vizier of Egypt (v 43); the vizier was known as "seal-bearer of the king of Lower Egypt." Another authentic detail is the gold chain, a symbol of high office in ancient Egypt.

41, 43: Abrek: apparently a cry of homage, though the word's derivation and actual meaning are uncertain.

41, 45: Zaphenath-paneah: a Hebrew transcription of an Egyptian name meaning "the god speaks and he (the new-

f: Ps 105, 20.   g: Gn 40, 8.   h: Acts 7, 10.   i: Ps 105, 21; Wis 10, 14; 1 Mc 2, 53; Acts 7, 10.

of Zaphenath-paneah* on Joseph, and he gave him in marriage Asenath, the daughter of Potiphera, priest of Heliopolis. ⁴⁶Joseph was thirty years old when he entered the service of Pharaoh, king of Egypt.

After Joseph left Pharaoh's presence, he traveled throughout the land of Egypt. ⁴⁷During the seven years of plenty, when the land produced abundant crops, ⁴⁸he husbanded all the food of these years of plenty that the land of Egypt was enjoying and stored it in the towns, placing in each town the crops of the fields around it. ⁴⁹Joseph garnered grain in quantities like the sands of the sea, so vast that at last he stopped measuring it, for it was beyond measure.

⁵⁰Before the famine years set in, Joseph became the father of two sons, born to him by Asenath, daughter of Potiphera, priest of Heliopolis.ʲ ⁵¹He named his first-born Manasseh,* meaning, "God has made me forget entirely the sufferings I endured at the hands of my family"; ⁵²and the second he named Ephraim,* meaning, "God has made me fruitful in the land of my affliction."

⁵³When the seven years of abundance enjoyed by the land of Egypt came to an end, ⁵⁴the seven years of famine set in, just as Joseph had predicted. Although there was famine in all the other countries, food was available throughout the land of Egypt.ᵏ ⁵⁵When hunger came to be felt throughout the land of Egypt and the people cried to Pharaoh for bread, Pharaoh directed all the Egyptians to go to Joseph and do whatever he told them. ⁵⁶When the famine had spread throughout the land, Joseph opened all the cities that had grain and rationed it to the Egyptians, since the famine had gripped the land of Egypt. ⁵⁷In fact, all the world came to Joseph to obtain rations of grain, for famine had gripped the whole world.

CHAPTER 42

The Brothers' First Journey to Egypt. See RG 60-61
¹When Jacob learned that grain rations were available in Egypt, he said to his sons: "Why do you keep gaping at one another? ²I hear," he went on, "that rations of grain are available in Egypt. Go down there and buy some for us, that we may stay alive rather than die of hunger."ˡ ³So ten of Joseph's brothers went down to buy an emergency supply of grain from Egypt. ⁴It was only Joseph's full brother Benjamin that Jacob did not send with the rest, for he thought some disaster might befall him. ⁵Thus, since there was famine in the land of Canaan also, the sons of Israel were among those who came to procure rations.ᵐ

⁶It was Joseph, as governor of the country, who dispensed the rations to all the people. When Joseph's brothers came and knelt down before him with their faces to the ground,ⁿ ⁷he recognized them as soon as he saw them. But he concealed his own identity from them and spoke sternly to them. "Where do you come from?" he asked them. They answered, "From the land of Canaan, to procure food."

⁸When Joseph recognized his brothers, although they did not recognize him, ⁹he was reminded of the dreams he had about them. He said to them: "You are spies.ᵒ You have come to see the nakedness of the land."* ¹⁰"No, my lord," they replied. "On the contrary, your servants have come to procure food. ¹¹All of us are sons of the same man. We are honest men; your servants have never been spies." ¹²But he answered them: "Not so! You have come to see the nakedness of the land." ¹³"We your servants," they said, "were twelve brothers, sons of a certain man in Canaan; but the youngest one is at present with our father, and the other one is gone."ᵖ ¹⁴"It is just as I said," Joseph per-

---

born child) lives." Asenath: means "belonging to (the Egyptian goddess) Neith." Potiphera: means "he whom Ra (the Egyptian god) gave"; a shorter form of the same name was borne by Joseph's master (Gn 37, 36). Heliopolis: in Hebrew, On, a city seven miles northeast of modern Cairo, site of the chief temple of the sun god; it is mentioned also in v 50; Gn 46, 20; Ez 30, 17.

41, 51: Manasseh: allusion to this name is in the Hebrew expression, nishshani, "he made me forget."

41, 52: Ephraim: related to the Hebrew expression hiphrani, "(God) has made me fruitful."

42, 9. 12: The nakedness of the land: the military weakness of the land, like human nakedness, should not be seen by strangers.

---

j: Gn 46, 20; 48, 5.   k: Ps 105, 16; Acts 7, 11.   l: Acts 7, 12.   m: Jdt 5, 10; Acts 7, 11.   n: Ps 105, 21.   o: Gn 37, 5.   p: Gn 44, 20.

sisted; "you are spies. [15]This is how you shall be tested: unless your youngest brother comes here, I swear by the life of Pharaoh that you shall not leave here. [16]So send one of your number to get your brother, while the rest of you stay here under arrest. Thus shall your words be tested for their truth; if they are untrue, as Pharaoh lives, you are spies!" [17]With that, he locked them up in the guardhouse for three days.

[18]On the third day Joseph said to them: "Do this, and you shall live; for I am a God-fearing man. [19]If you have been honest, only one of your brothers need be confined in this prison, while the rest of you may go and take home provisions for your starving families. [20]But you must come back to me with your youngest brother. Your words will thus be verified, and you will not die." To this they agreed.[q] [21]To one another, however, they said: "Alas, we are being punished because of our brother. We saw the anguish of his heart when he pleaded with us, yet we paid no heed; that is why this anguish has now come upon us."[r] [22]"Didn't I tell you," broke in Reuben, "not to do wrong to the boy? But you wouldn't listen! Now comes the reckoning for his blood."[s] [23]They did not know, of course, that Joseph understood what they said, since he spoke with them through an interpreter. [24]But turning away from them, he wept. When he was able to speak to them again, he had Simeon taken from them and bound before their eyes. [25]Then Joseph gave orders to have their containers filled with grain, their money replaced in each one's sack, and provisions given them for their journey. After this had been done for them, [26]they loaded their donkeys with the rations and departed.

[27]*At the night encampment, when one of them opened his bag to give his donkey some fodder, he was surprised to see his money in the mouth of his bag. [28]"My money has been returned!" he cried out to his brothers. "Here it is in my bag!" At that their hearts sank. Trembling, they asked one another, "What is this that God has done to us?"

[29]When they got back to their father Jacob in the land of Canaan, they told him all that had happened to them. [30]"The man who is lord of the country," they said, "spoke to us sternly and put us in custody as if we were spying on the land. [31]But we said to him: 'We are honest men; we have never been spies. [32]There were twelve of us brothers, sons of the same father; but one is gone, and the youngest one is at present with our father in the land of Canaan.' [33]Then the man who is lord of the country said to us: 'This is how I shall know if you are honest men: leave one of your brothers with me, while the rest of you go home with rations for your starving families. [34]When you come back to me with your youngest brother, and I know that you are honest men and not spies, I will restore your brother to you, and you may move about freely in the land.' "

[35]When they were emptying their sacks, there in each one's sack was his moneybag! At the sight of their moneybags, they and their father were dismayed. [36]Their father Jacob said to them: "Must you make me childless? Joseph is gone, and Simeon is gone, and now you would take away Benjamin! Why must such things always happen to me!" [37]Then Reuben told his father: "Put him in my care, and I will bring him back to you. You may kill my own two sons if I do not return him to you." [38]But Jacob replied: "My son shall not go down with you. Now that his full brother is dead, he is the only one left. If some disaster should befall him on the journey you must make, you would send my white head down to the nether world in grief."[t]

CHAPTER 43 *

The Second Journey to Egypt. [1]Now the famine in the land grew more severe. [2]So when they had used up all the rations they

See RG 60-61

42, 27-28: These two verses are from the Yahwist source, whereas the rest of the chapter is from the Elohist source, in which the men find the money in their sacks (not "bags"—a different Hebrew word) only when they arrive home (v 35); cf Gn 43, 21.

---

q: Gn 43, 5.   *r:* Gn 37, 18-27.   *s:* Gn 37, 22.   *t:* Gn 37, 35.

had brought from Egypt, their father said to them, "Go back and procure us a little more food." [3]But Judah replied: "The man strictly warned us, 'You shall not appear in my presence unless your brother is with you.'[u] [4]If you are willing to let our brother go with us, we will go down to procure food for you. [5]But if you are not willing, we will not go down, because the man told us, 'You shall not appear in my presence unless your brother is with you.' "[v] [6]Israel demanded, "Why did you bring this trouble on me by telling the man that you had another brother?" [7]They answered: "The man kept asking about ourselves and our family: 'Is your father still living? Do you have another brother?' We had to answer his questions. How could we know that he would say, 'Bring your brother down here'?"

[8]Then Judah urged his father Israel: "Let the boy go with me, that we may be off and on our way if you and we and our children are to keep from starving to death.[w] [9]I myself will stand surety for him. You can hold me responsible for him. If I fail to bring him back, to set him in your presence, you can hold it against me forever.[x] [10]Had we not dilly-dallied, we could have been there and back twice by now!"

[11]Their father Israel then told them: "If it must be so, then do this: Put some of the land's best products in your baggage and take them down to the man as gifts: some balm and honey, gum and resin, and pistachios and almonds.[y] [12]Also take extra money along, for you must return the amount that was put back in the mouths of your bags; it may have been a mistake. [13]Take your brother, too, and be off on your way back to the man. [14]May God Almighty dispose the man to be merciful toward you, so that he may let your other brother go, as well as Benjamin. As for me, if I am to suffer bereavement, I shall suffer it."

[15]So the men got the gifts, took double the amount of money with them, and, accompanied by Benjamin, were off on their way down to Egypt to present themselves to Joseph. [16]When Joseph saw Benjamin with them, he told his head steward, "Take these men into the house, and have an animal slaughtered and prepared, for they are to dine with me at noon." [17]Doing as Joseph had ordered, the steward conducted the men to Joseph's house. [18]But on being led to his house, they became apprehensive. "It must be," they thought, "on account of the money put back in our bags the first time, that we are taken inside; they want to use it as a pretext to attack us and take our donkeys and seize us as slaves." [19]So they went up to Joseph's head steward and talked to him at the entrance of the house. [20]"If you please, sir," they said, "we came down here once before to procure food.[z] [21]But when we arrived at a night's encampment and opened our bags, there was each man's money in the mouth of his bag— our money in the full amount! We have now brought it back.[a] [22]We have brought other money to procure food with. We do not know who put the first money in our bags." [23]"Be at ease," he replied; "you have no need to fear. Your God and the God of your father must have put treasures in your bags for you. As for your money, I received it." With that, he led Simeon out to them.

[24]The steward then brought the men inside Joseph's house. He gave them water to bathe their feet, and got fodder for their donkeys. [25]Then they set out their gifts to await Joseph's arrival at noon, for they had heard that they were to dine there. [26]When Joseph came home, they presented him with the gifts they had brought inside, while they bowed down before him to the ground. [27]After inquiring how they were, he asked them, "And how is your aged father, of whom you spoke? Is he still in good health?"[b] [28]"Your servant our father is thriving and still in good health," they said, as they bowed respectfully. [29]When Joseph's eye fell on his full brother Benjamin, he asked, "Is this your youngest brother, of whom you told me?" Then he said to him, "May God be

43, 1-34: This chapter and the following one are from the Yahwist source, in which Judah, not Reuben as in the Elohist source, volunteers to go surety for Benjamin.

u: Gn 44, 23.   *v:* Gn 42, 20.   *w:* Gn 42, 37.   *x:* Gn 44, 32.   *y:* Gn 45, 23.   *z:* Gn 42, 3.   *a:* Gn 42, 27f.   *b:* Tb 7, 4.

gracious to you, my boy!"[c] [30]With that, Joseph had to hurry out, for he was so overcome with affection for his brother that he was on the verge of tears. He went into a private room and wept there.

[31]After washing his face, he reappeared and, now in control of himself, gave the order, "Serve the meal." [32]It was served separately to him,[*] to the brothers, and to the Egyptians who partook of his board. (Egyptians may not eat with Hebrews; that is abhorrent to them.) [33]When they were seated by his directions according to their age, from the oldest to the youngest, they looked at one another in amazement; [34]and as portions were brought to them from Joseph's table, Benjamin's portion was five times as large as[*] anyone else's. So they drank freely and made merry with him.

CHAPTER 44

See RG 60–61 *Final Test.* [1][*]Then Joseph gave his head steward these instructions: "Fill the men's bags with as much food as they can carry, and put each man's money in the mouth of his bag. [2]In the mouth of the youngest one's bag put also my silver goblet, together with the money for his rations." The steward carried out Joseph's instructions. [3]At daybreak the men and their donkeys were sent off. [4]They had not gone far out of the city when Joseph said to his head steward: "Go at once after the men! When you overtake them, say to them, 'Why did you repay good with evil? Why did you steal the silver goblet from me? [5]It is the very one from which my master drinks and which he uses for divination.[*] What you have done is wrong.' "

[6]When the steward overtook them and repeated these words to them, [7]they remonstrated with him: "How can my lord say such things? Far be it from your servants to do such a thing! [8]We even brought back to you from the land of Canaan the money that we found in the mouths of our bags. Why, then, would we steal silver or gold from your master's house? [9]If any of your servants is found to have the goblet, he shall die, and as for the rest of us, we shall become my lord's slaves." [10]But he replied, "Even though it ought to be as you propose, only the one who is found to have it shall become my slave, and the rest of you shall be exonerated." [11]Then each of them eagerly lowered his bag to the ground and opened it; [12]and when a search was made, starting with the oldest and ending with the youngest, the goblet turned up in Benjamin's bag. [13]At this, they tore their clothes. Then, when each man had reloaded his donkey, they returned to the city.

[14]As Judah and his brothers reentered Joseph's house, he was still there; so they flung themselves on the ground before him. [15]"How could you do such a thing?" Joseph asked them. "You should have known that such a man as I could discover by divination what happened." [16]Judah replied: "What can we say to my lord? How can we plead or how try to prove our innocence? God has uncovered your servants' guilt.[*] Here we are, then, the slaves of my lord—the rest of us no less than the one in whose possession the goblet was found." [17]"Far be it from me to act thus!" said Joseph. "Only the one in whose possession the goblet was found shall become my slave; the rest of you may go back safe and sound to your father."

[18]Judah then stepped up to him and said: "I beg you, my lord, let your servant speak earnestly to my lord, and do not become angry with your servant, for you are the equal of Pharaoh. [19][*]My lord asked your servants,

---

43, 32: Separately to him: that Joseph did not eat with the other Egyptians was apparently a matter of rank.

43, 34: Five times as large as: probably an idiomatic expression for "much larger than."

44, 1f: Replacement of the money in the men's bags is probably a redactional addition here, taken from the Yahwist account of the first visit. It is only the goblet in Benjamin's bag, not any replaced money, that plays a part in the rest of the chapter.

44, 5: Divination: seeking omens through liquids poured into a cup or bowl was a common practice in the ancient Near

East; cf v 15. Even though divination was frowned on in later Israel (Lv 19, 31), it is in this place an authentic touch which the sacred author does not hesitate to ascribe to Joseph, the wisest man in Egypt.

44, 16: Guilt: in trying to do away with Joseph when he was young.

44, 19: My lord . . . your servants: such frequently repeated expressions in Judah's speech show the formal court style used by a subject in speaking to a high official.

---

c: Gn 42, 13.

'Have you a father, or another brother?' [20]So we said to my lord, 'We have an aged father, and a young brother, the child of his old age. This one's full brother is dead, and since he is the only one by that mother who is left, his father dotes on him.'[d] [21]Then you told your servants, 'Bring him down to me that my eyes may look on him.' [22]We replied to my lord, 'The boy cannot leave his father; his father would die if he were to leave him.' [23]But you told your servants, 'Unless your youngest brother comes back with you, you shall not come into my presence again.'[e] [24]When we returned to your servant our father, we reported to him the words of my lord.

[25]"Later, our father told us to come back and buy some food for the family. [26]So we reminded him, 'We cannot go down there; only if our youngest brother is with us can we go, for we may not see the man if our youngest brother is not with us.' [27]Then your servant our father said to us, 'As you know, my wife bore me two sons. [28]One of them, however, disappeared, and I had to conclude that he must have been torn to pieces by wild beasts; I have not seen him since.[f] [29]If you now take this one away from me, too, and some disaster befalls him, you will send my white head down to the nether world in grief.'

[30]"If then the boy is not with us when I go back to your servant my father, whose very life is bound up with his, he will die as soon as he sees that the boy is missing; [31]and your servants will thus send the white head of our father down to the nether world in grief. [32]Besides, I, your servant, got the boy from his father by going surety for him, saying, 'If I fail to bring him back to you, father, you can hold it against me forever.'[g] [33]Let me, your servant, therefore, remain in place of the boy as the slave of my lord, and let the boy go back with his brothers. [34]How could I go back to my father if the boy were not

with me? I could not bear to see the anguish that would overcome my father."

CHAPTER 45

See RG 60-61

The Truth Revealed. [1]Joseph could no longer control himself in the presence of all his attendants, so he cried out, "Have everyone withdraw from me!" Thus no one else was about when he made himself known to his brothers. [2]But his sobs were so loud that the Egyptians heard him, and so the news reached Pharaoh's palace. [3h]"I am Joseph," he said to his brothers. "Is my father still in good health?" But his brothers could give him no answer, so dumbfounded were they at him.

[4]"Come closer to me," he told his brothers. When they had done so, he said: "I am your brother Joseph, whom you once sold into Egypt. [5]But now do not be distressed, and do not reproach yourselves for having sold me here. It was really for the sake of saving lives that God sent me here ahead of you.[i] [6]For two years now the famine has been in the land, and for five more years tillage will yield no harvest. [7]God, therefore, sent me on ahead of you to ensure for you a remnant on earth and to save your lives in an extraordinary deliverance. [8]So it was not really you but God who had me come here; and he has made of me a father to Pharaoh,* lord of all his household, and ruler over the whole land of Egypt.

[9]*"Hurry back, then, to my father and tell him: 'Thus says your son Joseph: God has made me lord of all Egypt; come to me without delay.[j] [10]You will settle in the region of Goshen,* where you will be near me—you and your children and grandchildren, your flocks and herds, and everything that you own. [11]Since five years of famine still lie ahead, I will provide for you there, so that you and your family and all that are yours may not suffer want.' [12]Surely, you can see for your-

45, 8: Father to Pharaoh: a term applied to a vizier in ancient Egypt.

45, 9-15: In these verses, as in Gn 46, 31—47, 5a, all from the Yahwist source, Joseph in his own name invites his father and brothers to come to Egypt. Only after their arrival is Pharaoh informed of the fact. On the other hand, in 45, 16-20 from the Elohist source, it is Pharaoh himself who invites Joseph's

kinsmen to migrate to his domain.

45, 10: The region of Goshen: modern Wadi Tumilat in the eastern part of the Nile Delta.

d: Gn 42, 13.   *e:* Gn 43, 3.   *f:* Gn 37, 20. 33.   *g:* Gn 43, 9.   *h:* 3f: Acts 7, 13.   *i:* Gn 50, 20; Sir 49, 15.   *j:* Acts 7, 14.

Joseph Discloses His Identity

A central teaching of the Joseph story now unfolds: Despite the evil intent of Joseph's brothers, God has worked to ensure the realization of the divine promise (45, 7.8). The lesson here is that final judgment cannot be passed on unfavorable events of the moment. Sometimes people find that when they look back over what seemed like a terrible situation at the time, much good came from it.

selves, and Benjamin can see for himself, that it is I, Joseph, who am speaking to you. [13]Tell my father all about my high position in Egypt and what you have seen. But hurry and bring my father down here." [14]Thereupon he flung himself on the neck of his brother Benjamin and wept, and Benjamin wept in his arms. [15]Joseph then kissed all his brothers, crying over each of them; and only then were his brothers able to talk with him.

[16]When the news reached Pharaoh's palace that Joseph's brothers had come, Pharaoh and his courtiers were pleased. [17]So Pharaoh told Joseph: "Say to your brothers: 'This is what you shall do: Load up your animals and go without delay to the land of Canaan. [18]There get your father and your families, and then come back here to me; I will assign you the best land in Egypt, where you will live off the fat of the land.'[k] [19]Instruct them further: 'Do this. Take wagons from the land of Egypt for your children and your wives and to transport your father on your way back here. [20]Do not be concerned about your belongings, for the best in the whole land of Egypt shall be yours.' "

[21]The sons of Israel acted accordingly. Joseph gave them the wagons, as Pharaoh had ordered, and he supplied them with provisions for the journey. [22]He also gave to each of them fresh clothing, but to Benjamin he gave three hundred shekels of silver and five sets of garments. [23]Moreover, what he sent to his father was ten jackasses loaded with the finest products of Egypt and ten jennies loaded with grain and bread and other provisions for his journey. [24]As he sent his broth-

ers on their way, he told them, "Let there be no recriminations on the way."

[25]So they left Egypt and made their way to their father Jacob in the land of Canaan. [26]When they told him, "Joseph is still alive—in fact, it is he who is ruler of all the land of Egypt," he was dumbfounded; he could not believe them. [27]But when they recounted to him all that Joseph had told them, and when he saw the wagons that Joseph had sent for his transport, the spirit of their father Jacob revived. [28]"It is enough," said Israel. "My son Joseph is still alive! I must go and see him before I die."

CHAPTER 46

See RG 60–61

Migration to Egypt. [1]Israel set out with all that was his. When he arrived at Beer-sheba, he offered sacrifices to the God of his father Isaac. [2]There God, speaking to Israel in a vision by night, called, "Jacob! Jacob!" "Here I am," he answered. [3]Then he said: "I am God,[*] the God of your father. Do not be afraid to go down to Egypt, for there I will make you a great nation. [4]Not only will I go down to Egypt with you; I will also bring you back here, after Joseph has closed your eyes."

[5]So Jacob departed from Beer-sheba, and the sons of Israel put their father and their wives and children on the wagons that Pharaoh had sent for his transport. [6]They took with them their livestock and the possessions they had acquired in the land of Canaan. Thus Jacob and all his descendants migrated to Egypt.[l] [7]His sons and his grandsons, his daughters and his grand-

---

46, 3: I am God: more precisely according to the Hebrew text, "I am El." "El" is here a divine name, not the common noun "god."

k: Acts 7, 14.   l: Ex 1, 1; Jos 24, 4; Jdt 5, 10; Acts 7, 15.

Shepherds Are Abhorrent

Goshen is a pasture land in the Nile River delta isolated from the rest of Egypt. Shepherds were abhorrent (46, 34) because Egyptian agriculture was based more on crops and field agriculture that would be ruined by their wandering herds of grazing animals.

daughters—all his descendants—he took with him to Egypt.

*8*These are the names of the Israelites, Jacob and his descendants, who migrated to Egypt.

*Reuben, Jacob's first-born,*m* *9*and the sons of Reuben: Hanoch, Pallu, Hezron and Carmi.*n* *10*The sons of Simeon: Nemuel, Jamin, Ohad, Jachin, Zohar, and Shaul, son of a Canaanite woman.*o* *11*The sons of Levi: Gershon, Kohath and Merari.*p* *12*The sons of Judah: Er, Onan, Shelah, Perez and Zerah—but Er and Onan had died in the land of Canaan; and the sons of Perez were Hezron and Hamul.*q* *13*The sons of Issachar: Tola, Puah, Jashub and Shimron.*r* *14*The sons of Zebulun: Sered, Elon and Jahleel.*s* *15*These were the sons whom Leah bore to Jacob in Paddan-aram, along with his daughter Dinah—thirty-three persons in all, male and female.

*16*The sons of Gad: Zephon, Haggi, Shuni, Ezbon, Eri, Arod and Areli.*t* *17*The sons of Asher: Imnah, Ishvah, Ishvi and Beriah, with their sister Serah; and the sons of Beriah: Heber and Malchiel.*u* *18*These were the descendants of Zilpah, whom Laban had given to his daughter Leah; these she bore to Jacob—sixteen persons in all.

*19*The sons of Jacob's wife Rachel: Joseph and Benjamin. *20*In the land of Egypt Joseph became the father of Manasseh and Ephraim, whom Asenath, daughter of Potiphera, priest of Heliopolis, bore to him.*v* *21*The sons of Benjamin: Bela, Becher, Ashbel, Gera, Naaman, Ahiram, Shupham, Hupham and Ard.*w* *22*These were the sons

whom Rachel bore to Jacob—fourteen persons in all.

*23*The sons of Dan: Hushim.*x* *24*The sons of Naphtali: Jahzeel, Guni, Jezer and Shillem.*y* *25*These were the sons of Bilhah, whom Laban had given to his daughter Rachel; these she bore to Jacob—seven persons in all.

*26*Jacob's people who migrated to Egypt—his direct descendants, not counting the wives of Jacob's sons—numbered sixty-six persons in all.*z* *27*Together with Joseph's sons who were born to him in Egypt—two persons—all the people comprising Jacob's family who had come to Egypt amounted to seventy persons* in all.*a*

*28*Israel had sent Judah ahead to Joseph, so that he might meet him in Goshen. On his arrival in the region of Goshen, *29*Joseph hitched the horses to his chariot and rode to meet his father Israel in Goshen. As soon as he saw him, he flung himself on his neck and wept a long time in his arms. *30*And Israel said to Joseph, "At last I can die, now that I have seen for myself that Joseph is still alive."

*31*Joseph then said to his brothers and his father's household: "I will go and inform Pharaoh, telling him: 'My brothers and my father's household, whose home is in the land of Canaan, have come to me. *32*The men are shepherds, having long been keepers of livestock; and they have brought with them their flocks and herds, as well as everything else they own.' *33*So when Pharaoh summons you and asks what your occupation is, *34*you must answer, 'We your servants, like our ancestors, have been keepers of livestock from

46, 8-27: This genealogical list has here been inserted by a redactor who based it on the clan lists (Nm 26, 5-50) at the time of Moses. Therefore it includes some of Jacob's grandchildren, who would hardly have been born when Joseph was still a relatively young man. The number fourteen (v 22) is based on a garbled version of the genealogical list.

46, 27: Seventy persons: either to be understood as a round number, or arrived at by including Jacob and Joseph with the preceding persons, who add up to sixty-eight.

m: Ex 1, 2. *n:* Ex 6, 14; Nm 26, 5; 1 Chr 5, 3. *o:* Ex 6, 15; Nm 26, 12; 1 Chr 4, 24. *p:* Ex 6, 16; Nm 3, 17; 26, 57; 1 Chr 6, 1. *q:* Gn 38, 3-10. 29f; Nm 26, 19; Rv 4, 18-22; 1 Chr 2, 5. *r:* Nm 26, 23f; 1 Chr 7, 1. *s:* Nm 26, 26. *t:* Nm 26, 15f. *u:* Nm 26, 44; 1 Chr 7, 30f. *v:* Gn 41, 50; Nm 26, 28. 35. *w:* Nm 26, 38; 1 Chr 7, 6; 8, 1-4. *x:* Nm 26, 42. *y:* Nm 26, 48f; 1 Chr 7, 13. *z:* Ex 1, 5. *a:* Ex 1, 5; Dt 10, 22; Acts 7, 14.

the beginning until now,' in order that you may stay in the region of Goshen, since all shepherds are abhorrent to the Egyptians."

CHAPTER 47

See RG 60–61

Settlement in Goshen. [1]Joseph went and told Pharaoh, "My father and my brothers have come from the land of Canaan, with their flocks and herds and everything else they own; and they are now in the region of Goshen." [2]He then presented to Pharaoh five of his brothers whom he had selected from their full number. [3]When Pharaoh asked them what their occupation was, they answered, "We, your servants, like our ancestors, are shepherds. [4]We have come," they continued, "in order to stay in this country, for there is no pasture for your servants' flocks in the land of Canaan, so severe has the famine been there. Please, therefore, let your servants settle in the region of Goshen."[b] [5]Pharaoh said to Joseph, "They may settle in the region of Goshen; and if you know any of them to be qualified, you may put them in charge of my own livestock."

Thus, when Jacob and his sons came to Joseph in Egypt, and Pharaoh, king of Egypt, heard about it, Pharaoh said to Joseph, "Now that your father and brothers have come to you, [6]the land of Egypt is at your disposal; settle your father and brothers in the pick of the land." [7]Then Joseph brought his father Jacob and presented him to Pharaoh. After Jacob had paid his respects to Pharaoh, [8]Pharaoh asked him, "How many years have you lived?" [9]Jacob replied: "The years I have lived as a wayfarer amount to a hundred and thirty. Few and hard have been these years of my life, and they do not compare with the years that my ancestors lived as wayfarers."[*] [10]Then Jacob bade Pharaoh farewell and withdrew from his presence.

[11]As Pharaoh had ordered, Joseph settled his father and brothers and gave them holdings in Egypt on the pick of the land, in the region of Rameses.[*] [12]And Joseph sustained his father and brothers and his father's whole household, down to the youngest, with food.

Joseph's Land Policy. [13]Since there was no food in any country because of the extreme severity of the famine, and the lands of Egypt and Canaan were languishing from hunger, [14]Joseph gathered in, as payment for the rations that were being dispensed, all the money that was to be found in Egypt and Canaan, and he put it in Pharaoh's palace. [15]When all the money in Egypt and Canaan was spent, all the Egyptians came to Joseph, pleading, "Give us food or we shall perish under your eyes; for our money is gone." [16]"Since your money is gone," replied Joseph, "give me your livestock, and I will sell you bread in return for your livestock." [17]So they brought their livestock to Joseph, and he sold them food in return for their horses, their flocks of sheep and herds of cattle, and their donkeys. Thus he got them through that year with bread in exchange for all their livestock. [18]When that year ended, they came to him in the following one and said: "We cannot hide from my lord that, with our money spent and our livestock made over to my lord, there is nothing left to put at my lord's disposal except our bodies and our farm land. [19]Why should we and our land perish before your very eyes? Take us and our land in exchange for food, and we will become Pharaoh's slaves and our land his property; only give us seed, that we may survive and not perish, and that our land may not turn into a waste."

[20]Thus Joseph acquired all the farm land of Egypt for Pharaoh, since with the famine too much for them to bear, every Egyptian sold his field; so the land passed over to Pharaoh, [21]and the people were reduced to slavery, from one end of Egypt's territory to the other. [22]Only the priests' lands Joseph did not take over. Since the priests had a fixed allowance from Pharaoh and lived off the allowance Pharaoh had granted them, they did not have to sell their land.

47, 9: Wayfarer . . . wayfarers: man is merely a sojourner on earth; cf Ps 39, 13.

47, 11: The region of Rameses: same as the region of Goshen; see note on Gn 45, 10. The name Rameses, however, is an anachronism, since this royal name did not come into use before the end of the fourteenth century B.C., long after the time of Joseph.

b: Ex 23, 9; Dt 23, 8.

²³Joseph told the people: "Now that I have acquired you and your land for Pharaoh, here is your seed for sowing the land. ²⁴But when the harvest is in, you must give a fifth of it to Pharaoh, while you keep four-fifths as seed for your fields, and as food for yourselves and your families [and as food for your children]." ²⁵"You have saved our lives!" they answered. "We are grateful to my lord that we can be Pharaoh's slaves." ²⁶Thus Joseph made it a law for the land in Egypt, which is still in force, that a fifth of its produce should go to Pharaoh. Only the land of the priests did not pass over to Pharaoh.

Jacob Blesses Ephraim and Manasseh. ²⁷Thus Israel settled in the land of Egypt, in the region of Goshen. There they acquired property, were fertile, and increased greatly.ᶜ ²⁸Jacob lived in the land of Egypt for seventeen years; the span of his life came to a hundred and forty-seven years. ²⁹When the time approached for Israel to die, he called his son Joseph and said to him: "If you really wish to please me, put your hand under my thigh as a sign of your constant loyalty to me; do not let me be buried in Egypt. ³⁰When I lie down with my ancestors, have me taken out of Egypt and buried in their burial place."ᵈ ³¹"I will do as you say," he replied. But his father demanded, "Swear it to me!" So Joseph swore to him. Then Israel bowed at the head of the bed.*

See RG 60–61

CHAPTER 48

¹Some time afterward, Joseph was informed, "Your father is failing." So he took along with him his two sons, Manasseh and Ephraim. ²When Jacob was told, "Your son Joseph has come to you," he rallied his strength and sat up in bed.

³ᵉJacob then said to Joseph: "God Almighty appeared to me at Luz* in the land of Canaan, and blessing me, ⁴he said, 'I will make you fertile and numerous and raise you into an assembly of tribes, and I will give this land to your descendants after you as a permanent possession.' ⁵Your two sons, therefore, who were born to you in the land of Egypt before I joined you here, shall be mine; Ephraim and Manasseh shall be mine as much as Reuben and Simeon are mine. ⁶Progeny born to you after them shall remain yours; but their heritage shall be recorded in the names of their two brothers. ⁷ᶠI do this because, when I was returning from Paddan, your mother Rachel died, to my sorrow, during the journey in Canaan, while we were still a short distance from Ephrath; and I buried her there on the way to Ephrath [that is, Bethlehem].'*

⁸When Israel saw Joseph's sons, he asked, "Who are these?" ⁹"They are my sons," Joseph answered his father, "whom God has given me here." "Bring them to me," said his father, "that I may bless them." ¹⁰(Now Israel's eyes were dim from age, and he could not see well.) When Joseph brought his sons close to him, he kissed and embraced them. ¹¹Then Israel said to Joseph, "I never expected to see your face again, and now God has allowed me to see your descendants as well!"

¹²Joseph removed them from his father's knees and bowed down before him with his face to the ground. ¹³Then Joseph took the two, Ephraim with his right hand, to Israel's left, and Manasseh with his left hand, to Israel's right, and led them to him. ¹⁴But Israel, crossing his hands, put out his right hand and laid it on the head of Ephraim, although he was the younger, and his left hand on the head of Manasseh, although he was the first-born. ¹⁵Then he blessed them with these words:

"May the God in whose ways
     my fathers Abraham and Isaac walked,
The God who has been my shepherd
     from my birth to this day,ᵍ

47, 31: Israel bowed at the head of the bed: meaning perhaps that he gave a nod of assent and appreciation as he lay on his bed. By reading with different vowels the Hebrew word for "bed," the Greek version translated it as "staff," and understood the phrase to mean that he bowed in worship, leaning on the top of his staff; it is thus quoted in Heb 11, 21.

48, 3: Luz: an older name of Bethel (Gn 28, 19).

48, 7: Since her early death prevented Rachel from bearing more than two sons, Jacob feels justified in treating her two grandsons as if they were her own offspring.

ᶜ: Ex 1, 7.   ᵈ: Gn 50, 5.   ᵉ: 3f: Gn 28, 12-15; 35, 6.   ᶠ: Gn 35, 19   ᵍ: Heb 11, 21.

[16] The Angel who has delivered me from all
    harm,
        bless these boys
    That in them my name be recalled,
        and the names of my fathers, Abraham
            and Isaac,
    And they may become teeming
        multitudes
            upon the earth!"

[17]When Joseph saw that his father had laid his right hand on Ephraim's head, this seemed wrong to him; so he took hold of his father's hand, to remove it from Ephraim's head to Manasseh's, [18]saying, "That is not right, father; the other one is the first-born; lay your right hand on his head!" [19]But his father resisted. "I know it, son," he said, "I know. That one too shall become a tribe, and he too shall be great. Nevertheless, his younger brother shall surpass him, and his descendants shall become a multitude of nations." [20]So when he blessed them that day and said, "By you shall the people of Israel pronounce blessings; may they say, 'God make you like Ephraim and Manasseh,' " he placed Ephraim before Manasseh.[h]

[21]Then Israel said to Joseph: "I am about to die. But God will be with you and will restore you to the land of your fathers. [22i]As for me, I give to you, as to the one above his brothers, Shechem, which I captured from the Amorites with my sword and bow."[*]

CHAPTER 49

See RG
60-61
Jacob's Testament. [1]Jacob called his sons and said: "Gather around, that I may tell you what is to happen to you in days to come.

[2] "Assemble and listen, sons of Jacob,
        listen to Israel, your father.

[3] "You, Reuben, my first-born,
        my strength and the first fruit of my
            manhood,
        excelling in rank and excelling in
            power!
[4] Unruly as water, you shall no longer excel,
        for you climbed into your father's bed
        and defiled my couch to my sorrow.[j]

[5] "Simeon and Levi, brothers indeed,
        weapons of violence are their knives.[*]
[6] Let not my soul enter their council,
        or my spirit be joined with their
            company;
    For in their fury they slew men,
        in their willfulness they maimed oxen.[k]
[7] Cursed be their fury so fierce,
        and their rage so cruel!
    I will scatter them in Jacob,
        disperse them throughout Israel.

[8] "You, Judah, shall your brothers praise
        —your hand on the neck of your
            enemies;
        the sons of your father shall bow down
            to you.
[9] Judah, like a lion's whelp,
        you have grown up on prey, my son.
    He crouches like a lion recumbent,
        the king of beasts—who would dare
            rouse him?[l]
[10] The scepter shall never depart from Judah,
        or the mace from between his legs,
    While tribute is brought to him,[*]
        and he receives the people's homage.
[11] He tethers his donkey to the vine,
        his purebred ass to the choicest stem.
    In wine he washes his garments,

48, 22: Both the meaning of the Hebrew and the historical reference in this verse are obscure. By taking the Hebrew word for Shechem as a common noun meaning shoulder or mountain slope, some translators render the verse, "I give you one portion more than your brothers, which I captured . . ." The reference may be to the capture of Shechem by the sons of Jacob (Gn 34, 24-29). Shechem lay near the border separating the tribal territory of Manasseh from that of Ephraim (Jos 16, 4-9; 17, 1f. 7).

49, 5: Knives: if this is the meaning of the obscure Hebrew word here, the reference may be to the knives used in circumcising the men of Shechem (Gn 34, 24; cf Jos 5, 2).

49, 10: While tribute is brought to him: this translation is based on a slight change in the Hebrew text, which, as it stands would seem to mean, "until he comes to Shiloh." A somewhat different reading of the Hebrew text would be, "until he comes to whom it belongs." This last has been traditionally understood in a Messianic sense. In any case, the passage foretells the supremacy of the tribe of Judah, which found its fulfillment in the Davidic dynasty and ultimately in the Messianic Son of David, Jesus Christ.

49, 11: In wine . . . the blood of grapes: Judah's clothes are poetically pictured as soaked with grape juice from trampling in the wine press, the rich vintage of his land; cf Is 63, 2.

h: Heb 11, 21.   *i:* Jos 17, 14. 17f; Jn 4. 5.   *j:* Gn 35, 22; 1 Chr 5, 1f.   *k:* Gn 34, 25.   *l:* 1 Chr 5, 2.

his robe in the blood of grapes.*

[12] His eyes are darker than wine,
and his teeth are whiter than milk.

[13] "Zebulun shall dwell by the seashore
[This means a shore for ships],
and his flank shall be based on Sidon.

[14] "Issachar is a rawboned ass,
crouching between the saddlebags.
[15] When he saw how good a settled life was,
and how pleasant the country,
He bent his shoulder to the burden
and became a toiling serf.

[16] "Dan shall achieve justice* for his
kindred
like any other tribe of Israel.
[17] Let Dan be a serpent by the roadside,
a horned viper by the path,
That bites the horse's heel,
so that the rider tumbles backward.

[18] "[I long for your deliverance, O LORD!]

[19] "Gad shall be raided by raiders,
but he shall raid at their heels.*

[20] "Asher's produce is rich,
and he shall furnish dainties for kings.

[21] "Naphtali is a hind let loose,
which brings forth lovely fawns.

[22] "Joseph is a wild colt,
a wild colt by a spring,
a wild ass on a hillside.
[23] Harrying and attacking,
the archers opposed him;
[24] But each one's bow remained stiff,
as their arms were unsteady,
By the power of the Mighty One of Jacob,
because of the Shepherd, the Rock of
Israel,
[25] The God of your father, who helps you,*
God Almighty, who blesses you,
With the blessings of the heavens above,
the blessings of the abyss that
crouches below,
The blessings of breasts and womb,

[26] the blessings of fresh grain and
blossoms,
The blessings of the everlasting
mountains,
the delights of the eternal hills.
May they rest on the head of Joseph,
on the brow of the prince among his
brothers.

[27] "Benjamin is a ravenous wolf;
mornings he devours the prey,
and evenings he distributes the spoils."

Farewell and Death. [28] All these are the twelve tribes of Israel, and this is what their father said about them, as he bade them farewell and gave to each of them an appropriate message. [29] Then he gave them this charge: "Since I am about to be taken to my kindred, bury me with my fathers in the cave that lies in the field of Ephron the Hittite, [30] the cave in the field of Machpelah, facing on Mamre, in the land of Canaan, the field that Abraham bought from Ephron the Hittite for a burial ground.[m] [31] There Abraham and his wife Sarah are buried, and so are Isaac and his wife Rebekah, and there, too, I buried Leah— [32] the field and the cave in it that had been purchased from the Hittites."

[33] When Jacob had finished giving these instructions to his sons, he drew his feet into the bed, breathed his last, and was taken to his kindred.

CHAPTER 50

See RG
60-61

Jacob's Funeral. [1] Joseph threw himself on his father's face and wept over him as he kissed him. [2] Then he ordered the physicians in his service to embalm his father. When they embalmed Israel, [3] they spent forty days at it, for that is the full period of embalming; and the Egyptians mourned him for seventy days. [4] When that period of mourning was over, Joseph spoke to Pharaoh's courtiers. "Please do me this favor," he said, "and convey to Pharaoh this request of mine. [5] Since my father, at the point of death,

49, 16: In Hebrew the verb for achieve justice is from the same root as the name Dan.

49, 19: In Hebrew there is a certain assonance between the name Gad and the words for "raided," "raiders" and "raid."

49, 25f: A very similar description of the agricultural riches of the tribal land of Joseph is given in Dt 33, 13-16.

m: Gn 23, 17.

Good and Evil

The brothers' words "Let us be your slaves!" (50, 18) unintentionally anticipate the slavery of the Israelites in Egypt. Joseph's words in v. 20 sound the overriding theme of the Joseph story: the divine ability to guide events and to turn evil into good.

made me promise on oath to bury him in the tomb that he had prepared for himself in the land of Canaan, may I go up there to bury my father and then come back?"[n] [6]Pharaoh replied, "Go and bury your father, as he made you promise on oath."

[7]So Joseph left to bury his father; and with him went all of Pharaoh's officials who were senior members of his court and all the other dignitaries of Egypt, [8]as well as Joseph's whole household, his brothers, and his father's household; only their children and their flocks and herds were left in the region of Goshen. [9]Chariots, too, and charioteers went up with him; it was a very large retinue.

[10]When they arrived at Goren-ha-atad,[*] which is beyond the Jordan, they held there a very great and solemn memorial service; and Joseph observed seven days of mourning for his father. [11]When the Canaanites who inhabited the land saw the mourning at Goren-ha-atad, they said, "This is a solemn funeral the Egyptians are having." That is why the place was named Abel-mizraim. It is beyond the Jordan.

[12]Thus Jacob's sons did for him as he had instructed them. [13]They carried him to the land of Canaan and buried him in the cave in the field of Machpelah, facing on Mamre, the field that Abraham had bought for a burial ground from Ephron the Hittite.[o]

[14]After Joseph had buried his father he returned to Egypt, together with his brothers and all who had gone up with him for the burial of his father.

Plea for Forgiveness. [15]Now that their father was dead, Joseph's brothers became fearful and thought, "Suppose Joseph has been nursing a grudge against us and now plans to pay us back in full for all the wrong we did him!" [16]So they approached Joseph and said: "Before your father died, he gave us these instructions: [17]'You shall say to Joseph, Jacob begs you to forgive the criminal wrongdoing of your brothers, who treated you so cruelly.' Please, therefore, forgive the crime that we, the servants of your father's God, committed." When they spoke these words to him, Joseph broke into tears. [18]Then his brothers proceeded to fling themselves down before him and said, "Let us be your slaves!" [19]But Joseph replied to them: "Have no fear. Can I take the place of God? [20]Even though you meant harm to me, God meant it for good, to achieve his present end, the survival of many people.[p] [21]Therefore have no fear. I will provide for you and for your children." By thus speaking kindly to them, he reassured them.[q]

[22]Joseph remained in Egypt, together with his father's family. He lived a hundred and ten years. [23]He saw Ephraim's children to the third generation, and the children of Manasseh's son Machir were also born on Joseph's knees.[r]

Death of Joseph. [24]Joseph said to his brothers: "I am about to die. God will surely take care of you and lead you out of this land to the land that he promised on oath to Abraham, Isaac and Jacob."[s] [25]Then, putting the sons of Israel under oath, he continued, "When God thus takes care of you, you must bring my bones up with you from this place."[t] [26]Joseph died at the age of a hundred and ten. He was embalmed and laid to rest in a coffin in Egypt.[u]

50, 10f: Goren-ha-atad: "Threshing Floor of the Brambles." Abel-mizraim: although the name really means "watercourse of the Egyptians," it is understood here, by a play on the first part of the term, to mean "mourning of the Egyptians." The site has not been identified through either reading of the name. But it is difficult to see why the mourning rites should have been held in the land beyond the Jordan when the burial was at He-bron. Perhaps an earlier form of the story placed the mourning rites beyond the Wadi of Egypt, the traditional boundary between Canaan and Egypt (Nm 34, 5; Jos 15, 4. 47).

---

n: Gn 47, 30.   o: Gn 23, 16; Acts 7, 16.   p: Gn 45, 5; Sir 49, 15.   q: Gn 47, 12.   r: Nm 32, 39; Jos 17, 1.   s: Ex 3, 8; Jos 24, 32; Heb 11, 22.   t: Ex 13, 19; Heb 11, 22.   u: Sir 49, 15.

See RG
62–73

The Book of Exodus

The second book of the Pentateuch is called Exodus from the Greek word for "departure," because the central event narrated in it is the departure of the Israelites from Egypt. It continues the history of the chosen people from the point where the Book of Genesis leaves off. It recounts the oppression by the Egyptians of the ever-increasing descendants of Jacob and their miraculous deliverance by God through Moses, who led them across the Red Sea to Mount Sinai where they entered into a special covenant with the Lord.

These events were of prime importance to the chosen people, for they became thereby an independent nation and enjoyed a unique relationship with God. Through Moses God gave to the Israelites at Mount Sinai the "law": the moral, civil and ritual legislation by which they were to become a holy people, in whom the promise of a Savior for all mankind would be fulfilled.

The principal divisions of Exodus are:

I: The Israelites in Egypt (1, 1—12, 36).

II: The Exodus from Egypt and the Journey to Sinai (12, 37—18, 27).

III: The Covenant at Mount Sinai (19, 1—24, 18).

IV: The Dwelling and Its Furnishings (25, 1—40, 38).

I: The Israelites In Egypt

CHAPTER 1

See RG
64

Jacob's Descendants in Egypt. *¹*These are the names of the sons of Israel* who, accompanied by their households, migrated with Jacob into Egypt: *²*Reuben, Simeon, Levi and Judah; *³*Issachar, Zebulun and Benjamin; *⁴*Dan and Naphtali; Gad and Asher. *⁵*The total number of the direct descendants* of Jacob was seventy.*ᵃ* Joseph was already in Egypt.

*⁶*Now Joseph and all his brothers and that whole generation died.*ᵇ* *⁷*But the Israelites were fruitful and prolific. They became so numerous and strong that the land was filled with them.

The Oppression. *⁸*Then a new king, who knew nothing of Joseph,* came to power in Egypt.*ᶜ* *⁹*He said to his subjects, "Look how numerous and powerful the Israelite people are growing, more so than we ourselves! *¹⁰*Come, let us deal shrewdly with them to stop their increase; otherwise, in time of war they too may join our enemies to fight against us, and so leave our country."

*¹¹*Accordingly, taskmasters were set over the Israelites to oppress them with forced labor.*ᵈ* Thus they had to build for Pharaoh* the supply cities of Pithom and Raamses. *¹²*Yet the more they were oppressed, the more they multiplied and spread. The Egyptians, then, dreaded the Israelites *¹³*and reduced them to cruel slavery, *¹⁴*making life bitter for them with hard work in mortar* and brick and all kinds of field work—the whole cruel fate of slaves.

Command to the Midwives. *¹⁵*The king of Egypt told the Hebrew midwives, one of whom was called Shiphrah and the other Puah, *¹⁶*"When you act as midwives for the Hebrew women and see them giving birth,* if it is a boy, kill him; but if it is a girl, she may live." *¹⁷*The midwives, however, feared God; they did not do as the king of Egypt had ordered them, but let the boys live. *¹⁸*So the

---

1, 1: Sons of Israel: here literally the first-generation sons of Jacob. Cf v 5. However, beginning with Ex 1, 7 the same Hebrew phrase refers to the more remote descendants of Jacob; hence, from there on, it is ordinarily rendered as "the Israelites." Households: the family in its fullest sense, including wives, children and servants.

1, 2: The sons of Jacob are listed here according to the respective mothers. Cf Gn 29, 31; 30, 30; 35, 16-26.

1, 5: Direct descendants: literally, persons coming from the loins of Jacob; hence, wives and servants are here excluded. Cf Gn 46, 26.

1, 8: Who knew nothing of Joseph: this king ignored the

services that Joseph had rendered to Egypt.

1, 11: Pharaoh: not a personal name, but a title common to all the kings of Egypt.

1, 14: Mortar: either the wet clay with which the bricks were made, as in Na 3, 14, or the cement used between the bricks in building, as in Gn 11, 3.

1, 16: And see them giving birth: the Hebrew text is uncertain.

---

a: Gn 46, 27; Dt 10, 22; Acts 7, 14.   *b:* Gn 50, 26.   *c:* 8ff. Acts 7, 18.   *d:* Dt 26, 6.

Moses Is Born and Saved from the Nile River

This story of Moses' birth and rescue from the river includes parallels to other birth stories of heroes, especially the Legend of King Sargon of Akkad (ninth century B.C.). Moses is born of parents from the Israelite tribe of Levi. The Levites became a tribe of priests or servants dedicated to the worship of God (32, 25–29). The family tree for the tribe of Levi in Exodus 6, 14–27 names Moses' parents as Amram and Jochebed, his brother as Aaron, and his sister as Miriam. Micah 6, 4 lists these three siblings—Moses, Aaron, and Miriam—as the leaders of Israel in their wilderness trek from Egypt to the Promised Land of Canaan.

Pharaoh's own daughter conspires with Hebrew women to resist her father's vicious program against Israelite children (2, 10). In a satisfying twist of fate, Pharaoh's daughter will pay wages to Moses' mother for nursing the mother's own child (v. 9). The name Moses (*Mosheh*) plays on the verb "to draw out" (*mashah*).

king summoned the midwives and asked them, "Why have you acted thus, allowing the boys to live?" [19]The midwives answered Pharaoh, "The Hebrew women are not like the Egyptian women. They are robust and give birth before the midwife arrives." [20]Therefore God dealt well with the midwives. The people, too, increased and grew strong. [21]And because the midwives feared God, he built up families for them. [22]Pharaoh then commanded all his subjects, "Throw into the river* every boy that is born to the Hebrews,[e] but you may let all the girls live."

See RG 64–65

CHAPTER 2

Birth and Adoption of Moses. [1]Now a certain man of the house of Levi married a Levite woman,[f] [2]who conceived and bore a son. Seeing that he was a goodly child, she hid him for three months.[g] [3]When she could hide him no longer, she took a papyrus basket,* daubed it with bitumen and pitch, and putting the child in it, placed it among the reeds on the river bank. [4]His sister stationed herself at a distance to find out what would happen to him.

[5]Pharaoh's daughter came down to the river to bathe, while her maids walked along the river bank. Noticing the basket among the reeds, she sent her handmaid to fetch it. [6]On opening it, she looked, and lo, there was a baby boy, crying! She was moved with pity for him and said, "It is one of the Hebrews' children." [7]Then his sister asked Pharaoh's daughter, "Shall I go and call one of the Hebrew women to nurse the child for you?" [8]"Yes, do so," she answered. So the maiden went and called the child's own mother. [9]Pharaoh's daughter said to her, "Take this child and nurse it for me, and I will repay you." The woman therefore took the child and nursed it. [10]When the child grew,* she brought him to Pharaoh's daughter, who adopted him as her son[h] and called him Moses; for she said, "I drew him out of the water."

Moses' Flight to Midian. [11]On one occasion, after Moses had grown up,* when he visited his kinsmen[i] and witnessed their forced labor, he saw an Egyptian striking a Hebrew, one of his own kinsmen. [12]Looking about and seeing no one, he slew the Egyp-

1, 22: The river: the Nile, which was "the" river for the Egyptians.

2, 3: Basket: literally, "chest" or "ark"; the same Hebrew word was used in Gn 6, 14 for Noah's ark. Here, however, the chest was made of papyrus stalks.

2, 10: When the child grew: probably when he was weaned or a little later. Moses: in Hebrew, Mosheh; the Hebrew word for "draw out" is mashah. The explanation of the name is not intended as a scientific etymology but as a play on words. The name is probably derived from an Egyptian

word for "has been born," referring the birth to a god thought to be its sponsor.

2, 11: After Moses had grown up: Acts 7, 23 indicates that this was after an interval of nearly forty years. Cf Ex 7, 7. Striking: probably in the sense of "flogging"; according to some, "slaying."

e: Acts 7, 19.   f: Ex 6, 20; Nm 26, 59.   g: Acts 7, 20; Heb 11, 23.   h: Acts 7, 21; Heb 11, 24.   i: 11-14: Acts 7, 23-28.

tian and hid him in the sand. [13]The next day he went out again, and now two Hebrews were fighting! So he asked the culprit, "Why are you striking your fellow Hebrew?" [14]But he replied, "Who has appointed you ruler and judge over us? Are you thinking of killing me as you killed the Egyptian?" Then Moses became afraid and thought, "The affair must certainly be known."

[15]Pharaoh, too, heard of the affair and sought to put him to death. But Moses fled from him and stayed in the land of Midian.[j] As he was seated there by a well, [16]seven daughters of a priest of Midian came to draw water and fill the troughs to water their father's flock. [17]But some shepherds came and drove them away. Then Moses got up and defended them and watered their flock. [18]When they returned to their father Reuel,[*] he said to them, "How is it you have returned so soon today?" [19]They answered, "An Egyptian[*] saved us from the interference of the shepherds. He even drew water for us and watered the flock!" [20]"Where is the man?" he asked his daughters. "Why did you leave him there? Invite him to have something to eat." [21]Moses agreed to live with him, and the man gave him his daughter Zipporah in marriage. [22]She bore him a son, whom he named Gershom;[*] for he said, "I am a stranger in a foreign land."[k]

The Burning Bush. [23]A long time passed, during which the king of Egypt died. Still the Israelites groaned and cried out because of their slavery. As their cry for release went up to God,[l] [24]he heard their groaning and was mindful of his covenant[m] with Abraham, Isaac and Jacob. [25]He saw the Israelites and knew. . . .

CHAPTER 3

See RG 64-65

[1]Meanwhile Moses was tending the flock of his father-in-law Jethro, the priest of Midian. Leading the flock across the desert, he came to Horeb, the mountain of God.[*] [2]There an angel of the LORD[*] appeared to him in fire flaming out of a bush.[n] As he looked on, he was surprised to see that the bush, though on fire, was not consumed. [3]So Moses decided, "I must go over to look at this remarkable sight, and see why the bush is not burned."

The Call of Moses. [4]When the LORD saw him coming over to look at it more closely, God called out to him from the bush, "Moses! Moses!" He answered, "Here I am." [5]God said, "Come no nearer![o] Remove the sandals from your feet, for the place where you stand is holy ground. [6][p]I am the God of your father," he continued, "the God of Abraham, the God of Isaac, the God of Jacob."[*] Moses hid his face, for he was afraid to look at God. [7]But the LORD said, "I have witnessed the affliction of my people in Egypt and have heard their cry of complaint against their slave drivers, so I know well what they are suffering. [8]Therefore I have come down[*] to rescue them from the hands of the Egyptians and lead them out of that land into a good and spacious land, a land flowing with milk and honey, the country of the Canaanites, Hittites, Amorites, Perizzites, Hivites

---

2, 18: Reuel: he was also called Jethro. Cf Ex 3, 1; 4, 18; 18, 1.

2, 19: An Egyptian: Moses was probably wearing Egyptian dress, or spoke Egyptian to Reuel's daughters.

2, 22: Gershom: the name is explained as if it came from the Hebrew word ger, "stranger," joined to the Hebrew word sham, "there." Some Greek and Latin manuscripts add here a passage taken from Ex 18, 4.

3, 1: The mountain of God: probably given this designation because of the divine apparitions which took place there, such as on this occasion and when the Israelites were there after the departure from Egypt.

3, 2: An angel of the LORD: the visual form under which God appeared and spoke to men is referred to indifferently in some Old Testament texts either as God's angel or as God himself. Cf Gn 16, 7. 13; Ex 14, 19. 24f; Nm 22, 22-35; Jgs 6, 11-18.

3, 6: The God of Abraham . . . Jacob: cited by Christ in proof of the resurrection since the patriarchs, long dead, live on in God who is the God of the living. Cf Mt 22, 32; Mk 12, 26; Lk 20, 37. Afraid: The appearance of God caused fear of death, since it was believed that no one could see God and live; cf Gn 32, 30.

3, 8: I have come down: a figure of speech signifying an extraordinary divine intervention in human affairs. Cf Gn 11, 5. 7. Flowing with milk and honey: an expression denoting agricultural prosperity, which seems to have been proverbial in its application to Palestine. Cf Ex 13, 5; Nm 13, 27; Jos 5, 6; Jer 11, 5; 32, 22; Ez 20, 6. 15.

---

j: Acts 7, 29; Heb 11, 27.   k: Ex 18, 3.   l: Ex 3, 7. 9; Dt 26. 7.   m: Ex 6, 5; Pss 105, 8f; 106, 44f.   n: 2-10: Acts 7, 30-35.   o: Jos 5, 15.   p: Ex 4, 5; Mt 22, 32; Mk 12, 36; Lk 20, 37.

and Jebusites.*q* *9*So indeed the cry of the Israelites has reached me, and I have truly noted that the Egyptians are oppressing them. *10*Come, now! I will send you to Pharaoh to lead my people, the Israelites, out of Egypt."

*11*But Moses said to God, "Who am I* that I should go to Pharaoh and lead the Israelites out of Egypt?" *12*He answered, "I will be with you; and this shall be your proof that it is I who have sent you: when you bring my people out of Egypt, you will worship God on this very mountain." *13*"But," said Moses to God, "when I go to the Israelites and say to them, 'The God of your fathers has sent me to you,' if they ask me, 'What is his name?' what am I to tell them?" *14*God replied, "I am who am."* Then he added, "This is what you shall tell the Israelites: I AM sent me to you."

*15*God spoke further to Moses, "Thus shall you say to the Israelites: The LORD, the God of your fathers, the God of Abraham, the God of Isaac, the God of Jacob, has sent me to you.

"This is my name forever;*r*
this is my title for all generations.

16"Go and assemble the elders* of the Israelites, and tell them: The LORD, the God of your fathers, the God of Abraham, Isaac and Jacob, has appeared to me and said: I am concerned about you and about the way you are being treated in Egypt; *17*so I have decided to lead you up out of the misery of Egypt into the land of the Canaanites, Hittites, Amorites, Perizzites, Hivites and Jebusites, a land flowing with milk and honey. *18*"Thus they will heed your message. Then you and the elders of Israel shall go to the king of Egypt and say to him:*s* The LORD,

the God of the Hebrews, has sent us word. Permit us, then, to go a three-days' journey in the desert, that we may offer sacrifice to the LORD, our God.

19"Yet I know that the king of Egypt will not allow you to go unless he is forced. *20*I will stretch out my hand, therefore, and smite Egypt by doing all kinds of wondrous deeds there. After that he will send you away. *21*I will even make the Egyptians so well-disposed toward this people that, when you leave, you will not go empty-handed. *22t*Every woman shall ask her neighbor and her house guest for silver and gold articles* and for clothing to put on your sons and daughters. Thus you will despoil the Egyptians."

CHAPTER 4

Confirmation of Moses' Mission. See RG 64-65
1"But," objected Moses, "suppose they will not believe me, nor listen to my plea? For they may say, 'The LORD did not appear to you.' " *2*The LORD therefore asked him, "What is that in your hand?" "A staff," he answered. *3*The LORD then said, "Throw it on the ground." When he threw it on the ground it was changed into a serpent,*u* and Moses shied away from it. *4*"Now, put out your hand," the LORD said to him, "and take hold of its tail." So he put out his hand and laid hold of it, and it became a staff in his hand. *5*"This will take place so that they may believe," he continued, "that the LORD, the God of their fathers, the God of Abraham, the God of Isaac, the God of Jacob, did appear to you."

*6*Again the LORD said to him, "Put your hand in your bosom." He put it in his bosom, and when he withdrew it, to his surprise his

---

3, 11: Who am I: besides naturally shrinking from such a tremendous undertaking, Moses realized that, as a fugitive from Pharaoh, he could hardly hope to carry out a mission to him. Perhaps he also recalled that on one occasion even his own kinsmen questioned his authority. Cf Ex 2, 14.

3, 14: I am who am: apparently this utterance is the source of the word Yahweh, the proper personal name of the God of Israel. It is commonly explained in reference to God as the absolute and necessary Being. It may be understood of God as the Source of all created beings. Out of reverence for this name, the term Adonai, "my Lord," was later used as a substitute. The word Lord in the present version represents this tra-

ditional usage. The word "Jehovah" arose from a false reading of this name as it is written in the current Hebrew text.

3, 16: Elders: the Israelite leaders, who were usually older men. They were representatives of the people.

3, 22: Articles: probably jewelry. Despoil: this was permissible, that the Israelites might compensate themselves for their many years of servitude; besides, the Egyptians would give these things willingly. Cf Ex 12, 33-36.

---

q: 8f: Gn 15, 19ff.   *r:* Ps 135, 13.   *s:* Ex 5, 3.   *t:* 21f: Ex 11, 2f; 12, 35f.   *u:* Ex 7, 10.

hand was leprous, like snow. [7]The LORD then said, "Now, put your hand back in your bosom." Moses put his hand back in his bosom, and when he withdrew it, to his surprise it was again like the rest of his body. [8]"If they will not believe you, nor heed the message of the first sign, they should believe the message of the second. [9]And if they will not believe even these two signs, nor heed your plea, take some water from the river and pour it on the dry land. The water you take from the river will become blood on the dry land."[v]

Aaron's Office as Assistant. [10]Moses, however, said to the LORD, "If you please, Lord, I have never been eloquent, neither in the past, nor recently, nor now that you have spoken to your servant; but I am slow of speech and tongue."[w] [11]The LORD said to him, "Who gives one man speech and makes another deaf and dumb? Or who gives sight to one and makes another blind? Is it not I, the LORD? [12]Go, then! It is I who will assist you in speaking and will teach you what you are to say." [13]Yet he insisted, "If you please, Lord, send someone else!"[*] [14]Then the LORD became angry with Moses and said, "Have you not your brother, Aaron the Levite? I know that he is an eloquent speaker. Besides, he is now on his way to meet you. [15]When he sees you, his heart will be glad. You are to speak to him, then, and put the words in his mouth. I will assist both you and him in speaking and will teach the two of you what you are to do. [16]He shall speak to the people for you: he shall be your spokesman,[*] and you shall be as God to him.[x] [17]Take this staff[*] in your hand; with it you are to perform the signs."

Moses' Return to Egypt. [18]After this Moses returned to his father-in-law Jethro and said to him, "Let me go back, please, to my kinsmen in Egypt, to see whether they are still living." Jethro replied, "Go in peace."[*] [19]In Midian the LORD said to Moses, "Go back to Egypt, for all the men who sought your life are dead." [20]So Moses took his wife and his sons, and started back to the land of Egypt, with them riding the ass. The staff of God he carried with him. [21]The LORD said to him, "On your return to Egypt, see that you perform before Pharaoh all the wonders I have put in your power. I will make him obstinate,[*] however, so that he will not let the people go. [22]So you shall say to Pharaoh: Thus says the LORD: Israel is my son, my first-born. [23]Hence I tell you: Let my son go, that he may serve me. If you refuse to let him go, I warn you, I will kill your son, your first-born."[a]

[24][*]On the journey, at a place where they spent the night, the Lord came upon Moses and would have killed him. [25][b]But Zipporah took a piece of flint and cut off her son's foreskin and, touching his person, she said, "You are a spouse of blood to me." [26]Then God let Moses go. At that time she said, "A spouse of blood," in regard to the circumcision.

[27]The LORD said to Aaron, "Go into the desert to meet Moses." So he went, and when they met at the mountain of God, Aaron kissed him. [28]Moses informed him of all the LORD had said in sending him, and of the various signs he had enjoined upon him. [29]Then Moses and Aaron went and assembled all the elders of the Israelites. [30]Aaron told them everything the LORD had said to Moses, and he performed the signs before the people. [31]The people believed, and when they heard that the LORD was concerned about them and had seen their affliction, they bowed down in worship.

4, 13: Send someone else: literally, "Send by means of him whom you will send," that is, "Send whom you will."

4, 16: Spokesman: literally, "mouth"; Aaron was to serve as a mouthpiece for Moses, as a prophet does for God; hence the relation between Moses and Aaron is compared to that between God and his prophet. Cf Ex 7, 1.

4, 17: This staff: probably the same as that of vv 2ff; but some understand it here of a new staff now given by God to Moses.

4, 18: Moses did not tell his father-in-law his main reason for returning to Egypt, but this secondary motive which he of-

fered was also true.

4, 21: Make him obstinate: literally, "harden his heart." God permitted Pharaoh to be stubborn in his opposition to the departure of the Israelites. Cf Rom 9, 17f.

4, 24ff: Apparently God was angry with Moses for having failed to keep the divine command given to Abraham in Gn 17, 10ff. Moses' life is spared when his wife circumcises their son.

v: Ex 7, 17. 19f.   *w*: Ex 6, 12.   *x*: 15f: Ex 7, 1.   *y*: Ex 2, 15. 23.   *z*: Sir 36, 11.   *a*: Ex 11, 5; 12, 29.   *b*: Is 6, 2; 7, 20.

Moses and Aaron Confront Pharaoh for the First Time

Pharaoh's words "I do not know the LORD" (5, 2) introduce a theme that recurs throughout this book of the Bible (7, 5.17; 8, 6; 9, 14; 14, 18); hints of things to come are common in ch 5. The threat of pestilence or sword points indirectly to the plagues that will begin soon. The need to stop working to worship the LORD (v. 5) will become a defining practice of the Israelite community with the commandment concerning the Sabbath (20, 9–11; Dt 5, 12–15). Bad odor with the Pharaoh (v. 21) foreshadows the bad odor that will accompany the first two plagues (7, 21; 8, 13–14). Verses 22–23 give an example of Moses' bold willingness to speak words of resistance, correction, or complaint to God (chs 3–4; 32, 11–14; 33, 12–23).

See RG 65–67

CHAPTER 5

Pharaoh's Obduracy. ¹After that, Moses and Aaron went to Pharaoh and said, "Thus says the LORD, the God of Israel: Let my people go, that they may celebrate a feast to me in the desert." ²Pharaoh answered, "Who is the LORD, that I should heed his plea to let Israel go? I do not know the LORD; even if I did, I would not let Israel go." ³They replied, "The God of the Hebrews has sent us word. Let us go a three days' journey in the desert, that we may offer sacrifice to the LORD, our God;*c* otherwise he will punish us with pestilence or the sword."

⁴The king of Egypt answered them, "What do you mean, Moses and Aaron, by taking the people away from their work? Off to your labor! ⁵Look how numerous the people of the land are already," continued Pharaoh, "and yet you would give them rest from their labor!"

⁶That very day Pharaoh gave the taskmasters and foremen* of the people this order: ⁷"You shall no longer supply the people with straw for their brickmaking* as you have previously done. Let them go and gather straw themselves! ⁸Yet you shall levy upon them the same quota of bricks as they have previously made. Do not reduce it. They are lazy; that is why they are crying, 'Let us go to offer sacrifice to our God.' ⁹Increase the work for the men, so that they keep their mind on it and pay no attention to lying words."

¹⁰So the taskmasters and foremen of the people went out and told them, "Thus says Pharaoh: I will not provide you with straw. ¹¹Go and gather the straw yourselves, wherever you can find it. Yet there must not be the slightest reduction in your work." ¹²The people, then, scattered throughout the land of Egypt to gather stubble for straw, ¹³while the taskmasters kept driving them on, saying, "Finish your work, the same daily amount as when your straw was supplied."

Complaint of the Foremen. ¹⁴The foremen of the Israelites, whom the taskmasters of Pharaoh had placed over them, were beaten, and were asked, "Why have you not completed your prescribed amount of bricks yesterday and today, as before?"

¹⁵Then the Israelite foremen came and made this appeal to Pharaoh: "Why do you treat your servants in this manner? ¹⁶No straw is supplied to your servants, and still we are told to make bricks. Look how your servants are beaten! It is you who are at fault." ¹⁷Pharaoh answered, "It is just because you are lazy that you keep saying, 'Let us go and offer sacrifice to the LORD.' ¹⁸Off to work, then! Straw shall not be provided for you, but you must still deliver your quota of bricks."

¹⁹The Israelite foremen knew they were in a sorry plight, having been told not to reduce the daily amount of bricks. ²⁰When, therefore, they left Pharaoh and came upon Moses and Aaron, who were waiting to meet them, ²¹they said to them, "The LORD look upon

---

5, 6: The taskmasters and foremen: the former were higher officials and probably Egyptians; the latter were lower officials, chosen from the Israelites themselves. Cf v 14.

5, 7: Straw was mixed with the clay to give the sun-dried bricks greater consistency.

c: Ex 3, 18.

Genealogy

The genealogy or family tree in ch 6 traces the family line of Jacob's three oldest sons: Reuben (v. 14), Simeon (v. 15), and Levi (vv. 16–25). The focus is clearly on the descendants of Levi, a family of priests. The family tree of Levi has two functions: to identify Moses and Aaron as Levites and brothers, and to trace the priestly line through Aaron to his son Eleazar (vv. 23–24) and his grandson Phinehas (v. 25). Eleazar takes over Aaron's role as high priest in Numbers 20, 22–29. God commissions Phinehas and his descendants as priests in Numbers 25, 6–13.

you and judge! You have brought us into bad odor with Pharaoh and his servants and have put a sword in their hands to slay us."

Renewal of God's Promise. *22*Moses again had recourse to the LORD and said, "Lord, why do you treat this people so badly? And why did you send me on such a mission? *23*Ever since I went to Pharaoh to speak in your name, he has maltreated this people of yours, and you have done nothing to rescue them."

See RG 65-67

CHAPTER 6

*1*Then the LORD answered Moses, "Now you shall see what I will do to Pharaoh. Forced by my mighty hand, he will send them away; compelled by my outstretched arm, he will drive them from his land."

*2*God also said to Moses, "I am the LORD. *3*As God the Almighty I appeared*d* to Abraham, Isaac and Jacob, but my name, LORD, I did not make known to them. *4*I also established my covenant with them, to give them the land of Canaan, the land in which they were living as aliens.*e* *5*And now that I have heard the groaning of the Israelites, whom the Egyptians are treating as slaves, I am mindful of my covenant.*f* *6*Therefore, say to the Israelites: I am the LORD. I will free you from the forced labor of the Egyptians and will deliver you from their slavery. I will rescue you by my outstretched arm and with mighty acts of judgment. *7*I will take you as my own people, and you shall have me as your God.*g* You will know that I, the LORD, am your God when I

free you from the labor of the Egyptians *8*and bring you into the land which I swore to give to Abraham, Isaac and Jacob. I will give it to you as your own possession—I, the LORD!" *9*But when Moses told this to the Israelites, they would not listen to him because of their dejection and hard slavery.

*10*Then the LORD said to Moses, *11*"Go and tell Pharaoh, king of Egypt, to let the Israelites leave his land." *12*But Moses protested to the LORD, "If the Israelites would not listen to me, how can it be that Pharaoh will listen to me, poor speaker*h* that I am!" *13*Still, the LORD, to bring the Israelites out of Egypt, spoke to Moses and Aaron and gave them his orders regarding both the Israelites and Pharaoh, king of Egypt.

Genealogy of Moses and Aaron. *14*These are the heads of the ancestral houses.* The sons of Reuben,*i* the first-born of Israel, were Hanoch, Pallu, Hezron and Carmi; these are the clans of Reuben. *15*The sons of Simeon*j* were Jemuel, Jamin, Ohad, Jachin, Zohar and Shaul, who was the son of a Canaanite woman; these are the clans of Simeon. *16*The names of the sons of Levi,*k* in their genealogical order, are Gershon, Kohath and Merari. Levi lived one hundred and thirty-seven years.

*17*The sons of Gershon,*l* as heads of clans, were Libni and Shimei. *18*The sons of Kohath*m* were Amram, Izhar, Hebron and Uzziel. Kohath lived one hundred and thirty-three years. *19*The sons of Merari*n* were Mahli and Mushi. These are the clans of Levi in their genealogical order.

6, 14: The purpose of the genealogy here is to give the line from which Moses and Aaron sprang. Reuben and Simeon are first mentioned because, as older brothers of Levi, their names occur before his in the genealogy.

---

d: Gn 17, 1; 35, 11.   *e:* Gn 15, 18; 17, 4-8.   *f:* Ex 2, 24.   *g:* Lv 26, 12.   *h:* Ex 6, 30.   *i:* Nm 26. 5f; 1 Chr 5, 3   *j:* Nm 26, 12; 1 Chr 4, 24.   *k:* Nm 3, 17; 1 Chr 6, 1. 16; 23, 6.   *l:* Nm 3, 21; 1 Chr 6, 17; 23, 7.   *m:* Nm 3, 27; 1 Chr 6, 2. 18.   *n:* Nm 3, 20; 1 Chr 5, 19; 23, 21.

The Ten Plagues

The number "ten" is nowhere explicitly stated, and the ten plagues are the result of the combination of several overlapping plague accounts, none of which narrated all ten plagues. Alternative traditions, with fewer plagues, in different order, are preserved in Psalms 78, 44–51; 105, 28–36. Some of the plagues could be natural phenomena. Yet for the biblical writers they are clearly extraordinary manifestations of divine power (see Ex 9, 18.24; 10, 6.14; 11, 6).

[20] Amram married his aunt* Jochebed,[o] who bore him Aaron, Moses and Miriam. Amram lived one hundred and thirty-seven years. [21] The sons of Izhar were Korah, Nepheg and Zichri. [22] The sons of Uzziel were Mishael, Elzaphan and Sithri. [23] Aaron married Amminadab's[p] daughter, Elisheba, the sister of Nahshon; she bore him Nadab, Abihu, Eleazar and Ithamar. [24] The sons of Korah were Assir, Elkanah and Abiasaph. These are the clans of the Korahites. [25] Aaron's son, Eleazar, married one of Putiel's daughters, who bore him Phinehas. These are the heads of the ancestral clans of the Levites. [26] This is the Aaron and this the Moses to whom the LORD said, "Lead the Israelites from the land of Egypt, company by company." [27] These are the ones who spoke to Pharaoh, king of Egypt, to bring the Israelites out of Egypt—the same Moses and Aaron.

Moses and Aaron before Pharaoh. [28] On the day the LORD spoke to Moses in Egypt [29] he said, "I am the LORD. Repeat to Pharaoh, king of Egypt, all that I tell you." [30] But Moses protested to the LORD, "Since I am a poor speaker,[q] how can it be that Pharaoh will listen to me?"

CHAPTER 7

See RG 65-67

[1] The LORD answered him, "See! I have made you as God to Pharaoh,[r] and Aaron your brother shall act as your prophet.* [2] You shall tell him all that I command you. In turn, your brother Aaron shall tell Pharaoh to let the Israelites leave his land. [3] Yet I will make Pharaoh so obstinate that, despite the many signs and wonders that I will work in the land of Egypt, [4] he will not listen to you. Therefore I will lay my hand on Egypt and by great acts of judgment I will bring the hosts of my people, the Israelites, out of the land of Egypt, [5] so that the Egyptians may learn that I am the LORD, as I stretch out my hand against Egypt and lead the Israelites out of their midst."

[6] Moses and Aaron did as the LORD had commanded them. [7] Moses was eighty years old and Aaron eighty-three when they spoke to Pharaoh.

The Staff Turned into a Snake. [8] The LORD told Moses and Aaron, [9] "If Pharaoh demands that you work a sign or wonder, you shall say to Aaron: Take your staff and throw it down before Pharaoh, and it will be changed into a snake."[s] [10] Then Moses and Aaron went to Pharaoh and did as the LORD had commanded. Aaron threw his staff down before Pharaoh and his servants, and it was changed into a snake. [11] Pharaoh, in turn, summoned wise men and sorcerers, and they also, the magicians[t] of Egypt, did likewise by their magic arts. [12] Each one threw down his staff, and it was changed into a snake. But Aaron's staff swallowed their staffs. [13] Pharaoh, however, was obstinate and would not listen to them, just as the LORD had foretold.

First Plague: Water Turned into Blood. [14] *Then the LORD said to Moses, "Pharaoh is

---

6, 20: His aunt: more exactly, "his father's sister." Later on such a marriage was forbidden. Cf Lv 18, 12. Hence, the Greek and Latin versions render here, "his cousin."

7, 1: Just as God had his prophets to speak to men in his name, so Moses had Aaron as his "prophet" to speak to Pharaoh. Cf Ex 4, 16.

7, 14: Most of the ten plagues of Egypt seem to be similar

to certain natural phenomena of that country; but they are represented as supernatural at least in their greater intensity and in their occurring exactly to Moses' commands.

o: Nm 26, 59.   p: Ru 4, 19f; 1 Chr 2, 10.   q: Ex 6, 12.   r: Ex 4, 15f.   s: Ex 4, 3.   t: 2 Tm 3, 8.

The First Plague: The Nile Turns to Blood

The Nile River was the primary source of water and life for Egypt. However, the Egyptians had earlier used the Nile as an instrument of death when Pharaoh ordered every Hebrew baby boy to be thrown into the river (1, 22). This first plague recalls that previous atrocity. The plague also foreshadows one of the first miraculous signs God gave to Moses to convince the Israelites of God's power (4, 9).

obdurate in refusing to let the people go. [15]Tomorrow morning, when he sets out for the water, go and present yourself by the river bank, holding in your hand the staff that turned into a serpent. [16]Say to him: The LORD, the God of the Hebrews, sent me to you with the message: Let my people go to worship me in the desert. But as yet you have not listened. [17]The LORD now says: This is how you shall know that I am the LORD. I will strike the water of the river with the staff I hold, and it shall be changed into blood.[u] [18]The fish in the river shall die, and the river itself shall become so polluted that the Egyptians will be unable to drink its water."

[19]The LORD then said to Moses, "Say to Aaron: Take your staff and stretch out your hand over the waters of Egypt—their streams and canals and pools, all their supplies of water—that they may become blood. Throughout the land of Egypt there shall be blood, even in the wooden pails and stone jars."

[20]Moses and Aaron did as the LORD had commanded. Aaron raised his staff and struck the waters of the river in full view of Pharaoh and his servants, and all the water of the river was changed into blood. [21]The fish in the river died, and the river itself became so polluted that the Egyptians could not drink its water. There was blood throughout the land of Egypt. [22]But the Egyptian magicians did the same by their magic arts. So Pharaoh remained obstinate and would not listen to Moses and Aaron, just as the LORD had foretold. [23]He turned away and went into his house, with no con-

cern even for this. [24]All the Egyptians had to dig in the neighborhood of the river for drinking water, since they could not drink the river water.

Second Plague: the Frogs. [25]Seven days passed after the LORD had struck the river. [26]*Then the LORD said to Moses, "Go to Pharaoh and tell him:[v] Thus says the LORD: Let my people go to worship me. [27]If you refuse to let them go, I warn you, I will send a plague of frogs over all your territory. [28]The river will teem with frogs. They will come up into your palace and into your bedroom and onto your bed, into the houses of your servants, too, and your subjects, even into your ovens and your kneading bowls. [29]The frogs will swarm all over you and your subjects and your servants."

CHAPTER 8

See RG 65-67

[1]The LORD then told Moses, "Say to Aaron: Stretch out your hand and your staff over the streams and canals and pools, to make frogs overrun the land of Egypt." [2]Aaron stretched out his hand over the waters of Egypt, and the frogs came up and covered the land of Egypt. [3]But the magicians did the same by their magic arts. They, too, made frogs overrun the land of Egypt.

[4]Then Pharaoh summoned Moses and Aaron and said, "Pray the LORD to remove the frogs from me and my subjects, and I will let the people go to offer sacrifice to the LORD." [5]Moses answered Pharaoh, "Do me the favor of appointing the time when I am to pray for you and your servants and your subjects, that the frogs may be taken away from you and your houses and be left only in

---

7, 26—8, 28: This is Ex 8, 1-32 in the verse enumeration of the Vulgate.

u: 17-21: Ex 4, 9; Pss 78, 44; 105, 29; Wis 11, 5-7. *v:* 26-29: Pss 78, 45; 105, 30.

the river." ⁶"Tomorrow," said Pharaoh. Then Moses replied, "It shall be as you have said, so that you may learn that there is none like the LORD, our God. ⁷The frogs shall leave you and your houses, your servants and your subjects; only in the river shall they be left."

⁸After Moses and Aaron left Pharaoh's presence, Moses implored the LORD to fulfill the promise he had made to Pharaoh about the frogs; ⁹and the LORD did as Moses had asked. The frogs in the houses and courtyards* and fields died off. ¹⁰Heaps and heaps of them were gathered up, and there was a stench in the land. ¹¹But when Pharaoh saw that there was a respite, he became obdurate and would not listen to them, just as the LORD had foretold.

Third Plague: the Gnats. ¹²Thereupon the LORD said to Moses, "Tell Aaron to stretch out his staff and strike the dust of the earth, that it may be turned into gnatsʷ throughout the land of Egypt."* ¹³They did so. Aaron stretched out his hand, and with his staff he struck the dust of the earth, and gnats came upon man and beast. The dust of the earth was turned into gnats throughout the land of Egypt. ¹⁴Though the magicians tried to bring forth gnats by their magic arts, they could not do so.ˣ As the gnats infested man and beast, ¹⁵the magicians said to Pharaoh, "This is the finger of God."* Yet Pharaoh remained obstinate and would not listen to them, just as the LORD had foretold.

Fourth Plague: the Flies. ¹⁶Again the LORD told Moses, "Early tomorrow morning present yourself to Pharaoh when he goes forth to the water, and say to him: Thus says the LORD: Let my people go to worship me. ¹⁷If you will not let my people go, I warn you, I will loose swarms of flies upon you and your servants and your subjects and your houses. The houses of the Egyptians and the very ground on which they stand shall be filled with swarms of flies. ¹⁸But on that day I will make an ex-

ception of the land of Goshen: there shall be no flies where my people dwell, that you may know that I am the LORD in the midst of the earth. ¹⁹I will make this distinction between my people and your people. This sign shall take place tomorrow." ²⁰This the LORD did. Thick swarms of flies entered the house of Pharaoh and houses of his servants; throughout Egypt the land was infested with flies.ʸ

²¹Then Pharaoh summoned Moses and Aaron and said to them, "Go and offer sacrifice to your God in this land." ²²But Moses replied, "It is not right to do so, for the sacrifices we offer to the LORD, our God, are an abomination to the Egyptians.* If before their very eyes we offer sacrifices which are an abomination to them, will not the Egyptians stone us? ²³We must go a three days' journey in the desert to offer sacrifice to the LORD, our God, as he commands us." ²⁴"Well, then," said Pharaoh, "I will let you go to offer sacrifice to the LORD, your God, in the desert, provided that you do not go too far away and that you pray for me." ²⁵Moses answered, "As soon as I leave your presence I will pray to the LORD that the flies may depart tomorrow from Pharaoh and his servants and his subjects. Pharaoh, however, must not play false again by refusing to let the people go to offer sacrifice to the LORD." ²⁶When Moses left Pharaoh's presence, he prayed to the LORD; ²⁷and the LORD did as Moses had asked. He removed the flies from Pharaoh and his servants and subjects. Not one remained. ²⁸But once more Pharaoh became obdurate and would not let the people go.

CHAPTER 9

See RG
65-67

Fifth Plague: the Pestilence. ¹Then the LORD said to Moses, "Go to Pharaoh and tell him: Thus says the LORD, the God of the Hebrews: Let my people go to worship me. ²If you refuse to let them go and persist in

8, 9: Courtyards: some render "farmhouses."

8, 12. 17: Gnats, flies: it is uncertain what species of troublesome insects are here meant.

8, 15: The finger of God: understood by the magicians as the staff mentioned in Ex 8, 13. Cf Lk 11, 20.

8, 22: The Egyptians would fiercely resent the sacrifice of

any animal they considered sacred. Certain animals were worshiped in Egypt, at least as the symbols of various deities.

w: 12f: Ps 105, 31.   x: Wis 17, 7.   y: Pss 78, 45; 105, 31; Wis 16, 9.

holding them, [3]I warn you, the LORD will afflict all your livestock in the field—your horses, asses, camels, herds and flocks—with a very severe pestilence. [4]But the LORD will distinguish between the livestock of Israel and that of Egypt, so that none belonging to the Israelites will die." [5]And setting a definite time, the LORD added, "Tomorrow the LORD shall do this in the land." [6]And on the next day the LORD did so. All the livestock of the Egyptians died,[z] but not one beast belonging to the Israelites. [7]But though Pharaoh's messengers informed him that not even one beast belonging to the Israelites had died, he still remained obdurate and would not let the people go.

Sixth Plague: the Boils. [8]Then the LORD said to Moses and Aaron, "Take a double handful of soot from a furnace, and in the presence of Pharaoh let Moses scatter it toward the sky. [9]It will then turn into fine dust over the whole land of Egypt and cause festering boils on man and beast throughout the land."

[10]So they took soot from a furnace and stood in the presence of Pharaoh. Moses scattered it toward the sky, and it caused festering boils on man and beast. [11]The magicians could not stand in Moses' presence, for there were boils on the magicians no less than on the rest of the Egyptians. [12]But the LORD made Pharaoh obstinate, and he would not listen to them, just as the LORD had foretold to Moses.

Seventh Plague: the Hail. [13]Then the LORD told Moses, "Early tomorrow morning present yourself to Pharaoh and say to him: Thus says the LORD, the God of the Hebrews: Let my people go to worship me, [14]or this time I will hurl all my blows upon you and your servants and your subjects, that you may know that there is none like me anywhere on earth. [15]For by now I would have stretched out my hand and struck you and your subjects with such pestilence as would wipe you from the earth. [16]But this is why I have spared you: to show you[*] my power and to make my name resound throughout the earth![a] [17]Will you still block the way for my people by refusing to let them go? [18]I warn you, then, tomorrow at this hour I will rain down such fierce hail as there has never been in Egypt from the day the nation was founded up to the present. [19]Therefore, order all your livestock and whatever else you have in the open fields to be brought to a place of safety. Whatever man or beast remains in the fields and is not brought to shelter shall die when the hail comes upon them." [20]Some of Pharaoh's servants feared the warning of the LORD and hurried their servants and livestock off to shelter. [21]Others, however, did not take the warning of the LORD to heart and left their servants and livestock in the fields.

[22]The LORD then said to Moses, "Stretch out your hand toward the sky, that hail may fall upon the entire land of Egypt, on man and beast and every growing thing in the land of Egypt." [23]When Moses stretched out his staff toward the sky, the LORD sent forth hail[b] and peals of thunder. Lightning flashed toward the earth, and the LORD rained down hail upon the land of Egypt; [24]and lightning constantly flashed through the hail, such fierce hail as had never been seen in the land since Egypt became a nation. [25]It struck down every man and beast that was in the open throughout the land of Egypt; it beat down every growing thing and splintered every tree in the fields. [26]Only in the land of Goshen, where the Israelites dwelt, was there no hail.

[27]Then Pharaoh summoned Moses and Aaron and said to them, "I have sinned again! The LORD is just; it is I and my subjects who are at fault. [28]Pray to the LORD, for we have had enough of God's thunder and hail. Then I will let you go; you need stay no longer." [29]Moses replied, "As soon as I leave the city I will extend my hands to the LORD; the thunder will cease, and there will be no more hail. Thus you shall learn that the earth

---

9, 16: To show you: some ancient versions read, "to show through you." Cf Rom 9, 17.

---

z: Ps 78, 48.   a: Rom 9, 17.   b: 23f: Pss 78, 47; 105, 32f.

is the LORD's. *30*But you and your servants, I know, do not yet fear the LORD God."

*31*Now the flax and the barley were ruined, because the barley was in ear and the flax in bud. *32*But the wheat and the spelt were not ruined, for they grow later.

*33*When Moses had left Pharaoh's presence and had gone out of the city, he extended his hands to the LORD. Then the thunder and the hail ceased, and the rain no longer poured down upon the earth. *34*But Pharaoh, seeing that the rain and hail and thunder had ceased, sinned again: he with his servants became obdurate, *35*and in his obstinacy he would not let the Israelites go, as the LORD had foretold through Moses.

CHAPTER 10

See RG 65–67

Eighth Plague: the Locusts. *1*Then the LORD said to Moses, "Go to Pharaoh, for I have made him and his servants obdurate in order that I may perform these signs of mine among them *2*and that you may recount to your son and grandson how ruthlessly I dealt with the Egyptians and what signs I wrought among them, so that you may know that I am the LORD."*c*

*3*So Moses and Aaron went to Pharaoh and told him, "Thus says the LORD, the God of the Hebrews: How long will you refuse to submit to me? Let my people go to worship me. *4*If you refuse to let my people go, I warn you, tomorrow I will bring locusts into your country. *5*They shall cover the ground, so that the ground itself will not be visible. They shall eat up the remnant you saved unhurt from the hail, as well as all the foliage that has since sprouted in your fields. *6*They shall fill your houses and the houses of your servants and of all the Egyptians; such a sight your fathers or grandfathers have not seen from the day they first settled on this soil up to the present day." With that he turned and left Pharaoh.

*7*But Pharaoh's servants said to him, "How long must he be a menace to us? Let the men go to worship the LORD, their God. Do you not yet realize that Egypt is being destroyed?" *8*So Moses and Aaron were brought back to Pharaoh, who said to them, "You may go and worship the LORD, your God. But how many of you will go?" *9*"Young and old must go with us," Moses answered, "our sons and daughters as well as our flocks and herds must accompany us. That is what a feast of the LORD means to us." *10*"The LORD help you,"* Pharaoh replied, "if I ever let your little ones go with you! Clearly, you have some evil in mind. *11*No, no! Just you men can go and worship the LORD.* After all, that is what you want." With that they were driven from Pharaoh's presence.

*12*The LORD then said to Moses, "Stretch out your hand over the land of Egypt, that locusts*d* may swarm over it and eat up all the vegetation and whatever the hail has left." *13*So Moses stretched out his staff over the land of Egypt, and the LORD sent an east wind* blowing over the land all that day and all that night. At dawn the east wind brought the locusts. *14*They swarmed over the whole land of Egypt and settled down on every part of it. Never before had there been such a fierce swarm of locusts, nor will there ever be. *15*They covered the surface of the whole land, till it was black with them. They ate up all the vegetation in the land and the fruit of whatever trees the hail had spared. Nothing green was left on any tree or plant throughout the land of Egypt.

*16*Hastily Pharaoh summoned Moses and Aaron and said, "I have sinned against the LORD, your God, and against you. *17*But now, do forgive me my sin once more, and pray the LORD, your God, to take at least this deadly pest from me." *18*When Moses left the presence of Pharaoh, he prayed to

---

10, 10: The LORD help you . . . : literally, "May the LORD be with you in the same way as I let you . . ."; a sarcastic blessing intended as a curse.

10, 11: Pharaoh realized that if the men alone went they would have to return to their families. He suspected that the Hebrews had no intention of returning.

10, 13: East wind: coming across the desert from Arabia, the strong east wind brings Egypt the burning sirocco and, at times, locusts. Cf Ex 14, 21.

c: Dt 6, 20ff.   *d:* 12ff: Pss 78, 46; 105, 34f.

Moses Insists

Pharaoh will permit the people to go but not their flocks (10, 24), as if to undermine the purpose for which the Israelites are leaving—to sacrifice, which requires animals from the flocks. Moses counters by demanding that Pharaoh provide the sacrificial animals from his own livestock, while continuing to insist that the Israelite livestock also go with them. Moses seeks Pharaoh's total capitulation to God.

the LORD, [19]and the LORD changed the wind to a very strong west wind, which took up the locusts and hurled them into the Red Sea.* But though not a single locust remained within the confines of Egypt, [20]the LORD made Pharaoh obstinate, and he would not let the Israelites go.

Ninth Plague: the Darkness. [21]Then the LORD said to Moses, "Stretch out your hand toward the sky, that over the land of Egypt there may be such intense darkness* that one can feel it." [22]So Moses stretched out his hand toward the sky, and there was dense darkness[e] throughout the land of Egypt for three days. [23]Men could not see one another, nor could they move from where they were, for three days. But all the Israelites had light where they dwelt.

[24]Pharaoh then summoned Moses and Aaron and said, "Go and worship the LORD. Your little ones, too, may go with you. But your flocks and herds must remain." [25]Moses replied, "You must also grant us sacrifices and holocausts to offer up to the LORD, our God. [26]Hence, our livestock also must go with us. Not an animal must be left behind. Some of them we must sacrifice to the LORD, our God, but we ourselves shall not know which ones we must sacrifice to him until we arrive at the place itself." [27]But the LORD made Pharaoh obstinate, and he would not let them go. [28]"Leave my presence," Pharaoh said to him, "and see to it that you do not appear before me again! The day you appear before me you shall die!" [29]Moses replied, "Well said! I will never appear before you again."

CHAPTER 11

See RG 65-67

Tenth Plague: the Death of the First-born. [1]Then the LORD told Moses, "One more plague will I bring upon Pharaoh and upon Egypt. After that he will let you depart. In fact, he will not merely let you go; he will drive you away. [2]Instruct your people that every man is to ask his neighbor, and every woman her neighbor, for silver and gold articles and for clothing."[f] [3]The LORD indeed made the Egyptians well-disposed toward the people; Moses himself was very highly regarded by Pharaoh's servants and the people in the land of Egypt.

[4]Moses then said, "Thus says the LORD: At midnight I will go forth through Egypt.[g] [5]Every first-born in this land shall die,[h] from the first-born of Pharaoh on the throne to the first-born of the slave-girl at the handmill, as well as all the first-born of the animals. [6]Then there shall be loud wailing throughout the land of Egypt, such as has never been, nor will ever be again. [7]But among the Israelites and their animals not even a dog shall growl, so that you may know how the LORD distinguishes between the Egyptians and the Israelites. [8i]All these servants of yours shall then come down to me, and prostrate before me, they shall beg me, 'Leave us, you and all your followers!' Only then will I depart." With that he left Pharaoh's presence in hot anger.

[9]The LORD said to Moses, "Pharaoh refuses to listen to you that my wonders may be multiplied in the land of Egypt." [10]Thus, although Moses and Aaron performed these

---

10, 19: The Red Sea: according to the traditional translation, but the Hebrew is literally, "the Reed Sea"; hence the Red Sea of Exodus was probably a body of shallow water somewhat to the north of the present deep Red Sea.

10, 21: Darkness: at times a storm from the south, called the khamsin, blackens the sky of Egypt with sand from the

Sahara; the dust in the air is then so thick that the darkness can, in a sense, "be felt."

e: Ps 105, 28. f: 2f; Ex 3, 21f; 12, 35f. g: Ex 12, 12. h: 5f; Ex 12, 29f. i: Ex 12, 31ff.

The Lord Provides Instructions for the Annual Festivals of Passover and Unleavened Bread

The flow of the exodus story is interrupted in ch 12 by instructions for celebrating the two festivals of Passover and Unleavened Bread. The immediate purpose of the Passover is to mark every Israelite home with blood so that it will be protected from the effects of the final plague, the death of all Egyptian first-born. After Israel leaves Egypt, the annual festivals of Passover and Unleavened Bread will enable future generations to remember and identify the story of the exodus as their own (vv. 14–17). Passover comes from the smearing of the lamb's blood on the doorposts and lintel, or upper door frame, to mark the house as Israelite and thus protect it from the plague, which will kill all the Egyptian first-born (vv. 12–13. 21–23). The verb pass over (*pasah*) is the basis for the festival's name, Passover (*pesah,* v. 11). Unleavened bread, or biscuits without yeast, is quickly baked bread. Verses 33–34 provide the connection with the exodus: The Israelites could not wait for their bread dough to rise. The bitter herbs recall the bitterness of Israel's slavery. The lamb is to be roasted rather than eaten raw or boiled to ensure all of its blood is drained. The blood is the essence of life and must be returned to the deity and not eaten in recognition that life belongs to God (Gn 9, 4; Lv 17, 10–14).

various wonders in Pharaoh's presence, the LORD made Pharaoh obstinate, and he would not let the Israelites leave his land.

CHAPTER 12

See RG 65–67

The Passover Ritual Prescribed. [1] The LORD said to Moses and Aaron in the land of Egypt, [2] "This month* shall stand at the head of your calendar; you shall reckon it the first month of the year.[j] [3] Tell the whole community of Israel: On the tenth of this month every one of your families must procure for itself a lamb, one apiece for each household. [4] If a family is too small for a whole lamb, it shall join the nearest household in procuring one and shall share in the lamb* in proportion to the number of persons who partake of it. [5] The lamb must be a year-old male and without blemish. You may take it from either the sheep or the goats. [6] You shall keep it until the fourteenth day of this month, and then, with the whole assembly of Israel present, it shall be slaughtered during the evening twilight.

[7] They shall take some of its blood and apply it to the two doorposts and the lintel of every house in which they partake of the lamb. [8] That same night they shall eat its roasted flesh with unleavened bread and bitter herbs. [9] It shall not be eaten raw or boiled, but roasted whole, with its head and shanks and inner organs. [10] None of it must be kept beyond the next morning; whatever is left over in the morning shall be burned up.

[11] "This is how you are to eat it: with your loins girt, sandals on your feet and your staff in hand, you shall eat like those who are in flight. It is the Passover* of the LORD. [12] For on this same night I will go through Egypt, striking down every first-born of the land, both man and beast, and executing judgment on all the gods of Egypt—I, the LORD! [13] But the blood will mark the houses where you are. Seeing the blood, I will pass over you; thus, when I strike the land of Egypt, no destructive blow will come upon you.[k]

[14] "This day shall be a memorial feast for

12, 2: This month: Abib, the month of "ripe grain." Cf Ex 13, 4; 23, 15; 34, 18; Dt 16, 1. It occurred near the vernal equinox, March–April. Later it was known by the Babylonian name of Nisan. Cf Neh 2, 1; Est 3, 7.

12, 4: Share in the lamb: probably, in the expenses of its purchase. Some explain, "reckon for the lamb the number of persons required to eat it." Cf Ex 12, 10.

12, 11: Passover: in Hebrew, pesach, in Aramaic, pascha.

In the following verses the same root is used in the verb "to pass over." The word may be originally Egyptian, pesach, "the blow," i.e., the final plague which destroyed the Egyptian first-born.

[j]: 2-20: Lv 23, 5-8; Nm 9, 2-5; 28, 16ff; Dt 16, 1-8. [k]: Heb 11, 28.

you, which all your generations shall celebrate with pilgrimage to the LORD, as a perpetual institution. [15]For seven days you must eat unleavened bread. From the very first day you shall have your houses clear of all leaven. Whoever eats leavened bread from the first day to the seventh shall be cut off from Israel. [16]On the first day you shall hold a sacred assembly, and likewise on the seventh. On these days you shall not do any sort of work, except to prepare the food that everyone needs.

[17]"Keep, then, this custom of the unleavened bread.[l] Since it was on this very day that I brought your ranks out of the land of Egypt, you must celebrate this day throughout your generations as a perpetual institution. [18]From the evening of the fourteenth day of the first month until the evening of the twenty-first day of this month you shall eat unleavened bread. [19]For seven days no leaven may be found in your houses. Anyone, be he a resident alien or a native, who eats leavened food shall be cut off from the community of Israel. [20]Nothing leavened may you eat; wherever you dwell you may eat only unleavened bread."

Promulgation of the Passover. [21]Moses called all the elders of Israel and said to them, "Go and procure lambs for your families, and slaughter them as Passover victims. [22]Then take a bunch of hyssop,[*] and dipping it in the blood that is in the basin, sprinkle the lintel and the two doorposts with this blood.[m] But none of you shall go outdoors until morning. [23]For the LORD will go by, striking down the Egyptians. Seeing the blood on the lintel and the two doorposts, the LORD will pass over that door and not let the destroyer come into your houses to strike you down.

[24]"You shall observe this as a perpetual ordinance for yourselves and your descendants. [25]Thus, you must also observe this rite when you have entered the land which the LORD will give you as he promised. [26]When your children ask you, 'What does this rite of yours mean?'[n] [27]you shall reply, 'This is the Passover sacrifice of the LORD, who passed over the houses of the Israelites in Egypt; when he struck down the Egyptians, he spared our houses.' "

Then the people bowed down in worship, [28]and the Israelites went and did as the LORD had commanded Moses and Aaron.

Death of the First-born. [29]At midnight the LORD slew every first-born in the land of Egypt,[o] from the first-born of Pharaoh on the throne to the first-born of the prisoner in the dungeon, as well as all the first-born of the animals. [30]Pharaoh arose in the night, he and all his servants and all the Egyptians; and there was loud wailing throughout Egypt, for there was not a house without its dead.

Permission To Depart. [31]During the night Pharaoh summoned Moses and Aaron and said, "Leave my people at once, you and the Israelites with you! Go and worship the LORD as you said. [32]Take your flocks, too, and your herds, as you demanded, and begone; and you will be doing me a favor.'

[33]The Egyptians likewise urged the people on, to hasten their departure from the land; they thought that otherwise they would all die. [34]The people, therefore, took their dough before it was leavened, in their kneading bowls wrapped in their cloaks on their shoulders. [35]The Israelites did as Moses had commanded: they asked the Egyptians for articles of silver and gold and for clothing.[p] [36]The LORD indeed had made the Egyptians so well-disposed toward the people that they let them have whatever they asked for. Thus did they despoil the Egyptians.

II: The Exodus From Egypt and the Journey to Sinai

Departure from Egypt. [37]The Israelites set out from Rameses[q] for Succoth, about six hundred thousand men on foot, not counting the children. [38]A crowd of mixed ancestry[*]

12, 22: Hyssop: a plant with many woody branchlets that make a convenient sprinkler.
12, 38: Mixed ancestry: half-Hebrew and half-Egyptian. Cf Nm 11, 4; Lv 24, 10f.

---

l: Ex 13, 3.   m: 22f: Ex 12, 7. 13.   n: 26f: Ex 13, 8. 14; Dt 6, 20f.   o: 29f: Ex 11, 4ff; Pss 78, 51; 105, 36; 136, 10; Wis 18, 10-16.
p: 35f: Ex 3, 21f; 11, 2f; Ps 105, 37f.   q: Nm 33, 3ff.

also went up with them, besides their livestock, very numerous flocks and herds. ³⁹Since the dough they had brought out of Egypt was not leavened, they baked it into unleavened loaves. They had been rushed out of Egypt and had no opportunity even to prepare food for the journey.

⁴⁰The time the Israelites had stayed in Egypt* was four hundred and thirty years.^r ⁴¹At the end of four hundred and thirty years, all the hosts of the LORD left the land of Egypt on this very date. ⁴²This was a night of vigil for the LORD, as he led them out of the land of Egypt; so on this same night all the Israelites must keep a vigil for the LORD throughout their generations.

Passover Regulations. ⁴³The LORD said to Moses and Aaron, "These are the regulations for the Passover. No foreigner may partake of it. ⁴⁴However, any slave who has been bought for money may partake of it, provided you have first circumcised him. ⁴⁵But no transient alien or hired servant may partake of it. ⁴⁶It must be eaten in one and the same house; you may not take any of its flesh outside the house.^s You shall not break any of its bones.* ⁴⁷The whole community of Israel must keep this feast. ⁴⁸If any aliens^t living among you wish to celebrate the Passover of the LORD, all the males among them must first be circumcised, and then they may join in its observance just like the natives. But no man who is uncircumcised may partake of it. ⁴⁹The law shall be the same for the resident alien as for the native."

⁵⁰All the Israelites did just as the LORD had commanded Moses and Aaron. ⁵¹On that same day the LORD brought the Israelites out of Egypt company by company.

CHAPTER 13

See RG
67–68 **Consecration of First-born.** ¹The LORD spoke to Moses and said, ²"Consecrate to me every first-born that opens the womb among the Israelites,^u both of man and beast, for it belongs to me."

³Moses said to the people, "Remember this day on which you came out of Egypt, that place of slavery.^v It was with a strong hand that the LORD brought you away. Nothing made with leaven must be eaten. ⁴This day of your departure is in the month of Abib. ⁵Therefore, it is in this month that you must celebrate this rite, after the LORD, your God, has brought you into the land of the Canaanites, Hittites, Amorites, Hivites and Jebusites, which he swore to your fathers he would give you, a land flowing with milk and honey. ⁶For seven days you shall eat unleavened bread, and the seventh day shall also be a festival to the LORD. ⁷Only unleavened bread may be eaten during the seven days; no leaven and nothing leavened may be found in all your territory. ⁸On this day you shall explain to your son, 'This is because of what the LORD did for me when I came out of Egypt.' ⁹It shall be as a sign on your hand and as a reminder on your forehead;^w thus the law of the LORD will ever be on your lips, because with a strong hand the LORD brought you out of Egypt. ¹⁰Therefore, you shall keep this prescribed rite at its appointed time from year to year.

¹¹"When the LORD, your God, has brought you into the land of the Canaanites, which he swore to you and your fathers he would give you, ¹²you shall dedicate to the LORD every son that opens the womb;^x and all the male firstlings of your animals shall belong to the LORD. ¹³Every first-born of an ass you shall redeem with a sheep. If you do not redeem it, you shall break its neck. Every first-born son you must redeem. ¹⁴If your son should ask you later on, 'What does this mean?' you shall tell him, 'With a strong hand the LORD brought us out of Egypt, that place of slavery. ¹⁵When Pharaoh stubbornly refused to let us go, the LORD killed every first-born in the land of Egypt, every first-born of man and of

---

12, 40: In Egypt: according to some ancient sources, "in Canaan and Egypt," thus reckoning from the time of Abraham. Cf Gal 3, 17.

12, 46: You shall not break any of its bones: the application of these words to our Lord on the cross shows that the Paschal lamb was a prophetic type of Christ, immolated to free men from the bondage of sin. Cf also 1 Cor 5, 7; 1 Pt 1, 19.

r: Gn 15, 13; Acts 7, 6; Gal 3, 17. *s:* Nm 9, 12; Jn 19, 36.
t: 47f; Nm 9, 14. *u:* Ex 13, 12-15. *v:* 3-10; Ex 12, 2-20.
w: Ex 13, 16; Dt 6, 8; 11, 18. *x:* 12-15; Ex 13, 2; 22, 29f; 34, 19f;
Nm 3, 12f; 8, 16; 18, 15; Dt 15, 19.

beast. That is why I sacrifice to the LORD everything of the male sex that opens the womb, and why I redeem every first-born of my sons.' *16*Let this, then, be as a sign on your hand and as a pendant on your forehead: with a strong hand the LORD brought us out of Egypt."*y*

Toward the Red Sea. *17*Now, when Pharaoh let the people go, God did not lead them by way of the Philistines' land,* though this was the nearest; for he thought, should the people see that they would have to fight, they might change their minds and return to Egypt. *18*Instead, he rerouted them toward the Red Sea by way of the desert road. In battle array the Israelites marched out of Egypt. *19*Moses also took Joseph's bones* along, for Joseph had made the Israelites swear solemnly that, when God should come to them, they would carry his bones away with them.

*20*Setting out from Succoth, they camped at Etham*a* near the edge of the desert.

*21*The LORD preceded them, in the daytime by means of a column of cloud to show them the way, and at night by means of a column of fire* to give them light.*b* Thus they could travel both day and night. *22*Neither the column of cloud by day nor the column of fire by night ever left its place in front of the people.

See RG 67-68

CHAPTER 14

*1*Then the LORD said to Moses, *2**"Tell the Israelites to turn about and camp before Pi-hahiroth, between Migdol and the sea.*c* You shall camp in front of Baal-zephon, just opposite, by the sea. *3*Pharaoh will then say, 'The Israelites are wandering about aimlessly in the land. The desert has closed in on them.' *4*Thus will I make Pharaoh so obstinate that he will pursue them. Then I will receive glory through Pharaoh and all his army, and the Egyptians will know that I am the LORD."

This the Israelites did. *5*When it was reported to the king of Egypt that the people had fled, Pharaoh and his servants charged their minds about them. "What have we done!" they exclaimed. "Why, we have released Israel from our service!" *6*So Pharaoh made his chariots ready and mustered his soldiers— *7*six hundred first-class chariots and all the other chariots of Egypt, with warriors on them all. *8*So obstinate had the LORD made Pharaoh that he pursued*d* the Israelites even while they were marching away in triumph. *9*The Egyptians, then, pursued them; Pharaoh's whole army, his horses, chariots and charioteers, caught up with them as they lay encamped by the sea, at Pi-hahiroth, in front of Baal-zephon.

Crossing of the Red Sea. *10*Pharaoh was already near when the Israelites looked up and saw that the Egyptians were on the march in pursuit of them. In great fright they cried out to the LORD. *11*And they complained to Moses, "Were there no burial places in Egypt that you had to bring us out here to die in the desert? Why did you do this to us? Why did you bring us out of Egypt? *12*Did we not tell you this in Egypt, when we said, 'Leave us alone. Let us serve the Egyptians'? Far better for us to be the slaves of the Egyptians than to die in the desert." *13*But Moses answered the people, "Fear not! Stand your ground, and you will see the victory the LORD will win for you today. These Egyptians whom you see today you will never see again. *14*The LORD himself will fight for you; you have only to keep still."

*15*Then the LORD said to Moses, "Why are you crying out to me? Tell the Israelites to go forward. *16*And you, lift up your staff and, with hand outstretched over the sea, split the sea in two, that the Israelites may pass through it on dry land. *17*But I will make the

---

13, 17: By way of the Philistines' land: the most direct route from Egypt to Palestine, along the shore of the Mediterranean.

13, 21: A column of cloud . . . a column of fire: probably one and the same preternatural phenomenon, a central nucleus of fire surrounded by smoke; only at night was its luminous nature visible. Cf Ex 40, 38.

14, 2: These places have not been definitively identified. Even the relative position of Pi-hahiroth and Baal-zephon is

not clear; perhaps the former was on the west shore of the sea, where the Israelites were, and the latter on the opposite shore.

y: Ex 13, 9. *z:* Gn 50, 25; Jos 24, 32. *a:* Nm 33, 6. *b:* 21f: Ex 40, 33; Nm 9, 15-22; Dt 1, 33; Neh 9, 19; Pss 78, 14; 105, 39; Wis 10, 17. *c:* Nm 33, 7f. *d:* 5-8: Wis 19, 3; 1 Mc 4, 9.

Egyptians so obstinate that they will go in after them. Then I will receive glory through Pharaoh and all his army, his chariots and charioteers. [18]The Egyptians shall know that I am the LORD, when I receive glory through Pharaoh and his chariots and charioteers."

[19]The angel of God, who had been leading Israel's camp, now moved and went around behind them. The column of cloud also, leaving the front, took up its place behind them, [20]so that it came between the camp of the Egyptians and that of Israel. But the cloud now became dark,* and thus the night passed without the rival camps coming any closer together all night long. [21]Then Moses stretched out his hand over the sea, and the LORD swept the sea with a strong east wind throughout the night and so turned it into dry land.[e] When the water was thus divided, [22]the Israelites marched into the midst of the sea on dry land, with the water like a wall to their right and to their left.

Destruction of the Egyptians. [23]The Egyptians followed in pursuit; all Pharaoh's horses and chariots and charioteers went after them right into the midst of the sea. [24]In the night watch just before dawn the LORD cast through the column of the fiery cloud upon the Egyptian force a glance that threw it into a panic; [25]and he so clogged their chariot wheels that they could hardly drive. With that the Egyptians sounded the retreat before Israel, because the LORD was fighting for them against the Egyptians.

[26]Then the LORD told Moses, "Stretch out your hand over the sea, that the water may flow back upon the Egyptians, upon their chariots and their charioteers." [27]So Moses stretched out his hand over the sea, and at dawn the sea flowed back to its normal depth. The Egyptians were fleeing head on toward the sea, when the LORD hurled them into its midst. [28]As the water flowed back, it covered the chariots and the charioteers of Pharaoh's whole army[f] which had followed the Israelites into the sea. Not a single one of them escaped. [29]But the Israelites had marched on dry land through the midst of the sea, with the water like a wall to their right and to their left. [30]Thus the LORD saved Israel on that day from the power of the Egyptians. When Israel saw the Egyptians lying dead on the seashore [31]and beheld the great power that the LORD had shown against the Egyptians, they feared the LORD and believed in him[g] and in his servant Moses.

CHAPTER 15

See RG 67–68

[1]Then Moses and the Israelites sang[h] this song to the LORD:*

I will sing to the LORD, for he is
    gloriously triumphant;
    horse and chariot he has cast into the sea.
[2] My strength and my courage is the LORD,
    and he has been my savior.
He is my God, I praise him;
    the God of my father, I extol him.[i]
[3] The LORD is a warrior,
    LORD is his name!
[4] Pharaoh's chariots and army he hurled
    into the sea;
    the elite of his officers were
    submerged in the Red Sea.

[5] The flood waters covered them,
    they sank into the depths like a stone.[j]

[6] Your right hand, O LORD, magnificent in
    power,
    your right hand, O LORD, has shattered
    the enemy.
[7] In your great majesty you overthrew your
    adversaries;
    you loosed your wrath to consume
    them like stubble.
[8] At a breath of your anger the waters piled up,
    the flowing waters stood like a mound,

14, 20: The cloud now became dark: the light which it ordinarily cast at night would now have been a help to the Egyptians; its present obscurity serves as a shield for the Israelites. However, the reading of the original text here is not quite certain.

15, 1-21: This canticle (used in Christian liturgy) celebrates God's saving power, miraculously delivering his people from their enemies, and leading them to the victorious conquest of the Promised Land.

e: 21f: Ex 15, 19; Pss 66, 6; 78, 13; 136, 13f; Wis 10, 18; 19, 7f; Is 63, 12f; Heb 11, 29. *f:* 28f: Dt 11, 4; Ps 106, 11. *g:* 31f: Ps 106, 12; Wis 10, 20. *h:* Ex 15, 21. *i:* Ps 118, 14; Is 12, 2. *j:* Neh 9, 11.

Moses and Miriam Sing Songs of Victory

The songs of Moses and Miriam in ch 15 represent some of the earliest traditions of the Bible. The elevated language of Hebrew poetry in the songs contains many examples of parallelism or doubling of thoughts and images in consecutive lines. A recurring image in the poem is the stone. Israel's enemy sinks or freezes in fear like a stone (vv. 5, 10, 16) in contrast to being "planted" in the eternal security of God's mountain sanctuary (vv. 17–18). The Song of Moses (vv. 1–18) retells the story of ch 14 with some differences in details. For example, Israel's crossing the sea on dry land (14, 22) is not described in the song.

the flood waters congealed in the
  midst of the sea.
9 The enemy boasted, "I will pursue and
  overtake them;
I will divide the spoils and have my
  fill of them;
I will draw my sword; my hand shall
  despoil them!"
10 When your wind blew, the sea covered
  them;
like lead they sank in the mighty
  waters.

11 Who is like to you among the gods,
  O LORD?
Who is like to you, magnificent in
  holiness?
O terrible in renown, worker of wonders,
12   when you stretched out your right
  hand, the earth swallowed them!
13 In your mercy you led the people you
  redeemed;
in your strength you guided them to
  your holy dwelling.
14 The nations heard and quaked:
  anguish gripped the dwellers in
  Philistia.
15 Then were the princes of Edom
  dismayed;
  trembling seized the chieftains of Moab;
All the dwellers in Canaan melted away;
16   terror and dread fell upon them.[k]
By the might of your arm they were
  frozen like stone,

while your people, O LORD, passed
  over,
while the people you had made your
  own passed over.
17 And you brought them in and planted
  them on the mountain of your
  inheritance—
the place where you made your seat,
  O LORD,
the sanctuary, O LORD, which your
  hands established.
18 The LORD shall reign forever and ever.

19 They sang thus because Pharaoh's horses and chariots and charioteers had gone into the sea, and the LORD made the waters of the sea flow back upon them, though the Israelites had marched on dry land through the midst of the sea.[l] 20 The prophetess Miriam, Aaron's sister, took a tambourine in her hand, while all the women went out after her with tambourines, dancing; 21 and she led them[*] in the refrain:

Sing to the LORD, for he is gloriously
  triumphant;
  horse and chariot he has cast into the
  sea.[m]

At Marah and Elim. 22[n] Then Moses led Israel forward from the Red Sea, and they marched out to the desert of Shur. After traveling for three days through the desert without finding water, 23 they arrived at Marah,

15, 21: She led them: Miriam's refrain re-echoes the first verse of this song and was probably sung as an antiphon after each verse.

k: 16f: Ps 78, 53ff.   l: Ex 14, 21-29.   m: Ex 15, 1.   n: 22f: Nm 33, 8.

Quail and Manna

Quail migrating, often in great numbers, between Africa and Europe in the spring and fall often drop exhausted in the Sinai and are caught by hunters. This provision of meat was repeated in Numbers 11, 31–32 but was not a daily occurrence, as was the occurrence of manna. The quail were also not a miraculous phenomenon, but the Israelites saw their timely appearance at God's promise as an instance of divine providence. The manna (named in 16, 31) was a fine and flaky substance. If there is a natural explanation for manna, it is probably the sweet, edible honeydew (still called "manna" in Arabic) found in parts of the Sinai in June and July.

where they could not drink the water, because it was too bitter. Hence this place was called Marah. ²⁴As the people grumbled against Moses, saying, "What are we to drink?" ²⁵he appealed to the LORD, who pointed out to him a certain piece of wood. When he threw this into the water, the water became fresh.ᵒ

It was here that the LORD, in making rules and regulations for them, put them to the test. ²⁶"If you really listen to the voice of the LORD, your God," he told them, "and do what is right in his eyes: if you heed his commandments and keep all his precepts, I will not afflict you with any of the diseases with which I afflicted the Egyptians;ᵖ for I, the LORD, am your healer."

²⁷Then they came to Elim, where there were twelve springs of water and seventy palm trees, and they camped there near the water.�q

See RG 68

CHAPTER 16

The Desert of Sin. ¹Having set out from Elim, the whole Israelite community came into the desert of Sin, which is between Elim and Sinai, on the fifteenth day of the second month* after their departure from the land of Egypt. ²Here in the desert the whole Israelite community grumbled against Moses and Aaron. ³The Israelites said to them, "Would that we had died at the LORD's hand

in the land of Egypt, as we sat by our fleshpots and ate our fill of bread! But you had to lead us into this desert to make the whole community die of famine!"

The Quail and Manna. ⁴Then the LORD said to Moses,ʳ "I will now rain down bread from heaven* for you. Each day the people are to go out and gather their daily portion; thus will I test them, to see whether they follow my instructions or not. ⁵On the sixth day, however, when they prepare what they bring in, let it be twice as much as they gather on the other days." ⁶So Moses and Aaron told all the Israelites, "At evening you will know that it was the LORD who brought you out of the land of Egypt; ⁷and in the morning you will see the glory of the LORD, as he heeds your grumbling against him.ˢ But what are we that you should grumble against us? ⁸When the LORD gives you flesh to eat in the evening," continued Moses, "and in the morning your fill of bread, as he heeds the grumbling you utter against him, what then are we? Your grumbling is not against us, but against the LORD."

⁹Then Moses said to Aaron, "Tell the whole Israelite community: Present yourselves before the LORD, for he has heard your grumbling." ¹⁰When Aaron announced this to the whole Israelite community, they turned toward the desert, and lo, the glory of the LORD appeared in the cloud! ¹¹The LORD

16, 1: On the fifteenth day of the second month: just one full month after their departure from Egypt. Cf Ex 12, 2. 51; Nm 33, 3f. They encamped in the desert of Sin on a Friday; the murmuring (vv 2f) occurred on the sabbath, the arrival of the quail (v 13) the evening before Sunday, followed by six mornings (vv 14-27) of collecting manna before the next sabbath.

16, 4: Bread from heaven: as a gift from God, the manna

is said to come down from the sky. Cf Ps 78, 25; Wis 16, 20. Perhaps it was similar to a natural substance that is still found in small quantities on the Sinai peninsula, but here it is, at least in part, clearly miraculous. Our Lord referred to the manna as a type of the Blessed Eucharist. Cf Jn 6, 32. 49-52.

o: Sir 38, 5.   *p:* Dt 7, 15.   *q:* Nm 33, 9.   *r:* Pss 78, 24f; 105, 40; Jn 6, 31f; 1 Cor 10, 3.   *s:* 6f: Ex 16, 12.

spoke to Moses and said, *12*"I have heard the grumbling of the Israelites. Tell them: In the evening twilight you shall eat flesh, and in the morning you shall have your fill of bread, so that you may know that I, the LORD, am your God."

*13*In the evening quail*t* came up and covered the camp. In the morning a dew lay all about the camp, *14*and when the dew evaporated, there on the surface of the desert were fine flakes like hoarfrost on the ground. *15*On seeing it, the Israelites asked one another, "What is this?"* for they did not know what it was. But Moses told them, "This is the bread which the LORD has given you to eat.*u*

Regulations Regarding the Manna. *16*"Now, this is what the LORD has commanded. So gather it that everyone has enough to eat, an omer for each person, as many of you as there are, each man providing for those of his own tent." *17*The Israelites did so. Some gathered a large and some a small amount. *18**But when they measured it out by the omer, he who had gathered a large amount did not have too much, and he who had gathered a small amount did not have too little.*v* They so gathered that everyone had enough to eat. *19*Moses also told them, "Let no one keep any of it over until tomorrow morning." *20*But they would not listen to him. When some kept a part of it over until the following morning, it became wormy and rotten. Therefore Moses was displeased with them.

*21*Morning after morning they gathered it, till each had enough to eat; but when the sun grew hot, the manna melted away. *22*On the sixth day they gathered twice as much food, two omers for each person. When all the leaders of the community came and reported this to Moses, *23*he told them, "That is what the LORD prescribed. Tomorrow is a day of complete rest, the sabbath, sacred to the LORD. You may either bake or boil the manna, as you please; but whatever is left put away and keep for the morrow." *24*When they put it away for the morrow, as Moses commanded, it did not become rotten or wormy. *25*Moses then said, "Eat it today, for today is the sabbath of the LORD. On this day you will not find any of it on the ground. *26*On the other six days you can gather it, but on the seventh day, the sabbath, none of it will be there." *27*Still, on the seventh day some of the people went out to gather it, although they did not find any. *28*Then the LORD said to Moses, "How long will you refuse to keep my commandments and laws? *29*Take note! The LORD has given you the sabbath. That is why on the sixth day he gives you food for two days. On the seventh day everyone is to stay home and no one is to go out." *30*After that the people rested on the seventh day.

*31*The Israelites called this food manna.*w* It was like coriander seed,* but white, and it tasted like wafers made with honey.

*32*Moses said, "This is what the LORD has commanded. Keep an omerful of manna for your descendants, that they may see what food I gave you to eat in the desert when I brought you out of the land of Egypt." *33*Moses then told Aaron, "Take an urn* and put an omer of manna in it. Then place it before the LORD in safekeeping for your descendants."*x* *34*So Aaron placed it in front of the commandments* for safekeeping, as the LORD had commanded Moses.

*35*The Israelites ate this manna for forty years, until they came to settled land;*y* they ate manna until they reached the borders of Canaan. *36*[An omer is one tenth of an ephah.]

CHAPTER 17

Water from the Rock. *1*From the desert of Sin the whole Israelite community

!ee RG 68

16, 15: What is this: the original man hu is thus rendered by the ancient versions, which understood the phrase as a popular etymology of the Hebrew word man, "manna"; some render, "This is manna."

16, 18: St. Paul cites this passage as an example of equitable sharing. Cf 2 Cor 8, 15.

16, 31: Coriander seed: small, round, aromatic seeds of bright brown color; the comparison, therefore, refers merely to the size and shape, not to the taste or color of the manna.

16, 33: Urn: according to the Greek translation, which is followed in Heb 9, 4, this was a golden vessel.

16, 34: The commandments: the two tablets of the ten commandments, which were kept in the ark. Cf Ex 25, 16. 21f.

t: Nm 11, 31; Ps 78, 27f.   *u*: Dt 8, 3.   *v*: 2 Cor 8, 15.   *w*: Nm 11, 7.   *x*: Heb 9, 4.   *y*: Jos 5, 12.

journeyed by stages, as the LORD directed, and encamped at Rephidim.[z]

Here there was no water for the people to drink. [2]They quarreled, therefore, with Moses and said, "Give us water to drink."[a] Moses replied, "Why do you quarrel with me? Why do you put the LORD to a test?" [3]Here, then, in their thirst for water, the people grumbled against Moses, saying, "Why did you ever make us leave Egypt? Was it just to have us die here of thirst with our children and our livestock?" [4]So Moses cried out to the LORD, "What shall I do with this people? A little more and they will stone me!" [5]The LORD answered Moses, "Go over there in front of the people, along with some of the elders of Israel, holding in your hand, as you go, the staff with which you struck the river. [6]I will be standing there in front of you on the rock in Horeb. Strike the rock, and the water will flow from it for the people to drink."[b] This Moses did, in the presence of the elders of Israel. [7]The place was called Massah and Meribah,[*] because the Israelites quarreled there and tested the LORD, saying, "Is the LORD in our midst or not?"[c]

Battle with Amalek. [8]At Rephidim, Amalek[*] came and waged war against Israel.[d] [9]Moses, therefore, said to Joshua, "Pick out certain men, and tomorrow go out and engage Amalek in battle. I will be standing on top of the hill with the staff of God in my hand." [10]So Joshua did as Moses told him: he engaged Amalek in battle after Moses had climbed to the top of the hill with Aaron and Hur. [11]As long as Moses kept his hands raised up, Israel had the better of the fight, but when he let his hands rest, Amalek had the better of the fight. [12]Moses' hands, however, grew tired; so they put a rock in place for him to sit on. Meanwhile Aaron and Hur supported his hands, one on one side and one on the other, so that his hands remained steady till sunset. [13]And Joshua mowed

down Amalek and his people with the edge of the sword.

[14]Then the LORD said to Moses, "Write this down in a document as something to be remembered, and recite it in the ears of Joshua.[e] I will completely blot out the memory of Amalek from under the heavens." [15]Moses also built an altar there, which he called Yahweh-nissi;[*] [16]for he said, "The LORD takes in hand his banner; the LORD will war against Amalek through the centuries."

CHAPTER 18

See RG 68

Meeting with Jethro. [1]Now Moses' father-in-law Jethro, the priest of Midian, heard of all that God had done for Moses and for his people Israel: how the LORD had brought Israel out of Egypt. [2]So his father-in-law Jethro took along Zipporah, Moses' wife, whom Moses had sent back to him, [3]and her two sons. One of these was called Gershom;[f] for he said, "I am a stranger in a foreign land." [4]The other was called Eliezer; for he said, "My father's God is my helper; he has rescued me from Pharaoh's sword." [5]Together with Moses' wife and sons, then, his father-in-law Jethro came to him in the desert where he was encamped near the mountain of God, [6]and he sent word to Moses, "I, Jethro, your father-in-law, am coming to you, along with your wife and her two sons."

[7]Moses went out to meet his father-in-law, bowed down before him, and kissed him. Having greeted each other, they went into the tent. [8]Moses then told his father-in-law of all that the LORD had done to Pharaoh and the Egyptians for the sake of Israel, and of all the hardships they had had to endure on their journey, and how the LORD had come to their rescue. [9]Jethro rejoiced over all the goodness that the LORD had shown Israel in rescuing them from the hands of the Egyptians. [10]"Blessed be the LORD," he said, "who has rescued his people from the hands of Pharaoh and the Egyptians. [11]Now I know

---

17, 7: Massah . . . Meribah: Hebrew words meaning respectively, "the (place of the) test," and "the (place of the) quarreling."
17, 8: Amalek: the Amalekites were an aboriginal people of southern Palestine and the Sinai peninsula. Cf Nm 24, 20.
17, 15: Yahweh-nissi: meaning, "the LORD is my banner."

---

z: Nm 33, 12ff.   a: 2-7: Nm 20, 2-13.   b: 5f: Dt 8, 15; Pss 78, 15f; 105, 41; Wis 11, 4; Is 43, 20; 48, 21.   c: Ps 95, 8f.   d: Dt 25, 17; 1 Sm 15, 2.   e: Nm 24, 20; 1 Sm 15, 3. 20.   f: Ex 2, 22.

The Great Sea
(Mediterranean)

PHILISTIA

CANAAN

Nile
Delta

The Negeb

MOAB

Rameses
Sile
GOSHEN
Pithom
Succoth

Wilderness
of Shur

Kadesh-
barnea

EDOM

Isthmus of Suez

Wilderness
of Paran

E G Y P T

River Nile

Bitter
Lakes

Marah?
Elim

Wilderness
of Etham

Sinai Peninsula

Marah?
Elim

Ezion-geber

Wilderness
of Sin/Sinai

M I D I A N

Rephidim?

Taberah?

Mt. Sinai
(Horeb)?

Red Sea

Probable Exodus Route according to the Bible

that the LORD is a deity great beyond any other; for he took occasion of their being dealt with insolently to deliver the people from the power of the Egyptians." [12]Then Jethro, the father-in-law of Moses, brought a holocaust and other sacrifices to God, and Aaron came with all the elders of Israel to participate with Moses' father-in-law in the meal before God.

Appointment of Minor Judges. [13]The next day Moses sat in judgment for the people, who waited about him from morning until evening. [14]When his father-in-law saw all that he was doing for the people, he inquired, "What sort of thing is this that you are doing for the people? Why do you sit alone while all the people have to stand

about you from morning till evening?" [15]Moses answered his father-in-law, "The people come to me to consult God. [16]Whenever they have a disagreement, they come to me to have me settle the matter between them and make known to them God's decisions and regulations."

[17]"You are not acting wisely," his father-in-law replied. [18]"You will surely wear yourself out, and not only yourself but also these people with you. The task is too heavy for you;[g] you cannot do it alone. [19]Now, listen to me, and I will give you some advice, that God may be with you. Act as the people's representative before God, bringing to him whatever they have to say. [20]Enlighten them in regard to the decisions and regulations,

g: Nm 11, 14.

97

Israel Prepares for the Covenant with the LORD

Chapter 19 begins a major new section within the book of Exodus, chs 19–24. God initiates a formal relationship or covenant agreement with Israel. This covenant includes lists of obligations for Israel in the form of the Ten Commandments (20, 1–17) and the laws in the Book of the Covenant (20, 22—23, 19). Israel will remain encamped in this area at Sinai until Numbers 10, 11–12.

---

showing them how they are to live and what they are to do. ²¹But you should also look among all the people for able and God-fearing men, trustworthy men who hate dishonest gain, and set them as officers over groups of thousands, of hundreds, of fifties, and of tens.ʰ ²²Let these men render decisions for the people in all ordinary cases. More important cases they should refer to you, but all the lesser cases they can settle themselves. Thus, your burden will be lightened, since they will bear it with you. ²³If you do this, when God gives you orders you will be able to stand the strain, and all these people will go home satisfied."

²⁴Moses followed the advice of his father-in-law and did all that he had suggested. ²⁵He picked out able men from all Israel and put them in charge of the people as officers over groups of thousands, of hundreds, of fifties, and of tens. ²⁶They rendered decisions for the people in all ordinary cases. The more difficult cases they referred to Moses, but all the lesser cases they settled themselves. ²⁷Then Moses bade farewell to his father-in-law, who went off to his own country.

III: The Covenant at Mount Sinai

CHAPTER 19

See RG
69-70

Arrival at Sinai. ¹¹In the third month after their departure from the land of Egypt, on its first day, the Israelites came to the desert of Sinai. ²After the journey from Rephidim to the desert of Sinai, they pitched camp.

While Israel was encamped here in front of the mountain, ³Moses went up the mountain to God. Then the LORD called to him and said, "Thus shall you say to the house of Jacob; ⁴tell the Israelites: You have seen for yourselves how I treated the Egyptians and how I bore you up on eagle wings and brought you here to myself.ʲ ⁵Therefore, if you hearken to my voice and keep my covenant, you shall be my special possession, dearer to me than all other people,ᵏ though all the earth is mine. ⁶You shall be to me a kingdom of priests,* a holy nation.ˡ That is what you must tell the Israelites." ⁷So Moses went and summoned the elders of the people. When he set before them all that the LORD had ordered him to tell them, ⁸the people all answered together, "Everything the LORD has said, we will do." Then Moses brought back to the LORD the response of the people.

⁹The LORD also told him, "I am coming to you in a dense cloud,ᵐ so that when the people hear me speaking with you, they may always have faith in you also." When Moses, then, had reported to the LORD the response of the people, ¹⁰the LORD added, "Go to the people and have them sanctify themselves today and tomorrow. Make them wash their garments ¹¹and be ready for the third day; for on the third day the LORD will come down on Mount Sinai before the eyes of all the people. ¹²Set limits for the people all around the mountain,ⁿ and tell them: Take care not to go up the mountain, or even to touch its base. If anyone touches the moun-

---

19, 6: Kingdom of priests: inasmuch as the whole Israelite nation was consecrated to God in a special way, it formed a race of royal priests who participated in the liturgical sacrifices, even though the actual offering of the sacrifices was the exclusive prerogative of the Aaronic priesthood. The same condition exists in the New Dispensation as regards the whole Christian people and the Christian priesthood in the strict sense. Cf Is 61, 6; 1 Pt 2, 5. 9.

h: 21. 25: Dt 1, 15; 16, 18. *i:* 1f: Nm 33, 15. *j:* Dt 32, 11. *k:* Dt 7, 6; 14, 2; 26, 18f; 32, 8f. *l:* 1 Pt 2, 9. *m:* Ex 20, 21; 24, 15-18. *n:* 12f: Ex 34, 3; Heb 12, 18f.

The Decalogue

The Decalogue is the initial stipulation of the covenant. (*Decalogue*, Greek for "ten words" or "ten statements," is a more literal rendition of the Hebrew *aseret hadevarim* than "Ten Commandments"; see Ex 34, 28.) It is addressed directly to the people. No punishments are stated; obedience is motivated not by fear, but by God's absolute authority and the people's desire to live in accordance with his will.

The items in the Decalogue are arranged in two groups. Duties to God come first. Each commandment in this group contains the phrase, "the LORD, your God." The second group contains duties toward fellow humans, which are depicted as being of equal concern to God. The first five are accompanied by explanatory comments or exhortations. The remaining five, as widely recognized ethical requirements, need no such support.

tain he must be put to death. *13*No hand shall touch him; he must be stoned to death or killed with arrows. Such a one, man or beast, must not be allowed to live. Only when the ram's horn resounds may they go up to the mountain." *14*Then Moses came down from the mountain to the people and had them sanctify themselves and wash their garments. *15*He warned them, "Be ready for the third day. Have no intercourse with any woman."

The Great Theophany. *16*On the morning of the third day there were peals of thunder and lightning, and a heavy cloud over the mountain, and a very loud trumpet blast, so that all the people in the camp trembled. *17*But Moses led the people out of the camp to meet God, and they stationed themselves at the foot of the mountain.*o* *18*Mount Sinai was all wrapped in smoke, for the LORD came down upon it in fire. The smoke rose from it as though from a furnace, and the whole mountain trembled violently. *19*The trumpet blast grew louder and louder, while Moses was speaking and God answering him with thunder.

*20*When the LORD came down to the top of Mount Sinai, he summoned Moses to the top of the mountain, and Moses went up to him. *21*Then the LORD told Moses, "Go down and warn the people not to break through toward the LORD in order to see him; otherwise many of them will be struck down. *22*The priests, too, who approach the LORD must sanctify themselves; else he will vent his anger upon them." *23*Moses said to the LORD, "The people cannot go up to Mount Sinai, for you yourself warned us to set limits around the mountain to make it sacred." *24*The LORD repeated, "Go down now! Then come up again along with Aaron. But the priests and the people must not break through to come up to the LORD; else he will vent his anger upon them." *25*So Moses went down to the people and told them this.

CHAPTER 20

See RG 69-70

The Ten Commandments. *1*Then God delivered all these commandments:*

2p"I, the LORD, am your God, who brought you out of the land of Egypt,*q* that place of slavery. *3*You shall not have other gods besides me. *4*You shall not carve idols*r* for yourselves in the shape of anything in the sky above or on the earth below or in the waters beneath the earth; *5*you shall not bow down before them or worship them.*s* For I, the LORD, your God, am a jealous* God, inflicting punishment for their fathers' wickedness on the children of those who hate me, down

20, 1-17: The precise division of these precepts into "ten commandments" is somewhat uncertain. Traditionally among Catholics vv 1-6 are considered as only one commandment, and v 17 as two. Cf Dt 5, 6-21.

20, 5: Jealous: demanding exclusive allegiance, such as a wife must have for her husband.

o: 16ff: Dt 4, 10ff.   *p:* 2-17: Dt 5, 6-21.   *q:* Lv 26, 13; Ps 81, 10; Hos 13, 4.   *r:* Ex 34, 17; Lv 26, 1; Dt 4, 15-19; 27, 15.   *s:* Ex 34, 7. 14; Nm 14, 18; Dt 4, 24; 6, 15.

to the third and fourth generation; [6]but bestowing mercy down to the thousandth generation, on the children of those who love me and keep my commandments.

[7]"You shall not take the name of the LORD, your God, in vain.[t] For the LORD will not leave unpunished him who takes his name in vain.

[8]"Remember to keep holy the sabbath day. [9]Six days you may labor and do all your work, [10]but the seventh day is the sabbath of the LORD, your God.[u] No work may be done then either by you, or your son or daughter, or your male or female slave, or your beast, or by the alien who lives with you. [11]In six days the LORD made the heavens and the earth, the sea and all that is in them; but on the seventh day he rested.[v] That is why the LORD has blessed the sabbath day and made it holy.

[12w]"Honor your father and your mother, that you may have a long life in the land which the Lord, your God, is giving you.[x]

[13]"You shall not kill.[y]

[14]"You shall not commit adultery.[z]

[15]"You shall not steal.[a]

[16]"You shall not bear false witness against your neighbor.[b]

[17]"You shall not covet your neighbor's house. You shall not covet your neighbor's wife, nor his male or female slave, nor his ox or ass, nor anything else that belongs to him."[c]

The Fear of God. [18]When the people witnessed the thunder and lightning, the trumpet blast and the mountain smoking, they all feared and trembled.[d] So they took up a position much farther away [19]and said to Moses, "You speak to us, and we will listen; but let not God speak to us, or we shall die." [20]Moses answered the people, "Do not be afraid, for God has come to you only to test you and put his fear upon you, lest you should sin." [21]Still the people remained at a distance, while Moses approached the cloud where God was.

[22]The LORD told Moses, "Thus shall you speak to the Israelites: You have seen for yourselves that I have spoken to you from heaven. [23]Do not make anything to rank with me; neither gods of silver nor gods of gold shall you make for yourselves.[e]

[24]"An altar of earth you shall make for me, and upon it you shall sacrifice your holocausts and peace offerings, your sheep and your oxen.[f] In whatever place I choose for the remembrance of my name[*] I will come to you and bless you. [25]If you make an altar of stone for me,[g] do not build it of cut stone, for by putting a tool to it you desecrate it. [26]You shall not go up by steps to my altar, on which you must not be indecently uncovered.

CHAPTER 21

See RG 69–70

Laws Regarding Slaves. [1]"These are the rules[*] you shall lay before them. [2h]When you purchase a Hebrew slave, he is to serve you for six years, but in the seventh year he shall be given his freedom without cost. [3]If he comes into service alone, he shall leave alone; if he comes with a wife, his wife shall leave with him. [4]But if his master gives him a wife and she bears him sons or daughters, the woman and her children shall remain the master's property and the man shall leave alone. [5]If, however, the slave declares, 'I am devoted to my master and my wife and children; I will not go free,' [6]his master shall bring him to God[*] and there, at the door or doorpost, he shall pierce his ear with an awl, thus keeping him as his slave forever.

20, 24: I choose for the remembrance of my name: literally, "where I make my name to be remembered": at the sacred site where God wishes to be worshiped and his name revered.

21, 1: Rules: judicial precedents to be used in settling questions of law and custom. This introductory phrase serves as the title of the following collection of civil and religious laws (chapters 21–23) which is called in Ex 24, 7, the book of the covenant.

21, 6: To God: to the sanctuary; or perhaps the phrase is to be rendered, "to the gods," in the sense of "to the judges." Cf Ps 82, 1. Since the expression "to have an open ear" meant to

"obey," a pierced ear lobe was an ancient symbol of obedience. Cf Ps 40, 7.

---

t: Lv 19, 12; 24. 16.   *u:* 8ff: Ex 23, 12; 31, 13-16; 34, 21; 35, 2; Lv 23, 3.   *v:* Ex 31, 17; Gn 2, 2f.   *w:* 12-16: Mt 19, 18f; Mk 10, 19; Lk 18, 20; Rom 13, 9.   *x:* Mt 15, 4; Mk 7, 10; Eph 6, 2f.   *y:* Mt 5, 21.   *z:* Lv 18, 20; 20, 10; Dt 22, 22; Mt 5, 27.   *a:* Lv 19, 11.   *b:* Ex 23, 1; Dt 19, 16ff; Prv 19, 5. 9; 24, 28.   *c:* Rom 7, 7.   *d:* 18-21: Dt 4, 11; 5, 22-27; 18, 16; Heb 12, 18f.   *e:* Ex 20, 3f.   *f:* Dt 12, 5. 11; 14, 23; 16, 6.   *g:* Dt 27, 5; Jos 8, 31.   *h:* 2-6: Lv 25, 39ff; Dt 15, 12-18; Jer 34, 14.

7"When a man sells his daughter as a slave, she shall not go free as male slaves do. 8But if her master, who had destined her* for himself, dislikes her, he shall let her be redeemed. He has no right to sell her to a foreigner, since he has broken faith with her. 9If he destines her for his son, he shall treat her like a daughter. 10If he takes another wife, he shall not withhold her food, her clothing, or her conjugal rights. 11If he does not grant her these three things, she shall be given her freedom absolutely, without cost to her.

Personal Injury. 12"Whoever strikes a man a mortal blow must be put to death.[i] 13He, however, who did not hunt a man down, but caused his death by an act of God, may flee to a place which I will set apart for this purpose. 14But when a man kills another after maliciously scheming to do so, you must take him even from my altar and put him to death. 15Whoever strikes his father or mother shall be put to death.

16"A kidnaper, whether he sells his victim or still has him when caught, shall be put to death.[j]

17"Whoever curses his father or mother shall be put to death.[k]

18"When men quarrel and one strikes the other with a stone or with his fist, not mortally, but enough to put him in bed, 19the one who struck the blow shall be acquitted, provided the other can get up and walk around with the help of his staff. Still, he must compensate him for his enforced idleness and provide for his complete cure.

20"When a man strikes his male or female slave with a rod so hard that the slave dies under his hand, he shall be punished. 21If, however, the slave survives for a day or two, he is not to be punished, since the slave is his own property.

22"When men have a fight and hurt a pregnant woman, so that she suffers a miscarriage, but no further injury, the guilty one shall be fined as much as the woman's husband demands of him, and he shall pay in the presence of the judges.[l] 23*But if injury ensues, you shall give life for life, 24eye for eye, tooth for tooth, hand for hand, foot for foot, 25burn for burn, wound for wound, stripe for stripe.

26"When a man strikes his male or female slave in the eye and destroys the use of the eye, he shall let the slave go free in compensation for the eye. 27If he knocks out a tooth of his male or female slave, he shall let the slave go free in compensation for the tooth.

28"When an ox gores a man or a woman to death, the ox must be stoned; its flesh may not be eaten. The owner of the ox, however, shall go unpunished. 29But if an ox was previously in the habit of goring people and its owner, though warned, would not keep it in; should it then kill a man or a woman, not only must the ox be stoned, but its owner also must be put to death. 30If, however, a fine is imposed on him, he must pay in ransom for his life whatever amount is imposed on him. 31This law applies if it is a boy or a girl that the ox gores. 32But if it is a male or a female slave that it gores, he must pay the owner of the slave thirty shekels of silver, and the ox must be stoned.

Property Damage. 33"When a man uncovers or digs a cistern and does not cover it over again, should an ox or an ass fall into it, 34the owner of the cistern must make good by restoring the value of the animal to its owner; the dead animal, however, he may keep.

35"When one man's ox hurts another's ox so badly that it dies, they shall sell the live ox and divide this money as well as the dead animal equally between them. 36But if it was known that the ox was previously in the habit of goring and its owner would not keep it in, he must make full restitution, an ox for an ox; but the dead animal he may keep.

37*"When a man steals an ox or a sheep and slaughters or sells it, he shall restore five oxen for the one ox, and four sheep for the one sheep.[m]

21, 8: Destined her: intended her as a wife of second rank.

21, 23ff: This section is known as the lex talionis, the law of tit for tat. The purpose of this law was not merely the enforcement of rigorous justice, but also the prevention of greater penalties than would be just. Christ refers to this passage when he exhorts Christians to cede their lawful rights for the sake of charity. Cf Mt 5, 38ff.

21, 37—22, 30: In the Vulgate, 22, 1-31.

i: 12ff: Lv 24, 17; Nm 35, 15-29; Dt 4, 41f; 19, 2-5. *j:* Dt 24, 7. *k:* Lv 20, 9; Prv 20, 20; Mt 15, 4; Mk 7, 10. *l:* 22-25: Lv 24, 18-21; Dt 19, 21; Mt 5, 38. *m:* 2 Sm 12, 6.

CHAPTER 22

See RG
69–70

1"[If a thief is caught* in the act of housebreaking and beaten to death, there is no bloodguilt involved. *2*But if after sunrise he is thus beaten, there is bloodguilt.] He must make full restitution. If he has nothing, he shall be sold to pay for his theft. *3*If what he stole is found alive in his possession, be it an ox, an ass or a sheep, he shall restore two animals for each one stolen.

4"When a man is burning over a field or a vineyard, if he lets the fires spread so that it burns in another's field, he must make restitution with the best produce of his own field or vineyard. *5*If the fire spreads further, and catches on to thorn bushes, so that shocked grain or standing grain or the field itself is burned up, the one who started the fire must make full restitution.

Trusts and Loans. *6*"When a man gives money or any article to another for safekeeping and it is stolen from the latter's house, the thief, if caught, must make twofold restitution. *7*If the thief is not caught, the owner of the house shall be brought to God,* to swear that he himself did not lay hands on his neighbor's property. *8*In every question of dishonest appropriation, whether it be about an ox, or an ass, or a sheep, or a garment, or anything else that has disappeared, where another claims that the thing is his, both parties shall present their case before God; the one whom God convicts must make two-fold restitution to the other.

9"When a man gives an ass, or an ox, or a sheep, or any other animal to another for safekeeping, if it dies, or is maimed or snatched away, without anyone witnessing the fact, *10*the custodian shall swear by the Lord that he did not lay hands on his neighbor's property; the owner must accept the oath, and no restitution is to be made. *11*But if the custodian is really guilty of theft, he must make restitution to the owner. *12*If it has been killed by a wild beast, let him bring it as evidence, and he need not make restitution for the mangled animal.*n*

13"When a man borrows an animal from his neighbor, if it is maimed or dies while the owner is not present, the man must make restitution. *14*But if the owner is present, he need not make restitution. If it was hired, this was covered by the price of its hire.

Social Laws. *15*"When a man seduces a virgin who is not betrothed, and lies with her, he shall pay her marriage price and marry her.*o* *16*If her father refuses to give her to him, he must still pay him the customary marriage price for virgins.*

17"You shall not let a sorceress live.*p*

18"Anyone who lies with an animal shall be put to death.*q*

19"Whoever sacrifices to any god, except to the Lord alone, shall be doomed.*r*

20"You shall not molest or oppress an alien, for you were once aliens yourselves in the land of Egypt.*s* *21*You shall not wrong any widow or orphan. *22*If ever you wrong them and they cry out to me, I will surely hear their cry. *23*My wrath will flare up, and I will kill you with the sword; then your own wives will be widows, and your children orphans.

24"If you lend money to one of your poor neighbors among my people, you shall not act like an extortioner toward him by demanding interest from him. *25*If you take your neighbor's cloak as a pledge, you shall return it to him before sunset; *26*for this cloak of his is the only covering he has for his body. What else has he to sleep in? If he cries out to me, I will hear him; for I am compassionate.

22, 1f: If a thief is caught: this seems to be a fragment of what was once a longer law on housebreaking, which has been inserted here into the middle of a law on stealing animals. At night the householder would be justified in killing a burglar outright, but not so in the daytime, when the burglar could more easily be caught alive. He must make full restitution: this stood originally immediately after 21, 37.

22, 4: The Greek and Latin versions understood this verse as a prohibition against allowing one's cattle to graze in the field of another.

22, 7: Brought to God: see note on Ex 21, 6. Cf also Ex 22, 10.

22, 16: The customary marriage price for virgins: fifty shekels according to Dt 22, 29.

n: Gn 31, 39. *o:* 15f: Dt 22, 28f. *p:* Lv 19, 26. 31; 20. 6. 27; Dt 18, 10f. *q:* Lv 18, 23; Dt 27, 21. *r:* Dt 13; 17, 2-7. *s:* 20-23: Ex 23, 9; Lv 19, 33f; Dt 10, 18f; 24, 17f; 27, 19; Zec 7, 10. *t:* 24-26: Lv 25, 35-38; Dt 23, 19f; 24, 10-13; Ez 18, 7f. 17f.

[27]"You shall not revile God,* nor curse a prince of your people.[u]

[28]"You shall not delay the offering of your harvest and your press. You shall give me the first-born of your sons. [29]You must do the same with your oxen and your sheep; for seven days the firstling may stay with its mother, but on the eighth day you must give it to me.[v]

[30]"You shall be men sacred to me. Flesh torn to pieces in the field you shall not eat; throw it to the dogs.[w]

See RG 69–70

CHAPTER 23

[1]"You shall not repeat a false report. Do not join the wicked in putting your hand, as an unjust witness, upon anyone.[x] [2]Neither shall you allege the example of the many as an excuse for doing wrong, nor shall you, when testifying in a lawsuit, side with the many in perverting justice. [3]You shall not favor a poor man in his lawsuit.[y]

[4]"When you come upon your enemy's ox or ass going astray, see to it that it is returned to him.[z] [5]When you notice the ass of one who hates you lying prostrate under its burden, by no means desert him; help him, rather, to raise it up.

[6]"You shall not deny one of your needy fellow men his rights in his lawsuit. [7]You shall keep away from anything dishonest. The innocent and the just you shall not put to death, nor shall you acquit the guilty. [8]Never take a bribe, for a bribe blinds even the most clear-sighted and twists the words even of the just.[a] [9]You shall not oppress an alien; you well know how it feels to be an alien, since you were once aliens yourselves in the land of Egypt.[b]

Religious Laws. [10c]"For six years you may sow your land and gather in its produce. [11]But the seventh year you shall let the land lie untilled and unharvested, that the poor among you may eat of it and the beasts of the field may eat what the poor leave. So also shall you do in regard to your vineyard and your olive grove.

[12]"For six days you may do your work, but on the seventh day you must rest,[d] that your ox and your ass may also have rest, and that the son of your maidservant and the alien may be refreshed. [13]Give heed to all that I have told you.

"Never mention the name of any other god; it shall not be heard from your lips.

[14e]"Three times a year you shall celebrate a pilgrim feast to me.* [15]You shall keep the feast of Unleavened Bread. As I have commanded you, you must eat unleavened bread for seven days at the prescribed time in the month of Abib, for it was then that you came out of Egypt. No one shall appear before me* empty-handed. [16]You shall also keep the feast of the grain harvest with the first of the crop that you have sown in the field; and finally, the feast at the fruit harvest at the end of the year, when you gather in the produce from the fields. [17]Thrice a year shall all your men appear before the LORD God.

[18]"You shall not offer the blood of my sacrifice with leavened bread;[f] nor shall the fat of my feast be kept overnight till the next day. [19]The choicest first fruits of your soil you shall bring to the house of the LORD, your God.

"You shall not boil a kid in its mother's milk.*

Reward of Fidelity. [20]"See, I am sending an angel[g] before you, to guard you on the way and bring you to the place I have prepared. [21]Be attentive to him and heed his voice. Do not rebel against him, for he will not forgive your sin. My authority resides in him.* [22]If you heed his voice and carry out all I tell you, I will be an enemy to your enemies and a foe to your foes.

22, 27: God: or perhaps "the gods," in the sense of "the judges," as the parallel with a prince of your people suggests.

23, 14: These three feasts are elsewhere called the Passover, Pentecost and Booths. Cf Ex 34, 18-26; Lv 23; Dt 16.

23, 15: Appear before me: the original expression was "see my face"; so also in several other places, as Ex 23, 17; 34, 23f; Dt 16, 16; 31, 11.

23, 19: Boil a kid in its mother's milk: this was part of a Ca-naanite ritual; hence it is forbidden here as a pagan ceremony.

23, 21: My authority resides in him: literally, "My name is within him."

u: Acts 23, 5. v: Ex 13, 2; 34, 19; Lv 22, 27; Dt 15, 19. w: Lv 7, 24; 17, 15; 22, 8. x: 1f: Dt 19, 16ff. y: Lv 19, 15. z: Dt 22, 1ff. a: Dt 16, 19; 27, 25; Sir 20, 28. b: Ex 22, 21. c: 10f: Lv 25, 3-7. d: Ex 20, 8. e: 14-17: Ex 34, 18. 22ff; Lv 23; Dt 16, 1-17. f: 18f: Ex 34, 25f. g: Ex 14, 19; 32, 34; 33, 2.

23"My angel will go before you and bring you to the Amorites, Hittites, Perizzites, Canaanites, Hivites and Jebusites; and I will wipe them out. 24Therefore, you shall not bow down in worship before their gods, nor shall you make anything like them;* rather, you must demolish them and smash their sacred pillars.*h* 25The LORD, your God, you shall worship; then I will bless your food and drink, and I will remove all sickness from your midst; 26no woman in your land will be barren or miscarry; and I will give you a full span of life.

27"I will have the fear of me precede you, so that I will throw into panic every nation you reach.*i* I will make all your enemies turn from you in flight, 28and ahead of you I will send hornets* to drive the Hivites, Canaanites and Hittites out of your way. 29But not in one year will I drive them all out before you; else the land will become so desolate that the wild beasts will multiply against you. 30Instead, I will drive them out little by little before you, until you have grown numerous enough to take possession of the land. 31j*I will set your boundaries from the Red Sea to the sea of the Philistines,* and from the desert to the River; all who dwell in this land I will hand over to you to be driven out of your way. 32You shall not make a covenant with them or their gods. 33They must not abide in your land, lest they make you sin against me by ensnaring you into worshiping their gods."*k*

See RG 69-70

CHAPTER 24

Ratification of the Covenant. *1*Moses himself was told, "Come up to the LORD, you and Aaron, with Nadab, Abihu, and seventy of the elders of Israel. You shall all worship at some distance, 2but Moses alone is to come close to the LORD; the others shall not come too near, and the people shall not come up at all with Moses."

3When Moses came to the people and related all the words and ordinances of the LORD, they all answered with one voice, "We will do everything that the LORD has told us."*l* 4Moses then wrote down all the words of the LORD and, rising early the next day, he erected at the foot of the mountain an altar and twelve pillars* for the twelve tribes of Israel. 5Then, having sent certain young men of the Israelites to offer holocausts and sacrifice young bulls as peace offerings to the LORD, 6Moses took half of the blood and put it in large bowls; the other half he splashed on the altar. 7Taking the book of the covenant, he read it aloud to the people, who answered, "All that the LORD has said, we will heed and do." 8Then he took the blood and sprinkled it on the people, saying, "This is the blood of the covenant which the LORD has made with you in accordance with all these words of his."*m*

9Moses then went up with Aaron, Nadab, Abihu, and seventy elders of Israel, 10and they beheld the God of Israel. Under his feet there appeared to be sapphire tilework, as clear as the sky itself. 11Yet he did not smite these chosen Israelites. After gazing on God,* they could still eat and drink.

Moses on the Mountain. *12*The LORD said to Moses, "Come up to me on the mountain and, while you are there, I will give you the stone tablets*n* on which I have written the commandments intended for their instruction." 13So Moses set out with Joshua, his aide, and went up to the mountain of God. 14The elders, however, had been told by him, "Wait here for us until we return to you. Aaron

---

23, 24: Make anything like them: some render, "act according to their conduct." Sacred pillars: objects of religious veneration at Canaanite sanctuaries.

23, 28: Hornets: some understand this figuratively of various troublesome afflictions; others translate the Hebrew word as "leprosy." Cf Dt 7, 20; Jos 24, 12; Wis 12, 8.

23, 31: The sea of the Philistines: the Mediterranean. The River: the Euphrates. Only in the time of David and Solomon did the territory of Israel come near to reaching such distant borders.

24, 4: Pillars: stone shafts or slabs, erected as symbols of the fact that each of the twelve tribes had entered into this covenant

with God; not idolatrous as in Ex 23, 24, although the same Hebrew word is used in both passages. See note on Gn 28, 18.

24, 11: After gazing on God: the ancients thought that the sight of God would bring instantaneous death. Cf Ex 33, 20; Gn 16, 13; 32, 31; Jgs 6, 22f; 13, 22. Eat and drink: partake of the sacrificial meal.

---

h: 23f: Ex 34, 10-16; Nm 33, 51f; Dt 7, 24ff. *i:* 27ff: Dt 2, 25; 7, 20ff. *j:* Gn 15, 18; Dt 11, 24; Jos 1, 4. *k:* 32f: Ex 34, 12-16; Dt 7, 2ff. *l:* Ex 19, 8. *m:* 5-8: Heb 9, 18ff. *n:* Ex 31, 18; 32, 15f; Dt 5, 22.

Structure of the Tabernacle

and Hur are staying with you. If anyone has a complaint, let him refer the matter to them." [15]After Moses had gone up, a cloud covered the mountain. [16]The glory of the LORD settled upon Mount Sinai. The cloud covered it for six days, and on the seventh day he called to Moses from the midst of the cloud.[o] [17]To the Israelites the glory of the LORD was seen as a consuming fire on the mountaintop.[p] [18]But Moses passed into the midst of the cloud as he went up on the mountain; and there he stayed for forty days and forty nights.[q]

IV: The Dwelling and Its Furnishings

CHAPTER 25

See RG 70

Collection of Materials. [1]This is what the LORD then said to Moses:[r] [2]"Tell the Israelites to take up a collection for me. From every man you shall accept the contribution that his heart prompts him to give me. [3]These are the contributions you shall accept from them: gold, silver and bronze;[s] [4]violet, purple and scarlet yarn; fine linen and goat hair; [5]rams' skins dyed red, and tahash* skins; acacia wood; [6]oil for the light; spices for the anointing oil and for the fragrant incense; [7]onyx stones and other gems for mounting on the ephod and the breastpiece.

[8]"They shall make a sanctuary for me, that I may dwell in their midst.[t] [9]This Dwelling and all its furnishings you shall make exactly according to the pattern that I will now show you.[u]

Plan of the Ark. [10]"You shall make an ark of acacia wood,[v] two and a half cubits long, one and a half cubits wide, and one and a half cubits high. [11]Plate it inside and outside with pure gold, and put a molding of gold around the top of it. [12]Cast four gold rings and fasten them on the four supports of the ark, two rings on one side and two on the opposite side. [13]Then make poles of acacia wood and plate them with gold. [14]These poles you are to put through the rings on the

25, 5: Tahash: perhaps the name of a marine animal, such as the dugong or the porpoise. The Greek and Latin versions took it for the color hyacinth.

o: Sir 45, 4. *p:* Ex 19, 18; Heb 12, 18. *q:* Ex 34, 28; Dt 9, 9. *r:* 1-7: Ex 35, 4-9. 20-29. *s:* Ex 35, 4-9. *t:* 8f: Ex 26, 1-30; 36, 8-38. *u:* Acts 7, 44. *v:* 10-22: Ex 37, 1-9; Heb 9, 1-5.

The Ark of the Covenant

The wooden ark (25, 10–22) is a container that functions as throne or footstool for the divine presence. The two tablets of stone that contain the Ten Commandments are the covenant that will be carried in the ark. The gold and silver and other finery used to construct it derive presumably from what the Egyptians gave to the Israelites as they fled Egypt (12, 35–36). Cherubim are half-human and half-animal creatures with wings. The head is human, and the body is usually a lion or bull. They guard holy areas as well as kings. The propitiatory is the throne for the deity's presence.

sides of the ark, for carrying it; 15they must remain in the rings of the ark and never be withdrawn. 16In the ark you are to put the commandments which I will give you.

17"You shall then make a propitiatory* of pure gold, two cubits and a half long, and one and a half cubits wide. 18Make two cherubim* of beaten gold for the two ends of the propitiatory, 19fastening them so that one cherub springs direct from each end. 20The cherubim shall have their wings spread out above, covering the propitiatory with them; they shall be turned toward each other, but with their faces looking toward the propitiatory. 21This propitiatory you shall then place on top of the ark. In the ark itself you are to put the commandments which I will give you. 22There I will meet you and there, from above the propitiatory, between the two cherubim on the ark of the commandments, I will tell you all the commands that I wish you to give the Israelites.

The Table. 23"You shall also make a table of acacia*w* wood, two cubits long, a cubit wide, and a cubit and a half high. 24Plate it with pure gold and make a molding of gold around it. 25Surround it with a frame,* a handbreadth high, with a molding of gold around the frame. 26You shall also make four

rings of gold for it and fasten them at the four corners, one at each leg, 27on two opposite sides of the frame as holders for the poles to carry the table. 28These poles for carrying the table you shall make of acacia wood and plate with gold. 29Of pure gold you shall make its plates* and cups, as well as its pitchers and bowls for pouring libations. 30On the table you shall always keep showbread set before me.*x*

The Lampstand. 31"You shall make a lampstand of pure beaten gold*y*—its shaft and branches—with its cups and knobs and petals springing directly from it. 32Six branches are to extend from the sides of the lampstand, three branches on one side, and three on the other. 33*On one branch there are to be three cups, shaped like almond blossoms, each with its knob and petals; on the opposite branch there are to be three cups, shaped like almond blossoms, each with its knob and petals; and so for the six branches that extend from the lampstand. 34On the shaft there are to be four cups,* shaped like almond blossoms, with their knobs and petals, 35including a knob below each of the three pairs of branches that extend from the lampstand. 36Their knobs and

25, 17: Propitiatory: this traditional rendering of the Hebrew term, which may mean merely "cover," is derived from its connection with the ceremony of the Day of Atonement whereby God was rendered "propitious." Cf Lv 16, 14ff.

25, 18ff: Cherubim: probably in the form of human-headed winged lions. The cherubim over the ark formed the throne for the invisible Lord. Cf Ps 80, 2. For a more detailed description of the somewhat different cherubim in the temple of Solomon, see 1 Kgs 6, 23-28; 2 Chr 3, 10-13.

25, 25: A frame: probably placed near the bottom of the legs to keep them steady. The golden table of Herod's temple is pictured thus on the Arch of Titus.

25, 29f: The plates held the showbread, that is, the holy bread which was placed upon the table every sabbath as an of-

fering to God, and was later eaten by the priests. The cups held the incense which was strewn upon the bread. Cf Lv 24, 5-9. The libation wine was poured from the pitchers into the bowls. All these vessels were kept on the golden table.

25, 33: In keeping with the arrangement of the ornaments on the shaft, the three sets of ornaments on each branch were probably so placed that one was at the top and the other two equally spaced along the length of the branch. Knob: the cup-shaped seed capsule at the base of a flower.

25, 34f: Of the four ornaments on the shaft, one was at the top and one was below each of the three sets of side branches.

w: 23-30: Ex 37, 10-16.   *x:* Lv 24, 5ff.   *y:* 31-40: Ex 37, 17-24.

branches shall so spring from it that the whole will form but a single piece of pure beaten gold. *37**You shall then make seven lamps² for it and so set up the lamps that they shed their light on the space in front of the lampstand. *38*These, as well as the trimming shears and trays,* must be of pure gold. *39*Use a talent of pure gold for the lampstand and all its appurtenances. *40*See that you make them according to the pattern shown you on the mountain.*a*

See RG 70

CHAPTER 26

The Tent Cloth. *1*"The Dwelling itself you shall make out of sheets* woven of fine linen twined and of violet, purple and scarlet yarn, with cherubim embroidered on them.*b* *2*The length of each shall be twenty-eight cubits, and the width four cubits; all the sheets shall be of the same size. *3*Five of the sheets are to be sewed together, edge to edge; and the same for the other five. *4*Make loops of violet yarn along the edge of the end sheet in one set, and the same along the edge of the end sheet in the other set. *5*There are to be fifty loops along the edge of the end sheet in the first set, and fifty loops along the edge of the corresponding sheet in the second set, and so placed that the loops are directly opposite each other. *6*Then make fifty clasps of gold, with which to join the two sets of sheets, so that the Dwelling forms one whole.

7"Also make sheets woven of goat hair, to be used as a tent covering* over the Dwelling. *8*Eleven such sheets are to be made; the length of each shall be thirty cubits, and the width four cubits: all eleven sheets shall be of the same size. *9*Sew five of the sheets, edge to edge, into one set, and the other six sheets into another set. Use the sixth sheet double at the front of the tent.* *10*Make fifty loops along the edge of the end sheet in one set, and fifty loops along the edge of the end sheet in the second set. *11*Also make fifty bronze clasps and put them into the loops, to join the tent into one whole. *12*There will be an extra half sheet of tent covering, which shall be allowed to hang down over the rear of the Dwelling. *13*Likewise, the sheets of the tent will have an extra cubit's length to be left hanging down on either side of the Dwelling to protect it. *14*Over the tent itself you shall make a covering of rams' skins dyed red, and above that, a covering of tahash skins.

The Wooden Walls. *15c*"You shall make boards of acacia wood as walls for the Dwelling. *16*The length of each board is to be ten cubits, and its width one and a half cubits. *17*Each board shall have two arms* that shall serve to fasten the boards in line. In this way all the boards of the Dwelling are to be made. *18*Set up the boards of the Dwelling as follows: twenty boards on the south side, *19*with forty silver pedestals under the twenty boards, so that there are two pedestals under each board, at its two arms; *20*twenty boards on the other side of the Dwelling, the north side, *21*with their forty silver pedestals, two under each board; *22*six boards for the rear of the Dwelling, to the west; *23*and two boards for the corners at the rear of the Dwelling. *24*These two shall be double at the bottom, and likewise double at the top, to the first ring. That is how both boards in the corners are to be made. *25*Thus, there shall be in the rear eight boards, with their sixteen silver pedestals, two pedestals under each board. *26*Also make bars of acacia wood: five for the boards on one side of the Dwelling, *27*five for those on the other

---

25, 37: The lamps were probably shaped like small boats, with the wick at one end; the end with the wick was turned toward the front of the lampstand.

25, 38: Trays: small receptacles for the burnt-out wicks.

26, 1: Sheets: strips of tapestry, woven of white linen, the colored threads being used for the cherubim which were embroidered on them. These sheets were stretched across the top of the Dwelling to form a roof, their free ends hanging down inside the boards which formed walls.

26, 7: Tent covering: the cloth made of sheets of goat hair to cover the Dwelling.

26, 9: Half the width of the end strip was folded back at the front of the Dwelling, thus leaving another half-strip to hang down at the rear. Cf v 12.

26, 17: Arms: literally, "hands." According to some, they served as "tongue and groove" to mortise the boards together; according to others, they were pegs at the bottom of the boards and fitted into sockets in the pedestals.

z: Lv 24, 2ff; Nm 8, 2. *a:* Heb 8, 5. *b:* 1-14: Ex 36. 8-19. *c:* 15-30: Ex 36, 20-34.

side, and five for those at the rear, toward the west. ²⁸The center bar, at the middle of the boards, shall reach across from end to end. ²⁹Plate the boards with gold, and make gold rings on them as holders for the bars, which are also to be plated with gold. ³⁰You shall erect the Dwelling according to the pattern shown you on the mountain.

The Veils. ³¹"You shall have a veil woven of violet, purple and scarlet yarn,*d* and of fine linen twined, with cherubim embroidered on it.*e* ³²It is to be hung on four gold-plated columns of acacia wood, which shall have hooks* of gold and shall rest on four silver pedestals. ³³Hang the veil from clasps. The ark of the commandments you shall bring inside, behind this veil which divides the holy place from the holy of holies. ³⁴Set the propitiatory on the ark of the commandments in the holy of holies.

³⁵"Outside the veil you shall place the table and the lampstand, the latter on the south side of the Dwelling, opposite the table, which is to be put on the north side. ³⁶For the entrance of the tent make a variegated* curtain of violet, purple and scarlet yarn and of fine linen twined. ³⁷Make five columns of acacia wood for this curtain; have them plated with gold, with their hooks of gold; and cast five bronze pedestals for them.

See RG 70

CHAPTER 27

The Altar of Holocausts. ¹"You shall make an altar*f* of acacia wood, on a square, five cubits long and five cubits wide; it shall be three cubits high. ²At the four corners there are to be horns, so made that they spring directly from the altar. You shall then plate it with bronze. ³Make pots for removing the ashes, as well as shovels, basins, forks and fire pans, all of which shall be of bronze. ⁴Make a grating* of bronze network

for it; this to have four bronze rings, one at each of its four corners. ⁵Put it down around the altar, on the ground. This network is to be half as high as the altar. ⁶You shall also make poles of acacia wood for the altar, and plate them with bronze. ⁷These poles are to be put through the rings, so that they are on either side of the altar when it is carried. ⁸Make the altar itself in the form of a hollow* box, just as it was shown you on the mountain.

Court of the Dwelling. ⁹"You shall also make a court for the Dwelling. On the south side the court shall have hangings a hundred cubits long, woven of fine linen twined, ¹⁰with twenty columns and twenty pedestals of bronze; the hooks and bands on the columns shall be of silver. ¹¹On the north side there shall be similar hangings, a hundred cubits long, with twenty columns and twenty pedestals of bronze; the hooks and bands on the columns shall be of silver. ¹²On the west side, across the width of the court, there shall be hangings, fifty cubits long, with ten columns and ten pedestals. ¹³The width of the court on the east side shall be fifty cubits. ¹⁴On one side there shall be hangings to the extent of fifteen cubits, with three columns and three pedestals; ¹⁵on the other side there shall be hangings to the extent of fifteen cubits, with three columns and three pedestals.

¹⁶"At the entrance of the court there shall be a variegated curtain, twenty cubits long, woven of violet, purple and scarlet yarn and of fine linen twined. It shall have four columns and four pedestals.

¹⁷"All the columns around the court shall have bands and hooks of silver, and pedestals of bronze. ¹⁸The enclosure of the court is to be one hundred cubits long, fifty cubits wide, and five cubits high. Fine linen twined must be used, and the pedestals must be of bronze. ¹⁹All the fittings of the

---

26, 32: Hooks: probably placed near the tops of the columns, to hold the rope from which the veils and curtains hung.

26, 36: Variegated: without definite designs such as the cherubim on the inner veil.

27, 4: Grating: it is not clear whether this was flush with the altar or at some small distance from it; in the latter case the space between the altar and the grating would be filled with

stones and serve as a platform around the altar, which would otherwise be too high for the priest to reach conveniently.

27, 8: Hollow: probably filled with earth or stones when in use. Cf Ex 20, 24f.

---

d: 2 Chr 3, 14.   *e:* 31-37: Ex 36, 35-38.   *f:* 1-8: Ex 38, 1-7.
g: 9-19: Ex 38, 9-20.

Dwelling, whatever be their use, as well as all its tent pegs and all the tent pegs of the court, must be of bronze.

Oil for the Lamps. [20]"You shall order the Israelites to bring you clear oil of crushed olives, to be used for the light, so that you may keep lamps burning regularly.[h] [21]From evening to morning Aaron and his sons shall maintain them before the LORD in the meeting tent, outside the veil which hangs in front of the commandments. This shall be a perpetual ordinance for the Israelites throughout their generations.

See RG 70

CHAPTER 28

The Priestly Vestments. [1]"From among the Israelites have your brother Aaron, together with his sons Nadab, Abihu, Eleazar and Ithamar, brought to you, that they may be my priests. [2]For the glorious adornment of your brother Aaron you shall have sacred vestments made. [3]Therefore, to the various expert workmen whom I have endowed with skill, you shall give instructions to make such vestments for Aaron as will set him apart for his sacred service as my priest. [4]These are the vestments they shall make: a breastpiece, an ephod, a robe, a brocaded tunic, a miter and a sash. In making these sacred vestments which your brother Aaron and his sons are to wear in serving as my priests, [5]they shall use gold, violet, purple and scarlet yarn and fine linen.

The Ephod and Breastpiece. [6]"The ephod* they shall make of gold thread and of violet, purple and scarlet yarn, embroidered on cloth of fine linen twined.[j] [7]It shall have a pair of shoulder straps joined to its two upper ends. [8]The embroidered belt on the ephod shall extend out from it and, like it, be made of gold thread, of violet, purple and scarlet yarn, and of fine linen twined.

[9]"Get two onyx stones and engrave on them the names of the sons of Israel: [10]six of their names on one stone, and the other six on the other stone, in the order of their birth. [11]As a gem-cutter engraves a seal, so shall you have the two stones engraved with the names of the sons of Israel and then mounted in gold filigree work. [12]Set these two stones on the shoulder straps of the ephod as memorial stones of the sons of Israel. Thus Aaron shall bear their names on his shoulders as a reminder before the LORD. [13]Make filigree rosettes of gold,[k] [14]as well as two chains of pure gold, twisted like cords, and fasten the cordlike chains to the filigree rosettes.

[15]"The breastpiece* of decision you shall also have made, embroidered like the ephod with gold thread and violet, purple and scarlet yarn on cloth of fine linen twined. [16]It is to be square when folded double, a span high and a span wide. [17]*On it you shall mount four rows of precious stones: in the first row, a carnelian, a topaz and an emerald; [18]in the second row, a garnet, a sapphire and a beryl; [19]in the third row, a jacinth, an agate and an amethyst; [20]in the fourth row, a chrysolite, an onyx and a jasper. These stones are to be mounted in gold filigree work, [21]twelve of them to match the names of the sons of Israel, each stone engraved like a seal with the name of one of the twelve tribes.

[22]"When the chains of pure gold, twisted like cords, have been made for the breastpiece, [23]you shall then make two rings of gold for it and fasten them to the two upper ends of the breastpiece. [24]The gold cords are then to be fastened to the two rings at the upper ends of the breastpiece, [25]the other two ends of the cords being fastened in front to the two filigree rosettes which are attached to the shoulder straps of the ephod. [26]Make two other rings of gold and put them on the two lower ends of the breastpiece, on its

28, 6: Ephod: this Hebrew word is retained in the translation because it is the technical term for a peculiar piece of the priestly vestments, the exact nature of which is uncertain. It seems to have been a sort of apron that hung from the shoulders of the priest by shoulder straps (v 7) and was tied around his waist by the loose ends of the attached belt (v 8).

28, 15-30: Breastpiece: in shape like a modern altar burse, it was a pocketlike receptacle for holding the Urim and Thummim (v 30), and formed an integral part of the ephod,

to which it was attached by an elaborate system of rings and chains. Both the ephod and its breastpiece were made of brocaded linen.

28, 17-20: The translation of the Hebrew names of some of these gems is quite conjectural.

h: 20f: Lv 24, 1-4.   *i:* 1-5: Ex 39, 1; Sir 45, 7.   *j:* 6-12: Ex 39, 2-7; Sir 45, 8-14.   *k:* 13f: Ex 28, 22. 25; 39, 15. 18.   *l:* 15-21: Ex 39, 15-21.

edge that faces the ephod. [27]Then make two more rings of gold and fasten them to the bottom of the shoulder straps next to where they join the ephod in front, just above its embroidered belt. [28]Violet ribbons shall bind the rings of the breastpiece to the rings of the ephod, so that the breastpiece will stay right above the embroidered belt of the ephod and not swing loose from it.

[29]"Whenever Aaron enters the sanctuary, he will thus bear the names of the sons of Israel on the breastpiece of decision over his heart as a constant reminder before the LORD. [30]In this breastpiece of decision[m] you shall put the Urim and Thummim,* that they may be over Aaron's heart whenever he enters the presence of the LORD. Thus he shall always bear the decisions for the Israelites over his heart in the LORD's presence.

Other Vestments. [31]"The robe of the ephod[n] you shall make entirely of violet material. [32]It shall have an opening for the head in the center, and around this opening there shall be a selvage, woven as at the opening of a shirt, to keep it from being torn. [33]All around the hem at the bottom you shall make pomegranates, woven of violet, purple and scarlet yarn and fine linen twined, with gold bells between them; [34]first a gold bell, then a pomegranate, and thus alternating all around the hem of the robe. [35]Aaron shall wear it when ministering, that its tinkling may be heard as he enters and leaves the LORD's presence in the sanctuary; else he will die.

[36]"You shall also make a plate of pure gold and engrave on it, as on a seal engraving, "Sacred to the LORD." [37]This plate is to be tied over the miter with a violet ribbon in such a way that it rests on the front of the miter,[o] [38]over Aaron's forehead. Since Aaron bears whatever guilt the Israelites may incur in consecrating any of their sacred gifts, this plate must always be over his forehead, so that they may find favor with the LORD.

[39][p]"The tunic of fine linen shall be brocaded. The miter shall be made of fine linen. The sash shall be of variegated work.

[40]"Likewise, for the glorious adornment of Aaron's sons you shall have tunics and sashes and turbans made. [41]With these you shall clothe your brother Aaron and his sons. Anoint and ordain them,* consecrating them as my priests. [42]You must also make linen drawers for them, to cover their naked flesh from their loins to their thighs.[q] [43]Aaron and his sons shall wear them whenever they go into the meeting tent or approach the altar to minister in the sanctuary, lest they incur guilt and die. This shall be a perpetual ordinance for him and for his descendants.

CHAPTER 29

See RG 70

Consecration of the Priests. [1]"This is the rite you shall perform in consecrating them as my priests.[r] Procure a young bull and two unblemished rams. [2]With fine wheat flour make unleavened cakes mixed with oil, and unleavened wafers spread with oil, [3]and put them in a basket. Take the basket of them along with the bullock and the two rams. [4]Aaron and his sons you shall also bring to the entrance of the meeting tent, and there wash them with water. [5]Take the vestments and clothe Aaron with the tunic, the robe of the ephod, the ephod itself, and the breastpiece, fastening the embroidered belt of the ephod around him. [6]Put the miter on his head, the sacred diadem on the miter. [7]Then take the anointing oil and anoint him with it, pouring it on his head. [8]Bring forward his sons also and clothe them with the tunics, [9]gird them with the sashes, and tie the turbans on them.[s] Thus shall the priesthood be theirs by perpetual law, and thus shall you ordain Aaron and his sons.

Ordination Sacrifices. [10]"Now bring forward the bullock in front of the meeting tent. There Aaron and his sons shall lay their

---

28, 30: Urim and Thummim: both the meaning of these Hebrew words and the exact nature of the objects so designated are uncertain. They were apparently lots of some kind which were drawn or cast by the priest to ascertain God's decision in doubtful matters. Hence, the burse in which they were kept was called "the breastpiece of decision."

28, 41: Ordain them: literally, "fill their hands," a technical expression used solely for the installation of priests. The phrase probably originated in the custom of placing in the priests' hands the instruments or other symbols of the sacerdotal office.

m: Lv 8, 8; Sir 45, 11.   *n:* 31-35: Ex 39, 20ff; Lv 8, 9; Sir 45, 10.   *o:* Ex 39, 31; Lv 8, 9.   *p:* 39-43: Ex 39, 27ff.   *q:* Ez 44, 18.   *r:* 1-8: Lv 8, 1-9.   *s:* Lv 8, 13.   *t:* 10-26: Lv 8, 14-30.

hands on its head. [11]Then slaughter the bullock before the LORD, at the entrance of the meeting tent. [12]Take some of its blood and with your finger put it on the horns of the altar. All the rest of the blood you shall pour out at the base of the altar. [13]All the fat that covers its inner organs, as well as the lobe of its liver and its two kidneys, together with the fat that is on them, you shall take and burn on the altar. [14]But the flesh and hide and offal of the bullock you must burn up outside the camp, since this is a sin offering.[u]

[15]"Then take one of the rams, and after Aaron and his sons have laid their hands on its head, [16]slaughter it. The blood you shall take and splash on all the sides of the altar. [17]Cut the ram into pieces; its inner organs and shanks you shall first wash, and then put them with the pieces and with the head. [18]The entire ram shall then be burned on the altar, since it is a holocaust, a sweet-smelling oblation to the LORD.

[19]"After this take the other ram, and when Aaron and his sons have laid their hands on its head, [20]slaughter it. Some of its blood you shall take and put on the tip of Aaron's right ear and on the tips of his sons' right ears and on the thumbs of their right hands and the great toes of their right feet. Splash the rest of the blood on all the sides of the altar. [21]Then take some of the blood that is on the altar, together with some of the anointing oil, and sprinkle this on Aaron and his vestments, as well as on his sons and their vestments, that his sons and their vestments may be sacred.

[22]"Now, from this ram you shall take its fat: its fatty tail,[*] the fat that covers its inner organs, the lobe of its liver, its two kidneys with the fat that is on them, and its right thigh, since this is the ordination ram; [23]then, out of the basket of unleavened food that you have set before the LORD, you shall take one of the loaves of bread, one of the cakes made with oil, and one of the wafers.

[24]All these things you shall put into the hands of Aaron and his sons, so that they may wave them as a wave offering[*] before the LORD. [25]After you have received them back from their hands, you shall burn them on top of the holocaust on the altar as a sweet-smelling oblation to the LORD. [26]Finally, take the breast of Aaron's ordination ram and wave it as a wave offering before the LORD; this is to be your own portion.

[27]"Thus shall you set aside the breast of whatever wave offering is waved,[v] as well as the thigh of whatever raised offering is raised up, whether this be the ordination ram or anything else belonging to Aaron or to his sons. [28]Such things are due to Aaron and his sons from the Israelites by a perpetual ordinance as a contribution. From their peace offerings, too, the Israelites shall make a contribution, their contribution to the LORD.

[29]"The sacred vestments[w] of Aaron shall be passed down to his descendants, that in them they may be anointed and ordained. [30]The descendant who succeeds him as priest and who is to enter the meeting tent to minister in the sanctuary shall be clothed with them for seven days.

[31x]"You shall take the flesh of the ordination ram and boil it in a holy place. [32]At the entrance of the meeting tent Aaron and his sons shall eat the flesh of the ram and the bread that is in the basket. [33]They themselves are to eat of these things by which atonement was made at their ordination and consecration; but no layman may eat of them, since they are sacred. [34]If some of the flesh of the ordination sacrifice or some of the bread remains over on the next day, this remnant must be burned up; it is not to be eaten, since it is sacred. [35]Carry out all these orders in regard to Aaron and his sons just as I have given them to you.[y]

"Seven days you shall spend in ordaining them, [36z]sacrificing a bullock each day as a

---

29, 22: Fatty tail: the thick layer of fat surrounding the tails of sheep and rams bred in Palestine even today. It is regarded as a choice food. Cf Lv 3, 9.

29, 24-26: Wave offering: the portions of a peace offering, breast and right thigh, which the officiating priest moved to and fro (waved) in the presence of the Lord. They were reserved for Aaron and his sons.

29, 27-30: These verses are a parenthetical interruption of the ordination ritual; v 31 belongs logically immediately after v 26.

u: Heb 13, 11.   *v:* 27f: Lv 7, 31-34; 10, 14f; Nm 18, 18f; Dt 18, 3.   *w:* Nm 20, 26. 28.   *x:* 31-34: Lv 8, 31f.   *y:* Lv 8, 36. *z:* 36f: Lv 8, 33ff.

sin offering, to make atonement. Thus also shall you purge the altar* in making atonement for it; you shall anoint it in order to consecrate it. [37]Seven days you shall spend in making atonement for the altar and in consecrating it. Then the altar will be most sacred, and whatever touches it will become sacred.

[38]*"Now, this is what you shall offer on the altar: two yearling lambs[a] as the sacrifice established for each day; [39]one lamb in the morning and the other lamb at the evening twilight. [40]With the first lamb there shall be a tenth of an ephah of fine flour mixed with a fourth of a hin of oil of crushed olives and, as its libation, a fourth of a hin of wine. [41]The other lamb you shall offer at the evening twilight, with the same cereal offering and libation as in the morning. You shall offer this as a sweet-smelling oblation to the LORD. [42]Throughout your generations this established holocaust shall be offered before the LORD at the entrance of the meeting tent, where I will meet you and speak to you.

[43]"There, at the altar, I will meet the Israelites; hence, it will be made sacred by my glory.[b] [44]Thus I will consecrate the meeting tent and the altar, just as I also consecrate Aaron and his sons to be my priests. [45]I will dwell in the midst of the Israelites and will be their God. [46]They shall know that I, the LORD, am their God who brought them out of the land of Egypt, so that I, the LORD, their God, might dwell among them.

CHAPTER 30

See RG 70

Altar of Incense. [1]"For burning incense you shall make an altar of acacia wood,[c] [2]with a square surface, a cubit long, a cubit wide, and two cubits high, with horns that spring directly from it. [3]Its grate on top, its walls on all four sides, and its horns you shall plate with pure gold. Put a gold molding around it. [4]Underneath the molding you shall put gold rings, two on one side and two on the opposite side, as holders for the poles used in carrying it. [5]Make the poles, too, of acacia wood and plate them with gold. [6]This altar you are to place in front of the veil that hangs before the ark of the commandments where I will meet you.[d]

[7]"On it Aaron shall burn fragrant incense. Morning after morning, when he prepares the lamps, [8]and again in the evening twilight, when he lights the lamps, he shall burn incense. Throughout your generations this shall be the established incense offering before the LORD. [9]On this altar you shall not offer up any profane incense, or any holocaust or cereal offering; nor shall you pour out a libation upon it. [10]Once a year Aaron shall perform the atonement rite on its horns.[e] Throughout your generations this atonement is to be made once a year with the blood of the atoning sin offering. This altar is most sacred to the LORD."

Census Tax. [11]The LORD also said to Moses, [12]"When you take a census[f] of the Israelites who are to be registered, each one, as he is enrolled, shall give the LORD a forfeit for his life, so that no plague may come upon them for being registered. [13]Everyone who enters the registered group must pay a half-shekel, according to the standard of the sanctuary shekel, twenty gerahs to the shekel. This payment of a half-shekel is a contribution to the LORD.[g] [14]Everyone of twenty years or more who enters the registered group must give this contribution to the LORD. [15]The rich need not give more, nor shall the poor give less, than a half-shekel in this contribution to the LORD to pay the forfeit for their lives. [16h]When you receive this forfeit money from the Israelites, you shall donate it to the service of the meeting tent, that there it may be the Israelites' reminder, before the LORD, of the forfeit paid for their lives."

The Laver. [17]The LORD said to Moses, [18]"For ablutions you shall make a bronze laver with a bronze base. Place it between the meeting tent and the altar, and put water in it.[i] [19]Aaron and his sons shall use it in washing

---

29, 36f: Purge the altar: the construction of an altar by profane hands rendered it impure. The anointing and consecration of the altar purified it and made it sacred.

29, 38-42: A parenthesis inserted into the rubrics for consecrating the altar; v 43 belongs directly after v 37.

a: 38-42: Nm 28, 3-8.   b: Ex 25, 22.   c: 1-5: Ex 37, 25-28.   d: Ex 40, 26.   e: Lv 16, 18.   f: Nm 1, 2f; 26, 2.   g: Mt 17, 24-27.   h: Ex 38, 25.   i: Ex 38, 8; 40, 7. 30.

their hands and feet.[j] [20]When they are about to enter the meeting tent, they must wash with water, lest they die. Likewise when they approach the altar in their ministry, to offer an oblation to the LORD, [21]they must wash their hands and feet, lest they die. This shall be a perpetual ordinance for him and his descendants throughout their generations."

The Anointing Oil. [22]The LORD said to Moses, [23]"Take the finest spices: five hundred shekels of free-flowing myrrh; half that amount, that is, two hundred and fifty shekels, of fragrant cinnamon; two hundred and fifty shekels of fragrant cane; [24]five hundred shekels of cassia—all according to the standard of the sanctuary shekel; together with a hin of olive oil; [25]and blend them into sacred anointing oil,[k] perfumed ointment expertly prepared. [26]With this sacred anointing oil you shall anoint the meeting tent and the ark of the commandments, [27]the table and all its appurtenances, the lampstand and its appurtenances, the altar of incense [28]and the altar of holocausts with all its appurtenances, and the laver with its base. [29]When you have consecrated them, they shall be most sacred; whatever touches them shall be sacred. [30]Aaron and his sons you shall also anoint and consecrate as my priests.[m] [31]To the Israelites you shall say: As sacred anointing oil this shall belong to me throughout your generations. [32]It may not be used in any ordinary anointing of the body, nor may you make any other oil of a like mixture. It is sacred, and shall be treated as sacred by you. [33]Whoever prepares a perfume like this, or whoever puts any of this on a layman, shall be cut off from his kinsmen."

The Incense. [34n]The LORD told Moses, "Take these aromatic substances: storax and onycha and galbanum, these and pure frankincense in equal parts; [35]and blend them into incense. This fragrant powder, expertly prepared, is to be salted and so kept pure and sacred. [36]Grind some of it into fine dust and put this before the commandments in the meeting tent where I will meet you. This incense

shall be treated as most sacred by you. [37]You may not make incense of a like mixture for yourselves; you must treat it as sacred to the LORD. [38]Whoever makes an incense like this for his own enjoyment of its fragrance, shall be cut off from his kinsmen."

CHAPTER 31

See RG 70

Choice of Artisans. [1o]The LORD said to Moses, [2]"See, I have chosen Bezalel, son of Uri, son of Hur, of the tribe of Judah, [3]and I have filled him with a divine spirit of skill and understanding and knowledge in every craft: [4]in the production of embroidery, in making things of gold, silver or bronze, [5]in cutting and mounting precious stones, in carving wood, and in every other craft. [6]As his assistant I have appointed Oholiab, son of Ahisamach, of the tribe of Dan. I have also endowed all the experts with the necessary skill to make all the things I have ordered you to make: [7p]the meeting tent, the ark of the commandments with the propitiatory on top of it, all the furnishings of the tent, [8]the table with its appurtenances, the pure gold lampstand with all its appurtenances, the altar of incense, [9]the altar of holocausts with all its appurtenances, the laver with its base, [10]the service cloths,* the sacred vestments for Aaron the priest, the vestments for his sons in their ministry, [11]the anointing oil, and the fragrant incense for the sanctuary. All these things they shall make just as I have commanded you."

Sabbath Laws. [12q]The LORD said to Moses, [13]"You must also tell the Israelites: Take care to keep my sabbaths, for that is to be the token between you and me throughout the generations, to show that it is I, the LORD, who make you holy. [14]Therefore, you must keep the sabbath as something sacred. Whoever desecrates it shall be put to death. If anyone does work on that day, he must be rooted out of his people. [15]Six days there are for doing work, but the seventh day is the sabbath of complete rest, sacred to the LORD. Anyone who does work on the sabbath day shall be put to death. [16]So shall the Israelites

---

31, 10: The service cloths: so the Greek. They were perhaps the colored cloths mentioned in Nm 4, 4-15.

j: 19ff: Ex 40, 31f.   k: Ex 37, 29.   l: 26-29: Ex 40, 9ff; Lv 8, 10; Nm 7, 1.   m: Ex 29, 7; Lv 8, 12.   n: 34ff: Ex 25, 6; 37, 29.   o: 1-6: Ex 35, 30-35.   p: 7-11: Ex 35, 10-19.   q: 12-17: Ex 20, 8-11; 35, 1-3.

observe the sabbath, keeping it throughout their generations as a perpetual covenant. [17]Between me and the Israelites it is to be an everlasting token; for in six days the LORD made the heavens and the earth, but on the seventh day he rested at his ease."

[18]When the LORD had finished speaking to Moses on Mount Sinai, he gave him the two tablets of the commandments, the stone tablets inscribed by God's own finger.[r]

See RG 70

CHAPTER 32

The Golden Calf. [1]When the people became aware of Moses' delay in coming down from the mountain, they gathered around Aaron and said to him, "Come, make us a god who will be our leader; as for the man Moses who brought us out of the land of Egypt, we do not know what has happened to him."[s] [2]Aaron replied, "Have your wives and sons and daughters take off the golden earrings they are wearing, and bring them to me." [3]So all the people took off their earrings and brought them to Aaron, [4]who accepted their offering, and fashioning this gold with a graving tool, made a molten calf. Then they cried out, "This is your God, O Israel, who brought you out of the land of Egypt."[t] [5]On seeing this, Aaron built an altar before the calf and proclaimed, "Tomorrow is a feast of the LORD."[*] [6]Early the next day the people offered holocausts and brought peace offerings. Then they sat down to eat and drink, and rose up to revel.[u]

[7]With that, the LORD said to Moses, "Go down at once to your people, whom you brought out of the land of Egypt, for they have become depraved. [8v]They have soon turned aside from the way I pointed out to them, making for themselves a molten calf and worshiping it, sacrificing to it and crying out, 'This is your God, O Israel, who brought you out of the land of Egypt!' [9]I see how stiff-necked this people is,"[w] continued the LORD to Moses. [10]"Let me alone, then, that my wrath may blaze up against them to consume them. Then I will make of you a great nation."

[11]But Moses implored the LORD, his God, saying,[x] "Why, O LORD, should your wrath blaze up against your own people, whom you brought out of the land of Egypt with such great power and with so strong a hand? [12]Why should the Egyptians say, 'With evil intent he brought them out, that he might kill them in the mountains and exterminate them from the face of the earth'? Let your blazing wrath die down; relent in punishing your people. [13]Remember your servants Abraham, Isaac and Israel, and how you swore to them by your own self, saying,[y] 'I will make your descendants as numerous as the stars in the sky; and all this land that I promised, I will give your descendants as their perpetual heritage.' " [14]So the LORD relented in the punishment he had threatened to inflict on his people.

[15]Moses then turned and came down the mountain with the two tablets of the commandments in his hands,[z] tablets that were written on both sides, front and back; [16]tablets that were made by God, having inscriptions on them that were engraved by God himself.[a] [17]Now, when Joshua heard the noise of the people shouting, he said to Moses, "That sounds like a battle in the camp." [18]But Moses answered, "It does not sound like cries of victory, nor does it sound like cries of defeat; the sounds that I hear are cries of revelry." [19]As he drew near the camp, he saw the calf and the dancing. With that, Moses' wrath flared up, so that he threw the tablets down and broke them on the base of the mountain.[b] [20]Taking the calf they had made, he fused it in the fire and then ground it down to powder, which he scattered on the water[*] and made the Israelites drink.[c]

[21]Moses asked Aaron, "What did this people ever do to you that you should lead them

---

32, 5: The calf . . . a feast of the LORD: from this it is clear that the golden calf was intended as an image, not of a false god, but of the Lord himself, his strength being symbolized by the strength of a young bull. The Israelites, however, had been forbidden to represent the Lord under any visible form. Cf Ex 20, 4.

32, 20: The water: the stream that flowed down Mount Sinai. Cf Dt 9, 21.

r: Ex 24, 12; 32, 15f; Dt 5, 22. s: Ex 32, 23; Acts 7, 40. t: Ex 32, 8; 1 Kgs 12, 28. u: 1 Cor 10, 7. v: 7f; Dt 9, 12. 16. w: 9f: Dt 9, 13; Ps 106, 23. x: 11f: Nm 14, 13ff; Dt 9, 28. y: Gn 22, 16f. z: Dt 9, 15. a: Ex 31, 18. b: Dt 9, 16f. c: Dt 9, 21.

into so grave a sin?" Aaron replied, "Let not my lord be angry. *22* You know well enough how prone the people are to evil. *23* They said to me, 'Make us a god to be our leader; as for the man Moses who brought us out of the land of Egypt, we do not know what has happened to him.' *24* So I told them, 'Let anyone who has gold jewelry take it off.' They gave it to me, and I threw it into the fire, and this calf came out."

25 When Moses realized that, to the scornful joy of their foes, Aaron had let the people run wild, *26* he stood at the gate of the camp and cried, "Whoever is for the LORD, let him come to me!" All the Levites*d* then rallied to him, *27* and he told them, "Thus says the LORD, the God of Israel: Put your sword on your hip, every one of you! Now go up and down the camp, from gate to gate, and slay your own kinsmen,* your friends and neighbors!" *28* The Levites carried out the command of Moses, and that day there fell about three thousand of the people. *29* Then Moses said, "Today you have been dedicated to the LORD,* for you were against your own sons and kinsmen, to bring a blessing upon yourselves this day."

The Atonement. *30* On the next day Moses said to the people,*e* "You have committed a grave sin. I will go up to the LORD, then; perhaps I may be able to make atonement for your sin." *31* So Moses went back to the LORD and said, "Ah, this people has indeed committed a grave sin in making a god of gold for themselves! *32* If you would only forgive their sin! If you will not, then strike me out of the book that you have written."* *33* The LORD answered, "Him only who has sinned against me will I strike out of my book. *34* Now, go and lead the people whither I have told you. My angel will go before you. When it is time for me to punish, I will punish them for their sin."

35 Thus the LORD smote the people for having had Aaron make the calf for them.

CHAPTER 33

See RG 70

1 The LORD told Moses, "You and the people whom you have brought up from the land of Egypt, are to go up from here to the land which I swore to Abraham, Isaac and Jacob I would give to their descendants.*f* *2* Driving out the Canaanites, Amorites, Hittites, Perizzites, Hivites and Jebusites, I will send an angel before you*g* *3* to the land flowing with milk and honey. But I myself will not go up in your company, because you are a stiff-necked people; otherwise I might exterminate you on the way." *4* When the people heard this bad news, they went into mourning, and no one wore his ornaments.

5 The LORD said to Moses, "Tell the Israelites: You are a stiff-necked people. Were I to go up in your company even for a moment, I would exterminate you. Take off your ornaments, therefore; I will then see what I am to do with you." *6* So, from Mount Horeb onward, the Israelites laid aside their ornaments.

Moses' Intimacy with God. *7* The tent,*h* which was called the meeting tent,* Moses used to pitch at some distance away, outside the camp. Anyone who wished to consult the LORD would go to this meeting tent outside the camp. *8* Whenever Moses went out to the tent, the people would all rise and stand at the entrance of their own tents, watching Moses until he entered the tent. *9* As Moses entered the tent, the column of cloud would come down and stand at its entrance while the LORD spoke with Moses. *10* On seeing the column of cloud stand at the entrance of the tent, all the people would rise and worship at the entrance of their own tents. *11* The LORD used to speak to Moses face to face,*i* as one man speaks to another. Moses would then

---

32, 27: Slay your own kinsmen: those who were especially guilty of the idolatry.

32, 29: Dedicated to the LORD: because of their zeal for the true worship of the Lord, the Levites were chosen to be special ministers of the ritual service. However, the meaning of the Hebrew here is somewhat disputed.

32, 32: The book that you have written: the list of God's intimate friends. In a similar sense St. Paul wished to be anathema from Christ for the sake of his brethren. Cf Rom 9, 3.

33, 7-11: The meeting tent is mentioned here by anticipation; its actual construction is described in the following chapters.

d: 26-29: Dt 33, 8f.   *e:* 30-34: Dt 9, 18ff.   *f:* Gn 12, 7.   *g:* Ex 23, 23.   *h:* Ex 29, 42f.   *i:* Nm 12, 8; Dt 34, 10; Sir 45, 4-6.

return to the camp, but his young assistant, Joshua, son of Nun, would not move out of the tent.

¹²Moses said to the LORD, "You, indeed, are telling me to lead this people on;ʲ but you have not let me know whom you will send with me. Yet you have said, 'You are my intimate friend,' and also, 'You have found favor with me.' ¹³Now, if I have found favor with you, do let me know your ways so that, in knowing you, I may continue to find favor with you. Then, too, this nation is, after all, your own people." ¹⁴"I myself,"* the LORD answered, "will go along, to give you rest." ¹⁵Moses replied, "If you are not going yourself, do not make us go up from here. ¹⁶For how can it be known that we, your people and I, have found favor with you, except by your going with us? Then we, your people and I, will be singled out from every other people on the earth." ¹⁷The LORD said to Moses, "This request, too, which you have just made, I will carry out, because you have found favor with me and you are my intimate friend."

¹⁸Then Moses said, "Do let me see your glory!" ¹⁹He answered, "I will make all my beauty pass before you, and in your presence I will pronounce my name, 'LORD'; I who show favors to whom I will, I who grant mercy to whom I will.ᵏ ²⁰But my face you cannot see,ˡ for no man sees me and still lives. ²¹Here," continued the LORD, "is a place near me where you shall station yourself on the rock. ²²When my glory passes I will set you in the hollow of the rock and will cover you with my hand until I have passed by. ²³Then I will remove my hand, so that you may see my back;* but my face is not to be seen."

CHAPTER 34

See RG 70

Renewal of the Tablets. ¹The LORD said to Moses, "Cut two stone tablets like the former,ᵐ that I may write on them the commandments which were on the former tablets that you broke. ²Get ready for tomorrow morning, when you are to go up Mount Sinai and there present yourself to me on the top of the mountain. ³No one shall come up with you, and no one is even to be seen on any part of the mountain;ⁿ even the flocks and the herds are not to go grazing toward this mountain." ⁴Moses then cut two stone tablets like the former, and early the next morning he went up Mount Sinai as the LORD had commanded him, taking along the two stone tablets.

⁵Having come down in a cloud, the LORD stood with him there and proclaimed his name, "LORD." ⁶Thus the LORD passed before him and cried out, "The LORD, the LORD, a merciful and gracious God, slow to anger and rich in kindness and fidelity, ⁷continuing his kindness for a thousand generations, and forgiving wickedness and crime and sin; yet not declaring the guilty guiltless, but punishing children and grandchildren to the third and fourth generation for their fathers' wickedness!"ᵒ ⁸Moses at once bowed down to the ground in worship. ⁹Then he said, "If I find favor with you, O LORD, do come along in our company. This is indeed a stiff-necked people; yet pardon our wickedness and sins, and receive us as your own."

Religious Laws. ¹⁰"Here, then," said the LORD, "is the covenant I will make. Before the eyes of all your people I will work such marvels as have never been wrought in any nation anywhere on earth, so that this people among whom you live may see how awe-inspiring are the deeds which I, the LORD, will do at your side. ¹¹But you, on your part, must keep the commandments I am giving you today.ᵖ

"I will drive out before you the Amorites, Canaanites, Hittites, Perizzites, Hivites, and Jebusites. ¹²�q Take care, therefore, not to make a covenant with these inhabitants of the land that you are to enter; else they will

---

33, 14: I myself: literally, "my face," that is, "my presence." To give you rest: in the Promised Land; some understand, "to put your mind at rest"; others, by a slight emendation in the text, render, "to lead you."

33, 23: You may see my back: man can see God's glory as reflected in creation, but his "face," that is, God as he is in himself, mortal man cannot behold. Cf 1 Cor 13, 12.

j: Ex 32, 34. k: Rom 9, 15. l: Jn 1, 18; 1 Tm 6, 16. m: Dt 10, 1f. n: Ex 19, 12f. 21. o: 6f: Ex 20, 5f; Nm 14, 18; Dt 5, 9f; Jer 32, 18. p: Ex 13, 5; 33, 2. q: 12-16: Ex 23, 32f; Dt 7, 1-5; 12, 2f.

Accenting God's Mercy over God's Judgment

Israel's worship of the golden calf (32, 8) broke the covenant with God. The new covenant between God and Israel revealed a deeper aspect of God's character: God's mercy and compassion. This deeper revelation is evident when we compare the description of God's character in Exodus 20, 5–6 with that in Exodus 34, 6–7:

> For I, the LORD, your God, am a jealous God, inflicting punishment for their fathers' wickedness on the children of those who hate me, down to the third and fourth generation; but bestowing mercy down to the thousandth generation, on the children of those who love me and keep my commandments. (20, 5–6)

> The LORD, the LORD, a merciful and gracious God, slow to anger and rich in kindness and fidelity, continuing his kindness for a thousand generations, and forgiving wickedness and crime and sin; yet not declaring the guilty guiltless, but punishing children and grandchildren to the third and fourth generation for their fathers' wickedness! (34, 6–7)

We can see a number of differences between these two similar texts. The excerpt from ch 20 emphasizes God's punishment as the first element of God's character, whereas the excerpt from ch 34 puts this aspect in second place. The kindness and mercy of God, in second place in ch 20, moves to the front in ch 34. Chapter 34 also expands the description of God's compassionate nature: slow to anger, rich in kindness and fidelity. The condition that God loves "those who love" God in ch 20 is removed in ch 34, where also God forgives wickedness.

Variations of this important description of God's nature occur elsewhere: Nm 14, 18; Neh 9, 17; Ps 103, 8; Jl 2, 13; Jon 4, 2. Because it appears in so many places, this description seems to have been a creed or confession of faith in God for the ancient Israelites.

become a snare among you. [13]Tear down their altars; smash their sacred pillars, and cut down their sacred poles.* [14]You shall not worship any other god, for the LORD is 'the Jealous One';* a jealous God is he. [15]Do not make a covenant with the inhabitants of that land; else, when they render their wanton worship to their gods and sacrifice to them, one of them may invite you and you may partake of his sacrifice. [16]Neither shall you take their daughters as wives for your sons; otherwise, when their daughters render their wanton worship to their gods, they will make your sons do the same.

[17]"You shall not make for yourselves molten gods.[r]

[18]"You shall keep the feast of Unleavened Bread.[s] For seven days at the prescribed time in the month of Abib you are to eat unleavened bread, as I commanded you; for in the month of Abib you came out of Egypt.

[19]"To me belongs every first-born male that opens the womb among all your livestock, whether in the herd or in the flock.[t] [20]The firstling of an ass you shall redeem with one of the flock; if you do not redeem it, you must break its neck. The first-born among your sons you shall redeem.

"No one shall appear before me empty-handed.

[21]"For six days you may work,[u] but on the seventh day you shall rest; on that day you must rest even during the seasons of plowing and harvesting.

[22]"You shall keep the feast of Weeks* with the first of the wheat harvest; likewise,

---

34, 13: Sacred poles: "Ashera" was the name of a Canaanite goddess. In her honor wooden poles (asheroth) were erected, just as stone pillars (massebot) were erected in honor of the god Baal. Both were placed near the altar in a Canaanite shrine.

34, 14: The LORD is 'the Jealous One': see note on Ex 20,

5. Some, by a slight emendation, render, "The LORD is jealous for his name." Cf Ez 39, 25.

34, 22: Feast of Weeks: the festival of thanksgiving for

r: Lv 19, 4; Dt 5, 8f.   *s:* Ex 12, 15ff; 13, 3f.   *t:* 19f: Ex 13. 2. 12f; 23, 15.   *u:* Ex 20, 9f.   *v:* 22f: Ex 23, 16f; Dt 16, 10. 13. 16.

the feast at the fruit harvest at the close of the year. [23]Three times a year all your men shall appear before the Lord, the LORD God of Israel. [24]Since I will drive out the nations before you to give you a large territory, there will be no one to covet your land when you go up three times a year to appear before the LORD, your God.

[25]"You shall not offer me the blood of sacrifice with leavened bread, nor shall the sacrifice of the Passover feast be kept overnight for the next day.

[26]"The choicest first fruits of your soil you shall bring to the house of the LORD, your God.

"You shall not boil a kid in its mother's milk."[w]

Radiance of Moses' Face. [27]Then the LORD said to Moses, "Write down these words, for in accordance with them I have made a covenant with you and with Israel." [28]So Moses stayed there with the LORD for forty days and forty nights,[x] without eating any food or drinking any water, and he wrote on the tablets the words of the covenant, the ten commandments.

[29]As Moses came down from Mount Sinai with the two tablets of the commandments in his hands, he did not know that the skin of his face had become radiant while he conversed with the LORD. [30]When Aaron, then, and the other Israelites saw Moses and noticed how radiant the skin of his face had become, they were afraid to come near him. [31]Only after Moses called to them did Aaron and all the rulers of the community come back to him. Moses then spoke to them. [32]Later on, all the Israelites came up to him, and he enjoined on them all that the LORD had told him on Mount Sinai. [33]When he finished speaking with them, he put a veil over his face.[*] [34]Whenever Moses entered the presence of the LORD to converse with him,

he removed the veil until he came out again.[y] On coming out, he would tell the Israelites all that had been commanded. [35]Then the Israelites would see that the skin of Moses' face was radiant; so he would again put the veil over his face until he went in to converse with the LORD.

CHAPTER 35

See RG 70

Sabbath Regulations. [1]Moses assembled the whole Israelite community and said to them,[z] "This is what the LORD has commanded to be done. [2]On six days work may be done, but the seventh day shall be sacred to you as the sabbath of complete rest to the LORD. Anyone who does work on that day shall be put to death. [3]You shall not even light a fire in any of your dwellings on the sabbath day."

Collection of Materials. [4]Moses told the whole Israelite community, "This is what the LORD has commanded: [5a]Take up among you a collection for the LORD. Everyone, as his heart prompts him, shall bring, as a contribution to the LORD, gold, silver and bronze; [6]violet, purple and scarlet yarn; fine linen and goat hair; [7]rams' skins dyed red, and tahash skins; acacia wood; [8]oil for the light; spices for the anointing oil and for the fragrant incense; [9]onyx stones and other gems for mounting on the ephod and on the breastpiece.

Call for Artisans. [10b]"Let every expert among you come and make all that the LORD has commanded: [11]the Dwelling, with its tent, its covering, its clasps, its boards, its bars, its columns and its pedestals; [12]the ark, with its poles, the propitiatory, and the curtain veil; [13]the table, with its poles and all its appurtenances, and the showbread; [14]the lampstand, with its appurtenances, the lamps, and the oil for the light; [15]the altar of incense, with its poles; the anointing oil, and

---

the harvest, celebrated seven weeks or fifty days after the beginning of the harvest. It was also called Pentecost (fiftieth) and coincided with the giving of the law on Mount Sinai, fifty days after the offering of the first fruits; cf Lv 23, 10f; Dt 16, 9.

34, 33: He put a veil over his face: St. Paul sees in this a symbol of the failure of the Jews to recognize Jesus as the promised Messiah. The true spiritual meaning of the writings

of Moses and the prophets is still veiled from the unbelieving Jews. Cf 2 Cor 3, 7-18.

w: 25f: Ex 23, 18f. *x:* Ex 24, 18; Dt 9, 9. 18; 10, 2. 4. *y:* 33f: 2 Cor 3, 13. 16. *z:* 1-3: Ex 31, 13-17. *a:* 5-9: Ex 25, 2-7. *b:* 10-19: Ex 31, 6-11.

the fragrant incense; the entrance curtain for the entrance of the Dwelling; [16]the altar of holocausts, with its bronze grating, its poles, and all its appurtenances; the laver, with its base; [17]the hangings of the court, with their columns and pedestals; the curtain for the entrance of the court; [18]the tent pegs for the Dwelling and for the court, with their ropes; [19]the service cloths for use in the sanctuary; the sacred vestments for Aaron, the priest, and the vestments worn by his sons in their ministry."

The Contribution. [20]When the whole Israelite community left Moses' presence, [21]everyone, as his heart suggested and his spirit prompted, brought a contribution to the LORD for the construction of the meeting tent, for all its services, and for the sacred vestments. [22]Both the men and the women, all as their hearts prompted them, brought brooches, earrings, rings, necklaces and various other gold articles.[c] Everyone who could presented an offering of gold to the LORD. [23]Everyone who happened to have violet, purple or scarlet yarn, fine linen or goat hair, rams' skins dyed red or tahash skins, brought them. [24]Whoever could make a contribution of silver or bronze offered it to the LORD; and everyone who happened to have acacia wood for any part of the work, brought it. [25]All the women who were expert spinners brought hand-spun violet, purple and scarlet yarn and fine linen thread. [26]All the women who possessed the skill, spun goat hair. [27]The princes brought onyx stones and other gems for mounting on the ephod and on the breastpiece; [28]as well as spices, and oil for the light, anointing oil, and fragrant incense. [29]Every Israelite man and woman brought to the LORD such voluntary offerings as they thought best, for the various kinds of work which the LORD had commanded Moses to have done.

The Artisans. [30]Moses said to the Israelites,[d] "See, the LORD has chosen Bezalel, son of Uri, son of Hur, of the tribe of Judah, [31]and has filled him with a divine spirit of skill and understanding and knowledge in every craft: [32]in the production of embroidery, in making things of gold, silver or bronze, [33]in cutting and mounting precious stones, in carving wood, and in every other craft. [34]He has also given both him and Oholiab, son of Ahisamach, of the tribe of Dan, the ability to teach others. [35]He has endowed them with skill to execute all types of work: engraving, embroidering, the making of variegated cloth of violet, purple and scarlet yarn and fine linen thread, weaving, and all other arts and crafts.

CHAPTER 36

See RG 70

[1]"Bezalel, therefore, will set to work with Oholiab and with all the experts whom the LORD has endowed with skill and understanding in knowing how to execute all the work for the service of the sanctuary, just as the LORD has commanded."[e]

[2]Moses then called Bezalel and Oholiab and all the other experts whom the LORD had endowed with skill, men whose hearts moved them to come and take part in the work. [3]They received from Moses all the contributions which the Israelites had brought for establishing the service of the sanctuary. Still, morning after morning the people continued to bring their voluntary offerings to Moses. [4]Thereupon the experts who were executing the various kinds of work for the sanctuary, all left the work they were doing, [5]and told Moses, "The people are bringing much more than is needed to carry out the work which the LORD has commanded us to do." [6]Moses, therefore, ordered a proclamation to be made throughout the camp: "Let neither man nor woman make any more contributions for the sanctuary." So the people stopped bringing their offerings; [7]there was already enough at hand, in fact, more than enough, to complete the work to be done.

The Tent Cloth and Coverings. [8f]The various experts who were executing the work, made the Dwelling with its ten sheets woven of fine linen twined, having cherubim embroidered on them with violet, purple and scarlet yarn. [9]The length of each sheet was

c: 22-28: Ex 25, 3-7.   d: 30-35: Ex 31, 1-6.   e: 1f: Ex 31, 1. 6.   f: 8-19: Ex 26, 1-14.

twenty-eight cubits, and the width four cubits; all the sheets were of the same size. [10]Five of the sheets were sewed together, edge to edge; and the same for the other five. [11]Loops of violet yarn were made along the edge of the end sheet in the first set, and the same along the edge of the end sheet in the second set. [12]Fifty loops were thus put on one inner sheet, and fifty loops on the inner sheet in the other set, with the loops directly opposite each other. [13]Then fifty clasps of gold were made, with which the sheets were joined so that the Dwelling formed one whole.

[14]Sheets of goat hair were also woven as a tent over the Dwelling. Eleven such sheets were made. [15]The length of each sheet was thirty cubits and the width four cubits; all eleven sheets were of the same size. [16]Five of these sheets were sewed edge to edge into one set; and the other six sheets into another set. [17]Fifty loops were made along the edge of the end sheet in one set, and fifty loops along the edge of the corresponding sheet in the other set. [18]Fifty bronze clasps were made with which the tent was joined so that it formed one whole. [19]A covering for the tent was made of rams' skins dyed red, and above that, a covering of tahash skins.

The Boards. [20g]Boards of acacia wood were made as walls for the Dwelling. [21]The length of each board was ten cubits, and the width one and a half cubits. [22]Each board had two arms, fastening them in line. In this way all the boards of the Dwelling were made. [23]They were set up as follows: twenty boards on the south side, [24]with forty silver pedestals under the twenty boards, so that there were two pedestals under each board, at its two arms; [25]twenty boards on the other side of the Dwelling, the north side, [26]with their forty silver pedestals, two under each board; [27]six boards at the rear of the Dwelling, to the west; [28]and two boards at the corners in the rear of the Dwelling. [29]These were double at the bottom, and likewise double at the top, to the first ring. That is how both boards in the corners were made. [30]Thus, there were in the rear eight boards, with their sixteen silver pedestals,

two pedestals under each board. [31]Bars of acacia wood were also made, five for the boards on one side of the Dwelling, [32]five for those on the other side, and five for those at the rear, to the west. [33]The center bar, at the middle of the boards, was made to reach across from end to end. [34]The boards were plated with gold, and gold rings were made on them as holders for the bars, which were also plated with gold.

The Veil. [35h]The veil was woven of violet, purple and scarlet yarn, and of fine linen twined, with cherubim embroidered on it. [36]Four gold-plated columns of acacia wood, with gold hooks, were made for it, and four silver pedestals were cast for them.

[37]The curtain for the entrance of the tent was made of violet, purple and scarlet yarn, and of fine linen twined, woven in a variegated manner. [38]Its five columns, with their hooks as well as their capitals and bands, were plated with gold; their five pedestals were of bronze.

CHAPTER 37

See RG 70

The Ark. [1]Bezalel made the ark of acacia wood, two and a half cubits long, one and a half cubits wide, and one and a half cubits high. [2]The inside and outside were plated with gold, and a molding of gold was put around it. [3]Four gold rings were cast and put on its four supports, two rings for one side and two for the opposite side. [4]Poles of acacia wood were made and plated with gold; [5]these were put through the rings on the sides of the ark, for carrying it.

[6]The propitiatory was made of pure gold, two and a half cubits long and one and a half cubits wide. [7]Two cherubim of beaten gold were made for the two ends of the propitiatory, [8]one cherub fastened at one end, the other at the other end, springing directly from the propitiatory at its two ends. [9]The cherubim had their wings spread out above, covering the propitiatory with them. They were turned toward each other, but with their faces looking toward the propitiatory.[i]

The Table. [10j]The table was made of acacia wood, two cubits long, one cubit wide,

g: 20-34: Ex 26, 15-29.   h: 35-38: Ex 26, 31-37.   i: 1-9: Ex 25, 10-22.   j: 10-16: Ex 25, 23-30.

and one and a half cubits high. [11]It was plated with pure gold, and a molding of gold was put around it. [12]A frame a handbreadth high was also put around it, with a molding of gold around the frame. [13]Four rings of gold were cast for it and fastened, one at each of the four corners. [14]The rings were alongside the frame as holders for the poles to carry the table. [15]These poles were made of acacia wood and plated with gold. [16]The vessels that were set on the table, its plates and cups, as well as its pitchers and bowls for pouring libations, were of pure gold.

The Lampstand. [17k]The lampstand was made of pure beaten gold—its shaft and branches as well as its cups and knobs and petals springing directly from it. [18]Six branches extended from its sides, three branches on one side and three on the other. [19]On one branch there were three cups, shaped like almond blossoms, each with its knob and petals; on the opposite branch there were three cups, shaped like almond blossoms, each with its knob and petals; and so for the six branches that extended from the lampstand. [20]On the shaft there were four cups, shaped like almond blossoms, with their knobs and petals, [21]including a knob below each of the three pairs of branches that extended from the lampstand. [22]The knobs and branches sprang so directly from it that the whole formed but a single piece of pure beaten gold. [23]Its seven lamps, as well as its trimming shears and trays, were made of pure gold. [24]A talent of pure gold was used for the lampstand and its various appurtenances.

The Altar of Incense. [25l]The altar of incense was made of acacia wood, on a square, a cubit long, a cubit wide, and two cubits high, having horns that sprang directly from it. [26]Its grate on top, its walls on all four sides, and its horns were plated with pure gold; and a molding of gold was put around it. [27]Underneath the molding gold rings were placed, two on one side and two on the opposite side, as holders for the poles to carry

it. [28]The poles, too, were made of acacia wood and plated with gold.

[29]The sacred anointing oil and the fragrant incense were prepared in their pure form by a perfumer.[m]

CHAPTER 38

See RG 70

The Altar of Holocausts. [1]The altar of holocausts[n] was made of acacia wood, on a square, five cubits long and five cubits wide; its height was three cubits. [2]At the four corners horns were made that sprang directly from the altar. The whole was plated with bronze. [3]All the utensils of the altar, the pots, shovels, basins, forks and fire pans, were likewise made of bronze. [4]A grating of bronze network was made for the altar and placed round it, on the ground, half as high as the altar itself. [5]Four rings were cast for the four corners of the bronze grating, as holders for the poles, [6]which were made of acacia wood and plated with bronze. [7]The poles were put through the rings on the sides of the altar for carrying it. The altar was made in the form of a hollow box.

[8]The bronze laver,[o] with its bronze base, was made from the mirrors of the women who served* at the entrance of the meeting tent.

The Court. [9p]The court was made as follows. On the south side of the court there were hangings, woven of fine linen twined, a hundred cubits long, [10]with twenty columns and twenty pedestals of bronze, the hooks and bands of the columns being of silver. [11]On the north side there were similar hangings, one hundred cubits long, with twenty columns and twenty pedestals of bronze, the hooks and bands of the columns being of silver. [12]On the west side there were hangings, fifty cubits long, with ten columns and ten pedestals, the hooks and bands of the columns being of silver. [13]On the east side the court was fifty cubits long. [14]Toward one side there were hangings to the extent of fifteen cubits, with three columns and three pedestals; [15]toward the

---

38, 8: The reflecting surface of ancient mirrors was usually of polished bronze. The women who served: cf 1 Sm 2. 22.

k: 17-24: Ex 25, 31-39. l: 25-28: Ex 30, 1-5. m: Ex 30, 23ff. 34ff. n: 1-7: Ex 27, 1-8; 2 Chr 1, 5. o: Ex 30, 18-21. p: 9-20: Ex 27, 9-19.

other side, beyond the entrance of the court, there were likewise hangings to the extent of fifteen cubits, with three columns and three pedestals. [16]The hangings on all sides of the court were woven of fine linen twined. [17]The pedestals of the columns were of bronze, while the hooks and bands of the columns were of silver; the capitals were silver-plated, and all the columns of the court were banded with silver.

[18]At the entrance of the court there was a variegated curtain, woven of violet, purple and scarlet yarn and of fine linen twined, twenty cubits long and five cubits wide, in keeping with the hangings of the court. [19]There were four columns and four pedestals of bronze for it, while their hooks were of silver. [20]All the tent pegs for the Dwelling and for the court around it were of bronze.

Amount of Metal Used. [21]The following is an account of the various amounts used on the Dwelling, the Dwelling of the commandments, drawn up at the command of Moses by the Levites under the direction of Ithamar, son of Aaron the priest. [22]However, it was Bezalel, son of Uri,[q] son of Hur, of the tribe of Judah, who made all that the Lord commanded Moses, [23]and he was assisted by Oholiab, son of Ahisamach, of the tribe of Dan, who was an engraver, an embroiderer, and a weaver of variegated cloth of violet, purple and scarlet yarn and of fine linen.

[24]All the gold used in the entire construction of the sanctuary, having previously been given as an offering, amounted to twenty-nine talents and seven hundred and thirty shekels, according to the standard of the sanctuary shekel. [25]The amount of the silver received from the community was one hundred talents and one thousand seven hundred and seventy-five shekels, according to the standard of the sanctuary shekel; [26]one bekah apiece, that is, a half-shekel apiece, according to the standard of the sanctuary shekel, was received from every man of twenty years or more who entered the registered group; the number of these was six hundred and three thousand five hundred and fifty men.[r] [27]One

hundred talents of silver were used for casting the pedestals of the sanctuary and the pedestals of the veil, one talent for each pedestal, or one hundred talents for the one hundred pedestals. [28]The remaining one thousand seven hundred and seventy-five shekels were used for making the hooks on the columns, for plating the capitals, and for banding them with silver. [29]The bronze, given as an offering, amounted to seventy talents and two thousand four hundred shekels. [30]With this were made the pedestals at the entrance of the meeting tent, the bronze altar with its bronze gratings and all the appurtenances of the altar, [31]the pedestals around the court, the pedestals at the entrance of the court, and all the tent pegs for the Dwelling and for the court around it.

CHAPTER 39

See RG 70

The Vestments. [1]With violet, purple and scarlet yarn were woven the service cloths for use in the sanctuary, as well as the sacred vestments[s] for Aaron, as the LORD had commanded Moses.

[2t]The ephod was woven of gold thread and of violet, purple and scarlet yarn and of fine linen twined. [3]Gold was first hammered into gold leaf and then cut up into threads, which were woven with the violet, purple and scarlet yarn into an embroidered pattern on the fine linen. [4]Shoulder straps were made for it and joined to its two upper ends. [5]The embroidered belt on the ephod extended out from it, and like it, was made of gold thread, of violet, purple and scarlet yarn, and of fine linen twined, as the LORD had commanded Moses. [6]The onyx stones were prepared and mounted in gold filigree work; they were engraved like seal engravings with the names of the sons of Israel. [7]These stones were set on the shoulder straps of the ephod as memorial stones of the sons of Israel, just as the LORD had commanded Moses.

[8u]The breastpiece was embroidered like the ephod, with gold thread and violet, purple and scarlet yarn on cloth of fine linen twined. [9]It was square and folded double, a

q: 22f: Ex 31, 2. 6; 35, 30. 34; 36, 1.   *r:* Nm 1, 46.   *s:* Ex 31, 10.   *t:* 2-10: Ex 28, 6-12.   *u:* 8-14: Ex 28, 15-21.

span high and a span wide in its folded form. [10]Four rows of precious stones were mounted on it: in the first row a carnelian, a topaz and an emerald; [11]in the second row, a garnet, a sapphire and a beryl; [12]in the third row a jacinth, an agate and an amethyst; [13]in the fourth row a chrysolite, an onyx and a jasper. They were mounted in gold filigree work. [14]These stones were twelve, to match the names of the sons of Israel, and each stone was engraved like a seal with the name of one of the twelve tribes.

[15v]Chains of pure gold, twisted like cords, were made for the breastpiece, [16]together with two gold filigree rosettes and two gold rings. The two rings were fastened to the two upper ends of the breastpiece. [17]The two gold chains were then fastened to the two rings at the ends of the breastpiece. [18]The other two ends of the two chains were fastened in front to the two filigree rosettes, which were attached to the shoulder straps of the ephod. [19]Two other gold rings were made and put on the two lower ends of the breastpiece, on the edge facing the ephod. [20]Two more gold rings were made and fastened to the bottom of the two shoulder straps next to where they joined the ephod in front, just above its embroidered belt. [21]Violet ribbons bound the rings of the breastpiece to the rings of the ephod, so that the breastpiece stayed right above the embroidered belt of the ephod and did not swing loose from it. All this was just as the LORD had commanded Moses.

The Other Vestments. [22]The robe of the ephod was woven entirely of violet yarn, [23]with an opening in its center like the opening of a shirt, with selvage around the opening to keep it from being torn. [24]At the hem of the robe pomegranates were made of violet, purple and scarlet yarn and of fine linen twined; [25]bells of pure gold were also made and put between the pomegranates all around the hem of the robe: [26]first a bell, then a pomegranate, and thus alternating all around the hem of the robe which was to be worn in performing the ministry—all this, just as the LORD had commanded Moses.

[27]For Aaron and his sons there were also woven tunics of fine linen;[w] [28]the miter of fine linen; the ornate turbans of fine linen; drawers of linen [of fine linen twined]; [29]and sashes of variegated work made of fine linen twined and of violet, purple and scarlet yarn, as the LORD had commanded Moses. [30]The plate of the sacred diadem was made of pure gold[x] and inscribed, as on a seal engraving: "Sacred to the LORD." [31]It was tied over the miter with a violet ribbon, as the LORD had commanded Moses.

Presentation of the Work to Moses. [32]Thus the entire work of the Dwelling of the meeting tent was completed. The Israelites did the work just as the LORD had commanded Moses. [33]They then brought to Moses the Dwelling, the tent with all its appurtenances, the clasps, the boards, the bars, the columns, the pedestals, [34]the covering of rams' skins dyed red, the covering of tahash skins, the curtain veil; [35]the ark of the commandments with its poles, the propitiatory, [36]the table with all its appurtenances and the showbread, [37]the pure gold lampstand with its lamps set up on it and with all its appurtenances, the oil for the light, [38]the golden altar, the anointing oil, the fragrant incense; the curtain for the entrance of the tent, [39]the altar of bronze with its bronze grating, its poles and all its appurtenances, the laver with its base, [40]the hangings of the court with their columns and pedestals, the curtain for the entrance of the court with its ropes and tent pegs, all the equipment for the service of the Dwelling of the meeting tent; [41]the service cloths for use in the sanctuary, the sacred vestments for Aaron the priest, and the vestments to be worn by his sons in their ministry. [42]The Israelites had carried out all the work just as the LORD had commanded Moses. [43]So when Moses saw that all the work was done just as the LORD had commanded, he blessed them.

CHAPTER 40

See RG 70

Erection of the Dwelling. [1]Then the LORD said to Moses, [2y]"On the first day of the first month* you shall erect the Dwelling

---

40, 2: On the first day of the first month: almost a year after the departure of the Israelites from Egypt. Cf v 17.

v: 15-21: Ex 28, 31-35.   w: 27ff: Ex 28, 39-42.   x: 30f: Ex 28, 36f.   y: 2-8: Ex 40, 16-33.

The Climax of the Book

Now that Moses has carried out all of God's instructions (40, 33), everything is finally ready so that God may reside among the people (cf. Ex 25, 8; 29, 42–46). The cloud and the glory are signs of God's presence "tabernacling," that is, dwelling, with Israel. The column of cloud by day and the column of fire by night that have led Israel thus far (Ex 13, 21–22) take their place over the tabernacle, because they will accompany Israel on the rest of its journey (Nm 9, 15–23). As the cloud covered the top of Mount Sinai (Ex 24, 15–18), so it now covers the tabernacle and will guide Israel to the Promised Land. God is on the march.

of the meeting tent.[z] [3]Put the ark of the commandments in it, and screen off the ark with the veil.[a] [4]Bring in the table and set it. Then bring in the lampstand and set up the lamps on it. [5]Put the golden altar of incense in front of the ark of the commandments, and hang the curtain at the entrance of the Dwelling. [6]Put the altar of holocausts in front of the entrance of the Dwelling of the meeting tent. [7]Place the laver between the meeting tent and the altar, and put water in it. [8]Set up the court round about, and put the curtain at the entrance of the court.

[9b]"Take the anointing oil and anoint the Dwelling and everything in it, consecrating it and all its furnishings, so that it will be sacred. [10]Anoint the altar of holocausts and all its appurtenances, consecrating it, so that it will be most sacred. [11]Likewise, anoint the laver with its base, and thus consecrate it.

[12c]"Then bring Aaron and his sons to the entrance of the meeting tent, and there wash them with water. [13]Clothe Aaron with the sacred vestments and anoint him, thus consecrating him as my priest. [14]Bring forward his sons also, and clothe them with the tunics. [15]As you have anointed their father, anoint them also as my priests. Thus, by being anointed, they shall receive a perpetual priesthood throughout all future generations."

[16]Moses did exactly as the LORD had commanded him. [17]On the first day of the first month of the second year the Dwelling was erected. [18]It was Moses who erected the Dwelling. He placed its pedestals, set up its boards, put in its bars, and set up its columns. [19]He spread the tent over the Dwelling and put the covering on top of the tent, as the LORD had commanded him. [20d]He took the commandments and put them in the ark; he placed poles alongside the ark and set the propitiatory upon it. [21]He brought the ark into the Dwelling and hung the curtain veil, thus screening off the ark of the commandments, as the LORD had commanded him. [22]He put the table in the meeting tent, on the north side of the Dwelling, outside the veil, [23]and arranged the bread on it before the LORD, as the LORD had commanded him.[e] [24]He placed the lampstand in the meeting tent, opposite the table, on the south side of the Dwelling, [25]and he set up the lamps before the LORD, as the LORD had commanded him. [26]He placed the golden altar in the meeting tent, in front of the veil, [27]and on it he burned fragrant incense, as the LORD had commanded him. [28]He hung the curtain at the entrance of the Dwelling. [29]He put the altar of holocausts in front of the entrance of the Dwelling of the meeting tent, and offered holocausts and cereal offerings on it, as the LORD had commanded him. [30f]He placed the laver between the meeting tent and the altar, and put water in it for washing. [31]Moses and Aaron and his sons used to wash their hands and feet there, [32]for they washed themselves whenever they went into the meeting tent or approached the altar, as the LORD commanded Moses. [33]Finally, he set up the court around the Dwelling and the altar and hung the curtain at the entrance of the court. Thus Moses finished all the work.

God's Presence in the Dwelling. [34g]Then

z: Ex 26, 30.   a: 3ff: Ex 26, 33ff.   b: 9ff: Ex 30, 26-29.   c: 12-15: Ex 28, 41; 29, 4-9; Lv 8, 1-13.   d: 20ff: Ex 25, 16. 21; 26, 33ff.
e: Ex 25, 30.   f: 30ff: Ex 30, 18ff.   g: 34-38: Nm 9, 15-22.

the cloud covered the meeting tent, and the glory of the LORD filled the Dwelling. [35]Moses could not enter the meeting tent, because the cloud settled down upon it and the glory of the LORD filled the Dwelling. [36]Whenever the cloud rose from the Dwelling, the Israelites would set out on their journey. [37]But if the cloud did not lift, they would not go forward; only when it lifted did they go forward. [38]In the daytime the cloud of the LORD was seen over the Dwelling; whereas at night, fire was seen in the cloud by the whole house of Israel in all the stages of their journey.

See RG
73–80

The Book of Leviticus

The name "Leviticus" was bestowed on the third book of the Pentateuch by the ancient Greek translators because a good part of this book consists of sacrificial and other ritual laws prescribed for the priests of the tribe of Levi.

Continuing the legislation given by God to Moses at Mount Sinai, Leviticus is almost entirely legislative in character; the rare narrative portions are subordinate to the main legislative theme. Generally speaking, the laws contained in this book serve to teach the Israelites that they should always keep themselves in a state of legal purity, or external sanctity, as a sign of their intimate union with the Lord. Accordingly, the central idea of Leviticus is contained in its oft-repeated injunction: "You shall be holy, because I, the LORD, am holy."

The main divisions of Leviticus are:

I: Ritual of Sacrifices (1—7).
II: Ceremony of Ordination (8—10).
III: Laws regarding Legal Purity (11—16).
IV: Code of Legal Holiness (17—26).
V: Redemption of Offerings (27).

I: Ritual of Sacrifices

CHAPTER 1

See RG
76–77

Holocausts. [1]The LORD called Moses, and from the meeting tent gave him this message: [2a]"Speak to the Israelites and tell them: When any one of you wishes to bring an animal offering to the LORD, such an offering must be from the herd or from the flock.*

[3]"If his holocaust* offering is from the herd, it must be a male without blemish [b] To find favor with the LORD, he shall bring it to the entrance of the meeting tent [4]and there lay his hand on the head of the holocaust, so that it may be acceptable to make atonement for him.[c] [5]He shall then slaughter the bull before the LORD, but Aaron's sons, the priests, shall offer up its blood by splashing it on the sides of the altar which is at the entrance of the meeting tent.[d] [6]Then he shall skin the holocaust and cut it up into pieces. [7]After Aaron's sons, the priests, have put some burning embers on the altar and laid some wood on them, [8]they shall lay the pieces of meat, together with the head and the suet, on top of the wood and embers on the altar. [9]The inner organs and the shanks, however, the offerer shall first wash with water. The priest shall then burn the whole offering on the altar as a holocaust, a sweet-smelling oblation to the LORD.[e]

[10]"If his holocaust offering is from the flock, that is, a sheep or a goat, he must bring a male without blemish. [11]This he shall slaughter before the LORD at the north side of the altar. Then Aaron's sons, the priests, shall splash its blood on the sides of the altar. [12]When the offerer has cut it up into pieces, the priest shall lay these, together with the head and suet, on top of the wood and the fire on the altar. [13]The inner organs and the shanks, however, the offerer shall first wash with water. The priest shall offer

---

1, 2: From the herd or from the flock: the only animals which could be used as sacrificial victims were either of the bovine class (bulls, cows and calves) or the ovine class (sheep and lambs, goats and kids). Excluded, therefore, were not only all wild animals, but also such "unclean" domestic animals as the camel and the ass. See note on Lv 11, 1ff.

1, 3: Holocaust: from the Greek word meaning "wholly burned," this is the technical term for the special type of sacrifice in which an entire animal except its hide was consumed in the fire on the altar. The primary purpose of this complete gift was to render glory and praise to God.

a: Lv 22, 18. 19. *b:* Ex 12, 5. *c:* Lv 3, 2. 8. 13; 4, 15; 8, 14. 22; 16, 21; Ex 29, 10. 15. *d:* Lv 3, 8. *e:* Lv 3, 5. 16; Ex 29, 18.

Even after the destruction of the temple and the cessation of sacrificial worship and temple ritual, Leviticus remains at the foundation of Jewish life. Among the institutions still central to Judaism, which have their biblical origins in Leviticus, are most of the dietary laws (the permitted and forbidden animals and the blood prohibition); many of the festival rituals; most of the laws regulating sex, marriage, and family purity; and the commandments governing the seventh year, still applicable in the land of Israel. Moreover, the religious life of the congregation, centered upon the synagogue and the daily prayers offered at fixed times and in precisely ordained ritual forms, is a direct outgrowth of, and according to rabbinic tradition a substitute for, the temple ritual as envisioned in Leviticus.

All the institutions that ultimately shaped Israel's national and religious existence—the law, the priesthood, the forms of temple worship, and the tribal foundations of its society—are said to have been ordained and established during the years immediately after the exile.

them up and then burn the whole offering on the altar as a holocaust, a sweet-smelling oblation to the Lord.

¹⁴"If he offers a bird as a holocaust to the LORD, he shall choose a turtledove or a pigeon as his offering.ᶠ ¹⁵Having brought it to the altar where it is to be burned, the priest shall snap its head loose and squeeze out its blood against the side of the altar.ᵍ ¹⁶Its crop and feathers shall be removed and thrown on the ash heap at the east side of the altar. ¹⁷Then, having split the bird down the middle without separating the halves, the priest shall burn it on the altar, over the wood on the fire, as a holocaust, a sweet-smelling oblation to the LORD.

CHAPTER 2

See RG 76–77

Cereal Offerings. ¹"When anyone wishes to bring a cereal offering to the LORD, his offering must consist of fine flour. He shall pour oil on it and put frankincense over it.ʰ ²When he has brought it to Aaron's sons, the priests, one of them shall take a handful of this fine flour and oil, together with all the frankincense, and this he shall burn on the altar as a token offering,* a sweet-smelling oblation to the LORD.ⁱ ³The rest of the cereal offering belongs to Aaron and his sons. It is a most sacred oblation to the LORD.ʲ

⁴"When the cereal offering you present is baked in an oven, it must be in the form of unleavened cakes made of fine flour mixed with oil, or of unleavened wafers spread with oil. ⁵If you present a cereal offering that is fried on a griddle, it must be of fine flour mixed with oil and unleavened.ᵏ ⁶Such a cereal offering must be broken into pieces, and oil must be poured over it. ⁷If you present a cereal offering that is prepared in a pot, it must be of fine flour, deep-fried in oil. ⁸A cereal offering that is made in any of these ways you shall bring to the LORD, offering it to the priest, who shall take it to the altar. ⁹Its token offering the priest shall then lift from the cereal offering and burn on the altar as a sweet-smelling oblation to the LORD. ¹⁰The rest of the cereal offering belongs to Aaron and his sons. It is a most sacred oblation to the LORD.

¹¹"Every cereal offering that you present to the LORD shall be unleavened, for you shall not burn any leaven or honey as an oblation to the LORD.ˡ ¹²Such you may indeed present to the LORD in the offering of first fruits, but they are not to be placed on the altar for a pleasing odor. ¹³However, every cereal offering that you present to the LORD shall be seasoned with salt.ᵐ Do not let the salt of the covenant of your

2, 2: Token offering: literally, "reminder." Instead of burning the whole cereal offering, they burned only this part of it on the altar; it thus corresponded to the fat of the peace offering. See note on Lv 3, 1.

f: Lv 5, 7; 12, 8; Lk 2, 24.   g: Lv 5, 8.   h: Nm 15, 4.   i: Lv 6, 15.   j: Lv 7, 9f; Sir 7, 31; 1 Cor 9, 13.   k: 1 Chr 23, 29.   l: Lv 6, 16f; Mt 16, 12; Mk 8, 15; Lk 12, 1; 1 Cor 5, 7; Gal 5, 9.   m: Ez 43, 24.

God* be lacking from your cereal offering. On every offering you shall offer salt.

[14]"If you present a cereal offering of first fruits to the LORD, you shall offer it in the form of fresh grits of new ears of grain, roasted by fire. [15]On this cereal offering you shall put oil and frankincense. [16]For its token offering the priest shall then burn some of the grits and oil, together with all the frankincense, as an oblation to the LORD.

See RG 76-77

CHAPTER 3

Peace Offerings. [1]"If someone in presenting a peace offering* makes his offering from the herd, he may offer before the LORD either a male or a female animal, but it must be without blemish.[n] [2]He shall lay his hand on the head of his offering,[o] and then slaughter it at the entrance of the meeting tent; but Aaron's sons, the priests, shall splash its blood on the sides of the altar. [3]From the peace offering he shall offer as an oblation to the LORD the fatty membrane over the inner organs, and all the fat that adheres to them,[p] [4]as well as the two kidneys, with the fat on them near the loins, and the lobe of the liver,* which he shall sever above the kidneys. [5]All this Aaron's sons shall then burn on the altar with the holocaust,[q] on the wood over the fire, as a sweet-smelling oblation to the LORD.

[6]"If the peace offering he presents to the LORD is from the flock, he may offer either a male or a female animal, but it must be without blemish. [7]If he presents a lamb as his offering, he shall bring it before the LORD, [8]and after laying his hand on the head of his offering, he shall slaughter it before the meeting tent; but Aaron's sons shall splash its blood on the sides of the altar. [9]As an oblation to the LORD he shall present the fat of the peace offering: the whole fatty tail,* which he must sever close to the spine, the fatty membrane over the inner organs, and all the fat that adheres to them,[r] [10]as well as the two kidneys, with the fat on them near the loins, and the lobe of the liver, which he must sever above the kidneys. [11]All this the priest shall burn on the altar as the food of the LORD's oblation.

[12]"If he presents a goat, he shall bring it before the LORD, [13]and after laying his hand on its head, he shall slaughter it before the meeting tent; but Aaron's sons shall splash its blood on the sides of the altar. [14]From it he shall offer as an oblation to the LORD the fatty membrane over the inner organs, and all the fat that adheres to them, [15]as well as the two kidneys, with the fat on them near the loins, and the lobe of the liver, which he must sever above the kidneys. [16]All this the priest shall burn on the altar as the food of the sweet-smelling oblation. All the fat belongs to the LORD. [17]This shall be a perpetual ordinance for your descendants wherever they may dwell. You shall not partake of any fat* or any blood."[s]

CHAPTER 4

See RG 76-77

Sin Offerings: For Priests. [1]The LORD said to Moses, [2]"Tell the Israelites: When a person inadvertently commits a sin* against some command of the LORD by doing one of the forbidden things,[t] [3]if it is the anointed priest* who thus sins and thereby makes the people also become guilty, he shall present to the LORD a young, unblemished bull as a

---

2, 13: The salt of the covenant of your God: the partaking in common of salt by those seated together at table was an ancient symbol of friendship and alliance. Cf Mk 9, 49 and Col 4, 6; and see note on Nm 18, 19.

3, 1: Peace offering: thus the ancient versions have rendered the Hebrew word, which perhaps means more exactly, "fulfillment sacrifice," offered up in fulfillment of a vow. Cf Prv 7, 14. Its characteristic feature was the sacred banquet at which the offerer and his guests partook of the meat of the sacrificed animal. Cf Lv 7, 11-21.

3, 4: The lobe of the liver: some render, "the fatty covering of the liver."

3, 9: The whole fatty tail: see note on Ex 29, 22.

3, 17: Any fat: only the fat mentioned in vv 9f. 14f is meant; other fat could be eaten by the Israelites.

4, 2: A sin: not necessarily a moral fault; included are all the cases of ritual uncleanness which people necessarily incurred in certain unavoidable circumstances.

4, 3: The anointed priest: his violation of the ceremonial law brought a sort of collective guilt on all the people whom he represented before God. Sin offering: more exactly, "sacrifice for remitting sin"; sin is here understood as explained above.

n: Lv 22, 21.   *o:* Lv 1, 4.   *p:* Ex 29, 13. 22.   *q:* Lv 6, 12.   *r:* Lv 9, 19.   *s:* Lv 17, 10-14; Gn 9, 4; Dt 12, 16. 23; 15, 23.   *t:* Lv 5, 15. 17; Nm 15, 22-29.

sin offering for the sin he committed.[u] [4]Bringing the bullock to the entrance of the meeting tent, before the LORD, he shall lay his hand on its head and slaughter it before the LORD.[v] [5]The anointed priest shall then take some of the bullock's blood and bring it into the meeting tent, [6]where, dipping his finger in the blood, he shall sprinkle it seven times before the LORD, toward the veil of the sanctuary.[w] [7]The priest shall also put some of the blood on the horns of the altar[x] of fragrant incense which is before the LORD in the meeting tent. The rest of the bullock's blood he shall pour out at the base of the altar of holocausts which is at the entrance of the meeting tent. [8]From the sin-offering bullock he shall remove all the fat: the fatty membrane over the inner organs, and all the fat that adheres to them, [9]as well as the two kidneys, with the fat on them near the loins, and the lobe of the liver, which he must sever above the kidneys. [10]This is the same as is removed from the ox of the peace offering; and the priest shall burn it on the altar of holocausts. [11]The hide of the bullock and all its flesh, with its head, legs, inner organs and offal,[y] [12]in short, the whole bullock, shall be brought outside the camp to a clean place where the ashes are deposited and there be burned up in a wood fire. At the place of the ash heap, there it must be burned.

For the Community. [13]"If the whole community of Israel inadvertently and without even being aware of it does something that the LORD has forbidden and thus makes itself guilty,[z] [14]should it later on become known that the sin was committed, the community shall present a young bull as a sin offering. They shall bring it before the meeting tent, [15]and here, before the LORD, the elders of the community shall lay their hands on the bullock's head.[a] When the bullock has been slaughtered before the LORD, [16]the anointed priest shall bring some of its blood into the meeting tent, [17]and dipping his finger in the blood, he shall sprinkle it seven times before the LORD, toward the veil. [18]He shall also put some of the blood on the horns

of the altar of fragrant incense which is before the LORD in the meeting tent. The rest of the blood he shall pour out at the base of the altar of holocausts which is at the entrance of the meeting tent. [19]All of its fat he shall take from it and burn on the altar, [20]doing with this bullock just as he did with the other sin-offering bullock. Thus the priest shall make atonement for them, and they will be forgiven. [21]This bullock must also be brought outside the camp and burned, just as has been prescribed for the other one. This is the sin offering for the community.

For the Princes. [22]"Should a prince commit a sin inadvertently by doing one of the things which are forbidden by some commandment of the LORD, his God, and thus become guilty, [23]if later on he learns of the sin he committed, he shall bring as his offering an unblemished male goat. [24]Having laid his hands on its head, he shall slaughter the goat as a sin offering before the LORD, in the place where the holocausts are slaughtered. [25]The priest shall then take some of the blood of the sin offering on his finger and put it on the horns of the altar of holocausts. The rest of the blood he shall pour out at the base of this altar. [26]All of the fat he shall burn on the altar like the fat of the peace offering.[b] Thus the priest shall make atonement for the prince's sin, and it will be forgiven.

For Private Persons. [27]"If a private person commits a sin inadvertently[c] by doing one of the things which are forbidden by the commandments of the LORD, and thus becomes guilty, [28]should he later on learn of the sin he committed, he shall bring an unblemished she-goat as the offering for his sin. [29]Having laid his hand on the head of the sin offering,[d] he shall slaughter it at the place of the holocausts. [30]The priest shall then take some of its blood on his finger and put it on the horns of the altar of holocausts. The rest of the blood he shall pour out at the base of the altar. [31]All the fat shall be removed, just as the fat is removed from the peace offering, and the priest shall burn it on the altar for an odor pleasing to the LORD.[e] Thus the

u: Heb 7, 27. *v:* Lv 1, 3f. *w:* Lv 8, 11. *x:* Lv 8, 15; 9, 9; 16, 18; Ex 29, 12. *y:* Lv 8, 17; 9, 11; Ex 29, 14; Nm 19, 5. *z:* Lv 5, 2-4; Nm 15, 24-26. *a:* Lv 1, 4. *b:* Lv 3, 3-5. *c:* Nm 15, 27. *d:* Lv 1, 4. *e:* Lv 1, 9; 3, 3-5.

Two connected concepts give the meaning and significance for both the codes of law and the practices of worship in the Temple. These concepts are *holiness* and *sacrifice*.

The Hebrew word for "holy"—*qadosh*—comes from a root that means "separate" or "set apart." Something holy is set apart from other, ordinary things. The original and definitive holy being is God: although God made the creation, God is separate from it. Ultimately, the Israelite people as a whole are to be holy, set apart from the other nations of the world because of their service to God and their status as God's people: "Be holy, for I, the LORD, your God, am holy" (Lv 19, 2). Something can become holy by being associated with God in some way. The established way to do that, in Hebrew worship, is to offer it to God by setting it apart and putting it beyond the use of the person offering it.

This making holy or setting apart is a "sacrifice," from the Latin words that mean "to make holy." Something could be sacrificed by burning it (Lv 1, 9); giving it to someone else (the priest) to eat (Lv 2, 3); chasing it into the wilderness (Lv 16, 22); and, in the case of liquids, splashing them against the altar (Lv 1, 11) or pouring them on the ground (Lv 4, 18; see also Dt 12, 16). In each case, the offering had become God's possession; the particular action was a way of demonstrating this.

The Hebrew words for the different kinds of sacrifices indicate how the sacrifice is carried out or what its aim is. One word—*zebach*—means "slaughter [for sacrifice]," and is the term used in "peace offering" (see NAB note on 3, 1 for the alternative translation "fulfillment sacrifice"). Another—*olah*—is translated "holocaust" in the New American Bible and means "a whole burnt offering." In this sacrifice, the entire animal (except the skin) is consumed by fire. The name comes from a verb that means "ascend, go up" because the smoke from the sacrifice rises to the presence of God. The word *minchah* means "gift" or "tribute" as from an inferior to a superior, and refers to the "cereal offering" where cakes made of oil and flour were burnt or eaten by the priests.

These sacrifices—peace offering, holocaust, and cereal offering—are voluntary offerings from the individual to praise God, give thanks for a blessing, fulfill a vow, pray for healing or deliverance, and so on. The first three chapters deal with these.

In chs 4–5 the sacrifices are those brought about by wrongdoing, either deliberate or accidental, and are required, not voluntary. The first is *chattat* (NAB "sin offering" [4, 3]). This means "that which misses," like an arrow that falls short of its target. The point of the sacrifice, however, is to restore the right relationship between God and the person offering it, and to remove the sin. This atonement (Hebrew *kipper*, which means "wipe clean"; the same word names the Jewish holiday Yom Kippur, "Day of Atonement") is brought about by the sacrifice, which purges or purifies the offerer. (See NAB note on 4, 3, suggesting that this is a "sacrifice for remitting sin.") The second type of sacrifice for wrongdoing is the *asham*, which originally meant a penalty incurred and came to mean "offense" or "guilt." That is the basis for the translation "guilt offering" (Lv 5, 15). The emphasis, however, is not so much on the guilt of the offender but on the restoration (Lv 5, 16) or restitution (Lv 5, 24) of what has been wrongfully taken. Instead of "guilt offering" a better translation might be "reparation offering." The one who is offering is trying to make up for a past offense.

Thus, the Israelites maintained their relationship with God by offering sacrifices: setting something aside for God (making it holy), whether in thanksgiving or penitence.

priest shall make atonement for him, and he will be forgiven.

32"If, however, for his sin offering he presents a lamb, he shall bring an unblemished female. 33Having laid his hand on its head, he shall slaughter this sin offering in the place where the holocausts are slaughtered. 34The priest shall then take some of the blood of the sin offering on his finger and put it on the horns of the altar of holocausts. The rest of the blood he shall pour out at the base of the altar. 35All the fat shall be removed, just as the fat is removed from the peace-offering lamb,ʲ and the priest shall burn it on the altar with the other oblations of the LORD. Thus the priest shall make atonement for the man's sin, and it will be forgiven.

CHAPTER 5

See RG
76–77

For Special Cases. ¹"If any person refuses to give the information which, as a witness of something he has seen or learned, he has been adjured to give, and thus commits a sin and has guilt to bear;ᵍ ²or if someone, without being aware of it, touches any unclean thing, as the carcass of an unclean wild animal,ʰ or that of an unclean domestic animal, or that of an unclean swarming creature, and thus becomes unclean and guilty; ³or if someone, without being aware of it, touches some human uncleanness, whatever kind of uncleanness this may be, and then recognizes his guilt; ⁴or if someone, without being aware of it, rashly utters an oathⁱ to do good or evil, such as men are accustomed to utter rashly, and then recognizes that he is guilty of such an oath; ⁵then whoever is guilty in any of these cases shall confess the sin he has incurred,ʲ ⁶and as his sin offering for the sin he has committed he shall bring to the LORD a female animal from the flock, a ewe lamb or a she-goat. The priest shall then make atonement for his sin.

7"If, however, he cannot afford an animal of the flock, he shall bring to the LORD as the sin offering for his sin two turtledoves or two pigeons, one for a sin offering and the other for a holocaust.ᵏ ⁸He shall bring them to the priest, who shall offer the one for the sin offering first. Snapping its head loose at the neck, yet without breaking it off completely,ˡ ⁹he shall sprinkle some of the blood of the sin offering against the side of the altar.ᵐ The rest of the blood shall be squeezed out against the base of the altar. Such is the offering for sin. ¹⁰The other bird shall be offered as a holocaust in the usual way. Thus the priest shall make atonement for the sin the man committed, and it will be forgiven.

11"If he is unable to afford even two turtledoves or two pigeons, he shall present as a sin offering for his sin one tenth of an ephah of fine flour. He shall not put oil or frankincense on it, because it is a sin offering. ¹²When he has brought it to the priest, the latter shall take a handful of this flour as a token offering, and this he shall burn as a sin offering on the altar with the other oblations of the LORD. ¹³Thus the priest shall make atonement for the sin that the man committed in any of the above cases, and it will be forgiven.ⁿ The rest of the flour, like the cereal offerings, shall belong to the priest."

Guilt Offerings. ¹⁴The LORD said to Moses, ¹⁵"If someone commits a sin by inadvertently cheating* in the LORD's sacred dues, he shall bring to the LORD as his guilt offering an unblemished ram from the flock, valued at two silver shekels according to the standard of the sanctuary shekel. ¹⁶He shall also restore what he has sinfully withheld from the sanctuary, adding to it a fifth of its value.ᵒ This is to be given to the priest, who shall then make atonement for him with the guilt-offering ram, and he will be forgiven.

17ᵖ"If someone, without being aware of it,* commits such a sin by doing one of the things

---

5, 15: Cheating: not offering the full amount in tithes, first fruits, etc. Guilt offering: its characteristic was a certain additional penalty imposed as reparation for the injustice involved in the fault which was atoned for by this sacrifice. However, in certain passages, e.g., Lv 14, 12f; Nm 6, 12; Ezr 10, 19, the term "guilt offering" is used for more important cases of "sin offerings" where no apparent injustice is involved.

5, 17: Without being aware of it: the case naturally presupposes that later on the offender learns of his mistake. Cf Lv 4, 13f.

f: Lv 3, 3. 9. *g:* Prv 29, 24. *h:* Lv 11, 24. 31. 39; 12; 13; 15. *i:* Jgs 11, 30f; 1 Sm 14, 24; Mk 6, 23; Acts 23, 12. *j:* Lv 26, 40; Nm 5, 7. *k:* Lv 12, 8; Lk 2, 24. *l:* Lv 1, 15. 17. *m:* Lv 1, 15. *n:* Lv 4, 26. 35. *o:* Lv 22, 14. *p:* Lv 4, 2.

which are forbidden by some commandment of the LORD, that he incurs guilt for which he must answer, [18]he shall bring as a guilt offering to the priest an unblemished ram of the flock of the established value. The priest shall then make atonement for the fault which was unwittingly committed, and it will be forgiven. [19]Such is the offering for guilt; the penalty of the guilt must be paid to the LORD."

[20]The LORD said to Moses, [21]"If someone commits a sin of dishonesty against the LORD by denying his neighbor a deposit or a pledge for a stolen article, or by otherwise retaining his neighbor's goods unjustly, [22]or if, having found a lost article, he denies the fact and swears falsely about it with any of the sinful oaths that men make in such cases, [23]he shall therefore, since he has incurred guilt by his sin, restore the thing that was stolen or unjustly retained by him or the deposit left with him or the lost article he found [24]or whatever else he swore falsely about; on the day of his guilt offering he shall make full restitution of the thing itself, and in addition, give the owner one fifth of its value. [25]As his guilt offering he shall bring to the LORD an unblemished ram of the flock of the established value. When he has presented this as his guilt offering to the priest, [26]the latter shall make atonement for him before the LORD, and he will be forgiven whatever guilt he may have incurred."

CHAPTER 6

See RG
76-77

The Daily Holocaust. [1]The LORD said to Moses, [2]"Give Aaron and his sons the following command: This is the ritual* for holocausts. The holocaust is to remain on the hearth of the altar all night until the next morning, and the fire is to be kept burning on the altar. [3]The priest, clothed in his linen robe and wearing linen drawers on his body, shall take away the ashes to which the fire has reduced the holocaust on the altar, and lay them at the side of the altar. [4]Then, having taken off these garments and put on other

garments, he shall carry the ashes to a clean place outside the camp. [5]The fire on the altar is to be kept burning; it must not go out. Every morning the priest shall put firewood on it. On this he shall lay out the holocaust and burn the fat of the peace offerings. [6]The fire is to be kept burning continuously on the altar; it must not go out.

Daily Cereal Offering. [7]"This is the ritual of the cereal offering. One of Aaron's sons shall first present it before the LORD, in front of the altar. [8]Then he shall take from it a handful of its fine flour and oil, together with all the frankincense that is on it, and this he shall burn on the altar as its token offering, a sweet-smelling oblation to the LORD. [9]The rest of it Aaron and his sons may eat; but it must be eaten in the form of unleavened cakes and in a sacred place: in the court of the meeting tent they shall eat it. [10]It shall not be baked with leaven. I have given it to them as their portion from the oblations of the LORD; it is most sacred, like the sin offering and the guilt offering. [11]All the male descendants of Aaron may partake of it as their rightful share in the oblations of the LORD perpetually throughout your generations. Whatever touches the oblations becomes sacred."

[12]*The LORD said to Moses, [13]"This is the offering that Aaron and his sons shall present to the LORD [on the day he is anointed]: one tenth of an ephah of fine flour for the established cereal offering, half in the morning and half in the evening. [14]It shall be well kneaded and fried in oil on a griddle when you bring it in. Having broken the offering into pieces, you shall present it as a sweet-smelling oblation to the LORD. [15]Aaron's descendant who succeeds him as the anointed priest shall do likewise. This is a perpetual ordinance: for the Lord the whole offering shall be burned. [16]Every cereal offering of a priest shall be a whole burnt offering; it may not be eaten."

Sin Offerings. [17]The LORD said to Moses,

6, 2: Ritual: literally, "law, instruction." Here, and in the following paragraphs, are given additional prescriptions for various kinds of sacrifices which were, in part, treated of in the preceding chapters.

6, 12-16: This is another law about the daily or "established"

cereal offering. It differs in some respects from the preceding law (vv 7-11) and also from the law in Ex 29, 38-42. Hence, the words on the day he is anointed were probably added by some later scribe in order to avoid the difficulty of harmonizing this law with the other two laws on the same matter.

[18]"Tell Aaron and his sons: This is the ritual for sin offerings. At the place where holocausts are slaughtered, there also, before the LORD, shall the sin offering be slaughtered.[q] It is most sacred. [19]The priest who presents the sin offering may partake of it; but it must be eaten in a sacred place,[r] in the court of the meeting tent. [20]Whatever touches its flesh shall become sacred. If any of its blood is spilled on a garment, the stained part must be washed in a sacred place. [21]A clay vessel in which it has been cooked shall thereafter be broken;[s] if it is cooked in a bronze vessel, this shall be scoured afterward and rinsed with water. [22]All the males of the priestly line may partake of the sin offering, since it is most sacred.[t] [23]But no one may partake of any sin offering of which some blood has been brought into the meeting tent[u] to make atonement in the sanctuary; such an offering must be burned up in the fire.

CHAPTER 7

See RG 76–77

Guilt Offerings. [1]"This is the ritual for guilt offerings, which are most sacred. [2]At the place where the holocausts are slaughtered, there also shall the guilt offering be slaughtered.[v] Its blood shall be splashed on the sides of the altar. [3w]All of its fat shall be taken from it and offered up: the fatty tail, the fatty membrane over the inner organs, [4]as well as the two kidneys with the fat on them near the loins, and the lobe of the liver, which must be severed above the kidneys. [5]All this the priest shall burn on the altar as an oblation to the LORD. This is the guilt offering. [6]All the males of the priestly line may partake of it; but it must be eaten in a sacred place, since it is most sacred.[x]

[7]"Because the sin offering and the guilt offering are alike, both having the same ritual, the guilt offering likewise belongs to the priest who makes atonement with it. [8]Similarly, the priest who offers a holocaust for someone may keep for himself the hide of the holocaust that he has offered. [9y]Also, every cereal offering that is baked in an oven or deep-fried in a pot or fried on a griddle shall belong to the priest who offers it, [10]whereas all cereal offerings[z] that are offered up dry or mixed with oil shall belong to all of Aaron's sons without distinction.

Peace Offerings. [11]"This is the ritual for the peace offerings that are presented to the LORD. [12]When anyone makes a peace offering in thanksgiving, together with his thanksgiving sacrifice he shall offer unleavened cakes mixed with oil, unleavened wafers spread with oil, and cakes made of fine flour mixed with oil and well kneaded. [13]His offering shall also include loaves of leavened bread* along with the victim of his peace offering for thanksgiving. [14]From each of his offerings he shall present one portion as a contribution to the LORD; this shall belong to the priest who splashes the blood of the peace offering.

[15a]"The flesh of the thanksgiving sacrifice shall be eaten on the day it is offered; none of it may be kept till the next day. [16]However, if the sacrifice is a votive or a free-will offering, it should indeed be eaten on the day the sacrifice is offered, but what is left over may be eaten on the next day. [17]Should any flesh from the sacrifice be left over on the third day, it must be burned up in the fire. [18]If, therefore, any of the flesh of the peace offering is eaten on the third day, it shall not win favor for him nor shall it be reckoned to his credit; rather, it shall be considered as refuse, and anyone who eats of it shall have his guilt to bear. [19]Should the flesh touch anything unclean, it may not be eaten, but shall be burned up in the fire.

"All who are clean may partake of this flesh. [20]If, however, someone while in a state of uncleanness eats any of the flesh of a peace offering belonging to the LORD, that person shall be cut off from his people. [21]Likewise, if someone touches anything unclean, whether the uncleanness be of human or of animal origin or from some loathsome

---

7, 13: Leavened bread: these loaves were not burned on the altar (cf Lv 2, 11), but were eaten at the "communion" meal which followed the sacrifice. See note on Lv 3, 1.

q: Lv 7, 2.   *r:* Lv 10, 17.   *s:* Lv 11, 33; 15, 12.   *t:* Lv 7, 6; Nm 18, 10.   *u:* Lv 4, 5; Heb 13, 11.   *v:* Lv 6, 18.   *w:* 3-5: Lv 3, 4. 9f. 14-16; 4, 8f.   *x:* Lv 6, 22.   *y:* Lv 2, 3-10; Nm 18, 9; Ez 44, 29.   *z:* Lv 2, 14f.   *a:* 15-18: Lv 19, 6f.

crawling creature, and then eats of a peace offering belonging to the LORD, that person, too, shall be cut off from his people."

Prohibition against Blood and Fat. ²²The LORD said to Moses, ²³"Tell the Israelites: You shall not eat the fat* of any ox or sheep or goat.^b ²⁴Although the fat of an animal that has died a natural death or has been killed by wild beasts may be put to any other use, you may not eat it.^c ²⁵If anyone eats the fat of an animal from which an oblation is made to the LORD, such a one shall be cut off from his people. ²⁶Wherever you dwell, you shall not partake of any blood, be it of bird or of animal. ²⁷Every person who partakes of any blood shall be cut off from his people."^d

The Portions for Priests. ²⁸The LORD said to Moses, ²⁹"Tell the Israelites: He who presents a peace offering to the LORD shall bring a part of it as his special offering to him, ³⁰carrying in with his own hands the oblations to the LORD. The fat is to be brought in, together with the breast, which is to be waved as a wave offering* before the LORD. ³¹The priest shall burn the fat on the altar,^e but the breast belongs to Aaron and his sons. ³²Moreover, from your peace offering you shall give to the priest the right leg as a raised offering. ³³The descendant of Aaron who offers up the blood and fat of the peace offering shall have the right leg as his portion, ³⁴for from the peace offerings of the Israelites I have taken the breast that is waved and the leg that is raised up, and I have given them to Aaron, the priest, and to his sons by a perpetual ordinance as a contribution from the Israelites."^f

³⁵This is the priestly share* from the oblations of the LORD, allotted to Aaron and his sons on the day he called them to be the priests of the LORD; ³⁶on the day he anointed them the LORD ordered the Israelites to give

them this share by a perpetual ordinance throughout their generations.

³⁷This is the ritual for holocausts, cereal offerings, sin offerings, guilt offerings, [ordination offerings] and peace offerings, ³⁸which the LORD enjoined on Moses at Mount Sinai at the time when he commanded the Israelites in the wilderness of Sinai to bring their offerings to the LORD.

II: Ceremony of Ordination

CHAPTER 8

Ordination of Aaron and His Sons.

See RG 77

¹The LORD ^g said to Moses,* ²"Take Aaron and his sons, together with the vestments,* the anointing oil, the bullock for a sin offering, the two rams, and the basket of unleavened food. ³Then assemble the whole community at the entrance of the meeting tent." ⁴And Moses did as the LORD had commanded. When the community had assembled at the entrance of the meeting tent, ⁵Moses told them what the LORD had ordered to be done. ⁶Bringing forward Aaron and his sons, he first washed them with water.^h ⁷Then he put the tunic on Aaron,ⁱ girded him with the sash, clothed him with the robe, placed the ephod on him, and girded him with the embroidered belt of the ephod, fastening it around him. ⁸He then set the breastpiece on him, with the Urim and Thummim* in it, ⁹and put the miter on his head, attaching the gold plate, the sacred diadem, over the front of the miter, at his forehead, as the LORD had commanded him to do.

¹⁰Taking the anointing oil, Moses anointed and consecrated the Dwelling, with all that was in it.^j ¹¹Then he sprinkled some of this oil seven times on the altar, and anointed the altar, with all its appurtenances, and the laver, with its base, thus consecrating them. ¹²He also poured some of the anointing oil

---

7, 23: The fat: only the particular portions specified in Lv 3, 9f. 14f are meant. Ox or sheep or goat: such animals as could be sacrificed; the fat of other clean animals could be eaten.

7, 30-34: A wave offering . . . a raised offering: these ceremonies are described in Ex 29, 24-28. The Hebrew word for "raised offering" is also rendered, in certain contexts, as "contribution."

7, 35: The priestly share: literally, "the anointed part."

8, 1—9, 21: Though presented in the form of a narrative,

this description of Aaron's ordination was intended to serve as a guide for all future ordinations.

8, 2: The vestments, etc.: already described in Ex 28– 29.

8, 8: The Urim and Thummim: see note on Ex 28, 30.

---

b: Lv 3, 17.   c: Lv 22, 8.   d: Lv 17, 10.   e: Lv 3, 11. 16.   f: Ex 29, 27f.   g: 1-36: cf Ex 29.   h: 6f: Ex 40, 12f.   i: 7ff: Sir 45, 8-13.   j: Ex 28, 30.   k: Ex 28, 36.   l: Ex 30, 26.

The Consecration of Aaron and His Sons

In ch 8, Aaron and his sons are consecrated to the priesthood. According to the priestly source, God, many months earlier, had informed Moses that Aaron and his sons were to become his priests (Ex 28) and outlined the details of this ceremony (Ex 29). Now the consecration is to take place.

on Aaron's head, thus consecrating him.[m] [13]Moses likewise brought forward Aaron's sons, clothed them with tunics, girded them with sashes, and put turbans on them, as the LORD had commanded him to do.

Ordination Sacrifices. [14]When he had brought forward the bullock for a sin offering, Aaron and his sons laid their hands on its head. [15]Then Moses slaughtered it, and taking some of its blood, with his finger he put it on the horns around the altar, thus purifying the altar. He also made atonement for the altar by pouring out the blood at its base when he consecrated it.[n] [16]Taking all the fat that was over the inner organs, as well as the lobe of the liver and the two kidneys with their fat,[o] Moses burned them on the altar. [17]The bullock, however, with its hide and flesh and offal he burned in the fire outside the camp, as the LORD had commanded him to do.

[18]He next brought forward the holocaust ram, and Aaron and his sons laid their hands on its head. [19]When he had slaughtered it, Moses splashed its blood on all sides of the altar. [20]After cutting up the ram into pieces, he burned the head, the cut-up pieces and the suet; [21]then, having washed the inner organs and the shanks with water, he also burned these remaining parts of the ram on the altar as a holocaust, a sweet-smelling oblation to the LORD, as the LORD had commanded him to do.

[22]Then he brought forward the second ram, the ordination ram, and Aaron and his sons laid their hands on its head. [23]When he had slaughtered it, Moses took some of its blood and put it on the tip of Aaron's right ear, on the thumb of his right hand, and on the big toe of his right foot.[p] [24]Moses had the sons of Aaron also come forward, and he put some of the blood on the tips of their right

ears, on the thumbs of their right hands, and on the big toes of their right feet. The rest of the blood he splashed on the sides of the altar. [25]He then took the fat: the fatty tail and all the fat over the inner organs, the lobe of the liver and the two kidneys with their fat, and likewise the right leg; [26]from the basket of unleavened food that was set before the LORD he took one unleavened cake, one loaf of bread made with oil, and one wafer; these he placed on top of the portions of fat and the right leg. [27]He then put all these things into the hands of Aaron and his sons, whom he had wave them as a wave offering before the LORD. [28]When he had received them back, Moses burned them with the holocaust on the altar as the ordination offering, a sweet-smelling oblation to the LORD. [29]He then took the breast and waved it as a wave offering before the LORD; this was Moses' own portion of the ordination ram. All this was in keeping with the LORD's command to Moses. [30]Taking some of the anointing oil and some of the blood that was on the altar, Moses sprinkled with it Aaron and his vestments, as well as his sons and their vestments, thus consecrating both Aaron and his vestments and his sons and their vestments.

[31]Finally, Moses said to Aaron and his sons, "Boil the flesh at the entrance of the meeting tent, and there eat it with the bread that is in the basket of the ordination offering, in keeping with the command I have received: 'Aaron and his sons shall eat of it.' [32]What is left over of the flesh and the bread you shall burn up in the fire. [33]Moreover, you are not to depart from the entrance of the meeting tent for seven days, until the days of your ordination are completed; for your ordination is to last for seven days. [34]*The

8, 34: The sense is not quite clear. Either the verse gives merely the reason why God ordered this ceremony, or it contains

m: Sir 45, 15. n: Lv 4, 7; Heb 9, 22. o: 16f: Lv 3, 4; 4, 8-11. p: Lv 14, 14.

LORD has commanded that what has been done today be done to make atonement for you. [35]Hence you must remain at the entrance of the meeting tent day and night for seven days, carrying out the prescriptions of the LORD; otherwise you shall die; for this is the command I have received." [36]So Aaron and his sons did all that the LORD had commanded through Moses.

CHAPTER 9

See RG 77

Octave of the Ordination. [1]On the eighth day Moses summoned Aaron and his sons, together with the elders of Israel, [2]and said to Aaron, "Take a calf for a sin offering and a ram for a holocaust, both without blemish, and offer them before the LORD. [3]Tell the elders of Israel, too: Take a he-goat for a sin offering, a calf and a lamb, both unblemished yearlings, for a holocaust, [4]and an ox and a ram for a peace offering, to sacrifice them before the LORD, along with a cereal offering mixed with oil; for today the LORD will reveal himself to you." [5]So they brought what Moses had ordered. When the whole community had come forward and stood before the LORD, [6]Moses said, "This is what the LORD orders you to do, that the glory of the LORD may be revealed to you. [7]Come up to the altar," Moses then told Aaron, "and offer your sin offering and your holocaust in atonement for yourself and for your family; then present the offering of the people in atonement for them, as the LORD has commanded."

[8]Going up to the altar, Aaron first slaughtered the calf that was his own sin offering. [9]When his sons presented the blood to him, he dipped his finger in the blood and put it on the horns of the altar. The rest of the blood he poured out at the base of the altar. [10]He then burned on the altar the fat, the kidneys and the lobe of the liver that were taken from the sin offering, as the LORD had commanded Moses; [11]but the flesh and the hide he burned up in the fire outside the camp. [12]Then Aaron slaughtered his holocaust.

When his sons brought him the blood he splashed it on all sides of the altar. [13]They then brought him the pieces and the head of the holocaust, and he burned them on the altar. [14]Having washed the inner organs and the shanks, he burned these also with the holocaust on the altar.

[15]Thereupon he had the people's offering brought up. Taking the goat that was for the people's sin offering, he slaughtered it and offered it up for sin as before. [16]Then he brought forward the holocaust, other than the morning holocaust, and offered it in the usual manner. [17]He then presented the cereal offering; taking a handful of it, he burned it on the altar. [18]Finally he slaughtered the ox and the ram, the peace offering of the people. When his sons brought him the blood, Aaron splashed it on all sides of the altar. [19]The portions of fat from the ox and from the ram, the fatty tail, the fatty membrane over the inner organs, the two kidneys, with the fat that is on them, and the lobe of the liver,[q] [20]he placed on top of the breasts and burned them on the altar, [21]having first waved the breasts and the right legs as a wave offering before the LORD, in keeping with the LORD's command to Moses.

Revelation of the Lord's Glory. [22]Aaron then raised his hands over the people and blessed them. When he came down from offering the sin offering and holocaust and peace offering, [23]Moses and Aaron went into the meeting tent.[s] On coming out they again blessed the people. Then the glory of the LORD was revealed to all the people. [24]Fire came forth from the LORD's presence[t] and consumed the holocaust and the remnants of the fat on the altar. Seeing this, all the people cried out and fell prostrate.

CHAPTER 10

See RG 77

Nadab and Abihu. [1]During this time Aaron's sons Nadab and Abihu* took their censers and, strewing incense on the fire they had put in them,[u] they offered up before

God's command that the same ceremony be used in all future ordinations, or it decrees a repetition of the entire ceremony on each of the seven days. At least a sin offering for atonement was made on each of these days. Cf Ex 29, 29-36.

10, 1: Nadab and Abihu: the older sons of Aaron. Cf Ex 6, 23f.

q: 19f: Lv 3, 3ff.   r: Lv 7, 31f.   s: Nm 6, 23-26.   t: 1 Kgs 18, 38; 2 Chr 7, 1.   u: Lv 16, 1; Nm 3, 4; 26, 61; 1 Chr 24, 2.

the LORD profane fire, such as he had not authorized. [2]Fire* therefore came forth from the LORD's presence and consumed them,[v] so that they died in his presence. [3]Moses then said to Aaron, "This is as the LORD said:

Through those who approach me I will
    manifest my sacredness;*
In the sight of all the people I will
    reveal my glory."[w]

But Aaron said nothing. [4]Then Moses summoned Mishael and Elzaphan, the sons of Aaron's uncle Uzziel, with the order, "Come, remove your kinsmen from the sanctuary and carry them to a place outside the camp." [5]So they went in and took them, in their tunics,* outside the camp, as Moses had commanded.

Conduct of the Priests. [6]Moses said to Aaron and his sons Eleazar and Ithamar, "Do not bare your heads* or tear your garments,[x] lest you bring not only death on yourselves but God's wrath also on the whole community. Your kinsmen, the rest of the house of Israel, shall mourn for those whom the LORD's fire has smitten; [7]but do not you go beyond the entry of the meeting tent, else you shall die; for the anointing oil of the LORD is upon you." So they did as Moses told them.

[8]The LORD said to Aaron, [9]"When you are to go to the meeting tent, you and your sons are forbidden under pain of death, by a perpetual ordinance throughout your generations, to drink any wine or strong drink.[y] [10]You must be able to distinguish between what is sacred and what is profane, between what is clean and what is unclean;[z] [11]you must teach the Israelites all the laws that the LORD has given them through Moses."[a]

The Eating of the Priestly Portions. [12]Moses said to Aaron and his surviving sons, Eleazar and Ithamar, "Take the cereal offering left over from the oblations of the LORD, and eat it beside the altar in the form of unleavened cakes.[b] Since it is most sacred, [13]you must eat it in a sacred place. This is your due from the oblations of the LORD, and that of your sons; such is the command I have received. [14c]With your sons and daughters you shall also eat the breast of the wave offering and the leg of the raised offering, in a clean place; for these have been assigned to you and your children as your due from the peace offerings of the Israelites. [15]The leg of the raised offering and the breast of the wave offering shall first be brought in with the oblations, the fatty portions, that are to be waved as a wave offering before the LORD. Then they shall belong to you and your children by a perpetual ordinance, as the LORD has commanded."

[16]*When Moses inquired about the goat of the sin offering, he discovered that it had all been burned. So he was angry with the surviving sons of Aaron, Eleazar and Ithamar, and said, [17d]"Why did you not eat the sin offering in the sacred place, since it is most sacred? It has been given to you that you might bear the guilt of the community and make atonement for them before the LORD. [18]If its blood was not brought into the inmost part of the sanctuary, you should certainly have eaten the offering in the sanctuary, in keeping with the command I had received." [19]Aaron answered Moses, "Even though they presented their sin offering and holocaust before the LORD today, yet this misfortune has befallen me. Had I then eaten of the sin offering today,

---

10, 2: Fire: perhaps after the manner of lightning.

10, 3: I will manifest my sacredness: the presence of God is so sacred that it strikes dead those who approach him without the proper holiness. Cf Nm 20, 13; Ez 28, 22.

10, 5: In their tunics: they were buried just as they were, with no shroud or funeral solemnities.

10, 6: Bare your heads: go without the customary head covering, as a sign of mourning. Some interpreters, however, understand it as the cutting off of one's hair, which ordinarily all the Israelites, men as well as women, let grow long. Cf Is 15, 2; Jer 7, 29. Still others understand the verb to mean "to let one's hair hang loose and wild." Cf Lv 13, 45; 21, 10, where the same phrase is used.

10, 16-19: Eleazar and Ithamar burned the entire goat of the sin offering (Lv 9, 15) instead of eating it in a sacred place (Lv 6, 19) to bear the guilt of the community. Aaron defends this action of his sons against Moses' displeasure by implying that they did not have sufficient sanctity to eat the flesh of the victim and thus perform the expiation of the people. They themselves still labored under the blow of the divine anger which struck their brothers Nadab and Abihu.

---

v: Nm 16, 35.   w: Lv 21, 17. 21.   x: Lv 21, 10.   y: Ez 44, 21.   z: Lv 11, 47; 20, 25; Ez 22, 26; 44, 23.   a: Sir 45, 16.   b: Lv 6, 16.   c: 14f: Lv 7, 34.   d: Lv 6, 18f.

would it have been pleasing to the LORD?" 20On hearing this, Moses was satisfied.

III: Laws Regarding Legal Purity

CHAPTER 11

See RG
77-78

Clean and Unclean Food. 1The LORD said to Moses and Aaron,* 2"Speak to the Israelites and tell them: Of all land animals these are the ones you may eat: 3any animal that has hoofs you may eat, provided it is cloven-footed and chews the cud. 4But you shall not eat any of the following that only chew the cud or only have hoofs: the camel, which indeed chews the cud, but does not have hoofs and is therefore unclean for you; 5the rock badger,* which indeed chews the cud, but does not have hoofs and is therefore unclean for you; 6the hare, which indeed chews the cud, but does not have hoofs and is therefore unclean for you; and the pig, 7which does indeed have hoofs and is cloven-footed, but does not chew the cud and is therefore unclean for you. 8Their flesh you shall not eat, and their dead bodies you shall not touch; they are unclean for you.

9"Of the various creatures that live in the water, you may eat the following: whatever in the seas or in river waters has both fins and scales you may eat. 10But of the various creatures that crawl or swim in the water, whether in the sea or in the rivers, all those that lack either fins or scales are loathsome for you, 11and you shall treat them as loathsome. Their flesh you shall not eat, and their dead bodies you shall loathe. 12Every water creature that lacks fins or scales is loathsome for you.

13"Of the birds, these you shall loathe and, as loathsome, they shall not be eaten:* the eagle, the vulture, the osprey, 14the kite, the various species of falcons, 15the various species of crows, 16the ostrich, the nightjar, the gull, the various species of hawks, 17the owl, the cormorant, the screech owl, 18the barn owl, the desert owl, the buzzard, 19the stork, the various species of herons, the hoopoe, and the bat.*

20"The various winged insects that walk on all fours are loathsome for you. 21But of the various winged insects that walk on all fours you may eat those that have jointed legs for leaping on the ground; 22hence of these you may eat the following: the various kinds of locusts,* the various kinds of grasshoppers, the various kinds of katydids, and the various kinds of crickets. 23All other winged insects that have four legs are loathsome for you.

24"Such is the uncleanness that you contract, that everyone who touches their dead bodies shall be unclean until evening, 25and everyone who picks up any part of their dead bodies shall wash his garments and be unclean until evening. 26All hoofed animals that are not cloven-footed* or do not chew the cud are unclean for you; everyone who touches them becomes unclean. 27Of the various quadrupeds, all those that walk on paws* are unclean for you; everyone who touches their dead bodies shall be unclean until evening, 28and everyone who picks up their dead bodies shall wash his garments and be unclean until evening. Such is their uncleanness for you.

29"Of the creatures that swarm on the ground, the following are unclean for you: the rat, the mouse, the various kinds of lizards,

---

11, 1ff: These distinctions between edible and inedible meats were probably based on traditional ideas of hygiene, but they are here given a moral, religious basis: the inedible varieties are classified as "unclean" to remind the Israelites that they are to be a pure and holy people, dedicated to the Lord.

11, 5f: According to modern zoology, the rock badger (hyrax Syriacus) is classified as an ungulate, and the hare as a rodent; neither is a ruminant. They appear to chew their food as the true ruminants do, and it is upon this appearance that the classification in the text is based.

11, 13-19. 30: The identification of the various Hebrew names for these birds and reptiles is in many cases uncertain.

11, 19: The bat: actually a mammal, but listed here with the birds because of its wings.

11, 22: The Hebrew distinguishes four classes of edible locust-like insects, but the difference between them is quite uncertain. Cf Mt 3, 4.

11, 24-28: This paragraph sharpens the prohibition against unclean animals: not only is their meat unfit for food, but contact with their dead bodies makes a person ritually unclean.

11, 26: All hoofed animals that are not cloven-footed: such as the horse and the ass.

11, 27: All those that walk on paws: such as dogs and cats.

Purity, Cleanliness, and Ritual

In the thinking of the ancient Israelites, there were certain boundaries within nature that should not be crossed or confused. These boundaries separated things of one kind from things of another kind, and things that went together were seen to have certain characteristics in common. Take, for instance, the category of "creatures that live in the water" (11, 9): along with living in the water, these creatures were supposed to have fins and scales. If a creature—such as an oyster or a lobster—lived in the waters but did not have fins and scales, it did not fulfill all of the characteristics of its kind, and it therefore confused the boundaries of "creatures that live in the water" and was unclean. In the same way, the Israelites believed that animals that chewed the cud—ruminants, such as the cow—should have cloven, or divided, hoofs. The cow has divided hoofs, so it is clean. But the pig, which has divided hoofs, does not chew the cud, so it is unclean. It has confused a natural category, and is therefore to be avoided. See also Deuteronomy 14, 3-21.

The clearest and strongest boundary was the one between life and death, and one had to be very careful when dealing with anything that was dead.

³⁰the gecko, the chameleon, the agama, the skink, and the mole. ³¹Among the various swarming creatures, these are unclean for you. Everyone who touches them when they are dead shall be unclean until evening. ³²Everything on which one of them falls when dead becomes unclean. Any such article that men use, whether it be an article of wood, cloth, leather or goat hair, must be put in water and remain unclean until evening, when it again becomes clean. ³³Should any of these creatures fall into a clay vessel, everything in it becomes unclean, and the vessel itself you must break. ³⁴Any solid food that was in contact with water, and any liquid that men drink, in any such vessel become unclean. ³⁵Any object on which one of their dead bodies falls, becomes unclean; if it is an oven or a jar-stand, this must be broken to pieces; they are unclean and shall be treated as unclean by you. ³⁶However, a spring or a cistern for collecting water remains clean; but whoever touches the dead body* becomes unclean. ³⁷Any sort of cultivated grain remains clean even though one of their dead bodies falls on it; ³⁸but if the grain has become moistened, it becomes unclean when one of these falls on it.

³⁹"When one of the animals that you could otherwise eat, dies of itself, anyone who touches its dead body shall be unclean until evening; ⁴⁰and anyone who eats of its dead body shall wash his garments and be unclean until evening;ᵉ so also, anyone who removes its dead body shall wash his garments and be unclean until evening.

⁴¹"All the creatures that swarm on the ground are loathsome and shall not be eaten. ⁴²Whether it crawls on its belly, goes on all fours, or has many legs, you shall eat no swarming creature: they are loathsome. ⁴³Do not make yourselves loathsome or unclean with any swarming creature through being contaminated by them.ᶠ ⁴⁴For I, the LORD, am your God; and you shall make and keep yourselves holy, because I am holy.ᵍ You shall not make yourselves unclean, then, by any swarming creature that crawls on the ground. ⁴⁵Since I, the LORD, brought you up from the land of Egypt that I might be your God, you shall be holy, because I am holy.

⁴⁶"This is the law for animals and birds and for all the creatures that move about in the water or swarm on the ground, ⁴⁷that you may distinguish between the clean and the unclean, between creatures that may be eaten and those that may not be eaten."ʰ

11, 36: Whoever touches the dead body: to remove the dead insect from the water supply.

e: Lv 17, 15; 22, 8. *f:* 43f: Lv 20, 25f. *g:* Lv 19, 2; 20, 7. 26; Mt 5, 48; 1 Pt 1, 16. *h:* Lv 10, 10.

CHAPTER 12

See RG
77-78

Uncleanness of Childbirth. [1]The
LORD said to Moses, [2]"Tell the Israelites:
When a woman has conceived and gives
birth to a boy, she shall be unclean* for seven
days, with the same uncleanness as at her
menstrual period.[i] [3]On the eighth day, the
flesh of the boy's foreskin shall be circumcised,[j] [4]and then she shall spend thirty-three
days more in becoming purified of her
blood; she shall not touch anything sacred
nor enter the sanctuary till the days of her
purification are fulfilled. [5]If she gives birth
to a girl, for fourteen days she shall be as unclean as at her menstruation, after which she
shall spend sixty-six days in becoming purified of her blood.

[6]"When the days of her purification for a
son or for a daughter are fulfilled,[k] she shall
bring to the priest at the entrance of the
meeting tent a yearling lamb for a holocaust
and a pigeon or a turtledove for a sin offering. [7]The priest shall offer them up before
the LORD to make atonement for her, and
thus she will be clean again after her flow of
blood. Such is the law for the woman who
gives birth to a boy or a girl child. [8]*If, however, she cannot afford a lamb, she may take
two turtledoves or two pigeons,[l] the one for
a holocaust and the other for a sin offering.
The priest shall make atonement for her, and
thus she will again be clean."

CHAPTER 13

See RG
77-78

Leprosy. [1]The LORD said to Moses
and Aaron, [2m]"If someone has on his skin* a
scab or pustule or blotch which appears to be
the sore of leprosy, he shall be brought to
Aaron, the priest, or to one of the priests
among his descendants, [3]who shall examine
the sore on his skin. If the hair on the sore
has turned white and the sore itself shows
that it has penetrated below the skin, it is indeed the sore of leprosy; the priest, on seeing this, shall declare the man unclean. [4]If,
however, the blotch on the skin is white, but
does not seem to have penetrated below the
skin, nor has the hair turned white, the priest
shall quarantine the stricken man for seven
days. [5]On the seventh day the priest shall
again examine him. If he judges that the sore
has remained unchanged and has not spread
on the skin, the priest shall quarantine him
for another seven days, [6]and once more examine him on the seventh day. If the sore is
now dying out and has not spread on the
skin, the priest shall declare the man clean; it
was merely eczema. The man shall wash his
garments and so become clean. [7]But if, after
he has shown himself to the priest to be declared clean, the eczema spreads at all on his
skin, he shall once more show himself to the
priest. [8]Should the priest, on examining it,
find that the eczema has indeed spread on
the skin, he shall declare the man unclean; it
is leprosy.

[9]"When someone is stricken with leprosy,
he shall be brought to the priest. [10]Should
the priest, on examining him, find that there
is a white scab on the skin which has turned
the hair white and that there is raw flesh in it,
[11]it is skin leprosy that has long developed.
The priest shall declare the man unclean
without first quarantining him, since he is
certainly unclean. [12]If leprosy breaks out on
the skin* and, as far as the priest can see,
covers all the skin of the stricken man from
head to foot, [13]should the priest then, on examining him, find that the leprosy does
cover his whole body, he shall declare the
stricken man clean; since it has all turned

12, 2f: The uncleanness of the woman was more serious
during the first period, the seven days after the birth of a boy
or the fourteen days after the birth of a girl; only during this
period would the rules given in Lv 15, 19-24 apply.

12, 8: Forty days after the birth of Jesus, his Virgin
Mother made this offering of the poor (Lk 2, 22. 24);
since the holocaust was offered in thanksgiving for the birth
of the child, this was most fittingly offered by Mary.
However, because of her miraculous delivery, she was not
really obliged to make the sin offering of purification.

13, 2ff: Various kinds of skin blemishes are treated here

which were not contagious but simply disqualified their subjects from association with others, especially in public worship, until they were declared ritually clean. The Hebrew term
used does not refer to Hansen's disease, currently called leprosy.

13, 12ff: If leprosy breaks out on the skin: the symptoms
described here point to a form of skin disease which is merely
on the surface and therefore easily cured.

---

i: Lv 15, 19. *j:* Gn 17, 12; Jn 7, 22. *k:* Lk 2, 22. *l:* Lv 1, 14;
Lk 2, 24. *m:* Dt 24, 8.

white, the man is clean. [14]But as soon as raw flesh appears on him, he is unclean; [15]on observing the raw flesh, the priest shall declare him unclean, because raw flesh is unclean; it is leprosy. [16]If, however, the raw flesh again turns white, he shall return to the priest; [17]should the latter, on examining him, find that the sore has indeed turned white, he shall declare the stricken man clean, and thus he will be clean.

[18]"If a man who had a boil on his skin which later healed, [19]should now in the place of the boil have a white scab or a pink blotch, he shall show himself to the priest. [20]If the latter, on examination, sees that it is deeper than the skin and that the hair has turned white, he shall declare the man unclean: it is the sore of leprosy that has broken out in the boil. [21]But if the priest, on examining him, finds that there is no white hair in it and that it is not deeper than the skin and is already dying out, the priest shall quarantine him for seven days. [22]If it has then spread on the skin, the priest shall declare him unclean; the man is stricken. [23]But if the blotch remains in its place without spreading, it is merely the scar of the boil; the priest shall therefore declare him clean.

[24]"If a man had a burn on his skin, and the proud flesh of the burn now becomes a pink or a white blotch, [25]the priest shall examine it. If the hair has turned white on the blotch and this seems to have penetrated below the skin, it is leprosy that has broken out in the burn; the priest shall therefore declare him unclean and stricken with leprosy. [26]But if the priest, on examining it, finds that there is no white hair on the blotch and that this is not deeper than the skin and is already dying out, the priest shall quarantine him for seven days. [27]Should the priest, when examining it on the seventh day, find that it has spread at all on the skin, he shall declare the man unclean and stricken with leprosy. [28]But if the blotch remains in its place without spreading on the skin and is already dying out, it is merely the scab of the burn; the priest shall

therefore declare the man clean, since it is only the scar of the burn.

[29]"When a man or a woman has a sore on the head or cheek, [30]should the priest, on examining it, find that the sore has penetrated below the skin and that there is fine yellow hair on it, the priest shall declare the person unclean, for this is scall,* a leprous disease of the head or cheek. [31]But if the priest, on examining the scall sore, finds that it has not penetrated below the skin, though the hair on it may not be black, the priest shall quarantine the person with scall sore for seven days, [32]and on the seventh day again examine the sore. If the scall has not spread and has no yellow hair on it and does not seem to have penetrated below the skin, [33]the man shall shave himself, but not on the diseased spot. Then the priest shall quarantine him for another seven days. [34]If the priest, when examining the scall on the seventh day, finds that it has not spread on the skin and that it has not penetrated below the skin, he shall declare the man clean; the latter shall wash his garments, and thus he will be clean. [35]But if the scall spreads at all on his skin after he has been declared clean, [36]the priest shall again examine it. If the scall has indeed spread on the skin, he need not look for yellow hair; the man is surely unclean. [37]If, however, he judges that the scall has remained in its place and that black hair has grown on it, the disease has been healed; the man is clean, and the priest shall declare him clean.

[38]"When the skin of a man or a woman is spotted with white blotches, [39]the priest shall make an examination. If the blotches on the skin are white and already dying out, it is only tetter* that has broken out on the skin, and the person therefore is clean.

[40]"When a man loses the hair of his head, he is not unclean merely because of his bald crown. [41]So too, if he loses the hair on the front of his head, he is not unclean merely because of his bald forehead. [42]But when there is a pink sore on his bald crown or bald forehead, it is leprosy that is breaking out

---

13, 30: Scall: a scabby or scaly eruption of the scalp. According to some, "ringworm."
13, 39: Tetter: vitiligo, a harmless form of skin disease.

there. [43]The priest shall examine him; and if the scab on the sore of the bald spot has the same pink appearance as that of skin leprosy of the fleshy part of the body, [44]the man is leprous and unclean, and the priest shall declare him unclean by reason of the sore on his head.

[45]"The one who bears the sore of leprosy shall keep his garments rent and his head bare, and shall muffle his beard; he shall cry out, 'Unclean, unclean!' [46]As long as the sore is on him he shall declare himself unclean, since he is in fact unclean.[n] He shall dwell apart, making his abode outside the camp.

Leprosy of Clothes. [47]"When a leprous infection* is on a garment of wool or of linen, [48]or on woven or knitted material of linen or wool, or on a hide or anything made of leather, [49]if the infection on the garment or hide, or on the woven or knitted material, or on any leather article is greenish or reddish, the thing is indeed infected with leprosy and must be shown to the priest. [50]Having examined the infection, the priest shall quarantine the infected article for seven days.

[51]"On the seventh day the priest shall again examine the infection. If it has spread on the garment, or on the woven or knitted material, or on the leather, whatever be its use, the infection is malignant leprosy, and the article is unclean. [52]He shall therefore burn up the garment, or the woven or knitted material of wool or linen, or the leather article, whatever it may be, which is infected; since it has malignant leprosy, it must be destroyed by fire. [53]But if the priest, on examining the infection, finds that it has not spread on the garment, or on the woven or knitted material, or on the leather article, [54]he shall give orders to have the infected article washed and then quarantined for another seven days.

[55]"Then the priest shall again examine the infected article after it has been washed. If the infection has not changed its appearance, even though it may not have spread, the article is unclean and shall be destroyed by fire. [56]But if the priest, on examining the infection, finds that it is dying out after the washing, he shall tear the infected part out of the garment, or the leather, or the woven or knitted material. [57]If, however, the infection again appears on the garment, or on the woven or knitted material, or on the leather article, it is still virulent and the thing infected shall be destroyed by fire. [58]But if, after the washing, the infection has left the garment, or the woven or knitted material, or the leather article, the thing shall be washed a second time, and thus it will be clean. [59]This is the law for leprous infection[o] on a garment of wool or linen, or on woven or knitted material, or on any leather article, to determine whether it is clean or unclean."

CHAPTER 14

See RG 77-78

Purification after Leprosy. [1]The LORD said to Moses, [2,p]"This is the law for the victim of leprosy at the time of his purification. He shall be brought to the priest, [3]who is to go outside the camp to examine him. If the priest finds that the sore of leprosy has healed in the leper, [4]he shall order the man who is to be purified, to get two live, clean birds, as well as some cedar wood, scarlet yarn,* and hyssop. [5]The priest shall then order him to slay one of the birds over an earthen vessel with spring water* in it. [6]Taking the living bird with the cedar wood, the scarlet yarn and the hyssop, the priest shall dip them all in the blood of the bird that was slain over the spring water, [7]and then sprinkle seven times the man to be purified from his leprosy. When he has thus purified him, he shall let the living bird fly away over the countryside. [8]The man being purified shall then wash his garments and shave off all his hair and bathe in water; only when he is thus made clean may he come inside the camp; but he shall still remain outside his

---

13, 47: A leprous infection: some mold or fungus growth resembling human leprosy.

14, 4: Scarlet yarn: probably used for tying the hyssop sprig to the cedar branchlet.

14, 5: Spring water: literally, "living water," taken from some source of running water, not from a cistern.

---

n: Nm 5, 2; 12, 14f; 2 Kgs 15, 5; Lk 17, 12.   o: Lv 14, 54.   p: Mt 8, 4; Mk 1, 44; Lk 5, 14.

tent for seven days. [9]On the seventh day he shall again shave off all the hair of his head, his beard, his eyebrows, and any other hair he may have, and also wash his garments and bathe his body in water; and so he will be clean.

Purification Sacrifices. [10]"On the eighth day he shall take two unblemished male lambs, one unblemished yearling ewe lamb, three tenths of an ephah of fine flour mixed with oil for a cereal offering, and one log of oil. [11]The priest who performs the purification ceremony shall place the man who is being purified, as well as all these offerings, before the LORD at the entrance of the meeting tent. [12]Taking one of the male lambs, the priest shall present it as a guilt offering, along with the log of oil, waving them as a wave offering before the LORD. [13](This lamb he shall slaughter in the sacred place where the sin offering and the holocaust are slaughtered; because, like the sin offering, the guilt offering belongs to the priest and is most sacred.) [14]Then the priest shall take some of the blood of the guilt offering and put it on the tip of the man's right ear, the thumb of his right hand, and the big toe of his right foot.[q] [15]The priest shall also take the log of oil and pour some of it into the palm of his own left hand; [16]then, dipping his right forefinger in it, he shall sprinkle it seven times before the LORD. [17]Of the oil left in his hand the priest shall put some on the tip of the man's right ear, the thumb of his right hand, and the big toe of his right foot, over the blood of the guilt offering. [18]The rest of the oil in his hand the priest shall put on the head of the man being purified. Thus shall the priest make atonement for him before the LORD. [19]Only after he has offered the sin offering in atonement for the man's uncleanness shall the priest slaughter the holocaust [20]and offer it, together with the cereal offering, on the altar before the LORD. When the priest has thus made atonement for him, the man will be clean.

Poor Leper's Sacrifice. [21]"If a man is poor and cannot afford so much, he shall take one male lamb for a guilt offering, to be used as a wave offering in atonement for himself, one tenth of an ephah of fine flour mixed with oil for a cereal offering, a log of oil, [22]and two turtledoves* or pigeons, which he can more easily afford, the one as a sin offering and the other as a holocaust. [23]On the eighth day of his purification he shall bring them to the priest, at the entrance of the meeting tent before the LORD. [24]Taking the guilt-offering lamb, along with the log of oil, the priest shall wave them as a wave offering before the LORD. [25]When he has slaughtered the guilt-offering lamb, he shall take some of its blood, and put it on the tip of the right ear of the man being purified, on the thumb of his right hand, and on the big toe of his right foot. [26]The priest shall then pour some of the oil into the palm of his own left hand [27]and with his right forefinger sprinkle it seven times before the LORD. [28]Some of the oil in his hand the priest shall also put on the tip of the man's right ear, the thumb of his right hand, and the big toe of his right foot, over the blood of the guilt offering. [29]The rest of the oil in his hand the priest shall put on the man's head. Thus shall he make atonement for him before the LORD. [30]Then, of the turtledoves or pigeons, such as the man can afford, [31]the priest shall offer up one as a sin offering and the other as a holocaust, along with the cereal offering. Thus shall the priest make atonement before the LORD for the man who is to be purified. [32]This is the law for one afflicted with leprosy who has insufficient means for his purification."

Leprosy of Houses. [33]The LORD said to Moses and Aaron, [34]"When you come into the land of Canaan, which I am giving you to possess, if I put a leprous infection on any house of the land you occupy, [35]the owner of the house shall come and report to the priest, 'It looks to me as if my house were infected.' [36]The priest shall then order the house to be cleared out before he goes in to examine the infection, lest everything in the house become unclean. Only after this is he to go in

---

14, 22: Two turtledoves: substitutes for the two additional lambs, similar to the offering of a poor woman after childbirth. Cf Lv 12, 8.

q: Lv 8, 23f.

to examine the house. *37*If the priest, on examining it, finds that the infection on the walls of the house consists of greenish or reddish depressions which seem to go deeper than the surface of the wall, *38*he shall close the door of the house behind him and quarantine the house for seven days. *39*On the seventh day the priest shall return to examine the house again. If he finds that the infection has spread on the walls, *40*he shall order the infected stones to be pulled out and cast in an unclean place outside the city. *41*The whole inside of the house shall then be scraped, and the mortar that has been scraped off shall be dumped in an unclean place outside the city. *42*Then new stones shall be brought and put in the place of the old stones, and new mortar shall be made and plastered on the house.

43"If the infection breaks out once more after the stones have been pulled out and the house has been scraped and replastered, *44*the priest shall come again; and if he finds that the infection has spread in the house, it is corrosive leprosy, and the house is unclean. *45*It shall be pulled down, and all its stones, beams and mortar shall be hauled away to an unclean place outside the city. *46*Whoever enters a house while it is quarantined shall be unclean until evening. *47*Whoever sleeps or eats in such a house shall also wash his garments. *48*If the priest finds, when he comes to examine the house, that the infection has in fact not spread after the plastering, he shall declare the house clean, since the infection has been healed. *49*To purify the house, he shall take two birds, as well as cedar wood, scarlet yarn, and hyssop. *50*One of the birds he shall slay over an earthen vessel with spring water in it. *51*Then, taking the cedar wood, the hyssop and the scarlet yarn, together with the living bird, he shall dip them all in the blood of the slain bird and the spring water, and sprinkle the house seven times. *52*Thus shall he purify the house with the bird's blood and the spring water, along with the living bird, the cedar wood, the hyssop, and the scarlet yarn. *53*He shall then let the living bird fly away over the countryside outside the city. When he has thus made atonement for it, the house will be clean.

54"This is the law for every kind of human leprosy and scall, *55r*for leprosy of garments and houses, *56*as well as for scabs, pustules and blotches, *57*so that it may be manifest when there is a state of uncleanness and when a state of cleanness. This is the law for leprosy."

CHAPTER 15

Personal Uncleanness. *1*The LORD said to Moses and Aaron, *2*"Speak to the Israelites and tell them: Every man who is afflicted with a chronic flow from his private parts is thereby unclean.*s* *3*Such is his uncleanness from this flow that it makes no difference whether the flow drains off or is blocked up; his uncleanness remains. *4*Any bed on which the man afflicted with the flow lies, is unclean, and any piece of furniture on which he sits, is unclean. *5*Anyone who touches his bed shall wash his garments, bathe in water, and be unclean until evening. *6*Whoever sits on a piece of furniture on which the afflicted man was sitting, shall wash his garments, bathe in water, and be unclean until evening. *7*Whoever touches the body of the afflicted man shall wash his garments, bathe in water, and be unclean until evening. *8*If the afflicted man spits on a clean man, the latter shall wash his garments, bathe in water, and be unclean until evening. *9*Any saddle on which the afflicted man rides, is unclean. *10*Whoever touches anything that was under him shall be unclean until evening; whoever lifts up any such thing shall wash his garments, bathe in water, and be unclean until evening. *11*Anyone whom the afflicted man touches with unrinsed hands shall wash his garments, bathe in water, and be unclean until evening. *12*Earthenware touched by the afflicted man shall be broken; and every wooden article shall be rinsed with water.

13"When a man who has been afflicted with a flow becomes free of his affliction, he shall wait seven days for his purification. Then he shall wash his garments and bathe his body in fresh water, and so he will be clean. [14]On the eighth day he shall take two turtledoves or two pigeons, and going before the LORD, to the entrance of the meeting tent, he shall give them to the priest, [15]who shall offer them up, the one as a sin offering and the other as a holocaust. Thus shall the priest make atonement before the LORD for the man's flow.

[16]"When a man has an emission of seed, he shall bathe his whole body in water and be unclean until evening. [17]Any piece of cloth or leather with seed on it shall be washed with water and be unclean until evening.

[18]"If a man lies carnally with a woman, they shall both bathe in water and be unclean until evening.

[19]"When a woman has her menstrual flow, she shall be in a state of impurity for seven days.[t] Anyone who touches her shall be unclean until evening. [20]Anything on which she lies or sits during her impurity shall be unclean. [21]Anyone who touches her bed shall wash his garments, bathe in water, and be unclean until evening. [22]Whoever touches any article of furniture on which she was sitting, shall wash his garments, bathe in water, and be unclean until evening. [23]*But if she is on the bed or on the seat when he touches it, he shall be unclean until evening. [24]If a man dares to lie with her, he contracts her impurity and shall be unclean for seven days;[u] every bed on which he then lies also becomes unclean.

[25]"When a woman is afflicted with a flow of blood for several days outside her menstrual period, or when her flow continues beyond the ordinary period,[v] as long as she suffers this unclean flow she shall be unclean, just as during her menstrual period. [26]Any bed on which she lies during such a flow becomes unclean, as it would during her menstruation, and any article of furniture on which she sits becomes unclean just

as during her menstruation. [27]Anyone who touches them becomes unclean; he shall wash his garments, bathe in water, and be unclean until evening.

[28]"If she becomes freed from her affliction, she shall wait seven days, and only then is she to be purified. [29]On the eighth day she shall take two turtledoves or two pigeons and bring them to the priest at the entrance of the meeting tent. [30]The priest shall offer up one of them as a sin offering and the other as a holocaust. Thus shall the priest make atonement before the LORD for her unclean flow.

[31]"You shall warn the Israelites of their uncleanness, lest by defiling my Dwelling, which is in their midst, their uncleanness be the cause of their death.

[32]"This is the law for the man who is afflicted with a chronic flow, or who has an emission of seed, and thereby becomes unclean; [33]as well as for the woman who has her menstrual period, or who is afflicted with a chronic flow; the law for male and female; and also for the man who lies with an unclean woman."

CHAPTER 16

See RG 78

The Day of Atonement. [1]After the death of Aaron's two sons, who died when they approached the LORD's presence, the LORD spoke to Moses [2]and said to him,[w] "Tell your brother Aaron that he is not to come whenever he pleases into the sanctuary, inside the veil,* in front of the propitiatory on the ark; otherwise, when I reveal myself in a cloud above the propitiatory, he will die. [3]Only in this way may Aaron enter the sanctuary. He shall bring a young bullock for a sin offering and a ram for a holocaust. [4]He shall wear the sacred linen tunic, with the linen drawers next his flesh, gird himself with the linen sash and put on the linen miter. But since these vestments are sacred, he shall not put them on until he has first bathed his body

---

15, 23: What is added to the legislation by this verse is uncertain in both the Hebrew and the Greek.

16, 2: The sanctuary, inside the veil: the innermost part of the sanctuary, known also as "the holy of holies." Cf Ex 26, 33f. Here the high priest was allowed to enter only once a year, on Yom Kippur, the Day of Atonement. In Heb 9, 3-12

this ceremony is applied to Christ's single act of Redemption, whereby he won for us an everlasting atonement. Propitiatory: see note on Ex 25, 17.

t: Lv 12, 2. 5.   *u:* Lv 18, 19.   *v:* Mt 9, 20; Mk 5, 25; Lk 8, 43.   *w:* Heb 9, 6-12.

in water. [5]From the Israelite community he shall receive two male goats for a sin offering and one ram for a holocaust.[x]

[6]"Aaron shall bring in the bullock, his sin offering to atone for himself and for his household. [7]Taking the two male goats, and setting them before the LORD at the entrance of the meeting tent, [8]he shall cast lots to determine which one is for the LORD and which for Azazel.[*] [9]The goat that is determined by lot for the LORD, Aaron shall bring in and offer up as a sin offering. [10]But the goat determined by lot for Azazel he shall set alive before the LORD, so that with it he may make atonement by sending it off to Azazel in the desert.

[11]"Thus shall Aaron offer up the bullock, his sin offering, to atone for himself and for his family. When he has slaughtered it, [12]he shall take a censer full of glowing embers from the altar before the LORD, as well as a double handful of finely ground fragrant incense, and bringing them inside the veil, [13]there before the LORD he shall put incense on the fire, so that a cloud of incense may cover the propitiatory over the commandments; else he will die.[*] [14]Taking some of the bullock's blood, he shall sprinkle it with his finger on the fore part of the propitiatory and likewise sprinkle some of the blood with his finger seven times in front of the propitiatory.[y]

[15]"Then he shall slaughter the people's sin-offering goat, and bringing its blood inside the veil, he shall do with it as he did with the bullock's blood, sprinkling it on the propitiatory and before it.[z] [16]Thus he shall make atonement for the sanctuary because of all the sinful defilements and faults of the Israelites. He shall do the same for the meeting tent, which is set up among them in the midst of their uncleanness. [17]No one else may be in the meeting tent from the time he enters the sanctuary to make atonement until he departs. When he has made atonement for himself and

his household, as well as for the whole Israelite community, [18]he shall come out to the altar before the LORD and make atonement for it also. Taking some of the bullock's and the goat's blood, he shall put it on the horns around the altar,[a] [19]and with his finger sprinkle some of the blood on it seven times. Thus he shall render it clean and holy, purged of the defilements of the Israelites.

The Scapegoat. [20]"When he has completed the atonement rite for the sanctuary, the meeting tent and the altar, Aaron shall bring forward the live goat. [21]Laying both hands on its head, he shall confess over it all the sinful faults and transgressions of the Israelites, and so put them on the goat's head.[b] He shall then have it led into the desert by an attendant. [22]Since the goat is to carry off their iniquities to an isolated region, it must be sent away into the desert.[c]

[23]*"After Aaron has again gone into the meeting tent, he shall strip off and leave in the sanctuary the linen vestments he had put on when he entered there. [24]After bathing his body with water in a sacred place, he shall put on his vestments, and then come out and offer his own and the people's holocaust, in atonement for himself and for the people, [25]and also burn the fat of the sin offering on the altar.

[26]"The man who has led away the goat for Azazel shall wash his garments and bathe his body in water; only then may he enter the camp. [27]The sin-offering bullock and goat whose blood was brought into the sanctuary to make atonement, shall be taken outside the camp,[d] where their hides and flesh and offal shall be burned up in the fire. [28]The one who burns them shall wash his garments and bathe his body in water; only then may he enter the camp.

The Fast. [29e]"This shall be an everlasting ordinance for you: on the tenth day of the seventh month every one of you, whether a native or a resident alien, shall mortify himself[*] and

16, 8: Azazel: perhaps a name of Satan, used only in this chapter. The ancient versions translated this word as "the escaping goat," whence the English word "scapegoat."

16, 13: Else he will die: the smoke is to conceal the resplendent majesty of God, the sight of which would strike any man dead.

16, 23: This verse is best read after v 25. According to later Jewish practice the high priest again went into the holy of holies to remove the censer.

16, 29: Mortify himself: literally, "afflict his soul"; traditionally understood by the Jews as signifying abstinence from all food. This is the only fast day prescribed in the Mosaic law.

x: Nm 29, 11. y: Heb 9, 13. 25. z: Heb 5, 1; 6, 19. a: Ex 30, 12. b: Is 53, 6; 2 Cor 5, 21. c: Is 53, 11. 12; Jn 1, 29; 1 Pt 2, 24. d: Heb 13, 11. e: Lv 23, 27. 32; Nm 29, 7.

shall do no work. [30]Since on this day atonement is made for you to make you clean, so that you may be cleansed of all your sins before the LORD, [31]by everlasting ordinance it shall be a most solemn sabbath for you, on which you must mortify yourselves.

[32]"This atonement is to be made by the priest who has been anointed and ordained to the priesthood in succession to his father. He shall wear the linen garments, the sacred vestments, [33]and make atonement for the sacred sanctuary, the meeting tent and the altar, as well as for the priests and all the people of the community. [34]This, then, shall be an everlasting ordinance for you: once a year atonement shall be made for all the sins of the Israelites."[f]

Thus was it done, as the LORD had commanded Moses.

IV: Code of Legal Holiness

CHAPTER 17

See RG
79

Sacredness of Blood. [1]The LORD said to Moses, [2]"Speak to Aaron and his sons, as well as to all the Israelites, and tell them: This is what the LORD has commanded. [3]*Any Israelite who slaughters an ox or a sheep or a goat, whether in the camp or outside of it, [4]without first bringing it to the entrance of the meeting tent to present it as an offering to the LORD in front of his Dwelling, shall be judged guilty of bloodshed; and for this, such a man shall be cut off from among his people. [5]Therefore, such sacrifices as they used to offer up in the open field the Israelites shall henceforth offer to the LORD, bringing them to the priest at the entrance of the meeting tent and sacrificing them there as peace offerings to the LORD. [6]The priest shall splash the blood on the altar of the LORD at the entrance of the meeting

tent and there burn the fat for an odor pleasing to the LORD. [7]No longer shall they offer their sacrifices to the satyrs to whom they used to render their wanton worship.[g] This shall be an everlasting ordinance for them and their descendants.

[8]"Tell them, therefore: Anyone, whether of the house of Israel or of the aliens residing among them, who offers a holocaust or sacrifice [9]without bringing it to the entrance of the meeting tent to offer it to the LORD, shall be cut off from his kinsmen. [10]And if anyone, whether of the house of Israel or of the aliens residing among them, partakes of any blood, I will set myself against that one who partakes of blood and will cut him off from among his people.[h] [11i]Since the life of a living body is in its blood, I have made you put it on the altar, so that atonement may thereby be made for your own lives,* because it is the blood, as the seat of life, that makes atonement. [12]That is why I have told the Israelites: No one among you, not even a resident alien, may partake of blood.

[13]"Anyone hunting, whether of the Israelites or of the aliens residing among them, who catches an animal or a bird that may be eaten, shall pour out its blood and cover it with earth. [14]Since the life of every living body is its blood, I have told the Israelites: You shall not partake of the blood of any meat.[j] Since the life of every living body is its blood, anyone who partakes of it shall be cut off.

[15k]Everyone, whether a native or an alien, who eats of an animal that died of itself or was killed by a wild beast, shall wash his garments, bathe in water, and be unclean until evening, and then he will be clean. [16]If he does not wash or does not bathe his body, he shall have the guilt to bear."

17, 3ff: The ancients considered blood the seat and sign of life, and therefore something sacred, even in animals. Cf Gn 9, 4f. Hence, even the ordinary butchering of an animal for meat was looked upon as having a sacrificial character, so that it should be performed at the sanctuary. This law, however, could not be carried out without great difficulty when the Israelites were scattered throughout Palestine, and so was modified in Dt 12, 20ff.

17, 11: That atonement may thereby be made for your

own lives: hence, the sacrifice of an animal was a symbolic act which substituted the victim's life for the life of the offerer, who thus acknowledged that he deserved God's punishments for his sins. This idea of sacrifice is applied in Heb 9–10 to the death of Christ, inasmuch as "without the shedding of blood there is no forgiveness" (Heb 9, 22).

f: Heb 9, 7. 25.   *g:* Ex 34, 15; Dt 32, 17; 2 Chr 11, 15; 1 Cor 10, 20.   *h:* Lv 3, 17.   *i:* Gn 9, 4.   *j:* Lv 7, 26f.   *k:* Lv 11, 39f; 22, 8.

See RG
79

CHAPTER 18

The Sanctity of Sex. [1]The LORD said to Moses, [2]"Speak to the Israelites and tell them: I, the LORD, am your God. [3]You shall not do as they do in the land of Egypt, where you once lived, nor shall you do as they do in the land of Canaan, where I am bringing you; do not conform to their customs. [4]My decrees you shall carry out, and my statutes you shall take care to follow. I, the LORD, am your God. [5]Keep, then, my statutes and decrees, for the man who carries them out will find life through them. I am the LORD.[l]

[6]*"None of you shall approach a close relative to have sexual intercourse with her. I am the LORD. [7m]You shall not disgrace your father by having intercourse with your mother. Besides, since she is your own mother, you shall not have intercourse with her. [8]You shall not have intercourse with your father's wife,[n] for that would be a disgrace to your father. [9]You shall not have intercourse with your sister, your father's daughter or your mother's daughter, whether she was born in your own household or born elsewhere. [10]You shall not have intercourse with your son's daughter or with your daughter's daughter, for that would be a disgrace to your own family. [11]You shall not have intercourse with the daughter whom your father's wife bore to him, since she, too, is your sister. [12o]You shall not have intercourse with your father's sister, since she is your father's relative. [13]You shall not have intercourse with your mother's sister, since she is your mother's relative. [14]You shall not disgrace your father's brother by being intimate with his wife,[p] since she, too, is your aunt. [15]You shall not have intercourse with your daughter-in-law; she is your son's wife, and therefore you shall not disgrace her. [16]You shall not have intercourse with your brother's wife,* for that would be a disgrace to your brother.[q] [17]You shall not have intercourse with a woman and also with her daughter, nor shall you marry and have intercourse with her son's daughter or her daughter's daughter; this would be shameful, because they are related to her. [18]While your wife is still living you shall not marry her sister as her rival; for thus you would disgrace your first wife.

[19]"You shall not approach a woman to have intercourse with her while she is unclean from menstruation. [20]You shall not have carnal relations with your neighbor's wife, defiling yourself with her. [21r]You shall not offer any of your offspring to be immolated to Molech,* thus profaning the name of your God. I am the LORD. [22]You shall not lie with a male as with a woman; such a thing is an abomination.[s] [23]You shall not have carnal relations with an animal, defiling yourself with it; nor shall a woman set herself in front of an animal to mate with it; such things are abhorrent.[t]

[24]"Do not defile yourselves by any of these things by which the nations whom I am driving out of your way have defiled themselves. [25]Because their land has become defiled, I am punishing it for its wickedness, by making it vomit out its inhabitants. [26]You, however, whether natives or resident aliens, must keep my statutes and decrees forbidding all such abominations [27]by which the previous inhabitants defiled the land; [28]otherwise the land will vomit you out also for having defiled it, just as it vomited out the nations before you. [29]Everyone who does any of these abominations shall be cut off from among his people. [30]Heed my charge, then, not to defile yourselves by observing the abominable customs that have been observed before you.[u] I, the LORD, am your God."

18, 6-18: These laws are formulated as directed to the male Israelites only, but naturally the same norms of consanguinity and affinity would apply to the women as well. Marriage, as well as casual intercourse, is here forbidden between men and women of the specified degrees of relationship.

18, 16: With your brother's wife: it was the violation of this law which aroused the wrath of John the Baptist against Herod Antipas. Cf Mk 6, 18. An exception to this law is made in Dt 25, 5.

18, 21: Immolated to Molech: the reference is to the Canaanite custom of sacrificing children to the god Molech. The little victims were first slain and then cremated. Cf Ez 16, 20ff; 20, 26. 31; 23, 37.

l: Gal 3, 12.   m: 7-16: Lv 20, 11-21.   n: Dt 23, 1; 27, 20; 1 Cor 5, 1.   o: 12f: Lv 20, 19.   p: Lv 20, 20.   q: Lv 20, 21; Mt 14, 3f; Mk 6, 18.   r: Lv 20, 2-5; Dt 18, 10; 2 Kgs 16, 3; 21, 6.   s: Lv 20, 13; Rom 1, 27; 1 Cor 6, 9f.   t: Lv 20, 15f; Ex 22, 18.   u: Lv 20, 23; Dt 18, 9.

See RG
79

CHAPTER 19

Various Rules of Conduct. ¹The LORD said to Moses, ²"Speak to the whole Israelite community and tell them: Be holy, for I, the LORD, your God, am holy.ᵛ ³Revere your mother and father,ʷ and keep my sabbaths. I, the LORD, am your God.

⁴"Do not turn aside to idols, nor make molten gods for yourselves.ˣ I, the LORD, am your God.

⁵"When you sacrifice your peace offering to the LORD, if you wish it to be acceptable, ⁶it must be eaten on the very day of your sacrifice or on the following day. Whatever is left over until the third day shall be burned up in the fire. ⁷If any of it is eaten on the third day, the sacrifice will be unacceptable as refuse;ʸ ⁸whoever eats of it then shall pay the penalty for having profaned what is sacred to the LORD. Such a one shall be cut off from his people.

⁹"When you reap the harvest of your land, you shall not be so thorough that you reap the field to its very edge, nor shall you glean the stray ears of grain.ᶻ ¹⁰Likewise, you shall not pick your vineyard bare, nor gather up the grapes that have fallen. These things you shall leave for the poor and the alien. I, the LORD, am your God.

¹¹"You shall not steal. You shall not lie or speak falsely to one another.ᵃ ¹²You shall not swear falsely by my name, thus profaning the name of your God.ᵇ I am the LORD.

¹³"You shall not defraud or rob your neighbor. You shall not withhold overnight the wages of your day laborer.ᶜ ¹⁴You shall not curse the deaf, or put a stumbling block in front of the blind, but you shall fear your God. I am the LORD.

¹⁵"You shall not act dishonestly in rendering judgment. Show neither partiality to the weak nor deference to the mighty, but judge your fellow men justly.ᵈ ¹⁶You shall not go about spreading slander among your kinsmen; nor shall you stand by idly when your neighbor's life is at stake. I am the LORD.

¹⁷"You shall not bear hatred for your brother in your heart.ᵉ Though you may have to reprove your fellow man, do not incur sin because of him. ¹⁸Take no revenge and cherish no grudge against your fellow countrymen. You shall love your neighbor as yourself.* I am the LORD.ᶠ

¹⁹"Keep my statutes: do not breed any of your domestic animals with others of a different species; do not sow a field of yours with two different kinds of seed; and do not put on a garment woven with two different kinds of thread.

²⁰*"If a man has carnal relations with a female slave who has already been living with another man but has not yet been redeemed or given her freedom, they shall be punished but not put to death, because she is not free. ²¹The man, moreover, shall bring to the entrance of the meeting tent a ram as his guilt offering to the LORD. ²²With this ram the priest shall make atonement before the LORD for the sin he has committed, and it will be forgiven him.

²³"When you come into the land and plant any fruit tree there, first look upon its fruit as if it were uncircumcised.* For three years, while its fruit remains uncircumcised, it may not be eaten. ²⁴In the fourth year, however, all of its fruit shall be sacred to the LORD as a thanksgiving feast to him. ²⁵Not until the fifth year may you eat its fruit. Thus it will continue its yield for you. I, the LORD, am your God.

²⁶"Do not eat meat with the blood still in

19, 18: You shall love your neighbor as yourself: cited by our Lord as the second of the two most important commandments of God. Cf Mt 22, 39; Mk 12, 31. Although in the present context the word "neighbor" is restricted to "fellow countrymen," in Lk 10, 29-37 Christ extends its meaning to embrace all men, even enemies. Cf also Mt 5, 43ff.

19, 20ff: This law seems out of its proper context here; perhaps it stood originally after Lv 20, 12. Female slave . . . given her freedom: reference is to the case treated of in Ex 21, 7-11.

19, 23ff: Uncircumcised: by analogy with a newborn boy,

the newly planted tree was considered impure until "circumcised" by offering to the Lord all the fruit it bore in the fourth year.

v: Lv 11, 44; Mt 5, 48; 1 Pt 1, 16. *w:* Ex 20, 12. *x:* Lv 26, 1; Ex 20, 3-5; 34, 17; Dt 27, 15. *y:* Lv 7, 18. *z:* Lv 23, 22; Dt 24, 19ff. *a:* Ex 20, 15f. *b:* Ex 20, 7; Mt 5, 33. *c:* Dt 24, 14f. *d:* Ex 23, 2f; Dt 1, 17; 16, 19; Ps 82, 2; Prv 24, 23. *e:* Mt 18, 15; Lk 17, 3; Gal 6, 1; 1 Jn 3, 14. *f:* Mt 5, 43; 19, 19; 22, 39; Mk 12, 31; Rom 13, 9; Gal 5, 14; Jas 2, 8.

it.*g* Do not practice divination or soothsaying. *27**Do not clip your hair at the temples, nor trim the edges of your beard.*h* *28*Do not lacerate your bodies for the dead, and do not tattoo yourselves. I am the LORD.

29"You shall not degrade your daughter by making a prostitute of her; else the land will become corrupt and full of lewdness. *30*Keep my sabbaths, and reverence my sanctuary.*i* I am the LORD.

31"Do not go to mediums or consult fortune-tellers, for you will be defiled by them.*j* I, the LORD, am your God.

32"Stand up in the presence of the aged, and show respect for the old; thus shall you fear your God. I am the LORD.

33"When an alien resides with you in your land, do not molest him.*k* *34*You shall treat the alien who resides with you no differently than the natives born among you; have the same love for him as for yourself; for you too were once aliens in the land of Egypt.*l* I, the LORD, am your God.

35"Do not act dishonestly in using measures of length or weight or capacity. *36*You shall have a true scale and true weights, an honest ephah and an honest hin.*m* I, the LORD, am your God, who brought you out of the land of Egypt. *37*Be careful, then, to observe all my statutes and decrees. I am the LORD."

See RG
79

CHAPTER 20

Penalties for Various Sins. *1*The LORD said to Moses, *2*"Tell the Israelites: Anyone, whether an Israelite or an alien residing in Israel, who gives any of his offspring to Molech shall be put to death.*n* Let his fellow citizens stone him. *3o*I myself will turn against such a man and cut him off from the body of his people; for in giving his offspring to Molech, he has defiled my sanctuary and profaned my holy name. *4*Even if his fellow citizens connive at such a man's crime of giving his offspring to Molech, and fail to put him to death, *5*I myself will set my face against that man and his family and will cut off from their people both him and all who join him in his wanton worship of Molech. *6*Should anyone turn to mediums and fortune-tellers and follow their wanton ways,*p* I will turn against such a one and cut him off from his people. *7*Sanctify yourselves, then, and be holy; for I, the LORD, your God, am holy.*q* *8*Be careful, therefore, to observe what I, the LORD, who make you holy, have prescribed.

9"Anyone who curses his father or mother shall be put to death;*r* since he has cursed his father or mother, he has forfeited his life. *10*If a man commits adultery with his neighbor's wife, both the adulterer and the adulteress shall be put to death.*s* *11*If a man disgraces his father*t* by lying with his father's wife, both the man and his stepmother shall be put to death; they have forfeited their lives. *12*If a man lies with his daughter-in-law,*u* both of them shall be put to death; since they have committed an abhorrent deed, they have forfeited their lives. *13*If a man lies with a male as with a woman,*v* both of them shall be put to death for their abominable deed; they have forfeited their lives. *14*If a man marries a woman and her mother also,*w* the man and the two women as well shall be burned to death for their shameful conduct, so that such shamefulness may not be found among you. *15*If a man has carnal relations with an animal, the man shall be put to death,*x* and the animal shall be slain. *16*If a woman goes up to any animal to mate with it,*y* the woman and the animal shall be slain; let them both be put to death; their lives are forfeit. *17*If a man consummates marriage with his sister or his half-sister,*z* they shall be publicly cut off from their people for this shameful deed; the man shall pay the penalty of having had intercourse with his own sister. *18*If a man lies in sexual intercourse with a woman during her menstrual

19, 27: See note on Lv 21, 5.

g: Lv 3, 17; Dt 18, 10; 2 Kgs 17, 17; 21, 6; 2 Chr 33, 6.　h: Lv 21, 5.　i: Lv 26, 2; Ex 20, 8.　j: Lv 20, 6. 27; Dt 18, 11; Is 8, 19.　k: Ex 22, 20; 23, 9; Jer 22, 3; Mal 3, 5.　l: Dt 10, 19.　m: Dt 25, 13. 15; Prv 11, 1; 16, 11; 20, 10; Ez 45, 10.　n: Lv 18, 21.　o: Ez 23, 39. p: Lv 19, 31.　q: Lv 11, 44; 19, 2; 1 Pt 1, 16.　r: Ex 21, 17; Prv 20, 20; Mt 15, 4; Mk 7, 10.　s: Lv 18, 20; Dt 22, 22; Jn 8, 5.　t: Lv 18, 7f.　u: Lv 18, 15.　v: Lv 18, 22.　w: Lv 18, 17; Dt 27, 23.　x: Ex 22, 18; Dt 27, 21.　y: Lv 18, 23.　z: Lv 18, 9; Dt 27, 22 period,[a] both of them shall be cut off from their people, because they have laid bare the flowing fountain of her blood. [19]You shall not have intercourse with your mother's sister or your father's sister;[b] whoever does so shall pay the penalty of incest. [20]If a man disgraces his uncle by having intercourse with his uncle's wife, the man and his aunt shall pay the penalty by dying childless. [21]If a man marries his brother's wife and thus disgraces his brother, they shall be childless because of this incest.

[22]"Be careful to observe all my statutes and all my decrees; otherwise the land where I am bringing you to dwell will vomit you out. [23]Do not conform, therefore, to the customs of the nations[c] whom I am driving out of your way, because all these things that they have done have filled me with disgust for them. [24]But to you I have said:[d] Their land shall be your possession, a land flowing with milk and honey. I am giving it to you as your own, I, the LORD, your God, who have set you apart from the other nations. [25e]You, too, must set apart, then, the clean animals from the unclean, and the clean birds from the unclean, so that you may not be contaminated with the uncleanness of any beast or bird or of any swarming creature in the land that I have set apart for you. [26]To me, therefore, you shall be sacred; for I, the LORD, am sacred,[f] I, who have set you apart from the other nations to be my own.

[27]*"A man or a woman who acts as a medium or fortune-teller[g] shall be put to death by stoning; they have no one but themselves to blame for their death."

See RG 79

CHAPTER 21

Sanctity of the Priesthood. [1]The LORD said to Moses, "Speak to Aaron's sons, the priests, and tell them: None of you shall make himself unclean for any dead person* among his people,[h] [2]except for his nearest relatives, his mother or father, his son or daughter, his brother [3]or his maiden sister, who is of his own family while she remains unmarried; for these he may make himself unclean. [4]But for a sister who has married out of his family he shall not make himself unclean; this would be a profanation.

[5]*"The priests shall not make bare the crown of the head, nor shave the edges of the beard,[i] nor lacerate the body. [6]To their God they shall be sacred,* and not profane his name; since they offer up the oblations of the LORD, the food of their God, they must be holy.

[7]"A priest shall not marry a woman who has been a prostitute or has lost her honor, nor a woman who has been divorced by her husband; for the priest is sacred to his God.[j] [8]Honor him as sacred who offers up the food of your God; treat him as sacred, because I, the LORD, who have consecrated him, am sacred.

[9]"A priest's daughter who loses her honor by committing fornication and thereby dishonors her father also, shall be burned to death.

[10]"The most exalted of the priests, upon whose head the anointing oil has been poured and who has been ordained to wear the special vestments, shall not bare his head* or rend his garments, [11]nor shall he go near any dead person. Not even for his father or mother may he thus become unclean [12]or leave the sanctuary;[k] otherwise he will profane the sanctuary of his God, for with the anointing oil upon him, he is dedicated to his God, to me, the LORD.

[13]"The priest shall marry a virgin. [14]Not a widow or a woman who has been divorced or a woman who has lost her honor as a prostitute, but a virgin, taken from his own people, shall he marry;[l] [15]otherwise he will have

---

20, 27: This verse is best read immediately after v 6.

21, 1: Unclean for any dead person: by preparing the corpse for burial. Cf Nm 6, 6; 19, 11-19.

21, 5: Such mourning customs of the Canaanites were forbidden to all the Israelites, but especially to the priests. Cf Lv 19, 27f.

21, 6: Sacred: the same Hebrew word has both the active meaning of "holy," that is, keeping oneself free from profane impurities, and the passive meaning of "sacred," that is, set

apart from what is profane and therefore treated with religious reverence.

21, 10: Bare his head: see note on Lv 10, 6.

---

a: Lv 18, 19. *b:* Lv 18, 12f. *c:* Lv 18, 30. *d:* Ex 3, 8. 17; 6, 8.
e: Lv 11, 2-47; Dt 14, 4-20. *f:* Lv 11, 44; Ex 19, 6; 1 Pt 1, 16.
g: Lv 19, 31; Ex 22, 17; Dt 18, 11. *h:* Ez 44, 25. *i:* Ez 44, 20.
j: Ez 44, 22. *k:* Lv 10, 7. *l:* Ez 44, 22.

Worship and Holiness

Whereas earlier chapters were concerned with the proper procedure for sacrifice (chs 1–7, 17) and with the prompt disposal of impurity (chs 11–16), this section revolves primarily around holiness, that of the priests (ch 21) and that of sacrificial offerings (22, 1–16). The sacred, which belongs to the divine sphere and has been saturated with holiness is vulnerable to attack and is subject to desecration if not kept apart from impurity, disqualifying imperfections, and unauthorized contact or use. Desecration of the holy redounds to God, profaning his abode and his holy name, and brings disastrous consequences in its wake.

base offspring among his people. I, the LORD, have made him sacred."

Irregularities. [16]The LORD said to Moses, [17]"Speak to Aaron and tell him: None of your descendants, of whatever generation, who has any defect shall come forward to offer up the food of his God. [18]Therefore, he who has any of the following defects may not come forward: he who is blind, or lame, or who has any disfigurement or malformation, [19]or a crippled foot or hand, [20]or who is humpbacked or weakly or walleyed, or who is afflicted with eczema, ringworm or hernia. [21]No descendant of Aaron the priest who has any such defect may draw near to offer up the oblations of the LORD; on account of his defect he may not draw near to offer up the food of his God. [22]He may, however, partake of the food of his God: of what is most sacred as well as of what is sacred. [23]Only, he may not approach the veil nor go up to the altar on account of his defect; he shall not profane these things that are sacred to me, for it is I, the LORD, who make them sacred."

[24]Moses, therefore, told this to Aaron and his sons and to all the Israelites.

CHAPTER 22

See RG
79

Sacrificial Banquets. [1]The LORD said to Moses, [2]"Tell Aaron and his sons to respect the sacred offerings which the Israelites consecrate to me; else they will profane my holy name. I am the LORD.

[3]"Tell them: If any one of you, or of your descendants in any future generation, dares, while he is in a state of uncleanness, to draw near the sacred offerings which the Israelites consecrate to the LORD, such a one shall be cut off from my presence. I am the LORD.

[4]"No descendant of Aaron who is stricken with leprosy, or who suffers from a flow, may eat of these sacred offerings, unless he again becomes clean.[m] Moreover, if anyone touches a person who has become unclean by contact with a corpse, or if anyone has had an emission of seed, [5]or if anyone touches[n] any swarming creature or any man whose uncleanness, of whatever kind it may be, is contagious, [6]the one who touches such as these shall be unclean until evening and may not eat of the sacred portions until he has first bathed his body in water;[o] [7]then, when the sun sets, he again becomes clean. Only then may he eat of the sacred offerings, which are his food. [8]He shall not make himself unclean by eating of any animal that has died of itself or has been killed by wild beasts.[p] I am the LORD.

[9]"They shall keep my charge and not do wrong in this matter; else they will die for their profanation. I am the LORD who have consecrated them.

[10]"Neither a lay person nor a priest's tenant or hired servant may eat of any sacred offering.[q] [11]But a slave whom a priest acquires by purchase or who is born in his house may eat of his food. [12]A priest's daughter who is married to a layman may not eat of the sacred contributions. [13]But if a priest's daughter is widowed or divorced and, having no children, returns to her father's house, she may then eat of her father's food as in her youth. No layman, however, may eat of it.

m: Lv 7, 20; 15, 16.   *n:* Lv 11, 24. 43.   *o:* Heb 10, 22.   *p:* Lv 17, 15; Dt 14, 21; Ez 44, 31.   *q:* 1 Sm 21, 6; Mt 12, 4.

[14r]If such a one eats of a sacred offering through inadvertence, he shall make restitution to the priest for the sacred offering, with an increment of one fifth of the amount. [15]The sacred offerings which the Israelites contribute to the LORD the priests shall not allow to be profaned[s] [16]nor in the eating of the sacred offering shall they bring down guilt that must be punished; it is I, the LORD, who make them sacred."

Unacceptable Victims. [17]The LORD said to Moses, [18]"Speak to Aaron and his sons and to all the Israelites, and tell them: When anyone of the house of Israel, or any alien residing in Israel, who wishes to offer a sacrifice, brings a holocaust as a votive offering or as a free-will offering to the LORD, [19]if it is to be acceptable, the ox or sheep or goat that he offers must be an unblemished male.[t] [20]You shall not offer one that has any defect, for such a one would not be acceptable for you.[u] [21]When anyone presents a peace offering[v] to the LORD from the herd or the flock in fulfillment of a vow, or as a free-will offering, if it is to find acceptance, it must be unblemished; it shall not have any defect. [22]One that is blind or crippled or maimed, or one that has a running sore or mange or ringworm, you shall not offer to the LORD; do not put such an animal on the altar as an oblation to the LORD. [23]An ox or a sheep that is in any way ill-proportioned or stunted you may indeed present as a free-will offering, but it will not be acceptable as a votive offering. [24]One that has its testicles bruised or crushed or torn out or cut off you shall not offer to the LORD. You shall neither do this in your own land [25]nor receive from a foreigner any such animals to offer up as the food of your God; since they are deformed or defective,[w] they will not be acceptable for you."

[26]The LORD said to Moses, [27]"When an ox or a lamb or a goat is born, it shall remain with its mother for seven days; only from the eighth day onward will it be acceptable, to be offered as an oblation to the LORD.[x] [28]You shall not slaughter an ox or a sheep on one and the same day with its young. [29]Whenever you offer a thanksgiving sacrifice to the LORD, so offer it that it may be acceptable for you; [30]it must, therefore, be eaten on the same day; none of it shall be left over until the next day.[y] I am the LORD.

[31]"Be careful to observe the commandments which I, the LORD, give you, [32]and do not profane my holy name; in the midst of the Israelites I, the LORD, must be held as sacred. It is I who made you sacred [33]and led you out of the land of Egypt, that I, the LORD, might be your God."

CHAPTER 23

See RG 79

Holy Days. [1]The LORD said to Moses, [2]"Speak to the Israelites and tell them: The following are the festivals of the LORD, my feast days, which you shall celebrate with a sacred assembly.

[3]"For six days work may be done; but the seventh day is the sabbath rest, a day for sacred assembly, on which you shall do no work. The sabbath shall belong to the LORD wherever you dwell.[z]

Passover. [4]"These, then, are the festivals of the LORD which you shall celebrate at their proper time with a sacred assembly.[a] [5]The Passover of the LORD falls on the fourteenth day of the first month, at the evening twilight.[b] [6]The fifteenth day of this month is the LORD's feast of Unleavened Bread. For seven days you shall eat unleavened bread.[c] [7]On the first of these days you shall hold a sacred assembly and do no sort of work.[d] [8]On each of the seven days you shall offer an oblation to the LORD. Then on the seventh day you shall again hold a sacred assembly and do no sort of work."

[9]The LORD said to Moses, [10]"Speak to the Israelites and tell them: When you come into the land which I am giving you, and reap your harvest, you shall bring a sheaf of the first fruits of your harvest to the priest, [11]who

---

r: Lv 5, 16; 27, 13. 15. 19.   s: Lv 19, 8; Nm 18, 32.   t: Lv 1, 3. 10.   u: Dt 15, 21; 17, 1; Mal 1, 8. 14.   v: Lv 3, 1. 6.   w: Mal 1, 14.
x: Ex 22, 29.   y: Lv 7, 15.   z: Ex 20, 8-11; 23, 12; 31, 14f; 34, 21; Dt 5, 12-15; Lk 13, 14.   a: Ex 23, 14-19.   b: Nm 9, 2f; 28, 16.
c: Ex 12, 18; 13, 3. 10; 23, 15; 34, 18.   d: Ex 12, 15; Nm 28, 18. 25.

Sacred Times

In Lv 23, God conveys to Moses, in five speeches, the laws of the weekly Sabbath and the annual holy days. Each of the Torah law collections contains a calendar of annual festivities, and most include a Sabbath law (some mention the Sabbath more than once). The command to abstain from labor on the Sabbath is found in all the collections, as is the tradition of festivals coinciding with the major events in the agricultural year: the early grain ripening, the reaping of the first produce, and the final gathering.

shall wave the sheaf before the LORD that it may be acceptable for you. On the day after the sabbath* the priest shall do this. *12*On this day, when your sheaf is waved, you shall offer to the LORD for a holocaust an unblemished yearling lamb. *13*Its cereal offering shall be two tenths of an ephah of fine flour mixed with oil, as a sweet-smelling oblation to the LORD; and its libation shall be a fourth of a hin of wine. *14*Until this day, when you bring your God this offering, you shall not eat any bread* or roasted grain or fresh kernels. This shall be a perpetual statute for you and your descendants wherever you dwell.

Pentecost. *15*"Beginning with the day after the sabbath, the day on which you bring the wave-offering sheaf, you shall count seven full weeks,*e* *16*and then on the day after the seventh week, the fiftieth* day,*f* you shall present the new cereal offering to the LORD. *17*For the wave offering of your first fruits to the LORD, you shall bring with you from wherever you live two loaves of bread made of two tenths of an ephah of fine flour and baked with leaven. *18*Besides the bread, you shall offer to the LORD a holocaust of seven unblemished yearling lambs, one young bull, and two rams, along with their cereal offering and libations, as a sweet-smelling oblation to the LORD. *19*One male goat shall be sacrificed as a sin offering, and two yearling lambs as a peace offering.*g* *20*The priest shall wave the bread of the first fruits and the two lambs as a wave

offering before the LORD; these shall be sacred to the LORD and belong to the priest. *21*On this same day you shall by proclamation have a sacred assembly, and no sort of work may be done. This shall be a perpetual statute for you and your descendants wherever you dwell.

22"When you reap the harvest of your land, you shall not be so thorough that you reap the field to its very edge, nor shall you glean the stray ears of your grain. These things you shall leave for the poor and the alien. I, the LORD, am your God."

New Year's Day. *23*The LORD said to Moses, *24*"Tell the Israelites: On the first day of the seventh month you shall keep a sabbath rest, with a sacred assembly and with the trumpet blasts as a reminder; *25*you shall then do no sort of work, and you shall offer an oblation to the LORD."

The Day of Atonement. *26h*The LORD said to Moses, *27*"The tenth of this seventh month is the Day of Atonement,*i* when you shall hold a sacred assembly and mortify yourselves and offer an oblation to the LORD. *28*On this day you shall not do any work, because it is the Day of Atonement, when atonement is made for you before the LORD, your God. *29*Anyone who does not mortify himself on this day shall be cut off from his people; *30*and if anyone does any work on this day, I will remove him from the midst of his people. *31*This is a perpetual statute for you and your descendants wherever you

23, 11: The sabbath: according to the Jewish tradition this was the feast day itself, the fifteenth of Nisan, which was a special day of rest. Cf v 7. However, some understand here the Saturday of the Passover week, or even the Saturday following it; cf Jn 19, 31.

23, 14: Any bread: made from the new grain. The harvest had first to be sanctified for man's use by this offering to God.

23, 16: The fiftieth: from the Greek word for this we have the name "Pentecost." Cf 2 Mc 12, 31; Acts 2, 1. It was also

called "the feast of the Seven Weeks," or simply "the feast of Weeks" (Nm 28, 26; Dt 16, 10; Tb 2, 1). The new cereal offering: of flour made from the new grain. Pentecost was the thanksgiving feast at the end of the grain harvest, which began after Passover. Later tradition made it a commemoration of the giving of the law at Sinai.

e: Ex 34, 22; Nm 28, 26; Dt 16, 9.   *f:* Acts 2, 1.   *g:* Nm 28, 30.
h: Lv 25, 9.   *i:* Lv 16, 29f; Nm 29, 7.

dwell: you shall do no work, [32]but shall keep a sabbath of complete rest and mortify yourselves. Beginning on the evening of the ninth of the month, you shall keep this sabbath of yours from evening to evening."

The Feast of Booths. [33]The LORD said to Moses, [34]"Tell the Israelites: The fifteenth day of this seventh month[j] is the LORD's feast of Booths,* which shall continue for seven days. [35]On the first day there shall be a sacred assembly, and you shall do no sort of work. [36]For seven days you shall offer an oblation to the LORD, and on the eighth day you shall again hold a sacred assembly and offer an oblation to the LORD. On that solemn closing you shall do no sort of work.

[37]"These, therefore, are the festivals of the LORD on which you shall proclaim a sacred assembly, and offer as an oblation to the LORD holocausts and cereal offerings, sacrifices and libations, as prescribed for each day, [38]in addition to those of the LORD's sabbaths, your donations, your various votive offerings and the free-will offerings that you present to the LORD.

[39]"On the fifteenth day, then, of the seventh month, when you have gathered in the produce of the land,[k] you shall celebrate a pilgrim feast of the LORD for a whole week. The first and the eighth day shall be days of complete rest. [40]On the first day you shall gather foliage* from majestic trees, branches of palms and boughs of myrtles and of valley poplars, and then for a week you shall make merry before the LORD, your God. [41]By perpetual statute for you and your descendants you shall keep this pilgrim feast of the LORD for one whole week[l] in the seventh month of the year. [42]During this week every native Israelite among you shall dwell in booths, [43]that your descendants[m] may realize that, when I led the Israelites out of the land of Egypt, I made them dwell in booths. I, the LORD, am your God."

[44]Thus did Moses announce to the Israelites the festivals of the LORD.

CHAPTER 24

See RG 79

The Sanctuary Light. [1]The LORD said to Moses, [2]"Order the Israelites to bring you clear oil of crushed olives for the light, so that you may keep lamps burning regularly.[n] [3]In the meeting tent, outside the veil that hangs in front of the commandments, Aaron shall set up the lamps to burn before the LORD regularly, from evening till morning. Thus, by a perpetual statute for you and your descendants, [4]the lamps shall be set up on the pure gold lampstand,[o] to burn regularly before the LORD.

The Showbread. [5]"You shall take fine flour and bake it[p] into twelve cakes, using two tenths of an ephah of flour for each cake. [6]These you shall place in two piles, six in each pile, on the pure gold table before the LORD. [7]On each pile put some pure frankincense, which shall serve as an oblation to the LORD, a token offering for the bread. [8]Regularly on each sabbath day this bread shall be set out afresh[q] before the LORD, offered on the part of the Israelites by an everlasting agreement. [9]It shall belong to Aaron and his sons, who must eat it in a sacred place, since, as something most sacred among the various oblations to the LORD, it is his by perpetual right."

Punishment of Blasphemy. [10]Among the Israelites there was a man born of an Israelite mother (Shelomith, daughter of Dibri, of the tribe of Dan) and an Egyptian father. [11]This man quarreled publicly with another Israelite and cursed and blasphemed the LORD's name. So the people brought him to Moses, [12]who kept him in custody till a decision from the LORD should settle the case

---

23, 34: Feast of Booths: the joyful observance of the vintage and fruit harvest. Cf Dt 16, 13. During the seven days of the feast the Israelites camped in booths of branches erected on the roofs of their houses or in the streets in commemoration of their wanderings in the desert, where they dwelt in booths.
23, 40: Foliage: literally, "fruit," but here probably used in the general sense of "produce, growth." These branches were used for constructing the "booths" or huts in which the people lived during the feast. Cf Neh 8, 15. However, from about the time of Christ on, the Jews have understood this of "fruit" in the strict sense; hence, branches of lemons and oranges were carried with the other branches in joyous procession.

---

j: Nm 29, 12; Dt 16, 13; 2 Mc 1, 9. 18; Jn 7, 2.   *k:* Ex 23, 16; Dt 16, 13.   *l:* Nm 29, 12-38.   *m:* Dt 31, 10-13.   *n:* Ex 27, 20f.   *o:* Ex 25, 31.   *p:* Ex 25, 30; 1 Kgs 7, 48; 2 Chr 4, 19; 13, 11; Heb 9, 2.   *q:* 1 Chr 9, 32.

for them. [13]The LORD then said to Moses, [14]"Take the blasphemer outside the camp, and when all who heard him have laid their hands on his head, let the whole community stone him. [15]Tell the Israelites: Anyone who curses his God shall bear the penalty of his sin; [16]whoever blasphemes the name of the LORD shall be put to death.[r] The whole community shall stone him; alien and native alike must be put to death for blaspheming the LORD's name.

[17]"Whoever takes the life of any human being shall be put to death;[s] [18]whoever takes the life of an animal shall make restitution of another animal. A life for a life![t] [19]Anyone who inflicts an injury on his neighbor shall receive the same in return. [20]Limb for limb, eye for eye, tooth for tooth! The same injury that a man gives another shall be inflicted on him in return.[u] [21]Whoever slays an animal shall make restitution, but whoever slays a man shall be put to death. [22]You shall have but one rule, for alien and native alike.[v] I, the LORD, am your God."

[23]When Moses told this to the Israelites, they took the blasphemer outside the camp and stoned him;[w] they carried out the command that the LORD had given Moses.

See RG 79

CHAPTER 25

The Sabbatical Year. [1]The LORD said to Moses on Mount Sinai, [2]"Speak to the Israelites and tell them: When you enter the land that I am giving you, let the land, too, keep a sabbath for the LORD. [3]For six years you may sow your field, and for six years prune your vineyard, gathering in their produce.[x] [4]But during the seventh year the land shall have a complete rest, a sabbath for the LORD,[y] when you may neither sow your field nor prune your vineyard. [5]*The aftergrowth of your harvest you shall not reap, nor shall you pick the grapes of your untrimmed vines

in this year of sabbath rest for the land. [6]While the land has its sabbath, all its produce will be food equally for you yourself and for your male and female slaves, for your hired help and the tenants who live with you, [7]and likewise for your livestock and for the wild animals on your land.

The Jubilee Year. [8]"Seven weeks of years shall you count—seven times seven years—so that the seven cycles amount to forty-nine years. [9]Then, on the tenth day of the seventh month let the trumpet resound; on this, the Day of Atonement, the trumpet blast shall re-echo throughout your land. [10]This fiftieth year* you shall make sacred by proclaiming liberty in the land for all its inhabitants.[z] It shall be a jubilee for you, when every one of you shall return to his own property, every one to his own family estate. [11]In this fiftieth year, your year of jubilee, you shall not sow, nor shall you reap the aftergrowth or pick the grapes from the untrimmed vines. [12]Since this is the jubilee, which shall be sacred for you, you may not eat of its produce, except as taken directly from the field.

[13]"In this year of jubilee, then, every one of you shall return to his own property. [14]Therefore, when you sell any land to your neighbor or buy any from him, do not deal unfairly. [15]On the basis of the number of years since the last jubilee shall you purchase the land from him;[a] and so also, on the basis of the number of years for crops, shall he sell it to you. [16]When the years are many, the price shall be so much the more; when the years are few, the price shall be so much the less. For it is really the number of crops that he sells you. [17]Do not deal unfairly, then; but stand in fear of your god. I, the LORD, am your God.

[18]"Observe my precepts and be careful to keep my regulations, for then you will dwell securely in the land. [19]The land will yield its

---

25, 5ff: As long as the produce of the sabbatical year remains on the field, it remains available to everyone; cf v 12. In Ex 23, 10f the poor and the wild beasts that have no other source of nourishment are alone mentioned.

25, 10: Fiftieth year: to arrive at this number, the preceding year of jubilee is included in the count, and therefore this is more exactly the forty-ninth year, the seventh sabbatical year. Liberty: Israelite slaves were set free (v 50) and landed property was returned to its original owner (v 13): two im-

portant laws for preserving the social and economic equilibrium. Jubilee: derived from the Hebrew word yobel, "ram's horn," which was blown on this occasion.

r: 1 Kgs 21, 10. 13; Mt 26, 65f; Jn 10, 33. *s:* Gn 9, 5f; Ex 21, 12; Nm 35, 31; Dt 19, 11f. *t:* Ex 21, 33f. *u:* Dt 19, 21; Mt 5, 38. *v:* Lv 19, 34; Ex 12, 49; Nm 15, 16. *w:* Acts 7, 57f. *x:* Ex 23, 10f. *y:* 1 Mc 6, 49. 53. *z:* Nm 36, 4; Is 61, 2; Ez 46, 17; Lk 4, 19. *a:* Lv 27, 18. 23.

fruit and you will have food in abundance, so that you may live there without worry.[b] [20]Therefore, do not say, 'What shall we eat in the seventh year, if we do not then sow or reap our crop?'[c] [21]I will bestow such blessings on you in the sixth year that there will then be crop enough for three years. [22]When you sow in the eighth year, you will continue to eat from the old crop; and even into the ninth year, when the crop comes in, you will still have the old to eat from.[d]

Redemption of Property. [23e]"The land shall not be sold in perpetuity; for the land is mine, and you are but aliens who have become my tenants. [24]Therefore, in every part of the country that you occupy, you must permit the land to be redeemed. [25]When one of your countrymen is reduced to poverty and has to sell some of his property, his closest relative, who has the right to redeem it, may go and buy back what his kinsman has sold.[f] [26]If, however, the man has no relative to redeem his land, but later on acquires sufficient means to buy it back in his own name, [27]he shall make a deduction from the price in proportion to the number of years since the sale, and then pay back the balance to the one to whom he sold it, so that he may thus regain his own property. [28]But if he does not acquire sufficient means to buy back his land, what he has sold shall remain in the possession of the purchaser until the jubilee, when it must be released and returned to its original owner.[g]

[29]"When someone sells a dwelling in a walled town, he has the right to buy it back during the time of one full year from its sale. [30]But if such a house in a walled town has not been redeemed at the end of a full year, it shall belong in perpetuity to the purchaser and his descendants; nor shall it be released in the jubilee. [31]However, houses in villages that are not encircled by walls shall be considered as belonging to the surrounding farm land; they may be redeemed at any time, and in the jubilee they must be released.

[32]"In levitical cities the Levites shall always have the right to redeem the town houses that are their property. [33]Any town house of the Levites in their cities that had been sold and not redeemed, shall be released in the jubilee; for the town houses of the Levites are their hereditary property in the midst of the Israelites. [34]Moreover, the pasture land belonging to their cities shall not be sold at all;[h] it must always remain their hereditary property.

[35]"When one of your fellow countrymen is reduced to poverty and is unable to hold out beside you, extend to him the privileges of an alien or a tenant, so that he may continue to live with you.[i] [36]Do not exact interest from your countryman either in money or in kind, but out of fear of God let him live with you. [37j]You are to lend him neither money at interest nor food at a profit. [38]I, the LORD, am your God, who brought you out of the land of Egypt to give you the land of Canaan and to be your God.

[39]"When, then, your countryman becomes so impoverished beside you that he sells you his services, do not make him work as a slave.[k] [40]Rather, let him be like a hired servant or like your tenant, working with you until the jubilee year, [41]when he, together with his children, shall be released from your service and return to his kindred and to the property of his ancestors. [42]Since those whom I brought out of the land of Egypt are servants of mine, they shall not be sold as slaves to any man. [43]Do not lord it over them harshly, but stand in fear of your God.

[44]"Slaves, male and female, you may indeed possess, provided you buy them from among the neighboring nations. [45]You may also buy them from among the aliens who reside with you and from their children who are born and reared in your land. Such slaves you may own as chattels, [46]and leave to your sons as their hereditary property, making them perpetual slaves. But you shall not lord it harshly over any of the Israelites, your kinsmen.[l]

[47]"When one of your countrymen is reduced to such poverty that he sells himself to a wealthy alien who has a permanent or a

b: Lv 26, 5.   *c:* Mt 6, 25. 31; Lk 12, 22. 29.   *d:* Lv 26, 10.   *e:* 1 Pt 2, 11.   *f:* Ru 2, 20; 4, 4. 6; Jer 32, 7f.   *g:* Lv 27, 24.   *h:* Nm 35, 3. *i:* Dt 15, 7. 8.   *j:* Dt 23, 19.   *k:* 1 Kgs 9, 22.   *l:* Is 14, 1f.

temporary residence among you, or to one of the descendants of an immigrant family, [48]even after he has thus sold his services he still has the right of redemption; he may be redeemed by one of his own brothers, [49]or by his uncle or cousin, or by some other relative or fellow clansman; or, if he acquires the means, he may redeem himself. [50]With his purchaser he shall compute the years from the sale to the jubilee, distributing the sale price over these years as though he had been hired as a day laborer. [51]The more such years there are, the more of the sale price he shall pay back as ransom; [52]the fewer years there are left before the jubilee year, the more he has to his credit; in proportion to his years of service shall he pay his ransom. [53]The alien shall treat him as a servant hired on an annual basis, and he shall not lord it over him harshly under your very eyes. [54]If he is not thus redeemed, he shall nevertheless be released, together with his children, in the jubilee year.[m] [55]For to me the Israelites belong as servants; they are servants of mine, because I brought them out of the land of Egypt, I, the LORD, your God.

CHAPTER 26

See RG 79

The Reward of Obedience. [1]"Do not make false gods for yourselves. You shall not erect an idol or a sacred pillar for yourselves, nor shall you set up a stone figure for worship in your land;[n] for I, the LORD, am your God. [2]Keep my sabbaths,[o] and reverence my sanctuary. I am the LORD.

[3]"If you live in accordance with my precepts and are careful to observe my commandments, [4]I will give you rain in due season, so that the land will bear its crops, and the trees their fruit;[p] [5]your threshing will last till vintage time, and your vintage till the time for sowing, and you will have food to eat in abundance, so that you may dwell securely in your land. [6]I will establish peace in the land, that you may lie down to rest without anxiety. I will rid the country of ravenous beasts, and keep the sword of war from sweeping across your land. [7]You will rout your enemies and lay them low with your sword. [8]Five of you will put a hundred of your foes to flight, and a hundred of you will chase ten thousand of them, till they are cut down by your sword. [9]I will look with favor upon you, and make you fruitful and numerous, as I carry out my covenant with you. [10]So much of the old crops will you have stored up for food that you will have to discard them to make room for the new.[q] [11]I will set my Dwelling among you, and will not disdain you. [12]Ever present in your midst, I will be your God, and you will be my people; [13]for it is I, the LORD, your God, who brought you out of the land of the Egyptians and freed you from their slavery, breaking the yoke they had laid upon you and letting you walk erect.

Punishment of Disobedience. [14]"But if you do not heed me and do not keep all these commandments, [15]if you reject my precepts and spurn my decrees, refusing to obey all my commandments and breaking my covenant, [16]then I, in turn, will give you your deserts. I will punish you with terrible woes—with wasting and fever to dim the eyes and sap the life. You will sow your seed in vain, for your enemies will consume the crop. [17]I will turn against you, till you are beaten down before your enemies and lorded over by your foes. You will take to flight though no one pursues you.[s]

[18]"If even after this you do not obey me, I will increase the chastisement for your sins sevenfold, [19]to break your haughty confidence. I will make the sky above you as hard as iron, and your soil as hard as bronze, [20]so that your strength will be spent in vain; your land will bear no crops, and its trees no fruit. [21]"If then you become defiant in your unwillingness to obey me, I will multiply my blows another sevenfold, as your sins de-

---

26, 3-45: Since God's covenant was with the Israelite nation as a whole, these promises and threats are made primarily to the entire community. The rewards and punishments are of a temporal nature because the community as such exists only here on earth, not in the hereafter.

m: Ex 21, 2f.   *n:* Lv 19, 4; Ex 20, 4; Nm 33, 52; Dt 5, 8.   *o:* Ex 20, 8.   *p:* Ps 85, 13.   *q:* Lv 25, 22.   *r:* 11f: Ex 29, 45; Ez 39. 26ff; 2 Cor 6, 16.   *s:* Dt 28, 25.

serve. [22]I will unleash the wild beasts against you, to rob you of your children and wipe out your livestock, till your population dwindles away and your roads become deserted.

[23]"If, with all this, you still refuse to be chastened by me and continue to defy me, [24]I, too, will defy you and will smite you for your sins seven times harder than before.[t] [25]I will make the sword, the avenger of my covenant, sweep over you. Though you then huddle together in your walled cities, I will send in pestilence among you, till you are forced to surrender to the enemy. [26]And as I cut off your supply of bread, ten women will need but one oven for baking all the bread they dole out to you in rations[u]—not enough food to still your hunger.

[27]"If, despite all this, you still persist in disobeying and defying me, [28]I, also, will meet you with fiery defiance and will chastise you with sevenfold fiercer punishment for your sins, [29v]till you begin to eat the flesh of your own sons and daughters.* [30]I will demolish your high places,[w] overthrow your incense stands, and cast your corpses on those of your idols. In my abhorrence of you, [31]I will lay waste your cities and devastate your sanctuaries, refusing to accept your sweet-smelling offerings. [32]So devastated will I leave the land that your very enemies who come to live there will stand aghast at the sight of it.[x] [33]You yourselves I will scatter among the nations[y] at the point of my drawn sword, leaving your countryside desolate and your cities deserted. [34]Then shall the land retrieve its lost sabbaths during all the time it lies waste, while you are in the land of your enemies; then shall the land have rest and make up for its sabbaths[z] [35]during all the time that it lies desolate, enjoying the rest that you would not let it have on the sabbaths when you lived there.

[36]"Those of you who survive in the lands of their enemies I will make so fainthearted that, if leaves rustle behind them, they will flee headlong, as if from the sword, though no one pursues them; [37]stumbling over one another as if to escape a weapon, while no one is after them—so helpless will you be to take a stand against your foes! [38]You will be lost among the Gentiles, swallowed up in your enemies' country. [39]Those of you who survive in the lands of their enemies will waste away for their own and their fathers' guilt.[a]

[40]"Thus they will have to confess that they and their fathers were guilty of having rebelled against me and of having defied me, [41]so that I, too, had to defy them and bring them into their enemies' land. Then, when their uncircumcised hearts are humbled and they make amends for their guilt, [42]I will remember my covenant with Jacob, my covenant with Isaac, and my covenant with Abraham;[b] and of the land, too, I will be mindful. [43]But the land must first be rid of them, that in its desolation it may make up its lost sabbaths, and that they, too, may make good the debt of their guilt for having spurned my precepts and abhorred my statutes. [44]Yet even so, even while they are in their enemies' land, I will not reject or spurn them, lest, by wiping them out, I make void my covenant with them; for I, the LORD, am their God. [45]I will remember them because of the covenant I made with their forefathers, whom I brought out of the land of Egypt under the very eyes of the Gentiles,[c] that I, the LORD, might be their God."

[46]*These are the precepts, decrees and laws which the LORD had Moses promulgate on Mount Sinai in the pact between himself and the Israelites.

V: Redemption of Offerings

CHAPTER 27

See RG 79

Redemption of Votive Offerings. [1]The LORD said to Moses, [2]"Speak to the Israelites

---

26, 29: Eat the flesh of your own sons and daughters: extreme famine in cities under siege often forced their inhabitants to such dire means of subsistence. Cf Dt 28, 53; Jer 19, 9; Ez 5, 10; 2 Kgs 6, 28f.

26, 46: The Book of Leviticus seems originally to have ended here; the following chapter is an appendix.

t: 24f: Jer 2, 30; Ez 5, 17; 14, 17.   *u:* Is 9, 19; Ez 4, 16; 5, 16; 14, 13; Mi 6, 14.   *v:* Is 9, 18.   *w:* 2 Chr 14, 5; 34, 3. 4. 7; Ez 6, 3-6. *x:* 1 Kgs 9, 8; Jer 9, 11; 18, 16; 19, 8; 25, 18; Ez 5, 15.   *y:* Jer 9, 16; Zec 7, 14.   *z:* Lv 25, 2; 2 Chr 36, 21.   *a:* Ez 4, 17; 24, 23; 33, 10.   *b:* Ex 6, 5; 2 Kgs 13, 23; Ps 106, 45; Ez 16, 60.   *c:* Ex 12, 51.

and tell them: When anyone fulfills a vow of offering one or more persons to the LORD, who are to be ransomed at a fixed sum of money, ³for persons between the ages of twenty and sixty, the fixed sum, in sanctuary shekels, shall be fifty silver shekels for a man, ⁴and thirty shekels for a woman; ⁵for persons between the ages of five and twenty, the fixed sum shall be twenty shekels for a youth, and ten for a maiden; ⁶for persons between the ages of one month and five years, the fixed sum shall be five silver shekels for a boy, and three for a girl; ⁷for persons of sixty or more, the fixed sum shall be fifteen shekels for a man, and ten for a woman. ⁸However, if the one who took the vow is too poor to meet the fixed sum, the person must be set before the priest, who shall determine the sum for his ransom in keeping with the means of the one who made the vow.

⁹"If the offering vowed to the LORD is an animal that may be sacrificed, every such animal, when vowed to the LORD, becomes sacred. ¹⁰The offerer shall not present a substitute for it by exchanging either a better for a worse one or a worse for a better one. If he attempts to offer one animal in place of another, both the original and its substitute shall be treated as sacred. ¹¹If the animal vowed to the LORD is unclean and therefore unfit for sacrifice, it must be set before the priest, ¹²who shall determine its value* in keeping with its good or bad qualities, and the value set by the priest shall stand. ¹³If the offerer wishes to redeem the animal, he shall pay one fifth more than this valuation.ᵈ

¹⁴"When someone dedicates his house as sacred to the LORD, the priest shall determine its value in keeping with its good or bad points, and the value set by the priest shall stand. ¹⁵If the one who dedicated his house wishes to redeem it, he shall pay one fifth more than the price thus established, and then it will again be his.

¹⁶"If the object which someone dedicates to the LORD is a piece of his hereditary land, its valuation shall be made according to the amount of seed required to sow it, the acreage sown with a homer of barley seed being valued at fifty silver shekels. ¹⁷If the dedication of a field is made at the beginning of a jubilee period, the full valuation shall hold; ¹⁸but if it is some time after this, the priest shall estimate its money value according to the number of years left until the next jubilee year, with a corresponding rebate on the valuation.ᵉ ¹⁹If the one who dedicated his field wishes to redeem it, he shall pay one fifth more than the price thus established, and so reclaim it. ²⁰If, instead of redeeming such a field, he sells it to someone else, it may no longer be redeemed; ²¹but at the jubilee it shall be released as sacred to the LORD; like a field that is doomed, it shall become priestly property.

²²"If the field that some man dedicates to the LORD is one he had purchased and not a part of his hereditary property, ²³the priest shall compute its value in proportion to the number of years until the next jubilee, and on the same day the price thus established shall be given as sacred to the LORD; ²⁴at the jubilee,ᶠ however, the field shall revert to the hereditary owner of this land from whom it had been purchased.

²⁵"Every valuation shall be made according to the standard of the sanctuary shekel. There are twenty gerahs to the shekel.

Offerings Not To Be Redeemed. ²⁶"Note that a first-born animal,ᵍ which as such already belongs to the LORD, may not be dedicated by vow to him. If it is an ox or a sheep, it shall be ceded to the LORD; ²⁷but if it is an unclean animal,* it may be redeemed by paying one fifth more than its fixed value. If it is not redeemed, it shall be sold at its fixed value.

²⁸"Note, also, that any one of his posses-

27, 12: Determine its value: fix the price at which the animal may be sold to someone else. Only the original owner must pay the twenty percent tax, as a penalty for buying back what he had vowed to God. So also for houses and fields that are vowed to the Lord, as treated of in the following verses. The money from the sale or from the redemption of such vowed property naturally goes to the sanctuary.

27, 27: An unclean animal: such as the first-born of an ass, which was unfit for sacrifice. According to Ex 13, 13; 34, 20, a first-born ass was to be redeemed by offering a sheep in its stead, or was to have its neck broken. The present law is probably a later modification of the earlier one.

---

d: Lv 22, 14.   *e:* Lv 25, 15f.   *f:* Lv 25, 10. 28. 41.   *g:* Ex 13, 2.

sions which a man vows as doomed to the LORD, whether it is a human being or an animal or a hereditary field, shall be neither sold nor ransomed; everything that is thus doomed becomes most sacred to the LORD.*h* 29All human beings that are doomed* lose the right to be redeemed; they must be put to death.

30"All tithes of the land, whether in grain from the fields or in fruit from the trees, belong to the LORD, as sacred to him.*i* 31If someone wishes to buy back any of his tithes, he shall pay one fifth more than their value.

32The tithes of the herd and the flock shall be determined by ceding to the LORD as sacred every tenth animal as they are counted by the herdsman's rod. 33It shall not matter whether good ones or bad ones are thus chosen, and no exchange may be made. If any exchange is attempted, both the original animal and its substitute shall be treated as sacred, without the right of being bought back."

34These are the commandments which the LORD gave Moses on Mount Sinai for the Israelites.

27, 29: All human beings that are doomed: according to some interpreters, this signifies the idolatrous Canaanites, who were doomed to destruction by divine authority; according to others, this drastic law was enacted for the purpose of discouraging private persons from rashly vowing their slaves or other dependents as offerings to God. Cf Ex 22, 19; Dt 13, 13-19.

h: 1 Sm 15, 21. *i:* Nm 18, 21. 24; 2 Chr 31, 5f. 12; Mal 3, 8. 10.

The Book of Numbers

See RG 80–85

The Book of Numbers derives its name from the account of the two censuses of the Hebrew people taken, one near the beginning and the other toward the end of the journey in the desert (chapters 1 and 26). It continues the story of that journey, begun in Exodus, and describes briefly the experiences of the Israelites for a period of thirty-eight years, from the end of their encampment at Sinai to their arrival at the border of the Promised Land. Numerous legal ordinances are interspersed in the account, making the book a combination of law and history.

The various events described clearly indicate the action of God, who punishes the murmuring of the people by prolonging their stay in the desert, at the same time preparing them by this discipline to be his witnesses among the nations.

In the New Testament Christ and the Apostles derive useful lessons from such events in the Book of Numbers as the brazen serpent (Jn 3, 14f), the sedition of Korah and its consequences (1 Cor 10, 10), the prophecies of Balaam (2 Pt 2, 15f), and the water gushing from the rock (1 Cor 10, 4).

The chief divisions of the Book of Numbers are as follows:

I: Preparation for the Departure from Sinai (1, 1—10, 10).
II: From Sinai to the Plains of Moab (10, 11—22, 1).
III: On the Plains of Moab (22, 2—36, 13).

I: Preparation for the Departure from Sinai

CHAPTER 1

See RG 80–85

The Census. 1In the year following that of the Israelites' departure from the land of Egypt, on the first day of the second month, the LORD said to Moses in the meeting tent in the desert of Sinai: 2*"Take a census of the whole community of the Israelites,*a* by clans and ancestral houses, registering each male individually. 3You and Aaron shall enroll in companies all the men in Israel of twenty years or more who are fit for military service.

Moses' Assistants. 4"To assist you there shall be a man from each tribe, the head of his ancestral house. 5bThese are the names of those who are to assist you:

from Reuben: Elizur, son of Shedeur;

1, 2: All Israel was divided into tribes, each tribe into clans, and each clan into ancestral houses.

a: 2f: Nm 14, 29; 26, 2-51. *b:* 5-15: Nm 10, 14-27.

[6] from Simeon: Shelumiel, son of Zurishaddai;

[7] from Judah: Nahshon, son of Amminadab;

[8] from Issachar: Nethanel, son of Zuar;

[9] from Zebulun: Eliab, son of Helon;

[10] from Ephraim: Elishama, son of Ammihud, and from Manasseh: Gamaliel, son of Pedahzur, for the descendants of Joseph;

[11] from Benjamin: Abidan, son of Gideoni;

[12] from Dan: Ahiezer, son of Ammishaddai;

[13] from Asher: Pagiel, son of Ochran;

[14] from Gad: Eliasaph, son of Reuel;

[15] from Naphtali: Ahira, son of Enan."

[16c]These were councilors of the community, princes of their ancestral tribes, chiefs of the troops* of Israel. [17]So Moses and Aaron took these men who had been designated, [18]and assembled the whole community on the first day of the second month. Every man of twenty years or more then declared his name and lineage according to clan and ancestral house, [19]as the LORD had commanded Moses.

Count of the Twelve Tribes. This is their census as taken in the desert of Sinai. [20]Of the descendants of Reuben, the first-born of Israel, registered by lineage in clans and ancestral houses: when all the males of twenty years or more who were fit for military service were polled, [21]forty-six thousand five hundred were enrolled in the tribe of Reuben.

[22]Of the descendants of Simeon, registered by lineage in clans and ancestral houses: when all the males of twenty years or more who were fit for military service were polled, [23]fifty-nine thousand three hundred were enrolled in the tribe of Simeon.

[24]Of the descendants of Gad, registered by lineage in clans and ancestral houses: when all the males of twenty years or more who were fit for military service were polled, [25]forty-five thousand six hundred and fifty were enrolled in the tribe of Gad.

[26]Of the descendants of Judah, registered by lineage in clans and ancestral houses: when all the males of twenty years or more who were fit for military service were polled, [27]seventy-four thousand six hundred were enrolled in the tribe of Judah.

[28]Of the descendants of Issachar, registered by lineage in clans and ancestral houses: when all the males of twenty years or more who were fit for military service were polled, [29]fifty-four thousand four hundred were enrolled in the tribe of Issachar.

[30]Of the descendants of Zebulun, registered by lineage in clans and ancestral houses: when all the males of twenty years or more who were fit for military service were polled, [31]fifty-seven thousand four hundred were enrolled in the tribe of Zebulun.

[32]Of the descendants of Joseph—

Of the descendants of Ephraim, registered by lineage in clans and ancestral houses: when all the males of twenty years or more who were fit for military service were polled, [33]forty thousand five hundred were enrolled in the tribe of Ephraim.

[34]Of the descendants of Manasseh, registered by lineage in clans and ancestral houses: when all the males of twenty years or more who were fit for military service were polled, [35]thirty-two thousand two hundred were enrolled in the tribe of Manasseh.

[36]Of the descendants of Benjamin, registered by lineage in clans and ancestral houses: when all the males of twenty years or more who were fit for military service were polled, [37]thirty-five thousand four hundred were enrolled in the tribe of Benjamin.

[38]Of the descendants of Dan, registered by lineage in clans and ancestral houses: when all the males of twenty years or more who were fit for military service were polled, [39]sixty-two thousand seven hundred were enrolled in the tribe of Dan.

[40]Of the descendants of Asher, registered by lineage in clans and ancestral houses: when all the males of twenty years or more who were fit for military service were

---

1, 16: Troops: literally "thousands"; this division of the Israelites, with its subdivisions of "hundreds, fifties and tens," was primarily for military and judicial purposes. Cf Ex 18, 21: 2 Sm 18, 1.

c: Ex 18, 21. 25.

polled, [41]forty-one thousand five hundred were enrolled in the tribe of Asher.

[42]Of the descendants of Naphtali, registered by lineage in clans and ancestral houses: when all the males of twenty years or more who were fit for military service were polled, [43]fifty-three thousand four hundred were enrolled in the tribe of Naphtali.

[44]It was these who were registered, each according to his ancestral house, in the census taken by Moses and Aaron and the twelve princes of Israel. [45]The total number of the Israelites of twenty years or more who were fit for military service, registered by ancestral houses, [46]was six hundred and three thousand five hundred and fifty.

Levites Omitted in the Census. [47]The Levites, however, were not registered[d] by ancestral tribe with the others.* [48]For the LORD had told Moses, [49]"The tribe of Levi alone you shall not enroll nor include in the census along with the other Israelites. [50]You are to give the Levites charge of the Dwelling of the commandments with all its equipment and all that belongs to it. It is they who shall carry the Dwelling with all its equipment and who shall be its ministers.[e] They shall therefore camp around the Dwelling. [51]When the Dwelling is to move on, the Levites shall take it down; when the Dwelling is to be pitched, it is the Levites who shall set it up.[f] Any layman who comes near it shall be put to death. [52]While the other Israelites shall camp by companies, each in his own division of the camp,[g] [53]the Levites shall camp around the Dwelling of the commandments.[h] Otherwise God's wrath will strike the Israelite community. The Levites, then, shall have charge of the Dwelling of the commandments." [54]All this the Israelites fulfilled as the LORD had commanded Moses.

See RG 80-85

CHAPTER 2

Arrangement of the Tribes. [1]The LORD said to Moses and Aaron: [2]"The Israelites shall camp, each in his own division, under the ensigns of their ancestral houses.[i] They shall camp around the meeting tent, but at some distance from it.

[3]"Encamped on the east side, toward the sunrise, shall be the divisional camp of Judah, arranged in companies. [The prince of the Judahites was Nahshon, son of Amminadab, [4]and his soldiers amounted in the census to seventy-four thousand six hundred.] [5]With Judah shall camp the tribe of Issachar [their prince was Nethanel, son of Zuar, [6]and his soldiers amounted in the census to fifty-four thousand four hundred] [7]and the tribe of Zebulun. [Their prince was Eliab, son of Helon, [8]and his soldiers amounted in the census to fifty-seven thousand four hundred. [9]The total number of those registered by companies in the camp of Judah was one hundred and eighty-six thousand four hundred.] These shall be first on the march.

[10]"On the south side shall be the divisional camp of Reuben, arranged in companies. [Their prince was Elizur, son of Shedeur, [11]and his soldiers amounted in the census to forty-six thousand five hundred.] [12]Beside them shall camp the tribe of Simeon [their prince was Shelumiel, son of Zurishaddai, [13]and his soldiers amounted in the census to fifty-nine thousand three hundred] [14]and next the tribe of Gad. [Their prince was Eliasaph, son of Reuel, [15]and his soldiers amounted in the census to forty-five thousand six hundred and fifty. [16]The total number of those registered by companies in the camp of Reuben was one hundred and fifty-one thousand four hundred and fifty.] These shall be second on the march.

[17]"Then the meeting tent and the camp of the Levites shall set out in the middle of the line. As in camp, so also on the march, every man shall be in his proper place, with his own division.

[18]"On the west side shall be the divisional

1, 47: The Levites were not enrolled in this census, which was principally for military purposes, but a separate census was made of them. Cf Nm 3, 15f. 39.

2, 3-31: A similar arrangement of the tribes around the central sanctuary in the ideal Israelite state is given in Ez 48.

d: Nm 2, 33; 3, 14-39; 26, 57-62.   e: Nm 3, 7f; 4, 2-49; 1 Chr 6, 48.   f: Nm 3, 10. 38; 18, 7; 2 Sm 6, 6f; 1 Chr 13, 10.   g: Nm 2, 2. 34.   h: Nm 3, 7f. 38; 8, 19; 18, 4f.   i: Nm 1, 52.

camp of Ephraim, arranged in companies. [Their prince was Elishama, son of Ammihud, [19]and his soldiers amounted in the census to forty thousand five hundred.] [20]Beside them shall camp the tribe of Manasseh [their prince was Gamaliel, son of Pedahzur, [21]and his soldiers amounted in the census to thirty-two thousand two hundred] [22]and the tribe of Benjamin. [Their prince was Abidan, son of Gideoni, [23]and his soldiers amounted in the census to thirty-five thousand four hundred. [24]The total number of those registered by companies in the camp of Ephraim was one hundred and eight thousand one hundred.] These shall be third on the march.

[25]"On the north side shall be the divisional camp of Dan, arranged in companies. [Their prince was Ahiezer, son of Ammishaddai, [26]and his soldiers amounted in the census to sixty-two thousand seven hundred.] [27]Beside them shall camp the tribe of Asher [their prince was Pagiel, son of Ochran, [28]and his soldiers amounted in the census to forty-one thousand five hundred] [29]and next the tribe of Naphtali. [Their prince was Ahira, son of Enan, [30]and his soldiers amounted in the census to fifty-three thousand four hundred. [31]The total number of those registered by companies in the camp of Dan was one hundred and fifty-seven thousand six hundred.] These shall be the last of the divisions on the march."

[32]^j This was the census of the Israelites taken by ancestral houses. The total number of those registered by companies in the camps was six hundred and three thousand five hundred and fifty. [33]The Levites, however, were not registered with the other Israelites, for so the LORD had commanded Moses. [34]The Israelites did just as the LORD had commanded Moses; both in camp and on the march they were in their own divisions, every man according to his clan and his ancestral house.

CHAPTER 3

See RG 80–85

The Sons of Aaron. [1]The following were the descendants of Aaron and Moses at the time that the LORD spoke to Moses on Mount Sinai. [2]The sons of Aaron were Nadab his first-born, Abihu, Eleazar, and Ithamar.^k [3]These are the names of the sons of Aaron, the anointed priests who were ordained to exercise the priesthood. [4]But when Nadab and Abihu offered profane fire before the LORD in the desert of Sinai, they met death^l in the presence of the LORD, and left no sons. Thereafter only Eleazar and Ithamar performed the priestly functions under the direction of their father Aaron.

Levites in Place of the First-born. [5]Now the LORD said to Moses: [6]"Summon the tribe of Levi and present them to Aaron the priest, as his assistants.^m [7]They shall discharge his obligations and those of the whole community before the meeting tent^n by serving at the Dwelling. [8]They shall have custody of all the furnishings of the meeting tent and discharge the duties of the Israelites in the service of the Dwelling. [9]You shall give the Levites to Aaron and his sons;^o they have been set aside from among the Israelites as dedicated to me. [10]But only Aaron and his descendants shall you appoint to have charge of the priestly functions.^p Any layman who comes near shall be put to death."

[11]The LORD said to Moses, [12]"It is I who have chosen the Levites from the Israelites in place of every first-born that opens the womb among the Israelites.^q The Levites, therefore, are mine, [13]because every first-born is mine. When I slew all the first-born in the land of Egypt, I made all the first-born in Israel sacred to me, both of man and of beast. They belong to me; I am the LORD."

Census of the Levites. [14]The LORD said to Moses in the desert of Sinai, [15]"Take a census of the Levites by ancestral houses and clans, registering every male of a month or more."^r [16]Moses, therefore, took their census in accordance with the command the LORD had given him.

[17]^s The sons of Levi were named Gershon, Kohath and Merari. [18]The descendants of

j: 32-33: Nm 1, 46-49. k: Ex 6, 23. l: Nm 26, 61; Lv 10, 1f; 1 Chr 24, 2. m: Nm 18, 2. n: Nm 8, 24. o: Nm 8, 19. p: Nm 1, 51; 18, 7. q: 12f: Nm 3, 41; 8, 16f; Ex 13, 2. 12. 15. r: Nm 3, 39; 26. 62. s: 17-20: Nm 26, 57; Gn 46, 11; Ex 6, 16-19; 1 Chr 6, 1f. 16-19.

Gershon, by clans, were named Libni and Shimei. ¹⁹The descendants of Kohath, by clans, were Amram, Izhar, Hebron and Uzziel. ²⁰The descendants of Merari, by clans, were Mahli and Mushi. These were the clans of the Levites by ancestral houses.

Duties of the Levitical Clans. ²¹To Gershon belonged the clan of the Libnites and the clan of the Shimeites; these were the clans of the Gershonites. ²²When all their males of a month or more were registered, they numbered seven thousand five hundred. ²³The clans of the Gershonites camped behind the Dwelling, to the west. ²⁴The prince of their ancestral house was Eliasaph, son of Lael. ²⁵ᵗAt the meeting tent they had charge of whatever pertained to the Dwelling,* the tent and its covering, the curtain at the entrance of the meeting tent, ²⁶the hangings of the court, the curtain at the entrance of the court enclosing both the Dwelling and the altar, and the ropes.

²⁷To Kohath belonged the clans of the Amramites, the Izharites, the Hebronites, and the Uzzielites; these were the clans of the Kohathites. ²⁸When all their males of a month or more were registered, they numbered eight thousand three hundred. They had charge of the sanctuary. ²⁹The clans of the Kohathites camped at the south side of the Dwelling. ³⁰The prince of their ancestral house was Elizaphan, son of Uzziel. ³¹They had charge of whatever pertained to the ark, the table, the lampstand, the altars, the utensils with which the ministry of the sanctuary was exercised, and the veil.* ³²The chief prince of the Levites, however, was Eleazar, son of Aaron the priest; he was supervisor over those who had charge of the sanctuary.

³³To Merari belonged the clans of the Mahlites and the Mushites; these were the clans of Merari. ³⁴When all their males of a month or more were registered, they numbered six thousand two hundred. ³⁵The prince of the ancestral house of the clans of Merari was Zuriel, son of Abihail. They camped at the north side of the Dwelling. ³⁶*The Merarites were charged with the care of whatever pertained to the boards of the Dwelling, its bars, columns, pedestals, and all its fittings, ³⁷as well as the columns of the surrounding court with their pedestals, pegs and ropes.

³⁸East of the Dwelling, that is, in front of the meeting tent, toward the sunrise, were camped Moses and Aaron and the latter's sons. They discharged the obligations of the sanctuary for the Israelites. Any layman who came near was to be put to death.

³⁹The total number of male Levites a month old or more whom Moses had registered by clans in keeping with the LORD's command, was twenty-two thousand.

Census and Ransom of First-born. ⁴⁰The LORD then said to Moses, "Take a census of all the first-born males of the Israelites a month old or more, and compute their total number. ⁴¹Then assign the Levites to me, the LORD, in place of all the first-born of the Israelites, as well as their cattle in place of all the first-born among the cattle of the Israelites." ⁴²So Moses took a census of all the first-born of the Israelites, as the LORD had commanded him. ⁴³When all the first-born males of a month or more were registered, they numbered twenty-two thousand two hundred and seventy-three.

⁴⁴The LORD said to Moses: ⁴⁵"Take the Levites in place of all the first-born of the Israelites, and the Levites' cattle in place of their cattle, that the Levites may belong to me. I am the LORD. ⁴⁶As ransom for the two hundred and seventy-three first-born of the Israelites who outnumber the Levites, ⁴⁷you shall take five shekels for each individual, according to the standard of the

---

3, 25f: The Gershonites had two wagons for transporting these things; cf Nm 7, 7. For a description of the Dwelling, see Ex 26, 1-6; the tent, Ex 26, 7-13; its covering, Ex 26, 14; the curtain at the entrance, Ex 26, 36; the hangings of the court, Ex 27, 9-15; the curtain at the entrance of the court, Ex 27, 16; the ropes of the Dwelling, Ex 35, 18.

3, 31: The Kohathites had to carry these sacred objects on their shoulders; cf Nm 7, 9. For a description of the ark, see

Ex 25, 10-22; the table, Ex 25, 23-30; the lampstand, Ex 25, 31-40; the altars, Ex 27, 1-8; 30, 1-10.

3, 36f: The Merarites had four wagons for transporting this heavy material; cf Nm 7, 8. For a description of the boards, bars, etc., of the Dwelling, see Ex 26, 15-30; the columns, pedestals, etc., of the court, Ex 27, 9-19.

t: 25-26: Ex 26, 7. 14. 36; 36, 14.

The Ark of the Commandments

The ark is a wooden box holding the stone tablets of the Ten Commandments that also serves as a throne or footstool for the divine presence (Ex 25, 10–22). The ark is housed in the inner room of the tabernacle within the meeting tent (see Ex 25—27; 30). The warning concerning the special danger to the Kohathites (Nm 4, 17–20) stems from their responsibility to handle the most holy things (4, 4).

sanctuary shekel, twenty gerahs to the shekel.^{u} ^{48}Give this silver to Aaron and his sons as ransom for the extra number." ^{49}So Moses took the silver as ransom from those who were left when the rest had been redeemed by the Levites. ^{50}From the firstborn of the Israelites he received in silver one thousand three hundred and sixty-five shekels according to the sanctuary standard. ^{51}He then gave this ransom silver to Aaron and his sons, as the LORD had commanded him.

CHAPTER 4

See RG
80-85

Duties Further Defined. ^{1}The LORD said to Moses and Aaron: ^{2}"Among the Levites take a total of the Kohathites, by clans and ancestral houses, all the men of the Kohathites ^{3}between thirty* and fifty years of age; these are to undertake obligatory tasks in the meeting tent.^{v}

^{4}"The service of the Kohathites in the meeting tent concerns the most sacred objects. ^{5}In breaking camp, Aaron and his sons shall go in and take down the screening curtain* and cover the ark of the commandments with it. ^{6}Over these they shall put a cover of tahash skin, and on top of this spread an all-violet cloth. They shall then put the poles in place. ^{7}On the table of the Presence they shall spread a violet cloth and put on it the plates and cups, as well as the bowls and pitchers for libations; the established bread offering shall remain on the table. ^{8}Over these they shall spread a scarlet cloth and cover all this with tahash skin. They shall then put the poles in place. ^{9}They shall use a violet cloth to cover the lampstand with its lamps, trimming shears. and trays, as well as the various containers of oil from which it is supplied. ^{10}The lampstand with all its utensils they shall then enclose in a covering of tahash skin, and place on a litter. ^{11}Over the golden altar* they shall spread a violet cloth, and cover this also with a covering of tahash skin. They shall then put the poles in place. ^{12}Taking the utensils of the sanctuary service, they shall wrap them all in violet cloth and cover them with tahash skin. They shall then place them on a litter. ^{13}After cleansing the altar* of its ashes, they shall spread a purple cloth over it. ^{14}On this they shall put all the utensils with which it is served: the fire pans, forks,* shovels, basins, and all the utensils of the altar. They shall then spread a covering of tahash skin over this, and put the poles in place.

^{15}"Only after Aaron and his sons have finished covering the sacred objects and all their utensils on breaking camp, shall the Kohathites enter to carry them. But they shall not touch the sacred objects; if they do they will die.^{w} These, then, are the objects in the meeting tent that the Kohathites shall carry.

^{16}"Eleazar, son of Aaron the priest, shall be in charge of the oil for the light, the fragrant incense, the established cereal offer-

---

4, 3: Thirty: at a later period the Levites began to serve when they were twenty-five (Nm 8, 24) or even only twenty years old (1 Chr 23, 24. 27; 2 Chr 31, 17; Ezr 3, 8; but cf 1 Chr 23, 3).

4, 5: The screening curtain: the veil between the inner and the outer rooms of the sanctuary. Cf Ex 26, 31-33.

4, 11: The golden altar: the altar of incense. Cf Ex 30, 1-6.

4, 13: The altar: the bronze altar of holocausts. Cf Ex 27. 1-8.

4, 14: Forks: used in turning over the sacrificed animal on the fire of the altar. Basins: to receive the sacrificial blood; cf Zec 9, 15.

---

u: Nm 18, 16; Ex 30, 13; Lv 27, 25; Ez 45, 12.   *v:* Nm 8, 24; 1 Chr 23, 24-27.   *w:* 2 Sm 6, 6f; 1 Chr 13, 9f.

ing, and the anointing oil. He shall be in charge of the whole Dwelling with all the sacred objects and utensils that are in it."

17The LORD said to Moses and Aaron: 18"Do not let the group of Kohathite clans perish from the body of the Levites. 19That they may live and not die when they approach the most sacred objects, this is what you shall do for them: Aaron and his sons shall go in and assign to each of them his task and what he must carry; 20but the Kohathites shall not go in to look upon the sacred objects, even for an instant; if they do, they will die."x

21The LORD said to Moses, 22"Take a total among the Gershonites also, by ancestral houses and clans, 23of all the men between thirty and fifty years of age; these are to undertake obligatory tasks in the meeting tent. 24This is the task of the clans of the Gershonites, what they must do and what they must carry: 25they shall carry the sheets of the Dwelling, the meeting tent with its covering and the outer wrapping of tahash skin, the curtain at the entrance of the meeting tent, 26the hangings of the court, the curtain at the entrance of the court that encloses both the Dwelling and the altar, together with their ropes and all other objects necessary in their use. Whatever is to be done with these things shall be their task. 27The service of the Gershonites shall be entirely under the direction of Aaron and his sons, with regard to what they must do and what they must carry; you shall make each man of them responsible for what he is to carry. 28This, then, is the task of the Gershonites in the meeting tent; and they shall be under the supervision of Ithamar, son of Aaron the priest.

29"Among the Merarites, too, you shall enroll by clans and ancestral houses 30all their men between thirty and fifty years of age; these are to undertake obligatory tasks in the meeting tent. 31yThis is what they shall be responsible for carrying, all the years of their service in the meeting tent: the boards of the Dwelling with its bars, columns and pedestals, 32and the columns of the surrounding court with their pedestals, pegs and

ropes. You shall designate for each man of them all the objects connected with his service, which he shall be responsible for carrying. 33This, then, is the task of the clans of the Merarites during all their service in the meeting tent under the supervision of Ithamar, son of Aaron the priest."

Number of Adult Levites. 34So Moses and Aaron and the princes of the community made a registration among the Kohathites, by clans and ancestral houses, 35of all the men between thirty and fifty years of age. These were to undertake obligatory tasks in the meeting tent; 36as registered by clans, they numbered two thousand seven hundred and fifty. 37Such was the census of all the men of the Kohathite clans who were to serve in the meeting tent, which Moses took, together with Aaron, as the LORD bade him.

38The registration was then made among the Gershonites, by clans and ancestral houses, 39of all the men between thirty and fifty years of age. These were to undertake obligatory tasks in the meeting tent; 40as registered by clans and ancestral houses, they numbered two thousand six hundred and thirty. 41Such was the census of all the men of the Gershonite clans who were to serve in the meeting tent, which Moses took, together with Aaron, at the LORD's bidding.

42Then the registration was made among the Merarites, by clans and ancestral houses, 43of all the men from thirty up to fifty years of age. These were to undertake obligatory tasks in the meeting tent; 44as registered by clans, they numbered three thousand two hundred. 45Such was the census of the men of the Merarite clans which Moses took, together with Aaron, as the LORD bade him.

46Therefore, when Moses and Aaron and the Israelite princes had completed the registration among the Levites, by clans and ancestral houses, 47of all the men between thirty and fifty years of age who were to undertake tasks of service or transport of the meeting tent, 48the total number registered was eight thousand five hundred and eighty. 49According to the LORD's bidding to Moses, they gave them their individual assign-

x: 1 Sm 6, 19.   y: Nm 3, 36f.

ments for service and for transport; so the LORD had commanded Moses.

See RG 80–85

CHAPTER 5

The Unclean Expelled. [1]The LORD said to Moses: [2]"Order the Israelites to expel from camp every leper, and everyone suffering from a discharge, and everyone who has become unclean by contact with a corpse.*[z] [3]Male and female alike, you shall compel them to go out of the camp; they are not to defile the camp in which I dwell."[a] [4]The Israelites obeyed the command that the LORD had given Moses; they expelled them from the camp.

Unjust Possession. [5]*The LORD said to Moses, [6]b"Tell the Israelites: If a man (or woman) commits a fault against his fellow man and wrongs him, thus breaking faith with the LORD, [7]he shall confess the wrong he has done, restore his ill-gotten goods in full, and in addition give one fifth of their value to the one he has wronged. [8]However, if the latter has no next of kin* to whom restoration of the ill-gotten goods can be made, the goods to be restored shall be the LORD's and shall fall to the priest; this is apart from the atonement ram with which the priest makes amends for the guilty man. [9]Likewise, every sacred contribution that the Israelites are bound to make shall fall to the priest.[c] [10]Each Israelite man may dispose of his own sacred contributions; they become the property of the priest to whom he gives them."[d]

Ordeal for a Suspected Adulteress. [11]The LORD said to Moses, [12]"Speak to the Israelites and tell them: If a man's wife goes astray and becomes unfaithful to him [13]by having intercourse with another man,[e] though her husband has not sufficient evidence of the fact, so that her impurity remains unproved for lack of a witness who might have caught her in the act; [14]or if a man is overcome by a feeling of jealousy that makes him suspect his wife, whether she was actually impure or not: [15]he shall bring his wife to the priest and shall take along as an offering for her a tenth of an ephah of barley meal. However, he shall not pour oil on it nor put frankincense over it, since it is a cereal offering of jealousy, a cereal offering for an appeal in a question of guilt.

[16]"The priest shall first have the woman come forward and stand before the LORD. [17]In an earthen vessel he shall meanwhile put some holy water,* as well as some dust that he has taken from the floor of the Dwelling.[f] [18]Then, as the woman stands before the LORD, the priest shall uncover her head and place in her hands the cereal offering of her appeal,* that is, the cereal offering of jealousy, while he himself shall hold the bitter water that brings a curse. [19]Then he shall adjure the woman, saying to her, 'If no other man has had intercourse with you, and you have not gone astray by impurity while under the authority of your husband, be immune to the curse brought by this bitter water. [20]But if you have gone astray while under the authority of your husband and have acted impurely by letting a man other than your husband have intercourse with you'— [21]so shall the priest adjure the woman with this oath of imprecation—'may the LORD make you an example of malediction and imprecation* among your people by causing your thighs to waste away and your belly to swell! [22]May this water, then, that brings a curse, enter your body to make your belly

---

5, 2: For the laws regarding victims of leprosy, see Lv 13–14; those suffering from a discharge, Lv 15; the unclean by contact with a corpse, Nm 19, 11-22; Lv 21, 1-4.

5, 5-10: The basic law on unjust possession is given in Lv 5, 14-26. The new item here concerns the case where the injured party has died and left no heirs, in which case the restitution must be made to the priest.

5, 8: Next of kin: literally, "redeemer," a technical term denoting the nearest relative, upon whom devolved the obligation of "redeeming" the family property, in order to keep it within the family. Cf Lv 25, 25; Ru 4, 1-6.

5, 17: Holy water: water from the laver that stood in the court of the Dwelling.

5, 18: Appeal: by which she invokes the Lord and refers her case to his decision.

5, 21: An example of malediction and imprecation: the woman's name would be used in curses and oaths to invoke a similar misfortune on another person or on oneself. Cf Is 65, 15; Jer 29, 22.

z: Nm 19, 11. 13; Lv 13, 46; 21, 1; 22, 4. a: Nm 35, 34. b: 6ff: Lv 5, 21-25. c: Dt 18, 3f; Ex 44, 29f. d: Lv 10, 12-15. e: Lv 18, 20; Jn 8, 4. f: Nm 19, 17.

swell and your thighs waste away!'^{g} And the woman shall say, 'Amen, amen!'* ^{23}The priest shall put these imprecations in writing and shall then wash them off into the bitter water, ^{24}which he is to have the woman drink, so that it may go into her with all its bitter curse. ^{25}But first he shall take the cereal offering of jealousy from the woman's hand, and having waved this offering before the Lord, shall put it near the altar, ^{26}where he shall take a handful of the cereal offering as its token offering and burn it on the altar.^{h} Only then shall he have the woman drink the water. ^{27}Once she has done so, if she has been impure and unfaithful to her husband, this bitter water that brings a curse will go into her, and her belly will swell and her thighs will waste away, so that she will become an example of imprecation among her people. ^{28}If, however, the woman has not defiled herself, but is still pure, she will be immune and will still be able to bear children.

^{29}"This, then, is the law for jealousy: When a woman goes astray while under the authority of her husband and acts impurely, ^{30}or when such a feeling of jealousy comes over a man that he becomes suspicious of his wife, he shall have her stand before the Lord, and the priest shall apply this law in full to her. ^{31}The man shall be free from guilt,* but the woman shall bear such guilt as she may have."

CHAPTER 6

See RG
80-85

Laws Concerning Nazirites. ^{1}The Lord said to Moses: ^{2}"Speak to the Israelites and tell them: When a man (or a woman) solemnly takes the nazirite* vow to dedicate himself to the Lord, ^{3}he shall abstain from wine and strong drink;^{i} he may neither drink wine vinegar, other vinegar, or any kind of grape juice, nor eat either fresh or dried grapes. ^{4}As long as he is a nazirite he shall not eat anything of the produce of the vine; not even unripe grapes or grapeskins. ^{5}While he is under the nazirite vow, no razor shall touch his hair.^{j} Until the period of his dedication to the Lord is over, he shall be sacred, and shall let the hair of his head grow freely. ^{6}As long as he is dedicated to the Lord, he shall not enter where a dead person is.^{k} ^{7}Not even for his father or mother, his sister or brother, should they die, may he become unclean, since his head bears his dedication to God. ^{8}As long as he is a nazirite he is sacred to the Lord.

^{9}"If someone dies very suddenly in his presence, so that his dedicated head becomes unclean, he shall shave his head on the day of his purification, that is, on the seventh day. ^{10}On the eighth day he shall bring two turtledoves or two pigeons to the priest at the entrance of the meeting tent. ^{11}The priest shall offer up the one as a sin offering and the other as a holocaust, thus making atonement for him for the sin he has committed by reason of the dead person. On the same day he shall reconsecrate his head ^{12}and begin anew the period of his dedication to the Lord as a nazirite, bringing a yearling lamb as a guilt offering. The previous period is not valid, because his dedicated head became unclean.

^{13}"This is the ritual for the nazirite:^{l} On the day he completes the period of his dedication he shall go to the entrance of the meeting tent, ^{14}bringing as his offering to the Lord one unblemished yearling lamb for a holocaust, one unblemished yearling ewe lamb for a sin offering, one unblemished ram as a peace offering, along with their cereal offerings and libations, ^{15}and a basket of unleav-

---

5, 22: Amen: a Hebrew word meaning, "certainly, truly," used to give assent to a statement, a curse, a blessing, a prayer, or the like; in this sense of "so be it," the Christian liturgy also uses it after prayers and blessings.

5, 31: Free from guilt: by fulfilling his obligation of obtaining a decision in the matter.

6, 1ff: Nazirite: from the Hebrew word nazir, meaning "set apart as sacred, dedicated, vowed." The nazirite vow could be either for a limited period or for life. Those bound by this vow had to abstain from all the products of the grapevine, from cutting or shaving their hair, and from con-

tact with a corpse. They were regarded as men of God like the prophets; cf Am 2, 11f. Examples of lifelong nazirites were Samson (Jgs 13, 4f. 7; 16, 17), Samuel (1 Sm 1, 11), and John the Baptizer (Lk 1, 15). At the time of Christ the practice of taking the nazirite vow for a limited period seems to have been quite common, even among the early Christians; cf Acts 18, 18; 21, 23f. 26.

g: Ps 109, 18.   h: Lv 5, 12.   i: 3f: Jgs 13, 7. 14.   j: Jgs 13, 5; 16, 17; 1 Sm 1, 11.   k: Nm 19, 11. 16; Lv 21, 11.   l: Acts 21, 24. 26.

The Priestly Blessing

Priests concluded communal worship with the words of blessing and peace in 6, 24–26. Two silver cylinders discovered by archaeologists and dated to 600 B.C. contain portions of this ancient priestly blessing written in Hebrew. To let one's face shine and look upon someone kindly (lit. "lift up the face") are images of protection, favor, and graciousness (6, 25–26; see Ps 67, 1–2; Jb 34, 29). Peace ("shalom") connotes well-being and wholeness in all aspects of one's life (6, 26). Putting the divine name upon the Israelites implies that they belong exclusively to the LORD and that the LORD will care for them.

ened cakes of fine flour mixed with oil and of unleavened wafers spread with oil. [16]The priest shall present them before the LORD, and shall offer up the sin offering and the holocaust for him. [17]He shall then offer up the ram as a peace offering to the LORD, with its cereal offering and libation, and the basket of unleavened cakes. [18]Then at the entrance of the meeting tent the nazirite shall shave his dedicated head,[m] collect the hair, and put it in the fire that is under the peace offering. [19]After the nazirite has shaved off his dedicated hair, the priest shall take a boiled shoulder of the ram, as well as one unleavened cake and one unleavened wafer from the basket, and shall place them in the hands of the nazirite. [20]The priest shall then wave them as a wave offering before the LORD. They become sacred and shall belong to the priest, along with the breast of the wave offering and the leg of the raised offering. Only after this may the nazirite drink wine.

[21]"This, then, is the law for the nazirite; this is the offering to the LORD which is included in his vow of dedication apart from anything else which his means may allow. Thus shall he carry out the law of his dedication in keeping with the vow he has taken."

The Priestly Blessing. [22]The LORD said to Moses: [23]"Speak to Aaron and his sons and tell them: This is how you shall bless the Israelites. Say to them:

[24] The LORD bless you and keep you!

[25] The LORD let his face shine* upon you,
and be gracious to you!
[26] The LORD look upon you kindly and give
you peace!*

[27]So shall they invoke my name upon the Israelites, and I will bless them."

CHAPTER 7

See RG 80-85

Offerings of Princes. [1]Now, when Moses had completed the erection of the Dwelling and had anointed and consecrated it with all its equipment[n] (as well as the altar with all its equipment), [2]an offering was made by the princes of Israel, who were heads of ancestral houses; the same princes of the tribes who supervised the census. [3]The offering they brought before the LORD consisted of six baggage wagons and twelve oxen, that is, a wagon for every two princes, and an ox for every prince. These they presented as their offering before the Dwelling.

[4]The LORD then said to Moses, [5]"Accept their offering, that these things may be put to use in the service of the meeting tent. Assign them to the Levites, to each group in proportion to its duties." [6]So Moses accepted the wagons and oxen, and assigned them to the Levites. [7]He gave two wagons and four oxen to the Gershonites[o] in proportion to their duties, [8]and four wagons and eight oxen to the Merarites in proportion to their duties, under the supervision of Ithamar, son of Aaron the priest. [9]He gave none to the Kohathites, because they had to carry

6, 25: Let his face shine: a Hebrew idiom for "smile."
6, 26: Peace: the Hebrew word includes the idea of "prosperity, happiness."

m: Acts 18, 18; 21, 24.   *n:* Ex 40, 17.   *o:* 7f: Nm 4, 24-33.

on their shoulders the sacred objects which were their charge.*p*

¹⁰For the dedication of the altar also, the princes brought offerings before the altar on the day it was anointed.*q* ¹¹But the LORD said to Moses, "Let one prince a day present his offering for the dedication of the altar."

¹²*The one who presented his offering on the first day was Nahshon, son of Amminadab, prince of the tribe of Judah. ¹³His offering consisted of one silver plate weighing a hundred and thirty shekels according to the sanctuary standard and one silver basin weighing seventy shekels, both filled with fine flour mixed with oil for a cereal offering; ¹⁴one gold cup of ten shekels' weight filled with incense; ¹⁵one young bull, one ram, and one yearling lamb for a holocaust; ¹⁶one goat for a sin offering; ¹⁷and two oxen, five rams, five goats, and five yearling lambs for a peace offering. This was the offering of Nahshon, son of Amminadab.

¹⁸On the second day Nethanel, son of Zuar, prince of Issachar, made his offering. ¹⁹He presented as his offering one silver plate weighing a hundred and thirty shekels according to the sanctuary standard and one silver basin weighing seventy shekels, both filled with fine flour mixed with oil for a cereal offering; ²⁰one gold cup of ten shekels' weight filled with incense; ²¹one young bull, one ram, and one yearling lamb for a holocaust; ²²one goat for a sin offering; ²³and two oxen, five rams, five goats, and five yearling lambs for a peace offering. This was the offering of Nethanel, son of Zuar.

²⁴On the third day it was the turn of Eliab, son of Helon, prince of the Zebulunites. ²⁵His offering consisted of one silver plate weighing a hundred and thirty shekels according to the sanctuary standard and one silver basin weighing seventy shekels, both filled with fine flour mixed with oil for a cereal offering; ²⁶one gold cup of ten shekels' weight filled with incense; ²⁷one young bull, one ram, and one yearling lamb for a holocaust; ²⁸one goat for a sin offering; ²⁹and two oxen, five rams, five goats, and five yearling lambs for a peace offering. This was the offering of Eliab, son of Helon.

³⁰On the fourth day it was the turn of Elizur, son of Shedeur, prince of the Reubenites. ³¹His offering consisted of one silver plate weighing a hundred and thirty shekels according to the sanctuary standard and one silver basin weighing seventy shekels, both filled with fine flour mixed with oil for a cereal offering; ³²one gold cup of ten shekels' weight filled with incense; ³³one young bull, one ram, and one yearling lamb for a holocaust; ³⁴one goat for a sin offering; ³⁵and two oxen, five rams, five goats, and five yearling lambs for a peace offering. This was the offering of Elizur, son of Shedeur.

³⁶On the fifth day it was the turn of Shelumiel, son of Zurishaddai, prince of the Simeonites. ³⁷His offering consisted of one silver plate weighing a hundred and thirty shekels according to the sanctuary standard and one silver basin weighing seventy shekels, both filled with fine flour mixed with oil for a cereal offering; ³⁸one gold cup of ten shekels' weight filled with incense; ³⁹one young bull, one ram, and one yearling lamb for a holocaust; ⁴⁰one goat for a sin offering; ⁴¹and two oxen, five rams, five goats, and five yearling lambs for a peace offering. This was the offering of Shelumiel, son of Zurishaddai.

⁴²On the sixth day it was the turn of Eliasaph, son of Reuel, prince of the Gadites. ⁴³His offering consisted of one silver plate weighing a hundred and thirty shekels according to the sanctuary standard and one silver basin weighing seventy shekels, both filled with fine flour mixed with oil for a cereal offering; ⁴⁴one gold cup of ten shekels' weight filled with incense; ⁴⁵one young bull, one ram, and one yearling lamb for a holocaust; ⁴⁶one goat for a sin offering; ⁴⁷and two oxen, five rams, five goats, and five yearling lambs for a peace offering. This was the offering of Eliasaph, son of Reuel.

⁴⁸On the seventh day it was the turn of Elishama, son of Ammihud, prince of the

7, 12-88: The repetitive account of the same offerings brought by each of the twelve tribal princes and the summary of them are characteristic of an official registration.

p: Nm 3, 31; 4, 4-15.   *q:* Nm 7, 84.

Ephraimites. [49]His offering consisted of one silver plate weighing a hundred and thirty shekels according to the sanctuary standard and one silver basin weighing seventy shekels, both filled with fine flour mixed with oil for a cereal offering; [50]one gold cup of ten shekels' weight filled with incense; [51]one young bull, one ram, and one yearling lamb for a holocaust; [52]one goat for a sin offering; [53]and two oxen, five rams, five goats, and five yearling lambs for a peace offering. This was the offering of Elishama, son of Ammihud.

[54]On the eighth day it was the turn of Gamaliel, son of Pedahzur, prince of the Manassehites. [55]His offering consisted of one silver plate weighing a hundred and thirty shekels according to the sanctuary standard and one silver basin weighing seventy shekels, both filled with fine flour mixed with oil for a cereal offering; [56]one gold cup of ten shekels' weight filled with incense; [57]one young bull, one ram, and one yearling lamb for a holocaust; [58]one goat for a sin offering; [59]and two oxen, five rams, five goats, and five yearling lambs for a peace offering. This was the offering of Gamaliel, son of Pedahzur.

[60]On the ninth day it was the turn of Abidan, son of Gideoni, prince of the Benjaminites. [61]His offering consisted of one silver plate weighing a hundred and thirty shekels according to the sanctuary standard and one silver basin weighing seventy shekels, both filled with fine flour mixed with oil for a cereal offering; [62]one gold cup of ten shekels' weight filled with incense; [63]one young bull, one ram, and one yearling lamb for a holocaust; [64]one goat for a sin offering; [65]and two oxen, five rams, five goats, and five yearling lambs for a peace offering. This was the offering of Abidan, son of Gideoni.

[66]On the tenth day it was the turn of Ahiezer, son of Ammishaddai, prince of the Danites. [67]His offering consisted of one silver plate weighing a hundred and thirty shekels according to the sanctuary standard and one silver basin weighing seventy shekels, both filled with fine flour mixed with oil for a cereal offering; [68]one gold cup of ten shekels' weight filled with incense; [69]one young bull, one ram, and one yearling lamb for a holocaust; [70]one goat for a sin offering; [71]and two oxen, five rams, five goats, and five yearling lambs for a peace offering. This was the offering of Ahiezer, son of Ammishaddai.

[72]On the eleventh day it was the turn of Pagiel, son of Ochran, prince of the Asherites. [73]His offering consisted of one silver plate weighing a hundred and thirty shekels according to the sanctuary standard and one silver basin weighing seventy shekels, both filled with fine flour mixed with oil for a cereal offering; [74]one gold cup of ten shekels' weight filled with incense; [75]one young bull, one ram, and one yearling lamb for a holocaust; [76]one goat for a sin offering; [77]and two oxen, five rams, five goats, and five yearling lambs for a peace offering. This was the offering of Pagiel, son of Ochran.

[78]On the twelfth day it was the turn of Ahira, son of Enan, prince of the Naphtalites. [79]His offering consisted of one silver plate weighing a hundred and thirty shekels according to the sanctuary standard and one silver basin weighing seventy shekels, both filled with fine flour mixed with oil for a cereal offering; [80]one gold cup of ten shekels' weight filled with incense; [81]one young bull, one ram, and one yearling lamb for a holocaust; [82]one goat for a sin offering; [83]and two oxen, five rams, five goats, and five yearling lambs for a peace offering. This was the offering of Ahira, son of Enan.

[84]These were the offerings for the dedication of the altar, given by the princes of Israel on the occasion of its anointing: twelve silver plates, twelve silver basins, and twelve gold cups. [85]Each silver plate weighed a hundred and thirty shekels, and each silver basin seventy, so that all the silver of these vessels amounted to two thousand four hundred shekels, according to the sanctuary standard. [86]The twelve gold cups that were filled with incense weighed ten shekels apiece, according to the sanctuary standard, so that all the gold of the cups amounted to one hundred and twenty shekels. [87]The animals for the holocausts

were, in all, twelve young bulls, twelve rams, and twelve yearling lambs, with their cereal offerings; those for the sin offerings were twelve goats. [88]The animals for the peace offerings were, in all, twenty-four oxen, sixty rams, sixty goats, and sixty yearling lambs. These, then, were the offerings for the dedication of the altar after it was anointed.

The Voice. [89]When Moses entered the meeting tent to speak with him, he heard the voice addressing him from above the propitiatory[r] on the ark of the commandments, from between the two cherubim; and it spoke to him. . . ,

See RG 80-85

CHAPTER 8

The Lamps Set Up. [1]The LORD spoke to Moses, and said, [2]"Give Aaron this command: When you set up the seven lamps,[s] have them throw their light toward the front of the lampstand." [3]Aaron did so, setting up the lamps to face toward the front of the lampstand, just as the LORD had commanded Moses. [4]The lampstand was made of beaten gold[t] in both its shaft and its branches, according to the pattern which the LORD had shown Moses.

Purification of the Levites. [5]The LORD said to Moses: [6]"Take the Levites from among the Israelites and purify them.[*] [7]This is what you shall do to them to purify them. Sprinkle them with the water of remission;[*] then have them shave their whole bodies and wash their clothes, and so purify themselves. [8]They shall take a young bull, along with its cereal offering of fine flour mixed with oil; you shall take another young bull for a sin offering. [9]Then have the Levites come forward in front of the meeting tent, where you shall assemble also the whole community of the Israelites. [10]While the Levites are present before the LORD, the Israelites shall lay their hands upon them. [11]Let Aaron then offer the Levites before the LORD as a wave of-

fering from the Israelites, thus devoting them to the service of the LORD. [12]The Levites in turn shall lay their hands on the heads of the bullocks, which shall then be immolated, the one as a sin offering and the other as a holocaust to the LORD, in atonement for the Levites. [13]Thus, then, shall you have the Levites stand before Aaron and his sons, to be offered as a wave offering to the LORD; [14]and thus shall you set aside the Levites from the rest of the Israelites, that they may be mine.[u]

[15]"Only then shall the Levites enter upon their service in the meeting tent. You shall purify them and offer them as a wave offering; [16]because they, among the Israelites, are strictly dedicated to me; I have taken them for myself in place of every first-born that opens the womb among the Israelites.[v] [17]Indeed, all the first-born among the Israelites, both of man and of beast, belong to me; I consecrated them to myself on the day I slew all the first-born in the land of Egypt.[w] [18]But in place of all the first-born Israelites I have taken the Levites; [19]and I have given these dedicated Israelites to Aaron and his sons[x] to discharge the duties of the Israelites in the meeting tent and to make atonement for them, so that no plague may strike among the Israelites should they come near the sanctuary."

[20]Thus, then, did Moses and Aaron and the whole community of the Israelites deal with the Levites, carrying out exactly the command which the LORD had given Moses concerning them. [21]When the Levites had cleansed themselves of sin[*] and washed their clothes, Aaron offered them as a wave offering before the LORD, and made atonement for them to purify them. [22]Only then did they enter upon their service in the meeting tent under the supervision of Aaron and his sons. The command which the LORD had given Moses concerning the Levites was carried out.

8, 6: Purify them: in the language of the Pentateuch only the priests were "consecrated," that is, made sacred or set aside for the Lord, in an elaborate ceremony described in Ex 29; Lv 8. The Levites were merely "purified," that is, made ritually clean for their special work.

8, 7: Water of remission: literally, "water of sin," that is,

for the remission of sin.

8, 21: Cleansed themselves of sin: by having the "water of remission" sprinkled on them as prescribed in v 7.

---

r: Ex 25, 22. s: Ex 25, 37. t: Ex 25, 31. 40. u: Nm 3, 45. v: Nm 3, 12. 45. w: Nm 3, 13; 13, 2; Lk 2, 23. x: Nm 3, 9f.

Age Limits for Levitical Service. ²³The LORD said to Moses: ²⁴"This is the rule for the Levites. Each from his twenty-fifth year onward shall perform the required service in the meeting tent.ʸ ²⁵When he is fifty years old, he shall retire from the required service and work no longer. ²⁶His service with his fellow Levites shall consist in sharing their responsibilities in the meeting tent, but he shall not do the work. This, then, is how you are to regulate the duties of the Levites."

CHAPTER 9

See RG
80–85

Second Passover. ¹In the first month of the year following their departure from the land of Egypt, the LORD said to Moses in the desert of Sinai, ²"Tell the Israelites to celebrate the Passover at the prescribed time. ³The evening twilight of the fourteenth day of this monthᶻ is the prescribed time when you shall celebrate it, observing all its rules and regulations." ⁴Moses, therefore, told the Israelites to celebrate the Passover. ⁵And they did so, celebrating the Passover in the desert of Sinai during the evening twilight of the fourteenth day of the first month, just as the LORD had commanded Moses.

⁶There were some, however, who were unclean because of a human corpse and so could not keep the Passover that day. These men came up to Moses and Aaron that same day ⁷and said, "Although we are unclean because of a corpse, why should we be deprived of presenting the LORD's offering at its proper time along with the other Israelites?" ⁸Moses answered them, "Wait until I learn what the LORD will command in your regard."

⁹The LORD then said to Moses: ¹⁰"Speak to the Israelites and say: If any one of you or of your descendants is unclean because of a corpse, or if he is absent on a journey, he may still keep the LORD's Passover. ¹¹But he shall keep it in the second month,ᵃ during the evening twilight of the fourteenth day of that month, eating it with unleavened bread and bitter herbs, ¹²and not leaving any of it over till morning, nor breaking any of its bones,ᵇ but observing all the rules of the Passover. ¹³However, anyone who is clean and not away on a journey, who yet fails to keep the Passover, shall be cut off from his people, because he did not present the LORD's offering at the prescribed time. That man shall bear the consequences of his sin.

¹⁴"If an alien* who lives among you wishes to keep the LORD's Passover, he too shall observe the rules and regulations for the Passover. You shall have the same law for the resident alien as for the native of the land."ᶜ

The Fiery Cloud. ¹⁵On the day when the Dwelling was erected, the cloud* covered the Dwelling, the tent of the commandments; but from evening until morning it took on the appearance of fire over the Dwelling.ᵈ ¹⁶It was always so: during the day the Dwelling was covered by the cloud, which at night had the appearance of fire. ¹⁷Whenever the cloud rose from the tent, the Israelites would break camp; wherever the cloud came to rest, they would pitch camp.ᵉ ¹⁸At the bidding of the LORD the Israelites moved on, and at his bidding they encamped.ᶠ As long as the cloud stayed over the Dwelling, they remained in camp. ¹⁹Even when the cloud tarried many days over the Dwelling, the Israelites obeyed the LORD and would not move on; ²⁰yet sometimes the cloud was over the Dwelling only for a few days. It was at the bidding of the LORD that they stayed in camp, and it was at his bidding that they departed. ²¹Sometimes the cloud remained there only from evening until morning; and when it rose in the morning, they would depart. Or if the cloud lifted during the day, or even at night, they would then set out. ²²Whether the cloud tarried over the Dwelling for two days or for a month or longer, the Israelites remained in camp and did not depart; but when it lifted, they moved on. ²³Thus, it was always at the

---

9, 14: An alien: this passage presupposes that he is already circumcised as prescribed in Ex 12, 48.

9, 15: The cloud: already mentioned at the departure from Egypt; cf Ex 13, 21f.

---

y: Nm 4, 3. 23.   z: Ex 12, 6; Lv 23, 5.   a: 2 Chr 30, 2-15.   b: Ex 12, 46; Jn 19, 36.   c: Ex 12, 48f.   d: Ex 13, 21.   e: Wis 18, 3.
f: 1 Cor 10, 1.

The Two Silver Trumpets

The two silver trumpets (ch 10) are sacred instruments blown by priests for four purposes: to call together the whole congregation or the leaders for an assembly (vv. 3–4), to provide a signal to set out from camp on the wilderness sojourn (vv. 5–6), to sound an alarm at the time of war (v. 9), and to call a celebration on "your days of celebration" (v. 10). According to the ancient Jewish historian Josephus and as depicted on ancient Jewish coins, the silver trumpets are about twelve inches long with a slender body and wide mouth.

bidding of the LORD that they encamped, and at his bidding that they set out; ever heeding the charge of the LORD, as he had bidden them through Moses.

See RG 80–85

CHAPTER 10

The Silver Trumpets. ¹The LORD said to Moses: ²"Make two trumpets of beaten silver, which you shall use in assembling the community and in breaking camp. ³When both are blown, the whole community shall gather round you at the entrance of the meeting tent; ⁴but when one of them is blown, only the princes, the chiefs of the troops of Israel, shall gather round you. ⁵When you sound the first alarm, those encamped on the east side shall set out; ⁶when you sound the second alarm, those encamped on the south side shall set out; when you sound the third alarm, those encamped on the west side shall set out; when you sound the fourth alarm, those encamped on the north side shall set out. Thus shall the alarm be sounded for them to depart. ⁷But in calling forth an assembly you are to blow an ordinary blast, without sounding the alarm.

⁸"It is the sons of Aaron, the priests, who shall blow the trumpets; and the use of them is prescribed by perpetual statute for you and your descendants. ⁹ᵍWhen in your own land you go to war against an enemy that is attacking you, you shall sound the alarm on the trumpets, and the LORD, your God, will remember you and save you from your foes. ¹⁰On your days of celebration,* your festivals, and your new-moon feasts, you shall blow the trumpets over your holocausts and your peace offerings;ʰ this will serve as a reminder of you before your God. I, the LORD, am your God."

II: From Sinai to the Plains of Moab

Departure from Sinai. ¹¹In the second year, on the twentieth day of the second month, the cloud rose from the Dwelling of the commandments. ¹²The Israelites moved on from the desert of Sinai by stages, until the cloud came to rest in the desert of Paran.

¹³The first time that they broke camp at the bidding of the LORD through Moses, ¹⁴ⁱthe camp of the Judahites, under its own standard and arranged in companies, was the first to set out. Nahshon, son of Amminadab, was over their host, ¹⁵and Nethanel, son of Zuar, over the host of the tribe of Issachar, ¹⁶and Eliab, son of Helon, over the host of the tribe of Zebulun. ¹⁷Then, after the Dwelling was dismantled, the clans of Gershon and Merari set out, carrying the Dwelling. ¹⁸The camp of the Reubenites, under its own standard and arranged in companies, was the next to set out, with Elizur, son of Shedeur, over their host, ¹⁹and Shelumiel, son of Zurishaddai, over the host of the tribe of Simeon, ²⁰and Eliasaph, son of Reuel, over the host of the tribe of Gad. ²¹The clan of Kohath then set out, carrying the sacred objects for the Dwelling, which was to be erected before their arrival. ²²The camp of the Ephraimites next set out, under its own standard and arranged in companies, with Elishama, son of Ammihud, over their host, ²³and Gamaliel, son of Pedahzur, over the host of the tribe of

10, 10: Days of celebration: special holidays, such as the occasion of a victory. Festivals: the great annual feasts of the Passover, Pentecost and Booths described in Lv 23; Nm 28–29.

g: 2 Chr 13, 14.   *h:* Nm 29, 1; 2 Chr 29, 26ff.   *i:* 14ff: Nm 2, 3. 5. 7.

Manasseh, [24]and Abidan, son of Gideoni, over the host of the tribe of Benjamin. [25]Finally, as rear guard for all the camps, the camp of the Danites set out, under its own standard and arranged in companies, with Ahiezer, son of Amishaddai, over their host, [26]and Pagiel, son of Ochran, over the host of the tribe of Asher, [27]and Ahira, son of Enan, over the host of the tribe of Naphtali. [28]This was the order of departure for the Israelites, company by company.

Hobab as Guide. As they were setting out, [29]Moses said to his brother-in-law Hobab, son of Reuel the Midianite, "We are setting out for the place which the LORD has promised to give us. Come with us, and we will be generous toward you, for the LORD has promised prosperity to Israel." [30]*But he answered, "No, I will not come. I am going instead to my own country and to my own kindred." [31]Moses said, "Please, do not leave us; you know where we can camp in the desert, and you will serve as eyes for us. [32]If you come with us, we will share with you the prosperity the LORD will bestow on us."

Into the Desert. [33]jThey moved on from the mountain of the LORD,* a three days' journey, and the ark of the covenant of the LORD which was to seek out their resting place went the three days' journey with them. [34]And when they set out from camp, the cloud of the LORD was over them by day. [35]Whenever the ark set out, Moses would say,

"Arise, O LORD, that your enemies may
be scattered,
and those who hate you may flee
before you."

[36]And when it came to rest, he would say,

"Return, O LORD, you who ride upon the
clouds,
to the troops of Israel."

CHAPTER 11

See RG 80–85

Discontent of the People. [1]Now the people complained in the hearing of the LORD;k and when he heard it his wrath flared up so that the fire of the LORD burned among them and consumed the outskirts of the camp. [2]But when the people cried out to Moses, he prayed to the LORD and the fire died out. [3]Hence that place was called Taberah,* because there the fire of the LORD burned among them.

[4]The foreign elements among them were so greedy for meat that even the Israelites lamented again,[l] "Would that we had meat for food! [5]We remember the fish we used to eat without cost in Egypt, and the cucumbers, the melons, the leeks, the onions, and the garlic. [6]But now we are famished; we see nothing before us but this manna."m

[7]nManna was like coriander seed* and had the appearance of bdellium. [8]When they had gone about and gathered it up, the people would grind it between millstones or pound it in a mortar, then cook it in a pot and make it into loaves, which tasted like cakes made with oil. [9]At night, when the dew fell upon the camp, the manna also fell.o

[10]When Moses heard the people, family after family, crying at the entrance of their tents, so that the LORD became very angry, he was grieved. [11]"Why do you treat your servant so badly?" Moses asked the LORD. "Why are you so displeased with me that you burden me with all this people? [12]Was it I who conceived all this people? or was it I who gave them birth, that you tell me to carry them at my bosom, like a foster father carrying an infant, to the land you have promised under oath to their fathers? [13]Where can I get meat to give to all this people? For they are crying to me, 'Give us meat for our food.' [14]I cannot carry all this people by myself, for they are too heavy for me. [15]If this is the way

---

10, 30ff: Hobab wished to be coaxed before granting the favor. From Jgs 1, 16 it seems probable that he did accede to Moses' request.

10, 33: The mountain of the LORD: Sinai (Horeb), elsewhere always called "the mountain of God."

11, 3: Taberah: means "the burning."

11, 7: Coriander seed: see note on Ex 16, 31. Bdellium: a

transparent, amber-colored gum resin, which is also mentioned in Gn 2, 12.

---

j: Dt 1, 33. *k:* Dt 9, 22. *l:* Ps 78, 18. *m:* 5f: Nm 21, 5; Ex 16, 3; Acts 7, 39. *n:* 7f: Ex 16, 14f. 31; Ps 78, 24; Wis 16, 20; Jn 6, 31. *o:* Ex 16, 14f.

you will deal with me, then please do me the favor of killing me at once, so that I need no longer face this distress."

The Seventy Elders. [16]Then the LORD said to Moses, "Assemble for me seventy of the elders of Israel, men you know for true elders and authorities among the people, and bring them to the meeting tent. When they are in place beside you, [17]I will come down and speak with you there. I will also take some of the spirit that is on you and will bestow it on them, that they may share the burden of the people with you. You will then not have to bear it by yourself.

[18]"To the people, however, you shall say: Sanctify yourselves for tomorrow, when you shall have meat to eat. For in the hearing of the LORD you have cried, 'Would that we had meat for food! Oh, how well off we were in Egypt!' Therefore the LORD will give you meat for food, [19]and you will eat it, not for one day, or two days, or five, or ten, or twenty days, [20]but for a whole month—until it comes out of your very nostrils and becomes loathsome to you. For you have spurned the LORD who is in your midst, and in his presence you have wailed, 'Why did we ever leave Egypt?'"

[21]But Moses said, "The people around me include six hundred thousand soldiers; yet you say, 'I will give them meat to eat for a whole month.' [22]Can enough sheep and cattle be slaughtered for them? If all the fish of the sea were caught for them, would they have enough?" [23]The LORD answered Moses, "Is this beyond the LORD's reach? You shall see now whether or not what I have promised you takes place."

The Spirit on the Elders. [24]So Moses went out and told the people what the LORD had said. Gathering seventy elders of the people, he had them stand around the tent. [25]The LORD then came down in the cloud and spoke to him. Taking some of the spirit that was on Moses, he bestowed it on the seventy elders; and as the spirit came to rest on them, they prophesied.*

[26]Now two men, one named Eldad and the other Medad, were not in the gathering but had been left in the camp. They too had been on the list, but had not gone out to the tent; yet the spirit came to rest on them also, and they prophesied in the camp. [27]So, when a young man quickly told Moses, "Eldad and Medad are prophesying in the camp," [28]Joshua, son of Nun, who from his youth had been Moses' aide, said, "Moses, my lord, stop them." [29]But Moses answered him, "Are you jealous for my sake? Would that all the people of the LORD were prophets! Would that the LORD might bestow his spirit on them all!" [30]Then Moses retired to the camp, along with the elders of Israel.

The Quail. [31]There arose a wind[p] sent by the LORD, that drove in quail from the sea and brought them down over the camp site at a height of two cubits from the ground* for the distance of a day's journey all around the camp. [32][q]All that day, all night, and all the next day the people gathered in the quail. Even the one who got the least gathered ten homers of them. Then they spread them out* all around the camp. [33]But while the meat was still between their teeth, before it could be consumed, the LORD's wrath flared up against the people, and he struck them with a very great plague. [34]So that place was named Kibroth-hattaavah,* because it was there that the greedy people were buried.

[35]From Kibroth-hattaavah the people set out for Hazeroth.

CHAPTER 12   See RG 80–85

Jealousy of Aaron and Miriam. While they were in Hazeroth, [1]Miriam and Aaron spoke against Moses on the pretext of

---

11, 25: They prophesied: in the sense, not of foretelling the future, but of speaking in enraptured enthusiasm. Such manifestations of mystic exaltation occurred in the early days of Hebrew prophecy (1 Sm 10, 10ff; 19, 20ff) and in the first years of the Church (Acts 2, 6-11. 17; 19, 6; 1 Cor 12–14).

11, 31: At a height of two cubits from the ground: exhausted by the storm, the quail could take but short, low flights, so that they were easily captured. To give food to the hungry people, God may have used the natural phenomenon

of the annual migration of quail across the Sinai Peninsula. In the spring large flocks of these birds cross the Gulf of Aqabah flying toward the west; in the fall they fly back eastward from the Mediterranean. The sea mentioned here probably refers to the former body of water.

11, 32: They spread them out: to cure by drying.

11, 34: Kibroth-hattaavah: means "graves of greed."

p: Ps 78, 26ff.   q: 32f; 78, 26-31; 1 Cor 10, 6-7.

the marriage he had contracted with a Cushite woman.* ²They complained,* "Is it through Moses alone that the LORD speaks? Does he not speak through us also?" And the LORD heard this. ³ʳNow, Moses himself was by far the meekest man on the face of the earth. ⁴So at once the LORD said to Moses and Aaron and Miriam, "Come out, you three, to the meeting tent." And the three of them went. ⁵Then the LORD came down in the column of cloud, and standing at the entrance of the tent, called Aaron and Miriam. When both came forward, ⁶he said, "Now listen to the words of the LORD:

Should there be a prophet among you,
    in visions will I reveal myself to him,
    in dreams will I speak to him;
⁷ Not so with my servant Moses!
Throughout my house he bears my trust:ˢ
⁸   face to face I speak to him,ᵗ
    plainly and not in riddles.
The presence of the LORD he beholds.

Why, then, did you not fear to speak against my servant Moses?"

Miriam's Leprosy. ⁹So angry was the LORD against them that when he departed, ¹⁰and the cloud withdrew from the tent, there was Miriam,ᵘ a snow-white leper!* When Aaron turned and saw her a leper, ¹¹"Ah, my lord!" he said to Moses, "please do not charge us with the sin that we have foolishly committed! ¹²Let her not thus be like the stillborn babe that comes forth from its mother's womb with its flesh half consumed." ¹³Then Moses cried to the LORD, "Please, not this! Pray, heal her!" ¹⁴But the LORD answered Moses, "Suppose her father had spit in her face, would she not hide in shame for seven days? Let her be confined outside the camp for seven days; only then may she be brought back." ¹⁵So Miriam was confined outside the camp for seven days,

and the people did not start out again until she was brought back.

¹⁶After that the people set out from Hazeroth and encamped in the desert of Paran.

CHAPTER 13

The Twelve Scouts. ¹The LORD said to Moses, ²"Send men to reconnoiter the land of Canaan, which I am giving the Israelites. You shall send one man from each ancestral tribe, all of them princes." ³ᵛSo Moses dispatched them from the desert of Paran, as the LORD had ordered. All of them were leaders among the Israelites; ⁴by name they were:

Shammua, son of Zaccur, of the tribe of
    Reuben;
⁵ Shaphat, son of Hori, of the tribe of
    Simeon;
⁶ Caleb, son of Jephunneh, of the tribe of
    Judah;
⁷ Igal [son of Joseph] of the tribe of
    Issachar;
¹⁰ Gaddiel, son of Sodi, of the tribe of
    Zebulun;
¹¹ Gaddi, son of Susi, of the tribe of
    Manasseh, for the Josephites,
    with
⁸ Hoshea, son of Nun, of the tribe of
    Ephraim;
⁹ Palti, son of Raphu, of the tribe of
    Benjamin;
¹² Ammiel, son of Gemalli, of the tribe of
    Dan;
¹³ Sethur, son of Michael, of the tribe of
    Asher;
¹⁴ Nahbi, son of Vophsi, of the tribe of
    Naphtali;
¹⁵ Geuel, son of Machi, of the tribe of Gad.

¹⁶These are the names of the men whom Moses sent out to reconnoiter the land. But Hoshea, son of Nun, Moses called Joshua.*

See RG 80-85

12, 1: Cushite woman: apparently Zipporah, the Midianitess, is meant; cf Ex 2, 21. Perhaps the term is used here merely in the sense of "despised foreigner."

12, 2: The real reason for Miriam's quarrel with her brother Moses was her jealousy of his superior position; his Cushite wife served only as an occasion for the dispute. Aaron merely followed his sister in her rebellion; hence she alone was punished.

12, 10: A snow-white leper: afflicted with "white leprosy," a skin disease that generally is not serious or of long duration. Cf Lv 13, 3-6.

13, 16: Joshua: in Hebrew, "Jehoshua," which was later modified to "Jeshua," the Hebrew pronunciation of the name "Jesus." Hoshea and Joshua are variants of one original name meaning "the LORD saves." Cf Mt 1, 21.

r: Sir 45, 1f.   s: Sir 45, 3; Heb 3, 2. 5.   t: Ex 33, 11; Dt 34, 10.   u: Dt 24, 9.   v: 3-33: Dt 1, 22-28.

[17]In sending them to reconnoiter the land of Canaan, Moses said to them, "Go up here in the Negeb, up into the highlands, [18]and see what kind of land it is. Are the people living there strong or weak, few or many? [19]Is the country in which they live good or bad? Are the towns in which they dwell open or fortified? [20]Is the soil fertile or barren, wooded or clear? And do your best to get some of the fruit of the land." It was then the season for early grapes.

[21]So they went up and reconnoitered the land from the desert of Zin* as far as where Rehob adjoins Labo of Hamath. [22w]Going up by way of the Negeb, they reached Hebron, where Ahiman, Sheshai and Talmai, descendants of the Anakim,* were living. [Hebron had been built seven years before Zoan in Egypt.] [23]They also reached the Wadi Eshcol,* where they cut down a branch with a single cluster of grapes on it, which two of them carried on a pole, as well as some pomegranates and figs. [24]It was because of the cluster the Israelites cut there that they called the place Wadi Eshcol.[x]

Their Return. [25]After reconnoitering the land for forty days they returned, [26y]met Moses and Aaron and the whole community of the Israelites in the desert of Paran at Kadesh, made a report to them all, and showed them the fruit of the country. [27]They told Moses: "We went into the land to which you sent us. It does indeed flow with milk and honey, and here is its fruit. [28]However, the people who are living in the land are fierce, and the towns are fortified and very strong.[z] Besides, we saw descendants of the Anakim there. [29]Amalekites live in the region of the Negeb; Hittites, Jebusites and Amorites dwell in the highlands, and Canaanites along the seacoast and the banks of the Jordan."

[30]Caleb, however, to quiet the people toward Moses, said, "We ought to go up and seize the land, for we can certainly do so." [31]But the men who had gone up with him said, "We cannot attack these people; they are too strong for us." [32]So they spread discouraging reports[a] among the Israelites about the land they had scouted, saying, "The land that we explored is a country that consumes its inhabitants. And all the people we saw there are huge men, [33b]veritable giants* [the Anakim were a race of giants]; we felt like mere grasshoppers, and so we must have seemed to them."

CHAPTER 14

See RG
80-85

Threats of Revolt. [1]At this, the whole community broke out with loud cries, and even in the night the people wailed. [2c]All the Israelites grumbled against Moses and Aaron, the whole community saying to them, "Would that we had died in the land of Egypt, or that here in the desert we were dead! [3]Why is the LORD bringing us into this land only to have us fall by the sword? Our wives and little ones will be taken as booty. Would it not be better for us to return to Egypt?" [4]So they said to one another, "Let us appoint a leader and go back to Egypt."

[5]But Moses and Aaron fell prostrate before the whole assembled community of the Israelites; [6]while Joshua, son of Nun, and Caleb, son of Jephunneh, who had been in the party that scouted the land, tore their garments [7]and said to the whole community of the Israelites,[d] "The country which we went through and explored is a fine, rich land. [8]If the LORD is pleased with us, he will bring us in and give us that land, a land flowing with milk and honey. [9e]But do not rebel against the LORD! You need not be afraid of the peo-

---

13, 21: The desert of Zin: north of Paran and southwest of the Dead Sea. It is quite distinct from "the desert of Sin" near the border of Egypt (Ex 16, 1; 17, 1; Nm 33, 11). Labo of Hamath: a town near Riblah (Jer 39, 5f) at the southern border of Hamath, an independent kingdom in southern Syria. David's conquests extended as far as Hamath (2 Sm 8, 9ff), and Labo thus formed the northern border of the ideal extent of Israel's possessions (Nm 34, 7ff; Ez 47, 15; 48, 1). Some commentators think that this verse is a later addition to the text; cf Dt 1, 24.

13, 22. 28: Anakim: an aboriginal race in southern Palestine, largely absorbed by the Canaanites before the Israelite

invasion. Either because of their tall stature or because of the massive stone structures left by them the Israelites regarded them as giants.

13, 23: Eshcol: means "cluster."

13, 33: Giants: in Hebrew, "nephilim." Cf Gn 6, 4.

14, 9: They are but food for us: that is, "we can easily consume and destroy them." This is the answer to the pessimistic

w: Jos 11, 21f.   x: Nm 32, 9; Dt 1, 24f.   y: 26f: Ex 3, 8. 17. z: 28f: Dt 9, 1f.   a: Nm 32, 9; Jos 14, 8.   b: Dt 2, 10.   c: Ex 16, 3; Ps 106, 25.   d: 7f: Dt 1, 25.   e: Dt 7, 18.

The Decisive Rebellion: The Previous Generation's Refusal to Enter the Promised Land

This key narrative forms the basis for the overall structure of the book of Numbers, which divides into the death of the old generation of the wilderness (chs 1–25) and the birth of a new generation of hope on the edge of the Promised Land (chs 26–36). The old rebellious generation is condemned to wander for forty years and die in the wilderness (14, 22–23, 29–30). Only the new generation of "little ones" (along with the two faithful spies Caleb and Joshua) will be allowed to enter the land of Canaan (vv. 24, 30–31).

ple of that land; they are but food for us!* Their defense has left them, but the LORD is with us. Therefore, do not be afraid of them." [10]In answer, the whole community threatened to stone them.

The Lord's Sentence. But then the glory of the LORD appeared at the meeting tent to all the Israelites. [11]And the LORD said to Moses, "How long will this people spurn me? How long will they refuse to believe in me, despite all the signs I have performed among them?[f] [12]I will strike them with pestilence and wipe them out. Then I will make of you a nation greater and mightier than they."[g]

[13][h]But Moses said to the LORD: "Are the Egyptians to hear of this? For by your power you brought out this people from among them. [14]And are they to tell of it to the inhabitants of this land? It has been heard that you, O LORD, are in the midst of this people; you, LORD, who plainly reveal yourself! Your cloud stands over them, and you go before them by day in a column of cloud and by night in a column of fire.[i] [15]If now you slay this whole people, the nations who have heard such reports of you will say, [16]'The LORD was not able to bring this people into the land he swore to give them; that is why he slaughtered them in the desert.'[j] [17]Now then, let the power of my Lord be displayed in its greatness, even as you have said, [18][k]'The LORD is slow to anger and rich in

kindness, forgiving wickedness and crime; yet not declaring the guilty guiltless, but punishing children to the third and fourth generation for their fathers' wickedness.' [19]Pardon, then, the wickedness of this people in keeping with your great kindness, even as you have forgiven them from Egypt until now."[l]

[20]The LORD answered: "I pardon them as you have asked. [21]Yet, by my life and the LORD's glory that fills the whole earth, [22]of all the men who have seen my glory and the signs I worked in Egypt and in the desert,[m] and who nevertheless have put me to the test ten times already and have failed to heed my voice, [23]not one shall see the land which I promised on oath to their fathers. None of these who have spurned me shall see it. [24]But because my servant Caleb has a different spirit and follows me unreservedly,[n] I will bring him into the land where he has just been, and his descendants shall possess it. [25]But now, since the Amalekites and Canaanites are living in the valleys,* turn away tomorrow and set out in the desert on the Red Sea road."

[26]The LORD also said to Moses and Aaron: [27]"How long will this wicked community grumble against me?[o] I have heard the grumblings of the Israelites against me. [28]Tell them:* By my life, says the LORD, I will do to you just what I have heard you

report that this land "consumes its inhabitants" (Nm 13, 32).

14, 25: The valleys: the low-lying plains in the Negeb and along the seacoast and in the Jordan depression as well as the higher valleys in the mountains farther north; cf Nm 14, 45.

14, 28f: God punished the malcontents by giving them their wish; cf v 2. Their lack of faith and of confidence in God is cited in 1 Cor 10, 10, and Heb 3, 12-18, as a warning for Christians.

f: Ps 78, 22. 32.   g: Ex 32, 10.   h: 13-16: Ex 32, 12; Dt 9, 26ff; Ps 106, 23.   i: Ex 13, 21; Jos 2, 9f.   j: Ex 32, 12; Dt 9, 28.   k: Ex 20, 5; 34, 6f; Pss 103, 8; 145, 8.   l: Ps 78, 38.   m: 22f: Dt 1, 35.   n: Jos 14, 8f.   o: Ex 16, 7. 12.

say. [29]Here in the desert[p] shall your dead bodies fall. Of all your men of twenty years or more, registered in the census, who grumbled against me, [30]not one shall enter the land where I solemnly swore to settle you, except Caleb, son of Jephunneh, and Joshua, son of Nun. [31]Your little ones, however, who you said would be taken as booty, I will bring in, and they shall appreciate the land you spurned.[q] [32]But as for you, your bodies shall fall here in the desert, [33]here where your children must wander for forty years, suffering for your faithlessness, till the last of you lies dead in the desert.[r] [34]Forty days you spent in scouting the land; forty years shall you suffer for your crimes: one year for each day. Thus you will realize what it means to oppose me. [35]I, the LORD, have sworn to do this to all this wicked community that conspired against me: here in the desert they shall die to the last man."

[36]And so it happened to the men whom Moses had sent to reconnoiter the land[s] and who on returning had set the whole community grumbling against him by spreading discouraging reports about the land; [37]these men who had given out the bad report about the land were struck down by the LORD and died. [38]Of all the men who had gone to reconnoiter the land, only Joshua, son of Nun, and Caleb, son of Jephunneh, survived.[t]

Unsuccessful Invasion. [39]When Moses repeated these words to all the Israelites, the people felt great remorse. [40]Early the next morning they started up into the foothills, saying, "Here we are, ready to go up to the place that the LORD spoke of:[u] for we were indeed doing wrong." [41]But Moses said, "Why are you again disobeying the LORD's orders? This cannot succeed. [42]Do not go up, because the LORD is not in your midst; if you go, you will be beaten down before your enemies.[v] [43]For there the Amalekites and Canaanites face you, and you will fall by the sword. You

have turned back from following the LORD; therefore the LORD will not be with you."

[44]Yet they dared to go up into the foothills,[w] even though neither the ark of the covenant of the LORD nor Moses left the camp. [45]And the Amalekites and Canaanites who dwelt in that hill country came down and defeated them, beating them back as far as Hormah.[*]

CHAPTER 15

See RG 80-85

Secondary Offerings. [1]The LORD said to Moses, [2]*"Give the Israelites these instructions: When you have entered the land that I will give you for your homesteads, [3]if you make to the LORD a sweet-smelling oblation from the herd or from the flock, in holocaust, in fulfillment of a vow, or as a freewill offering, or for one of your festivals, [4]whoever does so shall also present to the LORD a cereal offering consisting of a tenth of an ephah of fine flour mixed with a fourth of a hin of oil, [5]as well as a libation of a fourth of a hin of wine, with each lamb sacrificed in holocaust or otherwise. [6]With each sacrifice of a ram you shall present a cereal offering of two tenths of an ephah of fine flour mixed with a third of a hin of oil, [7]and a libation of a third of a hin of wine, thus making a sweet-smelling offering to the LORD. [8]When you sacrifice an ox as a holocaust, or in fulfillment of a vow, or as a peace offering to the LORD, [9]with it you shall present a cereal offering of three tenths of an ephah of fine flour mixed with half a hin of oil, [10]and a libation of half a hin of wine, as a sweet-smelling oblation to the LORD. [11]The same is to be done for each ox, ram, lamb or goat. [12]Whatever the number you offer, do the same for each of them.

[13]"All the native-born shall make these offerings in the same way, whenever they present a sweet-smelling oblation to the LORD. [14]Likewise, in any future generation, any alien residing with you permanently or for a time, who presents a sweet-smelling

---

14, 45: Hormah: one of the Canaanite royal cities in southern Judea (Jos 12, 14), known at this time as "Zephath"; the origin of the later name is told in Nm 21, 3; Jgs 1, 17.

15, 2-16: These laws on sacrifice are complementary to those of Lv 1–3. Since the food of the Israelites consisted not only of meat but also of bread, oil and wine, so, besides the animal oblations, they offered flour, wine and oil in sacrifice to the Lord.

---

p: Dt 1, 35; Heb 3, 17.   *q:* Dt 1, 39.   *r:* 33f: Nm 13, 26; 32, 13; Ps 95, 10; Ez 4, 6.   *s:* 36f: Nm 13, 17. 32f; 1 Cor 10, 10.   *t:* Nm 26, 65.   *u:* Nm 13, 18; Dt 1, 42.   *v:* Dt 1, 42.   *w:* Dt 1, 43.

oblation to the LORD, shall do as you do. [15]There is but one rule for you and for the resident alien, a perpetual rule for all your descendants. Before the LORD you and the alien are alike, [16]with the same law and the same application of it for the alien residing among you as for yourselves."

[17]The LORD said to Moses, [18]"Speak to the Israelites and tell them: When you enter the land into which I will bring you [19]and begin to eat of the food of that land, you shall offer the LORD a contribution [20]consisting of a cake of your first batch of dough.* You shall offer it just as you offer a contribution from the threshing floor.[x] [21]Throughout your generations you shall give a contribution to the LORD from your first batch of dough.

Sin Offerings. [22]*"When through inadvertence you fail to carry out any of these commandments which the LORD gives to Moses,[y] [23]and through Moses to you, from the time the LORD first issues the commandment down through your generations: [24]if the community itself unwittingly becomes guilty of the fault of inadvertence, the whole community shall offer the holocaust of one young bull as a sweet-smelling oblation pleasing to the LORD, along with its prescribed cereal offering and libation, as well as one he-goat as a sin offering. [25z]Then the priest shall make atonement for the whole Israelite community; thus they will be forgiven the inadvertence for which they have brought their holocaust as an oblation to the LORD. [26]Not only the whole Israelite community, but also the aliens residing among you, shall be forgiven, since the fault of inadvertence affects all the people.

[27]"However, if it is an individual who sins inadvertently,[a] he shall bring a yearling she-goat as a sin offering, [28]and the priest shall make atonement before the LORD for him who sinned inadvertently; when atonement has been made for him, he will be forgiven. [29]You shall have but one law for him who sins inadvertently, whether he be a native Israelite or an alien residing with you.

[30]"But anyone who sins defiantly,[b] whether he be a native or an alien, insults the LORD, and shall be cut off from among his people. [31c]Since he has despised the word of the LORD and has broken his commandment, he must be cut off. He has only himself to blame."

The Sabbath-breaker. [32]While the Israelites were in the desert, a man was discovered gathering wood on the sabbath day. [33]Those who caught him at it brought him to Moses and Aaron and the whole assembly. [34]But they kept him in custody, for there was no clear decision* as to what should be done with him.[d] [35]Then the LORD said to Moses, "This man shall be put to death; let the whole community stone him outside the camp." [36]So the whole community led him outside the camp and stoned him to death, as the LORD had commanded Moses.

Tassels on the Cloak. [37]The LORD said to Moses, [38]"Speak to the Israelites and tell them that they and their descendants must put tassels* on the corners of their garments, fastening each corner tassel with a violet cord.[e] [39]When you use these tassels, let the sight of them remind you to keep all the commandments of the LORD, without going wantonly astray after the desires of your hearts and eyes. [40]Thus you will remember to keep all my commandments and be holy to your God. [41]I, the LORD, am your God who, as God, brought you out of Egypt that I, the LORD, may be your God."[f]

15, 20: Dough: some render, "barley grits." This word is used elsewhere only in Ez 44, 30 and Neh 10, 33; a related Hebrew word is used in Lv 2, 14.

15, 22ff: Although no moral guilt is incurred by an inadvertent violation of God's commandments, the sanctity of the law can require some reparation even for such violations.

15, 34: No clear decision: they already knew that a willful violation of the sabbath was a capital offense, but they did not yet know how the death penalty was to be inflicted.

15, 38: Tassels: at the time of Christ these tassels were worn by all pious Jews, including our Lord (Mt 9, 20f; Mk 6, 56): the Pharisees wore very large ones in ostentation of their zeal for the law (Mt 23, 5).

x: 19-20: Ez 44, 30. *y:* 22f: Lv 4, 13f. *z:* Lv 4, 20. *a:* 27f: Lv 4, 27f. *b:* Dt 17, 12. *c:* Prv 13, 13. *d:* Lv 24, 12. *e:* Dt 22, 12. *f:* Lv 22, 32f.

CHAPTER 16

See RG
80–85

Rebellion of Korah. [1]Korah, son of Izhar, son of Kohath, son of Levi,* [and Dathan and Abiram, sons of Eliab, son of Pallu, son of Reuben] took [2]two hundred and fifty Israelites who were leaders in the community, members of the council and men of note. They stood before Moses, [3]and held an assembly against Moses and Aaron, to whom they said,[g] "Enough from you! The whole community, all of them, are holy; the LORD is in their midst. Why then should you set yourselves over the LORD's congregation?"

[4]When Moses heard this, he fell prostrate. [5]Then he said to Korah and to all his band, "May the LORD make known tomorrow morning who belongs to him and who is the holy one and whom he will have draw near to him! Whom he chooses, he will have draw near him. [6]Do this: take your censers [Korah and all his band] [7]and put fire in them and place incense in them before the LORD tomorrow. He whom the LORD then chooses is the holy one. Enough from you Levites!"

[8]Moses also said to Korah, "Listen to me, you Levites! [9h]Is it too little for you that the God of Israel has singled you out from the community of Israel, to have you draw near him for the service of the LORD's Dwelling and to stand before the community to minister for them? [10]He has allowed you and your kinsmen, the descendants of Levi, to approach him, and yet you now seek the priesthood too. [11]It is therefore against the LORD that you and all your band are conspiring. For what has Aaron done that you should grumble against him?"

Rebellion of Dathan and Abiram. [12]Moses summoned Dathan and Abiram, sons of Eliab, but they answered, "We will not go.* [13]Are you not satisfied with having led us here away from a land flowing with milk and honey, to make us perish in the desert, that you must now lord it over us? [14]Far from bringing us to a land flowing with milk and honey, or giving us fields and vineyards for our inheritance, will you also gouge out our eyes?* No, we will not go."

[15]Then Moses became very angry and said to the LORD, "Pay no heed to their offering. I have never taken a single ass from them, nor have I wronged any one of them."[i]

Korah. [16]Moses said to Korah, "You and all your band shall appear before the LORD tomorrow—you and they and Aaron too. [17]Then each of your two hundred and fifty followers shall take his own censer, put incense in it, and offer it to the LORD; and you and Aaron, each with his own censer, shall do the same." [18]So they all took their censers, and laying incense on the fire they had put in them, they took their stand by the entrance of the meeting tent along with Moses and Aaron. [19]Then, when Korah had assembled all his band against them at the entrance of the meeting tent, the glory of the LORD appeared to the entire community, [20]and the LORD said to Moses and Aaron, [21]"Stand apart from this band, that I may consume them at once." [22]But they fell prostrate and cried out, "O God, God of the spirits of all mankind, will one man's sin make you angry with the whole community?" [23]The LORD answered Moses, [24]"Speak to the community and tell them: Withdraw from the space around the Dwelling" [of Korah, Dathan and Abiram].

Punishment of Dathan and Abiram. [25]Mo-

16, 1ff: The evidence seems to show that there were two distinct rebellions: one of Korah and his band (Nm 27, 3) and the other of Dathan and Abiram (Dt 11, 6); cf Ps 106. The present account combines both events into one narrative; but even here it is rather easy to separate the two, once certain proper names (vv 1. 6. 24. 32. 35) have been identified as glosses. The rebellion of the Reubenites, Dathan and Abiram, was of a political nature, against Moses alone as the civil leader; these rebels were punished by being swallowed alive in an earthquake. The rebellion of Korah was of a religious nature, against the religious leadership of both Moses and Aaron; about two hundred and fifty malcontents joined Korah's band; they were punished by fire. The parts of the present section which refer to the rebellion of Dathan and Abiram are vv 12-15 and vv 25-34 of chapter 16; the rest of chapter 16 and all of chapter 17 concern the rebellion of Korah.

16, 12: We will not go: to appear before Moses' tribunal.

16, 14: Gouge out our eyes: blind us to the real state of affairs.

16, 25: Since Dathan and Abiram had refused to go to Moses (vv 12ff), he, with the elders as witnesses, was obliged to go to their tent.

g: Ps 106, 16ff; Sir 45, 19; 1 Cor 10, 10.   h: Dt 10, 8.   i: 1 Sm 12, 3.

ses, followed by the elders of Israel, arose and went to Dathan and Abiram.* [26]Then he warned the community, "Keep away from the tents of these wicked men and do not touch anything that is theirs: otherwise you too will be swept away because of all their sins." [27]When Dathan and Abiram had come out and were standing at the entrances of their tents with their wives and sons and little ones, [28]Moses said, "This is how you shall know that it was the LORD who sent me to do all I have done, and that it was not I who planned it: [29]if these men die an ordinary death, merely suffering the fate common to all mankind, then it was not the LORD who sent me. [30]But if the LORD does something entirely new, and the ground opens its mouth and swallows them alive down into the nether world, with all belonging to them, then you will know that these men have defied the LORD." [31]jNo sooner had he finished saying all this than the ground beneath them split open, [32]and the earth opened its mouth and swallowed them and their families [and all of Korah's men] and all their possessions. [33]They went down alive to the nether world with all belonging to them; the earth closed over them, and they perished from the community. [34]But all the Israelites near them fled at their shrieks, saying, "The earth might swallow us too!"

Punishment of Korah. [35]So they withdrew from the space around the Dwelling [of Korah,* Dathan and Abiram]. And fire from the LORD came forth which consumed the two hundred and fifty men who were offering the incense.

CHAPTER 17

See RG 80-85

[1]The LORD said to Moses, [2]"Tell Eleazar, son of Aaron the priest, to remove the censers from the embers; and scatter the fire some distance away, [3]*for these sinners have consecrated the censers at the cost of their lives. Have them hammered into plates to cover the altar, because in being presented before the LORD they have become sacred. In this way they shall serve as a sign to the Israelites." [4]So Eleazar the priest had the bronze censers of those burned during the offering hammered into a covering for the altar, [5]in keeping with the orders which the LORD had given him through Moses. This cover was to be a reminder to the Israelites that no layman, no one who was not a descendant of Aaron, should approach the altar to offer incense before the LORD, lest he meet the fate of Korah and his band.

[6]The next day the whole Israelite community grumbled against Moses and Aaron, saying, "It is you who have slain the LORD's people." [7]But while the community was deliberating against them, Moses and Aaron turned toward the meeting tent, and the cloud now covered it and the glory of the LORD appeared. [8]Then Moses and Aaron came to the front of the meeting tent, °and the LORD said to Moses and Aaron, [10]"Depart from this community, that I may consume them at once." But they fell prostrate.

[11]Then Moses said to Aaron, "Take your censer, put fire from the altar in it, lay incense on it, and bring it quickly to the community to make atonement for them; for wrath has come forth from the LORD and the blow is falling."k [12]Obeying the orders of Moses, Aaron took his censer and ran in among the community, where the blow was already falling on the people. Then, as he offered the incense and made atonement for the people, [13]standing there between the living and the dead, the scourge was checked. [14]Yet fourteen thousand seven hundred died from the scourge, in addition to those who died because of Korah. [15]When the scourge had been checked, Aaron returned to Moses at the entrance of the meeting tent.

Aaron's Staff. [16]The LORD now said to Moses, [17]"Speak to the Israelites and get one staff* from them for each ancestral house,

---

16, 35: This verse continues v 24; the first sentence is transposed from v 27.

17, 3: Whatever was brought into intimate contact with something sacred shared in its sacredness. See note on Nm 19, 20.

17, 17: The staff was not merely an article of practical use, but also a symbol of authority; cf Gn 49, 10; Nm 24, 17; Jer 48, 17. Hence, the staff of a leader of a tribe was considered the emblem of his tribe; in fact, certain Hebrew words for "staff" also means "tribe." Perhaps for this reason, to avoid confusion, the author here uses the term "ancestral house" instead of the ordinary word for "tribe."

j: 31ff: Nm 26, 10; Lv 10, 2; Dt 11, 6; Ps 106, 7f. *k:* Wis 18, 20f.

twelve staffs in all, one from each of their tribal princes. Mark each man's name on his staff; [18]and mark Aaron's name on Levi's staff,* for the head of Levi's ancestral house shall also have a staff. [19]Then lay them down in the meeting tent, in front of the commandments, where I meet you. [20]There the staff of the man of my choice shall sprout. Thus will I suppress from my presence the Israelites' grumbling against you."

[21]So Moses spoke to the Israelites, and their princes gave him staffs, twelve in all, one from each tribal prince; and Aaron's staff was with them. [22]Then Moses laid the staffs down before the LORD in the tent of the commandments. [23]The next day, when Moses entered the tent, Aaron's staff, representing the house of Levi, had sprouted and put forth not only shoots, but blossoms as well, and even bore ripe almonds! [24]Moses thereupon brought out all the staffs from the LORD's presence to the Israelites. After each prince identified his own staff and took it, [25]the LORD said to Moses, "Put back Aaron's staff in front of the commandments, to be kept there as a warning to the rebellious, so that their grumbling may cease before me; if it does not, they will die." [26]And Moses did as the LORD had commanded him.

Charge of the Sacred Things. [27]*Then the Israelites cried out to Moses, "We are perishing; we are lost, we are all lost! [28]Every time anyone approaches the Dwelling of the LORD, he dies! Are we to perish to the last man?"

See RG 80–85

CHAPTER 18

[1]The LORD said to Aaron,* "You and your sons as well as the other members of your ancestral house shall be responsible for the sanctuary; but the responsibility of the priesthood shall rest on you and your sons alone. [2]Bring with you also your other kinsmen of the tribe of Levi, your ancestral tribe, as your associates* and assistants, while you and your sons are in front of the tent of the commandments. [3]They shall look after your persons and the whole tent; however, they shall not come near the sacred vessels or the altar, lest both they and you die. [4]As your associates they shall have charge of all the work connected with the meeting tent. But no layman* shall come near you. [5]You shall have charge of the sanctuary and of the altar, that wrath may not fall again upon the Israelites.

[6]"Remember, it is I who have taken your kinsmen, the Levites, from the body of the Israelites; they are a gift to you,[l] dedicated to the LORD for the service of the meeting tent. [7m]But only you and your sons are to have charge of performing the priestly functions in whatever concerns the altar and the room within the veil.* I give you the priesthood as a gift. Any layman who draws near shall be put to death."

The Priests' Share of the Sacrifices. [8]The LORD said to Aaron,* "I myself have given you charge of the contributions made to me in the various sacred offerings of the Israelites;[n] by perpetual ordinance I have assigned them to you and to your sons as your priestly share. [9]You shall have the right to share in the oblations that are most sacred, in whatever they offer me as cereal offerings or sin offerings or guilt offerings; these shares shall accrue to you and to your sons. [10]In eating them you shall treat them

---

17, 18: Levi's staff: it is not clear whether this is considered as one of the twelve mentioned in the preceding verse, or as a thirteenth staff. Sometimes Levi is reckoned as one of the twelve tribes (e.g., Dt 27, 12f), but more often the number twelve is arrived at by counting the two sub-tribes of Joseph, i.e., Ephraim and Manasseh, as distinct tribes. In this passage also it seems probable that the tribe of Levi is considered apart from the other twelve.

17, 27f: Logically these two verses belong immediately after Nm 16, 35.

18, 1ff: This law, which kept unqualified persons from contact with sacred things, is the answer to the Israelites' cry in Nm 17, 28. It is followed by other laws concerning priests and Levites.

18, 2: Associates: in Hebrew this word alludes to the popular etymology of the name "Levi." Cf Gn 29, 34.

18, 4: Layman: here, "one who is not a Levite"; in v 7, "one who is not a priest."

18, 7: Veil: the outer veil, or "curtain," is probably meant.

18, 8ff: Two classes of offerings are here distinguished: the most sacred offering, which only the male members of the priestly families could eat (vv 8ff), and the other offerings, which even the women of the priestly families could eat (vv 11-19).

l: Nm 3, 9; 8, 19.   *m:* Nm 3, 10.   *n:* Nm 5, 9.

The Duties and Support of the Priests and Levites

C hapter 18 makes a crucial distinction between Aaron and his sons as the Levites who serve as high priests and the other members of the tribe of Levi, who serve as assistants to Aaron and his sons (Nm 3, 5–10).

as most sacred; every male among you may partake of them. As sacred, they belong to you.

[11]"You shall also have what is removed from the gift in every wave offering* of the Israelites; by perpetual ordinance I have assigned it to you and to your sons and daughters.[o] All in your family who are clean may partake of it. [12]I have also assigned to you all the best[p] of the new oil and of the new wine and grain that they give to the Lord as their first fruits; [13]and likewise, of whatever grows on their land, the first products that they bring in to the Lord shall be yours; all of your family who are clean may partake of them. [14]Whatever is doomed* in Israel shall be yours. [15]Every living thing that opens the womb, whether of man or of beast, such as are to be offered to the Lord, shall be yours;[q] but you must let the first-born of man, as well as of unclean animals, be redeemed. [16]The ransom for a boy is to be paid when he is a month old; it is fixed at five silver shekels according to the sanctuary standard, twenty gerahs to the shekel. [17]But the first-born of cattle, sheep or goats shall not be redeemed; they are sacred. Their blood you must splash on the altar and their fat you must burn as a sweet-smelling oblation to the Lord. [18r]Their meat, however, shall be yours, just as the breast and the right leg of the wave offering belong to you. [19]By perpetual ordinance I have assigned to you and to your sons and daughters all the contributions from the sacred gifts which the Israel-

ites make to the Lord; this is an inviolable covenant* to last forever before the Lord, for you and for your descendants." [20s]Then the Lord said to Aaron,* "You shall not have any heritage in the land of the Israelites nor hold any portion among them; I will be your portion and your heritage among them.

Tithes Due the Levites. [21]"To the Levites, however, I hereby assign all tithes in Israel as their heritage in recompense for the service they perform in the meeting tent.[t] [22]The Israelites may no longer approach the meeting tent; else they will incur guilt deserving death. [23]Only the Levites are to perform the service of the meeting tent, and they alone shall be held responsible; this is a perpetual ordinance for all your generations. The Levites, therefore, shall not have any heritage among the Israelites, [24]for I have assigned to them as their heritage the tithes which the Israelites give as a contribution to the Lord. That is why I have ordered that they are not to have any heritage among the Israelites."

Tithes Paid by the Levites. [25]The Lord said to Moses, [26]"Give the Levites these instructions: When you receive from the Israelites the tithes I have assigned you from them as your heritage, you are to make a contribution from them to the Lord, a tithe of the tithes; [27]and your contribution will be credited to you as if it were grain from the threshing floor or new wine from the press. [28]Thus you too shall make a contribution from all the tithes you receive from the Israelites, handing over to Aaron the priest the

---

18, 11: Wave offering: this included the breast and right leg (v 18), the shoulder of the peace offering (Lv 7, 30-34), and portions of the nazirite sacrifice (Nm 6, 19f).

18, 14: Doomed: in Hebrew, herem, which means here "set aside from profane use and made sacred to the Lord." Cf Lv 27, 21. 28.

18, 19: An inviolable covenant: literally, "a covenant of salt." Cf 2 Chr 13, 5. The reference may perhaps be to the preservative power of salt (cf Mt 5, 13); but more likely the phrase refers to the custom of partaking of the same salt in common to

render a contract unbreakable. See note on Lv 2, 13.

18, 20: The priests and Levites were forbidden to own hereditary land such as the other Israelites possessed; therefore in the allotment of the land they were not to receive any portion of it. Certain cities, however, were assigned to them for their residence; cf Nm 35, 1-8.

---

o: Ex 29, 27f; Lv 7, 34; 10, 14. p: 12f; Dt 18, 4; 26, 2. q: Ex 13, 2. r: Lv 7, 31-34. s: Dt 10, 9; 18, 1f; Jos 13, 33; Ez 44, 28. t: Heb 7, 5.

part to be contributed to the LORD. [29]From all the gifts that you receive, and from the best parts, you are to consecrate to the LORD your own full contribution.

[30]"Tell them also: Once you have made your contribution from the best part, the rest of the tithes will be credited to you Levites as if it were produce of the threshing floor or of the wine press. [31]Your families, as well as you, may eat them anywhere, since they are your recompense for service at the meeting tent. [32]You will incur no guilt so long as you make a contribution of the best part. Do not profane the sacred gifts of the Israelites and so bring death on yourselves."

CHAPTER 19

See RG
80-85

Ashes of the Red Heifer. [1]The LORD said to Moses and Aaron: [2]"This is the regulation which the law of the LORD prescribes. Tell the Israelites to procure for you a red heifer that is free from every blemish and defect and on which no yoke has ever been laid. [3]This is to be given to Eleazar the priest, to be led outside the camp* and slaughtered in his presence. [4]Eleazar the priest shall take some of its blood on his finger and sprinkle it seven times toward the front of the meeting tent.* [5]Then the heifer shall be burned in his sight, with its hide and flesh, its blood and offal; [6]and the priest shall take some cedar wood, hyssop and scarlet yarn and throw them into the fire in which the heifer is being burned. [7]The priest shall then wash his garments and bathe his body in water. He remains unclean until the evening, and only afterward may he return to the camp. [8]Likewise, he who burned the heifer shall wash his garments, bathe his body in water, and be unclean until evening. [9]Finally, a man who is clean shall gather up the ashes of the heifer and deposit them in a clean place outside the camp. There they are to be kept for preparing lustral water

for the Israelite community. The heifer is a sin offering. [10]He who has gathered up the ashes of the heifer shall also wash his garments and be unclean until evening. This is a perpetual ordinance, both for the Israelites and for the aliens residing among them.

Use of the Ashes. [11]"Whoever touches the dead body of any human being shall be unclean for seven days; [12]he shall purify himself with the water on the third and on the seventh day, and then he will be clean again. But if he fails to purify himself on the third and on the seventh day, he will not become clean. [13]u Everyone who fails to purify himself after touching the body of any deceased person, defiles the Dwelling of the LORD and shall be cut off from Israel. Since the lustral water has not been splashed over him, he remains unclean: his uncleanness still clings to him.

[14]"This is the law: When a man dies in a tent, everyone who enters the tent, as well as everyone already in it, shall be unclean for seven days; [15]likewise, every vessel that is open, or with its lid unfastened, shall be unclean. [16]Moreover, everyone who in the open country touches a dead person, whether he was slain by the sword or died naturally, or who touches a human bone or a grave, shall be unclean for seven days. [17]*For anyone who is thus unclean, ashes from the sin offering shall be put in a vessel, and spring water shall be poured on them. [18]Then a man who is clean shall take some hyssop, dip it in this water, and sprinkle it on the tent and on all the vessels and persons that were in it, or on him who touched a bone, a slain person or other dead body, or a grave. [19]The clean man shall sprinkle the unclean on the third and on the seventh day; thus purified on the seventh day, he shall wash his garments and bathe his body in water, and in the evening he will be clean again. [20]*Any un-

---

19, 3: Outside the camp: several Fathers of the Church saw in this a prefiguring of the sacrificial death of Christ outside the walls of Jerusalem; cf Jn 19, 20; Heb 13, 12; in the purifying water, into which the ashes of the red heifer were put, they saw a type of the water of Baptism.

19, 4: Toward the front of the meeting tent: since the tabernacle faced the east (Ex 26, 15-30), the killing of the heifer took place east of the camp; in later times it was done on the Mount of Olives, east of the Temple.

19, 17ff: "If . . . the sprinkled ashes of a heifer sanctify the unclean unto the cleansing of the flesh, how much more will the blood of Christ . . . cleanse your conscience from dead works?" (Heb 9, 13f).

19, 20: Ritual uncleanness is, as it were, contagious; so also sacredness; see note on Nm 17, 3.

u: Lv 15, 31.

Water from the Rock and the LORD's Anger

The LORD's angry response and punishment of Moses and Aaron in Nm 20, 12ff is surprising and difficult to explain. Commentators have offered many possible solutions, but no clear explanation emerges out of the narrative itself. Did Moses' act of striking the rock disobey the LORD's instructions only to "order the rock" (v. 8)? Did Moses and Aaron in some way take credit themselves and away from the LORD (v. 10)? Did Moses and Aaron in some way imply that the LORD was unable or unwilling to give water to the people (v. 10)? Both Moses and Aaron are condemned to join the older generation in death outside the Promised Land of Canaan. Aaron's death is recorded in Numbers 20, 22–29, and Moses' death is recorded in Deuteronomy 34, 1–8.

clean man who fails to have himself purified shall be cut off from the community, because he defiles the sanctuary of the LORD. As long as the lustral water has not been splashed over him, he remains unclean. *21*This shall be a perpetual ordinance for you.

"One who sprinkles the lustral water shall wash his garments, and anyone who comes in contact with this water shall be unclean until evening. *22*Moreover, whatever the unclean person touches becomes unclean itself, and anyone who touches it becomes unclean until evening."

CHAPTER 20

See RG
80-85

Death of Miriam. *1*The whole Israelite community arrived in the desert of Zin in the first month,* and the people settled at Kadesh. It was here that Miriam died, and here that she was buried.

Water Famine at Kadesh. *2*As the community had no water, they held a council against Moses and Aaron. *3*The people contended with Moses, exclaiming, "Would that we too had perished with our kinsmen in the LORD's presence! *4*Why have you brought the LORD's community into this desert where we and our livestock are dying? *5*Why did you lead us out of Egypt, only to bring us to this wretched place which has neither grain nor figs nor vines nor pomegranates? Here there is not even water to drink!" *5*But Moses and Aaron went away from the assembly to the entrance of the meeting tent, where they fell prostrate.

Sin of Moses and Aaron. Then the glory of the LORD appeared to them, *7*and the LORD said to Moses, *8*"Take the staff and assemble the community, you and your brother Aaron, and in their presence order the rock to yield its waters. From the rock you shall bring forth water for the community and their livestock to drink." *9*So Moses took the staff from its place before the LORD, as he was ordered. *10*He and Aaron assembled the community in front of the rock, where he said to them,*v* "Listen to me, you rebels! Are we to bring water for you out of this rock?" *11w*Then, raising his hand, Moses struck the rock twice* with his staff, and water gushed out in abundance for the community and their livestock to drink. *12*But the LORD said to Moses and Aaron, "Because you were not faithful to me in showing forth my sanctity before the Israelites, you shall not lead this community into the land I will give them."

*13*These are the waters of Meribah,*x* where the Israelites contended against the LORD, and where he revealed his sanctity among them.

20, 1: The desert of Zin: a barren region with a few good oases, southwest of the Dead Sea. See note on Nm 13, 21. The first month: we would expect the mention also of the day and of the year (after the exodus) when this took place; cf similar dates in Nm 1, 1; 10, 11; 33, 38; Dt 1, 3. Here the full date seems to have been lost. Probably the Israelites arrived in Kadesh in the third year after the exodus. Cf Dt 1, 46.

20, 11: Twice: perhaps because he had not sufficient faith to work the miracle with the first blow. Cf v 12.

20, 12f: The sin of Moses and Aaron consisted in doubting God's mercy toward the ever-rebellious people. In showing forth my sanctity: God's sacred power and glory: an allusion to the name of the place, Kadesh, which means "sanctified, sacred." Meribah means "contention." Cf Ex 17, 7.

v: Ex 17, 5f. *w:* Ps 78, 15f; Wis 11, 4; 1 Cor 10, 4. *x:* Nm 27, 14; Ex 17, 7.

Edom's Refusal. [14]From Kadesh Moses sent men to the king of Edom with the message: "Your brother Israel* has this to say: You know of all the hardships that have befallen us, [15]how our fathers went down to Egypt, where we stayed a long time, how the Egyptians maltreated us and our fathers, [16]and how, when we cried to the LORD,[y] he heard our cry and sent an angel who led us out of Egypt. Now here we are at the town of Kadesh at the edge of your territory. [17]Kindly let us pass through your country. We will not cross any fields or vineyards, nor drink any well water, but we will go straight along the royal road* without turning to the right or to the left, until we have passed through your territory."

[18]But Edom answered him, "You shall not pass through here; if you do, I will advance against you with the sword." [19]The Israelites insisted, "We want only to go up along the highway. If we or our livestock drink any of your water, we will pay for it. Surely there is no harm in merely letting us march through." [20]But Edom still said, "No, you shall not pass through,"[z] and advanced against them with a large and heavily armed force. [21]Therefore, since Edom refused to let them pass through their territory, Israel detoured around them.

Death of Aaron. [22a]Setting out from Kadesh, the whole Israelite community came to Mount Hor.* [23]There at Mount Hor, on the border of the land of Edom, the LORD said to Moses and Aaron, [24]"Aaron is about to be taken to his people; he shall not enter the land I am giving to the Israelites, because you both rebelled against my commandment at the waters of Meribah. [25]Take Aaron and his son Eleazar and bring them up on Mount Hor.[b] [26]Then strip Aaron of his garments and put them on his son Eleazar; for there Aaron shall be taken in death."

[27]Moses did as the LORD commanded. When they had climbed Mount Hor in view of the whole community, [28]Moses stripped Aaron of his garments and put them on his son Eleazar. Then Aaron died there on top of the mountain.[c] When Moses and Eleazar came down from the mountain, [29]all the community understood that Aaron had passed away; and for thirty days the whole house of Israel mourned him.

CHAPTER 21

See RG 80-85

Victory over Arad. [1]When the Canaanite king of Arad,* who lived in the Negeb,[d] heard that the Israelites were coming along the way of Atharim, he engaged them in battle and took some of them captive. [2]Israel then made this vow to the LORD: "If you deliver this people into my hand, I will doom their cities."[e] [3]Later, when the LORD heeded Israel's prayer and delivered up the Canaanites,[f] they doomed them and their cities. Hence that place was named Hormah.*

The Bronze Serpent. [4]From Mount Hor they set out on the Red Sea road, to bypass the land of Edom. But with their patience worn out by the journey, [5]the people complained[g] against God and Moses, "Why have you brought us up from Egypt to die in this desert, where there is no food or water? We are disgusted with this wretched food!"*

[6]In punishment the LORD sent among the people saraph* serpents, which bit[h] the

20, 14: Your brother Israel: the Edomites were descended from Esau, the brother of Jacob. Their country, to the southeast of the Dead Sea, was also known as Seir; cf Gn 25, 24ff; 36, 1. 8f.

20, 17: The royal road: an important highway, running north and south along the plateau east of the Dead Sea. In ancient times it was much used by caravans and armies; later it was improved by the Romans, and large stretches of it are still clearly recognizable.

20, 22: Mount Hor: not definitively identified, but probably to be sought in the vicinity of Kadesh. According to Dt 10, 6, Aaron died at Moserah (cf "Moseroth" in Nm 33, 30f), which is apparently the name of the region in which Mount Hor is situated.

21, 1-3: The account of this episode seems to be a later insertion here, for Nm 21, 4, belongs logically immediately after Nm 20, 29. Perhaps this is the same event as that mentioned in Jgs 1, 16f.

21, 3: Hormah: related to the Hebrew word herem, meaning "doomed." See notes on Nm 14, 45; 18, 14.

21, 5: This wretched food: apparently the manna is meant.

21, 6: Saraph: the Hebrew name for a certain species of venomous snakes; the word probably signifies "the fiery one," these snakes being so called from the burning effect of their poisonous bite.

y: Ex 2, 23.   z: Jgs 11, 17.   a: 21f: Nm 33, 37.   b: 25f: Dt 32, 50.   c: Nm 33, 38.   d: Nm 33, 40.   e: Jos 6, 17; Jgs 1, 17. f: Nm 14, 45.   g: Nm 11, 6; Ex 16, 3.   h: Dt 8, 15; Wis 16, 5; 1 Cor 10, 9.

people so that many of them died. ⁷Then the people came to Moses and said, "We have sinned in complaining against the LORD and you. Pray the LORD to take the serpents from us." So Moses prayed for the people, ⁸and the LORD said to Moses, "Make a saraph and mount it on a pole, and if anyone who has been bitten looks at it, he will recover."* ⁹Moses accordingly made a bronze serpent* and mounted it on a pole, and whenever anyone who had been bitten by a serpent looked at the bronze serpent, he recovered.ⁱ

Journey around Moab. ¹⁰The Israelites moved on and encamped in Oboth.ʲ ¹¹Setting out from Oboth, they encamped in Iyeabarim* in the desert fronting Moab on the east. ¹²Setting out from there, they encamped in the Wadi Zered. ¹³Setting out from there, they encamped on the other side of the Arnon, in the desert that extends from the territory of the Amorites; for the Arnon forms Moab's boundary with the Amorites. ¹⁴Hence it is said in the "Book of the Wars of the LORD"*:

"Waheb in Suphah and the wadies,
¹⁵ Arnon and the wadi gorges
That reach back toward the site of Ar
and slant to the border of Moab."

¹⁶From there they went to Beer,* where there was the well of which the LORD said to Moses, "Bring the people together, and I will give them water." ¹⁷Then it was that Israel sang this song:

"Spring up, O well!—so sing to it—
¹⁸ The well that the princes sank,

that the nobles of the people dug,
with their scepters and their staffs."

From Beer they went to Mattanah, ¹⁹from Mattanah to Nahaliel, from Nahaliel to Bamoth, ²⁰from Bamoth to the cleft in the plateau of Moab at the headland of Pisgah that overlooks Jeshimon.*

Victory over Sihon. ²¹Now Israel sent men to Sihon, king of the Amorites, with the message, ²²"Let us pass through your country. We will not turn aside into any field or vineyard, nor will we drink any well water, but we will go straight along the royal road until we have passed through your territory." ²³Sihon,ᵏ however, would not let Israel pass through his territory, but mustered all his forces and advanced into the desert against Israel. When he reached Jahaz, he engaged Israel in battle. ²⁴But Israel defeated him at the point of the sword, and took possession of his land from the Arnon to the Jabbok and as far as the country of the Ammonites, whose boundary was at Jazer. ²⁵ˡIsrael seized all the towns here and settled in these towns of the Amorites, in Heshbon and all its dependencies. ²⁶Now Heshbon was the capital of Sihon, king of the Amorites, who had fought against the former king of Moab and had seized all his land from Jazer to the Arnon. ²⁷That is why the poets say:

"Come to Heshbon, let it be rebuilt,
let Sihon's capital be firmly
constructed.
²⁸ For fire went forth from Heshbon
and a blaze from the city of
Sihon;
It consumed the cities of Moab

21, 8: If anyone who has been bitten looks at it, he will recover: "and as Moses lifted up the serpent in the desert, even so must the Son of Man be lifted up, that those who believe in him may not perish, but may have life everlasting" (Jn 3, 14f).

21, 9: King Hezekiah, in his efforts to abolish idolatry, "smashed the bronze serpent which Moses had made" (2 Kgs 18, 4).

21, 11: Iye-abarim: probably means "the ruins in the Abarim (Mountains)." See note on Nm 27, 12.

21, 14: The "Book of the Wars of the LORD": an ancient collection of Israelite songs, now lost. Waheb in Suphah: since neither place is mentioned elsewhere, it is quite uncertain whether these dubious Hebrew words are even to be con-

sidered as place names; some Hebrew words apparently lost must have preceded this phrase.

21, 16: Beer: means a well.

21, 20: Jeshimon: "the wasteland"; in 1 Sm 23, 19. 24. and 26, 1. 3, this is the desert of Judah, on the western side of the Dead Sea, but here and in Nm 23, 28, it seems to refer to the southern end of the Jordan valley where Beth-jeshimoth was situated.

---

i: Wis 16, 6f. 10; Jn 3, 14f.   j: Nm 33, 43f.   k: Dt 2, 32; Jgs 11, 20.   l: 25f; Jos 21, 39; Jgs 11, 26.

and swallowed up the high places of the Arnon.

29 Woe to you, O Moab!
   You are ruined, O people of
      Chemosh!*
   He let his sons become fugitives
      and his daughters be taken captive
   by the Amorite king Sihon.

30 Their plowland is ruined from Heshbon
      to Dibon;
   Ar is laid waste; fires blaze as far as
      Medeba."

31 When Israel had settled in the land of the Amorites, 32 Moses sent spies to Jazer; Israel then captured it with its dependencies and dispossessed the Amorites who were there.

Victory over Og. 33m Then they turned and went up along the road to Bashan. But Og, king of Bashan, advanced against them with all his people to give battle at Edrei. 34 The LORD, however, said to Moses, "Do not be afraid of him; for into your hand I will deliver him with all his people and his land. Do to him as you did to Sihon, king of the Amorites, who lived in Heshbon."n 35 So they struck him down with his sons and all his people, until not a survivor was left to him, and they took possession of his land.

See RG
80-85

CHAPTER 22

1 Then the Israelites moved on and encamped in the plains of Moab* on the other side of the Jericho stretch of the Jordan.

III: On the Plains of Moab

Balaam Summoned. 2 Now Balak, son of Zippor, saw all that Israel did to the Amorites. 3 Indeed, Moab feared the Israelites greatly because of their numbers, and detested them. 4 So Moab said to the elders of Midian, "Soon this horde will devour all the country around us as an ox devours the grass of the field."

And Balak, Zippor's son, who was king of Moab at that time, 5 sent messengers to Balaam, son of Beor, at Pethor on the Euphrates, in the land of the Amawites, summoning him with these words, "A people has come here from Egypt who now cover the face of the earth and are settling down opposite us! 6 Please come and curse this people for us;* they are stronger than we are. We may then be able to defeat them and drive them out of the country. For I know that whoever you bless is blessed and whoever you curse is cursed." 7 Then the elders of Moab and of Midian left with the divination fee in hand and went to Balaam. When they had given him Balak's message, 8 he said to them in reply, "Stay here overnight, and I will give you whatever answer the LORD gives me." So the princes of Moab lodged with Balaam.

9 Then God came to Balaam and said, "Who are these men visiting you?" 10 Balaam answered God, "Balak, son of Zippor, king of Moab, sent me the message: 11 'This people that came here from Egypt now cover the face of the earth. Please come and lay a curse on them for us; we may then be able to give them battle and drive them out.' " 12 But God said to Balaam, "Do not go with them and do not curse this people, for they are blessed." 13 The next morning Balaam arose and told the princes of Balak, "Go back to your own country, for the LORD has refused to let me go with you." 14 So the princes of Moab went back to Balak with the report, "Balaam refused to come with us."

Second Appeal to Balaam. 15 Balak again sent princes, who were more numerous and more distinguished than the others. 16 On coming to Balaam they told him, "This is what Balak, son of Zippor, has to say: Please do not refuse to come to me. 17 I will reward you very handsomely and will do anything you ask of me. Please come and lay a curse on this people for me." 18o But Balaam

---

21, 29: Chemosh: the chief god of the Moabites, and mentioned as such in the famous inscription of Mesha, king of Moab, who was the contemporary of the dynasty of Omri in Israel. Cf 1 Kgs 11, 7. 33; 2 Kgs 23, 13; Jer 48, 7. 13.

22, 1: The plains of Moab: the lowlands to the northeast of the Dead Sea, between the Jordan and the foothills below Mount Nebo. Here the Israelites remained until they crossed the

Jordan, as told in Jos 1–4. Jericho lay to the west of the Jordan.

22, 6: Curse this people for us: Balak believed that if Balaam forecast an evil omen for Israel, this evil would come to pass, as if by magic. Balaam was a soothsayer or foreteller; cf Jos 13, 22.

m: Dt 3, 1ff.   n: Ps 136, 17ff.   o: Nm 24, 13.

replied to Balak's officials, "Even if Balak gave me his house full of silver and gold, I could not do anything, small or great, contrary to the command of the LORD, my God. ¹⁹But, you too shall stay here overnight, till I learn what else the LORD may tell me."

²⁰That night God came to Balaam and said to him, "If these men have come to summon you, you may go with them; yet only on the condition that you do exactly as I tell you." ²¹So the next morning when Balaam arose, he saddled his ass, and went off with the princes of Moab.

The Talking Ass. ²²But now the anger of God flared up* at him for going, and the angel of the LORD stationed himself on the road to hinder him as he was riding along on his ass, accompanied by two of his servants. ²³When the ass saw the angel of the LORD standing on the road with sword drawn, she turned off the road and went into the field, and Balaam had to beat her to bring her back on the road. ²⁴Then the angel of the LORD took his stand in a narrow lane between vineyards with a stone wall on each side. ²⁵When the ass saw the angel of the LORD there, she shrank against the wall; and since she squeezed Balaam's leg against it, he beat her again. ²⁶The angel of the LORD then went ahead, and stopped next in a passage so narrow that there was no room to move either to the right or to the left. ²⁷When the ass saw the angel of the LORD there, she cowered under Balaam. So, in anger, he again beat the ass with his stick.

²⁸ᵖBut now the LORD opened the mouth of the ass, and she asked Balaam, "What have I done to you that you should beat me these three times?" ²⁹"You have acted so willfully against me," said Balaam to the ass, "that if I but had a sword at hand, I would kill you here and now." ³⁰But the ass said to Balaam, "Am I not your own beast, and have you not always ridden upon me until now? Have I been in the habit of treating you this way before?" "No," replied Balaam.

³¹Then the LORD removed the veil from Balaam's eyes, so that he too saw the angel of the LORD standing on the road with sword drawn; and he fell on his knees and bowed to the ground. ³²But the angel of the LORD said to him, "Why have you beaten your ass these three times? It is I who have come armed to hinder you because this rash journey of yours is directly opposed to me. ³³When the ass saw me, she turned away from me these three times. If she had not turned away from me, I would have killed you; her I would have spared." ³⁴Then Balaam said to the angel of the LORD, "I have sinned. Yet I did not know that you stood against me to oppose my journey. Since it has displeased you, I will go back home." ³⁵But the angel of the LORD said to Balaam, "Go with the men; but you may say only what I tell you." So Balaam went on with the princes of Balak.

³⁶When Balak heard that Balaam was coming, he went out to meet him at the boundary city Ir-Moab on the Arnon at the end of the Moabite territory. ³⁷And he said to Balaam, "I sent an urgent summons to you! Why did you not come to me? Did you think I could not reward you?" ³⁸Balaam answered him, "Well, I have come to you after all. But what power have I to say anything? I can speak only what God puts in my mouth." ³⁹Then Balaam went with Balak, and they came to Kiriath-huzoth. ⁴⁰Here Balak slaughtered oxen and sheep, and sent portions to Balaam and to the princes who were with him.

The First Oracle. ⁴¹The next morning Balak took Balaam up on Bamoth-baal, and from there he saw some of the clans.

CHAPTER 23

See RG 80-85

¹Then Balaam said to Balak, "Build me seven altars, and prepare seven bullocks and seven rams for me here." ²So he did as Balaam had ordered, offering a bullock and a ram on each altar. And Balak said to him, "I have erected the seven altars, and have offered a bullock and a ram on each." ³Balaam

---

22, 22: The anger of God flared up: not merely because Balaam was going to Balak, for he had God's permission for the journey (v 20), but perhaps because he was tempted by avarice to curse Israel against God's command. "They have followed the way of Balaam, son of Bosor, who loved the wages of wrongdoing" (2 Pt 2, 15); "and have rushed on thoughtlessly into

p: 2 Pt 2, 16.

then said to him, "Stand here by your holocaust while I go over there. Perhaps the LORD will meet me, and then I will tell you whatever he lets me see." He went out on the barren height, *4*and God met him. *5*When he had put an utterance in Balaam's mouth, the LORD said to him, "Go back to Balak, and speak accordingly." *6*So he went back to Balak, who was still standing by his holocaust together with all the princes of Moab. *7*Then Balaam gave voice to his oracle:

From Aram* has Balak brought me here,
　Moab's king, from the Eastern
　　Mountains:*q*
"Come and lay a curse for me on Jacob,
　come and denounce Israel."
8 How can I curse whom God has not
　　cursed?
　How denounce whom the LORD has
　　not denounced?
9 For from the top of the crags I see him,
　from the heights I behold him.
Here is a people that lives apart*
　and does not reckon itself among the
　　nations.
10 Who has ever counted the dust of Jacob,
　or numbered Israel's wind-borne
　　particles?*
May I die the death of the just,
　may my descendants be as many as
　　theirs!

11"What have you done to me?" cried Balak to Balaam. "It was to curse my foes that I brought you here; instead, you have even blessed them." *12*Balaam replied, "Is it not what the LORD puts in my mouth that I must repeat with care?"

The Second Oracle. *13*Then Balak said to him, "Please come with me to another place* from which you can see only some and not all of them, and from there curse them for me." *14*So he brought him to the lookout field on the top of Pisgah, where he built seven altars and offered a bullock and a ram on each of them. *15*Balaam then said to Balak, "Stand here by your holocaust, while I seek a meeting over there." *16*Then the LORD met Balaam, and having put an utterance in his mouth, he said to him, "Go back to Balak, and speak accordingly." *17*So he went back to Balak, who was still standing by his holocaust together with the princes of Moab. When Balak asked him, "What did the LORD say?" *18*Balaam gave voice to his oracle:

Be aroused, O Balak, and hearken;
　give ear to my testimony, O son of
　　Zippor!
19 God is not man that he should speak
　　falsely,
　nor human, that he should change his
　　mind.
Is he one to speak and not act,
　to decree and not fulfill?
20 It is a blessing I have been given to
　　pronounce;
　a blessing which I cannot restrain.
21 Misfortune is not observed in Jacob,
　nor misery* seen in Israel.
The LORD, his God, is with him;
　with him is the triumph of his King.
22 It is God who brought him out of
　　Egypt,*r*
　a wild bull of towering might.*
23 No, there is no sorcery against Jacob,
　nor omen against Israel.
It shall yet be said of Jacob,

the error of Balaam for the sake of gain" (Jude 11). Cf v 32 and compare Ex 4, 18-26.

23, 7: Aram: the ancient name of the region later known as Syria. The Eastern Mountains: the low ranges in the Syrian desert near the Euphrates and Balaam's town of Pethor; cf Nm 22, 5.

23, 9: A people that lives apart: Israel, as the chosen people of God, occupied a unique place among the nations, from which they kept themselves aloof.

23, 10: The dust of Jacob . . . Israel's wind-borne particles: the Israelites will be as numerous as dust in a desert sandstorm. May I . . . as many as theirs: a formula by which

Balaam swears he is speaking the truth; he sees the reward of virtue in having numerous descendants.

23, 13: To another place: Balak thought that if Balaam would view Israel from a different site, he could forecast a different kind of omen.

23, 21: Misfortune . . . misery: Balaam admits that he is unable to predict any evils for Israel.

23, 22: A wild bull of towering might: the reference is to Israel, rather than to God.

---

q: Nm 22, 6.　　*r:* Nm 24, 8.

and of Israel, "Behold what God has wrought!"

²⁴ Here is a people that springs up like a lioness,
and stalks forth like a lion;
It rests not till it has devoured its prey
and has drunk the blood of the slain.^s

²⁵ "Even though you cannot curse them," said Balak to Balaam, "at least do not bless them." ²⁶ But Balaam answered Balak, "Did I not warn you that I must do all that the LORD tells me?"

The Third Oracle. ²⁷ Then Balak said to Balaam, "Come, let me bring you to another place; perhaps God will approve of your cursing them for me from there." ²⁸ So he took Balaam to the top of Peor, that overlooks Jeshimon. ²⁹ Balaam then said to him, "Here build me seven altars; and here prepare for me seven bullocks and seven rams." ³⁰ And Balak did as Balaam had ordered, offering a bullock and a ram on each altar.

CHAPTER 24

See RG 80-85

¹Balaam, however, perceiving that the LORD was pleased to bless Israel, did not go aside as before to seek omens, but turned his gaze toward the desert. ²When he raised his eyes and saw Israel encamped, tribe by tribe, the spirit of God came upon him, ³and he gave voice to his oracle:

The utterance of Balaam, son of Beor,
the utterance of the man whose eye is true,
⁴ The utterance of one who hears what God says,
and knows what the Most High knows,
Of one who sees what the Almighty sees,
enraptured, and with eyes unveiled:
⁵ How goodly are your tents, O Jacob;
your encampments, O Israel!
⁶ They are like gardens beside a stream,
like the cedars planted by the LORD.

⁷ His wells shall yield free-flowing waters,
he shall have the sea within reach;
His king shall rise higher than. . . .
and his royalty shall be exalted.
⁸ It is God who brought him out of Egypt,
a wild bull of towering might.
He shall devour the nations like grass,
their bones he shall strip bare.^t
⁹ He lies crouching like a lion,
or like a lioness; who shall arouse him?
Blessed is he who blesses you,
and cursed is he who curses you!^u

¹⁰Balak beat his palms* together in a blaze of anger at Balaam and said to him, "It was to curse my foes that I summoned you here; yet three times now you have even blessed them instead!^v ¹¹Be off at once, then, to your home. I promised to reward you richly, but the LORD has withheld the reward from you!" ¹²Balaam replied to Balak, "Did I not warn the very messengers whom you sent to me, ¹³'Even if Balak gave me his house full of silver and gold, I could not of my own accord do anything, good or evil, contrary to the command of the LORD'? Whatever the LORD says I must repeat.^w

The Fourth Oracle. ¹⁴"But now that I am about to go to my own people, let me first warn you what this people will do to your people in the days to come." ¹⁵Then Balaam gave voice to his oracle:

The utterance of Balaam, son of Beor,
the utterance of the man whose eye is true,
¹⁶ The utterance of one who hears what God says,
and knows what the Most High knows,
Of one who sees what the Almighty sees,
enraptured and with eyes unveiled
¹⁷ I see him, though not now;
I behold him, though not near:
A star shall advance from Jacob,
and a staff* shall rise from Israel,

24, 10: Balak beat his palms: a sign of disclaiming any responsibility for paying the promised reward.

24, 17: A star . . . a staff: many of the Fathers have understood this as a Messianic prophecy, although it is not referred to anywhere in the New Testament; in this sense the star is Christ himself, just as he is the staff from Israel; cf Is 11, 1. But it is

doubtful whether this passage is to be connected with the "star of the Magi" in Mt 2, 1-12. The Shuthites: mentioned in other documents of this period as nomads on the border of Palestine.

s: Nm 24, 9; Gn 49, 9. *t:* Nm 23, 22. *u:* Nm 23, 24; Gn 12, 3; 27, 29; 49, 9. *v:* Nm 23, 11. *w:* Nm 22, 18.

That shall smite the brows of Moab,[x]
and the skulls of all the Shuthites,
[18] Till Edom is dispossessed,
and no fugitive is left in Seir.
Israel shall do valiantly,
[19] and Jacob shall overcome his foes.

[20]Upon seeing Amalek, Balaam gave voice to his oracle:

First[*] of the peoples was Amalek,
but his end is to perish forever.[y]

[21]Upon seeing the Kenites,[*] he gave voice to his oracle:

Your abode is enduring, O smith,
and your nest is set on a cliff;
[22] Yet destined for burning—
even as I watch—are your
inhabitants.

[23]Upon seeing . . . he gave voice to his oracle:

[*]Alas, who shall survive of Ishmael,
[24]   to deliver his people from the hands of
the Kittim?
When they have conquered Asshur and
conquered Eber,
He too shall perish forever.

[25]Then Balaam set out on his journey home; and Balak also went his way.

See RG
80-85

CHAPTER 25

Worship of Baal of Peor. [1]While Israel was living at Shittim,[*] the people degraded themselves by having illicit relations with the Moabite women.[z] [2]These then invited the people to the sacrifices of their god, and the people ate of the sacrifices[a] and worshiped their god. [3]When Israel thus submitted to the rites of Baal of Peor,[b] the LORD's anger flared up against Israel, [4c]and he said to Moses, "Gather all the leaders of the people, and hold a public execution[*] of the guilty ones before the LORD, that his blazing wrath may be turned away from Israel." [5]So Moses told the Israelite judges, "Each of you shall kill those of his men who have submitted to the rites of Baal of Peor."

Zeal of Phinehas. [6]Yet a certain Israelite came and brought in a Midianite woman[*] to his clansmen in the view of Moses and of the whole Israelite community, while they were weeping at the entrance of the meeting tent. [7d]When Phinehas, son of Eleazar, son of Aaron the priest, saw this, he left the assembly, and taking a lance in hand, [8]followed the Israelite into his retreat where he pierced the pair of them, the Israelite and the woman. Thus the slaughter of Israelites was checked; [9]but only after twenty-four thousand had died.

[10]Then the LORD said to Moses, [11]"Phinehas, son of Eleazar, son of Aaron the priest, has turned my anger from the Israelites by his zeal for my honor[*] among them; that is why I did not put an end to the Israelites for the offense to my honor. [12e]Announce, therefore, that I hereby give him my pledge of friendship, [13]which shall be for him and for his descendants after him the pledge of an

---

24, 20: First: literally "the beginning." Amalek was an aboriginal people in Palestine and therefore considered as of great antiquity. There is a deliberate contrast here between the words first and end.

24, 21: The Kenites lived in high strongholds in the mountains of southern Palestine and the Sinai Peninsula, and were skilled in working the various metals found in their territory. Their name is connected, at least by popular etymology, with the Hebrew word for "smith"; of similar sound is the Hebrew word for "nest"—hence the play on words in the present passage.

24, 23f: The translation of this short oracle is based on a reconstructed text and is rather uncertain. Ishmael: the survival of Ishmael is indicated in Gn 17, 20; 21, 13. 18.

25, 1: Shittim: the full name was Abel-shittim, a locality at the foot of the mountains in the northeastern corner of the plains of Moab (Nm 33, 49). Illicit relations: perhaps as part of the licentious worship of Baal of Peor.

25, 4: Hold a public execution: the same phrase occurs in 2 Sm 21, 6-14, where the context shows that at least a part of the penalty consisted in being denied honorable burial. In both passages, dismemberment as a punishment for the breaking of covenant pledges is a current understanding of the phrase.

25, 6: Midianite woman: at this time the Midianites were leagued with the Moabites in opposing Israel; cf Nm 22, 4. 7. Balaam had induced both the Midianites (Nm 31, 16) and the Moabites (Rv 2, 14) to lure the Israelites to the obscene rites of Baal of Peor. They were weeping: on account of the plague that had struck them; cf v 8.

25, 11: For my honor: by taking vengeance on those who had made Baal of Peor a rival of the Lord.

x: 2 Sm 8, 2.   y: Ex 17, 14; 1 Sm 15, 3.   z: Nm 31, 16.   a: Ex 34, 15f.   b: Ps 106, 28; Hos 9, 10.   c: Dt 4, 3.   d: Ps 106, 30.   e: 12f: Sir 45, 23f; Ps 106, 31; 1 Mc 2, 26. 54.

everlasting priesthood, because he was zealous on behalf of his God and thus made amends for the Israelites."

14 *The Israelite slain with the Midianite woman was Zimri, son of Salu, prince of an ancestral house of the Simeonites. *15* The slain Midianite woman was Cozbi, daughter of Zur, who was head of a clan, an ancestral house, in Midian.

Vengeance on the Midianites. *16* *The LORD then said to Moses, *17f* "Treat the Midianites as enemies and crush them, *18* for they have been your enemies by their wily dealings with you as regards Peor and as regards their kinswoman Cozbi, the daughter of the Midianite prince, who was killed at the time of the slaughter because of Peor."

See RG
80-85

CHAPTER 26

The Second Census. *19* After the slaughter* *1* the LORD said to Moses and Eleazar, son of Aaron the priest, *2* "Take a census, by ancestral houses, throughout the community of the Israelites of all those of twenty years or more who are fit for military service in Israel."*& 3* So on the plains of Moab along the Jericho stretch of the Jordan, Moses and the priest Eleazar registered *4* those of twenty years or more, as the LORD had commanded Moses.

The Israelites who came out of the land of Egypt were as follows:

5h Of Reuben, the first-born of Israel, the Reubenites by clans were: through Hanoch the clan of the Hanochites, through Pallu the clan of the Palluites, *6* through Hezron the clan of the Hezronites, through Carmi the clan of the Carmites. *7* These were the clans of the Reubenites, of whom forty-three thousand seven hundred and thirty men were registered.

8 From Pallu descended Eliab, *9* and the descendants of Eliab were Dathan and Abiram*i*—the same Dathan and Abiram, councilors of the community, who revolted

against Moses and Aaron [like Korah's band when it rebelled against the LORD]. *10* The earth opened its mouth and swallowed them as a warning [Korah too and the band that died when the fire consumed two hundred and fifty men. *11* The descendants of Korah, however, did not die out].

12 The Simeonites by clans were: through Nemuel* the clan of the Nemuelites, through Jamin the clan of the Jaminites, through Jachin the clan of the Jachinites, *13* through Sohar the clan of the Soharites, through Shaul the clan of the Shaulites. *14* These were the clans of the Simeonites, of whom twenty-two thousand two hundred men were registered.

15 The Gadites by clans were: through Zephon the clan of the Zephonites, through Haggi the clan of the Haggites, through Shuni the clan of the Shunites, *16* through Ozni the clan of the Oznites, through Eri the clan of the Erites, *17* through Arod the clan of the Arodites, through Areli the clan of the Arelites. *18* These were the clans of the Gadites, of whom forty thousand five hundred men were registered.

19 The sons of Judah who died in the land of Canaan were Er and Onan.*j* *20* The Judahites by clans were: through Shelah the clan of the Shelahites, through Perez the clan of the Perezites, through Zerah the clan of the Zerahites. *21* The Perezites were: through Hezron the clan of the Hezronites, through Hamul the clan of the Hamulites. *22* These were the clans of Judah, of whom seventy-six thousand five hundred men were registered.

23 The Issacharites by clans were: through Tola the clan of the Tolaites, through Puvah the clan of the Puvahites, *24* through Jashub the clan of the Jashubites, through Shimron the clan of the Shimronites. *25* These were the clans of Issachar, of whom sixty-four thousand three hundred men were registered.

26 The Zebulunites by clans were: through Sered the clan of the Seredites, through Elon

---

25, 14f: The nobility of the slain couple is mentioned in order to stress the courage of Phinehas in punishing them. The zeal of Phinehas became proverbial; cf Ps 106, 30; Sir 45, 23; 1 Mc 2, 26. 54.

25, 16ff: The account of the execution of this command is given in Nm 31, 1-18.

26, 19: This is the last verse of Ch 25.

26, 12: Nemuel: so also in Gn 46, 10; 1 Chr 4, 24. In Ex 6, 15, the same man is called "Jemuel"; it is uncertain which form is correct.

f: 17f: Nm 31, 2-12.   *g:* Nm 1, 2f.   *h:* 5f: 1 Chr 5, 3.   *i:* 9f: Nm 16, 1. 32.   *j:* Gn 38, 7. 10; 46, 12; 1 Chr 2, 3.

the clan of the Elonites, through Jahleel the clan of the Jahleelites. [27]These were the clans of the Zebulunites, of whom sixty thousand five hundred men were registered.

[28]The sons of Joseph were Manasseh, and Ephraim. [29]The Manassehites by clans were: through Machir the clan of the Machirites, through Gilead, a descendant of Machir, the clan of the Gileadites. [30]The Gileadites were: through Abiezer the clan of the Abiezrites, through Helek the clan of the Helekites, [31]through Asriel the clan of the Asrielites, through Shechem the clan of the Shechemites, [32]through Shemida the clan of the Shemidaites, through Hepher the clan of the Hepherites. [33k]Zelophehad, son of Hepher, had no sons, but only daughters, whose names were Mahlah, Noah, Hoglah, Milcah and Tirzah. [34]These were the clans of Manasseh, of whom fifty-two thousand seven hundred men were registered.

[35]The Ephraimites by clans were: through Shuthelah the clan of the Shuthelahites, through Becher the clan of the Bechrites, through Tahan the clan of the Tahanites. [36]The Shuthelahites were: through Eran the clan of the Eranites. [37]These were the clans of the Ephraimites, of whom thirty-two thousand five hundred men were registered.

These were the descendants of Joseph by clans.

[38]The Benjaminites by clans were: through Bela the clan of the Belaites, through Ashbel the clan of the Ashbelites, through Ahiram the clan of the Ahiramites, [39]through Shupham the clan of the Shuphamites, through Hupham the clan of the Huphamites. [40]The descendants of Bela were Arad and Naaman: through Arad the clan of the Aradites, through Naaman the clan of the Naamanites. [41]These were the Benjaminites by clans, of whom forty-five thousand six hundred men were registered.

[42]The Danites by clans were: through Shuham the clan of the Shuhamites. These were the clans of Dan, [43]of whom sixty-four thousand four hundred men were registered.

[44]The Asherites by clans were: through Imnah the clan of the Imnites, through Ishvi the clan of the Ishvites, through Beriah the clan of the Beriites, [45]through Heber the clan of the Heberites, through Malchiel the clan of the Malchielites. [46]The name of Asher's daughter was Serah. [47]These were the clans of Asher, of whom fifty-three thousand four hundred men were registered.

[48]The Naphtalites by clans were: through Jahzeel the clan of the Jahzeelites, through Guni the clan of the Gunites, [49]through Jezer the clan of the Jezerites, through Shillem the clan of the Shillemites. [50]These were the clans of Naphtali, of whom forty-five thousand four hundred men were registered.

[51]These six hundred and one thousand seven hundred and thirty were the Israelites who were registered.

Allotment of the Land. [52]*The LORD said to Moses, [53]"Among these groups the land shall be divided as their heritage in keeping with the number of individuals in each group. [54m]To a large group you shall assign a large heritage, to a small group a small heritage, each group receiving its heritage in proportion to the number of men registered in it. [55]But the land shall be divided by lot, as the heritage of the various ancestral tribes. [56]As the lot falls shall each group, large or small, be assigned its heritage."

Census of the Levites. [57]The Levites registered by clans were: through Gershon the clan of the Gershonites, through Kohath the clan of the Kohathites, through Merari the clan of the Merarites. [58]These also were clans of Levi: the clan of the Libnites, the clan of the Hebronites, the clan of the Mahlites, the clan of the Mushites, the clan of the Korahites.

Among the descendants of Kohath was Amram, [59]whose wife was named Jochebed. She also was of the tribe of Levi, born to the

---

26, 52-56: The division of Canaan among the various tribes and clans and families was determined partly by the size of each group and partly by lot. Perhaps the lots determined the respective locality of each tribal land and the section reserved for each clan, while the relative size of the allotted locality and section depended on the numerical strength of each group. The Hebrews considered the outcome of the drawing of lots as an expression of God's will; cf Acts 1, 23-26.

k: Nm 27, 1; 36, 11; Jos 17, 3.   l: Jos 11, 23.   m: Nm 33, 54; 35, 8.

The Daughters of Zelophehad and the Inheritance of the Land

The legal case presented in Nm 27, 1–11, involves the conflict between two principles. On one hand, Israelite land normally passed from father to son and not to daughters. On the other hand, a high priority was given to maintaining a given land allotment within a particular family or clan to maintain a fair distribution of the land among family groups. On the basis of priority of this latter principle, the five daughters of a man named Zelophehad argue that they ought to receive their father's allotment of land as an inheritance. In the end, the LORD and Moses agree. In Numbers 36, the case is taken up again with some restrictions on whom the daughters of Zelophehad can marry to preserve the land in the family group.

tribe in Egypt. To Amram she bore Aaron and Moses and their sister Miriam. *60*To Aaron were born Nadab and Abihu, Eleazar and Ithamar. *61*But Nadab and Abihu died when they offered profane fire before the LORD.

*62*The total number of male Levites one month or more of age, who were registered, was twenty-three thousand.*n* They were not registered with the other Israelites, however, for no heritage was given them among the Israelites.

*63*These, then, were the men registered by Moses and the priest Eleazar in the census of the Israelites taken on the plains of Moab along the Jericho stretch of the Jordan. *64*Among them there was not a man of those who had been registered by Moses and the priest Aaron in the census of the Israelites taken in the desert of Sinai. *65o*For the LORD had told them that they would surely die in the desert, and not one of them was left except Caleb, son of Jephunneh, and Joshua, son of Nun.

See RG 80–85

CHAPTER 27

Zelophehad's Daughters. *1*Zelophehad, son of Hepher, son of Gilead, son of Machir, son of Manasseh, son of Joseph, had daughters named Mahlah, Noah, Hoglah, Milcah and Tirzah.*p* They came forward, *2*and standing in the presence of Moses, the priest Eleazar, the princes, and the whole community at the entrance of the meeting tent, said: *3*"Our father died in the desert. Although he did not join those who banded together against the LORD* [in Korah's band], he died for his own sin without leaving any sons. *4*But why should our father's name be withdrawn from his clan merely because he had no son? Let us, therefore, have property among our father's kinsmen."

Laws Concerning Heiresses. *5*When Moses laid their case before the LORD, *6*the LORD said to him, *7*"The plea of Zelophehad's daughters is just; you shall give them hereditary property among their father's kinsmen, letting their father's heritage pass on to them. *8*Therefore, tell the Israelites: If a man dies without leaving a son, you shall let his heritage pass on to his daughter; *9*if he has no daughter, you shall give his heritage to his brothers; *10*if he has no brothers, you shall give his heritage to his father's brothers; *11*if his father had no brothers, you shall give his heritage to his nearest relative in his clan, who shall then take possession of it." This is the legal norm for the Israelites, as the LORD commanded Moses.*q*

Joshua To Succeed Moses. *12*The LORD said to Moses, "Go up here into the Abarim Mountains* and view the land that I am giving to the Israelites.*r* *13*When you have viewed it, you too shall be taken to your people, as was your brother Aaron,*s* *14*because in

27, 3: He did not join . . . against the Lord: had he done so, he and his heirs could have rightly been deprived of the privilege of receiving a portion in the Promised Land.

27, 5-11: The purpose of this law, as also that of the related laws in Nm 36, 2-10 (heiresses to marry within the same tribe), Dt 25, 5-10 (levirate marriage), and Lv 25, 10 (return of property in the jubilee year), was to keep the landed prop-erty within the proper domain of each tribe.

27, 12: The Abarim Mountains: the range on the eastern side of the Dead Sea.

n: Nm 3, 39. *o*: Nm 14, 22ff. 29. *p*: Nm 26, 33; Jos 17, 3. *q*: Jer 32, 6-9. *r*: Dt 3, 27; 32, 49; 34, 1. *s*: 13f; Nm 20, 12. 24.

the rebellion of the community in the desert of Zin you both rebelled against my order to manifest my sanctity to them by means of the water."[1] [This is the water of Meribah of Kadesh in the desert of Zin.]

[15]Then Moses said to the LORD, [16]"May the LORD, the God of the spirits of all mankind,* set over the community a man [17]who shall act as their leader in all things, to guide them in all their actions; that the LORD's community may not be like sheep without a shepherd." [18]And the LORD replied to Moses, "Take Joshua, son of Nun,[u] a man of spirit,* and lay your hand upon him. [19]Have him stand in the presence of the priest Eleazar and of the whole community, and commission him before their eyes. [20]Invest him with some of your own dignity, that the whole Israelite community may obey him. [21]He shall present himself to the priest Eleazar, to have him seek out for him the decisions of the Urim* in the LORD's presence; and as he directs, Joshua, all the Israelites with him, and the community as a whole shall perform all their actions."

[22]Moses did as the LORD had commanded him. Taking Joshua and having him stand in the presence of the priest Eleazar and of the whole community, [23]he laid his hands on him and gave him his commission, as the LORD had directed through Moses.

CHAPTER 28

See RG 80–85

General Sacrifices. [1]The LORD said to Moses, [2]"Give the Israelites this commandment: At the times I have appointed, you shall be careful to present to me the food offerings that are offered to me as sweet-smelling oblations.

Each Morning and Evening. [3]"You shall tell them therefore: This is the oblation which you shall offer to the LORD: two unblemished yearling lambs each day as the established holocaust,* [4]offering one lamb in the morning and the other during the evening twilight, [5]each with a cereal offering of one tenth of an ephah of fine flour mixed with a fourth of a hin of oil of crushed olives.* [6]This is the established holocaust that was offered at Mount Sinai as a sweet-smelling oblation to the LORD. [7]And as the libation for the first lamb, you shall pour out to the LORD in the sanctuary* a fourth of a hin of wine. [8]The other lamb, to be offered during the evening twilight, you shall offer with the same cereal offering and the same libation as in the morning, as a sweet-smelling oblation to the LORD.

On the Sabbath. [9]"On the sabbath day you shall offer two unblemished yearling lambs, with their cereal offering, two tenths of an ephah of fine flour mixed with oil, and with their libations. [10]Each sabbath there shall be the sabbath holocaust in addition to the established holocaust and its libation.

At the New Moon Feast. [11]"On the first of each month* you shall offer as a holocaust to the LORD two bullocks, one ram, and seven unblemished yearling lambs, [12]with three tenths of an ephah of fine flour mixed with oil as the cereal offering for each bullock, two tenths of an ephah of fine flour mixed with oil as the cereal offering for the ram, [13]and one tenth of an ephah of fine flour mixed with oil as the cereal offering for each lamb, that the holocaust may be a sweet-smelling oblation to the LORD. [14]Their libations shall be half a hin of wine for each bullock, a third of a hin for the ram, and a fourth

27, 16: The God of the spirits of all mankind: the sense is either that God knows the character and abilities of all men and therefore knows best whom to appoint (cf Acts 1, 24), or, more probably, that God is Master of life and death and therefore can call Moses from this world whenever he wishes; cf the same phrase in Nm 16, 22, where "spirit" evidently means "the life principle."

27, 18: A man of spirit: literally, "a man in whom there is spirit": one who has the qualities of a good leader—courage, prudence, and strength of will. Cf Gn 41, 38; Dt 34, 9.

27, 21: The Urim: certain sacred objects which the Hebrew priests employed to ascertain the divine will, probably by obtaining a positive or negative answer to a given question. The full expression was "the Urim and Thummim"; cf

Ex 28, 30; Lv 8, 8; Dt 33, 8; Ezr 2, 63; Neh 7, 65. Joshua was ordinarily not to receive direct revelations from God as Moses had received them.

28, 3: The established holocaust: "the tamid holocaust," the technical term for the daily sacrifice.

28, 5: Oil of crushed olives: this oil, made in a mortar, was purer and more expensive than oil extracted in the olive press.

28, 7: In the sanctuary: according to Sir 50, 15, it was at the base of the altar.

28, 11: On the first of each month: literally, "at the new moons"; beginning on the evening when the crescent of the new moon first appeared.

t: Dt 32, 51.   *u:* Dt 34, 9.   *v:* 3-8: Ex 29, 38-42.

of a hin for each lamb. This is the new moon holocaust for every new moon of the year. [15]Moreover, one goat shall be sacrificed as a sin offering to the LORD. These are to be offered in addition to the established holocaust and its libation.

At the Passover. [16]"On the fourteenth day* of the first month falls the Passover of the LORD,[w] [17]and the fifteenth day of this month is the pilgrimage feast. For seven days unleavened bread is to be eaten. [18]On the first of these days you shall hold a sacred assembly, and do no sort of work.[x] [19]As an oblation you shall offer a holocaust to the LORD, which shall consist of two bullocks, one ram, and seven yearling lambs that you are sure are unblemished, [20]with their cereal offerings of fine flour mixed with oil, offering three tenths of an ephah for each bullock, two tenths for the ram, [21]and one tenth for each of the seven lambs; [22]and offer one goat as a sin offering in atonement for yourselves. [23]These offerings you shall make in addition to the established morning holocaust: [24]you shall make exactly the same offerings each day for seven days as food offerings, in addition to the established holocaust with its libation, for a sweet-smelling oblation to the LORD. [25]On the seventh day you shall hold a sacred assembly, and do no sort of work.[y]

At Pentecost. [26]"On the day of first fruits,* on your feast of Weeks,[z] when you present to the LORD the new cereal offering, you shall hold a sacred assembly, and do no sort of work. [27]You shall offer as a sweet-smelling holocaust to the LORD two bullocks, one ram, and seven yearling lambs that you are sure are unblemished, [28]with their cereal offerings of fine flour mixed with oil; offering three tenths of an ephah for each bullock, two tenths for the ram, [29]and

one tenth for each of the seven lambs. [30]Moreover, one goat shall be offered as a sin offering in atonement for yourselves. [31]You shall make these offerings, together with their libations, in addition to the established holocaust with its cereal offering.

CHAPTER 29

See RG 80-85

On New Year's Day. [1]"On the first day of the seventh month* you shall hold a sacred assembly, and do no sort of work; it shall be a day on which you sound the trumpet.[a] [2]You shall offer as a sweet-smelling holocaust to the LORD one bullock, one ram, and seven unblemished yearling lambs, [3]with their cereal offerings of fine flour mixed with oil; offering three tenths of an ephah for the bullock, two tenths for the ram, [4]and one tenth for each of the seven lambs. [5]Moreover, one goat shall be offered as a sin offering in atonement for yourselves. [6]These are to be offered in addition to the ordinary new moon holocaust with its cereal offering, and in addition to the established holocaust with its cereal offering, together with the libations prescribed for them, as a sweet-smelling oblation to the LORD.

On the Day of Atonement. [7]"On the tenth day of this seventh month* you shall hold a sacred assembly, and mortify yourselves, and do no sort of work.[b] [8]You shall offer as a sweet-smelling holocaust to the LORD one bullock, one ram, and seven yearling lambs that you are sure are unblemished, [9]with their cereal offerings of fine flour mixed with oil; offering three tenths of an ephah for the bullock, two tenths for the ram, [10]and one tenth for each of the seven lambs. [11]Moreover, one goat shall be sacrificed as a sin offering. These are to be offered in addition to the atonement sin offering,* the es-

---

28, 16: On the fourteenth day: toward evening at the end of this day; cf Ex 12, 6. 18.

28, 26: The day of first fruits: a unique term for this feast, which is usually called "the feast of Weeks"; it was celebrated as a thanksgiving for the wheat harvest seven weeks after the barley harvest (Passover). In the time of Christ it was commonly known by the Greek word "Pentecost," that is, "fiftieth" (day after the Passover); see note on Lv 23, 16.

29, 1: The first day of the seventh month: (about September-October) is now the Jewish New Year's Day. In the older calendar the year began with the first of Nisan (March-April);

cf Ex 12, 2.

29, 7: The tenth day of this seventh month: the Day of Atonement. Mortify yourselves: literally, "afflict your souls," that is, with fasting.

29, 11: The atonement sin offering: the bullock prescribed in Lv 16, 11f.

---

w: Ex 12, 18; Lv 23, 5; Dt 16, 1.   x: Ex 12, 16; Lv 23, 7.   y: Ex 12, 16; 13, 6; Lv 23, 8.   z: Ex 34, 22.   a: Nm 10, 10; Lv 23, 24.   b: Lv 16, 29; 23, 27f. 32.

tablished holocaust with its cereal offering, and their libations.

On the Feast of Booths. *12*"On the fifteenth day of the seventh month you shall hold a sacred assembly,*c* and do no sort of work; then, for seven days following, you shall celebrate a pilgrimage feast to the LORD. *13*You shall offer as a sweet-smelling holocaust to the LORD thirteen bullocks,* two rams, and fourteen yearling lambs that are unblemished, *14*with their cereal offerings of fine flour mixed with oil; offering three tenths of an ephah for each of the thirteen bullocks, two tenths for each of the two rams, *15*and one tenth for each of the fourteen lambs. *16*Moreover, one goat shall be sacrificed as a sin offering. These are to be offered in addition to the established holocaust with its cereal offering and libation.

17"On the second day you shall offer twelve bullocks, two rams, and fourteen unblemished yearling lambs, *18*with their cereal offerings and libations as prescribed for the bullocks, rams and lambs in proportion to their number, *19*as well as one goat for a sin offering, besides the established holocaust with its cereal offering and libation.

20"On the third day you shall offer eleven bullocks, two rams, and fourteen unblemished yearling lambs, *21*with their cereal offerings and libations as prescribed for the bullocks, rams and lambs in proportion to their number, *22*as well as one goat for a sin offering, besides the established holocaust with its cereal offering and libation.

23"On the fourth day you shall offer ten bullocks, two rams, and fourteen unblemished yearling lambs, *24*with their cereal offerings and libations as prescribed for the bullocks, rams and lambs in proportion to their number, *25*as well as one goat for a sin offering, besides the established holocaust with its cereal offering and libation.

26"On the fifth day you shall offer nine bullocks, two rams, and fourteen unblemished yearling lambs, *27d*with their cereal offerings and libations as prescribed for the bullocks, rams and lambs in proportion to their number, *28*as well as one goat for a sin offering, besides the established holocaust with its cereal offering and libation.

29"On the sixth day you shall offer eight bullocks, two rams, and fourteen unblemished yearling lambs, *30*with their cereal offerings and libations as prescribed for the bullocks, rams and lambs in proportion to their number, *31*as well as one goat for a sin offering, besides the established holocaust with its cereal offering and libation.

32"On the seventh day you shall offer seven bullocks, two rams, and fourteen unblemished yearling lambs, *33*with their cereal offerings and libations as prescribed for the bullocks, rams and lambs in proportion to their number, *34*as well as one goat for a sin offering, besides the established holocaust with its cereal offering and libation.

35"On the eighth day*e* you shall hold a solemn meeting,* and do no sort of work. *36*You shall offer up in holocaust as a sweet-smelling oblation to the LORD one bullock, one ram, and seven unblemished yearling lambs, *37*with their cereal offerings and libations as prescribed for the bullocks, rams and lambs in proportion to their number, *38*as well as one goat for a sin offering, besides the established holocaust with its cereal offering and libation.

39"These are the offerings you shall make to the LORD on your festivals, besides whatever holocausts, cereal offerings, libations, and peace offerings you present as your votive or free-will offerings."

CHAPTER 30

See RG 80-85

*1*Moses then gave the Israelites these instructions, just as the LORD had ordered him.

Validity and Annulment of Vows. *2*Moses said to the heads of the Israelite tribes, "This

---

29, 12: This feast of Booths celebrating the vintage harvest was the most popular of all and therefore had the most elaborate ritual. See note on Lv 23, 34.

29, 13: Thirteen bullocks: the number of bullocks sacrificed before the octave day was seventy, arranged on a descending scale so that the number on the seventh day was the sacred number seven.

29, 35: A solemn meeting: the Hebrew word is the technical term for the closing celebration of the three major feasts of the Passover, Pentecost and Booths, or of other special feasts that lasted for a week. Cf Lv 23, 36; Dt 16, 8; 2 Chr 7, 9; Neh 8, 18.

c: Lv 23, 34f. *d:* Nm 29, 30. 37. *e:* Lv 23, 36; Jn 7, 37.

is what the LORD has commanded: [3]When a man makes a vow to the LORD or binds himself under oath to a pledge* of abstinence, he shall not violate his word, but must fulfill exactly the promise he has uttered.[f]

[4]"When a woman, while still a maiden in her father's house, makes a vow to the LORD, or binds herself to a pledge, [5]if her father learns of her vow or the pledge to which she bound herself and says nothing to her about it, then any vow or any pledge she has made remains valid. [6]But if on the day he learns of it her father expresses to her his disapproval, then any vow or any pledge she has made becomes null and void; and the LORD releases her from it, since her father has expressed to her his disapproval.

[7]"If she marries while under a vow or under a rash pledge to which she bound herself, [8]and her husband learns of it, yet says nothing to her that day about it, then the vow or pledge she had made remains valid. [9]But if on the day he learns of it her husband expresses to her his disapproval, he thereby annuls the vow she had made or the rash pledge to which she had bound herself, and the LORD releases her from it. [10]The vow of a widow or of a divorced woman, or any pledge to which such a woman binds herself, is valid.

[11]"If it is in her husband's house* that she makes a vow or binds herself under oath to a pledge, [12]and her husband learns of it yet says nothing to express to her his disapproval, then any vow or any pledge she has made remains valid. [13]But if on the day he learns of them her husband annuls them, then whatever she has expressly promised in her vow or in her pledge becomes null and void; since her husband has annulled them, the LORD releases her from them.

[14]"Any vow or any pledge that she makes under oath to mortify herself, her husband can either allow to remain valid or render null and void. [15]But if her husband, day after day, says nothing at all to her about them, he thereby allows as valid any vow or any pledge she has made; he has allowed them to remain valid, because on the day he learned of them he said nothing to her about them. [16]If, however, he countermands them* some time after he first learned of them, he is responsible for her guilt."

[17]These are the statutes which the LORD prescribed through Moses concerning the relationship between a husband and his wife, as well as between a father and his daughter while she is still a maiden in her father's house.

CHAPTER 31

Extermination of the Midianites. See RG 80-85
[1]The LORD said to Moses,* [2]"Avenge the Israelites on the Midianites, and then you shall be taken to your people." [3]So Moses told the people, "Select men from your midst and arm them for war, to attack the Midianites and execute the LORD's vengeance on them. [4]From each of the tribes of Israel you shall send a band of one thousand men to war." [5]From the clans of Israel, therefore, a thousand men of each tribe were levied, so that there were twelve thousand men armed for war. [6]Moses sent them out on the campaign, a thousand from each tribe, with Phinehas, son of Eleazar, the priest for the campaign, who had with him the sacred vessels and the trumpets for sounding the alarm. [7]They waged war against the Midianites, as the LORD had commanded Moses, and killed every male among them. [8]Besides those slain in battle, they killed the five Midianite kings:* Evi, Rekem, Zur, Hur and Reba; and they also executed Balaam, son of Beor, with the sword. [9]But the Israelites kept the women of the Midianites with their little ones as captives, and all their herds and flocks and wealth as spoil, [10]while they set on fire all the towns where they had settled and all their en-

---

30, 3: A vow . . . a pledge: here the former signifies the doing of some positive good deed, in particular the offering of some sacrifice; the latter signifies the abstaining from some otherwise licit action or pleasure; cf v 14.

30, 11: In her husband's house: after her marriage. This contrasts with the case given in vv 7ff.

30, 16: He countermands them: he prevents their fulfillment. Since he has first allowed the vows to remain valid, he

can no longer annul them.

31, 1ff: The narrative of Israel's relations with Midian, which was interrupted after Nm 25, 18, is now resumed.

31, 8: The five Midianite kings: they are called "Midianite princes, Sihon's vassals" in Jos 13, 21.

---

[f]: Dt 23, 22; Eccl 5, 3f.

campments. [11]Then they took all the booty, with the people and beasts they had captured, and brought the captives, together with the spoils and booty, [12]to Moses and the priest Eleazar and to the Israelite community at their camp on the plains of Moab, along the Jericho stretch of the Jordan.

Treatment of the Captives. [13]When Moses and the priest Eleazar, with all the princes of the community, went outside the camp to meet them, [14]Moses became angry with the officers of the army, the clan and company commanders, who were returning from combat. [15]"So you have spared all the women!" he exclaimed. [16]"Why, they are the very ones who on Balaam's advice prompted the unfaithfulness of the Israelites toward the LORD in the Peor affair,[g] which began the slaughter of the LORD's community. [17]*Slay, therefore, every male child and every woman who has had intercourse with a man. [18]But you may spare and keep for yourselves all girls who had no intercourse with a man.

Purification after Combat. [19]"Moreover, you shall stay outside the camp for seven days, and those of you who have slain anyone or touched anyone slain in battle shall purify yourselves on the third and on the seventh day. This applies both to you and to your captives. [20]You shall also purify every article of cloth, leather, goats' hair, or wood."

[21]Eleazar the priest told the soldiers who had returned from combat: "This is what the law, as prescribed by the LORD to Moses, ordains: [22]Whatever can stand fire, such as gold, silver, bronze, iron, tin and lead, [23]you shall put into the fire, that it may become clean; however, it must also be purified with lustral water.* But whatever cannot stand fire you shall put into the water. [24]On the seventh day you shall wash your clothes, and then you will again be clean. After that you may enter the camp."

Division of the Booty. [25]The LORD said to Moses: [26]"With the help of the priest Eleazar and of the heads of the ancestral houses, count up all the human captives and the beasts that have been taken; [27]then divide them evenly,* giving half to those who took active part in the war by going out to combat, and half to the rest of the community. [28]You shall levy a tax for the LORD on the warriors who went out to combat: one out of every five hundred persons, oxen, asses and sheep [29]in their half of the spoil you shall turn over to the priest Eleazar as a contribution to the LORD. [30]From the Israelites' half you shall take one out of every fifty persons, and the same from the different beasts, oxen, asses and sheep, and give them to the Levites, who have charge of the LORD's Dwelling." [31]So Moses and the priest Eleazar did this, as the LORD had commanded Moses.

Amount of Booty. [32]This booty, what was left of the loot which the soldiers had taken, amounted to six hundred and seventy-five thousand sheep, [33]seventy-two thousand oxen, [34]sixty-one thousand asses, [35]and thirty-two thousand girls who were still virgins.

[36]The half that fell to those who had gone out to combat was: three hundred and thirty-seven thousand five hundred sheep, [37]of which six hundred and seventy-five fell as tax to the LORD; [38]thirty-six thousand oxen, of which seventy-two fell as tax to the LORD; [39]thirty thousand five hundred asses, of which sixty-one fell as tax to the LORD; [40]and sixteen thousand persons, of whom thirty-two fell as tax to the LORD. [41]The taxes contributed to the LORD, Moses gave to the priest Eleazar, as the LORD had commanded him.

[42]The half for the other Israelites, which fell to the community when Moses had taken it from the soldiers, was: [43]three hundred and thirty-seven thousand five hundred

---

31, 17: There are later references to Midian in Jgs 6–8; 1 Kgs 11, 18; Is 60, 6. The present raid was only against those Midianites who were dwelling at this time near the encampment of the Israelites.

31, 23: Lustral water: water mixed with the ashes of the red heifer as prescribed in Nm 19, 9.

31, 27: Divide them evenly: for a similar division of the booty into two equal parts, between those who engaged in the fray and those who stayed with the baggage, cf 1 Sm 30, 24. But note that here the tax on the booty of the non-combatants is ten times as much as that on the soldier's booty.

g: 2 Pt 2, 15; Rv 2, 14.

sheep, [44]thirty-six thousand oxen, [45]thirty thousand five hundred asses, [46]and sixteen thousand persons. [47]From this, the Israelites' share, Moses, as the LORD had ordered, took one out of every fifty, both of persons and of beasts, and gave them to the Levites, who had charge of the LORD's Dwelling.

Gifts of the Officers. [48]Then the officers who had been clan and company commanders of the army came up to Moses [49]and said to him, "Your servants have counted up the soldiers under our command, and not one is missing. [50]*So, to make atonement for ourselves before the LORD, each of us will bring as an offering to the LORD some gold article he has picked up, such as an anklet, a bracelet, a ring, an earring, or a necklace." [51]Moses and the priest Eleazar accepted this gold from them, all of it in well-wrought articles. [52]The gold that they gave as a contribution to the LORD amounted in all to sixteen thousand seven hundred and fifty shekels. This was from the clan and company commanders; [53]what the common soldiers had looted each one kept for himself. [54]Moses, then, and the priest Eleazar accepted the gold from the clan and company commanders, and put it in the meeting tent as a memorial for the Israelites before the LORD.

See RG 80–85

CHAPTER 32

Request of Gad and Reuben. [1]Now the Reubenites and Gadites had a very large number of livestock. Noticing that the land of Jazer and of Gilead* was grazing country, [2]they came to Moses and the priest Eleazar and to the princes of the community and said, [3]*"The region of Ataroth, Dibon, Jazer, Nimrah, Heshbon, Elealeh, Sebam, Nebo and Baal-meon, [4]which the LORD has laid low before the community of Israel, is grazing country. Now, since your servants have

livestock," [5]they continued, "if we find favor with you, let this land be given to your servants as their property. Do not make us cross the Jordan."

Moses' Rebuke. [6]But Moses answered the Gadites and Reubenites: "Are your kinsmen, then, to engage in war, while you remain here? [7]Why do you wish to discourage the Israelites from crossing to the land the LORD has given them? [8]That is just what your fathers did when I sent them from Kadesh-barnea to reconnoiter the land.[h] [9]They went up to the Wadi Eshcol and reconnoitered the land, then so discouraged the Israelites that they would not enter the land the LORD had given them. [10i]At that time the wrath of the LORD flared up, and he swore, [11]'Because they have not followed me unreservedly, none of these men of twenty years or more who have come up from Egypt shall ever see this country I promised under oath to Abraham and Isaac and Jacob, [12j]except the Kenizzite* Caleb, son of Jephunneh, and Joshua, son of Nun, who have followed the LORD unreservedly.' [13]So in his anger with the Israelites the LORD made them wander in the desert forty years, until the whole generation that had done evil in the sight of the LORD had died out. [14]And now here you are, a brood of sinners, rising up in your fathers' place to add still more to the LORD's blazing wrath against the Israelites. [15]If you turn away from following him, he will make them stay still longer in the desert, and so you will bring about the ruin of this whole nation."

Counter Proposal. [16]But they were insistent with him: "We wish only to build sheepfolds here for our flocks, and towns for our families; [17]but we ourselves will march as troops in the van of the Israelites,[k] until we have led them to their destination. Meanwhile our families can remain here in the fortified towns, safe from attack by the

---

31, 50: The precise nature and use of some of these articles of gold is not certain.

32, 1: Gilead: the name of the western part of the plateau east of the Jordan, sometimes signifying the whole region from the Yarmuk to the Jordan, sometimes only the northern part of this region, and sometimes, as here, only its southern part. Jazer lay to the east of southern Gilead.

32, 3: The places named in this verse, as well as the additional ones given in vv 34-38, were all in the former kingdom

of Sihon, that is, in the region between the Jabbok and the Arnon. Cf Nm 21, 23f; Jos 13, 19-21. 24-27.

32, 12: Kenizzite: a member of the clan of Kenaz, which, according to Gn 36, 11. 15. 42, was Edomitic; hence, although Caleb belonged to the tribe of Judah (Nm 13, 6; 34, 19), he must have had Edomite blood in his veins; cf also Jos 14, 6. 14.

h: 8f: Nm 13, 31ff; Dt 1, 22. *i:* 10f: Dt 1, 34f. *j:* Nm 14, 24; Dt 1, 36. *k:* Jos 4, 12f.

natives. [18]We will not return to our homes until every one of the Israelites has taken possession of his heritage, [19]and will not claim any heritage with them [once we cross the Jordan, so long as we receive a heritage for ourselves on this eastern side of the Jordan."

Agreement Reached. [20]*Moses said to them in reply: "If you keep your word to march as troops in the LORD's vanguard [21]and to cross the Jordan in full force before the LORD until he has driven his enemies out of his way [22]and the land is subdued before him, then you may return here, quit of every obligation to the LORD and to Israel, and this region shall be your possession before the LORD.[m] [23]But if you do not do this, you will sin against the LORD, and you can be sure that you will not escape the consequences of your sin. [24]Build the towns, then, for your families, and the folds for your flocks, but also fulfill your express promise."

[25]The Gadites and Reubenites answered Moses, "Your servants will do as you command, my lord. [26n]While our wives and children, our herds and other livestock remain in the towns of Gilead, [27]all your servants will go across as armed troops to battle before the LORD, just as your lordship says."

[28]Moses, therefore, gave this order in their regard to the priest Eleazar, to Joshua, son of Nun, and to the heads of the ancestral tribes of the Israelites: [29]"If all the Gadites and Reubenites cross the Jordan with you as combat troops before the LORD, you shall give them Gilead as their property when the land has been subdued before you. [30]But if they will not go across with you as combat troops before the LORD, you shall bring their wives and children and livestock across before you into Canaan, and they shall have their property with you in the land of Canaan."

[31]To this the Gadites and Reubenites replied, "We will do what the LORD has commanded us, your servants. [32]We ourselves will go across into the land of Canaan as troops before the LORD, but we will retain our hereditary property on this side of the Jordan." [33]So Moses gave them [*the Gadites and Reubenites, as well as half the tribe of Manasseh, son of Joseph, the kingdom of Sihon, king of the Amorites, and the kingdom of Og, king of Bashan,] the land with its towns and the districts that surrounded them.[o]

[34]The Gadites rebuilt the fortified towns of Dibon, Ataroth, Aroer, [35]Atroth-shophan, Jazer, Jogbehah, [36]Beth-nimrah and Beth-haran, and they built sheepfolds. [37]The Reubenites rebuilt Heshbon, Elealeh, Kiriathaim, [38]Nebo, Baal-meon [names to be changed!],* and Sibmah. These towns, which they rebuilt, they called by their old names.

Other Conquests. [39]The descendants of Machir, son of Manasseh, invaded Gilead and captured it, driving out the Amorites who were there. [40][Moses gave Gilead to Machir,[p] son of Manasseh, and he settled there.] [41]Jair,[q] a Manassehite clan, campaigned against the tent villages, captured them and called them Havvoth-jair. [42]Nobah also campaigned against Kenath, captured it with its dependencies and called it Nobah after his own name.

CHAPTER 33

See RG 80-85

Stages on the Journey. [1]The following are the stages by which the Israelites journeyed up by companies from the land of Egypt under the guidance of Moses and Aaron.* [2]By the LORD's command Moses

---

32, 20ff: Since the ark of the Lord was borne into battle with the Israelite army, the vanguard was said to march before the Lord.

32, 33: The preceding is concerned solely with the two tribes of Gad and Reuben and with the land of the former kingdom of Sihon; hence it seems probable that the sudden reference here to the half-tribe of Manasseh and to their territory in Bashan, the former kingdom of Og, is a later addition to the text.

32, 38: The phrase in brackets is a gloss, warning the reader either to change the order of the preceding names, or, more probably, to read some other word, such as bosheth, "shame," for Baal. They called them by their old names: literally,

"they called by their names" (see Textual Notes); however, some understand the current Hebrew text to mean, "they called by new names."

33, 1ff: This list of camping sites was drawn up by Moses, as v 2 expressly states. However, in its present form it probably includes some glosses. Moreover, a comparison with the more detailed accounts of the journey as given elsewhere shows that this is not complete. It records just forty camping sites, not counting the starting place, Rameses, and

l: Jos 13, 8.   *m:* Jos 1, 15.   *n:* Jos 1, 14.   *o:* Dt 3, 12; 29, 7; Jos 12, 6; 13, 8.   *p:* Dt 3, 15.   *q:* Dt 3, 14.

Journey from the Wilderness to Canaan

recorded the starting places of the various stages. The starting places of the successive stages were:

3 *They set out from Rameses in the first month,
    on the fifteenth day of the first month.
On the Passover morrow the Israelites went forth
    in triumph, in view of all Egypt,
4 While the Egyptians buried their first-born
    all of whom the Lord had struck down;
    on their gods, too, the Lord executed judgments.*r*

From Egypt to Sinai. *5*Setting out from Rameses, the Israelites camped at Succoth. *6*Setting out from Succoth, they camped at Etham near the edge of the desert. *7*Setting out from Etham, they turned back to Pi-hahiroth, which is opposite Baal-zephon, and they camped opposite Migdol.*s* *8*Setting out from Pi-hahiroth, they crossed over through the sea into the desert,*t* and after a three days' journey in the desert of Etham, they camped at Marah. *9*Setting out from Marah, they came to Elim, where there were twelve springs of water and seventy palm trees, and they camped there.*u* *10*Setting out from Elim, they camped beside the Red Sea. *11*Setting out from the Red Sea, they camped in the desert of Sin. *12*Setting out from the desert of Sin, they camped at Dophkah. *13*Setting out from Dophkah, they camped at Alush. *14*Setting out from Alush, they camped at Rephidim, where there was no water for the people to drink.*v* *15*Setting out from Rephidim, they camped in the desert of Sinai.*w*

the terminus, the plains of Moab. This number, which corresponds exactly to the forty years of wandering in the desert, is probably a schematic device. Besides, it seems that in its present form the order of some of these names has been disturbed. Several names listed here are not recorded elsewhere.

33, 3f: These two verses were probably borrowed from some ancient song celebrating the exodus from Egypt.

r: 4f: Ex 12, 12. 29. 37.   *s:* Ex 14, 2.   *t:* Ex 15, 22.   *u:* Ex 15, 27.   *v:* Ex 17, 1.   *w:* Ex 19, 2.

From Sinai to Kadesh. ¹⁶Setting out from the desert of Sinai, they camped at Kibroth-hattaavah. ¹⁷Setting out from Kibroth-hattaavah, they camped at Hazeroth.ˣ ¹⁸Setting out from Hazeroth, they camped at Rithmah. ¹⁹Setting out from Rithmah, they camped at Rimmon-perez. ²⁰Setting out from Rimmon-perez, they camped at Libnah. ²¹Setting out from Libnah, they camped at Rissah. ²²Setting out from Rissah, they camped at Kehelathah. ²³Setting out from Kehelathah, they camped at Mount Shepher. ²⁴Setting out from Mount Shepher, they camped at Haradah. ²⁵Setting out from Haradah, they camped at Makheloth. ²⁶Setting out from Makheloth, they camped at Tahath. ²⁷Setting out from Tahath, they camped at Terah. ²⁸Setting out from Terah, they camped at Mithkah. ²⁹Setting out from Mithkah, they camped at Hashmonah. ³⁰*Setting out from Hashmonah,—

From Mount Hor to Ezion-geber. They camped at Moseroth. ³¹Setting out from Moseroth, they camped at Bene-jaakan. ³²Setting out from Bene-jaakan, they camped at Mount Gidgad. ³³Setting out from Mount Gidgad, they camped at Jotbathah. ³⁴Setting out from Jotbathah, they camped at Abronah. ³⁵Setting out from Abronah, they camped at Ezion-geber. ³⁶Setting out from Ezion-geber,—

From Kadesh to Mount Hor. They camped in the desert of Zin, at Kadesh.ʸ ³⁷Setting out from Kadesh, they camped at Mount Hor on the border of the land of Edom. ³⁸[Aaron the priest ascended Mount Hor.ᶻ at the LORD's command, and there he died in the fortieth year from the departure of the Israelites from the land of Egypt, on the first day of the fifth month. ³⁹Aaron was a hundred and twenty-three years old when he died on Mount Hor. ⁴⁰*Now, when the Canaanite king of Arad, who lived in the Negeb in the land of Canaan, heard that the Israelites were coming. . . .] ⁴¹Setting out from Mount Hor,—

*From Ezion-geber to the Plains of Moab.** They camped at Zalmonah. ⁴²Setting out from Zalmonah, they camped at Punon. ⁴³Setting out from Punon, they camped at Oboth. ⁴⁴Setting out from Oboth, they camped at Iye-abarim on the border of Moab. ⁴⁵Setting out from Iye-abarim, they camped at Dibon-gad. ⁴⁶Setting out from Dibon-gad, they camped at Almon-diblathaim. ⁴⁷Setting out from Almon-diblathaim, they camped in the Abarim Mountains opposite Nebo. ⁴⁸Setting out from the Abarim Mountains, they camped on the plains of Moab along the Jericho stretch of the Jordan. ⁴⁹Their camp along the Jordan on the plains of Moab extended from Beth-jeshimoth to Abel-shittim.

Conquest and Division of Canaan. ⁵⁰The LORD spoke to Moses on the plains of Moab beside the Jericho stretch of the Jordan and said to him: ⁵¹"Tell the Israelites: When you go across the Jordan into the land of Canaan, ⁵²drive out all the inhabitants of the land before you; destroy all their stone figures and molten images, and demolish all their high places.ᵃ

⁵³"You shall take possession of the land and settle in it, for I have given you the land as your property. ⁵⁴You shall apportion the land among yourselves by lot, clan by clan, assigning a large heritage to a large group and a small heritage to a small group.ᵇ Wherever anyone's lot falls, there shall his property be within the heritage of his ancestral tribe.

⁵⁵"But if you do not drive out the inhabitants of the land before you, those whom you allow to remain will become as barbs in your eyes and thorns in your sides, and they will harass you in the country where you live,ᶜ ⁵⁶and I will treat you as I had intended to treat them."

33, 30-36: Moseroth is mentioned in Dt 10, 6 (in the form of "Moserah"), as the place where Aaron died. It must therefore have been close to Mount Hor; cf Nm 20, 22ff. It seems very probable that the section vv 36b-41a stood originally immediately after v 30a.

33, 40: The verse begins the same account of the victory over Arad as is given in Nm 21, 1ff, where it also follows the account of Aaron's death.

33, 41b-49: It seems that this section stood originally immediately after v 36a.

x: 17f: Nm 11, 34f.   *y:* 36f: Nm 20, 1. 22.   *z:* Nm 20, 25; Dt 32, 50.   *a:* Ex 23, 31; 34, 13; Dt 7, 5; 12, 3.   *b:* Nm 26, 53ff.   *c:* Jos 23, 13; Jgs 2, 3.

CHAPTER 34

See RG
80-85

The Boundaries. ¹The LORD said to Moses, ²"Give the Israelites this order: When you enter the land of Canaan, this is the territory that shall fall to you as your heritage— the land of Canaan with its boundaries:

³"Your southern boundary shall be at the desert of Zin along the border of Edom;ᵈ on the east it shall begin at the end of the Salt Sea, ⁴and turning south of the Akrabbim Pass, it shall cross Zin, and extend south of Kadesh-barnea to Hazar-addar; thence it shall cross to Azmon,ᵉ ⁵and turning from Azmon to the Wadi of Egypt, shall terminate at the Sea.ᶠ

⁶"For your western boundary you shall have the Great Sea* with its coast; this shall be your western boundary.

⁷"The following shall be your boundary on the north: from the Great Sea you shall draw a line to Mount Hor,* ⁸and shall continue it from Mount Hor to Labo in the land of Hamath, with the boundary extending through Zedad. ⁹Thence the boundary shall reach to Ziphron and terminate at Hazarenan. This shall be your northern boundary.

¹⁰"For your eastern boundary you shall draw a line from Hazar-enan to Shepham. ¹¹From Shepham the boundary shall go down to Ar-Baal, east of Ain, and descending further, shall strike the ridge on the east side of the Sea of Chinnereth; ¹²thence the boundary shall continue along the Jordan and terminate with the Salt Sea.

"This is the land that shall be yours, with the boundaries that surround it."

¹³Moses also gave this order to the Israelites: "This is the land, to be apportioned among you by lot, which the LORD has commanded to be given to the nine and one half tribes. ¹⁴For all the ancestral houses of the tribe of Reuben, and the ancestral houses of the tribe of Gad, as well as half of the tribe of Manasseh, have already received their heritage; ¹⁵these two and one half tribes have received their heritage on the eastern side of the Jericho stretch of the Jordan, toward the sunrise."

Supervisors of the Allotment. ¹⁶The LORD said to Moses, ¹⁷"These are the names of the men who shall apportion the land among you: Eleazar the priest, and Joshua, son of Nun, ¹⁸ᵍand one prince from each of the tribes whom you shall designate for this task. ¹⁹These shall be as follows:

from the tribe of Judah: Caleb, son of Jephunneh;
²⁰ from the tribe of Simeon: Samuel, son of Ammihud;
²¹ from the tribe of Benjamin: Elidad, son of Chislon;
²² from the tribe of Dan: Bukki, son of Jogli;
²³ from the tribe of Manasseh: Hanniel, son of Ephod; and
²⁴ from the tribe of Ephraim: Kemuel, son of Shiphtan, for the descendants of Joseph;
²⁵ from the tribe of Zebulun: Elizaphan, son of Parnach;
²⁶ from the tribe of Issachar: Paltiel, son of Azzan;
²⁷ from the tribe of Asher: Ahihud, son of Shelomi;
²⁸ from the tribe of Naphtali: Pedahel, son of Ammihud."

²⁹These are they whom the LORD commanded to assign the Israelites their heritage in the land of Canaan.

CHAPTER 35

See RG
80-85

Cities for the Levites. ¹The LORD gave these instructions to Moses on the plains of Moab beside the Jericho stretch of the Jordan: ²ʰ"Tell the Israelites that out of their hereditary property they shall give the Levites cities for homes, as well as pasture lands around the cities. ³The cities shall serve them to dwell in, and the pasture lands shall serve their herds and flocks and other animals. ⁴The pasture lands of the cities to

---

34, 6: The Great Sea: the Mediterranean.

34, 7f: Mount Hor: different from the one where Aaron died; cf Nm 20, 22; 33, 37f.

---

d: Jos 15, 1f.   e: Jos 15, 3.   f: Jos 15, 4.   g: Nm 1, 4.   h: Jos 14, 3f; 21, 2.

be assigned the Levites shall extend a thousand cubits from the city walls in each direction. [5]Thus you shall measure out two thousand cubits outside the city along each side—east, south, west and north—with the city lying in the center. This shall serve them as the pasture lands of their cities.

[6i]"Now these are the cities you shall give to the Levites: the six cities of asylum which you must establish as places where a homicide can take refuge, and in addition forty-two other cities— [7]a total of forty-eight cities with their pasture lands to be assigned the Levites. [8*]In assigning the cities from the property of the Israelites, take more from a larger group and fewer from a smaller one, so that each group will cede cities to the Levites in proportion to its own heritage."

Cities of Asylum. [9]The LORD said to Moses, [10]"Tell the Israelites: When you go across the Jordan into the land of Canaan, [11]select for yourselves cities[j] to serve as cities of asylum, where a homicide who has killed someone unintentionally may take refuge. [12]These cities shall serve you as places of asylum from the avenger of blood,[*] so that a homicide shall not be put to death unless he is first tried before the community. [13]Six cities of asylum shall you assign: [14]three beyond the Jordan, and three in the land of Canaan. [15]These six cities of asylum shall serve not only the Israelites but all the resident or transient aliens among them, so that anyone who has killed another unintentionally may take refuge there.

Murder and Manslaughter. [16*]"If a man strikes another with an iron instrument and causes his death, he is a murderer and shall be put to death.[k] [17]If a man strikes another with a death-dealing stone in his hand and causes his death, he is a murderer and shall be put to death. [18]If a man strikes another with a death-dealing club in his hand and causes his death, he is a murderer and shall be put to death. [19]The avenger of blood may

execute the murderer, putting him to death on sight.

[20]"If a man pushes another out of hatred, or after lying in wait for him throws something at him, and causes his death,[l] [21]or if he strikes another out of enmity and causes his death, he shall be put to death as a murderer. The avenger of blood may execute the murderer on sight.

[22m]"However, if a man pushes another accidentally and not out of enmity, or if without lying in wait for him he throws some object at him, [23]or without seeing him throws a death-dealing stone which strikes him and causes his death, although he was not his enemy nor seeking to harm him: [24]then the community, deciding the case between the slayer and the avenger of blood in accordance with these norms, [25]shall free the homicide from the avenger of blood and shall remand him to the city of asylum where he took refuge;[n] and he shall stay there until the death of the high priest who has been anointed with sacred oil. [26]If the homicide of his own accord leaves the bounds of the city of asylum where he has taken refuge, [27]and the avenger of blood finds him beyond these bounds and kills him, the avenger incurs no blood-guilt; [28]the homicide was bound to stay in his city of asylum until the death of the high priest. Only after the death of the high priest may the homicide return to his own district.

[29]"These shall be norms for you and all your descendants, wherever you live, for rendering judgment.

Witnesses. [30]"Whenever someone kills another, the evidence of witnesses is required for the execution of the murderer.[o] The evidence of a single witness is not sufficient for putting a person to death.

No Indemnity. [31]"You shall not accept indemnity in place of the life of a murderer who deserves the death penalty; he must be put to death. [32]Nor shall you accept indemnity to allow a refugee to leave his city of

---

35, 8: This provision was hardly observed in the actual assignment of the levitical cities as narrated in Jos 21.

35, 12: The avenger of blood: one of the close relatives of the slain (2 Sm 14, 7) who, as executor of public justice, had the right and duty to take the life of the murderer; cf Dt 19, 6. 12; Jos 20, 3. 5. 9.

35, 16-25: Here, as also in Dt 19, 1-13, there is a casuistic development of the original law as stated in Ex 21, 12ff.

i: Dt 4, 41f; Jos 20, 2. *j:* 10ff; Dt 19, 2; Jos 20, 2ff. *k:* Ex 21, 12; Lv 24, 17. *l:* Ex 21, 14; Dt 19, 11. *m:* Jos 20, 3. *n:* Jos 20, 6. *o:* Dt 17, 6; 19, 15; Jn 8, 17; 2 Cor 13, 1; 1 Tm 5, 19.

asylum and again dwell elsewhere in the land before the death of the high priest. ³³You shall not desecrate the land where you live. Since bloodshed desecrates the land, the land can have no atonement for the blood shed on it except through the blood of him who shed it. ³⁴Do not defile the land in which you live and in the midst of which I dwell;ᵖ for I am the LORD who dwells in the midst of the Israelites."

See RG 80-85

CHAPTER 36

Property of Heiresses. ¹The heads of the ancestral houses in the clan of descendants of Gilead, son of Machir, son of Manasseh—one of the Josephite clans—came up and laid this plea before Moses and the priest Eleazar and before the princes who were the heads of the ancestral houses of the other Israelites. ²They said: "The LORD commanded you, my lord, to apportion the land by lot among the Israelites;�q and you, my lord, were also commanded by the LORD to give the heritage of our kinsman Zelophehad to his daughters. ³But if they marry into one of the other Israelite tribes, their heritage will be withdrawn from our ancestral heritage and will be added to that of the tribe into which they marry; thus the heritage that fell to us by lot will be diminished. ⁴When the Israelites celebrate the jubilee year,* the heritage of these women will be permanently added to that of the tribe into which

they marry and will be withdrawn from that of our ancestral tribe."

⁵*So Moses gave this regulation to the Israelites according to the instructions of the LORD: "The tribe of the Josephites are right in what they say. ⁶This is what the LORD commands with regard to the daughters of Zelophehad: They may marry anyone they please, provided they marry into a clan of their ancestral tribe, ⁷so that no heritage of the Israelites will pass from one tribe to another, but all the Israelites will retain their own ancestral heritage. ⁸Therefore, every daughter who inherits property in any of the Israelite tribes shall marry someone belonging to a clan of her own ancestral tribe, in order that all the Israelites may remain in possession of their own ancestral heritage. ⁹Thus, no heritage can pass from one tribe to another, but all the Israelite tribes will retain their own ancestral heritage."

¹⁰The daughters of Zelophehad obeyed the command which the LORD had given to Moses. ¹¹Mahlah, Tirzah, Hoglah, Milcah and Noah, Zelophehad's daughters, married relatives on their father's side ¹²within the clans of the descendants of Manasseh, son of Joseph; hence their heritage remained in the tribe of their father's clan.

Conclusion. ¹³These are the commandments and decisions which the LORD prescribed for the Israelites through Moses, on the plains of Moab beside the Jericho stretch of the Jordan.

36, 4: Before the jubilee year various circumstances, such as divorce, could make such property revert to its original tribal owners; but in the jubilee year it became irrevocably attached to its new owners.
36, 5-9: This is a supplement to the law given in Nm 27, 5-11.

p: Ex 29, 45.   *q:* Nm 26, 55; 27, 6; Jos 17, 3f.

See RG 85-89

The Book of Deuteronomy

The fifth and last book of the Pentateuch is called Deuteronomy, meaning "second law." In reality, what it contains is not a new law but a partial repetition, completion and explanation of the law proclaimed on Mount Sinai. The historical portions of the book are also a résumé of what is related elsewhere in the Pentateuch. The chief characteristic of this book is its vigorous oratorical

style. In a series of eloquent discourses Moses presents the theme of covenant renewal in a vital religious framework. He exhorts, corrects and threatens his people, appealing to their past glory, their historic mission, and the promise of future triumph. His aim is to enforce among the Israelites the Lord's claim to their obedience, loyalty and love. The events contained in the Book of

The story begins just as the Israelites, encamped on the plains of Moab, stand poised finally to enter the Promised Land. The entry into Canaan would provide the long-awaited climax of the story that had begun with the promises to the ancestors in Genesis. The enslavement in Egypt and the wandering in the wilderness had delayed its fulfillment. Now, Moses, on the eve both of his death and of the nations' entry into the land without him, is portrayed as Deuteronomy's speaker. He delivers a series of three speeches, grouped together as a long address. He reviews the nation's history, expounds upon their laws, and instructs them about the importance of loyalty to God. He also tells the nation to uphold this combination of law and theological instruction as a covenant upon the plains of Moab, one that supplements the one previously sworn at Horeb (Deuteronomy's name for Sinai; 28, 69). Only after the conclusion of these three discourses and a following appendix (chs 31–34) does the story line resume with the account of the nation's entry into Canaan in Joshua and Judges.

Deuteronomy took place in the plains of Moab (1, 5) between the end of the wanderings in the desert (1, 3) and the crossing of the Jordan River (Jos 4, 19), a period of no more than forty days. The Book of Deuteronomy, written after the Israelites had for centuries been resident in the Land of Promise, takes the form of a testament of Moses, the great leader and legislator, to his people on the eve of his death. At the time of our Lord's coming, it shared with the Psalms a preeminent religious influence among the Old Testament books. The Savior quoted passages of Deuteronomy in overcoming the threefold temptation of Satan in the desert (Mt 4; Dt 6, 13. 16; 8, 3; 10, 20), and in explaining to the lawyer the first and greatest commandment (Mt 22, 35-39; Dt 6, 4).

The book is divided as follows:

I: Historical Review and Exhortation (1, 1—4, 43).

II: God and His Covenant (4, 44—11, 32).

III: Exposition of the Law (12, 1—26, 19).

IV: Final Words of Moses (27, 1—34, 12).

I: Historical Review and Exhortation

CHAPTER 1

See RG 85–89

Introduction. [1]These are the words which Moses spoke to all Israel beyond the Jordan [*in the desert, in the Arabah, opposite Suph, between Paran and Tophel, Laban, Hazeroth and Dizahab; [2]it is a journey of eleven days from Horeb to Kadesh-barnea by way of the highlands of Seir].

[3]In the fortieth year, on the first day of the eleventh month, Moses spoke to the Israelites all the commands that the LORD had given him in their regard. [4]After he had defeated Sihon, king of the Amorites, who lived in Heshbon,*a* and Og, king of Bashan, who lived in Ashtaroth and in Edrei, [5]Moses began to explain the law in the land of Moab beyond the Jordan, as follows:

Departure from Horeb. [6]"The LORD, our God, said to us at Horeb, 'You have stayed long enough at this mountain. [7]*Leave here and go to the hill country of the Amorites and to all the surrounding regions,*b* the land of the Canaanites in the Arabah, the mountains, the foothills, the Negeb and the seacoast; to Lebanon, and as far as the Great River [the

1, 1: The local setting of all these discourses is in the land of Moab beyond the Jordan (cf v 5), also known as the plains of Moab (Nm 36, 13).

1, 7: The Amorites and the Canaanites formed the principal part of the pre-Israelite population of Palestine. The foothills: the hills on the western slope of the Judean mountain range. The Arabah: the valley of the Jordan and the depression south of the Dead Sea. The Negeb: the arid land in southern Palestine.

a: Dt 3, 2; Nm 21, 21-35.   *b:* Nm 13, 29.

Euphrates]. [8]I have given that land over to you.[c] Go now and occupy the land I swore to your fathers, Abraham, Isaac and Jacob, I would give to them and to their descendants.'

Appointment of Elders. [9]"At that time I said to you, 'Alone, I am unable to carry you.* [10]The LORD, your God, has so multiplied you that you are now as numerous as the stars in the sky.[d] [11]May the LORD, the God of your fathers, increase you a thousand times over, and bless you as he promised! [12]But how can I alone bear the crushing burden that you are, along with your bickering? [13e]Choose wise, intelligent and experienced men from each of your tribes, that I may appoint them as your leaders.' [14]You answered me, 'We agree to do as you have proposed.' [15]So I took outstanding men of your tribes, wise and experienced, and made them your leaders as officials over thousands, over hundreds, over fifties and over tens, and other tribal officers. [16]I charged your judges at that time, 'Listen to complaints among your kinsmen, and administer true justice to both parties even if one of them is an alien.[f] [17]In rendering judgment, do not consider who a person is; give ear to the lowly and to the great alike, fearing no man, for judgment is God's. Refer to me any case that is too hard for you and I will hear it.' [18]Thereupon I gave you all the commands you were to fulfill.

The Twelve Scouts. [19]"Then, in obedience to the command of the LORD, our God, we set out from Horeb and journeyed through the whole desert, vast and fearful as you have seen,[g] in the direction of the hill country of the Amorites. We had reached Kadesh-barnea [20]when I said to you, 'You have come to the hill country of the Amorites, which the LORD, our God, is giving us. [21]The LORD, your God, has given this land over to you. Go up and occupy it, as the LORD, the God of your fathers, commands you. Do not fear or lose heart.' [22h]Then all of you came up to me and said, 'Let us send men ahead to reconnoiter the land for us and report to us on the road we must follow and the cities we must take.' [23]Agreeing with the proposal, I chose twelve men from your number, one from each tribe. [24]They set out into the hill country as far as the Wadi Eshcol, and explored it. [25]Then, taking along some of the fruit of the land, they brought it down to us and reported, 'The land which the LORD, our God, gives us is good.'

Threats of Revolt. [26]"But you refused to go up,[i] and after defying the command of the LORD, your God, [27]you set to murmuring in your tents,* 'Out of hatred for us the LORD has brought us up out of the land of Egypt,[j] to deliver us into the hands of the Amorites and destroy us. [28]What shall we meet with up there? Our kinsmen have made us faint-hearted by reporting that the people are stronger and taller than we, and their cities are large and fortified to the sky; besides, they saw the Anakim there.'[k]

[29]"But I said to you, 'Have no dread or fear of them. [30]The LORD, your God, who goes before you, will himself fight for you, just as he took your part before your very eyes in Egypt, [31]as well as in the desert, where you saw how the LORD, your God, carried you, as a man carries his child, all along your journey until you arrived at this place.' [32]Despite this, you would not trust the LORD, your God, [33]who journeys before you to find you a resting place—by day in the cloud, and by night in the fire, to show the way you must go.[l] [34]When the LORD heard your words, he was angry; [35]and he swore, 'Not one man of this evil generation shall look upon the good land I swore to give to your fathers,[m] [36]except Caleb,* son of Jephunneh; he shall see it. For to him and to his sons I will give the land he trod upon, be-

1, 9: Carry you: cf v 31.

1, 27: In your tents: among yourselves.

1, 36: Except Caleb: Joshua also was allowed to enter, but he is not referred to here because special mention is made of him in v 38 as the successor of Moses.

c: Gn 12, 7; 15, 18; 17, 7f; 28, 13f. *d:* Dt 10, 22; Gn 15, 5. *e:* 13ff: Ex 18, 21-25. *f:* 16f: Ex 18, 26; 2 Chr 19, 6f; Prv 24, 23; Jn 7, 24; Jas 2, 9. *g:* Dt 8, 15; 32, 10. *h:* 22-28: Nm 13, 2-34. *i:* Dt 9, 23. *j:* Dt 9, 28; Nm 14, 1-4; Ps 106, 25. *k:* Dt 9, 1f. *l:* Ex 13, 21; Nm 10, 33f; 14, 14. *m:* 34ff: Nm 14, 22f. 28-38; Jos 14, 9.

cause he has followed the LORD unreservedly.'

37"The LORD was angered against me also on your account, and said, 'Not even you shall enter there,*n* *38*but your aide Joshua,*o* son of Nun, shall enter. Encourage him, for he is to give Israel its heritage. *39*Your little ones, who you said would become booty, and your children, who as yet do not know good from bad—they shall enter; to them I will give it, and they shall occupy it.*p* *40*But as for yourselves: turn about and proceed into the desert on the Red Sea road.'

Unsuccessful Invasion. *41q*"In reply you said to me, 'We have sinned against the LORD. We will go up ourselves and fight, just as the LORD, our God, commanded us.' And each of you girded on his weapons, making light of going up into the hill country. *42*But the LORD said to me, 'Warn them: Do not go up and fight, lest you be beaten down before your enemies, for I will not be in your midst.' *43*I gave you this warning but you would not listen. In defiance of the LORD's command you arrogantly marched off into the hill country. *44*Then the Amorites living there came out against you and, like bees, chased you, cutting you down in Seir as far as Hormah. *45*On your return you wept before the LORD, but he did not listen to your cry or give ear to you. *46*That is why you had to stay as long as you did at Kadesh.

CHAPTER 2

See RG 85–89

Northward along Edom. *1*"When we did turn and proceed into the desert on the Red Sea road,*r* as the LORD had commanded me, we circled around the highlands of Seir for a long time. *2*Finally the LORD said to me, *3*'You have wandered round these highlands long enough; turn and go north. *4*Give this order to the people: You are now about to pass through the territory of your kinsmen, the descendants of Esau, who live in Seir. Though they are afraid of you, be very careful *5*not to come in conflict with them, for I will not give you so much as a foot of their land, since I have already given Esau

possession of the highlands of Seir. *6*You shall purchase from them with silver the food you eat and the well water you drink. *7*The LORD, your God, has blessed you in all your undertakings; he has been concerned about your journey through this vast desert. It is now forty years that he has been with you, and you have never been in want.'*s*

Along Moab. *8*"Then we left behind us the Arabah route, Elath, Ezion-geber, and Seir, where our kinsmen, the descendants of Esau, live; and we went on toward the desert of Moab.*t* *9*And the LORD said to me, 'Do not show hostility to the Moabites or engage them in battle, for I will not give you possession of any of their land, since I have given Ar to the descendants of Lot as their own.*u* *10*[Formerly the Emim lived there, a people strong and numerous and tall like the Anakim;*v* *11*like them they were considered Rephaim. It was the Moabites who called them Emim. *12*In Seir, however, the former inhabitants were the Horites;*w* the descendants of Esau dispossessed them, clearing them out of the way and taking their place, just as the Israelites have done in the land of their heritage which the LORD has given them.] *13*Get ready, then, to cross the Wadi Zered.'*x* So we crossed it. *14*Thirty-eight years had elapsed between our departure from Kadesh-barnea and that crossing; in the meantime the whole generation of soldiers had perished from the camp, as the LORD had sworn they should.*y* *15*For it was the LORD's hand that was against them, till he wiped them out of the camp completely.

Along Ammon. *16*"When at length death had put an end to all the soldiers among the people, *17*the LORD said to me, *18*'You are now about to leave Ar and the territory of Moab behind. *19*As you come opposite the Ammonites,*z* do not show hostility or come in conflict with them, for I will not give you possession of any land of the Ammonites, since I have given it to the descendants of Lot as their own. *20*[This also was considered a country of the Rephaim from its former inhabitants, whom the Ammonites called Zamzummim,

n: Dt 4, 21; 34, 4; Nm 20, 12.   o: Dt 31, 3. 7; Nm 27, 18ff; 34, 17.   p: 39f: Nm 14, 31.   q: 41-45: Nm 14, 40. 42-45.   r: Dt 1, 40; Nm 14, 25; 21, 4.   s: Dt 8, 2ff.   t: Jgs 11, 18.   u: Gn 19, 36f.   v: Dt 1, 28.   w: Gn 36, 20f.   x: Nm 21, 12.   y: Nm 14, 29. 33. 35. z: Gn 19, 38.

[21]a people strong and numerous and tall like the Anakim. But these, too, the LORD cleared out of the way for the Ammonites, who ousted them and took their place. [22]He had done the same for the descendants of Esau, who dwell in Seir, by clearing the Horites out of their way, so that the descendants of Esau have taken their place down to the present. [23]So also the Caphtorim,* migrating from Caphtor, cleared away the Avvim, who once dwelt in villages as far as Gaza, and took their place.]

Defeat of Sihon. [24]" 'Advance now across the Wadi Arnon.[a] I now deliver into your hands Sihon, the Amorite king of Heshbon, and his land. Begin the occupation; engage him in battle. [25]This day I will begin to put a fear and dread of you into every nation under the heavens, so that at the mention of your name they will quake and tremble before you.'

[26]"So I sent messengers from the desert of Kedemoth to Sihon, king of Heshbon, with this offer of peace: [27]'Let me pass through your country by the highway; I will go along it without turning aside to the right or to the left. [28]For the food I eat which you will supply, and for the water you give me to drink, you shall be paid in silver. Only let me march through, [29]as the descendants of Esau who dwell in Seir[b] and the Moabites who dwell in Ar have done, until I cross the Jordan into the land which the LORD, our God, is about to give us.' [30]But Sihon, king of Heshbon, refused to let us pass through his land, because the LORD, your God, made him stubborn in mind and obstinate in heart that he might deliver him up to you, as indeed he has now done.

[31]"Then the LORD said to me, 'Now that I have already begun to hand over to you Sihon and his land, begin the actual occupation.' [32]So Sihon and all his people advanced against us to join battle at Jahaz; [33]but since the LORD, our God, had delivered him to us,

we defeated him and his sons and all his people.[c] [34]At that time we seized all his cities and doomed* them all, with their men, women and children; we left no survivor.[d] [35]Our only booty was the livestock and the loot of the captured cities. [36]From Aroer on the edge of the Wadi Arnon and from the city in the wadi itself, as far as Gilead,[e] no city was too well fortified for us to whom the LORD had delivered them up. [37]However, in obedience to the command of the LORD, our God, you did not encroach upon any of the Ammonite land, neither the region bordering on the Wadi Jabbok, nor the cities of the highlands.[f]

CHAPTER 3

See RG 85-89

Defeat of Og. [1]"Then we turned and proceeded toward Bashan. But Og, king of Bashan,[g] advanced against us with all his people to give battle at Edrei. [2]The LORD, however, said to me,[h] 'Do not be afraid of him, for I have delivered him into your hand with all his people and his land. Do to him as you did to Sihon, king of the Amorites, who lived in Heshbon.' [3]And thus the LORD, our God, delivered into our hands Og, king of Bashan, with all his people. We defeated him so completely that we left him no survivor. [4]At that time we captured all his cities, none of them eluding our grasp, the whole region of Argob, the kingdom of Og in Bashan: sixty cities in all, [5]to say nothing of the great number of unwalled towns. All the cities were fortified with high walls and gates and bars. [6i]As we had done to Sihon, king of Heshbon, so also here we doomed all the cities, with their men, women and children; [7]but all the livestock and the loot of each city we took as booty for ourselves.

[8]"And so at that time we took from the two kings of the Amorites beyond the Jordan the territory from the Wadi Arnon to Mount Hermon [9][which is called Sirion by the Sidonians and Senir by the Amorites], [10]comprising all the cities of the plateau and all

2, 23: The Caphtorim: members of one of the groups of sea peoples who invaded the coast of Egypt and the southern part of Palestine about 1200 B.C. Caphtor: the ancient name of the island of Crete. Cf Am 9, 7.

2, 34: Doomed: see notes on Nm 18, 14; 21, 3.

a: Nm 21, 13; Jgs 11, 19-22.   *b:* Dt 2, 5. 8f; Jgs 11, 17.   *c:* Dt 29, 7; Nm 21, 23-32.   *d:* Dt 3, 6; 29, 7f.   *e:* Dt 3, 12; Jos 13. 9. 16; Jgs 11, 26.   *f:* Nm 21, 24; Jos 12, 2.   *g:* Dt 29, 6; Nm 21, 33.   *h:* 2f: Nm 21, 34f.   *i:* Ps 135, 10ff.

Gilead and all the cities of the kingdom of Og in Bashan including Salecah and Edrei. [11][Og, king of Bashan, was the last remaining survivor of the Rephaim. He had a bed of iron,* nine regular cubits long and four wide, which is still preserved in Rabbah of the Ammonites.]

Allotment of the Conquered Lands. [12][j]"When we occupied the land at that time, I gave Reuben and Gad the territory from Aroer, on the edge of the Wadi Arnon, halfway up into the highlands of Gilead, with the cities therein. [13]The rest of Gilead and all of Bashan, the kingdom of Og, the whole Argob region, I gave to the half-tribe of Manasseh. [All this region of Bashan was once called a land of the Rephaim. [14]Jair, a Manassehite clan,[k] took all the region of Argob as far as the border of the Geshurites and Maacathites, and called it after his own name Bashan Havvoth-jair, the name it bears today.] [15]To Machir I gave Gilead, [16]and to Reuben and Gad the territory from Gilead to the Wadi Arnon—including the wadi bed and its banks—and to the Wadi Jabbok, which is the border of the Ammonites, [17]as well as the Arabah with the Jordan and its eastern banks from Chinnereth to the Salt Sea of the Arabah, under the slopes of Pisgah.[l]

[18]"At that time I charged them* as follows: 'The LORD, your God, has given you this land as your own. But all you troops equipped for battle must cross over in the vanguard of your brother Israelites.[m] [19]Only your wives and children, as well as your livestock, of which I know you have a large number, shall remain behind in the towns I have given you,[n] [20]until the LORD has settled your kinsmen as well, and they too possess the land which the LORD, your God, will give them on the other side of the Jordan.[o] Then you may all return to the possessions I have given you.'

[21]"It was then that I instructed Joshua, 'Your eyes have seen all that the LORD, your God, has done to both these kings; so, too, will the LORD do to all the kingdoms which you will encounter over there. [22]Fear them not, for the LORD, your God, will fight for you.'

Refusal to Moses. [23]"And it was then that I besought the LORD, [24]'O Lord GOD, you have begun to show to your servant your greatness and might. For what god in heaven or on earth can perform deeds as mighty as yours? [25]Ah, let me cross over and see this good land beyond the Jordan, this fine hill country, and the Lebanon!' [26]But the LORD was angry with me on your account and would not hear me.[p] 'Enough!' the LORD said to me. 'Speak to me no more of this. [27]Go up to the top of Pisgah and look out to the west, and to the north, and to the south, and to the east. Look well, for you shall not cross this Jordan.[q] [28]Commission Joshua,[r] and encourage and strengthen him, for he shall cross at the head of this people and shall put them in possession of the land you are to see.' [29]This was while we were in the ravine opposite Beth-peor.

CHAPTER 4

See RG 85–89

Advantages of Fidelity. [1]"Now, Israel, hear the statutes and decrees which I am teaching you to observe, that you may live, and may enter in and take possession of the land which the LORD, the God of your fathers, is giving you. [2]In your observance of the commandments of the LORD, your God,[s] which I enjoin upon you, you shall not add to what I command you nor subtract from it. [3]You have seen with your own eyes what the LORD did at Baal-peor:[t] the LORD, your God, destroyed from your midst everyone that followed the Baal of Peor; [4]but you, who clung to the LORD, your God, are all alive today. [5]Therefore, I teach you the statutes and decrees as the LORD, my God, has commanded me, that you may observe them in the land you are entering to occupy. [6]Observe them carefully, for thus will you give evidence of

---

3, 11: Bed of iron: some translate, "a sarcophagus of basalt."

3, 18: I charged them: the words which follow were spoken to the men of Reuben and Gad (cf Nm 32).

---

j: 12f: Nm 32, 29. 32f; Jos 13, 8. 29.   *k:* Nm 32, 41; Jos 13, 11. 13.   *l:* Dt 4, 49; Jos 12, 3.   *m:* Jos 1, 14; 4, 12.   *n:* Nm 32, 1. 4; Jos 1, 14.   *o:* Jos 22, 4.   *p:* Dt 4, 21.   *q:* Dt 34, 4; Nm 27, 12f.   *r:* Dt 1, 38; 31, 7; Nm 27, 22f.   *s:* Dt 13, 1.   *t:* Nm 25, 3-9.

The New Generations

The paired instructions not to forget the powerful experience of God's actions and to undertake the education of "your children," so that the past becomes "present" also to them, represent a prominent aim of Deuteronomy: to overcome the historical distance of the past and to maintain it as a source of identity (Dt 4, 23. 25; 6, 2. 7. 20–25; 8, 11; 9, 7; 31, 13; 32, 18). The actual generation of the exodus had died off and been replaced by this new one, who had experienced none of the events here being recounted (Dt 2, 14–15). Moses addresses those who had not witnessed the events as if they had, while insisting that they pass on the events to posterity (Dt 5, 3–4. 23; 11, 7; 29, 13–14). Deuteronomy's theology of history treats all members of the community as if they were present when the community underwent its formative experiences. This may seem paradoxical to us, but we can find an analogy in our experience of the Mass, where we recount and relive the sacrifice of Jesus Christ as the followers of Jesus experienced it at the Last Supper and on Calvary.

your wisdom and intelligence to the nations, who will hear of all these statutes and say, 'This great nation is truly a wise and intelligent people.' [7u]"For what great nation is there that has gods so close to it as the LORD, our God, is to us whenever we call upon him? [8]Or what great nation has statutes and decrees that are as just as this whole law which I am setting before you today?

Revelation at Horeb. [9]"However, take care and be earnestly on your guard not to forget the things which your own eyes have seen, nor let them slip from your memory as long as you live, but teach them to your children[v] and to your children's children: [10]*There was the day on which you stood before the LORD, your God, at Horeb, and he said to me,[w] 'Assemble the people for me; I will have them hear my words, that they may learn to fear me as long as they live in the land and may so teach their children.' [11]You came near and stood at the foot of the mountain,[x] which blazed to the very sky with fire and was enveloped in a dense black cloud. [12]Then the LORD spoke to you from the midst of the fire.[y] You heard the sound of the words, but saw no form; there was only a voice. [13]He proclaimed to you his covenant, which he commanded you to keep: the ten commandments, which he wrote on two tablets of stone. [14]The LORD charged me at that time to teach you the statutes and decrees which you are to observe over in the land you will occupy.

Danger of Idolatry. [15]"You saw no form at all on the day the LORD spoke to you at Horeb from the midst of the fire.[z] Be strictly on your guard, therefore, [16]not to degrade yourselves by fashioning an idol to represent any figure, whether it be the form of a man or of a woman,[a] [17]of any animal on the earth or of any bird that flies in the sky, [18]of anything that crawls on the ground or of any fish in the waters under the earth. [19]And when you look up to the heavens and behold the sun or the moon or any star among the heavenly hosts, do not be led astray into adoring them and serving them.[b] These the LORD, your God, has let fall to the lot of all other nations under the heavens; [20]but you he has taken and led out of that iron foundry,* Egypt, that you might be his very own people, as you are today.[c] [21]Since the LORD was angered against me on your account[d] and

4, 10: Beginning here and continuing on for several verses (at least to the end of v 14) is the "reminiscence," the account of the things that the Israelites should recall and teach their children.

4, 20: Egypt is called an iron foundry, or furnace for smelting iron, because God allowed the Israelites to be afflicted there for the sake of their spiritual purification; the same expression for Egypt occurs also in 1 Kgs 8, 51; Jer 11, 4; compare the expression, "the furnace of affliction," in Is 48, 10

u: 2 Sm 7, 23.   v: Dt 11, 19; Ps 78, 3-6.   w: Heb 12, 18f.   x: Ex 19, 17f.   y: Dt 4, 33. 36; 5, 4.   z: Ex 24, 12; 31, 18; 34, 28.   a: Dt 5, 8; Ex 20, 4.   b: Dt 17, 3; Jb 31, 26ff.   c: 1 Kgs 8, 51; Jer 11, 4.   d: Dt 1, 37; 3, 26.

swore that I should not cross the Jordan nor enter the good land which he is giving you as a heritage, 22I myself shall die in this country without crossing the Jordan; but you will cross over and take possession of that good land.e 23Take heed, therefore, lest, forgetting the covenant which the LORD, your God, has made with you, you fashion for yourselves against his command an idol in any form whatsoever.f 24For the LORD, your God, is a consuming fire, a jealous God.

God's Fidelity. 25"When you have children, and have grown old* in the land, should you then degrade yourselves by fashioning an idol in any form and by this evil done in his sight provoke the LORD, your God, 26I call heaven and earth this day to witness against you, that you shall all quickly perish from the land which you will occupy when you cross the Jordan. You shall not live in it for any length of time but shall be promptly wiped out. 27The LORD will scatter you among the nations, and there shall remain but a handful of you among the nations to which the LORD will lead you.g 28There you shall serve gods fashioned by the hands of man out of wood and stone, gods which can neither see nor hear, neither eat nor smell.h 29Yet there too you shall seek the LORD, your God; and you shall indeed find him when you search after him with your whole heart and your whole soul.i 30In your distress, when all these things shall have come upon you, you shall finally return to the LORD, your God, and heed his voice. 31Since the LORD, your God, is a merciful God, he will not abandon and destroy you, nor forget the covenant which under oath he made with your fathers.j

Proofs of God's Love. 32"Ask now of the days of old, before your time, ever since God created man upon the earth; ask from one end of the sky to the other: Did anything so great ever happen before? Was it ever heard of? 33Did a people ever hear the voice of God speaking from the midst of fire, as you did, and live?k 34Or did any god venture to go and take a nation for himself from the midst of another nation, by testings,* by signs and wonders,l by war, with his strong hand and outstretched arm, and by great terrors, all of which the LORD, your God, did for you in Egypt before your very eyes? 35All this you were allowed to see that you might know the LORD is God and there is no other. 36Out of the heavens he let you hear his voice to discipline you; on earth he let you see his great fire, and you heard him speaking out of the fire. 37For love of your fathers he chose their descendants and personally led you out of Egypt by his great power, 38driving out of your way nations greater and mightier than you, so as to bring you in and to make their land your heritage, as it is today. 39This is why you must now know, and fix in your heart, that the LORD is God in the heavens above and on earth below, and that there is no other.m 40You must keep his statutes and commandments which I enjoin on you today, that you and your children after you may prosper, and that you may have long life on the land which the LORD, your God, is giving you forever."n

Cities of Refuge. 41oThen Moses set apart three cities in the region east of the Jordan, 42that a homicide might take refuge there if he unwittingly killed his neighbor to whom he had previously borne no malice, and that he might save his life by fleeing to one of these cities: 43Bezer in the desert, in the region of the plateau, for the Reubenites; Ramoth in Gilead for the Gadites; and Golan in Bashan for the Manassehites.

II: God and His Covenant

Introduction. 44This is the law which Moses set before the Israelites. 45These are the

---

4, 25: Grown old: Israel will lose the freshness of its youthful fervor.
4, 34: Testings: the demonstrations of God's power as in the ten great plagues of Egypt; cf Dt 7, 19; 29, 2.

---

e: Dt 3, 27.   f: Dt 4, 16.   g: 27f; Dt 28, 36. 62. 64.   h: Ps 135, 15ff; Is 44, 9.   i: Jer 29, 13.   j: Dt 31, 8.   k: Dt 4, 36; 5, 24. 26; Ex 20, 19.   l: Dt 7, 19; 26, 8; 29, 2; Ex 7, 3; 15, 3-10; Jer 32, 21.   m: Dt 4, 35.   n: Dt 6, 2f; 12, 28.   o: 41ff: Dt 19, 2-13; Nm 35, 6-29; Jos 20, 8; 21, 27. 36f; 1 Chr 6, 71. 80.

		Hellenistic Judaism	
Command	Rabbinic Judaism	and Church Fathers	Catholic/Lutheran
1	Self-Identification of God as separate command (v. 6)	Other Gods (vv. 6–7)	Other Gods + Images (vv. 6–10)
2	Other Gods + Images (vv. 7–10)	Images (vv. 8–10)	False Oath (v. 11)
3	False Oath (v. 11)	False Oath (v. 11)	Sabbath (vv. 12–15)
4	Sabbath (vv. 12–15)	Sabbath (vv. 12–15)	Parents (v. 16)
5	Parents (v. 16)	Parents (v. 16)	Murder (v. 17)
6	Murder (v. 17)	Murder (v. 17)	Adultery (v. 18)
7	Adultery (v. 17)	Adultery (v. 17)	Theft (v. 19)
8	Theft (v. 17)	Theft (v. 17)	False Witness (v. 20)
9	False Witness (v. 17)	False Witness (v. 17)	Coveting Wife (v. 21)
10	Coveting (v. 18)	Coveting (v. 18)	Coveting Property (v. 21)

The Analysis of the Decalogue in Deuteronomy 5, 6–21

ordinances, statutes and decrees which he proclaimed to them when they had come out of Egypt 46and were beyond the Jordan in the ravine opposite Beth-peor, in the land of Sihon, king of the Amorites, who dwelt in Heshbon and whom Moses and the Israelites defeated after coming out of Egypt. 47They occupied his land and the land of Og, king of Bashan, as well—the land of these two kings of the Amorites in the region east of the Jordan: 48from Aroer on the edge of the Wadi Arnon to Mount Sion* (that is, Hermon) 49and all the Arabah east of the Jordan, as far as the Arabah Sea under the slopes of Pisgah.p

See RG 85–89

CHAPTER 5

The Covenant at Horeb. 1Moses summoned all Israel and said to them, "Hear, O Israel, the statutes and decrees which I proclaim in your hearing this day, that you may learn them and take care to observe them. 2The LORD, our God, made a covenant with us at Horeb;q 3not with our fathers did he make this covenant, but with us, all of us who are alive here this day. 4The LORD spoke with you face to face on the mountain from the midst of the fire. 5rSince you were afraid of the fire and would not go up the mountain, I stood between the LORD and you at that time, to announce to you these words of the LORD:

The Decalogue. 6s'I, the LORD, am your God, who brought you out of the land of Egypt,t that place of slavery. 7uYou shall not have other gods besides me. 8You shall not carve idols for yourselvesv in the shape of anything in the sky above or on the earth below or in the waters beneath the earth; 9*you shall not bow down before them or worship them. For I, the LORD, your God, am a jealous God,w inflicting punishments for their fathers' wickedness on the children of those who hate me, down to the third and fourth generation 10but bestowing mercy, down to the thousandth generation,x on the children

4, 48: Sion: another name for Mount Hermon, besides those mentioned in Dt 3, 9.

5, 9f: God does not punish us for another's sins, but because of the solidarity of human society, the good or evil deeds of one generation may make their effects felt even in later generations. Yet note how God's mercy allows the good effects of virtue to last much longer than the bad effects of vice: a thousand generations compared to three or four.

p: Dt 3, 17.   q: Dt 28, 69.   r: Ex 24, 2.   s: 6-21: Ex 20, 2-17.   t: Ps 81, 11.   u: Ps 81, 10.   v: Dt 27, 15; Lv 26, 1; Ps 97, 7.   w: Ex 34, 14.   x: Dt 7, 9; Ex 20, 6.

of those who love me and keep my commandments.

11 'You shall not take the name of the LORD, your God, in vain.*y* For the LORD will not leave unpunished him who takes his name in vain.

12 'Take care to keep holy the sabbath day as the LORD, your God, commanded you. *13* Six days you may labor and do all your work; *14* but the seventh day is the sabbath of the LORD, your God.*z* No work may be done then, whether by you, or your son or daughter, or your male or female slave, or your ox or ass or any of your beasts, or the alien who lives with you. Your male and female slave should rest as you do. *15* For remember that you too were once slaves in Egypt,*a* and the LORD, your God, brought you from there with his strong hand and outstretched arm. That is why the LORD, your God, has commanded you to observe the sabbath day.

16b 'Honor your father and your mother, as the LORD, your God, has commanded you, that you may have a long life and prosperity in the land which the LORD, your God, is giving you.

17c 'You shall not kill.

18 'You shall not commit adultery.

19 'You shall not steal.

20 'You shall not bear dishonest witness against your neighbor.

21 'You shall not covet your neighbor's wife.

'You shall not desire your neighbor's house or field, nor his male or female slave, nor his ox or ass, or anything that belongs to him.'

Moses as Mediator. *22* "These words, and nothing more, the LORD spoke with a loud voice to your entire assembly on the mountain from the midst of the fire and the dense cloud. He wrote them upon two tablets of stone and gave them to me. *23* But when you heard the voice from the midst of the darkness, while the mountain was ablaze with fire, you came to me in the person of all your tribal heads and elders, *24* and said, 'The LORD, our God, has indeed let us see his glory and his majesty! We have heard his voice from the midst of the fire*d* and have found out today that a man can still live after God has spoken with him. *25* But why should we die now? Surely this great fire will consume us. If we hear the voice of the LORD, our God, any more, we shall die.*e* *26* For what mortal has heard, as we have, the voice of the living God speaking from the midst of fire, and survived? *27* Go closer, you, and hear all that the LORD, our God, will say, and then tell us what the LORD, our God, tells you; we will listen and obey.'*f*

28 "The LORD heard your words as you were speaking to me and said to me, 'I have heard the words these people have spoken to you, which are all well said.*g* *29* Would that they might always be of such a mind, to fear me and to keep all my commandments! Then they and their descendants would prosper forever. *30* Go, tell them to return to their tents. *31* Then you wait here near me and I will give you all the commandments, the statutes and decrees you must teach them, that they may observe them in the land which I am giving them to possess.'

32 "Be careful, therefore, to do as the LORD, your God, has commanded you, not turning aside to the right or to the left, *33* but following exactly the way prescribed for you by the LORD, your God, that you may live and prosper, and may have long life in the land which you are to occupy.*h*

CHAPTER 6

See RG 85-89

1 "These then are the commandments, the statutes and decrees*i* which the LORD, your God, has ordered that you be taught to observe in the land into which you are crossing for conquest, *2* so that you and your son and your grandson may fear the LORD, your God, and keep, throughout the days of your lives, all his statutes and commandments*j* which I enjoin on you, and thus have long life. *3* Hear then, Israel, and be careful to observe them, that you may grow and prosper the more, in keeping with the promise of the LORD, the God of your

y: Mt 5, 33.   z: Gn 2, 2; Ex 20, 8; 23, 12; Heb 4, 4.   a: Dt 15, 15; 16, 12; 24, 18. 22.   b: Sir 3, 2-16; Mt 15, 4; Mk 7, 10; Lk 18, 20; Eph 6, 2.   c: 17-20: Mt 5, 21. 27; Lk 18, 20; Jas 2, 11.   d: Dt 4, 33.   e: Dt 18, 16.   f: Ex 20, 19.   g: Dt 18, 17.   h: Dt 4, 40.   i: Dt 4, 1; 5, 31; 12, 1.   j: Dt 4, 40; 5, 29; 10, 12f.

"Hear, O Israel"

This statement of belief (6, 4–9) is the most important one for Israel, and is also partly quoted in the New Testament by Jesus (Mark 12, 29-30). It is known as the *Shema*, from its first word in Hebrew, the command "Hear!"

fathers, to give you a land flowing with milk and honey.

The Great Commandment. *4*"Hear, O Israel! The LORD is our God, the LORD alone!*k* *5*Therefore, you shall love the LORD, your God, with all your heart, and with all your soul, and with all your strength.*l* *6*Take to heart these words which I enjoin on you today. *7*Drill them into your children.*m* Speak of them at home and abroad, whether you are busy or at rest. *8*Bind them at your wrist as a sign* and let them be as a pendant on your forehead.*n* *9*Write them on the doorposts of your houses and on your gates.*o*

Fidelity in Prosperity. *10*"When the LORD, your God, brings you into the land which he swore to your fathers, Abraham, Isaac and Jacob, that he would give you, a land with fine, large cities that you did not build,*p* *11*with houses full of goods of all sorts that you did not garner, with cisterns that you did not dig, with vineyards and olive groves that you did not plant; and when, therefore, you eat your fill, *12*take care not to forget the LORD, who brought you out of the land of Egypt, that place of slavery. *13*The LORD, your God, shall you fear; him shall you serve,* and by his name shall you swear. *14*You shall not follow other gods, such as those of the surrounding nations, *15*lest the wrath of the LORD, your God, flare up against you and he destroy you from the face of the land;*s* for the LORD,

your God, who is in your midst, is a jealous God.

16"You shall not put the LORD, your God, to the test, as you did at Massah. *17*But keep the commandments of the LORD, your God, and the ordinances and statutes he has enjoined on you. *18*Do what is right and good in the sight of the LORD, that you may, according to his word, prosper, and may enter in and possess the good land which the LORD promised on oath to your fathers, *19*thrusting all your enemies out of your way.*u*

Instruction to Children. *20*"Later on, when your son asks you what these ordinances, statutes and decrees mean*v* which the LORD, our God, has enjoined on you, *21*you shall say to your son, 'We were once slaves of Pharaoh in Egypt, but the LORD brought us out of Egypt with his strong hand*w* *22*and wrought before our eyes signs and wonders, great and dire, against Egypt and against Pharaoh and his whole house. *23*He brought us from there to lead us into the land he promised on oath to our fathers, and to give it to us. *24*Therefore, the LORD commanded us to observe all these statutes in fear of the LORD, our God, that we may always have as prosperous and happy a life as we have today; *25*and our justice before the LORD, our God, is to consist in carefully observing all these commandments he has enjoined on us.'

6, 4f: This passage contains the basic principle of the whole Mosaic law, the keynote of the Book of Deuteronomy: since the Lord alone is God, we must love him with an undivided heart. Christ cited these words as "the greatest and the first commandment," embracing in itself the whole law of God (Mt 22, 37f and parallels).

6, 8: Bind them . . . as a sign: these injunctions were probably meant merely in a figurative sense; cf Ex 13, 9. 16. However, the later Jews understood them literally, and tied on their wrists and foreheads "phylacteries," boxes containing strips of parchment on which the words were inscribed;

cf Mt 23, 5.

6, 13: Him shall you serve: here, to "serve" God means especially to "worship" him; in this sense it is quoted by our Lord (Mt 4, 10) as an argument against worshiping the devil.

k: Mk 12, 29. *l:* Dt 10, 12; 11, 13; Mt 22, 37; Mk 12, 30; Lk 10, 27. *m:* 6f: Dt 4, 9; 11, 18; 32, 46. *n:* Dt 11, 18; Ex 13, 9. 16; Mt 23, 5. *o:* Dt 11, 20. *p:* 10f: Jos 24, 13. *q:* Dt 5, 6. *r:* Dt 10, 20; Mt 4, 10; Lk 4, 8. *s:* 14f: Dt 8, 19; 11, 16. 28. *t:* Nm 20, 1-13. *u:* Ex 23, 27; 34, 11. *v:* Ex 12, 26; 13, 14. *w:* Ex 20, 2.

See RG
85–89

CHAPTER 7

Destruction of Pagans. *1*"When the LORD, your God, brings you into the land which you are to enter and occupy, and dislodges great nations before you—the Hittites, Girgashites, Amorites, Canaanites, Perizzites, Hivites and Jebusites:*x* seven nations more numerous and powerful than you— *2*and when the LORD, your God, delivers them up to you and you defeat them, you shall doom them. Make no covenant with them*y* and show them no mercy. *3*You shall not intermarry with them, neither giving your daughters to their sons nor taking their daughters for your sons.*z* *4*For they would turn your sons from following me to serving other gods, and then the wrath of the LORD would flare up against you and quickly destroy you.

5"But this is how you must deal with them:*a* Tear down their altars, smash their sacred pillars, chop down their sacred poles,* and destroy their idols by fire. *6*For you are a people sacred to the LORD, your God; he has chosen you from all the nations on the face of the earth to be a people peculiarly his own.*b* *7*It was not because you are the largest of all nations that the LORD set his heart on you and chose you, for you are really the smallest of all nations. *8*It was because the LORD loved you and because of his fidelity to the oath he had sworn to your fathers, that he brought you out with his strong hand from the place of slavery, and ransomed you from the hand of Pharaoh, king of Egypt. *9c*Understand, then, that the LORD, your God, is God indeed, the faithful God who keeps his merciful covenant down to the thousandth generation toward those who love him and keep his commandments, *10*but who repays with destruction the person who hates him; he does not dally with such a one, but makes him personally pay for it. *11*You shall therefore carefully observe the commandments, the statutes and the decrees which I enjoin on you today.

Blessings of Obedience. *12d*"As your reward for heeding these decrees and observing them carefully, the LORD, your God, will keep with you the merciful covenant which he promised on oath to your fathers. *13*He will love and bless and multiply you; he will bless the fruit of your womb and the produce of your soil, your grain and wine and oil, the issue of your herds and the young of your flocks, in the land which he swore to your fathers he would give you.*e* *14*You will be blessed above all peoples; no man or woman among you shall be childless nor shall your livestock be barren. *15*The LORD will remove all sickness from you; he will not afflict you with any of the malignant diseases that you know from Egypt, but will leave them with all your enemies.

16"You shall consume all the nations which the LORD, your God, will deliver up to you. You are not to look on them with pity, lest you be ensnared into serving their gods. *17*Perhaps you will say to yourselves,*f* 'These nations are greater than we. How can we dispossess them?' *18*But do not be afraid of them. Rather, call to mind what the LORD, your God, did to Pharaoh and to all Egypt: *19*the great testings which your own eyes have seen, the signs and wonders, his strong hand and outstretched arm with which the LORD, your God, brought you out.*g* The same also will he do to all the nations of whom you are now afraid. *20*Moreover, the LORD, your God, will send hornets among them, until the survivors who have hidden from you are destroyed.*h* *21*Therefore, do not be terrified by them, for the LORD, your God, who is in your midst, is a great and awesome God. *22*He will dislodge these nations before you little by little. You cannot exterminate them all at once, lest the wild beasts become too numerous for you.*i* *23*The LORD, your God, will deliver them up to you and will rout them utterly until they are annihilated.*j* *24*He will deliver their kings into your hand, that you may make their names perish from

7, 5: Sacred pillars . . . poles: see note on Ex 34, 13.

x: Ex 23, 23; 33, 2. *y:* Ex 34, 12. *z:* 3f: Ex 34, 16; 1 Kgs 11, 1f. *a:* Dt 12, 3; Ex 34, 13. *b:* Dt 14, 2; 26, 18; Ex 19, 6. *c:* 9f: Dt 5, 9f. *d:* 12-16: Dt 28, 1-14; Ex 23, 22-26; Lv 26, 3-13. *e:* Dt 30, 9. *f:* 17f: Dt 1, 28ff. *g:* Dt 4, 34. *h:* Ex 23, 28ff. *i:* Ex 23, 29f. *j:* Dt 7, 2.

under the heavens. No man will be able to stand up against you,[k] till you have put an end to them. [25]The images of their gods you shall destroy by fire. Do not covet the silver or gold on them, nor take it for yourselves, lest you be ensnared by it; for it is an abomination to the LORD, your God. [26]You shall not bring any abominable thing into your house, lest you be doomed with it; loathe and abhor it utterly as a thing that is doomed.

CHAPTER 8

See RG 85–89

God's Care. [1]"Be careful to observe all the commandments[l] I enjoin on you today, that you may live and increase, and may enter in and possess the land which the LORD promised on oath to your fathers. [2]Remember how for forty years now the LORD, your God, has directed all your journeying in the desert,[m] so as to test you by affliction and find out whether or not it was your intention to keep his commandments. [3]He therefore let you be afflicted with hunger, and then fed you with manna,[n] a food unknown to you and your fathers, in order to show you that not by bread alone* does man live, but by every word that comes forth from the mouth of the LORD. [4]The clothing did not fall from you in tatters, nor did your feet swell these forty years.[o] [5]So you must realize that the LORD, your God, disciplines you even as a man disciplines his son.

Danger of Prosperity. [6]"Therefore, keep the commandments of the LORD, your God, by walking in his ways and fearing him. [7]For the LORD, your God, is bringing you into a good country,[p] a land with streams of water, with springs and fountains welling up in the hills and valleys, [8]a land of wheat and barley, of vines and fig trees and pomegranates, of olive trees and of honey, [9]a land where you can eat bread without stint and where you will lack nothing, a land whose stones contain iron and in whose hills you can mine copper. [10]But when you have eaten your fill, you must bless the LORD, your God, for the

good country he has given you. [11]Be careful not to forget the LORD, your God, by neglecting his commandments and decrees and statutes which I enjoin on you today: [12]lest, when you have eaten your fill, and have built fine houses and lived in them, [13]and have increased your herds and flocks, your silver and gold, and all your property, [14]you then become haughty of heart and unmindful of the LORD, your God, who brought you out of the land of Egypt, that place of slavery; [15]who guided you through the vast and terrible desert with its saraph serpents and scorpions, its parched and waterless ground; who brought forth water for you from the flinty rock[q] [16]and fed you in the desert with manna, a food unknown to your fathers, that he might afflict you and test you, but also make you prosperous in the end. [17]Otherwise, you might say to yourselves,[r] 'It is my own power and the strength of my own hand that has obtained for me this wealth.' [18]Remember then, it is the LORD, your God, who gives you the power to acquire wealth, by fulfilling, as he has now done, the covenant which he swore to your fathers. [19]But if you forget the LORD, your God, and follow other gods, serving and worshiping them,[s] I forewarn you this day that you will perish utterly. [20]Like the nations which the LORD destroys before you, so shall you too perish for not heeding the voice of the LORD, your God.

CHAPTER 9

See RG 85–89

Unmerited Success. [1]"Hear, O Israel! You are now about to cross the Jordan to enter in and dispossess nations greater and stronger than yourselves, having large cities fortified to the sky,[t] [2]the Anakim, a people great and tall.[u] You know of them and have heard it said of them, 'Who can stand up against the Anakim?' [3]Understand, then, today that it is the LORD, your God, who will cross over before you as a consuming fire; he it is who will reduce them to nothing and subdue them before you, so that you can drive them out and

---

8, 3: Not by bread alone, etc.: quoted by our Lord in Mt 4, 4. The sense is: God takes care of those who love him even when natural means seem to fail them.

k: Dt 11, 25.   *l:* Dt 4, 1; 6, 1.   *m:* Dt 2, 7; 29, 4; Am 2, 10.   *n:* Ex 16, 12-15. 35; Nm 11, 6-9; Mt 4, 4; Lk 4, 4.   *o:* Dt 29, 4; Neh 9, 21.   *p:* Dt 11, 10ff.   *q:* Wis 11, 4.   *r:* Dt 9, 4.   *s:* Dt 4, 25f; 30, 18.   *t:* Dt 1, 28; 4, 38.   *u:* Nm 13, 33.

destroy them quickly, as the LORD promised you.[v] [4]After the LORD, your God, has thrust them out of your way, do not say to yourselves, 'It is because of my merits that the LORD has brought me in to possess this land';[w] for it is really because of the wickedness of these nations that the LORD is driving them out before you. [5]No, it is not because of your merits or the integrity of your heart that you are going in to take possession of their land; but the LORD, your God, is driving these nations out before you on account of their wickedness and in order to keep the promise which he made on oath to your fathers, Abraham, Isaac and Jacob. [6]Understand this, therefore: it is not because of your merits that the LORD, your God, is giving you this good land to possess, for you are a stiff-necked people.

The Golden Calf. [7]"Bear in mind and do not forget how you angered the LORD, your God, in the desert. From the day you left the land of Egypt until you arrived in this place, you have been rebellious toward the LORD.[x] [8]At Horeb you so provoked the LORD that he was angry enough to destroy you,[y] [9]when I had gone up the mountain to receive the stone tablets of the covenant which the LORD made with you.[z] Meanwhile I stayed on the mountain forty days and forty nights without eating or drinking, [10]till the LORD gave me the two tablets of stone inscribed, by God's own finger,[a] with a copy of all the words that the LORD spoke to you on the mountain from the midst of the fire on the day of the assembly. [11]Then, at the end of the forty days and forty nights, when the LORD had given me the two stone tablets of the covenant, [12]he said to me,[b] 'Go down from here now, quickly, for your people whom you have brought out of Egypt have become depraved; they have already turned aside from the way I pointed out to them and have made for themselves a molten idol. [13]I have seen now how stiff-necked this people is,' the LORD said to me. [14]'Let me be, that I may destroy them and blot out their name from under the heavens. I will then make of you a nation mightier and greater than they.'

[15]"When I had come down again from the blazing, fiery mountain, with the two tablets of the covenant in both my hands,[c] [16]I saw how you had sinned against the LORD, your God: you had already turned aside from the way which the LORD had pointed out to you by making for yourselves a molten calf! [17]Raising the two tablets with both hands I threw them from me and broke them before your eyes.[d] [18]Then, as before, I lay prostrate before the LORD for forty days and forty nights without eating or drinking, because of all the sin you had committed in the sight of the LORD and the evil you had done to provoke him.[e] [19]For I dreaded the fierce anger of the LORD against you: his wrath would destroy you.[f] Yet once again the LORD listened to me. [20]With Aaron, too, the LORD was deeply angry, and would have killed him had I not prayed for him also at that time. [21]Then, taking the calf, the sinful object you had made, and fusing it with fire, I ground it down to powder as fine as dust, which I threw into the wadi that went down the mountainside.[g]

[22]"At Taberah, at Massah, and at Kibroth-hattaavah likewise, you provoked the LORD to anger.[h] [23]And when he sent you up from Kadesh-barnea to take possession of the land he was giving you, you rebelled against this command of the LORD, your God, and would not trust or obey him.[i] [24]Ever since I have known you, you have been rebels against the LORD.

[25]"Those forty days, then, and forty nights, I lay prostrate before the LORD, because he had threatened to destroy you. [26]This was my prayer to him: O Lord GOD, destroy not your people, the heritage which your majesty has ransomed and brought out of Egypt with your strong hand. [27]Remember your servants, Abraham, Isaac and Jacob. Look not upon the stubbornness of this people nor upon their wickedness and sin, [28]lest the people from whose land you have brought us say, 'The LORD was not able to bring them into the land he promised them'; or 'Out of hatred for them he brought them

v: Dt 31, 3; Ex 23, 27.   w: Dt 8, 17.   x: Dt 31, 27; Ex 14, 11; Nm 14, 11.   y: Ex 32, 4; Ps 106, 19.   z: Ex 24, 12. 18; 34, 28.   a: Ex 31, 18.   b: 12ff; Ex 32, 7-10.   c: Ex 32, 15.   d: 16f; Ex 32, 19.   e: Ex 32, 31; 34, 28.   f: Dt 10, 10; Ex 32, 10.   g: Ex 32, 20.   h: Ex 17, 7; Nm 11, 1ff. 34.   i: Nm 14, 1-4; Ps 106, 24f.

out to slay them in the desert.'[j] [29]They are, after all, your people and your heritage, whom you have brought out by your great power and with your outstretched arm.[k]

See RG
85–89

CHAPTER 10

[1]"At that time the LORD said to me, 'Cut two tablets of stone like the former;[l] then come up the mountain to me. Also make an ark of wood. [2]I will write upon the tablets the commandments that were on the former tablets that you broke, and you shall place them in the ark.' [3]So I made an ark of acacia wood, and cut two tablets of stone like the former, and went up the mountain carrying the two tablets.[m] [4n]The LORD then wrote on them, as he had written before, the ten commandments which he spoke to you on the mountain from the midst of the fire on the day of the assembly. After the LORD had given them to me, [5]I turned and came down the mountain, and placed the tablets in the ark I had made.[o] There they have remained, in keeping with the command the LORD gave me.

[6][The Israelites set out from Beeroth Bene-jaakan[p] for Moserah, where Aaron died and was buried, his son Eleazar succeeding him in the priestly office. [7]From there they set out for Gudgodah, and from Gudgodah for Jotbathah,[q] a region where there is water in the wadies.]

[8]"At that time the LORD set apart the tribe of Levi to carry the ark of the covenant of the LORD,[r] to be in attendance before the LORD and minister to him, and to give blessings in his name, as they have done to this day. [9]For this reason, Levi has no share in the heritage with his brothers;[s] the LORD himself is his heritage, as the LORD, your God, has told him.

[10]"After I had spent these other forty days and forty nights on the mountain, and the LORD had once again heard me and decided not to destroy you, [11]he said to me, 'Go now and set out at the head of your people,[t] that they may enter in and occupy the land which I swore to their fathers I would give them.'

The Lord's Majesty. [12]"And now, Israel, what does the LORD, your God, ask of you but to fear the LORD, your God, and follow his ways exactly, to love and serve the LORD, your God, with all your heart and all your soul,[u] [13]to keep the commandments and statutes of the LORD which I enjoin on you today for your own good? [14]Think! The heavens, even the highest heavens,* belong to the LORD, your God, as well as the earth and everything on it.[v] [15]Yet in his love for your fathers the LORD was so attached to them as to choose you, their descendants, in preference to all other peoples, as indeed he has now done.[w] [16]Circumcise your hearts,* therefore, and be no longer stiff-necked. [17]For the LORD, your God, is the God of gods, the LORD of lords, the great God, mighty and awesome, who has no favorites, accepts no bribes;[x] [18]who executes justice for the orphan and the widow, and befriends the alien, feeding and clothing him. [19]So you too must befriend the alien, for you were once aliens yourselves in the land of Egypt.[y] [20]The LORD, your God, shall you fear, and him shall you serve; hold fast to him and swear by his name.[z] [21]He is your glory, he, your God, who has done for you those great and terrible things which your own eyes have seen. [22]Your ancestors went down to Egypt seventy strong,[a] and now the LORD, your God, has made you as numerous as the stars of the sky.

CHAPTER 11

See RG
85–89

The Wonders of the Lord. [1]"Love the LORD, your God, therefore, and always heed

10, 14: Even the highest heavens: literally, "and the heavens of the heavens"; compare the phrase, "the third heaven," in 2 Cor 12, 2.

10, 16: Circumcise your hearts: cf Dt 30, 6; Jer 4, 4; Rom 2, 29. The "uncircumcised heart" (Lv 26, 41; Jer 9, 25; Ez 44, 7. 9) is closed and unreceptive to divine grace and guidance, just as "uncircumcised ears" (Jer 6, 10) are closed to sound, and "uncircumcised lips" (Ex 6, 12. 30) do not open well in speech.

j: Nm 14, 14ff. *k:* Dt 4, 20; Ex 6, 6f. *l:* Ex 34, 1. *m:* Ex 34, 4. *n:* Ex 20, 1-17; 34, 28. *o:* Ex 40, 20; 1 Kgs 8, 9. *p:* Nm 33, 31. *q:* Nm 33, 32f. *r:* Nm 3, 6; 6, 23-27; 16, 9. *s:* Nm 18, 20. *t:* Ex 32, 34; 33, 1. *u:* Dt 6, 2. 5. *v:* Neh 9, 6. *w:* Dt 7, 6ff. *x:* 2 Chr 19, 7; Jb 34, 19; Wis 6, 7; Acts 10, 34; Rom 2, 11; Gal 2, 6. *y:* Ex 22, 21; 23, 9; Lv 19, 33f. *z:* Dt 6, 13; Mt 4, 10; Lk 4, 8. *a:* Gn 46, 27; Ex 1, 5; Acts 7, 14.

Community Responsibility

L oyalty to the covenant provides the condition for life in Canaan. The punishments and rewards in chapter 11 are predominantly addressed to a plural "you," stressing communal rather than individual responsibility.

his charge: his statutes, decrees and commandments. ²It is not your children, who have not known it from experience, but you yourselves who must now understand the discipline of the LORD, your God; his majesty, his strong hand and outstretched arm; ³the signs and deeds he wrought among the Egyptians, on Pharaoh, king of Egypt, and on all his land;*b* ⁴what he did to the Egyptian army and to their horses and chariots, engulfing them in the water of the Red Sea as they pursued you,*c* and bringing ruin upon them even to this day; ⁵what he did for you in the desert until you arrived in this place; ⁶and what he did to the Reubenites Dathan and Abiram, sons of Eliab, when the ground opened its mouth and swallowed them up out of the midst of Israel, with their families and tents and every living thing that belonged to them.*d* ⁷With your own eyes you have seen all these great deeds that the LORD has done. ⁸Keep all the commandments, then, which I enjoin on you today, that you may be strong enough to enter in and take possession of the land into which you are crossing, ⁹and that you may have long life on the land which the LORD swore to your fathers he would give to them and their descendants, a land flowing with milk and honey.

The Gift of Rain. ¹⁰"For the land which you are to enter and occupy is not like the land of Egypt from which you have come, where you would sow your seed and then water it by hand, as in a vegetable garden. ¹¹*e*No, the land into which you are crossing for conquest is a land of hills and valleys that drinks in rain from the heavens, ¹²a land which the LORD, your God, looks after; his

eyes are upon it continually from the beginning of the year to the end. ¹³*If, then, you truly heed my commandments which I enjoin on you today, loving and serving the LORD, your God, with all your heart and all your soul,*f* ¹⁴I will give the seasonal rain to your land, the early rain* and the late rain, that you may have your grain, wine and oil to gather in; ¹⁵and I will bring forth grass in your fields for your animals.*g* Thus you may eat your fill. ¹⁶But be careful lest your heart be so lured away that you serve other gods and worship them.*h* ¹⁷For then the wrath of the LORD will flare up against you and he will close up the heavens, so that no rain will fall, and the soil will not yield its crops, and you will soon perish from the good land he is giving you.

Reward of Fidelity. ¹⁸*i*"Therefore, take these words of mine into your heart and soul. Bind them at your wrist as a sign, and let them be a pendant on your forehead. ¹⁹Teach them to your children, speaking of them at home and abroad, whether you are busy or at rest. ²⁰And write them on the doorposts of your houses and on your gates, ²¹so that, as long as the heavens are above the earth, you and your children may live on in the land which the LORD swore to your fathers he would give them.

²²"For if you are careful to observe all these commandments I enjoin on you, loving the LORD, your God, and following his ways exactly, and holding fast to him, ²³the LORD will drive all these nations out of your way,*j* and you will dispossess nations greater and mightier than yourselves. ²⁴*k*Every place where you set foot shall be yours: from the

---

11, 13ff: As often in the Prophets, the discourse passes into the words of God himself. Cf Dt 7, 4; 17, 3; 28, 20; 29, 4f.

11, 14: The early rain: the rains which begin in October or November and continue intermittently throughout the winter. The late rain: the heavy showers of March and April. In Palestine the crops are sown in the autumn and reaped in the spring.

b: Dt 6, 22; Ps 78, 42-51.   *c:* Ex 14, 26ff; 15, 9; Pss 78, 53; 106, 11.   *d:* Nm 16, 31ff.   *e:* 11f: Dt 8, 7.   *f:* 13f: Dt 10, 12; Lv 26, 4. *g:* Ps 104, 14.   *h:* 16f: Dt 4, 25f; 6, 14.   *i:* 18-21: Dt 6, 6-9.   *j:* Dt 7, 1; 9, 1.   *k:* Ex 23, 31.

desert and from Lebanon, from the Euphrates River to the Western Sea,* shall be your territory. [25]None shall stand up against you; the LORD, your God, will spread the fear and dread of you through any land where you set foot, as he promised you.[l]

A Blessing and a Curse. [26m]"I set before you here, this day, a blessing and a curse: [27]a blessing for obeying the commandments of the LORD, your God, which I enjoin on you today; [28]a curse if you do not obey the commandments of the LORD, your God, but turn aside from the way I ordain for you today, to follow other gods, whom you have not known. [29]When the LORD, your God, brings you into the land which you are to enter and occupy, then you shall pronounce the blessing on Mount Gerizim,[n] the curse* on Mount Ebal. [30][Are they not beyond the Jordan, on the other side of the western road in the country of the Canaanites who live in the Arabah, opposite the Gilgal beside the terebinth of Moreh?] [31]For you are about to cross the Jordan to enter and occupy the land which the LORD, your God, is giving you. When therefore, you take possession of it and settle there, [32]be careful to observe all the statutes and decrees that I set before you today.

III: Exposition of the Law

CHAPTER 12

See RG
85–89

One Sanctuary. [1]"These are the statutes and decrees which you must be careful to observe in the land which the LORD, the God of your fathers, has given you to occupy, as long as you live on its soil. [2]Destroy without fail every place on the high mountains, on the hills, and under every leafy tree where the nations you are to dispossess worship their gods.[o] [3]Tear down their altars, smash their sacred pillars, destroy by fire their sacred poles, and shatter the idols of their gods, that you may stamp out the remembrance of them in any such place.

[4]"That is not how you are to worship the LORD, your God. [5]Instead,[p] you shall resort to the place which the LORD, your God, chooses out of all your tribes and designates as his dwelling [6]and there you shall bring your holocausts and sacrifices, your tithes and personal contributions, your votive and freewill offerings, and the firstlings of your herds and flocks. [7]There, too, before the LORD, your God, you and your families shall eat and make merry over all your undertakings, because the LORD, your God, has blessed you. [8]You shall not do as we are now doing; here, everyone does what seems right to himself, [9]since you have not yet reached your resting place, the heritage which the LORD, your God, will give you. [10]But after you have crossed the Jordan and dwell in the land which the LORD, your God, is giving you as a heritage, when he has given you rest from all your enemies round about and you live there in security, [11]then to the place which the LORD, your God, chooses as the dwelling place for his name you shall bring all the offerings I command you: your holocausts and sacrifices, your tithes and personal contributions, and every special offering you have vowed to the LORD. [12]You shall make merry before the LORD, your God, with your sons and daughters, your male and female slaves, as well as with the Levite who belongs to your community but has no share of his own in your heritage. [13]Take care not to offer up your holocausts in any place you fancy, [14]but offer them up in the place which the LORD chooses from among your tribes; there you shall make whatever offerings I enjoin upon you.

Profane and Sacred Meals. [15]"However, in any of your communities you may slaughter and eat to your heart's desire as much meat as the LORD, your God, has blessed you with; and the unclean as well as the clean may eat it, as they do the gazelle or the deer. [16]Only, you shall not partake of the blood,

---

11, 24: The Western Sea: the Mediterranean.

11, 29: You shall pronounce the blessing . . . the curse: for the full ceremony, see chapters 27 and 28. Gerizim . . . Ebal: adjacent mountains in Samaria with a deep ravine between them. Their summits command an excellent view of the entire country.

l: Dt 2, 25; 7, 24; Ex 23, 27.   *m:* 26ff: Dt 28, 2-45; 30, 1. 15. 19.   *n:* Dt 27, 12f.   *o:* 2f: Dt 7, 5; Ex 23, 24; 34, 13.   *p:* 5-7. 11f: Dt 14, 22-26; 15, 19f; 16, 2. 10f. 14f; 26, 2.

Worship at a Central Sanctuary

Having a central place for sacrifice is Deuteronomy's most distinctive demand. Sacrificial worship was to take place only at a single, central sanctuary and at a location to be chosen by the Lord (Dt 12, 5.11.14.18.26). Earlier practice had permitted sacrifice at many local altars scattered around the country (Ex 20, 24). Deuteronomy never identifies the site of this central sanctuary because at the time Moses was supposedly speaking, the conquest of the land, and particularly of Jerusalem, had not yet taken place. This radical reform of centralized worship was imposed on Judah by King Josiah, who considered Jerusalem to be the Lord's chosen place (2 Kgs 23, 4–20).

but must pour it out on the ground like water.�q ¹⁷Moreover, you shall not, in your own communities, partake of your tithe of grain or wine or oil, of the first-born of your herd or flock, of any offering you have vowed, of your freewill offerings, or of your personal contributions. ¹⁸These you must eat before the Lord, your God, in the place he chooses, along with your son and daughter, your male and female slave, and the Levite who belongs to your community; and there, before the Lord, you shall make merry over all your undertakings. ¹⁹Take care, also, that you do not neglect the Levite as long as you live in the land.ʳ

²⁰"After the Lord, your God, has enlarged your territory, as he promised you,ˢ when you wish meat for food,* you may eat it at will, to your heart's desire; ²¹and if the place which the Lord, your God, chooses for the abode of his name is too far, you may slaughter in the manner I have told you any of your herd or flock that the Lord has given you, and eat it to your heart's desire in your own community. ²²You may eat it as you would the gazelle or the deer: the unclean and the clean eating it alike. ²³But make sure that you do not partake of the blood; for blood is life, and you shall not consume this seat of life with the flesh. ²⁴Do not partake of the blood, therefore, but pour it out on the ground like water. ²⁵Abstain from it, that you and your children after you may prosper for doing what is right in the sight of the

Lord. ²⁶However, any sacred gifts or votive offerings that you may have, you shall bring with you to the place which the Lord chooses, ²⁷and there you must offer both the flesh and the blood of your holocausts on the altar of the Lord, your God; of your other sacrifices the blood indeed must be poured out against the altar of the Lord, your God,ᵗ but their flesh may be eaten. ²⁸Be careful to heed all these commandments I enjoin on you, that you and your descendants may always prosper for doing what is good and right in the sight of the Lord, your God.

Pagan Rites. ²⁹"When the Lord, your God, removes the nations from your way as you advance to dispossess them, be on your guard! Otherwise, once they have been wiped out before you and you have replaced them and are settled in their land, ³⁰you will be lured into following them. Do not inquire regarding their gods, 'How did these nations worship their gods? I, too, would do the same.' ³¹You shall not thus worship the Lord, your God, because they offered to their gods every abomination that the Lord detests, even burning their sons and daughters to their gods.ᵘ

CHAPTER 13

See RG 85–89

Penalties for Idolatry. ¹"Every command that I enjoin on you, you shall be careful to observe, neither adding to it nor subtracting from it.

²"If there arises among you a prophet or a

12, 20: Meat for food: as on special feasts. Meat was not eaten every day in Israel, even by the wealthy.

q: Dt 15, 23; Gn 9, 4; Lv 3, 17.   r: Dt 14, 27.   s: Dt 19, 8; Gn 28, 14; Ex 34, 24.   t: Lv 17, 11.   u: Lv 18, 21; Jer 7, 31.

dreamer* who promises you a sign or wonder, *3*urging you to follow other gods, whom you have not known, and to serve them: even though the sign or wonder he has foretold you comes to pass, *4*pay no attention to the words of that prophet or that dreamer; for the LORD, your God, is testing you to learn whether you really love him with all your heart and with all your soul. *5*The LORD, your God, shall you follow, and him shall you fear; his commandment shall you observe, and his voice shall you heed, serving him and holding fast to him alone. *6v*But that prophet or that dreamer shall be put to death, because, in order to lead you astray from the way which the LORD, your God, has directed you to take, he has preached apostasy from the LORD, your God, who brought you out of the land of Egypt and ransomed you from that place of slavery. Thus shall you purge the evil from your midst.

7"If your own full brother, or your son or daughter, or your beloved wife, or your intimate friend, entices you secretly to serve other gods, whom you and your fathers have not known, *8*gods of any other nation, near at hand or far away, from one end of the earth to the other: *9*do not yield to him or listen to him, nor look with pity upon him, to spare or shield him, *10*but kill him. Your hand shall be the first raised to slay him; the rest of the people shall join in with you. *11*You shall stone him to death, because he sought to lead you astray from the LORD, your God, who brought you out of the land of Egypt, that place of slavery. *12*And all Israel, hearing of it, shall fear and never again do such evil as this in your midst.

13"If, in any of the cities which the LORD, your God, gives you to dwell in, you hear it said *14*that certain scoundrels have sprung up among you and have led astray the inhabitants of their city to serve other gods whom you have not known, *15*you must inquire carefully into the matter and investigate it thoroughly. If you find that it is true and an established fact that this abomination has been committed in your midst, *16w*you shall put the inhabitants of that city to the sword, dooming the city and all life that is in it, even its cattle, to the sword. *17*Having heaped up all its spoils in the middle of its square, you shall burn the city with all its spoils as a whole burnt offering to the LORD, your God. Let it be a heap of ruins forever, never to be rebuilt. *18*You shall not retain anything that is doomed, that the blazing wrath of the LORD may die down and he may show you mercy and in his mercy for you may multiply you as he promised your fathers on oath; *19*because you have heeded the voice of the LORD, your God, keeping all his commandments which I enjoin on you today, doing what is right in his sight.

CHAPTER 14

Pagan Mourning Rites. *1*"You are children of the LORD, your God. You shall not gash yourselves nor shave the hair above your foreheads for the dead.*x* *2*For you are a people sacred to the LORD, your God, who has chosen you from all the nations on the face of the earth to be a people peculiarly his own.*y*

Clean and Unclean Animals. *3*"You shall not eat any abominable thing.*z* *4a*These are the animals you may eat: the ox, the sheep, the goat, *5*the red deer, the gazelle, the roe deer, the ibex, the addax, the oryx,* and the mountain sheep. *6*Any animal that has hoofs you may eat, provided it is cloven-footed and chews the cud. *7*But you shall not eat any of the following that only chew the cud or only have cloven hoofs: the camel, the hare and the rock badger, which indeed chew the cud, but do not have hoofs and are therefore unclean for you; *8*and the pig, which indeed has hoofs and is cloven-footed,

---

13, 2. 4. 6: Dreamer: a false prophet who pretended to have received revelations from God in his dreams; cf Jer 23, 25-32; Zec 10, 2. But dreams could also be a channel of true prophecy (Nm 12, 6; Jl 3, 1) and of genuine revelations (Gn 20, 3. 6; 31, 10. 24; 37, 5. 9; Mt 1, 20; 2, 12f. 19; etc.).

14, 5: The gazelle, the addax, the oryx: species of an-

telopes. The ibex: a species of wild goat.

v: 6-10. 14: Dt 6, 14; 17, 2-7. *w:* 16f: Jos 6, 18. 24; 7, 26; 8, 28. *x:* Lv 19, 28. *y:* Dt 7, 6. *z:* Ez 4, 14; Acts 10, 14. *a:* 4-20: Lv 11, 2-23.

Ritual Purity

Israel's purity system categorized persons, objects, and foods (14, 3–21). It had nothing to do with modern notions of hygiene. Those who ate unclean food became ritually unclean. They were excluded from social contact and the worship assembly until their impurity was removed. A similar list of clean and unclean animals is given in Leviticus 11.

but does not chew the cud and is therefore unclean for you. Their flesh you shall not eat, and their dead bodies you shall not touch.[b]

9"Of the various creatures that live in the water, whatever has both fins and scales you may eat, 10but all those that lack either fins or scales you shall not eat; they are unclean for you.

11"You may eat all clean birds. 12But you shall not eat any of the following: the eagle, the vulture, the osprey, 13the various kites and falcons, 14all the various species of crows, 15the ostrich, the nightjar, the gull, the various species of hawks, 16the owl, the screech owl, the ibis, 17the desert owl, the buzzard, the cormorant, 18the stork, the various species of herons, the hoopoe, and the bat. 19*All winged insects, too, are unclean for you and shall not be eaten. 20But you may eat any clean winged creatures.

21"You must not eat any animal that has died of itself, for you are a people sacred to the LORD, your God.[c] But you may give it to an alien who belongs to your community, and he may eat it, or you may sell it to a foreigner.

"You shall not boil a kid in its mother's milk.*

Tithes. 22"Each year you shall tithe all the produce that grows in the field you have sown;[d] 23then in the place which the LORD, your God, chooses as the dwelling place of his name[e] you shall eat in his presence your tithe of the grain, wine and oil, as well as the firstlings of your herd and flock, that you may learn always to fear the LORD, your God. 24If, however, the journey is too much for you and you are not able to bring your tithe, because the place which the LORD, your God, chooses for the abode of his name is too far for you, considering how the LORD has blessed you,* 25you may exchange the tithe for money and, with the purse of money in hand, go to the place which the LORD, your God, chooses. 26You may then exchange the money for whatever you desire, oxen or sheep, wine or strong drink, or anything else you would enjoy, and there before the LORD, your God, you shall partake of it and make merry with your family. 27But do not neglect the Levite who belongs to your community, for he has no share in the heritage with you.[f]

28"At the end of every third year you shall bring out all the tithes of your produce for that year and deposit them in community stores, 29that the Levite who has no share in the heritage with you, and also the alien, the orphan and the widow who belong to your community, may come and eat their fill;[g] so that the LORD, your God, may bless you in all that you undertake.

CHAPTER 15

See RG 85–89

Debts and the Poor. 1"At the end of every seven-year period* you shall have a relaxation of debts,[h] 2which shall be observed as follows. Every creditor shall relax his

---

14, 19f: The apparent contradiction is to be resolved in the light of Lv 11, 20-23; the unclean winged insects are those that walk on the ground; the clean winged creatures are those that leap on the ground, such as certain species of locusts.

14, 21: Boil a kid in its mother's milk: see note on Ex 23, 19.

14, 24: Considering how the LORD has blessed you: should the Israelite farmer be blessed with an abundant harvest, a tenth of this would be too much to transport for a great distance.

15, 1: At the end of every seven-year period: in every seventh, or sabbatical, year. Cf Dt 15, 9; 31, 10; and compare Jer 34, 14 with Dt 15, 12. A relaxation of debts: it is uncertain whether a full cancellation of debts is meant, or merely a suspension of payment on them or on their interest among the Israelites. Cf Ex 23, 11 where the same Hebrew root is used of a field that is "let lie fallow" in the sabbatical year.

b: Lv 11, 26.   c: Ex 22, 30; 23, 19; 34, 26.   d: Lv 27, 30.   e: 23f; Dt 12, 5ff.   f: Dt 12, 12. 19.   g: 28f; Dt 26, 12.   h: Neh 10, 31.

Feeding the Disadvantaged

One out of every three years, the tithe law is shifted away from the central sanctuary to focus on the needs of the disadvantaged and the marginalized in the local community, to ensure they too may eat their fill (14, 29).

claim on what he has loaned his neighbor; he must not press his neighbor, his kinsman, because a relaxation in honor of the LORD has been proclaimed. [3]You may press a foreigner, but you shall relax the claim on your kinsman for what is yours.[i] [4]Nay, more! since the LORD, your God, will bless you abundantly in the land he will give you to occupy as your heritage, there should be no one of you in need. [5]If you but heed the voice of the LORD, your God, and carefully observe all these commandments which I enjoin on you today, [6]you will lend to many nations, and borrow from none;[j] you will rule over many nations, and none will rule over you, since the LORD, your God, will bless you as he promised. [7]If one of your kinsmen in any community is in need in the land which the LORD, your God, is giving you, you shall not harden your heart nor close your hand to him in his need. [8]Instead, you shall open your hand to him and freely lend him enough to meet his need.[k] [9]Be on your guard lest, entertaining the mean thought that the seventh year, the year of relaxation, is near, you grudge help to your needy kinsman and give him nothing; else he will cry to the LORD against you and you will be held guilty. [10]When you give to him, give freely and not with ill will; for the LORD, your God, will bless you for this in all your works and undertakings. [11]The needy will never be lacking* in the land; that is why I command you to open your hand to your poor and needy kinsman in your country.[l]

Hebrew Slaves. [12]"If your kinsman, a Hebrew man or woman, sells himself to you, he is to serve you for six years, but in the seventh year you shall dismiss him from your service, a free man.[m] [13]When you do so, you shall not send him away empty-handed, [14]but shall weight him down with gifts from your flock and threshing floor and wine press, in proportion to the blessing the LORD, your God, has bestowed on you. [15]For remember that you too were once slaves in the land of Egypt, and the LORD, your God, ransomed you. That is why I am giving you this command today.[n] [16]If, however, he tells you that he does not wish to leave you, because he is devoted to you and your household, since he fares well with you, [17]you shall take an awl and thrust it through his ear* into the door, and he shall then be your slave forever.[o] Your female slave, also, you shall treat in the same way. [18]You must not be reluctant to let your slave go free, since the service he has given you for six years was worth twice a hired man's salary; then also the LORD, your God, will bless you in everything you do.

Firstlings. [19][p]"You shall consecrate to the LORD, your God, all the male firstlings of your herd and of your flock. You shall not work the firstlings of your cattle, nor shear the firstlings of your flock. [20]Year after year you and your family shall eat them before the LORD, your God, in the place he chooses.[q] [21]If, however, a firstling is lame or blind or has any other serious defect, you shall not sacrifice it to the LORD, your God, [22]but in your own communities you may eat it, the unclean and the clean eating it alike, as you would a gazelle or a deer. [23]Only, you shall not partake of its blood,

---

15, 11: The needy will never be lacking: compare the words of Christ, "The poor you have always with you" (Mt 26, 11).
15, 17: His ear: cf Ex 21, 6 and the note there.

i: Dt 23, 20.   *j:* Dt 28, 12f.   *k:* Lv 25, 35; Sir 29, 1f; Mt 5, 42.   *l:* Dt 15, 8; Sir 29, 12.   *m:* Ex 21, 2; Jer 34, 14.   *n:* Dt 5, 15.   *o:* 16f: Ex 21, 5f.   *p:* Ex 13, 11.   *q:* Dt 14, 23.

which must be poured out on the ground like water.[r]

CHAPTER 16

See RG
85-89

Feast of the Passover. [1]"Observe the month of Abib* by keeping the Passover of the LORD, your God,[s] since it was in the month of Abib that he brought you by night out of Egypt. [2]You shall offer the Passover sacrifice from your flock or your herd to the LORD, your God, in the place which he chooses as the dwelling place of his name. [3t]You shall not eat leavened bread with it. For seven days you shall eat with it only unleavened bread, the bread of affliction, that you may remember as long as you live the day of your departure from the land of Egypt; for in frightened haste you left the land of Egypt. [4]Nothing leavened may be found in all your territory for seven days, and none of the meat which you sacrificed on the evening of the first day shall be kept overnight for the next day.

[5]"You may not sacrifice the Passover in any of the communities which the LORD, your God, gives you; [6]only at the place which he chooses as the dwelling place of his name, and in the evening at sunset, on the anniversary of your departure from Egypt, shall you sacrifice the Passover. [7]You shall cook and eat it at the place the LORD, your God, chooses; then in the morning you may return to your tents. [8]For six days you shall eat unleavened bread, and on the seventh there shall be a solemn meeting in honor of the LORD, your God; on that day you shall not do any sort of work.

Feast of Weeks. [9u]"You shall count off seven weeks, computing them from the day when the sickle is first put to the standing grain. [10]You shall then keep the feast of Weeks* in honor of the LORD, your God, and the measure of your own freewill offering shall be in proportion to the blessing the LORD, your God, has bestowed on you. [11]In the place which the LORD, your God, chooses as the dwelling place of his name,[v] you shall make merry in his presence together with your son and daughter, your male and female slave, and the Levite who belongs to your community, as well as the alien, the orphan and the widow among you. [12]Remember that you too were once slaves in Egypt, and carry out these statutes carefully.

Feast of Booths. [13w]"You shall celebrate the feast of Booths for seven days, when you have gathered in the produce from your threshing floor and wine press.* [14]You shall make merry at your feast,[x] together with your son and daughter, your male and female slave, and also the Levite, the alien, the orphan and the widow who belong to your community. [15]For seven days you shall celebrate this pilgrim feast in honor of the LORD, your God, in the place which he chooses; since the LORD, your God, has blessed you in all your crops and in all your undertakings, you shall do naught but make merry.

[16]"Three times a year,[y] then, every male among you shall appear before the LORD, your God, in the place which he chooses: at the feast of Unleavened Bread, at the feast of Weeks, and at the feast of Booths. No one shall appear before the LORD empty-handed, [17]but each of you with as much as he can give, in proportion to the blessings which the LORD, your God, has bestowed on you.

Judges. [18]"You shall appoint judges and officials throughout your tribes to administer true justice for the people in all the communities which the LORD, your God, is giving you. [19]You shall not distort justice; you must be impartial.[z] You shall not take a bribe; for a bribe blinds the eyes even of the wise and twists the words even of the just. [20]Justice and justice alone shall be your aim, that you

---

16, 1: Abib: "ear of grain, ripe grain," the name of the month in which the barley harvest fell, corresponding to our March and April; at a later period this month received the Babylonian name of "Nisan."

16, 10: Feast of Weeks: later known more commonly as "Pentecost."

16, 13: See note on Lv 23, 34.

---

r: 21ff; Dt 12, 15f; Lv 22, 20. *s:* 1-8: Ex 12, 2-20; 23, 15; Nm 28, 16ff. 24f. *t:* 3f: Ex 13, 6f; 34, 18. *u:* 9-12: Lv 23, 15-21. *v:* Dt 12, 5. 7. 12. 18. *w:* 13-15: Ex 23, 16; Lv 23, 34-43; Nm 29, 12-38. *x:* Dt 16, 11. *y:* Ex 23, 14f. 17; 34, 23; 2 Chr 8, 13. *z:* Dt 1, 17; Ex 23, 8.

Solomon's Offenses

The offenses specified in Dt 17, 16–18, allude to the warnings against royal autocracy outlined in the very founding of the monarchy (1 Sm 8, 10–18). They almost certainly presuppose Solomon's trade in horses (1 Kgs 10, 26–29) and his multiple marital alliances with foreign wives (1 Kgs 11, 1–8). Here, the author understood those marriages to lead to the corruption of Israelite religion, with the breakup of the united monarchy the divine punishment for these transgressions (1 Kgs 11, 9–13).

may have life and may possess the land which the LORD, your God, is giving you.

Pagan Worship. *21**"You shall not plant a sacred pole of any kind of wood beside the altar of the LORD, your God, which you will build;*a* *22*nor shall you erect a sacred pillar,* such as the LORD, your God, detests.

CHAPTER 17

See RG
85-89
1"You shall not sacrifice to the LORD, your God, from the herd or from the flock an animal with any serious defect;*b* that would be an abomination to the LORD, your God.

2c"If there is found among you, in any one of the communities which the LORD, your God, gives you, a man or a woman who does evil in the sight of the LORD, your God, and transgresses his covenant, *3*by serving other gods, or by worshiping the sun or the moon or any of the host of the sky, against my command;*d* *4*and if, on being informed of it, you find by careful investigation that it is true and an established fact that this abomination has been committed in Israel: *5*you shall bring the man (or woman) who has done the evil deed out to your city gates* and stone him to death. *6*The testimony of two or three witnesses is required for putting a person to death;*e* no one shall be put to death on the testimony of only one witness. *7*At the execution, the witnesses are to be the first to raise their hands against him; afterward all the people are to join in.*f* Thus shall you purge the evil from your midst.

Judges. *8*"If in your own community there is a case at issue which proves too complicated for you to decide, in a matter of bloodshed or of civil rights or of personal injury, you shall then go up to the place which the LORD, your God, chooses, *9*to the levitical priests or to the judge who is in office at that time. They shall study the case and then hand down to you their decision.*g* *10*According to this decision that they give you in the place which the LORD chooses, you shall act, being careful to do exactly as they direct. *11*You shall carry out the directions they give you and the verdict they pronounce for you, without turning aside to the right or to the left from the decision they hand down to you. *12*Any man who has the insolence to refuse to listen to the priest* who officiates there in the ministry of the LORD, your God, or to the judge, shall die. Thus shall you purge the evil from your midst. *13*And all the people, on hearing of it, shall fear, and never again be so insolent.

The King. *14*"When you have come into the land which the LORD, your God, is giving you, and have occupied it and settled in it, should you then decide to have a king over you like all the surrounding nations,*h* *15*you shall set that man over you as your king whom the LORD, your God, chooses.*i* He whom you set over you as king must be your kinsman; a foreigner, who is no kin of yours, you may not set over you. *16*But he shall not have a great number of horses;* nor

16, 21—17, 7: This section seems to be out of its proper place, since it interrupts the natural sequence of the laws for the judges (Dt 16, 18-20 and 17, 8-13). It probably belongs to the similar section, Dt 12, 29—14, 2.

16, 21f: Sacred pole . . . sacred pillar: see note on Ex 34, 13.

17, 5: Out to your city gates: outside the gates in an unclean place; cf Lv 24, 14; Nm 15, 36; Acts 7, 58; Heb 13, 12.

17, 12: The priest: the high priest; the judge: a layman. The former presided over the court in cases which directly

concerned religion, the latter in cases of a more secular nature; cf 2 Chr 19, 8-11.

17, 16: Horses: chariotry for war. The LORD's warning: the same warning is also referred to in Dt 28, 68, although it is not

a: 1 Kgs 14, 15; 2 Chr 33, 3. *b:* Lv 22, 20. *c:* 2-7: Dt 13, 6-15. *d:* Dt 4, 19. *e:* Dt 19, 15; Nm 35, 30; Mt 18, 16; Jn 8, 17; 2 Cor 13, 1. *f:* Dt 13, 10. *g:* Dt 21, 5; 2 Chr 19, 8. *h:* 1 Sm 8, 5. 19f. *i:* 1 Sm 9, 16; 10, 24; 16, 12.

shall he make his people go back again to Egypt to acquire them, against the LORD's warning that you must never go back that way again.*j* *17*Neither shall he have a great number of wives, lest his heart be estranged,*k* nor shall he accumulate a vast amount of silver and gold. *18*When he is enthroned in his kingdom, he shall have a copy of this law made from the scroll that is in the custody of the levitical priests.*l* *19*He shall keep it with him and read it all the days of his life that he may learn to fear the LORD, his God, and to heed and fulfill all the words of this law and these statutes. *20*Let him not become estranged from his countrymen through pride, nor turn aside to the right or to the left from these commandments. Then he and his descendants will enjoy a long reign in Israel.

CHAPTER 18

See RG 85–89

Priests. *1*"The whole priestly tribe of Levi shall have no share in the heritage with Israel; they shall live on the oblations of the LORD and the portions due to him.*m* *2*Levi shall have no heritage among his brothers; the LORD himself is his heritage, as he has told him. *3*The priests shall have a right to the following things from the people: from those who are offering a sacrifice, whether the victim is from the herd or from the flock, the priest shall receive the shoulder, the jowls and the stomach. *4*You shall also give him the first fruits of your grain and wine and oil,*n* as well as the first fruits of the shearing of your flock; *5*for the LORD, your God, has chosen him and his sons out of all your tribes to be always in attendance to minister in the name of the LORD.

6"When a Levite goes from one of your communities anywhere in Israel in which he ordinarily resides, to visit, as his heart may desire, the place which the LORD chooses, *7*he may minister there in the name of the LORD, his God, like all his fellow Levites who are in attendance there before the LORD. *8*He shall then receive the same portions to eat as the rest, along with his monetary offerings and heirlooms.

Prophets. *9*"When you come into the land which the LORD, your God, is giving you, you shall not learn to imitate the abominations of the peoples there.*o* *10*Let there not be found among you anyone who immolates his son or daughter*p* in the fire,* nor a fortune-teller, soothsayer, charmer, diviner, *11*or caster of spells, nor one who consults ghosts and spirits or seeks oracles from the dead. *12*Anyone who does such things is an abomination to the LORD, and because of such abominations the LORD, your God, is driving these nations out of your way.*q* *13*You, however, must be altogether sincere toward the LORD, your God. *14*Though these nations whom you are to dispossess listen to their soothsayers and fortune-tellers, the LORD, your God, will not permit you to do so.

15"A prophet like me* will the LORD, your God, raise up for you from among your own kinsmen; to him you shall listen.*r* *16*This is exactly what you requested of the LORD, your God, at Horeb on the day of the assembly, when you said, 'Let us not again hear the voice of the LORD, our God, nor see this great fire any more, lest we die.'*s* *17*And the LORD said to me, 'This was well said. *18*I will raise up for them a prophet like you from among their kinsmen, and will put my

---

mentioned explicitly elsewhere in the Pentateuch. We know from other sources that Egypt used to export war horses to Palestine. The danger envisioned here is that some king might make Israel a vassal of Egypt for the sake of such military aid.

18, 10f: Immolates his son or daughter in the fire: to Molech. See note on Lv 18, 21. Such human sacrifices are classed here with other pagan superstitions because they were believed to possess magical powers for averting a calamity; cf 2 Kgs 3, 27. Three other forms of superstition are listed here: augury (by a fortune-teller, a soothsayer or a diviner); black magic (by a charmer . . . or caster of spells); and necromancy (by one who consults ghosts and spirits or seeks oracles from the dead).

18, 15: A prophet like me: from the context (opposition to

the pagan soothsayers) it seems that Moses is referring in general to all the true prophets who were to succeed him. But since Christ is the Great Prophet in whom the prophetic office finds its fulfillment and completion, this passage was understood in a special Messianic sense both by the Jews (Jn 6, 14; 7, 40) and by the Apostles (Acts 3, 22; 7, 37).

---

j: Dt 28, 68; 1 Kgs 4, 26; 10, 26.   *k:* 1 Kgs 11, 3f; Neh 13, 26.   *l:* Dt 31, 9. 26.   *m:* Nm 18, 8f. 20-24; 1 Cor 9, 13.   *n:* Nm 18, 12; 2 Chr 31, 5.   *o:* Dt 12, 29ff; Lv 18, 26-30.   *p:* 10f: Lv 18, 21; 19, 31; 20, 27; 1 Sm 28, 7; 2 Kgs 17, 17; 21, 6.   *q:* Dt 9, 4.   *r:* Jn 1, 45; 6, 14; Acts 3, 22; 7, 37.   *s:* Ex 20, 19.

words into his mouth; he shall tell them all that I command him. [19]If any man will not listen to my words which he speaks in my name, I myself will make him answer for it.[t] [20]But if a prophet presumes to speak in my name[u] an oracle that I have not commanded him to speak, or speaks in the name of other gods, he shall die.'

[21]"If you say to yourselves, 'How can we recognize an oracle which the LORD has spoken?', [22]know that, even though a prophet speaks in the name of the LORD, if his oracle is not fulfilled or verified, it is an oracle which the LORD did not speak. The prophet has spoken it presumptuously, and you shall have no fear of him.

CHAPTER 19

See RG 85–89

Cities of Refuge. [1]"When the LORD, your God, removes the nations whose land he is giving you, and you have taken their place and are settled in their cities and houses, [2v]you shall set apart three cities* in the land which the LORD, your God, is giving you to occupy. [3]You shall thereby divide into three regions the land which the LORD, your God, will give you as a heritage, and so arrange the routes that every homicide will be able to find a refuge.

[4]"It is in the following case that a homicide may take refuge in such a place to save his life: when someone unwittingly kills his neighbor to whom he had previously borne no malice.[w] [5]For example, if he goes with his neighbor to a forest to cut wood, and as he swings his ax to fell a tree, its head flies off the handle and hits his neighbor a mortal blow, he may take refuge in one of these cities to save his life. [6]Should the distance be too great, the avenger of blood* may in the heat of his anger pursue the homicide and overtake him and strike him dead, even though he does not merit death since he had previously borne

the slain man no malice. [7]That is why I order you to set apart three cities.

[8x]"But if the LORD, your God, enlarges your territory, as he swore to your fathers, and gives you all the land he promised your fathers he would give [9]in the event that you carefully observe all these commandments which I enjoin on you today, loving the LORD, your God, and ever walking in his ways: then add three cities to these three. [10]Thus, in the land which the LORD, your God, is giving you as a heritage, innocent blood will not be shed and you will not become guilty of bloodshed.

[11y]"However, if someone lies in wait for his neighbor out of hatred for him, and rising up against him, strikes him mortally, and then takes refuge in one of these cities, [12]the elders of his own city shall send for him and have him taken from there, and shall hand him over to be slain by the avenger of blood. [13]Do not look on him with pity, but purge from Israel the stain of shedding innocent blood, that you may prosper.

Removal of Landmarks. [14]"You shall not move your neighbor's landmarks erected by your forefathers in the heritage you receive in the land which the LORD, your God, is giving you to occupy.[z]

False Witnesses. [15]"One witness alone shall not take the stand against a man in regard to any crime or any offense of which he may be guilty; a judicial fact shall be established only on the testimony of two or three witnesses.[a]

[16]"If an unjust witness takes the stand against a man to accuse him of a defection from the law, [17]the two parties in the dispute shall appear before the LORD in the presence of the priests or judges in office at that time;[b] [18]and if after a thorough investigation the judges find that the witness is a false witness and has accused his kinsman falsely, [19]you

19, 2: Set apart three cities: the Israelites were to have at least six cities of refuge, three in the land east of the Jordan and three in the land of Canaan west of the Jordan (Nm 35, 9-34); but since the three cities east of the Jordan had now been appointed (Dt 4, 41-43), reference is made here only to the three west of the Jordan. The execution of this command is narrated in Jos 20.

19, 6: The avenger of blood: see note on Nm 35, 12.

t: Acts 3, 23.   u: 20. 22: Dt 13, 2ff.   v: Dt 4, 41ff; Ex 21, 13; Nm 35, 10-15; Jos 20, 2. 8.   w: Dt 4, 42; Nm 35, 15; Jos 20, 3. 5.   x: Gn 15, 18-21; 28, 14; Ex 23, 31; 34, 24.   y: 11ff; Ex 21, 12. 14; Nm 35, 20f.   z: Dt 27, 17; Prv 23, 10; Hos 5, 10.   a: Dt 17, 6; Nm 35, 30; Mt 18, 16; Jn 8, 17; 2 Cor 13, 1.   b: Dt 17, 8f.

Rules for Waging Holy War

In contrast to other legal collections, which include only brief sections concerning military engagement (Ex 23, 23–33; 34, 11–16), Deuteronomy concerns itself extensively with the laws of holy war. God as divine warrior directly confronts the adversary on behalf of the nation, and God's presence in the camp imposes additional purity requirements on the people (Dt 23, 10–14).

shall do to him as he planned to do to his kinsman.[c] Thus shall you purge the evil from your midst. [20]The rest, on hearing of it, shall fear, and never again do a thing so evil among you. [21]Do not look on such a man with pity. Life for life, eye for eye, tooth for tooth, hand for hand, and foot for foot![d]

CHAPTER 20

See RG 85–89

Courage in War. [1]"When you go out to war against your enemies and you see horses and chariots and an army greater than your own, do not be afraid of them, for the LORD, your God, who brought you up from the land of Egypt, will be with you. [2]"When you are about to go into battle, the priest shall come forward and say to the soldiers: [3]'Hear, O Israel! Today you are going into battle against your enemies. Be not weakhearted or afraid; be neither alarmed nor frightened by them. [4]For it is the LORD, your God, who goes with you to fight for you against your enemies and give you victory.'[e] [5]"Then the officials shall say to the soldiers,[f] 'Is there anyone who has built a new house and not yet had the housewarming? Let him return home, lest he die in battle and another dedicate it. [6]Is there anyone who has planted a vineyard and never yet enjoyed its fruits? Let him return home, lest he die in battle and another enjoy its fruits in his stead. [7]Is there anyone who has betrothed a woman and not yet taken her as his wife? Let him return home, lest he die in battle and another take her to wife.'[g] [8]In fine, the officials shall say to the soldiers, 'Is there anyone who is afraid and weakhearted?[h] Let him return home, lest he make his fellows as fainthearted as himself.'

[9]"When the officials have finished speaking to the soldiers, military officers shall be appointed over the army.

Cities of the Enemy. [10]"When you march up to attack a city, first offer it terms of peace. [11]If it agrees to your terms of peace and opens its gates to you, all the people to be found in it shall serve you in forced labor. [12]But if it refuses to make peace with you and instead offers you battle, lay siege to it, [13]and when the LORD, your God, delivers it into your hand, put every male in it to the sword; [14]but the women and children and livestock and all else in it that is worth plundering you may take as your booty, and you may use this plunder of your enemies which the LORD, your God, has given you.[i]

[15]"That is how you shall deal with any city at a considerable distance from you, which does not belong to the peoples of this land. [16]But in the cities of those nations which the LORD, your God, is giving you as your heritage, you shall not leave a single soul alive. [17]You must doom them all—the Hittites, Amorites, Canaanites, Perizzites, Hivites and Jebusites[j]—as the LORD, your God, has commanded you, [18]lest they teach you to make any such abominable offerings as they make to their gods, and you thus sin against the LORD, your God.

Trees of a Besieged City. [19]"When you are at war with a city and have to lay siege to it for a long time before you capture it, you shall not destroy its trees by putting an ax to them. You may eat their fruit, but you must not cut down the trees. After all, are the trees of the field men, that they should be included in your siege? [20]However, those trees which you know are not fruit trees you may

c: 18f: Dn 13, 61f.   d: Ex 21, 23f; Lv 24, 20; Mt 5, 38.   e: Dt 1, 30; 3, 22; Jos 23, 10.   f: 5ff: 1 Mc 3, 56.   g: Dt 24, 5.   h: Jgs 7, 3.   i: 13f: Nm 31, 7. 9. 11; Jos 22, 8.   j: 16f: Dt 7, 1f; Jos 10, 40; 11, 14.

destroy, cutting them down to build siege-works with which to reduce the city that is resisting you.

CHAPTER 21

See RG 85–89

Expiation of Untraced Murder. ¹"If the corpse of a slain man* is found lying in the open on the land which the LORD, your God, is giving you to occupy, and it is not known who killed him, ²your elders and judges shall go out and measure the distances to the cities that are in the neighborhood of the corpse. ³When it is established which city is nearest the corpse, the elders of that city shall take a heifer that has never been put to work as a draft animal under a yoke, ⁴and bringing it down to a wadi with an ever-flowing stream at a place that has not been plowed or sown, they shall cut the heifer's throat there in the wadi.* ⁵The priests, the descendants of Levi, shall also be present, for the LORD, your God, has chosen them to minister to him and to give blessings in his name, and every case of dispute or violence must be settled by their decision.ᵏ ⁶Then all the elders of that city nearest the corpse shall wash their hands* over the heifer whose throat was cut in the wadi, ⁷and shall declare, 'Our hands did not shed this blood,* and our eyes did not see the deed. ⁸Absolve, O LORD, your people Israel, whom you have ransomed, and let not the guilt of shedding innocent blood remain in the midst of your people Israel.' Thus they shall be absolved from the guilt of bloodshed, ⁹and you shall purge from your midst the guilt of innocent blood, that you may prosper for doing what is right in the sight of the LORD.

Marriage with a Female Captive. ¹⁰"When you go out to war against your enemies and the LORD, your God, delivers them into your hand, so that you take captives, ¹¹if you see a comely woman among the captives and become so enamored of her that you wish to have her as wife, ¹²you may take her home to your house. But before she may live there, she must shave her head* and pare her nails ¹³and lay aside her captive's garb. After she has mourned her father and mother for a full month, you may have relations with her, and you shall be her husband and she shall be your wife. ¹⁴However, if later on you lose your liking for her, you shall give her her freedom, if she wishes it; but you shall not sell her or enslave her, since she was married to you under compulsion.

Rights of the First-born. ¹⁵"If a man with two wives loves one and dislikes the other; and if both bear him sons, but the first-born is of her whom he dislikes: ¹⁶when he comes to bequeath his property to his sons he may not consider as his first-born the son of the wife he loves, in preference to his true first-born, the son of the wife whom he dislikes. ¹⁷On the contrary, he shall recognize as his first-born the son of her whom he dislikes, giving him a double share of whatever he happens to own, since he is the first fruits of his manhood, and to him belong the rights of the first-born.

The Incorrigible Son. ¹⁸"If a man has a stubborn and unruly son who will not listen to his father or mother, and will not obey them even though they chastise him, ¹⁹his father and mother shall have him apprehended and brought out to the elders at the gate* of his home city, ²⁰where they shall say to those city elders, 'This son of ours is a stubborn and unruly fellow who will not lis-

---

21, 1-9: This paragraph is best read immediately after Dt 19, 21. The slain man may not necessarily have been murdered; he may have been killed by a wild beast. But the blood of the slain cries out to God from the soil where it was shed; cf Gn 4, 10. Therefore a religious ceremony of propitiation is here prescribed in order to avert God's anger on the community.

21, 4: They shall cut the heifer's throat there in the wadi: its blood is to be carried away by the stream, signifying thereby the removal of the human blood from the soil. This is not a sacrifice but a symbolic action; the priests are present merely as official witnesses.

21, 6: Wash their hands: a symbolic gesture in protesta-

tion of one's own innocence when human blood is unjustly shed; cf Mt 27, 24.

21, 7: This blood: the blood of the slain man as symbolized by the heifer's blood.

21, 12f: Shave her head . . . : these symbolic actions are meant to signify the purification of the woman from her pagan defilement or perhaps the end of her period of mourning for her previous husband.

21, 19: The gate: in the city walls. This open space served as the forum for the administration of justice. Cf Dt 22, 15; 25, 7; Ru 4, 1f. 11; Is 29, 21; Am 5, 10. 12. 15.

k: Dt 19, 17.

The Rebellious Son

While the Decalogue requirement to honor the parents (Dt 5, 16; Ex 20, 12) carries no explicit punishment, in Dt 21, 18–21, flagrant and sustained disobedience is a capital offense.

ten to us; he is a glutton and a drunkard.' [21]Then all his fellow citizens shall stone him to death. Thus shall you purge the evil from your midst, and all Israel, on hearing of it, shall fear.

Corpse of a Criminal. [22]"If a man guilty of a capital offense is put to death and his corpse hung on a tree,* [23]it shall not remain on the tree overnight.[l] You shall bury it the same day; otherwise, since God's curse rests on him who hangs on a tree,* you will defile the land which the LORD, your God, is giving you as an inheritance.

CHAPTER 22

See RG 85-89 **Care for Lost Animals.** [1]"You shall not see your kinsman's ox or sheep driven astray without showing concern about it; see to it that it is returned to your kinsman.[m] [2]If this kinsman does not live near you, or you do not know who he may be, take it to your own place and keep it with you until he claims it; then give it back to him. [3]You shall do the same with his ass, or his garment, or anything else which your kinsman loses and you happen to find; you may not be unconcerned about them. [4]You shall not see your kinsman's ass or ox foundering on the road without showing concern about it; see to it that you help him lift it up.

Various Precepts. [5]"A woman shall not wear an article proper to a man, nor shall a man put on a woman's dress; for anyone who does such things is an abomination to the LORD, your God.

[6]"If, while walking along, you chance upon a bird's nest with young birds or eggs in it, in any tree or on the ground, and the mother bird is sitting on them, you shall not take away the mother bird along with her brood; [7]you shall let her go, although you may take her brood away. It is thus that you shall have prosperity and a long life.

[8]"When you build a new house, put a parapet around the roof; otherwise, if someone falls off, you will bring blood-guilt upon your house.

[9n]"You shall not sow your vineyard with two different kinds of seed; if you do, its produce shall become forfeit,* both the crop you have sown and the yield of the vineyard. [10]You shall not plow with an ox and an ass harnessed together. [11]You shall not wear cloth of two different kinds of thread, wool and linen, woven together.

[12]"You shall put twisted cords* on the four corners of the cloak that you wrap around you.[o]

Crimes against Marriage. [13]"If a man, after marrying a woman and having relations with her, comes to dislike her, [14]and makes monstrous charges against her and defames her by saying, 'I married this woman, but when I first had relations with her I did not find her a virgin,' [15]the father and mother of the girl shall take the evidence of her virginity* and bring it to the elders at the city gate. [16]There the father of the girl shall say to the elders, 'I gave my daughter to this man in marriage, but he has come to dislike her, [17]and now brings monstrous charges against her, saying: I did not find your

---

21, 22: Hung on a tree: some understand, "impaled on a stake." In any case the hanging or impaling was not the means used to execute the criminal; he was first put to death by the ordinary means, stoning, and his corpse was then exposed on high as a salutary warning for others. Cf Jos 8, 29; 10, 26; 1 Sm 31, 10; 2 Sm 21, 9.

21, 23: God's curse rests on him who hangs on a tree: St. Paul quotes these words in Gal 3, 13, where he applies them to the crucified Savior, who "redeemed us from the curse of the law, becoming a curse for us."

22, 9: Become forfeit: to the sanctuary; cf Lv 19, 19; Jos 6, 19.

22, 12: Twisted cords: referred to as "tassels" on "violet cords" in Nm 15, 38. See note there.

22, 15: The evidence of her virginity: the bridal garment or sheet stained with a little blood from the first nuptial relations.

l: Gal 3, 13.   *m:* 1-4: Ex 23, 4f.   *n:* 9. 11: Lv 19, 19.   *o:* Nm 15, 38; Mt 23, 5.

daughter a virgin. But here is the evidence of my daughter's virginity!' And they shall spread out the cloth before the elders of the city. [18]Then these city elders shall take the man and chastise him,[*] [19]besides fining him one hundred silver shekels, which they shall give to the girl's father, because the man defamed a virgin in Israel. Moreover, she shall remain his wife, and he may not divorce her as long as he lives.

[20]"But if this charge is true, and evidence of the girl's virginity is not found, [21]they shall bring the girl to the entrance of her father's house and there her townsmen shall stone her to death, because she committed a crime against Israel by her unchasteness in her father's house. Thus shall you purge the evil from your midst.

[22]"If a man is discovered having relations with a woman who is married to another, both the man and the woman with whom he has had relations shall die.[p] Thus shall you purge the evil from your midst.

[23]"If within the city a man comes upon a maiden who is betrothed,[*] and has relations with her, [24]you shall bring them both out to the gate of the city and there stone them to death: the girl because she did not cry out for help though she was in the city, and the man because he violated his neighbor's wife. Thus shall you purge the evil from your midst.

[25]"If, however, it is in the open fields that a man comes upon such a betrothed maiden, seizes her and has relations with her, the man alone shall die. [26]You shall do nothing to the maiden, since she is not guilty of a capital offense. This case is like that of a man who rises up against his neighbor and murders him: [27]it was in the open fields that he came upon her, and though the betrothed maiden may have cried out for help, there was no one to come to her aid.

[28q]"If a man comes upon a maiden that is not betrothed, takes her and has relations with her, and their deed is discovered, [29]the man who had relations with her shall pay the girl's father fifty silver shekels and take her as his wife, because he has deflowered her. Moreover, he may not divorce her as long as he lives.

CHAPTER 23

See RG 85–89

[1]"A man shall not marry his father's wife,[*] nor shall he dishonor his father's bed.

Membership in the Community. [2]"No one whose testicles have been crushed or whose penis has been cut off, may be admitted into the community of the LORD. [3]No child of an incestuous union may be admitted into the community of the LORD, nor any descendant of his even to the tenth generation. [4r]No Ammonite or Moabite may ever be admitted into the community of the LORD, nor any descendants of theirs even to the tenth generation, [5s]because they would not succor you with food and water on your journey after you left Egypt, and because Moab hired Balaam, son of Beor, from Pethor in Aram Naharaim, to curse you; [6]though the LORD, your God, would not listen to Balaam and turned his curse into a blessing for you, because he loves you. [7]Never promote their peace and prosperity as long as you live. [8t]But do not abhor the Edomite, since he is your brother, nor the Egyptian, since you were an alien in his country. [9]Children born to them may in the third generation be admitted into the community of the LORD.

Cleanliness in Camp. [10]"When you are in camp during an expedition against your enemies, you shall keep yourselves from everything offensive. [11]If one of you becomes unclean because of a nocturnal emission, he shall go outside the camp, and not return until, [12]toward evening, he has bathed in water; then, when the sun has set, he may come back into the camp. [13]Outside the camp you shall have a place set aside to be used as a latrine. [14]You shall also keep a trowel in your equipment and with it, when you go outside

---

22, 18: Chastise him: flog him, as prescribed in Dt 25, 1-3.
22, 23: A maiden who is betrothed: a girl who is married but not yet brought to her husband's home and whose marriage is therefore still unconsummated.
23, 1: Father's wife: stepmother. Dishonor: cf Dt 27, 20.

p: Lv 20, 10; Jn 8, 4f.　　*q:* 28f: Ex 22, 16.　　*r:* Neh 13, 1f.　　*s:* Nm 24, 10.　　*t:* Gn 25, 24ff.

to ease nature, you shall first dig a hole and afterward cover up your excrement. *15*Since the LORD, your God, journeys along within your camp to defend you and to put your enemies at your mercy, your camp must be holy; otherwise, if he sees anything indecent in your midst, he will leave your company.

Various Precepts. *16*"You shall not hand over to his master a slave who has taken refuge from him with you. *17*Let him live with you wherever he chooses, in any one of your communities* that pleases him. Do not molest him. *18**"There shall be no temple harlot among the Israelite women, nor a temple prostitute among the Israelite men.*u* *19*You shall not offer a harlot's fee or a dog's price as any kind of votive offering in the house of the LORD, your God; both these things are an abomination to the LORD, your God.

20"You shall not demand interest from your countrymen on a loan of money or of food or of anything else on which interest is usually demanded.*v* *21*You may demand interest from a foreigner, but not from your countryman, so that the LORD, your God, may bless you in all your undertakings on the land you are to enter and occupy.

22"When you make a vow to the LORD, your God, you shall not delay in fulfilling it; otherwise you will be held guilty, for the LORD, your God, is strict in requiring it of you. *23*Should you refrain from making a vow, you will not be held guilty. *24*But you must keep your solemn word and fulfill the votive offering you have freely promised to the LORD.

25"When you go through your neighbor's vineyard, you may eat as many of his grapes as you wish, but do not put them in your basket. *26*When you go through your neighbor's grainfield, you may pluck some of the ears with your hand, but do not put a sickle to your neighbor's grain.

CHAPTER 24

See RG 85-89

Marriage Laws. *1*"When a man,* after marrying a woman and having relations with her, is later displeased with her because he finds in her something indecent,* and therefore he writes out a bill of divorce and hands it to her, thus dismissing her from his house: *2*if on leaving his house she goes and becomes the wife of another man, *3*and the second husband, too, comes to dislike her and dismisses her from his house by handing her a written bill of divorce; *4*or if this second man who has married her, dies; then her former husband, who dismissed her, may not again take her as his wife after she has become defiled. That would be an abomination before the LORD, and you shall not bring such guilt upon the land which the LORD, your God, is giving you as a heritage.

5w"When a man is newly wed, he need not go out on a military expedition, nor shall any public duty be imposed on him. He shall be exempt for one year for the sake of his family, to bring joy to the wife he has married.

Justice, Equity and Charity. *6**"No one shall take a hand mill or even its upper stone as a pledge for debt, for he would be taking the debtor's sustenance as a pledge.

7"If any man is caught kidnaping a fellow Israelite in order to enslave him and sell him, the kidnaper shall be put to death.*x* Thus shall you purge the evil from your midst.

8y"In an attack of leprosy you shall be

23, 17: In any one of your communities: from this it would seem that the slave in question is a fugitive from a foreign country.

23, 18f: The pagans believed that they could enter into special relationship with their gods and goddesses by having sexual relations with the pagan priests and priestesses who prostituted themselves for this purpose. The money paid for this was considered a sort of votive offering made to the pagan sanctuary. Such abominations were naturally forbidden in Israel. A dog's price: the money paid the pagan priest for his indecent service.

24, 1-4: This law is directly concerned only with forbidding divorced couples to remarry each other, and indirectly with checking hasty divorces, by demanding sufficient cause and certain legal formalities. Divorce itself is taken for granted and tolerated as an existing custom whose evils this law seeks to lessen. Cf Dt 22, 19. 29; Mal 2, 14ff. Christ gave the authentic interpretation of this law: "Moses, by reason of the hardness of your heart, permitted you to put away your wives; but it was not so from the beginning" (Mt 19, 8f).

24, 1: Something indecent: a rather indefinite phrase, meaning perhaps "immodest conduct." At the time of Christ the rabbis differed in opinion concerning the sufficient grounds for divorce; cf Mt 19, 3.

24, 6: Since the Israelites ground their grain into flour only in sufficient quantity for their current need, to deprive a debtor of his hand mill was virtually equivalent to condemning him to starve to death.

u: 1 Kgs 14, 24; 22, 46; 2 Kgs 23, 7.   *v:* Ex 22, 25; Lv 25, 37; Lk 6, 34f.   *w:* Dt 20, 7.   *x:* Ex 21, 16.   *y:* Lv 13, 1-14.

careful to observe exactly and to carry out all the directions of the levitical priests. Take care to act in accordance with the instructions I have given them. ⁹ᶻRemember what the LORD, your God, did to Miriam on the journey after you left Egypt.

¹⁰*"When you make a loan of any kind to your neighbor, you shall not enter his house to receive a pledge from him, ¹¹but shall wait outside until the man to whom you are making the loan brings his pledge outside to you. ¹²If he is a poor man, you shall not sleep in the mantle he gives as a pledge, ¹³but shall return it to him at sunset that he himself may sleep in it.ᵃ Then he will bless you, and it will be a good deed of yours before the LORD, your God.

¹⁴"You shall not defraud a poor and needy hired servant, whether he be one of your own countrymen or one of the aliens who live in your communities. ¹⁵You shall pay him each day's wages before sundown on the day itself, since he is poor and looks forward to them.ᵇ Otherwise he will cry to the LORD against you, and you will be held guilty.

¹⁶"Fathers shall not be put to death for their children, nor children for their fathers; only for his own guilt shall a man be put to death.ᶜ

¹⁷"You shall not violate the rights of the alien or of the orphan, nor take the clothing of a widow as a pledge.ᵈ ¹⁸For, remember, you were once slaves in Egypt, and the LORD, your God, ransomed you from there; that is why I command you to observe this rule.

¹⁹ᵉ"When you reap the harvest in your field and overlook a sheaf there, you shall not go back to get it; let it be for the alien, the orphan or the widow, that the LORD, your God, may bless you in all your undertakings. ²⁰When you knock down the fruit of your olive trees, you shall not go over the branches a second time; let what remains be for the alien, the orphan and the widow. ²¹When you pick your grapes, you shall not go over the vineyard a second time; let what remains be for the alien, the orphan, and the widow. ²²For remember that you were once slaves in Egypt; that is why I command you to observe this rule.

CHAPTER 25

See RG 85–89

¹"When men have a dispute and bring it to court, and a decision is handed down to them acquitting the innocent party and condemning the guilty party, ²if the latter deserves stripes, the judge shall have him lie down and in his presence receive the number of stripes his guilt deserves. ³Forty stripes* may be given him, but no more;ᶠ lest, if he were beaten with more stripes than these, your kinsman should be looked upon as disgraced because of the severity of the beating.

⁴*"You shall not muzzle an ox when it is treading out grain.ᵍ

Levirate Marriage. ⁵"When brothers live together* and one of them dies without a son, the widow of the deceased shall not marry anyone outside the family; but her husband's brother shall go to her and perform the duty of a brother-in-law by marrying her.ʰ ⁶The first-born son she bears shall continue the line of the deceased brother, that his name may not be blotted out from Israel. ⁷If, however, a man does not care to marry his brother's wife, she shall go up to the elders at the gate and declare, 'My brother-in-law does not intend to perform his duty toward me and refuses to perpetuate his brother's name in Israel.' ⁸Thereupon the elders of his city shall summon him and admonish him. If he persists in saying, 'I am not willing to marry her,' ⁹*his sister-in-law, in the presence of the elders, shall go up to him and strip his sandal from

24, 10f: The debtor had the right to select the pledge that the creditor demanded as a guarantee for his loan.

25, 3: Forty stripes: a relatively mild punishment in ancient times. Later Jewish practice limited the number to thirty-nine; cf 2 Cor 11, 24.

25, 4: St Paul argues from this verse that a laborer has the right to live on the fruits of his labor; cf 1 Cor 9, 9; 1 Tm 5, 18.

25, 5: When brothers live together: when relatives of the same clan, though married, hold their property in common. It was only in this case that the present law was to be observed, since one of its purposes was to keep the property of the de-

ceased within the same clan. Such a marriage of a widow with her brother-in-law is known as a "levirate" marriage from the Latin word levir, meaning "a husband's brother."

25, 9f: The penalty decreed for a man who refuses to comply with this law of family loyalty is public disgrace (the widow is to spit in his face) and the curse of poverty;

z: Nm 12, 10-15. a: Ex 22, 26. b: 14f: Lv 19, 13; Tb 4, 15; Sir 34, 25f; Jer 22, 13. c: 2 Kgs 14, 6; 2 Chr 25, 4; Ez 18, 20. d: Ex 22, 22; 23, 9. e: 19ff: Lv 19, 9f; 23, 22. f: 2 Cor 11, 24. g: 1 Cor 9, 9; 1 Tm 5, 18. h: Mt 22, 24; Mk 12, 19; Lk 20, 28. i: 6-9: Ru 4, 5-10.

his foot and spit in his face, saying publicly, 'This is how one should be treated who will not build up his brother's family!' [10]And his lineage shall be spoken of in Israel as 'the family of the man stripped of his sandal.'

Various Precepts. [11]"When two men are fighting and the wife of one intervenes to save her husband from the blows of his opponent, if she stretches out her hand and seizes the latter by his private parts, [12]you shall chop off her hand without pity.

[13]"You shall not keep two differing weights in your bag, one large and the other small;[j] [14]nor shall you keep two different measures in your house, one large and the other small. [15]But use a true and just weight, and a true and just measure, that you may have a long life on the land which the LORD, your God, is giving you. [16]Everyone who is dishonest in any of these matters is an abomination to the LORD, your God.

[17]"Bear in mind what Amalek did to you on the journey after you left Egypt,[k] [18]how without fear of any god he harassed you along the way, weak and weary as you were, and cut off at the rear all those who lagged behind. [19]Therefore, when the LORD, your God, gives you rest from all your enemies round about in the land which he is giving you to occupy as your heritage, you shall blot out the memory of Amalek from under the heavens.[l] Do not forget!

CHAPTER 26

See RG
85–89

Thanksgiving for the Harvest. [1]"When you have come into the land which the LORD, your God, is giving you as a heritage, and have occupied it and settled in it, [2]you shall take some first fruits[m] of the various products of the soil which you harvest from the land which the LORD, your God, gives you, and putting them in a basket, you shall go to the place which the LORD, your God, chooses for the dwelling place of his name. [3]There you shall go to the priest in office at that time and say to him, 'Today I acknowledge to the LORD, my God, that I have indeed come into the land which he swore to our fathers he would give us.' [4]The priest shall then receive the basket from you and shall set it in front of the altar of the LORD, your God. [5]Then you shall declare before the LORD, your God, 'My father was a wandering Aramean* who went down to Egypt with a small household and lived there as an alien.[n] But there he became a nation great, strong and numerous. [6o]When the Egyptians maltreated and oppressed us, imposing hard labor upon us, [7]we cried to the LORD, the God of our fathers, and he heard our cry and saw our affliction, our toil and our oppression. [8]He brought us out of Egypt with his strong hand and outstretched arm, with terrifying power, with signs and wonders;[p] [9]and bringing us into this country, he gave us this land flowing with milk and honey.[q] [10]Therefore, I have now brought you the first fruits of the products of the soil which you, O LORD, have given me.' And having set them before the LORD, your God, you shall bow down in his presence. [11]Then you and your family, together with the Levite and the aliens who live among you, shall make merry over all these good things which the LORD, your God, has given you.[r]

Prayer with the Tithes. [12]"When you have finished setting aside all the tithes of your produce in the third year,[s] the year of the tithes, and you have given them to the Levite,* the alien, the orphan and the widow, that they may eat their fill in your own community, [13]you shall declare before the LORD, your God, 'I have purged my house of the

---

sandals were proverbially a man's cheapest possession (cf Am 2, 6; 8, 6), and therefore "a man without sandals" was the poorest of the poor. Some commentators, however, connect this symbolic act with the ceremony mentioned in Ru 4, 7f.

25, 17-19: This attack on Israel by Amalek is not mentioned elsewhere in the Old Testament, although it probably was connected with the battle mentioned in Ex 17, 8. A campaign against Amalek was carried out by Saul; cf 1 Sm 15.

26, 5: Aramean: either in reference to the origin of the pa-

triarchs from Aram Naharaim (cf Gn 24, 10; 25, 20; 28, 5; 31, 20. 24), or merely in the sense of "nomad," in the same way as "Arab" was later used; cf Jer 3, 2.

26, 12: And you have given them to the Levite . . . : as prescribed in Dt 14, 28f.

---

j: 13ff: Lv 19, 35f; Prv 16, 11; Ez 45, 10; Mi 6, 11. k: Ex 17, 8. l: Ex 17, 14; 1 Sm 15, 2f. m: Ex 23, 19; 34, 26. n: Gn 46, 6f; Acts 7, 14f. o: 6f: Ex 1, 8-22; 2, 23ff; 3, 9; Nm 20, 15f. p: Ex 12, 51. q: Ex 3, 8. r: Dt 12, 7. 12. s: Dt 14, 28f.

sacred portion and I have given it to the Levite, the alien, the orphan and the widow, just as you have commanded me. In this I have not broken or forgotten any of your commandments: *14*I have not eaten any of the tithe as a mourner; I have not brought any of it out as one unclean; I have not offered any of it to the dead. I have thus hearkened to the voice of the LORD, my God, doing just as you have commanded me. *15*Look down, then, from heaven, your holy abode, and bless your people Israel and the soil you have given us in the land flowing with milk and honey which you promised on oath to our fathers.'

The Covenant. *16*"This day the LORD, your god, commands you to observe these statutes and decrees. Be careful, then, to observe them with all your heart and with all your soul. *17*Today you are making this agreement with the LORD: he is to be your God and you are to walk in his ways and observe his statutes, commandments and decrees, and to hearken to his voice.*t* *18*And today the LORD is making this agreement with you: you are to be a people peculiarly his own,*u* as he promised you; and provided you keep all his commandments, *19*he will then raise you high in praise and renown and glory above all other nations he has made, and you will be a people sacred to the LORD, your God, as he promised."

IV: Final Words of Moses

CHAPTER 27

See RG
85-89

Ceremonies. *1*Then Moses, with the elders of Israel, gave the people this order: "Keep all these commandments which I enjoin on you today. *2*On the day you cross the Jordan into the land which the LORD, your God, is giving you, set up some large stones and coat them with plaster. *3*Also write on them,*v* at the time you cross, all the words of this law, that you may thus enter into the land

flowing with milk and honey, which the LORD, your God, and the God of your fathers, is giving you as he promised you. *4*When, moreover, you have crossed the Jordan, besides setting up on Mount Ebal these stones concerning which I command you today, and coating them with plaster, *5*you shall also build to the LORD, your God, an altar made of stones that no iron tool has touched.*w* *6*You shall make this altar of the LORD, your God, with undressed stones, and shall offer on it holocausts to the LORD, your God. *7*You shall also sacrifice peace offerings and eat them there, making merry before the LORD, your God. *8*On the stones* you shall inscribe all the words of this law very clearly."

*9*Moses, with the levitical priests, then said to all Israel: "Be silent, O Israel, and listen! This day you have become the people of the LORD, your God.*x* *10*You shall therefore hearken to the voice of the LORD, your God, and keep his commandments and statutes which I enjoin on you today."

*11*That same day Moses gave the people this order: *12*"When you cross the Jordan, Simeon, Levi, Judah, Issachar, Joseph and Benjamin shall stand on Mount Gerizim*y* to pronounce blessings over the people, *13*while Reuben, Gad, Asher, Zebulun, Dan and Naphtali shall stand on Mount Ebal to pronounce curses.

The Twelve Curses. *14*"The Levites shall proclaim aloud to all the men of Israel: *15*'Cursed be the man who makes a carved or molten idol*z*—an abomination to the LORD, the product of a craftsman's hands—and sets it up in secret!' And all the people shall answer, 'Amen!'*

16'Cursed be he who dishonors his father or his mother!'*a* And all the people shall answer, 'Amen!'

17'Cursed be he who moves his neighbor's landmarks!'*b* And all the people shall answer, 'Amen!'

18'Cursed be he who misleads a blind man

26, 14: These are allusions to pagan religious practices.
27, 8: On the stones: cf vv 3f; not the stones of the altar.
27, 15-26: Amen: see note on Nm 5, 22.

t: Ex 24, 7.   *u:* 18f: Dt 7, 6; 14, 2; 28, 1; Ex 19, 5.   *v:* Jos 8, 32.   *w:* Ex 20, 25; Jos 8, 31.   *x:* Dt 26, 17ff.   *y:* 12f: Dt 11, 29; Jos 8, 33f.   *z:* Ex 20, 4. 23; Lv 19, 4; Wis 14, 8.   *a:* Dt 21, 18-21; Ex 21, 17; Lv 20, 9.   *b:* Dt 19, 14.

on his way!'*c* And all the people shall answer, 'Amen!'

¹⁹'Cursed be he who violates the rights of the alien, the orphan or the widow!'*d* And all the people shall answer, 'Amen!'

²⁰'Cursed be he who has relations with his father's wife, for he dishonors his father's bed!'*e* And all the people shall answer, 'Amen!'

²¹'Cursed be he who has relations with any animal!'*f* And all the people shall answer, 'Amen!'

²²'Cursed be he who has relations with his sister or his half-sister!'*g* And all the people shall answer, 'Amen!'

²³'Cursed be he who has relations with his mother-in-law!'*h* And all the people shall answer, 'Amen!'

²⁴'Cursed be he who slays his neighbor in secret!'*i* And all the people shall answer, 'Amen!'

²⁵'Cursed be he who accepts payment for slaying an innocent man!' And all the people shall answer, 'Amen!'

²⁶'Cursed be he who fails to fulfill any of the provisions of this law!'*j* And all the people shall answer, 'Amen!'

CHAPTER 28*

See RG 85-89

Blessings for Obedience. ¹"Thus, then,*k* shall it be:*l* if you continue to heed the voice of the LORD, your God, and are careful to observe all his commandments which I enjoin on you today, the LORD, your God, will raise you high above all the nations of the earth.*m* ²When you hearken to the voice of the LORD, your God, all these blessings will come upon you and overwhelm you:

³ "May you be blessed in the city,
　　and blessed in the country!
⁴ "Blessed be the fruit of your womb,

the produce of your soil and the
　　offspring of your livestock,
the issue of your herds and the young
　　of your flocks!*n*
⁵ "Blessed be your grain bin and your
　　kneading bowl!
⁶ "May you be blessed in your coming in,
　　and blessed in your going out!*

Victory and Prosperity. ⁷"The LORD will beat down before you the enemies that rise up against you; though they come out against you from but one direction, they will flee before you in seven.* ⁸The LORD will affirm his blessing upon you, on your barns and on all your undertakings, blessing you in the land that the LORD, your God, gives you. ⁹Provided that you keep the commandments of the LORD, your God, and walk in his ways, he will establish you as a people sacred to himself, as he swore to you;*o* ¹⁰so that, when all the nations of the earth see you bearing the name of the LORD,* they will stand in awe of you.*p* ¹¹The LORD will increase in more than goodly measure the fruit of your womb, the offspring of your livestock, and the produce of your soil, in the land which he swore to your fathers he would give you. ¹²The LORD will open up for you his rich treasure house of the heavens, to give your land rain in due season, blessing all your undertakings, so that you will lend to many nations and borrow from none.*q* ¹³The LORD will make you the head, not the tail,* and you will always mount higher and not decline, as long as you obey the commandments of the LORD, your God, which I order you today to observe carefully; ¹⁴not turning aside to the right or to the left from any of the commandments which I now give you, in order to follow other gods and serve them.

Curses for Disobedience. ¹⁵"But if you do not hearken to the voice of the LORD, your

---

28, 1-69: This chapter would read better immediately after chapter 26.

28, 6: In your coming in . . . in your going out: at the beginning and end of every action, or in all actions in general.

28, 7. 25: From but one direction . . . in seven: in one compact mass, contrasted with many scattered groups.

28, 10: You bearing the name of the LORD: literally, "The LORD's name is called over you," an expression signifying ownership and protection. Cf 2 Sm 12, 28; 1 Kgs 8, 43; Is 4, 1; 63, 19; Jer 7, 10f; 14, 9; 15, 16; 25, 29; Am 9, 12.

28, 13: The head, not the tail: in the honorable position as leader. Cf Is 9, 14; 19, 15.

c: Lv 19, 14.　*d:* Dt 24, 17; Ex 22, 21f.　*e:* Dt 22; 23, 1; Lv 18, 8; 20, 11.　*f:* Ex 22, 18; Lv 18, 23; 20, 15.　*g:* Lv 18, 9; 20, 17.　*h:* Lv 18, 17; 20, 14.　*i:* Ex 20, 13; 21, 12; Nm 35, 20f.　*j:* Gal 3, 10.　*k:* 1-68: Lv 26, 1-45.　*l:* 1-14: Dt 7, 12-16.　*m:* Dt 26, 19.　*n:* Dt 7, 13; 30, 9.　*o:* Dt 26, 18; Ex 19, 5f.　*p:* Dt 2, 25; 11, 25.　*q:* Dt 15, 6.

Curses

The preponderance of curses over blessings in Dt 28 emphasizes the urgent need to reform. Note how the curses in vv. 16–19 correspond to the blessings of vv. 3–6; vv. 23–24 oppose the blessing of v. 12; and vv. 43–44 counter vv. 12–13. In vv. 45–46, a temporary conclusion is reached, summing up both the cause and effect of this long litany (disobedience leads to destruction), but ever more curses follow.

God,[r] and are not careful to observe all his commandments which I enjoin on you today, all these curses shall come upon you and overwhelm you:

[16] "May you be cursed in the city,
and cursed in the country!

[17] "Cursed be your grain bin and your
kneading bowl!

[18] "Cursed be the fruit of your womb,
the produce of your soil and the
offspring of your livestock,
the issue of your herds and the young
of your flocks!

[19] "May you be cursed in your coming in,
and cursed in your going out!

Sickness and Defeat. [20]"The LORD will put a curse on you, defeat and frustration in every enterprise you undertake, until your are speedily destroyed and perish for the evil you have done in forsaking me. [21]The LORD will bring a pestilence upon you that will persist until he has exterminated you from the land you are entering to occupy. [22]The LORD will strike you with wasting and fever, with scorching, fiery drought, with blight and searing wind, that will plague you until you perish. [23]The sky over your heads will be like bronze and the earth under your feet like iron.[s] [24]For rain the LORD will give your land powdery dust, which will come down upon you from the sky until you are destroyed. [25]The LORD will let you be beaten down before your enemies; though you advance against them from one direction, you will flee before them in seven, so that you will become a terrifying example to all the kingdoms of the earth.[t] [26]Your carcasses will become food for all the birds of the air and for the beasts of the field, with no one to frighten them off. [27]The LORD will strike you with Egyptian boils[u] and with tumors, eczema and the itch, until you cannot be cured. [28]And the LORD will strike you with madness, blindness and panic, [29]so that even at midday you will grope like a blind man in the dark, unable to find your way.

Despoilment. "You will be oppressed and robbed continually, with no one to come to your aid. [30]Though you betroth a wife, another man will have her. Though you build a house, you will not live in it. Though you plant a vineyard, you will not enjoy its fruits. [31]Your ox will be slaughtered before your eyes, and you will not eat of its flesh. Your ass will be stolen in your presence, but you will not recover it. Your flocks will be given to your enemies, with no one to come to your aid. [32]Your sons and daughters will be given to a foreign nation while you look on and grieve for them in constant helplessness. [33]A people whom you do not know will consume the fruit of your soil and of all your labor, and you will be oppressed and crushed at all times without surcease, [34]until you are driven mad by what your eyes must look upon. [35]*The LORD will strike you with malignant boils of which you cannot be cured, on your knees and legs, and from the soles of your feet to the crown of your head.

Exile. [36]v"The LORD will bring you, and your king whom you have set over you, to a nation which you and your fathers have not

---

28, 35: This verse is best read with v 27.

r: Bar 1, 20; Dn 9, 11; Mal 2, 2.   s: 22f: Lv 26, 19.   t: Lv 26, 17. 37.   u: Ex 9, 9ff.   v: 1 Kgs 9, 7ff; 2 Chr 7, 20ff; 33, 11; 36, 6. 20.

known, and there you will serve strange gods of wood and stone, [37]and will call forth amazement, reproach and barbed scorn from all the nations to which the LORD will lead you.

Fruitless Labors. [38]"Though you spend much seed on your field, you will harvest but little, for the locusts will devour the crop.[w] [39]Though you plant and cultivate vineyards, you will not drink or store up the wine, for the grubs will eat the vines clean.[x] [40]Though you have olive trees throughout your country, you will have no oil for ointment, for your olives will drop off unripe.[y] [41]Though you beget sons and daughters, they will not remain with you, but will go into captivity.[z] [42]Buzzing insects will infest all your trees and the crops of your soil. [43]The alien residing among you will rise higher and higher above you, while you sink lower and lower. [44]He will lend to you, not you to him. He will become the head, you the tail.

[45]"All these curses will come upon you, pursuing you and overwhelming you, until you are destroyed, because you would not hearken to the voice of the LORD, your God, nor keep the commandments and statutes he gave you. [46]They will light on you and your descendants as a sign and a wonder* for all time. [47]Since you would not serve the LORD, your God, with joy and gratitude for abundance of every kind, [48]therefore in hunger and thirst, in nakedness and utter poverty, you will serve the enemies whom the LORD will send against you. He will put an iron yoke on your neck, until he destroys you.

Invasion and Siege. [49a]"The LORD will raise up against you a nation from afar, from the end of the earth, that swoops down like an eagle, a nation whose tongue you do not understand, [50]a nation of stern visage, that shows neither respect for the aged nor pity for the young. [51]They will consume the offspring of your livestock and the produce of your soil, until you are destroyed; they will leave you no grain or wine or oil, no issue of your herds or young of your flocks, until they have brought about your ruin. [52]They will besiege you in each of your communities, until the great, unscalable walls you trust in come tumbling down all over your land. They will so besiege you in every community throughout the land which the LORD, your God, has given you, [53]that in the distress of the siege to which your enemy subjects you, you will eat the fruit of your womb, the flesh of your own sons and daughters[b] whom the LORD, your God, has given you. [54]The most refined and fastidious man among you will begrudge his brother and his beloved wife and his surviving children [55]any share in the flesh of his children that he himself is using for food when nothing else is left him in the straits of the siege to which your enemy will subject you in all your communities. [56]The most refined and delicate woman among you, so delicate and refined that she would not venture to set the sole of her foot on the ground, will begrudge her beloved husband and her son and daughter [57]the afterbirth that issues from her womb and the infant she brings forth when she secretly uses them for food for want of anything else, in the straits of the siege to which your enemy will subject you in your communities.

Plagues. [58]"If you are not careful to observe every word of the law which is written in this book, and to revere the glorious and awesome name of the LORD, your God, [59]he will smite you and your descendants with severe and constant blows, malignant and lasting maladies. [60]He will again afflict you with all the diseases of Egypt* which you dread, and they will persist among you.[c] [61]Should there be any kind of sickness or calamity not mentioned in this book of the law, that too the LORD will bring upon you until you are destroyed. [62]Of you who were numerous as the stars in the sky,[d] only a few

---

28, 46: A sign and a wonder: an ominous example, attracting attention; cf Dt 29, 21-28.

28, 60: He will again afflict you with all the diseases of Egypt: such as the Lord had promised to remove from his people; cf Dt 7, 15.

---

w: Mi 6, 15; Hg 1, 6.   x: Zep 1, 13.   y: Mi 6, 15.   z: Lam 1, 5.   a: 49-52: Jer 5, 15ff; Bar 4, 15f.   b: Lv 26, 29; 2 Kgs 6, 28f; Jer 19, 9; Lam 4, 10; Bar 2, 3.   c: Dt 28, 27.   d: Dt 1, 10; Jer 42, 2.

will be left, because you would not hearken to the voice of the LORD, your God.

Exile. ⁶³"Just as the LORD once took delight in making you grow and prosper,ᵉ so will he now take delight in ruining and destroying you, and you will be plucked out of the land you are now entering to occupy. ⁶⁴The LORD will scatter you among all the nations from one end of the earth to the other,ᶠ and there you will serve strange gods of wood and stone, such as you and your fathers have not known. ⁶⁵Among these nations you will find no repose, not a foot of ground to stand upon, for there the LORD will give you an anguished heart and wasted eyes* and a dismayed spirit. ⁶⁶You will live in constant suspense and stand in dread both day and night, never sure of your existence. ⁶⁷In the morning you will say, 'Would that it were evening!' and in the evening you will say, 'Would that it were morning!' for the dread that your heart must feel and the sight that your eyes must see. ⁶⁸The LORD will send you back in galleys* to Egypt, to the region I told you that you were never to see again;ᵍ and there you will offer yourselves for sale to your enemies as male and female slaves, but there will be no buyer."

⁶⁹These are the words of the covenant which the LORD ordered Moses to make with the Israelites in the land of Moab, in addition to the covenant which he made with them at Horeb.

CHAPTER 29

See RG 85–89

Past Favors Recalled. ¹Moses summoned all Israel and said to them, "You have seen all that the LORD did in the land of Egypt before your very eyes to Pharaoh and all his servants and to all his land; ²the great testings your own eyes have seen, and those great signs and wonders.ʰ ³But not even at the present day has the LORD yet given you a mind to understand, or eyes to see, or ears to

hear.* ⁴'I led you for forty years in the desert.ⁱ Your clothes did not fall from you in tatters nor your sandals from your feet; ⁵bread was not your food, nor wine or beer your drink. Thus you should know that I, the LORD, am your God.' ⁶ʲWhen we came to this place, Sihon, king of Heshbon, and Og, king of Bashan, came out to engage us in battle, but we defeated them ⁷and took over their land, which we then gave as a heritage to the Reubenites, Gadites, and half the tribe of Manasseh.ᵏ ⁸Keep the terms of this covenant, therefore, and fulfill them, that you may succeed in whatever you do.

All Israel Bound to the Covenant. ⁹"You are all now standing before the LORD, your God—your chiefs and judges, your elders and officials, and all of the men of Israel, ¹⁰together with your wives and children and the aliens who live in your camp, down to those who hew wood and draw water for you— ¹¹that you may enter into the covenant of the LORD, your God, which he concluded with you today under this sanction of a curse;* ¹²so that he may now establish you as his people and he may be your God, as he promised you and as he swore to your fathers Abraham, Isaac and Jacob. ¹³But it is not with you alone that I am making this covenant, under this sanction of a curse; ¹⁴it is just as much with those who are not here among us* today as it is with those of us who are now here present before the LORD, our God.

Warning against Idolatry. ¹⁵"You know in what surroundings we lived in the land of Egypt and what we passed by in the nations we traversed, ¹⁶and you saw the loathsome idols of wood and stone, of gold and silver, that they possess. ¹⁷Let there be, then, no man or woman, no clan or tribe among you, who would now turn away their hearts from the LORD, our God, to go and serve these pagan gods! Let there be no root that would bear such poison and wormwood among

---

28, 65: Wasted eyes: worn out and disappointed in their longing gaze.

28, 68: In galleys: in the ships of the Phoenician slave traders (Ez 27, 13; Jl 4, 6; Am 1, 9), who also dealt with Egypt (Is 23, 3).

29, 3: Eyes to see . . . ears to hear: with inner, spiritual discernment. Cf Mt 13, 43.

29, 11: Sanction of a curse: the present pact binds under penalty of the curses mentioned in this book. Cf v 20.

29, 14: Not here among us: this includes their descendants.

e: Dt 30, 9. f: Lv 26, 33. g: Hos 8, 13; 9, 3. h: Dt 4, 34; Ex 19, 4. i: Dt 8, 2. 4. j: Dt 2, 24. 32; 3, 1; Nm 21, 33ff. k: Dt 3, 16; Nm 32, 33.

you! *18*If any such person, upon hearing the words of this curse, should beguile himself into thinking that he can safely persist in his stubbornness of heart, as though to sweep away both the watered soil and the parched ground,* *19*the LORD will never consent to pardon him. Instead, the LORD's wrath and jealousy will flare up against that man, and every curse mentioned in this book will alight on him. The LORD will blot out his name from under the heavens *20*and will single him out from all the tribes of Israel for doom, in keeping with all the curses of the covenant inscribed in this book of the law.

Punishment for Infidelity. *21*"Future generations, your own descendants who will rise up after you, as well as the foreigners who will come here from far-off lands, when they see the calamities of this land and the ills with which the LORD has smitten it— *22*all its soil being nothing but sulphur and salt, a burnt-out waste, unsown and unfruitful, without a blade of grass, destroyed like Sodom and Gomorrah,*l* Admah and Zeboiim, which the LORD overthrew in his furious wrath— *23*they and all the nations will ask, 'Why has the LORD dealt thus with this land? Why this fierce outburst of wrath?'*m* *24*And the answer will be, 'Because they forsook the covenant which the LORD, the God of their fathers, had made with them when he brought them out of the land of Egypt, *25*and they went and served other gods and adored them, gods whom they did not know and whom he had not let fall to their lot: *26*that is why the LORD was angry with this land and brought on it all the imprecations listed in this book; *27*in his furious wrath and tremendous anger the LORD uprooted them from their soil and cast them out into a strange land,*n* where they are today.' *28*[Both what is still hidden* and what has already been revealed concern us and our descendants forever, that we may carry out all the words of this law.]

CHAPTER 30

See RG 85–89

Mercy for the Repentant. *1*"When all these things which I have set before you, the blessings and the curses, are fulfilled in you,*o* and from among whatever nations the LORD, your God, may have dispersed you, you ponder them in your heart: *2*then, provided that you and your children return to the LORD, your God, and heed his voice with all your heart and all your soul,*p* just as I now command you, *3*the LORD, your God, will change your lot; and taking pity on you, he will again gather you from all the nations wherein he has scattered you. *4*Though you may have been driven to the farthest corner of the world, even from there will the LORD, your God, gather you; even from there will he bring you back. *5*The LORD, your God, will then bring you into the land which your fathers once occupied, that you too may occupy it, and he will make you more prosperous and numerous than your fathers. *6*The LORD, your God, will circumcise your hearts* and the hearts of your descendants,*q* that you may love the LORD, your God, with all your heart and all your soul, and so may live. *7*But all those curses the LORD, your God, will assign to your enemies and the foes who persecuted you. *8*You, however, must again heed the LORD's voice and carry out all his commandments which I now enjoin on you. *9*Then the LORD, your God, will increase in more than goodly measure the returns from all your labors, the fruit of your womb, the offspring of your livestock, and the produce of your soil;*r* for the LORD, your God, will again take delight in your prosperity, even as he took delight in your fathers', *10*if only you heed the voice of the LORD, your God, and keep his commandments and statutes that are written in this book of the law, when you return to the LORD, your God, with all your heart and all your soul.

29, 18: To sweep away both the watered soil and the parched ground: apparently a proverb signifying that such an unfaithful Israelite will cause God to punish the good with the wicked, to root out the good plants growing in irrigated soil, together with the worthless plants growing in the dry ground.

29, 28: What is still hidden: the events of the future. What has already been revealed: God's law and the punishments in store for those who break it. Leave the future to God; our business is to keep his law.

30, 6: Circumcise your hearts: see note on Dt 10, 16.

l: Gn 14, 10f; 19, 24f. *m:* 23f: 1 Kgs 9, 8f; Jer 22, 8f. *n:* Dn 9, 11-14. *o:* Dt 11, 26ff. *p:* 2f: Neh 1, 9. *q:* Dt 6, 5. *r:* Dt 28, 11.

God's Command Clear. [11]*"For this command which I enjoin on you today is not too mysterious and remote for you. [12]It is not up in the sky, that you should say, 'Who will go up in the sky to get it for us and tell us of it, that we may carry it out?' [13]Nor is it across the sea, that you should say, 'Who will cross the sea to get it for us and tell us of it, that we may carry it out?' [14]No, it is something very near to you, already in your mouths* and in your hearts; you have only to carry it out.

The Choice before Israel. [15]"Here, then, I have today set before you life and prosperity, death and doom. [16]If you obey the commandments of the LORD, your God, which I enjoin on you today, loving him, and walking in his ways, and keeping his commandments, statutes and decrees, you will live and grow numerous, and the LORD, your God, will bless you in the land you are entering to occupy. [17]If, however, you turn away your hearts and will not listen, but are led astray and adore and serve other gods, [18]I tell you now that you will certainly perish; you will not have a long life on the land which you are crossing the Jordan to enter and occupy. [19]I call heaven and earth today to witness against you:[s] I have set before you life and death, the blessing and the curse.[t] Choose life, then, that you and your descendants may live, [20]by loving the LORD, your God, heeding his voice, and holding fast to him. For that will mean life for you, a long life for you to live on the land which the LORD swore he would give to your fathers Abraham, Isaac and Jacob."

See RG
85–89

CHAPTER 31

The Lord's Leadership. [1]When Moses had finished speaking these words to all Israel, [2]he said to them, "I am now one hundred and twenty years old[u] and am no longer able to move about freely; besides, the LORD has told me that I shall not cross this Jordan. [3]It is the LORD your God, who will cross before you; he will destroy these nations before you, that you may supplant them.[v] [It is Joshua who will cross before you, as the LORD promised.] [4w]The LORD will deal with them just as he dealt with Sihon and Og, the kings of the Amorites whom he destroyed, and with their country. [5]When, therefore, the LORD delivers them up to you, you must deal with them exactly as I have ordered you.[x] [6]Be brave and steadfast; have no fear or dread of them, for it is the LORD, your God, who marches with you; he will never fail you or forsake you."[y]

Call of Joshua. [7]Then Moses summoned Joshua and in the presence of all Israel said to him,[z] "Be brave and steadfast, for you must bring this people into the land which the LORD swore to their fathers he would give them; you must put them in possession of their heritage. [8]It is the LORD who marches before you; he will be with you and will never fail you or forsake you. So do not fear or be dismayed."

The Reading of the Law. [9]When Moses had written down this law, he entrusted it to the levitical priests who carry the ark of the covenant of the LORD, and to all the elders of Israel, [10]giving them this order: "On the feast of Booths,[a] at the prescribed time in the year of relaxation* which comes at the end of every seven-year period, [11]when all Israel goes to appear before the LORD, your God, in the place which he chooses, you shall read this law* aloud in the presence of all Israel. [12]Assemble the people—men, women and children, as well as the aliens who live in your communities—that they may hear it and learn it, and so fear the LORD, your God, and carefully observe all the words of this law. [13]Their children also, who do not know it yet, must hear it and learn it, that they too may fear the LORD, your God, as long as you

---

30, 11-14: God has revealed his will so clearly that ignorance of his law can be no excuse. St. Paul in Rom 10, 6-10, applies these words to the ease with which we can come to faith and salvation in Christ.

30, 14: In your mouths: that you may readily talk about it; cf Dt 6, 7; 11, 19. And in your hearts: that you may easily remember it; cf Dt 6, 6; 11, 18.

31, 10: The year of relaxation: cf Dt 15, 1ff and the note there.

31, 11ff: Reading the law not only instructed the people but also consoled them by the assurance of the divine goodness.

s: Dt 4, 26.   *t:* Dt 11, 26ff; 28, 2. 15.   *u:* Dt 34, 7; Nm 20, 12.   *v:* Dt 9, 3.   *w:* Nm 21, 21-35.   *x:* Dt 7, 2.   *y:* Dt 20, 3f.   *z:* 7f: Jos 1, 6f. 9.   *a:* 10f: Dt 16, 13ff.

Covenant Responsibility

Stipulating that the Torah is taught to women, minors, and aliens (Dt 29, 10), the law does not restrict the responsibility to observe the covenant to males (contrast Ex 19, 15).

live on the land which you will cross the Jordan to occupy."

Commission of Joshua. [14]The LORD said to Moses, "The time is now approaching for you to die. Summon Joshua, and present yourselves at the meeting tent that I may give him his commission." So Moses and Joshua went and presented themselves at the meeting tent.* [15]And the LORD appeared at the tent in a column of cloud, which stood still at the entrance of the tent.

A Command to Moses. [16]The LORD said to Moses, "Soon you will be at rest with your fathers, and then this people will take to rendering wanton worship to the strange gods among whom they will live in the land they are about to enter.[b] They will forsake me and break the covenant which I have made with them. [17]At that time my anger will flare up against them; I will forsake them and hide my face from them, so that they will become a prey to be devoured, and many evils and troubles will befall them. At that time they will indeed say, 'Is it not because our God is not among us that these evils have befallen us?' [18]Yet I will be hiding my face from them at that time only because of all the evil they have done in turning to other gods. [19]Write out this song,[c] then, for yourselves. Teach it to the Israelites and have them recite it, so that this song may be a witness for me against the Israelites. [20]For when I have brought them into the land flowing with milk and honey which I promised on oath to their fathers, and they have eaten their fill and grown fat, if they turn to other gods and serve them, despising me and breaking my covenant; [21]then, when many evils and troubles befall them, this song, which their descendants will not have forgotten to recite, will bear witness against them. For I know what they are inclined to do even

at the present time, before I have brought them into the land which I promised on oath to their fathers." [22]So Moses wrote this song that same day, and he taught it to the Israelites.

Commission of Joshua. [23]Then the LORD commissioned Joshua, son of Nun, and said to him, "Be brave and steadfast, for it is you who must bring the Israelites into the land which I promised them on oath.[d] I myself will be with you."

The Law Placed in the Ark. [24]When Moses had finished writing out on a scroll the words of the law in their entirety, [25]he gave the Levites[e] who carry the ark of the covenant of the LORD this order: [26]"Take this scroll of the law and put it beside the ark of the covenant of the LORD, your God, that there it may be a witness against you. [27]For I already know how rebellious and stiff-necked you will be. Why, even now, while I am alive among you, you have been rebels against the LORD! How much more, then, after I am dead! [28f]Therefore, assemble all your tribal elders and your officials before me, that I may speak these words for them to hear, and so may call heaven and earth to witness against them. [29g]For I know that after my death you are sure to become corrupt and to turn aside from the way along which I directed you, so that evil will befall you in some future age because you have done evil in the LORD's sight, and provoked him by your deeds."

The Song of Moses. [30]Then Moses recited the words of this song from beginning to end, for the whole assembly of Israel to hear:

CHAPTER 32

A

[1] Give ear, O heavens, while I speak;*
 let the earth hearken to the words of
  my mouth!

See RG 85–89

31, 14f. 23: V 23 is best read immediately after v 15; perhaps the original order was vv 7-8. 14-15. 23.

32, 1-43: In the style of the great prophets, the speaker is often God himself. The whole song is a poetic sermon, having for its theme God's benefits to Israel (vv 1-14) and Is-

b: Jgs 2, 12. 17.   c: Dt 31, 21; 32, 1-43.   d: Dt 31, 7f; Jos 1, 5ff.   e: 24f: Dt 31, 9.   f: Dt 32, 1-43.   g: Jgs 2, 19.

2 May my instruction soak in like the rain,
and my discourse permeate like the
dew,
Like a downpour upon the grass,
like a shower upon the crops:
3 For I will sing the LORD's renown.
Oh, proclaim the greatness of our God!
4 The Rock—how faultless are his deeds,
how right all his ways!
A faithful God, without deceit,
how just and upright he is!*h*

5 Yet basely has he been treated by his
degenerate children,
a perverse and crooked race!*i*
6 Is the LORD to be thus repaid by you,
O stupid and foolish people?
Is he not your father who created you?
Has he not made you and established
you?*j*

7 Think back on the days of old,
reflect on the years of age upon age.
Ask your father and he will inform you,
ask your elders and they will tell you:*k*
8 When the Most High assigned the
nations their heritage,
when he parceled out the descendants
of Adam,*l*
He set up the boundaries of the peoples
after the number of the sons of
God;*
9 While the LORD's own portion was
Jacob,
his hereditary share was Israel.*m*

10 He found them in a wilderness,
a wasteland of howling desert.
He shielded them and cared for them,
guarding them as the apple of his eye.*n*

11 As an eagle incites its nestlings forth
by hovering over its brood,
So he spread his wings to receive them
and bore them up on his pinions.*o*
12 The LORD alone was their leader,
no strange god was with him.
13 He had them ride triumphant over the
summits of the land*
and live off the products of its fields,
Giving them honey to suck from its rocks
and olive oil from its hard, stony
ground;

14 Butter from its cows and milk from its
sheep,
with the fat of its lambs and rams;
Its Bashan* bulls and its goats,
with the cream of its finest wheat;
and the foaming blood of its grapes
you drank.

B

15 [So Jacob ate his fill,]
the darling* grew fat and frisky;
you became fat and gross and gorged.
They spurned the God who made them
and scorned their saving Rock.*p*
16 They provoked him with strange gods
and angered him with abominable
idols.*q*
17 They offered sacrifice to demons, to
"no-gods,"
to gods whom they had not known
before,
To newcomers just arrived,
of whom their fathers had never stood
in awe.
18 You were unmindful of the Rock that
begot you,

rael's ingratitude and idolatry in turning to the gods of the
pagans, which sins will be punished by the pagans themselves (vv 15-29); in turn, the foolish pride of the pagans
will be punished, and the Lord's honor will be vindicated
(vv 30-43).

32, 8: The sons of God: the angels; cf Jb 1, 6; 2, 1; 38,
7; Ps 89, 7f. Here the various nations are portrayed as
having their respective guardian angels. Cf Dn 10, 20f;
12, 1.

32, 13: The land: Canaan.

32, 14: Bashan: a fertile grazing land east of the Jordan,

famous for its strong cattle. Cf Ps 22, 13; Ez 39, 18;
Am 4, 1.

32, 15: The darling: a probable meaning of the Hebrew
word yeshurun, a term of endearment for "Israel." Cf Dt 33,
5. 26; Is 44, 2.

h: Ps 92, 15; Rv 15, 3. *i:* Dt 31, 29; Ps 78, 8; Lk 9, 41. *j:* Ex 4,
22; Is 63, 16; 64, 8; Jer 31, 9. *k:* Dt 4, 32; Ps 44, 2. *l:* Gn 10,
1-32; Acts 17, 26. *m:* Ex 19, 5; Ps 33, 12. *n:* Dt 8, 15; Jer 2, 6;
Zec 2, 8. *o:* Ex 19, 4. *p:* Dt 31, 20. *q:* Nm 25, 2f; Ps 78, 58.

You forgot the God who gave you
birth.[r]

19 When the LORD saw this, he was filled
with loathing
and anger toward his sons and
daughters.

20 "I will hide my face from them," he said,
"and see what will then become of
them.
What a fickle race they are,
sons with no loyalty in them![s]

21 "Since they have provoked me with their
'no god'
and angered me with their vain idols,
I will provoke them with a 'no-people';
with a foolish nation I will anger
them.[t]

22 "For by my wrath a fire is enkindled
that shall rage to the depths of the
netherworld,
Consuming the earth with its yield,
and licking with flames the roots of
the mountains.[u]

23 I will spend on them woe upon woe
and exhaust all my arrows against
them:

24 "Emaciating hunger and consuming fever
and bitter pestilence,
And the teeth of wild beasts I will send
among them,
with the venom of reptiles gliding in
the dust.

25 "Snatched away by the sword in the
street
and by sheer terror at home
Shall be the youth and the maiden alike,
the nursing babe as well as the hoary
old man.[v]

26 "I would have said, 'I will make an end
of them
and blot out their name from men's
memories,'

27 Had I not feared the insolence of their
enemies,
feared that these foes would
mistakenly boast,
'Our own hand won the victory;
the LORD had nothing to do with it.' "

28 For they are a people devoid of reason,[*]
having no understanding.

29 If they had insight they would realize
what happened,
they would understand their future and
say,

C

30 "How could one man rout a thousand,
or two men put ten thousand to flight,
Unless it was because their Rock sold
them
and the LORD delivered them up?"

31 Indeed, their "rock" is not like our Rock,
and our foes are under condemnation.

32 They are a branch of Sodom's
vine-stock,
from the vineyards of Gomorrah.
Poisonous are their grapes
and bitter their clusters.

33 Their wine is the venom of dragons
and the cruel poison of cobras.

34 "Is not this preserved in my treasury,
sealed up in my storehouse,

35 Against the day of vengeance and
requital,
against the time they lose their
footing?"
Close at hand is the day of their disaster,
and their doom is rushing upon them!

36 Surely, the LORD shall do justice for his
people;
on his servants he shall have pity.
When he sees their strength failing,
and their protected and unprotected[*]
alike disappearing,[w]

32, 28-35: The reference is to the pagan nations, not to Israel.
32, 36: Their protected and unprotected: the meaning of the Hebrew is uncertain; according to some, the idea is "slaves and freemen."

r: Jer 2, 32.   s: Dt 31, 17.   t: Rom 10, 19.   u: Lam 4, 11.   v: Lv 26, 25.   w: 2 Mc 7, 6.

250

³⁷ He will say, "Where are their gods*
    whom they relied on as their 'rock'?
³⁸ Let those who ate the fat of your sacrifices
    and drank the wine of your libations
Rise up now and help you!
    Let them be your protection!

³⁹ "Learn then that I, I alone, am God,
    and there is no god besides me.
It is I who bring both death and life,
    I who inflict wounds and heal them,
    and from my hand there is no rescue.*

⁴⁰ "To the heavens I raise my hand and swear:
    As surely as I live forever,

⁴¹ I will sharpen my flashing sword,
    and my hand shall lay hold of my quiver.

"With vengeance I will repay my foes
    and requite those who hate me.
⁴² I will make my arrows drunk with blood,
    and my sword shall gorge itself with
        flesh—
With the blood of the slain and the
        captured,
    Flesh from the heads of the enemy
        leaders."

⁴³ Exult with him, you heavens,
    glorify him, all you angels of God;
For he avenges the blood of his servants
    and purges his people's land.

⁴⁴ So Moses, together with Joshua, son of
Nun, went and recited all the words of this
song for the people to hear.

Final Appeal. ⁴⁵ When Moses had finished
speaking all these words to all Israel, ⁴⁶ he
said,² "Take to heart all the warning which I
have now given you and which you must impress on your children, that you may carry
out carefully every word of this law. ⁴⁷ For
this is no trivial matter for you; rather, it

means your very life, since it is by this means
that you are to enjoy a long life on the land
which you will cross the Jordan to occupy."

Moses to View Canaan. ⁴⁸ On that very
day the LORD said to Moses, ⁴⁹ "Go up on
Mount Nebo, here in the Abarim Mountains
[it is in the land of Moab facing Jericho], and
view the land of Canaan, which I am giving
to the Israelites as their possession.ᵃ ⁵⁰ Then
you shall die on the mountain you have
climbed, and shall be taken to your people,
just as your brother Aaron died on Mount
Hor and there was taken to his people;ᵇ ⁵¹ because both of you broke faith with me
among the Israelites at the waters of Meribath-kadesh in the desert of Zin by failing to
manifest my sanctity among the Israelites.ᶜ
⁵² You may indeed view the land at a distance, but you shall not enter that land which
I am giving to the Israelites."ᵈ

CHAPTER 33

Blessing upon the Tribes. ¹ This is the
blessing which Moses, the man of God, pronounced upon the Israelites before he died.
² He said:

See RG
85–89

"The LORD came from Sinai*
    and dawned on his people from Seir;
He shone forth from Mount Paran
    and advanced from Meribath-kadesh,
While at his right hand a fire blazed forth
    and his wrath devastated the nations.ᵉ
³ But all his holy ones were in his hand;*
    they followed at his feet
    and he bore them up on his pinions.
⁴ A law he gave to us;
    he made the community of Jacob his
        domain,ᶠ
⁵   and he became king of his darling,*
When the chiefs of the people assembled
    and the tribes of Israel came together.
⁶ "May Reuben live and not die out,ᵍ
    but let his men be few."*

33, 2-5. 26-29: These verses seem to form an independent
hymn describing, in the form of a theophany, the conquest of
Canaan. The first section of this hymn (vv 2-5) serves here as
an introduction to the various "blessings"; the second section
(vv 26-29), as their conclusion.

33, 3: His holy ones were in his hand: the Israelites were
protected by the Lord.

33, 5. 26: The darling: see note on Dt 32, 15.

33, 6: In keeping with the other blessings, probably this
verse was once introduced by the phrase, "Of Reuben he said."
It is to be noted that there is no blessing here for Simeon.

---

x: 37f: Jgs 10, 14; Jer 2, 28. y: Dt 4, 35; Tb 13, 2; Wis 16, 13.
z: Dt 4, 9. a: Nm 27, 12; 33, 47f. b: Nm 20, 24ff. 28; 27, 13;
33, 38. c: Nm 20, 12; 27, 14. d: Dt 3, 27; 34, 4. e: Ex 19, 18.
20; Jgs 5, 4f. f: Jn 1, 17; 7, 19. g: Gn 49, 3f.

7 The following is for Judah. He said:
"The LORD hears the cry of Judah;
    you will bring him to his people.*
His own hands defend his cause
    and you will be his help against his
        foes."[h]

8 Of Levi he said:
"To Levi belong your Thummim,
    to the man of your favor your Urim;*
For you put him to the test at Massah
    and you contended with him at the
        waters of Meribah.[i]
9 He said of his father, 'I regard him not';
    his brothers he would not
        acknowledge,
    and his own children he refused to
        recognize.
Thus the Levites keep your words,
    and your covenant they uphold.*
10 They promulgate your decisions to Jacob
    and your law to Israel.
They bring the smoke of sacrifice to your
        nostrils,
    and burnt offerings to your altar.[j]
11 Bless, O LORD, his possessions
    and accept the ministry of his hands.
Break the backs of his adversaries
    and of his foes, that they may not rise."

12 Of Benjamin he said:
"Benjamin is the beloved of the LORD,
    who shelters him all the day,
    while he abides securely at his
        breast."[k]

13 Of Joseph he said:[l]
"Blessed by the LORD is his land
    with the best of the skies above
    and of the abyss crouching beneath;

14 With the best of the produce of the year,
    and the choicest sheaves of the
        months;
15 With the finest gifts of the age-old
        mountains
    and the best from the timeless hills;
16 With the best of the earth and its fullness,
    and the favor of him who dwells in the
        bush.*
These shall come upon the head of
        Joseph
    and upon the brow of the prince
        among his brothers,
17 The majestic bull, his father's first-born,
    whose horns are those of the wild ox
With which to gore the nations,
    even those at the ends of the earth."
[These are the myriads of Ephraim,
    and these the thousands of Manasseh.]

18 Of Zebulun he said:[m]
"Rejoice, O Zebulun, in your pursuits,
    and you, Issachar, in your tents!
19 You who invite the tribes to the
        mountains
    where feasts are duly held,
Because you suck up the abundance of
        the seas*
    and the hidden treasures of the sand."

20 Of Gad he said:[n]
"Blessed be he who has made Gad so vast!
He lies there like a lion
    that has seized the arm and head of the
        prey.
21 He saw that the best should be his
    when the princely portion* was
        assigned,
    while the heads of the people were
        gathered.

33, 7: Bring him to his people: this probably refers to the isolated position of the tribe of Judah during the conquest of the Promised Land (cf Jgs 1, 17-19); according to some commentators the reference is to the divided kingdom.

33, 8: Thummim . . . Urim: see note on Ex 28, 30.

33, 9: The reference is probably to the Levites' slaughter of their brethren after the affair of the golden calf in the desert; cf Ex 32, 27-29.

33, 16: Him who dwells in the bush: a title given to the Lord because of his appearance to Moses in the burning bush; cf Ex 3.

33, 19: The abundance of the seas: perhaps the wealth that

comes from sea-borne trade or from fishing. The hidden treasures of the sand: possibly an allusion to the valuable purple dye extracted from certain marine shells found on the coast of northern Palestine.

33, 21: The princely portion: Moses gave the tribe of Gad their land on the east of the Jordan only on condition that they would help the other tribes conquer the land west of the river; cf Nm 32; Jos 22.

h: Gn 49, 8-12.   i: Gn 49, 5; Ex 17, 7; 28, 30; Nm 20, 13.   j: Ex 30, 7f.   k: Gn 49, 27.   l: 13-17: Gn 49, 22-26.   m: 18f: Gn 49, 13ff.   n: 20f: Gn 49, 19.

He carried out the justice of the
LORD
and his decrees respecting Israel."*o*

22 Of Dan he said:
"Dan is a lion's whelp,*p*
that springs forth from Bashan!"*

23 Of Naphtali he said:
"Naphtali is enriched with favors
and filled with the blessings of the
LORD;
The lake* and south of it are his
possession!"*q*

24 Of Asher he said:*r*
"More blessed than the other sons be
Asher!
May he be the favorite among his
brothers,
as the oil of his olive trees runs over
his feet!*

25 May your bolts be of iron and bronze;
may your strength endure through all
your days!"

26 "There is no god like the God of the
darling,
who rides the heavens in his power,
and rides the skies in his majesty;

27 He spread out the primeval tent;
he extended the ancient canopy.
He drove the enemy out of your way
and the Amorite he destroyed.

28 Israel has dwelt securely,
and the fountain of Jacob has been
undisturbed.
In a land of grain and wine,
where the heavens drip with dew.*s*

29 How fortunate you are, O Israel!
Where else is a nation victorious in the
LORD?
The LORD is your saving shield,

and his sword is your glory.
Your enemies fawn upon you,
as you stride upon their heights."*t*

CHAPTER 34

See RG
85–89

Death and Burial of Moses. *1*Then
Moses went up from the plains of Moab to
Mount Nebo,*u* the headland of Pisgah which
faces Jericho, and the LORD showed him all
the land—Gilead, and as far as Dan, *2*all
Naphtali, the land of Ephraim and Manasseh, all the land of Judah as far as the Western Sea, *3*the Negeb, the circuit of the Jordan
with the lowlands at Jericho, city of palms,
and as far as Zoar. *4*The LORD then said to
him, "This is the land*v* which I swore to
Abraham, Isaac and Jacob that I would give
to their descendants. I have let you feast
your eyes upon it, but you shall not cross
over." *5*So there, in the land of Moab, Moses,
the servant of the LORD, died*w* as the LORD
had said; *6*and he was buried in the ravine
opposite Beth-peor in the land of Moab, but
to this day no one knows the place of his burial. *7*Moses was one hundred and twenty
years old*x* when he died, yet his eyes were
undimmed and his vigor unabated. *8*For
thirty days the Israelites wept for Moses in
the plains of Moab, till they had completed
the period of grief and mourning for Moses.

*9*Now Joshua, son of Nun,*y* was filled with
the spirit of wisdom, since Moses had laid
his hands upon him; and so the Israelites
gave him their obedience, thus carrying out
the LORD's command to Moses.

*10z*Since then no prophet has arisen in Israel like Moses, whom the LORD knew face
to face. *11a*He had no equal in all the signs
and wonders the LORD sent him to perform
in the land of Egypt against Pharaoh and all
his servants and against all his land, *12*and
for the might and the terrifying power that
Moses exhibited in the sight of all Israel.

33, 22: The sense is, "May he leap up like a lion of Bashan"; the heavily wooded hills of Bashan were notorious for their lions, but the tribe of Dan was not settled in this region.

33, 23: The lake: the Lake of Gennesaret on which the land of this tribe bordered.

33, 24: The land of the tribe of Asher was covered with olive groves.

---

o: Nm 32, 1. 5. 16-19. 31f; Jos 1, 12-15; 1 Chr 5, 18-22. *p:* Gn 49, 16f. *q:* Gn 49, 21; Jos 19, 32-39. *r:* 24f: Gn 49, 20. *s:* Gn 27, 28. *t:* Dt 4, 7f. *u:* Dt 3, 27. *v:* Dt 3, 27; 32, 52; Gn 12, 7; 15, 18. *w:* Dt 32, 50. *x:* Dt 31, 2. *y:* Nm 27, 18. 23; Jos 1, 17. *z:* Ex 33, 11. *a:* Dt 4, 34.

See RG
93–99

The Book of Joshua

The Book of Joshua derives its name from the successor of Moses, with whose deeds it is principally concerned. The purpose of the book is to demonstrate God's fidelity in giving to the Israelites the land he had promised them for an inheritance (Gn 15, 18ff; Jos 1, 2ff; 21, 41ff; 23, 14ff).

Their occupation of the country is begun with the crossing of the Jordan and the conquest of Jericho (ch 1–6), in both of which the LORD intervenes on their behalf. This is followed by a first foothold on the Palestinian mountain range, at Ai, Bethel and Gibeon (ch 7–9), and two sweeping campaigns against the city-states in the south of the country (ch 10) and in the north (ch 11), with a summary in Jos 12. The broad claim to total sovereignty thus established is spelled out by a combined list of tribal boundaries and of the towns contained within each area or administrative district (ch 13–19), including cities of asylum and cities for the Levites (ch 20, 21). The book closes with a narrative about the tribes east of the Jordan (ch 22), a warning speech by Joshua (ch 23), and a renewal at Shechem (ch 24) of the covenant with the LORD, already affirmed there near the beginning (8, 30-35) of the conquest.

Like the books which precede it, the Book of Joshua was built up by a long and complex process of editing traditional materials. Both Jewish and Christian believers have always regarded it as inspired.

The entire history of the conquest of the Promised Land is a prophecy of the spiritual conquest of the world through the Church under the leadership of Jesus the Messiah.

The Book of Joshua may be divided as follows:

I: Conquest of Canaan

CHAPTER 1

See RG
94

Divine Promise of Assistance. [1]After Moses, the servant of the LORD, had died, the LORD said to Moses' aid Joshua, son of Nun: [2]"My servant Moses is dead. So prepare to cross the Jordan here, with all the people, into the land I will give the Israelites. [3]As I promised Moses, I will deliver to you every place where you set foot. [4]*Your domain is to be all the land of the Hittites, from the desert and from Lebanon east to the great river Euphrates and west to the Great Sea.[a] [5]No one can withstand you while you live. I will be with you as I was with Moses:[b] I will not leave you nor forsake you. [6]Be firm and steadfast, so that you may give this people possession of the land which I swore to their fathers I would give them. [7]Above all, be firm and steadfast, taking care to observe the entire law which my servant Moses enjoined on you. Do not swerve from it either to the right or to the left, that you may succeed wherever you go. [8]Keep this book of the law on your lips. Recite it by day and by night, that you may observe carefully all that is written in it; then you will successfully attain your goal. [9]I command you: be firm and steadfast! Do not fear nor be dismayed, for the LORD, your God, is with you wherever you go."[c]

[10]So Joshua commanded the officers of the people: [11]"Go through the camp and instruct the people, 'Prepare your provisions, for three days from now you shall cross the Jordan here, to march in and take possession of the land which the LORD, your God, is giving you.' "[d]

The Transjordan Tribes. [12]Joshua reminded the Reubenites, the Gadites, and the half-tribe of Manasseh: [13]"Remember what

---

1, 4: The ideal frontiers are given: in the south the desert of Sinai, in the north the Lebanon range, in the east the Euphrates, and in the west the Great Sea, the Mediterranean.

a: 3f: Jos 14, 9; Gn 15, 18; Dt 11, 24.   *b:* Dt 31, 8; Heb 13, 5.   *c:* 7. 9: Dt 31, 7f.   *d:* Dt 11, 31.

> **Do not fear nor be dismayed, for the LORD, your God, is with you wherever you go.**
>
> This thought from Joshua 1, 9 has been treasured through the years by readers of this passage. When you are uncertain about what to do, or challenged to do something difficult, it can be a source of courage and comfort at the same time.

Moses, the servant of the LORD, commanded you when he said, 'The LORD, your God, will permit you to settle in this land.' *14*Your wives, your children, and your livestock shall remain in the land Moses gave you here beyond the Jordan.*e* But all the warriors among you must cross over armed ahead of your kinsmen and you must help them *15*until the LORD has settled your kinsmen, and they like you possess the land which the LORD, your God, is giving them. Afterward you may return and occupy your own land, which Moses, the servant of the LORD, has given you east of the Jordan."*f* *16*"We will do all you have commanded us," they answered Joshua, "and we will go wherever you send us. We will obey you as completely as we obeyed Moses. *17*But may the LORD, your God, be with you as he was with Moses. *18*If anyone rebels against your orders and does not obey every command you give him, he shall be put to death. But be firm and steadfast."

See RG 94

CHAPTER 2

Spies Saved by Rahab. *1*Then Joshua, son of Nun, secretly sent out two spies from Shittim, saying, "Go, reconnoiter the land and Jericho." When the two reached Jericho, they went into the house of a harlot* named Rahab,*g* where they lodged. *2*But a report was brought to the king of Jericho that some Israelites had come there that night to spy out the land. *3*So the king of Jericho sent Rahab the order, "Put out the visitors who have entered your house, for they have come to spy out the entire land." *4*The woman*h* had taken the two men and hidden them, so she said, "True, the men you speak of came to me, but I did not know where they came from. *5*At dark, when it was time for the gate to be shut, they left, and I do not know where they went. You will have to pursue them immediately to overtake them." *6*Now, she had led them to the roof, and hidden them among her stalks of flax spread out* there. *7*But the pursuers set out along the way to the fords of the Jordan, and once they had left, the gate was shut.

*8*Before the spies fell asleep, Rahab* came to them on the roof *9*and said: "I know that the LORD has given you the land, that a dread of you has come upon us, and that all the inhabitants of the land are overcome with fear of you.*i* *10*For we have heard how the LORD dried up the waters of the Red Sea before you when you came out of Egypt,*j* and how you dealt with Sihon and Og, the two kings of the Amorites beyond the Jordan, whom you doomed to destruction. *11*At these reports, we are disheartened; everyone is discouraged because of you, since the LORD, your God, is God in heaven above and on earth below.*k* *12*Now then, swear to me by the LORD that, since I am showing kindness to you, you in turn will show kindness to my family;*l* and give me an unmistakable token *13*that you are to spare my father and mother, brothers and sisters, and all their kin, and save us from death." *14*"We pledge our lives for yours," the men answered her. "If you do not betray this

---

2, 1: Harlot: this is the regular equivalent of the Hebrew word, but perhaps it is used here of Rahab in the broader sense of a woman who kept a public house. Joshua's spies hoped to remain undetected at such an inn.

2, 6: Stalks of flax spread out: to dry in the sun, after they had been soaked in water, according to the ancient process of preparing flax for linen-making. In the Near East the flax harvest occurs near the time of the feast of the Passover (Jos 4,

19; 5, 10); cf Ex 9, 31.

2, 8-11: Rahab's faith and good works are praised in the New Testament; cf Heb 11, 31; Jas 2, 25.

e: Nm 32, 26. *f:* Jos 22, 4; Dt 3, 20. *g:* Mt 1, 5; Jas 2, 25. *h:* Jos 6, 17. *i:* Ex 15, 15f; 23, 27. *j:* Jos 4, 23; Ex 14, 21; Nm 21, 23-26. 33ff. *k:* Dt 4, 39. *l:* Jos 2, 18; 6, 23. 25.

errand of ours, we will be faithful in showing kindness to you when the LORD gives us the land."

[15]Then she let them down through the window with a rope; for she lived in a house built into the city wall.* [16]"Go up into the hill country," she suggested to them, "that your pursuers may not find you. Hide there for three days, until they return; then you may proceed on your way." [17]The men answered her, "This is how we will fulfill the oath you made us take: [18]When we come into the land, tie this scarlet cord in the window through which you are letting us down; and gather your father and mother, your brothers and all your family into your house. [19]Should any of them pass outside the doors of your house, he will be responsible for his own death, and we shall be guiltless. But we shall be responsible if anyone in the house with you is harmed. [20]If, however, you betray this errand of ours, we shall be quit of the oath you have made us take." [21]"Let it be as you say," she replied, and bade them farewell. When they were gone, she tied the scarlet cord in the window.

[22]They went up into the hills, where they stayed three days until their pursuers, who had sought them all along the road without finding them, returned. [23]Then the two came back down from the hills, crossed the Jordan to Joshua, son of Nun, and reported all that had befallen them. [24]They assured Joshua, "The LORD has delivered all this land into our power; indeed, all the inhabitants of the land are overcome with fear of us."

CHAPTER 3

See RG 94
Preparations for Crossing the Jordan.
[1]Early the next morning, Joshua[m] moved with all the Israelites from Shittim to the Jordan, where they lodged before crossing over. [2]Three days later the officers went through the camp [3]and issued these instructions to the people: "When you see the ark of the covenant of the LORD, your God, which the levitical priests will carry, you must also break camp and follow it, [4]that you may know the way to take, for you have not gone over this road before. But let there be a space of two thousand cubits between you and the ark. Do not come nearer to it." [5]Joshua also said to the people, "Sanctify yourselves, for tomorrow the LORD will perform wonders among you." [6]And he directed the priests to take up the ark of the covenant and go on ahead of the people; and they did so.

[7]Then the LORD said to Joshua, "Today I will begin to exalt you in the sight of all Israel, that they may know I am with you, as I was with Moses.[n] [8]Now command the priests carrying the ark of the covenant to come to a halt in the Jordan when they reach the edge of the waters."

[9]So Joshua said to the Israelites, "Come here and listen to the words of the LORD, your God." [10]He continued: "This is how you will know that there is a living God in your midst, who at your approach will dispossess the Canaanites, Hittites, Hivites, Perizzites, Girgashites, Amorites and Jebusites.[o] [11]The ark of the covenant of the LORD of the whole earth will precede you into the Jordan. [12][Now choose twelve men,[p] one from each of the tribes of Israel.] [13]When the soles of the feet of the priests carrying the ark of the LORD, the Lord of the whole earth, touch the water of the Jordan, it will cease to flow; for the water flowing down from upstream will halt in a solid bank."

The Crossing Begun. [14]The people struck their tents to cross the Jordan, with the priests carrying the ark of the covenant ahead of them. [15]No sooner had these priestly bearers of the ark waded into the waters at the edge of the Jordan, which overflows all its banks during the entire season of the harvest,*

2, 15: A house built into the city wall: such houses, which used the city wall for their own inner walls, have been found at ancient sites. The upper story of Rahab's house was evidently higher than the city wall. It was through the window of such a house that St. Paul escaped from Damascus; cf Acts 9, 25; 2 Cor 11, 33.

3, 15: Season of the harvest: toward the end of March

and the beginning of April, when the grain and other crops that grew during the rainy season of winter were reaped. The crossing took place "on the tenth day of the first month" of the Hebrew year, which began with the first new moon after the spring equinox; cf Jos 4, 19. At this

m: Jos 2, 1.   n: Jos 1, 5; 4, 14.   o: Ex 33, 2; Dt 7, 1.   p: Jos 4, 2. 4.

The Ark and Crossing the Jordan

The Ark of the Covenant served as a container for the scroll of the law according to Deuteronomy 31, 26. As the powerful physical symbol of God's presence among the people, it could be protective in battle (see Nm 10, 33–35; 1 Sm 4, 3–5). The Jordan symbolizes all the borders of the Promised Land, and crossing a river into Israel's territory echoes the people's passage through water (the Red Sea) under the leadership of Moses at the outset of the journey. This strengthens the depiction of Joshua as a new Moses, with great authority. The Jordan also functions primarily as a symbol representing the boundary between landlessness and settled peoplehood.

[16]than the waters flowing from upstream halted, backing up in a solid mass[q] for a very great distance indeed, from Adam, a city in the direction of Zarethan; while those flowing downstream toward the Salt Sea of the Arabah disappeared entirely.* Thus the people crossed over opposite Jericho. [17]While all Israel crossed over on dry ground, the priests carrying the ark of the covenant of the LORD remained motionless on dry ground in the bed of the Jordan[r] until the whole nation had completed the passage.

See RG 94

CHAPTER 4

Memorial Stones. [1]After the entire nation had crossed the Jordan, the LORD said to Joshua, [2]"Choose twelve men[s] from the people, one from each tribe, [3]and instruct them to take up twelve stones from this spot in the bed of the Jordan where the priests have been standing motionless.[t] Carry them over with you, and place them where you are to stay tonight."

[4]Summoning the twelve men whom he had selected from among the Israelites, one from each tribe, [5]Joshua said to them: "Go to the bed of the Jordan in front of the ark of the LORD, your God; lift to your shoulders one stone apiece, so that they will equal in number the tribes of the Israelites. [6]In the future, these are to be a sign among you. When your children

ask you what these stones mean to you, [7]you shall answer them, 'The waters of the Jordan ceased to flow before the ark of the covenant of the LORD when it crossed the Jordan.'[u] Thus these stones are to serve as a perpetual memorial to the Israelites." [8]The twelve Israelites did as Joshua had commanded: they took up as many stones from the bed of the Jordan as there were tribes of the Israelites, and carried them along to the camp site, where they placed them, according to the LORD's direction. [9]Joshua also had twelve stones set up in the bed of the Jordan on the spot where the priests stood who were carrying the ark of the covenant. They are there to this day.

[10]*The priests carrying the ark remained in the bed of the Jordan until everything had been done that the LORD had commanded Joshua to tell the people. The people crossed over quickly, [11]and when all had reached the other side, the ark of the LORD, borne by the priests, also crossed to its place in front of them. [12]The Reubenites, Gadites, and half-tribe of Manasseh, armed, marched in the vanguard of the Israelites, as Moses had ordered.[v] [13]About forty thousand troops equipped for battle passed over before the LORD to the plains of Jericho.

[14]That day the LORD exalted Joshua in the sight of all Israel,[w] and thenceforth during his whole life they respected him as they had respected Moses.

---

time of the year the Jordan would be swollen as a result of the winter rains and the melting snow of Mount Hermon.

3, 16: The sudden damming of the river could have been caused by a landslide, as has happened on other occasions. The miraculous character of this event would not thereby be removed because God, who foretold it (Jos 3, 13), also caused it to take place at precisely the right moment (Jos 3, 15),

whether or not he used natural forces to accomplish his will.

4, 10-18: After the digression about the two sets of memorial stones, the author resumes the narrative by briefly repeating the story of the crossing, which he had already told in Jos 3, 14-17.

---

q: Ps 114, 3.   r: Jos 4, 7. 22.   s: Jos 3, 12.   t: Jos 3, 13; 4, 8f; Dt 27, 2.   u: Jos 3, 13. 16.   v: Dt 3, 18.   w: Jos 3, 7.

[15]Then the LORD said to Joshua, [16]"Command the priests carrying the ark of the commandments to come up from the Jordan."[x] [17]Joshua did so, [18]and when the priests carrying the ark of the covenant of the LORD had come up from the bed of the Jordan, as the soles of their feet regained the dry ground, the waters of the Jordan resumed their course and as before overflowed all its banks.

[19]The people came up from the Jordan on the tenth day of the first month, and camped in Gilgal on the eastern limits of Jericho. [20]At Gilgal Joshua set up the twelve stones which had been taken from the Jordan, [21]saying to the Israelites, "In the future, when the children among you ask their fathers what these stones mean, [22]you shall inform them, 'Israel crossed the Jordan here on dry ground.' [23]For the LORD, your God, dried up the waters of the Jordan in front of you until you crossed over, just as the LORD, your God, had done at the Red Sea, which he dried up in front of us until we crossed over;[y] [24]in order that all the peoples of the earth may learn that the hand of the LORD is mighty, and that you may fear the LORD, your God, forever."

CHAPTER 5

See RG 94–97

Rites at Gilgal. [1]When all the kings of the Amorites to the west of the Jordan and all the kings of the Canaanites by the sea heard that the LORD had dried up the waters of the Jordan before the Israelites until they crossed over, they were disheartened and lost courage at their approach.

[2]On this occasion the LORD said to Joshua, "Make flint knives and circumcise the Israelite nation for the second time." [3]So Joshua made flint knives and circumcised the Israelites at Gibeath-haaraloth,* [4]under these circumstances: Of all the people who came out of Egypt, every man of military age had died in the desert[z] during the journey after they left Egypt. [5]Though all the men who came out were circumcised, none of those born in the desert during the journey after the departure from Egypt were circumcised. [6]Now the Israelites had wandered forty years in the desert, until all the warriors among the people that came forth from Egypt died off because they had not obeyed the command of the LORD.[a] For the LORD swore[b] that he would not let them see the land flowing with milk and honey which he had promised their fathers he would give us. [7c]It was the children whom he raised up in their stead whom Joshua circumcised, for these were yet with foreskins, not having been circumcised on the journey. [8]When the rite had been performed, the whole nation remained in camp where they were, until they recovered. [9]Then the LORD said to Joshua, "Today I have removed the reproach of Egypt from you."[d] Therefore the place is called Gilgal* to the present day.

[10e]While the Israelites were encamped at Gilgal on the plains of Jericho, they celebrated the Passover on the evening of the fourteenth of the month.* [11]On the day after the Passover they ate of the produce of the land in the form of unleavened cakes and parched grain. On that same day [12]after the Passover on which they ate of the produce of the land, the manna ceased. No longer was there manna for the Israelites, who that year ate of the yield of the land of Canaan.[f]

Siege at Jericho. [13]*While Joshua was near Jericho, he raised his eyes and saw one who stood facing him, drawn sword in hand.[g] Joshua went up to him and asked, "Are you one of us or of our enemies?" [14]He replied, "Neither. I am the captain of the

---

5, 3: Gibeath-haaraloth: "Hill of the Foreskins."

5, 9: The place is called Gilgal: by popular etymology, because of the similarity of sound with the Hebrew word gallothi, "I have removed." Gilgal probably means "(the place of) the circle of standing stones." Cf Jos 4, 4-8.

5, 10: The month: the first month of the year, later called Nisan; see note on Jos 3, 15. The crossing of the Jordan occurred, therefore, about the same time of the year as did the equally miraculous crossing of the Red Sea; cf Ex 12–14.

5, 13—6, 26: The account of the siege of Jericho embraces: (1) the command of the LORD, through his angel, to

Joshua (Jos 5, 13—6, 5); (2) Joshua's instructions to the Israelites, with a brief summary of how these orders were carried out (Jos 6, 6-11); (3) a description of the action on each of the first six days (Jos 6, 12-14); (4) the events on the seventh day (Jos 6, 15-26).

x: Jos 3, 6.   y: Ex 14, 21.   z: Nm 14, 29; 26, 64f; Dt 2, 16; Ps 106, 26; 1 Cor 10, 5.   a: Nm 14, 29.   b: Heb 3, 11. 17.   c: Dt 1, 39.
d: Jos 4, 19.   e: Ex 12, 6; Lv 23, 5; Nm 9, 3-5.   f: Ex 16, 35.
g: Ex 23, 20.

host of the LORD and I have just arrived." Then Joshua fell prostrate to the ground in worship, and said to him, "What has my lord to say to his servant?" [15]The captain of the host of the LORD replied to Joshua, "Remove your sandals from your feet, for the place on which you are standing is holy."[h] And Joshua obeyed.

CHAPTER 6

See RG 95-97

[1]Now Jericho was in a state of siege because of the presence of the Israelites, so that no one left or entered. [2]And to Joshua the LORD said, "I have delivered Jericho and its king into your power. [3]Have all the soldiers circle the city, marching once around it. Do this for six days, [4i]with seven priests carrying ram's horns ahead of the ark. On the seventh day march around the city seven times, and have the priests blow the horns. [5]When they give a long blast on the ram's horns and you hear that signal, all the people shall shout aloud. The wall of the city will collapse, and they will be able to make a frontal attack."

[6]Summoning the priests, Joshua, son of Nun, then ordered them to take up the ark of the covenant with seven of the priests carrying ram's horns in front of the ark of the LORD. [7]And he ordered the people to proceed in a circle around the city, with the picked troops marching ahead of the ark of the LORD. [8]At this order they proceeded, with the seven priests who carried the ram's horns before the LORD blowing their horns, and the ark of the covenant of the LORD following them. [9]In front of the priests with the horns marched the picked troops; the rear guard followed the ark, and the blowing of horns was kept up continually as they marched. [10]But the people had been commanded by Joshua not to shout or make any noise or outcry until he gave the word: only then were they to shout. [11]So he had the ark of the LORD circle the city, going once around it, after which they returned to camp for the night.

[12]Early the next morning, Joshua had the priests take up the ark of the LORD. [13]The seven priests bearing the ram's horns marched in front of the ark of the LORD, blowing their horns. Ahead of these marched the picked troops, while the rear guard followed the ark of the LORD; and the blowing of horns was kept up continually. [14]On this second day they again marched around the city once before returning to camp; and for six days in all they did the same.

[15]On the seventh day, beginning at daybreak, they marched around the city seven times in the same manner; on that day only did they march around the city seven times. [16]The seventh time around, the priests blew the horns and Joshua said to the people, "Now shout, for the LORD has given you the city [17]and everything in it.[j] It is under the LORD's ban. Only the harlot Rahab and all who are in the house with her are to be spared, because she hid the messengers we sent. [18k]But be careful not to take, in your greed, anything that is under the ban;[*] else you will bring upon the camp of Israel this ban and the misery of it. [19]All silver and gold, and the articles of bronze or iron, are sacred to the LORD. They shall be put in the treasury of the LORD."

The Fall of Jericho. [20]As the horns blew, the people began to shout. When they heard the signal horn, they raised a tremendous shout. The wall collapsed,[*] and the people stormed the city in a frontal attack and took it.[l] [21]They observed the ban by putting to the sword all living creatures[m] in the city: men and women, young and old, as well as oxen, sheep and asses.

[22]Joshua directed the two men who had spied out the land, "Go into the harlot's house and bring out the woman with all her kin, as you swore to her you would do."[n]

6, 18: That is under the ban: that is doomed to destruction; see notes on Lv 27, 29; Nm 18, 14; 21, 3.

6, 20: The wall collapsed: by the miraculous intervention of God. The blowing of the horns and the shouting of the people were a customary feature of ancient warfare, here intended by God as a test of the people's obedience and of their faith in his promise; cf Heb 11, 30.

h: Ex 3, 5; Acts 7, 33.   i: Nm 10, 8f.   j: Jos 2, 4; Dt 20, 17; Heb 11, 31.   k: Jos 7, 12. 25; Dt 13, 18.   l: 2 Mc 12, 15; Heb 11, 30. m: Dt 7, 2.   n: Jos 2, 14.

The Destruction of Jericho

The LORD gives specific instructions to Joshua in language combining ritual with warfare. Joshua then carries out the commands, defeating Jericho and instituting the "herem," the complete annihilation of the enemy, but sparing Rahab and her family. In this way the story of Jericho makes clear that it is God who is leading the conquest; the deliverance of the land to the Israelites is God's gift, not something they earned by their own efforts.

*23*The spies entered and brought out Rahab, with her father, mother, brothers, and all her kin.*o* Her entire family they led forth and placed them outside the camp of Israel. *24*The city itself they burned with all that was in it,*p* except the silver, gold, and articles of bronze and iron, which were placed in the treasury of the house of the LORD. *25**Because Rahab the harlot had hidden the messengers whom Joshua had sent to reconnoiter Jericho, Joshua spared her with her family and all her kin, who continue in the midst of Israel to this day.

*26q*On that occasion Joshua imposed the oath: Cursed before the LORD be the man who attempts to rebuild this city, Jericho. He shall lose his first-born when he lays its foundation, and he shall lose his youngest son when he sets up its gates.*

*27*Thus the LORD was with Joshua so that his fame spread throughout the land.*r*

See RG 95-97

CHAPTER 7

Defeat at Ai. *1*But the Israelites violated the ban; Achan, son of Carmi, son of Zerah, son of Zara of the tribe of Judah, took goods that were under the ban,*s* and the anger of the LORD flared up against the Israelites.

*2*Joshua next sent men from Jericho to Ai, which is near Bethel on its eastern side, with instructions to go up and reconnoiter the land. When they had explored Ai, *3*they returned to Joshua and advised, "Do not send all the people up; if only about two or three thousand go up, they can overcome Ai. The enemy there are few; you need not call for an effort from all the people." *4*About three thousand of the people made the attack, but they were defeated by those at Ai, *5*who killed some thirty-six of them. They pressed them back across the clearing in front of the city gate till they broke ranks, and defeated them finally on the descent, so that the confidence of the people melted away like water.

*6*Joshua, together with the elders of Israel, rent his garments and lay prostrate before the ark of the LORD until evening; and they threw dust on their heads. *7*"Alas, O Lord GOD," Joshua prayed, "why did you ever allow this people to pass over the Jordan, delivering us into the power of the Amorites, that they might destroy us? Would that we had been content to dwell on the other side of the Jordan. *8*Pray, Lord, what can I say, now that Israel has turned its back to its enemies? *9*When the Canaanites and the other inhabitants of the land hear of it, they will close in around us and efface our name from the earth. What will you do for your great name?"

*10*The LORD replied to Joshua: "Stand up. Why are you lying prostrate? *11*Israel has sinned: they have violated the covenant which I enjoined on them. They have stealthily taken goods subject to the ban, and have deceitfully put them in their baggage. *12*If the Israelites cannot stand up to their enemies, but must turn their back to them, it is because they are under the ban.*u* I will not remain with you unless you remove from

---

6, 25: From Mt 1, 5, we learn that Rahab married Salmon of the tribe of Judah and thus became the great-great-grandmother of David, Christ's ancestor; cf Ru 4, 18-22.

6, 26: He shall lose his first-born . . . its gates: this curse was fulfilled when Hiel rebuilt Jericho as a fortified city during the reign of Ahab, king of Israel; cf 1 Kgs 16, 34. Till then Jericho was merely an unwalled village; cf Jos 18, 12. 21; Jgs 3, 13; 2 Sm 10, 5.

o: Jos 2, 13; Heb 11, 31.   *p:* Jos 8, 2.   *q:* 1 Kgs 16, 34.   *r:* Jos 1, 5.   *s:* Jos 6, 18; 22, 20; 1 Chr 2, 7.   *t:* Jos 6, 17-19.   *u:* Jos 6, 18.

among you whoever has incurred the ban. ¹³Rise, sanctify the people.^v Tell them to sanctify themselves before tomorrow, for the LORD, the God of Israel, says: You are under the ban, O Israel. You cannot stand up to your enemies until you remove from among you whoever has incurred the ban. ¹⁴In the morning you must present yourselves by tribes. The tribe which the LORD designates shall come forward by clans; the clan which the LORD designates shall come forward by families; the family which the LORD designates shall come forward one by one. ¹⁵He who is designated as having incurred the ban shall be destroyed by fire, with all that is his, because he has violated the covenant of the LORD and has committed a shameful crime in Israel."

Achan's Guilt and Punishment. ¹⁶Early the next morning Joshua had Israel come forward by tribes, and the tribe of Judah was designated.* ¹⁷Then he had the clans of Judah come forward, and the clan of Zerah was designated. He had the clan of Zerah^w come forward by families, and Zabdi was designated. ¹⁸Finally he had that family come forward one by one, and Achan, son of Carmi, son of Zabdi, son of Zerah of the tribe of Judah, was designated. ¹⁹Joshua said to Achan, "My son, give to the LORD, the God of Israel, glory and honor by telling me what you have done; do not hide it from me." ²⁰Achan answered Joshua, "I have indeed sinned against the LORD, the God of Israel. This is what I have done: ²¹Among the spoils, I saw a beautiful Babylonian mantle, two hundred shekels of silver, and a bar of gold fifty shekels in weight; in my greed I took them. They are now hidden in the ground inside my tent, with the silver underneath." ²²The messengers whom Joshua sent hastened to the tent and found them hidden there, with the silver underneath. ²³They took them

from the tent, brought them to Joshua and all the Israelites, and spread them out before the LORD.

²⁴Then Joshua and all Israel took Achan, son of Zerah, with the silver, the mantle, and the bar of gold, and with his sons and daughters, his ox, his ass and his sheep, his tent, and all his possessions, and led them off to the Valley of Achor. ²⁵Joshua said, "The LORD bring upon you today the misery with which you have afflicted us!"^x And all Israel stoned him to death ²⁶and piled a great heap of stones over him, which remains to the present day.^y Then the anger of the LORD relented. That is why the place is called the Valley of Achor* to this day.

CHAPTER 8

See RG 95–97

Capture of Ai. ¹The LORD then said to Joshua, "Do not be afraid or dismayed. Take all the army with you and prepare to attack Ai.^z I have delivered the king of Ai into your power, with his people, city, and land. ²Do to Ai and its king what you did to Jericho and its king; except that you may take its spoil and livestock as booty.^a Set an ambush behind the city." ³So Joshua and all the soldiers prepared to attack Ai. Picking out thirty thousand warriors,* Joshua sent them off by night ⁴with these orders: "See that you ambush the city from the rear, at no great distance; then all of you be on the watch. ⁵The rest of the people and I will come up to the city, and when they make a sortie against us as they did the last time, we will flee from them. ⁶They will keep coming out after us until we have drawn them away from the city, for they will think we are fleeing from them as we did the last time. When this occurs, ⁷rise from ambush and take possession of the city, which the LORD, your God, will deliver into your power. ⁸When you have taken the city, set it afire in

---

7, 16ff: Was designated: probably by means of the Urim and Thummim; cf 1 Sm 14, 38-42. See note on Ex 28, 30.

7, 26: Achor: "misery, affliction." The reference is to the saying of Joshua in v 25, with an allusion also to the similar-sounding name of Achan.

8, 3: Thirty thousand warriors: this figure of the Hebrew text, which seems extremely high, may be due to a copyist's error; some manuscripts of the Septuagint have "three thou-

sand," which is the number of the whole army in the first, unsuccessful attack (Jos 7, 4); the variant reading in v 12 mentions "five thousand."

---

v: Jos 3, 5; Lv 20, 7; 1 Sm 16, 5.   *w:* Nm 26, 20.   *x:* Jos 6, 18; 22, 20; 1 Chr 2, 7.   *y:* Jos 8, 29.   *z:* Jos 2, 24.   *a:* Jos 6, 21. 24; Dt 20, 14.

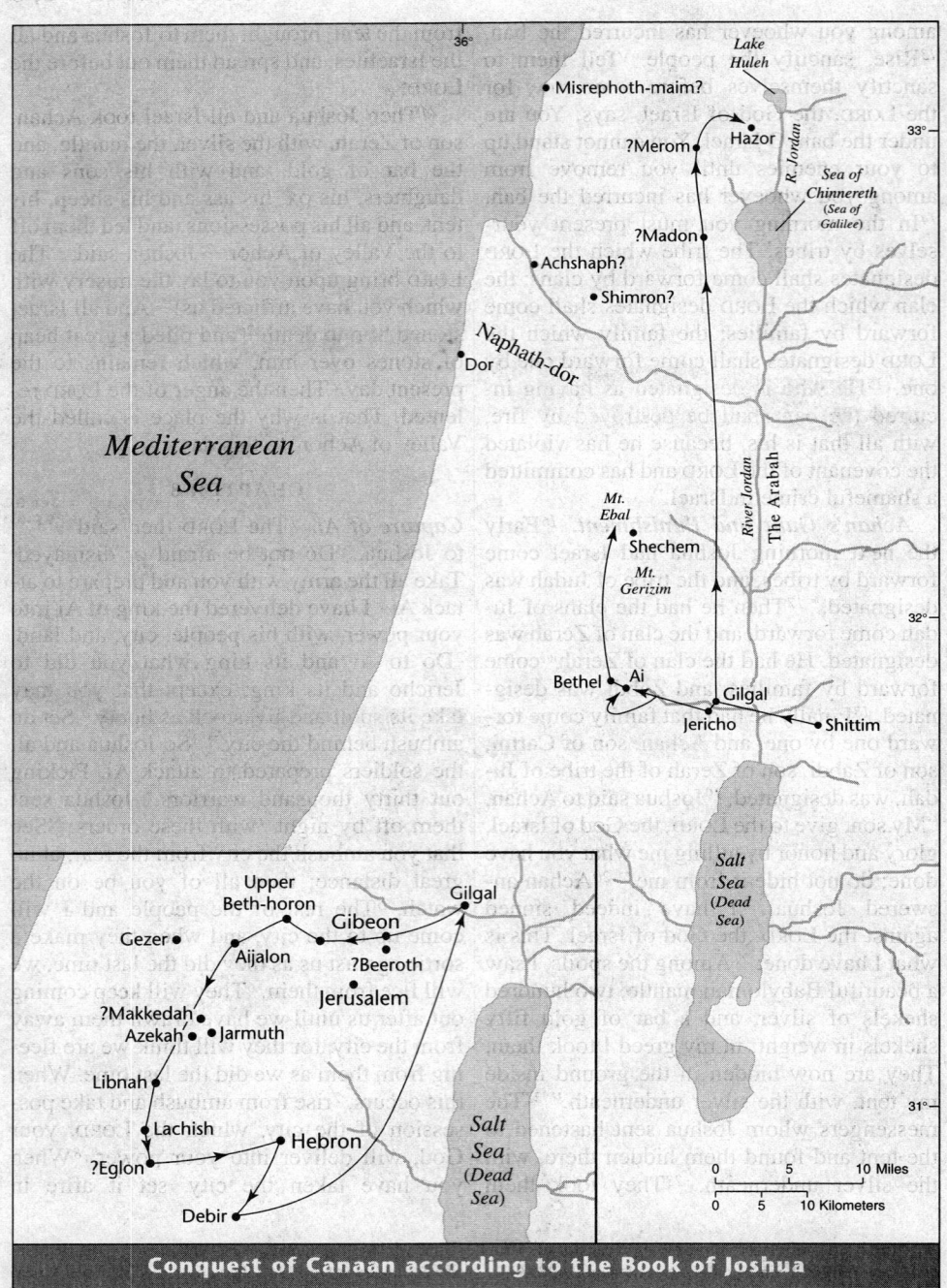

Mediterranean
Sea

Lake
Huleh

Misrephoth-maim?

?Merom   Hazor

Sea of
Chinnereth
(Sea of
Galilee)

?Madon

Achshaph?

Naphath-dor

Shimron?

Dor

Mt.
Ebal

Shechem

Mt.
Gerizim

Bethel   Ai   Gilgal

Jericho   Shittim

Salt
Sea
(Dead
Sea)

River Jordan

The Arabah

R. Jordan

Upper
Beth-horon   Gilgal

Gibeon

Gezer   Aijalon   ?Beeroth

?Makkedah   Jerusalem

Azekah   Jarmuth

Libnah

Lachish   Hebron

?Eglon

Debir

Salt
Sea
(Dead
Sea)

0   5   10 Miles

0   5   10 Kilometers

Conquest of Canaan according to the Book of Joshua

obedience to the LORD's command. These are my orders to you." [9]Then Joshua sent them away. They went to the place of ambush, taking up their position to the west of Ai, toward Bethel. Joshua, however, spent that night in the plain.

[10]Early the next morning Joshua mustered the army and went up to Ai at its head, with the elders of Israel. [11]When all the troops he led were drawn up in position before the city, they pitched camp north of Ai, on the other side of the ravine. [12][He took about five thousand men and set them in ambush between Bethel and Ai, west of the city.] [13]Thus the people took up their stations, with the main body north of the city and the ambush west of it, and Joshua waited overnight among his troops. [14]The king of Ai saw this, and he and all his army came out very early in the morning to engage Israel in battle at the descent toward the Arabah, not knowing that there was an ambush behind the city. [15]Joshua and the main body of the Israelites fled in seeming defeat toward the desert, [16]till the last of the soldiers in the city had been called out to pursue them. [17]Since they were drawn away from the city, with every man engaged in this pursuit of Joshua and the Israelites, not a soldier remained in Ai [or Bethel], and the city was open and unprotected.

[18]Then the LORD directed Joshua, "Stretch out the javelin in your hand toward Ai, for I will deliver it into your power." Joshua stretched out the javelin in his hand toward the city, [19]and as soon as he did so, the men in ambush rose from their post, rushed in, captured the city, and immediately set it on fire. [20]By the time the men of Ai looked back, the smoke from the city was already sky-high. Escape in any direction was impossible, because the Israelites retreating toward the desert now turned on their pursuers; [21]for when Joshua and the main body of Israelites saw that the city had been taken from ambush and was going up in smoke, they struck back at the men of Ai. [22]Since those in the city came out to intercept them, the men of Ai

were hemmed in by Israelites on either side, who cut them down without any fugitives or survivors[b] [23]except the king, whom they took alive and brought to Joshua.

[24]All the inhabitants of Ai who had pursued the Israelites into the desert were slain by the sword there in the open, down to the last man. Then all Israel returned and put to the sword those inside the city. [25]There fell that day a total of twelve thousand men and women, the entire population of Ai. [26c]Joshua kept the javelin in his hand stretched out until he had fulfilled the doom on all the inhabitants of Ai. [27]However, the Israelites took for themselves as booty the livestock and the spoil of that city, according to the command of the LORD issued to Joshua. [28]Then Joshua destroyed the place by fire, reducing it to an everlasting mound of ruins, as it remains today.[d] [29]He had the king of Ai hanged on a tree until evening;[e] then at sunset Joshua ordered the body removed from the tree and cast at the entrance of the city gate, where a great heap of stones was piled up over it, which remains to the present day.

Altar on Mount Ebal. [30]*Later Joshua built an altar to the LORD, the God of Israel, on Mount Ebal, [31]of unhewn stones on which no iron tool had been used,[f] in keeping with the command to the Israelites of Moses, the servant of the LORD, as recorded in the book of the law. On this altar they offered holocausts and peace offerings to the LORD. [32]There, in the presence of the Israelites, Joshua inscribed upon the stones a copy of the law written by Moses.[g] [33]And all Israel, stranger and native alike, with their elders, officers and judges, stood on either side of the ark facing the levitical priests who were carrying the ark of the covenant of the LORD.[h] Half of them were facing Mount Gerizim and half Mount Ebal, thus carrying out the instructions of Moses, the servant of the LORD, for the blessing of the people of Israel on this first occasion. [34i]Then were read aloud all the words of the law, the blessings and the

8, 30-35: These ceremonies were prescribed in Dt 11, 29, and Dt 27, 2-26. See notes on those passages.

b: Dt 7, 2.   *c:* Ex 17, 11ff.   *d:* Dt 13, 16.   *e:* Jos 10, 26f; Dt 21, 22f; Jn 19, 31.   *f:* Ex 20, 24f; Dt 27, 5f.   *g:* Dt 27, 2. 8.   *h:* Jos 3, 3; Dt 11, 27; 27, 12; 31, 9. 12.   *i:* Dt 28, 2-68; 30, 19; 31, 11; Neh 8, 2f.

curses, exactly as written in the book of the law. [35j]Every single word that Moses had commanded, Joshua read aloud to the entire community, including the women and children, and the strangers who had accompanied Israel.

See RG
95-97

CHAPTER 9

Confederacy against Israel. [1]When the news reached the kings west of the Jordan, in the mountain regions and in the foothills, and all along the coast of the Great Sea as far as Lebanon: Hittites, Amorites, Canaanites, Perizzites, Hivites and Jebusites,[k] [2]they all formed an alliance to launch a common attack against Joshua and Israel.

The Gibeonite Deception. [3]On learning what Joshua had done to Jericho and Ai, the inhabitants of Gibeon[l] [4]put into effect a device of their own. They chose provisions for a journey, making use of old sacks for their asses, and old wineskins, torn and mended. [5]They wore old, patched sandals and shabby garments; and all the bread they took was dry and crumbly. [6]Thus they journeyed to Joshua in the camp at Gilgal, where they said to him and to the men of Israel, "We have come from a distant land to propose that you make an alliance with us."[m] [7]But the men of Israel replied to the Hivites,* "You may be living in land that is ours. How, then, can we make an alliance with you?" [8]But they answered Joshua, "We are your servants." Then Joshua asked them, "Who are you? Where do you come from?" [9]They answered him, "Your servants have come from a far-off land, because of the fame of the LORD, your God. For we have heard reports of all that he did in Egypt[n] [10]and all that he did to the two kings of the Amorites beyond the Jordan,[o] Sihon, king of Heshbon, and Og, king of Bashan, who lived in Ashtaroth. [11]So our elders and all the inhabitants of our country

said to us, 'Take along provisions for the journey and go to meet them. Say to them: We are your servants; we propose that you make an alliance with us.' [12]This bread of ours was still warm when we brought it from home as provisions the day we left to come to you, but now it is dry and crumbled. [13]Here are our wineskins, which were new when we filled them, but now they are torn. Look at our garments and sandals, which are worn out from the very long journey." [14]Then the Israelite princes partook of their provisions, without seeking the advice of the LORD.[p] [15]So Joshua made an alliance with them and entered into an agreement to spare them,[q] which the princes of the community sealed with an oath.

Gibeonites Made Vassals. [16]Three days after the agreement was entered into, the Israelites learned that these people were from nearby, and would be living in Israel. [17]The third day on the road, the Israelites came to their cities of Gibeon, Chephirah, Beeroth and Kiriath-jearim, [18]but did not attack them, because the princes of the community had sworn to them by the LORD, the God of Israel. When the entire community grumbled against the princes, [19]these all remonstrated with the people, "We have sworn to them by the LORD, the God of Israel, and so we cannot harm them. [20]Let us therefore spare their lives and so deal with them that we shall not be punished for the oath we have sworn to them." [21]Thus the princes recommended that they be let live, as hewers of wood and drawers of water* for the entire community; and the community did as the princes advised them.

[22]Joshua summoned the Gibeonites and said to them, "Why did you lie to us and say that you lived at a great distance from us, when you will be living in our very midst? [23]For this are you accursed: every one of you shall always be a slave [hewers of wood and drawers of water] for the house of my God."

9, 7: The Hivites: apparently the Gibeonites belonged to this larger ethnic group (cf also Jos 11, 19), although in 2 Sm 21, 2 they are classed as Amorites; both groups are listed among the seven nations in Canaan whom the Israelites were to exterminate; cf Dt 7, 1f.

9, 21: Hewers of wood and drawers of water: proverbial

terms for the lowest social class in the Israelite community; cf Dt 29, 10f.

j: Dt 31, 12.   k: Jos 3, 10; Ex 3, 8. 17; 23, 23; Dt 1, 7.   l: Jos 6, 21. 24; 11, 19.   m: Ex 23, 32; Dt 7, 2.   n: Jos 2, 10.   o: Nm 21, 25. 33.   p: Nm 27, 21.   q: Jos 11, 19; 2 Sm 21, 2.

[24]They answered Joshua, "Your servants were fully informed of how the LORD, your God, commanded his servant Moses that you be given the entire land and that all its inhabitants be destroyed before you. Since, therefore, at your advance, we were in great fear for our lives, we acted as we did.[r] [25]And now that we are in your power, do with us what you think fit and right." [26]*Joshua did what he had decided: while he saved them from being killed by the Israelites, [27]at the same time he made them, as they still are, hewers of wood and drawers of water for the community and for the altar of the LORD, in the place of the LORD's choice.[s]

CHAPTER 10

See RG 95-97

The Siege of Gibeon. [1]Now Adonizedek, king of Jerusalem, heard that, in the capture and destruction of Ai, Joshua had done to that city and its king as he had done to Jericho and its king.[t] He heard also that the inhabitants of Gibeon had made their peace with Israel, remaining among them, [2]and that there was great fear abroad, because Gibeon was large enough for a royal city, larger even than the city of Ai, and all its men were brave. [3]So Adonizedek, king of Jerusalem, sent for Hoham, king of Hebron, Piram, king of Jarmuth, Japhia, king of Lachish, and Debir, king of Eglon, [4]to come to his aid for an attack on Gibeon, since it had concluded peace with Joshua and the Israelites.[u] [5]The five Amorite kings, of Jerusalem, Hebron, Jarmuth, Lachish and Eglon,* united all their forces and marched against Gibeon, where they took up siege positions. [6]Thereupon, the men of Gibeon sent an appeal to Joshua in his camp at Gilgal: "Do not abandon your servants. Come up here quickly and save us. Help us,

because all the Amorite kings of the mountain country have joined forces against us."[v]

Joshua's Victory. [7]So Joshua marched up from Gilgal with his picked troops and the rest of his soldiers. [8]Meanwhile the LORD said to Joshua, "Do not fear them, for I have delivered them into your power. Not one of them will be able to withstand you." [9]And when Joshua made his surprise attack upon them after an all-night march from Gilgal, [10]the LORD threw them into disorder before him. The Israelites inflicted a great slaughter on them at Gibeon and pursued them down the Beth-horon slope, harassing them as far as Azekah and Makkedah.

[11]While they fled before Israel along the descent from Beth-horon, the LORD hurled great stones from the sky* above them all the way to Azekah, killing many.[w] More died from these hailstones than the Israelites slew with the sword. [12]On this day, when the LORD delivered up the Amorites to the Israelites,

Joshua prayed to the LORD,
and said in the presence of Israel:
Stand still, O sun, at Gibeon,
O moon, in the valley of Aijalon!
[13] And the sun stood still,
and the moon stayed,
while the nation took vengeance on its
foes.[x]

Is this not recorded* in the Book of Jashar? The sun halted in the middle of the sky; not for a whole day did it resume its swift course. [14]Never before or since was there a day like this, when the LORD obeyed the voice of a man; for the LORD fought for Israel. [15][Then Joshua and all Israel returned to the camp at Gilgal.]

9, 26f: Later on, Saul violated the immunity of the Gibeonites, but David vindicated it; cf 2 Sm 21, 1-9.

10, 5: Hebron . . . Eglon: these four cities were to the south and southwest of Jerusalem.

10, 11: Great stones from the sky: the hailstones mentioned in the next sentence.

10, 13: Is this not recorded: the reference is to the preceding, poetic passage. Evidently the Book of Jashar, like the Book of the Wars of the LORD (Nm 21, 14), recounted in epic style the exploits of Israel's early heroes. The sun halted: though it is widely supposed that this passage describes in popular language and according to external appearances a

miraculous lengthening of the day, it is equally probable that Joshua's prayer was rather for an abrupt obscuration of the sun, which would impede his enemies in their flight homeward and also prevent them from rallying their forces; this request would have been answered by the hailstorm (cf Sir 46, 5) and by a darkness relieved only twenty-four hours later, well into the next day.

r: Ex 23, 27f; Dt 7, 1f.   *s:* Dt 12, 5.   *t:* Jos 9, 15; 6, 21. 24; 8, 26-29.   *u:* Jos 9, 15.   *v:* Jos 9, 6.   *w:* Jb 38, 22.   *x:* Sir 46, 4; Is 28, 21; Heb 3, 11.

Execution of Amorite Kings. [16]Meanwhile the five kings who had fled, hid in a cave at Makkedah. [17]When Joshua was told that the five kings had been discovered hiding in a cave at Makkedah, [18]he said, "Roll large stones to the mouth of the cave and post men over it to guard them. [19]But do not remain there yourselves. Pursue your enemies, and harry them in the rear. Do not allow them to escape to their cities, for the LORD, your God, has delivered them into your power."

[20]Once Joshua and the Israelites had finally inflicted the last blows in this very great slaughter, and the survivors had escaped from them into the fortified cities, [21]all the army returned safely to Joshua and the camp at Makkedah, no man uttering a sound against the Israelites. [22]Then Joshua said, "Open the mouth of the cave and bring out those five kings to me." [23]Obediently, they brought out to him from the cave the five kings, of Jerusalem, Hebron, Jarmuth, Lachish and Eglon. [24]When they had done so, Joshua summoned all the men of Israel and said to the commanders of the soldiers who had marched with him, "Come forward and put your feet on the necks of these kings." They came forward and put their feet upon their necks. [25]Then Joshua said to them, "Do not be afraid or dismayed, be firm and steadfast. This is what the LORD will do to all the enemies against whom you fight." [26y]Thereupon Joshua struck and killed them, and hanged them on five trees, where they remained hanging until evening. [27]At sunset they were removed from the trees at the command of Joshua and cast into the cave where they had hidden; over the mouth of the cave large stones were placed, which remain until this very day.

Conquest of Southern Canaan. [28z]Makkedah, too, Joshua captured and put to the sword at that time. He fulfilled the doom on the city, on its king, and on every person in it, leaving no survivors. Thus he did to the king of Makkedah what he had done to the king of Jericho. [29]Joshua then passed on with all Israel from Makkedah to Libnah, which he attacked. [30]Libnah also, with its king, the LORD delivered into the power of Israel. He put it to the sword with every person there, leaving no survivors. Thus he did to its king what he had done to the king of Jericho. [31]Joshua next passed on with all Israel from Libnah to Lachish, where they set up a camp during the attack. [32]The LORD delivered Lachish into the power of Israel, so that on the second day Joshua captured it and put it to the sword with every person in it, just as he had done to Libnah. [33]At that time Horam, king of Gezer, came up to help Lachish, but Joshua defeated him and his people, leaving him no survivors. [34]From Lachish, Joshua passed on with all Israel to Eglon; encamping near it, they attacked it [35]and captured it the same day, putting it to the sword. He fulfilled the doom that day on every person in it, just as he had done at Lachish. [36]From Eglon, Joshua went up with all Israel to Hebron, which they attacked [37]and captured. They put it to the sword with its king, all its towns, and every person there, leaving no survivors, just as Joshua had done to Eglon. He fulfilled the doom on it and on every person there. [38]Then Joshua and all Israel turned back to Debir and attacked it, [39]capturing it with its king and all its towns. They put them to the sword and fulfilled the doom on every person there, leaving no survivors. Thus was done to Debir and its king what had been done to Hebron, as well as to Libnah and its king.

[40a]Joshua conquered the entire country; the mountain regions, the Negeb, the foothills, and the mountain slopes, with all their kings. He left no survivors, but fulfilled the doom on all who lived there, just as the LORD, the God of Israel, had commanded. [41]Joshua conquered from Kadesh-barnea to Gaza, and all the land of Goshen* to Gibeon. [42]All these kings and their lands Joshua cap-

---

10, 41: Goshen: a town and its surrounding district at the southern end of the Judean mountains (cf Jos 11, 16; 15, 51); not to be confused with the land of Goshen in northeastern Egypt (Gen 45, 10), although in the current Hebrew Bible both names are spelled the same.

y: 26f: Jos 8, 29; Dt 21, 22f. z: Jos 6, 21. a: Dt 20, 16f.

tured in a single campaign, for the LORD, the God of Israel, fought for Israel. *43*Thereupon Joshua with all Israel returned to the camp at Gilgal.

CHAPTER 11

See RG 95-97

Northern Confederacy. *1*When Jabin, king of Hazor,* learned of this, he sent a message to Jobab, king of Madon, to the king of Shimron, to the king of Achshaph, *2*and to the northern kings in the mountain regions and in the Arabah near Chinneroth, in the foothills, and in Naphath-dor to the west.*b* *3*These were Canaanites to the east and west, Amorites, Hittites, Perizzites and Jebusites in the mountain regions, and Hivites at the foot of Hermon in the land of Mizpah. *4*They came out with all their troops, an army numerous as the sands on the seashore, and with a multitude of horses and chariots. *5*All these kings joined forces and marched to the waters of Merom,* where they encamped together to fight against Israel.

*6*The LORD said to Joshua, "Do not fear them, for by this time tomorrow I will stretch them slain before Israel. You must hamstring their horses and burn their chariots." *7*Joshua with his whole army came upon them at the waters of Merom in a surprise attack. *8*The LORD delivered them into the power of the Israelites, who defeated them and pursued them to Greater Sidon, to Misrephoth-maim,*c* and eastward to the valley of Mizpeh. They struck them all down, leaving no survivors. *9*Joshua did to them as the LORD had commanded: he hamstrung their horses and burned their chariots.

Conquest of Northern Canaan. *10*At that time Joshua, turning back, captured Hazor and slew its king with the sword; for Hazor formerly was the chief of all those kingdoms. *11*He also fulfilled the doom by putting every person there to the sword, till none was left alive. Hazor itself he burned. *12*Joshua thus captured all those kings with their cities and put them to the sword, fulfilling the doom on them, as Moses, the servant of the LORD, had commanded.*d* *13*However, Israel did not destroy by fire any of the cities built on raised sites, except Hazor, which Joshua burned. *14*The Israelites took all the spoil and livestock of these cities as their booty; but the people they put to the sword, until they had exterminated the last of them, leaving none alive. *15*As the LORD had commanded his servant Moses, so Moses commanded Joshua, and Joshua acted accordingly.*e* He left nothing undone that the LORD had commanded Moses should be done.

Survey of the Conquest. *16*So Joshua captured all this land: the mountain regions, the entire Negeb, all the land of Goshen, the foothills, the Arabah, as well as the mountain regions and foothills of Israel,*f* *17*from Mount Halak that rises toward Seir*g* as far as Baal-gad in the Lebanon valley at the foot of Mount Hermon. All their kings he captured and put to death. *18*Joshua waged war against all these kings for a long time. *19*With the exception of the Hivites who lived in Gibeon, no city made peace with the Israelites; all were taken in battle.*h* *20*For it was the design of the LORD to encourage them to wage war against Israel, that they might be doomed to destruction and thus receive no mercy, but be exterminated, as the LORD had commanded Moses.*i*

21*At that time Joshua penetrated the mountain regions and exterminated the Anakim in Hebron,*j* Debir, Anab, the entire mountain region of Judah, and the entire mountain region of Israel. Joshua fulfilled the doom on them and on their cities, *22*so that no Anakim were left in the land of the Israelites. However, some survived in

---

11, 1ff: Hazor, Madon, Shimron, and Chinneroth: cities and their surrounding districts in eastern Galilee. Achshaph and Naphath-dor: southwest of Galilee. The mountain regions: in central and northern Galilee.

11, 5: The waters of Merom: a stream in central Galilee that flows southeast to water the fertile Arabah, or plain of Chinneroth on the western shore of the lake of Gennesaret.

11, 21ff: Most of the land assigned to the tribe of Judah

was not conquered by it till the early period of the Judges. See note on Jgs 1, 1-36.

b: Jos 12, 3; Jgs 1, 27.   *c:* Jos 13, 6.   *d:* Dt 7, 2; 20, 16f.   *e:* Dt 7, 2.   *f:* Jos 10, 41; 12, 8.   *g:* Jos 12, 7; Dt 7, 24.   *h:* Jos 9, 3. 7. 15.   *i:* Dt 2, 30; 20, 16f.   *j:* Jos 15, 13f; Nm 13, 22; Dt 1, 28.

Gaza, in Gath, and in Ashdod. [23k]Thus Joshua captured the whole country, just as the LORD had foretold to Moses. Joshua gave it to Israel as their heritage, apportioning it among the tribes. And the land enjoyed peace.*

See RG 97-98

CHAPTER 12*

Lists of Conquered Kings. [1]The kings of the land east of the Jordan, from the River Arnon to Mount Hermon, including all the eastern section of the Arabah, whom the Israelites conquered and whose lands they occupied, were: [2l]First, Sihon, king of the Amorites, who lived in Heshbon. His domain extended from Aroer, which is on the bank of the Wadi Arnon, to include the wadi itself, and the land northward through half of Gilead to the Wadi Jabbok, [3]as well as the Arabah from the eastern side of the Sea of Chinnereth, as far south as the eastern side of the Salt Sea of the Arabah in the direction of Beth-jeshimoth,[m] to a point under the slopes of Pisgah. [4]Secondly, Og, king of Bashan, a survivor of the Rephaim, who lived at Ashtaroth and Edrei.[n] [5]He ruled over Mount Hermon, Salecah, and all Bashan as far as the boundary of the Geshurites and Maacathites, and over half of Gilead as far as the territory of Sihon, king of Heshbon. [6]After Moses, the servant of the LORD, and the Israelites conquered them, he assigned their land to the Reubenites, the Gadites, and the half-tribe of Manasseh, as their property.[o]

[7]This is a list of the kings whom Joshua and the Israelites conquered west of the Jordan and whose land, from Baal-gad in the Lebanon valley to Mount Halak which rises toward Seir, Joshua apportioned to the tribes of Israel. [8]It included the mountain regions and foothills, the Arabah, the slopes, the desert, and the Negeb, belonging to the Hittites, Amorites, Canaanites, Perizzites, Hivites and Jebusites. [9]They were the kings of Jericho,[p] Ai (which is near Bethel), [10]Jerusalem, Hebron, [11]Jarmuth, Lachish,[q] [12]Eglon, Gezer,[r] [13]Debir, Geder,[s] [14]Hormah, Arad, [15]Libnah, Adullam,[t] [16]Makkedah, Bethel,[u] [17]Tappuah, Hepher,[v] [18]Aphek, Lasharon,[w] [19]Madon, Hazor,[x] [20]Shimron, Achshaph,[y] [21]Taanach, Megiddo,[z] [22]Kedesh, Jokneam (at Carmel),[a] [23]and Dor (in Naphath-dor), the foreign king at Gilgal,[b] [24]and the king of Tirzah, thirty-one kings in all.

II: Division of the Land

CHAPTER 13

See RG 97-98

Division of Land Commanded. [1]When Joshua was old and advanced in years, the LORD said to him:[c] "Though now you are old and advanced in years, a very large part of the land still remains to be conquered. [2]This additional land includes all Geshur* and all the districts of the Philistines [3](from the stream adjoining Egypt to the boundary of Ekron in the north is reckoned Canaanite territory, though held by the five lords of the Philistines in Gaza, Ashdod, Ashkelon, Gath and Ekron); also where the Avvim are in the south;[d] [4]all the land of the Canaanites from Mearah of the Sidonians to Aphek, and the boundaries of the Amorites; [5]and the Gebalite territory; and all the Lebanon on the east, from Baal-gad at the foot of Mount Hermon to Labo in the land of Hamath. [6]At the advance of the Israelites I will drive out all the Sidonian

---

11, 23: The land enjoyed peace: of a limited and temporary nature. Many of the individual tribes had still to fight against the remaining Canaanites; cf Jos 15, 13-17; 17, 12f. This verse forms the conclusion to the first part of the book. Cf note on Jos 12, 1-24.

12, 1-24: This chapter, inserted between the two principal parts of the book (chapters 1-11 and 13-21), resembles the lists of conquered cities which are inscribed on monuments of the Egyptian and Assyrian monarchs. Perhaps it was copied here from some such public Israelite record.

13, 2: Geshur: not to be confused with the large Aramaean district of the same name in Bashan (vv 11-13; Dt 3, 14); here it is a region to the south of the Philistine country, since vv 2-5 list the unconquered lands along the coast from south to north; cf also 1 Sm 27, 8.

k: Jos 14, 1—19, 51; Nm 34, 2-12. l: 2-5: Nm 21, 21-26. 33ff. m: Jos 13, 20. n: Jos 13, 11f. o: Nm 32, 33; Dt 3, 12f. p: Jos 6, 2; 8, 23. q: 10f: Jos 10, 23. r: Jos 10, 23. 33. s: Jos 10, 38f; 15, 36. t: Jos 10, 29f; 15, 35. u: Jos 8, 17; 10, 28. v: Jos 15, 34. w: Jos 15, 53. x: Jos 11, 1: 10. y: Jos 11, 1. z: Jos 17, 11. a: Jos 19, 37. b: Jos 11, 2. c: Jos 23, 1. d: Jgs 3, 3.

inhabitants of the mountain regions between Lebanon and Misrephoth-maim;[e] at least include these areas in the division of the Israelite heritage, just as I have commanded you. [7]Now, therefore, apportion among the nine tribes and the half-tribe of Manasseh the land which is to be their heritage."

The Eastern Tribes. [8f] Now the other half of the tribe of Manasseh, as well as the Reubenites and Gadites, had received their heritage which Moses, the servant of the LORD, had given them east of the Jordan: [9]from Aroer on the bank of the Wadi Arnon and the city in the wadi itself, through the tableland of Medeba and Dibon, [10]with the rest of the cities of Sihon, king of the Amorites, who reigned in Heshbon, to the boundary of the Ammonites; [11]also Gilead and the territory of the Geshurites and Maacathites, all Mount Hermon, and all Bashan as far as Salecah, [12]the entire kingdom in Bashan of Og, a survivor of the Rephaim, who reigned at Ashtaroth and Edrei. Though Moses conquered and occupied these territories, [13]the Israelites did not dislodge the Geshurites and Maacathites, so that Geshur and Maacath survive in the midst of Israel to this day. [14g]However, to the tribe of Levi Moses assigned no heritage since, as the LORD had promised them, the LORD, the God of Israel, is their heritage.

Reuben. [15h]What Moses gave to the Reubenite clans:[i] [16]Their territory reached from Aroer, on the bank of the Wadi Arnon, and the city in the wadi itself, through the tableland about Medeba, [17]to include Heshbon and all its towns which are on the tableland, Dibon, Bamoth-baal, Beth-baal-meon, [18]Jahaz, Kedemoth, Mephaath, [19]Kiriathaim, Sibmah, Zereth-shahar on the knoll within the valley, [20]Beth-peor, the slopes of Pisgah, Beth-jeshimoth, [21]and the other cities of the tableland and, generally, of the kingdom of Sihon. This Amorite king, who reigned in Heshbon, Moses had killed, with his vassals, the princes of Midian, who were

settled in the land: Evi, Rekem, Zur, Hur and Reba;[j] [22]and among their slain followers the Israelites put to the sword also the soothsayer Balaam, son of Beor.[k] [23]The boundary of the Reubenites was the bank of the Jordan. These cities and their villages were the heritage of the clans of the Reubenites.

Gad. [24l]What Moses gave to the Gadite clans: [25]Their territory included Jazer, all the cities of Gilead, and half the land of the Ammonites as far as Aroer, toward Rabbah [26](that is, from Heshbon to Ramath-mizpeh and Betonim, and from Mahanaim to the boundary of Lodebar); [27]and in the Jordan valley: Beth-haram, Beth-nimrah, Succoth, Zaphon, the other part of the kingdom of Sihon, king of Heshbon, with the bank of the Jordan to the southeastern tip of the Sea of Chinnereth. [28]These cities and their villages were the heritage of the clans of the Gadites.

Manasseh. [29m]What Moses gave to the clans of the half-tribe of Manasseh: [30]Their territory included Mahanaim, all of Bashan, the entire kingdom of Og, king of Bashan, and all the villages of Jair, which are sixty cities in Bashan.[n] [31]Half of Gilead, with Ashtaroth and Edrei, once the royal cities of Og in Bashan, fell to the descendants of Machir, son of Manasseh, for half the clans descended from Machir.

[32]These are the portions which Moses gave when he was in the plains of Moab, beyond the Jordan east of Jericho. [33]However, Moses gave no heritage to the tribe of Levi, since the LORD himself, the God of Israel, is their heritage, as he promised.[o]

CHAPTER 14

See RG 97-98

The Western Tribes. [1]Here follow the portions which the Israelites received in the land of Canaan.[p] Eleazar the priest, Joshua, son of Nun, and the heads of families in the tribes of the Israelites determined [2]their heritage by lot, in accordance with the instructions the LORD had given through Moses concerning the remaining nine and a half tribes.[q] [3]For to two and a half tribes

e: Jos 11, 8.   f: Jos 12, 6; Nm 32, 33.   g: Jos 14, 3f; Nm 18, 20-24.   h: 15-31: Dt 3, 12-17.   i: 15-23: Nm 21, 25-31; 32, 37f.   j: Nm 21, 24; 31, 8; Dt 3, 10.   k: Nm 31, 8.   l: 24-28: Nm 32, 34ff.   m: 29-31: Nm 32, 39ff.   n: Nm 32, 41.   o: Jos 18, 7; Nm 18, 20. p: Jos 17, 4; 21, 1; Nm 34, 17f.   q: Nm 26, 55; 33, 54; 34, 13.

Land Distribution

Joshua is joined by the priest Eleazar in 14, 1 because casting the sacred lot could only be done by a priest (Dt 33, 8). Distribution by lot confirms that the results are in accordance with divine will. The total number of allotments comes out to twelve because Joseph gave rise to two tribes and Levi received no territory. In the practice of casting lots, two options (groups, people, or answers) would be presented and the lot would be cast, not unlike flipping a coin, to indicate one of the two options over the other. Subsequent castings would gradually narrow the results until the final answer was determined. See 1 Samuel 14, 40–42 for such a progression.

Moses had already given a heritage beyond the Jordan; and though the Levites were given no heritage among the tribes,' [r] 4the descendants of Joseph formed two tribes, Manasseh and Ephraim. The Levites themselves received no share of the land except cities to live in, with their pasture lands for the cattle and flocks.[s]

5Thus, in apportioning the land, did the Israelites carry out the instructions of the LORD to Moses.

Caleb's Portion. 6[t]When the Judahites came up to Joshua in Gilgal, the Kenizzite Caleb, son of Jephunneh, said to him: "You know what the LORD said to the man of God, Moses, about you and me in Kadesh-barnea. 7uI was forty years old when the servant of the LORD, Moses, sent me from Kadesh-barnea to reconnoiter the land; and I brought back to him a conscientious report. 8vMy fellow scouts who went up with me discouraged the people, but I was completely loyal to the LORD, my God. 9On that occasion Moses swore this oath, 'The land where you have set foot shall become your heritage and that of your descendants forever, because you have been completely loyal to the LORD, my God.' 10Now, as he promised, the LORD has preserved me while Israel was journeying through the desert, for the forty-five years since the LORD spoke thus to Moses; and although I am now eighty-five years old,[w] 11I am still as strong today as I was the day Moses sent me forth, with no less vigor whether for war or for ordinary tasks.[x] 12Give me, therefore, this mountain region which the LORD promised me that day, as you yourself heard. True, the Anakim are there, with large fortified cities, but if the LORD is with me I shall be able to drive them out, as the LORD promised."[y] 13Joshua blessed Caleb, son of Jephunneh, and gave him Hebron as his heritage.[z] 14Therefore Hebron remains the heritage of the Kenizzite Caleb, son of Jephunneh, to the present day, because he was completely loyal to the LORD, the God of Israel. 15Hebron was formerly called Kiriath-arba, for Arba, the greatest among the Anakim.[a] And the land enjoyed peace.

CHAPTER 15

See RG 97–98

Boundaries of Judah. 1The lot for the clans of the Judahite tribe fell in the extreme south toward the boundary of Edom, the desert of Zin in the Negeb.[b] 2cThe boundary there ran from the bay that forms the southern end of the Salt Sea, 3southward below the pass of Akrabbim, across through Zin, up to a point south of Kadesh-barnea, across to Hezron, and up to Addar; from there, looping around Karka, 4it crossed to Azmon and then joined the Wadi of Egypt before coming out at the sea. [This is your southern boundary.] 5The eastern boundary was the Salt Sea as far as the mouth of the Jordan.

6dThe northern boundary climbed from the bay where the Jordan meets the sea, up to Beth-hoglah, and ran north of Beth-arabah, up to Eben-Bohan-ben-Reuben. 7Thence it climbed to Debir, north of the vale of Achor,[e] in the direction of the Gilgal that faces the pass of Adummim, on the south side of the

r: Jos 13, 8. 14. 33.   s: Jos 21, 3-40; Gn 48, 5.   t: Nm 14, 24. 30; 32, 12; Dt 1, 36. 38.   u: Nm 14, 6-9.   v: Nm 13, 31ff; 14, 24; 32, 12; Dt 1, 36.   w: Nm 14, 30.   x: Sir 46, 1ff.   y: Jos 11, 21.   z: Jos 10, 36f; 15, 13-19; 21, 11f.   a: Jgs 1, 10.   b: Nm 34, 3.   c: 2-4; Nm 34, 3ff.   d: Jos 18, 18f. 22.   e: Jos 7, 26; 18, 16ff: 2 Sm 17, 17.

wadi; from there it crossed to the waters of En-shemesh and emerged at En-rogel. [8]Climbing again to the Valley of Ben-Hinnom* on the southern flank of the Jebusites [that is, Jerusalem], the boundary rose to the top of the mountain at the northern end of the Valley of Rephaim,[f] which bounds the Valley of Hinnom on the west. [9]From the top of the mountain it ran to the fountain of waters of Nephtoah,[g] extended to the cities of Mount Ephron, and continued to Baalah, or Kiriath-jearim. [10]From Baalah the boundary curved westward to Mount Seir and passed north of the ridge of Mount Jearim (that is, Chesalon); thence it descended to Beth-shemesh, and ran across to Timnah. [11]It then extended along the northern flank of Ekron, continued through Shikkeron, and across to Mount Baalah, thence to include Jabneel, before it came out at the sea. [12]The western boundary was the Great Sea and its coast. This was the complete boundary of the clans of the Judahites.

Conquest by Caleb. [13h]As the LORD had commanded, Joshua gave Caleb, son of Jephunneh,[i] a portion among the Judahites, namely, Kiriath-arba (Arba was the father of Anak), that is, Hebron. [14j]And Caleb drove out from there the three Anakim, the descendants of Anak: Sheshai, Ahiman and Talmai. [15]From there he marched up against the inhabitants of Debir,[k] which was formerly called Kiriath-sepher. [16]Caleb said, "I will give my daughter Achsah in marriage to the one who attacks Kiriath-sepher and captures it." [17]*Othniel, son of Caleb's brother Kenaz, captured it, and so Caleb gave him his daughter Achsah in marriage. [18]On the day of her marriage to Othniel, she induced him to ask her father for some land. Then, as she alighted from the ass, Caleb asked her, "What is troubling you?" [19]She answered,

"Give me an additional gift! Since you have assigned to me land in the Negeb, give me also pools of water." So he gave her the upper and the lower pools.

Cities of Judah. [20]*This is the heritage of the clans of the tribe of Judahites: [21]The cities of the tribe of the Judahites in the extreme southern district toward Edom were: Kabzeel, Eder, Jagur, [22]Kinah, Dimonah, Adadah, [23]Kedesh, Hazor and Ithnan; [24]Ziph, Telem, Bealoth, [25]Hazor-hadattah, and Kerioth-hezron (that is, Hazor); [26]Amam, Shema, Moladah, [27]Hazar-gaddah, Heshmon, Beth-pelet, [28]Hazar-shual, Beer-sheba, and Biziothiah, [29]Baalah, Iim, Ezem, [30]Eltolad, Chesil, Hormah, [31]Ziklag,[l] Madmannah, Sansannah, [32]Lebaoth, Shilhim and En-rimmon; a total of twenty-nine cities with their villages.

[33]In the foothills:* Eshtaol, Zorah, Ashnah, [34]Zanoah, Engannim, Tappuah, Enam, [35]Jarmuth, Adullam, Socoh, Azekah, [36]Shaaraim, Adithaim, Gederah, and Gederothaim; fourteen cities and their villages. [37]Zenan, Hadashah, Migdal-gad, [38]Dilean, Mizpeh, Joktheel, [39]Lachish, Bozkath, Eglon, [40]Cabbon, Lahmam, Chitlish, [41]Gederoth, Beth-dagon, Naamah and Makkedah; sixteen cities and their villages. [42]Libnah, Ether, Ashan, [43]Iphtah, Ashnah, Nezib, [44]Keilah, Achzib and Mareshah; nine cities and their villages. [45]Ekron and its towns and villages; [46]from Ekron to the sea, all the towns that lie alongside Ashdod and their villages; [47]Ashdod and its towns and villages; Gaza and its towns and villages, as far as the Wadi of Egypt and the coast of the Great Sea.

[48]In the mountain regions: Shamir, Jattir, Socoh, [49]Dannah, Kiriath-sannah (that is, Debir), [50]Anab, Eshtemoh, Anim, [51]Goshen, Holon and Giloh; eleven cities and their villages. [52]Arab, Dumah, Eshan, [53]Janim, Beth-tappuah, Aphekah, [54]Humtah,

---

15, 8: The Valley of Ben-hinnom: the southern limit of Jerusalem. Ben-hinnom means "son of Hinnom." The place was also called Valley of Hinnom, in Hebrew ge-hinnom, whence the word "Gehenna" is derived.

15, 17-19: The story of Othniel is told again in Jgs 1, 13-15; cf also Jgs 3, 9-11.

15, 20-62: This elaborate list of the cities of Judah was probably taken from a document made originally for administrative purposes; the cities are divided into four provincial districts, some of which have further subdivisions. For simi-

lar lists of the cities of Judah, cf Jos 19, 2-7; 1 Chr 4, 28-32; Neh 11, 25-30. This list has suffered in transmission, so that the totals given in vv 32 and 36 are not exact, and some of the names are probably misspelled; many of the cities cannot be identified.

15, 33: In the foothills: see note on Dt 1, 7.

---

f: Jos 18, 16.   *g:* Jos 18, 15.   *h:* 13-19: Jgs 1, 10-15.   *i:* Jos 14, 13ff.   *j:* Nm 13, 22; Jgs 1, 20.   *k:* Jos 10, 38.   *l:* 1 Sm 27, 6.

Kiriath-arba (that is, Hebron), and Zior; nine cities and their villages. [55]Maon, Carmel, Ziph, Juttah, [56]Jezreel, Jokdeam, Zanoah, [57]Kain, Gibbeah and Timnah; ten cities and their villages. [58]Halhul, Beth-zur, Gedor, [59]Maarath, Beth-anoth and Eltekon; six cities and their villages. Tekoa, Ephrathah (that is, Bethlehem), Peor, Etam, Kulom, Tatam, Zores, Karim, Gallim, Bether and Manoko; eleven cities and their villages. [60]Kiriath-baal (that is, Kiriath-jearim) and Rabbah: two cities and their villages.[m]

[61]In the desert:* Beth-arabah, Middin, Secacah, [62]Nibshan, Ir-hamelah and En-gedi; six cities and their villages. [63][But the Jebusites who lived in Jerusalem the Judahites could not drive out; so the Jebusites dwell in Jerusalem beside the Judahites to the present day.[n]]

See RG 97–98

CHAPTER 16

The Joseph Tribes. [1]The lot that fell to the Josephites* extended from the Jordan at Jericho to the waters of Jericho east of the desert; then the boundary went up from Jericho to the heights at Bethel.* [2]Leaving Bethel for Luz, it crossed the ridge to the border of the Archites at Ataroth, [3]and descended westward to the border of the Japhletites, to that of Lower Beth-horon, and to Gezer, ending thence at the sea.[o]

Ephraim. [4]Within the heritage of Manasseh and Ephraim, sons of Joseph, [5]the dividing line* for the heritage of the clans of the Ephraimites ran from east of Ataroth-addar to Upper Beth-horon[p] [6]and thence to the sea. From Michmethath[q] on the north, their boundary curved eastward around Taanath-shiloh, and continued east of it to Janoah; [7]from there it descended to Ataroth and Naarah, and skirting Jericho, it ended at the Jordan. [8]From Tappuah[r] the boundary ran westward to the Wadi Kanah

and ended at the sea. This was the heritage of the clans of the Ephraimites, [9]including the villages that belonged to each city set aside for the Ephraimites within the territory of the Manassehites.[s] [10]But they did not drive out the Canaanites living in Gezer,[t] who live on within Ephraim to the present day, though they have been impressed as laborers.

CHAPTER 17

See RG 97–98

Manasseh. [1]Now as for the lot that fell to the tribe of Manasseh[u] as the firstborn of Joseph: since his eldest son, Machir, the father of Gilead, was a warrior, who had already obtained Gilead and Bashan, [2]the allotment was now made to the other descendants of Manasseh, the clans of Abiezer, Helek, Asriel, Shechem, Hepher and Shemida, the other male children of Manasseh, son of Joseph.

[3]Furthermore, Zelophehad, son of Hepher,[w] son of Gilead, son of Machir, son of Manasseh, had had no sons, but only daughters, whose names were Mahlah, Noah, Hoglah, Milcah, and Tirzah. [4]These presented themselves to Eleazar the priest, to Joshua, son of Nun, and to the princes, saying, "The LORD commanded Moses to give us a heritage among our kinsmen." So in obedience to the command of the LORD a heritage was given to each of them among their father's kinsmen.[x] [5]Thus ten shares fell to Manasseh apart from the land of Gilead and Bashan beyond the Jordan,[y] [6]since these female descendants of Manasseh received each a portion among his sons. The land of Gilead fell to the rest of the Manassehites.

[7]Manasseh bordered on Asher.* From Michmethath, near Shechem, another boundary ran southward to include the natives

---

15, 61: In the desert: in the Jordan rift near the Dead Sea.
16, 1—17, 18: The boundaries and cities of Judah, the most important tribe, having been given, the land of the next most important group, the two Josephite tribes of Ephraim and Manasseh, is now described, though it was separated from Judah by the territories of Benjamin (Jos 18, 11-20) and Dan (Jos 19, 40-48).
16, 1-3: This line formed the southern boundary of Ephraim and the northern boundaries of Benjamin and of Dan.
16, 5: The dividing line: separating Ephraim from Manas-

seh. Ephraim's northern border (v 5) is given in an east-to-west direction; its eastern border (v 6f) in a north-to-south direction.
17, 7: Manasseh bordered on Asher: only at the extreme northwestern section of Manasseh's territory. The boundary

m: Jos 18, 14. n: Jgs 1, 21; 2 Sm 5, 6. o: Jos 10, 10. 33. p: Jos 18, 13. q: Jos 17, 7. r: Jos 17, 7. s: Jos 17, 9. t: Jgs 1, 29. u: Gn 41, 51; 46, 20; 48, 18; 50, 23; Nm 26, 29; Dt 3, 13. 15. v: Nm 26, 29-32. w: Nm 26, 33; 27, 1; 36, 2. x: Nm 27, 6f; 36, 2. y: Jos 13, 30f.

of En-Tappuah, [8]because the district of Tappuah belonged to Manasseh, although Tappuah itself was an Ephraimite city on the border of Manasseh. [9]This same boundary continued down to the Wadi Kanah.[z] The cities that belonged to Ephraim from among the cities of Manasseh were those to the south of the wadi; thus the territory of Manasseh ran north of the wadi and ended at the sea. [10]The land on the south belonged to Ephraim and that on the north to Manasseh; with the sea as their common boundary, they reached Asher on the north and Issachar on the east.

[11a]Moreover, in Issachar and in Asher Manasseh was awarded Beth-shean[b] and its towns, Ibleam and its towns, Dor and its towns and the natives there, Endor and its towns and natives, Taanach and its towns and natives, and Megiddo and its towns and natives [the third is Naphath-dor]. [12]Since the Manassehites could not conquer these cities, the Canaanites persisted in this region. [13]When the Israelites grew stronger they impressed the Canaanites as laborers, but they did not drive them out.

Protest of Joseph Tribes. [14]The descendants of Joseph said to Joshua, "Why have you given us only one lot and one share as our heritage?[c] Our people are too many, because of the extent to which the LORD has blessed us." [15]Joshua answered them, "If you are too many, go up to the forest and clear out a place for yourselves there in the land of the Perizzites and Rephaim, since the mountain regions of Ephraim are so narrow." [16]For the Josephites said, "Our mountain regions are not enough for us; on the other hand, the Canaanites living in the valley region all have iron chariots, in particular those in Beth-shean and its towns, and those in the valley of Jezreel."[d] [17]Joshua therefore said to Ephraim and Manasseh, the house of Joseph, "You are a numerous people and very strong. You shall have not merely one share, [18]for the mountain region which is now forest shall be yours when you clear it. Its adjacent land shall also be yours if, despite their strength and iron chariots, you drive out the Canaanites."

CHAPTER 18

See RG 97–98

[1]After they had subdued the land, the whole community of the Israelites assembled at Shiloh, where they set up the meeting tent.[e]

The Seven Remaining Portions. [2]Seven tribes among the Israelites had not yet received their heritage. [3]Joshua therefore said to the Israelites, "How much longer will you put off taking steps to possess the land which the LORD, the God of your fathers, has given you? [4]Choose three men from each of your tribes; I will commission them to begin a survey of the land, which they shall describe for purposes of inheritance. When they return to me, [5]you shall divide it into seven parts. Judah is to retain its territory in the south,[f] and the house of Joseph its territory in the north. [6]You shall bring here to me the description of the land in seven sections. I will then cast lots for you here before the LORD, our God. [7]For the Levites have no share among you,[g] because the priesthood of the LORD is their heritage; while Gad, Reuben, and the half-tribe of Manasseh have already received the heritage east of the Jordan which Moses, the servant of the LORD, gave them."

[8]When those who were to map out the land were ready for the journey, Joshua instructed them to survey the land, prepare a description of it, and return to him; then he would cast lots for them there before the LORD in Shiloh. [9]So they went through the land, listed its cities in writing in seven sections, and returned to Joshua in the camp at Shiloh. [10]Joshua then divided up the land for the Israelites into their separate shares, casting lots for them before the LORD in Shiloh.

given in the following sentences (vv 7-10) is a more detailed description of the one already mentioned in Jos 16, 5ff, as separating Manasseh from Ephraim.

---

z: Jos 16, 8f.   a: 1 Chr 7, 29.   b: 11ff: Jgs 1, 27f.   c: Jos 16, 4; Gn 48, 19f. 22.   d: Jgs 6, 33.   e: Jos 19, 51.   f: Jos 15, 1—17, 18.   g: Jos 13, 8. 33.

Benjamin. [11]One lot fell to the clans of the tribe of Benjaminites. The territory allotted them lay between the descendants of Judah and those of Joseph. [12h]Their northern boundary* began at the Jordan and went over the northern flank of Jericho, up westward into the mountains, till it reached the desert of Beth-aven. [13]From there it crossed over to the southern flank of Luz (that is, Bethel). Then it ran down to Ataroth-addar, on the mountaintop south of Lower Beth-horon.[i] [14]For the western border, the boundary line swung south from the mountaintop opposite Beth-horon till it reached Kiriath-baal (that is, Kiriath-jearim), which city belonged to the Judahites. This was the western boundary. [15]The southern boundary began at the limits of Kiriath-jearim and projected to the spring at Nephtoah. [16]It went down to the edge of the mountain on the north of the Valley of Rephaim, where it faces the Valley of Ben-hinnom; and continuing down the Valley of Hinnom along the southern flank of the Jebusites, reached En-rogel.[j] [17]Inclining to the north, it extended to En-shemesh, and thence to Geliloth, opposite the pass of Adummim. Then it dropped to Eben-Bohan-ben-Reuben, [18]across the northern flank of the Arabah overlook, down into the Arabah.[k] [19]From there the boundary continued across the northern flank of Beth-hoglah and extended to the northern tip of the Salt Sea, at the southern end of the Jordan. This was the southern boundary. [20]The Jordan bounded it on the east. This was how the heritage of the clans of the Benjaminites was bounded on all sides.

[21]Now the cities belonging to the clans of the tribe of the Benjaminites were: Jericho, Beth-hoglah, Emek-keziz, [22]Beth-arabah, Zemaraim, Bethel, [23]Avvim, Parah, Ophra, [24]Chephar-ammoni, Ophni and Geba; twelve cities and their villages.

[25]Also Gibeon, Ramah, Beeroth, [26]Mizpeh, Chephirah, Mozah, [27]Rekem, Irpeel, Taralah, [28]Zela, Haeleph, the Jebusite city (that is, Jerusalem), Gibeah and Kiriath; fourteen cities and their villages. This was the heritage of the clans of Benjaminites.

CHAPTER 19

See RG 97-98

Simeon. [1]The second lot fell to Simeon. The heritage of the clans of the tribe of Simeonites lay within that of the Judahites. [2]For their heritage they received Beer-sheba, Shema, Moladah, [3]Hazar-shual, Balah, Ezem, [4]Eltolad, Bethul, Hormah, [5]Ziklag, Beth-marcaboth, Hazar-susah, [6]Beth-lebaoth and Sharuhen; thirteen cities and their villages. [7]Also En-rimmon, Ether and Ashan; four cities and their villages, [8]besides all the villages around these cities as far as Baalath-beer (that is, Ramoth-negeb). This was the heritage of the clans of the tribe of the Simeonites. [9]This heritage of the Simeonites was within the confines of the Judahites; for since the portion of the latter was too large for them, the Simeonites obtained their heritage within it.

Zebulun. [10]*The third lot fell to the clans of the Zebulunites. The limit of their heritage was at Sarid. [11]Their boundary went up west . . . and through Mareal, reaching Dabbe-sheth and the wadi that is near Jokneam. [12]From Sarid eastward it ran to the district of Chisloth-tabor, on to Daberath, and up to Japhia. [13]From there it continued eastward to Gath-hepher and to Eth-kazin, extended to Rimmon, and turned to Neah. [14]Skirting north of Hannathon, the boundary ended at the valley of Iphtahel. [15]Thus, with Kattath, Nahalal, Shimron, Idalah and Bethlehem, there were twelve cities and their villages [16]to comprise the heritage of the clans of the Zebulunites.

18, 12-20: Benjamin's northern boundary (vv 12f) corresponded to part of the southern boundary of Ephraim (Jos 16, 1f). Their western border (v 14) was the eastern border of Dan (cf Jos 19, 40-47). Their southern boundary (vv 15-19) corresponded to part of the northern boundary of Judah (Jos 15, 6-9).

19, 10-16: Zebulun's territory was in the central section of the Plain of Esdraelon and of southern Galilee; it was bounded on the south by Manasseh, on the southeast by Issachar, on the

northeast and north by Naphtali, and on the west by Asher. The site of the later city of Nazareth was within its borders. Bethlehem of Zebulun was, of course, distinct from the city of the same name in Judah. Twelve cities: apparently seven of the names are missing from v 15, unless some of the places mentioned in vv 12-14 are to be included in the number.

---

h: Jos 16, 1.   i: Jos 16, 2f. 5; Gn 28, 19.   j: Jos 15, 7f.   k: Jos 15, 6.   l: 2-8: 1 Chr 4, 28-33.

Issachar. [17]*The fourth lot fell to Issachar. The territory of the clans of the Issacharites [18]included Jezreel, Chesulloth, Shunem, [19]Hapharaim, Shion, Anaharath, [20]Rabbith, Kishion, Ebez, [21]Remeth, En-gannim, En-haddah and Beth-pazzez. [22]The boundary reached Tabor, Shahazumah and Beth-shemesh, ending at the Jordan. These sixteen cities and their villages [23]were the heritage of the clans of the Issacharites.

Asher. [24]*The fifth lot fell to the clans of the tribe of the Asherites. [25]Their territory included Helkath, Hali, Beten, Achshaph, [26]Allammelech, Amad and Mishal, and reached Carmel on the west, and Shihor-libnath. [27]In the other direction, it ran eastward of Beth-dagon, reached Zebulun and the valley of Iphtahel; then north of Beth-emek and Neiel, it extended to Cabul, [28]Mishal, Abdon, Rehob,[m] Hammon and Kanah, near Greater Sidon. [29]Then the boundary turned back to Ramah and to the fortress city of Tyre; thence it cut back to Hosah and ended at the sea. Thus, with Mahalab, Achzib, [30]Ummah, Acco, Aphek and Rehob, there were twenty-two cities and their villages [31]to comprise the heritage of the clans of the tribe of the Asherites.

Naphtali. [32]*The sixth lot fell to the Naphtalites. The boundary of the clans of the Naphtalites [33]extended from Heleph, from the oak at Zaanannim to Lakkum, including Adami-nekeb and Jabneel, and ended at the Jordan. [34]In the opposite direction, westerly, it ran through Aznoth-tabor and from there extended to Hukkok; it touched Zebulun on the south, Asher on the west, and the Jordan on the east. [35]The fortified cities were Ziddim, Zer, Hammath,

Rakkath, Chinnereth, [36]Adamah, Ramah, Hazor, [37]Kedesh, Edrei, En-hazor, [38]Yiron, Migdal-el, Horem, Beth-anath and Beth-shemesh;[n] nineteen cities and their villages, [39]to comprise the heritage of the clans of the tribe of the Naphtalites.

Dan. [40]*The seventh lot fell to the clans of the tribe of Danites. [41]Their heritage was the territory of Zorah, Eshtaol, Ir-shemesh, [42]Shaalabbin, Aijalon, Ithlah,[o] [43]Elon, Timnah, Ekron, [44]Eltekoh, Gibbethon, Baalath, [45]Jehud, Bene-berak, Gath-rimmon, [46]Mejarkon and Rakkon, with the coast at Joppa. [47]pBut the territory of the Danites was too small for them; so the Danites marched up and attacked Leshem,* which they captured and put to the sword. Once they had taken possession of Leshem, they renamed the settlement after their ancestor Dan. [48]These cities and their villages were the heritage of the clans of the tribe of the Danites.

Joshua's City. [49]When the last of them had received the portions of the land they were to inherit, the Israelites assigned a heritage in their midst to Joshua, son of Nun. [50]In obedience to the command of the LORD, they gave him the city which he requested, Timnah-serah[q] in the mountain region of Ephraim. He rebuilt the city and made it his home.

[51]These are the final portions into which Eleazar the priest, Joshua, son of Nun, and the heads of families in the tribes of the Israelites divided the land by lot in the presence of the LORD, at the door of the meeting tent in Shiloh.

CHAPTER 20

See RG
98

Cities of Asylum. [1]The LORD said to Joshua:* [2]"Tell the Israelites to designate the

---

19, 17-23: Issachar's land was on the eastern watershed of the Plain of Esdraelon, but also included the southeastern end of the Galilean mountains. It was surrounded by Manasseh on the south and east, by Naphtali on the north, and by Zebulun on the west. Jezreel (v 18) dominated the plain to which it gave its name, the later form of which was Esdraelon.

19, 24-31: Asher inherited the western slope of the Galilean hills as far as the sea, with Manasseh to the south, Zebulun and Naphtali to the east, and Phoenicia to the north.

19, 32-39: Naphtali received eastern Galilee; Asher was to the west and Zebulun and Issachar were to the south, while the upper Jordan and Mount Hermon formed the east-

ern border. Part of the tribe of Dan later on occupied the northern extremity of Naphtali's lands, at the sources of the Jordan (v 47).

19, 40-46: The original territory of Dan was a small enclave between Judah, Benjamin, Ephraim and the Philistines.

19, 47: Leshem: called Laish in Jgs 18, where the story of the migration of the Danites is told at greater length.

20, 1-9: The laws concerning the cities of refuge are given in Nm 35, 9-28; Dt 19, 1-13; see notes on Nm 35, 16-25; Dt 19, 2.

---

m: 28f: Jgs 1, 31.   n: Jgs 1, 33.   o: Jgs 1, 35.   p: Jgs 18, 27-29.
q: Jos 24, 30; Jgs 2, 9.

cities of which I spoke to them through Moses,[r] [3]to which one guilty of accidental and unintended homicide may flee for asylum from the avenger of blood. [4]To one of these cities the killer shall flee, and standing at the entrance of the city gate, he shall plead his case before the elders, who must receive him and assign him a place in which to live among them. [5]Though the avenger of blood pursues him, they are not to deliver up the homicide who slew his fellow man unintentionally and not out of previous hatred. [6]Once he has stood judgment before the community, he shall live on in that city till the death of the high priest who is in office at the time. Then the killer may go back home to his own city from which he fled."[s]

List of Cities. [7]So they set apart Kedesh in Galilee in the mountain region of Naphtali, Shechem in the mountain region of Ephraim, and Kiriath-arba (that is, Hebron) in the mountain region of Judah.[t] [8]And beyond the Jordan east of Jericho they designated Bezer on the open tableland in the tribe of Reuben, Ramoth in Gilead in the tribe of Gad, and Golan in Bashan in the tribe of Manasseh.[u] [9]These were the designated cities[v] to which any Israelite or stranger living among them who had killed a person accidentally might flee to escape death at the hand of the avenger of blood, until he could appear before the community.

CHAPTER 21

See RG 98

Levitical Cities. [1]The heads of the Levite families* came up to Eleazar the priest, to Joshua, son of Nun, and to the heads of families of the other tribes of the Israelites[w] [2]at Shiloh in the land of Canaan, and said to them, "The LORD commanded, through Moses, that cities be given us to dwell in, with pasture lands for our livestock."[x] [3]Out of their own heritage, in obedience to this command

of the LORD, the Israelites gave the Levites the following cities with their pasture lands.

[4]When the first lot among the Levites fell to the clans of the Kohathites, the descendants of Aaron the priest obtained thirteen cities by lot from the tribes of Judah, Simeon and Benjamin. [5]The rest of the Kohathites obtained ten cities by lot from the clans of the tribe of Ephraim, from the tribe of Dan, and from the half-tribe of Manasseh. [6]The Gershonites obtained thirteen cities by lot from the clans of the tribe of Issachar, from the tribe of Asher, from the tribe of Naphtali, and from the half-tribe of Manasseh. [7]The clans of the Merarites obtained twelve cities from the tribes of Reuben, Gad and Zebulun. [8]These cities with their pasture lands the Israelites allotted to the Levites in obedience to the LORD's command through Moses.[y]

Cities of the Priests. [9]From the tribes of the Judahites and Simeonites they designated the following cities, [10]and assigned them to the descendants of Aaron in the Kohathite clan of the Levites, since the first lot fell to them: [11]first, Kiriath-arba (Arba was the father of Anak), that is, Hebron, in the mountain region of Judah, with the adjacent pasture lands, [12]although the open country and villages belonging to the city had been given to Caleb, son of Jephunneh, as his property.[a] [13]Thus to the descendants of Aaron the priest were given the city of asylum for homicides at Hebron, with its pasture lands; also, Libnah with its pasture lands, [14]Jattir with its pasture lands, Eshtemoa with its pasture lands, [15]Holon with its pasture lands, Debir with its pasture lands, [16]Ashan with its pasture lands, Juttah with its pasture lands, and Beth-shemesh with its pasture lands: nine cities from the two tribes mentioned. [17]From the tribe of Benjamin they obtained the four

---

21, 1: The order to establish special cities for the Levites is given in Nm 35, 1-8. The forty-eight cities listed here were hardly the exclusive possession of the Levites; at least the more important of them, such as Hebron, Shechem and Ramoth in Gilead, were certainly peopled for the most part by the tribe in whose territory they were situated. But in all these cities the Levites had special prop-

erty rights which they did not possess in other cities; cf Lv 25, 32ff.

---

r: Ex 21, 13; Nm 35, 10-14; Dt 4, 41-43; 19, 2-9. s: Nm 35, 12. 24f. t: Jos 15, 13; 19, 37; 21, 21. u: Jos 21, 27. 36f. v: Nm 35, 15. w: Ex 6, 16-19; Nm 3, 17-20. x: Nm 35, 2. y: Nm 35, 2. z: 9-19: 1 Chr 6, 54-60. a: Jos 14, 14; 15, 13.

Levitical Cities

cities of Gibeon with its pasture lands, Geba with its pasture lands, [18]Anathoth[b] with its pasture lands, and Almon with its pasture lands. [19]These cities which with their pasture lands belonged to the priestly descendants of Aaron, were thirteen in all.

Cities of the Other Kohathites. [20c]The rest of the Kohathite clans among the Levites obtained by lot, from the tribe of Ephraim, four cities. [21]They were assigned, with its pasture lands, the city of asylum for homicides at Shechem in the mountain region of Ephraim; also Gezer with its pasture lands, [22]Kibzaim with its pasture lands, and Beth-horon with its pasture lands. [23]From the tribe of Dan they obtained the four cities of Elteke with its pasture lands, Gibbethon with its pasture lands, [24]Aijalon with its pasture lands, and Gath-rimmon with its pasture lands; [25]and from the half-tribe of Manasseh the two cities of Taanach with its pasture lands and Ibleam with its pasture lands. [26]These cities which with their pasture lands belonged to the rest of the Kohathite clans were ten in all.

Cities of the Gershonites. [27d]The Gershonite clan of the Levites received from the half-tribe of Manasseh two cities: the city of asylum for homicides at Golan with its pasture lands; and also Beth-Astharoth with its pasture lands. [28]From the tribe of Issachar they obtained the four cities of Kishion with its pasture lands, Daberath with its pasture lands, [29]Jarmuth with its pasture lands, and En-gannim with its pasture lands; [30]from the tribe of Asher, the four cities of Mishal with its pasture lands, Abdon with its pasture lands, [31]Helkath with its pasture lands, and Rehob with its pasture lands; [32]and from the tribe of Naphtali, three cities: the city of asylum for homicides at Kedesh in Galilee, with its pasture lands; also Hammath with its pasture lands, and Rakkath with its pasture lands. [33]These cities which with their pasture lands belonged to the Gershonite clans were thirteen in all.

Cities of the Merarites. [34e]The Merarite clans, the last of the Levites, received from the tribe of Zebulun the four cities of Jokneam with its pasture lands, Kartah with its pasture lands, [35]Rimmon with its pasture lands, and Nahalal with its pasture lands; [36]also, across the Jordan, from the tribe of Reuben, four cities: the city of asylum for homicides at Bezer with its pasture lands, Jahaz with its pasture lands, [37]Kedemoth with its pasture lands, and Mephaath with its pasture lands; [38]and from the tribe of Gad a total of four cities: the city of asylum for homicides at Ramoth in Gilead with its pasture lands, also Mahanaim with its pasture lands, [39]Heshbon with its pasture lands, and Jazer with its pasture lands. [40]The cities which were allotted to the Merarite clans, the last of the Levites, were therefore twelve in all.

[41]Thus the total number of cities[f] within the territory of the Israelites which, with their pasture lands, belonged to the Levites, was forty-eight. [42]With each and every one of these cities went the pasture lands round about it.

[43]And so the LORD gave Israel all the land he had sworn to their fathers he would give them.[g] Once they had conquered and occupied it, [44]the LORD gave them peace on every side, just as he had promised their fathers. Not one of their enemies could withstand them; the LORD brought all their enemies under their power. [45]Not a single promise[h] that the LORD made to the house of Israel was broken; every one was fulfilled.

III: Return of the Transjordan Tribes and Joshua's Farewell

CHAPTER 22

The Eastern Tribes Dismissed. [1]At that time Joshua summoned the Reubenites, the Gadites, and the half-tribe of Manasseh [2]and said to them:[i] "You have done all that Moses, the servant of the LORD, commanded you, and have obeyed every command I gave you. [3]For many years now you have not once abandoned your kinsmen, but have faithfully carried out the

See RG 98

---

b: Jer 1, 1.   *c:* 20-26: 1 Chr 6, 66-70.   *d:* 27-33: 1 Chr 6, 56-61.   *e:* 34-40: 1 Chr 6, 62-66.   *f:* Nm 35, 7.   *g:* Gn 12, 7; 13, 15; 15, 18; 26, 3; 28, 4. 13.   *h:* Jos 23, 14f.   *i:* Jos 1, 16f; Nm 32, 20ff; Dt 3, 18ff.

commands of the LORD, your God. [4]Since, therefore, the LORD, your God, has settled your kinsmen as he promised them, you may now return to your tents beyond the Jordan; to your own land, which Moses, the servant of the LORD, gave you.[j] [5]But be very careful to observe the precept and law which Moses, the servant of the LORD, enjoined upon you: love the LORD, your God;[k] follow him faithfully; keep his commandments; remain loyal to him; and serve him with your whole heart and soul." [6]Joshua then blessed them and sent them away to their own tents.

[7](For, to half the tribe of Manasseh Moses had assigned land in Bashan;[l] and to the other half Joshua had given a portion along with their kinsmen west of the Jordan.) What Joshua said to them when he sent them off to their tents with his blessing was, [8]"Now that you are returning to your own tents with great wealth, with very numerous livestock, with silver, gold, bronze and iron, and with a very large supply of clothing, divide these spoils of your enemies with your kinsmen there."[m] [9]So the Reubenites, the Gadites, and the half-tribe of Manasseh left the other Israelites at Shiloh in the land of Canaan and returned to the land of Gilead, their own property, which they had received according to the LORD's command through Moses.[n]

The Altar beside the Jordan. [10]When the Reubenites, the Gadites, and the half-tribe of Manasseh came to the region of the Jordan in the land of Canaan, they built there at the Jordan a conspicuously large altar. [11]The other Israelites heard the report[o] that the Reubenites, the Gadites, and the half-tribe of Manasseh had built an altar in the region of the Jordan

facing the land of Canaan,* across from them, [12]and therefore they assembled their whole community at Shiloh to declare war on them.*

Accusation of the Western Tribes. [13]First, however, they sent to the Reubenites, the Gadites, and the half-tribe of Manasseh in the land of Gilead an embassy consisting of Phinehas, son of Eleazar the priest,[p] [14]and ten princes, one from every tribe of Israel, each one being both prince and military leader of his ancestral house. [15]When these came to the Reubenites, the Gadites, and the half-tribe of Manasseh in the land of Gilead, they said to them: [16q]"The whole community of the LORD sends this message: What act of treachery is this you have committed against the God of Israel? You have seceded from the LORD this day, and rebelled against him by building an altar of your own! [17]For the sin of Peor, a plague came upon the community of the LORD.[r] [18]We are still not free of that; must you now add to it? You are rebelling against the LORD today and by tomorrow he will be angry with the whole community of Israel! [19]If you consider the land you now possess unclean,* cross over to the land the LORD possesses, where the Dwelling of the LORD stands,[s] and share that with us. But do not rebel against the LORD, nor involve us in rebellion, by building an altar of your own in addition to the altar of the LORD, our God. [20]When Achan, son of Zerah,[t] violated the ban, did not wrath fall upon the entire community of Israel? Though he was but a single man, he did not perish alone* for his guilt!"

Reply of the Eastern Tribes. [21]The Reubenites, the Gadites, and the half-tribe of Manasseh replied to the military leaders

---

22, 11: In the region of the Jordan facing the land of Canaan: on the eastern side of the Jordan valley. The river itself formed the boundary between these eastern tribes and the rest of the tribes who lived in what was formerly Canaan—though the term Canaan could also be used of both sides of the Jordan valley (cf v 10). The Transjordan tribes naturally built their altar in their own territory.

22, 12: To declare war on them: the western Israelites considered this altar, which seemed to violate the customary unity of the sanctuary (cf Lv 17, 1-9; Dt 12, 4-14), as a sign of secession and dangerous to national unity. The motives for the war were political as well as religious.

22, 19: Unclean: not sanctified by the Dwelling of the LORD.

22, 20: Achan . . . did not perish alone: his guilt caused the failure of the first attack on Ai (Jos 7, 4-23); this fact is adduced as an argument for the solidarity and mutual responsibility of all the Israelites.

j: Jos 1, 13; 13, 8; Nm 32, 33. k: Dt 6, 5f. 17; 10, 12; 11, 1. 13. 22. l: Jos 17, 5. m: Nm 31, 27. n: Jos 18, 1; Nm 32, 1. 26 29. o: Dt 13, 13ff. p: Ex 6, 25; Sir 45, 28. q: Lv 17, 8f. r: Nm 25, 3f; Dt 4, 3. s: Jos 18, 1. t: Jos 7, 1. 5.

of the Israelites: "The LORD is the God of gods. [22]The LORD, the God of gods,* knows and Israel shall know. If now we have acted out of rebellion or treachery against the LORD, our God, [23]and if we have built an altar of our own to secede from the LORD, or to offer holocausts, grain offerings or peace offerings upon it, the LORD himself will exact the penalty. [24]We did it rather out of our anxious concern lest in the future your children should say to our children: 'What have you to do with the LORD, the God of Israel? [25]For the LORD has placed the Jordan as a boundary between you and us. You descendants of Reuben and Gad have no share in the LORD.' Thus your children would prevent ours from revering the LORD. [26]So we decided to guard our interests by building this altar of our own: not for holocausts or for sacrifices, [27u]but as evidence for you on behalf of ourselves and our descendants, that we have the right to worship the LORD in his presence with our holocausts, sacrifices, and peace offerings. Now in the future your children cannot say to our children, 'You have no share in the LORD.' [28]Our thought was, that if in the future they should speak thus to us or to our descendants, we could answer: 'Look at the model of the altar of the LORD which our fathers made, not for holocausts or for sacrifices, but to witness* between you and us.' [29]Far be it from us to rebel against the LORD or to secede now from the LORD by building an altar for holocaust, grain offering, or sacrifice in addition to the altar of the LORD, our God, which stands before his Dwelling."

[30]When Phinehas the priest and the princes of the community, the military leaders of the Israelites, heard what the Reubenites, the Gadites and the Manassehites had to say, they were satisfied. [31]Phinehas, son of Eleazar the priest, said to the Reubenites, the Gadites and the Manassehites, "Now we know that the LORD is with us. Since you have not committed this act of treachery against the LORD, you have kept the Israelites free from punishment by the LORD."

[32]Phinehas, son of Eleazar the priest, and the princes returned from the Reubenites and the Gadites in the land of Gilead to the Israelites in the land of Canaan, and reported the matter to them. [33]The report satisfied the Israelites, who blessed God and decided against declaring war on the Reubenites and Gadites or ravaging the land they occupied.

[34]The Reubenites and the Gadites gave the altar its name* as a witness among them that the LORD is God.

CHAPTER 23

See RG 98

Joshua's Final Plea. [1]Many years later, after the LORD had given the Israelites rest from all their enemies round about them, and when Joshua was old and advanced in years,[v] [2]he summoned all Israel (including their elders, leaders, judges and officers) and said to them: "I am old and advanced in years. [3]You have seen all that the LORD, your God, has done for you against all these nations; for it has been the LORD, your God, himself who fought for you. [4w]Bear in mind that I have apportioned among your tribes as their heritage the nations that survive [as well as those I destroyed] between the Jordan and the Great Sea in the west. [5]The LORD, your God, will drive them out and dislodge them at your approach, so that you will take possession of their land as the LORD, your God, promised you. [6]Therefore strive hard to observe and carry out all that is written in the book of the law of Moses, not straying from it in any way,[x] [7]or mingling with these nations while they survive among you. You must

---

22, 22: The LORD, the God of gods: the Hebrew, which cannot be adequately rendered in English here, adds to the divine name Yahweh ("the LORD") two synonymous words for "God," el and elohim. The repetition of these three sacred words adds force to the protestations of fidelity and innocence.

22, 28: To witness: far from being destined to form a rival sanctuary, the model of the altar was intended by the eastern tribes solely as a means of teaching their children to be faithful to the one true sanctuary beyond the Jordan.

22, 34: The name of this altar was the Hebrew word for "witness," [c] ed.

u: Dt 12, 5f. 17f. *v:* Jos 13, 1. *w:* Jos 13, 2-7; 14, 2; 18, 10; Ps 78, 55. *x:* Jos 1, 7.

not invoke their gods, or swear by them, or serve them, or worship them,[y] [8]but you must remain loyal to the LORD, your God, as you have been to this day. [9]At your approach the LORD has driven out large and strong nations, and to this day no one has withstood you. [10]One of you puts to flight a thousand, because it is the LORD, your God, himself who fights for you,[z] as he promised you. [11]Take great care, however, to love the LORD, your God. [12]For if you ever abandon him and ally yourselves with the remnant of these nations while they survive among you, by intermarrying and intermingling with them,[a] [13]know for certain that the LORD, your God, will no longer drive these nations out of your way. Instead they will be a snare and a trap for you, a scourge for your sides and thorns for your eyes, until you perish from this good land which the LORD, your God, has given you.

[14]"Today, as you see, I am going the way of all men.* So now acknowledge with your whole heart and soul that not one of all the promises the LORD, your God, made to you has remained unfulfilled. Every promise has been fulfilled for you, with not one single exception. [15b]But just as every promise the LORD, your God, made to you has been fulfilled for you, so will he fulfill every threat,* even so far as to exterminate you from this good land which the LORD, your God, has given you. [16]If you transgress the covenant of the LORD, your God, which he enjoined on you, serve other gods and worship them, the anger of the LORD will flare up against you and you will quickly perish from the good land which he has given you."

CHAPTER 24

See RG 98

Reminder of the Divine Goodness. [1]Joshua gathered together all the tribes of Israel at Shechem, summoning their elders, their leaders, their judges and their officers. When they stood in ranks before God, [2]Joshua addressed all the people: "Thus says the LORD, the God of Israel: In times past your fathers, down to Terah,[c] father of Abraham and Nahor, dwelt beyond the River* and served other gods. [3]But I brought your father Abraham from the region beyond the River and led him through the entire land of Canaan.[d] I made his descendants numerous, and gave him Isaac. [4]To Isaac I gave Jacob and Esau.[e] To Esau I assigned the mountain region of Seir in which to settle, while Jacob and his children went down to Egypt.

[5]"Then I sent Moses and Aaron, and smote Egypt with the prodigies which I wrought in her midst.[f] [6]Afterward I led you out of Egypt, and when you reached the sea, the Egyptians pursued your fathers to the Red Sea with chariots and horsemen.[g] [7]Because they cried out to the LORD,[h] he put darkness between your people and the Egyptians, upon whom he brought the sea so that it engulfed them. After you witnessed what I did to Egypt, and dwelt a long time in the desert, [8i]I brought you into the land of the Amorites who lived east of the Jordan. They fought against you, but I delivered them into your power. You took possesion of their land, and I destroyed them [the two kings of the Amorites] before you. [9j]Then Balak, son of Zippor, king of Moab, prepared to war against Israel. He summoned Balaam, son of Beor, to curse you; [10k]but I would not listen to Balaam. On the contrary, he had to bless you, and I saved you from him. [11]Once you crossed the Jordan[l] and came to Jericho, the men of Jericho fought against you, but I delivered them also into your power. [12]And I sent the hornets* ahead of you which drove them [the Amorites, Perizzites, Canaanites, Hittites, Girgashites, Hivites and Jebusites]

23, 14: Going the way of all men: drawing near to death, the inevitable goal of all; cf 1 Kgs 2, 1f.
23, 15: Every threat: mentioned especially in Dt 28, 15-68.
24, 2: Beyond the River: east of the Euphrates; cf Gn 11, 28-31.
24, 12: The hornets: see note on Ex 23, 28.

y: Dt 7, 2ff. z: Ex 14, 14; Lv 26, 8; Dt 3, 22. a: Ex 34, 16; Dt 7, 3. b: Lv 26, 14-39; Dt 28, 15-68. c: Gn 11, 26. 31; 31, 53.
d: Gn 12, 1; Acts 7, 2-4. e: Gn 25, 24ff; 36, 8; 46, 1. 6; Acts 7, 15. f: Ex 3, 10; 7, 14—12, 30. g: Ex 12, 37. 51; 14, 9. h: Ex 14,
10. 20. 27f. i: Nm 21, 21-35. j: Nm 22, 2-5. k: Nm 23, 1—24, 25. l: Jos 3, 14; 6, 1.

out of your way; it was not your sword or your bow.[m]

[13]"I gave you a land which you had not tilled and cities which you had not built, to dwell in; you have eaten of vineyards and olive groves which you did not plant.[n]

[14]"Now, therefore, fear the LORD and serve him completely and sincerely. Cast out the gods your fathers served beyond the River and in Egypt, and serve the LORD. [15][p]If it does not please you to serve the LORD, decide today whom you will serve, the gods your fathers served[*] beyond the River or the gods of the Amorites in whose country you are dwelling. As for me and my household, we will serve the LORD."

Renewal of the Covenant. [16]But the people answered, "Far be it from us to forsake the LORD for the service of other gods. [17]For it was the LORD, our God, who brought us and our fathers up out of the land of Egypt, out of a state of slavery. He performed those great miracles before our very eyes and protected us along our entire journey and among all the peoples through whom we passed. [18]At our approach the LORD drove out [all the peoples, including] the Amorites who dwelt in the land. Therefore we also will serve the LORD, for he is our God."

[19]Joshua in turn said to the people, "You may not be able[*] to serve the LORD, for he is a holy God; he is a jealous God[q] who will not forgive your transgressions or your sins. [20]If, after the good he has done for you, you forsake the LORD and serve strange gods, he will do evil to you and destroy you."

[21]But the people answered Joshua, "We will still serve the LORD." [22]Joshua therefore said to the people, "You are your own witnesses that you have chosen to serve the LORD." They replied, "We are, indeed!" [23]"Now, therefore, put away the strange gods that are among you and turn your hearts to the LORD, the God of Israel." [24]Then the people promised Joshua, "We will serve the LORD, our God, and obey his voice."

[25]So Joshua made a covenant with the people that day and made statutes and ordinances for them at Shechem, [26]which he recorded in the book of the law of God. Then he took a large stone and set it up there under the oak that was in the sanctuary of the LORD.[r] [27]And Joshua said to all the people, "This stone shall be our witness,[s] for it has heard all the words which the LORD spoke to us. It shall be a witness against you, should you wish to deny your God." [28]Then Joshua dismissed the people, each to his own heritage.[t]

Death of Joshua. [29][u]After these events, Joshua, son of Nun, servant of the LORD, died at the age of a hundred and ten. [30]He was buried within the limits of his heritage at Timnath-serah[v] in the mountain region of Ephraim north of Mount Gaash. [31]Israel served the LORD during the entire lifetime of Joshua and that of the elders who outlived Joshua and knew all that the LORD had done for Israel. [32][w]The bones of Joseph,[*] which the Israelites had brought up from Egypt, were buried in Shechem in the plot of ground Jacob had bought from the sons of Hamor, father of Shechem, for a hundred pieces of money. This was a heritage of the descendants of Joseph. [33]When Eleazar, son of Aaron, also died, he was buried on the hill which had been given to his son Phinehas[x] in the mountain region of Ephraim.

24, 15: The gods your fathers served: Abraham's ancestors were polytheists.

24, 19: You may not be able: fidelity to God's service is not easy, and therefore those who take such solemn obligations on themselves must be ever vigilant against human weakness.

24, 32: The bones of Joseph: the mummified body of Joseph (Gn 50, 25f), which the Israelites took with them as they left Egypt (Ex 13, 19), was fittingly buried at the ancient city of Shechem, near the border between the two Josephite tribes of Ephraim and Manasseh.

m: Jos 11, 20; Ex 23, 28; Dt 7, 20. n: Dt 6, 10f. o: Dt 10, 12; 1 Sm 7, 3; 12, 24; Tb 14, 9. p: Dt 30, 15-19. q: Ex 20, 5; 23, 21; 34, 14; Lv 19, 2. r: Gn 28, 18; 31, 45; Jgs 9, 6. s: Gn 31, 48. 52; Dt 31, 19. 21. 26. t: Jgs 2, 6. u: 29ff; Jgs 2, 7ff. v: Jos 19, 50; Jgs 2, 9. w: Gn 33, 19; 50, 24; Ex 13, 19. x: Jos 22, 13.

The Book of Judges

See RG
100–107

The Book of Judges derives its title from the twelve heroes of Israel whose deeds it records. They were not magistrates, but military leaders sent by God to aid and to relieve his people in time of external danger. They exercised their activities in the interval of time between the death of Joshua and the institution of the monarchy in Israel. Six of them—Othniel, Ehud, Barak, Gideon, Jephthah and Samson—are treated in some detail and have accordingly been styled the Major Judges. The other six, of whose activities this book preserves but a summary record, are called the Minor Judges. There were two other judges, whose judgeships are described in 1 Samuel—Eli and Samuel, who seem to have ruled the entire nation of Israel just before the institution of the monarchy. The twelve judges of the present book, however, very probably exercised their authority, sometimes simultaneously, over one or another tribe of Israel, never over the entire nation.

The purpose of the book is to show that the fortunes of Israel depended upon the obedience or disobedience of the people to God's law. Whenever they rebelled against him, they were oppressed by pagan nations; when they repented, he raised up judges to deliver them (cf Jgs 2, 10-23).

The accounts of various events, whether written shortly after their occurrence or orally transmitted, were later skillfully unified according to the moral purpose of the redactor sometime during the Israelite monarchy.

The book is divided as follows:

I: Palestine after the Death of Joshua (1, 1—3, 6).
II: Stories of the Judges (3, 7—16, 31).
III: The Tribes of Dan and Benjamin in the Days of the Judges (17, 1—21, 25).

I: Palestine After the Death of Joshua

CHAPTER 1

See RG
101–102

Pagan Survivors in Palestine. [1]After the death of Joshua* the Israelites consulted the LORD, asking, "Who shall be first among us to attack the Canaanites and to do battle with them?"[a] [2]The LORD answered, "Judah shall attack: I have delivered the land into his power." [3]Judah then said to his brother Simeon, "Come up with me into the territory allotted to me, and let us engage the Canaanites in battle. I will likewise accompany you into the territory allotted to you." So Simeon went with him.

[4]When the forces of Judah attacked, the LORD delivered the Canaanites and Perizzites into their power, and they slew ten thousand of them in Bezek. [5]It was in Bezek that they came upon Adonibezek and fought against him. When they defeated the Canaanites and Perizzites, [6]Adonibezek fled. They set out in pursuit, and when they caught him, cut off his thumbs and his big toes. [7]At this Adonibezek said, "Seventy kings, with their thumbs and big toes cut off, used to pick up scraps under my table. As I have done, so has God repaid me." He was brought to Jerusalem, and there he died. [8][The Judahites fought against Jerusalem and captured it, putting it to the sword; then they destroyed the city by fire.]

[9b]Afterward the Judahites went down to fight against the Canaanites who lived in the mountain region, in the Negeb, and in the foothills, [10c]Judah also marched against the Canaanites who dwelt in Hebron, which was formerly called Kiriath-arba, and defeated Sheshai, Ahiman and Talmai.[d] [11]From there they marched against the inhabitants of Debir, which was formerly called Kiriath-sepher.

1, 1-36: This chapter summarizes events most of which occurred shortly after the death of Joshua. Perhaps because they were planned and inaugurated by him, they are also attributed to him in the last half of the preceding book (Jos 14—22).

a: Jgs 20, 18; Nm 27, 21.   *b:* Jos 10, 40; 11, 16; 12, 8.   *c:* Jos 15, 13-19.   *d:* Nm 13, 22; Jos 14, 15.

Judges: The judges of the Bible were not people who wore black robes and presided over a court. Rather, they were spirit-led, charismatic leaders who rose up in times of crisis to lead the nation in battle against a threatening enemy. A better term might be "warlords" or "military heroes." The personalities of these freedom fighters were often seriously flawed. The term "judge" is also applied to local elders who settled disputes among the tribes.

[12] And Caleb said, "I will give my daughter Achsah in marriage to the one who attacks Kiriath-sepher and captures it." [13e] Othniel, son of Caleb's younger brother Kenaz, captured it; so Caleb gave him his daughter Achsah in marriage. [14] On the day of her marriage to Othniel she induced him to ask her father for some land. Then, as she alighted from the ass, Caleb asked her, "What is troubling you?" [15] "Give me an additional gift," she answered. "Since you have assigned land in the Negeb to me, give me also pools of water." So Caleb gave her the upper and the lower pool. [16] The descendants of the Kenite, Moses' father-in-law,* came up with the Judahites from the city of palms to the desert at Arad [which is in the Negeb]. But they later left and settled among the Amalekites.[f]

[17g] Judah then went with his brother Simeon, and they defeated the Canaanites who dwelt in Zephath. After having doomed the city to destruction, they renamed it Hormah. [18h] Judah, however, did not occupy Gaza with its territory, Ashkelon with its territory, or Ekron with its territory. [19i] Since the LORD was with Judah, he gained possession of the mountain region. Yet he could not dislodge those who lived on the plain, because they had iron chariots. [20] As Moses had commanded, Hebron was given to Caleb, who then drove from it the three sons of Anak.[j]

[21] *The Benjaminites did not dislodge the Jebusites who dwelt in Jerusalem, with the result that the Jebusites live in Jerusalem beside the Benjaminites to the present day.[k]

[22] The house of Joseph, too, marched up against Bethel, and the LORD was with them. [23] The house of Joseph had a reconnaissance made of Bethel, which formerly was called Luz.[l] [24] The scouts saw a man coming out of the city and said to him, "Show us a way into the city, and we will spare you." [25] He showed them a way into the city, which they then put to the sword; but they let the man and his whole clan go free. [26] He then went to the land of the Hittites, where he built a city and called it Luz, as it is still called.

[27] Manasseh did not take possession of Beth-shean with its towns or of Taanach with its towns. Neither did he dislodge the inhabitants of Dor and its towns, those of Ibleam and its towns, or those of Megiddo and its towns.[m] The Canaanites kept their hold in this district. [28] When the Israelites grew stronger, they impressed the Canaanites as laborers, but did not drive them out. [29] Similarly, the Ephraimites did not drive out the Canaanites living in Gezer, and so the Canaanites live in Gezer in their midst.[n]

[30] Zebulun did not dislodge the inhabitants of Kitron or those of Nahalol; the Canaanites live among them, but have become forced laborers.

[31o] Nor did Asher drive out the inhabitants of Acco or those of Sidon, or take possession of Mahaleb, Achzib, Helbah, Aphik or Rehob. [32] The Asherites live among the Canaanite natives of the land, whom they have not dislodged.

[33p] Naphtali did not drive out the inhabitants of Beth-shemesh or those of Beth-anath, and so they live among the Canaanite natives of the land. However, the inhabitants of Beth-shemesh and Beth-anath have become forced laborers for them.

[34] The Amorites hemmed in the Danites in the mountain region, not permitting them to

1, 16: Moses' father-in-law: Reuel; cf Nm 10, 29-32 and note. City of palms: Jericho (cf Dt 34, 3), or a town in the Negeb.

1, 21: According to Jos 18, 16, Jerusalem was assigned to the tribe of Benjamin. But it was not actually taken from the Jebusites until David captured it (2 Sm 5, 6-9) and made it his capital, outside the tribal organization.

e: Jgs 3, 9.   *f:* Jgs 4, 11; Nm 10, 29-32.   *g:* Nm 21, 3.   *h:* Jos 11, 22.   *i:* Jos 17, 16ff.   *j:* Jos 14, 9. 13; 15, 14.   *k:* Jos 15, 63.   *l:* Gn 28, 19; 35, 6; 48, 3; Jos 18, 13.   *m:* 27f: Jos 17, 11ff.   *n:* Jos 16, 10.   *o:* 31f: Jos 19, 24-31.   *p:* Jos 19, 32-39.

go down into the plain.*q* *35*The Amorites had a firm hold in Harheres, Aijalon and Shaalbim, but as the house of Joseph gained the upper hand, they were impressed as laborers.

*36*The territory of the Amorites extended from the Akrabbim pass to Sela and beyond.

See RG
101-102

CHAPTER 2

Infidelities of the Israelites. *1r*An angel of the LORD went up from Gilgal to Bochim and said, "It was I who brought you up from Egypt and led you into the land which I promised on oath to your fathers. I said that I would never break my covenant with you, *2*but that you were not to make a pact with the inhabitants of this land, and you were to pull down their altars. Yet you have not obeyed me.*s* What did you mean by this? *3*For now I tell you, I will not clear them out of your way; they shall oppose you and their gods shall become a snare for you."*t*

*4*When the angel of the LORD had made these threats to all the Israelites, the people wept aloud; *5*and so that place came to be called Bochim.* They offered sacrifice there to the LORD.

*6u*When Joshua dismissed the people, each Israelite went to take possession of his own hereditary land. *7*The people served the LORD during the entire lifetime of Joshua, and of those elders who outlived Joshua and who had seen all the great work which the LORD had done for Israel. *8*Joshua, son of Nun, the servant of the LORD, was a hundred and ten years old when he died; *9*and they buried him within the borders of his heritage at Timnath-heres in the mountain region of Ephraim north of Mount Gaash.*v*

*10*But once the rest of that generation were gathered to their fathers, and a later generation arose that did not know the LORD, or what he had done for Israel, *11*the Israelites offended the LORD by serving the Baals.*w* *12*Abandoning the LORD,

the God of their fathers, who had led them out of the land of Egypt, they followed the other gods of the various nations around them, and by their worship of these gods provoked the LORD.

*13*Because they had thus abandoned him and served Baal and the Ashtaroth,* *14*the anger of the LORD flared up against Israel, and he delivered them over to plunderers who despoiled them. He allowed them to fall into the power of their enemies round about whom they were no longer able to withstand. *15*Whatever they undertook, the LORD turned into disaster for them, as in his warning he had sworn he would do, till they were in great distress.*x* *16*Even when the LORD raised up judges to deliver them from the power of their despoilers, *17*they did not listen to their judges, but abandoned themselves to the worship of other gods. They were quick to stray from the way their fathers had taken, and did not follow their example of obedience to the commandments of the LORD. *18*Whenever the LORD raised up judges for them, he would be with the judge and save them from the power of their enemies as long as the judge lived; it was thus the LORD took pity on their distressful cries of affliction under their oppressors. *19*But when the judge died, they would relapse and do worse than their fathers, following other gods in service and worship, relinquishing none of their evil practices or stubborn conduct.*y*

*20z*In his anger toward Israel the LORD said, "Inasmuch as this nation has violated my covenant which I enjoined on their fathers, and has disobeyed me, *21*I for my part will not clear away for them any more of the nations which Joshua left when he died." *22*Through these nations the Israelites were to be made to prove whether or not they would keep to the way of the LORD and continue in it as their fathers had done; *23*therefore the LORD allowed them to remain

---

2, 5: Bochim: the Hebrew word for "weepers."

2, 11: Baals: the chief god of the Canaanites and the Phoenicians was called "Baal," a word meaning "lord." He was honored by various titles, hence the plural form here, equivalent to "the pagan gods."

2, 13: Ashtaroth: the Canaanite Phoenician goddess of love and fertility was Astarte. The plural form used here

refers to her various titles and images and is equivalent to "goddesses."

q: Jcs 19, 47f. *r:* 1ff; Jgs 6, 8ff. *s:* Ex 34, 12f. 15; Dt 7, 2. 5; 21, 2f. *t:* Nm 33, 55; Jos 23, 13. *u:* 6-9; Jos 24, 28-31. *v:* Jos 19, 50. *w:* 11. 14: Jgs 3, 7f; 4, 1f; 6, 1; 10, 6f; 13, 1. *x:* Dt 28, 15-63. *y:* Jgs 3, 12; 4, 1; 6, 1; 8, 33. *z:* 20f: Jos 23, 16.

> The stories in the book of Judges show how the people repeat the same pattern of unfaithfulness:
>
> 1. Israel sins by turning to other gods;
> 2. The LORD punishes Israel by allowing an enemy to conquer it;
> 3. The people repent and beg God for help;
> 4. The LORD sends a deliverer (a judge) who rescues Israel from their foe.
>
> This "sin-punishment-cry for help-deliverance" pattern is the theological frame that surrounds the entire book. The pattern is repeated in the story of each judge.

instead of expelling them immediately, or delivering them into the power of Israel.

See RG 101–103

CHAPTER 3

¹The following are the nations which the LORD allowed to remain, so that through them he might try all those Israelites who had no experience of the battles with Canaan ²[just to instruct, by training them in battle, those generations only of the Israelites who would not have had that previous experience]: ³ᵃthe five lords of the Philistines;* and all the Canaanites, the Sidonians, and the Hivites who dwell in the mountain region of Lebanon between Baal-hermon and the entrance to Hamath. ⁴These served to put Israel to the test, to determine whether they would obey the commandments the LORD had enjoined on their fathers through Moses. ⁵Besides, the Israelites were living among the Canaanites, Hittites, Amorites, Perizzites, Hivites and Jebusites. ⁶In fact, they took their daughters in marriage, and gave their own daughters to their sons in marriage, and served their gods.

II: Stories of the Judges

Othniel. ⁷ᵇBecause the Israelites had offended the LORD by forgetting the LORD, their God, and serving the Baals and the Asherahs,* ⁸the anger of the LORD flared up against them, and he allowed them to fall into the power of Cushan-rishathaim, king of Aram Naharaim, whom they served for eight years. ⁹But when the Israelites cried out to the LORD, he raised up for them a savior, Othniel, son of Caleb's younger brother Kenaz, who rescued them. ¹⁰The spirit of the LORD came upon him, and he judged Israel.ᶜ When he went out to war, the LORD delivered Cushan-rishathaim, king of Aram, into his power, so that he made him subject. ¹¹The land then was at rest for forty years,ᵈ until Othniel, son of Kenaz, died.

Ehud. ¹²Again the Israelites offended the LORD, who because of this offense strengthened Eglon, king of Moab, against Israel. ¹³In alliance with the Ammonites and Amalekites, he attacked and defeated Israel, taking possession of the city of palms. ¹⁴The Israelites then served Eglon, king of Moab, for eighteen years.

¹⁵But when the Israelites cried out to the LORD, he raised up for them a savior, the Benjaminite Ehud, son of Gera, who was left-handed. It was by him that the Israelites sent their tribute to Eglon, king of Moab. ¹⁶Ehud made himself a two-edged dagger a foot long, and wore it under his clothes over his right thigh. ¹⁷He presented the tribute to Eglon, king of Moab, who was very fat, ¹⁸and after the presentation went off with the tribute bearers. ¹⁹He returned, however, from where the idols are, near Gilgal, and said, "I have a private message for you, O king." And the king said, "Silence!" Then when all his attendants had left his presence,

---

3, 3: The Philistines: non-Semitic invaders, who gave their name to all Palestine, although they occupied only its southwestern plains. Their confederation embraced the five leading cities of Gaza, Ashkelon, Ashdod, Gath and Ekron.

3, 7: Asherahs: elsewhere rendered "sacred poles." See note on Ex 34, 13 and on Dt 7, 5. Here the word seems to mean "goddesses."

a: Jos 13, 2-6.   b: Jgs 2, 11ff.   c: Jgs 6, 34; 11, 29; 13, 25; 14, 6. 19; 15, 14.   d: Jgs 5, 31; 8, 28.

²⁰and Ehud went in to him where he sat alone in his cool upper room, Ehud said, "I have a message from God for you." So the king rose from his chair, ²¹and then Ehud with his left hand drew the dagger from his right thigh, and thrust it into Eglon's belly. ²²The hilt also went in after the blade, and the fat closed over the blade because he did not withdraw the dagger from his body.

²³Then Ehud went out into the hall, shutting the doors of the upper room on him and locking them. ²⁴When Ehud had left and the servants came, they saw that the doors of the upper room were locked, and thought, "He must be easing himself in the cool chamber." ²⁵They waited until they finally grew suspicious. Since he did not open the doors of the upper room, they took the key and opened them. There on the floor, dead, lay their lord!

²⁶During their delay Ehud made good his escape and, passing the idols, took refuge in Seirah. ²⁷On his arrival he sounded the horn in the mountain region of Ephraim, and the Israelites went down from the mountains with him as their leader. ²⁸"Follow me," he said to them, "for the LORD has delivered your enemies the Moabites into your power." So they followed him down and seized the fords of the Jordan leading to Moab, permitting no one to cross.^e ²⁹On that occasion they slew about ten thousand Moabites, all of them strong and valiant men. Not a man escaped. ³⁰Thus was Moab brought under the power of Israel at that time; and the land had rest for eighty years.

Shamgar. ³¹After him there was Shamgar, son of Anath, who slew six hundred Philistines with an oxgoad. He, too, rescued Israel.

See RG 103–104

CHAPTER 4

Deborah and Barak. ¹After Ehud's death, however, the Israelites again offended the LORD. ²So the LORD allowed them to fall into the power of the Canaanite king, Jabin, who reigned in Hazor.^f The general of his army was Sisera, who dwelt in Harosheth-ha-goiim. ³But the Israelites cried out to the LORD; for with his nine hundred iron chariots he sorely oppressed the Israelites for twenty years.

⁴At this time the prophetess Deborah, wife of Lappidoth, was judging Israel. ⁵She used to sit under Deborah's palm tree, situated between Ramah and Bethel in the mountain region of Ephraim, and there the Israelites came up to her for judgment. ⁶She sent and summoned Barak, son of Abinoam,^g from Kedesh of Naphtali. "This is what the LORD, the God of Israel, commands," she said to him; "go, march on Mount Tabor, and take with you ten thousand Naphtalites and Zebulunites. ⁷I will lead Sisera, the general of Jabin's army, out to you at the Wadi Kishon,^h together with his chariots and troops, and will deliver them into your power." ⁸But Barak answered her, "If you come with me, I will go; if you do not come with me, I will not go." ⁹"I will certainly go with you," she replied, "but you shall not gain the glory in the expedition on which you are setting out, for the LORD will have Sisera fall into the power of a woman." So Deborah joined Barak and journeyed with him to Kedesh.

¹⁰Barak summoned Zebulun and Naphtali to Kedesh, and ten thousand men followed him. Deborah also went up with him.ⁱ ¹¹*Now the Kenite Heber had detached himself from his own people, the descendants of Hobab, Moses' brother-in-law,^j and had pitched his tent by the tere-binth of Zaanannim, which was near Kedesh.

¹²It was reported to Sisera that Barak, son of Abinoam, had gone up to Mount Tabor. ¹³So Sisera assembled from Harosheth-ha-goiim at the Wadi Kishon all nine hundred of his iron chariots and all his forces. ¹⁴Deborah then said to Barak, "Be off, for this is the day on which the LORD has delivered Sisera into your power. The LORD marches before

---

4, 11: Most of the Kenites occupied a district in the southern part of Judah (Jgs 1, 16). A group of them, however had detached themselves and settled in lower Galilee.

---

e: Jgs 4, 7. 14; 7, 9. 15. *f:* Jos 11, 1. 10; Ps 83, 10; 1 Sm 12, 9. *g:* Heb 11, 32. *h:* Jgs 5, 21; Ps 83, 10. *i:* Jgs 5, 18. *j:* Nm 10, 29.

Deborah, Jael, and Barak

Deborah the prophetess, Barak the army commander, and Jael wife of Heber the Kenite all contributed to achieving delivery from the Canaanite enemy. None of them is called the deliverer, because each of these human figures made only a partial contribution to the victory; in practice, the true deliverer was God (4, 23).

you." So Barak went down Mount Tabor, followed by his ten thousand men. [15]And the LORD put Sisera[k] and all his chariots and all his forces to rout before Barak. Sisera himself dismounted from his chariot and fled on foot. [16]Barak, however, pursued the chariots and the army as far as Harosheth-ha-goiim. The entire army of Sisera fell beneath the sword, not even one man surviving.

[17]*Sisera, in the meantime, had fled on foot to the tent of Jael, wife of the Kenite Heber, since Jabin, king of Hazor, and the family of the Kenite Heber were at peace with one another. [18]Jael went out to meet Sisera and said to him, "Come in, my lord, come in with me; do not be afraid." So he went into her tent, and she covered him with a rug. [19]He said to her, "Please give me a little water to drink. I am thirsty." But she opened a jug of milk for him to drink, and then covered him over.[l] [20]"Stand at the entrance of the tent," he said to her. "If anyone comes and asks, 'Is there someone here?' say, 'No!' " [21]Instead Jael, wife of Heber, got a tent peg and took a mallet in her hand. While Sisera was sound asleep, she stealthily approached him and drove the peg through his temple down into the ground, so that he perished in death.[m] [22]Then when Barak came in pursuit of Sisera, Jael went out to meet him and said to him, "Come, I will show you the man you seek." So he went in with her, and there lay Sisera dead, with the tent peg through his temple.

[23]Thus on that day God humbled the Canaanite king, Jabin, before the Israelites;

[24]their power weighed ever heavier upon him, till at length they destroyed the Canaanite king, Jabin.

CHAPTER 5

See RG 103–104

Canticle of Deborah. [1]On that day Deborah [and Barak, son of Abinoam] sang this song:

[2] Of chiefs who took the lead in Israel,*
    of noble deeds by the people who
        bless the LORD,
[3] Hear, O kings! Give ear, O princes!
    I to the LORD will sing my song,
    my hymn to the LORD, the God of
        Israel.

[4] O LORD, when you went out from Seir,
    when you marched from the land of
        Edom,
The earth quaked and the heavens were
        shaken,
    while the clouds sent down showers.
[5] Mountains trembled
    in the presence of the LORD, the One
        of Sinai,[n]
    in the presence of the LORD, the God
        of Israel.[o]

[6] In the days of Shamgar, son of Anath,[p]
    in the days of slavery caravans ceased;
Those who traveled the roads
    went by roundabout paths.
[7] Gone was freedom beyond the walls
    gone indeed from Israel.

When I, Deborah, rose,
    when I rose, a mother in Israel,

4, 17-22: It is to be noted that the sacred author merely records the fact of the murder of Sisera. We must not construe this as approval of Jael's action.

5, 2-31: This canticle is an excellent example of early

Hebrew poetry, even though some of its verses are now obscure.

k: Ps 83, 10. l: Jgs 5, 25. m: Jgs 5, 26. n: Dt 33, 2; 2 Sm 22, 8; Pss 18, 8; 68, 9. o: Ex 19, 16; Dt 4, 11; Ps 97, 5. p: Jgs 3, 31.

⁸ New gods* were their choice;
    then the war was at their gates.
Not a shield could be seen, nor a lance,
    among forty thousand in Israel!

⁹ My heart is with the leaders of Israel,
    nobles of the people who bless the
      LORD;
¹⁰ They who ride on white asses,
    seated on saddlecloths as they go their
      way;
¹¹ Sing of them to the strains of the harpers
    at the wells,
    where men recount the just deeds of
      the LORD,
    his just deeds that brought freedom to
      Israel.

¹² Awake, awake, Deborah!
    awake, awake, strike up a song.
Strength! arise, Barak,
    make despoilers your spoil, son of
      Abinoam.
¹³ Then down came the fugitives with the
    mighty,
    the people of the LORD came down for
      me as warriors.

¹⁴ From Ephraim, princes were in the
    valley;*
    behind you was Benjamin, among
      your troops.
From Machir came down commanders,
    from Zebulun wielders of the
      marshal's staff.

¹⁵ With Deborah were the princes of
    Issachar;
    Barak, too, was in the valley, his
      course unchecked.

Among the clans of Reuben
    great were the searchings of heart.�q
¹⁶ Why do you stay beside your hearths
    listening to the lowing of the herds?
Among the clans of Reuben
    great were the searchings of heart!

¹⁷ Gilead, beyond the Jordan, rests;
    why does Dan spend his time in ships?
Asher, who dwells along the shore,
    is resting in his coves.
¹⁸ Zebulun is the people defying death;
    Naphtali, too, on the open heights!ʳ

¹⁹ The kings came and fought;
    then they fought, those kings of
      Canaan,
At Taanach by the waters of Megiddo;
    no silver booty did they take.ˢ
²⁰ From the heavens the stars, too, fought;*
    from their courses they fought against
      Sisera.ᵗ

²¹ The Wadi Kishon swept them away;
    a wadi . . . , the Kishon.ᵘ
²² Then the hoofs of the horses pounded,
    with the dashing, dashing of his steeds.

²³ "Curse Meroz,"* says the LORD,
    "hurl a curse at its inhabitants!
For they came not to my help,
    as warriors to the help of the LORD."

²⁴ Blessed among women be Jael,
    blessed among tent-dwelling
      women.ᵛ
²⁵ He asked for water, she gave him milk;ʷ
    in a princely bowl she offered curds.
²⁶ With her left hand she reached for the peg,
    with her right, for the workman's mallet.

5, 8: New gods: pagan deities; cf Dt 32, 16-18. God punished the idolatry of the Israelites by leaving them relatively unarmed before the attacks of their enemies, who had better weapons, made of iron; cf 1 Sm 13, 19-22.

5, 14-22: Praise for the tribes which formed the Israelite league against Sisera: Ephraim, Benjamin, Manasseh (represented by Machir), Zebulun, Issachar, and Naphtali (led by Barak). The tribes of Reuben, Gad (Gilead), Dan, and Asher are chided for their lack of co-operation. The more distant tribes of Judah and Simeon are not mentioned.

5, 20f: It would seem that nature aided the Hebrews in some way. Perhaps the torrential rains swelled the waters of Kishon, which then overwhelmed the Canaanites.

5, 23: Meroz: an unknown locality in which Hebrews probably resided, since its inhabitants are cursed for their failure to proffer aid.

q: Jgs 4, 14. r: Jgs 4, 10. s: Jgs 1, 27; Jos 17, 11. t: Jgs 4, 15; Jos 10, 14. u: Jgs 4, 7. 13. v: Jgs 4, 17; Jdt 13, 17; Lk 1, 28. 42. w: 25f: Jgs 4, 19. 21.

The Poem: Song of Deborah

The poetic counterpart to the prose of Judges 4, 1–24, chapter 5 provides a more emotional celebration of the victory. Many scholars believe that this song is one of the oldest texts in the Bible. It is also one of the most obscure and difficult. It celebrates the LORD's role in the victory over Sisera through a sudden downpour that disabled the chariots in battle. Its primary attribution to a woman fits the role women have elsewhere in victory celebrations (Ex 15, 20–21; Jgs 11, 34; 1 Sm 18, 6–7).

She hammered Sisera, crushed his head;
   she smashed, stove in his temple.
27 At her feet he sank down, fell, lay still;
   down at her feet he sank and fell;
   where he sank down, there he fell,
      slain.

28 From the window peered down and
      wailed
   the mother of Sisera, from the lattice:
"Why is his chariot so long in coming?
   why are the hoofbeats of his chariots
      delayed?"
29 The wisest of her princesses answers her,
   and she, too, keeps answering herself:
30 "They must be dividing the spoil they
      took:
   there must be a damsel or two for each
      man,
Spoils of dyed cloth as Sisera's spoil,
   an ornate shawl or two for me in the
      spoil."
31 May all your enemies perish thus,
   O LORD!ˣ
   but your friends be as the sun rising in
      its might!

And the land was at rest for forty years.

See RG
104

CHAPTER 6

The Call of Gideon. ¹The Israelites offended the LORD, who therefore delivered them into the power of Midian for seven years, ²so that Midian held Israel subject. For fear of Midian the Israelites established the fire signals on the mountains, the caves for refuge, and the strongholds. ³And it used to be that when the Israelites had completed their sowing, Midian, Amalek and the Kedemites would come up,ʸ ⁴encamp opposite them, and destroy the produce of the land as far as the outskirts of Gaza, leaving no sustenance in Israel, nor sheep, oxen or asses. ⁵For they would come up with their livestock, and their tents would become as numerous as locusts; and neither they nor their camels could be numbered, when they came into the land to lay it waste. ⁶Thus was Israel reduced to misery by Midian, and so the Israelites cried out to the LORD.

⁷When Israel cried out to the LORD because of Midian, ⁸ᶻhe sent a prophet to the Israelites who said to them, "The LORD, the God of Israel, says: I led you up from Egypt; I brought you out of the place of slavery. ⁹I rescued you from the power of Egypt and of all your other oppressors. I drove them out before you and gave you their land. ¹⁰And I said to you: I, the LORD, am your God; you shall not venerate the gods of the Amorites in whose land you are dwelling. But you did not obey me."

¹¹Then the angel of the LORD came and sat under the terebinth in Ophrah that belonged to Joash the Abiezrite. While his son Gideon was beating out wheat in the wine press to save it from the Midianites, ¹²the angel of the LORD appeared to him and said, "The LORD is with you, O champion!" ¹³"My LORD," Gideon said to him, "if the LORD is with us, why has all this happened to us? Where are his wondrous deeds of which our fathers told us when they said, 'Did not the LORD bring us up from Egypt?' For now the LORD has abandoned us and has delivered us into the power of Midian." ¹⁴The LORD turned to him and said, "Go with the strength you have and save Israel from the power of Midian. It is I who send you." ¹⁵But he

---

x: Ps 83, 10-19.   y: 3f: Jgs 7, 12; Dt 28, 30ff.   z: 8ff: Jgs 2, 1f; 10, 11-14.

> The "sacred pole" (6, 25) is a symbol of the goddess Asherah. Using it as firewood would be a calculated desecration.

answered him, "Please, my lord, how can I save Israel? My family is the meanest in Manasseh, and I am the most insignificant in my father's house." ¹⁶"I shall be with you," the LORD said to him, "and you will cut down Midian to the last man." ¹⁷He answered him, "If I find favor with you, give me a sign that you are speaking with me. ¹⁸Do not depart from here, I pray you, until I come back to you and bring out my offering and set it before you." He answered, "I will await your return."

¹⁹So Gideon went off and prepared a kid and an ephah of flour in the form of unleavened cakes. Putting the meat in a basket and the broth in a pot, he brought them out to him under the terebinth and presented them. ²⁰The angel of God said to him, "Take the meat and unleavened cakes and lay them on this rock; then pour out the broth."ᵃ When he had done so, ²¹the angel of the LORD stretched out the tip of the staff he held, and touched the meat and unleavened cakes. Thereupon a fire came up from the rock which consumed the meat and unleavened cakes, and the angel of the LORD disappeared from sight. ²²ᵇGideon, now aware that it had been the angel of the LORD, said, "Alas, Lord GOD, that I have seen the angel of the LORD face to face!" ²³The LORD answered him, "Be calm, do not fear. You shall not die." ²⁴So Gideon built there an altar to the LORD and called it Yahweh-shalom.* To this day it is still in Ophrah of the Abiezrites.

²⁵That same night the LORD said to him, "Take the seven-year-old spare bullock and destroy your father's altar to Baal and cut down the sacred pole* that is by it. ²⁶You shall build, instead, the proper kind of altar to the LORD, your God, on top of this stronghold. Then take the spare bullock and offer it as a holocaust on the wood from the sacred pole you have cut down." ²⁷So Gideon took ten of his servants and did as the LORD had commanded him. But through fear of his family and of the townspeople, he would not do it by day, but did it at night. ²⁸Early the next morning the townspeople found that the altar of Baal had been destroyed, the sacred pole near it cut down, and the spare bullock offered on the altar that was built. ²⁹They asked one another, "Who did this?" Their inquiry led them to the conclusion that Gideon, son of Joash, had done it. ³⁰So the townspeople said to Joash, "Bring out your son that he may die, for he has destroyed the altar of Baal and has cut down the sacred pole that was near it." ³¹But Joash replied to all who were standing around him, "Do you intend to act in Baal's stead, or be his champion? If anyone acts for him, he shall be put to death by morning. If he whose altar has been destroyed is a god, let him act for himself!" ³²So on that day Gideon was called Jerubbaal,* because of the words, "Let Baal take action against him, since he destroyed his altar."ᶜ

³³Then all Midian and Amalek and the Kedemites mustered and crossed over into the valley of Jezreel, where they encamped. ³⁴The spirit of the LORD enveloped Gideon; he blew the horn that summoned Abiezer to follow him. ³⁵He sent messengers, too, throughout Manasseh, which also obeyed his summons; through Asher, Zebulun and Naphtali, likewise, he sent messengers and these tribes advanced to meet the others. ³⁶Gideon said to God, "If indeed you are going to save Israel through me, as you promised, ³⁷I am putting this woolen fleece on the

6, 24: Yahweh-shalom: Hebrew for "the LORD is peace," a reference to the Lord's words, "Be calm," literally, "Peace be to you!"

6, 25: The sacred pole: see note on Ex 34, 13.

6, 32: Jerubbaal: similar in sound to the Hebrew words meaning, "Let Baal take action."

a: Jgs 13, 19. b: 22f: Gn 32, 31; Dt 5, 24ff. c: 1 Sm 12, 11.

threshing floor. If dew comes on the fleece alone, while all the ground is dry, I shall know that you will save Israel through me, as you promised." ³⁸That is what took place. Early the next morning he wrung the dew from the fleece, squeezing out of it a bowlful of water. ³⁹Gideon then said to God, "Do not be angry with me if I speak once more. Let me make just one more test with the fleece. Let the fleece alone be dry, but let there be dew on all the ground." ⁴⁰That night God did so; the fleece alone was dry, but there was dew on all the ground.

See RG 104

CHAPTER 7

Defeat of Midian. ¹Early the next morning Jerubbaal*ᵈ* (that is, Gideon) encamped by Enharod with all his soldiers. The camp of Midian was in the valley north of Gibeath-hammoreh. ²The LORD said to Gideon, "You have too many soldiers with you for me to deliver Midian into their power, lest Israel vaunt itself against me and say, 'My own power brought me the victory.' ³Now proclaim to all the soldiers, 'If anyone is afraid or fearful, let him leave.' "*ᵉ* When Gideon put them to this test on the mountain, twenty-two thousand of the soldiers left, but ten thousand remained. ⁴The LORD said to Gideon, "There are still too many soldiers. Lead them down to the water and I will test them for you there. If I tell you that a certain man is to go with you, he must go with you. But no one is to go if I tell you he must not." ⁵*When Gideon led the soldiers down to the water, the LORD said to him, "You shall set to one side everyone who laps up the water as a dog does with its tongue; to the other, everyone who kneels down to drink." ⁶Those who lapped up the water raised to their mouths by hand numbered three hundred, but all the rest of the soldiers knelt down to drink the water. ⁷The LORD said to Gideon, "By means of the three hundred who lapped up the water I will save you and will deliver

Battles of Gideon

Midian into your power. So let all the other soldiers go home." ⁸Their horns, and such supplies as the soldiers had with them, were taken up, and Gideon ordered the rest of the Israelites to their tents, but kept the three hundred men. Now the camp of Midian was beneath him in the valley.

⁹That night the LORD said to Gideon, "Go, descend on the camp, for I have delivered it up to you. ¹⁰If you are afraid to attack, go down to the camp with your aide Purah. ¹¹When you hear what they are saying, you will have the courage to descend on the camp." So he went down with his aide Purah to the outposts of the camp. ¹²The Midianites, Amalekites, and all the Kedemites lay in the valley, as numerous as locusts. Nor could their camels be counted, for these were as many as the sands on the seashore. ¹³*When

7, 5: The Lord desired not numerous but reliable soldiers. Those who drank from their hands were alert, standing ready to resist attack, whereas the others were careless and undependable. The cowardly soldiers had already been dismissed (v 3); cf Dt 20, 8.

7, 13: The barley loaf represents the agricultural Hebrews while the tent refers to the nomadic Midianites. The overthrow

of the tent indicates the victory of the Hebrews over their Midianite oppressors.

d: Jgs 6, 32. *e:* Dt 20, 8.

Gideon arrived, one man was telling another about a dream. "I had a dream," he said, "that a round loaf of barley bread was rolling into the camp of Midian. It came to our tent and struck it, and as it fell it turned the tent upside down." *14*"This can only be the sword of the Israelite Gideon, son of Joash," the other replied. "God has delivered Midian and all the camp into his power." *15*When Gideon heard the description and explanation of the dream, he prostrated himself. Then returning to the camp of Israel, he said, "Arise, for the LORD has delivered the camp of Midian into your power."

*16*He divided the three hundred men into three companies, and provided them all with horns and with empty jars and torches inside the jars. *17*"Watch me and follow my lead," he told them. "I shall go to the edge of the camp, and as I do, you must do also. *18*When I and those with me blow horns, you too must blow horns all around the camp and cry out, 'For the LORD and for Gideon!' " *19*So Gideon and the hundred men who were with him came to the edge of the camp at the beginning of the middle watch,* just after the posting of the guards. They blew the horns and broke the jars they were holding. *20*All three companies blew horns and broke their jars. They held the torches in their left hands, and in their right the horns they were blowing, and cried out, "A sword for the LORD and Gideon!" *21*They all remained standing in place around the camp, while the whole camp fell to running and shouting and fleeing. *22*But the three hundred men kept blowing the horns, and throughout the camp the LORD set the sword of one against another.*f* The army fled as far as Beth-shittah in the direction of Zarethan, near the border of Abel-meholah at Tabbath.

*23*The Israelites were called to arms from Naphtali, from Asher, and from all Manasseh, and they pursued Midian. *24*Gideon also sent messengers throughout the mountain region of Ephraim to say, "Go down to confront Midian, and seize the water courses against them as far as Beth-barah, as well as the Jordan." So all the Ephraimites were called to arms, and they seized the water courses as far as Beth-barah, and the Jordan as well. *25g*They captured the two princes of Midian, Oreb and Zeeb, killing Oreb at the rock of Oreb and Zeeb at the wine press of Zeeb. Then they pursued Midian and carried the heads of Oreb and Zeeb to Gideon beyond the Jordan.

CHAPTER 8

See RG 104

*1*But the Ephraimites said to him, "What have you done to us, not calling us when you went to fight against Midian?" And they quarrelled bitterly with him. *2*"What have I accomplished now in comparison with you?" he answered them. "Is not the gleaning of Ephraim better than the vintage of Abiezer?*h* *3*Into your power God delivered the princes of Midian, Oreb and Zeeb. What have I been able to do in comparison with you?" When he said this, their anger against him subsided.

*4*When Gideon reached the Jordan and crossed it with his three hundred men, they were exhausted and famished. *5*So he said to the men of Succoth, "Will you give my followers some loaves of bread? They are exhausted, and I am pursuing Zebah and Zalmunna, kings of Midian." *6*But the princes of Succoth replied, "Are the hands of Zebah and Zalmunna already in your possession, that we should give food to your army?"* *7*Gideon said, "Very well; when the LORD has delivered Zebah and Zalmunna into my power, I will grind your flesh in with the thorns and briers of the desert." *8*He went up from there to Penuel and made the same request of them, but the men of Penuel answered him as had the men of Succoth. *9*So to the men of Penuel, too, he said, "When I return in triumph, I will demolish this tower."

7, 19: At the beginning of the middle watch: about two hours before midnight. The ancient Hebrews divided the night into three watches of about four hours each. At the beginning of a watch the sentinels were changed.

8, 6: Are the hands . . . in your possession . . . ?: i.e., can you already boast of victory? The hands as well as the heads of slain enemies were cut off and counted as trophies; cf 2 Sm 4, 8; 2 Kgs 10, 7f; and the Ugaritic Anath Epic, V AB, II 10ff.

f: 22f: Ps 83, 10; Is 9, 4.　*g:* Jgs 8, 3; Ps 83, 12; Is 10, 26.　*h:* Jg 6, 34.

¹⁰Now Zebah and Zalmunna were in Karkor with their force of about fifteen thousand men; these were all who were left of the whole Kedemite army, a hundred and twenty thousand swordsmen having fallen. ¹¹Gideon went up by the route of the nomads east of Nobah and Jogbehah, and attacked the camp when it felt secure. ¹²Zebah and Zalmunna fled. He pursued them and took the two kings of Midian, Zebah and Zalmunna, captive, throwing the entire army into panic.

¹³Then Gideon, son of Joash, returned from battle by the pass of Heres. ¹⁴He captured a young man of Succoth, who upon being questioned listed for him the seventy-seven princes and elders of Succoth. ¹⁵So he went to the men of Succoth and said, "Here are Zebah and Zalmunna, with whom you taunted me, 'Are the hands of Zebah and Zalmunna already in your possession, that we should give food to your weary followers?' " ¹⁶He took the elders of the city, and thorns and briers of the desert, and ground these men of Succoth into them. ¹⁷He also demolished the tower of Penuel and slew the men of the city.

¹⁸Then he said to Zebah and Zalmunna, "Where now are the men you killed at Tabor?" "They all resembled you," they replied. "They appeared to be princes." ¹⁹"They were my brothers, my mother's sons," he said. "As the LORD lives, if you had spared their lives, I should not kill you." ²⁰Then he said to his first-born, Jether, "Go, kill them." Since Jether was still a boy, he was afraid and did not draw his sword. ²¹Zebah and Zalmunna said, "Come, kill us yourself, for a man's strength is like the man." So Gideon stepped forward and killed Zebah and Zalmunna. He also took the crescents that were on the necks of their camels.

²²The Israelites then said to Gideon, "Rule over us—you, your son, and your son's son—for you rescued us from the power of Midian." ²³But Gideon answered them, "I will not rule over you, nor shall my son rule over you. The LORD must rule over you."

²⁴Gideon went on to say, "I should like to make a request of you. Will each of you give me a ring from his booty?" (For being Ishmaelites,* the enemy had gold rings.) ²⁵"We will gladly give them," they replied, and spread out a cloak into which everyone threw a ring from his booty. ²⁶The gold rings that he requested weighed seventeen hundred gold shekels, in addition to the crescents and pendants, the purple garments worn by the kings of Midian, and the trappings that were on the necks of their camels. ²⁷Gideon made an ephod out of the gold and placed it in his city Ophrah. However, all Israel paid idolatrous homage to it there, and caused the ruin of Gideon and his family.

²⁸Thus was Midian brought into subjection by the Israelites; no longer did they hold their heads high. And the land had rest for forty years, during the lifetime of Gideon.

Gideon's Son Abimelech. ²⁹Then Jerubbaal, son of Joash, went back home to stay. ³⁰ⁱNow Gideon had seventy sons, his direct descendants, for he had many wives. ³¹His concubine* who lived in Shechem also bore him a son, whom he named Abimelech. ³²At a good old age Gideon, son of Joash, died and was buried in the tomb of his father Joash in Ophrah of the Abiezrites. ³³But after Gideon was dead, the Israelites again abandoned themselves to the Baals, making Baal of Berith* their god ³⁴and forgetting the LORD, their God, who had delivered them from the power of their enemies all around them. ³⁵Nor were they grateful to the family of Jerubbaal [Gideon] for all the good he had done for Israel.

CHAPTER 9

See RG 104-105

¹Abimelech, son of Jerubbaal, went to his mother's kinsmen in Shechem,ʲ and said to them and to the whole clan to which his mother's family belonged, ²"Put this question to all the citizens of Shechem: 'Which is better for you: that seventy men, or all Jerubbaal's sons, rule over you, or that one man rule over you?' You must remember that I am

---

8, 24: Ishmaelites: here as in Gn 37, 25-28, the designation is not ethnic; it refers rather to their status as nomads.

8, 31: Concubine: a wife of secondary rank.

8, 33: Baal of Berith: one of the titles of Baal as worshiped by the Canaanites of Shechem, meaning "the lord of the covenant."

i: Jgs 9, 2. 5.   *j:* Jgs 8, 31.

Ambivalence to Monarchy

The Bible contains much evidence that Israel was always divided about the institution of the monarchy: Some saw it as a practical, logical, and necessary development in the nation's history; others saw it as evidence of an abandonment of the LORD, the one true king of Israel. The story of Abimelech clearly preserves some of the negative attitude toward kingship. But the observation that everyone "did as he thought best" indicates that strong leadership became increasingly necessary.

your own flesh and bone." ³When his mother's kin repeated these words to them on his behalf, all the citizens of Shechem sympathized with Abimelech, thinking, "He is our kinsman." ⁴They also gave him seventy silver shekels from the temple of Baal of Berith, with which Abimelech hired shiftless men and ruffians as his followers. ⁵He then went to his ancestral house in Ophrah, and slew his brothers, the seventy sons of Jerubbaal, on one stone. Only the youngest son of Jerubbaal, Jotham, escaped, for he was hidden. ⁶Then all the citizens of Shechem and all Beth-millo came together and proceeded to make Abimelech king by the terebinth at the memorial pillar in Shechem.

⁷When this was reported to him, Jotham went to the top of Mount Gerizim, and standing there, cried out to them in a loud voice: "Hear me, citizens of Shechem, that God may then hear you! ⁸Once the trees went to anoint a king over themselves. So they said to the olive tree, 'Reign over us.'ᵏ ⁹But the olive tree answered them, 'Must I give up my rich oil, whereby men and gods are honored,* and go to wave over the trees?' ¹⁰Then the trees said to the fig tree, 'Come; you reign over us!' ¹¹But the fig tree answered them, 'Must I give up my sweetness and my good fruit, and go to wave over the trees?' ¹²Then the trees said to the vine, 'Come you, and reign over us.' ¹³But the vine answered them, 'Must I give up my wine that cheers gods* and men, and

go to wave over the trees?' ¹⁴Then all the trees said to the buckthorn, 'Come; you reign over us!' ¹⁵But the buckthorn replied to the trees, 'If you wish to anoint me king over you in good faith, come and take refuge in my shadow. Otherwise, let fire come from the buckthorn and devour the cedars of Lebanon.'

¹⁶*"Now then, if you have acted in good faith and honorably in appointing Abimelech your king, if you have dealt well with Jerubbaal and with his family, and if you have treated him as he deserved— ¹⁷for my father fought for you at the risk of his life when he saved you from the power of Midian; ¹⁸but you have risen against his family this day and have killed his seventy sons upon one stone, and have made Abimelech, the son of his handmaid,ˡ king over the citizens of Shechem, because he is your kinsman— ¹⁹if, then, you have acted in good faith and with honor toward Jerubbaal and his family this day, rejoice in Abimelech and may he in turn rejoice in you. ²⁰But if not, let fire come forth from Abimelech to devour the citizens of Shechem and Beth-millo, and let fire come forth from the citizens and from Beth-millo to devour Abimelech." ²¹Then Jotham went in flight to Beer, where he remained for fear of his brother Abimelech.

²²When Abimelech had ruled Israel for three years, ²³God put bad feelings between Abimelech and the citizens of Shechem,

---

9, 9: Whereby men and gods are honored: oil was used in the worship both of the true God and of false gods; it was prescribed in the worship of Yahweh (Lv 2, 1. 6. 15; 24, 2). It was also used to consecrate prophets, priests and kings (Ex 30, 25. 30; 1 Sm 10, 1; 16, 13).

9, 13: Cheers gods: wine was used in the libations both of the Temple of Jerusalem and of pagan temples.

9, 16: Just as the noble trees refused the honor of royalty and were made subject to a mean plant, so did Abimelech of less noble birth than the seventy sons of Gideon now tyrannize over the people.

---

k: Jgs 8, 22f.   l: Jgs 8, 31.

who rebelled against Abimelech. ²⁴This was to repay the violence done to the seventy sons of Jerubbaal and to avenge their blood upon their brother Abimelech, who killed them, and upon the citizens of Shechem, who encouraged him to kill his brothers. ²⁵The citizens of Shechem then set men in ambush for him on the mountaintops, and these robbed all who passed them on the road. But it was reported to Abimelech.

²⁶Now Gaal, son of Ebed, came over to Shechem with his kinsmen. The citizens of Shechem put their trust in him, ²⁷and went out into the fields, harvested their grapes and trod them out. Then they held a festival and went to the temple of their god, where they ate and drank and cursed Abimelech. ²⁸Gaal, son of Ebed, said, "Who is Abimelech? And why should we of Shechem serve him? Were not the son of Jerubbaal and his lieutenant Zebul once subject to the men of Hamor, father of Shechem?ᵐ Why should we serve him? ²⁹Would that this people were entrusted to my command! I would depose Abimelech. I would say to Abimelech, 'Get a larger army and come out!' "

³⁰At the news of what Gaal, son of Ebed, had said, Zebul, the ruler of the city, was angry ³¹and sent messengers to Abimelech in Arumah with the information: "Gaal, son of Ebed, and his kinsmen have come to Shechem and are stirring up the city against you. ³²Now rouse yourself; set an ambush tonight in the fields, you and the men who are with you. ³³Promptly at sunrise tomorrow morning, make a raid on the city. When he and his followers come out against you, deal with him as best you can."

³⁴During the night Abimelech advanced with all his soldiers and set up an ambush for Shechem in four companies. ³⁵Gaal, son of Ebed, went out and stood at the entrance of the city gate. When Abimelech and his soldiers rose from their place of ambush, ³⁶Gaal saw them and said to Zebul, "There are men coming down from the hilltops!" But Zebul answered him, "You see the shadow of the hills as men." ³⁷But Gaal went on to say, "Men are coming down from the region of Tabbur-Haares, and one company is coming by way of Elon-Meonenim." ³⁸Zebul said to him, "Where now is the boast you uttered, 'Who is Abimelech that we should serve him?' Are these not the men for whom you expressed contempt? Go out now and fight with them." ³⁹So Gaal went out at the head of the citizens of Shechem and fought against Abimelech. ⁴⁰But Abimelech routed him, and he fled before him; and many fell slain right up to the entrance of the gate. ⁴¹Abimelech returned to Arumah, but Zebul drove Gaal and his kinsmen from Shechem, which they had occupied.

⁴²The next day, when the people were taking the field, it was reported to Abimelech, ⁴³who divided the men he had into three companies, and set up an ambush in the fields. He watched till he saw the people leave the city, and then rose against them for the attack. ⁴⁴Abimelech and the company with him dashed in and stood by the entrance of the city gate, while the other two companies rushed upon all who were in the field and attacked them. ⁴⁵That entire day Abimelech fought against the city, and captured it. He then killed its inhabitants and demolished the city, sowing the site with salt.*

⁴⁶When they heard of this, all the citizens of Migdal-shechem went into the crypt of the temple of El-berith. ⁴⁷It was reported to Abimelech that all the citizens of Migdal-shechem were gathered together. ⁴⁸So he went up Mount Zalmon with all his soldiers, took his ax in his hand, and cut down some brushwood. This he lifted to his shoulder, then said to the men with him, "Hurry! Do just as you have seen me do." ⁴⁹So all the men likewise cut down brushwood, and following Abimelech, placed it against the crypt. Then they set the crypt on fire over their heads, so that every one of the citizens of Migdal-shechem, about a thousand men and women, perished.

9, 45: Sowing the site with salt: a severe measure, which was a symbol of desolation, and even more, since it actually rendered the ground barren and useless.

m: Gn 34, 2. 6.

⁵⁰Abimelech proceeded to Thebez, which he invested and captured. ⁵¹Now there was a strong tower in the middle of the city, and all the men and women, in a word all the citizens of the city, fled there, shutting themselves in and going up to the roof of the tower. ⁵²Abimelech came up to the tower and fought against it, advancing to the very entrance of the tower to set it on fire. ⁵³But a certain woman cast the upper part of a millstone down on Abimelech's head, and it fractured his skull.ⁿ ⁵⁴He immediately called his armor-bearer and said to him, "Draw your sword and dispatch me, lest they say of me that a woman killed me."ᵒ So his attendant ran him through and he died. ⁵⁵When the Israelites saw that Abimelech was dead, they all left for their homes.

⁵⁶Thus did God requite the evil Abimelech had done to his father in killing his seventy brothers. ⁵⁷God also brought all their wickedness home to the Shechemites, for the curse of Jotham, son of Jerubbaal, overtook them.

CHAPTER 10

See RG 105

Tola. ¹After Abimelech there rose to save Israel the Issacharite Tola, son of Puah, son of Dodo, a resident of Shamir in the mountain region of Ephraim. ²When he had judged Israel twenty-three years, he died and was buried in Shamir.

Jair. ³Jair the Gileadite came after him and judged Israel twenty-two years. ⁴He had thirty sons who rode on thirty saddle-asses* and possessed thirty cities in the land of Gilead; these are called Havvoth-jair to the present day.ᵖ ⁵Jair died and was buried in Kamon.

Oppression by the Ammonites. ⁶The Israelites again offended the LORD, serving the Baals and Ashtaroths, the gods of Aram, the gods of Sidon, the gods of Moab, the gods of the Ammonites, and the gods of the Philistines. Since they had abandoned the LORD and would not serve him, ⁷the LORD became angry with Israel and allowed them to fall into the power of [the Philistines

The Twelve Judges

and] the Ammonites. ⁸For eighteen years they afflicted and oppressed the Israelites in Bashan, and all the Israelites in the Amorite land beyond the Jordan in Gilead. ⁹The Ammonites also crossed the Jordan to fight against Judah, Benjamin, and the house of Ephraim, so that Israel was in great distress.

¹⁰Then the Israelites cried out to the LORD, "We have sinned against you; we have forsaken our God and have served the Baals." ¹¹�q The LORD answered the Israelites: "Did not the Egyptians, the Amorites,ʳ the Ammonites, the Philistines, ¹²the Sidonians, the Amalekites, and the Midianites oppress you?ˢ Yet when you cried out to me, and I saved you from their grasp, ¹³you still forsook me and worshiped other gods. Therefore I will save you no more. ¹⁴Go and cry out to the gods you have chosen; let them save you now that you are in distress." ¹⁵But the Israelites said to the

10, 4: Saddle-asses: a sign of rank and wealth; cf Jgs 5, 10; 12, 14.

n: 2 Sm 11, 21.   *o:* 1 Sm 31, 4; 1 Chr 10, 4.   *p:* Dt 3, 14.   *q:* 11-14: Jgs 2, 1ff; 6, 8ff.   *r:* Nm 21-32.   *s:* Jgs 6, 3.

LORD, "We have sinned. Do to us whatever you please. Only save us this day." [16]And they cast out the foreign gods from their midst and served the LORD, so that he grieved over the misery of Israel.

[17]The Ammonites had gathered for war and encamped in Gilead, while the Israelites assembled and encamped in Mizpah.[t] [18]And among the people the princes of Gilead said to one another, "The one who begins the war against the Ammonites shall be leader of all the inhabitants of Gilead."[u]

CHAPTER 11

See RG 105

Jephthah. [1]There was a chieftain, the Gileadite Jephthah, born to Gilead of a harlot. [2]Gilead's wife had also borne him sons, and on growing up the sons of the wife had driven Jephthah away, saying to him, "You shall inherit nothing in our family, for you are the son of another woman." [3]So Jephthah had fled from his brothers and had taken up residence in the land of Tob. A rabble had joined company with him, and went out with him on raids.

[4]Some time later, the Ammonites warred on Israel. [5]When this occurred the elders of Gilead went to bring Jephthah from the land of Tob. [6]"Come," they said to Jephthah, "be our commander that we may be able to fight the Ammonites." [7]"Are you not the ones who hated me and drove me from my father's house?" Jephthah replied to the elders of Gilead. "Why do you come to me now, when you are in distress?" [8]The elders of Gilead said to Jephthah, "In any case, we have now come back to you; if you go with us to fight against the Ammonites, you shall be the leader of all of us who dwell in Gilead." [9]Jephthah answered the elders of Gilead, "If you bring me back to fight against the Ammonites and the LORD delivers them up to me, I shall be your leader." [10]The elders of Gilead said to Jephthah, "The LORD is witness between us that we will do as you say." [11]So Jephthah went with the elders of Gil-

ead, and the people made him their leader and commander.[v] In Mizpah, Jephthah settled all his affairs before the LORD. [12]Then he sent messengers to the king of the Ammonites to say, "What have you against me that you come to fight with me in my land?" [13]He answered the messengers of Jephthah, "Israel took away my land from the Arnon to the Jabbok and the Jordan when they came up from Egypt.[w] Now restore the same peaceably."

[14]Again Jephthah sent messengers to the king of the Ammonites, [15]saying to him, "This is what Jephthah says: Israel did not take the land of Moab or the land of the Ammonites.[x] [16]For when they came up from Egypt, Israel went through the desert to the Red Sea and came to Kadesh. [17]Israel then sent messengers to the king of Edom saying, 'Let me pass through your land.' But the king of Edom did not give consent. They also sent to the king of Moab, but he too was unwilling. So Israel remained in Kadesh.[y] [18]Then they went through the desert, and by-passing the land of Edom and the land of Moab, went east of the land of Moab and encamped across the Arnon.[z] Thus they did not go through the territory of Moab, for the Arnon is the boundary of Moab. [19a]Then Israel sent messengers to Sihon, king of the Amorites, king of Heshbon. Israel said to him, 'Let me pass through your land to my own place.' [20]But Sihon refused to let Israel pass through his territory. On the contrary, he gathered all his soldiers, who encamped at Jahaz and fought Israel. [21]But the LORD, the God of Israel, delivered Sihon and all his men into the power of Israel, who defeated them and occupied all the land of the Amorites dwelling in that region, [22]the whole territory from the Arnon to the Jabbok, from the desert to the Jordan. [23]If now the LORD, the God of Israel, has cleared the Amorites out of the way of his people, are you to dislodge Israel? [24]Should you not possess that which your god Chemosh* gave you to pos-

---

11, 24: Chemosh: the chief god of the Moabites—not of the Ammonites, whose leading deity was called Molech or Milcom; cf Nm 21, 29; 1 Kgs 11, 7; 2 Kgs 23, 13. The error is probably due to an ancient copyist. Jephthah argues from the viewpoint of his adversaries, the Ammonites, that they were entitled to all the land they had conquered with the aid of their god. It does not necessarily follow that Jephthah himself believed in the actual existence of this pagan god.

---

t: Jgs 11, 29. *u:* Jgs 11, 5-11. *v:* Jgs 10, 18. *w:* Nm 21, 13. 24ff. *x:* Dt 2, 9. 19. *y:* Nm 20, 1. 14. 18-21; Dt 1, 46. *z:* Nm 21, 4. 11. 13; 22, 36; Dt 2, 8 *a:* 19-22: Nm 21, 21-26; Dt 2, 26-36.

ARAM (SYRIA)

Harosheth-
ha-goiim?

Mt. Tabor

Hill of
Moreh

Wadi Kishon

V. of Jezreel

Hill Country
of Ephraim

Thebez?

Mediterranean
Sea

Sidon

Kedesh

Hazor

NAPHTALI

Bethlehem

ZEBULUN

ISSACHAR

MANASSEH

Shechem

Mt. Gerizim
Arumah

EPHRAIM

Ramah

Bethel

Ophrah

DAN

Aijalon

Mizpah

Timnah

Ekron

Zorah

Ashdod

Lehi?

Ashkelon

Gath?

PHILISTIA

Gaza

Zaphon?

Penuel

River Jabbok

Succoth

GILEAD

Jogbehah

AMMON

Heshbon

River Jordan

32°

Dead
Sea

R. Arnon

Karkor

MOAB

AMALEK

MIDIAN

31°

0   10   20 Miles

0   10   20 Kilometers

35°

36°

Important Cities Mentioned in Judges

299

sess, and should we not possess all that the LORD, our God, has cleared out for us?[b] [25]Again, are you any better than Balak, son of Zippor, king of Moab? Did he ever quarrel with Israel, or did he war against them[c] [26]when Israel occupied Heshbon and its villages, Aroer and its villages, and all the cities on the banks of the Arnon?[d] Three hundred years have passed; why did you not recover them during that time? [27]I have not sinned against you, but you wrong me by warring against me. Let the LORD, who is judge, decide this day between the Israelites and the Ammonites!" [28]But the king of the Ammonites paid no heed to the message Jephthah sent him.

Jephthah's Vow. [29]The spirit of the LORD came upon Jephthah. He passed through Gilead and Manasseh, and through Mizpah-Gilead as well, and from there he went on to the Ammonites. [30]*Jephthah made a vow to the LORD. "If you deliver the Ammonites into my power," he said, [31]"whoever comes out of the doors of my house to meet me when I return in triumph from the Ammonites shall belong to the LORD. I shall offer him up as a holocaust."

[32]Jephthah then went on to the Ammonites to fight against them, and the LORD delivered them into his power, [33]so that he inflicted a severe defeat on them, from Aroer to the approach of Minnith (twenty cities in all) and as far as Abel-keramim. Thus were the Ammonites brought into subjection by the Israelites. [34]When Jephthah returned to his house in Mizpah, it was his daughter who came forth, playing the tambourines and dancing. She was an only child: he had neither son nor daughter besides her. [35]When he saw her, he rent his garments and said, "Alas, daughter, you have struck me down and brought calamity upon me. For I have made a vow to the LORD and I cannot retract."[e] [36]"Father," she replied, "you have made a vow

to the LORD. Do with me as you have vowed, because the LORD has wrought vengeance for you on your enemies the Ammonites." [37]Then she said to her father, "Let me have this favor. Spare me for two months, that I may go off down the mountains to mourn my virginity* with my companions." [38]"Go," he replied, and sent her away for two months. So she departed with her companions and mourned her virginity on the mountains. [39]At the end of the two months she returned to her father, who did to her as he had vowed. She had not been intimate with man. It then became a custom in Israel [40]for Israelite women to go yearly to mourn the daughter of Jephthah the Gileadite for four days of the year.

CHAPTER 12

See RG 105

The Shibboleth Incident. [1]The men of Ephraim gathered together and crossed over to Zaphon. They said to Jephthah, "Why do you go on to fight with the Ammonites without calling us to go with you? We will burn your house over you."[f] [2]Jephthah answered them, "My soldiers and I were engaged in a critical contest with the Ammonites. I summoned you, but you did not rescue me from their power. [3]When I saw that you would not effect a rescue, I took my life in my own hand and went on to the Ammonites, and the LORD delivered them into my power. Why, then, do you come up against me this day to fight with me?"

[4]Then Jephthah called together all the men of Gilead and fought against Ephraim, whom they defeated; for the Ephraimites had said, "You of Gilead are Ephraimite fugitives in territory belonging to Ephraim and Manasseh." [5]The Gileadites took the fords of the Jordan toward Ephraim. When any of the fleeing Ephraimites said, "Let me pass," the men of Gilead would say to him,

---

11, 30-40: The text clearly implies that Jephthah vowed a human sacrifice, according to the custom of his pagan neighbors; cf 2 Kgs 3, 27. The inspired author merely records the fact; he does not approve of the action.

11, 37: Mourn my virginity: to bear children was woman's greatest pride; to be childless was regarded as a

great misfortune. Hence Jephthah's daughter asks permission to mourn the fact that she will be put to death before she can bear children.

b: Nm 21, 29; 1 Kgs 11, 7.   *c:* Nm 22, 2; Jos 24, 9; Mi 6, 5.
d: Nm 21, 25; Dt 2, 36.   *e:* Nm 30, 3.   *f:* Jgs 8, 1.

"Are you an Ephraimite?" If he answered, "No!" [6]they would ask him to say "Shibboleth."* If he said "Sibboleth," not being able to give the proper pronunciation, they would seize him and kill him at the fords of the Jordan. Thus forty-two thousand Ephraimites fell at that time.

[7]After having judged Israel for six years, Jephthah the Gileadite died and was buried in his city in Gilead.

Ibzan. [8]After him Ibzan of Bethlehem judged Israel. [9]He had thirty sons. He also had thirty daughters married outside the family, and he brought in as wives for his sons thirty young women from outside the family. After having judged Israel for seven years, [10]Ibzan died and was buried in Bethlehem.

Elon. [11]After him the Zebulunite Elon judged Israel. When he had judged Israel for ten years, [12]the Zebulunite Elon died and was buried in Elon in the land of Zebulun.

Abdon. [13]After him the Pirathonite Abdon, son of Hillel, judged Israel. [14]He had forty sons and thirty grandsons who rode on seventy saddle-asses. After having judged Israel for eight years, [15]the Pirathonite Abdon, son of Hillel, died and was buried in Pirathon in the land of Ephraim on the mountain of the Amalekites.

CHAPTER 13

See RG 105–106

The Birth of Samson. [1]The Israelites again offended the LORD, who therefore delivered them into the power of the Philistines for forty years.[g]

[2]There was a certain man from Zorah, of the clan of the Danites, whose name was Manoah. His wife was barren and had borne no children. [3]An angel of the LORD appeared to the woman and said to her, "Though you are barren and have had no children, yet you will conceive and bear a son.[h] [4]Now, then, be careful to take no wine or strong drink and to eat nothing unclean. [5]As for the son you will conceive and bear, no razor shall touch his head,[i] for this boy is to be consecrated* to God from the womb. It is he who will begin the deliverance of Israel from the power of the Philistines."

[6]The woman went and told her husband, "A man of God came to me; he had the appearance of an angel of God, terrible indeed. I did not ask him where he came from, nor did he tell me his name. [7]But he said to me, 'You will be with child and will bear a son. So take neither wine nor strong drink, and eat nothing unclean. For the boy shall be consecrated to God from the womb, until the day of his death.' " [8]Manoah then prayed to the LORD. "O LORD, I beseech you," he said, "may the man of God whom you sent, return to us to teach us what to do for the boy who will be born."

[9]God heard the prayer of Manoah, and the angel of God came again to the woman as she was sitting in the field. Since her husband Manoah was not with her, [10]the woman ran in haste and told her husband. "The man who came to me the other day has appeared to me," she said to him; [11]so Manoah got up and followed his wife. When he reached the man, he said to him, "Are you the one who spoke to my wife?" "Yes," he answered. [12]Then Manoah asked, "Now, when that which you say comes true, what are we expected to do for the boy?" [13]The angel of the LORD answered Manoah, "Your wife is to abstain from all the things of which I spoke to her. [14]She must not eat anything that comes from the vine, nor take wine or strong drink, nor eat anything unclean. Let her observe all that I have commanded her." [15]Then Manoah said to the angel of the LORD, "Can we persuade you to stay, while we prepare a kid for you?" [16]But the angel of the LORD answered Manoah, "Although you press me, I will

---

12, 6: Shibboleth: "an ear of grain." But this Hebrew word can also mean "flood water" as in Ps 69, 3. 16. Apparently the Gileadites engaged the Ephraimites in conversation about the "flood water" of the Jordan. Differences in enunciating the initial sibilant of the Hebrew word betrayed different tribal affinities.

13, 5: Consecrated: In Hebrew, nazir. Samson therefore was for life to be under the nazirite vow, which obliged him to abstain from drinking wine or having his hair cut; cf Nm 6, 2-8.

g: Jgs 10, 6. *h:* 3f: 1 Sm 1, 20; Lk 1, 31. *i:* Nm 6, 5.

Nazirite Vows

Nazirites, who could be male or female, took their three vows for a designated period of time or for life (Nm 6, 2–8):

1. Abstain from wine and strong drink;
2. Avoid contact with any dead body;
3. Refrain from cutting the hair.

Though he was best at vow number three, Samson breaks all the vows, for by revealing his secret he becomes indirectly responsible for having his hair cut by Delilah.

---

not partake of your food. But if you will, you may offer a holocaust to the LORD." Not knowing that it was the angel of the LORD, [17]Manoah said to him, "What is your name, that we may honor you when your words come true?" [18]The angel of the LORD answered him,[j] "Why do you ask my name, which is mysterious?"* [19k]Then Manoah took the kid with a cereal offering and offered it on the rock to the LORD, whose works are mysteries. While Manoah and his wife were looking on, [20]as the flame rose to the sky from the altar, the angel of the LORD ascended in the flame of the altar. When Manoah and his wife saw this, they fell prostrate to the ground; [21]but the angel of the LORD was seen no more by Manoah and his wife. Then Manoah, realizing that it was the angel of the LORD, [22]said to his wife, "We will certainly die, for we have seen God."[l] [23]But his wife pointed out to him, "If the LORD had meant to kill us, he would not have accepted a holocaust and cereal offering from our hands! Nor would he have let us see all this just now, or hear what we have heard."

[24]The woman bore a son and named him Samson.[m] The boy grew up and the LORD blessed him; [25]the spirit of the LORD first stirred him in Mahaneh-dan, which is between Zorah and Eshtaol.

CHAPTER 14

See RG 105–106

Marriage of Samson. [1]Samson went down to Timnah and saw there one of the Philistine women.* [2]On his return he told his father and mother, "There is a Philistine woman I saw in Timnah whom I wish you to get as a wife for me." [3]His father and mother said to him, "Can you find no wife among your kinsfolk or among all our people, that you must go and take a wife from the uncircumcised Philistines?" But Samson answered his father, "Get her for me, for she pleases me." [4n]Now his father and mother did not know that this had been brought about by the LORD, who was providing an opportunity against the Philistines; for at that time they had dominion over Israel.

[5]*So Samson went down to Timnah with his father and mother. When they had come to the vineyards of Timnah, a young lion came roaring to meet him. [6]But the spirit of the LORD came upon Samson, and although he had no weapons, he tore the lion in pieces as one tears a kid. [7]However, on the journey to speak for the woman, he did not mention to his father or mother what he had done. [8]Later, when he returned to marry the woman who pleased him, he stepped aside to look at the remains of the lion and found

---

13, 18: Mysterious: incomprehensible, above human understanding. Hence, the angel speaks in the name of the Lord himself, to whom Manoah at once offers a sacrifice.

14, 1-3: Marriages were arranged by the parents of the bridegroom as well as of the bride; cf Gn 24, 2-8; 34, 3-6. The Mosaic law specified only seven pagan nations, not including the Philistines, in the prohibition against mixed marriages; cf Dt 7, 1-4. But national and religious sentiment was against any marriage with a non-Israelite; cf Gn

28, 1f; 1 Kgs 11, 1-10.

14, 5ff: Although Samson was accompanied by his parents on the journey to Timnah, v 7 implies that he was not near them when he tore the lion in pieces.

j: Gn 32, 29.   k: 19f: Jgs 6, 19ff.   l: 21f: Jgs 6, 22f.   m: Heb 11, 32.   n: Jgs 15, 11.

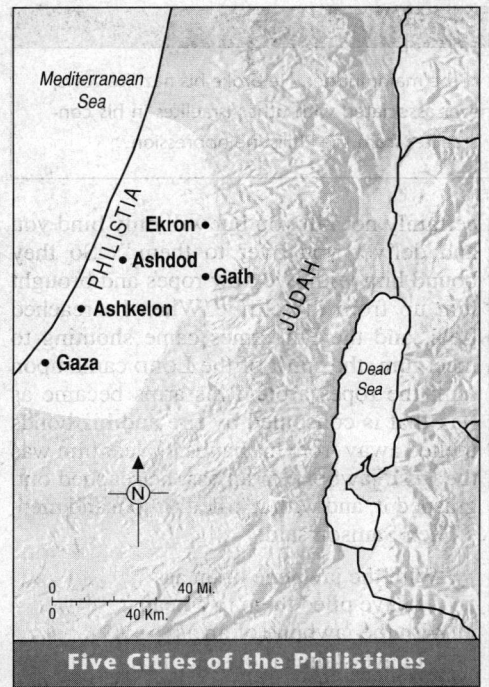

Mediterranean Sea

PHILISTIA

Ekron •

• Ashdod
• Gath

• Ashkelon

JUDAH

• Gaza

Dead Sea

N

| 0 | 40 Mi. |
| 0 | 40 Km. |

Five Cities of the Philistines

"Out of the eater came forth food,
and out of the strong came forth
sweetness."

After three days' failure to answer the riddle, ¹⁵they said on the fourth day to Samson's wife, "Coax your husband to answer the riddle for us, or we will burn you and your family. Did you invite us here to reduce us to poverty?" ¹⁶At Samson's side, his wife wept and said, "You must hate me; you do not love me, for you have proposed a riddle to my countrymen, but have not told me the answer." He said to her, "If I have not told it even to my father or my mother, must I tell it to you?" ¹⁷But she wept beside him during the seven days the feast lasted. On the seventh day, since she importuned him, he told her the answer, and he explained the riddle to her countrymen.

¹⁸On the seventh day, before the sun set, the men of the city said to him,

"What is sweeter than honey,
and what is stronger than a lion?"

He replied to them,

"If you had not plowed with my heifer,
you would not have solved my riddle."

¹⁹The spirit of the LORD came upon him, and he went down to Ashkelon, where he killed thirty of their men and despoiled them; he gave their garments to those who had answered the riddle. Then he went off to his own family in anger, ²⁰and Samson's wife was married to the one who had been best man at his wedding.^o

CHAPTER 15

Samson Defeats the Philistines. ¹After some time, in the season of the wheat harvest, Samson visited his wife, bringing a kid. But when he said, "Let me be with my wife in private," her father would not let him enter, ²saying, "I thought it certain you wished to repudiate her; so I gave her to your best man. Her younger

See RG 105–106

a swarm of bees and honey in the lion's carcass. ⁹So he scooped the honey out into his palms and ate it as he went along. When he came to his father and mother, he gave them some to eat, without telling them that he had scooped the honey from the lion's carcass.

¹⁰His father also went down to the woman, and Samson gave a banquet there, since it was customary for the young men to do this. ¹¹When they met him, they brought thirty men to be his companions.* ¹²Samson said to them, "Let me propose a riddle to you. If within the seven days of the feast you solve it for me successfully, I will give you thirty linen tunics and thirty sets of garments. ¹³But if you cannot answer it for me, you must give me thirty tunics and thirty sets of garments." "Propose your riddle," they responded; "we will listen to it." ¹⁴So he said to them,

14, 11: Companions: known at a later period as "the friends of the bridegroom" (1 Mc 9, 39; Mk 2, 19), the best man and his fellows. Here they are Philistines (v 16), appointed by the family of the bride, who would also have several bridesmaids; cf Mt 25, 1-13.

o: Jgs 15, 2. 6.

Samson

The final "deliverer" is the lowest moral point of the major judges. He broke his nazirite vows, had intercourse with non-Israelite women, never associated with other Israelites in his conflicts with the Philistines, and did not deliver the Israelites from the Philistine oppression.

sister is more beautiful than she; you may have her instead." ³Samson said to them, "This time the Philistines cannot blame me if I harm them." ⁴So Samson left and caught three hundred foxes. Turning them tail to tail, he tied between each pair of tails one of the torches he had at hand. ⁵He then kindled the torches and set the foxes loose in the standing grain of the Philistines, thus burning both the shocks and the standing grain, and the vineyards and olive orchards as well.

⁶ᵖWhen the Philistines asked who had done this, they were told, "Samson, the son-in-law of the Timnite, because his wife was taken and given to his best man." So the Philistines went up and destroyed her and her family by fire. ⁷Samson said to them, "If this is how you act, I will not stop until I have taken revenge on you." ⁸And with repeated blows, he inflicted a great slaughter on them. Then he went down and remained in a cavern of the cliff of Etam.

⁹The Philistines went up and, from a camp in Judah, deployed against Lehi. ¹⁰When the men of Judah asked, "Why have you come up against us?" they answered, "To take Samson prisoner; to do to him as he has done to us." ¹¹Three thousand men of Judah went down to the cavern in the cliff of Etam and said to Samson, "Do you not know that the Philistines are our rulers? Why, then, have you done this to us?" He answered them, "As they have done to me, so have I done to them." ¹²They said to him, "We have come to take you prisoner, to deliver you over to the Philistines." Samson said to them, "Swear to me that you will not kill me yourselves." ¹³"No," they replied, "we will

certainly not kill you but will only bind you and deliver you over to them."�q So they bound him with two new ropes and brought him up from the cliff. ¹⁴When he reached Lehi, and the Philistines came shouting to meet him, the spirit of the LORD came upon him: the ropes around his arms became as flax that is consumed by fire and his bonds melted away from his hands. ¹⁵Near him was the fresh jawbone of an ass; he reached out, grasped it, and with it killed a thousand men. ¹⁶Then Samson said,

"With the jawbone of an ass
    I have piled them in a heap;
With the jawbone of an ass
    I have slain a thousand men."

¹⁷As he finished speaking he threw the jawbone from him; and so that place was named Ramath-lehi.* ¹⁸Being very thirsty, he cried to the LORD and said, "You have granted this great victory by the hand of your servant. Must I now die of thirst or fall into the hands of the uncircumcised?" ¹⁹Then God split the cavity in Lehi, and water issued from it, which Samson drank till his spirit returned and he revived. Hence that spring in Lehi is called En-hakkore* to this day.

²⁰Samson judged Israel for twenty years in the days of the Philistines.ʳ

CHAPTER 16

See RG
106–107

¹Once Samson went to Gaza, where he saw a harlot and visited her. ²Informed that Samson had come there, the men of Gaza surrounded him with an ambush at the city gate all night long. And all the night they waited, saying, "Tomorrow morning we will kill him." ³Samson rested there until

---

15, 17: Ramath-lehi: "heights of the jawbone."
15, 19: En-hakkore: "the spring of him who cries out," an allusion to Samson's cry in v 18.

p: Jgs 14, 20.   q: Jgs 16, 11f.   r: Jgs 16, 31.

midnight. Then he rose, seized the doors of the city gate and the two gateposts, and tore them loose, bar and all. He hoisted them on his shoulders and carried them to the top of the ridge opposite Hebron.

Samson and Delilah. ⁴After that he fell in love with a woman in the Wadi Sorek whose name was Delilah. ⁵The lords of the Philistines came to her and said, "Beguile him and find out the secret of his great strength, and how we may overcome and bind him so as to keep him helpless. We will each give you eleven hundred shekels of silver."

⁶So Delilah said to Samson, "Tell me the secret of your great strength and how you may be bound so as to be kept helpless." ⁷"If they bind me with seven fresh bowstrings which have not dried," Samson answered her, "I shall be as weak as any other man." ⁸So the lords of the Philistines brought her seven fresh bowstrings which had not dried, and she bound him with them. ⁹She had men lying in wait in the chamber and so she said to him, "The Philistines are upon you, Samson!" But he snapped the strings as a thread of tow is severed by a whiff of flame;ˢ and the secret of his strength remained unknown.

¹⁰Delilah said to Samson, "You have mocked me and told me lies. Now tell me how you may be bound." ¹¹"If they bind me tight with new ropes, with which no work has been done," he answered her, "I shall be as weak as any other man."ᵗ ¹²So Delilah took new ropes and bound him with them. Then she said to him, "The Philistines are upon you, Samson!" For there were men lying in wait in the chamber. But he snapped them off his arms like thread.

¹³Delilah said to Samson again, "Up to now you have mocked me and told me lies. Tell me how you may be bound." He said to her, "If you weave my seven locks of hair into the web and fasten them with the pin, I shall be as weak as any other man." ¹⁴So while he slept, Delilah wove his seven locks of hair into the web, and fastened them in with the pin. Then she said, "The Philistines

are upon you, Samson!" Awakening from his sleep, he pulled out both the weaver's pin and the web.

¹⁵Then she said to him, "How can you say that you love me when you do not confide in me? Three times already you have mocked me, and not told me the secret of your great strength!" ¹⁶She importuned him continually and vexed him with her complaints till he was deathly weary of them. ¹⁷So he took her completely into his confidence and told her, "No razor has touched my head,ᵘ for I have been consecrated to God from my mother's womb. If I am shaved, my strength will leave me, and I shall be as weak as any other man!" ¹⁸When Delilah saw that he had taken her completely into his confidence, she summoned the lords of the Philistines, saying, "Come up this time, for he has opened his heart to me." So the lords of the Philistines came and brought up the money with them. ¹⁹She had him sleep on her lap, and called for a man who shaved off his seven locks of hair. Then she began to mistreat him, for his strength had left him. ²⁰When she said, "The Philistines are upon you, Samson!", and he woke from his sleep, he thought he could make good his escape as he had done time and again, for he did not realize that the LORD had left him. ²¹But the Philistines seized him and gouged out his eyes. Then they brought him down to Gaza and bound him with bronze fetters, and he was put to grinding in the prison. ²²But the hair of his head began to grow as soon as it was shaved off.

The Death of Samson. ²³ᵛThe lords of the Philistines assembled to offer a great sacrifice to their god Dagon* and to make merry. They said,

"Our god has delivered into our power
    Samson our enemy."

²⁵When their spirits were high, they said, "Call Samson that he may amuse us." So they called Samson from the prison, and he played the buffoon before them. ²⁴When the people saw him, they praised their god. For they said,

16, 23: Dagon was originally a Mesopotamian deity, whom the Philistines came to worship as their own god of grain.

s: Jgs 15, 14.   t: Jgs 15, 13.   u: Jgs 13, 5.   v: 1 Sm 5, 2-5.

"Our god has delivered into our power
our enemy, the ravager of our land,
the one who has multiplied our slain."

Then they stationed him between the columns. ²⁶Samson said to the attendant who was holding his hand, "Put me where I may touch the columns that support the temple and may rest against them." ²⁷The temple was full of men and women: all the lords of the Philistines were there, and from the roof about three thousand men and women looked on as Samson provided amusement. ²⁸Samson cried out to the LORD and said, "O Lord GOD, remember me! Strengthen me, O God, this last time that for my two eyes I may avenge myself once and for all on the Philistines." ²⁹Samson grasped the two middle columns on which the temple rested and braced himself against them, one at his right hand, the other at his left. ³⁰And Samson said, "Let me die with the Philistines!" He pushed hard, and the temple fell upon the lords and all the people who were in it. Those he killed at his death were more than those he had killed during his lifetime.

³¹All his family and kinsmen went down and bore him up for burial in the grave of his father Manoah between Zorah and Eshtaol. He had judged Israel for twenty years.^w

III: The Tribes of Dan and Benjamin in the Days of the Judges

CHAPTER 17

See RG 106–107

Micah and the Levite. ¹There was a man in the mountain region of Ephraim whose name was Micah. ²He said to his mother, "The eleven hundred shekels of silver over which you pronounced a curse in my hearing when they were taken from you, are in my possession. It was I who took them; so now I will restore them to you." ³When he re-

stored the eleven hundred shekels of silver to his mother, she took two hundred of them and gave them to the silversmith, who made of them a carved idol* overlaid with silver.^x ⁴Then his mother said, "May the LORD bless my son! I have consecrated the silver to the LORD as my gift in favor of my son, by making a carved idol overlaid with silver." It remained in the house of Micah. ⁵Thus the layman Micah had a sanctuary. He also made an ephod and household idols,^y and consecrated one of his sons, who became his priest. ⁶In those days there was no king in Israel; everyone did what he thought best.^z

⁷There was a young Levite who had resided within the tribe of Judah at Bethlehem of Judah. ⁸From that city he set out to find another place of residence. On his journey he came to the house of Micah in the mountain region of Ephraim. ⁹Micah said to him, "Where do you come from?" He answered him, "I am a Levite from Bethlehem in Judah, and am on my way to find some other place of residence." ¹⁰"Stay with me," Micah said to him. "Be father and priest to me,^a and I will give you ten silver shekels a year, a set of garments, and your food." ¹¹So the young Levite decided to stay with the man, to whom he became as one of his own sons. ¹²*Micah consecrated the young Levite, who became his priest, remaining in his house. ¹³Therefore Micah said, "Now I know that the LORD will prosper me, since the Levite has become my priest."

CHAPTER 18

See RG 106–107

Migration of the Danites. ¹At that time there was no king in Israel.^b Moreover the tribe of Danites were in search of a district to dwell in, for up to that time they had received no heritage among the tribes of Israel.*

²So the Danites sent from their clan a detail of five valiant men of Zorah and Eshtaol,

---

17, 3: Idol: an image, not of a pagan god, but of the Lord. The Mosaic law forbade the making of an image even of the true God.

17, 12f: According to Nm 18, 1-7 only those Levites who were descended from Aaron could be consecrated as priests.

18, 1: The tribe of Dan had been assigned a territory with definite limits in central Palestine. However they were unable to gain possession of the better portion of their land (Jgs 1, 34). So they now seek territory elsewhere in Palestine.

w: Jgs 15, 20. x: Ex 20, 4; Lv 19, 4. y: Jgs 18, 14. 17. z: Jgs 18, 1; 21, 25. a: Jgs 18, 19. b: Jos 19, 40-48.

Micah's House of God and the Temple of Dan

This story (17, 1—18, 31), focused upon cultic sites, serves to criticize the period of the judges by representing it as an age of anarchy: "In those days there was no king in Israel; every man did as he pleased." (This statement is repeated, in whole or in part, in Judges 17, 6; 18, 1; 19, 1; 21, 25.) In terms of chronology, the story is set at the beginning of the age of the judges (see Jgs 18, 30) but is placed at the end of the book to emphasize that the end of the period was similar to its beginning, and the judges were unable to correct the situation.

to reconnoiter the land and scout it. With their instructions to go and scout the land, they traveled as far as the house of Micah in the mountain region of Ephraim, where they passed the night. ³Near the house of Micah, they recognized the voice* of the young Levite[c] and turned in that direction. "Who brought you here and what are you doing here?" they asked him. "What is your interest here?" ⁴"This is how Micah treats me," he replied to them. "He pays me a salary and I am his priest."[d] ⁵They said to him, "Consult God, that we may know whether the undertaking we are engaged in will succeed." ⁶The priest said to them, "Go and prosper: the LORD is favorable to the undertaking you are engaged in."

⁷So the five men went on and came to Laish. They saw that the people dwelling there lived securely after the manner of the Sidonians, quiet and trusting, with no lack of any natural resources. They were distant from the Sidonians and had no contact with other people. ⁸When the five returned to their kinsmen in Zorah and Eshtaol and were asked for a report, ⁹they replied, "Come, let us attack them, for we have seen the land and it is very good. Are you going to hesitate? Do not be slothful about beginning your expedition to possess the land. ¹⁰Those against whom you go are a trusting people, and the land is ample. God has indeed given it into your power: a place where no natural resource is lacking."

¹¹So six hundred men of the clan of the Danites, fully armed with weapons of war, set out from where they were in Zorah and Eshtaol, ¹²and camped in Judah, up near Kiriath-jearim; hence to this day the place, which lies west of Kiriath-jearim, is called Mahaneh-dan.[e]

¹³From there they went on to the mountain region of Ephraim and came to the house of Micah. ¹⁴The five men who had gone to reconnoiter the land of Laish said to their kinsmen, "Do you know that in these houses there are an ephod, household idols, and a carved idol overlaid with silver?[f] Now decide what you must do!" ¹⁵So turning in that direction, they went to the house of the young Levite at the home of Micah and greeted him. ¹⁶The six hundred men girt with weapons of war, who were Danites, stood by the entrance of the gate, and the priest stood there also. ¹⁷Meanwhile the five men who had gone to reconnoiter the land went up and entered the house of Micah. ¹⁸When they had gone in and taken the ephod, the household idols, and the carved idol overlaid with silver, the priest said to them, "What are you doing?" ¹⁹They said to him, "Be still: put your hand over your mouth. Come with us and be our father and priest.[g] Is it better for you to be priest for the family of one man or to be priest for a tribe and a clan in Israel?" ²⁰The priest, agreeing, took the ephod, household idols, and carved idol and went off in the midst of the band. ²¹As they turned to depart, they placed their little ones, their livestock, and their goods at the head of the column.

²²The Danites had already gone some distance, when those in the houses near that of

---

18, 3: Recognized the voice: perhaps they noticed the peculiar pronunciation of his south Hebrew dialect.

c: Jgs 17, 7. d: Jgs 17, 10. e: Jgs 13, 25. f: Jgs 17, 4f. g: Jgs 17, 10.

Micah took up arms and overtook them. ²³They called to the Danites, who turned about and said to Micah, "What do you want, that you have taken up arms?" ²⁴"You have taken my god, which I made, and have gone off with my priest as well," he answered. "What is left for me? How, then, can you ask me what I want?" ²⁵The Danites said to him, "Let us hear no further sound from you, lest fierce men fall upon you and you and your family lose your lives." ²⁶The Danites then went on their way, and Micah, seeing that they were stronger than he, returned home.

²⁷Having taken what Micah had made, and the priest he had had, they attacked Laish, a quiet and trusting people; they put them to the sword and destroyed their city by fire. ²⁸No one came to their aid, since the city was far from Sidon and they had no contact with other people. The Danites then rebuilt the city, which was in the valley that belongs to Beth-rehob, and lived there. ²⁹They named it Dan after their ancestor Dan, son of Israel. However, the name of the city was formerly Laish. ³⁰The Danites set up the carved idol for themselves, and Jonathan, son of Gershom, son of Moses, and his descendants were priests for the tribe of the Danites until the time of the captivity of the land.* ³¹They maintained the carved idol Micah had made as long as the house of God was in Shiloh.

See RG 106–107

CHAPTER 19

The Levite from Ephraim. ¹At that time, when there was no king in Israel,^h there was a Levite residing in remote parts of the mountain region of Ephraim who had taken for himself a concubine from Bethlehem of Judah. ²His concubine was unfaithful to him and left him for her father's house in Bethlehem of Judah, where she stayed for some four months. ³Her husband then set out with his servant and a pair of asses, and went after her to forgive her and take her back. She

brought him into her father's house, and on seeing him, the girl's father joyfully made him welcome. ⁴He was detained by the girl's father, and so he spent three days with this father-in-law of his, eating and drinking and passing the night there. ⁵*On the fourth day they rose early in the morning and he prepared to go. But the girl's father said to his son-in-law, "Fortify yourself with a little food; you can go later on." ⁶So they stayed and the two men ate and drank together. Then the girl's father said to the husband, "Why not decide to spend the night here and enjoy yourself?" ⁷The man still made a move to go, but when his father-in-law pressed him he went back and spent the night there.

⁸On the fifth morning he rose early to depart, but the girl's father said, "Fortify yourself and tarry until the afternoon." When he and his father-in-law had eaten, ⁹and the husband was ready to go with his concubine and servant, the girl's father said to him, "It is already growing dusk. Stay for the night. See, the day is coming to an end. Spend the night here and enjoy yourself. Early tomorrow you can start your journey home." ¹⁰The man, however, refused to stay another night; he and his concubine set out with a pair of saddled asses, and traveled till they came opposite Jebus, which is Jerusalem. ¹¹Since they were near Jebus with the day far gone, the servant said to his master, "Come, let us turn off to this city of the Jebusites and spend the night in it." ¹²But his master said to him, "We will not turn off to a city of foreigners, who are not Israelites, but will go on to Gibeah.ⁱ ¹³Come," he said to his servant, "let us make for some other place, either Gibeah or Ramah, to spend the night."^j ¹⁴So they continued on their way till the sun set on them when they were abreast of Gibeah of Benjamin.

¹⁵*There they turned off to enter Gibeah for the night.^k The man waited in the public square of the city he had entered, but no one

***

18, 30: Until . . . land: about the year 734 B.C., when the Assyrian emperor Tiglath-pileser III subjected northern Palestine.

19, 5–9: Such importuning of guests to prolong their stay at the home of their host is characteristic of Oriental hospitality.

19, 15: Private hospitality was the customary means of providing comfort to travelers where public facilities were so rare.

h: Jgs 17, 6.   *i:* Jgs 1, 21.   *j:* Jos 18, 25.   *k:* Jgs 20, 4.

offered them the shelter of his home for the night. [16]In the evening, however, an old man came from his work in the field; he was from the mountain region of Ephraim, though he lived among the Benjaminite townspeople of Gibeah. [17]When he noticed the traveler in the public square of the city, the old man asked where he was going, and whence he had come. [18]He said to him, "We are traveling from Bethlehem of Judah far up into the mountain region of Ephraim, where I belong. I have been to Bethlehem of Judah and am now going back home; but no one has offered us the shelter of his house. [19]We have straw and fodder for our asses, and bread and wine for the woman and myself and for our servant; there is nothing else we need." [20]"You are welcome," the old man said to him, "but let me provide for all your needs, and do not spend the night in the public square." [21]So he led them to his house and provided fodder for the asses. Then they washed their feet, and ate and drank.[l]

The Outrage at Gibeah. [22m]While they were enjoying themselves, the men of the city, who were corrupt,* surrounded the house and beat on the door. They said to the old man whose house it was, "Bring out your guest, that we may abuse him." [23]The owner of the house went out to them and said, "No, my brothers; do not be so wicked. Since this man is my guest, do not commit this crime. [24]Rather let me bring out my maiden daughter or his concubine. Ravish them, or do whatever you want with them; but against the man you must not commit this wanton crime." [25]When the men would not listen to his host, the husband seized his concubine and thrust her outside to them. They had relations with her and abused her all night until the following dawn, when they let her go. [26]Then at daybreak the woman came and collapsed at the entrance of the house in which her husband was a guest, where she lay until the morning. [27]When her husband rose that day and opened the door of the house to start out again on his journey, there lay the woman, his concubine, at the entrance of the house with her hands on the threshold. [28]He said to her, "Come, let us go"; but there was no answer. So the man placed her on an ass and started out again for home.

[29]*On reaching home, he took a knife to the body of his concubine, cut her into twelve pieces, and sent them throughout the territory of Israel. [30n]Everyone who saw this said, "Nothing like this has been done or seen from the day the Israelites came up from the land of Egypt to this day. Take note of it, and state what you propose to do."

CHAPTER 20

See RG 106–107

Assembly of Israelites. [1]So all the Israelites came out as one man: from Dan to Beer-sheba,* and from the land of Gilead, the community was gathered to the LORD at Mizpah. [2]The leaders of all the people and all the tribesmen of Israel, four hundred thousand foot soldiers who were swordsmen, presented themselves in the assembly of the people of God. [3]Meanwhile, the Benjaminites heard that the Israelites had gone up to Mizpah. The Israelites asked to be told how the crime had taken place, [4]and the Levite, the husband of the murdered woman, testified: "My concubine and I went into Gibeah of Benjamin[o] for the night. [5p]But the citizens of Gibeah rose up against me by night and surrounded the house in which I was. Me they attempted to kill, and my concubine they abused so that she died. [6q]So I took my concubine and cut her up and sent her through every part of the territory of Israel, because of the monstrous crime they had committed in Israel. [7]*Now that you are

---

19, 22: Who were corrupt: literally "sons of Belial," indicating extreme perversion; cf Gn 19, 4-8. This crime and its punishment made the name Gibeah proverbial as a place of shameful wickedness; cf Hos 9, 9; 10, 9.

19, 29: A drastic means for arousing the tribes to avenge the unheard of crime of the Benjaminites.

20, 1: From Dan to Beer-sheba: from north to south. The land of Gilead: all the territory east of the Jordan.

20, 7: The Israelites were asked to decide at once what action to take concerning this crime; cf 2 Sm 16, 20. The Levite undoubtedly addressed the tribal heads who would speak in behalf of the multitude.

l: Gn 18, 4; 24, 32; 43, 24.   *m:* 22-25: Gn 19, 4-9.   *n:* Hos 9, 9; 10, 9.   *o:* Jgs 19, 14f.   *p:* Jgs 19, 22-27.   *q:* Jgs 19, 29.

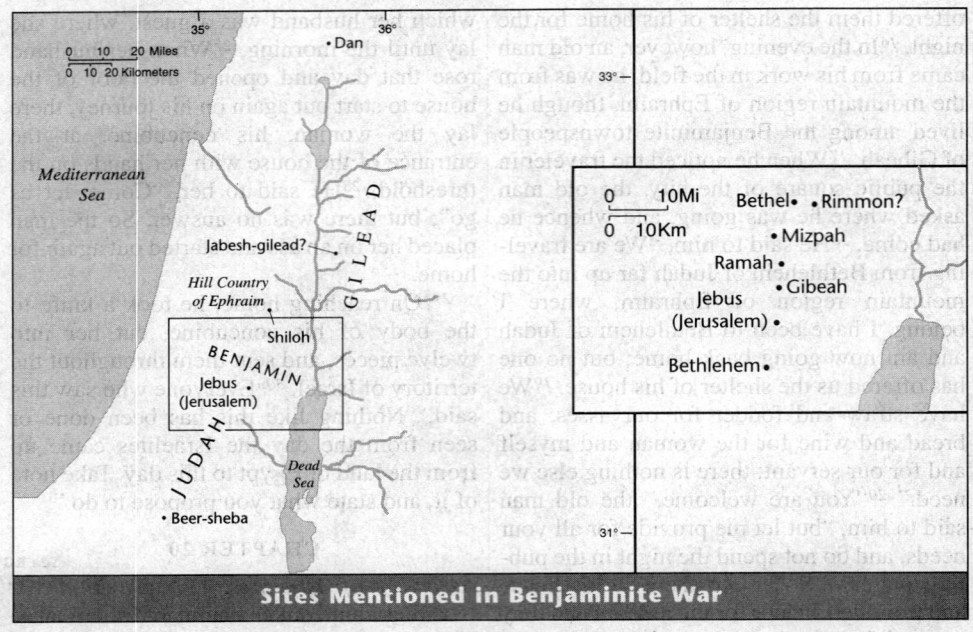

Sites Mentioned in Benjaminite War

all here, O Israelites, state what you propose to do."*r* *8*All the people rose as one man to say, "None of us is to leave for his tent or return to his home. *9*Now as for Gibeah, this is what we will do: We will proceed against it by lot, *10*taking from all the tribes of Israel ten men for every hundred, a hundred for every thousand, a thousand for every ten thousand, and procuring supplies for the soldiers who will go to deal fully and suitably with Gibeah of Benjamin for the crime it committed in Israel."

*11*When, therefore, all the men of Israel without exception were leagued together against the city, *12**the tribes of Israel sent men throughout the tribe of Benjamin to say, "What is this evil which has occurred among you? *13*Now give up these corrupt men of Gibeah, that we may put them to death and thus purge the evil from Israel." But the Benjaminites refused to accede to

the demand of their brothers, the Israelites. *14*Instead, the Benjaminites assembled from their other cities to Gibeah, to do battle with the Israelites. *15*The number of the Benjaminite swordsmen from the other cities on that occasion was twenty-six thousand, in addition to the inhabitants of Gibeah. *16*Included in this total were seven hundred picked men who were left-handed, every one of them able to sling a stone at a hair without missing. *17*Meanwhile the other Israelites who, without Benjamin, mustered four hundred thousand swordsmen ready for battle, *18*moved on to Bethel and consulted God. When the Israelites asked who should go first in the attack on the Benjaminites,*s* the LORD said, "Judah shall go first."** *19*The next day the Israelites advanced on Gibeah with their forces.

War with Benjamin. *20*On the day the Israelites drew up in battle array at Gibeah

---

20, 12: Before the crime at Gibeah was punished, the Benjaminites were invited to join their brethren, the Israelites, in punishing the crime. Since they failed to respond, special messengers were sent asking them to deliver up the guilty ones. They replied by gathering their forces for combat.

20, 18: Judah shall go first: the same response as in Jgs 1, 1f, but without the assurance of immediate success. Only after

the Israelites were punished at the hands of the Benjaminites for their own grossness, and had performed penance, did they succeed in punishing the latter for their part in the crime of rape and murder, by gaining the victory over them.

r: Jgs 19, 30.   *s:* Jgs 1, 1f.

for the combat with Benjamin, [21]the Benjaminites came out of the city and felled twenty-two thousand men of Israel. [23]Then the Israelites went up and wept before the LORD until evening. "Shall I again engage my brother Benjamin in battle?" they asked the LORD; and the LORD answered that they should. [22]But though the Israelite soldiers took courage and again drew up for combat in the same place as on the previous day, [24]when they met the Benjaminites for the second time, [25]once again the Benjaminites who came out of Gibeah against them felled eighteen thousand Israelites, all of them swordsmen. [26]So the entire Israelite army went up to Bethel, where they wept and remained fasting before the LORD until evening of that day, besides offering holocausts and peace offerings before the LORD. [27t]When the Israelites consulted the LORD (for the ark of the covenant of God was there in those days, [28]and Phinehas, son of Eleazar, son of Aaron, was ministering to him in those days), and asked, "Shall I go out again to battle with Benjamin, my brother, or shall I desist?" the LORD said, "Attack! for tomorrow I will deliver him into your power." [29u]So Israel set men in ambush around Gibeah.*

[30]The Israelites went up against the Benjaminites for the third time and formed their line of battle at Gibeah as on other occasions. [31]The Benjaminites went out to meet them, and in the beginning they killed off about thirty of the Israelite soldiers in the open field, just as on the other occasions. [32]Therefore the Benjaminites thought, "We are defeating them as before"; not realizing that disaster was about to overtake them. The Israelites, however, had planned the flight so as to draw them away from the city onto the highways. They were drawn away from the city onto the highways, of which the one led to Bethel, the other to Gibeon. [33]And then all the men of Israel rose from their places. They re-formed their ranks at Baaltamar, and the Israelites in ambush rushed from their place west of Gibeah, [34]ten thousand picked men from all Israel, and advanced against the city itself. In a fierce battle, [35]the LORD defeated Benjamin before Israel; and on that day the Israelites killed twenty-five thousand one hundred men of Benjamin, all of them swordsmen.

[36]To the Benjaminites it had looked as though the enemy were defeated, for the men of Israel gave ground to Benjamin, trusting in the ambush they had set at Gibeah. [37]But then the men in ambush made a sudden dash into Gibeah, overran it, and put the whole city to the sword. [38]Now, the other Israelites had agreed with the men in ambush on a smoke signal they were to send up from the city. [39]And though the men of Benjamin had begun by killing off some thirty of the men of Israel, under the impression that they were defeating them as surely as in the earlier fighting, the Israelites wheeled about to resist [40]as the smoke of the signal column began to rise up from the city. It was when Benjamin looked back and saw the whole city in flames against the sky [41]that the men of Israel wheeled about. Therefore the men of Benjamin were thrown into confusion, for they realized the disaster that had overtaken them. [42]They retreated before the men of Israel in the direction of the desert, with the fight being pressed against them. In their very midst, meanwhile, those who had been in the city were spreading destruction. [43]The men of Benjamin had been surrounded, and were now pursued to a point east of Gibeah, [44]while eighteen thousand of them fell, warriors to a man. [45]The rest turned and fled through the desert to the rock Rimmon.[v] But on the highways the Israelites picked off five thousand men among them, and chasing them up to Gidom, killed another two thousand of them there. [46]Those of

20, 29–46: This stratagem proved more useful to the Israelites than force, as in the siege of Ai (Jos 8, 3-21). In the parallel accounts the first (vv 29-35) is a summary of the second (vv 36-46).

t: 1 Sm 4, 3f. u: 29-46: Jos 8, 4-24. v: Jgs 21, 13.

Benjamin who fell on that day were in all twenty-five thousand swordsmen, warriors to a man. [47]But six hundred others who turned and fled through the desert reached the rock Rimmon, where they remained for four months.

[48]The men of Israel withdrew through the territory of the Benjaminites, putting to the sword the inhabitants of the cities, the livestock, and all they chanced upon. Moreover they destroyed by fire all the cities they came upon.

CHAPTER 21

See RG 106–107

Wives for the Survivors. [1]Now the men of Israel* had sworn at Mizpah that none of them would give his daughter in marriage to anyone from Benjamin. [2]So the people went to Bethel and remained there before God until evening, raising their voices in bitter lament.[w] [3]They said, "LORD, God of Israel, why has it come to pass in Israel that today one tribe of Israel should be lacking?" [4]Early the next day the people built an altar there and offered holocausts and peace offerings. [5]Then the Israelites asked, "Are there any among all the tribes of Israel who did not come up to the LORD for the assembly?" For they had taken a solemn oath that anyone who did not go up to the LORD at Mizpah should be put to death without fail.[x]

[6]*The Israelites were disconsolate over their brother Benjamin and said, "Today one of the tribes of Israel has been cut off. [7]What can we do about wives for the survivors, since we have sworn by the LORD not to give them any of our daughters in marriage?" [8]And when they asked whether anyone among the tribes of Israel had not come up to the LORD in Mizpah, they found that none of the men of Jabesh-gilead had come to the encampment for the assembly.

[9]A roll call of the army established that none of the inhabitants of that city were present. [10]The community, therefore, sent twelve thousand warriors with orders to go to Jabesh-gilead and put those who lived there to the sword, including the women and children. [11]They were told to include under the ban* all males and every woman who was not still a virgin.[y] [12]Finding among the inhabitants of Jabesh-gilead four hundred young virgins, who had had no relations with men, they brought them to the camp at Shiloh in the land of Canaan. [13z]Then the whole community sent a message to the Benjaminites at the rock Rimmon, offering them peace. [14]When Benjamin returned at that time, they gave them as wives the women of Jabesh-gilead whom they had spared; but these proved to be not enough for them.

[15]The people were still disconsolate over Benjamin because the LORD had made a breach* among the tribes of Israel. [16]And the elders of the community said, "What shall we do for wives for the survivors? For every woman in Benjamin has been put to death." [17]They said, "Those of Benjamin who survive must have heirs, else one of the Israelite tribes will be wiped out. [18]*Yet we cannot give them any of our daughters in marriage, because the Israelites have sworn, 'Cursed be he who gives a woman to Benjamin!' " [19]Then they thought of the yearly feast of the LORD at Shiloh, north of Bethel, east of the highway that goes up from Bethel to Shechem, and south of Lebonah. [20]And they instructed the Benjaminites, "Go and lie in wait in the vineyards. [21]When you see the girls of Shiloh come out to do their dancing, leave the vineyards and each of you seize one of the girls of Shiloh for a wife, and go to the land of Benjamin. [22]When their fathers or their brothers come to complain to

---

21, 1-3: The anger of the Israelites led them to destroy their brethren, the Benjaminites. Having realized their goal, however, they were soon filled with dismay, and sought to restore the tribe they had all but exterminated.

21, 6-9: This account is summarized in the parallel passage in vv 2-5.

21, 11: Under the ban: see note on Nm 21, 3.

21, 15: Had made a breach: what is here attributed to God was

in reality the free and deliberate act of the Israelites and happened only by the permissive will of God. The ancients attributed to the first primary cause what is more directly due to secondary causes.

21, 18: Regardless of the serious consequences of their vow, the Israelites considered themselves obliged to fulfill it; cf Jgs 11, 31. 35f. 39.

w: Jgs 20, 26.   x: Jgs 20, 8ff.   y: Nm 31, 17.   z: Jgs 20, 47.

us, we shall say to them, 'Release them to us as a kindness, since we did not take a woman apiece in the war. Had you yourselves given them these wives, you would now be guilty.' "

²³The Benjaminites did this; they carried off a wife for each of them from their raid on the dancers, and went back to their own territory, where they rebuilt and occupied the cities. ²⁴Also at that time the Israelites dispersed; each of them left for his own heritage in his own clan and tribe.

²⁵*In those days there was no king in Israel; everyone did what he thought best.ᵃ

21, 25: Cf Jgs 17, 6; 18, 1; 19, 1. The verse gives the reason why the lawlessness of the period of judges, and the events described herein, were possible.

a: Jgs 17, 6; 18, 1; 19, 1.

See RG
108–113

The Book of Ruth

The Book of Ruth is named after the Moabite woman who was joined to the Israelite people by her marriage with the influential Boaz of Bethlehem.

The book contains a beautiful example of filial piety, pleasing to the Hebrews especially because of its connection with King David, and useful both to Hebrews and to Gentiles. Its aim is to demonstrate the divine reward for such piety even when practiced by a stranger. Ruth's piety (2, 11), her spirit of self-sacrifice, and her moral integrity were favored by God with the gift of faith and an illustrious marriage whereby she became the ancestress of David and of Christ. In this, the universality of the messianic salvation is foreshadowed.

In the Greek and Latin canons the Book of Ruth is placed just after Judges, to which it is closely related because of the time of its action, and just before Samuel, for which it is an excellent introduction, since it traces the ancestry of the Davidic dynasty. One might characterize the literary form of this book as dramatic, since about two-thirds of it is in dialogue. Yet there is every indication that, as tradition has always held, it contains true history.

There is no certainty about the author of the book. It was written long after the events had passed (4, 7), which took place "in the time of the judges" (1, 1).

CHAPTER 1

See RG
110–111

Naomi in Moab. ¹Once in the time of the judges* there was a famine in the land; so a man from Bethlehem of Judah departed with his wife and two sons to reside on the plateau of Moab. ²The man was named Elimelech, his wife Naomi, and his sons Mahlon and Chilion; they were Ephrathites from Bethlehem of Judah. Some time after their arrival on the Moabite plateau, ³Elimelech, the husband of Naomi, died, and she was left with her two sons, ⁴who married Moabite women, one named Orpah, the other Ruth. When they had lived there about ten years, ⁵both Mahlon and Chilion died also, and the woman was left with neither her two sons nor her husband. ⁶She then made ready to go back from the plateau of Moab because word reached her there that the LORD had visited his people and given them food.

⁷She and her two daughters-in-law left the place where they had been living. Then as they were on the road back to the land of Judah, ⁸Naomi said to her two daughters-in-law, "Go back, each of you, to your mother's house!* May the LORD be kind to you as you were to the departed and to me! ⁹May the LORD grant each of you a husband and a home in which you will find rest." She kissed them good-by, but they wept with

1, 1f: In the time of the judges: three generations before the end of the period of Judges; cf Ru 4, 21f. Bethlehem of Judah: to distinguish it from the town of the same name in the tribe of Zebulun (Jos 19, 15). Ephrathites from Bethlehem: belonging to a Judean clan which settled in Bethlehem; cf 1 Sm 17, 12; 1 Chr 2, 50f; 4, 4.

1, 8: Mother's house: the women's part of the dwelling; cf Jgs 4, 17; Song 3, 4.

0 30 Mi.
0 30 Km.

Jericho •
Jebus
(Jerusalem) •
Heshbon •

Bethlehem •
(Ephratah)
Medeba •

Dead
Sea   REUBEN

JUDAH   Dibon •

Aroer •

MOAB

Kir Haraseth •

Places in Ruth

loud sobs, *¹⁰*and told her they would return with her to her people. *¹¹*"Go back, my daughters!" said Naomi. "Why should you come with me? Have I other sons in my womb who may become your husbands?* *¹²*Go back, my daughters! Go, for I am too old to marry again. And even if I could offer any hopes, or if tonight I had a husband or had borne sons, *¹³*would you then wait and deprive yourselves of husbands until those sons grew up? No, my daughters! my lot is too bitter for you, because the LORD has extended his hand against me." *¹⁴*Again they sobbed aloud and wept; and Orpah kissed her mother-in-law good-by, but Ruth stayed with her.

¹⁵"See now!" she said, "your sister-in-law has gone back to her people and her god. Go back after your sister-in-law!" *¹⁶**But Ruth said, "Do not ask me to abandon or forsake you! for wherever you go I will go, wherever you lodge I will lodge, your people shall be my people, and your God my God. *¹⁷*Wherever you die I will die, and there be buried. May the LORD do so and so to me, and more besides, if aught but death separates me from you!" *¹⁸*Naomi then ceased to urge her, for she saw she was determined to go with her.

The Return to Bethlehem. *¹⁹*So they went on together till they reached Bethlehem. On their arrival there, the whole city was astir over them, and the women asked, "Can this be Naomi?" *²⁰ᵃ*But she said to them, "Do not call me Naomi.* Call me Mara, for the Almighty has made it very bitter for me. *²¹*I went away with an abundance, but the LORD has brought me back destitute. Why should you call me Naomi, since the LORD has pronounced against me and the Almighty has brought evil upon me?" *²²*Thus it was that Naomi returned with the Moabite daughter-in-law, Ruth, who accompanied her back from the plateau of Moab. They arrived in Bethlehem at the beginning of the barley harvest.*

CHAPTER 2

See RG 111

The Meeting. *¹*Naomi had a prominent kinsman named Boaz,ᵇ of the clan of her husband Elimelech. *²*Ruth the Moabite said to Naomi, "Let me go and glean ears of grain* in the field of anyone who will allow me that favor."ᶜ Naomi said to her, "Go, my daughter," *³*and she went. The field she entered to glean after the harvesters happened to be the section belonging to Boaz of the clan of Elimelech. *⁴*Boaz himself came from Bethlehem and said to the harvesters, "The

---

1, 11: Have I other sons . . . husbands?: Naomi insisted that her daughters-in-law remain in their own country only for the sake of posterity. If she had had other sons, the levirate law would have obliged them to marry the widows of her deceased sons to perpetuate the names of the deceased; cf Gn 38, 8; Dt 25, 5f.

1, 16f: An example of heroic fidelity and piety. Ruth's decision, confirmed with an oath, to adhere to her mother-in-law impelled her to abandon her country and its pagan worship.

1, 20f: Naomi: means "amiable" or "pleasant," suggesting God's favor toward her. The Almighty has brought evil upon

me: the ancients regarded adversity as a punishment from God for personal sin, as if good and evil were always repaid in a temporal and material manner.

1, 22: Barley harvest: early April. This circumstance favored the events of the narrative that follow.

2, 2: Let me go and glean . . . grain: even the poor, the widow, the stranger, and the orphan had a right to glean at harvest time; cf Lv 19, 9f; 23, 22; Dt 24, 19-22.

a: Ex 15, 23.   *b:* Ru 3, 2. 12; 4, 21; Mt 1, 5.   *c:* Dt 24, 19.

LORD be with you!"* and they replied, "The LORD bless you!" ⁵Boaz asked the overseer of his harvesters, "Whose girl is this?" ⁶The overseer of the harvesters answered, "She is the Moabite girl who returned from the plateau of Moab with Naomi.ᵈ ⁷She asked leave to gather the gleanings into sheaves after the harvesters; and ever since she came this morning she has remained here until now, with scarcely a moment's rest."

⁸Boaz said to Ruth, "Listen, my daughter! Do not go to glean in anyone else's field; you are not to leave here. Stay here with my women servants. ⁹Watch to see which field is to be harvested, and follow them; I have commanded the young men to do you no harm. When you are thirsty, you may go and drink from the vessels the young men have filled." ¹⁰Casting herself prostrate upon the ground, she said to him, "Why should I, a foreigner, be favored with your notice?" ¹¹ᵉBoaz answered her: "I have had a complete account of what you have done for your mother-in-law after your husband's death; you have left your father and your mother and the land of your birth, and have come to a people whom you did not know previously. ¹²May the LORD reward what you have done! May you receive a full reward from the LORD, the God of Israel, under whose wings you have come for refuge." ¹³She said, "May I prove worthy of your kindness, my lord: you have comforted me, your servant, with your consoling words; would indeed that I were a servant of yours!" ¹⁴At mealtime Boaz said to her, "Come here and have some food; dip your bread in the sauce." Then as she sat near the reapers, he handed her some roasted grain and she ate her fill and had some left over. ¹⁵She rose to glean, and Boaz instructed his servants to let her glean among the sheaves themselves without scolding her, ¹⁶and even to let drop some handfuls and leave them for her to glean without being rebuked.

¹⁷She gleaned in the field until evening, and when she beat out what she had gleaned it came to about an ephah of barley, ¹⁸which she took into the city and showed to her mother-in-law. Next she brought out and gave her what she had left over from lunch. ¹⁹So her mother-in-law said to her, "Where did you glean today? Where did you go to work? May he who took notice of you be blessed!" Then she told her mother-in-law with whom she had worked. "The man at whose place I worked today is named Boaz," she said. ²⁰ᶠ"May he be blessed by the LORD, who is ever merciful to the living and to the dead," Naomi exclaimed to her daughter-in-law; and she continued, "He is a relative of ours, one of our next of kin."* ²¹"He even told me," added Ruth the Moabite, "that I should stay with his servants until they complete his entire harvest." ²²"You would do well, my dear," Naomi rejoined, "to go out with his servants; for in someone else's field you might be insulted." ²³So she stayed gleaning with the servants of Boaz until the end of the barley and wheat harvests.

CHAPTER 3

Ruth Again Presents Herself. When she was back with her mother-in-law, ¹Naomi said to her, "My daughter, I must seek a home for you that will please you. ²ᵍNow is not Boaz, with whose servants you were, a relative of ours? This evening he will be winnowing barley at the threshing floor. ³So bathe and anoint yourself; then put on your best attire and go down to the threshing floor. Do not make yourself known to the man before he has finished eating and drinking. ⁴But when he lies down, take note of the place where he does so. Then go, uncover a place at his feet,* and lie down. He will tell you what to do." ⁵"I will do whatever you advise," Ruth replied. ⁶So she went down to

See RG 111

2, 4: The Lord be with you: courtesy and religious feeling characterize the salutations of the Hebrews. This greeting is used in the Christian liturgy.

2, 20: One of our next of kin: literally "our redeemer," a near relative of the same clan who had the right and duty to restore the land which an impoverished kinsman had alienated (Lv 25, 25-28), and to marry the widow of a relative who

had died without male offspring so as to raise up posterity to his name (Dt 25, 5-10).

3, 4: Uncover a place at his feet . . . : confident of the virtue of Ruth and Boaz, Naomi advises this unusual expedient to her daughter-in-law for the purpose of introducing her claim.

d: Ru 1, 22. e: Ru 1, 14-17. f: Ru 3, 9. g: Ru 2, 1.

the threshing floor and did just as her mother-in-law had instructed her.

[7]Boaz ate and drank to his heart's content. Then when he went and lay down at the edge of the sheaves, she stole up, uncovered a place at his feet, and lay down. [8]In the middle of the night, however, the man gave a start and turned around to find a woman lying at his feet. [9]He asked, "Who are you?" And she replied, "I am your servant Ruth. Spread the corner of your cloak over me,* for you are my next of kin." [10]He said, "May the LORD bless you, my daughter! You have been even more loyal now than before in not going after the young men, whether poor or rich.[h] [11]So be assured, daughter, I will do for you whatever you say; all my townspeople know you for a worthy woman. [12][i]Now, though indeed I am closely related to you, you have another relative still closer.* [13]Stay as you are for tonight, and tomorrow, if he wishes to claim you, good! let him do so. But if he does not wish to claim you, as the LORD lives, I will claim you myself. Lie there until morning."[j] [14]So she lay at his feet until morning, but rose before men could recognize one another. Boaz said, "Let it not be known that this woman came to the threshing floor." [15]Then he said to her, "Take off your cloak and hold it out." When she did so, he poured out six measures of barley, helped her lift the bundle,[k] and left for the city.

[16]Ruth went home to her mother-in-law, who asked, "How have you fared, my daughter?" So she told her all the man had done for her, [17]and concluded, "He gave me these six measures of barley because he did not wish me to come back to my mother-in-law empty-handed!" [18]Naomi then said,

"Wait here, my daughter, until you learn what happens, for the man will not rest, but will settle the matter today."

CHAPTER 4

See RG 111–12

Boaz Marries Ruth. [1]Boaz went and took a seat at the gate;* and when he saw the closer relative[l] of whom he had spoken come along, he called to him by name, "Come and sit beside me!" And he did so. [2]Then Boaz picked out ten of the elders* of the city and asked them to sit nearby. When they had done this, [3]he said to the near relative: "Naomi, who has come back from the Moabite plateau, is putting up for sale the piece of land that belonged to our kinsman Elimelech. [4]*So I thought I would inform you, bidding you before those here present, including the elders of my people, to put in your claim for it if you wish to acquire it as next of kin.[m] But if you do not wish to claim it, tell me so, that I may be guided accordingly, for no one has a prior claim to yours, and mine is next." He answered, "I will put in my claim."

[5]*Boaz continued, "Once you acquire the field from Naomi, you must take also Ruth the Moabite,[n] the widow of the late heir, and raise up a family for the departed on his estate." [6]The near relative replied, "I cannot exercise my claim lest I depreciate my own estate. Put in a claim yourself in my stead, for I cannot exercise my claim." [7]Now it used to be the custom in Israel that, to make binding a contract of redemption or exchange, one party would take off his sandal* and give it to the other. This was the form of attestation in Israel. [8]So the near relative, in saying to Boaz, "Acquire it for yourself,"

3, 9: Spread the corner of your cloak over me: be my protector by marrying me according to the duty of a near kinsman; cf Dt 25, 5; Ez 16, 8.

3, 12: Relative still closer: who had a prior right and duty to marry Ruth.

4, 1: Took a seat at the gate: i.e., of the city, where business affairs were settled.

4, 2: Ten of the elders: to serve as judges in legal matters as well as witnesses of the settlement of business affairs; cf Dt 25, 7-9.

4, 4: Poverty had obliged Naomi to sell the land of her deceased husband. The law permitted the nearest kinsman to redeem the land and thus preserve the family patrimony; cf Lv 25, 25.

4, 5f: The heir of Elimelech's field had died without children (Ru 1, 5). The nearest of kin could now redeem the land but he must also take Ruth, the widow of the late heir, to wife to perpetuate the family of the deceased; cf Dt 25, 5f. The first male child of such a marriage would be the legal son of Mahlon and grandson of Elimelech.

4, 7: Take off his sandal . . . : by this act the near relative renounced his legal right, both to the field of Elimelech and to the marriage with Ruth. The custom mentioned in Dt 25, 6 is somewhat different.

---

h: Dt 25, 5.   i: Ru 4, 1.   j: Ru 4, 5; Dt 25, 5.   k: Ru 2, 17.   l: Ru 3, 12.   m: Lv 25, 25.   n: Ru 3, 13; Dt 25, 5.

The Well and the Gate

In various Bible scenes, meeting places play an important role. In Ruth, for instance, the climax of the story comes with the actions of Boaz in bringing about his betrothal to Ruth. The text makes clear that this takes place "at the gate" of the city (Ru 4, 1–12).

The gate was a narrow passageway through the defensive wall of a town or city. It was usually covered, with a barrier at one or both ends. Walls were thick because they were the main defense against invasion, and the passageway was narrow to impede the progress of any invaders who succeeded in getting past the outer barrier: They would have to walk in a narrow column through the passage. Often, a guardroom was built into the wall at one side of the passage, and places for the guards or others to sit outside lined both sides of the passage.

This gate would have been relatively shaded and cool and therefore was a pleasant place to gather. Because it was small, those of higher status would be favored for a place, and anyone of lower status would have to give way to a higher status person who came later. All of the people who gathered at the gate were men, and because of the presence of so many important members of the town, the gate became the place where the elders could pass judgment on questions put to them. In effect, the gate could become the town's court of justice, particularly for what we would call "civil actions": property disputes, debt collections, and the like.

In Ruth, Boaz brings up the complicated situation of the property of Naomi's family and the status of Ruth. The other relative with a claim on the property makes his declaration that he is abandoning the claim in the presence of the elders of the town, who serve as witnesses to make sure the declaration is binding. In Psalm 127, 5 the reference to "contending . . . at the gate," as the New American Bible notes point out, does not mean fighting off an invasion but, rather, making one's case in a legal dispute. In the book of Wisdom (6, 14), Wisdom herself (personified as a woman) is to be met "by [the] gate" where the wise gather. It may have been a slight shock to read about meeting a woman in the gate in this passage, because women did not gather there.

Women gathered at a different place: the well. Drawing and transporting water for household use was considered women's work, and this was so clearly understood that Jesus could tell his followers to go with "a man . . . carrying a jar of water" (Mk 14, 13; Lk 22, 10) to find the place of the Last Supper. A man with a water jar would have been a very distinctive figure, a signal that this guide had been arranged in advance. In Genesis 24, 10–14, Abraham's servant has been told to go to find a wife for Isaac, Abraham's son, in Abraham's ancestral land. The servant goes to the well to meet the local women, because he knows that that is where they will most likely be found. Saul and his servant, looking for the prophet Samuel, meet "some girls coming out to draw water" from whom they can ask directions (1 Sm 9, 11). And in the Gospel of John, Jesus' encounter with the woman of Samaria takes place at the well, where she had come to draw water (Jn 4, 7). The woman is drawing water at noon, rather than in the evening, which is unusual—perhaps because she wishes to avoid any meetings with the other women of the place, because her marital status is irregular. In her case, the social aspect of drawing water—the chance to meet and speak with other women—is a disadvantage.

drew off his sandal. ⁹Boaz then said to the elders and to all the people, "You are witnesses today that I have acquired from Naomi all the holdings of Elimelech, Chilion and Mahlon. ¹⁰I also take Ruth the Moabite, the widow of Mahlon, as my wife, in order to raise up a family for her late husband on his estate, so that the name of the departed may not perish among his kinsmen and fellow citizens. Do you witness this today?" ¹¹ᵒAll those at the gate, including the elders, said, "We do so. May the LORD make this wife come into your house like Rachel and Leah, who between them built up the house of Israel. May you do well in Ephrathah and win fame in Bethlehem. ¹²ᵖWith the offspring the LORD will give you from this girl, may your house become like the house of Perez, whom Tamar bore to Judah."*

¹³Boaz took Ruth. When they came together as man and wife, the LORD enabled her to conceive and she bore a son. ¹⁴Then the women said to Naomi, "Blessed is the LORD who has not failed to provide you today with an heir! May he become famous in Israel! ¹⁵He will be your comfort and the support of your old age, for his mother is the daughter-in-law who loves you. She is worth more to you than seven sons!" ¹⁶Naomi took the child, placed him on her lap,* and became his nurse. ¹⁷And the neighbor women gave him his name,�q at the news that a grandson had been born to Naomi. They called him Obed. He was the father of Jesse, the father of David.*

¹⁸ʳThese are the descendants of Perez: Perez was the father of Hezron,ˢ ¹⁹Hezron was the father of Ram, Ram was the father of Amminadab, ²⁰ᵗAmminadab was the father of Nahshon, Nahshon was the father of Salmon, ²¹Salmon was the father of Boaz, Boaz was the father of Obed, ²²ᵘObed was the father of Jesse, and Jesse became the father of David.

4, 12: Perez, whom Tamar bore to Judah: the right which Judah unwittingly satisfied for his daughter-in-law Tamar (Gn 38), Boaz willingly rendered to Ruth.

4, 16: Placed him on her lap: took him as her own; cf Gn 30, 3; 48, 12; Nm 11, 12.

4, 17: The father of Jesse, the father of David: indicating the place of Obed, Jesse and David in the line of Judah and the ancestry of Christ, the Messiah; cf Mt 1, 5f.

o: Gn 29, 31—30, 24; 35, 19. *p:* Gn 38, 29. *q:* Lk 1, 58. *r:* 18-22: 1 Chr 2, 4-15; Mt 1, 3-6. *s:* Gn 46, 12; 1 Chr 4, 1. *t:* Ex 6, 23; Nm 1, 7. *u:* 1 Sm 16, 10-13.

THE HISTORICAL BOOKS

See RG
90–167

The historical books include 1 and 2 Samuel, 1 and 2 Kings, 1 and 2 Chronicles, Ezra, Nehemiah, 1 and 2 Maccabees. To these are added the special literary group of Tobit, Judith, and Esther.

The Books of Tobit, Judith, and 1 and 2 Maccabees, as well as parts of Esther, are called deuterocanonical: they are not contained in the Hebrew canon but have been accepted by the Catholic Church as canonical and inspired.

By means of a series of episodes involving the persons of Samuel, Saul, and David, a century of history unfolds in 1 and 2 Samuel from the close of the period of Judges to the rise and establishment of the monarchy in Israel. Most important is God's promise to David of a lasting dynasty (2 Sm 7), from which royal messianism in the Bible developed.

In 1 and 2 Kings the religious history of Israel extends another four centuries, from the last days of David to the Babylonian captivity and the destruction of Jerusalem (587 B.C.). The various sources for these books are woven into a uniform pattern based on the principle of fidelity to Yahweh for rulers and people alike. The sequence of regnal chronicles in both books is interrupted by a cycle of traditions surrounding the prophets Elijah (1 Kgs) and Elisha (2 Kgs).

Chronicles, Ezra, and Nehemiah form a historical work, uniform in style and basic ideas. Chronicles records the long period from the reign of Saul to the return from exile, not so much with exactitude of detail as with concern for the meaning of the facts which demonstrate God's intervention in history. The Ezra-Nehemiah chronicle constitutes the most important source for the formation of the Jewish religious community after the Babylonian exile; the two persons most responsible for the reorganization of Jewish life were Ezra and Nehemiah.

1 and 2 Maccabees contain independent accounts of partially identical events which accompanied the attempted suppression of Judaism in Palestine in the second century B.C. Vigorous reaction to this attempt established for a time the religious and political independence of the Jews. 1 Maccabees portrays God as the eternal benefactor of the Jews and their unfailing source of help. The people are required to be devoted to his exclusive worship and to observe exactly the law he has given them. 2 Maccabees, besides supplementing the former volume, gives a theological interpretation of the history of the period and contains teaching on the resurrection from the dead, intercession of the saints, and suffrages for the dead.

Tobit, Judith, and Esther are examples of free composition—the religious novel used for purposes of edification and instruction. Interest in whatever historical data these books may contain is merely intensified by the addition of vivid details. Judith is a lesson in Providence: a pious reflection on the annual Passover observance to convey the reassurance that God is still the master of history who saves Israel from her enemies. Esther's purpose is the glorification of the Jewish people and the explanation of the origin, significance, and date of the feast of Purim. It is a literary development of the principle of reversal of fortune through punishment of the prosperous rich and reward for the virtuous who are oppressed.

Samuel to Maccabees demonstrates that before as well as during the millennium of history with which it is concerned, Israel was a covenanted people, bound to Yahweh, Lord of the universe, by the ties of faith and obedience. This required observance of the law and worship in his temple, the consequent rewards of which were divine favor and protection. In this way these books anticipate and prepare for the coming of him who would bring type and prophecy to fulfillment, history to term, and holiness to perfection: Christ, the Son of David and the promised Messiah.

The Books of Samuel

See RG
113–22

Originally but one book, the scroll of Samuel was early divided into two. The Greek translators called these the first and second Books of Kingdoms, a title St. Jerome later modified to "Kings." The Hebrew title, "Samuel," alludes to the leading figure in the first book, who was responsible for the enthronement of David. It is David's history that the second book recounts.

This sacred work thus comprises the history of about a century, describing the close of the age of the Judges and the beginnings of monarchy in Israel under Saul and David. It is not a complete and continuous history, nor a systematic account of the period, but rather a series of episodes centered around the persons of Samuel, Saul and David, the principal figures leading up to the establishment of the royal dynasty of David.

The final editor is unknown, nor are we certain of the time at which the various strands of the narrative were put together, though one may think of the period, perhaps late in the seventh century B.C., when the other volumes of the "Former Prophets," from Joshua through Kings, were built into a more or less continuous historical corpus.

The Samuel-Saul-David narratives clearly depend on several written sources: a Samuel cycle, two sets of stories about Saul and David, and a family history of David. This last (2 Sm 9—20; 1 Kgs 1—2), one of the most vivid historical narratives surviving from ancient times, probably originated early in the reign of Solomon.

One of the most significant theological contributions of the Old Testament is found in 2 Samuel 7, the oracle of Nathan. David is here promised an eternal dynasty, and this becomes the basis for the development of royal messianism throughout the Bible. With this promise to David one should compare 2 Chr 17; Pss 89, 20-38; 132, 11ff; Acts 2, 30; and Heb 1, 5.

The contents of this work may be divided as follows:

   I: History of the Last Judges, Eli and Samuel (1 Sm 1, 1—7, 17).

  II: Establishment of the Monarchy in Israel (1 Sm 8, 1—12, 25).

 III: Saul and David (1 Sm 13, 1—2 Sm 2, 7).

 IV: The Reign of David (2 Sm 2, 8—20, 26).

  V: Appendixes (2 Sm 21, 1—24, 25).

The First Book of Samuel

I: History of the Last Judges, Eli and Samuel

CHAPTER 1

See RG
114–15

Elkanah and His Family at Shiloh. [1]There was a certain man from Ramathaim, Elkanah by name, a Zuphite from the hill country of Ephraim. He was the son of Jeroham, son of Elihu, son of Tohu, son of Zuph, an Ephraimite.[a] [2]He had two wives, one named Hannah, the other Peninnah; Peninnah had children, but Hannah was childless. [3]This man regularly went on pilgrimage from his city to worship the LORD of hosts and to sacrifice to him at Shiloh, where the two sons of Eli, Hophni and Phinehas, were ministering as priests of the LORD.[b] [4]When the day came for Elkanah to offer sacrifice, he used to give a portion each to his wife Peninnah and to all her sons and daughters, [5]but a double portion to Hannah because he loved

a: 1 Chr 6, 19f. b: Ex 23, 14-17; 34, 23; Dt 16, 16; Jgs 21, 19.

her, though the LORD had made her barren.^c [c] ⁶Her rival, to upset her, turned it into a constant reproach to her that the LORD had left her barren.^d [d] ⁷This went on year after year; each time they made their pilgrimage to the sanctuary of the LORD, Peninnah would approach her, and Hannah would weep and refuse to eat. ⁸Her husband Elkanah used to ask her: "Hannah, why do you weep, and why do you refuse to eat? Why do you grieve? Am I not more to you than ten sons?"^e [e]

Hannah's Prayer. ⁹Hannah rose after one such meal at Shiloh, and presented herself before the LORD; at the time, Eli the priest was sitting on a chair near the doorpost of the LORD's temple. ¹⁰In her bitterness she prayed to the LORD, weeping copiously, ¹¹and she made a vow, promising: "O LORD of hosts, if you look with pity on the misery of your handmaid, if you remember me and do not forget me, if you give your handmaid a male child, I will give him to the LORD* for as long as he lives; neither wine nor liquor shall he drink, and no razor shall ever touch his head."^f [f] ¹²As she remained long at prayer before the LORD, Eli watched her mouth, ¹³for Hannah was praying silently; though her lips were moving, her voice could not be heard. Eli, thinking her drunk, ¹⁴said to her, "How long will you make a drunken show of yourself? Sober up from your wine!" ¹⁵"It isn't that, my lord," Hannah answered. "I am an unhappy woman. I have had neither wine nor liquor; I was only pouring out my troubles to the LORD. ¹⁶Do not think your handmaid a ne'er-do-well; my prayer has been prompted by my deep sorrow and misery." ¹⁷Eli said, "Go in peace, and may the God of Israel grant you what you have asked of him." ¹⁸She replied, "Think kindly of your maidservant," and left. She went to her quarters, ate and drank with her husband, and no longer appeared downcast. ¹⁹Early the next morning they worshiped before the LORD, and then returned to their home in Ramah.

Hannah Bears a Son. When Elkanah had relations with his wife Hannah, the LORD remembered her. ²⁰She conceived, and at the end of her term bore a son whom she called Samuel, since she had asked* the LORD for him. ²¹The next time her husband Elkanah was going up with the rest of his household to offer the customary sacrifice to the LORD and to fulfill his vows, ²²Hannah did not go, explaining to her husband, "Once the child is weaned, I will take him to appear before the LORD and to remain there forever; I will offer him as a perpetual nazirite." ²³Her husband Elkanah answered her: "Do what you think best; wait until you have weaned him. Only, may the LORD bring your resolve to fulfillment!" And so she remained at home and nursed her son until she had weaned him.

Samuel Is Offered to God. ²⁴Once he was weaned, she brought him up with her, along with a three-year-old bull, an ephah* of flour, and a skin of wine, and presented him at the temple of the LORD in Shiloh. ²⁵After the boy's father had sacrificed the young bull, Hannah, his mother, approached Eli ²⁶and said: "Pardon, my lord! As you live, my lord, I am the woman who stood near you here, praying to the LORD. ²⁷I prayed for this child, and the LORD granted my request. ²⁸Now I, in turn, give him to the LORD; as long as he lives, he shall be dedicated to the LORD." She left him there; *¹and as she worshiped the LORD, she said:

CHAPTER 2

See RG
114–15

"My heart exults in the LORD,*
   my horn* is exalted in my God.
I have swallowed up my enemies;
   I rejoice in my victory.^g [g]

1, 11: Give him to the Lord: some ancient texts call Samuel a nazir in this context; see note on Nm 6, 1ff.

1, 20: Since she had asked: this explanation would be more directly appropriate for the name Saul, which means "asked"; Samuel means "name of God."

1, 24: An ephah: a little more than a bushel.

1, 1: And . . . said: this belongs to ch 2.

2, 1-10: A hymn attributed to Hannah, the mother of Samuel, as her thanksgiving to God because she has borne a son despite her previous sterility. She praises God as the helper of the weak (1ff), who casts down the mighty and raises up the lowly (3ff), and who alone is the source of true strength (8ff); the hymn ends with a prayer for the king (v 10). This canticle has several points of resemblance with our Lady's Magnificat.

2, 1: Horn: the symbol of strength; cf Pss 18, 3; 75, 5; 89, 18; 112, 9.

c: Dt 21, 15ff. *d:* Gn 16, 4f. *e:* Ru 4, 15. *f:* Nm 6, 1-5; Jgs 13, 2-5; 16, 17; Lk 1, 15. *g:* Dt 33, 17; 2 Sm 22, 3; Ps 18, 2; Is 61, 10; Lk 1, 47. 69

The Song of Hannah

Biblical writers sometimes inserted poems into prose books where they seemed appropriate. In this case (2, 1–10) the poem seems to be considerably later than the surrounding context. It is a psalm of national thanksgiving, but its thankful tone appropriately reflects Hannah's sentiments. It was later used as a model for Mary's song in Luke 1, 46–55.

² There is no Holy One like the LORD;
    there is no Rock like our God.*h*

³ "Speak boastfully no longer,
    nor let arrogance issue from your
      mouths.*
For an all-knowing God is the LORD,
    a God who judges deeds.*i*
The bows of the mighty are broken,
    while the tottering gird on strength.*j*
⁵ The well-fed hire themselves out for
      bread,
    while the hungry batten on spoil.
The barren wife bears seven sons,
    while the mother of many languishes.
⁶ "The LORD puts to death and gives life;
    he casts down to the nether world;
    he raises up again.*k*
⁷ The LORD makes poor and makes rich,
    he humbles, he also exalts.
⁸ He raises the needy from the dust;
    from the ash heap he lifts up the poor,
To seat them with nobles
    and make a glorious throne their
      heritage.*l*
He gives to the vower his vow,
    and blesses the sleep of the just.

"For the pillars of the earth are the LORD's,
    and he has set the world upon them.
⁹ He will guard the footsteps of his faithful
      ones,
    but the wicked shall perish in the
      darkness.
For not by strength does man prevail;
¹⁰ the LORD's foes shall be shattered.
The Most High in heaven thunders;

the LORD judges the ends of the earth.
Now may he give strength to his king
    and exalt the horn of his anointed!"*m*

¹¹When Elkanah returned home to Ramah, the child remained in the service of the LORD under the priest Eli.

Wickedness of Eli's Sons. ¹²Now the sons of Eli were wicked; they had respect neither for the LORD ¹³nor for the priests' duties toward the people. When someone offered a sacrifice, the priest's servant would come with a three-pronged fork, while the meat was still boiling,*n* ¹⁴and would thrust it into the basin, kettle, caldron, or pot. Whatever the fork brought up, the priest would keep. That is how all the Israelites were treated who came to the sanctuary at Shiloh. ¹⁵In fact, even before the fat was burned, the priest's servant would come and say to the man offering the sacrifice, "Give me some meat to roast for the priest. He will not accept boiled meat from you, only raw meat." ¹⁶And if the man protested to him, "Let the fat be burned first as is the custom, then take whatever you wish," he would reply, "No, give it to me now, or else I will take it by force."*o* ¹⁷Thus the young men sinned grievously in the presence of the LORD; they treated the offerings to the LORD with disdain.

The Lord Rewards Hannah. ¹⁸Meanwhile the boy Samuel, girt with a linen apron,* was serving in the presence of the LORD. ¹⁹His mother used to make a little garment for him, which she would bring him each time she went up with her husband to offer the customary sacrifice. ²⁰And Eli would bless Elkanah and his wife, as they

---

    2, 3: Speak . . . mouths: addressed to the enemies mentioned in v 1.
    2, 18: Linen apron: called in Hebrew "ephod," but not the same as the high priest's ephod (Ex 28, 6-14) or the ephod used in divination (v 28). Samuel wore a simple apron such as was worn by the priests (1 Sm 22, 18), and on one occasion

also by David (2 Sm 6, 14).

h: 2 Sm 22, 3; Ps 18, 2.   *i:* Ps 75, 4.   *j:* Is 40, 29.   *k:* Dt 32, 39; Tb 4, 19; Jb 5, 11; Ps 30, 4; Wis 16, 13; Lk 1, 52.   *l:* Jb 9, 6; 38, 6; Ps 104, 5; 121, 3.   *m:* Ps 98, 9.   *n:* 13-15: Ex 29, 27f; Lv 7, 29-36; Dt 18, 3.   *o:* Lv 3, 3ff.

were leaving for home. He would say, "May the LORD repay you with children from this woman for the gift she has made to the LORD!" *21*The LORD favored Hannah so that she conceived and gave birth to three more sons and two daughters, while young Samuel grew up in the service of the LORD.*p*

Eli's Futile Rebuke. *22*When Eli was very old, he heard repeatedly how his sons were treating all Israel [and that they were having relations with the women serving at the entry of the meeting tent.]* *23*So he said to them: "Why are you doing such things? *24*No, my sons, you must not do these things! It is not a good report that I hear the people of the LORD spreading about you. *25*If a man sins against another man, one can intercede for him with the LORD; but if a man sins against the LORD, who can intercede for him?" But they disregarded their father's warning, since the LORD had decided on their death. *26*Meanwhile, young Samuel was growing in stature and in worth in the estimation of the LORD and of men.*q*

Doom of Eli's House.* *27*A man of God came to Eli and said to him: "This is what the LORD says: 'I went so far as to reveal myself to your father's family when they were in Egypt as slaves to the house of Pharaoh. *28*I chose them out of all the tribes of Israel to be my priests, to go up to my altar, to burn incense, and to wear the ephod* before me; and I assigned all the oblations of the Israelites to your father's family.*r* *29*Why do you keep a greedy eye on my sacrifices and on the offerings which I have prescribed? And why do you honor your sons in preference to me, fattening yourselves with the choicest part of every offering of my people Israel?' *30s*This, therefore, is the oracle of the LORD, the God of Israel: 'I said in the past that your family and your fa-

ther's family should minister in my presence forever. But now,' the LORD declares, 'away with this! for I will honor those who honor me, but those who spurn me shall be accursed. *31*Yes, the time is coming when I will break your strength and the strength of your father's family, so that no man in your family shall reach old age. *32*You shall witness as a disappointed rival all the benefits enjoyed by Israel, but there shall never be an old man in your family. *33*I will permit some of your family to remain at my altar, to wear out their eyes in consuming greed; but the rest of the men of your family shall die by the sword. *34*You shall have a sign in what will happen to your two sons, Hophni and Phinehas: both shall die on the same day.*t* *35*I will choose a faithful priest who shall do what I have in heart and mind. I will establish a lasting house for him which shall function in the presence of my anointed forever. *36*Then whoever is left of your family will come to grovel before him for a piece of silver or a loaf of bread, and will say: Appoint me, I beg you, to a priestly function, that I may have a morsel of bread to eat.' "*u*

CHAPTER 3

See RG 114–15

Revelation to Samuel. *1*During the time young Samuel was minister to the LORD under Eli, a revelation of the LORD was uncommon* and vision infrequent. *2*One day Eli was asleep in his usual place. His eyes had lately grown so weak that he could not see. *3*The lamp of God was not yet extinguished, and Samuel was sleeping in the temple of the LORD where the ark of God was.*v* *4*The LORD called to Samuel, who answered, "Here I am." *5*He ran to Eli and said, "Here I am. You called me." "I did not call you," Eli said. "Go back to sleep." So he went back to sleep. *6*Again the LORD called Samuel, who rose

---

2, 22: The bracketed words, which recall Ex 38, 8, are a gloss in the received text; they are lacking in the oldest Greek translation, and in a Hebrew manuscript from Qumran.

2, 27-36: These verses propose the punishment of Eli from a point of view contemporary with the reform of Josiah (2 Kgs 23, 9; cf v 36); they hint at the events recorded in 1 Sm 22, 18-23 and 1 Kgs 2, 27. The older story of this divine warning is that in 1 Sm 3, 11-14.

2, 28: Ephod: a portable container, presumably of cloth, for the lots used in ritual consultation of God during the days of the

Judges (Jgs 17, 5; 18, 14-15) and down into the time of David (1 Sm 14, 3ff; 23, 6ff; 30, 7f). The ephod of the high priest described in Ex 28, 6ff becomes a garment upon which a breastpiece of decision symbolizes, but no longer serves for, such consultation. The Exodus text codifies a later form of the tradition.

3, 1: Uncommon: prophetic communications from God were almost unknown.

p: 1 Sm 3, 19.   *q:* Lk 2, 52.   *r:* 1 Sm 23, 9; 30, 7f; Jgs 17, 5.   *s:* 30f: 2 Sm 22, 26; 1 Kgs 2, 27; Ps 18, 25.   *t:* 1 Sm 4, 11.   *u:* 2 Kgs 23, 9.   *v:* Ex 25, 22; 27, 20f; Lv 24, 2. 4; 2 Chr 13, 11.

Samuel's Call

Samuel's role as a prophet had not yet been established because "the LORD had not revealed anything to him as yet." In this story (3, 2–18), Samuel becomes "familiar with the LORD" by learning to recognize God's revelations. Samuel's bed was inside the temple near the inner sanctuary where the ark of God, representing God's presence, was kept. The lamp of God, which burned at night (Ex 27, 21), "was not yet extinguished," hence it was just before dawn when the LORD called to Samuel.

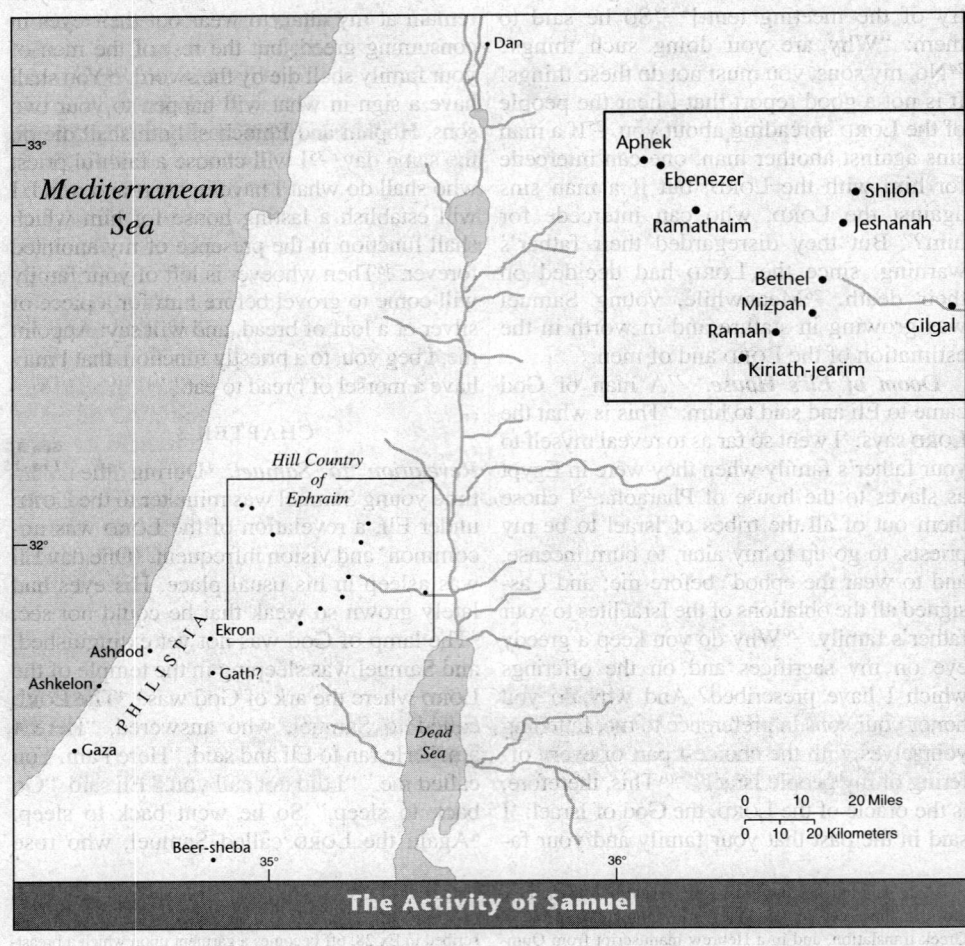

The Activity of Samuel

and went to Eli. "Here I am," he said. "You called me." But he answered, "I did not call you, my son. Go back to sleep."

[7]At that time Samuel was not familiar with the LORD, because the LORD had not revealed anything to him as yet. [8]The LORD called Samuel again, for the third time. Getting up and going to Eli, he said, "Here I am. You called me." Then Eli understood that the LORD was calling the youth. [9]So he said to Samuel, "Go to sleep, and if you are called, reply, 'Speak, LORD, for your servant is listening.' " When Samuel went to sleep in his place, [10]the LORD came and revealed his presence, calling out as before, "Samuel, Samuel!" Samuel answered, "Speak, for your servant is listening." [11]The LORD said to Samuel: "I am about to do something in Israel that will cause the ears of everyone who hears it to ring. [12]On that day I will carry out in full against Eli everything I threatened against his family. [13]I announce to him that I am condemning his family once and for all, because of this crime: though he knew his sons were blaspheming God, he did not reprove them.[w] [14]Therefore, I swear to the family of Eli that no sacrifice or offering will ever expiate its crime." [15]Samuel then slept until morning, when he got up early and opened the doors of the temple of the LORD. He feared to tell Eli the vision, [16]but Eli called to him, "Samuel, my son!" He replied, "Here I am." [17]Then Eli asked, "What did he say to you? Hide nothing from me! May God do thus and so to you[*] if you hide a single thing he told you." [18]So Samuel told him everything, and held nothing back. Eli answered, "He is the LORD. He will do what he judges best."

Samuel Acknowledged as Prophet. [19]Samuel grew up, and the LORD was with him, not permitting any word of his to be without effect.[x] [20y]Thus all Israel from Dan to Beer-sheba came to know that Samuel was

an accredited prophet of the LORD. [21]The LORD continued to appear at Shiloh; he manifested himself to Samuel at Shiloh through his word, [1*]and Samuel spoke to all Israel.

CHAPTER 4

See RG 115

Defeat of the Israelites. At that time, the Philistines gathered for an attack on Israel. Israel went out to engage them in battle and camped at Ebenezer, while the Philistines camped at Aphek. [2]The Philistines then drew up in battle formation against Israel. After a fierce struggle Israel was defeated by the Philistines, who slew about four thousand men on the battlefield. [3]When the troops retired to the camp, the elders of Israel said, "Why has the LORD permitted us to be defeated today by the Philistines? Let us fetch the ark of the LORD from Shiloh that it may go into battle among us and save us from the grasp of our enemies."

Loss of the Ark. [4]So the people sent to Shiloh and brought from there the ark of the LORD of hosts, who is enthroned upon the cherubim.[*] The two sons of Eli, Hophni and Phinehas, were with the ark of God.[z] [5]When the ark of the LORD arrived in the camp, all Israel shouted so loudly that the earth resounded. [6]The Philistines, hearing the noise of shouting, asked, "What can this loud shouting in the camp of the Hebrews mean?" On learning that the ark of the LORD had come into the camp, [7]the Philistines were frightened. They said, "Gods have come to their camp." They said also, "Woe to us! This has never happened before. [8]Woe to us! Who can deliver us from the power of these mighty gods?[*] These are the gods that struck the Egyptians with various plagues and with pestilence. [9]Take courage and be manly, Philistines; otherwise you will become slaves to the Hebrews, as they were your slaves. So fight manfully!" [10]The Philistines fought and Israel was defeated; every man fled to his own tent. It was a disastrous

---

3, 17: May God do thus and so to you: the Biblical writers avoid repeating for us the specific terms of a curse as the speaker would have uttered it.

3, 1: And . . . Israel: this belongs to ch 4.

4, 4: Enthroned upon the cherubim: this title of the Lord seems to have originated in the sanctuary at Shiloh; it represents the divine Majesty as seated upon a throne on which he

can be borne through the heavens by winged creatures somewhat as in the visions of Ez 1 and 10.

4, 8: These mighty gods: the Philistines, who were polytheists, are represented as supposing the Israelites honored several gods.

---

w: 1 Sm 2, 27-36.　x: 1 Sm 2, 21.　y: Jgs 20, 1.　z: Ex 25, 22.

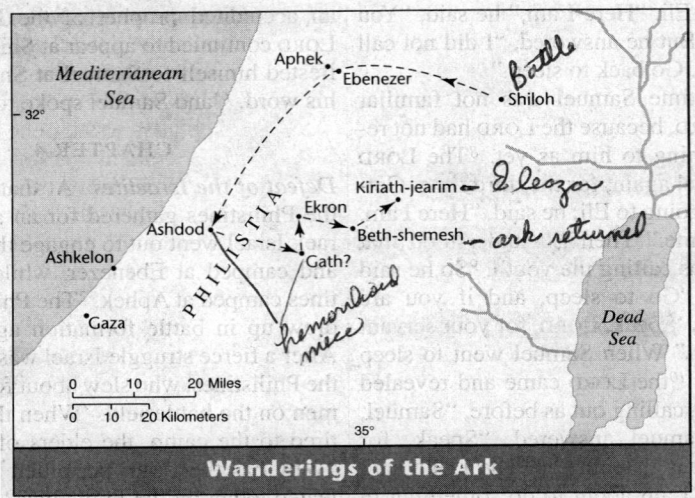

Wanderings of the Ark

(Map labels: Mediterranean Sea, 32°, Aphek, Ebenezer, Shiloh, *Battle*, Kiriath-jearim, *Eleazar*, Ekron, *ark returned*, Ashdod, Beth-shemesh, Ashkelon, Gath?, PHILISTIA, *hemorrhoids nice*, Gaza, Dead Sea, 35°, 0 10 20 Miles, 0 10 20 Kilometers)

defeat, in which Israel lost thirty thousand foot soldiers.*a* *11*The ark of God was captured, and Eli's two sons, Hophni and Phinehas, were among the dead.*b*

Death of Eli. *12*A Benjaminite fled from the battlefield and reached Shiloh that same day, with his clothes torn and his head covered with dirt.*c* *13*When he arrived, Eli was sitting in his chair beside the gate, watching the road, for he was troubled at heart about the ark of God. The man, however, went into the city to divulge his news, which put the whole city in an uproar. *14*Hearing the outcry of the men standing near him, Eli inquired, "What does this commotion mean?" *15*(Eli was ninety-eight years old, and his eyes would not focus, so that he could not see.) *16*The man quickly came up to Eli and said, "It is I who have come from the battlefield; I fled from there today." He asked, "What happened, my son?" *17*And the messenger answered: "Israel fled from the Philistines; in fact, the troops suffered heavy losses. Your two sons, Hophni and Phinehas, are among the dead, and the ark of God has been captured." *18*At this mention of the ark of God, Eli fell backward from his chair into the gateway; since he was an old man and heavy, he died of a broken neck. He had judged Israel for forty years.

*19*His daughter-in-law, the wife of Phinehas, was with child and at the point of giving birth. When she heard the news concerning the capture of the ark and the deaths of her father-in-law and her husband, she was seized with the pangs of labor, and gave birth. *20*She was about to die when the women standing around her said to her, "Never fear! You have given birth to a son." Yet she neither answered nor paid any attention.*d* *21*[She named the child Ichabod, saying, "Gone is the glory from Israel," with reference to the capture of the ark of God and to her father-in-law and her husband.] *22*She said, "Gone is the glory from Israel," because the ark of God had been captured.*e*

CHAPTER 5

See RG
115

The Ark in the Temple of Dagon. *1f*The Philistines, having captured the ark of God, transferred it from Ebenezer to Ashdod. *2*They then took the ark of God and brought it into the temple of Dagon, placing it beside Dagon. *3*When the people of Ashdod rose early the next morning, Dagon was lying prone on the ground before the ark of the LORD. So they picked Dagon up and replaced him. *4*But the next morning early, when they arose, Dagon lay prone on the

---

a: Ps 78, 61.   *b*: 1 Sm 2, 34.   *c*: Jos 7, 6; 2 Sm 1, 2; Jer 7, 12.   *d*: 1 Sm 14, 3; Gn 35, 16ff.   *e*: Ps 78, 61.   *f*: 1-5: Jgs 16, 23-30; Is 45, 5f. 20f.

The Ark Troubles the Philistines

In the ancient Near East, wars between nations were interpreted as contests between their re-spective gods. This story (5, 1–12) explains that although the Philistines defeated Israel, the LORD was superior to Dagon, a Philistine god.

ground before the ark of the LORD, his head and hands broken off and lying on the threshold, his trunk alone intact. *5*For this reason, neither the priests of Dagon nor any others who enter the temple of Dagon tread on the threshold of Dagon in Ashdod to this very day; they always step over it.

The Ark Is Carried About. *6*Now the LORD dealt severely with the people of Ashdod. He ravaged and afflicted the city and its vicinity with hemorrhoids; he brought upon the city a great and deadly plague of mice* that swarmed in their ships and overran their fields.*g* *7*On seeing how matters stood, the men of Ashdod decided, "The ark of the God of Israel must not remain with us, for he is handling us and our god Dagon severely." *8*So they summoned all the Philistine lords and in-quired of them, "What shall we do with the ark of the God of Israel?" The men of Gath replied, "Let them move the ark of the God of Israel on to us." *9*So they moved the ark of the God of Israel to Gath! But after it had been brought there, the LORD threw the city into ut-ter turmoil: he afflicted its inhabitants, young and old, and hemorrhoids broke out on them. *10*The ark of God was next sent to Ekron; but as it entered that city, the people there cried out, "Why have they brought the ark of the God of Israel here to kill us and our kindred?" *11*Then they, too, sent a summons to all the Philistine lords and pleaded: "Send away the ark of the God of Israel. Let it return to its own place, that it may not kill us and our kindred." A deadly panic had seized the whole city, since the hand of God had been very heavy upon it. *12*Those who escaped death were af-flicted with hemorrhoids, and the outcry from the city went up to the heavens.

CHAPTER 6

See RG 115

The Ark To Be Returned. *1*The ark of the LORD had been in the land of the Philis-tines seven months *2*when they summoned priests and fortune-tellers to ask, "What shall we do with the ark of the LORD? Tell us what we should send back with it." *3*They replied: "If you intend to send away the ark of the God of Israel, you must not send it alone, but must, by all means, make amends to him through a guilt offering.* Then you will be healed, and will learn why he contin-ues to afflict you." *4*When asked further, "What guilt offering should be our amends to him?", they replied:

"Five golden hemorrhoids and five golden mice to correspond to the number of Philistine lords, since the same plague has struck all of you and your lords. *5*Therefore, make images of the hemorrhoids and of the mice that are infesting your land and give them as a tribute to the God of Israel. Per-haps then he will cease to afflict you, your gods, and your land. *6*Why should you be-come stubborn, as the Egyptians and Phar-aoh were stubborn? Was it not after he had dealt ruthlessly with them that the Israelites were released and departed?*h* *7*So now set to work and make a new cart. Then take two milch cows that have not borne the yoke; hitch them to the cart, but drive their calves indoors away from them.*i* *8*You shall next take the ark of the LORD and place it on the cart, putting in a box beside it the golden ar-ticles that you are offering, as amends for your guilt. Start it on its way, and let it go. *9*Then watch! If it goes up to Beth-shemesh along the route to his own territory, he has

5, 6: Hemorrhoids . . . mice: a double calamity fell upon them—a plague of mice or rats, and a severe epidemic of pestilential tumors, probably the bubonic plague.

6, 3: A guilt offering: a propitiatory offering customary af-ter unwitting transgression of the ordinances of God regard-

ing holy things or property rights; cf Lv 6, 1ff.

g: Ps 78, 66. *h:* Ex 7, 14; 8, 15; 9, 34. *i:* Nm 19, 2; Dt 21, 3; 2 Sm 6, 3.

brought this great calamity upon us; if not, we will know it was not he who struck us, but that an accident happened to us."

The Ark in Beth-shemesh. [10]They acted upon this advice. Taking two milch cows, they hitched them to the cart but shut up their calves indoors. [11]Then they placed the ark of the LORD on the cart, along with the box containing the golden mice and the images of the hemorrhoids. [12]The cows went straight for the route to Beth-shemesh and continued along this road, mooing as they went, without turning right or left. The Philistine lords followed them as far as the border of Beth-shemesh. [13]The people of Beth-shemesh were harvesting the wheat in the valley. When they looked up and spied the ark, they greeted it with rejoicing. [14]The cart came to the field of Joshua the Beth-shemite and stopped there. At a large stone in the field, the wood of the cart was split up and the cows were offered as a holocaust to the LORD.[j] [15]The Levites, meanwhile, had taken down the ark of God and the box beside it, in which the golden articles were, and had placed them on the great stone. The men of Beth-shemesh also offered other holocausts and sacrifices to the LORD that day. [16]After witnessing this, the five Philistine lords returned to Ekron the same day.

Guilt Offering. [17]The golden hemorrhoids the Philistines sent back as a guilt offering to the LORD were as follows: one for Ashdod, one for Gaza, one for Ashkelon, one for Gath, and one for Ekron. [18]The golden mice, however, corresponded to the number of all the cities of the Philistines belonging to the five lords, including fortified cities and open villages. The large stone on which the ark of the LORD was placed is still in the field of Joshua the Beth-shemite at the present time.

Penalty for Irreverence. [19]The descendants of Jeconiah did not join in the celebration with the inhabitants of Beth-shemesh when they greeted the ark of the LORD, and seventy of them were struck down. The people went into mourning at this great calamity

with which the LORD had afflicted them. [20]The men of Beth-shemesh asked, "Who can stand in the presence of this Holy One? To whom shall he go from us?" [21]They then sent messengers to the inhabitants of Kiriath-jearim, saying, "The Philistines have returned the ark of the LORD; come down and get it."

CHAPTER 7

See RG 115-16

[1]So the inhabitants of Kiriath-jearim came for the ark of the LORD and brought it into the house of Abinadab on the hill, appointing his son Eleazar as guardian of the ark of the LORD.

Religious Reform. [2]From the day the ark came to rest in Kiriath-jearim a long time, twenty years, elapsed, and the whole Israelite population turned to the LORD. [3]Samuel said to them: "If you wish with your whole heart to return to the LORD, put away your foreign gods and your Ashtaroth, devote yourselves to the LORD, and worship him alone. Then he will deliver you from the power of the Philistines."[k] [4]So the Israelites put away their Baals and Ashtaroth, and worshiped the LORD alone. [5]Samuel then gave orders, "Gather all Israel to Mizpah, that I may pray to the LORD for you."[l] [6]When they were gathered at Mizpah, they drew water and poured it out on the ground* before the LORD, and they fasted that day, confessing, "We have sinned against the LORD." It was at Mizpah that Samuel began to judge the Israelites.[m]

Rout of the Philistines. [7]When the Philistines heard that the Israelites had gathered at Mizpah, their lords went up against Israel. Hearing this, the Israelites became afraid of the Philistines [8]and said to Samuel, "Implore the LORD our God unceasingly for us, to save us from the clutches of the Philistines."[n] [9]Samuel therefore took an unweaned lamb and offered it entire as a holocaust to the LORD.[o] He implored the LORD for Israel, and the LORD heard him. [10]While Samuel was offering the holocaust, the Philistines advanced to join battle with Israel. That day, however, the LORD thundered loudly against the Phi-

---

7, 6: Poured it out on the ground: for the symbolism, cf 2 Sm 14, 14.

j: 2 Sm 24, 21ff.   k: 1 Sm 12, 10. 20. 24; Jos 24, 23; Jgs 6, 6-10; 10, 10-16.   l: 1 Sm 10, 17; Jgs 20, 1.   m: Jgs 20, 26; Ps 22, 14; Lam 2, 19.   n: Ex 17, 9-13.   o: 9f: 2 Sm 22, 14f; Sir 46, 16ff.

listines, and threw them into such confusion that they were defeated by Israel. [11]Thereupon the Israelites sallied forth from Mizpah and pursued the Philistines, harrying them down beyond Beth-car. [12]Samuel then took a stone and placed it between Mizpah and Jeshanah; he named it Ebenezer,* explaining, "To this point has the LORD helped us." [13]Thus were the Philistines subdued, never again to enter the territory of Israel, for the LORD was severe with them as long as Samuel lived.[p] [14]The cities from Ekron to Gath which the Philistines had taken from Israel were restored to them. Israel also freed the territory of these cities from the dominion of the Philistines. Moreover there was peace between Israel and the Amorites.

[15]Samuel judged Israel as long as he lived. [16]He made a yearly journey, passing through Bethel, Gilgal and Mizpah and judging Israel at each of these sanctuaries. [17]Then he used to return to Ramah, for that was his home. There, too, he judged Israel and built an altar to the LORD.[q]

II: Establishment of the Monarchy in Israel

CHAPTER 8*

See RG 116

Request for a King. [1]In his old age Samuel appointed his sons judges over Israel. [2]His first-born was named Joel, his second son, Abijah; they judged at Beer-sheba. [3]His sons did not follow his example but sought illicit gain and accepted bribes, perverting justice.[r] [4]Therefore all the elders of Israel came in a body to Samuel at Ramah [5]and said to him, "Now that you are old, and your sons do not follow your example, appoint a king over us, as other nations have, to judge us."[s]

God Grants the Request. [6]Samuel was displeased when they asked for a king to judge them. He prayed to the LORD, however, [7]who said in answer: "Grant the people's every request. It is not you they reject, they are rejecting me as their king.[t] [8]As they have treated me constantly from the day I brought them up from Egypt to this day, deserting me and worshiping strange gods, so do they treat you too. [9]Now grant their request; but at the same time, warn them solemnly and inform them of the rights of the king who will rule them."

The Rights of a King. [10]Samuel delivered the message of the LORD in full to those who were asking him for a king. [11]He told them: "The rights of the king who will rule you will be as follows: He will take your sons and assign them to his chariots and horses, and they will run before his chariot.[u] [12]He will also appoint from among them his commanders of groups of a thousand and of a hundred soldiers. He will set them to do his plowing and his harvesting, and to make his implements of war and the equipment of his chariots.[v] [13]He will use your daughters as ointment-makers, as cooks, and as bakers. [14]He will take the best of your fields, vineyards, and olive groves, and give them to his officials.[w] [15]He will tithe your crops and your vineyards, and give the revenue to his eunuchs and his slaves. [16]He will take your male and female servants, as well as your best oxen and your asses, and use them to do his work. [17]He will tithe your flocks and you yourselves will become his slaves.[x] [18]When this takes place, you will complain against the king whom you have chosen, but on that day the LORD will not answer you."

Persistent Demand. [19]The people, however, refused to listen to Samuel's warning and said, "Not so! There must be a king over us.[y] [20]We too must be like other

---

7, 12: Ebenezer: or eben ha-ezer, means "stone of help."

8, 1: From this chapter on, the First Book of Samuel gives us two and sometimes three viewpoints on most of the events with which it is concerned, such as the appointment of Saul as king, the reasons for his downfall, his relationship with David, even the circumstances of Saul's death (1 Sm 31; 2 Sm 1). The choice of Saul as king is seen, in ch 8, followed by 10, 17-27 and ch 12, as motivated by the people's defection from the proper service of God; this later editorial approach incorporates not only narratives

with which it is consistent, but also early traditions (9, 1-10. 16; ch 11) which portray the events and their motivation quite differently.

---

p: Jgs 3, 30; 8, 28; 11, 33. q: 1 Sm 9, 12; 14, 35. r: Ex 23, 8; Dt 16, 19; Prv 17, 23. s: 5f: Dt 17, 14f; Hos 13, 10; Acts 13, 21. t: 7f: 1 Sm 12, 1. 12f; Jgs 8, 22f; 10, 13; 1 Kgs 9, 9. u: 1 Sm 10, 25; Dt 17, 14-20; 1 Kgs 12. v: 2 Sm 15, 1; 1 Kgs 1, 5. w: 1 Sm 22, 7; 1 Kgs 21, 1-24; Ez 46, 18. x: 1 Kgs 12, 4. y: 1 Sm 10, 19.

The Foundation of the Monarchy

No less than five chapters (8–12) are devoted to the foundation of the monarchy, which shows the importance attached to the subject. The attitude toward kingship is not consistent—in chapters 8; 10, 17–27; and 12 it is negative; in the other chapters, positive.

nations, with a king to rule us and to lead us in warfare and fight our battles." [21]When Samuel had listened to all the people had to say, he repeated it to the LORD, [22]who then said to him, "Grant their request and appoint a king to rule them." Samuel thereupon said to the men of Israel, "Each of you go to his own city."

See RG 116

CHAPTER 9

[1]There was a stalwart man from Benjamin named Kish, who was the son of Abiel, son of Zeror, son of Becorath, son of Aphiah, a Benjaminite.[z] [2]He had a son named Saul, who was a handsome young man. There was no other Israelite handsomer than Saul; he stood head and shoulders above the people.[a]

The Lost Asses. [3]Now the asses of Saul's father, Kish, had wandered off. Kish said to his son Saul, "Take one of the servants with you and go out and hunt for the asses." [4]Accordingly they went through the hill country of Ephraim, and through the land of Shalishah. Not finding them there, they continued through the land of Shaalim without success. They also went through the land of Benjamin, but they failed to find the animals. [5]When they came to the land of Zuph, Saul said to the servant who was with him, "Come, let us turn back, lest my father forget about the asses and become anxious about us." [6]The servant replied, "Listen! There is a man of God in this city, a man held in high esteem; all that he says is sure to come true. Let us go there now! Perhaps he can tell us how to accomplish our errand." [7b]But Saul said to his servant, "If we go,

what can we offer the man? There is no bread in our bags, and we have no present to give the man of God. What have we?" [8]Again the servant answered Saul, "I have a quarter of a silver shekel.* If I give that to the man of God, he will tell us our way." [10]Saul then said to his servant, "Well said! Come on, let us go!" And they went to the city where the man of God lived.

Quest for Samuel's Aid. [11c]As they were going up the ascent to the city, they met some girls coming out to draw water and inquired of them, "Is the seer in town?" [9d](In former times in Israel, anyone who sent to consult God used to say, "Come, let us go to the seer." For he who is now called prophet was formerly called seer.)* [12e]The girls answered, "Yes, there—straight ahead. Hurry now; just today he came to the city, because the people have a sacrifice today on the high place.* [13]When you enter the city, you may reach him before he goes up to the high place to eat. The people will not eat until he arrives; only after he blesses the sacrifice will the invited guests eat. Go up immediately, for you should find him right now."

Samuel's Revelation about Saul. [14]So they went up to the city. As they entered it, Samuel was coming toward them on his way to the high place. [15]The day before Saul's arrival, the LORD had given Samuel the revelation:[f] [16]"At this time tomorrow I will send you a man from the land of Benjamin whom you are to anoint as commander of my people Israel. He shall save my people from the clutches of the Philistines, for I have witnessed their misery and accepted their cry for help."[g] [17]When Samuel caught sight of

---

9, 8: A quarter of a silver shekel: about a tenth of an ounce of silver.

9, 9: This verse is a later explanation of the term seer, first used in the text in 1 Sm 9, 11.

9, 12: On the high place: the local sanctuary on the top of a hill, where the sacrifice was offered and the sacrificial meal eaten.

z: 1 Sm 14, 51; 1 Chr 8, 33.   a: 1 Sm 10, 23.   b: 7f: Nm 22, 7; 1 Kgs 14, 3; 2 Kgs 4, 42; 5, 15; 8, 8f.   c: Gn 24, 11ff; Ex 2, 16. d: Sir 46, 15.   e: 1 Sm 7, 17; 16, 2. 5; 20, 6. 29; Dt 12, 13; 1 Kgs 3, 2. 4.   f: Acts 13, 21.   g: 1 Sm 10, 1.

> *A*nointing: the rite that raised a commoner to kingship in Israel. Saul and David were anointed in secret (cf. 1 Sm 9, 26—10, 1; 16, 1–13) Later, it was a more formal and public act (see 1 Kings 1, 32–40).

Saul, the LORD assured him, "This is the man of whom I told you; he is to govern my people." [18]Saul met Samuel in the gateway and said, "Please tell me where the seer lives." [19]Samuel answered Saul: "I am the seer. Go up ahead of me to the high place and eat with me today. In the morning, before dismissing you, I will tell you whatever you wish. [20]As for the asses you lost three days ago, do not worry about them, for they have been found. Whom does Israel desire ardently if not you and your father's family?" [21]Saul replied: "Am I not a Benjaminite, of one of the smallest tribes of Israel, and is not my clan the least among the clans of the tribe of Benjamin? Why say such things to me?"[h]

[22]Samuel then took Saul and his servant and brought them to the room, where he placed them at the head of the guests, of whom there were about thirty. [23]He said to the cook, "Bring the portion I gave you and told you to put aside." [24]So the cook took up the leg and what went with it,[*] and placed it before Saul. Samuel said: "This is a reserved portion that has been set before you. Eat, for it was kept for you until your arrival; I explained that I was inviting some guests." Thus Saul dined with Samuel that day. [25]When they came down from the high place into the city, a mattress was spread for Saul on the roof, [26]and he slept there.

Saul's Anointing. At daybreak Samuel called to Saul on the roof, "Get up, and I will start you on your journey." Saul rose, and he and Samuel went outside the city together. [27]As they were approaching the edge of the town, Samuel said to Saul, "Tell the servant to go on ahead of us, but stay here yourself for the moment, that I may give you a message from God."

CHAPTER 10

See RG 116

[1]Then, from a flask he had with him, Samuel poured oil on Saul's head; he also kissed him, saying: "The LORD anoints you commander over his heritage. You are to govern the LORD's people Israel, and to save them from the grasp of their enemies roundabout.[i]

"This will be the sign for you that the LORD has anointed you commander over his heritage: [2]When you leave me today, you will meet two men near Rachel's tomb[*] at Zelzah in the territory of Benjamin, who will say to you, 'The asses you went to look for have been found. Your father is no longer worried about the asses, but is anxious about you and says, What shall I do about my son?'[j] [3]Farther on, when you arrive at the terebinth of Tabor, you will be met by three men going up to God at Bethel; one will be bringing three kids, another three loaves of bread, and the third a skin of wine. [4]They will greet you and offer you two wave offerings of bread, which you will take from them. [5k]After that you will come to Gibeath-elohim, where there is a garrison of the Philistines.[*] As you enter that

9, 24: And what went with it: a slight change would give "and the fatty tail" as perhaps the original reading. Sheep in the Near East are exceptionally fat-tailed, and such a portion would be thought a special delicacy by the Hebrews. However, the ritual legislation as we know it (Lv 3, 9) would require that the fat tail be burned on the altar. If this general rule was later than the time of Samuel, the present text may have been retouched so as not to seem to contravene it. A Qumran text has "the festive (leg)" here.

10, 2: Here, as in Jer 31, 15, Rachel's tomb is placed north of Jerusalem. Later tradition understood Gn 35, 19f in the sense given by Mt 2, 16ff, and placed the tomb at Bethlehem, farther south.

10, 5: A garrison of the Philistines: the Hebrew word for "garrison" has been explained alternatively to mean a pillar erected to mark the Philistine occupation, or an inspector or officer for the collection of taxes. In a prophetic state: in an ecstatic condition due to strong feelings of religious enthusiasm induced by a communal observance, possibly accompanied by music and dancing.

h: 1 Sm 15, 17.   i: 1 Sm 9, 16f; 24, 7; Jgs 9, 9; 1 Kgs 1, 39; Acts 13, 21.   j: Jer 31, 15; Mk 14, 13.   k: 5f: 1 Sm 13, 3; 16, 13; 19, 20f.

city, you will meet a band of prophets, in a prophetic state, coming down from the high place preceded by lyres, tambourines, flutes and harps. [6]The spirit of the LORD will rush upon you, and you will join them in their prophetic state and will be changed into another man.[l] [7]When you see these signs fulfilled, do whatever you judge feasible, because God is with you. [8m]Now go down ahead of me to Gilgal, for I shall come down to you, to offer holocausts and to sacrifice peace offerings. Wait seven days until I come to you; I shall then tell you what you must do."[*]

Fulfillment of the Signs. [9]As Saul turned to leave Samuel, God gave him another heart. That very day all these signs came to pass.... [10*]When they were going from there to Gibeah, a band of prophets met him, and the spirit of God rushed upon him, so that he joined them in their prophetic state.[n] [11]When all who had known him previously saw him in a prophetic state among the prophets, they said to one another, "What has happened to the son of Kish? Is Saul also among the prophets?"[o] [12]And someone from that district added, "And who is their father?" Thus the proverb arose, "Is Saul also among the prophets?" [13]When he came out of the prophetic state, he went home.

Silence about the Kingship. [14]Saul's uncle inquired of him and his servant, "Where have you been?" Saul replied, "To look for the asses. When we could not find them, we went to Samuel." [15]Then Saul's uncle said, "Tell me, then, what Samuel said to you." [16]Saul said to his uncle, "He assured us that the asses had been found." But he mentioned nothing to him of what Samuel had said about the kingship.

Saul Chosen King by Lot. [17]Samuel called the people together to the LORD at Mizpah[p]

[18]and addressed the Israelites: "Thus says the LORD, the God of Israel, 'It was I who brought Israel up from Egypt and delivered you from the power of the Egyptians and from the power of all the kingdoms that oppressed you.'[q] [19]But today you have rejected your God, who delivers you from all your evils and calamities, by saying to him, 'Not so, but you must appoint a king over us.' Now, therefore, take your stand before the LORD according to tribes and families."[r] [20]So Samuel had all the tribes of Israel come forward, and the tribe of Benjamin was chosen. [21]Next he had the tribe of Benjamin come forward in clans, and the clan of Matri was chosen, and finally Saul, son of Kish, was chosen. But they looked for him in vain. [22s]Again they consulted the LORD, "Has he come here?" The LORD answered, "He is hiding among the baggage." [23]They ran to bring him from there; and when he stood among the people, he was head and shoulders above all the crowd.[t] [24]Samuel said to all the people, "Do you see the man whom the LORD has chosen? There is none like him among all the people!" Then all the people shouted, "Long live the king!"[u]

[25]Samuel next explained to the people the law of royalty[*] and wrote it in a book, which he placed in the presence of the LORD. This done, Samuel dismissed the people, each to his own place.[v] [26]Saul also went home to Gibeah, accompanied by warriors whose hearts the LORD had touched. [27]But certain worthless men said, "How can this fellow save us?" They despised him and brought him no present.[w]

CHAPTER 11

See RG 116

Defeat of the Ammonites. [1]About a month later,[*] Nahash the Ammonite went up and laid siege to Jabesh-gilead. All the men

---

10, 8: By inserting this verse, with its seven days, an editor has prepared for one narrative of the rejection of Saul (1 Sm 13, 8-15) in the very context of Saul's anointing.

10, 10: The story has here been abridged by omitting the fulfillment of the first two signs given by Samuel (1 Sm 10, 2ff).

10, 25: The law of royalty: the charter defining the rights of the king.

11, 1: About a month later: there is ancient evidence for a longer introduction to this campaign. The time indication here may refer to its earlier stages rather than to the events of ch 10.

l: 1 Sm 11, 6; 16, 13; Jgs 14, 6. 19; 15, 14; 2 Kgs 3, 15. *m:* 1 Sm 13, 8; Lv 3, 1. *n:* 1 Sm 19, 20-24; Nm 11, 25. *o:* 1 Sm 19, 24. *p:* 1 Sm 7, 5. *q:* Ex 20, 2; Lv 11, 45; 25, 38; Nm 15, 41; Dt 5, 6; Jgs 6, 8f. *r:* 1 Sm 8, 19. *s:* 1 Sm 30, 24. *t:* 1 Sm 9, 2; 16, 7. *u:* 2 Sm 16, 16; 1 Kgs 1, 25; 2 Kgs 11, 12. *v:* 1 Sm 8, 11; Dt 17, 14-20. *w:* 1 Sm 11, 12.

of Jabesh begged Nahash, "Make a treaty with us, and we will be your subjects."ˣ ²But Nahash the Ammonite replied, "This is my condition for a treaty with you: I must gouge out every man's right eye, that I may thus bring ignominy on all Israel." ³The elders of Jabesh said to him: "Give us seven days to send messengers throughout the territory of Israel. If no one rescues us, we will surrender to you." ⁴When the messengers arrived at Gibeah of Saul, they related the news to the people, all of whom wept aloud. ⁵Just then Saul came in from the field, behind his oxen. "Why are the people weeping?" he asked. The message of the inhabitants of Jabesh was repeated to him. ⁶As he listened to this report, the spirit of God rushed upon him and he became very angry.ʸ ⁷Taking a yoke of oxen, he cut them into pieces, which he sent throughout the territory of Israel by couriers with the message, "If anyone does not come out to follow Saul [and Samuel], the same as this will be done to his oxen!" In dread of the LORD, the people turned out to a man.ᶻ ⁸When he reviewed them in Bezek, there were three hundred thousand Israelites and seventy thousand Judahites.

⁹To the messengers who had come he said, "Tell the inhabitants of Jabesh-gilead that tomorrow, while the sun is hot, they will be rescued." The messengers came and reported this to the inhabitants of Jabesh, who were jubilant, ¹⁰and said to Nahash, "Tomorrow we will surrender to you, and you may do whatever you please with us." ¹¹On the appointed day, Saul arranged his troops in three companies and invaded the camp during the dawn watch. They slaughtered Ammonites until the heat of the day; by then the survivors were so scattered that no two were left together.

Saul Accepted as King. ¹²*The people then said to Samuel: "Who questioned whether Saul should rule over us? Hand over the men and we will put them to death."ᵃ

¹³But Saul broke in to say, "No man is to be put to death this day, for today the LORD has saved Israel."ᵇ ¹⁴Samuel said to the people, "Come, let us go to Gilgal to inaugurate the kingdom there." ¹⁵So all the people went to Gilgal, where, in the presence of the LORD, they made Saul king. They also sacrificed peace offerings there before the LORD, and Saul and all the Israelites celebrated the occasion with great joy.

CHAPTER 12

See RG 116–17

Samuel's Integrity. ¹Samuel addressed all Israel: "I have granted your request in every respect," he said. "I have set a king over youᶜ ²and now the king is your leader. As for me, I am old and gray, and have sons among you. I have lived with you from my youth to the present day. ³Here I stand! Answer me in the presence of the LORD and of his anointed. Whose ox have I taken? Whose ass have I taken? Whom have I cheated? Whom have I oppressed? From whom have I accepted a bribe and overlooked his guilt? I will make restitution to you."ᵈ ⁴They replied, "You have neither cheated us, nor oppressed us, nor accepted anything from anyone." ⁵So he said to them, "The LORD is witness against you this day, and his anointed as well, that you have found nothing in my possession." "He is witness," they agreed.

Samuel Upbraids the People. ⁶Continuing, Samuel said to the people: "The LORD is witness, who appointed Moses and Aaron, and who brought your fathers up from the land of Egypt.ᵉ ⁷Now, therefore, take your stand, and I shall arraign you before the LORD, and shall recount for you all the acts of mercy the LORD has done for you and your fathers. ⁸When Jacob and his sons went to Egypt and the Egyptians oppressed them, your fathers appealed to the LORD, who sent Moses and Aaron to bring them out of Egypt, and he gave them this place to live in.ᶠ ⁹But they forgot the LORD their God; and he allowed them to fall

---

11, 12-14: With these verses, an editor has harmonized the account of the acknowledgment of Saul as king at Mizpah (1 Sm 10, 17-24) with the public acclamation at Gilgal (1 Sm 11, 15) after the defeat of the Ammonites (1 Sm 11, 1-11). The Greek text of 1 Sm 11, 15 reads "and Samuel anointed Saul as king," instead of they made Saul king.

---

x: 1 Sm 12, 12; 31, 11.   y: 1 Sm 16, 13; Jgs 14, 6. 19.   z: 1 Kgs 11, 30; 2 Kgs 13, 18.   a: 1 Sm 10, 27.   b: 2 Sm 19, 23.   c: 1 Sm 8, 7. 9. 22.   d: Ex 20, 17; 23, 8; Nm 16, 15; Dt 16, 19; Sir 46, 19.   e: Mi 6, 4.   f: Gn 46, 5; Ex 1, 11; 2, 23ff.

The Kingdom of Saul according to 1 Samuel

into the clutches of Sisera, the captain of the army of Jabin, king of Hazor, into the grasp of the Philistines, and into the grip of the king of Moab, who made war against them.g 10Each time they appealed to the LORD and said, 'We have sinned in forsaking the LORD and worshiping Baals and Ashtaroth; but deliver us now from the power of our enemies, and we will worship you.'h 11Accordingly, the LORD sent Jerubbaal, Barak, Jephthah, and Samson; he delivered you from the power of your enemies on every side, so that you were able to live in security.i 12Yet, when you saw Nahash, king of the Ammonites, advancing against you, you said to me, 'Not so, but a king must rule us,' even though the LORD your God is your king.j

Warnings for People and King. 13"Now you have the king you want, a king the LORD has given you.k 14If you fear the LORD and worship him, if you are obedient to him and do not rebel against the LORD's command, if both you and the king who rules you follow the LORD your God—well and good. 15But if you do not obey the LORD and if you rebel against his command, the LORD will deal severely with you and your king, and destroy you. 16Now then, stand ready to witness the great marvel the LORD is about to accomplish before your eyes. 17Are we not in the harvest time for wheat? Yet I shall call to the LORD, and he will send thunder and rain. Thus you will see and understand how greatly the LORD is displeased that you have asked for a king."l 18Samuel then called to the LORD, and the LORD sent thunder and rain that day.

Assistance Promised. As a result, all the people dreaded the LORD and Samuel. 19They said to Samuel, "Pray to the LORD your God for us, your servants, that we may not die for having added to all our other sins the evil of asking for a king." 20"Do not fear," Samuel answered them. "It is true you have

committed all this evil; still, you must not turn from the LORD, but must worship him with your whole heart. 21Do not turn to meaningless idols which can neither profit nor save; they are nothing.m 22For the sake of his own great name the LORD will not abandon his people, since the LORD himself chose to make you his people.n 23As for me, far be it from me to sin against the LORD by ceasing to pray for you and to teach you the good and right way.o 24But you must fear the LORD and worship him faithfully with your whole heart; keep in mind the great things he has done among you. 25If instead you continue to do evil, both you and your king shall perish."

III: Saul and David

CHAPTER 13

See RG 117

1[Saul was . . . years old when he became king and he reigned . . . (two) years over Israel.]*

Saul Offers Sacrifice. 2Saul chose three thousand men of Israel, of whom two thousand remained with him in Michmash and in the hill country of Bethel, and one thousand were with Jonathan in Gibeah of Benjamin. He sent the rest of the people back to their tents. 3Now Jonathan overcame the Philistine garrison* which was in Gibeah, and the Philistines got word of it. Then Saul sounded the horn throughout the land, with a proclamation, "Let the Hebrews hear!"p 4Thus all Israel learned that Saul had overcome the garrison of the Philistines and that Israel had brought disgrace upon the Philistines; and the soldiers were called up to Saul in Gilgal. 5The Philistines also assembled for battle, with three thousand chariots, six thousand horsemen, and foot soldiers as numerous as the sands of the seashore. Moving up against Israel, they encamped in Michmash, east of Beth-aven. 6Some Israelites, aware of the

13, 1: A formula like that of 2 Sm 5, 4 was introduced here at some time; but the age of Saul when he became king remains a blank, and the two years assigned for his reign in the received text cannot be correct. Tradition (Acts 13, 21) offers the round number, "forty years."

13, 3-4: The Philistine garrison: see note on 1 Sm 10, 5. Let the Hebrews hear: a different reading of these verses, based on the Greek, would yield: "And the Philistines heard that the Hebrews (or: the slaves) had revolted. Saul in the meantime sounded the trumpet throughout all the land (v 4), and all Israel heard that Saul. . . ."

g: Jgs 3, 12ff; 4, 2f; 10, 7; 13, 1.   h: 1 Sm 7, 3f.   i: Jgs 6, 14. 32; 11, 1.   j: 1 Sm 8, 6f. 19; 11, 1f; Jgs 8, 23.   k: 1 Sm 8, 7.   l: Ex 9, 23. 28ff; 1 Kgs 18, 1.   m: Dt 32, 37ff.   n: Jer 14, 21; Ez 20, 9; Dn 3, 34.   o: Ex 32, 11.   p: 1 Sm 14, 1-15; Jgs 3, 27; 6, 34; 2 Sm 20, 1f.

danger and of the difficult situation, hid themselves in caves, in thickets, among rocks, in caverns, and in cisterns,[q] [7]and other Hebrews passed over the Jordan into the land of Gad and Gilead. Saul, however, held out at Gilgal, although all his followers were seized with fear.* [8]He waited seven days— the time Samuel had determined. When Samuel did not arrive at Gilgal, the men began to slip away from Saul.[r] [9]He then said, "Bring me the holocaust and peace offerings," and he offered up the holocaust.

King Saul Reproved. [10]He had just finished this offering when Samuel arrived. Saul went out to greet him, [11]and Samuel asked him, "What have you done?" Saul replied: "When I saw that the men were slipping away from me, since you had not come by the specified time, and with the Philistines assembled at Michmash, [12]I said to myself, 'Now the Philistines will come down against me at Gilgal, and I have not yet sought the LORD's blessing.' So in my anxiety I offered up the holocaust." [13]Samuel's response was: "You have been foolish! Had you kept the command the LORD your God gave you, the LORD would now establish your kingship in Israel as lasting; [14]but as things are, your kingdom shall not endure. The LORD has sought out a man after his own heart and has appointed him commander of his people, because you broke the LORD's command."[s]

Philistine Invasion. [15]Then Samuel set out from Gilgal and went his own way; but the rest of the people went up after Saul to meet the soldiers, going from Gilgal to Gibeah of Benjamin. Saul then numbered the soldiers he had with him, who were about six hundred.[t] [16]Saul, his son Jonathan, and the soldiers they had with them were now occupying Geba of Benjamin, and the Philistines were encamped at Michmash. [17]Meanwhile, raiders left the camp of the Philistines in three bands.[u] One band took the Ophrah road toward the district of Shual; [18]another turned in the direction of Beth-horon; and the third took the road for Geba that overlooks the Valley of the Hyenas toward the desert.

Disarmament of Israel. [19]Not a single smith was to be found in the whole land of Israel, for the Philistines had said, "Otherwise the Hebrews will make swords or spears."[v] [20]All Israel, therefore, had to go down to the Philistines to sharpen their plowshares, mattocks, axes, and sickles. [21]The price for the plowshares and mattocks was two-thirds of a shekel, and a third of a shekel for sharpening the axes and for setting the ox-goads. [22]And so on the day of battle neither sword nor spear could be found in the possession of any of the soldiers with Saul or Jonathan. Only Saul and his son Jonathan had them.

Jonathan's Exploit. [23]An outpost of the Philistines had pushed forward to the pass of Michmash.[w]

CHAPTER 14

See RG 117-18

[1]One day Jonathan, son of Saul, said to his armor-bearer, "Come, let us go over to the Philistine outpost on the other side." But he did not inform his father.[x] [2](Saul's command post was under the pomegranate tree near the threshing floor on the outskirts of Geba; those with him numbered about six hundred men. [3]Ahijah, son of Ahitub, brother of Ichabod, who was the son of Phinehas, son of Eli, the priest of the LORD at Shiloh, was wearing the ephod.) Nor did the soldiers know that Jonathan had gone.[y] [4]Flanking the ravine through which Jonathan intended to get over to the Philistine outpost there was a rocky crag on each side, one called Bozez, the other Seneh. [5]One crag was to the north, toward Michmash, the other to the south, toward Geba. [6]Jonathan said to his armor-bearer: "Come, let us go over to that outpost of the uncircumcised. Perhaps the LORD will help us, because it is no more difficult for the LORD to grant victory through a few than through many."[z] [7]His armor-bearer replied, "Do whatever you

---

13, 7-15: These verses, like 1 Sm 10, 8, anticipate the rejection of Saul; a different occasion and motivation for this are given in ch 15, resumed in 1 Sm 28, 17f.

---

q: 1 Sm 14, 22. *r:* 1 Sm 10, 8. *s:* 1 Sm 25, 30; 2 Sm 7, 15f; Ps 78, 70; Acts 13, 22. *t:* 1 Sm 14, 2. *u:* 1 Sm 14, 15. *v:* Jgs 5, 8.
w: 1 Sm 14, 15. *x:* 1 Sm 13, 3. *y:* 1 Sm 2, 28; 4, 21; 14, 18; 23, 9; 30, 7. *z:* 1 Sm 17, 26. 36. 47; Sir 39, 18; 1 Mc 3, 19.

are inclined to do; I will match your resolve." [8]Jonathan continued: "We shall go over to those men and show ourselves to them. [9]If they say to us, 'Stay there until we can come to you,' we shall stop where we are; we shall not go up to them. [10]But if they say, 'Come up to us,' we shall go up, because the LORD has delivered them into our grasp. That will be our sign." [11]Accordingly, the two of them appeared before the outpost of the Philistines, who said, "Look, some Hebrews are coming out of the holes where they have been hiding." [12]The men of the outpost called to Jonathan and his armor-bearer. "Come up here," they said, "and we will teach you a lesson." So Jonathan said to his armor-bearer, "Climb up after me, for the LORD has delivered them into the grasp of Israel." [13]Jonathan clambered up with his armor-bearer behind him; as the Philistines turned to flee him, he cut them down, and his armor-bearer followed him and finished them off. [14]In this first exploit Jonathan and his armor-bearer slew about twenty men within half a furlong. [15]Then panic spread to the army and to the countryside, and all the soldiers, including the outpost and the raiding parties, were terror-stricken. The earth also shook, so that the panic was beyond human endurance.

Rout of the Philistines. [16]The lookouts of Saul in Geba of Benjamin saw that the enemy camp had scattered and were running about in all directions. [17]Saul said to those around him, "Count the troops and find out if any of us are missing." When they had investigated, they found Jonathan and his armor-bearer missing. [18]Saul then said to Ahijah, "Bring the ephod* here." (Ahijah was wearing the ephod in front of the Israelites at that time.) [19]While Saul was speaking to the priest, the tumult in the Philistine camp kept increasing. So he said to the priest, "Withdraw your hand." [20]And Saul and all his men shouted and rushed into the fight, where the Philistines, wholly confused, were thrusting swords at one another.[a] [21]In addition, the Hebrews who had previously sided with the Philistines and had gone up with them to the camp, turned to join the Israelites under Saul and Jonathan.[b] [22]Likewise, all the Israelites who were hiding in the hill country of Ephraim, on hearing that the Philistines were fleeing, pursued them in the rout.[c] [23]Thus the LORD saved Israel that day.

Saul's Oath. The battle continued past Beth-horon;* [24]the whole people, about ten thousand combatants, were with Saul, and there was scattered fighting in every town in the hill country of Ephraim. And Saul swore a very rash oath that day, putting the people under this ban: "Cursed be the man who takes food before evening, before I am able to avenge myself on my enemies." So none of the people tasted food. [25]Indeed, there was a honeycomb lying on the ground, [26]and when the soldiers came to the comb the swarm had left it; yet no one would raise a hand to his mouth from it, because the people feared the oath.

Violation of the Oath. [27]Jonathan, who had not heard that his father had put the people under oath, thrust out the end of the staff he was holding and dipped it into the honey. Then he raised it to his mouth and his eyes lit up. [28]At this one of the soldiers spoke up: "Your father put the people under a strict oath, saying, 'Cursed be the man who takes food this day!' As a result the people are weak." [29]Jonathan replied: "My father brings trouble to the land. Look how bright my eyes are from this small taste of honey I have had. [30]What is more, if the people had eaten freely today of their enemy's booty when they came across it, would not the slaughter of the Philistines by now have been the greater for it?"

Use of Flesh with Blood Forbidden. [21]After the Philistines were routed that day from Michmash to Aijalon, the people were completely exhausted. [32]So they pounced upon the spoil and took sheep, oxen and calves, slaughtering them on the ground and eating

---

14, 18: Ephod: to be used in consulting God; see note on v 41, and that on 1 Sm 2, 28 above.

14, 23: Past Beth-horon: this is a textual correction influenced by 1 Sm 13, 18; the received Hebrew text refers to Bethel (Bethaven), but the effect of the victory would seem to have been that the main ridge of mountains in the territories of Benjamin and Ephraim was cleared of Philistines.

a: Jgs 7, 22.　*b:* 1 Sm 29, 4.　*c:* 1 Sm 13, 6.

the flesh with blood.*d* *33*Informed that the people were sinning against the LORD by eating the flesh with blood, Saul said: "You have broken faith. Roll a large stone here for me." *34*He continued: "Mingle with the people and tell each of them to bring his ox or his sheep to me. Slaughter it here and then eat, but you must not sin against the LORD by eating the flesh with blood." So everyone brought to the LORD whatever ox he had seized, and they slaughtered them there; *35*and Saul built an altar to the LORD—this was the first time he built an altar to the LORD.*e*

Jonathan in Danger of Death. *36*Then Saul said, "Let us go down in pursuit of the Philistines by night, to plunder among them until daybreak and to kill them all off." They replied, "Do what you think best." But the priest said, "Let us consult God." *37*So Saul inquired of God: "Shall I go down in pursuit of the Philistines? Will you deliver them into the power of Israel?" But he received no answer on this occasion.*f* *38*Saul then said, "Come here, all officers of the army. We must investigate and find out how this sin was committed today. *39*As the LORD lives who has given victory to Israel, even if my son Jonathan has committed it, he shall surely die!" But none of the people answered him. *40*So he said to all Israel, "Stand on one side, and I and my son Jonathan will stand on the other." The people responded, "Do what you think best."*g* *41*And Saul said to the LORD, the God of Israel: "Why did you not answer your servant this time? If the blame for this resides in me or my son Jonathan, LORD, God of Israel, respond with Urim; but if this guilt is in your people Israel, respond with Thummim."* Jonathan and Saul were designated, and the people went free.*h* *42*Saul then said, "Cast lots between me and my son Jonathan." And Jonathan was designated. *43*Saul said to Jonathan,

"Tell me what you have done." Jonathan replied, "I only tasted a little honey from the end of the staff I was holding. Am I to die for this?" *44*Saul said, "May God do thus and so to me if you do not indeed die, Jonathan!"*i*

Rescue of Jonathan. *45*But the army said to Saul: "Is Jonathan to die, though it was he who brought Israel this great victory? This must not be! As the LORD lives, not a single hair of his head shall fall to the ground, for God was with him in what he did today!" Thus the soldiers were able to rescue* Jonathan from death.*j* *46*After that Saul gave up the pursuit of the Philistines, who returned to their own territory.

Wars and Victories. *47*After taking over the kingship of Israel, Saul waged war on all their surrounding enemies—Moab, the Ammonites, Aram, Beth-rehob, the king of Zobah, and the Philistines. Wherever he turned, he was successful*k* *48*and fought bravely. He defeated Amalek and delivered Israel from the hands of those who were plundering them.

Saul's Family. *49*The sons of Saul were Jonathan, Ishvi,* and Malchishua; his two daughters were named, the elder, Merob, and the younger, Michal.*l* *50*Saul's wife, who was named Ahinoam, was the daughter of Ahimaaz. The name of his general was Abner, son of Saul's uncle, Ner; *51*Kish, Saul's father, and Ner, Abner's father, were sons of Abiel.*m*

*52*An unremitting war was waged against the Philistines during Saul's lifetime. When Saul saw any strong or brave man, he took him into his service.

CHAPTER 15 See RG 117–18

*1*Samuel said to Saul: "It was I the LORD sent to anoint you king over his people Israel. Now, therefore, listen to the message of the LORD. *2*This is what the LORD of hosts has to say: 'I will punish what Amalek did to

---

14, 41: The Urim and Thummim, or sacred lots, were a device for ascertaining the will of God; they ceased to be used after the time of David. The material and the shape of these objects, and the manner in which they were used, are unknown. They gave a "yes" or "no" answer to specific questions.

14, 45: Rescue: the Hebrew word used is that for the "redemption" of the first-born (Ex 13, 13ff).

14, 49: Ishvi: known also as Ishbaal, in 2 Sm 2, 8 and elsewhere. The name may once have read "Ishyo" here.

d: 1 Sm 15, 19. 21; Lv 3, 17; 7, 26f; 17, 10-14; Acts 15, 20. 29. *e:* 1 Sm 7, 17; Jgs 6, 24. *f:* 1 Sm 28, 6. 15. *g:* Jos 7, 13ff. *h:* 1 Sm 28, 6; Ex 28, 30; Dt 33, 8. *i:* 1 Sm 3, 17; Ru 1, 17. *j:* 2 Sm 14, 11; 1 Kgs 1, 52. *k:* 2 Sm 1, 22; 8, 2-5. *l:* 1 Sm 18, 20. 25; 31, 2; 1 Chr 8, 33; 9, 39; 10, 2. *m:* 1 Sm 9, 1.

Israel when he barred his way as he was coming up from Egypt.[n] [3]Go, now, attack Amalek, and deal with him and all that he has under the ban.[*] Do not spare him, but kill men and women, children and infants, oxen and sheep, camels and asses.' "[o]

Disobedience of Saul. [4]Saul alerted the soldiers, and at Telaim reviewed two hundred thousand foot soldiers and ten thousand men of Judah.[*] [5]Saul went to the city of Amalek, and after setting an ambush in the wadi, [6][p]warned the Kenites: "Come! Leave Amalek and withdraw, that I may not have to destroy you with them, for you were kind to the Israelites when they came up from Egypt." After the Kenites left, [7]Saul routed Amalek from Havilah to the approaches of Shur, on the frontier of Egypt.[q] [8]He took Agag, king of Amalek, alive, but on the rest of the people he put into effect the ban of destruction by the sword. [9]He and his troops spared Agag and the best of the fat sheep and oxen, and the lambs. They refused to carry out the doom on anything that was worthwhile, dooming only what was worthless and of no account.

Saul Is Reproved. [10]Then the LORD spoke to Samuel: [11]"I regret[*] having made Saul king, for he has turned from me and has not kept my command." At this Samuel grew angry and cried out to the LORD all night. [12]Early in the morning he went to meet Saul, but was informed that Saul had gone to Carmel, where he erected a trophy in his own honor, and that on his return he had passed on and gone down to Gilgal. [13]When Samuel came to him, Saul greeted him: "The LORD bless you! I have kept the command of the LORD." [14]But Samuel asked, "What, then, is the meaning of this bleating of sheep that

comes to my ears, and the lowing of oxen that I hear?" [15]Saul replied: "They were brought from Amalek. The men spared the best sheep and oxen to sacrifice to the LORD, your God; but we have carried out the ban on the rest." [16]Samuel said to Saul: "Stop! Let me tell you what the LORD said to me last night." "Speak!" he replied. [17]Samuel then said: "Though little in your own esteem, are you not leader of the tribes of Israel? The LORD anointed you king of Israel[r] [18]and sent you on a mission, saying, 'Go and put the sinful Amalekites under a ban of destruction. Fight against them until you have exterminated them.'[s] [19]Why then have you disobeyed the LORD? You have pounced on the spoil, thus displeasing the LORD."[t] [20]Saul answered Samuel: "I did indeed obey the LORD and fulfill the mission on which the LORD sent me. I have brought back Agag, and I have destroyed Amalek under the ban. [21]But from the spoil the men took sheep and oxen, the best of what had been banned, to sacrifice to the LORD their God in Gilgal."[u] [22][v]But Samuel said:

"Does the LORD so delight in holocausts and sacrifices
   as in obedience to the command of the LORD?
Obedience is better than sacrifice,
   and submission than the fat of rams.[*]
[23] For a sin like divination is rebellion,
   and presumption is the crime of idolatry.
Because you have rejected the command of the LORD,
   he, too, has rejected you as ruler."

Saul Asks Forgiveness. [24]Saul replied to Samuel: "I have sinned, for I have disobeyed

---

15, 3: Under the ban: in such wars of extermination, all things (men, cities, beasts, etc.) were to be blotted out; nothing could be reserved for private use. The interpretation of God's will here attributed to Samuel is in keeping with the abhorrent practices of blood revenge prevalent among pastoral, seminomadic peoples such as the Hebrews had recently been. The slaughter of the innocent has never been in conformity with the will of God.

15, 4: The numbers here are not realistic; compare 1 Sm 14, 24 above.

15, 11: I regret: God manifests "regret" when, offended by

men, he takes away his benefits, graces and favors. It is not God, but men, who change, to their own detriment.

15, 22: Samuel is disapproving, not of sacrifices in general, but of merely external sacrifices offered in defiance of God's commandment and without heartfelt obedience.

n: Ex 17, 8-10. 16; Dt 25, 17ff.   *o:* 1 Sm 27, 8; 30, 17; Ex 17, 16; Nm 24, 20.   *p:* Nm 24, 21.   *q:* 1 Sm 27, 8.   *r:* 1 Sm 9, 21. *s:* 1 Sm 28, 18.   *t:* 1 Sm 14, 32.   *u:* Lv 27, 28.   *v:* Prv 21, 3; Hos 6, 6; Am 5, 21-25; Zec 10, 2; Mt 9, 13; 12, 7; Heb 10, 9.

command of the LORD and your instructions. In my fear of the people, I did what they said.[w] [25]Now forgive my sin, and return with me, that I may worship the LORD." [26]But Samuel said to Saul, "I will not return with you, because you rejected the command of the LORD and the LORD rejects you as king of Israel."[x] [27]As Samuel turned to go, Saul seized a loose end of his mantle, and it tore off.[y] [28]So Samuel said to him: "The LORD has torn the kingdom of Israel from you this day, and has given it to a neighbor of yours, who is better than you.[z] [29]The Glory of Israel neither retracts nor repents, for he is not man that he should repent."[a] [30]But he answered: "I have sinned, yet honor me now before the elders of my people and before Israel. Return with me that I may worship the LORD your God." [31]And so Samuel returned with him, and Saul worshiped the LORD.

Agag Is Cut Down. [32]Afterward Samuel commanded, "Bring Agag, king of Amalek, to me." Agag came to him struggling and saying, "So it is bitter death!" [33]And Samuel said,

"As your sword has made women
    childless,
so shall your mother be childless
    among women."

Then he cut Agag down before the LORD in Gilgal.[b]

[34]Samuel departed for Ramah, while Saul went up to his home in Gibeah of Saul. [35]Never again, as long as he lived, did Samuel see Saul. Yet he grieved over Saul, because the LORD regretted having made him king of Israel.[c]

CHAPTER 16

See RG
114

Samuel Sent to Bethlehem. [1d]The LORD said to Samuel: "How long will you grieve for Saul, whom I have rejected as king of Israel? Fill your horn with oil, and be on your way. I am sending you to Jesse of Bethlehem, for I have chosen my king from among his sons."* [2]But Samuel replied: "How can I go? Saul will hear of it and kill me." To this the LORD answered: "Take a heifer along and say, 'I have come to sacrifice to the LORD.' [3]Invite Jesse to the sacrifice, and I myself will tell you what to do; you are to anoint for me the one I point out to you."

[4]Samuel did as the LORD had commanded him. When he entered Bethlehem, the elders of the city came trembling to meet him and inquired, "Is your visit peaceful, O seer?" [5]He replied: "Yes! I have come to sacrifice to the LORD. So cleanse yourselves and join me today for the banquet." He also had Jesse and his sons cleanse themselves and invited them to the sacrifice.[e] [6]As they came, he looked at Eliab and thought, "Surely the LORD's anointed is here before him." [7]But the LORD said to Samuel: "Do not judge from his appearance or from his lofty stature, because I have rejected him. Not as man sees does God see, because man sees the appearance but the LORD looks into the heart."[f] [8g]Then Jesse called Abinadab and presented him before Samuel, who said, "The LORD has not chosen him." [9]Next Jesse presented Shammah, but Samuel said, "The LORD has not chosen this one either." [10]In the same way Jesse presented seven sons before Samuel, but Samuel said to Jesse, "The LORD has not chosen any one of these." [11]Then Samuel asked Jesse, "Are these all the sons you have?" Jesse replied, "There is still the youngest, who is tending the sheep." Samuel said to Jesse, "Send for him; we will not begin the sacrificial banquet until he arrives here."[h] [12]Jesse sent and had the young man brought to them. He was ruddy, a youth handsome to behold and making a splendid appearance. The LORD said, "There—anoint him, for this is he!"[i]

16, 1: The anointing here prepared for is unknown to David's brother Eliab in the next chapter (1 Sm 17, 28), and David is twice anointed after Saul's death (2 Sm 2, 4; 5, 3).

w: 1 Sm 26, 21.   *x:* 1 Kgs 11, 11. 30f.   *y:* 1 Sm 24, 6.   *z:* 1 Sm 28, 17; 2 Sm 7, 15f.   *a:* Nm 23, 19.   *b:* Ex 21, 23.   *c:* Gn 6, 6.
d: 1 Kgs 1, 39; Ru 4, 17-22; 1 Chr 11, 3; Is 11, 1; Lk 2, 4.   *e:* 1 Sm 9, 12f; 20, 26; Ex 19, 10; Jb 1, 5.   *f:* 1 Sm 10, 23f; 1 Chr 28, 9; Prv 15, 11; Jer 17, 10; 20, 12; Lk 16, 15; Acts 1, 24.   *g:* 8ff: 1 Sm 17, 12f; 1 Chr 2, 13ff.   *h:* 1 Sm 15. 28. 34; 2 Sm 7, 8.   *i:* 1 Sm 9, 2.

David's Anointing

In this first story about David in ch 16, 1–13, he still plays a passive role. Even his name is not mentioned until the last verse. His being chosen, though the youngest and the least esteemed of eight brothers, agrees with the biblical motif of the younger being preferred to the elder: Abel to Cain (Gn 4, 2–5), Isaac to Ishmael (Gn 21, 9–13), Jacob to Esau (Gn 27, 28–40), Joseph to Reuben (Gn 37, 3–11; 49, 3–4. 22–26). This indicates that not seniority, but suitability, is the decisive factor.

[13] Then Samuel, with the horn of oil in hand, anointed him in the midst of his brothers; and from that day on, the spirit of the LORD rushed upon David. When Samuel took his leave, he went to Ramah.[j]

Saul's Spirit of Melancholy. [14k] The spirit of the LORD had departed from Saul, and he was tormented by an evil spirit sent by the LORD.* [15] So the servants of Saul said to him: "Please! An evil spirit from God is tormenting you. [16] If your lordship will order it, we, your servants here in attendance on you, will look for a man skilled in playing the harp. When the evil spirit from God comes over you, he will play and you will feel better." [17] Saul then told his servants, "Find me a skillful harpist and bring him to me." [18l] A servant spoke up to say: "I have observed that one of the sons of Jesse of Bethlehem is a skillful harpist. He is also a stalwart soldier, besides being an able speaker, and handsome. Moreover, the LORD is with him."*

David Made Armor-Bearer. [19] Accordingly, Saul dispatched messengers to ask Jesse to send him his son David, who was with the flock. [20] Then Jesse took five loaves of bread, a skin of wine, and a kid, and sent them to Saul by his son David.[m] [21] Thus David came to Saul and entered his service. Saul became very fond of him, made him his armor-bearer,[n] [22] and sent Jesse the message, "Allow David to remain in my service, for he meets with my approval." [23] Whenever the spirit from God seized Saul, David would take the harp and play, and Saul would be relieved and feel better, for the evil spirit would leave him.

CHAPTER 17

See RG 114

The Challenge of Goliath. [1] The Philistines rallied their forces for battle at Socoh in Judah and camped between Socoh and Azekah at Ephes-dammim. [2] Saul and the Israelites also gathered and camped in the Vale of the Terebinth, drawing up their battle line to meet the Philistines. [3] The Philistines were stationed on one hill and the Israelites on an opposite hill, with a valley between them.

[4] A champion named Goliath of Gath came out from the Philistine camp; he was six and a half feet tall. [5] He had a bronze helmet on his head and wore a bronze corselet of scale armor weighing five thousand shekels, [6] and bronze greaves, and had a bronze scimitar* slung from a baldric. [7] The shaft of his javelin was like a weaver's heddle-bar, and its iron head weighed six hundred shekels.* His shield-bearer went before him.[o] [8] He stood and shouted to the ranks of Israel: "Why come out in battle formation? I am a Philistine, and you are Saul's servants. Choose one of your men, and have him come down to me. [9] If he beats me in combat and kills me, we will be your vassals; but if I beat him and kill him, you shall be our vassals and serve us."

16, 14: An evil spirit sent by the LORD: the LORD permitted Saul to be tormented with violent fits of rage.

16, 18: Of the two traditions which describe the coming of David into Saul's service, the oldest Greek translation retains only the one comprised in 1 Sm 16, 14-23; 17, 1-11. 32-54. This effort at consistency is not in accord with the character of the rest of the book; see note on 1 Sm 8, 1. Though square brackets are used in this edition to indicate the passages lacking in the oldest translation, this is meant only to help the reader follow one account at a time. Both are equally a part of the inspired text, as are also the various amplifications and retouchings of the narrative given within brackets in chs 18 and 19.

17, 6: Scimitar: the Hebrew word for this is rather rare, and the nature of the weapon was in doubt until recent years. It is not the same as the sword of v 45.

17, 7: Six hundred shekels: over 15 pounds.

j: 1 Sm 10, 6; 11, 6; Jgs 3, 10; 9, 9; Sir 46, 13.   *k:* 1 Sm 18, 10f.   *l:* 2 Sm 17, 8.   *m:* 1 Sm 9, 7f; 10, 4. 27; 16, 1; 17, 27ff.   *n:* 1 Sm 18, 2.   *o:* 2 Sm 21, 19; 1 Chr 11, 23; 20, 5.

*10*The Philistine continued: "I defy the ranks of Israel today. Give me a man and let us fight together." *11*Saul and all the men of Israel, when they heard this challenge of the Philistine, were dismayed and terror-stricken.

David Comes to the Camp.* *12*[David was the son of an Ephrathite named Jesse, who was from Bethlehem in Judah. He had eight sons, and in the days of Saul was old and well on in years.*p* *13*The three oldest sons of Jesse had followed Saul to war; these three sons who had gone off to war were named, the first-born Eliab, the second son Abinadab, and the third Shammah. *14*David was the youngest. While the three oldest had joined Saul, *15*David would go and come from Saul to tend his father's sheep at Bethlehem.*q*

16[Meanwhile the Philistine came forward and took his stand morning and evening for forty days.

17[Now Jesse said to his son David: "Take this ephah of roasted grain and these ten loaves for your brothers, and bring them quickly to your brothers in the camp. *18*Also take these ten cheeses for the field officer. Greet your brothers and bring home some token from them. *19*Saul, and they, and all Israel are fighting against the Philistines in the Vale of the Terebinth." *20*Early the next morning, having left the flock with a shepherd, David set out on his errand, as Jesse had commanded him. He reached the barricade of the camp just as the army, on their way to the battleground, were shouting their battle cry.*r* *21*The Israelites and the Philistines drew up opposite each other in battle array. *22*David entrusted what he had brought to the keeper of the baggage and hastened to the battle line where he greeted his brothers.*s* *23*While he was talking with them, the Philistine champion, by name Goliath of Gath, came up from the ranks of the Philistines and spoke as before, and David listened. *24*When the Israelites saw the man, they all retreated before him, very much afraid. *25*The Israelites had been saying: "Do you see this man coming up? He comes up to insult Is-

rael. If anyone should kill him, the king would give him great wealth, and his daughter as well, and would grant exemption to his father's family in Israel."*t* *26*David now said to the men standing by: "What will be done for the man who kills this Philistine and frees Israel of the disgrace? Who is this uncircumcised Philistine in any case, that he should insult the armies of the living God?"*u* *27*They repeated the same words to him and said, "That is how the man who kills him will be rewarded." *28*When Eliab, his oldest brother, heard him speaking with the men, he grew angry with David and said: "Why did you come down? With whom have you left those sheep in the desert meanwhile? I know your arrogance and your evil intent. You came down to enjoy the battle!" *29*David replied, "What have I done now?—I was only talking." *30*Yet he turned from him to another and asked the same question; and everyone gave him the same answer as before. *31*The words that David had spoken were overheard and reported to Saul, who sent for him.]

David Fights Goliath. *32*Then David spoke to Saul: "Let your majesty not lose courage. I am at your service to go and fight this Philistine." *33*But Saul answered David, "You cannot go up against this Philistine and fight with him, for you are only a youth, while he has been a warrior from his youth." *34v*Then David told Saul: "Your servant used to tend his father's sheep, and whenever a lion or bear came to carry off a sheep from the flock, *35*I would go after it and attack it and rescue the prey from its mouth. If it attacked me, I would seize it by the jaw, strike it, and kill it. *36*Your servant has killed both a lion and a bear, and this uncircumcised Philistine will be as one of them, because he has insulted the armies of the living God."

*37*David continued: "The LORD, who delivered me from the claws of the lion and the bear, will also keep me safe from the clutches of this Philistine." Saul answered David, "Go! the LORD will be with you."*w*

17, 12-31: An alternative account of how David came to undertake the combat with the Philistine is here inserted; it is continued in 1 Sm 17, 55—18, 6. See note on 1 Sm 16, 18.

p: 1 Sm 16, 1. 10; Ru 1, 2.   *q:* 1 Sm 18, 2; 2 Sm 7, 8.   *r:* 1 Sm 26, 5.   *s:* 1 Sm 25, 13.   *t:* 1 Sm 18, 17; Jos 15, 16.   *u:* 1 Sm 18, 25; Jgs 15, 18; 2 Kgs 19, 4; Is 37, 4.   *v:* 34f: Jgs 14, 6; Sir 47, 3.   *w:* Prv 28, 1.

Preparation for the Encounter. [38]Then Saul clothed David in his own tunic, putting a bronze helmet on his head and arming him with a coat of mail. [39]David also girded himself with Saul's sword over the tunic. He walked with difficulty, however, since he had never tried armor before. He said to Saul, "I cannot go in these, because I have never tried them before." So he took them off. [40]Then, staff in hand, David selected five smooth stones from the wadi and put them in the pocket of his shepherd's bag. With his sling also ready to hand, he approached the Philistine.

David's Victory. [41]With his shield-bearer marching before him, the Philistine also advanced closer and closer to David. [42]When he had sized David up, and seen that he was youthful, and ruddy, and handsome in appearance, he held him in contempt. [43]The Philistine said to David, "Am I a dog that you come against me with a staff?" Then the Philistine cursed David by his gods [44]and said to him, "Come here to me, and I will leave your flesh for the birds of the air and the beasts of the field."[x] [45]David answered him: "You come against me with sword and spear and scimitar, but I come against you in the name of the LORD of hosts, the God of the armies of Israel that you have insulted. [46]Today the LORD shall deliver you into my hand; I will strike you down and cut off your head. This very day I will leave your corpse and the corpses of the Philistine army for the birds of the air and the beasts of the field; thus the whole land shall learn that Israel has a God. [47]All this multitude, too, shall learn that it is not by sword or spear that the LORD saves. For the battle is the LORD's, and he shall deliver you into our hands."[y]

[48]The Philistine then moved to meet David at close quarters, while David ran quickly toward the battle line in the direction of the Philistine. [49]David put his hand into the bag and took out a stone, hurled it with the sling, and struck the Philistine on the forehead. The stone embedded itself in his brow, and he fell prostrate on the ground. [50][Thus David overcame the Philistine with sling and stone; he struck the Philistine mortally, and did it without a sword.][z] [51]Then David ran and stood over him; with the Philistine's own sword [which he drew from its sheath] he dispatched him and cut off his head.[a]

Flight of the Philistines. When they saw that their hero was dead, the Philistines took to flight. [52]Then the men of Israel and Judah, with loud shouts, went in pursuit of the Philistines to the approaches of Gath and to the gates of Ekron, and Philistines fell wounded along the road from Shaaraim as far as Gath and Ekron. [53]On their return from the pursuit of the Philistines, the Israelites looted their camp. [54b]David took the head of the Philistine and brought it to Jerusalem; but he kept Goliath's armor in his own tent.*

David Presented to Saul. [55][When Saul saw David go out to meet the Philistine, he asked his general Abner, "Abner, whose son is that youth?" Abner replied, "As truly as your majesty is alive, I have no idea." [56]And the king said, "Find out whose son the lad is." [57]So when David returned from slaying the Philistine, Abner took him and presented him to Saul. David was still holding the Philistine's head. [58]Saul then asked him, "Whose son are you, young man?" David replied, "I am the son of your servant Jesse of Bethlehem."

CHAPTER 18

See RG 114

David and Jonathan. [1][By the time David finished speaking with Saul, Jonathan had become as fond of David as if his life depended on him; he loved him as he loved himself.[c] [2]Saul laid claim to David that day and did not allow him to return to his father's house.[d] [3]And Jonathan entered into a bond with David, because he loved him as himself. [4]Jonathan divested himself of the mantle he was wearing and gave it to David, along with his military dress, and his sword,

---

17, 54: At the time supposed by this narrative, Jerusalem was still Jebusite, and David had no military tent of his own; the verse is a later gloss.

x: Dt 28, 26; Is 18, 6; Jer 15, 3. *y:* 1 Sm 14, 6; Ps 33, 16. *z:* Sir 47, 4; 1 Mc 4, 30. *a:* 1 Sm 21, 10. *b:* 1 Sm 31, 9. *c:* 1 Sm 19, 1-7; 20, 17; 23, 16; 2 Sm 1, 26; 9, 1. *d:* 1 Sm 16, 21; 17, 15.

his bow and his belt.*e* *5*David then carried out successfully every mission on which Saul sent him. So Saul put him in charge of his soldiers, and this was agreeable to the whole army, even to Saul's own officers.]

Saul's Jealousy. *6*At the approach of Saul and David (on David's return after slaying the Philistine), women came out from each of the cities of Israel to meet King Saul, singing and dancing, with tambourines, joyful songs, and sistrums.*f* *7*The women played and sang:

"Saul has slain his thousands,
　and David his ten thousands."*g*

*8*Saul was very angry and resentful of the song, for he thought: "They give David ten thousands, but only thousands to me. All that remains for him is the kingship." *9*[And from that day on, Saul was jealous of David.

10[*h* The next day an evil spirit from God came over Saul, and he raged in his house. David was in attendance, playing the harp as at other times, while Saul was holding his spear. *11*Saul poised the spear, thinking to nail David to the wall, but twice David escaped him.] *12*Saul then began to fear David, [because the LORD was with him, but had departed from Saul himself.] *13*Accordingly, Saul removed him from his presence by appointing him a field officer. So David led the people on their military expeditions, *14*and prospered in all his enterprises, for the LORD was with him. *15*Seeing how successful he was, Saul conceived a fear of David; *16*on the other hand, all Israel and Judah loved him, since he led them on their expeditions.*i*

17[Saul said to David, "There is my older daughter, Merob, whom I will give you in marriage if you become my champion and fight the battles of the LORD." Saul had in mind, "I shall not touch him; let the Philistines strike him."*j* *18*But David answered Saul: "Who am I? And who are my kin or my father's clan in Israel that I should become the king's son-in-law?" *19*However, when it was time for Saul's daughter Merob to be given to David, she was given in marriage to Adriel the Meholathite instead.]*k*

*20*Now Saul's daughter Michal loved David, and it was reported to Saul, who was pleased at this,*l* *21*for he thought, "I will offer her to him to become a snare for him, so that the Philistines may strike him." [Thus for the second time Saul said to David, "You shall become my son-in-law today."] *22*Saul then ordered his servants to speak to David privately and to say: "The king is fond of you, and all his officers love you. You should become the king's son-in-law." *23*But when Saul's servants mentioned this to David, he said: "Do you think it easy to become the king's son-in-law? I am poor and insignificant." *24*When his servants reported to him the nature of David's answer, *25*Saul commanded them to say this to David: "The king desires no other price for the bride than the foreskins of one hundred Philistines, that he may thus take vengeance on his enemies." Saul intended in this way to bring about David's death through the Philistines.*m* *26*When the servants reported this offer to David, he was pleased with the prospect of becoming the king's son-in-law. [Before the year was up,] *27*David made preparations and sallied forth with his men and slew two hundred Philistines. He brought back their foreskins and counted them out before the king, that he might thus become the king's son-in-law. So Saul gave him his daughter Michal in marriage. *28*Saul thus came to recognize that the LORD was with David; besides, his own daughter Michal loved David. *29*Therefore Saul feared David all the more [and was his enemy ever after].

30[The Philistine chiefs continued to make forays, but each time they took the field, David was more successful against them than any other of Saul's officers, and as a result acquired great fame.]

CHAPTER 19

See RG 118

Persecution of David. *1*Saul discussed his intention of killing David with his son Jonathan and with all his servants. But Saul's son Jonathan, who was very fond of David,*n* *2*told him: "My father Saul is trying

---

e: 2 Sm 1, 22.　*f:* Ex 15, 20f; Jgs 11, 34; Jdt 15, 12.　*g:* 1 Sm 21, 12; 29, 5; Sir 47, 6f.　*h:* 10f: 1 Sm 16, 14; 19, 9f; 20, 33; 22, 6; 26, 8.
i: 2 Sm 5, 2.　*j:* 1 Sm 14, 49; 17, 25.　*k:* 1 Sm 21, 8; 24, 16.　*l:* 1 Sm 14, 49; 25, 44; 26, 23; 2 Sm 3, 13.　*m:* 1 Sm 17, 26; Gn 34, 12.
n: 1 Sm 18, 1; 20, 1ff.

to kill you. Therefore, please be on your guard tomorrow morning; get out of sight and remain in hiding. ³I, however, will go out and stand beside my father in the countryside where you are, and will speak to him about you. If I learn anything, I will let you know."

⁴Jonathan then spoke well of David to his father Saul, saying to him: "Let not your majesty sin against his servant David, for he has committed no offense against you, but has helped you very much by his deeds. ⁵When he took his life in his hands and slew the Philistine, and the LORD brought about a great victory for all Israel through him, you were glad to see it. Why, then, should you become guilty of shedding innocent blood by killing David without cause?"ᵒ ⁶Saul heeded Jonathan's plea and swore, "As the LORD lives, he shall not be killed." ⁷So Jonathan summoned David and repeated the whole conversation to him. Jonathan then brought David to Saul, and David served him as before.

⁸When war broke out again, David went out to fight against the Philistines and inflicted a great defeat upon them, putting them to flight. ⁹ᵖThen an evil spirit from the LORD came upon Saul as he was sitting in his house with spear in hand and David was playing the harp nearby. ¹⁰Saul tried to nail David to the wall with the spear, but David eluded Saul, so that the spear struck only the wall, and David got away safe.

¹¹The same night, Saul sent messengers to David's house to guard it, that he might kill him in the morning. David's wife Michal informed him, "Unless you save yourself tonight, tomorrow you will be killed."* ¹²Then Michal let David down through a window, and he made his escape in safety.�q ¹³Michal took the household idol and laid it in the bed, putting a net of goat's hair at its head and covering it with a spread.ʳ ¹⁴When Saul sent messengers to arrest David, she said, "He is sick." ¹⁵Saul, however, sent the messengers back to see David and commanded them, "Bring him up to me in the bed, that I may kill him." ¹⁶But when the messengers entered, they found the household idol in the bed, with the net of goat's hair at its head. ¹⁷Saul therefore asked Michal: "Why did you play this trick on me? You have helped my enemy to get away!" Michal answered Saul: "He threatened me, 'Let me go or I will kill you.' "

David and Samuel in Ramah. ¹⁸Thus David got safely away; he went to Samuel in Ramah, informing him of all that Saul had done to him. Then he and Samuel went to stay in the sheds. ¹⁹When Saul was told that David was in the sheds near Ramah, ²⁰he sent messengers to arrest David. But when they saw the band of prophets, presided over by Samuel, in a prophetic frenzy, they too fell into the prophetic state.ˢ ²¹Informed of this, Saul sent other messengers, who also fell into the prophetic state. For the third time Saul sent messengers, but they too fell into the prophetic state.

Saul among the Prophets. ²²Saul then went to Ramah himself. Arriving at the cistern of the threshing floor on the bare hilltop, he inquired, "Where are Samuel and David?", and was told, "At the sheds near Ramah." ²³As he set out from the hilltop toward the sheds, the spirit of God came upon him also, and he continued on in a prophetic condition until he reached the spot. At the sheds near Ramah ²⁴he, too, stripped himself of his garments and he, too, remained in the prophetic state in the presence of Samuel; all that day and night he lay naked. That is why they say, "Is Saul also among the prophets?"ᵗ

CHAPTER 20

See RG 118

David Consults with Jonathan. ¹David fled from the sheds near Ramah, and went to Jonathan. "What have I done?" he asked him. "What crime or what offense does your father hold against me that he seeks my life?"ᵘ ²Jonathan answered him:

19, 11: This story in all probability originally followed 1 Sm 18, 29, placing the episode of David's escape on the night of his marriage with Michal.

o: Dt 19, 10; Ps 119, 109.   p: 9f: 1 Sm 16, 14; 18, 10f.   q: Jos 2, 15; Acts 9, 25; 2 Cor 11, 33.   r: Gn 31, 19; Jgs 17, 5; 18, 14. 18. 20.   s: 1 Sm 10, 5f. 10; Nm 11, 25.   t: 1 Sm 10, 10ff.   u: 1 Sm 19, 1-7. 11-17

"Heaven forbid that you should die! My father does nothing, great or small, without disclosing it to me. Why, then, should my father conceal this from me? This cannot be so!" ³But David replied: "Your father is well aware that I am favored with your friendship, so he has decided, 'Jonathan must not know of this lest he be grieved.' Nevertheless, as the LORD lives and as you live, there is but a step between me and death." ⁴Jonathan then said to David, "I will do whatever you wish." ⁵David answered: "Tomorrow is the new moon, when I should in fact dine with the king. Let me go and hide in the open country until evening.ᵛ ⁶If it turns out that your father misses me, say, 'David urged me to let him go on short notice to his city Bethlehem, because his whole clan is holding its seasonal sacrifice there.' ⁷If he says, 'Very well,' your servant is safe. But if he becomes quite angry, you can be sure he has planned some harm. ⁸ʷDo this kindness for your servant because of the LORD's bond between us, into which you brought me: if I am guilty, kill me yourself! Why should you give me up to your father?" ⁹But Jonathan answered: "Not I! If ever I find out that my father is determined to inflict injury upon you, I will certainly let you know." ¹⁰David then asked Jonathan, "Who will tell me if your father gives you a harsh answer?"

Mutual Agreement. ¹¹[Jonathan replied to David, "Come, let us go out into the field." When they were out in the open country together, ¹²Jonathan said to David: "As the LORD, the God of Israel, lives, I will sound out my father about this time tomorrow. Whether he is well disposed toward David or not, I will send you the information. ¹³ˣShould it please my father to bring any injury upon you, may the LORD do thus and so to Jonathan if I do not apprise you of it and send you on your way in peace. May the LORD be with you even as he was with my father. ¹⁴Only this: if I am still alive, may you show me the kindness of the LORD. But if I die, ¹⁵never withdraw your kindness from my house. And when the LORD exterminates all the enemies of David from the surface of the earth, ¹⁶the name of Jonathan must never be allowed by the family of David to die out from among you, or the LORD will make you answer for it." ¹⁷And in his love for David, Jonathan renewed his oath to him, because he loved him as his very self.]

¹⁸Jonathan then said to him: "Tomorrow is the new moon; and you will be missed, since your place will be vacant. ¹⁹On the following day you will be missed all the more. Go to the spot where you hid on the other occasion and wait near the mound there.ʸ ²⁰On the third day of the month I will shoot arrows, as though aiming at a target. ²¹I will then send my attendant to go and recover the arrows. If in fact I say to him, 'Look, the arrow is this side of you; pick it up,' come, for you are safe. As the LORD lives, there will be nothing to fear. ²²But if I say to the boy, 'Look, the arrow is beyond you,' go, for the LORD sends you away. ²³However, in the matter which you and I have discussed, the LORD shall be between you and me forever." ²⁴So David hid in the open country.

On the day of the new moon, when the king sat at table to dine, ²⁵taking his usual place against the wall, Jonathan sat facing him, while Abner sat at the king's side, and David's place was vacant. ²⁶ᶻSaul, however, said nothing that day, for he thought, "He must have become unclean by accident, and not yet have been cleansed."ˣ ²⁷On the next day, the second day of the month, David's place was vacant. Saul inquired of his son Jonathan, "Why has the son of Jesse not come to table yesterday or today?" ²⁸Jonathan answered Saul: "David urgently asked me to let him go to his city, Bethlehem. ²⁹'Please let me go,' he begged, 'for we are to have a clan sacrifice in our city, and my brothers insist on my presence. Now, therefore, if you think well of me, give me leave to visit my brothers.' That is why he has not

20, 26: The meal on the first day of the month would have religious overtones, and a ritual impurity (Lv 15, 16; Dt 23, 10ff) would bar David from sharing in it.

v: Nm 10, 10; 28, 11-15.   *w:* 8f: 1 Sm 23, 17f.   *x:* 13-16: 1 Sm 24, 22f; 2 Sm 9, 1-13; 21, 7.   *y:* 1 Sm 19, 1-7.   *z:* 1 Sm 16, 5; Lv 7, 20f; 15, 1ff.

come to the king's table." *30*But Saul was extremely angry with Jonathan and said to him: "Son of a rebellious woman, do I not know that, to your own shame and to the disclosure of your mother's shame, you are the companion of Jesse's son? *31*Why, as long as the son of Jesse lives upon the earth, you cannot make good your claim to the kingship! So send for him, and bring him to me, for he is doomed."*a* *32*But Jonathan asked his father Saul: "Why should he die? What has he done?" *33*At this Saul brandished his spear to strike him, and thus Jonathan learned that his father was resolved to kill David.*b* *34*Jonathan sprang up from the table in great anger and took no food that second day of the month, for he was grieved on David's account, since his father had railed against him.

Jonathan's Farewell. *35*The next morning Jonathan went out into the field with a little boy for his appointment with David. *36*There he said to the boy, "Run and fetch the arrow." And as the boy ran, he shot an arrow beyond him in the direction of the city. *37*When the boy made for the spot where Jonathan had shot the arrow, Jonathan called after him, "The arrow is farther on!" *38*Again he called to his lad, "Hurry, be quick, don't delay!" Jonathan's boy picked up the arrow and brought it to his master. *39*The boy knew nothing; only Jonathan and David knew what was meant. *40*Then Jonathan gave his weapons to this boy of his and said to him, "Go, take them to the city." *41*When the boy had left, David rose from beside the mound and prostrated himself on the ground three times before Jonathan in homage. They kissed each other and wept aloud together. *42c*At length Jonathan said to David, "Go in peace, in keeping with what we two have sworn by the name of the LORD: 'The LORD shall be between you and me, and between your posterity and mine forever.' "

CHAPTER 21

See RG 118

*1*Then David departed on his way, while Jonathan went back into the city.

The Holy Bread. *2*David went to Ahimelech, the priest of Nob, who came trembling to meet him and asked, "Why are you alone? Is there no one with you?"*d* *3*David answered the priest: "The king gave me a commission and told me to let no one know anything about the business on which he sent me or the commission he gave me. For that reason I have arranged a meeting place with my men. *4e*Now what have you on hand? Give me five loaves, or whatever you can find." *5*But the priest replied to David, "I have no ordinary bread on hand, only holy bread; if the men have abstained from women, you may eat some of that."* *6*David answered the priest: "We have indeed been segregated from women as on previous occasions. Whenever I go on a journey, all the young men are consecrated—even for a secular journey. All the more so today, when they are consecrated at arms!" *7*So the priest gave him holy bread, for no other bread was on hand except the showbread which had been removed from the LORD's presence and replaced by fresh bread when it was taken away.*f* *8*One of Saul's servants was there that day, detained before the LORD; his name was Doeg the Edomite, and he was Saul's chief henchman.

The Sword of Goliath. *9*David then asked Ahimelech: "Do you have a spear or a sword on hand? I brought along neither my sword nor my weapons, because the king's business was urgent." *10*The priest replied: "The sword of Goliath the Philistine, whom you killed in the Vale of the Terebinth, is here [wrapped in a mantle] behind an ephod. If you wish to take that, take it; there is no sword here except that one." David said: "There is none to match it. Give it to me!"*g*

David a Fugitive. *11*That same day David took to flight from Saul, going to Achish,

---

† **21, 5f:** From women: the high priest, willing to distribute the holy bread to David and his men, requires that they be free from ritual uncleanness, associated in Old Testament times (Lv 15. 18) with the marriage act. David's answer supposes the discipline of a military campaign under the conditions of "holy war" (Dt 23, 10).

a: 2 Sm 12, 5.   *b:* 1 Sm 18, 11.   *c:* 2 Sm 9, 1; 21, 7.   *d:* Is 10, 32; Mk 2, 26.   *e:* Lv 24, 5; 9.   *f:* 1 Sm 22, 9; Lv 24, 5-9; Mt 12, 3f; Mk 2, 26; Lk 6, 3ff.   *g:* 1 Sm 17, 51. 54.

king of Gath.[h] [12]But the servants of Achish said, "Is this not David, the king of the land? During their dances do they not sing,

'Saul has slain his thousands,
but David his ten thousands'?"[i]

[13]David took note of these remarks and became very much afraid of Achish, king of Gath. [14]So, as they watched, he feigned insanity and acted like a madman in their hands, drumming on the doors of the gate and drooling onto his beard. [15]Finally Achish said to his servants: "You see the man is mad. Why did you bring him to me? [16]Do I not have enough madmen, that you bring in this one to carry on in my presence? Should this fellow come into my house?"

CHAPTER 22

See RG
118

[1]David left Gath and escaped to the cave of Adullam. When his brothers and the rest of his family heard about it, they came down to him there.[j] [2]He was joined by all those who were in difficulties or in debt, or who were embittered, and he became their leader. About four hundred men were with him.

[3]From there David went to Mizpeh of Moab and said to the king of Moab, "Let my father and mother stay with you, until I learn what God will do for me." [4]He left them with the king of Moab, and they stayed with him as long as David remained in the refuge.*

[5]But the prophet Gad said to David: "Do not remain in the refuge. Leave, and go to the land of Judah." And so David left and went to the forest of Hereth.

Doeg Betrays Ahimelech. [6]Now Saul heard that David and his men had been located. At the time he was sitting in Gibeah under a tamarisk tree on the high place, holding his spear, while all his servants were standing by.[k] [7]So he said to them: "Listen, men of Benjamin! Will the son of Jesse give all of you fields and vineyards? Will he make each of you an officer over a thousand or a hundred men,[l] [8]that you have all con-

spired against me and no one tells me that my son has made an agreement with the son of Jesse? None of you shows sympathy for me or discloses to me that my son has stirred up my servant to be an enemy against me, as is the case today." [9m]Then Doeg the Edomite, who was standing with the officers of Saul, spoke up: "I saw the son of Jesse come to Ahimelech, son of Ahitub, in Nob. [10]He consulted the LORD for him and gave him supplies, and the sword of Goliath the Philistine as well."

Slaughter of the Priests. [11]At this the king sent a summons to Ahimelech the priest, son of Ahitub, and to all his family who were priests in Nob; and they all came to the king. [12]Then Saul said, "Listen, son of Ahitub!" He replied, "Yes, my lord." [13]Saul asked him, "Why did you conspire against me with the son of Jesse by giving him food and a sword and by consulting God for him, that he might rebel against me and become my enemy, as is the case today?" [14]Ahimelech answered the king: "And who among all your servants is as loyal as David, the king's son-in-law, captain of your bodyguard, and honored in your own house? [15]Is this the first time I have consulted God for him? No indeed! Let not the king accuse his servant or anyone in my family of such a thing. Your servant knows nothing at all, great or small, about the whole matter." [16]But the king said, "You shall die, Ahimelech, with all your family." [17]The king then commanded his henchmen standing by: "Make the rounds and kill the priests of the LORD, for they assisted David. They knew he was a fugitive and yet failed to inform me." But the king's servants refused to lift a hand to strike the priests of the LORD.[n]

[18]The king therefore commanded Doeg, "You make the rounds and kill the priests!" So Doeg the Edomite went from one to the next and killed the priests himself, slaying on that day eighty-five who wore the linen ephod. [19]Saul also put the priestly city of

---

22, 4-5: Refuge: seemingly connected with the cave complex spoken of in v 1.

h: 1 Sm 27, 2; 29, 5.   *i:* 1 Sm 18, 7; 29, 5.   *j:* 2 Sm 23, 13; Ps 63; Mi 1, 15.   *k:* Ps 52.   *l:* 1 Sm 8, 14.   *m:* 9f: 1 Sm 21, 2-10.
n: 1 Sm 2, 31. 33; 21, 7.

Nob to the sword, including men and women, children and infants, and oxen, asses and sheep.

Abiathar Escapes. *20*One son of Ahimelech, son of Ahitub, named Abiathar, escaped and fled to David.*o* *21*When Abiathar told David that Saul had slain the priests of the LORD, *22*David said to him: "I knew that day, when Doeg the Edomite was there, that he would surely tell Saul. I am responsible for the death of all your family. *23*Stay with me. Fear nothing; he that seeks your life must seek my life also. You are under my protection."

See RG 118

CHAPTER 23

Keilah Liberated. *1*David received information that the Philistines were attacking Keilah and plundering the threshing floors.*p* *2*So he consulted the LORD, inquiring, "Shall I go and defeat these Philistines?" The LORD answered, "Go, for you will defeat the Philistines and rescue Keilah."*q* *3*But David's men said to him: "We are afraid here in Judah. How much more so if we go to Keilah against the forces of the Philistines!" *4*Again David consulted the LORD, who answered, "Go down to Keilah, for I will deliver the Philistines into your power." *5*David then went with his men to Keilah and fought with the Philistines. He drove off their cattle and inflicted a severe defeat on them, and thus rescued the inhabitants of Keilah.

*6*Abiathar, son of Ahimelech, who had fled to David, went down with David to Keilah, taking the ephod with him.*r*

Flight from Keilah. *7*When Saul was told that David had entered Keilah, he said: "God has put him in my grip. Now he has shut himself in, for he has entered a city with gates and bars." *8*Saul then called all the people to war, in order to go down to Keilah and besiege David and his men. *9*When David found out that Saul was planning to harm him, he said to the priest Abiathar, "Bring forward the ephod."*s* *10*David then said: "O LORD God of Israel, your servant has heard a report that Saul plans to come to Keilah, to

destroy the city on my account. *11*Will they hand me over? And now: will Saul come down as your servant has heard? O LORD God of Israel, tell your servant." The LORD answered, "He will come down." *12*David then asked, "Will the citizens of Keilah deliver me and my men into the grasp of Saul?" And the LORD answered, "Yes." *13*So David and his men, about six hundred in number, left Keilah and wandered from place to place. When Saul was informed that David had escaped from Keilah, he abandoned the expedition.

David and Jonathan in Horesh. *14*David now lived in the refuges in the desert, or in the barren hill country near Ziph. Though Saul sought him continually, the LORD did not deliver David into his grasp. *15*David was apprehensive because Saul had come out to seek his life; but while he was at Horesh in the barrens near Ziph, *16*Saul's son, Jonathan, came down there to David and strengthened his resolve in the LORD.*t* *17*He said to him: "Have no fear, my father Saul shall not lay a hand to you. You shall be king of Israel and I shall be second to you. Even my father Saul knows this." *18*They made a joint agreement before the LORD in Horesh, where David remained, while Jonathan returned to his home.*u*

Treachery of the Ziphites. *19*Some of the Ziphites went up to Saul in Gibeah and said, "David is hiding among us, now in the refuges, and again at Horesh, or on the hill of Hachilah, south of the wasteland.*v* *20*Therefore, whenever the king wishes to come down, let him do so. It will be our task to deliver him into the king's grasp." *21*Saul replied: "The LORD bless you for your sympathy toward me.*w* *22*Go now and make sure once more! Take note of the place where he sets foot" (for he thought, perhaps they are playing some trick on me). *23*"Look around and learn in which of all the various hiding places he is holding out. Then come back to me with sure information, and I will go with you. If he is in the region, I will search him out among all the families of Judah." *24*So

---

o: 1 Sm 23, 6; 30, 7; 1 Kgs 2, 28f.   *p:* Jos 15, 44.   *q:* 1 Sm 28, 6.   *r:* 1 Sm 22, 20; 30, 7.   *s:* 1 Sm 2, 28.   *t:* 1 Sm 18, 1.   *u:* 1 Sm 18, 3; 20, 8.   *v:* 1 Sm 26, 1-3; Ps 54.   *w:* 2 Sm 2, 5.

they went off to Ziph ahead of Saul. At this time David and his men were in the desert below Maon, in the Arabah south of the wasteland.[x]

Escape from Saul. [25]When Saul and his men came looking for him, David got word of it and went down to the gorge in the desert below Maon. Saul heard of this and pursued David into the desert below Maon. [26]As Saul moved along one rim of the gorge, David and his men took to the other. David was in anxious flight to escape Saul, and Saul and his men were attempting to outflank David and his men in order to capture them, [27]when a messenger came to Saul, saying, "Come quickly, because the Philistines have invaded the land." [28]Saul interrupted his pursuit of David and went to meet the Philistines. This is how that place came to be called the Gorge of Divisions.

CHAPTER 24

See RG 118

David Spares Saul. [1]David then went up from there and stayed in the refuges behind Engedi. [2]And when Saul returned from the pursuit of the Philistines, he was told that David was in the desert near Engedi. [3]So Saul took three thousand picked men from all Israel and went in search of David and his men in the direction of the wild goat crags. [4]When he came to the sheepfolds along the way, he found a cave, which he entered to ease nature. David and his men were occupying the inmost recesses of the cave.[y]

[5]David's servants said to him, "This is the day of which the LORD said to you, 'I will deliver your enemy into your grasp; do with him as you see fit.' " So David moved up and stealthily cut off an end of Saul's mantle. [6]Afterward, however, David regretted that he had cut off an end of Saul's mantle.[z] [7]He said to his men, "The LORD forbid that I should do such a thing to my master, the LORD's anointed, as to lay a hand on him, for he is the LORD's anointed."[a] [8]With these words David restrained his men and would not permit them to attack Saul. Saul then left the cave and went on his way. [9]David also

stepped out of the cave, calling to Saul, "My lord the king!" When Saul looked back, David bowed to the ground in homage [10]and asked Saul: "Why do you listen to those who say, 'David is trying to harm you'? [11]You see for yourself today that the LORD just now delivered you into my grasp in the cave. I had some thought of killing you, but I took pity on you instead. I decided, 'I will not raise a hand against my lord, for he is the LORD's anointed and a father to me.' [12]Look here at this end of your mantle which I hold. Since I cut off an end of your mantle and did not kill you, see and be convinced that I plan no harm and no rebellion. I have done you no wrong, though you are hunting me down to take my life.[b] [13]The LORD will judge between me and you, and the LORD will exact justice from you in my case. I shall not touch you. [14]The old proverb says, 'From the wicked comes forth wickedness.' So I will take no action against you. [15]Against whom are you on campaign, O king of Israel? Whom are you pursuing? A dead dog, or a single flea! [16]The LORD will be the judge; he will decide between me and you. May he see this, and take my part, and grant me justice beyond your reach!"[c]

Saul's Remorse. [17]When David finished saying these things to Saul, Saul answered, "Is that your voice, my son David?" And he wept aloud. [18]Saul then said to David: "You are in the right rather than I; you have treated me generously, while I have done you harm. [19]Great is the generosity you showed me today, when the LORD delivered me into your grasp and you did not kill me. [20]For if a man meets his enemy, does he send him away unharmed? May the LORD reward you generously for what you have done this day. [21]And now, since I know that you shall surely be king and that sovereignty over Israel shall come into your possession,[d] [22]swear to me by the LORD that you will not destroy my descendants and that you will not blot out my name and family."[e] [23]David gave Saul his oath and Saul returned home, while David and his men went up to the refuge.

---

x: 1 Sm 25, 2. y: Ps 57. z: 1 Sm 15, 27. a: 1 Sm 10, 1; 31, 4; 2 Sm 1, 14. b: Rom 12, 19. c: 1 Sm 18, 19. 31; 26, 19; Pss 35, 1ff; 43, 1. d: 1 Sm 26, 25. e: 2 Sm 9, 1ff.

CHAPTER 25

See RG 118

Death of Samuel. *1*Samuel died, and all Israel gathered to mourn him; they buried him at his home in Ramah.*f*

Nabal and Abigail. *2*Then David went down to the desert of Maon. There was a man of Maon who had property in Carmel; he was very wealthy, owning three thousand sheep and a thousand goats. At this time he was present for the shearing of his flock in Carmel.*g* *3*The man was named Nabal, his wife, Abigail. The woman was intelligent and attractive, but Nabal himself, a Calebite, was harsh and ungenerous in his behavior.*h* *4*When David heard in the desert that Nabal was shearing his flock, *5*he sent ten young men, instructing them: "Go up to Carmel. Pay Nabal a visit and greet him in my name. *6*Say to him, 'Peace be with you, my brother, and with your family, and with all who belong to you. *7*I have just heard that shearers are with you. Now, when your shepherds were with us, we did them no injury, neither did they miss anything all the while they were in Carmel. *8*Ask your servants and they will tell you so. Look kindly on these young men, since we come at a festival time. Please give your servants and your son David whatever you can manage.' "

*9*When David's young men arrived, they delivered this message fully to Nabal in David's name, and then waited. *10*But Nabal answered the servants of David: "Who is David? Who is the son of Jesse? Nowadays there are many servants who run away from their masters. *11*Must I take my bread, my wine, my meat that I have slaughtered for my own shearers, and give them to men who come from I know not where?" *12*So David's young men retraced their steps and on their return reported to him all that had been said. *13*Thereupon David said to his men, "Let everyone gird on his sword." And so everyone, David included, girded on his sword. About four hundred men went up after David, while two hundred remained with the baggage.

*14*But Nabal's wife Abigail was informed of this by one of the servants, who said: "David sent messengers from the desert to greet our master, but he flew at them screaming. *15*Yet these men were very good to us. We were done no injury, neither did we miss anything all the while we were living among them during our stay in the open country. *16*For us they were like a rampart night and day the whole time we were pasturing the sheep near them. *17*Now, see what you can do, for you must realize that otherwise evil is in store for our master and for his whole family. He is so mean that no one can talk to him." *18*Abigail quickly got together two hundred loaves, two skins of wine, five dressed sheep, five seahs of roasted grain, a hundred cakes of pressed raisins, and two hundred cakes of pressed figs, and loaded them on asses. *19*She then said to her servants, "Go on ahead; I will follow you." But she did not tell her husband Nabal.

*20*As she came down through a mountain defile riding on an ass, David and his men were also coming down from the opposite direction. When she met them, *21*David had just been saying: "Indeed, it was in vain that I guarded all this man's possessions in the desert, so that he missed nothing. He has repaid good with evil. *22*May God do thus and so to David, if by morning I leave a single male alive among all those who belong to him."*i* *23*As soon as Abigail saw David, she dismounted quickly from the ass and, falling prostrate on the ground before David, did him homage. *24*As she fell at his feet she said:

"My lord, let the blame be mine. Please let your handmaid speak to you, and listen to the words of your handmaid. *25*Let not my lord pay attention to that worthless man Nabal, for he is just like his name. Fool is his name,* and he acts the fool. I, your handmaid, did not see the young men whom my lord sent. *26*Now, therefore, my lord, as the LORD lives, and as you live, it is the LORD who has kept you from shedding blood and from avenging yourself personally. May your enemies and those who seek to harm my lord become as Nabal!* *27*Accept this

25, 25: Fool is his name: Nabal in Hebrew means "a fool."
25, 26: Abigail anticipates that some misfortune will shortly overtake Nabal, as in fact it does (vv 37-38).

f: 1 Sm 28, 3; Sir 46, 13-20. *g:* 1 Sm 23, 24; Jos 15, 55. *h:* 1 Sm 27, 3; Jos 14, 6; 1 Chr 2, 42. 45. *i:* 1 Kgs 16, 11; 21, 21; 2 Kgs 9, 8.

Abigail

The placement of this story between the two accounts of David's chances to kill Saul (chs 24 and 26) is significant. While David avoids shedding Saul's blood, he is almost guilty of killing many innocent people in Nabal's household. Nabal is like Saul in many ways. He is "rich as a king" and was probably the chieftain among the Calebites, one of the leading clans of Judah. The name Nabal means "fool" or "brute." His wife, Abigail, on the other hand, is his complete opposite. The only other Abigail in the Bible is David's sister (1 Chr 2, 16).

present, then, which your maidservant has brought for my lord, and let it be given to the young men who follow my lord. [28]Please forgive the transgression of your handmaid, for the LORD shall certainly establish a lasting dynasty for my lord, because your lordship is fighting the battles of the LORD, and there is no evil to be found in you your whole life long. [29]If anyone rises to pursue you and to seek your life, may the life of my lord be bound in the bundle of the living* in the care of the LORD your God; but may he hurl out the lives of your enemies as from the hollow of a sling.[j] [30]And when the LORD carries out for my lord the promise of success he has made concerning you, and appoints you as commander over Israel,[k] [31]you shall not have this as a qualm or burden on your conscience, my lord, for having shed innocent blood or for having avenged yourself personally. When the LORD confers this benefit on your lordship, remember your handmaid." [32]David said to Abigail: "Blessed be the LORD, the God of Israel, who sent you to meet me today. [33]Blessed be your good judgment and blessed be you yourself, who this day have prevented me from shedding blood and from avenging myself personally. [34]Otherwise, as the LORD, the God of Israel, lives, who has restrained me from harming you, if you had not come so promptly to meet me, by dawn Nabal would not have had a single man or boy left alive." [35]David then took from her what she

had brought him and said to her: "Go up to your home in peace! See, I have granted your request as a personal favor."

Nabal's Death. [36]When Abigail came to Nabal, there was a drinking party in his house like that of a king, and Nabal was merry because he was very drunk. So she told him nothing at all before daybreak the next morning. [37]But then, when Nabal had become sober, his wife told him what had happened. At this his courage died within him, and he became like a stone. [38]About ten days later the LORD struck him and he died. [39]On hearing that Nabal was dead, David said: "Blessed be the LORD, who has requited the insult I received at the hand of Nabal, and who restrained his servant from doing evil, but has punished Nabal for his own evil deeds."

David Marries Abigail and Ahinoam. David then sent a proposal of marriage to Abigail. [40]When David's servants came to Abigail in Carmel, they said to her, "David has sent us to you that he may take you as his wife." [41]Rising and bowing to the ground, she answered, "Your handmaid would become a slave to wash the feet of my lord's servants." [42]She got up immediately, mounted an ass, and followed David's messengers, with her five maids following in attendance upon her. She became his wife, [43]l and David also married Ahinoam of Jezreel. Thus both of them were his wives; but Saul gave David's wife Michal, Saul's own daughter, to Palti, son of Laish, who was from Gallim.[m]

25, 29: The bundle of the living: the figure is perhaps taken from the practice of tying up valuables in a kerchief or bag for safekeeping. Abigail desires that David enjoy permanent peace and security, but that his enemies be subject to constant agitation and humiliation like a stone whirled about, cast out of the sling, and thereafter disregarded.

j: Ps 69, 28. *k:* 1 Sm 13, 14; 2 Sm 3, 10. *l:* 1 Sm 27, 3. *m:* 1 Sm 18, 20; 27, 3; 30, 5; 2 Sm 3, 2. 13ff; 1 Chr 3, 1.

CHAPTER 26

See RG 118

Saul's Life Again Spared. [1] [n] Men from Ziph came to Saul in Gibeah, reporting that David was hiding on the hill of Hachilah at the edge of the wasteland. [2] So Saul went off down to the desert of Ziph with three thousand picked men of Israel, to search for David in the desert of Ziph. [3] Saul camped beside the road on the hill of Hachilah, at the edge of the wasteland. David, who was living in the desert, saw that Saul had come into the desert after him [4] and sent out scouts, who confirmed Saul's arrival. [5] David himself then went to the place where Saul was encamped and examined the spot where Saul and Abner, son of Ner, the general, had their sleeping quarters. Saul's were within the barricade, and all his soldiers were camped around him. [o] [6] David asked Ahimelech the Hittite, and Abishai, son of Zeruiah and brother of Joab, "Who will go down into the camp with me to Saul?" Abishai replied, "I will." [p] [7] So David and Abishai went among Saul's soldiers by night and found Saul lying asleep within the barricade, with his spear thrust into the ground at his head and Abner and his men sleeping around him.

[8] Abishai whispered to David: "God has delivered your enemy into your grasp this day. Let me nail him to the ground with one thrust of the spear; I will not need a second thrust!" [q] [9] But David said to Abishai, "Do not harm him, for who can lay hands on the LORD's anointed and remain unpunished? [10] As the LORD lives," David continued, "it must be the LORD himself who will strike him, whether the time comes for him to die, or he goes out and perishes in battle. [11] But the LORD forbid that I touch his anointed! Now take the spear which is at his head and the water jug, and let us be on our way." [12] So David took the spear and the water jug from their place at Saul's head, and they got away without anyone's seeing or knowing or awakening. All remained asleep, because the LORD had put them into a deep slumber.

David Taunts Abner. [13] Going across to an opposite slope, David stood on a remote hilltop at a great distance from Abner, son of Ner, and the troops. [14] He then shouted, "Will you not answer, Abner?" And Abner answered, "Who is it that calls me?" [15] David said to Abner: "Are you not a man whose like does not exist in Israel? Why, then, have you not guarded your lord the king when one of his subjects went to kill the king, your lord? [16] This is no creditable service you have performed. As the LORD lives, you people deserve death because you have not guarded your lord, the LORD's anointed. Go, look: where are the king's spear and the water jug that was at his head?"

Saul Admits His Guilt. [17] Saul recognized David's voice and asked, "Is that your voice, my son David?" David answered, "Yes, my lord the king." [18] He continued: "Why does my lord pursue his servant? What have I done? What evil do I plan? [19] Please, now, let my lord the king listen to the words of his servant. If the LORD has incited you against me, let an offering appease him; but if men, may they be cursed before the LORD, because they have exiled me so that this day I have no share in the LORD's inheritance, [*] but am told: 'Go, serve other gods!' [r] [20] Do not let my blood flow to the ground far from the presence of the LORD. For the king of Israel has come out to seek a single flea as if he were hunting partridge in the mountains." [21] Then Saul said: "I have done wrong. Come back, my son David, I will not harm you again, because you have held my life precious today. Indeed, I have been a fool and have made a serious mistake." [22] But David answered: "Here is the king's spear. Let an attendant come over to get it. [23] The LORD will reward each man for his justice and faithfulness. Today, though the LORD delivered you into my grasp, I would not harm the LORD's anointed. [s] [24] As I valued your life highly today, so may the LORD value my life highly and deliver me from all difficulties." [25] Then Saul said to David: "Blessed are you,

---

26, 19: The LORD's inheritance: the land of Israel (Dt 32, 8f), under the Lord's special protection, where he could be freely worshiped.

n: 1f: 1 Sm 23, 19f; Ps 54.   o: 1 Sm 17, 20.   p: 1 Chr 2, 16.   q: 1 Sm 18, 11; 19, 10.   r: 1 Sm 24, 16.   s: 1 Sm 18, 20.

my son David! You shall certainly succeed in whatever you undertake." David went his way, and Saul returned to his home.[t]

CHAPTER 27

See RG
118

Refuge among Philistines. [1]But David said to himself: "I shall perish some day at the hand of Saul. I have no choice but to escape to the land of the Philistines; then Saul will give up his continuous search for me throughout the land of Israel, and I shall be out of his reach." [2]Accordingly, David departed with his six hundred men and went over to Achish, son of Maoch, king of Gath.[u] [3]David and his men lived in Gath with Achish; each one had his family, and David had his two wives, Ahinoam from Jezreel and Abigail, the widow of Nabal from Carmel.[v] [4]When Saul was told that David had fled to Gath, he no longer searched for him.

In Ziklag. [5]David said to Achish: "If I meet with your approval, let me have a place to live in one of the country towns. Why should your servant live with you in the royal city?" [6]That same day Achish gave him Ziklag, which has, therefore, belonged to the kings of Judah* up to the present time.[w] [7]In all, David lived a year and four months in the country of the Philistines.[x]

Raids on Israel's Foes. [8]David and his men went up and made raids on the Geshurites, Girzites, and Amalekites—peoples living in the land between Telam, on the approach to Shur, and the land of Egypt.[y] [9]In attacking the land David would not leave a man or woman alive, but would carry off sheep, oxen, asses, camels, and clothes. On his return he brought these to Achish, [10]who asked, "Whom did you raid this time?" And David answered, "The Negeb of Judah," or "The Negeb of Jarahmeel," or "The Negeb of the Kenites."[z] [11]But David would not leave a man or woman alive to be brought to Gath, fearing that they would betray him by

saying, "This is what David did." This was his custom as long as he lived in the country of the Philistines. [12]And Achish trusted David, thinking, "He must certainly be detested by his people Israel. I shall have him as my vassal forever."

CHAPTER 28

See RG
118-19

[1]In those days the Philistines mustered their military forces to fight against Israel. So Achish said to David, "You realize, of course, that you and your men must go out on campaign with me to Jezreel." [2]David answered Achish, "Good! Now you shall learn what your servant can do." Then Achish said to David, "I shall appoint you my permanent bodyguard."

[3]Now Samuel had died and, after being mourned by all Israel, was buried in his city, Ramah. Meanwhile Saul had driven mediums and fortune-tellers out of the land.[a]

Saul in Dismay. [4]The Philistine levies advanced to Shunem and encamped. Saul, too, mustered all Israel; they camped on Gilboa. [5]When Saul saw the camp of the Philistines, he was dismayed and lost heart completely. [6]He therefore consulted the LORD; but the LORD gave no answer, whether in dreams or by the Urim or through prophets.[b] [7]Then Saul said to his servants, "Find me a woman who is a medium, to whom I can go to seek counsel through her." His servants answered him, "There is a woman in Endor who is a medium."[c]

The Witch of Endor. [8]So he disguised himself, putting on other clothes, and set out with two companions. They came to the woman by night, and Saul said to her, "Tell my fortune through a ghost; conjure up for me the one I ask you to."[d] [9]But the woman answered him, "You are surely aware of what Saul has done, in driving the mediums and fortune-tellers out of the land. Why, then, are you laying snares for my life, to have me killed?" [10]But Saul swore to her by

27, 6: Has . . . belonged to the kings of Judah: as a personal holding, outside the system of tribal lands; Jerusalem, when taken by David, had a similar status (2 Sm 5, 7–9).

t: 1 Sm 24, 21. u: 1 Sm 21, 11-16. v: 1 Sm 25, 3. 44; 30, 3ff; 2 Sm 2, 3. w: 1 Sm 30, 1. x: 1 Sm 29, 3. y: 1 Sm 15, 3. 7. z: 1 Sm 30, 14. 29; 1 Chr 2, 9. 25. 42. a: 1 Sm 25, 1; Sir 46, 20. b: 1 Sm 14, 37. 41; Ex 28, 30; Lv 8, 8. c: Lv 19, 31; 20, 27; Dt 18, 10ff; 1 Chr 10, 13f; Acts 16, 16. d: 1 Kgs 14, 2.

Three Ways of Divining

Three means of divining (1 Sm 28, 6) were dreams, or incubation, in which one slept at a holy place, anticipating the answer to an inquiry; Urim or lots, used earlier in 14, 41; and prophets like the man of God in 9, 1—10, 16.

the LORD, "As the LORD lives, you shall incur no blame for this." *11*Then the woman asked him, "Whom do you want me to conjure up?" and he answered, "Samuel."

*Samuel Appears. 12*When the woman saw Samuel, she shrieked at the top of her voice and said to Saul, "Why have you deceived me? You are Saul!"* *13*But the king said to her, "Have no fear. What do you see?" The woman answered Saul, "I see a preternatural being rising from the earth." *14*"What does he look like?" asked Saul. And she replied, "It is an old man who is rising, clothed in a mantle." Saul knew that it was Samuel, and so he bowed face to the ground in homage.

*Saul's Doom. 15*Samuel then said to Saul, "Why do you disturb me by conjuring me up?" Saul replied: "I am in great straits, for the Philistines are waging war against me and God has abandoned me. Since he no longer answers me through prophets or in dreams, I have called you to tell me what I should do."*e 16*To this Samuel said: "But why do you ask me, if the LORD has abandoned you and is with your neighbor?*f 17*The LORD has done to you what he foretold through me: he has torn the kingdom from your grasp and has given it to your neighbor David.

18"Because you disobeyed the LORD's directive and would not carry out his fierce anger against Amalek, the LORD has done this to you today.*g 19*Moreover, the LORD will deliver Israel, and you as well, into the clutches of the Philistines. By tomorrow you and your sons will be with me, and the LORD will have delivered the army of Israel into the hands of the Philistines."*h*

*Saul's Despair. 20*Immediately Saul fell full length on the ground, for he was badly shaken by Samuel's message. Moreover, he had no bodily strength left, since he had eaten nothing all that day and night. *21*Then the woman came to Saul, and seeing that he was quite terror-stricken, said to him: "Remember, your maidservant obeyed you: I took my life in my hands and fulfilled the request you made of me. *22*Now you, in turn, please listen to your maidservant. Let me set something before you to eat, so that you may have strength when you go on your way." *23*But he refused, saying, "I will not eat." However, when his servants joined the woman in urging him, he listened to their entreaties, got up from the ground, and sat on a couch. *24*The woman had a stall-fed calf in the house, which she now quickly slaughtered. Then taking flour, she kneaded it and baked unleavened bread. *25*She set the meal before Saul and his servants, and they ate. Then they stood up and left the same night.

CHAPTER 29

See RG
118-19

*David's Aid Rejected. 1*Now the Philistines had mustered all their forces in Aphek, and the Israelites were encamped at the spring of Harod near Jezreel.*i 2*As the Philistine lords were marching their groups of a hundred and a thousand, David and his men were marching in the rear guard with Achish. *3*The Philistine chiefs asked, "What are those Hebrews doing here?" And Achish answered them: "Why, that is David, the officer of Saul, king of Israel. He has been with me now for a year or two, and I have no fault to find with him from the day he came over to me until the

28, 12: Human beings cannot communicate at will with the souls of the dead. God may, however, permit a departed soul to appear to the living and even to disclose things unknown to them. Saul's own prohibition of necromancy and divination (v 3) was in keeping with the consistent teaching of the Old Testament. If we are to credit the reality of the

apparition to Saul, it was due, not to the summons of the witch, but to God's will; the woman merely furnished the occasion.

e: Sir 46, 20. *f*: 1 Sm 15, 27f. *g*: 1 Sm 15, 18f. 26. *h*: 1 Sm 31, 2-6; Sir 46, 20. *i*: 1 Sm 4, 1.

present."[j] [4]But the Philistine chiefs were angered at this and said to him: "Send that man back! Let him return to the place you picked out for him. He must not go down into battle with us, lest during the battle he become our enemy. For how else can he win back his master's favor, if not with the heads of these men of ours?[k] [5]Is this not the David of whom they sing during their dances,

'Saul has slain his thousands,
    but David his ten thousands'?"[l]

[6]So Achish summoned David and said to him: "As the LORD lives, you are honest, and I should be pleased to have you active with me in the camp, for I have found nothing wrong with you from the day of your arrival to this day. But you are not welcome to the lords. [7]Withdraw peaceably, now, and do nothing that might displease the Philistine lords." [8]But David said to Achish: "What have I done? Or what have you against your servant from the first day I have been with you to this day, that I cannot go to fight against the enemies of my lord the king?" [9]"You know," Achish answered David, "that you are acceptable to me. But the Philistine chiefs have determined you are not to go up with us to battle. [10]So the first thing tomorrow, you and your lord's servants who came with you, go to the place I picked out for you. Do not decide to take umbrage at this; you are as acceptable to me as an angel of God. But make an early morning start, as soon as it grows light, and be on your way." [11]So David and his men left early in the morning to return to the land of the Philistines. The Philistines, however, went on up to Jezreel.

CHAPTER 30

See RG
118–19

Ziklag in Ruins. [1]Before David and his men reached Ziklag on the third day, the Amalekites had raided the Negeb and Ziklag, had stormed the city, and had set it on fire.[m] [2]They had taken captive the women and all who were in the city, young and old, killing no one; they had carried them off when they left. [3]David and his men arrived at the city to find it burned to the ground and their wives, sons and daughters taken captive. [4]Then David and those who were with him wept aloud until they could weep no more. [5]David's two wives, Ahinoam of Jezreel and Abigail, the widow of Nabal from Carmel, had also been carried off with the rest.[n] [6]Now David found himself in great difficulty, for the men spoke of stoning him, so bitter were they over the fate of their sons and daughters. But with renewed trust in the LORD his God, [7o]David said to Abiathar, the priest, son of Ahimelech, "Bring me the ephod!" When Abiathar brought him the ephod, [8]David inquired of the LORD, "Shall I pursue these raiders? Can I overtake them?" The LORD answered him, "Go in pursuit, for you shall surely overtake them and effect a rescue."

Raid of the Amalekites. [9]So David went off with his six hundred men and came as far as the Wadi Besor, where those who were to remain behind halted. [10]David continued the pursuit with four hundred men, but two hundred were too exhausted to cross the Wadi Besor and remained behind. [11]An Egyptian was found in the open country and brought to David. He was provided with food, which he ate, and given water to drink; [12]a cake of pressed figs and two cakes of pressed raisins were also offered to him. When he had eaten, he revived; he had not taken food nor drunk water for three days and three nights. [13]Then David asked him, "To whom do you belong, and where do you come from?" He replied: "I am an Egyptian, the slave of an Amalekite. My master abandoned me because I fell sick three days ago today. [14]We raided the Negeb of the Cherethites, the territory of Judah, and the Negeb of Caleb; and we set Ziklag on fire."[p] [15]David then asked him, "Will you lead me down to this raiding party?" He answered, "Swear to me by God that you will not kill me or deliver me to my master, and I will lead you to the raiding party." [16]He did lead them, and there were the Amalekites scattered all over the ground, eating, drinking, and in a festive mood because of all the

---

j: 1 Sm 27, 7.   *k:* 1 Chr 12, 19f.   *l:* 1 Sm 18, 6f; 21, 11.   *m:* 1 Sm 27, 6. 10; 1 Chr 12, 21.   *n:* 1 Sm 25, 42; 27, 3; 30, 5.   *o:* 7f: 1 Sm 2, 28; 23, 6; Ex 28, 30.   *p:* 1 Sm 27, 10; Ez 25, 16.

rich booty they had taken from the land of the Philistines and from the land of Judah.

The Booty Recovered. [17]From dawn to sundown David attacked them, putting them under the ban so that none escaped except four hundred young men, who mounted their camels and fled.[q] [18]David recovered everything the Amalekites had taken, and rescued his two wives. [19]Nothing was missing, small or great, booty or sons or daughters, of all that the Amalekites had taken. David brought back everything. [20]Moreover, David took all the sheep and oxen, and as they drove them before him, they shouted, "This is David's spoil."

Division of the Spoils. [21]When David came to the two hundred men who had been too exhausted to follow him, and whom he had left behind at the Wadi Besor, they came out to meet David and the men with him. On nearing them David greeted them. [22]But all the stingy and worthless men among those who had accompanied David spoke up to say, "Since they did not accompany us, we will not give them anything from the booty, except to each man his wife and children. Let them take those along and be on their way." [23]But David said: "You must not do this, my brothers, after what the LORD has given us. He has protected us and delivered into our grip the band that came against us. [24]Who could agree with this proposal of yours? Rather, the share of the one who goes down to battle and that of the one who remains with the baggage shall be the same; they shall share alike."[r] [25]And from that day forward he made it a law and a custom in Israel, as it still is today.[s]

David's Gifts to Judah. [26]When David came to Ziklag, he sent part of the spoil to the elders of Judah, city by city, saying, "This is a gift to you from the spoil of the enemies of the LORD": [27]to those in Bethel, to those in Ramoth-negeb, to those in Jattir, [28]to those in Aroer, to those in Siphmoth, to those in Eshtemoa, [29]to those in Racal, to those in the Jerahmeelite cities, to those in the Kenite cities,[t] [30]to those in Hormah, to those in Borashan, to those in Athach, [31]to those in Hebron, and to all the places frequented by David and his men.

CHAPTER 31

See RG
118–19

Death of Saul and His Sons. [1][u]As they pressed their attack on Israel, with the Israelites fleeing before them and falling mortally wounded on Mount Gilboa, [2]the Philistines pursued Saul and his sons closely, and slew Jonathan, Abinadab, and Malchishua, sons of Saul.[v] [3]The battle raged around Saul, and the archers hit him; he was pierced through the abdomen. [4]Then Saul said to his armorbearer, "Draw your sword and run me through, lest these uncircumcised come and make sport of me." But his armor-bearer, badly frightened, refused to do it. So Saul took his own sword and fell upon it.[w] [5]When the armor-bearer saw that Saul was dead, he too fell upon his sword and died with him.[x] [6]Thus Saul, his three sons, and his armorbearer died together on that same day.

[7]When the Israelites on the slope of the valley and those along the Jordan saw that the men of Israel had fled and that Saul and his sons were dead, they too abandoned their cities and fled. Then the Philistines came and lived in those cities.

[8]The day after the battle the Philistines came to strip the slain, and found Saul and his three sons lying on Mount Gilboa. [9]They cut off Saul's head and stripped him of his armor, and then sent the good news throughout the land of the Philistines to their idols and to the people.[y] [10]They put his armor in the temple of Astarte, but impaled his body on the wall of Beth-shan.

Burial of Saul. [11][z]When the inhabitants of Jabesh-gilead heard what the Philistines had done to Saul, [12]all their warriors set out, and after marching throughout the night, removed the bodies of Saul and his sons from the wall of Beth-shan, and brought

---

31, 5: This report of the suicidal act of Saul is presented as a part of his downfall, to be judged accordingly.

q: 1 Sm 15, 3; Jos 6, 17; Jgs 7, 12.   *r:* 1 Sm 17, 22; 25, 13.   *s:* Nm 31, 27.   *t:* 1 Sm 27, 10.   *u:* 1-13: 1 Chr 10, 1-12; 2 Sm 1, 1-16; 4, 4.   *v:* 1 Sm 14, 49; 28, 19; 1 Chr 10, 2f.   *w:* 1 Sm 24, 7; Jgs 9, 54; 1 Chr 10, 4.   *x:* 1 Sm 10, 1; 26, 9; 2 Mc 14, 42.   *y:* 1 Sm 17, 54; 2 Sm 1, 20; 2 Mc 15, 35.   *z:* 11ff: 1 Sm 11, 1-11; 2 Sm 2, 4-7.

them to Jabesh, where they cremated them.* [13]Then they took their bones and buried them under the tamarisk tree in Jabesh, and fasted for seven days.

31, 12: Cremated them: cremation was not normally practiced in Israel, though it was known in the country from pre-Israelite times.

See RG 113–22

The Second Book of Samuel

See RG 118–19

CHAPTER 1

Report of Saul's Death. [1] After the death of Saul, David returned from his defeat of the Amalekites and spent two days in Ziklag.[a] [2] On the third day a man came from Saul's camp, with his clothes torn and dirt on his head. Going to David, he fell to the ground in homage. [3] David asked him, "Where do you come from?" He replied, "I have escaped from the Israelite camp." [4] "Tell me what happened," David bade him. He answered that the soldiers had fled the battle and that many of them had fallen and were dead, among them Saul and his son Jonathan. [5] Then David said to the youth who was reporting to him, "How do you know that Saul and his son Jonathan are dead?" [6][b] The youthful informant replied: "It was by chance that I found myself on Mount Gilboa and saw Saul leaning on his spear, with chariots and horsemen closing in on him. [7] He turned around and, seeing me, called me to him. When I said, 'Here I am,' [8] he asked me, 'Who are you?' and I replied, 'An Amalekite.' [9] Then he said to me, 'Stand up to me, please, and finish me off, for I am in great suffering, yet fully alive.' [10] So I stood up to him and dispatched him, for I knew that he could not survive his wound. I removed the crown from his head and the armlet from his arm and brought them here to my lord."

[11]David seized his garments and rent them, and all the men who were with him did likewise.[c] [12]They mourned and wept and fasted until evening for Saul and his son Jonathan, and for the soldiers of the LORD of the clans of Israel, because they had fallen by the sword.[d] [13]Then David said to the young man who had brought him the information, "Where are you from?" He replied, "I am the son of an Amalekite immigrant." [14]David said to him, "How is it that you were not afraid to put forth your hand to desecrate the LORD's anointed?"[e] [15]David then called one of the attendants and said to him, "Come, strike him down"; and the youth struck him a mortal blow. [16]Meanwhile David said to him, "You are responsible for your own death, for you testified against yourself when you said, 'I dispatched the LORD's anointed.' "

Elegy for Saul and Jonathan. [17]Then David chanted this elegy for Saul and his son Jonathan, [18]which is recorded in the Book of Jashar to be taught to the Judahites. He sang:[f]

[19] "Alas! the glory of Israel, Saul,
  slain upon your heights;
how can the warriors have fallen!

[20] "Tell it not in Gath,
  herald it not in the streets of Ashkelon,
Lest the Philistine maidens rejoice,
  lest the daughters of the strangers exult![g]
[21] Mountains of Gilboa,
  may there be neither dew nor rain
    upon you,
  nor upsurgings of the deeps!*
Upon you lie begrimed the warriors'
    shields,
  the shield of Saul, no longer anointed
    with oil.[h]

[22]"From the blood of the slain,
  from the bodies of the valiant,

1, 21: Upsurgings of the deeps: this reading attempts to recover from an unintelligible Hebrew phrase the poetic parallel to dew and rain. The sense would be a wish that the mountain should have neither moisture from above nor water from springs or wells.

a: 1 Sm 30, 17-20; 31, 1-13. *b:* 6-10: 2 Sm 4, 10; 1 Sm 31, 1-4; 1 Chr 10, 1-4. *c:* 2 Sm 13, 31. *d:* 1 Sm 31, 13. *e:* 1 Sm 10, 1; 24, 7; Ps 105, 15. *f:* Jos 10, 13. *g:* Jgs 16, 23; 1 Sm 31, 9; Mi 1, 10. *h:* Gn 27, 28.

David's Wives' Influence

Davi d's two wives, Ahinoam and Abigail (2 Sm 2, 2) were both from the area around Hebron and were therefore important political assets for his gaining the throne of Judah. Through his marriage to Abigail, David had assumed the wealth and position of a prominent Calebite leader, perhaps their chieftain (1 Sm 25).

The bow of Jonathan did not turn back,
    or the sword of Saul return unstained.[i]
23 Saul and Jonathan, beloved and cherished,
    separated neither in life nor in death,
    swifter than eagles, stronger than lions!
24 Women of Israel, weep over Saul,
    who clothed you in scarlet and in finery,
    who decked your attire with ornaments
        of gold.

25 "How can the warriors have fallen—
    in the thick of the battle,
    slain upon your heights!
26 "I grieve for you, Jonathan my brother!
    most dear have you been to me;
More precious have I held love for you
    than love for women.[j]

27 "How can the warriors have fallen,
    the weapons of war have perished!"

CHAPTER 2

See RG 119

David Anointed King. [1]After this David inquired of the LORD, "Shall I go up into one of the cities of Judah?" The LORD replied to him, "Yes." Then David asked, "Where shall I go?" He replied, "To Hebron." [2]So David went up there accompanied by his two wives, Ahinoam of Jezreel and Abigail, the widow of Nabal of Carmel.[k] [3]David also brought up his men with their families, and they dwelt in the cities near Hebron. [4]Then the men of Judah came there and anointed David king of the Judahites.[l]

A report reached David that the men of Jabesh-gilead had buried Saul. [5]So David sent messengers to the men of Jabesh-gilead and said to them: "May you be blessed by the LORD for having done this kindness to your lord Saul in burying him. [6]And now may the LORD be kind and faithful to you. I, too, will be generous to you for having done this. [7]Take courage, therefore, and prove yourselves valiant men, for though your lord Saul is dead, the Judahites have anointed me their king."

IV: The Reign of David

Ishbaal King of Israel. [8]Abner, son of Ner, Saul's general, took Ishbaal, son of Saul, and brought him over to Mahanaim,[m] [9]where he made him king over Gilead, the Ashurites, Jezreel, Ephraim, Benjamin, and the rest of Israel. [10]Ishbaal, son of Saul, was forty years old when he became king over Israel, and he reigned for two years. The Judahites alone followed David. [11]In all, David spent seven years and six months in Hebron as king of the Judahites.[n]

Combat near Gibeon. [12]Now Abner, son of Ner, and the servants of Ishbaal, Saul's son, left Mahanaim for Gibeon. [13]Joab, son of Zeruiah, and David's servants also set out and met them at the pool of Gibeon. And they sat down, one group on one side of the pool and the other on the opposite side. [14]Then Abner said to Joab, "Let the young men rise and perform for us." Joab replied, "All right!" [15]So they rose and were counted off: twelve of the Benjaminites of Ishbaal, son of Saul, and twelve of David's servants. [16]Then each one grasped his opponent's head and thrust his sword into his opponent's side, and all fell down together.[*] And so that place, which is in Gibeon, was named the Field of the Sides.

Death of Asahel. [17]After a very fierce battle that day, Abner and the men of Israel

---

2, 16: The nature of this gruesome game is not clear, and the place name is variously given in the older texts.

---

i: 1 Sm 14, 47.   j: 1 Sm 18, 1; 1 Mc 9, 21.   k: 1 Sm 25, 42f.   l: 1 Sm 31, 11ff.   m: 1 Sm 14, 50.   n: 2 Sm 5, 5; 1 Kgs 2, 11.

were defeated by David's servants. [18]The three sons of Zeruiah were there—Joab, Abishai, and Asahel. Asahel, who was as fleet of foot as a gazelle in the open field,[o] [19]set out after Abner, turning neither right nor left in his pursuit.[p] [20]Abner turned around and said, "Is that you, Asahel?" He replied, "Yes." [21]Abner said to him, "Turn right or left; seize one of the young men and take what you can strip from him." But Asahel would not desist from his pursuit. [22]Once more Abner said to Asahel: "Stop pursuing me! Why must I strike you to the ground? How could I face your brother Joab?"[q] [23]Still he refused to stop. So Abner struck him in the abdomen with the heel of his javelin, and the weapon protruded from his back. He fell there and died on the spot. And all who came to the place where Asahel had fallen and died, came to a halt. [24]Joab and Abishai, however, continued the pursuit of Abner. The sun had gone down when they came to the hill of Ammah which lies east of the valley toward the desert near Geba.

Truce between Joab and Abner. [25]Here the Benjaminites rallied around Abner, forming a single group, and made a stand on the hilltop. [26]Then Abner called to Joab and said: "Must the sword destroy to the utmost? Do you not know that afterward there will be bitterness? How much longer will you refrain from ordering the people to stop the pursuit of their brothers?" [27]Joab replied, "As God lives, if you had not spoken, the soldiers would not have been withdrawn from the pursuit of their brothers until morning." [28]Joab then sounded the horn, and all the soldiers came to a halt, pursuing Israel no farther and fighting no more. [29]Abner and his men marched all night long through the Arabah, crossed the Jordan, marched all through the morning, and came to Mahanaim. [30]Joab, after interrupting the pursuit of Abner, assembled all the men. Besides Asahel, nineteen other servants of David were missing. [31]But David's servants had fatally wounded three hundred and sixty men of Benjamin, followers of Abner. [32]They took up Asahel and buried him in his father's tomb in Bethlehem.

Joab and his men made an all-night march, and dawn found them in Hebron.

CHAPTER 3

See RG 119

[1]There followed a long war between the house of Saul and that of David, in which David grew stronger, but the house of Saul weaker.

Sons Born in Hebron. [2r]Sons were born to David in Hebron: his first-born, Amnon, of Ahinoam from Jezreel; [3]the second, Chileab, of Abigail the widow of Nabal of Carmel; the third, Absalom, son of Maacah the daughter of Talmai, king of Geshur;[s] [4]the fourth, Adonijah, son of Haggith; the fifth, Shephatiah, son of Abital;[t] [5]and the sixth, Ithream, of David's wife Eglah. These were born to David in Hebron.

Ishbaal and Abner Quarrel. [6]During the war between the house of Saul and of David, Abner was gaining power in the house of Saul. [7]Now Saul had had a concubine, Rizpah, the daughter of Aiah. And Ishbaal, son of Saul, said to Abner, "Why have you been intimate with my father's concubine?"[u] [8]Enraged at the words of Ishbaal, Abner said, "Am I a dog's head in Judah? At present I am doing a kindness to the house of your father Saul, to his brothers and his friends, by keeping you out of David's clutches; yet this day you charge me with a crime involving a woman! [9]May God do thus and so to Abner if I do not carry out for David what the LORD swore to him[v]— [10]that is, take away the kingdom from the house of Saul and establish the throne of David over Israel and over Judah from Dan to Beersheba."[w] [11]In his fear of Abner, Ishbaal was no longer able to say a word to him.

Abner and David Reconciled. [12]Then Abner sent messengers to David in Telam, where he was at the moment, to say, "Make an agreement with me, and I will aid you by bringing all Israel over to you." [13]He replied, "Very well, I will make an agreement with you. But one thing I require of you. You must not appear before me unless you bring back Michal, Saul's daughter, when you come to present yourself to me."[x] [14]At the

---

o: 2 Sm 23, 24: 1 Chr 2, 16.   *p:* 1 Chr 27, 7.   *q:* 2 Sm 3, 27f. 30.   *r:* 2-5: 1 Chr 3, 14.   *s:* 2 Sm 13, 37; 15, 8.   *t:* 1 Kgs 1, 5.
u: 2 Sm 21, 8ff.   *v:* Ru 1, 17.   *w:* 2 Sm 5, 2; 1 Sm 25, 30.   *x:* 1 Sm 18, 20-27.

same time David sent messengers to Ishbaal, son of Saul, to say, "Give me my wife Michal, whom I espoused by paying a hundred Philistine foreskins." [15]Ishbaal sent for her and took her away from her husband Paltiel, son of Laish,[y] [16]who followed her weeping as far as Bahurim. But Abner said to him, "Go back!" And he turned back.

[17]Abner then said in discussion with the elders of Israel: "For a long time you have been seeking David as your king. [18]Now take action, for the LORD has said of David, 'By my servant David I will save my people Israel from the grasp of the Philistines and from the grasp of all their enemies.' " [19]Abner also spoke personally to Benjamin, and then went to make his own report to David in Hebron concerning all that would be agreeable to Israel and to the whole house of Benjamin. [20]When Abner, accompanied by twenty men, came to David in Hebron, David prepared a feast for Abner and for the men who were with him. [21]Then Abner said to David, "I will now go to assemble all Israel for my lord the king, that they may make an agreement with you; you will then be king over all whom you wish to rule." So David bade Abner farewell, and he went away in peace.

Death of Abner. [22]Just then David's servants and Joab were coming in from an expedition, bringing much plunder with them. Abner, having been dismissed by David, was no longer with him in Hebron but had gone his way in peace. [23]When Joab and the whole force he had with him arrived, he was informed, "Abner, son of Ner, came to David; he has been sent on his way in peace." [24]So Joab went to the king and said: "What have you done? Abner came to you. Why did you let him go peacefully on his way? [25]Are you not aware that Abner came to deceive you and to learn the ins and outs of all that you are doing?" [26]Joab then left David, and without David's knowledge sent messengers after Abner, who brought him back from the cistern of Sirah. [27]When Abner returned to Hebron, Joab took him aside within the city gate as though to speak with him privately. There he stabbed him in the abdomen, and he died

in revenge for the killing of Joab's brother Asahel.[z] [28]Later David heard of it and said: "Before the LORD, I and my kingdom are forever innocent.[a] [29]May the full responsibility for the death of Abner, son of Ner, be laid to Joab and to all his family. May the men of Joab's family never be without one suffering from a discharge, or a leper, or one unmanly, one falling by the sword, or one in need of bread!" [30][Joab and his brother Abishai had lain in wait for Abner because he killed their brother Asahel in battle at Gibeon.]

David Mourns Abner. [31]Then David said to Joab and to all the people who were with him, "Rend your garments, gird yourselves with sackcloth, and mourn over Abner." King David himself followed the bier.[b] [32]When they had buried Abner in Hebron, the king wept aloud at the grave of Abner, and the people also wept. [33]And the king sang this elegy over Abner:

"Would Abner have died like a fool?
[34] Your hands were not bound with chains,
    nor your feet placed in fetters;
As men fall before the wicked, you fell."

And all the people continued to weep for him. [35]Then they went to console David with food while it was still day. But David swore, "May God do thus and so to me if I eat bread or anything else before sunset."[c] [36]All the people noted this with approval, just as they were pleased with everything that the king did. [37]So on that day all the people and all Israel came to know that the king had no part in the killing of Abner, son of Ner. [38]The king then said to his servants: "You must recognize that a great general has fallen today in Israel. [39]Although I am the anointed king, I am weak this day, and these men, the sons of Zeruiah, are too ruthless for me. May the LORD requite the evildoer in accordance with his evil deed."[d]

CHAPTER 4

See RG 119

Death of Ishbaal. [1]When Ishbaal, son of Saul, heard that Abner had died in Hebron, he ceased to resist and all Israel was alarmed. [2]Ishbaal, son of Saul, had two company leaders named Baanah and Rechab, sons of

y: 1 Sm 25, 44.   *z:* 1 Kgs 2, 5. 32.   *a:* 28. 30: 2 Sm 2, 22f.   *b:* 2 Sm 21, 10.   *c:* Ru 1, 17.   *d:* Ps 28, 4; Is 3, 11.

361

Rimmon the Beerothite, of the tribe of Benjamin. [Beeroth, too, was ascribed to Benjamin:*e* ³the Beerothites fled to Gittaim, where they have been resident aliens to this day.*f* ⁴Jonathan, son of Saul, had a son named Meribbaal* with crippled feet. He was five years old when the news about Saul and Jonathan came from Jezreel, and his nurse took him up and fled. But in their hasty flight, he fell and became lame.]*g* ⁵The sons of Rimmon the Beerothite, Rechab and Baanah, came into the house of Ishbaal during the heat of the day, while he was taking his siesta. ⁶The portress of the house had dozed off while sifting wheat, and was asleep. So Rechab and his brother Baanah slipped past ⁷and entered the house while Ishbaal was lying asleep in his bedroom. They struck and killed him, and cut off his head. Then, taking the head, they traveled on the Arabah road all night long.

The Murder Avenged. ⁸They brought the head of Ishbaal to David in Hebron and said to the king: "This is the head of Ishbaal, son of your enemy Saul, who sought your life. Thus has the LORD this day avenged my lord the king on Saul and his posterity." ⁹But David replied to Rechab and his brother Baanah, sons of Rimmon the Beerothite: "As the LORD lives, who rescued me from all difficulty, ¹⁰in Ziklag I seized and put to death the man who informed me of Saul's death, thinking himself the bearer of good news for which I ought to give him a reward.*h* ¹¹How much more now, when wicked men have slain an innocent man in bed at home, must I hold you responsible for his death and destroy you from the earth!" ¹²So at a command from David, the young men killed them and cut off their hands and feet, hanging them up near the pool in Hebron. But he took the head of Ishbaal and buried it in Abner's grave in Hebron.*i*

CHAPTER 5

See RG 119

David King of Israel. ¹*j*All the tribes of Israel came to David in Hebron and said: "Here we are, your bone and your flesh. ²In days past, when Saul was our king, it was you who led the Israelites out and brought them back. And the LORD said to you, 'You shall shepherd my people Israel and shall be commander of Israel.' "*k* ³When all the elders of Israel came to David in Hebron, King David made an agreement with them there before the LORD, and they anointed him king of Israel. ⁴David was thirty years old when he became king, and he reigned for forty years: ⁵seven years and six months in Hebron over Judah, and thirty-three years in Jerusalem over all Israel and Judah.*l*

*Capture of Zion.** ⁶*m*Then the king and his men set out for Jerusalem against the Jebusites who inhabited the region. David was told, "You cannot enter here: the blind and the lame will drive you away!" which was their way of saying, "David cannot enter here."*n* ⁷But David did take the stronghold of Zion, which is the City of David. ⁸On that day David said: "All who wish to attack the Jebusites must strike at them through the water shaft. The lame and the blind shall be the personal enemies of David." That is why it is said, "The blind and the lame shall not enter the palace."*o* ⁹David then dwelt in the stronghold, which was called the City of David; he built up the area from Millo to the palace.*p* ¹⁰David grew steadily more powerful, for the LORD of hosts was with him.*q* ¹¹*r*Hiram, king of Tyre, sent ambassadors to David; he furnished cedar wood, as well as carpenters and masons, who built a palace for David.*s* ¹²And David knew that the LORD had established him as king of Israel and had exalted his rule for the sake of his people Israel.

4, 4: Saul's grandson Meribbaal is the subject of ch 9 below. The text of this verse may owe its present place to the fact that pre-Christian copies of the Books of Samuel tended to confuse his name with that of his uncle Ishbaal, Saul's son and successor, a principal figure in chapters 2–4.

5, 6-12: David's most important military exploit, the taking of Jerusalem, is here presented before his battles with the Philistines, vv 17-25, which were earlier in time. The sense of vv 6 and 8 is in doubt.

---

e: 2 Sm 9, 3; Jos 9, 17f. *f:* Jos 18, 25. *g:* 2 Sm 9, 3; 19, 25. *h:* 2 Sm 1, 6-10. 14. 16. *i:* Dt 21, 22f; 1 Sm 31, 10. *j:* 1ff: 1 Chr 11, 1ff. *k:* 2 Sm 3, 10; Dt 17, 15; 1 Sm 18, 16. *l:* 2 Sm 2, 11; 1 Kgs 2, 11; 1 Chr 3, 4. *m:* 6-10: 1 Chr 11, 4-9. *n:* Jos 15, 63; Jgs 1, 19. 21; Is 29, 3. *o:* Lv 21, 18; Mt 21, 14f. *p:* 1 Kgs 3, 1; 11, 27. *q:* Pss 78, 70ff. 89; 132, 13. *r:* 11-25: 1 Chr 14, 1-16. *s:* 11f: 1 Kgs 5, 15; 1 Chr 14, 1f.

Baal-hazor

Gilgal

Gezer
Gibeon
Geba

Ekron
Jerusalem

Gath?

Giloh
Tekoa

Hebron

Mediterranean
Sea

Tyre

Abel-beth-maacah

ZOBAH

ARAM (SYRIA)

Damascus

GESHUR

ISRAEL

Hill Country
of Ephraim

Mahanaim

AMMON

Rabbah

Ashdod
Ashkelon

Jerusalem

Gaza

PHILISTIA

JUDAH

MOAB

AMALEK

Valley of Salt

EDOM

0	25	50	75 Miles
0	40	80	120 Kilometers

The Kingdom of David according to 2 Samuel

David's Family in Jerusalem. [13]David took more concubines and wives in Jerusalem after he had come from Hebron, and more sons and daughters were born to him in Jerusalem. [14]These are the names of those who were born to him in Jerusalem: Shammua, Shobab, Nathan, Solomon, [15]Ibhar, Elishua, Nepheg, Japhia, [16]Elishama, Baaliada, and Eliphelet.

Rout of the Philistines. [17]When the Philistines heard that David had been anointed king of Israel, they all took the field in search of him. On hearing this, David went down to the refuge.* [18]The Philistines came and overran the valley of Rephaim.* [19]David inquired of the LORD, "Shall I attack the Philistines—will you deliver them into my grip?" The LORD replied to David, "Attack, for I will surely deliver the Philistines into your grip." [20]David then went to Baal-perazim,* where he defeated them. He said, "The LORD has scattered my enemies before me like waters that have broken free." That is why the place is called Baal-perazim. [21]They abandoned their gods there, and David and his men carried them away. [22]But the Philistines came up again and overran the valley of Rephaim. [23]So David inquired of the LORD, who replied: "You must not attack frontally, but circle their rear and meet them before the mastic trees. [24]When you hear a sound of marching* in the tops of the mastic trees, act decisively, for the LORD will have gone forth before you to attack the camp of the Philistines." [25]David obeyed the LORD's command and routed the Philistines from Gibeon as far as Gezer.

CHAPTER 6

See RG
119

The Ark Brought to Jerusalem. [1u]David again assembled all the picked men of Israel, thirty thousand in number. [2]Then David and all the people who were with him set out for Baala of Judah to bring up from there the ark of God, which bears the name of the LORD of hosts enthroned above the cherubim.[v] [3]The ark of God was placed on a new cart and taken away from the house of Abinadab on the hill. Uzzah and Ahio, sons of Abinadab, guided the cart,[w] [4]with Ahio walking before it, [5]while David and all the Israelites made merry before the LORD with all their strength, with singing and with citharas, harps, tambourines, sistrums and cymbals.[x] [6]When they came to the threshing floor of Nodan, Uzzah reached out his hand to the ark of God and steadied it, for the oxen were making it tip. [7]But the LORD was angry with Uzzah; God struck him on that spot, and he died there before God. [8]David was disturbed because the LORD had vented his anger on Uzzah. (The place has been called Perez-uzzah down to the present day.)[y] [9]David feared the LORD that day and said, "How can the ark of the LORD come to me?" [10]So David would not have the ark of the LORD brought to him in the City of David, but diverted it to the house of Obed-edom the Gittite.

[11]The ark of the LORD remained in the house of Obed-edom the Gittite for three months, and the LORD blessed Obed-edom and his whole house.[z] [12a]When it was reported to King David that the LORD had blessed the family of Obed-edom and all that belonged to him, David went to bring up the ark of God from the house of Obed-edom into the City of David amid festivities. [13]As soon as the bearers of the ark of the LORD had advanced six steps, he sacrificed an ox and a fatling. [14]Then David, girt with a linen apron, came dancing before the LORD with abandon,[b] [15]as he and all the Israelites were bringing up the ark of the LORD with shouts of joy and to the sound of the horn. [16]As the ark of the LORD was entering the City of David, Saul's daughter Michal looked down through the window and saw King David

---

5, 17: Refuge: probably near Adullam (1 Sm 22, 1-5).

5, 18-25: The successive defeats of the Philistines in the valley of Rephaim southwest of Jerusalem had the effect of blocking their access to the mountain ridge near Gibeon, and confining them to their holdings on the coast and in the foothills beyond Gezer to the west and south.

5, 20: Baal-perazim: means approximately "the lord of scatterings."

5, 24: Sound of marching: the wind in the treetops suggestive of the Lord's footsteps.

t: 13-16: 1 Chr 3, 5-8; 14, 3-7. u: 1-11: 1 Chr 13, 1-14. v: Ex 25, 10; Jos 15, 9; Ps 132, 8ff; 1 Chr 1, 4. w: 1 Sm 4, 3f; 6, 7f; 7, 1; Dn 3, 55. x: Pss 68, 25f; 150, 3. 5. y: 1 Kgs 8, 1. z: 1 Chr 26, 4. a: 12-23: 1 Chr 15, 1-29; Ps 24, 7-10. b: 1 Sm 2, 18.

Holy City

avid brings the ark of God to Jerusalem in 2 Sm 6, making the city not only his administrative center, but also his religious center. Thus, Jerusalem becomes the holy city, first in Judaism, where it is still the direction of prayer, and later also in Christianity and Islam, though for different reasons.

leaping and dancing before the LORD, and she despised him in her heart. *17c*The ark of the LORD was brought in and set in its place within the tent David had pitched for it. Then David offered holocausts and peace offerings before the LORD. *18*When he finished making these offerings, he blessed the people in the name of the LORD of hosts. *19*He then distributed among all the people, to each man and each woman in the entire multitude of Israel, a loaf of bread, a cut of roast meat, and a raisin cake. With this, all the people left for their homes.

*20*When David returned to bless his own family, Saul's daughter Michal came out to meet him and said, "How the king of Israel has honored himself today, exposing himself to the view of the slave girls of his followers, as a commoner might do!"*d* *21*But David replied to Michal: "I was dancing before the LORD. As the LORD lives, who preferred me to your father and his whole family when he appointed me commander of the LORD's people, Israel, not only will I make merry before the LORD,*e* *22*but I will demean myself even more. I will be lowly in your esteem, but in the esteem of the slave girls you spoke of I will be honored." *23*And so Saul's daughter Michal was childless to the day of her death.

CHAPTER 7

See RG 119–20

David's Concern for the Ark. *1f*When King David was settled in his palace, and the LORD had given him rest from his enemies on every side,*g* *2*he said to Nathan the prophet,

"Here I am living in a house of cedar, while the ark of God dwells in a tent!"*h* *3*Nathan answered the king, "Go, do whatever you have in mind, for the LORD is with you."*i* *4*But that night the LORD spoke to Nathan and said: *5*"Go, tell my servant David, 'Thus says the LORD: Should you build me a house to dwell in?*j* *6*I have not dwelt in a house from the day on which I led the Israelites out of Egypt to the present, but I have been going about in a tent under cloth. *7*In all my wanderings everywhere among the Israelites, did I ever utter a word to any one of the judges whom I charged to tend my people Israel, to ask: Why have you not built me a house of cedar?'

The Lord's Promises. *8*"Now then, speak thus to my servant David, 'The LORD of hosts has this to say:* It was I who took you from the pasture and from the care of the flock to be commander of my people Israel.*k* *9*I have been with you wherever you went, and I have destroyed all your enemies before you. And I will make you famous like the great ones of the earth.*l* *10*I will fix a place for my people Israel; I will plant them so that they may dwell in their place without further disturbance. Neither shall the wicked continue to afflict them as they did of old, *11*since the time I first appointed judges over my people Israel. I will give you rest from all your enemies. The LORD also reveals to you that he will establish a house for you.*m* *12n*And when your time comes and you rest with your ancestors, I will raise up your heir after you, sprung from your loins, and I will make his kingdom firm. *13*It is he

---

7, 8-16: The prophecy to David contained in these verses is cited again, in poetic form, in Ps 89, 20-38, and alluded to in Ps 132. The promise regarding the people of Israel, vv 10-11, is a part of the promise to David at least as old as the composition of this chapter of Samuel, where it is anticipated in vv 6-7, and alluded to in David's thanksgiving, vv 23-24; it applies to the people an expression used of David in Ps 89, 23. The prophecy to David is the basis for Jewish expectation of a messiah, son of David, which Jesus Christ

fulfilled in a transcendent way; cf Acts 2, 30; Heb 1, 5.

c: 17ff: Lv 1, 1-17; 3, 1-17; 1 Chr 16, 1ff. *d:* 1 Chr 16, 43. *e:* 1 Sm 13, 14; 15, 28. *f:* 1-29: 1 Chr 17, 1-27. *g:* 1 Kgs 5, 4. *h:* Dt 12, 10; 25, 19. *i:* Ps 132, 1-5. *j:* 1 Kgs 5, 17; 8, 16. 27; 1 Chr 22, 8; 28, 3; Is 66, 1; Acts 7, 48. *k:* 1 Sm 16, 13; 17, 15-20; Ps 78, 70f; Am 7, 14. *l:* Ps 89, 27. *m:* 2 Sm 23, 5; 1 Kgs 2, 4-24. *n:* 12ff: 1 Kgs 5, 19; 8, 19; 1 Chr 22, 10; 2 Chr 7, 18; Ps 89, 5. 27f. 30. 37f; Lk 1, 32; Heb 1, 5.

A Dynasty for David

There is a play throughout ch 7 on the word "house." The house David proposes to build is a temple. But the LORD declines David's offer and says instead that he will build David a house, that is, a dynasty.

who shall build a house for my name. And I will make his royal throne firm forever. [14]I will be a father to him, and he shall be a son to me. And if he does wrong, I will correct him with the rod of men and with human chastisements; [15]but I will not withdraw my favor from him as I withdrew it from your predecessor Saul, whom I removed from my presence.[o] [16]Your house and your kingdom shall endure forever before me; your throne shall stand firm forever.' "[p] [17]Nathan reported all these words and this entire vision to David.

King David's Prayer. [18]Then King David went in and sat before the LORD and said, "Who am I, Lord GOD, and who are the members of my house, that you have brought me to this point?[q] [19]Yet even this you see as too little, Lord GOD; you have also spoken of the house of your servant for a long time to come: this too you have shown to man,[*] Lord GOD! [20]What more can David say to you? You know your servant, Lord GOD! [21]For your servant's sake and as you have had at heart, you have brought about this entire magnificent disclosure to your servant. [22]And so—

"Great are you, Lord GOD! There is none like you and there is no God but you, just as we have heard it told.[r] [23]What other nation on earth is there like your people Israel, which God has led, redeeming it as his people; so that you have made yourself renowned by doing this magnificent deed, and by doing awe-inspiring things as you have cleared nations and their gods out of the way of your

people, which you redeemed for yourself from Egypt?[s] [24]You have established for yourself your people Israel as yours forever, and you, LORD, have become their God. [25]And now, LORD God, confirm for all time the prophecy you have made concerning your servant and his house, and do as you have promised. [26]Your name will be forever great, when men say, 'The LORD of hosts is God of Israel,' and the house of your servant David stands firm before you. [27]It is you, LORD of hosts, God of Israel, who said in a revelation to your servant, 'I will build a house for you.' Therefore your servant now finds the courage to make this prayer to you. [28]And now, Lord GOD, you are God and your words are truth; you have made this generous promise to your servant.[u] [29]Do, then, bless the house of your servant that it may be before you forever; for you, Lord GOD, have promised, and by your blessing the house of your servant shall be blessed forever."

CHAPTER 8

See RG 120

Summary of David's Wars. [1v]After this David attacked the Philistines and conquered them, wresting . . .[*] from the Philistines. [2]He also defeated Moab and then measured them with a line, making them lie down on the ground. He told off two lengths of line for execution, and a full length[*] to be spared. Thus the Moabites became tributary to David. [3w]Next David defeated Hadadezer, son of Rehob, king of Zobah, when he went

---

7, 19: This too you have shown to man: the text as transmitted has, rather, "and this is instruction for (or: the law of) mankind." The author of Chronicles (1 Chr 17, 17) saw approximately the same phrase, which he endeavored to fit into the context in a quite different sense. The above is conjectural; cf Dt 5, 24.

8, 1: Wresting . . .: the Hebrew text here gives "the bridle of the cubit"; 1 Chr 18, 1 understood "Gath and its dependent villages"; others implausibly read "dominion of the capital city."

8, 2: Two lengths . . . a full length: usually taken to mean that two-thirds of them were executed; but it could mean that

two-thirds were spared, if the line was used full length in their case but doubled on itself to make "two lines" for those to be put to death.

o: 2 Sm 23, 5; 1 Sm 13, 14; 15, 26. 28; 2 Kgs 19, 34; 1 Chr 17, 11-14; Ps 89, 34. *p:* 2 Sm 23, 5; Dn 2, 45; 1 Mc 2, 57; Mk 11, 10; Lk 1, 32f; Heb 1, 8. *q:* 1 Chr 17, 16. *r:* Ex 15, 11; Is 45, 5. *s:* Dt 4, 7. 34. *t:* 24f; Ex 6, 7; Dt 7, 6; 26, 17; 29, 12. *u:* Nm 23, 19; Jn 17, 17. *v:* 1-18: 1 Chr 18, 1-17. *w:* 3-8: 2 Sm 10, 15-19 to reestablish his dominion at the Euphrates River.[x] [4]David captured from him one thousand seven hundred horsemen and twenty thousand foot soldiers. And he hamstrung all the chariot horses, preserving only enough for a hundred chariots.[y] [5]When the Arameans of Damascus came to the aid of Hadadezer, king of Zobah, David slew twenty-two thousand of them. [6]David then placed garrisons in Aram of Damascus, and the Arameans became subjects, tributary to David. The LORD brought David victory in all his undertakings. [7]David also took away the golden shields used by Hadadezer's servants and brought them to Jerusalem. [These Shishak, king of Egypt, took away when he came to Jerusalem in the days of Rehoboam, son of Solomon.] [8]From Tebah and Berothai, towns of Hadadezer, King David removed a very large quantity of bronze. [9]When Toi, king of Hamath, heard that David had defeated all the forces of Hadadezer, [10]he sent his son Hadoram to King David to greet him and to congratulate him for his victory over Hadadezer in battle, because Toi had been in many battles with Hadadezer. Hadoram also brought with him articles of silver, gold, and bronze. [11]These, too, King David consecrated to the LORD, together with the silver and gold he had taken from every nation he had conquered: [12]from Edom and Moab, from the Ammonites, from the Philistines, from the Amalekites, and from the plunder of Hadadezer, son of Rehob, king of Zobah.

[13]On his return,[*] David became famous for having slain eighteen thousand Edomites in the Salt Valley;[z] [14]after which he placed garrisons in Edom. Thus all the Edomites became David's subjects, and the LORD brought David victory in all his undertakings.

David's Officials. [15a]David reigned over all Israel, judging and administering justice to all his people. [16]Joab, son of Zeruiah, was in command of the army. Jehoshaphat, son of Ahilud, was chancellor. [17]Zadok, son of Ahitub, and Ahimelech, son of Abiathar, were priests. Shawsha was scribe. [18]Benaiah, son of Jehoiada, was in command of the Cherethites and Pelethites. And David's sons were priests.[b]

CHAPTER 9

See RG 120

David and Meribbaal. [1]David asked, "Is there any survivor of Saul's house to whom I may show kindness for the sake of Jonathan?"[c] [2]Now there was a servant of the family of Saul named Ziba. He was summoned to David, and the king asked him, "Are you Ziba?" He replied, "Your servant."[d] [3]Then the king inquired, "Is there any survivor of Saul's house to whom I may show God's kindness?" Ziba answered the king, "There is still Jonathan's son, whose feet are crippled."[e] [4]The king said to him, "Where is he?" and Ziba answered, "He is in the house of Machir, son of Ammiel, in Lodebar."[f] [5]So King David sent for him and had him brought from the house of Machir, son of Ammiel, in Lodebar. [6]When Meribbaal, son of Jonathan, son of Saul, came to David, he fell prostrate in homage. David said, "Meribbaal," and he answered, "Your servant." [7]"Fear not," David said to him, "I will surely be kind to you for the sake of your father Jonathan. I will restore to you all the lands of your grandfather Saul, and you shall always eat at my table." [8]Bowing low, he answered, "What is your servant that you should pay attention to a dead dog like me?"[g] [9]The king then called Ziba, Saul's attendant, and said to him: "I am giving your lord's son all that belonged to Saul and to all his family. [10]You and your sons and servants must till the land for him. You shall bring in the produce, which shall be food for your lord's family to eat. But Meribbaal, your lord's son, shall always eat at my table." Ziba, who had fifteen sons and twenty servants, [11]said to the king, "Your servant shall

---

8, 13: On his return: possibly to Jerusalem, after the revolt of Absalom, a circumstance which this catalogue of victories would avoid mentioning. 1 Chr 18, 13 attributes the defeat of the Edomites to Abishai.

---

[x]: 2 Sm 10, 6; 1 Kgs 11, 23. [y]: Jos 11, 6. 9. [z]: 2 Kgs 14, 7. [a]: 15-18: 2 Sm 20, 23-26; 1 Kgs 4, 1-6; 1 Chr 18, 14-17. [b]: 2 Sm 15, 18; 20, 7. 23; 23, 20. [c]: 2 Sm 21, 7; 1 Sm 18, 1-4; 20, 8ff. 15f. 42. [d]: 2 Sm 16, 1-4; 19, 27. [e]: 2 Sm 4, 4. [f]: 2 Sm 17, 27. [g]: 1 Sm 24, 15.

do just as my lord the king has commanded him." And so Meribbaal ate at David's table like one of the king's sons.[h] [12]Meribbaal had a young son whose name was Mica; and all the tenants of Ziba's family worked for Meribbaal.[i] [13]But Meribbaal lived in Jerusalem, because he always ate at the king's table. He was lame in both feet.[j]

See RG 120

CHAPTER 10

Insult of the Ammonites. [1k]Some time later* the king of the Ammonites died, and his son Hanun succeeded him as king. [2]David thought, "I will be kind to Hanun, son of Nahash, as his father was kind to me." So David sent his servants with condolences to Hanun for the loss of his father. But when David's servants entered the country of the Ammonites, [3]the Ammonite princes said to their lord Hanun: "Do you think that David is honoring your father by sending men with condolences? Is it not rather to explore the city, to spy on it, and to overthrow it, that David has sent his messengers to you?" [4]Hanun, therefore, seized David's servants and, after shaving off half their beards and cutting away the lower halves of their garments at the buttocks, sent them away.[l] [5]When he was told of it, King David sent out word to them, since the men were quite ashamed. "Stay in Jericho until your beards grow," he said, "and then come back."

Ammonites Defeated. [6]*In view of the offense they had given to David, the Ammonites sent for and hired twenty thousand Aramean foot soldiers from Beth-rehob and Zobah, as well as the king of Maacah with one thousand men, and twelve thousand men from Tob.[m] [7]On learning this, David sent out Joab with the entire levy of trained soldiers.[n] [8]The Ammonites came out and drew up in battle formation at the entrance of their city gate, while the Arameans of Zobah and Rehob and the men of

Tob and Maacah remained apart in the open country. [9]When Joab saw the battle lines drawn up against him, both front and rear, he made a selection from all the picked troops of Israel and arrayed them against the Arameans. [10]He placed the rest of the soldiers under the command of his brother Abishai, who arrayed them against the Ammonites. [11]Joab said, "If the Arameans are stronger than I, you shall help me. But if the Ammonites are stronger than you, I will come to help you. [12]Be brave; let us prove our valor for the sake of our people and the cities of our God; the LORD will do what he judges best." [13]When Joab and the soldiers who were with him approached the Arameans for battle, they fled before him. [14]The Ammonites, seeing that the Arameans had fled, also fled from Abishai and withdrew into the city. Joab then ceased his attack on the Ammonites and returned to Jerusalem.

Arameans Defeated. [15o]Then the Arameans responded to their defeat by Israel with a full mustering of troops; [16]Hadadezer sent for and enlisted Arameans from beyond the Euphrates. They came to Helam, with Shobach, general of Hadadezer's army, at their head. [17]On receiving this news, David assembled all Israel, crossed the Jordan, and went to Helam. The Arameans drew up in formation against David and fought with him. [18]But the Arameans gave way before Israel, and David's men killed seven hundred charioteers and forty thousand of the Aramean foot soldiers. Shobach, general of the army, was struck down and died on the field. [19]All of Hadadezer's vassal kings, in view of their defeat by Israel, then made peace with the Israelites and became their subjects. And the Arameans were afraid to give further aid to the Ammonites.

CHAPTER 11

See RG 120

David's Sin. [1]At the turn of the year,* when kings go out on campaign, David sent

---

10, 1: Some time later: early in the reign of David, since Hanun's father had been ruling in Ammon at the beginning of Saul's reign (1 Sm 11) and Solomon was as yet unborn (2 Sm 11, 1; 12, 24).

10, 6-9: A Hebrew text from Qumran (4Q Samᵃ) comes closer in these verses to what is given in 1 Chr 19, 6-9. The scene of the conflict is more likely Rabbath-Ammon, with

Josephus (Ant., vii, 123), than Madeba, as in 1 Chr; compare ch 11.

11, 1: At the turn of the year: in the spring.

h: 2 Sm 19, 29. *i:* 1 Chr 8, 34. *j:* 2 Sm 21, 7. *k:* 1-19: 1 Chr 19, 1-19. *l:* Is 20, 4. *m:* 2 Sm 8, 3; 1 Sm 14, 47. *n:* 2 Sm 1[.], 1. *o:* 15-19: 2 Sm 8, 3-8; 1 Chr 9, 16-19.

Adultery and Murder

It is highly unusual for ancient literature to criticize powerful and successful kings. The way David's behavior is depicted and condemned in the Bible (cf. 2 Sm 11, 1—12, 25) shows the overriding importance it assigns to moral values.

out Joab along with his officers and the army of Israel, and they ravaged the Ammonites and besieged Rabbah. David, however, remained in Jerusalem.*p* *2*One evening David rose from his siesta and strolled about on the roof of the palace. From the roof he saw a woman bathing, who was very beautiful. *3*David had inquiries made about the woman and was told, "She is Bathsheba, daughter of Eliam, and wife of [Joab's armor-bearer] Uriah the Hittite."*q* *4*Then David sent messengers and took her. When she came to him, he had relations with her, at a time when she was just purified after her monthly period. She then returned to her house.*r* *5*But the woman had conceived, and sent the information to David, "I am with child."

*6*David therefore sent a message to Joab, "Send me Uriah the Hittite." So Joab sent Uriah to David. *7*When he came, David questioned him about Joab, the soldiers, and how the war was going, and Uriah answered that all was well. *8*David then said to Uriah, "Go down to your house and bathe your feet." Uriah left the palace, and a portion was sent out after him from the king's table. *9*But Uriah slept at the entrance of the royal palace with the other officers of his lord, and did not go down to his own house. *10*David was told that Uriah had not gone home. So he said to Uriah, "Have you not come from a journey? Why, then, did you not go down to your house?" *11*Uriah answered David, "The ark and Israel and Judah are lodged in tents, and my lord Joab and your majesty's servants are encamped in the open field. Can I go home to eat and to drink and to sleep with my wife? As the LORD lives and as you live, I will do no such thing."*s* *12*Then David

said to Uriah, "Stay here today also, I shall dismiss you tomorrow." So Uriah remained in Jerusalem that day. On the day following, *13*David summoned him, and he ate and drank with David, who made him drunk. But in the evening he went out to sleep on his bed among his lord's servants, and did not go down to his home. *14*The next morning David wrote a letter to Joab which he sent by Uriah. *15*In it he directed: "Place Uriah up front, where the fighting is fierce. Then pull back and leave him to be struck down dead." *16*So while Joab was besieging the city, he assigned Uriah to a place where he knew the defenders were strong. *17*When the men of the city made a sortie against Joab, some officers of David's army fell, and among them Uriah the Hittite died.

*18*Then Joab sent David a report of all the details of the battle, *19*instructing the messenger, "When you have finished giving the king all the details of the battle, *20*the king may become angry and say to you: 'Why did you go near the city to fight? Did you not know that they would shoot from the wall above? *21*Who killed Abimelech, son of Jerubbaal? Was it not a woman who threw a millstone down on him from the wall above, so that he died in Thebez? Why did you go near the wall?' Then you in turn shall say, 'Your servant Uriah the Hittite is also dead.' "*t* *22*The messenger set out, and on his arrival he relayed to David all the details as Joab had instructed him.* *23*He told David: "The men had us at a disadvantage and came out into the open against us, but we pushed them back to the entrance of the city gate. *24*Then the archers shot at your servants from the wall above, and some of the king's men were killed.

11, 22: After this verse, the Greek text, which is here the older form, has David, angry with Joab, repeat exactly the questions Joab had foreseen in vv 20ff. In v 24 of our oldest Greek text, the messenger specifies that about eighteen

p: 2 Sm 10, 7; 1 Chr 20, 1.   *q:* 2 Sm 23, 39.   *r:* Lv 15, 19.
s: 1 Sm 4, 3f.   *t:* Jgs 9, 50-54.

servants died, among them your servant Uriah." [25]David said to the messenger: "This is what you shall convey to Joab: 'Do not be chagrined at this, for the sword devours now here and now there. Strengthen your attack on the city and destroy it.' Encourage him."

[26]When the wife of Uriah heard that her husband had died, she mourned her lord. [27]But once the mourning was over, David sent for her and brought her into his house. She became his wife and bore him a son. But the LORD was displeased with what David had done.

See RG 120

CHAPTER 12

Nathan's Parable. [1]*The LORD sent Nathan to David, and when he came to him, he said: "Judge this case for me! In a certain town there were two men, one rich, the other poor.[u] [2]The rich man had flocks and herds in great numbers. [3]But the poor man had nothing at all except one little ewe lamb that he had bought. He nourished her, and she grew up with him and his children. She shared the little food he had and drank from his cup and slept in his bosom. She was like a daughter to him. [4]Now, the rich man received a visitor, but he would not take from his own flocks and herds to prepare a meal for the wayfarer who had come to him. Instead he took the poor man's ewe lamb and made a meal of it for his visitor." [5]David grew very angry with that man and said to Nathan: "As the LORD lives, the man who has done this merits death! [6]He shall restore the ewe lamb fourfold because he has done this and has had no pity."[v]

David's Punishment. [7]Then Nathan said to David: "You are the man! Thus says the LORD God of Israel: 'I anointed you king of Israel. I rescued you from the hand of Saul.[w] [8]I gave you your lord's house and your lord's wives for your own. I gave you the house of Israel and of Judah. And if this were not enough, I could count up for you still more. [9]Why have you spurned the LORD and done evil in his sight? You have cut down Uriah the Hittite with the sword; you took his wife

as your own, and him you killed with the sword of the Ammonites. [10]Now, therefore, the sword shall never depart from your house, because you have despised me and have taken the wife of Uriah to be your wife.'[x] [11]Thus says the LORD: 'I will bring evil upon you out of your own house. I will take your wives while you live to see it, and will give them to your neighbor. He shall lie with your wives in broad daylight.[y] [12]You have done this deed in secret, but I will bring it about in the presence of all Israel, and with the sun looking down.' "

David's Repentance. [13]Then David said to Nathan, "I have sinned against the LORD." Nathan answered David: "The LORD on his part has forgiven your sin: you shall not die.[z] [14]But since you have utterly spurned the LORD by this deed, the child born to you must surely die." [15]Then Nathan returned to his house.

The LORD struck the child that the wife of Uriah had borne to David, and it became desperately ill. [16]David besought God for the child. He kept a fast, retiring for the night to lie on the ground clothed in sackcloth. [17]The elders of his house stood beside him urging him to rise from the ground; but he would not, nor would he take food with them. [18]On the seventh day, the child died. David's servants, however, were afraid to tell him that the child was dead, for they said: "When the child was alive, we spoke to him, but he would not listen to what we said. How can we tell him the child is dead? He may do some harm!" [19]But David noticed his servants whispering among themselves and realized that the child was dead. He asked his servants, "Is the child dead?" They replied, "Yes, he is." [20]Rising from the ground, David washed and anointed himself, and changed his clothes. Then he went to the house of the LORD and worshiped. He returned to his own house, where at his request food was set before him, and he ate. [21]His servants said to him: "What is this you are doing? While the child was living, you

---

12, 1-4: This utterance of Nathan is in regular lines in Hebrew, resembling English blank verse.

u: Sir 47, 1. *v:* Ex 21, 37; Lk 19, 8. *w:* 1 Sm 16, 13. *x:* 2 Sm 13, 28f; 18, 14. *y:* 2 Sm 16, 11. 22. *z:* 1 Kgs 21, 29; Pss 32, 5; 50, 6; Sir 47, 11.

fasted and wept and kept vigil; now that the child is dead you rise and take food." ²²He replied: "While the child was living, I fasted and wept, thinking, 'Perhaps the LORD will grant me the child's life.' ²³But now he is dead. Why should I fast? Can I bring him back again? I shall go to him, but he will not return to me."ᵃ ²⁴Then David comforted his wife Bathsheba. He went and slept with her; and she conceived and bore him a son, who was named Solomon. The LORD loved him ²⁵and sent the prophet Nathan to name him Jedidiah, on behalf of the LORD.

Ammonite War Ends. ²⁶ᵇJoab fought against Rabbah of the Ammonites and captured this royal city. ²⁷He sent messengers to David with the word: "I have fought against Rabbah and have taken the water-city. ²⁸Therefore, assemble the rest of the soldiers, join the siege against the city and capture it, lest it be I that capture the city and it be credited to me." ²⁹So David assembled the rest of the soldiers and went to Rabbah. When he had fought against it and captured it, ³⁰he took the crown from Milcom's head. It weighed a talent,* of gold and precious stones; it was placed on David's head. He brought out immense booty from the city, ³¹and also led away the inhabitants, whom he assigned to work with saws, iron picks, and iron axes, or put to work at the brickmold. This is what he did to all the Ammonite cities. David and all the soldiers then returned to Jerusalem.

CHAPTER 13

See RG 120

The Crime of Amnon. ¹Some time later the following incident occurred. David's son Absalom had a beautiful sister named Tamar, and David's son Amnon loved her.ᶜ ²He was in such straits over his sister Tamar that he became sick; since she was a virgin, Amnon thought it impossible to carry out his designs toward her. ³Now Amnon had a friend named Jonadab, son of David's brother Shimeah, who was very clever.ᵈ ⁴He asked him, "Prince, why are you so dejected morning after morning? Why

not tell me?" So Amnon said to him, "I am in love with Tamar, my brother Absalom's sister." ⁵Then Jonadab replied, "Lie down on your bed and pretend to be sick. When your father comes to visit you, say to him, 'Please let my sister Tamar come and encourage me to take food. If she prepares something appetizing in my presence, for me to see, I will eat it from her hand.' " ⁶So Amnon lay down and pretended to be sick. When the king came to visit him, Amnon said to the king, "Please let my sister Tamar come and prepare some fried cakes before my eyes, that I may take nourishment from her hand."

⁷David then sent home a message to Tamar, "Please go to the house of your brother Amnon and prepare some nourishment for him." ⁸Tamar went to the house of her brother Amnon, who was in bed. Taking dough and kneading it, she twisted it into cakes before his eyes and fried the cakes. ⁹Then she took the pan and set out the cakes before him. But Amnon would not eat; he said, "Have everyone leave me." When they had all left him, ¹⁰Amnon said to Tamar, "Bring the nourishment into the bedroom, that I may have it from your hand." So Tamar picked up the cakes she had prepared and brought them to her brother Amnon in the bedroom. ¹¹But when she brought them to him to eat, he seized her and said to her, "Come! Lie with me, my sister!" ¹²But she answered him, "No, my brother! Do not shame me! That is an intolerable crime in Israel. Do not commit this insensate deed.ᵉ ¹³Where would I take my shame? And you would be a discredited man in Israel. So please, speak to the king; he will not keep me from you."ᶠ

¹⁴Not heeding her plea, he overpowered her; he shamed her and had relations with her. ¹⁵Then Amnon conceived an intense hatred for her, which far surpassed the love he had had for her. "Get up and leave," he said to her. ¹⁶She replied, "No, brother, because to drive me out would be far worse than the first injury you have done me." He would

---

12, 30: Weighed a talent: since this would be more than 75 pounds, some commentators picture the idol's crown as displaying a single precious stone of large size, which David took to wear; but the text does not say this.

---

a: Jb 7, 9.   *b:* 26-31: 1 Chr 20, 1-3.   *c:* 2 Sm 3, 2f; 1 Chr 3, 9.   *d:* 1 Sm 21, 21.   *e:* Lv 18, 9; 20, 17; Dt 27, 22.   *f:* Gn 34, 7.

not listen to her, [17]but called the youth who was his attendant and said, "Put her outside, away from me, and bar the door after her." [18]Now she had on a long tunic, for that is how maiden princesses dressed in olden days. When his attendant put her out and barred the door after her, [19]Tamar put ashes on her head and tore the long tunic in which she was clothed. Then, putting her hands to her head, she went away crying loudly. [20]Her brother Absalom said to her: "Has your brother Amnon been with you? Be still now, my sister; he is your brother. Do not take this affair to heart." But Tamar remained grief-stricken and forlorn in the house of her brother Absalom. [21]King David, who got word of the whole affair, became very angry. He did not, however, spark the resentment of his son Amnon, whom he favored because he was his first-born. [22]Absalom, moreover, said nothing at all to Amnon, although he hated him for having shamed his sister Tamar.

Absalom's Plot. [23]After a period of two years Absalom had shearers in Baal-hazor near Ephraim, and he invited all the princes. [24]Absalom went to the king and said: "Your servant is having shearers. Please, your majesty, come with all your retainers to your servant." [25]But the king said to Absalom, "No, my son, all of us should not go lest we be a burden to you." And though Absalom urged him, he refused to go and began to bid him goodbye. [26]Absalom then said, "If you will not come yourself, please let my brother Amnon come to us." The king asked him, "Why should he go to you?" [27]At Absalom's urging, however, he sent Amnon and all the other princes with him. Absalom prepared a banquet fit for royalty. [28g]But he had instructed his servants: "Now watch! When Amnon is merry with wine and I say to you, 'Kill Amnon,' put him to death. Do not be afraid, for it is I who order you to do it. Be resolute and act manfully."

Death of Amnon. [29]When the servants did to Amnon as Absalom had commanded, all the other princes rose, mounted their mules, and fled. [30]While they were still on the road,

a report reached David that Absalom had killed all the princes and that not one of them had survived. [31]The king stood up, rent his garments, and then lay on the ground. All his servants standing by him also rent their garments.[h] [32]But Jonadab, son of David's brother Shimeah, spoke up: "Let not my lord think that all the young princes have been killed! Amnon alone is dead, for Absalom was determined on this ever since Amnon shamed his sister Tamar. [33]So let not my lord the king put faith in the report that all the princes are dead. Amnon alone is dead." [34]Meanwhile, Absalom had taken flight. Then the servant on watch looked about and saw a large group coming down the slope from the direction of Bahurim. He came in and reported this, telling the king that he had seen some men coming down the mountainside from the direction of Bahurim. [35]So Jonadab said to the king: "There! The princes have come. It is as your servant said." [36]No sooner had he finished speaking than the princes came in, weeping aloud. The king, too, and all his servants wept very bitterly. [37]But Absalom, who had taken flight, went to Talmai, son of Ammihud, king of Geshur,[i] [38]and stayed in Geshur for three years.

Efforts for Absalom's Return. [39]The king continued during all that time to mourn over his son; but his longing reached out for Absalom as he became reconciled to the death of Amnon.

CHAPTER 14

See RG 120

[1]When Joab, son of Zeruiah, observed how the king felt toward Absalom, [2]he sent to Tekoa and brought from there a gifted woman, to whom he said: "Pretend to be in mourning. Put on mourning apparel and do not anoint yourself with oil, that you may appear to be a woman who has been long in mourning for a departed one. [3]Then go to the king and speak to him in this manner." And Joab instructed her what to say.

[4]So the woman of Tekoa went to the king and fell prostrate to the ground in homage, saying, "Help, your majesty!" [5j]The king said to her, "What do you want?" She

g: 28f: 2 Sm 12, 10.   h: 2 Sm 1, 11.   i: 2 Sm 3, 3; 15, 8.   j: 5f: 2 Kgs 6, 26f.

replied: "Alas, I am a widow; my husband is dead. 6Your servant had two sons, who quarreled in the field. There being no one to part them, one of them struck his brother and killed him. 7Then the whole clan confronted your servant and demanded: 'Give up the one who killed his brother. We must put him to death for the life of his brother whom he has slain; we must extinguish the heir also.' Thus they will quench my remaining hope* and leave my husband neither name nor posterity upon the earth."k 8The king then said to the woman: "Go home. I will issue a command on your behalf." 9The woman of Tekoa answered him, "Let me and my family be to blame, my lord king; you and your throne are innocent." 10Then the king said, "If anyone says a word to you, have him brought to me, and he shall not touch you again." 11But she went on to say, "Please, your majesty, keep in mind the LORD your God, that the avenger of blood may not go too far in destruction and that my son may not be done away with." He replied, "As the LORD lives, not a hair of your son shall fall to the ground."

12The woman continued, "Please let your servant say still another word to my lord the king." He replied, "Speak." 13So the woman said: "Why, then, do you think of this same kind of thing against the people of God? In pronouncing as he has, the king shows himself guilty, for not bringing back his own banished son. 14We must indeed die; we are then like water that is poured out on the ground and cannot be gathered up. Yet, though God does not bring back life, he does take thought how not to banish* anyone from him.l 15And now, if I have presumed to speak of this matter to your majesty, it is because the people have given me cause to fear. And so your servant thought: 'Let me speak to the king. Perhaps he will grant the petition of his maidservant. 16For the king must surely consent to free his servant from the grasp of one who would seek to destroy me and my son as well from God's inheritance.' " 17And the woman concluded: "Let the word of my lord the king provide a resting place;* indeed, my lord the king is like an angel of God, evaluating good and bad. The LORD your God be with you."m

18The king answered the woman, "Now do not conceal from me anything I may ask you!" The woman said, "Let my lord the king speak." 19So the king asked, "Is Joab involved with you in all this?" And the woman answered: "As you live, my lord the king, it is just as your majesty has said, and not otherwise. It was your servant Joab who instructed me and told your servant all these things she was to say. 20Your servant Joab did this to come at the issue in a roundabout way. But my lord is as wise as an angel of God, so that he knows all things on earth."

Absalom's Return. 21Then the king said to Joab: "I hereby grant this request. Go, therefore, and bring back young Absalom." 22Falling prostrate to the ground in homage and blessing the king, Joab said, "This day I know that I am in good favor with you, my lord the king, since the king has granted the request of his servant." 23Joab then went off to Geshur and brought Absalom to Jerusalem. 24But the king said, "Let him go to his own house; he shall not appear before me." So Absalom went off to his house and did not appear before the king.

25In all Israel there was not a man who could so be praised for his beauty as Absalom, who was without blemish from the sole of his foot to the crown of his head. 26When he shaved his head—which he used to do at the end of every year, because his hair became too heavy for him—the hair weighed two hundred shekels according to the royal standard. 27Absalom had three sons born to him, besides a daughter named Tamar, who was a beautiful woman.n

---

14, 7: Hope: literally, "glowing coal." The image is similar to that of the lighted lamp, e.g., Ps 89, 17, to keep alive the ancestral name.

14, 14: How not to banish: a possible allusion to the religious institution of cities of refuge for involuntary murderers; see Nm 35, 9-15.

14, 17: A resting place: cf Ps 95, 11; Heb 3, 7—4, 11. The reference here is to a return home for Absalom to Israel.

k: Nm 35, 19. l: Jb 7, 9; 14, 7-12; Ps 88, 5. 11ff. m: 17. 20: 1 Sm 29, 9. n: 2 Sm 18, 18.

Hebron and Absalom's Rebellion

Hebron was the capital of Judah, where David had been made king of both Judah and Israel and had ruled Judah for seven years. Absalom mirrored his father's rise by declaring himself king in Hebron (15, 7–12). His revolt, however, was not limited to Judah but spread throughout all the tribes of Israel (v. 10). Absalom would have become king on David's death. He either became too impatient or was embittered by the circumstances of the preceding years. Absalom's chariots, horses, and fifty henchmen (15, 1) gave him the airs of a king-to-be.

Absalom Is Pardoned. [28] Absalom lived in Jerusalem for two years without appearing before the king. [29] Then he summoned Joab to send him to the king, but Joab would not come to him. Although he summoned him a second time, Joab refused to come. [30] He therefore instructed his servants: "You see Joab's field that borders mine, on which he has barley. Go, set it on fire." And so Absalom's servants set the field on fire.[o] Joab's farmhands came to him with torn garments and reported to him what had been done. [31] At this, Joab went to Absalom in his house and asked him, "Why have your servants set my field on fire?" [32] Absalom answered Joab: "I was summoning you to come here, that I may send you to the king to say: 'Why did I come back from Geshur? I would be better off if I were still there!' Now, let me appear before the king. If I am guilty, let him put me to death." [33] Joab went to the king and reported this. The king then called Absalom, who came to him and in homage fell on his face to the ground before the king. Then the king kissed him.

CHAPTER 15

See RG 121

Absalom's Plot. [1] After this Absalom provided himself with chariots, horses, and fifty henchmen.[p] [2] Moreover, Absalom used to rise early and stand alongside the road leading to the gate. If someone had a lawsuit to be decided by the king, Absalom would call to him and say, "From what city are you?" And when he replied, "Your servant is of such and such a tribe of Israel," [3] Absalom would say to him, "Your suit is good and just, but there is no one to hear you in the king's name." [4] And he would continue:

"If only I could be appointed judge in the land! Then everyone who has a lawsuit to be decided might come to me and I would render him justice." [5] Whenever a man approached him to show homage, he would extend his hand, hold him, and kiss him. [6] By behaving in this way toward all the Israelites who came to the king for judgment, Absalom was stealing away the loyalties of the men of Israel.

Conspiracy in Hebron. [7] After a period of four years, Absalom said to the king: "Allow me to go to Hebron and fulfill a vow I made to the LORD. [8] For while living in Geshur in Aram, your servant made this vow: 'If the LORD ever brings me back to Jerusalem, I will worship him in Hebron.' "[q] [9] The king wished him a safe journey, and he went off to Hebron. [10] Then Absalom sent spies throughout the tribes of Israel to say, "When you hear the sound of the horn, declare Absalom king in Hebron." [11] Two hundred men had accompanied Absalom from Jerusalem. They had been invited and went in good faith, knowing nothing of the plan. [12] Absalom also sent to Ahithophel the Gilonite, David's counselor, an invitation to come from his town, Giloh, for the sacrifices he was about to offer. So the conspiracy gained strength, and the people with Absalom increased in numbers.[r]

David Flees Jerusalem. [13] An informant came to David with the report, "The Israelites have transferred their loyalty to Absalom."[s] [14] At this, David said to all his servants who were with him in Jerusalem: "Up! Let us take flight, or none of us will escape from Absalom. Leave quickly, lest he hurry and overtake us, then visit disaster upon us and put the city to the sword." [15] The king's

o: Jgs 15, 4f.   *p:* 1 Sm 8, 11; 1 Kgs 1, 5.   *q:* 2 Sm 3, 3; 13, 37.   *r:* 2 Sm 16, 23.   *s:* Ps 3.

officers answered him, "Your servants are ready, whatever our lord the king chooses to do." [16]Then the king set out, accompanied by his entire household, except for ten concubines whom he left behind to take care of the palace.[t] [17]As the king left the city, with all his officers accompanying him, they halted opposite the ascent of the Mount of Olives, at a distance, [18]while the whole army marched past him.[u]

David and Ittai. As all the Cherethites and Pelethites, and the six hundred men of Gath who had accompanied him from that city, were passing in review before the king, [19]he said to Ittai the Gittite: "Why should you also go with us? Go back and stay with the king, for you are a foreigner and you, too, are an exile from your own country. [20]You came only yesterday, and shall I have you wander about with us today, wherever I have to go? Return and take your brothers with you, and may the LORD be kind and faithful to you." [21]But Ittai answered the king, "As the LORD lives, and as my lord the king lives, your servant shall be wherever my lord the king may be, whether for death or for life."[v] [22]So the king said to Ittai, "Go, then, march on." And Ittai the Gittite, with all his men and all the dependents that were with him, marched on. [23]Everyone in the countryside wept aloud as the last of the soldiers went by, and the king crossed the Kidron Valley with all the soldiers moving on ahead of him by way of the Mount of Olives, toward the desert.

David and the Priests. [24]Zadok, too [with all the Levite bearers of the ark of the covenant of God], and Abiathar brought the ark of God to a halt until the soldiers had marched out of the city. [25]Then the king said to Zadok: "Take the ark of God back to the city. If I find favor with the LORD, he will bring me back and permit me to see it and its lodging. [26]But if he should say, 'I am not pleased with you,' I am ready; let him do to me as he sees fit."[w] [27]The king also said to the priest Zadok: "See to it that you and Abiathar return to the city in peace, and both

your sons with you, your own son Ahimaaz, and Abiathar's son Jonathan. [28]Remember, I shall be waiting at the fords near the desert until I receive information from you." [29]So Zadok and Abiathar took the ark of God back to Jerusalem and remained there.

[30]As David went up the Mount of Olives, he wept without ceasing. His head was covered, and he was walking barefoot. All those who were with him also had their heads covered and were weeping as they went.[x] [31]When David was informed that Ahithophel was among the conspirators with Absalom, he said, "O LORD, turn the counsel of Ahithophel to folly!"[y]

David and Hushai. [32]When David reached the top, where men used to worship God, Hushai the Archite was there to meet him, with rent garments and dirt upon his head.[z] [33]David said to him: "If you come with me, you will be a burden to me. [34]But if you return to the city and say to Absalom, 'Let me be your servant, O king; I was formerly your father's servant, but now I will be yours,' you will undo for me the counsel of Ahithophel.[a] [35]You will have the priests Zadok and Abiathar there with you. If you hear anything from the royal palace, you shall report it to the priests Zadok and Abiathar, [36]who have there with them both Zadok's son Ahimaaz and Abiathar's son Jonathan. Through them you shall send on to me whatever you hear." [37]So David's friend Hushai went into the city of Jerusalem as Absalom was about to enter it.

CHAPTER 16

See RG 121

David and Ziba. [1]David had gone a little beyond the top when Ziba, the servant of Meribbaal, met him with saddled asses laden with two hundred loaves of bread, an ephah of cakes of pressed raisins, an ephah of summer fruits, and a skin of wine.[b] [2]The king said to Ziba, "What do you plan to do with these?" Ziba replied: "The asses are for the king's household to ride on. The bread and summer fruits are for your servants to eat, and the wine for those to drink who are weary in the

---

t: 2 Sm 16, 21f; 20, 3.   *u:* 2 Sm 8, 18.   *v:* Ru 1, 16.   *w:* 2 Sm 16, 10.   *x:* 2 Sm 19, 5; Mi 1, 8.   *y:* 2 Sm 16, 23; 17, 14. 23.   *z:* 2 Sm 16, 16.   *a:* 2 Sm 16, 19.   *b:* 2 Sm 4, 4; 9, 1-13; 19, 18. 25.

desert." [3]Then the king said, "And where is your lord's son?" Ziba answered the king, "He is staying in Jerusalem, for he said, 'Now the Israelites will restore to me my father's kingdom.' "[c] [4]The king therefore said to Ziba, "So! Everything Meribbaal had is yours." Then Ziba said: "I pay you homage, my lord the king. May I find favor with you!"[d]

David and Shimei. [5]As David was approaching Bahurim, a man named Shimei, the son of Gera of the same clan as Saul's family, was coming out of the place, cursing as he came.[e] [6]He threw stones at David and at all the king's officers, even though all the soldiers, including the royal guard, were on David's right and on his left. [7]Shimei was saying as he cursed: "Away, away, you murderous and wicked man! [8]The LORD has requited you for all the bloodshed in the family of Saul,* in whose stead you became king, and the LORD has given over the kingdom to your son Absalom. And now you suffer ruin because you are a murderer." [9]Abishai, son of Zeruiah, said to the king: "Why should this dead dog curse my lord the king? Let me go over, please, and lop off his head."[f] [10]But the king replied: "What business is it of mine or of yours, sons of Zeruiah, that he curses? Suppose the LORD has told him to curse David; who then will dare to say, 'Why are you doing this?' "[g] [11]Then the king said to Abishai and to all his servants: "If my own son, who came forth from my loins, is seeking my life, how much more might this Benjaminite do so? Let him alone and let him curse, for the LORD has told him to.[h] [12]Perhaps the LORD will look upon my affliction and make it up to me with benefits for the curses he is uttering this day." [13]David and his men continued on the road, while Shimei kept abreast of them on the hillside, all the while cursing and throwing stones and dirt as he went.[i] [14]The king and all the soldiers with him arrived at the Jordan tired out, and stopped there for a rest.

Absalom's Counselors. [15]In the meantime Absalom, accompanied by Ahithophel, entered Jerusalem with all the Israelites. [16]When David's friend Hushai the Archite came to Absalom, he said to him: "Long live the king! Long live the king!"[j] [17]But Absalom asked Hushai: "Is this your devotion to your friend? Why did you not go with your friend?" [18]Hushai replied to Absalom: "On the contrary, I am his whom the LORD and all this people and all Israel have chosen, and with him I will stay. [19]Furthermore, as I was in attendance upon your father, so will I be before you. Whom should I serve, if not his son?"[k] [20]Then Absalom said to Ahithophel, "Offer your counsel on what we should do." [21]Ahithophel replied to Absalom: "Have relations with your father's concubines, whom he left behind to take care of the palace. When all Israel hears how odious you have made yourself to your father, all your partisans will take courage."[l] [22]So a tent was pitched on the roof for Absalom, and he visited his father's concubines in view of all Israel.[m]

Counsel of Ahithophel. [23]Now the counsel given by Ahithophel at that time was as though one had sought divine revelation. Such was all his counsel both to David and to Absalom.[n]

CHAPTER 17

See RG 121

[1]Ahithophel went on to say to Absalom: "Please let me choose twelve thousand men, and be off in pursuit of David tonight. [2]If I come upon him when he is weary and discouraged, I shall cause him to panic. When all the people with him flee, I shall strike down the king alone. [3]Then I can bring back the rest of the people to you, as a bride returns to her husband. It is the death of only one man you are seeking; then all the people will be at peace." [4]This plan was agreeable to Absalom and to all the elders of Israel.

Counsel of Hushai. [5]Then Absalom said, "Now call Hushai the Archite also; let us hear what he too has to say." [6]When Hushai came to Absalom, Absalom said to him: "This is what Ahithophel proposed. Shall

---

16, 8: Bloodshed . . . Saul: refers to the episode recounted in 2 Sm 21, 1-14.

c: 2 Sm 19, 26f.   d: 2 Sm 19, 30.   e: 2 Sm 3, 16; 19, 17. 22f; 1 Kgs 2, 8.   f: 2 Sm 19, 23. 29; 1 Sm 24, 15; 26, 6.   g: 2 Sm 15, 25f; 19, 23.   h: 2 Sm 12, 11.   i: 2 Sm 19, 19-24.   j: 2 Sm 15, 32-37.   k: 2 Sm 15, 34.   l: 2 Sm 15, 16; 20, 3.   m: 2 Sm 12, 11f.   n: 2 Sm 15, 12. 31; 17, 23.

we follow his proposal? If not, speak up." [7]Hushai replied to Absalom, "This time Ahithophel has not given good counsel." [8]And he went on to say: "You know that your father and his men are warriors, and that they are as fierce as a bear in the wild robbed of her cubs. Moreover, since your father is skilled in warfare, he will not spend the night with the people.[o] [9]Even now he lies hidden in one of the caves or in some other place. And if some of our soldiers should fall at the first attack, whoever hears of it will say, 'Absalom's followers have been slaughtered.' [10]Then even the brave man with the heart of a lion will lose courage. For all Israel knows that your father is a warrior and that those who are with him are brave.

[11]"This is what I counsel: Let all Israel from Dan to Beer-sheba, who are as numerous as the sands by the sea, be called up for combat; and go with them yourself. [12]We can then attack him wherever we find him, settling down upon him as dew alights on the ground. None shall survive—neither he nor any of his followers. [13]And if he retires into a city, all Israel shall bring ropes to that city and we can drag it into the gorge, so that not even a pebble of it can be found." [14]Then Absalom and all the Israelites pronounced the counsel of Hushai the Archite better than that of Ahithophel. For the LORD had decided to undo Ahithophel's good counsel, in order thus to bring Absalom to ruin.[p]

David Told of the Plan. [15]Then Hushai said to the priests Zadok and Abiathar: "This is the counsel Ahithophel gave Absalom and the elders of Israel, and this is what I counseled. [16]So send a warning to David immediately, not to spend the night at the fords near the desert, but to cross over without fail. Otherwise the king and all the people with him will be destroyed." [17]Now Jonathan and Ahimaaz were staying at En-rogel, since they could not risk being seen entering the city. A maidservant was to come with information for them, and they in turn were to go and report to King David. [18]But an attendant saw them and informed Absalom. They sped on their way and reached the house of a man in Bahurim who

had a cistern in his courtyard. They let themselves down into this, [19]and the housewife took the cover and spread it over the cistern, strewing ground grain on the cover so that nothing could be noticed. [20]When Absalom's servants came to the woman at the house, they asked, "Where are Ahimaaz and Jonathan?" The woman replied, "They went by a short while ago toward the water." They searched, but found no one, and so returned to Jerusalem. [21]As soon as they left, Ahimaaz and Jonathan came up out of the cistern and went on to inform King David. They said to him: "Leave! Cross the water at once, for Ahithophel has given the following counsel in regard to you." [22]So David and all his people moved on and crossed the Jordan. By daybreak, there was no one left who had not crossed.

[23]When Ahithophel saw that his counsel was not acted upon, he saddled his ass and departed, going to his home in his own city. Then, having left orders concerning his family, he hanged himself. And so he died and was buried in his father's tomb.[q]

[24]Now David had gone to Mahanaim when Absalom crossed the Jordan accompanied by all the Israelites. [25]Absalom had put Amasa in command of the army in Joab's place. Amasa was the son of an Ishmaelite named Ithra, who had married Abigail, daughter of Jesse and sister of Joab's mother Zeruiah.[r] [26]Israel and Absalom encamped in the territory of Gilead.

[27]When David came to Mahanaim, Shobi, son of Nahash from Rabbah of the Ammonites, Machir, son of Ammiel from Lodebar, and Barzillai, the Gileadite from Rogelim,[s] [28]brought couches, coverlets, basins and earthenware, as well as wheat, barley, flour, roasted grain, beans, lentils,[t] [29]honey, butter and cheese from the flocks and herds, for David and those who were with him to eat; for they said, "The people have been hungry and tired and thirsty in the desert."

CHAPTER 18

Preparation for Battle. [1]After mustering the troops he had with him, David placed officers in command of groups of a thousand

o: Hos 13, 8.   p: 2 Sm 15, 31.   q: 2 Sm 15, 31; 16, 23.   r: 2 Sm 19, 14; 20, 4-13.   s: 2 Sm 9, 4; 19, 32; 1 Kgs 2, 7.   t: 2 Sm 19, 32; Ezr 2, 61.

See RG
121

and groups of a hundred. [2]David then put a third part of the soldiers under Joab's command, a third under command of Abishai, son of Zeruiah and brother of Joab, and a third under command of Ittai the Gittite. The king then said to the soldiers, "I intend to go out with you myself." [3]But they replied: "You must not come out with us. For if we should flee, we shall not count; even if half of us should die, we shall not count. You are equal to ten thousand of us. Therefore it is better that we have you to help us from the city." [4]So the king said to them, "I will do what you think best"; and he stood by the gate as all the soldiers marched out in units of a hundred and of a thousand. [5]But the king gave this command to Joab, Abishai and Ittai: "Be gentle with young Absalom for my sake." All the soldiers heard the king instruct the various leaders with regard to Absalom.

Defeat of Absalom. [6]David's army then took the field against Israel, and a battle was fought in the forest near Mahanaim. [7]The forces of Israel were defeated by David's servants, and the casualties there that day were heavy—twenty thousand men. [8]The battle spread out over that entire region, and the thickets consumed more combatants that day than did the sword.

Death of Absalom. [9]Absalom unexpectedly came up against David's servants. He was mounted on a mule, and, as the mule passed under the branches of a large terebinth, his hair caught fast in the tree. He hung between heaven and earth while the mule he had been riding ran off. [10]Someone saw this and reported to Joab that he had seen Absalom hanging from a terebinth. [11]Joab said to his informant: "If you saw him, why did you not strike him to the ground on the spot? Then it would have been my duty to give you fifty pieces of silver and a belt." [12]But the man replied to Joab: "Even if I already held a thousand pieces of silver in my two hands, I would not harm the king's son, for the king charged you and Abishai and Ittai in our hearing to protect the youth Absalom for his sake. [13]Had I been disloyal and killed him, the whole matter would have come to the attention of the king, and you would stand aloof." [14]Joab replied, "I will not waste time with you in this way." And taking three pikes in hand, he thrust for the heart of Absalom, still hanging from the tree alive.[u] [15]Next, ten of Joab's young armor-bearers closed in on Absalom, and killed him with further blows. [16]Joab then sounded the horn, and the soldiers turned back from the pursuit of the Israelites, because Joab called on them to halt.[v] [17]Absalom was taken up and cast into a deep pit in the forest, and a very large mound of stones was erected over him. And all the Israelites fled to their own tents.[w]

[18]During his lifetime Absalom had taken a pillar and erected it for himself in the King's Valley, for he said, "I have no son to perpetuate my name." The pillar which he named for himself is called Yad-absalom to the present day.[x]

David Told of Absalom's Death. [19]Then Ahimaaz, son of Zadok, said, "Let me run to take the good news to the king that the LORD has set him free from the grasp of his enemies." [20]But Joab said to him: "You are not the man to bring the news today. On some other day you may take the good news, but today you would not be bringing good news, for in fact the king's son is dead." [21]Then Joab said to a Cushite, "Go, tell the king what you have seen." The Cushite bowed to Joab and sped away. [22]But Ahimaaz, son of Zadok, said to Joab again, "Come what may, permit me also to run after the Cushite." Joab replied: "Why do you want to run, my son? You will receive no reward." [23]But he insisted, "Come what may, I want to run." Joab said to him, "Very well." Ahimaaz sped off by way of the Jordan plain and outran the Cushite.

[24]Now David was sitting between the two gates, and a lookout mounted to the roof of the gate above the city wall, where he looked about and saw a man running all alone. [25]The lookout shouted to inform the king, who said, "If he is alone, he has good news to report." As he kept coming nearer, [26]the lookout spied another runner. From his place atop the

---

u: 2 Sm 12, 10; 13, 28f.   v: 2 Sm 20, 23-26.   w: Jos 7, 26; 8, 29; 10, 27.   x: 2 Sm 14, 27.

gate he cried out, "There is another man running by himself." And the king responded, "He, too, is bringing good news." [27]Then the lookout said, "I notice that the first one runs like Ahimaaz, son of Zadok." The king replied, "He is a good man; he comes with good news."[y] [28]Then Ahimaaz called out and greeted the king. With face to the ground he paid homage to the king and said, "Blessed be the LORD your God, who has delivered up the men who rebelled against my lord the king." [29]But the king asked, "Is the youth Absalom safe?" And Ahimaaz replied, "I saw a great disturbance when the king's servant Joab sent your servant on, but I do not know what it was." [30]The king said, "Step aside and remain in attendance here." So he stepped aside and remained there. [31]When the Cushite came in, he said, "Let my lord the king receive the good news that this day the LORD has taken your part, freeing you from the grasp of all who rebelled against you." [32]But the king asked the Cushite, "Is young Absalom safe?" The Cushite replied, "May the enemies of my lord the king and all who rebel against you with evil intent be as that young man!"

CHAPTER 19

See RG
121

[1]The king was shaken, and went up to the room over the city gate to weep. He said as he wept, "My son Absalom! My son, my son Absalom! If only I had died instead of you, Absalom, my son, my son!"

Joab Reproves David. [2]Joab was told that the king was weeping and mourning for Absalom; [3]and that day's victory was turned into mourning for the whole army when they heard that the king was grieving for his son. [4]The soldiers stole into the city that day like men shamed by flight in battle. [5]Meanwhile the king covered his face and cried out in a loud voice, "My son Absalom! Absalom! My son, my son!"[z] [6]Then Joab went to his residence and said: "Though they saved your life and your sons' and daughters' lives, also the lives of your wives and those of your concubines, you have put all your servants to shame today [7]by loving those who

hate you and hating those who love you. For you have shown today that officers and servants mean nothing to you. Indeed I am now certain that if Absalom were alive today and all of us dead, you would think that more suitable. [8]Now then, get up! Go out and speak kindly to your servants. I swear by the LORD that if you do not go out, not a single man will remain with you overnight, and this will be a far greater disaster for you than any that has afflicted you from your youth until now." [9]So the king stepped out and sat at the gate. When all the people were informed that the king was sitting at the gate, they came into his presence.

The Reconciliation. Now the Israelites had fled to their separate tents, [10]but throughout the tribes of Israel all the people were arguing among themselves, saying to one another: "The king delivered us from the clutches of our enemies, and it was he who rescued us from the grip of the Philistines. But now he has fled from the country before Absalom, [11]and Absalom, whom we anointed over us, died in battle. Why, then, should you remain silent about restoring the king to his palace?" When the talk of all Israel reached the king, [12]David sent word to the priests Zadok and Abiathar: "Say to the elders of Judah: 'Why should you be last to restore the king to his palace? [13]You are my brothers, you are my bone and flesh. Why should you be last to restore the king?' [14]Also say to Amasa: 'Are you not my bone and flesh? May God do thus and so to me, if you do not become my general permanently in place of Joab.' "[a] [15]He won over all the Judahites as one man, and so they summoned the king to return, with all his servants.

David and Shimei. [16]When the king, on his return, reached the Jordan, Judah had come to Gilgal to meet him and to escort him across the Jordan. [17]Shimei, son of Gera, the Benjaminite from Bahurim, hurried down with the Judahites to meet King David,[b] [18]accompanied by a thousand men from Benjamin. Ziba, too, the servant of the house of Saul, accompanied by his fifteen sons and twenty servants, hastened to the Jordan be-

y: 2 Kgs 9, 20.   z: 2 Sm 15, 30.   a: 2 Sm 17, 25; 20, 4.   b: 2 Sm 16, 5-13.

fore the king.[c] [19d]They crossed over the ford to bring the king's household over and to do whatever he wished. When Shimei, son of Gera, crossed the Jordan, he fell down before the king [20]and said to him: "May my lord not hold me guilty, and may he not remember and take to heart the wrong that your servant did the day my lord the king left Jerusalem. [21]For your servant knows that he has done wrong. Yet realize that I have been the first of the whole house of Joseph to come down today to meet my lord the king." [22]But Abishai, son of Zeruiah, countered: "Shimei must be put to death for this. He cursed the LORD's anointed." [23]David replied: "What has come between you and me, sons of Zeruiah, that you would create enmity for me this day? Should anyone die today in Israel? Am I not aware that today I am king of Israel?"[e] [24]Then the king said to Shimei, "You shall not die." And the king gave him his oath.

David and Meribbaal. [25]Meribbaal, son of Saul, also went down to meet the king. He had not washed his feet nor trimmed his mustache nor washed his clothes from the day the king left until he returned safely. [26]When he came from Jerusalem to meet the king, the king asked him, "Why did you not go with me, Meribbaal?"[f] [27]He replied: "My lord the king, my servant betrayed me. For your servant, who is lame, said to him, 'Saddle the ass for me, that I may ride on it and go with the king.'[g] [28]But he slandered your servant before my lord the king. But my lord the king is like an angel of God. Do what you judge best. [29]For though my father's entire house deserved only death from my lord the king, yet you placed your servant among the guests at your table. What right do I still have to make further appeal to the king?"[h] [30]But the king said to him: "Why do you go on talking? I say, 'You and Ziba shall divide the property.'"[i] [31]Meribbaal answered the king, "Indeed let him have it all, now that my lord the king has returned safely to his palace."

David and Barzillai. [32]Barzillai the Gileadite also came down from Rogelim and escorted the king to the Jordan for his crossing, taking leave of him there.[j] [33]It was Barzillai, a very old man of eighty and very wealthy besides, who had provisioned the king during his stay in Mahanaim. [34]The king said to Barzillai, "Cross over with me, and I will provide for your old age as my guest in Jerusalem." [35]But Barzillai answered the king: "How much longer have I to live, that I should go up to Jerusalem with the king? [36]I am now eighty years old. Can I distinguish between good and bad? Can your servant taste what he eats and drinks, or still appreciate the voices of singers and songstresses? Why should your servant be any further burden to my lord the king? [37]In escorting the king across the Jordan, your servant is doing little enough! Why should the king give me this reward? [38]Please let your servant go back to die in his own city by the tomb of his father and mother. Here is your servant Chimham. Let him cross over with my lord the king. Do for him whatever you will." [39]Then the king said to him, "Chimham shall come over with me, and I will do for him as you would wish. And anything else you would like me to do for you, I will do." [40]Then all the people crossed over the Jordan, but the king remained; he kissed Barzillai and bade him Godspeed as he returned to his own district. [41]Finally the king crossed over to Gilgal, accompanied by Chimham.

Israel and Judah Quarrel. All the people of Judah and half of the people of Israel had escorted the king across. [42]But all these Israelites began coming to the king and saying, "Why did our brothers the Judahites steal you away and escort the king and his household across the Jordan, along with all David's men?" [43]All the Judahites replied to the men of Israel: "Because the king is our relative. Why are you angry over this affair? Have we had anything to eat at the king's expense? Or have portions from his table been given to us?" [44]The Israelites answered the Judahites: "We have ten shares in the king.

---

c: 2 Sm 16, 1-4; 19, 25-31.   d: 19ff: 2 Sm 16, 13; Ex 22, 27; 1 Kgs 2, 8.   e: 2 Sm 16, 9f; 1 Sm 11, 13; 1 Kgs 2, 8. 38. 46.   f: 2 Sm 16, 3.   g: 2 Sm 9, 2-13; Dt 21, 12f.   h: 2 Sm 9, 9ff.   i: 2 Sm 16, 4.   j: 2 Sm 17, 27ff; 1 Kgs 2, 7; Ezr 2, 61.

Also, we are the first-born rather than you. Why do you slight us? Were we not first to speak of restoring the king?" Then the Judahites in turn spoke even more fiercely than the Israelites.[k]

See RG
121

CHAPTER 20

Sheba's Rebellion. [1]Now a rebellious individual from Benjamin named Sheba, the son of Bichri, happened to be there. He sounded the horn and cried out,

"We have no portion in David,
   nor any share in the son of Jesse.
Every man to his tent, O Israel!"[l]

[2]So all the Israelites left David for Sheba, son of Bichri. But from the Jordan to Jerusalem the Judahites remained loyal to their king. [3]When King David came to his palace in Jerusalem, he took the ten concubines whom he had left behind to take care of the palace and placed them in confinement. He provided for them, but had no further relations with them. And so they remained in confinement to the day of their death, lifelong widows.[m]

Amasa's Death. [4]Then the king said to Amasa: "Summon the Judahites for me within three days. Then present yourself here."[n] [5]Accordingly Amasa set out to summon Judah, but delayed beyond the time set for him by David. [6]Then David said to Abishai: "Sheba, son of Bichri, may now do us more harm than Absalom did. Take your lord's servants and pursue him, lest he find fortified cities and take shelter while we look on." [7]So Joab and the Cherethites and Pelethites and all the warriors marched out behind Abishai from Jerusalem to campaign in pursuit of Sheba, son of Bichri.[o] [8]*They were at the great stone in Gibeon when Amasa met them. Now Joab had a belt over his tunic, from which was slung, in its sheath near his thigh, a sword that could be drawn with a downward movement.[p] [9]And Joab asked Amasa, "How are you, my brother?"

With his right hand Joab held Amasa's beard as if to kiss him. [10]And since Amasa was not on his guard against the sword in Joab's other hand, Joab stabbed him in the abdomen with it, so that his entrails burst forth to the ground, and he died without receiving a second thrust. Then Joab and his brother Abishai pursued Sheba, son of Bichri.[q] [11]One of Joab's attendants stood by Amasa and said, "Let him who favors Joab and is for David follow Joab." [12]Amasa lay covered with blood in the middle of the highroad, and the man noticed that all the soldiers were stopping. So he removed Amasa from the road to the field and placed a garment over him, because all who came up to him were stopping. [13]When he had been removed from the road, everyone went on after Joab in pursuit of Sheba, son of Bichri.

Joab Pursues Sheba. [14]Sheba passed through all the tribes of Israel to Abel Beth-maacah. Then all the Bichrites assembled and they too entered the city after him. [15]So David's servants came and besieged him in Abel Beth-maacah. They threw up a mound against the city, and all the soldiers who were with Joab began battering the wall to throw it down. [16]Then a wise woman from the city stood on the outworks and called out, "Listen, listen! Tell Joab to come here, that I may speak with him." [17]When Joab had come near her, the woman said, "Are you Joab?" And he replied, "Yes." She said to him, "Listen to what your maidservant has to say." He replied, "I am listening." [18]Then she went on to say: "There is an ancient saying,* 'Let them ask if they will in Abel[r] [19]or in Dan whether loyalty is finished or ended in Israel.' You are seeking to beat down a city that is a mother in Israel. Why do you wish to destroy the inheritance of the LORD?" [20]Joab answered, "Not at all, not at all! I do not wish to destroy or to ruin anything. [21]That is not the case at all. A man named Sheba, son of Bichri, from the hill country of Ephraim has rebelled against King David. Surrender him alone, and I will

20, 8: The text of this verse is quite uncertain.
20, 18f: The proverbial expression here has been poorly transmitted, and its sense is doubtful.

k: 1 Kgs 11, 31.   l: 1 Kgs 12, 16.   m: 2 Sm 15, 16; 16, 20ff.   n: 2 Sm 17, 25; 19, 14.   o: 2 Sm 8, 18.   p: 2 Sm 2, 13.   q: 1 Kgs 2, 5.   r: Gn 49, 16.

withdraw from the city." Then the woman said to Joab, "His head shall be thrown to you across the wall." ²²She went to all the people with her advice, and they cut off the head of Sheba, son of Bichri, and threw it out to Joab. He then sounded the horn, and they scattered from the city to their own tents, while Joab returned to Jerusalem to the king.

David's Officials. ²³Joab was in command of the whole army of Israel. Banaiah, son of Jehoiada, was in command of the Cherethites and Pelethites.ˢ ²⁴Adoram was in charge of the forced labor. Jehoshaphat, son of Ahilud, was the chancellor. ²⁵Shawsha was the scribe. Zadok and Abiathar were priests.ᵗ ²⁶Ira the Jairite was also David's priest.

V: Appendixes

CHAPTER 21

See RG
121

Gibeonite Vengeance. ¹During David's reign there was a famine for three successive years. David had recourse to the LORD, who said, "There is bloodguilt on Saul and his family because he put the Gibeonites to death."ᵘ ²So the king called the Gibeonites and spoke to them. (Now the Gibeonites were not Israelites, but survivors of the Amorites; and although the Israelites had given them their oath, Saul had attempted to kill them off in his zeal for the men of Israel and Judah.)ᵛ ³David said to the Gibeonites, "What must I do for you and how must I make atonement, that you may bless the inheritance of the LORD?" ⁴The Gibeonites answered him, "We have no claim against Saul and his house for silver or gold, nor is it our place to put any man to death in Israel." Then he said, "I will do for you whatever you propose." ⁵They said to the king, "As for the man who was exterminating us and who intended to destroy us that we might have no place in all the territory of Israel, ⁶let seven men from among his descendants be given to us, that we may dismember them before the LORD in Gibeon, on the LORD's mountain." The king replied, "I will give them up." ⁷The king, however, spared Meribbaal, son of Jon-

athan, son of Saul, because of the LORD's oath that formed a bond between David and Saul's son Jonathan.ʷ ⁸But the king took Armoni and Meribbaal, the two sons that Aiah's daughter Rizpah had borne to Saul, and the five sons of Saul's daughter Merob that she had borne to Adriel, son of Barzillai the Meholathite,ˣ ⁹and surrendered them to the Gibeonites. They then dismembered them on the mountain before the LORD. The seven fell at the one time; they were put to death during the first days of the harvest—that is, at the beginning of the barley harvest.

¹⁰Then Rizpah, Aiah's daughter, took sackcloth and spread it out for herself on the rock from the beginning of the harvest until rain came down on them from the sky, fending off the birds of the sky from settling on them by day, and the wild animals by night.ʸ ¹¹When David was informed of what Rizpah, Aiah's daughter, the concubine of Saul, had done, ¹²he went and obtained the bones of Saul and of his son Jonathan from the citizens of Jabesh-gilead, who had carried them off secretly from the public square of Beth-shan, where the Philistines had hanged them at the time they killed Saul on Gilboa.ᶻ ¹³When he had brought up from there the bones of Saul and of his son Jonathan, the bones of those who had been dismembered were also gathered up. ¹⁴Then the bones of Saul and of his son Jonathan were buried in the tomb of his father Kish at Zela in the territory of Benjamin. After all that the king commanded had been carried out, God granted relief to the land.ᵃ

Exploits in Philistine Wars. ¹⁵There was another battle between the Philistines and Israel. David went down with his servants and fought the Philistines, but David grew tired. ¹⁶Dadu, one of the Rephaim, whose bronze spear weighed three hundred shekels, was about to take him captive. Dadu was girt with a new sword and planned to kill David, ¹⁷but Abishai, son of Zeruiah, came to his assistance and struck and killed the Philistine. Then David's men swore to him, "You must not go out to battle with us again, lest you quench the lamp of Israel."ᵇ

---

s: 2 Sm 8, 16ff; 23, 20.   *t:* 2 Sm 8, 17f.   *u:* 2 Sm 24, 13.   *v:* Jos 9, 3-27.   *w:* 2 Sm 9, 13; 1 Sm 18, 3; 20, 8ff. 15f. 42.   *x:* 2 Sm 3, 7.   *y:* 2 Sm 3, 31; 12, 16.   *z:* 1 Sm 31, 10-13.   *a:* 2 Sm 24, 25.   *b:* 1 Kgs 11, 36; 15, 4; 2 Kgs 8, 19.

^{18c}After this there was another battle with the Philistines in Gob. On that occasion Sibbecai, from Husha, killed Saph, one of the Rephaim.^d ^{19e}There was another battle with the Philistines in Gob, in which Elhanan, son of Jair from Bethlehem, killed Goliath of Gath, who had a spear with a shaft like a weaver's heddle-bar. ²⁰There was another battle at Gath in which there was a man of large stature with six fingers on each hand and six toes on each foot— twenty-four in all. He too was one of the Rephaim. ²¹And when he insulted Israel, Jonathan, son of David's brother Shimei, killed him.^f ²²These four were Rephaim in Gath, and they fell at the hands of David and his servants.

CHAPTER 22

See RG 121

Song of Thanksgiving.* ¹David sang the words of this song to the LORD when the LORD had rescued him from the grasp of all his enemies and from the hand of Saul.^g ²This is what he sang:^h

A

I

"O LORD, my rock, my fortress, my
    deliverer,
³   my God, my rock of refuge!
My shield, the horn of my salvation,*
    my stronghold, my refuge,
    my savior, from violence you keep me
    safe.ⁱ
⁴ 'Praised be the LORD,' I exclaim,
    and I am safe from my enemies.

II

⁵ "The breakers of death surged round
    about me,*
    the floods of perdition overwhelmed
    me;
⁶ The cords of the nether world enmeshed
    me,
    the snares of death overtook me.
⁷ In my distress I called upon the LORD
    and cried out to my God;
From his temple* he heard my voice,
    and my cry reached his ears.

III

⁸ "The earth swayed and quaked;*
    the foundations of the heavens
    trembled
    and shook when his wrath flared up.
⁹ Smoke rose from his nostrils,
    and a devouring fire from his mouth;
    he kindled coals into flame.
¹⁰ He inclined the heavens and came down,
    with dark clouds under his feet.^j
¹¹ He mounted a cherub* and flew,
    borne on the wings of the wind.^k
¹² He made darkness the shelter about him,
    with spattering rain and thickening
    clouds.
¹³ From the brightness of his presence
    coals were kindled to flame.
¹⁴ "The LORD thundered from heaven;
    the Most High gave forth his voice.
¹⁵ He sent forth arrows to put them to flight;
    he flashed lightning and routed them.^l
¹⁶ Then the wellsprings of the sea appeared,

22, 1-51: This song of thanksgiving is also given, with a few small variants, in Ps 18. In both places it is attributed to David. Two main sections can be distinguished. In the first part, after an introductory stanza of praise to God (2-4), David describes the peril he was in (5-7), and then poetically depicts, under the form of a theophany, God's intervention in his behalf (8-20), concluding with an acknowledgment of God's justice (21-31). In the second part, God is praised for having prepared the psalmist for war (32-35), given him victory over his enemies (36-39), whom he put to flight (40-43), and bestowed on him dominion over many peoples (44-46). The entire song ends with paean of grateful praise (47-51).

22, 3: The horn of my salvation: my strong savior. The horn, the dreadful weapon of an enraged bull, was a symbol of strength; cf Lk 1, 69.

22, 5f: These verses are to be understood figuratively.

22, 7: His temple: his heavenly abode.

22, 8ff: God's intervention is graphically portrayed under the figures of an earthquake (vv 8. 16) and a thunderstorm (vv 9-15); cf Jgs 5, 4f; Pss 29; 97, 2-6; Hb 3.

22, 11: He mounted a cherub: since God makes the winds his messengers, or "angels" (Ps 104, 4), he is spoken of poetically as riding on the clouds, or on the angelic creatures called "cherubim." His earthly throne above the ark of the covenant was likewise associated with two winged cherubim; cf Ex 37, 7ff. In both senses the Lord is enthroned upon the cherubim; cf Pss 79, 2; 99, 1.

c: 18-22: 1 Chr 20, 4-8. *d:* 2 Sm 23, 27. *e:* 19f: 1 Sm 17, 4. 7.
f: 2 Sm 13, 3. *g:* Ps 18, 1. *h:* 2-51: Ps 18, 3-51. *i:* 1 Sm 2, 1f.
j: Ps 144, 5. *k:* Ex 25, 18. *l:* Ps 144, 6.

the foundations of the earth were laid
bare,
At the rebuke of the LORD,
at the blast of the wind of his wrath.

17 "He reached out from on high and
grasped me;
he drew me out of the deep waters.*m*
18 He rescued me from my mighty enemy,
from my foes, who were too powerful
for me.
19 They attacked me on my day of calamity,
but the LORD came to my support.
20 He set me free in the open,
and rescued me, because he loves me.

IV
21 "The LORD rewarded me according to my
justice;
according to the cleanness of my
hands he requited me.
22 For I kept the ways of the LORD
and was not disloyal to my God.
23 For his ordinances were all present to me,
and his statutes I put not from me;
24 But I was wholehearted toward him,
and I was on my guard against guilt.
25 And the LORD requited me according to
my justice,
according to my innocence in his sight.

26 *n*"Toward the faithful you are faithful;*
toward the wholehearted you are
wholehearted;
27 Toward the sincere you are sincere;
but toward the crooked you are astute.
28 You save lowly people,
though on the lofty your eyes look
down.
29 You are my lamp,* O LORD!
O my God, you brighten the darkness
about me.
30 For with your aid I run against an armed
band,
and by the help of my God I leap over
a wall.
31 God's way is unerring;

the promise of the LORD is fire-tried;
he is a shield to all who take refuge in
him."*o*

B
I
32 "For who is God except the LORD?
Who is a rock save our God?
33 The God who girded me with strength
and kept my way unerring;
34 Who made my feet swift as those of hinds
and set me on the heights;*
35 Who trained my hands for war
till my arms could bend a bow of brass.

II
36 "You have given me your saving shield,
and your help has made me great.
37 You made room for my steps;
unwavering was my stride.
38 I pursued my enemies and destroyed
them,
nor did I turn again till I made an end
of them.
39 I smote them and they did not rise;
they fell beneath my feet.

III
40 "You girded me with strength for war;
you subdued my adversaries beneath
me.
41 My enemies you put to flight before me
and those who hated me I destroyed.
42 They cried for help—but no one saved
them;
to the LORD—but he answered them
not.
43 I ground them fine as the dust of the earth;
like the mud in the streets I trampled
them down.

IV
44 "You rescued me from the strife of my
people;
you made me head over nations.
A people I had not known became my
slaves;
45 as soon as they heard me, they obeyed.

22, 26f: Men are treated by God in the same way they treat
him and their fellow men.
22, 29: My lamp: a figure of life and happiness; cf 1 Kgs
11, 36.

22, 34: The heights: a natural stronghold safe from attack;
cf Ps 62, 3; Hb 3, 19.

m: Ps 144, 7.   n: 26f: 1 Sm 2, 30.   o: Prv 30, 5.

Words of David

There may have been a literary tradition in the Bible of ascribing poems to leading characters as their "last words" (see ch 23, 1–7). Compare the poems attributed to Jacob in Genesis 49 and to Moses in Deuteronomy 32—33. David's last words, though, do not consist of a benediction of Israel. Like Moses, David is portrayed as a prophet pronouncing an oracle (23, 1–2). The actual date of David's "last words" is uncertain. In contrast to ch 22, the poem in 23, 1–7 has no parallel in the Psalms. "Anointed" (v. 1) is a royal title, here referring to David, echoing the end of ch 22. "Mighty One of Israel" (v. 1) is an epithet for the LORD. The image of king as the sun (v. 4) was common in the ancient Near East, especially in Egypt, although less so in Israel. The "eternal covenant" (v. 5) was the LORD's promise of a dynasty for David in 7, 16 (cf. Ps 89, 28–29). The wicked are like thorns (v. 6) consumed by the sun's heat.

46 The foreigners fawned and cringed
      before me;
   they staggered forth from their
      fortresses."

C

47 "The LORD live! And blessed be my Rock!
   Extolled be my God, Rock of my
      salvation.
48 O God, who granted me vengeance,
   who made peoples subject to me
49   and helped me escape from my
      enemies,
   Above my adversaries you exalt me
   and from the violent man you rescue me.
50 Therefore will I proclaim you, O LORD,
      among the nations,
   and I will sing praise to your name,^{p}
51 You who gave great victories to your king
   and showed kindness to your anointed,
   to David and his posterity forever."

<blockquote>
See RG 121
</blockquote>

CHAPTER 23

The Last Words of David*

1 These are the last words of David:
"The utterance of David, son of Jesse;
   the utterance of the man God raised up,
Anointed of the God of Jacob,

   favorite of the Mighty One of Israel.^{q}
2 The spirit of the LORD spoke through me;
   his word was on my tongue.^{r}
3 The God of Israel spoke;
   of me the Rock of Israel said,
'He that rules over men in justice,
   that rules in the fear of God,^{s}
4 Is like the morning light at sunrise
   on a cloudless morning,
   making the greensward sparkle after
      rain.'^{t}
5 Is not my house firm before God?
   He has made an eternal covenant with me,
   set forth in detail and secured.^{u}
   Will he not bring to fruition
   all my salvation and my every desire?
6 But the wicked are all like thorns to be
      cast away;
   they cannot be taken up by hand.^{v}
7 He who wishes to touch them
   must arm himself with iron and the
      shaft of a spear,
   and they must be consumed by fire."

David's Warriors. 8These are the names of David's warriors.* Ishbaal, son of Hachamoni, was the first of the Three. It was he who brandished his battle-ax over eight hundred slain in a single encounter.^{w} 9Next to him,

23, 1-7: The text of this short composition in the spirit of the wisdom writers (Prv 30, 1-6) is difficult in places; it views David's career in retrospect.

23, 8ff: There are thirty-seven warriors in all mentioned in this list. First there are the Three warriors most noted for singlehanded exploits (vv 8-12). Then comes the story of a daring adventure by three unnamed members of the larger group (vv 13-17). Next come the commanders of the king's body-

guard, Abishai (vv 18-19) and Benaiah (vv 20-23), with whom must be counted Asahel (v 24) and Joab (vv 8. 24. 37), and finally the group of the Thirty (vv 24-39).

p: Ps 22, 23; Rom 15, 9. *q:* 1 Kgs 2, 3-9; Sir 47, 8. *r:* Is 59, 21; Jer 1, 9. *s:* Ps 72, 1-4. *t:* Jgs 5, 31; Ps 72, 6. *u:* 2 Sm 7, 11. 15f; Ps 89, 30; Is 55, 3. *v:* Dt 13, 14. *w:* 8-39: 1 Chr 11, 41; 27, 1-15.

among the Three warriors, was Eleazar, son of Dodo the Ahohite. He was with David at Ephesdammim when the Philistines assembled there for battle. The Israelites had retreated,[x] [10]but he stood his ground and fought the Philistines until his hand grew tired and became cramped, holding fast to the sword. The LORD brought about a great victory on that day; the soldiers turned back after Eleazar, but only to strip the slain. [11]Next to him was Shammah, son of Agee the Hararite. The Philistines had assembled at Lehi, where there was a plot of land full of lentils. When the soldiers fled from the Philistines,[y] [12]he took his stand in the middle of the plot and defended it. He slew the Philistines, and the LORD brought about a great victory. Such were the deeds of the Three warriors.

[13]During the harvest three of the Thirty went down to David in the cave of Adullam, while a Philistine clan was encamped in the Vale of Rephaim.[z] [14]At that time David was in the refuge, and there was a garrison of Philistines in Bethlehem. [15]Now David had a strong craving and said, "Oh, that someone would give me a drink of water from the cistern that is by the gate of Bethlehem!" [16]So the Three warriors broke through the Philistine camp and drew water from the cistern that is by the gate of Bethlehem. But when they brought it to David he refused to drink it, and instead poured it out to the LORD, [17]saying: "The LORD forbid that I do this! Can I drink the blood of these men who went at the risk of their lives?" So he refused to drink it.

[18]Abishai, brother of Joab, son of Zeruiah, was at the head of the Thirty. It was he who brandished his spear over three hundred slain. He was listed among the Thirty [19]and commanded greater respect than the Thirty, becoming their leader. However, he did not attain to the Three.

[20]Benaiah, son of Jehoiada, a stalwart from Kabzeel, was a man of great achievements. It was he who slew the two lions in Moab. He also went down and killed the lion in the cis-

tern at the time of the snow.[a] [21]It was he, too, who slew an Egyptian of large stature. Although the Egyptian was armed with a spear, he went against him with a club and wrested the spear from the Egyptian's hand, then killed him with his own spear. [22]Such were the deeds performed by Benaiah, son of Jehoiada. He was listed among the Thirty warriors [23]and commanded greater respect than the Thirty. However, he did not attain to the Three. David put him in command of his bodyguard.[b] [24]Asahel,[*] brother of Joab. . . .[c]

Among the Thirty were: Elhanan, son of Dodo, from Bethlehem; [25]Shammah from En-harod; Elika from En-harod; [26]Helez from Beth-pelet; Ira, son of Ikkesh, from Tekoa; [27]Abiezer from Anathoth; Sibbekai from Hushah;[d] [28]Zalmon from Ahoh; Maharai from Netophah; [29]Heled, son of Baanath, from Netophah; Ittai, son of Ribai, from Gibeah of the Benjaminites; [30]Benaiah from Pirathon; Hiddai from Nahale-gaash; [31]Abibaal from Beth-arabah; Azmaveth from Bahurim; [32]Eliahba from Shaalbon; Jashen the Gunite; Jonathan, [33]son of Shammah the Hararite; Ahiam, son of Sharar the Hararite; [34]Eliphelet, son of Ahasbai, from Beth-maacah; Eliam, son of Ahithophel, from Gilo; [35]Hezrai from Carmel; Paarai the Arbite; [36]Igal, son of Nathan, from Zobah; Bani the Gadite; [37]Zelek the Ammonite; Naharai from Beeroth, armor-bearer of Joab, son of Zeruiah; [38]Ira from Jattir; Gareb from Jattir; [39]Uriah the Hittite—thirty-seven in all.[e]

CHAPTER 24

See RG 121

Census of the People. [1]*The LORD's anger against Israel flared again,[f] and he incited David against the Israelites by prompting him to number Israel and Judah. [2]Accordingly the king said to Joab and the leaders of the army who were with him, "Tour all the tribes in Israel from Dan to Beer-sheba and register the people, that I may know their number." [3]But Joab said to the king: "May the LORD your God increase the number of people a hundredfold for your royal majesty to

---

23, 24: A more complete notice about Asahel, who died early in his career (2 Sm 2, 16-23), is to be presumed lost at this point. Elhanan is the first of the Thirty.

24, 1ff: This story was probably joined at one time to 2 Sm 21, 1-14.

---

x: 1 Sm 17, 1.   y: Jgs 15, 9.   z: 1 Sm 22, 1; Mi 1, 15.   a: 2 Sm 8, 18; 20, 23; Jgs 14, 6; 1 Kgs 2, 29f.   b: 1 Sm 22, 14.   c: 2 Sm 2, 18-23.   d: 2 Sm 21, 18.   e: 2 Sm 11, 3f.   f: 1-25: 1 Chr 21, 1-27.

see it with his own eyes. But why does it please my lord the king to order a thing of this kind?" [4]The king, however, overruled Joab and the leaders of the army, so they left the king's presence in order to register the people of Israel. [5]Crossing the Jordan, they began near Aroer, south of the city in the wadi, and went in the direction of Gad, toward Jazer. [6]They continued on to Gilead and to the district below Mount Hermon. Then they proceeded to Dan; from there they turned toward Sidon, [7]going to the fortress of Tyre and to all the cities of the Hivites and Canaanites, and ending up at Beer-sheba in the Negeb of Judah. [8]Thus they toured the whole country, reaching Jerusalem again after nine months and twenty days. [9]Joab then reported to the king the number of people registered: in Israel, eight hundred thousand men fit for military service; in Judah, five hundred thousand.

The Pestilence. [10]Afterward, however, David regretted having numbered the people, and said to the LORD: "I have sinned grievously in what I have done.[g] But now, LORD, forgive the guilt of your servant, for I have been very foolish."[*] [11]When David rose in the morning, the LORD had spoken to the prophet Gad, David's seer, saying: [12]"Go and say to David, 'This is what the LORD says: I offer you three alternatives; choose one of them, and I will inflict it on you.' " [13]Gad then went to David to inform him. He asked: "Do you want a three years' famine to come upon your land, or to flee from your enemy three months while he pursues you, or to have a three days' pestilence in your land? Now consider and decide what I must reply to him who sent me."[h] [14]David answered Gad: "I am in very serious difficulty. Let us fall by the hand of God, for he is most merciful; but let me not fall by the hand of man." [15]Thus David chose the pestilence. Now it was the time of the wheat harvest when the plague broke out among the people. [The LORD then sent a pestilence over Israel from morning until

the time appointed, and seventy thousand of the people from Dan to Beer-sheba died.] [16]But when the angel stretched forth his hand toward Jerusalem to destroy it, the LORD regretted the calamity and said to the angel causing the destruction among the people, "Enough now! Stay your hand." The angel of the LORD was then standing at the threshing floor of Araunah the Jebusite.[i] [17]When David saw the angel who was striking the people, he said to the LORD: "It is I who have sinned; it is I, the shepherd, who have done wrong. But these are sheep; what have they done? Punish me and my kindred."[*]

Sacrifice of Atonement. [18]On the same day Gad went to David and said to him, "Go up and build an altar to the LORD on the threshing floor of Araunah the Jebusite." [19]Following Gad's bidding, David went up as the LORD had commanded. [20]Now Araunah looked down and noticed the king and his servants coming toward him while he was threshing wheat. So he went out and paid homage to the king, with face to the ground. [21]Then Araunah asked, "Why does my lord the king come to his servant?" David replied, "To buy the threshing floor from you, to build an altar to the LORD, that the plague may be checked among the people." [22]But Araunah said to David: "Let my lord the king take and offer up whatever he may wish. Here are oxen for holocausts, and threshing sledges and the yokes of the oxen for wood. [23]All this does Araunah give to the king." Araunah then said to the king, "May the LORD your God accept your offering." [24]The king, however, replied to Araunah, "No, I must pay you for it, for I cannot offer to the LORD my God holocausts that cost nothing." So David bought the threshing floor and the oxen for fifty silver shekels. [25]Then David built an altar there to the LORD, and offered holocausts and peace offerings. The LORD granted relief to the country, and the plague was checked in Israel.

24, 10: The narrative supposes that since the people belonged to the Lord rather than to the king, only the Lord should know their exact number.

24, 17: Before this verse a Qumran manuscript (4Q Samª) gives the fuller text of 1 Chr 21, 16, an alternative to the words

"When David saw the angel who was striking the people."

g: 1 Sm 24, 6; 1 Chr 21, 7.   *h:* 2 Sm 21, 1.   *i:* Ex 12, 23; 2 Kgs 19, 35.   *j:* 22f: 1 Sm 6, 14; 1 Kgs 19, 21.

See RG
122–36

The Books of Kings

The two Books of Kings were originally, like 1 and 2 Samuel, a single historical work. In conjunction with the Books of Samuel, they extend the consecutive history of Israel from the birth of Samuel to the destruction of Jerusalem in 587 B.C. This combined work is designed as a religious history; hence in Kings the temple, which is the chosen site for the worship of Yahweh, occupies the center of attention.

The Books of Kings show clearly the theological bent of a Deuteronomic editor. In them, as already in Judges, material from various sources, such as the "book of the acts of Solomon" (1 Kgs 11, 41) and the "book of the chronicles of the kings of Israel" (1 Kgs 14, 19), is forged into structural unity by an editor whose principal interest is in the fidelity to Yahweh of rulers and people. The reigns of individual kings are adapted to an editorial framework consisting of a presentation and an obituary notice for each, in stereotyped formulas. In between, the achievements of the king are reported—above all, his fidelity or lack of fidelity to Yahweh. The faithful prosper; the unfaithful pay for their defections. Since this is basically a narrative of sin and retribution, it would not be inappropriate to entitle the Books of Kings "The Rise and Fall of the Israelite Monarchy."

Without minimizing the complexity of the process by which this material was transmitted for many centuries, one may speak of two editions of the Books: the first at some time between 621 B.C. and 597 B.C., and the second, final edi-tion during the Exile; probably shortly after Jehoiachin was released from his Babylonian prison (561 B.C.).

1 Kings carries the history of Israel from the last days and death of David to the accession in Samaria of Ahaziah, son of Ahab, near the end of the reign of Jehoshaphat, king of Judah. Judgment is passed on Ahaziah's reign but the details are given only later, in 2 Kings. We should note the two large cycles of traditions which grew up around the great prophetic figures of Elijah and Elisha, the former in 1 Kings and the latter chiefly in 2 Kings. These cycles, which interrupt the sequence of regnal chronicles, were very probably preserved and transmitted by the prophetic communities to which there are references in the same traditions. The Elijah cycle is the more important since it dramatically underscores Israel's critical struggle with the religion of Canaan.

The principal divisions of the Books of Kings are:

I: The Reign of Solomon (1 Kgs 1, 1—11, 43).

II: Judah and Israel to the Time of Ahab (1 Kgs 12, 1—16, 34).

III: Stories of the Prophets (1 Kgs 17, 1—22, 54).

IV: The Kingdoms of Israel and Judah (2 Kgs 1, 1—17, 41).

V: The Kingdom of Judah after 721 B.C. (2 Kgs 18, 1—25, 30).

See RG
126–29

The First Book of Kings

I: The Reign of Solomon

See RG
126

CHAPTER 1

¹When King David was old and advanced in years, though they spread covers over him he could not keep warm. ²His servants therefore said to him, "Let a young virgin be sought to attend you, lord king, and to nurse you. If she sleeps with your royal majesty, you will be kept warm." ³So they sought for a beautiful girl throughout the ter-ritory of Israel, and found Abishag the Shunamite, whom they brought to the king. ⁴The maiden, who was very beautiful, nursed the king and cared for him, but the king did not have relations with her.

Ambition of Adonijah. ⁵Adonijah, son of Haggith, began to display his ambition to be king. He acquired chariots, drivers, and fifty henchmen. ⁶Yet his father never rebuked him or asked why he was doing this. Adonijah was also very handsome, and next in age to Absalom by the same mother. ⁷He

Nathan and Bathsheba

It is surprising to find Nathan and Bathsheba in alliance with each other (1, 11ff). When they were mentioned together previously (2 Sm 11–12), Nathan was condemning David for his adultery with Bathsheba and the murder of her husband. Nathan advises Bathsheba on how to save her life and that of her son, Solomon. The lives of Bathsheba and Solomon were in danger if Adonijah became king, because new kings customarily killed off their potential rivals.

conferred with Joab, son of Zeruiah, and with Abiathar the priest, and they supported him. [8]However, Zadok the priest, Benaiah, son of Jehoiada, Nathan the prophet, and Shimei and his companions, the pick of David's army, did not side with Adonijah. [9]When he slaughtered sheep, oxen, and fatlings at the stone Zoheleth, near Enrogel,* Adonijah invited all his brothers, the king's sons, and all the royal officials of Judah. [10]But he did not invite the prophet Nathan, or Benaiah, or the pick of the army, or his brother Solomon.

Solomon Proclaimed King. [11]Then Nathan said to Bathsheba, Solomon's mother: "Have you not heard that Adonijah, son of Haggith, has become king without the knowledge of our lord David? [12]Come now, let me advise you so that you may save your life and that of your son Solomon. [13]Go, visit King David, and say to him, 'Did you not, lord king, swear to your handmaid: Your son Solomon shall be king after me and shall sit upon my throne? Why, then, has Adonijah become king?' [14]And while you are still there speaking to the king, I will come in after you and confirm what you have said."

[15]So Bathsheba visited the king in his room, while Abishag the Shunamite was attending him because of his advanced age. [16]Bathsheba bowed in homage to the king, who said to her, "What do you wish?" [17]She answered him: "My lord, you swore to me your handmaid by the LORD, your God, that my son Solomon should reign after you and sit upon your throne. [18]But now Adonijah has become king, and you, my lord king, do not know it. [19]He has slaughtered oxen, fatlings, and sheep in great numbers; he has invited all the king's sons, Abiathar the priest, and Joab, the general of the army, but not your servant Solomon. [20]Now, my lord king, all Israel is waiting for you to make known to them who is to sit on the throne after your royal majesty.* [21]If this is not done, when my lord the king sleeps with his fathers, I and my son Solomon will be considered criminals."

[22]While she was still speaking to the king, the prophet Nathan came in. [23]When he had been announced, the prophet entered the king's presence and, bowing to the floor, did him homage. [24]Then Nathan said: "Have you decided, my lord king, that Adonijah is to reign after you and sit on your throne? [25]He went down today and slaughtered oxen, fatlings, and sheep in great numbers; he invited all the king's sons, the commanders of the army, and Abiathar the priest, and they are eating and drinking in his company and saying, 'Long live King Adonijah!' [26]But me, your servant, he did not invite; nor Zadok the priest, nor Benaiah, son of Jehoiada, nor your servant Solomon. [27]Was this done by my royal master's order without my being told who was to succeed to your majesty's kingly throne?"

[28]King David answered, "Call Bathsheba here." When she re-entered the king's presence and stood before him, [29]the king swore, "As the LORD lives, who has delivered me from all distress, [30]this very day I will fulfill the oath I swore to you by the LORD, the God

---

1, 9: En-rogel: the modern Job's Well southeast of Jerusalem. It marked the ancient boundary between the tribes of Benjamin and Judah (Jos 15, 7; 18, 16). Here David's men sought information about Absalom's revolt

(2 Sm 17, 17).

1, 20: At this time, neither law nor the right of primogeniture, but the will of the ruling monarch, determined succession to the throne.

of Israel, that your son Solomon should reign after me and should sit upon my throne in my place." [31]Bowing to the floor in homage to the king, Bathsheba said, "May my lord, King David, live forever!" [32]Then King David summoned Zadok the priest, Nathan the prophet, and Benaiah, son of Jehoiada. When they had entered the king's presence, [33]he said to them: "Take with you the royal attendants. Mount my son Solomon upon my own mule and escort him down to Gihon. [34]There Zadok the priest and Nathan the prophet are to anoint him king of Israel, and you shall blow the horn and cry, 'Long live King Solomon!' [35]When you come back in his train, he is to go in and sit upon my throne and reign in my place. I designate him ruler of Israel and of Judah." [36]In answer to the king, Benaiah, son of Jehoiada, said: "So be it! May the LORD, the God of my lord the king, so decree! [37]As the LORD has been with your royal majesty, so may he be with Solomon, and exalt his throne even more than that of my lord, King David!"

[38]So Zadok the priest, Nathan the prophet, Benaiah, son of Jehoiada, and the Cherethites and Pelethites* went down, and mounting Solomon on King David's mule, escorted him to Gihon. [39]Then Zadok the priest took the horn of oil from the tent and anointed Solomon. They blew the horn and all the people shouted, "Long live King Solomon!" [40]Then all the people went up after him, playing flutes and rejoicing so much as to split open the earth with their shouting.

[41]Adonijah and all the guests who were with him heard it, just as they ended their banquet. When Joab heard the sound of the horn, he asked, "What does this uproar in the city mean?" [42]As he was speaking, Jonathan, son of Abiathar the priest, arrived. "Come," said Adonijah, "you are a man of worth and must bring good news." [43]"On the contrary!" Jonathan answered him. "Our lord,

King David, has made Solomon king. [44]The king sent with him Zadok the priest, Nathan the prophet, Benaiah, son of Jehoiada, and the Cherethites and Pelethites, and they mounted him upon the king's own mule. [45]Zadok the priest and Nathan the prophet anointed him king at Gihon, and they went up from there rejoicing, so that the city is in an uproar. That is the noise you heard. [46]Besides, Solomon took his seat on the royal throne, [47]and the king's servants went in and paid their respects to our lord, King David, saying, 'May God make Solomon more famous than you and exalt his throne more than your own!' And the king in his bed worshiped God, [48]and this is what he said: 'Blessed be the LORD, the God of Israel, who has this day seated one of my sons upon my throne, so that I see it with my own eyes.' "

[49]All the guests of Adonijah left in terror, each going his own way. [50]Adonijah, in fear of Solomon, also left; he went and seized the horns of the altar.* [51]It was reported to Solomon that Adonijah, in his fear of King Solomon, had seized the horns of the altar and said, "Let King Solomon first swear that he will not kill me, his servant, with the sword." [52]Solomon answered, "If he proves himself worthy, not a hair shall fall from his head. But if he is found guilty of crime, he shall die." [53]King Solomon sent to have him brought down from the altar, and he came and paid homage to the king. Solomon then said to him, "Go to your home."

CHAPTER 2

See RG 126

David's Last Instructions and Death.

[1]When the time of David's death drew near,* he gave these instructions to his son Solomon: [2]"I am going the way of all mankind. Take courage and be a man. [3]Keep the mandate of the LORD, your God, following his ways and observing his statutes, commands, ordinances, and decrees as they

---

1, 38: Cherethites and Pelethites: mercenaries in David's bodyguard. They became part of his retinue after he defeated the Philistines and established himself in Jerusalem; cf 2 Sm 8, 18; 15, 18; 20, 23.

1, 50: Horns of the altar: the protuberances on each of the four corners of the altar were surrounded with a special degree of holiness (Ex 27, 2; 29, 12), and constituted a place of asylum for transgressors of the law (Ex 21, 13f; 1 Kgs 2, 28).

2, 1-6. 8-9: Solomon is expected to remove from his father's family the imputation of blood guilt brought upon it by Joab in the unwarranted killings of Abner (2 Sm 3, 27-29) and Amasa (2 Sm 19, 9-10); and likewise to punish Shimei for his curse, the effects of which David had pledged himself not to avenge in person (2 Sm 19, 21-23). The standards of morality presumed in these verses are far from the Christian ones.

are written in the law of Moses, that you may succeed in whatever you do, wherever you turn,[a] [4]and the LORD may fulfill the promise he made on my behalf when he said, 'If your sons so conduct themselves that they remain faithful to me with their whole heart and with their whole soul, you shall always have someone of your line on the throne of Israel.'[b] [5]You yourself know what Joab, son of Zeruiah, did to me when he slew the two generals of Israel's armies, Abner, son of Ner, and Amasa, son of Jether. He took revenge for the blood of war in a time of peace, and put blood shed without provocation on the belt about my waist and on the sandal on my foot.[c] [6]Act with the wisdom you possess; you must not allow him to go down to the grave in peaceful old age.

[7]"But be kind to the sons of Barzillai the Gileadite, and have them eat at your table. For they received me kindly when I was fleeing your brother Absalom.[d]

[8]"You also have with you Shimei, son of Gera, the Benjaminite of Bahurim, who cursed me balefully when I was going to Mahanaim. Because he came down to meet me at the Jordan, I swore to him by the LORD that I would not put him to the sword.[e] [9]But you must not let him go unpunished. You are a prudent man and will know how to deal with him to send down his hoary head in blood to the grave."

[10]David rested with his ancestors and was buried in the City of David.[f] [11]The length of David's reign over Israel was forty years: he reigned seven years in Hebron and thirty-three years in Jerusalem.[g]

The Kingdom Made Secure. [12]When Solomon was seated on the throne of his father David, with his sovereignty firmly established, [13]Adonijah, son of Haggith, went to Bathsheba, the mother of Solomon. "Do you come as a friend?" she asked. "Yes," he answered, [14]and added, "I have something to say to you." She replied, "Say it." [15]So he said: "You know that the kingdom was mine,

and all Israel expected me to be king. But the kingdom escaped me and became my brother's, for the LORD gave it to him. [16]But now there is one favor I would ask of you. Do not refuse me." And she said, "Speak on." [17]He said, "Please ask King Solomon, who will not refuse you, to give me Abishag the Shunamite for my wife."* [18]"Very well," replied Bathsheba, "I will speak to the king for you."

[19]Then Bathsheba went to King Solomon to speak to him for Adonijah, and the king stood up to meet her and paid her homage. Then he sat down upon his throne, and a throne was provided for the king's mother, who sat at his right. [20]"There is one small favor I would ask of you," she said. "Do not refuse me." "Ask it, my mother," the king said to her, "for I will not refuse you." [21]So she said, "Let Abishag the Shunamite be given to your brother Adonijah for his wife." [22]"And why do you ask Abishag the Shunamite for Adonijah?" King Solomon answered his mother. "Ask the kingdom for him as well, for he is my elder brother and has with him Abiathar the priest and Joab, son of Zeruiah." [23]And King Solomon swore by the LORD: "May God do thus and so to me, and more besides, if Adonijah has not proposed this at the cost of his life. [24]And now, as the LORD lives, who has seated me firmly on the throne of my father David and made of me a dynasty as he promised, this day shall Adonijah be put to death." [25]Then King Solomon sent Benaiah, son of Jehoiada, who struck him dead.

[26]The king said to Abiathar the priest: "Go to your land in Anathoth. Though you deserve to die, I will not put you to death this time, because you carried the ark of the Lord GOD before my father David and shared in all the hardships my father endured." [27]So Solomon deposed Abiathar from his office of priest of the LORD, thus fulfilling the prophecy which the LORD had made in Shilon about the house of Eli.[h]

2, 17. 22-25: Abishag had been the concubine of King David (1 Kgs 1, 4). His successor, Solomon, inherited his father's harem. When Adonijah requested Abishag as his wife, he was subtly undermining the security of Solomon's throne and exposing himself to the suspicion of insurrection that would cost him his life; cf 2 Sm 3, 6-11; 16, 22.

a: Dt 17, 19. *b:* 2 Sm 7, 11-16; Ps 132, 11f. *c:* 2 Sm 3, 27; 20, 10. *d:* 2 Sm 19, 33ff. *e:* 2 Sm 16, 5; 19, 19. *f:* Acts 2, 29. *g:* 1 Chr 29, 27. *h:* 1 Sm 2, 31.

28When the news came to Joab, who had sided with Adonijah, though not with Absalom, he fled to the tent of the LORD and seized the horns of the altar. 29King Solomon was told that Joab had fled to the tent of the LORD and was at the altar. He sent Benaiah, son of Jehoiada, with the order, "Go, strike him down." 30Benaiah went to the tent of the LORD and said to him, "The king says, 'Come out.' " But he answered, "No! I will die here." Benaiah reported to the king, "This is what Joab said to me in reply." 31The king answered him: "Do as he has said. Strike him down and bury him, and you will remove from me and from my family the blood which Joab shed without provocation. 32The LORD will hold him responsible for his own blood, because he struck down two men better and more just than himself, and slew them with the sword without my father David's knowledge: Abner, son of Ner, general of Israel's army, and Amasa, son of Jether, general of Judah's army.i 33Joab and his descendants shall be responsible forever for their blood. But there shall be the peace of the LORD forever for David, and his descendants, and his house, and his throne." 34Benaiah, son of Jehoiada, went back, struck him down and killed him; he was buried in his house in the desert. 35The king appointed Benaiah, son of Jehoiada, over the army in his place, and put Zadok the priest in place of Abiathar.

36Then the king summoned Shimei and said to him: "Build yourself a house in Jerusalem and live there. Do not go anywhere else. 37For if you leave, and cross the Kidron Valley, be certain you shall die without fail. You shall be responsible for your own blood." 38Shimei answered the king: "I accept. Your servant will do just as the king's majesty has said." So Shimei stayed in Jerusalem for a long time. 39But three years later, two of Shimei's servants ran away to Achish, son of Maacah, king of Gath, and Shimei was informed that his servants were in Gath. 40So Shimei rose, saddled his ass, and went to Achish in Gath in search of his servants, whom he brought back. 41When Solomon was informed that Shimei had gone from Je-

rusalem to Gath, and had returned, 42the king summoned Shimei and said to him: "Did I not have you swear by the LORD to your clear understanding of my warning that, if you left and went anywhere else, you should die without fail? And you answered, 'I accept and obey.' 43Why, then, have you not kept the oath of the LORD and the command that I gave you?" 44And the king said to Shimei: "You know in your heart the evil that you did to my father David. Now the LORD requites you for your own wickedness. 45But King Solomon shall be blessed, and David's throne shall endure before the LORD forever." 46The king then gave the order to Benaiah, son of Jehoiada, who struck him dead as he left.

CHAPTER 3

See RG 126—29

Wisdom of Solomon. 1With the royal power firmly in his grasp, Solomon allied himself by marriage with Pharaoh, king of Egypt. The daughter of Pharaoh, whom he married, he brought to the City of David, until he should finish building his palace, and the temple of the LORD, and the wall around Jerusalem.j

2However, the people were sacrificing on the high places, for up to that time no temple had been built to the name of the LORD. 3Solomon loved the LORD, and obeyed the statutes of his father David; yet he offered sacrifice and burned incense on the high places.

4The king went to Gibeon to sacrifice there, because that was the most renowned high place. Upon its altar Solomon offered a thousand holocausts. 5In Gibeon the LORD appeared to Solomon in a dream at night. God said, "Ask something of me and I will give it to you." 6Solomon answered: "You have shown great favor to your servant, my father David, because he behaved faithfully toward you, with justice and an upright heart; and you have continued this great favor toward him, even today, seating a son of his on his throne. 7O LORD, my God, you have made me, your servant, king to succeed my father David; but I am a mere youth, not knowing at all how to act. 8I serve you in the midst of the people whom

i: 2 Sm 3, 27; 20, 10.   j: 1 Kgs 7, 8; 2 Chr 1, 1.

you have chosen, a people so vast that it cannot be numbered or counted. [9]Give your servant, therefore, an understanding heart to judge your people and to distinguish right from wrong. For who is able to govern this vast people of yours?"[k]

[10]The LORD was pleased that Solomon made this request. [11]So God said to him: "Because you have asked for this—not for a long life for yourself, nor for riches, nor for the life of your enemies, but for understanding so that you may know what is right— [12]I do as you requested. I give you a heart so wise and understanding that there has never been anyone like you up to now, and after you there will come no one to equal you. [13]In addition, I give you what you have not asked for, such riches and glory that among kings there is not your like.[l] [14]And if you follow me by keeping my statutes and commandments, as your father David did, I will give you a long life."

[15]When Solomon awoke from his dream, he went to Jerusalem, stood before the ark of the covenant of the LORD, offered holocausts and peace offerings, and gave a banquet for all his servants.

Solomon's Judgment. [16]Later, two harlots came to the king and stood before him. [17]One woman said: "By your leave, my lord, this woman and I live in the same house, and I gave birth in the house while she was present. [18]On the third day after I gave birth, this woman also gave birth. We were alone in the house; there was no one there but us two. [19]This woman's son died during the night; she smothered him by lying on him. [20]Later that night she got up and took my son from my side, as I, your handmaid, was sleeping. Then she laid him in her bosom, after she had laid her dead child in my bosom. [21]I rose in the morning to nurse my child, and I found him dead. But when I examined him in the morning light, I saw it was not the son whom I had borne."

[22]The other woman answered, "It is not so! The living one is my son, the dead one is yours." But the first kept saying, "No, the dead one is your child, the living one is mine!" Thus they argued before the king.

[23]Then the king said: "One woman claims, 'This, the living one, is my child, and the dead one is yours.' The other answers, 'No! The dead one is your child; the living one is mine.' " [24]The king continued, "Get me a sword." When they brought the sword before him, [25]he said, "Cut the living child in two, and give half to one woman and half to the other." [26]The woman whose son it was, in the anguish she felt for it, said to the king, "Please, my lord, give her the living child—please do not kill it!" The other, however, said, "It shall be neither mine nor yours. Divide it!" [27]The king then answered, "Give the first one the living child! By no means kill it, for she is the mother."

[28]When all Israel heard the judgment the king had given, they were in awe of him, because they saw that the king had in him the wisdom of God for giving judgment.

CHAPTER 4

See RG 126-29

Chief Officers of the Kingdom. [1]Solomon was king over all Israel, [2]and these were the officials he had in his service:

Azariah, son of Zadok, priest;
[3] Elihoreph and Ahijah, sons of Shisha, scribes;
Jehoshaphat, son of Ahilud, chancellor;
[4] [Benaiah, son of Jehoiada, commander of the army;
Zadok and Abiathar, priests;]
[5] Azariah, son of Nathan, chief of the commissaries;
Zabud, son of Nathan, companion to the king;
[6] Ahishar, major-domo of the palace; and Adoniram, son of Abda, superintendent of the forced labor.

Solomon's Royal State. [7]*Solomon had twelve commissaries for all Israel who supplied food for the king and his household, each having to provide for one month in the year. [8]Their names were:

4, 7-19: The administration of the kingdom thus initiated by Solomon continued in its main features for the duration of the monarchy in Israel and Judah.

k: 2 Chr 1, 10. *l:* Wis 7, 11; Mt 6, 29.

Mediterranean
Sea

ASHER

NAPHTALI

BASHAN

VIII

IX

NAPHATH-DOR

IV

ISSACHAR

X

Dor

Megiddo

Jezreel

Taanach

V

Beth-shean

Arubboth

Abel-meholah

Hepher

Socoh

III

EPHRAIM

I

GILEAD

VI

Ramoth-gilead

VII

Mahanaim

Shaalbim

Makaz

XI

Elon

BENJAMIN

Beth-shemesh

JERUSALEM

XII

JUDAH

Dead
Sea

33°

32°

31°

35°

36°

0   10   20 Miles

0   10   20 Kilometers

Solomon's Twelve Administrative Districts

the son of Hur in the hill country of
Ephraim;

⁹ the son of Deker in Makaz, Shaalbim,
Beth-shemesh, Elon and Beth-
hanan;

¹⁰ the son of Hesed in Arubboth, as well as
in Socoh and the whole region of
Hepher;

¹¹ the son of Abinadab, who was married to
Solomon's daughter Taphath, in
all the Naphath-dor;

¹² Baana, son of Ahilud, in Taanach and
Megiddo, and beyond Jokmeam,
and in all Beth-shean, and in the
country around Zarethan below
Jezreel from Beth-shean to Abel-
meholah;

¹³ the son of Geber in Ramoth-Gilead,
having charge of the villages of
Jair, son of Manasseh, in Gilead;
and of the district of Argob in
Bashan—sixty large walled cities
with gates barred with bronze;

¹⁴ Ahinadab, son of Iddo, in Mahanaim;

¹⁵ Ahimaaz, who was married to Basemath,
another daughter of Solomon, in
Naphtali;

¹⁶ Baana, son of Hushai, in Asher and along
the rocky coast;

¹⁷ Jehoshaphat, son of Paruah, in Issachar;

¹⁸ Shimei, son of Ela, in Benjamin;

¹⁹ Geber, son of Uri, in the land of Gilead,
the land of Sihon, king of the
Amorites, and of Og, king of
Bashan.

There was one prefect besides, in the
king's own land.*

CHAPTER 5

See RG
126-29
⁷These commissaries, one for each
month, provided food for King Solomon and
for all the guests at the royal table. They left
nothing unprovided. ⁸For the chariot horses
and draft animals also, each brought his
quota of barley and straw to the required
place.

²⁰*Judah and Israel were as numerous as
the sands by the sea; they ate and drank and
made merry. ¹Solomon ruled over all the
kingdoms from the River to the land of the
Philistines, down to the border of Egypt;
they paid Solomon tribute and were his vassals as long as he lived.ᵐ

²Solomon's supplies for each day were
thirty kors of fine flour, sixty kors of meal,
³ten fatted oxen, twenty pasture-fed oxen,
and a hundred sheep, not counting harts, gazelles, roebucks, and fatted fowl.

⁴He ruled over all the land west of the Euphrates, from Tiphsah to Gaza, and over all
its kings, and he had peace on all his borders
round about. ⁵Thus Judah and Israel lived in
security, every man under his vine or under
his fig tree from Dan to Beer-sheba, as long
as Solomon lived.

⁵Solomon had four thousand stalls for his
twelve thousand chariot horses.ⁿ

⁹ᵒMoreover, God gave Solomon wisdom
and exceptional understanding and knowledge, as vast as the sand on the seashore.
¹⁰Solomon surpassed all the Cedemites and
all the Egyptians in wisdom. ¹¹He was wiser
than all other men—than Ethan the Ezrahite,
or Heman, Chalcol, and Darda, the musicians—and his fame spread throughout the
neighboring nations. ¹²Solomon also uttered
three thousand proverbs, and his songs numbered a thousand and five.ᵖ ¹³He discussed
plants, from the cedar on Lebanon to the
hyssop growing out of the wall, and he
spoke about beasts, birds, reptiles, and
fishes. ¹⁴Men came to hear Solomon's wisdom from all nations, sent by all the kings of
the earth who had heard of his wisdom.

Preparations for the Temple. ¹⁵When Hiram, king of Tyre, heard that Solomon had
been anointed king in place of his father, he
sent an embassy to him; for Hiram had always been David's friend. ¹⁶Solomon sent
back this message to Hiram: ¹⁷"You know
that my father David, because of the enemies surrounding him on all sides, could not
build a temple in honor of the LORD, his

4, 19: One prefect . . . in the king's own land: the royal territory of Judah had its own peculiar administration different from
that of the twelve districts which had to supply the king and his
household with a month's provisions of food each year (v 7).

5, 20: This verse belongs to ch 4.

m: Sir 47, 15f; 2 Chr 9, 26.   *n:* 2 Chr 9, 25f.   *o:* 9-14: Sir 47, 16f.
p: 1 Kgs 3, 12.

God, until such a time as the LORD should put these enemies under the soles of his feet. [18]But now the LORD, my God, has given me peace on all sides. There is no enemy or threat of danger. [19]So I propose to build a temple in honor of the LORD, my God, as the LORD predicted to my father David when he said: 'It is your son whom I will put upon your throne in your place who shall build the temple in my honor.'[q] [20]Give orders, then, to have cedars from the Lebanon cut down for me. My servants shall accompany yours, since you know that there is no one among us who is skilled in cutting timber like the Sidonians, and I will pay you whatever you say for your servants' salary."

[21]When he had heard the words of Solomon, Hiram was pleased and said, "Blessed be the LORD this day, who has given David a wise son to rule this numerous people." [22]Hiram then sent word to Solomon, "I agree to the proposal you sent me, and I will provide all the cedars and fir trees you wish. [23]My servants shall bring them down from the Lebanon to the sea, and I will arrange them into rafts in the sea and bring them wherever you say. There I will break up the rafts, and you shall take the lumber. You, for your part, shall furnish the provisions I desire for my household."

[24]So Hiram continued to provide Solomon with all the cedars and fir trees he wished; [25]while Solomon every year gave Hiram twenty thousand kors of wheat to provide for his household, and twenty thousand measures of pure oil. [26]The LORD, moreover, gave Solomon wisdom as he promised him, and there was peace between Hiram and Solomon, since they were parties to a treaty.

[27]King Solomon conscripted thirty thousand workmen from all Israel. [28]He sent them to the Lebanon each month in relays of ten thousand, so that they spent one month in the Lebanon and two months at home. Adoniram was in charge of the draft. [29]Solomon had seventy thousand carriers and eighty thousand stonecutters in the mountain, [30]in addition to three thousand three hundred overseers, answerable to Solomon's prefects for the work, directing the people engaged in the work. [31]By order of the king, fine, large blocks were quarried to give the temple a foundation of hewn stone. [32]Solomon's and Hiram's builders, along with the Gebalites, hewed them out, and prepared the wood and stones for building the temple.

CHAPTER 6

See RG 126-29

Building of the Temple. [1]In the four hundred and eightieth year from the departure of the Israelites from the land of Egypt, in the fourth year of Solomon's reign over Israel, in the month of Ziv, which is the second month, the construction of the temple of the LORD* was begun.[r]

[2]The temple which King Solomon built for the LORD was sixty cubits long, twenty wide, and twenty-five high. [3]The porch in front of the temple was twenty cubits from side to side, along the width of the nave, and ten cubits deep in front of the temple. [4]Splayed windows with trellises were made for the temple, [5]and adjoining the wall of the temple, which enclosed the nave and the sanctuary, an annex of several stories was built. [6]Its lowest story was five cubits wide, the middle one six cubits wide, the third seven cubits wide, because there were offsets along the outside of the temple so that the beams would not be fastened into the walls of the temple. [7](The temple was built of stone dressed at the quarry, so that no hammer, axe, or iron tool was to be heard in the temple during its construction.) [8]The entrance to the lowest floor of the annex was at the right side of the temple, and stairs with intermediate landings led up to the middle story and from the middle story to the third. [9]When the temple was built to its full height, it was roofed in with rafters and boards of cedar. [10]The annex, with its lowest

6, 1: Construction of the temple of the Lord is here paralleled in importance with the founding of the nation after the departure from Egypt. In both, God is the central figure who chose Israel as his people, and now chooses the place where his temple should be built (Dt 12, 4-18. 26). The year is given in a round number, 480, which corresponds to twelve generations. The fourth year of Solomon's reign: c. 968 B.C.

q: 2 Sm 7, 13; 1 Chr 22, 10.   r: 2 Chr 3, 1.

The Temple and Palace of Solomon

story five cubits high, was built all along the outside of the temple, to which it was joined by cedar beams.

*11*This word of the LORD* came to Solomon: *12*"As to this temple you are building—if you observe my statutes, carry out my ordinances, keep and obey all my commands, I will fulfill toward you the promise I made to your father David.*s 13*I will dwell in the midst of the Israelites and will not forsake my people Israel."

*14*When Solomon finished building the temple, *15*its walls were lined from floor to ceiling beams with cedar paneling, and its floor was laid with fir planking. *16*At the rear

of the temple a space of twenty cubits was set off by cedar partitions from the floor to the rafters, enclosing the sanctuary, the holy of holies. *17*The nave, or part of the temple in front of the sanctuary, was forty cubits long. *18*The cedar in the interior of the temple was carved in the form of gourds and open flowers; all was of cedar, and no stone was to be seen.

*19*In the innermost part of the temple* was located the sanctuary to house the ark of the LORD's covenant, *20*twenty cubits long, twenty wide, and twenty high.* *21*Solomon overlaid the interior of the temple with pure gold. He made in front of the sanctuary a

6, 11ff: This word of the LORD . . . my people Israel: the oracle, which came as a climax at the completion of the work, was an expression of God's acceptance and approval. Nevertheless the fulfillment of God's promises to David and his royal descendants will depend on their observance of his ordinances and commands.

6, 19: The innermost part of the temple: the sanctuary or holy of holies reserved exclusively for the Lord. Here through his presence he dwelt as on a throne between the cherubim

above the ark of the covenant (2 Kgs 6, 23-28; 2 Chr 3, 10-13). See note on Ex 25, 18ff.

6, 20: Twenty (cubits) high: it is usually supposed that the holy of holies was of this height because it had a raised floor, five cubits above the floor level of the nave, rather than a dropped ceiling. The building was twenty-five cubits high (v 2) according to the reading here followed.

s: 2 Sm 7, 13. *t:* 1 Chr 22, 9f.

cedar altar, overlaid it with gold, and looped it with golden chains. ²²The entire temple was overlaid with gold so that it was completely covered with it; the whole altar before the sanctuary was also overlaid with gold. ²³In the sanctuary were two cherubim, each ten cubits high, made of olive wood. ²⁴Each wing of a cherub measured five cubits so that the space from wing tip to wing tip of each was ten cubits. ²⁵The cherubim were identical in size and shape, ²⁶and each was exactly ten cubits high. ²⁷The cherubim were placed in the inmost part of the temple, with their wings spread wide, so that one wing of each cherub touched a side wall while the other wing, pointing toward the middle of the room, touched the corresponding wing of the second cherub. ²⁸The cherubim, too, were overlaid with gold.

²⁹The walls on all sides of both the inner and the outer rooms had carved figures of cherubim, palm trees, and open flowers. ³⁰The floor of both the inner and the outer rooms was overlaid with gold. ³¹At the entrance of the sanctuary, doors of olive wood were made; the doorframes had beveled posts. ³²The two doors were of olive wood, with carved figures of cherubim, palm trees, and open flowers. The doors were overlaid with gold, which was also molded to the cherubim and the palm trees. ³³The same was done at the entrance to the nave, where the doorposts of olive wood were rectangular. ³⁴The two doors were of fir wood; each door was banded by a metal strap, front and back, ³⁵and had carved cherubim, palm trees, and open flowers, over which gold was evenly applied.

³⁶The inner court was walled off by means of three courses of hewn stones and one course of cedar beams.

³⁷The foundations of the LORD's temple were laid in the month of Ziv ³⁸in the fourth year, and it was completed in all particulars, exactly according to plan, in the month of Bul, the eighth month, in the eleventh year. Thus it took Solomon seven years to build it.

CHAPTER 7

See RG 126-29

Building of the Palace. ¹His own palace Solomon completed after thirteen years of construction.ᵘ ²He built the hall called the Forest of Lebanon one hundred cubits long, fifty wide, and thirty high; it was supported by four rows of cedar columns, with cedar capitals upon the columns. ³Moreover, it had a ceiling of cedar above the beams resting on the columns; these beams numbered forty-five, fifteen to a row. ⁴There were three window frames at either end, with windows in strict alignment. ⁵The posts of all the doorways were rectangular, and the doorways faced each other, three at either end. ⁶The porch of the columned hall he made fifty cubits long and thirty wide. The porch extended the width of the columned hall, and there was a canopy in front. ⁷He also built the vestibule of the throne where he gave judgment—that is, the tribunal; it was paneled with cedar from floor to ceiling beams. ⁸His living quarters were in another court, set in deeper than the tribunal and of the same construction. A palace like this tribunal was built for Pharaoh's daughter, whom Solomon had married.ᵛ

⁹All these buildings were of fine stones, hewn to size and trimmed front and back with a saw, from the foundation to the bonding course. ¹⁰(The foundation was made of fine, large blocks, some ten cubits and some eight cubits. ¹¹Above were fine stones hewn to size, and cedar wood.) ¹²The great court was enclosed by three courses of hewn stones and a bonding course of cedar beams. So also were the inner court of the temple of the LORD and the temple porch.

Furnishing of the Temple. ¹³King Solomon had Hiram brought from Tyre. ¹⁴He was a bronze worker, the son of a widow from the tribe of Naphtali; his father had been from Tyre. He was endowed with skill, understanding, and knowledge of how to produce any work in bronze. He came to King Solomon and did all his metal work.

¹⁵Two hollow bronze columns* were cast, each eighteen cubits high and twelve cubits

---

7, 15-21: The two hollow bronze columns, Jachin and Boaz (2 Chr 3, 17), stood free to the right and left of the temple porch. The names are related to God's power (Boaz)

founding (Jachin) the temple and his people.

u: 1 Kgs 9, 10.   *v:* 1 Kgs 3, 1.

in circumference; their metal was of four fingers' thickness.ʷ ¹⁶There were also two capitals cast in bronze, to place on top of the columns, each of them five cubits high. ¹⁷Two pieces of network with a chainlike mesh were made to cover the (nodes of the) capitals on top of the columns, one for each capital. ¹⁸Four hundred pomegranates were also cast; two hundred of them in a double row encircled the piece of network on each of the two capitals. ¹⁹The capitals on top of the columns were finished wholly in a lotus pattern ²⁰above the level of the nodes and their enveloping network. ²¹The columns were then erected adjacent to the porch of the temple, one to the right, called Jachin, and the other to the left, called Boaz. ²²Thus the work on the columns was completed.

²³*The sea was then cast; it was made with a circular rim, and measured ten cubits across, five in height, and thirty in circumference.ˣ ²⁴Under the brim, gourds encircled it, ten to the cubit all the way around; the gourds were in two rows and were cast in one mold with the sea. ²⁵This rested on twelve oxen, three facing north, three facing west, three facing south, and three facing east, with their haunches all toward the center, where the sea was set upon them. ²⁶It was a handbreadth thick, and its brim resembled that of a cup, being lily-shaped. Its capacity was two thousand measures.

²⁷Ten stands were also made of bronze, each four cubits long, four wide, and three high. ²⁸When these stands were constructed, panels were set within the framework. ²⁹On the panels between the frames there were lions, oxen, and cherubim; and on the frames likewise, above and below the lions and oxen, there were wreaths in relief.

³⁰Each stand had four bronze wheels and bronze axles. ³²The four wheels were below the paneling, and the axletrees of the wheels and the stand were of one piece. Each wheel was a cubit and a half high. ³³The wheels were constructed like chariot wheels; their axles, fellies, spokes, and hubs were all cast.

The four legs of each stand had cast braces, which were under the basin; they had wreaths on each side. ³⁴These four braces, extending to the corners of each stand, were of one piece with the stand.

³⁵On top of the stand there was a raised collar half a cubit high, with supports and panels which were of one piece with the top of the stand. ³¹This was surmounted by a crown one cubit high within which was a rounded opening to provide a receptacle a cubit and a half in depth. There was carved work at the opening, on panels that were angular, not curved. ³⁶On the surfaces of the supports and on the panels, wherever there was a clear space, cherubim, lions, and palm trees were carved, as well as wreaths all around. ³⁷This was how the ten stands were made, all of the same casting, the same size, the same shape. ³⁸Ten bronze basins were then made, each four cubits in diameter with a capacity of forty measures, one basin for the top of each of the ten stands. ³⁹The stands were placed, five on the south side of the temple and five on the north. The sea was placed off to the southeast from the south side of the temple.

⁴⁰When Hiram made the pots, shovels, and bowls, he therewith completed all his work for King Solomon in the temple of the LORD: ⁴¹two columns, two nodes for the capitals on top of the columns, two pieces of network covering the nodes for the capitals on top of the columns, ⁴²four hundred pomegranates in double rows on both pieces of network that covered the two nodes of the capitals where they met the columns, ⁴³ten stands, ten basins on the stands, ⁴⁴one sea, twelve oxen supporting the sea, ⁴⁵pots, shovels, and bowls. All these articles which Hiram made for King Solomon in the temple of the LORD were of burnished bronze. ⁴⁶The king had them cast in the neighborhood of the Jordan, in the clayey ground between Succoth and Zarethan. ⁴⁷Solomon did not weigh all the articles because they were so numerous; the weight of the bronze, therefore, was not determined.

⁴⁸Solomon had all the articles made for the interior of the temple of the LORD: the golden

7, 23-26: The sea . . . rested on twelve oxen: this was a large circular tank containing about twelve thousand gallons of water.

w: Jer 52, 21.   x: 2 Chr 4, 2.

altar; the golden table on which the show-bread lay; ⁴⁹the lampstands of pure gold, five to the right and five to the left before the sanctuary, with their flowers, lamps, and tongs of gold; ⁵⁰basins, snuffers, bowls, cups, and fire pans of pure gold; and hinges of gold for the doors of the inner room, or holy of holies, and for the doors of the outer room, the nave.

⁵¹When all the work undertaken by King Solomon in the temple of the LORD was completed, he brought in the dedicated offerings of his father David, putting the silver, gold, and other articles in the treasuries of the temple of the LORD.ʸ

CHAPTER 8

See RG
126-29

Dedication of the Temple. ¹At the order of Solomon, the elders of Israel and all the leaders of the tribes, the princes in the ancestral houses of the Israelites, came to King Solomon in Jerusalem, to bring up the ark of the LORD's covenant from the City of David [which is Zion].ᶻ ²All the men of Israel assembled before King Solomon during the festival in the month of Ethanim (the seventh month). ³When all the elders of Israel had arrived, the priests took up the ark; ⁴they carried the ark of the LORD and the meeting tent with all the sacred vessels that were in the tent. (The priests and Levites carried them.)

⁵King Solomon and the entire community of Israel present for the occasion sacrificed before the ark sheep and oxen too many to number or count. ⁶*The priests brought the ark of the covenant of the LORD to its place beneath the wings of the cherubim in the sanctuary, the holy of holies of the temple. ⁷The cherubim had their wings spread out over the place of the ark, sheltering the ark and its poles from above. ⁸The poles were so long that their ends could be seen from that part of the holy place adjoining the sanctuary; however, they could not be seen beyond. (They have remained there to this day.) ⁹There was nothing in the ark but the two stone tablets which Moses had put there at Horeb, when the LORD made a covenant with the Israelites at their departure from the land of Egypt.ᵃ

¹⁰When the priests left the holy place, the cloud filled the temple of the LORD ¹¹so that the priests could no longer minister because of the cloud, since the LORD's glory had filled the temple of the LORD. ¹²Then Solomon said, "The LORD intends to dwell in the dark cloud;ᵇ ¹³I have truly built you a princely house, a dwelling where you may abide forever."

¹⁴The king turned and greeted the whole community of Israel as they stood. ¹⁵He said to them: "Blessed be the LORD, the God of Israel, who with his own mouth made a promise to my father David and by his hand has brought it to fulfillment. It was he who said, ¹⁶'Since the day I brought my people Israel out of Egypt, I have not chosen a city out of any tribe of Israel for the building of a temple to my honor; but I choose David to rule my people Israel.' ¹⁷When my father David wished to build a temple to the honor of the LORD, the God of Israel,ᶜ ¹⁸the Lord said to him, 'In wishing to build a temple to my honor, you do well. ¹⁹It will not be you, however, who will build the temple; but the son who will spring from you, he shall build the temple to my honor.' ²⁰And now the LORD has fulfilled the promise that he made: I have succeeded my father David and sit on the throne of Israel, as the LORD foretold, and I have built this temple to honor the LORD, the God of Israel. ²¹I have provided in it a place for the ark in which is the covenant of the LORD, which he made with our fathers when he brought them out of the land of Egypt."

Solomon's Prayer. ²²Solomon stood before the altar of the LORD in the presence of the whole community of Israel, and stretching forth his hands toward heaven, ²³he said, "LORD, God of Israel, there is no God like you in heaven above or on earth below; you

---

8, 6-9: The transfer of the ark of the covenant into the newly constructed temple building, and the oracle of God's acceptance (1 Kgs 9, 3-9), and his act of possession (1 Kgs 8, 10-13), constituted the temple's solemn dedication, and made of it the abiding dwelling of God among his people for which David had hoped (2 Sm 6, 12-15; 7, 1-3). The concurrence of the feast of Booths marks an appropriate transition of God's dwelling among nomadic tribes to his permanent abode among a settled people.

y: 2 Chr 5, 1.   *z:* 2 Chr 5, 2.   *a:* Ex 34, 27; Heb 9, 4.   *b:* 2 Chr 6, 1.   *c:* 2 Sm 7, 5.

The Dedication of the Temple

The dedication of the temple occurred nearly a year after its completion, to coincide with the autumn new year celebration. The ark was carried by poles inside of rings on either side of the box that was the ark proper. The "LORD's glory" (8, 11) was the thick cloud that symbolized the LORD's presence. Solomon's speech (vv. 15–21) is a deuteronomistic composition. It links the promise to David of a dynasty (2 Sm 7) with that of rest for Israel (Dt 12, 10–12).

keep your covenant of kindness with your servants who are faithful to you with their whole heart. ²⁴You have kept the promise you made to my father David, your servant. You who spoke that promise, have this day, by your own power, brought it to fulfillment. ²⁵Now, therefore, LORD, God of Israel, keep the further promise you made to my father David, your servant, saying, 'You shall always have someone from your line to sit before me on the throne of Israel, provided only that your descendants look to their conduct so that they live in my presence, as you have lived in my presence.'ᵈ ²⁶Now, LORD, God of Israel, may this promise which you made to my father David, your servant, be confirmed.

²⁷"Can it indeed be that God dwells among men on earth? If the heavens and the highest heavens cannot contain you, how much less this temple which I have built! ²⁸Look kindly on the prayer and petition of your servant, O LORD, my God, and listen to the cry of supplication which I, your servant, utter before you this day. ²⁹May your eyes watch night and day over this temple, the place where you have decreed you shall be honored; may you heed the prayer which I, your servant, offer in this place. ³⁰Listen to the petitions of your servant and of your people Israel which they offer in this place. Listen from your heavenly dwelling and grant pardon.

³¹"If a man sins against his neighbor and is required to take an oath sanctioned by a curse, when he comes and takes the oath before your altar in this temple, ³²listen in heaven; take action and pass judgment on your servants. Condemn the wicked and punish him for his conduct, but acquit the just and establish his innocence.

³³"If your people Israel sin against you and are defeated by an enemy, and if then they return to you, praise your name, pray to you, and entreat you in this temple, ³⁴listen in heaven and forgive the sin of your people Israel, and bring them back to the land you gave their fathers.

³⁵"If the sky is closed, so that there is no rain, because they have sinned against you and you afflict them, and if then they repent of their sin, and pray, and praise your name in this place, ³⁶listen in heaven and forgive the sin of your servant and of your people Israel, teaching them the right way to live and sending rain upon this land of yours which you have given to your people as their heritage.

³⁷"If there is famine in the land or pestilence; or if blight comes, or mildew, or a locust swarm, or devouring insects; if an enemy of your people besieges them in one of their cities; whatever plague or sickness there may be, ³⁸if then any one [of your entire people Israel] has remorse of conscience and offers some prayer or petition, stretching out his hands toward this temple, ³⁹listen from your heavenly dwelling place and forgive. You who alone know the hearts of all men, render to each one of them according to his conduct; knowing their hearts, so treat them ⁴⁰that they may fear you as long as they live on the land you gave our fathers.

⁴¹"To the foreigner, likewise, who is not of your people Israel, but comes from a distant land to honor you ⁴²(since men will learn of your great name and your mighty

8, 33-34. 46-53: These references to deportation of Israelites to a hostile land are an expansion of Solomon's prayer dating from the Babylonian exile four centuries later.

d: 2 Sm 7, 12.

Solomon's prayer (8, 22–53) contains seven petitions, which address future problems and ask the LORD to heed prayers made in and toward the temple. This prayer may have been written after the exile. The idea behind the word "inheritance" (8, 53) is that each nation has its own god, and each god has his own people; the LORD's inheritance is Israel.

hand and your outstretched arm), when he comes and prays toward this temple, ⁴³listen from your heavenly dwelling. Do all that the foreigner asks of you, that all the peoples of the earth may know your name, may fear you as do your people Israel, and may acknowledge that this temple which I have built is dedicated to your honor.

⁴⁴"Whatever the direction in which you may send your people forth to war against their enemies, if they pray to you, O LORD, toward the city you have chosen and the temple I have built in your honor, ⁴⁵listen in heaven to their prayer and petition, and defend their cause.

⁴⁶"When they sin against you (for there is no man who does not sin), and in your anger against them you deliver them to the enemy, so that their captors deport them to a hostile land, far or near,^e ⁴⁷may they repent in the land of their captivity and be converted. If then they entreat you in the land of their captors and say, 'We have sinned and done wrong; we have been wicked'; ⁴⁸if with their whole heart and soul they turn back to you in the land of the enemies who took them captive, pray to you toward the land you gave their fathers, the city you have chosen, and the temple I have built in your honor, ⁴⁹listen from your heavenly dwelling. ⁵⁰Forgive your people their sins and all the offenses they have committed against you, and grant them mercy before their captors, so that these will be merciful to them. ⁵¹For they are your people and your inheritance, whom you brought out of Egypt, from the midst of an iron furnace.

⁵²"Thus may your eyes be open to the petition of your servant and to the petition of your people Israel. Hear them whenever they call upon you, ⁵³because you have set them apart among all the peoples of the earth for your inheritance, as you declared through

your servant Moses when you brought our fathers out of Egypt, O Lord GOD."

⁵⁴When Solomon finished offering this entire prayer of petition to the LORD, he rose from before the altar of the LORD, where he had been kneeling with his hands outstretched toward heaven. ⁵⁵He stood and blessed the whole community of Israel, saying in a loud voice: ⁵⁶"Blessed be the LORD who has given rest to his people Israel, just as he promised. Not a single word has gone unfulfilled of the entire generous promise he made through his servant Moses. ⁵⁷May the LORD, our God, be with us as he was with our fathers and may he not forsake us nor cast us off. ⁵⁸May he draw our hearts to himself, that we may follow him in everything and keep the commands, statutes, and ordinances which he enjoined on our fathers. ⁵⁹May this prayer I have offered to the LORD, our God, be present to him day and night, that he may uphold the cause of his servant and of his people Israel as each day requires, ⁶⁰that all the peoples of the earth may know the LORD is God and there is no other. ⁶¹You must be wholly devoted to the LORD, our God, observing his statutes and keeping his commandments, as on this day."

⁶²The king and all Israel with him offered sacrifices before the LORD. ⁶³Solomon offered as peace offerings to the LORD twenty-two thousand oxen and one hundred twenty thousand sheep. Thus the king and all the Israelites dedicated the temple of the LORD. ⁶⁴On that day the king consecrated the middle of the court facing the temple of the LORD; he offered there the holocausts, the cereal offerings, and the fat of the peace offerings, because the bronze altar before the LORD was too small to hold these offerings.

⁶⁵On this occasion Solomon and all the Israelites, who had assembled in large

e: 2 Chr 6, 36; Eccl 7, 20; 1 Jn 1, 8.

numbers from Labo of Hamath to the wadi of Egypt, celebrated the festival before the LORD, our God, for seven days. 66On the eighth day he dismissed the people, who bade the king farewell and went to their homes, rejoicing and happy over all the blessings the LORD had given to his servant David and to his people Israel.

See RG 126–29

CHAPTER 9

Promise and Warning to Solomon. 1After Solomon finished building the temple of the LORD, the royal palace, and everything else that he had planned, 2the LORD appeared to him a second time, as he had appeared to him in Gibeon.f 3The LORD said to him: "I have heard the prayer of petition which you offered in my presence. I have consecrated this temple which you have built; I confer my name upon it forever, and my eyes and my heart shall be there always. 4As for you, if you live in my presence as your father David lived, sincerely and uprightly, doing just as I have commanded you, keeping my statutes and decrees, 5I will establish your throne of sovereignty over Israel forever, as I promised your father David when I said, 'You shall always have someone from your line on the throne of Israel.'g 6But if you and your descendants ever withdraw from me, fail to keep the commandments and statutes which I set before you, and proceed to venerate and worship strange gods, 7I will cut off Israel from the land I gave them and repudiate the temple I have consecrated to my honor. Israel shall become a proverb and a byword among all nations, 8and this temple shall become a heap of ruins. Every passerby shall catch his breath in amazement, and ask, 'Why has the LORD done this to the land and to this temple?'h 9Men will answer: 'They forsook the LORD, their God, who brought their fathers out of the land of Egypt; they adopted strange gods which they worshiped and served. That is why the LORD has brought down upon them all this evil.' "

Other Acts of the King. 10After the twenty years during which Solomon built the two houses, the temple of the LORD and the palace of the king— 11Hiram, king of Tyre, supplying Solomon with all the cedar wood, fir wood, and gold he wished—King Solomon gave Hiram twenty cities in the land of Galilee. 12Hiram left Tyre to see the cities Solomon had given him, but was not satisfied with them. 13So he said, "What are these cities you have given me, my brother?" And he called them the land of Cabul, as they are called to this day. 14Hiram, however, had sent King Solomon one hundred and twenty talents of gold.*

15This is an account of the forced labor which King Solomon levied in order to build the temple of the LORD, his palace, Millo,* the wall of Jerusalem, Hazor, Megiddo, Gezer 16(Pharaoh king of Egypt, had come up and taken Gezer and, after destroying it by fire and slaying all the Canaanites living in the city, had given it as dowry to his daughter, Solomon's wife; 17Solomon then rebuilt Gezer), Lower Beth-horon, 18Baalath, Tamar in the desert of Judah, 19all his cities for supplies, cities for chariots and for horses, and whatever else Solomon decided should be built in Jerusalem, in Lebanon, and in the entire land under his dominion. 20All the non-Israelite people who remained in the land, descendants of the Amorites, Hittites, Perizzites, Hivites, and Jebusites 21whose doom the Israelites had been unable to accomplish, Solomon conscripted as forced laborers, as they are to this day. 22But Solomon enslaved none of the Israelites, for they were his fighting force, his ministers, commanders, adjutants, chariot officers, and charioteers. 23The supervisors of Solomon's works who policed the people engaged in the work numbered five hundred and fifty.

24As soon as Pharaoh's daughter went up from the City of David to her palace, which he had built for her, Solomon built Millo.

9, 14: One hundred and twenty talents of gold: approximately three million six hundred thousand dollars.

9, 15: Millo: probably means a filling, and may refer to an artificial earthwork or platform of stamped ground south of the temple area. It was begun by David (2 Sm 5, 9); cf

1 Kgs 9, 24; 11, 27.

f: 1 Kgs 3, 5; 11, 9; 2 Chr 7, 12.   g: 2 Sm 7, 12-16.   h: Dt 29, 23; Jer 22, 8.

²⁵Three times a year Solomon used to offer holocausts and peace offerings on the altar which he had built to the LORD, and to burn incense before the LORD; and he kept the temple in repair.

²⁶King Solomon also built a fleet at Eziongeber, which is near Elath on the shore of the Red Sea in the land of Edom.* ²⁷In this fleet Hiram placed his own expert seamen with the servants of Solomon. ²⁸They went to Ophir, and brought back four hundred and twenty talents of gold to King Solomon.

CHAPTER 10

See RG 126–29

Visit of the Queen of Sheba. ¹The queen of Sheba,* having heard of Solomon's fame, came to test him with subtle questions.ⁱ ²She arrived in Jerusalem with a very numerous retinue, and with camels bearing spices, a large amount of gold, and precious stones. She came to Solomon and questioned him on every subject in which she was interested. ³King Solomon explained everything she asked about, and there remained nothing hidden from him that he could not explain to her.

⁴When the queen of Sheba witnessed Solomon's great wisdom, the palace he had built, ⁵the food at his table, the seating of his ministers, the attendance and garb of his waiters, his banquet service, and the holocausts he offered in the temple of the LORD, she was breathless. ⁶"The report I heard in my country about your deeds and your wisdom is true," she told the king. ⁷"Though I did not believe the report until I came and saw with my own eyes, I have discovered that they were not telling me the half. Your wisdom and prosperity surpass the report I heard. ⁸Happy are your men, happy these servants of yours, who stand before you always and listen to your wisdom. ⁹Blessed be the LORD, your God, whom it has pleased to place you on the throne of Israel. In his enduring love for Israel, the LORD has made you king to carry out judgment and justice."

¹⁰Then she gave the king one hundred and twenty gold talents, a very large quantity of spices, and precious stones. Never again did anyone bring such an abundance of spices as the queen of Sheba gave to King Solomon.

¹¹Hiram's fleet, which used to bring gold from Ophir, also brought from there a large quantity of cabinet* wood and precious stones. ¹²With the wood the king made supports for the temple of the LORD and for the palace of the king, and harps and lyres for the chanters. No more such wood was brought or seen to the present day.

¹³King Solomon gave the queen of Sheba everything she desired and asked for, besides such presents as were given her from Solomon's royal bounty. Then she returned with her servants to her own country.

Solomon's Wealth. ¹⁴The gold that Solomon received every year weighed six hundred and sixty-six gold talents, ¹⁵in addition to what came from the Tarshish fleet, from the traffic of merchants, and from all the kings of Arabia and the governors of the country. ¹⁶Moreover, King Solomon made two hundred shields of beaten gold (six hundred gold shekels went into each shield)ʲ ¹⁷and three hundred bucklers of beaten gold (three minas of gold went into each buckler); and he put them in the hall of the Forest of Lebanon. ¹⁸The king also had a large ivory throne made, and overlaid it with refined gold. ¹⁹The throne had six steps, a back with a round top, and an arm on each side of the seat. Next to each arm stood a lion; ²⁰and twelve other lions stood on the steps, two to a step, one on either side of each step. Nothing like this was produced in any other kingdom. ²¹In addition, all King Solomon's drinking vessels were of gold, and all the utensils in the hall of the Forest of Lebanon were of pure gold. There was no silver, for in Solomon's time it was considered worthless. ²²The king had a fleet of Tarshish ships* at sea with Hiram's fleet.

9, 26: Ezion-geber . . . Edom: the first mention of maritime commerce in the Israelite kingdom (to which the land of Edom was subject after its conquest by King David; cf 2 Sm 8, 14).

10, 1: Queen of Sheba: women rulers among the Arabs are recorded in eighth-century-B.C. Assyrian inscriptions. Sheba was for centuries the leading principality in what is now the Yemen.

10, 11f: Cabinet: an unknown wood, probably fragrant.

10, 22: Tarshish ships: large, strong vessels for long voyages. Tarshish was the ancient Tartessus, a Phoenician colony in southern Spain, the name of which denotes a center for smelting metallic ore.

i: 2 Chr 9, 1; Mt 12, 42; Lk 11, 31. *j:* 1 Kgs 14, 26.

Once every three years the fleet of Tarshish ships would come with a cargo of gold, silver, ivory, apes, and monkeys. ²³Thus King Solomon surpassed in riches and wisdom all the kings of the earth. ²⁴And the whole world sought audience with Solomon, to hear from him the wisdom which God had put in his heart. ²⁵Each one brought his yearly tribute: silver or gold articles, garments, weapons, spices, horses and mules.

²⁶Solomon collected chariots and drivers; he had one thousand four hundred chariots and twelve thousand drivers; these he allocated among the chariot cities and to the king's service in Jerusalem.^k ²⁷The king made silver as common in Jerusalem as stones, and cedars as numerous as the sycamores of the foothills. ²⁸Solomon's horses were imported from Cilicia, where the king's agents purchased them. ²⁹A chariot imported from Egypt cost six hundred shekels, a horse one hundred and fifty shekels; they were exported at these rates to all the Hittite and Aramean kings.

CHAPTER 11

See RG
126-29

The Sins of Solomon. ¹*King Solomon loved many foreign women besides the daughter of Pharaoh (Moabites, Ammonites, Edomites, Sidonians, and Hittites),^l ²from nations with which the LORD had forbidden the Israelites to intermarry, "because," he said, "they will turn your hearts to their gods."^m ³But Solomon fell in love with them. He had seven hundred wives of princely rank and three hundred concubines, and his wives turned his heart.

⁴When Solomon was old his wives had turned his heart to strange gods, and his heart was not entirely with the LORD, his God, as the heart of his father David had been. ⁵By adoring Astarte, the goddess of the Sidonians, and Milcom, the idol of the Ammonites,

⁶Solomon did evil in the sight of the LORD; he did not follow him unreservedly as his father David had done. ⁷Solomon then built a high place to Chemosh, the idol of Moab, and to Molech, the idol of the Ammonites, on the hill opposite Jerusalem. ⁸He did the same for all his foreign wives who burned incense and sacrificed to their gods. ⁹The LORD, therefore, became angry with Solomon, because his heart was turned away from the LORD, the God of Israel, who had appeared to him twiceⁿ ¹⁰(for though the LORD had forbidden him this very act of following strange gods, Solomon had not obeyed him).

¹¹So the LORD said to Solomon: "Since this is what you want, and you have not kept my covenant and my statutes which I enjoined on you, I will deprive you of the kingdom and give it to your servant. ¹²I will not do this during your lifetime, however, for the sake of your father David; it is your son whom I will deprive.^o ¹³Nor will I take away the whole kingdom. I will leave your son one tribe for the sake of my servant David and of Jerusalem, which I have chosen."

¹⁴The LORD then raised up an adversary to Solomon: Hadad the Edomite, who was of the royal line in Edom. ¹⁵Earlier, when David had conquered Edom, Joab, the general of the army, while going to bury the slain, put to death every male in Edom.^p ¹⁶Joab and all Israel remained there six months until they had killed off every male in Edom. ¹⁷Meanwhile, Hadad, who was only a boy, fled toward Egypt with some Edomite servants of his father. ¹⁸They left Midian and passing through Paran, where they picked up additional men, they went into Egypt to Pharaoh, king of Egypt, who gave Hadad a house, appointed him rations, and assigned him land.

¹⁹Hadad won great favor with Pharaoh, so that he gave him in marriage the sister of

---

11, 1-3. 7: The glorious rise of Solomon, his piety and wisdom, administrative skill and wealth, the extension of his kingdom, his prestige among neighboring rulers, his reign of peace, above all his friendship with God—these are now eclipsed by his sins of intermarriage with great numbers of pagan wives and the consequent forbidden worship of their gods (Ex 34, 11-16; Dt 7, 1-5). His construction of temples in their honor merited the punishment of loss of a united kingdom to his posterity, and the opposition of adversaries to him-

self (vv 14. 23-27). Hadad the Edomite rebelled against Solomon at the beginning of his reign (v 25). Rezon of Syria established a new kingdom in Damascus; Jeroboam of Israel constituted the greatest threat because of his revolt from within. This threefold threat culminated in the breakup of Solomon's kingdom.

k: 2 Chr 1, 14. *l:* Dt 17, 17; Sir 47, 19f. *m:* Ex 34, 16. *n:* 1 Kgs 9, 2. *o:* 1 Kgs 12, 15. *p:* 2 Sm 8, 14.

Solomon's Apostasy

Solomon loved the LORD (3, 3); yet he also loved the daughter of Pharaoh (3, 1; 9, 16. 24) and many other women besides. Deuteronomy 6, 5; 10, 12. 20; and 11, 1. 22, however, speak of loving God as unswerving loyalty and obedience to God—the God who had forbidden intermarriage with foreign women (Dt 7, 3–4). A divided heart led Solomon in the end after other gods, including Astarte, a leading Canaanite goddess, and Milcom, the national god of the Ammonites. Solomon built sanctuaries on the Mount of Olives and elsewhere rivaling the temple.

Queen Tahpenes, his own wife. [20]Tahpenes' sister bore Hadad a son, Genubath. After his weaning, the queen kept him in Pharaoh's palace, where he then lived with Pharaoh's own sons. [21]When Hadad in Egypt heard that David rested with his ancestors and that Joab, the general of the army, was dead, he said to Pharaoh, "Give me leave to return to my own country." [22]Pharaoh said to him, "What do you lack with me, that you are seeking to return to your own country?" "Nothing," he said, "but please let me go!"

[23]God raised up against Solomon another adversary, in Rezon, the son of Eliada, who had fled from his lord, Hadadezer, king of Zobah, [24]when David defeated them with slaughter. Rezon gathered men about him and became leader of a band, went to Damascus, settled there, and became king in Damascus. [25]He was an enemy of Israel as long as Solomon lived; this added to the harm done by Hadad, who made a rift in Israel by becoming king over Edom.

[26]Solomon's servant Jeroboam, son of Nebat, an Ephraimite from Zeredah with a widowed mother, Zeruah, also rebelled against the king.[q] [27]This is why he rebelled. King Solomon was building Millo, closing up the breach of his father's City of David. [28]Jeroboam was a man of means, and when Solomon saw that he was also an industrious young man, he put him in charge of the entire labor force of the house of Joseph. [29]At that time Jeroboam left Jerusalem, and the prophet Ahijah the Shilonite met him on the road. The two were alone in the area, and the prophet was wearing a new cloak.[r] [30]Ahijah took off his new cloak, tore it into twelve pieces, [31]and said to Jeroboam:

"Take ten pieces for yourself; the LORD, the God of Israel, says: 'I will tear away the kingdom from Solomon's grasp and will give you ten of the tribes.[s] [32]One tribe shall remain to him for the sake of David my servant, and of Jerusalem, the city I have chosen out of all the tribes of Israel. [33]The ten I will give you because he has forsaken me and has worshiped Astarte, goddess of the Sidonians, Chemosh, god of Moab, and Milcom, god of the Ammonites; he has not followed my ways or done what is pleasing to me according to my statutes and my decrees, as his father David did. [34]Yet I will not take any of the kingdom from Solomon himself, but will keep him a prince as long as he lives for the sake of my servant David, whom I chose, who kept my commandments and statutes. [35]But I will take the kingdom from his son and will give it to you—that is, the ten tribes. [36]I will give his son one tribe, that my servant David may always have a lamp before me in Jerusalem, the city in which I choose to be honored. [37]I will take you; you shall reign over all that you desire and shall become king of Israel. [38]If, then, you heed all that I command you, follow my ways, and please me by keeping my statutes and my commandments like my servant David, I will be with you. I will establish for you, as I did for David, a lasting dynasty; I will give Israel to you. [39]I will punish David's line for this, but not forever.' "

q: 2 Chr 13, 6.   r: 1 Kgs 14, 2; 2 Chr 10, 15.   s: 1 Kgs 12, 15.

⁴⁰When Solomon tried to have Jeroboam killed for his rebellion, he escaped to King Shishak, in Egypt, where he remained until Solomon's death.

⁴¹The rest of the acts of Solomon, with all his deeds and his wisdom, are recorded in the book of the chronicles of Solomon. ⁴²The time that Solomon reigned in Jerusalem over all Israel was forty years. ⁴³Solomon rested with his ancestors; he was buried in his father's City of David, and his son Rehoboam succeeded him as king.

II: Judah and Israel to the Time of Ahab

See RG 129–34

CHAPTER 12

Secession of Israel. ¹Rehoboam went to Shechem,* where all Israel had come to proclaim him king.¹ ³They said to Rehoboam: ⁴"Your father put on us a heavy yoke. If you now lighten the harsh service and the heavy yoke your father imposed on us, we will serve you." ⁵"Come back to me in three days," he answered them. When the people had departed, ⁶King Rehoboam consulted the elders who had been in his father's service while he was alive, and asked, "What answer do you advise me to give this people?" ⁷They replied, "If today you will be the servant of this people and submit to them, giving them a favorable answer, they will be your servants forever." ⁸But he ignored the advice the elders had given him, and consulted the young men who had grown up with him and were in his service. ⁹He said to them, "What answer do you advise me to give this people, who have asked me to lighten the yoke my father imposed on them?" ¹⁰The young men who had grown up with him replied, "This is what you must say to this people who have asked you to lighten the yoke your father put on them: 'My little finger is thicker than my father's body. ¹¹Whereas my father put a heavy yoke on you, I will make it heavier. My father beat you with whips, but I will beat you with scorpions.' "

¹²On the third day all Israel came back to King Rehoboam, as he had instructed them to do. ¹³Ignoring the advice the elders had given him, the king gave the people a harsh answer. ¹⁴He said to them, as the young men had advised: "My father put on you a heavy yoke, but I will make it heavier. My father beat you with whips, but I will beat you with scorpions." ¹⁵The king did not listen to the people, for the LORD brought this about to fulfill the prophecy he had uttered to Jeroboam, son of Nebat, through Ahijah the Shilonite.ᵘ

¹⁶When all Israel saw that the king did not listen to them, the people answered the king:

"What share have we in David?*
We have no heritage in the son of Jesse.
To your tents, O Israel!
Now look to your own house, David."

So Israel went off to their tents, ¹⁷but Rehoboam reigned over the Israelites who lived in the cities of Judah. ¹⁸King Rehoboam then sent out Adoram, superintendent of the forced labor, but all Israel stoned him to death. Rehoboam managed to mount his chariot to flee to Jerusalem, ¹⁹and Israel went into rebellion against David's house to this day. ²Jeroboam, son of Nebat, who was still in Egypt, where he had fled from King Solomon, returned from Egypt as soon as he learned this. ²⁰When all Israel heard that Jeroboam had returned, they summoned him to an assembly and made him king over all Israel. None remained loyal to David's house except the tribe of Judah alone.

²¹On his arrival in Jerusalem, Rehoboam gathered together all the house of Judah and the tribe of Benjamin—one hundred eighty thousand seasoned warriors—to fight against the house of Israel, to restore the kingdom to Rehoboam, son of Solomon. ²²ᵛHowever, the LORD spoke to Shemaiah, a man of God:

12, 1: Shechem: chief city of the northern tribes, where a covenant of fidelity had previously been made between the Lord and his people and a stone of witness had been erected in memory of the event (Jos 24, 25ff).

12, 16: What share have we in David: even in David's

time the northern tribes seemed ready to withdraw from Judah (2 Sm 20, 1). The unreasonable attitude of Rehoboam toward them intensified the discontent caused by the oppression of Solomon (v 4) and thus precipitated the establishment

t: 2 Chr 10, 1.   *u:* 1 Kgs 11, 12. 31.   *v:* 22-24: 2 Chr 11, 2ff.

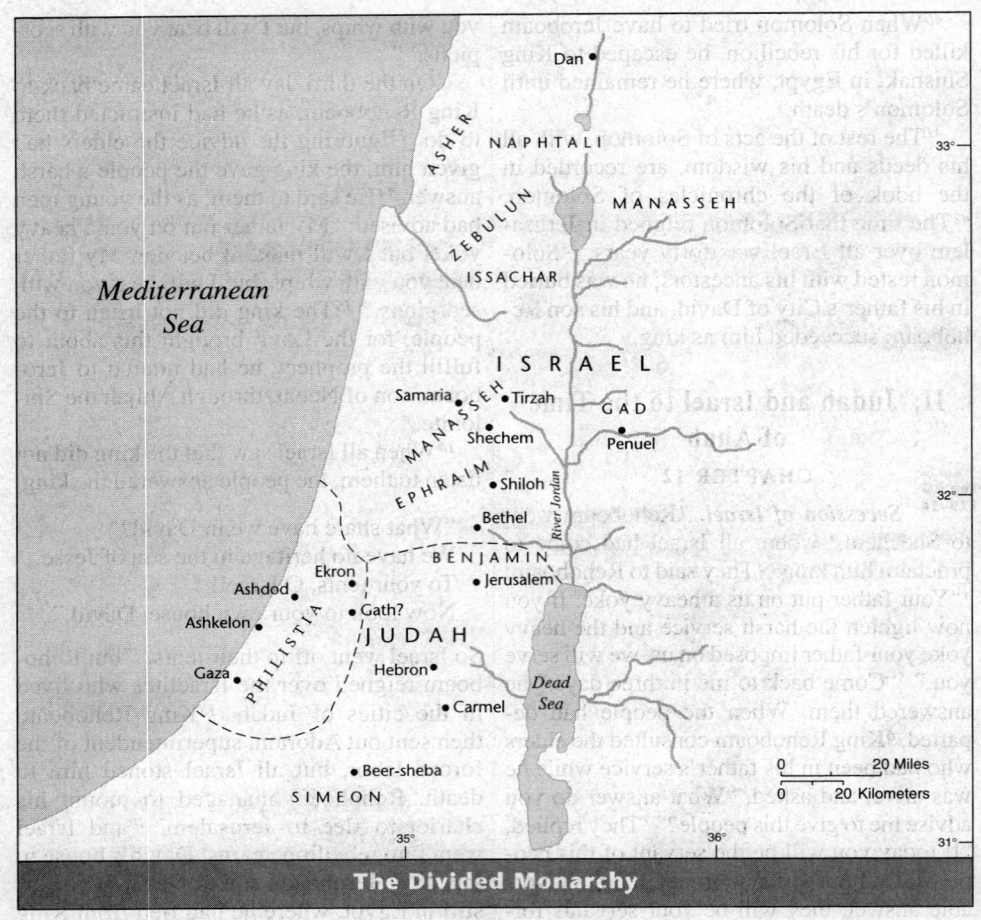

Dan

ASHER

NAPHTALI

33°—

ZEBULUN MANASSEH

ISSACHAR

*Mediterranean
Sea*

I S R A E L

Samaria MANASSEH •Tirzah GAD

• Shechem Penuel•

EPHRAIM • Shiloh

32°—

• Bethel

River Jordan

BENJAMIN

Ekron • Jerusalem

Ashdod •

PHILISTIA • Gath?

Ashkelon •

J U D A H

Gaza • Hebron • *Dead
Sea*

• Carmel

0   20 Miles

0   20 Kilometers

• Beer-sheba

SIMEON

35°   36°   31°—

The Divided Monarchy

23"Say to Rehoboam, son of Solomon, king of Judah, and to the house of Judah and to Benjamin, and to the rest of the people: 24'Thus says the LORD: You must not march out to fight against your brother Israelites. Let every man return home, for I have brought this about.' " They accepted this message of the LORD and gave up the expedition accordingly.

25Jeroboam built up Shechem in the hill country of Ephraim and lived there. Then he left it and built up Penuel.

*Religious Rebellion.** 26Jeroboam thought to himself: "The kingdom will return to David's house. 27If now this people go up to offer sacrifices in the temple of the LORD in Jerusalem, the hearts of this people will return to their master, Rehoboam, king of Judah, and they will kill me." 28After taking counsel, the king made two calves of gold and said to the people: "You have been going up to Jerusalem long enough. Here is your God, O Israel, who brought you up from the land of Egypt."w

of a rival monarchy (v 20).

12, 26-32: Jeroboam feared reunification of the divided kingdom through worship in the single temple in Jerusalem. To prevent this he encouraged shrines on the high places, and appointed false priests to supplement those of levitical descent. The golden bullocks he installed in two

of his sanctuaries, though probably intended as bearers of the invisible Divine Majesty, quickly became occasions for idolatry. Thus Jeroboam caused Israel to sin, and sealed his doom and that of his royal house (1 Kgs 13, 34; 14, 7-14).

w: Tb 1, 5; Ex 32, 8.

The Sins of Jeroboam

Jeroboam made two "calves of gold" (12, 28) and offered them to the people to worship. Images of calves and bulls were commonly used in the ancient Near East to represent deities, especially fertility gods like Baal.

Jeroboam also built "temples on the high places" (v. 31), which were probably shrines to the LORD. However, they and the calves were in Bethel and Dan, and the writer regards Jerusalem as the only legitimate place to worship the LORD. Another aspect of Jeroboam's apostasy was the appointment of non-Levites as priests (v. 31).

29And he put one in Bethel, the other in Dan.* 30This led to sin, because the people frequented these calves in Bethel and in Dan. 31He also built temples on the high places and made priests from among the people who were not Levites.x 32Jeroboam established a feast in the eighth month on the fifteenth day of the month to duplicate in Bethel the pilgrimage feast of Judah, with sacrifices to the calves he had made; and he stationed in Bethel priests of the high places he had built.

Message of the Prophet from Judah. 33Jeroboam ascended the altar he built in Bethel on the fifteenth day of the eighth month, the month in which he arbitrarily chose to establish a feast for the Israelites; he was going to offer sacrifice.

See RG 129-34

CHAPTER 13

1A man of God came from Judah to Bethel by the word of the LORD, while Jeroboam was standing at the altar to offer sacrifice. 2He cried out against the altar the word of the LORD: "O altar, altar, the LORD says, 'A child shall be born to the house of David, Josiah by name, who shall slaughter upon you the priests of the high places who offer sacrifice upon you, and he shall burn human bones upon you.' "y 3He gave a sign that same day and said: "This is the sign that the LORD has spoken: The altar shall break up and the ashes on it shall be strewn about."

4When King Jeroboam heard what the man of God was crying out against the altar, he stretched forth his hand from the altar and said, "Seize him!" But the hand he stretched forth against him withered, so that he could not draw it back. 5Moreover, the altar broke up and the ashes from it were strewn about—the sign the man of God had given as the word of the LORD. 6Then the king appealed to the man of God. "Entreat the LORD, your God," he said, "and intercede for me that I may be able to withdraw my hand." So the man of God entreated the LORD, and the king recovered the normal use of his hand. 7"Come home with me for some refreshment," the king invited the man of God, "and I will give you a present." 8"If you gave me half your kingdom," the man of God said to the king, "I would not go with you, nor eat bread or drink water in this place. 9For I was instructed by the word of the LORD not to eat bread or drink water and not to return by the way I came." 10So he departed by another road and did not go back the way he had come to Bethel.

11There was an old prophet living in the city, whose sons came and told him all that the man of God had done that day in Bethel. When they repeated to their father the words he had spoken to the king, 12the father asked them, "Which way did he go?" And his sons pointed out to him the road taken by the man of God who had come from Judah. 13Then he said to his sons, "Saddle the ass for me." When they had saddled it, he mounted 14and followed the man of God, whom he found seated under a terebinth. When he asked him, "Are you the

12, 29: Bethel . . . Dan: at the southern and northern boundaries of the separate kingdom of Israel, where sanctuaries had existed in the past (Gn 12, 8; 13, 3; 18, 10-22; 25, 1-16; Jgs 18, 1-31).

x: 2 Chr 11, 15.   y: 2 Kgs 23, 16.

man of God who came from Judah?" he answered, "Yes." [15]Then he said, "Come home with me and have some bread." [16]"I cannot go back with you, and I cannot eat bread or drink water with you in this place," he answered, [17]"for I was told by the word of the LORD neither to eat bread nor drink water here, and not to go back the way I came." [18]But he said to him, "I, too, am a prophet like you, and an angel told me in the word of the LORD to bring you back with me to my house and to have you eat bread and drink water." He was lying to him, however.

[19]So he went back with him, and ate bread and drank water in his house. [20]But while they were sitting at table, the LORD spoke to the prophet who had brought him back, [21]and he cried out to the man of God who had come from Judah: "The LORD says, 'Because you rebelled against the command of the LORD and did not keep the command which the LORD, your God, gave you, [22]but returned and ate bread and drank water in the place where he told you to do neither, your corpse shall not be brought to the grave of your ancestors.' "

[23]After he had eaten bread and drunk water, the ass was saddled for him, and he again [24]set out. But a lion met him on the road, and killed him. His corpse lay sprawled on the road, and the ass remained standing by it, and so did the lion. [25]Some passers-by saw the body lying in the road, with the lion standing beside it, and carried the news to the city where the old prophet lived. [26]On hearing it, the prophet who had brought him back from his journey said: "It is the man of God who rebelled against the command of the LORD. He has delivered him to a lion, which mangled and killed him, as the LORD predicted to him." [27]Then he said to his sons, "Saddle the ass for me." When they had saddled it, [28]he went off and found the body lying in the road with the ass and the lion standing beside it. The lion had not eaten the body nor had it harmed the ass. [29]The prophet lifted up the body of the man of God and put it on the ass, and brought it back to the city to mourn over it and to bury it. [30]He laid the man's body in his own grave, and they mourned over it:

"Alas, my brother!" [31]After he had buried him, he said to his sons, "When I die, bury me in the grave where the man of God is buried. Lay my remains beside his. [32]For the word of the LORD which he proclaimed against the altar in Bethel and against all the shrines on the high places in the cities of Samaria shall certainly come to pass."

[33]Jeroboam did not give up his evil ways after this event, but again made priests for the high places from among the common people. Whoever desired it was consecrated and became a priest of the high places. [34]This was a sin on the part of the house of Jeroboam for which it was to be cut off and destroyed from the earth.

CHAPTER 14

See RG 129-34

Death of Abijah. [1]At that time Abijah, son of Jeroboam, took sick. [2]So Jeroboam said to his wife, "Get ready and disguise yourself so that none will recognize you as Jeroboam's wife. Then go to Shiloh, where you will find the prophet Ahijah. It is he who predicted my reign over this people.[z] [3]Take along ten loaves, some cakes, and a jar of preserves, and go to him. He will tell you what will happen to the child." [4]The wife of Jeroboam obeyed. She made the journey to Shiloh and entered the house of Ahijah who could not see because age had dimmed his sight.

[5]The LORD had said to Ahijah: "Jeroboam's wife is coming to consult you about her son, for he is sick. This is what you must tell her. When she comes, she will be in disguise." [6]So Ahijah, hearing the sound of her footsteps as she entered the door, said, "Come in, wife of Jeroboam. Why are you in disguise? I have been commissioned to give you bitter news. [7]Go, tell Jeroboam, 'This is what the LORD, the God of Israel, says: I exalted you from among the people and made you ruler of my people Israel. [8]I deprived the house of David of the kingdom and gave it to you. Yet you have not been like my servant David, who kept my commandments and followed me with his whole heart, doing only what pleased me. [9]You have done worse than all who preceded you: you have gone and

z: 1 Kgs 11, 29.

made for yourself strange gods and molten images to provoke me; but me you have cast behind your back. [10]Therefore, I am bringing evil upon the house of Jeroboam: I will cut off every male in Jeroboam's line, whether slave or freeman in Israel, and will burn up the house of Jeroboam completely, as though dung were being burned.[a] [11]When one of Jeroboam's line dies in the city, dogs will devour him; when one of them dies in the field, he will be devoured by the birds of the sky. For the LORD has spoken!'[b] [12]So leave; go home! As you step inside the city, the child will die, [13]and all Israel will mourn him and bury him, for he alone of Jeroboam's line will be laid in the grave, since in him alone of Jeroboam's house has something pleasing to the LORD, the God of Israel, been found. [14]Today, at this very moment, the LORD will raise up for himself a king of Israel who will destroy the house of Jeroboam. [15]The LORD will strike Israel like a reed tossed about in the water and will pluck out Israel from this good land which he gave their fathers, scattering them beyond the River, because they made sacred poles for themselves and thus provoked the LORD. [16]He will give up Israel because of the sins Jeroboam has committed and caused Israel to commit."

[17]So Jeroboam's wife started back; when she reached Tirzah and crossed the threshold of her house, the child died. [18]He was buried with all Israel mourning him, as the LORD had prophesied through his servant the prophet Ahijah.

[19]The rest of the acts of Jeroboam, with his warfare and his reign, are recorded in the book of the chronicles of the kings of Israel. [20]The length of Jeroboam's reign was twenty-two years. He rested with his ancestors, and his son Nadab succeeded him as king.

Reign of Rehoboam. [21]Rehoboam, son of Solomon, reigned in Judah. He was forty-one years old when he became king, and he reigned seventeen years in Jerusalem, the city in which, out of all the tribes of Israel, the LORD chose to be honored. His mother was the Ammonite named Naamah.[c]

[22]Judah did evil in the sight of the LORD, and by their sins angered him even more than their fathers had done. [23]They, too, built for themselves high places, pillars, and sacred poles, upon every high hill and under every green tree. [24]There were also cult prostitutes in the land. Judah imitated all the abominable practices of the nations whom the LORD had cleared out of the Israelites' way.

[25]In the fifth year of King Rehoboam, Shishak, king of Egypt, attacked Jerusalem.* [26]He took everything, including the treasures of the temple of the LORD and those of the royal palace, as well as all the gold shields made under Solomon.[d] [27]To replace them, King Rehoboam had bronze shields made, which he entrusted to the officers of the guard on duty at the entrance of the royal palace. [28]Whenever the king visited the temple of the LORD, those on duty would carry the shields, and then return them to the guardroom.

[29]The rest of the acts of Rehoboam, with all that he did, are recorded in the book of the chronicles of the kings of Judah. [30]There was constant warfare between Rehoboam and Jeroboam. [31]Rehoboam rested with his ancestors; he was buried with them in the City of David. His mother was the Ammonite named Naamah. His son Abijam succeeded him as king.

CHAPTER 15

See RG 129-34

Reign of Abijam. [1]In the eighteenth year of King Jeroboam, son of Nebat, Abijam became king of Judah;[e] [2]he reigned three years in Jerusalem. His mother's name was Maacah, daughter of Abishalom. [3]He imitated all the sins his father had committed before him, and his heart was not entirely with the LORD, his God, like the heart of his grandfather David. [4]Yet for David's sake the LORD, his God, gave him a lamp in Jerusa-

---

14, 25: In the fifth year . . . Shishak, king of Egypt, attacked Jerusalem: c. 926 B.C. According to 2 Chr 12, 1-12, the repentance of King Rehoboam and of the princes of Israel after the warning of the prophet Shemaiah diverted the actual attack on Jerusalem. Shishak, however, carried off the treasures of the temple of the Lord and of the king's palace (2 Chr 12, 9). A bas-relief of this Pharaoh in the temple of Aman at Karnak commemorates his conquest of some hundred and fifty Palestinian and Trans-Jordanian cities and towns.

a: 1 Kgs 15, 29. *b:* 1 Kgs 16, 4. *c:* 2 Chr 12, 13. *d:* 1 Kgs 10, 16. *e:* 2 Chr 13, 1f.

lem, raising up his son after him and permitting Jerusalem to endure; [5]because David had pleased the LORD and did not disobey any of his commands as long as he lived, except in the case of Uriah the Hittite.[f]

[7]The rest of Abijam's acts, with all that he did, are written in the book of the chronicles of the kings of Judah.[g] [6]There was war between Abijam and Jeroboam. [8]Abijam rested with his ancestors; he was buried in the City of David, and his son Asa succeeded him as king.

Reign of Asa. [9]In the twentieth year of Jeroboam, king of Israel, Asa, king of Judah, began to reign; [10]he reigned forty-one years in Jerusalem. His grandmother's name was Maacah, daughter of Abishalom. [11]Asa pleased the LORD like his forefather David, [12]banishing the temple prostitutes from the land and removing all the idols his father had made. [13]He also deposed his grandmother Maacah from her position as queen mother, because she had made an outrageous object for Asherah. Asa cut down this object and burned it in the Kidron Valley. [14]The high places did not disappear; yet Asa's heart was entirely with the LORD as long as he lived. [15]He brought into the temple of the LORD his father's and his own votive offerings of silver, gold, and various utensils.

[16]There was war between Asa and Baasha, king of Israel, as long as they both reigned. [17]Baasha, king of Israel, attacked Judah and fortified Ramah to prevent communication with Asa, king of Judah.[h] [18]Asa then took all the silver and gold remaining in the treasuries of the temple of the LORD and of the royal palace. Entrusting them to his ministers, King Asa sent them to Ben-hadad, son of Tabrimmon, son of Hezion, king of Aram,[*] resident in Damascus. He said: [19]"There is a treaty between you and me, as there was between your father and my father. I am sending you a present of silver and gold. Go, break your treaty with Baasha, king of Israel, that he may withdraw from me." [20]Ben-hadad agreed with King Asa and sent the leaders of his troops against the cities of Israel. They attacked Ijon, Dan, Abel-beth-maacah, and all Chinnereth, besides all the land of Naphtali. [21]When Baasha heard of it, he left off fortifying Ramah, and stayed in Tirzah. [22]Then King Asa summoned all Judah without exception, and they carried away the stones and beams with which Baasha was fortifying Ramah. With them King Asa built Geba of Benjamin and Mizpeh.

[23]The rest of the acts of Asa, with all his valor and accomplishments, and the cities he built, are written in the book of the chronicles of the kings of Judah. In his old age, Asa had an infirmity in his feet. [24]He rested with his ancestors; he was buried in his forefather's City of David, and his son Jehoshaphat succeeded him as king.[i]

Reign of Nadab. [25]In the second year of Asa, king of Judah, Nadab, son of Jeroboam, became king of Israel; he reigned over Israel two years. [26]He did evil in the LORD's sight, imitating his father's conduct and the sin which he had caused Israel to commit. [27]Baasha, son of Ahijah, of the house of Issachar, plotted against him and struck him down at Gibbethon of the Philistines, which Nadab and all Israel were besieging. [28]Baasha killed him in the third year of Asa, king of Judah, and reigned in his stead. [29]Once he was king, he killed off the entire house of Jeroboam, not leaving a single soul to Jeroboam but destroying him utterly, according to the warning which the LORD had pronounced through his servant, Ahijah the Shilonite,[j] [30]because of the sins Jeroboam committed and caused Israel to commit, by which he provoked the LORD, the God of Israel, to anger.

[31]The rest of the acts of Nadab, with all that he did, are written in the book of the chronicles of the kings of Israel. [32][There was war between Asa and Baasha, king of Israel, as long as they lived.]

Reign of Baasha. [33]In the third year of Asa, king of Judah, Baasha, son of Ahijah, began his twenty-four-year reign over Israel in Tirzah. [34]He did evil in the LORD's sight,

---

15, 18: Ben-hadad . . . king of Aram: Ben-hadad I, third successor of Rezon, who had thrown off the yoke of the Israelites during the reign of Solomon and become king of Aram (11, 23f).

f: 2 Sm 11, 4. *g:* 2 Chr 13, 2. *h:* 2 Chr 16, 1. *i:* 2 Chr 17, 1. *j:* 1 Kgs 14, 10; 21, 22.

imitating the conduct of Jeroboam and the sin he had caused Israel to commit.

See RG
129–34

CHAPTER 16

[1]The LORD spoke against Baasha to Jehu, son of Hanani, and said: [2]"Inasmuch as I lifted you up from the dust and made you ruler of my people Israel, but you have imitated the conduct of Jeroboam and have caused my people Israel to sin, provoking me to anger by their sins, [3]I will destroy you, Baasha, and your house;[k] [4]I will make your house like that of Jeroboam, son of Nebat. If anyone of Baasha's line dies in the city, dogs shall devour him; if he dies in the field, he shall be devoured by the birds of the sky."[l]

[5]The rest of the acts of Baasha, with all his valor and accomplishments, are written in the book of the chronicles of the kings of Israel.[m] [6]Baasha rested with his ancestors; he was buried in Tirzah; and his son Elah succeeded him as king. [7][Through the prophet Jehu, son of Hanani, the LORD had threatened Baasha and his house, because of all the evil Baasha did in the sight of the LORD, provoking him to anger by his evil deeds, so that he became like the house of Jeroboam; and because he killed Nadab.]

Reign of Elah. [8]In the twenty-sixth year of Asa, king of Judah, Elah, son of Baasha, began his two-year reign over Israel in Tirzah. [9]His servant Zimri, commander of half his chariots, plotted against him. As he was in Tirzah, drinking to excess in the house of Arza, superintendent of his palace in Tirzah, [10]Zimri entered; he struck and killed him in the twenty-seventh year of Asa, king of Judah, and reigned in his place.[n] [11]Once he was seated on the royal throne, he killed off the whole house of Baasha, not sparing a single male relative or friend of his. [12]Zimri destroyed the entire house of Baasha, as the LORD had prophesied to Baasha through the prophet Jehu, [13]because of all the sins which Baasha and his son Elah committed and caused Israel to commit, provoking the LORD, the God of Israel, to anger by their idols.

[14]The rest of the acts of Elah, with all that he did, are written in the book of the chronicles of the kings of Israel.

Reign of Zimri. [15]In the twenty-seventh year of Asa, king of Judah, Zimri reigned seven days in Tirzah. The army was besieging Gibbethon of the Philistines [16]when they heard that Zimri had formed a conspiracy and had killed the king. So that day in the camp all Israel proclaimed Omri, general of the army, king of Israel. [17]Omri marched up from Gibbethon, accompanied by all Israel, and laid siege to Tirzah. [18]When Zimri saw the city was captured, he entered the citadel of the royal palace and burned down the palace over him. He died [19]because of the sins he had committed, doing evil in the sight of the LORD by imitating the sinful conduct of Jeroboam, thus causing Israel to sin.

[20]The rest of the acts of Zimri, with the conspiracy he carried out, are written in the book of the chronicles of the kings of Israel.

[21]At that time the people of Israel were divided, half following Tibni, son of Ginath, to make him king, and half for Omri. [22]The partisans of Omri prevailed over those of Tibni, son of Ginath. Tibni died and Omri became king.

Reign of Omri. [23]In the thirty-first year of Asa, king of Judah, Omri became king; he reigned over Israel twelve years, the first six of them in Tirzah. [24]He then bought the hill of Samaria from Shemer for two silver talents and built upon the hill, naming the city he built Samaria after Shemer, the former owner. [25]But Omri did evil in the LORD's sight beyond any of his predecessors. [26]He closely imitated the sinful conduct of Jeroboam, son of Nebat, causing Israel to sin and to provoke the LORD, the God of Israel, to anger by their idols.

[27]The rest of the acts of Omri, with all his valor and accomplishments, are written in the book of the chronicles of the kings of Israel. [28]Omri rested with his ancestors; he was buried in Samaria, and his son Ahab succeeded him as king.

Reign of Ahab. [29]In the thirty-eighth year of Asa, king of Judah, Ahab, son of Omri,

---

k: 1 Kgs 21, 22.   *l:* 1 Kgs 14, 11.   *m:* 2 Chr 16, 1.   *n:* 2 Kgs 9, 31.

Elijah and the Drought

The major theme of chs 12–16 has been that God is in control of history, rather than kings or other gods whom the kings worship. Everything comes to pass just as the prophets say. The Elijah and Elisha cycles, placed at the center of 1–2 Kings, further establish this perspective. In chs 17–18, in particular, the most sinful of Israel's kings, Ahab, is forced to reckon with the most powerful of prophetic interventions in the person of Elijah.

The name Elijah means "Yahweh is my God," and it sets the theme for the following chapters. These chapters make clear that Baal is no more a god in any real sense than are Jeroboam's calves. The divinely ordained drought (17, 1) provides the context for showing that it is the LORD and not Baal who controls both life and death, both fertility and infertility.

became king of Israel; he reigned over Israel in Samaria for twenty-two years. *30*Ahab, son of Omri, did evil in the sight of the LORD more than any of his predecessors. *31*It was not enough for him to imitate the sins of Jeroboam, son of Nebat. He even married Jezebel, daughter of Ethbaal, king of the Sidonians, and went over to the veneration and worship of Baal. *32*Ahab erected an altar to Baal in the temple of Baal which he built in Samaria, *33*and also made a sacred pole. He did more to anger the LORD, the God of Israel, than any of the kings of Israel before him.

*34o*During his reign, Hiel from Bethel rebuilt Jericho. He lost his first-born son, Abiram, when he laid the foundation, and his youngest son, Segub, when he set up the gates, as the LORD had foretold through Joshua, son of Nun.

III: Stories of the Prophets

CHAPTER 17

See RG 129-34 *Drought Predicted by Elijah.* *1*Elijah the Tishbite,* from Tishbe in Gilead, said to Ahab: "As the LORD, the God of Israel, lives, whom I serve, during these years there shall be no dew or rain except at my word."*p* *2*The

LORD then said to Elijah: *3*"Leave here, go east and hide in the Wadi Cherith, east of the Jordan. *4*You shall drink of the stream, and I have commanded ravens to feed you there." *5*So he left and did as the LORD had commanded. He went and remained by the Wadi Cherith, east of the Jordan. *6*Ravens brought him bread and meat in the morning, and bread and meat in the evening, and he drank from the stream.

Elijah and the Widow. *7*After some time, however, the brook ran dry, because no rain had fallen in the land. *8*So the LORD said to him: *9*"Move on to Zarephath of Sidon and stay there. I have designated a widow there to provide for you." *10*He left and went to Zarephath. As he arrived at the entrance of the city, a widow was gathering sticks there; he called out to her, "Please bring me a small cupful of water to drink."*q* *11*She left to get it, and he called out after her, "Please bring along a bit of bread." *12*"As the LORD, your God, lives," she answered, "I have nothing baked; there is only a handful of flour in my jar and a little oil in my jug. Just now I was collecting a couple of sticks, to go in and prepare something for myself and my son; when we have eaten it, we shall die." *13*"Do not be afraid," Elijah said to her. "Go and do as you propose. But first make me a little cake and

---

17, 1: Elijah the Tishbite: one of the most important figures in Old Testament history. As his name indicates ("Yahweh is my God"), Elijah was the successful leader in the struggle to preserve the knowledge and worship of Yahweh against the encroaching worship of Baal introduced into Israel by Jezebel, the Tyrian wife of Ahab. The Elijah cycle of narratives includes, besides the above struggle, miracle stories, denunciations of kings, and a preparation for the prophet's role as eschatological forerunner of the "great day of the Lord"; cf Mal 3, 23-24; Mt 17, 10-13; Lk 1, 17.

---

o: Jos 6, 26.   *p:* Sir 48, 3; Jas 5, 17.   *q:* Lk 4, 26.

bring it to me. Then you can prepare something for yourself and your son. [14]For the LORD, the God of Israel, says, 'The jar of flour shall not go empty, nor the jug of oil run dry, until the day when the LORD sends rain upon the earth.' " [15]She left and did as Elijah had said. She was able to eat for a year, and he and her son as well; [16]the jar of flour did not go empty, nor the jug of oil run dry, as the LORD had foretold through Elijah.

[17]Some time later the son of the mistress of the house fell sick, and his sickness grew more severe until he stopped breathing. [18]So she said to Elijah, "Why have you done this to me, O man of God? Have you come to me to call attention to my guilt and to kill my son?" [19]"Give me your son," Elijah said to her. Taking him from her lap, he carried him to the upper room where he was staying, and laid him on his own bed. [20]He called out to the LORD: "O LORD, my God, will you afflict even the widow with whom I am staying by killing her son?" [21]Then he stretched himself out upon the child three times and called out to the LORD: "O LORD, my God, let the life breath return to the body of this child." [22]The LORD heard the prayer of Elijah; the life breath returned to the child's body and he revived. [23]Taking the child, Elijah brought him down into the house from the upper room and gave him to his mother. "See!" Elijah said to her, "your son is alive." [24]"Now indeed I know that you are a man of God," the woman replied to Elijah. "The word of the LORD comes truly from your mouth."

CHAPTER 18

See RG 129-34

Elijah and the Prophets of Baal.
[1]Long afterward, in the third year, the LORD spoke to Elijah. "Go, present yourself to Ahab," he said, "that I may send rain upon the earth." [2]So Elijah went to present himself to Ahab.

[3]Now the famine in Samaria was bitter, [4]and Ahab had summoned Obadiah, his vizier, who was a zealous follower of the LORD. When Jezebel was murdering the prophets of the LORD, Obadiah took a hundred prophets, hid them away fifty each in two caves, and supplied them with food and drink. [5]Ahab said to Obadiah, "Come, let us go through the land to all sources of water and to all the streams. We may find grass and save the horses and mules, so that we shall not have to slaughter any of the beasts." [6]Dividing the land to explore between them, Ahab went one way by himself, Obadiah another way by himself.

[7]As Obadiah was on his way, Elijah met him. Recognizing him, Obadiah fell prostrate and asked, "Is it you, my lord Elijah?" [8]"Yes," he answered. "Go tell your master, 'Elijah is here!' " [9]But Obadiah said, "What sin have I committed, that you are handing me over to Ahab to have me killed? [10]As the LORD, your God, lives, there is no nation or kingdom where my master has not sent in search of you. When they replied, 'He is not here,' he made each kingdom and nation swear they could not find you. [11]And now you say, 'Go tell your master: Elijah is here!' [12]After I leave you, the spirit of the LORD will carry you to some place I do not know, and when I go to inform Ahab and he does not find you, he will kill me. Your servant has revered the LORD from his youth. [13]Have you not been told, my lord, what I did when Jezebel was murdering the prophets of the LORD—that I hid a hundred of the prophets of the LORD, fifty each in two caves, and supplied them with food and drink? [14]And now you say, 'Go tell your master: Elijah is here!' He will kill me!" [15]Elijah answered, "As the LORD of hosts lives, whom I serve, I will present myself to him today."

[16]So Obadiah went to meet Ahab and informed him. Ahab came to meet Elijah, [17]and when he saw Elijah, said to him, "Is it you, you disturber of Israel?" [18]"It is not I who disturb Israel," he answered, "but you and your family, by forsaking the commands of the LORD and following the Baals. [19]Now summon all Israel to me on Mount Carmel, as well as the four hundred and fifty prophets of Baal and the four hundred prophets of Asherah who eat at Jezebel's table." [20]So Ahab sent to all the Israelites and had the prophets assemble on Mount Carmel.

[21]Elijah appealed to all the people and said, "How long will you straddle the issue? If the LORD is God, follow him; if Baal, follow him." The people, however, did not answer

Mediterranean Sea

Sidon

Zarephath

Damascus

ARAM
(SYRIA)

R. Jordan

Sea of
Chinnereth

Aphek

Wadi (R.) Kishon

Mt. Carmel

Shunem
Jezreel

Ramoth-gilead

Tishbe

Wadi (Brook) Cherith

Samaria

I S R A E L

Baal-shalishah

G I L E A D

Bethel

Gilgal

Jericho

Ekron

Jerusalem

Sea of
Arabah
(Dead Sea)

J U D A H

M O A B

Beer-sheba

Kir-hareseth

0   10   20 Miles

0   10   20 Kilometers

35°

36°

32°

31°

E D O M

Places Associated with Elijah

him. ²²So Elijah said to the people, "I am the only surviving prophet of the LORD, and there are four hundred and fifty prophets of Baal. ²³Give us two young bulls. Let them choose one, cut it into pieces, and place it on the wood, but start no fire. I shall prepare the other and place it on the wood, but shall start no fire. ²⁴You shall call on your gods, and I will call on the LORD. The God who answers with fire is God." All the people answered, "Agreed!"

²⁵Elijah then said to the prophets of Baal, "Choose one young bull and prepare it first, for there are more of you. Call upon your gods, but do not start the fire." ²⁶Taking the young bull that was turned over to them, they prepared it and called on Baal from morning to noon, saying, "Answer us, Baal!" But there was no sound, and no one answering. And they hopped around the altar they had prepared. ²⁷When it was noon, Elijah taunted them: "Call louder, for he is a god and may be meditating, or may have retired, or may be on a journey. Perhaps he is asleep and must be awakened." ²⁸They called out louder and slashed themselves with swords and spears, as was their custom, until blood gushed over them. ²⁹Noon passed and they remained in a prophetic state until the time for offering sacrifice. But there was not a sound; no one answered, and no one was listening.

Elijah on Mount Horeb

Like Moses, Elijah fasts forty days and nights (19, 8), and he goes to Mount Horeb, the place where Moses received the law. Here the LORD appears to him. There is a strong wind, then an earthquake, then a fire. But the LORD does not appear in any of these violent forms, which might be associated with the storm god, Baal. Rather, the LORD appears quietly, in a "tiny whispering sound" (v.12).

³⁰Then Elijah said to all the people, "Come here to me." When they had done so, he repaired the altar of the LORD which had been destroyed. ³¹He took twelve stones, for the number of tribes of the sons of Jacob, to whom the LORD had said, "Your name shall be Israel." ³²He built an altar in honor of the LORD with the stones, and made a trench around the altar large enough for two seahs of grain. ³³When he had arranged the wood, he cut up the young bull and laid it on the wood. ³⁴"Fill four jars with water," he said, "and pour it over the holocaust and over the wood." "Do it again," he said, and they did it again. "Do it a third time," he said, and they did it a third time. ³⁵The water flowed around the altar, and the trench was filled with the water.

³⁶At the time for offering sacrifice, the prophet Elijah came forward and said, "LORD, God of Abraham, Isaac, and Israel, let it be known this day that you are God in Israel and that I am your servant and have done all these things by your command. ³⁷Answer me, LORD! Answer me, that this people may know that you, LORD, are God and that you have brought them back to their senses." ³⁸The LORD's fire came down and consumed the holocaust, wood, stones, and dust, and it lapped up the water in the trench. ³⁹Seeing this, all the people fell prostrate and said, "The LORD is God! The LORD is God!" ⁴⁰Then Elijah said to them, "Seize the prophets of Baal. Let none of them escape!" They were seized, and Elijah had them brought down to the brook Kishon and there he slit their throats.

⁴¹Elijah then said to Ahab, "Go up, eat and drink, for there is the sound of a heavy rain." ⁴²So Ahab went up to eat and drink, while Elijah climbed to the top of Carmel, crouched down to the earth, and put his head between his knees. ⁴³"Climb up and look out to sea," he directed his servant, who went up and looked, but reported, "There is nothing." Seven times he said, "Go, look again!" ⁴⁴And the seventh time the youth reported, "There is a cloud as small as a man's hand rising from the sea." Elijah said, "Go and say to Ahab, 'Harness up and leave the mountain before the rain stops you.' " ⁴⁵In a trice, the sky grew dark with clouds and wind, and a heavy rain fell. Ahab mounted his chariot and made for Jezreel. ⁴⁶But the hand of the LORD was on Elijah, who girded up his clothing and ran before Ahab as far as the approaches to Jezreel.

CHAPTER 19

Flight to Horeb. ¹Ahab told Jezebel all that Elijah had done—that he had put all the prophets to the sword. ²Jezebel then sent a messenger to Elijah and said, "May the gods do thus and so to me if by this time tomorrow I have not done with your life what was done to each of them." ³Elijah was afraid and fled for his life, going to Beer-sheba of Judah. He left his servant there ⁴and went a day's journey into the desert, until he came to a broom tree and sat beneath it. He prayed for death: "This is enough, O LORD! Take my life, for I am no better than my fathers." ⁵He lay down and fell asleep under the broom tree, but then an angel touched him and ordered him to get up and eat. ⁶He looked and there at his head was a hearth cake and a jug of water. After he ate and drank, he lay down again, ⁷but the angel of the LORD came back a second time, touched him, and ordered, "Get up and eat, else the journey will be too long for you!" ⁸He got up, ate and drank; then strengthened by that food, he walked forty days and forty nights to the mountain of God, Horeb.

See RG 129-34

⁹There he came to a cave, where he took shelter. But the word of the LORD came to him, "Why are you here, Elijah?" ¹⁰He answered: "I have been most zealous for the LORD, the God of hosts, but the Israelites have forsaken your covenant, torn down your altars, and put your prophets to the sword. I alone am left, and they seek to take my life." ¹¹*Then the LORD said, "Go outside and stand on the mountain before the LORD; the LORD will be passing by." A strong and heavy wind was rending the mountains and crushing rocks before the LORD—but the LORD was not in the wind. After the wind there was an earthquake—but the LORD was not in the earthquake. ¹²After the earthquake there was fire—but the LORD was not in the fire. After the fire there was a tiny whispering sound. ¹³When he heard this, Elijah hid his face in his cloak and went and stood at the entrance of the cave. A voice said to him, "Elijah, why are you here?" ¹⁴He replied, "I have been most zealous for the LORD, the God of hosts. But the Israelites have forsaken your covenant, torn down your altars, and put your prophets to the sword. I alone am left, and they seek to take my life."ʳ ¹⁵*"Go, take the road back to the desert near Damascus," the LORD said to him. "When you arrive, you shall anoint Hazael as king of Aram. ¹⁶Then you shall anoint Jehu, son of Nimshi, as king of Israel, and Elisha, son of Shaphat of Abel-meholah, as prophet to succeed you.ˢ ¹⁷If anyone escapes the sword of Hazael, Jehu will kill him. If he escapes the sword of Jehu, Elisha will kill him. ¹⁸Yet I will leave seven thousand men in Israel—all those who have not knelt to Baal or kissed him."ᵗ

Call of Elisha.* ¹⁹Elijah set out, and came upon Elisha, son of Shaphat, as he was plowing with twelve yoke of oxen; he was following the twelfth. Elijah went over to him and threw his cloak over him. ²⁰Elisha left the oxen, ran after Elijah, and said, "Please, let me kiss my father and mother goodbye, and I will follow you." "Go back!" Elijah answered. "Have I done anything to you?" ²¹Elisha left him and, taking the yoke of oxen, slaughtered them; he used the plowing equipment for fuel to boil their flesh, and gave it to his people to eat. Then he left and followed Elijah as his attendant.

CHAPTER 20

Ahab's Victories over Ben-hadad. ¹Ben-hadad, king of Aram, gathered all his forces, and accompanied by thirty-two kings with horses and chariotry, proceeded to invest and attack Samaria. ²He sent couriers to Ahab, king of Israel, within the city, ³and said to him, "This is Ben-hadad's message: 'Your silver and gold are mine, and your wives and your promising sons are mine.'" ⁴The king of Israel answered, "As you say, my lord king, I and all I have are yours." ⁵But the couriers came again and said, "This is Ben-hadad's message: 'I sent you word to give me your silver and gold, your wives and your sons. ⁶Now, however, at this time tomorrow I will send my servants to you, and they shall ransack your house and the houses of your servants. They shall seize and take away whatever they consider valuable.'"

⁷The king of Israel then summoned all the elders of the land and said: "Understand clearly that this man wants to ruin us. When he sent to me for my wives and sons, my silver and my gold, I did not refuse him." ⁸All the elders and all the people said to him, "Do

---

19, 11ff: Compare these divine manifestations to Elijah with those to Moses (Ex 19, 1-23; 33, 21ff; 34, 5) on the same Mount Horeb (Sinai) (Dt 4, 10-15). Though various phenomena, such as wind, storms, earthquakes, fire (Ex 19, 18f), herald the divine presence, they do not constitute the presence itself which, like the tiny whispering sound, is imperceptible and bespeaks the spirituality of God. It was fitting that Elijah, whose mission it was to reestablish the covenant and restore the pure faith, should have returned to Horeb where the covenant was revealed to Moses and through him to the Israelite people (Ex 3, 1-4. 17; 33, 18—34, 9). Moses and Elijah appeared with Christ at the time of his transfiguration (Mt 17, 1-9; Mk 9, 1-7; Lk 9, 28-36).

19, 15-17: Elijah himself carried out only the third of the commissions entrusted to him (vv 19-21); Elisha was deputed to perform the first in person (2 Kgs 8, 7-19), and the second through one of his followers (2 Kgs 9, 1-10).

19, 19-21: Elijah's act of throwing his mantle over the shoulders of Elisha expressed the divine call to share the prophetic mission. Elisha's prompt response through destruction of his plow and oxen is an example of total obedience and detachment from his former manner of living in order to promote the glory of God.

r: Rom 11, 3. *s*: 2 Kgs 9, 2. *t*: Rom 11, 4.

not listen. Do not give in." ⁹Accordingly he directed the couriers of Ben-hadad, "Say to my lord the king, 'I will do all that you demanded of your servant the first time. But this I cannot do.' " The couriers left and reported this. ¹⁰Ben-hadad then sent him the message, "May the gods do thus and so to me if there is enough dust in Samaria to make handfuls for all my followers." ¹¹The king of Israel replied, "Tell him, 'It is not for the man who is buckling his armor to boast as though he were taking it off.' " ¹²Ben-hadad was drinking in the pavilions with the kings when he heard this reply. "Prepare the assault," he commanded his servants; and they made ready to storm the city.

¹³Then a prophet came up to Ahab, king of Israel, and said: "The LORD says, 'Do you see all this huge army? When I deliver it up to you today, you will know that I am the LORD.' " ¹⁴But Ahab asked, "Through whom will it be delivered up?" He answered, "The LORD says, 'Through the retainers of the governors of the provinces.' " Then Ahab asked, "Who is to attack?" He replied, "You are." ¹⁵So Ahab called up the retainers of the governors of the provinces, two hundred thirty-two of them. Behind them he mustered all the Israelite soldiery, who numbered seven thousand. ¹⁶They marched out at noon, while Ben-hadad was drinking heavily in the pavilions with the thirty-two kings who were his allies. ¹⁷When the retainers of the governors of the provinces marched out first, Ben-hadad received word that some men had marched out of Samaria. ¹⁸He answered, "Whether they have come out for peace or for war, in any case take them alive." ¹⁹But when these had come out of the city—the soldiers of the governors of the provinces with the army following them— ²⁰each of them struck down his man. The Arameans fled with Israel pursuing them, while Ben-hadad, king of Aram, escaped on a chariot steed. ²¹The king of Israel went out, took the horses and chariots, and inflicted a severe defeat on Aram.

²²Then the prophet went up to the king of Israel and said to him: "Go, regroup your forces. Mark well what you do, for at the beginning of the year* the king of Aram will attack you." ²³On the other hand, the servants of the king of Aram said to him: "Their gods are gods of mountains. That is why they defeated us. But if we fight them on level ground, we shall be sure to defeat them. ²⁴This is what you must do: Take the kings from their posts and put prefects in their places. ²⁵Mobilize an army as large as the army that has deserted you, horse for horse, chariot for chariot. Let us fight them on level ground, and we shall surely defeat them." He took their advice and did this.

²⁶At the beginning of the year, Ben-hadad mobilized Aram and went up to Aphek to fight against Israel. ²⁷The Israelites, too, were called to arms and supplied with provisions; then they went out to engage the foe. The Israelites, encamped opposite them, seemed like a couple of small flocks of goats, while Aram covered the countryside. ²⁸A man of God came up and said to the king of Israel: "The LORD says, 'Because Aram has said the LORD is a god of mountains, not a god of plains, I will deliver up to you all this large army, that you may know I am the LORD.' " ²⁹They were encamped opposite each other for seven days. On the seventh day battle was joined, and the Israelites struck down one hundred thousand foot soldiers of Aram in one day. ³⁰The survivors, twenty-seven thousand of them, fled into the city of Aphek, and there the wall collapsed. Ben-hadad, too, fled, and took refuge within the city, in an inside room.

³¹His servants said to him: "We have heard that the kings of the land of Israel are merciful kings. Allow us, therefore, to garb ourselves in sackcloth, with cords around our heads, and go out to the king of Israel. Perhaps he will spare your life." ³²So they dressed in sackcloth girded at the waist, and wearing cords around their heads, they went to the king of Israel. "Your servant Ben-hadad pleads for his life," they said. "Is he still alive?" the king asked. "He is my brother." ³³Hearing this as a good omen, the men quickly took him at his word and said,

"Ben-hadad is your brother." He answered, "Go and get him." When Ben-hadad came out to him, the king had him mount his chariot. 34Ben-hadad said to him, "I will restore the cities which my father took from your father, and you may make yourself bazaars in Damascus, as my father did in Samaria." "On these terms," Ahab replied, "I will set you free." So he made an agreement with him and then set him free.

35One of the guild prophets was prompted by the LORD to say to his companion, "Strike me." But he refused to strike him. 36Then he said to him, "Since you did not obey the voice of the LORD, a lion will kill you when you leave me." When they parted company, a lion came upon him and killed him. 37The prophet met another man and said, "Strike me." The man struck him a blow and wounded him. 38The prophet went on and waited for the king on the road, having disguised himself with a bandage over his eyes. 39As the king was passing, he called out to the king and said, "Your servant went into the thick of the battle, and suddenly someone turned and brought me a man and said, 'Guard this man. If he is missing, you shall have to pay for his life with your life or pay out a talent of silver.' 40But while your servant was looking here and there, the man disappeared." The king of Israel said to him, "That is your sentence. You have decided it yourself." 41He immediately removed the bandage from his eyes, and the king of Israel recognized him as one of the prophets. 42He said to him: "The LORD says, 'Because you have set free the man I doomed to destruction, your life shall pay for his life, your people for his people.' " Disturbed and angry, the king of Israel went off homeward and entered Samaria.u

CHAPTER 21

See RG 129-34 *Seizure of Naboth's Vineyard.* 1Some time after this, as Naboth the Jezreelite had a vineyard in Jezreel next to the palace of Ahab, king of Samaria, 2Ahab said to Naboth, "Give me your vineyard to be my vegetable garden, since it is close by, next to my house. I will give you a better vineyard in exchange, or, if you prefer, I will give you its value in money." 3"The LORD forbid," Naboth answered him, "that I should give you my ancestral heritage." 4Ahab went home disturbed and angry at the answer Naboth the Jezreelite had made to him: "I will not give you my ancestral heritage." Lying down on his bed, he turned away from food and would not eat.

5His wife Jezebel came to him and said to him, "Why are you so angry that you will not eat?" 6He answered her, "Because I spoke to Naboth the Jezreelite and said to him, 'Sell me your vineyard, or, if you prefer, I will give you a vineyard in exchange.' But he refused to let me have his vineyard." 7"A fine ruler over Israel you are indeed!" his wife Jezebel said to him. "Get up. Eat and be cheerful. I will obtain the vineyard of Naboth the Jezreelite for you."

8So she wrote letters in Ahab's name and, having sealed them with his seal, sent them to the elders and to the nobles who lived in the same city with Naboth. 9This is what she wrote in the letters: "Proclaim a fast and set Naboth at the head of the people. 10Next, get two scoundrels to face him and accuse him of having cursed God and king. Then take him out and stone him to death." 11His fellow citizens—the elders and the nobles who dwelt in his city—did as Jezebel had ordered them in writing, through the letters she had sent them. 12They proclaimed a fast and placed Naboth at the head of the people. 13Two scoundrels came in and confronted him with the accusation, "Naboth has cursed God and king." And they led him out of the city and stoned him to death. 14Then they sent the information to Jezebel that Naboth had been stoned to death.

15When Jezebel learned that Naboth had been stoned to death, she said to Ahab, "Go on, take possession of the vineyard of Naboth the Jezreelite which he refused to sell you, because Naboth is not alive, but dead." 16On hearing that Naboth was dead, Ahab started off on his way down to the vineyard of Naboth the Jezreelite, to take possession of it.

_u:_ 1 Kgs 22, 35.

[17]But the LORD said to Elijah the Tishbite: [18]"Start down to meet Ahab, king of Israel, who rules in Samaria. He will be in the vineyard of Naboth, of which he has come to take possession. [19]*v This is what you shall tell him, 'The LORD says: After murdering, do you also take possession? For this, the LORD says: In the place where the dogs licked up the blood of Naboth, the dogs shall lick up your blood, too.' " [20]*"Have you found me out, my enemy?" Ahab said to Elijah. "Yes," he answered. "Because you have given yourself up to doing evil in the LORD's sight, [21]I am bringing evil upon you: I will destroy you and will cut off every male in Ahab's line, whether slave or freeman, in Israel.[w] [22]I will make your house like that of Jeroboam, son of Nebat, and like that of Baasha, son of Ahijah, because of how you have provoked me by leading Israel into sin."[x] [23](Against Jezebel, too, the LORD declared, "The dogs shall devour Jezebel in the district of Jezreel.")[y] [24]"When one of Ahab's line dies in the city, dogs will devour him; when one of them dies in the field, the birds of the sky will devour him." [25]Indeed, no one gave himself up to the doing of evil in the sight of the LORD as did Ahab, urged on by his wife Jezebel. [26]He became completely abominable by following idols, just as the Amorites had done, whom the LORD drove out before the Israelites.

[27]When Ahab heard these words, he tore his garments and put on sackcloth over his bare flesh. He fasted, slept in the sackcloth, and went about subdued. [28]Then the LORD said to Elijah the Tishbite, [29]"Have you seen that Ahab has humbled himself before me? Since he has humbled himself before me, I will not bring the evil in his time. I will bring the evil upon his house during the reign of his son."[z]

See RG 129-34

CHAPTER 22

Campaign against Ramoth-gilead.

[1]Three years passed without war between Aram and Israel.[a] [2]In the third year, however, King Jehoshaphat of Judah came down to the king of Israel, [3]who said to his servants, "Do you not know that Ramoth-gilead is ours and we are doing nothing to take it from the king of Aram?" [4]He asked Jehoshaphat, "Will you come with me to fight against Ramoth-gilead?" Jehoshaphat answered the king of Israel, "You and I are as one, and your people and my people, your horses and my horses as well." [5]Jehoshaphat also said to the king of Israel, "Seek the word of the LORD at once."

[5]The king of Israel gathered together the prophets, about four hundred of them, and asked, "Shall I go to attack Ramoth-gilead or shall I refrain?" "Go up," they answered. "The LORD will deliver it over to the king." [7]But Jehoshaphat said, "Is there no other prophet of the LORD here whom we may consult?" [8]The king of Israel answered, "There is one other through whom we might consult the LORD, Micaiah, son of Imlah; but I hate him because he prophesies not good but evil about me." Jehoshaphat said, "Let not your majesty speak of evil against you."

[9]So the king of Israel called an official and said to him, "Get Micaiah, son of Imlah, at once." [10]The king of Israel and King Jehoshaphat of Judah were seated, each on his throne, clothed in their robes of state on a threshing floor at the entrance of the gate of Samaria, and all the prophets were prophesying before them. [11]Zedekiah, son of Chenaanah, made himself horns of iron and said, "The LORD says, 'With these you shall

21, 19: The response of Ahab to this divine judgment is described in v 27, and the consequences are given in vv 28-29, and in 2 Kgs 9, 21-26.

21, 20-26: In these verses the Judean editor of the Books of Kings substitutes, for the message of Elijah prepared for in v 19, a sweeping and definitive judgment against the whole family of Ahab in the same terms as were used against the families of Jeroboam I (1 Kgs 14, 9-11) and Baasha (1 Kgs 16, 2-4). This judgment is the fruit of later theological reflec-

tion; it is not occasioned directly by the crime against Naboth, but by the idolatry of Ahab and Jezebel. The judgment on Jezebel herself (v 23) may have been uttered by Elijah during the Naboth episode; it finds its fulfillment in 2 Kgs 9, 36-37. Still another theological explanation for the death of Ahab is given by the north Israelite writer of 1 Kgs 20, 35-42 above.

v: 1 Kgs 22, 38.   w: 2 Kgs 9, 8.   x: 1 Kgs 15, 29; 16, 3.
y: 2 Kgs 9, 36.   z: 2 Kgs 9, 26.   a: 2 Chr 18, 1.

gore Aram until you have destroyed them.' " [12]The other prophets prophesied in a similar vein, saying: "Go up to Ramoth-gilead; you shall succeed. The LORD will deliver it over to the king."

[13]The messenger who had gone to call Micaiah said to him, "Look now, the prophets are unanimously predicting good for the king. Let your word be the same as any of theirs; predict good." [14]"As the LORD lives," Micaiah answered, "I shall say whatever the LORD tells me."

[15]When he came to the king, the king said to him, "Micaiah, shall we go to fight against Ramoth-gilead, or shall we refrain?" "Go up," he answered, "you shall succeed! The LORD will deliver it over to the king." [16]But the king answered him, "How many times must I adjure you to tell me nothing but the truth in the name of the LORD?" [17]So Micaiah said:

> "I see all Israel
> scattered on the mountains,
> like sheep without a shepherd,
> and the LORD saying, 'These have no
>   master!
> Let each of them go back home in
>   peace.' "

[18]The king of Israel said to Jehoshaphat, "Did I not tell you he prophesies not good but evil about me?" [19]*Micaiah continued: "Therefore hear the word of the LORD: I saw the LORD seated on his throne, with the whole host of heaven standing by to his right and to his left. [20]The LORD asked, 'Who will deceive Ahab, so that he will go up and fall at Ramoth-gilead?' And one said this, another that, [21]until one of the spirits came forth and presented himself to the LORD, saying, 'I will deceive him.' The LORD asked, 'How?' [22]He answered, 'I will go forth and become a lying spirit in the mouths of all his prophets.' The LORD replied, 'You shall succeed in deceiving him. Go forth and do this.' [23]So now, the LORD has put a lying spirit in the mouths of all these prophets of yours, but the LORD himself has decreed evil against you."

[24]Thereupon Zedekiah, son of Chenaanah, came up and slapped Micaiah on the cheek, saying, "Has the spirit of the LORD, then, left me to speak with you?" [25]"You shall find out," Micaiah replied, "on that day when you retreat into an inside room to hide." [26]The king of Israel then said, "Seize Micaiah and take him back to Amon, prefect of the city, and to Joash, the king's son, [27]and say, 'This is the king's order: Put this man in prison and feed him scanty rations of bread and water until I return in safety.' " [28]But Micaiah said, "If ever you return in safety, the LORD has not spoken through me."*

[29]The king of Israel and King Jehoshaphat of Judah went up to Ramoth-gilead, [30]and the king of Israel said to Jehoshaphat, "I will disguise myself and go into battle, but you put on your own clothes." So the king of Israel disguised himself and entered the fray. [31]In the meantime the king of Aram had given his thirty-two chariot commanders the order, "Do not fight with anyone at all except the king of Israel." [32]When the chariot commanders saw Jehoshaphat, they cried out, "That must be the king of Israel!" and shifted to fight him. But Jehoshaphat shouted his battle cry, [33]and the chariot commanders, aware that he was not the king of Israel, gave up pursuit of him. [34]Someone, however, drew his bow at random, and hit the king of Israel between the joints of his breastplate. He ordered his charioteer, "Rein about and take me out of the ranks, for I am disabled." [35]The battle grew fierce during the day, and the king, who was propped up in his chariot facing the Arameans, died in the evening. The blood from his wound flowed to the bottom of the chariot.[b] [36]At sunset a cry went through the army, "Every man to his city, every man to his land, [37]for the king is

---

22, 19-23: The prophet Micaiah uses as a last resort to deter Ahab from his foolhardy design of fighting against Ramoth-gilead the literary device of describing false prophets as messengers of a lying spirit which God, after holding counsel with his angels, permits to deceive them.

22, 28: A note in the Hebrew text after this verse attributes to Micaiah ben Imlah the first words of the book of a different Micaiah, the minor prophet of Moresheth.

b: 1 Kgs 20, 42.

dead!" So they went to Samaria, where they buried the king. [38]When the chariot was washed at the pool of Samaria, the dogs licked up his blood and harlots bathed there, as the LORD had prophesied.[c]

[39]The rest of the acts of Ahab, with all that he did, including the ivory palace and all the cities he built, are recorded in the book of the chronicles of the kings of Israel. [40]Ahab rested with his ancestors, and his son Ahaziah succeeded him as king.

Reign of Jehoshaphat. [41]Jehoshaphat, son of Asa, began to reign over Judah in the fourth year of Ahab, king of Israel. [42]Jehoshaphat was thirty-five years old when he began to reign, and he reigned twenty-five years in Jerusalem. His mother's name was Azubah, daughter of Shilhi. [43]He followed all the ways of his father Asa unswervingly, doing what was right in the LORD's sight. [44]Nevertheless, the high places did not disappear, and the people continued to sacrifice and to burn incense on the high places. [45]Jehoshaphat also made peace with the king of Israel. [46]The rest of the acts of Jehoshaphat, with his prowess, what he did and how he fought, are recorded in the book of the chronicles of the kings of Judah.

[47]He removed from the land the rest of the cult prostitutes who had remained in the reign of his father Asa. [48]There was no king in Edom, but an appointed regent. [49]Jehoshaphat made Tarshish ships to go to Ophir for gold; but in fact the ships did not go, because they were wrecked at Ezion-geber. [50]Then Ahaziah, son of Ahab, said to Jehoshaphat, "Let my servants accompany your servants in the ships." But Jehoshaphat would not agree. [51]Jehoshaphat rested with his ancestors; he was buried in his forefathers' City of David. His son Jehoram succeeded him as king.

Reign of Ahaziah. [52]Ahaziah, son of Ahab, began to reign over Israel in Samaria in the seventeenth year* of Jehoshaphat, king of Judah; he reigned two years over Israel. [53]He did evil in the sight of the LORD, behaving like his father, his mother, and Jeroboam, son of Nebat, who caused Israel to sin. [54]He served and worshiped Baal, thus provoking the LORD, the God of Israel, just as his father had done.

22, 52: Seventeenth year: so the present Hebrew text. More consistent with 2 Kgs 1, 17 would be a date in the twenty-fourth year of Jehoshaphat for Ahab's death; see note on 2 Kgs 1, 1.

c: 1 Kgs 21, 19.

See RG 122–36

The Second Book of Kings

See RG 129–34

I: The Kingdoms of Israel and Judah

CHAPTER 1

Ahaziah Consults Baalzebub. [1]After Ahab's death, Moab rebelled against Israel.[a] [2]Ahaziah had fallen through the lattice of his roof terrace at Samaria and had been injured. So he sent out messengers with the instructions: "Go and inquire of Baalzebub,* the god of Ekron, whether I shall recover from this injury."

[3]Meanwhile, the angel of the LORD said to Elijah the Tishbite: "Go, intercept the messengers of Samaria's king, and ask them, 'Is it because there is no God in Israel that you are going to inquire of Baalzebub, the god of Ekron?' [4]For this, the LORD says: 'You shall not leave the bed upon which you lie; instead, you shall die.' " And with that, Elijah departed. [5]The messengers then returned to

---

1, 2: Baalzebub: in this form, "Baal of flies." The name in the Hebrew text is a derisive alteration of Baalzebul, "Prince Baal." The best New Testament evidence supports the latter form in Mt 10, 25; Lk 11, 15. Later associations with Aramaic *beeldebaba,* "enemy," gave the ancient name its connotation of "devil."

a: 2 Kgs 3, 4-27.

Ahaziah, who asked them, "Why have you returned?" [6] "A man came up to us," they answered, "who said to us, 'Go back to the king who sent you and tell him: The LORD says, Is it because there is no God in Israel that you are sending to inquire of Baalzebub, the god of Ekron? For this you shall not leave the bed upon which you lie; instead, you shall die.' " [7] The king asked them, "What was the man like who came up to you and said these things to you?" [8] "Wearing a hairy garment,"* they replied, "with a leather girdle about his loins." "It is Elijah the Tishbite!" he exclaimed.[b]

Death of Two Captains. [9] Then the king sent a captain with his company of fifty men after Elijah. The prophet was seated on a hilltop when he found him. "Man of God," he ordered, "the king commands you to come down." [10] "If I am a man of God," Elijah answered the captain, "may fire come down from heaven and consume you and your fifty men." And fire came down from heaven and consumed him and his fifty men.[c] [11] Ahaziah sent another captain with his company of fifty men after Elijah. "Man of God," he called out to Elijah, "the king commands you to come down immediately." [12] "If I am a man of God," Elijah answered him, "May fire come down from heaven and consume you and your fifty men." And divine fire* came down from heaven, consuming him and his fifty men.

Death of the King. [13] Again, for the third time, Ahaziah sent a captain with his company of fifty men. When the third captain arrived, he fell to his knees before Elijah, pleading with him. "Man of God," he implored him, "let my life and the lives of these fifty men, your servants, count for something in your sight! [14] Already fire has come

down from heaven, consuming two captains with their companies of fifty men. But now, let my life mean something to you!" [15] Then the angel of the LORD said to Elijah, "Go down with him; you need not be afraid of him."

[16] So Elijah left and went down with him and stated to the king: "Thus says the LORD: 'Because you sent messengers to inquire of Baalzebub, the god of Ekron, you shall not leave the bed upon which you lie; instead you shall die.' "[d]

[17] Ahaziah died in fulfillment of the prophecy of the LORD spoken by Elijah. Since he had no son, his brother Joram* succeeded him as king, in the second year of Jehoram, son of Jehoshaphat, king of Judah. [18] The rest of the acts of Ahaziah are recorded in the book of chronicles of the kings of Israel.

CHAPTER 2

See RG 129–34

Elijah and Elisha. [1] When the LORD was about to take Elijah up to heaven in a whirlwind, he and Elisha were on their way from Gilgal.* [2] "Stay here, please," Elijah said to Elisha. "The LORD has sent me on to Bethel." "As the LORD lives, and as you yourself live," Elisha replied, "I will not leave you." So they went down to Bethel, [3] where the guild prophets went out to Elisha and asked him, "Do you know that the LORD will take your master from over you today?" "Yes, I know it," he replied. "Keep still."

[4] Then Elijah said to him, "Stay here, please, Elisha, for the LORD has sent me on to Jericho." "As the LORD lives, and as you yourself live," Elisha replied, "I will not leave you." [5] They went on to Jericho, where the guild prophets approached Elisha and asked him, "Do you know that the

---

1, 8: Hairy garment: a sign of ascetical and prophetic calling, imitated by John the Baptizer; see Mt 3, 4; Mk 1, 6.

1, 12: Divine fire: literally, "fire of God," which in Hebrew sounds quite like man of God. The play on words is the basis for Elijah's alleged retort. This story was told among the people to enhance the dignity of the prophet and to reflect the power of God whom he served. The mercy which God extends even to the wicked is described in Wis 11, 17—12, 22, and the prophet Elijah was well aware of it (1 Kgs 21, 28f).

1, 17: Joram: in the Second Book of Kings the name Joram (yoram), alternately Jehoram (yehoram), appears in numerous

passages to designate both the king of Judah, son and successor of Jehoshaphat (848–841 B.C.), and the contemporary king of Israel, son of Ahab (852–841 B.C.). For the convenience of the reader in distinguishing these two kings, the longer form, Jehoram, is used to designate the king of Judah and the shorter form, Joram, to designate the king of Israel. See note on 2 Kgs 3, 1.

2, 1: Gilgal: commonly identified with Jiljulieh, about seven miles north of Bethel, and different from the Gilgal in Dt 11, 30 near Shechem, and that in Jos 4 and 5, passim, near Jericho.

b: Zec 13, 4. *c:* Lv 10, 2; Sir 48, 3f; Lk 9, 54f. *d:* Sir 48, 6.

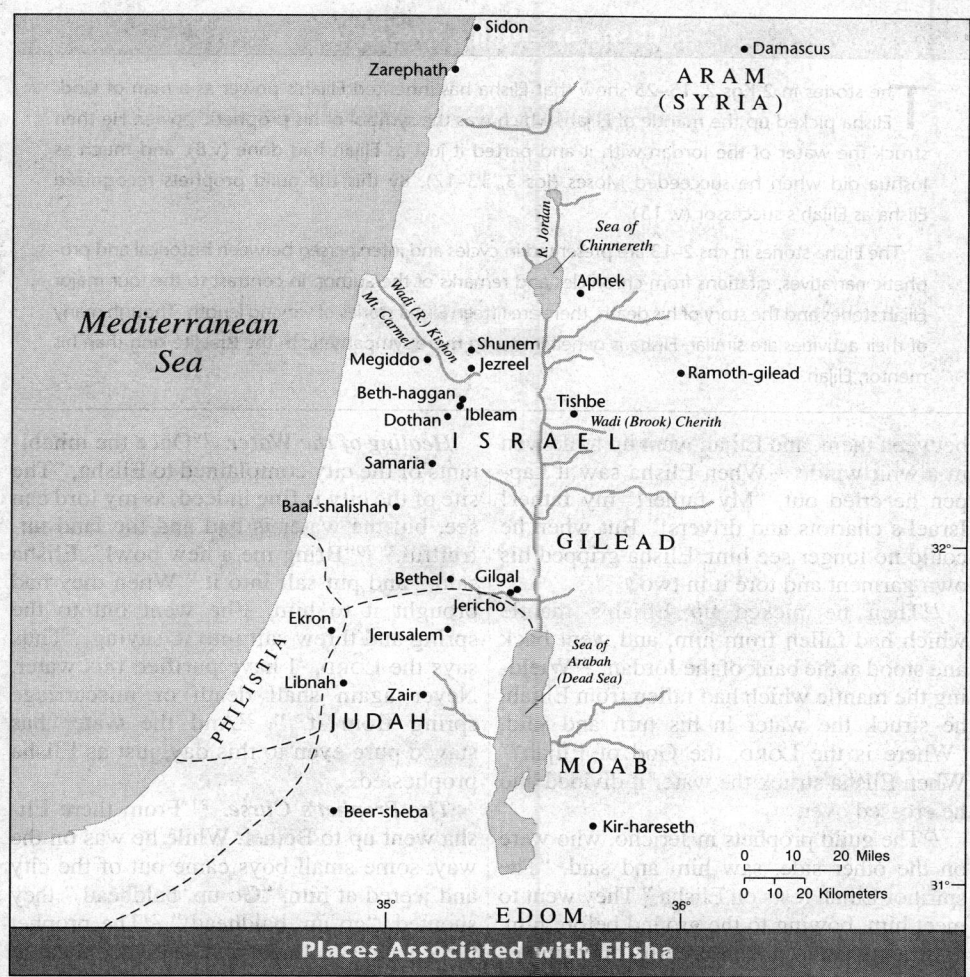

Places Associated with Elisha

LORD will take your master from over you today?" "Yes, I know it," he replied. "Keep still."

⁶Elijah said to Elisha, "Please stay here; the LORD has sent me on to the Jordan." "As the LORD lives, and as you yourself live," Elisha replied, "I will not leave you." And so the two went on together. ⁷Fifty of the guild prophets followed, and when the two stopped at the Jordan, stood facing them at a distance. ⁸Elijah took his mantle, rolled it up and struck the water, which divided, and both crossed over on dry ground.ᵉ

Elisha Succeeds Elijah. ⁹When they had crossed over, Elijah said to Elisha, "Ask for whatever I may do for you, before I am taken from you." Elisha answered, "May I receive a double portion of your spirit."* ¹⁰"You have asked something that is not easy," he replied. "Still, if you see me taken up from you, your wish will be granted; otherwise not."ᶠ ¹¹As they walked on conversing, a flaming chariot and flaming horses came

2, 9: Double portion of your spirit: as the first-born son inherited a double portion of his father's property (Dt 21, 17), so Elisha asks to inherit from Elijah his spirit of prophecy in the degree befitting his principal disciple. In

Nm 11, 17. 25, God bestows some of the spirit of Moses on others.

e: Ex 14, 16. 22.   f: Nm 11, 17. 25.

Elisha as Elijah's Successor

The stories in 2 Kgs 2, 13–25 show that Elisha has inherited Elijah's power as a man of God. Elisha picked up the mantle of Elijah, which was the symbol of his prophetic power. He then struck the water of the Jordan with it and parted it just as Elijah had done (v.8), and much as Joshua did when he succeeded Moses (Jos 3, 13–17). By this the guild prophets recognized Elisha as Elijah's successor (v. 15).

The Elisha stories in chs 2–13 are presented in cycles and interspersed between historical and prophetic narratives, citations from chronicles and remarks of the author. In contrast to the four major Elijah stories and the story of his death, there are fifteen Elisha stories of varying length. Though many of their activities are similar, Elisha is generally much more sympathetic to the Israelite king than his mentor, Elijah.

between them, and Elijah went up to heaven in a whirlwind.*g* *12*When Elisha saw it happen he cried out, "My father!* my father! Israel's chariots and drivers!" But when he could no longer see him, Elisha gripped his own garment and tore it in two.*h*

*13*Then he picked up Elijah's mantle which had fallen from him, and went back and stood at the bank of the Jordan.*i* *14*Wielding the mantle which had fallen from Elijah, he struck the water in his turn and said, "Where is the LORD, the God of Elijah?" When Elisha struck the water it divided and he crossed over.

*15*The guild prophets in Jericho, who were on the other side, saw him and said, "The spirit of Elijah rests on Elisha." They went to meet him, bowing to the ground before him. *16*"Among your servants are fifty brave men," they said. "Let them go in search of your master. Perhaps the spirit of the LORD has carried him away to some mountain or some valley." "Do not send them," he answered.*j* *17*However, they kept urging him, until he was embarrassed and said, "Send them." So they sent the fifty men, who searched for three days without finding him. *18*When they returned to Elisha in Jericho, where he was staying, he said to them, "Did I not tell you not to go?"

Healing of the Water. *19*Once the inhabitants of the city complained to Elisha, "The site of the city is fine indeed, as my lord can see, but the water is bad and the land unfruitful." *20*"Bring me a new bowl," Elisha said, "and put salt into it." When they had brought it to him, *21*he went out to the spring and threw salt into it, saying, "Thus says the LORD, 'I have purified this water. Never again shall death or miscarriage spring from it.' " *22*And the water has stayed pure even to this day, just as Elisha prophesied.

The Prophet's Curse. *23**From there Elisha went up to Bethel. While he was on the way, some small boys came out of the city and jeered at him. "Go up, baldhead," they shouted, "go up, baldhead!" *24*The prophet turned and saw them, and he cursed them in the name of the LORD. Then two she-bears came out of the woods and tore forty-two of the children to pieces.

*25*From there he went to Mount Carmel, and thence he returned to Samaria.

CHAPTER 3

Campaign of Joram against Moab. **See RG 129–34**
*1*Joram, son of Ahab, became king of Israel in Samaria [in the eighteenth year of Jehosha-

2, 12: My father: a religious title accorded prophetic leaders; cf 2 Kgs 6, 21; 8, 9. Israel's chariots and drivers: Elijah was worth more than a whole army in defending Israel and the true religion. King Joash of Israel uses the same phrase of Elisha himself (2 Kgs 13, 14).

2, 23f: This story, like the one about Elijah and the captains (ch 1), is preserved for us in Scripture to convey a popular understanding of the dignity of the prophet. Told in pop-

ular vein, it becomes a caricature, in which neither Elisha nor the bears behave in character. See note on 2 Kgs 1, 12 and the contrasting narrative in ch 4.

3, 1: The sequence of the reigns between Ahab and Jehu of Israel may be reconstructed as follows: Jehoshaphat of

g: Gn 5, 24; 1 Mc 2, 58; Acts 1, 9.   *h:* 2 Kgs 13, 14; Sir 48, 9. 12.   *i:* 1 Kgs 19, 19.   *j:* 1 Kgs 18, 12.

phat, king of Judah, and he reigned for twelve years].* [2]He did evil in the LORD's sight, though not as much as his father and mother. He did away with the pillar of Baal, which his father had made, [3]but he still clung to the sin to which Jeroboam, son of Nebat, had lured Israel; this he did not give up.

[4]Now Mesha, king of Moab, who raised sheep, used to pay the king of Israel as tribute a hundred thousand lambs and the wool of a hundred thousand rams. [5]But when Ahab died, the king of Moab had rebelled against the king of Israel. [6]Joram as king mustered all Israel, and when he set out on a campaign from Samaria, [7]he sent the king of Judah the message: "The king of Moab is in rebellion against me. Will you join me in battle against Moab?" "I will," he replied. "You and I shall be as one, your people and mine, and your horses and mine as well."[k] [8]They discussed the route for their attack, and settled upon the route through the desert of Edom.

[9]So the king of Israel set out, accompanied by the king of Judah and the king of Edom. After their roundabout journey of seven days the water gave out for the army and for the animals with them. [10]"Alas!" exclaimed the king of Israel. "The LORD has called together these three kings to put them in the grasp of Moab." [11]But the king of Judah asked, "Is there no prophet of the LORD here through whom we may inquire of the LORD?" One of the officers of the king of Israel replied, "Elisha, son of Shaphat, who poured water on the hands of Elijah, is here."[l] [12]"He has the word of the LORD," the king of Judah agreed. So the kings of Israel, Judah, and Edom went down to Elisha. [13]"What do you want with me?" Elisha asked the king of Israel. "Go to the prophets of your father and to the prophets of your mother." "No," the king of Israel replied. "The LORD has called these three kings together to put them in the grasp of Moab." [14]Then Elisha said, "As the LORD of hosts lives, whom I serve, were it not that I respect the king of Judah, I should neither look at you nor notice you at all.[m] [15]Now get me a minstrel."

When the minstrel played, the power of the LORD came upon Elisha [16]and he announced: "Thus says the LORD, 'Provide many catch basins in this wadi.' [17]For the LORD says, 'Though you will see neither wind nor rain, yet this wadi will be filled with water for you, your livestock, and your pack animals to drink.' [18]And since the LORD does not consider this enough, he will also deliver Moab into your grasp. [19]You shall destroy every fortified city, fell every fruit tree, stop up all the springs, and ruin every fertile field with stones."[n]

[20]In the morning, at the time of the sacrifice, water came from the direction of Edom and filled the land.[o] [21]Meanwhile, all Moab heard that the kings had come to give them battle; every man capable of bearing arms was called up and stationed at the border. [22]Early that morning, when the sun shone on the water, the Moabites saw the water at a distance as red as blood.* [23]"This is blood!" they exclaimed. "The kings have fought among themselves and killed one another. Quick! To the spoils, Moabites!" [24]But when they reached the camp of Israel, the Israelites rose up and attacked the Moabites, who fled from them. They ranged through the countryside striking down the Moabites, and [25]destroying

---

Judah outlived Ahab by a short time, so that Ahaziah of Israel was his contemporary. Jehoram of Judah succeeded his father Jehoshaphat while Ahaziah of Israel was still alive. Jehoram (Joram) of Israel became king, following his brother Ahaziah, in the second year of Jehoram of Judah (2 Kgs 1, 17); this is one datum on which the earliest Greek evidence and the standard Hebrew text are in agreement.

The two Jehorams were contemporary for much of their reigns; Jehoram of Judah was succeeded by Ahaziah something more than a year before Jehu did away with the rulers of both kingdoms (2 Kgs 9, 1-29).

The Moabite campaign of 2 Kgs 3, 4-27 is thus best placed under the two Kings Jehoram, before the Edomite rebellion mentioned in 2 Kgs 8, 20. In the received Hebrew text, Je-

hoshaphat has been made the Judahite protagonist in the campaign against Moab as a tribute to his piety; this assimilates the story of 2 Kgs 3 to that of 1 Kgs 22, but creates difficulties in the chronology which the extant data leave partly unresolved. An older practice for stories of the Israelite kings was to leave them and their fellow kings without identification by name; cf 2 Kgs 6, 8—7, 20. The name of Jehoshaphat has been omitted from a number of places in 2 Kgs 3-8 in this translation; cf 1 Kgs 22, 51.

3, 22: Red as blood: possibly caused by the red sandstone of the Wadi Zered (Dt 2, 13), south of Moab.

---

k: 1 Kgs 22, 4. l: 1 Kgs 22, 7. m: 1 Kgs 18, 15. n: Dt 20, 19. o: 1 Kgs 18, 29.

the cities; each of them cast stones onto every fertile field till they had loaded it down; all the springs they stopped up and every useful tree they felled. Finally only Kir-hareseth* was left behind its stone walls, and the slingers had surrounded it and were attacking it.ᵖ ²⁶When he saw that he was losing the battle, the king of Moab took seven hundred swordsmen to break through to the king of Aram, but he failed. ²⁷So he took his first-born, his heir apparent, and offered him as a holocaust upon the wall. The wrath against Israel* was so great that they gave up the siege and returned to their own land.�q

See RG
129–34

CHAPTER 4

The Widow's Oil. ¹ʳA certain woman, the widow of one of the guild prophets, complained to Elisha: "My husband, your servant, is dead. You know that he was a God-fearing man, yet now his creditor has come to take my two children as his slaves."* ²"How can I help you?" Elisha answered her. "Tell me what you have in the house." "This servant of yours has nothing in the house but a jug of oil," she replied. ³"Go out," he said, "borrow vessels from all your neighbors—as many empty vessels as you can. ⁴Then come back and close the door on yourself and your children; pour the oil into all the vessels, and as each is filled, set it aside." ⁵She went and did so, closing the door on herself and her children. As they handed her the vessels, she would pour in oil. ⁶When all the vessels were filled, she said to her son, "Bring me another vessel." "There is none left," he answered her. And then the oil stopped. ⁷She went and told the man of God, who said, "Go and sell the oil to pay off your creditor; with what remains, you and your children can live."

Elisha and the Shunammite. ⁸One day Elisha came to Shunem, where there was a woman of influence, who urged him to dine with her. Afterward, whenever he passed by,

he used to stop there to dine. ⁹So she said to her husband, "I know that he is a holy man of God. Since he visits us often, ¹⁰let us arrange a little room on the roof and furnish it for him with a bed, table, chair, and lamp, so that when he comes to us he can stay there." ¹¹Some time later Elisha arrived and stayed in the room overnight. ¹²Then he said to his servant Gehazi, "Call this Shunammite woman." He did so, and when she stood before Elisha, ¹³he told Gehazi, "Say to her, 'You have lavished all this care on us; what can we do for you? Can we say a good word for you to the king or to the commander of the army?' " She replied, "I am living among my own people." ¹⁴Later Elisha asked, "Can something be done for her?" "Yes!" Gehazi answered. "She has no son, and her husband is getting on in years." ¹⁵"Call her," said Elisha. When she had been called, and stood at the door, ¹⁶Elisha promised, "This time next year you will be fondling a baby son." "Please, my lord," she protested, "you are a man of God; do not deceive your servant."ˢ ¹⁷Yet the woman conceived, and by the same time the following year she had given birth to a son, as Elisha promised.

¹⁸The day came when the child was old enough to go out to his father among the reapers.ᵗ ¹⁹"My head hurts!" he complained to his father. "Carry him to his mother," the father said to a servant. ²⁰The servant picked him up and carried him to his mother; he stayed with her until noon, when he died in her lap. ²¹The mother took him upstairs and laid him on the bed of the man of God. Closing the door on him, she went out ²²and called to her husband, "Let me have a servant and a donkey. I must go quickly to the man of God, and I will be back." ²³"Why are you going to him today?" he asked. "It is neither the new moon nor the sabbath." But she bade him good-bye, ²⁴and when the donkey was saddled, said to her servant: "Lead on! Do not stop my donkey unless I tell you to."

3, 25: Kir-hareseth: modern Kerak, east of the Dead Sea; cf Is 16, 7. 11; Jer 48, 31. 36.

3, 27: The wrath against Israel: probably the wrath of Chemosh, the Moabite god to whom the child was offered. He was feared by the Israelites who lost heart on foreign soil.

4, 1: His creditor . . . slaves: Hebrew law permitted the selling of wife and children as chattels for debt; cf Ex 21, 7; Am 2, 6; 8, 6; Is 50.

p: Jb 5, 23.   q: Jgs 11, 30f.   r: 1 Kgs 17, 8-16.   s: Gn 18, 10.
t: 1 Kgs 17, 17-24.

Feeding the Hungry

A limited amount of food is once again multiplied (4, 42–44; see 4, 1–7). Compare the New Testament stories of Jesus' multiplication of the loaves (Mt 14, 13–21; 15, 32–38).

[25]She kept going till she reached the man of God on Mount Carmel. When he spied her at a distance, the man of God said to his servant Gehazi: "There is the Shunammite! [26]Hurry to meet her, and ask if all is well with her, with her husband, and with the boy." "Greetings,"* she replied. [27]But when she reached the man of God on the mountain, she clasped his feet. Gehazi came near to push her away, but the man of God said: "Let her alone, she is in bitter anguish; the LORD hid it from me and did not let me know." [28]"Did I ask my lord for a son?" she cried out. "Did I not beg you not to deceive me?" [29]"Gird your loins," Elisha said to Gehazi, "take my staff with you and be off; if you meet anyone, do not greet him,* and if anyone greets you, do not answer. Lay my staff upon the boy." [30]But the boy's mother cried out: "As the LORD lives and as you yourself live, I will not release you." So he started to go back with her. [31]uMeanwhile, Gehazi had gone on ahead and had laid the staff upon the boy, but there was no sound or sign of life. He returned to meet Elisha and informed him that the boy had not awakened. [32]When Elisha reached the house, he found the boy lying dead. [33]He went in, closed the door on them both, and prayed to the LORD.v [34]Then he lay upon the child on the bed, placing his mouth upon the child's mouth, his eyes upon the eyes, and his hands upon the hands. As Elisha stretched himself over the child, the body became warm. [35]He arose, paced up and down the room, and then once more lay down upon the boy, who now sneezed seven times and opened his eyes.w [36]Elisha summoned Gehazi and said, "Call the Shunammite." She came at his call, and Elisha said to her, "Take your son." [37]She came in and fell at his feet in gratitude; then she took her son and left the room.

The Poisoned Stew. [38]When Elisha returned to Gilgal, there was a famine in the land. Once, when the guild prophets were seated before him, he said to his servant, "Put the large pot on, and make some vegetable stew for the guild prophets." [39]Someone went out into the field to gather herbs and found a wild vine, from which he picked a clothful of wild gourds. On his return he cut them up into the pot of vegetable stew without anybody's knowing it. [40]The stew was poured out for the men to eat, but when they began to eat it, they exclaimed, "Man of God, there is poison in the pot!" And they could not eat it. [41]"Bring some meal," Elisha said. He threw it into the pot and said, "Serve it to the people to eat." And there was no longer anything harmful in the pot.

Multiplication of Loaves. [42]A man came from Baal-shalishah bringing the man of God twenty barley loaves made from the first-fruits, and fresh grain in the ear. "Give it to the people to eat," Elisha said. [43]But his servant objected, "How can I set this before a hundred men?" "Give it to the people to eat," Elisha insisted. "For thus says the LORD, 'They shall eat and there shall be some left over.'" [44]And when they had eaten, there was some left over, as the LORD had said.

CHAPTER 5

See RG 129–34

Cure of Naaman. [1]Naaman, the army commander of the king of Aram, was highly esteemed and respected by his master, for through him the LORD had brought victory to Aram. But valiant as he was, the man was a leper. [2]Now the Arameans had captured from the land of Israel in a raid a little girl, who became the servant of Naaman's wife. [3]"If only my master would present himself to the prophet in Samaria," she said to her mistress,

---

4, 26: Greetings: the conventional answer to Gehazi's question, which tells him nothing.

4, 29: Do not greet him: the profuse exchange of compliments among Orientals meeting and greeting one another consumed time. Urgency necessitated their omission, as our Lord counseled his disciples (Lk 10, 4).

u: 31-36: Acts 20, 10ff. *v:* 1 Kgs 17, 21-23. *w:* Heb 11, 35.

"he would cure him of his leprosy." [4]Naaman went and told his lord just what the slave girl from the land of Israel had said. [5]"Go," said the king of Aram. "I will send along a letter to the king of Israel." So Naaman set out, taking along ten silver talents, six thousand gold pieces, and ten festal garments. [6]To the king of Israel he brought the letter, which read: "With this letter I am sending my servant Naaman to you, that you may cure him of his leprosy."

[7]When he read the letter, the king of Israel tore his garments and exclaimed: "Am I a god with power over life and death, that this man should send someone to me to be cured of leprosy? Take note! You can see he is only looking for a quarrel with me!"[x] [8]When Elisha, the man of God, heard that the king of Israel had torn his garments, he sent word to the king: "Why have you torn your garments? Let him come to me and find out that there is a prophet in Israel."

[9]Naaman came with his horses and chariots and stopped at the door of Elisha's house. [10]The prophet sent him the message: "Go and wash seven times in the Jordan, and your flesh will heal, and you will be clean."[y] [11]But Naaman went away angry, saying, "I thought that he would surely come out and stand there to invoke the LORD his God, and would move his hand over the spot, and thus cure the leprosy. [12]Are not the rivers of Damascus, the Abana and the Pharpar, better than all the waters of Israel? Could I not wash in them and be cleansed?"[*] With this, he turned about in anger and left.

[13]But his servants came up and reasoned with him. "My father," they said, "if the prophet had told you to do something extraordinary, would you not have done it? All the more now, since he said to you, 'Wash and be clean,' should you do as he said." [14]So Naaman went down and plunged into the Jordan seven times at the word of the man of God. His flesh became again like the flesh of a little child, and he was clean.[z]

[15]He returned with his whole retinue to the man of God. On his arrival he stood before him and said, "Now I know that there is no God in all the earth, except in Israel. Please accept a gift from your servant." [16]"As the LORD lives whom I serve, I will not take it," Elisha replied; and despite Naaman's urging, he still refused. [17]Naaman said: "If you will not accept, please let me, your servant, have two mule-loads of earth,[*] for I will no longer offer holocaust or sacrifice to any other god except to the LORD. [18]But I trust the LORD will forgive your servant this: when my master enters the temple of Rimmon to worship there, then I, too, as his adjutant, must bow down in the temple of Rimmon. May the LORD forgive your servant this." [19]"Go in peace,"[*] Elisha said to him.

[20]Naaman had gone some distance when Gehazi, the servant of Elisha, the man of God, thought to himself: "My master was too easy with this Aramean Naaman, not accepting what he brought. As the LORD lives, I will run after him and get something out of him." [21]So Gehazi hurried after Naaman. Aware that someone was running after him, Naaman alighted from his chariot to wait for him. "Is everything all right?" he asked. [22]"Yes," Gehazi replied, "but my master sent me to say, 'Two young men have just come to me, guild prophets from the hill country of Ephraim. Please give them a talent of silver and two festal garments.' " [23]"Please take two talents," Naaman said, and pressed them upon him. He tied up these silver talents in bags and gave them, with the two festal garments, to two of his servants, who carried them before Gehazi. [24]When they reached the hill, Gehazi took what they had, carried it into the house, and sent the men on their way.

[25]He went in and stood before Elisha his master, who asked him, "Where have you been, Gehazi?" He answered, "Your servant has not gone anywhere." [26]But Elisha said to him: "Was I not present in spirit when the

---

5, 12: Wash in them and be cleansed: typical of the ambiguity in ritual healing or cleanliness. The muddy waters of the Jordan are no match hygienically for the mountain spring waters of Damascus; ritually, it is the other way around.

5, 17: Two mule-loads of earth: Israelite earth on which to erect in Aram an altar to the God of Israel.

5, 19: Go in peace: Elisha understands and approves the situation of Naaman who, though a proselyte as regards belief in and worship of the God of Israel, is required by his office to assist his master, the king, worshiping in the pagan temple of Rimmon.

x: Gn 30, 2; 1 Sm 2, 6; Jn 5, 21.   y: Jn 9, 7.   z: Lk 4, 27.

man alighted from his chariot to wait for you? Is this a time to take money or to take garments, olive orchards or vineyards, sheep or cattle, male or female servants? [27]The leprosy of Naaman shall cling to you and your descendants forever." And Gehazi left Elisha, a leper white as snow.[a]

See RG 129-34

④ CHAPTER 6

Recovery of the Lost Ax. [1]The guild prophets once said to Elisha: "There is not enough room for us to continue to live here with you. [2]Let us go to the Jordan, where by getting one beam apiece we can build ourselves a place to live." "Go," Elisha said. [3]"Please agree to accompany your servants," one of them requested. "Yes, I will come," he replied.

[4]So he went with them, and when they arrived at the Jordan they began to fell trees. [5]While one of them was felling a tree trunk, the iron axhead slipped into the water. "O master," he cried out, "it was borrowed!" [6]"Where did it fall?" asked the man of God. When he pointed out the spot, Elisha cut off a stick, threw it into the water, and brought the iron to the surface. [7]"Pick it up," he said. And the man reached down and grasped it.

Aramean Ambush. [8]When the king of Aram was waging war on Israel, he would make plans with his servants to attack a particular place. [9]But the man of God would send word to the king of Israel, "Be careful! Do not pass by this place, for Aram will attack there." [10]So the king of Israel would send word to the place which the man of God had indicated, and alert it; then they would be on guard. This happened several times.

[11]Greatly disturbed over this, the king of Aram called together his officers. "Will you not tell me," he asked them, "who among us is for the king of Israel?" [12]"No one, my lord king," answered one of the officers. "The Israelite prophet Elisha can tell the king of Israel the very words you speak in your bedroom." [13]"Go, find out where he is," he said, "so that I may take him captive."

Blinded Aramean Soldiers. Informed that Elisha was in Dothan, [14]he sent there a strong force with horses and chariots. They arrived by night and surrounded the city. [15]Early the next morning, when the attendant of the man of God arose and went out, he saw the force with its horses and chariots surrounding the city. "Alas!" he said to Elisha. "What shall we do, my lord?" [16]"Do not be afraid," Elisha answered. "Our side outnumbers theirs." [17]Then he prayed, "O LORD, open his eyes, that he may see." And the LORD opened the eyes of the servant, so that he saw the mountainside filled with horses and fiery chariots around Elisha.[b]

⑤ [18]When the Arameans came down to get him, Elisha prayed to the LORD, "Strike this people blind, I pray you." And in answer to the prophet's prayer the LORD struck them blind. [19]Then Elisha said to them: "This is the wrong road, and this is the wrong city. Follow me! I will take you to the man you want." And he led them to Samaria. [20]When they entered Samaria, Elisha prayed, "O LORD, open their eyes that they may see." The LORD opened their eyes, and they saw that they were inside Samaria. [21]When the king of Israel saw them, he asked, "Shall I kill them, my father?" [22]"You must not kill them," replied Elisha. "Do you slay those whom you have taken captive with your sword or bow?* Serve them bread and water. Let them eat and drink, and then go back to their master." [23]The king spread a great feast for them. When they had eaten and drunk he sent them away, and they went back to their master. No more Aramean raiders came into the land of Israel.

Siege of Samaria. [24]After this, Ben-hadad, king of Aram, mustered his whole army and laid siege to Samaria. [25]Because of the siege the famine in Samaria was so severe that an ass's head sold for eighty pieces of silver, and a fourth of a kab of wild onion for five pieces of silver. [26]One day, as the king of Israel was walking on the city wall, a woman cried out to him, "Help, my lord king!" [27]"No," he replied, "the

---

6, 22: With your sword or bow: since the king would not slay prisoners who had surrendered to his power, much less should he slay prisoners captured by God's power. By Oriental custom they became guests within Samaria's walls.

---

a: Ex 4, 6; Nm 12, 10. *b:* 2 Kgs 7, 6; Ps 67, 18.

LORD help you! Where could I find help for you: from the threshing floor or the wine-press?" [28]Then the king asked her, "What is your trouble?" She replied: "This woman said to me, 'Give up your son that we may eat him today; then tomorrow we will eat my son.'[c] [29]So we boiled my son and ate him. The next day I said to her, 'Now give up your son that we may eat him.' But she hid her son." [30]When the king heard the woman's words, he tore his garments. And as he was walking on the wall, the people saw that he was wearing sackcloth underneath, next to his skin.[d]

[31]"May God do thus and so to me," the king exclaimed, "if the head of Elisha, son of Shaphat, stays on him today!" [32]Meanwhile, Elisha was sitting in his house in conference with the elders. The king had sent a man ahead before he himself should come to him. Elisha had said to the elders: "Do you know that this son of a murderer is sending some-one to cut off my head? When the messenger comes, see that you close the door and hold it fast against him. His master's footsteps are echoing behind him." [33]While Elisha was still speaking, the king came down to him and said, "This evil is from the LORD. Why should I trust in the LORD any longer?"

CHAPTER 7

See RG 129-34

[1]Elisha said: "Hear the word of the LORD! Thus says the LORD, 'At this time to-morrow a seah of fine flour will sell for a shekel, and two seahs of barley for a shekel, in the market* of Samaria.' " [2]But the adjutant on whose arm the king leaned, answered the man of God, "Even if the LORD were to make windows in heaven, how could this happen?" "You shall see it with your own eyes," Elisha said, "but you shall not eat of it."[e]

The Lepers at the Gate. [3]At the city gate were four lepers who were deliberating, "Why should we sit here until we die?[f] [4]If we decide to go into the city, we shall die there, for there is famine in the city. If we remain here, we shall die too. Come, let us desert to the camp of the Arameans. If they spare us,

we live; if they kill us, we die." [5]At twilight they left for the Arameans; but when they reached the edge of the camp, no one was there. [6g]The LORD had caused the army of the Arameans to hear the sound of chariots and horses, the din of a large army, and they had reasoned among themselves, "The king of Is-rael has hired the kings of the Hittites and the kings of the borderlands* to fight us." [7]Then in the twilight they fled, abandoning their tents, their horses, and their asses, the whole camp just as it was, and fleeing for their lives.

[8]After the lepers reached the edge of the camp, they went first into one tent, ate and drank, and took silver, gold, and clothing from it, and went out and hid them. Back they came into another tent, took things from it, and again went out and hid them. [9]Then they said to one another: "We are not doing right. This is a day of good news, and we are keeping silent. If we wait until morn-ing breaks, we shall be blamed. Come, let us go and inform the palace."

[10]They came and summoned the city gate-keepers. "We went to the camp of the Arame-ans," they said, "but no one was there—not a human voice, only the horses and asses teth-ered, and the tents just as they were left." [11]The gatekeepers announced this and it was reported within the palace. [12]Though it was night, the king got up; he said to his servants: "Let me tell you what the Arameans have done to us. Knowing that we are in famine, they have left their camp to hide in the field, hoping to take us alive and enter our city when we leave it." [13]One of his servants, however, suggested: "Since those who are left in the city are no better off than all the throng that has perished, let some of us take five of the aban-doned horses and send scouts to investigate."

End of the Siege. [14]They took two chari-ots, and horses, and the king sent them to reconnoiter the Aramean army. "Go and find out," he ordered. [15]They followed the Ara-means as far as the Jordan, and the whole route was strewn with garments and other objects that the Arameans had thrown away

7, 1: Market: literally "gate," the principal place of trading in ancient walled cities in time of peace.

7, 6: Kings of the borderlands: from Musur in Anatolia rather than Egypt.

c: Dt 28, 53-57.   d: 1 Kgs 20, 31; 21, 27.   e: 2 Kgs 7, 17; Ps 78, 23; Is 24, 18.   f: Lv 13, 46.   g: 6f: 2 Kgs 6, 17; 19, 35f; 2 Sm 5, 24.

Elisha and the Shunammite

The woman who had helped Elisha (4, 8–13) now needs the help that Elisha had offered her in return. Chapter 8, 1–6 tells that she has followed his advice by leaving her homeland to avoid a famine, and while she was away, someone took her land. Just as she arrives at the royal court to appeal for her house and her land, Elisha's servant Gehazi is telling the king all about her. His words serve as the advocacy on her behalf that Elisha earlier had in mind (4, 13). God looks after those who look after his prophets.

in their haste. The messengers returned and told the king.

¹⁶The people went out and plundered the camp of the Arameans; and then a seah of fine flour sold for a shekel and two seahs of barley for a shekel, as the LORD had said.

¹⁷The king put in charge of the gate the officer who was his adjutant; but the people trampled him to death at the gate, just as the man of God had predicted when the king visited him. ¹⁸Thus was fulfilled the prophecy of the man of God to the king, "Two seahs of barley will sell for a shekel, and one seah of fine flour for a shekel at this time tomorrow at the gate of Samaria." ¹⁹The adjutant had answered the man of God, "Even if the LORD were to make windows in heaven, how could this happen?" And Elisha had replied, "You shall see it with your own eyes, but you shall not eat of it." ²⁰And that is what happened to him, for the people trampled him to death at the gate.

See RG 129–34

CHAPTER 8

Prediction of Famine. ¹Elisha once said to the woman whose son he had restored to life: "Get ready! Leave with your family and settle wherever you can, because the LORD has decreed a seven-year famine which is coming upon the land."^h ²The woman got ready and did as the man of God said, setting out with her family and settling in the land of the Philistines for seven years. ³At the end of the seven years, the woman returned from the land of the Philistines and went out to the king to claim her house and her field. ⁴The king was talking with Ge-

hazi, the servant of the man of God. "Tell me," he said, "all the great things that Elisha has done." ⁵Just as he was relating to the king how his master had restored a dead person to life, the very woman whose son Elisha had restored to life came to the king to claim her house and field. "My lord king," Gehazi said, "this is the woman, and this is that son of hers whom Elisha restored to life." ⁶The king questioned the woman, and she told him her story. With that the king placed an official[*] at her disposal, saying, "Restore all her property to her, with all that the field produced from the day she left the land until now."

Death of Ben-hadad Foretold. ⁷Elisha came to Damascus at a time when Ben-hadad, king of Aram, lay sick. When he was told that the man of God had come there, ⁸the king said to Hazael, "Take a gift with you and go call on the man of God. Have him consult the LORD as to whether I shall recover from this sickness." ⁹Hazael went to visit him, carrying a present, and with forty camel loads of the best goods of Damascus. On his arrival, he stood before the prophet and said, "Your son Ben-hadad, king of Aram, has sent me to ask you whether he will recover from his sickness." ¹⁰"Go and tell him," Elisha answered, "that he will surely recover. However, the LORD has showed me that he will in fact die." ¹¹Then he stared him down until Hazael became ill at ease. The man of God wept, ¹²and Hazael asked, "Why are you weeping, my lord?" Elisha replied, "Because I know the evil that you will inflict upon the Israelites. You will burn their fortresses, you will slay their youth with the sword, you will

8, 6: An official: Literally "eunuch," and perhaps actually so in this instance.

h: 2 Kgs 4, 36.

dash their little children to pieces, you will rip open their pregnant women."[i]

[13]Hazael exclaimed, "How can a dog like me, your servant,* do anything so important?" "The LORD has showed you to me as king over Aram," replied Elisha.[j]

[14]Hazael left Elisha and returned to his master. "What did Elisha tell you?" asked Ben-hadad. "He told me that you would surely recover," replied Hazael. [15]The next day, however, Hazael took a cloth, dipped it in water, and spread it over the king's face, so that he died. And Hazael reigned in his stead.

Reign of Jehoram of Judah. [16]In the fifth year of Joram, son of Ahab, king of Israel, Jehoram,* son of Jehoshaphat, king of Judah, became king. [17][k]He was thirty-two years old when he began to reign, and he reigned eight years in Jerusalem. [18]He conducted himself like the kings of Israel of the line of Ahab, since the sister of Ahab was his wife; and he did evil in the LORD's sight. [19]Even so, the LORD was unwilling to destroy Judah, because of his servant David. For he had promised David that he would leave him a lamp in the LORD's presence for all time.[l] [20]During Jehoram's reign, Edom revolted against the sovereignty of Judah and chose a king of its own. [21]Thereupon Jehoram with all his chariots crossed over to Zair. He arose by night and broke through the Edomites when they had surrounded him and the commanders of his chariots. Then his army fled homeward. [22]To this day Edom has been in revolt against the rule of Judah. Libnah also revolted at that time.[m] [23]The rest of the acts of Jehoram, with all that he did, are recorded in the book of the chronicles of the kings of Judah. [24]Jehoram rested with his ancestors and was buried with them in the City of David. His son Ahaziah succeeded him as king.

Accession of Ahaziah. [25]Ahaziah, son of Jehoram, king of Judah, became king in the twelfth year of Joram,* son of Ahab, king of Israel. [26]He was twenty-two years old when he began his reign, and he reigned one year in Jerusalem. His mother's name was Athaliah; she was the daughter of Omri, king of Israel. [27]He conducted himself like the house of Ahab, doing evil in the LORD's sight as they did, since he was related to them by marriage. [28]He joined Joram, son of Ahab, in battle against Hazael, king of Aram, at Ramoth-gilead, where the Arameans wounded Joram.[n] [29]King Joram returned to Jezreel to be healed of the wounds which the Arameans had inflicted on him at Ramah in his battle against Hazael, king of Aram. Then Ahaziah, son of Jehoram, king of Judah, went down to Jezreel to visit him there in his illness.

CHAPTER 9

See RG 129-34

Anointing of Jehu. [1]The prophet Elisha called one of the guild prophets and said to him: "Gird your loins, take this flask of oil with you, and go to Ramoth-gilead.[o] [2]When you get there, look for Jehu, son of Jehoshaphat, son of Nimshi. Enter and take him away from his companions into an inner chamber.[p] [3]From the flask you have, pour oil on his head, and say, 'Thus says the LORD: I anoint you king over Israel.' Then open the door and flee without delay."[q] [4]The young man (the guild prophet) went to Ramoth-gilead. [5]When he arrived, the commanders of the army were in session. "I have a message for you, commander," he said. "For which one of us?" asked Jehu. "For you, commander," he answered. [6]Jehu got up and went into the house. Then the young man poured the oil on his head and said, "Thus says the LORD, the God of Israel: 'I anoint you king over the people of the LORD, over Israel. [7]*You shall destroy the house of Ahab your master; thus will I avenge the blood of my servants the prophets, and the

---

8, 13: A dog . . . your servant: Hazael feigns humility (1 Sm 24, 14; 2 Sm 9, 8), without attending to the crimes he would commit after usurping the royal power as the prophet predicts. Anything so important: literally "a great deed" for a patriotic Syrian.

8, 16: Jehoram of Judah succeeded his father Jehoshaphat during the reign of Ahaziah of Israel. See note on 2 Kgs 3, 1.

8, 25: Twelfth year of Joram: i.e., of Israel, who probably reigned only eight years.

9, 7-10: The editors of the Books of Kings have here added

to the prophet's message the same type of indictment and sanctions against the family of Ahab as were invoked against the dynasties of Jeroboam (1 Kgs 14, 10f), Baasha (1 Kgs 16, 3f), and Ahab on a previous occasion (1 Kgs 21, 21–24).

---

i: 2 Kgs 13, 7. j: 2 Kgs 15, 16; 1 Kgs 19, 15. k: 17ff: 2 Chr 21, 5ff. l: 2 Sm 7, 11-16; 21, 17; 1 Kgs 11, 36; 15, 4; 2 Chr 21, 7. m: Gn 27, 40; 2 Chr 21, 8ff. n: 2 Kgs 9, 14f. o: 1 Kgs 21, 29; Hos 1, 4. p: 1 Kgs 19, 16. q: 1 Kgs 19, 16.

blood of all the other servants of the LORD shed by Jezebel, [8r]and by all the rest of the family of Ahab. I will cut off every male in Ahab's line, whether slave or freeman in Israel. [9]I will deal with the house of Ahab as I dealt with the house of Jeroboam, son of Nebat, and with the house of Baasha, son of Ahijah. [10]Dogs shall devour Jezebel at the confines of Jezreel, so that no one can bury her.' " Then he opened the door and fled.

[11]When Jehu rejoined his master's servants, they asked him, "Is all well? Why did that madman come to you?" "You know that kind of man and his talk," he replied. [12]But they said, "Not at all! Come, tell us." So he told them what the young man had said to him, and finally, "Thus says the LORD: 'I anoint you king over Israel.' " [13]At once each took his garment, spread it under Jehu on the bare steps, blew the trumpet, and cried out, "Jehu is king!"[s]

[14t]Thus Jehu, son of Jehoshaphat, son of Nimshi, formed a conspiracy against Joram. Joram, with all Israel, had been besieging Ramoth-gilead against Hazael, king of Aram, [15]but had returned to Jezreel to be healed of the wounds the Arameans had inflicted on him in the battle against Hazael, king of Aram.

Murder of Joram. "If you are truly with me," Jehu said, "see that no one escapes from the city to report in Jezreel." [16]Then Jehu mounted his chariot and drove to Jezreel, where Joram lay ill and Ahaziah, king of Judah, had come to visit him.

[17]The watchman standing on the tower in Jezreel saw the troop of Jehu coming and reported, "I see chariots." "Get a driver," Joram said, "and send him to meet them and to ask whether all is well." [18]So a driver went out to meet him and said, "The king asks whether all is well." "What does it matter to you how things are?" Jehu said. "Get behind me." The watchman reported to the king, "The messenger has reached them, but is not returning."

[19]Joram sent a second driver, who went to them and said, "The king asks whether all is

well." "What does it matter to you how things are?" Jehu replied. "Get behind me." [20]The watchman reported, "The messenger has reached them, but is not returning. The driving is like that of Jehu, son of Nimshi, in its fury." [21]"Prepare my chariot," said Joram. When they had done so, Joram, king of Israel, and Ahaziah, king of Judah, set out, each in his own chariot, to meet Jehu. They reached him near the field of Naboth the Jezreelite. [22]When Joram recognized Jehu, he asked, "Is all well, Jehu?" "How can all be well," Jehu replied, "as long as the many fornications and witchcrafts* of your mother Jezebel continue?" [23]Joram reined about and fled, crying to Ahaziah, "Treason, Ahaziah!" [24]But Jehu drew his bow and shot Joram between the shoulders, so that the arrow went through his heart and he collapsed in his chariot. [25u]Then Jehu said to his adjutant Bidkar, "Take him and throw him into the field of Naboth the Jezreelite. For I remember that when we were driving teams behind his father Ahab, the LORD delivered this oracle against him: [26]'As surely as I saw yesterday the blood of Naboth and the blood of his sons,' says the LORD, 'I will repay you for it in that very plot of ground, says the LORD.' So now take him into this plot of ground, in keeping with the word of the LORD."

Death of Ahaziah. [27v]Seeing what was happening, Ahaziah, king of Judah, fled toward Beth-haggan. Jehu pursued him, shouting, "Kill him too!" And they pierced him as he rode through the pass of Gur near Ibleam. He continued his flight as far as Megiddo and died there. [28]His servants brought him in a chariot to Jerusalem and buried him in the tomb of his ancestors in the City of David. [29]Ahaziah had become king of Judah in the eleventh year of Joram, son of Ahab.

Death of Jezebel. [30]When Jezebel learned that Jehu had arrived in Jezreel, she shadowed her eyes, adorned her hair, and looked down from her window. [31]As Jehu came through the gate, she cried out, "Is all well, Zimri, murderer of your master?"[w] [32]Jehu

---

9, 22: Fornications and witchcrafts: the worship of foreign gods.

r: 8ff: 1 Kgs 14, 10f; 16, 3f; 21, 21-24.   *s:* Mt 21, 8.   *t:* 14f: 2 Kgs 8, 28f; 1 Kgs 22, 3f.   *u:* 25f: 1 Kgs 21, 9-16.   *v:* 27ff: 2 Chr 22, 7ff.   *w:* 1 Kgs 16, 9ff.

looked up to the window and shouted, "Who is on my side? Anyone?" At this, two or three eunuchs looked down toward him. [33]"Throw her down," he ordered. They threw her down, and some of her blood spurted against the wall and against the horses. Jehu rode in over her body [34]and, after eating and drinking, he said: "Attend to that accursed woman and bury her; after all, she was a king's daughter." [35]But when they went to bury her, they found nothing of her but the skull, the feet, and the hands. [36]They returned to Jehu, and when they told him, he said, "This is the sentence which the LORD pronounced through his servant Elijah the Tishbite: 'In the confines of Jezreel dogs shall eat the flesh of Jezebel.[x] [37]The corpse of Jezebel shall be like dung in the field in the confines of Jezreel, so that no one can say: This was Jezebel.' "

See RG 129-34

CHAPTER 10

Killing of Ahab's Descendants. [1]Ahab had seventy descendants in Samaria. Jehu prepared letters and sent them to the city rulers, to the elders, and to the guardians of Ahab's descendants in Samaria.[y] [2]"Since your master's sons are with you," he wrote, "and you have the chariots, the horses, a fortified city, and the weapons, when this letter reaches you [3]decide which is the best and the fittest of your master's offspring, place him on his father's throne, and fight for your master's house." [4]They were overcome with fright and said, "If two kings could not withstand him, how can we?" [5]So the vizier and the ruler of the city, along with the elders and the guardians, sent this message to Jehu: "We are your servants, and we will do everything you tell us. We will proclaim no one king; do whatever you think best." [6]So Jehu wrote them a second letter: "If you are on my side and will obey me, count the heads of your master's sons and come to me in Jezreel at this time tomorrow." [The seventy princes were in the care of prominent men of the city, who were rearing them.]

[7]When the letter arrived, they took the princes and slew all seventy of them, put their heads in baskets, and sent them to Jehu in Jezreel. [8]"They have brought the heads of the princes," a messenger came in and told him. "Pile them in two heaps at the entrance of the city until morning," he ordered. [9]Going out in the morning, he stopped and said to all the people: "You are not responsible, and although I conspired against my lord and slew him, yet who killed all these? [10]Know that not a single word which the LORD has spoken against the house of Ahab shall go unfulfilled. The LORD has accomplished all that he foretold through his servant Elijah."[z] [11]Thereupon Jehu slew all who were left of the family of Ahab in Jezreel, as well as all his powerful supporters, intimates, and priests, leaving him no survivor.[a]

Ahaziah's Kinsmen. [12b]Then he set out for Samaria, and at Beth-eked-haroim on the way, [13]he came across kinsmen of Ahaziah, king of Judah. "Who are you?" he asked. "We are kinsmen of Ahaziah," they replied. "We are going down to visit the princes and the family of the queen mother." [14]"Take them alive," Jehu ordered. They were taken alive, forty-two in number, then slain at the pit of Beth-eked. Not one of them was spared.

Jehu in Samaria. [15]When he had left there, Jehu met Jehonadab, son of Rechab, on the road. He greeted him and asked, "Are you sincerely disposed toward me, as I am toward you?" "Yes," replied Jehonadab. "If you are," continued Jehu, "give me your hand." Jehonadab gave him his hand, and Jehu drew him up into his chariot.[c] [16]"Come with me," he said, "and see my zeal for the LORD." And he took him along in his own chariot.

[17]When he arrived in Samaria, Jehu slew all who remained there of Ahab's line, doing away with them completely and thus fulfilling the prophecy which the LORD had spoken to Elijah.

Baal's Temple Destroyed. [18]Jehu gathered all the people together and said to them: "Ahab served Baal to some extent, but Jehu will serve him yet more.[d] [19]Now summon for me all Baal's prophets, all his worshipers, and all his priests. See that no one is absent, for I have a great sacrifice for Baal. Whoever is

---

x: 1 Kgs 21, 23.   *y:* Jgs 9, 5; 1 Kgs 15, 29; 16, 11.   *z:* 1 Kgs 21, 17-24. 29.   *a:* Hos 1, 4.   *b:* 12ff: 2 Chr 22, 8f.   *c:* 1 Chr 2, 55; Jer 35, 1-11.   *d:* 1 Kgs 16, 30ff.

absent shall not live." This Jehu did as a ruse, so that he might destroy the worshipers of Baal. ²⁰Jehu said further, "Proclaim a solemn assembly in honor of Baal." They did so, ²¹and Jehu sent word of it throughout the land of Israel. All the worshipers of Baal without exception came into the temple of Baal, which was filled to capacity. ²²Then Jehu said to the custodian of the wardrobe, "Bring out the garments for all the worshipers of Baal." When he had brought out the garments for them,^e ²³Jehu, with Jehonadab, son of Rechab, entered the temple of Baal and said to the worshipers of Baal, "Search and be sure that there is no worshiper of the LORD here with you, but only worshipers of Baal." ²⁴Then they proceeded to offer sacrifices and holocausts. Now Jehu had stationed eighty men outside with this warning, "If one of you lets anyone escape of those whom I shall deliver into your hands, he shall pay life for life." ²⁵As soon as he finished offering the holocaust, Jehu said to the guards and officers, "Go in and slay them. Let no one escape." So the guards and officers put them to the sword and cast them out. Afterward they went into the inner shrine of the temple of Baal, ²⁶took out the stele of Baal, and burned the shrine. ²⁷Then they smashed the stele of Baal, tore down the building, and turned it into a latrine, as it remains today.

²⁸Thus Jehu rooted out the worship of Baal from Israel. ²⁹However, he did not desist from the sins which Jeroboam, son of Nebat, had caused Israel to commit, as regards the golden calves at Bethel and at Dan.^f ³⁰The LORD said to Jehu, "Because you have done well what I deem right, and have treated the house of Ahab as I desire, your sons to the fourth generation shall sit upon the throne of Israel."^g ³¹But Jehu was not careful to observe wholeheartedly the law of the LORD, the God of Israel, since he did not desist from the sins which Jeroboam caused Israel to commit.

^{32h}At that time the LORD began to dismember Israel. Hazael defeated the Israelites throughout their territory ³³east of the Jordan (all the land of Gilead, of the Gadites, Reu-

benites and Manassehites), from Aroer on the river Arnon up through Gilead and Bashan. ³⁴The rest of the acts of Jehu, his valor and all his accomplishments, are written in the book of the chronicles of the kings of Israel. ³⁵Jehu rested with his ancestors and was buried in Samaria. His son Jehoahaz succeeded him as king. ³⁶The length of Jehu's reign over Israel in Samaria was twenty-eight years.

CHAPTER 11

See RG 129-34

Rule of Athaliah. ¹When Athaliah, the mother of Ahaziah, saw that her son was dead, she began to kill off the whole royal family.ⁱ ²But Jehosheba,* daughter of King Jehoram and sister of Ahaziah, took Joash, his son, and spirited him away, along with his nurse, from the bedroom where the princes were about to be slain. She concealed him from Athaliah, and so he did not die. ³For six years he remained hidden in the temple of the LORD, while Athaliah ruled the land.

^{4j}But in the seventh year, Jehoiada summoned the captains of the Carians and of the guards. He had them come to him in the temple of the LORD, exacted from them a sworn commitment, and then showed them the king's son. ⁵He gave them these orders: "This is what you must do: the third of you who come on duty on the sabbath shall guard the king's palace; ⁶another third shall be at the gate Sur; and the last third shall be at the gate behind the guards. ⁷The two of your divisions who are going off duty that week shall keep guard over the temple of the LORD for the king. ⁸You shall surround the king, each with drawn weapons, and if anyone tries to approach the cordon, kill him; stay with the king, whatever he may do."

^{9k}The captains did just as Jehoiada the priest commanded. Each one with his men, both those going on duty for the sabbath and those going off duty that week, came to Jehoiada the priest. ^{10l}He gave the captains King David's spears and shields, which were in the temple of the LORD. ¹¹And the guards,

11, 2: Jehosheba was the wife of Jehoida, the high priest; cf 2 Chr 22, 11.

e: 1 Kgs 16, 32.   *f:* 1 Kgs 12, 28f.   *g:* 2 Kgs 15, 12ff.   *h:* Am 1, 3.   *i:* Jgs 9, 5.   *j:* 4-8: 2 Chr 23, 1-7.   *k:* 9-12: 2 Chr 23, 8-11. *l:* 10ff: 2 Sm 8, 7; 1 Kgs 1, 33f.

with drawn weapons, lined up from the southern to the northern limit of the enclosure, surrounding the altar and the temple on the king's behalf. [12]Then Jehoiada led out the king's son and put the crown and the insignia upon him. They proclaimed him king and anointed him, clapping their hands and shouting, "Long live the king!"[m]

[13][n]Athaliah heard the noise made by the people, and appeared before them in the temple of the LORD. [14]When she saw the king standing by the pillar,* as was the custom, and the captains and trumpeters near him, with all the people of the land rejoicing and blowing trumpets, she tore her garments and cried out, "Treason, treason!" [15]Then Jehoiada the priest instructed the captains in command of the force: "Bring her outside through the ranks. If anyone follows her," he added, "let him die by the sword." He had given orders that she should not be slain in the temple of the LORD. [16]She was led out forcibly to the horse gate of the royal palace, where she was put to death.

[17][o]Then Jehoiada made a covenant between the LORD as one party and the king and the people as the other, by which they would be the LORD's people; and another covenant, between the king and the people. [18]Thereupon all the people of the land went to the temple of Baal and demolished it. They shattered its altars and images completely, and slew Mattan, the priest of Baal, before the altars. After appointing a detachment for the temple of the LORD, Jehoiada [19]with the captains, the Carians, the guards, and all the people of the land, led the king down from the temple of the LORD through the guards' gate to the palace, where Joash took his seat on the royal throne. [20]All the people of the land rejoiced and the city was quiet, now that Athaliah had been slain with the sword at the royal palace.

See RG 129–34

CHAPTER 12

Reign of Joash. [1]Joash was seven years old when he became king.[p] [2]Joash began to reign in the seventh year of Jehu, and he reigned forty years in Jerusalem. His mother, who was named Zibiah, was from Beer-sheba. [3]Joash did what was pleasing to the LORD as long as he lived, because the priest Jehoiada guided him. [4]Still, the high places did not disappear; the people continued to sacrifice and to burn incense there.

[5][q]For the priests Joash made this rule: "All the funds for sacred purposes that are brought to the temple of the LORD—the census tax, personal redemption money, and whatever funds are freely brought to the temple of the LORD— [6]the priests may take for themselves, each from his own clients. However, they must make whatever repairs on the temple may prove necessary." [7]Nevertheless, as late as the twenty-third year of the reign of King Joash, the priests had not made needed repairs on the temple. [8]Accordingly, King Joash summoned the priest Jehoiada and the other priests. "Why do you not repair the temple?" he asked them. "You must no longer take funds from your clients, but you shall turn them over for the repairs." [9][r]So the priests agreed that they would neither take funds from the people nor make the repairs on the temple.

[10]The priest Jehoiada then took a chest, bored a hole in its lid, and set it beside the stele, on the right as one entered the temple of the LORD. The priests who guarded the entry would put into it all the funds that were brought to the temple of the LORD. [11]When they noticed that there was a large amount of silver in the chest, the royal scribe [and the priest] would come up, and they would melt down all the funds that were in the temple of the LORD, and weigh them. [12]The amount thus realized they turned over to the master workmen in the temple of the LORD. They in turn would give it to the carpenters and builders working in the temple of the LORD, [13]and to the lumbermen and stone cutters, and for the purchase of the wood and hewn stone used in repairing the breaches, and for any other expenses that were necessary to repair the temple. [14]None of the funds brought to the temple

---

11, 14: By the pillar: see note on 2 Chr 23, 13.

m: 2 Sm 1, 10.   *n:* 13-16: 2 Chr 23, 12-15.   *o:* 17-20: 2 Chr 23, 16-21.   *p:* 1f: 2 Chr 24, 1f.   *q:* 5-8: 2 Chr 24, 5-10.   *r:* 9-16: 2 Chr 24, 11-14.

of the LORD were used there to make silver cups, snuffers, basins, trumpets, or any gold or silver article. [15]Instead, they were given to the workmen, and with them they repaired the temple of the LORD. [16]Moreover, no reckoning was asked of the men who were provided with the funds to give to the workmen, because they held positions of trust. [17]The funds from guilt-offerings and from sin-offerings, however, were not brought to the temple of the LORD; they belonged to the priests.

[18s]Then King Hazael of Aram mounted a siege against Gath. When he had taken it, Hazael decided to go on to attack Jerusalem.[t] [19]But King Jehoash of Judah took all the dedicated offerings presented by his forebears, Jehoshaphat, Jehoram, and Ahaziah, kings of Judah, as well as his own, and all the gold there was in the treasuries of the temple and the palace, and sent them to King Hazael of Aram, who then led his forces away from Jerusalem. [20]The rest of the acts of Joash, with all that he did, are recorded in the book of the chronicles of the kings of Judah. [21]Certain of his officials entered into a plot against him and killed him at Beth-millo. [22]Jozacar, son of Shimeath, and Jehozabad, son of Shomer, were the officials who killed him. He was buried in his forefathers' City of David, and his son Amaziah succeeded him as king.

See RG 129-34

CHAPTER 13

Reign of Jehoahaz of Israel. [1]In the twenty-third year of Joash, son of Ahaziah, king of Judah, Jehoahaz, son of Jehu, began his seventeen-year reign over Israel in Samaria. [2]He did evil in the LORD's sight, conducting himself like Jeroboam, son of Nebat, and not renouncing the sin he had caused Israel to commit. [3]The LORD was angry with Israel and for a long time left them in the power of Hazael, king of Aram, and of Ben-hadad, son of Hazael. [4]Then Jehoahaz entreated the LORD, who heard him, since he saw the oppression to which the king of Aram had subjected Israel.[u] [5]So the LORD gave Israel a savior,* and the Israelites, freed from the power of Aram, dwelt in their own homes as formerly. [6]Nevertheless, they did not desist from the sins which the house of Jeroboam had caused Israel to commit, but persisted in them. The sacred pole* also remained standing in Samaria.[v] [7]No soldiers were left to Jehoahaz, except fifty horsemen with ten chariots and ten thousand foot soldiers, since the king of Aram had destroyed them and trampled them like dust. [8]The rest of the acts of Jehoahaz, with all his valor and accomplishments, are recorded in the book of the chronicles of the kings of Israel. [9]Jehoahaz rested with his ancestors and was buried in Samaria. His son Joash succeeded him as king.

Reign of Joash of Israel. [10]In the thirty-seventh year of Joash, king of Judah, Jehoash, son of Jehoahaz, began his sixteen-year reign over Israel in Samaria. [11]He did evil in the sight of the LORD; he did not desist from any of the sins which Jeroboam, son of Nebat, had caused Israel to commit, but persisted in them. [12]*[The rest of the acts of Joash, the valor with which he fought against Amaziah, king of Judah, and all his accomplishments, are recorded in the book of the chronicles of the kings of Israel.[w] [13]Joash rested with his ancestors, and Jeroboam occupied the throne. Joash was buried with the kings of Israel in Samaria.]

[14]When Elisha was suffering from the sickness of which he was to die, King Joash of Israel went down to visit him. "My father, my father!"* he exclaimed, weeping over him. "Israel's chariots and horsemen!"[x] [15]"Take a bow and some arrows," Elisha said to him. When he had done so, [16]*Elisha said to the king of Israel, "Put your hand on the bow." As the king held the bow, Elisha placed his hands over the king's hands [17]and said, "Open the

---

13, 5: A savior: by this language, typical of the Book of Judges (Jgs 3, 9. 15), Jeroboam II of Israel is meant; cf 2 Kgs 14, 27.

13, 6: Sacred pole: see note on Ex 34, 13.

13, 12f: The conclusion to the reign of Joash is given again in 2 Kgs 14, 15f, where it is more appropriate.

13, 14: My father, my father: the king expresses here the same sentiments as those with which Elisha addressed Elijah.

13, 16-19: Symbolic acts similar to these are seen in Ex 17, 8ff; Jos 8, 18ff; Ez 4, 1ff.

s: 2 Kgs 8, 12.   t: 18-22: 2 Chr 24, 23-27.   u: 2 Kgs 14, 26f.
v: Ex 34, 13.   w: 2 Kgs 14, 8-16.   x: 2 Kgs 2, 12.

window toward the east." He opened it, Elisha said, "Shoot," and he shot. The prophet exclaimed, "The LORD's arrow of victory! The arrow of victory over Aram! You will completely conquer Aram at Aphec."

[18]Then he said to the king of Israel, "Take the arrows," which he did. Elisha said to him, "Strike the ground!" He struck the ground three times and stopped. [19]Angry with him, the man of God said: "You should have struck five or six times; you would have defeated Aram completely. Now, you will defeat Aram only three times."

[20]Elisha died and was buried. At the time, bands of Moabites used to raid the land each year. [21]Once some people were burying a man, when suddenly they spied such a raiding band. So they cast the dead man into the grave of Elisha, and everyone went off. But when the man came in contact with the bones of Elisha, he came back to life and rose to his feet.[y]

[22]King Hazael of Aram oppressed Israel during the entire reign of Jehoahaz. [23]But the LORD was merciful with Israel and looked on them with compassion because of his covenant with Abraham, Isaac, and Jacob. He was unwilling to destroy them or to cast them out from his presence.[z] [24]So when King Hazael of Aram died and his son Ben-hadad succeeded him as king, [25]Joash, son of Jehoahaz, took back from Ben-hadad, son of Hazael, the cities which Hazael had taken in battle from his father Jehoahaz. Joash defeated Ben-hadad three times, and thus recovered the cities of Israel.

CHAPTER 14

See RG 129-34

Amaziah of Judah.[*] [1]In the second year of Joash, son of Jehoahaz, king of Israel, Amaziah, son of Joash, king of Judah,

began to reign. [2a]He was twenty-five years old when he became king, and he reigned twenty-nine years in Jerusalem. His mother, whose name was Jehoaddin, was from Jerusalem. [3]He pleased the LORD, yet not like his forefather David, since he did just as his father Joash had done. [4]Thus the high places did not disappear, but the people continued to sacrifice and to burn incense on them. [5b]When Amaziah had the kingdom firmly in hand, he slew the officials who had murdered the king, his father. [6]But the children of the murderers he did not put to death, obeying the LORD's command written in the book of the law of Moses, "Fathers shall not be put to death for their children, nor shall children be put to death for their fathers; each one shall die for his own sin."[c]

[7]Amaziah slew ten thousand Edomites in the Salt Valley, and took Sela in battle. He renamed it Joktheel, the name it has to this day.[d]

[8]Then Amaziah sent messengers to Jehoash, son of Jehoahaz, son of Jehu, king of Israel, with this challenge, "Come, let us meet face to face."[e] [9]King Jehoash of Israel sent this reply to the king of Judah: "The thistle of Lebanon sent word to the cedar of Lebanon, 'Give your daughter to my son in marriage,' but an animal of Lebanon passed by and trampled the thistle underfoot. [10]You have indeed conquered Edom, and you have become ambitious. Enjoy your glory, but stay at home! Why involve yourself and Judah with you in misfortune and failure?"

[11]But Amaziah would not listen. King Jehoash of Israel then advanced, and he and King Amaziah of Judah met in battle at Beth-shemesh of Judah. [12]Judah was defeated by Israel, and all the Judean soldiery fled homeward. [13]King Jehoash of Israel captured Amaziah, son of Jehoash, son of

---

14, 1f: In the second year . . . twenty-nine years in Jerusalem: the reigns of the kings of Judah between Athaliah and Ahaz are assigned too many years in all to correspond to the reigns in Israel from Jehu to the fall of Samaria. It seems probable that Amaziah was murdered as soon as his son Azaiah was old enough to rule, and that Amaziah's reign was nearer nineteen than twenty-nine years. The correlation, in 2 Kgs 15, 1, of the beginning of Azariah's reign with the 27th year of Jeroboam II can hardly be correct; and the sixteen-year reign of Jotham of Judah (2 Kgs 15, 33) consisted for the most part of a regency during the illness of his father (2 Kgs 15, 5).

y: Sir 48, 14. z: Dt 9, 27. a: 2f: 2 Chr 25, 1f. b: 5f: 2 Chr 25, 3f. c: Dt 24, 16; Ez 18, 20. d: 2 Sm 8, 13f; 2 Chr 25, 11. e: 2 Kgs 13, 12; Jgs 9, 8-15.

Ahaziah, king of Judah, at Beth-shemesh. He went on to Jerusalem where he tore down four hundred cubits of the city wall, from the Gate of Ephraim to the Corner Gate. [14]He took all the gold and silver and all the utensils there were in the temple of the LORD and in the treasuries of the palace, and hostages as well. Then he returned to Samaria. [15]The rest of the acts of Jehoash, his valor, and how he fought Amaziah, king of Judah, are recorded in the book of the chronicles of the kings of Israel.[f] [16]Jehoash rested with his ancestors; he was buried in Samaria with the kings of Israel. His son Jeroboam succeeded him as king.

[17]Amaziah, son of Joash, king of Judah, survived Jehoash, son of Jehoahaz, king of Israel, by fifteen years.[*] [18]The rest of the acts of Amaziah are written in the book of the chronicles of the kings of Judah. [19]When a conspiracy was formed against him in Jerusalem, he fled to Lachish. But he was pursued to Lachish and killed there. [20]He was brought back on horses and buried with his ancestors in the City of David in Jerusalem. [21]Thereupon all the people of Judah took the sixteen-year-old Azariah[*] and proclaimed him king to succeed his father Amaziah.[g] [22]It was Azariah who rebuilt Elath and restored it to Judah, after King Amaziah rested with his ancestors.

Jeroboam II of Israel. [23]In the fifteenth year of Amaziah, son of Joash, king of Judah, Jeroboam, son of Joash, king of Israel, began his forty-one-year reign in Samaria. [24]He did evil in the sight of the LORD; he did not desist from any of the sins which Jeroboam, son of Nebat, had caused Israel to commit. [25]He restored the boundaries of Israel from Labo-of-Hamath to the sea of the Arabah,[*] just as the LORD, the God of Israel, had prophesied through his servant, the prophet Jonah, son of Amittai, from Gath-hepher. [26]For the LORD saw the very bitter affliction of Israel, where there was neither slave nor freeman, no one at all to help Israel.[h] [27]Since the LORD had not determined to blot out the name of Israel from under the heavens, he saved them through Jer-

oboam, son of Joash. [28]The rest of the acts of Jeroboam, his valor and all his accomplishments, how he fought with Damascus and turned back Hamath from Israel, are recorded in the book of the chronicles of the kings of Israel. [29]Jeroboam rested with his ancestors, the kings of Israel, and his son Zechariah succeeded him as king.

CHAPTER 15

Azariah of Judah. [1i]Azariah, son of Amaziah, king of Judah, became king in the twenty-seventh year[*] of Jeroboam, king of Israel. [2]He was sixteen years old when he began to reign, and he reigned fifty-two years in Jerusalem. His mother, whose name was Jecholiah, was from Jerusalem. [3]He pleased the LORD just as his father Amaziah had done. [4]Yet the high places did not disappear; the people continued to sacrifice and to burn incense on them. [5j]The LORD afflicted the king, and he was a leper to the day of his death. He lived in a house apart, while Jotham, the king's son, was vizier and regent for the people of the land. [6]The rest of the acts of Azariah, and all his accomplishments, are recorded in the book of the chronicles of the kings of Judah. [7]Azariah rested with his ancestors, and was buried with them in the City of David. His son Jotham succeeded him as king.

Zechariah of Israel. [8]In the thirty-eighth year of Azariah, king of Judah, Zechariah, son of Jeroboam, was king of Israel in Samaria for six months. [9]He did evil in the sight of the LORD as his fathers had done, and did not desist from the sins which Jeroboam, son of Nebat, had caused Israel to commit. [10]Shallum, son of Jabesh, conspired against Zechariah, attacked and killed him at Ibleam, and reigned in his place. [11]The rest of the acts of Zechariah are recorded in the book of the chronicles of the kings of Israel. [12]Thus the LORD's promise to Jehu, "Your descendants to the fourth generation shall sit upon the throne of Israel," was fulfilled.[k]

Shallum of Israel. [13]Shallum, son of Jabesh, became king in the thirty-ninth year of

See RG
129–34

14, 17: See note on 2 Kgs 14, 1f.
14, 21: Azariah: also called Uzziah in many texts.
14, 25: Sea of the Arabah: the Dead Sea. Jonah: see note on Jon 1, 1.

15, 1: Twenty-seventh year: see note on 2 Kgs 14, 1f.

f: 2 Kgs 13, 12f.   *g:* 2 Chr 26, 1f.   *h:* 2 Kgs 13, 4f; 1 Kgs 14, 10.   *i:* 1ff: 2 Chr 26, 3f.   *j:* 5ff: 2 Chr 26, 21ff.   *k:* 2 Kgs 10, 30.

Uzziah, king of Judah; he reigned one month in Samaria. [14]Menahem, son of Gadi, came up from Tirzah to Samaria, where he attacked and killed Shallum, son of Jabesh, and reigned in his place. [15]The rest of the acts of Shallum, and the fact of his conspiracy, are recorded in the book of the chronicles of the kings of Israel. [16]At that time, Menahem punished Tappuah, all the inhabitants of the town and of its whole district, because on his way from Tirzah they did not let him in. He punished them even to ripping open all the pregnant women.

Menahem of Israel. [17]In the thirty-ninth year of Azariah, king of Judah, Menahem, son of Gadi, began his ten-year reign over Samaria. [18]He did evil in the sight of the LORD, not desisting from the sins which Jeroboam, son of Nebat, had caused Israel to commit. During his reign, [19]Pul,* king of Assyria, invaded the land, and Menahem gave him a thousand talents of silver to have his assistance in strengthening his hold on the kingdom. [20]Menahem secured the money to give to the king of Assyria by exacting it from all the men of substance in the country, fifty silver shekels from each. The king of Assyria did not remain in the country but withdrew. [21]The rest of the acts of Menahem, and all his accomplishments, are recorded in the book of the chronicles of the kings of Israel. [22]Menahem rested with his ancestors, and his son Pekahiah succeeded him as king.

Pekahiah of Israel. [23]In the fiftieth year of Azariah, king of Judah, Pekahiah, son of Menahem, began his two-year reign over Israel in Samaria. [24]He did evil in the sight of the LORD, not desisting from the sins which Jeroboam, son of Nebat, had caused Israel to commit. [25]His adjutant Pekah, son of Remaliah, who had with him fifty men from Gilead, conspired against him, killed him within the palace stronghold in Samaria, and reigned in his place. [26]The rest of the acts of Pekahiah, and all his accomplishments, are

recorded in the book of the chronicles of the kings of Israel.

Pekah of Israel. [27]In the fifty-second year of Azariah, king of Judah, Pekah, son of Remaliah, began his twenty-year reign over Israel in Samaria.* [28]He did evil in the sight of the LORD, not desisting from the sins which Jeroboam, son of Nebat, had caused Israel to commit. [29]During the reign of Pekah, king of Israel, Tiglath-pileser, king of Assyria, came and took Ijon, Abel-beth-maacah, Janoah, Kedesh, Hazor, all the territory of Naphtali, Gilead, and Galilee, deporting the inhabitants to Assyria. [30]Hoshea, son of Elah, conspired against Pekah, son of Remaliah; he attacked and killed him, and reigned in his place [in the twentieth year of Jotham, son of Uzziah]. [31]The rest of the acts of Pekah, and all his accomplishments, are recorded in the book of the chronicles of the kings of Israel.

Jotham of Judah. [32]In the second year of Pekah, son of Remaliah, king of Israel, Jotham, son of Uzziah, king of Judah, began to reign. [33]He was twenty-five years old when he became king, and he reigned sixteen years in Jerusalem. His mother's name was Jerusha, daughter of Zadok. [34]He pleased the LORD, just as his father Uzziah had done. [35]Nevertheless the high places did not disappear and the people continued to sacrifice and to burn incense on them. It was he who built the Upper Gate* of the temple of the LORD. [36]The rest of the acts of Jotham, and all his accomplishments, are recorded in the book of the chronicles of the kings of Judah. [37]It was at that time that the LORD first loosed Rezin, king of Aram, and Pekah, son of Remaliah, against Judah. [38]Jotham rested with his ancestors and was buried with them in his forefather's City of David. His son Ahaz succeeded him as king.

CHAPTER 16

See RG 129–34

Ahaz of Judah. [1m]In the seventeenth year of Pekah, son of Remaliah,

---

15, 19: Pul: the Babylonian throne name of the Assyrian Tiglath-pileser III; cf 2 Kgs 15, 29.

15, 27: The twenty years here ascribed to Pekah are an impossibility; the calculation which made his reign, of five years at most, appear so long may have been based on the attempt to give Jotham of Judah a full sixteen-year reign independently of his regency. See 2 Kgs 16, 1 and the note on 2 Kgs 14, 1f.

15, 35: The Upper Gate: also the Gate of Benjamin; cf Jer 20, 2; Ez 9, 2.

l: 32-38: 2 Chr 27, 1-4. 7-9.   *m:* 1-4: 2 Chr 28, 1-4.

Ahaz, son of Jotham, king of Judah, began to reign. [2]Ahaz was twenty years old when he became king, and he reigned sixteen years in Jerusalem. He did not please the LORD, his God, like his forefather David, [3]but conducted himself like the kings of Israel, and even immolated his son by fire, in accordance with the abominable practice of the nations whom the LORD had cleared out of the way of the Israelites.[n] [4]Further, he sacrificed and burned incense on the high places, on hills, and under every leafy tree.[o]

[5]Then Rezin, king of Aram, and Pekah, son of Remaliah, king of Israel, came up to Jerusalem to attack it. Although they besieged Ahaz, they were unable to conquer him.[p] [6]At the same time the king of Edom recovered Elath for Edom, driving the Judeans out of it. The Edomites then entered Elath, which they have occupied until the present.[q]

[7]Meanwhile, Ahaz sent messengers to Tiglath-pileser, king of Assyria, with the plea: "I am your servant and your son. Come up and rescue me from the clutches of the king of Aram and the king of Israel, who are attacking me."[r] [8]Ahaz took the silver and gold that were in the temple of the LORD and in the palace treasuries and sent them as a present to the king of Assyria,[s] [9]who listened to him and moved against Damascus, which he captured. He deported its inhabitants to Kir and put Rezin to death.[*]

[10]King Ahaz went to Damascus to meet Tiglath-pileser, king of Assyria. When he saw the altar in Damascus, King Ahaz sent to Uriah the priest a model of the altar and a detailed design of its construction.

[11]Uriah the priest built an altar according to the plans which King Ahaz sent him from Damascus, and had it completed by the time the king returned home. [12]On his arrival from Damascus, the king inspected this altar, then went up to it and offered sacrifice on it, [13]burning his holocaust and cereal-offering, pouring out his libation, and sprinkling the blood of his peace-offerings on the altar.[t] [14]The bronze altar that stood before the LORD he brought from the front of the temple—that is, from the space between the new altar and the temple of the LORD—and set it on the north side of his altar. [15]"Upon the large altar," King Ahaz commanded Uriah the priest, "burn the morning holocaust and the evening cereal-offering, the royal holocaust and cereal-offering, as well as the holocausts, cereal-offerings, and libations of the people. You must also sprinkle on it all the blood of holocausts and sacrifices. But the old bronze altar shall be mine for consultation."[*] [16]Uriah the priest did just as King Ahaz had commanded. [17]King Ahaz detached the frames from the bases and removed the lavers from them; he also took down the bronze sea from the bronze oxen that supported it, and set it on a stone pavement.[v] [18]In deference to the king of Assyria he removed from the temple of the LORD the emplacement which had been built in the temple for a throne, and the outer entrance for the king.[*] [19]The rest of the acts of Ahaz are recorded in the book of the chronicles of the kings of Judah.[w] [20]Ahaz rested with his ancestors and was buried with them in the City of David. His son Hezekiah succeeded him as king.

16, 9: Firmly dated events bearing on chapters 16 through 20 are: the fall of Damascus (16, 9) in 732 B.C., the fall of Samaria (18, 9-11) in 721 B.C., and Sennacherib's invasion of Judah (18, 13) in 701 B.C., which is equated both in Kgs and in Is 36, 1 with the 14th year of Hezekiah. These data make it necessary to credit Ahaz with at least a twenty-year reign, between 735 and c. 715 B.C., and to exclude the correlations between Hoshea of Israel and Hezekiah in chapter 18.

If the 14th-year correspondence for 701 B.C. is given up, other arrangements are possible. The alleged ages of Jotham (15, 33), Ahaz (16, 2), and Hezekiah (18, 2) at their successive accessions to the throne do not argue for an early date for Hezekiah; but one or more of these may be artificial. Azariah (15, 1-7; Is 6, 1) was still on the throne of Judah in 743 B.C.

16, 15: For consultation: perhaps the introduction into Judah of the Babylonian practice of omen sacrifices; cf Ez 21, 16.

16, 18: Emplacement . . . for a throne, and the outer entrance for the king: signs of sovereignty for the Hebrew kings.

n: Lv 18, 21. o: Dt 12, 2. p: 2 Chr 28, 5f. q: 2 Chr 28, 17. r: 2 Chr 28, 16. s: 2 Chr 28, 21. t: 2 Chr 28, 23. u: Ex 29, 38f; Nm 28, 3f. v: 2 Chr 28, 24. w: 2 Chr 28, 26f.

CHAPTER 17

See RG
129-34

Hoshea of Israel. [1]In the twelfth year of Ahaz, king of Judah, Hoshea, son of Elah, began his nine-year reign over Israel in Samaria. [2]He did evil in the sight of the LORD, yet not to the extent of the kings of Israel before him. [3]Shalmaneser,* king of Assyria, advanced against him, and Hoshea became his vassal and paid him tribute.[x] [4]But the king of Assyria found Hoshea guilty of conspiracy for sending envoys to the king of Egypt at Sais, and for failure to pay the annual tribute to his Assyrian overlord. [5]For this, the king of Assyria arrested and imprisoned Hoshea; he then occupied the whole land and attacked Samaria, which he besieged for three years. [6]In the ninth year of Hoshea, the king of Assyria* took Samaria, and deported the Israelites to Assyria, settling them in Halah, at the Habor, a river of Gozan, and in the cities of the Medes.[y]

[7]This came about because the Israelites sinned against the LORD, their God, who had brought them up from the land of Egypt, from under the domination of Pharaoh, king of Egypt, and because they venerated other gods. [8]They followed the rites of the nations whom the LORD had cleared out of the way of the Israelites [and the kings of Israel whom they set up]. [9]They adopted unlawful practices toward the LORD, their God. They built high places in all their settlements, the watchtowers as well as the walled cities. [10]They set up pillars and sacred poles for themselves on every high hill and under every leafy tree.[z] [11]There, on all the high places, they burned incense like the nations whom the LORD had sent into exile at their coming. They did evil things that provoked the LORD, [12]and served idols, although the LORD had told them, "You must not do this."

[13]And though the LORD warned Israel and Judah by every prophet and seer, "Give up your evil ways and keep my commandments and statutes, in accordance with the entire law which I enjoined on your fathers and which I sent you by my servants the prophets," [14a]they did not listen, but were as stiff-necked as their fathers, who had not believed in the LORD, their God. [15]They rejected his statutes, the covenant which he had made with their fathers, and the warnings which he had given them. The vanity they pursued, they themselves became: they followed the surrounding nations whom the LORD had commanded them not to imitate.[b] [16]They disregarded all the commandments of the LORD, their God, and made for themselves two molten calves; they also made a sacred pole and worshiped all the host of heaven, and served Baal.[c] [17d]They immolated their sons and daughters by fire, practiced fortune-telling and divination, and sold themselves into evildoing in the LORD's sight, provoking him [18]till, in his great anger against Israel, the LORD put them away out of his sight. Only the tribe of Judah was left.

[19]Even the people of Judah, however, did not keep the commandments of the LORD, their God, but followed the rites practiced by Israel. [20]So the LORD rejected the whole race of Israel. He afflicted them and delivered them over to plunderers, finally casting them out from before him. [21]When he tore Israel away from the house of David, they made Jeroboam, son of Nebat, king: he drove the Israelites away from the LORD, causing them to commit a great sin.[e] [22]The Israelites imitated Jeroboam in all the sins he committed, nor would they desist from them. [23]Finally, the LORD put Israel away out of his sight as he had foretold through all his servants, the prophets; and Israel went into exile from their native soil to Assyria, an exile lasting to the present.[f]

[24]The king of Assyria brought people

17, 3: Shalmaneser: son and successor of Tiglath-pileser.

17, 6: The king of Assyria: Shalmaneser's successor and usurper, Sargon II.

x: 2 Kgs 18, 9; Tb 1, 2.   y: 2 Kgs 18, 10f.   z: Ex 23, 24; 34, 13; Dt 12, 2.   a: Jer 25, 5; Dt 9, 13.   b: Jer 2, 5.   c: 1 Kgs 12, 28; Ex 34, 13; Dt 4, 19; 17, 2f.   d: Lv 18, 21; Dt 18, 10.   e: 1 Kgs 12, 19f; 12, 26-33.   f: Jer 25, 9.

Haran
Carchemish · Gozan
· Nineveh
Aleppo · Tiphsah
Arvad · · Hamath   ASSYRIA
Byblos
Tyre · · Damascus
Mediterranean Sea
· SAMARIA

ARUBU (ARABS)

Caspian Sea
Lake Urmia

MEDIA

· Ecbatana
Behistun·

Tigris River
Euphrates River

Persian Gulf

Red Sea

N

0   100   200   300 Mi.
0 100 200 300 400 500 Km.

Exile of Northern Kingdom

from Babylon, Cuthah, Avva, Hamath, and Sepharvaim, and settled them in the cities of Samaria in place of the Israelites. They took possession of Samaria and dwelt in its cities. ²⁵When they first settled there, they did not venerate the LORD, so he sent lions among them that killed some of their number. ²⁶A report reached the king of Assyria: "The nations whom you deported and settled in the cities of Samaria do not know how to worship the God of the land, and he has sent lions among them that are killing them, since they do not know how to worship the God of the land." ²⁷The king of Assyria gave the order, "Send back one of the priests whom I deported, to go there and settle, to teach them how to worship the God of the land." ²⁸So one of the priests who had been deported from Samaria returned and settled in Bethel, and taught them how to venerate the LORD.

²⁹But these peoples began to make their own gods in the various cities in which they were living; in the shrines on the high places which the Samaritans had made, each people set up gods.ᵍ ³⁰Thus the Babylonians made Marduk and his consort; the men of Cuth made Nergal; the men of Hamath made Ashima; ³¹the men of Avva made Nibhaz and Tartak; and the men of Sepharvaim immolated their children by fire to their city gods, King Hadad and his consort Anath. ³²They also venerated the LORD, choosing from their number priests for the high places, who officiated for them in the shrines on the high places.ʰ ³³But, while venerating the LORD, they served their own gods, following the worship of the nations from among whom they had been deported.

³⁴To this day they worship according to their ancient rites.* [They did not venerate the LORD nor observe the statutes and regulations, the law and commandments, which the LORD enjoined on the descendants of Jacob,

17, 34-40: They did not . . . earlier manner: this passage is an adaptation of language denouncing the Israelites to make it applicable to the later Samaritan sect of postexilic times. The original bearing of the discourse (vv 13-15) can be seen by reading it between vv 22 and 23. Cf also 2 Kgs 18, 12.

g: Jn 4, 9.   h: 1 Kgs 12, 31.

445

whom he had named Israel.[i] [35]When he made a covenant with them, he commanded them: "You must not venerate other gods, nor worship them, nor serve them, nor offer sacrifice to them.[j] [36]The LORD, who brought you up from the land of Egypt with great power and outstretched arm: him shall you venerate, him shall you worship, and to him shall you sacrifice. [37]You must be careful to observe forever the statutes and regulations, the law and commandment, which he wrote for you, and you must not venerate other gods. [38]The covenant which I made with you, you must not forget; you must not venerate other gods. [39]But the LORD, your God, you must venerate; it is he who will deliver you from the power of all your enemies." [40]They did not listen, however, but continued in their earlier manner.] [41]Thus these nations venerated the LORD, but also served their idols. And their sons and grandsons, to this day, are doing as their fathers did.

II: The Kingdom of Judah after 721 B.C.

CHAPTER 18

See RG 134—35

Hezekiah. [1k]In the third year of Hoshea, son of Elah, king of Israel, Hezekiah, son of Ahaz, king of Judah, began to reign. [2]He was twenty-five years old when he became king, and he reigned twenty-nine years in Jerusalem. His mother's name was Abi, daughter of Zechariah. [3]He pleased the LORD, just as his forefather David had done. [4]It was he who removed the high places, shattered the pillars, and cut down the sacred poles. He smashed the bronze serpent called Nehushtan which Moses had made, because up to that time the Israelites were burning incense to it.[l] [5]He put his trust in the LORD, the God of Israel; and neither before him nor after him was there anyone like him among all the kings of Judah. [6]Loyal to the LORD, Hez-

ekiah never turned away from him, but observed the commandments which the LORD had given Moses. [7]The LORD was with him, and he prospered in all that he set out to do. He rebelled against the king of Assyria and did not serve him. [8]He also subjugated the watchtowers and walled cities of the Philistines, all the way to Gaza and its territory.

[9]In the fourth year of King Hezekiah, which was the seventh year of Hoshea, son of Elah, king of Israel, Shalmaneser, king of Assyria, attacked Samaria, laid siege to it,* [10m]and after three years captured it. In the sixth year of Hezekiah, the ninth year of Hoshea, king of Israel, Samaria was taken. [11]The king of Assyria then deported the Israelites to Assyria and settled them in Halah, at the Habor, a river of Gozan, and in the cities of the Medes. [12]This came about because they had not heeded the warning of the LORD, their God, but violated his covenant, not heeding and not fulfilling the commandments of Moses, the servant of the LORD.[n]

Invasion of Sennacherib. [13*]In the fourteenth year of King Hezekiah, Sennacherib,* king of Assyria, went on an expedition against all the fortified cities of Judah and captured them.[o] [14]Hezekiah, king of Judah, sent this message to the king of Assyria at Lachish: "I have done wrong. Leave me, and I will pay whatever tribute you impose on me." The king of Assyria exacted three hundred talents of silver and thirty talents of gold from Hezekiah, king of Judah. [15]Hezekiah paid him all the funds there were in the temple of the LORD and in the palace treasuries. [16]He broke up the door panels and the uprights of the temple of the LORD which he himself had ordered to be overlaid with gold, and gave the gold to the king of Assyria.[p]

[17]The king of Assyria sent the general, the lord chamberlain, and the commander* from Lachish with a great army to King Hezekiah at Jerusalem. They went up, and on their arrival

---

18, 9: See note on 2 Kgs 16, 9.

18, 13—20, 11: Duplication of Is 36, 1—38, 8. 21. 22.

18, 13: Sennacherib succeeded Sargon II as king of Assyria. His Judean campaign was waged in 701 B.C. See note on 2 Kgs 16, 9.

18, 17: General, the lord chamberlain . . . commander: the text lists three major functionaries by their Assyrian titles, of

which only the first, more nearly "lord lieutenant," is military in origin; the commander was technically the king's chief butler.

i: Gn 32, 29.   *j:* Ex 20, 3ff.   *k:* 1ff: 2 Chr 28, 27; 29, 1f.   *l:* Ex 23, 24; 34, 13; Nm 21, 9; Dt 12, 2; 2 Chr 31, 1; Wis 16, 6; Jn 3, 14.   *m:* 10f: 2 Kgs 17, 6; Tb 1, 2.   *n:* 2 Kgs 17, 7-18.   *o:* 2 Chr 32, 1ff; Sir 48, 18; Is 36, 1.   *p:* 1 Kgs 6, 20-22.

in Jerusalem, stopped at the conduit of the upper pool on the highway of the fuller's field.*q* *18*They called for the king, who sent out to them Eliakim, son of Hilkiah, the master of the palace; Shebnah the scribe; and the herald Joah, son of Asaph.*r* *19*The commander said to them, "Tell Hezekiah, 'Thus says the great king, the king of Assyria: On what do you base this confidence of yours? *20*Do you think mere words substitute for strategy and might in war? On whom, then, do you rely, that you rebel against me? *21*This Egypt, the staff on which you rely, is in fact a broken reed which pierces the hand of anyone who leans on it. That is what Pharaoh, king of Egypt, is to all who rely on him.*s* *22*But if you say to me, We rely on the LORD, our God, is not he the one whose high places and altars Hezekiah has removed, commanding Judah and Jerusalem to worship before this altar in Jerusalem?'

23"Now, make a wager with my lord, the king of Assyria: I will give you two thousand horses if you can put riders on them. *24*How then can you repulse even one of the least servants of my lord, relying as you do on Egypt for chariots and horsemen? *25*Was it without the LORD's will that I have come up to destroy this place? The LORD said to me, 'Go up and destroy that land!' "

*26*Then Eliakim, son of Hilkiah, and Shebnah and Joah said to the commander: "Please speak to your servants in Aramaic; we understand it. Do not speak to us in Judean within earshot of the people who are on the wall."

*27*But the commander replied: "Was it to your master and to you that my lord sent me to speak these words? Was it not rather to the men sitting on the wall, who, with you, will have to eat their own excrement and drink their urine?" *28*Then the commander stepped forward and cried out in a loud voice in Judean, "Listen to the words of the great king, the king of Assyria. *29*Thus says the king: 'Do not let Hezekiah deceive you, since he cannot deliver you out of my hand. *30*Let not Hezekiah induce you to rely on the LORD, saying, The LORD will surely save us; this city will not be handed over to the king of Assyria. *31*Do not listen to Hezekiah, for the

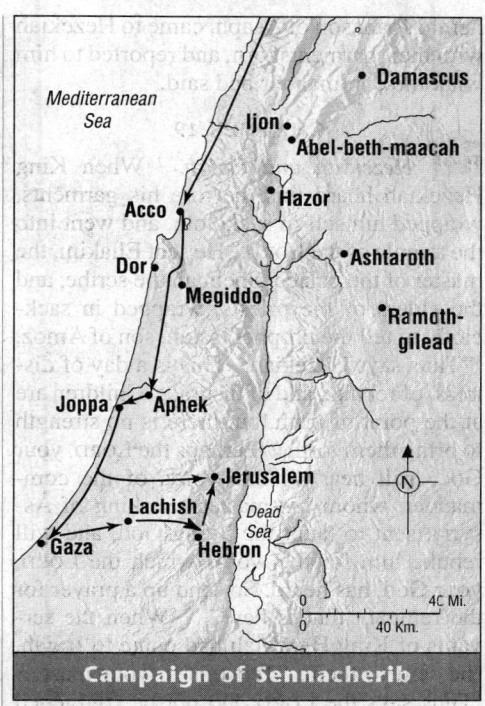

Campaign of Sennacherib

king of Assyria says: Make peace with me and surrender! Then each of you will eat of his own vine and of his own fig-tree, and drink the water of his own cistern, *32*until I come to take you to a land like your own, a land of grain and wine, of bread and orchards, of olives, oil and fruit syrup. Choose life, not death. Do not listen to Hezekiah when he would seduce you by saying, The LORD will rescue us. *33*Has any of the gods of the nations ever rescued his land from the hand of the king of Assyria? *34*Where are the gods of Hamath and Arpad? Where are the gods of Sepharvaim, Hena, and Avva? Where are the gods of the land of Samaria?*t* *35*Which of the gods for all these lands ever rescued his land from my hand? Will the LORD then rescue Jerusalem from my hand?' " *36*But the people remained silent and did not answer him one word, for the king had ordered them not to answer him.

*37*Then the master of the palace, Eliakim, son of Hilkiah, Shebnah the scribe, and the

q: 2 Chr 32, 9; Is 36, 1ff.   *r:* Is 22, 13-25.   *s:* Is 30, 1-7; 31, 1-3; Ez 29, 6-7.   *t:* 2 Kgs 17, 24.

herald Joah, son of Asaph, came to Hezekiah with their garments torn, and reported to him what the commander had said.

See RG 134–35

CHAPTER 19

Hezekiah and Isaiah. [1u]When King Hezekiah heard this, he tore his garments, wrapped himself in sackcloth, and went into the temple of the LORD. [2]He sent Eliakim, the master of the palace, Shebnah the scribe, and the elders of the priests, wrapped in sackcloth, to tell the prophet Isaiah, son of Amoz, [3]"Thus says Hezekiah: 'This is a day of distress, of rebuke, and of disgrace. Children are at the point of birth, but there is no strength to bring them forth.[*] [4]Perhaps the LORD, your God, will hear all the words of the commander, whom his master, the king of Assyria, sent to taunt the living God, and will rebuke him for the words which the LORD, your God, has heard. So send up a prayer for the remnant that is here.' " [5]When the servants of King Hezekiah had come to Isaiah, [6]he said to them, "Tell this to your master: 'Thus says the LORD: Do not be frightened by the words you have heard, with which the servants of the king of Assyria have blasphemed me.[v] [7]I am about to put in him such a spirit that, when he hears a certain report, he will return to his own land, and there I will cause him to fall by the sword.' "

[8]When the commander, on his return, heard that the king of Assyria had withdrawn from Lachish, he found him besieging Libnah. [9]The king of Assyria heard a report that Tirhakah, king of Ethiopia, had come out to fight against him. Again he sent envoys to Hezekiah with this message: [10]"Thus shall you say to Hezekiah, king of Judah: 'Do not let your God on whom you rely deceive you by saying that Jerusalem will not be handed over to the king of Assyria. [11]You have heard what the kings of Assyria have done to all other countries: they doomed them! Will you, then, be saved? [12]Did the gods of the nations whom my fathers destroyed save

them? Gozan, Haran, Rezeph, or the Edenites in Telassar?[w] [13]Where are the king of Hamath, the king of Arpad, or the kings of the cities Sepharvaim, Hena and Avva?' "[x]

[14y]Hezekiah took the letter from the hand of the messengers and read it; then he went up to the temple of the LORD, and spreading it out before him, [15]he prayed in the LORD's presence: "O LORD, God of Israel, enthroned upon the cherubim! You alone are God over all the kingdoms of the earth. You have made the heavens and the earth.[z] [16]Incline your ear, O LORD, and listen! Open your eyes, O LORD, and see! Hear the words of Sennacherib which he sent to taunt the living God. [17]Truly, O LORD, the kings of Assyria have laid waste the nations and their lands, [18]and cast their gods into the fire; they destroyed them because they were not gods, but the work of human hands, wood and stone.[a] [19]Therefore, O LORD, our God, save us from the power of this man, that all the kingdoms of the earth may know that you alone, O LORD, are God."[b]

Punishment of Sennacherib. [20]Then Isaiah, son of Amoz, sent this message to Hezekiah: "Thus says the LORD, the God of Israel, in answer to your prayer for help against Sennacherib, king of Assyria: I have listened! [21]This is the word the LORD has spoken concerning him:[*]

" 'She despises you, laughs you to scorn,
    the virgin daughter Zion!
Behind you she wags her head,
    daughter Jerusalem.
[22] Whom have you insulted and blasphemed,
    against whom have you raised your
        voice
And lifted up your eyes on high?
    Against the Holy One of Israel!
[23] Through your servants you have insulted
        the LORD.
    You said: With my many chariots
I climbed the mountain heights,
    the recesses of Lebanon;
I cut down its lofty cedars,

19, 3: See note on Is 37, 3.
19, 21-31: vv 21-28 are addressed to Sennacherib, vv 29-31 to Judah.

u: 1-7: Is 37, 1-7.   *v:* Is 10, 5-19.   *w:* 2 Kgs 17, 6.   *x:* 2 Kgs 18, 34.   *y:* 14-19: 2 Chr 32, 20; Is 37, 14-20.   *z:* Ex 25, 18.   *a:* Jer 10, 3.   *b:* 1 Kgs 18, 24.

its choice cypresses;
I reached the remotest heights,
    its forest park.
24 I dug wells and drank water in foreign
        lands;
I dried up with the soles of my feet
    all the rivers of Egypt.

25 " 'Have you not heard?
    Long ago I prepared it,
From days of old I planned it.
    Now I have brought it to pass:
That you should reduce fortified cities
    into heaps of ruins,
26 While their inhabitants, shorn of power,
    are dismayed and ashamed,
Becoming like the plants of the field, like
        the green growth,
    like the scorched grass on the
        housetops.
27 I am aware whether you stand or sit;
    I know whether you come or go,c
28   and also your rage against me.
Because of your rage against me
    and your fury which has reached my
        ears,
I will put my hook in your nose
    and my bit in your mouth,
    and make you return the way you came.

29 " 'This shall be a sign for you:
    this year you shall eat the aftergrowth,
    next year, what grows of itself;
But in the third year, sow and reap,
    plant vineyards and eat their fruit!
30 The remaining survivors of the house of
        Judah
    shall again strike root below
    and bear fruit above.
31 For out of Jerusalem shall come a
        remnant,
    and from Mount Zion, survivors.
    The zeal of the LORD of hosts shall do
        this.'

32"Therefore, thus says the LORD concerning the king of Assyria: 'He shall not
reach this city, nor shoot an arrow at it, nor
come before it with a shield, nor cast up siegeworks against it. 33He shall return by the same
way he came, without entering the city, says
the LORD. 34I will shield and save this city for
my own sake, and for the sake of my servant
David.' "d

35That night the angel of the LORD went
forth and struck down one hundred and
eighty-five thousand men in the Assyrian
camp. Early the next morning, there they
were, all the corpses of the dead.e 36So Sennacherib, the king of Assyria, broke camp,
and went back home to Nineveh.

37When he was worshiping in the temple
of his god Nisroch, his sons Adrammelech
and Sharezer slew him with the sword and
fled into the land of Ararat. His son Esarhaddon reigned in his stead.

CHAPTER 20

See RG
134-35

Hezekiah's Illness. 1f In those days,
when Hezekiah was mortally ill, the prophet
Isaiah, son of Amoz, came and said to him:
"Thus says the LORD: 'Put your house in order, for you are about to die; you shall not recover.' " 2He turned his face to the wall and
prayed to the LORD: 3"O LORD, remember
how faithfully and wholeheartedly I conducted myself in your presence, doing what
was pleasing to you!" And Hezekiah wept
bitterly.

4Before Isaiah had left the central courtyard, the word of the LORD came to him: 5"Go
back and tell Hezekiah, the leader of my people: 'Thus says the LORD, the God of your
forefather David: I have heard your prayer and
seen your tears. I will heal you. In three days
you shall go up to the LORD's temple; 6I will
add fifteen years to your life. I will rescue you
and this city from the hand of the king of Assyria; I will be a shield to this city for my own
sake, and for the sake of my servant David.' "

7Isaiah then ordered a poultice of figs to
be brought and applied to the boil, that he
might recover. 8Then Hezekiah asked Isaiah,
"What is the sign that the LORD will heal me
and that I shall go up to the temple of the
LORD on the third day?" 9Isaiah replied,

c: Ps 139, 2f.   d: 2 Sm 7, 12; Hos 1, 7.   e: Sir 48, 21; 2 Chr 32, 21f; Is 37, 36-38; 1 Mc 7, 41; 2 Mc 8, 19.   f: 1-9: 2 Chr 32, 24; Is 38, 1-8.

"This will be the sign for you from the LORD that he will do what he has promised: Shall the shadow go forward or back ten steps?"

10"It is easy for the shadow to advance ten steps," Hezekiah answered. "Rather, let it go back ten steps." *11*So the prophet Isaiah invoked the LORD, who made the shadow retreat the ten steps it had descended on the staircase to the terrace of Ahaz.

12*At that time, when Merodach-baladan, son of Baladan, king of Babylon, heard that Hezekiah had been ill, he sent letters and gifts to him.*g* *13*Hezekiah was pleased at this, and therefore showed the messengers his whole treasury, his silver, gold, spices and fine oil, his armory, and all that was in his storerooms; there was nothing in his house or in all his realm that Hezekiah did not show them.

*14*Then Isaiah the prophet came to King Hezekiah and asked him: "What did these men say to you? Where did they come from?" "They came from a distant land, from Babylon," replied Hezekiah. *15*"What did they see in your house?" the prophet asked. "They saw everything in my house," answered Hezekiah. "There is nothing in my storerooms that I did not show them."

*16*Then Isaiah said to Hezekiah: "Hear the word of the LORD: *17*The time is coming when all that is in your house, and everything that your fathers have stored up until this day, shall be carried off to Babylon; nothing shall be left, says the LORD. *18*Some of your own bodily descendants shall be taken and made servants in the palace of the king of Babylon."

*19*Hezekiah replied to Isaiah, "The word of the LORD which you have spoken is favorable." For he thought, "There will be peace and security in my lifetime."

*20*The rest of the acts of Hezekiah, all his valor, and his construction of the pool and conduit* by which water was brought into the city, are written in the book of the chronicles of the kings of Judah.*h* *21*Hezekiah rested with his ancestors and his son Manasseh succeeded him as king.

CHAPTER 21

Reign of Manasseh. *1i*Manasseh was See RG 134-35 twelve years old when he began to reign, and he reigned fifty-five years in Jerusalem. His mother's name was Hephzibah. *2*He did evil in the sight of the LORD, following the abominable practices of the nations whom the LORD had cleared out of the way of the Israelites. *3*He rebuilt the high places which his father Hezekiah had destroyed. He erected altars to Baal, and also set up a sacred pole, as Ahab, king of Israel, had done. He worshiped and served the whole host of heaven.*j* *4*He built altars in the temple of the LORD, about which the LORD had said, "I will establish my name in Jerusalem"— *5*altars for the whole host of heaven, in the two courts of the temple.*k*

*6*He immolated his son by fire. He practiced soothsaying and divination, and reintroduced the consulting of ghosts and spirits. He did much evil in the LORD's sight and provoked him to anger.

*7*The Asherah idol he had made, he set up in the temple, of which the LORD had said to David and to his son Solomon: "In this temple and in Jerusalem, which I have chosen out of all the tribes of Israel, I shall place my name forever.*l* *8*I will not in future allow Israel to be driven off the land I gave their fathers, provided that they are careful to observe all I have commanded them, the entire law which my servant Moses enjoined upon them." *9*But they did not listen, and Manasseh misled them into doing even greater evil than the nations whom the LORD had destroyed at the coming of the Israelites.

*10*Then the LORD spoke through his servants the prophets: *11*"Because Manasseh, king of Judah, has practiced these abominations and has done greater evil than all that was done by the Amorites before him, and has led Judah into sin by his idols,*m* *12*therefore thus says the LORD, the God of Israel: 'I will bring such evil on Jerusalem and Judah that, whenever anyone hears of it, his ears

20, 12–19: Duplication of Is 39, 1–8.

20, 20: Pool and conduit: Hezekiah's tunnel; cf 2 Chr 32, 30.

g: 12f: Is 39, 1f; 2 Chr 32, 27ff. *h:* 2 Chr 32, 30; Sir 48, 17. *i:* 1-10: 2 Chr 33, 1-10. *j:* 2 Kgs 17, 16; 1 Kgs 18, 4; 16, 32f. *k:* Lv 18, 21. *l:* 2 Sm 7, 13; 1 Kgs 8, 16; 9, 3. *m:* 1 Kgs 21, 26; Jer 15, 4.

Manasseh

Manasseh is credited with the longest reign, fifty-five years, of any king of Israel or Judah but he "did evil in the sight of the LORD" (21, 2). He set up a sacred pole, which was an important part of the worship of the Canaanite goddess Asherah. The host of heaven that he worshiped (v. 3) refers to the astral gods—sun, moon, and stars. He practiced child sacrifice and consulted ghosts and spirits. All such practices are condemned by the law (Dt 12, 29–31; 17, 3; 18, 10–12).

shall ring. [13]I will measure Jerusalem with the same cord as I did Samaria, and with the plummet I used for the house of Ahab. I will wipe Jerusalem clean as one wipes a dish, wiping it inside and out.[n] [14]I will cast off the survivors of my inheritance and deliver them into enemy hands, to become a prey and a booty for all their enemies, [15]because they have done evil in my sight and provoked me from the day their fathers came forth from Egypt until today.' "

[16]In addition to the sin which he caused Judah to commit, Manasseh did evil in the sight of the LORD, shedding so much innocent blood as to fill the length and breadth of Jerusalem. [17]The rest of the acts of Manasseh, the sin he committed and all that he did, are written in the book of the chronicles of the kings of Judah.[o] [18]Manasseh rested with his ancestors and was buried in his palace garden, the garden of Uzza. His son Amon succeeded him as king.

Reign of Amon. [19p]Amon was twenty-two years old when he began to reign, and he reigned two years in Jerusalem. His mother's name was Meshullemeth, daughter of Haruz of Jotbah. [20]He did evil in the sight of the LORD, as his father Manasseh had done. [21]He followed exactly the path his father had trod, serving and worshiping the idols his father had served. [22]He abandoned the LORD, the God of his fathers, and did not follow the path of the LORD. [23]Subjects of Amon conspired against him and slew the king in his palace, [24]but the people of the land then slew all who had conspired against King Amon, and proclaimed his son Josiah king in his stead. [25]The rest of the acts that Amon did are written in the book of the chronicles of the kings of Judah. [26]He was buried in his own grave in the garden of Uzza, and his son Josiah succeeded him as king.

CHAPTER 22

See RG
134-35

Reign of Josiah. [1q]Josiah was eight years old when he began to reign, and he reigned thirty-one years in Jerusalem. His mother's name was Jedidah, daughter of Adaiah of Bozkath. [2]He pleased the LORD and conducted himself unswervingly just as his ancestor David had done.

[3r]In his eighteenth year, King Josiah sent the scribe Shaphan,[*] son of Azaliah, son of Meshullam, to the temple of the LORD with orders to [4s]go to the high priest Hilkiah and have him smelt down the precious metals that had been donated to the temple of the LORD, which the doorkeepers had collected from the people. [5]They were to be consigned to the master workmen in the temple of the LORD, who should then pay them out to the carpenters, builders, and lumbermen making repairs on the temple, [6]and for the purchase of wood and hewn stone for the temple repairs. [7]No reckoning was asked of them regarding the funds consigned to them, because they held positions of trust.

The Book of the Law. [8]The high priest Hilkiah informed the scribe Shaphan, "I have found the book of the law in the temple of the

---

22, 3: Shaphan: head of a prominent family in the reign of Josiah, secretary to the king, bearer and reader of the newfound book of the law (vv 3-13; 2 Chr 34, 8f. 15-20). He and his sons favored the reform of King Josiah and supported the prophet Jeremiah; cf Jer 26, 24.

---

n: Is 34, 11; Am 7, 7-9; Lam 2, 8.   *o:* 2 Chr 33, 18ff.   *p:* 19-26: 2 Chr 33, 21-25.   *q:* 1f: 2 Chr 34, 1f.   *r:* 3-13: 2 Chr 34, 8-21.   *s:* 4-7: 2 Kgs 12, 11-16.

LORD." Hilkiah gave the book to Shaphan, who read it. [9]Then the scribe Shaphan went to the king and reported, "Your servants have smelted down the metals available in the temple and have consigned them to the master workmen in the temple of the LORD." [10]The scribe Shaphan also informed the king that the priest Hilkiah had given him a book, and then read it aloud to the king. [11]When the king had heard the contents of the book of the law, he tore his garments[t] [12]and issued this command to Hilkiah the priest, Ahikam, son of Shaphan, Achbor, son of Micaiah, the scribe Shaphan, and the king's servant Asaiah: [13]"Go, consult the LORD for me, for the people, for all Judah, about the stipulations of this book that has been found, for the anger of the LORD has been set furiously ablaze against us, because our fathers did not obey the stipulations of this book, nor fulfill our written obligations."

[14]So Hilkiah the priest, Ahikam, Achbor, Shaphan, and Asaiah betook themselves to the Second Quarter in Jerusalem, where the prophetess Huldah resided. She was the wife of Shallum, son of Tikvah, son of Harhas, keeper of the wardrobe. When they had spoken to her, [15]she said to them, "Thus says the LORD, the God of Israel: 'Say to the man who sent you to me, [16]Thus says the LORD: I will bring upon this place and upon its inhabitants all the evil that is threatened in the book which the king of Judah has read. [17]Because they have forsaken me and have burned incense to other gods, provoking me by everything to which they turn their hands, my anger is ablaze against this place and it cannot be extinguished.'

[18]"But to the king of Judah who sent you to consult the LORD, give this response: 'Thus says the LORD, the God of Israel: As for the threats you have heard, [19]because you were heartsick and have humbled yourself before the LORD when you heard my threats that this place and its inhabitants would become a desolation and a curse; because you tore your garments and wept before me; I in turn have listened, says the LORD. [20]I will therefore gather you to your ancestors; you shall go to your grave in peace, and your eyes shall not see all the evil I will bring upon this place.' " This they reported to the king.

CHAPTER 23

See RG 134-35

[1u]The king then had all the elders of Judah and of Jerusalem summoned together before him. [2]The king went up to the temple of the LORD with all the men of Judah and all the inhabitants of Jerusalem: priests, prophets, and all the people, small and great. He had the entire contents of the book of the covenant that had been found in the temple of the LORD, read out to them. [3]Standing by the column, the king made a covenant before the LORD that they would follow him and observe his ordinances, statutes and decrees with their whole hearts and souls, thus reviving the terms of the covenant which were written in this book. And all the people stood as participants in the covenant.

[4]Then the king commanded the high priest Hilkiah, his vicar, and the doorkeepers to remove from the temple of the LORD all the objects that had been made for Baal, Asherah, and the whole host of heaven. He had these burned outside Jerusalem on the slopes of the Kidron and their ashes carried to Bethel.[v] [5]He also put an end to the pseudo-priests whom the kings of Judah had appointed to burn incense on the high places in the cities of Judah and in the vicinity of Jerusalem, as well as those who burned incense to Baal, to the sun, moon, and signs of the Zodiac, and to the whole host of heaven.[w] [6]From the temple of the LORD he also removed the sacred pole, to the Kidron Valley, outside Jerusalem; there he had it burned and beaten to dust, which was then scattered over the common graveyard.[x] [7]He tore down the apartments of the cult prostitutes* which were in the temple of the LORD, and in which the women wove garments for the Asherah.[y]

[8]He brought in all the priests from the cities of Judah, and then defiled, from Geba to Beersheba, the high places where they had offered

---

23, 7: Cult prostitutes: of both sexes; cf 1 Kgs 14, 24.

t: 11-20: 2 Chr 34, 19-28.   *u:* 1-5: 2 Chr 34, 29-33.   *v:* 2 Chr 34, 3-5; Sir 49, 3.   *w:* Dt 17, 3ff.   *x:* Dt 16, 21; 1 Kgs 14, 23.   *y:* 1 Kgs 14, 24; Dt 23, 18f.

Topheth (23, 10) was a valley that marked Jerusalem's western border. Also known as the valley of Hinnom, it became Jerusalem's trash dump and was used by Jesus as the image for hell (Gehenna, see Mt 10, 28). It was despised because it had served as a place of child sacrifice to the Ammonite god Molech.

incense. He also tore down the high place of the satyrs, which was at the entrance of the Gate of Joshua, governor of the city, to the left as one enters the city gate.[z] [9]The priests of the high places could not function at the altar of the LORD in Jerusalem; but they, along with their relatives, ate the unleavened bread.

[10]The king also defiled Topheth in the Valley of Ben-hinnom, so that there would no longer be any immolation of sons or daughters by fire* in honor of Molech.[a] [11]He did away with the horses which the kings of Judah had dedicated to the sun; these were at the entrance of the temple of the LORD, near the chamber of Nathan-melech the eunuch, which was in the large building.* The chariots of the sun he destroyed by fire. [12]He also demolished the altars made by the kings of Judah on the roof (the roof terrace of Ahaz), and the altars made by Manasseh in the two courts of the temple of the LORD. He pulverized them and threw the dust into the Kidron Valley.[b] [13]The king defiled the high places east of Jerusalem, south of the Mount of Misconduct,* which Solomon, king of Israel, had built in honor of Astarte, the Sidonian horror, of Chemosh, the Moabite horror, and of Milcom, the idol of the Ammonites.[c] [14]He broke to pieces the pillars, cut down the sacred poles, and filled the places where they had been with human bones.[d] [15]Likewise the altar which was at Bethel, the high place built by Jeroboam, son of Nebat, who caused Israel to sin—this same altar and high place he tore down, breaking up the stones and grinding them to powder, and burning the Asherah.[e]

[16]When Josiah turned and saw the graves there on the mountainside, he ordered the bones taken from the graves and burned on the altar, and thus defiled it in fulfillment of the word of the LORD which the man of God had proclaimed as Jeroboam was standing by the altar on the feast day. When the king looked up and saw the grave of the man of God who had proclaimed these words, [17]he asked, "What is that tombstone I see?" The men of the city replied, "It is the grave of the man of God who came from Judah and predicted the very things you have done to the altar of Bethel." [18f]"Let him be," he said, "let no one move his bones." So they left his bones undisturbed together with the bones of the prophet who had come from Samaria.*

[19]Josiah also removed all the shrines on the high places near the cities of Samaria which the kings of Israel had erected, thereby provoking the LORD; he did the very same to them as he had done in Bethel.[g] [20]He slaughtered upon the altars all the priests of the high places that were at the shrines, and burned human bones upon them. Then he returned to Jerusalem.

[21]The king issued a command to all the people to observe the Passover of the LORD, their God, as it was prescribed in that book of the covenant.[h] [22]No Passover such as this had been observed during the period when the Judges ruled Israel, or during the entire period of the kings of Israel and the kings of Judah, [23]until the eighteenth year of King Josiah, when this Passover of the LORD was kept in Jerusalem.

23, 10: Topheth . . . by fire: condemned by Deuteronomic law and denounced by Jeremiah (Dt 12, 31; Jer 7, 29ff; Jer 19).

23, 11: Large building: to the west of the temple area (1 Chr 26, 18), named in the Hebrew by an Egyptian name for a similar construction.

23, 13: Mount of Misconduct: a paranomasia on "Mount of Olives" (in Hebrew Maschit/mishcheh) as suggested by the Targum. Cf Vulgate, "Mount of Offense." Horror . . . idol:

in all three phrases here the Hebrew uses a pejorative designation meaning "abomination."

23, 18: From Samaria: more narrowly, from Bethel; cf 1 Kgs 13, 31f.

z: Dt 12, 2f.   *a:* Lv 18, 21.   *b:* 2 Kgs 21, 5.   *c:* 1 Kgs 11, 7. *d:* Dt 16, 21f; 1 Kgs 14, 23.   *e:* 1 Kgs 12, 31f; 13, 32.   *f:* 1 Kgs 13, 31.   *g:* 2 Chr 34, 6f.   *h:* Dt 16, 1-8; 2 Chr 35, 1ff. 18f

The Reign and Reform of Josiah

Josiah, along with Hezekiah, is one of the good kings of Judah and one of the heroes of the deuteronomistic history. The temple repairs made by Josiah led to the discovery of a copy of the book of the law, which has long been identified as a form of the book of Deuteronomy. He is renowned for his obedience (22, 2; 23, 25) to the law book found in his reign.

²⁴Further, Josiah did away with the consultation of ghosts and spirits, with the household gods, idols,* and all the other horrors to be seen in the land of Judah and in Jerusalem, so that he might carry out the stipulations of the law written in the book that the priest Hilkiah had found in the temple of the LORD.ⁱ

²⁵Before him there had been no king who turned to the LORD as he did, with his whole heart, his whole soul, and his whole strength, in accord with the entire law of Moses; nor could any after him compare with him.ʲ

²⁶Yet, because of all the provocations that Manasseh had given, the LORD did not desist from his fiercely burning anger against Judah. ²⁷The LORD said: "Even Judah will I put out of my sight as I did Israel. I will reject this city, Jerusalem, which I chose, and the temple of which I said, 'There shall my name be.' "ᵏ

²⁸The rest of the acts of Josiah, with all that he did, are written in the book of the chronicles of the kings of Judah.ˡ ²⁹In his time Pharaoh Neco, king of Egypt, went up toward the river Euphrates to the king of Assyria. King Josiah set out to confront him, but was slain at Megiddo at the first encounter.ᵐ ³⁰His servants brought his body on a chariot from Megiddo to Jerusalem, where they buried him in his own grave. Then the people of the land* took Jehoahaz, son of Josiah, anointed him, and proclaimed him king to succeed his father.

Reign of Jehoahaz. ³¹Jehoahaz was twenty-three years old when he began to reign, and he reigned three months in Jerusalem. His mother, whose name was Hamutal, daughter of Jeremiah, was from Libnah.ⁿ

³²He did evil in the sight of the LORD, just as his forebears had done. ³³Pharaoh Neco took him prisoner at Riblah in the land of Hamath, thus ending his reign in Jerusalem. He imposed a fine upon the land of a hundred talents of silver and a talent of gold.* ³⁴Pharaoh Neco then appointed Eliakim, son of Josiah, king in place of his father Josiah; he changed his name to Jehoiakim. Jehoahaz he took away with him to Egypt, where he died. ³⁵Jehoiakim gave the silver and gold to Pharaoh, but taxed the land to raise the amount Pharaoh demanded. He exacted the silver and gold from the people of the land, from each proportionately, to pay Pharaoh Neco.

Reign of Jehoiakim. ³⁶ᵒJehoiakim was twenty-five years old when he began to reign, and he reigned eleven years in Jerusalem. His mother's name was Zebidah, daughter of Pedaiah, from Rumah. ³⁷He did evil in the sight of the LORD, just as his forebears had done.

CHAPTER 24

See RG 134-35

¹ᵖDuring his reign Nebuchadnezzar, king of Babylon, moved against him, and Jehoiakim became his vassal for three years. Then Jehoiakim turned and rebelled against him. ²The LORD loosed against him bands of Chaldeans, Arameans, Moabites, and Ammonites; he loosed them against Judah to destroy it, as the LORD had threatened through his servants the prophets.�q ³This befell Judah because the LORD had stated that he would inexorably put them out of his sight for the sins Manasseh had committed in all that he did; ⁴and especially because of the innocent

---

23, 24: Household gods, idols: teraphim. See note on Gn 31, 19.

23, 30. 35: People of the land: in this period, the phrase referred to "landed gentry"; in later times it meant "the poor." Cf 2 Kgs 24, 14.

23, 33: A talent of gold: some manuscripts of the Greek

and Syriac texts have "ten talents."

i: 2 Kgs 21, 6; Gn 31, 19; Dt 18, 11; Jgs 18, 14.   j: Dt 6, 5.
k: 2 Kgs 24, 2.   l: 2 Chr 35, 26f.   m: 2 Chr 35, 20-24.   n: 2 Chr 36, 2f.   o: 36f: 2 Chr 36, 4f.   p: 1-5: 2 Chr 36, 6ff.   q: 2 Kgs 23, 27.

All Jerusalem

The statement that all Jerusalem was taken captive (v. 14) is an obvious exaggeration. Evidently, the upper class was exiled. This wave of captives included King Jehoiachin and the prophet Ezekiel.

Nebuchadnezzar's Campaign

blood he shed, with which he filled Jerusalem, the LORD would not forgive.ʳ

⁵The rest of the acts of Jehoiakim, with all that he did, are written in the book of the chronicles of the kings of Judah.ˢ ⁶Jehoiakim rested with his ancestors, and his son Jehoiachin succeeded him as king. ⁷The king of Egypt did not again leave his own land, for the king of Babylon had taken all that belonged to the king of Egypt from the wadi of Egypt to the Euphrates River.

Reign of Jehoiachin. ⁸Jehoiachin was eighteen years old when he began to reign, and he reigned three months* in Jerusalem. His mother's name was Nehushta, daughter of Elnathan of Jerusalem. ⁹He did evil in the sight of the LORD, just as his forebears had done.

¹⁰At that time the officials of Nebuchadnezzar, king of Babylon, attacked Jerusalem, and the city came under siege.ᵗ ¹¹Nebuchadnezzar, king of Babylon, himself arrived at the city while his servants were besieging it. ¹²Then Jehoiachin, king of Judah, together with his mother, his ministers, officers, and functionaries, surrendered to the king of Babylon, who, in the eighth year of his reign, took him captive. ¹³He carried off all the treasures of the temple of the LORD and those of the palace, and broke up all the gold utensils that Solomon, king of Israel, had provided in the temple of the LORD, as the LORD had foretold.ᵘ ¹⁴He deported all Jerusalem: all the officers and men of the army, ten thousand in number, and all the craftsmen and smiths. None were left among the people of the land except the poor. ¹⁵He deported Jehoiachin to Babylon, and also led captive from Jerusalem to Babylon the king's mother and wives, his functionaries, and the chief men of the land.ᵛ ¹⁶The king of Babylon also led captive to Babylon all seven thousand men of the army, and a thousand craftsmen and smiths, all of them trained soldiers. ¹⁷In place of Jehoiachin, the king of Babylon appointed his uncle Mattaniah king, and changed his name to Zedekiah.

Reign of Zedekiah. ¹⁸Zedekiah was twenty-one years old when he became king, and he reigned eleven years in Jerusalem. His mother's name was Hamutal, daughter of Jeremiah of Libnah.ʷ ¹⁹He also did evil in the sight of the LORD, just as Jehoiakim had done. ²⁰The LORD's anger befell Jerusalem and Judah till he cast them out from his presence. Thus Zedekiah rebelled against the king of Babylon.ˣ

24, 8: He reigned three months: in the year 597 B.C.

r: 2 Kgs 21, 16. s: 2 Chr 36, 8. t: 2 Chr 36, 10; Dn 1, 1f. u: 2 Kgs 20, 17; Is 39, 6. v: Est A, 3; 2, 6. w: 2 Chr 36, 9; Jer 37, 1f; 52, 1ff. x: 2 Kgs 22, 17; 23, 27.

The Reign of Zedekiah and the Fall of Jerusalem

This section on Zedekiah (24, 18—25, 21) is very similar to Jer 52 and the first part of it to Jer 39, 1–10. Here the exile is blamed mostly on Zedekiah and his generation. Jerusalem fell to the Babylonians in 587 or 586 B.C. Jeremiah 52, 29 gives the number of captives from this deportation as 832.

CHAPTER 25

See RG
134–35

¹*ʸIn the tenth month of the ninth year of Zedekiah's reign, on the tenth day of the month, Nebuchadnezzar, king of Babylon, and his whole army advanced against Jerusalem, encamped around it, and built siege walls on every side. ²The siege of the city continued until the eleventh year of Zedekiah. ³On the ninth day of the fourth month, when famine had gripped the city, and the people had no more bread, ⁴the city walls were breached. Then the king and all the soldiers left the city by night through the gate between the two walls which was near the king's garden. Since the Chaldeans had the city surrounded, they went in the direction of the Arabah. ⁵But the Chaldean army pursued the king and overtook him in the desert near Jericho, abandoned by his whole army.

⁶The king was therefore arrested and brought to Riblah to the king of Babylon, who pronounced sentence on him. ⁷He had Zedekiah's sons slain before his eyes. Then he blinded Zedekiah, bound him with fetters, and had him brought to Babylon.

⁸On the seventh day of the fifth month (this was in the nineteenth year of Nebuchadnezzar, king of Babylon), Nebuzaradan, captain of the bodyguard, came to Jerusalem as the representative of the king of Babylon. ⁹He burned the house of the LORD, the palace of the king, and all the houses of Jerusalem; every large building was destroyed by fire.ᶻ ¹⁰Then the Chaldean troops who were with the captain of the guard tore down the walls that surrounded Jerusalem.

¹¹Then Nebuzaradan, captain of the guard, led into exile the last of the people remaining in the city, and those who had deserted* to the king of Babylon, and the last of the artisans. ¹²But some of the country's poor, Nebuzaradan, captain of the guard, left behind as vinedressers and farmers.

¹³The bronze pillars that belonged to the house of the LORD, and the wheeled carts and the bronze sea in the house of the LORD, the Chaldeans broke into pieces; they carried away the bronze to Babylon.ᵃ ¹⁴They took also the pots, the shovels, the snuffers, the bowls, the pans and all the bronze vessels used for service.ᵇ ¹⁵The fire-holders and the bowls which were of gold or silver the captain of the guard also carried off. ¹⁶The weight in bronze of the two pillars, the bronze sea, and the wheeled carts, all of them furnishings which Solomon had made for the house of the LORD, was never calculated. ¹⁷Each of the pillars was eighteen cubits high; a bronze capital five cubits high surmounted each pillar, and a network with pomegranates encircled the capital, all of bronze; and so for the other pillar, as regards the network.ᶜ

¹⁸The captain of the guard also took Seraiah the high priest, Zephaniah the second priest, and the three keepers of the entry. ¹⁹And from the city he took one courtier, a commander of soldiers, five men in the personal service of the king who were still in the city, the scribe of the army commander, who mustered the people of the land, and sixty of the common people still remaining in the city. ²⁰The captain of the guard, Nebuzaradan, arrested these and brought them to the king of Babylon at Riblah; ²¹the king had them struck down and put to death in Riblah, in the land of Hamath. Thus was Judah exiled from her land.

Governorship of Gedaliah. ²²ᵈAs for the people whom he had allowed to remain in the land of Judah, Nebuchadnezzar, king of Bab-

---

25, 1-30: This chapter parallels Jer 39 and 52; see notes to those parts of Jeremiah.

25, 11: Those who had deserted: perhaps on the advice of Jeremiah; cf Jer 38, 2f.

y: 1-21: Jer 39, 1-10; 52, 4-28.   z: 2 Chr 36, 19; Ps 74, 7.
a: 2 Kgs 16, 17; 1 Kgs 7, 15-39; 2 Chr 3, 15; 36, 18; Jer 27, 19.
b: 1 Kgs 7, 48ff.   c: 1 Kgs 7, 15; Jer 52, 21ff.   d: 22-26: Jer 40, 5. 7—41, 1-3.

ylon, appointed as their governor Gedaliah, son of Ahikam, son of Shaphan. ²³Hearing that the king of Babylon had appointed Gedaliah governor, all the army commanders with their men came to him at Mizpah: Ishmael, son of Nethaniah, Johanan, son of Kareah, Seraiah, son of Tanhumeth the Netophathite, and Jaazaniah, from Beth-maacah. ²⁴Gedaliah gave the commanders and their men his oath. "Do not be afraid of the Chaldean officials," he said to them. "Remain in the country and serve the king of Babylon, and all will be well with you."

²⁵But in the seventh month Ishmael, son of Nethaniah, son of Elishama, of royal descent, came with ten men, attacked Gedaliah and killed him, along with the Jews and Chaldeans who were in Mizpah with him.

²⁶Then all the people, great and small, left with the army commanders and went to Egypt for fear of the Chaldeans.

Release of Jehoiachin. ^{27e}In the thirty-seventh year of the exile of Jehoiachin, king of Judah, on the twenty-seventh day of the twelfth month, Evil-merodach, king of Babylon, in the inaugural year of his own reign, raised up Jehoiachin, king of Judah, from prison. ²⁸He spoke kindly to him and gave him a throne higher than that of the other kings who were with him in Babylon. ²⁹Jehoiachin took off his prison garb and ate at the king's table as long as he lived. ³⁰The allowance granted him by the king was a perpetual allowance, in fixed daily amounts, for as long as he lived.

e: 27-30: Jer 52, 31-34.

See RG 137–44

The First Book of Chronicles

Originally the two books of Chronicles formed, with the Books of Ezra and Nehemiah, a single historical work, uniform in style and basic ideas. The Greek title, *paraleipomena,* means "things omitted, or passed over (in Samuel and Kings)." The Books of Chronicles, however, are more than a supplement to Samuel and Kings; a comparison of the two histories discloses striking differences in scope and purpose. The Books of Chronicles record in some detail the lengthy span from the reign of Saul to the return from the Exile. Unlike the exact science of history today, wherein factual accuracy and impartiality of judgment are the standards for estimating what is of permanent worth, ancient biblical history, with rare exceptions, was less concerned with reporting in precise detail all the facts of a situation than with explaining the meaning of those facts. Such history was primarily interpretative and, in the Old Testament, its purpose was to disclose the action of the living God in the affairs of men. For this reason we speak of it as "sacred history"; its writer's first concern was to bring out the divine or supernatural dimension in history.

This is apparent when we examine the primary objective of the Chronicler in compiling his work. In view of the situation which confronted the Jew-ish people at this time (the end of the fifth century B.C.), the Chronicler realized that Israel's political greatness was a thing of the past. It would be a people under God, or nothing. Yet Israel's past held the key to her future. The Chronicler proposed to establish and defend the legitimate claims of the Davidic monarchy in Israel's history, and to underscore the place of Jerusalem and its divinely established temple worship as the center of religious life for the Jewish community of his day. If Judaism was to survive and prosper, it would have to heed the lessons of the past and devoutly serve Yahweh in the place where he had chosen to dwell, the temple of Jerusalem. From the Chronicler's point of view, David's reign was the ideal to which all subsequent rule in Judah must aspire.

The Chronicler was much more interested in David's religious and cultic influence than in his political power. There is little of royal messianism in his book. He apparently regarded as something of the distant past the prophet Zechariah's abortive attempt to have the Davidic kingdom reestablished in the time of Zerubbabel at the end of the sixth century B.C. (Zec 6, 9-15). He saw David's primary importance as deriving from the establishment of Jerusalem and its temple as the center of the true worship of the Lord.

Furthermore, he presented David as the one who had authorized the elaborate ritual (which, in point of fact, only gradually evolved in the temple built by Zerubbabel) and who had also appointed Levites to supervise the liturgical services there.

There are good reasons for believing that originally the Books of Ezra and Nehemiah formed the last part of a single literary work that began with 1 and 2 Chronicles. Some authors even regard Ezra himself as having been the anonymous Chronicler. In any case, the Chronicler's Hebrew as well as his religious and political outlook points to c. 400 B.C. as the time of composition of this work.

The Chronicler used sources in writing his history. Besides the canonical Books of Genesis, Exodus, Numbers, Joshua and Ruth, and especially the Books of Samuel and Kings, he cites the titles of many other works no longer extant. "The books of the kings of Israel," or "the books of the kings of Israel and Judah," "the history of Samuel the seer," "the history of Nathan the prophet," "the history of Gad the seer," "the commentary on the Books of Kings," are some of the documents mentioned as historical sources.

In addition, the Chronicler's work contains early preexilic material not found in the Books of Kings. At one time scholars discounted the value of this material, but modern research has shown that, even though the Chronicler may have at times treated the material rather freely, he derived it from authentic and reliable sources.

The principal divisions of 1 Chronicles are as follows:

I: Genealogical Tables (1, 1—9, 34).
II: The History of David (9, 35—29, 30).

I: Genealogical Tables

CHAPTER 1

See RG 138

From Adam to Abraham. [1a*] Adam, Seth, Enosh, [2b]Kenan, Mahalalel, Jared, [3]Enoch, Methuselah, Lamech,[c] [4]Noah, Shem, Ham, and Japheth.[d] [5e]The descendants of Japheth were Gomer, Magog, Madai, Javan, Tubal, Meshech, and Tiras. [6]The descendants of Gomer were Ashkenaz, Riphath, and Togarmah. [7]The descendants of Javan were Elishah, Tarshis, the Kittim, and the Rodanim.

[8f]The descendants of Ham were Cush, Mesraim, Put, and Canaan. [9]The descendants of Cush were Seba, Havilah, Sabta, Raama, and Sabteca. The descendants of Raama were Sheba and Dedan. [10]Cush became the father of Nimrod, who was the first to be a conqueror on the earth. [11g]Mesraim became the father of the Ludim, Anamim, Lehabim, Naphtuhim, [12]Pathrusim, Casluhim, and Caphtorim, from whom the Philistines sprang. [13]Canaan became the father of Sidon, his first-born, and Heth, [14]and the Jebusite, the Amorite, the Girgashite, [15]the Hivite, the Arkite, the Sinite, [16]the Arvadite, the Zemarite, and the Hamathite.

[17h]The descendants of Shem were Elam, Asshur, Arpachshad, Lud, and Aram. The descendants of Aram were Uz, Hul, Gether, and Mash. [18]Arpachshad became the father of Shelah, and Shelah became the father of Eber. [19]Two sons were born to Eber; the first was named Peleg (for in his time the world was divided), and his brother was Joktan. [20]Joktan became the father of Almodad, Sheleph, Hazarmaveth, Jerah, [21]Hadoram, Uzal, Diklah, [22]Ebal, Abimael, Sheba, [23]Ophir, Havilah, and Jobab; all these were the sons of Joktan.

[24i]Shem, Arpachshad, Shelah, [25]Eber,

1, 1—9, 34: The Chronicler set as his task the retelling, from his particular viewpoint, of the story of God's people from the beginning to his own day. Since his primary interest was the history of David and the Davidic dynasty of Judah, he presents through mere genealogical lists a summary of what preceded the reign of Saul, David's predecessor in the kingdom. The sources for these genealogies are mostly the canonical Hebrew Scriptures that were already in their present form

in his time. The cross references in this book indicate in each case the scriptural sources used.

---

a: 1 Chr 4, 25f; Gn 5, 3. 6. 9. *b*: 2ff; Gn 5, 9-32; 10, 2ff. *c*: Gn 4, 25. *d*: Gn 5, 32; 6, 10; 9, 18. *e*: 5ff; Gn 10, 2ff. *f*: Gn 10, 8. *g*: 11-16: Gn 10, 13-18. *h*: 17-23: Gn 10, 22-29; 11, 10-18. *i*: 24-27: Gn 11, 10-26; Lk 3, 34ff.

The Chronicler begins his history in a way similar to a number of ancient Greek histories by trying to show the internal connectedness of the nation. After tracing the nation's descent from a common stock of ancestors, the historian focuses on the tribe of Judah and the family line of David, which is of central importance to the destiny of Jerusalem.

Peleg, Reu, [26]Serug, Nahor, Terah, [27]Abram, who was Abraham.[j]

From Abraham to Jacob. [28]The sons of Abraham were Isaac and Ishmael.[k] [29]These were their descendants:[l]

Nebaioth, the first-born of Ishmael, then Kedar, Adbeel, Mibsam, [30]Mishma, Dumah, Massa, Hadad, Tema, [31]Jetur, Naphish, and Kedemah. These were the descendants of Ishmael.

[32m]The descendants of Keturah, Abraham's concubine: she bore Zimran, Jokshan, Medan, Midian, Ishbak, and Shuah. The sons of Jokshan were Sheba and Dedan. [33]The descendants of Midian were Ephah, Epher, Hanoch, Abida, and Eldaah. All these were the descendants of Keturah.

[34]Abraham became the father of Isaac. The sons of Isaac were Esau and Israel.[n]

[35o]The sons of Esau were Eliphaz, Reuel, Jeush, Jalam, and Korah. [36]The sons of Eliphaz were Teman, Omar, Zephi, Gatam, Kenaz, [Timna,] and Amalek. [37]The sons of Reuel were Nahath, Zerah, Shammah, and Mizzah.

[38p]The descendants of Seir* were Lotan, Shobal, Zibeon, Anah, Dishon, Ezer, and Dishan. [39]The sons of Lotan were Hori and Homam; Timna was the sister of Lotan. [40]The sons of Shobal were Alian, Manahath, Ebal, Shephi, and Onam. The sons of Zibeon were Aiah and Anah. [41]The sons of Anah: Dishon. The sons of Dishon were Hemdan, Eshban, Ithran, and Cheran. [42]The sons of Ezer were Bilhan, Zaavan, and Jaakan. The sons of Dishan were Uz and Aran.

[43q]The kings who reigned in the land of Edom before they had Israelite kings were the following: Bela, son of Beor, the name of whose city was Ninhabah. [44]When Bela died, Jobab, son of Zerah, from Bozrah, succeeded him.[r] [45]When Jobab died, Husham, from the land of the Temanites, succeeded him.[s] [46]Husham died and Hadad, son of Bedad, succeeded him. He overthrew the Midianites on the Moabite plateau, and the name of his city was Avith. [47]Hadad died and Samlah of Masrekah succeeded him. [48]Samlah died and Shaul from Rehoboth-han-nahar succeeded him. [49]When Shaul died, Baalhanan, son of Achbor, succeeded him. [50]Baalhanan died and Hadad succeeded him. The name of his city was Pai, and his wife's name was Mehetabel. She was the daughter of Matred, who was the daughter of Mezahab. [51t]After Hadad died. . . .

These were the chiefs of Edom: the chiefs of Timna, Aliah, Jetheth, [52]Oholibamah, Elah, Pinon, [53]Kenaz, Teman, Mibzar, [54]Magdiel, and Iram were the chiefs of Edom.

CHAPTER 2

See RG 138

[1]These were the sons of Israel: Reuben, Simeon, Levi, Judah, Issachar, Zebulun,[u] [2]Dan, Joseph, Benjamin, Naphtali, Gad, and Asher.[v]

Judah. [3]The sons of Judah* were: Er, Onan, and Shelah; these three were born to him of Bathshua, a Canaanite woman. But Judah's first-born, Er, was wicked in the sight of the LORD, so he killed him.[w] [4]Judah's daughter-in-law Tamar bore him Perez and Zerah, so that he had five sons in all.[x]

[5]The sons of Perez were Hezron and Hamul.[y] [6]The sons of Zerah were Zimri, Ethan, Heman, Calcol, and Darda—five in all.[z]

1, 38: Seir: another name for Esau (v 35) or Edom (v 43).

2, 3—4, 23: For two reasons, the Chronicler places the genealogy of the tribe of Judah before that of the other tribes, giving

---

j: Gn 17, 5; Neh 9, 7.   *k:* Gn 16, 11. 15; 21, 2f; Gal 4, 22f; Heb 11, 11.   *l:* 29ff: Gn 25, 13-16.   *m:* 32f: Gn 25, 1-4.   *n:* Gn 21, 2f; 25, 19. 25f; 32, 28f; Mt 1, 2; Lk 3, 34.   *o:* 35ff: Gn 36, 4f. 10-13. 15ff.   *p:* 38-42: Gn 36, 20-28.   *q:* 43-54: Gn 36, 31-43.   *r:* Is 34, 6; 63, 1; Jer 49, 13. 22.   *s:* Gn 36, 11; Jb 2, 11; Jer 49, 7. 20.   *t:* 51-54: Gn 36, 40-43.   *u:* Gn 29, 32-35; 30, 18. 20; 35, 23.   *v:* Gn 30, 6. 8. 11. 13. 24; 35, 18. 24ff.   *w:* 1 Chr 4, 21; Gn 38, 1-5; 46, 12.   *x:* Gn 38, 7. 13-30; 46, 12; Rv 4, 12. 18; Mt 1, 3.   *y:* Gn 46, 12.   *z:* 1 Kgs 5, 11.

> The term for "prince" (2, 10) had a variety of meanings in antiquity. Nahshon (Hebrew, nasi, meaning "prince") may be described in this way to highlight the line of David, because Nahshon's sister married Moses' brother Aaron (Ex 6, 23) and thus helped form the primary line of Israel's priesthood. Such a connection would tie the royal and priestly families together.

[7]The sons of Zimri: Carmi. The sons of Carmi: Achar, who brought trouble upon Israel by violating the ban.[a] [8]The sons of Ethan: Azariah. [9]The sons born to Hezron were Jerahmeel, Ram, and Chelubai.[b] *

[10]*Ram became the father of Amminadab, and Amminadab became the father of Nahshon, a prince of the Judahites.[c] [11]dNahshon became the father of Salma. Salma became the father of Boaz. [12]Boaz became the father of Obed. Obed became the father of Jesse. [13]eJesse became the father of Eliab, his first-born, of Abinadab, the second son, Shimea, the third,[f] [14]Nethanel, the fourth, Raddai, the fifth, [15]Ozem, the sixth, and David, the seventh. [16]Their sisters were Zeruiah and Abigail. Zeruiah had three sons: Abishai, Joab, and Asahel.[g] [17]Abigail bore Amasa, whose father was Jether the Ishmaelite.[h]

[18]*By his wife Azubah, Caleb, son of Hezron, became the father of a daughter, Jerioth. Her sons were Jesher, Shobab, and Ardon.[i] [19]When Azubah died, Caleb married Ephrath, who bore him Hur.[j] [20]Hur became the father of Uri, and Uri became the father of Bezalel.[k] [21]Then Hezron had relations with the daughter of Machir, the father of Gilead, having married her when he was sixty years old. She bore him Segub.[l] [22]Segub became the father of Jair,[m] who possessed twenty-three cities in the land of Gilead. [23]Geshur and Aram took from them the villages of Jair, that is, Kenath and its towns, sixty cities in all, which had belonged to the sons of Machir, the father of Gilead.[n] [24]After the death of Hezron, Caleb had relations with Ephrathah, the widow of his father Hezron, and she bore him Ashhur, the father of Tekoa.[o]

[25]The sons of Jerahmeel,* the first-born of Hezron, were Ram, the first-born, then Bunah, Oren, and Ozem, his brothers.[p] [26]Jerahmeel also had another wife, Atarah by name, who was the mother of Onam. [27]The sons of Ram, the first-born of Jerahmeel, were Maaz, Jamin, and Eker. [28]The sons of Onam were Shammai and Jada. The sons of Shammai were Nadab and Abishur. [29]Abishur's wife, who was named Abihail, bore him Ahban and Molid. [30]The sons of Nadab were Seled and Appaim. Seled died without sons. [31]The sons of Appaim: Ishi. The sons of Ishi: Sheshan. The sons of Sheshan: Ahlai.[q] [32]The sons of Jada, the brother of Shammai, were Jether and Jonathan. Jether died without sons. [33]The sons of Jonathan were Peleth and Zaza. These were the descendants of Jerahmeel. [34]Sheshan, who had no sons, only daughters, had an Egyptian slave named Jarha. [35]Sheshan gave his daughter in marriage to his slave Jarha, and she bore him Attai. [36]Attai became the father of Nathan.

it also at greater length than the others: because of his interest in David and because in the Chronicler's time the people of God were almost exclusively Jews. Both David and the Jews were of the tribe of Judah.

2, 9: Chelubai: a variant form of the name Caleb (vv 18. 42), distinct from Chelub of 1 Chr 4, 11.

2, 10-17: Immediate ancestors of David. A similar list is given in Ru 4, 19-22; each list, independent of the other, derives from a common source.

2, 18-24: Descendants of Caleb. In 1 Chr 4, 15, as is often the case in the Pentateuch (Nm 13, 6; 14, 6. 30; 26, 65; etc.), Caleb is called son of Jephunneh. Here he is called son of Hezron, perhaps because the Calebites were reckoned as part of the clan of the Hezronites.

a: Jos 7, 1. 18ff. 24f; 22, 20.   b: Rv 4, 19; Mt 1, 3.   c: Rv 4, 19; Mt 1, 4.   d: 11f: Nm 1, 7; Rv 4, 20f; Mt 1, 4f.   e: 13ff: 1 Sm 16, 6-13; 17, 13f.   f: 2 Chr 11, 18.   g: 2 Sm 2, 18.   h: 2 Sm 17, 25; 19, 14; 20, 4-13.   i: 1 Chr 2, 24.   j: 1 Chr 2, 24.   k: Ex 24, 14; 31, 2; 35, 30; 2 Chr 1, 5.   l: Nm 26, 29; 27, 1; 32, 32; Jos 13, 31; Jgs 5, 14.   m: Nm 32, 41; 1 Kgs 4, 13.   n: Dt 3, 14; Jos 13, 30; Jgs 10, 4.   o: 1 Chr 2, 19; 2 Sm 14, 2; 2 Chr 11, 6.   p: 1 Sm 27, 10; 30, 29; Jb 32, 2.   q: 1 Chr 4, 20.

Nathan became the father of Zabad. *37*Zabad became the father of Ephlal. Ephlal became the father of Obed. *38*Obed became the father of Jehu. Jehu became the father of Azariah. *39*Azariah became the father of Helez. Helez became the father of Eleasah. *40*Eleasah became the father of Sismai. Sismai became the father of Shallum. *41*Shallum became the father of Jekamiah. Jekamiah became the father of Elishama.

*42*The descendants of Caleb,* the brother of Jerahmeel: [Mesha] his first-born, who was the father of Ziph. Then the sons of Mareshah, who was the father of Hebron. *43*The sons of Hebron were Korah, Tappuah, Rekem, and Shema. *44*Shema became the father of Raham, who was the father of Jorkeam. Rekem became the father of Shammai. *45*The sons of Shammai: Maon, who was the father of Beth-zur. *46*Ephah, Caleb's concubine, bore Haran, Moza, and Gazez. Haran became the father of Gazez. *47*The sons of Jahdai were Regem, Jotham, Geshan, Pelet, Ephah, and Shaaph. *48*Maacah, Caleb's concubine, bore Sheber and Tirhanah. *49*She also bore Shaaph, the father of Madmannah, Sheva, the father of Machbenah, and the father of Gibea. Achsah was Caleb's daughter.*r*

*50*These were descendants of Caleb, sons of Hur,* the first-born of Ephrathah: Shobal, the father of Kiriath-jearim, *51*Salma, the father of Bethlehem, and Hareph, the father of Beth-gader. *52*The sons of Shobal, the father of Kiriath-jearim, were Reaiah, half the Manahathites, *53*and the clans of Kiriath-jearim: the Ithrites, the Puthites, the Shumathites, and the Mishraites. From these the people of Zorah and the Eshtaolites derived.*s* *54*The descendants of Salma were Bethlehem, the Netophathites, Atroth-beth-Joab, half the Manahath-

ites, and the Zorites. *55*The clans of the Sopherim dwelling in Jabez were the Tirathites, the Shimeathites, and the Sucathites. They were the Kenites, who came from Hammath of the ancestor of the Rechabites.

CHAPTER 3

See RG 138

*1u*The following* were the sons of David who were born to him in Hebron: the first-born, Amnon, by Ahinoam of Jezreel; the second, Daniel,* by Abigail of Carmel; *2*the third, Absalom, son of Maacah, who was the daughter of Talmai, king of Geshur; the fourth, Adonijah, son of Haggith; *3*the fifth, Shephatiah, by Abital; the sixth, Ithream, by his wife Eglah. *4*Six in all were born to him in Hebron, where he reigned seven years and six months. Then he reigned thirty-three years in Jerusalem,*v* *5w*where the following were born to him: Shimea,* Shobab, Nathan, Solomon—four by Bathsheba, the daughter of Ammiel,*x* *6*Ibhar, Elishua, Eliphelet, *7*Nogah, Nepheg, Japhia, *8*Elishama, Eliada, and Eliphelet—nine. *9*All these were sons of David, in addition to other sons by concubines; and Tamar was their sister.*y*

*10z*The son of Solomon was Rehoboam, whose son was Abijah, whose son was Asa, whose son was Jehoshaphat,*a* *11*whose son was Joram, whose son was Ahaziah, whose son was Joash,*b* *12*whose son was Amaziah, whose son was Azariah, whose son was Jotham,*c* *13*whose son was Ahaz, whose son was Hezekiah, whose son was Manasseh,*d* *14*whose son was Amon, whose son was Josiah.*e* *15*The sons of Josiah were: the first-born, Johanan; the second, Jehoiakim; the third, Zedekiah; the fourth, Shallum.*f* *16*The sons of Jehoiakim were: Jeconiah, his son; Zedekiah, his son.*g*

2, 25-41: The Jerahmeelites were a clan in the Negeb of Judah.

2, 42-49: Another list, dating from preexilic times, of the Calebites, a clan that inhabited the south of Judah.

2, 50-55: The Hurites, a clan dwelling to the south and west of Jerusalem and related to the Calebites.

3, 1-9: David's sons.

3, 1: Daniel: called Chileab in 2 Sm 3, 3.

3, 5: Shimea: called Shammua in 2 Sm 5, 14. Ammiel: called Eliam in 2 Sm 11, 3.

3, 10-16: The kings of Judah from Solomon to the destruction of Jerusalem by the Babylonians.

3, 15: Shallum: the same as Jehoahaz, Josiah's successor; cf Je- 22, 11.

r: Jos 15, 16; Jgs 1, 12. *s:* Jgs 18, 2. *t:* Nm 24, 21; Jgs 1, 16; 4, 11; 1 Sm 15, 6. *u:* 1-4: 2 Sm 3, 2-5. *v:* 2 Sm 2, 11; 5, 5. *w:* 5-8: 2 Sm 5, 14ff. *x:* 2 Sm 5, 5. *y:* 2 Sm 13, 1f. *z:* 10-17: Mt 1, 7-12. *a:* 1 Kgs 11, 43; 14, 31; 15, 1. 8. 24; 2 Chr 9, 31; 12, 16; 13, 23; 17, 1. *b:* 1 Kgs 22, 51; 2 Chr 21, 1; 22, 1; 24, 1. 27. *c:* 2 Kgs 12, 21; 14, 21; 15, 7; 2 Chr 25, 1; 26, 1. 23; 27, 1. *d:* 2 Kgs 15, 38; 16, 20; 20, 21; 2 Chr 28, 1. 27; 32, 33. *e:* 2 Kgs 21, 18. 26; 2 Chr 33, 20. 25. *f:* 2 Kgs 23, 34; 24, 17; 2 Chr 36, 4. 10. *g:* 2 Kgs 24, 6. 17; 2 Chr 36, 8. 10.

[17]The sons of Jeconiah[*] the captive were: Shealtiel,[h] [18]Malchiram, Pedaiah, Shenazzar,[*] Jekamiah, Shama, and Nedabiah. [19]The sons of Pedaiah were Zerubbabel[*] and Shimei. The sons of Zerubbabel were Meshullam and Hananiah; Shelomith was their sister. [20]The sons of Meshullam were Hashubah, Ohel, Berechiah, Hasadiah, Jushabhesed—five. [21]The sons of Hananiah were Pelatiah, Jeshaiah, Rephaiah, Arnan, Obadiah, and Shecaniah. [22i]The sons of Shecaniah were Shemiah, Hattush, Igal, Bariah, Neariah, Shaphat—six. [23]The sons of Neariah were Elioenai, Hizkiah, and Azrikam—three. [24]The sons of Elioenai were Hodaviah, Eliashib, Pelaiah, Akkub, Johanan, Delaiah, and Anani—seven.

CHAPTER 4

See RG
138 [1][*]The descendants of Judah were: Perez, Hezron, Carmi, Hur, and Shobal.[j] [2]Reaiah, the son of Shobal, became the father of Jahath, and Jahath became the father of Ahumai and Lahad. These were the clans of the Zorathites.

[3]These were the descendants of Hareph, the father of Etam: Jezreel, Ishma, and Idbash; their sister was named Hazzelelponi. [4]Penuel was the father of Gedor, and Ezer the father of Hushah. These were the descendants of Hur, the first-born of Ephrathah, the father of Bethlehem.

[5]Ashhur, the father of Tekoa, had two wives, Helah and Naarah.[k] [6]Naarah bore him Ahuzzam, Hepher, the Temenites and the Ahashtarites. These were the descendants of Naarah. [7]The sons of Helah were Zereth, Izhar, Ethnan, and Koz. [8]Koz became the father of Anub and Zobebah, as well as of the clans of Aharhel, son of Harum. [9]Jabez was the most distinguished of the brothers. His mother had named him Jabez, saying, "I bore him with pain." [10]Jabez prayed to the God of Israel: "Oh, that you may truly bless me and extend my boundaries! Help me and make me free of misfortune, without pain!" And God granted his prayer.

[11]Chelub, the brother of Shuhah, became the father of Mehir, who was the father of Eshton. [12]Eshton became the father of Beth-rapha, Paseah, and Tehinnah, the father of the city of Nahash. These were the men of Recah.

[13]The sons of Kenaz were Othniel and Seraiah. The sons of Othniel were Hathath and Meonothai;[l] [14]Meonothai became the father of Ophrah. Seraiah became the father of Joab, the father of Geharashim, so called because they were craftsmen. [15]The sons of Caleb, son of Jephunneh, were Ir, Elah, and Naam. The sons of Elah were . . . and Kenaz.[m] [16]The sons of Jehallelel were Ziph, Ziphah, Tiria, and Asarel. [17]The sons of Ezrah were Jether, Mered, Epher, and Jalon. Jether became the father of Miriam, Shammai, and Ishbah, the father of Eshtemoa. [. . . . . .][n] [18]His (Mered's) Egyptian wife bore Jared, the father of Gedor, Heber, the father of Soco, and Jekuthiel, the father of Zanoah. These were the sons of Bithiah, the daughter of Pharaoh, whom Mered married. [19]The sons of his Jewish wife, the sister of Naham, the father of Keilah, were Shimon the Garmite and Ishi the Maacathite. [20]The sons of Shimon were Amnon, Rinnah, Benhanan, and Tilon. The son of Ishi was Zoheth and the son of Zoheth. . . .

[21]The descendants of Shelah, son of Judah, were: Er, the father of Lecah; Laadah, the father of Mareshah; the clans of the linen weavers' guild in Beth-ashbea;[o] [22]Jokim; the men of Cozeba; and Joash and Saraph, who held property in Moab, but returned to Bethlehem. [These are events of old.] [23]They were

---

3, 17-24: The descendants of King Jeconiah up to the time of the Chronicler. If twenty-five years are allowed to each generation, the ten generations between Jeconiah and Anani (the last name on the list) would bring the birth of the latter to about 405 B.C.—an important item in establishing the approximate date of the Chronicler.

3, 18: Shenazzar: presumably the same as Sheshbazzar of Ezr 1, 8. 11; 5, 14ff, the prince of Judah who was the first Jewish governor of Judah after the exile. Both forms of the name probably go back to the Babylonian name Sin-ab-ussar signifying, "O [god] Sin, protect [our] father!"

3, 19: Zerubbabel: here called the son of Pedaiah, though elsewhere (Hg 1, 12. 14; 2, 2. 23; Ezr 3, 2. 8; 5, 2; Neh 12, 1) called son of Shealtiel. The latter term may merely mean that Zerubbabel succeeded Shealtiel as head of the house of David.

4, 1-43: The southern tribes.

h: 17. 19: Ezr 2, 2; 3, 2. 8; 5, 2; Sir 49, 11; Hg 1, 1. 12. 14; Mt 1, 12f; Lk 3, 27.   i: Neh 3, 29.   j: 1 Chr 2, 4f. 7. 9. 50; Gn 38, 29; 46, 12; Mt 1, 3.   k: 1 Chr 2, 24.   l: Jos 15, 17; Jgs 1, 13; 3, 9. 11.   m: Nm 13, 6; 14, 6; 32, 12; Jos 14, 6. 14.   n: 1 Sm 30, 28.   o: 1 Chr 2, 3; Gn 38, 5; 46, 12; Nm 26, 20.

The Tribe of Simeon

Because the author has begun with Judah (2, 3), it makes some sense to continue the examination of Israel by turning to the family group of Simeon (4, 24), a tribe connected with Judah both by birth (Judah and Simeon were Jacob's sons by the same mother) and by proximity.

potters and inhabitants of Netaim and Gederah, where they lived in the king's service.

Simeon. [24]The sons of Simeon were Nemuel, Jamin, Jachin, Zerah, and Shaul,[p] [25]whose son was Shallum, whose son was Mibsam, whose son was Mishma. [26]The descendants of Mishma were his son Hammuel, whose son was Zaccur, whose son was Shimei. [27]Shimei had sixteen sons and six daughters. His brothers, however, did not have many sons, and as a result all their clans did not equal the number of the Judahites.

[28q]They dwelt in Beer-sheba, Moladah, Hazar-shual, [29]Bilhah, Ezem, Tolad, [30]Bethuel, Hormah, Ziklag, [31]Beth-marcaboth, Hazar-susim, Bethbiri, and Shaaraim. Until David came to reign, these were their cities [32]and their villages. Etam, also, and Ain, Rimmon, Tochen, and Ashan—five cities, [33]together with all their outlying villages as far as Baal. Here is where they dwelt, and so it was inscribed of them in their family records.

[34]Meshobab, Jamlech, Joshah, son of Amaziah, [35]Joel, Jehu, son of Joshibiah, son of Seraiah, son of Asiel, [36]Elioenai, Jaakobath, Jeshohaiah, Asaiah, Adiel, Jesimiel, Benaiah, [37]Ziza, son of Shiphi, son of Allon, son of Jedaiah, son of Shimri, son of Shemaiah— [38]these just named were princes in their clans, and their ancestral houses spread out to such an extent[r] [39]that they went to the approaches of Gedor,* east of the valley, seeking pasture for their flocks. [40]They found abundant and good pastures, and the land was spacious, quiet, and peaceful. [41]They who have just been listed by name set out during the reign of Hezekiah, king of Judah, and attacked the tents of Ham (for Hamites dwelt there formerly) and also the Meunites who were there. They pronounced against them the ban that is still in force and dwelt in their place because they found pasture there for their flocks.[s]

[42]Five hundred of them (the Simeonites) went to Mount Seir under the leadership of Pelatiah, Neariah, Rephaiah, and Uzziel, sons of Ishi. [43]They attacked the surviving Amalekites who had escaped, and have resided there to the present day.[t]

CHAPTER 5

See RG 138

Reuben. [1]*The sons of Reuben, the first-born of Israel. (He was indeed the first-born, but because he disgraced the couch of his father his birthright was given to the sons of Joseph, son of Israel, so that he is not listed in the family records according to birthright.[u] [2]Judah, in fact, became powerful among his brothers, so that the ruler came from him, though the birthright had been Joseph's.)[v] [3]The sons of Reuben, the first-born of Israel, were Hanoch, Pallu, Hezron, and Carmi.[w] [4]His son was Joel, whose son was Shemaiah, whose son was Gog, whose son was Shimei, [5]whose son was Micah, whose son was Reaiah, whose son was Baal, [6]whose son was Beerah, whom Tiglath-pileser, the king of Assyria, took into exile; he was a prince of the Reubenites.[x] [7]His brothers who belonged to his clans, when they were listed in the family records according to their descendants, were: Jeiel, the chief, and Zechariah, [8]and Bela, son of Azaz, son of Shema, son of Joel. The Reubenites lived in Aroer and as far as Nebo and Baal-meon;[y] [9]toward the east they dwelt as far as the desert which extends from the Euphrates River, for they had

4, 39: Gedor: in the Greek, Gerar, no doubt correct.

5, 1-26: The Transjordan tribes.

p: Gn 46, 10; Ex 6, 15; Nm 26, 12f.   q: 28-32: Jos 19, 2-8.   r: Nm 1, 2.   s: 2 Kgs 18, 1f; 2 Chr 29, 1.   t: Ex 17, 8. 14; Dt 25, 17ff; 1 Sm 14, 48; 15, 3. 7f; 2 Sm 8, 12.   u: Gn 35, 22; 48, 5. 15-22; 49, 3f; Dt 33, 6.   v: 1 Chr 28, 4; Gn 49, 8ff.   w: Gn 46, 9; Ex 6, 14; Nm 26, 5f.   x: 2 Kgs 15, 29.   y: Jos 13, 9. 16f; Nm 32, 3. 38.

much livestock in the land of Gilead.*
[10]During the reign of Saul they waged war with the Hagrites, and when they had defeated them they occupied their tents throughout the region east of Gilead.*

Gad. [11]The Gadites lived alongside them in the land of Bashan as far as Salecah.* [12]Joel was chief, Shapham was second in command, and Janai was judge in Bashan.* [13]Their brothers, corresponding to their ancestral houses, were: Michael, Meshullam, Sheba, Jorai, Jacan, Zia, and Eber—seven. [14]These were the sons of Abihail, son of Huri, son of Jaroah, son of Gilead, son of Michael, son of Jeshishai, son of Jahdo, son of Buz. [15]Ahi, son of Abdiel, son of Guni, was the head of their ancestral houses. [16]They dwelt in Gilead, in Bashan and its towns, and in all the pasture lands of Sirion to the borders. [17]All were listed in the family records in the time of Jotham, king of Judah, and of Jeroboam, king of Israel.

[18]The Reubenites, Gadites, and half-tribe of Manasseh were warriors, men who bore shield and sword and who drew the bow, trained in warfare—forty-four thousand seven hundred and sixty men fit for military service. [19]When they waged war against the Hagrites and against Jetur, Naphish, and Nodab,* [20]they received help so that they mastered the Hagrites and all who were with them. For during the battle they called on God, and he heard them because they had put their trust in him.* [21]Along with one hundred thousand men they also captured their livestock: fifty thousand camels, two hundred fifty thousand sheep, and two thousand asses. [22]Many had fallen in battle, for victory is from God; and they took over their dwelling place until the time of the exile.*

East Manasseh. [23]The numerous members of the half-tribe of Manasseh lived in the land of Bashan as far as Baal-hermon,

Senir, and Mount Hermon. [24]The following were the heads of their ancestral houses: Epher, Ishi, Eliel, Azriel, Jeremiah, Hodaviah, and Jahdiel—men who were warriors, famous men, and heads over their ancestral houses.

[25]However, they offended the God of their fathers by lusting after the gods of the natives of the land, whom God had cleared out of their way.* [26]Therefore the God of Israel incited against them the anger of Pul,* king of Assyria, and of Tiglath-pileser, king of Assyria, who deported the Reubenites, the Gadites, and the half-tribe of Manasseh and brought them to Halah, Habor, and Hara, and to the river Gozan, where they have remained to this day.*

Levi. * [27]The sons of Levi were Gershon, Kohath, and Merari.* [28]The sons of Kohath were Amram, Izhar, Hebron, and Uzziel.* [29]The children of Amram were Aaron, Moses, and Miriam. The sons of Aaron were Nadab, Abihu, Eleazar, and Ithamar.* [30]*Eleazar became the father of Phinehas. Phinehas became the father of Abishua. [31]Abishua became the father of Bukki. Bukki became the father of Uzzi. [32]Uzzi became the father of Zerahiah. Zerahiah became the father of Meraioth. [33]Meraioth became the father of Amariah. Amariah became the father of Ahitub. [34]Ahitub became the father of Zadok. Zadok became the father of Ahimaaz. [35]Ahimaaz became the father of Azariah. Azariah became the father of Johanan. [36]Johanan became the father of Azariah, who served as priest in the temple Solomon built in Jerusalem. [37]Azariah became the father of Amariah. Amariah became the father of Ahitub. [38]Ahitub became the father of Zadok. Zadok became the father of Shallum. [39]Shallum became the father of Hilkiah. Hilkiah became the father of Azariah. [40]Azariah became the father of Seraiah. Seraiah became the father of Jehozadak. [41]Jehozadak was

5, 26: Pul: the name which the Assyrian king Tiglath-pileser III (745–727 B.C.) took as king of Babylon.

5, 27—6, 66: The tribe of Levi. The list gives special prominence to Levi's son Kohath, from whom were descended both the Aaronite priests (1 Chr 5, 28-41) and the leading group of temple singers (1 Chr 6, 18-23).

5, 30-41: The line of preexilic priests. The list seems to be confused in vv 36ff, which repeat the names, mostly in in-

verse order, that occur in vv 34f. A similar but shorter list is given, with variations, in Ezr 7, 1-5.

z: Jos 22, 9. a: Ps 83, 6. b: Jos 13, 11. 24-28. c: Gn 46, 16. d: 1 Chr 1, 31; 5, 10; Gn 25, 15; Ps 83, 6. e: Dt 33, 20f. f: Nm 32, 39; Dt 3, 8ff; Jgs 3, 3. g: Ex 34, 14ff; 2 Kgs 17, 7. h: 2 Kgs 15, 9. 29; 17, 6. i: 1 Chr 6, 1; 23, 6; Gn 46, 11; Ex 6, 16; Nm 26, 57. j: 1 Chr 6, 3; Ex 6, 18. k: Ex 6, 20; Nm 26, 59f.

Although David's son Solomon is the one who built the temple, the Chronicler asserts that all the main elements of temple worship, such as those entrusted with the choir services (6, 16), were put in place by David. He justifies this perspective by noting that such worship was instigated after the ark had "a permanent resting place," assuming that once the ark had been brought into Jerusalem, regular forms of worship would be required. While it is certainly possible that David authorized the formation of dedicated musicians prior to the foundation of the temple, this elaborate form of the organization suggests the Chronicler is referring to the temple music professionals of his own day.

one of those who went into the exile which the LORD inflicted on Judah and Jerusalem through Nebuchadnezzar.

CHAPTER 6

See RG 138

[1]The sons of Levi were Gershon, Kohath, and Merari.[l] [2]The sons of Gershon were named Libni and Shimei.[m] [3]The sons of Kohath were Amram, Izhar, Hebron, and Uzziel.[n] [4o]The sons of Merari were Mahli and Mushi.

The following were the clans of Levi, distributed according to their ancestors: [5]of Gershon: his son Libni, whose son was Jahath, whose son was Zimmah, [6]whose son was Joah, whose son was Iddo, whose son was Zerah, whose son was Jetherai.

[7]The descendants of Kohath were: his son Amminadab, whose son was Korah, whose son was Assir, [8]whose son was Elkanah, whose son was Ebiasaph, whose son was Assir, [9]whose son was Tahath, whose son was Uriel, whose son was Uzziah, whose son was Shaul. [10]The sons of Elkanah were Amasai and Ahimoth, [11]whose son was Elkanah, whose son was Zophai, whose son was Nahath, [12]whose son was Eliab, whose son was Jeroham, whose son was Elkanah, whose son was Samuel. [13]The sons of Samuel were Joel, the first-born, and Abijah, the second.

[14]The descendants of Merari were Mahli, whose son was Libni, whose son was Shimei, whose son was Uzzah,[p] [15]whose son was Shimea, whose son was Haggiah, whose son was Asaiah.

[16]The following were entrusted by David with the choir services[*] in the LORD's house

from the time when the ark had obtained a permanent resting place. [17]They served as singers before the Dwelling of the meeting tent until Solomon built the temple of the LORD in Jerusalem, and they performed their services in an order prescribed for them. [18]Those who so performed are the following, together with their descendants.

Among the Kohathites: Heman, the chanter, son of Joel, son of Samuel, [19]son of Elkanah, son of Jeroham, son of Eliel, son of Toah, [20]son of Zuth, son of Elkanah, son of Mahath, son of Amasi, [21]son of Elkanah, son of Joel, son of Azariah, son of Zephaniah, [22]son of Tahath, son of Assir, son of Ebiasaph, son of Korah,[q] [23]son of Izhar, son of Kohath, son of Levi, son of Israel.

[24]His brother Asaph stood at his right hand. Asaph was the son of Berechiah, son of Shimea, [25]son of Michael, son of Baaseiah, son of Malchijah, [26]son of Ethni, son of Zerah, son of Adaiah, [27]son of Ethan, son of Zimmah,[r] son of Shimei, [28]son of Jahath, son of Gershon, son of Levi.

[29]Their brothers, the Merarites, stood at the left: Ethan, son of Kishi, son of Abdi, son of Malluch, [30]son of Hashabiah, son of Amaziah, son of Hilkiah, [31]son of Amzi, son of Bani, son of Shemer, [32]son of Mahli, son of Mushi, son of Merari, son of Levi.[s]

[33]Their brother Levites were appointed to all other services of the Dwelling of the house of God.[t] [34]However, it was Aaron and his descendants who burnt the offerings on the altar of holocausts and on the altar of incense; they alone had charge of the holy of

---

6, 16-32: The origin of the choir services performed by the levitical families in the postexilic temple at the time of the Chronicler is here attributed to David, somewhat as all the laws in the Pentateuch are attributed to Moses.

---

l: 1 Chr 5, 27; 23, 6; Gn 46, 11; Ex 6, 16; Nm 26, 57.   *m:* Ex 6, 17.   *n:* Ex 6, 18; Nm 3, 19; 26, 59.   *o:* 1 Chr 6, 14; Ex 6, 19; Nm 3, 20; 26, 58.   *p:* 1 Chr 6, 4; Ex 6, 19; Nm 3, 20; 26, 58.   *q:* Ex 6, 24.   *r:* 1 Chr 6, 2. 5.   *s:* Ex 6, 19; Nm 26, 58.   *t:* 1 Chr 15, 17. 19; 16, 41f; 2 Chr 5, 12.

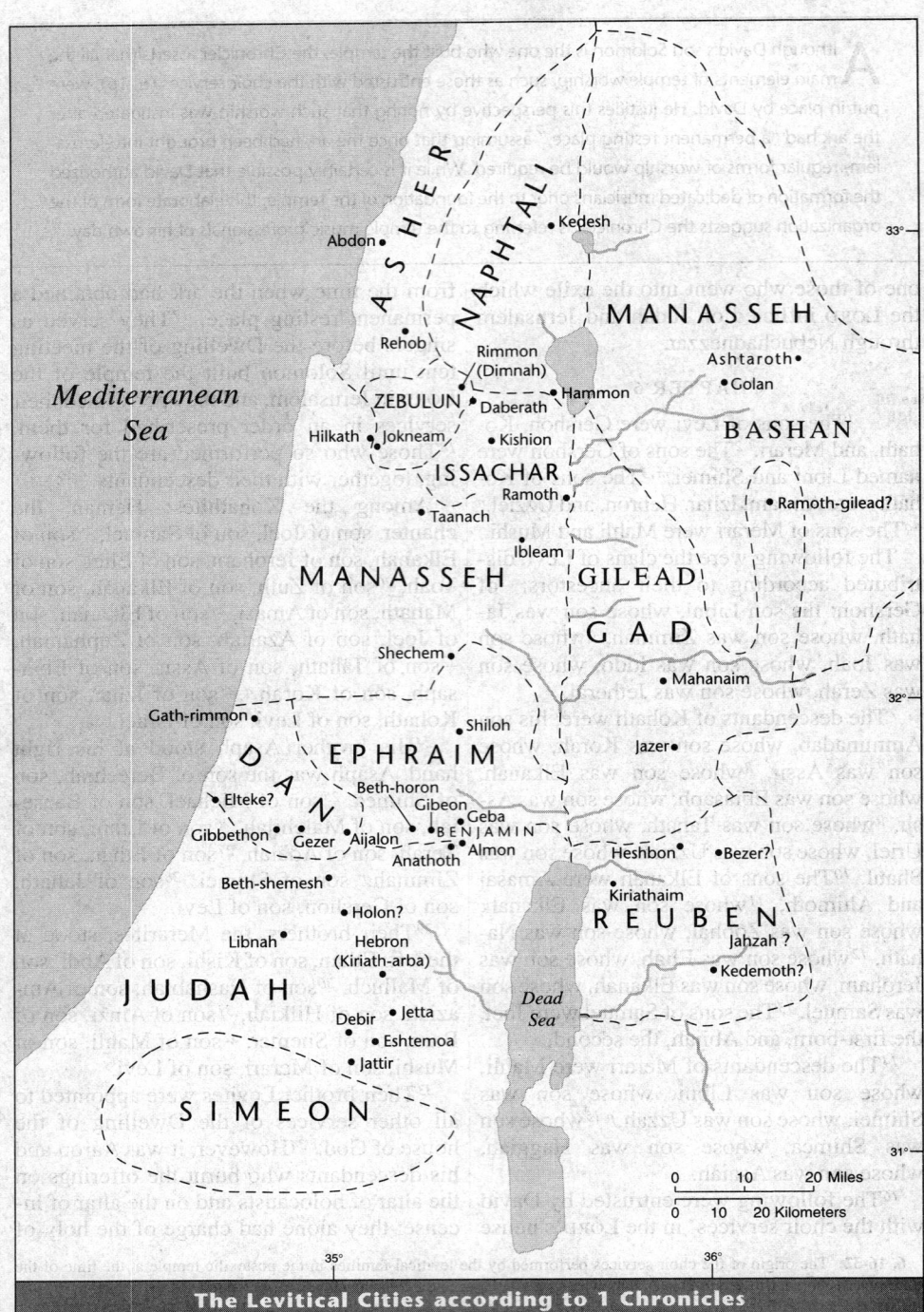

Mediterranean
Sea

ASHER

NAPHTALI

Kedesh

MANASSEH

Abdon

33°

Rehob

Ashtaroth

Rimmon
(Dimnah)

Golan

ZEBULUN   Daberath   Hammon

BASHAN

Hilkath   Jokneam   Kishion

ISSACHAR

Ramoth

Ramoth-gilead?

Taanach

Ibleam

MANASSEH   GILEAD

GAD

Shechem

Mahanaim

Gath-rimmon

Shiloh

Jazer

32°

D A N   EPHRAIM

Elteke?

Beth-horon

Gezer   Aijalon   Gibeon   Geba
Anathoth   BENJAMIN   Almon

Heshbon

Bezer?

Gibbethon

Kiriathaim

Beth-shemesh

Jahzah?

R E U B E N

Holon?

Libnah   Hebron
(Kiriath-arba)

Kedemoth?

Dead
Sea

JUDAH

Debir   Jetta

Eshtemoa

31°

Jattir

SIMEON

0   10   20 Miles

0   10   20 Kilometers

35°   36°

The Levitical Cities according to 1 Chronicles

466

Priests—Levite and Aaronides

The genealogy of Levi (6, 1–66), along with that of the tribe of Judah (2, 3—4, 23), represents the most elaborate portion of the genealogy. From the Chronicler's viewpoint, the tribe of Levi and the formal temple service responsibilities that only this family can undertake for Israel are of critical importance for Israel's destiny. By the time of the Chronicler's history, the priesthood of Israel had been segmented into various family lines with different responsibilities and social standings. Those who belonged to the sons of Aaron were eligible for the high priesthood, the chief administrative office of the temple. Those who belonged to the various lines of the Levites other than Aaron's had lesser roles in the temple.

One of the prime distinctions between the line of Aaron and the other members of the tribe of Levi is that it was the descendants of Aaron alone who could offer the sacrifice to atone for sin and purify the worshiper (v. 34).

holies and of making atonement for Israel, as Moses, the servant of God, had ordained.[u]

^{35}These were the descendants of Aaron: his son Eleazer, whose son was Phinehas, whose son was Abishua, ^{36}whose son was Bukki, whose son was Uzzi, whose son was Zerahiah, ^{37}whose son was Meraioth, whose son was Amariah, whose son was Ahitub, ^{38}whose son was Zadok, whose son was Ahimaaz.

^{39}*The following were their dwelling places to which their encampment was limited. To the descendants of Aaron who belonged to the clan of the Kohathites, since the first lot fell to them, ^{40}was assigned Hebron with its adjacent pasture lands in the land of Judah, ^{41}although the open country and the villages belonging to the city had been given to Caleb, the son of Jephunneh. ^{42}There were assigned to the descendants of Aaron: Hebron, a city of asylum, Libnah with its pasture lands, Jattir with its pasture lands, Eshtemoa with its pasture lands, ^{43}Holon with its pasture lands, Debir with its pasture lands, ^{44}Ashan with its pasture lands, Jetta with its pasture lands, and Beth-shemesh with its pasture lands. ^{45}Also from the tribe of Benjamin: Gibeon with its pasture lands, Geba with its pasture lands, Almon with its pasture lands, Anathoth with its pasture lands. In all, they had thirteen cities with their pasture lands. ^{49}The Israelites assigned these cities with their pasture lands to the Levites, ^{50}designating them by name and assigning them by lot from the tribes of the Judahites, Simeonites, and Benjaminites.

^{46}The other Kohathites obtained ten cities by lot for their clans from the tribe of Ephraim, from the tribe of Dan, and from the half-tribe of Manasseh. ^{47}The clans of the Gershonites obtained thirteen cities from the tribes of Issachar, Asher, and Naphtali, and from the half-tribe of Manasseh in Bashan. ^{48}The clans of the Merarites obtained twelve cities by lot from the tribes of Reuben, Gad, and Zebulun.

^{51}The clans of the Kohathites obtained cities by lot from the tribe of Ephraim. ^{52}They were assigned: Shechem in the mountain region of Ephraim, a city of asylum, with its pasture lands, Gezer with its pasture lands, ^{53}Kibzaim with its pasture lands, and Beth-horon with its pasture lands. ^{54}From the tribe of Dan: Elteke with its pasture lands, Gibbethon with its pasture lands, Aijalon with its pasture lands, and Gath-rimmon with its pasture lands. ^{55}From the half-tribe of Manasseh: Taanach with its pasture lands and Ibleam with its pasture lands. These belonged to the rest of the Kohathite clan.

^{56}The clans of the Gershonites received from the half-tribe of Manasseh: Golan in Bashan with its pasture lands and Ashtaroth with its pasture lands. ^{57}From the tribe of Issachar: Kedesh with its pasture lands, Daberath with its pasture lands, ^{58}Ramoth with

6, 39-66: Regarding the nature of the rights of Levites in the cities assigned to them, see note on Jos 21, 1.

u: 1 Chr 16, 39f.

its pasture lands, and Engannim with its pasture lands. [59]From the tribe of Asher: Mashal with its pasture lands, Abdon with its pasture lands, [60]Hilkath with its pasture lands, and Rehob with its pasture lands. [61]From the tribe of Naphtali: Kedesh in Galilee with its pasture lands, Hammon with its pasture lands, and Kiriathaim with its pasture lands.

[62]The rest of the Merarites received from the tribe of Zebulun: Jokneam with its pasture lands, Kartah with its pasture lands, Rimmon with its pasture lands, and Tabor with its pasture lands. [63]Across the Jordan at Jericho [that is, east of the Jordan] they received from the tribe of Reuben: Bezer in the desert with its pasture lands, Jahzah with its pasture lands, [64]Kedemoth with its pasture lands, and Mephaath with its pasture lands. [65]From the tribe of Gad: Ramoth in Gilead with its pasture lands, Mahanaim with its pasture lands, [66]Heshbon with its pasture lands, and Jazer with its pasture lands.

See RG
138

CHAPTER 7

Issachar.[*] [1]The sons of Issachar were Tola, Puah, Jashub, and Shimron: four.[v] [2]The sons of Tola were Uzzi, Rephaiah, Jeriel, Jahmai, Ibsam, and Shemuel, warrior heads of the ancestral houses of Tola. Their kindred numbered twenty-two thousand six hundred in the time of David.[w] [3]The sons of Uzzi: Izarahiah. The sons of Izarahiah were Michael, Obadiah, Joel, and Isshiah. All five of these were chiefs. [4]Their kindred, by ancestral houses, numbered thirty-six thousand men in organized military troops, since they had more wives and sons [5]than their fellow tribesmen. In all the clans of Issachar there was a total of eighty-seven thousand warriors in their family records.

Benjamin. [6]The sons of Benjamin were Bela, Becher, and Jediael—three.[x] [7]The sons of Bela were Ezbon, Uzzi, Uzziel, Jerimoth, and Iri—five. They were heads of their ancestral houses and warriors. Their family records listed twenty-two thousand and thirty-four. [8]The sons of Becher were Zemirah, Joash, Eliezer, Elioenai, Omri, Jeremoth, Abijah, Anathoth, and Alemeth—all these were sons of Becher.[y] [9]Their family records listed twenty thousand two hundred of their kindred who were heads of their ancestral houses and warriors. [10]The sons of Jediael: Bilhan. The sons of Bilhan were Jeush, Benjamin, Ehud, Chenaanah, Zethan, Tarshish, and Ahishahar. [11]All these were descendants of Jediael, heads of ancestral houses and warriors. They numbered seventeen thousand two hundred men fit for military service . . . Shupham and Hupham.[z]

Dan, Naphtali and Manasseh. [12a]The sons of Dan: Hushim. [13]The sons of Naphtali were Jahziel, Guni, Jezer, and Shallum. These were descendants of Bilhah. [14]The sons of Manasseh, whom his Aramean concubine bore:[b] she bore Machir, the father of Gilead.[c] [15]Machir took a wife whose name was Maacah; his sister's name was Molecheth. Manasseh's second son was named Zelophehad, but to Zelophehad only daughters were born.[d] [16]Maacah, Machir's wife, bore a son whom she named Peresh. He had a brother named Sheresh, whose sons were Ulam and Rakem. [17]The sons of Ulam: Bedan. These were the descendants of Gilead, the son of Machir, the son of Manasseh. [18]His sister Molecheth bore Ishhod, Abiezer, and Mahlah. [19]The sons of Shemida were Ahian, Shechem, Likhi, and Aniam.

Ephraim. [20e]The sons of Ephraim: Shuthelah, whose son was Bered, whose son was Tahath, whose son was Eleadah, whose son was Tahath, [21]whose son was Zabad. Ephraim's son Shuthelah, and Ezer and Elead, who were born in the land, were slain by the inhabitants of Gath because they had gone down to take away their livestock. [22]Their father Ephraim mourned a long time, but after his kinsmen had come and comforted him, [23]he visited his wife, who conceived and bore

7, 1-40: The northern tribes.

v: Gn 46, 13.   w: Nm 26, 23f; Jgs 10, 1.   x: 1 Chr 7, 6; Gn 46, 21; Nm 26, 38.   y: 1 Chr 7, 8.   z: Nm 26, 39.   a: 12f: Gn 46, 24; Nm 26, 48f.   b: 14-19: Nm 26, 29-32.   c: Nm 26, 29; Jos 17, 1.   d: Nm 26, 33; Jos 17, 3.   e: Nm 26, 35.

a son whom he named Beriah, since evil had befallen his house.*f 24*He had a daughter, Sheerah, who built lower and upper Beth-horon and Uzzen-sheerah. *25*Zabad's son was Rephah, whose son was Resheph, whose son was Telah, whose son was Tahan, *26*whose son was Ladan, whose son was Ammihud, whose son was Elishama,*g 27*whose son was Nun, whose son was Joshua.

*28*Their property and their dwellings were in Bethel and its towns, Naaran to the east, Gezer and its towns to the west, and also Shechem and its towns as far as Ayyah and its towns.*h 29*Manasseh, however, had possession of Beth-shean and its towns, Taanach and its towns, Megiddo and its towns, and Dor and its towns. In these dwelt the descendants of Joseph, the son of Israel.*i*

Asher. *30*The sons of Asher were Imnah, Iishvah, Ishvi, and Beriah; their sister was Serah.*j 31*Beriah's sons were Heber and Malchiel, who was the father of Birzaith. *32*Heber became the father of Japhlet, Shomer, Hotham, and their sister Shua. *33*The sons of Japhlet were Pasach, Bimhal, and Ashvath; these were the sons of Japhlet. *34*The sons of Shomer were Ahi, Rohgah, Jehubbah, and Aram. *35*The sons of his brother Hotham were Zophah, Imna, Shelesh, and Amal. *36*The sons of Zophah were Suah, Harnepher, Shual, Beri, Imrah, *37*Bezer, Hod, Shamma, Shilshah, Ithran, and Beera. *38*The sons of Jether were Jephunneh, Pispa, and Ara. *39*The sons of Ulla were Arah, Hanniel, and Rizia. *40*All these were descendants of Asher, heads of ancestral houses, distinguished men, warriors, and chiefs among the princes. Their family records numbered twenty-six thousand men fit for military service.

See RG 138

CHAPTER 8

*Benjamin.** *1*Benjamin became the father of Bela, his first-born, Ashbel, the second son, Aharah, the third,*k 2*Nohah, the fourth, and Rapha, the fifth. *3*The sons of Bela were Addar and Gera, the father of Ehud. *4*The sons of Ehud were Abishua, Naaman, Ahoah,*l 5*Gera, Shephuphan, and Huram. *6*These were the sons of Ehud, family heads over those who dwelt in Geba and were deported to Manahath. *7*Also Naaman, Ahijah, and Gera. The last, who led them into exile, became the father of Uzza and Ahihud. *8*Shaharaim became a father on the Moabite plateau after he had put away his wives Hushim and Baara. *9*By his wife Hodesh he became the father of Jobab, Zibia, Mesha, Malcam, *10*Jeuz, Sachia, and Mirmah. These were his sons, family heads. *11*By Hushim he became the father of Abitub and Elpaal. *12*The sons of Elpaal were Eber, Misham, Shemed, who built Ono and Lod with its nearby towns,*m 13*Beriah, and Shema. They were family heads of those who dwelt in Aijalon, and they put the inhabitants of Gath to flight. *14*Their brethren were Elpaal, Shashak, and Jeremoth. *15*Zebadiah, Arad, Eder, *16*Michael, Ishpah, and Joha were the sons of Beriah. *17*Zebadiah, Meshullam, Hizki, Heber, *18*Ishmerai, Izliah, and Jobab were the sons of Elpaal. *19*Jakim, Zichri, Zabdi, *20*Elienai, Zillethai, Eliel, *21*Adaiah, Beraiah, and Shimrath were the sons of Shimei. *22*Ishpan, Eber, Eliel, *23*Abdon, Zichri, Hanan, *24*Hananiah, Elam, Anthothijah, *25*Iphdeiah, and Penuel were the sons of Shashak. *26*Shamsherai, Shehariah, Athaliah, *27*Jaareshiah, Elijah, and Zichri were the sons of Jeroham. *28*These were family heads over their kindred, chiefs who dwelt in Jerusalem.

*29n*In Gibeon dwelt Jeiel, the founder of Gibeon, whose wife's name was Maacah; *30*also his first-born son, Abdon, and Zur, Kish, Baal, Ner, Nadab, *31*Gedor, Ahio, Zecher, and Mikloth. *32*Mikloth became the father of Shimeah. These, too, dwelt with their relatives in Jerusalem, opposite their fellow tribesmen. *33o*Ner became the father of Kish, and Kish became the father of Saul. Saul became the father of Jonathan, Malchishua, Abinadab, and Eshbaal.*p 34*The

---

8, 1-40: A second, variant list of the Benjaminites, with special prominence given to Saul's family (vv 33-40).

f: 1 Chr 8, 13.   *g:* Nm 1, 10; 2, 18; 7, 48; 10, 22.   *h:* Gn 12, 8; 1 Kgs 9, 16.   *i:* Jos 17, 11.   *j:* Gn 46, 17; Nm 26, 44ff.   *k:* 1 Chr 7, 6; Gn 46, 21; Nm 26, 38ff.   *l:* Jgs 3, 15.   *m:* Neh 11, 35.   *n:* 29-32: 1 Chr 9, 35-38.   *o:* 33-38: 1 Chr 9, 39-44.   *p:* 1 Chr 10, 2; 1 Sm 9, 1; 14, 49. 51; 31, 2.

son of Jonathan was Meribbaal, and Meribbaal became the father of Micah.*q* *35*The sons of Micah were Pithon, Melech, Tarea, and Ahaz. *36*Ahaz became the father of Jehoaddah, and Jehoaddah became the father of Alemeth, Azmaveth, and Zimri. Zimri became the father of Moza.*r* *37*Moza became the father of Binea, whose son was Raphah, whose son was Eleasah, whose son was Azel.*s* *38*Azel had six sons, whose names were Azrikam, his first-born, Ishmael, Sheariah, Azariah, Obadiah, and Hanan; all these were the sons of Azel. *39*The sons of Eshek, his brother, were Ulam, his first-born, Jeush, the second son, and Eliphelet, the third. *40*The sons of Ulam were combat archers, and many were their sons and grandsons: one hundred and fifty. All these were the descendants of Benjamin.

See RG 138

CHAPTER 9

*1*Thus all Israel was inscribed in its family records which are recorded in the book of the kings of Israel.*t*

Now Judah had been carried in captivity to Babylon because of its rebellion. *2u**The first to settle again in their cities and dwell there were certain lay Israelites, the priests, the Levites, and the temple slaves.*v*

Jerusalemites. *3*In Jerusalem lived Judahites and Benjaminites; also Ephraimites and Manassehites. *4*Among the Judahites was Uthai, son of Ammihud, son of Omri, son of Imri, son of Bani, one of the descendants of Perez, son of Judah. *5*Among the Shelanites were Asaiah, the first-born, and his sons. *6*Among the Zerahites were Jeuel and six hundred and ninety of their brethren. *7*Among the Benjaminites were Sallu, son of Meshullam, son of Hodaviah, son of Hassenuah; *8*Ibneiah, son of Jeroham; Elah, son of Uzzi, son of Michri; Meshullam, son of Shephatiah, son of Reuel, son of Ibnijah. *9*Their kindred of various families were nine hundred and fifty-six. All those named were heads of their ancestral houses.

*10*Among the priests were Jedaiah; Jehoiarib; Jachin; *11*Azariah, son of Hilkiah, son of Meshullam, son of Zadok, son of Meraioth, son of Ahitub, the ruler of the house of God; *12*Adaiah, son of Jeroham, son of Pashhur, son of Malchijah; Maasai, son of Adiel, son of Jahzerah, son of Meshullam, son of Meshillemith, son of Immer. *13*Their brethren, heads of their ancestral houses, were one thousand seven hundred and sixty, valiant for the work of the service of the house of God.

*14*Among the Levites were Shemaiah, son of Hasshub, son of Azrikam, son of Hashabiah, one of the descendants of Merari; *15*Bakbakkar; Heresh; Galal; Mattaniah, son of Mica, son of Zichri, a descendant of Asaph; *16*Obadiah, son of Shemaiah, son of Galal, a descendant of Jeduthun; and Berechiah, son of Asa, son of Elkanah, whose family lived in the villages of the Netophathites.

*17*The gatekeepers were Shallum, Akkub, Talmon, Ahiman, and their brethren; Shallum was the chief. *18*Previously they had stood guard at the king's gate on the east side; now they became gatekeepers for the encampments of the Levites. *19*Shallum, son of Kore, son of Ebiasaph, a descendant of Korah, and his brethren of the same ancestral house of the Korahites had as their assigned task the guarding of the threshold of the tent, just as their fathers had guarded the entrance to the encampment of the LORD. *20*Phinehas, son of Eleazar, had been their chief in times past—the LORD be with him!*w* *21*Zechariah, son of Meshelemiah, guarded the gate of the meeting tent.*x* *22*In all, those who were chosen for gatekeepers at the threshold were two hundred and twelve. They were inscribed in the family records of their villages. David and Samuel the seer had established them in their position of trust. *23*Thus they and their sons kept guard over the gates of the house of the LORD, the house which was then a tent. *24*The gatekeepers were stationed at the four sides, to

---

9, 2-34: The inhabitants of Jerusalem after the exile. A similar list, with many variants in the names, is given in Neh 11, 3-24.

q: 2 Sm 4, 4; 9, 6. 10. 12.　*r:* 1 Chr 9, 42.　*s:* 1 Chr 9, 43.　*t:* 2 Chr 16, 11; 20, 34; 25, 26; 27, 7; 33, 18; 36, 8.　*u:* 2-22: Neh 11, 3-19. *v:* Ezr 2, 70; 7, 7; Neh 11, 3.　*w:* Ex 6, 25; Nm 25, 7. 11; Jgs 20, 28.　*x:* 1 Chr 26, 2. 14.

The Organization of the Postexilic Community

Chapter 9 opens with a summary of what has gone before (vv. 1–2) and moves on to a detailed listing of those responsible for Jerusalem after the return from exile. The Chronicler places characteristic emphasis on the role of the Levites in maintaining proper worship in postexilic Yehud (the name for the Persian province of Jucah). In v. 2, the Israelites are all those in the population with no formal temple function; the priests are the sons of Aaron, those entitled to offer the sacrifices on behalf of the worshipers; the Levites are those with nonsacrificial responsibilities in the temple; and the temple servants are a class of persons assigned to assist in the mundane functions of the temple. The Chronicler spends a large portion of this section on those with a connection to the temple to underscore its importance.

the east, the west, the north, and the south.[y] [25]Their kinsmen who lived in their own villages took turns in assisting them for seven-day periods,[z] [26]while the four chief gate-keepers were on constant duty. These were the Levites who also had charge of the chambers and treasures of the house of God. [27]At night they lodged about the house of God, for it was in their charge and they had the duty of opening it each morning.

[28]Some of them had charge of the liturgical equipment, tallying it as it was brought in and taken out. [29]Others were appointed to take care of the utensils and all the sacred vessels, as well as the fine flour, the wine, the oil, the frankincense, and the spices. [30]It was the sons of priests, however, who mixed the spiced ointments.[a] [31b]Mattithiah, one of the Levites, the first-born of Shallum the Koreite, was entrusted with preparing the cakes. [32]Benaiah the Kohathite, one of their brethren, was in charge of setting out the showbread each sabbath.[c]

[33]These were the chanters and the gatekeepers, family heads over the Levites. They stayed in the chambers when free of duty, for day and night they had to be ready for service. [34]These were the levitical family heads over their kindred, chiefs who dwelt in Jerusalem.

II: The History of David

Genealogy of Saul. [35d]In Gibeon dwelt Jeiel, the founder of Gibeon, whose wife's name was Maacah. [36]His first-born son was Abdon; then came Zur, Kish, Baal, Ner, Nadab, [37]Gedor, Ahio, Zechariah, and Mikloth. [38]Mikloth became the father of Shimeam. These, too, with their brethren, dwelt opposite their brethren in Jerusalem. [39]Ner became the father of Kish, and Kish became the father of Saul. Saul became the father of Jonathan, Malchishua, Abinadab, and Eshbaal. [40]The son of Jonathan was Meribbaal, and Meribbaal became the father of Micah. [41]The sons of Micah were Pithon, Melech, Tahrea, and Ahaz. [42]Ahaz became the father of Jehoaddah, and Jehoaddah became the father of Alemeth, Azmaveth, and Zimri. Zimri became the father of Moza. [43]Moza became the father of Binea, whose son was Rephaiah, whose son was Eleasah, whose son was Azel. [44]Azel had six sons, whose names were Azrikam, his first-born, Ishmael, Sheariah, Azariah, Obadiah, and Hanan; these were the sons of Azel.

CHAPTER 10

See RG
138–40

His Death and Burial. [1e]Now the Philistines were at war with Israel; the Israelites fled before the Philistines, and a number of them fell, slain on Mount Gilboa. [2]The Philistines pressed hard after Saul and his sons. When the Philistines had killed Jonathan, Abinadab, and Malchishua, sons of Saul, [3]the whole fury of the battle descended upon Saul. Then the archers found him, and wounded him with their arrows.

[4]Saul said to his armor-bearer, "Draw your sword and thrust me through with it, that these uncircumcised may not come

y: 1 Chr 26, 13.   z: 2 Chr 23, 4f.   a: Ex 30, 22-33.   b: 31f: 1 Chr 23, 29; Lv 2, 1ff; 6, 13ff; 7, 11.   c: Ex 25, 30; Lv 24, 5-8.   d: 35-44: 1 Chr 8, 29-38.   e: 1-12: 1 Sm 31, 1-13.

Account of David's Reign

Chapters 10–20 sometimes repeat, and on occasion summarize, portions of the narratives of David's reign (2 Sm 5 through 1 Kgs 2). Many of these earlier accounts are completely left out by the Chronicler, and others are rewritten so thoroughly as to bear little resemblance to the earlier account. In these narratives, the Chronicler highlights David's success as king and his role in selecting Jerusalem as the capital, along with preparing for the construction and staffing of the temple.

and maltreat me." But the armor-bearer, in great fear, refused. So Saul took his own sword and fell on it; [5]and seeing him dead, the armor-bearer also fell on his sword and died. [6]Thus, with Saul and his three sons, his whole house died at one time. [7]When all the Israelites who were in the valley saw that Saul and his sons had died in the rout, they left their cities and fled; thereupon the Philistines came and occupied them.

[8]On the following day, when the Philistines came to strip the slain, they found Saul and his sons where they had fallen on Mount Gilboa. [9]They stripped him, cut off his head, and took his armor; these they sent throughout the land of the Philistines to convey the good news to their idols and their people. [10]His armor they put in the house of their gods, but his skull they impaled on the temple of Dagon.

[11]When all the inhabitants of Jabesh-gilead had heard what the Philistines had done to Saul, [12]its warriors rose to a man, recovered the bodies of Saul and his sons, and brought them to Jabesh. They buried their bones under the oak of Jabesh, and fasted seven days.[f]

[13]*Thus Saul died because of his rebellion against the LORD in disobeying his command, and also because he had sought counsel of a necromancer,[g] [14]and had not rather inquired of the LORD. Therefore the LORD slew him, and transferred his kingdom to David, the son of Jesse.[h]

CHAPTER 11

See RG 138–40

David Is Made King. [1][i]Then all Israel gathered about David in Hebron, and they said: "Surely, we are of the same bone and flesh as you. [2]Even formerly, when Saul was still the king, it was you who led Israel in all its battles. And now the LORD, your God, has said to you, 'You shall shepherd my people Israel and be ruler over them.' "[j] [3]Then all the elders of Israel came to the king at Hebron, and there David made a covenant with them in the presence of the LORD; and they anointed him king over Israel, in accordance with the word of the LORD as revealed through Samuel.[k]

Jerusalem Captured. [4]Then David and all Israel went to Jerusalem, that is, Jebus, where the natives of the land were called Jebusites.[l] [5]The inhabitants of Jebus said to David, "You shall not enter here." David nevertheless captured the fortress of Sion, which is the City of David. [6]David said, "Whoever strikes the Jebusites first shall be made the chief commander." Joab, the son of Zeruiah, was the first to go up; and so he became chief.[m] [7]David took up his residence in the fortress, which thenceforth was called the City of David. [8]He rebuilt the city on all sides, from the Millo all the way around, while Joab restored the rest of the city.[n] [9]David became more and more powerful, for the LORD of hosts was with him.

David's Warriors. [10][o]These were David's chief warriors who, together with all Israel, supported him in his reign in order to make him true king, even as the LORD had com-

10, 13f: The Chronicler's comment on why Saul met his tragic end: he had disobeyed the Lord's command given through the prophet Samuel (1 Sm 15, 3-9), and had sought counsel of a necromancer (1 Sm 28, 6-19), contrary to the Mosaic law against necromancy (Dt 18, 10f).

f: 2 Sm 2, 5.   *g:* Dt 18, 10ff; 1 Sm 13, 13f; 15, 3. 11. 26.   *h:* 1 Sm 15, 28; 2 Sm 3, 9f.   *i:* 1-9: 2 Sm 5, 1-10.   *j:* 1 Sm 18, 5. 13-16. 30; 19, 8.   *k:* 1 Sm 16, 1. 13; 2 Sm 2, 4.   *l:* Jos 15, 8; Jgs 1, 21; 19, 10f.   *m:* 2 Sm 2, 13ff; 8, 16.   *n:* 1 Kgs 9, 15. 24; 11, 27; 2 Chr 32, 5.   *o:* 10-41: 2 Sm 23, 8-39.

The Kingdom of David according to 1 Chronicles

manded concerning Israel. [11]Here is the list of David's warriors:

Ishbaal, the son of Hachamoni, chief of the Three.* He brandished his spear against three hundred, whom he slew in a single encounter. [12]Next to him Eleazar, the son of Dodo the Ahohite, one of the Three warriors.[p] [13]He was with David at Pasdammim, where the Philistines had massed for battle. The plowland was fully planted with barley, but its defenders were retreating before the Philistines.[q] [14]He made a stand on the sown ground, kept it safe, and cut down the Philistines. Thus the LORD brought about a great victory.

[15]Three of the Thirty chiefs went down to the rock, to David, who was in the cave of Adullam while the Philistines were encamped in the valley of Rephaim.[r] [16]David was then in the stronghold, and a Philistine garrison was at Bethlehem. [17]David expressed a desire: "Oh, that someone would give me a drink from the cistern that is by the gate at Bethlehem!" [18]Thereupon the Three broke through the encampment of the Philistines, drew water from the cistern by the gate at Bethlehem, and carried it back to David. But David refused to drink it. Instead, he poured it out as a libation to the LORD, [19]saying, "God forbid that I should do such a thing! Could I drink the blood of these men who risked their lives?" For at the risk of their lives they brought it; and so he refused to drink it. Such deeds as these the Three warriors performed.

[20s]Abishai, the brother of Joab. He was the chief of the Thirty;* he brandished his spear against three hundred, and slew them. Thus he had a reputation like that of the Three.[t] [21]He was twice as famous as any of the Thirty and became their commander, but he did not attain to the Three.

[22]Benaiah, the son of Jehoiada, a valiant man of mighty deeds, from Kabzeel. He killed the two sons of Ariel of Moab, and also, on a snowy day, he went down and killed the lion in the cistern. [23]He likewise slew the Egyptian, a huge man five cubits tall. The Egyptian carried a spear that was like a weaver's heddle-bar, but he came against him with a staff, wrested the spear from the Egyptian's hand, and killed him with his own spear. [24]Such deeds as these of Benaiah, the son of Jehoiada, gave him a reputation like that of the Three. [25]He was more famous than any of the Thirty, but he did not attain to the Three. David put him in charge of his bodyguard.[u]

[26]Also these warriors: Asahel, the brother of Joab; Elhanan, son of Dodo, from Bethlehem;[v] [27]Shammoth, from En-harod; Helez, from Palti; [28]Ira, son of Ikkesh, from Tekoa; Abiezer, from Anathoth; [29]Sibbecai, from Husha; Ilai, from Ahoh;[w] [30]Maharai, from Netophah; Heled, son of Baanah, from Netophah;[x] [31]Ithai, son of Ribai, from Gibeah of Benjamin; Benaiah, from Pirathon;[y] [32]Hurai, from the valley of Gaash; Abiel, from Betharabah; [33]Azmaveth, from Bahurim; Eliahba, from Shaalbon; [34]Jashen the Gunite; Jonathan, son of Shagee, from En-harod; [35]Ahiam, son of Sachar, from En-harod; Elipheleth, son of [36]Ahasabi, from Beth-maacah; Ahijah, from Gilo; [37]Hezro, from Carmel; Naarai, the son of Ezbai; [38]Joel, brother of Nathan, from Rehob, the Gadite; [39]Zelek the Ammonite; Naharai, from Beeroth, the armor-bearer of Joab, son of Zeruiah; [40]Ira, from Jattir; Gareb, from Jattir; [41]Uriah the Hittite; Zabad, son of Ahlai, [42]and, in addition to the Thirty, Adina, son of Shiza, the Reubenite, chief of the tribe of Reuben; [43]Hanan, from Beth-maacah; Joshaphat the Mithnite; [44]Uzzia, from Ashterath; Shama and Jeiel, sons of Hotham, from Aroer; [45]Jediael, son of Shimri, and Joha, his brother, the Tizite; [46]Eliel the Mahavite; Jeribai and Joshaviah, sons of Elnaam; Ithmah, from Moab; [47]Eliel, Obed, and Jaasiel the Mezobian.

11, 11f: The Three: the Chronicler names only two of them: Ishbaal and Eleazar. According to 2 Sm 23, 8-12, the Three were Ishbaal, Eleazar, and Shammah.

11, 20: The Thirty: listed by name in vv 26-47. The list given in 2 Sm 23, 8-39 often differs in names and spellings; for the numbers, see the note there.

p: 1 Chr 27, 4.　*q:* 1 Sm 17, 1.　*r:* 1 Chr 14, 9; 2 Sm 5, 18. 22.　*s:* 20f: 2 Sm 23, 18f.　*t:* 1 Chr 18, 12; 1 Sm 26, 6ff; 2 Sm 16, 9; 18, 2; 21, 17.　*u:* 2 Sm 8, 18; 20, 23.　*v:* 1 Chr 2, 16; 27, 7.　*w:* 1 Chr 27, 11.　*x:* 1 Chr 27, 13.　*y:* 1 Chr 27, 14.

The listing of troop strength in 12, 25ff seems grossly inflated. Some believe the author has misunderstood terms for "unit" and has understood it as a word for "thousand." Others have argued the numbers are symbolic rather than real.

See RG
138-40

CHAPTER 12

David's Early Followers. [1]The following men came to David in Ziklag while he was still under banishment from Saul, son of Kish; they, too, were among the warriors who helped him in his battles.[z] [2]They were archers who could use either the right or the left hand, both in slinging stones and in shooting arrows with the bow. They were some of Saul's kinsmen, from Benjamin. [3]Ahiezer was their chief, along with Joash, both sons of Shemaah of Gibeah; also Jeziel and Pelet, sons of Azmaveth; Beracah; Jehu, from Anathoth;[a] [4]Ishmaiah the Gibeonite, a warrior on the level of the Thirty, and in addition to their number: [5]Jeremiah; Jahaziel; Johanan; Jozabad, from Gederah; [6]Eluzai; Jerimoth; Bealiah; Shemariah; Shephatiah the Haruphite; [7]Elkanah, Isshiah, Azarel, Joezer, and Ishbaal, who were Korahites; [8]Joelah, finally, and Zebadiah, sons of Jeroham, from Gedor.

[9]Some of the Gadites also went over to David when he was at the stronghold in the wilderness. They were valiant warriors, experienced soldiers equipped with shield and spear, who bore themselves like lions, and were as swift as the gazelles on the mountains.[b] [10]Ezer was their chief, Obadiah was second, Eliab third, [11]Mishmannah fourth, Jeremiah fifth, [12]Attai sixth, Eliel seventh, [13]Johanan eighth, Elzabad ninth, [14]Jeremiah tenth, and Machbannai eleventh. [15]These Gadites were army commanders, the lesser placed over hundreds and the greater over thousands. [16]It was they who crossed over the Jordan when it was overflowing both its banks in the first month, and dispersed all who were in the valleys to the east and to the west.

[17]Some Benjaminites and Judahites also came to David at the stronghold. [18]David went out to meet them and addressed them in these words: "If you come peacefully, to help me, I am of a mind to have you join me. But if you have come to betray me to my enemies though my hands have done no wrong, may the God of our fathers see and punish you."

[19]Then spirit enveloped Amasai, the chief of the Thirty, who spoke:

"We are yours, O David,
we are with you, O son of Jesse.
Peace, peace to you,
and peace to him who helps you;
your God it is who helps you."

So David received them and placed them among the leaders of his troops.

[20]Men from Manasseh also deserted to David when he came with the Philistines to battle against Saul. However, he did not help the Philistines, for their lords took counsel and sent him home, saying, "At the cost of our heads he will desert to his master Saul." [21]As he was returning to Ziklag, therefore, these deserted to him from Manasseh: Adnah, Jozabad, Jediael, Michael, Jozabad, Elihu, and Zillethai, chiefs of thousands of Manasseh. [22]They helped David by taking charge of his troops, for they were all warriors and became commanders of his army. [23]And from day to day men kept coming to David's help until there was a vast encampment, like an encampment of angels.

The Assembly at Hebron. [24]This is the muster of the detachments of armed troops that came to David at Hebron to transfer to him Saul's kingdom, as the LORD had ordained. [25]*Judahites bearing shields and spears: six thousand eight hundred armed troops. [26]Of the Simeonites, warriors fit for

12, 25-38: The Chronicler fills out the pageantry of joyous occasions in keeping with his much later appreciation of the significance of the event in the history of God's people: the numbers in attendance at David's crowning in Hebron (cf 2 Sm 5, 1ff) are recounted in the same spirit of enthusiasm which in v 23 compares David's band of desert freebooters to a numerous encampment of angels.

z: 1 Sm 27, 1-7.   a: 1 Chr 27, 12.   b: Dt 33, 20.

battle: seven thousand one hundred. ²⁷Of the Levites: four thousand six hundred, ²⁸along with Jehoiada, leader of the line of Aaron, with another three thousand seven hundred, ²⁹and Zadok, a young warrior, with twenty-two princes of his father's house. ³⁰Of the Benjaminites, the brethren of Saul: three thousand—until this time, most of them had held their allegiance to the house of Saul. ³¹Of the Ephraimites: twenty thousand eight hundred warriors, men renowned in their ancestral houses. ³²Of the half-tribe of Manasseh: eighteen thousand, designated by name to come and make David king. ³³Of the Issacharites, their chiefs who were endowed with an understanding of the times and who knew what Israel had to do: two hundred chiefs, together with all their brethren under their command. ³⁴From Zebulun, men fit for military service, set in battle array with every kind of weapon for war: fifty thousand men rallying with a single purpose. ³⁵From Naphtali: one thousand captains, and with them, armed with shield and lance, thirty-seven thousand men. ³⁶Of the Danites, set in battle array: twenty-eight thousand six hundred. ³⁷From Asher, fit for military service and set in battle array: forty thousand. ³⁸From the other side of the Jordan, of the Reubenites, Gadites, and the half-tribe of Manasseh, men equipped with every kind of weapon of war: one hundred and twenty thousand.

³⁹All these soldiers, drawn up in battle order, came to Hebron with the resolute intention of making David king over all Israel. The rest of Israel was likewise of one mind to make David king. ⁴⁰They remained with David for three days, feasting and drinking, for their brethren had prepared for them. ⁴¹Moreover, their neighbors from as far as Issachar, Zebulun, and Naphtali came bringing food on asses, camels, mules, and oxen—provisions in great quantity of meal, pressed figs, raisins, wine, oil, oxen, and sheep. For there was rejoicing in Israel.

CHAPTER 13

See RG 138-40

Transfer of the Ark. ^{1c}After David had taken counsel with his commanders of thousands and of hundreds, that is to say, with every one of his leaders, ²he said to the whole assembly of Israel: "If it seems good to you, and is so decreed by the LORD our God, let us summon the rest of our brethren from all the districts of Israel, and also the priests and the Levites from their cities with pasture lands, that they may join us;^d ³and let us bring the ark of our God here among us, for in the days of Saul we did not visit it." ⁴And the whole assembly agreed to do this, for the idea was pleasing to all the people.

⁵Then David assembled all Israel, from Shihor of Egypt* to Labo of Hamath, to bring the ark of God from Kiriath-jearim.^e ⁶David and all Israel went up to Baalah, that is, to Kiriath-jearim, of Judah, to bring back the ark of God, which was known by the name "LORD enthroned upon the cherubim."^f ⁷They transported the ark of God on a new cart from the house of Abinadab; Uzzah and Ahio were guiding the cart, ⁸while David and all Israel danced before God with great enthusiasm, amid songs and music on lyres, harps, tambourines, cymbals, and trumpets.

⁹As they reached the threshing floor of Chidon,* Uzzah stretched out his hand to steady the ark, for the oxen were upsetting it. ¹⁰Then the LORD became angry with Uzzah and struck him; he died there in God's presence, because he had laid his hand on the ark. ¹¹David was disturbed because the LORD's anger had broken out against Uzzah. Therefore that place has been called Perezuzza* even to this day.

¹²David was now afraid of God, and he said, "How can I bring the ark of God with me?" ¹³Therefore he did not take the ark back with him to the City of David, but he took it instead to the house of Obed-edom

---

13, 5: Shihor of Egypt: the eastern branch of the Nile delta. Labo of Hamath: in southern Syria.

13, 9: Chidon: in 2 Sm 6, 6, Nodan.

13, 11: Perez-uzza: A Hebrew term meaning "the breaking out against Uzza."

---

c: 1-14: 2 Sm 6, 1-11. d: Nm 35, 1ff; Jos 14, 4; 21, 2ff. e: 1 Chr 15, 3; Jos 13, 3. 5; 1 Sm 6, 21; 7, 1f; 2 Sm 6, 1-11. f: Jos 15, 9; 18, 14; 1 Sm 4, 4; 7, 1.

Moving the Ark into Jerusalem

An important prelude to David's effectual rule from Jerusalem was bringing the ark of God into what will be the "chosen city" of Jerusalem (ch 13). Rearranging the order of his source (2 Sm 6, 1–11), the Chronicler has David acting to bring the divine presence as symbolized by the ark (Nm 10, 33–36) into the capital city even before beginning his own palace. The Chronicler's deliberate reformatting of the sequence of events highlights the importance the narrative will give to honoring God's presence in Jerusalem.

the Gittite. [14]The ark of God remained in the house of Obed-edom with his family for three months, and the LORD blessed Obed-edom's household and all that he possessed.[g]

See RG 138–40

CHAPTER 14

David in Jerusalem. [1h]Hiram, king of Tyre, sent envoys to David along with masons and carpenters, and cedar wood to build him a house.[i] [2]David now understood that the LORD had truly confirmed him as king over Israel, for his kingdom was greatly exalted for the sake of his people Israel. [3j]David took other wives in Jerusalem and became the father of more sons and daughters. [4]These are the names of those who were born to him in Jerusalem: Shammua, Shobab, Nathan, Solomon, [5]Ibhar, Elishua, Elpelet, [6]Nogah, Nepheg, Japhia, [7]Elishama, Beeliada, and Eliphelet.

The Philistine Wars. [8]When the Philistines had heard that David was anointed king over all Israel, they went up in unison to seek him out. But when David heard of this, he marched out against them. [9]Meanwhile the Philistines had come and raided the valley of Rephaim.[k] [10]David inquired of God, "Shall I advance against the Philistines, and will you deliver them into my power?" The LORD answered him, "Advance, for I will deliver them into your power." [11]They advanced, therefore, to Baal-perazim, and David defeated them there. Then David said, "God has used me to break through my enemies just as water breaks through a dam." Therefore that place was called Baal-perazim. [12]The Philistines

had left their gods there, and David ordered them to be burnt.[l]

[13]Once again the Philistines raided the valley, [14]and again David inquired of God. But God answered him: "Do not try to pursue them, but go around them and come upon them from the direction of the mastic trees. [15]When you hear the sound of marching in the tops of the mastic trees, then go forth to battle, for God has already gone before you to strike the army of the Philistines." [16]David did as God commanded him, and they routed the Philistine army from Gibeon to Gezer.

[17]Thus David's fame was spread abroad through every land, and the LORD made all the nations fear him.

CHAPTER 15

See RG 138–40

The Ark Brought to Jerusalem. [1]David built houses for himself in the City of David and prepared a place for the ark of God, pitching a tent for it there. [2]At that time he said, "No one may carry the ark of God except the Levites, for the LORD chose them to carry the ark of the LORD and to minister to him forever."[m] [3]Then David assembled all Israel in Jerusalem to bring the ark of the LORD to the place which he had prepared for it.[n] [4]David also called together the sons of Aaron and the Levites: [5]of the sons of Kohath, Uriel, their chief, and one hundred and twenty of his brethren; [6]of the sons of Merari, Asaiah, their chief, and two hundred and twenty of his brethren; [7]of the sons of Gershon, Joel, their chief, and one hundred and thirty of his brethren; [8]of the sons of Elizaphan, Shemaiah, their chief,

---

g: 1 Chr 26, 4f.   *h:* 1-16: 2 Sm 5, 11-25.   *i:* 1 Kgs 5, 1; 2 Chr 2, 3.   *j:* 3-7: 1 Chr 3, 5-8; 2 Sm 5, 13-16.   *k:* 1 Chr 11, 15.   *l:* Dt 7, 5. 25.   *m:* Nm 1, 50; 7, 9; Dt 10, 8; 31, 25; 1 Sm 6, 15; Jos 3, 8.   *n:* 1 Chr 13, 5; 2 Sm 6, 15. 17.

Chapter 15, v. 29 is an abridged version of 2 Samuel 6, 16–23, but without the observation that David's nakedness disturbed Michal. The Chronicler may be trying to draw another contrast between Saul and David by portraying Michal's displeasure at David's joy in bringing the ark to Jerusalem.

and two hundred of his brethren; [9]of the sons of Hebron, Eliel, their chief, and eighty of his brethren; [10]of the sons of Uzziel, Amminadab, their chief, and one hundred and twelve of his brethren.

[11]David summoned the priests Zadok and Abiathar, and the Levites Uriel, Asaiah, Joel, Shemaiah, Eliel, and Amminadab,[o] [12]and said to them: "You, the heads of the levitical families, must sanctify yourselves along with your brethren and bring the ark of the LORD, the God of Israel, to the place which I have prepared for it.[p] [13]Because you were not with us the first time, the wrath of the LORD our God burst upon us, for we did not seek him aright."[q] [14]Accordingly, the priests and the Levites sanctified themselves to bring up the ark of the LORD, the God of Israel. [15]The Levites bore the ark of God on their shoulders with poles, as Moses had ordained according to the word of the LORD.[r]

[16]David commanded the chiefs of the Levites to appoint their brethren as chanters, to play on musical instruments, harps, lyres, and cymbals, to make a loud sound of rejoicing.[s] [17]Therefore the Levites appointed Heman, son of Joel, and, among his brethren, Asaph, son of Berechiah; and among the sons of Merari, their brethren, Ethan, son of Kushaiah;[t] [18]and, together with these, their brethren of the second rank: the gatekeepers Zechariah, Uzziel, Shemiramoth, Jehiel, Unni, Eliab, Benaiah, Maaseiah, Mattithiah, Eliphelehu, Mikneiah, Obed-edom, and Jeiel. [19]The chanters, Heman, Asaph, and Ethan, sounded brass cymbals. [20]Zechariah, Uzziel, Shemiramoth, Jehiel, Unni, Eliab, Maaseiah, and Benaiah played on harps set to "Alamoth."[*] [21]But Mattithiah, Eliphelehu, Mikneiah, Obed-edom, and Jeiel led the chant on lyres set to "the eighth." [22]Chenaniah was the chief of the Levites in the chanting; he directed the chanting, for he was skillful.[u] [23]Berechiah and Elkanah were gatekeepers before the ark. [24]The priests, Shebaniah, Joshaphat, Nethanel, Amasai, Zechariah, Benaiah, and Eliezer, sounded the trumpets before the ark of God. Obed-edom and Jeiel were also gatekeepers before the ark.[v]

[25w]Thus David, the elders of Israel, and the commanders of thousands went to bring up the ark of the covenant of the LORD with joy from the house of Obed-edom. [26]While the Levites, with God's help, were bearing the ark of the covenant of the LORD, seven bulls and seven rams were sacrificed.[x] [27]David was clothed in a robe of fine linen, as were all the Levites who carried the ark, the singers, and Chenaniah, the leader of the chant; David was also wearing a linen ephod.[y] [28]Thus all Israel brought back the ark of the covenant of the LORD with joyful shouting, and to the sound of horns, trumpets, and cymbals, and the music of harps and lyres. [29]But as the ark of the covenant of the LORD was entering the City of David, Michal, daughter of Saul, looked down from her window, and when she saw King David leaping and dancing, she despised him in her heart.[z]

15, 20: Alamoth: a musical term (literally, "young women") of uncertain meaning, occurring also in Ps 46, 1, where it is rendered as virgins. Perhaps it may mean something like "soprano," whereas the term "eighth" (Hebrew sheminith, v 21) may then mean "bass"; cf Pss 6, 1; 12, 1.

o: 1 Chr 16, 39; 2 Sm 8, 17; 15, 29. 35.   p: 2 Chr 29, 5. 15. 34; 30, 3. 15. 24.   q: 1 Chr 13, 3.   r: Ex 25, 13ff; Nm 1, 50; 7, 9; 2 Chr 35, 3.   s: 1 Chr 13, 8; 16, 5; 2 Chr 5, 12; 29, 25; Neh 12, 27.   t: 1 Chr 6, 31-47; 25, 1-8.   u: 1 Chr 26, 29.   v: Nm 10, 8; Jos 6, 4ff. w: 25-29: 2 Sm 6, 12-16.   x: 2 Sm 6, 17; 2 Chr 29, 21.   y: 1 Sm 2, 18; 2 Sm 6, 14.   z: 2 Sm 6, 20ff.

CHAPTER 16

See RG
138-40

¹ᵃThey brought in the ark of God and set it within the tent which David had pitched for it. Then they offered up holocausts and peace offerings to God.ᵇ ²When David had finished offering up the holocausts and peace offerings, he blessed the people in the name of the LORD, ³and distributed to every Israelite, to every man and to every woman, a loaf of bread, a piece of meat, and a raisin cake.

The Ministering Levites. ⁴He now appointed certain Levites to minister before the ark of the LORD, to celebrate, thank, and praise the LORD, the God of Israel.ᶜ ⁵Asaph was their chief, and second to him were Zechariah, Uzziel, Shemira-moth, Jehiel, Mattithiah, Eliab, Benaiah, Obed-edom, and Jeiel. These were to play on harps and lyres, while Asaph was to sound the cymbals, ⁶and the priests Benaiah and Jahaziel were to be the regular trumpeters before the ark of the covenant of God.

⁷Then, on that same day, David appointed Asaph and his brethren to sing for the first time these praises of the LORD:

⁸ *Give thanks to the LORD, invoke his name;ᵈ
  make known among the nations his deeds.
⁹ Sing to him, sing his praise,
  proclaim all his wondrous deeds.
¹⁰ Glory in his holy name;
  rejoice, O hearts that seek the LORD!
¹¹ Look to the LORD in his strength;
  seek to serve him constantly.
¹² Recall the wondrous deeds that he has wrought,
  his portents, and the judgments he has uttered,
¹³ You descendants of Israel, his servants,
  sons of Jacob, his chosen ones!

¹⁴ He, the LORD, is our God;
  throughout the earth his judgments prevail.
¹⁵ He remembers forever his covenant

which he made binding for a thousand generations—
¹⁶ Which he entered into with Abraham
  and by his oath to Isaac;
¹⁷ Which he established for Jacob by statute,
  for Israel as an everlasting covenant,
¹⁸ Saying, "To you will I give the land of Canaan
  as your allotted inheritance."

¹⁹ When they were few in number,
  a handful, and strangers there,
²⁰ Wandering from nation to nation,
  from one kingdom to another people,
²¹ He let no one oppress them,
  and for their sake he rebuked kings:
²² "Touch not my anointed,
  and to my prophets do no harm."

²³ ᵉSing to the LORD, all the earth,
  announce his salvation, day after day.
²⁴ Tell his glory among the nations;
  among all peoples, his wondrous deeds.
²⁵ For great is the LORD and highly to be praised;
  and awesome is he, beyond all gods.
²⁶ For all the gods of the nations are things of nought,
  but the LORD made the heavens.
²⁷ Splendor and majesty go before him;
  praise and joy are in his holy place.

²⁸ Give to the LORD, you families of nations,
  give to the LORD glory and praise;
²⁹ Give to the LORD the glory due his name!
  Bring gifts, and enter his presence;
  worship the LORD in holy attire.
³⁰ Tremble before him, all the earth;
  he has made the world firm, not to be moved.

³¹ Let the heavens be glad and the earth rejoice;
  let them say among the nations: The LORD is king.
³² Let the sea and what fills it resound;
  let the plains rejoice and all that is in them!

16, 8-36: A hymn composed of parts, with textual variants, from several Psalms; vv 8-22 = Ps 105, 1-15; vv 23-33 = Ps 96, 1-13; vv 34-36 = Ps 106, 1. 47f.

a: 1-3: 2 Sm 6, 17ff.   *b:* 1 Chr 15, 1.   *c:* Sir 47, 9.   *d:* 8-22: Ps 105, 1-15.   *e:* 23-33: Ps 96, 1-13.

33 Then shall all the trees of the forest exult
    before the LORD, for he comes:
    he comes to rule the earth.

34 *f*Give thanks to the LORD, for he is good,
    for his kindness endures forever;
35 And say, "Save us, O God, our savior,
    gather us and deliver us from the
        nations,
    That we may give thanks to your holy
        name
    and glory in praising you."
36 Blessed be the LORD, the God of Israel,
    through all eternity!
    Let all the people say, Amen! Alleluia.

37Then David left Asaph and his brethren
there before the ark of the covenant of the
LORD to minister before the ark regularly according to the daily ritual; 38he also left there
Obed-edom and sixty-eight of his brethren,
including Obed-edom, son of Jeduthun, and
Hosah, to be gatekeepers.*g*
39But the priest Zadok and his priestly
brethren he left before the Dwelling of the
LORD on the high place at Gibeon,*h* 40to offer
holocausts to the LORD on the altar of holocausts regularly, morning and evening, and
to do all that is written in the law of the LORD
which he has decreed for Israel.*i* 41With them
were Heman and Jeduthun and the others
who were chosen and designated by name to
give thanks to the LORD, "because his kindness endures forever,"*j* 42with trumpets and
cymbals for accompaniment, and instruments for the sacred chant. The sons of Jeduthun kept the gate.*k*
43Then all the people departed, each to his
own home, and David returned to bless his
household.*l*

CHAPTER 17

See RG
138–40

The Oracle of Nathan. 1*m*After David
had taken up residence in his house, he said to
Nathan the prophet, "See, I am living in a
house of cedar, but the ark of the covenant of
the LORD dwells under tentcloth."*n* 2Nathan
replied to David, "Do, therefore, whatever
you desire, for God is with you."

3But that same night the word of God came
to Nathan: 4"Go and tell my servant David,
Thus says the LORD: It is not you who are to
build a house for me to dwell in.*o* 5For I have
never dwelt in a house, from the time when I
led Israel onward, even to this day, but I have
been lodging in tent or pavilion 6as long as I
have wandered about with all of Israel. Did I
ever say a word to any of the judges of Israel
whom I commanded to guide my people,
such as, 'Why have you not built me a house
of cedar?' 7Therefore, tell my servant David,
Thus says the LORD of hosts: I took you from
the pasture, from following the sheep, that
you might become ruler over my people Israel.*p* 8I was with you wherever you went,
and I cut down all your enemies before you. I
will make your name great like that of the
greatest on the earth. 9I will assign a place for
my people Israel and I will plant them in it to
dwell there henceforth undisturbed; nor shall
wicked men ever again oppress them, as they
did at first, 10and during all the time when I
appointed judges over my people Israel. And
I will subdue all your enemies. Moreover, I
declare to you that I, the LORD, will build you
a house; 11so that when your days have been
completed and you must join your fathers, I
will raise up your offspring after you who will
be one of your own sons, and I will establish
his kingdom.*q* 12He it is who shall build me a
house, and I will establish his throne forever.*r*
13I will be a father to him, and he shall be a
son to me, and I will not withdraw my favor
from him as I withdrew it from him who preceded you;*s* 14but I will maintain him in my
house and in my kingdom forever, and his
throne shall be firmly established forever."

15All these words and this whole vision
Nathan related exactly to David.

David's Thanksgiving. 16Then David came
in and sat in the LORD's presence, saying:
"Who am I, O LORD God, and what is my
family, that you should have brought me as
far as I have come? 17And yet, even this you
now consider too little, O God! For you have
made a promise regarding your servant's
family reaching into the distant future, and

f: 34ff: Ps 106, 1. 47f.   *g:* 1 Chr 15, 24.   *h:* 1 Kgs 3, 4.   *i:* Ex 29, 38-42; Lv 6, 9; Nm 28, 3. 6; 2 Chr 13, 11.   *j:* 2 Chr 5, 12; 7, 3. 6;
20, 21; Ezr 3, 11.   *k:* 2 Chr 29, 27.   *l:* 2 Sm 6, 19f.   *m:* 1-27: 2 Sm 7, 1-29.   *n:* 1 Chr 15, 1; 2 Sm 5, 11.   *o:* 1 Chr 28, 3; 1 Kgs 8,
19.   *p:* 1 Sm 16, 11.   *q:* 2 Sm 7, 12f.   *r:* 1 Chr 22, 10; 28, 6. 10.   *s:* 2 Sm 7, 14.

you have looked on me as henceforth the most notable of men, O LORD God.[t] [18]What more can David say to you? You know your servant. [19]O LORD, for your servant's sake and in keeping with your purpose, you have done this great thing. [20]O LORD, there is no one like you and there is no God but you, just as we have always understood.[u]

[21]"Is there, like your people Israel, whom you redeemed from Egypt, another nation on earth whom a god went to redeem as his people? You won for yourself a name for great and awesome deeds by driving out the nations before your people.[v] [22]You made your people Israel your own forever, and you, O LORD, became their God. [23]Therefore, O LORD, may the promise that you have uttered concerning your servant and his house remain firm forever. Bring about what you have promised, [24]that your renown as LORD of hosts, God of Israel, may be great and abide forever, while the house of David, your servant, is established in your presence.

[25]"Because you, O my God, have revealed to your servant that you will build him a house, your servant has made bold to pray before you.[w] [26]Since you, O LORD, are truly God and have promised this good thing to your servant, [27]and since you have deigned to bless the house of your servant, so that it will remain forever—since it is you, O LORD, who blessed it, it is blessed forever."[x]

CHAPTER 18

See RG 138–40

David's Victories. [1y]After this, David defeated the Philistines and subdued them; and he took Gath and its towns away from the control of the Philistines. [2]He also defeated Moab, and the Moabites became his subjects, paying tribute.

[3]David then defeated Hadadezer, king of Zobah toward Hamath, when the latter was on his way to set up his victory stele at the river Euphrates. [4]David took from him twenty thousand foot soldiers, one thousand chariots, and seven thousand horsemen. Of the chariot horses, David hamstrung all but one hundred.[z] [5]The Arameans of Damascus came to the aid of Hadadezer, king of Zobah, but David also slew twenty-two thousand of their men. [6]Then David set up garrisons in the Damascus region of Aram, and the Arameans became his subjects, paying tribute. Thus the LORD made David victorious in all his campaigns.

[7]David took the golden shields that were carried by Hadadezer's attendants and brought them to Jerusalem. [8]He likewise took away from Tibhath and Cun, cities of Hadadezer, large quantities of bronze, which Solomon later used to make the bronze sea and the pillars and the vessels of bronze.[a]

[9]When Tou, king of Hamath, heard that David had defeated the entire army of Hadadezer, king of Zobah, [10]he sent his son Hadoram to wish King David well and to congratulate him on having waged a victorious war against Hadadezer; for Hadadezer had been at war with Tou. He also sent David gold, silver and bronze utensils of every sort.[b] [11]These also King David consecrated to the LORD along with all the silver and gold that he had taken from the nations: from Edom, Moab, the Ammonites, the Philistines, and Amalek.

[12]Abishai, the son of Zeruiah, also slew eighteen thousand Edomites in the Valley of Salt.[c] [13]He set up garrisons in Edom, and all the Edomites became David's subjects. Thus the LORD made David victorious in all his campaigns.

David's Officials. [14d]David reigned over all Israel and dispensed justice and right to all his people. [15]Joab, son of Zeruiah, was in command of the army; Jehoshaphat, son of Ahilud, was herald;[e] [16]Zadok, son of Ahitub, and Ahimelech, son of Abiathar, were priests;*

18, 16: Zadok . . . and Ahimelech, son of Abiathar, were priests: as in the Chronicler's source, 2 Sm 8, 17. But according to 2 Sm 15, 24. 29. 35; 17, 15; 19, 11; 20, 25, and even 1 Chr 15, 11, it was Abiathar who shared the priestly office with Zadok, and he remained in this office even during the early years of Solomon's reign (1 Kgs 2, 26; 4, 4). Moreover, according to 1 Sm 22, 20; 23, 6; 30, 7, Ahimelech was the father, not the son, of Abiathar. If the text Ahimelech, son of Abiathar, is not due to a scribal change, one must assume that

Abiathar had a son who was named after his grandfather and who shared the priestly office with his father during the last years of David's reign.

t: 2 Sm 7, 19. u: Sir 36, 4. v: Dt 4, 7; 2 Sm 7, 23. w: 2 Sm 7, 27. x: Nm 22, 6. y: 1-13: 2 Sm 8, 1-14. z: 2 Sm 8, 14; Jos 11, 6. 9 a: 2 Sm 8, 8; 1 Kgs 7, 15. 23. 27. b: 2 Sm 8, 10. c: 2 Sm 8, 13; 2 Kgs 14, 7. d: 14-17: 2 Sm 8, 15-18. e: 1 Chr 11, 6; 2 Sm 8, 16; 1 Kgs 4, 3.

Shavsha was scribe;*f* *17*Benaiah, son of Jehoiada, was in command of the Cherethites and the Pelethites; and David's sons were the chief assistants to the king.*g*

See RG 138-40

CHAPTER 19

Campaigns against Ammon. *1h*Afterward Nahash, king of the Ammonites, died and his son succeeded him as king. *2*David said, "I will show kindness to Hanun, the son of Nahash, for his father treated me with kindness." Therefore he sent envoys to him to comfort him over the death of his father. But when David's servants had entered the land of the Ammonites to comfort Hanun, *3*the Ammonite princes said to Hanun, "Do you think David is doing this—sending you these consolers—to honor your father? Have not his servants rather come to you to explore the land, spying it out for its overthrow?" *4*Thereupon Hanun seized David's servants and had them shaved and their garments cut off half-way at the hips. Then he sent them away. *5*When David was informed of what had happened to his men, he sent messengers to meet them, for the men had been greatly disgraced. "Remain at Jericho," the king told them, "until your beards have grown again; and then you may come back here."

*6*When the Ammonites realized that they had put themselves in bad odor with David, Hanun and the Ammonites sent a thousand talents of silver to hire chariots and horsemen from Aram Naharaim, from Aram-maacah, and from Zobah. *7*They hired thirty-two thousand chariots along with the king of Maacah and his army, who came and encamped before Medeba. The Ammonites also assembled from their cities and came out for war.

*8*When David heard of this, he sent Joab and his whole army of warriors against them. *9*The Ammonites marched out and lined up for battle at the gate of the city, while the kings who had come to their help remained apart in the open field. *10*When Joab saw that there was a battle line both in front of and behind him, he chose some of the best fighters among the Israelites and set them in array against the Arameans;*i* *11*the rest of the army, which he placed under the command of his brother Abishai, then lined up to oppose the Ammonites.*j* *12*And he said: "If the Arameans prove too strong for me, you must come to my help; and if the Ammonites prove too strong for you, I will save you. *13*Hold steadfast and let us show ourselves courageous for the sake of our people and the cities of our God; then may the LORD do what seems best to him." *14*Joab therefore advanced with his men to engage the Arameans in battle; but they fled before him. *15*And when the Ammonites saw that the Arameans had fled, they also took to flight before his brother Abishai, and reentered the city. Joab then returned to Jerusalem.

*16*Seeing themselves vanquished by Israel, the Arameans sent messengers to bring out the Arameans from the other side of the River, with Shophach, the general of Hadadezer's army, at their head. *17*When this was reported to David, he gathered all Israel together, crossed the Jordan, and met them. With the army of David drawn up to fight the Arameans, they gave battle. *18*But the Arameans fled before Israel, and David slew seven thousand of their chariot fighters and forty thousand of their foot soldiers; he also killed Shophach, the general of the army. *19*When the vassals of Hadadezer saw themselves vanquished by Israel, they made peace with David and became his subjects. After this, the Arameans refused to come to the aid of the Ammonites.

CHAPTER 20

See RG 138-40

*1*At the beginning of the following year, the time when kings go to war, Joab led the army out in force, laid waste the land of the Ammonites, and went on to besiege Rabbah, while David himself remained in Jeru-

---

18, 17: David's sons were the chief assistants to the king: in the parallel passage, 2 Sm 8, 18, which was the Chronicler's source, David's sons were priests. The change is characteristic of the Chronicler, for whom only Aaron's descendants could be priests.

f: 1 Chr 24, 3. 6. 31; 2 Sm 8, 17. *g:* 1 Chr 11, 22; 2 Sm 8, 18; 1 Kgs 1, 38. 44. *h:* 1-19: 2 Sm 10, 1-19. *i:* 1 Chr 20, 23; 1 Kgs 2, 28. 34. *j:* 1 Chr 23, 18f.

salem. When Joab had attacked Rabbah and destroyed it, [2k]David took the crown of Milcom from the idol's head. It was found to weigh a talent of gold; and it contained precious stones, which David wore on his own head. He also brought out a great amount of booty from the city. [3]He deported the people of the city and set them to work with saws, iron picks, and axes. Thus David dealt with all the cities of the Ammonites. Then he and his whole army returned to Jerusalem.

Victories over the Philistines. [41]Afterward there was another battle with the Philistines, at Gezer. At that time, Sibbecai the Hushathite slew Sippai, one of the descendants of the Raphaim, and the Philistines were subdued.[m] [5]Once again there was war with the Philistines, and Elhanan, the son of Jair, slew Lahmi, the brother of Goliath* of Gath, whose spear shaft was like a weaver's heddle-bar.[n]

[6]In still another battle, at Gath, they encountered a giant, also a descendant of the Raphaim, who had six fingers to each hand and six toes to each foot; twenty-four in all. [7]He defied Israel, and Jonathan, the son of Shimea, David's brother, slew him. [8]These were the descendants of the Raphaim of Gath who died at the hands of David and his servants.

CHAPTER 21

See RG 138–40

David's Census; the Plague. [1o]A satan* rose up against Israel, and he enticed David into taking a census of Israel.[p] [2]David therefore said to Joab and to the other generals of the army, "Go, find out the number of the Israelites from Beer-sheba to Dan, and report back to me that I may know their number." [3]But Joab replied: "May the LORD increase his people a hundredfold! My lord king, are not all of them my lord's subjects? Why does my lord seek to do this thing? Why will he

bring guilt upon Israel?" [4]However, the king's command prevailed over Joab, who departed and traversed all of Israel, and then returned to Jerusalem. [5]Joab reported the result of the census to David: of men capable of wielding a sword, there were in all Israel one million one hundred thousand, and in Judah four hundred and seventy thousand. [6]Levi and Benjamin, however, he did not include in the census, for the king's command was repugnant to Joab.[q] [7]This command displeased God, who began to punish Israel. [8]Then David said to God, "I have sinned greatly in doing this thing. Take away your servant's guilt, for I have acted very foolishly."

[9]Then the LORD spoke to Gad, David's seer, in these words:[r] [10]"Go, tell David: Thus says the LORD: I offer you three alternatives; choose one of them, and I will inflict it on you." [11]Accordingly, Gad went to David and said to him: "Thus says the LORD: Decide now— [12]will it be three years of famine; or three months of fleeing your enemies, with the sword of your foes ever at your back; or three days of the LORD's own sword, a pestilence in the land, with the LORD's destroying angel in every part of Israel? Therefore choose: What answer am I to give him who sent me?" [13]Then David said to Gad: "I am in dire straits. But I prefer to fall into the hand of the LORD, whose mercy is very great, than into the hands of men."

[14]Therefore the LORD sent pestilence upon Israel, and seventy thousand men of Israel died. [15]God also sent an angel to destroy Jerusalem; but as he was on the point of destroying it, the LORD saw and decided against the calamity, and said to the destroying angel, "Enough now! Stay your hand!"[s]

Ornan's Threshing Floor. The angel of the LORD was then standing by the threshing

---

20, 5: Elhanan . . . slew Lahmi, the brother of Goliath: the Chronicler thus solves the difficulty of the apparent contradiction between 1 Sm 17, 49ff (David killed Goliath) and 2 Sm 21, 19 (Elhanan killed Goliath).

21, 1: A satan: in the parallel passage of 2 Sm 24, 1, the Lord's anger. The change in the term reflects the changed theological outlook of postexilic Israel, when evil could no longer be attributed directly to God. At an earlier period the Hebrew word satan ("adversary," or, especially in a court of law, "accuser"), when not used of men, designated an angel who ac-

cused men before God (Jb 1, 6-12; 2, 1-7; Zec 3, 1f). Here, as in later Judaism (Wis 2, 24) and in the New Testament, satan, or the "devil" (from the Greek translation of the word), designates an evil spirit who tempts men to wrongdoing.

---

k: 2f: 2 Sm 12, 30f.   *l:* 4-8: 2 Sm 21, 18-22.   *m:* 1 Chr 11, 29; 27, 11.   *n:* 1 Chr 11, 26; 1 Sm 17, 4. 23.   *o:* 1-7: 2 Sm 24, 1-25.   *p:* Zec 3, 1f.   *q:* 1 Chr 27, 24; Nm 1, 49.   *r:* 1 Chr 29, 29; 1 Sm 9, 9; 2 Chr 29, 25.   *s:* Gn 6, 6; Ex 32, 14; 2 Sm 24, 16; Jon 3, 10.

Transition in Reigns

While David is still clearly on the throne, chs 21–29 provide a number of points of continuity between David's reign, which is ending, and Solomon's, which is beginning. Along the way, David makes all the necessary provisions to ensure the successful completion of the temple and the continuing growth of Jerusalem. The Chronicler's version is in marked contrast to the opening chapters of 1 Kings, where Solomon apparently gains the throne at the last minute thanks to the resourceful intervention of the prophet Nathan and Solomon's mother Bathsheba.

---

floor of Ornan the Jebusite. *16*When David raised his eyes, he saw the angel of the LORD standing between earth and heaven, with a naked sword in his hand stretched out against Jerusalem. David and the elders, clothed in sackcloth, prostrated themselves face to the ground, *17*and David prayed to God: "Was it not I who ordered the census of the people? I am the one who sinned, I did this wicked thing. But these sheep, what have they done? O LORD, my God, strike me and my father's family, but do not afflict your people with this plague!"

*18*Then the angel of the LORD commanded Gad to tell David to go up and erect an altar to the LORD on the threshing floor of Ornan the Jebusite.*ᵗ* *19*David went up at Gad's command, given in the name of the LORD. *20*While Ornan was threshing wheat, he turned around and saw the king, and his four sons who were with him, without recognizing them. *21*But as David came on toward him, he looked up and saw that it was David. Then he left the threshing floor and bowed down before David, his face to the ground. *22*David said to Ornan: "Sell me the ground of this threshing floor, that I may build on it an altar to the LORD. Sell it to me at its full price, that the plague may be stayed from the people." *23*But Ornan said to David: "Take it as your own, and let my lord the king do what seems best to him. See, I also give you the oxen for

the holocausts, the threshing sledges for the wood, and the wheat for the cereal offering. I give it all to you." *24*But King David replied to Ornan: "No! I will buy it from you properly, at its full price. I will not take what is yours for the LORD, nor offer up holocausts that cost me nothing." *25*So David paid Ornan six hundred shekels of gold* for the place.

Altar of Holocausts. *26*David then built an altar there to the LORD, and offered up holocausts and peace offerings. When he called upon the LORD, he answered him by sending down fire from heaven upon the altar of holocausts.*ᵘ* *27*Then the LORD gave orders to the angel to return his sword to its sheath.

*28*Once David saw that the LORD had heard him on the threshing floor of Ornan the Jebusite, he continued to offer sacrifices there. *29*The Dwelling of the LORD, which Moses had built in the desert, and the altar of holocausts were at that time on the high place at Gibeon.*ᵛ* *30*But David could not go there to worship God, for he was fearful of the sword of the angel of the LORD. *1*Therefore David said, "This is the house of the LORD God, and this is the altar of holocausts for Israel."**w*

CHAPTER 22

See RG 138–40

Material for the Temple. *2*David then ordered that all the aliens who lived in the land of Israel be brought together, and he appointed them stonecutters to hew out stone

---

21, 25: Six hundred shekels of gold: about 10,000 dollars. According to 2 Sm 24, 24, David paid 50 shekels of silver, about 20 dollars, for Ornan's threshing floor; but for the Chronicler the site of the temple was much more precious than that.

21, 1: This belongs to ch 22.

22, 2ff: According to 1 Kgs 5, 15-32, it was Solomon who made the material preparations for building the temple, even though David had wished to do so (1 Kgs 5, 17ff). The

Chronicler, however, sought to have David, who was Israel's ideal king, more closely connected with Israel's most sacred sanctuary, the temple of Jerusalem.

t: 2 Chr 3, 1. *u:* Lv 9, 24; Jgs 6, 21; 1 Kgs 18, 38; 2 Chr 7, 1; 2 Mc 2, 10ff. *v:* 1 Chr 16, 39; 1 Kgs 8, 4; 2 Chr 1, 8. *w:* 1 Chr 21, 18. 26. 28; 2 Chr 3, 1.

Chapter 22, 12 is a reflection of 1 Kings 3, where God grants Solomon an understanding mind and the ability to discern between good and evil. The Chronicler's version narrows the scope of Solomon's fabled wisdom by defining its purpose as directing him in the law.

blocks for building the house of God.*x* *3*He also laid up large stores of iron to make nails for the doors of the gates, and clamps, together with so much bronze that it could not be weighed.*y* *4*and cedar trees without number. The Sidonians and Tyrians brought great stores of cedar logs to David,*z* *5*who said: "My son Solomon is young and immature; but the house that is to be built for the LORD must be made so magnificent that it will be renowned and glorious in all countries. Therefore I will make preparations for it." Thus before his death David laid up materials in abundance.*a*

Charge to Solomon. *6*Then he called for his son Solomon and commanded him to build a house for the LORD, the God of Israel. *7b*David said to Solomon: "My son, it was my purpose to build a house myself for the honor of the LORD, my God. *8*But this word of the LORD came to me: 'You have shed much blood, and you have waged great wars. You may not build a house in my honor, because you have shed too much blood upon the earth in my sight. *9*However, a son is to be born to you. He will be a peaceful man, and I will give him rest from all his enemies on every side. For Solomon shall be his name, and in his time I will bestow peace* and tranquility on Israel.*c* *10*It is he who shall build a house in my honor; he shall be a son to me, and I will be a father to him, and I will establish the throne of his kingship over Israel forever.'*d* *11*Now, my son, the LORD be with you, and may you succeed in building the house of the LORD your God, as he has said you shall. *12*May the LORD give you prudence and discernment when he brings

you to rule over Israel, so that you keep the law of the LORD, your God. *13*Only then shall you succeed, if you are careful to observe the precepts and decrees which the LORD gave Moses for Israel. Be brave and steadfast; do not fear or lose heart.*e* *14*See, with great effort I have laid up for the house of the LORD a hundred thousand talents of gold,* a million talents of silver, and bronze and iron in such great quantities that they cannot be weighed. I have also stored up wood and stones, to which you must add.*f* *15*Moreover, you have available an unlimited supply of workmen, stonecutters, masons, carpenters, and every kind of craftsman *16*skilled in gold, silver, bronze, and iron. Set to work, therefore, and the LORD be with you!"

Charge to the Leaders. *17*David also commanded all of Israel's leaders to help his son Solomon: *18*"Is not the LORD your God with you? Has he not given you rest on every side? Indeed, he has delivered the occupants of the land into my power, and the land is subdued before the LORD and his people.*g* *19*Therefore, devote your hearts and souls to seeking the LORD your God. Proceed to build the sanctuary of the LORD God, that the ark of the covenant of the LORD and God's sacred vessels may be brought into the house built in honor of the LORD."*h*

CHAPTER 23

See RG 138-40

The Levitical Classes. *1*When David had grown old and was near the end of his days, he made his son Solomon king over Israel.*i* *2*He then gathered together all the

22, 9: The Hebrew word for peace, shalom, is reflected in the name Solomon, in Hebrew, Shelomo. A contrast is drawn here between Solomon, the peaceful man, and David, who waged great wars (v 8). David was prevented from building the temple, not only because all his time was taken up in waging war (1 Kgs 5, 17), but also because he shed much blood (v 8), and in the eyes of the Chronicler this made him ritually unfit for the task.

22, 14: A hundred thousand talents of gold: about 3,775 tons of gold. A million talents of silver: about 37,750 tons of silver. The fantastically exaggerated figures are intended

merely to stress the inestimable value of the temple as the center of Israelite worship. More modest figures are given in 1 Kgs 9, 14. 28; 10, 10. 14.

x: 1 Kgs 5, 31f; 9, 20f; 2 Chr 2, 16f. *y:* 1 Chr 18, 8; 1 Kgs 7, 47. *z:* 1 Chr 10, 27; Ezr 3, 7. *a:* 1 Chr 29, 1. *b:* 7-10: 1 Chr 17, 1-14; 28, 2-7; 2 Sm 7, 1-16; 1 Kgs 5, 3ff; 8, 17-21. *c:* 2 Sm 12, 24. *d:* Heb 1, 5. *e:* 1 Chr 28, 7. 20; Dt 31, 6. 23; Jos 1, 6f. 9; 1 Kgs 2, 2f. *f:* 1 Chr 29, 2ff. *g:* 1 Chr 23, 25; Jos 21, 44; 23, 1; 2 Sm 7, 1. *h:* 1 Kgs 8, 6. 21; 2 Chr 5, 7; 6, 11. *i:* 1 Chr 28, 5; 1 Kgs 1, 30.

leaders of Israel, together with the priests and the Levites.

³The Levites thirty years old and above were counted, and their total number was found to be thirty-eight thousand men.ʲ ⁴Of these, twenty-four thousand were to direct the service of the house of the LORD, six thousand were to be officials and judges, ⁵four thousand were to be gatekeepers, and four thousand were to praise the LORD with the instruments which David had devised for praise.ᵏ ⁶David divided them into classes according to the sons of Levi: Gershon, Kohath, and Merari.ˡ

⁷To the Gershonites belonged Ladan and Shimei. ⁸The sons of Ladan: Jehiel the chief, then Zetham and Joel; three in all.ᵐ ⁹The sons of Shimei were Shelomoth, Haziel, and Haran; three. These were the heads of the families of Ladan. ¹⁰The sons of Shimei were Jahath, Zizah, Jeush, and Beriah; these were the sons of Shimei, four in all. ¹¹Jahath was the chief and Zizah was second to him; but Jeush and Beriah had not many sons, and therefore they were classed as a single family, fulfilling a single office.

¹²The sons of Kohath: Amram, Izhar, Hebron, and Uzziel; four in all.ⁿ ¹³The sons of Amran were Aaron and Moses. Aaron was set apart to be consecrated as most holy, he and his sons forever, to offer sacrifice before the LORD, to minister to him, and to bless his name forever.ᵒ ¹⁴As for Moses, however, the man of God, his sons were counted as part of the tribe of Levi. ¹⁵The sons of Moses were Gershon and Eliezer.ᵖ ¹⁶The sons of Gershon: Shubael the chief.�q ¹⁷The sons of Eliezer were Rehabiah the chief—Eliezer had no other sons, but the sons of Rehabiah were very numerous. ¹⁸The sons of Izhar: Shelomith the chief. ¹⁹The sons of Hebron: Jeriah, the chief, Amariah, the second, Jahaziel, the third, and Jekameam, the fourth.ʳ ²⁰The sons of Uzziel: Micah, the chief, and Isshiah, the second.ˢ

²¹The sons of Merari: Mahli and Mushi. The sons of Mahli: Eleazar and Kish.ᵗ ²²Ele-azar died leaving no sons, only daughters; the sons of Kish, their kinsmen, married them.ᵘ ²³The sons of Mushi: Mahli, Eder, and Jeremoth; three in all.ᵛ

²⁴These were the sons of Levi according to their ancestral houses, the family heads as they were enrolled one by one according to their names. They performed the work of service of the house of the LORD from twenty years of age upward,ʷ ²⁷for David's final orders were to enlist the Levites from the time they were twenty years old.

²⁵David said: "The LORD, the God of Israel, has given rest to his people, and has taken up his dwelling in Jerusalem.ˣ ²⁶Henceforth the Levites need not carry the Dwelling or any of its furnishings or equipment.ʸ ²⁸Rather, their duty shall be to assist the sons of Aaron in the service of the house of the LORD, having charge of the courts, the chambers, and the preservation of everything holy: they shall take part in the service of the house of God. ²⁹They shall also have charge of the showbread, of the fine flour for the cereal offering, of the wafers of unleavened bread, and of the baking and mixing, and of all measures of quantity and size.ᶻ ³⁰They must be present every morning to offer thanks and to praise the LORD, and likewise in the evening;ᵃ ³¹and at every offering of holocausts to the LORD on sabbaths, new moons, and feast days, in such numbers as are prescribed, they must always be present before the LORD.ᵇ ³²They shall observe what is prescribed for them concerning the meeting tent, the sanctuary, and the sons of Aaron, their brethren, in the service of the house of the LORD."ᶜ

CHAPTER 24

See RG
138-40

The Priestly Classes. ¹The descendants of Aaron also were divided into classes. The sons of Aaron were Nadab, Abihu, Eleazar, and Ithamar.ᵈ ²Nadab and Abihu died before their father, leaving no sons; therefore only Eleazar and Ithamar served as priests.ᵉ

j: Nm 4, 3. 23. 30. 35. 39. 43. 47; 8, 23–26; 2 Chr 31, 17.   k: 1 Chr 9, 22.   l: 1 Chr 6, 1. 16-30; 26, 1-19; Ex 6, 16; Nm 3, 17; 26, 57.
m: 1 Chr 26, 21f; 29, 8.   n: 1 Chr 26, 23; Ex 6, 18; Nm 3, 19; 26, 23ff.   o: 1 Chr 6, 49; Ex 6, 20; 28, 1; Nm 6, 23.   p: Ex 2, 22; 18, 3f.
q: 1 Chr 26, 24.   r: 1 Chr 24, 23.   s: 1 Chr 24, 24f.   t: 1 Chr 6, 29; 24, 26. 28f; Ex 6, 19; Nm 3, 20. 33.   u: 1 Chr 24, 28f.   v: 1 Chr 6,
47; 24, 30.   w: 2 Chr 31, 17; Ezr 3, 8.   x: 1 Chr 22, 18; Ps 132, 13.   y: 1 Chr 15, 15; 2 Chr 35, 3.   z: 1 Chr 9, 29. 31f; Lv 2, 1. 4f; 24,
5-8.   a: Nm 28, 3-8.   b: Nm 28, 2-29. 39.   c: Nm 3, 6-9; 18, 2-5.   d: Ex 6, 23; Nm 3, 2ff; 26, 60.   e: Lv 10, 1-7. 12; Nm 3, 2. 4.

³David, with Zadok, a descendant of Eleazar, and Ahimelech, a descendant of Ithamar, assigned the functions for the priestly service.ᶠ ⁴But since the descendants of Eleazar were found to be more numerous than those of Ithamar, the former were divided into sixteen groups, and the latter into eight groups, each under its family head. ⁵Their functions were assigned impartially by lot, for there were officers of the holy place, and officers of the divine presence, descended both from Eleazar and from Ithamar. ⁶The scribe Shemaiah, son of Nethanel, a Levite, made a record of it in the presence of the king, and of the leaders, of Zadok the priest, and of Ahimelech, son of Abiathar,* and of the heads of the ancestral houses of the priests and of the Levites, listing two successive family groups from Eleazar before each one from Ithamar.ᵍ

⁷ʰThe first lot fell to Jehoiarib, the second to Jedaiah, ⁸the third to Harim, the fourth to Seorim, ⁹the fifth to Malchijah, the sixth to Mijamin, ¹⁰the seventh to Hakkoz, the eighth to Abijah,ⁱ ¹¹the ninth to Jeshua, the tenth to Shecaniah, ¹²the eleventh to Eliashib, the twelfth to Jakim, ¹³the thirteenth to Huppah, the fourteenth to Ishbaal, ¹⁴the fifteenth to Bilgah, the sixteenth to Immer, ¹⁵the seventeenth to Hezir, the eighteenth to Happizzez, ¹⁶the nineteenth to Pethahiah, the twentieth to Jehezkel, ¹⁷the twenty-first to Jachin, the twenty-second to Gamul, ¹⁸the twenty-third to Delaiah, the twenty-fourth to Maaziah. ¹⁹This was the appointed order of their service when they functioned in the house of the Lᴏʀᴅ in keeping with the precepts given them by Aaron, their father, as the Lᴏʀᴅ, the God of Israel, had commanded him.ʲ

Other Levites. ²⁰ᵏOf the remaining Levites, there were Shubael, of the descendants of Amram, and Jehdeiah, of the descendants of Shubael; ²¹Isshiah, the chief, of the descendants of Rehabiah; ²²Shelomith of the Izharites, and Jahath of the descendants of Shelomith. ²³The descendants of Hebron were Jeriah, the chief, Amariah, the second, Jahaziel, the third, Jekameam, the fourth. ²⁴The descendants of Uzziel were Micah; Shamir, of the descendants of Micah; ²⁵Isshiah, the brother of Micah; and Zechariah, a descendant of Isshiah. ²⁶The descendants of Merari were Mahli, Mushi, and the descendants of his son Uzziah. ²⁷The descendants of Merari through his son Uzziah: Shoham, Zaccur, and Ibri. ²⁸Descendants of Mahli were Eleazar, who had no sons, ²⁹and Jerahmeel, of the descendants of Kish. ³⁰The descendants of Mushi were Mahli, Eder, and Jerimoth.

These were the descendants of the Levites according to their ancestral houses. ³¹They too, in the same manner as their relatives, the descendants of Aaron, cast lots in the presence of King David, Zadok, Ahimelech, and the heads of the priestly and levitical families; the more important family did so in the same way as the less important one.ˡ

CHAPTER 25

See RG 138-40

The Singers. ¹David and the leaders of the liturgical cult set apart for service the descendants of Asaph, Heman, and Jeduthun, as singers of inspired song to the accompaniment of lyres and harps and cymbals.ᵐ

This is the list of those who performed this service: ²*Of the sons of Asaph: Zaccur, Joseph, Nethaniah, and Asharelah, sons of Asaph, under the direction of Asaph, who sang inspired songs under the guidance of the king. ³Of Jeduthun, these sons of Jeduthun: Gedaliah, Zeri, Jeshaiah, Shimei, Hashabiah, and Mattithiah; six, under the direction of their father Jeduthun, who sang inspired songs to the accompaniment of a lyre, to give thanks and praise to the Lᴏʀᴅ. ⁴Of Heman, these sons of Heman: Bukkiah, Mattaniah, Uzziel, Shubael, and Jerimoth;

24, 6: Ahimelech, son of Abiathar: see note on 1 Chr 18, 16.

25, 2-31: This list of twenty-four classes of temple singers balances the list of the twenty-four classes of priests (1 Chr 24, 4-19). The last nine names in 1 Chr 25, 4, which seem to form a special group, appear to have been originally fragments or incipits of hymns. With some slight changes in the vocalization, the names would mean: "Have mercy on me, O Lord," "Have mercy on me," "You are my God," "I magnify," "I extol the help of . . . ," "Sitting in adversity," "I have fulfilled," "He made abundant," and "Visions."

f: 1 Chr 18, 16; 2 Sm 8, 17; 2 Chr 8, 14.   g: 1 Chr 18, 16; 2 Sm 8, 17.   h: 7-10: 1 Chr 9, 10ff; Ezr 2, 36ff; Neh 7, 39ff; 11, 10ff.   i: Lk 1, 5.
j: 2 Chr 23, 8.   k: 20-31: 1 Chr 23, 7-23.   l: 1 Chr 25, 8; 26, 13.   m: 1 Chr 6, 31ff; 15, 16f. 19; 16, 37; 2 Chr 5, 12; 35, 15; Neh 12, 27. 45.

Hananiah, Hanani, Eliathah, Giddalti, Romamti-ezer, Joshbekashah, Mallothi, Hothir, and Mahazioth. [5]All these were the sons of Heman, the king's seer in divine matters; to enhance his prestige, God gave Heman fourteen sons and three daughters.[n] [6]All these, whether of Asaph, Jeduthun, or Heman, were under their fathers' direction in the singing in the house of the LORD to the accompaniment of cymbals, harps and lyres, serving in the house of God, under the guidance of the king.[o] [7]Their number, together with that of their brethren who were trained in singing to the LORD, all of them skilled men, was two hundred and eighty-eight. [8]They cast lots for their functions equally, young and old, master and pupil alike.[p]

[9]The first lot fell to Asaph, the family of Joseph; he and his sons and his brethren were twelve. Gedaliah was the second; he and his brethren and his sons were twelve. [10]The third was Zaccur, his sons, and his brethren: twelve. [11]The fourth fell to Izri, his sons, and his brethren: twelve. [12]The fifth was Nethaniah, his sons, and his brethren: twelve. [13]The sixth was Bukkiah, his sons, and his brethren: twelve. [14]The seventh was Jesarelah, his sons, and his brethren: twelve. [15]The eighth was Jeshaiah, his sons, and his brethren: twelve. [16]The ninth was Mattaniah, his sons, and his brethren: twelve. [17]The tenth was Shimei, his sons, and his brethren: twelve. [18]The eleventh was Uzziel, his sons, and his brethren: twelve. [19]The twelfth fell to Hashabiah, his sons, and his brethren: twelve. [20]The thirteenth was Shubael, his sons, and his brethren: twelve. [21]The fourteenth was Mattithiah, his sons, and his brethren: twelve. [22]The fifteenth fell to Jeremoth, his sons, and his brethren: twelve. [23]The sixteenth fell to Hananiah, his sons, and his brethren: twelve. [24]The seventeenth fell to Joshbekashah, his sons, and his brethren: twelve. [25]The eighteenth fell to Hanani, his sons, and his brethren: twelve. [26]The nineteenth fell to Mallothi, his sons, and his brethren: twelve. [27]The twentieth fell to Eliathah, his sons, and his brethren: twelve. [28]The twenty-first fell to Hothir, his sons, and his brethren: twelve. [29]The twenty-second fell to Giddalti, his sons, and his brethren: twelve. [30]The twenty-third fell to Mahazioth, his sons, and his brethren: twelve. [31]The twenty-fourth fell to Romamti-ezer, his sons, and his brethren: twelve.

CHAPTER 26

See RG 138-40

Classes of Gatekeepers. [1q]As for the classes of gatekeepers. Of the Korahites was Meshelemiah, the son of Kore, one of the sons of Abiasaph. [2]Meshelemiah's sons: Zechariah, the first-born, Jediael, the second son, Zebadiah, the third, Jathniel, the fourth, [3]Elam, the fifth, Jehohanan, the sixth, Eliehoenai, the seventh. [4]Obed-edom's sons: Shemaiah, the first-born, Jehozabad, a second son, Joah, the third, Sachar, the fourth, Nethanel, the fifth, [5]Ammiel, the sixth, Issachar, the seventh, Peullethai, the eighth, for God blessed him. [6]To his son Shemaiah were born sons who ruled over their family, for they were warriors. [7]The sons of Shemaiah were Othni, Rephael, Obed, and Elzabad; also his brethren who were men of might, Elihu and Semachiah. [8]All these were of the sons of Obed-edom, who, together with their sons and their brethren, were mighty men, fit for the service. Of Obed-edom, sixty-two. [9]Of Meshelemiah, eighteen sons and brethren, mighty men.

[10]Hosah, a descendant of Merari, had these sons: Shimri, the chief (for though he was not the first-born, his father made him chief),[r] [11]Hilkiah, the second son, Tebaliah, the third, Zechariah, the fourth. All the sons and brethren of Hosah were thirteen.

[12]To these classes of gatekeepers, under their chief men, were assigned watches in the service of the house of the LORD, for each group in the same way. [13]They cast lots for each gate, the small and the large families alike. [14]When the lot was cast for the east side, it fell to Meshelemiah. Then they cast lots for his son Zechariah, a prudent counselor, and the north side fell to his lot.[s] [15]To Obed-edom fell the south side, and to his sons the storehouse. [16]To Hosah fell the west side with the Shallecheth gate at the

---

n: 2 Chr 35, 15.   *o:* 1 Chr 15, 16.   *p:* 1 Chr 24, 31.   *q:* 1 Chr 9, 19; 2 Chr 8, 14; 23, 19; 35, 15; Neh 12, 45.   *r:* 1 Chr 16, 38.
s: 1 Chr 9, 24.

ascending highway. For each family, watches were established. [17]On the east, six watched each day, on the north, four each day, on the south, four each day, and at the storehouse they were two and two; [18]as for the large building* on the west, there were four at the highway and two at the large building. [19]These were the classes of the gatekeepers, descendants of Kore and Merari.

Treasurers. [20]Their brother Levites superintended the stores for the house of God and the stores of votive offerings.[t] [21]Among the descendants of Ladan the Gershonite, the family heads were descendants of Jehiel: the descendants of Jehiel,[u] [22v]Zetham and his brother Joel, who superintended the treasures of the house of the LORD. [23]From the Amramites, Izharites, Hebronites, and Uzzielites, [24]Shubael, son of Gershon, son of Moses, was chief superintendent over the treasures. [25w]His associate pertained to Eliezer, whose son was Rehabiah, whose son was Jeshaiah, whose son was Joram, whose son was Zichri, whose son was Shelomith. [26]This Shelomith and his brethren superintended all the stores of the votive offerings dedicated by King David, the heads of the families, the commanders of thousands and of hundreds, and the commanders of the army,[x] [27]from the booty they had taken in the wars, for the enhancement of the house of the LORD. [28]Also, whatever Samuel the seer, Saul, son of Kish, Abner, son of Ner, Joab, son of Zeruiah, and all others had consecrated, was under the charge of Shelomith and his brethren.

Magistrates. [29]Among the Izharites, Chananiah and his sons were in charge of Israel's civil affairs as officials and judges.[y] [30]Among the Hebronites, Hashabiah and his brethren, one thousand seven hundred police officers, had the administration of Israel on the western side of the Jordan in all the work of the LORD and in the service of the king.[z] [31]Among the Hebronites, Jerijah was their chief according to their family

records. In the fortieth year of David's reign search was made, and there were found among them outstanding officers at Jazer of Gilead.[a] [32]His brethren were also police officers, two thousand seven hundred heads of families. King David appointed them to the administration of the Reubenites, the Gadites, and the half-tribe of Manasseh in everything pertaining to God and to the king.

CHAPTER 27

See RG 138–40

*Army Commanders.** [1]This is the list of the Israelite family heads, commanders of thousands and of hundreds, and other officers who served the king in all that pertained to the divisions, of twenty-four thousand men each, that came and went month by month throughout the year.

[2]Over the first division for the first month was Ishbaal, son of Zabdiel, and in his division were twenty-four thousand men; [3]a descendant of Perez, he was chief over all the commanders of the army for the first month. [4]Over the division of the second month was Eleazar, son of Dodo, from Ahoh, and in his division were twenty-four thousand men.[b] [5c]The third army commander, chief for the third month, was Benaiah, son of Jehoiada the priest, and in his division were twenty-four thousand men. [6]This Benaiah was a warrior among the Thirty and over the Thirty. His son Ammizabad was over his division. [7]Fourth, for the fourth month, was Asahel, brother of Joab, and after him his son Zebadiah, and in his division were twenty-four thousand men.[d] [8]Fifth, for the fifth month, was the commander Shamhuth, a descendant of Zerah, and in his division were twenty-four thousand men. [9]Sixth, for the sixth month, was Ira, son of Ikkesh, from Tekoa, and in his division were twenty-four thousand men. [10]Seventh, for the seventh month, was Helles, from Beth-pheleth, of the sons of Ephraim, and in his division were

---

26, 18: The large building (in the Hebrew text Parbar): see note on 2 Kgs 23, 11.

27, 1-15: This list of army commanders is similar to, but distinct from, the list of David's warriors as given in 1 Chr 11, 10-47. The schematic enumeration of the soldiers as presented here is, no doubt, artificial and grossly exaggerated (12 x 24,000 = 288,000 men!), unless the Hebrew word (eleph) for thousand is understood as designating a military

unit of much smaller size; see note on 1 Chr 12, 25-38.

t: 1 Chr 28, 12; 1 Kgs 7, 51. *u:* 1 Chr 23, 7f; 29, 8. *v:* 22ff: 1 Chr 23, 8. 12. 16. *w:* 1 Chr 23, 17f; 24, 21. *x:* 2 Sm 8, 11. *y:* 1 Chr 23, 4. *z:* 1 Chr 27, 17; Neh 11, 15f. *a:* 1 Chr 23, 19; 29, 27; Jos 13, 25. *b:* 1 Chr 9, 37; 11, 12; 2 Sm 23, 9. *c:* 5f: 1 Chr 11, 22ff; 18, 17; 2 Sm 23, 20ff. *d:* 2 Sm 2, 18; 23, 24.

twenty-four thousand men. *11*Eighth, for the eighth month, was Sibbecai the Hushathite, a descendant of Zerah, and in his division were twenty-four thousand men.*e* *12*Ninth, for the ninth month, was Abiezer from Anathoth, of Benjamin, and in his division were twenty-four thousand men. *13*Tenth, for the tenth month, was Maharai from Netophah, a descendant of Zerah, and in his division were twenty-four thousand men. *14*Eleventh, for the eleventh month, was Benaiah the Pirathonite, of Ephraim, and in his division were twenty-four thousand men. *15*Twelfth, for the twelfth month, was Heldai the Netophathite, of the family of Othniel, and in his division were twenty-four thousand men.

Tribal Heads. *16*Over the tribes of Israel, for the Reubenites the leader was Eliezer, son of Zichri; for the Simeonites, Shephatiah, son of Maacah; *17*for Levi, Hashabiah, son of Kemuel; for Aaron, Zadok; *18*for Judah, Eliab, one of David's brothers; for Issachar, Omri, son of Michael;*f* *19*for Zebulun, Ishmaiah, son of Obadiah; for Naphtali, Jeremoth, son of Azriel; *20*for the sons of Ephraim, Hoshea, son of Azaziah; for the half-tribe of Manasseh, Joel, son of Pedaiah; *21*for the half-tribe of Manasseh in Gilead, Iddo, son of Zechariah; for Benjamin, Jaasiel, son of Abner; *22*for Dan, Azarel, son of Jeroham. These were the commanders of the tribes of Israel.

*23*David did not count those who were twenty years of age or younger, for the LORD had promised to multiply Israel like the stars of the heavens.*g* *24*Joab, son of Zeruiah, began to take the census, but he did not complete it, for because of it wrath fell upon Israel. Therefore the number did not enter into the book of chronicles of King David.*h*

Overseers. *25*Over the treasures of the king was Azmaveth, the son of Adiel. Over the stores in the country, the cities, the villages,

and the towers was Jonathan, son of Uzziah.*i* *26*Over the farm workers who tilled the soil was Ezri, son of Chelub. *27*Over the vineyards was Shimei from Ramah, and over their produce for the wine cellars was Zabdi the Shiphmite. *28*Over the olive trees and sycamores of the foothills was Baal-hanan the Gederite, and over the stores of oil was Joash. *29*Over the cattle that grazed in Sharon was Shitrai the Sharonite, and over the cattle in the valleys was Shaphat, the son of Adlai; *30*over the camels was Obil the Ishmaelite; over the she-asses was Jehdeiah the Meronothite; *31*and over the flocks was Jaziz the Hagrite. All these were the overseers of King David's possessions.

David's Court. *32*Jonathan, David's uncle and a man of intelligence, was counselor and scribe; he and Jehiel, the son of Hachmoni, were tutors of the king's sons. *33*Ahithophel was also the king's counselor, and Hushai the Archite was the king's confidant.*j* *34*After Ahithophel* came Jehoiada, the son of Benaiah, and Abiathar. The commander of the king's army was Joab.

CHAPTER 28

See RG 138–40

The Assembly at Jerusalem. *1*David assembled at Jerusalem all the leaders of Israel, the heads of the tribes, the commanders of the divisions who were in the service of the king, the commanders of thousands and of hundreds, the overseers of all the king's estates and possessions, and his sons, together with the courtiers, the warriors, and every important man.*k* *2*King David rose to his feet and said: "Hear me, my brethren and my people. It was my purpose to build a house of repose myself for the ark of the covenant of the LORD, the footstool for the feet of our God;* and I was preparing to build it. *3*But God said to me, 'You may not build a house in my honor, for you are a man who fought wars and shed

---

27, 34: After Ahithophel: after his suicide (2 Sm 17, 23). Jehoiada then succeeded him as the king's counselor. Abiathar: the priest. The Chronicler does not mention his office because he regards only the Zadokites as legitimate high priests.

28, 2: The ark . . . the footstool . . . of our God: the Lord, who was invisibly enthroned upon the cherubim that were associated with the ark of the covenant at Shiloh and later in the Jerusalem temple, had the ark as his footstool; cf Pss 99, 5; 132, 7. The propitiatory (1 Chr 28, 11) and the chariot throne

(1 Chr 28, 18) reflect the different circumstances of the postexilic community, for whom only the place of the ark was a focal point of worship, though the ark itself was no longer present.

e: 1 Chr 11, 29; 20, 4; 2 Sm 21, 18. *f:* 1 Chr 2, 13. *g:* 1 Chr 22, 17. *h:* 2 Sm 24, 10. *i:* 2 Sm 23, 31. *j:* 2 Sm 15, 12. 32-37; 16, 16-19. 23; 17, 5-16. 23. *k:* 1 Chr 27, 2-22. 25-31; 11, 10ff. *l:* 2f; 1 Chr 17, 4; 22, 7ff; 2 Sm 7, 5; 1 Kgs 5, 3; Ps 132, 3-7.

David's Charge to Solomon

Employing the royal speech as a means of giving voice to his own concerns, the Chronicler has David offer the charge in ch 28 at the conclusion of organizing the community for the future. The end of v. 9 is the Chronicler's primary theology: "If you seek him, he will let himself be found by you; but if you abandon him, he will cast you off forever."

blood.' [4]However, the LORD, the God of Israel, chose me from all my father's family to be king over Israel forever. For he chose Judah as leader, then one family of Judah, that of my father; and finally, among all the sons of my father, it pleased him to make me king over all Israel.[m] [5]And of all my sons—for the LORD has given me many sons—he has chosen my son Solomon to sit on the LORD's royal throne over Israel.[n] [6]For he said to me: 'It is your son Solomon who shall build my house and my courts, for I have chosen him for my son, and I will be a father to him.[o] [7]I will establish his kingdom forever, if he perseveres in keeping my commandments and decrees as he keeps them now.' [8]Therefore in the presence of all Israel, the assembly of the LORD, and in the hearing of our God, I exhort you to keep and to carry out all the commandments of the LORD, your God, that you may continue to possess this good land and afterward leave it as an inheritance to your children forever.[p]

[9]"As for you, Solomon, my son, know the God of your father and serve him with a perfect heart and a willing soul, for the LORD searches all hearts and understands all the mind's thoughts. If you seek him, he will let himself be found by you; but if you abandon him, he will cast you off forever.[q] [10]See, then! The LORD has chosen you to build a house as his sanctuary. Take courage and set to work."

Temple Plans Given to Solomon. [11]Then David gave to his son Solomon the pattern of the portico and of the building itself, with its storerooms, its upper rooms and inner chambers, and the room with the propitiatory.[r] [12]He provided also the pattern for all else that he had in mind by way of courts for the house of the LORD, with the surrounding compartments for the stores for the house of God and the stores of the votive offerings, [13]as well as for the divisions of the priests and Levites, for all the work of the service of the house of the LORD, and for all the liturgical vessels of the house of the LORD. [14]He specified the weight of gold to be used in the golden vessels for the various services and the weight of silver to be used in the silver vessels for the various services; [15]likewise for the golden lampstands and their lamps he specified the weight of gold for each lampstand and its lamps, and for the silver lampstands he specified the weight of silver for each lampstand and its lamps, depending on the use to which each lampstand was to be put.[s] [16]He specified the weight of gold for each table to hold the showbread, and the silver for the silver tables; [17]the pure gold to be used for the forks and pitchers; the amount of gold for each golden bowl and the silver for each silver bowl; [18]the refined gold, and its weight, to be used for the altar of incense; and, finally, gold for what would suggest a chariot throne:* the cherubim that spread their wings and covered the ark of the covenant of the LORD.[t] [19]He had successfully committed to writing the exact specifications of the pattern, because the hand of the LORD was upon him.

[20]Then David said to his son Solomon: "Be firm and steadfast; go to work without fear or discouragement, for the LORD God, my God, is with you. He will not fail you or abandon you before you have completed all the work for the service of the house of the LORD.[u] [21]The classes of the priests and Levites are ready for all the service of the

28, 18: Chariot throne: probably suggested by Ez 1, 4-24; 10, 1-22.

m: 1 Chr 17, 23; Gn 49, 8ff; 1 Sm 16, 6-13.   *n:* 1 Chr 3, 1-9; 14, 3-7; 22, 9; 23, 1; Wis 9, 7.   *o:* 1 Chr 17, 11ff; 22, 9f; 2 Sm 7, 12f. *p:* Dt 4, 5.   *q:* 1 Chr 29, 17; 2 Chr 15, 2; 1 Kgs 8, 61.   *r:* Ex 25, 9. 40; 26, 30.   *s:* Ex 25, 31-37.   *t:* Ex 25, 18-22; 30, 1-10; 1 Kgs 6, 23-28.   *u:* 1 Chr 22, 13. 16; Jos 1, 5.

house of God; they will help you in all your work with all those who are eager to show their skill in every kind of craftsmanship. Also the leaders and all the people will do everything that you command."[v]

See RG
138–40

CHAPTER 29

Offerings for the Temple. [1]King David then said to the whole assembly: "My son Solomon, whom alone God has chosen, is still young and immature; the work, however, is great, for this castle is not intended for man, but for the LORD God.[w] [2]For this reason I have stored up for the house of my God, as far as I was able, gold for what will be made of gold, silver for what will be made of silver, bronze for what will be made of bronze, iron for what will be made of iron, wood for what will be made of wood, onyx stones and settings for them, carnelian and mosaic stones, every other kind of precious stone, and great quantities of marble.[x] [3]But now, because of the delight I take in the house of my God, in addition to all that I stored up for the holy house, I give to the house of my God my personal fortune in gold and silver: [4]three thousand talents of Ophir gold, and seven thousand talents of refined silver, for overlaying the walls of the rooms,[y] [5]for the various utensils to be made of gold and silver, and for every work that is to be done by artisans. Now, who else is willing to contribute generously this day to the LORD?"[z]

[6]Then the heads of the families, the leaders of the tribes of Israel, the commanders of thousands and of hundreds, and the overseers of the king's affairs came forward willingly[a] [7]and contributed for the service of the house of God five thousand talents and ten thousand darics of gold, ten thousand talents of silver, eighteen thousand talents of bronze, and one hundred thousand talents of iron.[b] [8]Those who had precious stones gave them into the keeping of Jehiel the Gershonite for the treasury of the house of the LORD.[c] [9]The people rejoiced over these free-will offerings, which had been contributed to the LORD wholeheartedly. King David also rejoiced greatly.[d]

David's Prayer. [10]Then David blessed the LORD in the presence of the whole assembly, praying in these words:

"Blessed may you be, O LORD,
    God of Israel our father,
    from eternity to eternity.

[11]"Yours, O LORD, are grandeur and
        power,
    majesty, splendor, and glory.
For all in heaven and on earth is yours;
    yours, O LORD, is the sovereignty;
    you are exalted as head over all.

[12]"Riches and honor are from you,
    and you have dominion over all.
In your hand are power and might;
    it is yours to give grandeur and
        strength to all.[e]
[13]Therefore, our God, we give you thanks
    and we praise the majesty of your
        name."

[14]"But who am I, and who are my people, that we should have the means to contribute so freely? For everything is from you, and we only give you what we have received from you. [15]For we stand before you as aliens: we are only your guests, like all our fathers. Our life on earth is like a shadow that does not abide.[f] [16]O LORD our God, all this wealth that we have brought together to build you a house in honor of your holy name comes from you and is entirely yours. [17]I know, O my God, that you put hearts to the test and that you take pleasure in uprightness. With a sincere heart I have willingly given all these things, and now with joy I have seen your people here present also giving to you generously. [18]O LORD, God of our fathers Abraham, Isaac, and Israel, keep such thoughts in the hearts and minds of your people forever, and direct their hearts toward you.[g] [19]Give to my son Solomon a

---

v: Ex 36, 1-5.   *w:* 1 Chr 22, 5; 28, 5.   *x:* 1 Chr 22, 14.   *y:* 2 Chr 9, 10; 1 Kgs 9, 28; 10, 11.   *z:* Ex 25, 2; 35, 5f.   *a:* 1 Chr 27, 1. 25-31; 28, 1.   *b:* Ezr 2, 69; 8, 27; Neh 7, 70ff.   *c:* 1 Chr 23, 8; 26, 21.   *d:* 2 Kgs 12, 4.   *e:* 2 Chr 20, 6; Wis 6, 3.   *f:* Lv 25, 23; Wis 2, 5; 5, 9.   *g:* Ex 3, 6. 15f; 4, 5; 1 Kgs 18, 36.

wholehearted desire to keep your commandments, precepts, and statutes, that he may carry out all these plans and build the castle for which I have made preparation."

²⁰Then David besought the whole assembly, "Now bless the LORD your God!" And the whole assembly blessed the LORD, the God of their fathers, bowing down and prostrating themselves before the LORD and before the king. ²¹On the following day they offered sacrifices and holocausts to the LORD, a thousand bulls, a thousand rams, and a thousand lambs, together with their libations and many other sacrifices for all Israel; ²²and on that day they ate and drank in the LORD's presence with great rejoicing.

Solomon Anointed. Then for a second time* they proclaimed David's son Solomon king, and they anointed him as the LORD's prince, and Zadok as priest. ²³Thereafter Solomon sat on the throne of the LORD as king in place of his father David; he pros-

pered, and all Israel obeyed him.ʰ ²⁴All the leaders and warriors, and also all the other sons of King David, swore allegiance to King Solomon. ²⁵And the LORD exalted Solomon greatly in the eyes of all Israel, giving him a glorious reign such as had not been enjoyed by any king over Israel before him.ⁱ

Death of David. ²⁶Thus David, the son of Jesse, had reigned over all Israel. ²⁷The time that he reigned over Israel was forty years: in Hebron he reigned seven years, and in Jerusalem thirty-three.ʲ ²⁸He died at a ripe old age, rich in years and wealth and glory, and his son Solomon succeeded him as king.ᵏ

²⁹Now the deeds of King David, first and last, can be found written in the history of Samuel the seer, the history of Nathan the prophet, and the history of Gad the seer,ˡ ³⁰together with the particulars of his reign and valor, and of the events that affected him and all Israel and all the kingdoms of the surrounding lands.

29, 22: For a second time: the first time is referred to in 1 Chr 23, 1. Here there is a solemn public ratification of David's earlier appointment of Solomon as his successor.

h: 1 Chr 28, 5; 2 Chr 9, 8; 1 Kgs 2, 10ff.   *i:* 2 Chr 1, 12; 1 Kgs 3, 13.   *j:* 2 Sm 5, 5; 1 Kgs 2, 11.   *k:* 1 Chr 23, 1.   *l:* 1 Chr 21, 9; 1 Sm 22, 5.

See RG
137–44

The Second Book of Chronicles

The Second Book of Chronicles takes up the history of the monarchy where the First Book breaks off. It begins with the account of the reign of Solomon from the special viewpoint of the Chronicler. The portrait of Solomon is an idealized one; he appears as second only to David. The great achievement of the building of the temple and the magnificence of Solomon's court are described in detail while the serious defects of his reign are passed over without comment. All this is in keeping with the Chronicler's purpose of stressing the supreme importance of the temple and its worship. He wishes to impress on his readers the splendor of God's dwelling and the magnificence of the liturgy of sacrifice, prayer and praise offered there. Judah's kings are judged by their attitude toward the temple and its cult. To this ideal of one people, united in the worship of the one true God at the

temple of Jerusalem founded by David and Solomon, the restored community would have to conform.

In treating the period of divided monarchy, the Chronicler gives practically all his attention to the kingdom of Judah. His omission of the northern Israelite kings is significant. In his view, the northern tribes of Israel were in religious schism as long as they worshiped Yahweh in a place other than the temple of Jerusalem. The Chronicler makes no mention of the important sanctuaries of Yahweh at Dan and Bethel—as though they had never existed. Nevertheless he retains the ancient ideal of "all Israel" (a phrase occurring forty-one times in Chronicles) as the people of God. The condition he places for a united people is that "the whole congregation of Israel" worship the Lord only in his temple at Jerusalem.

This explains his praise of Kings Hezekiah and Josiah for striving, after the fall of Samaria, to unite the remnants of the northern tribes of Israel into the kingdom of Judah.

At the end of the fifth century B.C., during the Chronicler's own time, "the people of the land" were the descendants of the people of all the tribes (including Judah) who had not gone into exile. These had become intermingled with aliens and had evolved a religion of Yahweh very different from the Judaism that developed during the Babylonian exile. Thus, religious and political cooperation between the returned exiles and these "people of the land" was out of the question for the Chronicler. This he clearly shows in the last part of his work, the Books of Ezra and Nehemiah.

The Second Book of Chronicles is divided as follows:

I: The Reign of Solomon (1, 1—9, 31).
II: The Monarchy before Hezekiah (10, 1—27, 9).
III: Reforms of Hezekiah and Josiah (28, 1—36, 1).
IV: End of the Kingdom (36, 2-23).

I: The Reign of Solomon

CHAPTER 1

See RG 141

Solomon at Gibeon. [1]Solomon, son of David, strengthened his hold on the kingdom, for the LORD, his God, was with him, constantly making him more renowned. [2]He sent a summons to all Israel, to the commanders of thousands and of hundreds, the judges, the princes of all Israel, and the family heads; [3a]and, accompanied by the whole assembly, he went to the high place at Gibeon, because the meeting tent of God, made in the desert by Moses, the LORD's servant, was there. [4](The ark of God, however, David had brought up from Kiriath-jearim to Jerusalem, where he had provided a place and pitched a tent for it.)

[5]The bronze altar made by Bezalel, son of Uri, son of Hur, he put in front of the LORD's Dwelling* on the high place. There Solomon and the assembly consulted the LORD,[b] [6]and Solomon offered sacrifice in the LORD's presence on the bronze altar at the meeting tent; he offered a thousand holocausts upon it.

[7]That night God appeared to Solomon and said to him, "Make a request of me, and I will grant it to you." [8]Solomon answered God: "You have shown great favor to my father David, and you have allowed me to succeed him as king. [9]Now, LORD God, may your promise to my father David be fulfilled, for you have made me king over a people as numerous as the dust of the earth. [10]Give me, therefore, wisdom and knowledge to lead this people, for otherwise who could rule this great people of yours?" [11]God then replied to Solomon: "Since this has been your wish and you have not asked for riches, treasures and glory, nor for the life of those who hate you, nor even for a long life for yourself, but have asked for wisdom and knowledge in order to rule my people over whom I have made you king, [12]wisdom and knowledge are given you; but I will also give you riches, treasures and glory, such as kings before you never had, nor will those have them who come after you."

Solomon's Wealth. [13]Solomon returned to Jerusalem from the high place at Gibeon, from the meeting tent, and became king over Israel. [14]He gathered together chariots and drivers, so that he had one thousand four hundred chariots and twelve thousand drivers he could station in the chariot cities and with the king in Jerusalem.[c] [15]The king made silver and gold as common in Jerusalem as stones, while cedars became as numerous as the sycamores of the foothills.[d] [16]Solomon also imported horses from Egypt and Cilicia.[e] The king's agents would acquire them by purchase from Cilicia,* [17]and would then

----

1, 5: The bronze altar . . . the Lord's Dwelling: the Chronicler justifies Solomon's worship at the high place of Gibeon. He pictures the Lord's Dwelling, i.e., the Mosaic meeting tent, and the bronze altar made at Moses' command (Ex 31, 1-9) as still at Gibeon after David had removed the ark of the covenant from there to a new tent in Jerusalem (1 Chr 15, 1. 25; 16, 1). The altar made by Bezalel is described as being of acacia wood plated with bronze (Ex 27, 1f). Solomon later made an all-bronze altar for the temple in Jerusalem (2 Chr 4, 1).

1, 16f: Egypt . . . Cilicia: it seems likely that the horses came from Cilicia and the chariots from Egypt. Some read the source of these data in 1 Kgs 10, 28f as containing the name (Musur) of a mountain district north of Cilicia, rather than of Egypt; but the author of Chronicles surely understood Egypt; cf 2 Chr 9, 28.

----

a: 3-12: 1 Kgs 3, 4-15; 1 Chr 21, 29. b: Ex 27, 1f; 31, 2; 1 Chr 2, 20. c: 2 Chr 9, 25; 10, 26-29. d: 1 Kgs 10, 27. e: 1 Kgs 10, 28.

bring up chariots from Egypt and export them at six hundred silver shekels, with the horses going for a hundred and fifty shekels. At these rates they served as middlemen for all the Hittite and Aramean kings.*f*

Preparations for the Temple. *18*Solomon gave orders for the building of a house to honor the LORD and also of a house for his own royal estate.

CHAPTER 2

See RG
141

*1*He conscripted seventy thousand men to carry stone and eighty thousand to cut the stone in the mountains, and over these he placed three thousand six hundred overseers.*g* *2h*Moreover, Solomon sent this message to Huram, king of Tyre: "As you dealt with my father David, sending him cedars to build a house for his dwelling, so deal with me. *3*I intend to build a house for the honor of the LORD, my God, and to consecrate it to him, for the burning of fragrant incense in his presence, for the perpetual display of the showbread, for holocausts morning and evening, and for the sabbaths, new moons, and festivals of the LORD, our God: such is Israel's perpetual obligation.*i* *4*And the house I intend to build must be large, for our God is greater than all other gods. *5*Yet who is really able to build him a house, since the heavens and even the highest heavens cannot contain him? And who am I that I should build him a house, unless it be to offer incense in his presence?*j* *6*Now, send me men skilled at work in gold, silver, bronze and iron, in purple, crimson, and violet fabrics, and who know how to do engraved work, to join the craftsmen who are with me in Judah and Jerusalem, whom my father David appointed. *7*Also send me boards of cedar, cypress and cabinet wood from Lebanon, for I realize that your servants know how to cut the wood of the Lebanon. My servants will labor with yours *8*in order to prepare for me a great quantity of wood, since the house I intend to build must be lofty and wonderful. *9*I will furnish as food for your servants, the hewers who cut the wood, twenty thousand kors of wheat, twenty thousand kors of barley, twenty thousand measures of wine, and twenty thousand measures of oil."*k*

*10*Huram, king of Tyre, wrote an answer which he sent to Solomon: "Because the LORD loves his people, he has placed you over them as king." *11*He added: "Blessed be the LORD, the God of Israel, who made heaven and earth, for having given King David a wise son of intelligence and understanding, who will build a house for the LORD and also a house for his royal estate.*l* *12*I am now sending you a craftsman of great skill, Huram-abi,*m* *13*son of a Danite woman* and of a father from Tyre; he knows how to work with gold, silver, bronze and iron, with stone and wood, with purple, violet, fine linen and crimson, and also how to do all kinds of engraved work and to devise every type of artistic work that may be given him and your craftsmen and the craftsmen of my lord David your father. *14n*And now, let my lord send to his servants the wheat, barley, oil and wine which he has promised. *15*For our part, we will cut trees on Lebanon, as many as you need, and float them down to you at the port of Joppa, whence you may take them up to Jerusalem."*o*

*16p*Thereupon Solomon took a census of all the alien men who were in the land of Israel (following the census David his father had taken of them), who were found to number one hundred fifty-three thousand six hundred. *17*Of these he made seventy thousand carriers and eighty thousand cutters in the mountains, and three thousand six hundred overseers to keep the people working.*q*

CHAPTER 3

See RG
141

Building of the Temple. *1r*Then Solomon began to build the house of the LORD in

---

2, 13: A Danite woman: a widow of the tribe of Naphtali (1 Kgs 7, 14). The Danites had settled in the northern section of Naphtali's territory (Jgs 18, 27ff). Bezalel's fellow craftsman was of the tribe of Dan (Ex 31, 6).

f: 1 Kgs 10, 29. *g:* 2 Chr 2, 17; 5, 29f. *h:* 2-9: 1 Kgs 5, 15-20; 1 Chr 14, 1. *i:* Lv 24, 5-8; Nm 28—29. *j:* 2 Chr 6, 18. *k:* 1 Kgs 5, 25; Ezr 3, 7. *l:* 1 Kgs 5, 21. *m:* 12f: 1 Kgs 7, 13f; Ex 31, 1-5. *n:* 14f: 1 Kgs 5, 22-26. *o:* Ezr 3, 7. *p:* 16f: 1 Chr 22, 2. *q:* 2 Chr 2, 1. *r:* 1f: Gn 22, 2; 1 Kgs 6, 1; 1 Chr 21, 22-26.

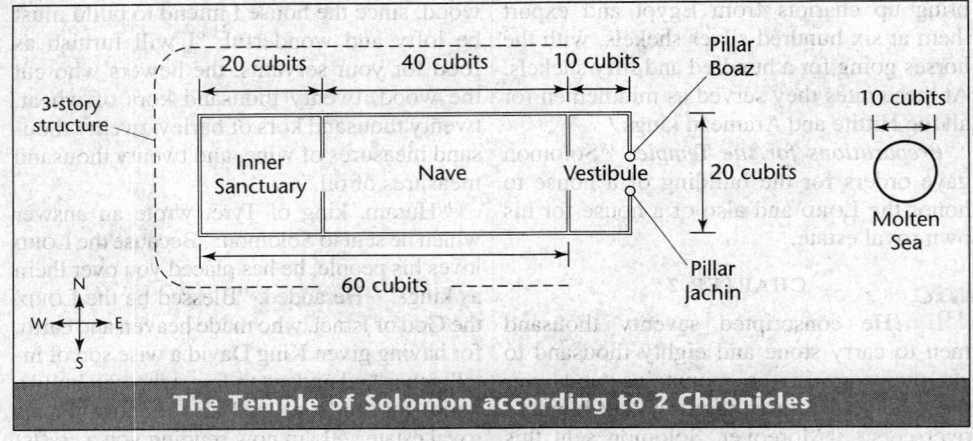

The Temple of Solomon according to 2 Chronicles

Jerusalem on Mount Moriah,* which had been pointed out to his father David, on the spot which David had selected, the threshing-floor of Ornan the Jebusite. ²He began to build in the second month of the fourth year of his reign. ³These were the specifications laid down by Solomon for building the house of God: the length was sixty cubits according to the old measure, and the width was twenty cubits;ˢ ⁴the porch which lay before the nave along the width of the house was also twenty cubits, and it was twenty cubits high.* He overlaid its interior with pure gold.ᵗ ⁵The nave he overlaid with cypress wood which he covered with fine gold, embossing on it palms and chains.ᵘ ⁶He also decorated the building with precious stones. ⁷The house; its beams and thresholds, as well as its walls and its doors, he overlaid with gold, and he engraved cherubim upon the walls. (The gold was from Parvaim.) ⁸He also made the room of the holy of holies. Its length corresponded to the width of the house, twenty cubits, and its width was also twenty cubits. He overlaid it with fine gold to the amount of six hundred talents.ᵛ

⁹The weight of the nails was fifty gold shekels. The upper chambers he likewise covered with gold.

¹⁰ʷFor the room of the holy of holies he made two cherubim of carved workmanship, which were then overlaid with gold. ¹¹The wings of the cherubim spanned twenty cubits: ¹²one wing of each cherub, five cubits in length, extended to a wall of the building, while the other wing, also five cubits in length, touched the corresponding wing of the second cherub. ¹³The combined wing-spread of the two cherubim was thus twenty cubits. They stood upon their own feet, facing toward the nave. ¹⁴He made the veil* of violet, purple, crimson and fine linen, and had cherubim embroidered upon it.ˣ

¹⁵ʸIn front of the building he set two columns thirty-five cubits high; the capital topping each was of five cubits. ¹⁶He worked out chains in the form of a collar with which he encircled the capitals of the columns, and he made a hundred pomegranates which he set on the chains. ¹⁷He set up the columns to correspond with the nave, one for the right

3, 1: Mount Moriah: the height in the land of Moriah (Gn 22, 2). This is the only place in the Bible where the temple mount is identified with the site where Abraham was to sacrifice Isaac.

3, 4: The porch . . . twenty cubits high: this measurement, not given in the Books of Kings, is here based on a variant Greek text that may be a later revision. The received Hebrew text says, "one hundred and twenty cubits high." The height of the two freestanding columns adjacent to the porch (1 Kgs 7, 15-16) is nearly doubled by the Chronicler (2 Chr 3, 15).

3, 14: The veil: at the entrance of the holy of holies, as also in the Mosaic meeting tent (Ex 26, 31f). Solomon's temple had doors at this place (1 Kgs 6, 31). Apparently there was a veil here in the temple of the Chronicler's time as there was also in Herod's temple (Mt 27, 51; Mk 15, 38; Lk 23, 45).

ˢ: 1 Kgs 6, 2; Ez 40, 5.   ᵗ: 1 Kgs 6, 3; Ez 40, 48.   ᵘ: 1 Kgs 6, 15; Ez 41, 1.   ᵛ: 1 Kgs 6, 16f. 20; Ez 41, 3.   ʷ: 10-13: 1 Kgs 6, 23-27.   ˣ: Mt 27, 51.   ʸ: 15ff: 1 Kgs 7, 15-22; Ez 40, 49.

side and the other for the left, and he called the one to the right Jachin and the one to the left Boaz.

CHAPTER 4

See RG 141

[1]Then he made a bronze altar twenty cubits long, twenty cubits wide and ten cubits high.[z] [2a]He also made the molten sea. It was perfectly round, ten cubits in diameter, five in depth, and thirty in circumference; [3]below the rim a ring of figures of oxen* encircled the sea, ten to the cubit, all the way around; there were two rows of these cast in the same mold with the sea. [4]It rested on twelve oxen, three facing north, three west, three south, and three east, with their haunches all toward the center; the sea rested on their backs. [5]It was a handbreadth thick, and its brim was made like that of a cup, being lily-shaped. It had a capacity of three thousand measures.*

[6]Then he made ten basins for washing, placing five of them to the right and five to the left. Here were cleansed the victims for the holocausts; but the sea was for the priests to wash in.[b]

[7]He made the lampstands of gold, ten of them as was prescribed, and placed them in the nave, five to the right and five to the left.[c] [8]He made ten tables and had them set in the nave, five to the right and five to the left; and he made a hundred golden bowls.[d] [9]He made the court of the priests and the great courtyard and the gates of the courtyard; the gates he overlaid with bronze.[e] [10]The sea was placed off to the southeast from the right side of the temple.[f]

[11g]Huram also made the pots, the shovels and the bowls. Huram thus completed the work he had to do for King Solomon in the house of God: [12]two columns, two nodes for the capitals topping these two columns, and two networks covering the nodes of the capitals topping the columns; [13]also four hundred pomegranates for the two networks, with two rows of pomegranates to each network, to cover the two nodes of the capitals topping the columns. [14]He made the stands, and the basins on the stands; [15]one sea, and the twelve oxen under it; [16]likewise the pots, the shovels and the forks. Huram-abi made all these articles for King Solomon from polished bronze for the house of the LORD. [17]The king had them cast in the Jordan region, in the clayey ground between Succoth and Zeredah. [18]Solomon made all these vessels, so many in number that the weight of the bronze was not ascertained.

[19]Solomon had all these articles made for the house of God: the golden altar, the tables on which the showbread lay, [20]the lampstands and their lamps of pure gold which were to burn according to prescription before the sanctuary, [21]flowers, lamps and gold tongs [this was the purest gold], [22]snuffers, bowls, cups and firepans of pure gold. As for the entry to the house, its inner doors to the holy of holies, as well as the doors to the nave, were of gold.

CHAPTER 5

See RG 141

Dedication of the Temple. [1h]When all the work undertaken by Solomon for the temple of the LORD had been completed, he brought in the dedicated offerings of his father David, putting the silver, the gold and all the other articles in the treasuries of the house of God. [2]At Solomon's order the elders of Israel and all the leaders of the tribes, the princes of the Israelite ancestral houses, came to Jerusalem to bring up the ark of the LORD's covenant from the City of David (which is Zion). [3]All the men of Israel assembled before the king during the festival of the seventh month. [4i]When all the elders of Israel had arrived, the Levites* took up the

---

4, 3: Oxen: in 1 Kgs 7, 24 this double row of ornaments is described as being gourds. The text of Kings available to the Chronicler may have been faulty on this point as the words are similar in sound. In 2 Chr 4, 16 the forks correspond in a similar way to bowls in the text of 1 Kings (7, 40).

4, 5: Three thousand measures: according to 1 Kgs 7, 26, "two thousand measures."

5, 4: The Levites: The parallel passage in 1 Kgs 8, 3 has the priests; but see 2 Chr 5, 5, where the Deuteronomic term levitical priests is used, as also in 2 Chr 23, 18; 30, 27.

z: Ez 43, 13-17. a: 2-5: 1 Kgs 7, 23-26; Ez 43, 13. b: 1 Kgs 7, 38f; Ez 40, 38. c: 1 Kgs 7, 49. d: 1 Kgs 7, 50; 1 Chr 23, 16. e: 1 Kgs 7, 12. f: 1 Kgs 7, 39. g: 11-22: 1 Kgs 7, 40-51. h: 1-14: 1 Kgs 7, 51—8, 13. i: 4f: 2 Chr 35, 3.

ark, [5]and they carried the ark and the meeting tent with all the sacred vessels that were in the tent; it was the levitical priests who carried them.

[6]King Solomon and the entire community of Israel gathered about him before the ark were sacrificing sheep and oxen so numerous that they could not be counted or numbered. [7]The priests brought the ark of the covenant of the LORD to its place beneath the wings of the cherubim in the sanctuary, the holy of holies of the temple. [8]The cherubim had their wings spread out over the place of the ark, sheltering the ark and its poles from above. [9]The poles were long enough so that their ends could be seen from that part of the holy place nearest the sanctuary; however, they could not be seen beyond. The ark has remained there to this day.* [10]There was nothing in it but the two tablets which Moses put there on Horeb, the tablets of the covenant which the LORD made with the Israelites at their departure from Egypt.

[11]When the priests came out of the holy place (all the priests who were present had purified themselves without reference to the rotation of their various classes), [12]the Levites who were singers, all who belonged to Asaph, Heman, Jeduthun, and their sons and brothers, clothed in fine linen, with cymbals, harps and lyres, stood east of the altar, and with them a hundred and twenty priests blowing trumpets.

[13]When the trumpeters and singers were heard as a single voice praising and giving thanks to the LORD, and when they raised the sound of the trumpets, cymbals and other musical instruments to "give thanks to the LORD, for he is good, for his mercy endures forever," the building of the LORD's temple was filled with a cloud. [14]The priests could not continue to minister because of the cloud, since the LORD's glory filled the house of God.[j]

CHAPTER 6

See RG 141

[1k]Then Solomon said: "The LORD intends to dwell in the dark cloud. [2]I have truly built you a princely house and dwelling, where you may abide forever." [3l]Turning about, the king greeted the whole community of Israel as they stood. [4]He said: "Blessed be the LORD, the God of Israel, who with his own mouth made a promise to my father David and by his own hands brought it to fulfillment. He said: [5]'Since the day I brought my people out of the land of Egypt, I have not chosen any city from among all the tribes of Israel for the building of a temple to my honor, nor have I chosen any man to be commander of my people Israel; [6]but now I choose Jerusalem, where I shall be honored, and I choose David to rule my people Israel.' [7]My father David wished to build a temple to the honor of the LORD, the God of Israel, [8]but the LORD said to him: 'In wishing to build a temple to my honor, you do well. [9]However, you shall not build the temple; rather, your son whom you will beget shall build the temple to my honor.'

[10]"Now the LORD has fulfilled the promise that he made. I have succeeded my father David and have taken my seat on the throne of Israel, as the LORD foretold, and I have built the temple to the honor of the LORD, the God of Israel. [11]And I have placed there the ark, in which abides the covenant of the LORD which he made with the Israelites."

Solomon's Prayer. [12m]Solomon then took his place before the altar of the LORD in the presence of the whole community of Israel and stretched forth his hands. [13]He had made a bronze platform five cubits long, five cubits wide, and three cubits high, which he had placed in the middle of the courtyard. Having ascended it, Solomon knelt in the presence of the whole of Israel and stretched forth his hands toward heaven.* [14]Thus he prayed: "LORD, God of Israel, there is no god like you in heaven or on earth; you keep your covenant

---

5, 9: The ark has remained there to this day: the Chronicler must have copied this from his source (1 Kgs 8, 8) without reflecting that the ark was lost in the Babylonian destruction of Jerusalem; cf 2 Mc 2, 4-8.

6, 13: This verse is not found in the Chronicler's source; cf 1 Kgs 8, 22f. He has Solomon praying on a bronze plat-

form . . . in the middle of the courtyard because at the time of the Chronicler only the priests prayed before the altar.

j: 2 Chr 7, 2; 1 Kgs 8, 10f.   *k:* 1f: 1 Kgs 8, 12f.   *l:* 3-11: 1 Kgs 8, 14-21.   *m:* 12-41: 1 Kgs 8, 22-53.

and show kindness to your servants who are wholeheartedly faithful to you. ¹⁵You have kept the promise you made to my father David, your servant. With your own mouth you spoke it, and by your own hand you have brought it to fulfillment this day. ¹⁶Now, therefore, LORD, God of Israel, keep the further promise you made to my father David, your servant, when you said, 'You shall always have someone from your line to sit before me on the throne of Israel, provided only that your descendants look to their conduct so as always to live according to my law, even as you have lived in my presence.' ¹⁷Now, LORD, God of Israel, may this promise which you made to your servant David be confirmed.

¹⁸"Can it indeed be that God dwells with mankind on earth? If the heavens and the highest heavens cannot contain you, how much less this temple which I have built! ¹⁹Look kindly on the prayer and petition of your servant, O LORD, my God, and listen to the cry of supplication your servant makes before you. ²⁰May your eyes watch day and night over this temple, the place where you have decreed you shall be honored; may you heed the prayer which I your servant offer toward this place. ²¹Listen to the petitions of your servant and of your people Israel which they direct toward this place. Listen from your heavenly dwelling, and when you have heard, pardon.

²²"When any man sins against his neighbor and is required to take an oath of execration against himself, and when he comes for the oath before your altar in this temple, ²³listen from heaven: take action and pass judgment on your servants, requiting the wicked man and holding him responsible for his conduct, but absolving the innocent and rewarding him according to his virtue. ²⁴When your people Israel have sinned against you and are defeated by the enemy, but afterward they return and praise your name, and they pray to you and entreat you in this temple, ²⁵listen from heaven and forgive the sin of your people Israel, and bring them back to the land which you gave them and their fathers. ²⁶When the sky is closed so that there is no rain, because they have sinned against you, but then they pray toward this place and praise your name,

and they withdraw from sin because you afflict them, ²⁷listen in heaven and forgive the sin of your servants and of your people Israel. But teach them the right way to live, and send rain upon your land which you gave your people as their heritage. ²⁸When there is famine in the land, when there is pestilence, or blight, or mildew, or locusts, or caterpillars; when their enemies besiege them at any of their gates; whenever there is a plague or sickness of any kind; ²⁹when any Israelite of all your people offers a prayer or petition of any kind, and in awareness of his affliction and pain, stretches out his hands toward this temple, ³⁰listen from your heavenly dwelling place, and forgive. Knowing his heart, render to everyone according to his conduct, for you alone know the hearts of men. ³¹So may they fear you and walk in your ways as long as they live on the land you gave our fathers.

³²"For the foreigner, too, who is not of your people Israel, when he comes from a distant land to honor your great name, your mighty power, and your outstretched arm, when they come in prayer to this temple, ³³listen from your heavenly dwelling place, and do whatever the foreigner entreats you, that all the peoples of the earth may know your name, fearing you as do your people Israel, and knowing that this house which I have built is dedicated to your honor.

³⁴"When your people go forth to war against their enemies, wherever you send them, and pray to you in the direction of this city and of the house I have built to your honor, ³⁵listen from heaven to their prayer and petition, and defend their cause. ³⁶When they sin against you (for there is no man who does not sin), and in your anger against them you deliver them to the enemy, so that their captors deport them to another land, far or near, ³⁷when they repent in the land where they are captive and are converted, when they entreat you in the land of their captivity and say, 'We have sinned and done wrong; we have been wicked,' ³⁸and with their whole heart and with their whole soul they turn back to you in the land of those who hold them captive, when they pray in the direction of their land which you gave their fathers, and of the city you have chosen, and of the house which I have built to

> For the Chronicler, the temple is important because God has consecrated the place by choosing it for himself. This interpretation by the Chronicler is related to the idea in Deuteronomy of God's choosing a place for his name to dwell (Dt 12, 11.14). The concept of a "house of sacrifice" (7, 12) places emphasis on the ritual aspects of temple service and its role as a place of mediation between God and the community.

your honor, [39]listen from your heavenly dwelling place, hear their prayer and petitions, and uphold their cause. Forgive your people who have sinned against you. [40]My God, may your eyes be open and your ears attentive to the prayer of this place. [41]And now,

"Advance, LORD God, to your resting place,
  you and the ark of your majesty.
May your priests, LORD God, be clothed with salvation,
  may your faithful ones rejoice in good things.
[42] LORD God, reject not the plea of your anointed,
  remember the devotion of David, your servant."

CHAPTER 7

See RG 141

[1n]When Solomon had ended his prayer, fire came down from heaven and consumed the holocaust and the sacrifices, and the glory of the LORD filled the house. [2]But the priests could not enter the house of the LORD, for the glory of the LORD had filled the house of the LORD.[o] [3]All the Israelites looked on while the fire came down and the glory of the LORD was upon the house, and they fell down upon the pavement with their faces to the earth and adored, praising the LORD, "for he is good, for his mercy endures forever." [4]The king and all the people were offering sacrifices before the LORD.[p] [5]King Solomon offered as sacrifice twenty-two thousand oxen, and one hundred twenty thousand sheep.[q]

End of the Dedication. [6]Thus the king and all the people dedicated the house of God. The priests were standing at their stations, as were the Levites, with the musical instruments of the LORD which King David had made for "praising the LORD, for his mercy endures forever," when David used them to accompany the hymns. Across from them the priests blew the trumpets and all Israel stood.[r]

[7]Then Solomon consecrated the middle part of the court which lay before the house of the LORD; there he offered the holocausts and the fat of the peace offerings, since the bronze altar which Solomon had made could not hold the holocausts, the cereal offerings and the fat.[s]

[8]On this occasion Solomon and with him all Israel, who had assembled in very large numbers from Labo of Hamath to the Wadi of Egypt, celebrated the festival for seven days.[t] [9u]On the eighth day they held a special meeting, for they had celebrated the dedication of the altar for seven days and the feast* for seven days. [10]On the twenty-third day of the seventh month he sent the people back to their tents, rejoicing and glad at heart at the good things the LORD had done for David, for Solomon, and for his people Israel. [11v]Solomon completed the house of the LORD and the royal palace; he successfully accomplished everything he had planned to do in regard to the house of the LORD and his own house.

God's Promise to Solomon. [12]The LORD appeared to Solomon during the night and said to him: "I have heard your prayer, and I

7, 9f: The feast: of Booths, celebrated on the fifteenth day of the seventh month and followed by a solemn octave lasting through the twenty-second day (Lv 23, 33-36; Nm 29, 12-35); the people are therefore sent home on the twenty-third day (v 10). The festival (v 8) for the dedication of the altar and of the temple lasted for seven days before the feast of Booths, from the seventh to the fourteenth day. According to 1 Kgs 8,

65f, the people are dismissed at the end of these seven days.

n: 1-10: 1 Kgs 8, 54-66; Jgs 6, 21; 1 Chr 21, 26; 2 Mc 2, 10. *o:* 2 Chr 5, 14; Ex 24, 16; 1 Kgs 8, 10f. *p:* 2 Chr 5, 13; 1 Kgs 8, 62; Ps 136, 1. *q:* 1 Kgs 8, 62f. *r:* Nm 10, 8. 10; Ps 136, 1. *s:* 1 Kgs 8, 64. *t:* 1 Kgs 8, 65. *u:* 9f: 1 Kgs 8, 66. *v:* 11-22: 1 Kgs 9, 1-9.

have chosen this place for my house of sacrifice. [13]If I close heaven so that there is no rain, if I command the locust to devour the land, if I send pestilence among my people, [14]and if my people, upon whom my name has been pronounced, humble themselves and pray, and seek my presence and turn from their evil ways, I will hear them from heaven and pardon their sins and revive their land. [15]Now my eyes shall be open and my ears attentive to the prayer of this place. [16]And now I have chosen and consecrated this house that my name may be there forever; my eyes and my heart also shall be there always.

[17]"As for you, if you live in my presence as your father David did, doing all that I have commanded you and keeping my statutes and ordinances, [18]I will establish your royal throne as I covenanted with your father David when I said, 'There shall never be lacking someone of yours as ruler in Israel.' [19]But if you turn away and forsake my statutes and commands which I placed before you, if you proceed to venerate and worship strange gods, [20]then I will uproot the people from the land I gave them; I will cast from my sight this house which I have consecrated to my honor, and I will make it a proverb and a byword among all peoples. [21]This temple which is so exalted—everyone passing by it will be amazed and ask: 'Why has the LORD done this to this land and to this house?' [22]And men will answer: 'They forsook the LORD, the God of their fathers, who brought them out of the land of Egypt, and they adopted strange gods and worshiped them and served them. That is why he has brought down upon them all this evil.' "

CHAPTER 8

See RG 141

Public Works. [1w]After the twenty years during which Solomon built the house of the LORD and his own house, [2]he built up the cities which Huram had given him,* and

settled Israelites there. [3]Then Solomon went to Hamath of Zoba and conquered it. [4]He built Tadmor* in the desert region and all the supply cities, which he built in Hamath. [5x]He built Upper Beth-horon and Lower Beth-horon, fortified cities with walls, gates and bars; [6]also Baalath, all the supply cities belonging to Solomon, and all the cities for the chariots, the cities for the horsemen, and whatever else Solomon decided should be built in Jerusalem, in the Lebanon, and in the entire land under his dominion. [7]All the people that remained of the Hittites, Amorites, Perizzites, Hivites, and Jebusites, who were not of Israel— [8]that is, their descendants remaining in the land, whom the Israelites had not destroyed—Solomon subjected to forced labor, as they continue to this day. [9]But Solomon did not enslave the Israelites for his works. They became soldiers, commanders of his warriors, and commanders of his chariots and his horsemen. [10]They were also King Solomon's two hundred and fifty overseers who had charge of the people.

Solomon's Piety. [11]Solomon brought the daughter of Pharaoh up from the City of David to the palace which he had built for her, for he said, "No wife of mine shall dwell in the house of David, king of Israel, for the places where the ark of the LORD has come are holy."

[12]In those times Solomon offered holocausts to the LORD upon the altar of the LORD which he had built in front of the porch, [13]as was required day by day according to the command of Moses, and in particular on the sabbaths, at the new moons, and on the fixed festivals three times a year: on the feast of the Unleavened Bread, the feast of Weeks and the feast of Booths.[y]

[14]And according to the ordinance of his father David he appointed the various classes of the priests for their service, and the Levites according to their functions of praise

---

8, 2: The cities which Huram had given him: according to 1 Kgs 9, 10-14, Solomon had ceded the cities as payment for the timber and gold received from Tyre. But since Huram was dissatisfied, he may have returned the cities to Solomon.

8, 4: Tadmor: later known as Palmyra, an important caravan city in the Syrian desert. The parallel passage in 1 Kgs 9,

18 has Tamar, in southern Judah; cf Ez 47, 19; 48, 28. But Solomon may well have fortified Tadmor against the Arameans.

---

w: f: 1 Kgs 9, 10f.   x: 5-12: 1 Kgs 9, 18-25.   y: 1 Kgs 9, 25; Ex 23, 14; Nm 28—29.

Mediterranean
Sea

ASHER

NAPHTALI

BASHAN

VIII

IX

ISSACHAR

X

Jezreel

Dor

NAPHATH-DOR

IV

Megiddo

Taanach

V

Beth-shean

Abel-meholah

VI

Ramoth-gilead

Hepher

Arubboth

III

Socoh

EPHRAIM

GILEAD

I

VII

Mahanaim

Shaalbim

XI

Makaz

II

Elon

BENJAMIN

Beth-shemesh

JERUSALEM

XII

JUDAH

Dead
Sea

0   10   20 Miles

0   10   20 Kilometers

33°

32°

31°

35°

36°

The Kingdom of Solomon according to 2 Chronicles

and ministry alongside the priests, as the daily duty required. The gatekeepers of the various classes stood guard at each gate, since such was the command of David, the man of God.*z* 15There was no deviation from the king's command in any respect relating to the priests and Levites or the treasuries. 16All of Solomon's work was carried out successfully from the day the foundation of the house of the LORD was laid until the house of the LORD had been completed in every detail.

Glories of the Court. 17In those times Solomon went to Ezion-geber and to Elath on the seashore of the land of Edom.*a* 18Huram, through his servants, sent him ships and crewmen acquainted with the sea, who accompanied Solomon's servants to Ophir and brought back from there four hundred and fifty talents of gold to King Solomon.*b*

See RG
141 **CHAPTER 9**

1When the queen of Sheba heard of Solomon's fame, she came to Jerusalem to test him with subtle questions, accompanied by a very numerous retinue and by camels bearing spices, much gold, and precious stones. She came to Solomon and questioned him on every subject in which she was interested.*c* 2Solomon explained to her everything she asked about, and there remained nothing hidden from Solomon that he could not explain to her.

3When the queen of Sheba witnessed Solomon's wisdom, the palace he had built, 4the food at his table, the seating of his ministers, the attendance of his servants and their dress, his cupbearers and their dress, and the holocausts he offered in the house of the LORD, it took her breath away. 5"The account I heard in my country about your deeds and your wisdom is true," she told the king. 6"Yet I did not believe the report until I came and saw with my own eyes. I have discovered that they did not tell me the half of your great wisdom; you have surpassed the stories I heard. 7Happy are your men, happy these servants of yours, who stand before you always and listen to your wisdom. 8Blessed be the LORD, your God, who has been so

pleased with you as to place you on his throne as king for the LORD, your God. Because your God has so loved Israel as to will to make it last forever, he has appointed you over them as king to administer right and justice." 9Then she gave the king one hundred and twenty gold talents and a very large quantity of spices, as well as precious stones. There was no other spice like that which the queen of Sheba gave to King Solomon.

10The servants of Huram and of Solomon who brought gold from Ophir also brought cabinet wood and precious stones. 11With the cabinet wood the king made stairs for the temple of the LORD and the palace of the king; also lyres and harps for the chanters. The like of these had not been seen before in the land of Judah.

12King Solomon gave the queen of Sheba everything she desired and asked him for, more than she had brought to the king. Then she returned to her own country with her servants.

13dThe gold that Solomon received each year weighed six hundred and sixty-six gold talents, 14in addition to what was collected from travelers and what the merchants brought. All the kings of Arabia also, and the governors of the country, brought gold and silver to Solomon.

15Moreover, King Solomon made two hundred large shields of beaten gold, six hundred shekels of beaten gold going into each shield, 16and three hundred bucklers of beaten gold, three hundred shekels of gold going into each buckler; these the king put in the hall of the Forest of Lebanon.

17King Solomon also made a large ivory throne which he overlaid with fine gold. 18The throne had six steps; a footstool of gold was fastened to it, and there was an arm on each side of the seat, with two lions standing beside the arms. 19Twelve other lions also stood there, one on either side of each step. Nothing like this had ever been produced in any other kingdom. 20Furthermore, all of King Solomon's drinking vessels were of gold, and all the utensils in the hall of the Forest of Lebanon were of pure

---

z: 1 Chr 23—26; Neh 12, 46.   *a:* 1 Kgs 9, 26; Mt 12, 42; Lk 11, 31.   *b:* 1 Kgs 9, 27f.   *c:* 1 Kgs 10, 1f; Mt 12, 42; Lk 11, 31.   *d:* 13-28: 1 Kgs 10, 14-28.

gold; silver was not considered of value in Solomon's time. [21]For the king had ships that went to Tarshish with the servants of Huram. Once every three years the fleet of Tarshish would return with a cargo of gold and silver, ivory, apes and monkeys. [22]Thus King Solomon surpassed all the other kings of the earth in riches as well as in wisdom.

[23]All the kings of the earth sought audience with Solomon, to hear from him the wisdom which God had put in his heart. [24]Year in and year out, each one would bring his tribute—silver and gold articles, garments, weapons, spices, horses and mules. [25]Solomon also had four thousand stalls of horses, chariots, and twelve thousand horsemen, which he assigned to the chariot cities and to the king in Jerusalem. [26]He was ruler over all the kings from the River to the land of the Philistines and down to the border of Egypt. [27]The king made silver as common in Jerusalem as stones, while cedars became as numerous as the sycamores of the foothills. [28]Horses were imported for Solomon from Egypt and from all the lands.[*]

The Death of Solomon. [29e]The rest of the acts of Solomon, first and last, are written, as is well known, in the acts of Nathan the prophet, in the prophecy of Ahijah the Shilonite, and in the visions of Iddo the seer which concern Jeroboam, son of Nebat. [30]Solomon reigned in Jerusalem over all Israel for forty years. [31]He rested with his ancestors; he was buried in his father's City of David, and his son Rehoboam succeeded him as king.

II: The Monarchy before Hezekiah

CHAPTER 10

See RG 141–42 **Division of the Kingdom.** [1f]Rehoboam went to Shechem, for all Israel* had come to Shechem to proclaim him king. [2]When Jeroboam, son of Nebat, heard of this in Egypt where he had fled from King Solomon, he re-

turned from Egypt. [3]Jeroboam was summoned to the assembly, and he and all Israel said to Rehoboam: [4]"Your father laid a heavy yoke upon us. If you now lighten the harsh service and the heavy yoke that your father imposed on us, we will serve you." [5]"In three days," he answered them, "come back to me."

When the people had departed, [6]King Rehoboam consulted the elders who had been in the service of his father during Solomon's lifetime, asking, "What answer do you advise me to give this people?" [7]They replied, "If you will deal kindly with this people and give in to them, acceding to their request, they will be your servants forever." [8]But he ignored the advice the elders had given him and consulted the young men who had grown up with him and were in his service. [9]He said to them, "What answer do you advise me to give this people, who have asked me to lighten the yoke my father imposed on them?" [10]The young men who had grown up with him replied: "This is the answer you should give to this people who have said to you, 'Your father laid a heavy yoke upon us, but do you lighten our yoke'; this you should say to them: 'My little finger is thicker than my father's body. [11]Whereas my father put a heavy yoke on you, I will make it heavier! My father beat you with whips, but I will beat you with scorpions!'"

[12]On the third day, Jeroboam and all the people came back to King Rehoboam as he had instructed them to do. [13]Ignoring the advice the elders had given him, the king gave them a harsh answer, [14]speaking to them according to the advice of the young men: "My father laid a heavy yoke on you, but I will make it heavier. My father beat you with whips, but I will beat you with scorpions." [15]The king would not listen to the people, for this turn of events was divinely ordained to fulfill the prophecy the LORD had uttered to Jeroboam, the son of Nebat, through Ahijah the Shilonite.[g]

9, 28: See note on 2 Chr 1, 16f.

10, 1: All Israel: as in the original source (1 Kgs 12, 1), the northern tribes, distinct from Judah and Benjamin. Contrast the Chronicler's own terms, those Israelites who lived in the cities of Judah (v 17), and all the Israelites [literally,

all Israel] in Judah and Benjamin (2 Chr 11, 3).

e: 29ff: 1 Kgs 11, 41ff. *f:* 1-14: 1 Kgs 12, 1-14. *g:* 1 Kgs 11, 29-39; 12, 15.

The Dissolution of Judah

Having described the high point of Israel under David and Solomon, the Chronicler turns his attention in chs 10 through 36 to the flow of Israel's history after the division of the kingdom into two parts. Writing in Jerusalem during the postexilic period, the Chronicler wants to present positive models for his own readership from Israel's past. These models share with David and Solomon a desire to ensure the proper worship of God in the temple and to instill in the community the idea of seeking God. Focused on the temple in Jerusalem, the Chronicler recounts the historical ebb and flow of the Davidic line that ruled Judah, only rarely incorporating any of the northern kingdom's history into his narrative.

[16h]When all Israel saw that the king would not listen to them, the people answered the king,

"What share have we in David?
  We have no heritage in the son of Jesse.
Everyone to your tents, O Israel!
  Now look to your own house, David!"

So all Israel went off to their tents. [17]Rehoboam, therefore, reigned over only those Israelites who lived in the cities of Judah. [18]King Rehoboam then sent out Hadoram, who was superintendent of the forced labor, but the Israelites stoned him to death. Rehoboam himself managed to mount his chariot and flee to Jerusalem. [19]Thus Israel has been in rebellion against David's house to this day.

CHAPTER 11

See RG 141–42

[1i]On his arrival in Jerusalem Rehoboam gathered together the house of Judah and Benjamin, a hundred and eighty thousand seasoned warriors, to have them fight against Israel and restore the kingdom to him. [2]However, the word of the LORD came to Shemiah, a man of God: [3]"Say to Rehoboam, son of Solomon, king of Judah, and to all the Israelites in Judah and Benjamin: [4]'Thus says the LORD: You must not march out to fight against your brothers. Let every man return home, for what has occurred I have brought about.'" They obeyed this message of the LORD and gave up the expedition against Jeroboam.

*Rehoboam's Works.** [5]Rehoboam took up residence in Jerusalem and built fortified cities in Judah. [6]He built up Bethlehem, Etam, Tekoa, [7]Beth-zur, Soco, Adullam, [8]Gath, Mareshah, Ziph, [9]Adoraim, Lachish, Azekah, [10]Zorah, Aijalon, and Hebron; these were fortified cities in Judah and Benjamin. [11]Then he strengthened the fortifications and put commanders in them, with supplies of food, oil and wine. [12]In every city were shields and spears, and he made them very strong. Thus Judah and Benjamin remained his.

Refugees from the North. [13]Now the priests and Levites throughout Israel presented themselves to him from all parts of their land, [14]for the Levites left their assigned pasture lands and their holdings and came to Judah and Jerusalem, because Jeroboam and his sons repudiated them as priests of the LORD.[j] [15]In their place, he himself appointed priests for the high places and satyrs and calves he had made.[k] [16]After them, all those of the Israelite tribes who firmly desired to seek the LORD, the God of Israel, came to Jerusalem to sacrifice to the LORD, the God of their fathers. [17]Thus they strengthened the kingdom of Judah and made Rehoboam, son of Solomon, prevail for three years; for they walked in the way of David and Solomon three years.

Rehoboam's Family. [18]Rehoboam took to himself as wife Mahalath, daughter of Jerimoth, son of David and of Abihail, daughter of Eliab, son of Jesse. [19]She bore him sons: Jehush, Shemariah and Zaham. [20]After her,

11, 5-12: These verses, though not found in 1 Kgs, are apparently based on a reliable, ancient source.

---

h: 16-19: 1 Kgs 12, 16-19.   i: 1-4: 1 Kgs 12, 21-24.   j: 1 Kgs 12, 32.   k: 1 Kgs 12, 32; Lv 17, 7.

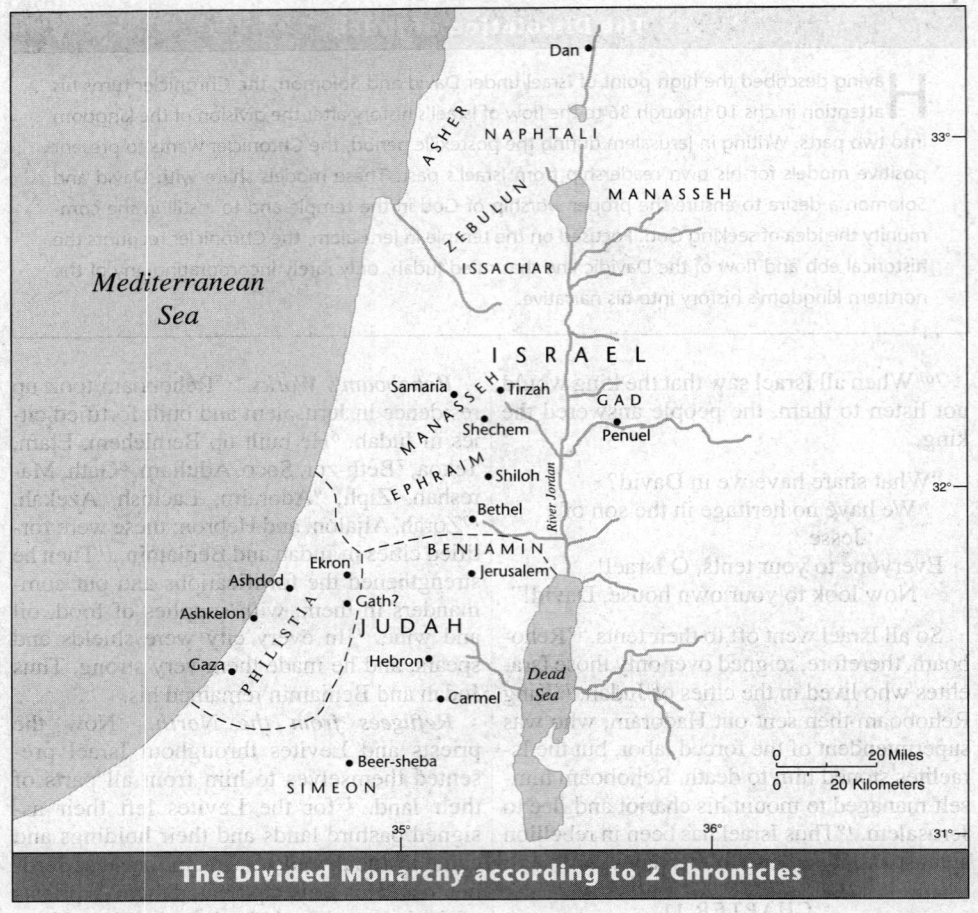

The Divided Monarchy according to 2 Chronicles

he married Maacah, daughter of Absalom, who bore him Abijah, Attai, Ziza and Shelomith.[l] [21]Rehoboam loved Maacah, daughter of Absalom, more than all his other wives and concubines; he had taken eighteen wives and sixty concubines, and he fathered twenty-eight sons and sixty daughters. [22]Rehoboam constituted Abijah, son of Maacah, commander among his brothers, for he intended to make him king. [23]He acted prudently, distributing various of his sons throughout all the districts of Judah and Benjamin, in all the fortified cities; and he furnished them with copious provisions and sought an abundance of wives for them.

CHAPTER 12

His Apostasy. [1]After Rehoboam had consolidated his rule and had become powerful, he abandoned the law of the LORD, he and all Israel with him.[m] [2]Thus it happened that in the fifth year of King Rehoboam, Shishak, king of Egypt, attacked Jerusalem, for they had been unfaithful to the LORD.[n] [3]He came up with twelve hundred chariots and sixty thousand horsemen, and there was no counting the army that came with him from Egypt—Libyans, Sukkites* and Ethiopians. [4]They captured the fortified cities of Judah and came as far as Jerusalem. [5]Then Shema-

See RG 141–42

12, 3: Sukkites: foreign mercenaries in the Egyptian army.

l: 1 Kgs 15, 2.   m: 1 Kgs 11, 4; 14, 22.   n: 1 Kgs 14, 25.

iah the prophet came to Rehoboam and the commanders of Judah who had gathered at Jerusalem because of Shishak, and said to them: "Thus says the LORD: 'You have abandoned me, and therefore I have abandoned you to the power of Shishak.' "*o*

⁶However, the commanders of Israel and the king humbled themselves, saying, "The LORD is just." ⁷When the LORD saw that they had humbled themselves, the word of the LORD came to Shemaiah: "Because they have humbled themselves, I will not destroy them; I will give them some deliverance, and my wrath shall not be poured out upon Jerusalem through Shishak. ⁸But they shall be his servants, that they may know what it is to serve me and what it is to serve earthly kingdoms." ⁹*p*Therefore Shishak, king of Egypt, attacked Jerusalem and carried off the treasures of the temple of the LORD and of the king's palace. He took everything, including the gold bucklers that Solomon had made. ¹⁰(To replace them, King Rehoboam made bronze bucklers, which he entrusted to the officers of the guard on duty at the entrance of the royal palace. ¹¹Whenever the king visited the temple of the LORD, the troops would come bearing them, and then they would return them to the guardroom.) ¹²Because he had humbled himself, the anger of the LORD turned from him so that it did not destroy him completely; and in Judah, moreover, good deeds were found.

¹³King Rehoboam consolidated his power in Jerusalem and continued to rule; he was forty-one years old when he became king, and he reigned seventeen years in Jerusalem, the city in which, out of all the tribes of Israel, the LORD chose to be honored. Rehoboam's mother was named Naamah, an Ammonite.*q* ¹⁴He did evil, for he had not truly resolved to seek the LORD. ¹⁵*r*The acts of Rehoboam, first and last, are written, as is well known, in the history of Shemaiah the prophet and of Iddo the seer [his family record]. There was war continually between Rehoboam and Jeroboam. ¹⁶Rehoboam rested with his ancestors;

he was buried in the City of David. His son Abijah succeeded him as king.

CHAPTER 13

War between Abijah and Jeroboam. See RG 141-42

¹*s*In the eighteenth year of King Jeroboam, Abijah became king of Judah; ²he reigned three years in Jerusalem. His mother was named Michaiah, daughter of Uriel of Gibeah. There was war between Abijah and Jeroboam.

³Abijah joined battle with a force of four hundred thousand picked warriors, while Jeroboam lined up against him in battle with eight hundred thousand picked and valiant warriors. ⁴*Abijah stood on Mount Zemaraim, which is in the highlands of Ephraim, and said: "Listen to me, Jeroboam and all Israel! ⁵Do you not know that the LORD, the God of Israel, has given the kingdom of Israel to David forever, to him and to his sons, by a covenant made in salt? ⁶Yet Jeroboam, son of Nebat, the servant of Solomon, son of David, has stood up and rebelled against his lord!*t* ⁷Worthless men, scoundrels, joined him and overcame Rehoboam, son of Solomon, when Rehoboam was young and unthinking, and no match for them. ⁸But now, do you think you are a match for the kingdom of the LORD commanded by the sons of David, simply because you are a huge multitude and have with you the golden calves which Jeroboam made you for gods?

⁹"Have you not expelled the priests of the LORD, the sons of Aaron, and the Levites, and made for yourselves priests like the peoples of foreign lands? Everyone who comes to consecrate himself with a young bull and seven rams becomes a priest of no-gods. ¹⁰But as for us, the LORD is our God, and we have not forsaken him. The priests ministering to the LORD are sons of Aaron, and the Levites also have their offices. ¹¹They burn holocausts to the LORD and fragrant incense morning after morning and evening after evening; they display the showbread on the pure table, and the lamps of

---

13, 4-12: This is a free composition of the Chronicler to show that this was a religious, rather than a political, war.

o: 2 Chr 11, 2.   *p:* 9ff: 1 Kgs 14, 25-28.   *q:* 1 Kgs 14, 21.   *r:* 15f: 1 Kgs 14, 29ff.   *s:* 1f: 1 Kgs 15, 1f.   *t:* 1 Kgs 11, 26.

the golden lampstand burn evening after evening; for we observe our duties to the LORD, our God, but you have abandoned him. ¹²See, God is with us, at our head, and his priests are here with trumpets to sound the attack against you. Do not battle against the LORD, the God of your fathers, O Israelites, for you will not succeed!"

¹³But Jeroboam had an ambush go around them to come at them from the rear; so that while his army faced Judah, his ambush lay behind them. ¹⁴When Judah turned and saw that they had to battle on both fronts, they cried out to the LORD and the priests sounded the trumpets. ¹⁵Then the men of Judah shouted; and when they did so, God defeated Jeroboam and all Israel before Abijah and Judah. ¹⁶The Israelites fled before Judah, and God delivered them into their hands. ¹⁷Abijah and his people inflicted a severe defeat upon them; five hundred thousand picked men of Israel fell slain. ¹⁸The Israelites were subdued on that occasion and the Judahites were victorious because they relied on the LORD, the God of their fathers. ¹⁹Abijah pursued Jeroboam and took cities from him: Bethel and its dependencies, Jeshanah and its dependencies, and Ephron and its dependencies. ²⁰Jeroboam did not regain power during the time of Abijah; the LORD struck him down and he died, ²¹while Abijah continued to grow stronger. He took to himself fourteen wives and fathered twenty-two sons and sixteen daughters.

Death of Abijah. ^{22u}The rest of Abijah's acts, his deeds and his words, are written in the midrash of the prophet Iddo. ²³Abijah rested with his ancestors; they buried him in the City of David. His son Asa succeeded him as king. During his time, ten years of peace began in the land.

CHAPTER 14

See RG 141–42 **Asa the Reformer.** ^{1v}Asa did what was good and pleasing to the LORD, his

God, ²removing the heathen altars and the high places, breaking to pieces the sacred pillars, and cutting down the sacred poles. ³He commanded Judah to seek the LORD, the God of their fathers, and to observe the law and its commands. ⁴He removed the high places and incense stands from all the cities of Judah, and under him the kingdom had peace. ⁵He built fortified cities in Judah, for the land had peace and no war was waged against him during these years, because the LORD had given him peace. ⁶He said to Judah: "Let us build these cities and surround them with walls, towers, gates and bars. The land is still ours, for we have sought the LORD, our God; we sought him, and he has given us rest on every side." So they built and prospered.

The Ethiopian Invasion. ⁷Asa had an army of three hundred thousand shield- and lance-bearers from Judah, and two hundred and eighty thousand from Benjamin who carried bucklers and were archers, all of them valiant warriors. ⁸Zerah the Ethiopian moved against them with a force of one million men and three hundred chariots, and he came as far as Mareshah.^w ⁹Asa went out to meet him and set himself in battle array in the valley of Zephathah, near Mareshah. ¹⁰Asa called upon the LORD, his God, praying: "O LORD, there is none like you to help the powerless against the strong. Help us, O LORD, our God, for we rely on you, and in your name we have come against this multitude. You are the LORD, our God; let no man prevail against you."^x ¹¹And so the LORD defeated the Ethiopians before Asa and Judah, and they fled.^y ¹²Asa and those with him pursued them as far as Gerar, and the Ethiopians fell until there were no survivors, for they were crushed before the LORD and his army, which carried away enormous spoils. ¹³Then the Judahites conquered all the cities around Gerar, for the fear of the LORD was upon them; they despoiled all the cities, for there

---

14, 7-14: An Ethiopian invasion of Judah is mentioned only in 1 Chronicles. This account may be a legend contrived to show how the pious King Asa was rewarded through divine assistance. There may, however, have been an incursion of nomads from the Negeb at this time; cf vv 13f.

u: 22f: 2 Chr 12, 15; 1 Kgs 7ff.   *v:* 1f: 2 Chr 33, 15; Ex 23, 24; 34, 13; 1 Kgs 15, 11f.   *w:* 2 Chr 16, 8.   *x:* 2 Chr 32, 8.   *y:* Pss 20, 7f; 60, 11f.

The Reign of Asa

In this classic expansion of his source in 1 Kings, the Chronicler takes a mere seven verses on the reign of Asa and develops three chapters (14–16) with complex plots and a rich theological content. The Chronicler portrays Asa as a model ruler who succeeds in bringing the community into peace, security, and joy by his devotion to God.

was much booty in them. *14*They attacked also the tents of the cattle-herders and carried off a great number of sheep and camels. Then they returned to Jerusalem.

CHAPTER 15

See RG 141-42

Cult Reform. *1*Upon Azariah, son of Oded, came the spirit of God. *2*He went forth to meet Asa and said to him: "Hear me, Asa and all Judah and Benjamin! The LORD is with you when you are with him, and if you seek him he will be present to you; but if you abandon him, he will abandon you.*z* *3*For a long time Israel had no true God, no priest-teacher and no law, *4*but when in their distress they turned to the LORD, the God of Israel, and sought him, he was present to them.*a* *5*In that former time there was no place for anyone to go or come, but there were many terrors upon the inhabitants of the lands. *6*Nation crushed nation and city crushed city, for God destroyed them by every kind of adversity.*b* *7*But as for you, be strong and do not relax, for your work shall be rewarded."*c*

*8*When Asa heard these words and the prophecy [Oded the prophet], he was encouraged to remove the detestable idols from the whole land of Judah and Benjamin and from the cities he had taken in the highlands of Ephraim, and to restore the altar of the LORD which was before the vestibule of the LORD. *9*Then he convened all Judah and Benjamin, together with those of Ephraim, Manasseh and Simeon who sojourned with them; for many had fled to him from Israel when they saw that the LORD, his God, was with him. *10**They gathered at Jerusalem in

the third month of the fifteenth year of Asa's reign, *11*and sacrificed to the LORD at that time seven hundred oxen and seven thousand sheep of the booty they had brought. *12*They entered into a covenant to seek the LORD, the God of their fathers, with all their heart and soul; *13*and everyone who would not seek the LORD, the God of Israel, was to be put to death, whether small or great, whether man or woman.*d* *14*They swore to the LORD with a loud voice, with shouting and with trumpets and horns. *15*All Judah rejoiced over the oath, for they had sworn with their whole heart and sought him with complete desire, so that he was present to them. And the LORD gave them rest on every side.*e*

*16*Maacah, the mother of King Asa, he deposed as queen mother because she had made an outrageous object for Asherah; Asa cut this down, smashed it, and burnt it in the Kidron Valley. *17*Although the high places did not disappear from Israel, yet Asa's heart was undivided as long as he lived. *18*He brought into the house of God his father's votive offerings and his own: silver, gold, and various utensils. *19*There was no war until the thirty-fifth year of Asa's reign.

CHAPTER 16

See RG 141-42

Asa's Infidelity. *1*In the thirty-sixth year of Asa's reign, Baasha, king of Israel, attacked Judah and fortified Ramah to prevent any communication with Asa, king of Judah. *2*Asa then brought out silver and gold from the treasuries of the temple of the LORD and of the royal palace and sent them to Ben-hadad, king of Aram, who lived in Damascus,

---

15, 10ff: With this description of a covenant ceremony in the third month of a year beginning in the spring, the Chronicler lays a foundation for celebrating the ancient feast of Pentecost (Weeks) as the time for a solemn renewal of the people's covenant with God on Mount Sinai; see Ex 19, 1ff; Lv 23, 16 and the note there. This is also the background for Pentecost as the "birthday of the Church."

z: Jer 29, 13f; Hos 3, 4f. *a:* Dt 4, 29f. *b:* Is 19, 2. *c:* Is 7, 4; Jer 31, 16. *d:* Neh 10, 30. *e:* Dt 4, 29. *f:* 16ff: 1 Kgs 15, 13ff. *g:* 1-5: 1 Kgs 15, 16-21.

with this message: ³"There is a treaty between you and me, as there was between your father and my father. See, I am sending you silver and gold. Go, break your treaty with Baasha, king of Israel, that he may withdraw from me." ⁴Ben-hadad agreed to King Asa's request and sent the leaders of his troops against the cities of Israel. They attacked Ijon, Dan, Abel-maim, and all the store cities of Naphtali. ⁵When Baasha heard of it, he left off fortifying Ramah; he stopped his work. ⁶Then King Asa commandeered all of Judah to carry away the stone and wood with which Baasha had been fortifying Ramah, and with them he fortified Geba and Mizpah.

⁷At that time Hanani the seer came to Asa, king of Judah, and said to him: "Because you relied on the king of Aram and did not rely on the LORD, your God, the army of the king of Aram has escaped* your hand. ⁸Were not the Ethiopians and Libyans a vast army, with great numbers of chariots and drivers? And yet, because you relied on the LORD, he delivered them into your power.ʰ ⁹The eyes of the LORD roam over the whole earth, to encourage those who are devoted to him wholeheartedly. You have acted foolishly in this matter, for from now on you will have wars."ⁱ ¹⁰But Asa became angry with the seer and imprisoned him in the stocks, so greatly was he enraged at him over this. Asa also oppressed some of his people at this time.

¹¹ʲNow the acts of Asa, first and last, can be found recorded in the book of the kings of Judah and Israel. ¹²In the thirty-ninth year of his reign, Asa contracted a serious disease in his feet. But even in his sickness he did not seek the LORD, but only the physicians. ¹³Asa rested with his ancestors; he died in the forty-first year of his reign. ¹⁴They buried him in the tomb he had hewn for himself in the City of David, having laid him upon a couch which was filled with spices and various kinds of aromatics compounded into an ointment. They also burned a very great funeral pyre for him.

CHAPTER 17

See RG 141-42

Zeal of Jehoshaphat for the Law. ¹His son Jehoshaphat succeeded him as king and strengthened his hold against Israel.ᵏ ²He placed armed forces in all the fortified cities of Judah, and put garrisons in the land of Judah and in the cities of Ephraim which his father Asa had taken. ³The LORD was with Jehoshaphat,* for he walked in the ways his father had pursued in the beginning, and he did not consult the Baals. ⁴Rather, he sought the God of his father and observed his commands, and not the practices of Israel. ⁵As a result, the LORD made his kingdom secure, and all Judah gave Jehoshaphat gifts, so that he enjoyed great wealth and glory. ⁶Thus he was encouraged to follow the LORD's ways, and again he removed the high places and the sacred poles from Judah.ˡ

⁷In the third year of his reign he sent his leading men, Ben-hail, Obadiah, Zechariah, Nethanel and Micaiah, to teach in the cities of Judah. ⁸With them he sent the Levites Shemaiah, Nethaniah, Zebadiah, Asahel, Shemiramoth, Jehonathan, Adonijah and Tobijah, together with the priests Elishama and Jehoram.ᵐ ⁹They taught in Judah, having with them the book containing the law of the LORD; they traveled through all the cities of Judah and taught among the people.ⁿ

His Power. ¹⁰Now the fear of the LORD was upon all the kingdoms of the countries surrounding Judah, so that they did not war against Jehoshaphat. ¹¹Some of the Philistines brought Jehoshaphat gifts and a tribute of silver; and the Arabs also brought him a flock of seven thousand seven hundred rams and seven thousand seven hundred he-goats.

¹²Jehoshaphat grew steadily greater. He built strongholds and store cities in Judah. ¹³He carried out many works in the cities of Judah, and he had soldiers, valiant warriors, in Jerusalem. ¹⁴This was their mustering ac-

---

16, 7: The king of Aram . . . escaped: according to the Lucianic recension, "the king of Israel escaped": this may well be the original reading; Asa was friendly with Aram.

17, 3: The LORD was with Jehoshaphat: along with Hezekiah and Josiah, Jehoshaphat was one of the Chronicler's favorite kings.

h: 2 Chr 14, 8-14.   i: Ps 33, 13ff.   j: 11-14: 1 Kgs 15, 23f.   k: 1 Kgs 15, 24.   l: 2 Chr 20, 33; Ex 34, 13.   m: 2 Chr 19, 8. n: Ezr 7, 25.

The Reign of Jehoshaphat

Chapters 17 to 20 are another example of the Chronicler's expansions of limited material in the narratives of 1 and 2 Kings. The Chronicler takes an initially positive assessment of Jehoshaphat and expands his role into a model of bringing the community into accord with God.

cording to their ancestral houses. Of Judah, the commanders of thousands: Adnah the commander, and with him three hundred thousand valiant warriors. *15*Next to him, Jehohanan the commander, and with him two hundred eighty thousand. *16*Next to him, Amasiah, son of Zichri, who offered himself to the LORD, and with him two hundred thousand valiant warriors. *17*From Benjamin: Eliada, a valiant warrior, and with him two hundred thousand armed with bow and buckler. *18*Next to him, Jozabad, and with him one hundred and eighty thousand equipped for war. *19*These were at the service of the king; in addition were those whom the king had placed in the fortified cities throughout all Judah.

See RG 141–42

CHAPTER 18

Alliance with Israel. *1o*Jehoshaphat therefore had wealth and glory in abundance; but he became related to Ahab by marriage. *2*After some years he went down to Ahab at Samaria; Ahab offered numerous sheep and oxen for him and the people with him, and persuaded him to go up against Ramoth-gilead. *3*Ahab, king of Israel, asked Jehoshaphat, king of Judah, "Will you come with me to Ramoth-gilead?" "You and I are as one," was his answer; "your people and my people as well. We will be with you in the battle." *4*But Jehoshaphat also said to the king of Israel, "Seek the word of the LORD at once."

The Prophets. *5*The king of Israel gathered his prophets, four hundred in number, and asked them, "Shall we go to attack Ramoth-gilead, or shall I refrain?" "Go up," they answered. "God will deliver it over to the king." *6*But Jehoshaphat said, "Is there no other prophet of the LORD here whom we

may consult?" *7*The king of Israel answered Jehoshaphat, "There is still another through whom we may consult the LORD, but I hate him, for he prophesies not good but always evil about me. That is Micaiah, son of Imlah." Jehoshaphat said, "Let not your Majesty speak of evil against you." *8*So the king of Israel called an official, to whom he said, "Get Micaiah, son of Imlah, at once." *9*The king of Israel and King Jehoshaphat of Judah were seated each on his throne, clothed in their robes of state on a threshing floor at the entrance of the gate of Samaria, and all the prophets were prophesying before them.

*10*Zedekiah, son of Chenaanah, made iron horns for himself and said: "The LORD says, 'With these you shall gore Aram until you have destroyed them.'" *11*The other prophets prophesied in the same vein, saying: "Go up to Ramoth-gilead. You shall succeed; the LORD will deliver it over to the king." *12**The messenger who had gone to call Micaiah said to him: "Look now, the prophets unanimously predict good for the king. Let your word, like each of theirs, predict good." *13**As the LORD lives," Micaiah answered, "I will say what my God tells me."

*14*When he came to the king, the king said to him, "Micaiah, shall we go to fight against Ramoth-gilead, or shall I refrain?" "Go up," he answered, "and succeed; they will be delivered into your power." *15*But the king said to him, "How many times must I adjure you to tell me nothing but the truth in the name of the LORD?" *16*Then Micaiah answered:

"I see all Israel
    scattered on the mountains,

18, 12-22: See note on 1 Kgs 22, 19-23.

o: 1-34: 1 Kgs 22, 1-35.

like sheep without a shepherd,
and the LORD saying, 'These have no
master!
Let each of them go back home in
peace.' "

[17]The king of Israel said to Jehoshaphat, "Did I not tell you that he prophesies no good about me, but only evil?" [18]But Micaiah continued: "Therefore hear the word of the LORD: I saw the LORD seated on his throne, with the whole host of heaven standing by to his right and to his left. [19]The LORD asked, 'Who will deceive Ahab, king of Israel, so that he will go up and fall at Ramoth-gilead?' And one said this, another that, [20]until a spirit came forward and presented himself to the LORD, saying, 'I will deceive him.' The LORD asked, 'How?' [21]He answered, 'I will go forth and become a lying spirit in the mouths of all his prophets.' The LORD agreed: 'You shall succeed in deceiving him. Go forth and do this.' [22]So now the LORD has put a lying spirit in the mouths of these your prophets, but the LORD himself has decreed evil against you."

[23]Thereupon Zedekiah, son of Chenaanah, came up and slapped Micaiah on the cheek, saying, "Which way did the spirit of the LORD go when he left me to speak to you?" [24]"You shall find out," Micaiah replied, "on that day when you enter an innermost chamber to hide." [25]The king of Israel then said: "Seize Micaiah and take him back to Amon, prefect of the city, and to Joash the king's son, [26]and say, 'This is the king's order: Put this man in prison and feed him scanty rations of bread and water until I return in safety!' " [27]But Micaiah said, "If ever you return in safety, the LORD has not spoken through me." And he said, "Hear, O peoples, all of you!"*

Ahab's Death. [28]The king of Israel and King Jehoshaphat of Judah went up to Ramoth-gilead [29]and the king of Israel said to Jehoshaphat, "I will go into battle disguised, but you put on your own clothes." So the king of Israel disguised himself and they entered the fray. [30]Meanwhile, the king of Aram had given his chariot commanders the order, "Fight with no one, small or great, except the king of Israel." [31]When the commanders saw Jehoshaphat, they exclaimed, "That must be the king of Israel!" and shifted to fight him. But Jehoshaphat cried out and the LORD helped him; God induced them to leave him. [32]The chariot commanders became aware that he was not the king of Israel and gave up their pursuit of him. [33]Someone, however, drew his bow at random and hit the king of Israel between the joints of his breastplate. He ordered his charioteer, "Rein about and take me out of the ranks, for I am disabled."[p] [34]The battle grew fierce during the day, and the king of Israel braced himself up on his chariot facing the Arameans until evening. He died as the sun was setting.

CHAPTER 19

See RG 141–42

Jehoshaphat Rebuked. [1]King Jehoshaphat of Judah returned in safety to his house in Jerusalem. [2]Jehu the seer, son of Hanani,* met King Jehoshaphat and said to him: "Should you help the wicked and love those who hate the LORD? For this reason, wrath is upon you from the LORD. [3]Yet some good things are to be found in you, since you have removed the sacred poles from the land and have been determined to seek God."

Judges Appointed. [4]Jehoshaphat dwelt in Jerusalem; but he went out again among the people from Beer-sheba to the highlands of Ephraim and brought them back to the LORD, the God of their fathers. [5]He appointed judges in the land, in all the fortified cities of Judah, city by city, [6]and he said to them: "Take care what you do, for you are judging, not on behalf of man, but on behalf of the LORD; he judges with you.[q] [7]And now, let the fear of the LORD be upon you. Act carefully, for with the LORD, our God, there is no injus-

---

18, 27: "Hear, O peoples, all of you!": this quotation, which appears in some texts of 1 Kgs 22, 28, ascribes to the prophets Micaiah ben Imlah the opening words of the prophetic utterance of Micah of Moresheth (Mi 1, 2), a century later.

19, 2: Jehu the seer, son of Hanani: hardly the same seer as Jehu, son of Hanani, who prophesied against Baasha almost 50 years earlier (1 Kgs 16, 1).

p: 2 Chr 35, 23; 1 Kgs 22, 34.   q: Dt 1, 16ff; 16, 19f.

tice, no partiality, no bribe-taking."[r] [8]In Jerusalem also, Jehoshaphat appointed some Levites and priests and some of the family heads of Israel to judge in the name of the LORD and to settle quarrels among the inhabitants of Jerusalem.[s] [9]He gave them this command: "You shall act faithfully and wholeheartedly in the fear of the LORD. [10]And in every dispute that your brethren living in their cities bring to you, whether it concerns bloodguilt or questions of law, command, statutes, or judgments, warn them lest they become guilty before the LORD and his wrath come upon you and your brethren. Do that and you shall be guiltless.[t] [11]See now, Amariah is high priest over you in everything that pertains to the LORD, and Zebadiah, son of Ishmael, is leader of the house of Judah in all that pertains to the king; and the Levites will be your officials. Act firmly, and the LORD will be with the good."

See RG 141-42

CHAPTER 20

Invasion from Edom.* [1]After this the Moabites, the Ammonites, and with them some Meunites came to fight against Jehoshaphat. [2]The message was brought to Jehoshaphat: "A great multitude is coming against you from across the sea, from Edom; they are already in Hazazon-tamar" (which is En-gedi). [3]Jehoshaphat was frightened, and he hastened to consult the LORD. He proclaimed a fast for all Judah. [4]Then Judah gathered to seek help from the LORD; from every one of the cities of Judah they came to seek the LORD.[u]

Prayer of Jehoshaphat. [5]Jehoshaphat stood up in the assembly of Judah and Jerusalem in the house of the LORD before the new court, [6]and he said: "LORD, God of our fathers, are you not the God in heaven, and do you not rule over all the kingdoms of the nations? In your hand is power and might, and no one can withstand you.[v] [7]Was it not you, our God, who drove out the inhabitants of this land before your people Israel and gave it forever to the descendants of Abraham, your friend?[w] [8]They have dwelt in it and they built in it a sanctuary to your honor, saying, [9]'When evil comes upon us, the sword of judgment, or pestilence, or famine, we will stand before this house and before you, for your name is in this house, and we will cry out to you in our affliction, and you will hear and save!' [10]And now, see the Ammonites, Moabites, and those of Mount Seir whom you did not allow Israel to invade when they came from the land of Egypt, but instead they passed them by and did not destroy them.[x] [11]See how they are now repaying us by coming to drive us out of the possession you have given us. [12]O our God, will you not pass judgment on them? We are powerless before this vast multitude that comes against us. We are at a loss what to do, hence our eyes are turned toward you."

Victory Prophesied. [13]All Judah was standing before the LORD, with their little ones, their wives, and their young sons. [14]And the spirit of the LORD came upon Jahaziel, son of Zechariah, son of Benaiah, son of Jeiel, son of Mattaniah, a Levite of the clan of Asaph, in the midst of the assembly, [15]and he said: "Listen, all of Judah, inhabitants of Jerusalem, and King Jehoshaphat! The LORD says to you: 'Do not fear or lose heart at the sight of this vast multitude, for the battle is not yours but God's. [16]Go down against them tomorrow. You will see them coming up by the ascent of Ziz, and you will come upon them at the end of the wadi which opens on the wilderness of Jeruel. [17]You will not have to fight in this encounter. Take your places, stand firm, and see how the LORD will be with you to deliver you, Judah and Jerusalem. Do not fear or lose heart. Tomorrow go out to meet them, and the LORD will be with you.' "[y] [18]Then Jehoshaphat knelt down with his face to the ground, and all Judah and the inhabitants of Jerusalem fell down before the

---

20, 1-30: Although the account here seems to be a free composition of the Chronicler, there is probably a basis in fact for it; there could well have been a raid of nomads against Judah in the reign of Jehoshaphat, similar to Zerah's attack on Asa (2 Chr 14, 8-14). The story may also, in some way, be connected with the campaign of Israel and Judah against Moab through the territory of Edom (2 Kgs 3, 4-27).

---

r: Dt 10, 17.   s: 2 Chr 17, 8f; Dt 17, 8-13; Ps 122, 3ff.   t: Nm 35, 19.   u: Jer 36, 6; Jb 1, 14.   v: 2 Chr 32, 7; Dt 4, 39.   w: Dn 3, 35.   x: Dt 2, 4f. 9f. 18f.   y: Is 8, 10.

LORD in worship. [19]Levites from among the Kohathites and Korahites rose to sing the praises of the LORD, the God of Israel, in a resounding chorus.

The Invaders Destroyed. [20]In the early morning they hastened out to the wilderness of Tekoa. As they were going out, Jehoshaphat halted and said: "Listen to me, Judah and inhabitants of Jerusalem! Trust in the LORD, your God, and you will be found firm. Trust in his prophets and you will succeed."[z] [21]After consulting with the people, he appointed some to sing to the LORD and some to praise the holy Appearance* as it went forth at the head of the army. They sang: "Give thanks to the LORD, for his mercy endures forever."[a] [22]At the moment they began their jubilant hymn, the LORD laid an ambush against the Ammonites, Moabites, and those of Mount Seir who were coming against Judah, so that they were vanquished. [23]For the Ammonites and Moabites set upon the inhabitants of Mount Seir and completely exterminated them. And when they had finished with the inhabitants of Seir, they began to destroy each other.[b]

[24]When Judah came to the watchtower of the desert and looked toward the throng, they saw only corpses fallen on the ground, with no survivors. [25]Jehoshaphat and his people came to take plunder, and they found an abundance of cattle and personal property, garments and precious vessels. They took so much that they were unable to carry it all; they were three days taking the spoil, so great was it. [26]On the fourth day they held an assembly in the Valley of Beracah—for there they blessed the LORD; therefore that place has ever since been called the Valley of Beracah.* [27]Then all the men of Judah and Jerusalem, with Jehoshaphat at their head, turned back toward Jerusalem celebrating the joyful victory the LORD had given them over their enemies. [28]They came to Jerusalem, to the house of the LORD, with harps, lyres and trumpets. [29]And the fear of God came upon all the kingdoms of the surrounding lands when they heard how the LORD had fought against the enemies of Israel. [30]Thereafter Jehoshaphat's kingdom enjoyed peace, for his God gave him rest on every side.

Jehoshaphat's Other Deeds. [31c]Thus Jehoshaphat reigned over Judah. He was thirty-five years old when he became king, and he reigned twenty-five years in Jerusalem. His mother was named Azubah, daughter of Shilhi. [32]He followed the path of his father Asa unswervingly, doing what was right in the LORD's sight. [33]But the high places were not removed, nor as yet had the people fixed their hearts on the God of their fathers.

[34]The rest of the acts of Jehoshaphat, first and last, can be found written in the chronicle of Jehu, son of Hanani, which is inserted in the book of the kings of Israel. [35]After this, King Jehoshaphat of Judah allied himself with King Ahaziah of Israel, who did evil. [36d]He joined with him in building ships to sail to Tarshish; the fleet was built at Ezion-geber. [37]But Eliezer, son of Dodavahu from Mareshah, prophesied against Jehoshaphat, saying, "Because you have joined with Ahaziah, the LORD will shatter your work." And the ships were wrecked and were unable to sail to Tarshish.

CHAPTER 21

See RG 141-42

[1]Jehoshaphat rested with his ancestors; he was buried with them in the City of David. Jehoram, his son, succeeded him as king.[e] [2]His brothers, sons of Jehoshaphat, were Azariah, Jehiel, Zechariah, Azariah, Michael and Shephatiah; all these were sons of King Jehoshaphat of Judah. [3]Their father gave them numerous gifts of silver, gold and precious objects, together with fortified cities in Judah, but the kingship he gave to Jehoram because he was the first-born.

Evil Deeds of Jehoram. [4]When Jehoram had come into his father's kingdom and had consolidated his power, he put to the sword

---

20, 21: Holy Appearance: the Lord, who is with the Israelite army (v 17), manifests himself (the same language is in Ps 29, 2) in bringing Israel the victory (Ex 14, 14. 24).

20, 26: Beracah: the Hebrew word for "blessing."

z: Is 7, 9.   a: Ps 136, 1.   b: Jos 6, 17; Ez 38, 21.   c: 31-34: 1 Kgs 22, 41-45.   d: 36f: 1 Kgs 22, 48f.   e: 1 Kgs 22, 51.

all his brothers and also some of the princes of Israel. *5f*Jehoram was thirty-two years old when he became king, and he reigned eight years in Jerusalem. *6*He conducted himself like the kings of Israel of the line of Ahab, because one of Ahab's daughters* was his wife. He did evil in the sight of the LORD, *7*but the LORD would not destroy the house of David because of the covenant he had made with David and because of his promise to give him and his sons a lamp for all time.*g*

*8h*During his time Edom revolted against the sovereignty of Judah; they chose a king of their own. *9*Thereupon Jehoram crossed over with his officers and all the chariots he had. He arose by night and broke through the Edomites when they had surrounded him and the commanders of his chariots. *10*However, Edom has continued in revolt against the sovereignty of Judah down to the present time. Libnah also revolted at that time against Jehoram's sovereignty because he had forsaken the LORD, the God of his fathers. *11*He also set up high places in the mountains of Judah; he led the inhabitants of Jerusalem into idolatry and seduced Judah.

Retribution. *12*He received a letter from the prophet Elijah* with this message: Thus says the LORD, the God of your ancestor David: 'Because you have not followed the path of your father Jehoshaphat, nor of Asa, king of Judah, *13*but instead have walked in the way of the kings of Israel and have led Judah and the inhabitants of Jerusalem into idolatry, as did the house of Ahab, and also because you have murdered your brothers of your father's house who were better than you, *14*the LORD will strike your people, your children, your wives, and all that is yours with a great plague; *15*and you shall have severe pains from a disease in your bowels, while your bowels issue forth because of the disease, day after day.' "

*16*Then the LORD stirred up against Jehoram the animosity of the Philistines and of the Arabs who bordered on the Ethiopians. *17*They came up against Judah, invaded it, and carried away all the wealth found in the king's palace, along with his sons and his wives; there was left to him only one son, Jehoahaz, his youngest. *18*After these events, the LORD afflicted him with an incurable disease of the bowels. *19*As time went on until a period of two years had elapsed, his bowels issued forth because of the disease and he died in great pain. His people did not make a pyre for him like that of his fathers. *20*He was thirty-two years old when he became king, and he reigned eight years in Jerusalem. He departed unloved and was buried in the City of David, but not in the tombs of the kings.*i*

CHAPTER 22

Ahaziah. *1j*Then the inhabitants of Jerusalem made Ahaziah, his youngest son, king in his stead, since all the older sons had been slain by the band that had come into the fort with the Arabs. Thus Ahaziah, son of Jehoram, reigned as king of Judah. *2*He was twenty-two years old when he became king, and he reigned one year in Jerusalem. His mother was named Athaliah, daughter of Omri. *3*He, too, followed the ways of the house of Ahab, because his mother counseled him to act sinfully. *4*To his own destruction, he did evil in the sight of the LORD, as did the house of Ahab, since they were his counselors after the death of his father.

*5*He was also following their counsel when he accompanied Jehoram, son of Ahab, king of Israel, to battle against Hazael, king of Aram, at Ramoth-gilead. There Jehoram was wounded by the Arameans. *6*He returned to Jezreel to be healed of the wounds he had received at Rama in his battle against Hazael, king of Aram. Because of this illness, Ahaziah, son of Jehoram, king of Judah, went down to visit Jehoram, son of Ahab, in Jezreel. *7*Now it was willed by God for Ahaziah's downfall that he should join Jehoram,

See RG 141–42

21, 6: One of Ahab's daughters: Athaliah. In 2 Chr 22, 2 (and its source, 2 Kgs 8, 26) she is called Omri's daughter; but this should probably be understood in the sense of granddaughter.

21, 12: Elijah: the only mention by the Chronicler of this prophet of the northern kingdom of Israel. It is doubtful that

Elijah was still living in the reign of Jehoram of Judah; in any case, the attribution of the letter to him is most likely an imaginative filling out of the narration.

f: 5f: 2 Kgs 8, 17ff.   *g:* 1 Kgs 11, 36; 2 Kgs 8, 19.   *h:* 8ff: Gn 27, 40; 2 Kgs 8, 20ff.   *i:* 2 Kgs 8, 24.   *j:* 1-6: 2 Kgs 8, 24-29.

for after his arrival he rode out with Jehoram to Jehu, son of Nimshi, whom the LORD had anointed to cut down the house of Ahab.[k] [8]While Jehu was executing judgment on the house of Ahab, he also encountered the princes of Judah and the nephews of Ahaziah who were his attendants, and he slew them.[l] [9]Then he looked for Ahaziah himself. They caught him where he was hiding in Samaria and brought him to Jehu, who put him to death. They buried him, for they said, "He was the grandson of Jehoshaphat, who sought the LORD with his whole heart."[m] There remained in Ahaziah's house no one powerful enough to wield the kingship.

Usurpation of Athaliah. [10][n]When Athaliah, mother of Ahaziah, learned that her son was dead, she proceeded to kill off all the royal offspring of the house of Judah. [11]But Jehosheba, a royal princess, secretly took Ahaziah's son Joash from among the king's sons who were about to be slain, and put him and his nurse in a bedroom. In this way Jehosheba, who was the daughter of King Jehoram, a sister of Ahaziah, and wife of Jehoiada the priest, hid the child from Athaliah's sight, so that she did not put him to death. [12]For six years he remained hidden with them in the house of God, while Athaliah ruled over the land.

CHAPTER 23

See RG 141–42

Athaliah Overthrown. [1][o]In the seventh year, Jehoiada took courage and entered a conspiracy with certain captains: Azariah, son of Jehoram; Ishmael, son of Jehohanan; Azariah, son of Obed; Masseiah, son of Adaiah; and Elishaphat, son of Zichri. [2]They journeyed about Judah, gathering the Levites from all the cities of Judah and also the heads of the Israelite families. When they had come to Jerusalem, [3]the whole assembly made a covenant with the king in the house of God. Jehoiada said to them: "Here is the king's son who must reign, as the LORD promised con-

cerning the sons of David. [4]This is what you must do: a third of your number, both priests and Levites, who come in on the sabbath must guard the thresholds, [5]another third must be at the king's palace, and the final third at the Foundation Gate, when all the people will be in the courts of the LORD's temple. [6]Let no one enter the LORD's house except the priests and those Levites who are ministering. They may enter because they are holy; but all the other people must observe the prescriptions of the LORD. [7]The Levites shall surround the king on all sides, each with his weapon drawn. Whoever tries to enter the house must be slain. Stay with the king wherever he goes."

[8]The Levites and all Judah did just as Jehoiada the priest commanded. Each brought his men, those who were to come in on the sabbath as well as those who were to depart on the sabbath, since Jehoiada the priest had not dismissed any of the divisions.[p] [9]Jehoiada the priest gave the captains the spears, shields and bucklers of King David which were in the house of God. [10]He stationed all the people, each with his spear in hand, from the southern to the northern extremity of the enclosure, around the altar and the temple on the king's behalf. [11]Then they brought out the king's son, set the crown and the insignia upon him, and made him king. Jehoiada and his sons anointed him, and they cried, "Long live the king!"

[12]When Athaliah heard the din of the people running and acclaiming the king, she went to the people in the temple of the LORD. [13]She looked, and there was the king standing beside his pillar* at the entrance, the officers and the trumpeters around him, and all the people of the land rejoicing and blowing trumpets, while the singers with their musical instruments were leading the acclaim. Athaliah tore her garments and cried out, "Treason! treason!" [14]Then Jehoiada the priest sent out the captains who were in command of the army;

22, 9: This account of the death of Ahaziah of Judah is not derived from 2 Kgs 9, 27f, with which it is at variance.

23, 13: Beside his pillar: the king had a special place in the eastern gateway of the temple court that contained the altar of holocausts. He occupied this place on feasts and sabbaths at the time of the statutory offerings, or when he made freewill

offerings of his own; cf 2 Kgs 11, 4 and also Ez 46, 1-8 for a later reflection of this.

k: 2 Kgs 9, 21; 10, 12ff. l: 2 Kgs 10, 12ff. m: 2 Kgs 9, 27f. n: 10ff: 2 Kgs 11, 1ff. o: 1-17. 19ff: 2 Kgs 11, 4-20. p: 2 Kgs 11, 9; 1 Chr 24, 19.

he said to them: "Take her outside through the ranks, and if anyone tries to follow her, let him die by the sword. For," the priest continued, "you must not put her to death in the LORD's temple." ¹⁵So they seized her, and when she arrived at the entrance to the Horse Gate of the palace, they put her to death there.

¹⁶Then Jehoiada made a covenant between himself and all the people and the king, that they should be the LORD's people. ¹⁷And all the people went to the temple of Baal and tore it down. They smashed its altars and images, and they slew Mattan, the priest of Baal, before the altars. ¹⁸Then Jehoiada gave the charge of the LORD's temple into the hands of the levitical priests, to whom David had assigned turns in the temple for offering the holocausts of the LORD, as is written in the law of Moses, with rejoicing and song, as David had provided.^q ¹⁹Moreover, he stationed guards at the gates of the LORD's temple, so that no one unclean in any respect might enter. ²⁰Then he took the captains, the nobles, the rulers among the people, and all the people of the land, and led the king out of the LORD's house. When they had come within the upper gate of the king's house, they seated the king upon the royal throne. ²¹All the people of the land rejoiced and the city was quiet, now that Athaliah had been put to death by the sword.

CHAPTER 24

See RG
141–42

The Temple Restored. ^{1r}Joash was seven years old when he became king, and he reigned forty years in Jerusalem. His mother, named Zibiah, was from Beersheba. ²Joash did what was pleasing to the LORD as long as Jehoiada the priest lived. ³Jehoiada provided him with two wives, and he became the father of sons and daughters.

⁴After some time, Joash decided to restore the LORD's temple. ⁵He called together the priests and Levites and said to them: "Go out to all the cities of Judah and collect money* from all Israel that you may repair the house

of your God over the years. You must hasten this affair." But the Levites did not hasten. ⁶Then the king summoned Jehoiada, who was in charge, and said to him: "Why have you not required the Levites to bring in from Judah and Jerusalem the tax levied by Moses, the servant of the LORD, and by the assembly of Israel, for the tent of the testimony?"^s ⁷For the wicked Athaliah and her sons had damaged the house of God and had even turned over to the Baals the dedicated resources of the LORD's temple.

⁸At the king's command, therefore, they made a chest, which they put outside the gate of the LORD's temple.^t ⁹They had it proclaimed throughout Judah and Jerusalem that the tax which Moses, the servant of God, had imposed on Israel in the desert should be brought to the LORD.^u ¹⁰All the princes and the people rejoiced; they brought what was asked and cast it into the chest until it was filled. ¹¹Whenever the chest was brought to the royal officials by the Levites and they saw that it contained much money, the royal scribe and an overseer for the high priest came, emptied the chest, then took it back and returned it to its place. This they did day after day until they had collected a large sum of money. ¹²Then the king and Jehoiada gave it to the workmen in charge of the labor on the LORD's temple, who hired masons and carpenters to restore the temple, and also iron- and bronze-smiths to repair it. ¹³The workmen labored, and the task of restoration progressed under their hands. They restored the house of God according to its original form, and reinforced it. ¹⁴After they had finished, they brought the rest of the money to the king and to Jehoiada, who had it made into utensils for the LORD's temple, utensils for the service and the holocausts, and basins and other gold and silver utensils. They offered holocausts in the LORD's temple continually throughout the lifetime of Jehoiada. ¹⁵Jehoiada lived to a ripe old age; he was a hundred and thirty years old when he died. ¹⁶He was buried in the City of David

---

24, 5: Collect money: according to 2 Kgs 12, 5, the people themselves brought the money to the temple; it consisted, at least in part, of voluntary contributions. At the time of the Chronicler (see Neh 10, 32) there was a fixed head tax for the upkeep of the temple (2 Chr 34, 9), based

on Ex 30, 12-16. This was still in force in New Testament times (Mt 17, 24f).

---

q: 1 Chr 23, 13.   r: 1-14: 2 Kgs 12, 1-13.   s: Ex 25, 1-9; Neh 10, 33.   t: 2 Chr 34, 9.   u: Ex 30, 13.

with the kings, because he had done good in Israel, in particular with respect to God and his temple.

Apostasy of King Joash. [17]After the death of Jehoiada, the princes of Judah came and paid homage to the king, and the king then listened to them. [18]They forsook the temple of the LORD, the God of their fathers, and began to serve the sacred poles and the idols; and because of this crime of theirs, wrath came upon Judah and Jerusalem.[v] [19]Although prophets were sent to them to convert them to the LORD, the people would not listen to their warnings. [20]Then the spirit of God possessed Zechariah, son of Jehoiada the priest. He took his stand above the people and said to them: "God says, 'Why are you transgressing the LORD's commands, so that you cannot prosper? Because you have abandoned the LORD, he has abandoned you.' " [21]But they conspired against him, and at the king's order they stoned him to death in the court of the LORD's temple. [22]Thus King Joash was unmindful of the devotion shown him by Jehoiada, Zechariah's father, and slew his son. And as he was dying, he said, "May the LORD see and avenge."

Retribution. [23]At the turn of the year a force of Arameans came up against Joash. They invaded Judah and Jerusalem, did away with all the princes of the people, and sent all their spoil to the king of Damascus.[w] [24]Though the Aramean force came with few men, the LORD surrendered a very large force into their power, because Judah had abandoned the LORD, the God of their fathers. So punishment was meted out to Joash.[x] [25y]After the Arameans had departed from him, leaving him in grievous suffering, his servants conspired against him because of the murder of the son of Jehoiada the priest. They killed him on his sickbed. He was buried in the City of David, but not in the tombs of the kings. [26]These conspired against him: Zabad, son of Shimeath from Ammon, and Jehozabad, son of Shimrith from Moab. [27]Of his sons, and the great tribute imposed on him, and of his rebuilding of the house of God,

there is a written account in the midrash of the book of the kings. His son Amaziah succeeded him as king.[z]

See RG 141–42

CHAPTER 25

Campaign in Edom. [1a]Amaziah was twenty-five years old when he became king, and he reigned twenty-nine years in Jerusalem. His mother, named Jehoaddan, was from Jerusalem. [2]He did what was pleasing in the sight of the LORD, though not wholeheartedly. [3]After he had strengthened his hold on the kingdom, he slew those of his servants who had killed the king, his father; [4]but he did not put their children to death, for he acted according to what is written in the law, in the Book of Moses, as the LORD commanded: "Fathers shall not be put to death for their children, nor children for their fathers; but only for his own guilt shall a man be put to death."[b]

[5]Amaziah mustered Judah and placed them, out of all Judah and Benjamin according to their ancestral houses, under leaders of thousands and of hundreds. When he had counted those of twenty years and over, he found them to be three hundred thousand picked men fit for war, capable of handling lance and shield. [6]He also hired a hundred thousand valiant warriors from Israel for a hundred talents of silver. [7]But a man of God came to him and said: "O king, let not the army of Israel go with you, for the LORD is not with Israel, with any Ephraimite. [8]Instead, go on your own, strongly prepared for the conflict; otherwise the LORD will defeat you in the face of the enemy. It is God who has the power to reinforce or to defeat." [9]Amaziah answered the man of God, "But what is to be done about the hundred talents that I paid for the troops of Israel?" The man of God replied, "The LORD can give you much more than that." [10]Amaziah then disbanded the troops that had come to him from Ephraim, and sent them home. They, however, became furiously angry with Judah, and returned home blazing with resentment.

[11]Amaziah now assumed command of his

v: Ex 34, 13.   w: 2 Kgs 12, 17f.   x: Dt 32, 30.   y: 25f: 2 Kgs 12, 21f.   z: 2 Kgs 12, 19. 22.   a: 1-4: 2 Kgs 14, 1-6.   b: Dt 24, 16; 2 Kgs 14, 5f; Ez 18, 20.

army. They proceeded to the Valley of Salt, and there they killed ten thousand men of Seir.[c] [12]The Judahites also brought back another ten thousand alive, whom they led to the summit of the Rock and then cast down, so that they were all crushed. [13]Meanwhile, the mercenaries whom Amaziah had dismissed from battle service with him raided the cities of Judah from Samaria to Beth-horon. They killed three thousand of the inhabitants and took away much booty.

Infidelity of Amaziah. [14]When Amaziah returned from his conquest of the Edomites he brought back with him the gods of the people of Seir, which he set up as his own gods; he bowed down before them and offered sacrifice to them. [15]Then the anger of the LORD blazed out against Amaziah, and he sent a prophet to him who said: "Why have you had recourse to this people's gods that could not save their own people from your hand?" [16]While he was still speaking, however, the king said to him: "Have you been made the king's counselor? Be silent! Why should it be necessary to kill you?" Therefore the prophet desisted. "I know, however," he said, "that God has let you take counsel to your own destruction, because you have done this thing and have refused to hear my counsel."

Retribution. [17d]Having taken counsel, King Amaziah of Judah sent messengers to Joash, son of Jehoahaz, son of Jehu, the king of Israel, saying, "Come, let us meet each other face to face." [18]King Joash of Israel sent this reply to King Amaziah of Judah: "The thistle of the Lebanon sent a message to the cedar of the Lebanon, saying, 'Give your daughter to my son for his wife.' But the wild beasts of the Lebanon passed by and trampled the thistle down.[e] [19]You are thinking, 'See, I have beaten Edom!', and thus ambition makes you proud. Remain at home. Why involve yourself, and Judah with you, in misfortune and failure?" [20]But Amaziah would not listen, for God had determined to hand them over because they had had recourse to the gods of Edom.

[21]Therefore King Joash of Israel advanced and he and King Amaziah met in battle at Beth-shemesh of Judah. [22]There Judah was defeated by Israel, and all the Judean soldiers fled homeward. [23]King Joash of Israel captured Amaziah, king of Judah, son of Joash, son of Jehoahaz, at Beth-shemesh and brought him to Jerusalem. Then he tore down the wall of Jerusalem from the Ephraim Gate to the Corner Gate, a distance of four hundred cubits. [24]He took away all the gold and silver and all the vessels he found in the house of God with Obed-edom,* together with the treasures of the palace, and hostages as well. Then he returned to Samaria.

[25f]Amaziah, son of Joash, king of Judah, survived Joash, son of Jehoahaz, king of Israel, by fifteen years. [26]The rest of the acts of Amaziah, first and last, can be found written, as is well known, in the book of the kings of Judah and Israel. [27]Now from the time that Amaziah ceased to follow the LORD, a conspiracy was formed against him in Jerusalem; hence he fled to Lachish. But they pursued him to Lachish and put him to death there. [28]They brought him back on horses and buried him with his ancestors in the City of Judah.*

CHAPTER 26

See RG 141-42

The Works of Uzziah. [1g]All the people of Judah chose Uzziah, though he was but sixteen years of age, and proclaimed him king to succeed his father Amaziah. [2]He rebuilt Elath and restored it to Judah; this was after King Amaziah had gone to rest with his ancestors. [3]Uzziah was sixteen years old when he became king, and he reigned fifty-two years in Jerusalem. His mother, named Jecoliah, was from Jerusalem. [4]He pleased the LORD, just as his father Amaziah had done.

25, 24: With Obed-edom: possibly a reference to the priest of an Edomite false worship (cf v 14), if not to a levitical family of gatekeepers; cf 1 Chr 15, 18; 26, 12-15.

25, 28: The City of Judah: in the parallel passage of 2 Kgs 14, 20, the City of David. The Chronicler is referring, by this term, to the capital of Judah, Jerusalem.

c: 2 Kgs 14, 7.   *d:* 17-24: 2 Kgs 14, 8-14.   *e:* Jgs 9, 7-15; 2 Kgs 14, 9.   *f:* 25-28: 2 Kgs 14, 17-20.   *g:* 1-4: 2 Kgs 14, 21f; 15, 1ff.

⁵He was prepared to seek God as long as Zechariah* lived, who taught him to fear God; and as long as he sought the LORD, God made him prosper.ʰ ⁶He went out and fought the Philistines and razed the walls of Gath, Jabneh and Ashdod [and built cities in the district of Ashdod and in Philistia].ⁱ ⁷God helped him against the Philistines, against the Arabs who dwelt in Gurbaal, and against the Meunites. ⁸The Ammonites paid tribute to Uzziah and his fame spread as far as Egypt, for he grew stronger and stronger. ⁹Moreover, Uzziah built towers in Jerusalem at the Corner Gate, at the Valley Gate, and at the Angle, and he fortified them. ¹⁰He built towers in the desert and dug numerous cisterns, for he had many cattle. He had plowmen in the foothills and the plains, and vinedressers in the highlands and the garden land. He was a lover of the soil.

¹¹Uzziah also had a standing army of fit soldiers divided into bands according to the number in which they were mustered by Jeiel the scribe and Maaseiah the recorder, under the command of Hananiah, one of the king's officials. ¹²The entire number of family heads over these valiant warriors was two thousand six hundred, ¹³and at their disposal was a mighty army of three hundred seven thousand five hundred fighting men of great valor to help the king against his enemies. ¹⁴Uzziah provided for them—for the entire army—bucklers, lances, helmets, breastplates, bows and slingstones. ¹⁵He also built machines in Jerusalem, devices contrived to stand on the towers and at the angles of the walls to shoot arrows and cast large stones. His fame spread far and wide, and his power was ascribed to the marvelous help he had received.

Pride and Fall. ¹⁶But after he had become strong, he became proud to his own destruction and broke faith with the LORD, his God. He entered the temple of the LORD to make an offering on the altar of incense. ¹⁷But Azariah the priest, and with him eighty other priests of the LORD, courageous men, followed him. ¹⁸They opposed King Uzziah, saying to him: "It is not for you, Uzziah, to burn incense to the LORD, but for the priests, the sons of Aaron, who have been consecrated for this purpose. Leave the sanctuary, for you have broken faith and no longer have a part in the glory that comes from the LORD God."ʲ ¹⁹Uzziah, who was holding a censer for burning the incense, became angry, but at the moment he showed his anger to the priests, while they were looking at him in the house of the LORD beside the altar of incense, leprosy broke out on his forehead.ᵏ ²⁰Azariah the chief priest and all the other priests examined him, and when they saw that his forehead was leprous, they expelled him from the temple. He himself fled willingly, for the LORD had afflicted him. ²¹King Uzziah remained a leper to the day of his death. As a leper he dwelt in a segregated house, for he was excluded from the house of the LORD. Therefore his son Jotham was regent of the palace and ruled the people of the land.

²²The prophet Isaiah, son of Amos, wrote the rest of the acts of Uzziah, first and last. ²³Uzziah rested with his ancestors; he was buried with them in the field adjoining the royal cemetery, for they said, "He was a leper." His son Jotham succeeded him as king.

CHAPTER 27

See RG 141-42

Jotham. ¹ᵐJotham was twenty-five years old when he became king, and he reigned sixteen years in Jerusalem. His mother was named Jerusa, daughter of Zadok. ²He pleased the LORD just as his father Uzziah had done, though he did not enter the temple of the LORD; the people, however, continued to act sinfully.

³He built the upper gate of the LORD's house and had much construction done on the wall of Ophel. ⁴Moreover, he built cities in the hill country of Judah, and in the forest land he set up fortresses and towers. ⁵He fought with the king of the Ammonites and conquered them. That year the Ammonites paid him one hundred talents of silver, together with ten thousand kors of wheat and

---

26, 5: Zechariah: this person, not otherwise identified, is referred to in language suggesting a pious layman rather than a priest or prophet; cf 2 Chr 29, 1.

---

h: 2 Chr 24, 2. *i:* Am 1, 8. *j:* Ex 30, 7. *k:* Nm 12, 10. *l:* 21ff: 2 Kgs 15, 5ff; Lv 13, 46; Nm 19, 20. *m:* 1-3: 2 Kgs 15, 32-35.

ten thousand of barley. They brought the same to him also in the second and in the third year. *6*Thus Jotham continued to grow strong because he lived resolutely in the presence of the LORD, his God. *7n*The rest of the acts of Jotham, his wars and his activities, can be found written in the book of the kings of Israel and Judah. *8*He was twenty-five years old when he became king, and he reigned sixteen years in Jerusalem. *9*Jotham rested with his ancestors and was buried in the City of David, and his son Ahaz succeeded him as king.

III: Reforms of Hezekiah and Josiah

CHAPTER 28

See RG 141–42 *Impiety of Ahaz.* *1o*Ahaz was twenty years old when he became king, and he reigned sixteen years in Jerusalem. He did not please the LORD as his forefather David had done, *2*but conducted himself like the kings of Israel and even made molten idols of the Baals. *3*Moreover, he offered sacrifice in the Valley of Ben-hinnom, and immolated his sons by fire according to the abominable practice of the nations which the LORD had cleared out before the Israelites.*p* *4*He offered sacrifice and incense on the high places, on hills, and under every leafy tree.

Retribution. *5*Therefore the LORD, his God, delivered him into the power of the king of Aram. The Arameans defeated him and carried away captive a large number of his people, whom they brought to Damascus. He was also delivered into the power of the king of Israel, who defeated him with great slaughter.*q* *6*For Pekah, son of Remaliah, slew one hundred and twenty thousand of Judah in a single day, all of them valiant men, because they had abandoned the LORD, the God of their fathers. *7*Zichri, an Ephraimite warrior, killed Maaseiah, the king's son, and Azrikam, the master of the palace, and also Elkanah, who was second to the king. *8*The Israelites took away as captives two hundred thousand of their brethren's wives, sons and daughters; they also took from them much plunder, which they brought to Samaria.

The Prophecy of Oded. *9*In Samaria there was a prophet of the LORD by the name of Oded. He went out to meet the army returning to Samaria and said to them: "It was because the LORD, the God of your fathers, was angry with Judah that he delivered them into your hands. You, however, have slaughtered them with a fury that has reached up to heaven. *10*And now you are planning to make the children of Judah and Jerusalem your slaves and bondwomen. Are not you yourselves, therefore, guilty of a crime against the LORD, your God? *11*Now listen to me: send back the captives you have carried off from among your brethren, for the burning anger of the LORD is upon you."

*12*At this, some of the Ephraimite leaders, Azariah, son of Johanan, Berechiah, son of Meshillemoth, Jehizkiah, son of Shallum, and Amasa, son of Hadlai, themselves stood up in opposition to those who had returned from the war. *13*They said to them: "Do not bring the captives here, for what you propose will make us guilty before the LORD and increase our sins and our guilt. Our guilt is already great, and there is a burning anger upon Israel." *14*Therefore the soldiers left their captives and the plunder before the princes and the whole assembly. *15*Then the men just named proceeded to help the captives. All of them who were naked they clothed from the booty; they clothed them, put sandals on their feet, gave them food and drink, anointed them, and all who were weak they set on asses. They brought them to Jericho, the city of palms, to their brethren. Then they returned to Samaria.*r*

Further Sins of Ahaz. *16*At that time King Ahaz sent an appeal for help to the kings of Assyria.*s* *17*The Edomites had returned, attacked Judah, and carried off captives.*t* *18*The Philistines too had raided the cities of the foothills and the Negeb of Judah; they captured Beth-shemesh, Aijalon, Gederoth, Soco and its dependencies, Timnah and its

n: 7-9: 2 Kgs 15, 36ff.   o: 1-4: 2 Kgs 16, 1-4.   p: 2 Kgs 16, 3; Lv 18, 21.   q: 2 Kgs 16, 5; Is 7, 1-9.   r: Lk 10, 25-37.   s: 2 Kgs 16, 7.   t: 2 Kgs 16, 6.

dependencies, and Gimzo and its dependencies, and occupied them. [19]For the LORD had brought Judah low because of Ahaz, king of Israel,* who let Judah go its own way and proved utterly faithless to the LORD. [20]Tilgath-pilneser, king of Assyria, did indeed come to him, but to oppress him rather than to help him.[u] [21]Though Ahaz plundered the LORD's house and the houses of the king and the princes to make payment to the king of Assyria, it availed him nothing.[v]

[22]While he was already in distress, the same King Ahaz became even more unfaithful to the LORD. [23]He sacrificed to the gods of Damascus who had defeated him, saying, "Since it was the gods of the kings of Aram who helped them, I will sacrifice to them that they may help me also." However, they only caused further disaster to him and to all Israel.[w] [24]Ahaz gathered up the utensils of God's house and broke them in pieces. He closed the doors of the LORD's house and had altars made for himself in every corner of Jerusalem.[x] [25]In every city throughout Judah he set up high places to offer sacrifice to other gods. Thus he angered the LORD, the God of his fathers.

[26y]The rest of his deeds and his activities, first and last, can be found written in the book of the kings of Judah and Israel. [27]Ahaz rested with his ancestors and was buried in Jerusalem—in the city, for they did not bring him to the tombs of the kings of Israel. His son Hezekiah succeeded him as king.

CHAPTER 29

See RG
141–42

Reforms of Hezekiah. [1z]Hezekiah was twenty-five years old when he became king, and he reigned twenty-nine years in Jerusalem. His mother was named Abia, daughter of Zechariah. [2]He pleased the LORD just as his forefather David had done. [3]It was he who, in the first month of the first year of his reign, opened the doors of the LORD's house and repaired them.[a] [4]He summoned the priests and Levites, gathered them in the open space to the east, [5]and said to them: "Listen to me, you Levites! Sanctify yourselves now and sanctify the house of the LORD, the God of your fathers, and clean out the filth from the sanctuary. [6]Our fathers acted faithlessly and did evil in the eyes of the LORD, our God. They abandoned him, turned away their faces from the LORD's dwelling, and turned their backs on him. [7]They also closed the doors of the vestibule, extinguished the lamps, and refused to burn incense and offer holocausts in the sanctuary to the honor of the God of Israel.[b] [8c]Therefore the anger of the LORD has come upon Judah and Jerusalem; he has made them an object of terror, astonishment and mockery, as you see with your own eyes. [9]For our fathers, as you know, fell by the sword, and our sons, our daughters and our wives have been taken captive because of this. [10]Now, I intend to make a covenant with the LORD, the God of Israel, that his burning anger may withdraw from us. [11]My sons, be not negligent any longer, for it is you whom the LORD has chosen to stand before him, to minister to him, to be his ministers and to offer incense."

[12]Then the Levites arose: Mahath, son of Amasai, and Joel, son of Azariah, descendants of the Kohathites; of the sons of Merari: Kish, son of Abdi, and Azariah, son of Jehallel; of the Gershonites: Joah, son of Zimmah, and Eden, son of Joah; [13]of the sons of Elizaphan: Shimri and Jeuel; of the sons of Asaph: Zechariah and Mattaniah; [14]of the sons of Heman: Jehuel and Shimei; of the sons of Jeduthun: Shemiah and Uzziel. [15]They gathered their brethren together and sanctified themselves; then they came as the king had ordered, to cleanse the LORD's house in keeping with his words.

[16]The priests entered the interior of the LORD's house to cleanse it; and whatever they found in the LORD's temple that was unclean they brought out to the court of the LORD's house, where the Levites took it from them

---

28, 19: Ahaz, king of Israel: in the period of the divided kingdom the term king of Israel would elsewhere mean "king of the northern Kingdom of Israel."

---

u: 2 Kgs 16, 10; Is 7, 17-20; 8, 5-8.   *v:* 2 Kgs 16, 8.   *w:* 2 Kgs 16, 12f; Is 10, 20.   *x:* 2 Chr 29, 3; 30, 14; 2 Kgs 16, 17.   *y:* 26f: 2 Kgs 16, 19f.   *z:* 1ff: 2 Kgs 18, 1ff.   *a:* 2 Chr 28, 24.   *b:* 2 Kgs 16, 15.   *c:* 8f: Lv 26, 32f; Dt 28, 25; Jer 25, 18.

The Reign of Hezekiah

One of the great narratives of the Chronicler's history is the account of Hezekiah in chs 29–32. Incorporating large portions of his source in 2 Kings 18–20, he adds considerable materials concerning Hezekiah's reforms and the great worshiping assemblies, in which the king tries to bring the community back into alignment with God.

---

and carried it out to the Kidron Valley. [17]They began the work of consecration on the first day of the first month, and on the eighth day of the month they arrived at the vestibule of the LORD; they consecrated the LORD's house during eight days, and on the sixteenth day of the first month, they had finished.

[18]Then they went inside to King Hezekiah and said: "We have cleansed the entire house of the LORD, the altar of holocausts with all its utensils, and the table for the showbread with all its utensils. [19]All the articles which King Ahaz during his reign had thrown away because of his apostasy, we have restored and consecrated, and they are now before the LORD's altar."

The Rite of Expiation. [20]Then King Hezekiah hastened to convoke the princes of the city and went up to the LORD's house. [21]Seven bulls, seven rams, seven lambs and seven he-goats were brought for a sin offering for the kingdom, for the sanctuary, and for Judah, and he ordered the sons of Aaron, the priests, to offer them on the altar of the LORD. [22]They slaughtered the bulls, and the priests collected the blood and cast it on the altar. Then they slaughtered the rams and cast the blood on the altar; then they slaughtered the lambs and cast the blood on the altar. [23]Then the he-goats for the sin offering were led before the king and the assembly, who laid their hands upon them. [24]The priests then slaughtered them and offered their blood on the altar to atone for the sin of all Israel; for "The holocaust and the sin offering," the king had said, "is for all Israel."

[25]He stationed the Levites in the LORD's house with cymbals, harps and lyres according to the prescriptions of David, of Gad the king's seer, and of Nathan the prophet; for the prescriptions were from the LORD through his prophets. [26]The Levites were stationed with the instruments of David, and the priests with the trumpets. [27]Then Hezekiah ordered the holocaust to be sacrificed on the altar, and in the same instant that the holocaust began, they also began the song of the LORD, to the accompaniment of the trumpets and the instruments of David, king of Israel. [28]The entire assembly prostrated itself, and they continued to sing the song and to sound the trumpets until the holocaust had been completed. [29]As the holocaust was completed, the king and all who were with him knelt and prostrated themselves. [30]King Hezekiah and the princes then commanded the Levites to sing the praises of the LORD in the words of David and of Asaph the seer. They sang praises till their joy was full, then fell down and prostrated themselves.

[31]Hezekiah now spoke out this command: "You have undertaken a work for the LORD. Approach, and bring forward the sacrifices and thank offerings for the house of the LORD." Then the assembly brought forward the sacrifices and thank offerings and all the holocausts which were free-will offerings. [32]The number of holocausts that the assembly brought forward was seventy oxen, one hundred rams, and two hundred lambs: all of these as a holocaust to the LORD. [33]As consecrated gifts there were six hundred oxen and three thousand sheep. [34]Since the priests were too few in number to be able to skin all the victims for the holocausts, their brethren the Levites assisted them until the task was completed and the priests had sanctified themselves; the Levites, in fact, were more willing than the priests to sanctify themselves.[d] [35]Also, the holocausts were many, along with the fat of the peace offerings and the libations for the holocausts. Thus the service of the house of the LORD was reestablished.

---

d: 1 Chr 15, 12.

36Hezekiah and all the people rejoiced over what God had reestablished for the people, and at how suddenly this had been done.

CHAPTER 30

See RG
141-42
Invitation to the Passover. ¹Hezekiah sent a message to all Israel and Judah, and even wrote letters to Ephraim and Manasseh saying that they should come to the house of the LORD in Jerusalem to celebrate the Passover in honor of the LORD, the God of Israel.*e 2f*The king, his princes, and the entire assembly in Jerusalem had agreed to celebrate the Passover during the second month, ³for they could not celebrate it at the time of the restoration: the priests had not sanctified themselves in sufficient numbers, and the people were not gathered at Jerusalem. ⁴When this proposal had been approved by the king and the entire assembly, ⁵they issued a decree to be proclaimed throughout all Israel from Beer-sheba to Dan, that everyone should come to Jerusalem to celebrate the Passover in honor of the LORD, the God of Israel; for not many had kept it in the manner prescribed. ⁶Accordingly the couriers, with the letters written by the king and his princes, traversed all Israel and Judah, and at the king's command they said: "Israelites, return to the LORD, the God of Abraham, Isaac and Israel, that he may return to you, the remnant left from the hands of the Assyrian kings. ⁷Be not like your fathers and your brethren who proved faithless to the LORD, the God of their fathers, so that he delivered them over to desolation, as you yourselves now see.*g* ⁸Be not obstinate, as your fathers were; extend your hands to the LORD and come to his sanctuary that he has consecrated forever, and serve the LORD, your God, that he may turn away his burning anger from you. ⁹For when you return to the LORD, your brethren and your children will find mercy with their captors and return to this land; for merciful and compassionate is the LORD, your God, and he will not turn away his face from you if you return to him."*h*

¹⁰So the couriers passed from city to city in the land of Ephraim and Manasseh and as far as Zebulun, but they were derided and scoffed at. ¹¹Nevertheless, some from Asher, Manasseh and Zebulun humbled themselves and came to Jerusalem. ¹²In Judah, however, the power of God brought it about that the people were of one mind to carry out the command of the king and the princes in accordance with the word of the LORD. ¹³Thus many people gathered in Jerusalem to celebrate the feast of Unleavened Bread in the second month; it was a very great assembly.

The Passover Celebrated. ¹⁴They proceeded to take down the altars that were in Jerusalem; also they removed all the altars of incense and cast them into the Kidron Valley.*i* ¹⁵They slaughtered the Passover on the fourteenth day of the second month. The priests and Levites, touched with shame, sanctified themselves and brought holocausts into the house of the LORD. ¹⁶They stood in the places prescribed for them according to the law of Moses, the man of God. The priests sprinkled the blood given them by the Levites; ¹⁷for many in the assembly had not sanctified themselves, and the Levites were in charge of slaughtering the Passover victims for all who were unclean and therefore could not consecrate them to the LORD.*j* ¹⁸The greater part of the people, in fact, chiefly from Ephraim, Manasseh, Issachar and Zebulun, had not cleansed themselves. Nevertheless they ate the Passover, contrary to the prescription; for Hezekiah prayed for them, saying, "May the LORD, who is good, grant pardon to ¹⁹everyone who has resolved to seek God, the LORD, the God of his fathers, though he be not clean as holiness requires." ²⁰The LORD heard Hezekiah and spared the people.

²¹Thus the Israelites who were in Jerusalem celebrated the feast of Unleavened Bread with great rejoicing for seven days, and the Levites and the priests sang the praises of the LORD day after day with all their strength. ²²Hezekiah spoke encouragingly to all the Levites who had shown themselves well skilled in the service of the LORD. And when they had completed the seven days of festival, slaying peace offer-

e: Ex 12, 1-28.   *f:* 2ff: Nm 9, 6-13.   *g:* Acts 7, 51.   *h:* 1 Kgs 8, 50.   *i:* 2 Chr 28, 42f.   *j:* 2 Chr 35, 6.

ings and singing praises to the LORD, the God of their fathers, [23]the whole assembly agreed to celebrate another seven days. With joy, therefore, they continued the festivity seven days longer. [24]King Hezekiah of Judah had contributed a thousand bulls and seven thousand sheep to the assembly, and the princes had contributed to the assembly a thousand bulls and ten thousand sheep. The priests sanctified themselves in great numbers, [25]and the whole assembly of Judah rejoiced, together with the priests and Levites and the rest of the assembly that had come from Israel, as well as the sojourners from the land of Israel and those that lived in Judah. [26]There was great rejoicing in Jerusalem, for since the days of Solomon, son of David, king of Israel, there had not been the like in the city. [27]Then the levitical priests rose and blessed the people; their voice was heard and their prayer reached heaven, God's holy dwelling.

CHAPTER 31

See RG 141–42

Liturgical Reform. [1]After all this was over, those Israelites who had been present went forth to the cities of Judah and smashed the sacred pillars, cut down the sacred poles, and tore down the high places and altars throughout Judah, Benjamin, Ephraim and Manasseh, until all were destroyed. Then the Israelites returned to their various cities, each to his own possession.[k]

[2]Hezekiah reestablished the classes of the priests and the Levites according to their former classification, assigning to each priest and Levite his proper service, whether in regard to holocausts or peace offerings, thanksgiving or praise, or ministering in the gates of the encampment of the LORD. [3]From his own wealth the king allotted a portion for holocausts, those of morning and evening and those on sabbaths, new moons and festivals, as prescribed in the law of the LORD.[l] [4]He also commanded the people living in Jerusalem to provide the support of the priests

and Levites, that they might devote themselves entirely to the law of the LORD.

[5]As soon as the order was promulgated, the Israelites brought, in great quantities, the best of their grain, wine, oil and honey, and all the produce of the fields; they gave a generous tithe of everything.[m] [6]Israelites and Judahites living in other cities of Judah also brought in tithes of oxen, sheep, and things that had been consecrated to the LORD, their God; these they brought in and set out in heaps.[n] [7]It was in the third month that they began to establish these heaps, and they completed them in the seventh month.[*] [8]When Hezekiah and the princes had come and seen the heaps, they blessed the LORD and his people Israel. [9]Then Hezekiah questioned the priests and the Levites concerning the heaps, [10]and the priest Azariah, head of the house of Zadoc, answered him, "Since they began to bring the offerings to the house of the LORD, we have eaten to the full and have had much left over, for the LORD has blessed his people. This great supply is what was left over."[o]

[11]Hezekiah then gave orders that chambers should be constructed in the house of the LORD. When this had been done, [12]the offerings, tithes and consecrated things were deposited there in safekeeping. The overseer of these things was Conaniah the Levite, and his brother Shimei was second in charge. [13]Jehiel, Azaziah, Nathan, Asahel, Jerimoth, Jozabad, Eliel, Ismachiah, Mahath and Benaiah were supervisors subject to Conaniah and his brother Shimei by appointment of King Hezekiah and of Azariah, the prefect of the house of God. [14]Kore, the son of Imnah, a Levite and the keeper of the eastern gate, was in charge of the free-will gifts made to God; he distributed the offerings made to the LORD and the most holy of the consecrated things. [15]Under him in the priestly cities were Eden, Miniamin, Jeshua, Shemaiah, Amariah and Shecaniah, who faithfully made the distribution to their brethren, great and small alike, according to their classes.

31, 7: Third month . . . seventh month: between the feast of Pentecost and that of Booths, an interval without rain in Palestine, at the end of which the problem of storage (v 11) would become more urgent.

k: 2 Chr 34, 3f; 2 Kgs 18, 4.   l: 1 Chr 29, 3; Ez 45, 17; Nm 28—29.   m: Nm 18, 8-24; Dt 14, 22f.   n: Nm 12, 44-47; 13, 10-13. o: Lv 25, 19-22.

¹⁶There was also a register by ancestral houses of males thirty years of age and over, for all priests who were eligible to enter the house of the LORD according to the daily rule to fulfill their service in the order of their classes.ᵖ ¹⁷The priests were inscribed in their family records according to their ancestral houses, and the Levites of twenty years and over according to their various offices and classes.�q ¹⁸A distribution was also made to all who were inscribed in the family records, for their little ones, wives, sons and daughters—thus for the entire assembly, since they were to sanctify themselves by sharing faithfully in the consecrated things. ¹⁹The sons of Aaron, the priests who lived on the lands attached to their cities, had in every city men designated by name to distribute portions to every male among the priests and to every Levite listed in the family records.

²⁰This Hezekiah did in all Judah. He did what was good, upright and faithful before the LORD, his God. ²¹Everything that he undertook, for the service of the house of God or for the law and the commandments, was to do the will of his God. He did this wholeheartedly, and he prospered.ʳ

See RG 141–42

CHAPTER 32

Invasion of Sennacherib. ¹But after he had proved his fidelity by such deeds, Sennacherib, king of Assyria, came. He invaded Judah, besieged the fortified cities, and proposed to take them by storm.ˢ ²When Hezekiah saw that Sennacherib was coming with the intention of attacking Jerusalem, ³he decided in counsel with his princes and warriors to stop the waters of the springs outside the city. When they had pledged him their support, ⁴¹a large crowd was gathered which stopped all the springs and also the running stream in the valley nearby. For they said, "Why should the kings of Assyria come and find an abundance of water?" ⁵He then looked to his defenses: he rebuilt the wall where it was broken down, raised towers upon it, and built another wall outside. He strengthened the Millo of the City of David and had a great number of spears and shields prepared.ᵘ ⁶Then he appointed army commanders over the people. He gathered them together in his presence in the open space at the gate of the city and encouraged them with these words: ⁷"Be brave and steadfast; do not be afraid or dismayed because of the king of Assyria and all the throng that is coming with him, for there is more with us than with him.ᵛ ⁸For he has only an arm of flesh, but we have the LORD, our God, to help us and to fight our battles." And the people took confidence from the words of King Hezekiah of Judah.ʷ

Threat of Sennacherib. ⁹ˣAfter this, while Sennacherib, king of Assyria, himself remained at Lachish with all his forces, he sent his officials to Jerusalem with this message for King Hezekiah of Judah, and all the Judahites who were in Jerusalem: ¹⁰"King Sennacherib of Assyria has this to say: On what are you relying, while you remain under siege in Jerusalem? ¹¹Has not Hezekiah deceived you, delivering you over to a death of famine and thirst, by his claim that 'the LORD, our God, will save us from the grasp of the king of Assyria'? ¹²Has not this same Hezekiah removed his high places and altars and commanded Judah and Jerusalem, 'You shall prostrate yourselves before one altar only, and on it alone you shall offer incense'? ¹³Do you not know what my fathers and I have done to all the peoples of other lands? Were the gods of the nations in those lands able to save their lands from my hand? ¹⁴Who among all the gods of those nations which my fathers put under the ban was able to save his people from my hand? Will your god, then, be able to save you from my hand? ¹⁵Let not Hezekiah mislead you further and deceive you in any such way. Do not believe him! Since no other god of any other nation or kingdom has been able to save his people from my hand or the hands of my fathers, how much the less shall your god save you from my hand!"

¹⁶His officials said still more against the LORD God and against his servant Hezekiah,

p: 1 Chr 23, 3f. q: 1 Chr 23, 6-24. r: Ps 119, 2f. s: 2 Kgs 18, 13. t: Is 22, 9. 11. u: Neh 2, 17f. v: 2 Chr 14, 10; 20, 6-12.
w: Is 31, 3. x: 9-20: 2 Kgs 18, 17-37; Is 36, 1-22.

[17]for he had written letters to deride the LORD, the God of Israel, speaking of him in these terms: "As the gods of the nations in other lands have not saved their people from my hand, neither shall Hezekiah's god save his people from my hand."[y] [18]In a loud voice they shouted in the Judean language to the people of Jerusalem who were on the wall, to frighten and terrify them so that they might capture their city. [19]They spoke of the God of Israel as though he were one of the gods of the other peoples of the earth, a work of human hands. [20]But because of this, King Hezekiah and the prophet Isaiah, son of Amos, prayed and called out to heaven.[z]

Defeat of Sennacherib. [21]Then the LORD sent an angel, who destroyed every valiant warrior, leader and commander in the camp of the Assyrian king, so that he had to return shamefaced to his own country. And when he entered the temple of his god, some of his own offspring struck him down there with the sword.[a] [22]Thus the LORD saved Hezekiah and the inhabitants of Jerusalem from the hand of Sennacherib, king of Assyria, as from every other power; he gave them rest on every side. [23]Many brought gifts for the LORD to Jerusalem and costly objects for King Hezekiah of Judah, who thereafter was exalted in the eyes of all the nations.[b]

Hezekiah's Other Deeds. [24]In those days Hezekiah became mortally ill. He prayed to the LORD, who answered him by giving him a sign.[c] [25]Hezekiah, however, did not then discharge his debt of gratitude, for he had become proud. Therefore anger descended upon him and upon Judah and Jerusalem. [26d]But then Hezekiah humbled himself for his pride—both he and the inhabitants of Jerusalem; and therefore the LORD did not vent his anger on them during the time of Hezekiah.

[27e]Hezekiah possessed very great wealth and glory. He had treasuries made for his silver, gold, precious stones, spices, jewels, and other precious things of all kinds; [28]also storehouses for the harvest of grain, for wine and oil, and barns for the various kinds of cattle and for the flocks. [29]He built cities for himself, and he acquired sheep and oxen in great numbers, for God gave him very great riches. [30]This same Hezekiah stopped the upper outflow of water from Gihon and led it underground westward to the City of David. Hezekiah prospered in all his undertakings.[f] [31]Nevertheless, in respect to the ambassadors [princes] sent to him from Babylon to investigate the sign that had occurred in the land, God forsook him to test him, that he might know all that was in his heart.

[32]The rest of Hezekiah's acts, including his pious works, can be found written in the Vision of the Prophet Isaiah, son of Amos, and in the book of the kings of Judah and Israel. [33]Hezekiah rested with his ancestors; he was buried at the approach to the tombs* of the descendants of David. All Judah and the inhabitants of Jerusalem paid him honor at his death. His son Manasseh succeeded him as king.

CHAPTER 33

See RG 141-42

Impiety of Manasseh. [1g]Manasseh was twelve years old when he became king, and he reigned fifty-five years in Jerusalem. [2]He did evil in the sight of the LORD, following the abominable practices of the nations whom the LORD had cleared out of the way of the Israelites. [3]He rebuilt the high places which his father Hezekiah had torn down, erected altars for the Baals, made sacred poles, and prostrated himself before the whole host of heaven and worshiped them. [4]He even built altars in the temple of the LORD, of which the LORD had said, "In Jerusalem shall my name be forever": [5]he built altars to the whole host of heaven in the two courts of the LORD's house. [6]It was he, too, who immolated his sons by fire in the Valley of Ben-hinnom. He practiced augury, divination and magic, and appointed necromancers and diviners of spirits, so that he provoked the LORD with the great evil that

---

32, 33: The approach to the tombs: literally, "the ascent of the tombs," which may mean "the upper section of the tombs," their most prominent and honored place.

y: 2 Kgs 19, 9-13; Is 37, 9-13.   z: 2 Kgs 19, 14-19; Is 37, 14-20.   a: 2 Kgs 19, 35ff; Is 37, 36ff.   b: 2 Chr 14, 6.   c: 2 Kgs 20, 1-11; Is 38, 1-8.   d: 26. 31: 2 Kgs 20, 12-19; Is 39, 1-8.   e: 27f: 2 Kgs 20, 13; Is 39, 2.   f: 2 Kgs 20, 20f.   g: 1-10: 2 Kgs 21, 1-9.

he did in his sight. [7]He placed an idol that he had carved in the house of God, of which God had said to David and his son Solomon: "In this house and in Jerusalem which I have chosen from all the tribes of Israel I shall place my name forever. [8]I will not again allow Israel's feet to leave the land which I assigned to your fathers, provided they are careful to observe all that I commanded them, keeping the whole law and the statutes and the ordinances given by Moses." [9]Manasseh misled Judah and the inhabitants of Jerusalem into doing even greater evil than the nations which the LORD had destroyed at the coming of the Israelites. [10]The LORD spoke to Manasseh and his people, but they paid no attention.

His Conversion. [11h]Therefore the LORD brought against them the army commanders of the Assyrian king; they took Manasseh with hooks, shackled him with chains, and transported him to Babylon.* [12]In this distress, he began to appease the LORD, his God. He humbled himself abjectly before the God of his fathers [13]and prayed to him.* The LORD let himself be won over: he heard his prayer and restored him to his kingdom in Jerusalem. Then Manasseh understood that the LORD is indeed God.

[14]Afterward he built an outer wall for the City of David to the west of Gihon in the valley, extending to the Fish Gate and encircling Ophel; he built it very high. He stationed army officers in all the fortified cities of Judah. [15]He removed the foreign gods and the idol from the LORD's house and all the altars he had built on the mount of the LORD's house and in Jerusalem, and he cast them outside the city.[i] [16]He restored the altar of the LORD, and sacrificed on it peace offerings and thank offerings, and commanded Judah to serve the

LORD, the God of Israel. [17]Though the people continued to sacrifice on the high places, they now did so to the LORD, their God.

[18j]The rest of the acts of Manasseh, his prayer to his God, and the words of the seers who spoke to him in the name of the LORD, the God of Israel, can be found written in the chronicles of the kings of Israel. [19]His prayer and how his supplication was heard, all his sins and his infidelity, the sites where he built high places and erected sacred poles and carved images before he humbled himself, all can be found written down in the history of his seers. [20]Manasseh rested with his ancestors and was buried in his own palace. His son Amon succeeded him as king.

Amon. [21k]Amon was twenty-two years old when he became king, and he reigned two years in Jerusalem. [22]He did evil in the sight of the LORD, just as his father Manasseh had done. Amon offered sacrifice to all the idols which his father Manasseh had made, and worshiped them. [23]Moreover, he did not humble himself before the LORD as his father Manasseh had done; on the contrary, Amon only increased his guilt. [24]His servants conspired against him and put him to death in his own house. [25]But the people of the land slew all those who had conspired against King Amon, and then they, the people of the land, made his son Josiah king in his stead.

CHAPTER 34

See RG 141-42

Reforms of Josiah. [11]Josiah was eight years old when he became king, and he reigned thirty-one years in Jerusalem. [2]He pleased the LORD, following the path of his ancestor David. [3m]In the eighth year of his reign, while he was still a youth, he began to seek after the God of his forefather David, and in his twelfth year*

33, 11: There is no evidence elsewhere for an imprisonment of King Manasseh in Babylon. However, according to the Assyrian inscriptions, he paid tribute to the Assyrian kings Esarhaddon (680–669 B.C.) and Asshurbanipal (668–627 B.C.). He may well have been obliged to go to Nineveh to take the oath of allegiance as vassal to the king of Assyria.

33, 13: And prayed to him: these words led an unknown writer to compose the apocryphal "Prayer of Manasseh," which is added as an appendix to many editions of the Vulgate Bible and is used in the public prayers of the church.

34, 3: In his twelfth year: c. 628 B.C., the year after Asshurbanipal's death, when Judah could free itself from

Assyrian domination. From 2 Kgs 22, 1—23, 25 alone, one might think that Josiah's reform began only after the discovery of the book of the law in the temple, in the eighteenth year of his reign. But the Chronicler is no doubt right in placing the beginning of the reform at an earlier period. The very repair of the temple, which led to the finding of the book of the law, must have been occasioned by a cultic reform.

---

h: Jb 36, 7f; Ez 19, 9. *i:* 2 Chr 14, 2. *j:* 18. 20: 2 Kgs 21, 17f.
k: 21-25: 2 Kgs 21, 19-26. *l:* 1f: 2 Kgs 22, 1f. *m:* 3-7: 2 Chr 14, 1-4; 31, 1; 2 Kgs 23, 4-20.

he began to purge Judah and Jerusalem of the high places, the sacred poles and the carved and molten images. [4]In his presence, the altars of the Baals were destroyed; the incense stands erected above them were torn down; the sacred poles and the carved and molten images were shattered and beaten into dust, which was strewn over the tombs of those who had sacrificed to them; [5]and the bones of the priests he burned upon their altars. Thus he purged Judah and Jerusalem. [6]He did likewise in the cities of Manasseh, Ephraim, Simeon, and in the ruined villages of the surrounding country as far as Naphtali; [7]he destroyed the altars, broke up the sacred poles and carved images and beat them into dust, and tore down the incense stands throughout the land of Israel. Then he returned to Jerusalem.

The Temple Restored. [8n]In the eighteenth year of his reign, in order to cleanse the temple as well as the land, he sent Shaphan, son of Azaliah, Maaseiah, the ruler of the city, and Joah, son of Joahaz, the chamberlain, to restore the house of the LORD, his God. [9]They came to Hilkiah the high priest and turned over the money brought to the house of God which the Levites, the guardians of the threshold, had collected from Manasseh, Ephraim, and all the remnant of Israel, as well as from all of Judah, Benjamin, and the inhabitants of Jerusalem.[o] [10]They turned it over to the master workmen in the house of the LORD, and these in turn used it to pay the workmen in the LORD's house who were restoring and repairing the temple. [11]They also gave it to the carpenters and the masons to buy hewn stone and timber for the tie beams and rafters of the buildings which the kings of Judah had allowed to fall into ruin. [12]The men worked faithfully at their tasks; their overseers were Jahath and Obadiah, Levites of the line of Merari, and Zechariah and Meshullam, of the Kohathites, who directed them. All those Levites who were skillful with musical instruments [13]were in charge of the men who carried the burdens, and they directed all the workers in every kind of labor. Some of the other Levites were scribes, officials and gatekeepers.

The Finding of the Law. [14p]When they brought out the money that had been deposited in the house of the LORD, Hilkiah the priest found the book of the law of the LORD given through Moses. [15]He reported this to Shaphan the scribe, saying, "I have found the book of the law in the house of the LORD." Hilkiah gave the book to Shaphan, [16]who brought it to the king at the same time that he was making his report to him. He said, "Your servants are doing everything that has been entrusted to them; [17]they have turned into bullion the metals deposited in the LORD's house and have handed it over to the overseers and the workmen." [18]Then Shaphan the scribe announced to the king, "Hilkiah the priest has given me a book." And Shaphan read from it before the king.

[19]When the king heard the words of the law, he tore his garments [20]and issued this command to Hilkiah, to Ahikam, son of Shaphan, to Abdon, son of Michah, to Shaphan the scribe, and to Asaiah, the king's servant: [21]"On behalf of myself and those who are left in Israel and Judah, go, consult the LORD concerning the words of the book that has been found. For the anger of the LORD has been set furiously ablaze against us, since our fathers have not kept the word of the LORD and have not done all that is written in this book." [22]Then Hilkiah and the other men from the king went to the prophetess Huldah, the wife of Shallum, son of Tokhath, son of Hasrah, the guardian of the wardrobe; she dwelt in Jerusalem, in the new quarter. They spoke to her as they had been instructed, [23]and she said to them: "Thus says the LORD, the God of Israel: 'Tell the one who sent you to me, [24]The LORD says: I am prepared to bring evil upon this place and upon its inhabitants, all the curses written in the book that has been read before the king of Judah. [25]Because they have abandoned me and have offered incense to other gods, provoking me by every deed that they have performed, my anger is ablaze against this place and cannot be extinguished.'

[26]"But to the king of Judah who sent you to consult the LORD, give this response: 'Thus

n: 8-13: 2 Kgs 22, 3-7.   *o*: 2 Chr 24, 8f.   *p*: 14-28: 2 Kgs 22, 8-20.

says the LORD, the God of Israel, concerning the threats you have heard: ²⁷Because you were heartsick and have humbled yourself before God on hearing his words spoken against this place and its inhabitants; because you have humbled yourself before me, have torn your garments, and have wept before me, I in turn have listened—so declares the LORD. ²⁸I will gather you to your ancestors and you shall be taken to your grave in peace. Your eyes shall not see all the evil I will bring upon this place and upon its inhabitants.' "

They brought back this message to the king.

Renewal of the Covenant. ²⁹�q The king now convened all the elders of Judah and Jerusalem. ³⁰He went up to the house of the LORD with all the men of Judah and the inhabitants of Jerusalem, the priests, the Levites, and all the people, great and small; and he had read aloud to them the entire text of the book of the covenant that had been found in the house of the LORD. ³¹Standing at his post,* the king made a covenant before the LORD to follow the LORD and to keep his commandments, decrees, and statutes with his whole heart and soul, thus observing the terms of the covenant written in this book. ³²He thereby committed all who were of Jerusalem and Benjamin, and the inhabitants of Jerusalem conformed themselves to the covenant of God, the God of their fathers. ³³Josiah removed every abominable thing from all the territory belonging to the Israelites, and he obliged all who were in Israel to serve the LORD, their God. During his lifetime they did not desert the LORD, the God of their fathers.ʳ

See RG
141-42

CHAPTER 35

The Passover. ¹ˢJosiah celebrated in Jerusalem a Passover to honor the LORD; the Passover sacrifice was slaughtered on the fourteenth day of the first month.ᵗ ²He reappointed the priests to their duties and encouraged them in the service of the LORD's house. ³He said to the Levites who were to instruct all Israel, and who were consecrated to the

LORD: "Put the holy ark in the house built by Solomon, son of David, king of Israel. It shall no longer be a burden on your shoulders. Serve now the LORD, your God, and his people Israel.ᵘ ⁴Prepare yourselves in your ancestral houses and your classes according to the prescriptions of King David of Israel and his son Solomon. ⁵Stand in the sanctuary according to the divisions of the ancestral houses of your brethren, the common people, so that the distribution of the Levites and the families may be the same.ᵛ ⁶Slay the Passover sacrifice, sanctify yourselves, and be at the disposition of your brethren, that all may be carried out according to the word of the LORD given through Moses."ʷ

⁷Josiah contributed to the common people a flock of lambs and kids, thirty thousand in number, each to serve as a Passover victim for any who were present, and also three thousand oxen; these were from the king's property.ˣ ⁸His princes also gave a free-will gift to the people, the priests and the Levites. Hilkiah, Zechariah and Jehiel, prefects of the house of God, gave to the priests two thousand six hundred Passover victims together with three hundred oxen.ʸ ⁹Conaniah and his brothers Shemaiah, Nethanel, Hashabiah, Jehiel and Jozabad, the rulers of the Levites, contributed to the Levites five thousand Passover victims, together with five hundred oxen.

¹⁰When the service had been arranged, the priests took their places, as did the Levites in their classes according to the king's command. ¹¹The Passover sacrifice was slaughtered, whereupon the priests sprinkled some of the blood and the Levites proceeded to the skinning. ¹²They separated what was destined for the holocaust and gave it to various groups of the ancestral houses of the common people to offer to the LORD, as is prescribed in the book of Moses. They did the same with the oxen. ¹³They cooked the Passover on the fire as prescribed, and also cooked the sacred meals in pots, cauldrons and pans, then brought them quickly to all the common people.ᶻ

34, 31: Standing at his post: see note on 2 Chr 23, 13.

q: 29-32: 2 Kgs 23, 1ff.   r: 2 Kgs 23, 4-20.   s: 1-19: 2 Kgs 23, 21ff.   t: Ex 12, 1-28; 2 Kgs 23, 21.   u: 2 Chr 5, 4; 1 Chr 15, 12. 15.
v: 1 Chr 24—26.   w: 2 Chr 30, 17.   x: Ex 12, 5.   y: Nm 7, 1-83.   z: Nm 12, 8f.

*14*Afterward they prepared the Passover for themselves and for the priests. Indeed the priests, the sons of Aaron, were busy offering holocausts and the fatty portions until night; therefore the Levites prepared for themselves and for the priests, the sons of Aaron. *15*The singers, the sons of Asaph, were at their posts as prescribed by David: Asaph, Heman and Jeduthun, the king's seer. The gatekeepers were at every gate; there was no need for them to leave their stations, for their brethren, the Levites, prepared for them. *16*Thus the entire service of the Lord was arranged that day so that the Passover could be celebrated and the holocausts offered on the altar of the Lord, as King Josiah had commanded. *17*The Israelites who were present on that occasion kept the Passover and the feast of the Unleavened Bread for seven days. *18a*No such Passover had been observed in Israel since the time of the prophet Samuel, nor had any king of Israel kept a Passover like that of Josiah, the priests and Levites, all of Judah and Israel that were present, and the inhabitants of Jerusalem. *19*It was in the eighteenth year of Josiah's reign that this Passover was observed.

Josiah's Reign Ends. *20*After Josiah had done all this to restore the temple, Neco, king of Egypt, came up to fight at Carchemish on the Euphrates, and Josiah went out to intercept him. *21*Neco sent messengers to him, saying: "What quarrel is between us, king of Judah? I have not come against you this day, for my war is with another kingdom, and God has told me to hasten. Do not interfere with God who is with me, as otherwise he will destroy you." *22*But Josiah would not withdraw from him, for he had sought a pretext for fighting with him. Therefore he would not listen to the words of Neco that came from the mouth of God, but went out to fight in the plain of Megiddo. *23*Then the archers shot King Josiah, who

said to his servants, "Take me away, for I am seriously wounded."*b* *24*His servants removed him from his own chariot, placed him in another he had in reserve, and brought him to Jerusalem, where he died. He was buried in the tombs of his ancestors, and all Judah and Jerusalem mourned him. *25*Jeremiah also composed a lamentation over Josiah,* which is recited to this day by all the male and female singers in their lamentations over Josiah. These have been made obligatory for Israel, and can be found written in the Lamentations.

*26c*The rest of the chronicle of Josiah, his pious deeds in regard to what is written in the law of the LORD, and his acts, first and last, can be found written in the book of the kings of Israel and Judah.

CHAPTER 36

*1d*The people of the land took Jehoahaz, son of Josiah, and made him king in Jerusalem in his father's stead.

See RG
141–42

IV: End of the Kingdom

Jehoahaz. *2*Jehoahaz was twenty-three years old when he became king, and he reigned three months in Jerusalem. *3*The king of Egypt deposed him in Jerusalem and fined the land one hundred talents of silver and a talent of gold. *4*Then the king of Egypt made his brother Eliakim king over Judah and Jerusalem, and changed his name to Jehoiakim. Neco took his brother Jehoahaz away and brought him to Egypt.

Jehoiakim. *5*Jehoiakim was twenty-five years old when he became king, and he reigned eleven years in Jerusalem. He did evil in the sight of the LORD, his God.*e* *6f*Nebuchadnezzar, king of Babylon, came up against him and bound him with chains to take him to Babylon.* *7*Nebuchadnezzar also

---

35, 25: The reference to a lamentation over Josiah composed by Jeremiah is not found either in 2 Kgs or Jer; but see note on Zec 12, 11. Their lamentations: probably a reference to the canonical Book of Lamentations.

36, 6: Nebuchadnezzar . . . bound him with chains to take him to Babylon: the Chronicler does not say that Jehoiakim was actually taken to Babylon. According to 2 Kgs 24, 1-6, Jehoiakim revolted after being Nebuchadnezzar's

vassal for three years; he died in Jerusalem before the Babylonian king could reach the city. However, Dn 1, 1f, apparently based on 2 Chr 36, 6f, speaks of Jehoiakim's deportation to Babylon.

---

a: 18f: 2 Kgs 23, 22f.   *b:* 2 Chr 18, 33f.   *c:* 2 Kgs 23, 28.   *d:* 1-4: 2 Kgs 23, 30-34; 1 Chr 3, 15f.   *e:* 2 Kgs 23, 36f; Jer 22, 18f.   *f:* 2 Kgs 24, 1f.

Exile of Southern Kingdom

carried away to Babylon some of the vessels of the house of the LORD and put them in his palace in Babylon. [8] The rest of the acts of Jehoiakim, the abominable things that he did, and what therefore happened to him, can be found written in the book of the kings of Israel and Judah. His son Jehoiachin succeeded him as king.[g]

Jehoiachin. [9] Jehoiachin was eighteen years old when he became king, and he reigned three months [and ten days] in Jerusalem. He did evil in the sight of the LORD.[h] [10] At the turn of the year, King Nebuchadnezzar sent for him and had him brought to Babylon, along with precious vessels from the temple of the LORD. He made his brother Zedekiah* king over Judah and Jerusalem.[i]

Zedekiah. [11] Zedekiah was twenty-one years old when he became king, and he reigned eleven years in Jerusalem.[j] [12] He did

evil in the sight of the LORD, his God, and he did not humble himself before the prophet Jeremiah, who spoke the word of the LORD.[k] [13] He also rebelled against King Nebuchadnezzar, who had made him swear by God. He became stiff-necked and hardened his heart rather than return to the LORD, the God of Israel.[l] [14] Likewise all the princes of Judah, the priests and the people added infidelity to infidelity, practicing all the abominations of the nations and polluting the LORD's temple which he had consecrated in Jerusalem.

Dissolution of Judah. [15] Early and often did the LORD, the God of their fathers, send his messengers to them, for he had compassion on his people and his dwelling place.[m] [16] But they mocked the messengers of God, despised his warnings, and scoffed at his prophets, until the anger of the LORD against

36, 10: His brother Zedekiah: Zedekiah was actually the brother of Jehoiakim and the uncle of Jehoiachin (2 Kgs 24, 17; Jer 37, 1), though scarcely older than his nephew (2 Kgs 24, 8. 18; 2 Chr 36, 9. 11).

g: 2 Kgs 24, 5.   *h:* 2 Kgs 24, 8f.   *i:* 2 Kgs 24, 10-16.   *j:* 2 Kgs 24, 18ff; Jer 52, 1ff.   *k:* Jer 37, 1ff.   *l:* 2 Kgs 25, 1; Jer 52, 4; Ex 17, 13-16.   *m:* Jer 7, 25; Heb 1, 1.

his people was so inflamed that there was no remedy.[n] [17]Then he brought up against them the king of the Chaldeans, who slew their young men in their own sanctuary building, sparing neither young man nor maiden, neither the aged nor the decrepit; he delivered all of them over into his grip.[o] [18]All the utensils of the house of God, the large and the small, and the treasures of the LORD's house and of the king and his princes, all these he brought to Babylon.[p] [19]They burnt the house of God, tore down the walls of Jerusalem, set all its palaces afire, and destroyed all its precious objects.[q] [20]Those who escaped the sword he carried captive to Babylon, where they became his and his sons' servants until the kingdom of the Persians came to power. [21]All this was to ful-

fill the word of the LORD spoken by Jeremiah: "Until the land has retrieved its lost sabbaths, during all the time it lies waste it shall have rest while seventy years are fulfilled."

Decree of Cyrus. [22]*In the first year of Cyrus, king of Persia, in order to fulfill the word of the LORD spoken by Jeremiah, the LORD inspired King Cyrus of Persia to issue this proclamation throughout his kingdom, both by word of mouth and in writing:[r] [23]"Thus says Cyrus, king of Persia: 'All the kingdoms of the earth the LORD, the God of heaven, has given to me, and he has also charged me to build him a house in Jerusalem, which is in Judah. Whoever, therefore, among you belongs to any part of his people, let him go up, and may his God be with him!' "

36, 22f: The words of these verses are identical with those of Ezr 1, 1-3a. Originally Ezra-Nehemiah formed the last part of the single work of the Chronicler, of which 1 and 2 Chronicles formed the first part. But when Ezra-Nehemiah was regarded as a natural sequence to the Books of Samuel and of Kings, it was separated from 1 and 2 Chronicles and placed before them. Thus, 1 and 2 Chronicles became the last part of the Hebrew Bible. To prevent this work from ending on a note of doom, Ezr 1, 1-3a was repeated as 2 Chr 36, 22f.

n: Mt 23, 34ff. *o:* Lam 1, 15; 5, 11-14. *p:* 2 Kgs 25, 14f. *q:* 2 Kgs 25, 9f; Lam 2, 8. *r:* Ezr 1, 1ff.

See RG 144-50

The Book of Ezra

The last four books of the Hebrew canon are Ezra, Nehemiah, 1 and 2 Chronicles, in that order. Originally, however, Ezra and Nehemiah followed the Books of Chronicles, and formed with them a unified historical work so homogeneous in spirit that one usually speaks of a single author for the four books. He is called "the Chronicler." The treatment of Ezra-Nehemiah as a single book by the earliest chroniclers was undoubtedly due to the fact that in ancient times the two books were put under the one name—Ezra. The combined work Ezra-Nehemiah is our most important literary source for the formation of the Jewish religious community after the Babylonian exile. This is known as the period of the Restoration, and the two men most responsible for the reorganization of Jewish life at this time were Ezra and Nehemiah.

In the present state of the Ezra-Nehemiah text, there are several dislocations of large sections so that the chronological or logical sequence is disrupted. The major instances are pointed out in the footnotes. Although Ezra appears before Nehemiah in this work, it seems probable that Nehemiah's activity preceded his.

What is known of Ezra and his work is due almost exclusively to Ezra 7—10 (the "Ezra Memoirs") and to Neh 8—9. Strictly speaking, the term "Ezra Memoirs" should be used only of that section in which Ezra speaks in the first person, i.e., Ezr 7, 27—9, 15. Compare the "Nehemiah Memoirs" in Neh 1, 1—7, 72a; 11, 1f; 12, 27-43; 13, 4-31. The Chronicler combined this material with other sources at his disposal. The personality of Ezra is less known than that of Nehemiah. Ben Sirach, in his praise of the fathers, makes no mention of Ezra. The genealogy of Ezra (7, 1–5) traces his priesthood back to Aaron, brother of Moses. This was the accepted way of establishing the legality of one's priestly office. He is also called *a scribe, well-versed in the law of Moses* (7, 6), indicating Ezra's dedication to the study of the Torah, which he sought to make the basic rule of life in the restored community. It was in religious and cultic reform rather than in political affairs that Ezra made his mark as a postexilic leader. Jewish tradition holds him in great honor; the Talmud even regards him as a second Moses, claiming that the Torah would have been given to Israel through Ezra had not Moses preceded him.

Utensils from the Temple

The return of these utensils from the temple of Solomon that had been destroyed by the Babylonians (v. 7) links that temple with the temple that will be built after the Exile.

Ezra is sometimes accused of having been a mere legalist who gave excessive attention to the letter of the law. His work, however, should be seen and judged within a specific historical context. He gave to his people a cohesion and spiritual unity which prevented the disintegration of the small Jewish community. Had it not been for the intransigence of Ezra and of those who adopted his ideal, it is doubtful that Judaism would have so effectively resisted Hellenism, then or in later centuries. Ezra set the tone of the postexilic community, and it was characterized by fidelity to the Torah, Judaism's authentic way of life. It is in this light that we can judge most fairly the work of Ezra during the Restoration.

The Book of Ezra is divided as follows:

I: The Return from Exile (1, 1—6, 22).

II: The Deeds of Ezra (7, 1—10, 44).

The following list of the kings of Persia, with the dates of their reigns, will be useful for dating the events mentioned in Ezra-Nehemiah:

Cyrus	538–529 B.C.
Cambyses	529–521 B.C.
Darius I	521–485 B.C.
Xerxes	485–464 B.C.
Artaxerxes I	464–423 B.C.
Darius II	423–404 B.C.
Artaxerxes II	404–358 B.C.
Artaxerxes III	358–337 B.C.
End of the Persian Empire	
(Defeat of Darius III)	331 B.C.

I: The Return from Exile

CHAPTER 1

See RG 145

The Decree of Cyrus. [1a]In the first year of Cyrus,* king of Persia, in order to fulfill the word of the LORD spoken by Jeremiah, the LORD inspired King Cyrus of Persia to issue this proclamation throughout his kingdom, both by word of mouth and in writing: [2]"Thus says Cyrus, king of Persia: 'All the kingdoms of the earth the LORD, the God of heaven, has given to me, and he has also charged me to build him a house in Jerusalem, which is in Judah. [3]Whoever, therefore, among you belongs to any part of his people, let him go up, and may his God be with him! [4]Let everyone who has survived, in whatever place he may have dwelt, be assisted by the people of that place with silver, gold, goods, and cattle, together with free will offerings for the house of God in Jerusalem.' "

[5]Then the family heads of Judah and Benjamin and the priests and Levites—everyone, that is, whom God had inspired to do so—prepared to go up to build the house of the LORD in Jerusalem. [6]All their neighbors gave them help in every way, with silver, gold, goods, and cattle, and with many precious gifts besides all their free-will offerings.[b] [7]King Cyrus, too, had the utensils of the house of the LORD brought forth which Nebuchadnezzar had taken away from Jerusalem and placed in the house of his god. [8]Cyrus, king of Persia, had them brought forth by the treasurer Mithredath, and counted out to Sheshbazzar,* the prince of Judah. [9]This was the inventory: sacks of goldware, thirty; sacks of silverware, one thousand and twenty-nine; [10]golden bowls, thirty; silver bowls, four hundred and ten; other ware, one thousand pieces. [11]Total of the gold- and silverware: five thousand four hundred pieces.* All these Sheshbazzar took

1, 1: In the first year of Cyrus: as sovereign over the world empire which began with his conquest of Babylon; that is, 538 B.C.

1, 8: Sheshbazzar: very probably the fourth son of Jehoiachin, king of Judah, taken captive to Babylon in 598 B.C., listed in 1 Chr 3, 18 as Senneser; if so, he was the uncle of Zerubbabel (Ezr 3, 2ff); see note on 1 Chr 3, 18.

1, 11: Total . . . five thousand four hundred pieces: either this figure or the figures given for one or more of the items listed (vv 9f) have been corrupted in the transmission of the text.

a: 1ff: 2 Chr 36, 22f; Jer 25, 11f; 29, 10; Zec 1, 12. *b:* Ex 3, 22; 11, 2; 12, 35.

The beginning of Ezra-Nehemiah seeks to establish the legitimacy of rebuilding the house of God, the temple. This is expressed by opening ch 1 with the imperial order to return to Jerusalem and rebuild the temple.

with him when the exiles were brought back from Babylon to Jerusalem.

CHAPTER 2

See RG 145

Census of the Province. *1**These are the inhabitants of the province who returned from the captivity of the exiles, whom Nebuchadnezzar, king of Babylon, had carried away to Babylon,*c* and who came back to Jerusalem and Judah, each man in his own city *2*(those who returned with Zerubbabel, Jeshua, Nehemiah, Seraiah, Reelaiah, Mordecai, Bilshan, Mispereth, Bigvai, Rehum, and Baanah):

The census of the men of Israel: *3*sons of Parosh, two thousand one hundred and seventy-two; *4*sons of Shephatiah, three hundred and seventy-two; *5*sons of Arah, seven hundred and seventy-five; *6*sons of Pahath-moab, who were sons of Jeshua and Joab, two thousand eight hundred and twelve; *7*sons of Elam, one thousand two hundred and fifty-four; *8*sons of Zattu, nine hundred and forty-five; *9*sons of Zaccai, seven hundred and sixty; *10*sons of Bani, six hundred and forty-two; *11*sons of Bebai, six hundred and twenty-three; *12*sons of Azgad, one thousand two hundred and twenty-two; *13*sons of Adonikam, six hundred and sixty-six; *14*sons of Bigvai, two thousand and fifty-six; *15*sons of Adin, four hundred and fifty-four; *16*sons of Ater, who were sons of Hezekiah, ninety-eight; *17*sons of Bezai, three hundred and twenty-three; *18*sons of Jorah, one hundred and twelve; *19*sons of Hashum, two hundred and twenty-three; *20*sons of Gibeon, ninety-five; *21*sons of Bethlehem, one hundred and twenty-three; *22*men of Netophah, fifty-six; *23*men of Anathoth, one hundred and twenty-eight; *24*men of Beth-azmaveth, forty-two; *25*men of Kiriath-jearim, Chephirah, and

Beeroth, seven hundred and forty-three; *26*men of Ramah and Geba, six hundred and twenty-one; *27*men of Michmas, one hundred and twenty-two; *28*men of Bethel and Ai, two hundred and twenty-three; *29*sons of Nebo, fifty-two; *30*sons of Magbish, one hundred and fifty-six; *31*sons of the other Elam, one thousand two hundred and fifty-four; *32*sons of Harim, three hundred and twenty; *33*sons of Lod, Hadid, and Ono, seven hundred and twenty-five; *34*sons of Jericho, three hundred and forty-five; *35*sons of Senaah, three thousand six hundred and thirty.

*35*The priests: sons of Jedaiah, who were of the house of Jeshua, nine hundred and seventy-three; *37*sons of Immer, one thousand and fifty-two; *38*sons of Pashhur, one thousand two hundred and forty-seven; *39*sons of Harim, one thousand and seventeen.

*40*The Levites: sons of Jeshua, Kadmiel, Binnui, and Hodaviah, seventy-four.*d*

*41*The singers: sons of Asaph, one hundred and twenty-eight.

*42*The gatekeepers: sons of Shallum, sons of Ater, sons of Talmon, sons of Akkub, sons of Hatita, sons of Shobai, one hundred and thirty-nine in all.

*43*The temple slaves: sons of Ziha, sons of Hasupha, sons of Tabbaoth, *44*sons of Keros, sons of Siaha, sons of Padon, *45*sons of Lebanah, sons of Hagabah, sons of Akkub, *46*sons of Hagab, sons of Shamlai, sons of Hanan, *47*sons of Giddel, sons of Gahar, sons of Reaiah, *48*sons of Rezin, sons of Nekoda, sons of Gazzam, *49*sons of Uzza, sons of Paseah, sons of Besai, *50*sons of Asnah, sons of the Meunites, sons of the Nephusites, *51*sons of Bakbuk, sons of Hakupha, sons of Harhur, *52*sons of Bazluth, sons of Mehida, sons of Harsha,

2, 1-67: As it now stands, this list is an expanded form of the lists of returned captives from the sixth century B.C.; see Neh 7, 6-72, where it reappears.

c: Neh 7, 6-67. *d:* Neh 12, 24.

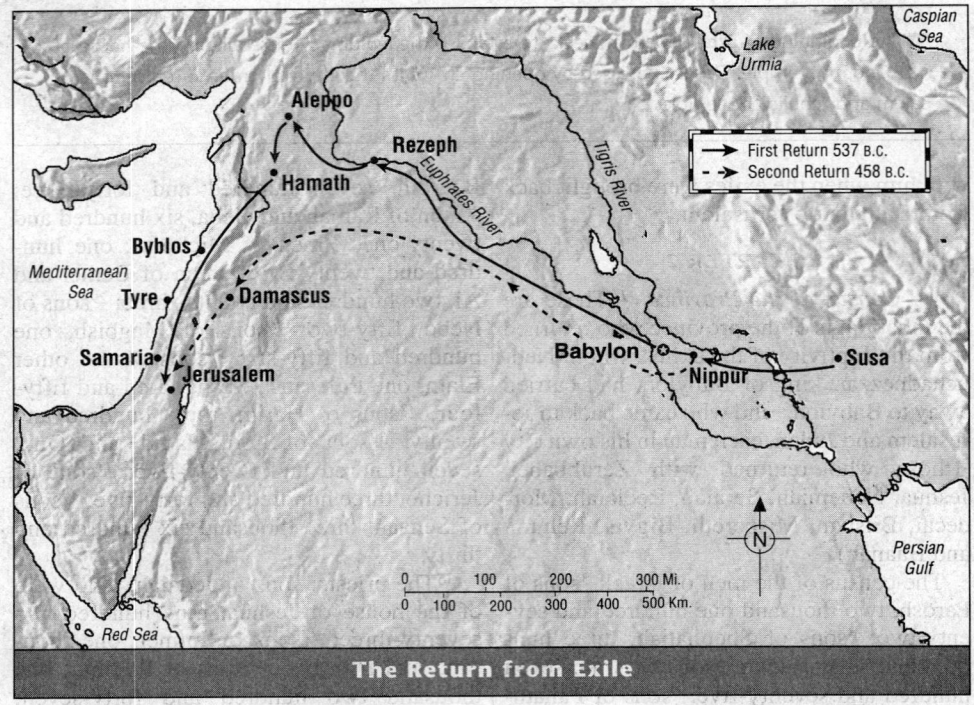

The Return from Exile

⁵³sons of Barkos, sons of Sisera, sons of Temah, ⁵⁴sons of Neziah, sons of Hatipha.

⁵⁵Descendants of the slaves of Solomon: sons of Sotai, sons of Hassophereth, sons of Peruda, ⁵⁶sons of Jaalah, sons of Darkon, sons of Giddel, ⁵⁷sons of Shephatiah, sons of Hattil, sons of Pochereth-hazzebaim, sons of Ami. ⁵⁸The total of the temple slaves and the descendants of the slaves of Solomon was three hundred and ninety-two.

⁵⁹The following who returned from Telmelah, Tel-harsha, Cherub, Addan, and Immer were unable to prove that their ancestral houses and their descent were Israelite: ⁶⁰sons of Delaiah, sons of Tobiah, sons of Nekoda, six hundred and fifty-two. ⁶¹Also, of the priests: sons of Habaiah, sons of Hakkoz, sons of Barzillai (he had married one of the daughters of Barzillai the Gileadite and became known by his name).^e ⁶²These men searched their family records, but their names could not be found written there; hence they

were degraded from the priesthood, ⁶³and His Excellency* ordered them not to partake of the most holy foods until there should be a priest bearing the Urim and Thummim.

⁶⁴The entire assembly taken together came to forty-two thousand three hundred and sixty, ⁶⁵not counting their male and female slaves, who were seven thousand three hundred and thirty-seven. They also had two hundred male and female singers. ⁶⁶Their horses were seven hundred and thirty-six, their mules two hundred and forty-five, ⁶⁷their camels four hundred and thirty-five, their asses six thousand seven hundred and twenty.

⁶⁸When they arrived at the house of the LORD in Jerusalem, some of the family heads made free-will offerings for the house of God, to rebuild it in its place. ⁶⁹According to their means they contributed to the treasury for the temple service: sixty-one thousand drachmas of gold, five thousand minas of silver, and one

---

2, 63: His Excellency: the deputy of the Persian government; from the context, he was one of the Jewish exile leaders. Nehemiah as governor receives the same title (Neh 8, 9;

10, 2). Urim and Thummim: see note on Ex 28, 30.

e: 2 Sm 17, 27; 19, 32f; 1 Kgs 2, 7.

The resumption of worship at the site of the ruined temple is described in 3, 1–7 as a prelude to building the temple according to rules on the composition of the altar found in Exodus 20, 25.

hundred garments for the priests. [70]The priests, the Levites, and some of the common people took up residence in Jerusalem; but the singers, the gatekeepers, and the temple slaves dwelt in their cities. Thus all the Israelites dwelt in their cities.

See RG 145

CHAPTER 3

Restoration of the Altar. [1]Now when the seventh month* came, after the Israelites had settled in their cities, the people gathered at Jerusalem as one man.[f] [2]Then Jeshua, son of Jozadak, together with his brethren the priests, and Zerrubbabel, son of Shealtiel, together with his brethren, set about rebuilding the altar of the God of Israel in order to offer on it the holocausts prescribed in the law of Moses, the man of God. [3]Despite their fear of the peoples of the land, they replaced the altar on its foundations and offered holocausts to the LORD on it, both morning and evening.[g] [4]They also kept the feast of Booths in the manner prescribed, and they offered the daily holocausts in the proper number required for each day.[h] [5]Thereafter they offered the established holocaust, the sacrifices prescribed for the new moons and all the festivals sacred to the LORD, and those which anyone might offer as a free-will gift to the LORD. [6]From the first day of the seventh month they began to offer holocausts to the LORD, though the foundation of the temple of the LORD had not yet been laid.

Founding of the Temple. [7]Then they hired stonecutters and carpenters, and sent food and drink and oil to the Sidonians and Tyrians that they might ship cedar trees from the Lebanon to the port of Joppa, as Cyrus, king of Persia, had authorized.[i] [8]In the year after their coming to the house of God in Jerusalem, in the second month, Zerubbabel, son of Shealtiel, and Jeshua, son of Jozadak, together with the rest of their brethren, the priests and Levites and all who had come from the captivity to Jerusalem, began by appointing the Levites twenty years of age and over to supervise the work on the house of the LORD. [9]Jeshua and his sons and brethren, with Kadmiel and Binnui, son of Henadad, and their sons and their brethren, the Levites, stood as one man to supervise those who were engaged in the work on the house of God. [10]When the builders had laid the foundation of the LORD's temple, the vested priests with the trumpets and the Levites, sons of Asaph, were stationed there with the cymbals to praise the LORD in the manner laid down by David, king of Israel.[j] [11]They alternated in songs of praise and thanksgiving to the LORD, "for he is good, for his kindness to Israel endures forever"; and all the people raised a great shout of joy, praising the LORD because the foundation of the LORD's house had been laid.[k] [12]Many of the priests, Levites, and family heads, the old men who had seen the former house, cried out in sorrow as they watched the foundation of the present house being laid.[l] Many others, however, lifted up their voices in shouts of joy, [13]and no one could distinguish the sound of the joyful shouting from the sound of those

---

3, 1f: The seventh month: Tishri (September–October), apparently of 538 B.C.; cf Ezr 1, 1; 4, 5. In this case, it was Sheshbazzar who erected the first altar, since he began the work on the foundations of the temple in Jerusalem; cf Ezr 5, 16. It was in the second year of Darius I, i.e., in 520 B.C., that Jeshua and Zerubbabel resumed the work on the temple that had been temporarily interrupted (Ezr 4, 24—5, 1; Hg 1, 1; 2, 1). The Chronicler or a later editor of the text here attributes to them the beginning of the work which, in reality, they

merely completed. Shealtiel: the oldest son of King Jehoiachin of Judah and the brother of Sheshbazzar (1 Chr 3, 18f); Zerubbabel was therefore the grandson of Jehoiachin; see note on Ezr 1, 8.

---

f: Neh 7, 73—8, 1. *g:* 1 Kgs 8, 64; Dn 9, 25. *h:* Ex 23, 16. Nm 28, 3-8. *i:* 1 Chr 22, 4; 2 Chr 2, 9. *j:* Ezr 2, 41. *k:* Pss 100, 5; 136; Jer 33, 11. *l:* Hg 2, 3.

who were weeping; for the people raised a mighty clamor which was heard afar off.[m]

CHAPTER 4

See RG 145

Samaritan Interference. [1]When the enemies of Judah and Benjamin heard that the exiles were building a temple for the LORD, the God of Israel, [2]they approached Zerubbabel and the family heads and said to them, "Let us build with you, for we seek your God just as you do, and we have sacrificed to him since the days of Esarhaddon, king of Assyria, who had us brought here." [3]But Zerubbabel, Jeshua, and the rest of the family heads of Israel answered them, "It is not your responsibility to build with us a house for our God, but we alone must build it for the LORD, the God of Israel, as King Cyrus of Persia has commanded us." [4]Thereupon the people of the land set out to intimidate and dishearten the people of Judah so as to keep them from building. [5]They also suborned counselors to work against them and thwart their plans during the remaining years of Cyrus, king of Persia, and until the reign of Darius,* king of Persia.

Later Hostility. [6]Also at the beginning of the reign of Ahashuerus they prepared a written accusation against the inhabitants of Judah and Jerusalem.

[7]Again, in the time of Artaxerxes, Mithredath wrote in concert with Tabeel and the rest of his fellow officials to Artaxerxes, king of Persia. The document was written in Aramaic* and was accompanied by a translation. [Aramaic:]

[8]*Then Rehum, the governor, and Shimshai, the scribe, wrote the following letter against Jerusalem to King Artaxerxes: [9]"Rehum, the governor, Shimshai, the scribe, and their fellow judges, officials, and agents from among the Persian, Urukian, Babylonian, Susian (that is, Elamite), [10]and the other peoples whom the great and illustrious Assurbanipal transported and settled in the city of Samaria and elsewhere in the province West-of-Euphrates, as follows. . . ." [11]This is a copy of the letter that they sent to him:

"To King Artaxerxes, your servants, the men of West-of-Euphrates, as follows: [12]Let it be known to the king that the Jews who came up from you to us have arrived at Jerusalem and are now rebuilding this rebellious and evil city. They are raising up its walls, and the foundations have already been laid. [13]Now let it be known to the king that if this city is rebuilt and its walls are raised up again, they will no longer pay taxes, tributes, or tolls; thus it can only result in harm to the throne. [14]Now, since we partake of the salt of the palace, we ought not simply to look on while the king is being dishonored. Therefore we have sent this message to inform you, O king, [15]so that inquiry may be made in the historical records of your fathers. In the historical records you can discover and verify that this city is a rebellious city which has proved fatal to kings and provinces, and that sedition has been fostered there since ancient times. For that reason this city was destroyed. [16]We inform you, O king, that if this city is rebuilt and its walls are raised up again, by that very fact you will no longer own any part of West-of-Euphrates."

[17]The king sent this answer: "To Rehum, the governor, Shimshai, the scribe, and their fellow officials living in Samaria and elsewhere in the province West-of-Euphrates, greetings and the following: [18]The communication which you sent us has been read plainly in my presence. [19]When at my command inquiry was made, it was verified that from ancient times this city has risen up against kings and that rebellion and sedition have been fostered there. [20]Powerful kings were once in Jerusalem who ruled over all

---

4, 5: Darius: Darius I (521–485 B.C.). The temple-building narrative continues in Ezr 4, 24. In between (Ezr 4, 6-23) is a series of notes about the opposition to the returned exiles voiced at the Persian court in the early fifth century B.C., after the temple had been reestablished.

4, 7: Aramaic: this word in the original text seems to be a note indicating a change of language from Hebrew to Aramaic, which in fact takes place here. The Aramaic section ends with Ezr 6, 18, but again in Ezr 7, 12-26 a royal letter is cited in Aramaic.

4, 8-23: The central question here is the rebuilding of the fortification walls of Jerusalem, not the building of the temple. The interruption of work on the city wall some time before 445 B.C. was the occasion for the coming of Nehemiah to Palestine (Neh 1, 1-4; 2, 1-5). Artaxerxes: Artaxerxes I (464–423 B.C.).

m: Tb 14, 5.

538

Opposition during the Reign of Artaxerxes

The correspondence in 4, 8 to 6, 18, mostly in Aramaic, is out of chronological order. In 4, 7–24 it serves thematic functions, documenting how adversaries successfully sabotaged Jewish activities and identifying the opponents as foreigners who displaced the legitimate inhabitants (v. 10).

West-of-Euphrates, and taxes, tributes, and tolls were paid to them. [21]Give orders, therefore, that will stop the work of these men. This city may not be rebuilt until a further decree has been issued by me. [22]Take care that you do not neglect this matter, lest the evil grow to the detriment of the throne."

[23]As soon as a copy of King Artaxerxes' letter had been read before Rehum, the governor, Shimshai, the scribe, and their fellow officials, they went in all haste to the Jews in Jerusalem and stopped their work by force of arms.[n]

Rebuilding of the Temple. [24]Thus it was that the work on the house of God in Jerusalem was halted. This inaction lasted until the second year of the reign of Darius,[*] king of Persia.

See RG
145

CHAPTER 5

[1]Then the prophets Haggai and Zechariah,[*] son of Iddo, began to prophesy to the Jews in Judah and Jerusalem in the name of the God of Israel.[o] [2]Thereupon Zerubbabel, son of Shealtiel, and Jeshua, son of Jozadak, began again to build the house of God in Jerusalem, with the prophets of God giving them support. [3]At that time there came to them Tattenai, governor of West-of-Euphrates, and Shethar-bozenai, and their fellow officials, who asked of them: "Who issued the decree for you to build this house and raise this edifice? [4]What are the names of the men who are building this structure?" [5]But their God watched over the elders of the Jews so that they were not hindered, until a report could go to Darius and then a written order be sent back concerning this matter.

[6]A copy of the letter sent to King Darius by Tattenai, governor of West-of-Euphrates,

and Shethar-bozenai, and their fellow officials from West-of-Euphrates; [7]they sent him a report in which was written the following:

"To King Darius, all good wishes! [8]Let it be known to the king that we have visited the province of Judah and the house of the great God: it is being rebuilt of cut stone and the walls are being reinforced with timber; the work is being carried on diligently and is making good progress under their hands. [9]We then questioned the elders, addressing to them the following words: 'Who issued the decree for you to build this house and raise this edifice?' [10]We also asked them their names, to report them to you in a list of the men who are their leaders. [11]This was their answer to us: 'We are the servants of the God of heaven and earth, and we are rebuilding the house built here long years ago, which a great king of Israel built and finished. [12]But because our fathers provoked the wrath of the God of heaven, he delivered them into the power of the Chaldean, Nebuchadnezzar, king of Babylon, who destroyed this house and led the people captive to Babylon. [13]However, in the first year of Cyrus, king of Babylon, King Cyrus issued a decree for the rebuilding of this house of God. [14]Moreover, the gold and silver utensils of the house of God which Nebuchadnezzar had taken from the temple in Jerusalem and carried off to the temple in Babylon, King Cyrus ordered to be removed from the temple in Babylon and consigned to a certain Sheshbazzar, whom he named governor. [15]And he commanded him: Take these utensils and deposit them in the temple of Jerusalem, and let the house of God be rebuilt on its former site. [16]Then this same Sheshbazzar

4, 24: The second year . . . of Darius: 520 B.C.; it marks the beginning of the successful restoration of the temple, which was accomplished within the five years following (Ezr 5, 1—6, 18).

5, 1: The prophets Haggai and Zechariah: two of the Mi-

nor Prophets, whose books record their role in the encouragement of this work.

n: Neh 1, 3.   o: Hg 1, 14—2, 9; Zec 4, 9.

The scroll with Cyrus' decree is found in Ecbatana, the summer residence of Persian kings, now Hamadan in Iran. This archival version of Cyrus' decree (6, 2–5) emphasizes building size and funding and is more generous than the public version (1, 1–4) in explicitly offering royal financial support. Darius' subsequent decree also provides funds from the royal treasury and gives extremely generous support (vv. 8–9).

came and laid the foundations of the house of God in Jerusalem. Since that time the building has been going on, and it is not yet completed.' *17*Now, if it please the king, let a search be made in the royal archives of Babylon to discover whether a decree really was issued by King Cyrus for the rebuilding of this house of God in Jerusalem. And may the king's pleasure in this matter be communicated to us.''

See RG
145

CHAPTER 6

The Decree of Darius. *1*Thereupon King Darius issued an order to search the archives in which the Babylonian records were stored away; *2p*and in Ecbatana, the stronghold in the province of Media, a scroll was found containing the following text: ''Memorandum. *3*In the first year of King Cyrus, King Cyrus issued a decree: The house of God in Jerusalem. The house is to be rebuilt as a place for offering sacrifices and bringing burnt offerings. Its height is to be sixty cubits and its width sixty cubits. *4*It shall have three courses of cut stone for each one of timber. The costs are to be borne by the royal palace. *5*Also, the gold and silver utensils of the house of God which Nebuchadnezzar took from the temple of Jerusalem and brought to Babylon are to be sent back: to be returned to their place in the temple of Jerusalem and deposited in the house of God.

6''Now, therefore, Tattenai, governor of West-of-Euphrates, and Shethar-bozenai, and you, their fellow officials in West-of-Euphrates, do not interfere in that place. *7*Let the governor and the elders of the Jews continue the work on that house of God; they are to rebuild it on its former site. *8*I also issue this decree concerning your dealing with these elders of the Jews in the rebuilding of

that house of God: From the royal revenue, the taxes of West-of-Euphrates, let these men be repaid for their expenses, in full and without delay. *9*Whatever else is required—young bulls, rams, and lambs for holocausts to the God of heaven, wheat, salt, wine, and oil, according to the requirements of the priests who are in Jerusalem—is to be delivered to them day by day without fail, *10*that they may continue to offer sacrifices of pleasing odor to the God of heaven and pray for the life of the king and his sons. *11*I also issue this decree: If any man violates this edict, a beam is to be taken from his house, and he is to be lifted up and impaled on it; and his house is to be reduced to rubble for this offense. *12*And may the God who causes his name to dwell there overthrow every king or people who may undertake to alter this or to destroy this house of God in Jerusalem. I, Darius, have issued this decree; let it be carefully executed.''

*13*Then Tattenai, the governor of West-of-Euphrates, and Shethar-bozenai, and their fellow officials carried out fully the instructions King Darius had sent them. *14*The elders of the Jews continued to make progress in the building, supported by the message of the prophets, Haggai and Zechariah, son of Iddo. They finished the building according to the command of the God of Israel and the decrees of Cyrus and Darius [and of Artaxerxes, king of Persia]. *15*They completed this house on the third day of the month Adar, in the sixth year of the reign of King Darius. *16*The Israelites—priests, Levites, and the other returned exiles—celebrated the dedication of this house of God with joy. *17*For the dedication of this house of God, they offered one hundred bulls, two hundred rams, and four hundred lambs, together with

p: 2-12: Ezr 1, 4-11.

The First Passover in the Rebuilt Temple

As a celebration of God's miraculous deliverance and the formation of the people into a nation, Passover was a powerful symbol of identity. Since some viewed the return as a second Exodus, those who had been exiled and returned clearly would be recognized as part of Israel. The population that remained behind joined the exiled community by separating from the surrounding peoples (6, 21).

twelve he-goats as a sin-offering for all Israel, in keeping with the number of the tribes of Israel. [18]Finally, they set up the priests in their classes and the Levites in their divisions for the service of God in Jerusalem, as is prescribed in the book of Moses.

The Passover. [19q]The exiles kept the Passover on the fourteenth day of the first month. [20]The Levites, every one of whom had purified himself for the occasion, sacrificed the Passover for the rest of the exiles, for their brethren the priests, and for themselves. [21]The Israelites who had returned from the exile partook of it together with all those who had separated themselves from the uncleanness of the peoples of the land to join them in seeking the LORD, the God of Israel.[r] [22]They joyfully kept the feast of Unleavened Bread for seven days, for the LORD had filled them with joy by making the king of Assyria* favorable to them, so that he gave them help in their work on the house of God, the God of Israel.

II: The Deeds of Ezra

CHAPTER 7

See RG
145-47

Ezra the Scribe. [1]After these events,* during the reign of Artaxerxes, king of Persia, Ezra, son of Seraiah, son of Azariah, son of Hilkiah, [2]son of Shallum, son of Zadok, son of Ahitub, [3]son of Amariah, son of Azariah, son of Meraioth, [4]son of Zerahiah, son of Uzzi, son of Bukki, [5]son of Abishua, son of Phinehas, son of Eleazar, son of the high priest Aaron— [6]this Ezra came up from Babylon. He was a scribe, well-versed in the law of Moses which was given by the LORD, the God of Israel. Because the hand of the LORD, his God, was upon him, the king granted him all that he requested.[s]

[7]Some of the Israelites and some priests, Levites, singers, gatekeepers, and temple slaves also came up to Jerusalem in the seventh year of King Artaxerxes. [8]Ezra came to Jerusalem in the fifth month of that seventh year of the king. [9]On the first day of the first month he resolved on the journey up from Babylon, and on the first day of the fifth month he arrived at Jerusalem, for the favoring hand of his God was upon him. [10]Ezra had set his heart on the study and practice of the law of the LORD and on teaching statutes and ordinances in Israel.[t]

The Decree of Artaxerxes. [11]This is a copy of the rescript which King Artaxerxes gave to Ezra the priest-scribe, the scribe of the text of the LORD's commandments and statutes for Israel:

[12u]"Artaxerxes, king of kings, to Ezra the priest, scribe of the law of the God of heaven (then, after greetings): [13]I have issued this decree, that anyone in my kingdom belonging to the people of Israel, its priests or Levites, who is minded to go up to Jerusalem with you, may do so. [14]You are the envoy from the king and his seven counselors to supervise Judah and Jerusalem in respect of the law of your God which is in your possession, [15]and to bring with you the silver and gold which the king and

6, 22: Assyria: used here in a broad sense for the Persian Empire.

7, 1-8: The date of Ezra's journey to Palestine is not known with certainty. The seventh year of King Artaxerxes I would be 458 B.C., and the present order of the text suggests that date. The narratives of Ezra and Nehemiah make it seem to many, however, that the arrival of Nehemiah in 445 B.C. should precede that of Ezra. If so, Ezra may be thought to have come in 398 B.C., the seventh year of King Artaxerxes II. Others argue for the thirty-seventh year of Artaxerxes I, that is, 428 B.C.; this would suppose that the date given in the text has suffered in transmission.

q: 19-22: Ex 12, 1-20.   r: Ps 47, 9.   s: Ezr 7, 28; 8, 18; Neh 2, 8. 13.   t: Ps 119, 45.   u: 12-17: Ezr 1, 2ff.

The Narrator's Introduction of Ezra

Ezra's long pedigree (7, 1–6) establishes his credentials as priest of the most distinguished line and scribe—two roles that will account for his stature and acceptance within the Jewish community. Ezra's goals of studying, teaching, and implementing the Torah (v. 10) account for his subsequent actions.

his counselors have freely contributed to the God of Israel, whose dwelling is in Jerusalem, ¹⁶as well as all the silver and gold which you may receive throughout the province of Babylon, together with the free-will offerings which the people and priests freely contribute for the house of their God in Jerusalem. ¹⁷You must take care, therefore, to use this money to buy bulls, rams, lambs, and the cereal offerings and libations proper to these, and offer them on the altar of the house of your God in Jerusalem. ¹⁸You and your brethren may do whatever seems best to you with the remainder of the silver and gold, conformably to the will of your God. ¹⁹The utensils consigned to you for the service of the house of your God you are to deposit before the God of Jerusalem. ²⁰Whatever else you may be required to supply for the needs of the house of your God, you may draw from the royal treasury. ²¹I, Artaxerxes the king, issue this decree to all the treasurers of West-of-Euphrates: Whatever Ezra the priest, scribe of the law of the God of heaven, requests of you, dispense to him accurately, ²²within these limits: silver, one hundred talents; wheat, one hundred kors; wine, one hundred baths; oil, one hundred baths; salt, without limit. ²³Let everything that is ordered by the God of heaven be carried out exactly for the house of the God of heaven, that wrath may not come upon the realm of the king and his sons. ²⁴We also inform you that it is not permitted to impose taxes, tributes, or tolls on any priest, Levite, singer, gatekeeper, temple slave, or any other servant of that house of God.

²⁵"As for you, Ezra, in accordance with the wisdom of your God* which is in your possession, appoint magistrates and judges to administer justice to all the people in West-of-Euphrates, to all, that is, who know the laws of your God. Instruct those who do not know these laws.^y ²⁶Whoever does not obey the law of your God and the law of the king, let strict judgment be executed upon him, whether death, or corporal punishment, or a fine on his goods, or imprisonment."

Ezra and His Companions. ²⁷Blessed be the LORD, the God of our fathers, who thus disposed the mind of the king to glorify the house of the LORD in Jerusalem, ²⁸and who let me find favor with the king, with his counselors, and with all the most influential royal officials. I therefore took courage and, with the hand of the LORD, my God, upon me, I gathered together Israelite family heads to make the return journey with me.^w

CHAPTER 8

See RG 145–47

¹This is the list of the family heads who returned with me from Babylon during the reign of King Artaxerxes:

²Of the sons of Phinehas, Gershon; of the sons of Ithamar, Daniel; of the sons of David, Hattush, ³son of Shecaniah; of the sons of Parosh, Zechariah, and with him one hundred and fifty males were enrolled; ⁴of the sons of Pahath-moab, Eliehoenai, son of Zerahiah, and with him two hundred males; ⁵of the sons of Zattu, Shecaniah, son of Jahaziel, and with him three hundred males; ⁶of the sons of Adin, Ebed, son of Jonathan, and with him fifty males; ⁷of the sons of Elam, Jeshaiah, son of Athaliah, and with him seventy males; ⁸of the sons of Shephatiah, Zebadiah, son of Michael, and with him eighty males; ⁹of the sons of Joab, Obadiah, son of Jehiel, and with him two hundred and eighteen males; ¹⁰of the sons of Bani, Shelomith, son of Josiphiah, and with him one hundred and sixty males; ¹¹of the sons of Bebai, Zechariah, son of Bebai, and with

---

7, 25: The wisdom of your God: the Mosaic law; cf vv 6, 14.

v: 2 Chr 17, 9.   w: Ezr 7, 6.

At first reading the statement in 6, 14 that the Israelites finished their building under the decrees of Kings Cyrus, Darius, and Artaxerxes seems incorrect; the physical temple was completed in the reign of Darius and Artaxerxes had nothing to do with it. However, the formation of the "house of God" (6, 16) involved not only rebuilding the temple, but also rebuilding the city and separating the community from the surrounding peoples by prohibiting intermarriages. These later steps, under reformers Ezra and Nehemiah, occurred in the time of Artaxerxes.

him twenty-eight males; [12] of the sons of Azgad, Johanan, son of Hakkatan, and with him one hundred and ten males; [13] of the sons of Adonikam, younger sons, whose names were Eliphelet, Jeiel, and Shemaiah, and with them sixty males; [14] of the sons of Bigvai, Uthai, son of Zakkur, and with him seventy males.

The Journey to Jerusalem. [15] I had them assemble by the river that flows toward Ahava,* where we made camp for three days. There I perceived that both laymen and priests were present, but I could not discover a single Levite. [16] Therefore I sent Eliezer, Ariel, Shemaiah, Jarib, Elnathan, Nathan, Zechariah, and Meshullam, wise leaders, [17] with a command for Iddo, the leader in the place Casiphia, instructing them what to say to Iddo and his brethren, and to the temple slaves in Casiphia, in order to procure for us ministers for the house of our God. [18] They sent to us—for the favoring hand of our God was upon us—a well-instructed man, one of the sons of Mahli, son of Levi, son of Israel, namely Sherebiah, with his sons and brethren, eighteen men.[x] [19] They also sent us Hashabiah, and with him Jeshaiah, sons of Merari, and their brethren and their sons, twenty men. [20] Of the temple slaves (those whom David and the princes appointed to serve the Levites) there were two hundred and twenty. All these men were enrolled by name.[y]

[21] Then I proclaimed a fast, there by the river of Ahava, that we might humble ourselves before our God to petition from him a safe journey for ourselves, our children, and all our possessions. [22] For I would have been ashamed to ask the king for troops and horsemen to protect us against enemies along the way, since we had said to the king, "The favoring hand of our God is upon all who seek him, but his mighty wrath is against all who forsake him."[z] [23] So we fasted, and prayed to our God for this, and our petition was granted. [24] Next I selected twelve of the priestly leaders along with Sherebiah, Hashabiah, and ten of their brethren, [25] and I weighed out before them the silver and the gold and the utensils offered for the house of our God by the king, his counselors, his officials, and all the Israelites of that region. I consigned it to them in these amounts: [26] silver, six hundred and fifty talents; silver utensils, one hundred; gold, one hundred talents; [27] twenty golden bowls valued at a thousand darics; two vases of excellent polished bronze, as precious as gold. [28] I addressed them in these words: "You are consecrated to the LORD, and the utensils are also consecrated; the silver and the gold are a free-will offering to the LORD, the God of your fathers. [29] Keep good watch over them till you weigh them out in Jerusalem in the presence of the chief priests and Levites and the family leaders of Israel, in the chambers of the house of the LORD." [30] The priests and the Levites then took over the silver, the gold, and the utensils that had been weighed out, to bring them to Jerusalem, to the house of our God.

[31] We set out for Jerusalem from the river of Ahava on the twelfth day of the first month. The hand of our God remained upon us, and he protected us from enemies and bandits along the way. [32] Thus we arrived at Jerusalem, where we first rested for three days. [33] On the fourth day, the silver, the gold, and the utensils were weighed out in the house of

8, 15: Ahava: a town at an unidentified site in Babylonia. The river that flowed toward it was probably a branch or canal of the Euphrates.

x: Ezr 7, 6.   y: Ezr 2, 43.   z: Neh 2, 9.

The Crisis of Mixed Marriages

The crisis in this second stage of reconstruction comes when men, including Jewish leaders, marry foreign women (9, 1–2). To ensure survival as a small minority in the midst of surrounding cultures, Ezra advocates this not be allowed.

our God and consigned to the priest Meremoth, son of Uriah, who was assisted by Eleazar, son of Phinehas; they were assisted by the Levites Jozabad, son of Jeshua, and Noadiah, son of Binnui. *34*Everything was in order as to number and weight, and the total weight was registered. At that same time, *35*those who had returned from the captivity, the exiles, offered as holocausts to the God of Israel twelve bulls for all Israel, ninety-six rams, seventy-seven lambs, and twelve goats as sin-offerings: all these as a holocaust to the LORD. *36*Finally, the orders of the king were presented to the king's satraps and to the governors in West-of-Euphrates, who gave their support to the people and to the house of God.*

See RG 145–47

CHAPTER 9

Denunciation of Mixed Marriages. *1a*When these matters had been concluded, the leaders approached me with this report: "Neither the Israelite laymen nor the priests nor the Levites have kept themselves aloof from the peoples of the land and their abominations [Canaanites, Hittites, Perizzites, Jebusites, Ammonites, Moabites, Egyptians, and Amorites]; *2*for they have taken some of their daughters as wives for themselves and their sons, and thus they have desecrated the holy race with the peoples of the land. Furthermore, the leaders and rulers have taken a leading part in this apostasy!"

Ezra's Exhortation. *3*When I had heard this thing, I tore my cloak and my mantle, plucked hair from my head and beard, and sat there stupefied.*b* *4*Around me gathered all who were in dread of the sentence of the God of Israel on this apostasy of the exiles, while I remained motionless until the evening sacrifice.*c* *5*Then,

at the time of the evening sacrifice, I rose in my wretchedness, and with cloak and mantle torn I fell on my knees, stretching out my hands to the LORD, my God.

*6*I said: "My God, I am too ashamed and confounded to raise my face to you, O my God, for our wicked deeds are heaped up above our heads and our guilt reaches up to heaven.*d* *7*From the time of our fathers even to this day great has been our guilt, and for our wicked deeds we have been delivered over, we and our kings and our priests, to the will of the kings of foreign lands, to the sword, to captivity, to pillage, and to disgrace, as is the case today.

8"And now, but a short time ago, mercy came to us from the LORD, our God, who left us a remnant and gave us a stake in his holy place; thus our God has brightened our eyes and given us relief in our servitude.*e* *9*For slaves we are, but in our servitude our God has not abandoned us; rather, he has turned the good will of the kings of Persia toward us. Thus he has given us new life to raise again the house of our God and restore its ruins, and has granted us a fence in Judah and Jerusalem.*f* *10*But now, O our God, what can we say after all this? For we have abandoned your commandments, *11*which you gave through your servants the prophets: the land which you are entering to take as your possession is a land unclean with the filth of the peoples of the land, with the abominations with which they have filled it from one end to the other in their uncleanness.*g* *12*Do not, then, give your daughters to their sons in marriage, and do not take their daughters for your sons. Never promote their peace and prosperity; thus you will

8, 36: The story of Ezra's mission is seemingly continued from this point by Neh 7, 72b—8, 18, which may be read before Ezr 9, 1.

9, 7: After this verse, the next part of the prayer attributed to Ezra is perhaps to be found in Neh 9, 6-37, which may be

read as leading up to Ezr 9, 8-15.

a: 1f: Dt 7, 1; Neh 9, 2.   *b:* Ps 119, 136.   *c:* Is 66, 2.   *d:* Ps 38, 4.   *e:* Is 4, 3.   *f:* Ps 106, 46.   *g:* Lv 18, 24f; Ez 36, 17.

Ezra's Prayer

More a sermon than a confession, the prayer in 9, 5–15 teaches values and history to alter community behavior. Like the prophets and the deuteronomistic history, Ezra interprets Israel's political devastation as the consequence of religious and moral failings by Israel and uses the fear of a recurrence to motivate the community.

grow strong, enjoy the produce of the land, and leave it as an inheritance to your children forever.[h]

[13]"After all that has come upon us for our evil deeds and our great guilt—though you, our God, have made less of our sinfulness than it deserved and have allowed us to survive as we do— [14]shall we again violate your commandments by intermarrying with these abominable peoples? Would you not become so angered with us as to destroy us without remnant or survivor? [15]O LORD, God of Israel, you are just; yet we have been spared, the remnant we are today. Here we are before you in our sins. Because of all this, we can no longer stand in your presence."

CHAPTER 10

See RG 145–47 *The People's Response.* [1]While Ezra prayed and acknowledged their guilt, weeping and prostrate before the house of God, a very large assembly of Israelites gathered about him, men, women, and children; and the people wept profusely. [2]Then Shecaniah, the son of Jehiel, one of the sons of Elam, made this appeal to Ezra: "We have indeed betrayed our God by taking as wives foreign women of the peoples of the land. Yet even now there remains a hope for Israel. [3]Let us therefore enter into a covenant before our God to dismiss all our foreign wives and the children born of them, in keeping with what you, my lord, advise, and those who fear the commandments of our God. Let the law be observed!

[4]Rise, then, for this is your duty! We will stand by you, so have courage and take action!"

[5]Ezra rose to his feet and demanded an oath from the chiefs of the priests, from the Levites and from all Israel that they would do as had been proposed; and they swore it. [6]Then Ezra retired from his place before the house of God and entered the chamber of Johanan, son of Eliashib,[*] where he spent the night neither eating food nor drinking water, for he was in mourning over the betrayal by the exiles. [7]A proclamation was made throughout Judah and Jerusalem that all the exiles should gather together in Jerusalem, [8]and that whoever failed to appear within three days would, according to the judgment of the leaders and elders, suffer the confiscation of all his possessions, and himself be excluded from the assembly of the exiles.

[9]All the men of Judah and Benjamin gathered together in Jerusalem within the three-day period: it was in the ninth month,[*] on the twentieth day of the month. All the people, standing in the open place before the house of God, were trembling both over the matter at hand and because it was raining. [10]Then Ezra, the priest, stood up and said to them: "Your unfaithfulness in taking foreign women as wives has added to Israel's guilt. [11]But now, give praise to the LORD, the God of your fathers, and do his will: separate yourselves from the peoples of the land and from these foreign women."[i] [12]In answer, the whole

10, 6: Johanan, son of Eliashib: actually, the grandson of Eliashib; the father of Johanan was Eliashib's son Joiada (Neh 12, 10f. 22). Since Eliashib was high priest at the time of Nehemiah (Neh 3, 1. 20f; 13, 4. 7) and Johanan, if not yet high priest, was at least old enough to have his own separate quarters (chamber) in the temple at the time of Ezra, it is practically certain that Nehemiah's activity in Jerusalem must have preceded that of Ezra.

10, 9: Ninth month: Chislev (November–December), during the "early rains" in Palestine. Since the assembly took place in the open . . . all the people . . . were trembling . . . because it was raining.

h: Dt 7, 3. i: Neh 9, 2.

Results: Compliance with Communal Decision

The issue of mixed marriages constitutes the first test of the new, legal status of the Torah, illustrating how an ancient book may shape the present and future through communal interpretive process. Verses 18–19 give an explicit report that the high priest's most powerful family fully complied with the communal decision. Given the power of that family over the community, its cooperation and compliance signal a crucial victory for this process.

assembly cried out with a loud voice: "Yes, it is our duty to do as you say! *13*But the people are numerous and it is the rainy season, so that we cannot remain out-of-doors; besides, this is not a task that can be performed in a single day or even two, for those of us who have sinned in this regard are many. *14*Let our leaders represent the whole assembly; then let all those in our cities who have taken foreign women for wives appear at appointed times, accompanied by the elders and magistrates of each city in question, till we have turned away from us our God's burning anger over this affair." *15*Only Jonathan, son of Asahel, and Jahzeiah, son of Tikvah, were against this proposal, with Meshullam and Shabbethai the Levite supporting them.

The Guilty. *16**The exiles did as agreed. Ezra appointed as his assistants men who were family heads, one for each family, all of them designated by name. They held sessions to examine the matter, beginning with the first day of the tenth month. *17*By the first day of the first month they had passed judgment on all the men who had taken foreign women for wives.

*18*Among the priests, the following were found to have taken foreign women for wives: Of the sons of Jeshua, son of Jozadak, and his brethren: Maaseiah, Eliezer, Jarib, and Gedaliah. *19*They pledged themselves to dismiss their wives, and as a guilt-offering for their guilt they gave a ram from the flock. *20*Of the sons of Immer: Hanani and Zebadiah; *21*of the sons of Harim: Maaseiah, Elijah, Shemaiah, Jehiel, and Uzziah; *22*of the

sons of Pashhur: Elioenai, Maaseiah, Ishmael, Nethanel, Jozabad, and Elasah.

*23*Of the Levites: Jozabad, Shemei, Kelaiah (also called Kelita), Pethahiah, Judah, and Eliezer.*j*

*24*Of the singers: Eliashib and Zakkur; of the gatekeepers: Shallum, Telem, and Uri.

*25*Among the other Israelites: Of the sons of Parosh: Ramiah, Izziah, Malchijah, Mijamin, Eleazar, Malchijah, and Benaiah; *26*of the sons of Elam: Mattaniah, Zechariah, Jehiel, Abdi, Jeremoth, and Elijah; *27*of the sons of Zattu: Elioenai, Eliashib, Mattaniah, Jeremoth, Zabad, and Aziza; *28*of the sons of Bebai: Jehohanan, Hananiah, Zabbai, and Athlai; *29*of the sons of Bani: Meshullam, Malluch, Adaiah, Jashub, Sheal, and Jeremoth; *30*of the sons of Pahath-moab: Adna, Chelal, Benaiah, Maaseiah, Mattaniah, Bezalel, Binnui, and Manasseh; *31*of the sons of Harim: Eliezer, Isshijah, Malchijah, Shemaiah, Shimeon, *32*Benjamin, Malluch, Shemariah; *33*of the sons of Hashum: Mattenai, Mattattah, Zabad, Eliphelet, Jeremai, Manasseh, Shimei; *34*of the sons of Begui: Maadai, Amram, Uel, *35*Benaiah, Bedeiah, Cheluhi, *36*Vaniah, Meremoth, Eliashib, *37*Mattaniah, Mattenai, and Jaasu; *38*of the sons of Binnui: Shimei, *39*Shelemiah, Nathan, and Adaiah; *40*of the sons of Zachai: Shashai, Sharai, *41*Azarel, Shelemiah, Shemariah, *42*Shallum, Amariah, Joseph; *43*of the sons of Nebo: Jeiel, Mattithiah, Zabad, Zebina, Jaddai, Joel, Benaiah.

*44*All these had taken foreign wives; but they sent them away, both the women and their children.*

10, 16f: The work of the committee lasted three months, from the first day of the tenth month, Tebet (December–January), to the first day of the first month, Nisan (March–April), of the following Jewish year.

10, 44: The account of the problem of mixed marriages at

the time of Ezra is continued in Neh 9, 1-5; this may be read immediately after Ezr 10, 44, though the date given in Neh 9, 1 fits more precisely after Ezr 10, 15; cf Hg 2, 10-14.

j: Neh 8, 7; 10, 1.

The Book of Nehemiah

Problems common to the combined Books Ezra-Nehemiah have been pointed out in the Introduction to the Book of Ezra. The achievements of the two men were complementary; each helped to make it possible for Judaism to maintain its identity during the difficult days of the Restoration. Nehemiah was the man of action who rebuilt the walls of Jerusalem and introduced necessary administrative reforms. Ezra in turn was the great religious reformer who succeeded in establishing the Torah as the constitution of the returned community.

The biblical sources for Nehemiah's life and work are the autobiographical portions scattered through the book. They are called the "Memoirs of Nehemiah," and have been used more extensively and effectively by "the Chronicler" than the "Memoirs of Ezra." No competent scholar questions the authenticity of Nehemiah's memoirs. From these and other sources, the picture emerges of a man dedicated to the single purpose of the welfare of his people. Despite temperamental shortcomings, Nehemiah was a man of good practical sense combined with deep faith in God. In view of his selfless service to a community capable of severely testing any leader, we can be indulgent toward his numerous appeals to God to credit him with the work he had done. Nehemiah was a layman, and his generous dedication of talents to the service of God and of God's people remains an example of undiminished force for laymen today.

The Book of Nehemiah is divided as follows:

I: The Deeds of Nehemiah (1, 1—7, 72).

II: Promulgation of the Law (8, 1—13, 31).

I: The Deeds of Nehemiah

CHAPTER 1

Nehemiah's Vocation. [1]The words of Nehemiah, the son of Hacaliah.*

In the month Chislev of the twentieth year, I was in the citadel of Susa [2]when Hanani, one of my brothers, came with other men from Judah. I asked them about the Jews, the remnant preserved after the captivity, and about Jerusalem, [3]and they answered me: "The survivors of the captivity there in the province are in great distress and under reproach. Also, the wall of Jerusalem lies breached, and its gates have been gutted with fire." [4]When I heard this report, I began to weep and continued mourning for several days; I fasted and prayed before the God of heaven.

[5]I prayed: "O LORD, God of heaven, great and awesome God, you who preserve your covenant of mercy toward those who love you and keep your commandments,[a] [6]may your ear be attentive, and your eyes open, to heed the prayer which I, your servant, now offer in your presence day and night for your servants the Israelites, confessing the sins which we of Israel have committed against you, I and my father's house included.[b] [7]Grievously have we offended you, not keeping the commandments, the statutes, and the ordinances which you committed to your servant Moses.[c] [8]But remember, I pray, the promise which you gave through Moses, your servant, when you said:[d] 'Should you prove faithless, I will scatter you among the nations; [9]but should you return to me and carefully keep my commandments, even though your outcasts have been driven to the farthest corner of the world, I will gather them from there, and bring them back to the place which I have chosen as the dwelling place for my name.' [10]They are your servants, your people, whom you freed by your great might and your strong hand.[e] [11]O LORD, may your ear be attentive to my prayer and that of all your willing servants who revere your name. Grant success to your servant this

1, 1: The first mission of Nehemiah, from the twentieth year of Artaxerxes I, lasted from the spring (Neh 2, 1) of 445 B.C. until 433 B.C. (Neh 5, 14). It is recounted in Neh 1, 1—6, 15; 12, 27-43; 6, 16—7, 5; 11, 1-21, which may be read in that order.

a: Dt 7, 9. 12; Dn 9, 4. b: 2 Chr 6, 40. c: Dn 3, 29f. d: 8f: Dt 30, 1-5. e: Dt 9, 29.

N ehemiah opens with a first-person narrative relating his concerns over Jerusalem and the Persian monarch's appointment of him as governor over the province. The bulk of the account covers the various incidents of Nehemiah's rule as governor as he attempted to rebuild the walls of Jerusalem.

day, and let him find favor with this man"— for I was cupbearer to the king.*f

See RG 148

CHAPTER 2

Appointment by the King. ¹In the month Nisan of the twentieth year of King Artaxerxes, when the wine was in my charge, I took some and offered it to the king. As I had never before been sad in his presence, ²the king asked me, "Why do you look sad? If you are not sick, you must be sad at heart." Though I was seized with great fear, ³I answered the king: "May the king live forever! How could I not look sad when the city where my ancestors are buried lies in ruins, and its gates have been eaten out by fire?" ⁴The king asked me, "What is it, then, that you wish?" I prayed to the God of heaven ⁵and then answered the king: "If it please the king, and if your servant is deserving of your favor, send me to Judah, to the city of my ancestors' graves, to rebuild it." ⁶Then the king, and the queen seated beside him, asked me how long my journey would take and when I would return. I set a date that was acceptable to him, and the king agreed that I might go.

⁷I asked the king further: "If it please the king, let letters be given to me for the governors of West-of-Euphrates, that they may afford me safe-conduct till I arrive in Judah; ⁸also

a letter for Asaph, the keeper of the royal park, that he may give me wood for timbering the gates of the temple-citadel and for the city wall and the house that I shall occupy." The king granted my requests, for the favoring hand of my God was upon me.g ⁹Thus I proceeded to the governors of West-of-Euphrates and presented the king's letters to them. The king also sent with me army officers and cavalry.h

¹⁰When Sanballat the Horonite* and Tobiah the Ammonite slave had heard of this, they were very much displeased that someone had come to seek the welfare of the Israelites.

Circuit of the City. ¹¹When I had arrived in Jerusalem, I first rested there for three days. ¹²Then I set out by night with only a few other men (for I had not told anyone what my God had inspired me to do for Jerusalem) and with no other animals but my own mount. ¹³*I rode out at night by the Valley Gate, passed by the Dragon Spring, and came to the Dung Gate, observing how the walls of Jerusalem lay in ruins and its gates had been eaten out by fire. ¹⁴Then I passed over to the Spring Gate and to the King's Pool. Since there was no room here for my mount to pass with me astride, ¹⁵I continued on foot up the wadi by night, inspecting the wall all the while till I once more reached the Valley Gate, by which I went back in. ¹⁶The magistrates knew

1, 11: Cupbearer to the king: an important official in the royal household. Because Nehemiah could appear in the queen's presence (Neh 2, 6), it is commonly presumed that he was a eunuch; but this is not necessarily so.

2, 10: Sanballat the Horonite: the governor of the province of Samaria (Neh 3, 33f), apparently a native of one of the Bethhorons. A letter from the Jews living at Elephantine in southern Egypt, dated 408–407 B.C., mentions "Delayah and Shelemyah, the sons of Sanballat, the governor of Samaria." Although his own name was Babylonian—Sin-uballit, i.e., "Sin (the moon god) has given life"—two sons had names referring to Yahweh. Tobiah, the Ammonite slave: the governor of the province of Ammon in Transjordan. His honorary title, "servant" (in Hebrew, ebed), i.e., of the king, could also be understood as slave, and Nehemiah no doubt meant it in this derogatory sense. The Tobiads remained a powerful family even in Maccabean times (2 Mc 3, 11). Sanballat and Tobiah

together with Geshem the Arab (Neh 2, 19; 6, 1f), who was probably in charge of Edom and the regions to the south and southeast of Judah, opposed the rebuilding of Jerusalem's walls on political grounds; the city was the capital of a rival province.

2, 13ff: Nehemiah left Jerusalem by the Valley Gate near the northwestern end of the old City of David and went south down the Tyropoean Valley toward the Dragon Spring (or the En-rogel of Jos 15, 7; 18, 16; 2 Sm 17, 17; 1 Kgs 1, 9, now known as Job's Well) at the juncture of the Valley of Hinnom and the Kidron Valley; he then turned north at the Dung Gate (or the Potsherd Gate of Jer 19, 2) at the southern end of the city and proceeded up the wadi, that is, the Kidron Valley, passing the Spring Gate (at the Spring of Gihon) and the King's Pool (unidentified); finally he turned west and then south to his starting point.

f: Ps 118, 25.   g: Ezr 7, 6.   h: Ezr 8, 22.

nothing of where I had gone or what I was doing, for as yet I had disclosed nothing to the Jews, neither to the priests, nor to the nobles, nor to the magistrates, nor to the others who would be concerned about the matter.

Rebuilding Jerusalem's Walls. *17*Afterward I said to them: "You see the evil plight in which we stand: how Jerusalem lies in ruins and its gates have been gutted by fire. Come, let us rebuild the wall of Jerusalem, so that we may no longer be an object of derision!" *18*Then I explained to them how the favoring hand of my God had rested upon me, and what the king had said to me. They replied, "Let us be up and building!" And they undertook the good work with vigor.*i*

*19*On hearing of this, Sanballat the Horonite, Tobiah the Ammonite slave, and Geshem the Arab mocked us and ridiculed us. "What is this that you are about?" they asked. "Are you rebelling against the king?" *20*My answer to them was this: "It is the God of heaven who will grant us success. We, his servants, shall set about the rebuilding; but for you there is to be neither share nor claim nor memorial* in Jerusalem.'"

CHAPTER 3

See RG 148

List of Workers.* *1*Eliashib the high priest and his priestly brethren took up the task of rebuilding the Sheep Gate. They timbered it and set up its doors, its bolts, and its bars, then continued the rebuilding to the Tower of Hananel.*j* *2*At their side the men of Jericho were rebuilding, and next to them was Zaccur, son of Imri. *3*The Fish Gate was rebuilt by the sons of Hassenaah; they timbered it and set up its doors, its bolts, and its bars.*k* *4*At their side Meremoth, son of Uriah, son of Hakkoz, carried out the work of repair; next to him was Meshullam, son of Berechiah, son of Meshezabel; and next to him was Zadok, son of Baana. *5*Next to him the Tekoites carried out the work of repair; however, some of

their outstanding men would not submit to the labor asked by their lords. *6*The New City Gate was repaired by Joiada, son of Paseah; and Meshullam, son of Besodeiah; they timbered it and set up its doors, its bolts, and its bars. *7*At their side were Melatiah the Gibeonite, Jadon the Meronothite, and the men of Gibeon and of Mizpah, who were under the jurisdiction of the governor of West-of-Euphrates. *8*Next to them the work of repair was carried out by Uzziel, son of Harhaiah, a member of the goldsmiths' guild, and at his side was Hananiah, one of the perfumers' guild. They restored Jerusalem as far as the wall of the public square.* *9*Next to them the work of repair was carried out by Rephaiah, son of Hur, leader of half the district of Jerusalem, *10*and at his side was Jedaiah, son of Harumaph, who repaired opposite his own house. Next to him Hattush, son of Hashabneiah, carried out the work of repair. *11*The adjoining sector, as far as the Oven Tower, was repaired by Malchijah, son of Harim, and Hasshub, of Pahath-moab. *12*At their side the work of repair was carried out by Shallum, son of Hallohesh, leader of half the district of Jerusalem, by himself and his daughters. *13*The Valley Gate was repaired by Hanun and the inhabitants of Zanoah; they rebuilt it and set up its doors, its bolts, and its bars. They also repaired a thousand cubits of the wall up to the Dung Gate. *14*The Dung Gate was repaired by Malchijah, son of Rechab, leader of the district of Beth-haccherem; he rebuilt it and set up its doors, its bolts, and its bars. *15*The Spring Gate was repaired by Shallum, son of Colhozeh, leader of the district of Mizpah; he rebuilt it, roofed it over, and set up its doors, its bolts, and its bars. He also repaired the wall of the Aqueduct Pool near the king's garden as far as the steps that lead down from the City of David. *16*After him, the work of repair was carried out by Nehemiah, son of Azbuk, leader of half the district of Beth-zur, to

---

2, 20: Neither share nor claim nor memorial: although Sanballat and Tobiah were Yahwist, Nehemiah would not let them participate in any of the rights of the religious community in Jerusalem.

3, 1-32: The construction work on the gates and walls of the city is described in counterclockwise direction, beginning and ending at the Sheep Gate (to the north of the temple). The ex-

act sites of many of the topographical points mentioned are uncertain.

3, 8: Wall of the public square: that is, the section of wall bounding the place of assembly outside the Gate of Ephraim, or New City Gate; cf Neh 3, 6; 8, 16.

i: Ezr 7, 6.   *j:* Jer 31, 38.   *k:* Ezr 2, 35; Zep 1, 10.

The Community Organizes to Rebuild

Chapter 3 marks the center point of the combined work Ezra-Nehemiah and places the emphasis squarely on the community's efforts. While having "the hand of God" (2, 8) on them marks Ezra and Nehemiah, the heroes of the narrative are the community members, elaborated in various lists, who willingly undertake the formation of the "house of God."

a place opposite the tombs of David, as far as the artificial pool and the barracks.

*17*After him, the Levites carried out the work of repair: Rehum, son of Bani. Next to him, for his own district, was Hashabiah, leader of half the district of Keilah. *18*After him, their brethren carried out the work of repair: Binnui, son of Henadad, leader of half the district of Keilah; *19*next to him Ezer, son of Jeshua, leader of Mizpah, who repaired the adjoining sector, the Corner, opposite the ascent to the arsenal. *20*After him, Baruch, son of Zabbai, repaired the adjoining sector from the Corner to the entrance of the house of Eliashib, the high priest. *21*After him, Meremoth, son of Uriah, son of Hakkoz, repaired the adjoining sector from the entrance of Eliashib's house to the end of the house.

*22*After him, the work of repair was carried out by the priests, men of the surrounding country. *23*After them, Benjamin and Hasshub carried out the repair in front of their houses; after them, Azariah, son of Maaseiah, son of Ananiah, made the repairs alongside his house. *24*After him, Binnui, son of Henadad, repaired the adjoining sector from the house of Azariah to the Corner [that is, to the Angle]. *25*After him, Palal, son of Uzai, carried out the work of repair opposite the Corner and the tower projecting from the Upper Palace at the quarters of the guard. After him, Pedaiah, son of Parosh, carried out the work of repair *26*to a point opposite the Water Gate on the east, and the projecting tower. *27*After him, the Tekoites repaired the adjoining sector opposite the great projecting tower, to the wall of Ophel [the temple slaves were dwelling on Ophel].

*28*Above the Horse Gate the priests carried out the work of repair, each before his own house. *29*After them Zadok, son of Immer, carried out the repair before his house, and after him the repair was carried out by Shemaiah, son of Shecaniah, keeper of the East Gate.*l* *30*After him, Hananiah, son of Shelemiah, and Hanun, the sixth son of Zalaph, repaired the adjoining sector; after them, Meshullam, son of Berechiah, repaired the place opposite his own lodging. *31*After him, Malchijah, a member of the goldsmiths' guild, carried out the work of repair as far as the quarters of the temple slaves and the merchants, before the Gate of Inspection and as far as the upper chamber of the Angle. *32*Between the upper chamber of the Angle and the Sheep Gate, the goldsmiths and the merchants carried out the work of repair.

Opposition from Judah's Foes. *33*When Sanballat heard that we were rebuilding the wall, it roused his anger and he became very much incensed. He ridiculed the Jews, *34*saying in the presence of his brethren and the troops of Samaria: "What are these miserable Jews trying to do? Will they complete their restoration in a single day? Will they recover these stones, burnt as they are, from the heaps of dust?" *35*Tobiah the Ammonite was beside him, and he said: "It is a rubble heap they are building. Any fox that attacked it would breach their wall of stones!" *36*Take note, O our God, how we were mocked! Turn back their derision upon their own heads and let them be carried away to a land of captivity! *37*Hide not their crime and let not their sin be blotted out in your sight, for they insulted the builders to their face!*m* *38*We, however, continued to build the wall, which was soon filled in and completed up to half its height. The people worked with a will.

l: Ezr 40, 6.   *m*: Jer 18, 23.

See RG
148

CHAPTER 4

*1*When Sanballat, Tobiah, the Arabs, the Ammonites, and the Ashdodites heard that the restoration of the walls of Jerusalem was progressing—for the gaps were beginning to be closed up—they became extremely angry. *2*Thereupon they all plotted together to come and fight against Jerusalem and thus to throw us into confusion. *3*We prayed to our God and posted a watch against them day and night for fear of what they might do. *4*Meanwhile the Judahites were saying:

"Slackened is the bearers' strength,
   there is no end to the rubbish;
Never shall we be able
   the wall to rebuild."

*5*Our enemies thought, "Before they are aware of it or see us, we shall come into their midst, kill them, and put an end to the work." *6*When the Jews who lived near them had come to us from one place after another, and had told us ten times over that they were about to attack us, *7*I stationed guards down below, behind the wall, near the exposed points, assigning them by family groups with their swords, their spears, and their bows. *8*I made an inspection, then addressed these words to the nobles, the magistrates, and the rest of the people: "Have no fear of them! Keep in mind the LORD, who is great and to be feared, and fight for your brethren, your sons and daughters, your wives and your homes." *9*When our enemies became aware that we had been warned and that God had upset their plan, we all went back, each to his own task at the wall.

*10*From that time on, however, only half my able men took a hand in the work, while the other half, armed with spears, bucklers, bows, and breastplates, stood guard behind the whole house of Judah*n* *11*as they rebuilt the wall. The load carriers, too, were armed; each did his work with one hand and held a weapon with the other. *12*Every builder, while he worked, had his sword girt at his side. Also, a trumpeter stood beside me, *13*for I had said to the nobles, the magistrates, and the rest of the people: "Our work is scattered and extensive, and we are widely separated from one another along the wall; *14*wherever you hear the trumpet sound, join us there; our God will fight with us." *15*Thus we went on with the work, half of the men with spears at the ready, from daybreak till the stars came out.

*16*At the same time I told the people to spend the nights inside Jerusalem, each man with his own attendant, so that they might serve as a guard by night and a working force by day. *17*Neither I, nor my kinsmen, nor any of my attendants, nor any of the bodyguard that accompanied me took off his clothes; everyone kept his weapon at his right hand.

CHAPTER 5

See RG
148

Antisocial Conduct. *1*Then there rose a great outcry of the common people and their wives against certain of their fellow Jews. *2*Some said: "We are forced to pawn our sons and daughters in order to get grain to eat that we may live." *3*Others said: "We are forced to pawn our fields, our vineyards, and our houses, that we may have grain during the famine." *4*Still others said: "To pay the king's tax we have borrowed money on our fields and our vineyards. *5*And though these are our own kinsmen and our children are as good as theirs, we have had to reduce our sons and daughters to slavery, and violence has been done to some of our daughters! Yet we can do nothing about it, for our fields and our vineyards belong to others."*p*

Nehemiah's Action. *6*I was extremely angry when I heard the reasons they had for complaint. *7*After some deliberation, I called the nobles and magistrates to account, saying to them, "You are exacting interest from your own kinsmen!"* I then rebuked them severely, *8*saying to them: "As far as we were able, we bought back our fellow Jews who had been sold to Gentiles; you, however, are selling your own brothers, to have

---

5, 7: You are exacting interest from your own kinsmen!: contrary to the Mosaic law (Dt 23, 20).

n: Ps 149, 6.   *o:* 1f: Jer 34, 8-22.   *p:* Ez 21, 7; Lv 25, 39.

Economic hardships, including the payment of heavy taxes to the Persian king (5, 4), are made worse by the actions of wealthier members of society who exploit the situation to their own profit. In response, Nehemiah initiates economic reforms. He reforms practices of the wealthy and contributes personally to the economy from his own funds (vv. 11–19).

them bought back by us." They remained silent, for they could find no answer.*q* *9*I continued: "What you are doing is not good. Should you not walk in the fear of our God, and put an end to the derision of our Gentile enemies? *10*I myself, my kinsmen, and my attendants have lent the people money and grain without charge. Let us put an end to this usury! *11*I ask that you return to them this very day their fields, their vineyards, their olive groves, and their houses, together with the interest on the money, the grain, the wine, and the oil that you have lent them." *12*They answered: "We will return everything and exact nothing further from them. We will do just what you ask." Then I called for the priests and had them administer an oath to these men that they would do as they had promised. *13*I also shook out the folds of my garment, saying, "Thus may God shake from his home and his fortune every man who fails to keep this promise, and may he thus be shaken out and emptied!" And the whole assembly answered, "Amen," and praised the LORD. Then the people did as they had promised.

Nehemiah's Lack of Self-Interest. *14*Moreover, from the time that King Artaxerxes appointed me governor in the land of Judah, from his twentieth to his thirty-second year—during these twelve years neither I nor my brethren lived from the governor's allowance. *15*The earlier governors, my predecessors, had laid a heavy burden on the people, taking from them each day forty silver shekels for their food; then too, their men oppressed the people. But I, because I feared God, did not act thus. *16*Moreover, though I had acquired no land of my own, I did my part in this work on the wall, and all my men were gathered there for the work. *17*Though I set my table for a hundred and fifty persons, Jews and magistrates, as well as those who came to us from the nations round about, *18*and though the daily preparations were made at my expense—one beef, six choice muttons, poultry—besides all kinds of wine in abundance every ten days, despite this I did not claim the governor's allowance, for the labor lay heavy upon this people. *19*Keep in mind, O my God, in my favor all that I did for this people.

CHAPTER 6

See RG 148

Plots against Nehemiah. *1*When it had been reported to Sanballat, Tobiah, Geshem the Arab, and our other enemies that I had rebuilt the wall and that there was no breach left in it (though up to that time I had not yet set up the doors in the gates), *2*Sanballat and Geshem sent me this message: "Come, let us hold council together at Caphirim in the plain of Ono." They were planning to do me harm. *3*However, I sent messengers to them with this reply: "I am engaged in a great enterprise and am unable to come down; why should the work stop, while I leave it to come down to you?" *4*Four times they sent me this same proposal, and each time I gave the same reply. *5*Then, the fifth time, Sanballat sent me the same message by one of his servants, who bore an unsealed letter *6*containing this text: "Among the nations it has been reported— Geshem is witness to this—that you and the Jews are planning a rebellion; that for this reason you are rebuilding the wall; and that you are to be their king"—and so on. *7*"Also, that you have set up prophets in Jerusalem to proclaim you king of Judah. Now, since matters like these must reach the ear of the king, come, let us hold council together." *8*I sent him this answer: "Nothing of what you report has taken place; rather, it is the invention of your own mind." *9*They were all trying to frighten

q: Lv 25, 48.

us, thinking, "Their hands will slacken in the work, and it will never be completed." But instead, I now redoubled my efforts.

[10]I went to the house of Shemaiah, son of Delaiah, son of Mehetabel, who was unable to go about, and he said:

"Let us meet in the house of God,
    inside the temple building;
    let us lock the doors of the temple.
For men are coming to kill you;
    by night they are coming coming to
        kill you."

[11]My answer was: "A man like me take flight? Can a man like me enter the temple to save his life? I will not go!" [12]For on consideration it was plain to me that God had not sent him; rather, because Tobiah and Sanballat had bribed him, he voiced this prophecy concerning me [13]that I might act on it out of fear and commit this sin. Then they would have had a shameful story with which to discredit me. [14]Keep in mind Tobiah and Sanballat, O my God, because of these things they did; keep in mind as well Noadiah the prophetess and the other prophets who were trying to frighten me.[r]

Conclusion of the Work. [15]The wall was finished on the twenty-fifth day of Elul;* it had taken fifty-two days. [16]When all our enemies had heard of this, and all the nations round about had taken note of it, our enemies lost much face in the eyes of the nations, for they knew that it was with our God's help that this work had been completed.[s] [17]*At that same time, however, many letters were going to Tobiah from the nobles of Judah, and Tobiah's letters were reaching them, [18]for many in Judah were in league with him, since he was the son-in-law of Shecaniah, son of Arah, and his son Jehohanan had married the daughter of Meshullam, son of Berechiah. [19]Thus they would praise his good deeds in my presence and re-

late to him whatever I said; and Tobiah sent letters trying to frighten me.

CHAPTER 7

See RG 148

[1]When the wall had been rebuilt, I had the doors set up, and the gatekeepers [and the singers and the Levites] were put in charge of them. [2]Over Jerusalem I placed Hanani, my brother, and Hananiah, the commander of the citadel, who was a more trustworthy and God-fearing man than most. [3]I said to them: "The gates of Jerusalem are not to be opened until the sun is hot, and while the sun is still shining they shall shut and bar the doors. Appoint as watchmen the inhabitants of Jerusalem, some at their watch posts, and others before their own houses."

Census of the Province. [4]Now the city was quite wide and spacious, but its population was small, and none of the houses had been rebuilt. [5]When my God had put it into my mind to gather together the nobles, the magistrates, and the common people, and to examine their family records, I came upon the family list of those who had returned in the earliest period. There I found the following written:

[6t]* These are the inhabitants of the province who returned from the captivity of the exiles whom Nebuchadnezzar, king of Babylon, had carried away, and who came back to Jerusalem and Judah, each man to his own city [7](those who returned with Zerubbabel, Jeshua, Nehemiah, Azariah, Raamiah, Nahamani, Mordecai, Bilshan, Mispereth, Bigvai, Nehum, and Baanah).

The census of the men of Israel: [8]sons of Parosh, two thousand one hundred and seventy-two; [9]sons of Shephatiah, three hundred and seventy-two; [10]sons of Arah, six hundred and fifty-two; [11]sons of Pahath-moab who were sons of Jeshua and Joab, two thousand eight hundred and eighteen; [12]sons of Elam, one thousand two hundred and fifty-four; [13]sons of Zattu, eight hundred and forty-five;

6, 15: Elul: the sixth month (August–September). Fifty-two days: according to Josephus (Antiquities XI, v 8), the rebuilding of the walls of Jerusalem by Nehemiah took two years and four months, which seems more probable.

6, 17ff: These verses should be read immediately after v 14.

7, 6-72a: See note on Ezr 2, 1-67.

r: Jer 23, 9-40; Zec 13, 3. s: Ps 118, 22f; 127, 1. t: 6-72: Ezr 2, 1-70.

14sons of Zaccai, seven hundred and sixty; 15sons of Binnui, six hundred and forty-eight; 16sons of Bebai, six hundred and twenty-eight; 17sons of Azgad, two thousand three hundred and twenty-two; 18sons of Adonikam, six hundred and sixty-seven; 19sons of Bigvai, two thousand and sixty-seven; 20sons of Adin, six hundred and fifty-five; 21sons of Ater who were sons of Hezekiah, ninety-eight; 22sons of Hashum, three hundred and twenty-eight; 23sons of Bezai, three hundred and twenty-four; 24sons of Hariph, one hundred and twelve; 25sons of Gibeon, ninety-five; 26men of Bethlehem and Netophah, one hundred and eighty-eight; 27men of Anathoth, one hundred and twenty-eight; 28men of Beth-azmaveth, forty-two; 29men of Kiriath-jearim, Chephirah, and Beeroth, seven hundred and forty-three; 30men of Ramah and Geba, six hundred and twenty-one; 31men of Michmas, one hundred and twenty-two; 32men of Bethel and Ai, one hundred and twenty-three; 33men of Nebo, fifty-two; 34sons of another Elam, one thousand two hundred and fifty-four; 35sons of Harim, three hundred and twenty; 36sons of Jericho, three hundred and forty-five; 37sons of Lod, Hadid, and Ono, seven hundred and twenty-one; 38sons of Senaah, three thousand nine hundred and thirty.

39The priests: sons of Jedaiah who were of the house of Jeshua, nine hundred and seventy-three; 40sons of Immer, one thousand and fifty-two; 41sons of Pashhur, one thousand two hundred and forty-seven; 42sons of Harim, one thousand and seventeen.

43The Levites: sons of Jeshua, Kadmiel, Binnui, Hodeviah, seventy-four.

44The singers: sons of Asaph, one hundred and forty-eight.

45The gatekeepers: sons of Shallum, sons of Ater, sons of Talmon, sons of Akkub, sons of Hatita, sons of Shobai, one hundred and thirty-eight.

46The temple slaves: sons of Ziha, sons of Hasupha, sons of Tabbaoth, 47sons of Keros, sons of Sia, sons of Padon, 48sons of Lebana, sons of Hagaba, sons of Shalmai, 49sons of Hanan, sons of Giddel, sons of Gahar, 50sons of Reaiah, sons of Rezin, sons of Nekoda, 51sons of Gazzam, sons of Uzza, sons of Paseah, 52sons of Besai, sons of the Meunites, sons of the Nephusites, 53sons of Bakbuk, sons of Hakupha, sons of Harhur, 54sons of Bazlith, sons of Mehida, sons of Harsha, 55sons of Barkos, sons of Sisera, sons of Temah, 56sons of Neziah, sons of Hatipha.

57Descendants of the slaves of Solomon: sons of Sotai, sons of Sophereth, sons of Perida, 58sons of Jaala, sons of Darkon, sons of Giddel, 59sons of Shephatiah, sons of Hattil, sons of Pochereth-hazzebaim, sons of Amon. 60The total of the temple slaves and the descendants of the slaves of Solomon was three hundred and ninety-two.

61The following who returned from Tel-melah, Tel-harsha, Cherub, Addon, and Immer were unable to prove that their ancestral houses and their descent were Israelite: 62sons of Delaiah, sons of Tobiah, sons of Nekoda, six hundred and forty-two. 63Also, of the priests: sons of Hobaiah, sons of Hakkoz, sons of Barzillai (he had married one of the daughters of Barzillai the Gileadite and became known by his name). 64These men searched their family records, but their names could not be found written there; hence they were degraded from the priesthood, 65and His Excellency* ordered them not to partake of the most holy foods until there should be a priest bearing the Urim and Thummim.

66The entire assembly taken together came to forty-two thousand three hundred and sixty, 67not counting their male and female slaves, who were seven thousand three hundred and thirty-seven. They also had two hundred male and female singers. Their horses were seven hundred and thirty-six, their mules two hundred and forty-five, 68their camels four hundred and thirty-five, their asses six thousand seven hundred and twenty.

69Certain of the family heads contributed to the service. His Excellency put into the treasury one thousand drachmas of gold, fifty basins, thirty garments for priests, and five hundred minas of silver. 70Some of the family heads contributed to the treasury for the temple service: twenty thousand drachmas of

---

7, 65. 69: His Excellency: see note on Ezr 2, 63.

gold and two thousand two hundred minas of silver. ⁷¹The contributions of the rest of the people amounted to twenty thousand drachmas of gold, two thousand minas of silver, and sixty-seven garments for priests.

⁷²The priests, the Levites, the gatekeepers, the singers, the temple slaves, and all Israel took up residence in their cities.

II: Promulgation of the Law

CHAPTER 8

See RG 149

Ezra Reads the Law.[*] Now when the seventh month came, ¹the whole people gathered as one man in the open space before the Water Gate, and they called upon Ezra the scribe to bring forth the book of the law of Moses which the LORD prescribed for Israel.^u ²On the first day of the seventh month, therefore, Ezra the priest brought the law before the assembly, which consisted of men, women, and those children old enough to understand. ³Standing at one end of the open place that was before the Water Gate, he read out of the book from daybreak till midday, in the presence of the men, the women, and those children old enough to understand; and all the people listened attentively to the book of the law. ⁴Ezra the scribe stood on a wooden platform that had been made for the occasion; at his right side stood Mattithiah, Shema, Anaiah, Uriah, Hilkiah, and Maaseiah, and on his left Pedaiah, Mishael, Malchijah, Hashum, Hashbaddanah, Zechariah, Meshullam. ⁵Ezra opened the scroll so that all the people might see it (for he was standing higher up than any of the people); and, as he opened it, all the people rose. ⁶Ezra blessed the LORD, the great God, and all the people, their hands raised high, answered, "Amen, amen!" Then they bowed down and prostrated themselves before the LORD, their faces to the ground. ⁷[The Levites Jeshua, Bani, Sherebiah, Jamin, Akkub, Shabbethai, Hodiah, Maaseiah, Kelita, Azariah, Jozabad, Hanan, and Pelaiah explained the law to the people, who remained in their places.]^v ⁸Ezra read plainly from the book of the law of God, interpreting it so that all could understand what was read.^w ⁹Then [Nehemiah, that is, His Excellency, and] Ezra the priest-scribe [and the Levites who were instructing the people] said to all the people: "Today is holy to the LORD your God. Do not be sad, and do not weep"—for all the people were weeping as they heard the words of the law. ¹⁰He said further: "Go, eat rich foods and drink sweet drinks, and allot portions to those who had nothing prepared; for today is holy to our LORD. Do not be saddened this day, for rejoicing in the LORD must be your strength!"^x ¹¹[And the Levites quieted all the people, saying, "Hush, for today is holy, and you must not be saddened."] ¹²Then all the people went to eat and drink, to distribute portions, and to celebrate with great joy, for they understood the words that had been expounded to them.

The Feast of Booths. ¹³On the second day, the family heads of the whole people and also the priests and the Levites gathered around Ezra the scribe and examined the words of the law more closely. ¹⁴They found it written in the law prescribed by the LORD through Moses that the Israelites must dwell in booths during the feast of the seventh month;^y ¹⁵and that they should have this proclamation made throughout their cities and in Jerusalem: "Go out into the hill country and bring in branches of olive trees, oleasters, myrtle, palm, and other leafy trees, to make booths, as the law prescribes."^z ¹⁶The people went out and brought in branches with which they made booths for themselves, on the roofs of their houses, in their courtyards, in the courts of the house of God, and in the open spaces of the Water Gate and the Gate of Ephraim. ¹⁷Thus the entire assembly of the returned exiles made booths and dwelt in them. Now the Israelites had done nothing of this sort

---

7, 72b—8, 18: to be read after Ezr 8, 36. The gloss mentioning Nehemiah in v 9 was inserted in this Ezra section after the dislocation of several parts of Ezra-Nehemiah had occurred. There is no clear evidence of a simultaneous presence of Nehemiah and Ezra in Jerusalem; Neh. 12, 26 and 12, 36 are also scribal glosses.

u: Ezr 3, 1.   v: Neh 10, 11.   w: Ezr 7, 6.   x: Est 9, 19.   y: Ex 23, 14; Lv 23, 33-36.   z: Ps 118, 27.

Celebration of Renewal and Reconstruction

The great celebration that inaugurates the reconstructed community extends over several weeks, at least from the first day of the seventh month (8, 2) to the twenty-fourth (9, 1), longer than any other celebration in the Bible. The narrative depicts four steps and a coda.

First step: reading and implementing the Torah (8, 1–18). The reconstruction culminates in this momentous event, as the community summons Ezra to bring the book of the law of Moses, the Torah. Chapter 8 signals the historical moment when the Pentateuch is publicly reintroduced and received communal sanction. This parallels the events at Mount Sinai in its impact as the receiving of God's teachings by the entire people, transforming them into "the people of the Book."

Second step: confession and commitment (9, 1—10, 39). The great communal confession rehearses Israel's shared history and leads to a renewed formal commitment to God's teaching. The community recalls the cycles of God's forbearance despite Israel's earlier infidelities and hopes to be worthy of it in the present dire circumstances.

Third step: repopulation and review (11, 1—12, 26). The restored community repopulates the rebuilt city. The lists of chs. 11–12 are compiled from different sources.

Fourth step: a service of dedication (12, 27—13, 3). Celebration, purification, procession, and separation are part of the service. The initiative for the grand finale again comes from the community (12, 27; cf 8, 1). Unique in the Hebrew Bible, the purification in 12, 30 signals that Israel is holy, and Jerusalem is a "holy city."

Coda (13, 4–31). Nehemiah's memoirs resume with a retrospective from a time after 433 B.C., after completing twelve years as governor. At some point after returning to King Artaxerxes, Nehemiah came back to Jerusalem, discovered violations of the communal pledge of ch 10, and took steps to restore order.

from the days of Jeshua, son of Nun, until this occasion; therefore there was very great joy. [18]Ezra read from the book of the law of God day after day, from the first day to the last. They kept the feast for seven days, and the solemn assembly on the eighth day, as was required.

CHAPTER 9

See RG 149 *Confession of the People.* [1a]* On the twenty-fourth day of this month, the Israelites gathered together fasting and in sackcloth, their heads covered with dust. [2]Those of Israelite descent separated themselves from all who were of foreign extraction, then stood forward and confessed their sins and the guilty deeds of their fathers.[b] [3]When they had taken their places, they read from the book of the law of the LORD their God, for a fourth part of the day, and during another fourth part they made their confession and prostrated themselves before the LORD their God. [4]Standing on the platform of the Levites were Jeshua, Binnui, Kadmiel, Shebaniah, Bunni, Sherebiah, Bani, and Chenani, who cried out to the LORD their God with a loud voice. [5]The Levites Jeshua, Kadmiel, Bani, Hashabneiah, Sherebiah, Hodiah, Shebaniah, and Pethahiah said,

9, 1-5: This is a continuation of the account concerning the problem of mixed marriages at the time of Ezra; it should be read immediately after Ezr 10, 44.

a: Dn 9, 3.   *b:* Ezr 9, 1f; 10, 11.

"Arise, bless the LORD, your God,
from eternity to eternity!"

The Israelites answered with the blessing,

"Blessed is your glorious name,
and exalted above all blessing and
praise."[c]

6*Then Ezra said: "It is you, O LORD, you are the only one; you made the heavens, the highest heavens and all their host, the earth and all that is upon it, the seas and all that is in them. To all of them you give life, and the heavenly hosts bow down before you.
7"You, O LORD, are the God who chose Abram, who brought him out from Ur of the Chaldees, and named him Abraham.[d] 8When you had found his heart faithful in your sight, you made the covenant with him to give to him and his posterity the land of the Canaanites, Hittites, Amorites, Perizzites, Jebusites, and Girgashites. These promises of yours you fulfilled, for you are just.[e]

9 "You saw the affliction of our fathers in
Egypt,
you heard their cry by the Red Sea;[f]
10 You worked signs and wonders against
Pharoah,
against all his servants and the people
of his land,
Because you knew of their insolence
toward them;
thus you made for yourself a name
even to this day.[g]
11 The sea you divided before them,
on dry ground they passed through the
midst of the sea;
Their pursuers you hurled into the depths,
like a stone into the mighty waters.[h]
12 With a column of cloud you led them by
day,
and by night with a column of fire,
To light the way of their journey,
the way in which they must travel.[i]
13 On Mount Sinai you came down,

you spoke with them from heaven;
You gave them just ordinances, firm laws,
good statutes, and commandments;[j]
14 Your holy sabbath you made known to
them,
commandments, statutes, and law you
prescribed for them,
by the hand of Moses your servant.[k]
15 Food from heaven you gave them in their
hunger,
water from a rock you sent them in
their thirst.
You bade them enter and occupy the land
which you had sworn with upraised
hand to give them.[l]

16"But they, our fathers, proved to be insolent; they held their necks stiff and would not obey your commandments. 17They refused to obey and no longer remembered the miracles you had worked for them. They stiffened their necks and turned their heads to return to their slavery in Egypt. But you are a God of pardons, gracious and compassionate, slow to anger and rich in mercy; you did not forsake them.[m] 18Though they made for themselves a molten calf, and proclaimed, 'Here is your God who brought you up out of Egypt,' and were guilty of great effronteries,[n] 19yet in your great mercy you did not forsake them in the desert. The column of cloud did not cease to lead them by day on their journey, nor did the column of fire by night cease to light for them the way by which they were to travel.

20"Your good spirit you bestowed on them, to give them understanding; your manna you did not withhold from their mouths, and you gave them water in their thirst.[o] 21Forty years in the desert you sustained them: they did not want; their garments did not become worn, and their feet did not become swollen.[p] 22You gave them kingdoms and peoples, which you divided up among them as border lands. They possessed the land of Sihon, king of Heshbon, and the land of Og, king of Bashan.[q]

9, 6-37: The prayer of Ezra which began in Ezr 9, 6f is here continued; see note on Ezr 9, 7.

c: Dn 2, 20; 3, 52.   d: Gn 12, 1; 17, 5.   e: Gn 15, 18f.   f: Ex 2, 23f.   g: Ex 7—11; 14.   h: Ex 15, 5. 10.   i: Ex 13, 21f.   j: Ex 19—20.   k: Ex 20, 8.   l: Ex 16, 4; 17, 1f.   m: Nm 14, 1-4; Ex 34, 6; Dn 9, 9.   n: Ex 32, 4.   o: Dt 2, 7.   p: Dt 8, 4.   q: Nm 21, 21-35; Dt 1, 4; 2, 26—3, 11.

²³"You made their children as numerous as the stars of the heavens, and you brought them into the land which you had commanded their fathers to enter and possess.ʳ ²⁴The sons went in to take possession of the land, and you humbled before them the Canaanite inhabitants of the land and delivered them over into their power, their kings as well as the peoples of the land, to do with them as they would. ²⁵They captured fortified cities and fertile land; they took possession of houses filled with all good things, cisterns already dug, vineyards, olive groves, and fruit trees in abundance. They could eat and have their fill, fatten and feast themselves on your immense good gifts.ˢ

²⁶"But they were contemptuous and rebellious: they cast your law behind their backs, they slew your prophets who bore witness against them in order to bring them back to you, and they were guilty of great effronteries.ᵗ ²⁷Therefore you delivered them into the power of their enemies, who oppressed them. But in the time of their oppression they would cry out to you, and you would hear them from heaven, and according to your great mercy give them saviors to deliver them from the power of their enemies.ᵘ

²⁸"As soon as they had relief, they would go back to doing evil in your sight. Then again you abandoned them to the power of their enemies, who crushed them. Then they cried out to you, and you heard them from heaven and delivered them according to your mercy, many times over. ²⁹You bore witness against them, in order to bring them back to your law. But they were insolent and would not obey your commandments; they sinned against your ordinances, from which men draw life when they practice them. They turned stubborn backs, stiffened their necks, and would not obey.ᵛ ³⁰You were patient with them for many years, bearing witness against them through your spirit, by means of your prophets; still they would not listen. Thus you delivered them over into the power of the peoples of the lands. ³¹Yet in your great mercy you did not completely destroy them and you did not forsake them, for you are a kind and merciful God.

³²"Now, therefore, O our God, great, mighty, and awesome God, you who in your mercy preserve the covenant, take into account all the disasters that have befallen us, our kings, our princes, our priests, our prophets, our fathers, and your entire people, from the time of the kings of Assyria until this day!ʷ ³³In all that has come upon us you have been just, for you kept faith while we have done evil.ˣ ³⁴Yes, our kings, our princes, our priests, and our fathers have not kept your law; they paid no attention to your commandments and the obligations of which you reminded them. ³⁵While they were yet in their kingdom, in the midst of the many good things that you had given them and in the wide and fertile land that you had spread out before them, they did not serve you nor did they turn away from their evil deeds. ³⁶But, see, we today are slaves; and as for the land which you gave our fathers that they might eat its fruits and good things— see, we have become slaves upon it! ³⁷Its rich produce goes to the kings whom you set over us because of our sins, who rule over our bodies and our cattle as they please. We are in great distress!"

CHAPTER 10

See RG 149

Agreement of the People. ¹*In view of all this, we are entering into a firm pact, which we are putting into writing. On the sealed document appear the names of our princes, our Levites, and our priests.ʸ

²On the sealed document: His Excellency Nehemiah, son of Hacaliah, and Zedekiah.

³Seraiah, Azariah, Jeremiah, ⁴Pashhur, Amariah, Malchijah, ⁵Hattush, Shebaniah, Malluch, ⁶Harim, Meremoth, Obadiah, ⁷Daniel, Ginnethon, Baruch, ⁸Meshullam, Abijah, Mijamin, ⁹Maaziah, Bilgai, Shemaiah: these are the priests.

10, 1-40: This section belongs to the Nehemiah narrative rather than to that of Ezra. It is best read after Neh 13, 31. In view of all this: considering the situation described in Neh 13, 4-31.

r: Dt 1, 10. *s:* Dt 3, 5; 6, 10f; 11, 11; 32, 15. *t:* Wis 2, 10-20. *u:* Dn 9, 19. *v:* Lv 18, 5; Dt 30, 16; 32, 47. *w:* Lam 5. *x:* Dn 3, 27; 9, 14. *y:* Neh 12, 12-26.

[10]The Levites: Jeshua, son of Azaniah; Binnui, of the sons of Henadad; Kadmiel; [11]and their brethren Shebaniah, Hodiah, Kelita, Pelaiah, Hanan,[z] [12]Mica, Rehob, Hashabiah, [13]Zaccur, Sherebiah, Shebaniah, [14]Hodiah, Bani, Beninu.

[15]The leaders of the people: Parosh, Pahath-moab, Elam, Zattu, Bani, [16]Bunni, Azgad, Be-bai, [17]Adonijah, Bigvai, Adin, [18]Ater, Heze-kiah, Azzur, [19]Hodiah, Hashum, Bezai, [20]Hariph, Anathoth, Nebai, [21]Magpiash, Me-shullam, Hazir, [22]Meshezabel, Zadok, Jaddua, [23]Pelatiah, Hanan, Anaiah, [24]Hoshea, Hana-niah, Hasshub, [25]Hallohesh, Pilha, Shobek, [26]Rehum, Hashabnah, Maaseiah, [27]Ahiah, Hanan, Anan, [28]Malluch, Harim, Baanah.

Provisions of the Pact. [29]The rest of the people, priests, Levites, gatekeepers, singers, temple slaves, and all others who have sepa-rated themselves from the peoples of the lands in favor of the law of God, with their wives, their sons, their daughters, all who are of the age of discretion, [30]join with their brethren who are their princes, and with the sanction of a curse take this oath to follow the law of God which was given through Mo-ses, the servant of God, and to observe care-fully all the commandments of the LORD, our Lord, his ordinances and his statutes.[a]

[31]Agreed, that we will not marry our daughters to the peoples of the land, and that we will not take their daughters for our sons.[b] [32]When the peoples of the land bring in merchandise or any kind of grain for sale on the sabbath day, we will not buy from them on the sabbath or on any other holy day. We will forgo the seventh year, as well as every kind of debt.[c]

[33]We impose these commandments on ourselves: to give a third of a shekel each year for the service of the house of our God,[d] [34]for the showbread, for the daily cereal of-fering, for the daily holocaust, for the sab-baths, new moons, and festivals, for the holy offerings, for sin offerings to make atone-ment for Israel, and for every service of the house of our God. [35]We, priests, Levites, and people, have determined by lot concerning the procurement of wood: it is to be brought to the house of our God by each of our fam-ily houses at stated times each year, to be burnt on the altar of the LORD, our God, as the law prescribes.[e] [36f]We have agreed to bring each year to the house of the LORD the first fruits of our fields and of our fruit trees, of whatever kind; [37]also, as is prescribed in the law, to bring to the house of our God, to the priests who serve in the house of our God, the first-born of our children and our animals, including the first-born of our flocks and herds. [38]The first batch of our dough, and our offerings of the fruit of every tree, of wine and of oil, we will bring to the priests, to the chambers of the house of our God. The tithe of our fields we will bring to the Levites; they, the Levites, shall take the tithe in all the cities of our service.[g] [39]An Aaronite priest shall be with the Levites when they take the tithe, and the Levites shall bring the tithe of the tithes to the house of our God, to the chambers of the treasury. [40]For to these chambers the Israelites and Levites bring the offerings of grain, wine, and oil; there also are housed the utensils of the sanctuary, and the ministering priests, the gatekeepers, and the singers. We will not neglect the house of our God.

CHAPTER 11

See RG 149

Repeopling of Jerusalem. [1]*The lead-ers of the people took up residence in Jeru-salem, and the rest of the people cast lots to bring one man in ten to reside in Jerusalem, the holy city, while the other nine would re-main in the other cities.[h] [2]The people ap-plauded all those men who willingly agreed to take up residence in Jerusalem.

The Residents of Jerusalem. [3i]These are the heads of the province who took up resi-dence in Jerusalem. (In the cities of Judah dwelt lay Israelites, priests, Levites, temple slaves, and the descendants of the slaves of

---

11, 1-19: This list of the family heads who lived in Jerusalem at the time of Nehemiah is best read after Neh 7, 72a. It is ba-sically the same as that given in 1 Chr 9, 2-17, but there are many differences between the two lists.

z: Ezr 10, 23. *a:* Neh 13, 23-27. *b:* Neh 13, 15-22. *c:* Neh 5, 1-13; Ex 20, 8; Lv 25, 2-7. *d:* 2 Chr 24, 6. 9f; Lv 24, 5-9. *e:* Neh 13, 31. *f:* 36f: Ex 13, 1. 11ff; Dt 26, 1. *g:* Neh 13, 10-14; Nm 18, 21. 24ff. *h:* Neh 7, 4. *i:* 3-19: 1 Chr 9, 2-34.

Solomon, each man on the property he owned in his own city.)

[4]In Jerusalem dwelt both Judahites and Benjaminites. Of the Judahites: Athaiah, son of Uzziah, son of Zechariah, son of Amariah, son of Shephatiah, son of Mehallalel, of the sons of Perez; [5]Maaseiah, son of Baruch, son of Colhozeh, son of Hazaiah, son of Adaiah, son of Joiarib, son of Zechariah, a son of the Shelanites. [6]The total of the sons of Perez who dwelt in Jerusalem was four hundred and sixty-eight valiant men.

[7]These were the Benjaminites: Sallu, son of Meshullam, son of Joed, son of Pedaiah, son of Kolaiah, son of Maaseiah, son of Ithiel, son of Jeshaiah, [8]and his brethren, warriors, nine hundred and twenty-eight in number. [9]Joel, son of Zichri, was their commander, and Judah, son of Hassenuah, was second in charge of the city.

[10]Among the priests were: Jedaiah; Joiarib; Jachin; [11]Seraiah, son of Hilkiah, son of Meshullam, son of Zadok, son of Meraioth, son of Ahitub, the ruler of the house of God, [12]and their brethren who carried out the temple service, eight hundred and twenty-two; Adaiah, son of Jeroham, son of Pelaliah, son of Amzi, son of Zechariah, son of Pashhur, son of Malchijah, [13]and his brethren, family heads, two hundred and forty-two; and Amasai, son of Azarel, son of Ahzai, son of Meshillemoth, son of Immer, [14]and his brethren, warriors, one hundred and twenty-eight. Their commander was Zabdiel, son of Haggadol.

[15]Among the Levites were Shemaiah, son of Hasshub, son of Azrikam, son of Hashabiah, son of Bunni; [16]Shabbethai and Jozabad, levitical chiefs who were placed over the external affairs of the house of God; [17]Mattaniah, son of Micah, son of Zabdi, son of Asaph, director of the psalms, who led the thanksgiving at prayer; Bakbukiah, second in rank among his brethren; and Abda, son of Shammua, son of Galal, son of Jeduthun. [18]The total of the Levites in the holy city was two hundred and eighty-four.

[19]The gatekeepers were Akkub, Talmon, and their brethren, who kept watch over the gates; one hundred and seventy-two in number.

[20]The rest of Israel, including priests and Levites, were in all the other cities of Judah, each man in his inheritance.

[21]The temple slaves lived on Ophel. Ziha and Gishpa were in charge of the temple slaves.

[22]The prefect of the Levites in Jerusalem was Uzzi, son of Bani, son of Hashabiah, son of Mattaniah, son of Mica; he was one of the sons of Asaph, the singers appointed to the service of the house of God[j] — [23]for they had been appointed by royal decree, and there was a fixed schedule for the singers assigning them their daily duties.

[24]Pethahiah, son of Meshezabel, a descendant of Zerah, son of Judah, was royal deputy in all affairs that concerned the people.

The Other Cities. [25]As concerns their villages in the country: Judahites lived in Kiriath-arba and its dependencies, in Dibon and its dependencies, in Jekabzeel and its villages, [26]in Jeshua, Moladah, Beth-pelet, [27]in Hazar-shual, in Beer-sheba and its dependencies, [28]in Ziklag, in Meconah and its dependencies, [29]in En-rimmon, Zorah, Jarmuth, [30]Zanoah, Adullam, and their villages, Lachish and its countryside, Azekah and its dependencies. They were settled from Beersheba to Ge-hinnom.

[31]Benjaminites were in Geba, Michmash, Aija, Bethel and its dependencies, [32]Anathoth, Nob, Ananiah, [33]Hazor, Ramah, Gittaim, [34]Hadid, Zeboim, Neballat, [35]Lod, Ono, and the Valley of the Artisans.

[36]Some sections of the Levites from Judah settled in Benjamin.

CHAPTER 12

See RG
149

Priests and Levites under Zerubbabel.
[1k]The following are the priests and Levites who returned with Zerubbabel, son of Shealtiel, and Jeshua: Seraiah, Jeremiah, Ezra, [2]Amariah, Malluch, Hattush, [3]Shecaniah, Rehum, Meremoth, [4]Iddo, Ginnethon, Abijah, [5]Mijamin, Maadiah, Bilgah, [6]Shemaiah, and Joiarib, Jedaiah, [7]Sallu, Amok, Hilkiah,

Jedaiah. These were the priestly heads and their brethren in the days of Jeshua.

[8]The Levites were Jeshua, Binnui, Kadmiel, Sherebiah, Judah, Mattaniah; the last-mentioned, together with his brethren, was in charge of the hymns, [9]while Bakbukiah and Unno and their brethren ministered opposite them by turns.

*High Priests.** [10]Jeshua became the father of Joiakim, Joiakim became the father of Eliashib, and Eliashib became the father of Joiada. [11]Joiada became the father of Johanan, and Johanan became the father of Jaddua.

Priests and Levites under Joiakim. [12l]In the days of Joiakim these were the priestly family heads: for Seraiah, Meraiah; for Jeremiah, Hananiah; [13]for Ezra, Meshullam; for Amariah, Jehohanan; [14]for Malluch, Jonathan; for Shebaniah, Joseph; [15]for Harim, Adna; for Meremoth, Helkai; [16]for Iddo, Zechariah; for Ginnethon, Meshullam; [17]for Abijah, Zichri; for Miamin, ...; for Maadiah, Piltai; [18]for Bilgah, Shammua; for Shemaiah, Jehonathan; [19]and for Joiarib, Mattenai; for Jedaiah, Uzzi; [20]for Sallu, Kallai; for Amok, Eber; [21]for Hilkiah, Hashabiah; for Jedaiah, Nethanel.

[22]In the time of Eliashib, Joiada, Johanan, and Jaddua, the family heads of the priests were written down in the Book of Chronicles, up until the reign of Darius the Persian. [23]The sons of Levi: the family heads were written down in the Book of Chronicles, up until the time of Johanan, the son of Eliashib.

[24]The heads of the Levites were Hashabiah, Sherebiah, Jeshua, Binnui, Kadmiel. Their brethren who stood opposite them to sing praises and thanksgiving in fulfillment of the command of David, the man of God,

one section opposite the other,[m] [25]were Mattaniah, Bakbukiah, Obadiah.

Meshullam, Talmon, and Akkub were gatekeepers. They kept watch over the storerooms at the gates.[n]

[26]All these lived in the time of Joiakim, son of Jeshua, son of Jozadak [and in the time of Nehemiah the governor and of Ezra the priest-scribe].

Dedication of the City Wall. [27*]At the dedication of the wall of Jerusalem, the Levites were sought out wherever they lived and were brought to Jerusalem to celebrate a joyful dedication with thanksgiving hymns and the music of cymbals, harps, and lyres. [28]The levitical singers gathered together from the region about Jerusalem, from the villages of the Netophathites, [29]from Beth-gilgal, and from the plains of Geba and Azmaveth (for the singers had built themselves settlements about Jerusalem). [30]The priests and Levites first purified themselves, then they purified the people, the gates, and the wall.

[31]I had the princes of Judah mount the wall, and I arranged two great choirs. The first of these proceeded to the right, along the top of the wall, in the direction of the Dung Gate, [32]followed by Hoshaiah and half the princes of Judah, [33]along with Azariah, Ezra, Meshullam, [34]Judah, Benjamin, Shemaiah, and Jeremiah, [35]priests with the trumpets, and also Zechariah, son of Jonathan, son of Shemaiah, son of Mattaniah, son of Micaiah, son of Zaccur, son of Asaph, [36]and his brethren Shemaiah, Azarel, Milalai, Gilalai, Maai, Nethanel, Judah, and Hanani, with the musical instruments of David, the man of God. [Ezra the scribe was at their head.] [37]At the Spring Gate they went straight up by the steps of the City of David and continued along the top of the wall

---

12, 10f: Jeshua, the high priest when Zerubbabel was governor, i.e., the last decades of the sixth century B.C. (Hg 1, 1. 12. 14; 2, 2. 4). He was the grandfather of Eliashib, the high priest at least in the early period of Nehemiah's governorship, i.e., 445–433 B.C. (Ezr 10, 6; Neh 3, 1. 20f; 13, 4. 7). Eliashib, in turn, was the grandfather of Johanan, a grown man, if not yet a high priest, at the time of Ezra, i.e., c. 400 B.C. (Ezr 10, 6, and note). According to Josephus (Antiquities XI, v), whose testimony here is doubtful, Jaddua, son of Johanan, died as an old man about the same time that Alexander the Great died, i.e., 323 B.C. If this list of the

postexilic high priests, at least as far as Johanan, comes, as seems probable (cf v 23), from the Chronicler himself and not from a later scribe, it is of prime importance for dating the Chronicler's work in the first decades of the fourth century B.C.

12, 27-43: The dedication of the wall of Jerusalem took place, no doubt, soon after the restoration of the wall and its gates had been completed. Therefore, this section is best read after Neh 6, 15.

l: 2-22: Neh 10, 3-9; 12, 1-6. m: Ezr 2, 40. n: Neh 11, 17.

above the house of David until they came to the Water Gate on the east.

[38]The second choir proceeded to the left, followed by myself and the other half of the princes of the people, along the top of the wall past the Oven Tower as far as the Broad Wall, [39]then past the Ephraim Gate [the New City Gate], the Fish Gate, the Tower of Hananel, and the Hundred Tower, as far as the Sheep Gate [and they came to a halt at the Prison Gate].

[40]The two choirs took up a position in the house of God; I, too, who had with me half the magistrates, [41]the priests Eliakim, Maaseiah, Minjamin, Micaiah, Elioenai, Zechariah, Hananiah, with the trumpets, [42]and Maaseiah, Shemaiah, Eleazar, Uzzi, Jehohanan, Malchijah, Elam, and Ezer. The singers were heard under the leadership of Jezrahiah. [43]Great sacrifices were offered on that day, and there was rejoicing over the great feast of the LORD in which they shared. The women and the children joined in, and the rejoicing at Jerusalem could be heard from afar off.

Offerings for Priests and Levites. [44o]At that time men were appointed over the chambers set aside for stores, offerings, first fruits, and tithes; in them they were to collect from the fields of the various cities the portions legally assigned to the priests and Levites. For Judah rejoiced in its appointed priests and Levites [45]who carried out the ministry of their God and the ministry of purification (as did the singers and the gatekeepers) in accordance with the prescriptions of David and of Solomon, his son. [46]For the heads of the families of the singers and the hymns of praise and thanksgiving to God came down from the days of David and Asaph in times of old.[p] [47]Thus all Israel, in

the days of Zerubbabel [and in the days of Nehemiah], gave the singers and the gatekeepers their portions, according to their daily needs. They made their consecrated offering to the Levites, and the Levites made theirs to the sons of Aaron.[q]

CHAPTER 13

See RG 149

Separation from Aliens. [1r*]At that time, when there was reading from the book of Moses in the hearing of the people, it was found written there that "no Ammonite or Moabite may ever be admitted into the assembly of God; [2]for they would not succor the Israelites with food and water, but they hired Balaam to curse them, though our God turned the curse into a blessing."[s] [3]When they had heard the law, they separated from Israel every foreign element.[t]

Reform in the Temple. [4*]Before this, the priest Eliashib, who had been placed in charge of the chambers of the house of our God and who was an associate of Tobiah, [5]had set aside for the latter's use a large chamber in which had previously been stored the cereal offerings, incense and utensils, the tithes in grain, wine, and oil allotted to the Levites, singers, and gatekeepers, and the offerings due the priests.[u] [6]During all this time I had not been in Jerusalem, for in the thirty-second year of Artaxerxes, king of Babylon, I had gone back to the king. After due time,* however, I asked leave of the king [7]and returned to Jerusalem, where I discovered the evil thing that Eliashib had done for Tobiah, in setting aside for him a chamber in the courts of the house of God. [8]This displeased me very much, and I had all of Tobiah's household goods thrown outside the chamber. [9]Then I gave orders to purify the chambers, and I had them replace there the

---

12, 44-47: This account of the provisions made for the temple services is apparently a composition of the Chronicler. At that time: a mere connective; no particular time is meant, but the account fits best after that of the restoration of the temple (Ezr 6, 13-18) in the days of Zerubbabel (v 47). The gloss mentioning Nehemiah is not in the ancient Greek version.

13, 1ff: These verses were composed by the Chronicler to serve as an introduction to the reforms that Nehemiah instituted during his second mission in Jerusalem (vv 4-31). The part of the book of Moses read to the people is freely quoted here from

13, 4-31: This is part of the "Memoirs of Nehemiah"; it is continued in Neh 10, 1-40.

13, 6: After due time: It is not known when Nehemiah returned to Jerusalem or how long his second period of activity there lasted, but it probably ended before Ezra came to Palestine; see note on Ezr 7, 1-8.

o: 44f: 1 Chr 23—26; 2 Chr 8, 14. *p:* 2 Chr 29, 30; 35, 15. *q:* Neh 13, 10f; 10, 39; Nm 18, 26. *r:* 1ff: Dt 23, 3-6. *s:* Nm 22—24. *t:* Neh 13, 23-28. *u:* Neh 12, 44.

utensils of the house of God, the cereal offerings, and the incense.

[10]I learned, too, that the portions due the Levites were no longer being given, so that the Levites and the singers who should have been carrying out the services had deserted, each man to his own field. [11]I took the magistrates to task, demanding, "Why is the house of God abandoned?" Then I brought the Levites together and had them resume their stations. [12]All Judah once more brought in the tithes of grain, wine, and oil to the storerooms;[y] [13]and in charge of the storerooms I appointed the priest Shelemiah, Zadok the scribe, and Pedaiah, one of the Levites, together with Hanan, son of Zaccur, son of Mattaniah, as their assistant; for these men were held to be trustworthy. It was their duty to make the distribution to their brethren. [14]Remember this to my credit, O my God! Let not the devotion which I showed for the house of my God and its services be forgotten!

Sabbath Observance. [15]In those days I perceived that men in Judah were treading the winepresses on the sabbath; that they were bringing in sheaves of grain, loading them on their asses, together with wine, grapes, figs, and every other kind of burden, and bringing them to Jerusalem on the sabbath day. I warned them to sell none of these victuals.[w] [16]In Jerusalem itself the Tyrians who were resident there were importing fish and every other kind of merchandise and selling it to the Judahites on the sabbath. [17]I took the nobles of Judah to task, demanding of them: "What is this evil thing that you are doing, profaning the sabbath day? [18]Did not your fathers act in this same way, with the result that our God has brought all this evil upon us and upon this city? Would you add to the wrath against Israel by once more profaning the sabbath?"

[19]When the shadows were falling on the gates of Jerusalem before the sabbath, I ordered the doors to be closed and forbade them to be reopened till after the sabbath. I posted some of my own men at the gates so that no

burden might enter on the sabbath day. [20]The merchants and sellers of various kinds of merchandise spent the night once or twice outside Jerusalem, [21]but then I warned them, saying to them: "Why do you spend the night alongside the wall? If you keep this up, I will lay hands on you!" From that time on, they did not return on the sabbath. [22]Then I ordered the Levites to purify themselves and to go and watch the gates, so that the sabbath day might be kept holy. This, too, remember in my favor, O my God, and have mercy on me in accordance with your great mercy!

Mixed Marriages. [23]Also in those days I saw Jews who had married Ashdodite, Ammonite, or Moabite wives.[x] [24]Of their children, half spoke Ashdodite,* and none of them knew how to speak Jewish; and so it was in regard to the languages of the various other peoples. [25]I took them to task and cursed them; I had some of them beaten and their hair pulled out; and I adjured them by God: "You shall not marry your daughters to their sons nor take any of their daughters for your sons or for yourselves! [26]Did not Solomon, the king of Israel, sin because of them? Though among the many nations there was no king like him, and though he was beloved of his God and God had made him king over all Israel, yet even he was made to sin by foreign women.[y] [27]Must it also be heard of you that you have done this same very great evil, betraying our God by marrying foreign women?"

[28]One of the sons of Joiada, son of Eliashib the high priest, was the son-in-law of Sanballat the Horonite! I drove him from my presence.[z] [29]Remember against them, O my God, how they defiled the priesthood and the covenant of the priesthood and the Levites!

[30]Thus I cleansed them of all foreign contamination. I established the various functions for the priests and Levites, so that each had his appointed task. [31]I also provided for the procurement of wood at stated times and for the first fruits. Remember this in my favor, O my God![a]

13, 24: Ashdodite: the language spoken at Ashdod, more likely an Aramaic rather than a Philistine dialect. Jewish: Hebrew as spoken in postexilic Judah.

v: Neh 10, 38f; 12, 44f. 47; 2 Chr 31, 6.   *w:* Neh 10, 32; Ex 20, 8.   *x:* Neh 10, 31; 13, 1ff; Dt 23, 3.   *y:* 1 Kgs 11, 1-13.   *z:* Neh 2, 10; 13, 4f. 7ff.   *a:* Neh 10, 35f.

See RG
151-53

The Book of Tobit

The Book of Tobit, named after its principal hero, combines specifically Jewish piety and morality with oriental folklore in a fascinating story that has enjoyed wide popularity in both Jewish and Christian circles. Prayers, psalms, and words of wisdom, as well as the skillfully constructed story itself, provide valuable insights into the faith and the religious milieu of its unknown author. The book was probably written early in the second century B.C.; it is not known where.

Tobit, a devout and wealthy Israelite living among the captives deported to Nineveh, from the northern kingdom of Israel in 721 B.C., suffers severe reverses and is finally blinded. Because of his misfortunes he begs the Lord to let him die. But recalling the large sum he had formerly deposited in far-off Media, he sends his son Tobiah there to bring back the money. In Media, at this same time, a young woman, Sarah, also prays for death, because she has lost seven husbands, each killed in turn on his wedding night by the demon Asmodeus. God hears the prayers of Tobit and Sarah, and sends the angel Raphael in disguise to aid them both.

Raphael makes the trip to Media with Tobiah. When Tobiah is attacked by a large fish as he bathes, Raphael orders him to seize it and to remove its gall, heart, and liver because they make "useful medicines." Later, at Raphael's urging, Tobiah marries Sarah, and uses the fish's heart and liver to drive Asmodeus from the bridal chamber. Returning to Nineveh with his wife and his father's money, Tobiah rubs the fish's gall into his father's eyes and cures them. Finally, Raphael reveals his true identity and returns to heaven. Tobit then utters his beautiful hymn of praise. Before dying, Tobit tells his son to leave Nineveh because God will destroy that wicked city. After Tobiah buries his father and mother, he and his family depart for Media, where he later learns that the destruction of Nineveh has taken place.

The inspired author of the book used the literary form of religious novel (as in Jonah and Ju-dith) for the purpose of instruction and edification. There may have been a historical nucleus around which the story was composed, but this possibility has nothing to do with the teaching of the book. The seemingly historical data—names of kings, cities, etc.—are used merely as vivid details to create interest and charm.

Although the Book of Tobit is usually listed with the historical books, it more correctly stands midway between them and the wisdom literature. It contains numerous maxims like those found in the wisdom books (cf 4, 3-19. 21; 12, 6-10; 14, 7. 9) as well as the customary sapiential themes: fidelity to the law, the intercessory function of angels, piety toward parents, the purity of marriage, reverence for the dead, and the value of almsgiving, prayer, and fasting. The book makes Tobit a relative of *Ahiqar,* a hero of ancient Near Eastern folklore.

Written in Aramaic, the original of the book was lost for centuries. The Greek translation, existing in three different recensions, is our primary source. In 1955, fragments of the book in Aramaic and in Hebrew were recovered from Cave IV at Qumran. These texts are in substantial agreement with the Greek recension that has served as the basis for the present translation. The divisions of the Book of Tobit are:

  I: Tobit's Ordeals (1, 3—3, 6).

  II: Sarah's Plight (3, 7-17).

  III: Tobiah's Journey and Marriage to Sarah (4, 1—9, 6).

  IV: Tobiah's Return; Cure of Tobit's Blindness (10, 1—11, 18).

  V: Raphael Reveals His Identity (12, 1-22).

  VI: Tobit's Song of Praise (13, 1-18).

  VII: Epilogue (14, 1-15).

————————

CHAPTER 1

See RG
152

Tobit. ¹This book tells the story of Tobit,* son of Tobiel, son of Hananiel, son of Aduel, son of Gabael of the family of Asiel,

---

1, 1: Tobit: in the fragments of the book found at Qumran, is given as Tobi, an abbreviated form of Tobiyah (v 9; Ezr 2, 60) or of Tobiyahu (2 Chr 17, 8), a name which means "Yahweh is good." Tobiel, "God is good"; Hananiel, "God is merciful." The book abounds in theophoric names.

of the tribe of Naphtali, ²who during the reign of Shalmaneser,* king of Assyria, was taken captive from Thisbe, which is south of Kedesh Naphtali in upper Galilee, above and to the west of Asser, north of Phogor.ᵃ

I: Tobit's Ordeals

His Virtue. ³I, Tobit, have walked all the days of my life on the paths of truth and righteousness. I performed many charitable works for my kinsmen and my people who had been deported with me to Nineveh, in Assyria. ⁴When I lived as a young man in my own country, Israel, the entire tribe of my forefather Naphtali had broken away from the house of David and from Jerusalem. This city had been singled out of all Israel's tribes, so that they all might offer sacrifice in the place where the temple, God's dwelling, had been built and consecrated for all generations to come. ⁵ᵇAll my kinsmen, like the rest of the tribe of my forefather Naphtali, used to offer sacrifice on all the mountains of Galilee as well as to the young bull which Jeroboam, king of Israel, had made in Dan.*

⁶ᶜI, for my part, would often make the pilgrimage alone to Jerusalem for the festivals, as is prescribed for all Israel by perpetual decree.* Bringing with me the first fruits of the field and the firstlings of the flock, together with a tenth of my income and the first shearings of the sheep,ᵈ I would hasten to Jerusalem ⁷ᵉand present them to the priests,

Aaron's sons, at the altar. To the Levites who were doing service in Jerusalem I would give the tithe of grain, wine, olive oil, pomegranates, figs, and other fruits. And except for sabbatical years, I used to give a second tithe in money, which each year I would go and disburse in Jerusalem. ⁸The third tithe I gave to orphans and widows, and to converts who were living with the Israelites. Every third year I would bring them this offering, and we ate it in keeping with the decree of the Mosaic law and the commands of Deborah, the mother of my father Tobiel; for when my father died, he left me an orphan.

⁹When I reached manhood, I married Anna, a woman of our own lineage. By her I had a son whom I named Tobiah. ¹⁰Now after I had been deported to Nineveh, all my brothers and relatives ate the food of heathens,ᶠ ¹¹but I refrained from eating that kind of food. ¹²Because of this wholehearted service of God, ¹³the Most High granted me favor and status with Shalmaneser, so that I became purchasing agent for all his needs.ᵍ ¹⁴Every now and then until his death I would go to Media to buy goods for him. I also deposited several pouches containing a great sum of money* with my kinsman Gabael, son of Gabri, who lived at Rages, in Media. ¹⁵But when Shalmaneser died and his son Sennacherib* succeeded him as king, the roads to Media became unsafe, so I could no longer go there.

Courage in Burying the Dead. ¹⁶During Shalmaneser's reign I performed many charitable works for my kinsmen and my people.

1, 2: Shalmaneser V (727–722 B.C.): began the siege of Samaria; the inhabitants of the northern kingdom were taken into captivity by his successor, Sargon II (722–705). Thisbe and Phogor: towns of Galilee that have not been identified; Thisbe in Gilead was perhaps the birthplace of Elijah. Kedesh: cf Jos 20, 7. Asser: Hazor (Jos 11, 1).

1, 5: Jeroboam established sanctuaries in Dan and Bethel so that the people would no longer go to Jerusalem for the festivals. The gold statues of bulls which he placed in the sanctuaries were considered the throne of Yahweh; but the people soon came to worship the images themselves. Jeroboam also encouraged the high places or hilltop shrines (1 Kgs 12, 26-33).

1, 6ff: Perpetual decree: Dt 12, 11. 13-14. Refusing to worship at Jeroboam's shrines, the faithful Tobit continued to bring his offerings to Jerusalem; see 2 Chr 11, 16. For the var-

ious tithes, cf Nm 18, 20-32; 2 Chr 31, 4-6; Dt 14, 22-29; 26, 12f.

1, 14: A great sum of money: literally, "ten silver talents," about ten thousand dollars. Rages: modern Rai, about five miles southeast of Teheran. Media: the northwestern part of modern Iran.

1, 15: Sennacherib (705–681 B.C.): the son of Sargon (722–705 B.C.); neither was descended from Shalmaneser. Inconsistencies such as this point to the fact that the Book of Tobit is a religious novel (see Introduction; also notes on 5, 6 and 14, 15).

---

a: 2 Kgs 17, 3; 18, 9ff. *b:* 1 Kgs 12, 26-32. *c:* Ex 23, 14f. 17; 34, 23. *d:* Dt 16, 16. *e:* 7f: Nm 18, 12f. 24; Dt 14, 22-29; 18, 4f. *f:* Lv 11; Dt 14, 3-21; Acts 15, 29; 1 Cor 8, 7ff. *g:* Dn 2, 48f.

> A dead body left unburied (1, 18) was considered a curse, a punishment for an evil life, which somehow affected the peace of the deceased. See 2 Kings 19, 35–36; Jeremiah 8, 2; Ecclesiasticus 44, 14.

*17h*I would give my bread to the hungry and my clothing to the naked. If I saw one of my people who had died and been thrown outside the walls of Nineveh, I would bury him.* *18*I also buried anyone whom Sennacherib slew when he returned as a fugitive from Judea during the days of judgment decreed against him by the heavenly King because of the blasphemies he had uttered. In his rage he killed many Israelites, but I used to take their bodies by stealth and bury them; so when Sennacherib looked for them, he could not find them. *19*But a certain citizen of Nineveh informed the king that it was I who buried the dead. When I found out that the king knew all about me and wanted to put me to death, I went into hiding; then in my fear I took to flight. *20*Afterward, all my property was confiscated; I was left with nothing. All that I had was taken to the king's palace, except for my wife Anna and my son Tobiah.

*21*But less than forty days later the king was assassinated by two of his sons, who then escaped into the mountains of Ararat. His son Esarhaddon,* who succeeded him as king, placed Ahiqar, my brother Anael's son, in charge of all the accounts of his kingdom, so that he took control over the entire administration.*i* *22*Then Ahiqar interceded on my behalf, and I was able to return to Nineveh. For under Sennacherib, king of Assyria, Ahiqar had been chief cupbearer, keeper of the seal, administrator, and treasurer; and Esarhaddon reappointed him. He was a close relative—in fact, my nephew.

CHAPTER 2

See RG 152

*1*Thus under King Esarhaddon I returned to my home, and my wife Anna and my son Tobiah were restored to me. Then on our festival of Pentecost, the feast of Weeks,* a fine dinner was prepared for me, and I reclined to eat.*j* *2*The table was set for me, and when many different dishes were placed before me, I said to my son Tobiah: "My son, go out and try to find a poor man from among our kinsmen exiled here in Nineveh. If he is a sincere worshiper of God, bring him back with you, so that he can share this meal with me. Indeed, son, I shall wait for you to come back."*

*3*Tobiah went out to look for some poor kinsman of ours. When he returned he exclaimed, "Father!" I said to him, "What is it, son?" He answered, "Father, one of our people has been murdered! His body lies in the market place where he was just strangled!" *4*I sprang to my feet, leaving the dinner untouched; and I carried the dead man from the street and put him in one of the rooms, so that I might bury him after sunset. *5*Returning to my own quarters, I washed myself* and ate my food in sorrow.*k* *6*I was reminded of the oracle pronounced by the prophet Amos against Bethel:*l*

> "Your festivals shall be returned into
> mourning,
> And all your songs into lamentation."

*7*And I wept. Then at sunset I went out, dug a grave, and buried him.

1, 17-18: Tobit risked his own life to bury the dead. Deprivation of burial was viewed with horror by the Jews. Cf Tb 4, 3-4; 6, 15; 14, 12-13.

1, 21: Esarhaddon: 681–669 B.C. Ahiqar: a hero of ancient folklore, known for his outstanding wisdom. The Story (or Wisdom) of Ahiqar was very popular in antiquity and is extant in many different forms: Aramaic, Syriac, Armenian, Arabic (Arabian Nights), Greek (Aesop's Fables), Slavonic, Ethiopic, and Romanian. The sacred author makes Tobit the uncle of the famous Ahiqar in order to enhance Tobit's own prestige. See note on Tb 14, 10.

2, 1: The feast of Weeks: also called by its Greek name Pentecost, was celebrated fifty days after the Passover. Cf Lv 23, 15-21; Dt 16, 9-12.

2, 2: Almsgiving and charity to the poor are important virtues taught by the book (Tb 4, 7-11. 16f; 12, 8f; 14, 10f).

2, 5: I washed myself: because of ritual defilement from touching a corpse (Nm 19, 11-13).

h: Jb 31, 16-20. *i:* 2 Kgs 19, 37; 2 Chr 32, 21; Sir 48, 21; Is 37, 38; 2 Mc 8, 19. *j:* Lv 23, 15-21; Nm 28, 26-31; Dt 16, 9-12. *k:* Nm 19, 11-22. *l:* Am 8, 10; 1 Mc 1, 39.

Tobit's Misfortunes

Tobit's charitable acts land him in trouble (1, 16–22). His zealous efforts to obey the law earn him the persecution of the pagans and the jeers of the other Jews (2, 8).

⁸The neighbors mocked me, saying to one another: "Will this man never learn! Once before he was hunted down for execution because of this very thing; yet now that he has escaped, here he is again burying the dead!"

Tobit's Blindness. ⁹That same night I bathed, and went to sleep next to the wall of my courtyard. Because of the heat I left my face uncovered. ¹⁰I did not know there were birds perched on the wall above me, till their warm droppings settled in my eyes, causing cataracts.* I went to see some doctors for a cure, but the more they anointed my eyes with various salves, the worse the cataracts became, until I could see no more. For four years I was deprived of eyesight, and all my kinsmen were grieved at my condition. Ahiqar, however, took care of me for two years, until he left for Elymais.

¹¹At that time my wife Anna worked for hire at weaving cloth, the kind of work women do. ¹²When she sent back the goods to their owners, they would pay her. Late in winter* she finished the cloth and sent it back to the owners. They paid her the full salary, and also gave her a young goat for the table. ¹³On entering my house the goat began to bleat. I called to my wife and said: "Where did this goat come from? Perhaps it was stolen! Give it back to its owners; we have no right to eat stolen food!" ¹⁴ᵐBut she said to me, "It was given to me as a bonus over and above my wages." Yet I would not believe her; and told her to give it back to its owners. I became very angry with her over

this. So she retorted: "Where are your charitable deeds now? Where are your virtuous acts? See! Your true character is finally showing itself!"*

CHAPTER 3

See RG 152

¹Grief-stricken in spirit, I groaned and wept aloud. Then with sobs I began to pray:

Tobit's Prayer for Death

² "You are righteous, O Lord,
   and all your deeds are just;
All your ways are mercy and truth;
   you are the judge of the world.ⁿ
³ And now, O Lord, may you be mindful
      of me,
   and look with favor upon me.
Punish me not for my sins,
   nor for my inadvertent offenses,
   nor for those of my fathers.ᵒ

"They sinned against you,
⁴   and disobeyed your commandments.
So you handed us over to plundering,
      exile, and death,
   till we were an object lesson, a
      byword, a reproach
   in all the nations among whom you
      scattered us.ᵖ

⁵ "Yes, your judgments are many and true
   in dealing with me as my sins
   and those of my fathers deserve.
For we have not kept your
      commandments,
   nor have we trodden the paths of truth
      before you.

2, 10: Cataracts: literally, "white scales, or films." Elymais: the Greek name of ancient Elam, a district northeast of the head of the Persian Gulf.

2, 12: Late in winter: literally, "seventh of Dystros," the Macedonian month which corresponds to the Jewish month of Shebat (January–February). For the table: literally, "for the hearth"; the gift had probably been made in view of some

springtime festival like the Jewish Purim.

2, 14: Anna's sharp rebuke calls to mind the words of Job's wife (Jb 2, 9).

---

m: Jb 2, 9. n: Pss 25, 10; 119, 137; Dn 3, 27. o: Ex 34, 7.
p: Dt 28, 15; Bar 1, 16-22; 2, 4f; 3, 8; Dn 9, 5f.

6 "So now, deal with me as you please,
  and command my life breath to be
    taken from me,
  that I may go from the face of the earth
    into dust.
It is better for me to die than to live,*
  because I have heard insulting
    calumnies,
  and I am overwhelmed with grief.*q*

"Lord, command me to be delivered
    from such anguish;
  let me go to the everlasting abode;
  Lord, refuse me not.
For it is better for me to die
  than to endure so much misery in life,
  and to hear these insults!"

II: Sarah's Plight

Sarah Falsely Accused. 7*On the same day, at
Ecbatana in Media, it so happened that
Raguel's daughter Sarah also had to listen to
abuse, from one of her father's maids. 8For
she had been married to seven husbands, but
the wicked demon Asmodeus* killed them off
before they could have intercourse with her,
as it is prescribed for wives. So the maid said
to her: "You are the one who strangles your
husbands! Look at you! You have already
been married seven times, but you have had
no joy with any one of your husbands. 9Why
do you beat us? Because your husbands are
dead? Then why not join them! May we never
see a son or daughter of yours!"

10That day she was deeply grieved in
spirit. She went in tears to an upstairs room
in her father's house with the intention of
hanging herself. But she reconsidered, saying to herself: "No! People would level this
insult against my father: 'You had only one

beloved daughter, but she hanged herself because of ill fortune!' And thus would I cause
my father in his old age to go down to the
nether world laden with sorrow. It is far better for me not to hang myself, but to beg the
Lord to have me die, so that I need no longer
live to hear such insults."*r*

11At that time, then, she spread out her
hands, and facing the window,* poured out
this prayer:

Sarah's Prayer for Death

"Blessed are you, O Lord, merciful God!
  Forever blessed and honored is your
    holy name;
  may all your works forever bless you.*s*
12 And now, O Lord, to you I turn my face
  and raise my eyes.
13 Bid me to depart from the earth,
  never again to hear such insults.

14 "You know, O Master, that I am innocent
  of any impure act with a man,
15 And that I have never defiled my own
    name
  or my father's name in the land of my
    exile.

"I am my father's only daughter,
  and he has no other child to make his
    heir,
Nor does he have a close kinsman or
    other relative
  whom I might bide my time to marry.
I have already lost seven husbands;
  why then should I live any longer?
But if it please you, Lord, not to slay me,
  look favorably upon me and have pity
    on me;
  never again let me hear these insults!"

An Answer to Prayer. 16At that very time,

3, 6: It is better for me to die than to live: in his distress Tobit uses the words of the petulant Jonah (Jon 4, 3. 8), who
wished to die because God did not destroy the hated Ninevites. In similar circumstances, Moses (Nm 11, 15), Elijah
(1 Kgs 19, 4), and Job (Jb 7, 15) also prayed for death. Everlasting abode: a reference to Sheol, the dismal abode of the
dead from which no one returns (Jb 7, 9-10; 14, 12; Is 26, 14).
The revelation of a blessed immortality had not yet been
made. See note on Tb 4, 6.

3, 7: From here on, the story is told in the third person. V
7 relates one of the several marvelous coincidences which the
story-teller uses to heighten interest; see also vv 16. 17; 4, 1;

5, 4. Ecbatana: Hamadan in modern Iran; this was the capital
of ancient Media. Raguel: "friend of God."

3, 8: Asmodeus: in Persian aeshma daeva, "demon of
wrath," adopted into Aramaic with the sense of "the Destroyer."
He will be subdued (Tb 8, 3) by Raphael (v 17), "God heals."

3, 11: Facing the window: that is, looking toward Jerusalem;
cf Dn 6, 11. Blessed are you and "Blessed be God" are traditional openings of Jewish prayers (Tb 8, 5. 15; 11, 14; 13, 1).

q: Nm 11, 15; 1 Kgs 19, 4; Jb 7, 15; Jon 4, 3. 8. *r:* Tb 6, 15; Gn
37, 35; 42, 38; 44, 29. 31. *s:* 1 Kgs 8, 44. 48; Pss 28, 2; 134, 2;
Dn 6, 11.

the prayer of these two suppliants was heard in the glorious presence of Almighty God. *17t*So Raphael was sent to heal them both: to remove the cataracts from Tobit's eyes, so that he might again see God's sunlight; and to marry Raguel's daughter Sarah to Tobit's son Tobiah, and then drive the wicked demon Asmodeus from her. For Tobiah had the right* to claim her before any other who might wish to marry her.

In the very moment that Tobit returned from the courtyard to his house, Raguel's daughter Sarah came downstairs from her room.

III: Tobiah's Journey and Marriage to Sarah

CHAPTER 4

See RG 152

A Father's Instruction. *1*That same day Tobit remembered the money he had deposited with Gabael at Rages in Media, and he thought, *2*"Now that I have asked for death, why should I not call my son Tobiah and let him know about this money before I die?" *3*So he called his son Tobiah; and when he came, he said to him:* "My son, when I die, give me a decent burial. Honor your mother, and do not abandon her as long as she lives. Do whatever pleases her, and do not grieve her spirit in any way.*u* *4*Remember, my son, that she went through many trials for your sake while you were in her womb. And when she dies, bury her in the same grave with me.

5"Through all your days, my son, keep the Lord in mind, and suppress every desire to sin or to break his commandments. Perform good works all the days of your life, and do not tread the paths of wrongdoing. *6v*For if you are steadfast in your service, your good works will bring success, not only to you, but also to all those who live uprightly.*

7"Give alms from your possessions. Do not turn your face away from any of the poor, and God's face will not be turned away from you.*w* *8*Son, give alms in proportion to what you own. If you have great wealth, give alms out of your abundance; if you have but little, distribute even some of that. But do not hesitate to give alms; *9*you will be storing up a goodly treasure for yourself against the day of adversity.*x* *10*Almsgiving frees one from death, and keeps one from going into the dark abode. *11*Alms are a worthy offering in the sight of the Most High for all who give them.*y*

12"Be on your guard, son, against every form of immorality, and above all, marry a woman of the lineage of your forefathers. Do not marry a stranger who is not of your father's tribe, because we are sons of the prophets. My boy, keep in mind Noah, Abraham, Isaac, and Jacob, our fathers from of old: all of them took wives from among their own kinsmen and were blessed in their children. Remember that their posterity shall inherit the land.*z* *13*Therefore, my son, love your kinsmen. Do not be so proudhearted toward your kinsmen, the sons and daughters of your people, as to refuse to take a wife for yourself from among them. For in such arrogance there is ruin and great disorder. Likewise, in worthlessness there is decay and dire poverty, for worthlessness is the mother of famine.

14"Do not keep with you overnight the wages of any man who works for you, but pay him immediately. If you thus behave as God's servant, you will receive your reward. Keep a close watch on yourself, my son, in everything you do, and discipline yourself in all your conduct.*a* *15*Do to no one what you yourself dislike. Do not drink wine till you become drunk, nor let drunkenness accompany you on your way.*b*

3, 17: Tobiah had the right: according to the patriarchal custom of marriage within the family group. Tobiah was Sarah's closest eligible relative (Tb 6, 12). Cf Tb 4, 12-13; Gn 24.

4, 3-19: A collection of maxims which parallel those in the wisdom literature, especially Prv and Sir (see Introduction): duties toward parents (3-4); cf also Tb 14, 13; perseverance in virtue and avoidance of evil (5-6. 14b); necessity and value of almsgiving and charity (7-11. 16-17); marriage to a kinsman (12-13a); industry (13b); prompt payment of wages (14a); the golden rule (15a); temperance (15b); docility (18); prayer (19).

4, 6: Before the revelation of retribution for all men in the

afterlife—a doctrine taught in the Book of Wisdom—Old Testament man believed that virtue guaranteed earthly prosperity, and sin earthly disaster (cf Dt 28).

t: Tt 4, 12f; 6, 12f; Gn 24, 3f. *u:* Ex 20, 12; Prv 23, 22; Sir 7, 27. *v:* Tb 13, 6; Jn 3, 21; Eph 4, 15. *w:* 7f; Tb 12, 8ff; Dt 15, 7f. 11; Prv 19, 17; Sir 4, 1-6; 14, 13; Lk 14, 13; 1 Jn 3, 17. *x:* Mt 6, 20f. *y:* Sir 3, 30; 29, 12. *z:* Tb 3, 15. 17; 6, 12; Gn 11, 29. 31; 25, 20; 28, 1-4; 29, 15-30; Ex 34, 16; Dt 7, 3; Jgs 14, 3. *a:* Lv 19, 13; Dt 24, 15. *b:* Mt 7, 12; Lk 6, 31.

Tobit Sends for His Son

Tobit's sage advice to Tobiah (4, 3–21) reflects the morals of Judaism of the Hellenistic period. Indeed, Tobit is the picture of virtue, speaking wisely, offering "Azariah" (5, 13) generous compensation, and keeping faith with God. Tobiah follows his example, and under the inspiration of the angel Raphael, saves himself from danger and brings healing to others.

16c"Give to the hungry some of your bread, and to the naked some of your clothing. Whatever you have left over, give away as alms; and do not begrudge the alms you give. 17dBe lavish with your bread and wine at the burial of the virtuous, but do not share them with sinners.*

18"Seek counsel from every wise man, and do not think lightly of any advice that can be useful. 19eAt all times bless the Lord God, and ask him to make all your paths straight and to grant success to all your endeavors and plans. For no pagan nation possesses good counsel, but the Lord himself gives all good things. If the Lord chooses, he raises a man up; but if he should decide otherwise, he casts him down to the deepest recesses of the nether world. So now, my son, keep in mind my commandments, and never let them be erased from your heart.*

20"And now, son, I wish to inform you that I have deposited a great sum of money with Gabri's son Gabael at Rages in Media. 21Do not be discouraged, my child, because of our poverty. You will be a rich man if you fear God, avoid all sin, and do what is right before the Lord your God."f

CHAPTER 5

See RG 152

The Angel Raphael. 1Then Tobiah replied to his father Tobit: "Everything that you have commanded me, father, I will do.

2But how shall I be able to obtain the money from him, since he does not know me nor do I know him? What can I show him to make him recognize me and trust me, so that he will give me the money? I do not even know which roads to take for the journey into Media!" 3Tobit answered his son Tobiah: "We exchanged signatures on a document* written in duplicate; I divided it into two parts, and each of us kept one; his copy I put with the money. Think of it, twenty years have already passed since I deposited that money! So now, my son, find yourself a trustworthy man who will make the journey with you. We will, of course, give him a salary when you return; but get back that money from Gabael."

4Tobiah went to look for someone acquainted with the roads who would travel with him to Media. As soon as he went out, he found the angel Raphael standing before him, though he did not know* that this was an angel of God.g 5Tobiah said to him, "Who are you, young man?" He replied, "I am an Israelite, one of your kinsmen. I have come here to work." Tobiah said, "Do you know the way to Media?" 6The other replied: "Yes, I have been there many times. I know the place well and I know all the routes. I have often traveled to Media; I used to stay with our kinsman Gabael, who lives at Rages in Media. It is a good two days' travel from Ecbatana to Rages,* for Rages is situated at the

4, 17: Tobit counsels his son either to give alms in honor of the dead, or, more probably, to give the "bread of consolation" to the family of the deceased. Cf Jer 16, 7; Ez 24, 17.

4, 19: Prayer is the foundation of a moral life.

5, 3: Document: in Greek cheirographon. In the Middle Ages, notably in England, a deed and its duplicate were written on one piece of parchment, with the Latin word chirographum inscribed across the top of the sheet or between the two copies of the text. The document was then cut in two in either a straight or a wavy line, the parts being given to the persons concerned. Perhaps this procedure derived from the present verse of Tobit. Duplicate documents, usually one open and

the other sealed, are well known from the ancient Near East.

5, 4: He did not know: the theme of an angel in disguise occurs frequently in folklore as well as in the Old Testament (Gn 18; cf Heb 13, 2).

5, 6: It is a good two days' travel from Ecbatana to Rages: Alexander's army took eleven days in forced marches to cover this distance, about 180 miles. The author is merely using popular impressions about faraway places; he is not teaching geography. (See notes on Tb 1, 15; 3, 7 and Introduction.)

c: Dt 15, 10; Is 58, 7; Mt 25, 35f; 2 Cor 9, 7.   d: Jer 16, 7; Lk 14, 13.   e: Dt 4, 6; Ps 119, 10.   f: 1 Tm 6, 6ff.   g: Heb 13, 2.

mountains, Ecbatana out on the plateau." [7]Tobiah said to him, "Wait for me, young man, till I go back and tell my father; for I need you to make the journey with me. I will, of course, pay you."[h] [8]Raphael replied, "Very well, I will wait for you; but do not be long."

[9]Tobiah went back to tell his father Tobit what had happened. He said to him, "I have just found a man who is one of our own Israelite kinsmen!" Tobit said, "Call the man, so that I may find out what family and tribe he comes from, and whether he is trustworthy enough to travel with you, son." Tobiah went out to summon the man saying, "Young man, my father would like to see you."

[10]When Raphael entered the house, Tobit greeted him first. Raphael said, "Hearty greetings* to you!" Tobit replied: "What joy is left for me any more? Here I am, a blind man who cannot see God's sunlight, but must remain in darkness, like the dead who no longer see the light! Though alive, I am among the dead. I can hear a man's voice, but I cannot see him." Raphael said, "Take courage! God has healing in store for you; so take courage!" Tobit then said: "My son Tobiah wants to go to Media. Can you go with him to show him the way? I will of course pay you, brother." Raphael answered: "Yes, I can go with him, for I know all the routes. I have often traveled to Media and crossed all its plains and mountains; so I know every road well." [11]Tobit asked, "Brother, tell me, please, what family and tribe are you from?" [12]Raphael said: "Why? Do you need a tribe and a family? Or are you looking for a hired man to travel with your son?" Tobit replied, "I wish to know truthfully whose son you are, brother, and what your name is."[i]

[13]Raphael answered, "I am Azariah,* son of Hananiah the elder, one of your own kinsmen." [14]Tobit exclaimed: "Welcome! God save you, brother! Do not be provoked with me, brother, for wanting to learn the truth about your family. So it turns out that you are a kinsman, and from a noble and good line! I knew Hananiah and Nathaniah, the two sons of Shemaiah the elder; with me they used to make the pilgrimage to Jerusalem, where we would worship together. No, they did not stray from the right path; your kinsmen are good men. You are certainly of good lineage, and welcome!"

[15]Then he added: "For each day you are away I will give you the normal wages,* plus expenses for you and for my son. If you go with my son, [16]I will even add a bonus to your wages!" Raphael replied: "I will go with him; have no fear. In good health we shall leave you, and in good health we shall return to you, for the way is safe." [17]Tobit said, "God bless you, brother." Then he called his son and said to him: "My son, prepare whatever you need for the journey, and set out with your kinsman. May God in heaven protect you on the way and bring you back to me safe and sound; and may his angel accompany you for safety, my son."

Before setting out on his journey, Tobiah kissed his father and mother. Tobit said to him, "Have a safe journey." [18]But his mother began to weep. She said to Tobit: "Why have you decided to send my child away? Is he not the staff to which we cling, ever there with us in all that we do? [19]I hope more money is not your chief concern! Rather let it be a ransom for our son! [20]What the Lord has given us to live on is certainly enough for us." [21]Tobit reassured her: "Have no such thought. Our son will leave in good health and come back to us in good health. Your own eyes will see the day when he returns to you safe and sound. [22]So, no such thought; do not worry about them, my love.* For a good angel will go with him, his journey will be successful, and he will return unharmed." [1]Then she stopped weeping.*

5, 10: Hearty greetings and what joy form a wordplay on the Greek verb chairein, "to greet" and "to be joyful."

5, 13-14: Azariah, "Yahweh helps"; Hananiah, "Yahweh is merciful"; Nathaniah, "Yahweh gives"; Shemaiah, "Yahweh hears."

5, 15: The normal wages: literally, "a drachma," about seventeen cents, a day's wage for a workingman.

5, 22: My love: literally, "sister," a term of endearment

applied to one's wife; cf Tb 7, 11. 15; 8, 4. 21; 10, 6. 13; Song 4, 9. 10. 12; 5, 1f. A good angel: a reference to the guardian angel, though Tobit does not know, of course, that Raphael himself, disguised as Azariah, is the good angel in this case.

5, 1: Then . . . weeping: this verse belongs to ch 6.

h: Tb 12, 2. i: Jgs 13, 17f.

CHAPTER 6

See RG
152

Journey to Rages. ²When the boy left home, accompanied by the angel, the dog followed Tobiah out of the house and went with him. The travelers walked till nightfall, and made camp beside the Tigris River. ³Now when the boy went down to wash his feet in the river, a large fish suddenly leaped out of the water and tried to swallow his foot. He shouted in alarm. ⁴But the angel said to him, "Take hold of the fish and don't let it get away!" The boy seized the fish and hauled it up on the shore. ⁵The angel then told him: "Cut the fish open and take out its gall, heart, and liver, and keep them with you; but throw away the entrails. Its gall, heart, and liver make useful medicines."* ⁶After the lad had cut the fish open, he put aside the gall, the heart, and liver. Then he broiled and ate part of the fish; the rest he salted and kept for the journey.

Raphael's Instructions. ⁷Afterward they traveled on together till they were near Media. The boy asked the angel this question: "Brother Azariah, what medicinal value is there in the fish's heart, liver, and gall?" ⁸He answered: "As regards the fish's heart and liver, if you burn them so that the smoke surrounds a man or a woman who is afflicted by a demon or evil spirit, the affliction will leave him completely, and no demons will ever return to him again. ⁹And as for the gall, if you rub it on the eyes of a man who has cataracts, blowing into his eyes right on the cataracts, his sight will be restored."

¹⁰When they had entered Media and were getting close to Ecbatana, ¹¹Raphael said to the boy, "Brother Tobiah!" He answered, "Yes, what is it?" Raphael continued: "Tonight we must stay with Raguel, who is a relative of yours. He has a daughter named Sarah, ¹²but no other child. Since you are Sarah's closest relative, you before all other men have the right to marry her. Also, her father's estate is rightfully yours to inherit.

Now the girl is sensible, courageous, and very beautiful; and her father loves her dearly."ʲ ¹³He continued: "Since you have the right to marry her, listen to me, brother. Tonight I will ask the girl's father to let us have her as your bride. When we return from Rages, we will hold the wedding feast for her. I know that Raguel cannot keep her from you or let her become engaged to another man; that would be a capital crime according to the decree in the Book of Moses,* and he knows that it is your right, before all other men, to marry his daughter. So heed my words, brother; tonight we must speak for the girl, so that we may have her engaged to you. And when we return from Rages, we will take her and bring her back with us to your house."

¹⁴Tobiah objected, however: "Brother Azariah, I have heard that this woman has already been married seven times, and that her husbands died in their bridal chambers. On the very night they approached her, they dropped dead. And I have heard it said that it was a demon who killed them. ¹⁵So now I too am afraid of this demon. Because he loves her, he does not harm her; but he does slay any man who wishes to come close to her. I am my father's only child. If I should die, I would bring my father and mother down to their grave in sorrow over me. And they have no other son to bury them!"ᵏ

¹⁶Raphael said to him: "Do you not remember your father's orders? He commanded you to marry a woman from your own family. So now listen to me, brother; do not give another thought to this demon, but marry Sarah. I know that tonight you shall have her for your wife! ¹⁷When you go into the bridal chamber, take the fish's liver and heart, and place them on the embers for the incense. ¹⁸As soon as the demon smells the odor they give off, he will flee and never again show himself near her. Then when you are about to have intercourse with her, both of you first rise up to pray.* Beg the Lord of heaven to show you mercy and grant you de-

---

6, 5: Its gall . . . medicines: belief in the healing power of these organs was common among even the physicians of antiquity.

6, 13: Raguel . . . Book of Moses: Nm 36, 6-8 prescribed marriage within the ancestral tribe, but no death penalty is

mentioned.

6, 18: Rise up to pray: prayer is needed to drive out the demon.

j: Tb 4, 12f; Nm 36, 8. *k:* Tb 3, 10.

Tobiah and Sarah Are Married

Similar marriage arrangements are related in Genesis 24, 14; 29, 9–12; Exodus 2, 16–21. The author strongly favors arranged marriages (see also Tb 6, 16), probably because in a foreign society romantic marriages were likely to involve non-Israelites or members of other tribes, thus weakening religious unity or tribal integrity.

liverance. But do not be afraid, for she was set apart for you before the world existed. You will save her, and she will go with you. And I suppose that you will have children by her, who will take the place of brothers for you. So do not worry."

When Tobiah heard Raphael say that she was his kinswoman, of his own family's lineage, he fell deeply in love with her, and his heart became set on her.

See RG 152

CHAPTER 7

At the House of Raguel. ¹When they entered Ecbatana, Tobiah said, "Brother Azariah, lead me straight to our kinsman Raguel." So he brought him to the house of Raguel, whom they found seated by his courtyard gate. They greeted him first. He said to them, "Greetings to you too, brothers! Good health to you, and welcome!" When he brought them into his home, ²he said to his wife Edna, "This young man looks just like my kinsman Tobit!" ³So Edna asked them, "Who are you, brothers?" They answered, "We are of the exiles from Naphtali at Nineveh." ⁴She said, "Do you know our kinsman Tobit?" They answered, "Indeed we do!" She asked, "Is he well?" ⁵They answered, "Yes, he is alive and well." Then Tobiah exclaimed, "He is my father!" ⁶Raguel sprang up and kissed him, shedding tears of joy. ⁷But when he heard that Tobit had lost his eyesight, he was grieved and wept aloud. He said to Tobiah: "My child, God bless you! You are the son of a noble and good father. But what a terrible misfortune that such a righteous and charitable man should be afflicted with blindness!" He continued to weep in the arms of his kinsman Tobiah. ⁸His wife Edna also wept for Tobit; and even their daughter Sarah began to weep.

Marriage of Tobiah and Sarah. ⁹Afterward, Raguel slaughtered a ram from the flock and gave them a cordial reception. When they had bathed and reclined to eat, Tobiah said to Raphael, "Brother Azariah, ask Raguel to let me marry my kinswoman Sarah." ¹⁰Raguel overheard the words; so he said to the boy: "Eat and drink and be merry tonight, for no man is more entitled to marry my daughter Sarah than you, brother. Besides, not even I have the right to give her to anyone but you, because you are my closest relative. But I will explain the situation to you very frankly. ¹¹I have given her in marriage to seven men, all of whom were kinsmen of ours, and all died on the very night they approached her. But now, son, eat and drink. I am sure the Lord will look after you both." Tobiah answered, "I will eat or drink nothing until you set aside what belongs to me."

Raguel said to him: "I will do it. She is yours according to the decree of the Book of Moses. Your marriage to her has been decided in heaven! Take your kinswoman; from now on you are her love, and she is your beloved. She is yours today and ever after. And tonight, son, may the Lord of heaven prosper you both. May he grant you mercy and peace." ¹²Then Raguel called his daughter Sarah, and she came to him. He took her by the hand and gave her to Tobiah with the words: "Take her according to the law. According to the decree written in the Book of Moses she is your wife. Take her and bring her back safely to your father. And may the God of heaven grant both of you peace and prosperity."[l] ¹³He then called her mother and told her to bring a scroll, so that he might draw up a marriage contract stating that he gave Sarah to Tobiah as his wife according to the decree of the Mosaic law. Her mother

l: Gn 24, 50f.

brought the scroll, and he drew up the contract, to which they affixed their seals.*m*

*14*Afterward they began to eat and drink. *15*Later Raguel called his wife Edna and said, "My love, prepare the other bedroom and bring the girl there." *16*She went and made the bed in the room, as she was told, and brought the girl there. After she had cried over her, she wiped away the tears and said: *17*"Be brave, my daughter. May the Lord of heaven grant you joy in place of your grief. Courage, my daughter." Then she left.

CHAPTER 8

See RG
152
Expulsion of the Demon. *1*When they had finished eating and drinking, the girl's parents wanted to retire. They brought the young man out of the dining room and led him into the bedroom. *2*At this point Tobiah, mindful of Raphael's instructions, took the fish's liver and heart from the bag which he had with him, and placed them on the embers for the incense.* *3*The demon, repelled by the odor of the fish, fled into Upper Egypt;* Raphael pursued him there and bound him hand and foot. Then Raphael returned immediately.

*4*When the girl's parents left the bedroom and closed the door behind them, Tobiah arose from bed and said to his wife, "My love, get up. Let us pray and beg our Lord to have mercy on us and to grant us deliverance." *5*She got up, and they started to pray and beg that deliverance might be theirs. He began with these words:

"Blessed are you, O God of our fathers;
	praised be your name forever and ever.
Let the heavens and all your creation
	praise you forever.*n*
6 You made Adam and you gave him his
		wife Eve
	to be his help and support;
	and from these two the human race
		descended.

You said, 'It is not good for the man to be
		alone;
	let us make him a partner like
		himself.'*o*
7 Now, Lord, you know that I take this
		wife of mine
	not because of lust,
	but for a noble purpose.
Call down your mercy on me and on her,
	and allow us to live together to a
		happy old age."

*8*They said together, "Amen, amen," *9*and went to bed for the night.

But Raguel got up and summoned his servants. With him they went out to dig a grave, *10*for he said, "I must do this, because if Tobiah should die, we would be subjected to ridicule and insult." *11*When they had finished digging the grave, Raguel went back into the house and called his wife, *12*saying, "Send one of the maids in to see whether Tobiah is alive or dead, so that if necessary we may bury him without anyone's knowing about it." *13*She sent the maid, who lit a lamp, opened the bedroom door, went in, and found them sound asleep together. *14*The maid went out and told the girl's parents that Tobiah was alive, and that there was nothing wrong. *15*Then Raguel praised the God of heaven in these words:

"Blessed are you, O God, with every
	holy and pure blessing!
Let all your chosen ones praise you;
	let them bless you forever!
16 Blessed are you, who have made me
		glad;
	what I feared did not happen.
Rather you have dealt with us
	according to your great mercy.
17 Blessed are you, for you were merciful
	toward two only children.
Grant them, Master, mercy and
		deliverance,
	and bring their lives to fulfillment

8, 2f: The manner of coping with demonic influences among the ancients seems quaint to us. However, the fish here is part of the story, and not a recipe for exorcism. It is clear that the author places primary emphasis on the value of prayer to God (Tb 6, 18; 8, 4-8), on the role of the angel as God's agent, and on the pious dispositions of Tobiah.

8, 3: Into Upper Egypt: to the desert there. The desert was considered the dwelling place of demons. Cf Is 13, 21; 34, 14; Mt 4, 1; 12, 43.

m: Tb 6, 12.	*n:* Dn 3, 26.	*o:* Gn 2, 18-23.

with happiness and mercy."

¹⁸Then he told his servants to fill in the grave before dawn.

Wedding Feast. ¹⁹He asked his wife to bake many loaves of bread; he himself went out to the herd and picked out two steers and four rams which he ordered to be slaughtered. So the servants began to prepare the feast. ²⁰He summoned Tobiah and made an oath in his presence, saying: "For fourteen days* you shall not stir from here, but shall remain here eating and drinking with me; and you shall bring joy to my daughter's sorrowing spirit. ²¹Take, to begin with, half of whatever I own when you go back in good health to your father; the other half will be yours when I and my wife die. Be of good cheer, my son! I am your father, and Edna is your mother; and we belong to you and to your beloved now and forever. So be happy, son!"

CHAPTER 9

See RG
152

The Money Recovered. ¹Then Tobiah called Raphael and said to him: ²"Brother Azariah, take along with you four servants and two camels and travel to Rages. Go to Gabael's house and give him this bond. Get the money and then bring him along with you to the wedding celebration. ⁴For you know that my father is counting the days. If I should delay my return by a single day, I would cause him intense grief. ³You witnessed the oath that Raguel has sworn; I cannot violate his oath." ⁵So Raphael, together with the four servants and two camels, traveled to Rages in Media, where they stayed at Gabael's house. Raphael gave Gabael his bond and told him about Tobit's son Tobiah, and that he had married and was inviting him to the wedding celebration. Gabael promptly checked over the sealed money-bags, and they placed them on the camels.

⁶The following morning they got an early start and traveled to the wedding celebration. When they entered Raguel's house, they found Tobiah reclining at table. He sprang up

and greeted Gabael, who wept and blessed him, exclaiming: "O noble and good child, son of a noble and good, upright and charitable man, may the Lord grant heavenly blessing to you and to your wife, and to your wife's father and mother. Blessed be God, because I have seen the very image of my cousin Tobit!"

IV: Tobiah's Return; Cure of Tobit's Blindness

CHAPTER 10

Anxiety of the Parents. ¹Meanwhile,

See RG
152

day by day, Tobit was keeping track of the time Tobiah would need to go and to return. When the number of days was reached and his son did not appear, ²he said, "I wonder what has happened. Perhaps he has been detained there; or perhaps Gabael is dead, and there is no one to give him the money." ³And he began to worry. ⁴His wife Anna said, "My son has perished and is no longer among the living!" And she began to weep aloud and to wail over her son: ⁵"Alas, my child, light of my eyes, that I let you make this journey!" ⁶But Tobit kept telling her: "Hush, do not think about it, my love; he is safe! Probably they have to take care of some unexpected business there. The man who is traveling with him is trustworthy, and is one of our own kinsmen. So do not worry over him, my love. He will be here soon." ⁷But she retorted, "Stop it, and do not lie to me! My child has perished!" She would go out and keep watch all day at the road her son had taken, and she ate nothing. At sunset she would go back home to wail and cry the whole night through, getting no sleep at all.^p

Departure from Ecbatana. Now at the end of the fourteen-day wedding celebration which Raguel had sworn to hold for his daughter, Tobiah went to him and said: "Please let me go, for I know that my father and mother do not believe they will ever see me again. So I beg you, father, let me go back to my father. I have already told you how I

8, 20: For fourteen days: because of the happy, and unexpected, turn of events, Raguel doubles the time of the wedding feast. When Tobiah returns home, the usual seven-day feast is held (Tb 11, 18). Cf Jgs 14, 12.

p: Gn 45, 26.

Tobiah and Sarah Leave Ecbatana

When Anna calls Tobiah the "light of my eyes" (10, 5), she is expressing the symbolic sight-blindness motif: Israel is blind to the meaning of history, but light will come at the end. See Tobit 11, 15. Tobiah's pleas to be allowed to go home are meant to be a model for all exiled Israelites who should yearn constantly for home.

left him." *8*Raguel said to Tobiah: "Stay, my child, stay with me. I am sending messengers to your father Tobit, and they will give him news of you." *9*But Tobiah insisted, "No, I beg you to let me go back to my father."

*10*Raguel then promptly handed over to Tobiah Sarah his wife, together with half of all his property: male and female slaves, oxen and sheep, asses and camels, clothing, money, and household goods. *11*Bidding them farewell, he let them go. He embraced Tobiah and said to him: "Good-bye, my son. Have a safe journey. May the Lord of heaven grant prosperity to you and to your wife Sarah. And may I see children of yours before I die!" *12*Then he kissed his daughter Sarah and said to her: "My daughter, honor your father-in-law and your mother-in-law, because from now on they are as much your parents as the ones who brought you into the world. Go in peace, my daughter; let me hear good reports about you as long as I live." Finally he said good-bye to them and sent them away.

*13*Then Edna said to Tobiah: "My child and beloved kinsman, may the Lord bring you back safely, and may I live long enough to see children of you and of my daughter Sarah before I die. Before the Lord, I entrust my daughter to your care. Never cause her grief at any time in your life. Go in peace, my child. From now on I am your mother, and Sarah is your beloved. May all of us be prosperous all the days of our lives." She kissed them both and sent them away in peace.

*14*When Tobiah left Raguel, he was full of happiness and joy, and he blessed the Lord of heaven and earth, the King of all, for making his journey so successful. Finally he said good-bye to Raguel and his wife Edna, and added, "May I honor you all the days of my life!"

q: Gn 33, 4; 45, 14; 46, 29f; Lk 15, 20.

CHAPTER 11

See RG 152

Homeward Journey. *1*Then they left and began their return journey. When they were near Kaserin, just before Nineveh, *2*Raphael said: "You know how we left your father. *3*Let us hurry on ahead of your wife to prepare the house while the rest of the party are still on the way." *4*So they both went on ahead and Raphael said to Tobiah, "Have the gall in your hand!" And the dog ran along behind them.

*5*Meanwhile, Anna sat watching the road by which her son was to come. *6*When she saw him coming, she exclaimed to his father, "Tobit, your son is coming, and the man who traveled with him!"

*7*Raphael said to Tobiah before he reached his father: "I am certain that his eyes will be opened. *8*Smear the fish gall on them. This medicine will make the cataracts shrink and peel off from his eyes; then your father will again be able to see the light of day."

Sight Restored. *9*Then Anna ran up to her son, threw her arms around him, and said to him, "Now that I have seen you again, son, I am ready to die!" And she sobbed aloud.*q* *10*Tobit got up and stumbled out through the courtyard gate. Tobiah went up to him *11*with the fish gall in his hand, and holding him firmly, blew into his eyes. "Courage, father," he said. *12*Next he smeared the medicine on his eyes, *13*and it made them smart. Then, beginning at the corners of Tobit's eyes, Tobiah used both hands to peel off the cataracts. When Tobit saw his son, he threw his arms around him *14*and wept. He exclaimed, "I can see you, son, the light of my eyes!" Then he said:

"Blessed be God,
and praised be his great name,

and blessed be all his holy angels.
May his holy name be praised
    throughout all the ages,
15 Because it was he who scourged me,
    and it is he who has had mercy on me.
Behold, I now see my son Tobiah!"

Then Tobit went back in, rejoicing and praising God with full voice. Tobiah told his father that his journey had been a success; that he had brought back the money; and that he had married Raguel's daughter Sarah, who would arrive shortly, for she was approaching the gate of Nineveh.*r*

*16*Rejoicing and praising God, Tobit went out to the gate of Nineveh to meet his daughter-in-law. When the people of Nineveh saw him walking along briskly, with no one leading him by the hand, they were amazed. *17*Before them all Tobit proclaimed how God had mercifully restored sight to his eyes. When Tobit reached Sarah, the wife of his son Tobiah, he greeted her: "Welcome, my daughter! Blessed be your God for bringing you to us, daughter! Blessed are your father and your mother. Blessed is my son Tobiah, and blessed are you, daughter! Welcome to your home with blessing and joy. Come in, daughter!" That day there was joy for all the Jews who lived in Nineveh. *18*Ahiqar and his nephew Nadab also came to rejoice with Tobit. They celebrated Tobiah's wedding feast for seven happy days, and he received many gifts.

V: Raphael Reveals His Identity

CHAPTER 12

See RG 152 *Raphael's Wages.** *1*When the wedding celebration came to an end, Tobit called his son Tobiah and said to him, "Son, see to it that you give what is due to the man who made the journey with you; give him a bonus too." *2*Tobiah said: "Father, how much shall I pay him? It would not hurt me at all to give him half of all the wealth he brought back with me.*s* *3*He led me back safe and sound; he cured my wife; he brought the money back with me; and he cured you. How much of a bonus should I give him?" *4*Tobit answered, "It is only fair, son, that he should receive half of all that he brought back." *5*So Tobiah called Raphael and said, "Take as your wages half of all that you have brought back, and go in peace."

*Exhortation.** *6*Raphael called the two men aside privately and said to them: "Thank God! Give him the praise and the glory. Before all the living, acknowledge the many good things he has done for you, by blessing and extolling his name in song. Before all men, honor and proclaim God's deeds, and do not be slack in praising him.* *7*A king's secret it is prudent to keep, but the works of God are to be declared and made known. Praise them with due honor. Do good, and evil will not find its way to you. *8*Prayer and fasting are good, but better than either is almsgiving accompanied by righteousness.* A little with righteousness is better than abundance with wickedness. It is better to give alms than to store up gold;*t* *9*for almsgiving saves one from death and expiates every sin. Those who regularly give alms shall enjoy a full life;*u* *10*but those habitually guilty of sin are their own worst enemies.

Raphael's Identity. *11*"I will now tell you the whole truth; I will conceal nothing at all from you. I have already said to you, 'A king's secret it is prudent to keep, but the works of God are to be made known with due honor.' *12v*I can now tell you that when you, Tobit, and Sarah prayed, it was I who presented and read the record of your prayer before the Glory of the Lord; and I did the same thing when you used to bury the dead.* *13*When you did not

12, 1-5: Tobit and his son generously agree to give Azariah far more than the wages agreed upon in Tb 5, 15-16.

12, 6-10: In the fashion of a wisdom teacher, Raphael gives the two men a short exhortation similar to the one Tobit gave his son in Tb 4, 3-19.

12, 6f: The Jews considered the duty of praising God their most esteemed privilege. Without praise of God, life was meaningless. Cf Is 38, 16-20.

12, 8: Prayer . . . fasting . . . almsgiving . . . righteousness:

these, together with the proper attitude toward wealth, are treated in great detail by Christ our Lord in the Sermon on the Mount (Mt 6).

12, 12. 15: Raphael is one of the seven specially designated intercessors who present man's prayers to God. Angelology was developing in this period. The names of two other angels

r: Tb 13, 2; Dt 32, 39; 1 Sm 2, 6.   *s:* Tb 5, 3. 7. 15f.   *t:* Tb 4, 7-11; Sir 29, 8-13.   *u:* Dn 4, 24.   *v:* Jb 33, 23f; Acts 10, 4; Rv 8, 3f.

The "whole truth" (12, 11) is that God's Providence works through human misfortune to test human beings, a theme that pervades Wisdom literature; see Wis 3, 6; Prv 17, 3.

hesitate to get up and leave your dinner in order to go and bury the dead, [14]I was sent to put you to the test.* At the same time, however, God commissioned me to heal you and your daughter-in-law Sarah. [15]I am Raphael, one of the seven angels who enter and serve before the Glory of the Lord."[w]

[16]Stricken with fear, the two men fell to the ground. [17]But Raphael said to them: "No need to fear; you are safe. Thank God now and forever. [18]As for me, when I came to you it was not out of any favor on my part, but because it was God's will. So continue to thank him every day; praise him with song. [19]Even though you watched me eat and drink, I did not really do so; what you were seeing was a vision. [20]So now get up from the ground and praise God. Behold, I am about to ascend to him who sent me; write down all these things that have happened to you."[x] [21]When Raphael ascended, they rose to their feet and could no longer see him. [22]They kept thanking God and singing his praises; and they continued to acknowledge these marvelous deeds which he had done when the angel of God appeared to them.

VI: Tobit's Song of Praise

CHAPTER 13

See RG 152 [1] Then Tobit composed this joyful prayer:*

Blessed be God who lives forever,
    because his kingdom lasts for all ages.[y]
[2] For he scourges and then has mercy;
    he casts down to the depths of the
        netherworld,
    and he brings up from the great abyss.

No one can escape his hand.[z]

[3] Praise him, you Israelites, before the
        Gentiles,
    for though he has scattered you among
        them,
[4]   he has shown you his greatness even
        there.
Exalt him before every living being,
    because he is the Lord our God,
    our Father and God forever.
[5] He scourged you for your iniquities,
    but will again have mercy on you all.
He will gather you from all the Gentiles
    among whom you have been
        scattered.[a]

[6] When you turn back to him with all your
        heart,
    to do what is right before him,
Then he will turn back to you,
    and no longer hide his face from you.[b]

So now consider what he has done for
        you,
    and praise him with full voice.
Bless the Lord of righteousness,
    and exalt the King of the ages.

In the land of my exile I praise him,
    and show his power and majesty to a
        sinful nation.
"Turn back, you sinners! do the right
        before him:
    perhaps he may look with favor upon
        you
    and show you mercy.
[7] "As for me, I exalt my God,

are given in the Bible: Gabriel (Dn 8, 16; 9, 21; Lk 1, 19. 26) and Michael (Dn 10, 13. 21; 12, 1; Jude 9; Rv 12, 7).

12, 14: I was sent . . . test: God often sends trials to purify his faithful servants further. Cf Jb 1—2.

13, 1-18: Tobit's hymn of praise (cf Ex 15, 1-18; Jdt 16, 1-17) is divided into two parts. The first part (vv 1-8) is a song of praise that echoes themes from the hymns and psalms of the kingdom; the second (vv 9-18) is addressed to Jerusalem in the style of the prophets who spoke of a new and ideal Jerusalem (Is 60); cf Rv 21.

w: Lk 1, 19; Rv 8, 2.   x: Jgs 13, 20.   y: Tb 3, 11; 8, 5. 15; 1 Chr 29, 10; Dn 3, 26.   z: Tb 11, 15; 13, 9; Dt 32, 39; 1 Sm 2, 6; Wis 16, 13.   a: Dt 30, 3; Neh 1, 9.   b: Dt 30, 2.

and my spirit rejoices in the King of
heaven.
[8] Let all men speak of his majesty,
and sing his praises in Jerusalem."

[9] O Jerusalem, holy city,
he scourged you for the works of your
hands,*
but will again pity the children of the
righteous.[c]
[10] Praise the Lord for his goodness,
and bless the King of the ages,
so that his tent may be rebuilt in you
with joy.
May he gladden within you all who were
captives;
all who were ravaged may he cherish
within you
for all generations to come.[d]

[11] A bright light will shine to all parts of the
earth;
many nations shall come to you from
afar,
And the inhabitants of all the limits of
the earth,
drawn to you by the name of the Lord
God,
Bearing in their hands their gifts for the
King of heaven.
Every generation shall give joyful praise
in you,
and shall call you the chosen one,
through all ages forever.[e]

[12] Accursed are all who speak a harsh word
against you;
accursed are all who destroy you
and pull down your walls,
And all who overthrow your towers
and set fire to your homes;
but forever blessed are all those who
build you up.[f]

[13] Go, then, rejoice over the children of the
righteous,

who shall all be gathered together
and shall bless the Lord of the ages.
[14] Happy are those who love you,
and happy those who rejoice in your
prosperity.

Happy are all the men who shall grieve
over you,
over all your chastisements,
For they shall rejoice in you
as they behold all your joy forever.[g]

[15] My spirit blesses the Lord, the great King;
[16] Jerusalem shall be rebuilt as his home
forever.
Happy for me if a remnant of my
offspring survive
to see your glory and to praise the
King of heaven!

The gates of Jerusalem shall be built with
sapphire and emerald,
and all your walls with precious stones.
The towers of Jerusalem shall be built
with gold,
and their battlements with pure gold.[h]
[17] The streets of Jerusalem shall be paved
with rubies and stones of Ophir;
[18] The gates of Jerusalem shall sing hymns
of gladness,
and all her houses shall cry out,
"Alleluia!"

"Blessed be God who has raised you up!
may he be blessed for all ages!"
For in you they shall praise his holy
name forever.

The end of Tobit's hymn of praise

VII: Epilogue
CHAPTER 14

Parting Advice. [1]Tobit died peacefully at the age of a hundred and twelve, and
received an honorable burial in Nineveh.

See RG
152

13, 9: Works of your hands: idols.

c: Tb 11, 15; Mi 7, 19; Rv 21.   *d:* Is 44, 26. 28; Am 9, 11; Zec 1, 16.   *e:* Is 2, 3f; 9, 1; 49, 6; 60, 1; Mi 4, 2; Zec 8, 22.   *f:* Bar 4, 31f.
g: Ps 122, 6; Is 66, 10.   *h:* Tb 14, 5; Is 54, 11-13; 62, 2; Rv 21, 10-21.

[2]He was sixty-two years old when he lost his eyesight, and after he recovered it he lived in prosperity, giving alms and continually blessing God and praising the divine Majesty.

[3]Just before he died, he called his son Tobiah and Tobiah's seven sons, and gave him this command: "Son, take your children[i] [4]and flee into Media, for I believe God's word which was spoken by Nahum* against Nineveh. It shall all happen, and shall overtake Assyria and Nineveh; indeed, whatever was said by Israel's prophets, whom God commissioned, shall occur. Not one of all the oracles shall remain unfulfilled, but everything shall take place in the time appointed for it. So it will be safer in Media than in Assyria or Babylon. For I know and believe that whatever God has spoken will be accomplished. It shall happen, and not a single word of the prophecies shall prove false.

"As for our kinsmen who dwell in Israel, they shall all be scattered and led away into exile from the Good Land. The entire country of Israel shall become desolate; even Samaria and Jerusalem shall become desolate! God's temple there shall be burnt to the ground and shall be desolate for a while.[j] [5]But God will again have mercy on them and bring them back to the land of Israel. They shall rebuild the temple, but it will not be like the first one, until the era when the appointed times shall be completed.* Afterward all of them shall return from their exile, and they shall rebuild Jerusalem with splendor. In her the temple of God shall also be rebuilt; yes, it will be rebuilt for all generations to come, just as the prophets of Israel said of her.[k] [6]All the nations of the world shall be converted and shall offer God true worship; all shall abandon their idols which have deceitfully led them into error,* [7]and shall bless the God of the ages in righteousness. Because all the Israelites who are to be saved in those days will truly be mindful of God, they shall be gathered together and go to Jerusalem; in security shall they dwell forever in the land of Abraham, which will be given over to them. Those who sincerely love God shall rejoice, but those who become guilty of sin shall completely disappear from the land.[m]

[9]"Now, children, I give you this command: serve God faithfully and do what is right before him; you must tell your children to do what is upright and to give alms, to be mindful of God and at all times to bless his name sincerely and with all their strength.

[8]"Now, as for you, my son, depart from Nineveh; do not remain here. [10]The day you bury your mother next to me, do not even stay overnight within the confines of the city. For I see that people here shamelessly commit all sorts of wickedness and treachery. Think, my son, of all that Nadab* did to Ahiqar, the very one who brought him up: Ahiqar went down alive into the earth! Yet God made Nadab's disgraceful crime rebound against him. Ahiqar came out again into the light, but Nadab went into the everlasting darkness, for he had tried to kill Ahiqar. Because Ahiqar had given alms to me, he escaped from the deadly trap Nadab had set for him. But Nadab himself fell into the deadly trap, and it destroyed him.[n] [11]So, my children, note well what almsgiving

14, 4f: Nahum: one of the minor prophets, whose book contains oracles of doom against Nineveh. Here, in keeping with the period to which he assigns his story, the sacred author makes Tobit speak as if the punishment of Nineveh, the destruction of Jerusalem (587 B.C.), the exile from Judah and the return, would all take place in the future. The technique of using the facts of past history as seemingly future predictions, is a frequent device of apocalyptic writers. The Good Land: a favorite name for the promised land. Cf Dt 1, 35; 3, 25; 4, 21. 22.

14, 5: Until the era . . . completed: a reference to the advent of messianic times, in which a new, more perfect temple was to be expected. Cf Heb 9, 1-14.

14, 6: Conversion of the Gentiles is also to come in the messianic era.

14, 10: Nadab: In the story of Ahiqar, the hero Ahiqar, chancellor under the Assyrian kings Sennacherib and Esarhaddon, adopts his nephew Nadab and prepares him to become his successor. But Nadab treacherously plots to have his uncle put to death. Ahiqar hides in a friend's house, and is finally vindicated (came out again into the light) when Nadab's scheme is discovered. Thereupon Nadab is thrown into a dungeon where he dies (went into everlasting darkness). It was Ahiqar's almsgiving that delivered him from death; see note on Tb 2, 2.

i: Gn 47, 29f.   j: Na 2, 2—3, 19.   k: Neh 12, 27; Jer 31, 38. l: Tb 45, 14; Is 60, 1-4.   m: Is 60, 21; Jer 32, 37; Ex 34, 28; 37, 25; 39, 26.   n: Tb 1, 21f.

does, and also what wickedness does—it kills! But now my spirit is about to leave me."

Death of Tobit and Tobiah. *12*They placed him on his bed and he died; and he received an honorable burial. When Tobiah's mother died, he buried her next to his father. He then departed with his wife and children for Media, where he settled in Ecbatana with his father-in-law Raguel.*o* *13*He took respectful care of his aging father-in-law and mother-in-law; and he buried them at Ecbatana in Media. Then he inherited Raguel's estate as well as that of his father Tobit. *14*He died at the venerable age of a hundred and seventeen. *15*But before he died, he heard of the destruction of Nineveh and saw its effects. He witnessed the exile of the city's inhabitants when Cyaxares,* king of Media, led them captive into Media. Tobiah praised God for all that he had done against the citizens of Nineveh and Assyria. Before dying he rejoiced over Nineveh's destruction, and he blessed the Lord God forever and ever. Amen.

14, 15: Cyaxares: Nabopolassar, king of Babylon, and Cyaxares conquered and destroyed Nineveh in 612 B.C.; see note on Tb 1, 15.

o: Tb 4, 4.

See RG
153–55

The Book of Judith

The Book of Judith is a vivid story relating how, in a grave crisis, God delivered the Jewish people through the instrumentality of a woman. The unknown author composed this edifying narrative of divine providence at the end of the second or the beginning of the first century B.C. The original was almost certainly written in Hebrew, but the Greek text shows so much freedom in adapting from the Septuagint the language of older biblical books that it must be regarded as having a literary character of its own. It is this Greek form of the book, accepted as canonical by the Catholic Church, which is translated here. St. Jerome, who prepared (with some reluctance) a Latin text of Judith, based his work on a secondary Aramaic text available to him in Palestine, combined with an older Latin rendering from the Greek. The long hymn of chapter 16 he took in its entirety from that earlier Latin text.

Since it is no longer possible to determine with any precision the underlying events which may have given rise to this narrative, it is enough to note that the author sought to strengthen the faith of his people in God's abiding presence among them. The Book of Judith is a tract for difficult times; the reader, it was hoped, would take to heart the lesson that God was still the Master of history, who could save Israel from her enemies. Note the parallel with the time of the Exodus: as God had delivered his people by the hand of Moses, so he could deliver them by the hand of the pious widow Judith (see note on 2, 12).

The story can be divided into two parts. In the first (cc 1—7), Holofernes, commander-in-chief of the armies of Nebuchadnezzar, leads an overwhelming Assyrian force in a punitive campaign against the vassals who refused to help in the Assyrian war against the Medes. The Jewish people stubbornly resist the enemy at Bethulia, guarding the route of access to Jerusalem. Despite the warning of Achior that the Jews cannot be conquered unless they sin against God, the proud general lays siege to the town and cuts off its water supply. After a siege of thirty-four days, the exhausted defenders are desperate and ready to surrender.

At this point, the climax of the story, Judith (the name means "Jewess") appears and promises to defeat the Assyrians. The rest of the story is too well known to repeat in detail. Having fasted and prayed, Judith dresses in her finest garments and proceeds to the Assyrian camp, where she succeeds in killing Holofernes while he lies in a drunken stupor. The Assyrians panic when they discover this, and the Jews are able to rout and slaughter them. The beautiful hymn of the people honoring Judith (15, 9-10) is often applied to Mary in the liturgy.

Nebuchadnezzar Wages War on Arphaxad

Nebuchadnezzar, king of the Babylonians from 605 to 561 B.C., directed the destruction of Jerusalem in 587 B.C. His father had conquered the Assyrians and destroyed Nineveh in 612 B.C. The historically impossible combination of Nebuchadnezzar and the Assyrians suggests that the author wished to combine Israel's traditional enemies to create a literary confrontation between faith and secular power.

Any attempt to read the book directly against the backdrop of Jewish history in relation to the empires of the ancient world is bound to fail. The story was written as a pious reflection on the meaning of the yearly Passover observance. It draws its inspiration from the Exodus narrative (especially Ex 14, 31) and from the texts of Isaiah and the Psalms portraying the special intervention of God for the preservation of Jerusalem. The theme of God's hand as the agent of this providential activity, reflected of old in the hand of Moses and now in the hand of Judith, is again exemplified at a later time in Jewish synagogue art. God's hand reaching down from heaven appears as part of the scene at Dura-Europos (before A.D. 256) in paintings of the Exodus, of the sacrifice of Isaac (Gn 22), and of Ezekiel's valley of dry bones (Ez 37).

The Book of Judith is divided as follows:

I: Peril of the Jews (1, 1—7, 32).
II: Deliverance of the Jews (8, 1—14, 10).
III: Victory (14, 11—16, 25).

I: Peril of the Jews

CHAPTER 1

See RG 154-56 *War against the Medes.* ¹It was the twelfth year of the reign of Nebuchadnezzar, king of the Assyrians in the great city of Nineveh. At that time Arphaxad ruled over the Medes in Ecbatana. ²Around this city he built a wall of blocks of stone, each three cubits in height and six in length. He made the wall seventy cubits high and fifty thick. ³At the gates he raised towers of a hundred cubits, with a thickness of sixty cubits at the base. ⁴The gateway he built to a height of seventy cubits, with an opening forty cubits wide for the passage of his chariot forces and the marshaling of his infantry. ⁵Then King Nebuchadnezzar waged war against King Arphaxad in the vast plain, in the district of Ragae. ⁶To him there rallied all the inhabitants of the mountain region, all who dwelt along the Euphrates, the Tigris, and the Hydaspes, and King Arioch of the Elamites, in the plain. Thus many nations came together to resist the people of Cheleoud.*

Ultimatum to the West. ⁷Now Nebuchadnezzar, king of the Assyrians, sent messengers to all the inhabitants of Persia, and to all those who dwelt in the West: to the inhabitants of Cilicia and Damascus, Lebanon and Anti-Lebanon, to all who dwelt along the seacoast, ⁸to the peoples of Carmel, Gilead, Upper Galilee, and the vast plain of Esdraelon, ⁹to all those in Samaria and its cities, and west of the Jordan as far as Jerusalem, Bethany, Chelous, Kadesh, and the River of Egypt; to Tahpanhes, Raamses, all the land of Goshen, ¹⁰Tanis, Memphis and beyond, and to all the inhabitants of Egypt as far as the borders of Ethiopia.

¹¹But the inhabitants of all that land disregarded the summons of Nebuchadnezzar, king of the Assyrians, and would not go with him to the war. They were not afraid of him but regarded him as a lone individual opposed to them, and turned away his envoys empty-handed, in disgrace. ¹²Then Nebuchadnezzar fell into a violent rage against all that land, and swore by his throne and his kingdom that he would avenge himself on all the territories of Cilicia and Damascus and Syria, and also destroy with his sword all the inhabitants of Moab, Ammon, the whole of

---

1, 6: Cheleoud: probably the Chaldeans are meant.

Nebuchadnezzar's designation of himself as "lord" without references to the rights of God (2, 5) makes this a battle between the ungodly and the God-fearing. The offering of earth and water (v. 7) was a Persian expression for the provisioning of an invading and conquering army by the occupied country.

Judea, and those living anywhere in Egypt as far as the borders of the two seas.*

Defeat of Arphaxad. *13*In the seventeenth year he proceeded with his army against King Arphaxad, and was victorious in his campaign. He routed the whole force of Arphaxad, his entire cavalry and all his chariots, *14*and took possession of his cities. He pressed on to Ecbatana and took its towers, sacked its marketplaces, and turned its glory into shame. *15*Arphaxad himself he overtook in the mountains of Ragae, ran him through with spears, and utterly destroyed him. *16*Then he returned home with all his numerous, motley horde of warriors; and there he and his army relaxed and feasted for a hundred and twenty days.*a*

See RG 154-56

CHAPTER 2

Council of War against the West. *1*In the eighteenth year, on the twenty-second day of the first month, there was a discussion in the palace of Nebuchadnezzar, king of the Assyrians, about taking revenge on the whole world, as he had threatened. *2*He summoned all his ministers and nobles, laid before them his secret plan, and urged the total destruction of those countries. *3*They decided to do away with all those who had refused to comply with the order he had issued.

*4*When he had completed his plan, Nebuchadnezzar, king of the Assyrians, summoned Holofernes, general in chief of his forces, second to himself in command, and said to him: *5b*"Thus says the great king, the lord of all the earth: Go forth from my presence, take with you men of proven valor, a hundred and twenty thousand infantry and twelve thousand

cavalry, *6*and proceed against all the land of the West, because they did not comply with the order I issued. *7*Tell them to have earth and water* ready, for I will come against them in my wrath; I will cover all the land with the feet of my soldiers, to whom I will deliver them as spoils. *8*Their slain shall fill their ravines and wadies, the swelling torrent shall be choked with their dead; *9*and I will deport them as exiles to the very ends of the earth.

10"You go before me and take possession of all their territories for me. If they surrender to you, guard them for me till the day of their punishment. *11*As for those who resist, show them no quarter, but deliver them up to slaughter and plunder in each country you occupy. *12*For as I live,* and by the strength of my kingdom, what I have spoken I will accomplish by my power. *13*Do not disobey a single one of the orders of your lord; fulfill them exactly as I have commanded you, and do it without delay."

Campaign of Holofernes. *14*So Holofernes left the presence of his lord, and summoned all the princes, and the generals and officers of the Assyrian army. *15*He mustered a hundred and twenty thousand picked troops, as his lord had commanded, and twelve thousand mounted archers, *16*and grouped them into a complete combat force. *17*He took along a very large number of camels, asses, and mules for their baggage; innumerable sheep, cattle, and goats for their food supply; *18*abundant provisions for each man, and much gold and silver from the royal palace.

*19*Then he and his whole army proceeded on their expedition in advance of King

1, 12: The two seas: the ancient rulers in Mesopotamia often designated the limits of their realm as extending from the Upper Sea (the Mediterranean) to the Lower Sea (the Persian Gulf).

2, 7: Earth and water: in the Persian period, the offering of these to a conqueror was a symbolic gesture of unconditional surrender.

2, 12: As I live: in the Old Testament, an oath proper to

divinity; cf Dt 32, 40. Nebuchadnezzar is making himself equal to God; see Jdt 6, 2. By my power: literally "by my hand." The hand of Nebuchadnezzar raised in opposition to God and to his people is the occasion for Judith's intervention by a woman's hand; cf Jdt 9, 9f; Is 10, 5-14.

a: Est 1, 3f. *b:* 5f: Est 3, 8f.

Nebuchadnezzar, to cover all the western region with their chariots and cavalry and regular infantry. [20] A huge, irregular force, too many to count, like locusts or the dust of the earth, went along with them.[c]

[21] After a three-day march from Nineveh, they reached the plain of Bectileth, and from Bectileth they next encamped near the mountains to the north of Upper Cilicia. [22] From there Holofernes took his whole force, the infantry, calvary, and chariots, and marched into the mountain region. [23] He devastated Put and Lud,* and plundered all the Rassisites and the Ishmaelites on the border of the desert toward the south of Chaldea.

[24] Then, following the Euphrates, he went through Mesopotamia, and battered down every fortified city along the Wadi Abron, until he reached the sea. [25] He seized the territory of Cilicia, and cut down everyone who resisted him. Then he proceeded to the southern borders of Japheth, toward Arabia. [26] He surrounded all the Midianites, burned their tents, and plundered their sheepfolds. [27] Descending to the plain of Damascus at the time of the wheat harvest, he set fire to all their fields, destroyed their flocks and herds, despoiled their cities, devastated their plains, and put all their youths to the sword.

[28] The fear and dread of him fell upon all the inhabitants of the coastland, upon those in Sidon and Tyre, and those who dwelt in Sur and Ocina, and the inhabitants of Jamnia. Those in Azotus and Ascalon also feared him greatly.

CHAPTER 3

See RG 154-56

Submission of the West. [1] They therefore sent messengers to him to sue for peace in these words: [2] "We, the servants of Nebuchadnezzar the great king, lie prostrate before you; do with us as you will. [3] Our dwellings and all our wheat fields, our flocks and herds, and all our encampments are at your disposal; make use of them as you please. [4] Our cities and their inhabitants are also at your service; come and deal with them as you see fit."

[5] After the spokesmen had reached Holofernes and given him this message, [6] he went down with his army to the seacoast, and stationed garrisons in the fortified cities; from them he impressed picked troops as auxiliaries. [7] The people of these cities and all the inhabitants of the countryside received him with garlands and dancing to the sound of timbrels. [8] Nevertheless, he devastated their whole territory and cut down their sacred groves, for he had been commissioned to destroy all the gods of the earth, so that every nation might worship Nebuchadnezzar alone, and every people and tribe invoke him as a god.[d] [9] At length Holofernes reached Esdraelon in the neighborhood of Dothan, the approach to the main ridge of the Judean mountains; [10] he set up his camp between Geba* and Scythopolis, and stayed there a whole month to refurbish all the equipment of his army.

CHAPTER 4

See RG 154-56

Israelite Defense. [1] When the Israelites who dwelt in Judea heard of all that Holofernes, commander in chief of Nebuchadnezzar, king of the Assyrians, had done to the nations, and how he had despoiled all their temples and destroyed them, [2] they were in extreme dread of him, and greatly alarmed for Jerusalem and the temple of the LORD, their God. [3] Now, they had lately returned from exile, and only recently had all the people of Judea been gathered together, and the vessels, the altar, and the temple been purified from profanation.* [4] So they sent word to the whole region of Samaria, to Kona, Beth-horon, Belmain, and Jericho, to Choba and Aesora, and to the valley of Salem. [5] The people there posted guards on all

---

2, 23: Put and Lud: the same as the "Put and Lud" mentioned in Ez 30, 5 as allies of Egypt, and in Ez 27, 10 as supplying mercenary soldiers to Tyre. Here they seem inserted to embellish the narrative with assonance and prophetic associations rather than to indicate definite localities.

3, 10: Geba: perhaps originally "Gelboe," the mountain range near the eastern end of which lay Scythopolis, the Greek name for ancient Beth-shean (Jos 17, 11).

4, 3: Returned from exile . . . profanation: these allusions are variously attributed—to the Persian period (538-323 B.C.), or even to a condition in the days of Antiochus Epiphanes (175-164 B.C.).

c: Jgs 7, 12.   d: Ex 34, 13.

Bethulia (4, 6), mentioned frequently in Judith, is not mentioned elsewhere in the Bible; this would be unthinkable if the story were historical. Betomesthaim is unknown.

the summits of the high mountains, fortified their villages, and since their fields had recently been harvested, stored up provisions in preparation for war.

⁶Joakim, who was high priest* in Jerusalem in those days, wrote to the inhabitants of Bethulia [and Betomesthaim], which is on the way to Esdraelon, facing the plain near Dothan, ⁷and instructed them to keep firm hold of the mountain passes, since these offered access to Judea. It would be easy to ward off the attacking forces, as the defile was only wide enough for two abreast. ⁸The Israelites carried out the orders given them by Joakim, the high priest, and the senate of the whole people of Israel, which met in Jerusalem.*

Prayer and Penance. ⁹All the men of Israel cried to God with great fervor and did penance— ¹⁰ᵉthey, along with their wives, and children, and domestic animals.* All their resident aliens, hired laborers, and slaves also girded themselves with sackcloth. ¹¹And all the Israelite men, women, and children who lived in Jerusalem prostrated themselves in front of the temple building,* with ashes strewn on their heads, displaying their sackcloth covering before the LORD. ¹²The altar, too, they draped in sackcloth; and with one accord they cried out fervently to the God of Israel not to allow their children to be seized, their wives to be taken captive, the cities of their inheritance to be ruined, or the sanctuary to be profaned and mocked for the nations to gloat over.ᶠ

¹³The LORD heard their cry and had regard for their distress. For the people observed a fast of many days' duration throughout Judea, and before the sanctuary of the LORD Almighty in Jerusalem.ᵍ ¹⁴The high priest Joakim, and all the priests in attendance on the LORD who served his altar, were also girded with sackcloth as they offered the daily holocaust, the votive offerings, and the free-will offerings of the people. ¹⁵With ashes upon their turbans, they cried to the LORD with all their strength to look with favor on the whole house of Israel.

CHAPTER 5

See RG 154–56

Council against the Israelites. ¹It was reported to Holofernes, commander in chief of the Assyrian army, that the Israelites were ready for battle, and had blocked the mountain passes, fortified the summits of all the higher peaks, and placed roadblocks in the plains. ²In great anger he summoned all the rulers of the Moabites, the generals of the Ammonites, and all the satraps of the seacoast ³and said to them: "Now tell me, you Canaanites, what sort of people is this that dwells in the mountains? Which cities do they inhabit? How large is their army? In what does their power and strength consist? Who has set himself up as their king and the leader of their army? ⁴Why have they refused to come out to meet me along with all the other inhabitants of the West?"

Achior's Speech. ⁵Then Achior, the leader of all the Ammonites, said to him: "My lord, hear this account from your servant; I will tell you the truth about this people that lives near you [that inhabits this mountain region]; no lie shall escape your servant's lips.ʰ

⁶*"These people are descendants of the Chaldeans. ⁷They formerly dwelt in Mesopotamia, for they did not wish to follow the gods of their forefathers who were born in the land of the Chaldeans.ⁱ ⁸Since they aban-

---

4, 6: Joakim, who was high priest: see Bar 1, 7 and the footnote on Bar 1, 8f; this name for a high priest cannot be used in dating the events in Jdt.

4, 8: The organization of the Jewish nation as subject to a high priest and a senate, or council of elders, was proper to the Greek period (after 323 B.C.), and is reflected in the coinage of John Hyrcanus (135–104 B.C.).

4, 10: Domestic animals: see note on Jon 3, 8.

4, 11: Prostrated themselves in front of the temple building; for a parallel to this ceremony of entreaty, see Jl 2, 13f; 2, 15ff, and the note on Jl 2, 17.

5, 6-9: Achior outlines the early history of the Hebrews, whose forefather, Abraham, first lived in Ur of the Chaldeans

e: 10f: Jon 3, 7f. *f:* Est 4, 1f. *g:* Est 4, 16. *h:* Jdt 11, 9-19. *i:* Gn 11, 31.

doned the way of their ancestors, and acknowledged with divine worship the God of heaven, their forefathers expelled them from the presence of their gods. So they fled to Mesopotamia and dwelt there a long time. ⁹Their God bade them leave their abode and proceed to the land of Canaan. Here they settled, and grew very rich in gold, silver, and a great abundance of livestock.ʲ ¹⁰Later, when famine had gripped the whole land of Canaan, they went down into Egypt. They stayed there as long as they found sustenance, and grew into such a great multitude that the number of their race could not be counted.ᵏ ¹¹The king of Egypt, however, rose up against them, shrewdly forced them to labor at brickmaking, oppressed and enslaved them. ¹²But they cried to their God, and he struck the land of Egypt with plagues for which there was no remedy. When the Egyptians expelled them, ¹³ᵐGod dried up the Red Sea before them, ¹⁴and led them along the route to Sinai and Kadesh-barnea. First they drove out all the inhabitants of the desert; ¹⁵then they settled in the land of the Amorites, destroyed all the Heshbonites by main force, crossed the Jordan, and took possession of the whole mountain region.ⁿ ¹⁶They expelled the Canaanites, the Perizzites, the Jebusites, the Shechemites, and all the Gergesites; and they lived in these mountains a long time.ᵒ

¹⁷ᵖ"As long as the Israelites did not sin in the sight of their God, they prospered, for their God, who hates wickedness, was with them. ¹⁸But when they deviated from the way he prescribed for them, they were ground down steadily, more and more, by frequent wars, and finally taken as captives into foreign lands. The temple of their God was razed to the ground, and their cities were occupied by their enemies.ᑫ ¹⁹But now that they have returned to their God, they have come back from the Dispersion wherein they were scattered, and have repossessed Jerusalem, where their sanctuary is, and have settled again in the mountain region which was unoccupied.

²⁰ʳ"So now, my lord and master, if these people are at fault, and are sinning against their God, and if we verify this offense of theirs, then we shall be able to go up and conquer them. ²¹But if they are not a guilty nation, then your lordship should keep his distance; otherwise their LORD and God will shield them, and we shall become the laughingstock of the whole world."

²²Now when Achior had concluded his recommendation, all the people standing round about the tent murmured; and the officers of Holofernes and all the inhabitants of the seacoast and of Moab alike said he should be cut to pieces. ²³"We are not afraid of the Israelites," they said, "for they are a powerless people, incapable of a strong defense. ²⁴Let us therefore attack them; your great army, Lord Holofernes, will swallow them up."ˢ

CHAPTER 6

See RG 154–56

Holofernes' Answer. ¹When the noise of the crowd surrounding the council had subsided, Holofernes, commander in chief of the Assyrian army, said to Achior, in the presence of the whole throng of coastland peoples, of the Moabites, and of the Ammonite mercenaries: ²"Who are you, Achior, to prophesy among us as you have done today, and to tell us not to fight against the Israelites because their God protects them? What god is there beside Nebuchadnezzar? He will send his force and destroy them from the face of the earth. Their God will not save them;ᵗ ³but we, the servants of Nebuchadnezzar, will strike them down as one man, for they will be unable to withstand the force of our cavalry.ᵘ ⁴We will overwhelm them with it, and the mountains shall be drunk with their blood, and their plains filled

(Gn 11, 28) and then migrated to Haran (Gn 11, 31) in Aram Naharaim (Gn 24, 10), which was called Mesopotamia by the Greeks. The gods of their forefathers were the pagan deities worshiped by Abraham's relatives (Jos 24, 2).

j: Gn 11, 31—12, 5.   *k:* Gn 42, 1-5; 46, 1-7; Ex 1, 7.   *l:* 11f: Ex 5, 4-21; 7, 1-9.   *m:* 13f: Ex 14, 21f. 29.   *n:* Nm 21, 21-32; Jos 2, 10.   *o:* Dt 7, 1.   *p:* 17f: Dt 28—30; Ps 106, 40-46; Is 59, 7.   *q:* 2 Kgs 25.   *r:* 20f: Jdt 8, 18ff; 11, 10.   *s:* Jdt 6, 2; 9, 7; 16, 2.   *t:* Jdt 3, 8; 9, 7.   *u:* Is 36, 18ff.

with their corpses. Not a trace of them shall survive our attack: they shall utterly perish, says King Nebuchadnezzar, lord of all the earth; for he has spoken, and his words shall not remain unfulfilled.[v] ⁵As for you, Achior, you Ammonite mercenary, for saying these things in a moment of perversity you shall not see my face after today, until I have taken revenge on this race of people from Egypt. ⁶Then at my return, the sword of my army or the spear of my servants will pierce your sides, and you shall fall among their slain.[w] ⁷My servants will now conduct you to the mountain region, and leave you at one of the towns along the ascent. ⁸You shall not die till you are destroyed together with them. ⁹If you still cherish the hope that they will not be taken, then there is no need for you to be downcast. I have spoken, and my words shall not prove false in any respect."

Achior in Bethulia. ¹⁰Then Holofernes ordered the servants who were standing by in his tent to seize Achior, conduct him to Bethulia, and hand him over to the Israelites. ¹¹So the servants took him in custody and brought him out of the camp into the plain. From there they led him into the mountain region till they reached the springs below Bethulia. ¹²When the men of the city saw them, they seized their weapons and ran out of the city to the crest of the ridge; and all the slingers blocked the ascent of Holofernes' servants by hurling stones upon them. ¹³So they took cover below the mountain, where they bound Achior and left him lying at the foot of the mountain; then they returned to their lord.

¹⁴The Israelites came down to him from their city, loosed him, and brought him into Bethulia. They haled him before the rulers of the city, ¹⁵who in those days were Uzziah, son of Micah of the tribe of Simeon, Chabris, son of Gothoniel, and Charmis, son of Melchiel. ¹⁶They then convened all the elders of the city; and all their young men, as well as the women, gathered in haste at the place of assembly. They placed Achior in the center of the throng, and Uzziah questioned him about what had happened. ¹⁷He replied by giving them an account of what was said in the council of Holofernes, and of all his own words among the Assyrian officers, and of all the boasting threats of Holofernes against the house of Israel.

¹⁸At this the people fell prostrate and worshiped God; and they cried out: ¹⁹"LORD, God of heaven, behold their arrogance! Have pity on the lowliness of our people, and look with favor this day on those who are consecrated to you."* ²⁰Then they reassured Achior and praised him highly. ²¹Uzziah brought him from the assembly to his home, where he gave a banquet for the elders. That whole night they called upon the God of Israel for help.

CHAPTER 7

See RG 154-56

Siege of Bethulia. ¹The following day Holofernes ordered his whole army, and all the allied troops that had come to his support, to move against Bethulia, seize the mountain passes, and engage the Israelites in battle. ²That same day all their fighting men went into action. Their forces numbered a hundred and seventy thousand infantry and twelve thousand horsemen, not counting the baggage train or the men who accompanied it on foot—a very great army. ³They encamped at the spring in the valley near Bethulia, and spread out in breadth toward Dothan as far as Balbaim, and in length from Bethulia to Cyamon, which faces Esdraelon.

⁴When the Israelites saw how many there were, they said to one another in great dismay: "Soon they will devour the whole country. Neither the high mountains nor the valleys and hills can support the mass of them." ⁵Yet they all seized their weapons, lighted fires on their bastions,* and kept watch throughout the night.

6, 19: The Latin Vulgate (6, 15) has a longer form of this prayer: "Lord, God of heaven and earth, behold their arrogance; regard our lowliness and look with favor on your holy ones; show that you do not abandon those who trust in you, but that you humble those who trust in themselves and glory in their own strength."

7, 5: Lighted fires on their bastions: to serve as signals for alerting the neighboring towns. Reference to fire signals in time of siege is made in the Lachish ostraca at the beginning of the sixth century B.C. Kept watch throughout the night: to prevent a surprise attack.

v: Jdt 6, 17. *w:* Jdt 5, 22.

⁶On the second day Holofernes led out all his cavalry in the sight of the Israelites who were in Bethulia. ⁷He reconnoitered the approaches to their city and located their sources of water; these he seized, stationing armed detachments around them, while he himself returned to his troops.

⁸All the commanders of the Edomites and all the leaders of the Ammonites, together with the generals of the seacoast, came to Holofernes and said: ⁹"Sir, listen to what we have to say, that there may be no losses among your troops. ¹⁰These Israelites do not rely on their spears, but on the height of the mountains where they dwell; it is not easy to reach the summit of their mountains.ˣ ¹¹Therefore, sir, do not attack them in regular formation; thus not a single one of your troops will fall. ¹²Stay in your camp, and spare all your soldiers. Have some of your servants keep control of the source of water that flows out at the base of the mountain, ¹³for that is where the inhabitants of Bethulia get their water. Then thirst will begin to carry them off, and they will surrender their city. Meanwhile, we and our men will go up to the summits of the nearby mountains, and encamp there to guard against anyone's leaving the city.ʸ ¹⁴They and their wives and children will languish with hunger, and even before the sword strikes them they will be laid low in the streets of their city. ¹⁵Thus you will render them dire punishment for their rebellion and their refusal to meet you peaceably."

¹⁶Their words pleased Holofernes and all his ministers, and he ordered their proposal to be carried out. ¹⁷Thereupon the Moabites moved camp, together with five thousand Assyrians. They encamped in the valley, and held the water supply and the springs of the Israelites. ¹⁸The Edomites and the Ammonites went up and encamped in the mountain region opposite Dothan; and they sent some of their men to the south and to the east opposite Egrebel, near Chusi, which is on Wadi Mochmur. The rest of the Assyrian army was encamped in the plain, covering the whole countryside.

Their enormous store of tents and equipment was spread out in profusion everywhere.

¹⁹The Israelites cried to the LORD, their God, for they were disheartened, since all their enemies had them surrounded, and there was no way of slipping through their lines.ᶻ ²⁰The whole Assyrian camp, infantry, chariots, and cavalry, kept them thus surrounded for thirty-four days. All the reservoirs of water failed the inhabitants of Bethulia, ²¹and the cisterns ran dry, so that on no day did they have enough to drink, but their drinking water was rationed. ²²Their children fainted away, and the women and youths were consumed with thirst and were collapsing in the streets and gateways of the city, with no strength left in them.

²³All the people, therefore, including youths, women, and children, went in a crowd to Uzziah and the rulers of the city. They set up a great clamor and said before the elders: ²⁴"God judge between you and us! You have done us grave injustice in not making peace with the Assyrians. ²⁵There is no help for us now! Instead, God has sold us into their power by laying us prostrate before them in thirst and utter exhaustion. ²⁶Therefore, summon them and deliver the whole city as booty to the troops of Holofernes and to all his forces; ²⁷we would be better off to become their prey. We should indeed be made slaves, but at least we should live, and not have to behold our little ones dying before our eyes and our wives and children breathing out their souls. ²⁸We adjure you by heaven and earth, and by our God, the LORD of our forefathers, who is punishing us for our sins and those of our forefathers, to do as we have proposed, this very day."

²⁹All in the assembly with one accord broke into shrill wailing and loud cries to the LORD their God. ³⁰But Uzziah said to them, "Courage, my brothers! Let us wait five days more for the LORD our God, to show his mercy toward us; he will not utterly forsake us. ³¹But if those days pass without help coming to us, I will do as you say." ³²Then he dispersed the men to their posts, and they

x: 1 Kgs 20, 23. 28.   y: Ex 5, 21.   z: Ps 106, 6.

returned to the walls and towers of the city; the women and children he sent to their homes. Throughout the city they were in great misery.

II: Deliverance of the Jews

CHAPTER 8

See RG 154–56

Judith. [1]Now in those days Judith, daughter of Merari, son of Joseph, son of Oziel, son of Elkiah, son of Ananias, son of Gideon, son of Raphain, son of Ahitob, son of Elijah, son of Hilkiah, son of Eliab, son of Nathanael, son of Salamiel, son of Sarasadai,* son of Simeon, son of Israel, heard of this. [2]Her husband, Manasseh, of her own tribe and clan, had died at the time of the barley harvest. [3]While he was in the field supervising those who bound the sheaves, he suffered sunstroke; and he died of this illness in Bethulia, his native city. He was buried with his forefathers in the field between Dothan and Balamon. [4]The widowed Judith remained three years and four months at home, [5]where she set up a tent* for herself on the roof of her house. She put sackcloth about her loins and wore widow's weeds. [6]She fasted all the days of her widowhood, except sabbath eves and sabbaths, new moon eves and new moons, feastdays and holidays of the house of Israel.[a] [7]She was beautifully formed and lovely to behold. Her husband, Manasseh, had left her gold and silver, servants and maids, livestock and fields, which she was maintaining. [8]No one had a bad word to say about her, for she was a very God-fearing woman.

Her Words to the Elders. [9]When Judith, therefore, heard of the harsh words which the people, discouraged by their lack of water, had spoken against their ruler, and of all that Uzziah had said to them in reply, swearing that he would hand over the city to the Assyrians at the end of five days, [10]she sent the maid who was in charge of all her things to ask Uzziah, Chabris, and Charmis, the elders of the city, to visit her. [11]When they came, she said to them: "Listen to me, you rulers of the people of Bethulia. What you said to the people today is not proper. When you promised to hand over the city to our enemies at the end of five days unless within that time the Lord comes to our aid, you interposed between God and yourselves this oath which you took. [12]Who are you, then, that you should have put God to the test this day, setting yourselves in the place of God in human affairs?[b] [13]It is the Lord Almighty for whom you are laying down conditions; will you never understand anything? [14]You cannot plumb the depths of the human heart or grasp the workings of the human mind; how then can you fathom God, who has made all these things, discern his mind, and understand his plan?[c]

"No, my brothers, do not anger the Lord our God. [15]For if he does not wish to come to our aid within the five days, he has it equally within his power to protect us at such time as he pleases, or to destroy us in the face of our enemies. [16]It is not for you to make the Lord our God give surety for his plans.

"God is not man that he should be moved
by threats,
nor human, that he may be given an
ultimatum.

[17]"So while we wait for the salvation that comes from him, let us call upon him to help us, and he will hear our cry if it is his good pleasure. [18]For there has not risen among us in recent generations, nor does there exist today, any tribe, or clan, or town, or city of ours that worships gods made by hands, as happened in former days.[d] [19]It was for such conduct that our forefathers were handed over to the sword and to pillage, and fell with great destruction before our enemies.[e] [20]But since we acknowledge no other god but the Lord, we hope that he will not disdain us or any of our people. [21]If we are taken, all Judea will fall, our sanctuary will be plundered, and God

---

8, 1: Salamiel, son of Sarasadai: head of the tribe of Simeon during the wanderings of the Israelites in the desert (Nm 1, 6).
8, 5: A tent: erected by Judith on the roof of her house (v 5); it was here that the elders came to confer with her (v 11).

a: Lk 2, 37.   b: Jb 38, 2; 40, 2. 7f; 42, 3.   c: Jb 41, 3; Prv 14, 10; Wis 9, 13; Is 40, 13; Rom 11, 33f; 1 Cor 2, 11   d: Jdt 5, 20f; 11, 10.   e: Pss 78, 56f; 106, 13f; Jer 7, 16-20; 14, 7.

Judith Upbraids the Magistrates

Judith's eloquent exhortation (8, 32–34) is an expression of what faith requires of Israel in the postexilic period of apparent abandonment by God. God puts Israel to the test by awaiting a response of fidelity. When faith interprets history, it tends to see suffering as a warning.

will make us pay for its profanation with our life's blood. ²²For the slaughter of our kinsmen, for the taking of exiles from the land, and for the devastation of our inheritance, he will lay the guilt on our heads. Wherever we shall be enslaved among the nations, we shall be a mockery and a reproach in the eyes of our masters. ²³Our enslavement will not be turned to our benefit, but the LORD our God will maintain it to our disgrace.

²⁴"Therefore, my brothers, let us set an example for our kinsmen. Their lives depend on us, and the defense of the sanctuary, the temple, and the altar rests with us. ²⁵ᶠBesides all this, we should be grateful to the LORD our God, for putting us to the test, as he did our forefathers. ²⁶Recall how he dealt with Abraham, and how he tried Isaac, and all that happened to Jacob in Syrian Mesopotamia while he was tending the flocks of Laban, his mother's brother. ²⁷Not for vengeance did the LORD put them in the crucible to try their hearts, nor has he done so with us. It is by way of admonition that he chastises those who are close to him."ᵍ

Uzziah's Response. ²⁸Then Uzziah said to her: "All that you have said was spoken with good sense, and no one can gainsay your words. ²⁹Not today only is your wisdom made evident, but from your earliest years all the people have recognized your prudence, which corresponds to the worthy dispositions of your heart. ³⁰The people, however, were so tortured with thirst that they forced us to speak to them as we did, and to bind ourselves by an oath that we cannot break. ³¹But now, God-fearing woman that you are, pray for us that the LORD may send rain to fill up our cisterns, lest we be weakened still further."

³²Then Judith said to them: "Listen to me! I will do something that will go down from generation to generation among the descendants of our race. ³³Stand at the gate tonight to let me pass through with my maid; and within the days you have specified before you will surrender the city to our enemies, the LORD will rescue Israel by my hand. ³⁴You must not inquire into what I am doing, for I will not tell you until my plan has been accomplished." ³⁵Uzziah and the rulers said to her, "Go in peace, and may the LORD God go before you to take vengeance upon our enemies!" ³⁶Then they withdrew from the tent and returned to their posts.

CHAPTER 9

See RG 154–56

The Prayer of Judith. ¹Judith threw herself down prostrate, with ashes strewn upon her head, and wearing nothing over her sackcloth. While the incense was being offered in the temple of God in Jerusalem that evening, Judith prayed to the LORD with a loud voice:ʰ ²"LORD, God of my forefather Simeon! You put a sword into his hand to take revenge upon the foreigners who had immodestly loosened the maiden's* girdle, shamefully exposed her thighs, and disgracefully violated her body. This they did, though you forbade it.ⁱ ³Therefore you had their rulers slaughtered; and you covered with their blood the bed in which they lay deceived, the same bed that had felt the shame of their own deceiving. You smote the slaves together with their princes, and the princes together with their servants.* ⁴Their wives you handed over to plunder, and their daughters to captivity; and all the spoils you divided among your favored sons, who

---

9, 2: The maiden's: Dinah, Jacob's daughter, who was violated by Shechem, the Hivite (Gn 34, 2).

9, 3: Because Shechem had deceived and violated Dinah, her brothers, Simeon and Levi, tricked Shechem and the men of his city into being circumcised, and then slew them while

they were confined to bed from the circumcision; cf Gn 34, 13-29.

f: 25f: Gn 22, 1-12; 29, 22-30.   *g:* Dt 4, 7.   *h:* Ex 30, 7f; Ps 141, 2.   *i:* Gn 34.

burned with zeal for you, and in their abhorrence of the defilement of their kinswoman, called on you for help.

[5]"O God, my God, hear me also, a widow. It is you who were the author of those events and of what preceded and followed them. The present, also, and the future you have planned. Whatever you devise comes into being;[j] [6]the things you decide on come forward and say, 'Here we are!' All your ways are in readiness, and your judgment is made with foreknowledge.[k]

[7]"Here are the Assyrians, a vast force, priding themselves on horse and rider, boasting of the power of their infantry, trusting in shield and spear, bow and sling. They do not know that

[8] " 'You, the LORD, crush warfare;
Lord is your name.'

"Shatter their strength in your might, and crush their force in your wrath; for they have resolved to profane your sanctuary, to defile the tent where your glorious name resides, and to overthrow with iron the horns of your altar. [9]See their pride, and send forth your wrath upon their heads. Give me, a widow, the strong hand to execute my plan.[m] [10]With the guile of my lips, smite the slave together with the ruler, the ruler together with his servant; crush their pride by the hand of a woman.

[11]"Your strength is not in numbers, nor does your power depend upon stalwart men; but you are the God of the lowly, the helper of the oppressed, the supporter of the weak, the protector of the forsaken, the savior of those without hope.

[12]"Please, please, God of my forefather, God of the heritage of Israel, LORD of heaven and earth, Creator of the waters, King of all you have created, hear my prayer! [13]Let my guileful speech bring wound and wale on those who have planned dire things against your covenant, your holy temple, Mount Zion, and the homes your children have inherited.[n] [14]Let your whole nation and all the tribes know clearly that you are the God of all

power and might, and that there is no other who protects the people of Israel but you alone."

CHAPTER 10

See RG 154-56

Judith's Departure. [1]As soon as Judith had thus concluded, and ceased her invocation to the God of Israel, [2]she rose from the ground. She called her maid and they went down into the house, which she used only on sabbaths and feast days. [3]She took off the sackcloth she had on, laid aside the garments of her widowhood, washed her body with water, and anointed it with rich ointment. She arranged her hair and bound it with a fillet, and put on the festive attire she had worn while her husband, Manasseh, was living.[o] [4]She chose sandals for her feet, and put on her anklets, bracelets, rings, earrings, and all her other jewelry. Thus she made herself very beautiful, to captivate the eyes of all the men who should see her.[p]

[5]She gave her maid a leather flask of wine and a cruse of oil. She filled a bag with roasted grain, fig cakes, bread and cheese; all these provisions she wrapped up and gave to the maid to carry.[q]

[6]Then they went out to the gate of the city of Bethulia and found Uzziah and the elders of the city, Chabris and Charmis, standing there. [7]When these men saw Judith transformed in looks and differently dressed, they were very much astounded at her beauty and said to her, [8]"May the God of our fathers bring you to favor, and make your undertaking a success, for the glory of the Israelites and the exaltation of Jerusalem."

Judith bowed down to God. Then she said to them, [9]"Order the gate of the city opened for me, that I may go to carry out the business we discussed." So they ordered the youths to open the gate for her as she requested. [10]When they did so, Judith and her maid went out. The men of the city kept her in view as she went down the mountain and crossed the valley; then they lost sight of her.

Judith Captured. [11]As Judith and her maid walked directly across the valley, they

---

j: Is 44, 7.   *k:* Jb 38, 35; Is 46, 9-13; Bar 3, 35.   *l:* 7f: Jdt 5, 23; 6, 2; 16, 2.   *m:* Ps 33, 16.   *n:* Jdt 10, 4; 11, 20. 23; 16, 6. 9.   *o:* Jdt 8, 6ff.   *p:* Jdt 9, 13.   *q:* Jdt 12, 2.

Fatal Error

Holofernes guarantees freedom from danger to his prospective executioner (11, 1–4). The Bible delights in showing how God uses evil people to bring about positive results. "God will give you complete success" (v. 6) has an altogether different meaning for Judith than for Holofernes. Judith's conversation is full of such delightful ambiguities.

encountered the Assyrian outpost. *12*The men took her in custody and asked her, "To what people do you belong? Where do you come from, and where are you going?" She replied: "I am a daughter of the Hebrews, and I am fleeing from them, because they are about to be delivered up to you as prey.* *13*I have come to see Holofernes, the general in chief of your forces, to give him a trustworthy report; I will show him the route by which he can ascend and take possession of the whole mountain district without a single one of his men suffering injury or loss of life."*r*

*14*When the men heard her words and gazed upon her face, which appeared wondrously beautiful to them, they said to her, *15*"By coming down thus promptly to see our master, you have saved your life. Now go to his tent; some of our men will accompany you to present you to him. *16*When you stand before him, have no fear in your heart; give him the report you speak of, and he will treat you well." *17*So they detailed a hundred of their men as an escort for her and her maid, and these conducted them to the tent of Holofernes.

*18*When the news of her arrival spread among the tents, a crowd gathered in the camp. They came and stood around her as she waited outside the tent of Holofernes, while he was being informed about her. *19*They marveled at her beauty, regarding the Israelites with wonder because of her, and they said to one another, "Who can despise this people that has such women among them? It is not wise to leave one man of them alive, for if any were to be spared they could beguile the whole world."

Judith Meets Holofernes. *20*The guard of Holofernes and all his servants came out and ushered her into the tent. *21*Now Holofernes was reclining on his bed under a canopy with a netting of crimson and gold, emeralds and other precious stones. *22*When they announced her to him, he came out to the antechamber, preceded by silver lamps; *23*and when Holofernes and his servants beheld Judith, they all marveled at the beauty of her face. She threw herself down prostrate before him, but his servants raised her up.

CHAPTER 11

See RG 154-56

*1*Then Holofernes said to her: "Take courage, lady; have no fear in your heart! Never have I harmed anyone who chose to serve Nebuchadnezzar, king of all the earth. *2*Nor would I have raised my spear against your people who dwell in the mountain region, had they not despised me and brought this upon themselves. *3*But now tell me why you fled from them and came to us. In any case, you have come to safety. Take courage! Your life is spared tonight and for the future. *4*No one at all will harm you. Rather, you will be well treated, as are all the servants of my lord, King Nebuchadnezzar."

*5s*Judith answered him: "Listen to the words of your servant, and let your handmaid speak in your presence! I will tell no lie to my lord this night, *6*and if you follow out the words of your handmaid, God will give you complete success, and my lord will not fail in any of his undertakings. *7*By the life of Nebuchadnezzar, king of all the earth, and by the power of him who has sent you to set all creatures aright! not only do men serve him

10, 12f: The deceitful means used by Judith against Holofernes, here and in Jdt 11, 5-19, are to be judged in the light of the moral concepts of Old Testament times; cf Gn 27, 1-25; 34, 13-29; 37, 32ff; Jos 2, 1-7; Jgs 4, 17-22.

r: Jdt 11, 5f.   s: 5f: Jdt 10, 13.

through you; but even the wild beasts and the cattle and the birds of the air, because of your strength, will live for Nebuchadnezzar and his whole house.[t] [8]Indeed, we have heard of your wisdom and sagacity, and all the world is aware that throughout the kingdom you alone are competent, rich in experience, and distinguished in military strategy.

[9u]"As for Achior's speech in your council, we have heard of it. When the men of Bethulia spared him, he told them all he had said to you. [10]So then, my lord and master, do not disregard his word, but bear it in mind, for it is true. For our people are not punished, nor does the sword prevail against them, except when they sin against their God.[v] [11]But now their guilt has caught up with them by which they bring the wrath of their God upon them whenever they do wrong; so that my lord will not be repulsed and fail, but death will overtake them. [12]Since their food gave out and all their water ran low, they decided to kill their animals, and determined to consume all the things which God in his laws forbade them to eat. [13]They decreed that they would use up the first fruits of grain and the tithes of wine and oil which they had sanctified and reserved for the priests who minister in the presence of our God in Jerusalem: things which no layman should even touch with his hands. [14]They have sent messengers to Jerusalem to bring back to them authorization from the council of the elders; for the inhabitants there have also done these things. [15]On the very day when the response reaches them and they act upon it, they will be handed over to you for destruction.

[16]"As soon as I, your handmaid, learned all this, I fled from them. God has sent me to perform with you such deeds that people throughout the world will be astonished on hearing of them. [17]Your handmaid is, indeed, a God-fearing woman, serving the God of heaven night and day. Now I will remain with you, my lord; but each night your handmaid will go out to the ravine and pray to God. He will tell me when the Israelites have committed their crimes. [18]Then I will come and let you know, so that you may go out with your whole force, and not one of them will be able to withstand you. [19]I will lead you through Judea, till you come to Jerusalem, and there I will set up your judgment seat. You will drive them like sheep that have no shepherd, and not even a dog will growl at you. This was told me, and announced to me in advance, and I in turn have been sent to tell you."

[20]Her words pleased Holofernes and all his servants; they marveled at her wisdom and exclaimed,[w] [21]"No other woman from one end of the world to the other looks so beautiful and speaks so wisely!" [22]Then Holofernes said to her: "God has done well in sending you ahead of your people, to bring victory to our arms, and destruction to those who have despised my lord. [23]You are fair to behold, and your words are well spoken. If you do as you have said, your God will be my God; you shall dwell in the palace of King Nebuchadnezzar, and shall be renowned throughout the earth."[x]

CHAPTER 12

Judith's Conduct. [1]Then he ordered them to lead her into the room where his silverware was kept, and bade them set a table for her with his own delicacies to eat and his own wine to drink. [2]But Judith said, "I will not partake of them, lest it be an occasion of sin; but I shall be amply supplied from the things I brought with me."[y] [3]Holofernes asked her: "But if your provisions give out, where shall we get more of the same to provide for you? None of your people are with us." [4]Judith answered him, "As surely as you, my lord, live, your handmaid will not use up her supplies till the LORD accomplishes by my hand what he has determined."

[5]Then the servants of Holofernes led her into the tent, where she slept till midnight. In the night watch just before dawn, she rose [6]and sent this message to Holofernes, "Give orders, my lord, to let your handmaid go out for prayer." [7]So Holofernes ordered his

See RG 154–56

---

t: Jer 27, 6; Bar 3, 16f; Dn 2, 38.   *u:* 9f: Jdt 5, 5.   *v:* Jdt 5, 21; 8, 18.   *w:* Jdt 9, 13.   *x:* Jdt 9, 13.   *y:* Jdt 10, 5; Dn 1, 8.

bodyguard not to hinder her. Thus she stayed in the camp three days. Each night she went out to the ravine of Bethulia, where she washed herself at the spring of the camp. [8]After bathing, she besought the LORD, the God of Israel, to direct her way for the triumph of his people. [9]Then she returned purified to the tent, and remained there until her food was brought to her toward evening.

Holofernes' Banquet. [10]On the fourth day Holofernes gave a banquet for his servants alone, to which he did not invite any of the officers.* [11]And he said to Bagoas, the eunuch in charge of his household: "Go and persuade this Hebrew woman in your care to come and to eat and drink with us. [12]It would be a disgrace for us to have such a woman with us without enjoying her company. If we do not entice her, she will laugh us to scorn."

[13]So Bagoas left the presence of Holofernes, and came to Judith and said, "So fair a maiden should not be reluctant to come to my lord to be honored by him, to enjoy drinking wine with us, and to be like one of the Assyrian women who live in the palace of Nebuchadnezzar." [14]She replied, "Who am I to refuse my lord? Whatever is pleasing to him I will promptly do. This will be a joy for me till the day of my death."

[15]Thereupon she proceeded to put on her festive garments and all her feminine adornments. Meanwhile her maid went ahead and spread out on the ground for her in front of Holofernes the fleece Bagoas had furnished for her daily use in reclining at her dinner. [16]Then Judith came in and reclined on it. The heart of Holofernes was in rapture over her, and his spirit was shaken. He was burning with the desire to possess her, for he had been biding his time to seduce her from the day he saw her. [17]Holofernes said to her, "Drink and be merry with us!" [18]Judith replied, "I will gladly drink, my lord, for at no time since I was born have I ever enjoyed life as much as I do today." [19]She then took the things her maid had prepared, and ate and drank in his presence. [20]Holofernes, charmed by her, drank a great quantity of wine, more than he had ever drunk on one single day in his life.

CHAPTER 13

See RG 154–56

[1]When it grew late, his servants quickly withdrew. Bagoas closed the tent from the outside and excluded the attendants from their master's presence. They went off to their beds, for they were all tired from the prolonged banquet. [2]Judith was left alone in the tent with Holofernes, who lay prostrate on his bed, for he was sodden with wine. [3]She had ordered her maid to stand outside the bedroom and wait, as on the other days, for her to come out; she said she would be going out for her prayer. To Bagoas she had said this also.

Beheading of Holofernes. [4]When all had departed, and no one, small or great, was left in the bedroom, Judith stood by Holofernes' bed and said within herself: "O LORD, God of all might, in this hour look graciously on my undertaking for the exaltation of Jerusalem; [5]now is the time for aiding your heritage and for carrying out my design to shatter the enemies who have risen against us." [6]She went to the bedpost near the head of Holofernes, and taking his sword from it, [7]drew close to the bed, grasped the hair of his head, and said, "Strengthen me this day, O God of Israel!" [8]Then with all her might she struck him twice in the neck and cut off his head.ᶻ [9]She rolled his body off the bed and took the canopy from its supports. Soon afterward, she came out and handed over the head of Holofernes to her maid, [10]who put it into her food pouch; and the two went off together as they were accustomed to do for prayer.

The Return to Bethulia. They passed through the camp, and skirting the ravine, reached Bethulia on the mountain. As they approached its gates, [11]Judith shouted to the guards from a distance: "Open! Open the gate! God, our God, is with us. Once more he has made manifest his strength in Israel and his power against our enemies; he has done it this very day." [12]When the citizens heard her voice, they quickly descended to their city gate and

---

12, 10: Banquet for his servants alone . . . officers: Holofernes invited the officials of his household, but not the officers of his army who were needed for military duty.

z: Jgs 4, 21.

> Judith's victory is proof that power and violence can be conquered by faith and wisdom. The weak, oppressed, and demoralized postexilic Israel needs this reminder.

summoned the city elders. *13*All the people, from the least to the greatest, hurriedly assembled, for her return seemed unbelievable. They opened the gate and welcomed the two women. They made a fire for light; and when they gathered around the two, *14*Judith urged them with a loud voice: "Praise God, praise him! Praise God, who has not withdrawn his mercy from the house of Israel, but has shattered our enemies by my hand this very night." *15*Then she took the head out of the pouch, showed it to them, and said: "Here is the head of Holofernes, general in charge of the Assyrian army, and here is the canopy under which he lay in his drunkenness. The LORD struck him down by the hand of a woman.*a* *16*As the LORD lives, who has protected me in the path I have followed, I swear that it was my face that seduced Holofernes to his ruin, and that he did not sin with me to my defilement or disgrace."

*17*All the people were greatly astonished. They bowed down and worshiped God, saying with one accord, "Blessed are you, our God, who today have brought to nought the enemies of your people." *18*Then Uzziah said to her: "Blessed are you, daughter, by the Most High God, above all the women on earth; and blessed be the LORD God, the creator of heaven and earth, who guided your blow at the head of the chief of our enemies.*b* *19*Your deed of hope will never be forgotten by those who tell of the might of God. *20*May God make this redound to your everlasting honor, rewarding you with blessings, because you risked your life when your people were being oppressed, and you averted our disaster, walking uprightly before our God." And all the people answered, "Amen! Amen!"

See RG
154–56

CHAPTER 14

Judith's Counsel. *1*Then Judith said to them: "Listen to me, my brothers. Take this head and hang it on the parapet of your wall. *2*At daybreak, when the sun rises on the earth, let each of you seize his weapons, and let all the able-bodied men rush out of the city under command of a captain, as if about to go down into the plain against the advance guard of the Assyrians, but without going down. *3*They will seize their armor and hurry to their camp to awaken the generals of the Assyrian army. When they run to the tent of Holofernes and do not find him, panic will seize them, and they will flee before you. *4*Then you and all the other inhabitants of the whole territory of Israel will pursue them and strike them down in their tracks. *5*But before doing this, summon for me Achior the Ammonite, that he may see and recognize the one who despised the house of Israel and sent him here to meet his death."

*Achior Summoned.** *6*So they called Achior from the house of Uzziah. When he came and saw the head of Holofernes in the hand of one of the men in the assembly of the people, he fell forward in a faint. *7*Then, after they lifted him up, he threw himself at the feet of Judith in homage, saying: "Blessed are you in every tent of Judah; and in every foreign nation, all who hear of you will be struck with terror. *8*But now, tell me all that you did during these days." So Judith told him, in the presence of the people, all that she had been doing from the day she left till the time she began speaking to them. *9*When she finished her account, the people cheered loudly, and their city resounded with shouts of joy. *10*Now Achior, seeing all that the God of Israel had done, believed firmly in him. He had the flesh of his foreskin circumcised, and he has been united with the house of Israel to the present day.

14, 6–10: In recognizing the head of Holofernes, whom he had known personally, Achior was so overcome with the evidence of the Lord's power exerted through a woman that he believed in the God of Israel.

---

a: Jdt 14, 18. *b:* Jgs 5, 24; Lk 1, 28. 42.

III: Victory

Consternation in the Camp. *11*At daybreak they hung the head of Holofernes on the wall. Then all the Israelite men took up their arms and went to the slopes of the mountain. *12*When the Assyrians saw them, they notified their captains; these, in turn, went to the generals and division leaders and all their other commanders. *13*They came to the tent of Holofernes and said to the one in charge of all his things, "Waken our master, for the slaves have dared come down to give us battle, to their utter destruction." *14*Bagoas went in, and knocked at the entry of the tent, presuming that he was sleeping with Judith. *15*As no one answered, he parted the curtains, entered the bedroom, and found him lying on the floor, a headless corpse. *16*He broke into a loud clamor of weeping, groaning, and howling, and rent his garments. *17*Then he entered the tent where Judith had her quarters; and, not finding her, he rushed out to the troops and cried: *18*"The slaves have duped us! A single Hebrew woman has brought disgrace on the house of King Nebuchadnezzar. Here is Holofernes headless on the ground!"*c*

*19*When the commanders of the Assyrian army heard these words, they rent their tunics and were seized with consternation. Loud screaming and howling arose in the camp.

CHAPTER 15

See RG 154–56 *1*On hearing what had happened, those still in their tents were amazed, *2*and overcome with fear and trembling. No one kept ranks any longer; they scattered in all directions, and fled along every road, both through the valley and in the mountains. *3*Those also who were stationed in the mountain district around Bethulia took to flight. Then all the Israelite warriors overwhelmed them.

Pursuit. *4*Uzziah sent messengers to Betomasthaim, to Choba and Kona, and to the whole country of Israel to report what had happened, that all might fall upon the enemy and destroy them. *5*On hearing this, all the Israelites, with one accord, attacked them and cut them down as far as Choba. Even those from Jerusalem and the rest of the mountain region took part in this, for they too had been notified of the happenings in the camp of their enemies. The Gileadites and the Galileans struck the enemy's flanks with great slaughter, even beyond Damascus and its territory. *6*The remaining inhabitants of Bethulia swept down on the camp of the Assyrians, plundered it, and acquired great riches. *7*The Israelites who returned from the slaughter took possession of what was left, till the towns and villages in the mountains and on the plain were crammed with the enormous quantity of booty they had seized.*d*

*8*The high priest Joakim and the elders of the Israelites, who dwelt in Jerusalem, came to see for themselves the good things that the LORD had done for Israel, and to meet and congratulate Judith.*e* *9*When they had visited her, all with one accord blessed her, saying:

"You are the glory of Jerusalem,
　the surpassing joy of Israel;
　you are the splendid boast of our
　　people.*
10 With your own hand you have done all
　　this;
　you have done good to Israel,
　and God is pleased with what you
　　have wrought.
May you be blessed by the LORD
　　Almighty
forever and ever!"

And all the people answered, "Amen!"

*11*For thirty days the whole populace plundered the camp, giving Judith the tent of Holofernes, with all his silver, his couches, his dishes, and all his furniture, which she accepted. She harnessed her mules, hitched her wagons to them, and loaded these things on them.

15, 9: You are the glory of Jerusalem, the surpassing joy of Israel; you are the splendid boast of our people: these words are used in the liturgy of the Church in regard to the Blessed Virgin Mary.

---

c: Jdt 13, 15; 16, 5-9; Jgs 9, 54.　*d:* Est 9, 5. 16.　*e:* Est 9, 10.

¹²All the women of Israel gathered to see her; and they blessed her and performed a dance in her honor. She took branches in her hands and distributed them to the women around her,ᶠ ¹³and she and the other women crowned themselves with garlands of olive leaves. At the head of all the people, she led the women in the dance, while the men of Israel followed in their armor, wearing garlands and singing hymns.

Hymn of Praise. ¹⁴Judith led all Israel in this song of thanksgiving, and the people swelled this hymn of praise:

CHAPTER 16

See RG 154-56

¹"Strike up the instruments,
a song to my God with timbrels,
chant to the LORD with cymbals;
Sing to him a new song,
exalt and acclaim his name.ᵍ
² For the LORD is God; he crushes warfare,
and sets his encampment among his people;
he snatched me from the hands of my persecutors.ʰ

³ "The Assyrian came from the mountains of the north,
with the myriads of his forces he came;
Their numbers blocked the torrents, their horses covered the hills.
⁴ He threatened to burn my land,
put my youths to the sword,
Dash my babes to the ground,
make my children a prey,
and seize my virgins as spoil.

⁵ "But the LORD Almighty thwarted them,
by a woman's hand he confounded them.ⁱ
⁶ Not by youths was their mighty one struck down,
nor did titans bring him low,
nor huge giants attack him;
But Judith, the daughter of Merari,
by the beauty of her countenance disabled him.ʲ

⁷ She took off her widow's garb
to raise up the afflicted in Israel.
She anointed her face with fragrant oil;
⁸ with a fillet she fastened her tresses
and put on a linen robe to beguile him.
⁹ Her sandals caught his eyes,
and her beauty captivated his mind.
The sword cut through his neck.ᵏ

¹⁰ "The Persians were dismayed at her daring,
the Medes appalled at her boldness.
¹¹ When my lowly ones shouted, they were terrified;
when my weaklings cried out, they trembled;
at the sound of their war cry, they took to flight.
¹² The sons of slave girls pierced them through;
the supposed sons of rebel mothers cut them down;
they perished before the ranks of my LORD.

¹³ "A new hymn I will sing to my God.
O LORD, great are you and glorious,
wonderful in power and unsurpassable.ˡ
¹⁴ Let your every creature serve you;
for you spoke, and they were made.
You sent forth your spirit, and they were created;
no one can resist your word.ᵐ
¹⁵ The mountains to their bases, and the seas, are shaken;
the rocks, like wax, melt before your glance.ⁿ

"But to those who fear you,
you are very merciful.
¹⁶ Though the sweet odor of every sacrifice is a trifle,
and the fat of all holocausts but little in your sight,
one who fears the LORD is forever great.ᵒ

---

f: Ex 15, 20f; Jgs 11, 34; 1 Sm 18, 6; Jer 31, 4. 13.   g: Pss 81, 2f; 135, 1ff. 149, 1ff.   h: Jdt 5, 23; 6, 2; 9, 7f; Ex 15, 3; Ps 46, 10.   i: Jdt 14, 8.   j: Jdt 9, 13.   k: Jdt 9, 13.   l: Ps 144, 9.   m: Pss 33, 9; 104, 30; 148, 5.   n: Jgs 5, 5; Ps 97, 5.   o: Ps 86, 11; Sir 34, 13-17.

[17] "Woe to the nations that rise against my
people!
The LORD Almighty will requite
them;
in the day of judgment he will punish
them:
He will send fire and worms into their
flesh,*
and they shall burn and suffer
forever."[p]

Thanksgiving. [18]The people then went to
Jerusalem to worship God; when they were
purified, they offered their holocausts, free-
will offerings, and gifts. [19]Judith dedicated,
as a votive offering to God, all the things of
Holofernes that the people had given her, as
well as the canopy that she herself had taken
from his bedroom.[q] [20]For three months the
people continued their celebration in Jerusalem before the sanctuary, and Judith remained with them.

Judith's Renown. [21]When those days
were over, each one returned to his inheritance. Judith went back to Bethulia and remained on her estate. For the rest of her life
she was renowned throughout the land.
[22]Many wished to marry her, but she gave
herself to no man all the days of her life from
the time of the death and burial of her husband, Manasseh. [23]She lived to be very old
in the house of her husband, reaching the advanced age of a hundred and five. She died
in Bethulia, where they buried her in the
tomb of her husband, Manasseh;[r] [24]and the
house of Israel mourned her for seven days.
Before she died, she distributed her goods to
the relatives of her husband, Manasseh, and
to her own relatives; and to the maid she
gave her freedom.

[25s]During the life of Judith and for a long
time after her death, no one again disturbed
the Israelites.*

16, 17: Fire and worms into their flesh: see footnote on
Is 66, 24.

16, 25: The Vulgate adds: "The feast day of this victory
was adopted by the Hebrews into the calendar of their holy
days, and has been celebrated by the Jews from that time to
the present." However, there is no other evidence of such a

festivity; and it is the ancient feast of Passover to which the
narrative is especially suited.

---

p: Is 66, 24.   *q:* Nm 31, 48-54; Dt 13, 13-18; Jos 6, 18f.   *r:* Gn
23, 19; 49, 29-32.   *s:* Jgs 3, 11. 30; 5, 31; 8, 28.

See RG
156–59

The Book of Esther

The Book of Esther is named after its Jewish heroine. It tells the story of the plot of Haman the Agagite, jealous and powerful vizier of King Xerxes
(Ahasuerus) of Persia (485–464 B.C.), to destroy
in a single day all the Jews living in the Persian
Empire. He is moved to this out of hatred for the
Jewish servant Mordecai, who for religious motives refuses to render him homage. The day of the
proposed massacre is determined by lot. Meanwhile Esther, niece and adopted daughter of Mordecai, is chosen queen by King Xerxes in place of
Vashti. She averts the pogrom planned against her
people and has the royal decree of extermination
reversed against Haman and the enemies of the
Jews. Mordecai replaces Haman, and together
with Esther, works for the welfare of their people.
The event is celebrated with feasting and great
joy, and the memory of it is to be perpetuated by
the annual observance of the feast of Purim (lots),
when the lot of destruction for the Jews was

reversed for one of deliverance and triumph by
Queen Esther and her uncle Mordecai.

The purpose of the book is didactic: the glorification of the Jewish people and the explanation
of the origin, significance and date of the feast of
Purim on the fourteenth and fifteenth of Adar
(February–March). The book was intended as a
consolation for Israel, a reminder that God's
providence continually watches over them,
never abandoning them when they serve him
faithfully or turn to him in sincere repentance.
There is no justification for interpreting the story
in mythological or cultic terms, as though Mordecai and Esther represented Marduk and Ishtar
in their mythological triumph over two Elamite
deities.

The Hebrew text of Esther is found in the Hebrew Bible, where it is the last of the five
megilloth (scrolls) read on special feasts of the
Jewish liturgical year.

The book is a free composition—not a historical document, despite the Achaemenian coloring of the narrative. Its time of composition may well have been at the end of the Persian Empire, toward the close of the fourth century B.C. The author shows skill in developing his story and in using the art of contrast for instruction and edification. The solution to the difficulties of the book is to be found in its literary presentation rather than in a forced attempt to square detailed data of the narrative with facts. The evident literary motif of the reversal of fortune of the prosperous wicked and the oppressed virtuous through eventual punishment of the former and triumph of the latter finds parallels in the story of Joseph (Gn 37; 39—45) and of Judith (8—16). The book is vindictive, but it should be remembered that the precept of love of enemies had not yet been taught by the word and example of Christ.

The text of Esther, written originally in Hebrew, was transmitted in two forms: a short Hebrew form and a longer Greek version. The latter contains 107 additional verses, inserted at appropriate places within the Hebrew form of the text. A few of these seem to have a Hebrew origin while the rest are Greek in original composition. It is possible that the Hebrew form of the text is original throughout. If it systematically omits reference to God and his Providence over Israel, this is perhaps due to fear of irreverent response (see note on 4, 14). The Greek text with the above-mentioned additions is probably a later literary paraphrase in which the author seeks to have the reader share his sentiments. This standard Greek text is pre-Christian in origin. The church has accepted the additions as equally inspired with the rest of the book.

In the present translation, the portions preceded by the letters A through F indicate the underlying Greek additions referred to above. The regular chapter numbers apply to the Hebrew text.

The book may be divided as follows:

I: Prologue (A, 1-17).

II: Elevation of Esther (1, 1—2, 23).

III: Haman's Plot against the Jews (3, 1-13; B, 1-7; 3, 14—4, 8; B, 8; 4, 9-16; C, 1—D, 16; 5, 1-14).

IV: Vindication of the Jews (6, 1—8, 12; E, 1-24; 8, 13—10, 3).

V: Epilogue (F, 1-11).

The order of the Vulgate text in relation to the order of the Greek text is as follows:

Vulg. 11, 2—12, 6 = A, 1-17 at the beginning of the book.

13, 1-7 = B, 1-7 after 3, 13.

13, 8—15, 3-19 = C, 1—D, 16 after 4, 16.

15, 1-2 = B, 8. 9 after 4, 8.

16, 1-24 = E, 1-24 after 8, 12.

10, 4—10, 13 = F, 1-10 after 10, 3.

I: Prologue

CHAPTER A

See RG 157–59

Dream of Mordecai. *¹*In the second year of the reign of the great King Ahasuerus,* on the first day of Nisan, Mordecai, son of Jair, son of Shimei, son of Kish, of the tribe of Benjamin, had a dream.*ᵃ* *²*He was a Jew residing in the city of Susa, a prominent man who served at the king's court, *³*and one of the captives whom Nebuchadnezzar, king of Babylon, had taken from Jerusalem with Jeconiah, king of Judah.*ᵇ*

*⁴ᶜ*This was his dream.* There was noise and tumult, thunder and earthquake—confusion upon the earth. *⁵*Two great dragons came on, both poised for combat. They uttered a mighty cry, *⁶*and at their cry every nation prepared for war, to fight against the race of the just. *⁷*It was a dark and gloomy day. Tribulation and distress, evil and great confusion, lay upon the earth. *⁸*The whole race of the just were dismayed with fear of the evils to come upon them, and were at the point of destruction. *⁹ᵈ*Then they cried out to

A, 1: King Ahasuerus: Xerxes I (485–464 B.C.). Mordecai: a Babylonian name, after the God Marduk. The genealogy of Mordecai is designed to reflect opposition to Israel's enemy, as narrated in 1 Sm 15, 7ff, where Saul (whose father's name was Kish, of the Tribe of Benjamin) conquered Agag the Amalekite; in A, 17 Haman is said to be the son of an Agagite. Further emphasis on the Benjaminite-Agagite opposition can be seen in Shimei, the Benjaminite who reviled David (2 Sm 16, 5ff). Jair

appears to be the minor Judge, a Transjordan Manassehite (Jgs 10, 3). The chronology of the book would make Mordecai well over one hundred years old, since he was deported with Jehoiachin about 598 B.C.; cf Est 2, 5f.

A, 4: The interpretation of this dream is given in Est F, 1-6.

a: Est 2, 5. *b:* Est 2, 6; 2 Kgs 24, 15; 2 Chr 36, 9f; Jer 22, 24ff; 24, 1; 29, 1f. *c:* 4ff: Est F, 2. 4ff. *d:* 9f: Est F, 3.

Vashti Deposed

The wise men (1, 13) are possibly the king's seven counselors (Ezr 7, 14). Reference to irrevocable laws (Est 1, 19) is also made in Est 8, 8 and in Dn 6, 9. There may be some irony in the allusion that in both Esther and Daniel the irrevocable decrees against the Jews are ineffective.

God, and as they cried, there appeared to come forth a great river, a flood of water from a little spring. *10*The light of the sun broke forth; the lowly were exalted and they devoured the nobles.

*11*Having seen this dream and what God intended to do, Mordecai awoke. He kept it in mind, and tried in every way, until night, to understand its meaning.

The Plot Discovered. *12e*Mordecai lodged at the court with Bagathan and Thares, two eunuchs of the king who were court guards. *13*He overheard them plotting, investigated their plans, and discovered that they were preparing to lay hands on King Ahasuerus. So he informed the king about them, *14*and the king had the two eunuchs questioned and, upon their confession, put to death. *15*Then the king had these things recorded; Mordecai, too, put them into writing. *16*The king also appointed Mordecai to serve at the court, and rewarded him* for his actions.*f*

*17*Haman, however, son of Hammedatha the Agagite,* who was in high honor with the king, sought to harm Mordecai and his people because of the two eunuchs of the king.*g*

II: Elevation of Esther

CHAPTER 1

See RG
157-59 *The Banquet of Ahasuerus.* *1*During the reign of Ahasuerus—this was the Ahasuerus who ruled over a hundred and twenty-seven provinces from India to Ethiopia*— *2*while he was occupying the royal throne in the stronghold of Susa,* *3*in the third year of his reign, he presided over a feast for all his officers and ministers: the Persian and Median aristocracy, the nobles, and the governors of the provinces.*h* *4*For as many as a hundred and eighty days, he displayed the glorious riches of his kingdom and the resplendent wealth of his royal estate.

*5*At the end of this time the king gave a feast of seven days in the garden court of the royal palace for all the people, great and small, who were in the stronghold of Susa. *6*There were white cotton draperies and violet hangings, held by cords of crimson byssus from silver rings on marble pillars. Gold and silver couches were on the pavement, which was of porphyry, marble, mother-of-pearl, and colored stones. *7*Liquor was served in a variety of golden cups, and the royal wine flowed freely, as befitted the king's munificence. *8*By ordinance of the king the drinking was unstinted, for he had instructed all the stewards of his household to comply with the good pleasure of everyone.

*9*Queen Vashti* also gave a feast for the women inside the royal palace of King Ahasuerus.

Deposal of Vashti. *10*On the seventh day, when the king was merry with wine, he instructed Mehuman, Biztha, Harbona, Bigtha, Abagtha, Zethar, and Carkas, the seven eunuchs who attended King Ahasuerus,*i* *11*to bring Queen Vashti into his presence wearing the royal crown, that he might display her beauty to the populace and the officials,

---

A, 16: Rewarded him: this reward comes only later; see the sequence of events from the Hebrew text of Esther at 2, 22f, and 6, 3, below.

A, 17: Haman . . . the Agagite: opposed Mordecai the Benjaminite, by whom, however, he was overcome (Est 7, 9f), just as King Agag the Amalekite, was conquered by King Saul ancestor of Mordecai (1 Sm 15, 7ff).

1, 1: From India to Ethiopia: from western India to Upper Egypt, the greatest extent of the Persian Empire achieved under Darius the Great, father of Ahasuerus.

1, 2: Susa: ancient capital of Elam (Gn 14, 1); under the Achaemenid kings, one of the two capitals of the Persian Empire. The other was Persepolis, the summer palace of the kings.

1, 9: Queen Vashti: Herodotus (Histories 7, 61) relates that the wife of Ahasuerus was Amestris.

---

e: 12-15: Est 2, 21ff; 6, 1ff.   *f:* Est 6, 3.   *g:* Est 3, 1-15; B, 1-7; E, 13.   *h:* Jdt 1, 16.   *i:* Dn 5, 1.

The Persian Empire

for she was lovely to behold. ¹²But Queen Vashti refused to come at the royal order issued through the eunuchs. At this the king's wrath flared up, and he burned with fury. ¹³He conferred with the wise men versed in the law, because the king's business was conducted in general consultation with lawyers and jurists. ¹⁴He summoned Carshena, Shethar, Admatha, Tarshish, Meres, Marsena and Memucan, the seven Persian and Median officials who were in the king's personal service and held first rank in the realm,ʲ ¹⁵and asked them, "What is to be done by law with Queen Vashti for disobeying the order of King Ahasuerus issued through the eunuchs?"

¹⁶In the presence of the king and of the officials, Memucan answered: "Queen Vashti has not wronged the king alone, but all the officials and the populace throughout the provinces of King Ahasuerus. ¹⁷For the queen's conduct will become known to all the women, and they will look with disdain upon their husbands when it is reported, 'King Ahasuerus commanded that Queen Vashti be ushered into his presence, but she would not come.' ¹⁸This very day the Persian and Median ladies who hear of the queen's conduct will rebel against all the royal officials, with corresponding disdain and rancor. ¹⁹If it please the king, let an irrevocable royal decree* be issued by him and inscribed among the laws of the Persians and Medes, forbidding Vashti to come into the presence of King Ahasuerus and authorizing the king to give her royal dignity to one more worthy than she.ᵏ ²⁰Thus, when the decree which the king will issue is published throughout his realm, vast as it is, all wives will honor their husbands, from the greatest to the least."

²¹This proposal found acceptance with the king and the officials, and the king acted on

---

1, 19: Irrevocable royal decree: the historian Siculus indicates that such a concept of irrevocable laws existed in the time of Darius III (335–331 B.C.), the last of the Persian kings, cf Est 8, 8.

ʲ: Ezr 7, 14.   ᵏ: Est 8, 5. 8; Dn 6, 8f.

the advice of Memucan. [22]He sent letters to all the royal provinces, to each province in its own script and to each people in its own language,* to the effect that every man should be lord in his own home.

CHAPTER 2

See RG 157-59

Esther Made Queen. [1]After this, when King Ahasuerus' wrath had cooled, he thought over what Vashti had done and what had been decreed against her. [2]Then the king's personal attendants suggested: "Let beautiful young virgins be sought for the king. [3]Let the king appoint commissaries in all the provinces of his realm to bring together all beautiful young virgins to the harem in the stronghold of Susa. Under the care of the royal eunuch Hegai, custodian of the women, let cosmetics be given them. [4]Then the girl who pleases the king shall reign in place of Vashti." This suggestion pleased the king, and he acted accordingly.

[5]There was in the stronghold of Susa a certain Jew named Mordecai, son of Jair, son of Shimei, son of Kish, a Benjaminite, [6]who had been exiled from Jerusalem with the captives taken with Jeconiah, king of Judah, whom Nebuchadnezzar, king of Babylon, had deported.[l] [7]He was foster father to Hadassah,* that is, Esther, his cousin; for she had lost both father and mother. The girl was beautifully formed and lovely to behold. On the death of her father and mother, Mordecai had taken her as his own daughter.[m]

[8]When the king's order and decree had been obeyed and many maidens brought together to the stronghold of Susa under the care of Hegai, Esther also was brought in to the royal palace under the care of Hegai, custodian of the women. [9]The girl pleased him and won his favor. So he promptly furnished her with cosmetics and provisions. Then picking out seven maids for her from the royal palace, he transferred both her and her maids to the best place in the harem. [10]Esther did not reveal her nationality or family, for Mordecai had commanded her not to do so.

[11]Day by day Mordecai would walk about in front of the court of the harem, to learn how Esther was faring and what was to become of her.

[12]Each girl went in turn to visit King Ahasuerus after the twelve months' preparation decreed for the women. Of this period of beautifying treatment, six months were spent with oil of myrrh, and the other six months with perfumes and cosmetics. [13]Then, when the girl was to visit the king, she was allowed to take with her from the harem to the royal palace whatever she chose. [14]She would go in the evening and return in the morning to a second harem under the care of the royal eunuch Shaashgaz, custodian of the concubines. She could not return to the king unless he was pleased with her and had her summoned by name.[n]

[15]As for Esther, daughter of Abihail and adopted daughter of his nephew Mordecai, when her turn came to visit the king, she did not ask for anything but what the royal eunuch Hegai, custodian of the women, suggested. Yet she won the admiration of all who saw her. [16]Esther was led to King Ahasuerus in his palace in the tenth month, Tebeth, in the seventh year of his reign. [17]The king loved Esther more than all other women, and of all the virgins she won his favor and benevolence. So he placed the royal diadem on her head and made her queen in place of Vashti. [18]Then the king gave a great feast in honor of Esther to all his officials and ministers, granting a holiday* to the provinces and bestowing gifts with royal bounty.

The Plot Discovered.* [19o][To resume: From the time the virgins had been brought together, and while Mordecai was passing

---

1, 22: To each province . . . script and to each people . . . language: many languages were spoken in the Persian Empire, the principal ones being Persian, Elamite, Babylonian, Aramaic, Phoenician, Egyptian, and Greek. Each of them had its own script.

2, 7: Hadassah (the feminine form of hadas, myrtle), was the name by which this woman would be known among her Jewish compatriots. Esther is a variant of the name of the

Babylonian goddess Ishtar.

2, 18: A holiday: or perhaps, "a remission of taxes."

2, 19-23: This is a resumption, in a slightly different form, of the story already told in Est A, 12-15.

---

l: Est A, 3; 2 Kgs 24, 15; 2 Chr 36, 9f; Jer 22, 24ff; 24, 1; 29, 1f. *m:* Est 2, 15. *n:* Est 2, 19f; 4, 11. 16. *o:* 19f: Est 2, 14.

his time at the king's gate, [20]Esther had not revealed her family or nationality, because Mordecai had told her not to; and Esther continued to follow Mordecai's instructions, just as she had when she was being brought up by him. [21p]And during the time that Mordecai spent at the king's gate,* Bagathan and Thares, two of the royal eunuchs who guarded the entrance, had plotted in anger to lay hands on King Ahasuerus. [22]When the plot became known to Mordecai, he told Queen Esther, who in turn informed the king for Mordecai. [23]The matter was investigated and verified, and both of them were hanged on a gibbet.* This was written in the annals for the king's use.]

III: Haman's Plot Against the Jews

CHAPTER 3

See RG 157-59

Mordecai Refuses To Honor Haman. [1]After these events King Ahasuerus raised Haman, son of Hammedatha the Agagite, to high rank, seating him above all his fellow officials.[q] [2]All the king's servants who were at the royal gate would kneel and bow down to Haman, for that is what the king had ordered in his regard.[r] Mordecai, however, would not kneel and bow down.* [3]The king's servants who were at the royal gate said to Mordecai, "Why do you disobey the king's order?"[s] [4]When they had reminded him day after day and he would not listen to them, they informed Haman, to see whether Mordecai's explanation was acceptable, since he had told them that he was a Jew.

Haman's Reprisal. [5]When Haman observed that Mordecai would not kneel and bow down to him, he was filled with anger. [6]Moreover, he thought it was not enough to lay hands on Mordecai alone. Since they had told Haman of Mordecai's nationality, he sought to destroy all the Jews, Mordecai's people, throughout the realm of King Ahasuerus. [7]In the first month, Nisan, in the twelfth year of King Ahasuerus, the pur,* or lot, was cast in Haman's presence, to determine the day and the month for the destruction of Mordecai's people on a single day, and the lot fell on the thirteenth day of the twelfth month, Adar.[t]

Decree against the Jews. [8]Then Haman said to King Ahasuerus: "Dispersed among the nations throughout the provinces of your kingdom, there is a certain people living apart, with laws differing from those of every other people. They do not obey the laws of the king, and so it is not proper for the king to tolerate them.[u] [9]If it please the king, let a decree be issued to destroy them; and I will deliver to the procurators ten thousand silver talents for deposit in the royal treasury."[v] [10]The king took the signet ring* from his hand and gave it to Haman, son of Hammedatha the Agagite, the enemy of the Jews.[w] [11]"The silver you may keep," the king said to Haman, "but as for this people, do with them whatever you please."

[12]So the royal scribes were summoned; and on the thirteenth day of the first month they wrote, at the dictation of Haman, an order to the royal satraps, the governors of every province, and the officials of every people, to each province in its own script and to each people in its own language. It was written in the name of King Ahasuerus and sealed with the royal signet ring. [13]Letters were sent by couriers to all the royal provinces, that all the Jews, young and old, including women and children, should be killed, destroyed, wiped out in one day, the thirteenth day of the twelfth

---

2, 21: Mordecai . . . at the king's gate: to exercise watchful care for Esther. Some understand this to mean that Mordecai was stationed at the gate to render royal service; cf Est A, 2.

2, 23: Hanged on a gibbet: impaled, perhaps, after the Babylonian manner.

3, 2: Mordecai . . . would not kneel and bow down: in order not to render to man, the homage which he regarded as belonging to God alone; cf Est C, 5ff.

3, 7: Pur: a Babylonian word which the Hebrew translates as goral, "lot." This word is preserved in the text because its plural, purim, became the name of the feast of Pu-

rim commemorating the deliverance of the Jews; cf Est 9, 24. 26.

3, 10: Signet ring: a ring containing a seal which was impressed on documents to authenticate them. By giving this ring to Haman, the king bestowed on him the power to authenticate royal decrees.

---

p: 21ff: Est A, 12-15; 6, 1ff. q: Est B, 3; 5, 11; E, 11. r: Est C, 5; 5, 9. 13; 6, 10. 12. s: Est 4, 16. t: Est 9, 24ff; F, 10. u: Est 3, 13; B, 4; E, 24; Dn 3, 8-12; Wis 2, 14f. v: Est 7, 4. w: Gn 41, 42.

month, Adar, and that their goods should be seized as spoil.^{x}

See RG 157-59

CHAPTER B

^{1}This is a copy of the letter:

"The great King Ahasuerus writes to the satraps of the hundred and twenty-seven provinces from India to Ethiopia, and the governors subordinate to them, as follows: ^{2}When I came to rule many peoples and to hold sway over the whole world, I determined not to be carried away with the sense of power, but always to deal fairly and with clemency; to provide for my subjects a life of complete tranquillity; and by making my government humane and effective as far as the borders, to restore the peace desired by all men.^{y} ^{3}When I consulted my counselors as to how this might be accomplished, Haman, who excels among us in wisdom, who is outstanding for constant devotion and steadfast loyalty, and who has gained the second rank in the kingdom,^{z} ^{4}brought it to our attention that, mixed in with all the races throughout the world, there is one people of bad will, which by its laws is opposed to every other people and continually disregards the decrees of kings, so that the unity of empire blamelessly designed by us cannot be established.^{a}

^{5}"Having noted, therefore, that this most singular people is continually at variance with all men, lives by divergent and alien laws, is inimical to our interests, and commits the worst crimes, so that stability of government cannot be obtained, ^{6}we hereby decree that all those who are indicated to you in the letters of Haman, who is in charge of the administration and is a second father to us, shall, together with their wives and children, be utterly destroyed by the swords of their enemies, without any pity or mercy, on the fourteenth day* of the twelfth month, Adar, of the current year;^{b} ^{7}so that when these people, whose present ill will is of long standing, have gone down into the nether

world by a violent death on one same day, they may at last leave our affairs stable and undisturbed for the future."

(CHAPTER 3)

See RG 157-59

^{14}A copy of the decree to be promulgated as law in every province was published to all the peoples, that they might be prepared for that day. ^{15}The couriers set out in haste at the king's command; meanwhile, the decree was promulgated in the stronghold of Susa. The king and Haman then sat down to feast, but the city of Susa was thrown into confusion.

CHAPTER 4

Esther's Aid Sought by Mordecai.

See RG 157-59

^{1}When Mordecai learned all that was happening, he tore his garments, put on sackcloth and ashes, and walked through the city, crying out loudly and bitterly,^{c} ^{2}till he came before the royal gate, which no one clothed in sackcloth might enter. ^{3}(Likewise in each of the provinces, wherever the king's legal enactment reached, the Jews went into deep mourning, with fasting, weeping, and lament; they all slept on sackcloth and ashes.)

^{4}Queen Esther's maids and eunuchs came and told her. Overwhelmed with anguish, she sent garments for Mordecai to put on, so that he might take off his sackcloth; but he refused. ^{5}Esther then summoned Hathach, one of the king's eunuchs whom he had placed at her service, and commanded him to find out what this action of Mordecai meant and the reason for it. ^{6}So Hathach went out to Mordecai in the public square in front of the royal gate, ^{7}and Mordecai told him all that had happened, as well as the exact amount of silver Haman had promised to pay to the royal treasury for the slaughter of the Jews. ^{8}He also gave him a copy of the written decree for their destruction which had been promulgated in Susa, to show and explain to Esther. He was to instruct her to go to the king; she was to plead and intercede with him in behalf of her people. ^{8*}"Remember the days of your

---

B, 6: Fourteenth day: the Hebrew text, as in Est 2, 13 above, and the Greek text here translated do not agree on the day of the month specified by the king; in fact, a two-day celebration is decreed in chapter 9, and the 13th, 14th and 15th of Adar are all mentioned; see Est 9, 15. 18.

4, 8: This verse belongs to ch B.

x: Est B, 6; 7, 4. y: Est E, 8f. z: Est 3, 1; 5, 11; E, 11. a: Est 3, 8; E, 24. b: Est 3, 13; 7, 4; E, 11ff. c: Jdt 4, 12.

lowly estate," Mordecai had him say, "when you were brought up in my charge; for Haman, who is second to the king, has asked for our death. [9]Invoke the LORD and speak to the king for us; save us from death."

Hathach returned to Esther and told her what Mordecai had said. [10]Then Esther replied to Hathach and gave him this message for Mordecai: [11]"All the servants of the king and the people of his provinces know that any man or woman who goes to the king in the inner court without being summoned, suffers the automatic penalty of death, unless the king extends to him the golden scepter, thus sparing his life. Now as for me, I have not been summoned to the king for thirty days."[d]

[12]When Esther's words were reported to Mordecai, [13]he had this reply brought to her: "Do not imagine that because you are in the king's palace, you alone of all the Jews will escape. [14]Even if you now remain silent, relief and deliverance will come to the Jews from another source;[*] but you and your father's house will perish. Who knows but that it was for a time like this that you obtained the royal dignity?"

[15]Esther sent back to Mordecai the response: [16]"Go and assemble all the Jews who are in Susa; fast on my behalf, all of you, not eating or drinking, night or day, for three days. I and my maids will also fast in the same way. Thus prepared, I will go to the king, contrary to the law. If I perish, I perish!"[e]

CHAPTER C

See RG
157-59

Prayer of Mordecai. Mordecai went away and did exactly as Esther had commanded. [1]Recalling all that the LORD had done, he prayed to him [2]and said: "O Lord God, almighty King, all things are in your power, and there is no one to oppose you in your will to save Israel. [3]You made heaven and earth and every wonderful thing under the heavens. [4]You are LORD of all, and there is no one who can resist you, LORD. [5f]You

know all things. You know, O LORD, that it was not out of insolence or pride or desire for fame that I acted thus in not bowing down to the proud Haman. [6]Gladly would I have kissed the soles of his feet for the salvation of Israel. [7]But I acted as I did so as not to place the honor of man above that of God. I will not bow down to anyone but you, my LORD. It is not out of pride that I am acting thus. [8]And now, LORD God, King, God of Abraham, spare your people, for our enemies plan our ruin and are bent upon destroying the inheritance that was yours from the beginning. [9]Do not spurn your portion, which you redeemed for yourself out of Egypt. [10]Hear my prayer; have pity on your inheritance and turn our sorrow into joy: thus we shall live to sing praise to your name, O LORD. Do not silence those who praise you."

[11]All Israel, too, cried out with all their strength, for death was staring them in the face.

Prayer of Esther. [12g]Queen Esther, seized with mortal anguish, likewise had recourse to the LORD. [13]Taking off her splendid garments, she put on garments of distress and mourning. In place of her precious ointments she covered her head with dirt and ashes. She afflicted her body severely; all her festive adornments were put aside, and her hair was wholly disheveled.

[14]Then she prayed to the LORD, the God of Israel, saying: "My LORD, our King, you alone are God. Help me, who am alone and have no help but you, [15]for I am taking my life in my hand.[h] [16]As a child I was wont to hear from the people of the land of my forefathers that you, O LORD, chose Israel from among all peoples, and our fathers from among all their ancestors, as a lasting heritage, and that you fulfilled all your promises to them.[i] [17]But now we have sinned in your sight, and you have delivered us into the hands of our enemies, [18]because we worshiped their gods. You are just, O LORD. [19]But now they are not satisfied with our bitter servitude, but have

---

4, 14: From another source: very probably Mordecai refers to divine aid; the Greek additions (C) are explicit about this.

d: Est 2, 14; 4, 12; D, 12.   e: Est C, 12f.   f: 5ff: Est 3, 2; 5, 9.   g: 12f: Est 4, 16.   h: Est 4, 16.   i: Dt 4, 20; 7, 6; 9, 29; 14, 2; 26, 18; 32, 9.

undertaken [20]to do away with the decree you have pronounced, and to destroy your heritage; to close the mouths of those who praise you, and to extinguish the glory of your temple and your altar; [21]to open the mouths of the heathen to acclaim their false gods, and to extol an earthly king forever.

[22]"O Lord, do not relinquish your scepter to those that are nought. Let them not gloat over our ruin, but turn their own counsel against them and make an example of our chief enemy. [23]Be mindful of us, O Lord. Manifest yourself in the time of our distress and give me courage, King of gods and Ruler of every power. [24]Put in my mouth persuasive words in the presence of the lion and turn his heart to hatred for our enemy, so that he and those who are in league with him may perish. [25]Save us by your power, and help me, who am alone and have no one but you, O Lord.

"You know all things. [26]You know that I hate the glory of the pagans, and abhor the bed of the uncircumcised or of any foreigner. [27]You know that I am under constraint, that I abhor the sign of grandeur which rests on my head when I appear in public; abhor it like a polluted rag, and do not wear it in private. [28]I, your handmaid, have never eaten at the table of Haman, nor have I graced the banquet of the king or drunk the wine of libations.* [29]From the day I was brought here till now, your handmaid has had no joy except in you, O Lord, God of Abraham. [30]O God, more powerful than all, hear the voice of those in despair. Save us from the power of the wicked, and deliver me from my fear."

See RG 157-59

CHAPTER D

Esther Is Received by the King. [1]On the third day, putting an end to her prayers, she took off her penitential garments and arrayed herself in her royal attire. [2]In making her state appearance, after invoking the all-seeing God and savior, she took with her two maids; [3]on the one she leaned gently for support, [4]while the other followed her, bearing her train. [5]She glowed with the perfection of her beauty and her countenance was as joyous as it was lovely, though her heart was shrunk with fear. [6]She passed through all the portals till she stood face to face with the king, who was seated on his royal throne, clothed in full robes of state, and covered with gold and precious stones, so that he inspired great awe. [7]As he looked up, his features ablaze with the height of majestic anger, the queen staggered, changed color, and leaned weakly against the head of the maid in front of her. [8]But God changed the king's anger to gentleness. In great anxiety he sprang from his throne, held her in his arms until she recovered, and comforted her with reassuring words. [9]"What is it, Esther?" he said to her. "I am your brother. Take courage! [10]You shall not die because of this general decree of ours. [11]Come near!" [12]Raising the golden scepter, he touched her neck with it, embraced her, and said, "Speak to me." [j]

[13]She replied: "I saw you, my lord, as an angel of God, and my heart was troubled with fear of your majesty. [14]For you are awesome, my lord, though your glance is full of kindness." [15]As she said this, she fainted. [16]The king became troubled and all his attendants tried to revive her.

CHAPTER 5

See RG 157-59

[1]*[Now on the third day, Esther put on her royal garments and stood in the inner courtyard, looking toward the royal palace, while the king was seated on his royal throne in the audience chamber, facing the palace doorway. [2]He saw Queen Esther standing in the courtyard, and made her welcome by extending toward her the golden staff which he held. She came up to him, and touched the top of the staff.]

[3]Then the king said to her, "What is it, Queen Esther? What is your request? Even if it is half of my kingdom, it shall be granted

---

C, 28: Wine of libations: offered in sacrifice to the gods.
5, 1f: The Hebrew text here translated is a short form of the account already given in Greek.

j: Est 4, 11.

Royal Gifts

The bestowal of the royal robe (6, 8) was common in ancient times (cf Gn 41, 42). Horses wearing royal crowns are pictured on Persian monuments.

you."[k] [4]"If it please your majesty," Esther replied, "come today with Haman to a banquet I have prepared." [5]And the king ordered, "Have Haman make haste to fulfill the wish of Esther."

First Banquet of Esther. So the king went with Haman to the banquet Esther had prepared. [6]During the drinking of the wine, the king said to Esther, "Whatever you ask for shall be granted, and whatever request you make shall be honored, even if it is for half my kingdom."[l] [7]Esther replied: "This is my petition and request: [8]if I have found favor with the king and if it pleases your majesty to grant my petition and honor my request, come with Haman tomorrow to a banquet which I shall prepare for you; and then I will do as you ask."

Haman's Plot against Mordecai. [9]That day Haman left happy and in good spirits. But when he saw that Mordecai at the royal gate did not rise, and showed no fear of him, he was filled with anger toward him.[m] [10]Haman restrained himself, however, and went home, where he summoned his friends and his wife Zeresh. [11]He recounted the greatness of his riches, the large number of his sons, and just how the king had promoted him and placed him above the officials and royal servants.[n] [12]"Moreover," Haman added, "Queen Esther invited no one but me to the banquet with the king; again tomorrow I am to be her guest, with the king. [13]Yet none of this satisfies me as long as I continue to see the Jew Mordecai sitting at the royal gate."[o] [14]His wife Zeresh and all his friends said to him, "Have a gibbet set up, fifty cubits in height, and in the morning ask the king to have Mordecai hanged on it. Then go to the banquet with the king in good cheer." This suggestion pleased Haman, and he had the gibbet erected.[p]

IV: Vindication of the Jews

CHAPTER 6

Mordecai's Reward from the King. See RG 157-59

[1]That night the king, unable to sleep, asked that the chronicle of notable events be brought in. While this was being read to him, [2]the passage occurred in which Mordecai reported Bagathan and Teresh, two of the royal eunuchs who guarded the entrance, for seeking to lay hands on King Ahasuerus.[q] [3]The king asked, "What was done to reward and honor Mordecai for this?" The king's attendants replied, "Nothing was done for him."[r]

[4]"Who is in the court?" the king asked. Now Haman had entered the outer court of the king's palace to suggest to the king that Mordecai should be hanged on the gibbet he had raised for him.[s] [5]The king's servants answered him, "Haman is waiting in the court." "Let him come in," the king said. [6]When Haman entered, the king said to him, "What should be done for the man whom the king wishes to reward?" Now Haman thought to himself, "Whom would the king more probably wish to reward than me?" [7]So he replied to the king: "For the man whom the king wishes to reward [8]there should be brought the royal robe which the king wore and the horse on which the king rode when the royal crown was placed on his head. [9]The robe and the horse should be consigned to one of the noblest of the king's officials, who must clothe the man the king wishes to reward, have him ride on the horse in the public square of the city, and cry out before him, 'This is what is done for the man whom the king wishes to reward.' "[t] [10]Then the king said to Haman: "Hurry! Take the robe and horse as you have

---

k: Est 5, 6; 7, 2; 9, 12.   l: Est 5, 3.   m: Est 3, 2f; C, 5ff; 6, 10. 12.   n: Est 3, 1; B, 3; E, 11; 9, 6-10.   o: Est 3, 2f; 6, 10. 12.   p: Est 6, 4; 7, 9f.   q: Est A, 12ff; 2, 21ff.   r: Est A, 16.   s: Est 5, 14; 7, 9f.   t: Gn 41, 42f; 1 Kgs 1, 33; Dn 5, 29.

proposed, and do this for the Jew Mordecai, who is sitting at the royal gate. Do not omit anything you proposed."[u] [11]So Haman took the robe and horse, clothed Mordecai, had him ride in the public square of the city, and cried out before him, "This is what is done for the man whom the king wishes to reward."

[12]Mordecai then returned to the royal gate, while Haman hurried home, his head covered in grief.[v] [13]When he told his wife Zeresh and all his friends everything that had happened to him, his advisers and his wife Zeresh said to him, "If Mordecai, before whom you are beginning to decline, is of the Jewish race, you will not prevail against him, but will surely be defeated by him."

Esther's Second Banquet. [14]While they were speaking with him, the king's eunuchs arrived and hurried Haman off to the banquet Esther had prepared.

CHAPTER 7

See RG 157–59

[1]So the king and Haman went to the banquet with Queen Esther. [2]Again, on this second day, during the drinking of the wine, the king said to Esther, "Whatever you ask, Queen Esther, shall be granted you. Whatever request you make shall be honored, even for half the kingdom."[w] [3]Queen Esther replied: "If I have found favor with you, O king, and if it pleases your majesty, I ask that my life be spared, and I beg that you spare the lives of my people. [4]For my people and I have been delivered to destruction, slaughter, and extinction. If we were to be sold into slavery I would remain silent, but as it is, the enemy will be unable to compensate for the harm done to the king."[x] [5]"Who and where," said King Ahasuerus to Queen Esther, "is the man who has dared to do this?"[y] [6]Esther replied, "The enemy oppressing us is this wicked Haman." At this, Haman was seized with dread of the king and queen.

[7]The king left the banquet in anger and went into the garden of the palace, but Haman stayed to beg Queen Esther for his life, since he saw that the king had decided on his doom. [8]When the king returned from the garden of the palace to the banquet hall, Haman had thrown himself on the couch on which Esther was reclining; and the king exclaimed, "Will he also violate the queen while she is with me in my own house!" Scarcely had the king spoken, when the face of Haman was covered over.

Punishment of Haman. [9]Harbona, one of the eunuchs who attended the king, said, "At the house of Haman stands a gibbet fifty cubits high. Haman prepared it for Mordecai, who gave the report that benefited the king." The king answered, "Hang him on it." [10]So they hanged Haman on the gibbet which he had made ready for Mordecai, and the anger of the king abated.

CHAPTER 8

See RG 157–59

[1]That day King Ahasuerus gave the house of Haman, enemy of the Jews, to Queen Esther; and Mordecai was admitted to the king's presence, for Esther had revealed his relationship to her.[a] [2]The king removed his signet ring from Haman, and transferred it into the keeping of Mordecai; and Esther put Mordecai in charge of the house of Haman.[b]

The Second Royal Decree. [3]In another audience with the king, Esther fell at his feet and tearfully implored him to revoke the harm done by Haman the Agagite, and the plan he had devised against the Jews. [4]The king stretched forth the golden scepter to Esther. So she rose and, standing in his presence, [5]said: "If it pleases your majesty and seems proper to you, and if I have found favor with you and you love me, let a document be issued to revoke the letters which that schemer Haman, son of Hammedatha the Agagite, wrote for the destruction of the Jews in all the royal provinces.[c] [6]For how can I witness the evil that is to befall my people, and how can I behold the destruction of my race?"

[7]King Ahasuerus then said to Queen Esther and to the Jew Mordecai: "Now that I

---

u: Est 2, 21; 3, 2f; 5, 9. 13.   *v:* Est 2, 21; 3, 2f; 5, 9. 13.   *w:* Est 5, 3.   *x:* Est 3, 13; B, 6.   *y:* Est 3, 8f.   *z:* 9f: Est 5, 14; 6, 4.   *a:* Est 9, 1; Prv 11, 8; 26, 27; Mt 7, 2.   *b:* Prv 13, 22; Dn 2, 48f.   *c:* Est 1, 19.

A Persian king would hardly have allowed a slaughter of his people, as told in Esther 8, 9–12; this section is not history, but theology, emphasizing retributive justice.

have given Esther the house of Haman, and they have hanged him on the gibbet because he attacked the Jews, *8d*you in turn may write in the king's name what you see fit concerning the Jews and seal the letter with the royal signet ring." For whatever is written in the name of the king and sealed with the royal signet ring cannot be revoked.*

⁹At that time, on the twenty-third day of the third month, Sivan, the royal scribes were summoned. Exactly as Mordecai dictated, they wrote to the Jews and to the satraps, governors, and officials of the hundred and twenty-seven provinces from India to Ethiopia: to each province in its own script and to each people in its own language, and to the Jews in their own script and language. ¹⁰These letters, which he wrote in the name of King Ahasuerus and sealed with the royal signet ring, he sent by mounted couriers riding thoroughbred royal steeds. *11e*In these letters the king authorized the Jews in each and every city to group together and defend their lives, and to kill, destroy, wipe out, along with their wives and children, every armed group of any nation or province which should attack them, and to seize their goods as spoil *12*throughout the provinces of King Ahasuerus, on a single day, the thirteenth of the twelfth month, Adar.

CHAPTER E

See RG
157–59

¹The following is a copy of the letter:

"King Ahasuerus the Great to the governors of the provinces in the hundred and twenty-seven satrapies from India to Ethiopia, and to those responsible for our interests: Greetings!

²"Many have become the more ambitious the more they were showered with honors

through the bountiful generosity of their patrons. ³Not only do they seek to do harm to our subjects; incapable of bearing such greatness, they even begin plotting against their own benefactors. ⁴Not only do they drive out gratitude from among men; with the arrogant boastfulness of those to whom goodness has no meaning, they suppose they will escape the vindictive judgment of the all-seeing God.

⁵"Often, too, the fair speech of friends entrusted with the administration of affairs has induced many placed in authority to become accomplices in the shedding of innocent blood, and has involved them in irreparable calamities ⁶by deceiving with malicious slander the sincere good will of rulers. ⁷This can be verified in the ancient stories that have been handed down to us, but more fully when one considers the wicked deeds perpetrated in your midst by the pestilential influence of those undeserving of authority. *8f*We must provide for the future, so as to render the kingdom undisturbed and peaceful for all men, ⁹taking advantage of changing conditions and deciding always with equitable treatment matters coming to our attention.

¹⁰"For instance, Haman, son of Hammedatha, a Macedonian,* certainly not of Persian blood, and very different from us in generosity, was hospitably received by us. ¹¹He so far enjoyed the good will which we have toward all peoples that he was proclaimed 'father of the king,' before whom everyone was to bow down; he attained the rank second to the royal throne.*g* ¹²But, unequal to this dignity, he strove to deprive us of kingdom and of life; ¹³and by weaving intricate webs of deceit, he demanded the destruction of Mordecai, our savior and constant benefactor, and of Esther,

---

8, 8: Whatever is written . . . cannot be revoked: the king cannot directly grant Esther's request (v 5) to revoke the previous decree against the Jews because of the irrevocable character of the laws of the Medes and Persians (Est 1, 19; Dn 6, 9); but he empowers Esther to issue a new decree which renders the earlier decree without effect; cf Est 3, 12f.

E, 10: Macedonian: a redactor of the book in the Hel-

lenistic period used the designation Macedonian, here and in v 14 to express, after Macedonia's conquest of Persia, the most odious kind of man that a Persian ruler could be supposed to think of; the Hebrew text, for a similar reason, called Haman an Agagite. See note on Est A, 17.

d: Est 1, 19.   *e:* 11f: Est 9, 1-4.   *f:* 8f: Est B, 2.   *g:* Est B, 3. 6.

our blameless royal consort, together with their whole race.[h] [14]For by such measures he hoped to catch us defenseless and to transfer the rule of the Persians to the Macedonians. [15]But we find that the Jews, who were doomed to extinction by this arch-criminal, are not evildoers, but rather are governed by very just laws [16]and are the children of the Most High, the living God of majesty, who has maintained the kingdom in a flourishing condition for us and for our forebears.

[17]"You will do well, then, to ignore the letter sent by Haman, son of Hammedatha, [18]for he who composed it has been hanged, together with his entire household, before the gates of Susa. Thus swiftly has God, who governs all, brought just punishment upon him.[i]

[19]"You shall exhibit a copy of this letter publicly in every place, to certify that the Jews may follow their own laws, [20]and that you may help them on the day set for their ruin, the thirteenth day of the twelfth month, Adar, to defend themselves against those who attack them. [21]For God, the ruler of all, has turned that day for them from one of destruction of the chosen race into one of joy. [22]Therefore, you too must celebrate this memorable day among your designated feasts with all rejoicing, [23]so that both now and in the future it may be, for us and for loyal Persians, a celebration of victory, and for those who plot against us a reminder of destruction.

[24]"Every city and province, without exception, that does not observe this decree shall be ruthlessly destroyed with fire and sword, so that it will be left not merely untrodden by men, but even shunned by wild beasts and birds forever."[j]

(CHAPTER 8)

See RG
157-59

[13]A copy of the letter to be promulgated as law in each and every province was published among all the peoples, so that the Jews might be prepared on that day to avenge themselves on their enemies.* [14]Couriers mounted on royal steeds sped forth in haste

at the king's order, and the decree was promulgated in the stronghold of Susa.

[15]Mordecai left the king's presence clothed in a royal robe of violet and of white cotton, with a large crown of gold and a cloak of crimson byssus. The city of Susa shouted with joy,[k] [16]and there was splendor and merriment for the Jews, exultation and triumph. [17]In each and every province and in each and every city, wherever the king's order arrived, there was merriment and exultation, banqueting and feasting for the Jews. And many of the peoples of the land embraced Judaism, for they were seized with a fear of the Jews.[l]

CHAPTER 9

See RG
157-59

Victory of the Jews. [1m]When the day arrived on which the order decreed by the king was to be carried out, the thirteenth day of the twelfth month, Adar, on which the enemies of the Jews had expected to become masters of them, the situation was reversed: the Jews became masters of their enemies. [2]The Jews mustered in their cities throughout the provinces of King Ahasuerus to attack those who sought to do them harm, and no one could withstand them, but all peoples were seized with a fear of them. [3]Moreover, all the officials of the provinces, the satraps, governors, and royal procurators supported the Jews from fear of Mordecai; [4]for Mordecai was powerful in the royal palace, and the report was spreading through all the provinces that he was continually growing in power.

[5]The Jews struck down all their enemies with the sword, killing and destroying them; they did to their enemies as they pleased.[n] [6o]In the stronghold of Susa, the Jews killed and destroyed five hundred men. [7]They also killed Parshandatha, Dalphon, Aspatha, [8]Porathai, Adalia, Aridatha, [9]Parmashta, Arisai, Aridai, and Vaizatha, [10p]the ten sons of Haman, son of Hammedatha, the foe of the Jews. However, they did not engage in plundering.*

[11]On the same day, when the number of those killed in the stronghold of Susa was

---

8, 13: Avenge themselves on their enemies: partly in self-defense (Est E, 20), and partly to express the fact that the extreme cruelty designed against the Jews by their enemies now recoiled upon the latter as a punishment. Cf 9, 1f.

9, 10: They did not engage in plundering: in contrast to the

Israelites who fought Agag (1 Sm 15, 9); cf also vv 15f.

h: Est A, 17.   *i:* Est 7, 10; 9, 14.   *j:* Est 3, 8f; B, 4.   *k:* Dn 5, 7.   *l:* Est 9, 27.   *m:* 1f: Est 8, 11f.   *n:* Jdt 15, 6.   *o:* 6-10: Est 5, 11; B, 3; E, 11.   *p:* Est 9, 15; Jdt 15, 7. 11.

Purim Celebrations

In keeping with the book's strong emphasis on banqueting, both ancient and modern Purim observances include gifts of food (9, 19) to friends and charities. Because Purim is not found in the Torah, its acceptance would have needed explanation and support.

reported to the king, [12] he said to Queen Esther: "In the stronghold of Susa the Jews have killed and destroyed five hundred men, as well as the ten sons of Haman. What must they have done in the other royal provinces! You shall again be granted whatever you ask, and whatever you request shall be honored." [13] So Esther said, "If it pleases your majesty, let the Jews in Susa be permitted again tomorrow to act according to today's decree, and let the ten sons of Haman be hanged on gibbets." [14] The king then gave an order to this effect, and the decree was published in Susa. So the ten sons of Haman were hanged,[q] [15] and the Jews in Susa mustered again on the fourteenth of the month of Adar and killed three hundred men in Susa.* However, they did not engage in plundering.[r]

[16] The other Jews, who dwelt in the royal provinces, also mustered and defended themselves, and obtained rest from their enemies. They killed seventy-five thousand* of their foes, without engaging in plunder,[s] [17] on the thirteenth day of the month of Adar. On the fourteenth of the month they rested, and made it a day of feasting and rejoicing.

[18] (The Jews in Susa, however, mustered on the thirteenth and fourteenth of the month. But on the fifteenth they rested, and made it a day of feasting and rejoicing.) [19] That is why the rural Jews, who dwell in villages, celebrate the fourteenth of the month of Adar as a day of rejoicing and feasting, a holiday on which they send gifts of food to one another.

The Feast of Purim. [20] Mordecai recorded these events and sent letters to all the Jews, both near and far, in all the provinces of King Ahasuerus. [21] He ordered them to celebrate every year both the fourteenth and the fifteenth of the month of Adar [22] as the day on which the Jews obtained rest from their enemies and as the month which was turned for them from sorrow into joy, from mourning into festivity. They were to observe these days with feasting and gladness, sending food to one another and gifts to the poor. [23] The Jews took upon themselves for the future this observance which they instituted at the written direction of Mordecai.[t]

[24] "Haman, son of Hammedatha the Agagite, the foe of all the Jews, had planned to destroy them and had cast the pur, or lot, for the time of their defeat and destruction. [25] Yet, when Esther entered the royal presence, the king ordered in writing that the wicked plan Haman had devised against the Jews should instead be turned against Haman and that he and his sons should be hanged on gibbets.[v] [26] And so these days have been named Purim after the word pur.

Thus, because of all that was contained in this letter, and because of what they had witnessed and experienced in this affair, [27] the Jews established and took upon themselves, their descendants, and all who should join them, the inviolable obligation of celebrating these two days every year in the manner prescribed by this letter, and at the time appointed.[w] [28] These days were to be commemorated and kept in every generation, by every clan, in every province, and in every city. These days of Purim were never to fall into disuse among the Jews, nor into oblivion among their descendants.

9, 15: This second slaughter explains the two dates (13th and 14th) of the Purim celebration by Jews in Susa (v 18).
9, 16: Seventy-five thousand: according to the Greek text this number was fifteen thousand.

q: Est 7, 10; E, 18.   *r:* Est 9, 10.   *s:* Jdt 15, 6.   *t:* Est 9, 29.   *u:* 24ff: Est 3, 7; F, 10.   *v:* Est 6, 5-13.   *w:* Est 8, 12. 17.

[29]Queen Esther, daughter of Abihail and of Mordecai* the Jew, wrote to confirm with full authority this second letter about Purim, [30]when Mordecai sent documents concerning peace and security to all the Jews in the hundred and twenty-seven provinces of Ahasuerus' kingdom.[x] [31]Thus were established, for their appointed time, these days of Purim which Mordecai the Jew and Queen Esther had designated for the Jews, just as they had previously enjoined upon themselves and upon their race the duty of fasting and supplication.* [32]The command of Esther confirmed these prescriptions for Purim and was recorded in the book.

CHAPTER 10

See RG 157-59

[1]King Ahasuerus laid tribute on the land and on the islands of the sea. [2]All the acts of his power and valor, as well as a detailed account of the greatness of Mordecai, whom the king promoted, are recorded in the chronicles of the kings of Media and Persia. [3]The Jew Mordecai was next in rank to King Ahasuerus, in high standing among the Jews, and was regarded with favor by his many brethren, as the promoter of his people's welfare and the herald of peace for his whole race.[y]

V: Epilogue

CHAPTER F

See RG 157-59

Mordecai's Dream Fulfilled. [1z]Then Mordecai said: "This is the work of God. [2]I recall the dream I had about these very things, and not a single detail has been left unfilled— [3]the tiny spring that grew into a river, the light of the sun, the many waters. The river is Esther, whom the king married and made queen. [4]The two dragons are myself and Haman. [5]The nations are those who assembled to destroy the name of the Jews, [6]but my people is Israel, who cried to God and was saved.

"The LORD saved his people and delivered us from all these evils. God worked signs and great wonders, such as have not occurred among the nations. [7]For this purpose he arranged two lots:* one for the people of God, the second for all the other nations. [8]These two lots were fulfilled in the hour, the time, and the day of judgment before God and among all the nations. [9]God remembered his people and rendered justice to his inheritance.[a]

[10]"Gathering together with joy and happiness before God, they shall celebrate these days on the fourteenth and fifteenth of the month Adar throughout all future generations of his people Israel."*

9, 29: Queen Esther, daughter of Abihail and of Mordecai: the natural offspring of Abihail and adopted daughter of Mordecai; cf Est 2, 15. This second letter: for the burden of this letter see Est 9, 20ff. It was endorsed by Queen Esther. The first letter, written in the king's name, is referred to in Est 8, 9.

9, 31: Fasting and supplication: as the Jews had previously undertaken the duty of fasting and supplication to prevent the impending disaster, they now observe days of festival to commemorate their deliverance—in both cases (cf Est 4, 3. 15f) at the request of Mordecai and Esther.

F, 7: Two lots: in this passage of the Greek text, which gives a more religious interpretation of the feast, the two lots are drawn by God to determine, respectively, the destiny of Israel and that of the nations. In Est 3, 7 above, translated

from the Hebrew text, the feast is called Purim because of the lots which Aman cast to determine the day for the extinction of the Jews.

F, 10: The Greek text of Esther contains a postscript as follows: In the fourth year of the reign of Ptolemy and Cleopatra, Dositheus, who said he was a priest and Levite, and his son Ptolemy brought the present letter of Purim, saying that it was genuine and that Lysimachus, son of Ptolemy, of the community of Jerusalem, had translated it. The date referred to in this postscript is most probably 78-77 B.C., in the reign of Ptolemy XII and Cleopatra V.

x: Est 9, 23-26.   *y:* 2 Mc 15, 14.   *z:* 1-6: Est A, 4-10.   *a:* Est 3, 7; 9, 17f. 21. 24-28.

See RG 160-64

The First Book of Maccabees

The name Maccabee, probably meaning "hammer," is actually applied in the Books of Maccabees to only one man, Judas, third son of the priest Mattathias and first leader of the revolt against the Seleucid kings who persecuted the Jews (1 Mc 2, 4. 66; 2 Mc 8, 5. 16; 10, 1. 16). Traditionally the name has come to be applied to the brothers of Judas, his supporters, and even to other Jewish heroes of the period, such as the seven brothers (2 Mc 7).

The two Books of Maccabees, placed last in the Douai version of the Old Testament, contain independent accounts of events in part identical which accompanied the attempted suppression of Judaism in Palestine in the second century B.C. The vigorous reaction to this attempt established for a time the religious and political independence of the Jews.

1 Maccabees was written about 100 B.C., in Hebrew, but the original has not come down to us. Instead, we have an early, pre-Christian, Greek translation full of Hebrew idioms. The author, probably a Palestinian Jew, is unknown. He was familiar with the traditions and sacred books of his people and had access to much reliable information on their recent history (from 175 to 134 B.C.). He may well have played some part in it himself in his youth. His purpose in writing is to record the salvation of Israel which God worked through the family of Mattathias (5, 62)—especially through his three sons, Judas, Jonathan, and Simon, and his grandson, John Hyrcanus. Implicitly the writer compares their virtues and their exploits with those of the ancient heroes, the Judges, Samuel, and David.

There are seven poetic sections in the book which imitate the style of classical Hebrew poetry: four laments (1, 25-28. 36-40; 2, 8-13; 3, 45), and three hymns of praise of "our fathers" (2, 51-64), of Judas (3, 3-9), and of Simon (14, 4-15).

The doctrine expressed in the book is the customary belief of Israel, without the new developments which appear in 2 Maccabees and Daniel. The people of Israel have been specially chosen by the one true God as his covenant-partner, and they alone are privileged to know him and worship him. He is their eternal benefactor and their unfailing source of help. The people, in turn, must be loyal to his exclusive worship and must observe exactly the precepts of the law he has given them.

There is no doctrine of individual immortality except in the survival of one's name and fame, nor does the book express any messianic expectation, though messianic images are applied historically to "the days of Simon" (14, 4–17). In true deuteronomic tradition, the author insists on fidelity to the law as the expression of Israel's love for God. The contest which he describes is a struggle, not simply between Jew and Gentile, but between those

who would uphold the law and those, Jews or Gentiles, who would destroy it. His severest condemnation goes, not to the Seleucid politicians, but to the lawless apostates among his own people, adversaries of Judas and his brothers, who are models of faith and loyalty.

1 Maccabees has importance also for the New Testament. Salvation is paralleled with Jewish national aspirations (1 Mc 4, 46—14, 41), in contrast to the universal reign of God taught by Christ in the Gospel (Mt 13, 47-50; 22, 1-14). Also, destruction of the wall of the temple separating Jew from Gentile is an act of desecration in 1 Mc 9, 54 but in Eph 2, 14, an act of redemption and unification of both through Christ. On the other hand, association, in 1 Mc 2, 52, of Abraham's offering up of Isaac (Gn 22) with his justification by God (Gn 15, 6) is reflected in Jn 2, 21f, just as the Scriptures are regarded as a source of consolation in 1 Mc 12, 9 and in Rom 15, 4.

The Books of Maccabees, though regarded by Jews and Protestants as apocryphal, i.e., not inspired Scripture, because not contained in the Palestinian Canon or list of books drawn up at the end of the first century A.D., have nevertheless always been accepted by the Catholic Church as inspired, on the basis of apostolic tradition.

1 Maccabees is divided as follows:

I: Introduction: Hellenism in Asia Minor (1, 1-9).

II: The Maccabean Revolt (1, 10—2, 70).

III: Leadership of Judas Maccabeus (3, 1— 9, 22).

IV: Leadership of Jonathan (9, 23—12, 54).

V: Simon, High Priest and Ethnarch (13, 1— 16, 24).

I: Introduction: Hellenism in Asia Minor

CHAPTER 1

See RG 162–63

Conquests and Death of Alexander. [1a]After Alexander the Macedonian, Philip's son, who came from the land of Kittim,[*] had defeated Darius, king of the Persians and

---

1, 1: Land of Kittim: Greece. The name referred originally to inhabitants of Kiti, capital of the isle of Cyprus, then to any Cypriots (Is 23, 1; Jer 2, 10), later to Greeks in general, and finally even to Romans. See note on Dn

11, 30. Darius: Darius III, Codoman (336–331 B.C.).

---

a: 1-10: Dn 8, 20ff; 11, 3f. 21.

Alexander the Great

Verses 1 to 10 summarize the history from Alexander to Antiochus IV. Alexander planned a universal empire dominated by Greek culture.

Medes, he became king in his place, having first ruled in Greece. ²He fought many campaigns, captured fortresses, and put kings to death. ³He advanced to the ends of the earth, gathering plunder from many nations; the earth fell silent before him, and his heart became proud and arrogant. ⁴He collected a very strong army and conquered provinces, nations, and rulers, and they became his tributaries. ⁵But after all this he took to his bed, realizing that he was going to die. ⁶He therefore summoned his officers, the nobles, who had been brought up with him from his youth, to divide his kingdom among them while he was still alive. ⁷Alexander had reigned twelve years* when he died.

⁸So his officers took over his kingdom, each in his own territory, ⁹and after his death they all put on royal crowns, and so did their sons after them for many years, causing much distress over the earth.

II: The Maccabean Revolt

Pact between Jews and Gentiles. ¹⁰There sprang from these a sinful offshoot, Antiochus Epiphanes, son of King Antiochus, once a hostage at Rome. He became king in the year one hundred and thirty-seven* of the kingdom of the Greeks.ᵇ

¹¹In those days there appeared in Israel men who were breakers of the law, and they seduced many people, saying: "Let us go and make an alliance with the Gentiles all around us; since we separated from them, many evils have come upon us."ᶜ ¹²The proposal was agreeable; ¹³ᵈsome from among the people promptly went to the king, and he authorized them to introduce the way of living of the Gentiles. ¹⁴Thereupon they built a gymnasium* in Jerusalem according to the Gentile custom. ¹⁵They covered over the mark of their circumcision and abandoned the holy covenant; they allied themselves with the Gentiles and sold themselves to wrongdoing.ᵉ

Egyptian Campaign of Antiochus. ¹⁶When his kingdom seemed secure, Antiochus proposed to become king of Egypt, so as to rule over both kingdoms. ¹⁷He invaded Egypt with a strong force, with chariots and elephants,* and with a large fleet,ᶠ ¹⁸to make war on Ptolemy, king of Egypt. Ptolemy was frightened at his presence and fled, leaving many casualties. ¹⁹The fortified cities in the land of Egypt were captured, and Antiochus plundered the land of Egypt.

Persecution of the Jews. ²⁰ᵍAfter Antiochus had defeated Egypt in the year one hundred and forty-three,* he returned and went up to Israel and to Jerusalem with a strong force. ²¹He insolently invaded the sanctuary and took away the golden altar, the lampstand for the light with all its fixtures, ²²the offering table, the cups and the bowls, the golden censers, the curtain, the crowns, and the golden ornament on the façade of the temple.

1, 7: Twelve years: 336–323 B.C.

1, 10: The year one hundred and thirty-seven: Antiochus IV seized the throne in September, 175 B.C. Dates are given in this book according to the Seleucid era, which however was reckoned in two different ways. Antiochians considered this date to be October, 312 B.C. (Syrian calendar), while Babylonians and Jewish priests accepted April, 311 B.C. as the commencement of the era (temple calendar). The author of 1 Mc dates political events by the Syrian calendar but religious events by the temple calendar. Accordingly, the civil New Year occurred variously in September or October, the religious New Year in March or April.

1, 14: Gymnasium: symbol and center of athletic and intellectual life, it was the chief instrument of Hellenistic propaganda. Jewish youth were attracted by sports and encouraged to join youth clubs. They received training in military skills and in the duties of citizens. Through participation in the intellectual life, many were gradually won over to paganism.

1, 17: Elephants: an important part of Seleucid armament. About 300 B.C. Seleucus I, founder of the dynasty, procured five hundred of them from India; cf 1 Mc 6, 34-37.

1, 20: Defeated Egypt in the year one hundred and forty-three: 169 B.C. No mention is made in 1 Mc of the second expedition to Egypt a year later, described in 2 Mc 5, 1. 11. Dn 11, 25. 29 records both.

b: 2 Mc 4, 7. *c:* 2 Mc 4, 9-17. *d:* 13ff: 2 Mc 4, 7-17. *e:* 1 Cor 7, 18. *f:* 2 Mc 5, 1; Dn 11, 25-28. *g:* 20-24: 2 Mc 5, 11-21.

Antiochus Epiphanes

After his successful invasion of Egypt, Epiphanes plundered the temple of Jerusalem (a sacrilegious act), simply to replenish his funds (1, 20–24). (This is also reported by Josephus, *Against Apion* 2, 83–84.)

He stripped off everything, ²³and took away the gold and silver and the precious vessels; he also took all the hidden treasures he could find. ²⁴Taking all this, he went back to his own country, after he had spoken with great arrogance and shed much blood.

²⁵ And there was great mourning for Israel,
 in every place where they dwelt,
²⁶ and the rulers and the elders
  groaned.
Virgins and young men languished,
 and the beauty of the women was
  disfigured.
²⁷ Every bridegroom took up lamentation,
 she who sat in the bridal chamber
  mourned,
²⁸ And the land was shaken on account of
  its inhabitants,
 and all the house of Jacob was covered
  with shame.

^{29h}Two years later, the king sent the Mysian commander to the cities of Judah, and he came to Jerusalem with a strong force. ³⁰He spoke to them deceitfully in peaceful terms, and won their trust. Then he attacked the city suddenly, in a great onslaught, and destroyed many of the people in Israel. ³¹He plundered the city and set fire to it, demolished its houses and its surrounding walls, ³²took captive the women and children, and seized the cattle. ³³Then they built up the City of David* with a high, massive wall and strong towers, and it became their citadel.ⁱ ³⁴There they installed a sinful race, perverse men, who fortified themselves inside it, ³⁵storing up weapons and provisions, and depositing there the plunder they had collected from Jerusalem. And they became a great threat.

³⁶ The citadel became an ambush against
 the sanctuary,
 and a wicked adversary to Israel at all
  times.
³⁷ And they shed innocent blood around the
  sanctuary;
 they defiled the sanctuary.
³⁸ Because of them the inhabitants of
  Jerusalem fled away,
 and she became the abode of strangers.
She became a stranger to her own
  offspring,
 and her children forsook her.
³⁹ Her sanctuary was as desolate as a
  wilderness;^j
 her feasts were turned into mourning,
Her sabbaths to shame,
 her honor to contempt.
⁴⁰ Her dishonor was as great as her glory
  had been,
 and her exaltation was turned into
  mourning.

Prohibitions against Religion. ⁴¹Then the king wrote to his whole kingdom that all should be one people, ⁴²each abandoning his particular customs. All the Gentiles conformed to the command of the king, ⁴³and many Israelites were in favor of his religion; they sacrificed to idols and profaned the sabbath.

^{44k}The king sent messengers with letters to Jerusalem and to the cities of Judah, ordering them to follow customs foreign to their land: ⁴⁵to prohibit holocausts, sacrifices, and libations in the sanctuary, to profane the sabbaths and feast days, ^{46 l}to desecrate

---

1, 33: City of David: not Mount Zion on the eastern hill of Jerusalem, which David captured from the Jebusites (2 Sm 5, 7), but a new fortress built on the western hill and overlooking the temple and its courts on Mount Zion. It was occupied for twenty-six years by the Syro-Macedonian garrison, together with apostate Jews, and was a continual threat to the temple and the Jewish people (v 36); cf 1 Mc 13, 49ff.

h: 29-32: 2 Mc 5, 24ff. *i:* 1 Mc 6, 18. *j:* 39f: Tb 2, 6; Am 8, 10. *k:* 44-63: 2 Mc 6, 1-11. *l:* 2 Mc 6, 2; Dn 9, 27.

Mattathias

Mattathias is not mentioned in 2 Maccabees. His prominence in 1 Maccabees 2 has the effect of exalting the whole family, not just Judas.

the sanctuary and the sacred ministers, to build pagan altars and temples and shrines, [47]to sacrifice swine and unclean animals, [48]to leave their sons uncircumcised, and to let themselves be defiled with every kind of impurity and abomination, [49]so that they might forget the law and change all their observances. [50]Whoever refused to act according to the command of the king should be put to death.[m]

[51]Such were the orders he published throughout his kingdom. He appointed inspectors over all the people, and he ordered the cities of Judah to offer sacrifices, each city in turn. [52]Many of the people, those who abandoned the law, joined them and committed evil in the land. [53]Israel was driven into hiding, wherever places of refuge could be found.

[54]On the fifteenth day of the month Chislev, in the year one hundred and forty-five,* the king erected the horrible abomination upon the altar of holocausts, and in the surrounding cities of Judah they built pagan altars.[n] [55]They also burnt incense at the doors of houses and in the streets. [56]Any scrolls of the law* which they found they tore up and burnt. [57]Whoever was found with a scroll of the covenant, and whoever observed the law, was condemned to death by royal decree.[o] [58]So they used their power against Israel, against those who were caught, each month, in the cities. [59]On the twenty-fifth day of each month they sacrificed on the altar erected over the altar of holocausts. [60p]Women who had had their children cir-

cumcised were put to death, in keeping with the decree, [61]with the babies hung from their necks; their families also and those who had circumcised them were killed. [62]But many in Israel were determined and resolved in their hearts not to eat anything unclean; [63]they preferred to die rather than to be defiled with unclean food or to profane the holy covenant; and they did die. Terrible affliction was upon Israel.[q]

CHAPTER 2

Mattathias and His Sons. [1]In those days Mattathias, son of John, son of Simeon, a priest of the family of Joarib, left Jerusalem and settled in Modein.* [2]He had five sons: John, who was called Gaddi;[r] [3]Simon, who was called Thassi; [4]Judas, who was called Maccabeus; [5]Eleazar, who was called Avaran; and Jonathan, who was called Apphus. [6]When he saw the sacrileges that were being committed in Judah and in Jerusalem, [7]he said: "Woe is me! Why was I born to see the ruin of my people and the ruin of the holy city, and to sit idle while it is given into the hands of enemies, and the sanctuary into the hands of strangers?

See RG 162-63

[8] "Her temple has become like a man
    disgraced,
[9] her glorious ornaments have been
    carried off as spoils,
Her infants have been murdered in her
    streets,
  her young men by the sword of the
    enemy.[s]

1, 54: Fifteenth day of the month Chislev, in the year one hundred and forty-five: early December, 167 B.C. Horrible abomination: in the original Hebrew, a contemptuous pun on the title "Lord of heaven" given to the god Zeus Olympios, to whom an image or perhaps an altar was erected upon the altar of holocausts in the temple of Jerusalem; cf Dn 9, 27; 11, 31.

1, 56f: Scrolls of the law: one or more of the first five books of the Old Testament.

2, 1: Modein: a village twenty miles northwest of Jerusalem.

m: 2 Mc 6, 18—7, 41. n: 1 Mc 6, 7; Dn 9, 27; 11, 31. o: 2 Mc 2, 14. p: 60f: 2 Mc 6, 10. q: 2 Mc 6, 10. r: 1 Chr 24, 7. s: Lam 2, 11. 21.

Zeal for the Law

When the Syrians had first conquered Jerusalem, the Jews had been given the right to follow their ancestral laws (2, 21). This right was very widely recognized in the Hellenistic and Roman worlds. In Numbers 25, Phinehas shows his zeal for the law by driving his spear through an Israelite man and Midianite woman in the act of intercourse. For this God gave him a covenant of perpetual priesthood. He became the prototypical zealot whose example legitimized religious violence. The fate of the zealots in the wilderness (2, 31–38) highlights the dilemma of the observant Jew. Strict observance of the law forbids fighting on the sabbath. The Maccabees resolved this dilemma by making an exception in the case of this commandment.

10 What nation has not taken its share of her realm,
and laid its hand on her possessions?
11 All her adornment has been
taken away.
From being free, she has become
a slave.
12 We see our sanctuary and our beauty
and our glory laid waste,
And the Gentiles have defiled them!
13 Why are we still alive?"

*14*Then Mattathias and his sons tore their garments, put on sackcloth, and mourned bitterly. ***Pagan Worship Refused.*** *15*The officers of the king in charge of enforcing the apostasy came to the city of Modein to organize the sacrifices. *16*Many of Israel joined them, but Mattathias and his sons gathered in a group apart. *17*Then the officers of the king addressed Mattathias: "You are a leader, an honorable and great man in this city, supported by sons and kinsmen. *18*Come now, be the first to obey the king's command, as all the Gentiles and the men of Judah and those who are left in Jerusalem have done. Then you and your sons shall be numbered among the King's Friends,* and shall be enriched with silver and gold and many gifts." *19*But Mattathias answered in a loud voice: "Although all the Gentiles in the king's realm obey him, so that each forsakes the religion of his fathers and consents to the king's orders, *20*yet I and my sons and my kinsmen will keep to the covenant of our fathers. *21*God forbid that we should forsake the law and the commandments. *22*We will not obey the words of the king nor depart from our religion in the slightest degree."

*23*As he finished saying these words, a certain Jew came forward in the sight of all to offer sacrifice on the altar in Modein according to the king's order. *24*When Mattathias saw him, he was filled with zeal; his heart was moved and his just fury was aroused; he sprang forward and killed him upon the altar. *25*At the same time, he also killed the messenger of the king who was forcing them to sacrifice, and he tore down the altar. *26*Thus he showed his zeal for the law, just as Phinehas did with Zimri, son of Salu.*t*

*27*Then Mattathias went through the city shouting, "Let everyone who is zealous for the law and who stands by the covenant follow after me!" *28*Thereupon he fled to the mountains with his sons, leaving behind in the city all their possessions.*u* *29*Many who sought to live according to righteousness and religious custom went out into the desert* to settle there, *30*they and their sons, their wives and their cattle, because misfortunes pressed so hard on them.

*31*It was reported to the officers and soldiers of the king who were in the City of David, in Jerusalem, that certain men who had flouted the king's order had gone out to the hiding places in the desert. *32v*Many hurried out after them, and having caught up with them, camped opposite and

---

2, 18: The King's Friends: a regular order of nobility at Hellenistic courts. The various grades are frequently mentioned in this book: Friends, Chief Friends, Kinsmen.

2, 29: The desert: the sparsely inhabited mountain country southward from Jerusalem and west of the Dead Sea. It was an arid region with some perennial springs and a fair amount of rain in winter.

t: 1 Mc 2, 54; Nm 25, 6-14. *u:* 2 Mc 5, 27. *v:* 32-38: 2 Mc 6, 11.

prepared to attack them on the sabbath. [33]"Enough of this!" the pursuers said to them. "Come out and obey the king's command, and your lives will be spared." [34]But they replied, "We will not come out, nor will we obey the king's command to profane the sabbath." [35]Then the enemy attacked them at once; [36]but they did not retaliate; they neither threw stones, nor blocked up their own hiding places. [37]They said, "Let us all die without reproach; heaven and earth are our witnesses that you destroy us unjustly." [38]So the officers and soldiers attacked them on the sabbath, and they died with their wives, their children and their cattle, to the number of a thousand persons.

[39]When Mattathias and his friends heard of it, they mourned deeply for them. [40]"If we all do as our kinsmen have done," they said to one another, "and do not fight against the Gentiles for our lives and our traditions, they will soon destroy us from the earth." [41]On that day they came to this decision: "Let us fight against anyone who attacks us on the sabbath, so that we may not all die as our kinsmen died in the hiding places."

[42]Then they were joined by a group of Hasideans,* valiant Israelites, all of them devout followers of the law. [43]And all those who were fleeing from the disaster joined them and supported them. [44]They gathered an army and struck down sinners in their anger and lawbreakers in their wrath, and the survivors fled to the Gentiles for safety.[w] [45]Mattathias and his friends went about and tore down the pagan altars; [46]they also forcibly circumcised any uncircumcised boys whom they found in the territory of Israel. [47]They put to flight the arrogant, and the work prospered in their hands. [48]They saved the law from the hands of the Gentiles and of the kings and did not let the sinner triumph.

Death of Mattathias. [49]When the time came for Mattathias to die, he said to his sons: "Arrogance and scorn have now grown strong; it is a time of disaster and violent anger. [50]Therefore, my sons, be zealous for the law and give your lives for the covenant of our fathers.

[51] "Remember the deeds that our fathers did
    in their times,
    and you shall win great glory and an
        everlasting name.
[52] Was not Abraham found faithful in trial,
    and it was reputed to him as
        uprightness?[x]
[53] Joseph, when in distress, kept the
        commandment,
    and he became master of Egypt.[y]
[54] Phinehas our father, for his burning zeal,
    received the covenant of an everlasting
        priesthood.[z]
[55] Joshua, for executing his commission,
    became a judge in Israel.[a]
[56] Caleb, for bearing witness before the
        assembly,
    received an inheritance in the land.[b]
[57] David, for his piety,
    received as a heritage a throne of
        everlasting royalty.[c]
[58] Elijah, for his burning zeal for the law,
    was taken up to heaven.[d]
[59] Hananiah, Azariah and Mishael, for their
        faith,
    were saved from the fire.[e]
[60] Daniel, for his innocence,
    was delivered from the jaws of lions.[f]
[61] And so, consider this from generation to
        generation,
    that none who hope in him shall fail in
        strength.
[62] Do not fear the words of a sinful man,
    for his glory ends in corruption and
        worms.
[63] Today he is exalted, and tomorrow he is
        not to be found,
    because he has returned to his dust,
    and his schemes have perished.

2, 42: Hasideans: in Hebrew hasidim, "pious ones," a religious group devoted to the strict observance of the law. They were the forerunners of both the Pharisees and the Essenes. They first supported the Maccabean movement, but subsequently opposed it, regarding it as too political.

w: Is 63, 3.   x: Gn 15, 6; 22, 1ff.   y: Gn 39, 7-10; 41, 39-43.   z: Nm 25, 10-13; Sir 45, 28ff.   a: Jos 1, 2. 5.   b: Nm 13, 30; 14, 6-9. 24; Jos 14, 14.   c: 2 Sm 2, 4; 7, 16.   d: 1 Kgs 19, 10. 14; 2 Kgs 2, 11.   e: Dn 3, 50.   f: Dn 6, 23; 14, 31-42.

The Early Victories of Judas

The idea that God can give victory to the few over the many (3, 18–19) is a popular biblical motif. Compare the story of Gideon in Judges 7 or Jonathan's statement in 1 Samuel 14, 6: " . . . it is no more difficult for the LORD to grant victory through a few than through many." Judas is careful to observe ritual as well as military preparation for battle. The victory is not attributed to superior tactics, but to the miraculous power of God.

64 Children! be courageous and strong in
keeping the law,
for by it you shall be glorified.

65"Here is your brother Simeon who I know is a wise man; listen to him always, and he will be a father to you. *66*And Judas Maccabeus, a warrior from his youth, shall be the leader of your army and direct the war against the nations. *67*You shall also gather about you all who observe the law, and you shall avenge the wrongs of your people. *68*Pay back the Gentiles what they deserve, and observe the precepts of the law."

*69*Then he blessed them, and he was united with his fathers. *70*He died in the year one hundred and forty-six,* and was buried in the tombs of his fathers in Modein, and all Israel mourned him greatly.

III: Leadership of Judas Maccabeus

CHAPTER 3

See RG
163
Defeat of Apollonius and Seron. *1*Then his son Judas, who was called Maccabeus, took his place. *2*All his brothers and all who had joined his father supported him, and they carried on Israel's war joyfully.

3 He spread abroad the glory of his people,
and put on his breastplate like a giant.
He armed himself with weapons of war;
he planned battles and protected the
camp with his sword.*g*
4 In his actions he was like a lion,
like a young lion roaring for prey.

5 He pursued the wicked, hunting them out,
and those who troubled his people he
destroyed by fire.
6 The lawbreakers were cowed by fear of
him,
and all evildoers were dismayed.
By his hand redemption was happily
achieved,
7 and he afflicted many kings;
He made Jacob glad by his deeds,
and his memory is blessed forever.
8 He went about the cities of Judah
destroying the impious there.
He turned away wrath from Israel
9 and was renowned to the ends of the
earth;
he gathered together those who were
perishing.

*10*Then Apollonius* gathered the Gentiles, together with a large army from Samaria, to fight against Israel. *11*When Judas learned of it, he went out to meet him and defeated and killed him. Many fell wounded, and the rest fled. *12*Their possessions were seized and the sword of Apollonius was taken by Judas, who fought with it the rest of his life.

*13*But Seron, commander of the Syrian army, heard that Judas had gathered many about him, an assembly of faithful men ready for war. *14*So he said, "I will make a name for myself and win glory in the kingdom by defeating Judas and his followers, who have despised the king's command." *15*And again a large company of renegades advanced with him to help him take revenge on the Israelites. *16*When he reached the ascent of Beth-horon,*

2, 70: In the year one hundred and forty-six: 166 B.C.

3, 10: Apollonius: the Mysian commander mentioned in 1 Mc 1, 29 and in 2 Mc 5, 24.

3, 16: Beth-horon: the famous pass leading up from the coastal plain to the Judean hill country. Here Joshua won an important battle (Jos 10, 10f), and in 66 A.D. a Roman force under Cestius was trapped and massacred.

---

g: 2 Mc 8, 5.

Sidon

Damascus

Tyre

PHOENICIA

Ladder
of Tyre

Kadesh

Hazor

33°

Maked

*Mediterranean
Sea*

GALILEE

Ptolemais

Baskama

Arbela

*Lake
Gennesaret*

Chaspo

Carnaim

Bosor

The Great Plain

Dor

Ephron

GILEAD

River Jordan

Beth-shan
(Scythopolis)

SAMARIA

Samaria

Joppa

Adida
(Hadid)

Jamnia

Azotus
(Ashdod)

LAND OF PHILISTINES

Askalon
(Ashkelon)

Gaza

Jazer

32°

AMMON

Jericho

Jerusalem

JUDAH (JUDEA)

Medeba

NABATEANS

Dead
Sea

(Detail on facing page)

| 0 | 10 | 20 Miles |
| 0 | 10 | 20 Kilometers |

IDUMEA

35°

36°

The Campaigns of the Maccabees and Hasmoneans

Judas went out to meet him with a few men. ¹⁷But when they saw the army coming against them, they said to Judas: "How can we, few as we are, fight such a mighty host as this? Besides, we are weak today from fasting." ¹⁸But Judas said: "It is easy for many to be overcome by a few; in the sight of Heaven there is no difference between deliverance by many or by few; ¹⁹for victory in war does not depend upon the size of the army, but on strength that comes from Heaven.[h] ²⁰With great presumption and lawlessness they come

h: 1 Sm 14, 16.

The Jerusalem Vicinity

Map labels: Rathamin, Lydda, Modein, Bethel, Beth-horon, Mizpah, Gazara (Gezer), Capharsalama, Michmash, Emmaus, Berea, Adasa, Ekron, Jerusalem, Bethbasi, Beth-zechariah, Beth-zaith, Tekoa, Marisa, Beth-zur, Adora (Adoraim), Hebron

32°, 35°, 0 — 10 Miles, 0 — 10 Kilometers

against us to destroy us and our wives and children and to despoil us; [21]but we are fighting for our lives and our laws. [22]He himself* will crush them before us; so do not be afraid of them." [23]When he finished speaking, he rushed suddenly upon Seron and his army, who were crushed before him. [24]He pursued Seron down the descent of Beth-horon into the plain. About eight hundred* of their men fell, and the rest fled to the country of the Philistines.[i] [25]Then Judas and his brothers began to be feared, and dread fell upon the Gentiles about them. [26]His fame reached the king, and all the Gentiles talked about the battles of Judas.

Regency of Lysias. [27]When Antiochus heard about these events, he was angry; so he ordered a muster of all the forces of his kingdom, a very strong army. [28]He opened his treasure chests, gave his soldiers a year's pay, and commanded them to be prepared for anything. [29]He then found that this exhausted the money in his treasury; moreover the income from the province was small, because of the dissension and distress he had brought upon the land by abolishing the laws which had been in effect from of old. [30]He feared that, as had happened more than once, he would not have enough for his expenses and for the gifts that he had previously given with a more liberal hand than the preceding kings. [31]Greatly perplexed, he decided to go to Persia and levy tribute on those provinces, and so raise a large sum of money. [32]He left Lysias, a nobleman of royal blood, in charge of the king's affairs from the Euphrates River to the frontier of Egypt, [33]and commissioned him to take care of his son Antiochus until his own return. [34]He entrusted to him half of the army, and the elephants, and gave him instructions concerning everything he wanted done. As for the inhabitants of Judea and Jerusalem, [35]Lysias was to send an army against them to crush and destroy the power of Israel and the remnant of Jerusalem and efface their memory from the land. [36]He was to settle foreigners in all their territory and distribute their land by lot.

[37]The king took the remaining half of the army and set out from Antioch, his capital, in the year one hundred and forty-seven; he crossed the Euphrates River and advanced inland.*

The Victories of Judas. [38][j]Lysias chose Ptolemy, son of Dorymenes, and Nicanor* and Gorgias, capable men among the King's Friends,[k] [39]and with them he sent forty thousand men and seven thousand cavalry to invade the land of Judah and

---

3, 22: He himself: out of reverence for God, the author of 1 Mc prefers to use this and other expressions, such as "Heaven," instead of the divine name. Cf 1 Mc 3, 50.

3, 24: About eight hundred: the figures given in this book for strength of armies and number of casualties are not to be taken literally. In accordance with biblical usage, they indicate rather the importance of the battle described or the greatness of the victory.

3, 37: This expedition, in the spring of 165 B.C., resulted in failure; cf ch 6.

3, 38: Nicanor: the leader of another attack against the Jews four years later. He was finally killed by Judas; cf 1 Mc 7, 26-46.

i: Jos 10, 10. *j:* 38-44: 2 Mc 8, 8-15. *k:* 38f: 1 Mc 7, 26; 2 Mc 4, 45; 8, 8f; 10, 14.

> It was common practice in the ancient world to sell people captured in battle into slavery (3, 41). See Joel 4, 6 where Tyre and Sidon are accused of selling Judeans to the Greeks. See also 2 Maccabees 8, 10.

ravage it according to the king's orders. [40]Setting out with all their forces, they came and pitched their camp near Emmaus* in the plain. [41]When the merchants of the country heard of their fame, they came to the camp, bringing fetters and a large sum of silver and gold, to buy the Israelites as slaves. A force from Idumea and from Philistia joined with them.

[42]Judas and his brothers saw that the situation had become critical now that armies were encamped within their territory; they knew of the orders which the king had given to destroy and utterly wipe out the people. [43]So they said to one another, "Let us restore our people from their ruined estate, and fight for our people and our sanctuary!"

[44]The assembly gathered together to prepare for battle and to pray and implore mercy and compassion.

[45] Jerusalem was uninhabited, like a desert;
    not one of her children entered or
        came out.
The sanctuary was trampled on,
    and foreigners were in the citadel;
    it was a habitation of Gentiles.
Joy had disappeared from Jacob,
    and the flute and the harp were silent.

[46]Thus they assembled and went to Mizpah near Jerusalem, because there was formerly at Mizpah a place of prayer for Israel.* [47]That day they fasted and wore sackcloth; they sprinkled ashes on their heads and tore their clothes. [48]They unrolled the scroll of the law, to learn about the things for which the Gentiles consulted the images of their idols.* [49]They brought with them the priestly vestments, the first fruits, and the tithes; and they brought forward the nazirites* who had completed the time of their vows.[m] [50]And they cried aloud to Heaven: "What shall we do with these men, and where shall we take them? [51]For your sanctuary has been trampled on and profaned, and your priests are in mourning and humiliation. [52]Now the Gentiles are gathered together against us to destroy us. You know what they plot against us. [53]How shall we be able to resist them unless you help us?" [54]Then they blew the trumpets and cried out loudly.

[55]After this Judas appointed officers among the people, over thousands, over hundreds, over fifties, and over tens. [56]He proclaimed that those who were building houses, or were just married, or were planting vineyards, and those who were afraid, could each return to his home, according to the law.[n] [57]Then the army moved off, and they camped to the south of Emmaus. [58]Judas said: "Arm yourselves and be brave; in the morning be ready to fight these Gentiles who have assembled against us to destroy us and our sanctuary. [59]It is better for us to die in battle than to witness the ruin of our nation and our sanctuary. Whatever Heaven wills, he will do."[o]

CHAPTER 4

See RG 163

[1]Now Gorgias took five thousand infantry and a thousand picked cavalry, and this detachment set out at night [2]in order to attack the camp of the Jews and take them by surprise. Some men from the citadel were

---

3, 40: Emmaus: probably not the village mentioned in Lk 24, 13, but a settlement about twenty miles west of Jerusalem at the edge of the hill country.

3, 46: . . . Mizpah a place of prayer for Israel: a holy place established of old eight miles north and slightly west of Jerusalem. It was here that Samuel began to judge the Israelites (1 Sm 7, 5-11; 10, 17).

3, 48: To learn . . . idols: favorable omens for the coming battle. A contrast is intended between the idol worship of the pagans and the consultation of the word of God by the Jews; cf 2 Mc 8, 23.

3, 49: Nazirites: see note on Nm 6, 1ff.

---

l: 46ff: 1 Sm 7, 5f; 2 Mc 8, 16-23.   *m:* Nm 6, 2-5.   *n:* Dt 20, 5-8; Jgs 7, 3.   *o:* 1 Mc 2, 21f.

their guides. ³Judas heard of it, and himself set out with his soldiers to attack the king's army at Emmaus, ⁴while the latter's forces were still scattered away from the camp. ⁵During the night Gorgias came into the camp of Judas, and found no one there; so he began to hunt for them in the mountains, saying, "They are fleeing from us."

⁶But at daybreak Judas appeared in the plain with three thousand men, who lacked such armor and swords as they would have wished. ⁷They saw the army of the Gentiles, strong and breastplated, flanked with cavalry, and made up of expert soldiers. ⁸Judas said to the men with him: "Do not be afraid of their numbers or dread their attack. ⁹Remember how our fathers were saved in the Red Sea, when Pharaoh pursued them with an army.ᵖ ¹⁰So now let us cry to Heaven in the hope that he will favor us, remember his covenant with our fathers, and destroy this army before us today.�q ¹¹All the Gentiles shall know that there is One who redeems and delivers Israel."

¹²When the foreigners looked up and saw them marching toward them, ¹³they came out of their camp for battle, and the men with Judas blew the trumpet. ¹⁴The battle was joined and the Gentiles were defeated and fled toward the plain. ¹⁵Their whole rearguard fell by the sword, and they were pursued as far as Gazara* and the plains of Judea, to Azotus and Jamnia. About three thousand of their men fell.

¹⁶When Judas and the army returned from the pursuit, ¹⁷he said to the people: "Do not be greedy for the plunder, for there is a fight ahead of us, ¹⁸and Gorgias and his army are near us on the mountain. But now stand firm against our enemies and overthrow them. Afterward you can freely take the plunder."

¹⁹As Judas was finishing this speech, a detachment appeared, looking down from the mountain. ²⁰They saw that their army had been put to flight and their camp was being burned. The smoke that could be seen indicated what had happened. ²¹When they realized this, they were terrified; and when they also saw the army of Judas in the plain ready to attack, ²²they all fled to Philistine territory.*

²³Then Judas went back to plunder the camp, and his men collected much gold and silver, violet and crimson cloth, and great treasure. ²⁴As they returned, they were singing hymns and glorifying Heaven, "for he is good, for his mercy endures forever."ʳ ²⁵Thus Israel had a great deliverance that day.

Victory over Lysias. ²⁶ˢBut those of the foreigners who had escaped went and told Lysias all that had occurred. ²⁷When he heard it he was disturbed and discouraged, because things in Israel had not turned out as he intended and as the king had ordered.

²⁸So the following year he gathered together sixty thousand picked men and five thousand cavalry, to subdue them. ²⁹They came into Idumea and camped at Beth-zur,* and Judas met them with ten thousand men. ³⁰Seeing that the army was strong, he prayed thus:

"Blessed are you, O Savior of Israel, who broke the rush of the mighty one by the hand of your servant David and delivered the camp of the Philistines into the hand of Jonathan, the son of Saul, and his armor-bearer.ᵗ ³¹Give this army into the hands of your people Israel; make them ashamed of their troops and their cavalry. ³²Strike them with fear, weaken the boldness of their strength, and let them tremble at their own destruction. ³³Strike them down by the sword of those who love you, that all who know your name may hymn your praise."

³⁴Then they engaged in battle, and about five thousand of Lysias' men fell in hand-to-hand fighting. ³⁵When Lysias saw his ranks

---

4, 15: Gazara: Gezer of the Hebrew Bible, five miles northwest of Emmaus: Azotus, Hebrew Ashdod, lay to the southwest; and Jamnia, Hebrew Jabneel (Jos 15, 11) or Jabneh (2 Chr 26, 6), to the west of Gazara.

4, 22: Philistine territory: the coastal cities of southern Palestine, traditionally hostile to Jerusalem. Jamnia in particular was an important base for the Seleucid power.

4, 29: Beth-zur: an important frontier city in the mountain area, fifteen miles southwest of Jerusalem. Its inhabitants were sympathetic to the Maccabees and refused to receive Lysias.

p: Ex 14, 21ff.   q: 1 Mc 2, 21.   r: Ps 118, 1ff. 29.   s: 26-35: 2 Mc 11, 1-12.   t: 1 Sm 17, 48ff.

> The high point of Judas's career is the purification of the temple. This is the event commemorated in the Jewish festival of Hanukkah (Hebrew for "dedication"; see 4, 59).

beginning to give way, and the increased boldness of Judas, whose men were ready either to live or to die bravely, he withdrew to Antioch and began to recruit mercenaries so as to return to Judea with greater numbers.*

Purification of the Temple. *36u*Then Judas and his brothers said, "Now that our enemies have been crushed, let us go up to purify the sanctuary* and rededicate it." *37*So the whole army assembled, and went up to Mount Zion. *38*They found the sanctuary desolate, the altar desecrated, the gates burnt, weeds growing in the courts as in a forest or on some mountain, and the priests' chambers demolished.*v* *39*Then they tore their clothes and made great lamentation; they sprinkled their heads with ashes *40*and fell with their faces to the ground. And when the signal was given with trumpets, they cried out to Heaven.

*41*Judas appointed men to attack those in the citadel, while he purified the sanctuary. *42*He chose blameless priests, devoted to the law; *43*these purified the sanctuary and carried away the stones of the Abomination to an unclean place. *44*They deliberated what ought to be done with the altar of holocausts that had been desecrated.*w* *45*The happy thought came to them to tear it down, lest it be a lasting shame to them that the Gentiles had defiled it; so they tore down the altar.*x* *46*They stored the stones in a suitable place on the temple hill, until a prophet should come and decide what to do with them. *47*Then they took uncut stones, according to the law, and built a new altar like the former one.*y* *48*They also repaired the sanctuary and the interior of the temple and purified the courts. *49*They made new sacred vessels and brought the lampstand, the altar of incense, and the table into the temple.*z* *50*Then they burned incense on the altar and lighted the lamps on the lampstand, and these illuminated the temple.*a* *51*They also put loaves on the table and hung up the curtains. Thus they finished all the work they had undertaken.

*52*Early in the morning on the twenty-fifth day of the ninth month, that is, the month of Chislev, in the year one hundred and forty-eight,* *53*they arose and offered sacrifice according to the law on the new altar of holocausts that they had made.*b* *54*On the anniversary of the day on which the Gentiles had defiled it, on that very day it was reconsecrated with songs, harps, flutes, and cymbals. *55*All the people prostrated themselves and adored and praised Heaven, who had given them success.

*56*For eight days they celebrated the dedication of the altar and joyfully offered holocausts and sacrifices of deliverance and praise. *57*They ornamented the façade of the temple with gold crowns and shields; they repaired the gates and the priests' chambers and furnished them with doors. *58*There was great joy among the people now that the disgrace of the Gentiles was removed. *59*Then Judas and his brothers and the entire congregation of Israel decreed that the days of the dedication* of the altar should be observed with joy and gladness on the anniversary every year for eight days, from the twenty-fifth day of the month Chislev.*c*

*60*At that time they built high walls and strong towers around Mount Zion, to prevent the Gentiles from coming and trampling over it as they had done before. *61*Judas also placed a garrison there to protect it, and likewise fortified Beth-zur, that the people might have a stronghold facing Idumea.

4, 35: According to 2 Mc 11, 13-15, peace negotiations followed between Lysias and Judas.

4, 36: The sanctuary: the whole temple area with its walls, courts and outbuildings, to be distinguished from the temple proper, the oblong edifice with porch, main room and inner shrine.

4, 52: Twenty-fifth day of the ninth month . . . in the year one hundred and forty-eight: December 14, 164 B.C.

4, 59: Days of the dedication . . . Chislev: institution of the feast of Hanukkah, also called the feast of Dedication (Jn 10, 22). Josephus Flavius calls it the feast of Lights.

---

u: 36-59: 2 Mc 10, 1-8. *v:* Ps 74, 2-7. *w:* 1 Kgs 8, 64. *x:* 1 Mc 6, 7. *y:* Ex 20, 25. *z:* Ex 25, 23-39; 30, 1-6. *a:* Ex 30, 7ff. *b:* 53. 56: Ex 30, 10; Ez 43, 18-27. *c:* Jn 10, 22.

See RG
163

CHAPTER 5*

Punishment of Hostile Acts. *1d*When the Gentiles round about heard that the altar had been rebuilt and the sanctuary consecrated as before, they were very angry. *2*So they decided to destroy the descendants of Jacob who were among them, and they began to massacre and persecute the people. *3e*Then Judas attacked the sons of Esau at Akrabattene* in Idumea, because they were blockading Israel; he defeated them heavily, overcame and despoiled them. *4*He also remembered the malice of the sons of Baean,* who had become a snare and a stumbling-block to the people by ambushing them along the roads. *5*He forced them to take refuge in towers, which he besieged; he vowed their annihilation and burned down the towers along with all the persons in them. *6*Then he crossed over to the Ammonites, where he found a strong army and a large body of people with Timothy as their leader. *7*He fought many battles with them, routed them, and struck them down. *8*After seizing Jazer and its villages, he returned to Judea.

Liberation of Galilean Jews. *9*The Gentiles in Gilead assembled to attack and destroy the Israelites who were in their territory; these then fled to the stronghold of Dathema. *10*They sent a letter to Judas and his brothers saying: "The Gentiles around us have combined against us to destroy us, *11*and they are preparing to come and seize this stronghold to which we have fled. Timothy is the leader of their army. *12*Come at once and rescue us from them, for many of us have fallen. *13*All our kinsmen who were among the Tobiads have been killed; the Gentiles have carried away their wives and children and their goods, and they have slain there about a thousand men."*f*

*14*While they were reading this letter, suddenly other messengers, in torn clothes, arrived from Galilee to deliver a similar message: *15*that the inhabitants of Ptolemais,* Tyre, and Sidon, and the whole of Gentile Galilee had joined forces to destroy them. *16*When Judas and the people heard this, a great assembly convened to consider what they should do for their unfortunate kinsmen who were being attacked by enemies.

*17*Judas said to his brother Simon: "Choose men for yourself, and go, rescue your kinsmen in Galilee; I and my brother Jonathan will go to Gilead." *18*In Judea he left Joseph, son of Zechariah, and Azariah, leader of the people, with the rest of the army to guard it. *19*"Take charge of these people," he commanded them, "but do not fight against the Gentiles until we return." *20*Three thousand men were allotted to Simon, to go into Galilee, and eight thousand men to Judas, for Gilead.

*21*Simon went into Galilee and fought many battles with the Gentiles. They were crushed before him, *22*and he pursued them to the very gate of Ptolemais. About three thousand men of the Gentiles fell, and he gathered their spoils. *23*He took with him the Jews who were in Galilee and in Arbatta, with their wives and children and all that they had, and brought them to Judea with great rejoicing.

Rescue in Gilead. *24g*Judas Maccabeus and his brother Jonathan crossed the Jordan and marched for three days through the desert. *25*There they met some Nabateans,* who received them peacefully and told them all that had happened to the Jews in Gilead: *26*"Many of them have been imprisoned in Bozrah, in Bosor near Alema, in Chaspho, Maked, and

5, 1: The events of this chapter occurred within the year 163 B.C.

5, 3: Akrabattene: a district southwest of the Dead Sea.

5, 4: Sons of Baean: 2 Mc 10, 15-23 calls them simply Idumeans.

5, 6ff: This summary anticipates the order of events and would fit better between vv 36 and 37. It corresponds to 2 Mc 12, 17-23. The action was probably a reprisal for the massacre referred to in v 13. Timothy was the Seleucid governor of Transjordan. Jazer: a town on the road from the Jordan to Amman.

5, 15: Ptolemais: Hebrew Acco (Jgs 1, 31), modern Acre, on the coast north of Haifa.

5, 25: Nabateans: an Arab people who acquired wealth and power as caravan merchants in the final two centuries B.C. They settled down, established Petra as their capital, and for a time controlled all of Transjordan, even as far as Damascus. It was from a Nabatean governor that St. Paul escaped about 38 A.D. (2 Cor 11, 32f).

d: 1f: 1 Mc 13, 6.   e: 3ff: 2 Mc 10, 15-23.   f: 2 Mc 12, 17.
g: 24-36: 2 Mc 12, 10ff.

Carnaim"—all of these are large, fortified cities— 27"and some have been imprisoned in the other cities of Gilead. Tomorrow their enemies plan to attack the strongholds and to seize and destroy all these people in one day."

28Thereupon Judas suddenly changed direction with his army, marched across the desert to Bozrah, and captured the city. He slaughtered all the male population, took all their possessions, and set fire to the city. 29He led his army from that place by night, and they marched toward the stronghold of Dathema. 30When morning came, they looked ahead and saw a countless multitude of people, with ladders and devices for capturing the stronghold, and beginning to attack the people within. 31When Judas perceived that the struggle had begun and that the noise of the battle was resounding to heaven with trumpet blasts and loud shouting, 32he said to the men of his army, "Fight for our kinsmen today."

33He came up behind them with three columns blowing their trumpets and shouting in prayer. 34When the army of Timothy realized that it was Maccabeus, they fell back before him, and he inflicted on them a crushing defeat. About eight thousand of their men fell that day. 35Then he turned toward Alema and attacked and captured it; he killed all the male population, plundered the place, and burned it down. 36From there he moved on and took Chaspho, Maked, Bosor, and the other cities of Gilead.

37hAfter these events Timothy assembled another army and camped opposite Raphon, on the other side of the stream. 38Judas sent men to spy on the camp, and they reported to him: "All the Gentiles around us have rallied to him, making a very large force; 39they have also hired Arabs to help them, and have camped beyond the stream, ready to attack you." So Judas went forward to attack them.

40As Judas and his army were approaching the running stream, Timothy said to the officers of his army: "If he crosses over to us first, we shall not be able to resist him; he will certainly defeat us.i 41But if he is afraid and camps on the other side of the river, we will cross over to him and defeat him."

42But when Judas reached the running stream, he stationed the officers of the people beside the stream and gave them this order: "Do not allow any man to pitch a tent; all must go into battle." 43He was the first to cross to the attack, with all the people behind him, and the Gentiles were crushed before them; they threw away their arms and fled to the temple enclosure at Carnaim. 44The Jews captured that city and burnt the enclosure with all who were in it. So Carnaim was subdued, and Judas met with no more resistance.j

45Then he assembled all the Israelites, great and small, who were in Gilead, with their wives and children and their goods, a great crowd of people, to go into the land of Judah. 46kWhen they reached Ephron,* a large and strongly fortified city along the way, they found it impossible to encircle it on either the right or the left; they would have to march right through it. 47But the men in the city shut them out and blocked up the gates with stones.l 48Then Judas sent them his peaceful message: "We wish to cross your territory in order to reach our own; no one will harm you; we will only march through." But they would not open to him.

49So Judas ordered a proclamation to be made in the camp that everyone make an attack from the place where he was. 50When the men of the army took up their positions, he assaulted the city all that day and night, and it was delivered to him. 51He slaughtered every male, razed and plundered the city, and passed through it over the slain.

52Then they crossed the Jordan to the great plain in front of Beth-shan; 53and Judas kept rounding up the stragglers and encouraging the people the whole way, until he reached the land of Judah. 54They ascended Mount Zion in joy and gladness and offered holocausts, because not one of them had fallen; they returned in safety.

5, 46: Ephron: a city in Trans-jordan opposite Beth-shan, about five miles east of the Jordan River. Situated on a height, it dominated the valleys of the two tributaries of the Jordan.

h: 37-44: 2 Mc 12, 20-26.   *i:* 1 Sm 14, 9f.   *j:* 2 Mc 12, 21.   *k:* 46-54: 2 Mc 12, 27-31.   *l:* Nm 20, 17-21; 21, 21-25.

Joseph and Azariah Defeated. [55]During the time that Judas and Jonathan were in the land of Gilead, and Simon his brother was in Galilee opposite Ptolemais, [56]Joseph, son of Zechariah, and Azariah, the leaders of the army, heard about the brave deeds and the fighting that they were doing. [57]They said, "Let us also make a name for ourselves by going out and fighting against the Gentiles around us."

[58]They gave orders to the men of their army who were with them, and marched toward Jamnia. [59]But Gorgias and his men came out of the city to meet them in battle. [60]Joseph and Azariah were beaten, and were pursued to the frontiers of Judea, and about two thousand Israelites fell that day. [61]It was a bad defeat for the people, because they had not obeyed Judas and his brothers, thinking that they would do brave deeds. [62]But they did not belong to the family of those men to whom it was granted to achieve Israel's salvation. [63]The valiant Judas and his brothers were greatly renowned in all Israel and among all the Gentiles, wherever their name was heard; [64]and men gathered about them and praised them.

[65]Then Judas and his brothers went out and attacked the sons of Esau* in the country toward the south; he took Hebron and its villages, and he destroyed its strongholds and burned the towers around it. [66]He then set out for the land of the Philistines and passed through Marisa. [67]At that time some priests fell in battle who had gone out rashly to fight in their desire to distinguish themselves. [68]Judas then turned toward Azotus in the land of the Philistines. He destroyed their altars and burned the statues of their gods; and after plundering their cities he returned to the land of Judah.

See RG 163

CHAPTER 6

Defeat and Death of Antiochus IV. [1m]As King Antiochus was traversing the inland provinces, he heard that in Persia there was a city called Elymais,* famous for its wealth in silver and gold, [2]and that its temple was very rich, containing gold helmets, breastplates, and weapons left there by Alexander, son of Philip, king of Macedon, the first king of the Greeks. [3]He went therefore and tried to capture and pillage the city. But he could not do so, because his plan became known to the people of the city [4]who rose up in battle against him. So he retreated and in great dismay withdrew from there to return to Babylon.

[5]While he was in Persia, a messenger brought him news that the armies sent into the land of Judah had been put to flight; [6]that Lysias had gone at first with a strong army and been driven back by the Israelites; that they had grown strong by reason of the arms, men, and abundant possessions taken from the armies they had destroyed; [7]that they had pulled down the Abomination which he had built upon the altar in Jerusalem; and that they had surrounded with high walls both the sanctuary, as it had been before, and his city of Beth-zur.[n]

[8]When the king heard this news, he was struck with fear and very much shaken. Sick with grief because his designs had failed, he took to his bed. [9]There he remained many days, overwhelmed with sorrow, for he knew he was going to die.

[10]So he called in all his Friends and said to them: "Sleep has departed from my eyes, for my heart is sinking with anxiety. [11]I said to myself: 'Into what tribulation have I come, and in what floods of sorrow am I now! [12]Yet I was kindly and beloved in my rule.' But I now recall the evils I did in Jerusalem, when I carried away all the vessels of gold and silver that were in it, and for no cause gave orders that the inhabitants of Judah be destroyed. [13]I know that this is why these evils have overtaken me; and now I am dying, in bitter grief, in a foreign land."

[14]Then he summoned Philip, one of his Friends, and put him in charge of his whole

---

5, 65: Sons of Esau: Idumeans.

6, 1: Elymais: the mountainous region of Elam, north of the Persian Gulf. This section continues the story from 1 Mc 3, 37 and pertains to events preceding those in 1 Mc 4, 37ff.

m: 1-13: 2 Mc 1, 12-17; 9, 1-29.   *n:* 1 Mc 1, 54; 4, 41ff. 60f.

The Death of Epiphanes

There are three distinct accounts of the death of Antiochus Epiphanes in the Maccabean books: 1 Mc 6, 1–17; 2 Mc 1, 11–17; and 9, 1–29. The first two agree that Epiphanes was trying to rob a temple but differ in attributing his death to remorse over what he had done in Jerusalem. Second Maccabees 9 goes further in claiming that Epiphanes repented on his deathbed and wanted to become a Jew. First Maccabees assumes that the death of the king is divine punishment for what he did in Jerusalem.

kingdom. [15]He gave him his crown, his robe, and his signet ring, so that he might guide the king's son Antiochus and bring him up to be king. [16]King Antiochus died in Persia in the year one hundred and forty-nine.*

The Citadel Besieged. [17]When Lysias learned that the king was dead, he set up the king's son Antiochus,* whom he had reared as a child, to be king in his place; and he gave him the title Eupator.[o]

[18]The men in the citadel were hemming in Israel around the sanctuary, continually trying to harm them and to strengthen the Gentiles.[p] [19]But Judas planned to destroy them, and called all the people together to besiege them. [20]So in the year one hundred and fifty* they assembled and stormed the citadel, for which purpose he constructed catapults and other devices. [21]Some of the besieged escaped, joined by impious Israelites; [22]they went to the king and said:

"How long will you fail to do justice and avenge our kinsmen? [23]We agreed to serve your father and to follow his orders and obey his edicts. [24]And for this the sons of our people have become our enemies; they have put to death as many of us as they could find and have plundered our estates. [25]They have acted aggressively not only against us, but throughout their whole territory. [26]Look! They have now besieged the citadel in Jerusalem in order to capture it, and they have fortified the sanctuary and Beth-zur. [27]Unless you quickly forestall them, they will do even worse things than these, and you will not be able to stop them."

Campaign against Judas. [28q]When the king heard this he was angry, and he called together all his Friends, the officers of his army, and the commanders of the cavalry.[r] [29]Mercenary forces also came to him from other kingdoms and from the islands of the seas. [30]His army numbered a hundred thousand foot-soldiers, twenty thousand cavalry, and thirty-two elephants trained for war. [31]They passed through Idumea and camped before Beth-zur. For many days they attacked it; they constructed siege-devices, but the besieged made a sortie and burned these, and they fought bravely.

[32]Then Judas marched away from the citadel and moved his camp to Beth-zechariah, on the way to the king's camp. [33]The king, rising before dawn, moved his force hastily along the road to Beth-zechariah; and the armies prepared for battle, while the trumpets sounded. [34]They made the elephants drunk on grape and mulberry wine to provoke them to fight. [35]The beasts were distributed along the phalanxes, each elephant having assigned to it a thousand men in coats of mail, with bronze helmets, and five hundred picked cavalry. [36]These anticipated the beast wherever it was; and wherever it moved, they moved too and never left it. [37]A strong wooden tower covering each elephant, and fastened to it by a harness,

---

6, 16: The year one hundred and forty-nine: September 22, 164, to October 9, 163 B.C. A Babylonian list of the Seleucid kings indicates that Antiochus died in November or early December of 164.

6, 17: The king's son Antiochus: Antiochus V Eupator, then about nine years old. He was in Antioch, still in the charge of Lysias, who proceeded to govern and wage wars in his name. Both were put to death two years later, when

Demetrius, brother of Antiochus IV, arrived to claim the kingship; cf 1 Mc 7, 1ff.

6, 20: The year one hundred and fifty: October, 163, to September, 162 B.C.

---

o: 2 Mc 10, 10f. p: 1 Mc 1, 33ff. q: 28-54: 2 Mc 13, 1-23. r: 28ff: 2 Mc 13, 1f.

held, besides the Indian mahout, three soldiers who fought from it. *38*The remaining cavalry were stationed on one or the other of the two flanks of the army, to harass the enemy and to be protected from the phalanxes. *39*When the sun shone on the gold and bronze shields, the mountains gleamed with their brightness and blazed like flaming torches. *40*Part of the king's army extended over the heights, while some were on low ground, but they marched forward steadily and in good order. *41*All who heard the noise of their numbers, the tramp of their marching, and the clashing of the arms, trembled; for the army was very great and strong.

*42*Judas with his army advanced to fight, and six hundred men of the king's army fell. *43*Eleazar, called Avaran, saw one of the beasts bigger than any of the others and covered with royal armor, and he thought the king must be on it.*s* *44*So he gave up his life to save his people and win an everlasting name for himself. *45*He dashed up to it in the middle of the phalanx, killing men right and left, so that they fell back from him on both sides. *46*He ran right under the elephant and stabbed it in the belly, killing it. The beast fell to the ground on top of him, and he died there.

*47*When the Jews saw the strength of the royal army and the ardor of its forces, they retreated from them. *48t*A part of the king's army went up to Jerusalem to attack them, and the king established camps in Judea and at Mount Zion. *49u*He made peace with the men of Beth-zur, and they evacuated the city, because they had no food there to enable them to stand a siege, for that was a sabbath year in the land.* *50*The king took Beth-zur and stationed a garrison there to hold it. *51*For many days he besieged the sanctuary, setting up artillery and machines, fire-throwers, catapults and mechanical bows for shooting arrows and slingstones. *52*The Jews countered by setting up machines of their own, and kept up the fight a long time. *53*But there were no provisions in the storerooms, because it was the seventh year, and the tide-over provisions had been eaten up by those who had been rescued from the Gentiles and brought to Judea. *54*Few men remained in the sanctuary; the rest scattered, each to his own home, for the famine was too much for them.

Peace Treaty. *55v*Lysias heard that Philip, whom King Antiochus, before his death, had appointed to train his son Antiochus to be king, *56*had returned from Persia and Media with the army that accompanied the king, and that he was seeking to take over the government. *57*So he hastily resolved to withdraw. He said to the king, the leaders of the army, and the soldiers: "We are growing weaker every day, our provisions are scanty, the place we are besieging is strong, and it is our duty to take care of the affairs of the kingdom.*w* *58*Therefore let us now come to terms with these men, and make peace with them and all their nation. *59*Let us grant them freedom to live according to their own laws as formerly; it was on account of their laws, which we abolished, that they became angry and did all these things."

*60*The proposal found favor with the king and the leaders; he sent peace terms to the Jews, and they accepted. *61*So the king and the leaders swore an oath to them, and on these terms they evacuated the fortification. *62*But when the king entered Mount Zion and saw how the place was fortified, he broke the oath he had sworn and gave orders for the encircling wall to be destroyed. *63*Then he departed in haste and returned to Antioch, where he found Philip in possession of the city. He fought against him and took the city by force.

CHAPTER 7

Expedition of Bacchides and Alcimus. *1x*In the year one hundred and fifty-one,* Demetrius, son of Seleucus, set out from Rome,

See RG 163

6, 49: A sabbath year in the land: when sowing and reaping were prohibited (Ex 23, 10f; Lv 25, 2-7). The year without a harvest (autumn of 164 to autumn of 163) was followed by a food shortage.

7, 1ff: The year one hundred and fifty-one: the spring of 161 B.C. Demetrius, son of Seleucus, was the lawful heir to the kingdom; but when only nine years old, he was taken as a hostage at Rome in place of his uncle, who ruled as Antiochus

IV Epiphanes. At the age of twenty-five Demetrius fled secretly from Rome and, with the support of the Syrians, overcame his rival Antiochus V and put him to death. The royal palace: at Antioch.

s: 2 Mc 13, 15.   *t:* 48f: 2 Mc 13, 22-23.   *u:* Lv 25, 2.   *v:* 55-63: 2 Mc 13, 23-26.   *w:* 2 Mc 11, 13ff.   *x:* 1-7: 2 Mc 14, 1-11.

arrived with a few men in a city on the sea-coast, and began to rule there. [2]As he was preparing to enter the royal palace of his ancestors, the soldiers seized Antiochus and Lysias to bring them to him. [3]When he was informed of this, he said, "Do not show me their faces." [4]So the soldiers killed them, and Demetrius sat on the royal throne.

[5]Then all the lawless and impious men of Israel came to him. They were led by Alcimus,* who desired to be high priest. [6]They made this accusation to the king against the people: "Judas and his brothers have destroyed all your friends and have driven us out of our country. [7]So now, send a man whom you trust to go and see all the havoc Judas has done to us and to the king's land, and let him punish them and all their supporters."

[8]Then the king chose Bacchides, one of the King's Friends, governor of West-of-Euphrates, a great man in the kingdom, and faithful to the king. [9y]He sent him and the impious Alcimus, to whom he granted the high priesthood, with orders to take revenge on the Israelites. [10]They set out and, on arriving in the land of Judah with a great army, sent messengers who spoke deceitfully to Judas and his brothers in peaceful terms. [11]But these paid no attention to their words, seeing that they had come with a great army. [12]A group of scribes, however, gathered about Alcimus and Bacchides to ask for a just agreement. [13z]The Hasideans were the first among the Israelites to seek peace with them, [14]for they said, "A priest of the line of Aaron has come with the army, and he will not do us any wrong." [15]He spoke with them peacefully and swore to them, "We will not try to injure you or your friends." [16]So they trusted him. But he arrested sixty of them and killed them in one day, according to the text of Scripture:

[17] "The flesh of your saints they have
strewn,

and their blood they have shed round
about Jerusalem,
and there was no one to bury them."[a]

[18]Then fear and dread of them came upon all the people, who said: "There is no truth or justice among them; they violated the agreement and the oath that they swore."

[19]Bacchides withdrew from Jerusalem and pitched his camp in Beth-zaith.* He had many of the men arrested who deserted to him, throwing them into the great pit. [20]He handed the province over to Alcimus, leaving troops to help him, while he himself returned to the king.

[21]Alcimus spared no pains to maintain his high priesthood, [22]and all those who were disturbing their people gathered about him. They took possession of the land of Judah and caused great distress in Israel. [23]When Judas saw all the evils that Alcimus and his men were bringing upon the Israelites, more than even the Gentiles had done, [24]he went about all the borders of Judea and took revenge on the men who had deserted, preventing them from going out into the country. [25]But when Alcimus saw that Judas and his followers were gaining strength and realized that he could not oppose them, he returned to the king and accused them of grave crimes.

Defeat of Nicanor. [26b]Then the king sent Nicanor, one of his famous officers, who was a bitter enemy of Israel, with orders to destroy the people. [27]Nicanor came to Jerusalem with a large force and deceitfully sent to Judas* and his brothers this peaceable message: [28]"Let there be no fight between me and you. I will come with a few men to meet you peaceably." [29]So he came to Judas, and they greeted one another peaceably. But Judas' enemies were prepared to seize him. [30]When he became aware that Nicanor had come to him with treachery in mind, Judas was afraid and would not meet him again.[c] [31]When Nicanor

---

7, 5f: Alcimus: a renegade Jew hostile to the Maccabees, who became high priest after the death of Menelaus (2 Mc 14, 3). He received confirmation in his office from the new King Demetrius (v 9), and brought malicious charges against Judas and his brothers and the people (v 6). He wrought more evils on the Israelites than the Gentiles had done (v 23).

7, 19: Beth-zaith: about three miles north of Beth-zur and twelve miles south of Jerusalem.

7, 27: Nicanor . . . deceitfully sent to Judas: a more favorable picture of Nicanor, as an honest man who became a personal friend of Judas, is given in 2 Mc 14, 17-25. Their friendship was broken by the intrigues of Alcimus (2 Mc 14, 26-30).

y: 9ff: 2 Mc 14, 46.   *z:* 13f: 1 Mc 2, 42.   *a:* Ps 79, 1ff.
b: 26f: 1 Mc 3, 38; 2 Mc 8, 9; 14, 12f.   *c:* 2 Mc 14, 30.

The Defeat of Nicanor

The display of Nicanor's head (7, 47) is shocking to modern sensibilities. However, it is a practice that has continued intermittently down to modern times, designed to terrorize the enemy and bolster the morale of one's own troops.

saw that his plan had been discovered, he went out to fight Judas near Caphar-salama.* ³²About five hundred men of Nicanor's army fell; the rest fled to the City of David.

³³ᵈAfter this, Nicanor went up to Mount Zion. Some of the priests from the sanctuary and some of the elders of the people came out to greet him peaceably and to show him the holocaust that was being offered for the king. ³⁴But he mocked and ridiculed them, defiled them,* and spoke disdainfully. ³⁵In a rage he swore: "If Judas and his army are not delivered to me at once, when I return victorious I will burn this temple down." He went away in great anger. ³⁶The priests, however, went in and stood before the altar and the sanctuary.ᵉ They wept and said: ³⁷"You have chosen this house to bear your name, to be a house of prayer and petition for your people. ³⁸Take revenge on this man and his army, and let them fall by the sword. Remember their blasphemies, and do not let them continue."

³⁹Nicanor left Jerusalem and pitched his camp at Beth-horon, where the Syrian army joined him. ⁴⁰But Judas camped in Adasa* with three thousand men. Here Judas uttered this prayer: ⁴¹"When they who were sent by the king blasphemed, your angel went out and killed a hundred and eighty-five thousand of them.ᶠ ⁴²In the same way, crush this army be-

fore us today, and let the rest know that Nicanor spoke wickedly against your sanctuary; judge him according to his wickedness."ᵍ

⁴³The armies met in battle on the thirteenth day of the month Adar. Nicanor's army was crushed, and he himself was the first to fall in the battle.ʰ ⁴⁴When his army saw that Nicanor was dead, they threw down their arms and fled. ⁴⁵The Jews pursued them a day's journey, from Adasa to near Gazara, blowing the trumpets behind them as signals. ⁴⁶From all the surrounding villages of Judea people came out and closed in on them. They hemmed them in, and all the enemies fell by the sword; not a single one escaped.

⁴⁷Then the Jews collected the spoils and the booty; they cut off Nicanor's head and his right arm, which he had lifted up so arrogantly. These they brought to Jerusalem and displayed there. ⁴⁸The people rejoiced greatly, and observed that day as a great festival. ⁴⁹They decreed that it should be observed every year on the thirteenth of Adar.* ⁵⁰And for a short time* the land of Judah was quiet.

CHAPTER 8

See RG 163

*Treaty with the Romans.** ¹Judas had heard of the reputation of the Romans. They were valiant fighters and acted

---

7, 31: Caphar-salama: a village seven miles north-north-west of Jerusalem, on the road leading to Beth-horon.

7, 34: Defiled them: spitting on the priests caused them to become legally defiled.

7, 40: Adasa: a village southeast of Caphar-salama.

7, 49: The thirteenth of Adar: March 27, 160 B.C. This day in the Jewish calendar was called the "Day of Nicanor" (2 Mc 15, 36), but it was not long celebrated by the Jews.

7, 50: A short time: about one month following the death of Nicanor. After that began the attack of Bacchides resulting in the death of Judas (1 Mc 9, 1-18).

8, 1: This chapter contains the account of the embassy which Judas sent to Rome, probably before the death of Nicanor, to conclude a treaty of alliance between Rome and the Jewish nation. Without precise chronology, the pertinent data are gathered into a unified theme.

The image of the Roman Republic greatly impressed the smaller Eastern peoples seeking support against their overlords (1-16), because of Roman success in war (2-11) and effective aid to their allies (12-13). Numerous interventions by Rome in the politics of the Near East bear witness to its power and prestige in the second century B.C. Cf 1 Mc 1, 10; 7, 2; 12, 3; 15, 15-24; 2 Mc 11, 34. With the Roman control of Palestine in 63 B.C., the Republic and later the Empire became heartily detested. The eulogy of Rome in this chapter is one of the reasons why 1 Maccabees was not preserved by the Palestinian Jews of the century that followed.

---

d: 33-38: 2 Mc 14, 31-36.   *e:* Jl 2, 17.   *f:* 41f: 2 Mc 8, 19; 15, 22ff.   *g:* Is 37, 36ff.   *h:* 2 Mc 15, 25-35.

The Treaty with Rome

Rome is admired for its might and organization, despite the general hostility of 1 Maccabees toward the Gentiles. The authenticity of the letter in 8, 23–32 is sometimes disputed, but it is probably genuine. The Romans promised little and made no effort to intervene on behalf of the Jews, but they were gaining a potential foothold in the Near East. Judas gained some international recognition and moral support. The short-term results were harmless. When the Romans actually intervened in Judea a century later, the results were disastrous for the Jews.

amiably to all who took their side. They established a friendly alliance with all who applied to them. ²He was also told of their battles and the brave deeds that they had performed against the Gauls,* conquering them and forcing them to pay tribute. ³They had gotten possession of the silver and gold mines in Spain, ⁴and by planning and persistence had conquered the whole country, although it was very remote from their own. They had crushed the kings who had come against them from the far corners of the earth and had inflicted on them severe defeat, and the rest paid tribute to them every year. ⁵Philip* and Perseus, king of the Macedonians, and the others who opposed them in battle had been overwhelmed and subjugated. ⁶Antiochus* the Great, king of Asia, who had fought against them with a hundred and twenty elephants and with cavalry and chariots and a very great army, had been defeated by them. ⁷They had taken him alive and obliged him and the kings who succeeded him to pay a heavy tribute, to give hostages and a section of ⁸Lycia, Mysia,* and Lydia from among their best provinces. The Romans took these from

him and gave them to King Eumenes. ⁹*When the men of Greece had planned to come and destroy them, ¹⁰the Romans discovered it, and sent against the Greeks a single general who made war on them. Many were wounded and fell, and the Romans took their wives and children captive. They plundered them, took possession of their land, tore down their strongholds and reduced them to slavery even to this day. ¹¹All the other kingdoms and islands that had ever opposed them they destroyed and enslaved; ¹²with their friends, however, and those who relied on them, they maintained friendship. They had conquered kings both far and near, and all who heard of their fame were afraid of them. ¹³In truth, those whom they desired to help to a kingdom became kings, and those whom they wished to depose they deposed; and they were greatly exalted. ¹⁴Yet with all this, none of them put on a crown or wore purple as a display of grandeur. ¹⁵They had made for themselves a senate house, and every day three hundred and twenty men took counsel, deliberating on all that concerned the people and their well-being. ¹⁶They entrusted

8, 2: Gauls: probably the Celts of northern Italy and southern France, subdued by the Romans in 222 B.C., and again in 200–191 B.C.; but perhaps also those in Asia Minor (the Galatians), whom the Romans defeated in 189 B.C.

8, 5: Philip: Philip V of Macedonia, defeated by a Graeco-Roman alliance at Cynoscephalae in 197 B.C. Perseus, his son, was defeated at Pydna in 168 B.C., and died a prisoner. With this, the kingdom of Macedonia came to an end.

8, 6: Antiochus: Antiochus III, greatest of the Seleucid kings. He was defeated at Magnesia in 190 B.C. By the Treaty of Apamea in 189, he was obliged to pay Rome a crushing indemnity of 15,000 talents. It was the weakening of Antiochene power and the growing military and economic

influence of Rome that led Antiochus IV to adopt the policy of political, religious and cultural unification of Syria and Palestine.

8, 8: Lycia, Mysia: regions in western Asia Minor. These names are restored here by conjectural emendation; the Greek text has "India, Media," most likely through scribal error. Eumenes: Eumenes II (197–158), king of Pergamum, an ally of Rome who benefited greatly from Antiochus' losses.

8, 9f: The revolt of the Achaean League, inserted here, occurred in 146 B.C., after Judas' time. It was crushed by the Roman consul Lucius Mummius and marked the end of Greek independence. The author regards all Greeks as the enemies of God.

their government to one man* every year, to rule over their entire country, and they all obeyed that one, and there was no envy or jealousy among them.

[17]So Judas chose Eupolemus, son of John, son of Accos, and Jason, son of Eleazar, and sent them to Rome to establish an alliance of friendship with them.[i] [18]He did this to get rid of the yoke, for it was obvious that the kingdom of the Greeks was subjecting Israel to slavery. [19]After making a very long journey to Rome, the envoys entered the senate and spoke as follows: [20]"Judas, called Maccabeus, and his brothers, with the Jewish people, have sent us to you to make a peaceful alliance with you, and to enroll ourselves among your allies and friends." [21]The proposal pleased the Romans, [22]and this is a copy of the reply they inscribed on bronze tablets and sent to Jerusalem,* to remain there with the Jews as a record of peace and alliance:[j]

[23]"May it be well with the Romans and the Jewish nation at sea and on land forever; may sword and enemy be far from them. [24]But if war is first made on Rome, or any of its allies in any of its dominions, [25]the Jewish nation will help them wholeheartedly, as the occasion shall demand; [26]and to those who wage war they shall not give nor provide grain, arms, money, or ships; this is Rome's decision. They shall fulfill their obligations without receiving any recompense. [27]In the same way, if war is made first on the Jewish nation, the Romans will help them willingly, as the occasion shall demand, [28]and to those who are attacking them there shall not be given grain, arms, money, or ships; this is Rome's decision. They shall fulfill their obligations without deception. [29]On these terms the Romans have made an agreement with the Jewish people. [30]But if both parties hereafter decide to add or take away anything, they shall do as they choose, and whatever they shall add or take away shall be valid.

[31]"Moreover, concerning the wrongs that King Demetrius has done to them, we have written to him thus: 'Why have you made your yoke heavy upon our friends and allies the Jews? [32]If they complain about you again, we will do them justice and make war on you by land and sea.' "

CHAPTER 9

Invasion of Judah. [1]When Demetrius See RG 163 heard that Nicanor and his army had fallen in battle, he again sent Bacchides and Alcimus into the land of Judah, along with the right wing of his army. [2]They took the road to Galilee, and camping opposite the ascent at Arbela, they captured it* and killed many people. [3]In the first month of the year one hundred and fifty-two,* they encamped against Jerusalem. [4]Then they set out for Berea with twenty thousand men and two thousand cavalry. [5]Judas, with three thousand picked men, had camped at Elasa. [6]When his men saw the great number of the troops, they were very much afraid, and many slipped away from the camp, until only eight hundred men remained.

[7]As Judas saw that his army was melting away just when the battle was imminent, he was panic-stricken, because he had no time to gather them together. [8]But in spite of his discouragement, he said to those who remained: "Let us go forward to meet our enemies; perhaps we can put up a good fight against them." [9]They tried to dissuade him, saying: "We certainly cannot. Let us save our lives now, and come back with our

---

8, 16: They entrusted their government to one man: actually the Roman Republic always had two consuls as joint heads of the government. Presumably, a single one dealt with embassies and answered letters, hence the impression the Jews received; cf 1 Mc 15, 16.

8, 22: The reply . . . on bronze tablets and sent to Jerusalem: the decree of the Senate would be inscribed on bronze and kept in the Roman Capitol, with only a copy in letter form sent to Jerusalem. The translation of the decree into Hebrew and then into Greek, as found here in 1 Mc, may have occasioned this error.

9, 2: They took the road . . . Arbela, they captured it: this

passage is restored, in part, by conjectural emendation. The present Greek text could be translated, "They took the road to Gilgal, and camping opposite Mesaloth at Arbela, they captured it." But Arbela (modern Khirbet Irbid) was in Galilee—on a high hill overlooking the western shore of the Sea of Galilee. Gilgal, on the contrary, was in the Jordan valley near Jericho. "Mesaloth" is probably a corrupt form of a Hebrew word meaning "steps, ascent."

9, 3: The first month of the year one hundred and fifty-two: April/May 160 B.C., by the temple calendar.

i: 1 Mc 12, 1f; 15, 15-22. *j:* 1 Mc 14, 18.

kinsmen, and then fight against them. Now we are too few." [10]But Judas said: "Far be it from me to do such a thing as to flee from them! If our time has come, let us die bravely for our kinsmen and not leave a stain upon our glory!"

Death of Judas. [11]Then the army of Bacchides moved out of camp and took its position for combat. The cavalry were divided into two squadrons, and the slingers and the archers came on ahead of the army, and all the valiant men were in the front line. [12]Bacchides was on the right wing. Flanked by the two squadrons, the phalanx attacked as they blew their trumpets. Those who were on Judas' side also blew their trumpets. [13]The earth shook with the noise of the armies, and the battle raged from morning until evening. [14]Seeing that Bacchides was on the right, with the main force of his army, Judas, with all the most stouthearted rallying to him, [15]drove back the right wing and pursued them as far as the mountain slopes.* [16]But when the men on the left wing saw that the right wing was driven back, they turned and followed Judas and his men, taking them in the rear. [17]The battle was fought desperately, and many on both sides fell wounded. [18]Then Judas fell, and the rest fled.

[19]Jonathan and Simon took their brother Judas and buried him in the tomb of their fathers at Modein. [20]All Israel bewailed him in great grief. They mourned for him many days, and they said, [21]"How the mighty one has fallen, the savior of Israel!"[k] [22]The other acts of Judas, his battles, the brave deeds he performed, and his greatness have not been recorded; but they were very many.

IV: Leadership of Jonathan

Bacchides and Jonathan. [23]After the death of Judas, the transgressors of the law raised their heads in every part of Israel, and all kinds of evildoers appeared. [24]In those days there was a very great famine, and the country deserted to them. [25]Bacchides chose impious men and made them masters of the country. [26]These sought out and hunted down the friends of Judas and brought them to Bacchides, who punished and derided them. [27]There had not been such great distress in Israel since the time prophets ceased to appear among the people.

[28]Then all the friends of Judas came together and said to Jonathan: [29]"Since your brother Judas died, there has been no one like him to oppose our enemies, Bacchides and those who are hostile to our nation. [30]Now therefore we have chosen you today to be our ruler and leader in his place, and to fight our battle." [31]From that moment Jonathan accepted the leadership, and took the place of Judas his brother.

[32]When Bacchides learned of it, he sought to kill him. [33]But Jonathan and his brother Simon and all the men with him discovered this, and they fled to the desert of Tekoa* and camped by the waters of the pool of Asphar.*

[35]Jonathan sent his brother* as leader of the convoy to ask permission of his friends, the Nabateans, to deposit with them their great quantity of baggage.[l] [36]But the sons of Jambri from Medaba* made a raid and seized and carried off John and everything he had. [37]After this, word was brought to Jonathan and his brother Simon: "The sons of Jambri are celebrating a great wedding, and with a large escort they are bringing the bride, the daughter of one of the great princes of Canaan, from Nadabath." [38]Remembering the blood of John their brother, they went up and hid themselves under cover of the mountain. [39]They watched, and suddenly saw a noisy crowd with baggage; the bridegroom and his friends and kinsmen had come out to meet the bride's party with tambourines and musicians and much equipment. [40]The Jews rose up against them from their ambush and killed them. Many fell wounded, and after the

---

9, 15: As far as the mountain slopes: conjectural emendation. The Greek text has "as far as Mount Azotus"; this is most unlikely. Apparently the Greek translator mistook the Hebrew word ashdot, "slopes," for asdod, "Azotus."

9, 33: Tekoa: Home of the prophet Amos in the wild country above the Dead Sea, southeast of Jerusalem.

9, 34: Omitted, it is a dittography of verse 43.

9, 35: Jonathan sent his brother: this was John who was called Gaddi (1 Mc 2, 2; cf 9, 36. 38).

9, 36: Medaba: northeast of the Dead Sea.

---

k: 2 Sam 1, 27.　　*l:* 1 Mc 5, 25.

survivors fled toward the mountain, all their spoils were taken. *41*Thus the wedding was turned into mourning, and the sound of music into lamentation. *42*Having taken their revenge for the blood of their brother, the Jews returned to the marshes of the Jordan.

*43*When Bacchides heard of it, he came on the sabbath to the banks of the Jordan with a large force. *44*Then Jonathan said to his companions, "Let us get up now and fight for our lives, for today is not like yesterday and the day before. *45*The battle is before us, and behind us are the waters of the Jordan on one side, marsh and thickets on the other, and there is no way of escape.* *46*Cry out now to Heaven for deliverance from our enemies." *47*When they joined battle, Jonathan raised his arm to strike Bacchides, but Bacchides backed away from him. *48*Jonathan and his men jumped into the Jordan and swam across to the other side, but the enemy did not pursue them across the Jordan. *49*A thousand men on Bacchides' side fell that day.

*50*On returning to Jerusalem, Bacchides built strongholds in Judea: the Jericho fortress, as well as Emmaus, Beth-horon, Bethel, Timnath, Pharathon, and Tephon, with high walls and gates and bars.* *51*In each he put a garrison to oppose Israel. *52*He fortified the city of Beth-zur, Gazara and the citadel, and put soldiers in them and stores of provisions. *53*He took as hostages the sons of the leaders of the country and put them in custody in the citadel at Jerusalem.*m*

*54*In the year one hundred and fifty-three, in the second month,* Alcimus ordered the wall of the inner court of the sanctuary to be torn down, thus destroying the work of the prophets. But he only began to tear it down. *55*Just at that time he had a stroke, and his work was interrupted; his mouth was closed and he was paralyzed, so that he could no longer utter a word to give orders concerning his house. *56*Finally he died in great agony. *57*Seeing that Alcimus was dead, Bacchides returned

to the king, and the land of Judah was quiet for two years.

*58*Then all the transgressors of the law held a council and said: "Jonathan and his companions are living in peace and security. Now then, let us have Bacchides return, and he will capture all of them in a single night." *59*So they went and took counsel with him. *60*When Bacchides was setting out with a large force, he sent letters secretly to all his allies in Judea, telling them to seize Jonathan and his companions. They were not able to do this, however, because their plot became known. *61*In fact, Jonathan's men seized about fifty of the men of the country who were ringleaders in the mischief and put them to death. *62*Then Jonathan and Simon and their companions withdrew to Bethbasi* in the desert; they rebuilt and strengthened its fortifications that had been demolished. *63*When Bacchides learned of this, he gathered together his whole force and sent word to those who were in Judea. *64*He came and pitched his camp before Bethbasi, and constructing siege-machines, he fought against it for many days.

*65*Leaving his brother Simon in the city, Jonathan, accompanied by a small group of men, went out into the field. *66*He struck down Odomera and his kinsmen and the sons of Phasiron in their encampment; these men had set out to go up to the siege with their forces. *67*Simon and his men then sallied forth from the city and set fire to the machines. *68*They fought against Bacchides, and he was beaten. This caused him great distress. Because the enterprise he had planned came to naught, *69*he was angry with the lawless men who had advised him to invade the province. He killed many of them and resolved to return to his own country.

*70*Jonathan learned of this and sent ambassadors to make peace with him and to obtain the release of the prisoners. *71*He agreed to do as Jonathan had asked. He

9, 45: Jonathan's force was apparently trapped in one of the many oxbows of the lower Jordan. Bacchides had crossed and caught them still on the east bank.

9, 50: These sites constitute a ring on the edges of the province of Judea.

9, 54: In the year . . . second month: May 159 B.C.

9, 62: Bethbasi: two miles east of Bethlehem, and six miles north of Tekoa.

m: 1 Mc 10, 9.

swore an oath to him that he would never try to injure him for the rest of his life; [72]and he released the prisoners he had previously taken from the land of Judah. He returned to his own country and never came into their territory again.

[73]Then the sword ceased in Israel. Jonathan settled in Michmash; he began to judge* the people, and he destroyed the impious in Israel.

CHAPTER 10

See RG 163

Revolt of Alexander. [1]In the year one hundred and sixty,* Alexander, who was called Epiphanes, son of Antiochus, came up and took Ptolemais. He was accepted and began to reign there. [2]When King Demetrius heard of it, he mustered a very large army and marched out to engage him in combat. [3]Demetrius sent a letter to Jonathan written in peaceful terms, to pay him honor; [4]for he said: "Let us be the first to make peace with him, before he makes peace with Alexander against us, [5]since he will remember all the wrongs we have done to him, his brothers, and his nation."

[6]So Demetrius authorized Jonathan, as his ally, to gather an army and procure arms; and he ordered that the hostages in the citadel be released to him. [7]Accordingly Jonathan went up to Jerusalem and read the letter to all the people. The men in the citadel [8]were struck with fear when they heard that the king had given him authority to gather an army. [9]They released the hostages to Jonathan, and he gave them back to their parents.[n] [10]Thereafter Jonathan dwelt in Jerusalem, and began to build and restore the city. [11]He ordered the workmen to build the walls and encircle Mount Zion with square stones for its fortification, which they did. [12]The foreigners in the strongholds that Bacchides had built,

took flight; [13]each one of them left his place and returned to his own country. [14]Only in Beth-zur did some remain of those who had abandoned the law and the commandments, for they used it as a place of refuge.

Jonathan Supports Alexander. [15]King Alexander heard of the promises that Demetrius had made to Jonathan; he was also told of the battles and valiant deeds of Jonathan and his brothers and the troubles that they had endured. [16]He said, "Shall we ever find another man like him? Let us now make him our friend and ally." [17]So he sent Jonathan a letter written in these terms: [18]"King Alexander sends greetings to his brother Jonathan. [19]We have heard of you, that you are a mighty warrior and worthy to be our friend. [20]We have therefore appointed you today to be high priest of your nation; you are to be called the King's Friend, and you are to look after our interests and preserve amity with us." He also sent him a purple robe and a crown of gold.[o]

[21]Jonathan put on the sacred vestments in the seventh month of the year one hundred and sixty at the feast of Booths,* and he gathered an army and procured many arms. [22]When Demetrius heard of these things, he was distressed and said: [23]"Why have we allowed Alexander to get ahead of us by gaining the friendship of the Jews and thus strengthening himself? [24]I too will write them conciliatory words and offer dignities and gifts, so that they may be an aid to me."

[25]So he sent them this message: "King Demetrius sends greetings to the Jewish nation. [26]We have heard how you have kept the treaty with us and continued in our friendship and not gone over to our enemies, and we are glad. [27]Continue, therefore, to keep faith with us, and we will reward you with favors in return for what you do in our

---

9, 73: Began to judge: exercise the governing authority as in the book of Judges. With Jerusalem and the garrison towns (v 50) firmly in Seleucid hands, Jonathan's freedom of action was greatly restricted. Michmash, southeast of Bethel, famous for the exploit of the former Jonathan, son of Saul; cf 1 Sm 14.

10, 1: The year one hundred and sixty: 152 B.C. Alexander . . . Antiochus: Alexander Balas claimed to be a son of Antiochus IV. He had the backing of the Romans, who had never forgiven Demetrius for becoming king without their permission. The latter meanwhile had become unpopular with his

own people as well as with the Jews.

10, 21: Jonathan . . . feast of Booths: Jonathan began to discharge the office of high priest October 23-30, 152 B.C. For seven years after the death of Alcimus there had been no high priest in Jerusalem. It was taken for granted that the king, though a Gentile, had the power to appoint one. The Maccabees, though a priestly family, were not of the line of Zadok, and some in Israel regarded Jonathan's tenure as a usurpation.

n: 1 Mc 9, 53.   *o:* 1 Mc 2, 18.

Jonathan and the Syrian Pretenders

Jonathan acknowledged the authority of the Syrian king when it worked to his advantage (10, 6) Then Alexander made Jonathan a better offer: He appointed him high priest (10, 20). Jonathan was not a legitimate high priest any more than Menelaus had been, but he accepted the office from a king whose own legitimacy was questionable. Many scholars think that Jonathan's acceptance of the high priesthood caused the Dead Sea sect to break away from the Jerusalem temple and its cult, and that he is the figure who is called "The Wicked Priest" in the Pesher (commentary) on Habakkuk from the Dead Sea Scrolls. The destruction of the temple of Dagon and those who had sought asylum there (v. 84) was in violation of all law and custom in the ancient world. Presumably 1 Maccabees regards the action as justifiable because the temple was pagan. Even while Jonathan fraternizes with the Gentile kings, he is still represented as hostile to pagan religion.

behalf. [28]We will grant you many exemptions and will bestow gifts on you.

[29]"I now free you, as I also exempt all the Jews, from the tribute, the salt tax, and the crown levies.[p] [30q]Instead of collecting the third of the grain and the half of the fruit of the trees that should be my share, I renounce the right from this day forward. Neither now nor in the future will I collect them from the land of Judah or from the three districts annexed from Samaria.[*] [31]Let Jerusalem and her territory, her tithes and her tolls, be sacred and free from tax. [32]I also yield my authority over the citadel in Jerusalem, and I transfer it to the high priest, that he may put in it such men as he shall choose to guard it. [33]Every one of the Jews who has been carried into captivity from the land of Judah into any part of my kingdom I set at liberty without ransom; and let all their taxes, even those on their cattle, be canceled. [34]Let all feast days, sabbaths, new moon festivals, appointed days, and the three days that precede each feast day, and the three days that follow, be days of immunity and exemption for every Jew in my kingdom. [35]Let no man have authority to exact payment from them or to molest any of them in any matter.

[36]"Let thirty thousand Jews be enrolled in the king's army and allowances be given them, as is due to all the king's soldiers. [37]Let some of them be stationed in the king's principal strongholds, and of these let some be given positions of trust in the affairs of the kingdom. Let their superiors and their rulers be taken from among them, and let them follow their own laws, as the king has commanded in the land of Judah.

[38]"Let the three districts that have been added to Judea from the province of Samaria be incorporated with Judea so that they may be under one man and obey no other authority than the high priest. [39]Ptolemais and its confines I give as a present to the sanctuary in Jerusalem for the necessary expenses of the sanctuary. [40]I make a yearly personal grant of fifteen thousand silver shekels out of the royal revenues, from appropriate places. [41]All the additional funds that the officials did not hand over as they had done in the first years, shall henceforth be handed over for the services of the temple. [42]Moreover, the dues of five thousand silver shekels that used to be taken from the revenue of the sanctuary every year shall be canceled, since these funds belong to the priests who perform the services. [43]Whoever takes refuge in the temple of Jerusalem or in any of its precincts, because of money he owes the king, or because of any other debt, shall be released, together with all the goods he possesses in my kingdom. [44]The cost of rebuilding and restoring the structures of the sanctuary shall be covered out of the royal revenue. [45]Likewise the cost of building

10, 30: The three districts annexed from Samaria: mentioned by name in 1 Mc 11, 34. The present Greek text, by a scribal error, has added "and Galilee" after "Samaria."

p: 1 Mc 11, 28f. 35.   q: 1 Mc 11, 28. 34.

the walls of Jerusalem and fortifying it all around, and of building walls in Judea, shall be donated from the royal revenue."

⁴⁶When Jonathan and the people heard these words, they neither believed nor accepted them, for they remembered the great evil that Demetrius had done in Israel, and how sorely he had afflicted them. ⁴⁷They therefore decided in favor of Alexander, for he had been the first to address them peaceably, and they remained his allies for the rest of his life.

⁴⁸King Alexander gathered together a large army and encamped opposite Demetrius. ⁴⁹The two kings joined battle, and when the army of Demetrius fled, Alexander pursued him, and overpowered his soldiers. ⁵⁰He pressed the battle hard until sunset, and Demetrius fell that day.

Treaty of Ptolemy and Alexander. ⁵¹Alexander sent ambassadors to Ptolemy, king of Egypt, with this message: ⁵²"Now that I have returned to my realm, taken my seat on the throne of my fathers, and established my rule by crushing Demetrius and gaining control of my country— ⁵³for I engaged him in battle, defeated him and his army, and recovered the royal throne— ⁵⁴let us now establish friendship with each other. Give me your daughter for my wife; and as your son-in-law, I will give to you and to her gifts worthy of you."

⁵⁵King Ptolemy answered in these words: "Happy the day on which you returned to the land of your fathers and took your seat on their royal throne! ⁵⁶I will do for you what you have written; but meet me in Ptolemais, so that we may see each other, and I will become your father-in-law as you have proposed."

⁵⁷So Ptolemy with his daughter Cleopatra* set out from Egypt and came to Ptolemais in the year one hundred and sixty-two. ⁵⁸There King Alexander met him, and Ptolemy gave him his daughter Cleopatra in marriage. Their wedding was celebrated at Ptolemais with great splendor according to the custom of kings.

⁵⁹King Alexander also wrote to Jonathan to come and meet him. ⁶⁰So he went with pomp to Ptolemais, where he met the two kings and gave them and their friends silver and gold and many gifts and thus won their favor.ʳ ⁶¹Some pestilent Israelites, transgressors of the law, united against him to accuse him, but the king paid no heed to them. ⁶²He ordered Jonathan to be divested of his ordinary garments and to be clothed in royal purple; and so it was done. ⁶³The king also had him seated at his side. He said to his magistrates: "Go with him to the center of the city and make a proclamation that no one is to bring charges against him on any grounds or be troublesome to him in any way."

⁶⁴ˢWhen his accusers saw the honor paid to him in the proclamation, and the purple with which he was clothed, they all fled. ⁶⁵The king also honored him by numbering him among his Chief Friends and made him military commander and governor of the province. ⁶⁶So Jonathan returned in peace and happiness to Jerusalem.

Victory over Apollonius. ⁶⁷In the year one hundred and sixty-five,* Demetrius, son of Demetrius, came from Crete to the land of his fathers. ⁶⁸When King Alexander heard of it he was greatly troubled, and returned to Antioch. ⁶⁹Demetrius appointed Apollonius governor of Coelesyria. Having gathered a large army, Apollonius pitched his camp at Jamnia. From there he sent this message to Jonathan the high priest:

⁷⁰"You are the only one who resists us. I am laughed at and put to shame on your account. Why are you displaying power against us in the mountains? ⁷¹If you have confidence in your forces, come down now to us in the plain, and let us test each other's strength there; the city forces are on my side. ⁷²Inquire and learn who I am and who the others are who are helping me. Men say that you cannot make a stand against us because your fathers were twice put to flight in their own land. ⁷³Now you too will be unable to withstand our cavalry and such a force as

---

10, 57: Cleopatra: Cleopatra Thea, then about fifteen years old. She later married Demetrius II, and later still, his brother Antiochus VII. The year one hundred and sixty-two. 151/150 B.C.

10, 67: The year one hundred and sixty-five: 147 B.C. Demetrius: Demetrius II Nicator.

---

r: 1 Mc 2, 18.   s: 64f: 1 Mc 2, 18; 11, 27.

this in the plain, where there is not a stone or a pebble or a place to flee."

[74]When Jonathan heard the message of Apollonius, he was roused. Choosing ten thousand men, he set out from Jerusalem, and Simon his brother joined him to help him. [75]He pitched camp near Joppa, but the men in the city shut him out because Apollonius had a garrison there. When the Jews besieged it, [76]the men of the city became afraid and opened the gates, and so Jonathan took possession of Joppa.*

[77]When Apollonius heard of it, he drew up three thousand horsemen and an innumerable infantry. He marched on Azotus as though he were going on through the country, but at the same time he advanced into the plain, because he had such a large number of horsemen to rely on. [78]Jonathan followed him to Azotus, and they engaged in battle. [79]Apollonius, however, had left a thousand cavalry in hiding behind them. [80]When Jonathan discovered that there was an ambush behind him, his army was surrounded. From morning until evening they showered his men with arrows. [81]But his men held their ground, as Jonathan had commanded, whereas the enemy's horses became tired out. [82]When the horsemen were exhausted, Simon attacked the phalanx, overwhelmed it and put it to flight. [83]The horsemen too were scattered over the plain. The enemy fled to Azotus and entered Beth-dagon, the temple of their idol, to save themselves. [84]But Jonathan burned and plundered Azotus with its neighboring towns, and destroyed by fire both the temple of Dagon and the men who had taken refuge in it.[t] [85]Those who fell by the sword, together with those who were burned alive, came to about eight thousand men. [86]Then Jonathan left there and pitched his camp at Ashkalon, and the people of that city came out to meet him with great pomp. [87]He and his men then returned to Jerusalem, laden with much booty. [88]When King Alexander heard of these events, he accorded new honors to Jonathan. [89]He sent him a gold buckle, such as is usually given to King's Kinsmen;* he also gave him Ekron and all its territory as a possession.

CHAPTER 11

See RG 163

Alliance of Demetrius and Ptolemy.
[1]The king of Egypt gathered his forces, as numerous as the sands of the seashore, and many ships; and he sought by deceit to take Alexander's kingdom and add it to his own. [2]He entered Syria with peaceful words, and the people in the cities opened their gates to welcome him, as King Alexander had ordered them to do, since Ptolemy was his father-in-law. [3]But when Ptolemy entered the cities, he stationed garrison troops in each one. [4]When he reached Azotus, he was shown the temple of Dagon destroyed by fire, Azotus and its suburbs demolished, corpses lying about, and the charred bodies of those burned by Jonathan in the war and stacked up along his route.[u] [5]To prejudice the king against Jonathan, he was told what the latter had done; but the king said nothing. [6]Jonathan met the king with pomp at Joppa, and they greeted each other and spent the night there. [7]Jonathan accompanied the king as far as the river called Eleutherus* and then returned to Jerusalem.

[8]Plotting evil against Alexander, King Ptolemy took possession of the cities along the seacoast as far as Seleucia-by-the-Sea.* [9]He sent ambassadors to King Demetrius, saying: "Come, let us make a pact with each other; I will give you my daughter whom Alexander has married, and you shall reign over your father's kingdom. [10]I regret that I gave him my daughter, for he has sought to kill me."* [11]His real reason for accusing

---

10, 76: Joppa: about forty miles northwest of Jerusalem. For the first time the Maccabees took possession of a seaport; nominally it was on behalf of King Alexander.

10, 89: Kinsmen: a class higher than Chief Friends.

11, 7: Eleutherus: modern Nahr el-Kebir, the northern border of modern Lebanon; in the second century B.C. the northern limit of Coelesyria.

11, 8: Seleucia-by-the-Sea: at the mouth of the Orontes,

the port city of Antioch.

11, 10: I regret . . . to kill me: according to Josephus, Ammonius, a friend of Alexander, had tried to assassinate Ptolemy, and the latter claimed that Alexander was the instigator, thus calumniating him to gain his kingdom (v 11).

t: 1 Mc 11, 4; 1 Sm 5, 2-5.   u: 1 Mc 10, 84.

Dynastic Struggles

In ch 11, the king of Egypt was Ptolemy VI Philometor, who was known for his sympathy to the Jews, and who allowed the exiled High Priest Onias IV to build a temple at Leontopolis in Egypt. His campaign in Asia is of interest to 1 Maccabees, because it led to the death of Alexander Epiphanes, who had been Jonathan's patron.

Alexander, however, was that he coveted Alexander's kingdom. [12]After taking his daughter away and giving her to Demetrius, Ptolemy broke with Alexander; their enmity became open. [13]Then Ptolemy entered Antioch and assumed the crown of Asia; he thus wore two crowns on his head, that of Egypt and that of Asia.

Deaths of Alexander and Ptolemy. [14]King Alexander was in Cilicia at that time, because the people of that region had revolted. [15]When Alexander heard the news, he came to challenge Ptolemy in battle. Ptolemy marched out and met him with a strong force and put him to flight. [16]Alexander fled to Arabia to seek protection. King Ptolemy's triumph was complete [17]when the Arab Zabdiel cut off Alexander's head and sent it to Ptolemy. [18]But three days later King Ptolemy himself died, and his men in the fortified cities were killed by the inhabitants of the strongholds. [19]Thus Demetrius became king in the year one hundred and sixty-seven.[*]

Pact with Demetrius. [20]At that time Jonathan gathered together the men of Judea to attack the citadel in Jerusalem, and they set up many machines against it. [21]Some transgressors of the law, enemies of their own nation, went to the king and informed him that Jonathan was besieging the citadel. [22]When Demetrius heard this, he was furious, and set out immediately for Ptolemais. He wrote to Jonathan to discontinue the siege and to meet him for a conference at Ptolemais as soon as possible.

[23]On hearing this, Jonathan ordered the siege to continue. He selected some elders and priests of Israel and exposed himself to danger [24]by going to the king at Ptolemais. He brought with him silver, gold apparel, and many other presents, and found favor with the king. [25]Although some impious men of his own nation brought charges against him, [26]the king treated him just as his predecessors had done and showed him great honor in the presence of all his Friends. [27]He confirmed him in the high priesthood and in all the honors he had previously held, and had him enrolled among his Chief Friends.

[28]Jonathan asked the king to exempt Judea and the three districts of Samaria from tribute, promising him in return three hundred talents.[v] [29]The king agreed and wrote the following letter to Jonathan about all these matters:

[30w]"King Demetrius sends greetings to his brother[*] Jonathan and to the Jewish nation. [31]We are sending you, for your information, a copy of the letter that we wrote to Lasthenes[*] our kinsman concerning you. [32]'King Demetrius sends greetings to his father Lasthenes. [33]Because of the good will they show us, we have decided to bestow benefits on the Jewish nation, who are our friends and who observe their obligations to us. [34x]Therefore we confirm their possession, not only of the territory of Judea, but also of the three districts of Aphairema,[*] Lydda, and Ramathaim. These districts, together with all their dependencies, were transferred from Samaria

---

11, 19: The year one hundred and sixty-seven: 146/145 B.C. The two deaths (vv 17-18) occurred in the summer of 145 B.C.

11, 30: Brother: this title and father in v 32 are honorific titles used of the Kinsmen.

11, 31: Lasthenes: leader of the mercenary troops who had come with Demetrius from Crete. He was now the young king's chief minister and was apparently responsible for the disastrous policy (v 38) of disbanding the national army.

11, 34: Aphairema: the Ophrah of Jos 18, 23; 1 Sm 23, 6; the Ephron of 2 Chr 13, 19; and the Ephraim of Jn 11, 54—modern et-Taiyibeh, five miles northeast of Bethel. Lydda: the Lod of the post-exilic Jews (Ez 2, 33; Neh 11, 35) and the hometown of Aeneas, who was cured by Peter (Acts 9, 32ff).

v: 1 Mc 10, 29; 11, 34.   *w:* 30-37: 1 Mc 10, 26-45.   *x:* 34f: 1 Mc 10, 29; 11, 28.

Jonathan sent troops to suppress a revolt against Demetrius in Antioch (11, 47). Jewish soldiers often acted as mercenaries in the service of foreign kings. This action in turn often led to anti-Jewish sentiment on the part of the opponents of those kings.

to Judea in favor of all those who offer sacrifices for us in Jerusalem instead of paying the royal taxes that formerly the king received from them each year from the produce of the soil and the fruit of the trees. *35*From this day on we grant them release from payment of all other things that would henceforth be due to us, that is, of tithes and tribute and of the tax on the salt pans and the crown tax. *36*Henceforth none of these provisions shall ever be revoked. *37*Be sure, therefore, to have a copy of these instructions made and given to Jonathan, that it may be displayed in a conspicuous place on the holy hill.' "

The Intrigue of Trypho. *38*When King Demetrius saw that the land was peaceful under his rule and that he had no opposition, he dismissed his entire army, every man to his home, except the foreign troops which he had hired from the islands of the nations. So all the soldiers who had served under his predecessors hated him. *39*When a certain Trypho, who had previously belonged to Alexander's party, saw that all the troops were grumbling at Demetrius, he went to Imalkue the Arab, who was bringing up Alexander's young son Antiochus.*y* *40*Trypho kept urging Imalkue to hand over the boy to him, that he might make him king in his father's place. During his stay there of many days, he told him of all that Demetrius had done and of the hatred that his soldiers had for him.

Jonathan Aids Demetrius. *41*Meanwhile Jonathan sent the request to King Demetrius to withdraw his troops from the citadel of Jerusalem and from the other strongholds, for they were constantly hostile to Israel. *42*Demetrius, in turn, sent this word to Jonathan: "I will not only do this for you and your nation, but I will greatly honor you and your nation when I find the opportunity. *43*Do me

the favor, therefore, of sending men to fight for me, because all my troops have revolted."

*44*So Jonathan sent three thousand good fighting men to him at Antioch. When they came to the king, he was delighted over their arrival, *45*for the populace, one hundred and twenty thousand strong, had massed in the center of the city in an attempt to kill him. *46*But he took refuge in the palace, while the populace gained control of the main streets and began to fight. *47*So the king called the Jews to his aid. They all rallied around him and spread out through the city. On that day they killed about a hundred thousand men in the city, *48*which, at the same time, they set on fire and plundered on a large scale. Thus they saved the king's life. *49*When the populace saw that the Jews held the city at their mercy, they lost courage and cried out to the king in supplication, *50*"Give us your terms and let the Jews stop attacking us and our city." So they threw down their arms and made peace. *51*The Jews thus gained glory in the eyes of the king and all his subjects, and they became renowned throughout his kingdom. Finally they returned to Jerusalem with much spoil.

*52*But when King Demetrius was sure of his royal throne, and the land was peaceful under his rule, *53*he broke all his promises and became estranged from Jonathan. Instead of rewarding Jonathan for all the favors he had received from him, he caused him much trouble.

Alliance with Trypho. *54*After this, Trypho returned and brought with him the young boy Antiochus, who became king and wore the royal crown.*z* *55*All the soldiers whom Demetrius had discharged rallied around Antiochus and fought against Demetrius, who was routed and fled. *56*Trypho captured the elephants and occupied

It is ten miles southeast of Joppa. Ramathaim: the Ramathaim-zophim of 1 Sm 1, 1, and the Arimathea of Mt 27, 57—modern Rentis, nine miles northeast of Lydda.

y: 1 Mc 12, 39.   *z:* 1 Mc 11, 39; 12, 39.

Antioch. [57]Then young Antiochus wrote to Jonathan: "I confirm you in the high priesthood and appoint you ruler over the four districts and wish you to be one of the King's Friends." [58]He also sent him gold dishes and a dinner service, gave him the right to drink from gold cups, to dress in royal purple, and to wear a gold buckle.[a] [59]Likewise, he made Jonathan's brother Simon governor of the region from the Ladder of Tyre* to the frontier of Egypt.

[60]Jonathan set out and traveled through West-of-Euphrates* and its cities, and all the forces of Syria espoused his cause as allies. When he arrived at Ashkalon, the citizens welcomed him with pomp. [61]But when he set out for Gaza, the people of Gaza locked their gates against him. So he besieged it and burned and plundered its suburbs. [62]Then the people of Gaza appealed to him for mercy, and he granted them peace. He took the sons of their chief men as hostages and sent them to Jerusalem. He then traveled on through the province as far as Damascus.

War with Demetrius. [63]Jonathan heard that the generals of Demetrius had come with a strong force to Kadesh in Galilee, intending to remove him from office. [64]So he went to meet them, leaving his brother Simon in the province. [65]Simon besieged Beth-zur, attacked it for many days, and blockaded the inhabitants. [66]When they sued for peace, he granted it to them. He expelled them from the city, took possession of it, and put a garrison there.

[67]Meanwhile, Jonathan and his army pitched their camp near the waters of Gennesaret, and at daybreak they went to the plain of Hazor.* [68]There, in front of him on the plain, was the army of the foreigners. This army attacked him in the open, having first detached an ambush against him in the mountains. [69]Then the men in ambush rose out of their places and joined in the battle. [70]All of Jonathan's men fled; no one stayed

except the army commanders Mattathias, son of Absalom, and Judas, son of Chalphi. [71]Jonathan tore his clothes, threw earth on his head, and prayed. [72]Then he went back to the combat and so overwhelmed the enemy that they took to flight. [73]Those of his men who were running away saw it and returned to him; and with him they pursued the enemy as far as their camp in Kadesh, where they pitched their own camp. [74]Three thousand of the foreign troops fell on that day. Then Jonathan returned to Jerusalem.

CHAPTER 12

Alliances with Rome and Sparta. [1]When Jonathan saw that the times favored him, he sent selected men to Rome to confirm and renew his friendship with the Romans.[b] [2]He also sent letters to Sparta and other places for the same purpose.

[3]After reaching Rome, the men entered the senate chamber and said, "The high priest Jonathan and the Jewish people have sent us to renew the earlier friendship and alliance between you and them." [4]The Romans gave them letters addressed to the authorities in the various places, requesting them to provide the envoys with safe conduct to the land of Judah.

[5]This is a copy of the letter that Jonathan wrote to the Spartans: [6]"Jonathan the high priest, the senate of the nation, the priests, and the rest of the Jewish people send greetings to their brothers the Spartans. [7]Long ago a letter was sent to the high priest Onias* from Arius, who then reigned over you, stating that you are our brothers, as the attached copy shows.[c] [8]Onias welcomed the envoy with honor and received the letter, which clearly referred to alliance and friendship. [9][d]Though we have no need of these things, since we have for our encouragement the sacred books that are in our possession,* [10]we have ventured to send word to you for the renewal of brotherhood and

---

11, 59: Ladder of Tyre: modern Ras en-Naquurah, on the border between Lebanon and Israel, where the mountains reach the sea, so that the coastal road must ascend in a series of steps.

11, 60: West-of-Euphrates: refers here to the territory of Palestine and Coelesyria, but not Upper Syria; cf 1 Mc 3, 32; 7, 8.

11, 67: Plain of Hazor: the site of the ancient Canaanite city (Jos 11, 10), ten miles north of the Lake of Gennesaret.

12, 7: Onias: Onias I, high priest from 323–300 or 290 B.C. Arius: Arius I, king from 309 to 265 B.C. The letter was sent long ago, i.e., a century and a half before.

12, 9: The sacred books . . . in our possession: a reference to "the law, the prophets and other books," as mentioned in the Prologue to Sirach (v 1), after 132 B.C.

a: 1 Mc 2, 18.   b: 1 Mc 8, 17.   c: 1 Mc 12, 20-23.   d: Rom 15, 4.

The Capture of Jonathan

Jonathan's remarkable success in the world of Hellenistic politics ultimately led to his downfall (12, 39–53). He was too powerful to be ignored by an ambitious climber like Trypho. His fatal mistake was unwarranted trust. The Pesher (commentary) on Habakkuk from the Dead Sea Scrolls says that God delivered the Wicked Priest into the hands of his enemies to destroy him. Many scholars think the reference is to Jonathan. If this is indeed the case, it gives an evaluation of Jonathan that is very different from that of 1 Maccabees.

friendship, so as not to become strangers to you altogether; a long time has passed since your mission to us. [11]We, on our part, have never ceased to remember you in the sacrifices and prayers that we offer on our feasts and other appropriate days, as it is right and proper to remember brothers. [12]We likewise rejoice in your renown. [13]But many hardships and wars have beset us, and the kings around us have attacked us. [14]We did not wish to be troublesome to you and to the rest of our allies and friends in these wars; [15]with the help of Heaven for our support, we have been saved from our enemies, and they have been humbled. [16]So we have chosen Numenius, son of Antiochus, and Antipater, son of Jason, and we have sent them to the Romans to renew our former friendship and alliance with them.[e] [17]We have also ordered them to come to you and greet you, and to deliver to you our letter about the renewal of our brotherhood. [18]Therefore kindly send us an answer on this matter."

[19]This is a copy of the letter that was sent to Onias: [20f]"Arius, king of the Spartans, sends greetings to Onias the high priest. [21]A document has been found stating that the Spartans and the Jews are brothers; both nations descended from Abraham. [22]Now that we have learned this, kindly write to us about your welfare. [23]We, on our part, are informing you that your cattle and your possessions are ours, and ours are yours. We have, therefore, given orders that you should be told of this."

Demetrius Repelled. [24]Jonathan heard that the generals of Demetrius had returned to attack him with a stronger army than before. [25]He set out from Jerusalem and went into the country of Hamath[*] to meet them, giving them no time to enter his province. [26]The spies he had sent into their camp came back and reported that the enemy had made ready to attack the Jews that very night. [27]Therefore, when the sun set, Jonathan ordered his men to be on guard and to remain armed, ready for combat, throughout the night. He also set outposts all around the camp. [28]When the enemy heard that Jonathan and his men were ready for battle, their hearts sank with fear and dread. They lighted fires and then withdrew. [29]But because Jonathan and his men were watching the lights burning, they did not know what had happened until morning. [30]Then Jonathan pursued them, but he could not overtake them, for they had crossed the river Eleutherus. [31]So Jonathan turned aside against the Arabs who are called Zabadeans, overwhelming and plundering them. [32]Then he marched on to Damascus and traversed that whole region.

[33]Simon also set out and went as far as Ashkalon and its neighboring strongholds. He then turned to Joppa and occupied it, [34]for he heard that its men had intended to hand over this stronghold to the supporters of Demetrius. He left a garrison there to guard it.

[35]When Jonathan returned, he assembled the elders of the people, and with them he made plans for building strongholds in Judea, [36]for making the walls of Jerusalem still higher, and for erecting a high barrier between

12, 25: Country of Hamath: the Seleucid territory of Upper Syria northeast of Coelesyria and separated from it by the Eleutherus River. The latter territory was under the command of Jonathan (1 Mc 11, 59f).

e: 1 Mc 14, 22; 15, 15.   f: 20-23: 1 Mc 12, 6f.

the citadel and the city, that would isolate the citadel and so prevent its garrison from commerce with the city. [37]The people therefore worked together on building up the city, for part of the east wall above the ravine had collapsed. The quarter called Chaphenatha was also repaired. [38]Simon likewise built up Adida in the Shephelah, and strengthened its fortifications by providing them with gates and bars.

Capture of Jonathan. [39]Trypho was determined to become king of Asia, assume the crown, and do away with King Antiochus.[g] [40]But he was afraid that Jonathan would not permit him, but would fight against him. Looking for a way to seize and kill him, he set out and reached Beth-shan. [41]Jonathan marched out against him with forty thousand picked fighting men and came to Beth-shan. [42]But when Trypho saw that Jonathan had arrived with a large army, he was afraid to offer him violence. [43]Instead, he received him with honor, introduced him to all his friends, and gave him presents. He also ordered his friends and soldiers to obey him as they would himself. [44]Then he said to Jonathan: "Why have you put all your soldiers to so much trouble when we are not at war? [45]Pick out a few men to stay with you, send the rest back home, and then come with me to Ptolemais. I will hand it over to you together with other strongholds and their garrisons, as well as the officials, then I will leave and go home. That is why I came here."

[46]Jonathan believed him and did as he said. He dismissed his troops, and they returned to the land of Judah. [47]But he kept with him three thousand men, of whom he sent two thousand to Galilee while one thousand accompanied him. [48]Then as soon as Jonathan had entered Ptolemais, the men of the city closed the gates and seized him; all who had entered with him, they killed with the sword.

[49]Trypho sent soldiers and cavalry to Galilee and the Great Plain* to destroy all Jonathan's men. [50]These, upon learning that Jonathan had been captured and his companions killed, encouraged one another and went out in compact body ready to fight.

[51]As their pursuers saw that they were ready to fight for their lives, they turned back. [52]Thus all these men of Jonathan came safely into the land of Judah. They mourned over Jonathan and his men, and were in great fear, and all Israel fell into deep mourning.

[53]All the nations round about sought to destroy them. They said, "Now that they have no leader to help them, let us make war on them and wipe out their memory from among men."[h]

V: Simon, High Priest and Ethnarch

CHAPTER 13

See RG 163

Simon, Leader of the Jews. [1]When Simon heard that Trypho was gathering a large army to invade and ravage the land of Judah, [2]and saw that the people were in dread and terror, he went up to Jerusalem. There he assembled the people [3]and exhorted them in these words: "You know what I, my brothers, and my father's house have done for the laws and the sanctuary; what battles and disasters we have been through. [4]It was for the sake of these, for the sake of Israel, that all my brothers have perished, and I alone am left. [5]Far be it from me, then, to save my own life in any time of distress, for I am not better than my brothers. [6]Rather will I avenge my nation and the sanctuary, as well as your wives and children, for all the nations out of hatred have united to destroy us."[i]

[7]As the people heard these words, their spirit was rekindled. [8]They shouted in reply: "You are our leader in place of your brothers Judas and Jonathan. [9]Fight our battles, and we will do everything that you tell us." [10]So Simon mustered all the men able to fight, and quickly completing the walls of Jerusalem, fortified it on every side. [11]He sent Jonathan, son of Absalom, to Joppa with a large force; Jonathan drove out the occupants and remained there.

Deceit and Treachery of Trypho. [12]Then Trypho moved from Ptolemais with a large

---

12, 49: The Great Plain: of Beth-shan (v 41), where Jonathan's disbanded troops remained.

g: 1 Mc 11, 39f. 54f.   *h:* 1 Mc 5, 2; 13, 6.   *i:* 1 Mc 5, 2; 12, 53.

army to invade the land of Judah, bringing Jonathan with him as prisoner. *13*But Simon pitched his camp at Adida, facing the plain. *14*When Trypho learned that Simon had succeeded his brother Jonathan, and that he intended to fight him, he sent envoys to him with this message: *15*"We have detained your brother Jonathan on account of the money that he owed the royal treasury in connection with the offices that he held. *16*Therefore, if you send us a hundred talents of silver, and two of his sons as hostages to guarantee that when he is set free he will not revolt against us, we will release him."

*17*Although Simon knew that they were speaking deceitfully to him, he gave orders to get the money and the boys, for fear of provoking much hostility among the people, who might say *18*that Jonathan perished because Simon would not send Trypho the money and the boys. *19*So he sent the boys and the hundred talents; but Trypho broke his promise and would not let Jonathan go. *20**Next he began to invade and ravage the country. His troops went around by the road that leads to Adora, but Simon and his army moved along opposite him everywhere he went. *21*The men in the citadel sent messengers to Trypho, urging him to come to them by way of the desert, and to send them provisions. *22*Although Trypho got all his cavalry ready to go, there was a heavy fall of snow that night, and he could not go. So he left for Gilead. *23*When he was approaching Baskama,* he had Jonathan killed and buried there. *24*Then Trypho returned to his own country.

Jonathan's Tomb. *25*Simon sent for the remains of his brother Jonathan, and buried him in Modein, the city of his fathers. *26*All Israel bewailed him with solemn lamentation, mourning over him for many days. *27*Then Simon erected over the tomb of his father and his brothers a monument of stones, polished front and back, and raised high enough to be seen at a distance. *28*He set up seven pyramids facing one another for his father and his mother and his four brothers. *29*For the pyramids he devised a setting of big columns, on which he carved suits of armor as a perpetual memorial, and next to the armor he placed carved ships, which could be seen by all who sailed the sea. *30*This tomb which he built at Modein is there to the present day.

Pact between Simon and Demetrius. *31*Trypho dealt treacherously with the young King Antiochus. He killed him *32*and assumed the kingship in his place, putting on the crown of Asia. Thus he brought much evil on the land. *33*Simon, on his part, built up the strongholds of Judea, strengthening their fortifications with high towers, thick walls, and gates with bars, and he stored up provisions in the fortresses. *34*Simon also sent chosen men to King Demetrius with the request that he grant the land a release from taxation, for all that Trypho did was to plunder the land. *35*In reply, King Demetrius sent him the following letter:

36"King Demetrius sends greetings to Simon the high priest, the friend of kings, and to the elders and the Jewish people. *37*We have received the gold crown and the palm branch that you sent. We are willing to be on most peaceful terms with you and to write to our official to grant you release from tribute. *38*Whatever we have guaranteed to you remains in force, and the strongholds that you have built shall remain yours. *39*We remit any oversights and defaults incurred up to now, as well as the crown tax that you owe. Any other tax that may have been collected in Jerusalem shall no longer be collected there. *40*If any of you are qualified for enrollment in our service, let them be enrolled. Let there be peace between us."

*41*Thus in the year one hundred and seventy,* the yoke of the Gentiles was removed from Israel, *42*and the people began to write in their records and contracts, "In the first year of Simon, high priest, governor, and leader of the Jews."

Capture of Gazara and the Citadel. *43*In those days Simon besieged Gazara* and

---

13, 20f: The invaders made a wide flanking movement to invade Judea from the south. Adora was a few miles southwest of Beth-zur. They would avoid Beth-zur itself and other strongholds of the Maccabees by following the way of the desert.

13, 23: Baskama: northeast of the Sea of Galilee.

13, 41: The year one hundred and seventy: March, 142, to April, 141 B.C., by the temple calendar.

13, 43: Gazara: a key position in the Shephelah, fortified by Bacchides in 160 B.C.; cf 1 Mc 9, 52.

surrounded it with troops. He made a siege machine, pushed it up against the city, and attacked and captured one of the towers.[j] ⁴⁴The men who had been on the siege machine jumped down into the city and caused a great tumult there. ⁴⁵The men of the city, joined by their wives and children, went up on the wall, with their garments rent, and cried out in loud voices, begging Simon to grant them peace. ⁴⁶"Do not treat us according to our evil deeds," they said, "but according to your mercy."

⁴⁷So Simon came to terms with them and did not destroy them. He made them leave the city, however, and he purified the houses in which there were idols. Then he entered the city with hymns and songs of praise. ⁴⁸After removing from it everything that was impure, he settled there men who observed the law. He improved its fortifications and built himself a residence.

⁴⁹The men in the citadel in Jerusalem were prevented from going out into the country and back for the purchase of food; they suffered greatly from hunger, and many of them died of starvation. ⁵⁰They finally cried out to Simon for peace, and he gave them peace. He expelled them from the citadel and cleansed it of impurities. ⁵¹On the twenty-third day of the second month,* in the year one hundred and seventy-one, the Jews entered the citadel with shouts of jubilation, waving of palm branches, the music of harps and cymbals and lyres, and the singing of hymns and canticles, because a great enemy of Israel had been destroyed.[k] ⁵²Simon decreed that this day should be celebrated every year with rejoicing. He also strengthened the fortifications of the temple hill alongside the citadel, and he and his companions dwelt there. ⁵³Seeing that his son John* was now a grown man, Simon made him commander of all his soldiers, with his residence in Gazara.

CHAPTER 14

See RG 163

Capture of Demetrius. ¹In the year one hundred and seventy-two,* King Demetrius assembled his army and marched into Media to obtain help so that he could fight Trypho. ²When Arsaces,* king of Persia and Media, heard that Demetrius had invaded his territory, he sent one of his generals to take him alive. ³The general went forth and defeated the army of Demetrius; he captured him and brought him to Arsaces, who put him in prison.

Glory of Simon

⁴ The land was at rest all the days of
    Simon,
    who sought the good of his nation.
His people were delighted with his power
    and his magnificence throughout his
    reign.[l]
⁵ As his crowning glory he captured the
    port of Joppa
    and made it a gateway to the isles of
    the sea.
⁶ He enlarged the borders of his nation
    and gained control of the country.[m]
⁷ He took many enemies prisoners of war
    and made himself master of Gazara,
    Beth-zur, and the citadel.

He cleansed the citadel of its impurities;
    there was no one to withstand him.
⁸ The people cultivated their land in peace;
    the land yielded its produce
    and the trees of the field their fruit.[n]
⁹ Old men sat in the squares,
    all talking about the good times,
    while the young men wore the glorious
    apparel of war.[o]
¹⁰ He supplied the cities with food
    and equipped them with means of
    defense,

13, 51: The twenty-third day of the second month: June 3, 141 B.C.

13, 53: John: John Hyrcanus, who was to succeed his father as ruler and high priest; cf 1 Mc 16, 23f.

14, 1: The year one hundred and seventy-two: 141–140 B.C. The expedition began most probably in the spring of 140.

14, 2: Arsaces: Arsaces VI, also called Mithridates I, the

Parthian king (171–138 B.C.). Parthians had overrun Persia and now held Babylonia, both of which had hitherto belonged to the Seleucid empire. The Greeks and Macedonians in these countries had appealed to Demetrius for help.

j: 2 Mc 10, 32-38.   *k:* 1 Mc 1, 36.   *l:* 1 Mc 3, 3-9.   *m:* Ex 34, 24.   *n:* Zec 8, 12.   *o:* Zec 8, 4f.

> The gift sent to Rome (14, 25) was very substantial for a small nation, indicating a strong desire on the part of Simon for friendship with Rome.

till his glorious name reached the ends
of the earth.

[11] He brought peace to the land,
and Israel was filled with happiness.p

[12] Every man sat under his vine and his fig
tree,
with no one to disturb him.q

[13] No one was left to attack them in their
land;
the kings in those days were crushed.

[14] He strengthened all the lowly among his
people
and was zealous for the law;
he suppressed all the lawless and the
wicked.

[15] He made the temple splendid
and enriched its equipment.

Alliance with Rome and Sparta. [16]When
people heard in Rome and even in Sparta that
Jonathan had died, they were deeply grieved.[*]
[17]But when the Romans heard that his brother
Simon had been made high priest in his place
and was master of the country and the cities,
[18]they sent him inscribed tablets of bronze to
renew with him the friendship and alliance
that they had established with his brothers Judas and Jonathan.r [19]These were read before
the assembly in Jerusalem.

[20]This is a copy of the letter that the Spartans sent: "The rulers and the citizens of
Sparta send greetings to Simon the high
priest, the elders, the priests, and the rest of
the Jewish people, our brothers. [21]The envoys you sent to our people have informed us
of your glory and fame, and we were happy
that they came. [22]In accordance with what
they said we have recorded the following in
the public decrees: Since Numenius, son of
Antiochus, and Antipater, son of Jason, envoys of the Jews, have come to us to renew

their friendship with us.s [23]the people have
voted to receive the men with honor, and to
deposit a copy of their words in the public archives, so that the people of Sparta may have
a record of them. A copy of this decree has
been made for Simon the high priest."

[24]After this, Simon sent Numenius to
Rome with a great gold shield weighing a
thousand minas, to confirm the alliance with
the Romans.t

Decree of Honor. [25]When the people
heard of these things, they said, "How can
we thank Simon and his sons? [26]He and his
brothers and his father's house have stood
firm and repulsed Israel's enemies. They
have thus preserved its liberty." So they
made an inscription on bronze tablets, which
they affixed to pillars on Mount Zion. [27]The
following is a copy of the inscription:
"On the eighteenth day of Elul,[*] in the
year one hundred and seventy-two, that is,
the third year under Simon the high priest in
Asaramel, [28]in a great assembly of priests,
people, rulers of the nation, and elders of the
country, the following proclamation was
made:

[29]" 'Since there have often been wars in
our country, Simon, son of the priest Mattathias, descendant of Joarib, and his brothers
have put themselves in danger and resisted
the enemies of their nation, so that their sanctuary and law might be maintained, and they
have thus brought great glory to their nation.
[30]After Jonathan had rallied his nation and
become their high priest, he was gathered to
his kinsmen. [31]When the enemies of the Jews
sought to invade and devastate their country
and to lay hands on their temple, [32]Simon
rose up and fought for his nation, spending
large sums of his own money to equip the
men of his nation's armed forces and giving

14, 16: The embassy to Rome and Sparta was sent soon
after Simon's accession to power, and the replies were received before Demetrius' expedition (vv 1-3)—probably in
142 B.C.
14, 27: Eighteenth day of Elul: September 13, 140 B.C.

Asaramel: a Hebrew name meaning "court of the people of
God."

p: Lv 26, 6.   q: Mi 4, 4; Zec 3, 10.   r: Mc 8, 22   s: 1 Mc
12, 16; 15, 15.   t: 1 Mc 12, 16; 15, 15.

them their pay. [33]He fortified the cities of Judea, especially the frontier city of Beth-zur, where he stationed a garrison of Jewish soldiers, and where previously the enemy's arms had been stored. [34]He also fortified Joppa by the sea and Gazara on the border of Azotus, a place previously occupied by the enemy; these cities he resettled with Jews, and furnished them with all that was necessary for their restoration. [35]When the Jewish people saw Simon's loyalty and the glory he planned to bring to his nation, they made him their leader and high priest because of all he had accomplished and the loyalty and justice he had shown his nation. In every way he sought to exalt his people.

[36]" 'In his time and under his guidance they succeeded in driving the Gentiles out of their country, especially those in the City of David in Jerusalem, who had built for themselves a citadel from which they used to sally forth to defile the environs of the temple and inflict grave injury on its purity. [37]In this citadel he stationed Jewish soldiers, and he strengthened its fortifications for the defense of the land and the city, while he also raised the wall of Jerusalem to a greater height. [38]Consequently, King Demetrius confirmed him in the high priesthood, [39]umade him one of his Friends, and conferred the highest honors on him. [40]He had indeed heard that the Romans had addressed the Jews as friends, allies, and brothers and that they had received Simon's envoys with honor.

[41]" 'The Jewish people and their priest have, therefore, made the following decisions. Simon shall be their permanent leader and high priest until a true prophet arises. [42]He shall act as governor general over them, and shall have charge of the temple, to make regulations concerning its functions and concerning the country, its weapons and strongholds; [43]he shall be obeyed by all. All contracts made in the country shall be dated by his name. He shall have the right to wear royal purple and gold ornaments. [44]It shall not be lawful for any of the people or priests to nullify any of these decisions, or to contradict the orders given by him, or to convene an assembly in the country without his consent, to be clothed in royal purple or wear an official gold brooch. [45]Whoever acts otherwise or violates any of these prescriptions shall be liable to punishment.

[46]" 'All the people approved of granting Simon the right to act in accord with these decisions, [47]and Simon accepted and agreed to act as high priest, governor general, and ethnarch* of the Jewish people and priests and to exercise supreme authority over all.' "

[48]It was decreed that this inscription should be engraved on bronze tablets, to be set up in a conspicuous place in the precincts of the temple, [49]and that copies of it should be deposited in the treasury, where they would be available to Simon and his sons.

CHAPTER 15

See RG
163

Letter of Antiochus. [1]Antiochus,* son of King Demetrius, sent a letter from the islands of the sea to Simon, the priest and ethnarch of the Jews, and to all the nation, [2]which read as follows:

"King Antiochus sends greetings to Simon, the priest and ethnarch, and to the Jewish nation. [3]Whereas certain villains have gained control of the kingdom of my ancestors, I intend to reclaim it, that I may restore it to its former state. I have recruited a large number of mercenary troops and equipped warships [4]to make a landing in my country and take revenge on those who have ruined it and laid waste many cities in my realm.

[5]"Now, therefore, I confirm to you all the tax exemptions that the kings before me granted you and whatever other privileges they conferred on you. [6]I authorize you to coin your own money, as legal tender in your country. [7]Jerusalem and its temple shall be free. All the weapons you have prepared and all the strongholds you have built and now occupy shall remain in your possession. [8]All

---

14, 47: Ethnarch: a subaltern ruler over a racial group whose office needed confirmation by a higher authority within the empire.

15, 1: Antiochus: Antiochus VII Sidetes, son of Demetrius I, and younger brother of Demetrius II, now a prisoner of the Parthians. At the age of twenty he set out from the island of Rhodes to take his brother's place and drive out the usurper Trypho.

u: 39f: 1 Mc 2, 18.

debts, present or future, due to the royal treasury shall be canceled for you, now and for all time. ⁹When we recover our kingdom, we will greatly honor you and your nation and the temple, so that your glory will be manifest in all the earth."

¹⁰In the year one hundred and seventy-four,* Antiochus invaded the land of his ancestors, and all the troops rallied to him, so that few were left with Trypho. ¹¹Pursued by Antiochus, Trypho fled to Dor, by the sea,* ¹²realizing what a mass of troubles had come upon him now that his soldiers had deserted him. ¹³Antiochus encamped before Dor with a hundred and twenty thousand infantry and eight thousand horsemen. ¹⁴While he invested the city, his ships closed in along the coast, so that he blockaded it by land and sea and let no one go in or out.

Roman Alliance Renewed. ¹⁵Meanwhile, Numenius and his companions left Rome with letters such as this addressed to various kings and countries:ᵛ

¹⁶"Lucius,* Consul of the Romans, sends greetings to King Ptolemy. ¹⁷Certain envoys of the Jews, our friends and allies, have come to us to renew their earlier alliance of friendship. They had been sent by Simon the high priest and the Jewish people, ¹⁸and they brought with them a gold shield worth a thousand minas.ʷ ¹⁹Therefore we have decided to write to various kings and countries, that they are not to harm them, or wage war against them or their cities or their country, and are not to assist those who fight against them. ²⁰We have also decided to accept the shield from them. ²¹If, then, any troublemakers from their country take refuge with you, hand them over to Simon the high priest, so that he may punish them according to their law."

²²The consul sent similar letters to Kings Demetrius, Attalus,* Ariarthes and Arsaces; ²³to all the countries—Sampsames, Sparta, Delos, Myndos, Sicyon, Caria, Samos, Pamphylia, Lycia, Halicarnassus, Rhodes, Phaselis, Cos, Side, Aradus, Gortyna, Cnidus, Cyprus, and Cyrene. ²⁴A copy of the letter was also sent to Simon the high priest.

Hostility of Antiochus. ²⁵When King Antiochus was encamped before Dor, he assaulted it continuously both with troops and with the siege machines he had made. He blockaded Trypho by preventing anyone from going in or out. ²⁶Simon sent to Antiochus' support two thousand elite troops, together with gold and silver and much equipment. ²⁷But he refused to accept the aid; in fact, he broke all the agreements he had previously made with Simon and became hostile toward him.

²⁸He sent Athenobius, one of his Friends, to confer with Simon and say: "You are occupying Joppa and Gazara and the citadel of Jerusalem; these are cities of my kingdom. ²⁹You have laid waste their territories, done great harm to the land, and taken possession of many districts in my realm. ³⁰Therefore, give up the cities you have seized and the tribute money of the districts outside the territory of Judea of which you have taken possession; ³¹or instead, pay me five hundred talents of silver for the devastation you have caused and five hundred talents more for the tribute money of the cities. If you do not do this, we will come and make war on you."

³²So Athenobius, the king's Friend, came to Jerusalem, and on seeing the splendor of Simon's court, the gold and silver plate on the sideboard, and the rest of his rich display, he was amazed. When he gave him the king's message, ³³Simon said to him in reply:

"We have not seized any foreign land; what we took is not the property of others, but our ancestral heritage which for a time had been unjustly held by our enemies. ³⁴Now that we have the opportunity, we are holding on to the heritage of our ancestors. ³⁵As for Joppa and Gazara, which you demand, the men of these cities were doing great harm to our people and laying waste

---

15, 10: The year one hundred and seventy-four: 138 B.C.

15, 11: Dor, by the sea: a fortress on the Palestinian coast, fifteen miles south of Carmel.

15, 16: Lucius: perhaps Lucius Caecilius Metellus, consul in 142 B.C., or Lucius Calpurnius Piso, consul in 140–139 B.C. This document pertains to Simon's first year as leader.

15, 22: Attalus: Attalus II of Pergamum, reigned 159–138 B.C. Ariarthes: Ariarthes V of Cappadocia, reigned 162–130 B.C. Arsaces: see note on 1 Mc 14, 2.

v: 1 Mc 8, 17; 12, 16; 14, 22. 24.   w: 1 Mc 14, 24.

our country; however, we are willing to pay you a hundred talents for these cities."

³⁶Athenobius made no reply, but returned to the king in anger. When he told him of Simon's words, of his splendor, and of all he had seen, the king fell into a violent rage.

Victory over Cendebeus. ³⁷Trypho had gotten aboard a ship and escaped to Orthosia.* ³⁸Then the king appointed Cendebeus commander in chief of the seacoast, and gave him infantry and cavalry forces. ³⁹He ordered him to move his troops against Judea and to fortify Kedron* and strengthen its gates, so that he could launch attacks against the Jewish people. Meanwhile the king went in pursuit of Trypho. ⁴⁰When Cendebeus came to Jamnia, he began to harass the people and to make incursions into Judea, where he took people captive or massacred them. ⁴¹As the king ordered, he fortified Kedron and stationed horsemen and infantry there, so that they could go out and patrol the roads of Judea.

CHAPTER 16

See RG
163

¹John then went up from Gazara and told his father Simon what Cendebeus was doing. ²Simon called his two oldest sons, Judas and John, and said to them: "I and my brothers and my father's house have fought the battles of Israel from our youth until today, and many times we succeeded in saving Israel. ³I have now grown old, but you, by the mercy of Heaven, have come to man's estate. Take my place and my brother's, and go out and fight for our nation; and may the help of Heaven be with you!"

⁴John then mustered in the land twenty thousand warriors and horsemen. Setting out against Cendebeus, they spent the night at Modein, ⁵rose early, and marched into the plain. There, facing them, was an immense army of foot soldiers and horsemen, and between the two armies was a stream. ⁶John and his men took their position against the enemy. Seeing that his men were afraid to cross the stream, John crossed first. When his men saw this, they crossed over after him. ⁷Then he divided his infantry into two corps and put his cavalry between them, for the enemy's horsemen were very numerous. ⁸They blew the trumpets, and Cendebeus and his army were put to flight; many of them fell wounded, and the rest fled toward the stronghold. ⁹It was then that John's brother Judas fell wounded; but John pursued them until Cendebeus reached Kidron, which he had fortified. ¹⁰Some took refuge in the towers on the plain of Azotus, but John set fire to these, and about two thousand of the enemy perished. He then returned to Judea in peace.

Murder of Simon and His Sons. ¹¹Ptolemy, son of Abubus, had been appointed governor of the plain of Jericho, and he had much silver and gold, ¹²being the son-in-law of the high priest. ¹³But he became ambitious and sought to get control of the country. So he made treacherous plans to do away with Simon and his sons. ¹⁴As Simon was inspecting the cities of the country and providing for their needs, he and his sons Mattathias and Judas went down to Jericho in the year one hundred and seventy-seven, in the eleventh month* (that is, the month Shebat). ¹⁵The son of Abubus gave them a deceitful welcome in the little stronghold called Dok* which he had built. While serving them a sumptuous banquet, he had his men hidden there. ¹⁶Then, when Simon and his sons had drunk freely, Ptolemy and his men sprang up, weapons in hand, rushed upon Simon in the banquet hall, and killed him, his two sons, and some of his servants. ¹⁷By this vicious act of treason he repaid good with evil.

¹⁸Then Ptolemy wrote an account of this and sent it to the king, asking that troops be sent to help him and that the country be turned over to him. ¹⁹He sent other men to Gazara to do away with John. To the army officers he sent letters inviting them to come to

---

15, 37: Orthosia: a port between Tripoli and the Eleutherus River.

15, 39: Kedron: a few miles southeast of Jamnia and facing the fortress of Gazara held by John Hyrcanus.

16, 14: In the year one hundred and seventy-seven, in the eleventh month: January-February, 134 B.C., by the temple calendar.

16, 15: Dok: a fortress built on a cliff three miles northwest of Jericho, near modern Ain Duq.

The Death of Simon

Like all his brothers, Simon met a violent death, treacherously murdered by his own son-in-law (16, 11–24). His death was also ignominious, because he was drunk. This episode also recalls a statement about the Wicked Priest in the Pesher on Habakkuk from the Dead Sea Scrolls (column 11): "Its interpretation concerns the Priest whose shame has exceeded his glory because he . . . walked on paths of drunkenness to slake his thirst; but the cup of God's anger will engulf him." The death of Simon is a somber conclusion to 1 Maccabees, but the survival of John Hyrcanus provides a note of hope for the future.

him so that he might present them with silver, gold, and gifts. [20]He also sent others to seize Jerusalem and the mount of the temple. [21]But someone ran ahead and brought word to John at Gazara that his father and his brothers had perished, and that Ptolemy had sent men to kill him also. [22]On hearing this, John was utterly astounded. When the men came to kill him, he had them arrested and put to death, for he knew what they meant to do. [23]*Now the rest of the history of John, his wars and the brave deeds he performed, his rebuilding of the walls, and his other achievements— [24]these things are recorded in the chronicle of his pontificate, from the time that he succeeded his father as high priest.

16, 23f: John Hyrcanus was ruler and high priest from 134 B.C. till his death in 104 B.C. These verses suggest that the book was written, or at least completed, only after he died.

See RG 164–67

The Second Book of Maccabees

Although this book, like the preceding one, receives its title from its protagonist, Judas Maccabee (or Maccabeus), it is not a sequel to 1 Maccabees. The two differ in many respects. Whereas the first covers the period from the beginning of the reign of Antiochus IV (175 B.C.) to the accession of John Hyrcanus I (134 B.C.), this present book treats of the events in Jewish history from the time of the high priest Onias III and King Seleucus IV (c. 180 B.C.) to the defeat of Nicanor's army (161 B.C.).

The author of 2 Maccabees states (2, 23) that his one-volume work is an abridgment of a certain five-volume work by Jason of Cyrene; but since this latter has not survived, it is difficult to determine its relationship to the present epitome. One does not know how freely the anonymous epitomizer may have rewritten his shorter composition, or how closely he may have followed the wording of the original in the excerpts he made. Some parts of the text here, clearly not derived from Jason's work, are the Preface (2, 19-32), the Epilogue (15, 37-39), and probably also certain moralizing reflections (e. g., 5, 17-20; 6, 12-17). It is certain, however, that both works were written in Greek, which explains why the Second Book of Maccabees was not included in the canon of the Hebrew Bible.

The book is not without genuine historical value in supplementing I Maccabees, and it contains some apparently authentic documents (11, 16-38). Its purpose, whether intended by Jason himself or read into it by the compiler, is to give a theological interpretation to the history of the period. There is less interest, therefore, in the actual exploits of Judas Maccabeus than in God's marvelous interventions. These direct the course of events, both to punish the sacrilegious and blasphemous pagans, and to purify God's holy temple and restore it to his faithful people. The author sometimes effects his purpose by transferring events from their proper chronological order, and giving exaggerated figures for the size of armies and the numbers killed in battle; he also places long, edifying discourses and prayers in the mouths of his heroes, and inclines to elaborate descriptions of celestial apparitions (3, 24-34; 5, 2ff; 10, 29f; 15, 11-16). He is the earliest known composer of stories that glorify God's holy martyrs (6, 18—7, 42; 14, 37-46).

The First Letter

The purpose of the letter in 1, 1–10 is to urge the Jews of Egypt to celebrate the festival of Hanukkah, to commemorate the rededication of the temple by Judas. The covenant with Abraham, Isaac, and Jacob (v. 2) is the basis for unity between the different branches of Judaism. This should not be set over against the covenant with Moses, because the latter entails observance of the law and commandments (v. 4).

Of theological importance are the author's teachings on the resurrection of the just on the last day (7, 9. 11. 14. 23; 14, 46), the intercession of the saints in heaven for people living on earth (15, 11-16), and the power of the living to offer prayers and sacrifices for the dead (12, 39-46).

The beginning of 2 Maccabees consists of two letters sent by the Jews of Jerusalem to their coreligionists in Egypt. They deal with the observance of the feast commemorating the central event of the book, the purification of the temple. It is uncertain whether the author or a later scribe prefixed these letters to the narrative proper. If the author is responsible for their insertion, he must have written his book some time after 124 B.C., the date of the more recent of the two letters. In any case, Jason's five-volume work very likely continued the history of the Jews well into the Hasmonean period, so that 2 Maccabees would probably not have been produced much before the end of the second century B.C.

The main divisions of 2 Maccabees are:

I: Letters to the Jews in Egypt (1, 1—2, 18).
II: Author's Preface (2, 19-32).
III: Heliodorus' Attempt To Profane the Temple (3, 1-40).
IV: Profanation and Persecution (4, 1—7, 42).
V: Victories of Judas and Purification of the Temple (8, 1—10, 8).
VI: Renewed Persecution (10, 9—15, 36).
VII: Epilogue (15, 37-39).

I: Letters to the Jews In Egypt

CHAPTER 1

See RG 165

First Letter 124 B.C. [1]The Jews in Jerusalem and in the land of Judea send greetings to their brethren, the Jews in Egypt, and wish them true peace! [2]May God bless you and remember his covenant with his faithful servants, Abraham, Isaac and Jacob. [3]May he give to all of you a heart to worship him and to do his will readily and generously. [4]May he open your heart to his law and his commandments and grant you peace. [5]May he hear your prayers, and be reconciled to you, and never forsake you in time of adversity. [6]Even now we are praying for you here.

[7]In the reign of Demetrius,[*] the year one hundred and sixty-nine, we Jews wrote to you during the trouble and violence that overtook us in those years after Jason and his followers had revolted against the holy land and the kingdom,[a] [8]setting fire to the gatehouse and shedding innocent blood. But we prayed to the LORD, and our prayer was heard;[*] we offered sacrifices and fine flour; we lighted the lamps and set out the loaves of bread.[b] [9]We are now reminding you to celebrate the feast of Booths in the month of Chislev.[*] [10]Dated in the year one hundred and eighty-eight.[*]

1, 7: Demetrius: Demetrius II, king of Syria (145–139, 129–125 B.C.). The year one hundred and sixty-nine of the Seleucid era, 143 B.C. Regarding the dates in 1 and 2 Mc, see note on 1 Mc 1, 10. On the troubles caused by Jason and his revolt against the kingdom, i.e., the rule of the legitimate high priest, see 2 Mc 4, 7-22.

1, 8: Our prayer was heard: in the ultimate victory of the Maccabees.

1, 9: Feast of Booths in the month of Chislev: really the feast of the Dedication of the temple (2 Mc 10, 1-8), cele-

brated on the twenty-fifth of Chislev (Nov.-Dec.). Its solemnity resembles that of the true feast of Booths (Lv 23, 33-43), celebrated on the fifteenth of Tishri (Sept.-Oct.); cf 2 Mc 1, 18.

1, 10: 124 B.C. The date pertains to the preceding, not the following letter. King Ptolemy: Ptolemy VI Philometor, ruler of Egypt from 180 to 145 B.C.; he is mentioned also in 1 Mc 1, 18; 10, 51-59.

a: 2 Mc 4, 7-20.   *b:* 1 Mc 4, 38.

The Second Letter

The letter in 1, 10—2, 18 presents itself as having been sent in the time of Judas, but it was probably inserted in the first century B.C. It is filled with legendary details and has no historical value, but it attempts to reinforce the importance of Hanukkah by associating the festival not only with Judas, but also with traditions about Nehemiah and even Solomon.

Festival Letter 164 B.C. The people of Jerusalem and Judea, the senate, and Judas send greetings and good wishes to Aristobulus, counselor of King Ptolemy and member of the family of the anointed priests, and to the Jews in Egypt. *11*Since we have been saved by God from grave dangers, we give him great thanks for having fought on our side against the king;* *12c*it was he who drove out those who fought against the holy city. *13*When their leader arrived in Persia with his seemingly irresistible army, they were cut to pieces in the temple of the goddess Nanea* through a deceitful stratagem employed by Nanea's priests. *14*On the pretext of marrying the goddess, Antiochus with his Friends had come to the place to get its great treasures by way of dowry. *15*When the priests of the Nanaeon had displayed the treasures, Antiochus with a few attendants came to the temple precincts. As soon as he entered the temple, the priests locked the doors. *16*Then they opened a hidden trapdoor in the ceiling, hurled stones at the leader and his companions and struck them down. They dismembered the bodies, cut off their heads and tossed them to the people outside. *17*Forever blessed be our God, who has thus punished the wicked!

*18*We shall be celebrating the purification of the temple on the twenty-fifth day of the month Chislev, so we thought it right to inform you that you too may celebrate the feast of Booths and of the fire that appeared when Nehemiah, the rebuilder of the temple* and the altar, offered sacrifices. *19*When our fathers were being exiled to Persia,* devout priests of the time took some of the fire from the altar and hid it secretly in the hollow of a dry cistern, making sure that the place would be unknown to anyone. *20*Many years later, when it so pleased God, Nehemiah, commissioned by the king of Persia, sent the descendants of the priests who had hidden the fire to look for it. *21*When they informed us that they could not find any fire, but only muddy water, he ordered them to scoop some out and bring it. After the material for the sacrifices had been prepared, Nehemiah ordered the priests to sprinkle with the water the wood and what lay on it. *22*When this was done and in time the sun, which had been clouded over, began to shine, a great fire blazed up, so that everyone marveled. *23*While the sacrifice was being burned, the priests recited a prayer, and all present joined in with them, Jonathan leading and the rest responding with Nehemiah.

*24*The prayer was as follows: "LORD, LORD God, creator of all things, awesome and strong, just and merciful, the only king and benefactor, *25*who alone are gracious, just, almighty, and eternal, Israel's savior from all evil, who chose our forefathers and sanctified them: *26*accept this sacrifice on behalf of all your people Israel and guard and sanctify your heritage. *27*Gather together

---

1, 11f: The king: Antiochus IV of Syria, the bitter persecutor of the Jews, who, as leader of the Syrian army that invaded Persia, perished there in 164 B.C.

1, 13: Nanea: an oriental goddess comparable to Artemis of the Greeks.

1, 14-17: A different account of the death of Antiochus IV is given in 2 Mc 9, 1-29, and another variant account in 1 Mc 6, 1-16. The writer of this letter had probably heard a distorted rumor of the king's death. This fact and other indications show that the letter was written very soon after Antiochus IV died, hence in 164 B.C.

1, 18-36: This purely legendary account of Nehemiah's miraculous fire is incorporated in the letter because of its connection with the temple and its rededication.

1, 18: Nehemiah, the rebuilder of the temple: he rebuilt the walls of Jerusalem, but the temple had been rebuilt by Zerubbabel almost a century before.

1, 19: Persia: actually Babylonia, which later became part of the Persian Empire.

c: 12-17: 2 Mc 9, 1-29; 1 Mc 6, 1-13.

Verses 13 and 14 mention collections of books by Nehemiah and Judas. There is no other evidence that Nehemiah founded a library or established a canon. Some scholars credit Judas with forming the canon of Hebrew Scriptures. He does not appear, however, to have made judgments about the authority of texts, but simply to have collected books that were in danger of being lost.

our scattered people, free those who are the slaves of the Gentiles, look kindly on those who are despised and detested, and let the Gentiles know that you are our God. ²⁸Punish those who tyrannize over us and arrogantly mistreat us. ²⁹Plant your people in your holy place, as Moses promised."ᵈ

³⁰Then the priests began to sing hymns. ³¹After the sacrifice was burned, Nehemiah ordered the rest of the liquid to be poured upon large stones. ³²As soon as this was done, a flame blazed up, but its light was lost in the brilliance cast from a light on the altar. ³³When the event became known and the king of the Persians was told that, in the very place where the exiled priests had hidden the fire, a liquid was found with which Nehemiah and his people had burned the sacrifices, ³⁴the king, after verifying the fact, fenced the place off and declared it sacred. ³⁵To those on whom the king wished to bestow favors he distributed the large revenues he received there. ³⁶Nehemiah and his companions called the liquid nephthar, meaning purification, but most people name it naphtha.*

CHAPTER 2

See RG 165

¹*You will find in the records, not only that Jeremiah the prophet ordered the deportees to take some of the aforementioned fire with them, ²but also that the prophet, in giving them the law, admonished them not to forget the commandments of the LORD or be led astray in their thoughts, when seeing the gold and silver idols and their ornaments.ᵉ ³With other similar words he urged them not to let the law depart from their hearts. ⁴ᶠThe same document also tells how the prophet, following a divine revelation, ordered that the tent and the ark should accompany him and how he went off to the mountain* which Moses climbed to see God's inheritance. ⁵When Jeremiah arrived there, he found a room in a cave in which he put the tent, the ark, and the altar of incense; then he blocked up the entrance. ⁶Some of those who followed him came up intending to mark the path, but they could not find it. ⁷When Jeremiah heard of this, he reproved them: "The place is to remain unknown until God gathers his people together again and shows them mercy. ⁸Then the LORD will disclose these things, and the glory of the LORD will be seen in the cloud, just as it appeared in the time of Moses and when Solomon prayed that the Place* might be gloriously sanctified."ᵍ

⁹It is also related how Solomon in his wisdom offered a sacrifice at the dedication and the completion of the temple. ¹⁰Just as Moses prayed to the LORD and fire descended from the sky and consumed the sacrifices, so Solomon also prayed and fire came down and burned up the holocausts.ʰ ¹¹Moses had said,ⁱ "Because it had not been eaten, the sin offering was burned up."* ¹²Solomon also celebrated the feast in the same way for eight days.

¹³Besides these things, it is also told in the records and in Nehemiah's Memoirs* how he collected the books about the kings, the writings of the prophets and of David, and the royal letters about sacred offerings. ¹⁴In like manner Judas also collected for us the

1, 36: By a play on words, the Greek term naphtha (petroleum) is assimilated to some Semitic word, perhaps nephthar, meaning "loosened."

2, 1-8: This legendary account of how Jeremiah hid the sacred tent (which was not mentioned after the time of Solomon!), the ark and the altar is given for the purpose of explaining why the postexilic temple was the legitimate place of worship even without these sacred objects.

2, 4: The mountain: Nebo; cf Dt 34, 1.

2, 8: The Place: the temple of Jerusalem.

2, 11: The statement attributed here to Moses seems to be based on Lv 10, 16-20.

2, 13: Nehemiah's Memoirs: a lost apocryphal work.

d: 2 Mc 2, 18; Dt 30, 3ff. e: Bar 6, 3-72. f: 4f: Dt 32, 49; 34, 1; Rv 11, 19. g: 1 Kgs 8, 11. h: Lv 9, 23f; 2 Chr 7, 1. i: Lv 10, 16-20.

books that had been scattered because of the war, and we now have them in our possession.[j] [15]If you need them, send messengers to get them for you.

[16]As we are about to celebrate the feast of the purification of the temple, we are writing to you requesting you also to please celebrate the feast. [17]It is God who has saved all his people and has restored to all of them their heritage, the kingdom, the priesthood, and the sacred rites, [18]as he promised through the law. We trust in God, that he will soon have mercy on us and gather us together from everywhere under the heavens to his holy Place, for he has rescued us from great perils and has purified his Place.[k]

II: Author's Preface

[19]This is the story of Judas Maccabeus and his brothers, of the purification of the great temple, the dedication of the altar, [20]the campaigns against Antiochus Epiphanes and his son Eupator,* [21]and of the heavenly manifestations accorded to the heroes who fought bravely for Judaism, so that, few as they were, they seized the whole land, put to flight the barbarian hordes, [22]regained possession of the world-famous temple, liberated the city, and reestablished the laws that were in danger of being abolished, while the LORD favored them with all his generous assistance. [23]All this, which Jason of Cyrene set forth in detail in five volumes, we will try to condense into a single book.

Purpose and Method. [24]In view of the flood of statistics, and the difficulties encountered by those who wish to plunge into historical narratives where the material is abundant, [25]we have aimed to please those who prefer simple reading, as well as to make it easy for the studious who wish to commit things to memory, and to be helpful to all. [26]For us who

have taken upon ourselves the labor of making this digest, the task, far from being easy, is one of sweat and of sleepless nights, [27]just as the preparation of a festive banquet is no light matter for one who thus seeks to give enjoyment to others. Similarly, to win the gratitude of many we will gladly endure these inconveniences, [28]while we leave the responsibility for exact details to the original author, and confine our efforts to giving only a summary outline. [29]As the architect of a new house must give his attention to the whole structure, while the man who undertakes the decoration and the frescoes has only to concern himself with what is needed for ornamentation, so I think it is with us. [30]To enter into questions and examine them thoroughly from all sides is the task of the professional historian; [31]but the man who is making an adaptation should be allowed to aim at brevity of expression and to omit detailed treatment of the matter. [32]Here, then, we shall begin our account without further ado; it would be nonsense to write a long preface to a story and then abbreviate the story itself.

III: Heliodorus' Attempt to Profane the Temple*

CHAPTER 3

See RG 165-67

Treachery of Simon. [1]While the holy city lived in perfect peace and the laws were strictly observed because of the piety of the high priest Onias* and his hatred of evil, [2]the kings themselves honored the Place and glorified the temple with the most magnificent gifts. [3]Thus Seleucus,* king of Asia, defrayed from his own revenues all the expenses necessary for the sacrificial services. [4]But a certain Simon, of the priestly course of Bilgah,* who had been appointed superintendent of the temple, had a quarrel with the high priest about the supervision of the

---

2, 20: For the account of the campaigns against Antiochus IV Epiphanes, see 2 Mc 4, 7—10, 9; and for the account of those against his son Antiochus V Eupator, see 2 Mc 10, 10—13, 26.

3, 1-40: This legendary episode about Heliodorus is recounted here for the purpose of stressing the inviolability of the temple of Jerusalem; its later profanation was allowed by God because of the people's sins; cf 2 Mc 5, 17f.

3, 1: The high priest Onias: Onias III, who was priest from 196 to 175 B.C., and died in 171 B.C. He was the son of Simon, whose praises are sung in Sir 50, 1-21.

3, 3: Seleucus: Seleucus IV Philopator, who reigned from 187 to 175 B.C.

3, 4: Bilgah: a priestly family mentioned in Neh 12, 5. 18.

j: 1 Mc 1, 57. *k:* Dt 30, 3ff. *l:* 1ff: 2 Mc 5, 19f; 15, 12.

city market.*m* *5*Since he could not prevail against Onias, he went to Apollonius of Tarsus, who at that time was governor of Coelesyria and Phoenicia, *6*and reported to him that the treasury in Jerusalem was so full of untold riches that the total sum of money was incalculable and out of all proportion to the cost of the sacrifices, and that it would be possible to bring it all under the control of the king.

Mission of Heliodorus. *7*When Apollonius had an audience with the king, he informed him about the riches that had been reported to him. The king chose his minister Heliodorus and sent him with instructions to expropriate the aforesaid wealth. *8*So Heliodorus immediately set out on his journey, ostensibly to visit the cities of Coelesyria and Phoenicia, but in reality to carry out the king's purpose. *9*When he arrived in Jerusalem and had been graciously received by the high priest of the city, he told him about the information that had been given, and explained the reason for his presence, and he asked if these things were really true. *10*The high priest explained that part of the money was a care fund for widows and orphans,*n* *11*and a part was the property of Hyrcanus, son of Tobias,* a man who occupied a very high position. Contrary to the calumnies of the impious Simon, the total amounted to four hundred talents of silver and two hundred of gold. *12*He added that it was utterly unthinkable to defraud those who had placed their trust in the sanctity of the Place and in the sacred inviolability of a temple venerated all over the world. *13*But because of the orders he had from the king, Heliodorus said that in any case the money must be confiscated for the royal treasury. *14*So on the day he had set he went in to take an inventory of the funds.

Anguish of the Faithful. There was great distress throughout the city. *15*Priests prostrated themselves in their priestly robes before the altar, and loudly begged him in heaven who had given the law about deposits to keep the deposits safe for those who had

made them. *16*Whoever saw the appearance of the high priest was pierced to the heart, for the changed color of his face manifested the anguish of his soul. *17*The terror and bodily trembling that had come over the man clearly showed those who saw him the pain that lodged in his heart. *18*People rushed out of their houses in crowds to make public supplication, because the Place was in danger of being profaned. *19*Women, girded with sackcloth below their breasts, filled the streets; maidens secluded indoors ran together, some to the gates, some to the walls, others peered through the windows, *20*all of them with hands raised toward heaven, making supplication. *21*It was pitiful to see the populace variously prostrated in prayer and the high priest full of dread and anguish.

Divine Intervention. *22*While they were imploring the almighty LORD to keep the deposits safe and secure for those who had placed them in trust, *23*Heliodorus went on with his plan. *24*But just as he was approaching the treasury with his bodyguards, the LORD of spirits who holds all power manifested himself in so striking a way that those who had been bold enough to follow Heliodorus were panic-stricken at God's power and fainted away in terror. *25*There appeared to them a richly caparisoned horse, mounted by a dreadful rider. Charging furiously, the horse attacked Heliodorus with its front hoofs. The rider was seen to be wearing golden armor. *26*Then two other young men, remarkably strong, strikingly beautiful, and splendidly attired, appeared before him. Standing on each side of him, they flogged him unceasingly until they had given him innumerable blows. *27*Suddenly he fell to the ground, enveloped in great darkness. Men picked him up and laid him on a stretcher. *28*The man who a moment before had entered that treasury with a great retinue and his whole bodyguard was carried away helpless, having dearly experienced the sovereign power of God. *29*While he lay speechless and deprived of all hope of aid, due to an

---

3, 11: Son of Tobias: a member of the Tobiad family of Transjordan (Neh 2, 10; 6, 17ff; 13, 4-8). Hyrcanus' father was Joseph, whose mother was the sister of the high priest Onias II.

m: 2 Mc 4, 23.   *n:* Dt 14, 29.

act of God's power, [30]the Jews praised the LORD who had marvelously glorified his holy Place; and the temple, charged so shortly before with fear and commotion, was filled with joy and gladness, now that the almighty LORD had manifested himself.

[31]Soon some of the companions of Heliodorus begged Onias to invoke the Most High, praying that the life of the man who was about to expire might be spared. [32]Fearing that the king might think that Heliodorus had suffered some foul play at the hands of the Jews, the high priest offered a sacrifice for the man's recovery. [33]While the high priest was offering the sacrifice of atonement, the same young men in the same clothing again appeared and stood before Heliodorus. "Be very grateful to the high priest Onias," they told him. "It is for his sake that the LORD has spared your life. [34]Since you have been scourged by Heaven, proclaim to all men the majesty of God's power." When they had said this, they disappeared.

Testimony of Heliodorus. [35]After Heliodorus had offered a sacrifice to the LORD and made most solemn vows to him who had spared his life, he bade Onias farewell, and returned with his soldiers to the king. [36]Before all men he gave witness to the deeds of the most high God that he had seen with his own eyes. [37]When the king asked Heliodorus who would be a suitable man to be sent to Jerusalem next, he answered: [38]"If you have an enemy or a plotter against the government, send him there, and you will receive him back well-flogged, if indeed he survives at all; for there is certainly some special divine power about the Place. [39]He who has his dwelling in heaven watches over that Place and protects it, and he strikes down and destroys those who come to harm it." [40]This was how the matter concerning Heliodorus and the preservation of the treasury turned out.

IV: Profanation and Persecution

CHAPTER 4

See RG 165-67

Onias Appeals to the King. [1]The Simon mentioned above as the informer about the funds against his own country, made false accusations that it was Onias who threatened Heliodorus and instigated the whole miserable affair. [2]He dared to brand as a plotter against the government the man who was a benefactor of the city, a protector of his compatriots, and a zealous defender of the laws. [3]When Simon's hostility reached such a point that murders were being committed by one of his henchmen, [4]Onias saw that the opposition was serious and that Apollonius, son of Menestheus, the governor of Coelesyria and Phoenicia, was abetting Simon's wickedness. [5]So he had recourse to the king, not as an accuser of his countrymen, but as a man looking to the general and particular good of all the people. [6]He saw that, unless the king intervened, it would be impossible to have a peaceful government, and that Simon would not desist from his folly.

Jews Led by Jason To Apostatize. [7]But Seleucus died,* and when Antiochus surnamed Epiphanes succeeded him on the throne, Onias' brother Jason obtained the high priesthood by corrupt means:[o] [8]in an interview, he promised the king three hundred and sixty talents of silver, as well as eighty talents from another source of income. [9]Besides this he agreed to pay a hundred and fifty more, if he were given authority to establish a gymnasium and a youth club* for it and to enroll men in Jerusalem as Antiochians.

[10]When Jason received the king's approval and came into office, he immediately initiated his countrymen into the Greek way of life. [11]He set aside the royal concessions granted to the Jews through the mediation of John, father of Eupolemus* (that Eupolemus who would

---

4, 7: Seleucus died: he was murdered by Heliodorus. Antiochus Epiphanes was his younger brother. Onias' brother showed his love for the Greek way of life (v 10) by changing his Hebrew name Joshua, or Jesus, to the Greek name Jason.

4, 9: Youth club: an educational institution in which young men were trained both in Greek intellectual culture and in physical fitness. Antiochians: honorary citizens of An-

tioch, a Hellenistic city of the Seleucid Kingdom that had a corporation of such Antiochians, who enjoyed certain political and commercial privileges.

4, 11: Eupolemus: one of the two envoys sent to Rome by Judas Maccabeus (1 Mc 8, 17).

o: 2 Mc 1, 7; 1 Mc 1, 10.

The Hellenistic Reform

It is possible that Jason had a genuine desire to improve the lot of his people by adopting the Greek way of life (v. 10) but would hardly have paid such substantial sums of money if he did not stand to gain in return. The existing royal concessions that he did away with (v. 11) had been granted by Antiochus III when he gained control of Jerusalem in 198 B.C. They guaranteed the Jews the right to live according to their ancestral laws.

later go on an embassy to the Romans to establish a treaty of friendship with them); he abrogated the lawful institutions and introduced customs contrary to the law.*p* *12*He quickly established a gymnasium* at the very foot of the acropolis, where he induced the noblest young men to wear the Greek hat.*q* *13*The craze for Hellenism and foreign customs reached such a pitch, through the outrageous wickedness of the ungodly pseudo-high-priest Jason, *14*that the priests no longer cared about the service of the altar. Disdaining the temple and neglecting the sacrifices, they hastened, at the signal for the discus-throwing, to take part in the unlawful exercises on the athletic field. *15*They despised what their ancestors had regarded as honors, while they highly prized what the Greeks esteemed as glory. *16*Precisely because of this, they found themselves in serious trouble: the very people whose manner of life they emulated, and whom they desired to imitate in everything, became their enemies and oppressors. *17*It is no light matter to flout the laws of God, as the following period will show.

*18*When the quinquennial games were held at Tyre in the presence of the king, *19*the vile Jason sent envoys as representatives of the Antiochians of Jerusalem, to bring there three hundred silver drachmas for the sacrifice to Hercules. But the bearers themselves decided that the money should not be spent on a sacrifice, as that was not right, but should be used for some other purpose. *20*So the contribution destined by the sender for the sacrifice to Hercules was in fact applied, by those who brought it, to the construction of triremes.*

*21*When Apollonius, son of Menestheus, was sent to Egypt for the coronation of King Philometor,* Antiochus learned that the king was opposed to his policies; so he took measures for his own security. *22*After going to Joppa, he proceeded to Jerusalem. There he was received with great pomp by Jason and the people of the city, who escorted him with torchlights and acclamations; following this, he led his army into Phoenicia.

Menelaus Supplants Jason. *23*Three years later Jason sent Menelaus,* brother of the aforementioned Simon, to deliver the money to the king, and to obtain decisions on some important matters. *24*When he had been introduced to the king, he flattered him with such an air of authority that he secured the high priesthood for himself, outbidding Jason by three hundred talents of silver. *25*He returned with the royal commission, but with nothing that made him worthy of the high priesthood; he had the temper of a cruel tyrant and the rage of a wild beast. *26*Then Jason, who had cheated his own brother and now saw himself cheated by another man, was driven out as a fugitive to the country of the Ammonites.

*27*Although Menelaus had obtained the office, he did not make any payments of the money he had promised to the king, *28*in spite of the demand of Sostratus, the commandant of the citadel, whose duty it was to collect the taxes. For this reason, both were summoned before the king. *29*Menelaus left his brother

4, 12: Since the gymnasium, where the youth exercised naked (Greek *gymnos*), lay in the Tyropoeon Valley to the east of the citadel, it was directly next to the temple on its eastern side. The Greek hat: a wide-brimmed hat, traditional headgear of Hermes, the patron god of athletic contests; it formed part of the distinctive costume of the members of the "youth club."

4, 20: Triremes: war vessels with three banks of oars.
4, 21: Philometor: Ptolemy VI, king of Egypt, c. 172 to c. 145 B.C.
4, 23: Menelaus: Jewish high priest from c. 172 to his execution in 162 B.C. (2 Mc 13, 3-8).

p: 1 Mc 8, 17.   *q:* 1 Mc 1, 14.

Corruption of the High Priesthood

The years of persecution under Antiochus were precipitated by the strife over the high priesthood recorded in chs 4 and 5. Jason "obtained the priesthood by corrupt means" (4, 7) and then Menelaus "secured the high priesthood for himself, outbidding Jason by three hundred talents of silver" (v. 24).

Lysimachus as his substitute in the high priesthood, while Sostratus left Crates, commander of the Cypriots, as his substitute.

Murder of Onias. [30]While these things were taking place, the people of Tarsus and Mallus* rose in revolt, because their cities had been given as a gift to Antiochis, the king's mistress. [31]The king, therefore, went off in haste to settle the affair, leaving Andronicus, one of his nobles, as his deputy. [32]Then Menelaus, thinking this a good opportunity, stole some gold vessels from the temple and presented them to Andronicus; he had already sold some other vessels in Tyre and in the neighboring cities. [33]When Onias had clear evidence of the facts, he made a public protest, after withdrawing to the inviolable sanctuary at Daphne, near Antioch. [34]Thereupon Menelaus approached Andronicus privately and asked him to lay hands on Onias. So Andronicus went to Onias, and by treacherously reassuring him through sworn pledges with right hands joined, persuaded him, in spite of his suspicions, to leave the sanctuary. Then, without any regard for justice, he immediately put him to death.

[35]As a result, not only the Jews, but many people of other nations as well, were indignant and angry over the unjust murder of the man. [36]When the king returned from the region of Cilicia, the Jews of the city,* together with the Greeks who detested the crime, went to see him about the murder of Onias. [37]Antiochus was deeply grieved and full of pity; he wept as he recalled the prudence and noble conduct of the deceased. [38]Inflamed with anger, he immediately stripped Andronicus of his purple robe, tore off his other garments, and had him

led through the whole city to the very place where he had committed the outrage against Onias; and there he put the murderer to death. Thus the LORD rendered him the punishment he deserved.

Riot against Lysimachus. [39]Many sacrilegious thefts had been committed by Lysimachus in the city* with the connivance of Menelaus. When word was spread that a large number of gold vessels had been stolen, the people assembled in protest against Lysimachus. [40]As the crowds, now thoroughly enraged, began to riot, Lysimachus launched an unjustified attack against them with about three thousand armed men under the leadership of Auranus, a man as advanced in folly as he was in years. [41]Reacting against Lysimachus' attack, the people picked up stones or pieces of wood or handfuls of the ashes lying there and threw them in wild confusion at Lysimachus and his men. [42]As a result, they wounded many of them and even killed a few, while they put all the rest to flight. The sacrilegious thief himself they slew near the treasury.

[43]Charges about this affair were brought against Menelaus. [44]When the king came to Tyre, three men sent by the senate* presented to him the justice of their cause. [45]But Menelaus, seeing himself on the losing side, promised Ptolemy, son of Dorymenes, a substantial sum of money if he would win the king over.[r] [46]So Ptolemy retired with the king under a colonnade, as if to get some fresh air, and persuaded him to change his mind. [47]Menelaus, who was the cause of all the trouble, the king acquitted of the charges, while he condemned to death those poor men who would have been declared innocent even if they had pleaded

4, 30: Mallus: a city of Cilicia (v 36) in southeastern Asia Minor, about thirty miles east of Tarsus.

4, 36: The city: Antioch. But some understand the Greek to mean "each city."

4, 39: The city: Jerusalem. Menelaus was still in Syria.

4, 44: The senate: the council of Jewish elders at Jerusalem. cf 1 Mc 12, 6.

r: 2 Mc 8, 8; 1 Mc 3, 38.

their case before Scythians. *48*Thus, those who had prosecuted the case for the city, for the people, and for the sacred vessels, quickly suffered unjust punishment. *49*For this reason, even some Tyrians were indignant over the crime and provided sumptuously for their burial. *50*But Menelaus, thanks to the covetousness of the men in power, remained in office, where he grew in wickedness and became the chief plotter against his fellow citizens.

CHAPTER 5

See RG 165–67 *Sedition and Death of Jason.* *1*About this time Antiochus sent his second expedition* into Egypt.*s* *21*It then happened that all over the city, for nearly forty days, there appeared horsemen charging in midair, clad in garments interwoven with gold—companies fully armed with lances *3*and drawn swords; squadrons of cavalry in battle array, charges and countercharges on this side and that, with brandished shields and bristling spears, flights of arrows and flashes of gold ornaments, together with armor of every sort. *4*Therefore all prayed that this vision might be a good omen.

*5*But when a false rumor circulated that Antiochus was dead, Jason* gathered fully a thousand men and suddenly attacked the city. As the defenders on the walls were forced back and the city was finally being taken, Menelaus took refuge in the citadel. *6*Jason then slaughtered his fellow citizens without mercy, not realizing that triumph over one's own kindred was the greatest failure, but imagining that he was winning a victory over his enemies, not his fellow countrymen. *7*Even so, he did not gain control of the government, but in the end received only disgrace for his treachery, and once again took refuge in the country of the Ammonites. *8*At length he met a miserable end. Called to account before Aretas,* king of the Arabs, he

fled from city to city, hunted by all men, hated as a transgressor of the laws, abhorred as the butcher of his country and his countrymen. After being driven into Egypt, *9*he crossed the sea to the Spartans, among whom he hoped to find protection because of his relations with them. There he who had exiled so many from their country perished in exile; *10*and he who had cast out so many to lie unburied went unmourned himself with no funeral of any kind or any place in the tomb of his ancestors.

The City Ravaged. *11u*When these happenings were reported to the king, he thought that Judea was in revolt. Raging like a wild animal, he set out from Egypt and took Jerusalem by storm. *12*He ordered his soldiers to cut down without mercy those whom they met and to slay those who took refuge in their houses. *13*There was a massacre of young and old, a killing of women and children, a slaughter of virgins and infants. *14*In the space of three days, eighty thousand were lost, forty thousand meeting a violent death, and the same number being sold into slavery. *15*Not satisfied with this, the king dared to enter the holiest temple in the world; Menelaus, that traitor both to the laws and to his country, served as guide. *16*He laid his impure hands on the sacred vessels and gathered up with profane hands the votive offerings made by other kings for the advancement, the glory, and the honor of the Place. *17*Puffed up in spirit, Antiochus did not realize that it was because of the sins of the city's inhabitants that the LORD was angry for a little while and hence disregarded the holy Place.*v* *18*If they had not become entangled in so many sins, this man, like Heliodorus, who was sent by King Seleucus to inspect the treasury, would have been flogged and turned back from his presumptuous action as soon as he approached. *19w*The LORD, however, had not chosen the people for the sake of the Place, but the Place for the sake of the people.*

5, 1: Second expedition: the first invasion of Egypt by Antiochus in 169 B.C. (1 Mc 1, 16-20) is not mentioned in 2 Mc, unless the coming of the Syrian army to Palestine (2 Mc 4, 21f) is regarded as the first invasion. The author of 2 Mc apparently combines the first pillage of Jerusalem in 169 B.C. after Antiochus' first invasion of Egypt (1 Mc 1, 20-28; cf 2 Mc 5, 5ff) with the second pillage of the city two years later (167 B.C.), following the king's second invasion of Egypt in 168 B.C. (1 Mc 1, 29-35; cf 2 Mc 5, 24ff).

5, 5: Jason: brother of Onias III, was claimant of the high

priesthood (2 Mc 4, 7-10). Later he was supplanted by Menelaus who drove him into Transjordan (2 Mc 4, 26).

5, 8: Aretas: King Aretas I of the Nabateans; cf 1 Mc 5, 25.

5, 19: Man is more important than even the most sacred institutions; cf Mk 2, 27.

---

s: 1 Mc 1, 17.   *t:* 2f: 2 Mc 3, 24ff; 10, 29f; 11, 8.   *u:* 11-21: 1 Mc 1, 20-24.   *v:* 2 Mc 6, 12-16; 7, 16-19. 32-38.   *w:* 19ff: 2 Mc 3, 1ff; 1 Chr 17, 9; Mk 2, 27.

The Intervention of Antiochus

Jason's attempt to recover the high priesthood resulted in the wholesale massacre of Jewish citizens (5, 6). That Antiochus took this to mean that Judea was in revolt is perhaps the most plausible explanation of his violent intervention in Jerusalem. His rage was also stirred up because he had been humiliated in Egypt; see 1 Mc 1, 20.

[20]Therefore, the Place itself, having shared in the people's misfortunes, afterward participated in their good fortune; and what the Almighty had forsaken in his anger was restored in all its glory, once the great Sovereign became reconciled.

[21]Antiochus carried off eighteen hundred talents from the temple, and hurried back to Antioch. In his arrogance he planned to make the land navigable and the sea passable on foot, so carried away was he with pride.[x] [22]But he left governors to harass the nation: at Jerusalem, Philip, a Phrygian by birth,[*] and in character more cruel than the man who appointed him; [23]at Mount Gerizim,[*] Andronicus; and besides these, Menelaus, who lorded it over his fellow citizens worse than the others did. Out of hatred for the Jewish citizens, [24y]the king sent Apollonius,[*] commander of the Mysians, at the head of an army of twenty-two thousand men, with orders to kill all the grown men and sell the women and young men into slavery. [25]When this man arrived in Jerusalem, he pretended to be peacefully disposed and waited until the holy day of the sabbath; then, finding the Jews refraining from work, he ordered his men to parade fully armed. [26]All those who came out to watch, he massacred, and running through the city with armed men, he cut down a large number of people.

[27]But Judas Maccabeus with about nine others withdrew to the wilderness where he and his companions lived like wild animals in the hills, continuing to eat what grew wild to avoid sharing the defilement.[z]

CHAPTER 6

See RG 165-67

The Temple Desecrated. [1a]Not long after this the king sent an Athenian senator to force the Jews to abandon the customs of their ancestors and live no longer by the laws of God; [2]also to profane the temple in Jerusalem and dedicate it to Olympian Zeus,[*] and that on Mount Gerizim to Zeus the Hospitable, as the inhabitants of the place requested.[b] [3]This intensified the evil in an intolerable and utterly disgusting way. [4]The Gentiles filled the temple with debauchery and revelry; they amused themselves with prostitutes[*] and had intercourse with women even in the sacred court. They also brought into the temple things that were forbidden, [5]so that the altar was covered with abominable offerings prohibited by the laws.

Abolition of the Law. [6]A man could not keep the sabbath or celebrate the traditional feasts, nor even admit that he was a Jew. [7]Moreover, at the monthly celebration of the king's birthday the Jews had, from bitter necessity, to partake of the sacrifices, and when the festival of Dionysus[*] was celebrated, they were compelled to march in his procession, wearing wreaths of ivy.

[8]At the suggestion of the citizens of Ptolemais, a decree was issued ordering the neighboring Greek cities to act in the same way against the Jews: oblige them to partake of the sacrifices, [9]and put to death those who

5, 22: Philip, a Phrygian by birth: the Philip of 2 Mc 6, 11 and 8, 8, but probably not the same as Philip the regent of 2 Mc 9, 29 and 1 Mc 6, 14.

5, 23: Mount Gerizim: the sacred mountain of the Samaritans at Shechem; cf 2 Mc 6, 2.

5, 24: Apollonius: the Mysian commander of 1 Mc 1, 29; mentioned also in 2 Mc 3, 5; 4, 4.

6, 2: Olympian Zeus: equated with the Syrian Baal shomem ("the lord of the heavens"), a term which the Jews rendered as "Shiqqus shomem," horrible abomination (Dn 9, 27; 11, 31; 12, 11; 1 Mc 1, 54).

6, 4: Amused themselves with prostitutes: as in the fertility cults of the ancient Near East; see notes on Bar 6, 10. 42f.

6, 7: Dionysus: called also Bacchus the god of the grape harvest and of wine; ivy was one of his symbols.

x: 1 Mc 1, 23f. y: 24ff; 1 Mc 1, 29f. z: 1 Mc 2, 28. a: 1-11: 1 Mc 1, 44-63. b: 1 Mc 1, 46; Dn 9, 27.

The Religious Persecution

It was common in the Hellenistic world to identify the deities of one culture with those of another (6, 2). Olympian Zeus was presumably regarded as equivalent to "God Most High." The Letter of Aristeas, a Jewish document written in Greek in the second century B.C., says that the Jews worship the same God, Zeus, as the Greeks, but by a different name. What is at issue here is not the suppression of all Jewish religion, but its translation and adaptation to Hellenistic categories. Gentiles sometimes thought that Jewish worship was related to that of Dionysus (v. 7), god of wine, because Jews drank wine in ritual celebration.

would not consent to adopt the customs of the Greeks. It was obvious, therefore, that disaster impended. [10]Thus, two women who were arrested for having circumcised their children were publicly paraded about the city with their babies hanging at their breasts and then thrown down from the top of the city wall.[c] [11]Others, who had assembled in nearby caves to observe the sabbath in secret, were betrayed to Philip and all burned to death. In their respect for the holiness of that day, they had scruples about defending themselves.[d]

Purpose of Divine Judgment. [12e]Now I beg those who read this book not to be disheartened by these misfortunes, but to consider that these chastisements were meant not for the ruin but for the correction of our nation. [13]It is, in fact, a sign of great kindness to punish sinners promptly instead of letting them go for long. [14f]Thus, in dealing with other nations, the LORD patiently waits until they reach the full measure of their sins before he punishes them; but with us he has decided to deal differently, [15]in order that he may not have to punish us more severely later, when our sins have reached their fullness. [16]He never withdraws his mercy from us. Although he disciplines us with misfortunes, he does not abandon his own people. [17]Let these words suffice for recalling this truth. Without further ado we must go on with our story.

Martyrdom of Eleazar. [18]Eleazar, one of the foremost scribes, a man of advanced age and noble appearance, was being forced to open his mouth to eat pork.[g] [19]But preferring a glorious death to a life of defilement, he spat out the meat, and went forward of his own accord to the instrument of torture, [20]as men ought to do who have the courage to reject the food which it is unlawful to taste even for love of life. [21]Those in charge of that unlawful ritual meal took the man aside privately, because of their long acquaintance with him, and urged him to bring meat of his own providing, such as he could legitimately eat, and to pretend to be eating some of the meat of the sacrifice prescribed by the king; [22]in this way he would escape the death penalty, and be treated kindly because of their old friendship with him. [23]But he made up his mind in a noble manner, worthy of his years, the dignity of his advanced age, the merited distinction of his gray hair, and of the admirable life he had lived from childhood; and so he declared that above all he would be loyal to the holy laws given by God.

He told them to send him at once to the abode of the dead, explaining: [24]"At our age it would be unbecoming to make such a pretense; many young men would think the ninety-year-old Eleazar had gone over to an alien religion. [25]Should I thus dissimulate for the sake of a brief moment of life, they would be led astray by me, while I would bring shame and dishonor on my old age. [26]Even if, for the time being, I avoid the punishment of men, I shall never, whether alive or dead, escape the hands of the Almighty. [27]There-

6, 18—7, 42: The stories of Eleazar and of the mother and her seven sons, among the earliest models of "martyrology," were understandably popular among the Christians of the early centuries. Written originally to encourage God's people in times of persecution, they add gruesome details to the record of tortures, and place long speeches in the mouths of the martyrs.

c: 1 Mc 1, 60f.   *d:* 1 Mc 2, 32-38.   *e:* 12-16: 2 Mc 5, 17; 7, 16-19. 32-38.   *f:* Wis 11, 9f; 12, 2.22.   *g:* Lv 11, 7f; Heb 11, 35.

The Martyrdom of Eleazar

Death with honor, rather than life without it (6, 19), was an ideal of Greek culture, beginning with Achilles in the Trojan War. Compare the decision of Judas Maccabee that led to his death in 1 Maccabees 9, 10. Eleazar refuses any subterfuge that might save his life (6, 23), partly for reasons of honor, and partly because of the example he would set.

fore, by manfully giving up my life now, I will prove myself worthy of my old age, [28]and I will leave to the young a noble example of how to die willingly and generously for the revered and holy laws."

He spoke thus, and went immediately to the instrument of torture. [29]Those who shortly before had been kindly disposed, now became hostile toward him because what he had said seemed to them utter madness. [30]When he was about to die under the blows, he groaned and said: "The LORD in his holy knowledge knows full well that, although I could have escaped death, I am not only enduring terrible pain in my body from this scourging, but also suffering it with joy in my soul because of my devotion to him." [31]This is how he died, leaving in his death a model of courage and an unforgettable example of virtue not only for the young but for the whole nation.

See RG 165–67

CHAPTER 7

Martyrdom of a Mother and Her Sons. [1]It also happened that seven brothers with their mother were arrested and tortured with whips and scourges by the king, to force them to eat pork in violation of God's law.[h] [2]One of the brothers, speaking for the others, said: "What do you expect to achieve by questioning us? We are ready to die rather than transgress the laws of our ancestors." [3]At that the king, in a fury, gave orders to have pans and caldrons heated. [4]While they were being quickly heated, he commanded his executioners to cut out the tongue of the one who had spoken for the others, to scalp him and cut off his hands and feet, while the rest of his broth-

ers and his mother looked on. [5]When he was completely maimed but still breathing, the king ordered them to carry him to the fire and fry him. As a cloud of smoke spread from the pan, the brothers and their mother encouraged one another to die bravely, saying such words as these: [6]"The LORD God is looking on, and he truly has compassion on us, as Moses declared in his canticle, when he protested openly with the words, 'And he will have pity on his servants.' "[i]

[7]When the first brother had died in this manner, they brought the second to be made sport of. After tearing off the skin and hair of his head, they asked him, "Will you eat the pork rather than have your body tortured limb by limb?" [8]Answering in the language of his forefathers, he said, "Never!" So he too in turn suffered the same tortures as the first. [9]At the point of death he said: "You accursed fiend, you are depriving us of this present life, but the King of the world will raise us up* to live again forever. It is for his laws that we are dying."[j]

[10]After him the third suffered their cruel sport. He put out his tongue at once when told to do so, and bravely held out his hands, [11]as he spoke these noble words: "It was from Heaven that I received these; for the sake of his laws I disdain them; from him I hope to receive them again."[k] [12]Even the king and his attendants marveled at the young man's courage, because he regarded his sufferings as nothing.

[13]After he had died, they tortured and maltreated the fourth brother in the same way. [14]When he was near death, he said, "It is my choice to die at the hands of men with

7, 9: The King of the world will raise us up: here, and in vv 11. 14. 23. 29. 36, belief in the future resurrection of the body, at least for the just, is clearly stated; cf also 2 Mc 12, 44; 14, 46; Dn 12, 2.

h: Jer 15, 9.   i: Dt 32, 36.   j: 2 Mc 12, 44; 14, 46.   k: 2 Mc 12, 43ff.

The Seven Brothers

Variants of the story of the mother with seven sons (ch 7) are found in rabbinic literature, set in Roman times. The story is a legend. The quotation from the Song of Moses (Dt 32) sheds light on the motivation of the martyrs, where it is said that God "avenges the blood of his servants and purges his people's land" (v. 43). The second brother introduces another consideration: the hope of resurrection (2 Mc 7, 9). The third brother gives the resurrection a very physical character: He hopes to get his limbs back (v. 11). Such a physical view of resurrection is exceptional in Jewish texts of the second century B.C. (Daniel, 1 Enoch), most of which envisage a resurrection of the spirit. The mother grounds the hope for resurrection in the doctrine of creation. If God gave life once, he can do so again (v. 23).

the God-given hope of being restored to life by him; but for you, there will be no resurrection to life."

[15]They next brought forward the fifth brother and maltreated him. [16]Looking at the king, he said:[l] "Since you have power among men, mortal though you are, do what you please. But do not think that our nation is forsaken by God. [17]Only wait, and you will see how his great power will torment you and your descendants."

[18]After him they brought the sixth brother. When he was about to die, he said: "Have no vain illusions. We suffer these things on our own account, because we have sinned against our God; that is why such astonishing things have happened to us. [19]Do not think, then, that you will go unpunished for having dared to fight against God."[m]

[20]Most admirable and worthy of everlasting remembrance was the mother, who saw her seven sons perish in a single day, yet bore it courageously because of her hope in the LORD. [21]Filled with a noble spirit that stirred her womanly heart with manly courage, she exhorted each of them in the language of their forefathers with these words: [22]"I do not know how you came into existence in my womb; it was not I who gave you the breath of life, nor was it I who set in order the elements of which each of you is composed. [23]Therefore, since it is the Creator of the universe who shapes each

man's beginning, as he brings about the origin of everything, he, in his mercy, will give you back both breath and life, because you now disregard yourselves for the sake of his law."

[24]Antiochus, suspecting insult in her words, thought he was being ridiculed. As the youngest brother was still alive, the king appealed to him, not with mere words, but with promises on oath, to make him rich and happy if he would abandon his ancestral customs: he would make him his Friend and entrust him with high office. [25]When the youth paid no attention to him at all, the king appealed to the mother, urging her to advise her boy to save his life. [26]After he had urged her for a long time, she went through the motions of persuading her son. [27]In derision of the cruel tyrant, she leaned over close to her son and said in their native language: "Son, have pity on me, who carried you in my womb for nine months, nursed you for three years, brought you up, educated and supported you to your present age. [28]I beg you, child, to look at the heavens and the earth and see all that is in them; then you will know that God did not make them out of existing things;[*] and in the same way the human race came into existence. [29]Do not be afraid of this executioner, but be worthy of your brothers and accept death, so that in the time of mercy I may receive you again with them."

[30]She had scarcely finished speaking when

7, 28: God did not make them out of existing things: that is, God made all things solely by his omnipotent will and his creative word; cf Heb 11, 3.

l: 16-19: 2 Mc 5, 17; 6, 12-16.   m: Acts 5, 39.

the youth said: "What are you waiting for? I will not obey the king's command. I obey the command of the law given to our forefathers through Moses. [31]But you, who have contrived every kind of affliction for the Hebrews, will not escape the hands of God. [32n]We, indeed, are suffering because of our sins. [33]Though our living LORD treats us harshly for a little while to correct us with chastisements, he will again be reconciled with his servants. [34]But you, wretch, vilest of all men! do not, in your insolence, concern yourself with unfounded hopes, as you raise your hand against the children of Heaven. [35]You have not yet escaped the judgment of the almighty and all-seeing God. [36]My brothers, after enduring brief pain, have drunk of never-failing life, under God's covenant, but you, by the judgment of God, shall receive just punishments for your arrogance. [37]Like my brothers, I offer up my body and my life for our ancestral laws, imploring God to show mercy soon to our nation, and by afflictions and blows to make you confess that he alone is God. [38]Through me and my brothers, may there be an end to the wrath of the Almighty that has justly fallen on our whole nation." [39]At that, the king became enraged and treated him even worse than the others, since he bitterly resented the boy's contempt. [40o]Thus he too died undefiled, putting all his trust in the LORD. [41]The mother was last to die, after her sons.

[42]Enough has been said about the sacrificial meals and the excessive cruelties.

V: Victories of Judas and Purification of the Temple

CHAPTER 8

See RG
165-67

Judas Maccabeus. [1p]Judas Maccabeus and his companions entered the villages secretly, summoned their kinsmen, and by also enlisting others who remained faithful to Judaism, assembled about six thousand men. [2]They implored the LORD to look kindly upon his people, who were being oppressed on all sides; to have pity on the temple, which was profaned by godless men; [3]to have mercy on the city, which was being destroyed and about to be leveled to the ground; to hearken to the blood that cried out to him; [4]to remember the criminal slaughter of innocent children and the blasphemies uttered against his name; and to manifest his hatred of evil. [5q]Once Maccabeus got his men organized, the Gentiles could not withstand him, for the LORD's wrath had now changed to mercy. [6]Coming unexpectedly upon towns and villages, he would set them on fire. He captured strategic positions, and put to flight a large number of the enemy. [7]He preferred the nights as being especially helpful for such attacks. Soon the fame of his valor spread everywhere.

First Victory over Nicanor.* [8]When Philip saw that Judas was gaining ground little by little and that his successful advances were becoming more frequent, he wrote to Ptolemy, governor of Coelesyria and Phoenicia, to come to the aid of the king's government.[r] [9]Ptolemy promptly selected Nicanor, son of Patroclus, one of the Chief Friends, and sent him at the head of at least twenty thousand armed men of various nations to wipe out the entire Jewish race. With him he associated Gorgias, a professional military commander, well-versed in the art of war.[s] [10]Nicanor planned to raise the two thousand talents of tribute owed by the king to the Romans by selling captured Jews into slavery. [11]So he immediately sent word to the coastal cities, inviting them to buy Jewish slaves and promising to deliver ninety slaves for a talent—little did he dream of the punishment that was to fall upon him from the Almighty.

[12]When Judas learned of Nicanor's advance and informed his companions about the approach of the army, [13]the cowardly and those who lacked faith in God's justice deserted and got away. [14]But the others sold

---

8, 8-29. 34ff: This account of the campaign of Nicanor and Gorgias against Judas is paralleled, with certain differences, in 1 Mc 3, 38—4, 24.

n: 32. 38: 2 Mc 5, 17; 6, 12-16; 17, 16-19. *o:* 40f: Heb 11, 35. *p:* 1-7: 2 Mc 5, 27; 1 Mc 3, 10-26. *q:* 5ff: 1 Mc 3, 3-9. *r:* 2 Mc 4, 45; 1 Mc 3, 38. *s:* 1 Mc 7, 26.

everything they had left, and at the same time besought the LORD to deliver those whom the ungodly Nicanor had sold before even meeting them. [15]They begged the LORD to do this, if not for their sake, at least for the sake of the covenants made with their forefathers, and because they themselves bore his holy, glorious name. [16]Maccabeus assembled his men, six thousand strong, and exhorted them not to be panic-stricken before the enemy, nor to fear the large number of the Gentiles attacking them unjustly, but to fight courageously, [17]keeping before their eyes the lawless outrage perpetrated by the Gentiles against the holy Place and the affliction of the humiliated city, as well as the subversion of their ancestral way of life. [18]"They trust in weapons and acts of daring," he said, "but we trust in almighty God, who can by a mere nod destroy not only those who attack us, but the whole world." [19]He went on to tell them of the times when help had been given their ancestors: both the time of Sennacherib, when a hundred and eighty-five thousand of his men were destroyed,[t] [20]and the time of the battle in Babylonia against the Galatians, when only eight thousand Jews fought along with four thousand Macedonians; yet when the Macedonians were hard pressed, the eight thousand routed one hundred and twenty thousand and took a great quantity of booty, because of the help they received from Heaven. [21]With such words he encouraged them and made them ready to die for their laws and their country.

Then Judas divided his army into four, [22]placing his brothers, Simon, Joseph,* and Jonathan, each over a division, assigning to each fifteen hundred men. [23](There was also Eleazar.) After reading to them from the holy book and giving them the watchword, "The Help of God," he himself took charge of the first division and joined in battle with Nicanor.[u] [24]With the Almighty as their ally, they killed more than nine thousand of the enemy, wounded and disabled the greater part of Nicanor's army, and put all of them to flight. [25]They also seized the money of those who had come to buy them as slaves. When they had pursued the enemy for some time, [26]they were obliged to return by reason of the late hour. It was the day before the sabbath, and for that reason they could not continue the pursuit. [27]They collected the enemy's arms and stripped them of their spoils, and then observed the sabbath with fervent praise and thanks to the LORD who kept them safe for that day on which he let descend on them the first dew of his mercy. [28]After the sabbath, they gave a share of the booty to the persecuted and to widows and orphans; the rest they divided among themselves and their children. [29]When this was done, they made supplication in common, imploring the merciful LORD to be completely reconciled with his servants.

Timothy and Bacchides Defeated. [30]They also challenged the forces of Timothy and Bacchides, killed more than twenty thousand of them, and captured some very high fortresses. They divided the enormous plunder, allotting half to themselves and the rest to the persecuted, to orphans, widows, and the aged. [31]They collected the enemies' weapons and carefully stored them in suitable places; the rest of the spoils they carried to Jerusalem. [32]They also killed the commander of Timothy's forces, a most wicked man, who had done great harm to the Jews. [33]While celebrating the victory in their ancestral city, they burned both those who had set fire to the sacred gates and Callisthenes, who had taken refuge in a little house; so he received the reward his wicked deeds deserved.

Humiliation of Nicanor. [34v]The accursed Nicanor, who had brought the thousand slave dealers to buy the Jews, [35]after being humbled through the LORD's help by those whom he had thought of no account, laid aside his fine clothes and fled alone across country like a runaway slave, until he reached Antioch. He was eminently success-

---

8, 22: Joseph: called John in 1 Mc 2, 2; 9, 36. 38. This paragraph interrupts the story of Nicanor's defeat, which is resumed in v 34. The purpose of the author apparently is to group together the defeats suffered by the Syrians on various occasions. Battles against Timothy are recounted in

1 Mc 5, 37-44 and 2 Mc 12, 10-25; against Bacchides in 1 Mc 7, 8-20.

---

t: 2 Mc 15, 22; 2 Kgs 19, 35; Is 37, 36.   u: 1 Mc 3, 48.   v: 34f; 2 Mc 8, 23f; 1 Mc 7, 26.

The Death of Antiochus Epiphanes

The attempt to "command the waves of the sea" (9, 8) was a classic instance act of hubris or wildly excessive pride, associated with the Persian king Xerxes by the fifth-century tragedian Aeschylus. Only God could "weigh the mountaintops in his scales" (see Is 40, 12). Later Jewish tradition preserved a similar account of the death of Herod the Great.

The most fantastic part of Epiphanes' (fictitious) deathbed conversion (v. 17) is the promise that he would become a Jew. There was one notable case of conversion in the first century A.D., involving the royal house of Adiabene, but the fantasy of royal conversion is often found in Jewish writings. Usually, however, the king in question stops short of becoming a Jew (compare Nebuchadnezzar in Dn 4).

ful in destroying his own army. *36*So he who had promised to provide tribute for the Romans by the capture of the people of Jerusalem testified that the Jews had a champion, and that they were invulnerable for the very reason that they followed the laws laid down by him.

See RG 165–67

CHAPTER 9

Punishment and Death of Antiochus.[*] *1w*About that time Antiochus retreated in disgrace from the region of Persia. *2*He had entered the city called Persepolis and attempted to rob the temple and gain control of the city. Thereupon the people had swift recourse to arms, and Antiochus' men were routed, so that in the end Antiochus was put to flight by the natives and forced to beat a shameful retreat. *3*On his arrival in Ecbatana, he learned what had happened to Nicanor and to Timothy's forces. *4*Overcome with anger, he planned to make the Jews suffer for the injury done by those who had put him to flight. Therefore he ordered his charioteer to drive without stopping until he finished the journey.

Yet the condemnation of Heaven rode with him, since he said in his arrogance, "I will make Jerusalem the common graveyard of the Jews as soon as I arrive there." *5*So the all-seeing LORD, the God of Israel, struck him down with an unseen but incurable blow; for scarcely had he uttered those words when he was seized with excruciating pains in his bowels and sharp internal torment,*x* *6*a fit punishment for him who had tortured the bowels of others with many barbarous torments. *7*Far from giving up his insolence, he was all the more filled with arrogance. Breathing fire in his rage against the Jews, he gave orders to drive even faster. As a result he hurtled from the dashing chariot, and every part of his body was racked by the violent fall. *8y*Thus he who previously, in his superhuman presumption, thought he could command the waves of the sea, and imagined he could weigh the mountaintops in his scales, was now thrown to the ground and had to be carried on a litter, clearly manifesting to all the power of God. *9z*The body of this impious man swarmed with worms, and while he was still alive in hideous torments, his flesh rotted off, so that the entire army was sickened by the stench of his corruption. *10*Shortly before, he had thought that he could reach the stars of heaven, and now, no one could endure to transport the man because of this intolerable stench.

*11*At last, broken in spirit, he began to give up his excessive arrogance, and to gain some understanding, under the scourge of God, for he was racked with pain unceasingly. *12*When he could no longer bear his own stench, he said, "It is right to be subject to God, and not

9, 1-28: In order to keep together the various accounts of God's punishment of the persecutors of his people, the author places here the stories of Antiochus' illness and death (in actuality the king died only after the purification of the temple; cf 1 Mc 4, 36-59; 6, 1-16; 2 Mc 10, 1-8); of Judas' campaigns in Idumea and Transjordan (cf 2 Mc 5, 1-51; 2 Mc 10, 14-38); and of the first expedition of Lysias (1 Mc 4, 26-35; 2 Mc 11, 1-15).

w: 1-29: 2 Mc 1, 12-17; 1 Mc 6, 1-13. *x:* Acts 12, 20-23. *y:* Jb 38, 8-11; Ps 65, 6f; Is 40, 12. *z:* Acts 12, 23.

to think one's mortal self divine." [13]Then this vile man vowed to the LORD, who would no longer have mercy on him, [14]that he would set free the holy city, toward which he had been hurrying with the intention of leveling it to the ground and making it a common graveyard; [15]he would put on perfect equality with the Athenians all the Jews, whom he had judged not even worthy of burial, but fit only to be thrown out with their children to be eaten by vultures and wild animals; [16]he would adorn with the finest offerings the holy temple which he had previously despoiled; he would restore all the sacred vessels many times over; and would provide from his own revenues the expenses required for the sacrifices. [17]Besides all this, he would become a Jew himself and visit every inhabited place to proclaim there the power of God. [18]But since God's punishment had justly come upon him, his sufferings were not lessened, so he lost hope for himself and wrote the following letter to the Jews in the form of a supplication. It read thus:

[19]*"To my esteemed Jewish citizens, Antiochus, their king and general, sends hearty greetings and best wishes for their health and happiness. [20]If you and your children are well and your affairs are going as you wish, I thank God very much, for my hopes are in heaven. [21]Now that I am ill, I recall with affection the esteem and good will you bear me. On returning from the regions of Persia, I fell victim to a troublesome illness; so I thought it necessary to form plans for the general welfare of all. [22]Actually, I do not despair about my health, since I have great hopes of recovering from my illness. [23]Nevertheless, I know that my father, whenever he went on campaigns in the hinterland, would name his successor, [24]so that, if anything unexpected happened or any unwelcome news came, the people throughout the realm would know to whom the government had been entrusted, and so not be disturbed. [25]I am also bearing in mind that the neighboring rulers, especially those on the borders of our kingdom, are on the watch for opportunities and waiting to see what will happen. I have therefore appointed as king my son Antiochus, whom I have often before entrusted and commended to most of you, when I made hurried visits to the outlying provinces. I have written to him the letter copied below.* [26]Therefore I beg and entreat each of you to remember the general and individual benefits you have received, and to continue to show good will toward me and my son. [27]I am confident that, following my policy, he will treat you with mildness and kindness in his relations with you."

[28]So this murderer and blasphemer, after extreme sufferings, such as he had inflicted on others, died a miserable death in the mountains of a foreign land. [29]His foster brother Philip brought the body home; but fearing Antiochus' son, he later withdrew into Egypt, to Ptolemy Philometor.

CHAPTER 10

See RG 165-67

Purification of Temple and City. [1a]When Maccabeus and his companions, under the LORD's leadership, had recovered the temple and the city, [2]they destroyed the altars erected by the Gentiles in the marketplace and the sacred enclosures. [3]After purifying the temple, they made a new altar. Then, with fire struck from flint, they offered sacrifice for the first time in two years,* burned incense, and lighted lamps. They also set out the showbread. [4]When they had done this, they prostrated themselves and begged the LORD that they might never again fall into such misfortunes, and that if they should sin at any time, he might chastise them with moderation and not hand them over to blasphemous and barbarous Gentiles. [5]On the anniversary of the day on which the temple had been profaned by the

---

9, 19-27: Despite the statement in v 18, this letter is not really a supplication. It is rather a notification to all the king's subjects of the appointment of his son as his successor and a request that they be loyal to the new king. Apparently the same letter, which has every appearance of being authentic, was sent to the various peoples throughout the kingdom, with only a few words of address changed for

each group.
9, 25: The letter copied below: not included in the text of 2 Mc.
10, 3: Two years: three years according to 1 Mc 1, 54 and 4, 52.

a: 1-8: 1 Mc 4, 36-59.

Gentiles, that is, the twenty-fifth of the same month Chislev, the purification of the temple took place. ⁶The Jews celebrated joyfully for eight days as on the feast of Booths, remembering how, a little while before, they had spent the feast of Booths living like wild animals in caves on the mountains. ⁷Carrying rods entwined with leaves, green branches and palms, they sang hymns of grateful praise to him who had brought about the purification of his own Place. ⁸By public edict and decree they prescribed that the whole Jewish nation should celebrate these days every year.

VI: Renewed Persecution

Death of Ptolemy. ⁹Such was the end of Antiochus surnamed Epiphanes.*ᵇ* ¹⁰Now we shall relate what happened under Antiochus Eupator, the son of that godless man, and shall give a summary of the chief evils caused by the wars. ¹¹When Eupator succeeded to the kingdom, he put a certain Lysias in charge of the government as commander in chief of Coelesyria and Phoenicia. ¹²Ptolemy, surnamed Macron,* had taken the lead in treating the Jews fairly because of the previous injustice that had been done them, and he endeavored to have peaceful relations with them. ¹³As a result, he was accused before Eupator by the King's Friends. In fact, on all sides he heard himself called a traitor for having abandoned Cyprus, which Philometor had entrusted to him, and for having gone over to Antiochus Epiphanes. Since he could not command the respect due to his high office, he ended his life by taking poison.

*Victory over the Idumeans.** ¹⁴When Gorgias became governor of the region, he employed foreign troops and used every opportunity to attack the Jews. ¹⁵ᶜAt the same time the Idumeans, who held some important strongholds, were harassing the Jews; they welcomed fugitives from Jerusalem and endeavored to continue the war. ¹⁶Maccabeus and his companions, after public prayers asking God to be their ally, moved quickly against the strongholds of the Idumeans. ¹⁷Attacking vigorously, they gained control of the places, drove back all who manned the walls, and cut down those who opposed them, killing as many as twenty thousand men. ¹⁸When at least nine thousand took refuge in two very strong towers, containing everything necessary to sustain a siege, ¹⁹Maccabeus left Simon and Joseph, along with Zacchaeus and his men, in sufficient numbers to besiege them, while he himself went off to places where he was more urgently needed. ²⁰But some of the men in Simon's force who were money lovers let themselves be bribed by some of the men in the towers; on receiving seventy thousand drachmas, they allowed a number of them to escape. ²¹When Maccabeus was told what had happened, he assembled the rulers of the people and accused those men of having sold their kinsmen for money by setting their enemies free to fight against them. ²²So he put them to death as traitors, and without delay captured the two towers. ²³As he was successful at arms in all his undertakings, he destroyed more than twenty thousand men in the two strongholds.

Victory over Timothy. ²⁴Timothy, who had previously been defeated by the Jews,* gathered a tremendous force of foreign troops and collected a large number of cavalry from Asia; then he appeared in Judea, ready to conquer it by force. ²⁵At his approach, Maccabeus and his men made supplication to God, sprinkling earth upon their heads and girding their loins in sackcloth. ²⁶Lying prostrate at the foot of the altar, they begged him to be gracious to them, and to be an enemy to their enemies, and a foe to their foes, as the law declares.*ᵈ*

²⁷After the prayer, they took up their arms and advanced a considerable distance from the city, halting when they were close to the

---

10, 12: Ptolemy, surnamed Macron: son of Dorymenes (2 Mc 4, 45), was formerly hostile to the Jews (2 Mc 6, 8).

10, 14-23: Probably the same campaign of Judas against the Idumeans that is mentioned in 1 Mc 5, 1-3.

10, 24: Timothy . . . previously . . . defeated by the Jews: as recounted in 2 Mc 8, 30ff.

b: 2 Mc 2, 21; 1 Mc 6, 17.   *c:* 15-23: 1 Mc 5, 3ff.   *d:* Ex 23, 22.

Peace with the Syrians

First Maccabees gives no indication that Lysias thought the Hebrews were invincible (11, 13). He returns undaunted in 2 Mc 13. Second Maccabees never acknowledges the defeats of the Maccabees at Bethzechariah (1 Mc 6, 32–47) or at Mount Azotus where Judas was killed (1 Mc 9, 11–22).

enemy. [28] As soon as dawn broke,* the armies joined battle, the one having as pledge of success and victory not only their valor but also their reliance on the LORD, and the other taking fury as their leader in the fight.

[29e] In the midst of the fierce battle, there appeared to the enemy from the heavens five majestic men riding on golden-bridled horses, who led the Jews on. [30] They surrounded Maccabeus, and shielding him with their own armor, kept him from being wounded. They shot arrows and hurled thunderbolts at the enemy, who were bewildered and blinded, thrown into confusion and routed. [31] Twenty-five hundred of their foot soldiers and six hundred of their horsemen were slain. [32] Timothy, however, fled to a well-fortified stronghold called Gazara, where Chaereas was in command.[f] [33] For four days Maccabeus and his men eagerly besieged the fortress. [34] Those inside, relying on the strength of the place, kept repeating outrageous blasphemies and uttering abominable words. [35] When the fifth day dawned, twenty young men in the army of Maccabeus, angered over such blasphemies, bravely stormed the wall and with savage fury cut down everyone they encountered. [36] Others who climbed up the same way swung around on the defenders, taking the besieged in the rear; they put the towers to the torch, spread the fire and burned the blasphemers alive. Still others broke down the gates and let in the rest of the troops, who took possession of the city. [37] Timothy had hidden in a cistern, but they killed* him, along with his brother

Chaereas, and Apollophanes. [38] On completing these exploits, they blessed, with hymns of grateful praise, the LORD who shows great kindness to Israel and grants them victory.

CHAPTER 11

See RG 165–67

*Defeat of Lysias.** [1g] Very soon afterward, Lysias, guardian and kinsman of the king and head of the government, being greatly displeased at what had happened, [2] mustered about eighty thousand infantry and all his cavalry and marched against the Jews. His plan was to make Jerusalem a Greek settlement; [3] to levy tribute on the temple, as he did on the sanctuaries of the other nations; and to put the high priesthood up for sale every year. [4] He did not take God's power into account at all, but felt exultant confidence in his myriads of foot soldiers, his thousands of horsemen, and his eighty elephants. [5] So he invaded Judea, and when he reached Beth-zur, a fortified place about twenty miles from Jerusalem, launched a strong attack against it. [6] When Maccabeus and his men learned that Lysias was besieging the strongholds, they and all the people begged the LORD with lamentations and tears to send a good angel to save Israel.[h] [7] Maccabeus himself was the first to take up arms, and he exhorted the others to join him in risking their lives to help their kinsmen. Then they resolutely set out together. [8] Suddenly, while they were still near Jerusalem, a horseman appeared at their head, clothed in white garments and brandishing gold weapons.[i] [9] Then all of them together thanked God for

---

10, 28: As soon as dawn broke: the same battle at dawn as in 1 Mc 5, 30-34.

10, 37: Timothy . . . they killed: apparently, the same Timothy is still alive in 2 Mc 12, 2. 18-25. The present passage is not in chronological order, Gazara, v 32 (Gezer) was not captured by the Jews until much later (cf 1 Mc 9, 50ff; 13, 53).

11, 1-12: The defeat of Lysias at Beth-zur probably occurred before the purification of the temple; cf 1 Mc 4, 26-35.

---

e: 29f: 2 Mc 3, 24ff; 5, 2f; 10, 29f; 11, 8.   *f:* 1 Mc 13, 43-48.
g: 1-12: 1 Mc 4, 26-35.   *h:* Ex 23, 20.   *i:* 2 Mc 3, 24ff; 5, 2f; 10, 29f.

Four Letters

The documents inserted in vv.16–38 are authentic letters, but the chronology is confused. The first, third, and fourth letters are dated to the year 148 of the Seleucid era, or 165–164 B.C., at the beginning of the revolt against Epiphanes. The second letter is authored by Antiochus V Eupator after the death of Epiphanes. The letter of Eupator formally abandons the attempt to compel the Jews to follow a Greek way of life. The third letter documents an earlier attempt by Epiphanes to put an end to the persecution and war, at the urging of Menelaus. This letter may represent the first contact between the Romans and the Jews. It implies recognition of the Jews as a people and sets the stage for their later treaty with Rome (1 Mc 8).

his mercy, and their hearts were filled with such courage that they were ready to assault not only men, but the most savage beasts, yes, even walls of iron. *10*Now that the LORD had shown his mercy toward them, they advanced in battle order with the aid of their heavenly ally. *11*Hurling themselves upon the enemy like lions, they laid low eleven thousand foot soldiers and sixteen hundred horsemen, and put all the rest to flight. *12*Most of those who got away were wounded and stripped of their arms, while Lysias himself escaped only by shameful flight.

Peace with the Syrians. *13 j*But Lysias was not a stupid man. He reflected on the defeat he had suffered, and came to realize that the Hebrews were invincible because the mighty God was their ally. He therefore sent a message *14*persuading them to settle everything on just terms, and promising to persuade the king also, and to induce him to become their friend. *15*Maccabeus, solicitous for the common good, agreed to all that Lysias proposed; and the king, on his part, granted in behalf of the Jews all the written requests of Maccabeus to Lysias.

Official Letters. *16*These are the terms of the letter which Lysias wrote to the Jews: "Lysias sends greetings to the Jewish people. *17*John and Absalom, your envoys, have presented your signed communication and asked about the matters contained in it. *18*Whatever had to be referred to the king I called to his attention, and the things that

were acceptable he has granted. *19*If you maintain your loyalty to the government, I will endeavor to further your interests in the future. *20*On the details of these matters I have authorized my representatives, as well as your envoys, to confer with you. *21*Farewell." The year one hundred and forty-eight,* the twenty-fourth of Dioscorinthius.

*22*The king's letter read thus: "King Antiochus sends greetings to his brother Lysias. *23*Now that our father has taken his place among the gods, we wish the subjects of our kingdom to be undisturbed in conducting their own affairs. *24*We understand that the Jews do not agree with our father's policy concerning Greek customs but prefer their own way of life. They are petitioning us to let them retain their own customs. *25*Since we desire that this people too should be undisturbed, our decision is that their temple be restored to them and that they live in keeping with the customs of their ancestors. *26*Accordingly, please send them messengers to give them our assurances of friendship, so that, when they learn of our decision, they may have nothing to worry about but may contentedly go about their own business."

*27*The king's letter to the people was as follows: "King Antiochus sends greetings to the Jewish senate and to the rest of the Jews. *28*If you are well, it is what we desire. We too are in good health. *29*Menelaus has told us of your wish to return home and attend to your

11, 21: The year one hundred and forty-eight: 164 B.C. The reading of the name of the month and its position in the calendar are uncertain.

j: 13-33: 1 Mc 6, 57-61.

The Massacre at Joppa

Second Maccabees is careful to point out that the Jews were willing to live quietly and at peace. The incident in ch 12 at Joppa, modern Tel Aviv, is one of the earliest outright attacks on a Jewish community in a Greek city.

own affairs. *30*Therefore, those who return by the thirtieth of Xanthicus will have our assurance of full permission *31*to observe their dietary laws and other laws, just as before, and none of the Jews shall be molested in any way for faults committed through ignorance. *32*I have also sent Menelaus to reassure you. *33*Farewell." In the year one hundred and forty-eight, the fifteenth of Xanthicus.*

*34*The Romans also sent them a letter as follows: "Quintus Memmius and Titus Manius, legates of the Romans, send greetings to the Jewish people. *35*Whatever Lysias, kinsman of the king, has granted you, we also approve. *36*But the matters on which he passed judgment should be submitted to the king. As soon as you have considered them, send someone to us with your decisions so that we may present them to your advantage, for we are on our way to Antioch. *37*Make haste, then, to send us those who can inform us of your intentions. *38*Farewell." In the year one hundred and forty-eight, the fifteenth of Xanthicus.*

See RG 165–67

CHAPTER 12

Persecution Renewed. *1*After these agreements were made, Lysias returned to the king, and the Jews went about their farming. *2*But some of the local governors, Timothy and Apollonius, son of Gennaeus,* as also Hieronymus and Demophon, to say nothing of Nicanor, the commander of the Cyprians, would not allow them to live in peace.

*3*Some people of Joppa also committed this outrage: they invited the Jews who lived among them, together with their wives and children, to embark on boats which they had provided. There was no hint of enmity toward them: *4*this was done by public vote of the city. When the Jews, not suspecting treachery and wishing to live on friendly terms, accepted the invitation, the people of Joppa took them out to sea and drowned at least two hundred of them.

Activity of Judas. *5*As soon as Judas heard of the barbarous deed perpetrated against his countrymen, he summoned his men; *6*and after calling upon God, the just judge, he marched against the murderers of his kinsmen. In a night attack he set the harbor on fire, burnt the boats, and put to the sword those who had taken refuge there. *7*When the gates of the town were shut, he withdrew, intending to come back later and wipe out the entire population of Joppa.

*8*On hearing that the men of Jamnia planned to give like treatment to the Jews who lived among them, *9*he attacked the Jamnian populace by night, setting fire to the harbor and the fleet, so that the glow of the flames was visible as far as Jerusalem, thirty miles away.

*10k*When the Jews had gone about a mile from there* in the campaign against Timothy, they were attacked by Arabs numbering at least five thousand foot soldiers, and five hundred horsemen. *11*After a hard fight, Judas and his companions, with God's help, were victorious. The defeated nomads begged Judas to make friends with them and

---

11, 33: The date, which is the same as the date of the Romans' letter (v 38) cannot be correct. The king's letter must be connected with the peace treaty of the year 149 of the Seleucid era, i.e., 163 B.C. Perhaps the mention of the month of Xanthicus in the body of the letter (v 30) caused the date of the Romans' letter to be transferred to this one.

11, 38: The date is April 12, 164 B.C.

12, 2: Apollonius, son of Gennaeus: not the Apollonius

who was the son of Menestheus (2 Mc 4, 21). Nicanor: probably distinct from the Nicanor of 2 Mc 14, 2.

12, 10: From there: not from the aforesaid Jamnia (vv 8f) or Joppa (vv 3-7), but from a place in Transjordan; vv 10-26 parallel the account given in 1 Mc 5, 9-13. 24-54 of Judas' campaign in northern Transjordan.

---

k: 10-16: 1 Mc 5, 24-36.

promised to supply the Jews with cattle and to help them in every other way. [12]Realizing that they could indeed be useful in many respects, Judas agreed to make peace with them. After the pledge of friendship had been exchanged, the Arabs withdrew to their tents.

[13]He also attacked a certain city called Caspin, fortified with earthworks and ramparts and inhabited by a mixed population of Gentiles. [14]Relying on the strength of their walls and their supply of provisions, the besieged treated Judas and his men with contempt, insulting them and even uttering blasphemies and profanity. [15]But Judas and his men invoked the aid of the great Sovereign of the world, who, in the day of Joshua, overthrew Jericho without battering-ram or siege machine; then they furiously stormed the ramparts.[l] [16]Capturing the city by the will of God, they inflicted such indescribable slaughter on it that the adjacent pool, which was about a quarter of a mile wide, seemed to be filled with the blood that flowed into it.

[17m]When they had gone on some ninety miles, they reached Charax,[n] where there were certain Jews known as Toubiani.[*] [18]But they did not find Timothy in that region, for he had already departed from there without having done anything except to leave behind in one place a very strong garrison. [19]But Dositheus and Sosipater, two of Maccabeus' captains, marched out and destroyed the force of more than ten thousand men that Timothy had left in the stronghold. [20]Meanwhile, Maccabeus divided his army into cohorts, with a commander over each cohort, and went in pursuit of Timothy, who had a force of a hundred and twenty thousand foot soldiers and twenty-five hundred horsemen. [21]When Timothy learned of the approach of Judas, he sent on ahead of him the women and children, as well as the baggage, to a place called Karnion, which was hard to besiege and even hard to reach because of the difficult terrain of that region. [22]But when Judas' first cohort appeared, the enemy was overwhelmed with fear and terror at the manifestation of the All-seeing. Scattering in every direction, they rushed away in such headlong flight that in many cases they wounded one another, pierced by the swords of their own men. [23]Judas pressed the pursuit vigorously, putting the sinners to the sword and destroying as many as thirty thousand men.

[24]Timothy himself fell into the hands of the men under Dositheus and Sosipater; but with great cunning, he asked them to spare his life and let him go, because he had in his power the parents and relatives of many of them, and could make these suffer. [25]When he had fully confirmed his solemn pledge to restore them unharmed, they let him go for the sake of saving their brethren.

Further Successes. [26]Judas then marched to Karnion and the shrine of Atargatis,[*] where he killed twenty-five thousand people. [27o]After the defeat and destruction of these, he moved his army to Ephron, a fortified city inhabited by people of many nationalities. Robust young men took up their posts in defense of the walls, from which they fought valiantly; inside were large supplies of machines and missiles. [28]But the Jews, invoking the Sovereign who forcibly shatters the might of his enemies, got possession of the city and slaughtered twenty-five thousand of the people in it. [29]Then they set out from there and hastened on to Scythopolis,[*] seventy-five miles from Jerusalem. [30]But when the Jews who lived there testified to the good will shown by the Scythopolitans and to their kind treatment even in times of adversity, [31]Judas and his men thanked them and exhorted them to be well disposed to their race in the future also. Finally they arrived in Jerusalem, shortly before the feast of Weeks.

[32]After this feast called Pentecost, they lost no time in marching against Gorgias, governor of Idumea, [33]who opposed them with three thousand foot soldiers and four hundred horsemen. [34]In the ensuing battle, a few of the Jews were slain. [35]A man called

12, 17: Certain Jews known as Toubiani: because they lived "in the land of Tob" (1 Mc 5, 13).
12, 26: Atargatis: a Syrian goddess, represented by the body of a fish.
12, 29: Scythopolis: the Greek name of the city of Beth-shan; cf 1 Mc 5, 52.

l: Jos 6, 1-21. m: 17-26: 1 Mc 5, 37-44. n: 1 Mc 5, 13. o: 27-31: 2 Mc 5, 45-54.

Dositheus, a powerful horseman and one of Bacenor's men,* caught hold of Gorgias, grasped his military cloak and dragged him along by main strength, intending to capture the vile wretch alive, when a Thracian horseman attacked Dositheus and cut off his arm at the shoulder. Then Gorgias fled to Marisa. [36]After Esdris and his men had been fighting for a long time and were weary, Judas called upon the LORD to show himself their ally and leader in the battle. [37]Then, raising a battle cry in his ancestral language, and with songs, he charged Gorgias' men when they were not expecting it and put them to flight.

Expiation for the Dead. [38]Judas rallied his army and went to the city of Adullam. As the week was ending, they purified themselves according to custom and kept the sabbath there. [39]On the following day, since the task had now become urgent, Judas and his men went to gather up the bodies of the slain and bury them with their kinsmen in their ancestral tombs. [40]But under the tunic of each of the dead they found amulets sacred to the idols of Jamnia, which the law forbids the Jews to wear. So it was clear to all that this was why these men had been slain.[p] [41]They all therefore praised the ways of the LORD, the just judge who brings to light the things that are hidden. [42]*Turning to supplication, they prayed that the sinful deed might be fully blotted out. The noble Judas warned the soldiers to keep themselves free from sin, for they had seen with their own eyes what had happened because of the sin of those who had fallen. [43]He then took up a collection among all his soldiers, amounting to two thousand silver drachmas, which he sent to Jerusalem to provide for an expiatory sacrifice. In doing this he acted in a very excellent and noble way, inasmuch as he had

the resurrection of the dead in view; [44]for if he were not expecting the fallen to rise again, it would have been useless and foolish to pray for them in death. [45]But if he did this with a view to the splendid reward that awaits those who had gone to rest in godliness, it was a holy and pious thought. [46]Thus he made atonement for the dead that they might be freed from this sin.

CHAPTER 13

See RG 165–67

The Syrians Invade Judea. [1]In the year one hundred and forty-nine,* Judas and his men learned that Antiochus Eupator was invading Judea with a large force, [2]and that with him was Lysias, his guardian, who was in charge of the government. They led* a Greek army of one hundred and ten thousand foot soldiers, fifty-three hundred horsemen, twenty-two elephants, and three hundred chariots armed with scythes.[q]

Death of Menelaus. [3]Menelaus also joined them, and with great duplicity kept urging Antiochus on, not for the welfare of his country, but in the hope of being established in office. [4]But the King of kings aroused the anger of Antiochus against the scoundrel. When the king was shown by Lysias that Menelaus was to blame for all the trouble, he ordered him to be taken to Beroea* and executed there in the customary local method.[r] [5]There is at that place a tower seventy-five feet high, full of ashes,* with a circular rim sloping down steeply on all sides toward the ashes. [6]A man guilty of sacrilege or notorious for certain other crimes is brought up there and then hurled down to destruction. [7]In such a manner was Menelaus, the transgressor of the law, fated to die; he was deprived even of decent burial. [8]It was altogether just that he who had committed so

---

12, 35: One of Bacenor's men: certain ancient witnesses to the text have "one of the Toubiani"; cf v 17.

12, 42-46: This is the earliest statement of the doctrine that prayers (v 42) and sacrifices (v 43) for the dead are beneficial. The statement is made here, however, only for the purpose of proving that Judas believed in the resurrection of the just (2 Mc 7, 9. 14. 23. 36). That is, he believed that expiation could be made for certain sins of otherwise good men—soldiers who had given their lives for God's cause. Thus, they could share in the resurrection. His belief was similar to, but not quite the same as, the Catholic doctrine of

purgatory.

13, 1: In the year one hundred and forty-nine: 163–162 B.C.

13, 2: They led: the Greek means literally "Each (of them) led," but it is unlikely that the author meant the already immense numbers to be doubled; the numbers are similar to those in 1 Mc 6, 30.

13, 4: Beroea: the Greek name of Aleppo.

13, 5: Ashes: probably smoldering ashes; the tower resembles the ancient Persian fire towers.

---

p: Dt 7, 25.   q: 1 Mc 6, 30.   r: 1 Tm 6, 15; Rv 17, 14; 19, 16.

many sins against the altar with its pure fire and ashes should meet his death in ashes.

Skirmish near Modein. [9]The king was advancing, his mind full of savage plans for inflicting on the Jews worse things than those they suffered in his father's time. [10]When Judas learned of this, he urged the people to call upon the LORD night and day, to help them now, if ever, [11]when they were about to be deprived of their law, their country, and their holy temple; and not to allow this nation, which had just begun to revive, to be subjected again to blasphemous Gentiles. [12]When they had all joined in doing this, and had implored the merciful LORD continuously with weeping and fasting and prostrations for three days, Judas encouraged them and told them to stand ready. [13]After a private meeting with the elders, he decided that, before the king's army could invade Judea and take possession of the city, the Jews should march out and settle the matter with God's help. [14]Leaving the outcome to the Creator of the world, and exhorting his followers to fight nobly to death for the laws, the temple, the city, the country, and the government, he pitched his camp near Modein. [15]Giving his men the battle cry "God's Victory," he made a night attack on the king's pavilion with a picked force of the bravest young men and killed about two thousand in the camp. They also slew* the lead elephant and its rider.[s] [16]Finally they withdrew in triumph,* having filled the camp with terror and confusion. [17]Day was just breaking when this was accomplished with the help and protection of the LORD.

Treaty with Antiochus V. [18t]The king, having had a taste of the Jews' daring, tried to take their positions by a stratagem. [19]So he marched against Beth-zur, a strong fortress of the Jews; but he was driven back, checked, and defeated. [20]Judas then sent supplies to the men inside, [21]but Rhodocus, of the Jewish army, betrayed military secrets* to the

enemy. He was found out, arrested, and imprisoned. [22]The king made a second attempt by negotiating with the men of Beth-zur. After giving them his pledge and receiving theirs, he withdrew [23]and attacked Judas and his men. But he was defeated. Next he heard that Philip, who was left in charge of the government in Antioch, had rebelled. Dismayed, he parleyed with the Jews, submitted to their terms, and swore to observe their rights. Having come to this agreement, he offered a sacrifice, and honored the temple with a generous donation. [24]He approved of Maccabeus and left him as military and civil governor of the territory from Ptolemais to the region of the Gerrenes.* [25]When he came to Ptolemais, the people of that city were angered by the peace treaty; in fact they were so indignant that they wanted to annul its provisions. [26]But Lysias took the platform, defended the treaty as well as he could, and won them over by persuasion. After calming them and gaining their good will, he returned to Antioch.

That is how the king's attack and withdrawal went.

CHAPTER 14

See RG 165-67

Antagonism of Alcimus. [1u]Three years later,* Judas and his men learned that Demetrius, son of Seleucus, had sailed into the port of Tripolis with a powerful army and a fleet, [2]and that he had occupied the country, after doing away with Antiochus and his guardian Lysias.

[3]A certain Alcimus, a former high priest, who had willfully incurred defilement at the time of the revolt, realized that there was no way for him to salvage his position and regain access to the holy altar. [4]So he went to King Demetrius in the year one hundred and fifty-one and presented him with a gold crown and a palm branch, as well as some of the customary olive branches from the temple. On that occasion he kept quiet.[v] [5]But he

---

13, 15: Slew: literally "stabbed"; the deed was done by Eleazar (1 Mc 6, 43-46).

13, 16: They withdrew in triumph: according to 1 Mc 6, 47 they fled.

13, 21: Military secrets: probably about the lack of provisions in the besieged city; cf 1 Mc 6, 49.

13, 24: The Greek text is uncertain and may be rendered: "He approved of Maccabeus, then left Hegemonides as gov-

ernor of the territory . . ." Gerrenes: probably the inhabitants of Gerar, southeast of Gaza.

14, 1: Three years later: actually, Demetrius (I Soter), son of Seleucus (IV), landed at Tripolis in the year 151 of the Seleucid era (v 4), i.e., 162–161 B.C.; cf 1 Mc 7, 1-7.

s: 1 Mc 6, 43-46.   *t:* 18-23: 1 Mc 6, 48-53.   *u:* 1-11: 1 Mc 7, 1-7.   *v:* 1 Mc 7, 7. 25.

Alcimus and Nicanor

Second Maccabees ignores the slaughter of the Hasidim, perhaps because it was a setback for the Jews. Chapter 14 identifies the Hasidim closely with Judas (v. 6) and ignores that they were the first to make peace. A Hellenizer like Alcimus may well have overlooked differences within the resistance movement.

found an opportunity to further his mad scheme when he was invited to the council by Demetrius and questioned about the dispositions and intentions of the Jews. He replied: 6"Those Jews called Hasideans, led by Judas Maccabeus, are warmongers, who stir up sedition and keep the kingdom from enjoying peace and quiet. 7For this reason, now that I am deprived of my ancestral dignity, that is to say, the high priesthood, I have come here— 8first, out of my genuine concern for the king's interests, and secondly, out of consideration for my own countrymen, since our entire nation is suffering great affliction from the unreasonable conduct of the people just mentioned. 9When you have informed yourself in detail on these matters, O king, act in the interest of our country and its hard-pressed people with the same gracious consideration that you show toward all. 10As long as Judas is around, it is impossible for the state to enjoy peace." 11When he had said this, the other Friends who were hostile to Judas quickly added fuel to Demetrius' indignation.

Dealings with Nicanor. 12wThe king immediately chose Nicanor, who had been in command of the elephants, and appointed him governor of Judea. He sent him off 13with orders to put Judas to death, to disperse his followers, and to set up Alcimus as high priest of the great temple. 14The Gentiles from Judea, who would have banished Judas,* came flocking to Nicanor, thinking that the misfortunes and calamities of the Jews would mean prosperity for themselves. 15xWhen the Jews heard of Nicanor's coming, and that the Gentiles were rallying to him, they sprinkled themselves with earth and prayed to him who

established his people forever, and who always comes to the aid of his heritage. 16At their leader's command, they set out at once and came upon the enemy at the village of Adasa. 17Judas' brother Simon had engaged Nicanor, but because of the sudden appearance of the enemy suffered a slight repulse. 18However, when Nicanor heard of the valor of Judas and his men, and the great courage with which they fought for their country, he shrank from deciding the issue by bloodshed. 19So he sent Posidonius, Theodotus and Mattathias to arrange an agreement. 20After a long discussion of the terms, each leader communicated them to his troops; and when general agreement was expressed, they assented to the treaty. 21A day was set on which the leaders would meet by themselves. From each side a chariot came forward and thrones were set in place. 22Judas had posted armed men in readiness at suitable points for fear that the enemy might suddenly carry out some treacherous plan. But the conference was held in the proper way. 23Nicanor stayed on in Jerusalem, where he did nothing out of place. He got rid of the throngs of ordinary people who gathered around him; 24but he always kept Judas in his company, for he had a cordial affection for the man. 25He urged him to marry and have children; so Judas married, settled down, and shared the common life.

Threats against Judas. 26When Alcimus saw their friendship for each other, he took the treaty that had been made, went to Demetrius, and said that Nicanor was plotting against the state, and that he had appointed Judas, the conspirator against the kingdom, to be his successor. 27Stirred up by the villain's calumnies, the king became enraged.

14, 14: Who would have banished Judas: the meaning of the Greek is uncertain; some render it: "who had fled before Judas."

w: 12f: 2 Mc 8, 9; 1 Mc 3, 38f.   x: 15-19: 1 Mc 7, 26-32.

He wrote to Nicanor, stating that he was displeased with the treaty, and ordering him to send Maccabeus as a prisoner to Antioch without delay. ²⁸When this message reached Nicanor he was dismayed, for he hated to break his agreement with a man who had done no wrong. ²⁹However, there was no way of opposing the king, so he watched for an opportunity to carry out this order by a stratagem. ³⁰But Maccabeus noticed that Nicanor was becoming cool in his dealings with him, and acting with unaccustomed rudeness when they met; he concluded that this coldness betokened no good. So he gathered together a large number of his men, and went into hiding from Nicanor.

³¹ʸWhen Nicanor realized that he had been disgracefully outwitted by the man, he went to the great and holy temple, at a time when the priests were offering the customary sacrifices, and ordered them to surrender Judas. ³²As they declared under oath that they did not know where the wanted man was, ³³he raised his right hand toward the temple and swore this oath: "If you do not hand Judas over to me as prisoner, I will level this shrine of God to the ground; I will tear down the altar, and erect here a splendid temple to Dionysus." ³⁴With these words he went away. The priests stretched out their hands toward heaven, calling upon the unfailing defender of our nation in these words: ³⁵"LORD of all, though you are in need of nothing, you have approved of a temple for your dwelling place among us.ᶻ ³⁶Therefore, O holy One, LORD of all holiness, preserve forever undefiled this house, which has been so recently purified."

The Story of Razis.* ³⁷A certain Razis, one of the elders of Jerusalem, was denounced to Nicanor as a patriot. A man highly regarded, he was called a father of the Jews because of his love for them. ³⁸In the early days of the revolt, he had been convicted of Judaism, and had risked body and life in his ardent zeal for it. ³⁹Nicanor, to show his detestation of the Jews, sent more than five hundred soldiers to arrest him. ⁴⁰He thought that by arresting such a man he would deal the Jews a hard blow. ⁴¹But when these troops, on the point of capturing the tower, were forcing the outer gate and calling for fire to set the door ablaze, Razis, now caught on all sides, turned his sword against himself, ⁴²preferring to die nobly rather than fall into the hands of vile men and suffer outrages unworthy of his noble birth. ⁴³In the excitement of the struggle he failed to strike exactly. So while the troops rushed in through the doors, he gallantly ran up to the top of the wall and with manly courage threw himself down into the crowd. ⁴⁴But as they quickly drew back and left an opening, he fell into the middle of the empty space. ⁴⁵Still breathing, and inflamed with anger, he got up and ran through the crowd, with blood gushing from his frightful wounds. ⁴⁶Then, standing on a steep rock, as he lost the last of his blood, he tore out his entrails and flung them with both hands into the crowd, calling upon the LORD of life and of spirit to give these back to him again. Such was the manner of his death.ᵃ

CHAPTER 15

See RG 165–67

Nicanor's Blasphemy. ¹When Nicanor learned that Judas and his companions were in the territory of Samaria, he decided to attack them in all safety on the day of rest. ²The Jews who were forced to follow him pleaded, "Do not massacre them in that way, like a savage barbarian, but show respect for the day which the All-seeing has exalted with holiness above all other days." ³At this the thrice-sinful wretch asked if there was a ruler in heaven who prescribed the keeping of the sabbath day.ᵇ ⁴When they replied that there was indeed such a ruler in heaven, the living LORD himself, who commanded the observance of the sabbath day, ⁵he said, "I, on my part, am ruler on earth, and my orders are that you take up arms and carry out the king's business." Nevertheless he did not succeed in carrying out his cruel plan.

14, 37-46: The story of Razis belongs to the "martyrology" class of literature; it is similar to the stories in 2 Mc 6, 18—7, 42.

y: 31-36: 1 Mc 7, 33-38.   z: Acts 17, 25.   a: 2 Mc 7, 9ff.   b: 1 Mc 7, 34.

Fresh Hope

Judas's trust in the LORD is contrasted with the hubris of Nicanor (15, 6–7). Onias III, the murdered high priest, was glorified in the early chapters of 2 Maccabees. By the time the book was written, however, the high priesthood had been usurped by the Maccabees; 2 Maccabees nonetheless claims the support of the dead high priest. Jeremiah is included because of his association with the temple at the time of the Babylonian attack, and because the sword is the dominant image in an oracle attributed to him in Jeremiah 50, 35–38. Ironically, Jeremiah, noted for his opposition to militant resistance, said that God would turn the swords of the defenders against themselves (Jer 21, 4).

Fresh Hope. [6]In his utter boastfulness and arrogance Nicanor had determined to erect a public monument of victory* over Judas and his men. [7]But Maccabeus remained confident, fully convinced that he would receive help from the LORD. [8]He urged his men not to fear the enemy, but mindful of the help they had received from Heaven in the past, to expect that now, too, victory would be given them by the Almighty. [9]By encouraging them with words from the law and the prophets,* and by reminding them of the battles they had already won, he filled them with fresh enthusiasm. [10]Having stirred up their courage, he gave his orders and pointed out at the same time the perfidy of the Gentiles and their violation of oaths. [11]When he had armed each of them, not so much with the safety of shield and spear as with the encouragement of noble words, he cheered them all by relating a dream, a kind of vision, worthy of belief.

[12]What he saw was this: Onias, the former high priest,* a good and virtuous man, modest in appearance, gentle in manners, distinguished in speech, and trained from childhood in every virtuous practice, was praying with outstretched arms for the whole Jewish community.[c] [13]Then in the same way another man appeared, distinguished by his white hair and dignity, and with an air about him of extraordinary, majestic authority.

[14]Onias then said of him, "This is God's prophet Jeremiah,* who loves his brethren and fervently prays for his people and their holy city." [15]Stretching out his right hand, Jeremiah presented a gold sword to Judas. As he gave it to him he said, [16]"Accept this holy sword as a gift from God; with it you shall crush your adversaries."

Defeat and Death of Nicanor. [17]Encouraged by Judas' noble words, which had power to instill valor and stir young hearts to courage, the Jews determined not to delay, but to charge gallantly and decide the issue by hand-to-hand combat with the utmost courage, since their city and its temple with the sacred vessels were in danger. [18]They were not so much concerned about their wives and children or their brothers and kinsmen; their first and foremost fear was for the consecrated sanctuary.[d] [19]Those who remained in the city suffered a like agony, anxious as they were about the battle in the open country.

[20]Everyone now awaited the decisive moment. The enemy were already drawing near with their troops drawn up in battle line, their elephants placed in strategic positions, and their cavalry stationed on the flanks. [21]Maccabeus, contemplating the hosts before him, their elaborate equipment, and the fierceness of their elephants, stretched out his hands toward heaven and called upon the LORD who

---

15, 6: Public monument of victory: a heap of stones covered with the arms and armor of the fallen enemy.

15, 9: The law and the prophets: the first of the three parts of the Hebrew Scriptures, called the sacred books (1 Mc 12, 9).

15, 12: Onias, the former high priest: Onias III (2 Mc 3, 1–40). Evidently the author believed that the departed just were in some way alive even before the resurrection.

15, 14: Jeremiah: regarded by the postexilic Jews as one of the greatest figures in their history; cf 2 Mc 2, 1; Mt 16, 14. Who . . . prays for his people: a clear belief in the intercession of the saints.

c: 2 Mc 3, 1ff.   *d:* 1 Mc 4, 36.

works miracles; for he knew that it is not through arms but through the LORD's decision that victory is won by those who deserve it. ²²ᵉHe prayed to him thus: "You, O LORD, sent your angel in the days of King Hezekiah of Judea, and he slew a hundred and eighty-five thousand men of Sennacherib's army. ²³Sovereign of the heavens, send a good angel now to spread fear and dread before us. ²⁴By the might of your arm may those be struck down who have blasphemously come against your holy people!" With this he ended his prayer.

²⁵ᶠNicanor and his men advanced to the sound of trumpets and battle songs. ²⁶But Judas and his men met the army with supplication and prayers. ²⁷Fighting with their hands and praying to God with their hearts, they laid low at least thirty-five thousand, and rejoiced greatly over this manifestation of God's power. ²⁸When the battle was over and they were joyfully departing, they discovered Nicanor lying there in all his armor; ²⁹so they raised tumultuous shouts in their native tongue in praise of the divine Sovereign.

³⁰Then Judas, who was ever in body and soul the chief defender of his fellow citizens, and had maintained from youth his affection for his countrymen, ordered Nicanor's head and whole right arm to be cut off and taken to Jerusalem. ³¹When he arrived there, he assembled his countrymen, stationed the priests before the altar, and sent for those in the citadel.* ³²He showed them the vile Nicanor's head and the wretched blasphemer's

arm that had been boastfully stretched out against the holy dwelling of the Almighty. ³³He cut out the tongue of the godless Nicanor, saying he would feed it piecemeal to the birds and would hang up the other wages of his folly opposite the temple. ³⁴At this, everyone looked toward heaven and praised the LORD who manifests his divine power, saying, "Blessed be he who has kept his own Place undefiled!"

³⁵Judas hung up Nicanor's head on the wall of the citadel, a clear and evident proof to all of the Lord's help.ᵍ ³⁶By public vote it was unanimously decreed never to let this day pass unobserved,ʰ but to celebrate it on the thirteenth day of the twelfth month, called Adar in Aramaic, the eve of Mordecai's Day.*

VII: Epilogue

Author's Apology. ³⁷Since Nicanor's doings ended in this way, with the city remaining in possession of the Hebrews from that time on, I will bring my own story to an end here too. ³⁸If it is well written and to the point, that is what I wanted; if it is poorly done and mediocre, that is the best I could do. ³⁹Just as it is harmful to drink wine alone or water alone, whereas mixing wine with water makes a more pleasant drink that increases delight, so a skillfully composed story delights the ears of those who read the work. Let this, then, be the end.

15, 31: Those in the citadel: presumably Jewish soldiers; actually, the citadel was still in the possession of the Syrians.
15, 36: Mordecai's Day: the feast of Purim, celebrated on the fourteenth and fifteenth days of Adar (Est 9, 17-22).

e: 22f: 2 Mc 8, 19; 2 Kgs 19, 35; Is 37, 36; 1 Mc 7, 40f.   *f:* 25-36: 2 Mc 8, 39-50.   *g:* 1 Sm 31, 9f.   *h:* 1 Mc 7, 49.

See RG
168-69

THE WISDOM BOOKS

The Books of Job, Psalms, Proverbs, Ecclesiastes, the Song of Songs, Wisdom, and Sirach, are all versified by the skillful use of parallelism, that is, of the balanced and symmetrical phrases peculiar to Hebrew poetry. With the exception of the Psalms, the majority of which are devotional lyrics, and the Song of Songs, a nuptial hymn, these books belong to the general class of wisdom or didactic literature, strictly so called because their chief purpose is instruction.

The wisdom literature of the Bible is the fruit of a movement among ancient oriental people to gather, preserve and express, usually in aphoristic style, the results of human experience as an aid toward understanding and solving the problems of life. In Israel especially, the movement concerned itself with such basic and vital problems as man's origin and destiny, his quest for happiness, the problem of suffering, of good and evil in human conduct, of death, and the state beyond the grave. Originating with oral tradition, these formulations found their way into the historical books of the Old Testament in the shape of proverbs, odes, chants, epigrams, and also into those psalms intended for instruction.

The developed compositions of this literature form the sapiential books. The Book of Proverbs is a collection of sentences or practical norms for moral conduct. The Book of Job is an artistic dialogue skillfully handling the problem of suffering though only from the standpoint of temporal life. Ecclesiastes examines a wide range of human experience only to conclude that all things are vanity except the fear of the Lord and observance of his commandments, and that God requites man in his own good time. Sirach gathers and presents the fruits of past experience, thus preparing for the Book of Wisdom, which sees for the just man seeking happiness the full hope of immortality (Wis 3, 4).

Those who cultivated wisdom were called sages. Men of letters, scribes, skilled in the affairs of government, and counselors to rulers, they were instructors of the people, especially of youth (Sir 51, 13-30). In times of crisis they guided the people by revaluating tradition, thus helping to preserve unity, peace and good will. The most illustrious of the sages, and the originator of wisdom literature in Israel, was Solomon. Because of his fame, some of the wisdom books of which he was not the author bear his name.

Despite numerous resemblances, sometimes exaggerated, between the sapiential literature of pagan nations and the wisdom books of the Bible, the former are often replete with vagaries and abound in polytheistic conceptions; the latter remained profoundly human, universal, fundamentally moral, and essentially religious and monotheistic. Under the influence of the law and the prophets, wisdom became piety and virtue; impiety and vice were folly. The teachers of wisdom were regarded as men of God, and their books were placed beside the law and the prophets. The highest wisdom became identified with the spirit of God through which the world was created and preserved (Prv 8, 22-31), and mankind was enlightened.

The limitations of Old Testament wisdom served to crystalize the problems of human life and destiny, thus preparing for their solution through New Testament revelation. Ecclesiastes' vain search for success and happiness on earth ends when the Savior assures these things to his followers, not in this world but in the bliss of heaven. The anxiety in the Book of Job over reconciling God's justice and wisdom with the suffering of the innocent is relieved by the account of the crucified and risen Redeemer in the gospel. By fulfilling all that the Psalms foretold concerning him, Jesus makes the Psalter his prayer book and that of the Church for all time. The love of God for the chosen people which underlies the Song of Songs is perfected in the union of Christ with his Church. The personification of the wisdom of Proverbs, Wisdom and Sirach shines forth in resplendent reality in the Word who was with God, and who was God, and who became incarnate to dwell among us; cf Jn 1, 2. 14.

See RG
169-73

The Book of Job

The Book of Job, named after its protagonist, is an exquisite dramatic poem which treats the problem of the suffering of the innocent, and of retribution. The contents of the book, together with its artistic structure and elegant style, place it among the literary masterpieces of all time.

Job, an oriental chieftain, pious and upright, richly endowed in his own person and in domestic prosperity, suffers a sudden and complete reversal of fortune. He loses his property and his children; a loathsome disease afflicts his body; and sorrow oppresses his soul. Nevertheless, Job does not complain against God. When some friends visit him to condole with him, Job protests his innocence and does not understand why he is afflicted. He curses the day of his birth and longs for death to bring an end to his sufferings. The debate which ensues consists of three cycles of speeches. Job's friends insist that his plight can only be a punishment for personal wrongdoing and an invitation from God to repentance. Job rejects their inadequate explanation and calls for a response from God himself. At this point the speeches of a youth named Elihu (chs 32—37) interrupt the development.

In response to Job's plea that he be allowed to see God and hear from him the cause of his suffering, God answers, not by justifying his action before men, but by referring to his own omniscience and almighty power. Job is content with this. He recovers his attitude of humility and trust in God, which is deepened now and strengthened by his experience of suffering.

The author of the book is not known; it was composed some time between the 7th and 5th centuries B.C. Its literary form, with speeches, prologue and epilogue disposed according to a studied plan, indicates that the purpose of the writing is didactic. The lesson is that even the just may suffer here, and their sufferings are a test of their fidelity. They shall be rewarded in the end. Man's finite mind cannot probe the depths of the divine omniscience that governs the world. The problems we encounter can be solved by a broader and deeper awareness of God's power, presence (42, 5) and wisdom.

The divisions of the Book of Job are as follows:

I: Prologue (1, 1—2, 13).
II: First Cycle of Speeches (3, 1—14, 22).
III: Second Cycle of Speeches (15, 1—21, 34).
IV: Third Cycle of Speeches (22, 1—28. 28).
V: Job's Final Summary of His Cause (29, 1—31, 37).
VI: Elihu's Speeches (32, 1—37, 24).
VII: The Lord's Speech (38, 1—42, 6).
VIII: Epilogue (42, 7-17)

I: Prologue

CHAPTER 1

See RG
169-73

Job's Wealth and Piety. [1]In the land of Uz* there was a blameless and upright man named Job,[a] who feared God and avoided evil. [2]*Seven sons and three daughters were born to him; [3]and he had seven thousand sheep, three thousand camels, five hundred yoke of oxen, five hundred she-asses, and a great number of work animals,

---

1, 1: Uz: somewhere in Edom or Arabia. Job: a not uncommon name in ancient Semitic circles; its original meaning was "enemy."

1, 2f: The numbers mentioned here indicate Job's

great wealth and happiness, external proof of God's friendship.

---

a: Jb 2, 3.

Who Is Job the Just?

Job is a venerable hero, well known beyond the confines of Israel. His homeland, Uz, is outside the holy land, located to the east, probably in Edom, an area south of the Dead Sea. Job was "blameless and upright," meaning that Job "feared God" and "avoided evil" (1, 1).

so that he was greater than any of the men of the East.* ⁴His sons used to take turns giving feasts, sending invitations to their three sisters to eat and drink with them. ⁵And when each feast had run its course, Job would send for them and sanctify them, rising early and offering holocausts for every one of them. For Job said, "It may be that my sons have sinned and blasphemed God in their hearts." This Job did habitually.

⁶ᵇOne day, when the sons of God* came to present themselves before the LORD, Satan also came among them.ᶜ ⁷And the LORD said to Satan, "Whence do you come?" Then Satan answered the LORD and said,ᵈ "From roaming the earth and patrolling it." ⁸And the LORD said to Satan, "Have you noticed my servant Job, and that there is no one on earth like him, blameless and upright, fearing God and avoiding evil?" ⁹But Satan answered the LORD and said, "Is it for nothing that Job is God-fearing? ¹⁰Have you not surrounded him and his family and all that he has with your protection? You have blessed the work of his hands, and his livestock are spread over the land. ¹¹ᵉBut now put forth your hand and touch anything that he has, and surely he will blaspheme you to your face." ¹²And the LORD said to Satan, "Behold, all that he has is in your power; only do not lay a hand upon his person." So Satan went forth from the presence of the LORD.

The First Trial. ¹³And so one day, while his sons and his daughters were eating and drinking wine in the house of their eldest brother, ¹⁴a messenger came to Job and said, "The oxen were plowing and the asses grazing beside them, ¹⁵and the Sabeans* carried them off in a raid. They put the herdsmen to the sword, and I alone have escaped to tell you." ¹⁶While he was yet speaking, another came and said, "Lightning* has fallen from heaven and struck the sheep and their shepherds and consumed them; and I alone have escaped to tell you." ¹⁷While he was yet speaking, another came and said, "The Chaldeans formed three columns, seized the camels, carried them off, and put those tending them to the sword, and I alone have escaped to tell you." ¹⁸While he was yet speaking, another came and said, "Your sons and daughters were eating and drinking wine in the house of their eldest brother, ¹⁹when suddenly a great wind came across the desert and smote the four corners of the house. It fell upon the young people and they are dead; and I alone have escaped to tell you." ²⁰Then Job began to tear his cloak and cut off his hair. He cast himself prostrate upon the ground, ²¹and said,

"Naked I came forth from my mother's womb,ᶠ
and naked shall I go back again.*
The LORD gave and the LORD has taken away;
blessed be the name of the LORD!"

²²In all this Job did not sin,ᵍ nor did he say anything disrespectful of God.

1, 3: Men of the East: that is, east of Palestine.
1, 6: Sons of God: angels. Satan: literally, "adversary."
1, 15: Sabeans: from southern Arabia.
1, 16: Lightning: literally, "God's fire."
1, 21: Go back again: to the earth; cf Gn 2, 7;

Sir 40, 1.

---

b: 6ff: Jb 2, 1ff. c: Gn 6, 2. 4; Zec 3, 1; Lk 22, 31; Rv 12, 9. d: 1 Pt 5, 8. e: Jb 2, 5. f: Eccl 5, 14; 1 Tm 6, 7. g: Jb 2, 10; Jas 5, 11.

God Tests Job

People imagined the heavenly court on the model of an earthly one: Courtiers present themselves before the king and officials report to the LORD (1, 6—2). Satan, literally, "the Satan" or adversary, is not the enemy of God as in later biblical books, but a member of the court whose particular task it is to watch the actions of humans and report back to the LORD. God is pleased by the utterly just actions of Job, but Satan cynically intimates that Job is doing them only for the abundant blessings he receives in return. God allows Satan to test Job to see whether he, when "touched" (v. 11), will curse God. The reader knows two things that the friends of Job do not: Job is genuinely just, and God is testing him.

CHAPTER 2

See RG 169–73

The Second Trial. ¹Once again the sons of God[h] came to present themselves before the LORD, and Satan also came with them. ²And the LORD said to Satan, "Whence do you come?" And Satan answered the LORD and said, "From roaming the earth and patrolling it." ³And the LORD said to Satan, "Have you noticed my servant Job, and that there is no one on earth like him, faultless and upright, fearing God and avoiding evil?[i] He still holds fast to his innocence although you incited me against him to ruin him without cause." ⁴And Satan answered the LORD and said, "Skin for skin!* All that a man has will he give for his life. ⁵[j]But now put forth your hand and touch his bone and his flesh, and surely he will blaspheme you to your face." ⁶And the LORD said to Satan, "He is in your power; only spare his life." ⁷So Satan went forth from the presence of the LORD and smote Job with severe boils from the soles of his feet to the crown of his head. ⁸And he took a potsherd to scrape himself, as he sat among the ashes. ⁹Then his wife said to him,[k] "Are you still holding to your innocence? Curse God and die."* ¹⁰But he said to her, "Are even you going to speak as senseless women do? We accept good things from God; and should we not accept evil?" Through all this, Job said nothing sinful.[l]

Job's Three Friends. ¹¹Now when three of Job's friends heard of all the misfortune that had come upon him, they set out each one from his own place: Eliphaz from Teman, Bildad from Shuh, and Zophar from Naamath.* They met and journeyed together to give him sympathy and comfort. ¹²But when, at a distance, they lifted up their eyes and did not recognize him, they began to weep aloud; they tore their cloaks and threw dust upon their heads. ¹³Then they sat down upon the ground with him seven days and seven nights, but none of them spoke a word to him; for they saw how great was his suffering.

II: First Cycle of Speeches

CHAPTER 3

See RG 169–73

Job's Plaint. ¹After this, Job opened his mouth and cursed his day. ²Job spoke out and said:

³ Perish the day on which I was born,[m]
the night when they said, "The child is
a boy!"
⁴ May that day be darkness:
let not God above call for it,
nor light shine upon it!
⁵ May darkness and gloom claim it,
clouds settle upon it,
the blackness of night affright it!
⁶ May obscurity seize that day;
let it not occur among the days of the
year,

2, 4: Skin for skin: an expression which, as applied to Job, means that he has borne his suffering patiently thus far only because he seeks to avoid greater suffering and to receive greater favors from God.

2, 9: Curse God and die: you have nothing to hope for from God and therefore nothing to live for.

2, 11: The names of Job's friends suggest Edomite origin. The Edomites (Ob 8f) and more specifically the Temanites (Jer 49, 7) enjoyed a reputation for wisdom.

h: Jb 1, 6.   i: Jb 1, 1.   j: Jb 1, 11.   k: Jb 19, 17.   l: Jb 1, 22; Sir 2, 4; Jas 5, 11.   m: Jer 20, 14.

nor enter into the count of the
months!

7 May that night be barren;
let no joyful outcry greet it!

8 Let them curse it who curse the sea,
the appointed disturbers of
Leviathan!*

9 May the stars of its twilight be
darkened;
may it look for daylight, but have
none,
nor gaze on the eyes of the dawn,

10 Because it kept not shut the doors of the
womb
to shield my eyes from trouble!

11 Why did I not perish at birth,[n]
come forth from the womb and
expire?

16 Or why was I not buried away like an
untimely birth,*
like babes that have never seen the
light?

12 Wherefore did the knees receive
me?
or why did I suck at the breasts?

13 For then I should have lain down and
been tranquil;
had I slept, I should then have been at
rest

14 With kings and counselors of
the earth
who built where now there are
ruins

15 Or with princes who had gold
and filled their houses with silver.

17 There* the wicked cease from
troubling,
there the weary are at rest.

18 There the captives are at ease
together,
and hear not the voice of the slave
driver.

19 Small and great are there the
same,
and the servant is free from his
master.

20 Why is light given to the toilers,
and life to the bitter in spirit?

21 They wait for death and it comes not;
they search for it rather than for hidden
treasures,

22 Rejoice in it exultingly,
and are glad when they reach the
grave:

23 Men whose path is hidden from
them,
and whom God has hemmed in!

24 For sighing comes more readily to me
than food,
and my groans well forth like
water.

25 For what I fear overtakes me,
and what I shrink from comes upon
me.

26 I have no peace nor ease;
I have no rest, for trouble comes!

CHAPTER 4

Eliphaz's First Speech. [1]Then spoke
Eliphaz the Temanite, who said:

See RG 169-73

2 If someone attempts a word with you,
will you mind?
For how can anyone refrain from
speaking?

3 Behold, you have instructed many,
and have made firm their feeble
hands.

4 Your words have upheld the
stumbler;
you have strengthened his faltering
knees.

5 But now that it comes to you, you are
impatient;

3, 8: Leviathan: in Jb 40, 25, the crocodile; here the reference is probably to a mythological sea monster symbolizing primeval chaos. Cf Jb 9, 13; 26, 13; Pss 74, 13f; 104, 26; Is 27, 1.

3, 16: This verse has been placed between vv 11 and 12 where it probably stood originally. There is reason to believe that here, as well as in several other places in Job, the original order of the poetic lines was accidentally disturbed in the early transmission of the text; so in chapters 12-15;

19-21; 24-31; 34; 36; 38-42. The verse numbers given in such cases are always those of the current Hebrew text, though the arrangement may differ. The footnotes will advise the reader of the difficulties and provide him with further indications for following the progress of thought in the book.

3, 17: There: in death.

---

n: Jb 10, 18f.

Eliphaz begins with an attack on Job's motives without bothering to listen to his words. The deterioration of Job's relationship to his friends increases his interest in exploring his relationship to God.

when it touches yourself, you are dismayed.

6 Is not your peity a source of confidence, and your integrity of life your hope?

7 Reflect now, what innocent person perishes?*o*
Since when are the upright destroyed?

8 As I see it, those who plow for mischief and sow trouble, reap the same.

9 By the breath of God they perish,*p*
and by the blast of his wrath they are consumed.

10 Though the lion* roars, though the king of beasts cries out,
yet the teeth of the young lions are broken;

11 The old lion perishes for lack of prey, and the cubs of the lioness are scattered.

12 For a word was stealthily brought to me,*
and my ear caught a whisper of it.

13 In my thoughts during visions of the night,*q*
when deep sleep falls on men,

14 Fear came upon me, and shuddering, that terrified me to the bones.

15 Then a spirit passed before me, and the hair of my flesh stood up.

16 It paused, but its likeness I could not discern;
a figure was before my eyes, and I heard a still voice:

17 "Can a man be righteous as against God?*r*
Can a mortal be blameless against his Maker?

18 Lo, he puts no trust in his servants,*s*
and with his angels he can find fault.

19 How much more with those that dwell in houses of clay,

whose foundation is in the dust, who are crushed more easily than the moth!

20 Morning or evening they may be shattered; with no heed paid to it, they perish forever.

21 The pegs of their tent are plucked up; they die without knowing wisdom."

CHAPTER 5

See RG 169–73

1 Call now! Will anyone respond to you?
To which of the holy ones will you appeal?

2 Nay, impatience kills the fool and indignation slays the simpleton.

3 I have seen a fool spreading his roots,*t*
but his household suddenly decayed.

4 His children shall be far from safety; they shall be crushed at the gate* without a rescuer.

5 What they have reaped the hungry shall eat up;
[or God shall take it away by blight;] and the thirsty shall swallow their substance.

6 For mischief comes not out of the earth,
nor does trouble spring out of the ground;

7 But man himself begets mischief, as sparks* fly upward.

8 In your place, I would appeal to God,
and to God I would state my plea.*

10 He gives rain upon the earth and sends water upon the fields;

11 *u*He sets up on high the lowly,

4, 10: The lion: used figuratively here for the violent, rapacious sinner who cannot prevail against God.

4, 12-21: A dramatic presentation of the idea of man's nothingness in contrast to God's greatness.

5, 4: At the gate: of the city, where justice was administered.

5, 7: Sparks: in Hebrew, "sons of resheph," which the ancient versions took as the name of a bird.

5, 9: Omitted here; it is a duplicate of Jb 9, 10.

o: Ps 37, 25. *p:* Ps 18, 16; Is 11, 4; 2 Thes 2, 8. *q:* Jb 33, 15. *r:* Jb 9, 2; 15, 14ff; 25, 4; Pss 130, 3; 143, 2. *s:* Jb 15, 15; 2 Pt 2, 4; Jude 6. *t:* Ps 37, 35f. *u:* 1 Sm 2, 7; Ps 113, 7; Lk 1, 52.

and those who mourn he exalts to
safety.

12 He frustrates the plans of the cunning,
so that their hands achieve no success;

13 He catches the wise in their own ruses,[v]
and the designs of the crafty are routed.

14 They meet with darkness in the daytime,
and at noonday they grope as though it
were night.

15 But the poor from the edge of the sword
and from the hand of the mighty, he
saves.

16 Thus the unfortunate have hope,
and iniquity closes her mouth.

17 Happy is the man whom God reproves!
The Almighty's chastening do not
reject.

18 For he wounds, but he binds up;[w]
he smites, but his hands give healing.

19 Out of six troubles he will deliver you,
and at the seventh* no evil shall touch
you.

20 In famine he will deliver you from death,
and in war from the threat of the
sword;

21 From the scourge of the tongue you shall
be hidden,
and shall not fear approaching ruin.

22 At destruction and want you shall laugh;
the beasts of the earth you need not
dread.

23 You shall be in league with the stones of
the field,
and the wild beasts shall be at peace
with you.

24 And you shall know that your tent is
secure;
taking stock of your household, you
shall miss nothing.

25 You shall know that your descendants are
many,
and your offspring as the grass of the
earth.

26 You shall approach the grave in full vigor,
as a shock of grain comes in at its
season.

27 Lo, this we have searched out; so it is!
This we have heard, and you should
know.

CHAPTER 6

See RG
169-73

Job's First Reply. 1Then Job answered
and said:

2 Ah, could my anguish but be measured
and my calamity laid with it in the
scales,

3 They would now outweigh the sands of
the sea!
Because of this I speak without
restraint.

4 For the arrows of the Almighty pierce
me,[x]
and my spirit drinks in their poison;
the terrors of God are arrayed against
me.

5 Does the wild ass bray when he has
grass?*
Does the ox low over his fodder?

6 Can a thing insipid be eaten without salt?
Is there flavor in the white of an egg?

7 I refuse to touch them;
they are loathsome food to me.

8 Oh, that I might have my request,
and that God would grant what I long
for:

9 Even that God would decide to crush me,
that he would put forth his hand and
cut me off!

10 Then I should still have consolation
and could exult through unremitting
pain,
because I have not transgressed the
commands of the Holy One.

11 What strength have I that I should endure,
and what is my limit that I should be
patient?

12 Have I the strength of stones,
or is my flesh of bronze?

13 Have I no helper,[y]
and has advice deserted me?

14 A friend owes kindness to one in despair,

5, 19: Six . . . the seventh: proverbial expression for any
large number; cf Prv 24, 16; Lk 17, 4.

6, 5f: Job would not complain if his life were as pleasant
to him as fodder to a hungry animal; but his life is as dis-
agreeable as insipid food. White of an egg: thus the obscure

Hebrew has been understood in Jewish tradition; some render
it "mallow juice."

---

v: 1 Cor 3, 19.   w: Hos 6, 1f.   x: Ps 88, 17.   y: Jb 19, 14f.

though he have forsaken the fear of the Almighty.

15 My brethren are undependable as a brook,
as watercourses that run dry in the wadies;

16 Though they may be black with ice,
and with snow heaped upon them,

17 Yet once they flow, they cease to be;
in the heat, they disappear from their place.

18 Caravans turn aside from their routes;
they go into the desert and perish.

19 The caravans of Tema* search,
the companies of Sheba have hopes;

20 They are disappointed, though they were confident;
they come there and are frustrated.

21 It is thus that you have now become for me;
you see a terrifying thing and are afraid.

22 Have I asked you to give me anything,
to offer a gift for me from your possessions,

23 Or to deliver me from the enemy,
or to redeem me from oppressors?

24 Teach me, and I will be silent;
prove to me wherein I have erred.

25 How agreeable are honest words;
yet how unconvincing is your argument!

26 Do you consider your words as proof,
but the sayings of a desperate man as wind?

27 You would even cast lots for the orphan,
and would barter away your friend!

28 Come, now, give me your attention;
surely I will not lie to your face.

29 Think it over; let there be no injustice.
Think it over; I still am right.

30 Is there insincerity on my tongue,
or cannot my taste discern falsehood?

CHAPTER 7

See RG 169-73

1 zIs not man's life on earth a drudgery?*

Are not his days those of a hireling?

2 He is a slave who longs for the shade,
a hireling who waits for his wages.

3 So I have been assigned months of misery,
and troubled nights have been told off for me.

4 If in bed I say, "When shall I arise?"
then the night drags on;
I am filled with restlessness until the dawn.

5 My flesh is clothed with worms and scabs;a
my skin cracks and festers;

6 My days are swifter than a weaver's shuttle;
they come to an end without hope.

7 Remember that my life is like the wind;b
I shall not see happiness again.

8 The eye that now sees me shall no more behold me;
as you look at me, I shall be gone.

9 As a cloud dissolves and vanishes,c
so he who goes down to the nether world shall come up no more.

10 He shall not again return to his house;
his place shall know him no more.

11 My own utterance I will not restrain;
I will speak in the anguish of my spirit;
I will complain in the bitterness of my soul.

12 *Am I the sea, or a monster of the deep,
that you place a watch over me?*
Why have you set me up as an object of attack?
or why should I be a target for you?

13 When I say, "My bed shall comfort me,
my couch shall ease my complaint,"

14 Then you affright me with dreams
and with visions terrify me,

15 So that I should prefer choking
and death rather than my pains.

16 I waste away: I cannot live forever;d
let me alone, for my days are but a breath.

17 What is man, that you make much of him,
or pay him any heed?

6, 19: Tema: in northwest Arabia. Sheba: see note on Jb 1, 15.

7, 1: Drudgery: taken by some to refer to military service; cf also Jb 14, 14.

7, 12: An allusion in poetic imagery to primeval chaos as a monstrous ocean vanquished by God at the world's creation.

7, 12-21: Job now speaks, not to his friends, but to God.

z: Jb 14, 14. a: Jb 2, 7f. b: Pss 8, 5; 144, 3. c: 9f: Jb 10, 21; 14, 10ff; 2 Sm 12, 23; 14, 14; Wis 2, 1. d: Jb 14, 1ff. 5.

¹⁸ You observe him with each new day*e*
and try him at every moment!
¹⁹ How long will it be before you look
away from me,
and let me alone long enough to
swallow my spittle?
²⁰ Though I have sinned, what can I do to you,
O watcher of men?
²¹ Why do you not pardon my offense,
or take away my guilt?
For soon I shall lie down in the dust;
and should you seek me I shall then be
gone.

CHAPTER 8

See RG
169–73

Bildad's First Speech. ¹Bildad the
Shuhite spoke out and said:

² How long will you utter such things?
The words from your mouth are like a
mighty wind!
³ Does God pervert judgment,*f*
and does the Almighty distort justice?
⁴ If your children have sinned against
him
and he has left them in the grip of their
guilt,
⁵ Still, if you yourself have recourse to
God
and make supplication to the
Almighty,
⁶ Should you be blameless and upright,
surely now he will awake for you
and restore your rightful domain;
⁷ Your former state will be of little
moment,
for in time to come you will flourish
indeed.
⁸ If you inquire of the former generations,
and give heed to the experience of the
fathers*g*
⁹ (As we are but of yesterday and have no
knowledge,
because our days on earth are but a
shadow),*h*
¹⁰ Will they not teach you and tell you

and utter their words of
understanding?
¹¹ Can the papyrus grow up without mire?*
Can the reed grass flourish without
water?
¹² While it is yet green and uncut,
it withers quicker than any grass.
¹³ So is the end of everyone who forgets
God,
and so shall the hope of the godless
man perish.
¹⁴ His confidence is but a gossamer thread
and his trust is a spider's web.
¹⁵ He shall rely upon his family, but it shall
not last;
he shall cling to it, but it shall not
endure.
¹⁶ He is full of sap before sunrise,
and beyond his garden his shoots go
forth;
¹⁷ About a heap of stones are his roots
entwined;
among the rocks he takes hold.
¹⁸ Yet if one tears him from his place,
it will disown him: "I have never seen
you!"
¹⁹ There he lies rotting beside the road,
and out of the soil another sprouts.
²⁰ Behold, God will not cast away the upright;
neither will he take the hand of the
wicked.
²¹ Once more will he fill your mouth with
laughter,
and your lips with rejoicing.
²² They that hate you shall be clothed with
shame,
and the tent of the wicked shall be no
more.

CHAPTER 9

Job's Second Reply. ¹Then Job answered and said:

See RG
169–73

² I know well that it is so;
but how can a man be justified before
God?

8, 11ff: As marsh plants need water, so man needs God. These verses are taken by some as a quotation from the teaching
of the forefathers; cf v 10.

---

e: Ps 17, 3.   *f:* Jb 34, 10ff.   *g:* Dt 4, 32; 32, 7.   *h:* Jb 14, 2; Pss 102, 12; 109, 23; 144, 4; Wis 2, 5.

³ Should one wish to contend with him,
    he could not answer him once in a
        thousand times.
⁴ God is wise in heart and mighty in
    strength;
    who has withstood him and remained
        unscathed?
⁵ He removes the mountains before they
    know it;
    he overturns them in his anger.
⁶ He shakes the earth out of its place,ⁱ
    and the pillars beneath it tremble.
⁷ He commands the sun, and it rises not;
    he seals up the stars.
⁸ He alone stretches out the heavens^j
    and treads upon the crests of the sea.
⁹ He made the Bear and Orion,
    the Pleiades and the constellations of
        the south;
¹⁰ He does great things past finding out,
    marvelous things beyond reckoning.
¹¹ Should he come near me, I see him not;
    should he pass by, I am not aware of
        him;
¹² Should he seize me forcibly, who can say
    him nay?
    Who can say to him, "What are you
        doing?"
¹³ He is God and he does not relent;
    the helpers of Rahab* bow beneath him.
¹⁴ How much less shall I give him any
    answer,
    or choose out arguments against him!
¹⁵ Even though I were right, I could not
    answer him,^k
    but should rather beg for what was due
        me.
¹⁶ If I appealed to him and he answered my
    call,
    I could not believe that he would
        hearken to my words;
¹⁷ With a tempest he might overwhelm me,
    and multiply my wounds without
        cause;
¹⁸ He need not suffer me to draw breath,
    but might fill me with bitter griefs.

¹⁹ If it be a question of strength, he is
    mighty;
    and if of judgment, who will call him
        to account?
²⁰ Though I were right, my own mouth
    might condemn me;^l
    were I innocent, he might put me in
        the wrong.
²¹ Though I am innocent, I myself cannot
    know it;
    I despise my life.
²² It is all one! therefore I say:
    Both the innocent and the wicked he
        destroys.^m
²³ When the scourge slays suddenly,
    he laughs at the despair of the innocent.
²⁴ The earth is given into the hands of the
    wicked;
    he covers the faces of its judges.
    If it is not he, who then is it?
²⁵ My days are swifter than a runner,
    they flee away; they see no happiness;ⁿ
²⁶ They shoot by like skiffs of reed,
    like an eagle swooping upon its prey.
²⁷ If I say: I will forget my complaining,
    I will lay aside my sadness and be of
        good cheer,
²⁸ Then I am in dread of all my pains;
    I know that you* will not hold me
        innocent.
²⁹ If I must be accounted guilty,
    why then should I strive in vain?
³⁰ If I should wash myself with snow
    and cleanse my hands with lye,
³¹ Yet you would plunge me in the ditch,
    so that my garments would abhor me.
³² For he is not a man like myself, that I
    should answer him,
    that we should come together in
        judgment.
³³ Would that there were an arbiter between
    us,
    who could lay his hand upon us both
³⁴   and withdraw his rod from me.
    Would that his terrors did not frighten
        me;

9, 13: Rahab: cf Jb 26, 12. See note on Ps 89, 11.
9, 28-31: You: refers to God.

i: Jb 26, 11.   *j:* Ps 104, 2; Is 40, 22.   *k:* Jb 10, 15.   *l:* Jb 15, 6.   *m:* Eccl 9, 2.   *n:* Jb 7, 6.

35 that I might speak without being afraid
of him.
Since this is not the case with me,
1 *I loathe my life.^o

CHAPTER 10

See RG
169–73 I will give myself up to complaint;
I will speak from the bitterness of my
soul.
2 I will say to God: Do not put me in the
wrong!
Let me know why you oppose me.
3 Is it a pleasure for you to oppress,
to spurn the work of your hands,
and smile on the plan of the wicked?
4 Have you eyes of flesh?
Do you see as man sees?
5 Are your days as the days of a mortal,^p
and are your years as a man's lifetime,
6 That you seek for guilt in me
and search after my sins,
7 Even though you know that I am not
wicked,^q
and that none can deliver me out of
your hand?
8 Your hands have formed me and
fashioned me;
will you then turn and destroy me?
9 Oh, remember that you fashioned me
from clay!^r
Will you then bring me down to dust
again?
10 Did you not pour me out as milk,
and thicken me like cheese?
11 With skin and flesh you clothed me,
with bones and sinews knit me
together.
12 Grace and favor you granted me,
and your providence has preserved my
spirit.
13 Yet these things you have hidden in your
heart;
I know that they are your purpose:
14 If I should sin, you would keep a watch
against me,
and from my guilt you would not
absolve me.

15 If I should be wicked, alas for me!
if righteous, I dare not hold up my
head,
filled with ignominy and sodden with
affliction!
16 Should it lift up, you hunt me like a lion:
repeatedly you show your wondrous
power against me,
17 You renew your attack upon me
and multiply your harassment of me;
in waves your troops come against me.
18 Why then did you bring me forth from
the womb?^s
I should have died and no eye have
seen me.
19 I should be as though I had never lived;
I should have been taken from the
womb to the grave.
20 Are not the days of my life few?
Let me alone, that I may recover a little
21 Before I go whence I shall not return,^t
to the land of darkness and of gloom,
22 The black, disordered land
where darkness is the only light.

CHAPTER 11

Zophar's First Speech. ¹And Zophar See RG
169–73
the Naamathite spoke out and said:

2 Should not the man of many words be
answered,
or must the garrulous man necessarily
be right?
3 Shall your babblings keep men silent,
and shall you deride and no one give
rebuke?
4 Shall you say: "My teaching is pure,
and I am clean in your sight"?
5 But oh, that God would speak,
and open his lips against you,
6 And tell you that the secrets of wisdom
are twice as effective:
So you might learn that God
will make you answer for your guilt.
7 Can you penetrate the designs of God?^u
Dare you vie with the perfection of the
Almighty?

10, 1: I loathe my life: this is the first verse of ch 10.

o: Jb 9, 21.   *p:* Jb 36, 26.   *q:* Jb 2, 3. 9; Dt 32, 39; Wis 16, 15.   *r:* Jb 4, 19; 33, 6; Gn 2, 7; 3, 19; Ps 146, 4.   *s:* Jb 3, 3. 11.   *t:* Jb 7,
9f; 16, 22.   *u:* Rom 11, 33.

⁸ It is higher than the heavens; what can
   you do?
   It is deeper than the nether world; what
   can you know?
⁹ It is longer than the earth in measure,
   and broader than the sea.
¹⁰ If he seize and imprison
   or call to judgment, who then can say
   him nay?
¹¹ For he knows the worthlessness of men
   and sees iniquity; will he then ignore
   it?
¹² Will empty man then gain understanding,
   and the wild jackassᵛ be made docile?
¹³ If you set your heart aright
   and stretch out your hands toward him,
¹⁴ If you remove all iniquity from your
   conduct,
   and let not injustice dwell in your tent,
¹⁵ Surely then you may lift up your face in
   innocence;
   you may stand firm and unafraid.
¹⁶ For then you shall forget your misery,
   or recall it like waters that have ebbed
   away.
¹⁷ Then your life shall be brighter than the
   noonday;
   its gloom shall become as the
   morning,
¹⁸ And you shall be secure, because there is
   hope;
   you shall look round you and lie down
   in safety,ʷ
¹⁹   and you shall take your rest with none
   to disturb.
   Many shall entreat your favor,
²⁰   but the wicked, looking on, shall be
   consumed with envy.
   Escape shall be cut off from them,
   they shall wait to expire.

CHAPTER 12

See RG
169-73 *Job's Third Reply.* ¹Then Job replied
and said:

² No doubt you are the intelligent folk,

and with you wisdom shall die!
³ But I have intelligence as well as you;ˣ
   for who does not know such things as
   these?
⁴ I have become the sport of my neighbors:*
   "The one whom God answers when he
   calls upon him,
   the just, the perfect man," is a
   laughingstock;ʸ
⁵ The undisturbed esteem my downfall a
   disgrace
   such as awaits unsteady feet;
⁶ Yet the tents of robbers are prosperous,
   and those who provoke God are
   secure.
⁷ But now ask the beasts to teach you,
   and the birds of the air to tell you;
⁸ Or the reptiles on earth to instruct you,
   and the fish of the sea to inform you.
⁹ Which of all these does not know
   that the hand of God has done this?
¹⁰ In his hand is the soul of every living
   thing,ᶻ
   and the life breath of all mankind.
¹¹ Does not the ear judge words
   as the mouth tastes food?ᵃ
¹² So with old age is wisdom,ᵇ
   and with length of days
   understanding.
¹³ With him are wisdom and might;
   his are counsel and understanding.
¹⁴ If he breaks a thing down, there is no
   rebuilding;ᶜ
   if he imprisons a man, there is no
   release.
¹⁵ He holds back the waters and there is
   drought;ᵈ
   he sends them forth and they
   overwhelm the land.
¹⁸ He loosens the bonds imposed by kings
   and leaves but a waistcloth to bind the
   king's own loins.*
²¹ He breaks down the barriers of the
   streams
¹⁹   and lets their never-failing waters flow
   away.

12, 4f: The Hebrew is somewhat obscure, but the general
sense is that the wicked mock at the pious when the latter appear to be abandoned by God; cf Ps 22, 7ff; Mt 27, 39-43.
12, 18: Waistcloth . . . loins: he reduces kings to the condition of slaves, who wear only a cloth wrapped about the waist

v: Jb 39, 5-8. w: Lv 26, 6; Ps 4, 9. x: Jb 13, 2; 15, 9. y: Jb 21,
3; 30, 1. z: Acts 17, 28. a: Jb 34, 3. b: Jb 32, 7. c: Rv 3, 7.
d: Gn 7, 11-24.

¹⁶ With him are strength and prudence;
  the misled and the misleaders are his.
¹⁷ He sends counselors away barefoot,
  and of judges he makes fools.
²⁰ He silences the trusted adviser,
  and takes discretion from the aged.
²² The recesses of the darkness he discloses,
  and brings the gloom forth to the light.
²³ He makes nations great and he destroys
      them;
  he spreads peoples abroad and he
      abandons them.
²⁴ He takes understanding from the leaders
      of the land,
²⁵   till they grope in the darkness without
      light;
  he makes them stagger like drunken
      men.

CHAPTER 13

See RG 169–73

¹Lo, all this my eye has seen;
  my ear has heard and perceived it.
² What you know, I also know;^e
  I fall not short of you.
³ But I would speak with the Almighty;^f
  I wish to reason with God.
⁴ You are glossing over falsehoods
  and offering vain remedies, every one
      of you!
⁵ Oh, that you would be altogether silent!
  This for you would be wisdom.
⁶ Hear now the rebuke I shall utter
  and listen to the reproof from my lips.
⁷ Is it for God that you speak falsehood?
  Is it for him that you utter deceit?
⁸ Is it for him that you show partiality?
  Do you play advocate on behalf of
      God?
⁹ Will it be well when he shall search you
      out?
  Would you impose on him as one does
      on men?
¹⁰ He will openly rebuke you
  if even in secret you show partiality.
¹¹ Surely will his majesty affright you

and the dread of him fall upon you.
¹² Your reminders are ashy maxims,
  your fabrications are mounds of clay.
¹³ Be silent, let me alone! that I may speak
  and give vent to my feelings.
¹⁴ I will carry my flesh between my teeth,
  and take my life in my hand.[*]
¹⁵ Slay me though he might,^g I will wait for
      him;
  I will defend my conduct before him.
¹⁶ And this shall be my salvation,
  that no impious man can come into his
      presence.
¹⁷ Pay careful heed to my speech,
  and give my statement a hearing.
¹⁸ Behold, I have prepared my case,^h
  I know that I am in the right.
¹⁹ If anyone can make a case against me,
  then I shall be silent and die.
²⁰ These things only do not use against me,[*]
  then from your presence I need not hide:
²¹ Withdraw your hand far from me,
  and let not the terror of you frighten me.
²² Then call me, and I will respond;
  or let me speak first, and answer me.
²³ What are my faults and my sins?
  My misdeeds and my sins make
      known to me!
²⁴ Why do you hide your faceⁱ
  and consider me your enemy?
²⁵ Will you harass a wind-driven leaf,
  or pursue a withered straw?
²⁶ For you draw up bitter indictments
      against me,
  and punish in me the faults of my youth.
²⁷ You put my feet in the stocks;
  you watch all my paths
  and trace out all my footsteps.

CHAPTER 14

See RG 169–73

¹ Man born of woman
  is short-lived and full of trouble,^j
² Like a flower that springs up and fades,^k
  swift as a shadow that does not abide.
³ Upon such a one will you cast your eyes

13, 14: The second half of the verse is a common biblical expression for risking one's life; cf Jgs 12, 3; 1 Sm 19, 5; 28, 21; Ps 119, 109; the first half of the verse must have a similar meaning. Job is so confident of his innocence that he is willing to risk his life by going to judgment with God.

13, 20: From here to the end of chapter 14, Job pleads his case, addressing God rather than his three friends.

e: Jb 12, 3; 15, 9.　f: Jb 23, 4.　g: Jb 27, 5.　h: Jb 33, 9.　i: Jb 19, 11; 33, 10.　j: Jb 10, 20; 15, 14; Pss 39, 5f; 89, 46; Wis 2, 1.　k: Jb 8, 9; Pss 90, 6; 102, 12; 103, 15; 109, 23; 144, 4; Is 40, 6f; Jas 1, 10.

Life Is Brief

Just as Psalm 103 reminds us that our days pass by like grass and the flowers that bloom and then die, so too Job underlines the brevity of human life (14, 1–2). He asks how God can possibly bring such a miserable creature into judgment (vv. 3–4). Job draws a comparison between the brief human life span and mountains worn slowly away by water. In between he entertains the impossible hope that he might escape the constraints of mortality and be enabled to speak with God beyond the grave (vv. 10–17).

---

so as to bring him into judgment
    before you,
28 Though he wears out like a leather bottle,
    like a garment that the moth has
        consumed?*
4 Can a man be found who is clean of
    defilement?*l
    There is none, 5however short his days.
You know the number of his months;
    you have fixed the limit which he
        cannot pass.
6 Look away from him and let him be,
    while, like a hireling, he completes his
        day.
7 For a tree there is hope,
    if it be cut down, that it will sprout again
    and that its tender shoots will not cease.
8 Even though its root grow old in the earth,
    and its stump die in the dust,
9 Yet at the first whiff of water it may
        flourish again
    and put forth branches like a young plant.
10 But when a man dies, all vigor leaves him;m
    when man expires, where then is he?
11 As when the waters of a lake fail,
    or a stream grows dry and parches,
12 So men lie down and rise not again.
    Till the heavens are no more, they
        shall not awake,
    nor be roused out of their sleep.n
13 Oh, that you would hide me in the nether
        world
    and keep me sheltered till your wrath
        is past;
    would fix a time for me, and then
        remember me!
14 When a man has died, were he to live
        again,

all the days of my drudgery I would wait,o
    until my relief should come.
15 You would call, and I would answer you;
    you would esteem the work of your hands.
16 Surely then you would count my steps,p
    and not keep watch for sin in me.
17 My misdeeds would be sealed up in a
        pouch,*
    and you would cover over my guilt.
18 But as a mountain falls at last
    and its rock is moved from its place,
19 As waters wear away the stones
    and floods wash away the soil of the land,
    so you destroy the hope of man.
20 You prevail once for all against him and
        he passes on;
    with changed appearance you send
        him away.
21 If his sons are honored, he is not aware of it;
    if they are in disgrace, he does not
        know about them.
22 Only his own flesh pains him,
    and his soul grieves for him.

III: Second Cycle of Speeches
CHAPTER 15

Second Speech of Eliphaz. 1Then Eliphaz the Temanite spoke and said:

> See RG 169-73

2 Should a wise man answer with airy
        opinions,
    or puff himself up with wind?
3 Should he argue in speech which does
        not avail,
    and in words which are to no profit?
4 You in fact do away with piety,
    and you lessen devotion toward God,

14, 28: This verse has been transposed from ch 13.
14, 17: Sealed up in a pouch: hidden away and forgotten.

l: Ps 51, 4. 7.   *m:* Jb 20, 7.   *n:* Jb 7, 10.   *o:* Jb 7, 1.   *p:* Jb 31, 4; 34, 21.

5 Because your wickedness instructs your
mouth,
and you choose to speak like the
crafty.
6 Your own mouth condemns you, not I;*q*
your own lips refute you.
7 Are you indeed the first-born of
mankind,
or were you brought forth before the
hills?
8 Are you privy to the counsels of God,*r*
and do you restrict wisdom to
yourself?
9 What do you know that we do not know?*s*
What intelligence have you which we
have not?
10 There are gray-haired old men among us
more advanced in years than your
father.
11 Are the consolations of God not enough
for you,
and speech that deals gently with you?
12 Why do your notions carry you away,
and why do your eyes blink,
13 So that you turn your anger against God
and let such words escape your mouth!
14 What is a man that he should be
blameless,*t*
one born of woman that he should be
righteous?*u*
15 If in his holy ones God places no
confidence,*v*
and if the heavens are not clean in his
sight,
16 How much less so is the abominable, the
corrupt:
man, who drinks in iniquity like water!
17 I will show you, if you listen to me;
what I have seen I will tell—
18 What wise men relate
and have not contradicted since the
days of their fathers,
19 To whom alone the land was given,
when no foreigner moved among
them.
20 The wicked man is in torment all his
days,

and limited years are in store for the
tyrant;
21 The sound of terrors is in his ears;
when all is prosperous, the spoiler
comes upon him.
22 He despairs of escaping the darkness,
and looks ever for the sword;
23 A wanderer, food for the vultures,
he knows that his destruction is
imminent.
24 By day the darkness fills him with dread;
distress and anguish overpower him.
25 Because he has stretched out his hand
against God
and bade defiance to the Almighty,
26 One shall rush sternly upon him
with the stout bosses of his shield,
like a king prepared for the charge.
27 Because he has blinded himself with his
crassness,
padding his loins with fat,
28 He shall dwell in ruinous cities,
in houses that are deserted,
That are crumbling into clay
29 with no shadow to lengthen over the
ground.
He shall not be rich, and his possessions
shall not endure;
31 for vain shall be his bartering.
30 A flame shall wither him up in his early
growth,
and with the wind his blossoms shall
disappear.
32 His stalk shall wither before its time,
and his branches shall be green no
more.
33 He shall be like a vine that sheds its
grapes unripened,
and like an olive tree casting off its
bloom.
34 For the breed of the impious shall be
sterile,*w*
and fire shall consume the tents of
extortioners.
35 They conceive malice and bring forth
emptiness;*x*
they give birth to failure.*

15, 35: They give birth to failure: their wicked plans yield nothing but futile results. Cf Ps 7, 15; Is 59, 4.

q: Jb 9, 20.   *r*: Jb 11, 7; Wis 9, 13; Jer 23, 18; Rom 11, 34; 1 Cor 2, 11.16.   *s*: Jb 12, 3; 13, 2.   *t*: 14ff; Jb 25, 4ff.   *u*: Jb 14, 4.   *v*: Jb 4, 18f.   *w*: Wis 3, 11. 18.   *x*: Ps 7, 15; Is 59, 4.

See RG
169–73

CHAPTER 16

Job's Fourth Reply. ¹Then Job answered and said:

² I have heard this sort of thing many
  times.ʸ
 Wearisome comforters are you all!
³ Is there no end to windy words?
 Or what sickness have you that you
  speak on?
⁴ I also could talk as you do,
 were you in my place.
 I could declaim over you,
  or wag my head at you;
⁵ I could strengthen you with talk,
 or shake my head with silent lips.
⁶ If I speak, this pain I have will not be
  checked;
 if I leave off, it will not depart from
  me.
⁷ But now that I am exhausted and stunned,
 all my company has closed in on me.
⁸ As a witness there rises up
 my traducer, speaking openly against
  me;
⁹ I am the prey his wrath assails,
 he gnashes his teeth against me.
 My enemies lord it over me;
¹⁰ their mouths are agape to bite me.
 They smite me on the cheek insultingly;
 they are all enlisted against me.
¹¹ God has given me over to the impious;
 into the clutches of the wicked he has
  cast me.
¹² I was in peace, but he dislodged me;
 he seized me by the neck and dashed
  me to pieces.
 He has set me up for a target;
¹³ his arrows strike me from all
  directions,
 He pierces my sides without mercy,
 he pours out my gall upon the ground.
¹⁴ He pierces me with thrust upon thrust;
 he attacks me like a warrior.
¹⁵ I have fastened sackcloth over my skin,
 and have laid my brow in the dust.

¹⁶ My face is inflamed with weeping
 and there is darkness over my eyes,
¹⁷ Although my hands are free from
  violence,
 and my prayer is sincere.
¹⁸ O earth, cover not my blood,
 nor let my outcry come to rest!*
¹⁹ Even now, behold, my witness* is in
  heaven,
 and my spokesman is on high.
²⁰ My friends it is who wrong me;
 before God my eyes drop tears,
²¹ That he may do justice for a mortal in his
  presence
 and decide between a man and his
  neighbor.
²² For my years are numbered now,
 and I am on a journey from which I
  shall not return.

CHAPTER 17

See RG
169–73

¹ My spirit is broken, my lamp of
  life extinguished;
 my burial is at hand.
² I am indeed mocked,
 and, as their provocation mounts, my
  eyes grow dim.
³ Grant me one to offer you a pledge on
  my behalf:*
 who is there that will give surety for
  me?
⁴ You darken their minds to knowledge;
 therefore they do not understand.
⁵ My lot is described as evil,
⁶ and I am made a byword of the
  people;ᶻ
 their object lesson I have become.
⁷ My eye has grown blind with anguish,
 and all my frame is shrunken to a
  shadow.
⁸ Upright men are astonished at this,
 and the innocent aroused against the
  wicked.
⁹ Yet the righteous shall hold to his way,
 and he who has clean hands increase in
  strength.
¹⁰ But turn now, and come on again;

16, 18: As the blood of those who were unjustly slain cries to heaven for vengeance (Gn 4, 10; Ez 24, 6-9), so Job's sufferings demand redress.

16, 19: Witness: refers either to God or, more probably, to

Job's prayer.
17, 3: Addressed to God; v 10 to Job's friends.

y: Jb 12, 3. z: Jb 30, 9.

for I shall not find a wise man among you!

11 My days are passed away, my plans are at an end,
the cherished purposes of my heart.

12 Such men change the night into day;
where there is darkness they talk of approaching light.

13 If I look for the nether world as my dwelling,
if I spread my couch in the darkness,

14 If I must call corruption "my father,"
and the maggot "my mother" and "my sister,"

15 Where then is my hope,
and my prosperity, who shall see?

16 Will they descend with me into the nether world?
Shall we go down together into the dust?

CHAPTER 18

See RG
169–73
Bildad's Second Speech. ¹Then Bildad the Shuhite replied and said:

2 When will you put an end to words?
Reflect, and then we can have discussion.

3 Why are we accounted like the beasts,
their equals in your sight?

4 You who tear yourself in your anger,*
shall the earth be neglected on your account
[or the rock be moved out of its place]?

5 Truly, the light of the wicked is extinguished;
no flame brightens his hearth.

6 The light is darkened in his tent;
in spite of him, his lamp goes out.ᵃ

7 His vigorous steps are hemmed in,
and his own counsel casts him down.

8 For he rushes headlong into a net,
and he wanders into a pitfall.

9 A trap seizes him by the heel,
and a snare lays hold of him.

10 A noose for him is hid on the ground,
and the toils for him on the way.

11 On every side terrors affright him;ᵇ
they harry him at each step.

12 Disaster is ready at his side,

13 the first-born of death* consumes his limbs.

14 Fiery destruction lodges in his tent,
and marches him off to the king of terrors.*
He is plucked from the security of his tent;

15 over his abode brimstone is scattered.

16 Below, his roots dry up,
and above, his branches wither.

17 His memory perishes from the land,ᶜ
and he has no name on the earth.

18 He is driven from light into darkness,
and banished out of the world.

19 He has neither son nor grandson among his people,
nor any survivor where once he dwelt.

20 They who come after shall be appalled at his fate;
they who went before are struck with horror.

21 So is it then with the dwelling of the impious man,
and such is the place of him who knows not God!

CHAPTER 19

Job's Fifth Reply. ¹Then Job answered and said:
See RG
169–73

2 How long will you vex my soul,
grind me down with words?

3 These ten times you have reviled me,
have assailed me without shame!

4 Be it indeed that I am at fault
and that my fault remains with me.

5 Even so, if you would vaunt yourselves against me
and cast up to me my reproach,

18, 4: Job himself is portrayed as having the heedless rage of wild beasts, despite which God does not forsake the usual course of Divine Providence.

18, 13: First-born of death: that is, disease, plague.

18, 14: The king of terrors: of the nether world, death;

however, the Hebrew is obscure.

a: Jb 21, 17; Prv 13, 9; 24, 20. *b:* Jb 15, 20-24; 27, 20. *c:* Ps 34, 17; Prv 2, 22; 10, 7.

⁶ Know then that God has dealt unfairly
    with me,
  and compassed me round with his net.
⁷ If I cry out "Injustice!" I am not heard.ᵈ
  I cry for help, but there is no redress.
⁸ He has barred my way and I cannot pass;
  he has veiled my path in darkness;
⁹ He has stripped me of my glory,
  and taken the diadem from my brow.
¹⁰ He breaks me down on every side, and I
    am gone;
  my hope he has uprooted like a tree.
¹¹ His wrath he has kindled against me;
  he counts me among his enemies.ᵉ
¹² His troops advance as one man;
  they build up their road to attack me,
  and they encamp around my tent.
¹³ My brethren have withdrawn from me,ᶠ
  and my friends are wholly estranged.
¹⁴ My kinsfolk and companions neglect me,
  and my guests have forgotten me.
¹⁵ Even my handmaids treat me as a
    stranger;
  I am an alien in their sight.
¹⁶ I call my servant, but he gives no answer,
  though in my speech I plead with him.
¹⁷ My breath is abhorred by my wife;ᵍ
  I am loathsome to the men of my
    family.
¹⁸ The young children, too, despise me;
  when I appear, they speak against me.
¹⁹ All my intimate friends hold me in horror;
  those whom I loved have turned
    against me!ʰ
²⁰ My bones cleave to my skin,
  and I have escaped with my flesh
    between my teeth.*
²¹ Pity me, pity me, O you my friends,
  for the hand of God has struck me!
²² Why do you hound me as though you
    were divine,*

and insatiably prey upon me?
²³ Oh, would that my words were written
    down!ⁱ
  Would that they were inscribed in a
    record:*
²⁴ That with an iron chisel and with lead
  they were cut in the rock forever!
²⁵ But as for me, I know that my Vindicator
    lives,*
  and that he will at last stand forth upon
    the dust;ʲ
²⁷ Whom I myself shall see:
  my own eyes, not another's, shall
    behold him,
²⁶ And from my flesh I shall see God;
  my inmost being is consumed with
    longing.
²⁸ But you who say, "How shall we
    persecute him,
  seeing that the root of the matter is
    found in him?"
²⁹ Be afraid of the sword for yourselves,
  for these crimes deserve the sword;
  that you may know that there is a
    judgment.

CHAPTER 20

Zophar's Second Speech. ¹Then Zophar the Naamathite spoke and said:

See RG
169–73

³ A rebuke which puts me to shame I hear,
²   and because of this I am disturbed.
  So now my thoughts provide me with an
    answer,
  and from my understanding a spirit
    gives me a reply.
⁴ Do you not know this from olden time,
  since man was placed upon the earth,
⁵ That the triumph of the wicked is short
  and the joy of the impious but for a
    moment?ᵏ

19, 20: With my flesh between my teeth: meaning perhaps that Job has been reduced to such an extremity that he scarcely has thin lips over his teeth. But the current Hebrew text of this line is probably corrupt.

19, 22: Divine: possessing God's attributes of judgment and authority to punish.

19, 23f: Job regards what he is about to say as so important that he wishes it recorded in a permanent manner.

19, 25. 27: The meaning of this passage is obscure because the original text has been poorly preserved and the ancient versions do not agree among themselves. It is certain

that Job expresses his belief in a future vindication by God (called here in the Hebrew "Goel"), but the time and manner of this vindication are undefined. In the Vulgate Job is made to indicate a belief in physical resurrection after death, but the Hebrew and the other ancient versions are less specific.

d: Jb 30, 20. e: Jb 13, 24; 33, 10. f: Jb 6, 13. g: Jb 2, 9.
h: Sir 6, 8. i: Jb 31, 35. j: 25ff: Phil 3, 20; Ti 2, 13. k: Jb 21,
13; Ps 37, 35f.

6 Though his pride mount up to the
        heavens
    and his head reach to the clouds,
7 Yet he perishes forever like the fuel of
        his fire,
    and the onlookers say, "Where is he?"*l*
8 Like a dream he takes flight and is not
        found again;
    he fades away like a vision of the
        night.
9 The eye which saw him does so no more;
    nor shall his dwelling again behold
        him.
11 Though his frame is full of youthful
        vigor,
    this shall lie with him in the dust.
12 Though wickedness is sweet in his
        mouth,
    and he hides it under his tongue,
13 Though he retains it and will not let it go
    but keeps it still within his mouth,
14 Yet in his stomach the food shall turn;
    it shall be venom of asps inside him.
15 The riches he swallowed he shall
        disgorge;
    God shall compel his belly to disown
        them.
16 The poison of asps he shall drink in;
    the viper's fangs shall slay him.
17 He shall see no streams of oil,*
    no torrents of honey or milk.
18 Restoring his gains, he shall not enjoy
        them;
    though his wealth increases, he shall
        not rejoice.
19 Because he has oppressed the poor,
    and stolen a patrimony he had not built
        up,
21 Therefore his prosperity shall not endure,
10   and his hands shall yield up his
        riches.*m*
20 Though he has known no quiet in his
        greed,
    his treasures shall not save him.*n*
22 *o*When he abounds to overflowing, he
        shall be brought into straits,

and nought shall be left of his goods.
23 God shall send against him the fury of
        his wrath
    and rain down his missiles of war
        upon him.
24 Should he escape the iron weapon,
    the bow of bronze shall pierce him
        through;
25 The dart shall come out of his back;
    terrors shall fall upon him.
26 Complete darkness is in store for him;
    the fire which shall consume him
        needs not to be fanned.*p*
27 The heavens shall reveal his guilt,
    and the earth shall rise up against him.
28 The flood shall sweep away his house
    with the waters that run off in the day
        of God's anger.
29 This is the portion of a wicked man,
    and the heritage appointed him by
        God.*q*

CHAPTER 21

Job's Sixth Reply. ¹Then Job said in
reply:

See RG
169–73

2 At least listen to my words,*r*
    and let that be the consolation you offer.
3 Bear with me while I speak;
    and after I have spoken, you can
        mock!
4 Is my complaint toward man?
    And why should I not be impatient?
5 Look at me and be astonished,
    put your hands over your mouths.
6 When I think of it, I am dismayed,
    and horror takes hold on my flesh.
7 Why do the wicked survive,
    grow old, become mighty in power?*s*
8 Their progeny is secure in their sight;
    they see before them their kinsfolk and
        their offspring.
9 Their homes are safe and without fear,
    nor is the scourge of God upon them.
10 Their bulls gender without fail;

20, 17: Oil: olive oil, one of the main agricultural products of Palestine, a land proverbially rich in honey and milk.

l: Jb 14, 10; Ps 37, 10, 36.   *m:* Jb 27, 14.   *n:* Eccl 5, 9; Lk 12, 20.   *o:* Jb 15, 20-35.   *p:* Dt 32, 22.   *q:* Jb 27, 13.   *r:* Jb 13, 17.
s: Jb 12, 6; Pss 37, 35; 73, 3; Eccl 8, 14; Jer 12, 1f; Mal 3, 14f.

their cows calve and do not miscarry.
¹¹ These folk have infants numerous as
lambs,
and their children dance.
¹² They sing to the timbrel and harp,
and make merry to the sound of the
flute.
¹³ They live out their days in prosperity,
and tranquilly go down to the nether
world.^t
¹⁴ Yet they say to God, "Depart from us,^u
for we have no wish to learn your
ways!
¹⁵ What is the Almighty that we should
serve him?
And what gain shall we have if we
pray to him?"^v
¹⁶ If their happiness is not in their own
hands
and if the counsel of the wicked is
repulsive to God,^w
¹⁷ How often is the lamp of the wicked put
out?
How often does destruction come
upon them,
the portion he allots in his anger?

¹⁸ Let them be like straw before the wind,
and like chaff which the storm
snatches away!
¹⁹ May God not store up the man's misery
for his children;
let him requite the man himself so that
he feels it,
²⁰ Let his own eyes see the calamity,
and the wrath of the Almighty let him
drink!
²¹ For what interest has he in his family
after him,
when the number of his months is
finished?

²³ One dies in his full vigor,
wholly at ease and content;
²⁴ His figure is full and nourished,
and his bones are rich in marrow.
²⁵ Another dies in bitterness of soul,

having never tasted happiness.
²⁶ Alike they lie down in the dust,
and worms cover them both.

²⁷ Behold, I know your thoughts,
and the arguments you rehearse
against me.
²⁸ For you say, "Where is the house of the
magnate,
and where the dwelling place of the
wicked?"
²⁹ Have you not asked the wayfarers
and do you not recognize their
monuments?
³⁰ Nay, the evil man is spared calamity
when it comes;
³² and on the day he is carried to the grave
³¹ Who will charge him with his conduct to
his face,
and for what he has done who will
repay him?
³³ Sweet to him are the clods of the valley,
and over him the funeral mound keeps
watch,
While all the line of mankind follows
him,
and the countless others who have
gone before.
³⁴ How then can you offer me vain
comfort,
while in your answers perfidy remains?

IV: Third Cycle of Speeches
CHAPTER 22

See RG
169-73

Eliphaz's Third Speech. ¹Then Eliphaz the Temanite answered and said:

² Can a man be profitable to God?^x
Though to himself a wise man be
profitable!
²² Can anyone teach God knowledge,
seeing that he judges those on high?*
³ Is it of advantage to the Almighty if you
are just?^y
Or is it a gain to him if you make your
ways perfect?

21, 22: Those on high: the angels. (This verse has been transposed from ch 21.)

t: Jb 34, 20.   *u:* Jb 22, 17.   *v:* Mal 3, 14.   *w:* Jb 22, 18.   *x:* Jb 9, 2.   *y:* Jb 35, 7.

⁴ Is it because of your piety that he
        reproves you—
    that he enters with you into judgment?
⁵ Is not your wickedness manifold?
    Are not your iniquities endless?

⁶ You have unjustly kept your kinsmen's
        goods in pawn,*
    left them stripped naked of their
        clothing.ᶻ
⁷ To the thirsty you have given no water to
        drink,
    and from the hungry you have
        withheld bread;
⁸ As if the land belonged to the man of
        might,
    and only the privileged were to dwell
        in it.
⁹ You have sent widows away empty-
        handed,
    and the resources of orphans you have
        destroyed.ᵃ
¹⁰ Therefore snares are round about you,ᵇ
    and a sudden terror causes you
        dismay,
¹¹ Or darkness, in which you cannot see;
    a deluge of waters covers you.

¹² Does not God, in the heights of the
        heavens,ᶜ
    behold the stars, high though they are?
¹³ Yet you say, "What does God know?ᵈ
    Can he judge through the thick
        darkness?
¹⁴ Clouds hide him so that he cannot see;
    he walks upon the vault of the
        heavens!"

¹⁵ Do you indeed keep to the ancient way
    trodden by worthless men,
¹⁶ Who were snatched away before their
        time;
    whose foundations a flood swept
        away?

¹⁷ These men said to God, "Depart from us!"
    and, "What can the Almighty do
        to us?"
¹⁸ [Yet he had filled their houses with good
        things!ᵉ
    But far be from me the mind of the
        impious!]*
¹⁹ The just look on and are gladdened,
    and the innocent deride them:ᶠ
²⁰ "Truly these have been destroyed where
        they stood,
    and such as were left, fire has
        consumed!"

²¹ Come to terms with him to be at peace.
    In this shall good come to you:
²² Receive instruction from his mouth,
    and lay up his words in your heart.
²³ If you return to the Almighty, you will
        be restored;
    if you put iniquity far from your tent,
²⁴ And treat raw gold like dust,
    and the fine gold of Ophir* as pebbles
        from the brook,
²⁵ Then the Almighty himself shall be your
        gold
    and your sparkling silver.

²⁶ For then you shall delight in the
        Almighty
    and you shall lift up your face toward
        God.
²⁷ You shall entreat him and he will hear
        you,ᵍ
    and your vows you shall fulfill.
²⁸ When you make a decision, it shall
        succeed for you,
    and upon your ways the light shall
        shine.
²⁹ For he brings down the pride of the
        haughty,
    but the man of humble mien he
        saves.ʰ
³⁰ God delivers him who is innocent;

22, 6ff: This criticism of Job by Eliphaz is altogether untrue, but it is made to dramatize the latter's argument that God always acts justly when he causes someone to suffer. Verse 8 is misplaced.

22, 18: A gloss, taken partly from Jb 21, 16.

22, 24: Ophir: cf note to Ps 45, 10.

z: Jb 24, 3; Dt 24, 6. 17; Ez 18, 12. 16.   a: Dt 24, 17; 27, 19.   b: Jb 18, 8ff.   c: Jb 11, 8.   d: 13f: Pss 10, 11; 73, 11; 94, 7; Is 29, 15;
Ez 8, 12; 9, 9.   e: Jb 21, 16.   f: Ps 107, 42.   g: Jb 33, 26.   h: Ps 138, 6; Prv 29, 23; Mt 23, 12; Lk 1, 52; Jas 4, 10; 1 Pt 5, 5.

you shall be delivered through cleanness of hands.[i]

See RG 169-73

CHAPTER 23

Job's Seventh Reply. [1] Again Job answered and said:

[2] Though I know my complaint is bitter, his hand is heavy upon me in my groanings.
[3] Oh, that today I might find him, that I might come to his judgment seat!
[4] I would set out my cause before him, and fill my mouth with arguments;
[5] I would learn the words with which he would answer, and understand what he would reply to me.
[6] Even should he contend against me with his great power, yet, would that he himself might heed me!
[7] There the upright man might reason with him, and I should once and for all preserve my rights.

[8] But if I go to the east, he is not there; or to the west, I cannot perceive him;
[9] Where the north enfolds him, I behold him not; by the south he is veiled, and I see him not.
[10] Yet he knows my way; if he proved me, I should come forth as gold.[j]
[11] My foot has always walked in his steps; his way I have kept and have not turned aside.
[12] From the commands of his lips I have not departed; the words of his mouth I have treasured in my heart.
[13] But he has decided, and who can say him nay? What he desires, that he does.[k]

[14] For he will carry out what is appointed for me; and many such things may yet be in his mind.
[15] Therefore am I dismayed before him; when I take thought, I fear him.
[16] Indeed God has made my courage fail; the Almighty has put me in dismay.
[17] Yes, would that I had vanished in darkness, and that thick gloom were before me to conceal me.

CHAPTER 24

See RG 169-73

[1] Why are not times set by the Almighty, and why do his friends not see his days?*
[2] The wicked remove landmarks; they steal away herds and pasture them.
[3] The asses of orphans they drive away; they take the widow's ox for a pledge.
[4] They force the needy off the road; all the poor of the land are driven into hiding.
[5] Like wild asses in the desert, these go forth to their task of seeking food; The steppe provides food for the young among them;
[6] they harvest at night in the untilled land.
[7] They pass the night naked, without clothing, for they have no covering against the cold;
[8] They are drenched with the rain of the mountains, and for want of shelter they cling to the rock.
[11] Between the rows they press out the oil; they glean in the vineyard of the wicked. They tread the wine presses, yet suffer thirst,
[10] and famished are those who carry the sheaves.

24, 1: Why does not God favor his friends by the speedy punishment of his enemies? (The text and order of verses in this chapter are not certain; note the omission of v 9 which duplicates words of vv 2-4.)

i: Jb 17, 9; Ps 18, 21.25.   *j:* Ps 66, 10; Prv 17, 3; Mal 3, 3; 1 Pt 1, 7.   *k:* Jb 42, 2; Pss 115, 3; 135, 6.

12 From the dust the dying groan,
  and the souls of the wounded cry out
  [yet God does not treat it as unseemly].
13 There are those who are rebels against
    the light;[l]
  they know not its ways;
  they abide not in its paths.
14 When there is no light the murderer rises,
  to kill the poor and needy.
15 The eye of the adulterer watches for the
    twilight;[m]
  he says, "No eye will see me."
In the night the thief roams about,
  and he puts a mask over his face;
16   in the dark he breaks into houses.
By day they shut themselves in;
  none of them know the light,
17   for daylight they regard as darkness.*

* * *

18 Their portion in the land is accursed,
20   and wickedness is splintered like
       wood.
19.21 . . . .
22 To him who rises without assurance of
    his life
23   he gives safety and support.
He sustains the mighty by his strength,
  and his eyes are on their ways.
24 They are exalted for a while, and then
       they are gone;
  they are laid low and, like all others,
    are gathered up;
  like ears of grain they shrivel.

* * *

25 If this be not so, who will confute me,
  and reduce my argument to nought?

CHAPTER 25

See RG 169–73

Bildad's Third Speech. [1]Then Bildad
the Shuhite answered and said:

2 Dominion and awesomeness are his
  who brings about harmony in his
    heavens.
3 Is there any numbering of his troops?*
  Yet to which of them does not his light
    extend?
4 How can a man be just in God's sight,[n]
  or how can any woman's child be
    innocent?
5 Behold, even the moon is not bright
  and the stars are not clear in his sight.
6 How much less man, who is but a maggot,
  the son of man, who is only a worm?[o]

CHAPTER 26

See RG 169–73

Job's Reply. [1]Then Job spoke again
and said:*

2 What help you give to the powerless,
  what strength to the feeble arm!
3 How you counsel, as though he had no
    wisdom;
  how profuse is the advice you offer!
4 With whose help have you uttered those
    words,
  and whose is the breath that comes
    forth from you?[p]
5 The shades* beneath writhe in terror,[q]
  the waters, and their inhabitants.
6 Naked before him is the nether world,*
  and Abaddon has no covering.[r]
7 He stretches out the North* over empty
    space,
  and suspends the earth over nothing at all;

24, 17: The asterisks which follow this verse mark off a passage (vv 18-24) which cannot be ascribed to Job with certainty. Vv 17-24 are in general poorly preserved; and much of vv 18-21 has not been translated because these verses are obscure. St. Jerome renders them as follows: (18) "He is light upon the face of the water, cursed be his portion on the earth; let him not walk by the way of vineyards. (19) Let him pass from the snow waters to excessive heat, and his sin even to hell. (20) Let mercy forget him; may worms be his sweetness; let him be remembered no more, but be broken in pieces as an unfruitful tree. (21) For he has fed the barren that bears not, and to the widow he has done no good."

25, 3: His troops: the heavenly hosts, the stars or the angels. His light: compare the wording in Jb 24, 13:

those who are rebels against the light.

26, 1-14: Probably to be read as Job's reply to Bildad's short speech. Some, however, would make it the reply to Zophar (Jb 27, 13-21); it would thus lead up to the poem of ch 28.

26, 5: Shades: the dead in Sheol, the nether world; cf Pss 6, 6; 88, 11.

26, 6: Nether world: cf note to Ps 6, 6. Abaddon: Hebrew for "(place of) destruction," a synonym for nether world: cf Jb 28, 22; Rv 9, 11.

26, 7: The North: used here as a synonym for the firmament, the heavens; cf Is 14, 13.

l: Jn 3, 19f. *m:* Prv 7, 9f. *n:* Jb 4, 17ff; 9, 2. *o:* Jb 4, 19; 15, 16. *p:* Gn 2, 7. *q:* Prv 9, 18. *r:* Ps 139, 7-12.

⁸ He binds up the waters in his clouds,
  yet the cloud is not rent by their weight;
⁹ He holds back the appearance of the full
    moon
  by spreading his clouds before it.

¹⁰ He has marked out a circle* on the
    surface of the deepˢ
  as the boundary of light and darkness.
¹¹ The pillars of the heavens trembleᵗ
  and are stunned at his thunderous
    rebuke;
¹² By his power he stirs up the sea,
  and by his might he crushes Rahab;*
¹³ With his angry breath he scatters the water,
  and he hurls the lightning against it
    relentlessly;
  His hand pierces the fugitive dragon*
  as from his hand it strives to flee.ᵘ
¹⁴ Lo, these are but the outlines of his ways,
  and how faint is the word we hear!

CHAPTER 27

See RG
169-73
Job's Reply

¹¹I will teach you the manner of
    God's dealings,
  and the way of the Almighty I will not
    conceal.
² As God lives,* who withholds my deserts,ᵛ
  the Almighty, who has made bitter my
    soul,
³ So long as I still have life in me
  and the breath of God is in my nostrils,
⁴ My lips shall not speak falsehood,
  nor my tongue utter deceit!
⁵ Far be it from me to account you right;
  till I die I will not renounce my
    innocence.ʷ
⁶ My justice I maintain and I will not
    relinquish it;
  my heart does not reproach me for any
    of my days.

⁷ Let my enemy be as the wicked
  and my adversary as the unjust!
⁸ For what can the impious man expect
    when he is cut off,
  when God requires his life?
⁹ Will God then attend to his cry
  when calamity comes upon him?
¹⁰ Will he then delight in the Almighty
  and call upon him constantly?
¹² Behold, you yourselves have all seen it;
  why then do you spend yourselves in
    idle words!

* * *

¹³ *This is the portion of a wicked man
    from God,
  the inheritance an oppressor receives
    from the Almighty:ˣ
¹⁴ Though his children be many, the sword
    is their destiny.
  His offspring shall not be filled with
    bread.
¹⁵ His survivors, when they die, shall have
    no burial,
  and their widows shall not be
    mourned.
¹⁶ Though he heap up silver like dust
  and store away mounds of clothing,
¹⁷ What he has stored the just man shall wear,
  and the innocent shall divide the silver.
¹⁸ He builds his house as of cobwebs,
  or like a booth put up by the
    vinekeeper.
¹⁹ He lies down a rich man, one last time;
  he opens his eyes and nothing remains
    to him.ʸ
²⁰ Terrors rush upon him by day;
  at night the tempest carries him off.
²¹ The storm wind seizes him and he
    disappears;
  it sweeps him out of his place.*

* * *

26, 10: Circle: the horizon of the ocean which serves as the boundary for the activity of light and darkness.
26, 12: Rahab: cf Jb 9, 13; see note on Ps 89, 11.
26, 13: The fugitive dragon: the same term occurs in Is 27, 1 in apposition to Leviathan; see note on Jb 3, 8. This is actually Jb 27, 22.
27, 2-12: This is probably to be read as Job's reply to Zophar's speech of Jb 27, 13-21. In the current Hebrew text the heading for this chapter (Jb 27, 1, here omitted) is identical with Jb 29, 1; we should expect rather such a heading as is Jb 21, 1; 23, 1; 26, 1.
27, 13-21: This is probably to be read as Zophar's third speech. The asterisks are present to indicate it is not likely that the sacred writer intended these words to be ascribed to Job.
27, 21: The Hebrew has two more verses: v 22 (read above with Jb 26, 13); and v 23, which is a variant form of v 21.

---

s: Jb 38, 8-11; Prv 8, 29. t: Jb 9, 6. u: Is 27, 1. v: Jb 34, 5.
w: Jb 2, 3. 9; 13, 15; 33, 9. x: Jb 20, 4-29. y: Pss 49, 18; 76, 6.

Poem on Wisdom

The anonymous poem of ch 28 breaks the cycle of speeches of Job and his three friends that began in ch 3. Some consider it a later insertion, but it is original to the story because it heightens the drama by retarding the action and by raising important questions in the reader's mind. For example, by declaring wisdom inaccessible to human beings, the poem suggests what the reader already suspects, that the dialogue between Job and his friends cannot provide a satisfactory answer to his problem. It suggests that the answer must come from a nonhuman source, pointing toward the divine response of chs 39–42.

See RG
169–73

CHAPTER 28

The Inaccessibility of Wisdom

¹ There is indeed a mine for silver,*
    and a place for gold which men
      refine.
² Iron is taken from the earth,
    and copper is melted out of stone.
⁴ . . . .
⁵ The earth, though out of it comes forth
      bread,
    is in fiery upheaval underneath.
⁶ Its stones are the source of sapphires,
    and there is gold in its dust.

¹² But whence can wisdom be obtained,
    and where is the place of
      understanding?ᶻ
¹³ Man knows nothing to equal it,
    nor is it to be had in the land of the
      living.
¹⁵ Solid gold cannot purchase it,
    nor can its price be paid with
      silver.ᵃ
¹⁶ It cannot be bought with gold of
      Ophir,*
    with the precious onyx or the
      sapphire.
¹⁷ Gold or crystal cannot equal it,
    nor can golden vessels reach its
      worth.

¹⁸ Neither coral nor jasper should be
      thought of;
    it surpasses pearls and ¹⁹Arabian
      topaz.

²⁰ Whence, then, comes wisdom,
    and where is the place of
      understanding?
²¹ It is hid from the eyes of any beast;
    from the birds of the air it is
      concealed.
⁷ The path to it no bird of prey knows,
    nor has the hawk's eye seen that path.
⁸ The proud beasts have not trodden it,
    nor has the lion gone that way.
¹⁴ The abyss declares, "It is not in me";
    and the sea says, "I have it not."
²² Abaddon* and Death say,
    "Only by rumor have we heard of it."

²³ God knows the way to it;ᵇ
    it is he who is familiar with its place.ᶜ
²⁴ For he beholds the ends of the earth
    and sees all that is under the heavens.
³ He has set a boundary for the darkness;
    to the farthest confines he penetrates.
⁹ He sets his hand to the flinty rock,
    and overturns the mountains at their
      foundations.
¹⁰ He splits channels in the rocks;
    his eyes behold all that is precious.

28, 1-28: Note the changed order of verses; v 4 is uncertain. This chapter contains a beautifully vivid description of that Wisdom which is beyond the attainment of creatures; known only to God, it is reflected in the order and majesty of his creation. Man, however, can, in a way, participate in this Wisdom by fearing the Lord and avoiding evil. Scholars are not agreed regarding the authorship of this poem, though it is altogether worthy of the author of the Book of Job. Used here as a counterpoise to ch 3 at the beginning of the dialogue, it may have been first conceived as an independent poem.

28, 16: Ophir: cf note to Ps 45, 10.

28, 22: Abaddon: cf note to Jb 26, 6.

z: Eccl 7, 24f; Bar 3, 14f. 29-33. a: Prv 3, 14; 8, 10f. 19; 16, 16; Wis 7, 11. b: 23-27: Prv 8, 22-31. c: Prv 2, 6; Sir 1, 1; Jas 1, 5.

¹¹ He probes the wellsprings of the streams,
and brings hidden things to light.
²⁵ He has weighed out the wind,
and fixed the scope of the waters;
²⁶ When he made rules for the rain
and a path for the thunderbolts,ᵈ
²⁷ Then he saw wisdom and appraised it,
gave it its setting, knew it through and
through.
²⁸ And to man he said:
Behold, the fear of the LORD is wisdom;
and avoiding evil is understanding.ᵉ

V: Job's Final Summary
of His Cause
CHAPTER 29

**See RG
169-73** ¹Job took up his theme anew and
said:

² Oh, that I were as in the months past!
as in the days when God watched over
me,ᶠ
³ While he kept his lamp shining above my
head,
and by his light I walked through
darkness;
⁴ As I was in my flourishing days,
when God sheltered my tent;
⁵ When the Almighty was yet with me,
and my children were round about
me;
⁶ When my footsteps were bathed in
milk,
and the rock flowed with streams of
oil;*
⁷ When I went forth to the gate of the city
and set up my seat in the square—

⁸ Then the young men saw me and
withdrew,
while the elders rose up and stood;
⁹ The chief men refrained from speaking
and covered their mouths with their
hands;ᵍ
¹⁰ The voice of the princes was silenced,

and their tongues stuck to the roofs of
their mouths.
²¹ For me they listened and waited;
they were silent for my counsel.
²² Once I spoke, they said no more,
but received my pronouncement drop
by drop.
²³ They waited for me as for the rain;
they drank in my words like the spring
rains.

²⁴ When I smiled on them they were
reassured;
²⁵ mourners took comfort from my
cheerful glance.
I chose out their way and presided;
I took a king's place in the armed
forces.
¹¹ Whoever heard of me blessed me;
those who saw me commended me.

¹² For I rescued the poor who cried out for
help,
the orphans, and the unassisted;
¹³ The blessing of those in extremity came
upon me,
and the heart of the widow I made
joyful.
¹⁴ I wore my honesty like a garment;
justice was my robe and my turban.
¹⁵ I was eyes to the blind,
and feet to the lame was I;
¹⁶ I was a father to the needy;
the rights of the stranger I studied,
¹⁷ And I broke the jaws of the wicked man;
from his teeth I forced the prey.

¹⁸ Then I said: "In my own nest I shall grow
old;
I shall multiply years like the
phoenix.*
¹⁹ My root is spread out to the waters;
the dew rests by night on my branches.
²⁰ My glory is fresh within me,
and my bow is renewed in my hand!"

29, 6: Hyperbole to express abundance; see note on Jb
20, 17.

29, 18: Phoenix: a legendary bird which, after several
centuries of life, consumed itself in fire, then rose from its
ashes in youthful freshness. This meaning, originally in-

tenced in the Greek, later came to mean "palm tree." Some
render the Hebrew as "sand."

---

d: Jb 38, 25; Prv 3, 20. e: Ps 111, 10; Prv 1, 7; 9, 10; Sir 1, 16.
f: Jb 1, 10. g: Wis 8, 10ff.

CHAPTER 30

See RG
169–73

¹ But now they hold me in derision
who are younger in years than I;ʰ
Whose fathers I should have disdained
to rank with the dogs of my flock.
² Such strength as they had, to me meant
nought;
they were utterly destitute.

³ In want and hunger was their lot,ⁱ
they who fled to the parched
wastelands:
⁴ They plucked saltwort* and shrubs;
the roots of the broom plant were their
food.
⁵ They were banished from among men,
with an outcry like that against a
thief—
⁶ To dwell on the slopes of the wadies,
in caves of sand and stone;
⁷ Among the bushes they raised their
raucous cry;
under the nettles they huddled
together.
⁸ Irresponsible, nameless men,
they were driven out of the land.

⁹ Yet now they sing of me in mockery;
I am become a byword among them.ʲ
¹⁰ They abhor me, they stand aloof from
me,
they do not hesitate to spit in my face!
¹¹ Indeed, they have loosed their bonds;
they lord it over me,
and have thrown off restraint in my
presence.

¹² To subvert my paths they rise up;
they build their approaches for my
ruin.
¹³ To destroy me, they attack with none to
stay them;
¹⁴ as through a wide breach they
advance.
Amid the uproar they come on in waves;

¹⁵ over me rolls the terror.
My dignity is borne off on the wind,
and my welfare vanishes like a cloud.
¹⁸ One with great power lays hold of my
clothing;*
by the collar of my tunic he seizes me:
¹⁹ He has cast me into the mire;
I am leveled with the dust and ashes.

²⁰ I cry to you, but you do not answer me;ᵏ
you stand off and look at me,
²¹ Then you turn upon me without mercy
and with your strong hand you buffet
me.
²² You raise me up and drive me before the
wind;
I am tossed about by the tempest.
²³ Indeed I know you will turn me back in
death
to the destined place of everyone
alive.ˡ
²⁴ Yet should not a hand be held out
to help a wretched man in his
calamity?
²⁵ Or have I not wept for the hardships of
others;
was not my soul grieved for the
destitute?ᵐ
²⁶ Yet when I looked for good, then evil
came;
when I expected light, then came
darkness.

¹⁶ My soul ebbs away from me;
²⁷ days of affliction have overtaken me.
¹⁷ My frame takes no rest by night;
my inward parts seethe and will not be
stilled.
²⁸ I go about in gloom, without the sun;
I rise up in public to voice my grief.

²⁹ I have become the brother of jackals,
companion to the ostrich.
³⁰ My blackened skin falls away from me;
the heat scorches my very frame.
³¹ My harp is turned to mourning,

30, 4: Saltwort: found in salt marshes and very sour to the taste; eaten by the extremely poor as a cooked vegetable. Broom plant: the juniper or brushwood; cf Ps 120, 4; a figure of bitterness and poverty, because of its bitter-tasting roots which are practically inedible.

30, 18-23: Job here refers to God's stern treatment of him.

h: Jb 12, 4; 19, 18. *i:* 3-8: Jb 24, 5f. *j:* Jb 17, 6. *k:* Jb 19, 7.
l: Heb 9, 27. *m:* Jb 29, 12-16.

and my reed pipe to sounds of weeping.

CHAPTER 31

See RG
169–73

2 But what is man's lot from God above,
his inheritance from the Almighty on high?
3 Is it not calamity for the unrighteous, and woe for evildoers?
4 Does he not see my ways, and number all my steps?[n]
6 Let God weigh me in the scales of justice; thus will he know my innocence![o]

5 If I have walked in falsehood*
and my foot has hastened to deceit;
7 If my steps have turned out of the way, and my heart has followed my eyes, or any stain clings to my hands,
8 Then may I sow, but another eat of it, or may my planting be rooted up!

38 If my land has cried out against me till its very furrows complained;
39 If I have eaten its produce without payment
and grieved the hearts of its tenants;
40 Then let the thistles grow instead of wheat
and noxious weeds instead of barley!
1 If I have made an agreement with my eyes*
and entertained any thoughts against a maiden;
9 If my heart has been enticed toward a woman,
and I have lain in wait at my neighbor's door;
10 Then may my wife grind for another, and may others cohabit with her!

11 For that would be heinous, a crime to be condemned;[p]
12 A fire that should burn down to the abyss till it consumed all my possessions to the roots.[q]
13 Had I refused justice to my manservant or to my maid, when they had a claim against me,
14 What then should I do when God rose up; what could I answer when he demanded an account?
15 Did not he who made me in the womb make him?
Did not the same One fashion us before our birth?
16 If I have denied anything to the poor,[r] or allowed the eyes of the widow to languish
17 While I ate my portion alone, with no share in it for the fatherless,
18 Though like a father God has reared me from my youth,
guiding me even from my mother's womb—
19 If I have seen a wanderer without clothing, or a poor man without covering,
20 Whose limbs have not blessed me when warmed with the fleece of my sheep;
21 If I have raised my hand against the innocent
because I saw that I had supporters at the gate—*
22 Then may my arm fall from the shoulder, my forearm be broken at the elbow!
23 For the dread of God will be upon me, and his majesty will overpower me.
24 Had I put my trust in gold or called fine gold my security;
25 Or had I rejoiced that my wealth was great, or that my hand had acquired abundance—
26 Had I looked upon the sun as it shone,[s] or the moon in the splendor of its progress,*
27 And had my heart been secretly enticed to waft them a kiss with my hand;

31, 5-34: Job's final protestation of his innocence.
31, 1. 9: Note the gradation: avoidance of sinful glances and thoughts against a maiden; desire for another's wife.
31, 21: Gate: cf notes on Jb 5, 4; Ru 4, 1.
31, 26ff: Job never sinned by worshiping the sun or the moon; waft them a kiss: an act of idolatrous worship.

n: Jb 14, 16; 34, 21; Ps 139, 3; Prv 5, 21.   o: Jb 23, 10.   p: Ex 20, 14; Lv 20, 10; Dt 22, 22.   q: Sir 9, 8f.   r: 16-23: Jb 29, 12-16.   s: 26f: Dt 4, 19.

28 This too would be a crime for
    condemnation,
  for I should have denied God above.[t]

29 Had I rejoiced at the destruction of my
    enemy
  or exulted when evil fell upon him,[u]

30 Even though I had not suffered my
    mouth to sin
  by uttering a curse against his life—

31 Had not the men of my tent exclaimed,
    "Who has not been fed with his
    meat!"[*]

32 Because no stranger lodged in the street,
  but I opened my door to wayfarers—

33 Had I, out of human weakness, hidden
    my sins
  and buried my guilt in my bosom[*]

34 Because I feared the noisy multitude
  and the scorn of the tribes terrified
    me—
  then I should have remained silent,
    and not come out of doors!

35 Oh, that I had one to hear my case,
  and that my accuser would write out
    his indictment![v]

36 Surely, I should wear it on my
    shoulder[*]
  or put it on me like a diadem;

37 Of all my steps I should give him an
    account;
  like a prince[*] I should present myself
    before him.

This is my final plea; let the Almighty answer me!
  The words of Job are ended.

VI: Elihu's Speeches

CHAPTER 32

See RG 169-73

[1]Then the three men ceased to answer Job, because he was righteous[w] in his own eyes. [2][x]But the anger of Elihu,[*] son of Barachel the Buzite, of the family of Ram, was kindled. He was angry with Job for considering himself rather than God to be in the right. [3][y]He was angry also with the three friends because they had not found a good answer and had not condemned Job. [4]But since these men were older than he, Elihu bided his time before addressing Job. [5]When, however, Elihu saw that there was no reply in the mouths of the three men, his wrath was inflamed. [6]So Elihu, son of Barachel the Buzite, spoke out and said:

I am young and you are very old;
    therefore I held back and was afraid
    to declare to you my knowledge.
7 Days should speak, I thought,
    and many years teach wisdom![z]
8 But it is a spirit in man,[a]
    the breath of the Almighty, that gives
    him understanding.
9 It is not those of many days who are
    wise,
    nor the aged who understand the
    right.
10 Therefore I say, hearken to me;
    let me too set forth my knowledge!

11 Behold, I have waited for your
    discourses,
    and have given ear to your
    arguments.
12 Yes, I followed you attentively

31, 31: The members of his household will testify to his hospitality.

31, 33f: Job's present protest is made, not in spite of hidden sins which he had been unwilling to disclose, but out of genuine innocence.

31, 36: On my shoulder: i.e., boldly, proudly.

31, 37: Like a prince: not as a frightened criminal. Final plea: literally, "tau," the last letter of the Hebrew alphabet; in the current Hebrew text this line is in v 35, while the following one ends v 40.

32, 2: Elihu means "My God is he." This speaker was from Buz, which, according to Jer 25, 23, was near Tema

and Dedan. A young man, he impetuously and impatiently upbraids Job for his boldness toward God, and the three friends for not successfully answering Job. He undertakes to defend God's absolute justice and to explain more clearly why there is suffering. While fundamentally his position is the same as that of the three friends, he does locate more definitely, though not perfectly, the place of suffering in the divine plan.

t: Dt 17, 2-7. *u:* Prv 24, 17. *v:* Jb 19, 23; 23, 3-7. *w:* Jb 33, 9. *x:* Jb 13, 18; 27, 6; 34, 5; 35, 2. *y:* Jb 22, 5. *z:* Jb 12, 12. *a:* Jb 33, 4.

as you searched out what to say;
And behold, there is none who has
    convicted Job,
    not one of you who could refute his
        statements.
¹³ Yet do not say, "We have met wisdom.*
    God may vanquish him but not man!"
¹⁴ For had he addressed his words to me,
    I should not then have answered him
        as you have done.

¹⁵ They are dismayed, they make no more
        reply;
    words fail them.
¹⁶ Must I wait? Now that they speak no
        more,
    and have ceased to make reply,
¹⁷ I too will speak my part;
    I also will show my knowledge!

¹⁸ For I am full of matters to utter;
    the spirit within me compels me.
¹⁹ Like a new wineskin with wine under
        pressure,
    my bosom is ready to burst.
²⁰ Let me speak and obtain relief;
    let me open my lips, and make reply.
²¹ I would not be partial to anyone,
    nor give flattering titles to any.
²² For I know nought of flattery;
    if I did, my Maker would soon take me
        away.

CHAPTER 33

See RG
169-73 ¹Therefore, O Job, hear my discourse,
    and hearken to all my words.
² Behold, now I open my mouth;
    my tongue and my voice form
        words.
³ I will state directly what is in my
        mind,
    my lips shall utter knowledge
        sincerely;
⁴ For the spirit of God has made me,
    the breath of the Almighty keeps me
        alive.ᵇ

⁵ If you are able, refute me;
    draw up your arguments and stand
        forth.
⁶ Behold I, like yourself, have been taken
    from the same clay by God.ᶜ
⁷ Therefore no fear of me should dismay
        you,
    nor should my presence weigh heavily
        upon you.

⁸ But you have said in my hearing,
    as I listened to the sound of your words:
⁹ "I am clean and without transgression;
    I am innocent; there is no guilt in me.ᵈ
¹⁰ Yet he invents pretexts against me
    and reckons me as his enemy.ᵉ
¹¹ He puts my feet in the stocks;
    he watches all my ways!"ᶠ

¹² In this you are not just, let me tell you;
    for God is greater than man.
¹³ Why, then, do you make complaint
        against him
    that he gives no account of his doings?ᵍ
¹⁴ For God does speak, perhaps once,
    or even twice, though one perceive it
        not.

¹⁵ In a dream, in a vision of the night,
    [when deep sleep falls upon men]
    as they slumber in their beds,
¹⁶ It is then he opens the ears of men
    and as a warning to them, terrifies
        them;
¹⁷ By turning man from evil
    and keeping pride away from him,
¹⁸ He withholds his soul from the pit
    and his life from passing to the grave.

¹⁹ Or a man is chastened on his bed by pain
    and unceasing suffering within his
        frame,
²⁰ So that to his appetite food becomes
        repulsive,
    and his senses reject the choicest
        nourishment.ʰ

32, 13: Met wisdom: in Job's arguments.

---

b: Jb 32, 8.   c: Jb 31, 15.   d: Jb 10, 7; 13, 18; 27, 5f; 29, 14; 32, 1; 34. 5.   e: Jb 13, 24; 19, 11.   f: Jb 13, 27; 31, 4.   g: Jb 31, 35.
h: Jb 6, 7.

21 His flesh is wasted so that it cannot be seen,
   and his bones, once invisible, appear;
22 His soul draws near to the pit,
   his life to the place of the dead.

23 If then there be for him an angel,*
   one out of a thousand, a mediator,
To show him what is right for him
   and bring the man back to justice,
24 He will take pity on him and say,
   "Deliver him from going down to the
   pit;
   I have found him a ransom."

25 Then his flesh shall become soft as a boy's;
   he shall be again as in the days of his
   youth.
26 He shall pray and God will favor him;
   he shall see God's face with rejoicing.i
27 He shall sing before men and say,
   "I sinned and did wrong,
   yet he has not punished me accordingly.
28 He delivered my soul from passing to the
   pit,
   and I behold the light of life."

29 Lo, all these things God does,
   twice, or thrice, for a man,
30 Bringing back his soul from the pit
   to the light, in the land of the living.
31 Be attentive, O Job; listen to me!
   Be silent and I will speak.
32 If you have aught to say, then answer me.
   Speak out! I should like to see you
   justified.
33 If not, then do you listen to me;
   be silent while I teach you wisdom.

CHAPTER 34

See RG
169-73   1 Then Elihu continued and said:

2 Hear, O wise men, my discourse,
   and you that have knowledge, hear
   me!
3 For the ear tests words,

as the taste does food.j
4 Let us discern for ourselves what is right;
   let us learn between us what is good.
5 For Job has said, "I am innocent,
   but God has taken what is my due.k
6 Notwithstanding my right I am set at
   nought;
   in my wound the arrow rankles, sinless
   though I am."l

7 What man is like Job?
   He drinks in blasphemies like water,
8 Keeps company with evildoers
   and goes along with wicked men,
9 When he says, "It profits a man nought
   that he is pleasing to God."m

10 Therefore, men of understanding,
   hearken to me:
   far be it from God to do wickedness;
   far from the Almighty to do wrong!n
11 Rather, he requites men for their conduct,
   and brings home to a man his way of
   life.o
12 Surely, God cannot act wickedly,
   the Almighty cannot violate justice.p
13 Who gave him government over the earth,
   or who else set all the land in its place?q
14 If he were to take back his spirit to himself,
   withdraw to himself his breath,
15 All flesh would perish together,
   and man would return to the dust.r

16 Now, do you, O Job, hear this!
   Hearken to the words I speak!
17 Can an enemy of justice indeed be in
   control,
   or will you condemn the supreme Just
   One,
18 Who says to a king, "You are worthless!"
   and to nobles, "You are wicked!"
19 Who neither favors the person of princes,
   nor respects the rich more than the
   poor?
   For they are all the work of his hands;s

33, 23: Angel: one of the thousands who stand between God and man as intermediaries, reminding man of his duties and giving God an account of their fulfillment.

---

i: Jb 22, 26-29. j: Jb 12, 11. k: Jb 33, 9f. l: Jb 9, 20. m: Jb 9, 22f. 30f; 21, 15; 35, 3. n: Jb 36, 23. o: Ps 62, 13; Prv 24, 12;
Mt 16, 27; Rom 2, 6; 2 Cor 5, 10; Rv 22, 12. p: Jb 8, 3. q: Jb 38, 4-7. r: Jb 10, 9. s: Dt 10, 17; 2 Chr 19, 7; Wis 6, 7; Acts 10,
34; Rom 2, 11; Eph 6, 9; Col 3, 25; 1 Pt 1, 17.

²⁰ in a moment they die, even at
midnight.^t
He brings on nobles, and takes them away,
removing the powerful without lifting
a hand;
²¹ For his eyes are upon the ways of man,
and he beholds all his steps.

²² There is no darkness so dense
that evildoers can hide in it.
²⁵ Therefore he discerns their works;
he turns at night and crushes them.
²³ For he forewarns no man of his time
to come before God in judgment.
²⁴ Without a trial he breaks the mighty,^u
and sets others in their stead,
²⁷ Because they turned away from him
and heeded none of his ways,
²⁸ But caused the cries of the poor to reach
him,
so that he heard the plea of the
afflicted.

²⁹ If he remains tranquil, who then can
condemn?*
If he hides his face, who then can
behold him?
³⁰ . . . .
³¹ When anyone says to God,
"I was misguided; I will offend no
more.
³² Teach me wherein I have sinned;
if I have done wrong, I will do so no
more,"
³³ Would you then say that God must
punish,
since you reject what he is doing?
It is you who must choose, not I;
speak, therefore, what you know.

³⁴ Men of understanding will say to me,
every wise man who hears my views:
³⁵ "Job speaks without intelligence,
and his words are without sense."^v
³⁶ Let Job be tried to the limit,

since his answers are those of the
impious;
³⁷ For he is adding rebellion to his sin
by brushing off our arguments
and addressing many words to God.

CHAPTER 35

See RG
169-73

¹Then Elihu proceeded and said:

² Do you think it right to say,
"I am just rather than God"?^w
³ To say, "What does it profit me;
what advantage have I more than if I
had sinned?"^x
⁴ I have words for a reply to you*
and your three companions as well.
⁵ Look up to the skies and behold;
regard the heavens high above you.
⁶ If you sin, what injury do you do to God?
Even if your offenses are many, how
do you hurt him?
⁷ If you are righteous, what do you give him,
or what does he receive from your
hand?^y
⁸ Your wickedness can affect only a man
like yourself;
and your justice only a fellow human
being.

⁹ In great oppression men cry out;
they call for help because of the power
of the mighty,
¹⁰ Saying, "Where is God, my Maker,
who has given visions in the night,
¹¹ Taught us rather than the beasts of the
earth,
and made us wise rather than the birds
of the heavens?"
¹² Though thus they cry out, he answers not
against the pride of the wicked.
¹³ But it is idle to say God does not hear
or that the Almighty does not take
notice.
¹⁴ Even though you say that you see him
not,*

34, 26. 29f: The extant Hebrew text of these verses contains several added phrases which either represent duplication or are very obscure.

35, 4: A reply to you: Elihu refers to Job's statement that the innocent suffer as much as the wicked, and especially to Eliphaz's words in Jb 22, 2f.

35, 14f: The text here is uncertain. It seems to indicate that Job should have realized God's indifference is only apparent, and that, because he has not done so, God will punish him.

t: Jb 21, 3. u: Ps 2, 9. v: Jb 35, 16; 38, 2; 42, 3. w: Jb 32, 2.
x: Jb 34, 9. y: Jb 22, 3; 41, 2; Lk 17, 10; Rom 11, 35.

the case is before him; with trembling
should you wait upon him.

[15] But now that you have done otherwise,
God's anger punishes,
nor does he show concern that a man
will die.

[16] Yet Job to no purpose opens his mouth,
and without knowledge multiplies
words.[z]

CHAPTER 36

See RG
169–73 [1]Elihu proceeded further and said:

[2] Wait yet a little and I will instruct you,
for there are still words to be said on
God's behalf.

[3] I will bring my knowledge from afar,
and to my Maker I will accord the
right.

[4] For indeed, my theme cannot fail me:
the one perfect in knowledge I set
before you.

[5] Behold, God rejects the obstinate in
heart;[*]
he preserves not the life of the wicked,

[6] He withholds not the just man's rights,
but grants vindication to the
oppressed[a]

[7] And with kings upon thrones
he sets them, exalted forever.[b]

[8] Or if they are bound with fetters
and held fast by bonds of affliction,

[9] Then he makes known to them what they
have done
and their sins of boastful pride.

[10] He opens their ears to correction
and exhorts them to turn back from
evil.

[11] If they obey and serve him,
they spend their days in prosperity,
their years in happiness.

[12] But if they obey not, they perish;
they die for lack of knowledge.[*]

[13] The impious in heart lay up anger for
themselves;
they cry not for help when he enchains
them;

[14] Therefore they expire in youth,
and perish among the reprobate.[*]

[15] But he saves the unfortunate through
their affliction,
and instructs them through distress.[*]

[16-20] . . . .[*]

[21] Take heed, turn not to evil;
for you have preferred carousal to
affliction.

[22] Behold, God is sublime in his power.
What teacher is there like him?

[23] Who prescribes for him his conduct,
or who can say, "You have done
wrong"?[c]

[24] Remember, you should extol his work,
which men have praised in song.

[25] All men contemplate it;
man beholds it from afar.

[26] Lo, God is great beyond our knowledge;
the number of his years is past
searching out.

[27] He holds in check the waterdrops
that filter in rain through his mists,

[28] Till the skies run with them
and the showers rain down on
mankind.

[31] For by these[*] he nourishes the nations,
and gives them food in abundance.

[29.30]Lo! he spreads the clouds in layers
as the carpeting of his tent.[*]

36, 5-21: Perhaps this section should be read between vv
6 and 7 of chapter 34.

36, 12: Knowledge: practical wisdom in serving God,
which they lack because they refused it when warned (cf v 10).

36, 14: Reprobate: cf Dt 23, 18f.

36, 16-20: The Hebrew text here is in disorder. The Vulgate has: "(16) Therefore he will give you most ample salvation from the narrow mouth which has no foundations beneath it; but the repose of your table will be filled with
fatness. (17) Your case has been judged as that of the wicked;
case and judgment you will receive. (18) Let no wrath, then,

overcome you, that you oppress anyone; nor let numerous
gifts mislead you. (19) Lay down your greatness without
tribulation, and all who are mighty in strength. (20) Do not
draw out the night, that people may go in place of them."

36, 31: These: refers to the showers of v 28, if the verse order indicated above is correct.

36, 29f: Because of the uncertainty of the text, no translation
of these verses has received unanimous approval from exegetes.

z: Jb 34, 35; 38, 2; 42, 3. *a*: Ps 72, 4. 12f. *b*: Ps 113, 7f. *c*: Jb
34, 10; Is 40, 13.

³² In his hands he holds the lightning,
    and he commands it to strike the
    mark.
³³ His thunder speaks for him
    and incites the fury of the storm.

CHAPTER 37

See RG
169-73
¹At this my heart trembles
    and leaps out of its place,
² To hear his angry voice*
    as it rumbles forth from his mouth!
³ Everywhere under the heavens he sends
    it,
    with his lightning, to the ends of the
    earth.
⁴ Again his voice roars—
    the majestic sound of his thunder.
⁵ He does great things beyond our
    knowing;
    wonders past our searching out.
⁶ For he says to the snow, "Fall to the
    earth";
    likewise to his heavy, drenching
    rain.
⁷ He shuts up all mankind indoors;
⁸   the wild beasts take to cover
    and remain quietly in their dens.

⁹ Out of its chamber* comes forth the
    tempest;
    from the north winds, the cold.
¹⁰ With his breath God brings the frost,
    and the broad waters become
    congealed.ᵈ
¹¹ With hail, also, the clouds are laden,
    as they scatter their flashes
    of light.
¹² He it is who changes their rounds,*
    according to his plans,
    in their task upon the surface of the
    earth,

¹³   whether for punishment or mercy, as
    he commands.
¹⁴ Hearken to this, O Job!
    Stand and consider the wondrous
    works of God!
¹⁵ Do you know how God lays his
    commands upon them,
    and makes the light shine forth from
    his clouds?
¹⁶ Do you know how the clouds are
    banked,
    the wondrous work of him who is
    perfect in knowledge?
¹⁷ You, whom the streams of water fail
    when a calm from the south comes
    over the land,
¹⁸ Do you spread out with him the
    firmament of the skies,
    hard as a brazen mirror?*
¹⁹ Teach us then what we shall say
    to him;
    we cannot, for the darkness, make our
    plea.
²⁰ Will he be told about it when
    I speak,
    or when a man says he is being
    destroyed?*
²¹ Nay, rather, it is as the light which men
    see not
    while it is obscured among the
    clouds,
    till the wind comes by and sweeps the
    clouds away.*
²² From the North the splendor comes,*
    surrounding God's awesome
    majesty!
²³ The Almighty! we cannot discover him,
    pre-eminent in power and judgment;

37, 2: Voice: the thunder.

37, 9: Chamber: where it was popularly believed storms were kept enclosed.

37, 12: Their rounds: of rain (Jb 36, 27), of clouds (Jb 36, 29f), of lightning and thunder (Jb 36, 32f), of snow (Jb 37, 6), of winds (Jb 37, 9).

37, 18: The firmament . . . mirror: the ancients thought of the sky as a ceiling above which were the "upper waters" (cf Gn 1, 6f; 7, 11); when this ceiling became as hard as metal, the usual rain failed to fall on the earth (cf Lv 26, 19; Dt 28, 23).

37, 20: Will an angel bring this to God's attention?

37, 21: Even though God seems not to know our circumstances, he does know them, just as surely as the sun shines, unseen by man, behind the clouds.

37, 22: Now the storms of doubt and ignorance disappear, and from the North, used here as a symbol for God's mysterious abode, comes the splendor of the manifestation of God's majestic ways.

d: Ps 148, 17.

God's Two Speeches to Job

The LORD's sudden appearance in the storm never fails to astonish even though the ground has been laid for it in Job's oaths and demands of chs 27 and 29–31 and, in an ironic way, by Elihu's "appearance" and final statement. God answers Job out of the storm in two speeches (chs 38–39 and 40–41), even evoking a brief response by Job (40, 3–5 and 42, 1–6). The structure and the meaning of the speeches have puzzled scholars. Some believe the speeches are deliberately incoherent, irrational divine blasts showing there is no answer to Job's questions except inscrutable divine will. Others rearrange the text, but no rearrangement has won wide acceptance. Most, however, find some kind of logic, even though the speeches are also an example of the mysterious communications of creator to creature. The first speech shows that the world has a design (God is wise, is able to govern), and the second demonstrates the world is just (God upholds the righteous and puts down the wicked).

his great justice owes no one an
    accounting.
24 Therefore men revere him,
    though none can see him, however
      wise their hearts.

VII: The Lord's Speech

CHAPTER 38

See RG
169–73 ¹Then the LORD* addressed Job out of
the storm and said:

2 Who is this that obscures divine plans
    with words of ignorance?
3 Gird up your loins* now, like a man;
    I will question you, and you tell me the
      answers!ᵉ
4 Where were you when I founded the earth?
    Tell me, if you have understanding.
5 Who determined its size; do you know?
    Who stretched out the measuring line
      for it?
6 Into what were its pedestals sunk,
    and who laid the cornerstone,
7 While the morning stars sang in chorus
    and all the sons of God* shouted for joy?

8 And who shut within doors the sea,

when it burst forth from the womb;ᶠ
9 When I made the clouds its garment
    and thick darkness its swaddling bands?
10 When I set limits for it
    and fastened the bar of its door,
11 And said: Thus far shall you come but no
      farther,
    and here shall your proud waves be
      stilled!

12 Have you ever in your lifetime
      commanded the morning
    and shown the dawn its place
13 For taking hold of the ends of the earth,
    till the wicked are shaken from its
      surface?
14 The earth is changed as is clay by the seal,
    and dyed as though it were a
      garment;
15 But from the wicked the light is withheld,
    and the arm of pride is shattered.

16 Have you entered into the sources of the
      sea,
    or walked about in the depths of the
      abyss?
17 Have the gates of death been shown to
      you,

38, 1: Now the Lord enters the debate and addresses two discourses (38—39 and 40—41) to Job, in which he speaks of his wisdom and power, which are altogether beyond the capacity of Job, who therefore should never dare to demand a reason for the divine actions. Out of the storm: frequently the background of the appearances of the Lord in the Old Testament; cf Pss 18; 50; Na 1, 3; Hb 3.

38, 3: Gird up your loins: prepare for combat—figuratively, be ready to defend yourself in debate.

38, 7: Sons of God: angels; cf Jb 1, 6.

e: Jb 40, 1. f: Gn 1, 9.

or have you seen the gates of darkness?
¹⁸ Have you comprehended the breadth of
the earth?
Tell me, if you know all:
¹⁹ Which is the way to the dwelling place of
light,
and where is the abode of darkness,
²⁰ That you may take them to their
boundaries
and set them on their homeward paths?
²¹ You know, because you were born before
them,
and the number of your years is great!*
²² Have you entered the storehouse of the
snow,
and seen the treasury of the hail
²³ Which I have reserved for times of stress,
for the days of war* and of battle?
²⁴ Which way to the parting of the winds,
whence the east wind spreads over the
earth?
²⁵ Who has laid out a channel for the
downpour
and for the thunderstorm a path
²⁶ To bring rain to no man's land,
the unpeopled wilderness;
²⁷ To enrich the waste and desolate ground
till the desert blooms with verdure?
²⁸ Has the rain a father;
or who has begotten the drops of
dew?
²⁹ Out of whose womb comes the ice,
and who gives the hoarfrost its birth in
the skies,
³⁰ When the waters lie covered as though
with stone
that holds captive the surface of the
deep?
³¹ Have you fitted a curb to the Pleiades,*
or loosened the bonds of Orion?
³² Can you bring forth the Mazzaroth in
their season,
or guide the Bear with its train?

³³ Do you know the ordinances of the
heavens;
can you put into effect their plan on
the earth?
³⁴ Can you raise your voice among the
clouds,
or veil yourself in the waters of the
storm?*
³⁵ Can you send forth the lightnings on
their way,
or will they say to you, "Here we are"?*
³⁷ Who counts the clouds in his wisdom?
Or who tilts the water jars of heaven
³⁸ So that the dust of earth is fused into a
mass
and its clods made solid?
³⁹ Do you hunt the prey for the lioness
or appease the hunger of her cubs,
⁴⁰ While they crouch in their dens,
or lie in wait in the thicket?
³⁶ Who puts wisdom in the heart,
and gives the cock its understanding?*
⁴¹ Who provides nourishment for the ravens
when their young ones cry out to God,ᵍ
and they rove abroad without food?

CHAPTER 39

¹Do you know about the birth of the
mountain goats,
watch for the birth pangs of the hinds,
² Number the months that they must fulfill,
and fix the time of their bringing
forth?
³ They crouch down and bear their young;
they deliver their progeny in the
desert.
⁴ When their offspring thrive and grow,
they leave and do not return.

⁵ Who has given the wild ass his freedom,
and who has loosed him from bonds?
⁶ I have made the wilderness his home
and the salt flats his dwelling.

See RG
169–73

38, 21: Divine irony.
38, 22f: Hail . . . of war: thus God used a hailstorm to
rout Joshua's foes in the battle of Gibeon; cf Jos 10, 11; Sir
46, 5.
38, 31f: Pleiades . . . Orion . . . Bear: cf Jb 9, 9. Mazzaroth:
it is uncertain what astronomical group is meant by this Hebrew word; perhaps a southern constellation (cf Jb 9, 9).

38, 34: Veil yourself . . . storm: wrap yourself in a cloud,
as God comes in a theophany; cf Ps 18, 12.
38, 35: Here we are: at your service.
38, 36: Understanding: the reflection of divine Wisdom
discernible in the created animal instincts of the cock.

---

g: Ps 147, 9.

7 He scoffs at the uproar of the city,
and hears no shouts of a driver.
8 He ranges the mountains for pasture,
and seeks out every patch of green.

9 Will the wild ox consent to serve you,
and to pass the nights by your manger?
10 Will a rope bind him in the furrow,
and will he harrow the valleys after
you?
11 Will you trust him for his great strength
and leave to him the fruits of your toil?
12 Can you rely on him to thresh out your
grain
and gather in the yield of your
threshing floor?
13 The wings of the ostrich* beat idly;
her plumage is lacking in pinions.
14 When she leaves her eggs on the ground*
and deposits them in the sand,
15 Unmindful that a foot may crush them,
that the wild beasts may trample them,
16 She cruelly disowns her young
and ruthlessly makes nought of her
brood;
17 For God has withheld wisdom from her
and has given her no share in
understanding.
18 Yet in her swiftness of foot
she makes sport of the horse and his
rider.

19 Do you give the horse his strength,*
and endow his neck with splendor?
20 Do you make the steed to quiver
while his thunderous snorting spreads
terror?
21 He jubilantly paws the plain
and rushes in his might against the
weapons.
22 He laughs at fear and cannot be deterred;
he turns not back from the sword.
23 Around him rattles the quiver,
flashes the spear and the javelin.
24 Frenzied and trembling he devours the
ground;

he holds not back at the sound of the
trumpet,
25 but at each blast he cries, "Aha!"
Even from afar he scents the battle,
the roar of the chiefs and the shouting.

26 Is it by your discernment that the hawk
soars,
that he spreads his wings toward the
south?
27 Does the eagle fly up at your command
to build his nest aloft?
28 On the cliff he dwells and spends the night,
on a spur of the cliff or the fortress.
29 From thence he watches for his prey;
his eyes behold it afar off.
30 His young ones greedily drink blood;
where the slain are, there is he.[h]

CHAPTER 40

See RG
169–73

1 The LORD then said to Job:

2 Will we have arguing with the Almighty
by the critic?
Let him who would correct God give
answer![i]

3 Then Job answered the LORD and said:

4 Behold, I am of little account; what can I
answer you?
I put my hand over my mouth.
5 Though I have spoken once, I will not do
so again;
though twice, I will do so no more.

6 Then the LORD addressed Job out of the
storm and said:

7 Gird up your loins now, like a man.
I will question you, and you tell me the
answers!
8 Would you refuse to acknowledge my
right?
Would you condemn me that you may
be justified?

9 Have you an arm like that of God,

39, 13: The wings of the ostrich cannot raise her from the ground, but they help her to run swiftly.

39, 14ff: It was popularly believed that, because the ostrich laid her eggs on the sand, she was thereby cruelly aban-

doning them; cf Lam 4, 3.

39, 19-25: The famous description of a war horse.

h: Mt 24, 28; Lk 17, 37.   i: Jb 38, 3.

or can you thunder with a voice like
his?
¹⁰ Adorn yourself with grandeur and
majesty,
and array yourself with glory and
splendor.
¹¹ Let loose the fury of your wrath;
¹² tear down the wicked and shatter them.
Bring down the haughty with a glance;
¹³ bury them in the dust together;
in the hidden world imprison them.
¹⁴ Then will I too acknowledge
that your own right hand can save you.

¹⁵ See, besides you I made Behemoth,*
that feeds on grass like an ox.
¹⁶ Behold the strength in his loins,
and his vigor in the sinews of his belly.
¹⁷ He carries his tail like a cedar;
the sinews of his thighs are like cables.
¹⁸ His bones are like tubes of bronze;
his frame is like iron rods.

¹⁹ He came at the beginning of God's ways,
and was made the taskmaster of his
fellows;
²⁰ For the produce of the mountains is
brought to him,
and of all wild animals he makes sport.
²¹ Under the lotus trees he lies,
in coverts of the reedy swamp.
²² The lotus trees cover him with their
shade;
all about him are the poplars on the
bank.
²³ If the river grows violent, he is not
disturbed;
he is tranquil though the torrent surges
about his mouth.
²⁴ Who can capture him by his eyes,
or pierce his nose* with a trap?

²⁵ Can you lead about Leviathan* with a
hook,
or curb his tongue with a bit?

²⁶ Can you put a rope into his nose,
or pierce through his cheek with a
gaff?
²⁷ Will he then plead with you, time after
time,
or address you with tender
words?
²⁸ Will he make an agreement with you
that you may have him as a slave
forever?
²⁹ Can you play with him, as with a bird?
Can you put him in leash for your
maidens?
³⁰ Will the traders bargain for him?
Will the merchants* divide him up?
³¹ Can you fill his hide with barbs,
or his head with fish spears?
³² Once you but lay a hand upon him,
no need to recall any other conflict!

CHAPTER 41

See RG
169-73

² Is he not relentless when aroused;
who then dares stand before him?*
¹ Whoever might vainly hope to do so
need only see him to be overthrown.
³ Who has assailed him and come off
safe—
who under all the heavens?

⁴ I need hardly mention his limbs,
his strength, and the fitness of his
armor.
⁵ Who can strip off his outer garment,
or penetrate his double corselet?
⁶ Who can force open the doors of his
mouth,
close to his terrible teeth?
⁷ Rows of scales are on his back,
tightly sealed together;
⁸ They are fitted each so close to
the next
that no space intervenes;
⁹ So joined one to another
that they hold fast and cannot be
parted.

40, 15: Behemoth: the hippopotamus.
40, 24: Eyes . . . nose: the only exposed parts of the submerged beast.
40, 25: Leviathan here is the crocodile. But cf Jb 3, 8.
40, 30: Merchants: literally, "Canaanites," whose reputation for trading was so widespread that their name came to be used for merchants; cf Prv 31, 24. The meaning of this verse is that the crocodile is too powerful a creature to be sold like common fish.
41, 2: Before him: some read, "before me," i.e., God; also in v 3.

Telling the Truth

Job, who protested and accused God of attacking an innocent man, is declared to have told the truth about God, whereas the friends, who defended God and divine justice and wisdom without regard for truth, are judged to have acted out of folly and incur God's anger. Job is once again an effective intercessor (42, 10; cf 1, 5).

10 When he sneezes, light flashes forth;
    his eyes are like those of the dawn.
11 Out of his mouth go forth firebrands;
    sparks of fire leap forth.
12 From his nostrils issues steam,
    as from a seething pot or bowl.
13 His breath sets coals afire;
    a flame pours from his mouth.
14 Strength abides in his neck,
    and terror leaps before him.

15.16 His heart is hard as stone:
    his flesh, as the lower millstone.
17 When he rises up, the mighty are afraid;
    the waves of the sea fall back.*
18 Should the sword reach him, it will not
    avail;
    nor will the spear, nor the dart, nor the
    javelin.
19 He regards iron as straw,
    and bronze as rotten wood.
20 The arrow will not put him to flight;
    slingstones used against him are but
    straws.
21 Clubs he esteems as splinters;
    he laughs at the crash of the spear.

22 His belly is sharp as pottery fragments;
    he spreads like a threshing sledge
    upon the mire.
23 He makes the depths boil like a pot;
    the sea he churns like perfume in a
    kettle.
24 Behind him he leaves a shining path;
    you would think the deep had the
    hoary head of age.

25 Upon the earth there is not his like,
    intrepid he was made.
26 All, however lofty, fear him;
    he is king over all proud beasts.

CHAPTER 42

See RG 169-73

1 Then Job answered the LORD and said:

2 I know that you can do all things,*
    and that no purpose of yours can be
    hindered.
3 I have dealt with great things that I do
    not understand;
    things too wonderful for me, which I
    cannot know.j
5 I had heard of you by word of mouth,
    but now my eye has seen you.
6 Therefore I disown what I have said,
    and repent in dust and ashes.

VIII: Epilogue

Job's Restoration. 7 And it came to pass after the LORD had spoken these words to Job, that the LORD said to Eliphaz the Temanite, "I am angry with you and with your two friends;* for you have not spoken rightly concerning me, as has my servant Job. 8 Now, therefore, take seven bullocks and seven rams, and go to my servant Job, and offer up a holocaust for yourselves; and let my servant Job pray for you;* for his prayer I will accept, not to punish you severely. For you have not spoken rightly concerning me, as has my servant Job." 9 Then Eliphaz the Temanite, and Bildad the Shuhite, and Zophar the Naamathite, went and did as

---

41, 17: The text here is uncertain.

42, 2-6: In the current Hebrew text, this final utterance of Job is interrupted by words ascribed to God (vv 3f) which are in large part a duplication of Jb 38, 2f.

42, 7: The three friends of Job (Elihu is ignored in the Epilogue) are criticized by the Lord because they had (even though in good faith) leveled false charges against him.

42, 8: Job becomes the intercessor for his friends, as were other great Old Testament characters, e.g., Abraham and Moses, and as our Lord would be, whom he prefigured. Seven: a symbolic number.

j: Jb 34, 35; 35, 16; 38, 2.

the LORD had commanded them. And the LORD accepted the intercession of Job.

[10]Also, the LORD restored the prosperity of Job, after he had prayed for his friends; the LORD even gave to Job twice as much as he had before. [11]Then all his brethren and his sisters came to him, and all his former acquaintances, and they dined with him in his house. They condoled with him and comforted him for all the evil which the LORD had brought upon him; and each one gave him a piece of money* and a gold ring.

[12]kThus the LORD blessed the latter days of Job more than his earlier ones. For he had fourteen thousand sheep, six thousand camels, a thousand yoke of oxen, and a thousand she-asses. [13]And he had seven sons and three daughters, [14]of whom* he called the first Jemimah, the second Keziah, and the third Keren-happuch. [15]In all the land no other women were as beautiful as the daughters of Job; and their father gave them an inheritance* among their brethren. [16]After this, Job lived a hundred and forty years;* and he saw his children, his grandchildren, and even his great-grandchildren.l [17]Then Job died, old and full of years.

42, 11: A piece of money: the term is the same as that used in Gn 33, 19; Jos 24, 32. Gold ring: for the nose or ear.

42, 14: Job's daughters had names symbolic of their charms: Jemimah, dove; Keziah, precious perfume (cf Ps 45, 9); Kerenhappuch, cosmetic jar—more precisely, a container for a black powder that was used like modern mascara.

42, 15: Ordinarily daughters did not inherit property unless there were no sons; cf Nm 27, 1-11.

42, 16: As his other rewards were twice as much as he had before (v 10), so Job's hundred and forty years were double the expected span of human life; cf Ps 90, 10.

k: Jb 1, 3. l: Jb 5, 25f.

See RG
174–79

The Book of Psalms

The Hebrew Psalter numbers 150 songs. The corresponding number in the LXX differs because of a different division of certain psalms. Hence the numbering in the Greek Psalter (which was followed by the Latin Vulgate) is usually one digit behind the Hebrew. In *The New American Bible* the numbering of the verses follows the Hebrew numbering; many of the traditional English translations are often a verse number behind the Hebrew because they do not count the superscriptions as a verse.

The superscriptions derive from pre-Christian Jewish tradition, and they contain technical terms, many of them apparently liturgical, which are no longer known to us. Seventy-three psalms are attributed to David, but there is no sure way of dating any psalm. Some are preexilic (before 587), and others are postexilic (after 539), but not as late as the Maccabean period (ca. 165). The psalms are the product of many individual collections (e.g., Songs of Ascents, Pss 120—134), which were eventually combined into the present work in which one can detect five "books," because of the doxologies which occur at 41, 14; 72, 18-19; 89, 53; 106, 48.

Two important features of the psalms deserve special notice. First, the majority were composed originally precisely for liturgical worship. This is shown by the frequent indication of liturgical leaders interacting with the community (e.g., Ps 118, 1-4). Secondly, they follow certain distinct patterns or literary forms. Thus, the hymn is a song of praise, in which a community is urged joyfully to sing out the praise of God. Various reasons are given for this praise (often introduced by "for" or "because"): the divine work of creation and sustenance (Pss 8; 104), or the divine acts in Israel's favor (Pss 135, 1-12; 136). Some of the hymns have received a more specific classification, based on content. The "Songs of Zion" are so called because they exalt Zion, the city in which God dwells among the people (Pss 46; 48). Others are termed "enthronement" psalms because they re-enact or re-present in the liturgy the kingship of the Lord (Pss 47; 96—99). Characteristic of the songs of praise is the joyful summons to get involved in the activity; Ps 104 is an exception to this, although it remains universal in its thrust.

Another type of psalm is similar to the hymn: the thanksgiving psalm. This too is a song of praise acknowledging the Lord as the rescuer of the psalmist from a desperate situation. Very often the psalmist will give a flash-back, recounting the past distress, and the plea that was uttered (Pss 30; 116). The setting for such prayers seems to have been the offering of a *todah* (a "praise" sacrifice) with friends in the Temple.

There are more psalms of lament than of any other type. They may be individual (e.g., Pss 3—7; 22) or communal (e.g., Ps 44). Although they usually begin with a cry for help, they develop in various ways. The description of the distress is couched in the broad imagery typical of the Bible (one is in Sheol, the Pit, or is afflicted by enemies or wild beasts, etc.)—in such a way that one cannot pinpoint the exact nature of the psalmist's plight. However, Ps 51 (cf also Ps 130) seems to refer clearly to deliverance from sin. Several laments end on a note of certainty that the Lord has heard the prayer (cf Ps 7, but contrast Ps 88), and the Psalter has been characterized as a movement from lament to praise. If this is somewhat of an exaggeration, it serves at least to emphasize the frequent expressions of trust which characterize the lament. In some cases it would seem as if the theme of trust has been lifted out to form a literary type all its own; cf Pss 23; 62; 91. Among the communal laments can be counted Pss 74 and 79. They complain to the Lord about some national disaster, and try to motivate God to intervene in favor of the suffering people.

Other psalms are clearly classified on account of content, and they may be in themselves laments or psalms of thanksgiving. Among the "royal" psalms, that deal directly with the currently reigning king, are Pss 20; 21 and 72. Many of the royal psalms were given a messianic interpretation by Christians. In Jewish tradition they were preserved, even after kingship had disappeared, because they were read in the light of the Davidic covenant reported in 2 Samuel 7. Certain psalms are called wisdom psalms because they seem to betray the influence of the concerns of the ages (cf. Pss 37; 49), but there is no general agreement as to the number of these prayers. Somewhat related to the wisdom psalms are the "torah" psalms, in which the torah (instruction or law) of the Lord is glorified (Pss 1; 19, 8-14; 119). Pss 78; 105 and 106 can be considered as "historical" psalms. Although the majority of the psalms have a liturgical setting, there are certain prayers that may be termed "liturgies," so clearly does their structure reflect a liturgical incident (e.g., Pss 15; 24).

It is obvious that not all of the psalms can be pigeon-holed into neat classifications, but even a brief sketch of these types helps us to catch the structure and spirit of the psalms we read. It has been rightly said that the psalms are "a school of prayer." They not only provide us with models to follow, but inspire us to voice our own deepest feelings and aspirations.

————

First Book: Psalms 1—41

PSALM 1*

True Happiness in God's Law

See RG 176

I
[1] Happy those* who do not follow
the counsel of the wicked,
Nor go the way* of sinners,
nor sit in company with scoffers.[a]
[2] Rather, the law of the LORD* is their joy;
God's law they study day and night.[b]
[3] They are like a tree[c]
planted near streams of water,
that yields its fruit in season;
Its leaves never wither;
whatever they do prospers.

II
[4] But not the wicked!*
They are like chaff driven by the wind.[d]
[5] Therefore the wicked will not survive
judgment,

Ps 1: A preface to the whole Book of Psalms, contrasting with striking similes the destiny of the good and the wicked. The psalm views life as activity, as choosing either the good or the bad. Each "way" brings its inevitable consequences. The wise through their good actions will experience rootedness and life, and the wicked, rootlessness and death.

1, 1: Those: literally, "the man." That word is used here and in many of the Psalms as typical, and therefore is translated "they." **The way:** a common biblical term for manner of living or moral conduct (Pss 32, 8; 101, 2. 6; Prv 2, 20; 1 Kgs 8, 36).

1, 2: The law of the LORD: either the Torah, the first five books of the Bible, or, more probably, divine teaching or instruction.

1, 4: The wicked: those who by their actions distance themselves from God's life-giving presence.

———

a: Pss 26, 4-5; 40, 5. *b:* Jos 1, 8; Ps 119; Sir 39, 1. *c:* Pss 52, 10; 92, 13-15; Jer 17, 8. *d:* Pss 35, 5; 83, 14-16; Jb 21, 18.

The Structure of the Book of Psalms

Psalms is divided into five "books," each of which ends with a verse or song of praise (a doxology).

Book 1, Psalms 1—41	Doxology is 41, 14
Book 2, Psalms 42—72	Doxology is 72, 18—19
Book 3, Psalms 73—89	Doxology is 89, 53
Book 4, Psalms 90—106	Doxology is 106, 48
Book 5, Psalms 107—150	Doxology is Psalm 150

Books 1, 4, and 5 tend to use "LORD" ("Yahweh") as the name of God; books 2 and 3 use "God" ("Elohim"). This indicates that there may have been two centers of collection for Psalms, and in one case—Psalms 14 and 53—we have a nearly identical Psalm with the different names for God.

nor will sinners in the assembly of the
  just.
⁶ The LORD watches over the way of the
  just,ᵉ
but the way of the wicked leads to ruin.

See RG 176

PSALM 2*

A Psalm for a Royal Coronation

¹ Why do the nations protest
  and the peoples grumble in vain?ᶠ
² Kings on earth rise up
  and princes plot together
  against the LORD and his anointed:ᵍ *
³ "Let us break their shackles
  and cast off their chains!"ʰ
⁴ The one enthroned in heaven laughs;
  the LORD derides them,ⁱ
⁵ Then speaks to them in anger,
  terrifies them in wrath:
⁶ "I myself have installed my king
  on Zion, my holy mountain."
⁷ I will proclaim the decree of the LORD,
  who said to me, "You are my son;

today I am your father.ʲ
⁸ Only ask it of me,
  and I will make your inheritance the
    nations,
  your possession the ends of the earth.
⁹ With an iron rod you shall shepherd
    them,
  like a clay pot you will shatter them."ᵏ
¹⁰ And now, kings, give heed;
  take warning, rulers on earth.
¹¹ Serve the LORD with fear;
  with trembling bow down in homage,
Lest God be angry and you perish from
    the way
  in a sudden blaze of anger.
Happy are all who take refuge in God!ˡ

PSALM 3*

See RG 175

Threatened but Trusting

¹ A psalm of David, when he fled from his
    son Absalom.ᵐ *

I

² How many are my foes, LORD!
  How many rise against me!

Ps 2: A royal psalm. To rebellious kings (1-3) God responds vigorously (4-6). A speaker proclaims the divine decree (in the legal adoption language of the day), making the Israelite king the earthly representative of God (7-9) and warning kings to obey (10-11). The psalm has a messianic meaning for the Church; the New Testament understands it of Christ (Acts 4, 25-27; 13, 33; Heb 1, 5).

2, 2: Anointed: in Hebrew *mashiah*, "anointed"; in Greek *christos*, whence English Messiah and Christ. In Israel kings (Jgs 9, 8; 1 Sm 9, 16; 16, 12-13) and high priests (Lv 8, 12; Nm 3, 3) received the power of their office through anointing.

Ps 3: An individual lament complaining of enemies who

deny that God will come to the rescue (2-3). Despite such taunts the psalmist hopes for God's protection even in sleep (4-7). The psalm prays for an end to the enemies' power to speak maliciously (8) and closes peacefully with an expression of trust (9).

3, 1: The superscription, added later, relates the psalm to an incident in the life of David.

e: Ps 37, 18.   *f:* Rv 11, 18.   *g:* Ps 83, 6.   *h:* Ps 149, 8.
i: Pss 37, 13; 59, 9; Wis 4, 18.   *j:* Pss 89, 27; 110, 2-3; Is 49, 1.
k: Rv 2, 27; 12, 5; 19, 15.   *l:* Pss 34, 9; 146, 5; Prv 16, 20.
m. 2 Sm 15, 13ff.

> Psalm 4 is an unusual individual petition: It is unclear what the petitioner's problem might be; it highlights the psalmist's confidence in God more than his troubles; and it focuses more on others than on the psalmist.

³ How many say of me,
    "God will not save that one."ⁿ   *Selah**
⁴ But you, LORD, are a shield around me;
    my glory, you keep my head high.ᵒ

II

⁵ Whenever I cried out to the LORD,
    I was answered from the holy
        mountain.   *Selah*
⁶ Whenever I lay down and slept,
    the LORD preserved me to rise again.ᵖ
⁷ I do not fear, then, thousands of people
    arrayed against me on every side.

III

⁸ Arise, LORD! Save me, my God!
    You will shatter the jaws of all my
        foes;
    you will break the teeth of the
        wicked.�q
⁹ Safety comes from the LORD!
    Your blessing for your people!ʳ   *Selah*

See RG 175

PSALM 4*

Trust in God

¹ For the leader;* with stringed instruments.
    A psalm of David.

I

² Answer when I call, my saving God.
    In my troubles, you cleared a way;
    show me favor; hear my prayer.ˢ

II

³ How long will you people mock my
        honor,
    love what is worthless, chase after
        lies?ᵗ   *Selah*

⁴ Know that the LORD works wonders for
    the faithful;
    the LORD hears when I call out.
⁵ Tremble* and do not sin;
    upon your beds ponder in silence.ᵘ
⁶ Offer fitting sacrifice
    and trust in the LORD.ᵛ

III

⁷ Many say, "May we see better times!
    LORD, show us the light of your
        face!"ʷ   *Selah*
⁸ But you have given my heart more joy
    than they have when grain and wine
        abound.
⁹ In peace I shall both lie down and
        sleep,ˣ
    for you alone, LORD, make me
        secure.

PSALM 5*

Prayer for Divine Help

See RG 175

¹ For the leader; with wind instruments.
    A psalm of David.

I

² Hear my words, O LORD;
    listen to my sighing.ʸ
³ Hear my cry for help,
    my king, my God!
    To you I pray, O LORD;
⁴   at dawn you will hear my cry;
    at dawn I will plead before you and
        wait.ᶻ

II

⁵ You are not a god who delights in evil;

3, 3. 5. 9: Selah: the term is generally considered a direction to the cantor or musicians but its exact meaning is not known. It occurs 71 times in 39 psalms.

Ps 4: An individual lament emphasizing trust in God. The petition is based upon the psalmist's vivid experience of God as savior (2). That experience of God is the basis for the warning to the wicked: revere God who intervenes on the side of the faithful (3-6). The faithful psalmist exemplifies the blessings given to the just (7-9).

4, 1: For the leader: many psalm headings contain this rubric. Its exact meaning is unknown but may signify that such psalms once stood together in a collection of "the choirmaster." Cf 1 Chr 15, 21.

4, 5: Tremble: be moved deeply with religious awe. The Greek translation understood the emotion to be anger, and it is so cited in Eph 4, 26.

Ps 5: A lament contrasting the security of the house of God (8-9. 12-13) with the danger of the company of evildoers (5-7. 10-11). The psalmist therefore prays that God will hear (2-4) and grant the protection and joy of the temple.

n: Ps 71, 11.   *o:* Pss 7, 11; 18, 3; 62, 7-8; Dt 33, 29; Is 60, 19.
p: Ps 4, 9; Prv 3, 24.   *q:* Ps 58, 7.   *r:* Ps 28, 9; Jon 2, 10.
s: Ps 118, 5.   *t:* Ps 62, 4.   *u:* Eph 4, 26.   *v:* Ps 51, 19.   *w:* Pss 31, 17; 44, 4; 67, 1; 80, 4; Jb 13, 24; Nm 6, 25; Dn 9, 17.   *x:* Ps 3, 6.   *y:* Pss 86, 6; 130, 1-2.   *z:* Wis 16, 28.

no wicked person finds refuge with
    you;

6 the arrogant cannot stand before
    you.
You hate all who do evil;

7 you destroy all who speak
    falsely.*a*
Murderers and deceivers
    the LORD abhors.

III

8 But I can enter your house
    because of your great love.
I can worship in your holy temple
    because of my reverence for you,
    LORD.*b*

9 Guide me in your justice because of my
    foes;
    make straight your way before me.*c*

IV

10 For there is no sincerity in their
    mouths;
    their hearts are corrupt.
Their throats* are open graves;*d*
    on their tongues are subtle lies.

11 Declare them guilty, God;
    make them fall by their own
    devices.*e*
Drive them out for their many sins;
    they have rebelled against you.

V

12 Then all who take refuge in you will be
    glad
    and forever shout for joy.*f*
Protect them that you may be the joy
    of those who love your name.

13 For you, LORD, bless the just;

you surround them with favor like a
    shield.

PSALM 6 *

Prayer in Distress

See RG
175

1 For the leader; with stringed instruments,
    "upon the eighth."* A psalm of David.

I

2 Do not reprove me in your anger,
    LORD,
    nor punish me in your wrath.*g*

3 Have pity on me, LORD, for I am weak;
    heal me, LORD, for my bones are
    trembling.*h*

4 In utter terror is my soul—
    and you, LORD, how long . . . ?*i* *

5 Turn, LORD, save my life;
    in your mercy* rescue me.

6 For who among the dead remembers
    you?
    Who praises you in Sheol?*j* *

II

7 I am wearied with sighing;
    all night long tears drench my bed;
    my couch is soaked with
    weeping.

8 My eyes are dimmed with sorrow,
    worn out because of all my foes.*k*

III

9 Away from me, all who do evil!*l*
    The LORD has heard my weeping.

10 The LORD has heard my prayer;
    the LORD takes up my plea.

11 My foes will be terrified and
    disgraced;
    all will fall back in sudden shame.*m*

5, 10: Their throats: their speech brings harm to their
hearers (cf Jer 5, 16). The verse mentions four parts of the
body, each a source of evil to the innocent.

Ps 6: The first of the seven Penitential Psalms (Pss 6; 32;
38; 51; 102; 130; 143), a designation dating from the seventh
century A.D. for psalms suitable to express repentance. The
psalmist does not, as in many laments, claim to be innocent
but appeals to God's mercy (5). Sin here, as often in the Bible,
is both the sinful act and its injurious consequences; here it is
physical sickness (3-4. 7-8) and the attacks of enemies (8. 9.
11). The psalmist prays that the effects of personal and social
sin be taken away.

6, 1: Upon the eighth: apparently a musical notation, now
lost.

6, 4: How long?: elliptical for "How long will it be before
you answer my prayer?" Cf Ps 13, 2-3.

6, 5: Mercy: Hebrew *hesed*, translated as "mercy" or

"love," describes God's affectionate fidelity to human beings,
which is rooted in divine and not human integrity.

6, 6: A motive for God to preserve the psalmist from
death: in the shadowy world of the dead no one offers you
praise. Sheol is the biblical term for the underworld where the
insubstantial souls of dead human beings dwelt. It was similar to the Hades of Greek and Latin literature. In the second
century B.C., biblical books begin to speak positively of life
with God after death (Dn 12, 1-3; Wis 3).

---

a: Ps 101, 7; Wis 14, 9; Hb 1, 13.   *b*: Ps 138, 2; Jon 2, 5.   *c*: Ps
23, 3; Prv 4, 11; Is 26, 7.   *d*: Rom 3, 13.   *e*: Ps 141, 10.   *f*: Ps
64, 11.   *g*: Ps 38, 2.   *h*: Jer 17, 14-15.   *i*: Pss 13, 2-3; 74, 10; 89,
47.   *j*: Pss 30, 10; 88, 11; 115, 17; Is 38, 18.   *k*: Pss 31, 10; 38, 11;
40, 13.   *l*: Ps 119, 115; Mt 7, 23; Lk 13, 27.   *m*: Pss 35, 4. 26; 40,
15; 71, 13.

See RG
175

PSALM 7*

God the Vindicator

1 A plaintive song of David, which he sang
to the LORD concerning Cush, the
Benjaminite.

I

2 LORD my God, in you I take refuge;
rescue me; save me from all who
pursue me,*n*
3 Lest they maul me like lions,
tear me to pieces with none to save.

II

4 LORD my God, if I am at fault in this,*
if there is guilt on my hands,
5 If I have repaid my friend with evil—
I spared even those who hated me
without cause—
6 Then let my enemy pursue and
overtake me,
trample my life to the ground,
and leave me dishonored in the dust.*o*
                      Selah

III

7 Rise up, LORD, in your anger;
rise against the fury of my foes.*p*
Wake to judge as you have decreed.
8 Have the assembly of the peoples gather
about you;
sit on your throne high above them,
9   O LORD, judge of the nations.
Grant me justice, LORD, for I am
blameless,
free of any guilt.
10 Bring the malice of the wicked to an end;
uphold the innocent,
O God of justice,
who tries hearts and minds.*q*

IV

11 A shield before me is God
who saves the honest heart.*r*
12 God is a just judge,
who rebukes in anger every day.
13 If sinners do not repent,
God sharpens his sword,
strings and readies the bow,*s*
14 Prepares his deadly shafts,
makes arrows blazing thunderbolts.*t*

V

15 Sinners conceive iniquity;
pregnant with mischief,
they give birth to failure.*u*
16 They open a hole and dig it deep,
but fall into the pit they have dug.*v*
17 Their mischief comes back upon
themselves;
their violence falls on their own heads.

VI

18 I praise the justice of the LORD;
I celebrate the name of the LORD Most
High.*w*

PSALM 8*

Divine Majesty and Human Dignity

See RG
175-76

1 For the leader; "upon the *gittith*."* A psalm
of David.

2 O LORD, our Lord,
how awesome is your name through
all the earth!
You have set your majesty above the
heavens!
3 Out of the mouths of babes*x* and infants*
you have drawn a defense* against
your foes,
to silence enemy and avenger.*

Ps 7: An individual lament. The psalmist flees to God's presence in the sanctuary for justice and protection (2-3) and takes an oath that only the innocent can swear (4-6). The innocent psalmist can thus hope for the just God's protection (7-14) and be confident that the actions of the wicked will come back upon their own heads (15-17). The justice of God leads the psalmist to praise (18).

7, 4: At fault in this: in the accusation the enemies have made against the psalmist.

Ps 8: While marvelling at the limitless grandeur of God (2-3), the psalmist is struck first by the smallness of human beings in creation (4-5), and then by the royal dignity and power that God has graciously bestowed upon them (6-10).

8, 1: Upon the gittith: probably the title of the melody to which the psalm was to be sung or a musical instrument.

8, 3: Babes and infants: the text is obscure. Some join this line to the last line of 2 (itself obscure) to read: "(you) whose majesty is exalted above the heavens / by the mouths of babes and infants." **Drawn a defense**: some prefer the Septuagint's "fashioned praise," which is quoted in Mt 21, 16. **Enemy and avenger**: probably cosmic enemies. The primeval powers of watery chaos are often personified in poetic texts (Pss 74, 13-14; 89, 11; Jb 9, 13; 26, 12-13; Is 51, 9).

---

n: Pss 6, 5; 22, 21.   *o:* Ps 143, 3.   *p:* Pss 9, 4; 19, 20.   *q:* Pss 17, 3; 26, 2; 35, 24; 43, 1; 139, 23; Jer 17, 10; 20, 12.   *r:* Ps 3, 4.   *s:* Ps 11, 2.   *t:* Is 50, 11.   *u:* Jb 15, 35; Is 59, 4.   *v:* Pss 9, 16; 35, 8; 57, 7; Prv 26, 27; Eccl 10, 8; Sir 27, 26.   *w:* Pss 18, 50; 30, 5; 135, 3; 146, 2.   *x:* Mt 21, 16; Wis 10, 21.

[4] When I see your heavens, the work of
   your fingers,
   the moon and stars that you set in
   place—
[5] What are humans that you are mindful of
   them,[y]
   mere mortals* that you care for them?[z]
[6] Yet you have made them little less than a
   god,*
   crowned them with glory and honor.
[7] You have given them rule over the works
   of your hands,[a]
   put all things at their feet:
[8] All sheep and oxen,
   even the beasts of the field,
[9] The birds of the air, the fish of the sea,
   and whatever swims the paths of the
   seas.
[10] O LORD, our Lord,
   how awesome is your name through
   all the earth!

See RG
175–76

PSALMS 9—10*

Thanksgiving for Victory and
Prayer for Justice

[1] For the leader; according to *Muth Labben.**
   A psalm of David.

A

I

[2] I will praise you, LORD, with all my
   heart;
   I will declare all your wondrous deeds.
[3] I will delight and rejoice in you;
   I will sing hymns to your name, Most
   High.
[4] For my enemies turn back;
   they stumble and perish before you.

II

[5] You upheld my right and my cause,
   seated on your throne, judging justly.
[6] You rebuked the nations, you destroyed
   the wicked;
   their name you blotted out for all time.[b]
[7] The enemies have been ruined forever;
   you destroyed their cities;
   their memory has perished.

III

[8] The LORD rules forever,
   has set up a throne for judgment.
[9] It is God who governs the world with
   justice,[c]
   who judges the peoples with fairness.
[10] The LORD is a stronghold for the
   oppressed,
   a stronghold in times of trouble.[d]
[11] Those who honor your name trust in you;
   you never forsake those who seek you,
   LORD.

IV

[12] Sing hymns to the LORD enthroned on
   Zion;
   proclaim God's deeds among the
   nations!
[13] For the avenger of bloodshed remembers,
   does not forget the cry of the
   afflicted.[e]

V

[14] Have mercy on me, LORD;
   see how my foes afflict me!
   You alone can raise me from the gates
   of death.[f]
[15] Then I will declare all your praises,
   sing joyously of your salvation
   in the gates of daughter Zion.*

8, 5: Humans . . . mere mortals: literally, "(mortal) person" . . . "son of man (in sense of a human being, Hebrew *'adam*)." The emphasis is on the fragility and mortality of human beings to whom God has given great dignity.

8, 6: Little less than a god: Hebrew *'elohim*, the ordinary word for "God" or "the gods" or members of the heavenly court. The Greek version translated *'elohim* by "angel, messenger"; several ancient and modern versions so translate. The meaning seems to be that God created human beings almost at the level of the beings in the heavenly world. Heb 2, 9 finds the eminent fulfillment of this verse in Jesus Christ, who was humbled before being glorified. Cf also 1 Cor 15, 27, where St. Paul applies to Christ the closing words of v 7.

Pss 9—10: Pss 9 and 10 in the Hebrew text have been transmitted as separate poems but they actually form a single

acrostic poem and are so transmitted in the Greek and Latin tradition. Each verse of the two psalms begins with a successive letter of the Hebrew alphabet (though several letters have no corresponding stanza). The psalm states loosely connected themes: the rescue of the helpless poor from their enemies, God's worldwide judgment and rule over the nations, the psalmist's own concern for rescue (14-15).

9, 1: Muth Labben: probably the melodic accompaniment of the psalm, now lost.

9, 15: Daughter Zion: an ancient Near Eastern city could sometimes be personified as a woman or a queen, the spouse of the god of the city.

y: Ps 144, 3; Jb 7, 17.   *z:* Heb 2, 6ff.   *a:* 7ff: Gn 1, 26. 28; Wis 9, 2, 1 Cor 15, 27.   *b:* Jb 18, 17.   *c:* Pss 96, 10; 98, 9.   *d:* Ps 37, 39; Is 25, 4.   *e:* Jb 16, 18.   *f:* Wis 16, 13.

VI

16 The nations fall into the pit they dig;
  in the snare they hide, their own foot is
    caught.
17 The LORD is revealed in this divine rule:
  by the deeds they do the wicked are
    trapped.ᵍ*   *Higgaion. Selah*

VII

18 To Sheol the wicked will depart,
  all the nations that forget God.
19 The needy will never be forgotten,
  nor will the hope of the afflicted ever
    fade.ʰ
20 Arise, LORD, let no mortal prevail;
  let the nations be judged in your
    presence.
21 Strike them with terror, LORD;
  show the nations they are mere
    mortals.   *Selah*

B

I

1 Why, LORD, do you stand at a distance
  and pay no heed to these troubled
    times?
2 Arrogant scoundrels pursue the poor;
  they trap them by their cunning
    schemes.ⁱ

II

3 The wicked even boast of their greed;
  these robbers curse and scorn the
    LORD.ʲ
4 In their insolence the wicked boast:
  "God doesn't care, doesn't even
    exist."ᵏ
5 Yet their affairs always succeed;
  they ignore your judgment on high;
  they sneer at all who oppose them.
6 They say in their hearts, "We will never
    fall;
  never will we see misfortune."
7 Their mouths are full of oaths, violence,
    and lies;
  discord and evil are under their
    tongues.ˡ

8 They wait in ambush near towns;
  their eyes watch for the helpless,
  to murder the innocent in secret.ᵐ
9 They lurk in ambush like lions in a thicket,
  hide there to trap the poor,
  snare them and close the net.ⁿ
10 The helpless are crushed, laid low;
  they fall into the power of the wicked,
11 Who say in their hearts, "God pays no
    attention,
  shows no concern, never bothers to
    look."ᵒ

III

12 Rise up, LORD God! Raise your arm!
  Do not forget the poor!
13 Why should the wicked scorn God,
  say in their hearts, "God doesn't care"?
14 But you do see;
  you do observe this misery and
    sorrow;ᵖ
  you take the matter in hand.
To you the helpless can entrust their cause;
  you are the defender of orphans.�q
15 Break the arms of the wicked and
    depraved;
  make them account for their crimes;
  let none of them survive.

IV

16 The LORD is king forever;ʳ
  the nations have vanished from God's
    land.
17 You listen, LORD, to the needs of the poor;
  you encourage them and hear their
    prayers.
18 You win justice for the orphaned and
    oppressed;ˢ
  no one on earth will cause terror again.

PSALM 11*

*Confidence in the Presence
of God*

See RG
175

1 For the leader. Of David.

I

In the LORD I take refuge;

9, 17: **The LORD is revealed in this divine rule**: God has so made the universe that the wicked are punished by the very actions they perform.

Ps 11: A song of trust. Though friends counsel flight to the mountain country (a traditional hideout) to escape trouble (1-3), the innocent psalmist reaffirms confidence in God, who protects those who seek asylum in the temple (4-7).

---

g: Sir 27, 26. h: Prv 23, 18. i: Is 32, 7. j: Ps 36, 2. k: Ps 14, 1; Jb 22, 13; Is 29, 15; Jer 5, 12; Zep 1, 12. l: Is 32, 7; Rom 3, 14.
m: Ps 11, 2; Jb 24, 14. n: Ps 17, 12; Prv 1, 11; Jer 5, 26. o: Pss 44, 25; 64, 6; 73, 11; 94, 7; Ez 9, 9. p: Pss 31, 8; 56, 9; 2 Kgs 20,
5; Is 25, 8; Rv 7, 17. q: Ex 22, 21-22. r: Ps 145, 13; Jer 10, 10. s: Dt 10, 18.

how can you say to me,
"Flee like a bird to the mountains!^{t}
2 See how the wicked string their bows,
fit their arrows to the string
to shoot from the shadows at the
upright.^{u}
3 When foundations* are being destroyed,
what can the upright do?"

II

4 The LORD is in his holy temple;
the LORD's throne is in heaven.^{v}
God's eyes keep careful watch;
they test all peoples.
5 The LORD tests the good and the bad,
hates those who love violence,
6 And rains upon the wicked
fiery coals and brimstone,
a scorching wind their allotted cup.^{w} *
7 The LORD is just and loves just deeds;
the upright shall see his face.

PSALM 12*

See RG 175

Prayer against Evil Tongues

1 For the leader; "upon the eighth."
A psalm of David.

I

2 Help, LORD, for no one loyal remains;
the faithful have vanished from the
human race.^{x}
3 Those who tell lies to one another
speak with deceiving lips and a double
heart.^{y}

II

4 May the LORD cut off all deceiving lips,
and every boastful tongue,
5 Those who say, "By our tongues we
prevail;
when our lips speak, who can lord it
over us?"^{z}

III

6 "Because they rob the weak, and the
needy groan,
I will now arise," says the LORD;
"I will grant safety to whoever longs
for it."^{a}

IV

7 The promises of the LORD are sure,
silver refined in a crucible,*
silver purified seven times.^{b}
8 LORD, protect us always;
preserve us from this generation.
9 On every side the wicked strut;
the shameless are extolled by all.

PSALM 13*

See RG 175

Prayer in Time of Illness

1 For the leader. A psalm of David.

I

2 How long, LORD? Will you utterly forget
me?
How long will you hide your face
from me?^{c}
3 How long must I carry sorrow in my
soul,
grief in my heart day after day?
How long will my enemy triumph over
me?

II

4 Look upon me, answer me, LORD, my
God!
Give light to my eyes lest I sleep in
death,
5 Lest my enemy say, "I have prevailed,"
lest my foes rejoice at my downfall.^{d}

III

6 I trust in your faithfulness.
Grant my heart joy in your help,
That I may sing of the LORD,

11, 3: Foundations: usually understood of public order. Cf Ps 82, 5.

11, 6: Their allotted cup: the cup that God gives people to drink is a common figure for their destiny. Cf Pss 16, 5; 75, 9; Mt 20, 22; 26, 39; Rv 14, 10.

Ps 12: A lament. The psalmist, thrown into a world where lying and violent people persecute the just (2-3), prays that the wicked be punished (4-5). The prayer is not simply for vengeance but arises from a desire to see God's justice appear on earth. V 6 preserves the word of assurance spoken by the priest to the lamenter; it is not usually transmitted in such psalms. In vv 7-9 the psalmist affirms the intention to live by the word of assurance.

12, 7: A crucible: literally "in a crucible in the ground."

The crucible was placed in the ground for support.

Ps 13: A lament in which the psalmist, seriously ill (4), expresses fear that enemies will interpret his or her death as a divine judgment. Hence the heartfelt prayer (2-3) for healing that will signal to those enemies that the psalmist enjoys God's favor (4-5). The poem ends with a confession of trust in God and a statement of praise (6).

t: Pss 55, 7; 91, 4. *u:* Pss 7, 13; 37, 14; 57, 5; 64, 4. *v:* Pss 14, 2; 102, 20; Hb 2, 20; Dt 26, 15; Is 66, 1; Mt 5, 34. *w:* Pss 120, 4; 140, 11; Prv 16, 27; Ez 38, 22; Rv 8, 5; 20, 10. *x:* Pss 3, 116, 11 Is 59, 15; Mi 7, 2. *y:* Pss 28, 3; 55, 22; Is 59, 3-4; Jer 9, 7. *z:* Sir 5, 3. *a:* Is 33, 10. *b:* Ps 18, 31; 19, 8; Prv 30, 5. *c:* Pss 6, 4; 44, 25; 77, 8; 79, 5; 89, 47; 94, 3; Lam 5, 20. *d:* Ps 38, 17.

"How good our God has been to
me!"e

PSALM 14*

A Lament over
Widespread Corruption

1 For the leader. Of David.

I

Fools* say in their hearts,
"There is no God."f
Their deeds are loathsome and corrupt;
not one does what is right.
2 The LORD looks down from heaven
upon the human race,g
To see if even one is wise,h
if even one seeks God.
3 All have gone astray;
all alike are perverse.
Not one does what is right,
not even one.i

II

4 Will these evildoers never learn?
They devour my people as they
devour bread;j
they do not call upon the LORD.k
5 They have good reason, then, to fear;
God is with the company of the just.
6 They would crush the hopes of the poor,
but the poor have the LORD as their
refuge.

III

7 Oh, that from Zion might come
the deliverance of Israel,
That Jacob may rejoice, and Israel be
glad

when the LORD restores his
people!l *

PSALM 15*

The Righteous Israelite

1 A psalm of David.

I

LORD, who may abide in your tent?
Who may dwell on your holy
mountain?m *

II

2 Whoever walks without blame,n
doing what is right,
speaking truth from the heart;
3 Who does not slander a neighbor,
does no harm to another,
never defames a friend;
4 Who disdains the wicked,
but honors those who fear the LORD;
Who keeps an oath despite the cost,
5 lends no money at interest,*
accepts no bribe against the innocent.o

III

Whoever acts like this
shall never be shaken.

PSALM 16*

God the Supreme Good

1 A miktam* of David.

I

Keep me safe, O God;
in you I take refuge.p
2 I say to the LORD,
you are my Lord,
you are my only good.

Ps 14: The lament (duplicated in Ps 53) depicts the world
as consisting of two types of people: "the fools" (= the
wicked, 1-3) and "the company of the just" (4-6; also called
"my people," and "the poor"). The wicked persecute the just,
but the psalm expresses the hope that God will punish the
wicked and reward the good.
14, 1: Fools: literally, "the fool." The singular is used
typically, hence the plural translation.
14, 7: Israel . . . Jacob . . . his people: the righteous poor
are identified with God's people.
Ps 15: The psalm records a liturgical scrutiny at the entrance to the temple court (cf Ps 24, 3-6; Is 33, 14b-16). The
Israelite wishing to be admitted had to ask the temple official
what conduct was appropriate to God's precincts. Note the
emphasis on virtues relating to one's neighbor.
15, 1: Your tent . . . your holy mountain: the temple could
be referred to as "tent" (Ps 61, 5; Is 33, 20), a reference to the
tent of the wilderness period and the tent of David (2 Sm 6, 17;

7, 2), predecessors of the temple. **Holy mountain:** a venerable
designation of the divine abode (Pss 2, 6; 3, 5; 43, 3; 48, 2, etc.).
15, 5: Lends no money at interest: lending money in the
Old Testament was often seen as assistance to the poor in
their distress, not as an investment; making money off the
poor by charging interest was thus forbidden (Ex 22, 24;
Lv 25, 36-37; Dt 23, 20).
Ps 16: In the first section, the psalmist rejects the futile
worship of false gods (2-5), preferring Israel's God (1), the
giver of the land (6). The second section reflects on the wise
and life-giving presence of God (7-11).
16, 1: Miktam: a term occurring six times in psalm superscriptions, always with "David." Its meaning is unknown.

e: Ps 116, 7.   f: Pss 10, 4; 36, 2; Is 32, 6; Jer 5, 12.   g: Pss 11, 4;
102, 20.   h: 2b-3: Rom 3, 11-12.   i: Ps 12, 1.   j: Ps 27, 2; Is 5,
11.   k: Ps 79, 6.   l: Ps 85, 2.   m: Is 56, 7.   n: Ps 119, 1.   o: Ex
22, 24; 23, 8.   p: Ps 25, 20.

³ Worthless are all the false gods of the
    land.
  Accursed are all who delight in them.
⁴ They multiply their sorrows
    who court other gods.
  Blood libations to them I will not pour
    out,
  nor will I take their names* upon my
    lips.
⁵ LORD, my allotted portion and my cup,
  you have made my destiny secure.�q
⁶ Pleasant places were measured out for
    me;*
  fair to me indeed is my inheritance.

            II

⁷ I bless the LORD who counsels me;
  even at night my heart exhorts me.
⁸ I keep the LORD always before me;
  with the Lord at my right, I shall
    never be shaken.ʳ
⁹ Therefore my heart is glad, my soul
    rejoices;
  my body also dwells secure,
¹⁰ For you will not abandon me to Sheol,
  nor let your faithful servant see the pit.ˢ *
¹¹ You will show me the path to life,
  abounding joy in your presence,
  the delights at your right hand forever.

PSALM 17*

See RG
175

*Prayer for Rescue from
Persecutors*

¹ A prayer of David.

            I

Hear, LORD, my plea for justice;
  pay heed to my cry;
Listen to my prayer
  spoken without guile.

² From you let my vindication come;
  your eyes see what is right.
³ You have tested my heart,
  searched it in the night.ᵗ
  You have tried me by fire,
  but find no malice in me.
  My mouth has not transgressed
⁴   as humans often do.
  As your lips have instructed me,
  I have kept the way of the law.
⁵ My steps have kept to your paths;
  my feet have not faltered.ᵘ

            II

⁶ I call upon you; answer me, O God.
  Turn your ear to me; hear my prayer.
⁷ Show your wonderful love,
  you who deliver with your right arm
  those who seek refuge from their
    foes.
⁸ Keep me as the apple of your eye;
  hide me in the shadow of your
    wings*
⁹   from the violence of the wicked.ᵛ

           III

  My ravenous enemies press upon me;ʷ
¹⁰   they close their hearts,*
  they fill their mouths with proud
    roaring.
¹¹ Their steps even now encircle me;
  they watch closely, keeping low to
    the ground,
¹² Like lions eager for prey,
  like young lions lurking in ambush.
¹³ Rise, O LORD, confront and cast them
    down;
  rescue me so from the wicked.
¹⁴ Slay them with your sword;
  with your hand, LORD, slay them;

16, 4: Take their names: to use the gods' names in oaths
and hence to affirm them as one's own gods.

16, 6: Pleasant places were measured out for me: the
psalmist is pleased with the plot of land measured out to the
family, which was to be passed on to succeeding generations
("my inheritance").

16, 10: Nor let your faithful servant see the pit: Hebrew
shahath means here the pit, a synonym for Sheol, the underworld. The Greek translation derives the word here and elsewhere from the verb *shahath*, "to be corrupt." On the basis of
the Greek, Acts 2, 25-32 and 13, 35-37 apply the verse to
Christ's resurrection, "Nor will you suffer your holy one to
see corruption."

Ps 17: A lament of an individual unjustly attacked who
has taken refuge in the temple. Confident of being found in-

nocent, the psalmist cries out for God's just judgment (1-5)
and requests divine help against enemies (6-9a). Those ravenous lions (9b-12) should be punished (13-14). The psalm
ends with a serene statement of praise (15). The Hebrew text
of vv 3-4 and 14 is uncertain.

17, 8: Apple of your eye . . . shadow of your wings: images of God's special care. Cf Dt 32, 10; Prv 7, 2; Is 49, 2.

17, 10-12. 14: An extended metaphor: the enemies are lions.

q: Pss 23, 5; 73, 26; Nm 18, 20; Lam 3, 24.   *r*: Pss 73, 23; 121, 5.
8-12; Acts 2, 25-28.   *s*: Pss 28, 1; 30, 4; 49, 16; 86, 13; Jon 2, 7; Acts
13, 35.   *t*: Pss 26, 2; 139, 23.   *u*: Ps 18, 36; Jb 23, 11-12.   *v*: Pss
36, 8; 57, 2; 63, 8; 91, 4; Dt 32, 10; Ru 2, 12; Zec 2, 12; Mt 23,
37.   *w*: 9b-12: Pss 10, 9; 22, 14. 22; 35, 17; 58, 7; Jb 4, 10-11.

snatch them from the world in their
    prime.
Their bellies are being filled with your
    friends;
    their children are satisfied too,
    for they share what is left with their
      young.
15 I am just—let me see your face;
    when I awake,* let me be filled with
      your presence.[x]

See RG
176

PSALM 18[*]

A King's Thanksgiving
for Victory

1 For the leader. Of David, the servant of the
LORD, who sang to the LORD the words of
this song after the LORD had rescued him
from the clutches of all his enemies and
from the hand of Saul. 2 He said:

I

I love you, LORD, my strength,
3   LORD, my rock, my fortress, my
    deliverer,[y]
My God, my rock of refuge,
    my shield, my saving horn,* my
      stronghold![z]
4 Praised be the LORD, I exclaim!
    I have been delivered from my
      enemies.

II

5 The breakers of death surged round
    about me;
    the menacing floods terrified me.
6 The cords* of Sheol tightened;
    the snares of death lay in wait for me.[a]

7 In my distress I called out: LORD!
    I cried out to my God.[b]
From his temple* he heard my voice;
    my cry to him reached his ears.
8 The earth rocked and shook;*
    the foundations of the mountains
      trembled;
    they shook as his wrath flared up.[c]
9 Smoke rose in his nostrils,
    a devouring fire poured from his
      mouth;
    it kindled coals into flame.
10 He parted the heavens and came down,
    a dark cloud under his feet.[d]
11 Mounted on a cherub* he flew,
    borne along on the wings of the wind.
12 He made darkness the cover about him;
    his canopy, heavy thunderheads.
13 Before him scudded his clouds,
    hail and lightning too.[e]
14 The LORD thundered from heaven;
    the Most High made his voice
      resound.[f]
15 He let fly his arrows* and scattered them;
    shot his lightning bolts and dispersed
      them.[g]
16 Then the bed of the sea appeared;
    the world's foundations lay bare,[h]
At the roar of the LORD,
    at the storming breath of his nostrils.
17 He reached down from on high and
    seized me;
    drew me out of the deep waters.[i]
18 He rescued me from my mighty enemy,
    from foes too powerful for me.

17, 15: When I awake: probably the psalmist has spent
the night in the sanctuary (cf 3) and hopes to wake to an oracle assuring God's protective presence.

Ps 18: A royal thanksgiving for a military victory, duplicated in 2 Sm 22. Thanksgiving psalms are in essence reports
of divine rescue. The psalm has two parallel reports of rescue,
the first told from a heavenly perspective (5-20), and the second from an earthly perspective (36-46). The first report
adapts old mythic language of a cosmic battle between sea
and rainstorm in order to depict God's rescue of the Israelite
king from his enemies. Each report has a short hymnic introduction (2-4. 32-35) and conclusion (21-31. 47-51).

18, 3: My saving horn: my strong savior. The horn referred to is the weapon of a bull and the symbol of fertility. Cf
1 Sm 2, 10; Ps 132, 17; Lk 1, 69.

18, 6: Cords: hunting imagery, the cords of a snare.

18, 7: His temple: his heavenly abode.

18, 8-16: God appears in the storm, which in Palestine

comes from the west. The introduction to the theophany (vv
8-9) is probably a description of a violent, hot, and dry east-
wind storm. In the fall transition period from the rainless
summer to the rainy winter, such storms regularly precede the
rains. Cf Ex 14, 21-22.

18, 11: Cherub: a winged creature, derived from myth, in
the service of the deity (Gn 3, 24; Ex 25, 18-20; 37, 6-9).
Cherubim were the throne bearers of the deity (Pss 80, 2; 99,
1; 1 Kgs 6, 23-28; 8, 6-8).

18, 15: Arrows: lightning.

x: Pss 4, 7; 31, 17; 67, 2; 80, 4; Nm 6, 25; Dn 9, 17.   y: 2-51: 2 Sm
22, 2-51.   z: Pss 3, 4; 31, 3-4; 42, 10; Gn 49, 24; Dt 32, 4.   a: Pss
88, 8; 93, 3-4; 116, 3-4.   b: Jon 2, 3.   c: Pss 97, 3-4; 99, 1; Jgs 5,
4-5; Is 64, 1; Hab 3, 9-11.   d: Pss 104, 3; 144, 5; Is 63, 19.   e: Ex
13, 21; 19, 16.   f: Pss 29; 77, 19; Ex 19, 19; Jb 37, 3-4.   g: Ps 144,
6; Wis 5, 21.   h: Ps 77, 17; Zec 9, 14.   i: Ps 144, 7.

¹⁹ They attacked me on a day of distress,
  but the LORD came to my support.
²⁰ He set me free in the open;
  he rescued me because he loves me.

III

²¹ The LORD acknowledged my
    righteousness,
  rewarded my clean hands.^j
²² For I kept the ways of the LORD;
  I was not disloyal to my God.
²³ His laws were all before me,
  his decrees I did not cast aside.
²⁴ I was honest toward him;
  I was on guard against sin.
²⁵ So the LORD rewarded my righteousness,
  the cleanness of my hands in his
    sight.
²⁶ Toward the faithful you are faithful;
  to the honest you are honest;^k
²⁷ Toward the sincere, sincere;
  but to the perverse you are devious.
²⁸ Humble people you save;
  haughty eyes you bring low.^l
²⁹ You, LORD, give light to my lamp;
  my God brightens the darkness about
    me.^m
³⁰ With you I can rush an armed band,
  with my God to help I can leap a wall.
³¹ God's way is unerring;
  the LORD's promise is tried and true;
  he is a shield for all who trust in him.ⁿ

IV

³² Truly, who is God except the LORD?
  Who but our God is the rock?^o
³³ This God who girded me with might,
  kept my way unerring,
³⁴ Who made my feet swift as a deer's,
  set me safe on the heights,^p
³⁵ Who trained my hands for war,
  my arms to bend even a bow of
    bronze.^q *

V

³⁶ You have given me your protecting
    shield;
  your right hand has upheld me;
  you stooped to make me great.

³⁷ You gave me room to stride;
  my feet never stumbled.^r
³⁸ I pursued my enemies and overtook
    them;
  I did not turn back till I destroyed
    them.
³⁹ I struck them down; they could not rise;
  they fell dead at my feet.
⁴⁰ You girded me with strength for war,
  subdued adversaries at my feet.
⁴¹ My foes you put to flight before me;
  those who hated me I destroyed.
⁴² They cried for help, but no one saved
    them;
  cried to the LORD but got no answer.
⁴³ I ground them fine as dust in the wind;
  like mud in the streets I trampled them
    down.
⁴⁴ You rescued me from the strife of
    peoples;
  you made me head over nations.
  A people I had not known became my
    slaves;
⁴⁵ as soon as they heard of me they
    obeyed.
  Foreigners cringed before me;
⁴⁶ their courage failed;
  they came trembling from their
    fortresses.^s

VI

⁴⁷ The LORD lives! Blessed be my rock!^t
  Exalted be God, my savior!
⁴⁸ O God who granted me vindication,
  made peoples subject to me,^u
⁴⁹ and preserved me from my enemies,
  Truly you have exalted me above my
    adversaries,
  from the violent you have rescued
    me.
⁵⁰ Thus I will proclaim you, LORD, among
    the nations;
  I will sing the praises of your name.^v
⁵¹ You have given great victories to your
    king,
  and shown kindness to your anointed,
  to David and his posterity forever.^w

18, 35: Bow of bronze: hyperbole for a bow difficult to bend and therefore capable of propelling an arrow with great force.

---

j: Ps 26; 1 Sm 26, 23. k: Ps 125, 4. l: Jb 22, 29; Prv 3, 34. m: Pss 27, 1; 36, 10; 43, 3; 119, 105; Jb 29, 3; Mi 7, 8. n: Pss 12, 6;
77, 13; Prv 30, 5. o: Is 44, 8; 45, 21. p: Hb 3, 19. q: Ps 144, 1. r: Ps 17, 5. s: Mi 7, 17. t: Ps 144, 1. u: Ps 144, 2. v: Pss
7, 18; 30, 5; 57, 9; 135, 3; 146, 2; Rom 15, 9. w: Pss 89, 28-37; 144, 10; 1 Sm 2, 10.

See RG
175

PSALM 19[*]

God's Glory in the Heavens and in the Law

1 For the leader. A psalm of David.

I

2 The heavens declare the glory of God;
the sky proclaims its builder's craft.[x]
3 One day to the next conveys that
message;
one night to the next imparts that
knowledge.
4 There is no word or sound;[*]
no voice is heard;
5 Yet their report goes forth through all the
earth,
their message, to the ends of the world.
God has pitched there a tent for the sun;[*]
6 it comes forth like a bridegroom from
his chamber,
and like an athlete joyfully runs its
course.
7 From one end of the heavens it comes
forth;
its course runs through to the other;
nothing escapes its heat.

II

8 The law of the LORD is perfect,
refreshing the soul.
The decree of the LORD is trustworthy,
giving wisdom to the simple.[y]
9 The precepts of the LORD are right,
rejoicing the heart.
The command of the LORD is clear,
enlightening the eye.
10 The fear of the LORD is pure,
enduring forever.
The statutes of the LORD are true,
all of them just;
11 More desirable than gold,
than a hoard of purest gold,
Sweeter also than honey
or drippings from the comb.[z]
12 By them your servant is instructed;[*]
obeying them brings much reward.

III

13 Who can detect heedless failings?
Cleanse me from my unknown faults.
14 But from willful sins keep your servant;
let them never control me.
Then shall I be blameless,
innocent of grave sin.
15 Let the words of my mouth meet with
your favor,
keep the thoughts of my heart before
you,
LORD, my rock and my redeemer.

PSALM 20[*]

Prayer for the King in Time of War

See RG
176

1 For the leader. A psalm of David.

I

2 The LORD answer you in time of
distress;
the name of the God of Jacob defend
you!
3 May God send you help from the
temple,
from Zion be your support.[a]
4 May God remember[*] your every offering,
graciously accept your
holocaust,   *Selah*
5 Grant what is in your heart,
fulfill your every plan.
6 May we shout for joy at your victory,[*]

Ps 19: The heavenly elements of the world, now beautifully arranged, bespeak the power and wisdom of their creator (2-7). The creator's wisdom is available to human beings in the law (8-11), toward which the psalmist prays to be open (12-15). The themes of light and speech unify the poem.

19, 4: No word or sound: the regular functioning of the heavens and the alternation of day and night inform humans without words of the creator's power and wisdom.

19, 5: The sun: in other religious literature the sun is a judge and lawgiver since it sees all in its daily course; 5b-7 form a transition to the law in 8-11. The six synonyms for God's revelation (8-11) are applied to the sun in comparable literature.

19, 12: Instructed: the Hebrew verb means both to shine and to teach. Cf Dn 12, 3.

Ps 20: The people pray for the king before battle. The people ask for divine help (2-6) and express confidence that such help will be given (7-10). A solemn assurance of divine help may well have been given between the two sections in the liturgy, something like the promises of Pss 12, 6 and 21, 9-13. The final verse (10) echoes the opening verse.

20, 4: Remember: God's remembering implies readiness to act. Cf Gn 8, 1; Ex 2, 24.

20, 6: Victory: the Hebrew root is often translated "salvation," "to save," but in military contexts it can have the specific meaning of "victory."

---

x: Pss 8, 1; 50, 6; 97, 6.   *y:* Pss 12, 7; 119.   *z:* Sir 24, 19.   *a:* Pss 128, 5; 134, 3.

raise the banners in the name of our
God.
The LORD grant your every prayer!

II

7 Now I know victory is given
to the anointed of the LORD.[b]
God will answer him from the holy
heavens
with a strong arm that brings victory.
8 Some rely on chariots, others on horses,
but we on the name of the LORD our
God.[c]
9 They collapse and fall,
but we stand strong and firm.[d]
10 LORD, grant victory to the king;
answer when we call upon you.

See RG
176

PSALM 21 *

Thanksgiving and Assurances
for the King

1 For the leader. A psalm of David.

I

2 LORD, the king finds joy in your power;[e]
in your victory how greatly he
rejoices!
3 You have granted him his heart's desire;
you did not refuse the prayer of his
lips.   Selah
4 For you welcomed him with goodly
blessings;
you placed on his head a crown of
pure gold.
5 He asked life of you;
you gave it to him,
length of days forever.[f]
6 Great is his glory in your victory;
majesty and splendor you confer upon
him.
7 You make him the pattern of blessings
forever,

you gladden him with the joy of your
presence.
8 For the king trusts in the LORD,
stands firm through the love of the
Most High.

II

9 Your hand will reach all your enemies;
your right hand will reach your foes!
10 At the time of your coming
you will drive them into a furnace.
Then the LORD's anger will consume
them,
devour them with fire.
11 Even their descendants you will wipe out
from the earth,
their offspring from the human race.
12 Though they intend evil against you,
devising plots, they will not succeed,
13 For you will put them to flight;
you will aim at them with your bow.

III

14 Arise, LORD, in your power![g]
We will sing and chant the praise of
your might.

PSALM 22 *

See RG
175, 178

The Prayer of an
Innocent Person

1 For the leader; according to "The deer of
the dawn."* A psalm of David.

I

2 My God, my God, why have you
abandoned me?
Why so far from my call for help,
from my cries of anguish?[h]
3 My God, I call by day, but you do not
answer;
by night, but I have no relief.[i]
4 Yet you are enthroned as the Holy One;
you are the glory of Israel.[j]

Ps 21: The first part of this royal psalm is a thanksgiving
(2-8), and the second is a promise that the king will triumph
over his enemies (9-14). The king's confident prayer (3. 5)
and trust in God (8) enable him to receive the divine gifts of
vitality, peace, and military success. V 14 reprises v 1. When
kings ceased in Israel after the sixth century B.C., the psalm
was sung of a future Davidic king.

Ps 22: A lament unusual in structure and in intensity of
feeling. The psalmist's present distress is contrasted with
God's past mercy in vv 2-12. In vv 13-22 enemies surround
the psalmist. The last third is an invitation to praise God (23-
27), becoming a universal chorus of praise (28-32). The

psalm is important in the New Testament. Its opening words
occur on the lips of the crucified Jesus (Mk 15, 34; Mt 27,
46), and several other verses are quoted, or at least alluded to,
in the accounts of Jesus' passion (Mt 27, 35. 43; Jn 19, 24).

22, 1: The deer of the dawn: apparently the title of the
melody.

b: Pss 18, 51; 144, 10; 1 Sm 2, 10.   c: Ps 147, 10-11; 2 Chr 14,
10; Prv 21, 31; 1 Sm 17, 45; Is 31, 1; 36, 9.   d: Is 40, 30.   e: Ps
63, 12.   f: 1 Kgs 3, 14.   g: Nm 10, 35.   h: Is 49, 14; 54, 7;
Mt 27, 46; Mk 15, 34.   i: Sir 2, 10.   j: Is 6, 3.

Psalm 22 opens with a plea from a person in dire straits. When his prayers are answered, he brings the offerings he vowed and gives public acclaim to God as he promised. God is praised for his care of all people, and all people, now and in the future, should praise God. Jesus quoted the beginning of this psalm from the cross (Mt 27, 46; Mk 15, 34); the ending of the psalm may shed new light on the meaning of the opening words.

5 In you our ancestors trusted;
   they trusted and you rescued them.
6 To you they cried out and they
     escaped;
   in you they trusted and were not
     disappointed.^k
7 But I am a worm, hardly human,*
   scorned by everyone, despised by the
     people.^l
8 All who see me mock me;
   they curl their lips and jeer;
   they shake their heads at me:^m
9 "You relied on the LORD—let him deliver
     you;
   if he loves you, let him rescue you."^n
10 Yet you drew me forth from the womb,
   made me safe at my mother's breast.
11 Upon you I was thrust from the womb;
   since birth you are my God.^o
12 Do not stay far from me,
   for trouble is near,
   and there is no one to help.^p

II

13 Many bulls* surround me;
   fierce bulls of Bashan* encircle me.
14 They open their mouths against me,
   lions that rend and roar.^q
15 Like water my life drains away;
   all my bones grow soft.
   My heart has become like wax,
   it melts away within me.

16 As dry as a potsherd is my throat;
   my tongue sticks to my palate;
   you lay me in the dust of death.*
17 Many dogs surround me;
   a pack of evildoers closes in on me.
   So wasted are my hands and feet
18   that I can count all my bones.^r
   They stare at me and gloat;
19   they divide my garments among
     them;
   for my clothing they cast lots.^s
20 But you, LORD, do not stay far off;
   my strength, come quickly to help me.
21 Deliver me from the sword,
   my forlorn life from the teeth of the
     dog.
22 Save me from the lion's mouth,
   my poor life from the horns of wild
     bulls.^t

III

23 Then I will proclaim your name to the
     assembly;
   in the community I will praise you:^u *
24 "You who fear the LORD, give praise!
   All descendants of Jacob, give
     honor;
   show reverence, all descendants of
     Israel!
25 For God has not spurned or disdained
   the misery of this poor wretch,
   Did not turn away* from me,

22, 7: **I am a worm, hardly human**: the psalmist's sense of isolation and dehumanization, an important motif of Ps 22, is vividly portrayed here.

22, 13-14: **Bulls**: the enemies of the psalmist are also portrayed in less-than-human form, as wild animals (cf 17, 21-22). **Bashan**: a grazing land east of the Jordan, famed for its cattle. Cf Dt 32, 14; Ez 39, 18; Am 4, 1.

22, 16: **The dust of death**: the netherworld, the domain of the dead.

22, 23: **In the community I will praise you**: the person who offered a thanksgiving sacrifice in the temple recounted to the other worshipers the favor received from God and invited them to share in the sacrificial banquet. The final sec-

tion (24-32) may be a summary or a citation of the psalmist's poem of praise.

22, 25: **Turn away**: literally, "hides his face from me," an important metaphor for God withdrawing from someone, e.g., Mi 3, 4; Is 8, 17; Pss 27, 9; 69, 18; 88, 15.

k: Ps 25, 3; Is 49, 23; Dn 3, 40.   l: Is 53, 3.   m: Ps 109, 25; Mt 27, 39; Mk 15, 29; Lk 23, 35.   n: Ps 71, 11; Wis 2, 18-20; Mt 27, 43.   o: Ps 71, 6; Is 44, 2; 46, 3.   p: Pss 35, 22; 38, 22; 71, 12. q: Ps 17, 12; Jb 4, 10; 1 Pt 5, 8.   r: Ps 109, 24.   s: Mt 27, 35; Mk 15, 24; Lk 23, 34; Jn 19, 24.   t: Pss 7, 2-3; 17, 12; 35, 17; 57, 5; 58, 7; 2 Tm 4, 17.   u: Pss 26, 12; 35, 18; 40, 10; 109, 30; 149, 1; 2 Sm 22, 50; Heb 2, 12.

but heard me when I cried out.
26 I will offer praise in the great assembly;
my vows I will fulfill before those
who fear him.
27 The poor* will eat their fill;
those who seek the LORD will offer
praise.
May your hearts enjoy life forever!"v

IV
28 All the ends of the earth
will worship and turn to the LORD;
All the families of nations
will bow low before you.w
29 For kingship belongs to the LORD,
the ruler over the nations.x
30 All who sleep in the earth
will bow low before God;
All who have gone down into the dust*
will kneel in homage.
31 And I will live for the LORD;
my descendants will serve you.
32 The generation to come will be told of
the Lord,
that they may proclaim to a people yet
unborn
the deliverance you have brought.y

See RG 175–76

PSALM 23*

The Lord, Shepherd and Host
1 A psalm of David.

I
The LORD is my shepherd;*
there is nothing I lack.z

2 In green pastures you let me graze;
to safe waters you lead me;
3 you restore my strength.
You guide me along the right path*
for the sake of your name.a
4 Even when I walk through a dark
valley,b *
I fear no harm for you are at my side;
your rod and staff give me courage.

II
5 You set a table before me*
as my enemies watch;*
You anoint my head with oil;c *
my cup overflows.d
6 Only goodness and love* will pursue me
all the days of my life;
I will dwell in the house of the LORDe
for years to come.

PSALM 24*

See RG 176

*The Glory of God in
Procession to Zion*
1 A psalm of David.

I
The earth is the LORD's and all
it holds,f
the world and those who live there.
2 For God founded it on the seas,
established it over the rivers.g

II
3 Who may go up the mountain of the
LORD?h
Who can stand in his holy place?

22, 27: The poor: originally the poor, who were dependent on God; the term (*'anawim*) came to include the religious sense of "humble, pious, devout."

22, 30: Hebrew unclear. The translation assumes that all on earth (28-29) and under the earth (30) will worship God.

Ps 23: God's loving care for the psalmist is portrayed under the figures of a shepherd for the flock (1-4) and a host's generosity toward a guest (5-6). The imagery of both sections is drawn from traditions of the exodus (Is 40, 11; 49, 10; Jer 31, 10).

23, 1: My shepherd: God as good shepherd is common in both the Old Testament and the New Testament (Ez 34, 11-16 and Jn 10, 11-18).

23, 3: The right path: connotes "right way" and "way of righteousness."

23, 4: A dark valley: a different division of the Hebrew consonants yields the translation "the valley of the shadow of death."

23, 5: You set a table before me: this expression occurs in an exodus context in Ps 78, 19. **As my enemies watch:** my

enemies see that I am God's friend and guest. **Oil**: a perfumed ointment made from olive oil, used especially at banquets (Ps 104, 15; Mt 26, 7; Lk 7, 37. 46; Jn 12, 2).

23, 6: Goodness and love: the blessings of God's covenant with Israel.

Ps 24: The psalm apparently accompanied a ceremony of the entry of God (invisibly enthroned upon the ark), followed by the people, into the temple. The temple commemorated the creation of the world (1-2). The people had to affirm their fidelity before being admitted into the sanctuary (3-6; cf Ps 15). A choir identifies the approaching God and invites the very temple gates to bow down in obeisance (7-10).

v: Pss 23, 5; 69, 33.   w: Ps 86, 9; Tb 13, 11; Is 45, 22; 52, 10; Zec 14, 16.   x: Ps 103, 19; Ob 21; Zec 14, 9.   y: Pss 48, 14-15; 71, 18; 78, 6; 102, 19; Is 53, 10.   z: Pss 80, 2; 95, 7; 100, 3; Dt 2, 7.   a: Prv 4, 11.   b: Jb 10, 21-22; Is 50, 10.   c: Ps 92, 11.   d: Ps 16, 5.   e: Ps 27, 4.   f: Pss 50, 12; 89, 12; Dt 10, 14; 1 Cor 10, 26.   g: Ps 136, 6; Is 42, 5.   h: Ps 15, 1.

4 "The clean of hand and pure of heart,*
   who are not devoted to idols,
   who have not sworn falsely.
5 They will receive blessings from the
   LORD,
   and justice from their saving God.
6 Such are the people that love the
   LORD,
   that seek the face of the God of
   Jacob."   Selah

III

7 Lift up your heads, O gates;
   rise up, you ancient portals,*
   that the king of glory may
   enter.*i*
8 Who is this king of glory?
   The LORD, a mighty warrior,
   the LORD, mighty in battle.
9 Lift up your heads, O gates;
   rise up, you ancient portals,
   that the king of glory may
   enter.
10 Who is this king of glory?
   The LORD of hosts is the king of
   glory.   Selah

See RG
175–76

PSALM 25*

Confident Prayer for Forgiveness and Guidance

1 Of David.

I

I wait for you, O LORD;
   I lift up my soul *2* to my God.*j*
In you I trust; do not let me be
   disgraced;*k*
   do not let my enemies gloat over me.
3 No one is disgraced who waits for you,*l*
   but only those who lightly break faith.
4 Make known to me your ways, LORD;
   teach me your paths.*m*

5 Guide me in your truth and teach me,
   for you are God my savior.
For you I wait all the long day,
   because of your goodness, LORD.*
6 Remember your compassion and love,
   O LORD;
   for they are ages old.*n*
7 Remember no more the sins of my
   youth;*o*
   remember me only in light of your
   love.

II

8 Good and upright is the LORD,
   who shows sinners the way,
9 Guides the humble rightly,
   and teaches the humble the way.
10 All the paths of the LORD are faithful
   love
   toward those who honor the covenant
   demands.
11 For the sake of your name, LORD,
   pardon my guilt, though it is great.
12 Who are those who fear the LORD?
   God shows them the way to choose.*p*
13 They live well and prosper,
   and their descendants inherit the land.*q*
14 The counsel of the LORD belongs to the
   faithful;
   the covenant instructs them.
15 My eyes are ever upon the LORD,
   who frees my feet from the snare.*r*

III

16 Look upon me, have pity on me,
   for I am alone and afflicted.*s*
17 Relieve the troubles of my heart;
   bring me out of my distress.
18 Put an end to my affliction and suffering;
   take away all my sins.
19 See how many are my enemies,
   see how fiercely they hate me.

24, 4-5: Literally, "the one whose hands are clean." The singular is used for the entire class of worshipers, hence the plural translation.

24, 7. 9: Lift up your heads, O gates . . . you ancient portals: the literal meaning is impossible since the portcullis (a gate that moves up and down) was unknown in the ancient world. Extra-biblical parallels suggest a full personification of the circle of gate towers: they are like a council of elders, bowed down and anxious, awaiting the return of the army and the Great Warrior gone to battle.

Ps 25: A lament. Each verse begins with a successive letter of the Hebrew alphabet. Such acrostic psalms are often a

series of statements only loosely connected. The psalmist mixes ardent pleas (1-2. 16-22) with expressions of confidence in God who forgives and guides.

25, 5: Because of your goodness, LORD: these words have been transposed from the end of 7 to preserve the pattern of two lines per letter of the Hebrew alphabet in the acrostic poem.

i: Ps 118, 19-20.   *j:* Pss 86, 4; 143, 8.   *k:* Ps 71, 1.   *l:* Ps 22, 6; Is 49, 23; Dn 3, 40.   *m:* Pss 27, 11; 86, 11; 119, 12. 35; 143, 8. 10.   *n:* Sir 51, 8.   *o:* Jb 13, 26; Is 64, 8.   *p:* Prv 19, 23.   *q:* Ps 37, 9. 29.   *r:* Pss 123, 1. 2; 141, 8.   *s:* Pss 86, 16; 119, 132.

P salm 25 is an individual's petition in acrostic form: The first line begins with the first letter of the Hebrew alphabet, the second line with the second letter of the alphabet, and so on to the final letter. Two letters are missing, and two are doubled, likely reflecting changes that the psalm has undergone in its transmission. The psalm is made up of alternating petitions and expressions of trust. It resembles wisdom literature in its concern with learning and finding the right path but has the religious concerns of Psalms in its hope for forgiveness and for deliverance from distress.

20 Preserve my life and rescue me;
    do not let me be disgraced, for I trust
        in you.
21 Let honesty and virtue preserve me;
    I wait for you, O LORD.
22 Redeem Israel, God,*
    from all its distress!

See RG 175

PSALM 26*

Prayer of Innocence

1 Of David.

I

Grant me justice, LORD!
    I have walked without blame.*t*
In the LORD I have trusted;
    I have not faltered.
2 Test me, LORD, and try me;
    search my heart and mind.*u*
3 Your love is before my eyes;
    I walk guided by your faithfulness.*v*

II

4 I do not sit with deceivers,
    nor with hypocrites do I mingle.
5 I hate the company of evildoers;
    with the wicked I do not sit.
6 I will wash my hands* in innocence*w*

and walk round your altar, LORD,
7 Lifting my voice in thanks,
    recounting all your wondrous deeds.
8 LORD, I love the house where you dwell,
    the tenting-place of your glory.*x*

III

9 Do not take me away with sinners,
    nor my life with the violent.*y*
10 Their hands carry out their schemes;
    their right hands are full of bribes.
11 But I walk without blame;*z*
    redeem me, be gracious to me!*a*
12 My foot stands on level ground;*
    in assemblies* I will bless the LORD.*b*

PSALM 27*

Trust in God

See RG 175

1 Of David

A

I

The LORD is my light and my salvation;*c*
    whom do I fear?
The LORD is my life's refuge;
    of whom am I afraid?
2 When evildoers come at me
    to devour my flesh,*d* *

25, 22: A final verse beginning with the Hebrew letter *pe* is added to the normal 22-letter alphabet. Thus the letters *aleph*, *lamed*, and *pe* open the first, middle (v 11), and last lines of the psalm. Together, they spell *aleph*, the first letter of the alphabet.

Ps 26: Like a priest washing before approaching the altar (Ex 30, 17-21), the psalmist seeks God's protection upon entering the temple. 1-3, matched by 11-12, remind God of past integrity while asking for purification; 4-5, matched by 9-10, pray for inclusion among the just; 6-8, the center of the poem, express the joy in God at the heart of all ritual.

26, 6: I will wash my hands: the washing of hands was a liturgical act (Ex 30, 19. 21; 40, 31-32), symbolic of inner as well as outer cleanness. Cf Is 1, 16.

26, 12: On level ground: in safety, where there is no danger of tripping and falling. **In assemblies:** at the temple. Hav-

ing walked around the altar, the symbol of God's presence, the psalmist blesses God.

Ps 27: Tradition has handed down the two sections of the psalm (1-6 and 7-14) as one psalm, though each part could be understood as complete in itself. Asserting boundless hope that God will bring rescue (1-3), the psalmist longs for the presence of God in the temple, protection from all enemies (4-6). In part B there is a clear shift in tone (7-12); the climax of the poem comes with "I believe" (13), echoing "I trust" (3).

27, 2: To devour my flesh: the psalmist's enemies are rapacious beasts (Pss 7, 3; 17, 12; 22, 14. 17).

t: Ps 7, 9.   *u:* Pss 17, 3; 139, 23.   *v:* Ps 86, 11.   *w:* Ps 73, 13.   *x:* Pss 29, 9; 63, 3; Ex 24, 16; 25, 8.   *y:* Ps 28, 3.   *z:* Ps 101, 6.   *a:* Ps 25, 16.   *b:* Pss 22, 23; 35, 18; 149, 1.   *c:* Pss 18, 29; 36, 10; 43, 3; Is 10, 17; Mi 7, 8.   *d:* Ps 14, 4.

These my enemies and foes
  themselves stumble and fall.
3 Though an army encamp against me,
  my heart does not fear;
Though war be waged against me,
  even then do I trust.

II

4 One thing I ask of the LORD;
  this I seek:
To dwell in the LORD's house
  all the days of my life,
To gaze on the LORD's beauty,
  to visit his temple.e
5 For God will hide me in his shelter
  in time of trouble,f
Will conceal me in the cover of his tent;
  and set me high upon a rock.
6 Even now my head is held high
  above my enemies on every side!
I will offer in his tent
  sacrifices with shouts of joy;
I will sing and chant praise to the LORD.

B

I

7 Hear my voice, LORD, when I call;
  have mercy on me and answer me.
8 "Come," says my heart, "seek God's
  face"; *
  your face, LORD, do I seek!g
9 Do not hide your face from me;
  do not repel your servant in anger.
You are my help; do not cast me off;
  do not forsake me, God my savior!
10 Even if my father and mother forsake me,
  the LORD will take me in.h

II

11 LORD, show me your way;
  lead me on a level path
  because of my enemies.i

12 Do not abandon me to the will of my
  foes;
  malicious and lying witnesses have
  risen against me.
13 But I believe I shall enjoy the LORD's
  goodness
  in the land of the living.j *
14 Wait for the LORD, take courage;
  be stouthearted, wait for the LORD!

PSALM 28 *

Petition and Thanksgiving

1 Of David.

I

To you, LORD, I call;
  my Rock, do not be deaf to me.k
If you fail to answer me,
  I will join those who go down to the
  pit.l *
2 Hear the sound of my pleading when I
  cry to you,
  lifting my hands toward your holy
  place.m *
3 Do not drag me off with the wicked,
  with those who do wrong,n
Who speak peace to their neighbors
  though evil is in their hearts.o
4 Repay them for their deeds,
  for the evil that they do.
For the work of their hands repay them;
  give them what they deserve.p
5 They pay no heed to the LORD's works,
  to the deeds of God's hands.q
God will tear them down,
  never to be rebuilt.

II

6 Blessed be the LORD,
  who has heard the sound of my
  pleading.*

See RG
175

27, 8: **Seek God's face** (literally: "to seek his face"): to commune with God in the temple. The idiom is derived from the practice of journeying to sacred places. Cf Hos 5, 15; 2 Sm 21, 1; Ps 24, 6.

27, 13: **In the land of the living**: or "in the land of life," an epithet of the Jerusalem temple (Pss 52, 7; 116, 9; Is 38, 11), where the faithful had access to the life-giving presence of God.

Ps 28: A lament asking that the psalmist, who has taken refuge in the temple (2), not be punished with the wicked, who are headed inevitably toward destruction (1. 3-5). The statement of praise is exceptionally lengthy and vigorous (6-7). The psalm ends with a prayer (8-9).

28, 1: **The pit**: a synonym for Sheol, the shadowy place of the dead.

28, 2: **Your holy place**: the innermost part of the temple, the holy of holies, containing the ark. Cf 1 Kgs 6, 16. 19-23; 8, 6-8.

28, 6: The psalmist shifts to fervent thanksgiving, probably responding to a priestly or prophetic oracle in 5cd (not usually transmitted) assuring the worshiper that the prayer has been heard.

e: Pss 23, 6; 61, 5. f: Ps 31, 21. g: Ps 24, 6; Hos 5, 15. h: Is 49, 15. i: Pss 25, 4; 86, 11. j: Ps 116, 9; Is 38, 11. k: Ps 18, 2. l: Pss 30, 4; 88, 5; 143, 7; Prv 1, 12. m: Ps 134, 2. n: Ps 26, 9. o: Pss 12, 2; 55, 22; 62, 5; Prv 26, 24-28. p: 2 Sm 3, 39. q: Is 5, 12.

7 The LORD is my strength and my shield,
    in whom my heart trusted and found
        help.
So my heart rejoices;
    with my song I praise my God.

III

8 LORD, you are the strength of your
        people,*
    the saving refuge of your anointed
        king.
9 Save your people, bless your
        inheritance;
    feed and sustain them forever!

See RG 175

PSALM 29*

The Lord of Majesty
Acclaimed as King of the World

1 A psalm of David.

I

Give to the LORD, you heavenly
        beings,*
    give to the LORD glory and might;
2 Give to the LORD the glory due God's
        name.
    Bow down before the LORD's holy
        splendor!ʳ

II

3 The voice of the LORD* is over the
        waters;
    the God of glory thunders,
    the LORD, over the mighty waters.
4 The voice of the LORD is power;

the voice of the LORD is splendor.ˢ
5 The voice of the LORD cracks the
        cedars;
    the LORD splinters the cedars of
        Lebanon,
6 Makes Lebanon leap like a calf,
    and Sirion* like a young bull.
7 The voice of the LORD strikes with fiery
        flame;
8   the voice of the LORD rocks the
        desert;
    the LORD rocks the desert of
        Kadesh.*
9 The voice of the LORD twists the oaks
    and strips the forests bare.
    All in his palace say, "Glory!"*

III

10 The LORD sits enthroned above the
        flood!ᵗ *
    The LORD reigns as king forever!
11 May the LORD give might to his
        people;*
    may the LORD bless his people with
        peace!ᵘ

PSALM 30*

Thanksgiving for Deliverance

See RG 175

1 A psalm. A song for the dedication of the
        temple.* Of David.

I

2 I praise you, LORD, for you raised me
        up

28, 8: Your people . . . your anointed king: salvation is more than individual, affecting all the people and their God-given leader.

Ps 29: The hymn invites the members of the heavenly court to acknowledge God's supremacy by ascribing glory and might to God alone (1-2a. 9b). Divine glory and might are dramatically visible in the storm (3-9a). The storm apparently comes from the Mediterranean onto the coast of Syria-Palestine and then moves inland. In 10 the divine beings acclaim God's eternal kingship. The psalm concludes with a prayer that God will impart the power just displayed to the Israelite king and through the king to Israel.

29, 1: You heavenly beings: literally "sons of God," i.e., members of the heavenly court who served Israel's God in a variety of capacities.

29, 3: The voice of the LORD: the sevenfold repetition of the phrase imitates the sound of crashing thunder and may allude to God's primordial slaying of Leviathan, the seven-headed sea monster of Canaanite mythology.

29, 6: Sirion: the Phoenician name for Mount Hermon. Cf Dt 3, 9.

29, 8: The desert of Kadesh: probably north of Palestine

in the neighborhood of Lebanon and Hermon.

29, 9b-10: Having witnessed God's supreme power (3-9a), the gods acknowledge the glory that befits the king of the divine and human world.

29, 10: The flood: God defeated the primordial waters and made them part of the universe. Cf Pss 89, 10-13 and 93, 3-4.

29, 11: His people: God's people, Israel.

Ps 30: An individual thanksgiving in four parts: praise and thanks for deliverance and restoration (2-4); an invitation to others to join in (5-6); a flashback to the time before deliverance (7-11); a return to praise and thanks (12-13). Two sets of images recur: 1) going down, death, silence; 2) coming up, life, praising. God has delivered the psalmist from one state to the other.

30, 1: For the dedication of the temple: a later adaptation of the psalm to celebrate the purification of the temple in 164 B.C. during the Maccabean Revolt.

---

r: Pss 68, 35; 96, 7-9.   s: Pss 46, 7; 77, 18-19; Jb 37, 4; Is 30, 30.
t. Bar 3, 3.   u: Ps 68, 36.

and did not let my enemies rejoice
over me.
3 O LORD, my God,
I cried out to you and you healed*
me.
4 LORD, you brought me up from Sheol;
you kept me from going down to the
pit.ᵛ*

II

5 Sing praise to the LORD, you
faithful;
give thanks to God's holy name.
6 For divine anger lasts but a moment;
divine favor lasts a lifetime.
At dusk weeping comes for the
night;
but at dawn there is rejoicing.

III

7 Complacent,* I once said,
"I shall never be shaken."
8 LORD, when you showed me favor
I stood like the mighty mountains.
But when you hid your face
I was struck with terror.ʷ
9 To you, LORD, I cried out;
with the Lord I pleaded for mercy:
10 "What gain is there from my
lifeblood,
from my going down to the grave?
Does dust give you thanks
or declare your faithfulness?*
11 Hear, O LORD, have mercy on me;
LORD, be my helper."

IV

12 You changed my mourning into
dancing;
you took off my sackcloth
and clothed me with gladness.ˣ
13 With my whole being I sing
endless praise to you.

O LORD, my God,
forever will I give you thanks.

PSALM 31*

Prayer in Distress and
Thanksgiving for Escape

See RG 175

1 For the leader. A psalm of David.

I

2 In you, LORD, I take refuge;ʸ
let me never be put to shame.
In your justice deliver me;
3   incline your ear to me;
make haste to rescue me!
Be my rock of refuge,
a stronghold to save me.
4 You are my rock and my fortress;ᶻ
for your name's sake lead and guide me.
5 Free me from the net they have set for me,
for you are my refuge.
6 Into your hands I commend my spirit;ᵃ*
you will redeem me, LORD, faithful
God.
7 You hate those who serve worthless idols,
but I trust in the LORD.
8 I will rejoice and be glad in your love,
once you have seen my misery,
observed my distress.ᵇ
9 You will not abandon me into enemy
hands,
but will set my feet in a free and open
space.

II

10 Be gracious to me, LORD, for I am in
distress;
with grief my eyes are wasted,
my soul and body spent.
11 My life is worn out by sorrow,
my years by sighing.
My strength fails in affliction;
my bones are consumed.ᶜ

30, 3: Healed: for God as healer, see also Pss 103, 3; 107, 20; Hos 6, 1; 7, 1; 11, 3; 14, 5.

30, 4: Sheol . . . pit: the shadowy underworld residence of the dead, here a metaphor for near death.

30, 7: Complacent: untroubled existence is often seen as a source of temptation to forget God. Cf Dt 8, 10-18; Hos 13, 6; Prv 30, 9.

30, 10: In the stillness of Sheol no one gives you praise; let me live and be among your worshipers. Cf Pss 6, 6; 88, 11-13; 115, 17; Is 38, 18.

Ps 31: A lament (2-19) with a strong emphasis on trust (4. 6. 15-16), ending with an anticipatory thanksgiving (20-25).

As is usual in laments, the affliction is couched in general terms. The psalmist feels overwhelmed by evil people but trusts in the "faithful God" (6).

31, 6: Into your hands I commend my spirit: in Lk 23, 46 Jesus breathes his last with this psalm verse. Stephen in Acts 7, 59 alludes to these words as he is attacked by enemies. The verse is used as an antiphon in the Divine Office at Compline, the last prayer of the day.

---

v: Ps 28, 1; Jon 2, 7.   w: Ps 104, 29.   x: Is 61, 3; Jer 31, 13.
y: 2-4: Ps 71, 1-3.   z: Ps 18, 2.   a: Lk 23, 46; Acts 7, 59.   b: Ps 10, 14.   c: Pss 32, 3; 38, 10-11.

¹² To all my foes I am a thing of scorn,
  to my neighbors, a dreaded sight,
  a horror to my friends.
 When they see me in the street,
  they quickly shy away.*d*

¹³ I am forgotten, out of mind like the dead;
  I am like a shattered dish.*

¹⁴ I hear the whispers of the crowd;
  terrors are all around me.*
 They conspire against me;
  they plot to take my life.

¹⁵ But I trust in you, LORD;
  I say, "You are my God."*e*

¹⁶ My times are in your hands;
  rescue me from my enemies,
  from the hands of my pursuers.

¹⁷ Let your face shine on your servant;*f*
  save me in your kindness.

¹⁸ Do not let me be put to shame,
  for I have called to you, LORD.
 Put the wicked to shame;
  reduce them to silence in Sheol.

¹⁹ Strike dumb their lying lips,
  proud lips that attack the just
  in contempt and scorn.*g*

III

²⁰ How great is your goodness, LORD,
  stored up for those who fear you.
 You display it for those who trust you,
  in the sight of all the people.

²¹ You hide them in the shelter of your
   presence,
  safe from scheming enemies.
 You keep them in your abode,
  safe from plotting tongues.*h*

²² Blessed be the LORD,
  who has shown me wondrous love,
  and been for me a city most secure.

²³ Once I said in my anguish,
  "I am shut out from your sight."*i*
 Yet you heard my plea,

when I cried out to you.

²⁴ Love the LORD, all you faithful.
 The LORD protects the loyal,
  but repays the arrogant in full.

²⁵ Be strong and take heart,
  all you who hope in the LORD.

PSALM 32*

Remission of Sin

See RG
175

¹ Of David. A *maskil*.

I

Happy the sinner whose fault is
   removed,
  whose sin is forgiven.*j*

² Happy those to whom the LORD imputes
   no guilt,
  in whose spirit is no deceit.

II

³ As long as I kept silent,* my bones
   wasted away;
  I groaned all the day.*k*

⁴ For day and night your hand was heavy
   upon me;
  my strength withered as in dry
   summer heat.   *Selah*

⁵ Then I declared my sin to you;
  my guilt I did not hide.*l*
 I said, "I confess my faults to the
   LORD,"
  and you took away the guilt of my
   sin.   *Selah*

⁶ Thus should all your faithful pray
  in time of distress.
 Though flood waters* threaten,
  they will never reach them.*m*

⁷ You are my shelter; from distress you
   keep me;
  with safety you ring me round. *Selah*

III

⁸ I will instruct you and show you the way
   you should walk,

31, 13: Like a shattered dish: a common comparison for something ruined and useless. Cf Is 30, 14; Jer 19, 11; 22, 28.

31, 14: Terrors are all around me: a cry used in inescapable danger. Cf Jer 6, 25; 20, 10; 46, 5; 49, 29.

Ps 32: An individual thanksgiving and the second of the seven Penitential Psalms (cf Ps 6). The opening declaration—the forgiven are blessed (1-2)—arises from the psalmist's own experience. At one time the psalmist was stubborn and closed, a victim of sin's power (3-4), and then became open to the forgiving God (5-7). Sin here, as often in the Bible, is not only the personal act of rebellion against God but also the

consequences of that act—frustration and waning of vitality. Having been rescued, the psalmist can teach others the joys of justice and the folly of sin (8-11).

32, 3: I kept silent: did not confess the sin before God.

32, 6: Flood waters: the untamed waters surrounding the earth, a metaphor for danger.

d. Jb 19, 13-19. *e:* Ps 140, 7; Is 25, 1. *f:* Ps 67, 1; Nm 6, 24.
g. Ps 12, 4. *h:* Ps 27, 5. *i:* Jon 2, 5. *j:* Is 1, 18; Ps 65, 3; Rom 4. 7-8. *k:* Ps 31, 11. *l:* Pss 38, 19; 51, 5. *m:* Ps 18, 5.

give you counsel and watch over you.
[9] Do not be senseless like horses or mules;
with bit and bridle their temper is
curbed,
else they will not come to you.

IV

[10] Many are the sorrows of the wicked,
but love surrounds those who trust in
the LORD.
[11] Be glad in the LORD and rejoice, you
just;
exult, all you upright of heart.[n]

See RG 175

PSALM 33[*]

Praise of the Lord's Power and Providence

I

[1] Rejoice, you just, in the LORD;
praise from the upright is fitting.[o]
[2] Give thanks to the LORD on the harp;
on the ten-stringed lyre offer praise.[p]
[3] Sing to God a new song;
skillfully play with joyful chant.
[4] For the LORD's word is true;
all his works are trustworthy.
[5] The LORD loves justice and right
and fills the earth with
goodness.[q]

II

[6] By the LORD's word the heavens were
made;
by the breath of his mouth all their
host.[r] [*]
[7] The waters of the sea were gathered as in
a bowl;[*]
in cellars the deep was confined.[s]

III

[8] Let all the earth fear the LORD;
let all who dwell in the world show
reverence.
[9] For he spoke, and it came to be,

commanded, and it stood in
place.[t]
[10] The LORD foils the plan of nations,
frustrates the designs of peoples.
[11] But the plan of the LORD stands
forever,
wise designs through all
generations.[u]
[12] Happy the nation whose God is the
LORD,
the people chosen as his very own.[v]

IV

[13] From heaven the LORD looks down
and observes the whole human
race,[w]
[14] Surveying from the royal throne
all who dwell on earth.
[15] The one who fashioned the hearts of
them all
knows all their works.

V

[16] A king is not saved by a mighty
army,
nor a warrior delivered by great
strength.
[17] Useless is the horse for safety;
its great strength, no sure escape.
[18] But the LORD's eyes are upon the
reverent,
upon those who hope for his gracious
help,
[19] Delivering them from death,
keeping them alive in times of
famine.

VI

[20] Our soul waits for the LORD,
who is our help and shield.[x]
[21] For in God our hearts rejoice;
in your holy name we trust.
[22] May your kindness, LORD, be upon us;
we have put our hope in you.

Ps 33: A hymn in which the just are invited (1-3) to praise God, who by a mere word (4-5) created the three-tiered universe of the heavens, the cosmic waters, and the earth (6-9). Human words, in contrast, effect nothing (10-11). The greatness of human beings consists in God's choosing them as a special people and their faithful response (12-22).

33, 6: All their host: the stars of the sky are commonly viewed as a vast army, e.g., Neh 9, 6; Is 40, 26; 45, 12; Jer 33, 22.

33, 7: The waters . . . as in a bowl: ancients sometimes

attributed the power keeping the seas from overwhelming land to a primordial victory of the storm-god over personified Sea. God confines the seas as easily as one puts water in a bowl.

n: Ps 33, 1.   *o:* Pss 32, 11; 147, 1.   *p:* Pss 92, 4; 144, 9.   *q:* Ps 119, 64.   *r:* Gn 2, 1.   *s:* Ps 78, 13; Gn 1, 9-10; Ex 15, 8.   *t:* Ps 148, 5; Gn 1, 3f; Jdt 16, 14.   *u:* Prv 19, 21; Is 40, 8.   *v:* Ps 144, 15; Ex 19, 6; Dt 7, 6.   *w:* Jb 34, 21; Sir 15, 19; Jer 16, 17; 32, 19.   *x:* Ps 115, 9.

See RG
176

PSALM 34*

Thanksgiving to God
Who Delivers the Just

1 Of David, when he feigned madness before
Abimelech,* who forced him to depart.

I

2 I will bless the LORD at all times;
praise shall be always in my mouth.*y*

3 My soul will glory in the LORD
that the poor may hear and be glad.

4 Magnify the LORD with me;
let us exalt his name together.

II

5 I sought the LORD, who answered me,
delivered me from all my fears.

6 Look to God that you may be radiant
with joy
and your faces may not blush for
shame.

7 In my misfortune I called,
the LORD heard and saved me from all
distress.

8 The angel of the LORD, who encamps
with them,
delivers all who fear God.*z*

9 Learn to savor how good the LORD is;
happy are those who take refuge in
him.*a*

10 Fear the LORD, you holy ones;
nothing is lacking to those who fear
him.*b*

11 The powerful* grow poor and hungry,
but those who seek the LORD lack no
good thing.

III

12 Come, children,* listen to me;*c*

I will teach you the fear of the LORD.

13 Who among you loves life,*d*
takes delight in prosperous days?

14 Keep your tongue from evil,
your lips from speaking lies.

15 Turn from evil and do good;*e*
seek peace and pursue it.

16 The LORD has eyes for the just*f*
and ears for their cry.

17 The LORD's face is against evildoers
to wipe out their memory from the
earth.

18 When the just cry out, the LORD hears
and rescues them from all distress.

19 The LORD is close to the brokenhearted,
saves those whose spirit is crushed.

20 Many are the troubles of the just,
but the LORD delivers from them all.

21 God watches over all their bones;
not a one shall be broken.*g*

22 Evil will slay the wicked;
those who hate the just are
condemned.

23 The LORD redeems loyal servants;
no one is condemned whose refuge is
God.

PSALM 35*

Prayer for Help against
Unjust Enemies

See RG
175

1 Of David.

I

Oppose, LORD, those who oppose me;*
war upon those who make war upon
me.

2 Take up the shield and buckler;
rise up in my defense.

Ps 34: A thanksgiving in acrostic form, each line beginning with a successive letter of the Hebrew alphabet. In this psalm one letter is missing and two are in reverse order. The psalmist, fresh from the experience of being rescued (5. 7), can teach the "poor," those who are defenseless, to trust in God alone (4. 12). God will make them powerful (5-11) and give them protection (12-23).

34, 1: Abimelech: a scribal error for Achish. In 1 Sm 21, 13-16, David feigned madness before Achish, not Abimelech.

34, 11: The powerful: literally, "lions." Fierce animals were sometimes metaphors for influential people.

34, 12: Children: the customary term for students in Wisdom literature.

Ps 35: A lament of a person betrayed by friends. The psalmist prays that the evildoers be publicly exposed as unjust (1-8), and gives thanks in anticipation of vindication (9-

10). Old friends are the enemies (11-16). May their punishment come quickly (17-21)! The last part (22-26) echoes the opening in praying for the destruction of the psalmist's persecutors. The psalm may appear vindictive, but one must keep in mind that the psalmist is praying for *public* redress now of a *public* injustice. There is at this time no belief in an afterlife in which justice will be redressed.

35, 1-6: The mixture of judicial, martial, and hunting images shows that the language is figurative. The actual injustice is false accusation of serious crimes (11. 15. 20-21). The psalmist seeks lost honor through a trial before God.

y: Ps 145, 2. *z:* Ex 14, 19. *a:* Ps 2, 12. *b:* Prv 3, 7. *c:* Prv 1, 8; 4, 1. *d:* 13-17: 1 Pt 3, 10-12. *e:* Ps 37, 27. *f:* Ps 33, 18. *g:* Jn 19, 36.

3 Brandish lance and battle-ax
    against my pursuers.
Say to my heart,
    "I am your salvation."
4 Let those who seek my life
    be put to shame and disgrace.
Let those who plot evil against me[h]
    be turned back and confounded.
5 Make them like chaff before the wind,[i]
    with the angel of the LORD driving
      them on.
6 Make their way slippery and dark,
    with the angel of the LORD pursuing
      them.

II

7 Without cause they set their snare for
    me;
  without cause they dug a pit for me.
8 Let ruin overtake them unawares;
    let the snare they have set catch
      them;
    let them fall into the pit they have
      dug.[j]
9 Then I will rejoice in the LORD,
    exult in God's salvation.
10 My very bones shall say,
    "O LORD, who is like you,[k]
Who rescue the afflicted from the
      powerful,
    the afflicted and needy from the
      despoiler?"

III

11 Malicious witnesses come forward,
    accuse me of things I do not know.
12 They repay me evil for good
    and I am all alone.[l]
13 Yet I, when they were ill, put on
    sackcloth,*
    afflicted myself with fasting,
    sobbed my prayers upon my bosom.
14 I went about in grief as for my brother,
    bent in mourning as for my mother.
15 Yet when I stumbled they gathered with
      glee,
    they gathered against me like
      strangers.

They slandered me without ceasing;
16   without respect they mocked me,
    gnashed their teeth against me.

IV

17 LORD, how long will you look on?
    Save me from roaring beasts,
    my precious life from lions![m]
18 Then I will thank you in the great
      assembly;
    I will praise you before the mighty
      throng.[n]
19 Do not let lying foes smirk at me,
    my undeserved enemies wink
      knowingly.[o]
20 They speak no words of peace,
    but against the quiet in the land
    they fashion deceitful speech.[p]
21 They open wide their mouths against
      me.
    They say, "Aha! Good!
    Our eyes relish the sight!"[q]
22 You see this, LORD; do not be silent;[r]
    Lord, do not withdraw from me.
23 Awake, be vigilant in my defense,
    in my cause, my God and my Lord.
24 Defend me because you are just, LORD;
    my God, do not let them gloat over
      me.
25 Do not let them say in their hearts,
    "Aha! Just what we wanted!"
Do not let them say,
    "We have devoured that one!"
26 Put to shame and confound
    all who relish my misfortune.
Clothe with shame and disgrace
    those who lord it over me.
27 But let those who favor my just cause
    shout for joy and be glad.
May they ever say, "Exalted be the
    LORD
    who delights in the peace of his loyal
      servant."
28 Then my tongue shall recount your
      justice,
    declare your praise, all the day
      long.[s]

35, 13. 15-17: The Hebrew is obscure.

h: Pss 40, 15; 71, 13. i: Pss 1, 4; 83, 14; Jb 21, 18. j: Pss 7, 16; 9, 16; 57, 7; Prv 26, 27; Eccl 10, 8; Sir 27, 26. k: Ps 86, 8; 89, 7.
9; Ex 15, 11. l: Pss 27, 12; 38, 20-21; 109, 5; Jer 18, 20. m: Pss 17, 12; 22, 22; 58, 7. n: Pss 22, 23; 26, 12; 35, 18; 40, 10; 149, 1.
o: Ps 38, 17. p: Ps 120, 6-7. q: Ps 40, 16; Lam 2, 16. r: Pss 22, 12; 38, 21; 109, 1. s: Ps 71, 15-16.

See RG
175–76

PSALM 36*

Human Wickedness and Divine Providence

1 For the leader. Of David, the servant of the LORD.

I

2 Sin directs the heart of the wicked;
  their eyes are closed to the fear of God.*t*

3 For they live with the delusion:
  their guilt will not be known and hated.*

4 Empty and false are the words of their mouth;
  they have ceased to be wise and do good.

5 In their beds they hatch plots;
  they set out on a wicked way;
  they do not reject evil.*u*

II

6 LORD, your love reaches to heaven;
  your fidelity, to the clouds.*v*

7 Your justice is like the highest mountains;
  your judgments,* like the mighty deep;
  all living creatures you sustain, LORD.

8 How precious is your love, O God!
  We take refuge in the shadow of your wings.*w* *

9 We feast on the rich food of your house;
  from your delightful stream*x* you give us drink.

10 For with you is the fountain of life,*y*
  and in your light we see light.*z*

11 Continue your kindness toward your friends,
  your just defense of the honest heart.

12 Do not let the foot of the proud overtake me,
  nor the hand of the wicked disturb me.

13 There make the evildoers fall;
  thrust them down, never to rise.

PSALM 37*

The Fate of Sinners and the Reward of the Just

See RG
176, 178

1 Of David.

ALEPH

Do not be provoked by evildoers;
  do not envy those who do wrong.*a*

2 Like grass they wither quickly;
  like green plants they wilt away.*b*

BETH

3 Trust in the LORD and do good
  that you may dwell in the land* and live secure.*c*

4 Find your delight in the LORD
  who will give you your heart's desire.*d*

GIMEL

5 Commit your way to the LORD;
  trust that God will act*e*

6 And make your integrity shine like the dawn,
  your vindication like noonday.*f*

DALETH

7 Be still before the LORD;
  wait for God.

Do not be provoked by the prosperous,
  nor by malicious schemers.

Ps 36: A psalm with elements of wisdom (2-5), the hymn (6-10), and the lament (11-13). The rule of sin over the wicked (2-5) is contrasted with the rule of divine love and mercy over God's friends (6-10). The psalm ends with a prayer that God's guidance never cease (11-13).

36, 3: Hated: punished by God.

36, 6-7: Love . . . judgments: God actively controls the entire world.

36, 8: The shadow of your wings: metaphor for divine protection. It probably refers to the winged cherubim in the holy of holies in the temple. Cf 1 Kgs 6, 23-28. 32; 2 Chr 3, 10-13; Ez 1, 4-9.

Ps 37: The psalm responds to the problem of evil, which the Old Testament often expresses as a question: Why do the wicked prosper and the good suffer? The psalm answers that the situation is only temporary. God will reverse things, rewarding the good and punishing the wicked here on earth. The perspective is concrete and earthbound: people's very actions place them among the ranks of the good or wicked. Each group or "way" has its own inherent dynamism—eventual frustration for the wicked, eventual reward for the just. The psalm is an acrostic, i.e., each section begins with a successive letter of the Hebrew alphabet. Each section has its own imagery and logic.

37, 3. 9. 11. 22. 27. 29. 34: The land: the promised land, Israel, which became for later interpreters a type or figure of heaven. Cf Heb 11, 9-10. 13-16. The New Testament Beatitudes (Mt 5, 3-12; Lk 6, 20-26) have been influenced by the psalm, especially their total reversal of the present and their interpretation of the happy future as possession of the land.

---

t: Rom 3, 18.   *u:* Mi 2, 1.   *v:* Pss 57, 11; 71, 19.   *w:* Ps 17, 8.   *x:* Gn 2, 8. 10.   *y:* Is 55, 1; Jn 4, 14.   *z:* Ps 80, 4. 8. 20.   *a:* Prv 3, 31; 23, 17; 24, 1. 19.   *b:* Pss 90, 5-6; 102, 12; 103, 15-16; Jb 14, 2; Is 40, 7.   *c:* Ps 128, 2.   *d:* Prv 10, 24.   *e:* Ps 55, 23; Prv 3, 5; 16, 3.   *f:* Wis 5, 6; Is 58, 10.

HE

8 Give up your anger, abandon your
   wrath;
   do not be provoked; it brings only
   harm.
9 Those who do evil will be cut off,
   but those who wait for the LORD will
   possess the land.*g*

WAW

10 Wait a little, and the wicked will be no
   more;
   look for them and they will not be
   there.
11 But the poor will possess the land,*h*
   will delight in great prosperity.

ZAYIN

12 The wicked plot against the just
   and grind their teeth at them;
13 But the LORD laughs at them,*i*
   knowing their day is coming.

HETH

14 The wicked draw their swords;
   they string their bows
   To fell the poor and oppressed,
   to slaughter those whose way is
   honest.*j*
15 Their swords will pierce their own
   hearts;
   their bows will be broken.

TETH

16 Better the poverty of the just
   than the great wealth of the wicked.*k*
17 The arms of the wicked will be broken;
   the LORD will sustain the just.

YODH

18 The LORD watches over the days of the
   blameless;
   their heritage lasts forever.
19 They will not be disgraced when times
   are hard;
   in days of famine they will have
   plenty.

KAPH

20 The wicked perish,
   the enemies of the LORD;
   Like the beauty of meadows they
   vanish;
   like smoke they disappear.*l*

LAMEDH

21 The wicked borrow but do not repay;
   the just are generous in giving.
22 For those blessed by the Lord will
   possess the land,
   but those accursed will be cut off.

MEM

23 Those whose steps are guided by the
   LORD;*m*
   whose way God approves,
24 May stumble, but they will never fall,
   for the LORD holds their hand.

NUN

25 Neither in my youth, nor now in old age
   have I ever seen the just abandoned*n*
   or their children begging bread.
26 The just always lend generously,
   and their children become a blessing.

SAMEKH

27 Turn from evil and do good,
   that you may inhabit the land forever.*o*
28 For the LORD loves justice
   and does not abandon the faithful.

AYIN

When the unjust are destroyed,
   and the children of the wicked cut off,
29 The just will possess the land
   and live in it forever.*p*

PE

30 The mouths of the just utter wisdom;*q*
   their tongues speak what is right.
31 God's teaching is in their hearts;*r*
   their steps do not falter.

SADHE

32 The wicked spy on the just
   and seek to kill them.
33 But the LORD does not leave the just in
   their power,
   nor let them be condemned when tried.

QOPH

34 Wait eagerly for the LORD,
   and keep to the way;*s*
   God will raise you to possess the land;
   you will gloat when the wicked are cut
   off.

RESH

35 I have seen ruthless scoundrels,
   strong as flourishing cedars.*t*

g: Ps 25, 13; Prv 2, 21; Is 57, 13.   h: Mt 5, 4.   i: Pss 2, 4; 59, 9; Wis 4, 18.   j: Pss 11, 2; 57, 5; 64, 4.   k: Prv 15, 16; 16, 8.   l: Wis
5, 14.   m: Prv 20, 24.   n: Jb 4, 7; Sir 2, 10.   o: Ps 34, 14-15; Am 5, 14.   p: Ps 25, 13; Prv 2, 21; Is 57, 13.   q: Prv 10, 31.   r: Ps
40, 9; Dt 6, 6; Is 51, 7; Jer 31, 33.   s: Ps 31, 24.   t: Ps 92, 8-9; Is 2, 13; Ez 31, 10-11.

36 When I passed by again, they were gone;
    though I searched, they could not be
    found.

SHIN
37 Observe the honest, mark the upright;
    those at peace with God have a future.ᵘ
38 But all sinners will be destroyed;
    the future of the wicked will be cut off.

TAW
39 The salvation of the just is from the LORD,
    their refuge in time of distress.ᵛ
40 The LORD helps and rescues them,
    rescues and saves them from the
    wicked,
    because in God they take refuge.

See RG 175

PSALM 38 *

Prayer of an Afflicted Sinner

¹ A psalm of David. For remembrance.

I

² LORD, punish me no more in your anger;
    in your wrath do not chastise me!ʷ
³ Your arrows have sunk deep in me;ˣ
    your hand has come down upon me.
⁴ My flesh is afflicted because of your
    anger;
    my frame aches because of my sin.ʸ
⁵ My iniquities overwhelm me,
    a burden beyond my strength.ᶻ

II

⁶ Foul and festering are my sores
    because of my folly.
⁷ I am stooped and deeply bowed;ᵃ
    all day I go about mourning.
⁸ My loins burn with fever;
    my flesh is afflicted.
⁹ I am numb and utterly crushed;
    I wail with anguish of heart.ᵇ
¹⁰ My Lord, my deepest yearning is before
    you;
    my groaning is not hidden from you.
¹¹ My heart shudders, my strength forsakes
    me;

the very light of my eyes has failed.ᶜ
¹² Friends and companions shun my pain;
    my neighbors stand far off.
¹³ Those who seek my life lay snares for
    me;
    they seek my misfortune, they speak
    of ruin;
    they plot treachery all the day.

III

¹⁴ But I am like the deaf, hearing nothing,
    like the dumb, saying nothing,
¹⁵ Like someone who does not hear,
    who has no answer ready.
¹⁶ LORD, I wait for you;
    O Lord, my God, answer me.ᵈ
¹⁷ For I fear they will gloat,
    exult over me if I stumble.

IV

¹⁸ I am very near to falling;
    my pain is with me always.
¹⁹ I acknowledge my guilt
    and grieve over my sin.ᵉ
²⁰ But many are my foes without cause,
    a multitude of enemies without reason,
²¹ Repaying me evil for good,
    harassing me for pursuing good.ᶠ
²² Forsake me not, O LORD;
    my God, be not far from me!ᵍ
²³ Come quickly to help me,ʰ
    my Lord and my salvation!

PSALM 39 *

See RG 175-76

The Vanity of Life

¹ For the leader, for Jeduthun.ⁱ
    A psalm of David.

I

² I said, "I will watch my ways,
    lest I sin with my tongue;
    I will set a curb on my mouth."
³ Dumb and silent before the wicked,
    I refrained from any speech.
    But my sorrow increased;
⁴   my heart smoldered within me.ʲ

Ps 38: In this lament, one of the Penitential Psalms (cf Ps 6), the psalmist acknowledges the sin that has brought physical and mental sickness and social ostracism. There is no one to turn to for help; only God can undo the past and restore the psalmist.

Ps 39: The lament of a mortally ill person who at first had resolved to remain silently submissive (2-4). But the grief was too much and now the psalmist laments the brevity and vanity of life (5-7), yet remaining hopeful (8-10). The

psalmist continues to express both acceptance of the illness and hope for healing in 11-14.

u: Prv 23, 18; 24, 14.   v: Ps 9, 10; Is 25, 4.   w: Ps 6, 2.   x: Jb 6, 4; Lam 3, 12; Pss 31, 11; 64, 7.   y: Is 1, 5-6.   z: Ps 40, 13; Ezr 9, 6.   a: Ps 35, 14.   b: Ps 102, 4-6.   c: Pss 6, 8; 31, 10.   d: Ps 13, 4.   e: Pss 32, 5; 51, 5.   f: Ps 109, 5.   g: Pss 22, 2. 12. 20; 35, 22.   h: Ps 40, 14.   i: 1 Chr 16, 41; Pss 62, 1; 77, 1.   j: Jer 20, 9.

In my thoughts a fire blazed up,
  and I broke into speech:

II

5 LORD, let me know my end, the number
    of my days,
  that I may learn how frail I am.
6 You have given my days a very short
    span;
  my life is as nothing before you.
  All mortals are but a breath.*k*   Selah
7 Mere phantoms, we go our way;
  mere vapor, our restless pursuits;
  we heap up stores without knowing for
    whom.
8 And now, Lord, what future do I have?
  You are my only hope.
9 From all my sins deliver me;
  let me not be the taunt of fools.

III

10 I was silent and did not open my
    mouth
  because you were the one who did
    this.
11 Take your plague away from me;
  I am ravaged by the touch of your
    hand.
12 You rebuke our guilt and chasten us;
  you dissolve all we prize like a
    cobweb.
  All mortals are but a breath.   Selah
13 Listen to my prayer, LORD, hear my
    cry;
  do not be deaf to my weeping!
  I sojourn with you like a passing
    stranger,
  a guest, like all my ancestors.*l*
14 Turn your gaze from me, that I may find
    peace
  before I depart to be no more.

PSALM 40 *

Gratitude and Prayer for Help

See RG 175–76

1 For the leader. A psalm of David.

A

I

2 I waited, waited for the LORD;
  who bent down and heard my cry,*m*
3 Drew me out of the pit of destruction,
  out of the mud of the swamp,*n*
  Set my feet upon rock,
  steadied my steps,
4 And put a new song* in my mouth,*o*
  a hymn to our God.
  Many shall look on in awe
  and they shall trust in the LORD.

II

5 Happy those whose trust is the LORD,
  who turn not to idolatry
  or to those who stray after
    falsehood.*p*
6 How numerous, O LORD, my God,
  you have made your wondrous
    deeds!
  And in your plans for us
  there is none to equal you.*q*
  Should I wish to declare or tell them,
  too many are they to recount.*r*

III

7 Sacrifice and offering you do not want;*s* *
  but ears open to obedience you gave
    me.
  Holocausts and sin-offerings you do not
    require;
8 so I said, "Here I am;
  your commands for me are written in
    the scroll.
9 To do your will is my delight;
  my God, your law is in my heart!"*t*

Ps 40: A thanksgiving (2-13) has been combined with a lament (14-18), that appears also in Ps 70. The psalmist describes the rescue in spatial terms—being raised up from the swampy underworld to firm earth where one can praise God (2-4). All who trust God will experience like protection (5-6)! The psalm stipulates the precise mode of thanksgiving: not animal sacrifice but open and enthusiastic proclamation of the salvation just experienced (7-11). A prayer for protection concludes (12-18).

40, 4: A new song: a song in response to the new action of God (cf Pss 33, 3; 96, 1; 144, 9; 149, 1; Is 42, 10). Giving thanks is not purely a human response but is itself a divine gift.

40, 7-9: Obedience is better than sacrifice (cf 1 Sm 15, 22; Is 1, 10-20; Hos 6, 6; Am 5, 22-25; Mi 6, 6-8; Acts 7, 42-43 [quoting Am 5, 25-26 LXX]). Heb 10, 5-9 quotes the somewhat different Greek version and interprets it as Christ's self-oblation.

k: Pss 62, 10; 90, 9-10; 144, 4; Jb 7, 6. 16; 14, 1. 5; Eccl 6, 12; Wis 2, 5. *l:* Ps 119, 19; Gn 23, 4; Heb 11, 13; 1 Pt 2, 11. *m:* Lam 3, 25. *n:* Pss 28, 1; 30, 4; 69, 3. 15-16; 88, 5; Prv 1, 12; Jon 2, 7. *o:* Ps 33, 3. *p:* Ps 1, 1; Prv 16, 20; Jer 17, 7. *q:* Ps 35, 10. *r:* Pss 71, 15; 139, 17-18. *s:* 7-9: Heb 10, 5-7; Ps 51, 18-19; Am 5, 22; Hos 6, 6; Is 1, 11-15. *t:* Ps 37, 31.

¹⁰ I announced your deed to a great
 assembly;
 I did not restrain my lips;
 you, LORD, are my witness.^u
¹¹ Your deed I did not hide within my heart;
 your loyal deliverance I have
 proclaimed.
 I made no secret of your enduring
 kindness
 to a great assembly.

B

I

¹² LORD, do not withhold your compassion
 from me;
 may your enduring kindness ever
 preserve me.^v
¹³ For all about me are evils beyond
 count;
 my sins so overcome me I cannot see.
 They are more than the hairs of my
 head;
 my courage fails me.^w

II

¹⁴ LORD, graciously rescue me!^x
 Come quickly to help me,
 LORD!
¹⁵ Put to shame and confound
 all who seek to take my life.
 Turn back in disgrace
 those who desire my ruin.^y
¹⁶ Let those who say "Aha!"^z
 know dismay and shame.
¹⁷ But may all who seek you
 rejoice and be glad in you.
 May those who long for your help
 always say, "The LORD be
 glorified."^a
¹⁸ Though I am afflicted and poor,
 the Lord keeps me in mind.

You are my help and deliverer;
 my God, do not delay!

PSALM 41[*]

Thanksgiving after Sickness

See RG 175

¹ For the leader. A psalm of David.

I

² Happy those concerned for the lowly and
 poor;[*]
 when misfortune strikes, the LORD
 delivers them.^b
³ The LORD keeps and preserves them,
 makes them happy in the land,
 and does not betray them to their
 enemies.
⁴ The LORD sustains them on their sickbed,
 allays the malady when they are ill.

II

⁵ Once I prayed, "LORD, have mercy on me;
 heal me, I have sinned against you.
⁶ My enemies say the worst of me:
 'When will that one die and be
 forgotten?'
⁷ When people come to visit me,
 they speak without sincerity.
 Their hearts store up malice;
 they leave and spread their vicious lies.^c
⁸ My foes all whisper against me;
 they imagine the worst about me:
⁹ I have a deadly disease, they say;
 I will never rise from my sickbed.
¹⁰ Even the friend who had my trust,
 who shared my table, has scorned me.^d [*]
¹¹ But you, LORD, have mercy and raise
 me up
 that I may repay them as they
 deserve."[*]

III

¹² By this I know you are pleased with me,

Ps 41: A thanksgiving for rescue from illness (4. 5. 9). Many people, even friends, have interpreted the illness as a divine punishment for sin and have ostracized the psalmist (5-11). The healing shows the return of God's favor and rebukes the psalmist's detractors (12-13).

41, 2: Happy those concerned for the lowly and poor: other psalms use the same formula ("Happy those") for those whom God favors. Cf Pss 32, 1-2; 34, 9; 40, 5; 65, 5. The psalmist's statement about God's love of the poor is based on the experience of being rescued (1-3).

41, 10: Even the friend . . . has scorned me: Jn 13, 18 cites this verse to characterize Judas as a false friend. **Scorned me:** an interpretation of the unclear Hebrew, "made

great the heel against me."

41, 11: That I may repay them as they deserve: the healing itself is an act of judgment through which God decides for the psalmist and against the false friends. The prayer is not necessarily for strength to punish enemies.

u: Pss 22, 23; 26, 12; 35, 18; 149, 1.   v: Ps 89, 34.   w: Ps 38, 5. 11; Ezr 9, 6.   x: 14-18: Pss 70, 2-6; 71, 12.   y: Ps 35, 4. 26. z: Ps 35, 21. 25.   a: Ps 35, 27.   b: Tb 4, 7-11.   c: Pss 31, 12; 38, 12-13; 88, 8; Jb 19, 13-19; Jer 20, 10.   d: Ps 55, 14-15; Jn 13, 18.

that my enemy no longer jeers at me.
13 For my integrity you have supported me
and let me stand in your presence
forever.

* * *

14 Blessed be the LORD, the God of Israel,
from all eternity and forever.
Amen. Amen.*e* *

Second Book: Psalms 42—72

See RG
175

PSALMS 42—43*

Longing for God's Presence
in the Temple

1 For the leader. A *maskil* of the Korahites.*

I

2 As the deer longs for streams of water,*f*
so my soul longs for you, O God.
3 My being thirsts for God, the living God.
When can I go and see the face of
God?*g* *
4 My tears have been my food day and
night,*h*
as they ask daily, "Where is your
God?"*i*
5 Those times I recall
as I pour out my soul,*j*
When I went in procession with the
crowd,
I went with them to the house of God,
Amid loud cries of thanksgiving,
with the multitude keeping festival.*k*
6 Why are you downcast, my soul;
why do you groan within me?
Wait for God, whom I shall praise again,
my savior and my God.

II

7 My soul is downcast within me;
therefore I will remember you
From the land of the Jordan* and Hermon,
from the land of Mount Mizar.*l*
8 Here deep calls to deep* in the roar of
your torrents.
All your waves and breakers sweep
over me.*m*
9 At dawn may the LORD bestow faithful
love
that I may sing praise through the night,
praise to the God of my life.
10 I say to God, "My rock,
why do you forget me?*n*
Why must I go about mourning
with the enemy oppressing me?"
11 It shatters my bones, when my
adversaries reproach me.
They say to me daily: "Where is your
God?"
12 Why are you downcast, my soul,
why do you groan within me?
Wait for God, whom I shall praise again,
my savior and my God.

III

1 Grant me justice, God;
defend me from a faithless people;
from the deceitful and unjust rescue me.*o*
2 You, God, are my strength.
Why then do you spurn me?
Why must I go about mourning,
with the enemy oppressing me?
3 Send your light and fidelity,*
that they may be my guide*p*
And bring me to your holy mountain,
to the place of your dwelling,*q*

41, 14: The doxology, not part of the psalm, marks the end
of the first of the five books of the Psalter. Compare Pss 72,
18-20; 89, 53; 106, 48.

Pss 42—43: Pss 42—43 form a single lament of three sections, each section ending in an identical refrain (42, 6. 12;
43, 5). The psalmist is in the extreme north of Israel, far from
Jerusalem, and longs for the divine presence that Israel experienced in the temple liturgy. Despite sadness, the psalmist
hopes once again to join the worshiping crowds.

42, 1: The Korahites: a major guild of temple singers
(2 Chr 20, 19) whose name appears in the superscriptions of
Pss 42; 44-49; 84-85; 87-88.

42, 3: See the face of God: "face" designates a personal presence (Gn 33, 10; Ex 10, 28-29; 2 Sm 17, 11). The expressions "see
God/God's face" occur elsewhere (Pss 11, 7; 17, 15; 63, 3; cf Ex
24, 10; 33, 7-11; Jb 33, 26) for the presence of God in the temple.

42, 7: From the land of the Jordan: the sources of the
Jordan are in the foothills of Mount Hermon in present-day
southern Lebanon. Mount Mizar is presumed to be a mountain in the same range.

42, 8: Here deep calls to deep: to the psalmist, the waters
arising in the north are overwhelming and far from God's presence, like the waters of chaos (Pss 18, 5; 69, 2-3. 15; Jon 2, 3-6).

43, 3: Your light and fidelity: a pair of divine attributes
personified as guides for the pilgrimage. The psalmist seeks
divine protection for the journey to Jerusalem.

e: Neh 9, 5. *f:* 2-3: Pss 63, 2; 84, 3; 143, 6; Is 26, 9. *g:* Ps 27,
4. *h:* Pss 80, 6; 102, 10. *i:* Ps 79, 10; Jl 2, 17. *j:* Lam 3, 20.
k: Ps 122, 5. *l:* Ps 43, 3. *m:* Pss 18, 5; 32, 6; 69, 2; 88, 8; Jon
2, 4. *n:* Pss 18, 2; 31, 3-4. *o:* Ps 119, 154. *p:* Pss 18, 29; 27,
1; 36, 10; Mi 7, 8. *q:* Ps 122, 1.

Covenants are mutual obligations; the psalmist is saying in 44, 18 that even though God has broken his side, the community continues to maintain its obligations.

⁴ That I may come to the altar of God,
  to God, my joy, my delight.
Then I will praise you with the harp,
  O God, my God.
⁵ Why are you downcast, my soul?
  Why do you groan within me?
Wait for God, whom I shall praise again,
  my savior and my God.

See RG 175, 177

PSALM 44*

God's Past Favor and Israel's Present Need

¹ For the leader. A *maskil* of the Korahites.

I

² O God, we have heard with our own ears;
  our ancestors have told us^r
The deeds you did in their days,
  with your own hand in days of old:
³ You rooted out nations to plant them,^s
  crushed peoples to make room for them.
⁴ Not with their own swords did they
    conquer the land,^t
  nor did their own arms bring victory;
It was your right hand, your own arm,
    the light of your face, for you favored
    them.^u
⁵ You are my king and my God,^v
  who bestows victories on Jacob.
⁶ Through you we batter our foes;
  through your name, trample our
    adversaries.
⁷ Not in my bow do I trust,
  nor does my sword bring me victory.
⁸ You have brought us victory over our
    enemies,
  shamed those who hate us.

⁹ In God we have boasted all the day long;
  your name we will praise forever.
                                                    Selah

II

¹⁰ But now you have rejected and
    disgraced us;^w
  you do not march out with our armies.^x
¹¹ You make us retreat* before the foe;
  those who hate us plunder us at will.^y
¹² You hand us over like sheep to be
    slaughtered,
  scatter us among the nations.^z
¹³ You sell your people for nothing;
  you make no profit from their sale.^a
¹⁴ You make us the reproach of our
    neighbors,^b
  the mockery and scorn of those around
    us.
¹⁵ You make us a byword among the nations;
  the peoples shake their heads at us.
¹⁶ All day long my disgrace is before me;
  shame has covered my face
¹⁷ At the sound of those who taunt and revile,
  at the sight of the spiteful enemy.

III

¹⁸ All this has come upon us,
  though we have not forgotten you,
  nor been disloyal to your covenant.
¹⁹ Our hearts have not turned back,*
  nor have our steps strayed from your
    path.
²⁰ Yet you have left us crushed,
  desolate in a place of jackals;^c *
  you have covered us with darkness.
²¹ If we had forgotten the name of our
    God,

Ps 44: In this lament the community reminds God of past favors which it has always acknowledged (2-9). But now God has abandoned Israel to defeat and humiliation (10-17), though the people are not conscious of any sin against the covenant (18-23). They struggle with being God's special people amid divine silence; yet they continue to pray (24-27).

44, 11: You make us retreat: the corollary of v 4. Defeat, like victory, is God's doing; neither Israel nor its enemies can claim credit (23).

44, 19: Our hearts have not turned back: Israel's defeat was not caused by its lack of fidelity.

44, 20: A place of jackals: following Israel's defeat and exile (11-12), the land lies desolate, inhabited only by jackals. Cf Is 13, 22; Jer 9, 10; 10, 22. Others take *tannim* as "sea monster" (cf Ez 29, 3; 32, 2) and render: "you crushed us as you did the sea monster."

r: Ps 78, 3. *s:* Pss 78, 55; 80, 9f. *t:* Dt 8, 17f; Jos 24, 12. *u:* Pss 4, 7; 31, 17; 67, 2; 80, 4; Nm 6, 25; Dn 9, 17. *v:* Ps 145, 1. *w:* 10-27. Ps 89, 39-52. *x:* Ps 60, 12. *y:* Lv 26, 17; Dt 28, 25. *z:* Lv 26, 33; Dt 28, 64. *a:* Dt 32, 30; Is 52, 3. *b:* 14-17: Pss 79, 4; 80, 7; 123, 3-4; Jb 12, 4; Dn 9, 16. *c:* Jer 9, 10.

stretched out our hands to another god,

22 Would not God have discovered this,
God who knows the secrets of the
heart?

23 For you we are slain all the day long,
considered only as sheep to be
slaughtered.[d]

IV

24 Awake! Why do you sleep, O Lord?
Rise up! Do not reject us forever![e]

25 Why do you hide your face;[f]
why forget our pain and misery?

26 We are bowed down to the ground;[g]
our bodies are pressed to the earth.

27 Rise up, help us!
Redeem us as your love demands.

See RG
176

PSALM 45[*]

Song for a Royal Wedding

1 For the leader; according to "Lilies."
A *maskil* of the Korahites. A love song.

I

2 My heart is stirred by a noble theme,
as I sing my ode to the king.
My tongue is the pen of a nimble
scribe.

II

3 You are the most handsome of men;
fair speech has graced your lips,
for God has blessed you forever.[h]

4 Gird your sword upon your hip, mighty
warrior!
In splendor and majesty ride on
triumphant![i]

5 In the cause of truth and justice
may your right hand show you
wondrous deeds.

6 Your arrows are sharp;
peoples will cower at your feet;

the king's enemies will lose heart.

7 Your throne, O god,[*] stands forever;[j]
your royal scepter is a scepter for
justice.

8 You love justice and hate wrongdoing;
therefore God, your God, has anointed
you
with the oil of gladness above your
fellow kings.

9 With myrrh, aloes, and cassia
your robes are fragrant.
From ivory-paneled palaces[*]
stringed instruments bring you joy.

10 Daughters of kings are your lovely wives;
a princess arrayed in Ophir's gold[*]
comes to stand at your right hand.

III

11 Listen, my daughter, and understand;
pay me careful heed.
Forget your people and your father's
house,[*]

12 that the king might desire your beauty.
He is your lord;

13 honor him, daughter of Tyre.
Then the richest of the people
will seek your favor with gifts.[k]

14 All glorious is the king's daughter as she
enters,[l]
her raiment threaded with gold;

15 In embroidered apparel she is led to the
king.
The maids of her train are presented to
the king.

16 They are led in with glad and joyous
acclaim;
they enter the palace of the king.

IV

17 The throne of your fathers your sons will
have;

Ps 45: A song for the Davidic king's marriage to a foreign princess from Tyre in Phoenicia. The court poet sings (2. 18) of God's choice of the king (3. 8), of his role in establishing divine rule (4-8), and of his splendor as he waits for his bride (9-10). The woman is to forget her own house when she becomes wife to the king (11-13). Her majestic beauty today is a sign of the future prosperity of the royal house (14-18). The psalm was retained in the collection when there was no reigning king, and came to be applied to the king who was to come, the messiah.

45, 7: O god: the king, in courtly language, is called "god," i.e., more than human, representing God to the people. Heb 1, 8-9 applies 7-8 to Christ.

45, 9: Ivory-paneled palaces: literally, "palaces of

ivory." Ivory paneling and furniture decoration have been found in Samaria and other ancient Near Eastern cities. Cf Am 3, 15.

45, 10: Ophir's gold: uncertain location, possibly a region on the coast of southern Arabia or eastern Africa, famous for its gold. Cf 1 Kgs 9, 28; 10, 11; Jb 22, 24.

45, 11: Forget your people and your father's house: the bride should no longer consider herself a daughter of her father's house, but the wife of the king—the queen.

---

d: Rom 8, 36. e: Pss 10, 1; 74, 1; 77, 8; 79, 5; 83, 2. f: Pss 10, 11; 89, 47; Jb 13, 24. g: Ps 119, 25. h: Song 5, 10-16. i: Ps 21, 5. j: 7-8: Heb 1, 8-9. k: Ps 72, 10-11; Is 60, 5f. l: 14-16: Ez 16, 10-13.

you shall make them princes through all the land.*m*

18 I will make your name renowned through all generations;
thus nations shall praise you forever.*n*

PSALM 46*

See RG 175

God, the Protector of Zion

1 For the leader. A song of the Korahites. According to *alamoth.**

I

2 God is our refuge and our strength,
an ever-present help in distress.*o*
3 Thus we do not fear, though earth be shaken*
and mountains quake to the depths of the sea,
4 Though its waters rage and foam
and mountains totter at its surging.*p*
The LORD of hosts is with us;*
our stronghold is the God of Jacob.
Selah

II

5 Streams of the river gladden the city of God,
the holy dwelling of the Most High.*q* *
6 God is in its midst; it shall not be shaken;
God will help it at break of day.*r*
7 Though nations rage and kingdoms totter,
God's voice thunders and the earth trembles.*s*
8 The LORD of hosts is with us;
our stronghold is the God of Jacob.
Selah

III

9 Come and see the works of the LORD,

who has done fearsome deeds on earth;*t*
10 Who stops wars to the ends of the earth,
breaks the bow, splinters the spear,
and burns the shields with fire;*u*
11 Who says:
"Be still and confess that I am God!
I am exalted among the nations,
exalted on the earth."*v*
12 The LORD of hosts is with us;
our stronghold is the God of Jacob.
Selah

PSALM 47*

The Ruler of All the Nations

See RG 175-76

1 For the leader. A psalm of the Korahites.

I

2 All you peoples, clap your hands;
shout to God with joyful cries.*w*
3 For the LORD, the Most High, inspires awe,
the great king over all the earth,*x*
4 Who made people subject to us,
brought nations under our feet,*y*
5 Who chose a land for our heritage,
the glory* of Jacob, the beloved.*z* *Selah*

II

6 God mounts the throne* amid shouts of joy;
the LORD, amid trumpet blasts.*a*
7 Sing praise to God, sing praise;
sing praise to our king, sing praise.

III

8 God is king over all the earth;*b*
sing hymns of praise.
9 God rules over the nations;
God sits upon his holy throne.

Ps 46: A song of confidence in God's protection of Zion with close parallels to Ps 48. The dominant note in Ps 46 is sounded by the refrain, **The LORD of hosts is with us** (4. 8. 12). The first strophe (2-4) sings of the security of God's presence even in utter chaos; the second (5-8), of divine protection of the city from its enemies; the third (9-12), of God's imposition of imperial peace.

46, 1: Alamoth: the melody of the psalm, now lost.

46, 3-4: Figurative ancient Near Eastern language to describe social and political upheavals.

46, 4b: The first line of the refrain is similar in structure and meaning to Isaiah's name for the royal child, Immanuel, **With us is God** (Is 7, 14; 8, 8. 10).

46, 5: Jerusalem is not situated on a river. This description derives from mythological descriptions of the divine abode and symbolizes the divine presence as the source of all life (cf Is 33, 21; Ez 47, 1-12; Jl 4, 18; Zec 14, 8; Rv 22, 1-2).

Ps 47: A hymn calling on the nations to acknowledge the universal rule of Israel's God (2-5) who is enthroned as king over Israel and the nations (6-10).

47, 5: Our heritage . . . the glory: the land of Israel (cf Is 58, 14), which God has given Israel in an act of sovereignty.

47, 6: God mounts the throne: "has gone up to the throne," according to the context (9). Christian liturgical tradition has applied the verse to the ascension of Christ.

m: Gn 17, 6. *n:* Is 60, 15. *o:* Ps 48, 4; Is 33, 2. *p:* Ps 93, 3-4; Jb 9, 5-6; Is 24, 18-20; 54, 10. *q:* Pss 48, 2-3; 76, 3. *r:* Is 7, 14. *s:* Pss 2, 1-5; 48, 5-8; 76, 7-9; Is 17, 12-14. *t:* Ps 48, 9-10. *u:* Ps 76, 4. *v:* Ps 48, 11. *w:* Ps 89, 16; Zep 3, 14. *x:* Ps 95, 3; Ex 15, 18; Is 24, 23; 52, 7. *y:* Ps 2, 8. *z:* Is 58, 14. *a:* Pss 24, 8. 10; 68, 18-19; 98, 6. *b:* 8-9: Pss 72, 11; 93, 1; 96, 10; 97, 1; 99, 1; Jer 10, 7.

¹⁰ The princes of the peoples assemble
    with the people of the God of Abraham.
For the rulers of the earth belong to God,
    who is enthroned on high.*c*

PSALM 48*

See RG
175

The Splendor of the Invincible City

¹ A psalm of the Korahites.* A song.

I

² Great is the LORD and highly praised
    in the city of our God:*d*
The holy mountain, ³ fairest of heights,
    the joy of all the earth,*e*
Mount Zion, the heights of Zaphon,*f* *
    the city of the great king.

II

⁴ God is its citadel,
    renowned as a stronghold.
⁵ See! The kings assembled,
    together they invaded.
⁶ When they looked* they were
        astounded;
    terrified, they were put to flight!*g*
⁷ Trembling seized them there,
    anguish, like a woman's labor,*h*
⁸ As when the east wind wrecks
    the ships of Tarshish!*

III

⁹ What we had heard we now see*
    in the city of the LORD of hosts,

In the city of our God,
    founded to last forever.   *Selah*
¹⁰ O God, within your temple
    we ponder your steadfast love.
¹¹ Like your name, O God,
    your praise reaches the ends of the
        earth.*i*
Your right hand is fully victorious.
¹²   Mount Zion is glad!
The cities of Judah rejoice
    because of your saving deeds!*j*

IV

¹³ Go about Zion, walk all around it,
    note the number of its towers.
¹⁴ Consider the ramparts, examine its
        citadels,
    that you may tell future generations:*k*
¹⁵ "Yes, so mighty is God,*
    our God who leads us always!"

PSALM 49*

Confidence in God rather than in Riches

See RG
176, 179

¹ For the leader. A psalm of
    the Korahites.*
² Hear this, all you peoples!
    Give ear, all who inhabit the world,
³ You of lowly birth or high estate,
    rich and poor alike.
⁴ My mouth shall speak wisdom,
    my heart shall offer insight.*l*

Ps 48: A Zion hymn, praising the holy city as the invincible dwelling place of God. Unconquerable, it is an apt symbol of God who has defeated all enemies. After seven epithets describing the city (2-3), the psalm describes the victory by the Divine Warrior over hostile kings (4-8). The second half proclaims the dominion of the God of Zion over all the earth (9-12) and invites pilgrims to announce that God is eternally invincible like Zion itself (13-15).

48, 1: Korahites: see note on Ps 42, 1.

48, 3: The heights of Zaphon: the mountain abode of the Canaanite storm-god Baal in comparable texts. To speak of Zion as if it were Zaphon was to claim for Israel's God what Canaanites claimed for Baal. Though topographically speaking Zion is only a hill, viewed religiously it towers over other mountains as the home of the supreme God (cf Ps 68, 16-17).

48, 6: When they looked: the kings are stunned by the sight of Zion, touched by divine splendor. The language is that of holy war, in which the enemy panics and flees at the sight of divine glory.

48, 8: The ships of Tarshish: large ships, named after the distant land or port of Tarshish, probably ancient Tartessus in southern Spain, although other identifications have been proposed. Cf Is 2, 16; 60, 9; Jon 1, 3.

48, 9: What we had heard we now see: the glorious things that new pilgrims had heard about the holy city—its beauty and awesomeness—they now see with their own eyes. The seeing here contrasts with the seeing of the hostile kings in 6.

48, 15: So mighty is God: Israel's God is like Zion in being eternal and invincible. The holy city is therefore a kind of "sacrament" of God.

Ps 49: The psalm affirms confidence in God (cf Pss 23; 27, 1-6; 62) in the face of the apparent good fortune of the unjust rich. Cf Pss 37; 73. Reliance on wealth is misplaced (8-10) for it is of no avail in the face of death (18-20). After inviting all to listen to this axiom of faith (2-5), the psalmist depicts the self-delusion of the ungodly (6-13), whose destiny is to die like ignorant beasts (13. 18; cf Prv 7, 21-23). Their wealth should occasion no alarm, for they will come to nought, whereas God will save the just (14-21).

49, 1: Korahites: see note on Ps 42, 1.

c: Ps 89, 19; Ex 3, 6; Is 2, 2-4.   *d*: Pss 96, 4; 145, 3.   *e*: Ps 50, 2; Lam 2, 15.   *f*: Is 14, 13.   *g*: Jgs 5, 19.   *h*: Ex 15, 14; Jer 4, 31.   *i*: Mal 1, 11.   *j*: Ps 97, 8.   *k*: Pss 22, 31-32; 71, 18.   *l*: Ps 78, 2; Mt 13, 35.

⁵ I will turn my attention to a problem,*
  expound my question* to the music of
  a lyre.

I

⁶ Why should I fear in evil days,
  when my wicked pursuers ring me
  round,
⁷ Those who trust in their wealth
  and boast of their abundant riches?ᵐ
⁸ One cannot redeem oneself,*
  pay to God a ransom.ⁿ
⁹ Too high the price to redeem a life;
  one would never have enough
¹⁰ To stay alive forever
  and never see the pit.
¹¹ Anyone can see that the wisest die,
  the fool and the senseless pass away
  too,ᵒ
  and must leave their wealth to
  others.ᵖ
¹² Tombs are their homes forever,
  their dwellings through all
  generations,
  though they gave their names to their
  lands.
¹³ For all their riches
  mortals do not abide;
  they perish like the beasts.�q

II

¹⁴ This is the destiny of those who trust in
  folly,
  the end of those so pleased with their
  wealth.   *Selah*
¹⁵ Like sheep they are herded into Sheol,
  where death will be their shepherd.
  Straight to the grave they descend,
  where their form will waste away,
  Sheol will be their palace.
¹⁶ But God will redeem my life,   *Selah*

will take me* from the power of
  Sheol.ʳ
¹⁷ Do not fear when others become rich,
  when the wealth of their houses grows
  great.
¹⁸ When they die they will take nothing
  with them,
  their wealth will not follow them
  down.ˢ
¹⁹ When living, they congratulate
  themselves and say:
  "All praise you, you do so well."
²⁰ But they will join the company of their
  forebears,
  never again to see the light.ᵗ
²¹ For all their riches,
  if mortals do not have wisdom,
  they perish like the beasts.

PSALM 50*

The Acceptable Sacrifice

See RG 175

¹ A psalm of Asaph.

I

The LORD, the God of gods,
  has spoken and summoned the earth
  from the rising of the sun to its
  setting.ᵘ
² From Zion God shines forth,ᵛ
  perfect in beauty.
³ Our God comes and will not be silent!
  Devouring fire precedes,
  storming fiercely round about.ʷ
⁴ God summons the heavens above
  and the earth to the judgment of his
  people:
⁵ "Gather my faithful ones before me,
  those who made a covenant with me
  by sacrifice."
⁶ The heavens proclaim divine justice,

49, 5: Problem: the psalmist's personal solution to the perennial biblical problem of the prosperity of the wicked. **Question**: parallel in meaning to **problem**; in Wisdom literature it means the mysterious way of how the world works.

49, 8: One cannot redeem oneself: an axiom. For the practice of redemption, cf Jb 6, 21-23. A play on the first Hebrew word of v 8 and v 16 relates the two verses.

49, 16: Will take me: the same Hebrew verb is used of God "taking up" a favored servant: Enoch in Gn 5, 24; Elijah in 2 Kgs 2, 11-12; the righteous person in Ps 73, 24. The verse apparently states the hope that God will rescue the faithful psalmist in the same manner.

Ps 50: A covenant lawsuit stating that the sacrifice God really wants is the sacrifice of praise accompanied by genuine obedience (cf Mi 6, 1-8). It begins with a theophany and the summoning of the court (1-6). Then in direct address God explains what is required of the faithful (7-15), rebukes the hypocritical worshiper (16-21), and concludes with a threat and a promise (22-23; cf Is 1, 19-20).

m· Jb 31, 24. n: Prv 10, 15; 11, 4; Ez 7, 19; Mt 16, 26. o: Eccl 2, 16. p: Ps 39, 7; Sir 11, 18-19. q: Eccl 3, 18-21. r: Pss 16, 10; 86, 13; 103, 4; 116, 8. s: Sir 11, 18-19; Eccl 5, 15; 1 Tm 6, 7. t: Jb 10, 21-22. u: Dt 10, 17; Jos 22, 22. v: Ps 48, 2. w· Ps 97, 3; Dn 7, 10.

for God alone is the judge.[x]   *Selah*

II

7 "Listen, my people, I will speak;
  Israel, I will testify against you;
  God, your God, am I.
8 Not for your sacrifices do I rebuke you,
  nor for your holocausts, set before me
    daily.
9 I need no bullock from your house,
  no goats from your fold.[y]
10 For every animal of the forest is mine,
  beasts by the thousands on my
    mountains.
11 I know every bird of the heavens;
  the creatures of the field belong to me.
12 Were I hungry, I would not tell you,
  for mine is the world and all that
    fills it.[z]
13 Do I eat the flesh of bulls
  or drink the blood of goats?
14 Offer praise as your sacrifice to God;[a]
  fulfill your vows to the Most High.
15 Then call on me in time of distress;[b]
  I will rescue you, and you shall honor
    me."

III

16 But to the wicked God says:
  "Why do you recite my commandments
  and profess my covenant with your
    lips?
17 You hate discipline;
  you cast my words behind you!
18 When you see thieves, you befriend
    them;
  with adulterers you throw in your lot.
19 You give your mouth free rein for evil;
  you harness your tongue to deceit.
20 You sit maligning your own kin,

slandering the child of your own
    mother.
21 When you do these things should I be
    silent?
  Or do you think that I am like you?
  I accuse you, I lay the charge before
    you."

IV

22 "Understand this, you who forget God,
  lest I attack you with no one to rescue.
23 Those who offer praise as a sacrifice
    honor me;
  to the obedient I will show the
    salvation of God."[c]

PSALM 51[*]

The Miserere:
Prayer of Repentance

See RG 175

1 For the leader. A psalm of David, 2 when
  Nathan the prophet came to him after his
    affair with Bathsheba.[d]

I

3 Have mercy on me, God, in your
    goodness;
  in your abundant compassion blot out
    my offense.
4 Wash away all my guilt;
  from my sin cleanse me.
5 For I know my offense;
  my sin is always before me.[e]
6 Against you alone have I sinned;
  I have done such evil in your sight
  That you are just in your sentence,
    blameless when you condemn.[f]
7 True, I was born guilty,
  a sinner, even as my mother conceived
    me.[g][*]
8 Still, you insist on sincerity of heart;

Ps 51: A lament, the most famous of the seven Penitential Psalms, prays for the removal of the personal and social disorders that sin has brought. The poem has two parts of approximately equal length: 3-10 and 11-19, and a conclusion in 20-21. The two parts interlock by repetition of "blot out" in the first verse of each section (3. 11), of "wash (away)" just after the first verse of each section (4) and just before the last verse (9) of the first section, and of "heart," "God," and "spirit" in 12 and 19. The first part (3-10) asks deliverance from sin, which is not just a past act but its emotional, physical, and social consequences. The second part (11-19) seeks something more profound than wiping the slate clean: nearness to God, living by the spirit of God (12-13), like the relation between God and people described in Jer 31, 33-34. Nearness to God brings joy and the authority to teach sinners

(15-16). Such proclamation is better than offering sacrifice (17-19). The last two verses ask for the rebuilding of Jerusalem (20-21).

51, 7: A sinner, even as my mother conceived me: literally, "In iniquity was I conceived," an instance of hyperbole: at no time was the psalmist ever without sin. Cf Ps 88, 16, "I am mortally afflicted since youth," i.e., I have always been afflicted. The verse does not imply that the sexual act of conception is sinful.

x: Pss 19, 2; 97, 6.   *y:* Ps 69, 32; Am 5, 21-22.   *z:* Pss 24, 1; 89, 12; Dt 10, 14; 1 Cor 10, 26.   *a:* Heb 13, 15.   *b:* Ps 77, 3. *c:* Ps 91, 16.   *d:* 2 Sm 12.   *e:* Pss 32, 5; 38, 19; Is 59, 12. *f:* Rom 3, 4.   *g:* Jb 14, 4.

in my inmost being teach me wisdom.
⁹ Cleanse me with hyssop,* that I may be
pure;
wash me, make me whiter than snow.ʰ
¹⁰ Let me hear sounds of joy and gladness;
let the bones you have crushed rejoice.

II

¹¹ Turn away your face from my sins;
blot out all my guilt.
¹² A clean heart create for me, God;
renew in me a steadfast spirit.ⁱ
¹³ Do not drive me from your presence,
nor take from me your holy spirit.ʲ
¹⁴ Restore my joy in your salvation;
sustain in me a willing spirit.
¹⁵ I will teach the wicked your ways,
that sinners may return to you.
¹⁶ Rescue me from death, God, my saving
God,
that my tongue may praise your
healing power.ᵏ
¹⁷ Lord, open my lips;
my mouth will proclaim your praise.
¹⁸ For you do not desire sacrifice;*
a burnt offering you would not
accept.ˡ
¹⁹ My sacrifice, God, is a broken spirit;
God, do not spurn a broken, humbled
heart.

III

²⁰ Make Zion prosper in your good
pleasure;*
rebuild the walls of Jerusalem.ᵐ
²¹ Then you will be pleased with proper
sacrifice,
burnt offerings and holocausts;
then bullocks will be offered on your
altar.

PSALM 52*

The Deceitful Tongue

See RG 175

¹ For the leader. A *maskil* of David,
² when Doeg the Edomite went and
told Saul, "David went to the house
of Ahimelech."ⁿ

I

³ Why do you glory in evil,
you scandalous liar?
All day long ⁴ you plot destruction;
your tongue is like a sharpened
razor,
you skillful deceiver.ᵒ
⁵ You love evil rather than good,
lies rather than honest speech.ᵖ   *Selah*
⁶ You love any word that destroys,
you deceitful tongue.�q

II

⁷ Now God will strike you down,
leave you crushed forever,
Pluck you from your tent,
uproot you from the land of the
living.ʳ   *Selah*
⁸ The righteous will look on with awe;
they will jeer and say:ˢ
⁹ "That one did not take God as a
refuge,
but trusted in great wealth,
relied on devious plots."ᵗ

III

¹⁰ But I, like an olive tree in the house of
God,ᵘ *
trust in God's faithful love forever.
¹¹ I will praise you always
for what you have done.
I will proclaim before the faithfulᵛ
that your name is good.

51, 9: Hyssop: a small bush whose many woody twigs make a natural sprinkler. It was prescribed in the Mosaic law as an instrument for sprinkling sacrificial blood or lustral water for cleansing. Cf Ex 12, 22; Lv 14, 4; Nm 19, 18.

51, 18: For you do not desire sacrifice: the mere offering of the ritual sacrifice apart from good dispositions is not acceptable to God. Cf Ps 50.

51, 20-21: Most scholars think that these verses were added to the psalm some time after the destruction of the temple in 587 B.C. The verses assume that the rebuilt temple will be an ideal site for national reconciliation.

Ps 52: A condemnation of the powerful and arrogant (3-6), who bring down upon themselves God's judgment (7). The just, those who trust in God alone, are gladdened and

strengthened by the downfall of their traditional enemies (8-11).

52, 10: Like an olive tree: the righteous will flourish in the house of God like a well-watered olive tree. Cf Pss 92, 14; 128, 3.

h: Jb 9, 30; Is 1, 18; Ez 36, 25.   i: Ez 11, 19.   j: Wis 1, 5; 9, 17; Is 63, 11; Hg 2, 5; Rom 8, 9.   k: Ps 30, 10.   l: Pss 40, 7; 50, 8; Am 5, 21-22; Hos 6, 6; Is 1, 11-15; Heb 10, 5-7.   m: Jer 31, 4; Ez 36, 33.   n: 1 Sm 21, 8; 22, 6ff.   o: Pss 12, 3; 59, 8; 120, 2-3; Sir 51, 3.   p: Jer 4, 22; Jn 3, 19-20.   q: Jer 9, 4.   r: Pss 27, 13; 28, 5; 55, 14; Jb 18, 14; Prv 2, 22; Is 38, 11.   s: Pss 44, 14; 64, 9. t: Jb 31, 24; Prv 11, 28.   u: Pss 1, 3; 92, 12-14; Jer 11, 16; 17, 8. v: Pss 22, 23; 26, 12; 35, 18; 149, 1.

PSALM 53*

See RG 175

A Lament over Widespread Corruption

¹ For the leader; according to *Mahalath.*
A *maskil* of David.

I

² Fools say in their hearts,ʷ
   "There is no God."ˣ
Their deeds are loathsome and
      corrupt;
   not one does what is right.
³ God looks down from heaven
      upon the human race,ʸ
To see if even one is wise,ᶻ
   if even one seeks God.
⁴ All have gone astray;
   all alike are perverse.
Not one does what is right, not even
      one.ᵃ

II

⁵ Will these evildoers never learn?
   They devour my people as they
      devour bread;ᵇ
   they do not call upon God.ᶜ
⁶ They have good reason to fear,
   though now they do not fear.
For God will certainly scatter
   the bones of the godless.
They will surely be put to shame,
   for God has rejected them.

III

⁷ Oh, that from Zion might come
   the deliverance of Israel,
That Jacob may rejoice and Israel be
      gladᵈ
   when God restores the
      people!

PSALM 54*

See RG 175

Confident Prayer in Great Peril

¹ For the leader. On stringed instruments.
A *maskil* of David, ² when the Ziphites came
and said to Saul, "David is hiding
among us."ᵉ

I

³ O God, by your name* save me.
   By your strength defend my cause.
⁴ O God, hear my prayer.
   Listen to the words of my mouth.
⁵ The arrogant have risen against me;
   the ruthless seek my life;
   they do not keep God before them.ᶠ
                                    Selah

II

⁶ God is present as my helper;ᵍ
   the Lord sustains my life.
⁷ Turn back the evil upon my foes;
   in your faithfulness, destroy them.ʰ
⁸ Then I will offer you generous sacrifice
   and praise your gracious name, LORD,
⁹ Because it has rescued me from every
      trouble,
   and my eyes look down on my foes.ⁱ

PSALM 55*

See RG 175

A Lament over Betrayal

¹ For the leader. On stringed instruments.
A *maskil* of David.

I

² Listen, God, to my prayer;ʲ
   do not hide from my pleading;
³   hear me and give answer.
I rock with grief; I groan
⁴   at the uproar of the enemy,

Ps 53: A lament of an individual, duplicated in Ps 14, except that "God" is used for "the LORD," and v 6 is different. See under Ps 14.

Ps 54: A lament in which the person under attack calls directly upon God for help (3-5). Refusing to despair, the psalmist hopes in God, who is active in history and just (6-7). The psalm ends with a serene promise to return thanks (8-9).

54, 3: By your name: one is present in one's name, hence God as revealed to humans.

Ps 55: The psalmist, betrayed by intimate friends (14-15. 21-22), prays that God punish those oath breakers and thus be acknowledged as the protector of the wronged. The sufferings of the psalmist include both ostracism (4) and mental turmoil (5-6), culminating in the wish to flee society (7-9). The wish for a sudden death for one's enemies (16) occurs elsewhere in

the psalms; an example of such a death is the earth opening under the wicked Dathan and Abiram (Nm 16, 31-32). The psalmist, confident of vindication, exhorts others to a like trust in the God of justice (23-24). The psalm is not so much for personal vengeance as for a public vindication of God's righteousness now. There was no belief in an afterlife where such vindication could take place.

w: 2-6a: Ps 14, 1-5a. *x*: Pss 10, 4; 36, 2; Is 32, 6; Jer 5, 12. *y*: Pss 11, 4; 102, 20. *z*: 2b-3: Rom 3, 11-12. *a*: Ps 12, 2. *b*: Ps 27, 2; Is 9, 11. *c*: Ps 79, 6. *d*: Ps 85, 2. *e*: 1 Sm 23, 19; 26, 1. *f*: Ps 86, 14. *g*: Ps 118, 7. *h*: Ps 143, 12. *i*: Pss 59, 11; 91, 8; 92, 12. *j*: 2-3: Pss 5, 2-3; 55, 2-3; 86, 6; 130, 1-2; Lam 3, 56; Jon 2, 3.

the clamor of the wicked.
They heap trouble upon me,
  savagely accuse me.
5 My heart pounds within me;
  death's terrors fall upon me.
6 Fear and trembling overwhelm me;
  shuddering sweeps over me.
7 I say, "If only I had wings like a dove
  that I might fly away and find rest.*k*
8 Far away I would flee;
  I would stay in the desert.*l*   Selah
9 I would soon find a shelter
  from the raging wind and storm."

II

10 Lord, check and confuse their scheming.
  I see violence and strife in the city
11   making rounds on its walls day and
      night.
  Within are mischief and evil;
12   treachery is there as well;
  oppression and fraud never leave its
      streets.*m*
13 If an enemy had reviled me,
  that I could bear;
  If my foe had viewed me with contempt,
  from that I could hide.
14 But it was you, my other self,
  my comrade and friend,*n*
15 You, whose company I enjoyed,
  at whose side I walked
  in procession in the house of God.

III

16 Let death take them by surprise;
  let them go down alive to Sheol,*o*
  for evil is in their homes and hearts.
17 But I will call upon God,
  and the LORD will save me.
18 At dusk, dawn, and noon
  I will grieve and complain,
  and my prayer will be heard.*p*
19 God will give me freedom and peace
  from those who war against me,
  though there are many who oppose me.

20 God, who sits enthroned forever,*q*
  will hear me and humble them.
  For they will not mend their ways;
  they have no fear of God.
21 They strike out at friends
  and go back on their promises.
22 Softer than butter is their speech,
  but war is in their hearts.
  Smoother than oil are their words,
  but they are unsheathed swords.*r*
23 Cast your care upon the LORD,
  who will give you support.
  God will never allow
  the righteous to stumble.*s*
24 But you, God, will bring them down
  to the pit of destruction.*t*
  These bloodthirsty liars
  will not live half their days,
  but I put my trust in you.*u*

PSALM 56*

Trust in God

See RG
175

1 For the director. According to *Yonath elem
  rehoqim.** A *miktam* of David, when the
  Philistines seized him at Gath.*v*

I

2 Have mercy on me, God,
  for I am treated harshly;
  attackers press me all the day.
3 My foes treat me harshly all the day;
  yes, many are my attackers.
  O Most High, 4 when I am afraid,
  in you I place my trust.
5 God, I praise your promise;
  in you I trust, I do not fear.*w*
  What can mere flesh do to me?*x*

II

6 All the day they foil my plans;
  their every thought is of evil against me.
7 They hide together in ambush;
  they watch my every step;
  they lie in wait for my life.*y*
8 They are evil; watch them, God!

Ps 56: Beset physically (2-3) and psychologically (6-7), the psalmist maintains a firm confidence in God (5. 9-10). Nothing will prevent the psalmist from keeping the vow to give thanks for God's gift of life (13-14). A refrain (5. 11-12) divides the psalm in two equal parts.

56, 1: **Yonath elem rehoqim:** Hebrew words probably designating the melody to which the psalm was to be sung.

k: Ps 11, 1. *l:* Jer 9, 1; Rv 12, 6. *m:* Jer 5, 1; 6, 6; Ez 22, 2; Hb 1, 3; Zep 3, 1. *n:* Ps 41, 10; Jer 9, 3; Mt 26, 21-24 par. *o:* Ps 49, 15; Nm 16, 33; Prv 1, 2; Is 5, 14. *p:* Dn 6, 11. *q:* Pss 29, 10; 93, 2; Ba~ 3, 3. *r:* Pss 12, 3; 28, 3; 57, 5; 62, 5; 64, 4; Prv 26, 24-28; Jer 9,7. *s:* Ps 37, 5; Prv 3, 5; 16, 3; 1 Pt 5, 7. *t:* Pss 28, 1; 30, 4; 40, 3; 88, 5; 143, 7; Prv 1, 12; Jon 2, 7. *u:* Pss 25, 2; 56, 4; 130, 5. *v:* 1 Sm 21, 10. *w:* Ps 130, 5. *x:* Ps 118, 6; Heb 13, 6. *y:* Ps 140 5-6.

Cast the nations down in your anger!
9 My wanderings you have noted;
  are my tears not stored in your vial,*
  recorded in your book?z
10 My foes turn back when I call on you.
  This I know: God is on my side.
11 God, I praise your promise;
12   in you I trust, I do not fear.
  What can mere mortals do to me?

III

13 I have made vows to you, God;
  with offerings I will fulfill them,a
14 Once you have snatched me from death,
  kept my feet from stumbling,
  That I may walk before God
  in the light of the living.

See RG
175

PSALM 57*

Confident Prayer for Deliverance

1 For the director. Do not destroy.* A *miktam*
  of David, when he fled from Saul into
  a cave.b

I

2 Have mercy on me, God,
  have mercy on me.
  In you I seek shelter.
  In the shadow of your wings* I seek shelter
  till harm pass by.c
3 I call to God Most High,
  to God who provides for me.
4 May God send help from heaven to save
  me,
  shame those who trample upon me.
  May God send fidelity and love. *Selah*

5 I must lie down in the midst of lions
  hungry for human prey.d
  Their teeth are spears and arrows;
  their tongue, a sharpened sword.e
6 Show yourself over the heavens, God;
  may your glory appear above all the
  earth.f

II

7 They have set a trap for my feet;
  my soul is bowed down;
  They have dug a pit before me.
  May they fall into it
    themselves!g   *Selah*
8 My heart is steadfast, God,
  my heart is steadfast.
  I will sing and chant praise.h
9 Awake, my soul;
  awake, lyre and harp!
  I will wake the dawn.i *
10 I will praise you among the peoples, Lord;
  I will chant your praise among the
  nations.j
11 For your love towers to the heavens;
  your faithfulness, to the skies.k
12 Show yourself over the heavens, God;
  may your glory appear above all the
  earth.

PSALM 58*

See RG
175

The Dethroning of Unjust Rulers

1 For the leader. Do not destroy.* A *miktam*
  of David.

I

2 Do you indeed pronounce justice, O gods;*

56, 9: Are my tears not stored in your vial: a unique saying in the Old Testament. The context suggests that the tears are saved because they are precious; God puts a high value on each of the psalmist's troubles.

Ps 57: Each of the two equal strophes contains a prayer for rescue from enemies, accompanied by joyful trust in God (2-5, 7-11). The refrain prays that God be manifested as saving (6, 12). Ps 108 is nearly identical to part of this psalm (57, 8-12 = 108, 2-6).

57, 1: Do not destroy: Probably the title of the melody to which the psalm was to be sung.

57, 2: The shadow of your wings: probably refers to the wings of the cherubim (powerful winged animals) whose wings spread over the ark in the inner chamber of the temple (1 Kgs 6, 23-28).

57, 9: I will wake the dawn: by a bold figure the psalmist imagines the sound of music and singing will waken a new day.

Ps 58: A lament expressing trust in God's power to dethrone

all powers obstructing divine rule of the world. First condemned are "the gods," the powers that were popularly imagined to control human destinies (2-3), then "the wicked," the human instruments of these forces (4-6). The psalmist prays God to prevent them from harming the just (7-10). The manifestation of justice will gladden the just; they will see that their God is with them (11-12). The psalm is less concerned with personal vengeance than with public vindication of God's justice now.

58, 1: Do not destroy: probably the title of the melody to which the psalm was to be sung.

58, 2: Gods: the Bible sometimes understands pagan gods to be lesser divine beings who are assigned by Israel's God to

z: Ps 10, 14; 2 Kgs 20, 5; Is 25, 8; Rv 7, 17. a: Nm 30, 3. b: 1 Sm 22, 1. c: Pss 17, 8; 36, 8. d: Pss 17, 11-12; 22, 22; 58, 7. e: Pss 11, 2; 64, 4. f: Ps 72, 19; Nm 14, 21. g: Pss 7, 15; 140, 5-6. h: Ps 108, 2. i: Jb 38, 12. j: Pss 9, 12; 18, 50. k: Pss 36, 6; 71, 19.

do you judge mortals fairly?[l]

3 No, you freely engage in crime;
your hands dispense violence to the
earth.

II

4 The wicked have been corrupt since
birth;
liars from the womb, they have gone
astray.

5 Their poison is like the poison of a
snake,*
like that of a serpent stopping its
ears,[m]

6 So as not to hear the voice of the
charmer
who casts such cunning spells.

III

7 O God, smash the teeth in their
mouths;
break the jaw-teeth of these lions,
LORD![n]

8 Make them vanish like water flowing
away;[o]
trodden down, let them wither like
grass.[p]

9 Let them dissolve like a snail that oozes
away,*
like an untimely birth that never sees
the sun.[q]

10 Suddenly, like brambles or thistles,
have the whirlwind snatch them
away.[r]

11 Then the just shall rejoice to see the
vengeance
and bathe their feet in the blood of the
wicked.[s]

12 Then it will be said:
"Truly there is a reward for the just;
there is a God who is judge on
earth!"

PSALM 59*

See RG
175

Complaint against
Bloodthirsty Enemies

1 For the director. Do not destroy.* A *miktam*
of David, when Saul sent people to watch
his house and kill him.[t]

I

2 Rescue me from my enemies, my God;
lift me out of reach of my foes.

3 Deliver me from evildoers;
from the bloodthirsty save me.

4 They have set an ambush for my life;
the powerful conspire against me.
For no offense or misdeed of mine,
LORD,

5 for no fault they hurry to take up arms.
Come near and see my plight!

6 You, LORD of hosts, are the God of
Israel!
Awake! Punish all the nations.
Have no mercy on these worthless
traitors.   *Selah*

7 Each evening they return,
growling like dogs, prowling the city.[u]

8 Their mouths pour out insult;
sharp words are on their lips.
They say: "Who is there to hear?"*

9 You, LORD, laugh at them;
you deride all the nations.[v]

10 My strength, for you I watch;
you, God, are my fortress, 11 my loving
God.

II

May God go before me,
and show me my fallen foes.

12 Slay them, God,
lest they deceive my people.
Shake them by your power;
Lord, our shield, bring them down.

rule the foreign nations. Here they are accused of injustice,
permitting the human judges under their patronage to abuse
the righteous. Cf Ps 82.

58, 5-6: The image is that of a poisonous snake that is controlled by the voice or piping of its trainer.

58, 9: A snail that oozes away: empty shells suggested
to ancients that snails melted away as they left a slimy
trail.

Ps 59: A lament in two parts (2-9. 11b-17), each ending in
a refrain (10. 18). Both parts alternate prayer for vindication
(2-3. 5b-6. 11b-14) with vivid depictions of the psalmist's enemies (4-5a. 7-8. 15-16). The near curse in 12-13 is not a

crude desire for revenge but a wish that God's just rule over
human affairs be recognized now.

59. 1: Do not destroy: probably the title of the melody to
which the psalm was to be sung.

59. 8: Who is there to hear?: a sample of the enemies'
godless reflection. The answer is that God hears their blasphemies.

l: Ps 82, 2; Dt 16, 19.   *m:* Pss 64, 4; 140, 3; Rom 3, 13.   *n:* Ps 3,
7.   *o:* Wis 16, 29.   *p:* Ps 37, 2.   *q:* Jb 3, 16.   *r:* Jb 21, 18; Hos
13, 3; Na 1, 10.   *s:* Ps 68, 24; Is 63, 1-6.   *t:* 1 Sm 19, 11.   *u:* Ps
55, 11.   *v:* Pss 2, 4; 37, 13; Wis 4, 18.

13 For the sinful words of their mouths
   and lips
   let them be caught in their pride.
   For the lies they have told under oath[w]
14   destroy them in anger,
   destroy till they are no more.
   Then people will know God rules over
   Jacob,
   yes, even to the ends of the
   earth.[x]   Selah
15 Each evening they return,
   growling like dogs, prowling the city.
16 They roam about as scavengers;
   if they are not filled, they howl.

III

17 But I shall sing of your strength,
   extol your love at dawn,
   For you are my fortress,
   my refuge in time of trouble.
18 My strength, your praise I will sing;
   you, God, are my fortress, my loving
   God.

PSALM 60[*]

See RG
175

Lament after Defeat in Battle

1 For the leader; according to "The Lily
   of . . . ." A *miktam* of David (for teaching),
2 when he fought against Aram-Naharaim
   and Aram-Zobah; and Joab, coming back,
   killed twelve thousand Edomites in the
   Valley of Salt.[y]

I

3 O God, you rejected us, broke our
   defenses;
   you were angry but now revive us.
4 You rocked the earth, split it open;[z]
   repair the cracks for it totters.
5 You made your people go through
   hardship,

made us stagger from the wine you
   gave us.[a]
6 Raise up a flag for those who revere you,
   a refuge for them out of
   bowshot.   Selah
7 Help with your right hand and answer us[*]
   that your loved ones may escape.

II

8 In the sanctuary God promised:
   "I will exult, will apportion Shechem;
   the valley of Succoth[*] I will measure
   out.[*]
9 Gilead is mine, mine is Manasseh;
   Ephraim is the helmet for my head,
   Judah, my own scepter.[*]
10 Moab is my washbowl;[*]
   upon Edom I cast my sandal.[b][*]
   I will triumph over Philistia."

III

11 Who will bring me to the fortified city?[*]
   Who will lead me into Edom?
12 Was it not you who rejected us, God?
   Do you no longer march with our
   armies?[c]
13 Give us aid against the foe;
   worthless is human help.
14 We will triumph with the help of God,
   who will trample down our foes.

PSALM 61[*]

See RG
175

Prayer of the King in
Time of Danger

1 For the leader; with stringed instruments.
   Of David.

I

2 Hear my cry, O God,
   listen to my prayer!
3 From the brink of Sheol[*] I call;
   my heart grows faint.

Ps 60: The community complains that God has let the enemy win the battle (3-5) and asks for an assurance of victory (6-7). In the oracle God affirms ownership of the land; the invasion of other nations is not permanent and will be reversed ultimately (8-10). With renewed confidence, the community resolves to fight again (11). The opening lament is picked up again (12-14), but this time with new awareness of God's power and human limitation.

60, 7-14: These verses occur again as the second half of Ps 108.

60, 8: I . . . will apportion . . . measure out: God lays claim to these places. **The valley of Succoth:** probably the lower stretch of the Jabbok valley.

60, 9: Judah, my own scepter: an allusion to the Testament of Jacob, Gn 49, 10.

60, 10: Moab is my washbowl: Moab borders the Dead

Sea, hence a metaphor for the country. **Upon Edom I cast my sandal:** an ancient legal gesture of taking possession of land.

60, 11: The fortified city: perhaps Bozrah, the fortified capital of Edom. Cf Is 34, 6; 63, 1; Am 1, 12.

Ps 61: A lament of the king who feels himself at the brink of death (3) and cries out for the strong and saving presence of God (3b-5). The king cites the prayer being made for him (7-8), and promises to give thanks to God.

61,3: Brink of Sheol: literally, "edge of the earth," "earth" being taken in its occasional meaning "the underworld." Cf Jon 2, 3.

w: Prv 12, 13; 18, 7.   x: Ps 83, 18-19; Ez 5, 13.   y: 2 Sm 8, 2. 3. 13; 1 Chr 18, 2. 3. 12.   z: Ps 75, 4; Is 24, 19.   a: Ps 75, 9; Is 51, 17. 21-22; Jer 25, 15.   b: Ru 4, 7-8.   c: Ps 44, 10.

Raise me up, set me on a rock,
4   for you are my refuge,
    a tower of strength against the foe.*d*
5 Then I will ever dwell in your tent,
    take refuge in the shelter of your
        wings.*e*   *Selah*

II

6 O God, when you accept my vows
    and hear the plea of those
    who revere your name in prayer:*
7 "Add to the days of the king's life;
    may his years be many generations;*f*
8 May he reign before God forever;*g*
    may your love and fidelity preserve
        him"—*h*
9 Then* I will sing your name forever,
    fulfill my vows day after day.

PSALM 62*

See RG
175

Trust in God Alone

1 For the leader; *'al Jeduthun.**
A psalm of David.

I

2 My soul rests in God alone,*i*
    from whom comes my salvation.
3 God alone is my rock and salvation,
    my secure height; I shall never fall.
4 How long will you set upon people,
    all of you beating them down,
As though they were a sagging fence
    or a battered wall?
5 Even from my place on high
    they plot to dislodge me.
They delight in lies;
    they bless with their mouths,
    but inwardly they curse.*j*   *Selah*

II

6 My soul, be at rest in God alone,
    from whom comes my hope.
7 God alone is my rock and my salvation,
    my secure height; I shall not fall.
8 My safety and glory are with God,*k*
    my strong rock and refuge.
9 Trust God at all times, my people!
    Pour out your hearts to God our
        refuge!   *Selah*

III

10 Mortals are a mere breath,
    the powerful but an illusion;*l*
On a balance they rise;*
    together they are lighter than air.
11 Do not trust in extortion;
    in plunder put no empty hope.
Though wealth increase,
    do not set your heart upon it.*m*
12 One thing God has said;
    two things* I have heard:*n*
Power belongs to God;
13   so too, Lord, does kindness,
And you render to each of us
    according to our deeds.*o*

PSALM 63*

Ardent Longing for God

See RG
175

1 A psalm of David, when he was in the
    wilderness of Judah.*p*

I

2 O God, you are my God—
    for you I long!
For you my body yearns;
    for you my soul thirsts,
Like a land parched, lifeless,

61, 6: In prayer: added for sense. Vv 7-8 express the plea of v 6.

61, 9: Then: Hebrew "just as," i.e., in accord with the vows referred to in v 6.

Ps 62: A song of trust displaying serenity from experiencing God's power (the refrains of 2-3 and 6-7) and anger toward unjust enemies (4-5). From the experience of being rescued, the psalmist can teach others to trust in God (10-13).

62, 1: 'Al Jeduthun: apparently the Hebrew name for the melody.

62, 10: On a balance they rise: precious objects were weighed by balancing two pans suspended from a beam. The lighter pan rises.

62, 12: One thing . . . two things: parallelism of numbers for the sake of variation, a common device in Semitic poetry. One should not literally add up the numbers. Cf Am 1, 3; Prv

6, 16-19; 30, 15. 18. 21.

Ps 63: A psalm expressing the intimate relationship between God and the worshiper. Separated from God (2), the psalmist longs for the divine life given in the temple (3-6), which is based on a close relationship with God (7-9). May all my enemies be destroyed and God's true worshipers continue in giving praise (10-12)!

---

d: Ps 46, 2.   *e:* Pss 17, 8; 36, 8; 57, 2.   *f:* Ps 21, 5.   *g.* Pss 72, 5; 89, 5. 30. 37.   *h:* Pss 85, 11; 89, 15. 25; Prv 20, 28.   *i:* 2-3. 6-7; Pss 18, 3; 31, 3-4; 42, 10; 118, 8; 146, 3.   *j:* Pss 12, 3. 28, 3; 55, 22; Prv 26, 24-25.   *k:* Ps 3, 3; Is 26, 4; 60, 19.   *l.* Pss 39, 6-7; 144, 4; Jb 7, 16; Wis 2, 5.   *m:* Jb 31, 25; Eccl 5, 9; Jer 17, 11; Mt 6, 19-21. 24.   *n:* Jb 40, 5.   *o:* Pss 28, 4; 31, 24; 2 Sm 3, 39; Jb 34, 11; Jer 17, 10; Mt 16, 27; Rom 2, 6; 2 Tm 4, 14.   *p:* 1 Sm 24.

and without water.*q*

3 So I look to you in the sanctuary
  to see your power and glory.
4 For your love is better than life;*
  my lips offer you worship!

II

5 I will bless you as long as I live;
  I will lift up my hands, calling on your
    name.
6 My soul shall savor the rich banquet of
    praise,
  with joyous lips my mouth shall honor
    you!
7 When I think of you upon my bed,
  through the night watches I will recall
8 That you indeed are my help,
  and in the shadow of your wings I
    shout for joy.*r*
9 My soul clings fast to you;
  your right hand upholds me.

III

10 But those who seek my life will come to
    ruin;
  they shall go down to the depths of the
    earth!
11 They shall be handed over to the sword
  and become the prey of jackals!
12 But the king shall rejoice in God;
  all who swear by the Lord* shall exult,
  for the mouths of liars will be shut!*s*

PSALM 64*

Treacherous Conspirators
Punished by God

1 For the leader. A psalm of David.

I

2 O God, hear my anguished voice;
  from the foes I dread protect my
    life.

3 Hide me from the malicious crowd,
  the mob of evildoers.
4 They sharpen their tongues like
    swords,
  ready their bows for arrows of poison
    words.*t*
5 They shoot at the innocent from
    ambush,
  shoot without risk, catch them
    unawares.*
6 They resolve on their wicked plan;
  they conspire to set snares;
  they say: "Who will see us?"
7 They devise wicked schemes,
  conceal the schemes they devise;
  the designs of their hearts are
    hidden.*u*

II

8 But God will shoot arrows at them
  and strike them unawares.*v*
9 They will be brought down by their own
    tongues;
  all who see them will shake their
    heads.*w*
10 Then all will fear and proclaim God's
    deed,
  pondering what has been done.
11 The just will rejoice and take refuge in
    the Lord;
  all the upright will glory in their God.*x*

PSALM 65*

Thanksgiving for God's
Blessings

1 For the leader. A psalm of David. A song.

I

2 To you we owe our hymn of praise,
  O God on Zion;
  To you our vows* must be fulfilled,

63, 4: For your love is better than life: only here in the
Old Testament is anything prized above life—in this case
God's love.

63, 12: All who swear by the Lord: to swear by a particular god meant that one was a worshiper of that god (Is 45,
23; 48, 1; Zep 1, 5).

Ps 64: A lament of a person overwhelmed by the malice of
the wicked who are depicted in the psalms as the enemies of
the righteous (2-7). When people see God bringing upon the
wicked the evil they intended against others, they will know
who is the true ruler of the world (8-10). The final verse is a
vow of praise (11).

64, 5: Catch them unawares: literally, "suddenly," i.e.,

"unexpectedly."

Ps 65: The community, aware of its unworthiness (3-4),
gives thanks for divine bounty (5), a bounty resulting from
God's creation victory (6-9). At God's touch the earth comes
alive with vegetation and flocks (10-14).

65, 2: Vows: the Israelites were accustomed to promising
sacrifices in the temple if their prayers were heard.

q: Pss 42, 2; 143, 6; Is 26, 9.   *r:* Pss 17, 8; 36, 8.   *s:* Ps 107, 42.
t: Pss 11, 2; 37, 14; 55, 22; 57, 5.   *u:* Ps 140, 3; Prv 6, 14.   *v:* Pss
7, 13-14; 38, 3; Dt 32, 42.   *w:* Pss 5, 11; 44, 14; 52, 6.   *x:* Pss
36, 8; 57, 2.

The beginning of Psalm 65 celebrates God and the temple, the place where vows are paid (vv. 2–5). The psalmist is thankful for the privilege of entering the temple—that is, coming into God's presence—to pay his vow (present an offering). The payment is made possible by the generous harvest that God has provided. The vow may have been to bring a special offering for a good harvest. The body of the psalm praises God for his power over the sources of water and his beneficence in providing water for irrigation. It is possible that this psalm was sung during Sukkoth, the Feast of Tabernacles, which marks the end of the summer harvest and the beginning of the rainy season. In post-biblical times it featured prayers for rain for the coming season.

3   you who hear our prayers.
    To you all flesh must come^y *
4   with its burden of wicked deeds.
    We are overcome by our sins;
      only you can pardon them.^{z}
5 Happy the chosen ones you bring
    to dwell in your courts.
 May we be filled with the good things of
      your house,
    the blessings of your holy temple!

II

6 You answer us with awesome deeds* of
      justice,
    O God our savior,
 The hope of all the ends of the
      earth
    and of far distant islands.^{a}
7 You are robed in power,
    you set up the mountains by your
      might.
8 You still the roaring of the seas,^{b}
    the roaring of their waves,
    the tumult of the peoples.^{c}
9 Distant peoples stand in awe of your
      marvels;
    east and west you make resound with
      joy.
10 You visit the earth and water it,*

make it abundantly fertile.^{d}
God's stream* is filled with water;
    with it you supply the world with grain.
Thus do you prepare the earth:
11   you drench plowed furrows,
    and level their ridges.
With showers you keep the ground soft,
    blessing its young sprouts.
12 You adorn the year with your bounty;
    your paths* drip with fruitful rain.
13 The untilled meadows also drip;
    the hills are robed with joy.
14 The pastures are clothed with flocks,
    the valleys blanketed with grain;
    they cheer and sing for joy.^{e}

PSALM 66*

See RG
176

Praise of God,
Israel's Deliverer

1 For the leader. A song; a psalm.

I

Shout joyfully to God, all you on earth;
2   sing of his glorious name;
    give him glorious praise.^{f}
3 Say to God: "How awesome your deeds!
    Before your great strength your
      enemies cringe.
4 All on earth fall in worship before you;^{g}

65, 3: **To you all flesh must come**: all must have recourse to God's mercy.

65, 6: **Awesome deeds**: the acts of creating—installing mountains, taming seas, restraining nations (7-8)—that are visible worldwide (6. 9).

65, 10-14: Apparently a description of the agricultural year, beginning with the first fall rains that soften the hard sun-baked soil (10-11).

65, 10: **God's stream**: the fertile waters of the earth derive from God's fertile waters in the heavenly world.

65, 12: **Paths**: probably the tracks of God's storm chariot dropping rain upon earth.

Ps 66: In the first part (1-12), the community praises

God for powerful acts for Israel, both in the past (the exodus from Egypt and the entry into the land [6]) and in the present (deliverance from a recent but unspecified calamity [8-12]). In the second part (13-20), an individual from the rescued community fulfills a vow to offer a sacrifice of thanksgiving. As often in thanksgivings, the rescued person steps forward to teach the community what God has done (16-20).

y: Is 66, 23. z: Pss 32, 1-2; 78, 38; Is 1, 18. a: Is 66, 19.
b: Pss 89, 10; 107, 29; Jb 38, 11; Mt 8, 26. c: Is 17, 12. d: Lv
26, 4; Is 30, 23. 25; Jl 2, 22-23. e: Is 44, 23. f: Ps 65, 14; Is 44,
23. g: 3-4: Ps 18, 45; Mi 7, 17.

they sing of you, sing of your name!"
         Selah

II

5 Come and see the works of God,*
  awesome in the deeds done for us.
6 He changed the sea to dry land;
  through the river they passed on foot.*h*
Therefore let us rejoice in him,
7   who rules by might forever,
Whose eyes are fixed upon the nations.
  Let no rebel rise to challenge!   *Selah*
8 Bless our God, you peoples;
  loudly sound his praise,
9 Who has kept us alive
  and not allowed our feet to slip.*i*
10 You tested us, O God,
  tried us as silver tried by fire.*j*
11 You led us into a snare;
  you bound us at the waist as captives.
12 You let captors set foot on our neck;*
  we went through fire and water;
  then you led us out to freedom.*k*

III

13 I will bring holocausts* to your house;
  to you I will fulfill my vows,
14 The vows my lips pronounced
  and my mouth spoke in distress.
15 Holocausts of fatlings I will offer you
  and burnt offerings of rams;
  I will sacrifice oxen and goats.   *Selah*
16 Come and hear, all you who fear God,
  while I recount what has been done for
  me.
17 I called to the Lord with my mouth;
  praise was upon my tongue.
18 Had I cherished evil in my heart,
  the Lord would not have heard.
19 But God did hear
  and listened to my voice in prayer.

20 Blessed be God, who did not refuse me
  the kindness I sought in prayer.

PSALM 67*

See RG 175

Harvest Thanks and Petition

1 For the leader; with stringed instruments.
  A psalm; a song.

I

2 May God be gracious to us* and bless us;
  may God's face shine upon us.*l*   *Selah*
3 So shall your rule be known upon the
    earth,
  your saving power among all the
    nations.*m*
4 May the peoples praise you, God;
  may all the peoples praise you!

II

5 May the nations be glad and shout for joy;
  for you govern the peoples justly,
  you guide the nations upon the
    earth.*n*   *Selah*
6 May the peoples praise you, God;
  may all the peoples praise you!

III

7 The earth has yielded its harvest;
  God, our God, blesses us.*o*
8 May God bless us still;
  that the ends of the earth may revere
    our God.

PSALM 68*

See RG 175-76

The Exodus and Conquest, Pledge of Future Help

1 For the leader. A psalm of David, a song.

I

2 God will arise for battle;*
  the enemy will be scattered;
  those who hate God will flee.*p*
3 The wind will disperse them like smoke;

66, 5-6: Cf the events described in Ex 14, 1—15, 21; Jos 3, 11—4, 24, and Ps 114.

66, 12: You let captors set foot on our neck: literally, "you let men mount our head." Conquerors placed their feet on the neck of their enemies as a sign of complete defeat. Cf Jos 10, 24. A ceremonial footstool of the Egyptian king Tutankhamen portrays bound and prostrate bodies of enemies ready for the king's feet on their heads, and one of Tutankhamen's ceremonial chariots depicts the king as a sphinx standing with paw atop the neck of an enemy.

66, 13: Holocausts: wholly burnt offerings. Cf Lv 1, 3-13; 6, 1-4; 22, 17-20.

Ps 67: A petition for a bountiful harvest (7), made in the

awareness that Israel's prosperity will persuade the nations to worship its God.

67, 2: May God be gracious to us: the people's petition echoes the blessing pronounced upon them by the priests. Cf Nm 6, 22-27.

Ps 68: The psalm is extremely difficult because the Hebrew text is badly preserved and the ceremony that it de-

---

h: Pss 74, 15; 114, 3; Ex 14, 21f; Jos 3, 14ff; Is 44, 27; 50, 2. *i:* Pss 91, 12; 121, 3; 1 Sm 2, 9; Prv 3, 23. *j:* Is 48, 10. *k:* Is 43, 2. *l:* Pss 4, 7; 31, 17; 44, 4; 80, 4; Dn 9, 17. *m:* Jer 33, 9. *n:* Ps 98, 9. *o:* Ps 85, 13; Lv 26, 4; Ez 34, 27; Hos 2, 23-24. *p:* Nm 10, 35.

as wax is melted by fire,
so the wicked will perish before God.*q*
4 Then the just will be glad;
they will rejoice before God;
they will celebrate with great joy.

II

5 Sing to God, praise the divine name;
exalt the rider of the clouds.*
Rejoice before this God
whose name is the LORD.*r*
6 Father of the fatherless, defender of
widows— *s*
this is the God whose abode is holy,
7 Who gives a home to the forsaken,
who leads prisoners out to prosperity,
while rebels live in the desert.*

III

8 God, when you went forth before your
people,*t*
when you marched through the
desert,   *Selah*
9 The earth quaked, the heavens shook,
before God, the One of Sinai,
before God, the God of Israel.
10 You claimed a land as your own, O God;
11   your people settled there.
There you poured abundant rains, God,
graciously given to the poor in their
need.

IV

12a The Lord announced the news of victory:*
13a   "The kings and their armies are in
desperate flight.*u*
12b All you people so numerous,
14a   will you stay by the sheepfolds?*v*
13b Every household will share the
booty,
14b   perhaps a dove sheathed with silver,
14c   its wings covered with yellow gold."
15 When the Almighty routed the kings
there,
the spoils were scattered like snow on
Zalmon.*

V

16 You high mountains of Bashan,
you rugged mountains of Bashan,
17 You rugged mountains, why look with
envy
at the mountain* where God has
chosen to dwell,
where the LORD resides forever?*w*
18 God's chariots were myriad, thousands
upon thousands;
from Sinai the Lord entered the holy
place.
19 You went up to its lofty height;
you took captives, received slaves as
tribute.*x*

scribes is uncertain. The translation assumes the psalm accompanied the early autumn Feast of Tabernacles (Sukkoth), which included a procession of the tribes (25-28). Israel was being oppressed by a foreign power, perhaps Egypt (31-32)—unless Egypt stands for any oppressor. The psalm may have been composed from segments of ancient poems, which would explain why the transitions are implied rather than explicitly stated. At any rate, v 2 is based on Nm 10, 35-36, and vv 8-9 are derived from Jgs 5, 4-5.

The argument develops in nine stanzas (each of three to five poetic lines): 1) confidence that God will destroy Israel's enemies (2-4); 2) call to praise God as savior (5-7); 3) God's initial rescue of Israel from Egypt (8), the Sinai encounter (9), and the settlement in Canaan (10-11) 4) the defeat of the Canaanite kings (12-15); 5) the taking of Jerusalem, where Israel's God will rule the world (16-19); 6) praise for God's past help and for the future interventions that will be modeled on the ancient exodus-conquest (20-24); 7) procession at the Feast of Tabernacles (25-28); 8) prayer that the defeated enemies bring tribute to the temple (29-32); 9) invitation for all kingdoms to praise Israel's God (33-36).

68, 2: The opening line alluding to Nm 10, 35 makes clear that God's assistance in the period of the exodus and conquest is the model and assurance of all future divine help.

68, 5: Exalt the rider of the clouds: God's intervention is

in the imagery of Canaanite myth in which the storm-god mounted the storm clouds to ride to battle. Such theophanies occur throughout the psalm: 2-3. 8-10. 12-15. 18-19. 22-24. 29-32. 34-35. See Dt 33, 26; Ps 18, 8-16; Is 19, 1.

68, 7: While rebels live in the desert: rebels must live in the arid desert, whereas God's people will live in the well-watered land (vv 8-11).

68, 12-15: The Hebrew text upon which the translation is based has apparently suffered dislocation and has been substantially rearranged for sense. The version of the defeat of the kings differs from that in the Book of Joshua, where the people play a significant role. Here God alone is responsible for the victory (though the actual battle is not described); Israel only gathers the spoils. God alone is the source of Israel's success; human effort is not important.

68, 15: Zalmon: generally taken as the name of a mountain where snow is visible in winter, perhaps to be located in the Golan Heights or in the mountains of Bashan or Hauran east of the Sea of Galilee.

68, 17: The mountain: Mount Zion, the site of the temple.

q: Ps 97, 5; Jdt 16, 15; Wis 5, 14; Mi 1, 4.   *r:* Pss 18, 10; 104, 3; Dt 33, 26; Is 19, 1.   *s:* 6-7: Pss 103, 6; 146, 7. 9; Ex 22, 20-22; Bar 6, 37.   *t:* 8-9: Pss 44, 10; 114, 4. 7; Jgs 5, 4-5; Heb 12, 26.
u: Jgs 5, 19. 22.   *v:* Jgs 5, 16.   *w:* Ps 132, 13-14; Ez 43, 7.
x: Ps 47, 8; Eph 4, 8-10.

No rebels can live in the presence of
God.

VI

20 Blessed be the Lord day by day,
God, our salvation, who carries
us.*y*   *Selah*
21 Our God is a God who saves;
escape from death is in the LORD
God's hands.
22 God will crush the skulls of the enemy,
the hairy heads of those who walk in
sin.*z*
23 The Lord has said:
"Even from Bashan I will fetch them,
fetch them even from the depths of the
sea.*
24 You will wash your feet in your enemy's
blood;
the tongues of your dogs will lap it up."*a*

VII

25 Your procession* comes into view,
O God,
your procession into the holy place,
my God and king.
26 The singers go first, the harpists follow;
in their midst girls sound the timbrels.*b*
27 In your choirs, bless God;
bless the LORD, you from Israel's
assemblies.
28 In the lead is Benjamin, few in number;
there the princes of Judah, a large
throng,
the princes of Zebulun, the princes of
Naphtali, too.*c*

VIII

29 Summon again, O God, your power,

the divine power you once showed for
us.
30 Show it from your temple on behalf of
Jerusalem,
that kings may bring you tribute.
31 Roar at the wild beast of the reeds,*
the herd of mighty bulls, the lords of
nations;
scatter the nations that delight in war.
32 Exact rich tribute from lower Egypt,*d*
from upper Egypt,* gold and silver;
make Ethiopia* extend its hands to God.*e*

IX

33 You kingdoms of the earth, sing to God;*f*
chant the praises of the Lord,   *Selah*
34 Who rides the heights of the ancient
heavens,
whose voice is thunder, mighty
thunder.
35 Confess the power of God,
whose majesty protects Israel,
whose power is in the sky.
36 Awesome is God in his holy place,
the God of Israel,
who gives power and strength to his
people.*g*
Blessed be God!

PSALM 69*

*A Cry of Anguish in
Great Distress*

See RG
175, 178

1 For the leader; according to "Lilies."*
Of David.

I

2 Save me, God,
for the waters* have reached my neck.*h*

**68, 23: Even from Bashan . . . from the depths of the
sea**: the heights and the depths, the farthest places where enemies might flee.

68, 25-28: Your procession: the procession renews God's
original taking up of residence on Zion, described in 16-19.

68, 31: The wild beast of the reeds: probably the Nile
crocodile, a symbol for Egypt; see 32 and Ez 29, 2-5.

68, 31-32: Lower Egypt is the delta area north of Cairo.
Upper Egypt is the Nile Valley from Cairo to Aswan.
Ethiopia is still further south.

Ps 69: A lament complaining of suffering in language both
metaphorical (2-3 and 15-16, the waters of chaos) and literal (4.
5. 9. 11-13, exhaustion, alienation from family and community,
false accusation). In the second part the psalmist prays with special emphasis that the enemies be punished for all to see (23-
29). Despite the pain, the psalmist does not lose hope that all be
set right, and promises public praise (30-37). The psalm, which

depicts the suffering of the innocent just person vividly, is cited
often by the New Testament especially in the passion accounts,
e.g., v 5 in Jn 15, 25; v 22 in Mk 15, 23. 36 and parallels and in
Jn 19, 29. The psalm prays not so much for personal vengeance
as for public vindication of God's justice. There was, at this
time, no belief in an afterlife where such vindication could take
place. Redress had to take place now, in the sight of all.

69, 1: "Lilies": apparently the name of the melody.

69, 2: Waters: the waters of chaos from which God created the world are a common metaphor for extreme distress.
Cf Pss 18, 5; 42, 8; 88, 8; Jon 2, 3-6.

y: Pss 34, 2; 145, 2; Is 46, 3-4; 63, 9.   *z*: Dt 32, 42.   *a*: Ps 58,
11; 1 Kgs 21, 19; 22, 38; Is 63, 1-6.   *b*: Pss 81, 2-3; 87, 7; 149, 3;
150, 3-5; 2 Sm 6, 5.   *c*: Is 8, 23.   *d*: Ez 29, 2ff.,   *e*: Is 18, 7; 45,
14.   *f*: Ps 138, 4.   *g*: Pss 28, 8; 29, 11.   *h*: Pss 18, 5; 93, 3-4; Jb
22, 11.

The gate of a city was the main public meeting place, where business and legal transactions took place. In Psalm 69, 13, those who "sit at the gate" are the leading officials of the city. At the other end of the spectrum, those who congregate publicly are the "drunkards."

³ I have sunk into the mire of the deep,
  where there is no foothold.
I have gone down to the watery depths;
  the flood overwhelms me.*i*
⁴ I am weary with crying out;
  my throat is parched.
My eyes have failed,
  looking for my God.*j*
⁵ More numerous than the hairs of my head
  are those who hate me without cause.*k*
Too many for my strength
  are my treacherous enemies.
Must I now restore
  what I did not steal?*

II

⁶ God, you know my folly;
  my faults are not hidden from you.
⁷ Let those who wait for you, LORD of
    hosts,
  not be shamed through me.
Let those who seek you, God of Israel,*l*
  not be disgraced through me.
⁸ For your sake I bear insult,
  shame covers my face.*m*
⁹ I have become an outcast to my kin,
  a stranger to my mother's children.*n*
¹⁰ Because zeal for your house consumes
    me,*
  I am scorned by those who scorn
    you.*o* *
¹¹ I have wept and fasted,*p*
  but this led only to scorn.
¹² I clothed myself in sackcloth;
  I became a byword for them.
¹³ They who sit at the gate gossip about me;
  drunkards make me the butt of their
    songs.

III

¹⁴ But I pray to you, LORD,
  for the time of your favor.
God, in your great kindness answer me
  with your constant help.*q*
¹⁵ Rescue me from the mire;*r*
  do not let me sink.
Rescue me from my enemies
  and from the watery depths.
¹⁶ Do not let the floodwaters overwhelm me,
  nor the deep swallow me,
  nor the mouth of the pit close over me.
¹⁷ Answer me, LORD, in your generous love;
  in your great mercy turn to me.
¹⁸ Do not hide your face from your servant;
  in my distress hasten to answer me.*s*
¹⁹ Come and ransom my life;
  because of my enemies redeem me.
²⁰ You know my reproach, my shame, my
    disgrace;
  before you stand all my foes.
²¹ Insult has broken my heart, and I am weak;
  I looked for compassion, but there was
    none,
  for comforters, but found none.*t*
²² Instead they put gall in my food;
  for my thirst they gave me vinegar.*u*

IV

²³ Make their own table a snare for them,
  a trap for their friends.*v*
²⁴ Make their eyes so dim they cannot see;
  keep their backs ever feeble.
²⁵ Pour out your wrath upon them;
  let the fury of your anger overtake
    them.
²⁶ Make their camp desolate,
  with none to dwell in their tents.*w*

69, 5: **What I did not steal**: the psalmist, falsely accused of theft, is being forced to make restitution.
69, 10: **Zeal for your house consumes me**: the psalmist's commitment to God's cause brings only opposition. Cf Jn 2, 17.
I am scorned by those who scorn you: Rom 15, 3 uses the verse as an example of Jesus' unselfishness.

i: Pss 40, 2; 124, 4-5. *j:* Pss 25, 15; 119, 82; 123, 2; 141, 8; Is 38, 14. *k:* Ps 40, 13; Lam 3, 52; Jn 15, 25. *l:* Ps 40, 17. *m:* Jer 15, 15. *n:* Jb 19, 13-15. *o:* Ps 119, 139; Jn 2, 17; Rom 15, 3. *p:* 11-13: Ps 109, 24-25; Jb 30, 9; Lam 3, 14. *q:* Is 49, 8. *r:* 15-16: Pss 28, 1; 30, 4; 32, 6; 40, 3; 88, 5; Prv 1, 12. *s:* Ps 102, 3; 143, 7. *t:* Lam 1, 2. *u:* Lam 3, 15; Mt 27, 34. 48; Mk 15, 23. *v:* Rom 11, 9-10. *w:* Acts 1, 20.

27 For they pursued the one you struck,
   added to the pain of the one you
   wounded.
28 Add that to their crimes;
   let them not attain to your reward.
29 Strike them from the book of the living;
   do not count them among the just!ˣ

V

30 But I am afflicted and in pain;
   let your saving help protect me, God,
31 That I may praise God's name in song*
   and glorify it with thanksgiving.
32 My song will please the LORD more than
   oxen,
   more than bullocks with horns and
   hooves:ʸ
33 "See, you lowly ones, and be glad;
   you who seek God, take heart!ᶻ
34 For the LORD hears the poor,
   does not spurn those in bondage.
35 Let the heavens and the earth sing praise,
   the seas and whatever moves in them!"

VI

36 God will rescue Zion,
   rebuild the cities of Judah.ᵃ
   God's servants shall dwell in the land
   and possess it;
37 it shall be the heritage of their
   descendants;
   those who love God's name shall
   dwell there.ᵇ

See RG
175

PSALM 70*

Prayer for Divine Help

1 For the leader; of David. For remembrance.

2 Graciously rescue me, God!ᶜ
   Come quickly to help me, LORD!ᵈ
3 Confound and put to shame
   those who seek my life.ᵉ

Turn back in disgrace
   those who desire my ruin.
4 Let those who say "Aha!"ᶠ
   turn back in their shame.
5 But may all who seek you
   rejoice and be glad in you.
   May those who long for your help
   always say, "God be glorified!"ᵍ
6 Here I am, afflicted and poor.
   God, come quickly!
   You are my help and deliverer.
   LORD, do not delay!

PSALM 71*

Prayer in Time of Old Age

See RG
175

I

1 In you, LORD, I take refuge;ʰ
   let me never be put to shame.ⁱ
2 In your justice rescue and deliver me;
   listen to me and save me!
3 Be my rock and refuge,
   my secure stronghold;
   for you are my rock and fortress.ʲ
4 My God, rescue me from the power of
   the wicked,
   from the clutches of the violent.ᵏ
5 You are my hope, Lord;
   my trust, GOD, from my youth.
6 On you I depend since birth;
   from my mother's womb you are my
   strength;ˡ
   my hope in you never wavers.
7 I have become a portent to many,*
   but you are my strong refuge!
8 My mouth shall be filled with your praise,
   shall sing your glory every day.

II

9 Do not cast me aside in my old age;
   as my strength fails, do not forsake me.
10 For my enemies speak against me;
   they watch and plot against me.ᵐ

69, 31: That I may praise God's name in song: the actual song is cited in 33-35, the word "praise" in 35 referring back to "praise" in 31.

Ps 70: A lament of a poor and afflicted person (6) who has no resource except God, and who cries out to be saved from the enemy. The psalm is almost identical to Ps 40, 14-18.

Ps 71: A lament of an old person (9. 18) whose afflictions are interpreted by enemies as a divine judgment (11). The first part of the psalm pleads for help (1-4) on the basis of a hope learned from a lifetime's experience of God; the second part describes the menace (9-13) yet remains buoyant (14-

16); the third develops the theme of hope and praise.

71, 7: A portent to many: the afflictions of the sufferer are taken as a manifestation of God's anger. Cf Dt 28, 46; Ps 31, 12.

x: Ps 139, 16; Ex 32, 32; Is 4, 3; Dn 12, 1; Mal 3, 16; Rv 3, 5. y: Pss 40, 7; 50, 8-9. 14; 51, 18; Is 1, 11-15; Hos 6, 6; Am 5, 21-22; Heb 10, 5-8. z: Pss 22, 27; 35, 27; 70, 5. a: Is 44, 26; Ez 36, 10. b: Ps 102, 29; Is 65, 9. c: 2-6: Ps 40, 14-18. d: Ps 71, 12. e: Ps 35, 4. 26. f: Ps 35, 21. 25. g: Ps 35, 27. h: 1-3: Ps 31, 2-4. i: Ps 25, 2. j: Ps 18, 3. k: Ps 140, 2. l: Ps 22, 11. m: Pss 3, 2; 22, 8.

[11] They say, "God has abandoned that one.
  Pursue, seize the wretch!
  No one will come to the rescue!"
[12] God, do not stand far from me;
  my God, hasten to help me.[n]
[13] Bring to a shameful end
    those who attack me;
  Cover with contempt and scorn
    those who seek my ruin.[o]
[14] I will always hope in you
  and add to all your praise.
[15] My mouth shall proclaim your just deeds,
    day after day your acts of deliverance,
  though I cannot number them all.[p]
[16] I will speak of the mighty works of the
      Lord;
  O GOD, I will tell of your singular
    justice.

III

[17] God, you have taught me from my youth;
  to this day I proclaim your wondrous
    deeds.
[18] Now that I am old and gray,[q]
  do not forsake me, God,
  That I may proclaim your might
    to all generations yet to come,[r]
  Your power [19] and justice, God,
    to the highest heaven.
  You have done great things;[s]
    O God, who is your equal?[t]
[20] You have sent me many bitter afflictions,
  but once more revive me.
  From the watery depths of the earth
    once more raise me up.
[21] Restore my honor;
  turn and comfort me,
[22] That I may praise you with the lyre
    for your faithfulness, my God,
  And sing to you with the harp,
    O Holy One of Israel!

[23] My lips will shout for joy as I sing your
    praise;
  my soul, too, which you have redeemed.
[24] Yes, my tongue shall recount
    your justice day by day.
  For those who sought my ruin
    will have been shamed and disgraced.

PSALM 72*

A Prayer for the King

| See RG 176 |

[1] Of Solomon.

I

O God, give your judgment to the king;
  your justice to the son of kings;[u] *
[2] That he may govern your people with
    justice,
  your oppressed with right judgment,[v]
[3] That the mountains may yield their
    bounty for the people,
  and the hills great abundance,[w]
[4] That he may defend the oppressed among
    the people,
  save the poor and crush the oppressor.

II

[5] May he live as long as the sun endures,
  like the moon, through all generations.[x]
[6] May he be like rain coming down upon
    the fields,
  like showers watering the earth,[y]
[7] That abundance may flourish in his days,
  great bounty, till the moon be no more.

III

[8] May he rule from sea to sea,
  from the river to the ends of the earth.[z] *
[9] May his foes kneel before him,
  his enemies lick the dust.[a]
[10] May the kings of Tarshish and the
    islands* bring tribute,
  the kings of Arabia and Seba* offer
    gifts.[b]

Ps 72: A royal psalm in which the Israelite king, as the representative of God, is the instrument of divine justice (1-4. 12-14) and blessing (5-7. 15-17) for the whole world. The king is human, giving only what he has received from God. Hence intercession must be made for him. The extravagant language is typical of oriental royal courts.

72, 1: The king . . . the son of kings: the crown prince is the king's son; the prayer envisages the dynasty.

72, 8: From sea to sea . . . the ends of the earth: the boundaries of the civilized world known at the time: from the Mediterranean Sea (the western sea) to the Persian Gulf (the eastern sea), and from the Euphrates (the river) to the islands

and lands of southwestern Europe, "the ends of the earth." The words may also have a mythic nuance—the earth surrounded by cosmic waters, hence everywhere.

72. 10: Tarshish and the islands: the far west (Ps 48, 6); **Arabia and Seba:** the far south (1 Kgs 10, 1).

n: Ps 22, 20. o: Pss 35, 4; 40, 15; 70, 3. p: Ps 35, 28. q: Is 46, 3-4. r: Pss 22, 31-32; 48, 14-15; 145, 4. s: Ps 72, 18. t: Ps 86, 8. u: Ps 99, 4; Jer 23, 5. v: Prv 31, 8-9. w: Is 52, 7; 55, 12. x: Ps 89, 37-38; Jer 31, 35. y: Dt 32, 2; Is 45, 8; Hos 6, 3. z: Dt 11, 24; Zec 9, 10. a: Is 49, 23; Mi 7, 17. b: Ps 68, 30; Is 60, 5-6; 1 Kgs 10, 1ff.

11 May all kings bow before him,
    all nations serve him.[c]
12 For he rescues the poor when they cry
    out,
    the oppressed who have no one to
    help.
13 He shows pity to the needy and the
    poor[d]
    and saves the lives of the poor.
14 From extortion and violence he frees
    them,
    for precious is their blood* in his
    sight.

IV

15 Long may he live, receiving gold from
    Arabia,
    prayed for without cease, blessed day
    by day.
16 May wheat abound in the land,
    flourish even on the mountain
    heights.
    May his fruit increase like Lebanon's,
    his wheat like the grasses of the
    land.[e] *
17 May his name be blessed forever;
    as long as the sun, may his name
    endure.[f]
    May the tribes of the earth give blessings
    with his name;*
    may all the nations regard him as
    favored.[g]

* * *

18 Blessed be the LORD, the God of Israel,*
    who alone does wonderful deeds.[h]
19 Blessed be his glorious name forever;
    may all the earth be filled with the
    LORD's glory.[i]
    Amen and amen.

20 The end of the psalms of David, son of
    Jesse.

Third Book: Psalms 73—89

PSALM 73 *

The Trial of the Just

1 A psalm of Asaph.

See RG
176

How good God is to the upright,
    the Lord, to those who are clean of
    heart!

I

2 But, as for me, I lost my balance;
    my feet all but slipped,
3 Because I was envious of the arrogant
    when I saw the prosperity of the
    wicked.[j]
4 For they suffer no pain;
    their bodies are healthy and sleek.
5 They are free of the burdens of life;
    they are not afflicted like others.
6 Thus pride adorns them as a necklace;
    violence clothes them as a robe.
7 Out of their stupidity comes sin;
    evil thoughts flood their hearts.[k]
8 They scoff and spout their malice;
    from on high they utter threats.[l]
9 They set their mouths against the heavens,*
    their tongues roam the earth.
10 So my people turn to them
    and drink deeply of their words.*
11 They say, "Does God really know?"
    "Does the Most High have any
    knowledge?"[m]
12 Such, then, are the wicked,
    always carefree, increasing their
    wealth.

72, 14: Their blood: cf Ps 116, 15.

72, 16: The translation of the difficult Hebrew is tentative.

72, 17: May the tribes of the earth give blessing with his name: an echo of the promise to the ancestors (Gn 12, 3; 26, 4; 28, 14), suggesting that the monarchy in Israel fulfilled the promise to Abraham, Isaac, and Jacob.

72, 18-19: A doxology marking the end of Book II of the Psalter.

Ps 73: The opening verse of this probing poem (cf Pss 37, 49) is actually the psalmist's hard-won conclusion from personal experience: God is just and good! The psalmist describes near loss of faith (2-3), occasioned by observing the wicked who blasphemed God with seeming impunity (4-12). Feeling abandoned despite personal righteousness, the psalmist could not bear the injustice until an experience of

God's nearness in the temple made clear how deluded the wicked were. Their sudden destruction shows their impermanence (13-20). The just can thus be confident, for, as the psalmist now knows, their security is from God (1. 23-28).

73, 9: They set their mouths against the heavens: in an image probably derived from mythic stories of half-divine giants, the monstrous speech of the wicked is likened to enormous jaws gaping wide, devouring everything in sight.

73, 10: The Hebrew is obscure.

---

c: Pss 47, 8.   d: Prv 31, 9.   e: Is 27, 6; Hos 14, 6-8; Am 9, 13.
f: Ps 21, 7.   g: Gn 12, 3; Zec 8, 13.   h: Pss 41, 14; 89, 53; 106,
48; 136, 4.   i: Ps 57, 5; Nm 14, 21.   j: Ps 37, 1; Jb 21, 13.   k: Jb
15, 27.   l: Ps 17, 10.   m: Ps 10, 11; Jb 22, 13.

II

¹³ Is it in vain that I have kept my heart
clean,
washed my hands in innocence?[n]
¹⁴ For I am afflicted day after day,
chastised every morning.
¹⁵ Had I thought, "I will speak as they do,"
I would have betrayed your people.
¹⁶ Though I tried to understand all this,
it was too difficult for me,
¹⁷ Till I entered the sanctuary of God
and came to understand their end.*

III

¹⁸ You set them, indeed, on a slippery
road;
you hurl them down to ruin.
¹⁹ How suddenly they are devastated;
undone by disasters forever!
²⁰ They are like a dream after waking,
Lord,
dismissed like shadows when you
arise.[o]

IV

²¹ Since my heart was embittered
and my soul deeply wounded,
²² I was stupid and could not understand;
I was like a brute beast in your
presence.
²³ Yet I am always with you;
you take hold of my right hand.[p]
²⁴ With your counsel you guide me,
and at the end receive me with honor.*
²⁵ Whom else have I in the heavens?
None beside you delights me on earth.
²⁶ Though my flesh and my heart fail,
God is the rock of my heart, my
portion forever.
²⁷ But those who are far from you perish;

you destroy those unfaithful to you.
²⁸ As for me, to be near God is my good,
to make the Lord GOD my refuge.
I shall declare all your works
in the gates of daughter Zion.

PSALM 74*

Prayer at the Destruction
of the Temple

¹ A *maskil* of Asaph.

I

Why, God, have you cast us off
forever?[q]*
Why does your anger burn against the
sheep of your pasture?[r]
² Remember your flock that you gathered
of old,
the tribe you redeemed as your very
own.
Remember Mount Zion where you
dwell.[s]
³ Turn your steps toward the utter ruins,
toward the sanctuary devastated by the
enemy.
⁴ Your foes roared triumphantly in your
shrine;
they set up their own tokens of victory.
⁵ They hacked away like foresters
gathering boughs,
swinging their axes in a thicket of
trees.
⁶ They smashed all your engraved work.
pounded it with hammer and pick.
⁷ They set your sanctuary on fire;
the abode of your name they razed and
profaned.[t]
⁸ They said in their hearts, "Destroy them
all!

73, 17: And came to understand their end: the psalmist
receives a double revelation in the temple: 1) the end of the
wicked comes unexpectedly (18-20); 2) God is with me.

73, 24: And at the end receive me with honor: a perhaps deliberately enigmatic verse. It is understood by some
commentators as reception into heavenly glory, hence the
traditional translation, "receive me into glory." The Hebrew
verb can indeed refer to mysterious divine elevation of a
righteous person into God's domain: Enoch in Gn 5, 24; Elijah in 2 Kgs 2, 11-12; the righteous psalmist in Ps 49, 16.
Personal resurrection in the Old Testament, however, is
clearly attested only in the second century B.C. The verse is
perhaps best left unspecified as a reference to God's nearness
and protection.

Ps 74: A communal lament sung when the enemy invaded

the temple; it would be especially appropriate at the destruction of Jerusalem in 587 B.C. Israel's God is urged to look
upon the ruined sanctuary and remember the congregation
who worshiped there (1-11). People and sanctuary are bound
together; an attack on Zion is an attack on Israel. In the second half of the poem, the community brings before God the
story of their origins—their creation (12-17)—in order to
move God to reenact that deed of creation now. Will God allow a lesser power to destroy the divine project (18-23)?

74, 1: Forever: the word implies that the disaster is already of long duration. Cf 74, 9 and note.

n: Ps 26, 6; Mal 3, 14. o: Jb 20, 8. p: Ps 121, 5. q: Pss 10, 1;
44, 24; 77, 8. r: Ps 80, 5. s: Pss 68, 17; 132, 13; Ex 15, 17; Jer
10, 15; 51, 19. t: Is 64, 10; Ps 79, 1.

Burn all the shrines of God in the land!"
⁹ Now we see no signs,*
  we have no prophets,ᵘ
  no one who knows how long.
¹⁰ How long, O God, shall the enemy jeer?ᵛ
  Shall the foe revile your name forever?
¹¹ Why draw back your right hand,
  why keep it idle beneath your cloak?

  II

¹² Yet you, God, are my king from of old,*
  winning victories throughout the earth.
¹³ You stirred up the sea in your might;ʷ
  you smashed the heads of the dragons
    on the waters.ˣ
¹⁴ You crushed the heads of Leviathan,ʸ
  tossed him for food to the sharks.
¹⁵ You opened up springs and torrents,
  brought dry land out of the primeval
    waters.
¹⁶ Yours the day and yours the night;
  you set the moon and sun in place.
¹⁷ You fixed all the limits of the earth;
  summer and winter you made.ᶻ
¹⁸ Remember how the enemy has jeered,
    O LORD,
  how a foolish people has reviled your
    name.
¹⁹ Do not surrender to beasts those who
    praise you;
  do not forget forever the life of your
    afflicted.
²⁰ Look to your covenant,
  for the land is filled with gloom;
  the pastures, with violence.
²¹ Let not the oppressed turn back in shame;
  may the poor and needy praise your
    name.

²² Arise, God, defend your cause;
  remember the constant jeers of the
    fools.
²³ Do not ignore the clamor of your foes,
  the unceasing uproar of your enemies.

PSALM 75*

God the Judge of the World

See RG 176

¹ For the leader. Do not destroy! A psalm of
    Asaph; a song.

  I

² We thank you, God, we give thanks;
  we call upon your name,
  declare your wonderful deeds.
  You said:*
³ "I will choose the time;
  I will judge fairly.
⁴ The earth and all its inhabitants will
    quake,
  but I have firmly set its pillars."ᵃ *Selah*

  II

⁵ So I say to the boastful: "Do not
    boast!"ᵇ
  to the wicked: "Do not raise your
    horns!"*
⁶ Do not raise your horns against heaven!
  Do not speak arrogantly against the
    Rock!"ᶜ
⁷ For judgment comes not from east or
    from west,
  not from the desert or from the
    mountains,ᵈ
⁸ But from God who decides,
  who brings some low and raises others
    high.ᵉ
⁹ Yes, a cup* is in the LORD's hand,
  foaming wine, fully spiced.*

74, 9: Now we see no signs: ancients often asked prophets to say for how long a divine punishment was to last. Cf 2 Sm 24, 13. Here no prophet has arisen to indicate the duration.

74, 12-17: Comparable Canaanite literature describes the storm-god's victory over all-encompassing Sea and its allies (dragons and Leviathan) and the subsequent peaceful arrangement of the universe, sometimes through the placement of paired cosmic elements (day and night, sun and moon). Cf Ps 89, 12-13. The psalm apparently equates the enemies attacking the temple with the destructive cosmic forces already tamed by God. Why then are those forces now raging untamed against your own people?

Ps 75: The psalmist gives thanks and rejoices (2. 10) for the direct intervention of God, which is promised in two oracles (3-4. 11). Expecting that divine intervention, the psalmist

warns evildoers to repent (5-9).

75, 2: You said: supplied for clarity here and in v 11. The translation assumes in both places that the psalmist is citing an oracle of God.

75, 5: Do not raise your horns!: the horn is the symbol of strength; to raise one's horn is to exalt one's own power as v 6 explains.

75, 9: A cup: "the cup of God's wrath" is the punishment inflicted on the wicked. Cf Is 51, 17; Jer 25, 15-29; 49, 12; Ez 23, 31-33. **Spiced**: literally, "a mixed drink"; spices or drugs were added to wine. Cf Prv 9, 2. 5.

---

u: Lam 2, 9. *v*: Ps 89, 47. *w*: Ps 89, 10. *x*: Is 51, 9-10. *y*: Jb 3, 8; 40, 25; Is 27, 1. *z*: 16-17: Gn 1. *a*: Pss 46, 3; 60, 4; 93, 1; 96, 10; 104, 5; 1 Sm 2, 8; Is 24, 19. *b*: 1 Sm 2, 3; Zec 2, 1-4. *c*: Jb 15, 25. *d*: Mt 24, 23-27. *e*: Jb 5, 11; 1 Sm 2, 7.

When God pours it out,
they will drain it even to the dregs;
all the wicked of the earth must
drink.*f*

[10] But I will rejoice forever;
I will sing praise to the God of Jacob,

[11] Who has said:
"I will break off all the horns of the
wicked,
but the horns of the just shall be lifted
up."*g*

See RG
175-76

PSALM 76*

God Defends Zion

[1] For the leader; a psalm with stringed
instruments. A song of Asaph.

I

[2] Renowned in Judah is God,*h*
whose name is great in Israel.

[3] On Salem* is God's tent, a shelter on Zion.

[4] There the flashing arrows were
shattered,
shield, sword, and weapons of war.*i*
Selah

II

[5] Terrible and awesome are you,
stronger than the ancient mountains.*

[6] Despoiled are the bold warriors;
they sleep their final sleep;
the hands of all the mighty have failed.*j*

[7] At your roar, O God of Jacob,
chariots and steeds lay still.

[8] So terrible and awesome are you;
who can stand before you and your
great anger?*k*

[9] From the heavens you pronounced
sentence;
the earth was terrified and reduced to
silence,

[10] When you arose, O God, for judgment
to deliver the afflicted of the
land.
Selah

[11] Even wrathful Edom praises you;
the remnant of Hamath* keeps your
feast.

III

[12] Make and keep vows to the LORD your
God.*l*
May all present bring gifts to this
awesome God,

[13] Who checks the pride of princes,
inspires awe among the kings of earth.

PSALM 77*

See RG
175

Confidence in God during
National Distress

[1] For the leader; 'al Jeduthun. A psalm
of Asaph.

I

[2] I cry aloud to God,
cry to God to hear me.

[3] On the day of my distress I seek the
Lord;
by night my hands are raised
unceasingly;*m*
I refuse to be consoled.

[4] When I think of God, I groan;
as I ponder, my spirit grows
faint.*n*
Selah

[5] My eyes cannot close in sleep;
I am troubled and cannot speak.

[6] I consider the days of old;
the years long past [7] I remember.*o*
In the night I meditate in my heart;
I ponder and my spirit broods:

[8] "Will the Lord reject us forever,*p*
never again show favor?

[9] Has God's love ceased forever?

Ps 76: A song glorifying Zion, the mountain of Jerusalem
where God destroyed Israel's enemies. Zion is thus the appropriate site to celebrate the victory (3-4), a victory described in parallel scenes (5-7. 8-11). Israel is invited to worship its powerful patron deity (12-13).

76, 3: Salem: an ancient name for Jerusalem, used here
perhaps on account of its allusion to the Hebrew word for
peace, *shalom*. Cf Gn 14, 18; Heb 7, 1-3.

76, 5: Ancient mountains: conjectural translation of a
difficult Hebrew phrase on the basis of Gn 49, 26. The mountains are part of the structure of the universe (Ps 89, 12-13).

76, 11: Edom . . . Hamath: conjectural translation. Israel's neighbors to the southeast and north.

Ps 77: A community lament in which the speaker ("I") describes the anguish of Israel at God's silence when its very existence is at stake (2-11). In response the speaker recites the
story of how God brought the people into existence (12-21).
The question is thus posed to God: Will you allow the people
you created to be destroyed?

f: Ps 60, 5; Jb 21, 20; Is 51, 17. 21-22; Jer 25, 15ff; Hb 2, 16.
g: Ps 92, 11. *h:* Hb 3, 2. *i:* Pss 46, 10; 122, 6-9. *j:* 2 Kgs 19,
35; Jer 51, 39; Na 3, 18. *k:* Dt 7, 21; 1 Sm 6, 20; Na 1, 6; Mal
3, 2. *l:* Nm 30, 3. *m:* Pss 50, 15; 88, 2. *n:* Jon 2, 8. *o:* Ps
143, 5; Dt 32, 7. *p:* 8-10: Pss 13, 2; 44, 24; 74, 1; 80, 5; 89, 47;
Lam 3, 31.

Has the promise failed for all ages?
[10] Has God forgotten mercy,
    in anger withheld compassion?" *Selah*
[11] I conclude:* "My sorrow is this,
    the right hand of the Most High has
    left us."*q*

II

[12] I will remember* the deeds of the LORD;
    yes, your wonders of old I will
    remember.*r*
[13] I will recite all your works;
    your exploits I will tell.
[14] Your way, O God, is holy;
    what god is as great as our God?*s*
[15] You alone are the God who did wonders;
    among the peoples you revealed your
    might.*t*
[16] With your arm you redeemed your
    people,
    the descendants of Jacob and
    Joseph.*u*   *Selah*
[17] The waters saw you, God;
    the waters saw you and lashed about,
    trembled even to their depths.*v*
[18] The clouds poured down their rains;
    the thunderheads rumbled;
    your arrows flashed back and forth.*w*
[19] The thunder of your chariot wheels
    resounded;
    your lightning lit up the world;
    the earth trembled and quaked.*x*
[20] Through the sea was your path;
    your way, through the mighty waters,
    though your footsteps were unseen.*y*
[21] You led your people like a flock
    under the care of Moses and Aaron.*z*

PSALM 78*

See RG
176

A New Beginning in Zion and David

[1] A *maskil* of Asaph.

I

Attend, my people, to my teaching;
    listen to the words of my mouth.
[2] I will open my mouth in story,*
    drawing lessons from of old.*a*
[3] We have heard them, we know them;
    our ancestors have recited them to us.*b*
[4] We do not keep them from our
    children;
    we recite them to the next generation,
The praiseworthy and mighty deeds of
    the LORD,
    the wonders that he performed.*c*
[5] God set up a decree in Jacob,
    established a law in Israel:*d*
What he commanded our ancestors,
    they were to teach their children;
[6] That the next generation might come to
    know,
    children yet to be born.*e*
In turn they were to recite them to their
    children,
[7] that they too might put their trust in
    God,
And not forget the works of God,
    keeping his commandments.
[8] They were not to be like their ancestors,
    a rebellious and defiant generation,*f*
A generation whose heart was not
    constant,*g*
    whose spirit was not faithful to God,

77, 11: I conclude: literally, "I said." The psalmist, after pondering the present distress and God's promises to Israel, has decided that God has forgotten the people.

77, 12: I will remember: the verb sometimes means to make present the great deeds of Israel's past by reciting them. Cf Pss 78, 42; 105, 5; 106, 7.

Ps 78: A recital of history to show that past generations did not respond to God's gracious deeds and were punished by God making the gift into a punishment. Will Israel now fail to appreciate God's new act—the choosing of Zion and of David? The tripartite introduction invites Israel to learn the lessons hidden in its traditions (1-4. 5-7. 8-11); each section ends with the mention of God's acts. There are two distinct narratives of approximately equal length: the wilderness events (12-39) and the movement from Egypt to Canaan (40-72). The structure of both is parallel: gracious act (12-16. 40-55), rebellion (17-20. 56-58), divine punishment (21-31. 59-64),

God's readiness to forgive and begin anew (32-39. 65-72). The psalm may reflect the reunification program of either King Hezekiah (late eighth century) or King Josiah (late seventh century) in that the Northern Kingdom (Ephraim, Joseph) is especially invited to accept Zion and the Davidic king.

78, 2: Story: Hebrew *mashal* literally means "comparison" and can signify a story with a hidden meaning. Mt 13, 35 cites the verse to explain Jesus' use of parables.

---

q: Ex 15, 6. 12; Pss 17, 7; 18, 36.   *r*: Ps 143, 5.   *s*: Ps 18, 31; Ex 15, 11.   *t*: Pss 86, 10; 89, 6.   *u*: Gn 46, 26-27; Neh 1, 10.   *v*: Pss 18, 16; 114, 3; Na 1, 4.   *w*: Pss 18, 14-15; 29; 144, 6; Jb 37, 3-4; Wis 5, 21; Hb 3, 10-11; Zec 9, 14.   *x*: Pss 18, 8; 97, 4; 99, 1; Ex 19, 16; Jgs 5, 4-5.   *y*: Neh 9, 11; Wis 14, 3; Is 51, 10; Hb 3, 15.   *z*: Ps 78, 52; Is 63, 11-14; Hos 12, 14; Mi 6, 4.   *a*: Ps 49, 5; Mt 13, 35.   *b*: Ps 44, 2.   *c*: Ex 10, 2; Dt 4, 9; Jb 8, 8.   *d*: Ps 147, 19; Dt 33, 4.   *e*: Ps 22, 31-32; Dt 4, 9; 6, 7.   *f*: Dt 31, 27; 32, 5.   *g*: Ps 95, 10.

⁹ Like the ranks of Ephraimite archers,*
   who retreated on the day of battle.
¹⁰ They did not keep God's covenant;
   they refused to walk by his law.
¹¹ They forgot his works,
   the wondrous deeds he had shown
   them.

II

A

¹² In the sight of their ancestors God did
   wonders,
   in the land of Egypt, the plain of
   Zoan.ʰ*
¹³ He split the sea and led them across,ⁱ
   piling up the waters rigid as walls.ʲ
¹⁴ God led them with a cloud by day,
   all night with the light of fire.ᵏ
¹⁵ He split rock in the desert,
   gave water to drink, abounding as the
   deep.ˡ
¹⁶ He made streams flow from crags,
   drew out rivers of water.

B

¹⁷ But they went on sinning against him,
   rebelling against the Most High in the
   desert.ᵐ
¹⁸ They tested God in their hearts,
   demanding the food they craved.ⁿ
¹⁹ They spoke against God, and said,
   "Can God spread a table in the
   desert?ᵒ
²⁰ True, when he struck the rock,
   water gushed forth,
   the wadis flooded.
   But can he also provide bread,
   give meat to his people?"

C

²¹ The LORD heard and grew angry;ᵖ
   fire blazed up against Jacob;
   anger flared up against Israel.
²² For they did not believe in God,
   did not trust in his saving power.

²³ So he commanded the skies above;*
   the doors of heaven he opened.
²⁴ God rained manna upon them for food:
   bread from heaven he gave them.�q
²⁵ All ate a meal fit for heroes;
   food he sent in abundance.
²⁶ He stirred up the east wind in the
   heavens;
   by his power God brought on the south
   wind.
²⁷ He rained meat upon them like dust,
   winged fowl like the sands of the sea,
²⁸ Brought them down in the midst of the
   camp,
   round about their tents.
²⁹ They ate and were well filled;
   he gave them what they had craved.
³⁰ But while they still wanted more,
   and the food was still in their
   mouths,
³¹ God's anger attacked them,
   killed their best warriors,
   laid low the youth of Israel.ʳ
³² In spite of all this they went on sinning.
   they did not believe in his wonders.

D

³³ God ended their days abruptly,
   their years in sudden death.
³⁴ When he slew them, they began to seek
   him;
   they again inquired of their God.ˢ
³⁵ They remembered* that God was their
   rock,
   God Most High, their redeemer.
³⁶ But they deceived him with their
   mouths,
   lied to him with their tongues.
³⁷ Their hearts were not constant toward
   him;
   they were not faithful to his covenant.ᵗ
³⁸ But God is merciful and forgave their
   sin;

78, 9: Ephraimite archers: Ephraim was the most important tribe of the Northern Kingdom. Its military defeat (here unspecified) demonstrates its infidelity to God, who otherwise would have protected it.

78, 12. 43: Zoan: a city on the arm of the Nile, a former capital of Egypt.

78, 23-31: On the manna and the quail, see Ex 16 and Nm 11. Unlike Ex 16, here both manna and quail are instruments of punishment, showing that a divine gift can become deadly because of Israel's apostasy.

78, 35: Remembered: invoked God publicly in worship. Their words were insincere (36).

---

h: Ps 106, 7.   i: 13-14: Ex 14-15; Ps 136, 13.   j: Ex 14, 22; 15, 8.   k: Ps 105, 39; Ex 13, 21; Wis 18, 3.   l: Pss 105, 41; 114 8; Ex 17, 1-7; Nm 20, 2-13; Dt 8, 15; Wis 11, 4; Is 48, 21.   m: Dt 9, 7; Ez 20, 13.   n: Ps 106, 14; Ex 16, 2-36.   o: Ps 23, 5.   p: 21f: Nm 11 Dt 32, 22.   q: Ps 105, 40; Ex 16, 4. 14; Dt 8, 3; Wis 16, 20; Jn 6, 31.   r: Nm 14, 29.   s: Dt 32, 15. 18; Is 26, 16.   t: Ps 95, 10; Is 29, 13.

he did not utterly destroy them.
Time and again he turned back his anger,
    unwilling to unleash all his rage.[u] *
[39] He was mindful that they were flesh,
    a breath that passes and does not return.

III

A

[40] How often they rebelled against God in
    the desert,
    grieved him in the wasteland.
[41] Again and again they tested God,
    provoked the Holy One of Israel.
[42] They did not remember his power,
    the day he redeemed them from the foe,[v]
[43] When he displayed his wonders in
    Egypt,*
    his marvels in the plain of Zoan.[w]
[44] God changed their rivers to blood;
    their streams they could not drink.
[45] He sent insects that devoured them,[x]
    frogs that destroyed them.
[46] He gave their harvest to the caterpillar,
    the fruits of their labor to the locust.
[47] He killed their vines with hail,[y]
    their sycamores with frost.
[48] He exposed their flocks to deadly hail,
    their cattle to lightning.[z]
[49] He unleashed against them his fiery
    breath,
    roar, fury, and distress,
    storming messengers of death.
[50] He cleared a path for his anger;
    he did not spare them from death;
    he delivered their beasts to the plague.
[51] He struck all the firstborn of Egypt,[a]
    love's first child in the tents of Ham.
[52] God led forth his people like sheep;
    he guided them through the desert like
    a flock.[b]
[53] He led them on secure and unafraid,
    but the sea enveloped their enemies.[c]
[54] He brought them to his holy land,

the mountain his right hand had won.[d]
[55] God drove out the nations before them,
    apportioned them a heritage by lot,
    settled the tribes of Israel in their tents.

B

[56] But they tested, rebelled against God
    Most High,
    his decrees they did not observe.
[57] They turned back, deceitful like their
    ancestors;
    they proved false like a bow with no
    tension.
[58] They enraged him with their high places;
    with their idols they goaded him.[e]

C

[59] God heard and grew angry;
    he rejected Israel completely.
[60] He forsook the shrine at Shiloh,[f] *
    the tent where he dwelt with humans.
[61] He gave up his might into captivity,
    his glorious ark into the hands of the
    foe.[g]
[62] God abandoned his people to the sword;
    he was enraged against his heritage.
[63] Fire consumed their young men;
    their young women heard no wedding
    songs.[h]
[64] Their priests fell by the sword;
    their widows made no lamentation.

D

[65] Then the Lord awoke as from sleep,
    like a warrior from the effects of wine.
[66] He put his enemies to flight;
    everlasting shame he dealt them.
[67] He rejected the tent of Joseph,
    chose not the tribe of Ephraim.
[68] God chose the tribe of Judah,*
    Mount Zion which he favored.[i]
[69] He built his shrine like the heavens,
    like the earth which he founded
    forever.
[70] He chose David his servant,

78, 38: God is always ready to forgive and begin anew, as in choosing Zion and David (65-72).

78, 43-55: Ex 7—12 records ten plagues. Here there are six divine attacks upon Egypt; the seventh climactic act is God's bringing Israel to the holy land.

78, 60: Shiloh: an important shrine in the north prior to Jerusalem. Despite its holy status, it was destroyed (60-64; cf Jer 7, 12. 14).

78, 68. 70: God's ultimate offer of mercy to the sinful helpless people is Zion and the Davidic king.

---

u: Ps 85, 4; Ex 32, 14; Is 48, 9; Ez 20, 22.   *v:* Ps 106, 21.   *w:* 43f; Pss 105, 27-36; 135, 9; Ex 7, 14—11, 10; 12, 29-36; Wis 16-18.
x: Ex 8, 17.   *y:* Wis 16, 16.   *z:* Ex 9, 23.   *a:* Pss 105, 36; 136, 10; Ex 12, 29.   *b:* Ps 77, 21.   *c:* Ex 14, 26-28.   *d:* Ex 15, 17.   *e:* Dt 32, 16. 21.   *f:* Jos 18, 1; 1 Sm 1, 3; Jer 7, 12; 26, 6.   *g:* 1 Sm 4, 11. 22.   *h:* Dt 32, 25; Jer 7, 34.   *i:* Pss 48, 2; 50, 2; Lam 2, 15.   *j:* Ps 89, 21; Ez 34, 23; 37, 24; 2 Chr 6, 6.

took him from the sheepfold.[j]

[71] From tending sheep God brought him,
to shepherd Jacob, his people,
Israel, his heritage.[k]

[72] He shepherded them with a pure heart;
with skilled hands he guided them.

PSALM 79[*]

See RG
175

A Prayer for Jerusalem

[1] A psalm of Asaph.

I

O God, the nations have invaded your
heritage;
they have defiled your holy temple,
have laid Jerusalem in ruins.[l]

[2] They have left the corpses of your
servants
as food for the birds of the heavens,
the flesh of your faithful for the beasts
of the earth.[m]

[3] They have spilled their blood like water
all around Jerusalem,
and no one is left to bury them.[n]

[4] We have become the reproach of our
neighbors,
the scorn and derision of those
around us.[o]

II

[5] How long, LORD? Will you be angry
forever?
Will your rage keep burning like
fire?[p]

[6] Pour out your wrath on nations that reject
you,
on kingdoms that do not call on your
name,[q]

[7] For they have devoured Jacob,
laid waste his home.

[8] Do not hold past iniquities against us;

may your compassion come quickly,
for we have been brought very low.[r]

III

[9] Help us, God our savior,
for the glory of your name.
Deliver us, pardon our sins
for your name's sake.[s]

[10] Why should the nations say,
"Where is their God?"[t]
Before our eyes make clear to the
nations
that you avenge the blood of your
servants.[u]

IV

[11] Let the groans of prisoners come before
you;
by your great power free those
doomed to death.[v]

[12] Lord, inflict on our neighbors sevenfold
the disgrace they inflicted on you.[w]

[13] Then we, your people, the sheep of your
pasture,
will give thanks to you forever;
through all ages we will declare your
praise.

PSALM 80[*]

Prayer to Restore God's
Vineyard

See RG
175

[1] For the leader; according to "Lilies."
Eduth.[*] A psalm of Asaph.

I

[2] Shepherd of Israel, listen,
guide of the flock of Joseph!
From your throne upon the cherubim
reveal yourself[x]

[3] to Ephraim, Benjamin, and
Manasseh.
Stir up your power, come to save us.

Ps 79: A communal lament complaining that the nations have defiled the temple and murdered the holy people, leaving their corpses unburied (1-4). The occasion is probably the destruction of Jerusalem by the Babylonian army in 587 B.C. The people ask how long the withdrawal of divine favor will last (5), pray for action now (6-7), and admit that their own sins have brought about the catastrophe (8-9). They seek to persuade God to act for reasons of honor: the nations who do not call upon the Name are running amok (6); the divine honor is compromised (1. 10. 12); God's own servants suffer (2-4. 11).

Ps 80: A community lament in time of military defeat. Using the familiar image of Israel as a vineyard, the people complain that God has broken down the wall protecting the once splendid vine brought from Egypt (9-14). They pray that God

will again turn to them and use the Davidic king to lead them to victory (15-20).

80, 1: Lilies . . . . Eduth: the first term is probably the title of the melody to which the psalm was to be sung; the second is unexplained.

k: 1 Sm 16, 11-13; 2 Sm 7, 8. l: 2 Kgs 25, 9-10; Lam 1, 10. m: Jer 7, 33. n: 1 Mc 7, 17; Jer 14, 16. o: Pss 44, 14; 80, 7; 123, 3-4; Jb 12, 4; Dn 9, 16; Zep 2, 8. p: Pss 13, 2; 44, 24; 89, 47; Dt 4, 24. q: Ps 14, 4; Jer 10, 25. r: Ps 142, 7. s: Ez 20, 44; 36, 22. t: Pss 42, 4; 115, 2; Jl 2, 17. u: Jl 4, 21. v: Ps 102, 21. w: Ps 89, 51-52. x: Pss 23, 1-3; 95, 7; 100, 3; Gn 48, 15; Ex 25, 22; 1 Sm 4, 4; 2 Sm 6, 2; Mi 7, 14.

4 O LORD of hosts, restore us;
Let your face shine upon us,
that we may be saved.[y]

II

5 LORD of hosts,
how long will you burn with anger
while your people pray?[z]
6 You have fed them the bread of tears,
made them drink tears in abundance.[a]
7 You have left us to be fought over by our
neighbors;
our enemies deride us.[b]
8 O LORD of hosts, restore us;
let your face shine upon us,
that we may be saved.

III

9 You brought a vine* out of Egypt;
you drove away the nations and
planted it.
10 You cleared the ground;
it took root and filled the land.
11 The mountains were covered by its
shadow,
the cedars of God by its branches.
12 It sent out boughs as far as the sea,*
shoots as far as the river.*
13 Why have you broken down the walls,
so that all who pass by pluck its fruit?[c]
14 The boar from the forest strips the vine;
the beast of the field feeds upon it.[d]
15 Turn again, LORD of hosts;
look down from heaven and see;
Attend to this vine,
16 the shoot your right hand has planted.
17 Those who would burn or cut it down—

may they perish at your rebuke.
18 May your help be with the man at your
right hand,
with the one* whom you once made
strong.
19 Then we will not withdraw from you;
revive us, and we will call on your
name.
20 LORD of hosts, restore us;
let your face shine upon us,
that we may be saved.

PSALM 81*

An Admonition to Fidelity

See RG
175

1 For the leader; "upon the *gittith*."*
Of Asaph.

I

2 Sing joyfully to God our strength;[e]
shout in triumph to the God of Jacob!
3 Take up a melody, sound the timbrel,
the sweet-sounding harp and lyre.
4 Blow the trumpet at the new moon,
at the full moon,* on our solemn
feast.[f]
5 For this is a law in Israel,
an edict of the God of Jacob,[g]
6 Who made it a decree for Joseph
when he came out of the land of Egypt.

II

I hear a new oracle:*
7 "I relieved their shoulders of the
burden;*
their hands put down the basket.[h] *
8 In distress you called and I rescued you;
unseen, I spoke to you in thunder;

80, 9: A vine: a frequent metaphor for Israel. Cf Is 5, 1-7; 27, 2-5; Jer 2, 21; Hos 10, 1; Mt 21, 33.

80, 12: The sea: the Mediterranean. **The river**: the Euphrates. Cf Gn 15, 18; 1 Kgs 5, 1. The terms may also have a mythic nuance—the seas that surround the earth; sea and river are sometimes paralleled in poetry.

80, 18: The man at your right hand ... the one: the Davidic king who will lead the army in battle.

Ps 81: At a pilgrimage feast, probably harvest in the fall, the people assemble in the temple in accord with the Sinai ordinances (2-6a). They hear a divine word (mediated by a temple speaker) telling how God rescued them from slavery in Egypt (7-9), gave them the fundamental commandment of fidelity (9-11), which would bring punishment if they refused to obey (12-13). But if Israel repents, God will be with them once again, bestowing protection and fertility (14-17).

81, 1: Upon the gittith: probably the title of the melody to which the psalm was to be sung or a muscial instrument.

81, 4: New moon . . . full moon: the pilgrimage feast of harvest began with a great assembly (Lv 23, 24; Nm 29, 1), used the new moon as a sign (Nm 29, 6), and included trumpets (Lv 23, 24).

81, 6: I hear a new oracle: literally, "a tongue I do not know I hear." A temple official speaks the word of God (6b-17), which is authoritative and unlike merely human words (cf Nm 24, 4. 16).

81, 7: I relieved their shoulders of the burden: literally, "his [Israel's] shoulder," hence the plural translation. A reference to the liberation of Israel from salvery in Egypt. **The basket**: for carrying clay to make bricks. Cf Ex 1, 14.

y: 4. 8. 20: Pss 4, 7; 31, 17; 67, 2; 85, 5; Nm 6, 25; Dn 9, 17. *z*: Pss 13, 2; 44, 24; 74, 1; 79, 5; 89, 47; Dt 4, 24. *a*: Pss 42, 4; 102, 10. *b*: Pss 44, 14; 79, 4; 123, 3-4; Jb 12, 4; Dn 9, 16; Zep 2, 8. *c*: Ps 89, 41. *d*: Hos 2, 14. *e*: Pss 43, 4; 68, 26; 149, 3; 150, 3-4; Jdt 16, 1. *f*: Lev 23, 24; Nm 29, 1. *g*: Ex 23, 14ff. *h*: Ex 1, 14; 6, 6.

At the waters of Meribah* I tested you
    and said:[i]   Selah
9 'Listen, my people, I give you warning!
    If only you will obey me, Israel![j]
10 There must be no foreign god among
    you;[k]*
    you must not worship an alien god.
11 I, the LORD, am your God,
    who brought you up from the land of
      Egypt.
    Open wide your mouth that I may fill
      it.'
12 But my people did not listen to my words;
    Israel did not obey me.
13 So I gave them over to hardness of heart;
    they followed their own designs.[l]
14 But even now if my people would listen,
    if Israel would walk in my paths,[m]
15 In a moment I would subdue their foes,
    against their enemies unleash my hand.[n]
16 Those who hate the LORD would tremble,
    their doom sealed forever.
17 But Israel I would feed with the finest
      wheat,
    satisfy them with honey from the
      rock."[o]

See RG 175-76

PSALM 82*

The Downfall of Unjust Gods

1 A psalm of Asaph.

I

God rises in the divine council,
    gives judgment in the midst of the
      gods.[p]
2 "How long will you judge unjustly

and favor the cause of the
    wicked?[q]   Selah
3 Defend the lowly and fatherless;
    render justice to the afflicted and needy.
4 Rescue the lowly and poor;
    deliver them from the hand of the
      wicked."[r]

II

5 The gods neither know nor understand,
    wandering about in darkness,
    and all the world's foundations shake.*
6 I declare: "Gods though you be,*
    offspring of the Most High all of you,
7 Yet like any mortal you shall die;
    like any prince you shall fall."
8 Arise, O God, judge the earth,*
    for yours are all the nations.

PSALM 83*

See RG 175-77

Prayer against a Hostile Alliance

1 A song; a psalm of Asaph.

I

2 God, do not be silent;
    God, be not still and unmoved![s]
3 See how your enemies rage;
    your foes proudly raise their heads.
4 They conspire against your people,
    plot against those you protect.[t]
5 They say, "Come, let us wipe out their
      nation;
    let Israel's name be mentioned no
      more!"
6 They scheme with one mind,
    in league against you:[u]

81, 8: Meribah: place of rebellion in the wilderness; cf Ex 17, 7; Nm 20, 13.

81, 10: There must be no foreign god among you: as in Pss 50 and 95, Israel is challenged to obey the first commandment of fidelity to God after the proclamation of the exodus.

Ps 82: As in Ps 58, the pagan gods are seen as subordinate divine beings to whom Israel's God had delegated oversight of the foreign countries in the beginning (Dt 32, 8-9 LXX). Now God arises in the heavenly assembly (1) to rebuke the unjust "gods" (2-4), who are stripped of divine status and reduced in rank to mortals (5-7). They are accused of misruling the earth by not upholding the poor. A short prayer for universal justice concludes the psalm (8).

82, 5: The gods are blind and unable to declare what is right. Their misrule shakes earth's foundations (cf Pss 11, 3; 75, 4), which God made firm in creation (Ps 96, 10).

82, 6: I declare: "Gods though you be": in Jn 10, 34 Jesus uses the verse to prove that those to whom the word of

God is addressed can fittingly be called "gods."

82, 8: Judge the earth: according to Dt 32, 8-9 LXX, Israel's God had originally assigned jurisdiction over the foreign nations to the subordinate deities, keeping Israel as a personal possession. Now God will directly take over the rulership of the whole world.

Ps 83: The community lament complains to God of the nations' attempts to wipe out the name of Israel (2-9). The psalmist sees all Israel's enemies throughout its history united in a conspiracy (3-9). May God destroy the current crop of enemies as the enemies of old were destroyed (10-13), and may they be pursued until they acknowledge the name of Israel's God (14-19).

---

i: Ps 95, 8; Ex 2, 23ff; 17, 7; 19, 16; Nm 20, 13; 27, 14. j: Ex 1, 14; 6, 6. k: 10-11: Ex 20, 2-6; Dt 5, 6-10. l: Jer 3, 17; 7, 24. m: Is 48, 18. n: Lv 26, 7-8. o: Ps 147, 14; Dt 32, 13-14. p: Is 3, 13-14. q: Ps 58, 2. r: Dt 1, 17. s: Pss 10, 1; 44, 24; 109, 1. t: Jer 11, 9. u: Ps 2, 2.

7 The tents of Ishmael and Edom,*
 the people of Moab and Hagar,[v] *
8 Gebal,* Ammon, and Amalek,[w]
 Philistia and the inhabitants of Tyre.[x]
9 Assyria, too, in league with them
 gives aid to the descendants of Lot.*
   Selah

II

10 Deal with them as with Midian;*
 as with Sisera and Jabin at the torrent
 Kishon,[y]
11 Those destroyed at Endor,
 who became dung for the ground.[z]
12 Make their nobles like Oreb and Zeeb,
 all their princes like Zebah and
 Zalmunna,
13 Who made a plan together,
 "Let us seize the pastures of God."
14 My God, turn them into withered grass,
 into chaff flying before the wind.[a]
15 As a fire raging through a forest,
 a flame setting mountains ablaze,[b]
16 Pursue them with your tempest;
 terrify them with your storm.[c]
17 Cover their faces with shame,
 till they pay you homage, LORD.
18 Let them be dismayed and shamed
 forever;
 let them perish in disgrace.
19 Show them you alone are the LORD,
 the Most High over all the earth.[d]

See RG 175

PSALM 84 *

Prayer of a Pilgrim to Jerusalem

1 For the leader; "upon the *gittith*." A psalm
 of the Korahites.

I

2 How lovely your dwelling,

O LORD of hosts![e]
3 My soul yearns and pines
 for the courts of the LORD.[f]
My heart and flesh cry out
 for the living God.
4 As the sparrow finds a home
 and the swallow a nest to settle her
 young,*
My home is by your altars,
 LORD of hosts, my king and my God![g]
5 Happy are those who dwell in your house!
 They never cease to praise you.   Selah

II

6 Happy are those who find refuge in you,
 whose hearts are set on pilgrim roads.
7 As they pass through the Baca valley,*
 they find spring water to drink.
Also from pools the Lord provides water
 for those who lose their way.
8 They pass through outer and inner wall
 and see the God of gods on Zion.

III

9 LORD of hosts, hear my prayer;
 listen, God of Jacob.   Selah
10 O God, look kindly on our shield;
 look upon the face of your anointed.[h] *

IV

11 Better one day in your courts
 than a thousand elsewhere.
Better the threshold of the house of my
 God
 than a home in the tents of the wicked.
12 For a sun and shield is the LORD God,
 bestowing all grace and glory.
The LORD withholds no good thing
 from those who walk without
 reproach.
13 O LORD of hosts,
 happy are those who trust in you!

83, 7-9: Apart from the Assyrians, all the nations listed here were neighbors of Israel. **The people of . . . Hagar:** a tribe of the desert regions east of **Ammon** and **Moab** (1 Chr 5, 10. 19-22). **Gebal** is the Phoenician city of Byblos or perhaps a mountain region south of the Dead Sea. **The descendants of Lot** are Moab and Edom (Gn 19, 36-38 and Dt 2, 9). These nations were never united against Israel in the same period; the psalm has lumped them all together.

83, 10-13: For the historical events, see Jgs 4—8.

Ps 84: Israelites celebrated three pilgrimage feasts in Jerusalem annually. The psalm expresses the sentiments of the pilgrims eager to enjoy the divine presence.

84, 4: The desire of a restless bird for a secure home is an image of the desire of a pilgrim for the secure house of God.

Cf Ps 42, 2-3, where the image for the desire of the pilgrim is the thirst of the deer for water.

84, 7: Baca valley: Hebrew obscure; probably a valley on the way to Jerusalem.

84, 10: Our shield . . . your anointed: the king had a role in the liturgical celebration. For the king as shield, cf Ps 89, 19.

v: Nm 20, 23; 1 Chr 5, 10. 19.   w: Ex 17, 8.   x: Jos 13, 2.   y: Ex 2, 15; Is 9, 3; 10, 26.   z: Jer 8, 2.   a: Pss 1, 4; 35, 5; 58, 10; Is 5, 24; 10, 17; 17, 13; 29, 5; Ez 21, 3.   b: Ps 50, 3.   c: Jb 25, 32; 27, 21.   d: Ps 97, 9; Dt 4, 39; Dn 3, 45.   e: Pss 43, 3-4; 122, 1.   f: Pss 42, 2-3; 63, 2-3; 143, 6; Is 26, 9.   g: Ps 5, 3.   h: Ps 89, 19.

See RG
175-76

PSALM 85*

Prayer for Divine Favor

[1] For the leader. A psalm of the Korahites.

I

[2] You once favored, LORD, your land,
restored the good fortune of Jacob.[i]

[3] You forgave the guilt of your people,
pardoned all their sins.   *Selah*

[4] You withdrew all your wrath,
turned back your burning anger.[j]

II

[5] Restore us once more, God our savior;
abandon your wrath against us.[k]

[6] Will you be angry with us forever,
drag out your anger for all generations?[l]

[7] Please give us life again,
that your people may rejoice in you.

[8] Show us, LORD, your love;
grant us your salvation.

III

[9] I will listen for the word of God;
surely the LORD will proclaim peace
To his people, to the faithful,
to those who trust in him.*

[10] Near indeed is salvation for the loyal;
prosperity will fill our land.

[11] Love and truth will meet;*
justice and peace will kiss.[m]

[12] Truth will spring from the earth;
justice will look down from heaven.[n]

[13] The LORD will surely grant abundance;
our land will yield its increase.[o]

[14] Prosperity will march before the LORD,
and good fortune will follow behind.

See RG
175-76

PSALM 86*

Prayer in Time of Distress

[1] A prayer of David.

I

Hear me, LORD, and answer me,
for I am poor and oppressed.

[2] Preserve my life, for I am loyal;
save your servant who trusts in you.

[3] You are my God; pity me, Lord;
to you I call all the day.

[4] Gladden the soul of your servant;
to you, Lord, I lift up my soul.[p]

[5] Lord, you are kind and forgiving,
most loving to all who call on you.[q]

[6] LORD, hear my prayer;
listen to my cry for help.[r]

[7] In this time of trouble I call,
for you will answer me.

II

[8] None among the gods can equal you,
O Lord;
nor can their deeds compare to yours.[s]

[9] All the nations you have made shall
come
to bow before you, Lord,
and give honor to your name.[t]

[10] For you are great and do wondrous
deeds;
and you alone are God.

III

[11] Teach me, LORD, your way
that I may walk in your truth,[u]
single-hearted and revering your
name.

[12] I will praise you with all my heart,
glorify your name forever, Lord my
God.

[13] Your love for me is great;
you have rescued me from the depths
of Sheol.[v]

[14] O God, the arrogant have risen against
me;
a ruthless band has sought my life;
to you they pay no heed.

[15] But you, Lord, are a merciful and
gracious God,

Ps 85: A national lament reminding God of past favors and forgiveness (2-4) and begging for forgiveness and grace now (5-8). A speaker represents the people who wait humbly with open hearts (9-10): God will be active on their behalf (11-14). The situation suggests the conditions of Judea during the early postexilic period, the fifth century B.C.; the thoughts are similar to those of postexilic prophets (Hg 1, 5-11; 2, 6-9).

85, 9: The prophet listens to God's revelation. Cf Hb 2, 1.
85, 11-14: Divine activity is personified as pairs of virtues.
Ps 86: An individual lament. The psalmist, "poor and op-

pressed" (1), "devoted" (2), "your servant" (2. 4. 16), "rescued from the depths of Sheol" (13), attacked by the ruthless (14), desires only God's protection (1-7. 11-17).

i: Pss 14, 7; 126, 4. j: Ps 78, 38; Ex 32, 14; Is 48, 9. k: Ps 80, 4. l: Pss 79, 5; 89, 47. m: Pss 89, 15; 97, 2. n: Is 45, 8. o: Ps 67, 7; Lv 26, 4; Ez 34, 27; Hos 2, 23-24; Zec 8, 12. p: Pss 25, 1; 143, 8. q: Jl 2, 13. r: Pss 5, 2; 130, 1-2. s: Pss 35, 10; 89, 9; Ex 15, 11; Dt 3, 24; Jer 10, 6. t: Ps 22, 28; Zec 14, 16; Rv 15, 4. u: Pss 25, 4; 26, 3; 27, 11; 119, 12. 35; 143, 8. 10. v: Pss 30, 4; 40, 3; Jon 2, 7.

Psalm 88 is a desperate complaint by a person who is mortally ill. Perhaps the complaint can be interpreted as symbolizing the national catastrophe, the destruction and exile (Sheol may represent the exile), which could potentially sever the connection between Israel and God. Prolonged thoughts of death dominate, with many synonyms for the place of the dead: Sheol, pit, grave, abyss, darkness. In the realm of the dead, humankind is cut off from God and completely forgotten; the sense of isolation and finality is overwhelming. The psalmist tries to remind God that it is to everyone's benefit if he escapes death: the dead cannot praise God. The psalm ends without hope or resolution; there is no expectation that God will cure the psalmist and no promise to praise God upon recovery.

slow to anger, most loving and true.[w]

16 Turn to me, have pity on me;
    give your strength to your servant;
    save this child of your handmaid.[x]

17 Give me a sign of your favor:
    make my enemies see, to their
        confusion,
    that you, LORD, help and comfort
        me.

See RG 175

PSALM 87[*]

Zion the True Birthplace of
Diaspora Pilgrims

1 A psalm of the Korahites. A song.

I

The LORD loves the city[y]
    founded on holy mountains,
2 Loves the gates[*] of Zion
    more than any dwelling in Jacob.
3 Glorious things are said of you,
    O city of God!   Selah

II

4 From Babylon and Egypt I count
    those who acknowledge the LORD.
Philistia, Ethiopia, Tyre,
    of them it can be said:
"This one was born there."
5 But of Zion it must be said:[*]
"They all were born here."[z]
The Most High confirms this;[a]

6 the LORD notes in the register of the
        peoples:
"This one was born here."[b]   Selah
7 So all sing in their festive dance:
"Within you is my true home."[c]

PSALM 88[*]

A Despairing Lament

See RG 175

1 A song; a psalm of the Korahites. For the
leader; according to Mahalath. For singing;
a maskil of Heman the Ezrahite.

I

2 LORD, my God, I call out by day;
    at night I cry aloud in your presence.[d]
3 Let my prayer come before you;
    incline your ear to my cry.[e]
4 For my soul is filled with troubles;[f][*]
    my life draws near to Sheol.
5 I am reckoned with those who go down
        to the pit;
    I am weak, without strength.
6 My couch is among the dead,
    with the slain who lie in the grave.
You remember them no more;
    they are cut off from your care.
7 You plunged me into the bottom of the pit,
    into the darkness of the abyss.
8 Your wrath lies heavy upon me;
    all your waves crash over me.[g]   Selah
9 Because of you my friends shun me;

Ps 87: A song of Zion, like Psalms 46, 48, 76, and 132. After the exile of the sixth century B.C., diaspora Jews from all over the world (4) made the long pilgrimage to Jerusalem, the city of God (1-3). Such Jews may have hailed from distant lands, but the psalm sees them as children of Zion (5-7). The original occasion may have been Pentecost, which always attracted a large number of diaspora Jews.

87, 2: The gates: the city itself, a common Hebrew idiom.

87, 5-6: The bond between the exile and the holy city was so strong as to override the exile's citizenship of lesser cities.

Ps 88: A lament in which the psalmist prays for rescue from

the alienation of approaching death. Each of the three stanzas begins with a call to God (2. 10b. 14) and complains of the death that separates one from God. The tone is persistently grim.

88, 4-8: In imagination the psalmist already experiences the alienation of Sheol.

w: Pss 103, 8; 130, 7; 145, 8; Ex 34, 6.   x: Pss 25, 16; 116, 16; Wis 9, 5.   y: 1-2: Pss 76, 2-3; 78, 68-69.   z: Gal 4, 26.   a: Ps 48, 9.   b: Is 4, 3.   c: Pss 68, 26; 149, 3.   d: Ps 77, 3.   e: Ps 119, 170.   f: 4-7: Pss 28, 1; 30, 4; 40, 3; 86, 13; 143, 7; Nm 16, 33; Jb 17, 1; Jon 2, 7.   g: Pss 18, 5; 32, 6; 42, 8; 69, 2; Jon 2, 4.

you make me loathsome to them;[h]
Caged in, I cannot escape;
[10]   my eyes grow dim from trouble.

II

All day I call on you, LORD;
I stretch out my hands to you.
[11] Do you work wonders for the dead?[*]
Do the shades arise and praise
you?[i]   *Selah*
[12] Is your love proclaimed in the grave,
your fidelity in the tomb?
[13] Are your marvels declared in the darkness,
your righteous deeds in the land of
oblivion?

III

[14] But I cry out to you, LORD;
in the morning my prayer comes
before you.
[15] Why do you reject me, LORD?
Why hide your face from me?
[16] I am mortally afflicted since youth;
lifeless, I suffer your terrible blows.
[17] Your wrath has swept over me;
your terrors have reduced me to
silence.[j]
[18] All the day they surge round like a flood;
from every side they close in on me.
[19] Because of you companions shun me;[k]
my only friend is darkness.

See RG 176

PSALM 89[*]

A Lament over God's Promise to David

[1] A *maskil* of Ethan the Ezrahite.

I

[2] The promises of the LORD I will sing
forever,[l]

proclaim your loyalty through all ages.
[3] For you said, "My love is established
forever;[*]
my loyalty will stand as long as the
heavens.
[4] I have made a covenant with my chosen
one;
I have sworn to David my servant:
[5] I will make your dynasty stand forever
and establish your throne through all
ages."[m]   *Selah*

II

[6] The heavens praise your marvels, LORD,
your loyalty in the assembly of the
holy ones.[n]
[7] Who in the skies ranks with the LORD?
Who is like the LORD among the
gods?[o] [*]
[8] A God dreaded in the council of the holy
ones,
greater and more awesome than all
who sit there!
[9] LORD, God of hosts, who is like you?
Mighty LORD, your loyalty is always
present.
[10] You rule the raging sea;[p]
you still its swelling waves.
[11] You crushed Rahab[*] with a mortal blow;
your strong arm scattered your foes.
[12] Yours are the heavens, yours the earth;
you founded the world and everything
in it.[q]
[13] Zaphon and Amanus[*] you created;
Tabor[*] and Hermon[*] rejoice in your
name.
[14] Mighty your arm, strong your hand,
your right hand is ever exalted.

88, 11-13: The psalmist seeks to persuade God to act out of concern for divine honor: the shades give you no worship, so keep me alive to offer you praise.

Ps 89: The community laments the defeat of the Davidic king, to whom God promised kingship as enduring as the heavens (2-5). The psalm narrates how God became king of the divine beings (6-9) and how the Davidic king became king of earthly kings (20-38). Since the defeat of the king calls into question God's promise, the community ardently prays God to be faithful to the original promise to David (39-52).

89, 3-5: David's dynasty is to be as long-lasting as the heavens, a statement reinforced by using the same verbs (establish, stand) both of the divine love and loyalty and of the Davidic dynasty and throne. Cf 29-30.

89, 7: The gods: literally, "the sons of gods," "the holy

ones" and "courtiers" of 6 and 8. These heavenly spirits are members of God's court.

89, 11: Rahab: a mythological sea monster whose name is used in the Bible mainly as a personification of primeval chaos. Cf Jb 9, 13; 26, 12; Ps 74, 13-14; Is 51, 9.

89, 13: Zaphon and Amanus: two sacred mountains in northern Syria. **Tabor:** a high hill in the valley of Jezreel in northern Israel. **Hermon:** a mountain in Lebanon, forming the southern spur of the Anti-Lebanon range.

h: Pss 38, 12; 79, 4; 80, 7; 123, 3-4; 142, 8; Jb 12, 4; 19, 13; Lam 3, 7; Dn 9, 16.   *i:* Pss 6, 6; 30, 10; 38, 18; 115, 17.   *j:* Jb 6, 4; 20, 25.   *k:* Jb 19, 13.   *l:* Is 63, 7.   *m:* Pss 61, 7-8; 132, 11; 2 Sm 7, 8-16.   *n:* Pss 29, 1; 82, 1; Jb 1, 6; 5, 1.   *o:* 7-9: Pss 35, 10; 86, 8; 113, 5; Ex 15, 11; Jer 10, 6.   *p:* 10-11: Pss 65, 8; 74, 13-15; 107, 29; Jb 7, 12; Is 51, 9-10.   *q:* Pss 24, 1-2; 50, 12; Dt 10, 14; 1 Cor 10, 26.

¹⁵ Justice and judgment are the foundation
  of your throne;
  love and loyalty march before you.^r
¹⁶ Happy the people who know you, LORD,
  who walk in the radiance of your face.
¹⁷ In your name they sing joyfully all the day;
  at your victory they raise the festal
  shout.^s
¹⁸ You are their majestic strength;
  by your favor our horn* is exalted.^t
¹⁹ Truly the LORD is our shield,
  the Holy One of Israel, our king!^u

III

²⁰ Once you spoke in vision;^v
  to your faithful ones you said:
  "I have set a leader over the warriors;
  I have raised up a hero from the army.
²¹ I have chosen David, my servant;
  with my holy oil I have anointed him.
²² My hand will be with him;^w
  my arm will make him strong.
²³ No enemy shall outwit him,
  nor shall the wicked defeat him.
²⁴ I will crush his foes before him,
  strike down those who hate him.
²⁵ My loyalty and love will be with him;
  through my name his horn will be
  exalted.
²⁶ I will set his hand upon the sea,
  his right hand upon the rivers.*
²⁷ He shall cry to me, 'You are my father,^x
  my God, the Rock that brings me
  victory!'
²⁸ I myself make him firstborn,
  Most High* over the kings of the earth.
²⁹ Forever I will maintain my love for him;^y
  my covenant with him stands firm.
³⁰ I will establish his dynasty forever,
  his throne as the days of the heavens.
³¹ If his descendants forsake my law,^z
  do not follow my decrees,

³² If they fail to observe my statutes,
  do not keep my commandments,
³³ I will punish their crime with a rod
  and their guilt with lashes.
³⁴ But I will not take my love from him,
  nor will I betray my bond of loyalty.^a
³⁵ I will not violate my covenant;
  the promise of my lips I will not alter.^b
³⁶ By my holiness I swore once for all:^c
  I will never be false to David.
³⁷ His dynasty will continue forever,^d
  his throne, like the sun before me.
³⁸ Like the moon it will stand eternal,
  forever firm like the sky!"*   *Selah*

IV

³⁹ But now you have rejected and spurned,^e
  been enraged at your anointed.
⁴⁰ You renounced the covenant with your
  servant,
  defiled his crown in the dust.
⁴¹ You broke down all his defenses,^f
  left his strongholds in ruins.
⁴² All who pass through seize plunder;
  his neighbors deride him.
⁴³ You have exalted the right hand of his
  foes,
  have gladdened all his enemies.^g
⁴⁴ You turned back his sharp sword,
  did not support him in battle.
⁴⁵ You brought to an end his splendor,
  hurled his throne to the ground.
⁴⁶ You cut short the days of his youth,
  covered him with shame.   *Selah*
⁴⁷ How long, LORD?
  Will you stay hidden forever?
  Must your wrath smolder like fire?^h
⁴⁸ Remember how brief is my life,
  how frail the race you created!ⁱ
⁴⁹ What mortal can live and not see death?
  Who can escape the power of
  Sheol?^j   *Selah*

89, 18. 25: Horn: a concrete noun for an abstract quality; horn is a symbol of strength.

89, 26: The sea . . . the rivers: geographically the limits of the Davidic Empire (the Mediterranean and the Euphrates); mythologically, the traditional forces of chaos. See note on v 11.

89, 28: Most High: a divine title, which is here extended to David as God's own king. Cf Ps 2, 7-9; Is 9, 5. As God rules over the members of the heavenly council (6-9), so David, God's surrogate, rules over earthly kings.

89, 37-38: Like the sun before me . . . like the sky: as enduring as the heavenly lights. Cf 2-5 and Ps 72, 5. 17.

r: Pss 85, 11-12; 97, 2.   *s:* Ps 47, 2; Zep 3, 14.   *t:* Pss 112, 9; 148, 14. *u:* Pss 47, 9; 96, 10; 97, 1; 99, 1; Is 6, 3.   *v:* 20-21: Pss 78, 70; 132, 11-12; 2 Sm 7, 4. 8-16; 1 Chr 17, 3. 7-14; Is 42, 1; Acts 13, 22   *w:* 22-25: 1 Sm 2, 9-10.   *x:* 27-28: Pss 2, 7; 110, 2-3; 2 Sm 7, 9. 14; Col 1, 15. 18; Rv 1, 5.   *y:* 29-30: Pss 18, 51; 61, 8; 144, 10; 2 Sm 7, 11; Is 55, 3.   *z:* 31-33: Lv 26, 14-33.   *a:* Ps 40, 12; Sir 47, 22.   *b:* Jer 33, 20-21.   *c:* Am 4, 2.   *d:* 37-38: Pss 61, 8; 72, 5; Sir 43, 6.   *e:* 39-47: Ps 44, 10-25.   *f:* 41-42: Ps 80, 13-14.   *g:* Lam 1, 5.   *h:* Pss 13, 2; 44, 25; 74, 10; 79, 5; Dt 4, 24.   *i:* Pss 39, 5-6; 62, 10; 90, 9-10; 144, 4; Jb 7, 6. 16; 14, 1. 5; Eccl 6, 12; Wis 2, 5.   *j:* Ps 90, 3.

⁵⁰ Where are your promises of old, Lord,
  the loyalty sworn to David?
⁵¹ Remember, Lord, the insults to your
    servants,
  how I bear all the slanders of the
    nations.ᵏ
⁵² Your enemies, Lᴏʀᴅ, insult your
    anointed;
  they insult my every endeavor.

* * *

⁵³ Blessed be the Lᴏʀᴅ forever! Amen and
  amen!ˡ *

Fourth Book: Psalms 90—106

PSALM 90 *

See RG 175

*God's Eternity and
Human Frailty*

¹ A prayer of Moses, the man of God.

I

Lord, you have been our refuge
  through all generations.
² Before the mountains were born,
  the earth and the world brought forth,
  from eternity to eternity you are
    God.ᵐ
⁴* A thousand years in your eyes
  are merely a yesterday,ⁿ
³ But humans you return to dust,
  saying, "Return,* you
    mortals!"ᵒ
⁴ᶜ Before a watch passes in the night,*
⁵   you have brought them to their end;ᵖ *
  They disappear like sleep at dawn;
    they are like grass that dies.
⁶ It sprouts green in the morning;

by evening it is dry and
  withered.�q *

II

⁷ Truly we are consumed by your
    anger,
  filled with terror by your wrath.
⁸ You have kept our faults before you,
  our hidden sins exposed to your
    sight.ʳ
⁹ Our life ebbs away under your
    wrath;ˢ
  our years end like a sigh.
¹⁰ Seventy is the sum of our years,
  or eighty, if we are strong;
Most of them are sorrow and toil;
  they pass quickly, we are all but
    gone.
¹¹ Who comprehends your terrible
    anger?
  Your wrath matches the fear it
    inspires.
¹² Teach us to count our days aright,
  that we may gain wisdom of heart.
¹³ Relent, O Lᴏʀᴅ! How long?
  Have pity on your servants!
¹⁴ Fill us at daybreak with your love,ᵗ
  that all our days we may sing for joy.
¹⁵ Make us glad as many days as you
    humbled us,
  for as many years as we have seen
    trouble.ᵘ
¹⁶ Show your deeds to your servants,
  your glory to their children.
¹⁷ May the favor of the Lord our God be
    ours.ᵛ
  Prosper the work of our hands!
  Prosper the work of our hands!

89, 53: The doxology at the end of the third book of the Psalms; it is not part of Ps 89.

Ps 90: A communal lament that describes only in general terms the cause of the community's distress. After confidently invoking God (1), the psalm turns to a complaint contrasting God's eternity with the brevity of human life (2-6) and sees in human suffering the punishment for sin (7-12). The psalm concludes with a plea for God's intervention (13-17).

90, 3: Return: one word of God is enough to return mortals to the dust from which they were created. Humans were created from earth in Gn 2, 7; 3, 19.

90, 4: The translation reverses the order of the difficult Hebrew verses 3 and 4 to get the probable original order. **A watch . . . in the night:** the night was divided into three sen-

try periods or watches. Cf Jgs 7, 19.

90, 5: You have brought them to their end: an interpretation of the unclear Hebrew.

90, 6: It is dry and withered: the transitory nature of the grass under the scorching sun was proverbial. Cf Ps 129, 6; Is 40, 6-8.

k: Ps 79, 12. l: Pss 41, 14; 72, 18; 106, 48. m: Pss 48, 15; 55, 20; 93, 2; 102, 13; Hb 1, 12. n: 2 Pt 3, 8. o: Pss 103, 14; 104, 29; 146, 4; Gn 3, 19; 1 Mc 2, 63; Jb 34, 14-15; Eccl 3, 20; 12, 7; Sir 40, 11. p: Ps 89, 48. q: Pss 37, 2; 102, 11; 103, 15-16; Jb 14, 1-2; Is 40, 6-8. r: Ps 109, 14-15; Hos 7, 2. s: 9-10: Pss 39, 5-7; 62, 10; 102, 24-25; 144, 4; Gn 6, 3; Jb 7, 6. 16; 14, 5; Prv 10, 27; Eccl 6, 12; Wis 2, 5; Sir 18, 8; Is 65, 20. t: Ps 17, 15. u: Nm 14, 34; Jer 31, 13. v: Ps 33, 22.

See RG 175

PSALM 91[*]

Security Under God's Protection

I

[1] You who dwell in the shelter of the Most
  High,[*]
  who abide in the shadow of the
  Almighty,[*]
[2] Say to the LORD, "My refuge and
  fortress,
  my God in whom I trust."[w]
[3] God will rescue you from the fowler's
  snare,
  from the destroying plague,
[4] Will shelter you with pinions,
  spread wings that you may take
  refuge;[x]
  God's faithfulness is a protecting
  shield.
[5] You shall not fear the terror of the night
  nor the arrow that flies by day,[y]
[6] Nor the pestilence that roams in
  darkness,
  nor the plague that ravages at noon.[z]
[7] Though a thousand fall at your side,
  ten thousand at your right hand,
  near you it shall not come.
[8] You need simply watch;
  the punishment of the wicked you will
  see.[a]
[9] You have the LORD for your refuge;
  you have made the Most High your
  stronghold.
[10] No evil shall befall you,
  no affliction come near your tent.[b]
[11] For God commands the angels[c] [*]
  to guard you in all your ways.[d]
[12] With their hands they shall support you,

lest you strike your foot against a
  stone.[e]
[13] You shall tread upon the asp and the
  viper,
  trample the lion and the dragon.[f]

II

[14] Whoever clings to me I will deliver;
  whoever knows my name I will set on
  high.[g]
[15] All who call upon me I will answer;[h]
  I will be with them in distress;[i]
  I will deliver them and give them
  honor.
[16] With length of days I will satisfy them
  and show them my saving power.[j]

PSALM 92[*]

A Hymn of Thanksgiving for God's Fidelity

See RG 175

[1] A psalm. A sabbath song.

I

[2] It is good to give thanks to the LORD,
  to sing praise to your name, Most
  High,[k]
[3] To proclaim your love in the morning,
  your faithfulness in the night,
[4] With the ten-stringed harp,
  with melody upon the lyre.[l]
[5] For you make me jubilant, LORD, by your
  deeds;
  at the works of your hands I shout for
  joy.

II

[6] How great are your works, LORD![m]
  How profound your purpose!
[7] A senseless person cannot know this;
  a fool cannot comprehend.
[8] Though the wicked flourish like grass
  and all sinners thrive,[n]

Ps 91: A prayer of someone who has taken refuge in the security of the temple (1-2). The psalmist is confident that God's presence will protect the people in every dangerous situation (3-13). The final verses are an oracle of salvation promising salvation to those who trust in God (14-16).

91, 1: The shelter of the Most High: basically "hiding place" but in the psalms a designation for the protected temple precincts. Cf Pss 27, 5; 31, 21; 61, 5. **The shadow of the Almighty:** literally, "the shadow of the wings of the Almighty." Cf Pss 17, 8; 36, 8; 57, 2; 63, 8. V 4 makes clear that the shadow is an image of the safety afforded by the outstretched wings of the cherubim in the holy of holies.

91, 11-12: The words are cited in Mt 4, 6; Lk 4, 10-11, as

Satan tempts Jesus in the desert.

Ps 92: A hymn of praise and thanks for God's faithful deeds (2-5). The wicked, deluded by their prosperity (6-9), are punished (10), whereas the psalmist has already experienced God's protection (11-16).

w: Pss 18, 3; 31, 3-4; 42, 10; 142, 6; 2 Sm 22, 3.   x: Pss 17, 8; 36, 8; 57, 2; 63, 8; Dt 32, 11; Ru 2, 12; Mt 23, 37.   y: Prv 3, 25; Song 3, 8.   z: Dt 32, 24.   a: Ps 92, 12.   b: Prv 12, 21; Dt 7, 15.   c: 11-12: Mt 4, 6; Lk 4, 10f.   d: Heb 1, 14.   e: Ps 121, 3; Prv 3, 23.   f: Is 11, 8; Lk 10, 19.   g: Pss 9, 11; 119, 132.   h: Jer 33, 3; Zec 13, 9.   i: Is 43, 2.   j: Prv 3, 2.   k: Pss 33, 1; 147, 1.   l: Pss 33, 2; 144, 9.   m: 6-7: Pss 131, 1; 139, 6. 17; Wis 13, 1; 17, 1.   n: Ps 37, 35.

They are destined for eternal
destruction;
⁹ for you, LORD, are forever on high.
¹⁰ Indeed your enemies, LORD,
indeed your enemies shall perish;
all sinners shall be scattered.ᵒ

III

¹¹ You have given me the strength of a wild
bull;ᵖ
you have poured rich oil upon me.�q
¹² My eyes look with glee on my wicked
enemies;
my ears delight in the fall of my foes.ʳ
¹³ The just shall flourish like the palm tree,
shall grow like a cedar of Lebanon.ˢ
¹⁴ Planted* in the house of the LORD,
they shall flourish in the courts of our
God.
¹⁵ They shall bear fruit even in old age,
always vigorous and sturdy,
¹⁶ As they proclaim: "The LORD is just;
our rock, in whom there is no wrong."ᵗ

PSALM 93*

See RG
175

God is a Mighty King

¹ The LORD is king,* robed with majesty;
the LORD is robed, girded with might.ᵘ
The world will surely stand in place,
never to be moved.ᵛ
² Your throne stands firm from of old;
you are from everlasting, LORD.ʷ
³ The flood* has raised up, LORD;
the flood has raised up its roar;
the flood has raised its pounding waves.

⁴ More powerful than the roar of many
waters,
more powerful than the breakers of the
sea,
powerful in the heavens is the LORD.
⁵ Your decrees are firmly established;
holiness belongs to your house, LORD,
for all the length of days.

PSALM 94*

See RG
175

*A Prayer for Deliverance
from the Wicked*

I

¹ LORD, avenging God,
avenging God, shine forth!ˣ
² Rise up, judge of the earth;
give the proud what they deserve.ʸ

II

³ How long, LORD, shall the wicked,
how long shall the wicked glory?ᶻ
⁴ How long will they mouth haughty
speeches,
go on boasting, all these evildoers?ᵃ
⁵ They crush your people, LORD,
torment your very own.
⁶ They kill the widow and alien;
the fatherless they murder.ᵇ
⁷ They say, "The LORD does not see;
the God of Jacob takes no notice."ᶜ

III

⁸ Understand, you stupid people!
You fools, when will you be wise?ᵈ
⁹ Does the one who shaped the ear not
hear?
The one who formed the eye not see?ᵉ

92, 14: Planted: the just are likened to trees growing in the sacred precincts of the temple, which is often seen as the source of life and fertility because of God's presence. Cf Ps 36, 9. 10; Ez 47, 1-12.

Ps 93: A hymn celebrating the kingship of God, who created the world (1-2) by defeating the sea (3-4). In the ancient myth that is alluded to here, Sea completely covered the land, making it impossible for the human community to live. Sea, or Flood, roars in anger against God, who is personified in the storm. God's utterances or decrees are given authority by the victory over Sea (5).

93, 1: The LORD is king: literally, "the LORD reigns." This psalm, and Pss 47 and 96—99, are sometimes called enthronement psalms. They may have been used in a special liturgy during which God's ascent to the throne was ritually reenacted. They have also been interpreted eschatologically, pointing to the coming of God as king at the end-time.

93, 3: The flood: the primordial sea was tamed by God in

the act of creation. It is a figure of chaos and rebellion. Cf Ps 46, 4.

Ps 94: A lament of an individual who is threatened by wicked people. The danger affects the whole community. Calling upon God as judge (1-2), the psalm complains about oppression of the holy community by people within (3-7). Bold declarations of faith follow: denunciation of evildoers (8-11) and assurance to the just (12-15). The psalm continues with further lament (16-19) and ends with strong confidence in God's response (20-23).

o: Pss 68, 1-2; 125, 5. *p:* Ps 75, 10; Dt 33, 17. *q:* Ps 23, 5. *r:* Ps 91, 8. *s:* Pss 1, 3; 52, 10; Jer 17, 8. *t:* Dt 32, 4. *u:* Pss 47, 8; 96, 10; 97, 1; 99, 1. *v:* Pss 75, 2-3; 104, 5. *w:* Pss 55, 20; 90, 2; 102, 13; Hb 1, 12. *x:* Na 1, 2. *y:* Jer 51, 56; Lam 3, 64. *z:* Pss 13, 2; 75, 5; Jer 12, 1. *a:* Ps 73; Mal 2, 17; 3, 14. *b:* Ex 22, 21-22; Dt 24, 17-22. *c:* Pss 10, 11; 64, 6; 73, 11; Jb 22, 13-14; Ez 9, 9. *d:* Prv 1, 22; 8, 5. *e:* Ex 4, 11; Prv 20, 12.

¹⁰ Does the one who guides nations not
    rebuke?
    The one who teaches humans not have
      knowledge?
¹¹ The LORD does know human plans;
    they are only puffs of air.*f*

IV

¹² Happy those whom you guide, LORD,*g*
    whom you teach by your instruction.
¹³ You give them rest from evil days,
    while a pit is being dug for the
      wicked.
¹⁴ You, LORD, will not forsake your people,
    nor abandon your very own.*h*
¹⁵ Judgment shall again be just,
    and all the upright of heart will
      follow it.

V

¹⁶ Who will rise up for me against the
    wicked?
    Who will stand up for me against
      evildoers?
¹⁷ If the LORD were not my help,
    I would long have been silent in the
      grave.*i*
¹⁸ When I say, "My foot is slipping,"
    your love, LORD, holds me up.*j*
¹⁹ When cares increase within me,
    your comfort gives me joy.

VI

²⁰ Can unjust judges be your allies,
    those who create burdens in the name
      of law,
²¹ Those who conspire against the just
    and condemn the innocent to death?
²² No, the LORD is my secure height,
    my God, the rock where I find refuge,
²³ Who will turn back their evil upon them*k*
    and destroy them for their wickedness.
    Surely the LORD our God will destroy
      them!*l*

PSALM 95[*]

See RG
176

*A Call to Praise and
Obedience*

I

¹ Come, let us sing joyfully to the LORD;
    cry out to the rock of our salvation.*m*
² Let us greet him with a song of praise,
    joyfully sing out our psalms.
³ For the LORD is the great God,
    the great king over all gods,*n*
⁴ Whose hand holds the depths of the earth;
    who owns the tops of the mountains.
⁵ The sea and dry land belong to God,
    who made them, formed them by hand.*o*

II

⁶ Enter, let us bow down in worship;
    let us kneel before the LORD who
      made us.
⁷ For this is our God,
    whose people we are,
    God's well-tended flock.*p*

III

Oh, that today you would hear his voice:*q*
⁸   Do not harden your hearts as at
      Meribah,[*]
    as on the day of Massah[*] in the desert.
⁹ There your ancestors tested me;
    they tried me though they had seen
      my works.*r*
¹⁰ Forty years I loathed that generation;
    I said: "This people's heart goes
      astray;
    they do not know my ways."*s*
¹¹ Therefore I swore in my anger:
    "They shall never enter my rest."[*]

PSALM 96[*]

See RG
175

God of the Universe

I

¹ Sing to the LORD a new song;*t*

Ps 95: Twice the psalm calls the people to praise and worship God (1-2. 6), the king of all creatures (3-5) and shepherd
of the flock (7ab). The last strophe warns the people to be
more faithful than were their ancestors in the journey to the
promised land (7c-11). This invitation to praise God regularly
opens the Church's official prayer, the Liturgy of the Hours.

95, 8: Meribah: literally, "contention"; the place where
the Israelites quarreled with God. **Massah:** "testing," the
place where they put God to the trial. Cf Ex 17, 7; Nm 20, 13.

95, 11: My rest: the promised land as in Dt 12, 9. Heb 4
applies the verse to the eternal rest of heaven.

Ps 96: A hymn inviting all humanity to praise the glories
of Israel's God (1-3), who is the sole God (4-6). To the just
ruler of all belongs worship (7-10); even inanimate creation

f: Ps 33, 15; 1 Cor 3, 20.   *g:* Ps 119, 71; Jb 5, 17.   *h:* 1 Sm 12,
22; Sir 47, 22.   *i:* Ps 115, 17.   *j:* Ps 145, 14.   *k:* Pss 7, 16; 9, 16;
35, 8; 57, 7; Prv 26, 27; Eccl 10, 8; Sir 27, 26.   *l:* Ps 107, 42.
m: Dt 32, 15.   *n:* Pss 47, 2; 135, 5.   *o:* Ps 24, 1-2.   *p:* Pss 23, 1-
3; 100, 3; Mi 7, 14.   *q:* 7c-11: Pss 81, 8; 106, 32; Heb 3, 7-11. 15;
4, 3. 5. 7.   *r:* Nm 14, 22; 20, 2-13; Dt 6, 16; 33, 8.   *s:* Ps 78, 8;
Nm 14, 34; Dt 32, 5.   *t:* Ps 98, 1; Is 42, 10.

sing to the LORD, all the earth.
² Sing to the LORD, bless his name;
announce his salvation day after day.
³ Tell God's glory among the nations;
among all peoples, God's marvelous
deeds.ᵘ

II

⁴ For great is the LORD and highly to be
praised,
to be feared above all gods.ᵛ *
⁵ For the gods of the nations all do
nothing,
but the LORD made the heavens.ʷ
⁶ Splendor and power go before him;
power and grandeur are in his holy
place.

III

⁷ Give to the LORD, you families of nations,
give to the LORD glory and might;
⁸ give to the LORD the glory due his
name!ˣ
Bring gifts and enter his courts;
⁹ bow down to the LORD, splendid in
holiness.
Tremble before God, all the earth;
¹⁰ say among the nations: The LORD is
king.ʸ
The world will surely stand fast, never to
be moved.
God rules the peoples with fairness.

IV

¹¹ Let the heavens be glad and the earth
rejoice;
let the sea and what fills it resound;ᶻ
¹² let the plains be joyful and all that is
in them.
Then let all the trees of the forest rejoice
¹³ before the LORD who comes,
who comes to govern the earth,ᵃ
To govern the world with justice

and the peoples with faithfulness.

PSALM 97*

The Divine Ruler of All

See RG
175

I

¹ The LORD is king; let the earth
rejoice;
let the many islands be glad.ᵇ
² Cloud and darkness surround the Lord;
justice and right are the foundation of
his throne.ᶜ
³ Fire goes before him;
everywhere it consumes the foes.
⁴ Lightning illumines the world;
the earth sees and trembles.ᵈ
⁵ The mountains melt like wax before the
LORD,
before the Lord of all the earth.ᵉ
⁶ The heavens proclaim God's justice;
all peoples see his glory.ᶠ

II

⁷ All who serve idols are put to shame,
who glory in worthless things;
all gods* bow down before you.ᵍ
⁸ Zion hears and is glad,
and the cities of Judah rejoice
because of your judgments,
O LORD.ʰ
⁹ You, LORD, are the Most High over all
the earth,ⁱ
exalted far above all gods.
¹⁰ The LORD loves those who hate evil,
protects the lives of the faithful,ʲ
rescues them from the hand of the
wicked.
¹¹ Light dawns for the just;
gladness, for the honest of heart.ᵏ
¹² Rejoice in the LORD, you just,
and praise his holy name.ˡ

is to offer praise (11-13). This psalm has numerous verbal and
thematic contacts with Is 40-55, as does Ps 98. Another version of the psalm is 1 Chr 16, 23-33.
  96, 4: For references to other gods, see comments on Pss
58 and 82.
  Ps 97: The hymn begins with God appearing in a storm, a
traditional picture of some ancient Near Eastern gods (1-6);
cf Ps 18, 8-16; Mi 1, 3-4; Hb 3, 3-15. Israel rejoices in the
overthrowing of idol worshipers and their gods (7-9) and the
rewarding of the faithful righteous (10-12).
  97, 7: All gods: divine beings thoroughly subordinate to

Israel's God. The Greek translates "angels," an interpretation
accepted by Heb 1, 6.

ᵘ: Pss 98, 4; 105, 1.   ᵛ: Pss 48, 2; 95, 3; 145, 3.   ʷ: Ps 97, 7; Is
40, 17; 1 Cor 8, 4.   ˣ: Ps 29, 2.   ʸ: Pss 75, 4; 93, 1.   ᶻ: Ps 98, 7.
ᵃ: Ps 98, 9.   ᵇ: Pss 75, 4; 93, 1; 96, 10.   ᶜ: Pss 85, 11; 89, 15; Ex
19, 6; Dt 4, 11; 5, 22; 1 Kgs 8, 12.   ᵈ: Pss 18, 8; 50, 3; 77, 18; 99,
1; Jgs 5, 4-5.   ᵉ: Jdt 16, 15; Mi 1, 4.   ᶠ: Ps 50, 6.   ᵍ: Ps 96, 5.
ʰ: Ps 48, 12.   ⁱ: Ps 83, 19.   ʲ: Ps 121, 7.   ᵏ: Ps 112, 4.   ˡ: Ps
30, 5.

See RG
175

PSALM 98*

The Coming of God

¹ A psalm.

I

Sing a new song to the LORD,
　who has done marvelous deeds,ᵐ
Whose right hand and holy arm*
　have won the victory.ⁿ
² The LORD has made his victory known;
　has revealed his triumph for the
　　nations to see,
³ Has remembered faithful love
　toward the house of Israel.
All the ends of the earth have seen
　the victory of our God.

II

⁴ Shout with joy to the LORD, all the
　earth;
　break into song; sing praise.
⁵ Sing praise to the LORD with the harp,
　with the harp and melodious song.
⁶ With trumpets and the sound of the horn
　shout with joy to the King, the LORD.ᵒ

III

⁷ Let the sea and what fills it resound,ᵖ
　the world and those who dwell there.
⁸ Let the rivers clap their hands,
　the mountains shout with them for joy,�q
⁹ Before the LORD who comes,
　who comes to govern the earth,ʳ
To govern the world with justice
　and the peoples with fairness.ˢ

See RG
175

PSALM 99*

The Holy King

I

¹ The LORD is king, the peoples tremble;

God is enthroned on the cherubim,*
　the earth quakes.ᵗ
² The LORD is great on Zion,
　exalted above all the peoples.
³ Let them praise your great and awesome
　　name:
　holy is God!ᵘ

II

⁴ O mighty king, lover of justice,
　you alone have established fairness;
　you have created just rule in Jacob.ᵛ
⁵ Exalt the LORD, our God;
　bow down before his footstool;ʷ*
　holy is God!

III

⁶ Moses and Aaron were among his priests,
　Samuel among those who called on
　　God's name;
　they called on the LORD, who
　　answered them.ˣ
⁷ From the pillar of cloud God spoke to
　　them;
　they kept the decrees, the law they
　　received.ʸ
⁸ O LORD, our God, you answered them;
　you were a forgiving God,
　though you punished their offenses.ᶻ
⁹ Exalt the LORD, our God;
　bow down before his holy mountain;
　holy is the LORD, our God.

PSALM 100*

Processional Hymn

See RG
175

¹ A psalm of thanksgiving.

Shout joyfully to the LORD, all you lands;
²　worship the LORD with cries of
　　gladness;

Ps 98: A hymn, similar to Ps 96, extolling God for Israel's victory (1-3). All nations (4-6) and even inanimate nature (7-8) are summoned to welcome God's coming to rule over the world (9).

98, 1: Marvelous deeds . . . victory: the conquest of all threats to the peaceful existence of Israel, depicted in the psalms variously as a cosmic force such as Sea, or nations bent on Israel's destruction, or evildoers seemingly triumphant. **Whose right hand and holy arm:** God is pictured as a powerful warrior.

Ps 99: A hymn to God as the king whose grandeur is most clearly seen on Mount Zion (2) and in the laws given to Israel (4). Israel is special because of God's word of justice, which was mediated by the revered speakers, Moses, Aaron, and Samuel (6-8). The poem is structured by the threefold statement that God is holy (3. 5. 9) and by the twice-repeated command to praise (5. 9).

99, 1: Enthroned on the cherubim: cherubim were

composite beings with animal and human features, common in ancient Near Eastern art. Two cherubim were placed on the ark (or box) of the covenant in the holy of holies. Upon them God was believed to dwell invisibly. Cf Ex 25, 20-22; 1 Sm 4, 4; 2 Sm 6, 2; Ps 80, 2.

99, 5: Footstool: a reference to the ark. Cf 1 Chr 28, 2; Ps 132, 7.

Ps 100: A hymn inviting the people to enter the temple courts with thank offerings for the God who created them.

m: Ps 96, 1; Is 42, 10.　n: Is 59, 16; 63, 5.　o: Ps 47, 6-7.　p: Ps 96, 11.　q: Is 44, 23; 55, 12.　r: Ps 96, 13.　s: Ps 67, 5.　t: Pss 18, 8-11; 80, 2; 93, 1; Ex 25, 22; 1 Sm 4, 4; 2 Sm 6, 2.　u: Is 6, 3. v: Pss 72, 1; 99, 4; Jer 23, 5.　w: Ps 132, 7.　x: Jer 15, 1.　y: Ex 33, 9; Nm 12, 5.　z: Ex 32, 11; Nm 20, 12.

come before him with joyful song.
³ Know that the LORD is God,
    our maker to whom we belong,
    whose people we are, God's well-
        tended flock.ᵃ *
⁴ Enter the temple gates with praise,
    its courts with thanksgiving.
Give thanks to God, bless his name;ᵇ
⁵   good indeed is the LORD,
Whose love endures forever,
    whose faithfulness lasts through every
        age.

See RG
176

PSALM 101 *

Norm of Life for Rulers

¹ A psalm of David.

I

I sing of love and justice;
    to you, LORD, I sing praise.
² I follow the way of integrity;ᶜ
    when will you come to me?
I act with integrity of heart
    within my royal court.ᵈ *
³ I do not allow into my presence
    anyone who speaks perversely.
Whoever acts shamefully I hate;
    no such person can be my friend.ᵉ
⁴ I shun the devious of heart;
    the wicked I do not tolerate.
⁵ Whoever slanders another in secret
    I reduce to silence.ᶠ
Haughty eyes and arrogant heartsᵍ
    I cannot endure.

II

⁶ I look to the faithful of the land; *
    they alone can be my companions.
Those who follow the way of integrity,ʰ

they alone can enter my service.
⁷ No one who practices deceit
    can hold a post in my court.
No one who speaks falsely
    can be among my advisors.ⁱ
⁸ Each morning* I clear the wicked from
        the land,*
    and rid the LORD's city of all evildoers.

PSALM 102 *

Prayer in Time of Distress

See RG
175

¹ The prayer of one afflicted and
wasting away whose anguish is poured out
before the LORD.

I

² LORD, hear my prayer;
    let my cry come to you.
³ Do not hide your face from me
    now that I am in distress.ʲ
Turn your ear to me;
    when I call, answer me quickly.
⁴ For my days vanish like smoke;ᵏ
    my bones burn away as in a furnace.
⁵ I am withered, dried up like grass,
    too wasted to eat my food.
⁶ From my loud groaning
    I become just skin and bones.
⁷ I am like a desert owl,
    like an owl among the ruins.
⁸ I lie awake and moan,
    like a lone sparrow on the roof.
⁹ All day long my enemies taunt me;
    in their rage, they make my name a
        curse.*
¹⁰ I eat ashes like bread,
    mingle my drink with tears.ˡ
¹¹ Because of your furious wrath,

100, 3: Although the people call on all the nations of the world to join in their hymn, they are conscious of being the chosen people of God.

Ps 101: The king, grateful at being God's chosen (1), promises to be a ruler after God's own heart (2-3), allowing into the royal service only the God-fearing (3-8).

101, 2: Within my royal court: the king promises to make his own household a model for Israel, banning all officials who abuse their power.

101, 6: I look to the faithful of the land: the king seeks companions only among those faithful to God.

101, 8: Each morning: the normal time for the administration of justice (2 Sm 15, 2; Jer 21, 12) and for the arrival of divine aid (Pss 59, 17; 143, 8; Is 33, 2). **I clear the wicked from the land:** the king, as God's servant, is responsible for seeing that divine justice is carried out.

Ps 102: A lament, one of the Penitential Psalms. The psalmist, experiencing psychic and bodily disintegration (4-12), cries out to God (1-3). In the temple precincts where God has promised to be present, the psalmist recalls God's venerable promises to save the poor (13-23). The final part (24-29) restates the original complaint and prayer, and emphasizes God's eternity.

102, 9: They make my name a curse: enemies use the psalmist's name in phrases such as, "May you be as wretched as this person!"

---

a: Pss 23, 1; 95, 7; Mi 7, 14; Is 64, 7. *b:* 4-5: Pss 105, 1: 107, 1; 118, 1; 136, 1; 138, 8; Jer 33, 11. *c:* Ps 26, 11. *d:* 1 Kgs 9, 4; Is 33, 15. *e:* Prv 11, 20. *f:* Prv 17, 20; 30, 10. *g:* Prv 21, 4. *h:* Ps 26, 11; Prv 20, 7. *i:* Ps 5, 5; Prv 25, 5. *j:* Pss 69, 18; 143, 7. *k:* 4-6: Ps 38, 7-9. *l:* Pss 42, 4; 80, 6.

you lifted me up just to cast me down.

[12] My days are like a lengthening shadow;[m]
  I wither like the grass.[n]

II

[13] But you, LORD, are enthroned forever;
  your renown is for all generations.[o]

[14] You will again show mercy to Zion;
  now is the time for pity;
  the appointed time has come.

[15] Its stones are dear to your servants;
  its dust moves them to pity.

[16] The nations shall revere your name, LORD,
  all the kings of the earth, your glory.[p]

[17] Once the LORD has rebuilt Zion
  and appeared in glory,

[18] Heeding the plea of the lowly,
  not scorning their prayer.

[19] Let this be written for the next
  generation,
  for a people not yet born,
  that they may praise the LORD:[q]

[20] "The LORD looked down from the holy
  heights,*
  viewed the earth from heaven,[r]

[21] To attend to the groaning of the prisoners,
  to release those doomed to die."[s]

[22] Then the LORD's name will be declared
  on Zion,
  the praise of God in Jerusalem,

[23] When all peoples and kingdoms gather
  to worship the LORD.[t]

III

[24] God has shattered my strength in
  mid-course,
  has cut short my days.

[25] I plead, O my God,
  do not take me in the midst of my
  days.[u] *
  Your years last through all generations.

[26] Of old you laid the earth's foundations;[v]
  the heavens are the work of your hands.

[27] They perish, but you remain;
  they all wear out like a garment;
  Like clothing you change them and they
  are changed,

[28] but you are the same, your years have
  no end.

[29] May the children of your servants live on;
  may their descendants live in your
  presence.[w]

PSALM 103 *

Praise of Divine Goodness

[1] Of David.

See RG
175-76

I

Bless the LORD, my soul;
  all my being, bless his holy name!

[2] Bless the LORD, my soul;
  do not forget all the gifts of God,

[3] Who pardons all your sins,
  heals all your ills,

[4] Delivers your life from the pit,[x]
  surrounds you with love and
  compassion,

[5] Fills your days with good things;
  your youth is renewed like the
  eagle's.*

II

[6] The LORD does righteous deeds,
  brings justice to all the oppressed.[y]

[7] His ways were revealed to Moses,
  mighty deeds to the people of Israel.

[8] Merciful and gracious is the LORD,
  slow to anger, abounding in kindness.[z]

[9] God does not always rebuke,
  nurses no lasting anger,

[10] Has not dealt with us as our sins merit,
  nor requited us as our deeds deserve.

III

[11] As the heavens tower over the earth,
  so God's love towers over the
  faithful.[a]

102, 20-23: Both 20-21 and 22-23 depend on 19.

102, 25: In the midst of my days: when the normal span of life is but half completed. Cf Is 38, 10; Jer 17, 11.

Ps 103: The speaker in this hymn begins by praising God for personal benefits (1-5), then moves on to God's mercy toward all the people (6-18). Even sin cannot destroy that mercy (11-13), for the eternal God is well aware of the people's human fragility (14-18). The psalmist invites the heavenly beings to join in praise (19-22).

103, 5: Your youth is renewed like the eagle's: because of the eagle's long life it was a symbol of perennial youth and

vigor. Cf Is 40, 31.

---

m: Pss 109, 23; 144, 4; Jb 8, 9; 14, 2; Eccl 6, 12; Wis 2, 5.   n: Ps 90, 5-6.   o: Pss 55, 20; 90, 2; 93, 2; 102, 13; 135, 13; 145, 13; Lam 5, 19; Hb 1, 12.   p: Is 59, 19; 66, 18.   q: Ps 22, 31-32.   r: Pss 11, 4; 14, 2.   s: Ps 79, 11.   t: Is 60, 3-4; Zec 2, 15; 8, 22.   u: Pss 39, 5; 90, 10; Jb 14, 5.   v: 26-28: Heb 1, 10-12.   w: Ps 69, 36-37.   x: Pss 28, 1; 30, 4; 40, 3; 69, 16; 88, 5; 143, 7; Prv 1, 12; Jon 2, 7.   y: Ps 146, 6-7.   z: Pss 86, 15; 145, 8; Ex 34, 6-7; Nm 14, 18; Jer 3, 12; Jl 2, 13; Jon 4, 2.   a: Is 55, 9.

¹² As far as the east is from the west,
so far have our sins been removed
from us.
¹³ As a father has compassion on his
children,
so the LORD has compassion on the
faithful.
¹⁴ For he knows how we are formed,
remembers that we are dust.ᵇ
¹⁵ Our days are like the grass;
like flowers of the field we blossom.ᶜ
¹⁶ The wind sweeps over us and we are
gone;
our place knows us no more.
¹⁷ But the LORD's kindness is forever,
toward the faithful from age to age.
He favors the children's children
¹⁸ of those who keep his covenant,
who take care to fulfill its precepts.

IV

¹⁹ The LORD's throne is established in
heaven;
God's royal power rules over all.
²⁰ Bless the LORD, all you angels,ᵈ
mighty in strength and attentive,
obedient to every command.
²¹ Bless the LORD, all you hosts,
ministers who do God's will.
²² Bless the LORD, all creatures,
everywhere in God's domain.
Bless the LORD, my soul!

See RG 175, 178

PSALM 104*

Praise of God the Creator

I

¹ Bless the LORD, my soul!
LORD, my God, you are great indeed!
You are clothed with majesty and glory,
² robed in light as with a cloak.
You spread out the heavens like a tent;ᵉ

³ you raised your palace upon the
waters.*
You make the clouds your chariot;
you travel on the wings of the wind.
⁴ You make the winds your messengers;
flaming fire, your ministers.ᶠ

II

⁵ You fixed the earth on its foundation,*
never to be moved.
⁶ The ocean covered it like a garment;
above the mountains stood the waters.
⁷ At your roar they took flight;
at the sound of your thunder they fled.ᵍ
⁸ They rushed up the mountains, down the
valleys
to the place you had fixed for them.
⁹ You set a limit they cannot pass;
never again will they cover the earth.ʰ

III

¹⁰ You made springs flow into channels
that wind among the mountains.
¹¹ They give drink to every beast of the
field;ⁱ
here wild asses quench their thirst.
¹² Beside them the birds of heaven nest;
among the branches they sing.
¹³ You water the mountains from your
palace;
by your labor the earth abounds.
¹⁴ You raise grass for the cattle
and plants for our beasts of burden.
You bring bread from the earth,
¹⁵ and wine to gladden our hearts,
Oil to make our faces gleam,
food to build our strength.
¹⁶ The trees of the LORD drink their fill,*
the cedars of Lebanon, which you
planted.
¹⁷ There the birds build their nests;
junipers are the home of the stork.ʲ

Ps 104: A hymn praising God who easily and skillfully made rampaging waters and primordial night into a world vibrant with life. The psalmist describes God's splendor in the heavens (1-4), how the chaotic waters were tamed to fertilize and feed the world (5-18), and how primordial night was made into a gentle time of refreshment (19-23). The picture is like Gn 1, 1-2: a dark and watery chaos is made dry and lighted so that creatures might live. The psalmist reacts to the beauty of creation with awe (24-34). May sin not deface God's work (35)!

104, 3: Your palace upon the waters: God's heavenly dwelling above the upper waters of the sky. Cf Gn 1, 6-7; Ps

29. 10.

104, 5-9: God places the gigantic disk of the earth securely on its foundation and then, as a warrior, chases away the enveloping waters and confines them under, above, and around the earth.

104, 16-18: Even the exotic flora and fauna of the high mountains of the Lebanon range receive adequate water.

b: Ps 90, 3. c: Pss 37, 2; 90, 5-6; Is 40, 7. d: Ps 148, 2; Dn 3, 58. e: Prv 8, 27-28; Jb 9, 8; Is 40, 22; Gn 1, 6-7; Am 9, 6. f: Heb 1, 7. g: Ps 29, 3. h: Jer 5, 22; Gn 9, 11-15. i. 11-14: Ps 147, 8-9. j: Ez 31, 6.

18 The high mountains are for wild goats;
    the rocky cliffs, a refuge for badgers.

IV

19 You made the moon to mark the seasons,[k]
    the sun that knows the hour of its
      setting.
20 You bring darkness and night falls,
    then all the beasts of the forest roam
      abroad.
21 Young lions roar for prey;
    they seek their food from God.[l]
22 When the sun rises, they steal away
    and rest in their dens.
23 People go forth to their work,
    to their labor till evening falls.

V

24 How varied are your works, LORD!
    In wisdom you have wrought them all;
    the earth is full of your creatures.[m]
25 Look at the sea, great and wide!
    It teems with countless beings,
    living things both large and small.[n]
26 Here ships ply their course;
    here Leviathan,* your creature, plays.[o]

VI

27 All of these look to you
    to give them food in due time.[p]
28 When you give to them, they gather;
    when you open your hand, they are
      well filled.
29 When you hide your face, they are lost.*
    When you take away their breath, they
      perish
    and return to the dust from which they
      came.[q]
30 When you send forth your breath, they
      are created,
    and you renew the face of the earth.

VII

31 May the glory of the LORD endure forever;
    may the LORD be glad in these works!
32 If God glares at the earth, it trembles;
    if God touches the mountains, they
      smoke![r]
33 I will sing to the LORD all my life;
    I will sing praise to my God while I
      live.[s]
34 May my theme be pleasing to God;
    I will rejoice in the LORD.
35 May sinners vanish from the earth,
    and the wicked be no more.
    Bless the LORD, my soul! Hallelujah!*

PSALM 105*

God's Fidelity to the Promise

See RG 176

I

1 Give thanks to the LORD, invoke his
    name;[t]
    make known among the peoples his
      deeds![u]
2 Sing praise, play music;
    proclaim all his wondrous deeds!
3 Glory in his holy name;
    rejoice, O hearts that seek the LORD!
4 Rely on the mighty LORD;
    constantly seek his face.[v]
5 Recall the wondrous deeds he has done,
    his signs and his words of judgment,
6 You descendants of Abraham his
      servant,
    offspring of Jacob the chosen one!

II

7 The LORD is our God
    who rules the whole earth.
8 He remembers forever his covenant,
    the pact imposed for a thousand
      generations,
9 Which was made with Abraham,
    confirmed by oath to Isaac,[w]

104, 26: **Leviathan**: a sea monster symbolizing primeval chaos. Cf Ps 74, 14; Is 27, 1; Jb 40, 25. God does not destroy chaos but makes it part of the created order.

104, 29-30: On one level, the spirit (or wind) of God is the fall and winter rains that provide food for all creatures. On another, it is the breath (or spirit) of God that makes beings live.

104, 35: **Hallelujah**: a frequent word in the last third of the Psalter. The word combines the plural imperative of praise (*hallelu*) with an abbreviated form of the divine name Yah(weh).

Ps 105: A hymn to God who promised the land of Canaan to the holy people. Cf Pss 78; 106; 136. Israel is invited to praise and seek the presence of God (1-6), who is faithful to the promise of land to the ancestors (7-11). In every phase of the national story—the ancestors in the land of Canaan (12-15), Joseph in Egypt (16-22), Israel in Egypt (23-38), Israel in the desert on the way to Canaan (39-45)—God remained faithful, reiterating the promise of the land to successive servants.

k: Sir 43, 6.   *l:* Jb 38, 39.   *m:* Ps 92, 6; Sir 39, 16.   *n:* Sir 43, 26.   *o:* Jb 3, 8; 40, 25.   *p:* Pss 136, 25; 145, 15-16.   *q:* Jb 34, 14-15; Eccl 3, 20; Ps 90, 3.   *r:* Ps 144, 5.   *s:* Ps 146, 2.   *t:* 1-15: 1 Chr 16, 8-22.   *u:* Pss 18, 50; 96, 3; 145, 5; Is 12, 4-5.   *v:* Pss 24, 6; 27, 8.   *w:* Gn 15, 1ff; 26, 3.

10 And ratified as binding for Jacob,
  an everlasting covenant for Israel:
11 "To you I give the land of Canaan,
  your own allotted heritage."x

III

12 When they were few in number,y
  a handful, and strangers there,
13 Wandering from nation to nation,
  from one kingdom to another,
14 He let no one oppress them;
  for their sake he rebuked kings:*
15 "Do not touch my anointed,
  to my prophets* do no harm."

IV

16 Then he called down a famine on the
  land,
  destroyed the grain that sustained
  them.z
17 He had sent a man ahead of them,
  Joseph, sold as a slave.a
18 They shackled his feet with chains;
  collared his neck in iron,b
19 Till his prediction came to pass,
  and the word of the LORD proved him
  true.c
20 The king sent and released him;
  the ruler of peoples set him free.d
21 He made him lord over his palace,
  ruler over all his possessions,e
22 To instruct his princes by his word,
  to teach his elders wisdom.

V

23 Then Israel entered Egypt;f
  Jacob lived in the land of Ham.*
24 God greatly increased his people,
  made them too many for their foes.g
25 He turned their hearts to hate his
  people,
  to treat his servants unfairly.h
26 He sent his servant Moses,
  Aaron whom he had chosen.i
27 They worked his signs in Egyptj *

and wonders in the land of Ham.
28 He sent darkness and it grew dark,
  but they rebelled against his word.
29 He turned their waters into blood
  and killed all their fish.
30 Their land swarmed with frogs,
  even the chambers of their kings.
31 He spoke and there came swarms of flies,
  gnats through all their country.
32 For rain he gave them hail,
  flashes of lightning throughout their
  land.
33 He struck down their vines and fig trees,
  shattered the trees of their country.
34 He spoke and the locusts came,
  grasshoppers without number.k
35 They devoured every plant in the land;
  they ravaged the crops of their fields.
36 He struck down every firstborn in the
  land,
  the first fruits of all their vigor.
37 He brought his people out,
  laden with silver and gold;l
  no stragglers among the tribes.
38 Egypt rejoiced when they left,
  for panic had seized them.

VI

39 He spread a cloud as a cover,
  and made a fire to light up the night.m
40 They asked and he brought them quail;
  with bread from heaven he filled
  them.n
41 He split the rock and water gushed
  forth;
  it flowed through the desert like a
  river.o
42 For he remembered his sacred word
  to Abraham his servant.
43 He brought his people out with joy,
  his chosen ones with shouts of
  triumph.
44 He gave them the lands of the nations,

105, 14: Kings: Pharaoh and Abimelech of Gerar. Cf Gn 12, 17; 20, 6-7.

105, 15: My anointed . . . my prophets: the patriarchs Abraham, Isaac, and Jacob, who were "anointed" in the sense of being consecrated and recipients of God's revelation.

105, 23. 27: The land of Ham: a synonym for Egypt. Cf Gn 10, 6.

105, 27-38: This psalm and Ps 78, 43-51 have an account of the plagues differing in number or in order from Ex 7,

14—12, 30. Several versions of the exodus story were current.

x: Gn 12, 7; 15, 18.   y: 12-13: Dt 4, 27; 26, 5.   z: Gn 41, 54. 57.
a: Gn 37, 28. 36; 45, 5.   b: Gn 39, 20.   c: Gn 40-41.   d: Gn 41, 14.
e: Gn 41, 41-44.   f: Gn 46, 1—47, 12; Acts 7, 15.   g: Ex 1, 7; Acts
7, 17.   h: Ex 1, 8-14.   i: Ex 3, 10; 4, 27.   j: 27-36: Ps 78, 43-51;
Ex 7-12.   k: Jl 1, 4.   l: Ex 12, 33-36.   m: Ps 78, 14; Ex 13, 21-22;
Wis 18, 3.   n: Ps 78, 24-28; Ex 16, 13-15; Nm 11, 31ff; Wis 16, 20.
o: Ps 78, 15-16; Ex 17, 1-7; Nm 20, 11.

the wealth of the peoples to own,*p*
45 That they might keep his laws
and observe his teachings.*q*
Hallelujah!

PSALM 106*

See RG
175

Israel's Confession of Sin

1 Hallelujah!

A

Give thanks to the LORD, who is good,
whose love endures forever.*r*
2 Who can tell the mighty deeds of the
LORD,
proclaim in full God's praise?
3 Happy those who do what is right,
whose deeds are always just.*s*
4 Remember me, LORD, as you favor your
people;
come to me with your saving help,*t*
5 That I may see the prosperity of your
chosen,
rejoice in the joy of your people,
and glory with your heritage.

B

6 We have sinned like our ancestors;*u*
we have done wrong and are guilty.

I

7 Our ancestors in Egypt
did not attend to your wonders.
They did not remember your great
love;
they defied the Most High at the Red
Sea.
8 Yet he saved them for his name's sake
to make his power known.*v*
9 He roared at the Red Sea and it dried up.

He led them through the deep as
through a desert.*w*
10 He rescued them from hostile hands,
freed them from the power of the
enemy.
11 The waters covered their oppressors;
not one of them survived.
12 Then they believed his words
and sang songs of praise.*x*

II

13 But they soon forgot all he had done;
they had no patience for his plan.
14 In the desert they gave way to their
cravings,
tempted God in the wasteland.*y*
15 So he gave them what they asked
and sent among them a wasting
disease.*z*

III

16 In the camp they challenged Moses*a*
and Aaron, the holy one of the LORD.
17 The earth opened and swallowed Dathan,
it closed on the followers of Abiram.
18 Against that company the fire blazed;
flames consumed the wicked.

IV

19 At Horeb they fashioned a calf,*b*
worshiped a metal statue.
20 They exchanged their glorious God
for the image of a grass-eating bull.
21 They forgot the God who saved them,
who did great deeds in Egypt,*c*
22 Amazing deeds in the land of Ham,
fearsome deeds at the Red Sea.
23 He would have decreed their destruction,
had not Moses, the chosen leader,
Withstood him in the breach*

Ps 106: Israel is invited to praise the God whose mercy
has always tempered judgment of Israel (1-3). The speaker,
on behalf of all, seeks solidarity with the people, who can always count on God's fidelity despite their sin (4-5). Confident of God's mercy, the speaker invites national repentance
(6) by reciting from Israel's history eight instances of sin,
judgment, and forgiveness. The sins are the rebellion at the
Red Sea (6-12; see Ex 14-15), the craving for meat in the
desert (13-15; see Nm 11), the challenge to Moses' authority
(16-18; see Nm 16), the golden calf episode (19-23; see Ex
32-34), the refusal to take Canaan by the southern route (24-
27; see Nm 13-14 and Dt 1-2), the rebellion at Baal-Peor (28-
31; see Nm 25, 1-10), the anger of Moses (32-33; see Nm 20,
1-13), and mingling with the nations (34-47). The last, as suggested by its length and generalized language, may be the sin
that invites the repentance of the present generation. The text
gives the site of each sin: Egypt (7), the desert (14), the camp
(16), Horeb (19), in their tents (25), Baal-Peor (28), the waters of Meribah (32), Canaan (38).

106, 23: Withstood him in the breach: the image is that
of Moses standing in a narrow break made in the wall to keep
anyone from entering.

p: Dt 4, 37-40.   *q:* Dt 6, 20-25; 7, 8-11.   *r:* Pss 100, 5; 107, 1;
1 Chr 16, 34; Jer 33, 11; Dn 3, 89.   *s:* Is 56, 1-2.   *t:* Ps 25, 7; Neh
5, 19.   *u:* 6-7: Ps 78, 11-17; Ex 14, 11; Lv 26, 40; 1 Kgs 8, 47;
Bar 2, 12; Dn 9, 5.   *v:* Ez 36, 20-22.   *w:* Ex 14, 21-31; Is 50, 2;
63, 11-14; Na 1, 4.   *x:* Ex 15, 1-21.   *y:* Ps 78, 18; Ex 15, 24; 16,
3; Nm 11, 1-6.   *z:* Ps 78, 26-31; Nm 11, 33.   *a:* 16-18: Nm 16;
Dt 11, 6; Is 26, 11.   *b:* 19-20: Ex 32; Dt 9, 8-21; Jer 2, 11; Acts 7,
41; Rom 1, 23.   *c:* Ps 78, 42-58; Dt 32, 18; Jer 2, 32.

to turn back his destroying anger.[d]

V

[24] Next they despised the beautiful land;[e]
  they did not believe the promise.
[25] In their tents they complained;
  they did not obey the LORD.
[26] So with raised hand he swore
  to destroy them in the desert,
[27] To scatter their descendants among the
  nations,
  disperse them in foreign lands.

VI

[28] They joined in the rites of Baal of Peor,[f]
  ate food sacrificed to dead gods.
[29] They provoked him by their actions,
  and a plague broke out among them.
[30] Then Phinehas rose to intervene,
  and the plague was brought to a halt.
[31] This was counted for him as a righteous
  deed
  for all generations to come.

VII

[32] At the waters of Meribah they angered
  God,[g]
  and Moses suffered because of them.*
[33] They so embittered his spirit
  that rash words crossed his lips.

VIII

[34] They did not destroy the peoples
  as the LORD had commanded them,[h]
[35] But mingled with the nations
  and imitated their ways.[i]
[36] They worshiped their idols
  and were ensnared by them.[j]
[37] They sacrificed to the gods*
  their own sons and daughters,
[38] Shedding innocent blood,
  the blood of their own sons and
  daughters,
  Whom they sacrificed to the idols of
  Canaan,

desecrating the land with bloodshed.
[35] They defiled themselves by their
  actions,
  became adulterers by their conduct.
[46] So the LORD grew angry with his people,
  abhorred his own heritage.
[41] He handed them over to the nations,
  and their adversaries ruled them.[k]
[42] Their enemies oppressed them,
  kept them under subjection.
[43] Many times did he rescue them,
  but they kept rebelling and scheming
  and were brought low by their own
  guilt.[l]
[44] Still God had regard for their affliction
  when he heard their wailing.
[45] For their sake he remembered his
  covenant
  and relented in his abundant love,[m]
[46] Winning for them compassion
  from all who held them captive.

C

[47] Save us, LORD, our God;
  gather us from among the nations
That we may give thanks to your holy
  name
  and glory in praising you.[n]

* * *

[48] Blessed be the LORD, the God of Israel,
  from everlasting to everlasting!
  Let all the people say, Amen![o]
Hallelujah!*

Fifth Book: Psalms 107—150

PSALM 107*

*God the Savior of Those
in Distress*

See RG
175

[1] "Give thanks to the LORD who is good,
  whose love endures forever!"[p]

106, 32: Moses suffered because of them: Moses was
not allowed to enter the promised land because of his rash
words (Nm 20, 12). According to Dt 1, 37, Moses was not allowed to cross because of the people's sin, not his own.

106, 37: The gods: Hebrew *shedim,* customarily translated
"demons," occurs in parallelism with "gods" in an important
inscription from Transjordan and hence is translated "gods."

106, 48: A doxology ending Book IV of the Psalter. It is
not part of the psalm.

Ps 107: A hymn inviting those who have been rescued by
God to give praise (1-3). Four archetypal divine rescues are

described, each ending in thanksgiving: from the sterile
desert (4-9), from imprisonment in gloom (10-16), from

d: Ex 32, 11; Dt 9, 25; Ez 22, 30. *e:* 24-27: Lv 26, 33; Nm 14;
Dt 1, 25-36; Ez 20, 15. 23. *f:* 28-31: Nm 25; Dt 26, 14; Sir 45,
23-24. g: 32-33: Ps 95, 8-9; Ex 17, 1-7; Nm 20, 2-13; Dt 6, 16;
33, 8. *h:* Dt 7, 1; Jgs 2, 1-5. *i:* Lv 18, 3; Jgs 1, 27-35; 3, 5.
j: 36-38: Lv 18, 21; Nm 35, 33; Dt 32, 17; Jgs 2, 11-13. 17. 19;
2 Kgs 16, 3; Bar 4, 7; 1 Cor 10, 20. *k:* Jgs 2, 14-23. *l:* Is 63, 7-
9. *m:* Lv 26, 42. *n:* 1 Chr 16, 35. *o:* Pss 41, 14; 72, 18; 89,
53; 1 Chr 16, 36; Neh 9, 5. *p:* Pss 100, 4-5; 106, 1; Jer 33, 11.

2 Let that be the prayer of the LORD's
   redeemed,
   those redeemed from the hand of the
   foe,*q*
3 Those gathered from foreign lands,
   from east and west, from north and
   south.*r*

I

4 Some had lost their way in a barren
   desert;
   found no path toward a city to live in.
5 They were hungry and thirsty;
   their life was ebbing away.*s*
6 In their distress they cried to the LORD,
   who rescued them in their peril,
7 Guided them by a direct path*t*
   so they reached a city to live in.*u*
8 Let them thank the LORD for such
   kindness,
   such wondrous deeds for mere mortals.
9 For he satisfied the thirsty,
   filled the hungry with good things.*v*

II

10 Some lived in darkness and gloom,
   in prison, bound with chains,
11 Because they rebelled against God's
   word,
   scorned the counsel of the Most
   High,*w*
12 Who humbled their hearts through
   hardship;
   they stumbled with no one to help.*x*
13 In their distress they cried to the LORD,
   who saved them in their peril,
14 Led them forth from darkness and gloom
   and broke their chains asunder.*y*
15 Let them thank the LORD for such
   kindness,
   such wondrous deeds for mere mortals.
16 For he broke down the gates of bronze
   and snapped the bars of iron.

III

17 Some fell sick from their wicked ways,
   afflicted because of their sins.
18 They loathed all manner of food;*z*
   they were at the gates of death.
19 In their distress they cried to the LORD,
   who saved them in their peril,
20 Sent forth the word to heal them,*a*
   snatched them from the grave.
21 Let them thank the LORD for such
   kindness,
   such wondrous deeds for mere mortals.
22 Let them offer a sacrifice in thanks,
   declare his works with shouts of joy.

IV

23 Some went off to sea in ships,
   plied their trade on the deep waters.*b*
24 They saw the works of the LORD,
   the wonders of God in the deep.
25 He spoke and roused a storm wind;
   it tossed the waves on high.*c*
26 They rose up to the heavens, sank to the
   depths;
   their hearts trembled at the danger.
27 They reeled, staggered like drunkards;
   their skill was of no avail.*d*
28 In their distress they cried to the LORD,
   who brought them out of their peril,
29 Hushed the storm to a murmur;
   the waves of the sea were stilled.*e*
30 They rejoiced that the sea grew calm,
   that God brought them to the harbor
   they longed for.
31 Let them thank the LORD for such
   kindness,
   such wondrous deeds for mere mortals.
32 Let them praise him in the assembly of
   the people,
   give thanks in the council of the elders.

V

33 God changed rivers into desert,*

mortal illness (17-22), and from the angry sea (23-32). The number four connotes totality, all the possible varieties of rescue. The same saving activity of God is shown in Israel's history (33-41); whenever the people were endangered God rescued them. The last verses invite people to ponder the persistent saving acts of God (42-43).

107, 33-41: God destroyed Sodom and Gomorrah in Gn 18-19, which the psalm sees as the destruction of the wicked inhabitants of Canaan to prepare the way for Israel (33-34). God then led Israel through the desert to give them

a fertile land (35-38) and protected them from every danger (39-41).

q: Is 63, 12.   r: Is 43, 5-6; 49, 12; Zec 8, 7.   s: Dt 8, 15; 32, 10; Is 49, 10.   t: Is 35, 8; 40, 3; 43, 19.   u: Dt 6, 10.   v: Lk 1, 53. w: Is 42, 7. 22; Jb 36, 8-9; Prv 1, 25.   x: Ps 106, 43.   y: Is 42, 7; 49, 9; 51, 14.   z: Jb 6, 6-7; 33, 20.   a: Ps 147, 15; Wis 16, 12; Is 55, 11; Mt 8, 8.   b: Sir 43, 25.   c: Jon 1, 4.   d: Is 29, 9.   e: Pss 65, 8; 89, 10; Mt 8, 26 par.

springs of water into thirsty ground,*f*
³⁴ Fruitful land into a salty waste,
because of the wickedness of its
people.*g*
³⁵ He changed the desert into pools of
water,
arid land into springs of water,*h*
³⁶ And settled the hungry there;
they built a city to live in.*i*
³⁷ They sowed fields and planted vineyards,
brought in an abundant harvest.*j*
³⁸ God blessed them, they became very
many,
and their livestock did not decrease.*k*
⁴⁰ But he poured out contempt on
princes,
made them wander the trackless
wastes,*l*
³⁹ Where they were diminished and brought
low
through misery and cruel oppression,
⁴¹ While the poor were released from their
affliction;
their families increased like their
flocks.*m*
⁴² The upright saw this and rejoiced;*n*
all wickedness shut its mouth.
⁴³ Whoever is wise will take note of these
things,*o*
will ponder the merciful deeds of the
LORD.

PSALM 108*

See RG 176

Prayer for Victory

¹ A song; a psalm of David.

I

² My heart is steadfast, God;*p*
my heart is steadfast.
I will sing and chant praise.
³ Awake, my soul; awake, lyre and harp!
I will wake the dawn.*q*

⁴ I will praise you among the peoples,
LORD;
I will chant your praise among the
nations.*r*
⁵ For your love towers to the heavens;
your faithfulness, to the skies.*s*
⁶ Appear on high over the heavens, God;
may your glory appear above all the
earth.
⁷ Help with your right hand and answer
us
that your loved ones may escape.

II

⁸ God promised in the sanctuary:*t*
"I will exult, I will apportion
Shechem;
the valley of Succoth I will measure
out.
⁹ Gilead is mine, mine is Manasseh;
Ephraim is the helmet for my head,
Judah, my own scepter.
¹⁰ Moab is my washbowl;
upon Edom I cast my sandal;*u*
I will triumph over Philistia."

III

¹¹ Who will bring me to the fortified city?
Who will lead me into Edom?
¹² Was it not you who rejected us, God?
Do you no longer march with our
armies?*v*
¹³ Give us aid against the foe;
worthless is human help.
¹⁴ We will triumph with the help of God,
who will trample down our foes.

PSALM 109*

See RG 175

Prayer of a Person Falsely Accused

¹ For the leader. A psalm of David.

I

O God, whom I praise, do not be silent,*w*

Ps 108: A prayer compiled from two other psalms: 2-6 are virtually the same as Ps 57, 8-12; 7-14 are the same as Ps 60, 7-14. An old promise of salvation (8-10) is combined with a confident assurance (1-6. 14) and petition (7. 12-13).

Ps 109: A lament notable for the length and vehemence of its prayer against evildoers (6-20); the cry to God (1) and the complaint (22-25) are brief in comparison. The psalmist is apparently the victim of a slander campaign, potentially devastating in a society where reputation and honor are paramount. In the emotional perspective of the psalm, there are only two types of people: the wicked and their poor victims.

The psalmist is a poor victim (22. 31) and by that fact a friend of God and enemy of the wicked. The psalmist seeks vindication not on the basis of personal virtue but because of God's promise to protect the poor.

f: Is 35, 7; 42, 15; 50, 2.   *g:* Gn 19, 23-28; Dt 29, 22; Sir 39, 23.   *h:* Ps 114, 8; Is 41, 8.   *i:* Ez 36, 35.   *j:* Is 65, 21; Jer 31. 5.   *k:* Dt 7, 13-14.   *l:* Jb 12, 23-25.   *m:* Ps 113, 7.   *n:* Pss 58, 11; 63, 12.   *o:* Hos 14, 10.   *p:* 2-6: Ps 57, 8-12.   *q:* Jb 38, 12.   *r:* Pss 9, 12; 18, 50; 148, 13.   *s:* Pss 36, 6; 71, 19.   *t:* 8-14: Ps 60, 8-14.   *u:* Ru 4, 7-8.   *v:* Ps 44, 10.   *w:* Pss 35, 22; 83, 1.

2 for wicked and treacherous mouths
    attack me.
They speak against me with lying tongues;
3   with hateful words they surround me,
    attacking me without cause.
4 In return for my love they slander me,
    even though I prayed for them.
5 They repay me evil for good,
    hatred for my love.*x*

II

My enemies say of me:
6 "Find a lying witness,
    an accuser* to stand by his right hand,
7 That he may be judged and found guilty,
    that his plea may be in vain.
8 May his days be few;
    may another take his office.*y*
9 May his children be fatherless,
    his wife, a widow.*z*
10 May his children be vagrant beggars,
    driven from their hovels.
11 May the usurer snare all he owns,
    strangers plunder all he earns.
12 May no one treat him kindly
    or pity his fatherless children.
13 May his posterity be destroyed,*a*
    his name cease in the next generation.
14 May the LORD remember his fathers'
    guilt;
    his mother's sin not be canceled.*b*
15 May their guilt be always before the
    LORD,*c*
    till their memory is banished from the
    earth,*d*
16 For he did not remember to show
    kindness,
    but hounded the wretched poor
    and brought death to the brokenhearted.
17 He loved cursing; may it come upon him;
    he hated blessing; may none come to
    him.
18 May cursing clothe him like a robe;

    may it enter his belly like water,
    seep into his bones like oil.
19 May it be near as the clothes he wears,
    as the belt always around him."

III

20 May the LORD bring all this* upon my
    accusers,
    upon those who speak evil against me.
21 But you, LORD, my God,
    deal kindly with me for your name's
    sake;
    in your great mercy rescue me.
22 For I am sorely in need;
    my heart is pierced within me.
23 Like a lengthening shadow I near my end,
    all but swept away like the locust.
24 My knees totter from fasting;*e*
    my flesh has wasted away.
25 I have become a mockery to them;
    when they see me, they shake their
    heads.
26 Help me, LORD, my God;
    save me in your kindness.
27 Make them know this is your hand,
    that you, LORD, have acted.
28 Though they curse, may you bless;
    shame my foes, that your servant may
    rejoice.
29 Clothe my accusers with disgrace;
    make them wear shame like a mantle.
30 I will give fervent thanks to the LORD;
    before all I will praise my God.*f*
31 For God stands at the right hand of the
    poor
    to defend them against unjust accusers.

PSALM 110*

God Appoints the King both King and Priest

1 A psalm of David.

The LORD says to you, my lord:*

109, 6: An accuser: Hebrew *satan*, a word occurring in Jb 1-2 and Zec 3, 1-2. In the latter passage Satan stands at the right hand of the high priest to bring false accusations against him before God. Here the accuser is human.

109, 20: May the LORD bring all this: the psalmist prays that God ratify the curses of 6-19 and bring them upon the wicked.

Ps 110: A royal psalm in which a court singer recites three oracles in which God assures the king that his enemies are

conquered (1-2), makes the king "son" in traditional adoption language (3), gives priestly status to the king and promises to be with him in future military ventures (4-7).

110, 1: The LORD says to you, my lord: literally, "The LORD says to my lord," a polite form of address of an inferior

x: Pss 35, 12; 38, 21; Prv 17, 13; Jer 18, 20.   *y:* Acts 1, 20.   *z:* Ex 22, 23; Jer 18, 21.   *a:* Ps 21, 11; Prv 10, 7.   *b:* Ex 20, 5.   *c:* Ps 90, 8.   *d:* Ps 34, 16.   *e:* 24-25: Ps 69, 11-13.   *f:* Ps 111, 1.

See RG 176, 178

Psalms 111 and 112, acrostic psalms introduced by "Hallelujah," are comprised of short lines that often quote traditional expressions containing wisdom ideas. They are somewhat disjointed and resemble answers to a student exercise: Compose a logical, complete acrostic of short lines using traditional statements. The simple style suggests that perhaps these were poems for teaching children. Stylistically, the two are so similar that they have been characterized as "twins."

"Take your throne at my right hand,
    while I make your enemies your
    footstool."*g* *
2 The scepter of your sovereign might
    the LORD will extend from Zion.
The LORD says: "Rule over your enemies!
3   Yours is princely power from the day
    of your birth.
In holy splendor before the daystar,*
    like the dew I begot you."*h* *
4 The LORD has sworn and will not waver:
    "Like Melchizedek* you are a priest
    forever."*i*
5 At your right hand is the Lord,
    who crushes kings on the day of wrath,*j*
6 Who, robed in splendor, judges nations,
    crushes heads across the wide earth,
7 Who drinks from the brook by the
    wayside*
    and thus holds high his head.*k*

See RG 175-76

PSALM 111*

Praise of God for Goodness to Israel

1 Hallelujah.

I will praise the LORD with all my heart*l*

in the assembled congregation of the
    upright.*
2 Great are the works of the LORD,
    to be treasured for all their delights.
3 Majestic and glorious is your* work,
    your wise design endures forever.
4 You won renown for your wondrous
    deeds;
    gracious and merciful is the LORD.*m*
5 You gave food to those who fear you,*
    mindful of your covenant forever.
6 You showed powerful deeds to your
    people,
    giving them the lands* of the nations.
7 The works of your hands are right and
    true,
    reliable all your decrees,
8 Established forever and ever,
    to be observed with loyalty and
    care.
9 You sent deliverance to your people,
    ratified your covenant forever;
    holy and awesome is your name.
10 The fear of the LORD* is the beginning of
    wisdom;*n*
    prudent are all who live by it.
    Your praise endures forever.

to a superior. Cf 1 Sm 25, 25; 2 Sm 1, 10. The court singer refers to the king. Jesus in the synoptic gospels (Mt 22, 41-46 and parallels) takes the psalmist to be David and hence "my lord" refers to the messiah, who must be someone greater than David. **Your footstool:** in ancient times victorious kings put their feet on the prostrate bodies of their enemies.

110, 3: Before the daystar: possibly an expression for before the world began (Prv 8, 22). **Like the dew I begot you:** an adoption formula as in Pss 2, 7; 89, 27-28.

110, 4: Like Melchizedek: Melchizedek was the ancient king of Salem (Jerusalem) who blessed Abraham (Gn 14, 18-20); like other kings of the time he performed priestly functions. Heb 7 sees in Melchizedek a type of Christ.

110, 7: Who drinks from the brook by the wayside: the meaning is uncertain. Some see an allusion to a rite of royal consecration at the Gihon spring (cf 1 Kgs 1, 33. 38). Others find here an image of the divine warrior (or king) pursuing enemies so relentlessly that he does not stop long enough to eat and drink.

Ps 111: A temple singer (1) tells how God is revealed in

Israel's history (2-10). The deeds reveal God's very self, powerful, merciful, faithful. The poem is an acrostic, each verse beginning with a successive letter of the Hebrew alphabet.

111, 1: In the assembled congregation of the upright: in the temple. Cf Ps 149, 1.

111, 3: Your: the psalm refers to God in the third person throughout; the shift to the second person is for the sake of inclusive language.

111, 5: Food to those who fear you: probably a reference to the manna in the desert, which elsewhere is seen as a type of the Eucharist. Cf Jn 6, 31-33. 49-51.

111, 6: Lands: literally, "inheritance, heritage."

111, 10: The fear of the LORD: reverence for God, the Hebrew term for religion.

g: Mt 22, 44; Acts 2, 34-35; 1 Cor 15, 25; Heb 1, 13; 8, 1; 10, 12-13; 1 Pt 3, 22. *h:* Pss 2, 7; 89, 27; Is 49, 1. *i:* Pss 89, 35; 132, 11; Gn 14, 18; Heb 5, 6; 7, 21. *j:* Ps 2, 9; Rv 2, 27; 12, 5; 19, 15. *k:* Ps 3, 4. *l:* Ps 138, 1. *m:* Ps 103, 8; 112, 4. *n:* Prv 1, 7; 9, 10; Sir 1, 16.

See RG
176

PSALM 112*

The Blessings of the Just

¹ Hallelujah!

Happy are those* who fear the LORD,
  who greatly delight in God's
    commands.º
² Their descendants shall be mighty in the
    land,
  a generation upright and blessed.
³ Wealth and riches shall be in their
    homes;
  their prosperity* shall endure forever.
⁴ They shine through the darkness, a light
    for the upright;ᵖ
  they are gracious, merciful, and just.
⁵ All goes well for those gracious in
    lending,
  who conduct their affairs with justice.
⁶ They shall never be shaken;
  the just shall be remembered
    forever.�q
⁷ They shall not fear an ill report;
  their hearts are steadfast, trusting the
    LORD.
⁸ Their hearts are tranquil, without fear,
  till at last they look down on their foes.
⁹ Lavishly they give to the poor;
  their prosperity shall endure forever;ʳ
  their horn* shall be exalted in honor.
¹⁰ The wicked shall be angry to see this;
  they will gnash their teeth and waste
    away;
  the desires of the wicked come to
    nothing.

See RG
175

PSALM 113*

*Praise of God's Care of
the Poor*

¹ Hallelujah!

I

Praise, you servants of the LORD,
  praise the name of the LORD.ˢ
² Blessed be the name of the LORD
  both now and forever.
³ From the rising of the sun to its setting
  let the name of the LORD be praised.

II

⁴ High above all nations is the LORD;
  above the heavens God's glory.ᵗ
⁵ Who is like the LORD,
  our God enthroned on high,
⁶   looking down on heaven and earth?ᵘ
⁷ The LORD raises the needy from the
    dust,
  lifts the poor from the ash heap,ᵛ
⁸ Seats them with princes,
  the princes of the people,
⁹ Gives the childless wife a home,
  the joyful mother of children.ʷ
Hallelujah!

See RG
175

PSALM 114*

*The Lord's Wonders at
the Exodus*

¹ When Israel came forth from Egypt,
  the house of Jacob from an alien people,
² Judah became God's holy place,
  Israel, God's domain.ˣ
³ The sea beheld and fled;*

Ps 112: An acrostic poem detailing the blessings received by those who remain close to God by obedience to the commandments. Among their blessings are children (2), wealth that enables them to be magnanimous (3. 5. 9), and virtue by which they encourage others (4). The just person is an affront to the wicked, whose hopes remain unfulfilled (10). The logic resembles Pss 1 and 111.

112, 1: Happy are those: literally, "Happy the person." "Person" is used typically, hence the plural translation.

112, 3: Prosperity: literally, "justice." In the Second Temple Period the word acquired the nuance of liberality and almsgiving. Cf Sir 3, 30; 7, 10; Mt 6, 1-4.

112, 9: Their horn: the symbol for vitality and honor.

Ps 113: A hymn exhorting the congregation to praise God's name, i.e., the way in which God is present in the world; the name is mentioned three times in 1-3. The divine name is especially honored in the temple (1) but its recognition is not limited by time (2) and space (3), for God is everywhere ac-

tive (4-5) especially in rescuing the lowly faithful (7-9).

Ps 114: A hymn celebrating Israel's escape from Egypt, journey through the wilderness, and entry into the promised land, and the miracles of nature that bore witness to God's presence in their midst. In the perspective of the psalm, the people proceed directly from Egypt into the promised land (1-2). Sea and Jordan, which stood like soldiers barring the people from their land, flee before the mighty God as the earth recoils from the battle (3-4). The poet taunts the natural elements as one taunts defeated enemies (5-6).

114, 3-4: Pairs of cosmic elements such as sea and rivers, mountains and hills, are sometimes mentioned in creation accounts. Personified here as warriors, the pairs tremble in fear

o: Pss 1, 1-2; 119, 1-2; 128, 1.   p: Pss 37, 6; 97, 11; Prv 13, 9; Is 58, 10.   q: Prv 10, 7; Wis 8, 13.   r: Prv 22, 9; 2 Cor 9, 9.   s: Ps 135, 1.   t: Ps 148, 13.   u: Ps 89, 7-9.   v: Ps 107, 41; 1 Sm 2, 7-8.   w: 1 Sm 2, 5; Is 54, 1.   x: Ex 19, 6.

the Jordan turned back.[y]

4 The mountains skipped like rams;
   the hills, like lambs of the flock.[z]

5 Why was it, sea, that you fled?
   Jordan, that you turned back?

6 You mountains, that you skipped like
   rams?
   You hills, like lambs of the flock?

7 Tremble, earth, before the Lord,[a]
   before the God of Jacob,

8 Who turned rock into pools of water,
   stone into flowing springs.[b] *

PSALM 115*

See RG 175

The Greatness of the True God

I

1 Not to us, Lord, not to us
   but to your name give glory
   because of your faithfulness and love.[c]

2 Why should the nations say,
   "Where is their God?"[d] *

3 Our God is in heaven;
   whatever God wills is done.[e]

II

4 Their idols are silver and gold,[f]
   the work of human hands.[g]

5 They have mouths but do not speak,
   eyes but do not see.

6 They have ears but do not hear,
   noses but do not smell.

7 They have hands but do not feel,
   feet but do not walk,
   and no sound rises from their throats.

8 Their makers shall be like them,

all who trust in them.

III

9 The house of Israel trusts in the Lord,[h]
   who is their help and shield.[i]

10 The house of Aaron trusts in the Lord,
   who is their help and shield.

11 Those who fear the Lord* trust in the
   Lord,
   who is their help and shield.

12 The Lord remembers us and will bless us,
   will bless the house of Israel,
   will bless the house of Aaron,

13 Will bless those who fear the Lord,
   small and great alike.

14 May the Lord increase your number,
   you and your descendants.

15 May you be blessed by the Lord,
   who made heaven and earth.

16 The heavens* belong to the Lord,
   but the earth is given to us.[j]

17 The dead do not praise the Lord,
   all those gone down into silence.[k] *

18 It is we who bless the Lord,
   both now and forever.
   Hallelujah!

PSALM 116*

Thanksgiving to God Who Saves from Death

See RG 175

I

1 I love the Lord, who listened
   to my voice in supplication,

2 Who turned an ear to me
   on the day I called.

---

before the Divine Warrior. The quaking also recalls the divine appearance in the storm at Sinai (Ex 19, 16-19) and elsewhere (Jgs 5, 4-5; Ps 18, 8-16).

114, 8: The miracles of giving drink to the people in the arid desert. Cf Ex 17, 1-7; Is 41, 17-18.

Ps 115: A response to the enemy taunt, "Where is your God?" This hymn to the glory of Israel's God (1-3) ridicules the lifeless idols of the nations (4-8), expresses in a litany the trust of the various classes of the people in God (9-11), invokes God's blessing on them as they invoke the divine name (12-15), and concludes as it began with praise of God. Ps 135, 15-18 similarly mocks the Gentile gods and has a similar litany and hymn (Ps 135, 19-21).

115, 2: Where is their God?: implies that God cannot help them.

115, 9-11: The house of Israel . . . the house of Aaron . . . those who fear the Lord: the laity of Israelite birth, the priests, and the converts to Judaism. Cf Pss 118, 2-4; 135, 19-21. In the New Testament likewise "those who fear the

Lord" means converts to Judaism (cf Acts 10, 2. 22. 35; 13, 16 26).

115, 16: The heavens: literally "the heaven of heavens" or "the highest heavens," i.e., above the firmament. See note on Ps 148, 4.

115, 17: See note on Ps 6, 6.

Ps 116: A thanksgiving in which the psalmist responds to divine rescue from mortal danger (3-4) and from near despair (10-11) with vows and temple sacrifices (13-14. 17-19). The Greek and Latin versions divide the psalm into two parts: 1-9 and 10-19, corresponding to its two major divisions.

---

y: Ex 14, 21f; Jos 3, 14ff; Pss 66, 6; 74, 15. z: Ps 29, 6; Wis 19, 9. a: Ps 68, 9. b: Ex 17, 6; Nm 20, 11. c: Ez 36, 22-23. d: Ps 79, 10. e: Ps 135, 6. f: 4-10: Ps 135, 15-19; Wis 15, 15-16; Is 44, 9f; Jer 10, 1-5. g: Is 40, 19. h: Ps 118, 2-4. i: Ps 33, 20. j: Gn 1, 28. k: Pss 6, 6; 88, 11ff; Sir 17, 22f; Is 38, 18.

[3] I was caught by the cords of death;[l][*]
    the snares of Sheol had seized me;
    I felt agony and dread.
[4] Then I called on the name of the LORD,
    "O LORD, save my life!"

II

[5] Gracious is the LORD and just;
    yes, our God is merciful.[m]
[6] The LORD protects the simple;
    I was helpless, but God saved me.
[7] Return, my soul, to your rest;
    the LORD has been good to you.[n]
[8] For my soul has been freed from death,
    my eyes from tears, my feet from
        stumbling.[o]
[9] I shall walk before the LORD
    in the land of the living.[p][*]

III

[10] I kept faith, even when I said,[*]
    "I am greatly afflicted!"[q]
[11] I said in my alarm,
    "No one can be trusted!"[r]
[12] How can I repay the LORD
    for all the good done for me?
[13] I will raise the cup of salvation[*]
    and call on the name of the LORD.
[14] I will pay my vows to the LORD
    in the presence of all his people.
[15] Too costly in the eyes of the LORD[*]
    is the death of his faithful.[s]
[16] LORD, I am your servant,
    your servant, the child of your
        maidservant;[t]
    you have loosed my bonds.
[17] I will offer a sacrifice of thanksgiving

and call on the name of the LORD.[u]
[18] I will pay my vows to the LORD[v]
    in the presence of all his people,
[19] In the courts of the house of the LORD,
    in your midst, O Jerusalem.
Hallelujah!

PSALM 117[*]

The Nations Called to Praise

See RG 175–76

[1] Praise the LORD, all you nations!
    Give glory, all you peoples![w]
[2] The LORD's love for us is strong;
    the LORD is faithful forever.
Hallelujah!

PSALM 118[*]

Hymn of Thanksgiving

See RG 179

I

[1] Give thanks to the LORD, who is good,[x]
    whose love endures forever.
[2] Let the house of Israel say:
    God's love endures forever.
[3] Let the house of Aaron say,
    God's love endures forever.
[4] Let those who fear the LORD say,[y]
    God's love endures forever.

II

[5] In danger I called on the LORD;
    the LORD answered me and set me free.
[6] The LORD is with me; I am not afraid;
    what can mortals do against me?[z]
[7] The LORD is with me as my helper;
    I shall look in triumph on my foes.
[8] Better to take refuge in the LORD[a]

116, 3: The cords of death: death is personified here; it attempts to capture the psalmist with snares and nets. Cf Ps 18, 6.

116, 9: The land of the living: the phrase elsewhere is an epithet of the Jerusalem temple (cf Pss 27, 13; 52, 7; Is 38, 11). Hence the psalmist probably refers to being present to God in the temple.

116, 10: I kept faith, even when I said: even in the days of despair, the psalmist did not lose all hope.

116, 13: The cup of salvation: probably the libation of wine poured out in gratitude for rescue. Cf Ex 25, 29; Nm 15, 5. 7. 10.

116, 15: Too costly in the eyes of the LORD: the meaning is that the death of God's faithful is grievous to God, not that God is pleased with the death. Cf Ps 72, 14. In Wis 3, 5-6 God accepts the death of the righteous as a sacrificial burnt offering.

Ps 117: This shortest of hymns calls on the nations to acknowledge God's supremacy. The supremacy of Israel's God has been demonstrated to them by the people's secure exis-

tence, which is owed entirely to God's gracious fidelity.

Ps 118: A thanksgiving liturgy accompanying a victory procession of the king and the people into the temple precincts. After an invocation in the form of a litany (1-4), the psalmist (very likely speaking in the name of the community) describes how the people confidently implored God's help (5-9) when hostile peoples threatened its life (10-14); vividly God's rescue is recounted (15-18). Then follows a dialogue at the temple gates between the priests and the psalmist as the latter enters to offer the thanksgiving sacrifice (19-25). Finally, the priests impart their blessing (26-27), and the psalmist sings in gratitude (28-29).

l: Ps 18, 5; Jon 2, 3. m: Ex 34, 6. n: Ps 13, 6. o: Ps 56, 14; Is 25, 8; Rv 21, 4. p: Pss 27, 13; 56, 14; Is 38, 11. q: 2 Cor 4, 13. r: Ps 12, 2. s: Ps 72, 14; Is 43, 4. t: Pss 86, 16; 143, 12; Wis 9, 5. u: Lv 7, 12ff. v: Jon 2, 10. w: Rom 15, 11. x: Pss 100, 5; 136, 1f. y: Ps 115, 9-11. z: Ps 27, 1; Heb 13, 6. a: 8f: Ps 146, 3.

than to put one's trust in mortals.
⁹ Better to take refuge in the LORD
than to put one's trust in princes.

III

¹⁰ All the nations surrounded me;
in the LORD's name I crushed them.
¹¹ They surrounded me on every side;
in the LORD's name I crushed them.
¹² They surrounded me like bees;ᵇ
they blazed like fire among thorns;
in the LORD's name I crushed them.
¹³ I was hard pressed and falling,
but the LORD came to my help.ᶜ
¹⁴ The LORD, my strength and might,
came to me as savior.ᵈ

IV

¹⁵ The joyful shout of deliverance
is heard in the tents of the victors:
"The LORD's right hand strikes with
power;
¹⁶ the LORD's right hand is raised;
the LORD's right hand strikes with
power."
¹⁷ I shall not die but live
and declare the deeds of the LORD.
¹⁸ The LORD chastised me harshly,
but did not hand me over to death.

V

¹⁹ Open the gates of victory;
I will enter and thank the LORD.ᵉ
²⁰ This is the LORD's own gate,
where the victors enter.*

²¹ I thank you for you answered me;
you have been my savior.
²² The stone the builders rejected*
has become the cornerstone.ᶠ
²³ By the LORD has this been done;
it is wonderful in our eyes.
²⁴ This is the day the LORD has made;
let us rejoice in it and be glad.
²⁵ LORD, grant salvation!*
LORD, grant good fortune!

VI

²⁶ Blessed is he
who comes in the name of the LORD.ᵍ
We bless you from the LORD's house.
²⁷ The LORD is God and has given us
light.
Join in procession with leafy branches
up to the horns of the altar.

VII

²⁸ You are my God, I give you thanks;
my God, I offer you praise.
²⁹ Give thanks to the LORD, who is good,
whose love endures forever.

PSALM 119*

A Prayer to God, the Lawgiver

See RG 176

ALEPH
¹ Happy those whose way is blameless,
who walk by the teaching of the
LORD.ʰ
² Happy those who observe God's decrees,
who seek the LORD with all their heart.ⁱ

118, 20: Where the victors enter: their victory has demonstrated that God favors them; they are "just" in the biblical sense.

118, 22: The stone the builders rejected: a proverb: what is insignificant to human beings has become great through divine election. The "stone" may originally have meant the foundation stone or capstone of the temple. The New Testament interpreted the verse as referring to the death and resurrection of Christ (Mt 21, 42; Acts 4, 11; cf Is 28, 16 and Rom 9, 33; 1 Pt 2, 7).

118, 25: Grant salvation: the Hebrew for this cry has come into English as "Hosanna." This cry and the words in 26 were used in the gospels to welcome Jesus entering the temple on Palm Sunday (Mk 11, 9-10).

Ps 119: This psalm, the longest by far in the Psalter, praises God for giving such splendid laws and instruction for people to live by. The author glorifies and thanks God for the Torah, prays for protection from sinners enraged by others' fidelity to the law, laments the cost of obedience, delights in the law's consolations, begs for wisdom to understand the precepts, and asks for the rewards of keeping them. Several expected ele-

ments do not appear in the psalm: Mount Sinai with its story of God's revelation and gift to Israel of instruction and commandments, the temple and other institutions related to revelation and laws (frequent in other psalms). The psalm is fascinated with God's word directing and guiding human life.

The poem is an acrostic; its twenty-two stanzas (of eight verses each) are in the order of the Hebrew alphabet. Each of the eight verses within a stanza begins with the same letter. Each verse contains one word for "instruction." The translation here given attempts to translate each Hebrew word for "instruction" with the same English word. There are, however, nine words for "instruction," not eight, so the principle of a different word for "instruction" in each verse cannot be maintained with perfect consistency. The nine words for "instruction" in the translation are: law, edict, command, precept, word, utterance, way, decree, and teaching.

---

b: Dt 1, 44.   *c*: Ps 129, 1-2.   *d*: Ex 15, 2; Is 12, 2.   *e*: Is 26, 2.
f: Mt 21, 42; Lk 20, 17; Acts 4, 11; Rom 9, 33; 1 Pt 2, 7.   *g*: Mt 21, 9; 23, 39.   *h*: Pss 1, 1-2; 15, 2; 112, 1.   *i*: Dt 4, 29.

3 They do no wrong;
   they walk in God's ways.
4 You have given them the command
   to keep your precepts with care.
5 May my ways be firm
   in the observance of your laws!
6 Then I will not be ashamed
   to ponder all your commands.
7 I will praise you with sincere heart
   as I study your just edicts.
8 I will keep your laws;
   do not leave me all alone.

BETH

9 How can the young walk without fault?
   Only by keeping your words.
10 With all my heart I seek you;
   do not let me stray from your
   commands.
11 In my heart I treasure your promise,
   that I may not sin against you.
12 Blessed are you, O LORD;
   teach me your laws.j
13 With my lips I recite
   all the edicts you have spoken.
14 I find joy in the way of your decrees
   more than in all riches.
15 I will ponder your precepts
   and consider your paths.
16 In your laws I take delight;
   I will never forget your word.

GIMEL

17 Be kind to your servant that I may live,
   that I may keep your word.
18 Open my eyes to see clearly
   the wonders of your teachings.
19 I am a sojourner in the land;k *
   do not hide your commands from me.
20 At all times my soul is stirred
   with longing for your edicts.
21 With a curse you rebuke the proud
   who stray from your commands.
22 Free me from disgrace and contempt,
   for I observe your decrees.
23 Though princes meet and talk against me,
   your servant studies your laws.
24 Your decrees are my delight;

they are my counselors.

DALETH

25 I lie prostrate in the dust;l
   give me life in accord with your word.
26 I disclosed my ways and you answered me;
   teach me your laws.
27 Make me understand the way of your
   precepts;
   I will ponder your wondrous deeds.
28 I weep in bitter pain;
   in accord with your word to strengthen
   me.
29 Lead me from the way of deceit;
   favor me with your teaching.
30 The way of loyalty I have chosen;
   I have set your edicts before me.
31 I cling to your decrees, LORD;
   do not let me come to shame.
32 I will run the way of your commands,
   for you open my docile heart.*

HE

33 LORD, teach me the way of your laws;
   I shall observe them with care.m
34 Give me insight to observe your
   teaching,
   to keep it with all my heart.
35 Lead me in the path of your commands,n
   for that is my delight.
36 Direct my heart toward your decrees
   and away from unjust gain.
37 Avert my eyes from what is worthless;
   by your way give me life.
38 For your servant fulfill your promise
   made to those who fear you.
39 Turn away from me the taunts I dread,
   for your edicts bring good.
40 See how I long for your precepts;
   in your justice give me life.

WAW

41 Let your love come to me, LORD,
   salvation in accord with your promise.
42 Let me answer my taunters with a word,
   for I trust in your word.
43 Do not take the word of truth from my
   mouth,
   for in your edicts is my hope.

119, 19: A sojourner in the land: like someone without the legal protection of a native inhabitant, the psalmist has a special need for the guidance of God's teaching.

119, 32: For you open my docile heart: literally, "you make broad my heart."

j: Pss 25, 4; 27, 11; 86, 11; 143, 8. 10.   k: Ps 39, 13.   l: Ps 44, 26.   m: Ps 19, 12.   n: Pss 25, 4; 27, 11; 86, 11; 143, 8. 10.

⁴⁴ I will keep your teachings always,
    for all time and forever.
⁴⁵ I will walk freely in an open space
    because I cherish your precepts.
⁴⁶ I will speak openly of your decrees
    without fear even before kings.
⁴⁷ I delight in your commands,
    which I dearly love.
⁴⁸ I lift up my hands to your commands;*
    I study your laws, which I love.
    ZAYIN
⁴⁹ Remember your word to your servant
    by which you give me hope.
⁵⁰ This is my comfort in affliction,
    your promise that gives me life.
⁵¹ Though the arrogant utterly scorn me,
    I do not turn from your teaching.
⁵² When I recite your edicts of old
    I am comforted, LORD.
⁵³ Rage seizes me because of the wicked;
    they forsake your teaching.
⁵⁴ Your laws become my songs
    wherever I make my home.
⁵⁵ Even at night I remember your name
    in observance of your teaching,
    LORD.
⁵⁶ This is my good fortune,
    for I have observed your precepts.
    HETH
⁵⁷ My portion is the LORD;
    I promise to keep your words.
⁵⁸ I entreat you with all my heart:
    have mercy on me in accord with your
    promise.
⁵⁹ I have examined my ways
    and turned my steps to your decrees.
⁶⁰ I am prompt, I do not hesitate
    in keeping your commands.
⁶¹ Though the snares of the wicked
    surround me,
    your teaching I do not forget.
⁶² At midnight I rise to praise you
    because your edicts are just.
⁶³ I am the friend of all who fear you,
    of all who keep your precepts.
⁶⁴ The earth, LORD, is filled with your love;ᵒ
    teach me your laws.

    TETH
⁶⁵ You have treated your servant well,
    according to your word, O LORD.
⁶⁶ Teach me wisdom and knowledge,
    for in your commands I trust.
⁶⁷ Before I was afflicted I went astray,
    but now I hold to your promise.
⁶⁸ You are good and do what is good;
    teach me your laws.
⁶⁹ The arrogant smear me with lies,
    but I observe your precepts with all
    my heart.
⁷⁰ Their hearts are gross and fat;ᵖ
    as for me, your teaching is my delight.
⁷¹ It was good for me to be afflicted,
    in order to learn your laws.
⁷² Teaching from your lips is more precious
    to me
    than heaps of silver and gold.
    YODH
⁷³ Your hands made me and fashioned me;
    give me insight to learn your
    commands.
⁷⁴ Those who fear you rejoice to see me,
    because I hope in your word.
⁷⁵ I know, LORD, that your edicts are just;
    though you afflict me, you are faithful.
⁷⁶ May your love comfort me
    in accord with your promise to your
    servant.
⁷⁷ Show me compassion that I may live,
    for your teaching is my delight.
⁷⁸ Shame the proud for oppressing me
    unjustly,
    that I may study your precepts.
⁷⁹ Let those who fear you turn to me,
    those who acknowledge your decrees.
⁸⁰ May I be wholehearted toward your
    laws,
    that I may not be put to shame.
    KAPH
⁸¹ My soul longs for your salvation;
    I put my hope in your word.�q
⁸² My eyes long to see your promise.ʳ
    When will you comfort me?
⁸³ I am like a wineskin shriveled by smoke,ˢ
    but I have not forgotten your laws.

119, 48: I lift up my hands to your commands: to lift up the hands was an ancient gesture of reverence to God. Here the picture is applied to God's law.

---

o: Ps 33, 5.   *p*: Pss 17, 10; 73, 7; Jb 15, 27.   *q*: Ps 130, 6.   *r*: Pss 25, 15; 123, 1-2; 141, 8.   *s*: Jb 30, 30.

84 How long can your servant survive?
    When will your edict doom my foes?
85 The arrogant have dug pits for me;
    defying your teaching.
86 All your commands are steadfast.
    Help me! I am pursued without cause.
87 They have almost ended my life on earth,
    but I do not forsake your precepts.
88 In your kindness give me life,
    to keep the decrees you have spoken.

LAMEDH
89 Your word, LORD, stands forever;[t] *
    it is firm as the heavens.
90 Through all generations your truth
        endures;
    fixed to stand firm like the earth.
91 By your edicts they stand firm to this
        day,
    for all things are your servants.
92 Had your teaching not been my delight,
    I would have perished in my affliction.
93 I will never forget your precepts;
    through them you give me life.
94 I am yours; save me,
    for I cherish your precepts.
95 The wicked hope to destroy me,
    but I pay heed to your decrees.
96 I have seen the limits of all perfection,
    but your command is without bounds.

MEM
97 How I love your teaching, LORD!
    I study it all day long.
98 Your command makes me wiser than my
        foes,
    for it is always with me.
99 I have more understanding than all my
        teachers,
    because I ponder your decrees.
100 I have more insight than my elders,
    because I observe your precepts.[u]
101 I keep my steps from every evil path,
    that I may obey your word.
102 From your edicts I do not turn,
    for you have taught them to me.
103 How sweet to my tongue is your
        promise,
    sweeter than honey to my mouth![v]

104 Through your precepts I gain insight;
    therefore I hate all false ways.

NUN
105 Your word is a lamp for my feet,
    a light for my path.[w]
106 I make a solemn vow
    to keep your just edicts.
107 I am very much afflicted, LORD;
    give me life in accord with your word.
108 Accept my freely offered praise;[x]
    LORD, teach me your decrees.
109 My life is always at risk,
    but I do not forget your teaching.
110 The wicked have set snares for me,
    but from your precepts I do not stray.
111 Your decrees are my heritage forever;
    they are the joy of my heart.
112 My heart is set on fulfilling your laws;
    they are my reward forever.

SAMEKH
113 I hate every hypocrite;
    your teaching I love.
114 You are my refuge and shield;
    in your word I hope.
115 Depart from me, you wicked,[y]
    that I may observe the commands of
        my God.
116 Sustain me by your promise that I may
        live;
    do not disappoint me in my hope.
117 Strengthen me that I may be safe,
    ever to contemplate your laws.
118 You reject all who stray from your laws,
    for vain is their deceit.
119 Like dross you regard all the wicked on
        earth;
    therefore I love your decrees.
120 My flesh shudders with dread of you;
    I hold your edicts in awe.

AYIN
121 I have fulfilled your just edict;
    do not abandon me to my oppressors.
122 Guarantee your servant's welfare;
    do not let the arrogant oppress me.
123 My eyes long to see your salvation
    and the justice of your promise.
124 Act with kindness toward your servant;

119, 89-91: God's word creates the world, which manifests that word by its permanence and reliability.

t: Is 40, 8.   u: Jb 32, 6; Wis 4, 8-9.   v: Ps 19, 11.   w: Ps 18, 29; Prv 6, 23.   x: Ps 50, 14. 23; Heb 13, 15.   y: Pss 6, 9; 139, 19; Jb 21, 14.

teach me your laws.
^{125}I am your servant; give me discernment
that I may know your decrees.
^{126}It is time for the LORD to act;
they have disobeyed your teaching.
^{127}Truly I love your commands
more than the finest gold.
^{128}Thus I follow all your precepts;
every wrong way I hate.

PE
^{129}Wonderful are your decrees;
therefore I observe them.
^{130}The revelation of your words sheds light,
gives understanding to the simple.
^{131}I sigh with open mouth,
yearning for your commands.
^{132}Turn to me and be gracious,^{z}
your edict for lovers of your name.
^{133}Steady my feet in accord with your
promise;
do not let iniquity lead me.
^{134}Free me from human oppression,
that I may keep your precepts.
^{135}Let your face shine upon your servant;
teach me your laws.
^{136}My eyes shed streams of tears
because your teaching is not followed.

SADHE
^{137}You are righteous, LORD,
and just are your edicts.^{a}
^{138}You have issued your decrees in justice
and in surpassing faithfulness.
^{139}I am consumed with rage,
because my foes forget your words.
^{140}Your servant loves your promise;
it has been proved by fire.
^{141}Though belittled and despised,
I do not forget your precepts.
^{142}Your justice is forever right,
your teaching forever true.
^{143}Though distress and anguish come upon
me,
your commands are my delight.
^{144}Your decrees are forever just;
give me discernment that I may live.

QOPH
^{145}I call with all my heart, O LORD;
answer me that I may observe your
laws.

^{146}I call to you to save me
that I may keep your decrees.
^{147}I rise before dawn and cry out;
I put my hope in your words.
^{148}My eyes greet the night watches
as I meditate on your promise.^{b}
^{149}Hear my voice in your love, O LORD;
by your edict give me life.
^{150}Malicious persecutors draw near me;
they are far from your teaching.
^{151}You are near, O LORD;
reliable are all your commands.
^{152}Long have I known from your decrees
that you have established them forever.

RESH
^{153}Look at my affliction and rescue me,
for I have not forgotten your teaching.
^{154}Take up my cause and redeem me;^{c}
for the sake of your promise give me
life.
^{155}Salvation is far from sinners
because they do not cherish your laws.
^{156}Your compassion is great, O LORD;
in accord with your edicts give me life.
^{157}Though my persecutors and foes are
many
I do not turn from your decrees.
^{158}I view the faithless with loathing,^{d}
because they do not heed your promise.
^{159}See how I love your precepts, LORD;
in your kindness give me life.
^{160}Your every word is enduring;
all your just edicts are forever.

SHIN
^{161}Princes persecute me without reason,
but my heart reveres only your word.
^{162}I rejoice at your promise,
as one who has found rich spoil.
^{163}Falsehood I hate and abhor;
your teaching I love.
^{164}Seven times a day I praise you
because your edicts are just.
^{165}Lovers of your teaching have much peace;^{e}
for them there is no stumbling block.
^{166}I look for your salvation, LORD,
and I fulfill your commands.
^{167}I observe your decrees;
I love them very much.
^{168}I observe your precepts and decrees;

z: Pss 25, 16; 86, 16.   a: Tb 3, 2.   b: Pss 63, 7; 77, 7.   c: Ps 43, 1.   d: Ps 139, 22.   e: Ps 72, 7.

all my ways are before you.

TAW

¹⁶⁹Let my cry come before you, LORD;*f*
   in keeping with your word give me
      discernment.
¹⁷⁰Let my prayer come before you;
   rescue me according to your promise.
¹⁷¹May my lips pour forth your praise,
   because you teach me your laws.
¹⁷²May my tongue sing of your promise,
   for all your commands are just.
¹⁷³Keep your hand ready to help me,
   for I have chosen your precepts.
¹⁷⁴I long for your salvation, LORD;
   your teaching is my delight.
¹⁷⁵Let me live to praise you;
   may your edicts give me help.
¹⁷⁶I have wandered like a lost sheep;
   seek out your servant,
      for I do not forget your commands.*g*

See RG
175–76

PSALM 120*

Prayer of a Returned Exile

¹ A song of ascents.*

I

The LORD answered me
   when I called in my distress:*h*
² LORD, deliver me from lying lips,
   from treacherous tongues.*i*

II

³ What will the Lord inflict on you,

O treacherous tongue,
   and what more besides?*
⁴ A warrior's sharpened arrows
   and fiery coals of brushwood!*j* *

III

⁵ Alas, I was an alien in Meshech,*
   I lived near the tents of Kedar!
⁶ Too long did I live
   among those who hated peace.
⁷ When I spoke of peace,
   they were for war.*k*

PSALM 121*

See RG
175–76

The Lord My Guardian

¹ A song of ascents.

I

I raise my eyes toward the mountains.*
   From where will my help come?*l*
² My help comes from the LORD,
   the maker of heaven and earth.*m*

II

³ God will not allow your foot to slip;*n*
   your guardian does not sleep.
⁴ Truly, the guardian of Israel
   never slumbers nor sleeps.
⁵ The LORD is your guardian;*
   the LORD is your shade
      at your right hand.*o*
⁶ By day the sun cannot harm you,
   nor the moon by night.*p*
⁷ The LORD will guard you from all evil,

Ps 120: A thanksgiving, reporting divine rescue (1) yet with fervent prayer for further protection against lying attackers (2-4). The psalmist is acutely conscious of living away from God's own land where divine peace prevails (5-7).

120, 1: Song of ascents: Pss 120–134 all begin with this superscription. Most probably these fifteen psalms once formed a collection of psalms sung when pilgrims went to Jerusalem, since one "ascended" to Jerusalem (1 Kgs 12, 28; Pss 24, 3; 122, 4; Lk 2, 42) or to the house of God or to an altar (1 Kgs 12, 33; 2 Kgs 23, 2; Ps 24, 3). Less probable is the explanation that these psalms were sung by the exiles when they "ascended" to Jerusalem from Babylonia (cf Ezr 7, 9). The idea, found in the Mishnah, that the fifteen steps on which the Levites sang corresponded to these fifteen psalms (*Middot* 2, 5) must underlie the Vulgate translation *canticum graduum*, "song of the steps" or "gradual song."

120, 3: More besides: a common curse formula in Hebrew was "May the Lord do such and such evils to you [the evils being specified], and add *still more* to them." Cf 1 Sm 3, 17; 14, 44; 25, 22. Here the psalmist is at a loss for a suitable malediction.

120, 4: Coals of brushwood: coals made from the stalk of the broom plant burn with intense heat. The psalmist thinks of lighted coals cast at his enemies.

120, 5: Meshech was in the far north (Gn 10, 2) and **Kedar** was a tribe of the north Arabian desert (Gn 25, 13). The psalmist may be thinking generally of all aliens living among inhospitable peoples.

Ps 121: A blessing given to someone embarking on a dangerous journey, whether a soldier going on a campaign or a pilgrim returning home from the temple. People look anxiously at the wooded hills. Will God protect them on their journey (1)? The speaker declares that God is not confined to a place or a time (2), that every step is guarded (3-4); night and day (5-6) God watches over their every movement (7-8).

121, 1: The mountains: possibly Mount Zion, the site of the temple and hence of safety, but more probably mountains as a place of dangers, causing anxiety to the psalmist.

121, 5-6: The image of shade, a symbol of protection, is apt: God as shade protects from the harmful effects that ancients believed were caused by the sun and moon.

f: Ps 88, 3.   *g:* Is 53, 6; Jer 50, 6; Lk 15, 1-7.   *h:* Jon 2, 3.   *i:* Ps 12, 3-5; Sir 51, 3.   *j:* Pss 11, 6; 140, 11; Prv 16, 27.   *k:* Pss 35, 20; 140, 3-4.   *l:* Jer 3, 23.   *m:* Pss 124, 8; 146, 6.   *n:* Pss 66, 9; 91, 12; 1 Sm 2, 9; Prv 3, 23.   *o:* Ps 16, 8; 73, 23.   *p:* Wis 18, 3; Is 25, 4; 49, 10.

will always guard your life.*q*
[8] The LORD will guard your coming and
going
both now and forever.*r*

See RG
175-76

PSALM 122*

A Pilgrim's Prayer for Jerusalem

[1] A song of ascents. Of David.

I

I rejoiced when they said to me,
"Let us go to the house of the LORD."*s*
[2] And now our feet are standing
within your gates, Jerusalem.
[3] Jerusalem, built as a city,
walled round about.*t* *
[4] Here the tribes have come,
the tribes of the LORD,
As it was decreed for Israel,
to give thanks to the name of the LORD.*u*
[5] Here are the thrones of justice,
the thrones of the house of David.

II

[6] For the peace of Jerusalem pray:
"May those who love you prosper!"
[7] May peace be within your ramparts,
prosperity within your towers."*v*
[8] For family and friends I say,
"May peace be yours."
[9] For the house of the LORD, our God, I pray,
"May blessings be yours."

See RG
175-76

PSALM 123*

Reliance on the Lord

[1] A song of ascents.

To you I raise my eyes,

to you enthroned in heaven.*w*
[2] Yes, like the eyes of a servant
on the hand of his master,
Like the eyes of a maid
on the hand of her mistress,
So our eyes are on the LORD our God,
till we are shown favor.
[3] Show us favor, LORD, show us favor,
for we have our fill of contempt.*x*
[4] We have our fill of insult from the
insolent,
of disdain from the arrogant.

PSALM 124*

See RG
176

God, the Rescuer of the People

[1] A song of ascents. Of David.

I

Had not the LORD been with us,
let Israel say,*y*
[2] Had not the LORD been with us,
when people rose against us,
[3] They would have swallowed us alive,*z*
for their fury blazed against us.
[4] The waters would have engulfed us,
the torrent overwhelmed us;*a*
[5] seething waters would have drowned
us.

II

[6] Blessed be the LORD, who did not leave
us
to be torn by their fangs.
[7] We escaped with our lives
like a bird from the fowler's snare;
the snare was broken and we escaped.
[8] Our help is the name* of the LORD,
the maker of heaven and earth.*b*

Ps 122: A song of Zion, sung by pilgrims obeying the law to visit Jerusalem three times on a journey. The singer anticipates joining the procession into the city (1-3). Jerusalem is a place of encounter, where the people praise God (4) and hear the divine justice mediated by the king (5). The very buildings bespeak God's power (cf Ps 48, 13-15). May the grace of this place transform the people's lives (6-9)!

122, 3: Walled round about: literally, "which is joined to it," probably referring both to the density of the buildings and to the dense population.

Ps 123: A lament that begins as a prayer of an individual (1), who expresses by a touching comparison exemplary confidence in God (2). The psalm ends in prayer that God relieve the people's humiliation at the hands of the arrogant (3-4).

Ps 124: A thanksgiving which teaches that Israel's very existence is owed to God who rescues them. In the first part Israel's enemies are compared to the mythic sea dragon (2b-3a; cf Jer 51, 34) and Flood (3b-5; cf Is 51, 9-10). The psalm heightens the malice of human enemies by linking them to the primordial enemies of God's creation. Israel is a bird freed from the trapper's snare (6-8)—freed originally from Pharaoh and now from the current danger.

124, 8: Our help is the name: for the idiom, see Ex 18, 4.

q: Ps 97, 10. *r:* Dt 28, 6. *s:* Pss 43, 3-4; 84, 2-5. *t:* Ps 48, 13-14. *u:* Dt 16, 16. *v:* Ps 128, 5. *w:* Pss 25, 15; 119, 82; 141, 8. *x:* Ps 44, 13-14; Jb 12, 4. *y:* Ps 129, 1. *z:* Prv 1, 12. *a:* Pss 18, 5; 69, 2. *b:* Pss 121, 2; 146, 6.

See RG
175-76

PSALM 125*

Israel's Protector

1 A song of ascents.

I

Like Mount Zion are they
   who trust in the LORD,
   unshakable, forever enduring.*c*
2 As mountains surround Jerusalem,
   the LORD surrounds his people
   both now and forever.*d*

II

3 The scepter of the wicked will not prevail
   in the land given to the just,*
Lest the just themselves
   turn their hands to evil.

III

4 Do good, LORD, to the good,
   to those who are upright of heart.*e*
5 But those who turn aside to crooked ways
   may the LORD send down with the
      wicked.*f*
Peace upon Israel!*g*

See RG
175-76

PSALM 126*

The Reversal of Zion's Fortunes

1 A song of ascents.

I

When the LORD restored the fortunes of
      Zion,*h*
   then we thought we were dreaming.
2 Our mouths were filled with laughter;
   our tongues sang for joy.*i*
Then it was said among the nations,
   "The LORD has done great things for
      them."

3 The LORD had done great things
      for us;
   Oh, how happy we were!
4 Restore again our fortunes, LORD,
   like the dry stream beds of the
      Negeb.*

II

5 Those who sow in tears
   will reap with cries of joy.*j*
6 Those who go forth weeping,
   carrying sacks of seed,
Will return with cries of joy,
   carrying their bundled sheaves.

PSALM 127*

The Need of God's Blessing

1 A song of ascents. Of Solomon.

See RG
176

I

Unless the LORD build the house,
   they labor in vain who build.
Unless the LORD guard the city,
   in vain does the guard keep watch.
2 It is vain for you to rise early
   and put off your rest at night,
To eat bread earned by hard toil—
   all this God gives to his beloved in
      sleep.*k*

II

3 Children too are a gift from the LORD,
   the fruit of the womb, a reward.*l*
4 Like arrows in the hand of a warrior
   are the children born in one's youth.
5   Blessed are they whose quivers are
      full.
They will never be shamed
   contending with foes at the gate.*

Ps 125: In response to exilic anxieties about the ancient promises of restoration, the psalm expresses confidence that God will surround the people as the mountains surround Zion (1-2). The just will not be contaminated by the wicked (3). May God judge between the two groups (4-5).

125, 3: The land given to the just: literally, "the lot of the just." The promised land was divided among the tribes of Israel by lot (Nm 26, 55; Jos 18). **The just** are the members of the people who are obedient to God. If the domination of the wicked were to continue in the land, even the just would be infected by their evil attitudes.

Ps 126: A lament probably sung shortly after Israel's return from exile. The people rejoice that they are in Zion (1-3) but mere presence in the holy city is not enough; they must pray for the prosperity and the fertility of the land (4). The last verses are probably an oracle of promise: the painful work of sowing will be crowned with life (5-6).

126, 4: Like the dry stream beds of the Negeb: the psalmist prays for rain in such abundance that the dry riverbeds will run.

Ps 127: The psalm puts together two proverbs (1-2 and 3-5) on God establishing "houses" or families. The prosperity of human groups is not the work of humans but the gift of God.

127, 5: At the gate: the reference is not to enemies besieging the walls of a city but to adversaries in litigation. Law courts functioned in the open area near the main city gate. The more adult sons a man had, the more forceful he would appear in disputes. Cf Prv 31, 23.

---

c: Prv 10, 25.   *d:* Dt 32, 11.   *e:* Ps 18, 25ff.   *f:* Prv 3, 32.   *g:* Ps 128, 6.   *h:* Ps 14, 7.   *i:* Jb 8, 21.   *j:* Bar 4, 23; Is 65, 19.   *k:* Eccl 2, 24.   *l:* Pss 115, 14; 128, 3; Dt 28, 11; Prv 17, 6.

See RG
176

PSALM 128*

The Happy Home of the Just

1 A song of ascents.

I

Happy are all who fear the LORD,*
  who walk in the ways of God.*m*
2 What your hands provide you will
    enjoy;
  you will be happy and prosper:*n*
3 Like a fruitful vine
    your wife within your home,
  Like olive plants
    your children around your table.*o*
4 Just so will they be blessed
    who fear the LORD.

II

5 May the LORD bless you from Zion,
    all the days of your life*p*
  That you may share Jerusalem's joy
6   and live to see your children's
    children.*q*
  Peace upon Israel!*r*

See RG
175-76

PSALM 129*

Against Israel's Enemies

1 A song of ascents.

I

Much have they oppressed me from my
    youth,
  now let Israel say.*s*
2 Much have they oppressed me from my
    youth,*t*
  yet they have not prevailed.

3 Upon my back the plowers plowed,
    as they traced their long furrows.*u*
4 But the just LORD cut me free
    from the ropes of the yoke of the
    wicked.*

II

5 May they be scattered in disgrace,
    all who hate Zion.
6 May they be like grass on the rooftops*
    withered in early growth,*v*
7 Never to fill the reaper's hands,
    nor the arms of the binders of
    sheaves,
8 With none passing by to call out:
  "The blessing of the LORD be upon
    you!*
  We bless you in the name of the
    LORD!"*w*

See RG
175-76

PSALM 130*

Prayer for Pardon and Mercy

1 A song of ascents.

I

Out of the depths* I call to you,
    LORD;
2   Lord, hear my cry!
  May your ears be attentive
    to my cry for mercy.*x*
3 If you, LORD, mark our sins,
    Lord, who can stand?*y*
4 But with you is forgiveness
    and so you are revered.*

II

5 I wait with longing for the LORD,

Ps 128: A statement that the ever-reliable God will bless
the reverent (1). God's blessing is concrete: satisfaction and
prosperity, a fertile spouse and abundant children (2-4). The
perspective is that of the adult male, ordinarily the ruler and
representative of the household to the community. The last
verses extend the blessing to all the people for generations to
come (5-6).

128, 1: All who fear the LORD: literally, singular: "the
one fearing," is used in a typical sense and so is translated by
the plural.

Ps 129: A psalm giving thanks for God's many rescues of
Israel over the long course of their history (1-4); the people
pray that their oppressors never know the joy of harvest (5-8).

129, 4: The ropes of the yoke of the wicked: usually understood as the rope for yoking animals to the plow. If it is
severed, the plowing (cf 3) comes to a halt.

129, 6: Like grass on the rooftops: after the spring rains,
grass would sprout from the coat of mud with which the flat
roofs of simple houses were covered, but when the dry sum-

mer began there was no moisture in the thin roof-covering to
sustain the grass.

129, 8: The blessing of the LORD be upon you: harvesters greeted one another with such blessings. Cf Ru 2, 4.

Ps 130: This lament, a Penitential Psalm, is the *De pro-
fundis* used in liturgical prayers for the faithful departed. In
deep sorrow the psalmist cries to God (1-2), asking for mercy
(3-4). The psalmist's trust (5-6) becomes a model for the
people (7-8).

130, 1: The depths: Sheol here is a metaphor of total misery. Deep anguish makes the psalmist feel "like those descending to the pit" (Ps 143, 7).

130, 4: And so you are revered: the experience of God's
mercy leads one to a greater sense of God.

---

m: Ps 112, 1.   *n:* Ps 112, 3.   *o:* Jb 29, 5; Ps 144, 12.   *p:* Pss 20,
3; 134, 3.   *q:* Jb 42, 16; Prv 17, 6.   *r:* Ps 125, 5.   *s:* Ps 124, 1.
t: Ps 118, 13.   *u:* Is 51, 23.   *v:* Is 37, 27.   *w:* Ps 118, 26.   *x:* Pss
5, 2-3; 55, 2-3; 86, 6; Lam 3, 55-56; Jon 2, 3.   *y:* Na 1, 6.

my soul waits for his word.[z]

6 My soul looks for the Lord
more than sentinels for daybreak.[a]
More than sentinels for daybreak,
7 let Israel look for the LORD,
For with the LORD is kindness,
with him is full redemption,[b]
8 And God will redeem Israel
from all their sins.[c]

**See RG
175-76**

PSALM 131 *

Humble Trust in God
1 A song of ascents. Of David.

LORD, my heart is not proud;
nor are my eyes haughty.
I do not busy myself with great matters,
with things too sublime for me.[d]
2 Rather, I have stilled my soul,
hushed it like a weaned child.
Like a weaned child on its mother's lap,
so is my soul within me.[e]
3 Israel, hope in the LORD,
now and forever.

**See RG
176**

PSALM 132 *

The Covenant between
David and God
1 A song of ascents.

I

LORD, remember David
and all his anxious care;*
2 How he swore an oath to the LORD,
vowed to the Mighty One of Jacob:*
3 "I will not enter the house where I live,[f]
nor lie on the couch where I sleep;
4 I will give my eyes no sleep,

my eyelids no rest,
5 Till I find a home for the LORD,
a dwelling for the Mighty One of
Jacob."
6 "We have heard of it in Ephrathah;*
we have found it in the fields of Jaar.*
7 Let us enter God's dwelling;
let us worship at God's footstool."[g]
8 "Arise, LORD, come to your resting
place,[h]
you and your majestic ark.
9 Your priests will be clothed with justice;
your faithful will shout for joy."
10 For the sake of David your servant,
do not reject your anointed.

II

11 The LORD swore an oath to David,
a pledge never to be broken:[i]
"Your own offspring[j] I will set upon
your throne.
12 If your sons observe my covenant,
the laws I shall teach them,
Their sons, in turn,
shall sit forever on your throne."
13 Yes, the LORD has chosen Zion,
desired it for a dwelling:
14 "This is my resting place forever;
here I will dwell, for I desire it.
15 I will bless Zion with meat;
its poor I will fill with bread.
16 I will clothe its priests with blessing;
its faithful shall shout for joy.[k]
17 There I will make a horn sprout for
David's line;[l] *
I will set a lamp for my anointed.
18 His foes I will clothe with shame,
but on him my crown shall gleam."

Ps 131: A song of trust, in which the psalmist gives up self-sufficiency (1), like a babe enjoying the comfort of its mother's lap (2), thus providing a model for Israel's faith (3).

Ps 132: A song for a liturgical ceremony in which the ark, the throne of Israel's God, was carried in procession to the temple. The singer asks that David's care for the proper housing of the ark be regarded with favor (1-5), and tells how it was brought to Jerusalem (6-10). There follows God's promise of favor to the Davidic dynasty (11-12) and to Zion (13-17). The transfer of the ark to the tent in Jerusalem is described in 2 Sm 6.

132, 1: All his anxious care: to build the temple. Cf 2 Sm 7, 1-17 and 1 Kgs 8, 17.

132, 2. 5: Mighty One of Jacob: one of the titles of Israel's God. Cf Gn 49, 24; Is 49, 26; 60, 16.

132, 6: Ephrathah: the homeland of David. Cf Ru 4, 11. The fields of Jaar: poetic for Kiriath-jearim, a town west of Jerusalem where the ark remained for several generations. Cf 1 Sm 7, 1-2; 2 Sm 6, 2; 1 Chr 13, 5-6.

132, 17: A horn sprout for David's line: the image of the horn, a symbol of strength, is combined with that of a "sprout," a term used for the Davidic descendant (cf Jer 23, 5; 33, 15; Zec 3, 8; 6, 12). Early Christians referred the latter designation to Christ as son of David (Lk 1, 69).

z: Ps 119, 81. a: Is 21, 11; 26, 9. b: Pss 86, 15; 100, 5; 103, 8. c: Ps 25, 22; Mt 1, 21. d: Ps 139, 6. e: Is 66, 12-13. f: 2 Sm 7; 1 Chr 28, 2. g: Ps 99, 5. h: 8-10: Pss 2, 2; 89, 21; 95, 11; Nm 10, 35; 2 Chr 6, 41-42; Sir 24, 7. i: Ps 110, 4; 2 Sm 7, 12. j: 11-14: Ps 68, 17; 1 Kgs 8, 13; Sir 24, 7. k: 2 Chr 6, 41; Is 61, 10. l: Is 11, 1; Jer 33, 15; Ez 29, 21; Zec 3, 8; Lk 1, 69.

PSALM 133*

See RG 176

A Vision of a Blessed Community

1 A song of ascents. Of David.

How good it is, how pleasant,
  where the people* dwell as one!
2 Like precious ointment* on
    the head,*m*
  running down upon the beard,
Upon the beard of Aaron,
  upon the collar of his robe.
3 Like dew* of Hermon* coming down
  upon the mountains of Zion.*n*
There the LORD has lavished blessings,
  life for evermore!*o*

PSALM 134*

See RG 176

Exhortation to the Night Watch to Bless God

1 A song of ascents.

Come, bless the LORD,
  all you servants of the LORD*
Who stand in the house of the LORD
  through the long hours of night.*p*
2 Lift up your hands toward the
    sanctuary,*q*
  and bless the LORD.
3 May the LORD who made heaven and
    earth*r*
  bless you from Zion.

PSALM 135*

See RG 175

Praise of God, the Ruler and Benefactor of Israel

1 Hallelujah!

I

Praise the name of the LORD!
  Praise, you servants of the LORD,*s*
2 Who stand in the house of the LORD,
  in the courts of the house of our God!*t*
3 Praise the LORD; the LORD is good!
  Sing to God's name; it is gracious!
4 For the LORD has chosen Jacob,
  Israel as a treasured possession.*u* *

II

5 I know that the LORD is great,
  our Lord is greater than all gods.*v*
6 Whatever the LORD wishes
  he does in heaven and on earth,
  in the seas and in all the deeps.*w*
7 He raises storm clouds from the end of
    the earth,
  makes lightning and rain,
  brings forth wind from the
    storehouse.*x*

III

8 He struck down Egypt's firstborn,*y*
  human and beast alike,
9 And sent signs and portents against you,
    Egypt,
  against Pharaoh and all his servants.
10 The Lord struck down many nations,*z*
  slew mighty kings—

Ps 133: A benediction over a peaceful community, most probably the people Israel, but appropriate too for Israelite families (1). The history of Israel, whether of its ancestors in the book of Genesis or of later periods, was a history of distinct groups struggling to live in unity. Here that unity is declared blessed, like the holy oils upon the priest Aaron or the dew of the rainless summer that waters the crops (2-3).

133, 1: The people: literally, "brothers," i.e., male and female members of a kin group or people—most probably, the people Israel.

133, 2: Ointment: oil was used at the consecration of the high priest (Ex 30, 22-33).

133, 3: Dew: dew was an important source of moisture in the dry climate (Gn 27, 28; Hos 14, 6). **Hermon**: the majestic snow-capped mountain visible in the north of Palestine.

Ps 134: A brief liturgy exhorting the temple singers to acknowledge the great deeds of God at a night service (cf Is 30, 29). Mount Zion is the place from which blessings affect the lives of humans, for there Israel's God dwells.

134, 1: Servants of the LORD: priests and Levites. Cf Dt 10, 8; Pss 113, 1; 135, 1; Dn 3, 84-85.

Ps 135: The hymn begins and ends with an invitation to praise God (1-3. 19-20) for the great act of choosing Israel (4). The story of Israel's emergence as a people is told in 5-14; God created and redeemed the people, easily conquering all opposition. God's defeat of hostile powers means that the powers themselves and their images are useless (15-18). The last three verses appear also in Ps 115, 4-8.

135, 4: Though all nations are God's, Israel has a special status as God's "treasured" people: Ex 19, 5; Dt 7, 6; 14, 2; 26, 18; Mal 3, 17.

---

m: Ex 30, 25. 30.   *n*: Hos 14, 6.   *o*: Dt 28, 8; 30, 20.   *p*: Ps 135, 1-2; 1 Chr 9, 33.   *q*: Pss 28, 2; 141, 2.   *r*: Pss 20, 3; 128, 5; Nm 6, 24.   *s*: Ps 113, 1.   *t*: Ps 134, 1.   *u*: Pss 33, 12; 144, 15; Ex 19, 6; Dt 7, 6.   *v*: Ps 95, 3; Ex 18, 11.   *w*: Ps 115, 3.   *x*: Ps 148, 8; Jer 10, 13; 51, 16; Jb 37, 9.   *y*: 8-9: Pss 78, 51; 105, 27. 36; 136, 10; Ex 12, 29.   *z*: 10-12: Nm 21, 21-35; Dt 2, 24—3, 17; Ps 136, 17-22.

Psalm 136 is known in Jewish liturgy as the Great Hallel and has been incorporated into the Passover Seder. Like 135, it is part of the introductory prayers to the morning service on Sabbath and festival days. The psalm is probably written to be chanted responsively, with the assembly chanting the refrain after each line. In Hebrew *hesed*, here translated "love," means a favor done out of loyalty. God's *hesed* to Israel is eternal. The psalm recounts in chronological order the many acts of *hesed* that God did for Israel in the past and the refrain confirms that these acts of *hesed* will continue.

¹¹ Sihon, king of the Amorites,
    Og, king of Bashan,
    all the kings of Canaan—
¹² And made their land a heritage,
    a heritage for Israel his people.
¹³ O LORD, your name is forever,
    your renown, from age to age!*a*
¹⁴ For the LORD defends his people,
    shows mercy to his servants.*b*

IV

¹⁵ The idols of the nations are silver and
    gold,*c*
    the work of human hands.
¹⁶ They have mouths but speak not;
    they have eyes but see not;
¹⁷ They have ears but hear not;
    no breath is in their mouths.
¹⁸ Their makers shall be like them,
    all who trust in them.

V

¹⁹ House of Israel, bless the LORD!*d*
    House of Aaron, bless the LORD!
²⁰ House of Levi, bless the LORD!
    You who fear the LORD, bless the
    LORD!
²¹ Blessed from Zion be the LORD,
    who dwells in Jerusalem!
    Hallelujah!

See RG 175

PSALM 136*

*Hymn of Thanksgiving for
God's Everlasting Love*

I

¹ Praise the LORD, who is so good;*e*

God's love endures forever;
² Praise the God of gods;
    God's love endures forever;
³ Praise the Lord of lords;
    God's love endures forever;

II

⁴ Who alone has done great wonders,*f*
    God's love endures forever;
⁵ Who skillfully made the heavens,*g*
    God's love endures forever;
⁶ Who spread the earth upon the waters,*h*
    God's love endures forever;
⁷ Who made the great lights,
    God's love endures forever;
⁸ The sun to rule the day,
    God's love endures forever;
⁹ The moon and stars to rule the night,*i*
    God's love endures forever;

III

¹⁰ Who struck down the firstborn of
    Egypt,*j*
    God's love endures forever;
¹¹ And led Israel from their midst,
    God's love endures forever;
¹² With mighty hand and outstretched
    arm,*k*
    God's love endures forever;
¹³ Who split in two the Red Sea
    God's love endures forever;
¹⁴ And led Israel through,
    God's love endures forever;
¹⁵ But swept Pharaoh and his army into the
    Red Sea,*l*
    God's love endures forever;

Ps 136: The hymn praises Israel's God ("the God of gods," 2), who has created the world in which Israel lives. The refrain occurring after every line suggests that a speaker and chorus sang the psalm in antiphonal fashion. A single act of God is described in 4-25: God arranges the heavens and the earth as the environment for human community, and then creates the community by freeing them and giving them land. In

the final section (23-25) God, who created the people and gave them land, continues to protect and nurture them.

a: Ps 102, 13; Ex 3, 15. *b:* Dt 32, 36. *c:* 15-18: Ps 115, 4-6. 8. *d:* 19-20: Ps 118, 2-4. *e:* Pss 100, 5; 118, 1. *f:* Ps 72, 18. *g:* Gn 1, 9-19. *h:* Ps 24, 2. *i:* Jer 31, 35. *j:* Ex 12, 29. 51; 14, 22. 27; 15, 22; Pss 78, 51-52; 135, 8. *k:* Dt 4, 34. *l:* Ex 14, 21f.

16 Who led the people through the desert,*m*
God's love endures forever;

IV

17 Who struck down great kings,*n*
God's love endures forever;

18 Slew powerful kings,
God's love endures forever;

19 Sihon, king of the Amorites,
God's love endures forever;

20 Og, king of Bashan,
God's love endures forever;

21 And made their lands a heritage,
God's love endures forever;

22 A heritage for Israel,* God's servant,
God's love endures forever.

V

23 The LORD remembered us in our misery,
God's love endures forever;

24 Freed us from our foes,
God's love endures forever;

25 And gives food to all flesh,
God's love endures forever.

VI

26 Praise the God of heaven,
God's love endures forever.

See RG
175

PSALM 137*

Sorrow and Hope in Exile

I

1 By the rivers of Babylon
we sat mourning and weeping
when we remembered Zion.*o*

2 On the poplars* of that land
we hung up our harps.*p*

3 There our captors asked us
for the words of a song;
Our tormentors, for a joyful song:

"Sing for us a song of Zion!"

4 But how could we sing a song of the
LORD
in a foreign land?

II

5 If I forget you, Jerusalem,
may my right hand wither.*q*

6 May my tongue stick to my palate
if I do not remember you,
If I do not exalt Jerusalem
beyond all my delights.

III

7 Remember, LORD, against Edom
that day at Jerusalem.
They said: "Level it, level it
down to its foundations!"*r*

8 Fair Babylon, you destroyer,
happy those who pay you back
the evil you have done us!*s*

9 Happy those who seize your
children
and smash them against a rock.*t* *

PSALM 138*

Hymn of a Grateful Heart

See RG
175

1 Of David.

I

I thank you, LORD, with all my
heart;*u*
before the gods* to you I sing.

2 I bow low toward your holy temple;
I praise your name for your fidelity
and love.
For you have exalted over all
your name and your promise.

3 When I cried out, you answered;
you strengthened my spirit.

136, 22: A heritage for Israel: the land was given to Israel by God to be handed on to future generations.

Ps 137: A temple singer refuses to sing the people's sacred songs in an alien land despite demands from Babylonian captors (1-4). The singer swears an oath by what is most dear to a musician—hands and tongue—to exalt Jerusalem always (5-6). The psalm ends with a prayer that the old enemies of Jerusalem, Edom and Babylon, be destroyed (7-9).

137, 2: Poplars: sometimes incorrectly translated "willow." The Euphrates poplar is a high tree common on riverbanks in the Orient.

137, 9: Happy those who seize your children and smash them against a rock: the infants represent the future generations, and so must be destroyed if the enemy is truly to be eradicated.

Ps 138: A thanksgiving to God, who came to the rescue of the psalmist. Divine rescue was not the result of the psalmist's virtues but of God's loving fidelity (1-3). The act is not a private transaction but a public act that stirs the surrounding nations to praise God's greatness and care for the people (4-6). The psalmist, having experienced salvation, trusts that God will always be there in moments of danger (7-8).

138, 1: Before the gods: i.e., heavenly beings, who were completely subordinate to Israel's God. The earthly temple represents the heavenly palace of God.

m: Dt 8, 2. 15.   *n:* 17-22: Ps 135, 10-12.   *o:* Ez 3, 15; Lam 3, 48. *p:* Is 24, 8; Lam 5, 14.   *q:* Jer 51, 50.   *r:* Jer 49, 7; Lam 4, 21-22; Ez 25, 12-14.   *s:* Is 47, 1-3; Jer 50-51.   *t:* Hos 14, 1.   *u:* Ps 9, 1.

II

4 All the kings of earth will praise you,
  LORD,
    when they hear the words of your
    mouth.
5 They will sing of the ways of the LORD:
    "How great is the glory of the
    LORD!"
6 The LORD is on high, but cares for the
    lowly;
    and knows the proud from afar.
7 Though I walk in the midst of dangers,
    you guard my life when my enemies
    rage.
  You stretch out your hand;
    your right hand saves me.
8 The LORD is with me to the end.
  LORD, your love endures forever.
  Never forsake the work of your
    hands!

See RG
176

PSALM 139*

The All-knowing and
Ever-present God

1 For the leader. A psalm of David.

I

LORD, you have probed me, you know me:
2   you know when I sit and stand;[w] *
    you understand my thoughts from afar.
3 My travels and my rest you mark;
    with all my ways you are familiar.
4 Even before a word is on my tongue,
  LORD, you know it all.
5 Behind and before you encircle me
    and rest your hand upon me.
6 Such knowledge is beyond me,
    far too lofty for me to reach.[x]

II

7 Where can I hide from your spirit?
    From your presence, where can I flee?
8 If I ascend to the heavens, you are there;
    if I lie down in Sheol, you are there too.[y]

9 If I fly with the wings of dawn*
    and alight beyond the sea,*
10 Even there your hand will guide me,
    your right hand hold me fast.
11 If I say, "Surely darkness shall hide me,
    and night shall be my light"—*
12 Darkness is not dark for you,
    and night shines as the day.
    Darkness and light are but one.[z]

III

13 You formed my inmost being;
    you knit me in my mother's womb.[a]
14 I praise you, so wonderfully you made
    me;
    wonderful are your works!
  My very self you knew;
15   my bones were not hidden from you,
  When I was being made in secret,
    fashioned as in the depths of the
    earth.*
16 Your eyes foresaw my actions;
    in your book all are written down;[b]
    my days were shaped, before one
    came to be.

IV

17 How precious to me are your designs,
    O God;
    how vast the sum of them!
18 Were I to count, they would outnumber
    the sands;
    to finish, I would need eternity.[c]
19 If only you would destroy the wicked,
    O God,
    and the bloodthirsty would depart
    from me![d]
20 Deceitfully they invoke your name;
    your foes swear faithless oaths.
21 Do I not hate, LORD, those who hate you?
    Those who rise against you, do I not
    loathe?[e]
22 With fierce hatred I hate them,
    enemies I count as my own.

Ps 139: A hymnic meditation on God's omnipresence and omniscience. The psalmist is keenly aware of God's all-knowing gaze (1-6), of God's presence in every part of the universe (7-12), and of God's control over the psalmist's very self (13-16). Summing up 1-16. 17-18 express wonder. There is only one place hostile to God's rule—wicked people. The psalmist prays to be removed from their company (19-24).

139, 2: When I sit and stand: in all my physical movement.
139, 9: Fly with the wings of dawn: go to the extremities of the east. **Beyond the sea:** uttermost bounds of the west; the

sea is the Mediterranean.
139, 11: Night shall be my light: night to me is what day is to others.
139, 15: The depths of the earth: figurative language for the womb, stressing the hidden and mysterious operations that occur there.

v: Lk 1, 51-52. w: 2 Kgs 19, 27; Jb 12, 3. x: Ps 131, 1. y: Jb 23, 8-9; Jer 23, 23-24. z: Jb 12, 22. a: Wis 7, 1; Eccl 11, 5; Jb 1, 21. b: Mal 3, 16. c: Jb 11, 7. d: Jb 21, 14. e: Ps 119, 158.

V

²³ Probe me, God, know my heart;
     try me, know my concerns.*

²⁴ See if my way is crooked,
     then lead me in the ancient paths.*

See RG
175

PSALM 140*

Prayer for Deliverance from
the Wicked

¹ For the leader. A psalm of David.

I

² Deliver me, LORD, from the wicked;
     preserve me from the violent,ᵍ

³ From those who plan evil in their
     hearts,
     who stir up conflicts every day,

⁴ Who sharpen their tongues like
     serpents,
     venom of asps upon their lips.ʰ * Selah

II

⁵ Keep me, LORD, from the clutches of the
     wicked;
     preserve me from the violent,
     who plot to trip me up.ⁱ

⁶ The arrogant have set a trap for me;
     villains have spread a net,*
     laid snares for me by the
     wayside.   Selah

⁷ I say to the LORD: You are my God;ʲ
     listen, LORD, to the words of my
     prayer.

⁸ My revered LORD, my strong helper,
     my helmet on the day of battle.

⁹ LORD, do not grant the desires of the
     wicked;
     do not let their plots succeed.   Selah

¹⁰ Around me they raise their proud
     heads;

may the mischief they threaten
     overwhelm them.

¹¹ May God rain burning coals upon
     them,ᵏ
     cast them into the grave never more to
     rise.

III

¹² Slanderers will not survive on earth;
     evil will quickly entrap the violent.

¹³ For I know the LORD will secure
     justice for the needy, their rights for
     the poor.

¹⁴ Then the just will give thanks to your
     name;
     the upright will dwell in your
     presence.ˡ

PSALM 141*

Prayer for Deliverance from
the Wicked

See RG
175, 179

¹ A psalm of David.

LORD, I call to you;
     come quickly to help me;
     listen to my plea when I call.

² Let my prayer be incense* before you:
     my uplifted hands* an evening
     sacrifice.ᵐ

³ Set a guard, LORD, before my mouth,
     a gatekeeper at my lips.ⁿ

⁴ Do not let my heart incline to evil,
     or yield to any sin.
     I will never feast upon
     the fine food of evildoers.

⁵ Let the just strike me; that is kindness;*
     let them rebuke me; that is oil for my
     head.ᵒ
     All this I shall not refuse,

139, 24: My way . . . the ancient paths: the manner of living of our ancestors, who were faithful to God's will. Cf Jer 6, 16.

Ps 140: A lament seeking rescue from violent and treacherous foes (2-6). The psalmist remains trusting (7-8), vigorously praying that the plans of the wicked recoil upon themselves (9-12). A serene statement of praise ends the psalm (13-14). The psalmist is content to be known as one of "the needy," "the poor," "the just," "the upright" (13-14), a class of people expecting divine protection.

140, 4: Similar metaphors for a wicked tongue are used in Pss 52, 4; 55, 22; 58, 5.

140, 6: Have set a trap . . . have spread a net: the same figure, of hunters setting traps, occurs in Pss 9, 16; 31, 5; 35, 7; 64, 6. Cf Mt 22, 15; Lk 11, 54.

Ps 141: A lament of an individual (1-2) who is keenly aware that only the righteous can worship God properly and who therefore prays to be protected from the doomed wicked (3-10).

141, 2: Incense: literally, "smoke," i.e., the fragrant fumes arising from the altar at the burning of sacrificial animals or of aromatic spices; also used in Rv 5, 8 as a symbol of prayer. **My uplifted hands**: the gesture of supplication. Cf Pss 28, 2; 63, 5; 88, 10; 134, 2; 143, 6.

141, 5-7: The Hebrew text is obscure.

f: Pss 17, 3; 26, 2.   g: Ps 71, 4.   h: Ps 64, 4; Rom 3, 13.   i: Jer 18, 22; Pss 56, 7; 57, 7.   j: Ps 31, 15.   k: Pss 11, 6; 120, 4; Gn 19, 24.   l: Pss 11, 7; 16, 11; 17, 15.   m: Ps 134, 2; Ex 30, 8. n: Sir 22, 27.   o: Prv 9, 8; 25, 12.

but will pray despite these trials.
6 When their leaders are cast over the
cliff,
all will learn that my prayers were
heard.
7 As when a farmer plows a field into
broken clods,
so their bones will be strewn at the
mouth of Sheol.
8 My eyes are upon you, O GOD, my
Lord;[p]
in you I take refuge; do not strip me of
life.
9 Guard me from the trap they have set for
me,
from the snares of evildoers.[q]
10 Into their own nets let all the wicked
fall,
while I make good my own escape.

PSALM 142[*]

See RG
175

A Prayer in Time of Trouble

1 A *maskil* of David, when he was in the
cave.[*] A prayer.

2 With full voice I cry to the LORD;
with full voice I beseech the LORD.
3 Before God I pour out my complaint,
lay bare my distress.
4 My spirit is faint within me,[r]
but you know my path.[s]
Along the way I walk
they have hidden a trap for me.[t]
5 I look to my right hand,[u]
but no friend is there.
There is no escape for me;
no one cares for me.
6 I cry out to you, LORD,
I say, You are my refuge,[v]

my portion in the land of the
living.[w]
7 Listen to my cry for help,
for I am brought very low.[x]
Rescue me from my pursuers,
for they are too strong for me.
8 Lead me out of my prison,
that I may give thanks to your name.
Then the just shall gather around me[*]
because you have been good to me.

PSALM 143[*]

See RG
175

A Prayer in Distress

1 A psalm of David.

LORD, hear my prayer;
in your faithfulness listen to my
pleading;
answer me in your justice.
2 Do not enter into judgment with your
servant;
before you no living being can be
just.[y]
3 The enemy has pursued me;
they have crushed[*] my life to the
ground.[z]
They have left me in darkness
like those long dead.[a]
4 My spirit is faint within me;
my heart is dismayed.[b]
5 I remember the days of old;
I ponder all your deeds;
the works of your hands I recall.[c]
6 I stretch out my hands to you;
I thirst for you like a parched
land.[d]   Selah
7 Hasten to answer me, LORD;
for my spirit fails me.
Do not hide your face from me,

Ps 142: In this lament imploring God for help (2-4b), the psalmist tells how enemies have set a trap (4c-5), and prays for rescue (6-8). The speaker feels utterly alone (5), exhausted (7), and may even be imprisoned (8a). Prison is possibly a metaphor for general distress. The last two verses are the vow of praise, made after receiving an assurance of divine help (8cd).

142, 1: In the cave: cf 1 Sm 22, 1; 24, 1-3; Ps 57, 1.

142, 8: Then the just shall gather around me: in the temple, when the psalmist offers a thanksgiving sacrifice.

Ps 143: One of the Church's seven Penitential Psalms, this lament is a prayer to be freed from death-dealing enemies. The psalmist addresses God, aware that there is no equality between God and humans; salvation is a gift (1-2). Victimized by evil people (3-4), the psalmist recites ("remembers") God's past actions on behalf of the innocent (5-6). The psalm continues with fervent prayer (7-9) and a strong desire for guidance and protection (10-12).

143, 3: They have crushed: literally, "he crushed"; the singular is used typically, hence the plural translation.

p: Pss 25, 15; 123, 1-2.   *q:* Ps 142, 4.   *r:* Ps 143, 4.   *s:* Ps 139, 24.   *t:* Ps 141, 9.   *u:* Pss 16, 8; 73, 23; 121, 5.   *v:* Ps 91, 2: 9.   *w:* Pss 16, 5; 27, 13; 116, 9; Is 38, 11.   *x:* Ps 79, 8.   *y:* Ecc 7, 20; Jb 4, 17; Rom 3, 20.   *z:* Ps 7, 6.   *a:* Lam 3, 6.   *b:* Ps 142, 4; Jb 17, 1.   *c:* Ps 77, 6. 12.   *d:* Pss 42, 2; 63, 2.

lest I become like those descending to
   the pit.*e*

8 At dawn let me hear of your kindness,
   for in you I trust.
Show me the path I should walk,
   for to you I entrust my life.*f*

9 Rescue me, LORD, from my foes,
   for in you I hope.

10 Teach me to do your will,
   for you are my God.
May your kind spirit guide me
   on ground that is level.

11 For your name's sake, LORD, give me
   life;
in your justice lead me out of distress.

12 In your kindness put an end to my foes;
   destroy all who attack me,
   for I am your servant.*g*

> See RG
> 176

PSALM 144*

A Prayer for Victory and Prosperity

1 Of David.

I

Blessed be the LORD, my rock,*
   who trains my hands for battle,
   my fingers for war;

2 My safeguard and my fortress,
   my stronghold, my deliverer,
My shield, in whom I trust,
   who subdues peoples under me.

II

3 LORD, what are mortals that you notice
   them;
   human beings, that you take thought of
   them?*h* *

4 They are but a breath;
   their days are like a passing
   shadow.*i* *

5 LORD, incline your heavens and come;*
   touch the mountains and make them
   smoke.*j*

6 Flash forth lightning and scatter my
   foes;
   shoot your arrows and rout them.

7 Reach out your hand from on high;
   deliver me from the many waters;
   rescue me from the hands of foreign
   foes.

8 Their mouths speak untruth;
   their right hands are raised in lying
   oaths.*

9 O God, a new song I will sing to you;
   on a ten-stringed lyre I will play for
   you.*k*

10 You give victory to kings;
   you delivered David your servant.*l*
From the menacing sword *11* deliver me;
   rescue me from the hands of foreign
   foes.
Their mouths speak untruth;
   their right hands are raised in lying
   oaths.

III

12 May our sons be like plants*m*
   well nurtured from their youth,
Our daughters, like carved columns,
   shapely as those of the temple.

13 May our barns be full
   with every kind of store.
May our sheep increase by thousands,
   by tens of thousands in our fields;
   may our oxen be well fattened.

14 May there be no breach in the walls,
   no exile, no outcry in our streets.*n*

15 Happy the people so blessed;
   happy the people whose God is the
   LORD.*o*

Ps 144: The psalm may reflect a ceremony in which the king, as leader of the army, asked God's help (1-8). In 9 the poem shifts abruptly from pleading to thanksgiving, and (except for 11) shifts again to prayer for the people. The first section (1-2) is a prayer of thanks for victory; the second (3-7a), a humble acknowledgment of human nothingness and a supplication that God show forth saving power; the third (9-11), a promise of future thanksgiving; the fourth (12-15), a wish for prosperity and peace. A prayer for deliverance from treacherous foes serves as a refrain after the second and third sections (7b-8. 11). Except for its final section, the psalm is made up almost entirely of verses from other psalms.

144, 1-2: Composed of phrases from Ps 18, 3. 35. 47-48.
144, 3: Similar to Ps 8, 5.
144, 4: Composed of phrases from Pss 39, 6; 102, 12.
144, 5-7: Adapted in large part from Pss 18, 10. 15. 17; 104, 32.
144, 8b. 11b: Their right hands are raised in lying oaths: the psalmist's enemies give false testimony.

e: Pss 28, 1; 30, 4; 88, 5; Prv 1, 12. *f:* Pss 25, 4; 27, 11; 86, 11; 119, 12. 35. *g:* Ps 116, 16. *h:* Jb 7, 17. *i:* Pss 62, 10; 90, 9-10; Jb 7, 16; Eccl 6, 12; Wis 2, 5. *j:* Is 63, 19. *k:* Ps 33, 2-3. *l:* Ps 18, 51. *m:* Ps 128, 3. *n:* Is 65, 19. *o:* Ps 33, 12.

See RG
175-76

PSALM 145[*]

The Greatness and Goodness
of God

[1] Praise. Of David.

I will extol you, my God and king;
    I will bless your name forever.
[2] Every day I will bless you;
    I will praise your name forever.[p]
[3] Great is the LORD and worthy of high
    praise;[q]
    God's grandeur is beyond
    understanding.
[4] One generation praises your deeds to the
    next
    and proclaims your mighty works.[r]
[5] They speak of the splendor of your
    majestic glory,
    tell of your wonderful deeds.[s]
[6] They speak of your fearsome power
    and attest to your great deeds.[t]
[7] They publish the renown of your
    abounding goodness
    and joyfully sing of your justice.
[8] The LORD is gracious and merciful,
    slow to anger and abounding in
    love.[u]
[9] The LORD is good to all,
    compassionate to every creature.[v]
[10] All your works give you thanks, O LORD
    and your faithful bless you.[w]
[11] They speak of the glory of your reign
    and tell of your great works,
[12] Making known to all your power,
    the glorious splendor of your rule.
[13] Your reign is a reign for all ages,
    your dominion for all generations.[x]
    The LORD is trustworthy in every word,
    and faithful in every work.

[14] The LORD supports all who are falling
    and raises up all who are bowed
    down.[y]
[15] The eyes of all look hopefully to you;
    you give them their food in due
    season.[z]
[16] You open wide your hand
    and satisfy the desire of every living
    thing.
[17] You, LORD, are just in all your ways,
    faithful in all your works.[a]
[18] You, LORD, are near to all who call upon
    you,
    to all who call upon you in truth.[b]
[19] You satisfy the desire of those who fear
    you;
    you hear their cry and save them.[c]
[20] You, LORD, watch over all who love you,
    but all the wicked you destroy.[d]
[21] My mouth will speak your praises, LORD;
    all flesh will bless your holy name
    forever.[e]

PSALM 146[*]

See RG
175

Trust in God the Creator and
Redeemer

[1] Hallelujah!

[2] Praise the LORD, my soul;
    I shall praise the LORD all my life,
    sing praise to my God while I live.[f]

I

[3] Put no trust in princes,
    in mere mortals powerless to save.[g]
[4] When they breathe their last, they return
    to the earth;
    that day all their planning comes to
    nothing.[h]

II

[5] Happy those whose help is Jacob's God,

Ps 145: A hymn in acrostic form; every verse begins
with a successive letter of the Hebrew alphabet. Acrostic
poems usually do not develop ideas but consist rather of
loosely connected statements. The singer invites all to
praise God (1-3. 21). The "works of God" make God present and invite human praise (4-7); they climax in a confession (8-9). God's mighty acts show forth divine kingship
(10-20), a major theme in the literature of early Judaism
and in Christianity.

Ps 146: A hymn of someone who has learned there is no
other source of strength except the merciful God. Only
God, not mortal humans (3-4), can help vulnerable and op-

pressed people (5-9). The first of the five hymns that conclude the Psalter.

p: Ps 34, 2.   q: Pss 48, 2; 95, 3; 96, 4; Jb 36, 26.   r: Pss 22, 31-
32; 48, 14-15; 71, 18; 78, 4; Ex 10, 2; Dt 4, 9.   s: Pss 96, 3; 105,
2.   t: Ps 66, 3.   u: Pss 86, 5. 15; 103, 8; Ex 34, 6; Sir 2, 11.
v: Ps 103, 13; Wis 11, 24.   w: Dn 3, 57.   x: Pss 10, 16; 102, 13;
146, 10; Lam 5, 19; Dn 3, 100; Rv 11, 15.   y: Pss 94, 18; 146, 8.
z: Pss 136, 25; 104, 27-28; Mt 6, 25-26.   a: Dt 32, 4.   b: Dt 4,
7; Is 55, 6; 58, 9.   c: Ps 34, 18.   d: Jgs 5, 31.   e: Sir 40, 35.
f: Pss 103, 1; 104, 33.   g: Ps 118, 8-9.   h: Pss 90, 3; 104, 29;
1 Mc 2, 63; Jb 34, 14-15; Eccl 3, 20; 12, 7; Sir 40, 11; Is 2, 22.

whose hope is in the LORD, their God,
⁶ The maker of heaven and earth,
the seas and all that is in them,ⁱ
Who keeps faith forever,
⁷   secures justice for the oppressed,^j
gives food to the hungry.
The LORD sets prisoners free;^k
⁸   the LORD gives sight to the blind.
The LORD raises up those who are
bowed down;^l
the LORD loves the righteous.
⁹ The LORD protects the stranger,
sustains the orphan and the widow,^m
but thwarts the way of the wicked.
¹⁰ The LORD shall reign forever,
your God, Zion, through all
generations!ⁿ
Hallelujah!

See RG
175–76

PSALM 147*

God's Word Restores Jerusalem

¹ Hallelujah!

I

How good to celebrate our God in song;
how sweet to give fitting praise.^o
² The LORD rebuilds Jerusalem,
gathers the dispersed of Israel,^p
³ Heals the brokenhearted,
binds up their wounds,^q
⁴ Numbers all the stars,
calls each of them by name.^r
⁵ Great is our Lord, vast in power,
with wisdom beyond measure.^s
⁶ The LORD sustains the poor,
but casts the wicked to the ground.^t

II

⁷ Sing to the LORD with thanksgiving;

with the lyre celebrate our God,^u
⁸ Who covers the heavens with clouds,*
provides rain for the earth,
makes grass sprout on the
mountains,^v
⁹ Who gives animals their food
and ravens what they cry for.^w
¹⁰ God takes no delight in the strength of
horses,*
no pleasure in the runner's stride.^x
¹¹ Rather the LORD takes pleasure in the
devout,
those who await his faithful care.

III

¹² Glorify the LORD, Jerusalem;
Zion, offer praise to your God,
¹³ Who has strengthened the bars of your
gates,
blessed your children within you,^y
¹⁴ Brought peace to your borders,
and filled you with finest wheat.^z
¹⁵ The LORD sends a command to earth;*
his word runs swiftly!^a
¹⁶ Thus snow is spread like wool,
frost is scattered like ash,^b
¹⁷ Hail is dispersed like crumbs;
before such cold the waters freeze.
¹⁸ Again he sends his word and they
melt;
the wind is unleashed and the waters
flow.
¹⁹ The LORD also proclaims his word to
Jacob,
decrees and laws to Israel.^c
²⁰ God has not done this for other nations;
of such laws they know nothing.
Hallelujah!

Ps 147: The hymn is divided into three sections by the calls to praise in 1, 7 and 12. The first section praises the powerful creator who restores exiled Judah (1-6); the second section, the creator who provides food to animals and humans; the third and climactic section exhorts the holy city to recognize it has been re-created and made the place of disclosure for God's word, a word as life-giving as water.

147, 8-9: God clothes the fields and feeds the birds. Cf Mt 6, 26. 30.

147, 10-11: Acknowledging one's dependence upon God rather than claiming self-sufficiency pleases God. Cf Pss 20, 8; 33, 16-19.

147, 15-19: God speaks through the thunder of nature and

the word of revealed law. Cf Is 55, 10-11. The weather phenomena are well known in Jerusalem: a blizzard of snow and hail followed by a thunderstorm that melts the ice.

---

i: Ex 20, 11; Pss 121, 2; 124, 8; Acts 14, 15; Rv 14, 7.   j: Ps 103, 6.   k: Ps 68, 7; Is 49, 9; 61, 1.   l: Ps 145, 14.   m: Ps 68, 6; Dt 10, 18.   n: Ps 145, 13; Lam 5, 19.   o: Pss 33, 1; 92, 2.   p: Is 11, 12; 56, 8; Jer 31, 10.   q: Jb 5, 18; Is 30, 26; 61, 1; Jer 33, 6.   r: Is 40, 26.   s: Jdt 16, 13; Jer 51, 15.   t: Ps 146, 9; 1 Sm 2, 7-8.   u: Ps 71, 22.   v: Ps 104, 13f; Jb 5, 10; Jer 14, 22; Jl 2, 23.   w: Jb 38, 41; Mt 6, 26.   x: Pss 20, 8; 33, 16-18.   y: Ps 48, 14.   z: Ps 81, 17.   a: Ps 33, 9.   b: Jb 6, 16; 37, 10; 38, 22.   c: Ps 78, 5; Bar 3, 37; Dt 4, 7-8.

PSALM 148*

*All Creation Summoned
to Praise*

1 Hallelujah!

I

Praise the LORD from the heavens;
 give praise in the heights.
2 Praise him, all you angels;
 give praise, all you hosts.*d*
3 Praise him, sun and moon;
 give praise, all shining stars.
4 Praise him, highest heavens,*
 you waters above the heavens.
5 Let them all praise the LORD's name;
 for the LORD commanded and they
  were created,*e*
6 Assigned them duties forever,
 gave them tasks that will never
  change.

II

7 Praise the LORD from the earth,
 you sea monsters and all deep
  waters;*f*
8 You lightning and hail, snow and
  clouds,
 storm winds that fulfill his command;
9 You mountains and all hills,
 fruit trees and all cedars;*g*
10 You animals wild and tame,
 you creatures that crawl and fly;*h*
11 You kings of the earth and all peoples,
 princes and all who govern on earth;
12 Young men and women too,
 old and young alike.
13 Let them all praise the LORD's name,
 for his name alone is exalted,

majestic above earth and heaven.*i*
14 The LORD has lifted high the horn of his
  people,*
 to the glory of all the faithful,
 of Israel, the people near to their God.
Hallelujah!

PSALM 149*

*Praise God with Song
and Sword*

1 Hallelujah!

Sing to the LORD a new song,
 a hymn in the assembly of the
  faithful.*j*
2 Let Israel be glad in their maker,
 the people of Zion rejoice in their king.
3 Let them praise his name in festive
  dance,
 make music with tambourine and
  lyre.*k* *
4 For the LORD takes delight in his people,
 honors the poor with victory.
5 Let the faithful rejoice in their glory,
 cry out for joy at their banquet,*
6 With the praise of God in their mouths,
 and a two-edged sword in their
  hands,*l*
7 To bring retribution on the nations,
 punishment on the peoples,*m*
8 To bind their kings with chains,
 shackle their nobles with irons,
9 To execute the judgments decreed for
  them—
 such is the glory* of all God's
  faithful.
Hallelujah!

Ps 148: A hymn inviting the beings of heaven (1-6) and of earth (7-14) to praise God. The hymn does not distinguish between inanimate and animate (and rational) nature.

148, 4: Highest heavens: literally, "the heavens of the heavens," i.e., the space above the firmament, where the "upper waters" are stored. Cf Gn 1, 6-7; Dt 10, 14; 1 Kgs 8, 27; Ps 104, 3. 13.

148, 14: The LORD has lifted high the horn of his people: horn = strength, the concrete noun for the abstract. Of all peoples God has chosen Israel to return praise and thanks in a special way.

Ps 149: A hymn inviting the people of Israel to celebrate their God in song and festive dance (1-3. 5) because God has chosen them and given them victory (4). The exodus and conquest are the defining acts of Israel; the people must be ready to

do again those acts in the future at the divine command (6-9).

149, 3: Make music with tambourine and lyre: the verse recalls the great exodus hymn of Ex 15, 20.

149, 5: At their banquet: literally, "upon their couches." The people reclined to banquet.

149, 9: The glory: what brings honor to the people is their readiness to carry out the divine will, here conceived as punishing injustice done by the nations.

---

d: Dn 3, 58-63; Ps 103, 20f.   *e:* Ps 33, 9; Gn 1, 3f; Jdt 16, 14.
f: Gn 1, 21; Ps 135, 6.   *g:* Is 44, 23.   *h:* Gn 1, 21. 24f; Ps 30, 5.
Dt 4, 7.   *i:* Ps 30, 5; Dt 4, 7.   *j:* Pss 22, 23; 26, 12; 35, 18; 40,
10; Jdt 16, 1.   *k:* Pss 68, 26; 81, 2-3; 87, 7; 150, 3-4.   *l:* Neh 4,
10-12; 2 Mc 15, 27.   *m:* Wis 3, 8.

> In Psalm 150, the command to "give praise," *hallelu*, occurs in every verse. This psalm concludes the section and the book of Psalms as a whole, capturing the essence of the book. Instead of closing with a doxological verse, the book closes with an entire chapter that serves as a doxology.

See RG
175

PSALM 150[*]

Final Doxology

1 Hallelujah!

Praise God in his holy sanctuary;[n] [*]
    give praise in the mighty dome of
        heaven.[*]
2 Give praise for his mighty deeds,[o]
    praise him for his great majesty.

3 Give praise with blasts upon the horn.[p]
    praise him with harp and lyre.
4 Give praise with tambourines and
        dance,
    praise him with flutes and strings.[q]
5 Give praise with crashing cymbals,
    praise him with sounding cymbals.
6 Let everything that has breath
    give praise to the LORD![r]
Hallelujah!

Ps 150: The psalm is a closing doxology both for the fifth book of the Psalms (107—149) and for the Psalter as a whole. Temple musicians and dancers are called to lead all beings on earth and in heaven in praise of God. The psalm proclaims to whom praise shall be given, and where (1); what praise shall be given, and why (2); how praise shall be given (3-5); and by whom (6).

150, 1: His holy sanctuary: God's temple on earth. **The**

mighty dome of heaven: literally, "[God's] strong vault"; heaven is here imagined as a giant plate separating the inhabited world from the waters of the heavens.

n: En 3, 53. *o:* Dt 3, 24. *p:* 3ff: Pss 81, 3-4; 149, 3; 2 Sm 6, 5; 1 Chr 13, 8; 16, 5. 42; 2 Chr 5, 12-13; 7, 6. *q:* Ps 68, 26; Ex 15, 20. *r:* Rv 5, 13.

See RG
180–82

The Book of Proverbs

The first word of this book, *MISHLE*, has provided the title by which it is generally designated in Jewish and Christian circles. The name "Proverbs," while not an exact equivalent of *MISHLE*, describes the main contents satisfactorily, even though it is hardly an adequate designation for such parts as 1, 1—9, 18 or 31, 10-31. Among some early Christian writers the book was also known by the name of "Wisdom," and in the Roman Missal it was referred to as a "Book of Wisdom."

The Book of Proverbs is an anthology of didactic poetry forming part of the sapiential literature of the Old Testament. Its primary purpose, indicated in the first sentence (1, 2f), is to teach wisdom. It is thus directed particularly to the young and inexperienced (1, 4); but also to those who desire advanced training in wisdom (1, 5). The wisdom which the book teaches covers a wide field of human and divine activity, ranging from matters purely secular to most lofty moral and religious truths, such as God's omniscience (5, 21; 15, 3-11), power (19, 21; 21, 30), provi-

dence (20, 1-24), goodness (15, 29), and the joy and strength resulting from abandonment to him (3, 5; 16, 20; 18, 10). The teaching of the entire book is placed on a firm religious foundation by the principle that "the fear of the LORD is the beginning of knowledge" (1, 7; cf 9, 10).

To Solomon are explicitly ascribed parts II and V of the book; he is the patron of Hebrew wisdom. Of Agur (part VI) and Lemuel (part VIII), nothing further is known. Parts III and IV are attributed to "the wise." The remaining parts are anonymous.

The manner of compilation is conjectural. Parts II and V may have circulated first as independent collections, compiled before the fall of Jerusalem, as the references to Solomon (10, 1) and Hezekiah (25, 1) suggest. Parts III, IV and VII would seem to belong together as a third collection of a similar kind. The author of the first nine chapters, a religious sage familiar with the earlier sacred books, was the editor of the whole as we have it, probably in the early part of the fifth century B.C.

Christ and the Apostles often expressly quoted the Proverbs (Jn 7, 38; Rom 12, 20; Jas 4, 6) or repeated their teaching; compare Lk 10, 14, and Prv 25, 7; 1 Pe 4, 8; Jas 5, 20 and Prv 10, 12. The book has an important place in the Latin and Greek liturgies.

On the basis of titles, subject matter, and poetic structure the Book of Proverbs may be divided as follows:

I: Introduction: The Value of Wisdom

CHAPTER 1

See RG 180–82

*Purpose of the Proverbs of Solomon**

[1] The proverbs of Solomon,[a] the son of David,
  king of Israel:
[2] That men may appreciate wisdom and discipline,*
  may understand words of intelligence;
[3] May receive training in wise conduct,
  in what is right, just and honest;
[4] That resourcefulness may be imparted to the simple,*
  to the young man knowledge and discretion.

[5] A wise man by hearing them will
    advance in learning,
  an intelligent man will gain sound
    guidance,
[6] That he may comprehend proverb and
    parable,
  the words of the wise and their riddles.

[7] The fear of the LORD* is the beginning of
    knowledge;[b]
  wisdom and instruction fools despise.

*The Path of the Wicked: Greed and Violence**

[8] Hear, my son, your father's instruction,
  and reject not your mother's teaching;
[9] A graceful diadem will they be for your
    head;
  a torque for your neck.
[10] My son, should sinners entice you, [11]and
    say,
  "Come along with us!
  Let us lie in wait for the honest man,
    let us, unprovoked, set a trap for the
    innocent;
[12] Let us swallow them up, as the nether
    world does, alive,
  in the prime of life, like those who go
    down to the pit!
[13] All kinds of precious wealth shall we gain,
  we shall fill our houses with booty;
[14] Cast in your lot with us,
  we shall all have one purse!"—

[15] My son, walk not in the way with them,
  hold back your foot from their path!
[16] [For their feet run to evil,
  they hasten to shed blood.[c]]
[17] It is in vain that a net is spread*
  before the eyes of any bird—
[18] These men lie in wait for their own
    blood,

1, 1-6: This prologue explains the purpose of the book: to educate the inexperienced in knowledge and right conduct, and to increase the learning of the wise man by proverbs, parables and riddles.

1, 2: Discipline: education or formation which dispels ignorance and corrects vice.

1, 4: Simple: immature and inexperienced, hence easily influenced for good or evil.

1, 7: Fear of the LORD: reverential fear and respect for God on account of his sovereignty, goodness and justice to-

ward men. This is the foundation of religion.

1, 8-19: A warning against association with the greedy and the violent who seek to destroy the honest man and to steal his possessions (11-14). The trap which the wicked set for the innocent (11), in the end (19) takes away the life of the wicked themselves.

1, 17: Instructed by the wise man, the youth (of v 4) will

a: Prv 10, 1; 25, 1; 1 Kgs 4, 32.   b: Prv 9, 10; Jb 28, 28; Ps 111, 10; Sir 1, 16.   c: Is 59, 7.

Parental Advice on Leaving Home

The opening scene of a youth leaving his parents and home to establish his own household (1, 8–19) sets the scene for the entire book of Proverbs. Every reader must establish a household in the sense of learning to live well as an adult, accepting traditional wisdom and discerning where true life is to be found.

they set a trap for their own lives.
¹⁹ This is the fate of everyone greedy of loot:
  unlawful gain takes away the life of him who acquires it.

Wisdom in Person Gives Warning*
²⁰ Wisdom cries aloud in the street,
  in the open squares she raises her voice;^d
²¹ Down the crowded ways she calls out,
  at the city gates she utters her words:
²² "How long, you simple ones, will you love inanity,
²³   how long will you turn away at my reproof?
Lo! I will pour out to you my spirit,
  I will acquaint you with my words.

²⁴ "Because I called and you refused,
  I extended my hand and no one took notice;^e
²⁵ Because you disdained all my counsel,
  and my reproof you ignored—
²⁶ I, in my turn, will laugh at your doom;
  I will mock when terror overtakes you;
²⁷ When terror comes upon you like a storm,
  and your doom approaches like a whirlwind;

when distress and anguish befall you.
²⁸ "Then they call me, but I answer not;
  they seek me, but find me not;*
²⁹ Because they hated knowledge,
  and chose not the fear of the Lord;
³⁰ They ignored my counsel,
  they spurned all my reproof;
And in their arrogance they preferred arrogance,
  and like fools they hated knowledge:

³¹ "Now they must eat the fruit of their own way,
  and with their own devices be glutted."*
³² For the self-will of the simple kills them,
  the smugness of fools destroys them.
³³ But he who obeys me dwells in security,
  in peace, without fear of harm."^f

CHAPTER 2*

The Blessings of Wisdom*

See RG 180–82

¹ My son, if you receive my words
  and treasure my commands,
² Turning your ear to wisdom,*
  inclining your heart to understanding;
³ Yes, if you call to intelligence,
  and to understanding raise your voice;
⁴ If you seek her like silver,

recognize the invitation of the wicked (11-14) as a net spread before him, and he will thus, like the bird, be protected against falling into it.

1, 20-33: Wisdom is here personified: with divine authority she sets forth and proclaims the moral order, instructing and threatening (24-33) the multitudes in the streets and places of assembly.

1, 28: Overtaken by doom, the foolish seek wisdom, but in vain because they do so too late. Cf Jn 7, 34; 8, 21.

1, 31: Sinners are punished by the bad fruits which their sins produce. Cf Wis 11, 16.

2—7: These chapters form an ordered discourse in seven "columns" of twenty-two verses each. Chapter 2 introduces the four topics about which the sage instructs his pupil: the service

of God (3, 1-12. 25-34), the search for wisdom (3, 13-24. 35; 4, 1-9), the avoidance of evil companions among men (4, 10-27; 5, 21-23), and among women (5, 1-20; 6, 20—7, 27). The last topic is treated at a length equal to the first three because the discourse is meant especially for youths (cf Prv 1, 4).

2, 1-22: The search for wisdom (1-4) leads to the protection of God (5-8) and of wisdom herself (9ff; cf Prv 1, 20-33) and to deliverance from evil men (12-15) and evil women (16-19), and so to lasting happiness (20ff).

2, 2f: Wisdom, understanding, intelligence: various names or aspects of the same gift.

d: Prv 8, 1-3; 9, 3. *e:* Is 65, 2. 12; 66, 4; Jer 7, 13. *f:* Prv 3, 33f.

The Blessings of Wisdom

Chapter 2 is an acrostic poem of twenty-two lines (the number of consonants in the Hebrew alphabet). The first letter of the Hebrew alphabet ("aleph") dominates the first half (vv. 1–11; "aleph" is the initial letter in vv. 1, 3, 4, 5, and 9). The middle letter of the Hebrew alphabet ("lamed") dominates the second half (vv. 12–22; "lamed" is the initial letter of vv. 12, 16, 20). The main point of the poem is that if you seek wisdom with all your strength, the LORD will give it to you, and wisdom will safeguard you from wicked men and seductive women with the result that you can walk on the blessed path. Wisdom will be given to anyone who earnestly seeks it. However, one cannot directly take wisdom; it must be given as a gift.

and like hidden treasures search her out:

5 Then will you understand the fear of the
   LORD;
   the knowledge of God you will find;
6 For the LORD gives wisdom,
   from his mouth come knowledge and
   understanding;*g*
7 He has counsel in store for the upright,
   he is the shield of those who walk
   honestly,
8 Guarding the paths of justice,
   protecting the way of his pious ones.

9 Then you will understand rectitude and
   justice,
   honesty, every good path;
10 For wisdom will enter your heart,
    knowledge will please your soul,
11 Discretion will watch over you,
    understanding will guard you;

12 Saving you from the way of evil men,
    from men of perverse speech,
13 Who leave the straight paths
    to walk in ways of darkness,
14 Who delight in doing evil,
    rejoice in perversity;
15 Whose ways are crooked,
    and devious their paths;

16 Saving you from the wife of another,

from the adulteress with her smooth
   words,*h*
17 Who forsakes the companion of her youth
    and forgets the pact with her God;
18 For her path sinks down to death,
    and her footsteps lead to the shades;*i*
19 None who enter thereon come back
    again,
    or gain the paths of life.

20 Thus you may walk in the way of good
    men,
    and keep to the paths of the just.
21 For the upright will dwell in the land,*j*
    the honest will remain in it;
22 But the wicked will be cut off from the
    land,
    the faithless will be rooted out of it.

CHAPTER 3

Attitude toward the Lord*

See RG
180–82

1 My son, forget not my teaching,
   keep in mind my commands;
2 For many days, and years of life,*k*
   and peace, will they bring you.

3 Let not kindness and fidelity leave you;
   bind them around your neck;
4 Then will you win favor and good esteem
   before God and man.

5 Trust in the LORD with all your heart,

3, 1-12: Many are the rewards for fidelity and trust in God, and for diffidence of self (1-8). Cf Dt 30, 20; Is 38, 19. The offering of material things for divine worship is blessed by an increase of such goods (9f). Even correction and chastisement are a mark of God's love and favor (11f).

g: Jb 32, 8; Wis 7, 25; Sir 1, 1; Jas 1, 5. *h:* Prv 5, 3. 20; 6, 24; 7, 5; 22, 14. *i:* Prv 5, 5f; 7, 27. *j:* 21f: Prv 10, 7. 30; Jb 18, 17; Pss 21, 9-13; 37, 22. 28. *k:* Prv 4, 10; 9, 11; 10, 27.

on your own intelligence rely not;
6 In all your ways be mindful of him,
  and he will make straight your paths.

7 Be not wise in your own eyes,[l]
  fear the LORD and turn away from evil;
8 This will mean health for your flesh
  and vigor for your bones.

9 Honor the LORD with your wealth,
  with first fruits of all your produce;[m]
10 Then will your barns be filled with
  grain,
  with new wine your vats will
  overflow.
11 The discipline of the LORD, my son,
  disdain not;[n]
  spurn not his reproof;
12 For whom the LORD loves he reproves,
  and he chastises the son he favors.[o]

The Value of Wisdom*
13 Happy the man who finds wisdom,
  the man who gains understanding![p]
14 For her profit is better than profit in
  silver,
  and better than gold is her revenue;
15 She is more precious than corals,*
  and none of your choice possessions
  can compare with her.[q]

16 Long life is in her right hand,
  in her left are riches and honor;
17 Her ways are pleasant ways,
  and all her paths are peace;
18 She is a tree of life* to those who grasp
  her,[r]
  and he is happy who holds her fast.

19 The LORD by wisdom founded the earth,

established the heavens by
  understanding;
20 By his knowledge the depths break open,
  and the clouds drop down dew.*
21 My son, let not these slip out of your
  sight:
  keep advice and counsel in view;
22 So will they be life to your soul,
  and an adornment for your neck.
23 Then you may securely go your way;
  your foot will never stumble;
24 When you lie down, you need not be
  afraid,
  when you rest, your sleep will be
  sweet.
35 Honor is the possession of wise men,
  but fools inherit shame.

Attitude toward Fellow Men*
25 Be not afraid of sudden terror,
  of the ruin of the wicked* when it
  comes;
26 For the LORD will be your confidence,
  and will keep your foot from the
  snare.

27 Refuse no one the good on which he has
  a claim
  when it is in your power to do it for him.
28 Say not to your neighbor, "Go, and come
  again,
  tomorrow I will give," when you can
  give at once.
29 Plot no evil against your neighbor,
  against him who lives at peace with
  you.
30 Quarrel not with a man without cause,
  with one who has done you no harm.
31 Envy not the lawless man
  and choose none of his ways:[s]

3, 13-24: Wisdom, or understanding, is more valuable than silver and gold. Its fruit is long life, riches, honor and happiness (13-18). Even the creation of the universe and its adornment (Gn 1) were not done without wisdom (19f). It is the life of the soul and gives security in work and in repose (21-24).

3, 15: Corals: some precious stone may be intended.
3, 18: A tree of life: cf Prv 11, 30; 13, 12; Gn 2, 9.
3, 20: For the Hebrews, the depths enclosed the great subterranean ocean; the rain and dew descended from the celestial ocean above the firmament; cf Gn 1, 6-10; Jb 26, 8. 12; Pss 18, 16; 24, 2.

3, 25-34: Serving God with confidence in him (25f) requires serving one's neighbor through kindness (27f), peace with the good (29ff), no envy of the wicked (31), because the Lord's friendship and kindness are with the just; his curse is with the wicked.

3, 25: The ruin of the wicked: i.e., the ruin that comes upon the wicked.

l: Rom 11, 25; 12, 16. m: Ex 34, 26; Lv 27, 30; Dt 26, 2; Sir 7, 31; 35, 7. n: Heb 12, 5f. o: Jdt 8, 27; Rv 3, 19. p: Prv 8. 34f. q: Prv 8, 11. 19; Wis 7, 8-11. r: Prv 4, 13; 8, 35; 11, 30; Gn 2, 9; 3, 22 s: Prv 23, 17; 24, 1. 19; Ps 37, 1.

The Two Ways

The process of gaining wisdom is essentially the same in all the instructions. One begins by memorizing the teaching and putting it into practice; then one receives wisdom as a gift. Proverbs 4, 10–19 develops the doctrine of the two ways, in which a person's moral life is dramatized as two competing paths, the way of wisdom (vv. 10–13) and the path of the wicked (vv. 14–17). Each has its inherent destiny, represented here by the symbols of light and darkness (vv. 18, 19). The two ways are not far removed from each other; one must struggle to stay on the right path. It is possible to leave one path and walk on the other.

32 To the LORD the perverse man is an
    abomination,
  but with the upright is his friendship.

33 The curse of the LORD is on the house of
    the wicked,
  but the dwelling of the just he blesses;
34 When he is dealing with the arrogant, he
    is stern,[t]
  but to the humble he shows kindness.

CHAPTER 4

See RG
180-82

Wisdom: the Supreme Guide of Men*

1 Hear, O children, a father's instruction,
  be attentive, that you may gain
    understanding!
2 Yes, excellent advice I give you;
  my teaching do not forsake.
3 When I was my father's child,
  frail, yet the darling of my mother,
4 He taught me, and said to me:
  "Let your heart hold fast my words:[u]
  keep my commands, that you may
    live!

5 "Get wisdom, get understanding!
  Do not forget or turn aside from the
    words I utter.
6 Forsake her not, and she will preserve
    you;
  love her, and she will safeguard you;

7 The beginning of wisdom is: get wisdom;
  at the cost of all you have, get
    understanding.
8 Extol her, and she will exalt you;
  she will bring you honors if you
    embrace her;
9 She will put on your head a graceful
    diadem;
  a glorious crown will she bestow on
    you."

The Good and the Evil Way*

10 Hear, my son, and receive my words,
  and the years of your life shall be
    many.[v]
11 On the way of wisdom I direct you,
  I lead you on straightforward paths.
12 When you walk, your step will not be
    impeded,
  and should you run, you will not
    stumble.
13 Hold fast to instruction, never let her go;
  keep her, for she is your life.

14 The path of the wicked enter not,
  walk not on the way of evil men;
15 Shun it, cross it not,
  turn aside from it, and pass on.
16 For they cannot rest unless they have
    done evil;
  to have made no one stumble steals
    away their sleep.

4, 1-9: The sage speaks as a father admonishing his children to secure wisdom at any cost.

4, 10-27: The way of wisdom leads directly to life (10-13); it is a light that grows brighter (18). The wise man is bound to shun (14-17) the dark and violent path of the wicked (19). Singleness of purpose and right conduct proceed from the heart of a wise man as from the source of life (23-26); they save him from destruction on evil paths (4, 27; 5, 21ff).

---

t: Prv 1, 26. *u:* 1 Kgs 2, 2ff. *v:* Prv 3, 2.

17 For they eat the bread of wickedness
and drink the wine of violence.
19 The way of the wicked is like darkness;
they know not on what they stumble.
18 But the path of the just is like shining
light,
that grows in brilliance till perfect
day.*

20 My son, to my words be attentive,
to my sayings incline your ear;
21 Let them not slip out of your sight,
keep them within your heart;
22 For they are life to those who find them,^w
to man's whole being they are health.

23 With closest custody, guard your heart,
for in it are the sources of life.
24 Put away from you dishonest talk,
deceitful speech put far from you.
25 Let your eyes look straight ahead
and your glance be directly forward.
26 Survey the path for your feet,
and let all your ways be sure.
27 Turn neither to right nor to left,
keep your foot far from evil.

See RG 180-82

CHAPTER 5

*Warning against Adultery**
1 My son, to my wisdom be attentive,
to my knowledge incline your ear,
2 That discretion may watch over you,
and understanding may guard you.
3 The lips of an adulteress drip with honey,
and her mouth is smoother than oil;^x
4 But in the end she is as bitter as
wormwood,
as sharp as a two-edged sword.
5 Her feet go down to death,
to the nether world her steps attain;^y
6 Lest you see before you the road to life,
her paths will ramble, you know not
where.

7 So now, O children, listen to me,
go not astray from the words of my
mouth.
8 Keep your way far from her,^z
approach not the door of her house,
9 Lest you give your honor* to others,^a
and your years to a merciless one;
10 Lest strangers have their fill of your
wealth,
your hard-won earnings go to an
alien's house;
11 And you groan in the end,
when your flesh and your body are
consumed;
12 And you say, "Oh, why did I hate
instruction,
and my heart spurn reproof!
13 Why did I not listen to the voice of my
teachers,
nor to my instructors incline my ear!
14 I have all but come to utter ruin,
condemned by the public assembly!'"

15 Drink water from your own cistern,
running water from your own well.
16 How may your water sources be
dispersed abroad,
streams of water in the streets?
17 Let your fountain be yours alone,
not one shared with strangers;
18 And have joy of the wife of your youth,
19 your lovely hind, your graceful doe.*
Her love will invigorate you always,
through her love you will flourish
continually,
22 When you lie down she will watch over
you,
and when you wake, she will share
your concerns;
wherever you turn, she will guide
you.*
20 Why then, my son, should you go astray
for another's wife

4, 18: Till perfect day: literally, "till the day is established"; this may refer to full daylight or to noonday.

5, 1-20: Understanding and discretion guard a man against the wiles of an adulteress, which lead astray and beget bitterness, bloodshed and death (1-6). They destroy honor, waste the years of life, despoil hard-earned wealth, consume the flesh, and bring remorse in the end (7-14). Conjugal fidelity and love for one wife only bring happiness and security (15-20). Cf Prv 6, 20—7, 27.

5, 9: Honor: the words "life" and "wealth" have also been read in this place. A merciless one: the offended husband; cf Prv 6, 34f.

5, 19: Lovely hind . . . graceful doe: oriental symbols of feminine beauty and charm; cf Song 2, 7. 9. 17.

5, 22: This is transposed from chapter 6, 22.

w: Prv 8, 35. x: Prv 7, 5. y: Prv 2, 18; 7, 27. z: Prv 7, 25. a: 9f: Sir 9, 6.

Four Short Pieces

Proverbs 6, 1–19 is often judged to be an addition on the grounds that its topics and style are very different from the surrounding instructions. It is possible, however, that the editors wanted to insert related but miscellaneous material at this point. Thematically, the section is concerned not with external obstacles to acquiring wisdom, such as violent men and seductive women, but with internal obstacles, such as poor judgment (vv. 1–5) and laziness (vv. 6–11). It also sketches an evil character (vv. 12–15), who is wholly unacceptable to the LORD (vv. 16–19).

and accept the embraces of an adulteress?

21 For each man's ways are plain to the LORD's sight;[*]
all their paths he surveys;[b]
22 By his own iniquities the wicked man will be caught,
in the meshes of his own sin he will be held fast;
23 He will die from lack of discipline,
through the greatness of his folly he will be lost.

See RG 180–82

CHAPTER 6

Miscellaneous Proverbs[*]

1 My son, if you have become surety to your neighbor,[c]
given your hand in pledge[*] to another,
2 You have been snared by the utterance of your lips,
caught by the words of your mouth;
3 So do this, my son, to free yourself,
since you have fallen into your neighbor's power:
Go, hurry, stir up your neighbor!
4 Give no sleep to your eyes,
nor slumber to your eyelids;
5 Free yourself as a gazelle from the snare,
or as a bird from the hand of the fowler.

6 Go to the ant,[d] O sluggard,

study her ways and learn wisdom;
7 For though she has no chief,
no commander or ruler,
8 She procures her food in the summer,
stores up her provisions in the harvest.
9 How long, O sluggard, will you rest?
when will you rise from your sleep?
10 A little sleep, a little slumber,
a little folding of the arms to rest—[*]
11 Then will poverty come upon you like a highwayman,
and want like an armed man.

12 A scoundrel, a villain, is he
who deals in crooked talk.
13 He winks his eyes,
shuffles his feet,
makes signs with his fingers;
14 He has perversity in his heart,
is always plotting evil,
sows discord.
15 Therefore suddenly ruin comes upon him;
in an instant he is crushed beyond cure.

16 There are six things the LORD hates,
yes, seven are an abomination to him;[*]
17 Haughty eyes, a lying tongue,
and hands that shed innocent blood;
18 A heart that plots wicked schemes,
feet that run swiftly to evil,
19 The false witness who utters lies,
and he who sows discord among brothers.

5, 21-23: These verses are best read after Prv 4, 27.

6, 1-19: These verses interrupt the discourse of chapters 2—7, which should be read apart from them; they contain four shorter proverbs akin to those in chapter 30.

6, 1: Given your hand in pledge: literally, "struck your hands"; this was probably the legal method for closing a contract.

6, 10: This verse may be regarded as the sluggard's reply

or as a continuation of the remonstrance.

6, 16-19: The seven vices symbolized for the most part by bodily organs are pride, lying, murder, intrigue, readiness to do evil, false witness, and the stirring up of discord.

b: Jb 14, 16; 31, 4; 34, 21. c: 1f: Prv 11, 15; 22, 26; Sir 8, 13; 29, 19. d: Prv 30, 25.

Warning against Adultery*

20 Observe, my son, your father's bidding,
and reject not your mother's teaching;

21 Keep them fastened over your heart
always,
put them around your neck;

23 For the bidding is a lamp, and the
teaching a light,
and a way to life are the reproofs of
discipline;

24 To keep you from your neighbor's wife,
from the smooth tongue of the
adulteress.e

25 Lust not in your heart after her beauty,
let her not captivate you with her
glance!f

26 For the price of a loose woman
may be scarcely a loaf of bread,
But if she is married,
she is a trap for your precious life.*

27 Can a man take fire to his bosom,
and his garments not be burned?

28 Or can a man walk on live coals,
and his feet not be scorched?

29 So with him who goes in to his
neighbor's wife—
none who touches her shall go
unpunished.g

30 Men despise not the thief if he steals
to satisfy his appetite when he is hungry;

31 Yet if he be caught he must pay back
sevenfold;
all the wealth of his house he may
yield up.

32 But he who commits adultery is a fool;
he who would destroy himself does it.

33 A degrading beating will he get,
and his disgrace will not be wiped away;

34 For vindictive is the husband's wrath,
he will have no pity on the day of
vengeance;

35 He will not consider any restitution,
nor be satisfied with the greatest
gifts.

CHAPTER 7

See RG
180-82

1 My son, keep my words,
and treasure my commands.

2 Keep my commands and live,
my teaching as the apple of your eye;

3 Bind them on your fingers,
write them on the tablet of your
heart.h

4 Say to Wisdom, "You are my sister!"
call Understanding, "Friend!"

5 That they may keep you from another's
wife,
from the adulteress with her smooth
words.i

6 For at the window of my house,
through my lattice I looked out—

7 And I saw among the simple ones,
I observed among the young men,
a youth with no sense,

8 Going along the street near the corner,
then walking in the direction of her
house—

9 In the twilight, at dusk of day,
at the time of the dark of night.

10 And lo! the woman comes to meet him,
robed like a harlot, with secret designs—

11 She is fickle and unruly,
in her home her feet cannot rest;

12 Now she is in the streets, now in the open
squares,
and at every corner she lurks in
ambush—

13 When she seizes him, she kisses him,
and with an impudent look says to him:

14 "I owed peace offerings,
and today I have fulfilled my vows;*

6, 20—7, 27: Parental training and the love of wisdom are
an invaluable and constant help for the young (6, 20-23; 7, 1-
4). They are the best defense against adultery (6, 24; 7, 5.
24f), which involves the guilty in many dangers and punishments (6, 26-35; 7, 6-27). Cf Prv 5, 1-20.

6, 26: Some interpret the verse in a progressive sense, i.e.,
to satisfy the increasing demands of a courtesan a man is reduced to poverty; if the woman is married, even his very life
is endangered.

7, 14: "Peace offerings . . . vows": a portion of the sacrifice reverted to the donor and had to be eaten on the same day
at a family festival (Lv 7, 11-15). In this figure, the adulteress
offers to share with the foolish young man the deadly feast of
her sensuality.

e: Prv 2, 16; 7, 5.   f: Ex 20, 17; Dt 5, 21; Sir 9, 8; 25, 20; Mt 5,
28.   g: Sir 9, 9.   h: Dt 6, 8.   i: Prv 2, 16; 6, 24.

15 So I came out to meet you,
   to look for you, and I have found you!
16 With coverlets I have spread my couch,
   with brocaded cloths of Egyptian
      linen;
17 I have sprinkled my bed with myrrh,
   with aloes, and with cinnamon.

18 "Come, let us drink our fill of love,
   until morning, let us feast on love!
19 For my husband is not at home,
   he has gone on a long journey;
20 A bag of money he took with him,
   not till the full moon will he return
      home."

21 She wins him over by her repeated
      urging,
   with her smooth lips she leads him
      astray;*j*
22 He follows her stupidly,
   like an ox that is led to slaughter;
   Like a stag that minces toward the net,
23   till an arrow pierces its liver;
   Like a bird that rushes into a snare,
      unaware that its life is at stake.

24 So now, O children, listen to me,
   be attentive to the words of my
      mouth!
25 Let not your heart turn to her ways,
   go not astray in her paths;
26 For many are those she has struck down
      dead,
   numerous, those she has slain.
27 Her house is made up of ways to the
      nether world,
   leading down into the chambers of
      death.*k*

CHAPTER 8

See RG
180-82

The Discourse of Wisdom*

1 Does not Wisdom call,

and Understanding raise her voice?*l*
2 On the top of the heights along the road,
   at the crossroads she takes her stand;
3 By the gates at the approaches of the
      city,
   in the entryways she cries aloud:
4 "To you, O men, I call;
   my appeal is to the children of men.
5 You simple ones, gain resource,
   you fools,* gain sense.
6 "Give heed! for noble things I speak;
   honesty opens my lips.
7 Yes, the truth my mouth recounts,*
   but wickedness my lips abhor.
8 Sincere are all the words of my mouth,
   no one of them is wily or crooked;
9 All of them are plain to the man of
      intelligence,
   and right to those who attain
      knowledge.
10 Receive my instruction in preference to
      silver,
   and knowledge rather than choice gold.
11 [For Wisdom is better than corals,
   and no choice possession can compare
      with her.*m*]

12 "I, Wisdom, dwell with experience,
   and judicious knowledge I attain.
13 [The fear of the LORD is to hate evil;]
   Pride, arrogance, the evil way,
   and the perverse mouth I hate.*n*
14 Mine are counsel and advice;
   mine is strength; I am understanding.*
15 By me kings reign,
   and lawgivers establish justice;
16 By me princes govern,
   and nobles; all the rulers of earth.

17 "Those who love me I also love,
   and those who seek me find me.
18 With me are riches and honor,*o*
   enduring wealth and prosperity.

8, 1-36: Wisdom is here personified as in Prv 1, 20-33, to confirm the words of the teacher of wisdom. She exalts her grandeur and origin, and invites all (1-11) to be attentive to her salutary influence in human society (12-21), for she was privileged to be present at the creation of the world (22-31). Finally, she promises life and the favor of God to those who find her, death to those who despise her.

8, 5: Simple ones . . . fools: see note on Prv 1, 4.
8, 7f: The truth and sincerity of wisdom are absolute be-

cause they are divine. They can neither deceive nor tolerate deception. An intelligent man understands and accepts them.

8, 14: What is here predicated of wisdom is elsewhere attributed to God (Jb 12, 13-16).

j: Prv 5, 3; 6, 24.   *k:* Prv 2, 18f; 5, 5.   *l:* Prv 1, 20f; 9, 3.   *m:* Prv 3, 15; Wis 7, 8.   *n:* Prv 6, 16f; 16, 5.   *o:* Prv 3, 16.

The Personification of Wisdom

One of the most striking features of Proverbs is its vivid personification of wisdom as a woman. Personification is a way of presenting an idea, a natural force, or an abstract concept as if it were a person. "Woman Wisdom" gives two lengthy speeches in the town square (1, 20–33 and 8, 1–36), and she invites passers-by to the banquet dedicating her newly built palace (9, 1–6).

The book of Proverbs presents a counter-figure to Woman Wisdom: the adulterous woman (2, 16–19; 5, 1–23; 6, 20–35; 7, 1–27) and the woman "Folly" (9, 13–18). Ultimately, derived from warnings to young men against the wrong kind of women, the adulterous woman has a metaphorical dimension in the book: She seeks to seduce her hearers with words, promising them life but dealing them death. The book thus presents the moral life in dramatic terms; there are two voices (Wisdom and Folly), and there are two ways (the way of the righteous and the way of the wicked). Each person must choose one or the other.

Woman Wisdom's speeches in Proverbs contain no specific advice. Rather, she invites her hearers to become her disciples—to trust and obey her, and even to wait at her gates like a dear friend (8, 32–36). She promises to bestow security (1, 33), authority, wealth, and success (8, 14–21). Her own authority rests on her intimacy and honored position with God; she was created before everything and has an intimate relationship with God. In fact, traditional love language is used to describe her relationship to God and to human beings (8, 30–31. 34).

The personification of wisdom gives Proverbs a metaphorical dimension. The moral life is not simply a series of right actions but a fundamental option—seeking wisdom before all else.

---

19 My fruit is better than gold, yes, than
  pure gold,
 and my revenue than choice
  silver.*p*
20 On the way of duty I walk,
 along the paths of justice,
21 Granting wealth to those who love me,
 and filling their treasuries.

22 "The LORD begot me, the first-born of his
  ways,*
 the forerunner of his prodigies of long
  ago;*q*
23 From of old I was poured forth,*
 at the first, before the earth.*r*

24 When there were no depths I was brought
  forth,*
 when there were no fountains or
  springs of water;
25 Before the mountains were settled into
  place,
 before the hills, I was brought forth;
26 While as yet the earth and the fields were
  not made,
 nor the first clods of the world.

27 "When he established the heavens I was
  there,*s*
 when he marked out the vault over the
  face of the deep;

8, 22-31: Wisdom is of divine origin. It is here represented as a being which existed before all things (22-26) and concurred with God when he planned and executed the creation of the universe, adorned it with beauty and variety, and established its wonderful order (27-30). Here that plurality of divine Persons is foreshadowed which was afterward to be fully revealed when Wisdom in the Person of Jesus Christ became incarnate.

8, 23: Poured forth: the exact meaning of the Hebrew is

uncertain; the expression must imply the equivalent of "born." The Hebrews likened the movement of air and of spirit to that of liquids.

8, 24-26: The formless mass from which God created the heavens and the earth; cf Gn 1, 1f; 2, 4ff.

p: Prv 3, 14. *q:* Wis 9, 9; Sir 1, 1; 24, 9. *r:* Sir 1, 4 *s:* Prv 3, 19 Sir 24, 4f.

28 When he made firm the skies above,
    when he fixed fast the foundations of
        the earth;
29 When he set for the sea its limit,
    so that the waters should not transgress
        his command;
30 Then was I beside him as his craftsman,*
    and I was his delight day by day,'
    Playing before him all the while,
31   playing on the surface of his earth;
    and I found delight in the sons of men.

32 "So now, O children, listen to me;
33   instruction and wisdom do not reject!
    Happy the man who obeys me,
    and happy those who keep my ways,
34 Happy the man watching daily at my
        gates,
    waiting at my doorposts;
35 For he who finds me finds life,ᵘ
    and wins favor from the LORD;
36 But he who misses me harms himself;
    all who hate me love death."

CHAPTER 9

See RG
180–82

*The Two Banquets**

1 Wisdom has built her house,
    she has set up her seven columns;
2 She has dressed her meat, mixed her
        wine,
    yes, she has spread her table.
3 She has sent out her maidens; she calls*
    from the heights out over the city:ᵛ
4 "Let whoever is simple turn in here;
    to him who lacks understanding, I
        say,
5 Come, eat of my food,
    and drink of the wine I have mixed!
6 Forsake foolishness that you may live;
    advance in the way of understanding.
11 For by me your days will be multiplied
    and the years of your life increased."ʷ

7 He who corrects an arrogant man earns
        insult;
    and he who reproves a wicked man
        incurs opprobrium.
8 Reprove not an arrogant man, lest he hate
        you;
    reprove a wise man, and he will love you.ˣ
9 Instruct a wise man, and he becomes still
        wiser;
    teach a just man, and he advances in
        learning.
10 The beginning of wisdom is the fear of
        the LORD,
    and knowledge of the Holy One is
        understanding.ʸ
12 If you are wise, it is to your own advantage;
    and if you are arrogant, you alone shall
        bear it.
13 The woman Folly is fickle,ᶻ
    she is inane, and knows nothing.
14 She sits at the door of her house
    upon a seat on the city heights,
15 Calling to passers-by
    as they go on their straight way:
16 "Let whoever is simple turn in here,
    or who lacks understanding; for to him
        I say,
17 Stolen water is sweet,
    and bread gotten secretly is pleasing!"*
18 Little he knows that the shades are there,
    that in the depths of the nether world
        are her guests!*

II: First Collection of the
Proverbs of Solomon*
CHAPTER 10

See RG
180–82

1 The Proverbs of Solomon:

A wise son makes his father glad,

8, 30: His craftsman: furnishing God with the plan, as it were, for the creation of all things; cf Jb 38, 1f; Wis 7, 22—8, 1. I was his delight: the ever-present object of God's complacency.

9, 1-6. 13-18: Wisdom and folly are represented as matrons, each inviting people to her banquet. Wisdom offers the food and drink of divine doctrine and virtue which give life (1-6). Unstable and senseless folly furnishes the stolen bread and water of deceit and vice which bring death to her guests.

9, 3: She calls: i.e., indirectly, through her maidens; but the text could also mean that wisdom herself publicly pro-

claims her invitation.

9, 17: The secrecy implies wrongdoing.

9, 18: The banquet chamber of folly is a tomb from which no one who enters it is released.

10, 1—22, 16: The varied contents of this first collection of Solomon's proverbs apply mostly to individual life. Each

t: Wis 9, 9. *u:* Prv 3, 13-18; 4, 22. *v:* Prv 8, 1f. *w:* Prv 3, 2. 16; 4, 10; 10, 27. *x:* Sir 10, 27. *y:* Prv 1, 7; Jb 28, 28; Ps 111, 10; Sir 1, 16. *z:* 13-18: Prv 7, 7-27.

The Proverbs of Solomon

Nearly all of chs 1–15 are antithetic proverbs, that is, the second line (B) restates the first line (A) in an opposite way. The section contrasts the wicked and the righteous person (treated as types) and emphasizes the consequences of human acts. Chapters 16–22, on the other hand, contain far fewer antitheses and many more exceptions to the rule. A key metaphor throughout all these chapters is founding or maintaining a house, which continues the same image as in chs 1–9. The chapters contain more than fifty references to father, mother, son, house, wife, or servant.

but a foolish son is a grief to his mother.*a*

2 Ill-gotten treasures profit nothing, but virtue saves from death.*b*

3 The LORD permits not the just to hunger, but the craving of the wicked he thwarts.

4 The slack hand impoverishes, but the hand of the diligent enriches.*c*

5 A son who fills the granaries in summer is a credit; a son who slumbers during harvest, a disgrace.

6 Blessings are for the head of the just, but a rod for the back of the fool.

7 The memory of the just will be blessed, but the name of the wicked will rot.

8 A wise man heeds commands, but a prating fool will be overthrown.

9 He who walks honestly walks securely, but he whose ways are crooked will fare badly.

10 He who winks at a fault causes trouble,

but he who frankly reproves promotes peace.

11 A fountain of life is the mouth of the just, but the mouth of the wicked conceals violence.

12 Hatred stirs up disputes, *d*but love covers all offenses.*

13 On the lips of the intelligent is found wisdom, [but the mouth of the wicked conceals violence].

14 Wise men store up knowledge, but the mouth of a fool is imminent ruin.

15 The rich man's wealth is his strong city; the ruination of the lowly is their poverty.*

16 The just man's recompense leads to life, the gains of the wicked, to sin.*e*

17 A path to life is his who heeds admonition, but he who disregards reproof goes astray.*f*

18 It is the lips of the liar that conceal hostility;

---

of its three hundred and seventy-five proverbs is meant to be distinct from the others, developing one idea through contrasting parallelism in chapters 10—15, and a climactic treatment in 16—22.

10, 12: Love covers all offenses: a favorite maxim of the Apostles; cf 1 Cor 13, 7; Jas 5, 20; 1 Pt 4, 8; also Prv 17, 9.

10, 15: The inspired author reflects upon the reality of the

power of money and the defeat of poverty, without approving these things.

a: Prv 1, 1; 15, 20; 17, 25; 19, 13; 25, 1; 29, 15. *b:* Prv 11, 4. 6.
c: Prv 6, 11; 12, 24; 13, 4; 20, 13; 28, 19. *d:* 1 Cor 13, 4–7; 1 Pt 4, 8. *e:* Prv 11, 18f. *f:* Prv 15, 10.

but he who spreads accusations is a fool.

19 Where words are many, sin is not
wanting;
but he who restrains his lips does
well.*g*

20 Like choice silver is the just man's
tongue;
the heart of the wicked is of little
worth.

21 The just man's lips nourish many,
but fools die for want of sense.

22 It is the LORD's blessing that brings
wealth,*h*
and no effort can substitute for it.*

23 Crime is the entertainment of the fool;
so is wisdom for the man of sense.

24 What the wicked man fears will befall
him,
but the desire of the just will be
granted.

25 When the tempest passes, the wicked
man is no more;
but the just man is established forever.

26 As vinegar to the teeth, and smoke to the
eyes,
is the sluggard to those who use him as
a messenger.

27 The fear of the LORD prolongs life,
but the years of the wicked are brief.*i*

28 The hope of the just brings them joy,
but the expectation of the wicked
comes to nought.

29 The LORD is a stronghold to him who
walks honestly,
but to evildoers, their downfall.

30 The just man will never be disturbed,
but the wicked will not abide in the
land.

31 The mouth of the just yields wisdom,
but the perverse tongue will be cut off.

32 The lips of the just know how to please,
but the mouth of the wicked, how to
pervert.

CHAPTER 11

See RG
180–82

1 False scales are an abomination
to the LORD,
but a full weight is his delight.*j*

2 When pride comes, disgrace comes;
but with the humble is wisdom.

3 The honesty of the upright guides them;
the faithless are ruined by their
duplicity.

4 Wealth is useless on the day of wrath,*k*
but virtue saves from death.*

5 The honest man's virtue makes his way
straight,
but by his wickedness the wicked man
falls.*l*

6 The virtue of the upright saves them,
but the faithless are caught in their
own intrigue.

7 When a wicked man dies his hope
perishes,*m*
and what is expected from strength
comes to nought.

8 The just man escapes trouble,
and the wicked man falls into it in his
stead.

9 With his mouth the impious man would
ruin his neighbor,*n*

10, 22: The blessing of God rather than our own industry crowns our efforts with success; cf Ps 127, 1f; Mt 6, 25-34.
11, 4: Wealth . . . death: not what a man is worth but what he is, counts before God.

g: Prv 17, 27; Sir 20, 17; Jas 1, 19.   *h:* Sir 11, 22.   *i:* Prv 3, 2; 4, 10; 9, 11; 14, 27.   *j:* Prv 16, 11; 20, 10; Lv 19, 35f.   *k:* Prv 10, 2.
l: Prv 28, 18.   *m:* Prv 10, 28; Wis 3, 18.   *n:* Prv 29, 5.

but through their knowledge the just
make their escape.

10 When the just prosper, the city rejoices;*o*
and when the wicked perish, there is
jubilation.

11 Through the blessing of the righteous the
city is exalted,
but through the mouth of the wicked it
is overthrown.

12 He who reviles his neighbor has no sense,
but the intelligent man keeps silent.

13 A newsmonger reveals secrets,*p*
but a trustworthy man keeps a
confidence.

14 For lack of guidance a people falls;
security lies in many counselors.*q*

15 He is in a bad way who becomes surety
for another,*r*
but he who hates giving pledges is
safe.

16 A gracious woman wins esteem,
but she who hates virtue is covered
with shame.

[The slothful become impoverished,
but the diligent gain wealth.]

17 A kindly man benefits himself,
but a merciless man harms himself.

18 The wicked man makes empty profits,
but he who sows virtue has a sure
reward.*s*

19 Virtue directs toward life,
but he who pursues evil does so to his
death.

20 The depraved in heart are an abomination
to the LORD,
but those who walk blamelessly are his
delight.

21 Truly the evil man shall not go
unpunished,
but those who are just shall
escape.

22 Like a golden ring in a swine's snout
is a beautiful woman with a rebellious
disposition.

23 The desire of the just ends only in good;
the expectation of the wicked is wrath.

24 One man is lavish yet grows still richer;
another is too sparing, yet is the
poorer.

25 He who confers benefits will be amply
enriched,
and he who refreshes others will
himself be refreshed.

26 Him who monopolizes grain, the people
curse—
but blessings upon the head of him
who distributes it!

27 He who seeks the good commands favor,
but he who pursues evil will have evil
befall him.

28 He who trusts in his riches will fall,
but like green leaves the just flourish.*t*

29 He who upsets his household has empty
air for a heritage;
and the fool will become slave to the
wise man.

30 The fruit of virtue is a tree of life,
but violence takes lives away.

31 If the just man is punished on earth,
how much more the wicked and the
sinner!*u*

CHAPTER 12

See RG
180–82

1 He who loves correction loves
knowledge,
but he who hates reproof is stupid.*v*

o: Prv 28, 12; 29, 2.   *p:* Prv 20, 19.   *q:* Prv 15, 22; 20, 18; 24, 6.   *r:* Prv 6, 1f.   *s:* Prv 10, 16.   *t:* Ps 52, 9f.   *u:* 1 Pt 4, 18.   *v:* Prv 15, 5. 10; 29, 1; Sir 19, 5; 21, 6.

2 The good man wins favor from the LORD,
   but the schemer is condemned by him.

3 No man is built up by wickedness,
   but the root of the just will never be
   disturbed.

4 A worthy wife is the crown of her
   husband,[w]
   but a disgraceful one is like rot in his
   bones.

5 The plans of the just are legitimate;
   the designs of the wicked are
   deceitful.

6 The words of the wicked are a deadly
   ambush,
   but the speech of the upright saves
   them.

7 The wicked are overthrown and are no
   more,
   but the house of the just stands firm.

8 According to his good sense a man is
   praised,
   but one with a warped mind is
   despised.

9 Better a lowly man who supports
   himself
   than one of assumed importance who
   lacks bread.[x]

10 The just man takes care of his beast,
    but the heart of the wicked is
    merciless.

11 He who tills his own land has food in
    plenty,
    but he who follows idle pursuits is a
    fool.[y]

12 The stronghold of evil men will be
    demolished,
    but the root of the just is enduring.

13 In the sin of his lips the evil man is
    ensnared,
    but the just comes free of trouble.

14 From the fruit of his words a man has his
    fill of good things,[z]
    and the work of his hands comes back
    to reward him.[*]

15 The way of the fool seems right in his
    own eyes,
    but he who listens to advice is wise.

16 The fool immediately shows his anger,
    but the shrewd man passes over an
    insult.

17 He tells the truth who states what he is
    sure of,
    but a lying witness speaks deceitfully.[a]

18 The prating of some men is like sword
    thrusts,
    but the tongue of the wise is healing.

19 Truthful lips endure forever,
    the lying tongue, for only a moment.

20 Deceit is in the hands of those who plot
    evil,
    but those who counsel peace have joy.

21 No harm befalls the just,
    but the wicked are overwhelmed with
    misfortune.

22 Lying lips are an abomination to the LORD,[b]
    but those who are truthful are his
    delight.

23 A shrewd man conceals his knowledge,
    but the hearts of fools gush forth folly.

24 The diligent hand will govern,
    but the slothful will be enslaved.[c]

25 Anxiety in a man's heart depresses it,

12, 14: Cf Mt 7, 17; Gal 6, 8.

w: Sir 26, 1. 16.   x: Sir 10, 26.   y: Prv 28, 19; Sir 20, 27.   z: Prv 13, 2; 18, 20.   a: Prv 14, 5.   b: Prv 6, 17.   c: Prv 10, 4; 13, 4.

but a kindly word makes it glad.*d*

26 The just man surpasses his neighbor,
    but the way of the wicked leads them
        astray.

27 The slothful man catches not his prey,
    but the wealth of the diligent man is
        great.

28 In the path of justice there is life,
    but the abominable way leads to death.

See RG
180–82

CHAPTER 13

1 A wise son loves correction,
    but the senseless one heeds no rebuke.

2 From the fruit of his words a man eats
        good things,*e*
    but the treacherous one craves
        violence.

3 He who guards his mouth protects his
        life;
    to open wide one's lips brings
        downfall.*f*

4 The soul of the sluggard craves in vain,
    but the diligent soul is amply satisfied.

5 Anything deceitful the just man hates,
    but the wicked brings shame and
        disgrace.

6 Virtue guards one who walks honestly,
    but the downfall of the wicked is sin.*g*

7 One man pretends to be rich, yet has
        nothing;
    another pretends to be poor, yet has
        great wealth.

8 A man's riches serve as ransom for his
        life,
    but the poor man heeds no rebuke.

9 The light of the just shines gaily,

but the lamp* of the wicked goes out.*h*

10 The stupid man sows discord by his
        insolence,
    but with those who take counsel is
        wisdom.

11 Wealth quickly gotten dwindles away,
    but amassed little by little, it
        grows.*i*

12 Hope deferred makes the heart sick,
    but a wish fulfilled is a tree of life.

13 He who despises the word* must pay for
        it,
    but he who reveres the commandment
        will be rewarded.

14 The teaching of the wise is a fountain of
        life,
    that a man may avoid the snares of
        death.

15 Good sense brings favor,
    but the way of the faithless is their ruin.

16 The shrewd man does everything with
        prudence,
    but the fool peddles folly.

17 A wicked messenger brings on disaster,
    but a trustworthy envoy is a healing
        remedy.

18 Poverty and shame befall the man who
        disregards correction,
    but he who heeds reproof is honored.

19 Lust indulged starves the soul,
    but fools hate to turn from evil.

20 Walk with wise men and you will
        become wise,
    but the companion of fools will fare
        badly.*j*

13, 9: Light . . . lamp: symbols of life and prosperity; cf Prv 4, 18f.
13, 13: Word: advice, or God's law.

d: Prv 15, 13; 17, 22.   *e:* Prv 12, 14; 18, 20.   *f:* Prv 18, 7; 21, 23.   *g:* Prv 11, 3. 5f.   *h:* Prv 24, 20.   *i:* Prv 28, 20. 22.   *j:* Sir 6, 34;
8, 8. 17.

²¹ Misfortune pursues sinners,
    but the just shall be recompensed with
      good.

²² The good man leaves an inheritance to
    his children's children,
    but the wealth of the sinner is stored
      up for the just.

²³ A lawsuit devours the tillage of the poor,
    but some men perish for lack of a law
      court.

²⁴ He who spares his rod hates his son,
    but he who loves him takes care to
      chastise him.^k

²⁵ When the just man eats, his hunger is
      appeased;
    but the belly of the wicked suffers
      want.

CHAPTER 14

See RG
180–82

¹ Wisdom builds her house,
    but Folly tears hers down with her
      own hands.

² He who walks uprightly fears the LORD,
    but he who is devious in his ways
      spurns him.

³ In the mouth of the fool is a rod for his
      back,
    but the lips of the wise preserve them.

⁴ Where there are no oxen, the crib
      remains empty;
    but large crops come through the
      strength of the bull.

⁵ A truthful witness does not lie,
    but a false witness utters lies.^l

⁶ The senseless man seeks in vain for
      wisdom,
    but knowledge is easy to the man of
      intelligence.

⁷ To avoid the foolish man, take steps!

But knowing lips one meets with by
    surprise.

⁸ The shrewd man's wisdom gives him
      knowledge of his way,
    but the folly of fools is their deception.

⁹ Guilt lodges in the tents of the arrogant,
    but favor in the house of the just.

¹⁰ The heart knows its own bitterness,
    and in its joy no one else shares.

¹¹ The house of the wicked will be
      destroyed,
    but the tent of the upright will
      flourish.^m

¹² Sometimes a way seems right to a man,
    but the end of it leads to death!ⁿ

¹³ Even in laughter the heart may be sad
    and the end of joy may be sorrow.

¹⁴ The scoundrel suffers the consequences
      of his ways,
    and the good man reaps the fruit of his
      paths.

¹⁵ The simpleton believes everything,
    but the shrewd man measures his
      steps.

¹⁶ The wise man is cautious and shuns
      evil;
    the fool is reckless and sure of himself.

¹⁷ The quick-tempered man makes a fool of
      himself,
    but the prudent man is at peace.

¹⁸ The adornment of simpletons is folly,
    but shrewd men gain the crown of
      knowledge.

¹⁹ Evil men must bow down before the
      good,
    and the wicked, at the gates of the
      just.

k: Prv 19, 18; 22, 15; 23, 13f; 29, 15; Sir 30, 1. 8-13.   l: Prv 12, 17.   m: Prv 3, 33; 12, 7; 15, 25.   n: Prv 16, 25.

20 Even by his neighbor the poor man is
hated,
but the friends of the rich are many.[o]

21 He sins who despises the hungry;
but happy is he who is kind to the
poor!

22 Do not those who plot evil go astray?
But those intent on good gain kindness
and constancy.

23 In all labor there is profit,
but mere talk tends only to penury.

24 The crown of the wise is resourcefulness;
the diadem of fools is folly.

25 The truthful witness saves lives,
but he who utters lies is a betrayer.

26 In the fear of the LORD is a strong
defense;
even for one's children he will be a
refuge.

27 The fear of the LORD is a fountain of
life,
that a man may avoid the snares of
death.

28 In many subjects lies the glory of the
king;
but if his people are few, it is the
prince's ruin.

29 The patient man shows much good
sense,
but the quick-tempered man displays
folly at its height.[p]

30 A tranquil mind gives life to the body,
but jealousy rots the bones.

31 He who oppresses the poor blasphemes
his Maker,
but he who is kind to the needy
glorifies him.[q]

32 The wicked man is overthrown by his
wickedness,
but the just man finds a refuge in his
honesty.

33 In the heart of the intelligent wisdom
abides,
but in the bosom of fools it is
unknown.

34 Virtue exalts a nation,
but sin is a people's disgrace.

35 The king favors the intelligent servant,
but the worthless one incurs his wrath.

CHAPTER 15

See RG
180-82

1 A mild answer calms wrath,[r]
but a harsh word stirs up anger.

2 The tongue of the wise pours out
knowledge,
but the mouth of fools spurts forth folly.

3 The eyes of the LORD are in every place,
keeping watch on the evil and the
good.

4 A soothing tongue is a tree of life,
but a perverse one crushes the spirit.

5 The fool spurns his father's admonition,
but prudent is he who heeds
reproof.[s]

6 In the house of the just there are ample
resources,
but the earnings of the wicked are in
turmoil.

7 The lips of the wise disseminate
knowledge,
but the heart of fools is perverted.

8 The sacrifice of the wicked is an
abomination to the LORD,[t]
but the prayer of the upright is his
delight.

o: Prv 19, 4. 7; Sir 6, 8. 12.   p: Prv 16, 32; 19, 11; Jas 1, 19.   q: Prv 17, 5.   r: Prv 25, 15; Sir 6, 5.   s: Prv 12, 1; 13, 18.   t: Prv 21,
27; Eccl 4, 17; Sir 34, 18ff; Is 1, 11-15.

⁹ The way of the wicked is an abomination
to the LORD,
but he loves the man who pursues
virtue.ᵘ

¹⁰ Severe punishment is in store for the man
who goes astray;
he who hates reproof will die.

¹¹ The nether world and the abyss* lie open
before the LORD;
how much more the hearts of men!

¹² The senseless man loves not to be
reproved;
to wise men he will not go.

¹³ A glad heart lights up the face,
but by mental anguish the spirit is
broken.ᵛ

¹⁴ The mind of the intelligent man seeks
knowledge,
but the mouth of fools feeds on folly.

¹⁵ Every day is miserable for the
depressed,
but a lighthearted man has a continual
feast.

¹⁶ Better a little with fear of the LORD*
than a great fortune with anxiety.

¹⁷ Better a dish of herbs where love is
than a fatted ox and hatred with it.

¹⁸ An ill-tempered man stirs up strife,ʷ
but a patient man allays discord.

¹⁹ The way of the sluggard is hemmed in as
with thorns,
but the path of the diligent is a
highway.

²⁰ A wise son makes his father glad,

but a fool of a man despises his
mother.ˣ

²¹ Folly is joy to the senseless man,
but the man of understanding goes the
straight way.

²² Plans fail when there is no counsel,
but they succeed when counselors are
many.ʸ

²³ There is joy for a man in his utterance;
a word in season, how good it is!ᶻ

²⁴ The path of life leads the prudent man
upward,
that he may avoid the nether world
below.

²⁵ The LORD overturns the house of the
proud,
but he preserves intact the widow's
landmark.

²⁶ The wicked man's schemes are an
abomination to the LORD,ᵃ
but the pure speak what is pleasing to
him.

²⁷ He who is greedy of gain brings ruin on
his own house,
but he who hates bribes will live.

²⁸ The just man weighs well his utterance,
but the mouth of the wicked pours out
evil.

²⁹ The LORD is far from the wicked,
but the prayer of the just he hears.

³⁰ A cheerful glance brings joy to the heart;
good news invigorates the bones.

³¹ He who listens to salutary reproofᵇ
will abide among the wise.

15, 11: Nether world . . . abyss: the abode of the dead, signifying the profound obscurity which is open nevertheless to the sight and power of God.

15, 16f: Not the amount of temporal goods but the virtue of their possessor makes them a source of happiness.

u: Prv 11, 20; 21, 21.   v: Prv 12, 25; 17, 22; Sir 30, 22.   w: Prv 26, 21; 29, 22; Sir 28, 11.   x: Prv 10, 1; 29, 3.   y: Prv 11, 14.   z: Prv 25, 11; Sir 20, 6.   a: Prv 6, 18.   b: Prv 25, 12.

³² He who rejects admonition despises his
    own soul,
but he who heeds reproof gains
    understanding.

³³ The fear of the LORD is training for
    wisdom,
and humility goes before honors.ᶜ

**See RG
180–82**

CHAPTER 16

¹Man may make plans in his heart,
but what the tongue utters is from the
    LORD.*

² All the ways of a man may be pure in his
    own eyes,
but it is the LORD who proves the
    spirit.ᵈ

³ Entrust your works to the LORD,
and your plans will succeed.

⁴ The LORD has made everything for his
    own ends,
even the wicked for the evil day.*

⁵ Every proud man is an abomination to
    the LORD;ᵉ
I assure you that he will not go
    unpunished.

⁶ By kindness and piety guilt is expiated,
and by the fear of the LORD man
    avoids evil.

⁷ When the LORD is pleased with a man's
    ways,
he makes even his enemies be at peace
    with him.

⁸ Better a little with virtue,
than a large income with injustice.

⁹ In his mind a man plans his course,
but the LORD directs his steps.ᶠ

¹⁰ The king's lips are an oracle;
no judgment he pronounces is false.*

¹¹ Balance and scales belong to the LORD;
all the weights used with them are his
    concern.ᵍ

¹² Kings have a horror of wrongdoing,
for by righteousness the throne
    endures.ʰ

¹³ The king takes delight in honest lips,
and the man who speaks what is right
    he loves.ⁱ

¹⁴ The king's wrath is like messengers of
    death,ʲ
but a wise man can pacify it.

¹⁵ In the light of the king's countenance is
    life,
and his favor is like a rain cloud in
    spring.

¹⁶ How much better to acquire wisdom than
    gold!
To acquire understanding is more
    desirable than silver.ᵏ

¹⁷ The path of the upright avoids
    misfortune;
he who pays attention to his way
    safeguards his life.

¹⁸ Pride goes before disaster,
and a haughty spirit before a fall.

¹⁹ It is better to be humble with the meek
than to share plunder with the proud.ˡ

²⁰ He who plans a thing will be successful;
happy is he who trusts in the LORD!

²¹ The wise man is esteemed for his
    discernment,

16, 1: Words, like actions, often produce results different from those which were planned.
16, 4: Even the wicked, in their punishment, cannot escape glorifying God's justice.
16, 10: Decisions of supreme judicial authority were presumed disinterested and correct.

c: Prv 1, 7; Sir 1, 24.   d: Prv 21, 2.   e: Prv 6, 16f; 8, 13.   f: Prv 19, 2 ; 20, 24.   g: Prv 11, 1.   h: Prv 25, 5.   i: Prv 14, 35; 22, 11.
j: Prv 19, 12; 20, 2.   k: Prv 8, 10f. 19.   l: Prv 11, 2.

yet pleasing speech increases his
    persuasiveness.

22 Good sense is a fountain of life to its
    possessor,
    but folly brings chastisement on fools.

23 The mind of the wise man makes him
    eloquent,
    and augments the persuasiveness of
    his lips.

24 Pleasing words are a honeycomb,
    sweet to the taste and healthful to the
    body.

25 Sometimes a way seems right to a man,
    but the end of it leads to death!*m*

26 The laborer's appetite labors for him,
    for his mouth urges him on.*n*

27 A scoundrel is a furnace of evil,
    and on his lips there is a scorching
    fire.

28 An intriguer sows discord,
    and a talebearer separates bosom
    friends.*o*

29 A lawless man allures his neighbor,
    and leads him into a way that is not
    good.

30 He who winks his eye is plotting
    trickery;
    he who compresses his lips has
    mischief ready.

31 Gray hair is a crown of glory;*p*
    it is gained by virtuous living.

32 A patient man is better than a warrior,
    and he who rules his temper, than he
    who takes a city.*q*

33 When the lot is cast into the lap,
    its decision depends entirely on the
    LORD.*

CHAPTER 17

See RG
180-82

1 Better a dry crust with peace
    than a house full of feasting with strife.

2 An intelligent servant will rule over a
    worthless son,
    and will share the inheritance with the
    brothers.*

3 The crucible for silver, and the furnace
    for gold,
    but the tester of hearts is the LORD.

4 The evil man gives heed to wicked lips,
    and listens to falsehood from a
    mischievous tongue.*

5 He who mocks the poor blasphemes his
    Maker;*r*
    he who is glad at calamity will not go
    unpunished.

6 Grandchildren are the crown of old men,
    and the glory of children is their
    parentage.

7 Fine words are out of place in a fool;
    how much more, lying words in a
    noble!

8 A man who has a bribe to offer rates it a
    magic stone;
    at every turn it brings him success.

9 He who covers up a misdeed fosters
    friendship,
    but he who gossips about it separates
    friends.

10 A single reprimand does more for a man
    of intelligence

16, 33: The favorable or unfavorable result of chance depends on God. Deciding strifes and doubts by lot was practiced by the ancient Hebrews; cf Ex 28, 15-30; Lv 16, 8; Jos 7, 14; 1 Sm 10, 20f.

17, 2: Intelligence and ability are esteemed more highly than nobility of blood.

17, 4: To justify his own evil ways, a wicked man judges evil of others. Cf Mt 7, 1-5.

m: Prv 14, 12.   *n:* Prv 10, 4.   *o:* Prv 6, 14. 19; 17, 9; 26, 22; Sir 28, 15.   *p:* Prv 20, 29.   *q:* Prv 14, 29.   *r:* Prv 14, 31.

than a hundred lashes for a fool.

11 On rebellion alone is the wicked man
bent,
but a merciless messenger will be sent
against him.

12 Face a bear robbed of her cubs,
but never a fool in his folly!

13 If a man returns evil for good,
from his house evil will not depart.*s*

14 The start of strife is like the opening of a
dam;
therefore, check a quarrel before it
begins!

15 He who condones the wicked,*t* he who
condemns the just,
are both an abomination to the LORD.

16 Of what use in the fool's hand are the
means
to buy wisdom, since he has no mind
for it?

17 He who is a friend is always a friend,
and a brother is born for the time of
stress.*u*

18 Senseless is the man who gives his hand
in pledge,
who becomes surety for his neighbor.*v*

19 He who loves strife loves guilt;*w*
he who builds his gate high* courts
disaster.

20 He who is perverse in heart finds no
good,
and a double-tongued man falls into
trouble.

21 To be a fool's parent is grief for a man;
the father of a numskull has no joy.

22 A joyful heart is the health of the body,
but a depressed spirit dries up the
bones.*x*

23 The wicked man accepts a concealed
bribe
to pervert the course of justice.

24 The man of intelligence fixes his gaze on
wisdom,*y*
but the eyes of a fool are on the ends
of the earth.

25 A foolish son is vexation to his father,
and bitter sorrow to her who bore him.*z*

26 It is wrong to fine an innocent man,
but beyond reason to scourge princes.

27 He who spares his words is truly wise,
and he who is chary of speech is a man
of intelligence.*a*

28 Even a fool, if he keeps silent, is
considered wise;
if he closes his lips, intelligent.

CHAPTER 18
See RG
180–82

1 In estrangement one seeks
pretexts:
with all persistence he picks a quarrel.

2 The fool takes no delight in
understanding,
but rather in displaying what he thinks.

3 With wickedness comes contempt,
and with disgrace comes scorn.

4 The words from a man's mouth are deep
waters,
but the source of wisdom is a flowing
brook.*b*

5 It is not good to be partial to the guilty,
and so to reject a rightful claim.*c*

17, 19: Builds . . . high: a symbol of arrogance.

---

s: Mt 5, 39; Rom 12, 17; 1 Thes 5, 15; 1 Pt 3, 9.   *t:* Prv 24, 24; Is 5, 23.   *u:* Prv 18, 24.   *v:* Prv 6, 1f; 11, 15.   *w:* Prv 15, 18.   *x:* Prv
12, 25; 15, 13.   *y:* Eccl 8, 1.   *z:* Prv 10, 1; 29, 15.   *a:* Prv 10, 19; Sir 1, 21; Jas 1, 19.   *b:* Prv 20, 5; Jn 7, 38.   *c:* Prv 24, 23; 28, 21.

6 The fool's lips lead him into strife,
    and his mouth provokes a beating.

7 The fool's mouth is his ruin;
    his lips are a snare to his life.*d*

8 The words of a talebearer are like dainty
        morsels
    that sink into one's inmost being.*e*

9 The man who is slack in his work
    is own brother to the man who is
        destructive.

10 The name of the LORD is a strong
        tower;*
    the just man runs to it and is safe.

11 The rich man's wealth is his strong city;*f*
    he fancies it a high wall.

12 Before his downfall a man's heart is
        haughty,*g*
    but humility goes before honors.*

13 He who answers before he hears*h* —
    his is the folly and the shame.*

14 A man's spirit sustains him in infirmity—
    but a broken spirit who can bear?

15 The mind of the intelligent gains
        knowledge,
    and the ear of the wise seeks
        knowledge.

16 A man's gift clears the way for him,
    and gains him access to great men.*i*

17 The man who pleads his case first seems
        to be in the right;
    then his opponent comes and puts him
        to the test.

18 The lot puts an end to disputes,
    and is decisive in a controversy
        between the mighty.*

19 A brother is a better defense than a strong
        city,
    and a friend is like the bars of a
        castle.

20 From the fruit of his mouth a man has his
        fill;*
    with the yield of his lips he sates
        himself.*j*

21 Death and life are in the power of the
        tongue;*k*
    those who make it a friend shall eat its
        fruit.

22 He who finds a wife finds happiness;
    it is a favor he receives from the
        LORD.*l*

23 The poor man implores,
    but the rich man answers harshly.

24 Some friends bring ruin on us,
    but a true friend is more loyal than a
        brother.*m*

CHAPTER 19

See RG
180–82

1 Better a poor man who walks in
        his integrity
    than he who is crooked in his ways
        and rich.*n*

2 Without knowledge even zeal is not
        good;
    and he who acts hastily, blunders.

3 A man's own folly upsets his way,
    but his heart is resentful against the
        LORD.

18, 10f: Religion is a strong support and sure refuge in the struggle of life. The rich foolishly rely on their wealth for such support.

18, 12: Compare the Savior's words: "Whoever exalts himself shall be humbled, but whoever humbles himself shall be exalted" (Mt 23, 12).

18, 13: To speak without first listening is characteristic of a fool; cf Prv 10, 14; Sir 11, 8.

18, 18: See note on Prv 16, 33.

18, 20f: Everyone must accept the consequences, of benefit or harm to himself, which his words produce.

d: Prv 10, 14; 12, 13; 13, 3; Eccl 10, 12.   *e:* Prv 26, 22.   *f:* Prv 10, 15.   *g:* Prv 11, 2; 16, 18; Sir 10, 15.   *h:* Sir 11, 8.   *i:* Prv 21, 14.   *j:* Prv 12, 14; 13, 2.   *k:* Sir 37, 18.   *l:* Prv 12, 4; 19, 14; Sir 7, 26.   *m:* Prv 17, 17.   *n:* Prv 28, 6.

⁴ Wealth adds many friends,
but the friend of the poor man deserts
him.ᵒ

⁵ The false witness will not go unpunished,
and he who utters lies will not escape.ᵖ

⁶ Many curry favor with a noble;
all are friends of the man who has
something to give.

⁷ All the poor man's brothers hate him;
how much more do his friends shun
him!

⁸ He who gains intelligence is his own best
friend;
he who keeps understanding will be
successful.

⁹ The false witness will not go unpunished,
and he who utters lies will perish.

¹⁰ Luxury is not befitting a fool;
much less should a slave rule over
princes.

¹¹ It is good sense in a man to be slow to
anger,
and it is his glory to overlook an
offense.

¹² The king's wrath is like the roaring of a
lion,
but his favor, like dew on the grass. q

¹³ The foolish son is ruin to his father,ʳ
and the nagging of a wife is a
persistent leak.

¹⁴ Home and possessions are an inheritance
from parents,
but a prudent wife is from the LORD.ˢ

¹⁵ Laziness plunges a man into deep sleep,
and the sluggard must go hungry.ᵗ

¹⁶ He who keeps the precept keeps his life,
but the despiser of the word will die.ᵘ

¹⁷ He who has compassion on the poor
lends to the LORD,ᵛ
and he will repay him for his good
deed.*

¹⁸ Chastise your son, for in this there is
hope;
but do not desire his death.ʷ

¹⁹ The man of violent temper pays the
penalty;
even if you rescue him, you will have
it to do again.

²⁰ Listen to counsel and receive
instruction,
that you may eventually become wise.

²¹ Many are the plans in a man's heart,
but it is the decision of the LORD that
endures.ˣ

²² From a man's greed comes his shame;
rather be a poor man than a liar.

²³ The fear of the LORD is an aid to life;
one eats and sleeps without being
visited by misfortune.

²⁴ The sluggard loses his hand in the dish;
he will not even lift it to his mouth.ʸ

²⁵ If you beat an arrogant man, the simple
learn a lesson;
if you rebuke an intelligent man, he
gains knowledge.ᶻ

²⁶ He who mistreats his father, or drives
away his mother,
is a worthless and disgraceful son.ᵃ

²⁷ If a son ceases to hear instruction,
he wanders from words of knowledge.

19, 17: Cf Mt 25, 34-40.

o: Prv 14, 20; Sir 13, 20ff. p: Dt 19, 16-20; Dn 13, 61. q: Prv 20, 2. r: Prv 10, 1; 17, 25. s: Prv 18, 22. t: Prv 6, 9ff. u: Prv 13, 13;
16, 17. v: Prv 14, 21; 22, 9; 28, 27. w: Prv 13, 24; 23, 13f. x: Prv 16, 9. y: Prv 26, 15. z: Prv 17, 10; 21, 11. a: Sir 3, 16.

28 An unprincipled witness perverts
justice,
and the mouth of the wicked pours out
iniquity.

29 Rods are prepared for the arrogant,
and blows for the backs of fools.*b*

CHAPTER 20

See RG
180–82
1Wine is arrogant, strong drink is
riotous;
none who goes astray for it is wise.*c*

2 The dread of the king is as when a lion
roars;*d*
he who incurs his anger forfeits his life.

3 It is honorable for a man to shun strife,
while every fool starts a quarrel.

4 In seedtime the sluggard plows not;
when he looks for the harvest, it is not
there.

5 The intention in the human heart is like
water far below the surface,
but the man of intelligence draws it
forth.*e*

6 Many are declared to be men of virtue:
but who can find one worthy of trust?

7 When a man walks in integrity and
justice,
happy are his children after him!

8 A king seated on the throne of judgment
dispels all evil with his glance.

9 Who can say, "I have made my heart
clean,*f*
I am cleansed of my sin"?*

10 Varying weights, varying measures,

are both an abomination to the LORD.*g*

11 Even by his manners the child betrays
whether his conduct is innocent and
right.

12 The ear that hears, and the eye that
sees—
the LORD has made them both.

13 Love not sleep, lest you be reduced to
poverty;
eyes wide open mean abundant food.

14 "Bad, bad!" says the buyer;
but once he has gone his way, he
boasts.*

15 Like gold or a wealth of corals,
wise lips are a precious ornament.

16 Take his garment who becomes surety
for another,*h*
and for strangers yield it up!*

17 The bread of deceit is sweet to a man,
but afterward his mouth will be filled
with gravel.

18 Plans made after advice succeed;
so with wise guidance wage your war.

19 A newsmonger reveals secrets;
so have nothing to do with a babbler!

20 If one curses his father or mother,
his lamp will go out* at the coming of
darkness.*i*

21 Possessions gained hastily at the outset
will in the end not be blessed.

22 Say not, "I will repay evil!"
Trust in the LORD and he will help you.*j*

20, 9: Man can be free of sin only by the power of God. Cf
1 Kgs 8, 46ff; Jb 4, 17; 14, 4; Pss 51, 2ff; 130, 3f; Rom 3, 23f;
1 Jn 1, 8.

20, 14: What one wishes to buy is valued cheaply in order
that it may be obtained at a low price; once purchased, it is
deemed more valuable.

20, 16: Caution is again advised in the matter of becoming
surety; cf Prv 6, 1ff.

20, 20: His lamp will go out: misfortune, even death,
awaits him; cf Prv 13, 9; Ex 21, 17.

---

b: Prv 26, 3. *c:* Prv 23, 29-35. *d:* Prv 19, 12. *e:* Prv 18, 4.
f: 1 Kgs 8, 46; 2 Chr 6, 36; Eccl 7, 20; 1 Jn 1, 8. *g:* Prv 11, 1; 20,
23. *h:* Prv 27, 13. *i:* Prv 30, 11. 17; Ex 21, 17; Lv 20, 9; Mt 15,
4. *j:* Prv 24, 29; Sir 28, 1; Mt 5, 39; Rom 12, 17. 19; 1 Thes 5,
15; 1 Pt 3, 9.

²³ Varying weights are an abomination to
the LORD,
and false scales are not good.ᵏ

²⁴ Man's steps are from the LORD;ˡ
how, then, can a man understand his
way?*

²⁵ Rashly to pledge a sacred gift is a trap for
a man,
or to regret a vow once made.*

²⁶ A wise king winnows the wicked,
and threshes them under the cartwheel.

²⁷ A lamp from the LORD is the breath of
man;
it searches through all his inmost
being.

²⁸ Kindness and piety safeguard the king,
and he upholds his throne by justice.ᵐ

²⁹ The glory of young men is their strength,
and the dignity of old men is gray
hair.ⁿ

³⁰ Evil is cleansed away by bloody lashes,
and a scourging to the inmost being.

See RG
180–82

CHAPTER 21

¹ Like a stream is the king's heart in
the hand of the Lord;
wherever it pleases him, he directs it.

² All the ways of a man may be right in his
own eyes,
but it is the LORD who proves hearts.ᵒ

³ To do what is right and justᵖ
is more acceptable to the LORD than
sacrifice.*

⁴ Haughty eyes and a proud heart—

the tillage of the wicked is sin.

⁵ The plans of the diligent are sure of
profit,
but all rash haste leads certainly to
poverty.

⁶ He who makes a fortune by a lying
tongue
is chasing a bubble over deadly
snares.

⁷ The oppression of the wicked will sweep
them away,
because they refuse to do what is right.

⁸ The way of the culprit is crooked,
but the conduct of the innocent is
right.

⁹ It is better to dwell in a corner of the
housetop
than in a roomy house with a
quarrelsome woman.�q

¹⁰ The soul of the wicked man desires evil;
his neighbor finds no pity in his eyes.

¹¹ When the arrogant man is punished, the
simple are the wiser;
when the wise man is instructed, he
gains knowledge.ʳ

¹² The just man appraises the house of the
wicked:
there is one who brings down the
wicked to ruin.

¹³ He who shuts his ear to the cry of the
poor
will himself also call and not be heard.

¹⁴ A secret gift allays anger,
and a concealed present, violent wrath.

20, 24: Man is dependent upon God and cannot fully foresee his own course.
20, 25: This verse cautions against making vows without proper reflection; cf Dt 23, 22ff; Eccl 5, 4f.
21, 3: External rites or sacrifices do not please God unless accompanied by internal worship and right moral conduct; cf Prv 15, 8; 21, 27; Is 1, 11-15; Am 5, 22; Mal 1, 12.

---

k: Prv 11, 1; 20, 10.   l: Prv 16, 9.   m: Prv 16, 12.   n: Prv 16, 31.   o: Prv 16, 2.   p: 1 Sm 15, 22; Hos 6, 6.   q: Prv 21, 19; 25, 24; 27, 15; Sir 25, 23.   r: Prv 19, 25.

15 To practice justice is a joy for the just,
   but terror for evildoers.[s]

16 The man who strays from the way of
      good sense
   will abide in the assembly of the
      shades.*

17 He who loves pleasure will suffer want;
   he who loves wine and perfume will
      not be rich.

18 The wicked man serves as ransom for the
      just,*
   and the faithless man for the righteous.[t]

19 It is better to dwell in a wilderness
   than with a quarrelsome and vexatious
      wife.

20 Precious treasure remains in the house of
      the wise,
   but the fool consumes it.

21 He who pursues justice and kindness
   will find life and honor.

22 The wise man storms a city of the mighty,
   and overthrows the stronghold in
      which it trusts.

23 He who guards his mouth and his tongue
   keeps himself from trouble.[u]

24 Arrogant is the name for the man of
      overbearing pride
   who acts with scornful effrontery.

25 The sluggard's propensity slays him,
   for his hands refuse to work.

26 Some are consumed with avarice all the
      day,
   but the just man gives unsparingly.

27 The sacrifice of the wicked is an
      abomination,
   the more so when they offer it with a
      bad intention.[v]

28 The false witness will perish,[w]
   but he who listens will finally have his
      say.

29 The wicked man is brazenfaced,
   but the upright man pays heed to his
      ways.

30 There is no wisdom, no understanding,
   no counsel, against the LORD.

31 The horse is equipped for the day of
      battle,
   but victory is the LORD's.

CHAPTER 22

See RG
180–82

1 A good name is more desirable
      than great riches,
   and high esteem, than gold and silver.[x]

2 Rich and poor have a common bond:
   the LORD is the maker of them all.[y]

3 The shrewd man perceives evil and hides,
   while simpletons continue on and
      suffer the penalty.[z]

4 The reward of humility and fear of the
      LORD
   is riches, honor and life.

5 Thorns and snares are on the path of the
      crooked;
   he who would safeguard his life will
      shun them.

6 Train a boy in the way he should go;
   even when he is old, he will not
      swerve from it.

21, 16: Assembly of the shades: cf note on Jb 26, 5.
  21, 18: Wicked . . . ransom for the just: exemplified in the history of God's chosen people whom he ransomed from Egypt at the cost of the life of Pharaoh and his army (Ex 14, 23-31), and from Babylon by giving to Cyrus, the Persian conqueror, Egypt, Ethiopia and Seba, the richest lands of the world (Is 43, 1ff).

s: Prv 10, 29. t: Prv 11, 8. u: Prv 13, 3. v: Prv 15, 8; Sir 34, 18ff. w: Prv 19, 5. 9. x: Eccl 7, 1. y: Prv 29, 13. z: Prv 27, 12.

7 The rich rule over the poor,
and the borrower is the slave of the
lender.

8 He who sows iniquity reaps calamity,*a*
and the rod destroys his labors.

9 The kindly man will be blessed,
for he gives of his sustenance to the poor.

10 Expel the arrogant man and discord goes
out;
strife and insult cease.

11 The LORD loves the pure of heart;*b*
the man of winning speech has the
king for his friend.

12 The eyes of the LORD safeguard
knowledge,
but he defeats the projects of the
faithless.

13 The sluggard says, "A lion is outside;*c*
in the streets I might be slain."*

14 The mouth of the adulteress is a deep
pit;*d*
he with whom the LORD is angry will
fall into it.

15 Folly is close to the heart of a child,
but the rod of discipline will drive it
far from him.

16 He who oppresses the poor to enrich
himself
will yield up his gains to the rich as
sheer loss.*

III: Sayings of the Wise*

17 The sayings of the wise:*

Incline your ear, and hear my words,*e*
and apply your heart to my doctrine;
18 For it will be well if you keep them in
your bosom,
if they all are ready on your lips.
19 That your trust may be in the LORD,
I make known to you the words of
Amen-em-Ope.*
20 Have I not written for you the "Thirty,"
with counsels and knowledge,
21 To teach you truly
how to give a dependable report to one
who sends you?

22 Injure not the poor because they are poor,
nor crush the needy at the gate;
23 For the LORD will defend their cause,*f*
and will plunder the lives of those who
plunder them.

24 Be not friendly with a hotheaded man,
nor the companion of a wrathful man,
25 Lest you learn his ways,
and get yourself into a snare.

26 Be not one of those who give their hand
in pledge,
of those who become surety for debts;*g*
27 For if you have not the means to pay,
your bed will be taken from under you.

28 Remove not the ancient landmark
which your fathers set up.*h*

29 You see a man skilled at his work?

22, 13: To avoid the effort required for doing good, the sluggard exaggerates the difficulties that must be overcome.

22, 16: Money gained by exploiting the poor is in turn lost to those who are more wealthy.

22, 17—24, 22: This collection of proverbs, introduced as sayings of the wise, is given in the more intimate and personal form of an address to a pupil called the son and is arranged in strophes instead of couplets.

22, 17—23, 35: The maxims warn against: oppression of the poor and defenseless (22, 22f), anger (24f), giving surety for debts (26f), bad manners at a king's table (23, 1f), anxiety for riches (4f), a grudging host (6ff), intemperance in food and drink (19ff. 29-35), and adultery (26ff). They exhort

to: careful workmanship (22, 29), respect for the rights of orphans (23, 10f), correction of the young (13f), filial piety (15f. 22-25), and fear of the Lord (17f).

22, 19f: Amen-em-Ope: an Egyptian scribe to whom is attributed a collection of maxims in Thirty chapters (v 20) composed for the instruction of his children and addressed to a young man who wishes to enter upon a career. The inspired editor of Proverbs does not translate these, but uses their materials in constructing a similar collection of proverbs.

a: Jb 4, 8; Sir 7, 3; Hos 8, 7.   *b:* Mt 5, 8.   *c:* Prv 26, 13.   *d:* Prv 23, 27.   *e:* Prv 5, 1.   *f:* Prv 23, 11.   *g:* Prv 6, 1f; 11, 15; 17, 18.
h: Prv 23, 10; Dt 19, 14; 27, 17.

He will stand in the presence of kings;
   he will not stand in the presence of
      obscure men.

CHAPTER 23

See RG
180–82 ¹When you sit down to dine with a
   ruler,
   keep in mind who is before you;
² And put a knife to your throat*
   if you have a ravenous appetite.
³ Do not desire his delicacies;
   they are deceitful food.
⁴ Toil not to gain wealth,
   cease to be concerned about it;
⁵ While your glance flits to it, it is gone!
   for assuredly it grows wings,
   like the eagle that flies toward heaven.

⁶ Do not take food with a grudging man,
   and do not desire his dainties;
⁷ For in his greed he is like a storm.
   "Eat and drink," he says to you,
   though his heart is not with you;
⁸ The little you have eaten you will vomit
   up,
   and you will have wasted your
      agreeable words.
⁹ Speak not for the fool's hearing;
   he will despise the wisdom of your
      words.ⁱ

¹⁰ Remove not the ancient landmark,ʲ
   nor invade the fields of orphans;
¹¹ For their redeemer is strong;
   he will defend their cause against you.ᵏ

¹² Apply your heart to instruction,
   and your ears to words of knowledge.

¹³ Withhold not chastisement from a
      boy;
   if you beat him with the rod, he will
      not die.ˡ
¹⁴ Beat him with the rod,ᵐ
   and you will save him from the nether
      world.

¹⁵ My son, if your heart be wise,
   my own heart also will rejoice;
¹⁶ And my inmost being will exult,
   when your lips speak what is right.

¹⁷ Let not your heart emulate sinners,ⁿ
   but be zealous for the fear of the Lᴏʀᴅ
      always;
¹⁸ For you will surely have a future,
   and your hope will not be cut off.ᵒ

¹⁹ Hear, my son, and be wise,
   and guide your heart in the right way.
²⁰ Consort not with winebibbers,
   nor with those who eat meat to
      excess;
²¹ For the drunkard and the glutton come to
      poverty,
   and torpor clothes a man in rags.

²² Listen to your father who begot you,
   and despise not your mother when she
      is old.
²³ Get the truth, and sell it not—
   wisdom, instruction and
      understanding.
²⁴ The father of a just man will exult with
      glee;
   he who begets a wise son will have joy
      in him.ᵖ
²⁵ Let your father and mother have joy;
   let her who bore you exult.

²⁶ My son, give me your heart,
   and let your eyes keep to my ways.
²⁷ For the harlot is a deep ditch,
   and the adulteress a narrow pit;
²⁸ Yes, she lies in wait like a robber,�q
   and increases the faithless among
      men.

²⁹ Who scream? Who shriek?*
   Who have strife? Who have anxiety?
   Who have wounds for nothing?
   Who have black eyes?
³⁰ Those who linger long over wine,

23, 2: Put a knife to your throat: a proverbial metaphor for self-restraint.
23, 29-35: A vivid description of the evil effects, physical and psychological, of drunkenness.

---

i: Prv 9, 7.   j: Prv 22, 28.   k: Prv 22, 23.   l: Prv 13, 24; 19, 18; Sir 30, 1.   m: Prv 29, 15. 17.   n: Prv 3, 31; 24, 1. 19.   o: Prv 24,
14.   p: Prv 10, 1.   q: Prv 7, 10-27.

those who engage in trials of blended
wine.ʳ

³¹ Look not on the wine when it is red,
when it sparkles in the glass.
It goes down smoothly;
³² but in the end it bites like a serpent,
or like a poisonous adder.
³³ Your eyes behold strange sights,
and your heart utters disordered
thoughts;
³⁴ You are like one now lying in the depths
of the sea,
now sprawled at the top of the mast.
³⁵ "They struck me, but it pained me not;
they beat me, but I felt it not;
When shall I awake
to seek wine once again?"*

CHAPTER 24

See RG
180–82
¹ Be not emulous of evil men,*
and desire not to be with them;ˢ
² For their hearts plot violence,
and their lips speak of foul play.

³ By wisdom is a house built,
by understanding is it made firm;
⁴ And by knowledge are its rooms filled
with every precious and pleasing
possession.
⁵ A wise man is more powerful than a
strong man,
and a man of knowledge than a man of
might;ᵗ
⁶ For it is by wise guidance that you wage
your war,
and the victory is due to a wealth of
counselors.ᵘ

⁷ For a fool, to be silent is wisdom;ᵛ
not to open his mouth at the gate.*
⁸ He who plots evil doing—
men call him an intriguer.

⁹ Beyond intrigue and folly and sin,
it is arrogance that men find
abominable.

¹⁰ If you remain indifferent* in time of
adversity,
your strength will depart from you.
¹¹ Rescue those who are being dragged to
death,*
and from those tottering to execution
withdraw not.
¹² If you say, "I know not this man!"
does not he who tests hearts perceive
it?
He who guards your life knows it,
and he will repay each one according
to his deeds.ʷ

¹³ If you eat honey, my son, because it is
good,
if virgin honey is sweet to your taste;
¹⁴ Such, you must know, is wisdom to your
soul.
If you find it, you will have a future,
and your hope will not be cut off.ˣ

¹⁵ Lie not in wait against the home of the
just man,
ravage not his dwelling place;
¹⁶ For the just man* falls seven times and
rises again,
but the wicked stumble to ruin.

¹⁷ Rejoice not when your enemy falls,
and when he stumbles, let not your
heart exult,
¹⁸ Lest the LORD see it, be displeased with
you,
and withdraw his wrath from your
enemy.

¹⁹ Be not provoked with evildoers,

23, 35: Wine makes the drunkard insensible to bodily and
moral harm. His one desire is to indulge again.

24, 1-22: These verses continue an exhortation to wisdom
(vv 3-7. 13f), and against: violence (1f), pride and intrigue
(8f), callousness (10-12), injustice (15f), joy in the failure of
others (17f) or scandal at their success (19f), and rebellion
against authority (21f).

24, 7: At the gate: of the city, where justice was administered and public affairs discussed; see note on Ru 4, 1. Cf
also Pss 69, 13; 127, 5; Prv 22, 22; 31, 23. 31.

24, 10: Indifferent: to those who suffer unjustly.

24, 11: Rescue . . . death: most probably refers to the legal rescue of those unjustly condemned to death.

24, 16: The just man overcomes every misfortune which
oppresses him. Seven times: i.e., an indefinite number; cf Mt
18, 21f; Lk 17, 4.

ʳ: Prv 20, 1; Sir 19, 2; Hos 4, 11.   ˢ: Prv 3, 31; 23, 17.   ᵗ: Prv 21,
22.   ᵘ: Prv 20, 18.   ᵛ: Sir 6, 21.   ʷ: Ps 62, 13; Sir 15, 12; Mt
16, 27; Rom 2, 6.   ˣ: Prv 23, 18.

nor envious of the wicked;
20 For the evil man has no future,
   the lamp of the wicked will be put out.ʸ

21 My son, fear the LORD and the king;*
   have nothing to do with those who
      rebel against them;
22 For suddenly arises the destruction they
      send,
   and the ruin from either one, who can
      measure?

IV: Other Sayings of the Wise*

23These also are sayings of the wise:

To show partiality in judgment is not good.ᶻ
24 He who says to the wicked man, "You
      are just"—
   men will curse him, people will
      denounce him;
25 But those who convict the evildoer will
      fare well,
   and on them will come the blessing of
      prosperity.
26 He gives a kiss on the lips*
   who makes an honest reply.

27 Complete your outdoor tasks,
   and arrange your work in the field;
   afterward you can establish your house.*

28 Be not a witness against your neighbor
      without just cause,ᵃ
   thus committing folly with your lips.
29 Say not, "As he did to me, so will I do to
      him;ᵇ
   I will repay the man according to his
      deeds."*

30 I passed by the field of the sluggard,

by the vineyard of the man without
      sense;
31 And behold! it was all overgrown with
      thistles;
   its surface was covered with nettles,
   and its stone wall broken down.
32 And as I gazed at it, I reflected;
   I saw and learned the lesson:
33 A little sleep, a little slumber,ᶜ
   a little folding of the arms to rest—
34 Then will poverty come upon you like a
      highwayman,
   and want like an armed man.

V: Second Collection of the Proverbs of Solomon

CHAPTER 25

See RG
180–82

1These also are proverbs of Solomon.ᵈ The men of Hezekiah,* king of Judah,
transmitted them.

2 God has glory in what he conceals,
   kings have glory in what they fathom.
3 As the heavens in height, and the earth in
      depth,
   the heart of kings is unfathomable.

4 Remove the dross from silver,
   and it comes forth perfectly purified;
5 Remove the wicked from the presence of
      the king,
   and his throne is made firm through
      righteousness.

6 Claim no honor in the king's presence,*
   nor occupy the place of great men;
7 For it is better that you be told, "Come
      up closer!"
   than that you be humbled before the
      prince.ᵉ

24, 21f: One owes obedience to God and to supreme civil authority (Mt 22, 21; Rom 13, 1ff; 1 Pt 2, 13f). The punishments for failure in either duty transcend the limits of private justice.

24, 23-34: This collection of sayings continues in the same vein as the preceding: it instructs in fairness (23-26) and preparation for the future (27); and warns against vengeance (28f) and slothfulness (30-34).

24, 26: He gives a kiss on the lips: shows himself a true friend.

24, 27: This verse is commonly interpreted as advocating careful and practical preparation for marriage.

24, 29: This verse indicates great progress from the prin-

ciple on the law of Talion (see note on Ex 21, 23ff) toward the teaching found in Rom 12, 17ff. Cf also Prv 25, 21ff.

25, 1: The men of Hezekiah: literary men at the royal court of Hezekiah who are represented as transcribing the proverbs from other collections. Hezekiah was a reformer of national religious life (2 Chr 29, 25-30).

25, 6f: Compare the lesson on humility which was taught by Christ (Lk 14, 7-11).

---

y: Prv 13, 9.   z: Prv 18, 5; 28, 21; Lv 19, 15; Dt 1, 17; 16, 19.
a: Prv 19, 5; 25, 18.   b: Prv 20, 22.   c: 33f: Prv 6, 10f.   d: Prv
1, 1.   e: Lk 14, 8ff.

8 What your eyes have seen
    bring not forth hastily against an
      opponent;
For what will you do later on
    when your neighbor puts you to
      shame?
9 Discuss your case with your neighbor,
    but another man's secret do not
      disclose;
10 Lest, hearing it, he reproach you,
    and your ill repute cease not.

11 Like golden apples in silver settings
    are words spoken at the proper time.

12 Like a golden earring, or a necklace of
      fine gold,
    is a wise reprover to an obedient ear.

13 Like the coolness of snow in the heat of
      the harvest
    is a faithful messenger for the one who
      sends him.
    [He refreshes the soul of his master.]

14 Like clouds and wind when no rain
      follows
    is the man who boastfully promises
      what he never gives.

15 By patience is a ruler persuaded,f
    and a soft tongue will break a bone.

16 If you find honey, eat only what you
      need,
    lest you become glutted with it and
      vomit it up.

17 Let your foot be seldom in your
      neighbor's house,
    lest he have more than enough of you,
    and hate you.

18 Like a club, or a sword, or a sharp arrow,
    is the man who bears false witness
      against his neighbor.

19 Like an infected tooth or an unsteady
      foot
    is [dependence on] a faithless man in
      time of trouble.

20 Like a moth in clothing, or a maggot in
      wood,
    sorrow gnaws at the human heart.g

21 If your enemy be hungry, give him food
      to eat,*
    if he be thirsty, give him to drink;h

22 For live coals you will heap on his
      head,
    and the LORD will vindicate you.

23 The north wind brings rain,
    and a backbiting tongue an angry
      countenance.

24 It is better to dwell in a corner of the
      housetop
    than in a roomy house with a
      quarrelsome woman.i

25 Like cool water to one faint from
      thirst
    is good news from a far country.

26 Like a troubled fountain or a polluted
      spring
    is a just man who gives way before the
      wicked.

27 To eat too much honey is not good;
    nor to seek honor after honor.*

28 Like an open city with no defenses
    is the man with no check on his
      feelings.

CHAPTER 26*

See RG
180-82

1 Like snow in summer, or rain in
      harvest,
    honor for a fool is out of place.

25, 21f: Charity is invaluable in resolving enmities and restoring peace. Live coals: i.e., either remorse and embarrassment for the harm done, or increased punishment for refusing reconciliation. Cf Mt 5, 44; Rom 12, 20.

25, 27: Nor . . . honor after honor: the text is uncertain.

26, 1-28: Concrete images describe the vices of fools (1-12), of sluggards (13-16), of meddlers (17-19), of talebearers (20ff), and of flatterers (23-28).

f: Prv 15, 1. 4.   g: Sir 30, 24.   h: Rom 12, 20.   i: Prv 21, 9.

2 Like the sparrow in its flitting, like the
   swallow in its flight,
   a curse uncalled-for arrives nowhere.

3 The whip for the horse, the bridle for the
   ass,
   and the rod for the back of fools.*j*

4 Answer not the fool according to his
   folly,*
   lest you too become like him.

5 Answer the fool according to his folly,
   lest he become wise in his own eyes.

6 He cuts off his feet, he drinks down
   violence,
   who sends messages by a fool.

7 A proverb in the mouth of a fool*
   hangs limp, like crippled legs.

8 Like one who entangles the stone in the
   sling
   is he who gives honor to a fool.

9 Like a thorn stick brandished by the hand
   of a drunkard
   is a proverb in the mouth of fools.

10 Like an archer wounding all who
    pass by
    is he who hires a drunken fool.

11 As the dog returns to his vomit,
    so the fool repeats his folly.*k*

12 You see a man wise in his own eyes?
    There is more hope for a fool than for
    him.

13 The sluggard says, "There is a lion in the
    street,
    a lion in the middle of the square!"*l*

14 The door turns on its hinges,

the sluggard, on his bed!

15 The sluggard loses his hand in the
    dish;
    he is too weary to lift it to his mouth.*m*

16 The sluggard imagines himself wiser
    than seven men who answer with good
    sense.

17 Like the man who seizes a passing dog
    by the ears
    is he who meddles in a quarrel not his
    own.

18 Like a crazed archer
    scattering firebrands and deadly
    arrows

19 Is the man who deceives his neighbor,
    and then says, "I was only joking."

20 For lack of wood, the fire dies out;
    and when there is no talebearer, strife
    subsides.

21 What a bellows is to live coals, what
    wood is to fire,
    such is a contentious man in
    enkindling strife.*n*

22 The words of a talebearer are like dainty
    morsels
    that sink into one's inmost being.*o*

23 Like a glazed finish on earthenware
    are smooth lips with a wicked heart.

24 With his lips an enemy pretends,
    but in his inmost being he maintains
    deceit;

25 When he speaks graciously, trust him
    not,*p*
    for seven abominations* are in his
    heart.

26, 4f: There is no contradiction between these two
proverbs. In any answer the wise man gives he must
protect his own interest against the fool.

26, 7ff: The fool abuses whatever knowledge he possesses.

26, 25: Seven abominations: many evil intentions.

j: Pv 19, 29; Sir 33, 25.   k: 2 Pt 2, 22.   l: Prv 22, 13.   m: Prv 19,
24.   n: Prv 15, 18; 29, 22.   o: Prv 18, 8.   p: Sir 12, 10; 27, 23.

²⁶ A man may conceal hatred under
      dissimulation,
    but his malice will be revealed in the
      assembly.

²⁷ He who digs a pit falls into it;
    and a stone comes back upon him who
      rolls it.^q

²⁸ The lying tongue is its owner's enemy,
    and the flattering mouth works ruin.

CHAPTER 27

^{See RG 180–82} ¹Boast not of tomorrow,
    for you know not what any day may
      bring forth.

² Let another praise you—not your own
      mouth;
    someone else—not your own lips.

³ Stone is heavy, and sand a burden,
    but a fool's provocation is heavier than
      both.^r

⁴ Anger is relentless, and wrath
      overwhelming—
    but before jealousy who can stand?

⁵ Better is an open rebuke
    than a love that remains hidden.

⁶ Wounds from a friend may be accepted
      as well meant,
    but the greetings of an enemy one
      prays against.

⁷ One who is full, tramples on virgin
      honey;
    but to the man who is hungry, any
      bitter thing is sweet.

⁸ Like a bird that is far from its nest
    is a man who is far from his home.

⁹ Perfume and incense gladden the heart,
but by grief the soul is torn asunder.

¹⁰ Your own friend and your father's friend
      forsake not;
    but if ruin befalls you, enter not a
      kinsman's house.
Better is a neighbor near at hand
    than a brother far away.

¹¹ If you are wise, my son, you will gladden
      my heart,
    and I will be able to rebut him who
      taunts me.

¹² The shrewd man perceives evil and
      hides;
    simpletons continue on and suffer the
      penalty.^s

¹³ Take his garment who becomes surety
      for another,^t
    and for the sake of a stranger, yield it up![*]

¹⁴ When one greets his neighbor with a
      loud voice in the early morning,
    a curse can be laid to his charge.[*]

¹⁵ For a persistent leak on a rainy day
    the match is a quarrelsome woman.^u

¹⁶ He who keeps her stores up a
      stormwind;
    he cannot tell north from south.

¹⁷ As iron sharpens iron,
    so man sharpens his fellow man.

¹⁸ He who tends a fig tree eats its fruit,
    and he who is attentive to his master
      will be enriched.

¹⁹ As one face differs from another,
    so does one human heart from
      another.

²⁰ The nether world and the abyss are never
      satisfied;^v

27, 13: See note on Prv 20, 16.
27, 14: The loud voice suggests hypocrisy in the greeting.

---

q: Eccl 10, 8; Sir 27, 25f.   r: Sir 22, 14f.   s: Prv 22, 3.   t: Prv 20, 16.   u: Prv 21, 9; 25, 24.   v: Prv 30, 16; Eccl 4, 8.

so too the eyes of men.

21 As the crucible tests silver and the
        furnace gold,
    so a man is tested by the praise he
        receives.

22 Though you should pound the fool to bits
        with the pestle, amid the grits in a
        mortar,
    his folly would not go out of him.

23 Take good care of your flocks,*
    give careful attention to your herds;

24 For wealth lasts not forever,
    nor even a crown from age to age.

25 When the grass is taken away and the
        aftergrowth appears,
    and the mountain greens are gathered
        in,

26 The lambs will provide you with clothing,
    and the goats will bring the price of a
        field,

27 And there will be ample goat's milk to
        supply you,
    to supply your household,
    and maintenance for your maidens.

CHAPTER 28

See RG
180-82

1 The wicked man flees although no
        one pursues him;
    but the just man, like a lion, feels sure
        of himself.

2 If a land is rebellious, its princes will be
        many;
    but with a prudent man it knows
        security.*

3 A rich man who oppresses the poor

is like a devastating rain that leaves no
        food.

4 Those who abandon the law* praise the
        wicked man,
    but those who keep the law war
        against him.

5 Evil men understand nothing of justice,
    but those who seek the LORD
        understand all.

6 Better a poor man who walks in his
        integrity
    than he who is crooked in his ways
        and rich.ʷ

7 He who keeps the law is a wise son,
    but the gluttons' companion disgraces
        his father.

8 He who increases his wealth by interest
        and overcharge*
    gathers it for him who is kind to the
        poor.

9 When one turns away his ear from
        hearing the law,ˣ
    even his prayer is an abomination.*

10 He who seduces the upright into an evil
        way
    will himself fall into his own pit.
    [And blameless men will gain
        prosperity.]

11 The rich man is wise in his own eyes,
    but a poor man who is intelligent sees
        through him.

12 When the just are triumphant, there is
        great jubilation;
    but when the wicked gain
        pre-eminence, people hide.

27, 23-27: The land of Palestine was very suitable for
flocks and herds, which formed the principal source of wealth
for their owners.

28, 2: The meaning of this poorly preserved verse seems
to be that frequent changes of rulers often result from moral
corruption and political disorder.

28, 4: The law: religious and moral teaching.

28, 8: Interest and overcharge were strictly forbidden in

the old law among Israelites because it was presumed that the
borrower was in distress; cf Ex 22, 25; Lv 25, 35ff; Dt 23, 19;
Ps 15, 5; Ez 18, 8. Civil and divine law will take the offender's wealth from him.

28, 9: Prayers offered in bad faith are displeasing to God.

---

w: Prv 19, 1.   x: Prv 21, 27.

¹³ He who conceals his sins
    prospers not,
  but he who confesses and forsakes
    them obtains mercy.

¹⁴ Happy the man who is always on his
    guard;
  but he who hardens his heart will fall
    into evil.

¹⁵ Like a roaring lion or a ravenous
    bear
  is a wicked ruler over a poor people.

¹⁶ The less prudent the prince, the more his
    deeds oppress.
  He who hates ill-gotten gain prolongs
    his days.

¹⁷ Though a man burdened with human blood
    were to flee to the grave, none should
    support him.

¹⁸ He who walks uprightly is safe,
  but he whose ways are crooked falls
    into the pit.

¹⁹ He who cultivates his land will have
    plenty of food,
  but from idle pursuits a man has his
    fill of poverty.ʸ

²⁰ The trustworthy man will be richly
    blessed;
  he who is in haste to grow rich will not
    go unpunished.ᶻ

²¹ To show partiality is never good:ᵃ
  for even a morsel of bread a man may
    do wrong.

²² The avaricious man is perturbed about
    his wealth,
  and he knows not when want will
    come upon him.

²³ He who rebukes a man gets more thanks
    in the end
  than one with a flattering tongue.

²⁴ He who defrauds father or mother and
    calls it no sin,ᵇ
  is a partner of the brigand.

²⁵ The greedy man stirs up disputes,
  but he who trusts in the LORD will
    prosper.

²⁶ He who trusts in himself is a fool,
  but he who walks in wisdom is safe.

²⁷ He who gives to the poor suffers no want,ᶜ
  but he who ignores them gets many a
    curse.

²⁸ When the wicked gain pre-eminence,
    other men hide;
  but at their fall the just flourish.

CHAPTER 29

See RG 180–82

¹ The man who remains stiff-necked
    and hates rebuke
  will be crushed suddenly beyond
    cure.

² When the just prevail, the people
    rejoice;
  but when the wicked rule, the people
    groan.ᵈ

³ He who loves wisdom makes his father
    glad,
  but he who consorts with harlots
    squanders his wealth.ᵉ

⁴ By justice a king gives stability to the
    land;
  but he who imposes heavy taxes ruins
    it.

⁵ The man who flatters his neighbor
  is spreading a net under his feet.

⁶ The wicked man steps into a snare,
  but the just man runs on joyfully.

⁷ The just man has a care for the rights of
    the poor;
  the wicked man has no such concern.

y: Prv 12, 11. z: Prv 13, 11. a: Prv 24, 23. b: Mk 7, 11ff. c: Prv 19, 17; Sir 4, 3-8. d: Prv 11, 10. e: Prv 5, 10; 10, 1.

8 Arrogant men set the city ablaze,
   but wise men calm the fury.*f*

9 If a wise man disputes with a fool,
   he may rage or laugh but can have no
      peace.

10 Bloodthirsty men hate the honest man,
   but the upright show concern for his
      life.

11 The fool gives vent to all his anger;
   but by biding his time, the wise man
      calms it.*g*

12 If a ruler listens to lying words,
   his servants all become wicked.

13 The poor and the oppressor* have a
      common bond:*h*
   the Lord gives light to the eyes of both.

14 If a king is zealous for the rights of the
      poor,
   his throne stands firm forever.

15 The rod of correction gives wisdom,
   but a boy left to his whims disgraces
      his mother.*i*

16 When the wicked prevail, crime increases;
   but their downfall the just will behold.

17 Correct your son, and he will bring you
      comfort,
   and give delight to your soul.

18 Without prophecy the people become
      demoralized;
   but happy is he who keeps the law.

19 By words no servant can be trained;*j*
   for he understands what is said, but
      obeys not.

20 Do you see a man hasty in his words?*k*
   More can be hoped for from a fool!

21 If a man pampers his servant from
      childhood,
   he will turn out to be stubborn.

22 An ill-tempered man stirs up disputes,
   and a hotheaded man is the cause of
      many sins.*l*

23 Man's pride causes his humiliation,
   but he who is humble of spirit obtains
      honor.*m*

24 The accomplice of a thief is his own
      enemy:*
   he hears himself put under a curse, yet
      discloses nothing.

25 The fear of man brings a snare,
   but he who trusts in the Lord is safe.

26 Many curry favor with the ruler,
   but the rights of each are from the
      Lord.

27 The evildoer is an abomination to the
      just,
   and he who walks uprightly is an
      abomination to the wicked.

VI: The Words of Agur

CHAPTER 30

See RG 180–82

1 The words of Agur,* son of Jakeh the
Massaite:

   The pronouncement of mortal man: "I
      am not God;*
   I am not God, that I should prevail.
2 Why, I am the most stupid of men,
   and have not even human intelligence;
3 Neither have I learned wisdom,

29, 13: God gives life to all classes of people; cf Prv 22, 2.
29, 24: Is his own enemy: because he not only incurs guilt
as an accomplice but, by his silence, brings down on himself
the curse invoked on the unknown guilty partner.

30, 1: Agur: an unknown person. Massaite: from Massa in
northern Arabia, elsewhere referred to as an encampment of
the Ishmaelites (Gn 25, 14). But the word may not be intended
as a place name; it might signify "an oracle," "a prophecy."

30, 1ff: Agur wishes to stress man's insignificance when
he is compared to God; cf Jb 38—39.

---

f: Prv 11, 11.   *g:* Prv 12, 16; 25, 28; Sir 21, 26.   *h:* Prv 22, 2.
i: Prv 13, 24; 22, 15; 23, 13f; Sir 22, 6; 30, 1.   *j:* Sir 33, 25f.
k: Eccl 5, 1.   *l:* Prv 15, 18; 26, 21.   *m:* Prv 11, 2; 16, 18; 18, 12;
Jb 22, 29.

nor have I the knowledge of the Holy
One.
⁴ Who has gone up to heaven and come
down again—
who has cupped the wind in his hands?
Who has bound up the waters in a
cloak—
who has marked out all the ends of the
earth?
What is his name, what is his son's name,
if you know it?"
⁵ Every word of God is tested;[n]
he is a shield to those who take refuge
in him.
⁶ Add nothing to his words,[o]
lest he reprove you, and you be
exposed as a deceiver.

VII: Numerical Proverbs

⁷ Two things I ask of you,
deny them not to me before I die:
⁸ Put falsehood and lying far from me,
give me neither poverty nor riches;
[provide me only with the food I need;]
⁹ Lest, being full, I deny you,
saying, "Who is the Lord?"
Or, being in want, I steal,
and profane the name of my God.

¹⁰ Slander not a servant to his master,
lest he curse you, and you have to pay
the penalty.

¹¹ There is a group of people that curses its
father,*
and blesses not its mother.[p]
¹² There is a group that is pure in its own
eyes,
yet is not purged of its filth.
¹³ There is a group—how haughty their eyes!
how overbearing their glance!
¹⁴ There is a group whose incisors are swords,

whose teeth are knives,
Devouring the needy from the earth,
and the poor from among men.

¹⁵ The two daughters of the leech are,
"Give, Give."*
Three things are never satisfied,
four never say, "Enough!"
¹⁶ The nether world, and the barren womb;[q]
the earth, that is never saturated with
water,
and fire, that never says, "Enough!"
¹⁷ The eye that mocks a father,
or scorns an aged mother,
Will be plucked out by the ravens in the
valley;
the young eagles will devour it.

¹⁸ Three things are too wonderful for me,*
yes, four I cannot understand:
¹⁹ The way of an eagle in the air,
the way of a serpent upon a rock,
The way of a ship on the high seas,
and the way of a man with a maiden.
²⁰ Such is the way of an adulterous
woman:
she eats, wipes her mouth,
and says, "I have done no wrong."*

²¹ Under three things the earth trembles,
yes, under four it cannot bear up:
²² Under a slave when he becomes king,
and a fool when he is glutted with
food;[r]
²³ Under an odious woman when she is
wed,
and a maidservant when she displaces
her mistress.

²⁴ Four things are among the smallest on
the earth,
and yet are exceedingly wise:
²⁵ Ants—a species not strong,

30, 11-14: Perverted people are here classified as unfilial (11), self-righteous (12), proud (13) and rapacious (14).

30, 15f: The two daughters . . . "Give, Give": the text is obscure but the sense seems to be that the leech is insatiable in its desire for blood, just as are the nether world for victims, the barren womb for offspring, the parched earth for water, and fire for fuel (16).

30, 18f: The soaring flight of the eagle, the mysterious

movement upon a rock of the serpent which has no feet, the path of the ship through the trackless deep, and the marvelous procreation of human life, excite great wonderment.

30, 20: This verse portrays the indifference of an adulterous woman who thinks there is no trace of her wicked act.

n: Ps 12, 7.   o: Dt 4, 2.   p: Prv 20, 20.   q: Prv 27, 20.   r: Prv 19 10; Eccl 10, 6f.

Praise of the Capable Wife

Chapter 31 (vv. 10–31) is an acrostic poem of twenty-two lines, each line beginning with a successive letter of the alphabet. It is an encomium or hymn praising the capable wife. A hymn does not dwell on the inner feelings or the physical appearance of its hero but describes the hero's mighty feats of valor, in this case the wife's extraordinarily wise management of her great household.

yet they store up their food in the
summer;
26 Rock-badgers*—a species not mighty,
yet they make their home in the crags;
27 Locusts—they have no king,
yet they migrate all in array;
28 Lizards—you can catch them with your
hands,
yet they find their way into kings'
palaces.

29 Three things are stately in their stride,
yes, four are stately in their carriage:
30 The lion, mightiest of beasts,
who retreats before nothing;
31 The strutting cock, and the he-goat,
and the king at the head of his people.

32 If you have foolishly been proud*
or presumptuous—put your hand on
your mouth;
33 For the stirring of milk brings forth curds,
and the stirring of anger brings forth
blood.

VIII: The Words of Lemuel

CHAPTER 31

See RG
180–82 1The words of Lemuel, king of
Massa. The advice which his mother gave
him:

2 What, my son, my first-born!
what, O son of my womb;
what, O son of my vows!
3 Give not your vigor to women,
nor your strength to those who ruin
kings.s

4 It is not for kings, O Lemuel,
not for kings to drink wine;
strong drink is not for princes!t
5 Lest in drinking they forget what the law
decrees,
and violate the rights of all who are in
need.
6 Give strong drink to one who is
perishing,
and wine to the sorely depressed;
7 When they drink, they will forget their
misery,
and think no more of their burdens.
8 Open your mouth in behalf of the dumb,
and for the rights of the destitute;
9 Open your mouth, decree what is just,
defend the needy and the poor!

IX: The Ideal Wife

10 When one finds a worthy wife,u
her value is far beyond pearls.
11 Her husband, entrusting his heart to her,
has an unfailing prize.
12 She brings him good, and not evil,*
all the days of her life.
13 She obtains wool and flax
and makes cloth with skillful hands.
14 Like merchant* ships,
she secures her provisions from afar.
15 She rises while it is still night,
and distributes food to her
household.
16 She picks out a field to purchase;
out of her earnings she plants a
vineyard.
17 She is girt about with strength,
and sturdy are her arms.

30, 26: Rock-badgers: cf note on Ps 104, 18.
30, 32f: The anger aroused by overweening pride threatens an awesome punishment.
31, 12: Good, and not evil: i.e., prosperity, not adversity.
31, 14: Merchant: literally, "Canaanite" (cf v 24), probably because the merchant class had been composed chiefly of Canaanites.

s: Prv 5, 9.   t: Prv 20, 1.   u: 10-31: Sir 26, 1ff. 13-18.

¹⁸ She enjoys the success of her dealings;
 at night her lamp is undimmed.*
¹⁹ She puts her hands to the distaff,
 and her fingers ply the spindle.
²⁰ She reaches out her hands to the poor,
 and extends her arms to the needy.
²¹ She fears not the snow for her household;
 all her charges are doubly clothed.
²² She makes her own coverlets;
 fine linen and purple are her clothing.
²³ Her husband is prominent at the city
 gates
 as he sits with the elders of the land.
²⁴ She makes garments and sells them,
 and stocks the merchants with belts.
²⁵ She is clothed with strength and dignity,

and she laughs at the days to come.*
²⁶ She opens her mouth in wisdom,
 and on her tongue is kindly counsel.
²⁷ She watches the conduct of her
 household,
 and eats not her food in idleness.
²⁸ Her children rise up and praise her;
 her husband, too, extols her:
²⁹ "Many are the women of proven worth,
 but you have excelled them all."
³⁰ Charm is deceptive and beauty fleeting;
 the woman who fears the LORD is to be
 praised.*
³¹ Give her a reward of her labors,
 and let her works praise her at the city
 gates.

31, 18: Her lamp is undimmed: indicates abundance of productive work and its accompanying prosperity; cf Prv 20, 20; Jb 18, 6.

31, 25: Laughs at the days to come: anticipates the future with gladness free from anxiety.

31, 30: The true charm of the ideal wife is her religious spirit, for she fears the Lord; cf note on Prv 1, 7.

See RG 183–87

The Book of Ecclesiastes

The title ECCLESIASTES given to this book is the Greek translation of the Hebrew name QOHELETH meaning, perhaps, "one who convokes an assembly." The book, however, does not consist of public addresses, but is a treatise, more or less logically developed, on the vanity of all things. Reflections in prose and aphorisms in verse are intermingled in Ecclesiastes, which contains, besides, an introduction and an epilogue.

The book is concerned with the purpose and value of human life. While admitting the existence of a divine plan, it considers such a plan to be hidden from man, who seeks happiness without ever finding it here below (3, 11; 8, 7. 17). Ecclesiastes applies his "Vanity of vanities" to everything "under the sun," even to that wisdom which seeks to find at last a semblance of good in the things of the world. Merit does not yield happiness for it is often tried by suffering. Riches and pleasures do not avail. Existence is monotonous, enjoyment fleeting and vain; darkness quickly follows. Life, then, is an enigma beyond human ability to solve.

While Ecclesiastes concedes that there is an advantage for man in the enjoyment of certain legitimate pleasures lest he lapse into pessimism and despair, he nevertheless considers this indulgence also vanity unless man returns due thanks

to the Creator who has given him all. Under this aspect, earthly wisdom would rise to the higher level of true spiritual wisdom. This true wisdom is not found "under the sun" but is perceived only by the light of faith, inasmuch as it rests with God, who is the final Judge of the good and the bad, and whose reign endures forever. The Epilogue gives the clue to this thought (12, 13f).

The moral teaching of the book is imperfect, like the Old Testament itself (Heb 7, 19), yet it marks an advance in the development of the doctrine of divine retribution. While rejecting the older solution of earthly rewards and punishments, Ecclesiastes looks forward to a more lasting one. The clear answer to the problem was to come with the light of Christ's teaching concerning future life.

The author of the book was a teacher of popular wisdom (12, 9). Qoheleth was obviously only his literary name. Because he is called "David's son, king in Jerusalem," it was commonly thought that he was King Solomon. Such personation, however, was but a literary device to lend greater dignity and authority to the book—a circumstance which does not in any way impugn its inspired character. The Epilogue seems to have been written by an editor, probably a disciple of Qoheleth.

The entire work differs considerably in language and style from earlier books of the Old Testament. It reflects a late period of Hebrew, and was probably written about three centuries before Christ.

See RG
183-87

CHAPTER 1

*1*The words of David's son, Qoheleth,* king in Jerusalem:*a*

Vanity of Toil without Profit

2 Vanity of vanities,* says Qoheleth,
vanity of vanities! All things are vanity!*b*

3 What profit has man from all the labor*c*
which he toils at under the sun?*

4 One generation passes and another comes,
but the world forever stays.

5 The sun rises and the sun goes down;
then it presses on to the place where it rises.

6 Blowing now toward the south, then
toward the north,
the wind turns again and again,
resuming its rounds.

7 All rivers go to the sea,
yet never does the sea become full.
To the place where they go,
the rivers keep on going.

8 All speech is labored;
there is nothing man can say.*
The eye is not satisfied with seeing
nor is the ear filled with hearing.*d*

*9*What has been, that will be; what has been done, that will be done. Nothing is new under the sun.*e* *10*Even the thing of which we say, "See, this is new!" has already existed in the ages that preceded us.*f* *11*There is no remembrance of the men of old;*g* nor of those to come will there be any remembrance among those who come after them.*

I: Qoheleth's Investigation of Life

Twofold Introduction. *12*I, Qoheleth, was king over Israel in Jerusalem, *13*and I applied my mind to search and investigate in wisdom all things that are done under the sun.*h*

A thankless task God has appointed
for men to be busied about.

*14*I have seen all things that are done under the sun,*i* and behold, all is vanity and a chase after wind.*

15 What is crooked cannot be made straight,
and what is missing cannot be supplied.

*16j*Though I said to myself, "Behold, I have become great and stored up wisdom beyond all who were before me in Jerusalem, and my mind has broad experience of wisdom and knowledge"; *17*yet when I applied my mind to know wisdom and knowledge, madness and folly, I learned that this also is a chase after wind.*k*

18 For in much wisdom there is much sorrow,
and he who stores up knowledge stores up grief.

CHAPTER 2

Study of Pleasure-seeking. *1*I said to myself,* "Come, now, let me try you with pleasure and the enjoyment of good things."*l* But behold, this too was vanity. *2*Of laughter I said: "Mad!" and of mirth: "What good does this do?" *3*I thought of beguiling my senses with wine, though my mind was concerned with wisdom,* and of taking up folly, until I should understand what is best for

See RG
183-87

1, 1: Qoheleth: see Introduction.

1, 2: Vanity of vanities: a Hebrew superlative expressing the supreme degree of futility and emptiness.

1, 3: Under the sun: used throughout this book to signify "on the earth."

1, 8: All speech . . . man can say: or "All things are wearisome beyond man's power to tell."

1, 11: Men remember nothing long; God, however, never forgets.

1, 14: Chase after wind: futility, like an attempt to corral the winds. Cf Hos 12, 2. The ancient versions understood "af-

fliction of spirit." These words are used to conclude sections of the discourse, as far as Eccl 6, 9.

2, 1-11: The author here assumes the role of Solomon.

2, 3: Though my mind . . . wisdom: while indulging in pleasure the author hopes to discover wherein man's true happiness consists.

a: Eccl 7, 27; 12, 8f. *b:* Eccl 12, 8. *c:* Eccl 2, 11. 22; 3, 9; 5, 15. *d:* Eccl 8, 17. *e:* Eccl 3, 15; 6, 10. *f:* Eccl 3, 15. *g:* Eccl 2, 16. *h:* Eccl 8, 9. *i:* Eccl 2, 11. 17. *j:* Eccl 2, 9. *k:* Eccl 2, 3; 7, 25. *l:* Wis 2, 6.

Ecclesiastes and Wisdom Literature

Like Job, the book of Ecclesiastes relates to the wisdom tradition in its own way. According to the tradition, as given for instance in the book of Proverbs, in the Wisdom of Solomon, and in Sirach (Ecclesiasticus), the regularity of life was what people relied on for guidance: "What a bellows is to live coals, what wood is to fire, such is a contentious man in enkindling strife" (Prv 26, 21). And just as human behavior follows in its regular course, good behavior regularly brings its reward: "He who tends a fig tree eats its fruit, and he who is attentive to his master will be enriched" (Prv 27, 18). The book of Job denies that reward inevitably follows goodness. Ecclesiastes takes the idea of inevitability and repetition in life and turns it around: Instead of being an image of reliability, such regular recurrences as the returning seasons are the image of futility, "vanity." We may attempt to escape such futility by the pursuit of pleasure (Eccl 2, 1–11); by attaining wisdom (vv. 12–17); or by working (vv. 18–26). But the realities of life will eventually bring us to recognize that all of these escapes are themselves futile. Implicitly, the argument of Ecclesiastes is that nothing in the natural life can be our ultimate goal: if we try to make it so, we will only learn that it is empty. Thus, without saying so, the book makes the point: Only God can truly satisfy every longing.

The issue of greed echoes through the centuries. One who seeks wealth for its own sake rather than for what it can provide when shared cannot be satisfied. Today we are still counseled to examine how we can share our time and our talent as well as our treasure. This can bring us closer to the wisdom taught here.

men to do under the heavens during the limited days of their life.

⁴ I undertook great works; I built myself houses and planted vineyards; ⁵ I made gardens and parks, and set out in them fruit trees of all sorts. ⁶ And I constructed for myself reservoirs to water a flourishing woodland. ⁷ I acquired male and female slaves, and slaves were born in my house. I also had growing herds of cattle and flocks of sheep, more than all who had been before me in Jerusalem. ⁸ I amassed for myself silver and gold, and the wealth of kings and provinces. I got for myself male and female singers and all human luxuries. ⁹ I became great, and I stored up more than all others before me in Jerusalem; my wisdom, too, stayed with me. ¹⁰ᵐ Nothing that my eyes desired did I deny them, nor did I deprive myself of any joy, but my heart rejoiced in the fruit of all my toil. This was my share for all my toil. ¹¹ⁿ But when I turned to all the works that my hands had wrought, and to the toil at which I had taken such pains, behold! all was vanity and a chase after wind, with

nothing gained under the sun. ¹² For what will the man do who is to come after the king? What men have already done!

Study of Wisdom and Folly. I went on to the consideration of wisdom, madness and folly. ¹³ And I saw that wisdom has the advantage over folly as much as light has the advantage over darkness.

¹⁴ The wise man has eyes in his head,
  but the fool walks in darkness.ᵒ

Yet I knew that one lot befalls both of them. ¹⁵ So I said to myself, if the fool's lot is to befall me also, why then should I be wise? Where is the profit for me? And I concluded in my heart that this too is vanity. ¹⁶ᵖ Neither of the wise man nor of the fool will there be an abiding remembrance, for in days to come both will have been forgotten. How is it that the wise man dies as well as the fool! ¹⁷ Therefore I loathed life, since for me the work that is done under the sun is evil; for all is vanity and a chase after wind.

m: Eccl 3, 22; 5, 18.   n: Eccl 1, 17; Sir 44, 9.   o: 14f: Eccl 6, 8; 9, 2f.   p: Eccl 1, 11; Wis 2, 4.

Study of the Fruits of Toil

To Others the Profits. [18]And I detested all the fruits of my labor under the sun, because I must leave them to a man who is to come after me. [19]And who knows whether he will be a wise man or a fool? Yet he will have control over all the fruits of my wise labor under the sun. This also is vanity. [20]So my feelings turned to despair of all the fruits of my labor under the sun. [21]For there is a man who has labored with wisdom and knowledge and skill, and to another, who has not labored over it, he must leave his property. This also is vanity and a great misfortune. [22q]For what profit comes to a man from all the toil and anxiety of heart with which he has labored under the sun? [23]All his days sorrow and grief are his occupation; even at night his mind is not at rest. This also is vanity.

[24r]There is nothing better for man than to eat and drink and provide himself with good things by his labors. Even this, I realized, is from the hand of God.* [25]For who can eat or drink apart from him? [26s]For to whatever man he sees fit he gives wisdom and knowledge and joy; but to the sinner he gives the task of gathering possessions to be given to whatever man God sees fit. This also is vanity and a chase after wind.

CHAPTER 3

See RG 183-87

Man Cannot Hit on the Right Time To Act

[1] There is an appointed time for everything,
and a time for every affair under the heavens.
[2] A time to be born, and a time to die;
a time to plant, and a time to uproot the plant.
[3] A time to kill, and a time to heal;
a time to tear down, and a time to build.
[4] A time to weep, and a time to laugh;
a time to mourn, and a time to dance.

[5] A time to scatter stones, and a time to gather them;
a time to embrace, and a time to be far from embraces.
[6] A time to seek, and a time to lose;
a time to keep, and a time to cast away.
[7] A time to rend, and a time to sew;
a time to be silent, and a time to speak.
[8] A time to love, and a time to hate;
a time of war, and a time of peace.

[9t]What advantage has the worker from his toil? [10]I have considered the task which God has appointed for men to be busied about. [11u]He has made everything appropriate to its time, and has put the timeless into their hearts, without men's ever discovering, from beginning to end, the work which God has done. [12]I recognized that there is nothing better than to be glad and to do well during life. [13v]For every man, moreover, to eat and drink and enjoy the fruit of all his labor is a gift of God. [14]I recognized that whatever God does will endure forever; there is no adding to it, or taking from it. Thus has God done that he may be revered. [15w]What now is has already been; what is to be, already is; and God restores* what would otherwise be displaced.

The Problem of Retribution. [16x]And still under the sun in the judgment place I saw wickedness, and in the seat of justice, iniquity. [17y]And I said to myself, both the just and the wicked God will judge, since there is a time for every affair and on every work a judgment. [18]I said to myself: As for the children of men, it is God's way of testing them and of showing that they are in themselves like beasts. [19]For the lot of man and of beast is one lot; the one dies as well as the other. Both have the same life-breath, and man has no advantage over the beast; but all is vanity. [20z]Both go to the same place; both were made from the dust, and to the dust they both return. [21a]Who knows if the life-breath of the children of men goes upward and the life-breath of beasts goes earthward? [22b]And I

2, 24: Unrestrained indulgence is not advocated here, but legitimate pleasure and the cheerfulness it begets.
3, 15: God restores: the meaning is probably that God allows no part of his creation to drop out of existence.

---

q: Eccl 1, 3.   *r:* Eccl 3, 12f. 22; 5, 17f; 8, 15.   *s:* Prv 13, 22.   *t:* Eccl 1, 3.   *u:* Eccl 8, 17; 11, 5; Gn 1, 31.   *v:* Eccl 2, 24.   *w:* Eccl 1, 9.
x: Eccl 4, 1.   *y:* Eccl 12, 14.   *z:* Eccl 12, 7; Gn 2, 7; 3, 19; Ps 103, 14; Wis 2, 3; Sir 10, 9; 17, 1; 40, 11.   *a:* Wis 2, 2.   *b:* Eccl 8, 7; 10, 14.

saw that there is nothing better for a man than to rejoice in his work; for this is his lot. Who will let him see what is to come after him?

CHAPTER 4

See RG 183–87

Vanity of Toil. [1]Again I considered all the oppressions that take place under the sun: the tears of the victims with none to comfort them! From the hand of their oppressors comes violence, and there is none to comfort them![c] [2]And those now dead, I declared more fortunate in death than are the living to be still alive.[d] [3]And better off than both is the yet unborn, who has not seen the wicked work that is done under the sun. [4]Then I saw that all toil and skillful work is the rivalry of one man for another. This also is vanity and a chase after wind.

[5] "The fool folds his arms
    and consumes his own flesh"*—
[6] Better is one handful with tranquility
    than two with toil and a chase after
    wind!

Companions and Successors. [7]Again I found this vanity under the sun: [8]a solitary man with no companion; with neither son nor brother. Yet there is no end to all his toil, and riches do not satisfy his greed. "For whom do I toil and deprive myself of good things?" This also is vanity and a worthless task. [9]Two are better than one: they get a good wage for their labor. [10]If the one falls, the other will lift up his companion. Woe to the solitary man! For if he should fall, he has no one to lift him up. [11]So also, if two sleep together, they keep each other warm. How can one alone keep warm? [12]Where a lone man may be overcome, two together can resist. A three-ply cord is not easily broken.

[13]Better is a poor but wise youth than an old but foolish king who no longer knows caution; [14]for from a prison house* one comes forth to rule, since even in his royalty he was poor at birth. [15]Then I saw all those who are to live and move about under the sun with the heir apparent who will succeed to his place.* [16]There is no end to all these people, to all over whom he takes precedence; yet the later generations will not applaud him. This also is vanity and a chase after wind.

Vanity of Many Words. [17e]Guard your step when you go to the house of God. Let your approach be obedience, rather than the fools' offering of sacrifice;* for they know not how to keep from doing evil.

CHAPTER 5

See RG 183–87

[1]Be not hasty in your utterance and let not your heart be quick to make a promise in God's presence. God is in heaven and you are on earth; therefore let your words be few.

[2] For nightmares* come with many cares,
    and a fool's utterance with many
    words.

[3f]When you make a vow to God, delay not its fulfillment. For God has no pleasure in fools; fulfill what you have vowed. [4]You had better not make a vow than make it and not fulfill it. [5]Let not your utterances make you guilty, and say not before his representative, "It was a mistake," lest God be angered by such words and destroy the works of your hands. [6g]Rather, fear God!

Gain and Loss of Goods. [7h]If you see oppression of the poor, and violation of rights and justice in the realm, do not be shocked by the fact, for the high official has another higher than he watching him and above these are others higher still—. [8]Yet an advantage for a country in every respect is a king for the arable land.*

[9i]The covetous man is never satisfied with money, and the lover of wealth reaps no fruit

---

4, 5: Consumes his own flesh: refuses to work for the necessities of life and consequently suffers hunger and impairs his bodily health.

4, 14: Prison house: probably his mother's womb, from which the king issues without possessions. Cf Eccl 5, 14.

4, 15: The king is no sooner dead than the people transfer their allegiance to his successor.

4, 17: The fools' . . . sacrifice: unacceptable to God because of their disobedience; cf 1 Sm 15, 22; Hos 6, 6.

5, 2: Nightmares: literally, "dreams."

5, 8: The wording of this verse has perhaps never been adequately explained.

---

c: Eccl 5, 7.   *d:* Eccl 7, 2.   *e:* 1 Sm 15, 22; Hos 6, 6.   *f:* Nm 30, 3; Dt 23, 23; Ps 50, 14.   *g:* Eccl 12, 13; Dt 10, 12.   *h:* Eccl 3, 16; 4, 1.   *i:* Prv 28, 22.

from it; so this too is vanity. [10]Where there are great riches, there are also many to devour them. Of what use are they to the owner except to feast his eyes upon? [11]Sleep is sweet to the laboring man, whether he eats little or much, but the rich man's abundance allows him no sleep.

[12j]This is a grievous evil which I have seen under the sun: riches kept by their owner to his hurt. [13]Should the riches be lost through some misfortune, he may have a son when he is without means. [14k]As he came forth from his mother's womb, so again shall he depart, naked as he came, having nothing from his labor that he can carry in his hand. [15]This too is a grievous evil, that he goes just as he came. What then does it profit him to toil for wind? [16]All the days of his life are passed in gloom and sorrow, under great vexation, sickness and wrath.

[17l]Here is what I recognize as good: it is well for a man to eat and drink and enjoy all the fruits of his labor under the sun during the limited days of the life which God gives him; for this is his lot. [18]Any man to whom God gives riches and property, and grants power to partake of them, so that he receives his lot and finds joy in the fruits of his toil, has a gift from God. [19]For he will hardly dwell on the shortness of his life, because God lets him busy himself with the joy of his heart.*

See RG 183-87

CHAPTER 6

Limited Worth of Enjoyment. [1]There is another evil which I have seen under the sun, and it weighs heavily upon man: [2m]there is the man to whom God gives riches and property and honor, so that he lacks none of all the things he craves; yet God does not grant him power to partake of them, but a stranger devours them. This is vanity and a dire plague. [3]Should a man have a hundred children and live many years, no matter

to what great age, still if he has not the full benefit of his goods, or if he is deprived of burial, of this man I proclaim that the child born dead is more fortunate than he.* [4]Though it came in vain and goes into darkness and its name is enveloped in darkness; [5]though it has not seen or known the sun, yet the dead child is at rest rather than such a man. [6]Should he live twice a thousand years and not enjoy his goods, do not both go to the same place?*

[7]All man's toil is for his mouth,* yet his desire is not fulfilled. [8]For what advantage has the wise man over the fool, or what advantage has the poor man in knowing how to conduct himself in life? [9]"What the eyes see is better than what the desires wander after."* This also is vanity and a chase after wind.

II: Qoheleth's Conclusions

[10]Whatever is, was long ago given its name, and the nature of man is known, and that he cannot contend in judgment with one who is stronger than he.* [11]For though there are many sayings that multiply vanity, what profit is there for a man? [12n]For who knows what is good for a man in life, the limited days of his vain life (which God has made like a shadow)? Because—who is there to tell a man what will come after him under the sun?

A. Man Cannot Find Out What Is Good for Him To Do

CHAPTER 7

Critique of Sages on the Day of Adversity

See RG 183-87

[1] A good name is better than good ointment,*
   and the day of death than the day of
      birth.[o]
[2] It is better to go to the house of mourning
   than to the house of feasting,

5, 19: The meaning is that the joys of life, though temporary, keep a man from dwelling on the ills which afflict humanity.

6, 3: A large family, a long life, an honorable burial, all were highly esteemed by the Hebrews, and it was considered a great misfortune to be deprived of them.

6, 6: Same place: the grave.

6, 7: Mouth: appetite, and therefore, body.

6, 9: Better . . . wander after: the good that is present to us

is better than that which is absent and, perhaps, unattainable.

6, 10: The one who is stronger than man is God.

7, 1: Ointment: applied to the child at birth; a good name remains even after death.

j: Jb 20, 20. *k:* Jb 1, 21; 1 Tm 6, 7. *l:* 17f: Eccl 2, 24. *m:* Eccl 2, 18f. *n:* Jb 8, 9; 14, 2; Ps 102, 12. *o:* Eccl 4, 2; Prv 22, 1; Sir 41, 13.

For that is the end of every man,
  and the living should take it to heart.ᵖ

³ Sorrow is better than laughter,
  because when the face is sad the heart
    grows wiser.

⁴ The heart of the wise is in the house of
  mourning,
  but the heart of fools is in the house of
    mirth.

⁵ It is better to hearken to the wise man's
  rebuke
  than to hearken to the song of fools;

⁶ For as the crackling of thorns under a
  pot,
  so is the fool's laughter.
    This also is vanity,

⁷ For oppression can make a fool of a wise
  man,
  and a bribe corrupts the heart.

⁸ Better is the end of speech than its
  beginning;
  better is the patient spirit than the lofty
    spirit.

⁹ Do not in spirit become quickly
  discontented,
  for discontent lodges in the bosom of a
    fool.

¹⁰Do not say: How is it that former times were better than these? For it is not in wisdom that you ask about this.

¹¹ Wisdom and an inheritance are good,
  and an advantage to those that see the
    sun.

¹²For the protection of wisdom is as the protection of money; and the advantage of knowledge is that wisdom preserves the life of its owner.

¹³Consider the work of God. Who can make straight what he has made crooked?

¹⁴On a good day enjoy good things, and on an evil day consider: Both the one and the other God has made, so that man cannot find fault with him in anything.

Critique of Sages on Justice and Wickedness. ¹⁵I have seen all manner of things in my vain days: a just man perishing in his justice, and a wicked one surviving in his wickedness. ¹⁶ᵃ"Be not just to excess, and be not overwise, lest you be ruined.*¹⁷Be not wicked to excess, and be not foolish. Why should you die before your time?"*¹⁸It is good to hold to this rule, and not to let that one* go; but he who fears God will win through at all events.

¹⁹Wisdom is a better defense for the wise man than would be ten princes in the city, ²⁰ʳyet there is no man on earth so just as to do good and never sin.* ²¹ˢDo not give heed to every word that is spoken lest you hear your servant speaking ill of you, ²²for you know in your heart that you have many times spoken ill of others.

²³All these things I probed in wisdom. I said, "I will acquire wisdom"; but it was beyond me. ²⁴What exists is far-reaching; it is deep, very deep: who can find it out? ²⁵ᵗI turned my thoughts toward knowledge; I sought and pursued wisdom and reason, and I recognized that wickedness is foolish and folly is madness.

Critique of Sages on Women. ²⁶ᵘMore bitter than death I find the woman who is a hunter's trap, whose heart is a snare and whose hands are prison bonds. He who is pleasing to God will escape her, but the sinner will be entrapped by her. ²⁷Behold, this have I found, says Qoheleth, adding one thing to another that I might discover the answer ²⁸which my soul still seeks and has not found: One man out of a thousand have I come upon, but a woman among them all I have not found.*

7, 16: St. Jerome explains the warning against excessive justice in reference to the self-righteous man who is so stern that he is never willing to forgive sin in others; cf vv 20ff.

7, 17: Untimely death was traditionally recognized as a divine punishment of the wicked; cf 1 Sm 2, 31-34; Jer 17, 11; Ps 55, 24; Prv 10, 27. This warning against presumptuous wickedness is not an endorsement of any lesser degree of misconduct.

7, 18: This rule . . . that one: the sayings cited in vv 16f. Others refer this and that to riches and wisdom (cf 7, 12), jus-

tice and wisdom, or justice and wickedness. This last supposition makes the author's thought hard to follow.

7, 20: This is to be understood in the sense of Rom 5, 12. See note there.

7, 28: The author found sincerity rare among men, but among women still more rare.

---

p: Eccl 4, 2.   q: 16f: Eccl 8, 12ff.   r: Jb 25, 4; Prv 20, 9; 1 Kgs 8, 46; Rom 3, 23; Jas 3, 2; 1 Jn 1, 8.   s: 21f: 1 Kgs 8, 46.   t: Eccl 1, 17.   u: Prv 5, 4.

²⁹Behold, only this have I found out: God made mankind straight, but men have had recourse to many calculations.*

See RG
183-87

CHAPTER 8

Critique of Sages on the Wise Man and the King

¹ Who is like the wise man,
and who knows the explanation of things?
A man's wisdom illumines his face,
but an impudent look is resented.

²Observe the precept of the king, and in view of your oath to God, ³be not hasty to withdraw from the king; do not join in with a base plot, for he does whatever he pleases, ⁴because his word is sovereign, and who can say to him, "What are you doing?"

⁵"He who keeps the commandment experiences no evil, and the wise man's heart knows times and judgments; ⁶for there is a time and a judgment for everything."—Yet it is a great affliction for man ^{7v}that he is ignorant of what is to come; for who will make known to him how it will be? ⁸There is no man who is master of the breath of life so as to retain it, and none has mastery of the day of death. There is no exemption from the struggle, nor are the wicked saved by their wickedness. ^{9w}All these things I considered and I applied my mind to every work that is done under the sun, while one man tyrannizes over another to his hurt.

The Problem of Retribution. ¹⁰Meanwhile I saw wicked men approach and enter; and as they left the sacred place, they were praised in the city for what they had done. This also is vanity.* ¹¹Because the sentence against evildoers is not promptly executed, therefore the hearts of men are filled with the desire to commit evil— ¹²because the sinner does evil a hundred times and sur-

vives. Though indeed I know that it shall be well with those who fear God, for their reverence toward him; ¹³and that it shall not be well with the wicked man, and he shall not prolong his shadowy* days, for his lack of reverence toward God.

¹⁴This is a vanity which occurs on earth: there are just men treated as though they had done evil and wicked men treated as though they had done justly. This, too, I say is vanity. ^{15x}Therefore I commend mirth, because there is nothing good for man under the sun except eating and drinking and mirth: for this is the accompaniment of his toil during the limited days of the life which God gives him under the sun.*

^{16y}When I applied my heart to know wisdom and to observe what is done on earth, ^{17z}I recognized that man is unable to find out all God's work that is done under the sun, even though neither by day nor by night do his eyes find rest in sleep. However much man toils in searching, he does not find it out; and even if the wise man says that he knows, he is unable to find it out.

B. Man Does Not Know What Is To Come

CHAPTER 9

See RG
183-87

¹All this I have kept in mind and recognized:* the just, the wise, and their deeds are in the hand of God. Love from hatred* man cannot tell; both appear equally vain, ^{2a}in that there is the same lot for all, for the just and the wicked, for the good and the bad, for the clean and the unclean, for him who offers sacrifice and him who does not. As it is for the good man, so it is for the sinner; as it is for him who swears rashly, so it is for him who fears an oath. ³Among all the things that happen under the sun, this is the worst, that things turn out the same for all. Hence the minds of men are filled with evil,

---

7, 29: Calculations: the many vain attempts and schemes of men to attain happiness by their own efforts.

8, 10: The text is obscure. The Latin has "wicked men buried, who, while still alive, were in the holy place, and were praised in the city as if their works were just."

8, 13: Shadowy: perhaps an addition here; cf Eccl 6, 12.

8, 15: See notes on Eccl 2, 24; 5, 19.

9, 1-10: These statements are based on a very imperfect

concept of life beyond the grave. With Christian revelation about the future life came the only satisfactory solution of the problem which so perplexed the author.

9, 1: Love from hatred: divine favor or disfavor.

---

v: Eccl 3, 22; 10, 14.   w: Eccl 1, 13f.   x: Eccl 2, 24; 9, 7.
y: Eccl 1, 13; 3, 10.   z: Eccl 3, 11.   a: Eccl 2, 14.

and madness is in their hearts during life; and afterward they go to the dead.

4Indeed, for any among the living there is hope; a live dog is better off than a dead lion. 5bFor the living know that they are to die, but the dead no longer know anything. There is no further recompense for them, because all memory of them is lost. 6For them, love and hatred and rivalry have long since perished. They will never again have part in anything that is done under the sun.

7cGo, eat your bread with joy and drink your wine with a merry heart, because it is now that God favors your works. 8At all times let your garments be white, and spare not the perfume for your head. 9Enjoy life with the wife whom you love, all the days of the fleeting life that is granted you under the sun. This is your lot in life, for the toil of your labors under the sun. 10Anything you can turn your hand to, do with what power you have; for there will be no work, nor reason, nor knowledge, nor wisdom in the nether world where you are going.

The Evil Time Not Known. 11Again I saw under the sun that the race is not won by the swift, nor the battle by the valiant, nor a livelihood by the wise, nor riches by the shrewd, nor favor by the experts; for a time of calamity comes to all alike. 12Man no more knows his own time* than fish taken in the fatal net, or birds trapped in the snare; like these the children of men are caught when the evil time falls suddenly upon them.

The Uncertain Future and the Sages. 13On the other hand I saw this wise deed under the sun, which I thought sublime. 14Against a small city with few men in it advanced a mighty king, who surrounded it and threw up great siegeworks about it. 15But in the city lived a man who, though poor, was wise, and he delivered it through his wisdom. Yet no one remembered this poor man. 16dThough I had said, "Wisdom is better than force," yet the wisdom of the poor man is despised and his words go unheeded.

17 "The quiet words of the wise are better heeded
than the shout of a ruler of fools"—!

18 "A fly that dies can spoil the perfumer's ointment,
and a single slip can ruin much that is good."

CHAPTER 10

See RG 183–87

1 More weighty than wisdom or wealth is a little folly!
2 The wise man's understanding turns him to his right;
the fool's understanding turns him to his left.*

When the fool walks through the street, in his lack of understanding he calls everything foolish.

Should the anger of the ruler burst upon you, forsake not your place; for mildness abates great offenses.

I have seen under the sun another evil, like a mistake that proceeds from the ruler: 6a fool put in lofty position while the rich sit in lowly places. 7I have seen slaves on horseback, while princes walked on the ground like slaves.

8 He who digs a pit may fall into it,e
and he who breaks through a wall may be bitten by a serpent.

9 He who moves stones may be hurt by them,
and he who chops wood is in danger from it.

10If the iron becomes dull, though at first he made easy progress, he must increase his efforts; but the craftsman has the advantage of his skill.

11 If the serpent bites because it has not been charmed,
then there is no advantage for the charmer.

9, 12: His own time: the time of death or sudden disaster.
10, 2: It is doubtful whether the author is endorsing either direction; cf Prv 4, 25ff.

b: Eccl 1, 11. c: Eccl 2, 1. 24; 8, 15; 11, 9. d: Prv 24, 5. e: 8f: Prv 26, 27; Sir 27, 29.

¹² Words from the wise man's mouth win
favor,
but the fool's lips consume him.*f*
¹³ The beginning of his words is folly,
and the end of his talk is utter
madness;
¹⁴   yet the fool multiplies words.
Man knows not what is to come,
for who can tell him what is to come
after him?*g*
¹⁵ When will the fool be weary of his
labor,
he who knows not the way to the
city?*

Man Does Not Know What Evil Will Come

¹⁶ Woe to you, O land, whose king was a
servant,
and whose princes dine in the
morning!
¹⁷ Blessed are you, O land, whose king is of
noble birth,
and whose princes dine at the right
time
(for vigor and not in drinking bouts).
¹⁸ When hands are lazy, the rafters sag;
when hands are slack, the house
leaks.
¹⁹ Bread and oil call forth merriment
and wine makes the living glad,
but money answers for everything.
²⁰ Even in your thoughts do not make light
of the king,
nor in the privacy of your bedroom
revile the rich,
Because the birds of the air may carry
your voice,
a winged creature may tell what you
say.

CHAPTER 11

**See RG
183–87**
¹ Cast your bread upon the waters;*
after a long time you may find it again.
² Make seven or eight portions;*
you know not what misfortune may
come upon the earth.

Man Does Not Know What Good
Will Come

³ When the clouds are full,
they pour out rain upon the earth.
Whether a tree falls to the south or to the
north,
wherever it falls, there shall it lie.
⁴ One who pays heed to the wind will not
sow,
and one who watches the clouds will
never reap.
⁵ Just as you know not how the breath of
life
fashions the human frame in the
mother's womb,
So you know not the work of God
which he is accomplishing in the
universe.*h*
⁶ In the morning sow your seed,
and at evening let not your hand be
idle:
For you know not which of the two will
be successful,
or whether both alike will turn out
well.

Poem on Youth and Old Age.
⁷Light is
sweet! and it is pleasant for the eyes to see
the sun. ⁸However many years a man may
live, let him, as he enjoys them all, remember that the days of darkness will be many.
All that is to come is vanity.

⁹ Rejoice, O young man, while you are
young,
and let your heart be glad in the days
of your youth.
Follow the ways of your heart,
the vision of your eyes;
Yet understand that as regards all this
God will bring you to judgment.
¹⁰ Ward off grief from your heart
and put away trouble from your
presence,
though the dawn of youth is fleeting.*

10, 15: He who . . . city: perhaps a proverbial expression
for supreme stupidity.

11, 1: This may refer to a spirit of adventure in business or
to generosity in almsgiving. Waters: of the ocean, which
sometimes carry lost treasures to the shore.

11, 2: This verse refers either to almsgiving or to the wis-

dom of not putting all one's cargo into a single vessel.

11, 10: Dawn . . . fleeting: literally, "youth and the dawn
[of life] are vanity."

---

f: Sir 21, 19.   *g:* Eccl 5, 2; 8, 7.   *h:* Eccl 8, 17.

See RG
183–87

CHAPTER 12

1 Remember your Creator in the days
of your youth,
before the evil days come
And the years approach of which you
will say,
I have no pleasure in them;
2 Before the sun is darkened,
and the light, and the moon, and the
stars,
while the clouds return* after the rain;
3 When the guardians* of the house
tremble,
and the strong men are bent,
And the grinders are idle because they
are few,
and they who look through the
windows grow blind;
4 When the doors* to the street are shut,
and the sound of the mill is low;
When one waits for the chirp of a bird,
but all the daughters of song are
suppressed;
5 And one fears heights,
and perils in the street;
When the almond tree blooms,*
and the locust grows sluggish
and the caper berry is without effect,
Because man goes to his lasting home,

and mourners go about the streets;
6 Before the silver cord is snapped
and the golden bowl* is broken,
And the pitcher is shattered at the spring,
and the broken pulley falls into the
well,
7 And the dust returns to the earth as it
once was,
and the life breath returns to God who
gave it.*i*
8 Vanity of vanities, says Qoheleth,
all things are vanity!*j*

Epilogue. *9*Besides being wise, Qoheleth
taught the people knowledge, and weighed,
scrutinized and arranged many proverbs.
*10*Qoheleth sought to find pleasing sayings,
and to write down true sayings with precision. *11*The sayings of the wise are like
goads; like fixed spikes are the topics given
by one collector.* *12k*As to more than these,
my son, beware. Of the making of many
books there is no end, and in much study
there is weariness for the flesh.
*13l*The last word, when all is heard: Fear
God and keep his commandments, for this is
man's all;* *14m*because God will bring to
judgment every work, with all its hidden
qualities, whether good or bad.

12, 2: The sun . . . return: the cloudy and rainy Palestinian
winter, a natural symbol of old age.

12, 3: Guardians: the arms; strong men: the legs; grinders:
the teeth; they who . . . windows: the eyes.

12, 4: Doors: the tightly compressed lips; sound of the mill:
perhaps the sound of mastication; daughters of song: the voice.

12, 5: The almond tree blooms: resembling the white hair of
age. The locust . . . sluggish: an image of the stiffness in movement of the aged. The caper berry: a stimulant for appetite.

12, 6: The golden bowl suspended by the silver cord was
a symbol of life; the snapping of the cord and the breaking of

the bowl, a symbol of death. The pitcher . . . the broken pulley: another pair of metaphors for life and its ending.

12, 11: Goads . . . one collector: the sayings were stimu-
lants to thought and also spikes or centers around which to
group correlated pronouncements of the wise.

12, 13: Man's all: St. Jerome explains: "Unto this is every
man born, that, knowing his Maker, he may revere him in
fear, honor, and the observance of his commandments."

i: Eccl 3, 20f; Jb 34, 15.   *j:* Eccl 1, 2.   *k:* Eccl 1, 18.   *l:* Eccl 5,
6.   *m:* Eccl 11, 9.

See RG
187–92

The Song of Songs

The Song of Songs, meaning the greatest of
songs (1, 1), contains in exquisite poetic form
the sublime portrayal and praise of the mutual
love of the Lord and his people. The Lord is the
Lover and his people are the beloved. Describing this relationship in terms of human love, the

author simply follows Israel's tradition. Isaiah
(5, 1-7; 54, 4-8), Jeremiah (2, 2f. 32), and Ezekiel (16; 23) all characterize the covenant
between the Lord and Israel as a marriage. Hosea the prophet sees the idolatry of Israel in the
adultery of Gomer (1—3). He also represents the

Lord speaking to Israel's heart (2, 16) and changing her into a new spiritual people, purified by the Babylonian captivity and betrothed anew to her divine Lover "in justice and uprightness, in love and mercy" (2, 21).

The author of the Song, using the same literary figure, paints a beautiful picture of the ideal Israel, the chosen people of the Old and New Testaments, whom the Lord led by degrees to an exalted spiritual union with himself in the bond of perfect love. When the Song is thus interpreted there is no reason for surprise at the tone of the poem, which employs in its descriptions the courtship and marriage customs of the author's time. Moreover, the poem is not an allegory in which each remark, e. g., in the dialogue of the lovers, has a higher meaning. It is a parable in which the true meaning of mutual love comes from the poem as a whole.

While the Song is thus commonly understood by most Catholic scholars, it is also possible to see in it an inspired portrayal of ideal human love. Here we would have from God a description of the sacredness and the depth of married union.

Although the poem is attributed to Solomon in the traditional title (1, 1), the language and style of the work, among other considerations, point to a time after the end of the Babylonian Exile (538 B.C.) as that in which an unknown poet composed this masterpiece. The structure of the Song is difficult to analyze; here it is regarded as a lyric dialogue, with dramatic movement and interest.

The use of marriage as a symbol, characteristic of the Song, is found extensively also in the New Testament (Mt 9, 15; 25, 1-13; Jn 3, 29; 2 Cor 11, 2; Eph 5, 23-32; Rv 19, 7ff; 21, 9ff). In Christian tradition, the Song has been interpreted in terms of the union between Christ and the Church and, particularly by St. Bernard, of the union between Christ and the individual soul. Throughout the liturgy, especially in the Little Office, there is a consistent application of the Song of Songs to the Blessed Virgin Mary.

I: The Song of Songs by Solomon*

CHAPTER 1

See RG 187–92

Love's Desires

2 B Let him kiss me with kisses of his
  mouth!*

More delightful is your love than wine!a
3   Your name spoken is a spreading
    perfume—
    that is why the maidens love you.
4 Draw me!—
  D   We will follow you eagerly!
  B Bring me, O king, to your chambers.

  D With you we rejoice and exult,
    we extol your love; it is beyond wine:b
    how rightly you are loved!

Love's Boast

5 B I am as dark—but lovely,
    O daughters of Jerusalem*—
  As the tents of Kedar,
    as the curtains of Salma.
6 Do not stare at me because I am swarthy,*
  because the sun has burned me.
My brothers have been angry with me;
    they charged me with the care of the
      vineyards:
    my own vineyard I have not cared for.

Love's Inquiry

7 B Tell me, you whom my heart loves,*
  where you pasture your flock,

1, 1: This title is actually the first verse of chapter 1.

1, 2ff: The marginal letters indicate the speaker of the verses: *B*—Bride; *D*—Daughters of Jerusalem; *G*—Bridegroom. In vv 2-7 the bride and the daughters address the bridegroom who appears here as a king, but more often in the poem as a shepherd. King and shepherd are familiar figures of the Lord in the Sacred Scriptures. Cf Ps 23, 1; Is 40, 11; Jn 10, 1-16.

1, 5: Daughters of Jerusalem: the chorus whom the bride addresses and who ask her questions (Song 5, 9; 6, 1), thus developing action within the poem. Kedar: a Syrian desert region whose name suggests blackness; tents were often made of black goat hair. Curtains: tent coverings of Salma, a region close to Kedar.

1, 6: Swarthy: tanned by the sun from working in her brothers' vineyards. My own vineyard: the bride herself; cf Is 5, 1-7, where Israel is designated as the vineyard and the Lord is the Lover.

1, 7: Here and elsewhere in the Song (3, 1; 5, 8; 6, 1), the bride expresses her desire to be in the company of her lover. These verses point to a certain tension in the poem. Only at the end (Song 8, 5ff) does mutual possession of the lovers become final.

a: 2f: Song 4, 10.   *b:* Song 4, 10.

where you give them rest at midday,
Lest I be found wandering
  after the flocks of your companions.

⁸ **G** If you do not know,
  O most beautiful among women,
Follow the tracks of the flock
  and pasture the young ones
  near the shepherds' camps.

Love's Vision

⁹ **G** To the steeds of Pharaoh's chariots*
  would I liken you, my beloved:
¹⁰ Your cheeks lovely in pendants,
  your neck in jewels.
¹¹ We will make pendants of gold for you,
  and silver ornaments.

Love's Union

¹² **B** For the king's banquet
  my nard* gives forth its fragrance.
¹³ My lover is for me a sachet of myrrh*
  to rest in my bosom.
¹⁴ My lover is for me a cluster of henna*
  from the vineyards of Engedi.

¹⁵ **G** Ah, you are beautiful, my beloved,ᶜ
  ah, you are beautiful; your eyes are
    doves!*

¹⁶ **B** Ah, you are beautiful, my lover—
  yes, you are lovely.
  Our couch, too, is verdant;*
¹⁷   the beams of our house are cedars,
  our rafters, cypresses.

**See RG
187–92**

CHAPTER 2

¹I am a flower of Sharon,*
  a lily of the valley.

² **G** As a lily among thorns,
  so is my beloved among women.
³ **B** As an apple tree among the trees of
    the woods,
  so is my lover among men.
I delight to rest in his shadow,
  and his fruit is sweet to my mouth.
⁴ He brings me into the banquet hall*
  and his emblem over me is love.ᵈ
⁵ Strengthen me with raisin cakes,
  refresh me with apples,
  for I am faint with love.ᵉ
⁶ His left hand is under my head
  and his right arm embraces me.ᶠ
⁷ I adjure you, daughters of Jerusalem,ᵍ
  by the gazelles and hinds* of the field,
Do not arouse, do not stir up love
  before its own time.

A Tryst in the Spring

⁸ **B** Hark! my lover—here he comes*
  springing across the mountains,
  leaping across the hills.
⁹ My lover is like a gazelle
  or a young stag.
Here he stands behind our wall,
  gazing through the windows,
  peering through the lattices.
¹⁰ My lover speaks; he says to me,
  "Arise, my beloved, my beautiful
    one,
  and come!
¹¹ "For see, the winter is past,
  the rains are over and gone.
¹² The flowers appear on the earth,
  the time of pruning the vines has come,
  and the song of the dove is heard in
    our land.
¹³ The fig tree puts forth its figs,

1, 9ff: The bridegroom compares the girl's beauty to the rich adornment of the royal chariot of Pharaoh.

1, 12: Nard: a precious perfume, a figure of the bride; cf Song 4, 14.

1, 13: Myrrh: produced from aromatic resin of balsam or roses.

1, 14: Henna: a plant which bears white scented flowers.

1, 15: Doves: suggesting innocence and charm.

1, 16f: Though the meeting place of the lovers is but a shepherd's hut of green branches, it becomes a palace with beams of cedar and rafters of cypress when adorned with their love.

2, 1: Flower of Sharon: probably the narcissus, which grows in the fertile Plain of Sharon lying between Mount Car-

mel and Jaffa on the Mediterranean coast.

2, 4ff: The banquet hall, the sweet things of the table, the embrace of the bride and bridegroom, express the delicacy of their affection and the intimacy of their love.

2, 7: By the gazelles and hinds: the swiftness of these animals and the luster and soft expression of their eyes are suggestive of love; cf Prv 5, 19.

2, 8ff: In this sudden change of scene, the bride pictures her lover hastening toward her dwelling until his voice is heard bidding her come to him.

c: Song 4, 1. 7. *d:* Song 1, 4. *e:* Song 5, 8. *f:* Song 8, 3.
g: Song 3, 5; 8, 4.

Her Nighttime Search

In ch 3 the man does not return, and the woman takes the initiative to seek him. The book has a strong feminine orientation, speaking of the mother's house (v. 4; see also 1, 6; 8, 1–2; Ru 1, 8) instead of the more normal house of the father. The woman seems to be at the center of every scene, either searching for her love, being praised by him, or in conversation with the daughters of Jerusalem.

and the vines, in bloom, give forth
    fragrance.
Arise, my beloved, my beautiful one,
    and come!

[14] "O my dove in the clefts of the rock,*
    in the secret recesses of the cliff,
Let me see you,
    let me hear your voice,
For your voice is sweet,
    and you are lovely."

[15] B Catch us the foxes, the little foxes*
    that damage the vineyards; for our
      vineyards are in bloom!

[16] My lover belongs to me and I to him;
    he browses among the lilies.[h]
[17] Until the day breathes cool* and the
      shadows lengthen,
    roam, my lover,
Like a gazelle or a young stag
    upon the mountains of Bether.[i]

See RG
187–92

CHAPTER 3
Loss and Discovery

[1] B On my bed at night I sought him*
    whom my heart loves—
    I sought him but I did not find him.[j]
[2] I will rise then and go about the city;
    in the streets and crossings I will
      seek
Him whom my heart loves.
    I sought him but I did not find him.
[3] The watchmen came upon me,

as they made their rounds of the city:
    Have you seen him whom my heart
      loves?
[4] I had hardly left them
    when I found him whom my heart
      loves.
I took hold of him and would not let him
      go
    till I should bring him to the home of
      my mother,[k]
    to the room of my parent.
[5] I adjure you, daughters of Jerusalem,
    by the gazelles and hinds of the field,
Do not arouse, do not stir up love
    before its own time.[l]

Regal State of the Bridegroom

[6] D What is this coming up from the
      desert,*
    like a column of smoke
Laden with myrrh, with frankincense,
    and with the perfume of every exotic
      dust?[m]
[7] Ah, it is the litter of Solomon;
    sixty valiant men surround it,
    of the valiant men of Israel:
[8] All of them expert with the sword,
    skilled in battle,
Each with his sword at his side
    against danger in the watches of the
      night.

[9] King Solomon made himself a carriage
    of wood from Lebanon.
[10] He made its columns of silver,

2, 14: The bride is addressed as though she were a dove in a mountain fastness out of sight and reach.

2, 15: A snatch of song in answer to the request of v 14; cf Song 8, 13f. Foxes: all who threaten to disturb the security of love symbolized by the vineyard; cf v 16.

2, 17: Breathes cool: in the evening when the sun is going down. Cf Gn 3, 8. Bether: a very obscure word; some interpret it in the sense of ruggedness; others, of spices; still oth-

ers, of sacrifice (Gn 15, 10).

3, 1ff: See the parallel in Song 5, 2-8.

3, 6ff: The lover is portrayed as King Solomon, escorted by sixty armed men, coming in royal procession to meet his bride.

h: Song 6, 3; 7, 10. i: Song 4, 6; 8, 14. j: 1ff: Song 5, 2ff.
k: Song 8, 2. l: Song 2, 7; 8, 4. m: Song 6, 10; 8, 5.

A Wedding Scene

The book of Songs' only description of a wedding, with Solomon present, occurs in 3, 6–11. These verses have been variously assessed 1) as a later insertion, modeled on Ps 45 and intended to strengthen the book's connection with Solomon; or 2) as an extended royal image, in which the woman compares the sight of her lover to that of the extravagant entourage of a king known for his love of women (1 Kgs 11, 1–3).

its roof of gold,
Its seat of purple cloth,
its framework inlaid with ivory.
[11] Daughters of Jerusalem, come forth
and look upon King Solomon
In the crown with which his mother has
crowned him
on the day of his marriage,
on the day of the joy of his heart.

See RG
187–92

CHAPTER 4

The Charms of the Beloved

[1] G Ah, you are beautiful, my beloved,[n]
ah, you are beautiful!
Your eyes are doves[o]
behind your veil.
Your hair is like a flock of goats
streaming down the mountains of
Gilead.
[2] Your teeth[*] are like a flock of ewes to be
shorn,
which come up from the washing,
All of them big with twins,
none of them thin and barren.
[3] Your lips are like a scarlet strand;
your mouth is lovely.
Your cheek is like a half-pomegranate[*]
behind your veil.

[4] Your neck is like David's tower[p]
girt with battlements;
A thousand bucklers hang upon it,
all the shields of valiant men.[*]

[5] Your breasts are like twin fawns,[q]
the young of a gazelle
that browse among the lilies.
[6] Until the day breathes cool and the
shadows lengthen,[r]
I will go to the mountain of myrrh,
to the hill of incense.[*]
[7] You are all-beautiful, my beloved,
and there is no blemish in you.[*]

[8] Come from Lebanon, my bride,
come from Lebanon, come!
Descend from the top of Amana,
from the top of Senir and
Hermon,[*]
From the haunts of lions,
from the leopards' mountains.
[9] You have ravished my heart, my sister,[*]
my bride;[s]
you have ravished my heart with one
glance of your eyes,
with one bead of your necklace.
[10] How beautiful is your love, my sister, my
bride,[t]
how much more delightful is your love
than wine,
and the fragrance of your ointments
than all spices!
[11] Your lips drip honey,[*] my bride,
sweetmeats and milk are under your
tongue;
And the fragrance of your garments
is the fragrance of Lebanon.

4, 2: Teeth: praised for whiteness and regularity.
4, 3: Pomegranate: a fruit somewhat like an orange, with a firm skin and deep red color. The girl's cheek is compared, in roundness and tint, to a half-pomegranate.
4, 4: The ornaments about her neck are compared to the trophies on the city walls. Cf 1 Kgs 10, 10; 14, 26ff; Ez 27, 10.
4, 6: Mountain of myrrh . . . hill of incense: spoken figuratively of the bride; cf Song 8, 14.
4, 7: Cf St. Paul's description of the church in Eph 5, 27. This verse is also applied to Our Lady, especially in the

liturgy of the feast of the Immaculate Conception.
4, 8: Amana . . . Senir and Hermon: these rugged heights symbolize obstacles that would separate the lovers; cf Song 2, 14.
4, 9: Sister: a term of endearment; it forms part of the conventional language of love used in this canticle.
4, 11: Honey: sweet words. Cf Prv 5, 3.

n: Song 1, 15.   o: 1ff: Song 6, 5ff.   p: Song 7, 5.   q: Song 7, 4.
r: Song 2, 17.   s: Song 6, 5.   t: Song 1, 2f.

The Lover and His Garden

12 **G** You are an enclosed garden, my sister,
    my bride,[u]
    an enclosed garden, a fountain
    sealed.*
13 You are a park that puts forth
    pomegranates,
    with all choice fruits;
14 Nard and saffron, calamus and
    cinnamon,
    with all kinds of incense;
  Myrrh and aloes,
    with all the finest spices.*
15 You are a garden fountain, a well of
    water
    flowing fresh from Lebanon.
16 Arise, north wind! Come, south
    wind!
    blow upon my garden*
    that its perfumes may spread
    abroad.
  B Let my lover come to his garden
    and eat its choice fruits.

CHAPTER 5

See RG
187–92

1 **G** I have come to my garden, my
    sister, my bride;[v]
  I gather my myrrh and my spices,
  I eat my honey and my sweetmeats,
  I drink my wine and my milk.

  D Eat, friends; drink!* Drink freely of
    love!

A Fruitless Search

2 **B** I was sleeping, but my heart kept
    vigil;*
  I heard my lover knocking:
  "Open to me, my sister, my beloved,
    my dove, my perfect one!"[w]
  For my head is wet with dew,
    my locks with the moisture of the
    night."
3 I have taken off my robe,*
    am I then to put it on?
  I have bathed my feet,
    am I then to soil them?

4 My lover put his hand through the
    opening;
    my heart trembled within me,
    and I grew faint when he spoke.
5 I rose to open to my lover,
    with my hands dripping myrrh:
  With my fingers dripping choice myrrh
    upon the fittings of the lock.
6 I opened to my lover—
    but my lover had departed, gone.[x]
  I sought him but I did not find him;
    I called to him but he did not answer
    me.*
7 The watchmen came upon me[y]
    as they made their rounds of the city;
  They struck me, and wounded me,
    and took my mantle from me,
    the guardians of the walls.*
8 I adjure you, daughters of Jerusalem,[z]
    if you find my lover—
  What shall you tell him?—
    that I am faint with love.

The Charms of the Lost Lover

9 **D** How does your lover differ from any
    other,
    O most beautiful among women?
  How does your lover differ from any
    other,
    that you adjure us so?

10 **B** My lover is radiant and ruddy;*
    he stands out among thousands.

4, 12: Enclosed garden . . . fountain sealed: reserved for the bridegroom alone. The bride's fidelity is implied. Cf Prv 5, 15-19.
4, 14: These plants are all known for their sweet scent.
4, 16: The last two lines of the verse are spoken by the girl, inviting her lover to herself, the garden.
5, 1: Eat, friends; drink!: the lovers are encouraged to enjoy the delights of their love, symbol of Christ's union with the church.
5, 2-8: A trial similar to that in Song 3, 1ff.
5, 3f: The bride's hesitation is due, not to levity, but to strong emotion.
5, 6: The disappearance of the lover seems to be a deliberate trial and test inflicted on the girl.
5, 7: The watchmen do not know the reason for the girl's appearance in the city streets; cf Song 3, 2ff.
5, 10f: In answer to the question of v 9, the girl sings her lover's praises (vv 10-16). Gold: indicates how precious the lover is. Palm fronds: his thick, luxuriant growth of hair.

u: Song 6, 2. 11.   *v:* Song 6, 2.   *w:* 2ff: Song 3, 1f.   *x:* Song 3, 1.   *y:* Song 3, 3.   *z:* Song 2, 5.

[11] His head is pure gold;
    his locks are palm fronds,
    black as the raven.
[12] His eyes are like doves
    beside running waters,
His teeth would seem bathed in milk,
    and are set like jewels.
[13] His cheeks are like beds of spice
    with ripening aromatic herbs.
His lips are red blossoms;
    they drip choice myrrh.

[14] His arms are rods of gold
    adorned with chrysolites.
His body is a work of ivory
    covered with sapphires.
[15] His legs are columns of marble
    resting on golden bases.
His stature is like the trees on Lebanon,
    imposing as the cedars.
[16] His mouth is sweetness itself;
    he is all delight.
Such is my lover, and such my friend,
    O daughters of Jerusalem.

See RG
187-92

CHAPTER 6

Discovery

[1] *D* Where has your lover gone,
    O most beautiful among women?
Where has your lover gone
    that we may seek him with you?*
[2] *B* My lover has come down to his
        garden,*
    to the beds of spice,
To browse in the garden[a]
    and to gather lilies.
[3] My lover belongs to me and I to him;
    he browses among the lilies.[b]

The Charms of the Beloved

[4] *G* You are as beautiful as Tirzah, my
        beloved,*

as lovely as Jerusalem,
    as awe-inspiring as bannered troops.
[5] Turn your eyes from me,[c]
    for they torment me.
Your hair is like a flock of goats
    streaming down from Gilead.
[6] Your teeth are like a flock of ewes[d]
    which come up from the washing,
All of them big with twins,
    none of them thin and barren.
[7] Your cheek is like a half-pomegranate
    behind your veil.

[8] There are sixty queens, eighty
        concubines,
    and maidens without number—
[9] One alone is my dove, my perfect one,
    her mother's chosen,
    the dear one of her parent.
The daughters saw her and declared her
        fortunate,
    the queens and concubines, and they
        sang her praises;
[10] *D* Who is this that comes forth like the
        dawn,[e]
    as beautiful as the moon, as
        resplendent as the sun,
    as awe-inspiring as bannered troops?

Love's Meeting

[11] *B* I came down to the nut garden[f]
    to look at the fresh growth of the
        valley,
To see if the vines were in bloom,
    if the pomegranates had blossomed.
[12] Before I knew it, my heart had made me
    the blessed one of my kinswomen.*

CHAPTER 7

See RG
187-92

The Beauty of the Bride

· *D* Turn, turn, O Shulammite,*
    turn, turn, that we may look at you!

6, 1: The daughters of Jerusalem are won by this description of the lover and offer their aid in seeking him.

6, 2f: Determined to share her lover with no one, the girl refuses the aid offered by the daughters in seeking him. She implies that she had never really lost him, for he has come down to his garden.

6, 4-9: The lover again celebrates her beauty. Tirzah: probably meaning "pleasant"; it was the early capital of the northern kingdom of Israel (1 Kgs 16).

6, 12: The text is obscure in Hebrew and in the ancient versions. The Vulgate reads: "I did not know; my soul disturbed me because of the chariots of Aminadab."

7, 1: Shulammite: so called either because the girl is considered to be from Shulam in the plain of Esdraelon (cf 1 Kgs 1, 3) or because the name may mean "the peaceful one," and

a: Song 4, 12; 5, 1. *b:* Song 2, 16; 7, 11. *c:* Song 4, 9. *d:* 6f:
Song 4, 1ff. *e:* Song 3, 6; 8, 5. *f:* Song 4, 12ff; 7, 13.

B Why would you look at the
    Shulammite
        as at the dance of the two companies?

2 *D* How beautiful are your feet in
        sandals,*
    O prince's daughter!
Your rounded thighs are like jewels,
    the handiwork of an artist.
3 Your navel is a round bowl
    that should never lack for mixed
        wine.
Your body is a heap of wheat
    encircled with lilies.
4 Your breasts are like twin fawns,
    the young of a gazelle.*g*
5 Your neck is like a tower of ivory.*h*
    Your eyes are like the pools in
        Heshbon
    by the gate of Bath-rabbim.
Your nose is like the tower on Lebanon
    that looks toward Damascus.*
6 Your head rises like Carmel;
    your hair is like draperies of purple;
    a king is held captive in its tresses.

Love's Desires

7 *G* How beautiful you are, how
        pleasing,
    my love, my delight!
8 Your very figure is like a palm tree,*
    your breasts are like clusters.
9 I said: I will climb the palm tree,
    I will take hold of its branches.
Now let your breasts be like clusters of
    the vine
    and the fragrance of your breath like
        apples,

10 And your mouth like an excellent
        wine—

Love's Union

B that flows smoothly for my lover,
    spreading over the lips and the teeth.*
11 I belong to my lover*
    and for me he yearns.*i*
12 Come, my lover, let us go forth to the
        fields
    and spend the night among the villages.
13 Let us go early to the vineyards, and see
    if the vines are in bloom,
If the buds have opened,
    if the pomegranates have blossomed;*j*
There will I give you my love.
14 The mandrakes* give forth fragrance,
    and at our doors are all choice fruits;
Both fresh and mellowed fruits, my lover,
    I have kept in store for you.

CHAPTER 8

See RG
187–92

1 Oh, that you were my brother,
    nursed at my mother's breasts!
If I met you out of doors, I would kiss you
    and none would taunt me.
2 I would lead you, bring you in
    to the home of my mother.*k*
There you would teach me to give you
    spiced wine to drink, and pomegranate
        juice.

3 His left hand is under my head
    and his right arm embraces me.*l*
4 I adjure you, daughters of Jerusalem,
    by the gazelles and hinds of the field,
Do not arouse, do not stir up love,
    before its own time.*m*

---

thus recall the name of Solomon. As at the dance of the two companies: the meaning is uncertain. The question in this verse could be construed as a refusal to dance; more probably, however, the girl accedes, as the following verses suggest.

7, 2-6: A flattering description of the girl's charms. Rounded . . . jewels: the meaning of these Hebrew words is not certain. Wine and wheat are symbolic of fertility; they are here associated with parts of the body which have a close relation to fruitfulness.

7, 5: The comparison emphasizes the stateliness and whiteness of the neck, and the limpidity of the eyes. Bath-rabbim: a proper name which occurs only here; there was a city of Rabbah northeast of Heshbon in Transjordan. Cf Jer 49, 3.

7, 8f: Palm tree: a figure of stateliness. The bridegroom is eager to enjoy the possession of his bride.

7, 10: The bride delicately turns his compliment into an expression of the love and tenderness she feels for him.

7, 11-14: The girl's answer assures him of her affection and invites him to return with her to the rural delights which are associated with their love and which recall the meeting described in Song 6, 11f.

7, 14: Mandrakes: herbs believed to have power to arouse love and promote fertility; cf Gn 30, 14ff.

---

g: Song 4, 5.   *h:* Song 4, 4.   *i:* Song 2, 16; 6, 3.   *j:* Song 6, 11.
k: Song 3, 4.   *l:* Song 2, 6.   *m:* Song 2, 7; 3, 5.

Homecoming

[5] *D* Who is this coming up from the desert,[n]
leaning upon her lover?[*]
G Under the apple tree I awakened you;
it was there that your mother
conceived you,
it was there that your parent
conceived.

True Love

[6] *B* Set me as a seal[*] on your heart,
as a seal on your arm;
For stern as death is love,
relentless as the nether world is
devotion;
its flames are a blazing fire.
[7] Deep waters cannot quench love,
nor floods sweep it away.
Were one to offer all he owns to purchase
love,
he would be roundly mocked.

Chastity and Its Welcome

[8] "Our sister is little[*]
and she has no breasts as yet.
What shall we do for our sister
when her courtship begins?
[9] If she is a wall,

we will build upon it a silver parapet;
If she is a door,
we will reinforce it with a cedar plank."
[10] I am a wall,
and my breasts are like towers.
So now in his eyes I have become
one to be welcomed.

The Bride and Her Dowry

[11] *B* Solomon had a vineyard at Baalhamon;[*]
he gave over the vineyard to caretakers.
For its fruit one would have to pay
a thousand silver pieces.
[12] My vineyard is at my own disposal;
the thousand pieces are for you,
O Solomon,
and two hundred for the caretakers of
its fruit.

Life Together

[13] *G* O garden-dweller,[*]
my friends are listening for your voice,
let me hear it!

[14] *B* Be swift, my lover,
like a gazelle or a young stag
on the mountains of spices![o]

8, 5: The lovers are pictured walking homeward, enjoying the fulfillment of the desire which the girl expressed in vv 1f. The groom speaks of their first meeting.

8, 6f: Seal: this could be worn bound to the arm, as here, or suspended at the neck, or as a ring (Jer 22, 24). It was used for identification and signatures. Stern . . . relentless: in human experience, death and the nether world are inevitable, unrelenting; in the end they always triumph. Love, which is just as certain of its victory, matches its strength against the natural enemies of life; waters cannot extinguish it nor floods carry it away. It is more priceless than all riches.

8, 8ff: The bride affirms her chastity. In 8, 9 she quotes the course of action which her elder brothers had decided on. While she is yet immature, they will shelter her in view of eventual marriage. If she is virtuous, she will be honored; if

she is unchaste, she will be kept under strict vigilance. In reply to this she proclaims her virtue and boasts of having found welcome from her lover.

8, 11f: These enigmatic verses have been variously interpreted. In v 11 the girl alludes to a vineyard of great value which is compared to her own self in v 12. Her enormous dowry, a thousand silver pieces, is in keeping with her intrinsic worth. She has been the generous lover, giving herself and a dowry to her lover, referred to as Solomon, and also smaller gifts to her brothers, the caretakers (cf vv 8ff).

8, 13f: As in Song 2, 14f, her lover asks for a word or a song and she replies in words similar to those found in Song 2, 17.

n: Song 3, 6; 6, 10.   *o:* Song 2, 9. 17; 4, 6.

See RG
192–97

The Book of Wisdom

The Book of Wisdom was written about a hundred years before the coming of Christ. Its author, whose name is not known to us, was a member of the Jewish community at Alexandria, in Egypt. He wrote in Greek, in a style patterned on that of Hebrew verse. At times he speaks in the person of

Solomon, placing his teachings on the lips of the wise king of Hebrew tradition in order to emphasize their value. His profound knowledge of the earlier Old Testament writings is reflected in almost every line of the book, and marks him, like Ben Sira, as an outstanding representative

The author assumes that human beings are composed of two parts, the *body* and the *soul* (1, 4). Such an assumption is different from the traditional view of the Hebrew Bible about the nature of human beings, in which the human person is understood as an integrated whole; souls and bodies cannot exist apart from one another. The philosophical position that there are two separate, underlying aspects of reality, neither of which can be derived from the other, is called "dualism." Body/soul dualism developed from a more fundamental dualism common in Platonic thought: The substance of spiritual things is completely different from that of matter. A person's physical body consists of matter, while a soul exists as a nonmaterial substance that is potentially imperishable.

of religious devotion and learning among the sages of postexilic Judaism.

The primary purpose of the sacred author was the edification of his co-religionists in a time when they had experienced suffering and oppression, in part at least at the hands of apostate fellow Jews. To convey his message he made use of the most popular religious themes of his time, namely the splendor and worth of divine wisdom (6, 22—11, 1), the glorious events of the Exodus (11, 2-16; 12, 23-27; 15, 18—19, 22), God's mercy (11, 17—12, 22), the folly of idolatry (13, 1—15, 17), and the manner in which God's justice is vindicated in rewarding or punishing the individual soul (1, 1—6, 21). The first ten chapters especially form a preparation for the fuller teachings of Christ and his Church. Many passages from this section of the book, notably 3, 1-8, are used by the Church in her liturgy.

The principal divisions of the Book of Wisdom are:

I: Reward of Justice (1, 1—6, 21).

II: Praise of Wisdom by Solomon (6, 22—11, 1).

III: Special Providence of God during the Exodus (11, 2-16; 12, 23-27; 15, 18—19, 22) with digressions on God's mercy (11, 17—12, 22) and on the folly and shame of idolatry (13, 1—15, 17).

I: The Reward of Justice

CHAPTER 1

See RG 194–95

Exhortation to Justice, the Key to Life

¹ Love justice,* you who judge the earth;ᵃ
  think of the LORD in goodness,
  and seek him in integrity of heart;ᵇ
² Because he is found by those who test him not,
  and he manifests himself to those who do not disbelieve him.ᶜ
³ For perverse counsels separate a man from God,
  and his power, put to the proof, rebukes the foolhardy;ᵈ
⁴ Because into a soul that plots evil wisdom enters not,
  nor dwells she in a body under debt of sin.ᵉ
⁵ For the holy spirit of discipline* flees deceit
  and withdraws from senseless counsels;
  and when injustice occurs it is rebuked.ᶠ
⁶ For wisdom is a kindly spirit,
  yet she acquits not the blasphemer of his guilty lips;
  Because God is the witness of his inmost selfᵍ
  and the sure observer of his heart

1, 1: Justice: not merely the cardinal virtue of that name (cf Wis 8, 7), but the universal moral quality which is the application of Wisdom to moral conduct.

1, 5: Discipline: here and elsewhere, another name for Wisdom; injustice: the opposite of the virtue in Wis 1, 1.

a: 1 Chr 29, 17; Ps 2, 10; Is 26, 9.   *b:* 1f; Sir 1, 25.   *c:* 1 Chr 28, 9.   *d:* Is 59, 2.   *e:* Sir 15, 7f; Rom 7, 14.   *f:* Is 63, 10.   *g:* Jer 17, 10.

Covenant with Death

In ch 1, v. 16, the author employs a rhetorical device from Hellenistic diatribe, a popular genre of the era intended for pedagogical purposes. The diatribe typically included dialogue with imaginary opponents. In this case the opponents represent those who deny that humans are immortal.

and the listener to his tongue.*h*

7 For the spirit of the LORD fills
    the world,*i*
is all-embracing, and knows what man
    says.*

8 Therefore no one who utters wicked
    things can go unnoticed,
nor will chastising condemnation pass
    him by.*j*

9 For the devices of the wicked man shall
    be scrutinized,
and the sound of his words shall reach
    the LORD,
for the chastisement of his
    transgressions;

10 Because a jealous ear hearkens to
    everything,*k*
and discordant grumblings are no
    secret.

11 Therefore guard against profitless
    grumbling,
and from calumny* withhold your
    tongues;
For a stealthy utterance does not go
    unpunished,
and a lying mouth slays the soul.

12 Court not death by your erring way of
    life,
nor draw to yourselves destruction by
    the works of your hands.

13 Because God did not make death,*l*
nor does he rejoice in the destruction
    of the living.

14 For he fashioned all things that they
    might have being;
and the creatures of the world are
    wholesome,
And there is not a destructive drug
    among them

nor any domain of the nether world on
    earth,

15 For justice is undying.*m*

The Wicked Reject Immortality and Justice Alike

16 It was the wicked who with hands and
    words invited death,
considered it a friend, and pined for it,
and made a covenant with it,
Because they deserve to be in its
    possession,*n*

CHAPTER 2

See RG 194-95

1 they who said among
    themselves, thinking not aright:
"Brief and troublous is our lifetime;*o*
    neither is there any remedy for man's
    dying,
nor is anyone known to have come
    back from the nether world.

2 For haphazard were we born,
    and hereafter we shall be as though we
    had not been;
Because the breath in our nostrils is a
    smoke
and reason is a spark at the beating of
    our hearts,

3 And when this is quenched, our body
    will be ashes
and our spirit will be poured abroad
    like unresisting air.*p*

4 Even our name will be forgotten in time,
    and no one will recall our deeds.
So our life will pass away like the traces
    of a cloud,
and will be dispersed like a mist
    pursued by the sun's rays
    and overpowered by its heat.

1, 7: This verse is applied to the Holy Spirit in the liturgy at Pentecost.
1, 11: Calumny: speech against God and his providence is meant.

h: 6f: Jer 23, 24f. *i:* Wis 12, 1. *j:* Prv 19, 5. *k:* 10f: Nm 14, 27f. *l:* 13f: Ez 18, 32; 33, 11; 2 Pt 3, 9. *m:* Is 51, 6ff. *n:* Is 28, 15.
o: Jb 14, 1; 7, 9. *p:* Jb 7, 9; Jas 4, 14.

[5] For our lifetime is the passing of a shadow;
and our dying cannot be deferred
because it is fixed with a seal; and no one returns.[q]

[6] Come, therefore, let us enjoy the good things that are real,
and use the freshness of creation avidly.[r]

[7] Let us have our fill of costly wine and perfumes,
and let no springtime blossom pass us by;

[8] let us crown ourselves with rosebuds ere they wither.

[9] Let no meadow be free from our wantonness;[*]
everywhere let us leave tokens of our rejoicing,
for this our portion is, and this our lot.[s]

[10] Let us oppress the needy just man;
let us neither spare the widow
nor revere the old man for his hair grown white with time.[t]

[11] But let our strength be our norm of justice;
for weakness proves itself useless.

[12] *Let us beset the just one, because he is obnoxious to us;
he sets himself against our doings,
Reproaches us for transgressions of the law*
and charges us with violations of our training.[u]

[13] He professes to have knowledge of God
and styles himself a child of the LORD.[v]

[14] To us he is the censure of our thoughts;
merely to see him is a hardship for us,[w]

[15] Because his life is not like other men's,
and different are his ways.

[16] He judges us debased;
he holds aloof from our paths as from things impure.
He calls blest the destiny of the just

and boasts that God is his Father.[x]

[17] Let us see whether his words be true;
let us find out what will happen to him.[y]

[18] For if the just one be the son of God, he will defend him
and deliver him from the hand of his foes.[z]

[19] With revilement and torture let us put him to the test
that we may have proof of his gentleness
and try his patience.

[20] Let us condemn him to a shameful death;
for according to his own words, God will take care of him."[a]

[21] These were their thoughts, but they erred;
for their wickedness blinded them,[b]

[22] And they knew not the hidden counsels of God;
neither did they count on a recompense of holiness
nor discern the innocent souls' reward.[c]

[23] For God formed man to be imperishable;
the image of his own nature he made him.[d]

[24] But by the envy of the devil, death entered the world,
and they who are in his possession experience it.[e]

CHAPTER 3

The Hidden Counsels of God

See RG 194–95

A. ON SUFFERING

[1] But the souls of the just are in the hand of God,[f]
and no torment shall touch them.[*]

[2] They seemed, in the view of the foolish, to be dead;
and their passing away was thought an affliction

[3] and their going forth from us, utter destruction.
But they are in peace.[g]

2, 9: Let no meadow . . . wantonness: the extant Greek Mss have "Let none of us be without part in our wanton doings." Most Latin Mss have both forms of this line.

2, 12-20: Often applied to the Passion of our Lord; many have understood these verses as a direct prophecy. Cf Mt 27, 41-44.

2, 12: Law: the law of Moses; training has the same meaning.

3, 1-8: Verses frequently applied to the martyrs.

q: Ps 144, 4.   r: Is 22, 13; 1 Cor 15, 32.   s: Jer 13, 25.   t: Ex 22, 22ff; Lv 19, 32.   u: Hos 8, 1.   v: Mt 27, 43; Jn 8, 55; 10, 36-39.   w: Mt 9, 4.   x: Jer 6, 30.   y: Gn 37, 20.   z: Ps 22, 9; Is 42, 1; Mt 27, 43; Jn 5, 18.   a: Jas 5, 6.   b: Rom 1, 21.   c: Ps 18, 24f; Prv 11, 18; Mt 11, 25.   d: Gn 1, 26f; Is 54, 16 LXX.   e: Gn 3, 1-24; Rom 5, 12.   f: Jb 12, 10; 5, 19.   g: Is 57, 2.

⁴ For if before men, indeed, they be
     punished,
     yet is their hope full of immortality;
⁵ Chastised a little, they shall be greatly
     blessed,
     because God tried them
     and found them worthy of himself.ʰ
⁶ As gold in the furnace, he proved them,
     and as sacrificial offerings* he took
     them to himself.ⁱ
⁷ In the time of their visitation* they shall
     shine,
     and shall dart about as sparks through
     stubble;ʲ
⁸ They shall judge nations and rule over
     peoples,
     and the LORD shall be their King
     forever.ᵏ
⁹ Those who trust in him shall understand
     truth,
     and the faithful shall abide with him in
     love:
     Because grace and mercy are with his
     holy ones,ˡ
     and his care is with his elect.
¹⁰ But the wicked shall receive a
     punishment to match their
     thoughts,*
     since they neglected justice and
     forsook the LORD.
¹¹ For he who despises wisdom and
     instruction is doomed.ᵐ
     Vain is their hope, fruitless are their
     labors,
     and worthless are their works.ⁿ
¹² Their wives are foolish and their
     children wicked;
     accursed is their brood.ᵒ

B. ON CHILDLESSNESS

¹³ Yes, blessed is she who, childless and
     undefiled,
     knew not transgression of the marriage
     bed;
     she shall bear fruit at the visitation of
     souls.*
¹⁴ So also the eunuch whose hand wrought
     no misdeed,
     who held no wicked thoughts against
     the LORD—
     For he shall be given fidelity's choice
     reward*
     and a more gratifying heritage in the
     LORD's temple.ᵖ
¹⁵ For the fruit of noble struggles is a
     glorious one;
     and unfailing is the root of
     understanding.�q
¹⁶ But the children of adulterers will remain
     without issue,
     and the progeny of an unlawful bed
     will disappear.ʳ
¹⁷ For should they attain long life, they will
     be held in no esteem,
     and dishonored will their old age be at
     last;
¹⁸ While should they die abruptly, they
     have no hope
     nor comfort in the day of scrutiny;
¹⁹   for dire is the end of the wicked
     generation.ˢ

CHAPTER 4

¹ Better is childlessness with virtue;
     for immortal is its memory:*
     because both by God is it
     acknowledged, and by men.ᵗ
² When it is present men imitate it,
     and they long for it when it is gone;
     And forever it marches crowned in
     triumph,
     victorious in unsullied deeds of
     valor.

See RG
194–95

3, 6: Offerings: the image is that of the holocaust, in which the victim is completely consumed by fire.

3, 7: Visitation: God's loving judgment of those who have been faithful to him; the same word is used in Wis 14, 11 for the punishment of the wicked at God's final judgment. Cf also Wis 3, 13.

3, 10: To match their thoughts: a fate as empty as that which they describe; cf Wis 2, 1-5.

3, 13: Visitation of souls: that is, the last judgment. Cf Wis 3, 7-9.

3, 14: Fidelity's choice reward: cf Is 56, 1-8. More grati-fying: better than sons and daughters; cf Is 56, 5.

4, 1: The Latin form of this line, "Oh, how fair is the chaste generation in its glory!" is a later adaptation, which is applied in the liturgy to the splendor of virginity.

h: Tb 12, 13; 2 Cor 4, 17; 1 Pt 1, 6f.   i: Ps 51, 19; Prv 17, 3; Sir 2, 5; Is 48, 10.   j: Dn 12, 3; Ob 18; Mal 3, 3; Mt 13, 43.   k: Wis 8, 14; Prv 8, 16; Dn 7, 22; 1 Cor 6, 2; Rv 20, 4.   l: Wis 3, 9; 4, 15; Jb 10, 12; Jn 15, 10.   m: Prv 1, 7.   n: 11f: Sir 41, 8.   o: Dt 28, 18ff.   p: Is 56, 2-5.   q: Sir 1, 18.   r: 2 Sm 12, 14.   s: Ps 34, 22.   t: Sir 16, 1ff; Prv 3, 3f.

Childlessness

In Wis 3, 13 to 4, 6 the author offers an impassioned diatribe against the traditional devaluation of childlessness. The inability to bear children was typically regarded as a curse and was grounds for a husband to divorce his wife. In traditional Israelite religion, the continuation of one's family line through one's progeny constitutes a form of immortality. Because the author of the Wisdom of Solomon advocates a belief in immortality for righteous individuals, producing heirs becomes less important.

³ But the numerous progeny of the wicked
    shall be of no avail;
    their spurious offshoots shall not strike
      deep root
    nor take firm hold.ᵘ
⁴ For even though their branches flourish
    for a time,
    they are unsteady and shall be rocked
      by the wind
    and, by the violence of the winds,
      uprooted;ᵛ
⁵ Their twigs shall be broken off
    untimely,
    and their fruit be useless, unripe for
      eating,
    and fit for nothing.
⁶ For children born of lawless unions
    give evidence of the wickedness of
      their parents, when they are
      examined.

C. ON EARLY DEATH

⁷ But the just man, though he die early,
    shall be at rest.ʷ
⁸ For the age that is honorable comes not
    with the passing of time,ˣ
    nor can it be measured in terms of years.
⁹ Rather, understanding is the hoary crown
    for men,
    and an unsullied life, the attainment of
      old age.
¹⁰ He who pleased God was loved;ʸ
    he who lived among sinners was
      transported—*
¹¹ Snatched away, lest wickedness pervert
    his mind

    or deceit beguile his soul;ᶻ
¹² For the witchery of paltry things
    obscures what is right
    and the whirl of desire transforms the
      innocent mind.ᵃ
¹³ Having become perfect in a short while,
    he reached the fullness of a long
      career;
¹⁴ for his soul was pleasing to the LORD,
    therefore he sped him out of the midst
      of wickedness.ᵇ
    But the people saw and did not
      understand,
    nor did they take this into account.*
¹⁶ Yes, the just man dead condemns the
    sinful who live,
    and youth swiftly completed
    condemns the many years of the
      wicked man grown old.ᶜ
¹⁷ For they see the death of the wise man
    and do not understand what the LORD
      intended for him,
    or why he made him secure.
¹⁸ They see, and hold him in contempt;
    but the LORD laughs them to scorn.ᵈ
¹⁹ And they shall afterward become
    dishonored corpsesᵉ
    and an unceasing mockery among the
      dead.
    For he shall strike them down speechless
      and prostrateᶠ
    and rock them to their foundations;
    They shall be utterly laid waste
    and shall be in grief
    and their memory shall perish.

4, 10f: There are allusions here to Enoch (Gn 5, 21-24), who was young by patriarchal standards, and to Lot (Gn 19, 10f; 2 Pt 2, 7f). Cf also Is 57, 1f.

4, 15: The verse here omitted repeats the last two lines of Wis 3, 9.

u: Sir 23, 25.   *v:* Sir 40, 15; Is 40, 24.   *w:* Wis 3, 3.   *x:* 8f; Jb 12, 12; 32, 9; Sir 25, 4ff.   *y:* Gn 5, 24; Sir 44, 16; Heb 11, 5.   *z:* Is 57, 1f.   *a:* Wis 2, 21; Dn 13, 9.   *b:* Gn 19, 22. 29; 2 Pt 2, 7.   *c:* Mt 12, 41f.   *d:* Ps 37, 13.   *e:* Neh 1, 10 LXX; Ps 18, 8; Is 14, 19; Jer 23, 39f.   *f:* 2 Mc 3, 29.

The Final Judgment of the Wicked

²⁰ Fearful shall they come, at the counting
    up* of their sins,
    and their lawless deeds shall convict
      them to their face.

CHAPTER 5

See RG 194–95

¹ Then shall the just one with great
    assurance confront^g
his oppressors who set at nought his
    labors.^h
² Seeing this, they shall be shaken with
    dreadful fear,
    and amazed at the unlooked-for
      salvation.
³ They shall say among themselves,
    rueful
    and groaning through anguish of
      spirit:
"This is he whom once we held as a
    laughingstock
    and as a type for mockery, ⁴fools that
      we were!
His life we accounted madness,
    and his death dishonored.
⁵ See how he is accounted among the sons
    of God;
    how his lot is with the saints!ⁱ
⁶ We, then, have strayed from the way of
    truth,^j
    and the light of justice did not shine
      for us,
    and the sun did not rise for us.^k
⁷ We had our fill of the ways of mischief
    and of ruin;
    we journeyed through impassable
      deserts,
    but the way of the LORD we knew
      not.
⁸ What did our pride avail us?
    What have wealth and its boastfulness
      afforded us?^l
⁹ All of them passed like a shadow
    and like a fleeting rumor;^m
¹⁰ Like a ship traversing the heaving
    water,

of which, when it has passed, no trace
    can be found,
    no path of its keel in the waves.
¹¹ Or like a bird flying through the air;
    no evidence of its course is to be
      found—
But the fluid air, lashed by the beat of
    pinions,
    and cleft by the rushing force
Of speeding wings, is traversed:
    and afterward no mark of passage can
      be found in it.
¹² Or as, when an arrow has been shot at a
    mark,
    the parted air straightway flows
      together again
    so that none discerns the way it went
      through—
¹³ Even so we, once born, abruptly came to
    nought
    and held no sign of virtue to display,
    but were consumed in our
      wickedness."ⁿ
¹⁴ Yes, the hope of the wicked is like
    thistledown borne on the wind,
    and like fine, tempest-driven foam;
Like smoke scattered by the wind,
    and like the passing memory of the
      nomad camping for a single day.^o
¹⁵ But the just live forever,
    and in the LORD is their recompense,
    and the thought of them is with the
      Most High.^p
¹⁶ Therefore shall they receive the splendid
    crown,
    the beauteous diadem, from the hand
      of the LORD—
For he shall shelter them with his right
    hand,
    and protect them with his arm.^q
¹⁷ He shall take his zeal for armor^r
    and he shall arm creation to requite the
      enemy;
¹⁸ He shall don justice for a breastplate
    and shall wear sure judgment for a
      helmet;

4, 20: Counting up: the last judgment.

---

g: 1f: 2 Thes 1, 6f.   h: Col 2, 15.   i: Acts 26, 18; Col 1, 12.   j: Prv 4, 18f; Jn 12, 35.   k: 6f: Is 59, 6-14.   l: Ps 49, 7; Prv 10, 2.
m: 9ff: 1 Chr 20, 15; Ps 144, 4; Jb 9, 25f LXX.   n: Ez 33, 10.   o: Jb 21, 18; Ps 1, 4; 37, 20; Is 17, 13.   p: Is 62, 11; Ez 18, 9.   q: Ex
33, 22; Is 62, 3; 2 Tm 4, 8; 1 Pt 5, 4.   r: 17: Is 59, 16.

19 He shall take invincible rectitude as a
shield[s]

20 and whet his sudden anger for a sword,
And the universe shall war with him
against the foolhardy.

21 Well-aimed shafts of lightnings shall go
forth
and from the clouds as from a well-
drawn bow shall leap to the mark;[t]

22 and as from his sling, wrathful
hailstones shall be hurled.
The water of the sea shall be enraged
against them
and the streams shall abruptly
overflow;[u]

23 A mighty wind shall confront them
and a tempest winnow them out;
Thus lawlessness shall lay the whole
earth waste
and evildoing overturn the thrones of
potentates.[v]

See RG 194-95

CHAPTER 6

Exhortation to Seek Wisdom

1 Hear, therefore, kings, and understand;[w]
learn, you magistrates of the earth's
expanse!

2 Hearken, you who are in power over the
multitude
and lord it over throngs of peoples!

3 Because authority was given you by the
LORD
and sovereignty by the Most High,
who shall probe your works and
scrutinize your counsels![x]

4 Because, though you were ministers of his
kingdom, you judged not rightly,
and did not keep the law,*
nor walk according to the will of
God,

5 Terribly and swiftly shall he come
against you,
because judgment is stern for the
exalted—

6 For the lowly may be pardoned out of
mercy[y]
but the mighty shall be mightily put to
the test.

7 For the Lord of all shows no partiality,
nor does he fear greatness,[z]
Because he himself made the great as
well as the small,
and he provides for all alike;

8 but for those in power a rigorous
scrutiny impends.

9 To you, therefore, O princes, are my
words addressed[a]
that you may learn wisdom and that
you may not sin.

10 For those who keep the holy precepts
hallowed shall be found holy,
and those learned in them will have
ready a response.*

11 Desire therefore my words;
long for them and you shall be
instructed.

12 Resplendent and unfading is Wisdom,
and she is readily perceived by those
who love her,
and found by those who seek her.[b]

13 She hastens to make herself known in
anticipation of men's desire;[c]

14 he who watches for her at dawn shall
not be disappointed,
for he shall find her sitting by his
gate.

15 For taking thought of her is the
perfection of prudence,
and he who for her sake keeps vigil
shall quickly be free from care;

16 Because she makes her own rounds,
seeking those worthy of her,
and graciously appears to them in the
ways,
and meets them with all solicitude.[d]

17 For the first step toward discipline is a
very earnest desire for her;[e]
then, care for discipline is love of her;

6, 4: Law: that of Moses; cf v 10; Wis 2, 12.

6, 10: Response: a suitable plea before the great Judge. Cf Prv 22, 21; Jb 31, 14; Hb 2, 1; Sir 8, 9.

---

s: 19f: Dt 32, 40ff.   t: Hb 3, 9ff.   u: Dt 11, 4.   v: Wis 11, 20; Sir 10, 13f.   w: 1f: Wis 1, 1; Sir 33, 19; Mi 3, 1. 9.   x: 2 Chr 36, 23;
Prv 8, 15f; Jn 19, 11; Rom 13, 1ff.   y: 6ff: Lk 12, 48.   z: Dt 1, 17; Prv 22, 2.   a: 9ff: Dt 4, 10; Ps 2, 12; Sir 32, 14; 1 Jn 3, 7.   b: Wis
7, 10; Prv 8, 17; Jer 29, 13.   c: 13ff: Prv 8, 3. 17. 34.   d: Prv 8, 20f; Sir 15, 1ff.   e: 17-21: Ps 2, 10ff; Prv 4, 4-9; 7, 1-4; 8, 15f; Dn
7, 27; Jn 14, 15. 21; 1 Jn 5, 3.

> Descriptions of wisdom personified as a female figure, "Sophia," such as in Wis 6, 12–21, are common in wisdom literature (e.g., see Prv 8; Sir 1, 1–10; 24, 1–22). Both the Greek word *sophia* and the Hebrew word *hokhma*, meaning "wisdom," are feminine.

18 love means the keeping of her laws;
To observe her laws is the basis for
incorruptibility;
19 and incorruptibility makes one close to
God;
20 thus the desire for Wisdom leads up to
a kingdom.
21 If, then, you find pleasure in throne and
scepter, you princes of the peoples,
honor Wisdom, that you may reign as
kings forever.

II: Praise of Wisdom by Solomon

Introduction
22 Now what Wisdom is, and how she came
to be, I shall relate;
and I shall hide no secrets from you,
But from the very beginning I shall
search out
and bring to light knowledge of her,
nor shall I diverge from the truth.*f*
23 Neither shall I admit consuming jealousy
to my company,
because that can have no fellowship
with Wisdom.*g*
24 A great number of wise men is the safety
of the world,
and a prudent king, the stability of his
people;*h*
25 so take instruction from my words, to
your profit.

See RG
195–96

CHAPTER 7

*Solomon Is Like All
Other Men*
1 I too am a mortal man, the same as all the
rest,*i*
and a descendant of the first man
formed of earth.*

And in my mother's womb I was molded
into flesh
2 in a ten-months' period*—body and
blood,
from the seed of man, and the pleasure
that accompanies marriage.
3 And I too, when born, inhaled the
common air,
and fell upon the kindred earth;
wailing, I uttered that first sound
common to all.
4 In swaddling clothes and with constant
care I was nurtured.
5 For no king has any different origin or
birth,
6 but one is the entry into life for all; and
in one same way they leave it.*j*

*Solomon Prayed and Wisdom and Riches
Came to Him*
7 Therefore I prayed, and prudence was
given me;
I pleaded, and the spirit of Wisdom
came to me.*k*
8 I preferred her to scepter and throne,*l*
And deemed riches nothing in
comparison with her,
9 nor did I liken any priceless gem to
her;
Because all gold, in view of her, is a little
sand,
and before her, silver is to be
accounted mire.
10 Beyond health and comeliness I loved
her,
And I chose to have her rather than the
light,
because the splendor of her never
yields to sleep.*m*

7, 1: First man formed of earth: Adam. The author omits throughout the book the proper names of the characters in sacred history of whom he speaks; see especially chapter 10.
7, 2: In a ten-months' period: thus the ancients were accustomed to reckon the period of pregnancy.

f: Tb 12, 7. 11; Mt 13, 11; Jn 15, 15.   *g:* Wis 7, 13; Jas 3, 14f.   *h:* Prv 24, 6; 29, 4; Sir 10, 1ff.   *i:* 1f: Wis 10, 1; Gn 2, 7; Jb 10, 9-12; 33, 6; 1 Cor 15, 47ff.   *j:* Jb 1, 21; 1 Tm 6, 7f.   *k:* 1 Kgs 3, 5-15; Prv 2, 3-11.   *l:* 8f: Wis 8, 5; 1 Kgs 10, 21; Prv 3, 14ff; 8, 10. 18f; Jb 28, 15-19.   *m:* Prv 6, 23.

11 Yet all good things together came to me
  in her company,[n]
  and countless riches at her hands;
12 And I rejoiced in them all, because
    Wisdom is their leader,
  though I had not known that she is the
    mother of these.[o]

Solomon Prays for Help To Speak
of Wisdom

13 Simply I learned about her, and
    ungrudgingly do I share—
  her riches I do not hide away;[p]
14 For to men she is an unfailing treasure;
  those who gain this treasure win the
    friendship of God,
  to whom the gifts they have from
    discipline* commend them.
15 Now God grant I speak suitably
  and value these endowments at their
    worth:
  For he is the guide of Wisdom
    and the director of the wise.
16 For both we and our words are in his
    hand,
  as well as all prudence and knowledge
    of crafts.[q]
17 For he gave me sound knowledge of
    existing things,
  that I might know the organization of
    the universe and the force of its
    elements,
18 The beginning and the end and the
    midpoint of times,
  the changes in the sun's course and the
    variations of the seasons.
19 Cycles of years, positions of the stars,
20   natures of animals, tempers of
    beasts,
  Powers of the winds and thoughts of
    men,
  uses of plants and virtues of roots—
21 Such things as are hidden I learned, and
    such as are plain;
22   for Wisdom, the artificer of all, taught
    me.[r]

Nature and Incomparable Dignity
of Wisdom

For in her is a spirit
  intelligent, holy, unique,
Manifold, subtle, agile,
  clear, unstained, certain,
Not baneful, loving the good, keen,[s]
  unhampered, beneficent, 23kindly,
Firm, secure, tranquil,
  all-powerful, all-seeing,
And pervading all spirits,
  though they be intelligent, pure and
    very subtle.
24 For Wisdom is mobile beyond all motion,
  and she penetrates and pervades all
    things by reason of her purity.[t]
25 For she is an aura of the might of God
  and a pure effusion of the glory of the
    Almighty;
  therefore nought that is sullied enters
    into her.
26 For she is the refulgence of eternal
    light,
  the spotless mirror of the power of God,
  the image of his goodness.[u]
27 And she, who is one, can do all things,
  and renews everything while herself
    perduring;
  And passing into holy souls from age to
    age,
  she produces friends of God and
    prophets.[v]
28 For there is nought God loves, be it not
  one who dwells with Wisdom.
29 For she is fairer than the sun[w]
  and surpasses every constellation of
    the stars.
  Compared to light, she takes precedence;
30   for that, indeed, night supplants,
  but wickedness prevails not over
    Wisdom.

CHAPTER 8

See RG
195–96

1 Indeed, she reaches from end to
    end* mightily
  and governs all things well.[x]

7, 14: Discipline: cf note on Wis 1, 5.
8, 1: End to end: from one end of the heavens to the other.

n: Prv 8, 21. o: Prv 8, 14f. p: Wis 6, 23. q: Wis 3, 1. r: Wis 14, 2; Prv 8, 30. s: 22f: Heb 4, 12f; Jas 3, 17. t: Wis 8, 1.
u: 2 Cor 4, 4; Col 1, 15; Heb 1, 3. v: Ex 33, 11; Jb 42, 2; Ps 104, 29; Jl 3, 1. w: 29f: Song 6, 3. 9. x: Wis 7, 24; 15, 1.

Solomon Sought Wisdom, the Source of Blessings

2 Her I loved and sought after from my youth;
  I sought to take her for my bride
    and was enamored of her beauty.*y*
3 She adds to nobility the splendor of companionship with God;
  even the LORD of all loved her.
4 For she is instructress in the understanding of God,
  the selector of his works.*z*
5 And if riches be a desirable possession in life,
  what is more rich than Wisdom, who produces all things?*a*
6 And if prudence renders service,*b*
  who in the world is a better craftsman than she?
7 Or if one loves justice,
  the fruits of her works are virtues;
  For she teaches moderation and prudence,
  justice and fortitude,*
  and nothing in life is more useful for men than these.
8 Or again, if one yearns for copious learning,
  she knows the things of old, and infers those yet to come.
  She understands the turns of phrases and the solutions of riddles;
  signs and wonders she knows in advance
  and the outcome of times and ages.*c*

Solomon Sought Wisdom as His Counselor and Comfort

9 So I determined to take her to live with me,
  knowing that she would be my counselor while all was well,
  and my comfort in care and grief.

10 For her sake I should have glory among the masses,*d*
  and esteem from the elders, though I be but a youth.
11 I should become keen in judgment,
  and should be a marvel before rulers.
12 They would abide my silence and attend my utterance;
  and as I spoke on further,
  they would place their hands upon their mouths.*
13 For her sake I should have immortality
  and leave to those after me an everlasting memory.*e*
14 I should govern peoples, and nations would be my subjects—*f*
15   terrible princes, hearing of me, would be afraid;
  in the assembly I should appear noble,
  and in war courageous.
16 Within my dwelling, I should take my repose beside her;
  For association with her involves no bitterness
  and living with her no grief,
  but rather joy and gladness.*g*

Solomon Realizes That Wisdom Is a Gift of God

17 Thinking thus within myself,
  and reflecting in my heart
  That there is immortality in kinship with Wisdom,*h*
18   and good pleasure in her friendship,
  and unfailing riches in the works of her hands,
  And that in frequenting her society there is prudence,
  and fair renown in sharing her discourses,
  I went about seeking to take her for my own.
19 Now, I was a well-favored child,*

8, 7: Moderation . . . fortitude: what are now known as the cardinal virtues.

8, 12: Hands upon their mouths: an oft-mentioned sign of respect among the ancients for unanswerable wisdom; cf Jb 40, 4.

8, 19f: Here the sacred writer mentions first bodily, then spiritual, excellence. To make it plain that the latter is the governing factor in the harmonious development of the hu-

man person, he then reverses the order.

y: 1 Kgs 3, 7ff; Ps 45, 12; Prv 5, 18; 8, 17. *z*: Prv 8, 27-31. *a*: Frv 8, 18f. *b*: 6f; Prv 8, 14f. *c*: Prv 1, 6; Sir 39, 1ff; 42, 19f; Dn 2, 21. *d*: 10ff; 1 Kgs 3, 28; Jb 29, 8ff. 21f. *e*: Sir 15, 6; 41, 12f; Is 56, 5. *f*: Wis 3, 8; Ps 18, 48; 47, 4. *g*: Prv 29, 6; Sir 15, 6; Ear 3, 38. *h*: Prv 3, 18.

and I came by a noble nature;

20 or rather, being noble, I attained an
  unsullied body.

21 And knowing that I could not otherwise
  possess her* except God gave it—
  and this, too, was prudence, to know
  whose is the gift—
  I went to the LORD and besought
  him,[i]
  and said with all my heart:

CHAPTER 9

See RG
195-96

Solomon's Prayer

1 God of my fathers, LORD of mercy,[j]
  you who have made all things by your
  word[k]

2 And in your wisdom have established
  man
  to rule the creatures produced by
  you,[l]

3 To govern the world in holiness and
  justice,
  and to render judgment in integrity of
  heart:[m]

4 Give me Wisdom, the attendant at your
  throne,
  and reject me not from among your
  children;[n]

5 For I am your servant, the son of your
  handmaid,
  a man weak and short-lived
  and lacking in comprehension of
  judgment and of laws.[o]

6 Indeed, though one be perfect among the
  sons of men,
  if Wisdom, who comes from you, be
  not with him,
  he shall be held in no esteem.[p]

7 You have chosen me king over your
  people
  and magistrate for your sons and
  daughters.[q]

8 You have bid me build a temple on your
  holy mountain
  and an altar in the city that is your
  dwelling place,
  a copy of the holy tabernacle which
  you had established from of old.[r]

9 Now with you is Wisdom, who knows
  your works
  and was present when you made the
  world;
  Who understands what is pleasing in
  your eyes
  and what is conformable with your
  commands.[s]

10 Send her forth from your holy heavens
  and from your glorious throne dispatch
  her
  That she may be with me and work with
  me,
  that I may know what is your
  pleasure,[t]

11 For she knows and understands all
  things,
  and will guide me discreetly in my
  affairs
  and safeguard me by her glory;[u]

12 Thus my deeds will be acceptable,
  and I shall judge your people justly
  and be worthy of my father's throne.[v]

13 For what man knows God's counsel,
  or who can conceive what the LORD
  intends?[w]

14 For the deliberations of mortals are
  timid,
  and unsure are our plans.

15 For the corruptible body burdens the
  soul
  and the earthen shelter weighs down
  the mind that has many
  concerns.[x]

16 And scarce do we guess the things on
  earth,
  and what is within our grasp we find
  with difficulty;
  but when things are in heaven, who
  can search them out?[y]

8, 21: Possess her: in the Latin, "be continent." Though this verse has often been cited in connection with the virtue of chastity, the original must certainly mean "be possessed of Wisdom."

---

i: 1 Kgs 3, 9; 4, 29; Prv 2, 6; Jas 1, 5. *j:* Ps 86, 15. *k:* 1f: Gn 1; Ps 33, 6; Prv 3, 19; Jer 10, 12; Jn 1, 3. 10. *l:* Ps 8, 7ff; Sir 17, 2ff.
m: 1 Kgs 3, 6; 9, 4f; Ps 9, 8f. *n:* 2 Chr 1, 10. *o:* 1 Kgs 3, 7; Ps 116, 16. *p:* Wis 3, 17; 1 Kgs 11, 4; 1 Cor 3, 18ff. *q:* 1 Chr 28, 5.
r: Ex 25, 8f; 2 Sm 7, 13; 1 Chr 28, 5; 2 Chr 6, 1f; 7, 7; Tb 1, 4; Pss 15, 1; 48, 2f. *s:* Dt 6, 17f; Prv 8, 22-31; Jn 1, 1ff. 10. *t:* Wis 18,
15; Mt 5, 34; Jn 3, 17; 20, 21. *u:* Wis 8, 8. *v:* 1 Kgs 3, 6-9. *w:* Is 40, 13; Bar 3, 31. *x:* Jb 4, 19. *y:* Sir 1, 3; Jn 3, 12.

The Wicked and the Just

In ch 10 there is richness in the presentation of Wisdom and the followers who are just, by contrasting how the unjust are destroyed and the just enriched. Cain and Noah (vv. 3–4) are contrasts of the wicked and the just. So, too, the stories of Abraham and the Tower of Babel are opposites (vv. 5–8).

¹⁷ Or who ever knew your counsel, except
    you had given Wisdom
  and sent your holy spirit from on
    high?^z
¹⁸ And thus were the paths of those on earth
    made straight,
  and men learned what was your
    pleasure,
  and were saved by Wisdom.^a

See RG
195–96

CHAPTER 10*

Wisdom Preserves Her Followers

¹ She preserved the first-formed father* of
    the world^b
  when he alone had been created;^c
And she raised him up from his fall,
²   and gave him power to rule all things.^d
³ But when the unjust man* withdrew from
    her in his anger,
  he perished through his fratricidal
    wrath.^e
⁴ When on his account the earth was
    flooded, Wisdom again saved it,
  piloting the just man* on frailest wood.^f
⁵ She, when the nations were sunk in
    universal wickedness,
  knew the just man,* kept him
    blameless before God,
  and preserved him resolute against
    pity for his child.^g
⁶ She delivered the just man* from among
    the wicked who were being
    destroyed,^h

  when he fled as fire descended upon
    Pentapolis—
⁷ Where as a testimony to its wickedness,
    there yet remain a smoking desert,
Plants bearing fruit that never ripens,
  and the tomb of a disbelieving soul,*
    a standing pillar of salt.ⁱ
⁸ For those who forsook Wisdom
  first were bereft of knowledge of the
    right,
And then they left mankind a memorial
    of their folly—
  so that they could not even be hidden
    in their fall.
⁹ But Wisdom delivered from tribulations
    those who served her.^j
¹⁰ She, when the just man fled from his
    brother's anger,^k
  guided him in direct ways,*
Showed him the kingdom of God
  and gave him knowledge of holy
    things;
She prospered him in his labors
  and made abundant the fruit of his
    works,
¹¹ Stood by him against the greed of his
    defrauders,
  and enriched him;^l
¹² She preserved him from foes,
  and secured him against ambush,
And she gave him the prize for his stern
    struggle
  that he might know that devotion to
    God* is mightier than all else.^m

10, 1-21: This chapter prepares for the following section (11, 2—19, 22) on the history of Israel in the Exodus, by reviewing the dealings of Wisdom with the patriarchs. It has a parallel in Sir 44—50; cf also Wis 18, 9.
  10, 1f: Adam.
  10, 3: Cain.
  10, 4: Noah.
  10, 5: Abraham.
  10, 6: Lot. Pentapolis: the five cities, including Sodom; cf Gn 14, 2.
  10, 7: Disbelieving soul: Lot's wife; cf Gn 19, 26.

  10, 10ff: Jacob.
  10, 12: Devotion to God: in the Greek this signifies "piety" or "religion," and is the equivalent of the Hebrew "fear of the Lord"; cf Prv 1, 7.

z: Jn 14, 26. *a:* Wis 10, 9; Prv 28, 26. *b:* 1-16: Heb 11, 17-27.
c: Wis 7, 1. *d:* Gn 1, 28. *e:* Gn 4, 1-16. *f:* Wis 14, 5f; Gn 6, 5-9. *g:* Gn 22, 7-10. *h:* Gn 18, 22-33; 19, 15-25; 2 P: 2, 6f.
i: Gn 19, 26; Lk 17, 32. *j:* Wis 16, 8. *k:* Gn 27, 43ff; 28, 12-15.
l: Gn 30, 29f; 31, 5-12. *m:* Gn 32, 24-29; 1 Tm 4, 8.

13 She did not abandon the just man* when he was sold,ⁿ
but delivered him from sin.ᵒ

14 She went down with him into the dungeon,
and did not desert him in his bonds,
Until she brought him the scepter of royalty
and authority over his oppressors,
Showed those who had defamed him false,
and gave him eternal glory.

15 The holy people and blameless race—it was she
who delivered them from the nation that oppressed them.ᵖ

16 She entered the soul of the LORD's servant,*
and withstood fearsome kings with signs and portents;�q

17 she gave the holy ones the recompense of their labors,ʳ
Conducted them by a wondrous road,
and became a shelter for them by day
and a starry flame by night.

18 She took them across the Red Sea
and brought them through the deep waters—

19 But their enemies she overwhelmed,
and cast them up* from the bottom of the depths.

20 Therefore the just despoiled the wicked;
and they sang, O LORD, your holy name
and praised in unison your conquering handˢ —

21 Because Wisdom opened the mouths of the dumb,

and gave ready speech to infants.ᵗ

CHAPTER 11

See RG 195–96

1 She made their affairs prosper through the holy prophet.ᵘ

III: Special Providence of God During the Exodus

Introduction

2 They journeyed through the uninhabited desert,*
and in solitudes they pitched their tents;ᵛ

3 they withstood enemies and took vengeance on their foes.ʷ

4 When they thirsted, they called upon you,
and water was given them from the sheer rock,
assuagement for their thirst from the hard stone.

5 For by the things through which their foes were punished
they in their need were benefited.ˣ

First Example: Water Punishes the Egyptians and Benefits the Israelites

6 Instead of a spring, when the perennial river*
was troubled with impure bloodʸ

7 as a rebuke to the decree for the slaying of infants,
You gave them abundant water in an unhoped-for way,

8 once you had shown by the thirst they then had
how you punished their adversaries.

10, 13f: Joseph.

10, 16: Moses.

10, 19: Cast them up: their bodies, on the shore.

11, 2ff: Few verses in these later chapters can be fully understood without consulting the passages in the Mosaic books which are indicated in the cross references. The theme of this part of the book is expressed in Wis 11, 5, and is illustrated in the following chapters by five examples drawn from Exodus events.

11, 6ff: The perennial river: the Nile; the contrast is between the first plague of Egypt (Ex 7, 17-24) and the wa-

ter drawn from the rock in Horeb (Ex 17, 5-7; Nm 20, 8-11).

n: 13f: Gn 37-45. o: Gn 39, 7-10. p: Ex 3, 9; 14, 30; 19, 6. q: Wis 1, 4; 7, 27; Ex 4, 10; Ps 76, 13. r: 17ff: Wis 14, 3; 19, 7; Ex 13, 21f; 14—15; Pss 77, 20f; 78, 13. 53; Is 4, 5f. s: Ex 12, 35f; 15, 1-21. t: Ex 4, 10-15; Ps 8, 3; Mt 11, 25. u: Dt 2, 7; Hos 12, 14. v: 2ff: Ex 17, 2-6; Nm 20, 1-13; Pss 63, 2; 107, 4-7; Jer 2, 6. w: Ex 17, 8-16; Nm 21, 1ff. 21-35; 31, 1-12; Ps 118, 10ff. x: Wis 16, 1f. y: 6ff: Wis 18, 5; Ex 1, 22; 7, 17-24.

⁹ For when they had been tried, though
only mildly chastised,ᶻ
they recognized how the wicked,
condemned in anger, were being
tormented.
¹¹ Both those afar off and those close by
were afflicted:ᵃ
¹⁰ the latter you tested, admonishing
them as a father;
the former as a stern king you probed
and condemned.
¹² For a twofold grief took hold of themᵇ
and a groaning at the remembrance of
the ones who had departed.
¹³ For when they heard that the cause of
their own torments
was a benefit to these others, they
recognized the LORD.
¹⁴ Him who of old had been cast out in
exposure they indeed mockingly
rejected;
but in the end of events, they marveled
at him,
since their thirst proved unlike that of
the just.ᶜ

Second Example: Animals Punish the Egyptians and Benefit the Israelites

¹⁵ And in return for their senseless, wicked
thoughts,
which misled them into worshiping
dumb* serpents and worthless
insects,
You sent upon them swarms of dumb
creatures for vengeance;ᵈ
¹⁶ that they might recognize that a man is
punished by the very things
through which he sins.ᵉ

Digression on God's Mercy

¹⁷ For not without means was your
almighty hand,ᶠ
that had fashioned the universe from
formless matter,

to send upon them a drove of bears or
fierce lions,
¹⁸ Or new-created, wrathful, unknown
beasts
to breathe forth fiery breath,
Or pour out roaring smoke,
or flash terrible sparks from their eyes.
¹⁹ Not only could these attack and
completely destroy them;
even their frightful appearance itself
could slay.
²⁰ Even without these, they could have been
killed at a single blast,
pursued by retribution
and winnowed out by your mighty
spirit;
But you have disposed all things by
measure and number and weight.ᵍ
²¹ For with you great strength abides
always;
who can resist the might of your arm?ʰ
²² Indeed, before you the whole universe is
as a grain from a balance,*
or a drop of morning dew come down
upon the earth.ⁱ
²³ But you have mercy on all, because you
can do all things;
and you overlook the sins of men that
they may repent.ʲ
²⁴ For you love all things that are
and loathe nothing that you have
made;
for what you hated, you would not
have fashioned.ᵏ
²⁵ And how could a thing remain, unless
you willed it;
or be preserved, had it not been called
forth by you?ˡ
²⁶ But you spare all things, because they are
yours, O LORD and lover of souls,ᵐ

CHAPTER 12

¹ for your imperishable spirit is in all
things!ⁿ

See RG 196

11, 15: Dumb: that is, irrational.
11, 22: Grain from a balance: a tiny particle used for weighing on sensitive scales.

z: 9ff: Wis 3, 5; 16, 3f; Dt 8, 2-5; Ps 6, 2; Prv 3, 12; 2 Mc 6, 12-16   a: Ps 6, 2.   b: 12f: Wis 16, 8; Ex 14, 4. 18.   c: Ex 2, 3.   d: Wis 12, 23f; 15, 18—16, 1; Ex 7, 26ff.   e: Wis 12, 23. 27; Ex 10, 16; Prv 1, 31f; 26, 27.   f: 17ff: Wis 12, 8f; 16, 1. 5; Gn 1, 1f; Dt 32, 24; 2 Kgs 17, 25f; Hos 13, 4-8.   g: Jb 4, 9.   h: Wis 12, 12; 2 Chr 20, 6.   i: Hos 13, 3.   j: Wis 12, 10; Dt 9, 27; Acts 17, 30; Rom 2, 4; 11, 32; 2 Pt 3, 9.   k: Ps 145, 9.   l: Is 41, 4.   m: Wis 12, 16; Is 63, 9.   n: Wis 1, 7.

2 Therefore you rebuke offenders little by
little,
warn them, and remind them of the
sins they are committing,
that they may abandon their
wickedness and believe in you, O
LORD!
3 For, truly, the ancient inhabitants of your
holy land,[o]
4 whom you hated for deeds most
odious—
Works of witchcraft and impious
sacrifices;
5 a cannibal feast of human flesh
and of blood, from the midst of . . . .*—
These merciless murderers of children,
6 and parents who took with their own
hands defenseless lives,[p]
You willed to destroy by the hands of our
fathers,
7 that the land that is dearest of all to
you
might receive a worthy colony of
God's children.[q]
8 But even these, as they were men, you
spared,
and sent wasps as forerunners of your
army
that they might exterminate them by
degrees.[r]
9 Not that you were without power to have
the wicked vanquished in battle
by the just,
or wiped out at once by terrible beasts
or by one decisive word;[s]
10 But condemning them bit by bit, you
gave them space for repentance.
You were not unaware that their race was
wicked
and their malice ingrained,[t]
And that their dispositions would never
change;

11 for they were a race accursed from the
beginning.
Neither out of fear for anyone
did you grant amnesty for their sins.[u]
12 For who can say to you, "What have you
done?"
or who can oppose your decree?
Or when peoples perish, who can
challenge you, their maker;
or who can come into your presence as
vindicator of unjust men?[v]
13 For neither is there any god besides you
who have the care of all,
that you need show you have not
unjustly condemned;[w]
14 Nor can any king or prince confront you
on behalf of those you have
punished.[x]
15 But as you are just, you govern all things
justly;
you regard it as unworthy of your
power
to punish one who has incurred no
blame.[y]
16 For your might is the source of justice;
your mastery over all things makes
you lenient to all.[z]
17 For you show your might when the
perfection of your power is
disbelieved;*
and in those who know you, you
rebuke temerity.[a]
18 But though you are master of might, you
judge with clemency,
and with much lenience you govern us;
for power, whenever you will, attends
you.
19 And you taught your people, by these
deeds,[b]
that those who are just must be kind;
And you gave your sons good ground for
hope

12, 5: And of blood, from the midst of . . . .: this line is obscure in the current Greek text and in all extant translations. Either one or two words would complete it. The horrible crimes here spoken of (cf Wis 14, 23) were not unheard of in the ancient pagan world.

12, 17: The brunt of God's anger and vindictive justice is borne by those who know him and yet defy his authority and might. Cf Wis 1, 2; 15, 2, but also Wis 12, 27; 18, 13.

o: 3ff: Wis 14, 23; Dt 18, 9-12; Pss 5, 6; 106, 28. 34-39; Jer 19, 4f; Ez 16, 3. 20f. 36.   p: Nm 33, 52.   q: Dt 11, 12.   r: Ex 23, 28ff; Dt 7, 17-24.   s: Wis 11, 18; 18, 15; Nm 16, 21.   t: Wis 11, 23; Ps 55, 20; Sir 16, 9.   u: Gn 9, 25.   v: 2 Sm 16, 10; Eccl 8, 4; Sir 46, 19; Is 45, 9; Dn 4, 32; Rom 9, 19ff.   w: Wis 6, 7; Dt 3, 24; 32, 39; Is 44, 6. 8.   x: Jer 49, 19; 50, 44.   y: Gn 18, 23ff; Dt 32, 4.   z: Wis 2, 11; 11, 26; Ps 103. 19.   a: Wis 15, 2f; Ex 9, 16.   b: 19f: Wis 11, 23; Sir 17, 24.

Worship of Creation, Rather Than Creator

In ch 13 the beauty of the natural world reflects the nature of God, or less specifically, the plan of an intelligent mind. This is known as the "argument from design," a proof for the existence of God used in many different eras. The argument in antiquity represents a well-known strategy for undermining nature worship to demonstrate that the invisible God lies behind the visible world; it appears in Stoic writings, in Philo, and in truncated form in Paul (Rom 1, 18–25).

that you would permit repentance for their sins.

²⁰ For these were enemies of your servants, doomed to death;
yet, while you punished them with such solicitude and pleading,
granting time and opportunity to abandon wickedness,

²¹ With what exactitude you judged your sons,
to whose fathers you gave the sworn covenants of goodly promises!^c

²² Us, therefore, you chastise, and our enemies with a thousand blows you punish,
that we may think earnestly of your goodness when we judge,
and, when being judged, may look for mercy.

Second Example Resumed

²³ Hence those unjust also, who lived a life of folly,
you tormented through their own abominations.^d

²⁴ For they went far astray in the paths of error,
taking for gods the worthless and disgusting among beasts,
deceived like senseless infants.^e

²⁵ Therefore as though upon unreasoning children,
you sent your judgment on them as a mockery;^f

²⁶ But they who took no heed of punishment which was but child's play

were to experience a condemnation worthy of God.

²⁷ For in the things through which they suffered distress,
since they were tortured by the very things they deemed gods,
They saw and recognized the true God whom before they had refused to know;
with this, their final condemnation came upon them.^g

Digression on False Worship

CHAPTER 13

See RG 196

A. NATURE WORSHIP

¹ For all men were by nature foolish who were in ignorance of God,
and who from the good things seen did not succeed in knowing him who is,[*]
and from studying the works did not discern the artisan;^h

² But either fire, or wind, or the swift air,
or the circuit of the stars, or the mighty water,
or the luminaries of heaven,[*] the governors of the world, they considered gods.ⁱ

³ Now if out of joy in their beauty they thought them gods,
let them know how far more excellent is the Lord than these;
for the original source of beauty fashioned them.^j

⁴ Or if they were struck by their might and energy,

13, 1: Him who is: the Hebrew sacred name of God; cf Ex 3, 14.

13, 2: Luminaries of heaven: the Latin interprets, "sun and moon"; governors: cf Gn 1, 16.

---

c: Wis 18, 22; Gn 50, 24; Dt 7, 6-14; Ps 105, 8ff.   d: Wis 11, 16; 16, 1.   e: Dt 11, 28; Jer 5, 28; Rom 1, 23.   f: Jer 4, 22.   g: Wis 16, 16; Ex 14, 4. 28.   h: Acts 14, 17; Eph 4, 17ff.   i: Gn 1, 14-19; Dt 4, 19; Jb 31, 26ff.   j: Ps 8, 4.

let them from these things realize how much more powerful is he who made them.[k]

5 For from the greatness and the beauty of created things
their original author, by analogy, is seen.

6 But yet, for these the blame is less;[*]
For they indeed have gone astray perhaps,
though they seek God and wish to find him.

7 For they search busily among his works,
but are distracted by what they see,
because the things seen are fair.

8 But again, not even these are pardonable.

9 For if they so far succeeded in knowledge
that they could speculate about the world,
how did they not more quickly find its LORD?

B. IDOLATRY

10 But doomed are they, and in dead things are their hopes,
who termed gods things made by human hands:
Gold and silver, the product of art, and likenesses of beasts,
or useless stone, the work of an ancient hand.[l]

The Carpenter and Wooden Idols

11 A carpenter may saw out a suitable tree[m]
and skillfully scrape off all its bark,
And deftly plying his art,
produce something fit for daily use,[n]

12 and use up the refuse from his handiwork in preparing his food,
and have his fill;

13 Then the good-for-nothing refuse from these remnants,
crooked wood grown full of knots,

he takes and carves to occupy his spare time.[o]
This wood he models with listless skill,
and patterns it on the image of a man

14 or makes it resemble some worthless beast.
When he has daubed it with red and crimsoned its surface with red stain,
and daubed over every blemish in it,[p]

15 He makes a fitting shrine for it
and puts it on the wall, fastening it with a nail.[q]

16 Thus lest it fall down he provides for it,
knowing that it cannot help itself;
for, truly, it is an image and needs help.[r]

17 But when he prays about his goods or marriage or children,[s]
he is not ashamed to address the thing without a soul.
And for vigor he invokes the powerless;

18 and for life he entreats the dead;
And for aid he beseeches the wholly incompetent,
and about travel, something that cannot even walk.

19 And for profit in business and success with his hands
he asks facility of a thing with hands completely inert.

CHAPTER 14

See RG 196

1 Again, one preparing for a voyage
and about to traverse the wild waves
cries out to wood more unsound than the boat that bears him.[t]

2 For the urge for profits devised this latter,
and Wisdom the artificer produced it.

3 But your providence, O Father! guides it,
for you have furnished even in the sea a road,
and through the waves a steady path,[u]

4 Showing that you can save from any danger,

13, 6: The blame is less: the greater blame is incurred by those mentioned in Wis 13, 10 and 15, 14ff.

---

k: Jer 10, 2; Bar 6, 39.   l: Wis 3, 11; 15, 5. 17; Dt 4, 25-28; 7, 25; 27, 15; Ps 115, 4; Hos 14, 4; Acts 17, 29.   m: 11-19: Is 44, 9-20.
n: Wis 15, 7; Bar 6, 58.   o: Dt 4, 16.   p: Jer 10, 9.   q: Is 40, 20; 41, 7; 44, 13.   r: 1 Sm 5, 3ff; Bar 6, 57.   s: 17ff: Wis 15, 15.   t: Is
46, 7.   u: Ps 107, 23-30; Is 43, 16.

so that even one without skill may
embark.[v]
⁵ But you will that the products of your
Wisdom be not idle;
therefore men trust their lives even to
frailest wood,
and have been safe crossing the surge
on a raft.[w]
⁶ For of old, when the proud giants were
being destroyed,
the hope of the universe, who took
refuge on a raft,*
left to the world a future for his race,
under the guidance of your hand.[x]
⁷ For blest is the wood through which
justice comes about;*
⁸   but the handmade idol is accursed, and
its maker as well:
he for having produced it, and it,
because though corruptible, it
was termed a god.[y]
⁹ Equally odious to God are the evildoer
and his evil deed;
¹⁰   and the thing made shall be punished
with its contriver.
¹¹ Therefore upon even the idols of the
nations shall a visitation come,
since they have become abominable
amid God's works,
Snares for the souls of men
and a trap for the feet of the senseless.[z]

The Origin and Evils of Idolatry
¹² For the source of wantonness is the
devising of idols;
and their invention was a corruption of
life.[a]
¹³ For in the beginning they were not,
nor shall they continue forever;[b]
¹⁴   for by the vanity of men they came
into the world,
and therefore a sudden end is devised
for them.
¹⁵ For a father, afflicted with untimely
mourning,

made an image of the child so quickly
taken from him,
And now honored as a god what was
formerly a dead man
and handed down to his subjects
mysteries and sacrifices.
¹⁶ Then, in time, the impious practice gained
strength and was observed as law,
and graven things were worshiped by
princely decrees.[c]
¹⁷ Men who lived so far away that they
could not honor him in his
presence
copied the appearance of the distant
king
And made a public image of him they
wished to honor,
out of zeal to flatter him when absent,
as though present.
¹⁸ And to promote this observance among
those to whom it was strange,
the artisan's ambition provided a
stimulus.
¹⁹ For he, mayhap in his determination to
please the ruler,
labored over the likeness to the best of
his skill;[d]
²⁰ And the masses, drawn by the charm of
the workmanship,
soon thought he should be worshiped
who shortly before was honored
as a man.[e]
²¹ And this became a snare for mankind,
that men enslaved to either grief or
tyranny
conferred the incommunicable Name
on stocks and stones.
²² Then it was not enough for them to err in
their knowledge of God;[f]
but even though they live in a great
war of ignorance,
they call such evils peace.[g]
²³ For while they celebrate either child-
slaying sacrifices or clandestine
mysteries,

14, 6: Noah.
14, 7: Often applied to the Cross of our Lord.

---

v: Wis 16, 8.   w: Wis 10, 4.   x: Gn 6, 4; 17, 1ff. 21f.   y: Rom 1, 23.   z: Wis 3, 7; 23, 33; Nm 33, 4; Jos 23, 13; Ps 115, 4; Jer 6, 15; 10, 15; 46, 25; Hos 9, 15.   a: Rom 1, 23ff.   b: Is 2, 18.   c: Dn 3, 4ff; 1 Mc 1, 47-50.   d: Is 44, 12f LXX.   e: Wis 15, 4.   f: 22-31: Jer 2, 20; 3, 1-25; Hos 4, 1f. 9-19; Rom 1, 26-31; Gal 5, 19ff; 1 Tm 1, 9f.   g: Jer 6, 14; Ez 13, 10.

Idol Worship

Both idol worship and deviant sexual behavior (14, 26–27) invert the proper social order. Jews often stereotyped Gentiles as sexually licentious and make a connection between idolatry and such behavior.

or frenzied carousals in unheard-of
    rites,[h]
24 They no longer safeguard either lives or
    pure wedlock;
    but each either waylays and kills his
        neighbor, or aggrieves him by
        adultery.
25 And all is confusion—blood and murder,
    theft and guile,[i]
    corruption, faithlessness, turmoil,
        perjury,
26 Disturbance of good men, neglect of
    gratitude,
    besmirching of souls, unnatural lust,
    disorder in marriage, adultery and
        shamelessness.
27 For the worship of infamous idols
    is the reason and source and extremity
        of all evil.[j]
28 For they either go mad with enjoyment,
    or prophesy lies,
    or live lawlessly or lightly forswear
        themselves.[k]
29 For as their trust is in soulless idols,
    they expect no harm when they have
        sworn falsely.
30 But on both counts shall justice overtake
    them:
    because they thought ill of God and
        devoted themselves to idols,[l]
    and because they deliberately swore
        false oaths, despising piety.*
31 For not the might of those that are sworn
    by
    but the retribution of sinners
    ever follows upon the transgression of
        the wicked.*

CHAPTER 15

See RG 196

1 But you, our God, are good and
    true,
    slow to anger, and governing all with
        mercy.[m]
2 For even if we sin, we are yours, and
    know your might;
    but we will not sin, knowing that we
        belong to you.[n]
3 For to know you well is complete justice,
    and to know your might is the root of
        immortality.[o]
4 For neither did the evil creation of men's
    fancy deceive us,
    nor the fruitless labor of painters,[p]
A form smeared with varied colors,
5   the sight of which arouses yearning in
        the senseless man,
    till he longs for the inanimate form of
        a dead image.
6 Lovers of evil things, and worthy of such
    hopes
    are they who make them and long for
        them and worship them.[q]

The Potter's Clay Idols
7 For truly the potter, laboriously working
    the soft earth,
    molds for our service each several
        article:
Both the vessels that serve for clean
    purposes
    and their opposites, all alike;
As to what shall be the use of each vessel
    of either class
    the worker in clay is the judge.[r]

14, 30: Piety: the sanctity of oaths.
14, 31: Perjury is a form of deceit which calls for punishment even though it be practiced in the name of a lifeless idol.

h: Wis 12, 4f; 14, 15; Is 57, 5. i: 25f: Jer 7, 8f; 22, 17. j: Ex 23, 13. k: Jer 5, 31; 29, 26. l: Wis 1, 8; 11, 20; Jer 5, 2. 7. m: Ex 34, 6f; Pss 86, 5. 15; 145, 8. 9. 14. n: Jb 10, 14f LXX. o: Wis 3, 15; Jn 17, 3. p: Wis 13, 14. q: Ps 115, 8. r: Wis 13, 11; Jer 18, 3f; Rom 9, 21; 2 Tm 2, 20f.

⁸ And with misspent toil he molds a
    meaningless god from the
    selfsame clay;
though he himself shortly before was
    made from the earth
And after a little, is to go whence he was
    taken,
when the life that was lent him is
    demanded back.ˢ
⁹ But his concern is not that he is to die
    nor that his span of life is brief;
Rather, he vies with goldsmiths and
    silversmiths
    and emulates molders of bronze,
    and takes pride in modeling
    counterfeits.ᵗ
¹⁰ Ashes his heart is! more worthless than
    earth is his hope,ᵘ
    and more ignoble than clay his life;
¹¹ Because he knew not the one who
    fashioned him,
    and breathed into him a quickening
    soul,
    and infused a vital spirit.ᵛ
¹² Instead, he esteemed our life a plaything,
    and our span of life a holiday for gain;
"For one must," says he, "make profit
    every way, be it even out of
    evil."ʷ
¹³ For this man more than any knows that
    he is sinning,
when out of earthen stuff he creates
    fragile vessels and idols alike.
¹⁴ But all quite senseless, and worse than
    childish in mind,
are the enemies of your people who
    enslaved them.ˣ
¹⁵ For they esteemed all the idols of the
    nations, gods,
which have no use of the eyes for
    vision,
    nor nostrils to snuff the air,
Nor ears to hear,

nor fingers on their hands for feeling;
even their feet are useless to walk
    with.ʸ
¹⁶ For a man made them;ᶻ
    one whose spirit has been lent him
    fashioned them.
For no man succeeds in fashioning a god
    like himself;
¹⁷ being mortal, he makes a dead thing
    with his lawless hands.
For he is better than the things he
    worships;
he at least lives, but never they.

Second Example Resumed
¹⁸ And besides, they worship* the most
    loathsome beasts—ᵃ
for compared as to folly, these are
    worse than the rest,*
¹⁹ Nor for their looks are they good or
    desirable beasts,
but they have escaped both the
    approval of God and his
    blessing.ᵇ

CHAPTER 16
¹ Therefore they* were fittingly
    punished by similar creatures,
and were tormented by a swarm of
    insects.ᶜ
² Instead of this punishment, you benefited
    your people
with a novel dish, the delight they
    craved,
by providing quail for their food;ᵈ
³ That those others, when they desired
    food,
since the creatures sent to plague them
    were so loathsome,
should be turned from even the
    craving of necessities,
While these, after a brief period of
    privation,

See RG
196

15, 18ff: The author here returns to the main theme of chapters 11—19, which was interrupted by the digression 13, 1—15, 17.

15, 18: For . . . rest: this may mean that the creatures worshiped by the Egyptians (e.g., crocodiles, serpents, scarabs, etc.) were more patently lacking in intelligence than the general run of beasts; cf Wis 11, 15; 12, 24.

16, 1: They: the Egyptian idolaters.

s: Gn 3, 19; Eccl 12, 7. t: Bar 6, 46. u: Jb 13, 12 LXX. v: Gn 2, 7; Zec 12, 1. w: Jas 4, 13f. x: Ex 1, 13. y: Wis 14, 11; Dt 4, 28; Pss 115, 4-7; 135, 15ff. z: 16f; Wis 13, 10. a: Wis 11, 15; 12, 24. b: Gn 1, 25; 3, 14. c: Wis 11, 15f; 12, 23. 27; Ex 7, 27; 8, 12. 17. d: Wis 11, 13; 19, 11f; Ex 16, 13; Nm 11, 31f; Ps 105, 4C.

partook of a novel dish.*

4 For upon those oppressors, inexorable want had to come;
but these needed only be shown how their enemies were being tormented.*

5 For when the dire venom of beasts came upon them*
and they were dying from the bite of crooked serpents,
your anger endured not to the end.

6 But as a warning, for a short time they were terrorized,
though they had a sign* of salvation, to remind them of the precept of your law.

7 For he who turned toward it was saved,
not by what he saw,
but by you, the savior of all.

8 And by this also you convinced our foes
that you are he who delivers from all evil.*

9 For the bites of locusts and of flies slew them,
and no remedy was found to save their lives
because they deserved to be punished by such means;*

10 But not even the fangs of poisonous reptiles overcame your sons,
for your mercy brought the antidote to heal them.*

11 For as a reminder of your injunctions, they were stung,
and swiftly they were saved,
Lest they should fall into deep forgetfulness
and become unresponsive to your beneficence.*

12 For indeed, neither herb nor application cured them,
but your all-healing word, O LORD!*

13 For you have dominion over life and death;*

you lead down to the gates of the nether world, and lead back.

14 Man, however, slays in his malice,
but when the spirit has come away, it does not return,
nor can he bring back the soul once it is confined.*

15 But your hand none can escape.

Third Example: A Rain of Manna for Israel instead of the Plague of Storms

16 For the wicked who refused to know you were punished by the might of your arm,
Pursued by unwonted rains and hailstorms and unremitting downpours,
and consumed by fire.*

17 For against all expectation, in water which quenches anything,
the fire grew more active;
For the universe fights on behalf of the just.*

18 For now the flame was tempered*
so that the beasts might not be burnt up that were sent upon the wicked,
but that these might see and know they were struck by the judgment of God;

19 And again, even in the water, fire blazed beyond its strength
so as to consume the produce of the wicked land.

20 Instead of this, you nourished your people with food of angels
and furnished them bread from heaven, ready to hand, untoiled-for,
endowed with all delights and conforming to every taste.*

21 For this substance of yours revealed your sweetness toward your children,
and serving the desire of him who received it,

16, 6: Sign: the brazen serpent; cf Nm 21, 9.
16, 14: Confined: in the nether world, in limbo.

---

e: Wis 11, 15; Ex 8, 10; 16, 3.   *f:* Wis 11, 8f.   *g:* 5f: Nm 21, 4-9; Dt 32, 24; Jer 8, 7 LXX.   *h:* Gn 48, 16; 2 Mc 1, 24f.   *i:* Ex 8, 16-28; 10, 4-19; Pss 78, 45f; 105, 31. 34; Rv 9, 1-11.   *j:* Dt 32, 33.   *k:* Ps 78, 11.   *l:* Ex 15, 26.   *m:* 13ff: Dt 32, 39; 1 Sm 2, 6; Tb 13, 2; Ps 78, 34. 39; Eccl 8, 8; Dn 5, 19; 2 Mc 6, 26; 7, 23.   *n:* Wis 11, 21; 12, 27; Ex 5, 2; 9, 29-34.   *o:* Wis 10, 20; 19, 20; Ex 9, 23-28; 2 Mc 8, 36; 14, 34.   *p:* 18f: Wis 19, 20f.   *q:* Ex 16, 4; Nm 11, 8; Ps 78, 24f; Jn 6, 31.

was blended to whatever flavor each one wished.[r]

22 Yet snow and ice* withstood fire and were not melted,
that they might know that their enemies' fruits
Were consumed by a fire that blazed in the hail
and flashed lightning in the rain.[s]

23 But this fire, again, that the just might be nourished,
forgot even its proper strength;[t]

24 For your creation, serving you, its maker, grows tense for punishment against the wicked,
but is relaxed in benefit for those who trust in you.[u]

25 Therefore at that very time, transformed in all sorts of ways,
it was serving your all-nourishing bounty
according to what they needed and desired;

26 That your sons whom you loved might learn, O LORD,
that it is not the various kinds of fruits that nourish man,
but it is your word that preserves those who believe you![v]

27 For what was not destroyed by fire, when merely warmed by a momentary sunbeam, melted;[w]

28 So that men might know that one must give you thanks before the sunrise,
and turn to you at daybreak.[x]

29 For the hope of the ingrate melts like a wintry frost
and runs off like useless water.[y]

CHAPTER 17

See RG 196

Fourth Example: Darkness Afflicts the Egyptians, While the Israelites Have Light

1 For great are your judgments, and hardly to be described;

therefore the unruly souls were wrong.[z]

2 For when the lawless thought to enslave the holy nation,
shackled with darkness, fettered by the long night,
they lay confined beneath their own roofs as exiles from the eternal providence.[a]

3 For they who supposed their secret sins were hid[b]
under the dark veil of oblivion
Were scattered in fearful trembling,
terrified by apparitions.

4 For not even their inner chambers kept them fearless,
for crashing sounds on all sides terrified them,
and mute phantoms with somber looks appeared.

5 No force, even of fire, was able to give light,
nor did the flaming brilliance of the stars
succeed in lighting up that gloomy night.[c]

6 But only intermittent, fearful fires* flashed through upon them;
And in their terror they thought beholding these was worse
than the times when that sight was no longer to be seen.[d]

7 And mockeries of the magic art were in readiness,
and a jeering reproof of their vaunted shrewdness.[e]

8 For they who undertook to banish fears and terrors from the sick soul
themselves sickened with a ridiculous fear.

9 For even though no monstrous thing frightened them,
they shook at the passing of insects and the hissing of reptiles,[f]

10 And perished trembling,

16, 22: Snow and ice: the manna; cf Wis 16, 27; 19, 21.
17, 6: Fires: that is, lightnings.

---

r: Ps 34, 9.   s: Ex 9, 25-31; 10, 12; Ps 148, 8.   t: Wis 19, 21.   u: Wis 5, 17. 20; 19, 6; Sir 39, 25ff.   v: Dt 8, 3; Mt 4, 4.   w: Ex 16, 21.
x: Pss 57, 9f; 92, 3.   y: Wis 5, 14; 2 Sm 14, 14.   z: Ex 6, 6 LXX.   a: Wis 18, 4; Ex 1, 13f; 19, 6; 10, 21ff.   b: 3f; Wis 1, 7f; 10, 8; 18,
17.   c: Wis 10, 17; Jer 23, 24 LXX.   d: Ex 9, 23f.   e: Wis 12, 25f; Ex 7, 11f. 22; 8, 3; 9, 11; 10, 2.   f: Wis 16, 1; Jer 26, 22 LXX

reluctant to face even the air that they
could nowhere escape.

11 For wickedness, of its nature cowardly,
testifies in its own condemnation,
and because of a distressed
conscience, always magnifies
misfortunes.*g*

12 For fear is nought but the surrender of
the helps that come from reason;

13 and the more one's expectation is of
itself uncertain,
the more one makes of not knowing
the cause that brings on torment.

14 So they, during that night, powerless
though it was,
that had come upon them from the
recesses of a powerless* nether
world,
while all sleeping the same sleep,

15 Were partly smitten by fearsome
apparitions
and partly stricken by their soul's
surrender;
for fear came upon them, sudden and
unexpected.*h*

16 Thus, then, whoever was there fell
into that unbarred prison and was kept
confined.*i*

17 For whether one was a farmer, or a
shepherd,
or a worker at tasks in the wasteland,
Taken unawares, he served out the
inescapable sentence;

18 for all were bound by the one bond of
darkness.*j*
And were it only the whistling wind,
or the melodious song of birds in the
spreading branches,
Or the steady sound of rushing water,

19 or the rude crash of overthrown rocks,
Or the unseen gallop of bounding
animals,
or the roaring cry of the fiercest beasts,
Or an echo resounding from the hollow
of the hills,

these sounds, inspiring terror,
paralyzed them.

20 For the whole world shone with brilliant
light*k*
and continued its works without
interruption;

21 Over them alone was spread oppressive
night,
an image of the darkness that next
should come upon them;
yet they were to themselves more
burdensome than the darkness.

CHAPTER 18

See RG 196

1 But your holy ones had very great
light;
And those others, who heard their voices
but did not see their forms,
since now they themselves had
suffered, called them blest;

2 And because they who formerly had been
wronged did not harm them, they
thanked them,
and pleaded with them, for the sake of
the difference between them.*

3 Instead of this, you furnished the flaming
pillar
which was a guide on the unknown
way,
and the mild sun for an honorable
migration.*l*

4 For those deserved to be deprived of
light and imprisoned by
darkness,
who had kept your sons confined
through whom the imperishable light
of the law was to be given to the
world.*m*

Fifth Example: Death of the Egyptian First-born; the Israelites Are Spared

5 When they determined to put to death the
infants of the holy ones,
and when a single boy* had been cast
forth but saved,

17, 14: Powerless: the nether world, the home of darkness, has no power against God, nor even against such men as do not submit to it of themselves; cf Wis 1, 14ff.

18, 2: The difference between them: God's distinctive manner of treating the Israelites and the Egyptians according to their respective merits.

18, 5: Single boy: Moses.

g: Wis 4, 6; 10, 7; Rom 2, 15.   h: Ex 11, 9f.   i: Wis 18, 4; Ex 10, 23.   j: 18f: Lv 26, 36.   k: 20f: Ex 10, 23; Is 9, 1; 60, 1ff; 2 Pt 2, 17.   l: Ex 13, 21.   m: Wis 17, 2; Ps 119, 105; Is 2, 3. 5.

As a reproof you carried off their
    multitude of sons
and made them perish all at once in the
    mighty water.*n*

6 That night was known beforehand to our
    fathers,
that, with sure knowledge of the oaths
    in which they put their faith, they
    might have courage.*o*

7 Your people awaited
the salvation of the just and the
    destruction of their foes.*p*

8 For when you punished our adversaries,
in this you glorified us whom you had
    summoned.*q*

9 For in secret the holy children of the
    good were offering sacrifice
and putting into effect with one accord
    the divine institution,
That your holy ones should share alike the
    same good things and dangers,*r*
having previously sung the praises of
    the fathers.*

10 But the discordant cry of their enemies
    responded,
and the piteous wail of mourning for
    children was borne to them.*s*

11 And the slave was smitten with the same
    retribution as his master;
even the plebeian suffered the same as
    the king.*t*

12 And all alike by a single death
    had countless dead;
For the living were not even sufficient
    for the burial,
since at a single instant their nobler
    offspring were destroyed.*u*

13 For though they disbelieved at every turn
    on account of sorceries,
at the destruction of the first-born they
    acknowledged that the people*
    was God's son.*v*

14 For when peaceful stillness compassed
    everything
and the night in its swift course was
    half spent,

15 Your all-powerful word from heaven's
    royal throne
bounded, a fierce warrior, into the
    doomed land,*w*

16   bearing the sharp sword of your
    inexorable decree.
And as he alighted, he filled every place
    with death;
he still reached to heaven, while he
    stood upon the earth.*x*

17 Then, forthwith, visions in horrible
    dreams perturbed them*y*
and unexpected fears assailed them;

18 And cast half-dead, one here, another
    there,
each was revealing the reason for his
    dying.

19 For the dreams that disturbed them had
    proclaimed this beforehand,
lest they perish unaware of why they
    suffered ill.

20 But the trial of death touched at one time
    even the just,
and in the desert a plague struck the
    multitude;
Yet not for long did the anger last.*z*

21 For the blameless man* hastened to be
    their champion,
bearing the weapon of his special
    office,
prayer and the propitiation of incense;
He withstood the wrath and put a stop to
    the calamity,
showing that he was your servant.*a*

22 And he overcame the bitterness
not by bodily strength, not by force of
    arms;
But by word he overcame the smiter,*

18, 9: Praises of the fathers: cf Sir 44—50; Wis 10.
18, 13: People: the Hebrews.
18, 21: Blameless man: Aaron acting according to his office of high priest and intercessor.
18, 22: Smiter: the destroying angel; cf v 25.

n: Wis 11, 7. 14; Ex 1, 16. 22; 2, 3. 6-10; 15, 10; Neh 9, 11.   *o:* Wis 12, 21; Ex 6, 8; 13, 5.   *p:* Ex 14, 13.   *q:* Wis 19, 22; Ex 3, 18;
Is 43, 3f.   *r:* Ex 12, 21-28; Sir 44—50.   *s:* Ex 12, 30; Jer 9, 17. 19.   *t:* Ex 11, 5; 12, 29.   *u:* Nm 33, 4.   *v:* Wis 17, 7; Ex 4, 22f; 12,
12. 29; 13, 2. 13. 15.   *w:* Wis 9, 10; Ex 15, 3.   *x:* 1 Chr 21, 16; Heb 4, 12; Rv 1, 16.   *y:* 17ff; Wis 17, 3f.   *z:* Wis 16, 5; Nm 17, 9-
15.   *a:* Wis 12, 21; Ex 32, 12f; Ps 20, 8.

recalling the sworn covenants with their fathers.*b*

23 For when corpses had already fallen one on another in heaps,
he stood in the midst and checked the anger,
and cut off the way to the living.*c*

24 For on his full-length robe was the whole world,
and the glories of the fathers were carved in four rows upon the stones,
and your grandeur* was on the crown upon his head.*d*

25 To these names the destroyer yielded, and these he feared;
for the mere trial of anger was enough.*e*

CHAPTER 19

See RG 196

1 But the wicked, merciless wrath assailed until the end.
For he* knew beforehand what they were yet to do:*f*

2 That though they themselves had agreed to the departure
and had anxiously sent them* on their way,
they would regret it and pursue them.*g*

3 For while they* were still engaged in funeral rites
and were mourning at the burials of the dead,
They adopted another senseless plan;
and those whom they had sent away with entreaty,
they pursued as fugitives.*h*

4 For a compulsion suited to this ending drew them on,
and made them forgetful of what had befallen them,

That they might fill out the torments of their punishment,

5 and your people might experience a glorious* journey
while those others met an extraordinary death.

6 For all creation, in its several kinds, was being made over anew,
serving its natural laws,
that your children might be preserved unharmed.*i*

7 The cloud overshadowed their camp;
and out of what had before been water, dry land was seen emerging:
Out of the Red Sea an unimpeded road,
and a grassy plain out of the mighty flood.*j*

8 Over this crossed the whole nation sheltered by your hand,
after they beheld stupendous wonders.

9 For they ranged about like horses,
and bounded about like lambs,
praising you, O Lord! their deliverer.*k*

10 For they were still mindful of what had happened in their sojourn:
how instead of the young of animals the land brought forth gnats,
and instead of fishes the river swarmed with countless frogs.*l*

11 And later they saw also a new kind of bird*m*
when, prompted by desire, they asked for pleasant foods;

12 For to appease them quail came to them from the sea.

13 And the punishments came upon the sinners
only after forewarnings from the violence of the thunderbolts.
For they justly suffered for their own misdeeds,

18, 24: Glories . . . grandeur: the name of God and the names of the tribes were inscribed on the high priest's apparel.
19, 1: He: i.e., God.
19, 2: Them: the Hebrews.
19, 3: They: the Egyptians.
19, 5: Glorious: more precisely, "wondrous," but the word reflects glorified in Wis 18, 8 and 19, 22.

b: 12, 21; Ex 32, 12f.   *c:* Nm 14, 29f.   *d:* Ex 28, 15-21. 31-38; Sir 45, 8-12; 50, 11.   *e:* 1 Chr 21, 15.   *f:* Ex 14, 4.   *g:* Ex 12, 33; 14, 5. 8.   *h:* Wis 18, 10. 12; Ex 12, 30ff.   *i:* Wis 5, 17; 16, 24.   *j:* Ex 14, 21-29.   *k:* Wis 10, 20; 16, 8; Ex 15, 1-18; Ps 114, 4-6.
l: Ex 7, 27ff; 8, 12-15; Ps 105, 30f.   *m:* 11f: Wis 16, 2; Ps 78, 18.

since indeed they treated their guests
   with the more grievous* hatred.[n]
[14] For those others did not receive
   unfamiliar visitors,[o]
but these were enslaving beneficent
   guests.
[15] And not that only; but what punishment
   was to be theirs*
since they received strangers
   unwillingly!
[16] Yet these, after welcoming them with
   festivities,
oppressed with awful toils
those who now shared with them the
   same rights.[p]
[17] And they were struck with blindness,
as those others had been at the portals
   of the just—
When, surrounded by yawning darkness,
   each sought the entrance of his own
   gate.[q]
[18] For the elements, in variable harmony
   among themselves,

like strings of the harp, produce new
   melody,
while the flow of music steadily
   persists.
And this can be perceived exactly from a
   review of what took place.
[19] For land creatures were changed into
   water creatures,
and those that swam went over on to
   the land.
[20] Fire in water maintained its own
   strength,[r]
and water forgot its quenching nature;
[21] Flames, by contrast, neither consumed
   the flesh
of the perishable animals that went
   about in them,
nor melted the icelike, quick-melting
   kind of ambrosial food.
[22] For every way, O LORD! you magnified
   and glorified your people;
unfailing, you stood by them in every
   time and circumstance.[s]

19, 13: More grievous: than that of the people of Sodom; cf Gn 19.
19, 15: Theirs: the people of Sodom.

n: 2 Mc 7, 18. 32. o: 14f: Gn 15, 13; Ex 2, 22. p: Gn 45, 17-20; 47, 4ff; Ex 1, 11. q: Wis 17, 2; Gn 19, 11. r: 20f: Wis 16, 17ff.
22f. 27. s: Wis 18, 8; Lv 26, 44; Ps 126, 3.

See RG
198–200

The Book of Sirach (Ecclesiasticus)

The Book of Sirach derives its name from the author, Jesus, son of Eleazar, son of Sirach (Sir 50, 27). Its earliest title seems to have been "Wisdom of the Son of Sirach." The designation "Liber Ecclesiasticus," meaning "Church Book," appended to some Greek and Latin manuscripts was due to the extensive use which the church made of this book in presenting moral teaching to catechumens and to the faithful.

The author, a sage who lived in Jerusalem, was thoroughly imbued with love for the law, the priesthood, the temple, and divine worship. As a wise and experienced observer of life he addressed himself to his contemporaries with the motive of helping them to maintain religious faith and integrity through study of the holy books, and through tradition.

The book contains numerous maxims formu-
lated with care, grouped by affinity, and dealing with a variety of subjects such as the individual, the family, and the community in their relations with one another and with God. It treats of friendship, education, poverty and wealth, the law, religious worship, and many other matters which reflect the religious and social customs of the time.

Written in Hebrew between 200 and 175 B.C., the text was translated into Greek sometime after 132 B.C. by the author's grandson, who also wrote a Foreword which contains information about the book, the author, and the translator himself. Until the close of the nineteenth century Sirach was known only in translations, of which this Greek rendering was the most important. From it the Latin version was made. Between 1896 and 1900, again in 1931, and several times since 1956, manuscripts were discovered containing in all about two thirds of the Hebrew text, which agrees substantially with the Greek. One such text, from Masada, is pre-Christian in date.

Though not included in the Hebrew Bible after the first century A.D., nor accepted by Protestants, the Book of Sirach has always been recognized by the Catholic Church as divinely inspired and canonical. The Foreword, though not inspired, is placed in the Bible because of its antiquity and importance.

The contents of Sirach are of a discursive nature, not easily divided into separate parts. Chapters 1—43 deal largely with moral instruction; 44, 1—50, 24 contain a eulogy of the heroes of Israel and some of the patriarchs. There are two appendices in which the author expresses his gratitude to God, and appeals to the unlearned to acquire true wisdom.

The church uses the Book of Sirach extensively in her liturgy.

FOREWORD

Many important truths have been handed down to us through the law, the prophets, and the later authors; and for these the instruction and wisdom of Israel merit praise. Now, those who are familiar with these truths must not only understand them themselves but, as lovers of wisdom, be able, in speech and in writing, to help others less familiar. Such a one was my grandfather, Jesus, who, having devoted himself for a long time to the diligent study of the law, the prophets, and the rest of the books of our ancestors, and having developed a thorough familiarity with them, was moved to write something himself in the nature of instruction and wisdom, in order that those who love wisdom might, by acquainting themselves with what he too had written, make even

greater progress in living in conformity with the divine law.

You therefore are now invited to read it in a spirit of attentive good will, with indulgence for any apparent failure on our part, despite earnest efforts, in the interpretation of particular passages. For words spoken originally in Hebrew are not as effective when they are translated into another language. That is true not only of this book but of the law itself, the prophets and the rest of the book[1] which differ no little when they are read in the original.

I arrived in Egypt in the thirty-eighth year of the reign of King Euergetes,[2] and while there, I found a reproduction of our valuable teaching.[3] I therefore considered myself in duty bound to devote some diligence and industry to the translation of this book. Many sleepless hours of close application have I devoted in the interval to finishing the book for publication, for the benefit of those living abroad who wish to acquire wisdom and are disposed to live their lives according to the standards of the law.

———

The Wisdom of Sirach

CHAPTER 1

*Praise of Wisdom**

See RG 198-200

[1] All wisdom* comes from the LORD
and with him it remains forever.[a]
[2] The sand of the seashore, the drops of rain,
the days of eternity: who can number these?
[3] Heaven's height, earth's breadth,
the depths of the abyss: who can explore these?
[4] Before all things else wisdom was created;

---

[1] The law, the prophets, and the rest of the books: the Sacred Scriptures of the Old Testament written before the time of Sirach, according to the threefold division of the present Hebrew Bible.

[2] Thirty-eighth . . . Euregetes: 132 B.C. The reference is to Ptolemy VII, Physkon Euergetes II (170–163; 145, 117 B.C.).

[3] Reproduction . . . teaching: may refer to the Septuagint (Greek) translation of Hebrew wisdom writings predating Sirach.

1, 1-8: The Lord is the source and preserver of wisdom

(1); he created her from eternity, before all things else (4-7); all his works reflect wisdom (2f. 8).

1, 1: Wisdom: here the author speaks of true wisdom, namely God's external revelation of himself. Throughout the book he describes in great detail just what wisdom is; sometimes it is divine; sometimes it is a synonym for God's law; sometimes it is human. But the author makes clear that even human wisdom, properly understood, comes from God.

———

a: 1 Kgs 3, 9.

The Fear of the LORD

Taking his cue from Psalm 111, 10, "The fear of the LORD is the beginning of wisdom," which is similarly stated in Sirach 1, 12, Ben Sirach equates the possession of wisdom with the fear of the LORD. Since the pursuit of wisdom is a common goal found across cultures, the fear of the LORD may be a way of specifying what counts as Jewish wisdom. Because Ben Sirach does not entertain the possibility of an afterlife, the rewards and blessings of wisdom are manifest in one's earthly life; they include happiness, long life, and lack of want (1, 11–20). Such a perspective is comparable to that of Deuteronomy 6. The teachings of Ben Sirach deal mostly with practical wisdom that could just as easily apply to Gentiles as well as Jews. The reference to the commandments (1, 23), which fills out the meaning of the fear of the LORD, helps maintain a connection between Ben Sirach's general instructions for living and the explicitly Jewish teachings of the Torah (see also 2, 16; 38, 34b—39, 1). One who lacks wisdom inevitably disobeys God, which results in dishonor (1, 25–28). Ben Sirach's ethical teachings are based on a system of honor and shame (dishonor). Dishonor is not an internal feeling of guilt but, rather, a diminishment of one's esteem in the eyes of others. God's way of punishing anyone guilty of secret transgressions is to expose and thereby shame the culprit publicly.

and prudent understanding, from
  eternity.
⁵ To whom has wisdom's root been
  revealed?
  Who knows her subtleties?ᵇ
⁶ There is but one, wise and truly
  awe-inspiring,
  seated upon his throne:
⁷ It is the LORD; he created her,
  has seen her and taken note of her.ᶜ
⁸ He has poured her forth upon all his
  works,
  upon every living thing according to
  his bounty;
  he has lavished her upon his friends.
⁹ *Fear of the LORD* is glory and splendor,
  gladness and a festive crown.
¹⁰ Fear of the LORD warms the heart,
  giving gladness and joy and length of
  days.
¹¹ He who fears the LORD will have a happy
  end;
  even on the day of his death he will be
  blessed.
¹² The beginning of wisdom is fear of the
  LORD,

which is formed with the faithful in
  the womb.ᵈ
¹³ With devoted men was she created from
  of old,
  and with their children her beneficence
  abides.
¹⁴ Fullness of wisdom is fear of the
  LORD;
  she inebriates men with her fruits.ᵉ
¹⁵ Her entire house she fills with choice
  foods,
  her granaries with her harvest.
¹⁶ Wisdom's garland is fear of the LORD,
  with blossoms of peace and perfect
  health.ᶠ
¹⁷ Knowledge and full understanding she
  showers down;
  she heightens the glory of those who
  possess her.
¹⁸ The root of wisdom is fear of the LORD;
  her branches are length of days.

¹⁹ One cannot justify unjust anger;*
  anger plunges a man to his downfall.
²⁰ A patient man need stand firm but for a
  time,

1, 9-18: Here are described the spiritual and temporal blessings that come during the lifetime of him who fears the Lord, i.e. practices true religion.

1, 9: Fear of the LORD: see note on Ps 111, 10.

1, 19-22: The disciple of wisdom shuns unjust anger which brings downfall. By patience and self-control he pre-

serves calm, recovers contentment, and receives public praise. The sinner, on the contrary, despises the restraints which religion imposes.

b: Bar 3, 15.   c: Jb 28, 27.   d: Jb 28, 28; Ps 111, 10; Prv 1, 7; 9, 10.   e: Eccl 12, 13.   f: Sir 21, 11.

and then contentment comes back to
him.
21 For a while he holds back his words,
then the lips of many herald his
wisdom.
22 Among wisdom's treasures is the
paragon of prudence;
but fear of the LORD is an abomination
to the sinner.
23 If you desire wisdom, keep the
commandments,
and the LORD will bestow her upon you;
24 For fear of the LORD is wisdom and
culture;
loyal humility is his delight.
25 Be not faithless to the fear of the LORD,*
nor approach it with duplicity of
heart.
26 Play not the hypocrite before men;
over your lips keep watch.
27 Exalt not yourself lest you fall
and bring upon you dishonor;
28 For then the LORD will reveal your
secrets
and publicly cast you down,
29 Because you approached the fear of the
LORD
with your heart full of guile.

CHAPTER 2

Duties toward God

See RG
198-200

1 My son, when you come to serve the
LORD,*
prepare yourself for trials.g
2 Be sincere of heart and steadfast,
undisturbed in time of adversity.
3 Cling to him, forsake him not;
thus will your future be great.
4 Accept whatever befalls you,
in crushing misfortune be patient;
5 For in fire gold is tested,
and worthy men in the crucible of
humiliation.h

6 Trust God and he will help you;
make straight your ways and hope in
him.
7 You who fear the LORD, wait for his
mercy,
turn not away lest you fall.
8 You who fear the LORD, trust him,
and your reward will not be lost.
9 You who fear the LORD, hope for good
things,
for lasting joy and mercy.
10 Study the generations long past and
understand;
has anyone hoped in the LORD and
been disappointed?
Has anyone persevered in his fear and
been forsaken?
has anyone called upon him and been
rebuffed?i
11 Compassionate and merciful is the LORD;
he forgives sins, he saves in time of
trouble.

12 Woe to craven hearts and drooping
hands,*
to the sinner who treads a double path!
13 Woe to the faint of heart who trust not,
who therefore will have no shelter!
14 Woe to you who have lost hope!
what will you do at the visitation of
the LORD?
15 Those who fear the LORD disobey not his
words;
those who love him keep his ways.j
16 Those who fear the LORD seek to please
him,
those who love him are filled with his
law.
17 Those who fear the LORD prepare their
hearts
and humble themselves before him.
18 Let us fall into the hands of the LORD

1, 25-29: Infidelity to religion, or the use of it for any but
the single purpose of serving God, is hypocrisy and self-exal-
tation, deserving of public disgrace.

2, 1-11: Serving God is not without its trials (1); moreover, it must be done with sincerity, steadfastness and fidelity
(2f). Misfortune and humiliation merely purify man and
prove his worth (4f). Patience and unwavering trust in God
are always rewarded with the benefits of God's mercy and of
lasting joy (6-11).

2, 12-18: A warning to those who compromise their religion in time of affliction; they fail in courage and trust and
therefore have no security (12ff). But those who fear the Lord
through obedience, reverence, love and humility find his
mercy equal to his majesty (15-18).

---

g: 2 Tm 3, 12.   h: Prv 17, 3; Wis 3, 6; 1 Pt 1, 7.   i: Pss 31, 2;
145, 18f.   j: Jn 14, 23.

and not into the hands of men,
For equal to his majesty
   is the mercy that he shows.[k]

See RG
198–200

CHAPTER 3

Duties toward Parents*

[1] Children, pay heed to a father's right;
   do so that you may live.
[2] For the LORD sets a father in honor over
   his children;
   a mother's authority he confirms over
   her sons.
[3] He who honors his father atones for sins;
[4]   he stores up riches who reveres his
   mother.
[5] He who honors his father is gladdened by
   children,
   and when he prays he is heard.
[6] He who reveres his father will live a long
   life;
   he obeys the LORD who brings comfort
   to his mother.

[7] He who fears the LORD honors his
   father,
   and serves his parents as rulers.
[8] In word and deed honor your father
   that his blessing may come upon
   you;[l]
[9] For a father's blessing gives a family
   firm roots,
   but a mother's curse uproots the
   growing plant.[m]
[10] Glory not in your father's shame,
   for his shame is no glory to you!
[11] His father's honor is a man's glory;
   disgrace for her children, a mother's
   shame.
[12] My son, take care of your father when he
   is old;
   grieve him not as long as he lives.[n]

[13] Even if his mind fail, be considerate with
   him;
   revile him not in the fullness of your
   strength.
[14] For kindness to a father will not be
   forgotten,
   it will serve as a sin offering—it will
   take lasting root.
[15] In time of tribulation it will be recalled to
   your advantage,
   like warmth upon frost it will melt
   away your sins.
[16] A blasphemer is he who despises his
   father;
   accursed of his Creator, he who angers
   his mother.[o]

Humility*

[17] My son, conduct your affairs with
   humility,
   and you will be loved more than a
   giver of gifts.
[18] Humble yourself the more, the greater
   you are,
   and you will find favor with God.[p]
[19] For great is the power of God;
   by the humble he is glorified.*
[20] What is too sublime for you, seek not,
   into things beyond your strength
   search not.[q]
[21] What is committed to you, attend to;
   for what is hidden is not your concern.
[22] With what is too much for you meddle
   not,
   when shown things beyond human
   understanding.
[23] Their own opinion has misled many,
   and false reasoning unbalanced their
   judgment.
[24] Where the pupil of the eye is missing,
   there is no light,

3, 1-16: Besides the virtues that must characterize our conduct toward God, special duties toward our neighbor are enjoined, such as honor and respect toward parents, with corresponding blessings (1-9). Even to old and infirm parents this respect is due (10-13); through it, the sins of children are pardoned (14f). Failure to render respect is blasphemy and merits a curse from God (16). Cf Ex 20, 12; Eph 6, 2f.

3, 17-27: Humility gives a true estimate of self (17ff). Through it a man performs duty, avoids what is beyond his understanding and strength (20ff). Pride, however, begets

false greatness, misjudgment, stubbornness, sorrow, affliction and perdition (23-27).

3, 19: An alternate or additional line would read: "For though many have been great in the course of time, it is to the humble he reveals his secrets." Cf Mt 11, 25f; 1 Cor 1, 26-29.

k: Sir 18, 3. l: Ex 20, 12; Dt 5, 16; Mt 15, 4; Mk 7, 10; Eph 6, 2.
m: Gn 27, 29; 49, 2-27. n: Prv 23, 22. o: Prv 19, 26: 30, 11. 14.
17. p: Mt 23, 12. q: Ps 131, 1.

Care for Those in Need

Care for those who of necessity depend on the good will of others for their survival (4, 1–10) reflects a standard of ethical piety that is well-represented in the various parts of the biblical tradition: in legal texts (Dt 24, 17–22); in the prophets (Am 2, 6–7); and elsewhere in wisdom literature (Jb 29, 12–20; Prv 19, 17, though compare Prv 19, 6–7; Sir 10, 26–31).

and where there is no knowledge,
there is no wisdom.

25 A stubborn man will fare badly in the end,
and he who loves danger will perish in it.
26 A stubborn man will be burdened with sorrow;
a sinner will heap sin upon sin.
27 For the affliction of the proud man there is no cure;
he is the offshoot of an evil plant.*r*
28 The mind of a sage appreciates proverbs,
and an attentive ear is the wise man's joy.

Alms for the Poor*

29 Water quenches a flaming fire,
and alms atone for sins.*s*
30 He who does a kindness is remembered afterward;
when he falls, he finds a support.

See RG
198-200

CHAPTER 4

1 My son, rob not the poor man of his livelihood:
force not the eyes of the needy* to turn away.*t*
2 A hungry man grieve not,
a needy man anger not;
3 Do not exasperate the downtrodden;
delay not to give to the needy.
4 A beggar in distress do not reject;
avert not your face from the poor.
5 From the needy turn not your eyes,

give no man reason to curse you;
6 For if in the bitterness of his soul he curse you,
his Creator will hear his prayer.
7 Endear yourself to the assembly;
before a ruler bow your head.
8 Give a hearing to the poor man,
and return his greeting with courtesy;
9 Deliver the oppressed from the hand of the oppressor;
let not justice be repugnant to you.
10 To the fatherless be as a father,
and help their mother as a husband would;
Thus will you be like a son to the Most High,
and he will be more tender to you than a mother.

The Rewards of Wisdom*

11 Wisdom instructs her children
and admonishes those who seek her.
12 He who loves her loves life;
those who seek her out win her favor.
13 He who holds her fast inherits glory;
wherever he dwells, the LORD bestows blessings.
14 Those who serve her serve the Holy One;
those who love her the LORD loves.*u*
15 He who obeys her judges nations;
he who hearkens to her dwells in her inmost chambers.
16 If one trusts her, he will possess her;
his descendants too will inherit her.
17 She walks with him as a stranger,
and at first she puts him to the test;

3, 29—4, 10: Mercy and kindness toward those in misfortune atone for sin and endear a man to God and to his fellow men.

4, 1: Eyes of the needy: when they look for help; cf Sir 18, 17.

4, 11-19: The Hebrew text presents wisdom speaking in the first person, as in ch 24. The precious fruits of wisdom: life, favor, glory, blessings, God's love, are intended to arouse

desire for her (11-14). Her disciples are like priests (14) and judges (15), even partners who possess her for themselves and their descendants (16). They enjoy happiness and penetrate her profound secrets after surviving her tests (17f). Those who fail her are abandoned to destruction (19).

r: Dt 32, 32; Wis 12, 10. *s:* Dn 4, 27. *t:* Tb 4, 7-11. *u:* Wis 7, 28.

Fear and dread she brings upon him
and tries him with her discipline;
With her precepts she puts him to the
proof,
until his heart is fully with her.
¹⁸ Then she comes back to bring him
happiness
and reveal her secrets to him.
¹⁹ But if he fails her, she will abandon him
and deliver him into the hands of
despoilers.

Sincerity and Justice*

²⁰ Use your time well; guard yourself from
evil,
and bring upon yourself no shame.
²¹ There is a sense of shame laden with
guilt,
and a shame that merits honor and
respect.
²² Show no favoritism to your own
discredit;
let no one intimidate you to your own
downfall.
²³ Refrain not from speaking at the proper
time,
and hide not away your wisdom;
²⁴ For it is through speech that wisdom
becomes known,
and knowledge through the tongue's
rejoinder.
²⁵ Never gainsay the truth,
and struggle not against the rushing
stream.
²⁶ Be not ashamed to acknowledge your
guilt,
but of your ignorance rather be
ashamed.
²⁷ Do not abase yourself before an impious
man,
nor refuse to do so before rulers.
²⁸ Even to the death fight for truth,

and the LORD your God will battle for
you.
²⁹ Be not surly in your speech,
nor lazy and slack in your deeds.
³⁰ Be not a lion at home,
nor sly and suspicious at work.
³¹ Let not your hand be open to receive
and clenched when it is time to give.

CHAPTER 5

See RG 198–200

Against Presumption*

¹ Rely not on your wealth;
say not: "I have the power."ᵛ
² Rely not on your strength
in following the desires of your heart.
³ Say not: "Who can prevail against me?"
for the LORD will exact the
punishment.
⁴ Say not: "I have sinned, yet what has
befallen me?"
for the LORD bides his time.
⁵ Of forgiveness be not overconfident,
adding sin upon sin.
⁶ Say not: "Great is his mercy;
my many sins he will forgive."
⁷ For mercy and anger alike are with him;
upon the wicked alights his wrath.
⁸ Delay not your conversion to the LORD,
put it not off from day to day;
⁹ For suddenly his wrath flames forth;
at the time of vengeance, you will be
destroyed.
¹⁰ Rely not upon deceitful wealth,
for it will be no help on the day of
wrath.ʷ

Sincerity in Speech

¹¹ Winnow not in every wind,
and start not off in every direction.*
¹² Be consistent in your thoughts;
steadfast be your words.*
¹³ Be swift to hear,

4, 20-31: Besides the interior trials of discipline and precept, the disciple of wisdom is warned against external dangers to his sincerity and justice, namely evil, human respect (20f), compromise of liberty in speech and action (22-25), false shame, and ignorance (26). He must fight for the truth (28), and avoid cynicism and laziness (29), and inconsistency in his conduct (30).

5, 1-10: The vices of the rich are pride and independence (1f), presumption (3), false security (4-7), and impenitence (8), which cannot escape the divine wrath (9f). Cf Prv 18, 23;

19, 1; 28, 6.
5, 11: A proverbial expression condemning inconstancy and advocating sincerity and honesty.
5, 12—6, 1: Proper use of the tongue requires constancy in speech (5, 12), prudence (13f), reserve (15), charity (6, 1), as well as the avoidance of detraction, calumny (16) and double talk, which bring shame and disgrace (5, 17; 6, 1).

v: Lk 12, 19.   *w:* Prv 10, 2; 11, 4. 28.

The Dangers of Money, Talk, and Passion

A twenty-two-line poem (5, 1—6, 4) provides an overview of three topics of central importance throughout the text of Sirach: wealth, speech, and desire. All three have the potential to bring ruin. Wealth should not be gained by thievery (5, 8.14b). Speech must not be double-tongued (5, 17), meaning it should never be deceitful or self-serving. Desire must be subordinate to wisdom.

but slow to answer.[x]

14 If you have the knowledge, answer your
neighbor;
if not, put your hand over your mouth.
15 Honor and dishonor through talking!
A man's tongue can be his downfall.
16 Be not called a detractor;
use not your tongue for calumny;
17 For shame has been created for the thief,
and the reproach of his neighbor for
the double-tongued.

CHAPTER 6

See RG
198–200
1 Say nothing harmful, small or great;
be not a foe instead of a friend;
A bad name and disgrace will you
acquire:
"That for the evil man with double
tongue!"*

2 Fall not into the grip of desire,[y]
lest, like fire, it consume your strength;
3 Your leaves it will eat, your fruits destroy,
and you will be left a dry tree,
4 For contumacious desire destroys its
owner
and makes him the sport of his enemies.

True Friendship*

5 A kind mouth multiplies friends,
and gracious lips prompt friendly
greetings.
6 Let your acquaintances be many,
but one in a thousand your confidant.
7 When you gain a friend, first test him,[z]

and be not too ready to trust him.
8 For one sort of friend is a friend when it
suits him,
but he will not be with you in time of
distress.
9 Another is a friend who becomes an
enemy,
and tells of the quarrel to your shame.
10 Another is a friend, a boon companion,
who will not be with you when sorrow
comes.
11 When things go well, he is your other self,
and lords it over your servants;
12 But if you are brought low, he turns
against you
and avoids meeting you.
13 Keep away from your enemies;
be on your guard with your friends.
14 A faithful friend is a sturdy shelter;
he who finds one finds a treasure.
15 A faithful friend is beyond price,
no sum can balance his worth.
16 A faithful friend is a life-saving remedy,
such as he who fears God finds;
17 For he who fears God behaves
accordingly,
and his friend will be like himself.

Blessings of Wisdom*

18 My son, from your youth embrace
discipline;
thus will you find wisdom with
graying hair.
19 As though plowing and sowing, draw
close to her;

6, 1: "That . . . double tongue!": people will say this against the man whose deceitful tongue has brought him to disgrace.

6, 5-17: True friends are discerned not by prosperity (11) but through the trials of adversity: distress, quarrels (9), sorrow (10) and misfortune (12). Such friends are rare and their value is beyond estimation, a gift from God (14-17).

6, 18-37: The various figures in each of the three strophes urge the search for wisdom through patience (19-23), docility (32-37), and perseverance in trials (25ff), promising rich rewards (28-31). Cf 4, 11-19.

x: Prv 29, 20; Jas 1, 19.   y: 2-3: Sir 9, 8; 23, 17; Jb 31, 12; Is 56, 3.   z: 7ff: Sir 12, 8f; 37, 1-5; Prv 19, 4.

then await her bountiful crops.
²⁰ For in cultivating her you will labor but
little,
and soon you will eat of her fruits.
²¹ How irksome she is to the unruly!
The fool cannot abide her.
²² She will be like a burdensome stone to
test him,
and he will not delay in casting her
aside.
²³ For discipline* is like her name,
she is not accessible to many.

²⁴ Listen, my son, and heed my advice;
refuse not my counsel.
²⁵ Put your feet into her fetters,
and your neck under her yoke.
²⁶ Stoop your shoulders and carry her
and be not irked at her bonds.
²⁷ With all your soul draw close to her;
with all your strength keep her ways.
²⁸ Search her out, discover her; seek her
and you will find her.
Then when you have her, do not let her
go;
²⁹ Thus will you afterward find rest in her,
and she will become your joy.
³⁰ Her fetters will be your throne of
majesty;
her bonds, your purple cord.
³¹ You will wear her as your robe of glory,ᵃ
bear her as your splendid crown.*

³² My son, if you wish, you can be taught;
if you apply yourself, you will be
shrewd.
³³ If you are willing to listen, you will
learn;
if you give heed, you will be wise.
³⁴ Frequent the company of the elders;
whoever is wise, stay close to him.
³⁵ Be eager to hear every godly discourse;
let no wise saying escape you.ᵇ

³⁶ If you see a man of prudence, seek him
out;
let your feet wear away his doorstep!
³⁷ Reflect on the precepts of the LORD,
let his commandments be your
constant meditation;
Then he will enlighten your mind,
and the wisdom you desire he will
grant.ᶜ

CHAPTER 7

Conduct in Public Life*

See RG 198–200

¹ Do no evil, and evil will not overtake you;
² avoid wickedness, and it will turn
aside from you.
³ Sow not in the furrows of injustice,
lest you harvest it sevenfold.ᵈ
⁴ Seek not from the LORD authority,
nor from the king a place of honor.
⁵ Parade not your justice before the LORD,
and before the king flaunt not your
wisdom.ᵉ
⁶ Seek not to become a judge
if you have not strength to root out
crime,
Or you will show favor to the ruler
and mar your integrity.
⁷ Be guilty of no evil before the city's
populace,
nor disgrace yourself before the
assembly.
⁸ Do not plot to repeat a sin;
not even for one will you go
unpunished.
⁹ Say not: "He will appreciate my many
gifts;
the Most High will accept my
offerings."ᶠ
¹⁰ Be not impatient in prayers,
and neglect not the giving of alms.
¹¹ Laugh not at an embittered man;
be mindful of him who exalts and
humbles.*

6, 23: Discipline (musar, in the sense of wisdom) is a perfect homonym for musar, "removed, withdrawn"; thus the path of discipline is inaccessible to many.

6, 31: Some forms of the text speak also of the "yoke" of wisdom under the imagery of golden ornaments.

7, 1-17: In the conduct of social relations wisdom forbids evil and injustice (1ff), pride (5. 15ff), ambition and human respect (4, 6), public disorder (7), presumption and impa-

tience toward God (9f), ridicule (11), mischief and deceit toward one's neighbor (8, 12f).

7, 11: Him who exalts and humbles: God; cf 1 Sm 2, 7; Ps 75, 8; Lk 1, 52.

a: Is 62, 3.   b: Sir 8, 9.   c: Ps 1, 2.   d: Prv 22, 8.   e: Jb 9, 2; Ps 143, 2; Prv 25, 6; 1 Cor 4, 4.   f: Sir 34, 18; 35, 12.

¹² Plot no mischief against your brother,
  nor against your friend and
    companion.
¹³ Delight not in telling lie after lie,
  for it never results in good.
¹⁴ Thrust not yourself into the deliberations
    of princes,ᵍ
  and repeat not the words of your prayer.*
¹⁵ Hate not laborious tasks,
  nor farming, which was ordained by
    the Most High.ʰ
¹⁶ Do not esteem yourself better than your
    fellows;
  remember, his wrath will not delay.
¹⁷ More and more, humble your pride;
  what awaits man is worms.ⁱ

Duties of Family Life, Religion and Charity*

¹⁸ Barter not a friend for money,
  nor a dear brother for the gold of Ophir.*
¹⁹ Dismiss not a sensible wife;
  a gracious wife is more precious than
    corals.
²⁰ Mistreat not a servant who faithfully
    serves,
  nor a laborer who devotes himself to
    his task.ʲ
²¹ Let a wise servant be dear to you as your
    own self;
  refuse him not his freedom.*
²² If you have livestock, look after them;
  if they are dependable, keep them.
²³ If you have sons, chastise them;
  bend their necks* from childhood.ᵏ
²⁴ If you have daughters, keep them chaste,
  and be not indulgent to them.ˡ
²⁵ Giving your daughter in marriage ends a
    great task;

but give her to a worthy man.ᵐ
²⁶ If you have a wife, let her not seem
    odious to you;
  but where there is ill-feeling, trust her
    not.
²⁷ With your whole heart honor your father;
  your mother's birthpangs forget not.ⁿ
²⁸ Remember, of these parents you were
    born;
  what can you give them for all they
    gave you?
²⁹ With all your soul, fear God,
  revere his priests.
³⁰ With all your strength, love your Creator,
  forsake not his ministers.
³¹ Honor God and respect the priest;
  give him his portion as you have been
    commanded:ᵒ
First fruits and contributions,
  due sacrifices and holy offerings.*
³² To the poor man also extend your hand,
  that your blessing may be complete;
³³ Be generous to all the living,
  and withhold not your kindness from
    the dead.*
³⁴ Avoid not those who weep,
  but mourn with those who mourn;ᵖ
³⁵ Neglect not to visit the sick—
  for these things you will be loved.�q
³⁶ In whatever you do, remember your last
    days,
  and you will never sin.

CHAPTER 8

See RG
198–200

Prudence in Dealing
with Other Men*

¹ Contend not with an influential man,
  lest you fall into his power.

7, 14: Repeat not . . . prayer: brevity of speech in dealings with superiors and more especially with God is a sign of reverence and respect; cf Eccl 5, 1; Mt 6, 7.

7, 18-36: The duties of respect and appreciation, justice and kindness should characterize relations toward members of the household (18-28), and also toward God and his priests (29ff), the poor and afflicted, the living and the dead (32-36).

7, 18: Ophir was the port, at present unidentified, to which the ships of Solomon sailed and from which they brought back gold and silver; cf note on Ps 45, 10.

7, 21: After six years of service a Hebrew slave was entitled to freedom; cf Ex 21, 2; Dt 15, 12-15.

7, 23: Bend their necks: keep them from rebellious pride; so with the Greek. Cf Sir 30, 12. The present Hebrew text, which is probably not original here, reads: "Choose wives for

them while they are young."

7, 31: First fruits . . . holy offerings: cf Ex 29, 27; Lv 7, 31-34; Nm 18, 8-20; Dt 18, 1-5.

7, 33: This seems to refer to the observances ordained toward the dead, that is, proper mourning and burial. Cf 2 Sm 21, 12ff; Tb 1, 20; 12, 12. When this verse is read in the light of later teaching, prayers for the souls of the deceased would also be recommended. Cf 2 Mc 12, 43ff.

8, 1-19: A prudent man will be circumspect, avoiding conflict with the powerful, the rich and insolent, the impious, the

g: Sir 32, 7ff; Mt 6, 7.   h: Gn 2, 15; 3, 17.   i: Is 66, 24.   j: Lv 19, 13; Dt 24, 14f; Jas 5, 4.   k: Sir 30, 8-13; Prv 13, 24.   l: Sir 42, 9ff.   m: 1 Cor 7, 36ff.   n: Ex 20, 12.   o: Lv 7, 31; Nm 18, 18.   p: Rom 12, 15.   q: Mt 25, 36.

² Quarrel not with a rich man,
　　lest he pay out the price of your
　　　downfall;
　　For gold has dazzled many,
　　　and perverts the character of
　　　　princes.ʳ
³ Dispute not with a man of railing speech,
　　heap no wood upon his fire.ˢ
⁴ Be not too familiar with an unruly man,
　　lest he speak ill of your forebears.
⁵ Shame not a repentant sinner;ᵗ
　　remember, we all are guilty.*
⁶ Insult no man when he is old,
　　for some of us, too, will grow old.
⁷ Rejoice not when a man dies;
　　remember, we are all to die.
⁸ Spurn not the discourse of the wise,ᵘ
　　but acquaint yourself with their
　　　proverbs;
　　From them you will acquire the training
　　　to serve in the presence of princes.
⁹ Reject not the tradition of old men
　　which they have learned from their
　　　fathers;
　　From it you will obtain the knowledge
　　　how to answer in time of need.
¹⁰ Kindle not the coals of a sinner,
　　lest you be consumed in his flaming
　　　fire.
¹¹ Let not the impious man intimidate you;
　　it will set him in ambush against you.*
¹² Lend not to one more powerful than
　　　yourself;
　　and whatever you lend, count it as lost.ᵛ
¹³ Go not surety beyond your means;
　　think any pledge a debt you must pay.
¹⁴ Contend not at law with a judge,
　　for he will settle it according to his
　　　whim.
¹⁵ Travel not with a ruthless man,
　　lest he weigh you down with calamity;

For he will go his own way straight,
　　and through his folly you will perish
　　　with him.
¹⁶ Provoke no quarrel with a quick-
　　　tempered man
　　nor ride with him through the desert;
　　For bloodshed is nothing to him;
　　　when there is no one to help you, he
　　　　will destroy you.
¹⁷ Take no counsel with a fool,
　　for he can keep nothing to himself.
¹⁸ Before a stranger do nothing that should
　　　be kept secret,
　　for you know not what it will
　　　engender.ʷ
¹⁹ Open your heart to no man,
　　and banish not your happiness.

CHAPTER 9

Advice concerning Women[*]
See RG 198–200

¹ Be not jealous of the wife of your
　　　bosom,
　　lest you teach her to do evil against
　　　you.*
² Give no woman power over you
　　to trample upon your dignity.ˣ
³ Be not intimate with a strange woman,
　　lest you fall into her snares.
⁴ With a singing girl be not familiar,
　　lest you be caught in her wiles.
⁵ Entertain no thoughts against a virgin,
　　lest you be enmeshed in damages for
　　　her.*
⁶ Give not yourself to harlots,
　　lest you surrender your inheritance.ʸ
⁷ Gaze not about the lanes of the city
　　and wander not through its squares;
⁸ Avert your eyes from a comely woman;
　　gaze not upon the beauty of another's
　　　wife—
　　Through woman's beauty many perish,

---

irascible, and with judges (1ff. 10ff. 14. 16). He will seek friendship not with the undisciplined (4. 12f) and the ruthless (15), nor with fools and strangers (17ff), but with the wise and the ancients of the people (8f).

8, 5: We all are guilty: cf 1 Kgs 8, 46; 2 Chr 6, 36; Eccl 7, 20; Rom 3, 9f; 1 Jn 1, 8.

8, 11: To give in to the wicked in one instance becomes an occasion of sin for the future.

9, 1-9: Prudence and reserve in dealing with women are the best defense of morality. To preserve the liberty and dignity of his person and the integrity of his possessions, a man

must avoid jealousy toward his own wife and familiarity toward all other women. Cf Sir 25, 12—26, 18.

9, 1: Unjust suspicions often engender hatred between husband and wife and may prompt a wife to commit those faults of which heretofore she had been innocent.

9, 5: Cf Ex 22, 15f; Dt 22, 28f; Jb 31, 1.

---

r: Sir 31, 6; Dt 16, 19.　s: Prv 26, 20.　t: 1 Kgs 8, 46; 1 Jn 1, 8.
u: 8f; Sir 6, 35.　v: Sir 29, 4-7; Prv 17, 18.　w: Prv 25, 9f.
x: Sir 25, 21.　y: Prv 5, 3-11; 6, 24; 29, 3.

for lust for it burns like fire.[z]

[9] With a married woman dine not,
  recline not at table to drink by her side,
Lest your heart be drawn to her
  and you go down in blood to the grave.

Choice of Friends*

[10] Discard not an old friend,
  for the new one cannot equal him.
A new friend is like new wine
  which you drink with pleasure only
  when it has aged.
[11] Envy not a sinner's fame,
  for you know not what disaster awaits
  him.
[12] Rejoice not at a proud man's
  success;
  remember he will not reach death
  unpunished.
[13] Keep far from the man who has power to
  kill,
  and you will not be filled with the
  dread of death.
But if you approach him, offend him not,
  lest he take away your life;
Know that you are stepping among
  snares
  and walking over a net.
[14] As best you can, take your neighbors'
  measure,
  and associate with the wise.
[15] With the learned be intimate;
  let all your conversation be about the
  law of the LORD.
[16] Have just men for your table
  companions;
  in the fear of God be your glory.

Concerning Rulers*

[17] Skilled artisans are esteemed for their
  deftness;

but the ruler of his people is the skilled
  sage.
[18] Feared in the city is the man of railing
  speech,
  and he who talks rashly is hated.

CHAPTER 10

See RG 198–200

[1] A wise magistrate lends stability to
  his people,
  and the government of a prudent man
  is well ordered.[a]
[2] As the people's judge, so are his
  ministers;[b]
  as the head of a city, its inhabitants.
[3] A wanton king destroys his people,
  but a city grows through the wisdom
  of its princes.[c]
[4] Sovereignty over the earth is in the hand
  of God,
  who raises up on it the man of the
  hour;
[5] Sovereignty over every man is in the
  hand of God,
  who imparts his majesty to the ruler.

The Sin of Pride*

[6] No matter the wrong, do no violence to
  your neighbor,
  and do not walk the path of
  arrogance.[d]
[7] Odious to the LORD and to men is
  arrogance,
  and the sin of oppression they both
  hate.
[8] Dominion is transferred from one people
  to another
  because of the violence of the
  arrogant.
[9] Why are dust and ashes proud?*
  even during life man's body decays;
[10] A slight illness—the doctor jests,

9, 10-16: In social relations, adherence to the law of the Lord should serve as a guide (15). Associate with true friends (10), with the just and the learned (14ff); avoid the company of the mighty and of sinners doomed to punishment (11ff). Cf Sir 8, 1-19.

9, 17—10, 5: Public office as conducted justly, or unjustly benefits or destroys the people, according to the axiom, "as the prince, so the people." Cf 24, 2. God, however, has sovereignty over both.

10, 6-18: Glory displayed through arrogance and pride is false and displeasing to God and men, because founded on

dust and ashes (6-11). It is the denial of the glory due to God, and therefore the source of all sin (12f). Even the memory of the proud is destroyed and God transfers their power to the lowly (14-18).

10, 9f: The text is uncertain. Its general implication is that man deteriorates physically even while alive: a slight illness today may be followed by death tomorrow. The uncertainty of life leaves no room for pride.

---

z: Sir 25, 20; 41, 21. a: Wis 6, 24. b: 2f: Prv 29, 12. c: Prv 29, 4. 8. d: Lv 19, 18.

a king today—tomorrow he is dead.

¹¹ When a man dies, he inherits corruption;
worms and gnats and maggots.*

¹² The beginning of pride is man's
stubbornness
in withdrawing his heart from his
Maker;

¹³ For pride is the reservoir of sin,
a source which runs over with vice;
Because of it God sends unheard-of
afflictions
and brings men to utter ruin.*

¹⁴ The thrones of the arrogant God
overturns
and establishes the lowly in their stead.

¹⁵ The roots of the proud God plucks up,
to plant the humble in their place:

¹⁶ He breaks down their stem to the level of
the ground,
then digs their roots from the earth.

¹⁷ The traces of the proud God sweeps
away
and effaces the memory of them from
the earth.

¹⁸ Insolence is not allotted to a man,
nor stubborn anger to one born of
woman.

True Glory*

¹⁹ Whose offspring can be in honor? Those
of men.
Which offspring are in honor? Those
who fear God.
Whose offspring can be in disgrace?
Those of men.
Which offspring are in disgrace?
Those who transgress the
commandments.

²⁰ Among brethren their leader is in honor;
he who fears God is in honor among
his people.

²¹ Be it tenant or wayfarer, alien or pauper,
his glory is the fear of the LORD.

²² It is not just to despise a man who is wise
but poor,
nor proper to honor any sinner.*

²³ The prince, the ruler, the judge are in
honor;
but none is greater than he who fears
God.

²⁴ When free men serve a prudent slave,
the wise man does not complain.*

²⁵ Flaunt not your wisdom in managing
your affairs,
and boast not in your time of need.

²⁶ Better the worker who has plenty of
everything
than the boaster who is without bread.*

²⁷ My son, with humility have self-esteem;
prize yourself as you deserve.

²⁸ Who will acquit him who condemns
himself?
who will honor him who discredits
himself?

²⁹ The poor man is honored for his wisdom
as the rich man is honored for his
wealth;

³⁰ Honored in poverty, how much more so
in wealth!
Dishonored in wealth, in poverty how
much the more!

CHAPTER 11

See RG
198-200

¹ The poor man's wisdom lifts his
head high
and sets him among princes.

² Praise not a man for his looks;
despise not a man for his appearance.

³ Least is the bee among winged things,
but she reaps the choicest of all
harvests.

⁴ Mock not the worn cloak
and jibe at no man's bitter day:
For strange are the works of the LORD,
hidden from men his deeds.

⁵ The oppressed often rise to a throne,
and some that none would consider
wear a crown.*

⁶ The exalted often fall into utter
disgrace;
the honored are given into enemy
hands.

10, 19—11, 6: Regardless of social barriers, genuine honor among men comes from fear of the Lord and a true estimate
of self. The Lord exalts the lowly and oppressed; transgressors of the commandments merit dishonor and disgrace.
11, 5: Cf 1 Sm 2, 8; Ps 105, 17-22; Lk 1, 52.

e: Jb 17, 14.   *f:* Prv 18, 12.   *g:* Jas 2, 1-4.   *h:* Prv 17, 2.   *i:* Prv 12, 9.

Who Is Deserving of Honor?

In contrast to the previous section, which described the proud and powerful who seemingly possess honor but ultimately lack it, Sirach 10, 19—11, 6 addresses those who genuinely deserve honor. The opening questions emphasize that all people are worthy of honor if they fear the Lord. The prince, the ruler and the judge (10, 23) should be honored not because of their professional station, but because they fear the Lord. Ben Sirach points out that the same man will be more honored if he is rich than if he is poor. Such a sentiment seems to contrast with other of Ben Sirach's teachings about the insignificance of wealth (11, 14–28), but it may simply reflect reality and his pragmatic approach to life (13, 21–24).

Moderation*

7 Before investigating, find no fault;
  examine first, then criticize.
8 Before hearing, answer not,
  and interrupt no one in the middle of
    his speech.*j*
9 Dispute not about what is not your
    concern;
  in the strife of the arrogant take no
    part.
10 My son, why increase your cares,
  since he who is avid for wealth will
    not be blameless?
  Even if you run after it, you will never
    overtake it;
  however you seek it, you will not find
    it.
11 One may toil and struggle and drive,
  and fall short all the more.*k*
12 Another goes his way a weakling and a
    failure,
  with little strength and great misery—
  Yet the eyes of the Lord look favorably
    upon him;
  he raises him free of the vile dust,
13 Lifts up his head and exalts him
  to the amazement of the many.
14 Good and evil, life and death,*l*
  poverty and riches, are from the
    Lord.*
15 Wisdom and understanding and
    knowledge of affairs,*

love and virtuous paths are from the
  Lord,
16 Error and darkness were formed with
    sinners from their birth,
  and evil grows old with evildoers.
17 The Lord's gift remains with the just;
  his favor brings continued success.
18 A man may become rich through a
    miser's life,
  and this is his allotted reward:
19 When he says: "I have found rest,*m*
  now I will feast on my possessions,"
  He does not know how long it will be
  till he dies and leaves them to others.*
20 My son, hold fast to your duty, busy
    yourself with it,
  grow old while doing your task.
21 Admire not how sinners live,
  but trust in the Lord and wait for his
    light;
  For it is easy with the Lord
  suddenly, in an instant, to make a poor
    man rich.
22 God's blessing is the lot of the just man,
  and in due time his hopes bear fruit.
23 Say not: "What do I need?
  What further pleasure can be mine?"
24 Say not: "I am independent.
  What harm can come to me now?"
25 The day of prosperity makes one forget
    adversity;

11, 7-25: Discretion regulates a man's conduct toward others and their affairs (7ff); as regards his own interests, a man should avoid solicitude for the passing external benefits of life and property (10-14. 18f. 21. 23ff), and cultivate the lasting inward gifts of wisdom and virtue (15. 17. 20. 22).

11, 14: Divine Providence ultimately governs the lives of men. Evil: misfortune and calamity sent by God either in punishment or as an incentive to repentance or to greater virtue.

11, 15f: Some ancient witnesses omit these two verses.

11, 19: Cf the parable of the rich man, Lk 12, 16-21.

j: Prv 18, 13. *k:* Ps 127, 2; Eccl 4, 8. *l:* Jb 1, 21; 2, 10. *m:* Eccl 4, 8; 6, 2; Lk 12, 19.

the day of adversity makes one forget
prosperity.[n]

26 For it is easy with the LORD on the day of
death*

to repay man according to his deeds.

27 A moment's affliction brings
forgetfulness of past delights;

when a man dies, his life is revealed.

28 Call no man happy before his death,

for by how he ends, a man is known.

Care in Choosing Friends

29 Bring not every man into your house,

for many are the snares of the crafty
one;

30 Though he seem like a bird confined in a
cage,

yet like a spy he will pick out the weak
spots.

31 The talebearer turns good into evil;

with a spark he sets many coals afire.

32 The evil man lies in wait for blood,

and plots against your choicest
possessions.

33 Avoid a wicked man, for he breeds only
evil,

lest you incur a lasting stain.

34 Lodge a stranger with you, and he will
subvert your course,

and make a stranger of you to your
own household.

CHAPTER 12

**See RG
198–200** 1If you do good, know for whom you
are doing it,*

and your kindness will have its effect.

2 Do good to the just man and reward will
be yours,

if not from him, from the LORD.

3 No good comes to him who gives
comfort to the wicked,*

nor is it an act of mercy that he does.

4 Give to the good man, refuse the sinner;[o]

refresh the downtrodden, give nothing
to the proud man.

5 No arms for combat should you give
him,

lest he use them against yourself;

6 With twofold evil you will meet

for every good deed you do for him.

7 The Most High himself hates sinners,

and upon the wicked he takes
vengeance.

8 In our prosperity we cannot know our
friends;*

in adversity an enemy will not remain
concealed.[p]

9 When a man is successful even his
enemy is friendly;

in adversity even his friend
disappears.[q]

10 Never trust your enemy,

for his wickedness is like corrosion in
bronze.

11 Even though he acts humbly and
peaceably toward you,

take care to be on your guard against
him.

Rub him as one polishes a brazen
mirror,*

and you will find that there is still
corrosion.

12 Let him not stand near you,

lest he oust you and take your place.

Let him not sit at your right hand,

lest he then demand your seat,

And in the end you appreciate my advice,

when you groan with regret, as I
warned you.

13 Who pities a snake charmer when he is
bitten,

or anyone who goes near a wild beast?

14 So is it with the companion of the proud
man,

who is involved in his sins:

11, 26ff: Sirach, writing before Christian revelation, did
not go beyond the hour of death to find full divine retribution.

12, 1-7: The limitations to the practice of charity here reflected were removed by Christ, who requires that good be
done even to enemies and to those who hate, persecute and
calumniate us (Mt 5, 43-48).

12, 3ff: The author advises against generosity to those

who would abuse it.

12, 8-18: Through adversity friends are distinguished
from enemies; to trust the latter or permit them intimacy
is to invite disaster. Cf note on Sir 6, 5-17.

12, 11: Brazen mirror: see note on Ex 38, 8.

n: Sir 18, 25. *o:* 4f: Gal 6, 10. *p:* Prv 17, 17. *q:* Prv 19, 4-7.

¹⁵ While you stand firm, he makes no bold
move;
but if you slip, he cannot hold back.
¹⁶ With his lips an enemy speaks sweetly,
but in his heart he schemes to plunge
you into the abyss.
Though your enemy has tears in his eyes,
if given the chance, he will never have
enough of your blood.
¹⁷ If evil comes upon you, you will find him
at hand;
feigning to help, he will trip you up,
¹⁸ Then he will nod his head and clap his
hands
and hiss repeatedly, and show his true
face.

CHAPTER 13

See RG
198–200 *Caution Regarding Associates**
¹ He who touches pitch blackens his hand;
he who associates with an impious
man learns his ways.
² Bear no burden too heavy for you;
go with no one greater or wealthier
than yourself.
How can the earthen pot go with the
metal cauldron?
When they knock together, the pot will
be smashed:
³ The rich man does wrong and boasts of it,
the poor man is wronged and begs
forgiveness.
⁴ As long as the rich man can use you he
will enslave you,
but when you are exhausted, he will
abandon you.
⁵ As long as you have anything he will
speak fair words to you,
and with smiles he will win your
confidence;
⁶ When he needs something from you he
will cajole you,
then without regret he will impoverish
you.
⁷ While it serves his purpose he will
beguile you,

then twice or three times he will terrify
you;
When later he sees you he will pass you by,
and shake his head over you.
⁸ Guard against being presumptuous;
be not as those who lack sense.
⁹ When invited by a man of influence,
keep your distance;
then he will urge you all the more.
¹⁰ Be not bold with him lest you be rebuffed,
but keep not too far away lest you be
forgotten.
¹¹ Engage not freely in discussion with him,
trust not his many words;
For by prolonged talk he will test you,
and though smiling he will probe you.
¹² Mercilessly he will make of you a
laughingstock,
and will not refrain from injury or
chains.
¹³ Be on your guard and take care
never to accompany men of violence.

¹⁴ Every living thing loves its own kind,
every man a man like himself.
¹⁵ Every being is drawn to its own kind;
with his own kind every man
associates.
¹⁶ Is a wolf ever allied with a lamb?
So it is with the sinner and the just.ʳ
¹⁷ Can there be peace between the hyena
and the dog?
Or between the rich and the poor can
there be peace?*
¹⁸ Lion's prey are the wild asses of the
desert;
so too the poor are feeding grounds for
the rich.
¹⁹ A proud man abhors lowliness;
so does the rich man abhor the poor.
²⁰ When a rich man stumbles he is
supported by a friend;
when a poor man trips he is pushed
down by a friend.
²¹ Many are the supporters for a rich man
when he speaks;

13, 1—14, 2: By means of various figures Sirach indicates
the practical impossibility of genuine and sincere companionship between the poor and the proud rich. He lays down
the principle of associating with equals (13, 15).

13, 17: The hostility between the dogs which guard the

flocks at night and the rapacious hyenas is proverbial in
Palestine.

r: 2 Cor 6, 14ff.

though what he says is odious, it wins
approval.
When a poor man speaks they make
sport of him;
he speaks wisely and no attention is
paid him.
22 A rich man speaks and all are silent,
his wisdom they extol to the clouds.
A poor man speaks and they say: "Who
is that?"
If he slips they cast him down.
23 Wealth is good when there is no sin;
but poverty is evil by the standards of
the proud.
24 The heart of a man changes his
countenance,
either for good or for evil.ˢ
25 The sign of a good heart is a cheerful
countenance;
withdrawn and perplexed is the
laborious schemer.

CHAPTER 14

See RG
198–200
1 Happy the man whose mouth
brings him no grief,
who is not stung by remorse for sin.ᵗ
2 Happy the man whose conscience does
not reproach him,
who has not lost hope.

The Use of Wealth

3 Wealth ill becomes the mean man;*
and to the miser, of what use is gold?
4 What he denies himself he collects for
others,
and in his possessions a stranger will
revel.ᵘ
5 To whom will he be generous who is
stingy with himself
and does not enjoy what is his own?
6 None is more stingy than he who is
stingy with himself;
he punishes his own miserliness.

7 If ever he is generous, it is by mistake;
and in the end he displays his greed.
8 In the miser's opinion his share is too
small;
9 he refuses his neighbor and brings ruin
on himself.
10 The miser's eye is rapacious for bread,
but on his own table he sets it stale.
11 My son, use freely whatever you have
and enjoy it as best you can;ᵛ
12 Remember that death does not tarry,
nor have you been told the grave's
appointed time.
13 Before you die, be good to your friend,
and give him a share in what you
possess.ʷ
14 Deprive not yourself of present good
things,
let no choice portion escape you.
15 Will you not leave your riches to others,
and your earnings to be divided by lot?
16 Give, take, and treat yourself well,
for in the nether world there are no
joys to seek.
17 All flesh grows old, like a garment;
the age-old law is: All must die.ˣ
18 As with the leaves that grow on a
vigorous tree:
one falls off and another sprouts—
So with the generations of flesh and
blood:
one dies and another is born.ʸ
19 All man's works will perish in decay,
and his handiwork will follow after
him.

The Search for Wisdom and Its Blessings*
20 Happy the man who meditates on
wisdom,
and reflects on knowledge;ᶻ
21 Who ponders her ways in his heart,
and understands her paths;
22 Who pursues her like a scout,

14, 3-16: The miser does no good even to himself (3-10);
wealth should be wisely used during life, for it must be left
behind at death (11-16). In the light of the gospel, generosity
has a higher motivation and promise of reward than the Old
Testament writer could propose. Cf Mt 6, 19ff; Lk 12, 32ff.

14, 20—15, 20: From his social teaching the sage now
turns to consider individual responsibility. Happiness is to be
found in the pursuit and possession of wisdom (14, 20—15,
5). Joy and honor are given, not to the sinner (7ff), but to him

who fears God and observes his law (1-6. 10). The sinner is
fully responsible for his conduct because God, who sees all
things (18f), is not the author of wickedness (11ff. 20): he
gives to every man the liberty to choose between good and evil
(14-17).

s: Prv 15, 13. t: Sir 19, 15; 25, 8; Jas 3, 2. u: Eccl 6, 2. v: Prv
3, 9. w: Sir 4, 1; Tb 4, 7. x: Ps 103, 14ff; Is 40, 6; Jas 1, 10; 1 Pt
1, 24. y: Eccl 1, 4. z: Ps 1, 2.

and lies in wait at her entry way;

23 Who peeps through her windows,
and listens at her doors;

24 Who encamps near her house,
and fastens his tent pegs next to her
walls;

25 Who pitches his tent beside her,
and lives as her welcome neighbor;

26 Who builds his nest in her leafage,
and lodges in her branches;

27 Who takes shelter with her from the heat,
and dwells in her home.

CHAPTER 15

See RG 198-200

1 He who fears the LORD will do
this;
he who is practiced in the law will
come to wisdom.

2 Motherlike she will meet him,
like a young bride she will embrace
him,

3 Nourish him with the bread of
understanding,
and give him the water of learning to
drink.ᵃ

4 He will lean upon her and not fall,
he will trust in her and not be put to
shame.

5 She will exalt him above his fellows;
in the assembly she will make him
eloquent.

6 Joy and gladness he will find,
an everlasting name inherit.ᵇ

7 Worthless men will not attain to her,
haughty men will not behold her.

8 Far from the impious is she,
not to be spoken of by liars.

9 Unseemly is praise on a sinner's lips,
for it is not accorded to him by God.

10 But praise is offered by the wise man's
tongue;
its rightful steward will proclaim it.

Man's Free Will

11 Say not: "It was God's doing that I fell
away";

for what he hates he does not do.

12 Say not: "It was he who set me astray";
for he has no need of wicked man.ᶜ

13 Abominable wickedness the LORD hates,
he does not let it befall those who fear
him.

14 When God, in the beginning, created man,
he made him subject to his own free
choice.ᵈ

15 If you choose you can keep the
commandments;
it is loyalty to do his will.

16 There are set before you fire and water;
to whichever you choose, stretch forth
your hand.

17 Before man are life and death,
whichever he chooses shall be given
him.ᵉ

18 Immense is the wisdom of the LORD;
he is mighty in power, and all-seeing.

19 The eyes of God see all he has made;
he understands man's every deed.ᶠ

20 No man does he command to sin,
to none does he give strength for lies.

CHAPTER 16

See RG 198-200

God's Punishment of Sinners*

1 Desire not a brood of worthless children,
nor rejoice in wicked offspring.

2 Many though they be, exult not in them
if they have not the fear of the LORD.

3 Count not on their length of life,ᵍ
have no hope in their future.
For one can be better than a thousand;
rather die childless than have godless
children!

4 Through one wise man can a city be
peopled;
through a clan of rebels it becomes
desolate.

5 Many such things has my eye seen,
even more than these has my ear heard.

6 Against a sinful band fire is enkindled,ʰ
upon a godless people wrath flames
out.*

16, 1-21: Sinful offspring are a great misfortune (1-4), for history and experience show how God punishes sin (5-10). He judges everyone according to his deeds (11ff); no one is hidden from him or escapes retribution at his hand (15-21).

16, 6: For Korah and his band (6a), see Nm 16, 35; Ps 106,

18; for the disgruntled Israelites (6b), Ps 78, 21f.

a: Jn 4, 10; 6, 31ff.   *b:* Sir 6, 29-32.   *c:* Jas 1, 13.   *d:* Gn 1, 27.
e: Dt 30, 15.   *f:* Pss 33, 18; 34, 16; Heb 4, 13.   *g:* 3f: Wis 4, 1f.
h: Sir 21, 9.

⁷ He forgave not the leaders of old*
    who rebelled long ago in their
        might;*ⁱ*
⁸ He spared not the neighbors of Lot*ʲ*
    whom he detested for their pride;*
⁹ Nor did he spare the doomed people*
    who were uprooted because of their
        sin;
¹⁰ Nor the six hundred thousand foot
        soldiers*ᵏ*
    who perished for the impiety of their
        hearts.*
¹¹ And had there been but one stiffnecked
        man,
    it were a wonder had he gone
        unpunished.
For mercy and anger alike are with him
    who remits and forgives, though on the
        wicked alights his wrath.
¹² Great as his mercy is his punishment;
    he judges men, each according to his
        deeds.
¹³ A criminal does not escape with his
        plunder;
    a just man's hope God does not leave
        unfulfilled.
¹⁴ Whoever does good has his reward,
    which each receives according to his
        deeds.
¹⁵ Say not: "I am hidden from God;
    in heaven who remembers me?
Among so many people I cannot be
        known;
    what am I in the world of spirits?
¹⁶ Behold, the heavens, the heaven of
        heavens,
    the earth and the abyss tremble at his
        visitation;
¹⁷ The roots of the mountains, the earth's
        foundations,
    at his mere glance, quiver and
        quake.

¹⁸ Of me, therefore, he will take no
        thought;
    with my ways who will concern
        himself?
¹⁹ If I sin, no eye will see me;
    if all in secret I am disloyal, who is to
        know?*ˡ*
²⁰ Who tells him of just deeds
    and what could I expect for doing my
        duty?"
²¹ Such are the thoughts of senseless men,
    which only the foolish knave will
        think.

*Divine Wisdom Seen in Creation**

²² Hearken to me, my son, take my advice,
    apply your mind to my words,
²³ While I propose measured wisdom,
    and impart accurate knowledge.
²⁴ When at the first God created his works
    and, as he made them, assigned their
        tasks,*ᵐ*
²⁵ He ordered for all time what they were to
        do
    and their domains from generation to
        generation.
They were not to hunger, nor grow
        weary,
    nor ever cease from their tasks.
²⁶ Not one should ever crowd its neighbor,
    nor should they ever disobey his
        word.
²⁷ Then the LORD looked upon the earth,
    and filled it with his blessings.*ⁿ*
²⁸ Its surface he covered with all manner of
        life
    which must return into it again.

CHAPTER 17

¹ The LORD from the earth created
        man,
    and in his own image he made him.*ᵒ*

See RG
198–200

16, 7: The leaders of old: the "mighty men of old" who were destroyed by the flood: Gn 6, 4; Wis 14, 6; Bar 3, 26ff.

16, 8: The people of Sodom and Gomorrah: Gn 19, 24f; Ez 16, 49f.

16, 9: The Canaanites: Ex 23, 23f. 27-31; 33, 2; Dt 7, 1; Wis 12, 3.

16, 10: The Israelites who murmured against Moses: Nm 11, 20; 14, 12. 22ff.

16, 22—17, 18: In harmony with Gn 1—2, the author describes God's wisdom in creating the universe and all things in it (22-28), endowing man with a moral nature, with wisdom and knowledge and freedom of will according to his own image (17, 1. 6), so that man may govern the earth (3f), praise God's name (8), obey his law (9-12), and render to him an account of his deeds (18). Cf Pss 19; 104.

i: Gr 6, 4; Wis 14, 6; Bar 3, 26ff.   *j:* Gn 19, 24ff.   *k:* Nm 14, 29.
l: Sir 23, 18.   *m:* Gn 1, 4ff.   *n:* Gn 1, 20ff.   *o:* Gn 2, 7; 3. 19.

2 Limited days of life he gives him[p]
   and makes him return to earth again.
3 He endows man with a strength of his
   own,
   and with power over all things else on
   earth.
4 He puts the fear of him in all flesh,
   and gives him rule over beasts and
   birds.
5 He forms men's tongues and eyes and ears,
   and imparts to them an understanding
   heart.
6 With wisdom and knowledge he fills
   them;
   good and evil he shows them.
7 He looks with favor upon their hearts,
   and shows them his glorious works,
8 That they may describe the wonders of
   his deeds
   and praise his holy name.
9 He has set before them knowledge,
   a law of life as their inheritance;
10 An everlasting covenant* he has made
   with them,
   his commandments he has revealed to
   them.
11 His majestic glory their eyes beheld,
   his glorious voice their ears heard.
12 He says to them, "Avoid all evil";
   each of them he gives precepts about
   his fellow men.
13 Their ways are ever known to him,
   they cannot be hidden from his eyes.
14 Over every nation he places a ruler,*
   but the LORD's own portion is Israel.[q]
15 All their actions are clear as the sun to
   him,
   his eyes are ever upon their ways.
16 Their wickedness cannot be hidden from
   him;

all of their sins are before the LORD.
17 A man's goodness God cherishes like a
   signet ring,
   a man's virtue, like the apple of his
   eye.
18 Later he will rise up and repay them,
   and requite each one of them as they
   deserve.[r]

Appeal for a Return to God*
19 But to the penitent he provides a way
   back,
   he encourages those who are losing
   hope!
20 Return to the LORD and give up sin,
   pray to him and make your offenses
   few.
21 Turn again to the Most High and away
   from sin,
   hate intensely what he loathes;
22 Who in the nether world can glorify the
   Most High[s]
   in place of the living who offer their
   praise?
23 No more can the dead give praise than
   those who have never lived;
   they glorify the LORD who are alive
   and well.
24 How great the mercy of the LORD,
   his forgiveness of those who return to
   him!
25 The like cannot be found in men,
   for not immortal is any son of man.
26 Is anything brighter than the sun? Yet it
   can be eclipsed.
   How obscure* then the thoughts of
   flesh and blood!
27 God watches over the hosts of highest
   heaven,
   while all men are dust and ashes.

17, 10: An everlasting covenant . . . his commandments:
the various covenants which God entered into with mankind,
e.g., Gn 2, 15ff; 17, 1-22, especially on Mount Sinai where
the people saw God's glory and heard his voice (Ex 19, 16—
24, 18).

17, 14: Ruler: this may refer to civil authority or to angels
placed over nations as guardians; see note on Dt 32, 8, and the
cross references above.

17, 19-27: Exhorting the sinner to return to God (19ff.
24ff), the author implies that the Lord will postpone death
for a repentant sinner so that he may fulfill his destiny of
praising God on earth (22f). In the light of Christian teach-

ing, the gift of final penitence extends this divine purpose
into life everlasting. See note on Ps 6, 6; cf also Ez 18, 23;
33, 11-16.

17, 26: Obscure: literally, evil; compare Gn 6, 5.
Though moral fault is not excluded, the thought here is the
inability to understand the merciful designs of God. Cf Wis
9, 14-18.

p: 2ff: Gn 1, 26ff; Ps 8, 4-8.   q: Ex 19, 5; Dt 4, 19f; 32, 8f; Dn
10, 13-21; 12, 1; Rom 13, 1.   r: Jb 19, 25; Jl 3, 4.   s: 22f: Pss 6,
6; 115, 17; Is 38, 18.

CHAPTER 18

See RG
198–200

The Divine Power and Mercy*

¹ The Eternal is the judge of all things
without exception;
the LORD alone is just.
² Whom has he made equal to describing
his works,
and who can probe his mighty deeds?
³ Who can measure his majestic power,
or exhaust the tale of his mercies?
⁴ One cannot lessen, nor increase,
nor penetrate the wonders of the LORD.
⁵ When a man ends he is only beginning,
and when he stops he is still
bewildered.
⁶ What is man, of what worth is he?
the good, the evil in him, what are these?
⁷ The sum of a man's days is great
if it reaches a hundred years:ᵗ
⁸ Like a drop of sea water, like a grain of
sand,
so are these few years among the days
of eternity.
⁹ That is why the LORD is patient with men
and showers upon them his mercy.
¹⁰ He sees and understands that their death
is grievous,
and so he forgives them all the more.
¹¹ Man may be merciful to his fellow man,
but the LORD's mercy reaches all flesh,
¹² Reproving, admonishing, teaching,
as a shepherd guides his flock;ᵘ
¹³ Merciful to those who accept his guidance,
who are diligent in his precepts.

The Necessity of Prudence

¹⁴ My son, to your charity add no reproach,*
nor spoil any gift by harsh words.
¹⁵ Like dew that abates a burning wind,
so does a word improve a gift.

¹⁶ Sometimes the word means more than
the gift;
both are offered by a kindly man.
¹⁷ Only a fool upbraids before giving;
a grudging gift wears out the expectant
eyes.ᵛ
¹⁸ Be informed before speaking;
before sickness prepare the cure.
¹⁹ Before you are judged, seek merit for
yourself,
and at the time of visitation you will
have a ransom.*
²⁰ Before you have fallen, humble
yourself;
when you have sinned, show
repentance.
²¹ Delay not to forsake sins,
neglect it not till you are in distress.
²² Let nothing prevent the prompt payment
of your vows;*
wait not to fulfill them when you are
dying.ʷ
²³ Before making a vow have the means to
fulfill it;
be not one who tries the LORD.
²⁴ Think of wrath and the day of death,
the time of vengeance when he will
hide his face.ˣ
²⁵ Remember the time of hunger in the time
of plenty,
poverty and want in the day of wealth.ʸ
²⁶ Between morning and evening the
weather changes;
before the LORD all things are fleeting.
²⁷ A wise man is circumspect in all things;
when sin is rife he keeps himself from
wrongdoing.
²⁸ Any learned man should make wisdom
known,*
and he who attains to her should
declare her praise;

18, 1-13: Not only are God's justice and power beyond man's understanding (1-5), his mercy also is boundless and surpasses all human compassion (6-13).
18, 14-27: The practice of charity is an art which avoids every offense to the recipient (14-18). Prudence directs the changing circumstances of daily life toward the attainment of its reward at the time of visitation, i.e., the day of reckoning (19-27).
18, 19: Merit . . . ransom: almsgiving is often portrayed in the Bible as a means of approach to the forgiving mercy of God. Cf Sir 3, 29f; 29, 11f; Tb 12, 12f; Dn 4, 24; Lk 16, 9;

Acts 10, 31.
18, 22f: The usual object of a vow in Old Testament times was the offering of a bloody sacrifice.
18, 28f: A general statement on the teaching of wisdom, serving either as a conclusion to the preceding section or as an introduction to the following one. The neighbors of the wise man are regarded as the field into which he channels the waters of wisdom to encourage growth. Cf Sir 24, 28-31.

t: Ps 90, 10.   u: Jn 10, 11.   v: Sir 20, 13.   w: Nm 30. 3; Dt 23, 22; Ps 50, 14; Prv 20, 25; Eccl 5, 4.   x: Sir 7, 16.   y: Sir 11, 25.

29 Those trained in her words must show
their wisdom,
dispensing sound proverbs like life-
giving waters.

Self-Control*

30 Go not after your lusts,[z]
but keep your desires in check.
31 If you satisfy your lustful appetites
they will make you the sport of your
enemies.
32 Have no joy in the pleasures of a moment
which bring on poverty redoubled;
33 Become not a glutton and a winebibber
with nothing in your purse.

CHAPTER 19

See RG
198–200 1 He who does so grows no richer;
he who wastes the little he has will be
stripped bare.
2 Wine and women make the mind giddy,
and the companion of harlots becomes
reckless.[a]
4 He who lightly trusts in them has no sense,
and he who strays after them sins
against his own life.
3 Rottenness and worms will possess him,
for contumacious desire destroys its
owner.

The Proper Use of Speech*

5 He who gloats over evil will meet with
evil,
and he who repeats an evil report has
no sense.
6 Never repeat gossip,
and you will not be reviled.[b]
7 Tell nothing to friend or foe;
if you have a fault, reveal it not,[c]
8 For he who hears it will hold it against
you,
and in time become your enemy.
9 Let anything you hear die within you;

be assured it will not make you burst.
10 When a fool hears something, he is in
labor,
like a woman giving birth to a child.
11 Like an arrow lodged in a man's thigh
is gossip in the breast of a fool.
12 Admonish your friend—he may not have
done it;
and if he did, that he may not do it
again.[d]
13 Admonish your neighbor—he may not
have said it;
and if he did, that he may not say it
again.
14 Admonish your friend—often it may be
slander;
every story you must not believe.
15 Then, too, a man can slip and not mean
it;
who has not sinned with his tongue?[e]
16 Admonish your neighbor before you
break with him;
thus will you fulfill the law of the
Most High.[f]

How To Recognize True Wisdom*

17 All wisdom is fear of the LORD;
perfect wisdom is the fulfillment of the
law.[g]
18 The knowledge of wickedness is not
wisdom,
nor is there prudence in the counsel of
sinners.
19 There is a shrewdness that is detestable,
while the simple man may be free
from sin.
20 There are those with little understanding
who fear God,
and those of great intelligence who
violate the law.
21 There is a shrewdness keen but
dishonest,
which by duplicity wins a judgment.

18, 30—19, 4: Inordinate gratification of the senses makes a man unreasonable, the slave of passion, the sport of his enemies. In the end it destroys him physically and spiritually.

19, 5-16: An excellent commentary on the eighth commandment of the Decalogue, forbidding intemperance in speech through calumny, rash judgment, and detraction (5f), and inculcating discreet silence in defense of self and of neighbor (7-11). Justice requires that an accused neighbor be given a hearing, and charity urges fraternal correction; both together

fulfill the law of the Most High (12-16); cf Mt 7, 1f; 18, 15f.

19, 17-26: True and false wisdom as here described are synonymous with virtue and vice, with the fulfillment of the law and the violation of it.

---

z: Rom 6, 12; 13, 14. a: Prv 20, 1; 23, 20ff. b: Prv 25, 10.
c: Sir 8, 18f. d: Lv 19, 17; Mt 18, 15; Lk 17, 3. e: Sir 14, 1; Jas
3, 2. f: Lv 19, 17. g: Sir 1, 1. 12. 14; Jb 28, 28; Ps 111, 10; Prv
1, 7; 9, 10.

²² There is the wicked man who is bowed in
grief,
but is full of guile within;
²³ He bows his head and feigns not to
hear,
but when not observed, he will take
advantage of you:
²⁴ Even though his lack of strength keeps
him from sinning,
when he finds the opportunity, he will
do harm.
²⁵ One can tell a man by his appearance;
a wise man is known as such when
first met.
²⁶ A man's attire, his hearty laughter and his
gait,
proclaim him for what he is.

See RG
198-200

CHAPTER 20

Conduct of the Wise and
the Foolish

¹ An admonition can be inopportune,*
and a man may be wise to hold his
peace.
² It is much better to admonish than to lose
one's temper,
for one who admits his fault will be
kept from disgrace.
³ Like a eunuch lusting for intimacy with a
maiden
is he who does right under
compulsion.*
⁴ One man is silent and is thought wise,
another is talkative and is disliked.
⁵ One man is silent because he has nothing
to say;
another is silent, biding his time.ʰ
⁶ A wise man is silent till the right time
comes,
but a boasting fool ignores the proper
time.
⁷ He who talks too much is detested;

he who pretends to authority is hated.

⁸ Some misfortunes bring success;*
some things gained are a man's loss.
⁹ Some gifts do one no good,
and some must be paid back double.*
¹⁰ Humiliation can follow fame,
while from obscurity a man can lift up
his head.
¹¹ A man may buy much for little,
but pay for it seven times over.
¹² A wise man makes himself popular by a
few words,
but fools pour forth their
blandishments in vain.
¹³ A gift from a rogue will do you no good,
for in his eyes his one gift is equal to
seven.
¹⁴ He gives little and criticizes often,
and like a crier he shouts aloud.
He lends today, he asks it back
tomorrow;
hateful indeed is such a man.
¹⁵ A fool has no friends,
nor thanks for his generosity;
¹⁶ Those who eat his bread have an evil
tongue.
How many times they laugh him to
scorn!

¹⁷ A fall to the ground is less sudden than a
slip of the tongue;*
that is why the downfall of the wicked
comes so quickly.
¹⁸ Insipid food is the untimely tale;
the unruly are always ready to offer it.
¹⁹ A proverb when spoken by a fool is
unwelcome,
for he does not utter it at the proper
time.
²⁰ A man through want may be unable to
sin,

20, 1-7: Wisdom indicates the proper times for speech and
silence, that is, the occasions when the most benefit can be
gained from them.

20, 3: The sense is that violence or force against a person
can prevent an external act of sin or compel a good deed without eliminating the internal sin or desire of wrongdoing. Cf
Sir 20, 20.

20, 8-16: In a series of paradoxes the author indicates
how much true and lasting values differ from apparent
ones.

20, 9: And some . . . double: or perhaps, "but some are
doubly precious."

20, 17-25: The ill-timed speech of the wicked, the unruly
and a fool is repulsive (17ff); human respect exposes one to
intimidation, rash promises and enmity (21f); lies bring dishonor and lasting disgrace (23ff).

h: Sir 20, 1; Prv 10, 19; 17, 28.

yet in this tranquility he cannot rest.
21 One may lose his life through shame,
and perish through a fool's
intimidation.
22 A man makes a promise to a friend out of
shame,
and has him for his enemy needlessly.
23 A lie is a foul blot in a man,
yet it is constantly on the lips of the
unruly.
24 Better a thief than an inveterate liar,
yet both will suffer disgrace;
25 A liar's way leads to dishonor,
his shame remains ever with him.
26 A wise man advances himself by his
words,*
a prudent man pleases the great.
27 He who works his land has abundant
crops,
he who pleases the great is pardoned
his faults.
28 Favors and gifts blind the eyes;
like a muzzle over the mouth they
silence reproof.*
29 Hidden wisdom and unseen treasure—
of what value is either?
30 Better the man who hides his folly
than the one who hides his wisdom.

CHAPTER 21

See RG
198–200

Sin Must Be Avoided*

1 My son, if you have sinned, do so no
more,
and for your past sins pray to be
forgiven.
2 Flee from sin as from a serpent
that will bite you if you go near it;
Its teeth are lion's teeth,
destroying the souls of men.

3 Every offense is a two-edged sword;
when it cuts, there can be no healing.
4 Violence and arrogance wipe out wealth;
so too a proud man's home is
destroyed.
5 Prayer from a poor man's lips is heard at
once,
and justice is quickly granted him.
6 He who hates correction walks the
sinner's path,
but he who fears the LORD repents in
his heart.
7 Widely known is the boastful speaker,
but the wise man knows his own
faults.
8 He who builds his house with another's
money
is collecting stones for his funeral
mound.
9 A band of criminals is like a bundle of
tow;
they will end in a flaming fire.j
10 The path of sinners is smooth stones
that end in the depths of the nether
world.*

The Wise and the Foolish Differ*

11 He who keeps the law controls his
impulses;
he who is perfect in fear of the LORD
has wisdom.
12 He can never be taught who is not
shrewd,
but one form of shrewdness is
thoroughly bitter.
13 A wise man's knowledge wells up in a
flood,
and his counsel, like a living spring;k
14 A fool's mind is like a broken jar—

20, 26-30: Unlike the fool who invites disaster through misuse of his tongue, the sage through prudent speech gains in honor and esteem among the great (26f). He must beware, however, of accepting bribes, lest he share in evil through silence when he should reprove (28ff).

21, 1-10: Under various figures the consequences of sin are described as destructive of wealth, and even of bodily life, and deserving of death and a place in the depths of the nether world (2ff. 6a. 8ff). Through prayer, forgiveness can be sought (1), and through fear of the Lord, repentance is achieved (1, 5. 6b).

21, 10: The path of sinners . . . nether world: eternal retribution is not yet proposed in this reference. It became clearly

revealed through the teaching of Christ; cf Mt 7, 13f; 25, 41-46; Lk 16, 19-31.

21, 11-28: The mind of the wise man is a fountain of knowledge (13. 15); his will is trained to keep the law (11); his words are gracious, valued, carefully weighed, sincere (16f. 25f); his conduct is respectful, cultured and restrained (20. 22ff). The fool's mind is devoid of knowledge and impenetrable to it (12. 14. 18f); his will rejects it (15); his talk is burdensome (16), his laughter unrestrained (20), his conversation shallow and meddlesome (25f); his conduct is bold and rude (22ff); his abuse of others redounds on himself (27f).

i: Ex 23, 8; Dt 16, 19. j: Ps 21, 9. k: Prv 13, 14; 16, 22.

no knowledge at all can it hold.

¹⁵ When an intelligent man hears words of
wisdom,
he approves them and adds to them;
The wanton hears them with scorn
and casts them behind his back.
¹⁶ A fool's chatter is like a load on a
journey,
but there is charm to be found upon
the lips of the wise.
¹⁷ The views of a prudent man are sought in
an assembly,
and his words are considered with
care.
¹⁸ Like a house in ruins is wisdom to a fool;
the stupid man knows it only as
inscrutable words.
¹⁹ Like fetters on the legs is learning to a
fool,
like a manacle on his right hand.
²⁰ A fool raises his voice in laughter,
but a prudent man at the most smiles
gently.ˡ
²¹ Like a chain of gold is learning to a wise
man,
like a bracelet on his right arm.

²² The fool steps boldly into a house,
while the well-bred man remains
outside;ᵐ
²³ A boor peeps through the doorway of a
house,
but a cultured man keeps his glance
cast down.
²⁴ It is rude for one to listen at a door;
a cultured man would be overwhelmed
by the disgrace of it.
²⁵ The lips of the impious talk of what is
not their concern,
but the words of the prudent are
carefully weighed.
²⁶ Fools' thoughts are in their mouths,

wise men's words are in their hearts.
²⁷ When a godless man curses his
adversary,*
he really curses himself.
²⁸ A slanderer besmirches himself,
and is hated by his neighbors.

CHAPTER 22

On Laziness and Foolishness

See RG 198–200

¹ The sluggard is like a stone in the mud;*
everyone hisses at his disgrace.
² The sluggard is like a lump of dung;
whoever touches him wipes his hands.
³ An unruly child is a disgrace to its
father;
if it be a daughter, she brings him to
poverty.ⁿ
⁴ A thoughtful daughter becomes a
treasure to her husband,
a shameless one is her father's grief.
⁵ A hussy shames her father and her
husband;
by both she is despised.
⁶ Like a song in time of mourning is
inopportune talk,*
but lashes and discipline are at all
times wisdom.
⁷ Teaching a fool is like gluing a broken pot,ᵒ
or like disturbing a man in the depths
of sleep;
⁸ He talks with a slumberer who talks with
a fool,
for when it is over, he will say, "What
was that?"
⁹ Weep over the dead man, for his light has
gone out;
weep over the fool, for sense has left
him.
¹⁰ Weep but a little over the dead man, for
he is at rest;
but worse than death is the life of a
fool.

21, 27: Adversary: this can be understood in the sense that, if a man curses one who led him into sin, he implicitly curses himself for having yielded to the sin; or in the sense that the enemy is the man's own sinful nature; or even in the sense that the enemy is the devil, since the Hebrew word used here is satan. Cf 1 Chr 21, 1; Zec 3, 2; 2 Pt 2, 12f; Jude 9.

22, 1-15: To Sirach, a lazy person and an unruly child are a cause of shame and disgrace; everyone wishes to be rid of them (1-5). A wicked fool is as senseless as a man asleep or

dead, but the grief he causes others lasts a lifetime (7-11). He is like a brute, troublesome and intolerable (12-15).

22, 6: Like a song . . . is . . . talk: some understand talk in the sense of a rebuke unheeded by the unruly as a joyful song is out of place among mourners. Corporal punishment, however, is always effective.

l: Eccl 7, 6.   *m:* Prv 25, 17.   *n:* Prv 17, 21; 19, 13.   *o:* 7-11: Prv 23, 9.

¹¹ Seven days of mourning for the dead,
  but for the wicked fool a whole
    lifetime.ᵖ

¹² Speak but seldom with the stupid man,
  be not the companion of a brute;
¹³ Beware of him lest you have trouble
  and be spattered when he shakes
    himself;
  Turn away from him and you will find
    rest
  and not be wearied by his lack of
    sense.
¹⁴ What is heavier than lead,
  and what is its name but "Fool"?
¹⁵ Sand and salt and an iron mass
  are easier to bear than a stupid man.�q

¹⁶ Masonry bonded with wooden beams*
  is not loosened by an earthquake;
  Neither is a resolve constructed with
    careful deliberation
  shaken in a moment of fear.
¹⁷ A resolve that is backed by prudent
    understanding
  is like the polished surface of a smooth
    wall.
¹⁸ Small stones lying on an open height
  will not remain when the wind blows;
  Neither can a timid resolve based on
    foolish plans
  withstand fear of any kind.

The Preservation of Friendship*
¹⁹ One who jabs the eye brings tears:
  he who pierces the heart bares its
    feelings.
²⁰ He who throws stones at birds drives
    them away,
  and he who insults a friend breaks up
    the friendship.

²¹ Should you draw a sword against a
    friend,
  despair not, it can be undone.
²² Should you speak sharply to a friend,
  fear not, you can be reconciled.
  But a contemptuous insult, a confidence
    broken,
  or a treacherous attack will drive away
    any friend.

²³ Make fast friends with a man while he is
    poor;
  thus will you enjoy his prosperity with
    him.
  In time of trouble remain true to him,
  so as to share in his inheritance when
    it comes.
²⁴ Before flames burst forth an oven
    smokes;
  so does abuse come before bloodshed.
²⁵ From a friend in need of support
  no one need hide in shame;
²⁶ But from him who brings harm to his
    friend
  all will stand aloof who hear of it.

Prayer*
²⁷ Who will set a guard over my mouth,
  and upon my lips an effective seal,
  That I may not fail through them,
  that my tongue may not destroy me?ʳ

CHAPTER 23

See RG
198–200

¹ LORD, Father and Master of my life,*
  permit me not to fall by them!
² Who will apply the lash to my thoughts,
  to my mind the rod of discipline,
  That my failings may not be spared,
  nor the sins of my heart overlooked;
³ Lest my failings increase,
  and my sins be multiplied;

22, 16ff: A prudent mind firmly resolved is undisturbed by violent and conflicting thoughts, whereas a foolish person is tossed about by the winds of fear, like small stones whipped about by high winds.

22, 19-26: As disputes and violence weaken friendship, and disloyalty and abuse of confidence destroy it utterly (19-22. 24. 26), so kindness to a poor man in time of poverty and adversity builds up friendship and merits a share in his prosperity and inheritance (23. 25).

22, 27—23, 6: The sage implores the divine assistance to preserve him through stern discipline from sins of the tongue

(22, 27; 23, 1); ignorance of mind and weakness of will (2f); and inclinations of the senses and the flesh, lest he fall into the hands of his enemies, or become a prey of shameful desires (3-6).

23, 1: LORD, Father and Master of my life: these words express the tender personal relationship between the author's soul and God, the need of his assistance, and the truth of his providence.

p: Gn 50, 10.   q: Prv 27, 3.   r: Ps 141, 3.

Lest I succumb to my foes,
and my enemy rejoice over me?
⁴ LORD, Father and God of my life,
abandon me not into their control!
⁵ A brazen look allow me not;
ward off passion from my heart,
⁶ Let not the lustful cravings of the flesh
master me,
surrender me not to shameless desires.

The Proper Use of the Tongue*

⁷ Give heed, my children, to the instruction
that I pronounce,
for he who keeps it will not be
enslaved.
⁸ Through his lips is the sinner ensnared;
the railer and the arrogant man fall
thereby.
⁹ Let not your mouth form the habit of
swearing,
or becoming too familiar with the
Holy Name.ˢ
¹⁰ Just as a slave that is constantly under
scrutiny*
will not be without welts,
So one who swears continually by the
Holy Name
will not remain free from sin.
¹¹ A man who often swears heaps up
obligations;
the scourge will never be far from his
house.
If he swears in error, he incurs guilt;
if he neglects his obligation, his sin is
doubly great.ᵗ
If he swears without reason he cannot be
found just,
and all his house will suffer affliction.
¹² There are words which merit death;
may they never be heard among
Jacob's heirs.

For all such words are foreign to the
devout,
who do not wallow in sin.
¹³ Let not your mouth become used to
coarse talk,
for in it lies sinful matter.
¹⁴ Keep your father and mother in mind
when you sit among the mighty,
Lest in their presence you commit a
blunder
and disgrace your upbringing,
By wishing you had never been born
or cursing the day of your birth.ᵘ
¹⁵ A man who has the habit of abusive
language
will never mature in character as long
as he lives.

Sins of the Flesh*

¹⁶ Two types of men multiply sins,
a third* draws down wrath;
For burning passion is a blazing fire,
not to be quenched till it burns itself
out:
A man given to sins of the flesh,
who never stops until the fire breaks
forth;
¹⁷ The rake to whom all bread is sweet
and who is never through till he dies;ᵛ
¹⁸ And the man who dishonors his marriage
bed
and says to himself, "Who can see me?
Darkness surrounds me, walls hide me;
no one sees me; why should I fear to
sin?"ʷ
Of the Most High he is not mindful,
¹⁹ fearing only the eyes of men;
He does not understand that the eyes of
the LORD,
ten thousand times brighter than the
sun,

23, 7-15: A warning against sins of the tongue through misuse of the Holy Name, thoughtless swearing which involves obligation and incurs guilt (7-11), blasphemy (12), talk that is coarse and blundersome (13f), and the incorrigible habit of abusive language (15).

23, 10: As a slave . . . under scrutiny, so is he who calls on God to witness the truth of what he says.

23, 16-27: From sins of the tongue the author proceeds to treat of sins of the flesh and their dire consequences. The passion of lust tyrannizes over its victims and, like fire, consumes and utterly destroys them (16f. 22-26). The

false security of the adulterer serves but to aggravate his inevitable fate (18-21). Only the fear of the Lord and observance of his commandments can assure moral safety (27).

23, 16: Two types . . . a third: three kinds of sins of impurity with increasing degrees of gravity: solitary sins (16), fornication (17) and adultery (18-21).

s: Ex 20, 7; Lv 19, 12; Dt 5, 11; Mt 5, 33ff.   t: Lv 5, 4ff.   u: Sir 7, 27; Ex 20, 12; Dt 5, 16.   v: Prv 9, 17.   w: Is 29, 15.

Observe every step a man takes
and peer into hidden corners.
20 He who knows all things before they
exist
still knows them all after they are
made.
21 Such a man will be punished in the
streets of the city;*
when he least expects it, he will be
apprehended.*

22 So also with the woman who is
unfaithful to her husband
and offers as heir her son by a
stranger.
23 First, she has disobeyed the law of the
Most High;
secondly, she has wronged her
husband;
Thirdly, in her wanton adultery
she has borne children by another
man.*
24 Such a woman will be dragged before the
assembly,*
and her punishment will extend to her
children;
25 Her children will not take root;
her branches will not bring forth
fruit.
26 She will leave an accursed memory;
her disgrace will never be blotted
out.
27 Thus all who dwell on the earth shall
know,
and all who inhabit the world shall
understand,
That nothing is better than the fear of the
LORD,
nothing more salutary than to obey his
commandments.*

CHAPTER 24

Praise of Wisdom

See RG
198–200

1 Wisdom sings her own praises,*
before her own people she proclaims
her glory;
2 In the assembly of the Most High she
opens her mouth,
in the presence of his hosts she
declares her worth:
3 "From the mouth of the Most High I
came forth,ᶻ
and mistlike covered the earth.
4 In the highest heavens did I dwell,
my throne on a pillar of cloud.
5 The vault of heaven I compassed alone,
through the deep abyss I wandered.
6 Over waves of the sea, over all the land,
over every people and nation I held
sway.
7 Among all these I sought a resting place;
in whose inheritance should I abide?

8 "Then the Creator of all gave me his
command,
and he who formed me chose the spot
for my tent,
Saying, 'In Jacob make your dwelling,
in Israel your inheritance.'
9 Before all ages, in the beginning, he
created me,
and through all ages I shall not cease
to be.
10 In the holy tent I ministered before him,
and in Zion I fixed my abode.
11 Thus in the chosen city he has given me
rest,
in Jerusalem is my domain.
12 I have struck root among the glorious
people,

23, 21: Cf Lv 20, 19; Dt 22, 22.

23, 23: The detailed evil of adultery includes disobedience to God's law (Ex 20, 14), injustice to a partner in marriage, and disgraceful offspring.

23, 24f: The judgment of the assembly determined the illegitimacy of children born of adultery or incest and excluded them from the "community of the Lord" (Dt 23, 3). Cf Wis 3, 16-19; 4, 3-6.

24, 1-27: In this chapter Wisdom speaks in the first person, describing her origin, her dwelling place in Israel, and the reward she gives her followers. As in Prv 8, Wisdom is de-

scribed as a being who comes from God and is distinct from him. While we do not say with certainty that this description applies to a personal being, it does foreshadow the beautiful doctrine of the Word of God later developed in St. John's Gospel (Jn 1, 1-14). In the liturgy this chapter is applied to the Blessed Virgin because of her constant and intimate association with Christ, the Incarnate Wisdom.

x: 21f: Lv 20, 10; Dt 22, 21.   y: Sir 1, 10-18. 24; Prv 3, 1f.
z: 3ff: Sir 1, 1; Prv 2, 6; 8, 22-36; Wis 7, 24f.

in the portion of the Lord, his heritage.

13 "Like a cedar on Lebanon I am raised
aloft,
like a cypress on Mount Hermon,
14 Like a palm tree in Engedi,
like a rosebush in Jericho,
Like a fair olive tree in the field,
like a plane tree growing beside the
water.
15 Like cinnamon, or fragrant balm, or
precious myrrh,
I give forth perfume;ª
Like galbanum and onycha and sweet
spices,
like the odor of incense in the holy
place.*
16 I spread out my branches like a terebinth,
my branches so bright and so graceful.
17 I bud forth delights like the vine,
my blossoms become fruit fair and
rich.
18 Come to me, all you that yearn for me,
and be filled with my fruits;*
19 You will remember me as sweeter than
honey,
better to have than the honeycomb.
20 He who eats of me will hunger still,*
he who drinks of me will thirst for
more;ᵇ
21 He who obeys me will not be put to
shame,
he who serves me will never fail."

22 All this is true of the book of the Most
High's covenant,ᶜ
the law which Moses commanded us
as an inheritance for the community of
Jacob.*

23 It overflows, like the Pishon, with
wisdom—ᵈ
like the Tigris in the days of the new
fruits.
24 It runs over, like the Euphrates, with
understanding,
like the Jordan at harvest time.
25 It sparkles like the Nile with knowledge,
like the Gihon* at vintage time.
26 The first man never finished
comprehending wisdom,
nor will the last succeed in fathoming
her.
27 For deeper than the sea are her
thoughts;
her counsels, than the great abyss.

28 Now I, like a rivulet from her stream,"
channeling the waters into a garden,
29 Said to myself, "I will water my plants,
my flower bed I will drench";
And suddenly this rivulet of mine
became a river,
then this stream of mine, a sea.
30 Thus do I send my teachings forth
shining like the dawn,
to become known afar off.
31 Thus do I pour out instruction like
prophecy
and bestow it on generations to come.

CHAPTER 25

*Those Who Are Worthy of Praise**

See RG
198-200

1 With three things I am delighted,
for they are pleasing to the Lord and
to men:
Harmony among brethren, friendship
among neighbors,

24, 15: These substances were associated with worship, being mentioned in Ex 30, 22f. 34 as the ingredients of the anointing oil and the sacred incense. Israel was a priestly nation.

24, 18: Compare the words of the Savior in Mt 11, 28ff.

24, 20: So pleasing is wisdom to man that, far from being satiated, he will always desire more.

24, 22: Here the author begins to speak once more, Wisdom having ended her discourse in the preceding verse. Wisdom and the law of Moses are now identified.

24, 25: Gihon: understood by some to have been a name for the Nile; cf Gn 2, 13.

24, 28-31: Spoken by the author. He had at first drawn a small portion of the water of wisdom for his own private ben-

efit, but finding it so useful, he soon began to let others share in this boon by teaching them the lessons of wisdom.

25, 1-11: While praising brotherly love, love of neighbor, and conjugal love, the sage condemns their opposites in the arrogant pauper who despises his brother, the fraudulent rich man who cheats his neighbor, and the lecherous old man unfaithful to his wife (1f). This last, sensual from his youth, lacks the mature blessings of judgment and wisdom in old age (3-6), and the joy of a peaceful household, where honesty and dignity friendship, wisdom and fear of God prevail (7-11).

a: Ex 30, 22-25. *b:* Is 55, 1; Jn 6, 35. *c:* Ex 24, 7. *d:* 23ff: Gn 2, 11-14.

and the mutual love of husband and
wife.

² Three kinds of men I hate;
    their manner of life I loathe indeed:
  A proud pauper, a rich dissembler,
    and an old man lecherous in his
      dotage.

³ What you have not saved in your
      youth,
    how will you acquire in your old age?
⁴ How becoming to the gray-haired is
      judgment,
    and a knowledge of counsel to those
      on in years!
⁵ How becoming to the aged is wisdom,
    understanding and prudence to the
      venerable!
⁶ The crown of old men is wide
      experience;
    their glory, the fear of the LORD.

⁷ There are nine who come to my mind as
      blessed,
    a tenth whom my tongue proclaims:
  The man who finds joy in his children,
    and he who lives to see his enemies'
      downfall.
⁸ Happy is he who dwells with a sensible
      wife,
    and he who plows not like a donkey
      yoked with an ox.*
  Happy is he who sins not with his
      tongue,
    and he who serves not his inferior.
⁹ Happy is he who finds a friend
    and he who speaks to attentive ears.
¹⁰ He who finds wisdom is great indeed,
    but not greater than he who fears the
      LORD.
¹¹ Fear of the LORD surpasses all else,
    its possessor is beyond compare.

Wicked and Virtuous Women*

¹² Worst of all wounds is that of the heart,
    worst of all evils is that of a woman.
¹³ Worst of all sufferings is that from one's
      foes,
    worst of all vengeance is that of one's
      enemies:
¹⁴ No poison worse than that of a serpent,
    no venom greater than that of a
      woman.
¹⁵ With a dragon or a lion I would rather
      dwell
    than live with an evil woman.
¹⁶ Wickedness changes a woman's looks,
    and makes her sullen as a female
      bear.
¹⁷ When her husband sits among his
      neighbors,
    a bitter sigh escapes him unawares.
¹⁸ There is scarce any evil like that in a
      woman;
    may she fall to the lot of the sinner!
¹⁹ Like a sandy hill to aged feet
    is a railing wife to a quiet man.
²⁰ Stumble not through woman's beauty,
    nor be greedy for her wealth;
²¹ The man is a slave, in disgrace and
      shame,
    when a wife supports her husband.
²² Depressed mind, saddened face,
    broken heart—this from an evil wife.
  Feeble hands and quaking knees—
    from a wife who brings no happiness
      to her husband.
²³ In woman was sin's beginning,
    and because of her we all die.*
²⁴ Allow water no outlet,
    and be not indulgent to an erring
      wife.
²⁵ If she walks not by your side,
    cut her away from you.

25, 8: Like a donkey yoked with an ox: incompatibility
between husband and wife.

25, 12-25: Wickedness in a woman is most grievous,
painful and bitter to her husband. Through it she becomes
vengeful, dangerous and intolerable, jealous, talkative, intemperate and unchaste. Even her very appearance is changed
(12-17). The worst of all evils, a source of grief, a snare and
a disgrace to her husband, she depresses his mind, saddens
and breaks his heart, destroys his strength (18-22). She must

not be indulged but made obedient or punished (24f).

25, 23: According to the account in Gn 3, to which Ben
Sirach refers, sin, the cause of death, originated in woman:
Eve, the first human being to sin, induced Adam to follow her
example. But it is through Adam, as head of the race, that
original sin and its punishment of spiritual death are presented by St. Paul (Rom 5) as having entered the world, to become the occasion for the redemptive work of Christ our
Lord.

See RG
198–200

CHAPTER 26

1 Happy the husband of a good wife,*
twice-lengthened are his days;*e*

2 A worthy* wife brings joy to her
husband,
peaceful and full is his life.

3 A good wife is a generous gift
bestowed upon him who fears the
LORD;*f*

4 Be he rich or poor, his heart is content,
and a smile is ever on his face.

5 There are three things at which my heart
quakes,
a fourth before which I quail:
Though false charges in public, trial
before all the people,
and lying testimony are harder to bear
than death,

6 A jealous wife is heartache and
mourning*
and a scourging tongue like the other
three.

7 A bad wife is a chafing yoke;
he who marries her seizes a scorpion.

8 A drunken wife arouses great anger,
for she does not hide her shame.

9 By her eyelids and her haughty stare
an unchaste wife can be recognized.

10 Keep a strict watch over an unruly wife,
lest, finding an opportunity, she make
use of it;*g*

11 Follow close if her eyes are bold,
and be not surprised if she betrays
you:

12 As a thirsty traveler with eager mouth
drinks from any water that he finds,
So she settles down before every tent
peg
and opens her quiver for every
arrow.

13 A gracious wife delights her husband,
her thoughtfulness puts flesh on his
bones;

14 A gift from the LORD is her governed
speech,
and her firm virtue is of surpassing
worth.

15 Choicest of blessings is a modest wife,
priceless her chaste person.

16 Like the sun rising in the LORD's
heavens,
the beauty of a virtuous wife is the
radiance of her home.

17 Like the light which shines above the
holy lampstand,*
are her beauty of face and graceful
figure.

18 Golden columns on silver bases
are her shapely limbs and steady
feet.*

Dangers to Integrity and Friendship

19 These two bring grief to my heart,
and the third arouses my horror:
A wealthy man reduced to want;
illustrious men held in contempt;
And the man who passes from justice to
sin,
for whom the LORD makes ready the
sword.*h*

26, 1-4. 13-18: A good wife is as a gift from God, bringing joy and peace, happiness and contentment to her husband (1-4) through her thoughtfulness, reserve, modesty and chastity, beauty, grace and virtue (13-18).

26, 2: Worthy: gifted spiritually, mentally and physically. Cf Prv 31, 10.

26, 6-12: A repetition of the thought expressed in Sir 25, 12-25.

26, 17f: The holy lampstand and the golden columns stood in the holy place of the ancient Tabernacle (Ex 25, 31-40; 26, 32).

26, 18: Among the additions found here in some manuscripts are the following lines:
"My son, take care in the prime of life
not to surrender your strength to strangers;
Single out from the land a goodly field
and there with confidence sow the seed of your increase;
So shall you have your offspring around you,
and in confidence shall they grow up.

"Though a woman for hire be thought of as a trifle,
a married woman is a deadly snare for those who
embrace her. [Cf Prv 6, 26.]

"A wife's complaint should be made in meekness,
and show itself in a slight flush;
But a loud-mouthed, scolding wife
is a trumpet signaling for battle;
Any human being who answers that challenge
will spend his life amid the turbulence of war."

---

e: Sir 25, 8; Prv 18, 22; 31, 10ff.   *f:* Sir 36, 24.   *g:* Sir 42, 11.
h: Ez 18, 24ff.

20 A merchant can hardly remain upright,*
   nor a shopkeeper free from sin;

See RG
198–200

CHAPTER 27

1 For the sake of profit many sin,
   and the struggle for wealth blinds the
   eyes.i
2 Like a peg driven between fitted stones,
   between buying and selling sin is
   wedged in.
3 Unless you earnestly hold fast to the fear
   of the LORD,
   suddenly your house will be thrown
   down.
4 When a sieve is shaken, the husks
   appear;
   so do a man's faults when he speaks.
5 As the test of what the potter molds is in
   the furnace,
   so in his conversation is the test of a
   man.j
6 The fruit of a tree shows the care it has
   had;
   so too does a man's speech disclose
   the bent of his mind.k
7 Praise no man before he speaks,
   for it is then that men are tested.
8 If you strive after justice you will attain it,
   and put it on like a splendid robe.
9 Birds nest with their own kind,
   and fidelity comes to those who live
   by it.
10 As a lion crouches in wait for prey,
   so do sins for evildoers.
11 Ever wise are the discourses of the
   devout,
   but the godless man, like the moon,
   is inconstant.
12 Limit the time you spend among fools,
   but frequent the company of
   thoughtful men.

13 The conversation of the wicked is
   offensive,
   their laughter is wanton guilt.
14 Their oath-filled talk makes the hair
   stand on end,
   their brawls make one stop one's ears.
15 Wrangling among the haughty ends in
   bloodshed,
   their cursing is painful to hear.l
16 He who betrays a secret cannot be
   trusted,*
   he will never find an intimate friend.m
17 Cherish your friend, keep faith with him;
   but if you betray his confidence,
   follow him not;
18 For as an enemy might kill a man,
   you have killed your neighbor's
   friendship.
19 Like a bird released from the hand,
   you have let your friend go and cannot
   recapture him;
20 Follow him not, for he is far away,
   he has fled like a gazelle from the trap.
21 A wound can be bound up, and an insult
   forgiven,
   but he who betrays secrets does
   hopeless damage.n

Malice, Anger and Vengeance
22 He who has shifty eyes plots mischief
   and no one can ward him off;
23 In your presence he uses honeyed talk,
   and admires your every word,
   But later he changes his tone
   and twists your words to your ruin.o
24 There is nothing that I hate so much,
   and the LORD hates him as well.p
25 As a stone falls back on him who throws
   it up,q
   so a blow struck in treachery injures
   more than one.

26, 20—27, 15: From proper conduct in family life, the author proceeds to social morality, warning especially against injustice in commerce (26, 20—27, 3), and perversity of speech in business (4-7). The pursuit of justice in these matters is all the more meritorious as it is difficult (8ff). The discourses of the devout are marked with wisdom, but the conversations of the wicked, with offense, swearing, cursing, quarrels and even bloodshed (11-15).

27, 16—28, 11: Betrayal of confidence through indiscretion destroys friendship and does irreparable harm (16-21); cf Sir 22, 22. False friendship based on hypocrisy and deceit is

hateful to God and man (22ff); it soon becomes a victim of its own treachery (25ff). The same fate awaits the malicious and vengeful (27, 28—28, 1). They can obtain mercy and forgiveness only by first forgiving their neighbor, being mindful of death and of the commandments of the Most High (28, 2-7). And they must avoid quarrels and strife (8-11).

---

i: Sir 7, 18; 31, 6; Prv 30, 8f.   j: 1 Pt 1, 7.   k: Mt 7, 20.   l: Sir 23, 9-15.   m: Prv 11, 13; 20, 19.   n: Sir 22, 20.   o: Prv 26, 24ff.   p: Prv 6, 13. 16.   q: 25f: Ps 7, 16f; Prv 26, 27; Eccl 10, 8.

²⁶ As he who digs a pit falls into it,
  and he who lays a snare is caught in it,
²⁷ Whoever does harm will be involved in it
  without knowing how it came upon him.

²⁸ Mockery and abuse will be the lot of the
  proud,
  and vengeance lies in wait for them
  like a lion.
²⁹ The trap seizes those who rejoice in
  pitfalls,
  and pain will consume them before
  they die;
³⁰ Wrath and anger are hateful things,
  yet the sinner hugs them tight.

CHAPTER 28

**See RG
198-200**

¹ The vengeful will suffer
  the LORD's vengeance,
  for he remembers their sins in detail.^r
² Forgive your neighbor's injustice;
  then when you pray, your own sins
  will be forgiven.^s
³ Should a man nourish anger against his
  fellows
  and expect healing from the LORD?^t
⁴ Should a man refuse mercy to his fellows,
  yet seek pardon for his own sins?
⁵ If he who is but flesh cherishes wrath,
  who will forgive his sins?
⁶ Remember your last days, set enmity
  aside;
  remember death and decay, and cease
  from sin!^u
⁷ Think of the commandments, hate not
  your neighbor;
  of the Most High's covenant, and
  overlook faults.

⁸ Avoid strife and your sins will be fewer,
  for a quarrelsome man kindles
  disputes,
⁹ Commits the sin of disrupting friendship
  and sows discord among those at
  peace.^v

¹⁰ The more wood, the greater the fire,^w
  the more underlying it, the fiercer the
  fight;
  The greater a man's strength, the sterner
  his anger,
  the greater his power, the greater his
  wrath.
¹¹ Pitch and resin make fires flare up,
  and insistent quarrels provoke
  bloodshed.

The Evil Tongue*

¹² If you blow upon a spark, it quickens into
  flame,
  if you spit on it, it dies out;
  yet both you do with your mouth!
¹³ Cursed be gossips and the double-
  tongued,
  for they destroy the peace of many.^x
¹⁴ A meddlesome tongue subverts many,
  and makes them refugees among the
  peoples;
  It destroys walled cities,
  and overthrows powerful dynasties.
¹⁵ A meddlesome tongue can drive virtuous
  women from their homes
  and rob them of the fruit of their toil;
¹⁶ Whoever heeds it has no rest,
  nor can he dwell in peace.

¹⁷ A blow from a whip raises a welt,
  but a blow from the tongue smashes
  bones;
¹⁸ Many have fallen by the edge of the
  sword,
  but not as many as by the tongue.^y
¹⁹ Happy he who is sheltered from it,
  and has not endured its wrath;
  Who has not borne its yoke
  nor been fettered with its chains;
²⁰ For its yoke is a yoke of iron
  and its chains are chains of bronze!
²¹ Dire is the death it inflicts,
  besides which even the nether world is
  a gain;

28, 12-26: Further treatment of sins of the tongue and their havoc; cf Sir 5, 12—6, 1; 19, 5-16; 20, 17-25; 23, 7-15. Gossips and the double-tongue destroy domestic peace (12-16). The whip, the sword, chains, even the nether world, are not so cruel as the suffering inflicted by an evil tongue (17-21). Not the just but those who forsake the Lord are victims of their evil tongues (22f). Therefore, guard your mouth and tongue as you would guard treasure against an enemy (24ff).

r: Dt 32, 35; Rom 12, 19.   *s:* Mt 6, 14.   *t:* Mt 18, 23ff.   *u:* Sir 7, 36; 38, 20.   *v:* Prv 15, 18.   *w:* 10ff: Prv 26, 20f.   *x:* Sir 5, 16f.   *y:* Jas 3, 5ff.

22 It will not take hold among the just
    nor scorch them in its flame,
23 But those who forsake the LORD will fall
        victims to it,
    as it burns among them unquenchably!
    It will hurl itself against them like a lion;
    like a panther, it will tear them to
        pieces.
24 As you hedge round your vineyard with
        thorns,
    set barred doors over your mouth;[z]
25 As you seal up your silver and gold,
    so balance and weigh your words.
26 Take care not to slip by your tongue
    and fall victim to your foe waiting in
        ambush.

CHAPTER 29

Loans, Alms and Surety*

See RG
198–200

1 He does a kindness who lends to his
        neighbor,
    and he fulfills the precepts who holds
        out a helping hand.[a]
2 Lend to your neighbor in his hour of
        need,
    and pay back your neighbor when a
        loan falls due;[b]
3 Keep your promise, be honest with him,
    and you will always come by what you
        need.
4 Many a man who asks for a loan
    adds to the burdens of those who help
        him;
5 When he borrows, he kisses the lender's
        hand
    and speaks with respect of his
        creditor's wealth;
    But when payment is due he disappoints
        him
    and says he is helpless to meet the
        claim.
6 If the lender is able to recover barely
        half,
    he considers this an achievement;
    If not, he is cheated of his wealth

and acquires an enemy at no extra
        charge;
    With curses and insults the borrower
        pays him back,
    with abuse instead of honor.
7 Many refuse to lend, not out of
        meanness,
    but from fear of being cheated.

8 To a poor man, however, be generous;
    keep him not waiting for your alms;
9 Because of the precept, help the needy,
    and in their want, do not send them
        away empty-handed.[c]
10 Spend your money for your brother and
        friend,
    and hide it not under a stone to perish;
11 Dispose of your treasure as the Most
        High commands,
    for that will profit you more than the
        gold.[d]
12 Store up almsgiving in your treasure
        house,
    and it will save you from every evil;
13 Better than a stout shield and a sturdy
        spear
    it will fight for you against the foe.

14 A good man goes surety for his neighbor,
    and only the shameless would play
        him false;[e]
15 Forget not the kindness of your backer,
    for he offers his very life for you.
16 The wicked turn a pledge on their behalf
        into misfortune,
    and the ingrate abandons his protector;
17 Going surety has ruined many
        prosperous men
    and tossed them about like waves of
        the sea;[f]
18 Has exiled men of prominence
    and sent them wandering through
        foreign lands.
19 The sinner through surety comes to grief,

29, 1-20: Some practical maxims concerning the use of
wealth. Give to a poor man (8f), lend to a needy neighbor, but
repay when a loan falls due lest the lender's burden be increased (1-5) and his kindness abused (6f); through charity
build up defense against evil (10-13). Go surety for your
neighbor according to your means, but take care (20) not to

fall, for the shameless play false and bring their protectors
and themselves to misfortune and ruin (14-19).

z: Sir 22, 27; Ps 141, 3.   a: Dt 15, 8; Ps 112, 5; Prv 19, 17.   b: Ex
22, 24ff; Lv 25, 36; Mt 5, 42.   c: Sir 4, 1ff; Lv 19, 9f; 23, 22; Dt
15, 8.   d: Sir 17, 17; Tb 4, 7ff.   e: Sir 8, 13.   f: Prv 6, 1f; 11, 15.

and he who undertakes too much falls into lawsuits.
²⁰ Go surety for your neighbor according to your means,
but take care lest you fall thereby.

Frugality and Its Rewards*
²¹ Life's prime needs are water, bread, and clothing,
a house, too, for decent privacy.ᵍ
²² Better a poor man's fare under the shadow of one's own roof
than sumptuous banquets among strangers.ʰ
²³ Be it little or much, be content with what you have,
and pay no heed to him who would disparage your home;
²⁴ A miserable life it is to go from house to house,
for as a guest you dare not open your mouth.
²⁵ The visitor has no thanks for filling the cups;
besides, you will hear these bitter words:
²⁶ "Come here, stranger, set the table, give me to eat the food you have!
²⁷ Away, stranger, for one more worthy; for my brother's visit I need the room!"
²⁸ Painful things to a sensitive man are abuse at home and insults from his creditors.

See RG 198–200

CHAPTER 30

The Training of Children*
¹ He who loves his son chastises him often,
that he may be his joy when he grows up.ⁱ

² He who disciplines his son will benefit from him,
and boast of him among his intimates.
³ He who educates his son makes his enemy jealous,
and shows his delight in him among his friends.
⁴ At the father's death, he will seem not dead,
since he leaves after him one like himself,
⁵ Whom he looks upon through life with joy,
and even in death, without regret:
⁶ The avenger he leaves against his foes,
and the one to repay his friends with kindness.

⁷ He who spoils his son will have wounds to bandage,
and will quake inwardly at every outcry.
⁸ A colt untamed turns out stubborn;
a son left to himself grows up unruly.
⁹ Pamper your child and he will be a terror for you,
indulge him and he will bring you grief.
¹⁰ Share not in his frivolity lest you share in his sorrow,
when finally your teeth are clenched in remorse.
¹¹ Give him not his own way in his youth,
and close not your eyes to his follies.
¹² Bend him to the yoke when he is young,
thrash his sides while he is still small,
Lest he become stubborn, disobey you,
and leave you disconsolate.ʲ
¹³ Discipline your son, make heavy his yoke,
lest his folly humiliate you.

Health of Soul and Body*
¹⁴ Better a poor man strong and robust,

29, 21-28: The man who provides his own basic needs of food, clothing and dwelling, and is content with what he has, preserves his freedom and self-respect (21ff). But if he lives as a guest, even among the rich, he exposes himself to insult and abuse (24-28).

30, 1-13: Sound discipline and careful education of children correct frivolity and stubbornness, prevent remorse and humiliation, and bring to parents lasting joy and delight, prestige among friends, jealousy of enemies, perpetuation and vindication of themselves through their offspring (1-6). Lack of discipline and overindulgence of children bring sorrow and

disappointment, terror and grief (7-13).

30, 14-25: Health of mind and body and joy of heart are judged more precious than wealth (14ff); bitterness, constant illness and affliction more difficult to bear than death (17-20). Sadness, resentment, anxiety, envy and anger shorten . . . life; they should be dispelled by cheerfulness and gladness of heart, which help to prolong one's days (21-25).

g: Sir 39, 26. h: Sir 40, 29. i: Prv 13, 24; 23, 13; 29, 15; Heb 12, 7. j: Sir 7, 23.

than a rich man with wasted frame.

15 More precious than gold is health and
well-being,
contentment of spirit than coral.

16 No treasure greater than a healthy body;
no happiness, than a joyful heart!

17 Preferable is death to a bitter life,*k*
unending sleep to constant illness.*

18 Dainties set before one who cannot eat
are like the offerings placed before a
tomb.*l*

19 What good is an offering to an idol
that can neither taste nor smell?

20 So it is with the afflicted man
who groans at the good things his eyes
behold!

21 Do not give in to sadness,
torment not yourself with brooding;*m*

22 Gladness of heart is the very life of man,
cheerfulness prolongs his days.

23 Distract yourself, renew your courage,
drive resentment far away from you;
For worry has brought death to many,
nor is there aught to be gained from
resentment.*n*

24 Envy and anger shorten one's life,
worry brings on premature old age.

25 One who is cheerful and gay while at
table
benefits from his food.*o*

See RG
198–200

CHAPTER 31

The Proper Attitude
toward Riches*

1 Keeping watch over riches wastes the
flesh,
and the care of wealth drives away
rest.

2 Concern for one's livelihood banishes
slumber;
more than a serious illness it disturbs
repose.*

3 The rich man labors to pile up wealth,
and his only rest is wanton pleasure;

4 The poor man toils for a meager
subsistence,
and if ever he rests, he finds himself in
want.

5 The lover of gold will not be free from
sin,
for he who pursues wealth is led astray
by it.

6 Many have been ensnared by gold,
though destruction lay before their
eyes;*p*

7 It is a stumbling block to those who are
avid for it,
a snare for every fool.

8 Happy the rich man found without fault,*
who turns not aside after gain!*q*

9 Who is he, that we may praise him?
he, of all his kindred, has done
wonders,

10 For he has been tested by gold and come
off safe,
and this remains his glory;
He could have sinned but did not,
could have done evil but would not,

11 So that his possessions are secure,
and the assembly recounts his praises.*r*

Table Etiquette*

12 If you are dining with a great man,
bring not a greedy gullet to his table,
Nor cry out, "How much food there is
here!"

30, 17: Preferable is death . . . constant illness: the true
value of human suffering was revealed through the passion
and death of Christ. It serves as reparation for sin, and when
united with Christ's suffering, as merit for eternal life.

31, 1-11: Solicitude for acquiring wealth and anxiety over
preserving it disturb repose and easily lead to sin and ruin (1-
7). Cf Mt 6, 25-34. A rich man who has not sinned or been seduced by wealth is worthy of praise (8-11).

31, 2: The Hebrew adds a verse that seems out of place
here: "A faithful comrade drives away reproach, and the
friend who keeps secrets is as dear as life."

31, 8ff: The church in her liturgy applies this passage to
holy confessors of the Faith.

31, 12—32, 13: A man observing etiquette at table avoids
greed and selfishness (31, 12f), is considerate of a neighbor's
likes and dislikes and generous toward him (14f. 23f), observes proper manners (16ff), is moderate in eating and
drinking (19-22. 25-30). A good host makes himself one with
his guests, is solicitous for them (32, 1f), provides conversation and diversion (3-6), is modest in speech (7f. 10), is respectful of elders (9), polite in comportment and grateful to
God for his favors (11ff).

k: Sir 41, 2.   l: Tb 4, 17.   m: Sir 38, 20; Prv 12, 25; 15, 13; 17,
22.   n: Sir 38, 18f.   o: Prv 15, 15.   p: Sir 8, 2.   q: Sir 5, 1. 10.
r: Prv 29, 14.

¹³ Remember that gluttony is evil.
No creature is greedier than the eye:
therefore it weeps for any cause.ˢ
¹⁵ Recognize that your neighbor feels as
you do,
and keep in mind your own dislikes:
¹⁴ Toward what he eyes, do not put out a
hand;
nor reach when he does for the same
dish.
¹⁶ Behave at table like a favored guest,
and be not greedy, lest you be
despised.
¹⁷ Be the first to stop, as befits good
manners;
gorge not yourself, lest you give
offense.ᵗ
¹⁸ If there are many with you at table,
be not the first to reach out your hand.
¹⁹ Does not a little suffice for a well-bred
man?
When he lies down, it is without
discomfort.ᵘ
²⁰ Distress and anguish and loss of sleep,
and restless tossing for the glutton!
Moderate eating ensures sound slumber
and a clear mind next day on rising.
²¹ If perforce you have eaten too much,
once you have emptied your stomach,*
you will have relief.
²² Listen to me, my son, and scorn me not;
later you will find my advice good.
In whatever you do, be moderate,
and no sickness will befall you.
²³ On a man generous with food, blessings
are invoked,
and this testimony to his goodness is
lasting;ᵛ
²⁴ He who is miserly with food is
denounced in public,
and this testimony to his stinginess is
lasting.
²⁵ Let not wine-drinking be the proof of
your strength,
for wine has been the ruin of many.
²⁶ As the furnace probes the work of the
smith,

so does wine the hearts of the insolent.
²⁷ Wine is very life to man
if taken in moderation.
Does he really live who lacks the wine
which was created for his joy?ʷ
²⁸ Joy of heart, good cheer and merriment
are wine drunk freely at the proper
time.
²⁹ Headache, bitterness and disgrace
is wine drunk amid anger and strife.
³⁰ More and more wine is a snare for the
fool;
it lessens his strength and multiplies
his wounds.
³¹ Rebuke not your neighbor when wine is
served,
nor put him to shame while he is merry;
Use no harsh words with him
and distress him not in the presence of
others.

CHAPTER 32

See RG
198-200

¹ If you are chosen to preside at
dinner, be not puffed up,
but with the guests be as one of
themselves;
Take care of them first before you sit
down;
² when you have fulfilled your duty,
then take your place,
To share in their joy
and win praise for your hospitality.
³ Being older, you may talk; that is only
your right,
but temper your wisdom, not to disturb
the singing.
⁴ When wine is present, do not pour out
discourse,
and flaunt not your wisdom at the
wrong time.
⁵ Like a seal of carnelian in a setting of gold
is a concert when wine is served.
⁶ Like a gold mounting with an emerald seal
is string music with delicious wine.
⁷ Young man, speak only when necessary,ˣ
when they have asked you more than
once;

31, 21: Emptied your stomach: the practice of induced vomiting, well-known among pagan Romans, and less well-known among the Jews, seems to be referred to here.

s: Sir 37, 28ff; Prv 23, 1f.   t: Sir 37, 29.   u: Eccl 5, 11.   v: Prv 22, 9.   w: Ps 104, 15; 1 Tm 5, 23.   x: 7ff; Sir 7, 14.

⁸ Be brief, but say much in those few words,
    be like the wise man, taciturn.
⁹ When among your elders be not forward,
    and with officials be not too insistent.
¹⁰ Like the lightning that flashes before a
    storm
    is the esteem that shines on modesty.
¹¹ When it is time to leave, tarry not;
    be off for home! There take your ease,
¹² And there enjoy doing as you wish,
    but without sin or words of pride.
¹³ Above all, give praise to your Creator,
    who showers his favors upon you.

The Providence of God

¹⁴ He who would find God must accept
    discipline;*
    he who seeks him obtains his request.ʸ
¹⁵ He who studies the law masters it,
    but the hypocrite finds it a trap.ᶻ
¹⁶ His judgment is sound who fears the
    LORD;
    out of obscurity he draws forth a clear
    plan.ᵃ
¹⁷ The sinner turns aside reproof
    and distorts the law to suit his purpose.ᵇ
¹⁸ The thoughtful man will not neglect
    direction;
    the proud and insolent man is deterred
    by nothing.
¹⁹ Do nothing without counsel,
    and then you need have no regrets.ᶜ
²⁰ Go not on a way that is set with snares,
    and let not the same thing trip you
    twice.
²¹ Be not too sure even of smooth roads,
²²   be careful on all your paths.
²³ Whatever you do, be on your guard,
    for in this way you will keep the
    commandments.
²⁴ He who keeps the law preserves himself;

and he who trusts in the LORD shall not
    be put to shame.

CHAPTER 33

See RG 198–200

¹ No evil can harm the man who
    fears the LORD;
    through trials, again and again he is
    safe.ᵈ
² He who hates the law is without wisdom,
    and is tossed about like a boat in a
    storm.
³ The prudent man trusts in the word of the
    LORD,
    and the law is dependable for him as a
    divine oracle.*
⁴ Prepare your words and you will be
    listened to;
    draw upon your training, and then give
    your answer.
⁵ Like the wheel of a cart is the mind of a
    fool;*
    his thoughts revolve in circles.
⁶ A fickle friend is like the stallion
    that neighs, no matter who the rider.
⁷ Why is one day more important than
    another,
    when it is the sun that lights up every
    day?
⁸ It is due to the LORD's wisdom that they
    differ;
    it is through him the seasons and feasts
    come and go.ᵉ
⁹ Some he dignifies and sanctifies,
    and others he lists as ordinary days.ᶠ
¹⁰ So too, all men are of clay,
    for from earth man was formed;ᵍ
¹¹ Yet with his great knowledge the LORD
    makes men unlike;
    in different paths he has them walk.
¹² Some he blesses and makes great,

32, 14—33, 4: God is shown to reveal himself through the discipline of his law, a clear and safe plan of life for the pious Jew of old. Direction and counsel are aids in following it (14ff. 18-24); 33, 1. 3f). Sinners and hypocrites, hating the law or distorting it, fail in wisdom and are devoid of security (32, 15. 17f; 33, 2).

33, 3: Oracle: as the answer given through the Urim and Thummim to the high priest is true, so the law proves itself true to him who obeys it. Cf Ex 28, 30; Nm 27, 21.

33, 5-15: Contrasts observable in the physical universe

as well as in the moral order serve the purposes of divine wisdom (5-9). All creatures are like clay . . . in the hands of their Creator—the fool and the wise man, the sinner, and the just (10-15). This does not imply that man is created to be a sinner: God is not the author of wickedness. Cf Jas 1, 13f.

y: Sir 4, 13.   z: Sir 2, 16.   a: Ps 37, 6.   b: Sir 21, 6; Prv 12, 1.
c: Sir 37, 16; Tb 4, 18.   d: Ps 91, 10.   e: Gn 1, 14.   f: Ex 20, 11.
g: Gn 2, 7.

some he sanctifies and draws to
  himself.
Others he curses and brings low,
  and expels them from their place.
13 Like clay in the hands of a potter,
  to be molded according to his pleasure,
So are men in the hands of their Creator,
  to be assigned by him their function.*h*
14 As evil contrasts with good, and death
    with life,
  so are sinners in contrast with the just;*i*
15 See now all the works of the Most High:
  they come in pairs, the one the
    opposite of the other.

16 Now I am the last to keep vigil,*
  like a gleaner after the vintage;
17 Since by the LORD's blessing I have
    made progress
  till like a vintager I have filled my
    winepress,
18 I would inform you that not for myself
    only have I toiled,
  but for every seeker after wisdom.

Property and Servants*

19 Listen to me, O leaders of the multitude;
  O rulers of the assembly, give ear!*j*
20 Let neither son nor wife, neither brother
    nor friend,
  have power over you as long as you
    live.
21 While breath of life is still in you,
  let no man have dominion over you.
Give not to another your wealth,
  lest then you have to plead with him;
22 Far better that your children plead with
    you
  than that you should look to their
    generosity.
23 Keep control over all your affairs;
  let no one tarnish your glory.
24 When your few days reach their limit,

at the time of death distribute your
  inheritance.
25 Fodder and whip and loads for an ass;
  the yoke and harness and the rod of his
    master.
27 Food, correction and work for a slave;
  and for a wicked slave, punishment in
    the stocks.
26 Make a slave work and he will look for
    his rest;
  let his hands be idle and he will seek to
    be free.*k*
28 Force him to work that he be not idle,
  for idleness is an apt teacher of
    mischief.
29 Put him to work, for that is what befits
    him;
  if he becomes unruly, load him with
    chains.
30 But never lord it over any human being,
  and do nothing unjust.
31 If you have but one slave, treat him like
    yourself,
  for you have acquired him with your
    life's blood;*l*
32 If you have but one slave, deal with him
    as a brother,
  for you need him as you need your life:
33 If you mistreat him and he runs away,
  in what direction will you look for him?

CHAPTER 34

Trust in the Lord and
Not in Dreams*

See RG
198-200

1 Empty and false are the hopes of the
    senseless,
  and fools are borne aloft by dreams.
2 Like a man who catches at shadows or
    chases the wind,
  is the one who believes in dreams.
3 What is seen in dreams is to reality

33, 16ff: Here the author refers to himself as the most recent of the writers who have endeavored to present true wisdom to their readers.

33, 19-33: Public officials should reject every influence that would restrict their freedom in the management of their affairs. They must make their own household subservient to them rather than be subservient to it (19-24). Slaves are to be given food and work and correction but never to be treated unjustly (25-29). Great care should be taken of good slaves (30-33).

34, 1-17: Confidence placed in dreams, divinations and omens is false because these are devoid of reality (1-8). True confidence is founded on knowledge and experience (9-12), and above all on the fear of the Lord, with its accompanying blessings of divine assistance and protection (13-17).

---

h: Wis 15, 7; Jer 18, 1-6; Rom 9, 20f.   *i:* Sir 42, 25.   *j:* Wis 6, 1f.
k: Prv 29, 19.   *l:* Sir 7, 21.

what the reflection of a face is to the
face itself.

4 Can the unclean produce the clean?
can the liar ever speak the truth?[m]

5 Divination, omens and dreams all are
unreal;
what you already expect, the mind
depicts.

6 Unless it be a vision specially sent by the
Most High,
fix not your heart on it;

7 For dreams have led many astray,
and those who believed in them have
perished.

8 The law is fulfilled without fail,
and perfect wisdom is found in the
mouth of the faithful man.

9 A man with training gains wide knowledge;
a man of experience speaks sense.

10 One never put to the proof knows little,
whereas with travel a man adds to his
resourcefulness.

11 I have seen much in my travels,
learned more than ever I could say.

12 Often I was in danger of death,
but by these attainments I was saved.

13 Lively is the courage of those who fear
the LORD,
for they put their hope in their savior;

14 He who fears the LORD is never alarmed,
never afraid; for the LORD is his hope.[n]

15 Happy the soul that fears the LORD!
In whom does he trust, and who is his
support?

16 The eyes of the LORD are upon those who
love him;
he is their mighty shield and strong
support,
A shelter from the heat, a shade from the
noonday sun,
a guard against stumbling, a help
against falling.[o]

17 He buoys up the spirits, brings a sparkle
to the eyes,
gives health and life and blessing.

True Worship of God*

18 Tainted his gifts who offers in sacrifice
ill-gotten goods!
Mock presents from the lawless win
not God's favor.[p]

19 The Most High approves not the gifts of
the godless,
nor for their many sacrifices does he
forgive their sins.

20 Like the man who slays a son in his
father's presence
is he who offers sacrifice from the
possessions of the poor.

21 The bread of charity is life itself for the
needy;[q]
he who withholds it is a man of blood.

22 He slays his neighbor who deprives him
of his living;
he sheds blood who denies the laborer
his wages.

23 If one man builds up and another tears
down,
what do they gain but trouble?

24 If one man prays and another curses,
whose voice will the LORD hear?

25 If a man again touches a corpse after he
has bathed,
what did he gain by the purification?[r]

26 So with a man who fasts for his sins,
but then goes and commits them again:
Who will hear his prayer,
and what has he gained by his
mortification?

CHAPTER 35*

1 To keep the law is a great oblation,[s]
and he who observes the
commandments sacrifices a peace
offering.

See RG 198–200

34, 18-26: To be acts of true religion, sacrifice and penance
must be accompanied by the proper moral dispositions. To offer to God goods taken from the poor (18-22), or to practice
penance without interior reform, is a mockery, worthless in the
sight of God (23-26). Cf Mt 15, 4-7; Mk 7, 9-13.

35, 1-24: Keeping the commandments of the law and
avoiding injustice constitute sacrifice pleasing and acceptable to God (1ff). Offerings also should be made to him,
cheerfully and generously; these he repays . . . sevenfold (4-

10). Extortion from widows and orphans is injustice, which
God quickly repays (11-18). Punishing the proud and the
merciless and coming to the aid of the distressed, he requites
all according to their deeds (19-24).

m: Jb 14, 4. n: Pss 23, 4; 112, 7f; Prv 3, 23ff; 28, 1. o: Pss 33,
18; 34, 16. p: Sir 35, 11; Prv 21, 27. q: 21f: Lv 19, 13; Dt 24,
14f; Tb 4, 14. r: Nm 19, 11f; Prv 26, 11; 2 Pt 2, 22. s: 1ff: 1 Sm
15, 22; Ps 51, 18f; Is 1, 11-18; Hos 6, 6; Am 5, 21-24.

2 In works of charity one offers fine flour,*
  and when he gives alms he presents
    his sacrifice of praise.
3 To refrain from evil pleases the LORD,
  and to avoid injustice is an atonement.
4 Appear not before the LORD empty-
    handed,
  for all that you offer is in fulfillment of
    the precepts.*
5 The just man's offering enriches the altar
  and rises as a sweet odor before the
    Most High.
6 The just man's sacrifice is most pleasing,
  nor will it ever be forgotten.
7 In generous spirit pay homage to the
    LORD,
  be not sparing of freewill gifts.*
8 With each contribution show a cheerful
    countenance,
  and pay your tithes in a spirit of joy.*
9 Give to the Most High as he has given to
    you,
  generously, according to your means.

10 For the LORD is one who always repays,
  and he will give back to you
    sevenfold.*
11 But offer no bribes, these he does not
    accept!
  Trust not in sacrifice of the fruits of
    extortion,*
12 For he is a God of justice,
  who knows no favorites.*
13 Though not unduly partial toward the
    weak,
  yet he hears the cry of the oppressed.*
14 He is not deaf to the wail of the orphan,*
  nor to the widow when she pours out
    her complaint;
15 Do not the tears that stream down her
    cheek
  cry out against him that causes them to
    fall?

16 He who serves God willingly is heard;
  his petition reaches the heavens.
17 The prayer of the lowly pierces the
    clouds;
  it does not rest till it reaches its goal,
18 Nor will it withdraw till the Most High
    responds,
  judges justly and affirms the right.
19 God indeed will not delay,
  and like a warrior, will not be still*
20 Till he breaks the backs of the merciless
  and wreaks vengeance upon the proud;
21 Till he destroys the haughty root and
    branch,
  and smashes the scepter of the wicked;
22 Till he requites mankind according to its
    deeds,
  and repays men according to their
    thoughts;
23 Till he defends the cause of his people,
  and gladdens them by his mercy.
24 Welcome is his mercy in time of distress
  as rain clouds in time of drought.

CHAPTER 36

A Prayer for God's People*

See RG 198-200

1 Come to our aid, O God of the universe,
  and put all the nations in dread of you!
2 Raise your hand against the heathen,
  that they may realize your power.
3 As you have used us to show them your
    holiness,
  so now use them to show us your glory.
4 Thus they will know, as we know,
  that there is no God but you.

5 Give new signs and work new wonders;
  show forth the splendor of your right
    hand and arm;
6 Rouse your anger, pour out wrath,
  humble the enemy, scatter the foe.*
7 Hasten the day, bring on the time;
9 crush the heads of the hostile rulers.

35, 2: Fine flour, together with oil and frankincense, was a prescribed offering to God; cf Lv 2, 1ff.
  35, 13: Cf Lv 19, 15.
  36, 1-17: Making an act of faith and hope in the supreme Lord of the universe, the author begs God to continue manifesting his holiness and mercy through Israel, his people (1ff. 10-13), and his power and justice through the punishment of the nations (2. 5-9), that all the earth may acknowledge him the eternal God (4. 14-17).

t: Ex 23, 15; 34, 20; Dt 16, 16. *u:* Sir 7, 31. *v:* 2 Cor 9, 7. *w:* Prv 19, 17. *x:* Sir 34, 18f; Prv 21, 27. *y:* Dt 10, 17; 2 Chr 19, 7; Jb 34, 19; Wis 6, 7; Acts 10, 34; Rom 2, 11; Gal 2, 6; 1 Pt 1, 17. *z:* 14f: Ex 22, 22. *a:* Is 42, 13ff; 2 Pt 3, 9. *b:* Ps 79, 6.

A Prayer for Israel

The prayer in ch 36 reflects a political and theological perspective different from the rest of Sirach. Typical of wisdom literature, Sirach generally does not contain teachings about the end times, but focuses on providing guidance for living out one's life in the world as it currently exists. This section of the text is a petition for the overturning of the present world. As such, it presages a time in Jewish history, immediately following the time of Ben Sirach, when Hellenistic rule reaches an intolerable level and results in the Maccabean revolt. It is difficult to know whether Ben Sirach prays generically for a utopian time in the distant future when all God's promises to Israel would be fulfilled, or whether he prays more particularly for immediate deliverance from the foreign domination of the Seleucid dynasty. Comments like "crush the heads of the hostile rulers" (v. 9) and "gather all the tribes of Jacob, that they may inherit the land as of old" (v. 10) sound explicitly political. They call for the reestablishment of Israel as a nation distinct from other nations and for the return of the Diaspora Jews, so that Israel in general and Jerusalem in particular can be restored to glory. Part of the motivation for the reestablishment of Israel is to demonstrate Israel's preeminent creed (Dt 6, 4)—that there is only one God, the God of Israel.

8 Let raging fire consume the fugitive,
　　and your people's oppressors meet
　　　　destruction.
10 Gather all the tribes of Jacob,
　　that they may inherit the land as of
　　　　old.
11 Show mercy to the people called by your
　　　　name;
　　Israel, whom you named your first-
　　　　born.c
12 Take pity on your holy city,
　　Jerusalem, your dwelling place.d
13 Fill Zion with your majesty,
　　your temple with your glory.
14 Give evidence of your deeds of old;
　　fulfill the prophecies spoken in your
　　　　name,
15 Reward those who have hoped in you,
　　and let your prophets be proved
　　　　true.
16 Hear the prayer of your servants,
　　for you are ever gracious to your
　　　　people;
17 Thus it will be known to the very ends of
　　　　the earth
　　that you are the eternal God.

Choice of Associates*
18 The throat can swallow any food,
　　yet some foods are more agreeable
　　　　than others;
19 As the palate tests meat by its savor,
　　so does a keen mind insincere words.
20 A deceitful character causes grief,
　　but an experienced man can turn the
　　　　tables on him.
21 Though any man may be accepted as a
　　　　husband,
　　yet one girl will be more suitable than
　　　　another:
22 A woman's beauty makes her husband's
　　　　face light up,
　　for it surpasses all else that charms the
　　　　eye;e
23 And if, besides, her speech is kindly,
　　his lot is beyond that of mortal men.
24 A wife is her husband's richest treasure,
　　a helpmate, a steadying column.f
25 A vineyard with no hedge will be
　　　　overrun;
　　a man with no wife becomes a
　　　　homeless wanderer.
26 Who will trust an armed band

36, 18—37, 15: In the choice of wife, friend or associate, experience is a discerner of character (18-21). Beauty and kindly speech make a woman desirable as wife (22f). The good wife becomes her husband's richest treasure, his help-mate in establishing his household (24-27). A true friend fights for his comrade and shares his spoils with him (37, 5f); a false one deceives and abandons him in time of need (1-4).

A true counselor and associate should be sought among those who keep the commandments, not among those who break them and seek their own advantage (7-12). In all things pray to God for light and follow conscience (13ff).

c: Ex 4, 22.　d: 2 Chr 6, 41; Ps 132, 8. 14; Is 2, 1ff; Mi 4, 1ff.
e: Sir 26, 13ff.　f: Gn 2, 18; Prv 18, 22.

that shifts from city to city?
²⁷ Or a man who has no nest,
but lodges where night overtakes him?ᵍ

CHAPTER 37

See RG
198–200 ¹Every friend declares his friendship,
but there are friends who are friends in
name only.ʰ
² Is it not a sorrow unto death
when your bosom companion becomes
your enemy?
³ "Alas, my companion! Why were you
created
to blanket the earth with deceit?"
⁴ A false friend will share your joys,
but in time of trouble he stands afar off.
⁵ A true friend will fight with you against
the foe,
against your enemies he will be your
shield-bearer.
⁶ Forget not your comrade during the battle,
and neglect him not when you
distribute your spoils.

⁷ Every counselor points out a way,
but some counsel ways of their own;
⁸ Be on the alert when one proffers
advice,
find out first of all what he wants.
For he may be thinking of himself
alone;
why should the profit fall to him?
⁹ He may tell you how good your way will
be,
and then stand by to watch your
misfortune.
¹⁰ Seek no advice from one who regards
you with hostility;
from those who envy you, keep your
intentions hidden.
¹¹ Speak not to a woman about her rival,
nor to a coward about war,
to a merchant about business,
to a buyer about value,
to a miser about generosity,
to a cruel man about mercy,

to a lazy man about work,
to a seasonal laborer about the harvest,
to an idle slave about a great task:
pay no attention to any advice they give.
¹² Instead, associate with a religious man,
who you are sure keeps the
commandments;
Who is like-minded with yourself
and will feel for you if you fall.
¹³ Then, too, heed your own heart's counsel;
for what have you that you can depend
on more?
¹⁴ A man's conscience can tell him his
situation
better than seven watchmen in a lofty
tower.
¹⁵ Most important of all, pray to God
to set your feet in the path of truth.

Wisdom and Temperance

¹⁶ A word is the source of every deed;*
a thought, of every act.ⁱ
¹⁷ The root of all conduct is the mind;
four branches it shoots forth:
¹⁸ Good and evil, death and life,
their absolute mistress is the tongue.ʲ
¹⁹ A man may be wise and benefit many,
yet be of no use to himself.
²⁰ Though a man may be wise, if his words
are rejected
he will be deprived of all enjoyment.
²¹ When a man is wise to his own advantage,
the fruits of his knowledge are seen in
his own person;
²² When a man is wise to his people's
advantage,
the fruits of his knowledge are
enduring:ᵏ
²³ Limited are the days of one man's life,
but the life of Israel is days without
number.
²⁴ One wise for himself has full enjoyment,
and all who see him praise him;
²⁵ One wise for his people wins a heritage
of glory,
and his name endures forever.ˡ

37, 16-25: Thoughts determine action. Wisdom is the source of good and life; folly, of evil and death (16ff). If the fruits of a man's wisdom benefit himself, he may be praised in his own lifetime; if they benefit his people, his praise endures after him, in their lives (19-25).

---

g: Prv 27, 8.   *h:* Sir 6, 7ff.   *i:* Sir 32, 19.   *j:* Prv 18, 21.   *k:* Sir 15, 1ff.   *l:* Sir 39, 9; 44, 13f.

26 My son, while you are well, govern your
appetite*
so that you allow it not what is bad for
you;
27 For not every food is good for everyone,
nor is everything suited to every
taste.^m
28 Be not drawn after every enjoyment,^n
neither become a glutton for choice
foods,
29 For sickness comes with overeating,
and gluttony brings on biliousness.
30 Through lack of self-control many have
died,
but the abstemious man prolongs his
life.

See RG
198–200

CHAPTER 38

Sickness and Death

1 Hold the physician in honor, for he is
essential to you,*
and God it was who established his
profession.
2 From God the doctor has his wisdom,
and the king provides for his sustenance.
3 His knowledge makes the doctor
distinguished,
and gives him access to those in
authority.
4 God makes the earth yield healing herbs
which the prudent man should not
neglect;
5 Was not the water sweetened by a twig
that men might learn his power?^o
6 He endows men with the knowledge
to glory in his mighty works,
7 Through which the doctor eases pain
and the druggist prepares his
medicines;
8 Thus God's creative work continues
without cease

in its efficacy on the surface of the earth.
9 My son, when you are ill, delay not,
but pray to God, who will heal you:^p
10 Flee wickedness; let your hands be just,
cleanse your heart of every sin;
11 Offer your sweet-smelling oblation and
petition,
a rich offering according to your means.^q
12 Then give the doctor his place
lest he leave; for you need him too.
13 There are times that give him an
advantage,
14 and he too beseeches God
That his diagnosis may be correct
and his treatment bring about a cure.
15 He who is a sinner toward his Maker
will be defiant toward the doctor.

16 My son, shed tears for one who is dead*
with wailing and bitter lament;
As is only proper, prepare the body,
absent not yourself from his burial:^r
17 Weeping bitterly, mourning fully,
pay your tribute of sorrow, as he
deserves,
18 One or two days, to prevent gossip;
then compose yourself after your grief,
19 For grief can bring on an extremity
and heartache destroy one's health.^s
20 Turn not your thoughts to him again;
cease to recall him; think rather of the
end.^t
21 Recall him not, for there is no hope of his
return;
it will not help him, but will do you
harm.^u
22 Remember that his fate will also be yours;
for him it was yesterday, for you today.^v
23 With the departed dead, let memory fade;
rally your courage, once the soul has
left.

37, 26-30: Temperance and self-control should govern a
man's appetite for food, which is intended not to destroy but
to preserve life.

38, 1-15: The profession of medicine comes from God,
who makes the earth yield healing herbs and gives the physician knowledge of their virtue (1-8). In illness the sick man
should cleanse his soul from sin and petition God for help
through an offering of sacrifice; the physician, too, does well
to invoke God that he may understand the illness and apply
the proper remedy (9-14). The sinner, in contrast, defies both
his Maker and the doctor (15).

38, 16-23: A period of mourning for the deceased and care
for their burial is becoming (16ff). But grief should not be excessive, for it neither helps the dead, who cannot return, nor
fails to harm the living. The mourner's own end will quickly
follow, and the time to prepare for it is now (19-23).

m: 1 Cor 6, 12; 10, 23.   n: 28f: Sir 31, 13. 16ff.   o: Ex 15, 25.
p: Is 38, 2f.   q: Lv 2, 1ff.   r: Sir 22, 9f.   s: Prv 12, 25; 15, 13;
17, 22.   t: Sir 7, 36; 18, 24; 30, 21.   u: 2 Sm 12, 23; Wis 2, 1.
v: Jas 4, 13ff.

Vocations of the Craftsman and the Scribe*

24 The scribe's profession increases his
  wisdom;
  whoever is free from toil can become a
  wise man.
25 How can he become learned who guides
  the plow,
  who thrills in wielding the goad like a
  lance,
  Who guides the ox and urges on the
  bullock,
  and whose every concern is for cattle?
26 His care is for plowing furrows,
  and he keeps a watch on the beasts in
  the stalls.

27 So with every engraver and designer
  who, laboring night and day,
  Fashions carved seals,
  and whose concern is to vary the pattern.
  His care is to produce a vivid impression,
  and he keeps watch till he finishes his
  design.
28 So with the smith standing near his anvil,
  forging crude iron.
  The heat from the fire sears his flesh,
  yet he toils away in the furnace heat.
  The clang of the hammer deafens his ears,
  his eyes are fixed on the tool he is
  shaping.
  His care is to finish his work,
  and he keeps watch till he perfects it in
  detail.

29 So with the potter sitting at his labor
  revolving the wheel with his feet.
  He is always concerned for his products,
  and turns them out in quantity.
30 With his hands he molds the clay,
  and with his feet softens it.
  His care is for proper coloring,
  and he keeps watch on the fire of his
  kiln.
31 All these men are skilled with their hands,
  each one an expert at his own task;

32 Without them no city could be lived in,
  and wherever they stay, they need not
  hunger.
33 They do not occupy the judge's bench,
  nor are they prominent in the assembly;
  They set forth no decisions or judgments,
  nor are they found among the rulers;
34 Yet they maintain God's ancient
  handiwork,
  and their concern is for exercise of
  their skill.

CHAPTER 39

See RG 198–200

1 How different the man who
  devotes himself
  to the study of the law of the Most
  High!
  He explores the wisdom of the men of old
  and occupies himself with the
  prophecies;
2 He treasures the discourses of famous
  men,
  and goes to the heart of involved
  sayings;
3 He studies obscure parables,
  and is busied with the hidden
  meanings of the sages.
4 He is in attendance on the great,
  and has entrance to the ruler.
5 He travels among the peoples of foreign
  lands
  to learn what is good and evil among
  men.
6 His care is to seek the LORD, his Maker,
  to petition the Most High,
  To open his lips in prayer,
  to ask pardon for his sins.
  Then, if it pleases the LORD Almighty,
  he will be filled with the spirit of
  understanding;
  He will pour forth his words of wisdom
  and in prayer give thanks to the LORD,
7 Who will direct his knowledge and his
  counsel,
  as he meditates upon his mysteries.

38, 24—39, 11: More excellent than the useful service of craftsmen—farmer, engraver, smith, potter (25-34)—is the profession of the scribe (24), who studies and meditates on the law of the Most High, seeks him in prayer of thanksgiving, petition and repentance for sin (39, 1. 6f), explores the wisdom of the past and present, travels abroad to observe the conduct of many peoples, and attends rulers and great men. Through the spirit of understanding granted by God, he will show forth his wisdom to the glory of God's law, gaining renown for generations to come (2-5. 8-11).

8 He will show the wisdom of what he has
learned
and glory in the law of the LORD's
covenant.
9 Many will praise his understanding;
his fame can never be effaced;
Unfading will be his memory,
through all generations his name will
live;ʷ
10 Peoples will speak of his wisdom,
and in assembly sing his praises.
11 While he lives he is one out of a thousand,
and when he dies his renown will not
cease.

Praise of God the Creator*

12 Once more I will set forth my theme
to shine like the moon in its fullness!
13 Listen, my faithful children: open up
your petals,
like roses planted near running waters;
14 Send up the sweet odor of incense,
break forth in blossoms like the lily.
Send up the sweet odor of your hymn of
praise;
bless the LORD for all he has done!
15 Proclaim the greatness of his name,
loudly sing his praises,
With music on the harp and all stringed
instruments;
sing out with joy as you proclaim:

16 The works of God are all of them good;
in its own time every need is supplied.ˣ
17 At his word the waters become still as in
a flask;
he had but to speak and the reservoirs
were made.ʸ
18 He has but to command and his will is
done;
nothing can limit his achievement.
19 The works of all mankind are present to
him;
not a thing escapes his eye.ᶻ

20 His gaze spans all the ages;
to him there is nothing unexpected.
21 No cause then to say: "What is the
purpose of this?"
Everything is chosen to satisfy a need.
22 His blessing overflows like the Nile;
like the Euphrates it enriches the
surface of the earth.
23 Again, his wrath expels the nations
and turns fertile land into a salt marsh.ᵃ
24 For the virtuous his paths are level,
to the haughty they are steep;
25 Good things for the good he provided
from the beginning,
but for the wicked good things and
bad.
26 Chief of all needs for human life
are water and fire, iron and salt,
The heart of the wheat, milk and honey,
the blood of the grape, and oil, and
cloth;ᵇ
27 For the good all these are good,
but for the wicked they turn out evil.
28 There are storm winds created to punish,
which in their fury can dislodge
mountains;
When destruction must be, they hurl all
their force
and appease the anger of their Maker.
29 In his treasury also, kept for the proper
time,
are fire and hail, famine, disease,
30 Ravenous beasts, scorpions, vipers,
and the avenging sword to exterminate
the wicked;
31 In doing his bidding they rejoice,
in their assignments they disobey not
his command.
32 So from the first I took my stand,
and wrote down as my theme:
33 The works of God are all of them good;
every need when it comes he fills.ᶜ
34 No cause then to say: "This is not as
good as that";

39, 12-35: The sage invites his disciples to join him in joyfully proclaiming his favorite theme: The works of God are all of them good; in its own time every need is supplied (12-16, 32-35). He describes God's omniscience, supreme power and wisdom, whereby all created things, good in themselves, are ever present to him, obey him, and fulfill their intended purpose (17-21), bringing blessing to the vir- tuous, but evil and punishment to the wicked who misuse them (22-31). Cf similar hymns of praise, Sir 36, 1-17; 42, 15—43, 35.

w: Sir 37, 25; 44, 14. x: Gn 1, 31; Eccl 3, 11. y: Gn 1, 6-10; Ex 14, 21f; Jos 3, 16. z: Sir 15, 19; 42, 20. a: Jos 1, 2-6. b: Sir 29, 21. c: Sir 39, 16; Gn 1, 31; Eccl 3, 11.

for each shows its worth at the proper
time.

³⁵ So now with full joy of heart proclaim
and bless the name of the Holy One.

CHAPTER 40

See RG
198–200

Joys and Miseries of Life

¹ A great anxiety has God allotted,*
and a heavy yoke, to the sons of men;^d
From the day one leaves his mother's
womb
to the day he returns to the mother of
all the living,*

² His thoughts, the fear in his heart,
and his troubled forebodings till the
day he dies—

³ Whether he sits on a lofty throne
or grovels in dust and ashes,

⁴ Whether he bears a splendid crown
or is wrapped in the coarsest of
cloaks—

⁵ Are of wrath and envy, trouble and dread,
terror of death, fury and strife.
Even when he lies on his bed to rest,
his cares at night disturb his sleep.

⁶ So short is his rest it seems like none,
till in his dreams he struggles as he did
by day,
Terrified by what his mind's eye sees,
like a fugitive being pursued;

⁷ As he reaches safety, he wakes up
astonished that there was nothing to
fear.

⁸ So it is with all flesh, with man and with
beast,
but for sinners seven times more.

⁹ Plague and bloodshed, wrath and the
sword,
plunder and ruin, famine and death:^e

¹⁰ For the wicked, these were created evil,
and it is they who bring on destruction.

¹¹ All that is of earth returns to earth,
and what is from above returns above.*

¹² All that comes from bribes or injustice
will be wiped out,
but loyalty remains for ages.

¹³ Wealth out of wickedness is like a wadi
in spate:
like a mighty stream with lightning
and thunder,

¹⁴ Which, in its rising, rolls along the
stones,
but suddenly, once and for all, comes
to an end.^f

¹⁵ The offshoot of violence will not
flourish,
for the root of the godless is on sheer
rock;

¹⁶ Or they are like reeds on the riverbank,
withered before all other plants.

¹⁷ But goodness will never be cut off,
and justice endures forever.

Wealth or wages can make life sweet,*
but better than either is finding a
treasure.

¹⁸ A child or a city will preserve one's
name,
but better than either, attaining
wisdom.^g

¹⁹ Sheepfolds and orchards bring
flourishing health;
but better than either, a devoted wife;

²⁰ Wine and music delight the soul,
but better than either, conjugal love.^h

²¹ The flute and the harp offer sweet
melody,
but better than either, a voice that is true.

²² Charm and beauty delight the eye,
but better than either, the flowers of
the field.ⁱ

²³ A friend, a neighbor, are timely guides,

40, 1-16: The former idyllic description of the universe is contrasted with the picture of the evils afflicting humanity. Every man, high or low, is burdened from birth to death with fears, anxieties and troubles, by day and often by night, the time appointed for rest (1-7). For sinners, the suffering is much greater (8ff). What they gained by violence and injustice is quickly destroyed; but justice endures forever (14ff).

40, 1: Mother of all the living: the earth from which man was taken. Cf Gn 2, 7; 3, 19f; Jb 1, 21; Ps 139, 15.

40, 11: All that is of earth . . . returns above: a reference to bodily mortality and to the divine origin of life from the Spirit

of God Cf Sir 41, 10; Gn 2, 7; 3, 19; Jb 34, 14f; Pss 104, 29f; 146, 4; Eccl 12, 7. The Greek and the Latin render the second half of the verse: "all waters shall return to the sea."

40, 17-27: Of the many treasures making life sweet, such as health, children, friends, music, vigor, the best are called true conjugal love, wisdom, and above all, fear of God; cf Sir 25, 6-1.

---

d: Gn 3, 17; Jb 7, 1; 14, 1; Eccl 2, 23.   *e:* Sir 39, 28ff.   *f:* Sir 23, 25; Wis 4, 3ff.   *g:* Prv 19, 14.   *h:* Ps 104, 15.   *i:* Mt 6, 28f.

but better than either, a prudent wife.
24 A brother, a helper, for times of stress;
but better than either, charity that
rescues.
25 Gold and silver make one's way secure,
but better than either, sound judgment.
26 Wealth and vigor build up confidence,
but better than either, fear of God.
Fear of the LORD leaves nothing wanting;
he who has it need seek no other
support:
27 The fear of God is a paradise of blessings;
its canopy, all that is glorious.[j]

28 My son, live not the life of a beggar,*
better to die than to beg;
29 When one has to look to another's table,
his life is not really a life.
His neighbor's delicacies bring revulsion
of spirit
to one who understands inward
feelings:[k]
30 In the mouth of the shameless man
begging is sweet,
but within him it burns like fire.

CHAPTER 41

See RG
198-200 1 O death! how bitter the thought of
you*
for the man at peace amid his
possessions,
For the man unruffled and always
successful,
who still can enjoy life's pleasures.
2 O death! how welcome your sentence
to the weak man of failing strength,
Tottering and always rebuffed,
with no more sight, with vanished hope.[l]
3 Fear not death's decree for you;
remember, it embraces those before
you, and those after.[m]
4 Thus God has ordained for all flesh;

why then should you reject the will of
the Most High?
Whether one has lived a thousand years,
a hundred, or ten,
in the nether world he has no claim on
life.

5 A reprobate line are the children of
sinners,[n]
and witless offspring are in the homes
of the wicked.
6 Their dominion is lost to sinners' children,
and reproach abides with their
descendants.
7 Children curse their wicked father,
for they suffer disgrace through him.
8 Woe to you, O sinful men,
who forsake the law of the Most High.
9 If you have children, calamity will seize
them;
you will beget them only for groaning.
When you stumble, there is lasting joy;
at death, you become a curse.
10 Whatever is of nought returns to nought,
so too the godless from void to void.[o]
11 Man's body is a fleeting thing,
but a virtuous name will never be
annihilated.[p]
12 Have a care for your name, for it will
stand by you
better than precious treasures in the
thousands;[q]
13 The boon of life is for limited days,
but a good name, for days without
number.*

True and False Shame*

14 My children, heed my instruction about
shame;
judge of disgrace only according to my
rules,
For it is not always well to be ashamed,

40, 28ff: Among the Jews, beggary was considered degrading to human dignity; it was agreeable only to the shameless, who had lost their sense of honor. Cf Sir 29, 22f.

41, 1-13: Whether death seems bitter to one who enjoys peace, success and pleasure, or welcome to one who is weak and in despair, it comes to all and must be accepted as the will of God (1-4). As the human body passes away (11), so do those who have sinned through the body and their offspring alike, who, needy and accursed, pass on with their parents as if they had never been (5-10). Only the good name of the vir-

tuous endures (11ff).

41, 13: After this verse many texts repeat Sir 20, 29f.

41, 14—42, 8: The author illustrates the subject of true and false shame with numerous and detailed examples of sin (14-24) and virtue (42, 1-8), following the norm of the commandments.

j: Is 4, 5.   k: Sir 29, 24.   l: Sir 30, 17.   m: Sir 38, 20ff.   n: 5ff: Sir 3, 9ff; Wis 3, 16-19.   o: Sir 40, 11; Wis 4, 19.   p: Prv 10, 7.   q: Prv 22, 1; Eccl 7, 1.

nor is it always the proper thing to blush:

¹⁵ Before father and mother be ashamed of immorality,
before master and mistress, of falsehood;

¹⁶ Before prince and ruler, of flattery;
before the public assembly, of crime;

¹⁷ Before friend and companion, of disloyalty,
and of breaking an oath or agreement.

¹⁸ Be ashamed of theft from the people where you settle,
and of stretching out your elbow when you dine;

¹⁹ Of refusing to give when asked,
of defrauding another of his appointed share,

²⁰ Of failing to return a greeting,
and of rebuffing a friend;

²¹ Of gazing at a married woman,
and of entertaining thoughts about another's wife;ʳ
Of trifling with a servant girl you have,
and of violating her couch;

²² Of using harsh words with friends,
and of following up your gifts with insults;ˢ

²³ Of repeating what you hear,
and of betraying secrets—ᵗ

²⁴ These are the things you should rightly avoid as shameful
if you would be looked upon by everyone with favor.

CHAPTER 42

See RG 198–200

¹ But of these things be not ashamed,
lest you sin through human respect:ᵘ

² Of the law of the Most High and his precepts,
or of the sentence to be passed upon the sinful;

³ Of sharing the expenses of a business or a journey,

or of dividing an inheritance or property;

⁴ Of accuracy of scales and balances,
or of tested measures and weights;ᵛ

⁵ Of acquiring much or little,
or of bargaining in dealing with a merchant;
Of constant training of children,
or of beating the sides of a disloyal servant;ʷ

⁶ Of a seal to keep an erring wife at home,
or of a lock placed where there are many hands;

⁷ Of numbering every deposit,
or of recording all that is given or received;

⁸ Of chastisement of the silly and the foolish,
or of the aged and infirm answering for wanton conduct.
Thus you will be truly cautious
and recognized by all men as discreet.

A Father's Care for His Daughter*

⁹ A daughter is a treasure that keeps her father wakeful,
and worry over her drives away rest:ˣ
Lest she pass her prime unmarried,
or when she is married, lest she be disliked;

¹⁰ While unmarried, lest she be seduced,
or, as a wife, lest she prove unfaithful;
Lest she conceive in her father's home,
or be sterile in that of her husband.

¹¹ Keep a close watch on your daughter,
lest she make you the sport of your enemies,
A byword in the city, a reproach among the people,
an object of derision in public gatherings.
See that there is no lattice in her room,
no place that overlooks the approaches to the house.ʸ

42, 9-14: The author considers a daughter to be a source of anxiety to her father, lest she fail to marry, or be seduced, or lest, marrying, she be disliked, prove unfaithful, or find herself sterile (9f). He is advised to keep a close watch on her at home, and on her companionship while abroad, lest he suf-fer on her account among the people (11-14).

r: Sir 9, 8; Mt 5, 28.   *s:* Sir 18, 14; 20, 13.   *t:* Sir 27, 16.   *u:* Prv 24, 23; Jas 2, 1.   *v:* Prv 11, 1.   *w:* Sir 30, 1-13; 33, 25-33.   *x:* Sir 7, 24f.   *y:* Sir 26, 10.

12 Let her not parade her charms before
    men,^z
  or spend her time with married
    women;
13 For just as moths come from
    garments,
  so harm to women comes from
    women:
14 Better a man's harshness than a woman's
    indulgence,
  and a frightened daughter than any
    disgrace.

The Works of God in Nature*

15 Now will I recall God's works;
  what I have seen, I will describe.
  At God's word were his works brought
    into being;
  they do his will as he has ordained for
    them.^a
16 As the rising sun is clear to all,
  so the glory of the LORD fills all his
    works;
17 Yet even God's holy ones must fail
  in recounting the wonders of the
    LORD,
  Though God has given these, his hosts,
    the strength
  to stand firm before his glory.
18 He plumbs the depths and penetrates the
    heart;
  their innermost being he
    understands.
  The Most High possesses all
    knowledge,
  and sees from of old the things that are
    to come:
19 He makes known the past and the
    future,
  and reveals the deepest secrets.
20 No understanding does he lack;
  no single thing escapes him.^b
21 Perennial is his almighty
    wisdom;
  he is from all eternity one and the
    same,

22 With nothing added, nothing taken
    away;
  no need of a counselor for him!^c
23 How beautiful are all his works!
  even to the spark and fleeting vision!
24 The universe lives and abides forever;
  to meet each need, each creature is
    preserved.
25 All of them differ, one from another,
  yet none of them has he made in
    vain,
  For each in turn, as it comes, is good;
  can one ever see enough of their
    splendor?^d

CHAPTER 43

See RG
198–200

1 The clear vault of the sky shines
    forth^e
  like heaven itself, a vision of glory.
2 The orb of the sun, resplendent at its
    rising:
  what a wonderful work of the Most
    High!
3 At noon it seethes the surface of the
    earth,
  and who can bear its fiery heat?
4 Like a blazing furnace of solid metal,
  it sets the mountains aflame with its
    rays;
  By its fiery darts the land is
    consumed;
  the eyes are dazzled by its light.
5 Great indeed is the LORD who made
    it,
  at whose orders it urges on its
    steeds.
6 The moon, too, that marks the changing
    times,
  governing the seasons, their lasting
    sign,^f
7 By which we know the feast days and
    fixed dates,
  this light-giver which wanes in its
    course:
8 As its name says, each month it renews
    itself;

42, 15—43, 35: These verses comprise a new section. In
them the author contemplates God's power, beauty and goodness as manifested in the mighty work of creating and preserving the universe (42, 15ff. 23. 25; 43, 1-27), his omniscience (42,
18ff), his perfect wisdom (21f), his eternity (24). The conclusion

is a fervent hymn of praise (43, 28-35). Cf Sir 16, 22—18, 13.

z: 12f: Sir 9, 1-9. a: Ps 77, 12f. b: Sir 39, 19; Wis 1, 6-10.
c: Is 40, 13; Rom 11, 34. d: Sir 33, 15. e: 1ff: Ps 19, 2f. f: Lv
23, 5; Nm 28, 11-14; Ps 81, 4.

how wondrous in this change!

9 The beauty, the glory, of the heavens are
the stars
that adorn with their sparkling the
heights of God,g

10 At whose command they keep their
place
and never relax in their vigils.
A weapon against the flood waters stored
on high,
lighting up the firmament by its
brilliance,

11 Behold the rainbow! Then bless its
Maker,
for majestic indeed is its splendor;h

12 It spans the heavens with its glory,
this bow bent by the mighty hand of
God.

13 His rebuke marks out the path for the
lightning,
and speeds the arrows of his judgment
to their goal.

14 At it the storehouse is opened,
and like vultures the clouds hurry forth.

15 In his majesty he gives the storm its
power
and breaks off the hailstones.

16 The thunder of his voice makes the earth
writhe;
before his might the mountains
quake.

17 A word from him drives on the south
wind,
the angry north wind, the hurricane
and the storm.

18 He sprinkles the snow like fluttering
birds;
it comes to settle like swarms of
locusts.

19 Its shining whiteness blinds the eyes,
the mind is baffled by its steady
fall.

20 He scatters frost like so much salt;
it shines like blossoms on the
thornbush.

21 Cold northern blasts he sends
that turn the ponds to lumps of ice.
He freezes over every body of
water,
and clothes each pool with a coat of
mail.

22 When the mountain growth is scorched
with heat,
and the flowering plains as though by
flames,

23 The dripping clouds restore them
all,
and the scattered dew enriches the
parched land.

24 His is the plan that calms the deep,
and plants the islands in
the sea.

25 Those who go down to the sea tell part of
its story,
and when we hear them we are
thunderstruck;i

26 In it are his creatures, stupendous,
amazing,
all kinds of life, and the monsters of
the deep.

27 For him each messenger succeeds,
and at his bidding accomplishes his
will.j

28 More than this we need not add;
let the last word be, he is all in all!*

29 Let us praise him the more, since we
cannot fathom him,
for greater is he than all his works;

30 Awful indeed is the LORD's majesty,
and wonderful is his power.

31 Lift up your voices to glorify
the LORD,
though he is still beyond your power
to praise;

32 Extol him with renewed strength,
and weary not, though you cannot
reach the end:

33 For who can see him and describe him?
or who can praise him as he is?k

34 Beyond these, many things lie hid;
only a few of his works have we
seen.

35 It is the LORD who has made all things,

43, 28: All in all: the perfections reflected in creation are found in a transcendent way in God, who alone is their source.

g: Ps 8, 4.   h: Gn 9, 13.   i: Ps 104, 25-30.   j: Ps 33, 6.   k: Ps 106, 2.

and to those who fear him he gives
wisdom.[l]

See RG
198–200

CHAPTER 44

Praise of Israel's Great Ancestors

[1] Now will I praise those godly men,*
our ancestors, each in his own
time:*
[2] The abounding glory of the Most High's
portion,
his own part, since the days of old.
Subduers of the land in kingly
fashion,
men of renown for their might,[m]
[3] Or counselors in their prudence,
or seers of all things in prophecy;[n]
[4] Resolute princes of the folk,
and governors with their staves;
Authors skilled in composition,
and forgers of epigrams with their
spikes;
[5] Composers of melodious psalms,
or discoursers on lyric themes;
[6] Stalwart men, solidly established
and at peace in their own estates—
[7] All these were glorious in their time,
each illustrious in his day.
[8] Some of them have left behind a name
and men recount their praiseworthy
deeds;
[9] But of others there is no memory,
for when they ceased, they ceased.
And they are as though they had not
lived,
they and their children after them.
[10] Yet these also were godly men
whose virtues have not been
forgotten;

[11] Their wealth remains in their families,
their heritage with their descendants;
[12] Through God's covenant with them their
family endures,
their posterity for their sake.
[13] And for all time their progeny will
endure,
their glory will never be blotted out;
[14] Their bodies are peacefully laid away,
but their name lives on and on.[o]
[15] At gatherings their wisdom is retold,
and the assembly proclaims their
praise.

The Early Patriarchs

[16] [ENOCH* walked with the LORD and was
taken up,[p]
that succeeding generations might
learn by his example.]
[17] NOAH, found just and perfect,
renewed the race in the time of
devastation.[q]
Because of his worth there were
survivors,
and with a sign to him the deluge
ended;
[18] A lasting agreement was made with
him,
that never should all flesh be
destroyed.
[19] ABRAHAM, father of many peoples,
kept his glory without stain:[r]
[20] He observed the precepts of the Most
High,
and entered into an agreement with
him;
In his own flesh he incised the
ordinance,*

44, 1—50, 24: As in the previous section God's wisdom shone forth in the works of nature, so in these chapters it is also revealed through the history of God's people as seen in the lives of their patriarchs, prophets, priests and rulers. The example of these great men, whose virtues are here recalled, constitutes a high point of the author's teaching and illustrates his belief in the canonical Scriptures.

44, 1-15: The reader is here introduced to those men of Israel, later mentioned by name, who through various achievements and beneficial social activities have acquired great renown (1-8. 14f); and also to those who, though forgotten, endure through the fruit of their virtues and through their families because of God's covenant with them (9-13).

44, 16: Enoch: because of his friendship with God and

also by reason of his unusual disappearance from the earth, this prophet's renown was great among the chosen people, particularly in the two centuries just before the coming of Christ; cf Gn 5, 21-24; Heb 11, 5. The present verse is an expansion of the original text; cf Sir 49, 14.

44, 20: In his own flesh . . . ordinance: the covenant of circumcision; cf Gn 17, 10-14. And when tested . . . loyal: Abraham's willingness to sacrifice his son Isaac at the Lord's command; cf Gn 22, 9-12.

l: Jb 28, 28.   m: Dt 32, 8f.   n: Sir 39, 1.   o: Wis 3, 3.   p: Sir 49, 14; Gn 5, 18-24; Heb 11, 5.   q: Gn 6, 8—9, 29; Heb 11, 7.   r: Gn 12, 1—25, 10; Gal 3, 6; Heb 11, 8-19.

Praise of the Heroes

The final chapters of Sirach form a distinct unit in which Ben Sirach sings the praises of Israel's heroes. It is the best-known passage in Sirach and represents a kind of finale. With the exception of the last hero, Simon son of Onias, all the heroes are known from biblical literature. Thus, this long poem of praise partly functions as a retelling of biblical history. Its primary function is to recall the legacy of these renowned men (no women are included on the list), because they illustrate what it means to be truly honored. They are the paradigmatic examples of Ben Sirach's claim that a good name lasts forever (41, 13).

and when tested he was found loyal.[s]

21 For this reason, God promised him with
    an oath
    that in his descendants the nations
      would be blessed,
That he would make him numerous as
    the grains of dust,
    and exalt his posterity like the stars;
That he would give them an inheritance
    from sea to sea,
    and from the River[*] to the ends of the
      earth.

22 And for ISAAC he renewed the same
    promise
    because of Abraham, his father.
The covenant with all his forebears was
    confirmed,
    and the blessing rested upon the head
      of JACOB.[t]

23 God acknowledged him as the
    firstborn,
    and gave him his inheritance.
He fixed the boundaries for his
    tribes,
    and their division into twelve.

**See RG
198–200**

CHAPTER 45

Praise of Moses, Aaron
and Phinehas

1 From him was to spring the man[*]
who won the favor of all:[u]
Dear to God and men,
    MOSES, whose memory is held in
      benediction.

2 God's honor[v] devolved upon
    him,[*]
    and the Lord strengthened him with
      fearful powers;[w]

3 God wrought swift miracles at his
    words
    and sustained him in the king's
      presence.
He gave him the commandments for his
    people,
    and revealed to him his glory.[x]

4 For his trustworthiness and
    meekness
God selected him from all
    mankind;[y]

5 He permitted him to hear his
    voice,
    and led him into the cloud,
Where, face to face,[*] he gave him the
    commandments,
    the law of life and
      understanding,
That he might teach his precepts to
    Jacob,
    his judgments and decrees to
      Israel.

44, 21: The River: the Euphrates; cf Gn 2, 14.

45, 1-5: Moses manifested God's power through miracles (1ff), God's authority through the promulgation of the commandments and the law (5), and God's mercy through the intimacy granted him by the Lord for his own faithfulness and meekness (4f). The very personification of the old covenant, Moses was also a type of Christ, the Prophet and Legislator of the new; cf Dt 18, 15.

45, 2: God's honor devolved upon him: Moses was actu-

ally God's substitute in dealing with Pharaoh, hence God entrusted his own honor to Moses.

45, 5: Face to face: on God's intimacy with Moses, see Ex 33, 11; Nm 12, 8. St. Paul alluded to this in 1 Cor 13, 12.

s: Gn 17, 10; 22, 1. t: Gn 26, 3. 5. 24; 27, 28f; 28, 14. u: Ex 2, 2; 11, 3; 33, 11; Nm 12, 7. v: Ex 7, 1—13, 22. w: 2-5: Ex 7— Dt 34. x: Ex 4, 17; 7, 1. y: Nm 12, 3. 7.

⁶ He raised up also, like Moses in
holiness,*
his brother AARON, of the tribe of
Levi.^z
⁷ He made him perpetual in his
office
when he bestowed on him the
priesthood* of his people;
He established him in honor
and crowned him with lofty
majesty;
⁸ He clothed him with splendid apparel,
and adorned him with the glorious
vestments:
Breeches and tunic and robe
with pomegranates around the hem,
⁹ And a rustle of bells round about,
through whose pleasing sound at each
step
He would be heard within the sanctuary,
and the children of his race would be
remembered;
¹⁰ The sacred vestments of gold, of violet,
and of crimson, wrought with
embroidery;
The breastpiece for decision, the ephod
and cincture
¹¹ with scarlet yarn, the work of the
weaver;
Precious stones with seal engravings
in golden settings, the work of the
jeweler,
To commemorate in incised letters
each of the tribes of Israel;
¹² On his turban the diadem of gold,
its plate wrought with the insignia of
holiness,
Majestic, glorious, renowned for
splendor,
a delight to the eyes, beauty supreme.
¹³ Before him, no one was adorned with
these,

nor may they ever be worn by any
Except his sons and them alone,
generation after generation, for all
time.
¹⁴ His cereal offering is wholly burnt
with the established sacrifice twice
each day;
¹⁵ For Moses ordained him
and anointed him with the holy oil,
In a lasting covenant with him
and with his family, as permanent as
the heavens,
That he should serve God in his
priesthood
and bless his people in his name.
¹⁶ He chose him from all mankind
to offer holocausts and choice
offerings,
To burn sacrifices of sweet odor for a
memorial,
and to atone for the people of Israel.
¹⁷ He gave to him his laws,
and authority to prescribe and to
judge:
To teach the precepts to his people,
and the ritual to the descendants of
Israel.
¹⁸ Men of other families were inflamed
against him,
were jealous of him in the desert,
The followers of Dathan and Abiram,
and the band of Korah in their
defiance.^a
¹⁹ But the LORD saw this and became
angry,
he destroyed them in his burning
wrath.
He brought down upon them a miracle,
and consumed them with his flaming
fire.
²⁰ Then he increased the glory of
Aaron^b

45, 6-21: The author here expresses his reverence and esteem for the priesthood of the old covenant. He recalls God's
choice of Aaron and his sons for this sublime office (6f), and
describes in detail the beauty of the high priest's vestments
(8-13). He relates the ordination of Aaron at the hands of Moses, his brother (15), and describes the priestly functions, of
offering sacrifice to God (16), and of blessing (15), teaching,
governing and judging the people (17); the inheritance of the
high priest (20ff); the punishment of those families who were

jealous of Aaron (18f); and the confirmation of the covenant
of the priesthood with Aaron's descendants through Phinehas
(23ff).
45, 7: The priesthood of Aaron was superseded by the
priesthood of Christ; cf Heb 7, 18-28.

---

z: 6ff: Ex 28f; Wis 18, 24.   a: Nm 16, 1ff.   b: 20f: Nm 18, 11-
21; Dt 10, 9.

and bestowed upon him his
   inheritance:
The sacred offerings he allotted to him,
   with the showbread as his portion;
21 The oblations of the LORD are his food,
   a gift to him and his descendants.
22 But he holds no land among the people
   nor shares with them their heritage;
For the LORD himself is his portion,
   his inheritance in the midst of Israel.

23 PHINEHAS too, the son of Eleazar,
   was the courageous third of his line
When, zealous for the God of all,
   he met the crisis of his people c
And, at the prompting of his noble heart,
   atoned for the children of Israel.
24 Therefore on him again God conferred
   the right,
   in a covenant of friendship, to provide
   for the sanctuary,
So that he and his descendants
   should possess the high priesthood
   forever.
25 For even his covenant with David,
   the son of Jesse of the tribe of Judah,
Was an individual heritage through one
   son alone;
   but the heritage of Aaron is for all his
   descendants.d

26 And now bless the LORD
   who has crowned you with glory!
May he grant you wisdom of heart
   to govern his people in justice,
Lest their welfare should ever be forgotten,
   or your authority, throughout all time.

CHAPTER 46

See RG
198-200
Joshua, Caleb and the Judges
1 Valiant leader was JOSHUA, son of
   Nun*

assistant to Moses in the prophetic
   office,
Formed to be, as his name implies,
   the great savior of God's chosen ones,
To punish the enemy
   and to win the inheritance for Israel.e
2 What glory was his when he raised his
   arm,
   to brandish his javelin against
   the city!f
3 And who could withstand him
   when he fought the battles of the LORD?*
4 Did he not by his power stop the sun,
   so that one day became two?g
5 He called upon the Most High God
   when his enemies beset him on all
   sides,
And God Most High gave answer to him
   in hailstones of tremendous power,
6 Which he rained down upon the hostile
   army
   till on the slope he destroyed the foe;
That all the doomed nations might know
   that the LORD was watching over his
   people's battles.
And because he was a devoted follower
   of God
7 and in Moses' lifetime showed himself
   loyal,
He and CALEB,* son of Jephunneh,
   when they opposed the rebel
   assembly,
Averted God's anger from the people
   and suppressed the wicked
   complaint— h
8 Because of this, they were the only two
   spared
   from the six hundred thousand
   infantry,
To lead the people into their
   inheritance,
   the land flowing with milk and honey.i

46, 1-6: Joshua: whose name means "the LORD is savior"
(1), was the instrument through which God delivered his
people in miraculous ways (2-6) by destroying their enemies, whose land he gave to the Israelites as an inheritance
(1).

46, 3: The battles of the LORD: cf Jos 6—10.

46, 7-10: Caleb, who with Joshua advised Moses and the
people in the desert to conquer Canaan, despite the counsel of
their companion scouts and the rebellion of the people, merited to lead the Israelites of the succeeding generation into the
Promised Land. Caleb in his old age received as his inheritance a portion of land which he himself had previously conquered; cf Jos 15, 13f.

c: Nm 25, 7-13; Ps 106, 30f; 1 Mc 2, 26. 54. d: 2 Sm 7, 12-16.
e: Ex 17, 9; Nm 27, 18; Dt 34, 9; Jos 1, 1-4. f: Jos 8, 18. g: Jos
10, 13. h: Nm 13, 30; 14, 6. i: Nm 14, 22-38.

9 And the strength he gave to Caleb
  remained with him even in his old age
Till he won his way onto the summits of
  the land;
  his family too received an
    inheritance,[j]
10 That all the people of Jacob might know
  how good it is to be a devoted follower
  of the LORD.
11 The JUDGES,* too, each one of them,
  whose hearts were not deceived,
Who did not abandon God:
  may their memory be ever blessed,[k]
12 Their bones return to life from their
    resting place,
  and their names receive fresh luster in
    their children!
13 Beloved of his people, dear to his
    Maker,
  dedicated from his mother's womb,
Consecrated to the LORD as a prophet,
  was SAMUEL, the judge and priest.
At God's word he established the
    kingdom
  and anointed princes to rule the
    people.[l]
14 By the law of the LORD he judged the
    nation,
  when he visited the encampments of
    Jacob.
15 As a trustworthy prophet he was sought
    out
  and his words proved him true as a
    seer.
16 He, too, called upon God,
  and offered him a suckling lamb;[m]
17 Then the LORD thundered forth from
    heaven,
  and the tremendous roar of his voice
    was heard.[n]
18 He brought low the rulers of the enemy

and destroyed all the lords of the
  Philistines.
19 When Samuel approached the end of his
    life,
  he testified before the LORD and his
    anointed prince,
"No bribe or secret gift have I taken from
    any man!"
  and no one dared gainsay him.[o]
20 Even when he lay buried, his guidance
    was sought;
  he made known to the king his fate,
And from the grave he raised his voice
  as a prophet, to put an end to
    wickedness.[p]

CHAPTER 47

Nathan, David and Solomon

See RG
198–200

1 After him came NATHAN*
  who served in the presence of David.[q]
2 Like the choice fat of the sacred
    offerings,
  so was DAVID in Israel.[r]
3 He made sport of lions as though they
    were kids,
  and of bears, like lambs of the flock.[s]
4 As a youth he slew the giant
  and wiped out the people's disgrace,
When his hand let fly the slingstone
  that crushed the pride of Goliath.[t]
5 Since he called upon the Most High God,
  who gave strength to his right arm
To defeat the skilled warrior
  and raise up the might of his people,
6 Therefore the women sang his praises
  and ascribed to him tens of thousands.
When he assumed the royal crown, he
    battled[u]
7   and subdued the enemy on every
    side.
He destroyed the hostile Philistines

46, 11-20: Of the Judges praised and blessed for their fidelity to God in opposing idolatry, Samuel, a man of spotless integrity, was the greatest (11f. 19). He was judge of the entire nation, and was also a prophet and priest who through his sacrificial offering obtained victory over the Philistines. He established the kingdom, anointed kings (13-18), and even after his death foretold the king's fate and put an end to wickedness (20).

47, 1-11: David, a youthful and fearless warrior, the favorite of all Israel, by defeating Goliath, the boastful Philistine giant, removed the people's disgrace and greatly

strengthened their power (1-7). With his whole being he loved and praised God, and his devotion to divine worship led him to develop liturgical cult. David fell into sin, but repenting, received pardon from God and the promise of an everlasting kingdom (8-11).

j: Jos 14, 6; 15, 13.   k: Jgs 1, 1—16, 31.   l: 1 Sm 1, 10ff; 8, 4ff; 10, 1; 16, 13.   m: 1 Sm 7, 9.   n: Sir 12, 18.   o: 1 Sm 12, 3. p: 1 Sm 28, 14.   q: 2 Sm 7, 2.   r: 1 Sm 16, 11.   s: 1 Sm 17, 35. t: 1 Sm 17, 49.   u: 1 Sm 18, 7.

and shattered their power till our own
day.[v]

8 With his every deed he offered thanks
to God Most High, in words of praise.
With his whole being he loved his
Maker
and daily had his praises sung;

9 He added beauty to the feasts
and solemnized the seasons of each
year
With string music before the altar,
providing sweet melody for the
psalms[w]

10 So that when the Holy Name was praised,
before daybreak the sanctuary would
resound.

11 The LORD forgave him his sins
and exalted his strength forever;
He conferred on him the rights of
royalty
and established his throne in Israel.[x]

12 Because of his merits he had as his
successor*
a wise son, who lived in security:[y]

13 SOLOMON reigned during an era of peace,
for God made tranquil all his borders.
He built a house to the name of God,
and established a lasting sanctuary.[z]

14 How wise you were when you were
young,
overflowing with instruction, like the
Nile in flood![a]

15 Your understanding covered the whole
earth,
and, like a sea, filled it with
knowledge.

16 Your fame reached distant coasts,
and their peoples came to hear you;

17 With song and story and riddle,

and with your answers, you astounded
the nations.

18 You were called by that glorious name
which was conferred upon Israel.*
Gold you gathered like so much iron,
you heaped up silver as though it were
lead;

19 But you abandoned yourself to women
and gave them dominion over your
body.[b]

20 You brought dishonor upon your
reputation,
shame upon your marriage,
Wrath upon your descendants,
and groaning upon your domain;

21 Thus two governments came into being,
when in Ephraim kingship was
usurped.[c]

22 But God does not withdraw his mercy,
nor permit even one of his promises to
fail.
He does not uproot the posterity of his
chosen one,
nor destroy the offspring of his friend.
So he gave to Jacob a remnant,
to David a root from his own family.[d]

23 Solomon finally slept with his fathers,
and left behind him one of his sons,
Expansive* in folly, limited in sense,
REHOBOAM, who by his policy made
the people rebel;
Until one arose who should not be
remembered,
the sinner who led Israel into sin,[e]
Who brought ruin to Ephraim

24 and caused them to be exiled from
their land.

Elijah and Elisha
Their sinfulness grew more and more,

47, 12-24: Solomon, son and successor of David, inherited peace through his father's conquests. He built the magnificent temple of Jerusalem (12f) and received from God the favor of unparalleled wisdom, through which he obtained great fame (14-17). Luxury and sensuality, however, brought disgrace upon him, and because of his oppressive burdens, he disposed the kingdom for division after his death (19-21. 23f). Nevertheless God did not withdraw his promise of establishing his throne in the descendants of David (22).

47, 18: Cf 2 Sm 12, 25, where Solomon is called Jedidiah, "beloved of the Lord." The same term is used of Israel in Jer 11, 15.

47, 23: Expansive: the name Rehoboam means "the people is expansive," that is, widespread. The sinner: Jeroboam; cf 1 Kgs 12, 2. 20. 26-32.

v: 2 Sm 5, 6-25. w: 1 Chr 16, 4ff; 23, 2ff; 25, 1-7. x: 2 Sm 12, 13; 7, 12-16. y: 1 Kgs 2, 12. z: 1 Kgs 5, 1. 5. a: 14-18: 1 Kgs 5, 9-14; 10, 14-28. b: 1 Kgs 11, 1ff. c: 1 Kgs 12, 1ff. d: 2 Sm 7, 15; Ps 89, 34ff. e: 1 Kgs 11, 43; 12, 13. 21; 13, 34; 2 Kgs 17, 6ff.

25 and they lent themselves to every evil,*

CHAPTER 48

See RG
198-200 [1]Till like a fire there appeared the
        prophet
    whose words were as a flaming
        furnace.[f]
2 Their staff of bread he shattered,
    in his zeal he reduced them to straits;
3 By God's word he shut up the heavens
    and three times brought down fire.[g]
4 How awesome are you, ELIJAH!
    Whose glory is equal to yours?
5 You brought a dead man back to life
    from the nether world, by the will of
        the LORD.[h]
6 You sent kings down to destruction,
    and nobles, from their beds of
        sickness.[i]
7 You heard threats at Sinai,
    at Horeb avenging judgments.[j]
8 You anointed kings who should inflict
        vengeance,
    and a prophet as your successor.[k]
9 You were taken aloft in a whirlwind,
    in a chariot with fiery horses.[l]
10 You are destined, it is written, in time to
        come
    to put an end to wrath before the day
        of the LORD,
    To turn back the hearts of fathers toward
        their sons,
    and to re-establish the tribes of
        Jacob.[m]
11 Blessed is he who shall have seen you
        before he dies,
12   O Elijah, enveloped in the whirlwind![n]

Then ELISHA, filled with a twofold
        portion of his spirit,*
    wrought many marvels by his mere
        word.
    During his lifetime he feared no one,
        nor was any man able to intimidate his
        will.
13 Nothing was beyond his power;[o]
    beneath him flesh was brought back
        into life.
14 In life he performed wonders,
    and after death, marvelous deeds.
15 Despite all this the people did not repent,
    nor did they give up their sins,
    Until they were rooted out of their land
        and scattered all over the earth.
    But Judah remained, a tiny people,
        with its rulers from the house of
        David.[p]
16 Some of these did what was right,
    but others were extremely sinful.

Hezekiah and Isaiah*

17 HEZEKIAH fortified his city
    and had water brought into it;[q]
    With iron tools he cut through the rock
        and he built reservoirs for water.
18 During his reign Sennacherib led an
        invasion,
    and sent his adjutant;
    He shook his fist at Zion
        and blasphemed God in his pride.[r]
19 The people's hearts melted within them,
    and they were in anguish like that of
        childbirth.
20 But they called upon the Most High God
    and lifted up their hands to him;

47, 25—48, 11: The prophetic ministry of Elijah amid
widespread idolatry is here described as a judgment by fire
(47, 25f). Through his preaching, miracles and vengeance
against God's enemies within and without Israel, the prophet
succeeded for a time in destroying idols and in restoring faith
and the worship of the true God (48, 2-8). His miraculous departure from this life gave rise to the belief that he did not die
but would return before the end of the world to put an end to
wrath and restore the tribes of Israel (9ff). Cf Mt 17, 9-13.

48, 12-16: Elisha fearlessly continued the work of his predecessor by numerous miracles (12ff), but the obstinacy of
the people eventually brought on the destruction of the kingdom of Israel and the dispersion of its subjects. Judah, however, survived under the rule of Davidic kings, both good and
bad (15f).

48, 17-25: The fidelity, trust and courage of King Hezekiah (17. 22), the zeal of the prophet Isaiah, and the prayer of
the people (20) availed with God. The Assyrian oppressors
were routed (18f. 21), the king's life was prolonged, and consolations were granted the people through Isaiah's prophecies
concerning the future (23ff), especially the coming of the
Messiah and the establishment of his kingdom; cf Is 7, 14; 9,
6f; 40—65.

f: 1 Kgs 17, 1.   g: 1 Kgs 17, 1; 2 Kgs 1, 9-14.   h: 1 Kgs 17, 22.
i: 1 Kgs 21, 19; 2 Kgs 1, 17.   j: 1 Kgs 19, 8ff.   k: 1 Kgs 19, 15ff.
l: 2 Kgs 2, 11.   m: Mal 3, 23f; Mt 17, 10.   n: 2 Kgs 2, 9; 3, 13.
o: 13f: 2 Kgs 13, 21.   p: 2 Kgs 15, 29; 18, 11.   q: 2 Kgs 20, 20;
2 Chr 32, 3ff. 30.   r: 2 Kgs 18, 13ff; Is 36, 1ff.

He heard the prayer they uttered,
   and saved them through ISAIAH.[s]
21 God struck the camp of the Assyrians
   and routed them with a plague.[t]
22 For Hezekiah did what was right
   and held fast to the paths of David,
As ordered by the illustrious prophet
   Isaiah, who saw the truth in visions.
23 In his lifetime he turned back the sun
   and prolonged the life of the king.[u]
24 By his powerful spirit he looked into the
     future[v]
   and consoled the mourners of Zion;
25 He foretold what should be till the end of
     time,
   hidden things yet to be fulfilled.

See RG
198-200

CHAPTER 49

*Josiah and the Prophets**

1 The name JOSIAH is like blended
   incense,
   made lasting by a skilled perfumer.[w]
Precious is his memory, like honey to the
   taste,
   like music at a banquet.
2 For he grieved over our betrayals
   and destroyed the abominable idols.
3 He turned to God with his whole heart,
   and, though times were evil, he
     practiced virtue.
4 Except for David, Hezekiah and Josiah,
   they all were wicked;
They abandoned the law of the Most High,
   these kings of Judah, right to the very
     end.
5 So he gave over their power to others,
   their glory to a foolish foreign nation
6 Who burned the holy city
   and left its streets desolate,
As JEREMIAH had foretold;[x] 7 for they had
   treated him badly

who even in the womb had been made
   a prophet,
To root out, pull down, and destroy,
   and then to build and to plant.[y]
8 EZEKIEL beheld the vision
   and described the different creatures of
     the chariot;[z]
9 He also referred to JOB,
   who always persevered in the right
     path.[a]
10 Then, too, the TWELVE PROPHETS—
   may their bones return to life from
     their resting place!—
Gave new strength to Jacob
   and saved him by their faith and hope.

The Heroes after the Exile

11 How can we fittingly praise
   ZERUBBABEL,*
   who was like a signet ring on God's
     right hand,[b]
12 And Jeshua, Jozadak's son?
   In their time they built the house of
     God;
They erected the holy temple,
   destined for everlasting glory.
13 Extolled be the memory of NEHEMIAH!
   He rebuilt our ruined walls,
Restored our shattered defenses,
   and set up gates and bars.[c]

The Earliest Patriarchs

14 Few on earth have been made the equal
   of ENOCH,*
   for he was taken up bodily.[d]
15 Was ever a man born like JOSEPH?
   Even his dead body was provided for.[e]
16 Glorious, too, were SHEM and SETH and
     ENOS;
   but beyond that of any living being
   was the splendor of ADAM.[f]

49, 1-10: The author's praise of King Josiah (1-3), of the prophets Jeremiah and Ezekiel and likewise the minor prophets (7-10) derives from their spirit of fidelity to the Lord and his law amid the infidelity of kings and people (4ff. 10).

49, 11ff: Zerubbabel and Jeshua, in rebuilding the temple, and Nehemiah, the governor, in repairing the walls of the Holy City, also restored what these constructions signify, namely, religious worship and civil authority as prescribed in the law.

49, 14ff: The patriarchs here mentioned were glorious be-

cause of their spirit of religion, i.e., their profound reverence for God and obedience to him. The splendor of Adam, moreover, was due to his direct origin from God.

s: 2 Kgs 19, 20.   *t:* 2 Kgs 19, 35; Is 37, 36.   *u:* 2 Kgs 20, 11; Is 38, 8.   *v:* 24f: 2 Kgs 20, 17; Is 40, 1ff; 42, 9; 46, 10; 48, 6; 61, 2. *w:* 2 Kgs 22, 1; 2 Chr 34, 1.   *x:* 2 Kgs 25, 9; 2 Chr 36, 19.   *y:* Jer 1, 5. 10.   *z:* Ez 1, 4ff.   *a:* Ez 14, 14. 20.   *b:* 11f: Ezr 3, 2; Hg 1, 12; Zec 3, 1.   *c:* Neh 1, 1; 3, 1.   *d:* Sir 44, 16; Gn 5, 18-24. *e:* Gn 37—50; Ex 13, 19; Jos 24, 32.   *f:* Gn 1, 27; 4, 25f.

CHAPTER 50

See RG
198–200

Simon, Son of Jochanan

1 The greatest among his brethren, the
glory of his people,
was SIMON the priest, son of Jochanan,*
In whose time the house of God was
renovated,
in whose days the temple was
reinforced.

2 In his time also the wall was built
with powerful turrets for the temple
precincts;

3 In his time the reservoir was dug,
the pool with a vastness like the sea's.

4 He protected his people against
brigands
and strengthened his city against the
enemy.

5 How splendid he was as he appeared
from the tent,
as he came from within the veil!

6 Like a star shining among the clouds,
like the full moon at the holyday
season;

7 Like the sun shining upon the temple,
like the rainbow appearing in the
cloudy sky;

8 Like the blossoms on the branches in
springtime,
like a lily on the banks of a stream;
Like the trees of Lebanon in summer,

9 like the fire of incense at the sacrifice;
Like a vessel of beaten gold,
studded with precious stones;

10 Like a luxuriant olive tree thick with fruit,
like a cypress standing against the
clouds;

11 Vested in his magnificent robes,
and wearing his garments of
splendor,*g*
As he ascended the glorious altar
and lent majesty to the court of the
sanctuary.

12 When he received the sundered victims
from the priests
while he stood before the sacrificial
wood,
His brethren ringed him about like a
garland,
like a stand of cedars on Lebanon;

13 All the sons of Aaron in their dignity
clustered around him like poplars,
With the offerings to the LORD in their
hands,
in the presence of the whole assembly
of Israel.

14 Once he had completed the services at
the altar
with the arranging of the sacrifices for
the Most High,

15 And had stretched forth his hand for the
cup,*h*
to offer blood of the grape,
And poured it out at the foot of the
altar,
a sweet-smelling odor to the Most
High God,

16 The sons of Aaron would sound a
blast,
the priests, on their trumpets of beaten
metal;
A blast to resound mightily
as a reminder before the Most High.*i*

17 Then all the people with one accord
would quickly fall prostrate to the
ground
In adoration before the Most High,
before the Holy One of Israel.

18 Then hymns would re-echo,
and over the throng sweet strains of
praise resound.

50, 1-21: The son of Jochanan here mentioned was Simon II, in whose time as high priest (219-196 B.C.) great works were accomplished for the benefit of public worship and welfare (1-4). The author, a contemporary of this high priest, describes in great detail and by numerous comparisons the impression of awful majesty received, the lofty joy aroused, at sight of the high priest fully vested entering the sanctuary, ascending the altar (6-11), and, in the presence of the whole assembly of Israel, encircled by assistant priests bearing offerings, sacrificing the burnt offering on the Day of Atonement, while the trumpets blast and the people bow down in adoration of the Most High (12-17). The hymnody, the joyful shouts of the multitude, and finally the high priest's blessing, in which he pronounces—once only in the year, on this occasion—the holy name of Yahweh, climax the description of this most solemn Jewish liturgical function (18-21).

g: Sir 45, 8-12; Ex 28, 2-5; 39, 1-21. *h:* 15f: Nm 15, 5; 28, 7.
i: Nm 10, 10.

^{19} All the people of the land would shout
for joy,
praying to the Merciful One,
As the high priest completed the services
at the altar
by presenting to God the sacrifice
due;
^{20} Then coming down he would raise his
hands
over all the congregation of Israel.^{j}
The blessing of the LORD would be upon
his lips,
the name of the LORD would be his
glory.
^{21} Then again the people would lie
prostrate
to receive from him the blessing of the
Most High.

^{22} And now, bless the God of all,*
who has done wondrous things on
earth;
Who fosters men's growth from their
mother's womb,
and fashions them according to his
will!
^{23} May he grant you joy of heart
and may peace abide among you;
^{24} May his goodness toward us endure in
Israel
as long as the heavens are above.

Epilogue and Canticles

^{25} My whole being loathes two nations,*
the third is not even a people:*
^{26} Those who live in Seir* and Philistia,
and the degenerate folk who dwell in
Shechem.^{k}

^{27} Wise instruction, appropriate proverbs,*
I have written in this book,

I, Jesus, son of Eleazar, son of Sirach,
as they gushed forth from my heart's
understanding.
^{28} Happy the man who meditates upon
these things,
wise the man who takes them to
heart!
^{29} If he puts them into practice, he can cope
with anything,
for the fear of the LORD is his lamp.

CHAPTER 51

**See RG
198–200**

^{1} I give you thanks, O God of my
father;*
I praise you, O God my savior!
I will make known your name, refuge of
my life;^{l}
^{2} you have been my helper against my
adversaries.
You have saved me from death,
and kept back my body from the pit,
From the clutches of the nether world
you have snatched my feet;^{m}
^{3} you have delivered me, in your great
mercy,
From the scourge of a slanderous tongue,
and from lips that went over to
falsehood;
From the snare of those who watched for
my downfall,
and from the power of those who
sought my life;^{n}
From many a danger you have saved me,
^{4} from flames that hemmed me in on
every side;^{o}
From the midst of unremitting fire,
^{5} from the deep belly of the nether
world;
From deceiving lips and painters of lies,
^{6} from the arrows of dishonest tongues.
I was at the point of death,

50, 22ff: Praise and thanksgiving are given to God for his wondrous works, and a blessing is invoked on man that he may enjoy peace and gladness of heart and the abiding goodness of the Most High.

50, 25f: The author's abhorrence of the pagan Edomites (Idumeans), Philistines and Samaritans can be understood in the light of Old Testament thinking, which does not always distinguish between hatred of evildoers and hatred of the evil they do.

50, 25: Not even a people: the Samaritans.

50, 26: Seir: Mount Seir in the territory of the Edomites.

Shechem: a city in Samaria.

50. 27ff: These verses contain the subscription of the author, Jesus, son of Eleazar, son of Sirach, to his long and beautiful treatise on wisdom as applying to all of human life, integrating it under the direction of the fear of the Lord.

51. 1-12: A canticle of praise and thanks to God for delivering the author from slander, dangers, destruction, death, the nether world, and evil of every kind.

---

j: Nm 6, 23-26.   *k:* 2 Kgs 17, 24; Jn 4, 9.   *l:* Ps 138, 1.   *m.:* Ps 91, 3.   *n:* Pss 40, 5; 91, 3.   *o:* Ps 66, 12.

my soul was nearing the depths of the
nether world;[p]
⁷ I turned every way, but there was no one
to help me,
I looked for one to sustain me, but
could find no one.[q]
⁸ But then I remembered the mercies of the
LORD,
his kindness through ages past;
For he saves those who take refuge in
him,
and rescues them from every evil.
⁹ So I raised my voice from the very earth,
from the gates of the nether world, my
cry.
¹⁰ I called out: O Lord, you are my father,
you are my champion and my savior;
Do not abandon me in time of trouble,
in the midst of storms and dangers.[r]
¹¹ I will ever praise your name
and be constant in my prayers to you.
Thereupon the LORD heard my voice,
he listened to my appeal;
¹² He saved me from evil of every kind
and preserved me in time of trouble.
For this reason I thank him and I praise
him;
I bless the name of the LORD.*

¹³ *When I was young and innocent,
I sought wisdom.[s]
¹⁴ She came to me in her beauty,
and until the end I will cultivate her.
¹⁵ As the blossoms yielded to ripening
grapes,
the heart's joy,
My feet kept to the level path
because from earliest youth I was
familiar with her.
¹⁶ In the short time I paid heed,
I met with great instruction.
¹⁷ Since in this way I have profited,
I will give my teacher grateful praise.
¹⁸ I became resolutely devoted to her—
the good I persistently strove for.
¹⁹ I burned with desire for her,
never turning back.
I became preoccupied with her,
never weary of extolling her.
My hand opened her gate
and I came to know her secrets.
²⁰ For her I purified my hands;
in cleanness I attained to her.
At first acquaintance with her, I gained
understanding
such that I will never forsake her.[t]

51, 12: After this verse the Hebrew text gives the litany of praise contained below. It is similar to Ps 136. Though not found in any versions, and therefore of doubtful authenticity, the litany seems from internal evidence to go back to the time of Sirach:

Give thanks to the Lord, for he is good, for his mercy endures forever;

Give thanks to the God of glory, for his mercy endures forever;

Give thanks to the guardian of Israel, for his mercy endures forever;

Give thanks to the creator of the universe, for his mercy endures forever;

Give thanks to the redeemer of Israel, for his mercy endures forever;

Give thanks to him who gathers the dispersed of Israel, for his mercy endures forever;

Give thanks to him who builds his city and his sanctuary, for his mercy endures forever;

Give thanks to him who makes a horn to sprout forth, for the house of David, for his mercy endures forever;

Give thanks to him who has chosen for his priests the sons of Zadok, for his mercy endures forever;

Give thanks to the shield of Abraham, for his mercy endures forever;

Give thanks to the rock of Isaac, for his mercy endures forever;

Give thanks to the mighty one of Jacob, for his mercy endures forever;

Give thanks to him who has chosen Zion, for his mercy endures forever;

Give thanks to the king over kings of kings, for his mercy endures forever;

He has lifted up the horn of his people, be this his praise from all his faithful ones,

From the children of Israel, the people close to him. Alleluia! (Cf Ps 148, 14.)

51, 13-30: An alphabetic canticle describing: a) the approach to wisdom through prayer, persistent study and instruction (13-17), purification from sin, enlightenment and ardent desire; b) the possession of wisdom (18-22). The author concludes with an urgent invitation to men to receive instruction in wisdom from him, and to live by it, because wisdom gives herself to those who seek her (23-26); and for their labor. God will reward them in the end (27-30). Cf Mt 11, 28; Eccl 12, 14.

In the Greek of 13f there is an expansion introducing Solomon as the speaker. This deviates from the original author's intent. It reads, "Publicly, in my prayer, facing the temple, I asked for her."

p: Pss 88, 4; 94, 17.   q: Pss 22, 12; 142, 5.   r: Ps 89, 27.   s: Sir 34, 11.   t: Prv 4, 6.

²¹ My whole being was stirred as I learned
    about her;
        therefore I have made her my prize
        possession.
²² The LORD has granted me my lips as a
    reward,
        and my tongue will declare his praises.

²³ Come aside to me, you untutored,
        and take up lodging in the house of
        instruction;ᵘ
²⁴ How long will you be deprived of
    wisdom's food,
        how long will you endure such bitter
        thirst?
²⁵ I open my mouth and speak of her:
        gain, at no cost, wisdom for
        yourselves.ᵛ

²⁶ Submit your neck to her yoke,
        that your mind may accept her
        teaching.
    For she is close to those who seek her,
        and the one who is in earnest finds
        her.ʷ
²⁷ See for yourselves! I have labored only a
    little,
        but have found much.
²⁸ Acquire but a little instruction;
        you will win silver and gold through
        her.
²⁹ Let your spirits rejoice in the mercy of
    God,
        and be not ashamed to give him praise.
³⁰ Work at your tasks in due season,
        and in his own time God will give you
        your reward.ˣ

u: Prv 8, 5.   v: Sir 6, 20.   w: Sir 6, 25.   x: Sir 2, 8; Jb 34, 11; Jn 9, 4.

THE PROPHETIC BOOKS

The prophetic books bear the names of the four major and twelve minor prophets, besides Lamentations and Baruch. The terms "major" and "minor" refer merely to the length of the respective compositions and not to any distinction in the prophetic office. Jonah is a story of the mission of the prophet rather than a collection of prophecies. Lamentations and Daniel are listed among the hagiographa in the Hebrew Bible, not among the prophetic books. The former contains a series of elegies on the fate of Jerusalem; the latter is apocalyptic in character. Daniel, who lived far removed from Palestine, was not called by God to preach; yet the book is counted as prophecy. Baruch, though excluded from the Hebrew canon, is found in the Septuagint version, and the church has always acknowledged it to be sacred and inspired.

The prophetic books, together with the oral preaching of the prophets, were the result of the institution of prophetism, in which a succession of Israelites chosen by God and appointed by him to be prophets received communications from him and transmitted them to the people in his name (Dt 18, 15-20). The prophets were spokesmen of God, intermediaries between him and his people. The communications they received from God came through visions, dreams, and ecstasies and were transmitted to the people through sermons, writings, and symbolic actions.

The office of prophet was due to a direct call from God. It was not the result of heredity, just as it was not a permanent gift but a transient one, subject entirely to the divine will. The prophets preserved and developed revealed religion (1 Sm 12, 6-25), denounced idolatry (1 Kgs 14, 1-13),

defended the moral law (2 Sm 12, 1-15), gave counsel in political matters (Is 31, 1ff), and often also in matters of private life (1 Sm 9, 6-9). At times miracles confirmed their preaching, and their predictions of the future intensified the expectation of the Messiah and of his kingdom.

The prophetic literature in this volume contains the substance of the prophets' authentic preaching, résumés, and genuine samples of such preaching. Some parts were recorded by the prophets themselves, some by persons other than the prophets who uttered them.

The prophecies express judgments of the people's moral conduct, on the basis of the Mosaic alliance between God and Israel. They teach sublime truths and lofty morals. They contain exhortations, threats, announcements of punishment, promises of deliverance, made with solemn authority and in highly imaginative language. In the affairs of men, their prime concern is the interests of God, especially in what pertains to the chosen people through whom the Messiah is to come; hence their denunciations of idolatry and of that externalism in worship which excludes the interior spirit of religion. They are concerned also with the universal nature of the moral law, with personal responsibility, with the person and office of the Messiah, and with the conduct of foreign nations.

In content, the literary genre of prophecy uses warning and threat besides exhortation and promise to declare in God's name events of the near and distant future (Is 8—9). In form, the divine source of prophetic declaration appears in: "The word (or oracle) of the LORD," or "Thus says the LORD," followed by the announcement of a coming event and its moral cause (Hos 4, 7-10). Divine exhortation and promise are introduced by such forms as: "Hear this word, O men of Israel, that the LORD pronounces over you" (Am 3, 1). Kindly and persuasive tones pervade the promises of reward and even the threats of punishment (Am 5, 14-15).

Disregard for exact chronological perspective in the prophecies is an additional characteristic. Predictions of the immediate and distant future are often interrelated, not on the basis of years separating the events but on the analogy of the pattern joining present with very distant, though similar, conditions and circumstances. This is prophetic compenetration, idealization in which persons and things of the more immediate present, in the prophet's day, fade into a wider and more perfect order of persons and things of the future; the former are figures and types of the latter. Thus, some details of what the Psalmist said of the kingdom of David and Solomon (Ps 72) went beyond what was fulfilled in these men, as St. Thomas points out, and found their realization only in the kingdom of Christ. St. Jerome before him, and still earlier the apostles themselves—Peter (Acts 2, 14-36) and Paul (Gal 4, 21-31)—taught us that through anticipation in types we discover in Sacred Scripture the truth of things to come.

Thus the universal blessing for mankind, often promised by God through the mouths of his prophets in figures and types, was in time to become personalized and to confer its full benefit on us through the Word made flesh, who became for us the New Covenant through his life, death, and resurrection, as the prophets had foretold.

The Book of Isaiah

See RG 204-212

The greatest of the prophets appeared at a critical moment of Israel's history. The second half of the eighth century B.C. witnessed the collapse of the northern kingdom under the hammerlike blows of Assyria (722), while Jerusalem itself saw the army of Sennacherib drawn up before its walls (701). In the year that Uzziah, king of Judah, died (742), Isaiah received his call to the prophetic office in the Temple of Jerusalem. Close attention should be given to chapter 6, where this divine summons to be the ambassador of the Most High is circumstantially described.

The vision of the Lord enthroned in glory stamps an indelible character on Isaiah's ministry and provides the key to the understanding of his message. The majesty, holiness and glory of the Lord took possession of his spirit and, conversely, he gained a new awareness of human pettiness and sinfulness. The enormous abyss between God's sovereign holiness and man's sin overwhelmed the prophet. Only the purifying coal of the seraphim could cleanse his lips and prepare him for acceptance of the call: "Here I am, send me!"

The ministry of Isaiah may be divided into three periods, covering the reigns of Jotham (742–735), Ahaz (735–715), and Hezekiah (715–687). To the first period belong, for the most part, the early oracles (1—5) which exposed the moral breakdown of Judah and its capital, Jerusalem. With the accession of Ahaz, the prophet became adviser to the king, whose throne was threatened by the Syro-Ephraimite coalition. Rejecting the plea of Isaiah for faith and courage, the weak Ahaz turned to Assyria for help. From this period came the majority of messianic oracles found in the section of Immanuel prophecies (6—12).

Hezekiah succeeded his father and undertook a religious reform which Isaiah undoubtedly supported. But the old intrigues began again, and the king was soon won over to the pro-Egyptian party. Isaiah denounced this "covenant with death" and again summoned Judah to faith in Yahweh as her only hope. But it was too late; the revolt had already begun. Assyria acted quickly and her army, after ravaging Judah, laid siege to Jerusalem (701). "I shut up Hezekiah like a bird in his cage," boasts the famous inscription of Sennacherib. But Yahweh delivered the city, as Isaiah had promised: God is the Lord of history, and Assyria but an instrument in his hands.

Little is known about the last days of this great religious leader, whose oracles, of singular poetic beauty and power constantly reminded his wayward people of their destiny and the fidelity of Yahweh to his promises.

The Indictment and Complaint

The poem in ch 1 consists of a legal complaint concerning covenant violation by the Israelites, who are depicted as ungrateful and also less intelligent than farm animals (vv. 2–4). In ancient Israelite thinking, heaven and earth serve as witnesses to the covenant between God and Israel (see Dt 4, 26; 32, 1); hence, God calls on them to hear the charges against Israel.

The complete Book of Isaiah is an anthology of poems composed chiefly by the great prophet, but also by disciples, some of whom came many years after Isaiah. In 1—39 most of the oracles come from Isaiah and faithfully reflect the situation in eighth-century Judah. To disciples deeply influenced by the prophet belong sections such as the Apocalypse of Isaiah (24—27), the oracles against Babylon (13—14), and probably the poems of 34—35.

Chapters 40—55, sometimes called the Deutero-Isaiah, are generally attributed to an anonymous poet who prophesied toward the end of the Babylonian exile. From this section come the great messianic oracles known as the songs of the Servant, whose mysterious destiny of suffering and glorification is fulfilled in the passion and glorification of Christ. Chapters 56—66 contain oracles from a later period and were composed by disciples who inherited the spirit and continued the work of the great prophet.

The principal divisions of the Book of Isaiah are the following:

A: The Book of Judgment:
 I: Indictment of Israel and Judah (1, 1—5, 30).
 II: Immanuel Prophecies (6, 1—12, 6).
 III: Oracles against the Pagan Nations (13, 1—23, 18).
 IV: Apocalypse of Isaiah (24, 1—27, 13).
 V: The Lord Alone, Israel's and Judah's Salvation (28, 1—33, 24).
 VI: The Lord, Zion's Avenger (34, 1—35, 10).
 VII: Historical Appendix (36, 1—39, 8).

B: The Book of Consolation:
 I: The Lord's Glory in Israel's Liberation (40, 1—48, 21).
 II: Expiation of Sin, Spiritual Liberation of Israel (49, 1—55, 13).
 III: Return of the First Captives (56, 1—66, 24).

A. The Book of Judgment

I: Indictment of Israel and Judah

CHAPTER 1

See RG 207-208

Israel's Sinfulness. [1]The vision* which Isaiah, son of Amoz, had concerning Judah and Jerusalem in the days of Uzziah, Jotham, Ahaz and Hezekiah, kings of Judah.

[2] Hear, O heavens, and listen, O earth,
 for the LORD speaks:
Sons have I raised and reared,
 but they have disowned me![a]
[3] An ox knows its owner,
 and an ass, its master's manger;
But Israel* does not know,
 my people has not understood.
[4] Ah! sinful nation, people laden with wickedness,
 evil race, corrupt children!
They have forsaken the LORD,
 spurned the Holy One of Israel,*
 apostatized.[b]
[5] Where would you yet be struck,*
 you that rebel again and again?

1, 1: The title of the book: an editorial addition. Isaiah: meaning "the salvation of the Lord," or "The Lord is salvation." Amoz: not the minor prophet. Judah: The southern kingdom of the tribes of Judah and Benjamin. Uzziah: also called Azariah; cf 2 Kgs 15, 1; 2 Chr 26, 1.

1, 3: Israel, not the northern kingdom, as in Is 9, 11, exclusively, which Isaiah usually calls "Ephraim" from the tribe bordering on the southern kingdom, but the entire chosen people; cf Is 8, 14.

1, 4: Holy One of Israel: a title used frequently by Isaiah, rarely by other writers.

1, 5-8: Sufferings inflicted upon God's people for their sins.

a: Dt 32, 1. 5f. *b:* Is 5, 24; Dt 32, 15.

Rite and Right

The sacrifices and prayers offered by Isaiah's contemporaries are useless because they are not accompanied by ethical action (vv. 10–20). This is a frequent prophetic theme; see especially Amos 5, 21–25; Isaiah 58, 1–9.

The whole head is sick,
  the whole heart faint.
[6] From the sole of the foot to the head
  there is no sound spot:
Wound and welt and gaping gash,
  not drained, or bandaged,
  or eased with salve.
[7] Your country is waste,
  your cities burnt with fire;
Your land before your eyes
  strangers devour
  [a waste, like Sodom overthrown]—
[8] And daughter Zion* is left
  like a hut in a vineyard,
Like a shed in a melon patch,
  like a city blockaded.

[9] Unless the LORD of hosts*
  had left us a scanty remnant,
We had become as Sodom,
  we should be like Gomorrah.[c]
[10] Hear the word of the LORD,
  princes of Sodom!
Listen to the instruction of our God,
  people of Gomorrah!
[11] What care I for the number of your
    sacrifices?*
says the LORD.
I have had enough of whole-burnt rams
  and fat of fatlings;
In the blood of calves, lambs and goats
  I find no pleasure.[d]

[12] When you come in to visit me,
  who asks these things of you?

[13] Trample my courts no more!
  Bring no more worthless offerings;
  your incense is loathsome to me.
New moon and sabbath, calling of
    assemblies,
  octaves with wickedness:* these I
    cannot bear.[e]
[14] Your new moons and festivals I detest;
  they weigh me down, I tire of the load.
[15] When you spread out your hands,*
  I close my eyes to you;
Though you pray the more,
  I will not listen.
Your hands are full of blood![f]
[16]   Wash yourselves clean!
Put away your misdeeds from before my
    eyes;
  cease doing evil; [17]learn to do good.
Make justice your aim: redress the
    wronged,
  hear the orphan's plea, defend the
    widow.[g]

[18] Come now, let us set things right,
  says the LORD:
Though your sins be like scarlet,
  they may become white as snow;
Though they be crimson red,
  they may become white as wool.[h]
[19] If you are willing, and obey,
  you shall eat the good things of the
    land;
[20] But if you refuse and resist,
  the sword shall consume you:
  for the mouth of the LORD has spoken!

1, 8: Daughter Zion: Jerusalem. Hut . . . shed: for the shelter of watchmen and laborers.

1, 9: LORD of hosts: God, who is the Creator and Ruler of the heavenly armies of the angels, stars, etc. Remnant: St. Paul uses this text in Rom 9, 29, where he speaks of God's saving mercy toward the Jews and Gentiles. Sodom . . . Gomorrah: cf Gn 19.

1, 11: The number of your sacrifices: however numerous, they are not acceptable without the right dispositions on the part of the worshipers.

1, 13: Octaves with wickedness: the solemnity of the feasts marred by evil deeds.

1, 15: Spread out your hands: in prayer.

c: Rom 9, 29. d: Ps 50, 8-13; Sir 34, 19; Mi 6, 7. e: Prv 15, 8; Jer 6, 20. f: Prv 1, 28; Sir 34, 21-25. g: Ex 23, 6; Dt 24, 17; Sir 4, 9f; Jer 22, 3; Ez 22, 7; Zec 7, 9f. h: Ps 51, 9.

21 How has she turned adulteress,
   the faithful city, so upright!*
Justice used to lodge within her,
   but now, murderers.[i]
22 Your silver is turned to dross,
   your wine is mixed with water.
23 Your princes are rebels
   and comrades of thieves;
Each one of them loves a bribe
   and looks for gifts.
The fatherless they defend not,
   and the widow's plea does not reach
      them.[j]
24 Now, therefore, says the Lord,
   the LORD of hosts, the Mighty One of
      Israel:
Ah! I will take vengeance on my foes
   and fully repay my enemies![k]
25 I will turn my hand against you,
   and refine your dross in the
      furnace,
   removing all your alloy.
26 I will restore your judges as at first,
   and your counselors as in the
      beginning;
After that you shall be called
   city of justice, faithful city.[l]

27 Zion shall be redeemed by judgment,
   and her repentant ones by justice.*
28 Rebels and sinners alike shall be
      crushed,
   those who desert the LORD shall be
      consumed.
29 You shall be ashamed of the terebinths
   which you prized,
   and blush for the groves which you
      chose.*
30 You shall become like a tree with falling
      leaves,

like a garden that has no water.
31 The strong man shall turn to tow,
   and his work shall become a spark;
Both shall burn together,
   and there shall be none to quench the
      flames.

CHAPTER 2

See RG 207-208

Zion, the Messianic Capital. [1]This
is what Isaiah, son of Amoz, saw concerning
Judah and Jerusalem.*

2   In days to come,*
   The mountain of the LORD's house[m]
      shall be established as the highest
         mountain
   and raised above the hills.
All nations shall stream toward it;[n]
3   many peoples shall come and say:
"Come, let us climb the LORD's
      mountain,
   to the house of the God of Jacob,
That he may instruct us in his ways,
   and we may walk in his paths."[o]
For from Zion shall go forth
      instruction,
   and the word of the LORD from
      Jerusalem.*
4 He shall judge between the nations,
   and impose terms on many peoples.
They shall beat their swords into
      plowshares
   and their spears into pruning hooks;
One nation shall not raise the sword
      against another,
   nor shall they train for war again.[p]

5 O house of Jacob, come,
   let us walk in the light of the
      LORD!

1, 21: A picture of Jerusalem, once so faithful to God. Apostasy from the covenant is often likened by the prophets to unfaithfulness to the marriage vow.

1, 27: This verse is the key to the whole Book of Isaiah. Zion's defiant persistence in sin has demanded a divine judgment, by which her survivors will be cleansed and will return to God in justice; cf Is 40, 2.

1, 29: Terebinths which you prized . . . groves which you chose: as popular shrines for idolatrous worship.

2, 1: An editorial addition introducing chapters 2—5.

2, 2-4: The messianic destiny which ensures Judah's later restoration. In the messianic kingdom the prophets generally see

the Lord's house as the seat of authority and the source of clear and certain doctrine; also, its rule willingly accepted by all peoples, maintained by spiritual sanctions, and tending to universal peace. This passage is found substantially unchanged in Mi 4, 1-3; it probably, although not certainly, has Isaiah as its author.

2, 3: Zion . . . Jerusalem: types of the earthly center of the messianic kingdom.

---

i: Jer 3, 8; Hos 2, 7.   *j:* Ex 23, 8; Dt 16, 19.   *k:* Dt 32, 41.   *l:* Jer 33, 7ff; Zec 8, 3.   *m:* 2ff: Mi 4, 1ff.   *n:* Is 56, 7.   *o:* Zec 8, 20-23.   *p:* Is 9, 7; 11, 4; Ps 72, 3f; Zec 9, 10.

Jerusalem of the Future and of the Present

This long section (2, 2—4, 6) begins and ends with a description of Jerusalem as it should and will be: a city of peace, equity, and divine presence. The prophet Micah shared this vision. The long middle section (2, 6—4, 1) focuses on the sinfulness of the current inhabitants and their grim fate. The nation's sins—magic; amassing extraordinary amounts of wealth; pursuing military power; pride; and idolatry—are criticized here. All these vices embody inappropriate confidence in humanity's own powers. This confidence is not only mistaken, but is offensive to God.

The Lord's Judgment against Idols

⁶ You have abandoned your people,
the house of Jacob,
Because they are filled with fortune-tellers
and soothsayers,* like the Philistines;
they covenant with strangers.�q
⁷ Their land is full of silver and gold,
and there is no end to their treasures;
Their land is full of horses,
and there is no end to their chariots.
⁸ Their land is full of idols;
they worship the works of their hands,
that which their fingers have made.ʳ

⁹ But man is abased,
each one brought low.
[Do not pardon them!]
¹⁰ Get behind the rocks,
hide in the dust,
From the terror of the LORD
and the splendor of his majesty!ˢ
¹¹ The haughty eyes of man will be
lowered,
the arrogance of men will be abased,
and the LORD alone will be exalted, on
that day.*
¹² For the LORD of hosts will have his day
against all that is proud and arrogant,
all that is high, and it will be brought
low;
¹³ Yes, against all the cedars of Lebanon*
and all the oaks of Bashan,
¹⁴ Against all the lofty mountains
and all the high hills,

¹⁵ Against every lofty tower
and every fortified wall,
¹⁶ Against all the ships of Tarshish*
and all stately vessels.
¹⁷ Human pride will be abased,
the arrogance of men brought low,
And the LORD alone will be exalted, on
that day.

¹⁸ The idols will perish forever.

¹⁹ Men will go into caves in the rocks
and into holes in the earth,
From the terror of the LORD
and the splendor of his majesty,
when he arises to overawe the earth.

²⁰On that day men will throw to the moles and the bats the idols of silver and gold which they made for worship.

²¹ They go into caverns in the rocks
and into crevices in the cliffs,
From the terror of the LORD
and the splendor of his majesty,
when he arises to overawe the earth.

²² As for you, let man alone,
in whose nostrils is but a breath;
for what is he worth?

CHAPTER 3

Judgment of Judah and Jerusalem

See RG
207–208

¹ The Lord, the LORD of hosts,*

2, 6: Fortune-tellers and soothsayers: divination was strictly forbidden; cf Dt 18, 9-14.

2, 11: That day: the day of the Lord, a day of retribution, often referred to, especially by the minor prophets, and described in terms of natural phenomena: earthquake, fire, storm.

2, 13: Lebanon: Mount Lebanon in Syria, famed for its cedars. Bashan: the wooded uplands east of the Jordan River.

2, 16: Tarshish: cf note on Ps 48, 8.

3, 1-12: Anarchy will reign in Jerusalem and Judah. In the prevailing desperation, even the most unworthy and the least qualified will be sought as rulers.

q: Is 8, 19; 19, 3.   r: Is 31, 1ff.   s: 2 Thes 1, 9.

Announcement of Judgment against the Women of Jerusalem

First, reasons for punishment are given in terms of the posture of the daughters of Zion (3, 16); next, a judgment is announced that fits the crime (vv. 17–24). The humiliations which the women will suffer are common to military defeat and exile. The list of finery is a prose elaboration of vv. 17, 24.

shall take away from Jerusalem and
  from Judah
support and prop [all supplies of bread
  and water]:[t]
2 Hero and warrior,
  judge and prophet, fortune-teller and
    elder,
3 The captain of fifty and the nobleman,
  counselor, skilled magician, and expert
    charmer.
4 I will make striplings their princes;
  the fickle shall govern them,
5 And the people shall oppress one
    another,
  yes, every man his neighbor.
The child shall be bold toward the elder,
  and the base toward the honorable.
6 When a man seizes his brother
  in his father's house, saying,
"You have clothes! Be our ruler,
  and take in hand this ruin!"—
7   Then shall he answer in that day:
"I will not undertake to cure this,
  when in my own house there is no
    bread or clothing!
You shall not make me ruler of the
    people."

8 Jerusalem is crumbling, Judah is falling;
  for their speech and their deeds are
    before the LORD,
  a provocation in the sight of his
    majesty.
9 Their very look bears witness against
    them;
  their sin like Sodom they vaunt,
They hide it not. Woe to them!
  they deal out evil to themselves.
10 Happy the just, for it will be well with
    them,

the fruit of their works they will eat.
11 Woe to the wicked man! All goes ill,
  with the work of his hands he will be
    repaid.
12 My people—a babe in arms will be their
    tyrant,
  and women will rule them!
O my people, your leaders mislead,
  they destroy the paths you should
    follow.

13 The LORD rises to accuse,
  standing to try his people.
14 The Lord enters into judgment
  with his people's elders and princes:
It is you who have devoured the
    vineyard;
  the loot wrested from the poor is in
    your houses.
15 What do you mean by crushing my
    people,
  and grinding down the poor when they
    look to you?
says the Lord, the God of hosts.[u]
16 The LORD said:[v]
  Because the daughters of Zion are
    haughty,
  and walk with necks outstretched
Ogling and mincing as they go,
  their anklets tinkling with every step,
17 The Lord shall cover the scalps of Zion's
    daughters with scabs,
  and the LORD shall bare their heads.[*]

18 On that day the LORD will do away with the finery of the anklets, sunbursts, and crescents; 19 the pendants, bracelets, and veils; 20 the headdresses, bangles, cinctures, perfume boxes, and amulets; 21 the signet rings, and the nose rings;[*] 22 the court dresses, wraps, cloaks,

3, 17: Bare their heads: a mark of social disgrace; cf Nm 5, 18.
3, 21: Nose rings: of gold, a feminine ornament in the East; cf note on Gn 24, 22.

t: Lv 26, 26; Ez 4, 16.   u: Lv 25, 42. 55.   v: 16ff: Is 32, 11f.

A Poem of Rebuke

Chapter 5 is a parable in which God is the farmer and Israel the vineyard. At first, the identity of the characters is not evident, and only gradually does the audience realize that it is they themselves who are being rebuked.

and purses; ²³the mirrors, linen tunics, turbans, and shawls.

²⁴ Instead of perfume there will be stench,
  instead of the girdle, a rope,
And for the coiffure, baldness;
  for the rich gown, a sackcloth skirt.
  Then, instead of beauty:
²⁵ Your men will fall by the sword,
  and your champions, in war;
²⁶ Her gates will lament and mourn,
  as the city sits desolate on the
  ground.

See RG
207–208

CHAPTER 4

¹ Seven women will take hold of one
  man*
  on that day, saying:
"We will eat our own food
  and wear our own clothing;
Only let your name be given us,
  put an end to our disgrace!"

The Messianic Branch

²   On that day,
The branch of the LORD* will be luster
  and glory,
  and the fruit of the earth will be honor
  and splendor
  for the survivors of Israel.^w
³ He who remains in Zion
  and he that is left in Jerusalem
Will be called holy:
  every one marked down for life* in
  Jerusalem.^x
⁴ When the Lord washes away
  the filth of the daughters of Zion,

And purges Jerusalem's blood from her
  midst
  with a blast of searing judgment,
⁵ Then will the LORD create,
  over the whole site of Mount Zion
  and over her place of assembly,
A smoking cloud by day
  and a light of flaming fire by night.^y
⁶ For over all, his glory will be shelter and
  protection:
  shade from the parching heat of day,
  refuge and cover from storm and rain.

CHAPTER 5

The Vineyard Song

See RG
207–208

¹ Let me now sing of my friend,
  my friend's song concerning his
  vineyard.
My friend had a vineyard*
  on a fertile hillside;
² He spaded it, cleared it of stones,
  and planted the choicest vines;
Within it he built a watchtower,
  and hewed out a wine press.
Then he looked for the crop of grapes,
  but what it yielded was wild grapes.

³ Now, inhabitants of Jerusalem and men
  of Judah,
  judge between me and my vineyard:
⁴ What more was there to do for my vineyard
  that I had not done?
Why, when I looked for the crop of grapes,
  did it bring forth wild grapes?
⁵ Now, I will let you know
  what I mean to do to my vineyard:
Take away its hedge, give it to grazing,

4, 1: Seven women . . . one man: the disproportion of the sexes due to war leaves the female population almost without male partners. The women are eager to marry, not for support, but to avoid the disgrace of being childless.

4, 2: Branch of the LORD: divine blessings in general, which later culminated in the Messiah; cf Jer 23, 5; Zec 3, 8; 6, 12.

4, 3: Marked down for life: in God's list of his elect; cf Ex 32, 32.

5, 1: My friend had a vineyard: the Lord and his chosen people.

w: Is 11, 1; Jer 23, 5; 33, 15.   x: Is 6, 13; 10, 20; Ob 17.   y: Ex 13, 21.

A Series of Woe Indictments

Each accusation in ch 5 begins with the cry "woe to" (vv. 8, 11, 18, 20, 21, 22). Isaiah 10, 1–4 may also belong to this series. Each unit describes a group in terms of its immoral actions, and fitting punishments are handed out: against the rich who take the land of the poor; against those whose pursuit of pleasure obscures their perception of the LORD's activity and the needs of the people; against those who dare the LORD to act; against those who reverse morality; against those who are proud of their wisdom; and against drunkards who pervert justice.

break through its wall, let it be
trampled!
6 Yes, I will make it a ruin:
it shall not be pruned or hoed,
but overgrown with thorns and
briers;
I will command the clouds
not to send rain upon it.
7 The vineyard of the LORD of hosts is the
house of Israel,
and the men of Judah are his cherished
plant;
He looked for judgment, but see,
bloodshed!
for justice, but hark, the outcry!*

Doom of the Unjust

8 Woe to you who join house to house,*
who connect field with field,
Till no room remains, and you are left to
dwell
alone in the midst of the land!z
9 In my hearing the LORD of hosts has
sworn:
Many houses shall be in ruins,
large ones and fine, with no one to live
in them.a
10 Ten acres* of vineyard
shall yield but one liquid measure,
And a homer of seed
shall yield but an ephah.
17 Lambs shall graze there at pasture,
and kids shall eat in the ruins of the
rich.

11 Woe to those who demand strong drink
as soon as they rise in the morning,
And linger into the night
while wine inflames them!
12 With harp and lyre, timbrel and flute,
they feast on wine;
But what the LORD does, they regard not,
the work of his hands they see not.b
13 Therefore my people go into exile,
because they do not understand;
Their nobles die of hunger,
and their masses are parched with
thirst.
14 Therefore the nether world* enlarges its
throat
and opens its maw without limit;
Down go their nobility and their masses,
their throngs and their revelry.c
15 Men shall be abased, each one brought
low,
and the eyes of the haughty lowered,
16 But the LORD of hosts shall be exalted by
his judgment,
and God the Holy shall be shown holy
by his justice.

18 Woe to those who tug at guilt with cords
of perversity,
and at sin as if with cart ropes!
19 To those who say, "Let him make haste
and speed his work, that we may
see it;
On with the plan of the Holy One of
Israel!

5, 7: Judgment . . . bloodshed . . . justice . . . outcry: in Hebrew, these adversative terms constitute a play on words.
5, 8-10: Land-grabbers who unjustly acquire property will be impoverished instead of enriched.
5, 10: Ten acres: a field requiring ten days of plowing by

a yoke of oxen. Liquid measure: in Hebrew, a "bath," i.e., about ten gallons. Homer: a dry measure of about ten bushels. Ephah: a dry measure of about one bushel.
5, 14: Nether world: cf note on Ps 6, 6.

z: Mi 2, 2.   a: Is 6, 12.   b: Am 6, 5f.   c: Hb 2, 5.

let it come to pass, that we may know
it!"*d*

20 Woe to those who call evil good, and
good evil,
who change darkness into light, and
light into darkness,
who change bitter into sweet, and
sweet into bitter!
21 Woe to those who are wise in their own
sight,
and prudent in their own esteem!*e*
22 Woe to the champions at drinking wine,
the valiant at mixing strong drink!*f*
23 To those who acquit the guilty for
bribes,
and deprive the just man of his
rights!*g*
24 Therefore, as the tongue of fire licks up
stubble,
as dry grass shrivels in the flame,
Even so their root shall become rotten
and their blossom scatter like dust;
For they have spurned the law of the
LORD of hosts,
and scorned the word of the Holy One
of Israel.
25 Therefore the wrath of the LORD blazes
against his people,
he raises his hand to strike them;
When the mountains quake,
their corpses shall be like refuse in the
streets.
For all this, his wrath is not turned back,
and his hand is still outstretched.

Invasion*

26 He will give a signal to a far-off nation,
and whistle to them from the ends of
the earth;
speedily and promptly will they come.

27 None of them will stumble with
weariness,
none will slumber and none will sleep.
None will have his waist belt loose,
nor the thong of his sandal broken.
28 Their arrows are sharp,
and all their bows are bent.
The hoofs of their horses seem like flint,
and their chariot wheels like the
hurricane.
29 Their roar is that of the lion,
like the lion's whelps they roar;
They growl and seize the prey,
they carry it off and none will rescue it.
30 [They will roar over it, on that day,
with a roaring like that of the sea.]*h*

II: Immanuel Prophecies

CHAPTER 6

See RG
207–208

Call of Isaiah. ¹In the year king
Uzziah died,* I saw the Lord seated on a high
and lofty throne,*i* with the train of his garment
filling the temple.* ²Seraphim were stationed
above; each of them had six wings: with two
they veiled their faces, with two they veiled
their feet, and with two they hovered aloft.*j*

³"Holy, holy, holy is the LORD of hosts!"
they cried one to the other. "All the earth is
filled with his glory!" ⁴*k*At the sound of that
cry, the frame of the door shook and the
house was filled with smoke.*

⁵Then I said, "Woe is me, I am doomed!*
For I am a man of unclean lips, living among
a people of unclean lips; yet my eyes have
seen the King, the LORD of hosts!"*l* ⁶Then one
of the seraphim flew to me, holding an ember
which he had taken with tongs from the altar.
⁷He touched my mouth with it. "See," he
said, "now that this has touched your lips,*

5, 26-30: A description of the invading Assyrian army,
God's instrument for punishing his people.

6, 1: In the year king Uzziah died: 742 B.C.

6, 1ff: Temple: the holy place, just in front of the holy of
holies. Seraphim: literally "the burning ones," are celestial beings who surround the throne of God. Each has six wings. Reverence for the divine majesty causes them to veil their faces with
two wings; modesty, to veil their extremities in similar fashion;
alacrity in God's service, to extend two wings in preparation for
flight. Holy, holy, holy: God's perfect interior holiness whose
exterior manifestation is his glory. These words are found in the
Roman liturgy just before the Canon of the Mass.

6, 4: Smoke: reminiscent of the clouds which surrounded
God at Mount Sinai; cf Ex 19, 16-19; Dt 4, 11f.

6, 5: Doomed: it was popularly believed that to see God
would lead to one's death; cf Gn 32, 31; Ex 33, 20; Jgs 13, 22.

6, 7: Touched your lips: Isaiah is thus symbolically purified to be worthy of his vocation as God's prophet. In the Roman liturgy, the celebrant at Mass makes reference to this incident just before he reads the gospel.

d: Jer 5, 12; 2 Pt 3, 4. *e:* Prv 3, 7; Rom 12, 16. *f:* Sir 31, 3. *g:* Ex
23, 8; Prv 17, 15. *h:* Is 8, 22. *i:* Jn 12, 41. *j:* Rv 4, 8. *k:* 1 Kgs
8, 10f; Rv 15, 8. *l:* Gn 32, 3; Ex 20, 19; 33, 20; Jgs 6, 22; 13, 22.

your wickedness is removed, your sin purged."*m*

8Then I heard the voice of the Lord saying, "Whom shall I send? Who will go for us?" "Here I am;" I said; "send me!" 9And he replied: Go and say to this people:*

Listen carefully, but you shall not
    understand!
Look intently, but you shall know
    nothing!*n*
10 You are to make the heart of this people
    sluggish,
to dull their ears and close their eyes;
Else their eyes will see, their ears hear,
    their heart understand,
    and they will turn and be healed.*o*

11"How long, O Lord?" I asked. And he replied:

Until the cities are desolate,
    without inhabitants,
Houses, without a man,
    and the earth is a desolate waste.
12 Until the LORD removes men far away,
    and the land is abandoned more and
    more.*
13 If there be still a tenth part in it,
    then this in turn shall be laid waste;
As with a terebinth or an oak
    whose trunk remains when its leaves
    have fallen.
[Holy offspring is the trunk.]*p*

**See RG
208**

CHAPTER 7

Birth of Immanuel. 1In the days of Ahaz,* king of Judah, son of Jotham, son of Uzziah, Rezin, king of Aram, and Pekah, king of Israel, son of Remaliah, went up to attack Jerusalem,*q* but they were not able to conquer it. 2When word came to the house of David that Aram was encamped in Ephraim, the heart of the king and the heart of the people trembled, as the trees of the forest tremble in the wind.

3*r*Then the LORD said to Isaiah: Go out to meet Ahaz, you and your son Shear-jashub,* at the end of the conduit of the upper pool, on the highway of the fuller's field, 4and say to him: Take care you remain tranquil and do not fear; let not your courage fail before these two stumps of smoldering brands [the blazing anger of Rezin and the Arameans, and of the son of Remaliah], 5because of the mischief that Aram [Ephraim and the son of Remaliah] plots against you, saying, 6"Let us go up and tear Judah asunder, make it our own by force, and appoint the son of Tabeel* king there."

7 Thus says the LORD:

This shall not stand, it shall not be!
8 Damascus is the capital of Aram,
    and Rezin the head of Damascus;
Samaria is the capital of Ephraim,
    and Remaliah's son the head of
        Samaria.
9 But within sixty years and five,*
    Ephraim shall be crushed, no longer a
        nation.
Unless your faith is firm
    you shall not be firm!*s*

10Again the LORD spoke to Ahaz: 11Ask for a sign from the LORD, your God; let it be deep as the nether world, or high as the sky!* 12But Ahaz answered, "I will not ask! I will not tempt the LORD!"* 13Then he said: Listen, O house of David! Is it not enough for you to

---

6, 9f: The truth that the nation will remain impenitent is vividly foretold, as if its obstinacy would be caused, instead of merely occasioned, by the prophet's warning. Cf Mt 13, 13ff; Mk 4, 12; Lk 8, 10.

6, 12: Several limited deportations in the time of Isaiah would later culminate in the Babylonian Exile.

7, 1: Days of Ahaz: who ruled from 735 to 715 B.C. This attack against Jerusalem by the kings of Aram (Syria) and Israel was occasioned by Ahaz' refusal to enter with them into an anti-Assyrian alliance; cf 2 Kgs 16.

7, 3: Shear-jashub: this name means "a remnant will return."

7, 6: Son of Tabeel: an adherent of Jerusalem's enemies. His appointment would interrupt the lawful succession from David.

7, 9: Within sixty years and five: if the text is correct, its reference is unknown.

7, 11: Deep . . . sky: an extraordinary or miraculous sign that would prove God's firm will to save the royal house of David from its oppressors.

7, 12: Tempt the LORD: Ahaz expresses in this hypocritical way his preference for depending upon the might of Assyria rather than upon God.

m: Jer 1, 9; Dn 10, 16.   *n:* Mt 13, 14f; Mk 4, 12; Lk 8, 10; Acts 28, 26f.   *o:* Jer 5, 21; Jn 12, 40.   *p:* Is 10, 22.   *q:* 2 Kgs 16, 5; 2 Chr 28, 5-15.   *r:* Is 36, 2; 2 Chr 32, 3.   *s:* Is 8, 6ff.

weary men, must you also weary my God? [14]Therefore the Lord himself will give you this sign:* the virgin shall be with child, and bear a son, and shall name him Immanuel. [15]He shall be living on curds and honey* by the time he learns to reject the bad and choose the good. [16]For before the child learns to reject the bad and choose the good, the land of those two kings whom you dread shall be deserted.

[17]The LORD shall bring upon you and your people and your father's house days worse than any since Ephraim seceded from Judah. [This means the king of Assyria.] [18]On that day

The LORD shall whistle
   for the fly that is in the farthest
      streams of Egypt,
   and for the bee in the land of Assyria.
[19] All of them shall come and settle
   in the steep ravines and in the rocky
      clefts,
   on all thornbushes and in all pastures.

[20]On that day the LORD shall shave with the razor hired from across the River [with the king of Assyria] the head, and the hair between the legs. It shall also shave off the beard.* [21]On that day a man shall keep a heifer or a couple of sheep, [22]and from their abundant yield of milk he shall live on curds; curds and honey shall be the food of all who remain in the land. [23]On that day every place

where there used to be a thousand vines, worth a thousand pieces of silver, shall be turned to briers and thorns. [24]Men shall go there with bow and arrows; for all the country shall be briers and thorns. [25]For fear of briers and thorns you shall not go upon any mountainside which used to be hoed with the mattock; they shall be grazing land for cattle and shall be trampled upon by sheep.

CHAPTER 8

See RG 208

The Son of Isaiah. [1]The LORD said to me: Take a large cylinder-seal, and inscribe on it in ordinary letters:* "Belonging to Maher-shalal-hash-baz." [2]And I took reliable witnesses,* Uriah the priest, and Zechariah, son of Jeberechiah. [3]Then I went to the prophetess* and she conceived and bore a son. The LORD said to me: Name him Maher-shalal-hash-baz, [4]for before the child knows how to call his father or mother by name, the wealth of Damascus and the spoil of Samaria shall be carried off by the king of Assyria.

[5]Again the LORD spoke to me:

[6] Because this people* has rejected
   the waters of Shiloah that flow gently,[t]
And melts with fear before the loftiness
   of Rezin and Remaliah's son,
[7] Therefore the LORD raises against them
   the waters of the River, great and
      mighty
   [the king of Assyria and all his power].

7, 14: The sign proposed by Isaiah was concerned with the preservation of Judah in the midst of distress (cf Is 7, 15. 17), but more especially with the fulfillment of God's earlier promise to David (2 Sm 7, 12-16) in the coming of Immanuel (meaning, "With us is God") as the ideal king (cf Is 9, 5-6; 11, 1-5). The church has always followed St. Matthew in seeing the transcendent fulfillment of this verse in Christ and his Virgin Mother. The prophet need not have known the full force latent in his own words; and some Catholic writers have sought a preliminary and partial fulfillment in the conception and birth of the future King Hezekiah, whose mother, at the time Isaiah spoke, would have been a young, unmarried woman (Hebrew, almah). The Holy Spirit was preparing, however, for another Nativity which alone could fulfill the divinely given terms of Immanuel's mission, and in which the perpetual virginity of the Mother of God was to fulfill also the words of this prophecy in the integral sense intended by the divine Wisdom.

7, 15: Curds and honey: the restricted diet of those who remain after devastation has changed the once fertile fields of Judah into grazing land; cf Is 7, 21-25.

7, 20: God will use the Assyrians from across the River (the Euphrates) as his instrument (razor) to inflict disgrace and suffering upon his people.

8, 1: Ordinary letters: easily read by all. Maher-shalal-hash-baz: a symbolic name to be given to another son of Isaiah (v 3); it means "quick spoils; speedy plunder," and describes what the Assyrians will do.

8, 2: Reliable witnesses: who would testify that Isaiah had indeed prophesied the future destruction. Uriah the priest: cf 2 Kgs 16, 10.

8, 3: The prophetess: wife of Isaiah.

8, 6ff: This people: Judah. Waters of Shiloah: the stream that flows into the pool of Shiloah in Jerusalem, its slow current symbolizing the silent, divine protection which Judah has rejected. God will therefore summon the mighty Assyrian army, symbolized by the River (Euphrates), to devastate Judah, which, however, will not be entirely destroyed, because it is the land of Immanuel.

t: Jn 9, 7.11.

It shall rise above all its channels,
and overflow all its banks;
8 It shall pass into Judah, and flood it all
throughout:
up to the neck it shall reach;
It shall spread its wings
the full width of your land, Immanuel!
9 Know, O peoples, and be appalled!
Give ear, all you distant lands!
Arm, but be crushed! Arm, but be
crushed!
10 Form a plan,* and it shall be thwarted;
make a resolve, and it shall not be
carried out,
for "With us is God!"

Disciples of Isaiah. 11For thus said the
LORD to me, taking hold of me and warning
me not to walk in the way of this people:*u*
12 Call not alliance what this people calls
alliance,
and fear not, nor stand in awe of what
they fear.
13 But with the LORD of hosts make your
alliance—
for him be your fear and your awe.
14 Yet he shall be a snare, an obstacle and a
stumbling stone
to both the houses of Israel,
A trap and a snare
to those who dwell in Jerusalem;*v*
15 And many among them shall stumble and
fall,
broken, snared, and captured.

16The record is to be folded and the sealed
instruction kept among my disciples.* 17For I
will trust in the LORD, who is hiding his face
from the house of Jacob; yes, I will wait for
him. 18Look at me and the children whom the
Lord has given me: we are signs* and portents
in Israel from the LORD of hosts who dwells
on Mount Zion. 19wAnd when they say to you,
"Inquire of mediums and fortune-tellers (who
chirp and mutter!*); should not a people inquire of their gods, apply to the dead on behalf
of the living!"— 20then this document will
furnish its instruction. That kind of thing they
will surely say.*

The Prince of Peace. 23First he degraded
the land of Zebulun and the land of
Naphtali;* but in the end he has glorified the
seaward road, the land west of the Jordan,
the District of the Gentiles.

Anguish has taken wing, dispelled is
darkness:
for there is no gloom where until now
there was distress.

CHAPTER 9

See RG
208

1 The people who walked in
darkness*x*
have seen a great light;
Upon those who dwelt in the land of gloom
a light has shone.
2 You have brought them abundant joy
and great rejoicing,
As they rejoice before you as at the
harvest,
as men make merry when dividing
spoils.
3 For the yoke that burdened them,
the pole on their shoulder,
And the rod of their taskmaster
you have smashed, as on the day of
Midian.
4 For every boot that tramped in battle,
every cloak rolled in blood,
will be burned as fuel for
flames.*y*

8, 10: The plan of Israel's enemies will be thwarted because, as the name "Immanuel" signifies, With us is God.

8, 16: Kept among my disciples: for preservation and
transmission.

8, 18: Signs: Isaiah and his sons had symbolic names.

8, 19: Chirp and mutter: a mocking reference to the
sounds uttered by necromancers, as if the dead were speaking; all such practices were forbidden.

8, 21f: These verses have been transposed and placed
within Is 14, 25, which affords the context in which they can
be understood.

8, 23: Zebulun . . . Naphtali: northern Palestine, which
was first to be attacked by the Assyrians; God, however, redeems it, as he redeems all his people. Seaward road: from
Damascus, across southern Galilee to the Mediterranean Sea.
District of the Gentiles: northern Galilee, inhabited by pagans; cf Jos 20, 7; Is 9, 1. Mt 4, 15f refers to this, since Jesus
began his public mission in Galilee.

---

u: Ez 3, 14.   v: Rom 9, 33; 1 Pt 2, 8.   w: Lv 19, 31; Dt 18, 10ff.
x: 1f: Mt 4, 15f.   y: Sir 39, 9.

5 For a child* is born to us, a son is given
　　us;
　upon his shoulder dominion rests.
They name him Wonder-Counselor,
　　God-Hero,
　Father-Forever, Prince of Peace.ᶻ
6 His dominion is vast
　and forever peaceful,
From David's throne, and over his
　　kingdom,
　which he confirms and sustains
By judgment and justice,
　both now and forever.
The zeal of the LORD of hosts will do
　this!ᵃ

Fall of the Northern Kingdom

7 The Lord has sent word against Jacob,
　it falls upon Israel;
8 And all the people know it,
　Ephraim and those who dwell in
　　Samaria,
　those who say in arrogance and pride
　　of heart,
9 "Bricks have fallen,
　but we will build with cut stone;
Sycamores are felled,
　but we will replace them with cedars."
10 But the LORD raises up their foes against
　　them
　and stirs up their enemies to action:
11 Aram* on the east and the Philistines on
　　the west
　devour Israel with open mouth.
For all this, his wrath is not turned
　　back,
　and his hand is still outstretched!

12 The people do not turn to him who struck
　　them,
　nor seek the LORD of hosts.
13 So the LORD severs from Israel head and
　　tail,

palm branch and reed in one day.
14 [The elder and the noble are the head,
　the prophet who teaches falsehood is
　　the tail.]
15 The leaders of this people mislead them
　and those to be led are engulfed.ᵇ
16 For this reason, the Lord does not spare
　　their young men,
　and their orphans and widows he does
　　not pity;
They are wholly profaned and sinful,
　and every mouth gives vent to folly.
For all this, his wrath is not turned back,
　his hand is still outstretched!

17 For wickedness burns like fire,
　devouring brier and thorn;
It kindles the forest thickets,
　which go up in columns of smoke.
18 At the wrath of the LORD of hosts the
　　land quakes,
　and the people are like fuel for fire;
No man spares his brother,
　each devours the flesh of his neighbor.
19 Though they hack on the right, they are
　　hungry;
　though they eat on the left, they are not
　　filled.
20 Manasseh devours Ephraim,* and
　　Ephraim Manasseh;
　together they turn on Judah.
For all this, his wrath is not turned back,
　his hand is still outstretched!

CHAPTER 10

See RG
208

Social Injustice

1 Woe to those who enact unjust statutes
　and who write oppressive decrees,ᶜ
2 Depriving the needy of judgment
　and robbing my people's poor of their
　　rights.
Making widows their plunder,
　and orphans their prey!ᵈ

9, 5: A child: the Immanuel of Is 7, 14 and 8, 8; cf Is 11,
1. 2. 9. In Christian tradition and liturgy, this passage is used
to refer to Christ. Upon his shoulder dominion rests: authority. Wonder-Counselor: remarkable for his wisdom and
prudence. God-Hero: a warrior and a defender of his people,
like God himself. Father-Forever: ever devoted to his people. Prince of Peace: his reign will be characterized by
peace.

9, 11: Aram: the Syrian kingdom, with its capital at Damascus.
9, 20: Manasseh ... Ephraim: two of the leading tribes of
the northern kingdom.

z: Ps 72, 7; Lk 2, 11. 14.　a: Jer 23, 5; Lk 1, 32f.　b: Is 28, 7; Jer
2, 8; 5, 31; 20, 6; 23, 13f; Ez 13, 1-7; 22, 28; Mi 3, 11.
c: Jer 8, 8.　d: Is 1, 23.

Assyria, Rod of God's Anger

Assyria is the LORD's means of punishing the people, but that nation also will be judged for its arrogance. God's purpose to punish Israel, carried out by Assyria, is just, but Assyria's own purpose is to plunder and conquer. While the king of Assyria boasts about his victories, God will destroy them when Assyria has served its purpose.

³ What will you do on the day of
    punishment,
  when ruin comes from afar?
To whom will you flee for help?
  Where will you leave your wealth,
⁴ Lest it sink beneath the captive
  or fall beneath the slain?
For all this, his wrath is not turned back,
  his hand is still outstretched!

Assyria the Unconscious Instrument of God
⁵ Woe to Assyria! My rod in anger,
  my staff in wrath.
⁶ Against an impious nation* I send him,
  and against a people under my wrath I
    order him
To seize plunder, carry off loot,
  and tread them down like the mud of
    the streets.
⁷ But this is not what he intends,
  nor does he have this
    in mind;
Rather, it is in his heart to destroy,
  to make an end of nations not a few.
⁸ "Are not my commanders all kings?" he
    says,
⁹   "Is not Calno like Carchemish,ᵉ
Or Hamath like Arpad,
  or Samaria like Damascus?*
¹⁰ Just as my hand reached out to idolatrous
    kingdoms
  that had more images than Jerusalem
    and Samaria,
¹¹ Just as I treated Samaria and her idols,
  shall I not do to Jerusalem and her
    graven images?"ᶠ

¹²*[But when the LORD has brought to an
end all his work on Mount Zion and in Jerusalem,

I will punish the utterance
  of the king of Assyria's proud heart,
¹³   and the boastfulness of his haughty
      eyes.
    For he says:]

"By my own power I have done it,
  and by my wisdom, for I am shrewd.
I have moved the boundaries of
    peoples,
  their treasures I have pillaged,
  and, like a giant, I have put down the
    enthroned.
¹⁴ My hand has seized like a nest
  the riches of nations;
As one takes eggs left alone,
  so I took in all the earth;
No one fluttered a wing,
  or opened a mouth, or chirped!"

¹⁵ Will the axe boast against him who hews
    with it?
  Will the saw exalt itself above him
    who wields it?
As if a rod could sway him who lifts it,
  or a staff him who is not wood!
¹⁶ Therefore the Lord, the LORD of hosts,
  will send among his fat ones* leanness,
And instead of his glory there will be
    kindling
  like the kindling of fire.
¹⁷ The Light of Israel will become a fire,
  Israel's Holy One a flame,
That burns and consumes his briers
  and his thorns in a single day.

10, 6f: Impious nation: Israel. It was God's intention to use Assyria merely to punish, not to destroy, his people.
10, 9: Calno . . . Damascus: cities captured by the Assyrians.
10, 16: His fat ones: the strong men of the king of Assyria.

e: Is 36, 19; Am 6, 2. *f:* Is 36, 20.

¹⁸ His splendid forests and orchards
  will be consumed, soul and body;
¹⁹ And the remnant of the trees in his
    forest
  will be so few,
Like poles set up for signals,
  that any boy can record them.
²⁰   On that day
The remnant of Israel,
  the survivors of the house of Jacob,
  will no more lean upon him who
    struck them;
But they will lean upon the LORD,
  the Holy One of Israel, in truth.
²¹ A remnant will return,* the remnant of
    Jacob,
  to the mighty God.
²² For though your people, O Israel,
  were like the sand of the sea,
Only a remnant of them will return;
  their destruction is decreed
  as overwhelming justice demands.ᵍ

²³Yes, the destruction he has decreed, the Lord, the GOD of hosts, will carry out within the whole land. ²⁴Therefore thus says the Lord, the GOD of hosts: O my people, who dwell in Zion, do not fear the Assyrian, though he strikes you with a rod, and raises his staff against you. ²⁵For only a brief moment more, and my anger shall be over; but them I will destroy in wrath. ²⁶Then the LORD of hosts will raise against them a scourge such as struck Midian at the rock of Oreb; and he will raise his staff over the sea as he did against Egypt.ʰ ²⁷On that day,*

His burden shall be taken from your
    shoulder,
  and his yoke shattered from your neck.

Sennacherib's Invasion
He has come up from the direction of
    Rimmon,

²⁸ he has reached Aiath, passed through
    Migron,
  at Michmash his supplies are stored.
²⁹ They cross the ravine:
  "We will spend the night at Geba."
Ramah is in terror,
  Gibeah of Saul has fled.
³⁰ Cry and shriek, O daughter of Gallim!
  Hearken, Laishah! Answer her,
    Anathoth!
³¹ Madmenah is in flight,
  the inhabitants of Gebim seek refuge.
³² Even today he will halt at Nob,*
  he will shake his fist at the mount of
    daughter Zion,
  the hill of Jerusalem!
³³ Behold, the Lord, the LORD of hosts,
  lops off the boughs with terrible
    violence;
The tall of stature are felled,
  and the lofty ones brought low;
³⁴ The forest thickets are felled with the axe,
  and Lebanon in its splendor
    falls.

CHAPTER 11
The Rule of Immanuel

See RG 208

¹ But a shoot shall sprout from the stump
    of Jesse,*
  and from his roots a bud shall blossom.ⁱ
² The spirit of the LORD shall rest upon
    him:ʲ
  a spirit of wisdom and of understanding,
A spirit of counsel and of strength,
  a spirit of knowledge and of fear of the
    LORD,*
³   and his delight shall be the fear of the
    LORD.
Not by appearance shall he judge,
  nor by hearsay shall he decide,
⁴ But he shall judge the poor with justice,
  and decide aright for the land's
    afflicted.ᵏ

10, 21: A remnant will return: in Hebrew, shear-jashub, an allusion to the name of Isaiah's son, Shear-jashub; cf Is 7, 3.

10, 27-32: A poetic description of the progress of the Assyrian army, advancing from the north through Judah to the gates of Jerusalem.

10, 32ff: Just when the enemy is about to capture Jerusalem, God intervenes and destroys the hostile army.

11, 1: Jesse: David's father. Shoot . . . stump: after the Babylonian exile only a stump of the Davidic dynasty will

remain; from it will arise the new shoot, the messianic King.

11, 2f: The source of the traditional names of the gifts of the Holy Spirit. The Septuagint and the Vulgate read "piety" for fear of the Lord in its first occurrence, thus listing seven gifts.

g: Rom 9, 27f. *h:* Jgs 7, 25. *i:* Lk 3, 32. *j:* Mt 3, 16; Mk 1, 10. *k:* Pss 72, 2. 4; 98, 9; 2 Thes 2, 8.

He shall strike the ruthless with the rod
of his mouth,
and with the breath of his lips he shall
slay the wicked.
5 Justice shall be the band around his waist,
and faithfulness a belt upon his hips.

6 Then the wolf shall be a guest of the lamb,*
and the leopard shall lie down with the
kid;
The calf and the young lion shall browse
together,
with a little child to guide them.[l]
7 The cow and the bear shall be neighbors,
together their young shall rest;
the lion shall eat hay like the ox.
8 The baby shall play by the cobra's den,
and the child lay his hand on the
adder's lair.
9 There shall be no harm or ruin on all my
holy mountain;
for the earth shall be filled with
knowledge of the LORD,
as water covers the sea.[m]

Union of Ephraim and Judah

10   On that day,
The root of Jesse,
set up as a signal for the nations,
The Gentiles shall seek out,
for his dwelling shall be glorious.[n]
11   On that day,
The Lord shall again take it in hand[o]
to reclaim the remnant of his people
that is left from Assyria and
Egypt,
Pathros, Ethiopia, and Elam,
Shinar, Hamath, and the isles of the
sea.*
12 He shall raise a signal to the nations
and gather the outcasts of Israel;
The dispersed of Judah he shall assemble
from the four corners of
the earth.

13 The envy of Ephraim shall pass away,
and the rivalry of Judah be removed;
Ephraim shall not be jealous of Judah,
and Judah shall not be hostile to
Ephraim;[p]
14 But they shall swoop down on the
foothills
of the Philistines to the west,
together they shall plunder the
Kedemites;*
Edom and Moab shall be their possessions,
and the Ammonites their subjects.
15 The LORD shall dry up the tongue of the
Sea of Egypt,*
and wave his hand over the Euphrates
in his fierce anger
And shatter it into seven streamlets,
so that it can be crossed in sandals.[q]
16 There shall be a highway for the remnant
of his people
that is left from Assyria,
As there was for Israel
when he came up from the land of
Egypt.

CHAPTER 12

Song of Thanksgiving*

1   On that day, you will say:
I give you thanks, O LORD;
though you have been angry with me,
your anger has abated, and you have
consoled me.
2 God indeed is my savior;
I am confident and unafraid.
My strength and my courage is the LORD,
and he has been my savior.[r]

3 With joy you will draw water
at the fountain of salvation, 4and say
on that day:
Give thanks to the LORD, acclaim his
name;
among the nations make known his
deeds,

See RG 208

11, 6-9: This picture of the idyllic harmony of paradise is
a dramatic symbol of the universal peace and justice of messianic times.

11, 11: Pathros . . . sea: where God's people lived in exile.
Pathros: upper Egypt. Elam: east of Babylonia. Shinar: Babylonia. Hamath: on the Orontes River in Syria. Isles: or coastlands, in the Mediterranean.

11, 14: Kedemites: tribes in the Arabian Desert.

11, 15: Tongue . . . Egypt: the body of water between
Egypt and Palestine.

12, 1-6: Israel's thanksgiving to the Lord, expressed in
language like that of the Psalms.

l: Is 65, 25.   *m:* Hb 2, 14.   *n:* Is 49, 22; Rom 15, 12.   *o:* Is 27,
13; Mi 7, 12; Zec 10, 10.   *p:* Ex 37, 16-17.   *q:* Ex 14, 29.   *r:* Ex
15, 2; Ps 118, 14.

A Song of Thanksgiving

Isaiah has been constructed to form a series of "books within books." In ch 12 a song of thanksgiving for the salvation of God that will surely come to Jerusalem concludes the section that began in Isaiah 5, 1. These shorter collections display a broad editorial structure where hope and promise follow threats and warnings. Even the punitive fires of judgment are placed within this larger context of the saving purpose of God.

proclaim how exalted is his name.
⁵ Sing praise to the LORD for his glorious achievement;
let this be known throughout all the earth.ˢ
⁶ Shout with exultation, O city of Zion,
for great in your midst
is the Holy One of Israel!ᵗ

III: Oracles Against the Pagan Nations

CHAPTER 13

See RG 209

Babylon. ¹An oracle concerning Babylon; a vision of Isaiah, son of Amoz.

² Upon the bare mountains set up a signal;
cry out to them,*
Wave for them to enter
the gates of the volunteers.ᵘ

³ I have commanded my dedicated soldiers,*
I have summoned my warriors,
eager and bold to carry out my anger.
⁴ Listen! the rumble on the mountains:
that of an immense throng!
Listen! the noise of kingdoms,
nations assembled!
The LORD of hosts is mustering
an army for battle.ᵛ
⁵ They come from a far-off country,
and from the end of the heavens,

The LORD and the instruments of his wrath,
to destroy all the land.

⁶ Howl, for the day of the LORD* is near;
as destruction from the Almighty it comes.ʷ
⁷ Therefore all hands fall helpless,ˣ
the bows of the young men fall from their hands.
Every man's heart melts ⁸in terror.
Pangs and sorrows take hold of them,
like a woman in labor they writhe;
They look aghast at each other,
their faces aflame.ʸ
⁹ Lo, the day of the LORD comes,
cruel, with wrath and burning anger;
To lay waste the land
and destroy the sinners within it!
¹⁰ The stars and constellations of the heavens
send forth no light;
The sun is dark when it rises,
and the light of the moon does not shine.ᶻ
¹¹ Thus I will punish the world for its evil
and the wicked for their guilt.
I will put an end to the pride of the arrogant,
the insolence of tyrants I will humble.ᵃ
¹² I will make mortals more rare than pure gold,
men, than gold of Ophir.*

13, 2: To them: the Medes (v 17) and Persians, who would destroy Babylon. Gates of the volunteers: the mustering places of Babylon's enemies for war against her.

13, 3: Dedicated soldiers: in the sense that they will wage a "holy war" and carry out God's plan.

13, 6ff: Day of the LORD: described often in prophetical writings, it generally signified the coming of the Lord in power and majesty to destroy his enemies and inaugurate his kingdom. Here it refers to the overthrow of Babylon. The figures used convey the idea of horror and destruction. Read vv 6-8 with vv 14-16.

13, 12: Ophir: cf note to Ps 45, 10.

s: Ex 15, 1. t: Is 41, 14. 16; 54, 1; Zep 3, 14; Zec 2, 10. u: Is 5, 26. v: Jer 50, 9. w: Jer 46, 10; Jl 1, 15. x: Ez 7, 17. y: Is 21, 3; Ps 48, 7; Mi 4, 9. z: Is 24, 23. a: Is 2, 17; Jer 50, 32.

Places Mentioned in the Oracles against the Nations

13 For this I will make the heavens tremble
and the earth shall be shaken from its
place,
At the wrath of the LORD of hosts
on the day of his burning anger.

14 Like a hunted gazelle,
or a flock that no one gathers,
Every man shall turn to his kindred
and flee to his own land.[b]

15 Everyone who is caught shall be run
through;
to a man, they shall fall by the sword.

16 Their infants shall be dashed to pieces in
their sight;
their houses shall be plundered
and their wives ravished.[c]

17 I am stirring up against them the Medes,

who think nothing of silver
and take no delight in gold.[d]

18 The fruit of the womb they shall not spare,
nor shall they have eyes of pity for
children.

19 And Babylon, the jewel of kingdoms,
the glory and pride of the Chaldeans,
Shall be overthrown by God
like Sodom and like Gomorrah.

20 She shall never be inhabited,
nor dwelt in, from age to age;
The Arab shall not pitch his tent there,
nor shepherds couch their flocks.[e]

21 But wildcats shall rest there
and owls shall fill the houses;
There ostriches shall dwell,
and satyrs* shall dance.[f]

22 Desert beasts shall howl in her castles,

13, 21: Satyrs: in the popular mind, demons of goatlike form dwelling in ruins, symbols of immorality; cf Lv 17, 7.

b: Jer 50, 16.   c: Na 3, 10.   d: Is 21, 2; Jer 51, 11. 28.   e: Jer 51, 62.   f: Is 34, 13f; 35, 7.

Isaiah 13, 15 is one of the only verses in First Isaiah (RG 205) that anticipates the Israelites and Judeans taking vengeance on their enemies. It contradicts not only the prediction of a nonviolent messianic age earlier in this chapter, but also the consistent rejection of national revenge in Isaiah's prophecies.

A Mocking Lament for the Death of the King of Babylon

The Babylonian threat occupies most of chs 40–55, so this great world power takes on a symbolic role as the supreme example of oppression. The editorial note in 14, 1–2 provides a summary of the message of hope (chs 56–66; see also Is 11, 12–16). In vv. 3–11, a brilliant, mocking lament for the death of the king of Babylon ironically contrasts the king's power in life and powerlessness in death and celebrates the passing of Babylon as a world power.

and jackals in her luxurious palaces.
Her time is near at hand
and her days shall not be prolonged.

CHAPTER 14

See RG 209

The King of Babylon. [1]When the LORD has pity on Jacob and again chooses Israel and settles them on their own soil, the aliens will join them and be counted with the house of Jacob.[g] [2]The house of Israel will take them and bring them along to its place, and possess them as male and female slaves on the Lord's soil, making captives of its captors and ruling over its oppressors.[h] [3]On the day the LORD relieves you of sorrow and unrest and the hard service in which you have been enslaved,[i] [4]you will take up this taunt-song* against the king of Babylon:[j]

How the oppressor has reached his end!
how the turmoil is stilled!
[5] The LORD has broken the rod of the wicked,
the staff of the tyrants
[6] That struck the peoples in wrath
relentless blows;
That beat down the nations in anger,
with oppression unchecked.
[7] The whole earth rests peacefully,
song breaks forth;
[8] The very cypresses rejoice over you,
and the cedars of Lebanon:
"Now that you are laid to rest,
there will be none to cut us down."[k]

[9] The nether world below is all astir
preparing for your coming;
It awakens the shades to greet you,
all the leaders of the earth;
It has the kings of all nations
rise from their thrones.
[10] All of them speak out
and say to you,
"You too have become weak like us,
you are the same as we.
[11] Down to the nether world your pomp is brought,
the music of your harps.
The couch beneath you is the maggot,
your covering, the worm."[l]

[12] How have you fallen from the heavens,
O morning star,* son of the dawn!
How are you cut down to the ground,
you who mowed down the nations!
[13] You said in your heart:[m]
"I will scale the heavens;
Above the stars of God
I will set up my throne;
I will take my seat on the Mount of Assembly,
in the recesses of the North.*
[14] I will ascend above the tops of the clouds;
I will be like the Most High!"[n]

[15] Yet down to the nether world you go
to the recesses of the pit!
[16] When they see you they will stare,
pondering over you:

14, 4-21: This taunt-song, or satire, is one of the finest in the Bible.
14, 12: Morning star: the king of Babylon. The Vulgate has "Lucifer," a name applied by the church Fathers to Satan.
14, 13: Recesses of the North: see note on Ps 48, 3.

g: Is 56, 3; 60, 4; Ps 102, 14; Jer 24, 6; Zec 1, 17.　h: Is 66, 20.　i: Jer 30, 10.　j: Hb 2, 6.　k: Ez 31, 16.　l: Sir 10, 13.　m: Jer 51, 53; Am 9, 2.　n: Ez 28, 2.

"Is this the man who made the earth
tremble,
and kingdoms quake?

17 Who made the world a desert,
razed its cities,
and gave his captives no release?

18 All the kings of the nations lie in glory,
each in his own tomb;

19 But you are cast forth without burial,
loathsome and corrupt,
Clothed as those slain at sword-point,
a trampled corpse.
Going down to the pavement of the pit,

20 you will never be one with them in the
grave."
For you have ruined your land,
you have slain your people!

Let him not be named forever,
that scion of an evil race!

21 Make ready to slaughter his sons
for the guilt of their fathers;
Lest they rise and possess the earth,
and fill the breadth of the world with
tyrants.

22I will rise up against them, says the
LORD of hosts, and cut off from Babylon
name and remnant, progeny and offspring,
says the LORD.^o 23I will make it a haunt of
hoot owls and a marshland; I will sweep it
with the broom of destruction, says the
LORD of hosts.

Assyria

24 The LORD of hosts has sworn:
As I have resolved,
so shall it be;
As I have proposed,
so shall it stand:

25 I will break the Assyrian in my land
and trample him on my mountains;

21*He shall pass through it hard-pressed and
hungry,
and in his hunger he shall become
enraged,
and curse his king and his gods.
He shall look upward,

but there shall be strict darkness
without any dawn;

22 He shall gaze at the earth,
but there shall be distress and darkness,
with the light blacked out by its clouds.

(25)Then his yoke shall be removed from
them,
and his burden from their shoulder.

26 This is the plan proposed for the whole
earth.
and this the hand outstretched over all
nations.

27 The LORD of hosts has planned;
who can thwart him?
His hand is stretched out;
who can turn it back?

Philistia. 28In the year that King Ahaz
died,* there came this oracle:

29 Rejoice not, O Philistia, not a man of
you,
that the rod* which smote you is
broken;
For out of the serpent's root shall come
an adder,
its fruit shall be a flying saraph.

30 In my pastures the poor shall eat,
and the needy lie down in safety;
But I will kill your root with famine
that shall slay even your
remnant.

31 Howl, O gate; cry out, O city!
Philistia, all of you melts away!
For there comes a smoke from the north,
without a straggler in the ranks.

32 What will one answer the messengers of
the nation?
"The LORD has established Zion,
and in her the afflicted of his people
find refuge."^p

CHAPTER 15

Moab

1 Oracle on Moab:
Laid waste in a night,
Ar of Moab is destroyed;
Laid waste in a night,

See RG
209

14, 21f: He . . . clouds: the two verses have been transposed from chap. 8.

14, 28: The year that King Ahaz died: 715 B.C.

14, 29: Rod: an Assyrian oppressor whose identity is uncertain. Flying saraph: a poisonous serpent, distinguished by
its speedy movement; cf note on Nm 21, 6.

o: Jer 51, 62.   *p:* Pss 87, 5; 102, 17f; Zep 3, 12.

Kir of Moab is destroyed.*q*

2 Up goes daughter Dibon*r*
    to the high places to weep;
Over Nebo and over Medeba
    Moab wails.
Every head is shaved,
    every beard sheared off.*

3 In the streets they wear sackcloth,
    lamenting and weeping;
On rooftops and in the squares
    everyone wails.

4 Heshbon and Elealeh cry out,
    they are heard as far as Jahaz.
At this the loins of Moab
      tremble,
    his soul quivers within him;*s*

5 The heart of Moab cries out,
    his fugitives reach Zoar
    [Eglath-shelishiyah].
The ascent of Luhith
    they climb weeping;
On the way to Horonaim*t*
    they utter rending cries.

6 The waters of Nimrim
    have become a waste;
The grass is withered,
    new growth is gone,
    nothing is green.

7 So now whatever they have acquired or
      stored away
    they carry across the Gorge of the
      Poplars,

8 For the cry has gone round
    the land of Moab;
As far as Eglaim the wailing,
    and to Beer-elim, the wail.

9 The waters of Dimon were filled with
      blood,*
    but I will bring still more upon
      Dimon:
Lions for those who are fleeing from
      Moab
    and for those who remain in the land!

CHAPTER 16

See RG 209

1 Send them forth, hugging the earth
    like reptiles,
    from Sela across the desert,
    to the mount of daughter Zion.

2 Like flushed birds,
    like startled nestlings,
Are the daughters of Moab
    at the fords of the Arnon.*

3 Offer counsel, take their part:*
    at high noon let your shadow be like
      the night,
To hide the outcasts,
    to conceal the fugitives.

4 Let the outcasts of Moab live with you,
    be their shelter from the destroyer.
When the struggle is ended, the ruin
      complete,
    and they have done with trampling the
      land,

5 A throne shall be set up in mercy,
    and on it shall sit in fidelity
    [in David's tent]
A judge upholding right
    and prompt to do justice.*u*

6 We have heard of the pride of Moab,
    how very proud he is,
With his haughty, arrogant insolence
    that his empty words do not match.*v*

7 Therefore Moab wails for Moab,*
    everywhere they wail;
For the raisin cakes* of Kir-hareseth
    they sigh, stricken with grief.*w*

8 The terraced slopes of Heshbon languish,
    the vines of Sibmah,
Whose clusters overpowered
    the lords of nations,
While they reached as far as Jazer
    and scattered over the desert,*
And whose branches spread forth
    and extended over the sea.

15, 2: Every head . . . sheared off: traditional signs of grief.

15, 9: There is in the Hebrew a play on words: Dimon and dam, the latter signifying "blood."

16, 2: The Arnon: principal river of Moab.

16, 3-5: Directed to Jerusalem, which should receive the suffering Moabites with mercy, as befits the city of David's family, who were partly descended from Ruth the Moabite.

16, 7-14: Moab had been prosperous; now it has become

a desert.

16, 7: Raisin cakes: masses of dried compressed grapes used as food (cf 2 Sm 6, 19; 1 Chr 16, 3; Song 2, 5), and also in pagan cult (Hos 3, 1).

16, 8: Desert: to the east. Sea: the Dead Sea.

q: Is 16, 7.   *r:* Jer 48, 38f.   *s:* Jer 48, 34.   *t:* Is 16, 9; Jer 48, 3.
u: Is 32, 1.   *v:* Jer 48, 29.   *w:* Is 15, 3.

⁹ Therefore I weep with Jazer
  for the vines of Sibmah;
I water you with tears,
  Heshbon and Elealeh;
For on your summer fruits and harvests
  the battle cry has fallen.ˣ
¹⁰ From the orchards are taken away
  joy and gladness,
In the vineyards there is no singing,
  no shout of joy;
In the wine presses no one treads grapes,
  the vintage shout is stilled.ʸ
¹¹ Therefore for Moab
  my breast moans like a lyre,
  and my heart for Kir-hareseth.ᶻ
¹² When Moab grows weary on the high
    places,ᵃ
  he shall enter his sanctuary to pray,
  but it shall avail him nothing.*

¹³*This is the word the LORD spoke against Moab in times past. ¹⁴But now the LORD has spoken: In three years, like those of a hireling, the glory of Moab shall be degraded despite all its great multitude; there shall be a remnant, very small and weak.

CHAPTER 17

See RG
209

Damascus

¹   Oracle on Damascus:*
Lo, Damascus shall cease to be a city
  and become a ruin;ᵇ
² Her cities shall be forever abandoned,
  given over to flocks to lie in undisturbed.
³ The fortress shall be lost to Ephraim*
  and the kingdom to Damascus;
 The remnant of Aram shall have the same
    glory
  as the Israelites,
  says the LORD of hosts.

⁴   On that day
The glory of Jacob shall fade,
  and his full body grow thin,ᶜ
⁵ Like the reaper's mere armful of stalks
  when he gathers the standing grain;
Or as when one gleans the ears
  in the Valley of Rephaim.*
⁶ Only a scattering of grapes shall be left!
  As when an olive tree has been beaten,
Two or three olives remain at the very
    top,
  four or five on its fruitful branches,*
  says the LORD, the God of Israel.ᵈ

⁷ On that day man shall look to his
    maker,
  his eyes turned toward the Holy One
    of Israel.ᵉ
⁸ He shall not look to the altars, his
    handiwork,
  nor shall he regard what his fingers
    have made:
  the sacred poles* or the incense stands.
⁹ On that day his strong cities shall be
  like those abandoned by the Hivites
    and Amorites
When faced with the children of Israel:
  they shall be laid waste.ᶠ
¹⁰ For you have forgotten God, your savior,
  and remembered not the Rock, your
    strength.
Therefore, though you plant your pagan
    plants*
  and set out your foreign vine slips,ᵍ
¹¹ Though you make them grow the day
    you plant them
  and make your sprouts blossom on the
    next morning.
The harvest shall disappear on the day of
  the grievous blow,

16, 12: In vain do the Moabites appeal to their god Chemosh.

16, 13f: A prose application of the preceding poetic oracle against Moab (15, 1—16, 12); cf Jer 4, 8. Like those of a hireling: who fulfills his period of service according to the shortest manner of reckoning; cf Is 21, 16.

17, 1: Damascus: capital of Syria, destroyed in 732 B.C.

17, 3: Ephraim: Israel, leagued with Syria against Assyria and Judah; destroyed in 721 B.C. Aram: Syria.

17, 5: Valley of Rephaim: a fertile plain to the southwest of Jerusalem; cf Jos 15, 8; 2 Sm 5, 18.

17, 6: Olives not easily picked by hand were knocked from the tree by means of a long stick; cf Is 24, 13.

17, 8: Sacred poles: see note on Ex 34, 13. Incense stands: small altars on which incense was burned in idolatrous worship; cf Is 27, 9; Lv 26, 30.

17, 10: Pagan plants: literally, "plants of delights," understood by some as planted in honor of the god of fertility.

x: Is 15, 5; Jer 48, 32. *y:* Is 24, 8. *z:* Is 15, 5; Jer 48, 36. *a:* Jer 48, 13. *b:* Jer 49, 23. *c:* Is 10, 16. *d:* Is 24, 13. *e:* Mi 5, 12. *f:* Is 27, 10. *g:* Jer 2, 32; Hos 8, 14.

the incurable blight.

12 Ah! the roaring of many peoples*
   that roar like the roar of the seas!
The surging of nations
   that surge like the surging of mighty
      waves!
13 But God shall rebuke them,
   and they shall flee far away;
Windswept, like chaff on the mountains,
   like tumbleweed in a storm.
14 In the evening, they spread terror,
   before morning, they are gone!
Such is the portion of those who despoil
   us,
   the lot of those who plunder us.

CHAPTER 18

Ethiopia

1 Ah, land of buzzing insects,*
   beyond the rivers of Ethiopia,
2 Sending ambassadors by sea,
   in papyrus boats* on the waters!
Go, swift messengers,
   to a nation tall and bronzed,
To a people dreaded near and far,
   a nation strong and conquering,
   whose land is washed by rivers.h
3 All you who inhabit the world,
   who dwell on earth,
When the signal is raised on the
   mountain, look!
When the trumpet blows, listen!
4 For thus says the LORD to me:
   I will quietly look on from where I
      dwell,
Like the glowing heat of sunshine,
   like a cloud of dew at harvest time.
5 Before the vintage, when the flowering is
   ended,
   and the blooms are succeeded by
      ripening grapes,
Then comes the cutting of branches with
   pruning hooks

and the discarding of the lopped-off
   shoots.
6 They shall all be left to the mountain
   birds of prey,
   and to the beasts in the land;
The birds of prey shall summer on them
   and on them all the beasts of the earth
      shall winter.

7Then will gifts be brought to the LORD of
hosts from a people tall and bronzed, from a
people dreaded near and far, a nation strong
and conquering, whose land is washed by
rivers—to Mount Zion where dwells the
name of the LORD of hosts.i

CHAPTER 19

Egypt

1   Oracle on Egypt:
   See, the LORD is riding on a swift cloud
      on his way to Egypt;
The idols of Egypt tremble before him,
   the hearts of the Egyptians melt within
      them.
2 I will rouse Egypt against Egypt:
   brother will war against brother,
Neighbor against neighbor,
   city against city, kingdom against
      kingdom.
3 The courage of the Egyptians ebbs away
      within them,
   and I will bring to nought their counsel;
They shall consult idols and charmers,
   ghosts and spirits.j
4 I will deliver Egypt
   into the power of a cruel master,*
A harsh king who shall rule over them,
   says the Lord, the LORD of hosts.k
5 The waters shall be drained from the sea,
   the river shall shrivel and dry up;l
6 Its streams shall become foul,
   and the canals of Egypt shall dwindle
      and dry up.
Reeds and rushes shall wither away,

17, 12f: Many peoples: the hordes that accompanied the invading Assyrians, whom God repels just as he vanquished the
primeval waters of chaos; see notes on Jb 3, 8; 7, 12; Ps 89, 11.
   18, 1: Land of buzzing insects: the region of the Upper
Nile where these multiplied with great rapidity.
   18, 2: Papyrus boats: light and serviceable vessels made
of bundles of papyrus stalks and sealed with pitch. Egypt,

ruled by a dynasty from Ethiopia, had invited Judah to join a
coalition against Assyria, but Isaiah bade the ambassadors return to their own people.
   19, 4: Cruel master: the king of Assyria.

---

h: Is 18, 7.   i: Is 45, 14; Zep 3, 10; Mal 1, 11.   j: Is 44, 25.
k: Ez 29, 19; 30, 10.   l: Ez 30, 12; 32, 2.

Threats concerning Egypt

Throughout the period when Assyria and Babylonia were assaulting Israel and Judah, Egypt repeatedly promised protection, yet consistently failed to carry through. Egypt's help was "futile and vain" (30, 7). The people famed throughout antiquity for learning and literary skill could offer no defense against a ruthless invader (19, 11–15). In spite of these failures, Judah's relations with Egypt were prolonged and often close. The prophet looks beyond the turmoil of Mesopotamian rule to the time when a community would dwell there who spoke the language of Canaan (v. 18) and swore allegiance to the LORD of hosts. Even Assyria would one day become with Egypt and Israel a blessing in the midst of the land (v. 24). This series of remarkable short prophecies builds on the aftermath of the disasters that befell Jerusalem at the hands of the Assyrians and Babylonians. Many citizens fled to Egypt, and, from the sixth century B.C. onward, substantial settlements of exiled Judeans took refuge there. In this bold look across the spiritual boundaries of the ancient world, a genuine religious universalism begins to appear (vv. 23–24). The knowledge of God revealed to Israel would be shared among other peoples, replacing the failed learning of the Egyptian sages (v. 11).

7 and bulrushes on the bank of the Nile;
  All the sown land along the Nile
    shall dry up and blow away, and be no
      more.
8 The fishermen shall mourn and lament,
    all who cast hook in the Nile;
  Those who spread their nets in the water
    shall pine away.
9 The linen-workers shall be disappointed,
    the combers and weavers shall turn
      pale;[m]
10 The spinners shall be crushed,
    all the hired laborers shall be
      despondent.
11 Utter fools are the princes of Zoan!*
    the wisest of Pharaoh's advisers give
      stupid counsel.
  How can you say to Pharaoh,
    "I am a disciple of wise men, of
      ancient kings"?
12 Where then are your wise men?
    Let them tell you and make known
  What the LORD of hosts has planned
    against Egypt.
13 The princes of Zoan have become fools,

  the princes of Memphis have been
    deceived.
  The chiefs of her tribes
    have led Egypt astray.
14 The LORD has prepared among them
    a spirit of dizziness,
  And they have made Egypt stagger in
    whatever she does,
    as a drunkard staggers in his vomit.
15 Egypt shall have no work to do[n]
    for head or tail, palm branch or
      reed.*

16 On that day the Egyptians shall be like women, trembling with fear, because of the LORD of hosts shaking his fist at them.[o] 17 And the land of Judah shall be a terror to the Egyptians. Every time they remember Judah, they shall stand in dread because of the plan which the LORD of hosts has in mind for them.[p]

18 On that day there shall be five cities* in the land of Egypt speaking the language of Canaan and swearing by the LORD of hosts; one shall be called "City of the Sun."

19, 11. 13: Zoan: later known as Tanis, and Memphis (in Hebrew Noph) were the key cities of the Nile Delta.
19, 15: Head or tail, palm branch or reed: the leaders or the people; cf Is 9, 13f.
19, 18: Five cities: colonies of Jews living together and speaking their languages, Hebrew and Aramaic; cf Jer, chap. 43. City of the Sun: the meaning is uncertain, but the reference seems to be to the city known later as Heliopolis.

m: Ez 27, 7.   n: Is 9, 14.   o: Na 3, 13.   p: Ex 14, 25.

¹⁹On that day there shall be an altar to the LORD in the land of Egypt, and a sacred pillar to the LORD near the boundary. ²⁰It shall be a sign and a witness to the LORD of hosts in the land of Egypt, when they cry out to the LORD against their oppressors, and he sends them a savior to defend and deliver them. ²¹The LORD shall make himself known to Egypt, and the Egyptians shall know the LORD in that day; they shall offer sacrifices and oblations, and fulfill the vows they make to the LORD.�q ²²Although the LORD shall smite Egypt severely, he shall heal them; they shall turn to the LORD and he shall be won over and heal them.

²³On that day there shall be a highway from Egypt to Assyria; the Assyrians shall enter Egypt, and the Egyptians enter Assyria, and Egypt shall serve Assyria.

²⁴On that day Israel shall be a third party with Egypt and Assyria, a blessing in the midst of the land,ʳ ²⁵when the LORD of hosts blesses it: "Blessed be my people Egypt, and the work of my hands Assyria, and my inheritance, Israel."

CHAPTER 20

See RG 209

Captivity of Egypt and Ethiopia. ¹In the year the general sent by Sargon, king of Assyria, fought against Ashdod and captured it, ²the LORD gave a warning through Isaiah,* the son of Amoz: Go and take off the sackcloth from your waist, and remove the sandals from your feet. This he did, walking naked and barefoot. ³Then the LORD said: Just as my servant Isaiah has gone naked and barefoot for three years as a sign and portent against Egypt and Ethiopia, ⁴so shall the king of Assyria lead away captives from Egypt, and exiles from Ethiopia, young and old, naked and barefoot, with buttocks uncovered [the shame of Egypt]. ⁵They shall be dismayed and ashamed because of Ethiopia,

their hope, and because of Egypt, their boast.ˢ ⁶The inhabitants of this coastland shall say on that day, "Look at our hope! We have fled here for help and deliverance from the king of Assyria; where can we flee now?"ᵗ

CHAPTER 21

See RG 209

Fall of Babylon

¹ Oracle on the wastelands by the sea:*
Like whirlwinds sweeping in waves
    through the Negeb,
there comes from the desert,
    from the fearful land,
² A cruel sight, revealed to me:
    the traitor betrays,
    the despoiler spoils.
"Go up, Elam; besiege, O Media;*
    I will put an end to all groaning!"ᵘ
³ Therefore my loins are filled with anguish,
    pangs have seized me like those of a
        woman in labor;
I am too bewildered to hear,
    too dismayed to look.ᵛ
⁴ My mind reels,
    shuddering assails me;
My yearning for twilight
    has turned into dread.
⁵ They set the table,
    spread out the rugs;
    they eat, they drink.*
Rise up, O princes,
    oil the shield!

⁶ For thus says my Lord to me:
    Go, station a watchman,
    let him tell what he sees.
⁷ If he sees a chariot,
    a pair of horses,
Someone riding an ass,
    someone riding a camel,
Then let him pay heed,
    very close heed.

20, 2-6: The symbolic act of the prophet conveyed the idea that Assyria would lead captive the Egyptians and Ethiopians. The Judeans and their allies would then realize the folly of having trusted in them.

21, 1: Wastelands by the sea: Babylonia. Negeb: the desert south of Judah.

21, 2: Elam . . . Media: nations which, under the leadership of Cyrus, captured Babylon in 538 B.C. End to all groan-

ing: those who were captives of Babylon shall be freed.

21, 5: Babylon is destroyed while its leaders are feasting; cf Dn 5. Oil the shield: shields were oiled and greased so as to divert blows more easily.

---

q: Zec 14, 16. 18.   *r:* Gn 12, 2.   *s:* Is 30, 3. 5.   *t:* Is 31, 3; 35, 6.
u: Is 13, 17.   *v:* Ps 38, 8.

8 Then the watchman cried,
"On the watchtower, O my Lord,
I stand constantly by day;
And I stay at my post
    through all the watches of the night."ʷ
⁹ Here he comes now:
    a single chariot,
    a pair of horses;
He calls out and says,
    'Fallen, fallen is Babylon,
And all the images of her gods
    are smashed to the ground.' "ˣ

¹⁰ O my people who have been threshed,
    beaten on my threshing floor!
What I have heard
    from the LORD of hosts,
The God of Israel,
    I have announced to you.ʸ

Edom

11 Oracle on Edom:
They call to me from Seir,*
    "Watchman, how much longer the
        night?
Watchman, how much longer the night?"
12 The watchman replies,
"Morning has come, and again night.
    If you will ask, ask; come back again."

Arabia

13 Oracle on Arabia:*
In the thicket in the nomad country spend
    the night,
O caravans of Dedanites.
¹⁴ Meet the thirsty, bring them water;
    you who dwell in the land of Tema,
    greet the fugitives with bread.
¹⁵ They flee from the sword,
    from the whetted sword;
From the taut bow,
    from the fury of battle.

¹⁶For thus says the Lord to me: In another
year, like those of a hireling,* all the glory of
Kedar shall come to an end. ¹⁷Few of Kedar's stalwart archers shall remain, for the
LORD, the God of Israel, has spoken.

CHAPTER 22

See RG
209

Jerusalem

1   Oracle of the Valley of Vision:*
What is the matter with you now, that
    you have gone up,
    all of you, to the housetops,
² O city full of noise and chaos,
    O wanton town!
Your slain are not slain with the sword,
    nor killed in battle.ᶻ
³ All your leaders fled away together,
    fled afar off;
All who were in you were captured
    together,
    captured without the use of a bow.ᵃ
⁴ At this I say: Turn away from me,
    let me weep bitterly;
Do not try to comfort me
    for the ruin of the daughter of my
        people.ᵇ
⁵ It is a day of panic, rout and confusion,
    from the Lord, the GOD of hosts, in the
        Valley of Vision.
Walls crash;
    they cry for help to the mountains.ᶜ
⁶ Elam* takes up the quivers,
    Aram mounts the horses,
    and Kir uncovers the shields.
⁷ Your choice valleys are filled with chariots,
    and horses are posted at the gates,
⁸   and shelter over Judah is removed.

*On that day you looked to the weapons in
the House of the Forest; ⁹you saw that the
breaches in the City of David were many;
you collected the water of the lower pool.

21, 11f: Seir: another name for Edom. The Edomites ask
the prophet how much longer they must suffer (the night of
suffering); he answers ambiguously: "Liberation (morning)
and further suffering (night)," but perhaps they will later receive a more encouraging answer (ask; come back again).

21, 13f: Arabia: that is, the nomad country. Dedanites: an
Arab tribe associated with Edom and Tema, and living east of
the Red Sea; cf Gn 10, 7; 25, 3; Jer 25, 23.

21, 16: Year . . . of a hireling: see note on Is 16, 14. Kedar:
a nomad tribe in Arabia; cf Is 42, 11; 60, 7; Ps 120, 5.

22, 1-8: Valley of Vision: while the people live in revelry and
disorder, the prophet foresees the impending doom of the city.
22, 6: Elam, Aram, Kir: all allies of Assyria. Kir: perhaps
the same people referred to in Am 1, 5.
22, 8-11: Defense measures, in which the inhabitants of
Jerusalem placed their trust instead of relying on God.
House of the Forest: an armory built by Solomon; its

---

w: Hb 2, 1.   *x:* Is 46, 1; Jer 50, 2; 51, 8; Rv 14, 8.   *y:* Is 51, 23. *z:* Is
32, 13.   *a:* 2 Kgs 25, 4.   *b:* Jer 6, 26; 9, 1; 14, 17.   *c:* Is 37, 3.

[10] You numbered the houses of Jerusalem, tearing some down to strengthen the wall; [11] you made a reservoir between the two walls for the water of the old pool. But you did not look to the city's Maker, nor did you consider him who built it long ago.

[12] On that day the Lord,
the GOD of hosts, called on you
To weep and mourn,
to shave your head and put on sackcloth.[d]
[13] But look! you feast and celebrate,
you slaughter oxen and butcher sheep,
You eat meat and drink wine:
"Eat and drink, for tomorrow we die!"[e]
[14] This reaches the ears of the LORD of hosts—
You shall not be pardoned this wickedness till you die,
says the Lord, the GOD of hosts.

Shebna and Eliakim

[15] Thus says the Lord, the GOD of hosts:
Up, go to that official,
Shebna,* master of the palace,
[16] Who has hewn for himself a sepulcher on a height
and carved his tomb in the rock:
"What are you doing here, and what people have you here,
that here you have hewn for yourself a tomb?"
[17] The LORD shall hurl you down headlong, mortal man!
He shall grip you firmly
[18] And roll you up and toss you like a ball into an open land
To perish there, you and the chariots you glory in,
you disgrace to your master's house!
[19] I will thrust you from your office

and pull you down from your station.
[20] On that day I will summon my servant Eliakim,* son of Hilkiah;[f]
[21] I will clothe him with your robe,
and gird him with your sash,
and give over to him your authority.
He shall be a father to the inhabitants of Jerusalem,
and to the house of Judah.
[22] I will place the key* of the House of David on his shoulder;
when he opens, no one shall shut,
when he shuts, no one shall open.[g]
[23] I will fix him like a peg in a sure spot,
to be a place of honor for his family;
[24] On him shall hang all the glory of his family:*
descendants and offspring,
all the little dishes, from bowls to jugs.

[25] On that day, says the LORD of hosts, the peg fixed in a sure spot shall give way, break off and fall, and the weight that hung on it shall be done away with; for the LORD has spoken.

CHAPTER 23

Tyre and Sidon

See RG 209

[1]   Oracle on Tyre:
Wail, O ships of Tarshish,*
for your port is destroyed;
From the land of the Kittim*
the news reaches them.
[2] Silence! you who dwell on the coast,
you merchants of Sidon,
Whose messengers crossed the sea
[3]   over the deep waters.
The grain of Shihor,* the harvest of the Nile, was her revenue,
and she the merchant among nations.
[4] Shame, O Sidon, fortress on the sea,
for the sea has spoken:*

---

columns of wood suggested the trees of a forest; cf 1 Kgs 7, 2; 10, 17.

22, 15: Shebna: referred to as the scribe in Is 36, 3.

22, 20: Eliakim: also referred to in Is 36, 3; he is described as loyal to God.

22, 22: Key: symbol of authority; cf Mt 16, 19; Rv 3, 7.

22, 24f: If Eliakim should anger God, he and his family (compared here to dishes, bowls and jugs) will suffer disaster.

23, 1-4. 12ff: These verses refer to Sidon, vv 5-11 to Tyre.

23, 1: Kittim: Cyprus.

23, 3: Shihor: a synonym for the Nile.

23, 4: The sea brings to distant coasts the news that Sidon must disown her children; her people are dispersed.

---

d: Jl 2, 17. e: Is 56, 12; Wis 2, 6; 1 Cor 15, 32. f: 2 Kgs 18, 18. 37. g: Rv 3, 7.

"I have not been in labor, nor given birth,
　　nor raised young men,
　　nor reared virgins."
5 When it is heard in Egypt
　　they shall be in anguish at the news of
　　　　Tyre.
6 Pass over to Tarshish, wailing,
　　you who dwell on the coast!
7 Is this your wanton city,
　　whose origin is from of old,
　　Whose feet have taken her
　　to dwell in distant lands?
8 Who has planned such a thing
　　against Tyre, the bestower of crowns,
　　Whose merchants are princes,
　　whose traders are the earth's honored
　　　　men?
9 The LORD of hosts has planned it,
　　to disgrace all pride of majesty,
　　to degrade all the earth's honored
　　　　men.*h*
10 Cross to your own land,
　　O ship of Tarshish;
　　the harbor is no more.
11 His hand he stretches out over the sea,
　　he shakes kingdoms;
　　The LORD has ordered the destruction
　　of Canaan's strongholds.*
12 You shall exult no more, he says,
　　you who are now oppressed, virgin
　　　　daughter Sidon.
　　Arise, pass over to the Kittim,
　　even there you shall find no rest.*i*
13 *[This people is the land of the Chaldeans,
not Assyria.]
　　She whom the impious founded,
　　setting up towers for her,
　　Has had her castles destroyed,
　　and has been turned into a ruin.*j*
14 Lament, O ships of Tarshish,
　　for your haven is destroyed.

15 On that day, Tyre shall be forgotten for
seventy years. With the days of another king,

at the end of seventy years,* it shall be for
Tyre as in the song about the harlot:*k*
16 Take a harp, go about the city,
　　O forgotten harlot;
　　Pluck the strings skillfully, sing many
　　　　songs,
　　that they may remember you.

17 At the end of the seventy years the LORD
shall visit Tyre. She shall return to her hire
and deal with all the world's kingdoms on
the face of the earth.*l* 18 But her merchandise
and her hire shall be sacred to the LORD. It
shall not be stored up or laid away, but from
her merchandise those who dwell before the
LORD shall eat their fill and clothe themselves in choice attire.*

IV: Apocalypse of Isaiah*

CHAPTER 24

See RG 209

Devastation of the World:
A Remnant Saved

1 Lo, the LORD empties the land and lays it
　　waste;
　　he turns it upside down,
　　scattering its inhabitants:*m*
2 Layman and priest alike,
　　servant and master,
　　The maid as her mistress,
　　the buyer as the seller,
　　The lender as the borrower,
　　the creditor as the debtor.
3 The earth is utterly laid waste, utterly
　　　　stripped,
　　for the LORD has decreed this thing.
4 The earth mourns and fades,
　　the world languishes and fades;
　　both heaven and earth languish.
5 The earth is polluted because of its
　　　　inhabitants,
　　who have transgressed laws, violated
　　　　statutes,

23, 11: Canaan's strongholds: the fortresses of Phoenicia.
23, 13: The gloss here identifies she whom the impious
founded with the land of the Chaldeans.
23, 15: Seventy years: a conventional period of time indicating simply a long disaster; cf Jer 25, 11 and 29, 10.
23, 18: Describes the conversion of Tyre.

24, 1—27, 13: This section, probably composed at a later
date, contains oracles on the day of the Lord, combined with
hymns of thanksgiving and of supplication.

h: Ez 28, 7.　i: Ez 28, 21f.　j: Ez 26, 7.　k: Jer 25, 11.　l: Ez 27,
12.　m: Is 13, 9; Hos 4, 9.

broken the ancient covenant.*

[6] Therefore a curse devours the earth,
 and its inhabitants pay for their guilt;
Therefore they who dwell on earth turn
 pale,
 and few men are left.
[7] The wine mourns, the vine languishes,
 all the merry-hearted groan.[n]
[8] Stilled are the cheerful timbrels,
 ended the shouts of the jubilant,
 stilled is the cheerful harp.[o]
[9] They cannot sing and drink wine;
 strong drink is bitter to those who
 partake of it.
[10] Broken down is the city of chaos,*
 shut against entry, every house.[p]
[11] In the streets they cry out for lack of wine;
 all joy has disappeared
 and cheer has left the land.[q]
[12] In the city nothing remains but ruin;
 its gates are battered and desolate.
[13] Thus it is within the land,
 and among the peoples,
As with an olive tree after it is beaten,
 as with a gleaning when the vintage is
 done.[r]
[14] These* lift up their voice in acclaim;
 from the sea they proclaim the majesty
 of the LORD:
[15] "For this, in the coastlands,
 give glory to the LORD!
In the coastlands of the sea,
 to the name of the LORD, the God of
 Israel!"[s]
[16] From the end of the earth we hear songs:
 "Splendor to the Just One!"
But I said, "I am wasted, wasted away.
 Woe is me! The traitors betray:
 with treachery have the traitors
 betrayed!
[17] Terror, pit, and trap[t]
 are upon you, inhabitant of the earth;
[18] He who flees at the sound of terror
 will fall into the pit;

He who climbs out of the pit
 will be caught in the trap.
For the windows on high will be opened
 and the foundations of the earth will
 shake.
[19] The earth will burst asunder,
 the earth will be shaken apart,
 the earth will be convulsed.
[20] The earth will reel like a drunkard,
 and it will sway like a hut;
Its rebellion will weigh it down,
 until it falls, never to rise again."[u]

[21] On that day the LORD will punish
 the host of the heavens* in the
 heavens,
 and the kings of the earth on the earth.[v]
[22] They will be gathered together
 like prisoners into a pit;
They will be shut up in a dungeon,
 and after many days they will be
 punished.
[23] Then the moon will blush[w]
 and the sun grow pale,
For the LORD of hosts will reign
 on Mount Zion and in Jerusalem,
 glorious in the sight of his elders.*

CHAPTER 25

See RG 209

[1] O LORD, you are my God,*
 I will extol you and praise your name;
For you have fulfilled your wonderful
 plans of old,
 faithful and true.[x]
[2] For you have made the city a heap,
 the fortified city a ruin;
The castle of the insolent is a city no
 more,
 nor ever to be rebuilt.[y]
[3] Therefore a strong people will honor you,
 fierce nations will fear you.
[4] For you are a refuge to the poor,
 a refuge to the needy in distress;
Shelter from the rain,

24, 5: Ancient covenant: God's commandments to all mankind.
24, 10: City of chaos: a symbol of godlessness as opposed to Jerusalem, the city of God.
24, 14: These: the saved.
24, 21: Host of the heavens: the stars, which were regarded by the pagans as gods; cf Dt 4, 19; Jer 8, 2.
24, 23: His elders: the heavenly courtiers surrounding the throne of God.
25, 1-8: Victory in messianic times.

n: Jl 1, 10.   o: Jer 7, 34; Hos 2, 13.   p: Is 25, 2.   q: Jer 48, 33; Lam 5, 14f.   r: Is 17, 6; Mi 7, 1.   s: Is 42, 10. 12; Zep 2, 11. t: 17f: Jer 48, 43f.   u: Is 9, 14.   v: Ps 76, 13.   w: Is 13, 10; Jl 3, 3f; 4, 15.   x: Ex 15, 2.   y: Jer 9, 11.

The Banquet of the LORD of Hosts

The great festival to be celebrated in Jerusalem on the holy mountain (ch 25) gives pictorial expression to the praise of God (vv. 1–5). Even in the most violent trouble, God is a refuge to the needy in distress (v. 4). The prophetic vision, however, recognizes that there are wrongs and sufferings on earth that cannot be put right by stilling the blast of the ruthless. The ultimate resolution of injustice can come only when God overcomes the power of death itself (vv. 7–8a; cf Is 26, 19).

shade from the heat.*z*
As with the cold rain,
5   as with the desert heat,
   even so you quell the uproar of the
      wanton.
6 On this mountain* the LORD of hosts
   will provide for all peoples
A feast of rich food and choice wines,
   juicy, rich food and pure, choice
      wines.
7 On this mountain he will destroy
   the veil that veils all peoples,
The web that is woven over all nations;*a*
8   he will destroy death forever.
The Lord GOD will wipe away
   the tears from all faces;
The reproach of his people he will
      remove
from the whole earth; for the LORD has
   spoken.

9   On that day it will be said:
"Behold our God, to whom we looked to
   save us!
This is the LORD for whom we looked;
let us rejoice and be glad that he has
   saved us!"*b*
10 For the hand of the LORD will rest on this
   mountain,
but Moab* will be trodden down
   as a straw is trodden down in the
      mire.*c*
11 He will stretch forth his hands in Moab
   as a swimmer extends his hands to
      swim;
He will bring low their pride

as his hands sweep over them.*d*
12 The high-walled fortress he will raze,
   and strike it down level with the earth,
      with the very dust.*e*

CHAPTER 26

See RG 209

The Divine Vindicator. *1*On that day
they will sing this song in the land of
Judah:

"A strong city have we;
   he sets up walls and ramparts to
      protect us.
2 Open up the gates
   to let in a nation that is just,
   one that keeps faith.*f*
3 A nation of firm purpose you keep in
      peace;
   in peace, for its trust in you."*g*

4 Trust in the LORD forever!
   For the LORD is an eternal Rock.*h*
5 He humbles those in high places,
   and the lofty city he brings down;
He tumbles it to the ground,
   levels it with the dust.*i*
6 It is trampled underfoot by the needy,
   by the footsteps of the poor.
7 The way of the just is smooth;
   the path of the just you make level.*j*
8 Yes, for your way and your judgments,
      O LORD,
   we look to you;
Your name and your title
   are the desire of our souls,
9 My soul yearns for you in the night,

25, 6: This mountain: Zion, symbol of the heavenly Jerusalem.
25, 10: Moab: symbol of God's enemies.

z: Is 14, 32; 32, 2; Na 1, 7. *a*: Is 60, 1. 3; 1 Cor 15, 53ff; Rv 7, 17; 21, 4. *b*: Is 30, 18f. *c*: Zep 2, 9f. *d*: Is 16, 6f. 14. *e*: Is 26, 5. *f*: Ps 118, 19f. *g*: Is 32, 17f; 54, 13. *h*: Is 30, 29; Ps 62, 8. *i*: Is 25, 12; 32, 19. *j*: Ps 23, 3f; Prv 11, 3. 5.

yes, my spirit within me keeps vigil
for you;
When your judgment dawns upon the
earth,
the world's inhabitants learn justice.*k*
¹⁰ The wicked man, spared, does not learn
justice;
in an upright land he acts perversely,
and sees not the majesty of the LORD.*l*
¹¹ O LORD, your hand is uplifted,
but they behold it not;
Let them be shamed when they see your
zeal for your people:
let the fire prepared for your enemies
consume them.
¹² O LORD, you mete out peace to us,
for it is you who have accomplished
all we have done.*m*
¹³ O LORD, our God, other lords than you
have ruled us;
it is from you only that we can call
upon your name.

¹⁴ Dead they are, they have no life,
shades that cannot rise;
For you have punished and destroyed
them,
and wiped out all memory of them.
¹⁵ You have increased the nation, O LORD,
increased the nation to your own
glory,
and extended far all the borders of the
land.*n*
¹⁶ O LORD, oppressed by your punishment,
we cried out in anguish under your
chastising.*o*
¹⁷ As a woman about to give birth
writhes and cries out in her pains,
so were we in your presence,
O LORD.*p*
¹⁸ We conceived and writhed in pain,
giving birth to wind;
Salvation we have not achieved for the
earth,

the inhabitants of the world cannot
bring it forth.
¹⁹ But your dead shall live, their corpses
shall rise;
awake and sing, you who lie in the dust.*q*
For your dew is a dew of light,
and the land of shades gives birth.*

Day of the Lord: Reward and Punishment

²⁰ Go, my people, enter your chambers,
and close your doors behind you;
Hide yourselves for a brief moment,
until the wrath is past.
²¹ See, the LORD goes forth from his place,
to punish the wickedness of the earth's
inhabitants;
The earth will reveal the blood upon her,
and no longer conceal her slain.*r*

CHAPTER 27

See RG
209

¹   On that day,
The LORD will punish with his sword
that is cruel, great, and strong,
Leviathan the fleeing serpent,
Leviathan the coiled serpent;
and he will slay the dragon* that is in
the sea.*s*
²   On that day—
The pleasant vineyard, sing about it!*t*
³   I, the LORD, am its keeper,
I water it every moment;
Lest anyone harm it,
night and day I guard it.*u*
⁴ I am not angry,
but if I were to find briers and thorns,
In battle I should march against them;
I should burn them all.*v*
⁸ Expunging and expelling, I should strive
against them,
carrying them off with my cruel wind
in time of storm.*w*
⁶ In days to come Jacob shall take root,
Israel shall sprout and blossom,
covering all the world with fruit.

26, 19: This verse refers to the restoration of Israel in messianic times under the figure of the resurrection of the dead; cf Ez, chap. 37.

27, 1: Leviathan . . . dragon: symbols of the forces of evil which God vanquishes even as he overcame primeval chaos; cf notes on Jb 3, 8; 7, 12.

---

k: Ps 94, 15.   *l:* Is 5, 12.   *m:* Jer 29, 11.   *n:* Is 54, 2f; Neh 9, 23.   *o:* Hos 6, 1.   *p:* Mi 4, 10.   *q:* Ez 37, 5f; Dn 12, 2; Hos 6, 2.
r: Mi 1, 3.   *s:* Jb 40, 25-32; Ez 32, 2.   *t:* Is 5, 1.   *u:* Is 5, 2ff; Ps 121, 4f.   *v:* Is 10, 17.   *w:* Jer 18, 17.

7 Is he to be smitten as his smiter was
smitten?
or slain as his slayer was slain?*

5 Or shall he cling to me for refuge?*
He must make peace with me;
peace shall he make with me!ˣ

9 This, then, shall be the expiation of
Jacob's guilt,
this the whole fruit of the removal of
his sin:
He shall pulverize all the stones of the
altars
like pieces of chalk;
no sacred poles or incense altars shall
stand.

10 For the fortified city* shall be desolate,
an abandoned pasture, a forsaken
wilderness,
where calves shall browse and lie.ʸ
Its boughs shall be destroyed,

11 its branches shall wither and be broken
off,
and women shall come to build a fire
with them.
This is not an understanding people;
therefore their maker shall not spare
them,
nor shall he who formed them have
mercy on them.ᶻ

12 On that day,
The LORD shall beat out the grain
between the Euphrates and the Wadi of
Egypt,*
and you shall be gleaned one by one,
O sons of Israel.

13 On that day,*
A great trumpet shall blow,
and the lost in the land of Assyria
and the outcasts in the land of
Egypt
Shall come and worship the LORD
on the holy mountain, in Jerusalem.ᵃ

V: The Lord Alone, Israel's and Judah's Salvation

CHAPTER 28

The Fate of Samaria

See RG
209

1 Woe to the majestic garland
of the drunkard Ephraim,*
To the fading blooms of his glorious
beauty,
on the head of him who is stupefied
with wine.ᵇ

2 Behold, the LORD has a strong one and a
mighty,*
who, like a downpour of hail, a
destructive storm,
Like a flood of water, great and
overflowing,
levels to the ground with violence;ᶜ

3 With feet that will trample
the majestic garland of the drunkard
Ephraim.

4 The fading blooms of his glorious beauty
on the head of the fertile valley
Will be like an early fig before summer:
when a man sees it,
he picks and swallows it at once.

5 On that day the LORD of hosts
will be a glorious crown
And a brilliant diadem
to the remnant of his people,

6 A spirit of justice
to him who sits in judgment,
And strength to those
who turn back the battle at the gate.

Against Judah

7 But these also stagger from wine
and stumble from strong drink:
Priest and prophet stagger from strong
drink,
overpowered by wine;

27, 7: God's people will not be treated as sternly as were
their enemies.

27, 5. 9: Israel will make peace with God and destroy all
signs of idolatrous worship.

27, 10f: The fortified city: symbol of the powers of evil;
see note on Is 24, 10.

27, 12: The Euphrates and the Wadi of Egypt: the ideal
borders of Israel; cf Gn 15, 18; 2 Kgs 24, 7.

27, 13: The triumph of God's people is described in es-

chatological language; they will gather in Jerusalem from Assyria and Egypt.

28, 1: Ephraim: the northern kingdom. Its capital, Samaria,
was built upon a hill, suggestive of a majestic garland adorning the head of the drunken kingdom.

28, 2: A strong one and a mighty: Assyria.

---

x: Is 37, 31; Rom 11, 12.   y: Is 6, 11.   z: Jer 4, 22.   a: Hos 11,
11.   b: Hos 7, 5; Am 6, 6.   c: Is 30, 30.

Led astray by strong drink,
staggering in their visions,
tottering when giving judgment.*d*

8 Yes, all the tables
are covered with filthy vomit,
with no place left clean.

9 "To whom would he impart knowledge?*
To whom would he convey the message?
To those just weaned from milk,
those taken from the breast? 10For he says,
'Command on command, command on command,
rule on rule, rule on rule,
here a little, there a little!' "

11 Yes, with stammering lips and in a
strange language*
he will speak to this people*e*

12 to whom he said:
This is the resting place,
give rest to the weary;
Here is repose—
but they would not listen.

13 So for them the word of the LORD shall be:
"Command on command, command
on command,
Rule on rule, rule on rule,
here a little, there a little!"
So that when they walk, they stumble
backward,
broken, ensnared, and captured.

14 Therefore, hear the word of the LORD,
you arrogant,
who rule this people in Jerusalem:

15 Because you say, "We have made a
covenant with death,

and with the nether world* we have
made a pact;
When the overwhelming scourge passes,
it will not reach us;
For we have made lies our refuge,
and in falsehood we have found a
hiding place,"—*f*

16 Therefore, thus says the Lord GOD:
See, I am laying a stone in Zion,*
a stone that has been tested,
A precious cornerstone as a sure
foundation;
he who puts his faith in it shall
not be shaken.*g*

17 I will make of right a measuring
line,
of justice a level.—
Hail shall sweep away the refuge of lies,
and waters shall flood the hiding place.

18 Your covenant with death shall be
canceled
and your pact with the nether world
shall not stand.
When the overwhelming scourge passes,
you shall be trampled down by it.

19 Whenever it passes, it shall take you;
morning after morning it shall pass,
By day and by night;
terror alone shall convey the message.

20 For the bed shall be too short to stretch
out in,
and the cover too narrow to wrap in.

21 For the LORD shall rise up as on Mount
Perazim,
bestir himself as in the Valley of Gibeon,*
To carry out his work, his singular work,
to perform his deed, his strange deed.*h*

28, 9f: The words of those who ridicule Isaiah. The Hebrew of v 10, by its very sound, conveys the idea of mocking imitation of what the prophet says, as though he spoke like a stammering child: SAU LASAU, SAU LASAU, CAU LACAU, CAU LACAU, ZE'ER SHAM, ZE'ER SHAM. But in v 13 God repeats these words in deadly earnest, putting them in the mouth of the victorious pagan army.

28, 11: God will answer the mockers and defend Isaiah. Strange language: spoken by the invading army.

28, 15. 18: A covenant with death, and with the nether world: an alliance with foreign powers, such as Egypt and Babylon, to prevent death and destruction. Have made lies . . . a hiding place: this confidence in human aid proves to be false and deceitful, incapable of averting the dreaded disaster. Overwhelming scourge: the flood of the Assyrian invasion; cf Is 8, 7f.

28, 16: A stone in Zion: the true and sure foundation of salvation promised by God to the Davidic dynasty (cf Is 7, 13-16; 9, 1-6), which the Apostles saw fulfilled in Christ the universal Savior; cf 1 Pt 2, 6-8; Rom 9, 33; 10, 9ff. Cornerstone: the assurance of salvation rejected by Israel in the prophet's time, is reflected by the psalmist (Ps 118, 22) and fulfilled in the Person of Christ; cf Mt 21, 42; Lk 20, 17; Acts 4, 11; Rom 9, 33; 1 Pt 2, 7.

28, 21: Mount Perazim . . . Valley of Gibeon: where David defeated the Philistines; cf 2 Sm 5, 20. 25; 1 Chr 14, 11. 16.

d: Is 36, 10. 12.   *e:* Jer 5, 15; 1 Cor 14, 21; Dt 28, 49; Bar 4, 15.
f: Wis 1, 16; Jer 5, 12.   *g:* Ps 118, 22; Mt 21, 42; Acts 4, 11; Rom 9, 33; 1 Pt 2, 6.   *h:* Jos 10, 10; 2 Sm 5, 20; 1 Chr 14, 11.

The Lesson of the Farmer's Year

One of the most instructive prophetic parables of the Hebrew Scriptures appears in 28, 23–29. The variety of activities that make up the farmer's year illustrates the force of vv. 21–22. To the question, "Would not destroying the city where the temple stands be a strange work for God the protector?" the prophet's answer is that, like the farmer, God has many varied tasks to perform—and judging a rebellious people is one of them.

22 Now, be arrogant no more
　　lest your bonds be tightened,
For I have heard from the Lord, the GOD
　　of hosts,
　　the destruction decreed for the whole
　　　earth.*i*
23 Give ear and hear my voice,*
　　pay attention and listen to what I say:
24 Is the plowman forever plowing,
　　always loosening and harrowing his
　　　land for planting?
25 When he has leveled the surface,
　　does he not scatter gith and sow cumin,*
Put in wheat and barley,
　　with spelt as its border?
26 He has learned this rule,
　　instructed by his God.
27 Gith is not threshed with a sledge,
　　nor does a cartwheel roll over cumin.
But gith is beaten out with a staff,
　　and cumin crushed for food with a rod.
28 No, he does not thresh it unendingly,
　　nor does he crush it
　　with his noisy cartwheels and horses.
29 This too comes from the LORD of hosts;
　　wonderful is his counsel and great his
　　　wisdom.

See RG 209

CHAPTER 29

The Fall of Jerusalem
1 Woe to Ariel, Ariel,*
　　the city where David encamped!
　Add year to year,
　　let the feasts come round.*j*

2 But I will bring distress upon Ariel,
　　with mourning and grief.
You shall be to me like Ariel,*k*
3 　I will encamp like David against
　　　you;
I will encircle you with outposts
　　and set up siege works against you.*l*
4 Prostrate you shall speak from the
　　　earth,
　　and from the base dust your words
　　　shall come.
Your voice shall be like a ghost's from
　　　the earth,
　　and your words like chirping* from the
　　　dust.
5 The horde of your arrogant shall be like
　　　fine dust,
　　the horde of the tyrants like flying
　　　chaff.
Then suddenly, in an instant,*m*
6 　you shall be visited by the LORD of
　　　hosts,
With thunder, earthquake, and great
　　　noise,
　　whirlwind, storm, and the flame of
　　　consuming fire.

7 Then like a dream,*
　　a vision in the night,
Shall be the horde of all the nations
　　who war against Ariel
　　with all the earthworks of her
　　　besiegers.

28, 23-29: The practical variation of the farmer's work taught him by God reflects God's dealing with his people, wisely adapted to circumstances; he does not crush their weakness altogether; cf ch 29.

28, 25: Gith . . . cumin: herbs used in seasoning food. Spelt: a variety of wheat.

29, 1f: Ariel: variously interpreted to mean "lion of God" or "hearth (altar) of God," a poetic name for Jerusalem; or perhaps to be read as Uru-el, "foundation of God," an archaic name for the Jebusite city of Jerusalem; like that Ariel, against which David encamped, it will be besieged by God.

29, 4: Chirping: see note on Is 8, 19.

29, 7f: Just when the Assyrians think their capture of Jerusalem to be certain, the Lord will snatch victory from their hands and save his city.

i: Is 10, 23.　*j:* 2 Sm 5, 9.　*k:* Is 33, 7.　*l:* 2 Kgs 25, 1; Ez 4, 2.　*m:* Is 17, 13; Ps 18, 43; Jb 21, 18.

[8] As when a hungry man dreams he is
    eating
and awakens with an empty stomach,
Or when a thirsty man dreams he is
    drinking
and awakens faint and dry,
So shall the horde of all the nations be,
who make war against Zion.

Blindness and Perversity

[9] Be irresolute, stupefied;*
blind yourselves and stay blind!
Be drunk, but not from wine,
stagger, but not from strong drink![n]
[10] For the LORD has poured out on you
a spirit of deep sleep.
He has shut your eyes [the prophets]
and covered your heads [the seers].[o]

[11]For you the revelation of all this has become like the words of a sealed scroll. When it is handed to one who can read, with the request, "Read this," he replies, "I cannot; it is sealed."[p] [12]When it is handed to one who cannot read, with the request, "Read this," he replies, "I cannot read."

[13]   The Lord said:
Since this people draws near with words
    only
and honors me with their lips alone,
though their hearts are far from me,
And their reverence for me has become
routine observance of the precepts of
    men,[q]
[14] Therefore I will again deal with this
    people
in surprising and wondrous fashion:
The wisdom of its wise men shall perish
and the understanding of its prudent
men be hid.[r]
[15] Woe to those who would hide their plans
too deep for the LORD!
Who work in the dark, saying,
"Who sees us, or who knows us?"[s]

[16] Your perversity is as though the potter
were taken to be the clay:
As though what is made should say of its
    maker,
"He made me not!"
Or the vessel should say of the potter,
"He does not understand."[t]

Redemption*

[17] But a very little while,
and Lebanon shall be changed into an
    orchard,
and the orchard be regarded as a
    forest![u]
[18] On that day the deaf shall hear
the words of a book;
And out of gloom and darkness,
the eyes of the blind shall see.[v]
[19] The lowly will ever find joy in the LORD,
and the poor rejoice in the Holy One
of Israel.[w]
[20] For the tyrant will be no more
and the arrogant will have gone;
All who are alert to do evil will be cut
    off,[x]
[21]   those whose mere word condemns a
        man,
Who ensnare his defender at the gate,
    and leave the just man with an empty
    claim.[y]
[22] Therefore thus says the LORD,
the God of the house of Jacob,
who redeemed Abraham:*
Now Jacob shall have nothing to be
    ashamed of,
nor shall his face grow pale.[z]
[23] When his children see
the work of my hands in his midst,
They shall keep my name holy;
they shall reverence the Holy One of
    Jacob,
and be in awe of the God of Israel.
[24] Those who err in spirit shall acquire
    understanding,

29, 9-12: Jerusalem in her blindness refuses to believe God's revelation that she will be saved.

29, 17-24: The prophet presents God's plan of redemption in terms of unheard-of natural phenomena as if such changes in nature took place, e. g., the change of the cedars of Lebanon into an orchard (v 17).

29, 22: Who redeemed Abraham: by freeing him from the idolatry of his native land.

n: Is 19, 14; 28, 7f. o: Is 6, 10; Rom 11, 8. p: Dn 12, 4. q: Ez 33, 31; Mt 15, 8f; Mk 7, 6f. r: Jer 49, 7; 1 Cor 1, 19. s: Is 30, 1; Ez 8, 12; Jn 3, 19f. t: Is 45, 9; Jer 18, 6; Rom 9, 20. u: Is 32, 15. v: Is 35, 5; 42, 6f. w: Is 61, 1. x: Is 28, 22. y: Am 5, 10. 12. z: Is 45, 17.

and those who find fault shall receive
instruction.

CHAPTER 30

See RG
209

Futile Alliance with Egypt

1 Woe to the rebellious children,
  says the LORD,
Who carry out plans that are not
    mine,
  who weave webs that are not inspired
    by me,
  adding sin upon sin.*a*
2 They go down to Egypt,
  but my counsel they do not seek.
They find their strength in Pharaoh's
    protection
  and take refuge in Egypt's shadow;*b*
3 Pharaoh's protection shall be your
    shame,
  and refuge in Egypt's shadow your
    disgrace.*c*
4 When their princes are at Zoan
  and their messengers reach Hanes,*d*
5 All shall be ashamed
  of a people that gain them nothing,
Neither help nor benefit,
  but only shame and reproach.*e*

6   [Oracle on the Beasts of the
        Negeb]

Through the distressed and troubled
    land
  of the lioness and roaring lion,
  of the viper and flying saraph,*
They carry their riches on the backs of
    asses
  and their treasures on the humps of
    camels
To a people good for nothing,
7   to Egypt whose help is futile and vain.
Therefore I call her
  "Rahab* quelled."
8 Now come, write it on a tablet they can
    keep,

inscribe it in a record;*
That it may be in future days
  an eternal witness:*f*
9 This is a rebellious people,
  deceitful children,
Children who refuse
  to obey the law of the LORD.*g*
10 They say to the seers, "Have no visions";
  to the prophets, "Do not descry for us
    what is right;
  speak flatteries to us, conjure up
    illusions.*h*
11 Out of the way! Out of our path!
  Let us hear no more
  of the Holy One of Israel."*i*
12 Therefore, thus says the Holy One of
    Israel:
  Because you reject this word,
  And put your trust in what is crooked and
    devious,
  and depend on it,
13 This guilt of yours shall be
  like a descending rift
Bulging out in a high wall
  whose crash comes suddenly, in an
    instant.*j*
14 It crashes like a potter's jar
  smashed beyond rescue,
And among its fragments cannot be
    found
  a sherd to scoop fire from the hearth
  or dip water from the cistern.*k*

15 For thus said the Lord GOD,
  the Holy One of Israel:
By waiting and by calm you shall be
    saved,
  in quiet and in trust your strength
    lies.
  But this you did not wish.*l*
16 "No," you said,
  "Upon horses we will flee."
  —Very well, flee!
  "Upon swift steeds we will ride."
  —Not so swift as your pursuers.*m*

30, 6: Flying saraph: see note on Nm 21, 6.

30, 7: Rahab: Egypt, here as elsewhere (cf Ps 87, 4), is
compared to the stormy, impetuous sea monster (cf Is 51, 9;
Jb 26, 12; Ps 89, 11), which yet, when asked for aid by Judah,
becomes silent, quelled.

30, 8: Isaiah will write down his condemnation of the peo-

ple so that (vv 12-18) its fulfillment may afterward be admitted.

a: Is 1, 4. *b:* Is 31, 1; 36, 6. *c:* Is 20, 5; Jer 2, 26f. *d:* Is 19,
11. *e:* 36, 6. *f:* Is 8, 1. 16; Jer 36, 2; Heb 2, 2. *g:* Is 1, 4; Jer
7, 28. *h:* Jer 5, 31. *i:* Jb 21, 14f. *j:* Ez 13, 14. *k:* Jer 19, 11.
l: Is 7, 4; Mi 7, 7. *m:* Is 31, 3.

Egypt was famous for palaces and monuments, and as the gateway to Africa for the caravans that brought wealth and luxuries (see 1 Kgs 10). In Is 30, 6–26, the prophet contrasts such exotic wealth with the worthlessness of the promises of Egyptian help. The description "it crashes like a potter's jar" (v. 14) emphasizes the suddenness and completeness of the disaster that is to come. Hezekiah's attempt to build security through an alliance with Egypt will prove disastrously misjudged. The poetry of waiting, calm, quiet and trust (v. 15) attests that God alone is the defense of Jerusalem.

17 A thousand shall tremble at the threat of
        one;
    if five threaten you, you shall flee,
Until you are left like a flagstaff on the
        mountaintop,
    like a flag on the hill.
18 Yet the LORD is waiting to show you
        favor,
    and he rises to pity you;
For the LORD is a God of justice:
    blessed are all who wait for him![n]

19 O people of Zion, who dwell in
        Jerusalem,
    no more will you weep;
He will be gracious to you when you cry
        out,
    as soon as he hears he will answer
        you.[o]
20 The Lord will give you the bread you
        need
    and the water for which you thirst.
No longer will your Teacher* hide
        himself,
    but with your own eyes you shall see
        your Teacher,
21 While from behind, a voice shall sound
        in your ears:
    "This is the way; walk in it,"
    when you would turn to the right or to
        the left.[p]
22 And you shall consider unclean your
        silver-plated idols
    and your gold-covered images;
You shall throw them away like filthy
        rags

to which you say, "Begone!"[q]

Zion's Future Prosperity
23 He will give rain for the seed
        that you sow in the ground,
    And the wheat that the soil produces
        will be rich and abundant.
    On that day your cattle will graze
        in spacious meadows;[r]
24 The oxen and the asses that till the
        ground
    will eat silage tossed to them
    with shovel and pitchfork.
25 Upon every high mountain and lofty
        hill
    there will be streams of running water.
    On the day of the great slaughter,
        when the towers fall,[s]
26 The light of the moon will be like that of
        the sun
    and the light of the sun will be seven
        times greater
    [like the light of seven days].
    On the day the LORD binds up the
        wounds of his people,
    he will heal the bruises left by his
        blows.[t]

Divine Judgment on Assyria*
27 See the name of the LORD coming from
        afar
    in burning wrath, with lowering
        clouds!
    His lips are filled with fury,
        his tongue is like a consuming fire;
28 His breath, like a flood in a ravine

30, 20: Teacher: God, who in the past taught in a veiled manner through his prophets, will in future help them to understand his teaching clearly. This was eminently true when the Son of God became Man.

30, 27-33: God's punishment of Assyria. The name of the

Lord: God himself; cf Ps 20, 2.

n: Ps 34, 9; Jer 17, 7.   o: Is 58, 9.   p: Jer 31, 33f.   q: Is 31, 7.
r: Lv 26, 3. 5.   s: Jl 4, 18.   t: Jer 30, 17.

that reaches suddenly to the neck,
Will winnow the nations with a
    destructive winnowing,
and with repeated winnowings will he
    battle against them
[and a bridle on the jaws of the
    peoples to send them astray].
30 The LORD will make his glorious voice
    heard,
and let it be seen how his arm
    descends
In raging fury and flame of consuming fire,
    in driving storm and hail.
31 When the LORD speaks, Assyria will be
    shattered,
    as he strikes with the rod;
32 While at every sweep of the rod
    which the LORD will bring down on
    him in punishment,
29 You will sing
    as on a night when a feast is observed,
And be merry of heart,
    as one marching along with a flute
Toward the mountain of the LORD,
    toward the Rock of Israel,
    accompanied by the timbrels and lyres.
33 For the pyre* has long been ready,
    prepared for the king;
Broad and deep it is piled
    with dry grass and wood in abundance,
And the breath of the LORD, like a stream
    of sulphur,
    will set it afire.

CHAPTER 31

See RG
209

Against the Egyptian Alliance

1Woe to those who go down to Egypt for
    help,
who depend upon horses;
Who put their trust in chariots because of
    their number,
and in horsemen because of their
    combined power,
But look not to the Holy One of Israel
    nor seek the LORD!u

2 Yet he too is wise and will bring disaster;
he will not turn from what he has
    threatened to do.
He will rise up against the house of the
    wicked
and against those who help evildoers.
3 The Egyptians are men, not God,
    their horses are flesh, not spirit;
When the LORD stretches forth his hand,
    the helper shall stumble, the one
    helped shall fall,
and both of them shall perish together.v

4   Thus says the LORD to me:
As a lion or a lion cub
    growling over its prey,
With a band of shepherds
    assembled against it,
Is neither frightened by their shouts
    nor disturbed by their noise,
So shall the LORD of hosts come down
    to wage war upon the mountain and
    hill of Zion.
5 Like hovering birds, so the LORD of
    hosts
    shall shield Jerusalem,
To protect and deliver,
    to spare and rescue it.w

6Return, O children of Israel, to him
whom you have utterly deserted.x 7On that
day each one of you shall spurn his sinful
idols of silver and gold, which he made with
his hands.y

Downfall of Assyria

8 Assyria shall fall by a sword not wielded
    by man,
no mortal sword shall devour him;
He shall flee before the sword,
    and his young men shall be impressed
    as laborers.z
9 He shall rush past his crag* in panic,
    and his princes shall flee in terror from
    his standard,

30, 29-33: Pyre: on which the corpse of the king of Assyria is burned. This is the occasion of festal rejoicing for the Israelites, who are now free from his yoke.

31, 9: Crag: the king as the rallying point of the princes.

---

u: Is 30, 2; 36, 6.   v: Ps 146, 3ff.   w: Ps 91, 4.   x: Jer 3, 12.   y: Is 30, 22.   z: Is 37, 36.

Says the LORD who has a fire in Zion
and a furnace in Jerusalem.

See RG
209

CHAPTER 32

The Kingdom of Justice

¹ See, a king will reign justly
and princes will rule rightly.*a*
² Each of them will be a shelter from the
wind,
a retreat from the rain.
They will be like streams of water in a
dry country,
like the shade of a great rock in a
parched land.*b*
³ The eyes of those who see will not be
closed;
the ears of those who hear will be
attentive.
⁴ The flighty will become wise and capable,
and the stutterers will speak fluently
and clearly.
⁵ No more will the fool be called noble,
nor the trickster be considered
honorable.
⁶ For the fool speaks foolishly,
planning evil in his heart:
How to do wickedness,
to speak perversely against the
LORD,
To let the hungry go empty
and the thirsty be without drink.*c*
⁷ And the trickster uses wicked trickery,
planning crimes:
How to ruin the poor with lies,
and the needy when they plead their
case.
⁸ But the noble man plans noble things,
and by noble things he stands.

The Women of Jerusalem

⁹ O complacent ladies, rise up and hear my
voice,
overconfident women, give heed to my
words.
¹⁰ In a little more than a year

you overconfident ones will be
shaken;
The vintage will fail,
there will be no harvest.*d*
¹¹ Tremble, you who are complacent!
Shudder, you who are overconfident!
Strip yourselves bare,
with only a loincloth to cover you.*e*
¹² Beat your breasts
for the pleasant fields, the fruitful vine,
¹³ And the soil of my people,
overgrown with thorns and briers;
For all the joyful houses,
the wanton city.*f*
¹⁴ Yes, the castle* will be forsaken,
the noisy city deserted;*g*
¹⁹ Down it comes, as trees come down in
the forest!
The city will be utterly laid low.
Hill and tower will become wasteland
forever
for wild asses to frolic in, and flocks to
pasture,
¹⁵ Until the spirit from on high*
is poured out on us.
Then will the desert become an orchard
and the orchard be regarded as a forest.*h*

¹⁶ Right will dwell in the desert
and justice abide in the orchard.
¹⁷ Justice will bring about peace;
right will produce calm and security.*i*
¹⁸ My people will live in peaceful country,
in secure dwellings and quiet resting
places.*j*
²⁰ Happy are you who sow beside every
stream,
and let the ox and the ass go freely!*k*

CHAPTER 33

Overthrow of Assyria

See RG
209

¹ Woe, O destroyer never destroyed,
O traitor never betrayed!
When you finish destroying, you will be
destroyed;

32, 14. 19: The castle: the citadel of Jerusalem. Hill and tower: the fortified hill, in Hebrew Ophel, with its stronghold called "the great projecting tower" in Neh 3, 27.

32, 15-18. 20: Extraordinary peace and prosperity will come to Israel under just rulers.

---

a: Is 16, 5; Ps 72, 2ff; Jer 23, 5.   *b:* Is 4, 6; 25, 4.   *c:* Prv 10, 32; Eccl 10, 12f.   *d:* Zep 1, 13.   *e:* Jer 4, 8.   *f:* Is 7, 23; 34, 15.   *g:* Is 27, 10.   *h:* Is 35, 1; 44, 3.   *i:* Is 54, 13f; Ps 72, 7; Jas 3, 18.   *j:* Mi 4, 4.   *k:* Is 30, 23.

Restoration of Zion

The catastrophes that had befallen Jerusalem had cast doubt on the future of the Davidic kingship. The message of Is 11, 1–5 reveals how eagerly the people awaited a descendant of Judah's royal dynasty, and this hope is repeated at the end of ch 33. Instead of the hated representatives of foreign domination—zealous only for plunder and gain (v. 18)—there would be a king upholding justice and building prosperity (v. 17).

when wearied with betraying, you will
be betrayed.
2 O LORD, have pity on us, for you we
wait.
Be our strength every morning,
our salvation in time of trouble![l]
3 At the roaring sound, peoples flee;
when you rise in your majesty, nations
are scattered.
4 Men gather spoil as caterpillars are
gathered up;
they rush upon it like the onrush of
locusts.[m]
5 The LORD is exalted, enthroned on high;
he fills Zion with right and justice.[n]
6 That which makes her seasons lasting,
the riches that save her, are wisdom
and knowledge;
the fear of the LORD is her treasure.[o]

7 See, the men of Ariel cry out in the streets,
the messengers of Shalem* weep
bitterly.
8 The highways are desolate,
travelers have quit the paths,
Covenants are broken, their terms are
spurned;
yet no man gives it a thought.[p]
9 The country languishes in mourning,
Lebanon withers with shame;
Sharon* is like the steppe,
Bashan and Carmel are stripped bare.[q]
10 Now will I rise up, says the LORD,
now will I be exalted, now be lifted up.
11 You conceive dry grass, bring forth
stubble;
my spirit shall consume you like fire.

12 The peoples shall be as in a limekiln,
like brushwood cut down for burning
in the fire.[r]
13 Hear, you who are far off, what I have
done;
you who are near, acknowledge my
might.
14 On Zion sinners are in dread,
trembling grips the impious:
"Who of us can live with the consuming
fire?
who of us can live with the everlasting
flames?"[s]
15 He who practices virtue and speaks
honestly,
who spurns what is gained by
oppression,
Brushing his hands free of contact with a
bribe,
stopping his ears lest he hear of
bloodshed,
closing his eyes lest he look on evil—[t]
16 He shall dwell on the heights,
his stronghold shall be the rocky
fastness,
his food and drink in steady supply.

Restoration of Zion

17 Your eyes will see a king* in his splendor,
they will look upon a vast land.
18 Your mind will dwell on the terror:
"Where is he who counted, where is he
who weighed?
Where is he who counted the towers?"
19 To the people of alien tongue you will
look no more,
the people of obscure speech,

33, 7: Ariel . . . Shalem: Jerusalem; cf Is 29, 1; Gn 14, 18.
33, 9: Sharon: the fertile plain near the Mediterranean.
33, 17: King: the messianic King, or God; cf v 22.

l: Is 25, 9.   m: 2 Chr 20, 25.   n: Is 1, 26.   o: Prv 9, 10.   p: Jgs 5, 6.   q: Na 1, 4.   r: Is 10, 17.   s: Na 1, 6.   t: Pss 15, 2-6; 24, 4f.

stammering in a language not
understood.

²⁰ Look to Zion, the city of our festivals;
let your eyes see Jerusalem
as a quiet abode, a tent not to be
struck,
Whose pegs will never be pulled up,
nor any of its ropes severed.
²² Indeed the LORD will be there with us,
majestic;
yes, the LORD our judge, the LORD our
lawgiver,
the LORD our king, he it is who will
save us.
²¹ In a place of rivers and wide streams
on which no boat is rowed,
where no majestic ship* passes,
²³ The rigging hangs slack;
it cannot hold the mast in place,
nor keep the sail spread out.
Then the blind will divide great spoils
and the lame will carry off the loot.
²⁴ No one who dwells there will say, "I am
sick";
the people who live there will be
forgiven their guilt.

VI: The Lord, Zion's Avenger
CHAPTER 34

See RG
209

Judgment upon Edom

¹ Come near, O nations, and hear;
be attentive, O peoples!
Let the earth and what fills it listen,
the world and all it produces.ᵘ
² The LORD is angry with all the nations
and is wrathful against all their host;
he has doomed them and given them
over to slaughter.
³ Their slain shall be cast out,
their corpses shall send up a stench;
The mountains shall run with their
blood,ᵛ
⁴ and all the hills shall rot;
The heavens shall be rolled up like a
scroll,

and all their host shall wither away.
As the leaf wilts on the vine,
or as the fig withers on the tree.ʷ
⁵ When my sword has drunk its fill in the
heavens,
lo, it shall come down in judgment
upon Edom, a people I have doomed.ˣ
⁶ The LORD has a sword filled with blood,ʸ
greasy with fat,
With the blood of lambs and goats,
with the fat of rams' kidneys;
For the LORD has a sacrifice in Bozrah,
a great slaughter in the land of Edom.
⁷ Wild oxen shall be struck down with
fatlings,
and bullocks with bulls;
Their land shall be soaked with blood,
and their earth greasy with fat.
⁸ For the LORD has a day of vengeance,
a year of requital by Zion's defender.ᶻ
⁹ Edom's streams shall be changed into
pitch
and her earth into sulphur,
and her land shall become burning
pitch;
¹⁰ Night and day it shall not be quenched,
its smoke shall rise forever.
From generation to generation she shall
lie waste,
never again shall anyone pass through
her.
¹¹ But the desert owl and hoot owl shall
possess her,
the screech owl and raven shall dwell
in her.
The LORD will measure her with line and
plummet
to be an empty waste
for satyrs* to dwell in.ᵃ

¹² Her nobles shall be no more,
nor shall kings be proclaimed there;
all her princes are gone.ᵇ
¹³ Her castles shall be overgrown with
thorns,

33, 21. 23: Boat . . . majestic ship: of a foreign oppressor.
34, 11: Satyrs: see note on Is 13, 21; cf Is 34, 14.

---

u: Dt 32, 1.   v: Ez 32, 4. 6.   w: Is 13, 10; Ez 32, 7f; 4, 15.   x: Jer 46, 10.   y: 6f: Jer 49, 12f.   z: Is 13, 9; 63, 4.   a: Is 14, 23; Zep
2, 14.   b: Ob 18.

her fortresses with thistles and briers.
She shall become an abode for jackals
and a haunt for ostriches.*c*

14 Wildcats shall meet with desert beasts,
satyrs shall call to one another;
There shall the lilith* repose,
and find for herself a place to rest.

15 There the hoot owl shall nest and lay
eggs,
hatch them out and gather them in her
shadow;
There shall the kites assemble,
none shall be missing its mate.

16 Look in the book of the LORD* and read:
No one of these shall be lacking,
For the mouth of the LORD has ordered it,
and his spirit shall gather them there.*d*

17 It is he who casts the lot for them,
and with his hand he marks off their
shares of her;
They shall possess her forever,
and dwell there from generation to
generation.

CHAPTER 35

**See RG
209**

Israel's Deliverance*

1 The desert and the parched land will
exult;
the steppe will rejoice and bloom.*e*

2 They will bloom with abundant flowers,
and rejoice with joyful song.
The glory of Lebanon will be given to
them,
the splendor of Carmel and Sharon;
They will see the glory of the LORD,
the splendor of our God.*f*

3 Strengthen the hands that are feeble,
make firm the knees that are weak,*g*

4 Say to those whose hearts are frightened:
Be strong, fear not!
Here is your God,
he comes with vindication;
With divine recompense

he comes to save you.*h*

5 Then will the eyes of the blind be
opened,
the ears of the deaf be cleared;*i*

6 Then will the lame leap like a stag,
then the tongue of the dumb will sing.*j*

Streams will burst forth in the desert,
and rivers in the steppe.

7 The burning sands will become pools,
and the thirsty ground, springs of
water;
The abode where jackals lurk
will be a marsh for the reed and
papyrus.

8 A highway will be there,
called the holy way;
No one unclean may pass over it,
nor fools go astray on it.

9 No lion will be there,
nor beast of prey go up to be met upon
it.
It is for those with a journey to make,
and on it the redeemed will walk.*k*

10 Those whom the LORD has ransomed will
return
and enter Zion singing,
crowned with everlasting joy;
They will meet with joy and gladness,
sorrow and mourning will flee.*l*

VII: Historical Appendix

CHAPTER 36

**See RG
209-210**

*Invasion of Sennacherib.** 1In the
fourteenth year of King Hezekiah, Sennacherib, king of Assyria, went on an expedition
against all the fortified cities of Judah and
captured them.*m* 2From Lachish the king of
Assyria sent his commander with a great
army to King Hezekiah in Jerusalem. When
he stopped at the conduit of the upper pool, on
the highway of the fuller's field, 3there came
out to him the master of the palace, Eliakim,

34, 14: Lilith: a female demon thought to roam about the desert.

34, 16: Book of the LORD: God's list of all his creatures; cf Ps 69, 29, "the book of the living"; Ps 139, 16, "your book."

35, 1-10: Similar to the description of the return from the Exile, as found in chaps. 40—55.

36, 1—39, 8: Except for 38, 9-20, this historical appendix describing the siege, etc., is paralleled in 2 Kgs 18, 13—20,

19, which, however, has certain details proper to itself. The events are also recorded in substantially the same way in the cuneiform inscriptions of Sennacherib.

c: Is 13, 21; Hos 9, 6. *d:* Jos 18, 10; Ps 78, 55. *e:* Is 55, 12f.
f: Is 60, 13; Ps 96, 12. *g:* Jb 4, 3f; Heb 12, 12. *h:* Is 41, 10; Zec
8, 13. *i:* Is 29, 18; 32, 3. *j:* Is 41, 18; 43, 10. 19. *k:* Is 62, 10;
Lv 26, 6. *l:* Is 51, 11. *m:* 2 Kgs 18, 13; 2 Chr 32, 1.

The Assyrian Empire

son of Hilkiah, and Shebna the scribe, and the herald Joah, son of Asaph. ⁴The commander said to them, "Tell King Hezekiah: Thus says the great king, the king of Assyria, 'On what do you base this confidence of yours? ⁵Do you think mere words substitute for strategy and might in war? On whom, then, do you rely, that you rebel against me? ⁶This Egypt, the staff on which you rely, is in fact a broken reed which pierces the hand of anyone who leans on it. That is what Pharaoh, king of Egypt, is to all who rely on him.*ⁿ* ⁷But if you say to me: "We rely on the LORD, our God," is not he the one whose high places and altars Hezekiah removed,* commanding Judah and Jerusalem to worship before this altar?'*ᵒ*

⁸"Now, make a wager with my lord the king of Assyria: 'I will give you two thousand horses, if you can put riders on them.' ⁹How then can you repulse even one of the least servants of my lord? And yet you rely on Egypt for chariots and horsemen! ¹⁰'Was it without the LORD's will that I have come up to destroy this land? The LORD said to me, "Go up and destroy that land!" ' "*ᵖ*

¹¹Then Eliakim and Shebna and Joah said to the commander, "Please speak to your servants in Aramaic; we understand it. Do not speak to us in Judean within earshot of the people who are on the wall."*

¹²But the commander replied, "Was it to you and your master that my lord sent me to speak these words? Was it not rather to the men sitting on the wall, who, with you, will have to eat their own excrement and drink their own urine?" ¹³Then the commander stepped forward and cried out in a loud voice in Judean, "Listen to the words of the great king, the king of Assyria. ¹⁴Thus says the king: 'Do not let Hezekiah deceive you,

36, 7: The Assyrians pretend that Hezekiah's removal of the high places and altars (illegal sanctuaries) was taken by the Lord as an insult. They declare to Jerusalem's emissaries that the city therefore no longer has a right to the Lord's protection and that they are the ones who truly carry out his will (cf v 10).

36, 11: The Jewish emissaries ask that the conversation be carried on in Aramaic, not in Judean, for they fear the effect of the Assyrian claims upon the morale of the people.

n: Is 30, 2.   *o:* 2 Kgs 18, 4.   *p:* Is 10, 5f.

1017

since he cannot deliver you. *15*Let not Hezekiah induce you to rely on the LORD, saying, "The LORD will surely save us; this city will not be handed over to the king of Assyria." ' *16*Do not listen to Hezekiah, for the king of Assyria says: 'Make peace with me and surrender! Then each of you will eat of his own vine and of his own fig tree, and drink the water of his own cistern,*q 17*until I come to take you to a land like your own, a land of grain and wine, of bread and vineyards. *18*Do not let Hezekiah seduce you by saying, "The LORD will save us." Has any of the gods of the nations ever rescued his land from the hand of the king of Assyria?*r 19*Where are the gods of Hamath and Arpad? Where are the gods of Sepharvaim? Where are the gods of Samaria? Have they saved Samaria from my hand?*s 20*Which of all the gods of these lands ever rescued his land from my hand? Will the LORD then save Jerusalem from my hand?' " *21*But they remained silent and did not answer him one word, for the king had ordered them not to answer him.

*22*Then the master of the palace, Eliakim, son of Hilkiah, Shebna the scribe, and the herald Joah, son of Asaph, came to Hezekiah with their garments torn, and reported to him what the commander had said.

CHAPTER 37

See RG
209-210 *1*When King Hezekiah heard this, he tore his garments, wrapped himself in sackcloth, and went into the temple of the LORD. *2*He sent Eliakim, the master of the palace, and Shebna the scribe, and the elders of the priests, wrapped in sackcloth, to tell the prophet Isaiah, son of Amoz: *3*"Thus says Hezekiah: 'This is a day of distress, of rebuke, and of disgrace. Children are at the point of birth, but there is no strength to bring them forth.* *4*Perhaps the LORD, your God, will hear the words of the commander,

whom his master, the king of Assyria, sent to taunt the living God, and will rebuke him for the words which the LORD, your God, has heard. Send up a prayer for the remnant that is here.' "

*5*When the servants of King Hezekiah had come to Isaiah, *6*he said to them: "Tell this to your master: 'Thus says the LORD: Do not be frightened by the words you have heard, with which the servants of the king of Assyria have blasphemed me.*t 7*I am about to put in him such a spirit that, when he hears a certain report, he will return to his own land, and there I will cause him to fall by the sword.' "

*8*When the commander returned to Lachish and heard that the king of Assyria had left there, he found him besieging Libnah. *9*The king of Assyria heard a report that Tirhakah,* king of Ethiopia, had come out to fight against him. Again he sent envoys to Hezekiah with this message: "Thus shall you say to Hezekiah, king of Judah: *10*'Do not let your God on whom you rely deceive you by saying that Jerusalem will not be handed over to the king of Assyria.*u 11*You yourself have heard what the kings of Assyria have done to all the countries: They doomed them! Will you, then, be saved? *12*Did the gods of the nations whom my fathers destroyed save them? Gozen, Haran, Rezeph, and the Edenites in Telassar? *13*Where is the king of Hamath, the king of Arpad, or a king of the cities of Sepharvaim, Hena or Ivvah?' "

*14*Hezekiah took the letter from the hand of the messengers and read it; then he went up to the temple of the LORD, and spreading it out before him, *15*he prayed to the LORD: *16*"O LORD of hosts, God of Israel, enthroned upon the cherubim! You alone are God over all the kingdoms of the earth. You have made the heavens and the earth.* *17*Incline your ear, O LORD, and listen! Open your eyes, O LORD, and see! Hear all the words of the letter that

---

37, 3: A proverbial expression. In the Bible the pangs of childbirth often typify extreme anguish; cf Is 13, 8; Jer 6, 24; Mi 4, 9f. In this instance there is reference to the desperate situation of Hezekiah from which he was scarcely able to free himself.

37, 9: Tirhakah: may have been general of the Egyptian army in 701 B.C.; later he became king, one of the Ethiopian dynasty of Egyptian kings (c. 690–664 B.C.). Many consider

that this account in Isaiah combines features of two originally distinct sieges of Jerusalem by Sennacherib.

37, 16: In contrast to the empty boasting of the Assyrians, Hezekiah proclaims the Lord as God over all the kingdoms of the earth.

---

q: 1 Kgs 4, 25; Zec 3, 10. *r:* Is 37, 11. *s:* Is 10, 9; 37, 13. *t:* Is 41, 10-14; 51, 7. *u:* Is 36, 14.

Sennacherib sent to taunt the living God. [18]Truly, O Lord, the kings of Assyria have laid waste all the nations and their lands, [19]and cast their gods into the fire; they destroyed them because they were not gods but the work of human hands, wood and stone.[v] [20]Therefore, O Lord, our God, save us from his hand, that all the kingdoms of the earth may know that you, O Lord, alone are God."

Punishment of Sennacherib. [21]Then Isaiah, son of Amoz, sent this message to Hezekiah: Thus says the Lord, the God of Israel: In answer to your prayer for help against Sennacherib, king of Assyria, [22]this is the word the Lord has spoken concerning him:[w]

She despises you, laughs you to scorn,
  the virgin daughter Zion;
Behind you she wags her head,
  daughter Jerusalem.
[23] Whom have you insulted and blasphemed,
  against whom have you raised your
    voice
And lifted up your eyes on high?
  Against the Holy One of Israel![x]
[24] Through your servants you have insulted
    the Lord:
  You said, "With my many chariots
I climbed the mountain heights,
  the recesses of Lebanon;
I cut down its lofty cedars,
  its choice cypresses;
I reached the remotest heights,
  its forest park.
[25] I dug wells and drank water in foreign
    lands;
  I dried up with the soles of my feet
  all the rivers of Egypt."

[26] Have you not heard?
  Long ago I prepared it,
From days of old I planned it,
  now I have brought it to pass:
That you should reduce fortified cities
  into heaps of ruins,

[27] While their inhabitants, shorn of power,
  are dismayed and ashamed,
Becoming like the plants of the field,
  like the green growth,
  like the scorched grass on the
    housetops.
[28] I am aware whether you stand or sit;
  I know whether you come or go,
  and also your rage against me.
[29] Because of your rage against me
  and your fury which has reached my
    ears,
I will put my hook in your nose
  and my bit in your mouth,
  and make you return the way you
    came.

[30] This shall be a sign for you:[*]
  this year you shall eat the aftergrowth,
  next year, what grows of itself;
But in the third year, sow and reap,
  plant vineyards and eat their fruit!
[31] The remaining survivors of the house of
    Judah
  shall again strike root below
  and bear fruit above.[y]
[32] For out of Jerusalem shall come a
    remnant,
  and from Mount Zion, survivors.
  The zeal of the Lord of hosts shall do
    this.

[33]Therefore, thus says the Lord concerning the king of Assyria: He shall not reach this city, nor shoot an arrow at it, nor come before it with a shield, nor cast up siegeworks against it. [34]He shall return by the same way he came, without entering the city, says the Lord[z] [35]I will shield and save this city for my own sake, and for the sake of my servant David.[a]

[36]The angel of the Lord went forth and struck down one hundred and eighty-five thousand in the Assyrian camp.[b] Early the next morning, there they were, all the corpses of the dead.[*] [37]So Sennacherib, the

---

37, 30: You: Hezekiah. A sign: it is difficult to know the nature of this sign. Either it is merely a proverbial expression to signify that prosperity follows adversity, or it indicates that after two years the normal conditions of life will be resumed.

37, 36: The destruction of Sennacherib's army is also recorded by Herodotus, a Greek historian of the fifth century

B.C. It was probably due to the bubonic plague, but the sacred author attributes it to its ultimate cause, God through his angel.

v: Jer 16, 20. w: 2 Kgs 19, 21. x: Is 1, 4. y: Is 27, 6. z: Is 37, 29. a: 1 Kgs 15, 4f. b: Is 10, 12; 17, 14.

king of Assyria, broke camp and went back home to Nineveh.[c]

[38]When he was worshiping in the temple of his god Nisroch, his sons Adrammelech and Sharezer slew him with the sword and fled into the land of Ararat.[*] His son Esarhaddon reigned in his stead.

CHAPTER 38

See RG 209-210 *Sickness and Recovery of Hezekiah.*[*]
[1]In those days,[*] when Hezekiah was mortally ill, the prophet Isaiah, son of Amoz, came and said to him: "Thus says the LORD: Put your house in order, for you are about to die; you shall not recover."[d] [2]Then Hezekiah turned his face to the wall and prayed to the LORD:

["3]O LORD, remember how faithfully and wholeheartedly I conducted myself in your presence, doing what was pleasing to you!" And Hezekiah wept bitterly.[e]

[4]Then the word of the LORD came to Isaiah: [5]"Go, tell Hezekiah:[*] Thus says the LORD, the God of your father David: I have heard your prayer and seen your tears. I will heal you: in three days you shall go up to the LORD's temple; I will add fifteen years to your life. [6]I will rescue you and this city from the hand of the king of Assyria; I will be a shield to this city."[f]

[21]Isaiah then ordered a poultice of figs to be taken and applied to the boil, that he might recover. [22]Then Hezekiah asked, "What is the sign that I shall go up to the temple of the LORD?"

[7][Isaiah answered:] "This will be the sign for you from the LORD that he will do what he has promised: [8]See, I will make the shadow cast by the sun on the stairway to the terrace of Ahaz[*] go back the ten steps it has advanced." So the sun came back the ten steps it had advanced.[g]

Hezekiah's Hymn of Thanksgiving. [9]The song of Hezekiah, king of Judah, after he had been sick and had recovered from his illness:

[10] Once I said,
 "In the noontime of life[*] I must depart!
To the gates of the nether world I shall be consigned
 for the rest of my years."[h]
[11] I said, "I shall see the LORD[*] no more
 in the land of the living.
No longer shall I behold my fellow men
 among those who dwell in the world."
[12] My dwelling, like a shepherd's tent,
 is struck down and borne away from me;
You have folded up my life, like a weaver
 who severs the last thread.[*]
Day and night you give me over to torment;[i]
[13] I cry out until the dawn.
Like a lion he breaks all my bones;
 [day and night you give me over to torment].
[14] Like a swallow I utter shrill cries;
 I moan like a dove.
My eyes grow weak, gazing heavenward:
 O Lord, I am in straits; be my surety!

[15] What am I to say or tell him?[*]

37, 38: The violent death of Sennacherib (681 B.C.) is also mentioned in non-biblical sources. It occurred twenty years after his invasion of Judea.

38, 1—39, 8: The events of this section—sickness and recovery of Hezekiah, embassy of Merodach-baladan—point forward to Babylon (cc 40—66). They occurred prior to the events of Is 36, 1—37, 38, which point back to Assyria (Is 1, 1—35, 10).

38, 1: In those days: a time prior to the siege of Jerusalem in 701 B.C.

38, 5: Since Hezekiah died in 687 B.C. this sickness of his seems to have been in 702 B.C., that is, fifteen years before.

38, 8: Stairway to the terrace of Ahaz: this interpretation is based on a reading of the Hebrew text revised according to the Dead Sea Scroll of Isaiah; cf 2 Kgs 23, 12. Many translate the phrase as "steps of Ahaz" and understand this as referring to a sundial.

38, 10: In the noontime of life: long before the end of a full span of life; cf Pss 55, 24; 102, 25.

38, 11: See the LORD: go to the temple and take part in its service.

38, 12: These two metaphors emphasize the suddenness and finality of death.

38, 15: What am I to say or tell him?: a rhetorical question, as if the poet were at a loss in giving fitting expression to his gratitude; cf Ps 116, 12. He has done it: accomplished the cure. Despite the bitterness: even though the one praying was previously so dejected.

---

c: 2 Kgs 19, 35f. *d:* 2 Kgs 20, 1. *e:* 2 Kgs 18, 5f. *f:* Is 37, 35. *g:* 2 Kgs 20, 9. 11. *h:* Jb 17, 11; Ps 102, 25. *i:* Jb 7, 6.

Hezekiah's Sickness and Recovery

Hezekiah's piety (38, 3) is illustrated in the story of his illness and recovery. His total submissiveness to the will of the LORD God and his subsequent recovery from the sickness are inseparably related to the wonderful deliverance of Jerusalem from the forces of Assyria (v. 6). Hezekiah's hymn of thanksgiving in vv. 10–20 is not included in 2 Kings 20, 1–11, but is added here as further evidence of the king's piety. It is a personal psalm of thanksgiving for recovery from serious illness. It includes a lamentation during the time of distress (vv. 10–15) and thanksgiving for recovery (vv. 16–20).

He has done it!
I shall go on through all my years
  despite the bitterness of my soul.
[16] Those live whom the LORD protects;
  yours . . . the life of my spirit.*
You have given me health and life;
[17]   thus is my bitterness transformed into
      peace.
You have preserved my life
  from the pit of destruction,
When you cast behind your back
  all my sins.*
[18] For it is not the nether world that gives
      you thanks,*
  nor death that praises you;
Neither do those who go down into the pit
  await your kindness.[j]
[19] The living, the living give you thanks,
  as I do today.
Fathers declare to their sons,
  O God, your faithfulness.
[20] The LORD is our savior;
  we shall sing to stringed instruments
In the house of the LORD
  all the days of our life.

CHAPTER 39

See RG
209-210 **Embassy from Merodach-baladan.**
[1] At that time when Merodach-baladan,* son of Baladan, king of Babylon, heard that Hez-

ekiah had recovered from his sickness, he sent letters and gifts to him.[k] [2]Hezekiah was pleased at this, and therefore showed the messengers his treasury, the silver and gold, the spices and fine oil, his whole armory, and everything that was in his storerooms; there was nothing in his house or in his whole realm that he did not show them.[l]

[3]Then Isaiah the prophet came to King Hezekiah and asked him, "What did these men say to you? Where did they come from?" Hezekiah answered, "They came to me from a distant land, from Babylon." [4]"What did they see in your house?" he asked. Hezekiah replied, "They saw everything in my house; there is nothing in my storerooms that I did not show them."

[5]Then Isaiah said to Hezekiah, "Hear the word of the LORD of hosts: [6]Behold, the days shall come when all that is in your house, and everything that your fathers have stored up until this day, shall be carried off to Babylon;* nothing shall be left, says the LORD.[m] [7]Some of your own bodily descendants shall be taken and made servants in the palace of the king of Babylon."[n] [8]Hezekiah replied to Isaiah, "The word of the LORD which you have spoken is favorable."* For he thought, "There will be peace and security in my lifetime."[o]

38, 16: Yours . . . the life of my spirit: the current Hebrew text is corrupt. The revised Latin psalter renders it: "You have revived my soul."

38, 17: You cast behind your back all my sins: figurative language to express the divine forgiveness of sins, as if God no longer saw or cared about them. This expression is ordinarily used of men forgetting God; cf 1 Kgs 14, 9; Ez 23, 35; Ps 50, 17.

38, 18f: See note on Ps 6, 6.

39, 1: Merodach-baladan: twice king of Babylon, probably from 721 to 710 B.C., and again for nine months, in 704–703. This visit of his messengers, certainly before 701,

was in reality a political one. Babylon hoped to lead an anti-Assyrian confederation composed of neighboring states

39, 6: Because Judah preferred to follow a pro-Babylonian policy, instead of trusting in God, it would later be exiled to Babylon.

39, 8: Favorable: for the Exile would not occur in his lifetime.

j: Pss 6, 6; 88, 11-13.   k: 1-8: 2 Kgs 20, 12.   l: 2 Chr 32, 25ff.
m: 2 Kgs 24, 13; 25, 13ff.   n: 2 Chr 33, 11; Dn 1, 2f.   o: 2 Chr 32, 26.

B. The Book of Consolation

I: The Lord's Glory in Israel's Liberation

CHAPTER 40

See RG 210

Promise of Salvation

¹ Comfort, give comfort to my people,
  says your God.
² Speak tenderly to Jerusalem, and
    proclaim to her
  that her service* is at an end,
    her guilt is expiated;
  Indeed, she has received from the hand
    of the LORD
  double for all her sins.ᵖ

³ A voice cries out:*
  In the desert prepare the way of the
    LORD!
  Make straight in the wasteland a
    highway for our God!�q
⁴ Every valley shall be filled in,
    every mountain and hill shall be made
    low;
  The rugged land shall be made a plain,
    the rough country, a broad valley.
⁵ Then the glory of the LORD shall be
    revealed,
    and all mankind shall see it together;
  for the mouth of the LORD has spoken.

⁶ A voice says, "Cry out!"
  I answer, "What shall I cry out?"
  "All mankind is grass,
    and all their glory like the flower of
    the field.ʳ
⁷ The grass withers, the flower wilts,
    when the breath of the LORD blows
    upon it.
  [So then, the people is the grass.]
⁸ Though the grass withers and the flower
    wilts,

the word of our God stands forever."

⁹ Go up onto a high mountain,
    Zion, herald of glad tidings;
  Cry out at the top of your voice,
    Jerusalem, herald of good news!
  Fear not to cry out
    and say to the cities of Judah:
    Here is your God!
¹⁰ Here comes with power
    the Lord GOD,
    who rules by his strong arm;
  Here is his reward with him,
    his recompense before him.
¹¹ Like a shepherd he feeds his flock;
    in his arms he gathers the lambs,
  Carrying them in his bosom,
    and leading the ewes with care.ˢ

Power of the Creator To Save His People

¹² Who has cupped in his hand the waters
    of the sea,
  and marked off the heavens with a
    span?*
  Who has held in a measure the dust of
    the earth,
  weighed the mountains in scales
    and the hills in a balance?
¹³ Who has directed the spirit of the LORD,
    or has instructed him as his
    counselor?ᵗ
¹⁴ Whom did he consult to gain knowledge?
  Who taught him the path of judgment,
    or showed him the way of
    understanding?

¹⁵ Behold, the nations count as a drop of the
    bucket,
    as dust on the scales;
  the coastlands weigh no more than
    powder.
¹⁶ Lebanon would not suffice for fuel,*
    nor its animals be enough for
    holocausts.

40, 2: Service: servitude and exile.

40, 3–5: The figurative language here describes the actual return of the exiles from Babylon to Jerusalem. It is the Lord who leads them; their road is made easy for them. Mt 3, 3 and parallels see in these verses a prophecy of the Baptizer and Christ.

40, 12: Span: the distance between the extended little finger and the thumb. Measure: literally, "third"; here a small container.

40, 16: Lebanon . . . fuel: the famed cedars would not be enough to keep the fires of sacrifice burning.

p: Is 50, 21.   q: Mt 3, 3; Jn 1, 23.   r: Jb 8, 12; 14, 2; Ps 37, 2; Sir 14, 18; Jas 1, 10; 1 Pt 1, 24.   s: Is 49, 9f; 63, 11; Ez 34, 23; 37, 24; Jn 10, 11.   t: Wis 9, 13; Rom 11, 34; 1 Cor 2, 16; Jb 38, 1ff.

¹⁷ Before him all the nations are as nought,
    as nothing and void he accounts them.

¹⁸ To whom can you liken God?ᵘ
    With what equal can you confront
        him?
¹⁹ An idol, cast by a craftsman,
    which the smith plates with gold
    and fits with silver chains?ᵛ
²⁰ Mulberry wood, the choice portion
    which a skilled craftsman picks out for
        himself,
Choosing timber that will not rot,
    to set up an idol that will not be
        unsteady?ʷ
⁶ One man helps another,*
    one says to the other, "Keep on!"
⁷ The craftsman encourages the goldsmith,
    the one who beats with the hammer,
        him who strikes on the anvil;
He says the soldering is good,
    and he fastens it with nails to steady it.

²¹ Do you not know? Have you not heard?
    Was it not foretold you from the
        beginning?
Have you not understood? Since the
        earth was founded
²² He sits enthroned above the vault of the
        earth,
    and its inhabitants are like
        grasshoppers;
He stretches out the heavens like a veil,
    spreads them out like a tent to dwell
        in.ˣ
²³ He brings princes to nought
    and makes the rulers of the earth as
        nothing.
²⁴ Scarcely are they planted or sown,
    scarcely is their stem rooted in the
        earth,
When he breathes upon them and they
        wither,
    and the stormwind carries them away
        like straw.

²⁵ To whom can you liken me as an equal?
    says the Holy One.
²⁶ Lift up your eyes on high
    and see who has created* these:
He leads out their army and numbers
        them,
    calling them all by name.
By his great might and the strength of his
        power
    not one of them is missing!ʸ
²⁷ Why, O Jacob, do you say,*
    and declare, O Israel,
"My way is hidden from the Lᴏʀᴅ,
    and my right is disregarded by my
        God"?
²⁸ Do you not know
    or have you not heard?
The Lᴏʀᴅ is the eternal God,
    creator of the ends of the earth.
He does not faint nor grow weary,
    and his knowledge is beyond
        scrutiny.
²⁹ He gives strength to the fainting;
    for the weak he makes vigor abound.
³⁰ Though young men faint and grow
        weary,
    and youths stagger and fall,
³¹ They that hope in the Lᴏʀᴅ will renew
        their strength,
    they will soar as with eagles' wings;
They will run and not grow weary,
    walk and not grow faint.

CHAPTER 41
The Liberator of Israel

See RG
210

¹ Keep silence before me, O coastlands:*
    you peoples, wait for my words!
Let them draw near and speak;
    let us come together for judgment.

² Who has stirred up from the East the
        champion of justice,*
    and summoned him to be his
        attendant?
To him he delivers the nations

40, 6-7: These two verses have been transposed from chap. 41.
40, 26: Created: see note on Gn 1, 1. By name: for he is their Creator.
40, 27f: God's people, here called Jacob and Israel, must not give way to discouragement: their Lord is the eternal God.
41, 1-4: It is generally agreed that these verses describe the vocation and victory of Cyrus, whom the Lord used as his instrument to redeem Israel.
41, 2: Cyrus is the champion of justice and God's attendant.

u: 18f: Acts 17, 29.   *v:* Ps 115, 4-7.   *w:* Is 44, 13.   *x:* Ps 104, 2.
y: Ps 147, 4f.

and subdues the kings;
With his sword he reduces them to dust,
with his bow, to driven straw.
3 He pursues them, passing on without
loss,
by a path his feet do not even tread.
4 Who has performed these deeds?
He who has called forth the
generations since the beginning.ᶻ

I, the LORD, am the first,
and with the last I will also be.
5 The coastlands see, and fear;
the ends of the earth tremble:
these things are near, they come to pass.
8 But you, Israel, my servant,ᵃ
Jacob, whom I have chosen,
offspring of Abraham my friend—
9 You whom I have taken from the ends of
the earth
and summoned from its far-off places,
You whom I have called my servant,
whom I have chosen and will not cast
off—
10 Fear not, I am with you;
be not dismayed; I am your God.
I will strengthen you, and help you,
and uphold you with my right hand of
justice.

11 Yes, all shall be put to shame and
disgrace
who vent their anger against you;
Those shall perish and come to nought
who offer resistance.
12 You shall seek out, but shall not find,
those who strive against you;
They shall be as nothing at all
who do battle with you.

13 For I am the LORD, your God,
who grasp your right hand;
It is I who say to you, "Fear not,
I will help you."
14 Fear not, O worm Jacob,
O maggot Israel;
I will help you, says the LORD;

your redeemer* is the Holy One of
Israel.
15 I will make of you a threshing sledge,
sharp, new, and double-edged,
To thresh the mountains and crush them,
to make the hills like chaff.
16 When you winnow them, the wind shall
carry them off
and the storm shall scatter them.
But you shall rejoice in the LORD,
and glory in the Holy One of Israel.
17 The afflicted and the needy seek water in
vain,
their tongues are parched with thirst.
I, the LORD, will answer them;
I, the God of Israel, will not forsake
them.
18 I will open up rivers on the bare heights,
and fountains in the broad valleys;
I will turn the desert into a marshland,
and the dry ground into springs of water.
19 I will plant in the desert the cedar,
acacia, myrtle, and olive;
I will set in the wasteland the cypress,
together with the plane tree and the pine,
20 That all may see and know,
observe and understand,
That the hand of the LORD has done this,
the Holy One of Israel has created it.

21 Present your case, says the LORD;*
bring forward your reasons, says the
King of Jacob.
22 Let them come near and foretell to us
what it is that shall happen!
What are the things of long ago?
Tell us, that we may reflect on them
And know their outcome;
or declare to us the things to come!
23 Foretell the things that shall come
afterward,
that we may know that you are gods!
Do something, good or evil,
that will put us in awe and in fear.
24 Why, you are nothing and your work is
nought!
To choose you is an abomination.

41, 14: Redeemer: in Hebrew, goel, one who frees another from slavery and avenges his sufferings; cf Lv 25, 48; Dt 19, 6. 12.
41, 21-24: An indictment of idols.

z: Is 44, 7; 46, 10. a: 8f: Is 44, 1f. 21; 45, 4.

25 I have stirred up one from the north, and
    he comes;
  from the east I summon him* by name;
He shall trample the rulers down like red
    earth,
    as the potter treads the clay.
26 Who announced this from the beginning,
    that we might know;
  beforehand, that we might say it is
    true?
Not one of you foretold it, not one spoke;
  no one heard you say,
27 "The first news for Zion: they are coming
    now,"
  or, "For Jerusalem I will pick out a
    bearer of the glad tidings."
28 When I look, there is not one,
  no one of them to give counsel,
  to make an answer when I question
    them.
29 Ah, all of them are nothing,
  their works are nought,
  their idols are empty wind!

CHAPTER 42

See RG
210

The Servant of the Lord

1 Here is my servant* whom I uphold,
  my chosen one with whom I am
    pleased,
Upon whom I have put my spirit;
  he shall bring forth justice to the
    nations,*b*
2 Not crying out, not shouting,
  not making his voice heard in the
    street.
3 A bruised reed he shall not break,
  and a smoldering wick he shall not
    quench,*
4 Until he establishes justice on the earth;
  the coastlands* will wait for his
    teaching.

5 Thus says God, the LORD,

who created the heavens and stretched
    them out,
who spreads out the earth with its
    crops,
Who gives breath to its people
  and spirit to those who walk on it:
6 I, the LORD, have called you for the
    victory of justice,
  I have grasped you by the hand;
I formed you, and set you
  as a covenant of the people,
  a light for the nations,*c*
7 To open the eyes of the blind,
  to bring out prisoners from
    confinement,
  and from the dungeon, those who live
    in darkness.
8 I am the LORD, this is my name;
  my glory I give to no other,
  nor my praise to idols.
9 See, the earlier things have come to pass,
  new ones I now foretell;
Before they spring into being,
  I announce them to you.

The Salvation of Israel despite Its Sins

10 Sing to the LORD a new song,
  his praise from the end of the earth:
Let the sea and what fills it resound,
  the coastlands, and those who dwell in
    them.
11 Let the steppe and its cities cry out,
  the villages where Kedar* dwells;
Let the inhabitants of Sela exult,
  and shout from the top of the
    mountains.
12 Let them give glory to the LORD,
  and utter his praise in the coastlands.
13 The LORD goes forth like a hero,
  like a warrior he stirs up his ardor;
He shouts out his battle cry,
  against his enemies he shows his
    might:*d*

41, 25: I summon him: Cyrus.

42, 1-4: Servant: there are three other "Servant-of-the-
Lord" oracles, Is 49, 1-7; 50, 4-11; 52, 13—53, 12. Many
identifications have been proposed, e.g., historical Israel,
ideal Israel, an Old Testament historical character before or
during the lifetime of the prophet, the prophet himself. The
New Testament and Christian tradition, however, have seen a
fulfillment of these prophecies in Jesus Christ.

42, 3: A reference to the mercy of Christ.

42, 4: Coastlands: the lands of the Mediterranean. In the
Old Testament the word often refers to the pagan lands of the
west.

42, 11: Kedar: cf footnote to Is 21, 16. Sela: Petra, the capital of Edom.

---

b: Is 45, 6; 49, 6.   *c:* Is 45, 13.   *d:* Ex 14, 3.

¹⁴ I have looked away, and kept silence,
    I have said nothing, holding myself in;
But now, I cry out as a woman in labor,
    gasping and panting.
¹⁵ I will lay waste mountains and hills,
    all their herbage I will dry up;
I will turn the rivers into marshes,
    and the marshes I will dry up.ᵉ
¹⁶ I will lead the blind on their journey;
    by paths unknown I will guide them.
I will turn darkness into light before
    them,
    and make crooked ways straight.
These things I do for them,
    and I will not forsake them.ᶠ
¹⁷ They shall be turned back in utter shame
    who trust in idols;
Who say to molten images,
    "You are our gods."
¹⁸ You who are deaf, listen,*
    you who are blind, look and see!
¹⁹ Who is blind but my servant,
    or deaf like the messenger I send?
²⁰ You see many things without taking note;
    your ears are open, but without
      hearing.
²¹ Though it pleased the LORD in his justice
    to make his law great and glorious,
²² This is a people* despoiled and
      plundered,
    all of them trapped in holes,
    hidden away in prisons.
They are taken as booty, with no one to
      rescue them,
    as spoil, with no one to demand their
      return.
²³ Who of you gives ear to this?
    Who listens and pays heed for the time
      to come?
²⁴ Who was it that gave Jacob to be
      plundered,
    Israel to the despoilers?*
Was it not the LORD, against whom we
    have sinned?
In his ways they refused to walk,
    his law they disobeyed.

²⁵ So he poured out wrath upon them,
    his anger, and the fury of battle;
It blazed round about them, yet they did
    not realize,
    it burned them, but they took it not to
      heart.

CHAPTER 43

See RG
210

Promises of Redemption
and Restoration

¹But now, thus says the LORD,
    who created you, O Jacob, and formed
    you, O Israel:
Fear not, for I have redeemed you;
    I have called you by name: you are
      mine.
² When you pass through the water, I will
      be with you;
    in the rivers you shall not drown.
When you walk through fire, you shall
      not be burned;
    the flames shall not consume you.
³ For I am the LORD, your God,
    the Holy One of Israel, your savior.
I give Egypt as your ransom,
    Ethiopia and Seba* in return for you.
⁴ Because you are precious in my eyes
    and glorious, and because I love you.
I give men in return for you
    and peoples in exchange for your
      life.ᵍ
⁵ Fear not, for I am with you;
    from the east I will bring back your
      descendants,
    from the west I will gather you.
⁶ I will say to the north: Give them up!
    and to the south: Hold not back!
Bring back my sons from afar,
    and my daughters from the ends of the
      earth:ʰ
⁷ Everyone who is named as mine,
    whom I created for my glory,
    whom I formed and made.
⁸ Lead out the people who are blind
    though they have eyes,
    who are deaf though they have ears.

42, 18-20: Because of their unbelief, the Lord rebukes his people, whom he calls his servant, his messenger.

42, 22: A people: Israel in exile.

42, 24: Despoilers: the Assyrians and Babylonians.

43, 3f: Egypt . . . Ethiopia and Seba: countries which God permitted the Persians to conquer in return for having given Israel its freedom.

e: Ex 9, 25; 10, 15; 14, 21; Ps 105, 33ff.   f: Ex 13, 21.   g: Dt 4, 37; Hos 11, 1.   h: Is 49, 22; Ez 16, 20.

⁹ Let all the nations gather together,
    let the peoples assemble!
Who among them could have revealed
        this,
    or foretold to us the earlier things?*
Let them produce witnesses to prove
        themselves right,
    that one may hear and say, "It is true!"
¹⁰ You are my witnesses, says the LORD,
    my servants whom I have chosen
To know and believe in me
    and understand that it is I.
Before me no god was formed,
    and after me there shall be none.

¹¹ It is I, I the LORD;
    there is no savior but me.
¹² It is I who foretold, I who saved;
    I made it known, not any strange god
        among you;
You are my witnesses, says the LORD.
    I am God, ¹³yes, from eternity I am He;
There is none who can deliver from my
        hand:
    who can countermand what I do?ⁱ

¹⁴ Thus says the LORD, your redeemer,*
    the Holy One of Israel:
For your sakes I send to Babylon;
    I will lower all the bars,
    and the Chaldeans shall cry out in
        lamentation.
¹⁵ I am the LORD, your Holy One,
    the creator of Israel, your King.
¹⁶ Thus says the LORD,
    who opens a way in the sea
    and a path in the mighty waters,ʲ
¹⁷ Who leads out chariots and horsemen,
    a powerful army,
Till they lie prostrate together, never to
        rise,
    snuffed out and quenched like a wick.ᵏ
¹⁸ Remember not the events of the past,
    the things of long ago consider not;*

¹⁹ See, I am doing something new!
    Now it springs forth, do you not
        perceive it?
In the desert I make a way,
    in the wasteland, rivers.
²⁰ Wild beasts honor me,
    jackals and ostriches,
For I put water in the desert
    and rivers in the wasteland
    for my chosen people to drink,
²¹ The people whom I formed for myself,
    that they might announce my praise.

²² Yet you did not call upon me, O Jacob,*
    for you grew weary of me, O Israel.
²³ You did not bring me sheep for your
        holocausts,
    nor honor me with your sacrifices.
I did not exact from you the service of
        offerings,
    nor weary you for frankincense.ⁱ
²⁴ You did not buy me sweet cane* for
        money,
    nor fill me with the fat of your
        sacrifices;
Instead, you burdened me with your
        sins,
    and wearied me with your crimes.
²⁵ It is I, I, who wipe out,
    for my own sake, your offenses;
    your sins I remember no more.
²⁶ Would you have me remember, have us
        come to trial?
    Speak up, prove your innocence!
²⁷ Your first father* sinned;
    your spokesmen rebelled against me
²⁸ Till I repudiated the holy gates,
    put Jacob under the ban,
    and exposed Israel to scorn.

CHAPTER 44

¹ Hear then, O Jacob, my servant,
    Israel, whom I have chosen.
² Thus says the LORD who made you,

See RG
210

43, 9: Only God can know and predict future events; cf Is 41, 1-5. 21-29.

43, 14-17: The destruction of Babylon.

43, 18: No need to think solely of the past wonders of the exodus from Egypt; equally great is the exodus from Babylon.

43, 22-28: The reason for the liberation of the Israelites is not their fidelity but rather God's mercy.

43, 24: Sweet cane: a fragrant substance used in making incense and the sacred anointing oil; cf Ex 30, 23; Jer 6, 20.

43, 27: First father: Adam or Jacob, or collectively "early ancestors." Spokesmen: leaders, priests, prophets.

i: Is 41, 4. j: Is 51, 10f; Ex 14, 21. k: Ex 15, 4. l: Jer 5, 20.

your help, who formed you from the
womb:
Fear not, O Jacob, my servant,
the darling* whom I have chosen.
³ I will pour out water upon the thirsty
ground,
and streams upon the dry land;
I will pour out my spirit upon your
offspring,
and my blessing upon your descendants.
⁴ They shall spring up amid the verdure
like poplars beside the flowing waters.ᵐ
⁵ One shall say, "I am the LORD's,"
another shall be named after Jacob,
And this one shall write on his hand,*
"The LORD's,"
and Israel shall be his surname.ⁿ

The True God and False Gods

⁶ Thus says the LORD, Israel's King
and redeemer, the LORD of hosts:
I am the first and I am the last;
there is no God but me.ᵒ
⁷ Who is like me? Let him stand up and
speak,
make it evident, and confront me with it.
Who of old announced future events?
Let them foretell to us the things to
come.
⁸ Fear not, be not troubled:
did I not announce and foretell it long
ago?
You are my witnesses! Is there a God
or any Rock* besides me?ᵖ

⁹*Idol makers all amount to nothing, and
their precious works are of no avail, as they
themselves give witness. To their shame,
they neither see nor know anything; and they
are more deaf than men are.�q ¹⁰Indeed, all
the associates of anyone who forms a god, or
casts an idol to no purpose, will be put to
shame; ¹¹they will all assemble and stand
forth, to be reduced to fear and shame.
¹²The smith fashions an iron image,

works it over the coals, shapes it with hammers, and forges it with his strong arm. He is
hungry and weak, drinks no water and becomes exhausted.ʳ

¹³The carpenter stretches a line and marks
with a stylus the outline of an idol. He shapes
it with a plane and measures it off with a compass, making it like a man in appearance and
dignity, to occupy a shrine. ¹⁴He cuts down
cedars, takes a holm or an oak, and lays hold
of other trees of the forest, which the Lord
had planted and the rain made grow ¹⁵to serve
man for fuel. With a part of their wood he
warms himself, or makes a fire for baking
bread; but with another part he makes a god
which he adores, an idol which he worships.
¹⁶Half of it he burns in the fire, and on its embers he roasts his meat; he eats what he has
roasted until he is full, and then warms himself and says, "Ah! I am warm, I feel the fire."
¹⁷Of what remains he makes a god, his idol,
and prostrate before it in worship, he implores
it, "Rescue me, for you are my god."

¹⁸The idols have neither knowledge nor reason; their eyes are coated so that they cannot
see, and their hearts so that they cannot understand. ¹⁹Yet he does not reflect, nor have the intelligence and sense to say, "Half of the wood
I burned in the fire, and on its embers I baked
bread and roasted meat which I ate. Shall I then
make an abomination out of the rest, or worship a block of wood?" ²⁰He is chasing
ashes*—a thing that cannot save itself when
the flame consumes it; yet he does not say, "Is
not this thing in my right hand a fraud?"

²¹ Remember this, O Jacob,
you, O Israel, who are my servant!
I formed you to be a servant to me;
O Israel, by me you shall never be
forgotten:
²² I have brushed away your offenses like a
cloud,
your sins like a mist;
return to me, for I have redeemed you.

44, 2: The darling: see note on Dt 32, 15; cf also Dt 33, 5.
26.

44, 5: Write on his hand: an allusion to the Babylonian
custom of tatooing the owner's name on the hand of his slave;
cf also Rv 13, 16.

44, 8: Rock: place of refuge; said of God in Dt 32, 4. 18;
1 Sm 2, 2; etc.

44, 9-20: Satire on the makers and worshipers of idols.
44, 20: Chasing ashes: exerting efforts in vain; cf Hos 12,
2; Eccl 1, 14; 2, 11. 17.

m: Is 54, 1ff.   n: Is 43, 7; 45, 14.   o: Is 41, 44; 43, 15; 45, 21; 48,
3. 12; 51, 15; 54, 5.   p: Is 43, 10. 12; Dt 32, 4.   q: Is 48, 5. 7.
r: Wis 13, 11ff.

The Election of Cyrus

The LORD announces that Israel will be ransomed through a foreign king. Cyrus, king of Persia (559–529 B.C.) and victor over Babylon (539 B.C.), issued the edict that Jerusalem and the temple be rebuilt; see Ezra 1, 1–4. Cyrus is the only non-Israelite called "anointed" (Is 45, 1) because he carried out God's purpose of liberating Israel. God leads Cyrus by the hand so that he may accomplish his task without fail.

23 Raise a glad cry, you heavens: the LORD
    has done this;
shout, you depths of the earth.
Break forth, you mountains, into song,
    you forest, with all your trees.
For the LORD has redeemed Jacob,
    and shows his glory through Israel.

Cyrus, Anointed of the Lord,
Liberator of Israel

24 Thus says the LORD, your redeemer,
    who formed you from the womb:
I am the LORD, who made all things,
    who alone stretched out the heavens;
when I spread out the earth, who was
    with me?s
25 It is I who bring to nought the omens of
    liars,
who make fools of diviners;
I turn wise men back
    and make their knowledge foolish.
26 It is I who confirm the words of my
    servants,
I carry out the plan announced by my
    messengers;
I say to Jerusalem: Be inhabited;
    to the cities of Judah: Be rebuilt;
I will raise up their ruins.
27 It is I who said to the deep: Be dry;
    I will dry up your wellsprings.t
28 I say of Cyrus:* My shepherd,
    who fulfills my every wish;
He shall say of Jerusalem, "Let her be
    rebuilt,"

and of the temple, "Let its foundations
    be laid."u

CHAPTER 45

See RG 210

1 Thus says the LORD to his anointed,*
    Cyrus,
whose right hand I grasp,
Subduing nations before him,
    and making kings run in his service,
Opening doors before him
    and leaving the gates unbarred:
2 I will go before you
    and level the mountains;
Bronze doors* I will shatter,
    and iron bars I will snap.v
3 I will give you treasures out of the
    darkness,
    and riches that have been hidden away,
That you may know that I am the LORD,
    the God of Israel, who calls you by
    your name.
4 For the sake of Jacob, my servant,
    of Israel my chosen one,
I have called you by your name,
    giving you a title, though you knew
    me not.w
5 I am the LORD and there is no other,
    there is no God besides me.
It is I who arm you, though you know me
    not,
6 so that toward the rising and the
    setting of the sun
    men may know that there is none
    besides me.*

44, 28: Cyrus: king of Persia (559–529 B.C.) and conqueror of Babylon (538 B.C.), who liberated the Jews, permitting them to return to their native land and to rebuild Jerusalem and the Temple.

45, 1: Anointed: in Hebrew, meshiah, from which the word "Messiah" is derived; from its Greek translation, Christos, we have the name "Christ." Applied to kings, "anointed" originally referred only to those of Israel, but it is here given

to Cyrus because he is the agent of the Lord.

45, 2: Bronze doors: of Babylon.

45, 6: The Gentiles will come to know the true God; cf also vv 20-25.

s: Is 40, 22; Jb 9, 8.   t: Is 42, 15; 51, 10.   u: Jer 3, 15; Ez 34, 23.
v: Ps 107, 16.   w: Is 40, 26.

I am the LORD, there is no other;
7 I form the light, and create the
   darkness,
I make well-being and create woe;*
   I, the LORD, do all these things.
8 Let justice descend, O heavens, like dew
   from above,
   like gentle rain let the skies drop it
   down.
Let the earth open and salvation bud forth;
   let justice also spring up!*
I, the LORD, have created this.ˣ
9 Woe to him who contends with his
   Maker;ʸ
   a potsherd among potsherds of the
   earth!*
Dare the clay say to its modeler, "What
   are you doing?"
   or, "What you are making has no
   hands"?
10 Woe to him who asks a father, "What are
   you begetting?"
   or a woman, "What are you giving
   birth to?"
11 Thus says the LORD,
   the Holy One of Israel, his maker:
You question me about my children,
   or prescribe the work of my hands for
   me!
12 It was I who made the earth
   and created mankind upon it;
It was my hands that stretched out the
   heavens;
   I gave the order to all their host.
13 It was I who stirred up one* for the
   triumph of justice;
   all his ways I make level.
He shall rebuild my city
   and let my exiles go free

Without price or ransom,
   says the LORD of hosts.
14   Thus says the LORD:
The earnings of Egypt, the gain of
   Ethiopia,
   and the Sabeans,* tall of stature,
Shall come over to you and belong to you;
   they shall follow you, coming in
   chains.
Before you they shall fall prostrate,
   saying in prayer:
"With you only is God, and nowhere else;
   the gods are nought.ᶻ
15 Truly with you God is hidden,*
   the God of Israel, the savior!ᵃ
16 Those are put to shame and disgrace
   who vent their anger against him;
Those go in disgrace
   who carve images.
17 Israel, you are saved by the LORD,
   saved forever!
You shall never be put to shame or
   disgrace
   in future ages."
18   For thus says the LORD,
The creator of the heavens,
   who is God,
The designer and maker of the earth
   who established it,
Not creating it to be a waste,*
   but designing it to be lived in:
I am the LORD, and there is no other.
19   I have not spoken from hiding
   nor from some dark place of the earth,
And I have not said to the descendants of
   Jacob,
   "Look for me in an empty waste."
I, the LORD, promise justice,
   I foretell what is right.

45, 7: Create woe: God permits evil for the sake of a greater good.

45, 8: The Vulgate rendering gives a more precise Messianic sense to this verse, using "just one" and "savior" in place of justice and salvation. The Advent liturgy uses the Vulgate form, Rorate coeli desuper . . . , to express the world's longing for the coming of Christ.

45, 9: No one may challenge God's freedom of action, exemplified here by the selection of Cyrus as his anointed.

45, 13: One: Cyrus, called by God for the deliverance and restoration of Israel.

45, 14: Egypt . . . Ethiopia . . . Sabeans: the Egyptians and their allies who, when conquered by Cyrus, are seen as ac-

knowledging the God of Israel to be the one true God; cf Is 43, 3.

45, 15: God is hidden: he dwells invisibly in the holy of holies.

45, 18: Waste: an allusion to the beginning of creation, when the earth was waste and void (Gn 1, 2), the same Hebrew word, tohu, being used in both passages. The further reference here is to Palestine, which God wishes again to be inhabited by the returning exiles.

x: Pss 72, 6; 85, 11.   y: Jer 18, 6; Rom 9, 20.   z: Is 43, 3.   a: Is 55, 8; Prv 25, 2.

20 Come and assemble, gather together,
    you fugitives from among the gentiles!
They are without knowledge who bear
    wooden idols*
    and pray to gods that cannot save.
21 Come here and declare
    in counsel together:
Who announced this from the beginning
    and foretold it from of old?
Was it not I, the LORD,
    besides whom there is no other God?
There is no just and saving God but me.
22 Turn to me and be safe,
    all you ends of the earth,
    for I am God; there is no other!
23 By myself I swear,
    uttering my just decree
    and my unalterable word:
To me every knee shall bend;
    by me every tongue shall swear,*b*
24 Saying, "Only in the LORD
    are just deeds and power.
Before him in shame shall come
    all who vent their anger against him.
25 In the LORD shall be the vindication and
    the glory
    of all the descendants of Israel."

See RG
210

CHAPTER 46

The Gods of Babylon

1 Bel bows down, Nebo* stoops,
    their idols are upon beasts and cattle;
They must be borne up on shoulders,
    carried as burdens by the weary.
2 They stoop and bow down together;
    unable to save those who bear them,
    they too go into captivity.

3 Hear me, O house of Jacob,
    all who remain of the house of Israel,
My burden since your birth,
    whom I have carried from your infancy.*c*
4 Even to your old age I am the same,
    even when your hair is gray I will bear
    you;

It is I who have done this, I who will
    continue,
    and I who will carry you to safety.

5 Whom would you compare me with, as
    an equal,
    or match me against, as though we
    were alike?
6 There are those who pour out gold from a
    purse
    and weigh out silver on the scales;
Then they hire a goldsmith to make it
    into a god
    before which they fall down in worship.
7 They lift it to their shoulders to carry;
    when they set it in place again, it stays,
    and does not move from the spot.
Although they cry out to it, it cannot
    answer;
    it delivers no one from distress.

8 Remember this and be firm,
    bear it well in mind, you rebels;
    remember the former things, those
    long ago:
9 I am God, there is no other;
    I am God, there is none like me.
10 At the beginning I foretell the outcome;
    in advance, things not yet done.
I say that my plan shall stand,
    I accomplish my every purpose.

11 I call from the east a bird of prey,*
    from a distant land, one to carry out
    my plan.
Yes, I have spoken, I will accomplish it;
    I have planned it, and I will do it.
12 Listen to me, you fainthearted,
    you who seem far from the victory of
    justice:
13 I am bringing on my justice, it is not far
    off,
    my salvation shall not tarry;
I will put salvation within Zion,
    and give to Israel my glory.

45, 20: Who bear wooden idols: in their religious processions. The gods of the pagans have feet but cannot walk; cf Ps 115, 7; Bar 6, 25.

46, 1: Bel . . . Nebo: gods of Babylon; their complete helplessness is here contrasted with God's omnipotence.

46, 11: From the east a bird of prey: Cyrus; cf Is 41, 2-4.

b: Rom 14, 11; Phil 2, 10.   *c:* Is 44, 2.

CHAPTER 47

See RG 210

The Fall of Babylon*

[1] Come down, sit in the dust,
   O virgin daughter Babylon;
Sit on the ground, dethroned,
   O daughter of the Chaldeans.
No longer shall you be called
   dainty and delicate.
[2] Take the millstone and grind flour,
   remove your veil;
Strip off your train, bare your legs,
   pass through the streams.
[3] Your nakedness shall be uncovered
   and your shame be seen;
I will take vengeance,
   I will yield to no entreaty,
   says our redeemer.
[4] Whose name is the LORD of hosts,
   the Holy One of Israel.

[5] Go into darkness and sit in silence,
   O daughter of the Chaldeans,
No longer shall you be called
   sovereign mistress of kingdoms.
[6] Angry at my people,
   I profaned my inheritance,
And I gave them into your hand;
   but you showed them no mercy,
And upon old men
   you laid a very heavy yoke.
[7] You said, "I shall remain always,
   a sovereign mistress forever!"
But you did not lay these things to heart,
   you disregarded their outcome.[d]
[8] Now hear this, voluptuous one,
   enthroned securely,
Saying to yourself,
   "I, and no one else!
I shall never be a widow,
   or suffer the loss of my children"—[e]
[9] Both these things shall come to you
   suddenly, in a single day:
Complete bereavement and widowhood
   shall come upon you
For your many sorceries
   and the great number of your spells;*

[10] Because you felt secure in your
   wickedness,
   and said, "No one sees me."
Your wisdom and your knowledge
   led you astray,
And you said to yourself,
   "I, and no one else!"
[11] But upon you shall come evil
   you will not know how to predict;
Disaster shall befall you
   which you cannot allay.
Suddenly there shall come upon you
   ruin which you will not expect.
[12] Keep up, now, your spells
   and your many sorceries;
Perhaps you can make them avail,
   perhaps you can strike terror!
[13] You wearied yourself with many
   consultations,
   at which you toiled from your youth;
Let the astrologers stand forth to save you,
   the stargazers who forecast at each
   new moon
what would happen to you.
[14] Lo, they are like stubble,
   fire consumes them;
They cannot save themselves
   from the spreading flames.
This is no warming ember,
   no fire to sit before.
[15] Thus do your wizards serve you
   with whom you have toiled from your
   youth;
Each wanders his own way,
   with none to save you.

CHAPTER 48

See RG 210

Exhortations to the Exiles

[1] Hear this, O house of Jacob
   called by the name Israel,
   sprung from the stock of Judah,
You who swear by the name of the LORD
   and invoke the God of Israel
   without sincerity or justice,
[2] Though you are named after the holy city
   and rely on the God of Israel,
   whose name is the LORD of hosts.

47, 1-15: A taunt-song, mocking Babylon, once queen of the nations, now made a slave girl.
47, 9. 13. 15: Babylon was known for its sorcery and astrology.

d: Is 14, 13f.   e: Zep 2, 15; Rv 18, 7.

³ Things of the past I foretold long ago,
    they went forth from my mouth, I let
      you hear of them;
    then suddenly I took action and they
      came to be.
⁴ Because I know that you are stubborn
    and that your neck is an iron sinew
    and your forehead bronze,
⁵ I foretold them to you of old;
    before they took place I let you hear of
      them,
    That you might not say, "My idol did
      them,
    my statue, my molten image
      commanded them."
⁶ Now that you have heard, look at all
      this;
    must you not admit it?*f*

From now on I announce new things to
    you,
    hidden events of which you knew not.
⁷ Now, not long ago, they are brought into
    being,
    and beforetime you did not hear of
      them,
    so that you cannot claim to have
      known them;
⁸ You neither heard nor knew,
    they did not reach your ears
      beforehand.
    Yes, I know you are utterly treacherous,
    a rebel you were called from birth.*g*
⁹ For the sake of my name I restrain my
    anger,
    for the sake of my renown I hold it
      back from you,
    lest I should destroy you.
¹⁰ See, I have refined you like silver,
    tested you in the furnace of affliction.*h*
¹¹ For my sake, for my own sake, I do
    this;
    why should I suffer profanation?
    My glory I will not give to another.

¹² Listen to me, Jacob,
    Israel, whom I named!

I, it is I who am the first,
    and also the last am I.*i*
¹³ Yes, my hand laid the foundations of the
      earth;
    my right hand spread out the heavens.
    When I call them,
    they stand forth at once.*j*

¹⁴ All of you assemble and listen:
    Who among you foretold these things?
    The LORD's friend* shall do his will
      against Babylon and the progeny of
      Chaldea.
¹⁵ I myself have spoken, I have called him,
    I have brought him, and his way
      succeeds!
¹⁶ Come near to me and hear this!
    Not from the beginning did I speak it
      in secret;
    At the time it comes to pass, I am
      present:
      "Now the Lord* GOD has sent me, and
      his spirit."
¹⁷ Thus says the LORD, your redeemer,
    the Holy One of Israel:
    I, the LORD, your God,
    teach you what is for your good,
    and lead you on the way you should go.
¹⁸ If you would hearken to my
      commandments,
    your prosperity would be like a river,
    and your vindication like the waves of
      the sea;
¹⁹ Your descendants would be like the sand,
    and those born of your stock like its
      grains,
    Their name never cut off
    or blotted out from my presence.
²⁰ Go forth from Babylon, flee from
      Chaldea!
    With shouts of joy proclaim this, make
      it known;
    Publish it to the ends of the earth, and say,
    "The LORD has redeemed his servant
      Jacob.
²¹ They did not thirst
    when he led them through dry lands;

48, 14: The LORD's friend: Cyrus, who carries out God's plans.
48, 16: "Now the Lord . . . spirit": said by Cyrus; cf v 14.

f: Is 42, 9. *g:* Is 43, 22ff. *h:* Is 1, 25; Jer 6, 29f; Zec 13, 9; Mal 3, 2. *i:* Is 41, 4; 44, 6; 48, 12; Rv 1, 8. 17. *j:* Is 40, 22. 26; 45, 12. 18.

Water from the rock he set flowing for
them;
he cleft the rock, and waters welled
forth."[k]
22 [There is no peace for the wicked,
says the LORD.]

II: Expiation of Sin, Spiritual Liberation of Israel

CHAPTER 49

See RG
210

The Servant of the Lord*

1 Hear me, O coastlands,
listen, O distant peoples.[l]
The LORD called me from birth,
from my mother's womb he gave me
my name.*
2 He made of me a sharp-edged sword
and concealed me in the shadow of his
arm.
He made me a polished arrow,
in his quiver he hid me.*
3 You are my servant, he said to me,
Israel,* through whom I show my
glory.

4 Though I thought I had toiled in vain,
and for nothing, uselessly, spent my
strength,
Yet my reward is with the LORD,
my recompense is with my God.[m]
5 For now the LORD has spoken
who formed me as his servant from the
womb,
That Jacob may be brought back to him
and Israel gathered to him;
And I am made glorious in the sight of
the LORD,
and my God is now my strength!
6 It is too little, he says, for you to be my
servant,

to raise up the tribes of Jacob,
and restore the survivors of Israel;[n]
I will make you a light to the nations,
that my salvation may reach to the
ends of the earth.*

7 Thus says the LORD,
the redeemer and the Holy One of
Israel,
To the one despised, whom the nations
abhor,
the slave of rulers:
When kings see you, they shall stand
up,
and princes shall prostrate themselves
Because of the LORD who is faithful,
the Holy One of Israel who has chosen
you.[o]

The Liberation and Restoration of Zion

8 Thus says the LORD:
In a time of favor I answer you,
on the day of salvation I help you,
To restore the land
and allot the desolate heritages,[p]
9 Saying to the prisoners: Come out!
To those in darkness: Show yourselves!
Along the ways they shall find pasture,
on every bare height shall their
pastures be.[q]
10 They shall not hunger or thirst,
nor shall the scorching wind or the sun
strike them;
For he who pities them leads them
and guides them beside springs of
water.[r]
11 I will cut a road through all my
mountains,
and make my highways level.[s]
12 See, some shall come from afar,
others from the north and the west,
and some from the land of Syene.*

49, 1-7: The second of the four "Servant-of-the-Lord" oracles.

49, 1: Gave me my name: designated me for a special office (cf Jer 1, 5), or perhaps, made me renowned (cf Ps 45, 18).

49, 2: The servant was made ready and fit for the preaching of God's word.

49, 3: Israel: the Servant is identified with the people of Israel as their ideal representative; however, since vv 5f seem to distinguish the Servant from Israel, some regard the word Israel here as a gloss.

49, 6: The Servant's vocation will be not only the restoration of Israel but the conversion of the world; cf Lk 2, 32.

49, 12: Syene: now called Aswan, at the first cataract of the Nile in southern Egypt.

---

k: Ex 17, 6; Nm 20, 11.   l: Is 41, 9; 43, 1; 44, 2. 24; 46, 3.   m: Is 40, 27.   n: Is 42, 1-6; 44, 5; 45, 14; Lk 2, 32; Acts 13, 46f.   o: Is 49, 23; 55, 5.   p: 2 Cor 6, 2.   q: Is 42, 7. 18ff.   r: Is 51, 14; Rv 7, 16.   s: Is 40, 3f.

¹³ Sing out, O heavens, and rejoice, O earth,
  break forth into song, you mountains.
For the LORD comforts his people
  and shows mercy to his afflicted.

¹⁴ But Zion said, "The LORD has forsaken
    me;
  my Lord has forgotten me."ᵗ
¹⁵ Can a mother forget her infant,
  be without tenderness for the child of
    her womb?
Even should she forget,
  I will never forget you.ᵘ
¹⁶ See, upon the palms of my hands I have
    written your name;*
  your walls are ever before me.
¹⁷ Your rebuilders make haste,
  as those who tore you down and laid
    you waste
  go forth from you;
¹⁸ Look about and see,
  they are all gathering and coming to you.
As I live, says the LORD,
  you shall be arrayed with them all as
    with adornments,
  like a bride you shall fasten them on
    you.

¹⁹ Though you were waste and desolate,
  a land of ruins,
Now you shall be too small for your
    inhabitants,
  while those who swallowed you up
    will be far away.
²⁰ The children whom you had lost
  shall yet say to you,
"This place is too small for me,
  make room for me to live in."
²¹ You shall ask yourself:
  "Who has borne me these?
I was bereft and barren
  [exiled and repudiated];
  who has reared them?
I was left all alone;
  where then do these come from?"ᵛ

²² Thus says the Lord GOD:
See, I will lift up my hand to the nations,
  and raise my signal to the peoples;
They shall bring your sons in their arms,
  and your daughters shall be carried on
    their shoulders.ʷ
²³ Kings shall be your foster fathers,
  their princesses your nurses;
Bowing to the ground, they shall worship
    you
  and lick the dust at your feet.
Then you shall know that I am the
    LORD,
  and those who hope in me shall never
    be disappointed.

²⁴ Thus says the LORD:
Can booty be taken from a warrior?
  or captives be rescued from a tyrant?
²⁵ Yes, captives can be taken from a
    warrior,
  and booty be rescued from a tyrant;
Those who oppose you I will oppose,
  and your sons I will save.
²⁶ I will make your oppressors eat their own
    flesh,
  and they shall be drunk with their own
    blood
  as with the juice of the grape.
All mankind shall know
  that I, the LORD, am your savior,
  your redeemer, the mighty one of
    Jacob.ˣ

CHAPTER 50

Salvation Only through the
Lord's Servant

¹ Thus says the LORD:
Where is the bill of divorce
  with which I dismissed your mother?*
Or to which of my creditors
  have I sold you?
It was for your sins that you were sold,
  for your crimes that your mother was
    dismissed.ʸ

See RG
210

49, 16: Upon the palms . . . name: for continual remembrance; cf Ex 13, 9. 16; Dt 6, 6-9.

50, 1: Responding to the people's complaint of utter abandonment by God, the prophet shows that their sins were responsible for their banishment. Since there was no bill of divorce, the bond between the Lord and his people still exists

and he will ultimately save them.

t: Is 40, 27. u: Is 43, 4; 44, 21; 46, 3f. v: Is 54, 1ff. w: Is 5, 26; 13, 2. x: Is 19, 2; Ez 38, 21; Zec 14, 13. y: Dt 24, 1-4; Mt 19, 3; Mk 10, 2ff; Is 54, 6ff.

2 Why was no one there when I came?
    Why did no one answer when I called?*
Is my hand too short to ransom?
    Have I not the strength to deliver?
Lo, with my rebuke I dry up the sea,
    I turn rivers into a desert;
Their fish rot for lack of water,
    and die of thirst.*z*

3 I clothe the heavens in mourning,
    and make sackcloth their vesture.

4 The Lord GOD has given me*
    a well-trained tongue,
That I might know how to speak to the
        weary
    a word that will rouse them.
Morning after morning
    he opens my ear that I may hear;
5 And I have not rebelled,
    have not turned back.*
6 I gave my back to those who beat me,
    my cheeks to those who plucked my
        beard;*
My face I did not shield
    from buffets and spitting.*a*

7 The Lord GOD is my help,
    therefore I am not disgraced;
I have set my face like flint,
    knowing that I shall not be put to
        shame.*b*
8 He is near who upholds my right;
    if anyone wishes to oppose me,
    let us appear together.
Who disputes my right?
    Let him confront me.
9 See, the Lord GOD is my help;
    who will prove me wrong?
Lo, they will all wear out like cloth,
    the moth will eat them up.*c*

10 Who among you fears the LORD,*
    heeds his servant's voice,

And walks in darkness
    without any light,
Trusting in the name of the LORD
    and relying on his God?*d*
11 All of you kindle flames
    and carry about you fiery darts;
Walk by the light of your own fire
    and by the flares you have burnt!
This is your fate from my hand:
    you shall lie down in a place of pain.

CHAPTER 51

Exhortation To Trust
in the Lord

See RG
210

1 Listen to me, you who pursue justice,
    who seek the LORD;
Look to the rock from which you were
        hewn,
    to the pit* from which you were
        quarried;*e*
2 Look to Abraham, your father,
    and to Sarah, who gave you birth;
When he was but one I called him,
    I blessed him and made him many.*f*
3 Yes, the LORD shall comfort Zion
    and have pity on all her ruins;
Her deserts he shall make like Eden,
    her wasteland like the garden of the
        LORD;
Joy and gladness shall be found in her,
    thanksgiving and the sound of song.

4 Be attentive to me, my people;*
    my folk, give ear to me.
For law shall go forth from my
        presence,
    and my judgment, as the light of the
        peoples.*g*
5 I will make my justice come speedily;
    my salvation shall go forth
    [and my arm shall judge the nations];
In me shall the coastlands hope,
    and my arm they shall await.

50, 2: Israel's faith in God is weak; she does not answer
his call, nor believe in his promises of deliverance.

50, 4-11: The third of the four "Servant-of-the-Lord" oracles; in vv 4-9 the Servant speaks; in vv 10f God reproves the
people for not following the Servant.

50, 5: The Servant does not refuse the divine vocation.

50, 6: He willingly submits to insults and beatings.
Plucked my beard: a grave insult.

50, 10f: Instead of trusting in the Lord and his Servant, the
people rely on their own devices, to their own destruction.

51, 1: Rock . . . pit: your glorious ancestry.

51, 4f: The conversion of the Gentiles.

z: Ex 7, 18; Ps 105, 29.   a: 2 Sm 10, 4ff; Mt 26, 67; 27, 30.
b: Ez 3, 9.   c: Is 51, 6-8; Ps 102, 27.   d: Is 43, 1f; 44, 1f.
e: Rom 9, 30f.   f: Ez 33, 24; Gn 12, 2ff; 22, 17.   g: Is 2, 3.

⁶ Raise your eyes to the heavens,
  and look at the earth below;
Though the heavens grow thin like smoke,
  the earth wears out like a garment
  and its inhabitants die like flies,
My salvation shall remain forever
  and my justice shall never be
    dismayed.*
⁷ Hear me, you who know justice,
  you people who have my teaching at
    heart:
Fear not the reproach of men,
  be not dismayed at their revilings.
⁸ They shall be like a garment eaten by
    moths,
  like wool consumed by grubs;
But my justice shall remain forever
  and my salvation, for all generations.ʰ

⁹ Awake, awake, put on strength,
  O arm of the LORD!
Awake as in the days of old,
  in ages long ago!
Was it not you who crushed Rahab,*
  you who pierced the dragon?ⁱ
¹⁰ Was it not you who dried up the sea,
  the waters of the great deep,*
Who made the depths of the sea into a way
  for the redeemed to pass over?
¹¹ Those whom the LORD has ransomed will
    return
  and enter Zion singing,
  crowned with everlasting joy;
They will meet with joy and gladness,
  sorrow and mourning will flee.
¹² I, it is I who comfort you.
  Can you then fear mortal man,
  who is human only, to be looked upon
    as grass,
¹³ And forget the LORD, your maker,
  who stretched out the heavens
  and laid the foundations of the earth?
All the day you are in constant dread
  of the fury of the oppressor;
But when he sets himself to destroy,
  what is there of the oppressor's fury?

¹⁴ The oppressed shall soon be released;
  they shall not die and go down into the
    pit,
  nor shall they want for bread.
¹⁵ For I am the LORD, your God,
  who stirs up the sea so that its waves
    roar;
  the LORD of hosts by name.ʲ
¹⁶ I have put my words into your mouth
  and shielded you in the shadow of my
    hand,
I, who stretched out the heavens,
  who laid the foundations of the earth,
  who say to Zion: You are my people.

The Cup of the Lord

¹⁷ Awake, awake!
  Arise, O Jerusalem,
You who drank at the LORD's hand
  the cup of his wrath;
Who drained to the dregs
  the bowl of staggering!ᵏ
¹⁸ She has no one to guide her
  of all the sons she bore;
She has no one to grasp her by the hand,
  of all the sons she reared!—
¹⁹ Your misfortunes are double;
  who is there to condole with you?
Desolation and destruction, famine and
    sword!
  Who is there to comfort you?
²⁰ Your sons lie helpless
  at every street corner
  like antelopes in a net.
They are filled with the wrath of the
    LORD,
  the rebuke of your God.
²¹ But now, hear this, O afflicted one,
  drunk, but not with wine,ˡ
²² Thus says the LORD, your Master,
  your God, who defends his people:
See, I am taking from your hand
  the cup of staggering;
The bowl of my wrath
  you shall no longer drink.

51, 6: God's salvation and justice are eternal, in contrast to the impermanence of the heavens and the earth: cf Mt 24, 35.
51, 9: Rahab: see note on Is 30, 7. The dragon: see notes on Is 27, 1; Ps 74, 13.
51, 10: Great deep: another reference to the primeval chaos of Gn 1, 2.

h: Is 50, 9.   *i:* Ex 15, 16; Jb 9, 13; 26, 12; Pss 74, 13; 89, 11.   *j:* Jer 31, 35.   *k:* Jer 25, 15ff; Ez 23, 32ff.   *l:* Is 29, 9.

23 I will put it into the hands of your
    tormentors,
  those who ordered you
  to bow down, that they might walk
    over you,
  While you offered your back like the
    ground,
  like the street for them to walk on.

See RG
210

CHAPTER 52

Let Zion Rejoice

1 Awake, awake!
  Put on your strength, O Zion;
  Put on your glorious garments,
    O Jerusalem, holy city.
  No longer shall the uncircumcised
  or the unclean enter you.
2 Shake off the dust,
    ascend to the throne, Jerusalem;
  Loose the bonds from your neck,
    O captive daughter Zion!
3   For thus says the LORD:
  You were sold for nothing,
    and without money you shall be
    redeemed.
4   Thus says the Lord GOD:
  To Egypt in the beginning my people
    went down,
    to sojourn there;
  Assyria, too, oppressed them for
    nought.
5 But now, what am I to do here?
    says the LORD.
  My people have been taken away without
    redress;
    their rulers make a boast of it, says the
    LORD;
  all the day my name is constantly
    reviled.
6 Therefore on that day my people shall
    know my renown,
    that it is I who have foretold it. Here I
    am!
7 How beautiful upon the mountains*

are the feet of him who brings glad
    tidings,
  Announcing peace, bearing good news,
    announcing salvation, and saying to
    Zion,
  "Your God is King!"[m]
8 Hark! Your watchmen raise a cry,
    together they shout for joy,
  For they see directly, before their eyes,
    the LORD restoring Zion.[n]
9 Break out together in song,
    O ruins of Jerusalem!
  For the LORD comforts his people,
    he redeems Jerusalem.
10 The LORD has bared his holy arm
    in the sight of all the nations;
  All the ends of the earth will behold
    the salvation of our God.

11 Depart, depart, come forth from there,
    touch nothing unclean!
  Out from there!* Purify yourselves,
    you who carry the vessels of the LORD.
12 Yet not in fearful haste will you come
    out,
    nor leave in headlong flight,
  For the LORD comes before you,
    and your rear guard is the God of Israel.[o]

*Suffering and Triumph of the Servant of the Lord**

13 See, my servant shall prosper,
    he shall be raised high and greatly
    exalted.
14 Even as many were amazed at him—
    so marred was his look beyond that of
    man,
    and his appearance beyond that of
    mortals—[p]
15 So shall he startle many nations,
    because of him kings shall stand
    speechless;
  For those who have not been told shall
    see,

52, 7-10: God leads his people back from Babylon to
Zion, from whose ruined walls watchmen . . . shout for joy;
cf Rom 10, 15.

52, 11: From there: from Babylon. Vessels of the LORD:
taken to Babylon by Nebuchadnezzar, now carried back by
the exiled priests returning in procession to Zion; cf Ezr 1, 7.

52, 13—53, 12: The last of the four "Servant-of-the-Lord"

oracles. An extraordinary description of the sinless Servant,
who by his voluntary suffering atones for the sins of his people, and saves them from just punishment at the hands of
God. Only in Jesus Christ is the prophecy perfectly fulfilled.

m: Is 40, 9; Rom 10, 15.   *n:* Is 62, 6.   *o:* Ex 12, 11.   *p:* Ps 69, 8.

The Suffering Servant

Israel, the servant of God, has suffered as a humiliated individual. However, the servant endured without complaint because it was suffering for others. Nations and kings (52, 15) will be surprised to see the unattractive, rejected servant exalted. In traditional Hebrew thought, the good person prospers like a tree by water, but the wicked is like a plant growing in parched ground; see Ps 1, 3–6. The phrase in Is 53, 3, "hide their faces" was used in relation to lepers, whose sickness was considered a sign of sin. In the end, however, this reviled, condemned character is restored and exalted for accepting punishment for the transgressions of others.

those who have not heard shall ponder
    it.*q*

CHAPTER 53

See RG 210

1 Who would believe what we have
    heard?
To whom has the arm of the LORD
    been revealed?*r*
2 He grew up like a sapling before him,*s*
    like a shoot from the parched earth;
There was in him no stately bearing to
    make us look at him,
    nor appearance that would attract us to
    him.*
3 He was spurned* and avoided by men,
    a man of suffering, accustomed to
    infirmity,
One of those from whom men hide their
    faces,
    spurned, and we held him in no
    esteem.*t*

4 Yet it was our infirmities that he bore,*
    our sufferings that he endured,
While we thought of him as stricken,
    as one smitten by God and afflicted.*u*
5 But he was pierced for our offenses,
    crushed for our sins,
Upon him was the chastisement that
    makes us whole,
    by his stripes we were healed.*v*
6 We had all gone astray like sheep,

each following his own way;
But the LORD laid upon him
    the guilt of us all.*w*
7 Though he was harshly treated, he
    submitted
    and opened not his mouth;
Like a lamb led to the slaughter
    or a sheep before the shearers,
    he was silent and opened not his
    mouth.*x*
8 Oppressed and condemned, he was taken
    away,
    and who would have thought any more
    of his destiny?
When he was cut off from the land of the
    living,
    and smitten for the sin of his people,
9 A grave was assigned him among the
    wicked
    and a burial place with evildoers,
Though he had done no wrong
    nor spoken any falsehood.*y*
10 [But the LORD was pleased*
    to crush him in infirmity.]

If he gives his life as an offering for
    sin,
    he shall see his descendants in a long
    life,
    and the will of the LORD shall be
    accomplished through him.
11 Because of his affliction

53, 2: Only God appreciated his Servant's true greatness.
53, 3: Because he suffered, he was regarded as a sinner and therefore as one to be spurned.
53, 4ff: He did indeed suffer but it was for the sins of mankind, and through his sufferings men are healed.
53, 10ff: Because he fulfilled the divine will by suffering for the sins of others, the Servant will be rewarded by the Lord. See the light: enjoy happiness. This line may originally

have read, "he shall drink and eat to the full"—at the thanksgiving sacrifice at which he shall divide the spoils (v 12).

q: Mi 7, 16.   *r:* Is 52, 10; Jn 12, 38; Rom 10, 16.   *s:* Is 11, 1.   *t:* Jb 19, 18; Ps 31, 11ff; Mk 9, 11.   *u:* Jer 10, 19; Mt 8, 17.   *v:* 1 Cor 15, 3; 1 Pt 2, 24.   *w:* Lv 16, 21ff.   *x:* Mt 26, 63; Acts 8, 32.   *y:* 1 Pt 2, 22f; 1 Jn 3, 5.

he shall see the light in fullness of
days;
Through his suffering, my servant shall
justify many,
and their guilt he shall bear.
[12] Therefore I will give him his portion
among the great,
and he shall divide the spoils with the
mighty,
Because he surrendered himself to death
and was counted among the wicked;
And he shall take away the sins of many,
and win pardon for their offenses.[z]

CHAPTER 54

See RG
210

The New Zion

[1] Raise a glad cry, you barren one* who did
not bear,
break forth in jubilant song, you who
were not in labor,
For more numerous are the children of
the deserted wife
than the children of her who has a
husband,
says the LORD.[a]
[2] Enlarge the space for your tent,
spread out your tent cloths
unsparingly;
lengthen your ropes and make firm
your stakes.[b]
[3] For you shall spread abroad to the right
and to the left;
your descendants shall dispossess the
nations
and shall people the desolate cities.
[4] Fear not, you shall not be put to shame;
you need not blush, for you shall not
be disgraced.
The shame of your youth you shall
forget,
the reproach of your widowhood no
longer remember.
[5] For he who has become your husband is
your Maker;
his name is the LORD of hosts;

Your redeemer* is the Holy One of Israel,
called God of all the earth.
[6] The LORD calls you back,
like a wife forsaken and grieved in
spirit,
A wife married in youth and then cast
off,
says your God.[c]
[7] For a brief moment I abandoned you,
but with great tenderness I will take
you back.
[8] In an outburst of wrath, for a moment
I hid my face from you;
But with enduring love I take pity on you,
says the LORD, your redeemer.

[9] This is for me like the days of Noah,
when I swore that the waters of Noah
should never again deluge the earth;
So I have sworn not to be angry with
you,
or to rebuke you.[d]
[10] Though the mountains leave their place
and the hills be shaken,
My love shall never leave you
nor my covenant of peace be shaken,
says the LORD, who has mercy on you.[e]

[11] O afflicted one, storm-battered and
unconsoled,*
I lay your pavements in carnelians,
and your foundations in sapphires;[f]
[12] I will make your battlements of rubies,
your gates of carbuncles,
and all your walls of precious stones.
[13] All your sons shall be taught by the
LORD,
and great shall be the peace of your
children.
[14] In justice shall you be established,
far from the fear of oppression,
where destruction cannot come near
you.
[15] Should there be any attack, it shall not be
of my making;

54, 1: Jerusalem, pictured as a wife who had been barren
and deserted, now suddenly finds herself with innumerable
children (the returning exiles); cf Gal 4, 27 for the application
of this text to the church, the New Zion.

54, 5: Redeemer: cf note on Is 41, 14.

54, 11f: Cf Rv 21. Afflicted one: Jerusalem; carnelians:

reddish quartz, hard and durable; carbuncles: another precious stone of red color.

z: Mk 15, 28; Lk 22, 37.   a: Gal 4, 27.   b: Is 49, 20.   c: Mal 2,
14f.   d: Gn 9, 15.   e: Pss 76, 5; 46, 3.   f: Rv 21, 18-21.

whoever attacks you shall fall before
you.
¹⁶ Lo, I have created the craftsman
who blows on the burning coals
and forges weapons as his work;
It is I also who have created
the destroyer to work havoc.
¹⁷ No weapon fashioned against you shall
prevail;
every tongue you shall prove false
that launches an accusation against you.
This is the lot of the servants of the LORD,
their vindication from me, says the
LORD.

See RG
210

CHAPTER 55

An Invitation to Grace

¹All you who are thirsty,*
come to the water!
You who have no money,
come, receive grain and eat;
Come, without paying and without cost,
drink wine and milk!ᵍ
² Why spend your money for what is not
bread;
your wages for what fails to satisfy?
Heed me, and you shall eat well,
you shall delight in rich fare.
³ Come to me heedfully,
listen, that you may have life.
I will renew with you the everlasting
covenant,
the benefits assured to David.ʰ
⁴ As I made him a witness to the peoples,
a leader and commander of nations,
⁵ So shall you summon a nation you knew
not,
and nations that knew you not shall
run to you,
Because of the LORD, your God,
the Holy One of Israel, who has
glorified you.ⁱ

⁶ Seek the LORD while he may be found,

call him while he is near.
⁷ Let the scoundrel forsake his way,
and the wicked man his thoughts;
Let him turn to the LORD for mercy;
to our God, who is generous in
forgiving.
⁸ For my thoughts are not your thoughts,
nor are your ways my ways, says the
LORD.
⁹ As high as the heavens are above the
earth,
so high are my ways above your ways
and my thoughts above your thoughts.
¹⁰ For just as from the heavens
the rain and snow come down
And do not return there
till they have watered the earth,
making it fertile and fruitful,
Giving seed to him who sows
and bread to him who eats,
¹¹ So shall my word be
that goes forth from my mouth;
It shall not return to me void,
but shall do my will,
achieving the end for which I sent it.

¹² Yes, in joy you shall depart,
in peace you shall be brought back;
Mountains and hills shall break out in
song before you,
and all the trees of the countryside
shall clap their hands.
¹³ In place of the thornbush, the cypress
shall grow,
instead of nettles,* the myrtle.
This shall be to the LORD's renown,
an everlasting imperishable sign.

III: Return of the First Captives

CHAPTER 56

*The Lord's House Open to All**

See RG
211

¹ Thus says the LORD:
Observe what is right, do what is just;

55, 1ff: God's salvation is freely extended to his people
and to all nations; through him will the benefits assured to
David be renewed; cf Is 12, 3; Jn 7, 37.

55, 13: Thornbush . . . nettles: suggestive of the desert and
therefore symbolic of suffering and hardship; cypress, myrtle:
suggestive of fertile land and therefore symbolic of joy and
strength.

56, 1-8: Participation in the future messianic salvation is
offered to all who believe in the Lord and keep his commandments, regardless of origin or social condition.

---

g: Jr 4, 10ff; 6, 35; 7, 37ff; Rv 21, 6; 22, 17.   h: 2 Sm 7, 12-16.
i: Acts 13, 34.

for my salvation is about to come,
my justice, about to be revealed.

2 Happy is the man who does this,
the son of man who holds to it;
Who keeps the sabbath free from
profanation,
and his hand from any evildoing.

3 Let not the foreigner say,
when he would join himself to the LORD,
"The LORD will surely exclude me
from his people";
Nor let the eunuch say,
"See, I am a dry tree."*

4 For thus says the LORD:
To the eunuchs who observe my sabbaths
and choose what pleases me
and hold fast to my covenant,[j]

5 I will give, in my house
and within my walls, a monument and
a name*
Better than sons and daughters;
an eternal, imperishable name will I
give them.

6 And the foreigners who join themselves
to the LORD,
ministering to him,
Loving the name of the LORD,
and becoming his servants—
All who keep the sabbath free from
profanation
and hold to my covenant,

7 Them I will bring to my holy mountain
and make joyful in my house of
prayer;
Their holocausts and sacrifices
will be acceptable on my altar,
For my house shall be called
a house of prayer for all peoples.[k]

8 Thus says the Lord GOD,
who gathers the dispersed of Israel:
Others will I gather to him
besides those already gathered.

Blind Leaders

9 *All you wild beasts* of the field,
come and eat,
all you beasts in the forest![l]

10 My watchmen are blind,
all of them unaware;
They are all dumb dogs,
they cannot bark;
Dreaming as they lie there,
loving their sleep.

11 They are relentless dogs,
they know not when they have
enough.
These are the shepherds
who know no discretion;
Each of them goes his own way,
every one of them to his own gain:

12 "Come, I will fetch some wine;
let us carouse with strong drink,
And tomorrow will be like today,
or even greater."[m]

CHAPTER 57

See RG
211

1 The just man perishes,
but no one takes it to heart;
Devout men are swept away,
with no one giving it a thought.
Though he is taken away from the
presence of evil,
the just man [2]enters into peace;
There is rest on his couch
for the sincere, straightforward man.

Faithless People

3 But you, draw near,
you sons of a sorceress,
adulterous, wanton race!

4 Of whom do you make sport,
at whom do you open wide your
mouth,
and put out your tongue?
Are you not rebellious children,
a worthless race;

56, 3: Eunuchs had originally been excluded from the community of the Lord; cf Dt 23, 2; Wis 3, 14. Dry tree: unable to produce the fruit of offspring.

56, 5: A monument and a name: a memorial inscription to prevent oblivion for one who had no children; cf 2 Sm 18, 18; Neh 7, 15; 13, 14.

56, 9—57, 13: This section is apparently preexilic, written

in the manner of the older prophets who condemned the pagan rites of Baal worship.

56, 9: Wild beasts: foreign nations, which are invited to come and ravage Israel.

---

j: Wis 3, 14f. k: 1 Kgs 8, 29f; Mt 21, 13. l: Ez 34, 5. m: Is 28, 7ff; Wis 2, 7.

5 You who are in heat among the
terebinths,
under every green tree;
You who immolate children in the
wadies,
behind the crevices in the cliffs?*n*

6 Among the smooth stones* of the wadi is
your portion,
these are your lot;
To these you poured out libations,
and brought offerings.
Should I decide not to punish these
things?
7 Upon a high and lofty mountain
you made your bed,
and there you went up to offer
sacrifice.*o*
8 Behind the door and the doorpost
you placed your indecent symbol.
Deserting me, you spread out
your high, wide bed;
And of those whose embraces you
love
you carved the symbol and gazed
upon it
9 While you approached the king* with
scented oil,
and multiplied your perfumes;
While you sent your ambassadors far
away,
down even to the nether world.
10 Though worn out by your many
misdeeds,
you never said, "It is hopeless";
New strength you found,
and so you did not weaken.

11 Of whom were you afraid? Whom did
you fear,
that you became false
And did not remember me
or give me any thought?
Was I to remain silent and unseeing,

so that you would not have me to
fear?
12 I will expose your justice*
and your works;
13 They shall not help you when you cry
out,
nor save you in your distress.
All these* the wind shall carry off,
the breeze shall bear away;
But he who takes refuge in me shall
inherit the land,
and possess my holy mountain.

Comfort for the Afflicted
14 Build up, build up, prepare the way,
remove the stumbling blocks from my
people's path.*p*
15 For thus says he who is high and exalted,
living eternally, whose name is the
Holy One:
On high I dwell, and in holiness,
and with the crushed and dejected in
spirit,
To revive the spirits of the dejected,
to revive the hearts of the crushed.*q*
16 I will not accuse forever,
nor always be angry;
For their spirits would faint before me,
the souls that I have made.
17 Because of their wicked avarice I was
angry,
and struck them, hiding myself in
wrath,
as they went their own rebellious way.*r*
18 I saw their ways,
but I will heal them and lead them;
I will give full comfort
to them and to those who mourn for
them,
19 I, the Creator, who gave them life.

Peace, peace to the far and the near,
says the LORD; and I will heal them.
20 But the wicked are like the tossing sea

57, 6: Smooth stones: the Hebrew word for this expression has the same consonants as the word for "portion"; instead of making the Lord their portion (cf Ps 16, 5), the people adored slabs of stone which they took from the streambeds in valleys and set up as idols; cf Jer 3, 9. Therefore, it is implied, they will be swept away as by a sudden torrent of waters carrying them down the rocky-bottomed gorge to destruction and death without burial.

57, 9: The king: the pagan god Moloch. Ambassadors: children sent to him through a sacrificial death.
57, 12: Justice: here used ironically.
57, 13: All these: the wicked mentioned in Is 57, 3–10.

---

n: Jer 7, 31; 19, 5; Ez 20, 28. 31.   *o:* Hos 4, 13; Jer 2, 20; Ez 6,
13.   *p:* Is 40, 3f.   *q:* Is 61, 2f.   *r:* Is 56, 11.

which cannot be calmed,
And its waters cast up mud and filth.
21 No peace for the wicked! says my
God.[s]

CHAPTER 58

See RG 211

True Fasting

1 Cry out full-throated and unsparingly,
lift up your voice like a trumpet blast;
Tell my people their wickedness,
and the house of Jacob their sins.[*]
2 They seek me day after day,[*]
and desire to know my ways,
Like a nation that has done what is just
and not abandoned the law of their
God;
They ask me to declare what is due them,
pleased to gain access to God.
3 "Why do we fast, and you do not see it?
afflict ourselves, and you take no note
of it?"

Lo, on your fast day you carry out your
own pursuits,
and drive all your laborers.
4 Yes, your fast ends in quarreling and
fighting,
striking with wicked claw.
Would that today you might fast
so as to make your voice heard on
high!
5 Is this the manner of fasting I wish,
of keeping a day of penance:
That a man bow his head like a reed,
and lie in sackcloth and ashes?
Do you call this a fast,
a day acceptable to the LORD?[t]
6 This, rather, is the fasting that I wish:
releasing those bound unjustly,
untying the thongs of the yoke;
Setting free the oppressed,
breaking every yoke;
7 Sharing your bread with the hungry,
sheltering the oppressed and the
homeless;
Clothing the naked when you see them,

and not turning your back on your
own.[u]
8 Then your light shall break forth like the
dawn,
and your wound shall quickly be
healed;
Your vindication shall go before you,
and the glory of the LORD shall be
your rear guard.
9 Then you shall call, and the LORD will
answer,
you shall cry for help, and he will say:
Here I am!
If you remove from your midst
oppression,
false accusation and malicious speech;
10 If you bestow your bread on the hungry
and satisfy the afflicted;
Then light shall rise for you in the
darkness,
and the gloom shall become for you
like midday;
11 Then the LORD will guide you always
and give you plenty even on the
parched land.
He will renew your strength,
and you shall be like a watered garden,
like a spring whose water never fails.[v]
12 The ancient ruins shall be rebuilt for your
sake,
and the foundations from ages past
you shall raise up;
"Repairer of the breach," they shall call
you,
"Restorer of ruined homesteads."[w]

13 If you hold back your foot on the sabbath
from following your own pursuits on
my holy day;
If you call the sabbath a delight,
and the LORD's holy day honorable;
If you honor it by not following your
ways,
seeking your own interests, or
speaking with malice—
14 Then you shall delight in the LORD,

58, 1: This command is directed to the prophet.
58, 2-14: Merely external worship does not avail with God; it must be joined to internal sincerity.

---

s: Is 48, 21.   t: Zec 7, 5.   u: Ez 18, 7. 16; Mt 25, 35.   v: Is 51, 3; Ps 24.   w: Is 61, 4.

and I will make you ride on the heights
of the earth;
I will nourish you with the heritage of
Jacob, your father,
for the mouth of the LORD has spoken.

CHAPTER 59

See RG 211

Sin and Confession

[1] Lo, the hand of the LORD is not too short
to save,
nor his ear too dull to hear.[x]
[2] Rather, it is your crimes
that separate you from your God,
It is your sins that make him hide his face
so that he will not hear you.
[3] For your hands are stained with blood,
your fingers with guilt;
Your lips speak falsehood,
and your tongue utters deceit.[y]
[4] No one brings suit justly,
no one pleads truthfully;
They trust in emptiness* and tell lies;
they conceive mischief and bring forth
malice.
[5] They hatch adders' eggs,*
and weave spiders' webs:
Whoever eats their eggs will die,
if one of them is pressed, it will hatch
as a viper;[z]
[6] Their webs cannot serve as clothing,
nor can they cover themselves with
their works.
Their works are evil works,
and deeds of violence come from their
hands.
[7] Their feet run to evil,
and they are quick to shed innocent
blood;
Their thoughts are destructive thoughts,
plunder and ruin are on their
highways.[a]
[8] The way of peace they know not,
and there is nothing that is right in
their paths;
Their ways they have made crooked,
whoever treads them knows no peace.

[9] That is why right is far from us*
and justice does not reach us.
We look for light, and lo, darkness;
for brightness, but we walk in gloom!
[10] Like blind men we grope along the wall,
like people without eyes we feel our
way.
We stumble at midday as at dusk,
in Stygian darkness, like the dead.
[11] We all growl like bears,
like doves we moan without ceasing.
We look for right, but it is not there;
for salvation, and it is far from us.[b]
[12] For our offenses before you are many,
our sins bear witness against us.
Yes, our offenses are present to us,
and our crimes we know:
[13] Transgressing, and denying the LORD,
turning back from following our God,
Threatening outrage, and apostasy,
uttering words of falsehood the heart
has conceived.
[14] Right is repelled,
and justice stands far off;
For truth stumbles in the public square,
uprightness cannot enter.
[15] Honesty is lacking,
and the man who turns from evil is
despoiled.

The Redeemer in Zion

The LORD saw this, and was aggrieved
that right did not exist.
[16] He saw that there was no one,
and was appalled that there was none
to intervene;
So his own arm brought about the
victory,
and his justice lent him its support.
[17] He put on justice as his breastplate,
salvation, as the helmet on his head;
He clothed himself with garments of
vengeance,
wrapped himself in a mantle of zeal.[c]
[18] He repays his enemies their deserts,
and requites his foes with wrath.

59, 4: Emptiness: things having no value.

59, 5f: A proverb signifying evil works—adders' eggs—and useless devices—spiders' webs; the former do positive harm to oneself and others, the latter serve no useful purpose.

59, 9-15: Spoken by the people through the mouth of the prophet.

---

x: Is 50, 2; Nm 11, 23.   *y:* Is 1, 15.   *z:* Jb 20, 12-16.   *a:* Rom 3, 15.   *b:* Is 38, 14.   *c:* Wis 5, 17ff; Eph 6, 14; 1 Thes 5, 8.

19 Those in the west shall fear the name of
the LORD,
and those in the east, his glory;
For it shall come like a pent-up river
which the breath of the LORD drives
on.
20 He shall come to Zion a redeemer
to those of Jacob who turn from sin,
says the LORD.*d*
21 This is the covenant with them
which I myself have made, says the
LORD:
My spirit which is upon you
and my words that I have put into your
mouth
Shall never leave your mouth,
nor the mouths of your children
Nor the mouths of your children's
children
from now on and forever, says the
LORD.

CHAPTER 60

Glory of the New Zion

See RG
211

1 Rise up in splendor! Your light has
come,*
the glory of the Lord shines upon you.
2 See, darkness covers the earth,
and thick clouds cover the peoples;
But upon you the LORD shines,
and over you appears his glory.
3 Nations shall walk by your light,
and kings by your shining radiance.*e*
4 Raise your eyes and look about;
they all gather and come to you:
Your sons come from afar,
and your daughters in the arms of their
nurses.*f*

5 Then you shall be radiant at what you
see,
your heart shall throb and overflow,
For the riches of the sea shall be emptied
out before you,
the wealth of nations shall be brought
to you.

6 Caravans of camels shall fill you,
dromedaries from Midian and Ephah;
All from Sheba shall come
bearing gold and frankincense,
and proclaiming the praises of the
LORD.
7 All the flocks of Kedar shall be gathered
for you,
the rams of Nebaioth shall be your
sacrifices;
They will be acceptable offerings on my
altar,
and I will enhance the splendor of my
house.

8 What are these that fly along like
clouds,
like doves* to their cotes?
9 All the vessels of the sea are assembled,
with the ships of Tarshish in the lead,
To bring your children from afar
with their silver and gold,
In the name of the LORD, your God,
the Holy One of Israel, who has
glorified you.

10 Foreigners shall rebuild your walls,
and their kings shall be your
attendants;
Though I struck you in my wrath,
yet in my good will I have shown you
mercy.
11 Your gates shall stand open constantly;
day and night they shall not be closed
But shall admit to you the wealth of
nations,
and their kings, in the vanguard.*g*
12 For the people or kingdom shall perish
that does not serve you;
those nations shall be utterly
destroyed.
13 The glory of Lebanon* shall come to you:
the cypress, the plane and the pine,
To bring beauty to my sanctuary,
and glory to the place where I set my
feet.*h*

60, 1-6: The Church makes use of these verses for the first
reading of the Mass on the feast of Epiphany, for she sees in
them symbols of her universality.

60, 8f: Like clouds, like doves: the white sails of the ships
of Tarshish; cf note on Ps 48, 8.

60, 13: Glory of Lebanon: the cedars, together with the
cypress, the plane and the pine, all precious, durable wood.

d: Rom 11, 26f.   *e:* Is 42, 6; 45, 14; 49, 6.   *f:* Is 49, 18.   *g:* Rv
21, 25.   *h:* Is 35, 2.

¹⁴ The children of your oppressors shall
come,
bowing low before you;
All those who despised you
shall fall prostrate at your feet.
They shall call you "City of the LORD,"
"Zion of the Holy One of Israel."

¹⁵ Once you were forsaken,
hated and unvisited,
Now I will make you the pride of the
ages,
a joy to generation after generation.ⁱ
¹⁶ You shall suck the milk of nations,
and be nursed at royal breasts;
You shall know that I, the LORD, am your
savior,
your redeemer, the mighty one of
Jacob.
¹⁷ In place of bronze I will bring gold,
instead of iron, silver;
In place of wood, bronze,
instead of stones, iron;
I will appoint peace your governor,
and justice your ruler.
¹⁸ No longer shall violence be heard of in
your land,
or plunder and ruin within your
boundaries.
You shall call your walls "Salvation"
and your gates "Praise."
¹⁹ No longer shall the sun
be your light by day,
Nor the brightness of the moon
shine upon you at night;
The LORD shall be your light forever,
your God shall be your glory.ʲ
²⁰ No longer shall your sun go down,
or your moon withdraw,
For the LORD will be your light
forever,
and the days of your mourning shall be
at an end.
²¹ Your people shall all be just,
they shall always possess the land,
They, the bud of my planting,
my handiwork to show my glory.

²² The smallest shall become a thousand,
the youngest, a mighty nation;
I, the LORD, will swiftly accomplish
these things
when their time comes.ᵏ

CHAPTER 61

The Mission to the Afflicted

¹ The spirit of the Lord GOD is upon me,*
because the LORD has anointed me;
He has sent me to bring glad tidings to
the lowly,
to heal the brokenhearted,
To proclaim liberty to the captives
and release to the prisoners,ˡ
² To announce a year of favor from the
LORD
and a day of vindication by our God,
to comfort all who mourn;ᵐ
³ To place on those who mourn in Zion
a diadem instead of ashes,
To give them oil of gladness in place of
mourning,
a glorious mantle instead of a listless
spirit.
They will be called oaks of justice,
planted by the LORD to show his
glory.

The Reward of Israel

⁴ They shall rebuild the ancient ruins,
the former wastes they shall raise up
And restore the ruined cities,
desolate now for generations.ⁿ
⁵ Strangers shall stand ready to pasture
your flocks,
foreigners shall be your farmers and
vinedressers.
⁶ You yourselves shall be named priests of
the LORD,
ministers of our God you shall be
called.
You shall eat the wealth of the
nations
and boast of riches from them.
⁷ Since their shame was double

See RG
211

61, 1f: This was spoken by the prophet in regard to the restoration of Zion, but quoted by Christ as referring to his mission; cf Lk 4, 18f. Year of favor . . . day of vindication: the time of God's salvation.

i: Ez 16.   j: Rv 21, 23; 22, 5.   k: Gn 12, 2; 17, 6.   l: Is 42, 1; 48, 16; Lk 4, 18f.   m: Mt 5, 5.   n: Is 58, 12.

and disgrace and spittle were their
portion,
They shall have a double inheritance in
their land,
everlasting joy shall be theirs.°
8 For I, the LORD, love what is right,
I hate robbery and injustice;
I will give them their recompense
faithfully,
a lasting covenant I will make with
them.ᵖ
9 Their descendants shall be renowned
among the nations,
and their offspring among the
peoples;
All who see them shall acknowledge
them
as a race the LORD has blessed.

10 I rejoice heartily in the LORD,
in my God is the joy of my soul;
For he has clothed me with a robe of
salvation,
and wrapped me in a mantle of justice,
Like a bridegroom adorned with a
diadem,
like a bride bedecked with her jewels.
11 As the earth brings forth its plants,
and a garden makes its growth spring
up,
So will the Lord GOD make justice and
praise
spring up before all the nations.

CHAPTER 62

See RG 211

Jerusalem the Lord's Bride

1 For Zion's sake I will not be silent,
for Jerusalem's sake I will not be
quiet,
Until her vindication shines forth like the
dawn
and her victory like a burning torch.

2 Nations shall behold your vindication,
and all kings your glory;
You shall be called by a new name*

pronounced by the mouth of the LORD.�q
3 You shall be a glorious crown in the hand
of the LORD,
a royal diadem held by your God.
4 No more shall men call you "Forsaken,"
or your land "Desolate,"
But you shall be called "My Delight,"
and your land "Espoused."
For the LORD delights in you,
and makes your land his spouse.ʳ
5 As a young man marries a virgin,
your Builder shall marry you;
And as a bridegroom rejoices in his bride
so shall your God rejoice in you.

Restoration of Zion

6 Upon your walls, O Jerusalem,
I have stationed watchmen;
Never, by day or by night,
shall they be silent.
O you who are to remind the LORD,*
take no rest
7 And give no rest to him,
until he re-establishes Jerusalem
And makes of it
the pride of the earth.

8 The LORD has sworn by his right hand
and by his mighty arm:
No more will I give your grain
as food to your enemies;
Nor shall foreigners drink your wine,
for which you toiled.ˢ
9 But you who harvest the grain shall eat it,
and you shall praise the LORD;
You who gather the grapes shall drink the
wine
in the courts of my sanctuary.ᵗ

10 Pass through, pass through the gates,
prepare the way for the people;ᵘ
Build up, build up the highway,
clear it of stones,
raise up a standard over the nations.*
11 See, the LORD proclaims
to the ends of the earth:

62, 2: New name: figurative expression for a new state of
happiness; cf Rv 2, 17; 3, 12.

62, 6f: Remind the LORD . . . give no rest to him: figuratively, as though to make certain that the Lord will remember
his pledge to Jerusalem. Cf Lk 11, 7f.

62, 10: The command is given to the workmen to begin
the reconstruction of the city.

o: Is 40, 2.   p: Is 55, 3; 59, 21.   q: Rv 2, 17; 3, 12.   r: Is 49, 15f;
54, 1ff.   s: Is 52, 10.   t: Dt 12, 17f; 14, 23.   u: Is 58, 14.

Say to daughter Zion,
  your savior comes!
Here is his reward with him,
  his recompense before him.[v]
[12] They shall be called the holy people,
  the redeemed of the LORD,
And you shall be called "Frequented,"
  a city that is not forsaken.[w]

See RG
211–12

CHAPTER 63

Punishment of Edom*

[1] Who is this that comes from Edom,
  in crimsoned garments, from Bozrah—
This one arrayed in majesty,
  marching in the greatness of his
    strength?
"It is I, I who announce vindication,
  I who am mighty to save."
[2] Why is your apparel red,
  and your garments like those of the
    wine presser?[x]

[3] "The wine press I have trodden alone,
  and of my people there was no one
    with me.
I trod them in my anger,
  and trampled them down in my wrath;
Their blood spurted on my garments;
  all my apparel I stained.
[4] For the day of vengeance was in my
    heart,
  my year for redeeming was at hand.[y]
[5] I looked about, but there was no one to
    help,
  I was appalled that there was no one to
    lend support;
So my own arm brought about the victory
  and my own wrath lent me its support.[z]
[6] I trampled down the peoples in my anger,
  I crushed them in my wrath,
  and I let their blood run out upon the
    ground."

Prayer for the Return of God's Favor*

[7] The favors of the LORD I will recall,

the glorious deeds of the LORD,
Because of all he has done for us;
  for he is good to the house of Israel,
He has favored us according to his
    mercy
  and his great kindness.[a]
[8] He said: They are indeed my people,
  children who are not disloyal;
So he became their savior
[9] in their every affliction.
It was not a messenger or an angel,
  but he himself who saved them.
Because of his love and pity
  he redeemed them himself,
Lifting them and carrying them
  all the days of old.[b]
[10] But they rebelled, and grieved
  his holy spirit;
So he turned on them like an enemy,
  and fought against them.

[11] Then they remembered the days of old
  and Moses, his servant;
Where is he who brought up out of the
    sea
  the shepherd of his flock?
Where is he who put his holy spirit
  in their midst;
[12] Whose glorious arm
  was the guide at Moses' right;
Who divided the waters before them,
  winning for himself eternal renown;
[13] Who led them without stumbling through
    the depths
  like horses in the open country,
[14] Like cattle going down into the plain,
  the spirit of the LORD guiding them?
Thus you led your people,
  bringing glory to your name.

[15] Look down from heaven and regard us
  from your holy and glorious palace!
Where is your zealous care and your
    might,
  your surge of pity and your mercy?[c]

63, 1-6: In a dramatic dialogue between God and the prophet, the Lord is portrayed as the sole avenger of justice against his enemies.

63, 7—64, 11: A prayer probably composed toward the end of the exile, in which the prophet, after recalling God's blessings on Israel in its past history (63, 7-10), especially at the Exodus (11-14), begs the Lord to come once more to the aid of his people (63, 15—64, 3), who now humbly confess their sins (4-11).

v: Is 40, 10. w: Is 62, 4. x: Rv 19, 13. y: Is 34, 8; 61, 2. z: Is 59, 16. a: Is 26, 15. b: Dt 4, 37f. c: Dt 26, 15; Bar 2, 16.

O Lord, hold not back,
16   for you are our father.
Were Abraham not to know us,
     nor Israel to acknowledge us,
You, LORD, are our father,
     our redeemer you are named forever.
17 Why do you let us wander, O LORD, from
          your ways,
     and harden our hearts so that we fear
          you not?
Return for the sake of your servants,
     the tribes of your heritage.
18 Why have the wicked invaded your holy
          place,
     why have our enemies trampled your
          sanctuary?
19 Too long have we been like those you do
          not rule,
     who do not bear your name.

Oh, that you would rend the heavens and
          come down,
     with the mountains quaking before you,

See RG
211–12

CHAPTER 64

1 As when brushwood is set ablaze,
     or fire makes the water boil!
Thus your name would be made known
          to your enemies
     and the nations would tremble before
          you,
2 While you wrought awesome deeds we
          could not hope for,
3   such as they had not heard of from of
          old.
No ear has ever heard, no eye ever seen,
     any God but you
     doing such deeds for those who wait
          for him.d
4 Would that you might meet us doing right,
     that we were mindful of you in our
          ways!
Behold, you are angry, and we are sinful;
5   all of us have become like unclean
          men,
     all our good deeds are like polluted rags;

We have all withered like leaves,
     and our guilt carries us away like the
          wind.
6 There is none who calls upon your name,
     who rouses himself to cling to you;
For you have hidden your face from us
     and have delivered us up to our guilt.
7 Yet, O LORD, you are our father;
     we are the clay and you the potter:
     we are all the work of your hands.
8 Be not so very angry, LORD,
     keep not our guilt forever in mind;
     look upon us, who are all your people.
9 Your holy cities have become a desert,
     Zion is a desert, Jerusalem a waste.e
10 Our holy and glorious temple
     in which our fathers praised you
Has been burned with fire;
     all that was dear to us is laid waste.
11 Can you hold back, O LORD, after all this?
     Can you remain silent, and afflict us so
          severely?

See RG
211–12

CHAPTER 65

Necessity of Punishment

1 I was ready to respond to those who
          asked me not,
     to be found by those who sought me not.
I said: Here I am! Here I am!
     To a nation that did not call upon my
          name.f
2 I have stretched out my hands all the day
     to a rebellious people,
Who walk in evil paths
     and follow their own thoughts,g
3 People who provoke me
     continually, to my face,
Offering sacrifices in the groves
     and burning incense on bricks,
4 Living among the graves
     and spending the night in caverns,
Eating swine's flesh,
     with carrion broth in their dishes,
5 Crying out, "Hold back,
     do not touch me; I am too sacred for
          you!"*

65, 5: I am too sacred for you: the uncleanness of pork, obvious to a Semite, is what these people claim has made them
sacred! The prophet ridicules them. Some translate: "I will
render you sacred," and understand this as referring to the

concept of sacredness as something contagious.

d: 1 Cor 2, 9.   e: Ps 79, 1.   f: Rom 10, 20.   g: Rom 10, 21.

These things enkindle my wrath,
a fire that burns all the day.
6 Lo, before me it stands written;
I will not be quiet until I have paid in
full
7 Your crimes and the crimes of your
fathers as well,
says the LORD.
Since they burned incense on the
mountains,
and disgraced me on the hills,
I will at once pour out in full measure
their recompense into their laps.

Fate of the Good and the Bad in Israel

8   Thus says the LORD:
When the juice is pressed from
grapes,
men say, "Do not discard them,
for there is still good in them";
Thus will I do with my servants:
I will not discard them all;
9 From Jacob I will save offspring,
from Judah, those who are to inherit
my mountains;
My chosen ones shall inherit the land,
my servants shall dwell there.
10 Sharon shall be a pasture for the
flocks
and the valley of Achor a resting place
for the cattle
of my people who have sought me.

11 But you who forsake the LORD,
forgetting my holy mountain,
You who spread a table for Fortune
and fill cups of blended wine for
Destiny,*
12 You I will destine for the sword;
you shall all go down in slaughter.
Since I called and you did not
answer,
I spoke and you did not listen,
But did what was evil in my sight
and preferred things which displease
me,[h]
13   therefore thus says the Lord GOD:
Lo, my servants shall eat,

but you shall go hungry;
My servants shall drink,
but you shall be thirsty;
My servants shall rejoice,
but you shall be put to shame;
14 My servants shall shout
for joy of heart,
But you shall cry out for grief of
heart
and howl for anguish of spirit.
15 The Lord GOD shall slay you,
and the name you leave
Shall be used by my chosen ones for
cursing;
but my servants shall be called by
another name
16 By which he will be blessed
on whom a blessing is invoked in the
land;
He who takes an oath in the land
shall swear by the God of truth;
For the hardships of the past shall be
forgotten,
and hidden from my eyes.

The World Renewed

17 Lo, I am about to create new heavens
and a new earth;
The things of the past shall not be
remembered
or come to mind.[i]
18 Instead, there shall always be rejoicing
and happiness
in what I create;
For I create Jerusalem to be a joy
and its people to be a delight;
19 I will rejoice in Jerusalem
and exult in my people.
No longer shall the sound of weeping be
heard there,
or the sound of crying;
20 No longer shall there be in it
an infant who lives but a few
days,
or an old man who does not round out
his full lifetime;
He dies a mere youth who reaches but a
hundred years,

65, 11f: Destiny: the Hebrew also has a play on the words: Destiny and destine; meni and manithi.

h: Is 66, 4; Prv 1, 24; Jer 7, 13.   i: Is 66, 22; Rv 21, 1.

and he who fails of a hundred shall be
  thought accursed.

21 They shall live in the houses they build,
  and eat the fruit of the vineyards they
    plant;
22 They shall not build houses for others to
    live in,
  or plant for others to eat.
As the years of a tree, so the years of my
    people;
  and my chosen ones shall long enjoy
    the produce of their hands.
23 They shall not toil in vain,
  nor beget children for sudden
    destruction;
For a race blessed by the LORD
  are they and their offspring.
24 Before they call, I will answer;
  while they are yet speaking, I will
    hearken to them.
25 The wolf and the lamb shall graze alike,
  and the lion shall eat hay like the ox
    [but the serpent's food shall be dust].*j*
None shall hurt or destroy
  on all my holy mountain, says the
    LORD.*

See RG
211–12

CHAPTER 66

True and False Worship

1   Thus says the LORD:
The heavens are my throne,
  the earth is my footstool.
What kind of house can you build for
    me;
  what is to be my resting place?*k*
2 My hand made all these things
  when all of them came to be, says the
    LORD.
This is the one whom I approve:
  the lowly and afflicted man who
    trembles at my word.

3 Merely slaughtering an ox is like slaying
    a man;

sacrificing a lamb, like breaking a
    dog's neck;
Bringing a cereal offering, like offering
    swine's blood;
  burning incense, like paying homage
    to an idol.
Since these have chosen their own
    ways
  and taken pleasure in their own
    abominations,*l*
4 I in turn will choose ruthless treatment
    for them*
  and bring upon them what they fear.

Because, when I called, no one
    answered,
  when I spoke, no one listened;
Because they did what was evil in my
    sight,
  and chose what gave me
    displeasure,*m*
5 Hear the word of the LORD,
  you who tremble at his word:
Your brethren who, because of my name,
  hate and reject you, say,
"Let the LORD show his glory
  that we may see your joy";
  but they shall be put to shame.
6 A sound of roaring from the city,
  a sound from the temple,
The sound of the LORD
  repaying his enemies their deserts!*n*

Mother Zion

7 Before she comes to labor,*
  she gives birth;*o*
Before the pains come upon her,
  she safely delivers a male child.
8 Who ever heard of such a thing,
  or saw the like?
Can a country be brought forth in one
    day,
  or a nation be born in a single
    moment?
Yet Zion is scarcely in labor

65, 25: See note on Is 11, 6-9.
66, 4f: Worship which is merely external is as evil as though it were idolatry.
66, 7-9: The absence of labor in Zion's childbearing is a symbol of the joyful begetting of the new people of God.

j: Is 11, 6-9. *k*: 2 Sm 7, 4ff; 1 Kgs 8, 27; Acts 7, 49; 17, 24. *l*: Lv 11, 7. *m*: Is 65, 12; Prv 1, 24; Jer 7, 13. *n*: Jl 4, 16; Am 1, 2.
o: 7-9: Is 49, 18-21; 54, 1.

when she gives birth to her children.
[9] Shall I bring a mother to the point of birth,
and yet not let her child be born? says the LORD;
Or shall I who allow her to conceive,
yet close her womb? says your God.

[10] Rejoice with Jerusalem and be glad
because of her,
all you who love her;
Exult, exult with her,
all you who were mourning over her!
[11] Oh, that you may suck fully
of the milk of her comfort,
That you may nurse with delight
at her abundant breasts!
[12]   For thus says the LORD:
Lo, I will spread prosperity over her like a river,
and the wealth of the nations like an overflowing torrent.
As nurslings, you shall be carried in her arms,
and fondled in her lap;
[13] As a mother comforts her son,
so will I comfort you;
in Jerusalem you shall find your comfort.

[14] When you see this, your heart shall rejoice,
and your bodies flourish like the grass;
The LORD's power shall be known to his servants,
but to his enemies, his wrath.

[15] Lo, the LORD shall come in fire,
his chariots like the whirlwind,
To wreak his wrath with burning heat
and his punishment with fiery flames.
[16] For the LORD shall judge all mankind
by fire and sword,
and many shall be slain by the LORD.

[17] They who sanctify and purify themselves to go to the groves, as followers of one who stands within, they who eat swine's flesh, loathsome things and mice, shall all perish with their deeds and their thoughts, says the LORD.[p]

Gathering of the Nations. [18] I come to gather nations of every language; they shall come and see my glory.* [19] I will set a sign among them; from them I will send fugitives to the nations: to Tarshish, Put and Lud, Mosoch, Tubal and Javan, to the distant coastlands that have never heard of my fame, or seen my glory; and they shall proclaim my glory among the nations. [20] They shall bring all your brethren from all the nations as an offering to the LORD, on horses and in chariots, in carts, upon mules and dromedaries, to Jerusalem, my holy mountain, says the LORD, just as the Israelites bring their offering to the house of the LORD in clean vessels. [21] Some of these I will take as priests and Levites, says the LORD.

Lasting Reward and Punishment
[22] As the new heavens and the new earth which I will make
Shall endure before me, says the LORD,
so shall your race and your name endure.[q]
[23] From one new moon to another,
and from one sabbath to another,
All mankind shall come to worship before me, says the LORD.
[24] They shall go out and see the corpses[r]
of the men who rebelled against me;
Their worm shall not die,
nor their fire be extinguished;
and they shall be abhorrent to all mankind.*

66, 18-21: God summons the neighboring nations to Zion and from among them will send some to far distant lands to proclaim his glory. All your brethren: Jews in exile.

66, 24: God's enemies lie dead outside the walls of the New Jerusalem; just as in the past, corpses, filth and refuse

lay in the Valley of Hinnom outside the city, where huge fires were constantly burning; cf Jos 15, 8; 2 Chr 28, 3; Mk 9, 45-48.

---

p: Lv 11, 29.   *q:* Is 65, 17; Rv 21, 1.   *r:* Mk 9, 45.

See RG
213–19

The Book of Jeremiah

The Book of Jeremiah combines history, biography, and prophecy. It portrays a nation in crisis and introduces the reader to an extraordinary leader upon whom the Lord placed the heavy burden of the prophetic office. Jeremiah was born about 650 B.C. of a priestly family from the little village of Anathoth, near Jerusalem. While still very young he was called to his task in the thirteenth year of King Josiah (628), whose reform, begun with enthusiasm and hope, ended with his death on the battlefield of Megiddo (609) as he attempted to stop the northward march of the Egyptian Pharaoh Neco.

The prophet heartily supported the reform of the pious King Josiah, which began in 629 B.C. Nineveh, the capital of Assyria, fell in 612, preparing the way for the new colossus, Babylon, which was soon to put an end to Judean independence.

After the death of Josiah the old idolatry returned. Jeremiah opposed it with all his strength. Arrest, imprisonment, and public disgrace were his lot. Jeremiah saw in the nation's impenitence the sealing of its doom. Nebuchadnezzar captured Jerusalem and carried King Jehoiachin into exile (22, 24).

During the years 598–587, Jeremiah attempted to counsel Zedekiah in the face of bitter opposition. The false prophet Hananiah proclaimed that the yoke of Babylon was broken and a strong pro-Egyptian party in Jerusalem induced Zedekiah to revolt. Nebuchadnezzar took swift and terrible vengeance; Jerusalem was destroyed in 587 and its leading citizens sent into exile. About this time Jeremiah uttered the great oracle of the "New Covenant" (31, 31-34) sometimes called "The Gospel before the Gospel." This passage contains his most sublime teaching and is a landmark in Old Testament theology.

The prophet remained amidst the ruins of Jerusalem, but was later forced into Egyptian exile by a band of conspirators. There, according to an old tradition, he was murdered by his own countrymen. The influence of Jeremiah was greater after his death than before. The exiled community read and meditated on the lessons of the prophet, and his influence can be seen in Ezekiel, certain of the psalms, and the second part of Isaiah. Shortly after the exile, the Book of Jeremiah as we have it today was published in a final edition.

It is divided as follows:

I: Oracles in the Days of Josiah (1, 1—6, 30).

II: Oracles Mostly in the Days of Jehoiaim (7, 1—20, 18).

III: Oracles in the Last Years of Jerusalem (21, 1—33, 26).

IV: Fall of Jerusalem (34, 1—45, 5).

V: Oracles against the Nations (46, 1—51, 64).

VI: Historical Appendix (52, 1-34).

I: Oracles in the Days of Josiah

CHAPTER 1

See RG
216

¹The words of Jeremiah, son of Hilkiah, of a priestly family in Anathoth,* in the land of Benjamin. ²The word of the LORD first came to him in the days of Josiah, son of Amon, king of Judah, in the thirteenth year of his reign,ᵃ ³and continued through the reign of Jehoiakim, son of Josiah, king of Judah, and until the downfall* and exile of Jerusalem in the fifth month of the eleventh year of Zedekiah, son of Josiah, king of Judah.ᵇ

Call of Jeremiah

⁴ The word of the LORD came to me thus:

1, 1: Anathoth: a village about three miles northeast of Jerusalem, where Solomon exiled Abiathar (1 Kgs 2, 26f); it is probable that Jeremiah belonged to the priestly family of Abiathar.

1, 3: Until the downfall: these words were originally prefixed as a title to a collection of Jeremiah's prophecies which lacked chapters 40—44. The new title in Jer 40, 1 and the oracles that follow clearly show that Jeremiah continued to prophesy after the destruction of Jerusalem in 587 B.C.

a: Jer 25, 3. b: Jer 25, 1.

To understand the book of Jeremiah, it is probably best first to skim the whole book to get a sense of the book's many voices and different kinds of literature. Then it will be helpful to return to the first chapter, Jeremiah's call, and think of it is as an introduction to the book's major themes. It is important to recall that the book is not arranged in sequence. Time does not move in a straight line. Events in the past, promises about the future, and appeals to the reader in the present are braided together. Memories about the past shape the present and remain alive in it, just as future hope changes perceptions of the present. This overlapping of time is particularly true for survivors of trauma and loss. The present and the past weave together, and hopeful anticipation for the future can burst in without preparation upon the present.

⁵ Before I formed you in the womb I knew
you,*
before you were born I dedicated you,
a prophet to the nations I appointed you.ᶜ
⁶ "Ah, Lord GOD!" I said,
"I know not how to speak; I am too
young."*
⁷ But the LORD answered me,
Say not, "I am too young."
To whomever I send you, you shall go;
whatever I command you, you shall
speak.
⁸ Have no fear before them,
because I am with you to deliver you,
says the LORD.

⁹Then the LORD extended his hand and touched my mouth, saying,

See, I place my words in your mouth!ᵈ
¹⁰ This day I set you
over nations and over kingdoms,
To root up and to tear down,
to destroy and to demolish,
to build and to plant.

¹¹The word of the LORD came to me with the question: What do you see, Jeremiah? "I see a branch of the watching-tree,"* I replied. ¹²Then the LORD said to me: Well have you seen, for I am watching to fulfill my word. ¹³ᵉA second time the word of the LORD came to me with the question: What do you see? "I see a boiling cauldron," I replied, "that appears from the north."*

¹⁴And from the north, said the LORD to me, evil will boil over upon all who dwell in the land.ᶠ

¹⁵ Lo, I am summoning
all the kingdoms of the north, says the
LORD;
Each king shall come and set up his
throne
at the gateways of Jerusalem,
Opposite her walls all around
and opposite all the cities of Judah.ᵍ
¹⁶ I will pronounce my sentence against
them
for all their wickedness in forsaking me,
And in burning incense to strange gods
and adoring their own handiwork.ʰ

¹⁷ But do you gird your loins;
stand up and tell them
all that I command you.

1, 5: Jeremiah was destined to the office of prophet before his birth; cf Is 49, 1. 5; Lk 1, 15; Gal 1, 15f. I knew you: I loved you and chose you. I dedicated you: I set you apart to be a prophet. Some Fathers and later theologians understand this to mean that Jeremiah was freed from original sin before his birth. The context does not justify this conclusion. The nations: the pagan neighbors of Judah, besides the great world powers—Assyria, Babylonia, Egypt—intimately associated with Judah's destiny.

1, 6: I am too young: Jeremiah's youth (he was less than thirty years old) must not be an obstacle to the responsibilities of the prophetic office; God will supply for his human defects (cf vv 7f).

1, 11: The watching-tree: the almond tree, which is the first to blossom in the springtime as though it had not slept. The Hebrew name contains a play on words with 'I am watching."

1, 13: Boiling cauldron . . . the north: symbol of an invasion from the north; cf vv 14f.

ᶜ: Jer 49, 1; Gal 1, 15f. ᵈ: Is 6, 7. ᵉ: Ez 11, 3. 7; 24. 3. ᶠ: Jer 4, 6; 6, 1. ᵍ: Jer 6, 22. ʰ: Is 2, 8.

Jeremiah's Call

The introductory verses of the book tell who Jeremiah was and when he prophesied. His call came during the time of King Josiah and extended until the fall of Jerusalem in 587 B.C., a 40-year period that symbolically links him with Moses' 40 years of leadership in the wilderness. Jeremiah is presented as a prophet like Moses, as promised in Deuteronomy 18, 18.

In a poetic conversation between God and Jeremiah (Jer 1, 4–10), Jeremiah receives his mission. His call before birth indicates that his prophecy was not his own invention but given to him by God. His resistance on the grounds that he is too young and so cannot speak properly also indicates that God has sent him; he has not chosen this task for himself. God tells him not to be afraid, promises to be with him, and touches his mouth. This gesture symbolizes the divine origin of the words Jeremiah speaks and the words recorded in this book. The short poem in verse 10 gives Jeremiah and his book authority in the face of opposition.

Jeremiah's mission gains substance from two visions written in prose. In verses 11–13, Jeremiah sees a branch of an almond tree, a *shaqed* in Hebrew. In a play on words, God says, "I am watching" (*shoqed*) "to fulfill my word." What God says through Jeremiah will happen. Next Jeremiah sees a "boiling cauldron, that appears from the north." The boiling pot is a symbol of destruction, overflowing and burning. The north may refer to a historical enemy, but more likely the threat from the north refers to a mythic enemy, coming like a superhuman monster. The tilting pot will spill out an army of invaders who will stream upon the land. God is "summoning all the kingdoms of the north" to invade Jerusalem. Only in Jeremiah 20, 4 will the foe from the north be identified as Babylon. Jeremiah himself should have courage to deliver God's judgment, for God will be with him.

Be not crushed on their account,
   as though I would leave you crushed
      before them;
[18] For it is I this day
   who have made you a fortified city,
A pillar of iron, a wall of brass,
   against the whole land:
Against Judah's kings and princes,
   against its priests and people.[i]
[19] They will fight against you, but not
      prevail over you,
   for I am with you to deliver you, says
      the LORD.

CHAPTER 2

See RG
216–17 *Infidelity of Israel.*[*] [1] This word of the
LORD came to me: [2] Go, cry out this message
for Jerusalem to hear!

I remember the devotion[*] of your youth,
   how you loved me as a bride,
Following me in the desert,
   in a land unsown.[j]
[3] Sacred to the LORD was Israel,
   the first fruits[*] of his harvest;
Should anyone presume to partake of them,
   evil would befall him, says the LORD.[k]

[4] Listen to the word of the LORD, O house
      of Jacob!
   All you clans of the house of Israel,
[5]   thus says the LORD:
What fault did your fathers find in me
   that they withdrew from me,
Went after empty idols,
   and became empty themselves?[l]
[6] They did not ask, "Where is the LORD

2, 1–3, 5: These verses probably contain the earliest of Jeremiah's preachings. The covenant relationship, symbolized by the figure of a marriage, was frequently broken by Israel, seen here as an unfaithful wife unworthy of reconciliation with God (Jer 3, 1-5).

2, 2: Devotion: Israel's gratitude, fidelity, and love for God.

2, 3: First fruits: an offering to God which became his exclusive property, and could therefore not be put to profane use; cf Lv 22, 1.

---

i: Jer 6, 27; 15, 20; Ex 3, 8.   *j:* Dt 2, 7; 32, 9-12; Mi 6, 4.   *k:* Jer 12, 14; Ex 4, 22; Dt 7, 6; 14, 2.   *l:* Is 5, 4; Mi 6, 3.

who brought us up from the land of
Egypt,
Who led us through the desert,
through a land of wastes and gullies,
Through a land of drought and darkness,
through a land which no one crosses,
where no man dwells?"*m*

7 When I brought you into the garden land
to eat its goodly fruits,
You entered and defiled my land,
you made my heritage loathsome.*n*
8 The priests asked not,
"Where is the LORD?"
Those who dealt with the law* knew me
not:
the shepherds rebelled against me.
The prophets prophesied by Baal,
and went after useless idols.*o*
9 Therefore will I yet accuse you, says the
LORD,
and even your children's children I
will accuse.*p*
10 Pass over to the coast of the Kittim* and
see,
send to Kedar and carefully inquire:
Where has the like of this been done?
11 Does any other nation change its gods?—
yet they are not gods at all!
But my people have changed their glory
for useless things.*q*
12 Be amazed at this, O heavens,
and shudder with sheer horror, says the
LORD.
13 Two evils have my people done:
they have forsaken me, the source of
living waters;
They have dug themselves cisterns,
broken cisterns, that hold no water.*r*

14 Is Israel a slave, a bondman by birth?*
Why then has he become booty?
15 Against him lions roar
full-throated cries.
They have made his land a waste;
his cities are charred ruins, without
inhabitant.*s*
16 Yes, the people of Memphis* and
Tahpanhes
shave the crown of your head.
17 Has not the forsaking of the LORD, your
God,
done this to you?*t*
18 And now, why go to Egypt,*
to drink the waters of the Nile?
Why go to Assyria,
to drink the waters of the Euphrates?
19 Your own wickedness chastises you,
your own infidelities punish you.
Know then, and see, how evil and bitter
is your forsaking the LORD, your God,
And showing no fear of me,
says the Lord, the GOD of hosts.*u*

20 Long ago you broke your yoke,*v*
you tore off your bonds.
"I will not serve," you said.
On every high hill, under every green tree,
you gave yourself to harlotry.*
21 I had planted you, a choice vine
of fully tested stock;
How could you turn out obnoxious to me,
a spurious vine?*w*
22 Though you scour it with soap,
and use much lye,
The stain of your guilt is still before me,
says the Lord GOD.*x*
23 How can you say, "I am not defiled,
I have not gone after the Baals"?

2, 8: Those who dealt with the law: the priests. The shepherds: the kings and nobles.

2, 10: Kittim: a Phoenician colony in Cyprus. Kedar: a nomad tribe of the Syrian desert. These two names represent West and East.

2, 14: Bondman by birth: a perpetual slave, different from the debt-slave, who was to be freed after six years; cf Ex 21, 2.

2, 16: Memphis: the capital of Lower Egypt. Tahpanhes: a frontier city of Egypt, east of the Delta. Shave the crown of your head: the spoliation of Judah at the hands of the Egyptians.

2, 18: Egypt and Assyria were the protecting foreign pow-

ers favored by rival parties within Judah. The desire for such foreign alliances is a further desertion of the Lord, the source of living waters (v 13), in favor of the above-named powers, symbolized by the Nile and the Euphrates rivers.

2, 20: Harlotry: idolatry (because Israel is the bride of God).

---

m: Ex 20, 2f; Dt 8, 14; Is 63, 11ff. *n:* Lv 18, 24f; Dt 8, 7–13; 32, 13f. *o:* Jer 8, 8ff; 23, 1. 13. *p:* Ex 20, 5. *q:* Jer 16, 20; Ps 106, 20. *r:* Jer 17, 13; Ps 36, 9; Is 1, 4. *s:* Jer 9, 11. *t:* Jer 4, 18; 30, 15. *u:* Prv 5, 22; Hos 5, 5. *v:* Jer 3, 6. 13; Jgs 10, 6. *w:* Ex 15, 17; Ps 80, 9; Is 5, 4. *x:* Jb 9, 30.

Consider your conduct in the Valley,*
  recall what you have done:
A frenzied she-camel, coursing near and
    far,
24 breaking away toward the desert,
Snuffing the wind in her ardor—
  who can restrain her lust?
No beasts need tire themselves seeking
    her;
  in her month they will meet her.

25 Stop wearing out your shoes
  and parching your throat!
But you say, "No use! no!
  I love these strangers,
  and after them I must go."ʸ
26 As the thief is shamed when caught,
  so shall the house of Israel be shamed:
They, their kings and their princes,
  their priests and their prophets;ᶻ
27 They who say to a piece of wood, "You
    are my father,"
  and to a stone, "You gave me birth."
They turn to me their backs, not their
    faces;
  yet, in their time of trouble they cry
    out,
  "Rise up and save us!"
28 Where are the gods you made for
    yourselves?
  Let them rise up!
  Will they save you in your time of
    trouble?
For as numerous as your cities
  are your gods, O Judah!
And as many as the streets of Jerusalem
  are the altars you have set up for Baal.ᵃ

29 How dare you still plead with me?
  You have all rebelled against me, says
    the LORD.
30 In vain I struck your children;
  the correction they did not take.
Your sword devoured your prophets
  like a ravening lion.ᵇ

31 You, of this generation,
  take note of the word of the Lord:
Have I been a desert to Israel,
  a land of darkness?
Why do my people say, "We have moved
    on,
  we will come to you no more"?
32 Does a virgin forget her jewelry,
  a bride her sash?
Yet my people have forgotten me
  days without number.ᶜ

33 How well you pick your way
  when seeking love!
You who, in your wickedness,
  have gone by ways unclean!
34 You, on whose clothing there is
  the life-blood of the innocent,
  whom you found committing no
    burglary;
35 Yet withal you say, "I am innocent;
  at least, his anger is turned away from
    me."
Behold, I will judge you
  on that word of yours, "I have not
    sinned."
36 How very base you have become
  in changing your course!
By Egypt will you be shamed,
  as you were shamed by Assyria.ᵈ
37 From there also shall you go away
  with hands upon your head;
For the LORD has rejected those in whom
    you trust,
  with them you will have no success.ᵉ

CHAPTER 3

See RG
216–17

1 If a man sends away his wifeᶠ
  and, after leaving him,
  she marries another man,
Does the first husband come back to her?
  Would not the land be wholly defiled?
But you have sinned with many lovers,
  and yet you would return to me! says
    the LORD.*

2, 23: The Valley: of Ben-hinnom, south of Jerusalem, site of the infamous sanctuary of Topheth where children were sacrificed to Molech; cf Jer 7, 31.

3, 1: Such remarriage of divorced spouses was forbidden by Dt 24, 1-4. Under this figure the prophet sees the presumption of Judah, the unfaithful spouse, who thinks she can return to the Lord after uniting herself to other gods.

y: Jer 18, 12. *z:* Jer 48, 27; Rom 6, 21. *a:* Jer 11, 13; Dt 32, 38; Jgs 10, 14. *b:* Jer 5, 3; Neh 9, 26. *c:* Jer 13, 25; Dt 32, 18. *d:* 2 Chr 28, 16-21. *e:* 2 Sm 13, 19. *f:* Dt 24, 1-4.

Chapters 2 and 3 use marriage and family symbolism to describe historical situations. Both the northern and southern kingdoms have betrayed God and been cast off. The northern kingdom of Israel fell to Assyria in 721 B.C., and the text explains that historical tragedy in the symbolic terms of betrayal in a marriage. The divine husband sends Jeremiah to speak to the first wife and invite her to return. The text reports no response from her. Then the invitation to return is addressed to the children (3, 14). Their father promises them restoration and reunification of the whole people in Jerusalem (vv. 15–18).

2 Lift your eyes to the heights, and see,
  where have men not lain with you?
By the waysides you waited for them
  like an Arab* in the desert.
You defiled the land
  by your wicked harlotry.g
3 Therefore the showers were withheld,
  the spring rain failed.
But because you have a harlot's brow,
  you refused to blush.h

4 Even now do you not call me, "My
    father,
  you who are the bridegroom of my
    youth"?
5 "Will he keep his wrath forever,
  will he hold his grudge to the end?"
This is what you say; yet you do
  all the evil you can.

Judah and Israel. 6The LORD said to me in the days of King Josiah: See now what rebellious Israel has done! She has gone up every high mountain, and under every green tree she has played the harlot.i 7And I thought, after she has done all this she will return to me. But she did not return. Then, even though her traitor sister Judah saw 8that for all the adulteries rebellious Israel had committed, I put her away and gave her a bill of divorce, nevertheless her traitor sister Judah was not frightened; she too went off and played the harlot.j 9Eager to sin, she polluted the land, committing adultery with stone and

wood.k 10With all this, the traitor sister Judah did not return to me wholeheartedly, but insincerely, says the LORD.

Restoration of Israel. 11Then the LORD said to me: Rebel Israel is inwardly more just than traitorous Judah.l 12Go, proclaim these words toward the north, and say:

Return, rebel Israel, says the LORD,
  I will not remain angry with you;
For I am merciful, says the LORD,
  I will not continue my wrath forever.m
13 Only know your guilt:
  how you rebelled against the LORD,
    your God,
How you ran hither and yon to strangers
  [under every green tree]
  and would not listen to my voice, says
    the LORD.n
14 Return, rebellious children, says the
    LORD,*
  for I am your Master;
I will take you, one from a city, two from
  a clan,
  and bring you to Zion.o
15 I will appoint over you shepherds after
    my own heart,
  who will shepherd you wisely and
    prudently.p
16 When you multiply and become fruitful
    in the land,
  says the LORD,
They will in those days no longer say,

3, 2: An Arab: a marauding nomad who lay in wait for caravans.

3, 14-18: A remnant of Israel (14) will reunite with Judah (18). The elementary cult of the Lord represented by the ark of the covenant will now be replaced by a more deeply spiritual and universal alliance, symbolized by his throne in the ideal Jerusalem around which all nations will be gathered together (17).

g: Ex 16, 24f. h: Jer 6, 15; 8, 12. i: Jer 2, 20; Dt 12, 2. j: 2 Kgs 17, 6. 18-23; Ez 23, 11. k: Jer 2, 27. l: Ez 16, 51; 23, 11. m: Dt 4, 29ff. n: Jer 2, 20. 25; Lv 26, 40. o: Jer 23, 3; Is 10, 21f. p: Ez 34, 23; Jn 21, 15.

"The ark of the covenant of the
  LORD!"
They will no longer think of it, or
  remember it,
  or miss it, or make another.

[17]At that time they will call Jerusalem the
LORD's throne; there all nations will be gathered together to honor the name of the LORD
at Jerusalem, and they will walk no longer in
their hardhearted wickedness.[q] [18]In those
days the house of Judah will join the house
of Israel; together they will come from the
land of the north to the land which I gave to
your fathers as a heritage.[r]

Conditions for Forgiveness

[19] I had thought:
    How I should like to treat you as sons,
And give you a pleasant land,
    a heritage most beautiful among the
      nations!
You would call me, "My Father," I
      thought,
    and never cease following me.[s]
[20] But like a woman faithless to her lover,
    even so have you been faithless to me,
    O house of Israel, says the LORD.[t]
[21] A cry is heard on the heights!
    the plaintive weeping of Israel's
      children,
Because they have perverted their ways
    and forgotten the LORD, their God.
[22] Return, rebellious children,
    and I will cure you of your rebelling.
  "Here we are, we now come to you
    because you are the LORD, our God.[u]
[23] Deceptive indeed are the hills,
    the thronging mountains;
In the LORD, our God, alone
    is the salvation of Israel.[v]
[24] The shame-god* has devoured
    our fathers' toil from our youth,
Their sheep and their cattle,
    their sons and their daughters.

[25] Let us lie down in our shame,
    let our disgrace cover us,
  for we have sinned against the LORD,
    our God,
From our youth to this day, we and our
    fathers also;
  we listened not to the voice of the
    LORD, our God."[w]

CHAPTER 4

See RG
216-17

[1] If you wish to return, O Israel,
    says the LORD,
    return to me.
If you put your detestable things out of
    my sight,
    and do not stray,[x]
[2] Then you can swear, "As the LORD lives,"*
    in truth, in judgment, and in justice;
Then shall the nations use his name in
    blessing,
    and glory in him.[y]

[3]For to the men of Judah and to Jerusalem,
thus says the LORD:

Till your untilled ground,
    sow not among thorns.[z]
[4] For the sake of the LORD, be
    circumcised,*
    remove the foreskins of your hearts,
    O men of Judah and citizens of
      Jerusalem;
Lest my anger break out like fire,
    and burn till none can quench it,
    because of your evil deeds.[a]

The Invasion from the North

[5] Proclaim it in Judah,
    make it heard in Jerusalem;
Blow the trumpet through the land,
    summon the recruits!
Say, "Fall in, let us march
    to the fortified cities."
[6] Bear the standard to Zion,
    seek refuge without delay!
Evil I bring from the north,

3, 24: Shame-god: literally, shame, a term commonly substituted for Baal, the Canaanite god with many local shrines.

4, 2: As the LORD lives: this oath, made sincerely, implies
Israel's return to God and loyal adherence to him. Thus the
ancient promises are fulfilled; cf Gn 12, 3; 18, 18; 22, 18; 26,
4; Ps 72, 17.

4, 4: The mere external rite of circumcision avails nothing

unless accompanied by the removal of blindness and obstinacy
of heart; cf Rom 2, 25. 29; 1 Cor 7, 19; Gal 5, 6; 6, 13. 15.

q: Is 2, 2. *r:* Jer 30, 3; 31, 8. *s:* Jer 31, 9. 20; Is 63, 16. *t:* Jer
5, 11. *u:* Hos 3, 5. *v:* Jer 14, 8. *w:* Jer 16, 11f; 22, 21. *x:* Jer
25, 5. *y:* Jer 12, 16; Dt 10, 20; Is 65, 16. *z:* Hos 10, 12; Mt 13,
7. 22. *a:* Jer 9, 24.

and great destruction.
7 Up comes the lion from his lair,
  the destroyer of nations has set out,
  has left his place,
To turn your land into desolation,
  till your cities lie waste and empty.*b*
8 So gird yourselves with sackcloth,
  mourn and wail:
"The blazing wrath of the LORD
  is not turned away from us."*c*

9   In that day, says the LORD,
The king will lose heart, and the princes;
  the priests will be amazed,
  and the prophets stunned.
10 "Alas! Lord GOD," they will say,
  "You only deceived us*
When you said: Peace shall be yours;
  for the sword touches our very soul."*d*
11 At that time it will be said
  of this people and of Jerusalem,
"From the glaring heights through the
    desert
  a wind comes toward the daughter of
    my people."
Not to winnow, not to cleanse,
12   does this wind from the heights come
    at my bidding;
And I myself now pronounce
  sentence upon them.*e*

13 See! like storm clouds he advances,
  like a hurricane his chariots;
Swifter than eagles are his steeds:
  "Woe to us! we are ruined."
14 Cleanse your heart of evil, O Jerusalem,
  that you may be saved.
How long must your pernicious
    thoughts
  lodge within you?
15 Listen! They proclaim it from Dan,
  from Mount Ephraim they announce
    destruction:
16 "Make this known to the nations,
  announce it to Jerusalem:

The besiegers are coming from the
    distant land,
  shouting their war cry against the
    cities of Judah."*f*
17 Like watchmen of the fields they
    surround her,
  for she has rebelled against me, says
    the LORD.*g*
18 Your conduct, your misdeeds, have done
    this to you;
  how bitter is this disaster of yours,
  how it reaches to your very heart!*h*

19 My breast! my breast! how I suffer!*
  The walls of my heart!
My heart beats wildly,
  I cannot be still;
For I have heard the sound of the
    trumpet,
  the alarm of war.
20 Ruin after ruin is reported;
  the whole earth is laid waste.
In an instant my tents are ravaged;
  in a flash, my shelters.*i*
21 How long must I see that signal,
  hear that trumpet sound!

22 Fools my people are,
  they know me not;
Senseless children they are,
  having no understanding;
They are wise in evil,
  but know not how to do good.*j*
23 I looked at the earth, and it was waste
    and void;
  at the heavens, and their light had gone
    out!*k*
24 I looked at the mountains, and they were
    trembling,
  and all the hills were crumbling!
25 I looked and behold, there was no man;
  even the birds of the air had flown
    away!
26 I looked and behold, the garden land was
    a desert,

4, 10: You only deceived us: the false prophets blame their deception on God; cf Jer 14, 13-16.
4, 19ff: Probably the prophet's own anguish at the coming destruction of Judah.

b: Jer 2, 15; 5, 6.   *c:* Jer 6, 26; Is 5, 25.   *d:* Jer 6, 14.   *e:* Jer 1, 16.   *f:* Jer 5, 15.   *g:* Jer 6, 3.   *h:* Jer 2, 17. 19.   *i:* Jer 10, 20.   *j:* Dt 32, 5f. 28.   *k:* Is 24, 1. 3.

with all its cities destroyed
before the LORD, before his blazing
wrath.[l]

27   For thus says the LORD:
Waste shall the whole land be;
    I will [not] wholly destroy it.[m]
28 Because of this the earth shall mourn,
    the heavens above shall darken;
I have spoken, I will not repent,
    I have resolved, I will not turn back.[n]
29 At the shout of horseman and
        bowman
    each city takes to flight;
They shrink into the thickets,
    they scale the rocks:
All the cities are abandoned,
    and no one dwells in them.
30 You now who are doomed, what do you
        mean
    by putting on purple,
    bedecking yourself with gold,
Shading your eyes with cosmetics,
    beautifying yourself in vain?
Your lovers spurn you,
    they seek your life.
31 Yes, I hear the moaning, as of a woman
        in travail,
    like the anguish of a mother with her
        first child—
The cry of daughter Zion gasping,
    as she stretches forth her hands:
"Ah, woe is me! I sink exhausted
    before the slayers!"[o]

See RG
216–17

CHAPTER 5

Universal Corruption

1 Roam the streets of Jerusalem,
    look about and observe,
Search through her public places,
    to find even one
Who lives uprightly
    and seeks to be faithful,
    and I will pardon her!
2 Though they say, "As the LORD lives,"
    they swear falsely.

3   O LORD, do your eyes not look for
        honesty?
You struck them, but they did not cringe;
    you laid them low, but they refused
        correction;
They set their faces harder than stone,
    and refused to return to you.[p]
4 It is only the lowly, I thought,
    who are foolish;
For they know not the way of the LORD,
    their duty to their God.[q]
5 I will go to the great ones
    and speak with them;
For they know the way of the LORD,
    their duty to their God.
But, one and all, they had broken the yoke,
    torn off the harness.[r]
6 Therefore lions from the forest slay them,
    wolves of the desert ravage them,
Leopards keep watch round their cities:
    all who come out are torn to pieces
For their many crimes
    and their numerous rebellions.
7 Why should I pardon you these things?
    Your sons have forsaken me,
    they swear by gods that are not.
I fed them, but they committed adultery;
    to the harlot's house they throng.
8 Lustful stallions they are,
    each neighs after another's wife.[s]
9 Shall I not punish them for these things?
    says the LORD;
On a nation such as this shall I not take
        vengeance?
10 Climb to her terraces, and ravage them,
    destroy them [not] wholly.
Tear away her tendrils,
    they do not belong to the LORD.[t]
11 For they have openly rebelled against me,
    both the house of Israel and the house
        of Judah,
    says the LORD,[u]
12 They denied the LORD,[*]
    saying, "Not he—
No evil shall befall us,

5, 12: They denied the LORD: the people act as though God does not exist and will not interfere.

l: Lv 26, 31.   m: Jer 5, 18.   n: Is 24, 4.   o: Jer 6, 24.   p: Jer 2, 30.   q: Jer 8, 7.   r: Jer 6, 13.   s: Jer 13, 27.   t: Jer 2, 21.   u: Jer 3, 20.

God's Reluctance to Send the Attackers

The loosely connected poems in ch 5 show that God does not wish to destroy the nation. Instead, the people are at fault because they will not act justly or repent. God is neither arbitrary nor whimsical in orchestrating the attack on the nation. In fact, God will not destroy the nation if Jeremiah can find one righteous person (v. 1). Though he runs up and down the streets of Jerusalem to the rich and the poor, Jeremiah's search is unsuccessful. God promises invasions by wild animals (v. 6), which symbolize the invading enemy.

neither sword nor famine shall we
    see.[v]
13 The prophets have become wind,
    and the word is not in them.
    May their threats be carried out against
      themselves!"

14 Now, for this that you have said,
    says the LORD, the God of hosts—
Behold, I make my words
    in your mouth, a fire,
And this people is the wood
    that it shall devour!—
15 Beware, I will bring against you
    a nation from afar,
O house of Israel, says the LORD;
A long-lived nation, an ancient nation,
    a people whose language you know not,
    whose speech you cannot understand.[w]
16 Their quivers are like open graves;
    all of them are warriors.
17 They will devour your harvest and your
      bread,
    devour your sons and your daughters,
Devour your sheep and cattle,
    devour your vines and fig trees;
They will beat flat with the sword
    the fortified city in which you trust.[x]

18 Yet even in those days, says the LORD, I will not wholly destroy you.[y] 19 And when they ask, "Why has the LORD done all these things to us?" say to them, "As you have forsaken me to serve strange gods in your own land, so shall you serve strangers in a land not your own."

20 Announce this to the house of Jacob,
    proclaim it in Judah:
21 Pay attention to this,
    foolish and senseless people
Who have eyes and see not,
    who have ears and hear not.[z]
22 Should you not fear me, says the LORD,
    should you not tremble before me?
I made the sandy shore the sea's limit,
    which by eternal decree it may not
      overstep.
Toss though it may, it is to no avail;
    though its billows roar, they cannot
      pass.[a]
23 But this people's heart is stubborn and
      rebellious;
    they turn and go away,
24 And say not in their hearts,
    "Let us fear the LORD, our God,
Who gives us rain
    early and late,* in its time;
Who watches for us
    over the appointed weeks of harvest."[b]
25 Your crimes have prevented these things,
    your sins have turned back these
      blessings from you.[c]
26 For there are among my people
      criminals;
    like fowlers they set traps,
    but it is men they catch.[d]
27 Their houses are as full of treachery
    as a bird-cage is of birds;
Therefore they grow powerful and rich,
28   fat and sleek.
They go their wicked way;

5, 24: Rain early and late: autumn and spring rains respectively. Appointed weeks of harvest: the seven weeks between the Passover (Dt 16, 9f) and Pentecost, during which it ordinarily did not rain.

v: Jer 14, 13; Is 28, 15.   w: Dt 28, 49.   x: Dt 28, 31.   y: Jer 4, 27.   z: Is 6, 9.   a: Jb 38, 10f.   b: Gn 8, 22; Dt 11, 14.   c: Jer 2, 17. 19.   d: Prv 1, 11.

justice they do not defend
By advancing the claim of the fatherless
   or judging the cause of the poor.[e]
29 Shall I not punish these things? says the
   LORD;
   on a nation such as this shall I not take
     vengeance?
30 A shocking, horrible thing
   has happened in the land:
31 The prophets prophesy falsely,
   and the priests teach as they wish;
Yet my people will have it so;
   what will you do when the end comes?[f]

CHAPTER 6

See RG
216–17

The Enemy at the Gates

1 Flee, sons of Benjamin,
   out of Jerusalem!
Blow the trumpet in Tekoa,
   raise a signal over Beth-haccherem;
For evil threatens from the north,
   and mighty destruction.[g]
2 O lovely and delicate
   daughter Zion, you are ruined!
3 Against her, shepherds come with their
     flocks;*
   all around, they pitch their tents,
   each one grazes his portion.[h]
4 "Prepare for war against her,
   Up! let us rush upon her at midday!
Alas! the day is waning,
   evening shadows lengthen;
5 Up! let us rush upon her by night,
   destroy her palaces!"[i]

6   For thus says the LORD of hosts:
Hew down her trees,
   throw up a siege mound against
     Jerusalem.
Woe to the city marked for punishment;
   nought but oppression within her![j]
7 As the well gushes out its waters,
   so she gushes out her wickedness.
Violence and destruction resound in her;
   ever before me are wounds and blows.[k]
8 Be warned, O Jerusalem,

   lest I be estranged from you;
Lest I turn you into a desert,
   a land where no man dwells.

9   Thus says the LORD of hosts:
Glean, glean like a vine
   the remnant of Israel;
Pass your hand, like a vintager,
   repeatedly over the tendrils.
10 To whom shall I speak?
   whom shall I warn, and be heard?
See! their ears are uncircumcised,
   they cannot give heed;
See, the word of the LORD has become
     for them
   an object of scorn, which they will not
     have.[l]
11 Therefore my wrath brims up within me,
   I am weary of holding it in;
I will pour it out upon the child in the
     street,
   upon the young men gathered together.
Yes, all will be taken, husband and wife,
   graybeard with ancient.[m]
12 Their houses will fall to strangers,
   their fields and their wives as well;
For I will stretch forth my hand
   against those who dwell in this land,
   says the LORD.[n]
13 Small and great alike, all are greedy for
     gain;
   prophet and priest, all practice fraud.[o]
14 They would repair, as though it were
     nought,*
   the injury to my people:
"Peace, peace!" they say,
   though there is no peace.[p]
15 They are odious; they have done
     abominable things,
   yet they are not at all ashamed,
   they know not how to blush.
Hence they shall be among those who
     fall;
   in their time of punishment they shall
     go down,
   says the LORD.[q]

6, 3: Shepherds . . . with their flocks: foreign invaders with their armies.
6, 14: As though it were nought: the false assurance of well-being given by priest and prophet cannot reduce the harm which

e: Jer 12, 1; Is 1, 23. *f:* Jer 14, 14; Mi 2, 11. *g:* Jer 1, 14f. *h:* Jer 4, 17. *i:* 2 Chr 36, 19. *j:* Jer 32, 24; Zep 3, 1-4. *k:* Is 57, 20.
l: Jer 7, 26; 20, 8. *m:* Ez 9, 6. *n:* Jer 8, 10; Dt 28, 30ff. *o:* Jer 8, 10; 23, 11. *p:* Jer 8, 11. *q:* Jer 3, 3; 8, 12.

¹⁶   Thus says the LORD:
Stand beside the earliest roads,
    ask the pathways of old*
Which is the way to good, and walk it;
    thus you will find rest for your souls.
But they said, "We will not walk it."^r
¹⁷ When I raised up watchmen* for them:
    "Hearken to the sound of the trumpet!"
    they said, "We will not hearken."
¹⁸ Therefore hear, O nations,
    and know, O earth,
    what I will do with them:
¹⁹ See, I bring evil upon this people,
    the fruit of their own schemes,
Because they heeded not my words,
    because they despised my law.^s
²⁰ Of what use to me incense that comes
        from Sheba,
    or sweet cane from far-off lands?
Your holocausts find no favor with me,
    your sacrifices please me not.^t
²¹   Therefore, thus says the LORD:
See, I will place before this people
    obstacles to bring them down;
Fathers and sons alike,
    neighbors and friends shall perish.^u

²²   Thus says the LORD:
See, a people comes from the land of the
        north,
    a great nation, roused from the ends of
        the earth.^v
²³ Bow and javelin they wield;
    cruel and pitiless are they.
They sound like the roaring sea
    as they ride forth on steeds,
Each in his place, for battle
    against you, daughter Zion.
²⁴ We hear the report of them;
    helpless fall our hands,
Anguish takes hold of us,
    throes like a mother's in childbirth.^w
²⁵ Go not forth into the field,
    step not into the street,

Beware of the enemy's sword;
    terror on every side!
²⁶ O daughter of my people, gird on
        sackcloth,
    roll in the ashes.
Mourn as for an only child
    with bitter wailing,
For sudden upon us
    comes the destroyer.^x

²⁷ A tester among my people I have
        appointed you,
    to search and test their way.^y
²⁸ Arch-rebels are they all,
    dealers in slander,
    all of them corrupt.
²⁹ The bellows roars,
    the lead is consumed by the fire;
In vain has the smelter refined,
    the wicked are not drawn off.
³⁰ "Silver rejected" they shall be called,
    for the LORD has rejected them.

II: Oracles Mostly in the Days of Jehoiakim
CHAPTER 7

See RG 217

The Temple Sermon.* ¹The following message came to Jeremiah from the LORD: ²Stand at the gate of the house of the LORD, and there proclaim this message: Hear the word of the LORD, all you of Judah who enter these gates to worship the LORD! ³Thus says the LORD of hosts, the God of Israel: Reform your ways and your deeds, so that I may remain with you in this place.^z ⁴Put not your trust in the deceitful words: "This is the temple of the LORD! The temple of the LORD! The temple of the LORD!"^a ⁵Only if you thoroughly reform your ways and your deeds; if each of you deals justly with his neighbor; ⁶if you no longer oppress the resident alien,* the orphan, and the widow; if you no longer shed innocent blood in this place, or follow

universal materialism and corruption have done to the people.

6, 16: Earliest roads . . . pathways of old: history and the lessons to be learned from it.

6, 17: Watchmen: the prophets who, like Jeremiah, had upheld God's moral law.

7, 1-15: The temple of the Lord will not serve as a place of refuge for the Jews against their enemies if they fail to

reform their evil ways.

7, 6: The resident alien: specially protected by law; cf Ex 20, 10; Nm 9, 14; 15, 14; Dt 5, 14; 28, 43.

r: Jer 7, 23f; 18, 15.   s: Prv 1, 31.   t: Is 1, 11; 43, 24.   u: Is 8, 14f.   v: Jer 1, 15; 5, 15.   w: Jer 4, 31.   x: Jer 25, 34; Am 8, 10.   y: Jer 1, 18.   z: Jer 18, 11; 26, 13.   a: Mi 3, 11.

The Temple Sermon

The long prose sermon in chs 7–8, which is presented by Jeremiah at the temple in Jerusalem, appears to interrupt the poetry of chs 1–10. The poetry contains multiple images and voices that intrude upon each other, but the prose sermon contains only the voice of Jeremiah as the divine spokesperson. The sermon's subject is the hypocrisy and arrogance of the people's worship, and it focuses attention on the people's sinfulness. The people themselves, not God, should be blamed for the destruction of the nation. Judah and its capital city, Jerusalem, fell to Babylon because their worship was false.

The sermon must have been immensely shocking for its original audience. Since the time of David, the king and the temple had been closely bound together in the people's thinking. When David came to the throne, God promised that David's son would build the temple and that David and his throne would be established forever (1 Sm 7, 1–7). A century earlier than Jeremiah, the prophet Isaiah had interpreted the promises to David as an unconditional assurance of Jerusalem's safety (Is 36–37). By the time of Jeremiah, the people of Judah seemed to think they were safe no matter what they did.

strange gods to your own harm,[b] [7]will I remain with you in this place, in the land which I gave your fathers long ago and forever.[c]

[8]But here you are, putting your trust in deceitful words to your own loss! [9]Are you to steal and murder, commit adultery and perjury, burn incense to Baal, go after strange gods that you know not,[d] [10]and yet come to stand before me in this house which bears my name, and say: "We are safe; we can commit all these abominations again"?[e] [11]Has this house which bears my name become in your eyes a den of thieves? I too see what is being done, says the LORD.[f] [12]You may go to Shiloh,* which I made the dwelling place of my name in the beginning. See what I did to it because of the wickedness of my people Israel.[g] [13]And now, because you have committed all these misdeeds, says the LORD, because you did not listen, though I spoke to you untiringly; because you did not answer, though I called you, [14]I will do to this house named after me, in which you trust, and to this place which I gave to you and your fathers, just as I did to Shiloh.[h] [15]I will cast you

away from me, as I cast away all your brethren, all the offspring of Ephraim.[i]

Abuses in Worship. [16]You, now, do not intercede for this people; raise not in their behalf a pleading prayer![j] Do not urge me, for I will not listen to you. [17]Do you not see what they are doing in the cities of Judah, in the streets of Jerusalem? [18]The children gather wood, their fathers light the fire, and the women knead dough to make cakes for the queen of heaven,* while libations are poured out to strange gods in order to hurt me.[k] [19]Is it I whom they hurt, says the LORD; is it not rather themselves, to their own confusion?[l] [20]See now, says the Lord GOD, my anger and my wrath will pour out upon this place, upon man and beast, upon the trees of the field and the fruits of the earth; it will burn without being quenched.[m]

[21]Thus says the LORD of hosts, the God of Israel: Heap your holocausts upon your sacrifices; eat up the flesh! [22]In speaking to your fathers on the day I brought them out of the land of Egypt, I gave them no command* concerning holocaust or sacrifice. [23]This rather is what I commanded them: Listen to

---

7, 12: Shiloh: original place of worship from the time of Joshua to that of Samuel. The sanctuary was later rejected by God and destroyed by the Philistines; cf 1 Sm 1, 9; 4, 3f; Ps 78, 60. 68f.

7, 18: Queen of heaven: the Assyro-Babylonian Ishtar, goddess of fertility, whose worship was introduced under King Manasseh and was revived after Josiah's death. Cakes shaped like stars (Ishtar was identified with the planet Venus) were offered in her honor.

7, 22: I gave them no command: right conduct rather than mere external cult was God's will concerning his people (v 23).

b: Ex 22, 21-24. *c:* Dt 4, 40. *d:* Jer 44, 17. *e:* Jer 32, 34. *f:* Mt 21, 13. *g:* Jos 18, 1. *h:* Jer 26, 9. *i:* 1 Kgs 9, 7; 2 Kgs 17, 23. *j:* Jer 11, 14; 14, 11. *k:* Jer 44, 17. 19. *l:* Jb 35, 6. *m:* Jer 36, 29; 2 Kgs 22, 17.

my voice; then I will be your God and you shall be my people. Walk in all the ways that I command you, so that you may prosper.[n]

[24]But they obeyed not, nor did they pay heed. They walked in the hardness of their evil hearts and turned their backs, not their faces, to me.[o] [25]From the day that your fathers left the land of Egypt even to this day, I have sent you untiringly all my servants the prophets.[p] [26]Yet they have not obeyed me nor paid heed; they have stiffened their necks and done worse than their fathers.[q] [27]When you speak all these words to them, they will not listen to you either; when you call to them, they will not answer you. [28]Say to them: This is the nation which does not listen to the voice of the LORD, its God, or take correction. Faithfulness has disappeared; the word itself is banished from their speech.

[29] Cut off your dedicated hair* and throw it
away!
   on the heights intone an elegy;
For the LORD has rejected and cast off
   the generation that draws down his
   wrath.[r]

[30]The people of Judah have done what is evil in my eyes, says the LORD. They have defiled the house which bears my name by setting up in it their abominable idols.[s] [31]In the Valley of Ben-hinnom they have built the high place of Topheth to immolate in fire their sons and their daughters, such a thing as I never commanded or had in mind. [32]Therefore, beware! days will come, says the LORD, when Topheth and the Valley of Ben-hinnom will no longer be called such, but rather the Valley of Slaughter. For lack of space, Topheth will be a burial place.[t] [33]The corpses of this people will be food for the birds of the sky and for the beasts of the field, which no one will drive away.[u] [34]In the cities of Judah and in the streets of Jerusalem I will silence the cry of joy, the cry of gladness, the voice of the bridegroom and the voice of the bride; for the land will be turned to rubble.[v]

CHAPTER 8

See RG 217

[1]At that time, says the LORD, the bones of the kings and princes of Judah, the bones of the priests and the prophets, and the bones of the citizens of Jerusalem will be emptied out of their graves[w] [2]and spread out before the sun and the moon and the whole army of heaven,* which they loved and served, which they followed, consulted, and worshiped. They will not be gathered up for burial, but will lie like dung upon the ground.[x] [3]Death will be preferred to life by all the survivors of this wicked race who remain in any of the places to which I banish them, says the LORD of hosts.

Israel's Conduct Incomprehensible
[4]   Tell them: Thus says the LORD:
When someone falls, does he not rise
   again?
   if he goes astray, does he not turn back?
[5] Why do these people rebel
   with obstinate resistance?
Why do they cling to deceptive idols,
   refuse to turn back?[y]
[6] I listen closely:
   they speak what is not true;
No one repents of his wickedness,
   saying "What have I done!"
Everyone keeps on running his course,
   like a steed dashing into battle.[z]
[7] Even the stork in the air
   knows its seasons;
Turtledove, swallow and thrush
   observe their time of return,
But my people do not know
   the ordinance of the LORD.[a]
[8] How can you say, "We are wise,[b]
   we have the law of the LORD"?
Why, that has been changed into falsehood
   by the lying pen of the scribes!*

7, 29: Dedicated hair: the unshorn hair of the nazirite, regarded as sacred because of a vow, temporary or permanent, to abstain from cutting or shaving the hair, from contact with a corpse, and from all products of the vine; cf Nm 6, 4-8. The cutting of this hair was a sign of extreme mourning.

8, 2: Army of heaven: the stars, worshiped by the pagan nations and even by the inhabitants of Jerusalem during the reigns of Manasseh and Amon.

8, 8f: Lying pen of the scribes: because the interpretations and ordinances of the scribes ran counter to the word of the Lord.

n: Jer 11, 4; Lv 26, 3. 12.   o: Jer 17, 23.   p: 2 Chr 36, 15f; Bar 1, 19.   q: Jer 19, 15; 2 Chr 30, 8.   r: Jer 9, 17-21.   s: Jer 32, 34.   t: Jer 19, 6; 32, 35.   u: Jer 16, 4; 34, 20.   v: Jer 16, 9.   w: Bar 2, 24.   x: Dt 4, 19.   y: Jer 5, 3; 7, 24. 26.   z: Jb 34, 31f.   a: Is 1, 3.   b: Mal 2, 8; Rom 2, 17-23.

Gilead (8, 22) is the part of Israel located to the east of the Jordan River, south of Bashan (Golan Heights) and north of Moab. It was apparently a site where balm and other healing substances could be extracted from local plants (see Gn 37, 25).

9 The wise are confounded,
    dismayed and ensnared;
Since they have rejected the word of the
        LORD,
    of what avail is their wisdom?[c]

Shameless in Their Crimes

10 Therefore, I will give their wives to
        strangers,
    their fields to spoilers.
Small and great alike, all are greedy for
        gain,
    prophet and priest, all practice fraud.[d]
11 They would repair, as though it were
        nought,
    the injury to the daughter of my people:*
"Peace, peace!" they say,
    though there is no peace.[e]
12 They are odious; they have done
        abominable things,
    yet they are not at all ashamed,
    they know not how to blush.
Hence they shall be among those who fall;
    in their time of punishment they shall
        go down,
    says the LORD.[f]

Threats of Punishment

13 I will gather them all in, says the LORD:
    no grapes on the vine,
No figs on the fig trees,
    foliage withered!
14 Why do we remain here?
    Let us form ranks and enter the walled
        cities,
    to perish there;
For the LORD has wrought our destruction,
    he has given us poison to drink,
    because we have sinned against the
        LORD.[g]
15 We wait for peace to no avail;

for a time of healing, but terror comes
    instead.[h]
16 From Dan is heard
    the snorting of his steeds;
The neighing of his stallions
    shakes the whole land.
They come devouring the land and all it
        contains,
    the city and those who dwell in it.
17 Yes, I will send against you
    poisonous snakes,
Against which no charm will work
    when they bite you, says the LORD.[i]

The Prophet's Grief over the People's Suffering

18 My grief is incurable,
    my heart within me is faint.
19 Listen! the cry of the daughter of my
        people,
    far and wide in the land!
Is the LORD no longer in Zion,
    is her King no longer in her midst?
[Why do they provoke me with their idols,
    with their foreign nonentities?][j]
20 "The harvest has passed, the summer is
        at an end,
    and yet we are not safe!"
21 I am broken by the ruin of the daughter
        of my people.
    I am disconsolate; horror has seized me.[k]
22 Is there no balm in Gilead,*
    no physician there?
Why grows not new flesh
    over the wound of the daughter of my
        people?[l]
23 Oh, that my head were a spring of water,
    my eyes a fountain of tears,
That I might weep day and night
    over the slain of the daughter of my
        people!

8, 11: Daughter of my people: the people itself personified as a woman.
8, 22: Gilead: noted for its healing balm but unable to heal the moral wound of the people.

c: 1 Cor 3, 20.   d: Jer 6, 13; Dt 28, 30.   e: Jer 6, 14.   f: Jer 6, 15.   g: Jer 9, 14; 23, 15.   h: Jer 14, 19.   i: Dt 32, 24.   j: Dt 32, 21;
Mi 4, 9.   k: Jer 14, 17.   l: Jer 46, 11.

See RG
217

CHAPTER 9

The Corruption of the People

1 Would that I had in the desert
   a travelers' lodge!
That I might leave my people
   and depart from them.
They are all adulterers,
   a faithless band.
2 They ready their tongues like a drawn bow;
   with lying, and not with truth,
   they hold forth in the land.
They go from evil to evil,
   but me they know not, says the LORD.
3 Be on your guard, everyone against his
   neighbor;
   put no trust in any brother.
Every brother apes Jacob, the supplanter,*
   every friend is guilty of slander.
4 Each one deceives the other,
   no one speaks the truth.
They have accustomed their tongues to
   lying,
   and are perverse, and cannot repent.ᵐ
5 Violence upon violence,
   deceit upon deceit:
They refuse to recognize me,
   says the LORD.
6   Therefore, thus says the LORD of
   hosts:
I will smelt them and test them;
   how else should I deal with their
   wickedness?
7 A murderous arrow is his tongue,
   his mouth utters deceit;
He speaks cordially with his friends,
   but in his heart he lays an ambush!ⁿ
8 For these things, says the LORD,
   shall I not punish them?
On a nation such as this
   shall I not take vengeance?ᵒ

Dirge over the Ravaged Land

9 Over the mountains, break out in cries of
   lamentation,
over the pasture lands, intone a dirge:
They are scorched, and no man crosses
   them,
   unheard is the bleat of the flock;
Birds of the air as well as beasts,
   all have fled, and are gone.ᵖ
10 I will turn Jerusalem into a heap of ruins,
   a haunt of jackals;
The cities of Judah I will make into a
   waste,
   where no one dwells.�q

11 Who is so wise that he can understand
this? Let him to whom the mouth of the
LORD has spoken make it known:

Why is the land ravaged,
   scorched like a wasteland
      untraversed?ʳ

12 The LORD answered: Because they have
abandoned my law, which I set before them,
and have not followed it or listened to my
voice, 13 but followed rather the hardness of
their hearts and the Baals, as their fathers
had taught them;ˢ 14 therefore, thus says the
LORD of hosts, the God of Israel: See now, I
will give them wormwood to eat and poison
to drink.ᵗ 15 I will scatter them among nations
whom neither they nor their fathers have
known; I will send the sword to pursue them
until I have completely destroyed them.ᵘ

16   Thus says the LORD of hosts:
Attention! tell the wailing women to come,
   summon the best of them;
17 Let them come quickly
   and intone a dirge for us,
That our eyes may be wet with weeping,
   our cheeks run with tears.ᵛ
18 The dirge is heard from Zion:
   Ruined we are, and greatly ashamed;
We must leave the land,
   give up our homes!
19 Hear, you women, the word of the LORD,
   let your ears receive his message.
Teach your daughters this dirge,

9, 3: Jacob, the supplanter: in Hebrew, a play on words. Jacob, as his name indicates ("he supplants"), deprived his brother Esau of his birthright; cf Gn 25, 26. 33.

m: Jer 12, 6.   n: Pss 28, 3; 62, 4.   o: Jer 5, 9. 29.   p: Jer 4, 25; 12, 4.   q: Is 13, 22.   r: Ps 107, 43; Hos 14, 10.   s: Jer 7, 24; 19, 4f.
t: Jer 23, 15.   u: Lv 26, 33; Dt 28, 36. 64.   v: Jer 14, 17.

and each other this lament.

²⁰ Death has come up through our windows,
has entered our palaces;
It cuts down the children in the street,
young people in the squares.ʷ

²¹ The corpses of the slain
lie like dung on a field,
Like sheaves behind the harvester,
with no one to gather them.

True Glory

²²   Thus says the LORD:
Let not the wise man glory in his wisdom,
nor the strong man glory in his strength,
nor the rich man glory in his riches;ˣ

²³ But rather, let him who glories, glory in
this,
that in his prudence he knows me,
Knows that I, the LORD, bring about
kindness,
justice and uprightness on the earth;
For with such am I pleased, says the LORD.
Circumcision Worthless. ²⁴See, days are
coming, says the LORD, when I will demand
an account of all those circumcised in their
flesh:ʸ ²⁵Egypt and Judah, Edom and the
Ammonites, Moab and the desert dwellers
who shave their temples.* For all these nations, like the whole house of Israel, are uncircumcised in heart.

CHAPTER 10

See RG 217

The Folly of Idolatry. ¹Hear the word
which the LORD speaks to you, O house of
Israel. ²Thus says the LORD:

Learn not the customs of the nations,
and have no fear of the signs of the
heavens,*
though the nations fear them.ᶻ

³ For the cult idols of the nations are nothing,
wood cut from the forest,
Wrought by craftsmen with the adze,ᵃ

⁴   adorned with silver and gold.
With nails and hammers they are fastened,
that they may not totter.ᵇ

⁵ Like a scarecrow in a cucumber field are
they,
they cannot speak;
They must be carried about,
for they cannot walk.
Fear them not, they can do no harm,
neither is it in their power to do good.ᶜ

⁶ No one is like you, O LORD,
great are you,
great and mighty is your name.ᵈ

⁷ Who would not fear you,
King of the nations,
for it is your due!

Among all the wisest of the nations,
and in all their domain,
there is none like you.ᵉ

⁸ One and all they are dumb and senseless,
these idols they teach about are wooden:

⁹ Silver strips brought from Tarshish,
and gold from Ophir,
The work of the craftsman
and the handiwork of the smelter,
Clothed with violet and purple—
all of them the work of artisans.

¹¹Thus shall you say of them: Let the gods
that did not make heaven and earth perish from
the earth, and from beneath these heavens!ᶠ

¹⁰ The LORD is true God,
he is the living God, the eternal King,
Before whose anger the earth quakes,
whose wrath the nations cannot endure:ᵍ

¹² He who made the earth by his power,
established the world by his wisdom,
and stretched out the heavens by his
skill.ʰ

¹³ When he thunders, the waters in the
heavens roar,
and he brings up clouds from the end
of the earth;
He makes the lightning flash in the rain,
and releases stormwinds from their
chambers.

9, 25: Desert dwellers . . . temples: Arab tribesmen who cut off their hair and shaved their temples in honor of the pagan god of Dushara. This was forbidden the Israelites (Lv 19, 27).

10, 2: Signs of the heavens: phenomena in the sky super-

stitiously regarded by the pagans as dire omens.

w: Jer 14, 16.   x: Prv 21, 30.   y: Jer 4, 4.   z: Bar 6, 6.   a: Wis 13, 11; Is 44, 9.   b: Is 40, 19; 41, 7.   c: Ps 115, 4-8; Bar 6, 15.   d: Ps 86, 8ff. e: Jer 5, 22; Ps 47, 2. 8.   f: Ps 96, 5.   g: Ps 10, 16.   h: Ps 104, 5.

Hymn of Praise

The first 16 verses of ch 10 contain a hymn that expresses loyalty to the one true God and makes fun of other gods as worthless idols. The hymn serves as a model of repentance and reconciliation for the exiles surviving the nation's collapse. The poem is similar in subject and worship style to the repentance of the children from the broken family (3, 22–25). The people should neither become like the nations around them nor adopt their idolatrous customs. Israel's God is the true king of the nations; by contrast, the gods of the nations are stupid, human creations. Only the God of Israel is the Creator whose wisdom made the world. Israel is God's special inheritance. In this hymn, creation's harmony is reestablished.

[14] Every man is stupid, ignorant;
  every artisan is put to shame by his idol:
He has molded a fraud,
  without breath of life.[i]
[15] Nothingness are they, a ridiculous work;
  they will perish in their time of punishment.
[16] Not like these is the portion of Jacob:
  he is the creator of all things;
Israel is his very own tribe,
  LORD of hosts is his name.[j]

Abandonment of Judah
[17] Lift your bundle and leave the land,
  O city living in a state of siege!
[18]   For thus says the LORD:
Behold, this time
  I will sling away the inhabitants of the land;
I will hem them in,
  that they may be taken.
[19] Woe is me! I am undone,
  my wound is incurable;
Yet I had thought:
  if I make light of my wound, I can bear it.
[20] My tent is ruined,
  all its cords are severed.
My sons have left me, they are no more:
  no one to pitch my tent,
  no one to raise its curtains.[k]
[21] Yes, the shepherds were stupid as cattle,
  the LORD they sought not;
Therefore they had no success,
  and all their flocks were scattered.[l]
[22] Listen! a noise! it comes closer,

a great uproar from the northern land:
To turn the cities of Judah
  into a desert haunt of jackals.

Prayer of Jeremiah
[23] You know, O LORD,
  that man is not master of his way;
Man's course is not within his choice,
  nor is it for him to direct his step.
[24] Punish us, O LORD, but with equity,
  not in anger, lest you have us dwindle away.
[25] Pour out your wrath on the nations that know you not,
  on the tribes that call not upon your name;
For they have devoured Jacob utterly,
  and laid waste his dwelling.[m]

CHAPTER 11

See RG 217

Plea for Fidelity to the Covenant. [1]The following message came to Jeremiah from the LORD: [2]Speak to the men of Judah and to the citizens of Jerusalem, [3]saying to them: Thus says the LORD, the God of Israel: Cursed be the man who does not observe the terms of this covenant,[n] [4]which I enjoined upon your fathers the day I brought them up out of the land of Egypt, that iron foundry, saying: Listen to my voice and do all that I command you. Then you shall be my people, and I will be your God.[o] [5]Thus I will fulfill the oath which I swore to your fathers, to give them a land flowing with milk and honey: the one you have today. "Amen, LORD," I answered.

i: Rom 1, 22f. *j*: Jer 31, 35. *k*: Jer 4, 20. *l*: Jer 23, 1; Ez 34, 5f. *m*: Ps 79, 6f. *n*: Dt 27, 26. *o*: Dt 4, 20; 1 Kgs 8, 51.

[6]Then the LORD said to me: Proclaim all these words in the cities of Judah and in the streets of Jerusalem: Hear the words of this covenant and obey them. [7]Urgently and constantly I warned your fathers to obey my voice, from the day I brought them up out of the land of Egypt even to this day. [8]But they did not listen or give ear. Each one followed the hardness of his evil heart, till I brought upon them all the threats of this covenant which they had failed to observe as I commanded them.[p]

[9]A conspiracy has been found, the LORD said to me, among the men of Judah and the citizens of Jerusalem. [10]They have returned to the crimes of their forefathers who refused to obey my words. They also have followed and served strange gods; the covenant which I had made with their fathers, the house of Israel and the house of Judah have broken.[q] [11]Therefore, thus says the LORD: See, I bring upon them misfortune which they cannot escape. Though they cry out to me, I will not listen to them.[r] [12]Then the cities of Judah and the citizens of Jerusalem will go and cry out to the gods to which they have been offering incense. But these gods will give them no help whatever when misfortune strikes.[s]

[13] For as numerous as your cities
    are your gods, O Judah!
And as many as the streets of Jerusalem
    are the altars for offering sacrifice to
        Baal.[t]

[14]Do not intercede on behalf of this people, nor utter a plea for them. I will not listen when they call to me at the time of their misfortune.[u]

Sacrifices of No Avail

[15] What right has my beloved in my house,
    while she prepares her plots?
Can vows and sacred meat turn away
    your misfortune from you?
Will you still be jubilant
[16]   when you hear the great invasion?
A spreading olive tree, goodly to behold,
    the LORD has named you;
Now he sets fire to it,
    its branches burn.

[17]The LORD of hosts who planted you has decreed misfortune for you because of the evil done by the house of Israel and by the house of Judah, who provoked me by sacrificing to Baal.[v]

The Plot against Jeremiah. [18]I knew it because the LORD informed me; at that time you, O LORD, showed me their doings.

See RG 217

CHAPTER 12

[1] You would be in the right, O LORD,
    if I should dispute with you;
    even so, I must discuss the case with
        you.
Why does the way of the godless prosper,
    why live all the treacherous in
        contentment?[w]
[2] You planted them; they have taken root,
    they keep on growing and bearing fruit.
You are upon their lips,
    but far from their inmost thoughts.[x]
[3] You, O Lord, know me, you see me,
    you have found that at heart I am with
        you.[y]
Pick them out like sheep for the slaughter,
    set them apart for the day of carnage.[*]
[4] How long must the earth mourn,
    the green of the whole countryside
        wither?
For the wickedness of those who dwell in it
    beasts and birds disappear,
    because they say, "God does not see
        our ways."

[5] If running against men has wearied you,
    how will you race against horses?
And if in a land of peace you fall headlong,
    what will you do in the thickets of the
        Jordan?

[6]For even your own brothers, the members of your father's house, betray you; they have

12, 3: Jeremiah does not seek private vengeance but the punishment of the wicked by the Lord; cf Jer 20, 12. Nevertheless, the prophet's reaction to persecution shows the difference between the spirit of the Old Testament and the New.

p: 2 Kgs 17, 14. *q*. Dt 31, 16; Ez 20, 21-30. *r*: Jer 14, 12; Mi 3, 4. *s*: Dt 32, 37f. *t*: Jer 2, 28; Hos 10, 1. *u*: Jer 7, 16; 14, 11.
v: Is 5, 2. *w*: Jb 21. 7; Mal 3, 15. *x*: Is 29, 13. *y*: Jer 17, 18; Jb 23, 10.

Jeremiah's Lament

Chapter 12 opens with the first of several laments of Jeremiah (12, 1–6.19–23; 15, 10–21; 17, 14–18; 18, 18–23; 20, 7–13; 20, 14–18), in which he complains to God concerning his own suffering for announcing divine judgment to the people. The language is typical of complaint language of the Psalms (e.g., Ps 7) and Lamentations, but it nevertheless provides an intimate glimpse of the prophet's own feelings. These laments, sometimes called "confessions," typify Jeremiah, in whose book there is more biographical information than in those of all of the other prophets combined.

recruited a force against you. Do not believe them, even if they are friendly to you in their words.[z]

[19]*Yet I, like a trusting lamb led to slaughter, had not realized that they were hatching plots against me: "Let us destroy the tree in its vigor; let us cut him off from the land of the living, so that his name will be spoken no more."[a]

[20] But, you, O LORD of hosts, O just Judge, searcher of mind and heart,
Let me witness the vengeance you take on them,
for to you I have entrusted my cause![b]

[21]Therefore, thus says the LORD concerning the men of Anathoth who seek your life, saying, "Do not prophesy in the name of the LORD; else you shall die by our hand."[c]
[22]Therefore, thus says the LORD of hosts: I am going to punish them. The young men shall die by the sword; their sons and daughters shall die by famine.[d] [23]None shall be spared among them, for I will bring misfortune upon the men of Anathoth, the year of their punishment.[e]

The Lord's Complaint
[7] I abandon my house,
cast off my heritage;
The beloved of my soul I deliver
into the hand of her foes.[f]
[8] My heritage has turned on me
like a lion in the jungle;
Because she has roared against me,
I treat her as an enemy.[g]
[9] My heritage is a prey for hyenas,
is surrounded by vultures;
Come, gather together, all you beasts of the field,
come and eat![h]
[10] Many shepherds have ravaged my vineyard,
have trodden my heritage underfoot;
The portion that delighted me they have turned
into a desert waste.[i]
[11] They have made it a mournful waste,
desolate it lies before me,
Desolate, all the land,
because no one takes it to heart.
[12] Upon every desert height
brigands have come up.
The LORD has a sword which consumes
the land, from end to end:
no peace for all mankind.[j]
[13] They have sown wheat and reaped thorns,
they have tired themselves out to no purpose;
They recoil before their harvest,
the flaming anger of the LORD.

Judah's Neighbors. [14]Thus says the LORD against all my evil neighbors* who plunder the heritage which I gave my people Israel as their own: See, I will pluck them up from their land; the house of Judah I will pluck up in their midst.[k] [15]But after plucking them up, I will pity them again and bring them back, each to his heritage, each to his land.[l] [16]And

12, 19-23: These verses have been transposed from ch 11.
12, 14: My evil neighbors: nations surrounding Israel, the land belonging to the Lord; cf Is 8, 8.

z: Jer 9, 4.   a: Jer 18, 18; 20, 10; Wis 2, 20.   b: Jer 15, 15.   c: Am 7, 13. 16.   d: Jer 18, 21f.   e: Jer 23, 12.   f: Ps 78, 62; Lam 2, 1f.   g: Ps 106, 40.   h: 2 Kgs 24, 2; Is 56, 9.   i: Jer 6, 3; Is 63, 18.   j: Is 42, 25; 57, 21.   k: 2 Kgs 24, 2.   l: Am 9, 14.

if they carefully learn my people's custom of swearing by my name, "As the LORD lives," they who formerly taught my people to swear by Baal shall be built up in the midst of my people.[m] [17]But if they do not obey, I will uproot and destroy that nation entirely, says the LORD.[n]

See RG
217

CHAPTER 13

Judah's Corruption.* [1]The LORD said to me: Go buy yourself a linen loincloth; wear it on your loins, but do not put it in water. [2]I bought the loincloth, as the LORD commanded, and put it on. [3]A second time the word of the LORD came to me thus: [4]Take the loincloth which you bought and are wearing, and go now to the Parath; there hide it in a cleft of the rock. [5]Obedient to the LORD's command, I went to the Parath and buried the loincloth. [6]After a long interval, he said to me: Go now to the Parath and fetch the loincloth which I told you to hide there. [7]Again I went to the Parath, sought out and took the loincloth from the place where I had hid it. But it was rotted, good for nothing! [8]Then the message came to me from the LORD: [9]Thus says the LORD: So also I will allow the pride of Judah to rot, the great pride of Jerusalem.[o] [10]This wicked people who refuse to obey my words, who walk in the stubbornness of their hearts, and follow strange gods to serve and adore them, shall be like this loincloth which is good for nothing.[p] [11]For, as close as the loincloth clings to a man's loins, so had I made the whole house of Israel and the whole house of Judah cling to me, says the LORD; to be my people, my renown, my praise, my beauty. But they did not listen.[q]

The Broken Wineflask. [12]Now speak to them this word: Thus says the LORD, the God of Israel: Every wineflask is meant to be filled with wine. If they reply, "Do we not know that every wineflask is meant to be filled with wine?" [13]say to them: Thus says the LORD: Beware! I am filling with drunkenness all the inhabitants of this land, the kings who succeed to David's throne, the priests and prophets, and all the citizens of Jerusalem.[r] [14]I will dash them against each other, fathers and sons together, says the LORD; I will show no compassion, I will not spare or pity, but will destroy them.[s]

A Last Warning
[15] Give ear, listen humbly,
  for the LORD speaks.
[16] Give glory to the LORD, your God,
  before it grows dark;
Before your feet stumble
  on darkening mountains;
Before the light you look for turns to
  darkness,
  changes into black clouds.[t]
[17] If you do not listen to this in your pride,
  I will weep in secret many tears;
My eyes will run with tears
  for the LORD's flock, led away to exile.[u]

Exile
[18] Say to the king and to the queen mother:
  come down from your throne;
From your heads fall
  your magnificent crowns.[v]
[19] The cities of the Negeb are besieged,
  with no one to relieve them;
All Judah is banished
  in universal exile.

Jerusalem's Disgrace
[20] Lift up your eyes and see
  men coming from the north.
Where is the flock entrusted to you,
  the sheep that were your glory?[w]
[21] What will you say when they place as
  rulers over you
  those whom you taught to be your
  lovers?
Will not pangs seize you
  like those of a woman giving birth?[x]

13, 1-11: This is probably a vision of the prophet symbolizing the religious corruption of Judah at the hands of the Babylonians, represented here by the river Parath, the Euphrates; though a spring of the same name, northeast of Anathoth, may be directly meant.

m: Dt 6, 13.　n: Is 60, 12.　o: Prv 16, 18.　p: Jer 2, 20; 7, 24; 16, 11.　q: Ex 19, 5; Dt 26, 18f.　r: Jer 25, 15-18; Is 51, 17.　s: Jer 19, 10f.　t: Prv 4, 18f; Is 5, 30; Am 8, 9.　u: Jer 14, 17; Ps 119, 136.　v: Jer 22, 26; 2 Kgs 24, 12. 15.　w: Jer 6, 22f.　x: 2 Kgs 16, 7.

22 If you ask in your heart
    why these things befall you:
For your great guilt your skirts are
        stripped away
    and you are violated.*y*

23 Can the Ethiopian change his skin?
    the leopard his spots?
As easily would you be able to do good,
    accustomed to evil as you are.*z*

24 I will scatter them like chaff that flies
    when the desert wind blows.*a*

25 This is your lot, the portion measured out
        to you
    from me, says the LORD.
Because you have forgotten me,
    and trusted in the lying idol,*b*

26 I now will strip off your skirts from
        you,
    so that your shame will appear.*c*

27 Your adulteries, your neighings,
    your shameless prostitutions:
On the hills in the highlands
    I see these horrible crimes of yours.
Woe to you, Jerusalem, how long will it
       yet be
    before you become clean!*d*

CHAPTER 14

See RG 217

The Great Drought. ¹The word of the LORD that came to Jeremiah concerning the drought:*e*

2 Judah mourns,
    her gates are lifeless;
Her people sink down in mourning:
    from Jerusalem ascends a cry of
        anguish.*f*

3 The nobles send their servants for
       water,
    but when they come to the cisterns
They find no water
    and return with empty jars.*g*
Ashamed, despairing, they cover their
       heads

4   because of the stricken soil;
Because there is no rain in the land
    the farmers are ashamed, they cover
       their heads.*h*

5 Even the hind in the field deserts her
       offspring
    because there is no grass.

6 The wild asses stand on the bare heights,
    gasping for breath like jackals;
Their eyes grow dim,
    because there is no vegetation to be
       seen.

7 Even though our crimes bear witness
       against us,
    take action, O LORD, for the honor of
       your name—
Even though our rebellions are many,
    though we have sinned against you.*i*

8 O Hope of Israel, O LORD,
    our savior in time of need!
Why should you be a stranger in this
       land,
    like a traveler who has stopped but for
       a night?

9 Why are you like a man dumbfounded,
    a champion who cannot save?
You are in our midst, O LORD,
    your name we bear:
    do not forsake us!*j*

10   Thus says the LORD of this people:
They so love to wander
    that they do not spare their feet.
The LORD has no pleasure in them;
    now he remembers their guilt,
    and will punish their sins.*k*

¹¹Then the LORD said to me: Do not intercede for this people.*l* ¹²If they fast, I will not listen to their supplication. If they offer holocausts or cereal offerings, I will not accept them. Rather, I will destroy them with the sword, famine, and pestilence.*m*

¹³Ah! Lord GOD, I replied, it is the prophets who say to them, "You shall not see the sword; famine shall not befall you. Indeed, I will give you lasting peace in this place."*n*

¹⁴Lies these prophets utter in my name, the LORD said to me. I did not send them; I gave them no command nor did I speak to them. Lying visions, foolish divination,

---

y: Is 47, 2f.   *z:* Ps 55, 20.   *a:* Pss 1, 4; 83, 14.   *b:* Jb 20, 29.   *c:* Ez 16, 32.   *d:* Jer 2, 20.   *e:* Lv 26, 19f.   *f:* Is 3, 26.   *g:* Am 4, 8.   *h:* Dt 28, 23.   *i:* Dn 9, 4-14.   *j:* Is 59, 1f; 63, 19.   *k:* Jer 2, 25.   *l.* Jer 11, 14; Ex 32, 10.   *m:* Jer 6, 20; Is 1, 11. 13.   *n:* Jer 4, 10; 5, 12.

Jeremiah's Lament over Jerusalem's Inevitable Punishment

The theme of Jerusalem's punishment continues in ch 15, and Jeremiah laments his task and the city's fate. Jerusalem's punishment is inevitable; not even Moses and Samuel, the great earlier prophetic intercessors, could convince God to reverse the decision. The four punishments—death, sword, famine, and captivity—represent a comprehensive list of punishments not unlike those mentioned in Ezekiel ch 5. Even animals participate in the judgment.

dreams of their own imagination, they prophesy to you.*o* *15*Therefore, thus says the LORD: Concerning the prophets who prophesy in my name, though I did not send them; who say, "Sword and famine shall not befall this land": by the sword and famine shall these prophets meet their end.*p* *16*The people to whom they prophesy shall be cast out into the streets of Jerusalem by famine and the sword. No one shall bury them, their wives, their sons, or their daughters, for I will pour out upon them their own wickedness.*q* *17*Speak to them this word:

Let my eyes stream with tears
    day and night, without rest,
Over the great destruction which
        overwhelms
    the virgin daughter of my people,
    over her incurable wound.*r*
18 If I walk out into the field,
    look! those slain by the sword;
If I enter the city,
    look! those consumed by hunger.
Even the prophet and the priest
    forage in a land they know not.

19 Have you cast Judah off completely?
    Is Zion loathsome to you?
Why have you struck us a blow
    that cannot be healed?
We wait for peace, to no avail;
    for a time of healing, but terror comes
        instead.*s*
20 We recognize, O LORD, our
        wickedness,
    the guilt of our fathers;

that we have sinned against you.*t*
21 For your name's sake spurn us not,
    disgrace not the throne of your glory;
    remember your covenant with us, and
        break it not.*u*
22 Among the nations' idols is there any that
        gives rain?
Or can the mere heavens send
        showers?
Is it not you alone, O LORD,
    our God, to whom we look?
    You alone have done all these things.*v*

CHAPTER 15

See RG 217

*1*The LORD said to me: Even if Moses and Samuel stood before me, my heart would not turn toward this people. Send them away from me.*w* *2*If they ask you where they should go, tell them, Thus says the LORD: Whoever is marked for death, to death; whoever is marked for the sword, to the sword; whoever is marked for famine, to famine; whoever is marked for captivity, to captivity.*x* *3*Four kinds of scourge I have decreed against them, says the LORD: the sword to slay them; dogs to drag them about; the birds of the sky and the beasts of the earth to devour and destroy them.*y* *4*And I will make them an object of horror to all the kingdoms of the earth because of what Manasseh, son of Hezekiah, king of Judah, did in Jerusalem.*z*

Scene of Tragedy

5 Who will pity you, Jerusalem,
    who will console you?
Who will stop to ask

o: Jer 5, 31; 23, 16.   p: Jer 5, 12f.   q: Jer 7, 33; 19, 7.   r: Jer 9, 17.   s: Jer 8, 15; 2 Chr 36, 16.   t: Ps 106, 6; Dn 9, 5. 8.   u: Jer 14, 7; Lv 26, 44; Ps 25, 11.   v: Jer 5, 24; Zec 10, 1.   w: Ps 99, 6; Ez 14, 14. 16.   x: Jer 14, 12; Ez 5, 12.   y: Ez 14, 21.   z: Jer 24, 9; 2 Kgs 21, 11-16; 23, 26; 24, 3f.

about your welfare?[a]

⁶ You have disowned me, says the LORD,
   turned your back upon me;
And so I stretched out my hand to
      destroy you,
   I was weary of sparing you.[b]
⁷ I winnowed them with the fan
   in every city gate.
I destroyed my people through
      bereavement;
   they returned not from their evil ways.[c]
⁸ Their widows were more numerous
      before me
   than the sands of the sea.
I brought against the mother of youths
   the spoiler at midday;
Suddenly I struck her
   with anguish and terror.
⁹ The mother of seven swoons away,
   gasping out her life;
Her sun sets in full day,
   she is disgraced, despairing.
Their survivors I will give to the sword
   before their enemies, says the LORD.[d]

Jeremiah's Complaint

¹⁰ Woe to me, mother, that you gave me
      birth!
   a man of strife and contention to all
      the land!
I neither borrow nor lend,
   yet all curse me.[e]
¹¹ Tell me, LORD, have I not served you for
      their good?
   Have I not interceded with you
   in the time of misfortune and anguish?[f]*
¹⁵   You know I have.
Remember me, LORD, visit me,
   and avenge me on my persecutors.
Because of your long-suffering banish
      me not;
   know that for you I have borne
      insult.[g]
¹⁶ When I found your words, I devoured
      them;

they became my joy and the happiness
   of my heart,
Because I bore your name,
   O LORD, God of hosts.
¹⁷ I did not sit celebrating
   in the circle of merrymakers;
Under the weight of your hand I sat alone
   because you filled me with indignation.[h]
¹⁸ Why is my pain continuous,
   my wound incurable, refusing to be
      healed?
You have indeed become for me a
      treacherous brook,*
   whose waters do not abide![i]
¹⁹   Thus the LORD answered me:
If you repent, so that I restore you,
   in my presence you shall stand;
If you bring forth the precious without
      the vile,
   you shall be my mouthpiece.
Then it shall be they who turn to you,
   and you shall not turn to them;
²⁰ And I will make you toward this people
   a solid wall of brass.
Though they fight against you,
   they shall not prevail,
For I am with you,
   to deliver and rescue you, says the
      LORD.[j]
²¹ I will free you from the hand of the
      wicked,
   and rescue you from the grasp of the
      violent.

CHAPTER 16

Jeremiah's Life a Warning.

See RG 217

¹This message came to me from the LORD: ²Do not marry any woman; you shall not have sons or daughters in this place, ³for thus says the LORD concerning the sons and daughters who will be born in this place, the mothers who will give them birth, the fathers who will beget them in this land: ⁴Of deadly disease they shall die. Unlamented and unburied they will lie like dung on the ground.

15, 12-14: These verses are omitted because v 12 is a dittography of 17, 1. Verses 13-14 are a dittography of 17, 3 f.

15, 18: A treacherous brook: that dries up when its waters are needed. The prophet complains that he cannot rely on God with unfailing assurance of his assistance.

a: Is 51, 19.   *b:* Am 7, 8.   *c:* Is 41, 16.   *d:* 1 Sm 2, 5.   *e:* Jer 20, 14.   *f:* Jer 39, 11-14.   *g:* Jer 11, 20; 12, 3; Ps 69, 8.   *h:* Ps 25, 4.
i: Jer 14, 19; 30, 15.   *j:* Jer 1, 18; 6, 27.

Sword and famine will make an end of them, and their corpses will become food for the birds of the sky and the beasts of the field.[k]

[5]Go not into a house of mourning, the LORD continued: go not there to lament or offer sympathy. For I have withdrawn my friendship from this people, says the LORD, my kindness and my pity.[l] [6]They shall die, the great and the lowly, in this land, and shall go unburied and unlamented.* No one will gash himself or shave his head for them.[m] [7]They will not break bread with the bereaved to console them in their bereavement; they will not give them the cup of consolation to drink over the death of father or mother.[n]

[8]Enter not a house where people are celebrating, to sit with them eating and drinking. [9]For thus says the LORD of hosts, the God of Israel: Before your very eyes and during your lifetime I will silence from this place the cry of joy and the cry of gladness, the voice of the bridegroom and the voice of the bride.[o]

[10]When you proclaim all these words to this people and they ask you: "Why has the LORD pronounced all these great evils against us? What is our crime? What sin have we committed against the LORD, our God?"[p] — [11q]you shall answer them: It is because your fathers have forsaken me, says the LORD, and followed strange gods, which they served and worshiped; but me they have forsaken, and my law they have not observed. [12]And you have done worse than your fathers. Here you are, every one of you, walking in the hardness of his evil heart instead of listening to me.[r] [13]I will cast you out of this land into a land that neither you nor your fathers have known; there you can serve strange gods day and night, because I will not grant you my mercy.

Return from Exile. [14]However, days will surely come, says the LORD, when it will no longer be said, "As the LORD lives, who brought the Israelites out of Egypt";[s] [15]but rather, "As the LORD lives, who brought the Israelites out of the land of the north and out of all the countries to which he had banished them." I will bring them back to the land which I gave their fathers.[t]

Double Punishment. [16]Look! I will send many fishermen, says the LORD, to catch them. After that, I will send many hunters to hunt them out from every mountain and hill and from the clefts of the rocks.[u] [17]For my eyes are upon all their ways; they are not hidden from me, nor does their guilt escape my view.[v] [18]I will at once repay them double for their crime and their sin of profaning my land with their detestable corpses of idols, and filling my heritage with their abominations.[w]

Conversion of the Heathen

[19] O LORD, my strength, my fortress,
  my refuge in the day of distress!
To you will the nations come
  from the ends of the earth, and say,
"Mere frauds are the heritage of our
    fathers,
  empty idols of no use."[x]
[20] Can man make for himself gods?
    These are not gods.[y]
[21] Look, then: I will give them knowledge;
    this time I will leave them in no doubt
Of my strength and my power:
  they shall know that my name is LORD.[z]

CHAPTER 17

The Sin of Judah and
Its Punishment

See RG 217

[1] The sin of Judah is written
  with an iron stylus,
Engraved with a diamond point
  upon the tablets of their hearts.[a]

[And the horns of their altars, [2]when their sons remember their altars and their sacred poles, beside the green trees, on the high hills, [3]the peaks in the highland.]

Your wealth and all your treasures
  I will give as spoil.

16, 6f: These verses refer to popular mourning practices, sometimes connected with pagan superstition; cf Dt 14, 1f.

---

k: Jer 7, 33; 22, 18.   l: Ez 24, 16f.   m: Lv 19, 28; Dt 14, 1.   n: Ez 24, 17.   o: Jer 7, 34; 25, 10.   p: Jer 2, 35; 5, 19; 13, 22.   q: Jer 22, 9; Dt 29, 25.   r: Jer 7, 24ff.   s: Jer 23, 7f.   t: Jer 24, 6.   u: 2 Kgs 24, 2; Lam 4, 19.   v: Jer 32, 19; Jb 34, 21.   w: Is 40, 2.   x: Jer 2, 11; Is 2, 2f.   y: Jer 2, 11; Gal 4, 8.   z: Am 5, 8.   a: Jb 19, 24.

In recompense for all your sins
    throughout your borders,
[4] You will relinquish your hold on your
    heritage
    which I have given you.
I will enslave you to your enemies
    in a land that you know not:
For a fire has been kindled by my wrath
    that will burn forever.[b]

True Wisdom

[5]   Thus says the LORD:
Cursed is the man who trusts in human
    beings,
    who seeks his strength in flesh,
    whose heart turns away from the
      LORD.[c]
[6] He is like a barren bush in the desert
    that enjoys no change of season,
But stands in a lava waste,
    a salt and empty earth.
[7] Blessed is the man who trusts in the LORD,
    whose hope is the LORD.[d]
[8] He is like a tree planted beside the waters
    that stretches out its roots to the
      stream:
It fears not the heat when it comes,
    its leaves stay green;
In the year of drought it shows no
    distress,
    but still bears fruit.[e]
[9] More tortuous than all else is the human
    heart,
    beyond remedy; who can understand
      it?
[10] I, the LORD, alone probe the mind
    and test the heart,
To reward everyone according to his ways,
    according to the merit of his deeds.[f]
[11] A partridge that mothers a brood not her
    own
    is the man who acquires wealth
      unjustly:
In midlife it will desert him;
    in the end he is only a fool.[g]

The Source of Life

[12] A throne of glory, exalted from the
    beginning,
    such is our holy place.[h]
[13] O hope of Israel, O LORD!
    all who forsake you shall be in disgrace;
The rebels in the land shall be put to
    shame;
    they have forsaken the source of living
    waters
    [the LORD].[i]

Prayer for Vengeance

[14] Heal me, LORD, that I may be healed;
    save me, that I may be saved,
    for it is you whom I praise.
[15] See how they say to me,
    "Where is the word of the LORD?
    Let it come to pass!"[j]
[16] Yet I did not press you to send calamity;
    the day without remedy I have not
      desired.
You know what passed my lips;
    it is present before you.
[17] Do not be my ruin,
    you, my refuge in the day of
      misfortune.[k]
[18] Let my persecutors, not me, be
    confounded;
    let them, not me, be broken.
Bring upon them the day of misfortune,
    crush them with repeated destruction.[l]

Observance of the Sabbath. [19]Thus said
the LORD to me: Go, stand at the Gate of
Benjamin,* where the kings of Judah enter
and leave, and at the other gates of Jerusalem.[m] [20]There say to them: Hear the word of
the LORD, you kings of Judah, and all Judah,
and all you citizens of Jerusalem who enter
these gates! [21]Thus says the LORD: As you
love your lives, take care not to carry burdens on the sabbath day, to bring them in
through the gates of Jerusalem.[n] [22]Bring no
burden from your homes on the sabbath. Do
no work whatever, but keep holy the sab-

17, 19: The Gate of Benjamin: probably the northern gate of the temple area and city wall of Jerusalem; cf Jer 20. 2; 37,
12; 38, 7.

b: Jer 5, 19; Dt 32, 22. c: Ps 146, 2f. d: Ps 1, 3. e: Is 58, 11. f: Jer 32, 19; 1 Sm 16, 7; Eccl 12, 14. g: Prv 13, 11; Lk 12, 20.
h: Jer 14, 21. i: Jer 2, 13. j: Is 5, 19; 2 Pt 3, 4. k: Jer 16, 19. l: Jer 15, 15; 18, 20-23; Ps 35, 5f. m: Jer 7, 2. n: Neh 13, 15-19.

bath, as I commanded your fathers,[o] [23]though they did not listen or give ear, but stiffened their necks so as not to hear or take correction.[p] [24]If you obey me wholeheartedly, says the LORD, and carry no burden through the gates of this city on the sabbath, keeping the sabbath holy and abstaining from all work on it,[q] [25]then, through the gates of this city, kings who sit upon the throne of David will continue to enter, riding in their chariots or upon their horses, along with their princes, and the men of Judah, and the citizens of Jerusalem. This city will remain inhabited forever.[r] [26]To it people will come from the cities of Judah and the neighborhood of Jerusalem, from the land of Benjamin and from the foothills, from the hill country and the Negeb, to bring holocausts and sacrifices, cereal offerings and incense and thank offerings to the house of the LORD.[s] [27]But if you do not obey me and keep holy the sabbath, if you carry burdens and come through the gates of Jerusalem on the sabbath, I will set unquenchable fire to its gates, which will consume the palaces of Jerusalem.[t]

CHAPTER 18

See RG 217

The Potter's Vessel.* [1]This word came to Jeremiah from the LORD: [2]Rise up, be off to the potter's house; there I will give you my message. [3]I went down to the potter's house and there he was, working at the wheel. [4]Whenever the object of clay which he was making turned out badly in his hand, he tried again, making of the clay another object of whatever sort he pleased.[u] [5]Then the word of the Lord came to me: [6]Can I not do to you, house of Israel, as this potter has done? says the LORD. Indeed, like clay in the hand of the potter, so are you in my hand, house of Israel.[v] [7w]Sometimes I threaten to uproot and tear down and destroy a nation or

a kingdom. [8]But if that nation which I have threatened turns from its evil, I also repent of the evil which I threatened to do.[x] [9]Sometimes, again, I promise to build up and plant a nation or a kingdom. [10]But if that nation does what is evil in my eyes, refusing to obey my voice, I repent of the good with which I promised to bless it.[y]

[11]And now, tell this to the men of Judah and the citizens of Jerusalem: Thus says the LORD: Take care! I am fashioning evil against you and making a plan. Return, each of you, from his evil way; reform your ways and your deeds.[z] [12]But they will say, "No use! We will follow our own devices; each one of us will behave according to the stubbornness of his evil heart!"[a]

Judah's Apostasy Unnatural

[13]   Therefore thus says the LORD:
Ask among the nations—
     who has ever heard the like?
Truly horrible things
     has virgin Israel done![b]
[14] Does the snow of Lebanon*
     desert the rocky heights?
Do the gushing waters dry up
     that flow fresh down the mountains?
[15] Yet my people have forgotten me:
     they burn incense to a thing that does
          not exist.
They stumble out of their ways,
     the paths of old,
To travel on bypaths,
     not the beaten track.[c]
[16] Their land shall be turned into a desert,
     an object of lasting ridicule:
All passers-by will be amazed,
     will shake their heads.[d]
[17] Like the east wind, I will scatter them
     before their enemies;
I will show them my back, not my face,
     in their day of disaster.[e]

18, 1-12: The lesson of the potter is not that God deals arbitrarily with his people, but that he is almighty to destroy or restore, accordingly as they disobey him or fulfill his plans.

18, 14: Lebanon: here apparently including Mount Hermon, whose snow-capped peak can be seen from parts of Palestine all year round. The prophet contrasts the certainties of nature with Israel's unnatural desertion of the Lord for idols (v 15).

o: Ex 20, 8; 23, 12.   p: Jer 5, 3; 7, 24.   q: Is 58, 14.   r: Jer 22, 4.   s: Jer 32, 44.   t: Ez 22, 8.   u: Rom 9, 20f.   v: Wis 15, 7; Is 45, 9.   w: Jer 1, 10.   x: Jer 26, 3; Is 55, 7; Ez 18, 21. 27.   y: Nm 14, 22f.   z: Jer 7, 3; 25, 5; 35, 15.   a: Jer 2, 25; 7, 24.   b: Jer 2, 10f; 5, 30.   c: Jer 2, 13. 32.   d: Jer 19, 8; Lv 26, 32; 1 Kgs 9, 8.   e: Prv 1, 24-31.

Another Prayer for Vengeance. [18]"Come," they said, "let us contrive a plot against Jeremiah. It will not mean the loss of instruction from the priests, nor of counsel from the wise, nor of messages from the prophets. And so, let us destroy him by his own tongue; let us carefully note his every word."[f]

[19] Heed me, O LORD,
    and listen to what my adversaries say.
[20] Must good be repaid with evil
    that they should dig a pit to take my life?
    Remember that I stood before you
      to speak in their behalf,
      to turn away your wrath from them.[g]
[21] So now, deliver their children to famine,[h]
    do away with them by the sword.
    Let their wives be made childless and
      widows;
    let their men die of pestilence,
    their young men be slain by the sword
      in battle.*
[22] May cries be heard from their homes,
    when suddenly you send plunderers
      against them.
    For they have dug a pit to capture me,
    they have hid snares for my feet;
[23] But you, O LORD, know
    all their plans to slay me.
    Forgive not their crime,
    blot not out their sin in your sight!
    Let them go down before you,
    proceed against them in the time of
      your anger.[i]

CHAPTER 19

See RG 217

Symbol of the Potter's Flask. [1]Thus said the LORD: Go, buy a potter's earthen flask. Take along some of the elders of the people and of the priests, [2]and go out toward the Valley of Ben-hinnom, at the entrance of the Potsherd Gate;* there proclaim the words which I will speak to you: [3]Listen to the word of the LORD, kings of Judah and citizens of Jerusalem: Thus says the LORD of hosts, the God of Israel: I am going to bring such evil upon this place that all who hear of it will feel their ears tingle. [4]This is because they have forsaken me and alienated this place by burning in it incense to strange gods which neither they nor their fathers knew; and the kings of Judah have filled this place with the blood of the innocent.[j] [5]They have built high places for Baal to immolate their sons in fire as holocausts to Baal: such a thing as I neither commanded nor spoke of, nor did it ever enter my mind.[k] [6]Therefore, days will come, says the LORD, when this place will no longer be called Topheth, or the Valley of Ben-hinnom, but rather, the Valley of Slaughter.[l] [7]In this place I will foil the plan of Judah and Jerusalem; I will make them fall by the sword before their enemies, by the hand of those that seek their lives. Their corpses I will give as food to the birds of the sky and the beasts of the field.[m] [8]I will make this city an object of amazement and derision. Because of all its wounds, every passer-by will be amazed and will catch his breath. [9]I will have them eat the flesh of their sons and daughters; they shall eat one another's flesh during the strict siege by which their enemies and those who seek their lives will confine them.[n]

[10]And you shall break the flask in the sight of the men who went with you, [11]and say to them: Thus says the LORD of hosts: Thus will I smash this people and this city, as one smashes a clay pot so that it cannot be repaired. And Topheth shall be a burial place, for lack of place to bury elsewhere.[o] [12]Thus I will do to this place and to its inhabitants, says the LORD; I will make this city like Topheth.[p] [13]And the houses of Jerusalem and the palaces of the kings of Judah shall be defiled like the place of Topheth, all the houses upon whose roofs they burnt incense to the whole host of heaven and poured out libations to strange gods.[q]

[14]When Jeremiah returned from Topheth,

18, 21: In the Old Testament a man's family was regarded as part of his personality, to be rewarded or punished along with him; cf Jos 7, 24ff.

19, 2: Potsherd Gate: in the south wall of Jerusalem, through which potsherds and other refuse were carried to the Valley of Ben-hinnom.

f: Jer 11, 19; Ps 35, 15f. g: Ps 35, 12. h: Ps 109, 9f. i: Neh 4, 5; Pss 35, 4; 37, 32f. j: Jer 1, 16; 2 Kgs 21, 16; 24, 4. k: Jer 7, 31f; 32, 35. l: Jer 7, 32. m: Jer 7, 33. n: Lv 26, 29. o: Jer 7, 32. p: 2 Kgs 23, 10. q: Jer 32, 29.

where the LORD had sent him to prophesy, he stood in the court of the house of God and said to all the people:[r] [15]Thus says the LORD of hosts, the God of Israel: I will surely bring upon this city all the evil with which I threatened it, because they have stiffened their necks and have not obeyed my words.[s]

See RG 217

CHAPTER 20

[1]Jeremiah was heard prophesying these things by the priest Pashhur,[t] son of Immer, chief officer in the house of the LORD.[*] [2]So he had the prophet scourged and placed in the stocks at the upper Gate of Benjamin in the house of the LORD.[u] [3]The next morning, after Pashhur had released Jeremiah from the stocks, the prophet said to him:[v] Instead of Pashhur, the LORD will name you "Terror on every side."[*] [4]For thus says the LORD: Indeed, I will deliver you to terror, you and all your friends. Your own eyes shall see them fall by the sword of their enemies. All Judah I will deliver to the king of Babylon,[*] who shall take them captive to Babylon or slay them with the sword. [5]All the wealth of this city, all it has toiled for and holds dear, all the treasures of the kings of Judah, I will give as plunder into the hands of their foes, who shall seize it and carry it away to Babylon.[w] [6]You, Pashhur, and all the members of your household shall go into exile. To Babylon you shall go, you and all your friends; there you shall die and be buried, because you have prophesied lies to them.[x]

Jeremiah's Interior Crisis

[7] You duped me,[*] O LORD, and I let myself be duped;
  you were too strong for me, and you triumphed.
All the day I am an object of laughter;

everyone mocks me.
[8] Whenever I speak, I must cry out,
  violence and outrage is my message;
The word of the LORD has brought me derision and reproach all the day.
[9] I say to myself, I will not mention him,
  I will speak in his name no more.
But then it becomes like fire burning in my heart,
  imprisoned in my bones;
I grow weary holding it in,
  I cannot endure it.[y]
[10] Yes, I hear the whisperings of many:
  "Terror on every side!
  Denounce! let us denounce him!"
All those who were my friends
  are on the watch for any misstep of mine.
"Perhaps he will be trapped; then we can prevail,
  and take our vengeance on him."[z]
[11] But the LORD is with me, like a mighty champion:
  my persecutors will stumble, they will not triumph.
In their failure they will be put to utter shame,
  to lasting, unforgettable confusion.[a]
[12] O LORD of hosts, you who test the just,
  who probe mind and heart,
Let me witness the vengeance you take on them,
  for to you I have entrusted my cause.[b]
[13] Sing to the LORD,
  praise the LORD,
For he has rescued the life of the poor
  from the power of the wicked![c]

[14] Cursed be the day[*]
  on which I was born!
May the day my mother gave me birth

20, 1: Chief officer in the house of the LORD: head of the temple police; cf Jer 29, 26. By entering the temple court (Jer 19, 14), Jeremiah had put himself under Pashhur's jurisdiction.

20, 3: Terror on every side: Pashhur will share the fate of doomed Jerusalem and will experience personally all that the people as a whole have had to endure.

20, 4: Babylon: mentioned here for the first time as the land of exile. The prophecy probably dates from after 605 B.C., when Nebuchadnezzar defeated Egypt and made the Chaldean empire dominant in Syria and Palestine.

20, 7: You duped me: to be understood in the light of Jer-

emiah's intimate dealings with God; cf Jer 15, 18.

20, 14-18: Deception, sorrow and terror have brought the prophet close to the point of despair; nevertheless he has expressed his utmost confidence in the triumph of God's will (vv 11ff); cf Jb 3, 3-12.

r: Jer 26, 2.   *s:* Jer 7, 26; Prv 29, 1.   *t:* Jer 21, 1.   *u:* Jer 29, 26.   *v:* Jer 6, 25.   *w:* 2 Kgs 20, 17; 24, 12-16.   *x:* Jer 14, 13f; 28, 15.   *y:* Jer 6, 11; Jb 32, 18.   *z:* Jb 19, 19; Ps 31, 13; Lk 20, 20.   *a:* Jer 1, 8; 15, 20.   *b:* Jer 11, 20.   *c:* Pss 35, 9f; 109, 30f.

A Curse

Jeremiah curses the day of his birth (20, 14), like Job (Jb 3). This curse closes the section on the covenant's destruction that was begun by the curse against the nation in ch 11. Jeremiah's curse speaks of the tragedy of his mission to announce disaster so that he wishes he had never been born. If his life represents that of the people, then his captivity, the fulfillment of his word, and his curse enact and bring about their captivity.

never be blessed!*d*

15 Cursed be the man who brought the news
   to my father, saying,
"A child, a son, has been born to you!"
   filling him with great joy.
16 Let that man be like the cities
   which the LORD relentlessly overthrew;
Let him hear war cries in the morning,
   battle alarms at noonday,*e*
17   because he did not dispatch me in the
      womb!
Then my mother would have been my
      grave,
   her womb confining me forever.*f*
18 Why did I come forth from the womb,
   to see sorrow and pain,
   to end my days in shame?*g*

III: Oracles in the Last Years of Jerusalem

CHAPTER 21

See RG 217 *Fate of Zedekiah and Jerusalem.*
*1*The message which came to Jeremiah from the LORD when King Zedekiah* sent him Pashhur, son of Malchiah, and the priest Zephaniah, son of Maaseiah, with this request: *2*Inquire for us of the LORD, because Nebuchadnezzar, king of Babylon, is attacking us. Perhaps the LORD will deal with us according to all his wonderful works, so that he will withdraw from us. *3*But Jeremiah answered them: This is what you shall report to Zedekiah: *4*Thus says the LORD, the God of

Israel: I will turn back in your hands the weapons with which you intend to fight the king of Babylon and the Chaldeans who besiege you outside the walls. These weapons I will pile up in the midst of this city,*h* *5*and I myself will fight against you with outstretched hand and mighty arm, in anger, and wrath, and great rage!*i* *6*I will strike the inhabitants of this city, both man and beast; they shall die in a great pestilence.*j* *7*After that, says the LORD, I will hand over Zedekiah, king of Judah, and his ministers and the people in this city who survive pestilence, sword, and famine, into the hand of Nebuchadnezzar, king of Babylon, into the hands of their enemies and those who seek their lives. He shall strike them with the edge of the sword, without quarter, without pity or mercy.*k* *8*And to this people you shall say: Thus says the LORD: See, I am giving you a choice between life and death.*l* *9*Whoever remains in this city shall die by the sword or famine or pestilence. But whoever leaves and surrenders to the besieging Chaldeans shall live and have his life as booty. *10*For I have turned against this city, for its woe and not for its good, says the LORD. It shall be given into the power of the king of Babylon who shall burn it with fire.*

Oracles regarding the Kings

11   To the royal house of Judah:*
   Hear the word of the LORD, *12*O house of
      David!
   Thus says the LORD:

21, 1: Zedekiah: brother of Jehoiakim, appointed king by Nebuchadnezzar after he had carried Jehoiachin away to captivity (2 Kgs 24, 17). Pashhur: different from the one in Jer 20, 1ff but also one of Jeremiah's enemies; cf Jer 38, 1. 4.

21, 10: Jeremiah consistently pointed out the uselessness of resistance to Babylon, since the Lord had delivered Judah to Nebuchadnezzar (Jer 27, 6). Because of this the prophet

was denounced and imprisoned as a traitor (Jer 37, 13f).

21, 11—23, 8: This section contains an editor's collection of Jeremiah's oracles against the kings of Judah. They are

d: Jer 15, 10; Jb 3, 1-10; 10, 18.   *e:* Gn 19, 25; Is 13, 19.   *f:* Jb 3, 10f; 10, 19.   *g:* Jb 14, 1.   *h:* Jer 37, 8ff.   *i:* Is 63, 10; Lam 2, 4f.
j: Jer 16, 4.   *k:* Jer 24, 8ff; Dt 28, 49f.   *l:* Jer 21, 9; Dt 30, 15. 19.

Each morning dispense justice,
> rescue the oppressed from the hand of
> > the oppressor,

Lest my fury break out like fire
> which burns without being quenched,
> because of the evil of your deeds.*m*

13 Beware! I am against you, Valley-site,
> Rock of the Plain,* says the LORD.

You who say, "Who will attack us,
> who can penetrate our retreats?"

14 I will punish you, says the LORD,
> as your deeds deserve!

I will kindle a fire in its forest*
> that shall devour all its surroundings."*n*

See RG 217 **CHAPTER 22**

1 The LORD told me this: Go down to the palace of the king of Judah and there deliver this message: 2 You shall say: Listen to the word of the LORD, king of Judah, who sit on the throne of David, you, your ministers, and your people that enter by these gates!*o* 3 Thus says the LORD: Do what is right and just. Rescue the victim from the hand of his oppressor. Do not wrong or oppress the resident alien, the orphan, or the widow, and do not shed innocent blood in this place.*p* 4 If you carry out these commands, kings who succeed to the throne of David will continue to enter the gates of this palace, riding in chariots or mounted on horses, with their ministers, and their people. 5 But if you do not obey these commands, I swear by myself, says the LORD: this palace shall become rubble. 6 For thus says the LORD concerning the palace of the king of Judah:

Though you be to me like Gilead,

like the peak of Lebanon,*
> I will turn you into a waste,
> > a city uninhabited.

7 Against you I will send destroyers,
> each with his axe:

They shall cut down your choice cedars,
> and cast them into the fire.*q*

8 Many people will pass by this city and ask one another: "Why has the LORD done this to so great a city?"*r* 9 And the answer will be given: "Because they have deserted their covenant with the LORD, their God, by worshiping and serving strange gods."*s*

Jehoahaz

10 Weep not for him who is dead,*
> mourn not for him!

Weep rather for him who is going away;
> never again will he see
> > the land of his birth.*t*

11 Thus says the LORD concerning Shallum,* son of Josiah, king of Judah, who succeeded his father as king. He has left this place never to return. 12 Rather, he shall die in the place where they exiled him; this land he shall not see again.

Jehoiakim

13 Woe to him who builds his house on
> > wrong,
> > his terraces on injustice;

Who works his neighbor without pay,*
> and gives him no wages.*u*

14 Who says, "I will build myself a spacious
> > house,
> > with airy rooms,"

---

placed in the chronological order of the kings, and are prefaced by the oracles against the kings of Judah in general (Jer 21, 11—22, 9).

21, 13: Valley-site, Rock of the Plain: Mount Zion, surrounded by valleys, was regarded by the royal house as impregnable. Despite this natural fortification, God shows derisively that it is no more than a rock rising from the plain, undefendable against the attack of his fury.

21, 14: Its forest: probably the royal palace, built of cedar wood; cf Jer 22, 14; in 1 Kgs 7, 2 the armory of Solomon's palace is called "the house of the forest of Lebanon."

22, 6: Gilead . . . Lebanon: both were known for their trees; cf v 7.

22, 10: Him who is dead: Josiah. His successor, Jehoahaz, who is going away, was deported by Pharaoh Neco to Egypt,

where he died (2 Kgs 23, 33f).

22, 11: Shallum: Jehoahaz is called this only here. Presumably it was his name at birth, while Jehoahaz was his royal name.

22, 13: Without pay: either by forced labor in public works, or in as much as workers were defrauded of their hire. Despite the impoverishment caused in Judah by the payment of foreign tribute, Jehoiakim embarked on a program of lavish building in Jerusalem (v 14). Social injustice is the cause of much of the prophetic condemnation of the kings (v 17).

m: Jer 4, 4; 22, 3; Zec 7, 9.   *n:* 2 Kgs 25, 9; 2 Chr 36, 19.   *o:* Jer 17, 20.   *p:* Jer 21, 12; Ex 22, 21-24; Dt 24, 17.   *q:* Jer 21, 14. *r:* Dt 29, 24ff.   *s:* Jer 19, 4; 40, 2f.   *t:* 2 Chr 35, 23ff.   *u:* Lv 19, 13; Dt 24, 14; Hb 2, 9. 12.

Who cuts out windows for it,
  panels it with cedar,
  and paints it with vermillion.
15 Must you prove your rank among
    kings*
  by competing with them in cedar?
Did not your father eat and drink?
  He did what was right and just,
  and it went well with him.v
16 Because he dispensed justice to the weak
    and the poor,
  it went well with him.
Is this not true knowledge of me?
  says the LORD.w
17 But your eyes and heart are set on
    nothing
  except on your own gain,
On shedding innocent blood,
  on practicing oppression and
  extortion.x

18Therefore, thus says the LORD concerning Jehoiakim, son of Josiah, king of Judah:

They shall not lament him,
  "Alas! my brother"; "Alas! sister."*
They shall not lament him,
  "Alas, Lord! alas, Majesty!"y
19 The burial of an ass* shall he be given,
  dragged forth and cast out
  beyond the gates of Jerusalem.z

Jeconiah
20 Scale Lebanon and cry out,*
  in Bashan lift up your voice;
Cry out from Abarim,

for all your lovers are crushed.a
21 I spoke to you when you were secure,
  but you answered, "I will not listen."
This has been your way from your youth,
  not to listen to my voice.
22 The wind shall shepherd all your
    shepherds,
  your lovers shall go into exile.
Surely then you shall be ashamed and
    confounded
  because of all your wickedness.
23 You who dwell on Lebanon,
  who nest in the cedars,
How you shall groan when pains come
    upon you,
  like the pangs of a woman in travail!

24As I live, says the LORD, if you, Coniah,* son of Jehoiakim, king of Judah, are a signet ring on my right hand, I will snatch you from it. 25I will deliver you into the hands of those who seek your life; the hands of those whom you fear; the hands of Nebuchadnezzar, king of Babylon, and the Chaldeans.b 26I will cast you out, you and the mother who bore you,* into a different land from the one you were born in; and there you shall die.c 27Neither of them shall come back to the land for which they yearn.d

28 Is this man Coniah a vessel despised, to
    be broken up,
  an instrument that no one wants?
Why are he and his descendants cast out?
  why thrown into a land they know
    not?

22, 15f: Josiah, the reforming king, prospered materially without oppressing his people; he embodied all the ideals of kingship.

22, 18: "Alas! my brother"; "Alas! sister": customary cries of mourning.

22, 19: The burial of an ass: no burial at all, except to be cast outside the city as refuse. This prophecy regards the popular feeling toward Jehoiakim rather than the actual circumstances of his burial. According to 2 Kgs 24, 5 he was buried with his fathers in Jerusalem. However, his grave may have been profaned by Nebuchadnezzar.

22, 20-23: The prophet first apostrophizes Jerusalem, which is bidden to scale Lebanon, Bashan, and Abarim, i.e., the highest surrounding mountains to the north, northeast, and southeast, to gaze on the ruin of its lovers, i.e., the false leaders of Judah, called its shepherds (22); cf Jer 2, 8. The year is 597 B.C., after Nebuchadnezzar's deportation of Jehoiachin. Jerusalem still stands (23), apparently as secure as

the heights of Lebanon, but destruction is to follow (cf v 6).

22, 24: Coniah: a shortened form of Jeconiah, the name which Jeremiah gives the king called elsewhere in the Bible Jehoiachin. A signet ring: the seal used by important men—in a sense, their most valuable possession—mounted in a ring worn constantly on the hand. The Lord says that even were Jehoiachin such a precious possession, he would reject him. The words in vv 24-30 date from the short three-month reign of Jehoiachin, before he was carried away by Nebuchadnezzar.

22, 26: You and the mother who bore you: the queen mother held a special position in the monarchy of Judah, and in the Books of Kings she is invariably mentioned by name along with the king (1 Kgs 15, 2; 2 Kgs 18, 2). Jehoiachin did indeed die in Babylon.

v: 2 Kgs 23, 25. w: Prv 31, 9. x: Ez 22, 13. 27. y: Jer 16, 4ff;
1 Kgs 13, 30. z: Jer 36, 30. a: Jer 30, 14f; Dt 32, 49. b: Jer
21, 7; 34, 20. c: 2 Kgs 24, 15. d: Jer 44, 14.

29 O land, land, land,
   hear the word of the LORD—
30   Thus says the LORD:
   Write this man down as one childless,
   who will never thrive in his lifetime!
No descendant of his shall achieve
   a seat on the throne of David
   as ruler again over Judah.

See RG 217

CHAPTER 23

Messianic Reign.* 1ʲWoe to the shepherds who mislead and scatter the flock of my pasture, says the LORD. ²Therefore, thus says the LORD, the God of Israel, against the shepherds who shepherd my people: You have scattered my sheep and driven them away. You have not cared for them, but I will take care to punish your evil deeds.ᵍ ³I myself will gather the remnant of my flock from all the lands to which I have driven them and bring them back to their meadow; there they shall increase and multiply.ʰ ⁴I will appoint shepherds for them who will shepherd them so that they need no longer fear and tremble; and none shall be missing, says the LORD.ⁱ

⁵ Behold, the days are coming, says the
   LORD,
   when I will raise up a righteous shoot
   to David;
As king he shall reign and govern wisely,
   he shall do what is just and right in the
   land.ʲ
⁶ In his days Judah shall be saved,
   Israel shall dwell in security.
This is the name they give him:
   "The LORD our justice."ᵏ

⁷ᶦTherefore, the days will come, says the LORD, when they shall no longer say, "As the LORD lives, who brought the Israelites out of the land of Egypt"; ⁸but rather, "As the LORD lives, who brought the descendants of the house of Israel up from the land of the north"—and from all the lands to which I banished them; they shall again live on their own land.

The False Prophets*

9   Concerning the prophets:
My heart within me is broken,
   my bones all tremble;
I am like a man who is drunk,
   overcome by wine,
Because of the LORD,
   because of his holy words.
¹⁰ With adulterers the land is filled;
   on their account the land mourns,
   the pasture ranges are seared.ᵐ
Theirs is an evil course,
   theirs is unjust power.
¹¹ Both prophet and priest are godless!
   In my very house I find their
      wickedness,
   says the LORD.ⁿ
¹² Hence their way shall become for them
      slippery ground.
In the darkness they shall lose their
      footing,
   and fall headlong;
Evil I will bring upon them:
   the year of their punishment, says the
      LORD.ᵒ
¹³ Among Samaria's prophets
   I saw unseemly deeds:
   They prophesied by Baal

22, 30: Childless: Jehoiachin is so considered because none of his descendants will be king. From the Book of Ezekiel, who dates his oracles according to Jehoiachin's fictitious regnal years, it is evident that the people expected Jehoiachin to return. The above prophecy of Jeremiah was uttered to dispel this hope (Jer 28, 4). Of the seven sons born to Jehoiachin in exile, none became king. His grandson Zerubbabel presided for a time over the Jewish community after the return from exile, but not as king.

23, 1-8: With the false rulers who have governed his people the Lord contrasts himself, the good shepherd, who will in the times of restoration appoint worthy rulers (1-4). A messianic King will arise from the line of David who will rule over Judah and Israel with the justice of the Lord, fulfilling all the kingly ideals (5f). "The Lord our justice" is probably

an ironic wordplay on the name of the weak King Zedekiah ("The Lord is justice"); the messianic King will be in reality what Zedekiah's name falsely proclaims him. The final verses, 7-8, were probably added during the exile.

23, 9-40: After the collection of oracles against the kings, the editor of the book placed this collection of oracles against the false prophets. With them are associated the priests, for both have betrayed their trust as instructors in the religion of the Lord; cf Jer 2, 8; 4, 9; 6, 13f.

e: Jer 36, 30; 1 Chr 3, 16f; Mt 1, 12. *f:* Jer 22, 22. *g:* Ez 34, 4ff; Zec 11, 16f. *h:* Jer 29, 14; 32, 37. *i:* Jer 3, 15; Ez 34, 11f. *j:* Jer 33, 14ff; Is 4, 2; 9, 5f; 11, 1-5. *k:* Dn 9, 24. *l:* 7f: Jer 16, 14f. *m:* Jer 4, 22; 5, 7f; 9, 2. 10. *n:* Jer 6, 13. *o:* Ps 35, 6.

and led my people Israel astray.*p*
[14] But among Jerusalem's prophets
I saw deeds still more shocking:
Adultery, living in lies,
siding with the wicked,
so that no one turns from evil;
To me they are all like Sodom,
its citizens like Gomorrah.*q*

[15] Therefore, thus says the LORD of hosts
against the prophets:

Behold, I will give them wormwood to
eat,
and poison to drink;
For from Jerusalem's prophets
ungodliness has gone forth into the
whole land.*r*
[16] Thus says the LORD of hosts:
Listen not to the words of your
prophets,
who fill you with emptiness;
Visions of their own fancy they speak,
not from the mouth of the LORD.*s*
[17] They say to those who despise the word
of the LORD,*
"Peace shall be yours";
And to everyone who walks in hardness
of heart,
"No evil shall overtake you."*t*
[18] Now, who has stood in the council of the
LORD,
to see him and to hear his word?
Who has heeded his word, so as to
announce it?*u*
[19] See, the storm of the LORD!
His wrath breaks forth
In a whirling storm
that bursts upon the heads of the
wicked.*v*
[20] The anger of the LORD shall not abate
until he has done and fulfilled
what he has determined in his heart.
When the time comes,
you shall fully understand.

[21] I did not send these prophets,
yet they ran;
I did not speak to them,
yet they prophesied.*w*
[22] Had they stood in my council,
and did they but proclaim to my
people my words,
They would have brought them back
from evil ways
and from their wicked deeds.
[23] Am I a God near at hand only, says the
LORD,*x*
and not a God far off?*
[24] Can a man hide in secret
without my seeing him? says the
LORD.
Do I not fill
both heaven and earth? says the LORD.

[25] I have heard the prophets who prophesy lies in my name say, "I had a dream! I had a dream!" [26] How long will this continue? Is my name in the hearts of the prophets who prophesy lies and their own deceitful fancies? [27] By their dreams which they recount to each other, they think to make my people forget my name, just as their fathers forgot my name for Baal.*y* [28] Let the prophet who has a dream recount his dream; let him who has my word speak my word truthfully!

What has straw to do with the wheat?*
says the LORD.*z*
[29] Is not my word like fire, says the LORD,
like a hammer shattering rocks?

[30] Therefore I am against the prophets, says the LORD, who steal my words from each other.*a* [31] Yes, I am against the prophets, says the LORD, who borrow speeches to pronounce oracles. [32] Yes, I am against the prophets who prophesy lying dreams, says the LORD, and who lead my people astray by recounting their lies and by their empty boasting. From me they have no mission or

23, 17-20: Not only are the false prophets personally immoral, but they encourage immorality by prophesying good of those who do evil. The true prophet, on the other hand, sees the inevitable consequences of sin.

23, 23: Near at hand only . . . far off: God knows not merely the present but also the future.

23, 28f: Straw . . . wheat: such is the contrast between false and true prophecy. True prophecy is like fire (cf Jer 5,

14; 20, 9), producing violent results (v 29); Jeremiah's own life is a testimony of this.

p: 1 Kgs 18, 19.   *q:* Jer 29, 21ff; Is 1, 9f.   *r:* Jer 8, 14; 9, 14.   *s:* Je: 14, 14.   *t:* Jer 5, 12; Ez 13, 10; Mi 3, 11; Zec 10, 2.   *u:* Jb 15, 8; Is 40, 13; 1 Cor 2, 16.   *v:* Jer 30, 23.   *w:* Jer 29, 9.   *x:* Jer 16, 17; Ps 139, 8.   *y:* Jgs 3, 7; 8, 33.   *z:* Nm 12, 6.   *a:* Dt 18, 20.

command, and they do this people no good at all, says the LORD.[b]

[33]*And when this people, or a prophet or a priest asks you, "What is the burden of the LORD?" you shall answer, "You are the burden, and I cast you off, says the LORD." [34]If a prophet or a priest or anyone else mentions "the burden of the LORD," I will punish that man and his house. [35]Thus you shall ask, when speaking to one another, "What answer did the LORD give?" or, "What did the LORD say?" [36]But the burden of the LORD you shall mention no more. For each man his own word becomes the burden so that you pervert the words of the living God, the LORD of hosts, our God. [37]Thus shall you ask the prophet, "What answer did the LORD give?" or, "What did the LORD say?" [38]But if you ask about "the burden of the LORD," then thus says the LORD: Because you use this phrase, "the burden of the LORD," though I forbade you to use it, [39]therefore I will lift you on high and cast you from my presence, you and the city which I gave to you and your fathers. [40]And I will bring upon you eternal reproach, eternal, unforgettable shame.[c]

CHAPTER 24

See RG 217

The Two Baskets of Figs.[*] [1]The LORD showed me two baskets of figs placed before the temple of the LORD.[d] —This was after Nebuchadnezzar, king of Babylon, had exiled from Jerusalem Jeconiah, son of Jehoiakim, king of Judah, and the princes of Judah, the artisans and the skilled workers, and brought them to Babylon.— [2]One basket contained excellent figs, the early-ripening kind. But the other basket contained very bad figs, so bad they could not be eaten. [3]Then the LORD said to me: What do you see, Jeremiah?[e] "Figs," I replied; "the good ones are very good, but the bad ones very bad, so bad they cannot be eaten." [4]Thereupon this word of the LORD came to me: [5]Thus says the LORD, the God of Israel: Like these good figs, even so will I regard with favor Judah's exiles whom I sent away from this place into the land of the Chaldeans.[f] [6]I will look after them for their good, and bring them back to this land, to build them up, not to tear them down; to plant them, not to pluck them out.[g] [7]I will give them a heart with which to understand that I am the LORD. They shall be my people and I will be their God, for they shall return to me with their whole heart.[h] [8]And like the figs that are bad, so bad they cannot be eaten—yes, thus says the LORD— even so will I treat Zedekiah, king of Judah, and his princes, the remnant of Jerusalem remaining in this land and those who have settled in the land of Egypt.[i] [9]I will make them an object of horror to all the kingdoms of the earth, a reproach and a byword, a taunt and a curse, in all the places to which I will drive them.[j] [10]I will send upon them the sword, famine, and pestilence, until they have disappeared from the land which I gave them and their fathers.[k]

CHAPTER 25

See RG 217

Seventy Years of Exile.[*] [1]The word that came to Jeremiah concerning all the people of Judah, in the fourth year of Jehoiakim,[*] son of Josiah, king of Judah (the first year of Nebuchadnezzar, king of Babylon).[l] [2]This word the prophet Jeremiah spoke to all the people of Judah and all the citizens of

---

23, 33-40: A wordplay on massa, which means both oracle (usually of woe) and burden. In 34ff it appears that the word massa itself is forbidden the people in the meaning of a divine oracle. Doubtless this was because of some association unknown to us. In Hos 2, 18 it is forbidden to call God "Baal" ("master"), because of the association of this title with the Canaanite god.

24, 1-10: Jeremiah, like Ezekiel, saw that no good could be expected from the people who had been left in Judah under Zedekiah or who had fled into Egypt; good was to be hoped for only from those who would pass through the purifying experience of the exile to form the new Israel.

25, 1-14: The fourth year of Jehoiakim: 605 B.C. Officially, the first year of Nebuchadnezzar began the following year; but as early as his victory over Egypt at Carchemish in 605, Nebuchadnezzar was the dominant power in the Near East, in whom Jeremiah now saw the fulfillment of his prophecy of the enemy to come from the north (cf Jer 1, 13; 6, 22ff). In vv 11f occurs for the first time the prophecy of the seventy years' exile; cf Jer 29, 10. This Jeremiah intends as a round number, to signify that the present generation must die out.

---

b: Jer 28, 15ff. *c:* Jer 20, 11. *d:* Am 8, 1f. *e:* Jer 1, 11. *f:* Jer 29, 11; Lv 26, 44f. *g:* Jer 12, 15; Am 9, 15. *h:* Jer 30, 22; 31, 1; 32, 37; Bar 2, 31. *i:* Jer 29, 18. *j:* Jer 15, 4; Dt 28, 37. *k:* Jer 14, 12. *l:* Jer 36, 1.

Jerusalem: ³Since the thirteenth year of Josiah, son of Amon, king of Judah, to this day—these three and twenty years—the word of the LORD has come to me and I spoke to you untiringly, but you would not listen.ᵐ ⁴Though you refused to listen or pay heed, the LORD has sent you without fail all his servants the prophetsⁿ ⁵with this message: Turn back, each of you, from your evil way and from your evil deeds; then you shall remain in the land which the LORD gave you and your fathers, from of old and forever. ⁶Do not follow strange gods to serve and adore them, lest you provoke me with your handiwork, and I bring evil upon you.ᵒ ⁷But you would not listen to me, says the LORD, and so you provoked me with your handiwork to your own harm.ᵖ ⁸Hence, thus says the LORD of hosts: Since you would not listen to my words, ⁹lo! I will send for and fetch all the tribes of the north, says the LORD (and I will send to Nebuchadnezzar, king of Babylon, my servant); I will bring them against this land, against its inhabitants, and against all these neighboring nations. I will doom them, making them an object of horror, of ridicule, of everlasting reproach.�q ¹⁰Among them I will bring to an end the song of joy and the song of gladness, the voice of the bridegroom and the voice of the bride, the sound of the millstone and the light of the lamp. ¹¹This whole land shall be a ruin and a desert. Seventy years these nations shall be enslaved to the king of Babylon;ʳ ¹²but when the seventy years have elapsed, I will punish the king of Babylon and the nation and the land of the Chaldeans for their guilt, says the LORD. Their land I will turn into everlasting desert.ˢ ¹³Against that land I will fulfill all the words I have spoken against it [all that is written in this book, which Jeremiah prophesied against all the nations]. ¹⁴They also shall be enslaved to great nations and mighty kings, and thus I will repay them according to their own deeds and according to their own handiwork.ᵗ

The Cup of Judgment on the Nations. ¹⁵For thus said the LORD, the God of Israel, to me:* Take this cup of foaming wine from my hand, and have all the nations to whom I will send you drink it.ᵘ ¹⁶They shall drink, and be convulsed, and go mad, because of the sword I will send among them.ᵛ ¹⁷I took the cup from the hand of the LORD and gave drink to all the nations to which the LORD sent me: ¹⁸[Jerusalem, the cities of Judah, her kings and her princes, to make them a ruin and a desert, an object of ridicule and cursing, as they are today;] ¹⁹Pharaoh, king of Egypt, and his servants, his princes, all the people under him, native ²⁰and foreign; all the kings of the land of Uz;* all the kings of the land of the Philistines: Ashkelon, Gaza, Ekron, and the remnant of Ashdod; ²¹Edom, Moab, and the Ammonites; ²²all the kings of Tyre, of Sidon, and of the shores beyond the sea;* ²³Dedan and Tema and Buz,* all the desert dwellers who shave their temples; ²⁴[all the kings of Arabia;] ²⁵all the kings of Zimri, of Elam, of the Medes; ²⁶all the kings of the north, near and far, one after the other; all the kingdoms upon the face of the earth [and after them the king of Sheshach* shall drink].

²⁷Tell them: Thus says the LORD of hosts, the God of Israel: Drink! become drunk and vomit; fall, never to rise, before the sword that I will send among you!ʷ ²⁸If they refuse to take the cup from your hand and drink, say to them: Thus says the LORD of hosts: You must drink!ˣ ²⁹For since with this city, which is called by my name, I begin to inflict evil, how can you possibly be spared? You shall not be spared! I will call down the sword upon all who inhabit the earth, says the LORD of hosts.

25, 15ff: Jeremiah is a prophet to the nations (cf 1, 5) as well as to his own people. All the nations mentioned here appear again in the more extensive collection of Jeremiah's oracles against the nations in chapters 46—51.

25, 20: Uz: the homeland of Job, in Edomite or Arabian territory.

25, 22: The shores beyond the sea: Phoenician commercial colonies planted throughout the Mediterranean world.

25, 23: Dedan and Tema and Buz: North Arabian tribes.

25, 26: Sheshach: Babylon. The word is formed from babel by substituting letters of the Hebrew alphabet in inverse order.

---

m: Jer 1, 2.   n: 2 Chr 36, 15.   o: Jer 7, 6f.   p: Jer 7, 17ff.   q: Jer 1, 15; 43, 10.   r: Lv 26, 32-35.   s: Is 13, 20ff.   t: Jer 27, 7; 50, 9. 41f; 51, 6. 24.   u: Rv 14, 10.   v: Jer 51, 7.   w: Ob 1, 16.   x: Jer 49, 12.

Jeremiah on Trial

Chapter 26 shows that Jeremiah faced great conflict but that he is the true prophet, and, hence, is to be heeded. The chapter refers to Jeremiah's temple sermon (7, 1—8, 3) and summarizes it. What is of interest here, however, is the community's response to the sermon. Some accept it; priests, prophets, and King Jehoiakim reject it. Some of the leaders put Jeremiah on trial. Jeremiah responds to the charges by claiming that it was God who sent him (v. 12). The trial concludes with a declaration of Jeremiah's innocence.

³⁰Prophesy against them all these things and say to them:

The LORD roars from on high,
   from his holy dwelling he raises his
      voice;
Mightily he roars over the range,
   a shout like that of vintagers over the
      grapes.ʸ
³¹ To all who inhabit the earth to its very
      ends
   the uproar spreads;
For the LORD has an indictment against
      the nations,
   he is to pass judgment upon all
      mankind:
The godless shall be given to the sword,
   says the LORD.
³²   Thus says the LORD of hosts:
Lo! calamity stalks
   from nation to nation;
A great storm is unleashed
   from the ends of the earth.

³³On that day, those whom the LORD has slain will be strewn from one end of the earth to the other. None will mourn them, none will gather them for burial; they shall lie like dung on the field.ᶻ

³⁴ Howl, you shepherds, and wail!
   roll in the dust, leaders of the flock!
The time for your slaughter has come;
   like choice rams you shall fall.
³⁵ There is no flight for the shepherds,
   no escape for the leaders of the flock.ᵃ
³⁶ Listen! Wailing from the shepherds,
   howling by the leaders of the flock!

For the LORD lays waste their grazing
      place,
³⁷   desolate lie the peaceful pastures;
³⁸ The lion leaves his lair,
   and their land is made desolate
By the sweeping sword,
   by the burning wrath of the LORD.ᵇ

CHAPTER 26

See RG
217

Jeremiah Threatened with Death. ¹In the beginning of the reign* of Jehoiakim, son of Josiah, king of Judah, this message came from the LORD: ²Thus says the LORD: Stand in the court of the house of the LORD and speak to the people of all the cities of Judah who come to worship in the house of the LORD; whatever I command you, tell them, and omit nothing.ᶜ ³Perhaps they will listen and turn back, each from his evil way, so that I may repent of the evil I have planned to inflict upon them for their evil deeds.ᵈ ⁴Say to them: Thus says the LORD: If you disobey me, not living according to the law I placed before you ⁵and not listening to the words of my servants the prophets, whom I send you constantly though you do not obey them,ᵉ ⁶I will treat this house like Shiloh, and make this the city which all the nations of the earth shall refer to when cursing another.ᶠ

⁷Now the priests, the prophets, and all the people heard Jeremiah speak these words in the house of the LORD. ⁸When Jeremiah finished speaking all that the LORD bade him speak to all the people, the priests and prophets laid hold of him, crying, "You must be put to death! ⁹Why do you prophesy in

26, 1: The beginning of the reign: a technical expression for the time between a king's accession to the throne and the beginning of his first official (calendar) year as king. Jehoiakim's first regnal year was 608 B.C.

y: Jer 51, 14.   z: Jer 8, 2; 16, 4. 6.   a: Jer 32, 4.   b: Jer 4, 7.   c: Jer 7, 2.   d: Jer 18, 3.   e: Jer 25, 4.   f: Jer 7, 12. 14.

the name of the LORD: 'This house shall be like Shiloh,' and 'This city shall be desolate and deserted'?" And all the people gathered about Jeremiah in the house of the LORD.

[10]When the princes of Judah were informed of these things, they came up from the king's palace to the house of the LORD and held court at the New Gate of the house of the LORD. [11]The priests and prophets said to the princes and to all the people, "This man deserves death; he has prophesied against this city, as you have heard with your own ears."[g] [12]Jeremiah gave this answer to the princes and all the people: "It was the LORD who sent me to prophesy against this house and city all that you have heard. [13]Now, therefore, reform your ways and your deeds; listen to the voice of the LORD your God, so that the LORD will repent of the evil with which he threatens you.[h] [14]As for me, I am in your hands; do with me what you think good and right. [15]But mark well: if you put me to death, it is innocent blood you bring on yourselves, on this city and its citizens. For in truth it was the LORD who sent me to you, to speak all these things for you to hear."

[16]Thereupon the princes and all the people said to the priests and the prophets, "This man does not deserve death; it is in the name of the LORD, our God, that he speaks to us." [17]At this, some of the elders of the land came forward and said to all the people assembled, [18]"Micah of Moresheth* used to prophesy in the days of Hezekiah, king of Judah, and he told all the people of Judah: Thus says the LORD of hosts:

Zion shall become a plowed field,
    Jerusalem a heap of ruins,
    and the temple mount a forest ridge.[i]

[19]Did Hezekiah, king of Judah, and all Judah condemn him to death? Did they not rather fear the LORD and entreat the favor of the LORD, so that he repented of the evil with which he had threatened them? But we are on the point of committing this great evil to our own undoing."[j]

The Fate of Uriah. [20]There was another man who prophesied in the name of the LORD, Uriah, son of Shemaiah, from Kiriath-jearim; he prophesied the same things against this city and land as Jeremiah did. [21]When King Jehoiakim and all his officers and princes were informed of his words, the king sought to kill him. But Uriah heard of it and fled in fear to Egypt. [22]Thereupon King Jehoiakim sent Elnathan, son of Achbor, and others with him into Egypt [23]to bring Uriah back to the king, who had him slain by the sword and his corpse cast into the common grave. [24]But Ahikam, son of Shaphan,* protected Jeremiah, so that he was not handed over to the people to be put to death.

CHAPTER 27

See RG 217

Serve Babylon or Perish.* [1][In the beginning of the reign of Jehoiakim, son of Josiah, king of Judah,]* . . . this message came to Jeremiah from the LORD: [2]Thus said the LORD to me: Make for yourself bands and yoke bars and put them over your shoulders. [3]Send to the kings of Edom, of Moab, of the Ammonites, of Tyre, and of Sidon, through the ambassadors who have come to Jerusalem to Zedekiah, king of Judah, [4]and charge them thus: Tell your masters: Thus says the LORD of hosts, the God of Israel: [5]It was I who made the earth, and man and beast on the face of the earth, by my great power, with my outstretched arm; and I can give them to whomever I think fit.[k] [6]Now I have given all these lands into the hand of Nebuchadnezzar, king of Babylon, my servant; even the beasts of the field I have given him for his use.[l] [7]All

---

26, 18: Micah of Moresheth: the prophet Micah, who appears among the canonical minor prophets (cf Mi 1, 1).

26, 24: Ahikam, son of Shaphan: one of Josiah's officials (2 Kgs 22, 12) and father of Gedaliah, Jeremiah's friend, who was governor of Judah after Zedekiah's deportation (cf Jer 39, 14; 40, 5ff).

27, 1—29, 32: A special collection of Jeremiah's prophecies dealing with false prophets. From stylistic peculiarities, quite evident in the Hebrew, it is plain that these three chapters once existed independently of the other prophecies of Jeremiah.

27, 1: [In the beginning of the reign of Jehoiakim . . . Judah]: this gloss cannot be correct because according to Jer 28, 1 the time is the fourth year of Zedekiah, 594 B.C., the occasion of an embassy of the neighboring states (v 3), doubtless for the purpose of laying plans against Nebuchadnezzar.

g: Jer 38, 4.   h: Jer 7, 3.   i: Mi 1, 1; 3, 12.   j: 2 Chr 32, 26.
k: Jer 32, 17.   l: Jer 25, 9; 43, 10; Ez 30, 21. 25.

How the Nation Will Survive

The first "book" (chs 1–25) accused Judah of infidelity, promised destruction and exile, and defended God from accusations of injustice. The second "book" (chs 26–52) presents stories and poems that reveal how to survive the period after the nation's fall to Babylon. The book's audience lives with the community's failure to repent. They themselves must repent and endure. Jeremiah appears here as a model of faithful endurance. Jeremiah's companion Baruch also appears in this part of the book. Baruch has traditionally been named as the writer of stories about Jeremiah, particularly in chs 37–45. The period of the exile was a time of great conflict about how to survive. This book insists that survival requires continued submission to Babylon, repentance, and obedience as set out in the book of Jeremiah.

nations shall serve him and his son and his grandson, until the time of his land, too, shall come. Then it in turn shall serve great nations and mighty kings.*m* *8*Meanwhile, if any nation or kingdom will not serve Nebuchadnezzar, king of Babylon, or will not bend its neck under the yoke of the king of Babylon, I will punish that nation with sword, famine, and pestilence, says the LORD, until I give them into his hand.*n*

*9*You, however, must not listen to your prophets,* to your diviners and dreamers, to your soothsayers and sorcerers, who say to you, "You need not serve the king of Babylon."*o* *10*For they prophesy lies to you, in order to drive you far from your land, to make me banish you so that you will perish.*p* *11*The people that submits its neck to the yoke of the king of Babylon to serve him I will leave in peace on its own land, says the LORD, to till it and dwell in it.*q*

*12*To Zedekiah, king of Judah, I spoke the same words: Submit your necks to the yoke of the king of Babylon; serve him and his people, so that you may live.*r* *13*Why should you and your people die by sword, famine, and pestilence, with which the LORD has threatened the nation that will not serve the king of Babylon?*s* *14*Do not listen to the words of those prophets who say, "You need not serve the king of Babylon," for they prophesy lies to you.*t* *15*I did not send them, says the LORD, but they prophesy falsely in my name, with the result that I must banish you, and you will perish, you and the prophets who are prophesying to you.*u*

*16v*To the priests and to all the people I spoke as follows: Thus says the LORD: Do not listen to the words of your prophets who prophesy to you: "The vessels of the house of the LORD will be brought back from Babylon soon now," for they prophesy lies to you. *17*Do not listen to them! Serve the king of Babylon that you may live; else this city will become a heap of ruins. *18*If they were prophets, if the word of the LORD were with them, they would intercede with the LORD of hosts, that the vessels which remain in the house of the LORD and in the palace of the king of Judah and in Jerusalem might not be taken to Babylon. *19*For thus says the LORD of hosts concerning the pillars, the bronze sea, the stands, and the rest of the vessels that remain in this city, *20*which Nebuchadnezzar, king of Babylon, did not take when he exiled Jeconiah, son of Jehoiakim, king of Judah, from Jerusalem to Babylon, along with all the nobles of Judah and Jerusalem— *21*yes, thus says the LORD of hosts, the God of Israel, concerning the vessels that remain in the house of the LORD, in the palace of the king of Judah, and in Jerusalem:*w* *22*To Babylon they shall be brought, and there they shall remain, until the day I look for them, says the LORD; then I will bring them back and restore them to this place.

27, 9: Your prophets: seers and diviners served the Gentile kings as the professional prophets served the kings of Judah.
27, 19-22: This prophecy was fulfilled after Zedekiah's disastrous defeat; cf 2 Kgs 25, 13ff.

m: Jer 25, 11; 2 Chr 36, 20. *n:* Jer 25, 9; Bar 2, 22. *o:* Jer 29, 8. *p:* Jer 14, 13-16. *q:* Bar 2, 21. *r:* Jer 38, 17. *s:* Jer 24, 8ff. *t:* Jer 14, 14; 23, 21. *u:* Jer 20, 6. *v:* Jer 28, 3; 2 Chr 36, 7. 10. 18. *w:* 21f: 2 Kgs 25, 13-17; 2 Chr 36, 18. 22.

CHAPTER 28

The Two Yokes. ¹That same year, in [the beginning of] the reign of Zedekiah, king of Judah, in the fifth month of the fourth year, the prophet Hananiah, son of Azzur, from Gibeon, said to me in the house of the LORD in the presence of the priests and all the people: ²"Thus says the LORD of hosts, the God of Israel: 'I will break the yoke of the king of Babylon. ³Within two years I will restore to this place all the vessels of the temple of the LORD which Nebuchadnezzar, king of Babylon, took away from this place to Babylon. ⁴And I will bring back to this place Jeconiah, son of Jehoiakim, king of Judah, and all the exiles of Judah who went to Babylon,' says the LORD, 'for I will break the yoke of the king of Babylon.' "

⁵The prophet Jeremiah answered the prophet Hananiah in the presence of the priests and all the people assembled in the house of the LORD, ⁶and said: Amen! thus may the LORD do! May he fulfill the things you have prophesied by bringing the vessels of the house of the LORD and all the exiles back from Babylon to this place! ⁷But now, listen to what I am about to state in your hearing and the hearing of all the people. ⁸From of old, the prophets who were before you and me prophesied war, woe, and pestilence against many lands and mighty kingdoms. ⁹But the prophet who prophesies peace is recognized as truly sent by the LORD only when his prophetic prediction is fulfilled.ˣ

¹⁰Thereupon the prophet Hananiah took the yoke from the neck of the prophet Jeremiah, broke it, ¹¹and said in the presence of all the people: "Thus says the LORD: 'Even so, within two years I will break the yoke of Nebuchadnezzar, king of Babylon, from off the neck of all the nations.' " At that, the prophet Jeremiah went away.

¹²Some time after the prophet Hananiah had broken the yoke from off the neck of the prophet Jeremiah, the word of the LORD came to Jeremiah: ¹³Go tell Hananiah this: Thus says the LORD: By breaking a wooden yoke, you forge an iron yoke! ¹⁴For thus says the LORD of hosts, the God of Israel: A yoke of iron I will place on the necks of all these nations serving Nebuchadnezzar, king of Babylon, and they shall serve him; even the beasts of the field I give him.ʸ

¹⁵To the prophet Hananiah the prophet Jeremiah said: Hear this, Hananiah! The LORD has not sent you, and you have raised false confidence in this people. ¹⁶For this, says the LORD, I will dispatch you from the face of the earth; this very year you shall die, because you have preached rebellion against the LORD.ᶻ ¹⁷That same year, in the seventh month, Hananiah the prophet died.

CHAPTER 29

Letter to the Exiles in Babylon. ¹This is the contents of the letter which the prophet Jeremiah sent from Jerusalem to the remaining elders among the exiles, to the priests, the prophets, and all the people who were exiled by Nebuchadnezzar from Jerusalem to Babylon. ²This was after King Jeconiah and the queen mother, the courtiers, the princes of Judah and Jerusalem, the artisans and the skilled workmen had left Jerusalem.ᵃ ³Delivered in Babylon by Elasah,* son of Shaphan, and by Gemariah, son of Hilkiah, whom Zedekiah, king of Judah, sent to the king of Babylon, the letter read:

⁴Thus says the LORD of hosts, the God of Israel, to all the exiles whom I exiled from Jerusalem to Babylon: ⁵Build houses to dwell in; plant gardens, and eat their fruits. ⁶Take wives and beget sons and daughters; find wives for your sons and give your daughters husbands, so that they may bear sons and daughters. There you must increase in number, not decrease. ⁷Promote the welfare of the city to which I have exiled you; pray for it to the LORD, for upon its welfare depends your own.ᵇ

¹⁰Thus says the LORD: Only after seventy

29, 3: Elasah: possibly the brother of Ahikam (cf Jer 26, 24). Gemariah: perhaps the son of the high priest Hilkiah; cf 2 Kgs 22, 4. Zedekiah had dispatched these men to Nebuchadnezzar for some other purpose, possibly the payment of tribute, but Jeremiah took advantage of their mission to send his letter by them.

x: Dt 18, 22.   y: Jer 27, 6f; Dt 28, 48.   z: Dt 13, 6.   a: 2 Kgs 24, 15.   b: 1 Tm 2, 1f.

years have elapsed for Babylon will I visit you and fulfill for you my promise to bring you back to this place.*c* *11*For I know well the plans I have in mind for you, says the LORD, plans for your welfare, not for woe! plans to give you a future full of hope. *12*When you call me, when you go to pray to me, I will listen to you.*d* *13*When you look for me, you will find me. Yes, when you seek me with all your heart, *14*you will find me with you, says the LORD, and I will change your lot; I will gather you together from all the nations and all the places to which I have banished you, says the LORD, and bring you back to the place from which I have exiled you.*e*

*16*Thus says the LORD concerning the king who sits on David's throne, and all the people who remain in this city, your brethren who did not go with you into exile; *17*thus says the LORD of hosts: I am sending against them sword, famine and pestilence. I will make them like rotten figs, too bad to be eaten. *18*I will pursue them with sword, famine, and pestilence, and make them an object of horror to all the kingdoms of the earth, of malediction, astonishment, ridicule, and reproach to all the nations among which I will banish them.*f* *19*For they did not listen to my words, says the LORD, though I kept sending them my servants the prophets, only to have them go unheeded, says the LORD.*g*

*20*You, now, listen to the word of the LORD, all you exiles whom I sent away from Jerusalem to Babylon. *15*As for your saying, "The LORD has raised up for us prophets here in Babylon"— *8*thus says the LORD of hosts, the God of Israel: Do not let yourselves be deceived by the prophets and diviners who are among you; do not listen to those among you who dream dreams.*h* *9*For they prophesy lies to you in my name; I did not send them, says the LORD.*i* *21*This is what the LORD of hosts, the God of Israel, has to say about those who prophesy lies to you in my name, Ahab, son of Kolaiah, and Zedekiah, son of Maaseiah: I am handing them over to Nebuchadnezzar, king of Babylon, who will slay them before your eyes.*j* *22*All the exiles of Judah in Babylon will pattern a curse after them: "May the LORD make you like Zedekiah and Ahab, whom the king of Babylon roasted in the flames." *23*For they are criminals in Israel, committing adultery with their neighbors' wives, and alleging in my name things I did not command. I know, I am witness, says the LORD.*k*

The False Prophet Shemaiah. *24*Say this to Shemaiah, the Nehelamite: *25*Thus says the LORD of hosts, the God of Israel: Because you sent letters on your own authority to all the people of Jerusalem, to all the priests and to Zephaniah, the priest, son of Maaseiah, with this message: *26**"The LORD has appointed you priest in place of the priest Jehoiada, so that there may be police officers in the house of the LORD, to take action against all madmen and those who pose as prophets, by putting them into the stocks or the pillory. *27*Why, then, do you not rebuke Jeremiah of Anathoth who poses as a prophet among you? *28*For he sent us in Babylon this message: It will be a long time; build houses to live in; plant gardens and eat their fruits. . . ."

*29*When the priest Zephaniah read this letter to the prophet, *30*the word of the LORD came to Jeremiah: *31*Send the message to all the exiles: Thus says the LORD concerning Shemaiah, the Nehelamite: Because Shemaiah prophesies to you without a mission from me, and raises false confidence, *32*says the LORD, I will therefore punish Shemaiah, the Nehelamite, and his offspring. None of them shall survive among this people to see the good I will do to this people, says the LORD, because he preached rebellion against the LORD.

29, 26-29: The words of Jeremiah to the false prophet Shemaiah are not fully preserved in the current Hebrew text, as is seen in the incomplete sentence of this translation (vv 25-28). In his letter to Zephaniah Shemaiah reminds him of his authority, as Pashhur's successor, to imprison Jeremiah. Zephaniah, however, merely reads the letter to Jeremiah but does not imprison him.

c: Jer 25, 11; 2 Chr 36, 21f; Ezr 1, 1; Dn 9, 2; Zec 1, 12; 7, 5.   *d:* Jer 33, 3.   *e:* Jer 23, 3. 8.   *f:* Jer 15, 4; 24, 9; 34, 17f.   *g:* Jer 25, 4.   *h:* Jer 27, 9. 14.   *i:* Jer 5, 31.   *j:* Jer 14, 14.   *k:* Jer 23, 14.

CHAPTER 30

See RG
217–18

The Restoration.* *¹The following
message came to Jeremiah from the LORD:
²Thus says the LORD, the God of Israel:
Write all the words I have spoken to you in a
book.*ˡ* ³For behold, the days will come, says
the LORD, when I will change the lot of my
people (of Israel and Judah, says the LORD),
and bring them back to the land which I gave
to their fathers; they shall have it as their
possession.*ᵐ*

⁴These are the words which the LORD
spoke to Israel and to Judah: ⁵thus says the
LORD:

A cry of dismay we hear;
    fear reigns, not peace.
⁶ Inquire, and see:
    since when do men bear children?
Why, then, do I see all these men,
    with their hands on their loins
    like women in childbirth?
Why have all their faces turned deathly
    pale?*ⁿ*
⁷ How mighty is that day—
    none like it!
A time of distress for Jacob,
    though he shall be saved from
      it.*ᵒ*

⁸On that day, says the LORD of hosts, "I
will break his yoke from off your necks and
snap your bonds." Strangers shall no longer
enslave them;*ᵖ* ⁹instead, they shall serve
the LORD, their God, and David, their king,*
whom I will raise up for them.*�q*

¹⁰ But you, my servant Jacob, fear not, says
    the LORD,
    be not dismayed, O Israel!
Behold, I will deliver you from the
    far-off land,

your descendants, from their land of
    exile;
Jacob shall again find rest,
    shall be tranquil and undisturbed,*ʳ*
¹¹   for I am with you, says the LORD, to
      deliver you.
I will make an end of all the nations
    among which I have scattered you;
    but of you I will not make an end.
I will chastise you as you deserve,
    I will not let you go unpunished.*ˢ*

¹²   For thus says the LORD:
Incurable is your wound,
    grievous your bruise;*ᵗ*
¹³ There is none to plead your cause,
    no remedy for your running sore,
    no healing for you.
¹⁴ All your lovers have forgotten you,
    they do not seek you.
I struck you as an enemy would strike,
    punished you cruelly;*ᵘ*
¹⁵ Why cry out over your wound?
    your pain is without relief.
Because of your great guilt,
    your numerous sins,
    I have done this to you.*ᵛ*
¹⁶ Yet all who devour you shall be devoured,
    all your enemies shall go into exile.
All who plunder you shall be plundered,
    all who pillage you I will hand over to
      pillage.*ʷ*
¹⁷ For I will restore you to health;
    of your wounds I will heal you, says
      the LORD.
"The outcast" they have called you,
    "with no avenger."*ˣ*

¹⁸   Thus says the LORD:
See! I will restore the tents of Jacob,
    his dwellings I will pity;
City shall be rebuilt upon hill,
    and palace restored as it was.*ʸ*

30, 1—31, 40: These two chapters do not belong chronologically to those that precede or follow. They contain mainly
oracles of salvation which Jeremiah originally uttered on behalf of the conquered remnants of the northern kingdom;
then, after Judah began to share Samaria's fate, the oracles
were extended to include Judah. Their composition is to be
placed early in Jeremiah's ministry, probably after the fall of
Nineveh (612 B.C.), when Josiah assumed power over the
North; cf 2 Kgs 23, 15ff.

30, 9: David, their king: the messianic King of the Davidic

line, often called David by the prophets; cf Ez 34, 23f; 37,
24f; Hos 3, 5.

l: Jer 36, 2; Hb 2, 2; Rv 1, 11.   *m:* Jer 29, 14; 31, 8. 10. 23. 32,
37. 44; Ez 39, 25; Am 9, 14.   *n:* Jer 6, 24; 50, 43.   *o:* Am 5. 18;
Zep 1. 14f.   *p:* Is 14, 5f; Ez 34, 27.   *q:* Ez 34, 23; 37, 24; Hos 3,
5; Lk 1, 69.   *r:* Jer 46, 27; Is 43, 5.   *s:* Jer 46, 28; Ez 11, 16f; Am
9, 8f.   *t:* Jer 10, 19; 14, 17; 15, 18.   *u:* Jer 22, 22; Lam 1, 19.
v: Jer 15, 18.   *w:* Jer 2, 3.   *x:* Jer 33, 6.   *y:* Jer 33, 7. 11; Ezr 6,
3-15; Ez 36, 10.

Little Book of Consolation

These chapters combine poetry (chs 30–31) and prose (chs 32–33) to depict a harmonious, idealized future for Israel and Judah. The placement of these chapters of hope and healing toward the center of the book is puzzling. Stories and poems of accusation and conflict surround them as if to temper the hope the chapters create. This structure may reflect the situation of the exilic audience, for whom escape from captivity remains a distant possibility. The chapters create a vision of what lies ahead, but they do not present a program for escape. Instead, they create unimagined possibilities that may help the community endure for a new day.

¹⁹ From them will resound songs of
    praise,
  the laughter of happy men.
I will make them not few, but many;
  they will not be tiny, for I will glorify
    them.^z
²⁰ His sons shall be as of old,
  his assembly before me shall stand
    firm;
I will punish all his oppressors.^a
²¹ His leader* shall be one of his own,
  and his rulers shall come from his
    kin.
When I summon him, he shall approach
    me;
  how else should one take the deadly
    risk
  of approaching me? says the LORD.
²² You shall be my people,
  and I will be your God.^b

²³ See, the storm of the LORD!
  His wrath breaks forth
In a whirling storm
  that bursts upon the heads of the
    wicked.^c
²⁴ The anger of the LORD will not abate
  until he has done and fulfilled
what he has determined in his
    heart.
When the time comes,
  you will fully understand.^d

CHAPTER 31

Good News of the Return

See RG 217–18

¹ At that time, says the LORD,
  I will be the God of all the tribes of
    Israel,
  and they shall be my people.^e
²   Thus says the LORD:
The people that escaped the sword*
  have found favor in the desert.
As Israel comes forward to be given his
    rest,
³   the LORD appears to him from afar:
With age-old love I have loved you;
  so I have kept my mercy toward you.^f
⁴ Again I will restore you, and you shall be
    rebuilt,
  O virgin Israel;
Carrying your festive tambourines,
  you shall go forth dancing with the
    merrymakers.
⁵ Again you shall plant vineyards
  on the mountains of Samaria;
  those who plant them shall enjoy the
    fruits.^g
⁶ Yes, a day will come when the watchmen
  will call out on Mount Ephraim:
"Rise up, let us go to Zion,
  to the LORD, our God."^h

The Road of Return

⁷   For thus says the LORD:

30, 21: His leader: probably not the messianic King, but simply any one of the rulers of the restored Israel, who will no longer be foreigners, and with whom the Lord will be on terms of intimacy, as with the whole people. The deadly risk of approaching me: to approach God unsummoned brings death; cf Lv 16, 1f.

31, 2: The people that escaped the sword: the exiles who were not killed but deported; they have found favor in the desert, across which they were driven into captivity. The

prophet alludes to the first desert wandering of Israel (Ex 16ff), in which the people found the Lord. His rest: the land of promise. The perfect fulfillment of this promised rest is found only in the New Testament (Heb chapters 3 and 4).

z: Is 35, 10; 51, 11.   a: Is 49, 26.   b: Jer 24, 7; 31, 1. 33; 32, 38; Lv 26, 12; Ez 11, 20; 36, 28.   c: Jer 23, 19.   d: Jer 23, 20. e: Jer 30, 22.   f: Dt 7, 8; 10, 15; Is 43, 4; 63, 9; Hos 11, 1. 4. g: Is 65, 21; Am 9, 14.   h: Is 2, 3; 27, 13; Mi 4, 2.

Israel as Rachel

The portrayal of Israel as Rachel weeping for her lost children (31, 15) draws upon the tragic tradition of Rachel, Jacob's beloved wife, who died while giving birth to Benjamin. Although Genesis 35, 16–21 places her tomb on the road to Bethlehem, where the current structure stands, 1 Samuel 10, 2 suggests that her tomb was on the road to Ramah, near modern Ramallah. The present text portrays Rachel weeping not for herself but for her lost children who have gone into exile.

Shout with joy for Jacob,
    exult at the head of the nations;
    proclaim your praise and say:
The LORD has delivered his people,
    the remnant of Israel.[i]
[8] Behold, I will bring them back
    from the land of the north;
I will gather them from the ends of the
    world,
    with the blind and the lame in their
    midst,
The mothers and those with child;
    they shall return as an immense
    throng.[j]
[9] They departed in tears,
    but I will console them and guide
    them;
I will lead them to brooks of water,
    on a level road, so that none shall
    stumble.
For I am a father to Israel,
    Ephraim is my first-born.[k]
[10] Hear the word of the LORD, O nations,
    proclaim it on distant coasts, and
    say:
He who scattered Israel, now gathers
    them together,
    he guards them as a shepherd his
    flock.
[11] The LORD shall ransom Jacob,
    he shall redeem him from the hand of
    his conqueror.[l]
[12] Shouting, they shall mount the heights of
    Zion,
    they shall come streaming to the
    LORD's blessings:
The grain, the wine, and the oil,

the sheep and the oxen;
They themselves shall be like watered
    gardens,
    never again shall they languish.[m]
[13] Then the virgins shall make merry and
    dance,
    and young men and old as well.
I will turn their mourning into joy,
    I will console and gladden them after
    their sorrows.
[14] I will lavish choice portions upon the
    priests,
    and my people shall be filled with my
    blessings,
says the LORD.

End of Rachel's Mourning

[15]   Thus says the LORD:
In Ramah* is heard the sound of
    moaning,
    of bitter weeping!
Rachel mourns her children,
    she refuses to be consoled
    because her children are no
    more.[n]
[16]   Thus says the LORD:
Cease your cries of mourning,
    wipe the tears from your eyes.
The sorrow you have shown shall have
    its reward,
    says the LORD,
    they shall return from the enemy's
    land.
[17] There is hope for your future, says the
    LORD;
    your sons shall return to their own
    borders.[o]

31, 15: Ramah: a village about five miles north of Jerusalem, where Rachel was buried (1 Sm 10, 2). Rachel: said to mourn for her children since she was the ancestress of Ephraim, the chief of the northern tribes. Mt 2, 18 applies this verse to the slaughter of the innocents by Herod.

i: Is 12, 6.   *j*: Jer 3, 18; 23, 3. 8; Is 35, 5f.   *k*: Ex 4, 22.   *l*: Is 44, 23; 48, 20.   *m*: Is 58, 11.   *n*: Mt 2, 18.   *o*: Jer 29, 10-14.

¹⁸ I hear, I hear Ephraim pleading:
  You chastised me, and I am chastened;
  I was an untamed calf.
If you allow me, I will return,
  for you are the LORD, my God.ᵖ
¹⁹ I turn in repentance;
  I have come to myself, I strike my
    breast;
I blush with shame,
  I bear the disgrace of my youth.�q
²⁰ Is Ephraim not my favored son,
  the child in whom I delight?
Often as I threaten him,
  I still remember him with favor;
My heart stirs for him,
  I must show him mercy, says the LORD.ʳ

Summons To Return Home

²¹ Set up road markers,
  put up guideposts;
Turn your attention to the highway,
  the road by which you went.
Turn back, O virgin Israel,
  turn back to these your cities.
²² How long will you continue to stray,
  rebellious daughter?
The LORD has created a new thing upon
    the earth:
  the woman must encompass the man*
    with devotion.

²³Thus says the LORD of hosts, the God of Israel: When I change their lot in the land of Judah and her cities, they shall again repeat this greeting: "May the LORD bless you, holy mountain, abode of justice!"ˢ ²⁴Judah and all her cities, the farmers and those who lead the flock, shall dwell there together. ²⁵For I will refresh the weary soul; every soul that languishes I will replenish. ²⁶Upon this I awoke and opened my eyes; but my sleep was sweet to me.*

²⁷The days are coming, says the LORD, when I will seed the house of Israel and the house of Judah with the seed of man and the seed of beast. ²⁸As I once watched over them to uproot and pull down, to destroy, to ruin, and to harm, so I will watch over them to build and to plant, says the LORD.ᵗ ²⁹In those days they shall no longer say,

"The fathers ate unripe grapes,ᵘ
  and the children's teeth are set on
    edge,"*

³⁰but through his own fault only shall anyone die: the teeth of him who eats the unripe grapes shall be set on edge.

The New Covenant.* ³¹The days are coming, says the LORD, when I will make a new covenant with the house of Israel and the house of Judah.ᵛ ³²It will not be like the covenant I made with their fathers the day I took them by the hand to lead them forth from the land of Egypt; for they broke my covenant and I had to show myself their master, says the LORD.ʷ ³³But this is the covenant which I will make with the house of Israel after those

---

31, 22: The woman must encompass the man: the words "with devotion," not in the Hebrew, are added for the sense. No fully satisfactory explanation has been given this text. Among the more probable are these: (a) Formerly the man (the Lord) encompassed the woman (Israel) with mercy and devotion; now in the spiritual religion of Israel which will follow on the restoration, this order will be reversed. (b) So secure will Israel be after the restoration that women will no longer need the natural protection of their husbands, but even weak women can protect men. (c) St. Jerome in his commentary on this verse understood it of Mary's virginal conception of Christ. "The Lord has created a new thing on earth; without seed of man, without carnal union and conception, 'a woman will encompass a man' within her womb—One who, though He will later appear to advance in wisdom and age through the stages of infancy and childhood, yet, while confined for the usual number of months in his mother's womb, will already be perfect man."

31, 26: I awoke . . . sweet to me: probably said by the prophet himself.

31, 29: "The fathers . . . on edge": a proverb used in Israel, expressing the idea that children suffer for the sins of their parents (cf Ez 18, 2). The Israel of the restoration will be characterized instead by personal responsibility and retribution for one's acts (v 30; cf vv 31-34).

31, 31-34: The new covenant to be made with Israel is a common theme of the prophets, beginning with Hosea. According to Jeremiah, the qualities of the new covenant that make it different from the old are: (a) It will not be broken, but will last forever; (b) Its law will be written in the heart, not merely on tablets of stone; (c) The knowledge of God will be so generally shown forth in the life of the people that it will no longer be necessary to put it into words of instruction. In the fullest sense, this prophecy was fulfilled only through the work of Jesus Christ; cf Lk 22, 20; 1 Cor 11, 25.

p: Lv 26, 40ff. *q:* Dt 30, 1ff. *r:* Hos 11, 8. *s:* Jer 30, 3; Ps 122, 8. *t:* Jer 1, 10; 18, 7. *u:* Dt 24, 16; Ez 18, 2. *v:* Jer 32, 40; Heb 9, 15. *w:* Ex 24, 7f; Dt 5, 2.

days, says the LORD. I will place my law within them, and write it upon their hearts; I will be their God, and they shall be my people.[x] [34]No longer will they have need to teach their friends and kinsmen how to know the LORD. All, from least to greatest, shall know me, says the LORD, for I will forgive their evildoing and remember their sin no more.[y]

Certainty of God's Promise

[35] Thus says the LORD,

He who gives the sun to light the day,
    moon and stars to light the night;
Who stirs up the sea till its waves roar,
    whose name is LORD of hosts:[z]
[36] If ever these natural laws give way
    in spite of me, says the LORD,
Then shall the race of Israel cease
    as a nation before me forever.[a]
[37] Thus says the LORD:
If the heavens on high can be
    measured,
    or the foundations below the earth be
    sounded,
Then will I cast off the whole race of
    Israel
    because of all they have done, says the
    LORD.

Rebuilding of Jerusalem. [38]The days are coming, says the LORD, when the city shall be rebuilt as the LORD's,[b] from the Tower of Hananel to the Corner Gate.* [39]The measuring line shall be stretched from there straight to the hill Gareb and then turn to Goah. [40]The whole valley of corpses and ashes,* all the slopes toward the Kidron Valley, as far as the corner of the Horse Gate at the east, shall

be holy to the LORD. Never again shall the city be rooted up or thrown down.

CHAPTER 32

See RG
217–18

Pledge of Restoration.* [1]This message came to Jeremiah from the LORD in the tenth year of Zedekiah,* king of Judah, the eighteenth year of Nebuchadnezzar. [2]At that time the army of the king of Babylon was besieging Jerusalem, and the prophet Jeremiah was imprisoned in the quarters of the guard, at the king's palace.[c] [3]Zedekiah, king of Judah, had imprisoned him there, remonstrating: "How dare you prophesy: Thus says the LORD: I am handing over this city to the king of Babylon, who will capture it.[d] [4]Neither shall Zedekiah, king of Judah, escape the hands of the Chaldeans; rather shall he be handed over to the king of Babylon. They shall meet and speak face to face,[e] [5]and Zedekiah shall be taken to Babylon. There he shall remain, until I attend to him, says the LORD; in fighting the Chaldeans, you cannot win!"[f]

[6]*This message came to me from the LORD, said Jeremiah: [7]Hanamel, son of your uncle Shallum, will come to you with the offer:[g] "Buy for yourself my field in Anathoth, since you, as nearest relative, have the first right of purchase."* [8]Then, as the LORD foretold, Hanamel, my uncle's son, came to me to the quarters of the guard and said, "Please buy my field in Anathoth, in the district of Benjamin; as nearest relative, you have the first claim to possess it; make it yours." I knew this was what the LORD meant, [9]so I bought the field in Anathoth from my cousin Hanamel, paying him the money, seventeen silver shekels.

31, 38: From the Tower of Hananel to the Corner Gate: from the northeast to the northwest.

31, 40: Valley of corpses and ashes: the Valley of Benhinnom, which joins the Kidron at the southeast of ancient Jerusalem. The Horse Gate: in the eastern city wall, at the southeast corner of the temple area.

32, 1-44: This chapter recounts a prophecy "in action." At the Lord's command, Jeremiah fulfills his family duty to purchase the land of his cousin, carrying out all the legal forms, including records, to testify that Judah will be restored and that the life of the past will be resumed.

32, 1: The tenth year of Zedekiah: 588 B.C. The eighteenth year of Nebuchadnezzar: dating his reign from his victory at Carchemish; see note on Jer 25, 1-14.

32, 6-9: Jeremiah's imprisonment by the weak-willed

Zedekiah was a technical custody that did not deprive him of all freedom of action. The siege maintained by the Chaldeans (v 2) was only now beginning (v 24), and could be bypassed by individual persons going to and fro between Jerusalem and nearby Anathoth.

32, 7: The first right of purchase: the obligation of the closest relative to redeem the property of one in economic distress, so that the ancestral land might remain within the family (Lv 25, 25-28); see note on Ru 2, 20.

---

x: Jer 32, 40; Ez 37, 26; Heb 10, 16.   y: Is 54, 13.   z: Gn 1, 14-18   a: Jer 33, 20f.   b: Neh 12, 38; Zec 14, 10f.   c: Jer 33, 1; 37, 20; 38, 6; 39, 14.   d: Jer 26, 9; 34, 2; 37, 6-10.   e: Jer 34, 3; 38, 18. 23; 39, 4-7.   f: Jer 39, 7; 52, 11.   g: Lv 25, 24-34; Ru 4, 4.

[10]When I had written and sealed the deed, called witnesses and weighed out the silver on the scales, [11]I accepted the deed of purchase, both the sealed copy, containing title and conditions, and the open one.* [12]This deed of purchase I gave to Baruch, son of Neriah, son of Mahseiah, in the presence of my cousin Hanamel and of the witnesses who had signed the deed, and before all the men of Judah who happened to be in the quarters of the guard.[h]

[13]In their presence I gave Baruch this charge: [14]Thus says the LORD of hosts, the God of Israel: Take these deeds, both the sealed and the open deed of purchase, and put them in an earthen jar,* so that they can be kept there a long time. [15]For thus says the LORD of hosts, the God of Israel: Houses and fields and vineyards shall again be bought in this land.

[16]After giving the deed of purchase to Baruch, son of Neriah, I prayed thus to the LORD: [17]Ah, Lord GOD, you have made heaven and earth by your great might, with your outstretched arm; nothing is impossible to you.[i] [18]You continue your kindness through a thousand generations; and you repay the fathers' guilt, even into the lap of their sons who follow them. O God, great and mighty, whose name is LORD of hosts,[j] [19]great in counsel, mighty in deed, whose eyes are open to all the ways of men, giving to each according to his ways, according to the fruit of his deeds:[k] [20]you have wrought signs and wonders in the land of Egypt and to this day, both in Israel and among all other men, until now you have gained renown.[l] [21]With strong hand and outstretched arm you brought your people Israel out of the land of Egypt amid signs and wonders and great terror. [22]This land you gave them, as you had promised their fathers under oath, a land flowing with milk and honey.[m] [23]They entered and took possession of it, but they

did not listen to your voice; by your law they did not live, and what you commanded they failed to do. Hence you let all these evils befall them.[n] [24]See, the siegeworks have arrived at this city to breach it; the city will be handed over to the Chaldeans who are attacking it, amid sword, famine, and pestilence. What you threatened has happened, you see it yourself;[o] [25]and yet you tell me, O Lord GOD: Buy the field with money, call in witnesses. But the city has already been handed over to the Chaldeans!

[26]Then this word of the LORD came to Jeremiah: [27]I am the LORD, the God of all mankind! Is anything impossible to me? [28]This now is what the LORD says: I will hand over this city to the Chaldeans, for Nebuchadnezzar, king of Babylon, to take. [29]The Chaldeans who are attacking it shall enter this city and set fire to it, burning it and its houses, on the roofs of which incense was burned to Baal and libations were poured out to strange gods as a provocation to me.[p] [30]The Israelites and the Judeans from their youth have done only what is evil in my eyes; the Israelites did nothing but provoke me with the works of their hands, says the LORD.[q] [31]From the day it was built to this day, this city has excited my anger and wrath, [32]so that I must put it out of my sight for all the wickedness the Israelites and Judeans, with their kings and their princes, their priests and their prophets, the men of Judah and the citizens of Jerusalem, have done to provoke me.[r] [33]They turned their backs to me, not their faces; though I kept teaching them, they would not listen to my correction.[s] [34]They defiled the house named after me by the horrid idols they set up in it.[t] [35]They built high places to Baal in the Valley of Ben-hinnom, and immolated their sons and daughters to Molech,* bringing sin upon Judah; this I never commanded them, nor

---

32, 11: The sealed copy . . . and the open one: the legal deed of sale was written on a scroll, which was then rolled up and sealed; about it was rolled another scroll, left unsealed, containing a copy or a summary of the first.

32, 14: In an earthen jar: the first of the Dead Sea Scrolls were found in such a jar.

32, 35: Molech: the god to whom human sacrifice was offered in the Valley of Ben-hinnom. Here, as in Jer 19, 5, he is

given the name Baal; see note on Lv 18, 21.

h: Jer 36, 4.   i: 2 Kgs 19, 15; Jb 42, 2.   j: Ex 20, 5f; Dt 5, 9.   k: Jb 34, 21; Ps 33, 13ff.   l: Ex 6, 6; Dt 4, 34; Ps 135, 9.   m: Jer 11, 5; Gn 15, 18; 17, 8; 26, 3.   n: Jer 7, 24ff; Dn 9, 10-14.   o: Jer 21, 5; 33, 4.   p: Jer 21, 10; 37, 8ff.   q: Jer 3, 25; 44, 8.   r: Jer 2, 26; Is 3, 8.   s: Jer 7, 24.   t: Jer 7, 30; 2 Kgs 21, 4f.

did it even enter my mind that they should practice such abominations.*

³⁶Now, therefore, thus says the LORD, the God of Israel, concerning this city, which as you say is handed over to the king of Babylon amid sword, famine, and pestilence: ³⁷Behold, I will gather them together from all the lands to which in anger, wrath, and great rage I banish them; I will bring them back to this place and settle them here in safety.ᵛ ³⁸They shall be my people, and I will be their God.ʷ ³⁹One heart and one way I will give them, that they may fear me always, to their own good and that of their children after them. ⁴⁰I will make with them an eternal covenant, never to cease doing good to them; into their hearts I will put the fear of me, that they may never depart from me.ˣ ⁴¹I will take delight in doing good to them: I will replant them firmly in this land, with all my heart and soul.ʸ

⁴²For thus says the LORD: Just as I brought upon this people all this great evil, so I will bring upon them all the good I promise them.ᶻ ⁴³Fields shall again be bought in this land, which you call a desert, without man or beast, handed over to the Chaldeans.ᵃ ⁴⁴Fields shall be bought with money, deeds written and sealed, and witnesses shall be used in the land of Benjamin, in the suburbs of Jerusalem, in the cities of Judah and of the hill country, in the cities of the foothills and of the Negeb, when I change their lot, says the LORD.ᵇ

CHAPTER 33

See RG 217–18

Restoration of Jerusalem. ¹The word of the LORD came to Jeremiah a second time while he was still imprisoned in the quarters of the guard: ²Thus says the LORD who made the earth and gave it form and firmness, whose name is LORD: ³Call to me, and I will answer you; I will tell you things great beyond reach of your knowledge.ᶜ ⁴Thus says the LORD, the God of Israel, concerning the houses of this city and the palaces of Judah's

kings, which are being destroyed in the face of siegeworks and the sword:ᵈ ⁵men come to battle the Chaldeans, and these houses will be filled with the corpses of those whom I slay in my anger and wrath, when I hide my face from this city for all their wickedness.ᵉ

⁶Behold, I will treat and assuage the city's wounds; I will heal them, and reveal to them an abundance of lasting peace.ᶠ ⁷I will change the lot of Judah and the lot of Israel, and rebuild them as of old.ᵍ ⁸I will cleanse them of all the guilt they incurred by sinning against me; all their offenses by which they sinned and rebelled against me, I will forgive.ʰ ⁹Then Jerusalem shall be my joy, my praise, my glory, before all the nations of the earth, as they hear of all the good I will do among them. They shall be in fear and trembling over all the peaceful benefits I will give her.

¹⁰Thus says the LORD: In this place of which you say, "How desolate it is, without man, without beast!" and in the cities of Judah, in the streets of Jerusalem that are now deserted, without man, without citizen, without beast, there shall yet be heardⁱ ¹¹the cry of joy, the cry of gladness, the voice of the bridegroom, the voice of the bride, the sound of those who bring thank offerings to the house of the LORD, singing, "Give thanks to the LORD of hosts, for the LORD is good; his mercy endures forever." For I will restore this country as of old, says the LORD.ʲ

¹²Thus says the LORD of hosts: In this place, now desolate, without man or beast, and in all its cities there shall again be sheepfolds for the shepherds to couch their flocks. ¹³In the cities of the hill country, of the foothills, and of the Negeb, in the land of Benjamin and the suburbs of Jerusalem, and in the cities of Judah, flocks will again pass under the hands of the one who counts them, says the LORD.

¹⁴*The days are coming, says the LORD, when I will fulfill the promise I made to the

---

33, 14-26: This is the longest continuous passage in the Book of Jeremiah that is lacking in the Greek. It appears to be the post-exilic composition of an inspired writer who used parts of the prophecies of Jeremiah—often, however, in a sense different from the prophet's. The prediction of an eternal Davidic dynasty (14-17) to fulfill the prophecy of Nathan (2 Sm 7, 11-16), and of a per-

u: Jer 7, 31; 19, 5; Ps 106, 37f. *v:* Jer 23, 3; 29, 14; Is 11, 12; Ez 11, 17. *w:* Jer 24, 7; 31, 33. *x:* Jer 31, 31ff. *y:* Dt 30, 9. *z:* Jer 33, 10-14; Zec 8, 13. *a:* Jer 33, 10. *b:* Jer 17, 26; 33, 7. *c:* Is 48, 6. *d:* Jer 32, 24. *e:* Jer 21, 4ff. *f:* Is 57, 18. *g:* Jer 30, 3; 32, 44. *h:* Ez 36, 25. *i:* Jer 32, 43. *j:* 1 Chr 16, 34; Ezr 3, 11; Ps 136, 1.

house of Israel and Judah. [15]In those days, in that time, I will raise up for David a just shoot; he shall do what is right and just in the land.[k] [16]In those days Judah shall be safe and Jerusalem shall dwell secure; this is what they shall call her: "The LORD our justice." [17]For thus says the LORD: Never shall David lack a successor on the throne of the house of Israel,[l] [18]nor shall priests of Levi ever be lacking, to offer holocausts before me, to burn cereal offerings, and to sacrifice victims.[m]

This word of the LORD also came to Jeremiah: [19]Thus says the LORD: [20]If you can break my covenant with day,[n] and my covenant with night, so that day and night no longer alternate in sequence, [21]then can my covenant with my servant David also be broken, so that he will not have a son to be king upon his throne, and my covenant with the priests of Levi who minister to me. [22]Like the host of heaven which cannot be numbered, and the sands of the sea which cannot be counted, I will multiply the descendants of my servant David and the Levites who minister to me.

[23]This word of the LORD came to Jeremiah: [24]Have you not noticed what these people are saying: "The LORD has rejected the two tribes which he had chosen"? They spurn my people as if it were no longer a nation in their eyes.[o] [25][p]Thus says the LORD: When I have no covenant with day and night, and have given no laws to heaven and earth, [26]then too will I reject the descendants of Jacob and of my servant David, so as not to take from his descendants rulers for the race of Abraham, Isaac, and Jacob. For I will change their lot and show them mercy.

IV: Fall of Jerusalem

CHAPTER 34

See RG
217 *Fate of Zedekiah.* [1]This word came

to Jeremiah from the LORD while Nebuchadnezzar, king of Babylon, and his armies and the earth's kingdoms subject to him, as well as the other peoples, were all attacking Jerusalem and all her cities:[q] [2]Thus says the LORD, the God of Israel: Go to Zedekiah, king of Judah, and tell him: Thus says the LORD: I am handing this city over to the king of Babylon; he will destroy it with fire.[r] [3]Neither shall you escape his hand; rather you will be captured and fall into his hands. You shall see the king of Babylon and speak to him face to face. Then you shall be taken to Babylon.[s]

[4]But if you obey the word of the LORD, Zedekiah, king of Judah, then, says the LORD to you, you shall not die by the sword. [5]You shall die in peace, and they will lament you as their lord, and burn spices for your burial as they did for your fathers, the kings who preceded you from the first; it is I who make this promise, says the LORD.

[6]The prophet Jeremiah told all these things to Zedekiah, king of Judah, in Jerusalem, [7]while the armies of the king of Babylon were attacking Jerusalem and the remaining cities of Judah, Lachish, and Azekah,* since these alone were left of the fortified cities of Judah.

The Pact Broken.* [8]This is the word that came to Jeremiah from the LORD after King Zedekiah had made an agreement with all the people in Jerusalem to issue an edict of emancipation. [9]Everyone was to free his Hebrew slaves, male and female, so that no one should hold a man of Judah, his brother, in slavery.[t] [10]All the princes and the others who entered the agreement consented to set free their male and female servants, so that they should be slaves no longer. But though they agreed and freed them, [11]afterward they took back their male and female slaves whom they had set free and again forced them into service.

---

petual priesthood and sacrifice (18), was not to be realized in the restoration of the Jewish nation. It finds its fulfillment only in Jesus of Nazareth, who combined with his messianic Davidic kingship an eternal priesthood; cf Heb 6, 20; 7, 24f.

34, 7: Lachish, and Azekah: fortress towns to the southwest of Jerusalem which Nebuchadnezzar besieged to prevent help coming to Jerusalem from Egypt. Between 1935 and 1938, archaeologists found at Lachish several letters written on pottery fragments which date from 598 or 588

B.C., and which mention both Lachish and Azekah.

34, 8-22: While the Chaldean siege of Jerusalem was in progress, the citizens of Jerusalem made a covenant at Zede-

k: Jer 23, 5; Ps 72, 1-4. 12ff; Is 11, 1. *l:* 2 Sm 7, 16; 1 Kgs 2, 4; Ps 89, 4f. 29. 36f. *m:* Ez 44, 15f. *n:* 20f: Jer 31, 36f; Ps 89, 37f. *o:* Rom 11, 1f. *p:* 25f: Jer 31, 36f; 32, 44. *q:* Jer 52, 4; 2 Kgs 25, 1. *r:* Jer 21, 10; 32, 3. 28. *s:* Jer 32, 4; 52, 11. *t:* Ex 21, 2ff; Lv 25, 39. 46; Dt 15, 12-15.

¹²Then this word of the LORD came to Jeremiah: ¹³Thus says the LORD, the God of Israel: The day I brought your fathers out of the land of Egypt, out of the place where they were slaves, I made this covenant with them: ¹⁴Every seventh year each of you shall set free his Hebrew brother who has sold himself to you; six years he shall serve you, but then you shall let him go free. Your fathers, however, did not heed me or obey me. ¹⁵Today you indeed repented and did what is right in my eyes by proclaiming the emancipation of your brethren and making an agreement before me in the house that is named after me. ¹⁶But then you changed your mind and profaned my name by taking back your male and female slaves to whom you had given their freedom; you forced them once more into slavery.ᵘ ¹⁷Therefore, thus says the LORD: You did not obey me by proclaiming your neighbors and kinsmen free. I now proclaim you free, says the LORD, for the sword, famine, and pestilence. I will make you an object of horror to all the kingdoms of the earth. ¹⁸*The men who violated my covenant and did not observe the terms of the agreement which they made before me, I will make like the calf which they cut in two, between whose two parts they passed. ¹⁹The princes of Judah and of Jerusalem, the courtiers, the priests, and the common people, who passed between the parts of the calf, ²⁰I will hand over, all of them, to their enemies, to those who seek their lives: their corpses shall be food for the birds of the air and the beasts of the field.ᵛ

²¹Zedekiah, too, king of Judah, and his princes, I will hand over to their enemies, to those who seek their lives, to the soldiers of the king of Babylon who have at present withdrawn from you.ʷ ²²I will give the command, says the LORD, and bring them back to this city. They shall attack and capture it, and destroy it with fire; the cities of Judah I will turn into a desert where no man dwells.ˣ

See RG 217

CHAPTER 35

The Faithful Rechabites. ¹This word came to Jeremiah from the LORD in the days of Jehoiakim, son of Josiah, king of Judah: ²Approach the Rechabites* and speak to them; bring them into the house of the LORD, to one of the rooms, and give them wine to drink. ³So I went and brought Jaazaniah, son of Jeremiah, son of Habazziniah, his brothers and all his sons, the whole company of the Rechabites, ⁴into the house of the LORD, to the room of the sons of Hanan,* son of Igdaliah, the man of God, next to the princes' room, above the room of Maaseiah, son of Shallum, keeper of the doorway. ⁵I set before these Rechabite men bowls full of wine and offered them cups to drink the wine.

⁵"We do not drink wine," they said to me: "Jonadab,* Rechab's son, our father, forbade us in these words: 'Neither you nor your children shall ever drink wine. ⁷Build no house and sow no seed; neither plant nor own a vineyard. You shall dwell in tents all your life, so that you may live long on the earth where you are wayfarers.' ⁸Now we have heeded Jonadab, Rechab's son, our father, in all his prohibitions. All our lives we have not drunk wine, neither we, nor our

---

kiah's instigation to free their brother Judeans who were in slavery. Doubtless this was both to provide additional free defenders for the city and to offer reparation for past violations of the law, according to which Hebrew slaves were to serve no longer than six years (Dt 15, 12-15). But when the siege was temporarily lifted, probably because of the help promised by Pharaoh Hophra (cf Jer 37, 5), the inhabitants of Jerusalem broke the covenant and once more pressed their brethren into slavery (v 11).

34, 18f: As the Bible (Gn 15, 10-17) and also contemporary inscriptions make clear, agreements were sometimes ratified by walking between the divided pieces of animals while the contracting parties invoked on themselves a fate similar to that of the slaughtered beast if they should fail to keep their word. The agreement: that mentioned in vv 10. 15.

35, 2: The Rechabites: reactionaries who believed that the Lord could not be well served except by maintaining the original nomadic conditions of Israel's life. Without sharing their convictions, the prophet holds up their fidelity to their ideals as an example to put to shame his faithless countrymen. In the days of Jehoiakim: probably in 599 or 598 B.C.

35, 4: The sons of Hanan: probably the disciples of this man of God or prophet. Maaseiah: possibly the father of the priest Zephaniah (Jer 29, 25; 37, 3). Keeper of the doorway: a priestly function of responsibility; cf Jer 52, 24.

35, 6: Jonadab: a contemporary of King Jehu; cf 2 Kgs 10, 15ff.

---

u: Lv 19, 12.   *v:* Jer 7, 33; 16, 4; 19, 7.   *w:* Jer 37, 5. 11.   *x:* Jer 37, 8; 52, 7-13; 2 Chr 36, 17. 19.

wives, nor our sons, nor our daughters. [9]We build no houses to live in; we own no vineyards or fields or crops, [10]and we live in tents; we obediently do everything our father Jonadab commanded us. [11]But when Nebuchadnezzar, king of Babylon, invaded this land, we decided to come into Jerusalem to escape the army of the Chaldeans and the army of Aram;* that is why we are now living in Jerusalem."

[12]Then this word of the LORD came to Jeremiah: [13]Thus says the LORD of hosts, the God of Israel: Go, say to the men of Judah and to the citizens of Jerusalem: Will you not take correction and obey my words? says the LORD.[y] [14]The advice of Jonadab, Rechab's son, by which he forbade his children to drink wine, has been followed: to this day they have not drunk it; they obeyed their father's command. Me, however, you have not obeyed, although I spoke to you untiringly and insistently.[z] [15]I kept sending you all my servants the prophets, telling you to turn back, all of you, from your evil way; to reform your conduct, and not follow strange gods or serve them, if you would remain on the land which I gave you and your fathers; but you did not heed me or obey me.[a] [16]Yes, the children of Jonadab, Rechab's son, observed the command which their father laid on them; but this people does not obey me! [17]Now, therefore, says the LORD God of hosts, the God of Israel: I will bring upon Judah and all the citizens of Jerusalem every evil that I threatened; because when I spoke they did not obey, when I called they did not answer.[b]

[18]But to the company of the Rechabites Jeremiah said: Thus says the LORD of hosts, the God of Israel: Since you have obeyed the command of Jonadab, your father, kept all his commands and done everything he commanded you, [19]thus therefore says the LORD of hosts, the God of Israel: Never shall there fail to be a descendant of Jonadab, Rechab's son, standing in my service.

CHAPTER 36

See RG 217

Baruch Writes the Prophecies of Jeremiah. [1]In the fourth year of Jehoiakim, son of Josiah, king of Judah, this word came to Jeremiah from the LORD: [2]Take a scroll and write on it all the words I have spoken to you against Israel, Judah, and all the nations, from the day I first spoke to you, in the days of Josiah, until today. [3]Perhaps, when the house of Judah hears all the evil I have in mind to do to them, they will turn back each from his evil way, so that I may forgive their wickedness and their sin.[c] [4]So Jeremiah called Baruch, son of Neriah, who wrote down on a scroll, as Jeremiah dictated, all the words which the LORD had spoken to him.

[9]In the ninth month, in the fifth year of Jehoiakim, son of Josiah, king of Judah, a fast to placate the LORD was proclaimed for all the people of Jerusalem and all who came from Judah's cities to Jerusalem. [5]Then Jeremiah charged Baruch: I cannot go to the house of the LORD; I am prevented* from doing so. [6]Do you go on the fast day and read publicly in the LORD's house the LORD's words from the scroll you wrote at my dictation; read them also to all the men of Judah who come up from their cities. [7]Perhaps they will lay their supplication before the LORD and will all turn back from their evil way; for great is the fury of anger with which the LORD has threatened this people.[d]

[8]Baruch, son of Neriah, did everything the prophet Jeremiah commanded; from the book-scroll he read the LORD's words in the LORD's house. [10]It was in the room of Gemariah,* son of the scribe Shaphan, in the upper court of the LORD's house, at the entrance of the New Temple-Gate, that Baruch publicly read the words of Jeremiah from his book.

[11]Now Micaiah, son of Gemariah, son of Shaphan, heard all the words of the LORD

35, 11: The army of Aram: Nebuchadnezzar enlisted the help of Judah's foreign neighbors in his assault on Jerusalem.

36, 5: I am prevented: probably because of his temple sermon (Jer 7, 1-15), or because of temporary ritual uncleanness.

36, 10: Gemariah: member of a family friendly to Jeremiah, which had rights to a room in the fortress of the temple gateway overlooking the court of the temple; from a window in this room Baruch read Jeremiah's prophetic sermon to the people.

y: Jer 32, 33.   *z:* Jer 7, 13; 25, 3; 2 Chr 36, 15f.   *a:* Jer 25, 4f. 7.
b: Jer 11, 8f.   *c:* Jer 26, 3; Is 55, 6f.   *d:* 2 Kgs 22, 13.

read from the book. [12]So he went down to the king's palace, into the scribe's chamber,* where the princes were just then in session: Elishama, the scribe, Delaiah, son of Shemaiah, Elnathan, son of Achbor, Gemariah, son of Shaphan, Zedekiah, son of Hananiah, and the other princes. [13]To them Micaiah reported all that he had heard Baruch read publicly from his book. [14]Thereupon the princes sent Jehudi, son of Nethaniah, son of Shelemiah, son of Cushi, to Baruch with the order: "Come, and bring with you the scroll you read publicly to the people." Scroll in hand, Baruch, son of Neriah, went to them. [15]"Sit down," they said to him, "and read it to us." Baruch read it to them, [16]and when they heard all its words, they were frightened and said to one another, "We must certainly tell the king all these things." [17]Then they asked Baruch: "Tell us, please, how you came to write down all these words." [18]"Jeremiah dictated all these words to me," Baruch answered them, "and I wrote them down with ink in the book." [19]At this the princes said to Baruch, "Go into hiding, you and Jeremiah; let no one know where you are."

[20]Leaving the scroll in safekeeping in the room of Elishama the scribe, they entered the room where the king was. When they told him everything that had happened, [21]he sent Jehudi to fetch the scroll. Jehudi brought it from the room of Elishama the scribe, and read it to the king and to all the princes who were in attendance on the king. [22]Now the king was sitting in his winter house, since it was the ninth month, and fire was burning in a brazier before him. [23]Each time Jehudi finished reading three or four columns, the king would cut off the piece with a scribe's knife* and cast it into the fire in the brazier, until the entire roll was consumed in the fire. [24]Hearing all these words did not frighten the king and his ministers or cause them to rend their garments. [25]And though Elnathan, Delaiah, and Gemariah urged the king not to burn the scroll,

he would not listen to them, [26]but commanded Jerahmeel, a royal prince, and Seraiah, son of Azriel, and Shelemiah, son of Abdeel, to arrest Baruch, the secretary, and the prophet Jeremiah. But the LORD kept them concealed.

[27]This word of the LORD came to Jeremiah, after the king burned the scroll with the text Jeremiah had dictated to Baruch: [28]Take another scroll, and write on it everything that the first scroll contained, which Jehoiakim, king of Judah, burned up. [29]And against Jehoiakim, king of Judah, say this: Thus says the LORD: You burned that scroll, saying, "Why did you write on it: Babylon's king shall surely come and lay waste this land and empty it of man and beast?" [30]The LORD now says of Jehoiakim, king of Judah:[e] No descendant of his shall succeed to David's throne; his corpse shall be cast out, exposed to the heat of day, to the cold of night.* [31]I will punish him and his descendants and his ministers for their wickedness; against them and the citizens of Jerusalem and the men of Judah I will fulfill all the threats of evil which went unheeded.

[32]Jeremiah took another scroll, and gave it to his secretary, Baruch, son of Neriah; he wrote on it at Jeremiah's dictation all the words contained in the book which Jehoiakim, king of Judah, had burned in the fire, and many others of the same kind in addition.

CHAPTER 37

See RG 217

Jeremiah in the Dungeon. [1]Coniah, son of Jehoiakim, was succeeded by King Zedekiah, son of Josiah; he was made king over the land of Judah by Nebuchadnezzar, king of Babylon.[f] [2]Neither he, nor his ministers, nor the people of the land would listen to the words of the LORD spoken by Jeremiah the prophet. [3]Yet King Zedekiah sent Jehucal, son of Shelemiah, and Zephaniah, son of Maaseiah the priest, to the prophet Jeremiah with this request: "Pray to the LORD, our God, for us."[g] [4]At this time Jere-

---

36, 12: The scribe's chamber: the office of the royal secretary.

36, 23: A scribe's knife: used to sharpen the reeds which were employed as pens.

36, 30: Jehoiakim's son Jehoiachin was named king, but reigned only three months; he was known better for his thirty-

seven-year exile in Babylon. His corpse shall be cast out: see note on Jer 22, 19.

e: Jer 22, 19.   f: Jer 52, 1; 2 Kgs 24, 17; 2 Chr 36, 10.   g: Jer 21, 1.

miah had not yet been put into prison;* he still came and went freely among the people. [5]Also, Pharaoh's army* had set out from Egypt, and when the Chaldeans who were besieging Jerusalem heard this report they marched away from the city.[h]

[6]This word of the LORD then came to the prophet Jeremiah: [7]Thus says the LORD, the God of Israel: Give this answer to the king of Judah who sent you to me to consult me: Pharaoh's army which has set out to help you will return to its own land, Egypt.[i] [8]The Chaldeans shall return to the fight against this city; they shall capture it and destroy it with fire.[j]

[9]Thus says the LORD: Do not deceive yourselves with the thought that the Chaldeans will leave you for good, because they shall not leave! [10]Even if you were to defeat the whole Chaldean army now attacking you, and only the wounded remained, each in his tent, these would rise up and destroy the city with fire.[k]

[11]When the Chaldean army lifted the siege of Jerusalem at the threat of the army of Pharaoh,[l] [12]Jeremiah set out from Jerusalem for the district of Benjamin, to take part with his family in the division of an inheritance. [13]But when he reached the Gate of Benjamin, he met the captain of the guard, a man named Irijah, son of Shelemiah, son of Hananiah; he seized the prophet Jeremiah, saying, "You are deserting to the Chaldeans!" [14]"That is a lie!" Jeremiah answered, "I am not deserting to the Chaldeans." Without listening, Irijah kept Jeremiah in custody and brought him to the princes.

[15]The princes were enraged, and had Jeremiah beaten and thrown into prison in the house of Jonathan the scribe, which they were using as a jail.[m] [16]And so Jeremiah entered the vaulted dungeon, where he remained a long time.

[17]Once King Zedekiah had him brought to his palace and he asked him secretly whether there was any message from the LORD. Yes! Jeremiah answered: you shall be handed over to the king of Babylon.[n] [18]Jeremiah then asked King Zedekiah: In what have I wronged you, or your ministers, or this people, that you should put me in prison?[o] [19]And where are your own prophets now, [20]who prophesied to you that the king of Babylon would not attack you or this land? Hear now, my lord king, and grant my petition: do not send me back into the house of Jonathan the scribe, or I shall die there.

[21]King Zedekiah ordered that Jeremiah be confined in the quarters of the guard, and given a loaf of bread each day from the bakers' shop until all the bread in the city was eaten up. Thus Jeremiah remained in the quarters of the guard.[p]

CHAPTER 38

See RG 217

Jeremiah in the Miry Cistern. [1]Shephatiah, son of Mattan, Gedaliah, son of Pashhur, Jucal, son of Shelemiah, and Pashhur, son of Malchiah, heard Jeremiah speaking these words to all the people:* [2]Thus says the LORD: He who remains in this city shall die by sword, or famine, or pestilence; but he who goes out to the Chaldeans shall live; his life shall be spared him as booty, and he shall live.[q] [3]Thus says the LORD: This city shall certainly be handed over to the army of the king of Babylon; he shall capture it.

[4]"This man ought to be put to death," the princes said to the king; "he demoralizes the soldiers* who are left in this city, and all the people, by speaking such things to them; he is not interested in the welfare of our people, but in their ruin."[r] [5]King Zedekiah answered: "He is in your power"; for the king could do nothing with them. [6]And so they

---

37, 4: Put into prison: as described in Jer 32, 1ff. Chronologically, the present episode follows Jer 34, 1-7.

37, 5: Pharaoh's army: the force sent by Pharaoh Hophra which caused the Chaldeans momentarily to lift the siege of Jerusalem (cf Jer 34, 21).

38, 1: Jeremiah enjoyed sufficient liberty in the quarters of the guard (Jer 37, 21) to speak to the people; cf Jer 32, 6-9. Gedaliah, son of Pashhur: the latter is possibly the Pashhur of

Jer 20, 1. Pashhur, son of Malchiah; mentioned in Jer 21, 1.

38, 4: He demoralizes the soldiers: literally, "he weakens their hands." One of the Lachish ostraca (see note on Jer 34, 7) uses the same expression of the princes in Jerusalem.

h: Ez 17, 15; 29, 6f. *i:* Ez 17, 17. *j:* Jer 34, 22. *k:* Jer 21, 4. *l:* Zec 14, 10. *m:* Jer 38, 6-13. *n:* Jer 21, 7; 32, 3; 34, 21. *o:* Jer 26, 19. *p:* Jer 32, 2; 38, 28. *q:* Jer 21, 9f; 39, 18; 45, 5. *r:* Jer 26, 11.

took Jeremiah and threw him into the cistern of Prince Malchiah, which was in the quarters of the guard, letting him down with ropes. There was no water in the cistern, only mud, and Jeremiah sank into the mud.[s]

[7]Now Ebed-melech, a Cushite,[*] a courtier in the king's palace, heard that they had put Jeremiah into the cistern. The king happened just then to be at the Gate of Benjamin, [8]and Ebed-melech went there from the palace and said to him, [9]"My lord king, these men have been at fault in all they have done to the prophet Jeremiah, casting him into the cistern. He will die of famine on the spot, for there is no more food in the city."[t] [10]Then the king ordered Ebed-melech the Cushite to take three men along with him, and draw the prophet Jeremiah out of the cistern before he should die. [11]Ebed-melech took the men along with him, and went first to the linen closet in the palace, from which he took some old, tattered rags; these he sent down to Jeremiah in the cistern, with ropes. [12]Then he said to Jeremiah, "Put the old, tattered rags between your armpits and the ropes." Jeremiah did so, [13]and they drew him up with the ropes out of the cistern. But Jeremiah remained in the quarters of the guard.

[14]Once King Zedekiah summoned the prophet Jeremiah to come to him at the third entrance to the house of the LORD. "I have a question to ask you," the king said to Jeremiah; "hide nothing from me."[u] Jeremiah answered Zedekiah: [15]If I tell you anything, you will have me killed, will you not? If I counsel you, you will not listen to me![v] [16]But King Zedekiah swore to Jeremiah secretly: "As the LORD lives who gave us the breath of life, I will not kill you; nor will I hand you over to these men who seek your life."

[17]Thereupon Jeremiah said to Zedekiah: Thus says the LORD God of hosts, the God of Israel: If you surrender to the princes of Babylon's king, you shall save your life; this city shall not be destroyed with fire,

and you and your family shall live.[w] [18]But if you do not surrender to the princes of Babylon's king, this city shall fall into the hands of the Chaldeans, who shall destroy it with fire, and you shall not escape their hands.[x]

[19]King Zedekiah, however, said to Jeremiah, "I am afraid of the men of Judah who have deserted to the Chaldeans; I may be handed over to them, and they will mistreat me."[y] [20]You will not be handed over, Jeremiah answered. Please obey the voice of the LORD and do as I tell you; then it shall go well with you, and your life will be spared.[z] [21]But if you refuse to surrender, this is what the LORD shows me: [22]All the women left in the house of Judah's king shall be brought out to the princes of Babylon's king, and they shall taunt you thus:

"They betrayed you, outdid you,
    your good friends!
Now that your feet are stuck in the mud,
    they slink away."[a]

[23]All your wives and sons shall be led forth to the Chaldeans, and you shall not escape their hands; you shall be handed over to the king of Babylon, and this city shall be destroyed with fire.[b]

[24]Then Zedekiah said to Jeremiah, "Let no one know about this conversation, or you shall die. [25]If the princes hear I spoke to you, if they come and ask you, 'Tell us what you said to the king; do not hide it from us, or we will kill you,' or, 'What did the king say to you?' [26]give them this answer: 'I petitioned the king not to send me back to Jonathan's house to die there.' " [27]When all the princes came to Jeremiah, they questioned him, and he answered them in the very words the king had commanded. They said no more to him, for nothing had been heard of the earlier conversation. [28]Thus Jeremiah stayed in the quarters of the guard till the day Jerusalem was taken.[c]

38, 7: A Cushite: an Ethiopian. Ebed-melech evidently held a position of some authority at court.

s: Jer 37, 14f.   *t:* Jer 52, 6.   *u:* Jer 37, 16.   *v:* Lk 22, 67f.   *w:* Jer 27, 12f; 2 Kgs 24, 12.   *x:* Jer 32, 4.   *y:* 1 Sm 31, 4.   *z:* 2 Chr 20, 20.   *a:* Jb 6, 15; 19, 13f. 19.   *b:* Jer 41, 10.   *c:* Jer 39, 14.

CHAPTER 39

See RG 217

Jeremiah and Gedaliah. When Jerusalem was taken. . . . [1]In the tenth month of the ninth year* of Zedekiah,[d] king of Judah, Nebuchadnezzar, king of Babylon, and all his army marched against Jerusalem and besieged it. [2]On the ninth day of the fourth month, in the eleventh year* of Zedekiah, a breach was made in the city's defenses. [3]All the princes of the king of Babylon came and occupied the middle gate: Nergal-sharezer, of Simmagir, the chief officer, Nebushazban, the high dignitary, and all the other princes of the king of Babylon. . . . [4]When Zedekiah, king of Judah, saw them, he and all his warriors fled by night, leaving the city on the Royal Garden Road* through the gate between the two walls. He went in the direction of the Arabah,[e] [5]but the Chaldean army pursued them, and overtook and captured Zedekiah in the desert near Jericho. He was brought to Riblah,* in the land of Hamath, where Nebuchadnezzar, king of Babylon, pronounced sentence upon him.[f] [6]As Zedekiah looked on, his sons were slain at Riblah by order of the king of Babylon, who slew also all the nobles of Judah.[g] [7]He then blinded Zedekiah and bound him in chains to bring him to Babylon.[h]

[8]The Chaldeans set fire to the king's palace and the houses of the people, and demolished the walls of Jerusalem.[i] [9]Nebuzaradan, chief of the bodyguard, deported to Babylon the rest of the people left in the city, those who had deserted to him, and the rest of the workmen.[j] [10]But some of the poor who had no property were left in the land of Judah by Nebuzaradan, chief of the bodyguard, and were given at the same time vineyards and farms.[k]

[11]Concerning Jeremiah, Nebuchadnezzar, king of Babylon, gave the following orders through Nebuzaradan, chief of the bodyguard: [12]"Take him and look after him; let no harm befall him, but treat him as he himself requests."[l] [13]Thereupon Nebuzaradan, chief of the bodyguard, and Nebushazban, the high dignitary, and Nergal-sharezer, the chief officer, and all the nobles of the king of Babylon, [14]had Jeremiah taken out of the quarters of the guard, and entrusted to Gedaliah, son of Ahikam, son of Shaphan, to be brought home. And so he remained among the people.[m]

A Word of Comfort for Ebed-melech. [15]While Jeremiah was still imprisoned in the quarters of the guard, the word of the LORD came to him: [16]Go, tell this to Ebed-melech the Cushite: Thus says the LORD of hosts, the God of Israel: Behold, I am now fulfilling the words I spoke against this city, for evil and not for good; and this before your very eyes.[n] [17]But on that day I will rescue you, says LORD; you shall not be handed over to the men of whom you are afraid. [18]I will make certain that you escape and do not fall by the sword. Your life shall be spared as booty, because you trusted in me, says the LORD.[o]

CHAPTER 40

See RG 217

Jeremiah Still in Judah. [1]This word* came to Jeremiah from the LORD, after Nebuzaradan, captain of the bodyguard, had released him in Ramah, where he had found him a prisoner in chains, among the captives of Jerusalem and Judah who were being exiled to Babylon.[p] [2]When the captain of the bodyguard took charge of Jeremiah, he said to him, "The LORD, your God, foretold the ruin of this place. [3]Now he has brought about in deed what he threatened; because

39, 1: The tenth month of the ninth year: the month Tebet (mid-December to mid-January) of the year 589/8 B.C.

39, 2: The ninth day of the fourth month, in the eleventh year: in July of 587 B.C.

39, 4: The Royal Garden Road: along the southeast side of the city; the royal garden was in the Kidron Valley. The gate between the two walls: the southernmost city gate, at the end of the Tyropoean Valley. The Arabah: the Jordan Valley. Zedekiah was attempting to escape across the Jordan when he was captured near Jericho.

39, 5: Riblah: Nebuchadnezzar's headquarters in Syria,

which had also been used by Pharaoh Neco (2 Kgs 23, 33).

40, 1: This word: actually, no further word of the Lord is recorded until Jer 42, 7ff. This is a title affixed to the following chapters after they were attached to an earlier form of the book ending with chapter 39.

d: 1f: Jer 52, 4-16; 2 Kgs 25, 1-12; Ez 24, 1. *e:* Jer 52, 7. *f:* Jer 32, 4f; 38, 18. *g:* Jer 34, 21. *h:* Jer 32, 4f; Ez 12, 13. *i:* Jer 21, 10; 34, 2; 52, 13. *j:* 2 Kgs 25, 11. *k:* 2 Kgs 25, 12. 22. *l:* Jer 40, 4. *m:* Jer 26, 24; 38, 28. *n:* Jer 21, 10; Dn 9, 12. *o:* Jer 45, 5; Pss 25, 3; 36, 40. *p:* Jer 39, 14.

you sinned against the LORD and did not obey his voice, this fate has befallen you. ⁴And now, I am freeing you today from the fetters that bind your hands; if it seems good to you to come with me to Babylon, you may come: I will look after you well. But if it does not please you to come to Babylon, you need not come. See, the whole land is before you; go wherever you think good and proper";*q* ⁵and then, before he left—"or go to Gedaliah, son of Ahikam, son of Shaphan, whom the king of Babylon has appointed ruler over the cities of Judah; stay with him among the people, or go wherever you please." The captain of the bodyguard gave him food and gifts and let him go.*r* ⁶Jeremiah went to Gedaliah, son of Ahikam, in Mizpah,* and stayed with him among the people left in the land.*s*

⁷When the army leaders who were still in the field with all their men heard that the king of Babylon had given Gedaliah, son of Ahikam, charge of the land, of men, women, and children, and of those poor who had not been led captive to Babylon, ⁸they came with their men to Gedaliah in Mizpah: Ishmael, son of Nethaniah; Johanan, son of Kareah; Seraiah, son of Tanhumeth; the sons of Ephai of Netophah; and Jezaniah* of Beth-maacah. ⁹Gedaliah, son of Ahikam, son of Shaphan, adjured them and their men not to be afraid to serve the Chaldeans: to stay in the land and submit to the king of Babylon, for their own welfare,*t* ¹⁰saying that he himself would remain in Mizpah, as their intermediary with the Chaldeans who should come to them. They were to collect the wine, the fruit, and the oil, to store them in jars, and to settle in the cities they occupied. ¹¹When the people of Judah in Moab, those among the Ammonites, those in Edom, and those in all other lands heard that the king of Babylon had left a remnant in Judah, and had appointed over them Gedaliah, son of Ahikam, son of Sha-

phan, ¹²they all returned to the land of Judah from the places to which they had scattered. They went to Gedaliah at Mizpah and had a rich harvest of wine and fruit.

Assassination of Gedaliah. ¹³Now Johanan, son of Kareah, and all the leaders of the armies in the field came to Gedaliah in Mizpah ¹⁴and asked him whether he did not know that Baalis, the king of the Ammonites,* had sent Ishmael, son of Nethaniah, to assassinate him.*u* ¹⁵But Gedaliah, son of Ahikam, would not believe them. Then Johanan, son of Kareah, said secretly to Gedaliah in Mizpah: "Let me go and kill Ishmael, son of Nethaniah; no one will know it. Why should he be allowed to kill you? All the Jews who have now rallied to you will be dispersed and the remnant of Judah will perish." ¹⁶Nevertheless, Gedaliah, son of Ahikam, answered Johanan, son of Kareah, "You shall do nothing of the kind; you have lied about Ishmael."

CHAPTER 41

See RG 217

¹In the seventh month Ishmael, son of Nethaniah, son of Elishama, of royal descent, one of the king's nobles, came with ten men to Gedaliah, son of Ahikam, at Mizpah.*v* And while they were together at table in Mizpah, ²Ishmael, son of Nethaniah, and the ten who were with him, rose up and attacked with swords Gedaliah, son of Ahikam, son of Shaphan, whom the king of Babylon had made ruler over the land; and they killed him. ³Ishmael also slew all the men of Judah of military age who were with Gedaliah and the Chaldean soldiers who were there.

⁴The second day after the murder of Gedaliah, before anyone knew of it, ⁵eighty men with beards shaved off, clothes in rags, and with gashes on their bodies came from Shechem, Shiloh, and Samaria, bringing food offerings and incense for the house of the LORD. ⁶Ishmael, son of Nethaniah, went out from Mizpah to meet them, weeping as he

---

40, 6: Mizpah: some five miles northwest of Jerusalem, where Israel chose its first king (1 Sm 10, 17-24). Presumably Jerusalem had been damaged too much by the Chaldean conquest to remain a seat of government.

40, 8: Jezaniah: the seal ring of a high official of this name was discovered in 1932 at the site usually identified with Mizpah, Tell en-Nasbe.

40, 14: The Ammonites: they resented the survival of

their ancient enemy, Judah. Ishmael: their willing tool, who doubtless aspired to rule over Judah himself, as he was of the house of David; cf Jer 41, 1.

q: Jer 39, 12. *r:* Jer 39, 14; 2 Kgs 25, 22. *s:* Jer 39, 14. *t:* Jer 27, 12f; 2 Kgs 25, 24. *u:* Jer 41, 1ff. 10. *v:* Jer 40, 14ff; 2 Kgs 25, 25.

went. [7]"Come to Gedaliah, son of Ahikam," he said as he met them. When they were once inside the city, Ishmael, son of Nethaniah, and his men slew them and threw them into the cistern. [8]But there were ten among them who pleaded with Ishmael: "Do not kill us; we have stores buried in the field: wheat and barley, oil and honey." And so he spared them and did not kill them, as he had killed their companions. [9]The cistern into which Ishmael threw all the corpses of the men he had killed was the large one made by King Asa to defend himself against Baasha, king of Israel; this cistern Ishmael, son of Nethaniah, filled with the slain.[w]

[10]Ishmael, son of Nethaniah, led away the remnant of the people left in Mizpah and the princesses,* whom Nebuzaradan, captain of the bodyguard, had confided to Gedaliah, son of Ahikam. With these captives, Ishmael, son of Nethaniah, set out to make his way to the Ammonites.

Flight to Egypt. [11]But when Johanan, son of Kareah, and the other army leaders with him heard of the crimes Ishmael, son of Nethaniah, had committed, [12]they took all their men and set out to attack Ishmael, son of Nethaniah. They overtook him at the Great Waters in Gibeon.* [13]At the sight of Johanan, son of Kareah, and the other army leaders, the people who were Ishmael's captives rejoiced. [14]All of those whom Ishmael had brought away from Mizpah went over to Johanan, son of Kareah. [15]But Ishmael, son of Nethaniah, escaped from Johanan and fled to the Ammonites with eight men. [16]Then Johanan, son of Kareah, and all his army leaders took charge of the remnant of the people, both the soldiers and the women and children with their guardians, whom Ishmael, son of Nethaniah, had brought away from Mizpah after he killed Gedaliah, son of Ahikim. From Gibeon, [17]they retreated to the lodging place of Chimham near Bethlehem, where they stopped, intending to flee into Egypt. [18]They were afraid of the Chaldeans, because

Ishmael, son of Nethaniah, had slain Gedaliah, son of Ahikam, whom the king of Babylon had made ruler in the land of Judah.

CHAPTER 42

See RG 217

[1]Then all the army leaders, Johanan, son of Kareah, Azariah, son of Hoshaiah, and all the people, high and low, approached the prophet Jeremiah [2]and said, "Grant our petition; pray for us to the LORD, your God, for all this remnant. We are now few who once were many, as you well see. [3]Let the LORD, your God, show us what way we should take and what we should do." [4]Very well! the prophet Jeremiah answered them: I will pray to the LORD, your God, as you desire; whatever the LORD answers you, I will tell you; I will withhold nothing from you.[x] [5]And they said to Jeremiah, "May the LORD be our witness: we will truly and faithfully follow all the instructions the LORD, your God, will send us.[y] [6]Whether it is pleasant or difficult, we will obey the command of the LORD, our God, to whom we are sending you, so that it will go well with us for obeying the command of the LORD, our God."[z]

[7]Ten days passed before the word of the LORD came to Jeremiah. [8]Then he called Johanan, son of Kareah, his army leaders, and all the people, high and low, [9]and said to them: Thus says the LORD, the God of Israel, to whom you sent me to offer your prayer: [10]If you remain quietly in this land I will build you up, and not tear you down; I will plant you, not uproot you; for I regret the evil I have done you.[a] [11]Do not fear the king of Babylon, before whom you are now afraid; do not fear him, says the LORD, for I am with you to save you, to rescue you from his power.[b] [12]I will grant you mercy, so that he will be sorry for you and let you return to your land.[c] [13]But if you disobey the voice of the LORD, your God, and decide not to remain in this land, [14]saying, "No, we will go to Egypt, where we will see no more of war, hear the trumpet alarm no longer, nor hunger for bread; there we will

---

41, 10: The princesses: of the royal house of Judah. They had not been deported to Babylon with the men of this house.

41, 12: Gibeon: today called El-Jib; it is northwest of Jerusalem. The most recent excavations have revealed the extensive dimensions of the city spring and well, called here the

Great Waters; cf 2 Sm 2, 12ff.

w: 1 Kgs 15, 16; 2 Chr 16, 6. x: 1 Sm 3, 18. y: Jgs 11, 10.
z: Jer 7, 23; Dt 5, 33; 6, 3. a: Jer 31, 28; 32, 41. b: Jer 30, 10f.
c: Ps 106, 45f; Prv 16, 7.

Emigration to Egypt

Jeremiah is an ally of Babylon and an opponent of Egypt in the international power struggles that afflict Judah at this time. Chapters 42–44 reflect anti-Egyptian viewpoints. They accuse survivors who go to Egypt of refusing to listen and engaging in idolatry. Paradoxically, Jeremiah and his scribe Baruch are also forced into exile.

live";[d] [15]then listen to the word of the LORD, remnant of Judah: Thus says the LORD of hosts, the God of Israel: If you are determined to go to Egypt, when you arrive there to stay, [16]the sword you fear shall reach you in the land of Egypt; the hunger you dread shall cling to you no less in Egypt, and there you shall die.[e] [17]All those men who determine to go to Egypt to stay, shall die by the sword, famine, and pestilence; not one shall survive or escape the evil that I will bring upon them.[f] [18]For thus says the LORD of hosts, the God of Israel: Just as my furious anger was poured out upon the citizens of Jerusalem, so shall my anger be poured out on you when you reach Egypt. You shall become an example of malediction and horror, a curse and a reproach, and you shall never see this place again.[g]

[19]It is the LORD who has spoken to you, remnant of Judah; do not go to Egypt! You can never say that I did not warn you this day. [20]At the cost of your lives you have deceived me, sending me to the LORD, your God, saying, "Pray for us to the LORD, our God; make known to us all that the LORD, our God, shall say, and we will do it." [21]Today I proclaim his message, but you obey the voice of the LORD, your God, in nothing that he has commissioned me to make known to you.[h] [22]Have no doubt of this, you shall die by the sword, famine, and pestilence in the place where you wish to go and settle.[i]

CHAPTER 43

See RG 217

[1]When Jeremiah finished speaking to the people all these words of the LORD, their God, with which the LORD had sent him to them, [2]Azariah, son of Hoshaiah, Johanan, son of Kareah, and all the insolent men shouted to Jeremiah: "You lie; it was not the LORD, our God, who sent you to tell us not to go to Egypt to settle. [3]It is Baruch, son of Neriah, who stirs you up against us, to hand us over to the Chaldeans to be killed or exiled to Babylon."[j]

[4]Johanan, son of Kareah, and the rest of the leaders and the people did not obey the LORD's command to stay in the land of Judah.[k] [5]Instead, Johanan, son of Kareah, and all the army leaders took along the whole remnant of Judah that had been dispersed among the nations and had returned thence to dwell again in the land of Judah: [6]men, women, and children, the princesses and everyone whom Nebuzaradan, captain of the bodyguard, had entrusted to Gedaliah, son of Ahikam, son of Shaphan; also Jeremiah, the prophet, and Baruch, son of Neriah.[l] [7]Against the LORD's command they went to Egypt, and arrived at Tahpanhes. . . .[m]

Jeremiah in Egypt. [8]This word of the LORD came to Jeremiah in Tahpanhes: [9]Take with you large stones and sink them in mortar in the brickyard at the entrance to the royal building* in Tahpanhes, while the men of Judah look on, [10]and then say to them: Thus says the LORD of hosts, the God of Israel: I will send for my servant Nebuchadnezzar, king of Babylon, and bring him here. He will set his throne upon these stones which I, Jeremiah, have sunk, and stretch his canopy over them.[n] [11]He shall come and strike the land of Egypt: with death, whoever is marked for death; with exile, everyone destined for exile; with the sword, all who are intended for the sword.[o] [12]He shall set fire to the temples of Egypt's gods, and

43, 9: The royal building: residence of the Egyptian governor.

---

d: Dt 28, 68.   e: Jer 44, 13f. 27.   f: Jer 29, 17f; 44, 14. 28.   g: Jer 44, 12.   h: Zec 7, 11f.   i: Jer 44, 12; Hos 9, 6.   j: Jer 38, 4.   k: Jer 41, 16.   l: Jer 41, 10.   m: Jer 42, 13f; 44, 1.   n: Jer 27, 6; Ez 29, 19.   o: Jer 46, 13; Ez 30, 10.

burn the gods or carry them off. As a shepherd delouses his cloak, he shall delouse the land of Egypt and depart victorious.[p] [13]He shall smash the obelisks of the temple of the sun in the land of Egypt and destroy with fire the temples of the Egyptian gods.

See RG
217

CHAPTER 44

[1]This word came to Jeremiah for all the people of Judah who were living in Egypt, at Migdol, Tahpanhes, and Memphis, and in Upper Egypt: [2]*Thus says the LORD of hosts, the God of Israel: You have seen all the evil I brought on Jerusalem and the other cities of Judah. Today they are ruins and uninhabited,[q] [3]because of the evil they did to provoke me, going after strange gods, serving them and sacrificing to them, gods which neither they, nor you, nor your fathers knew.[r] [4]Though I kept sending to you all my servants the prophets, with the plea not to commit this horrible deed which I hate, [5]they would not listen or accept the warning to turn away from the evil of sacrificing to strange gods.[s] [6]Therefore the fury of my anger poured forth in flame over the cities of Judah and the streets of Jerusalem, so that they became the ruinous waste they are today.

[7]Now thus says the LORD God of hosts, the God of Israel: Why do you inflict so great an evil upon yourselves? Will you root out from Judah man and wife, child and nursling, and not leave yourselves even a remnant? [8]Will you go on provoking me by the works of your hands, by sacrificing to strange gods here in the land of Egypt where you have come to live? Will you be rooted out and become a curse and a disgrace among all the nations of the earth?[t] [9]Have you forgotten the evil deeds which your fathers, and the kings of Judah and their wives, and you yourselves and your wives have done in the land of Judah and the streets of Jerusalem?[u] [10]To this day they have not been crushed; they do not fear or follow the law

and the statutes which I set before you and your fathers.[v]

[11]Hence, thus says the LORD of hosts, the God of Israel: I have determined evil against you; and I will uproot all Judah. [12]I will take away the remnant of Judah who insisted on coming to dwell in Egypt, so that they shall be wholly destroyed. In the land of Egypt they shall fall by the sword or be consumed by hunger. High and low, they shall die by the sword, or by hunger, and become an example of malediction, a horror, a curse and a reproach.[w] [13]Thus will I punish those who live in Egypt, just as I punished Jerusalem with sword, hunger, and pestilence. None of the remnant of Judah that have come to settle in the land of Egypt shall escape or survive.[x] [14]None shall return to the land of Judah, though they yearn to return and live there. Only scattered refugees shall return.

[15]From all the men who knew that their wives were burning incense to strange gods, from all the women who were present in the immense crowd, and from all the people who lived in Lower and Upper Egypt, Jeremiah received this answer: [16]"We will not listen to what you say in the name of the LORD.[y] [17]Rather will we continue doing what we had proposed; we will burn incense to the queen of heaven and pour out libations to her, as we and our fathers, our kings and princes have done in the cities of Judah and the streets of Jerusalem. Then we had enough food to eat and we were well off; we suffered no misfortune.[z] [18]But since we stopped burning incense to the queen of heaven and pouring out libations to her, we are in need of everything and are being destroyed by the sword and by hunger. [19]And when we burned incense to the queen of heaven and poured out libations to her, was it without our husbands' consent that we baked for her cakes in her image and poured out libations to her?"[a]

[20]To all the people, men and women, who gave him this answer, Jeremiah said: [21]Was

---

44, 2-30: Chronologically, this is the last of Jeremiah's prophecies to his countrymen. The narrative leaves him an old man nearing seventy, rejected by his people. According to tradition, he was murdered in Egypt by fellow Judeans.

p: Jer 46, 25; Ez 30, 13f.   q: Jer 34, 22; Lv 26, 32f.   r: Jer 11, 17; Dt 32, 17.   s: Jer 7, 24. 26; 19, 4.   t: Jer 25, 6f.   u: 1 Kgs 11, 1. 8; Ezr 9, 7. 14.   v: Jer 7, 24.   w: Jer 42, 15. 18. 22.   x: Jer 43, 11.   y: Jer 6, 16f.   z: Jer 5, 3; 7, 18.   a: Jer 7, 18.

Jeremiah's Journey to Egypt

it not this that the LORD remembered and brought to mind, that you burned incense in the cities of Judah and the streets of Jerusalem: you, your fathers, your kings and princes, and the people generally?[b] [22]The LORD could no longer bear your evil deeds, the horrible things which you were doing; and so your land became a waste, a desert, a thing accursed and without inhabitants, as it is today.[c] [23]Because you burned incense and sinned against the LORD, not obeying the voice of the LORD, not living by his law, his statutes, and his decrees, this evil has befallen you at the present day.[d]

[24]Jeremiah said further to all the people, including the women: Hear the word of the LORD, all you Judeans in the land of Egypt: [25]Thus says the LORD of hosts, the God of Israel: You and your wives have stated your intentions, and kept them in fact: "We will continue to fulfill the vows we have made to burn incense to the queen of heaven and to pour out libations to her." Very well! keep your vows, carry out your resolutions! [26]But listen then to the word of the LORD, all you people of Judah who live in Egypt; I swear by my own great name, says the LORD, in the whole land of Egypt no man of Judah shall henceforth pronounce my name, saying, "As the Lord GOD lives." [27]I am watching over them to do evil, not good. All the men of Judah in Egypt shall perish by the sword or famine until they are utterly destroyed.[e] [28]Those who escape the sword to return from the land of Egypt to the land of Judah shall be few in number. The whole remnant of Judah who came to settle in Egypt shall know whose word stands, mine or theirs.[f]

[29]That you may know how surely my threats of punishment for you shall be fulfilled, this shall be a sign to you, says the LORD, that I will punish you in this place. [30]Thus says the LORD: See! I will hand over

b: Jer 11, 13.   c: Jer 15, 6.   d: 2 Kgs 17, 15; Dn 9, 11f.   e: Ez 7, 3-7.   f: Dt 28, 62; Is 10, 22.

Pharaoh Hophra,* king of Egypt, to his enemies, to those who seek his life, just as I handed over Zedekiah, king of Judah, to his enemy and mortal foe, Nebuchadnezzar, king of Babylon.*g*

CHAPTER 45

See RG
217

*A Message to Baruch.** *1*This is the message that the prophet Jeremiah gave to Baruch, son of Neriah, when he wrote in a book the prophecies that Jeremiah dictated in the fourth year of Jehoiakim, son of Josiah, king of Judah:*h* *2*Thus says the LORD, God of Israel, to you, Baruch, *3*because you said, "Alas! the LORD adds grief to my pain;*i* I am weary from groaning, and can find no rest": *4*say this to him, says the LORD: What I have built, I am tearing down; what I have planted, I am uprooting: even the whole land.*j* *5*And do you seek great things for yourself? Seek them not! I am bringing evil on all mankind, says the LORD, but your life I will leave you as booty, wherever you may go.*k*

V: Oracles against the Nations*

CHAPTER 46

See RG
218

*1*This is the word of the LORD that came to the prophet Jeremiah against the nations.

Against Egypt. *2*Concerning Egypt. Against the army of Pharaoh Neco, king of Egypt, which was defeated at Carchemish on the Euphrates* by Nebuchadnezzar, king of Babylon, in the fourth year of Jehoiakim, son of Josiah, king of Judah:

3 Prepare shield and buckler!
  march to battle!

4 Harness the horses,
  mount, charioteers
Fall in with your helmets;
  polish your spears, put on your
    breastplates.
5 What do I see?
  With broken ranks
They fall back;
  their heroes are routed,
They flee headlong
  without making a stand.
Terror on every side,
  says the LORD!*l*
6 The swift cannot flee,
  nor the hero escape:
There in the north, on the Euphrates' bank,
  they stumble and fall.

7 Who is this that surges forward like the
    Nile,
  like rivers of billowing waters?
8 Egypt surges like the Nile,
  like rivers of billowing waters.
"I will surge forward," he says, "and
    cover the earth,
  destroying the city and its people.*m*
9 Forward, horses!
  drive madly, chariots!
Set out, warriors,
  Cush and Put, bearing your shields,
  Men of Lud, stretching your bows!"
10 But this is the day of the Lord GOD of
    hosts,
  a day of vengeance, vengeance on his
    foes!
The sword devours, is sated, drunk with
    their blood:
  for the Lord GOD of hosts holds a
    slaughter feast
  in the northland, on the Euphrates.*n*

44, 30: Hophra: killed by his own people. The ruler of Egypt at the time of its conquest by Nebuchadnezzar was Hophra's successor Amasis, who was also slain by his enemies.

45, 1-5: At the conclusion of his narrative, Baruch appends a prophecy given him personally by Jeremiah when he first wrote down Jeremiah's words (cf chap. 36). The future revealed by the prophet had depressed Baruch; this prophecy was to assure him of his personal safety, while repeating the Lord's determination to destroy Judah.

46—51: In these chapters most of Jeremiah's oracles against the foreign nations have been gathered together and placed at the end of his book; in the Greek text they appear with the other oracles against the nations, in chap. 25. In general, they are in chronological order: 46, 1—49, 33, from the fourth year of Jehoiakim; 49, 34-39, at the beginning of Zedekiah's reign; 50, 1—51, 64, from the fourth year of Zedekiah.

46, 2: Carchemish on the Euphrates: the western terminus of the Mesopotamian trade route, where Nebuchadnezzar defeated Neco in 605 B.C., thus gaining undisputed control of Syria and Palestine.

---

g: Jer 39, 5ff; 46, 25f; Ez 29, 3f; 30, 21. h: Jer 36, 4. 18. 32.
i: Lam 1, 3; 5, 5. j: Jer 18, 7; Is 5, 5f. k: Jer 25, 26-29. l: Jer 6,
25; 49, 29. m: Ez 29, 3; 32, 2. n: Dt 32, 42; Is 13, 9; Ez 39, 17-20.

Places Mentioned in the Oracles against the Nations

[labels on map: Mediterranean Sea; ISRAEL (EPHRAIM); Samaria; R. Jordan; PHILISTIA; Ashdod; Ekron; Gath?; Ashkelon; Gaza; JUDAH; Jerusalem; AMMON; Rabbah; Heshbon; Dead Sea; MOAB; The Negeb; Kir; EDOM (SEIR); 20 Miles; 20 Kilometers; Mediterranean Sea; Cyprus; Sidon; Tyre; ARAM; Damascus; Memphis; Migdol; Tahpanhes; EGYPT; R. Nile; Thebes; Kedar; Dumah; Tema; Dedan; OPHIR; Red Sea; ETHIOPIA; SHEBA; Carchemish; Nineveh; ASSYRIA; Asshur; R. Euphrates; R. Tigris; MEDIA; BABYLONIA; Babylon; ELAM; Persian Gulf; 200 Miles; 200 Kilometers]

[11] Go up to Gilead, and take balm,
  O virgin daughter Egypt!
No use to multiply remedies;
  for you there is no cure.[o]
[12] The nations hear of your shame,
  your cries fill the earth.
Warrior trips over warrior,
  both fall together.[p]

[13][q]The message which the LORD gave to the prophet Jeremiah concerning the advance of Nebuchadnezzar, king of Babylon, to attack the land of Egypt:[*]

[14] Announce it in Egypt, publish it in Migdol,
  proclaim it in Memphis and Tahpanhes!
Say: Take your stand, prepare yourselves,
  the sword has already devoured your neighbors.[r]

[15] Why has Apis[*] fled,
  your mighty one failed to stand?
The LORD thrust him down;
[16] he stumbled repeatedly, and fell.
They said one to another,
  "Up! let us return to our own people,
To the land of our birth,
  away from the destroying sword."[s]

[17] Call Pharaoh, king of Egypt, by the name
  "The noise that let its time go by."[*]
[18] As I live, says the King
  whose name is LORD of hosts,
Like Tabor among the mountains he shall come,
  like Carmel[*] above the sea.
[19] Pack your baggage for exile,
  capital city of daughter Egypt;
Memphis shall become a desert,
  an empty ruin.

46, 13: In 601 B.C. Nebuchadnezzar advanced against Egypt and even entered the country, but finally had to withdraw to Syria.

46, 15: Apis: the chief god of Memphis, venerated in the form of a black bull.

46, 17: "The noise . . . go by": in Hebrew there is word-play here on the name Hophra, who still made a pretense of power though his career was at an end.

46, 18: Tabor . . . Carmel: outstanding mountains of Palestine, symbols of strength, to which Nebuchadnezzar is compared.

o: Jer 8, 22; 51, 8; Ez 30, 21f.   *p:* Ez 32, 9-12.   *q:* Jer 43, 10f; 44, 30; Is 19, 1.   *r:* Jer 44, 1.   *s:* Lv 26, 37.

20 Egypt is a pretty heifer,
   from the north a horsefly lights upon
      her.
21 The mercenaries in her ranks
      are like fatted calves;
   They too turn and flee together,
      stand not their ground,
   When the day of their ruin comes upon
         them,
      the time of their punishment.
22 She sounds like a retreating reptile!
      Yes, they come in force;
   like woodchoppers, they attack her
      with axes.
23 They cut down her forest, says the
      LORD,
   impenetrable though it be;
   More numerous than locusts,
      they cannot be counted.
24 Disgraced is daughter Egypt,
   handed over to the people of the
      north.

25The LORD of hosts, the God of Israel,
has said: See! I will punish Amon* of
Thebes, and Egypt, her gods and her kings,
Pharaoh, and those who trust in him.[t] 26I will
hand them over to those who seek their lives,
to Nebuchadnezzar, king of Babylon, and
his ministers. But later on Egypt shall be inhabited again, as in times past, says the
LORD.[u]

27 But you, my servant Jacob, fear not;
   be not dismayed, O Israel.
   Behold, I will deliver you from the faroff
      land,
   your descendants, from their land of
      exile.
   Jacob shall again find rest,
      shall be tranquil and undisturbed.[v]
28 You, my servant Jacob, never fear, says
      the LORD,
   for I am with you;

I will make an end of all the nations
   to which I have driven you,
But of you I will not make an end:
   I will chastise you as you deserve,
   I will not let you go unpunished.[w]

CHAPTER 47

See RG
218

Against the Philistines. [1]This is the
word that came from the LORD to the
prophet Jeremiah concerning the Philistines,
before Pharaoh attacked Gaza:[x] [2]Thus says
the LORD:

*Behold: waters are rising from the north,
   a torrent in flood;
It shall flood the land and all that is in it,
   the cities and their people.
All the people of the land
   set up a wailing cry.
3 They hear the stamping hooves of his
      steeds,
   the rattling chariots, the rumbling
      wheels.
Fathers turn not to save their children;
   their hands fall helpless
4 Because of the day which has come
   to ruin all the Philistines,
And cut off from Tyre and Sidon*
   the last of their allies.
Yes, the LORD is destroying the
      Philistines,
   the remnant from the coasts of
      Caphtor.[y]
5 Gaza is shaved bald,[z]
   Ashkelon is reduced to silence;
Ashdod, the remnant of their strength,
   how long will you gash yourself?*
6 Alas, sword of the LORD!
   how long till you find rest?
Return into your scabbard;
   stop, be still!*
7 How can it find rest
   when the LORD has commanded it?

46, 25: Amon: the sun-god worshiped at Thebes, in Upper
Egypt.

47, 2-7: This prophecy was fulfilled in 605/4 B.C.

47, 4: Tyre and Sidon: Phoenician cities associated commercially with the Philistines, and enemies of Nebuchadnezzar; cf Jer 27, 1-4. Nebuchadnezzar carried out a thirteen-year
siege of Tyre which was only partially successful. Caphtor:
probably the island of Crete, the traditional place of origin of
the Philistines; cf Am 9, 7.

47, 5: Of the ancient Philistine cities, neither Gath nor Ekron (Jer 25, 20) is mentioned in this period of waning independence of the seacoast.

47, 6: Words of the Philistines.

t: Ez 30, 15f.   u: Jer 44, 30; Ez 30, 4; 32, 11f.   v: Jer 30, 10; 43,
5.   w: Jer 30, 11.   x: Ez 25, 15f; Zep 2, 4.   y: Jer 25, 22; Ez 25,
16f; Am 1, 8; 9, 7.   z: Am 1, 7.

Against Ashkelon and the seashore
he has appointed it.[a]

See RG
218

CHAPTER 48

*Against Moab.** [1]Concerning Moab,
thus says the LORD of hosts, the God of Israel:

Woe to Nebo, it is laid waste;
Kiriathaim is disgraced and captured,
Disgraced and overthrown is the
stronghold:
[2]   Moab's glory is no more.
Evil they plan against Heshbon:
"Come, let us put an end to her as a
people."
You, too, Madmen, shall be reduced to
silence;
behind you stalks the sword.
[3] Listen! a cry from Horonaim[b]
of ruin and great destruction!
[4] Moab is crushed,
their outcry is heard in Zoar.
[5] The ascent of Luhith
they climb weeping;
On the descent to Horonaim
the cry of destruction is heard.
[6] "Flee, save your lives,
to survive like the wild ass in the
desert!"
[7] Because you trusted in your works and
your treasures,
you also shall be captured.
Chemosh* shall go into exile,
his priests and princes with him.[c]
[8] The destroyer comes upon every city,
not a city escapes;
Ruined is the valley,
wasted the plain, as the LORD has said.
[9] Set up a memorial for Moab,
for it is an utter wasteland;
Its cities are turned into ruins
where no one dwells.
[10] [Cursed be he who does the LORD's work
remissly,
cursed he who holds back his sword
from blood.]

[11] Moab has been tranquil from his youth,
has rested upon his lees;
He was not poured from one flask to
another,
he went not into exile.
Thus he kept his taste,
and his scent was not lost.[d]

[12]Hence, the days shall come, says the
LORD, when I will send him coopers to turn
him over; they shall empty his flasks and
break his jars. [13]Chemosh shall disappoint
Moab, as Israel was disappointed by Bethel
in which they trusted.[e]

[14] How can you say, "We are heroes,
men valiant in war"?
[15] The ravager of Moab and his cities
advances,
the flower of his youth goes down to
be slaughtered,
says the King, the LORD of hosts by
name.
[16] Near at hand is Moab's ruin,
his disaster hastens apace.
[17] Mourn for him, all you his neighbors,
all you who knew him well!
Say: How the strong staff is broken,
the glorious rod!
[18] Come down from glory, sit on the
ground,
you that dwell in Dibon;
Moab's ravager has come up against you,
he has ruined your strongholds.[f]
[19] Stand by the wayside, watch closely,
you that dwell in Aroer;
Ask the man who flees, the woman who
tries to escape:
say to them, "What has happened?"[g]
[20] Moab is disgraced, yes, destroyed,
howl and cry out;
Publish it at the Arnon,
Moab is ruined![h]

[21]For judgment has come on the land of
the plateau: on Holon, Jahzah, and Mephaath,[i] [22]on Dibon, Nebo, and Beth-diblathaim,

---

48, 1–47: Moab was one of the Israelites' bitterest enemies. According to Flavius Josephus, Moab and Ammon were conquered by Nebuchadnezzar in this twenty-third year, 582 B.C., five years after the destruction of Jerusalem.
48, 7: Chemosh: chief god of the Moabites.

a: Zep 2, 5f. *b:* 3ff: Is 15, 5. *c:* Nm 21, 29. *d:* Zep 1, 12. *e:* Is 16, 12. *f:* Nm 21, 30. *g:* Dt 2, 36. *h:* Is 16, 7. *i:* Is 15, 4.

23on Kiriathaim, Beth-gamul, and Beth-meon, 24on Kerioth and on Bozrah: on all the cities of Moab, far and near.

25 Moab's strength is broken,
    his might is shattered, says the
    LORD.

26Because he boasted against the LORD, make Moab drunk so that he retches and vomits, and he too becomes a laughingstock. 27Is Israel a laughingstock to you? Was she caught among thieves, that you shake your head whenever you speak of her?*j*

28 Leave the cities, dwell in the crags,
    you that dwell in Moab.
Be like a dove that nests
    out of reach on the edge of a chasm.
29 We have heard of the pride of Moab,*k*
    pride beyond bounds:
His loftiness, his pride, his scorn,
    his insolence of heart.
30 I know, says the LORD, his arrogance;
    liar in boast, liar in deed.
31 And so I wail over Moab,
    over all Moab I cry,
    over the men of Kir-heres I moan.*l*
32 More than for Jazer I weep over you,
    vineyard of Sibmah.
Your tendrils trailed down to the sea,
    as far as Jazer they stretched.
Upon your harvest, upon your vintage,
    the ravager has fallen.*m*
33 Joy and jubilation are at an end
    in the fruit gardens of the land of
    Moab.
I drain the wine from the wine vats,
    the treader treads no more,
    the vintage shout is stilled.

34The cry of Heshbon and Elealeh is heard as far as Jahaz; they call from Zoar to Horonaim, and to Eglath-shelishiyah, for even the waters of Nimrim turn into a desert.*n* 35I will leave no one in Moab, says the LORD, to offer a holocaust on the high place, or to burn incense to his gods. 36Hence the wail of flutes for Moab is in my heart; for the men of Kir-heres the wail of flutes is in my heart:

the wealth they acquired has perished.*o* 37Every head has been made bald, every beard shaved; every hand is gashed, and the loins of all are clothed in sackcloth.*p* 38On every roof of Moab and in all his squares there is mourning; I have shattered Moab like a pot that no one wants, says the LORD. 39How terror seizes Moab, and wailing! How he turns his back in shame! Moab has become a laughingstock and a horror to all his neighbors! 40For thus says the LORD:

Behold, like an eagle he soars,
    spreads his wings over Moab.*q*
41 Cities are taken,
    strongholds seized:
On that day the hearts of Moab's heroes
    are like the heart of a woman in
    travail.*r*
42 Moab shall be destroyed, no more a
    people,
    because he boasted against the
    LORD.*s*
43 Terror, pit, and trap be upon you,
    people of Moab, says the LORD.*t*
44 He who flees from the terror
    falls into the pit;
He who climbs from the pit
    is caught in the trap;
For I will bring these things upon
    Moab
    in the year of their punishment, says
    the LORD.
45 In Heshbon's shadow stop short
    the exhausted refugees;
For fire breaks forth from Heshbon,
    and a blaze from the house of
    Sihon:
It consumes the brow of Moab,
    the skull of the noisemakers.*u*
46 Woe to you, O Moab,
    you are ruined, O people of
    Chemosh!
Your sons are taken into exile,
    your daughters into captivity.
47 But I will change the lot of Moab
    in the days to come, says the LORD.*v*
Thus far the judgment of Moab.

j: Zep 2, 8ff.   *k:* 29f: Is 16, 6.   *l:* Is 16, 7.   *m:* Is 16, 8f.   *n:* Is 15, 4f.   *o:* Is 16, 11.   *p:* Jer 47, 5; Is 15, 2f; Ez 7, 18.   *q:* Jer 49, 22.   *r:* Jer 6, 24; 30, 6.   *s:* Zep 2, 9f.   *t:* Is 24, 17f.   *u:* Nm 21, 28f.   *v:* Jer 49, 39.

CHAPTER 49

See RG
218

Against the Ammonites. [1]Concerning the Ammonites, thus says the LORD:

Has Israel no sons?
  has he no heir?
Why then has Milcom* disinherited Gad,
  why have his people settled in Gad's
    cities?
[2] But the days are coming, says the LORD,
  when against Rabbah of the Ammonites*
  I will sound the battle alarm;
She shall become a mound of ruins,
  and her daughter cities shall be
    destroyed by fire.
Israel shall inherit those who disinherited
  her,
  says the LORD.[w]
[3] Howl, Heshbon, for the ravager
    approaches,
  shriek, daughters of Rabbah!
Put on sackcloth and mourn,
  run to and fro, gashing yourselves;
For Milcom goes into exile
  along with his priests and captains.[x]
[4] Why do you glory in your strength,
  your ebbing strength, rebellious
    daughter?
You who trust in your treasures, saying,
  "Who can come against me?"
[5] I am bringing terror upon you,
  says the Lord GOD of hosts,
  from all round about you;
You shall be scattered, each man in
    headlong flight,
  with no one to rally the fugitives.[y]
[6] But afterward I will change the lot
  of the Ammonites, says the LORD.

Against Edom.* [7]Concerning Edom, thus says the LORD of hosts:

Is there no more wisdom in Teman,*
  has counsel perished from the prudent,
  has their wisdom become corrupt?
[8] Flee, retreat, hide in deep holes,
  you who live in Dedan:
For I will bring destruction upon Esau*
  when I come to punish him.[z]
[9] If vintagers came upon you,
  they would leave no gleanings;
If thieves by night,
  they would destroy as they pleased.[a]
[10] So I myself will strip Esau;
  I will uncover his retreats so that he
    cannot hide.
He is ruined: sons, and brothers,
  and neighbors, so that he is no more.[b]
[11] Leave your orphans behind, I will keep
    them alive;
  your widows, let them trust in me.[c]

[12]For thus says the LORD: Even those not sentenced to drink the cup must drink it! Shall you then go unpunished? You shall not go unpunished; you shall surely drink it.[d] [13]By my own self I have sworn, says the LORD: Bozrah* shall become an object of horror and a disgrace, a desolation and a curse; she and all her cities shall become ruins forever.[e]

[14] I have heard a report from the LORD,
  a herald has been sent among the
    nations:
Gather together, move against her,
  rise up for battle.
[15] Small will I make you among the
    nations,
  despised among men![f]
[16] The terror you spread beguiled you,
  and your presumption of heart;
You that live in rocky crags,
  that hold the heights of the hill:

49, 1: Milcom: chief god of the Ammonites. The Transjordan tribe of Gad bordered on Ammon, and after the collapse of the northern kingdom the Ammonites occupied its territory.

49, 2: Rabbah of the Ammonites: or Rabbath-Ammon, capital of the Ammonite kingdom. The modern Amman is the capital of the kingdom of Jordan.

49, 7-22: Edom: this implacable enemy from ancient times profited from Judah's downfall; cf Ob 11f.

49, 7: Teman: a district of Edom, used here for the whole country; it was famous for its wise men; cf Jb 2, 11.

49, 8: Esau: Jacob's brother, the traditional ancestor of the Edomites; cf Gn 36.

49, 13: Bozrah: capital of Edom, southeast of the Dead Sea.

w: Am 1, 14. x: Is 15, 2ff. y: Jer 48, 47. z: Ez 25, 13. a: Ob 5. b: Mal 1, 3. c: Dt 10, 18; Ps 68, 6. d: Jer 25, 15. 28; Lam 4, 21f. e: Is 34, 6; Ez 35, 3-9; Ob 16. f: Ob 2.

Though you build your nest high as the
  eagle,
  from there I will drag you down, says
    the LORD.[g]

[17]Edom shall become an object of horror.
Every passer-by shall be appalled and catch
his breath at all her wounds. [18]As when
Sodom, Gomorrah, and their neighbors were
overthrown, says the LORD, not a man shall
dwell there: no one shall visit there.[h]

[19] As when a lion comes up from the
    thicket of Jordan
  to the permanent feeding grounds,
So I, in an instant, will drive men off;
  and whom I choose I will establish
    there!
For who is like me? who can call me to
    account?
  What shepherd can stand against me?[i]
[20] Therefore, hear the counsel of the LORD,
  which he has taken against Edom;
Hear the plans he has made
  against those that live in Teman:
They shall be dragged away, even the
    smallest sheep,
  their own pasture shall be aghast
    because of them.
[21] At the noise of their fall the earth quakes,
  to the Red Sea the outcry is heard!
[22] See! like an eagle he soars aloft,
  and spreads his wings over Bozrah;
On that day the hearts of Edom's heroes
    shall be
  like the heart of a woman in travail.[j]

Against Damascus. Concerning Damascus:

[23] Hamath and Arpad* are covered with
    shame,
  they have heard bad news;
Worried, they toss like the sea
  which cannot rest.[k]
[24] Damascus is weakened, she turns to flee,

panic has seized her.
Distress and pangs take hold of her,
  like those of a woman in travail.
[25] How can the city of glory be forsaken,
  the town of delight!
[26] But now her young men shall fall in her
    streets,
  and all her warriors shall be stilled.
On that day, says the LORD of hosts,
[27] I will set fire to the wall of Damascus,
  and it shall devour the palaces of Ben-
    hadad.*

Against Arabia. [28]Of Kedar and the kingdoms of Hazor, defeated by Nebuchadnezzar, king of Babylon, thus says the LORD:

Rise up, attack Kedar,
  ravage the Easterners.[l]
[29] Their tents and herds shall be taken
    away,
  their tent curtains and all their goods;
Their camels they shall carry off for
    themselves,
  and shout from upon them, "Terror on
    every side!"[m]
[30] Flee! leave your homes, hide in deep
    holes,
  you that live in Hazor, says the LORD;
For counsel has been taken against you,
  a plan has been formed against you
  [Nebuchadnezzar, king of Babylon].
[31] Rise up! set out against a nation that is at
    peace,
  that lives secure, says the LORD,
That has no gates or bars,
  and dwells alone.
[32] Their camels shall be your booty,
  their many herds your spoil;
I will scatter to the winds those who
    shave their temples,
  from all sides I will bring ruin upon
    them,
  says the LORD.[n]
[33] Hazor shall become a haunt of jackals,
  a desert forever,

49, 23: Hamath and Arpad: independent Aramean states to the north of Damascus; the invasion is conceived as coming
from the north. The situation is of the eighth century B.C. Cf Is 10, 9ff.

49, 27: The palaces of Ben-hadad: the royal palaces in Damascus where at least three kings bore this name; cf 1 Kgs 15, 18. 20.

g: Jer 48, 29f.   *h:* Jer 50, 40; Dt 29, 23.   *i:* Jer 12, 5; 25, 9; 50, 44f.   *j:* Jer 4, 13.   *k:* Is 36, 19; 37, 13.   *l:* Is 21, 16.   *m:* Jer 4, 20.
n: Jer 9, 25.

Where no man lives,
no human being stays.

Against Elam. [34]The following word of the LORD against Elam* came to the prophet Jeremiah at the beginning of the reign of Zedekiah, king of Judah: [35]Thus says the LORD of hosts:

Behold, I will break the bow of Elam,
the mainstay of their might.
[36] I will bring upon Elam the four winds
from the four ends of the heavens:
I will scatter them to all these winds, till
there is no nation
to which the outcasts of Elam shall not
come.
[37] I will break Elam before their foes,
before those who seek their life;
I will bring evil upon them,
my burning wrath, says the LORD.
I will send the sword to pursue them
until I have completely made an end of
them;
[38] My throne I will set up in Elam
and destroy from there king and
princes,
says the LORD.
[39] But in the days to come I will change
the lot of Elam, says the LORD.

CHAPTER 50

See RG
218

The First Prophecy against Babylon.

[1]The word which the LORD spoke against Babylon,* against the land of the Chaldeans, through the prophet Jeremiah:[o]

[2] Announce and publish it among the
nations;
publish it, hide it not, but say:
Babylon is taken, Bel* confounded,
Merodach shattered;
her images are put to shame, her idols
shattered.

[3] A people from the north advances against
her
to turn her land into a desert,
So that no one shall live there,
because man and beast have fled
away.[p]
[4] In those days, at that time, says the LORD,
the men of Israel and of Judah shall
come,
Weeping as they come, to seek the LORD,
their God;[q]
[5] to their goal in Zion they shall ask the
way.
"Come, let us join ourselves to the LORD
with covenant everlasting, never to be
forgotten."[r]
[6] Lost sheep were my people,
their shepherds misled them,
straggling on the mountains;
From mountain to hill they wandered,
losing the way to their fold.[s]
[7] Whoever came upon them devoured
them,
and their enemies said, "We incur no
guilt,
Because they sinned against the LORD,
the hope of their fathers, their abode of
justice."[t]

[8] Flee from Babylon, leave the land of the
Chaldeans,
be like the rams at the head of the
flock.[u]
[9] See, I am stirring up against Babylon
a band of great nations from the north;
from there they advance, and she shall
be taken.
Their arrows are arrows of the skilled
warrior;
none shall return without effect.[v]
[10] Chaldea shall be their plunder,
and all her plunderers shall be
enriched,

49, 34: Elam: the ancient kingdom to the east of Babylonia.

50, 1—51, 58: A collection of miscellaneous prophecies against Babylon which now stands as the introduction to the story in Jer 51, 59-64. The Greek text of Jer 50, 1 omits through the prophet Jeremiah, and it is in fact likely that these oracles are not Jeremiah's, but were composed by other inspired writers after the fall of Jerusalem, who may have used some of Jeremiah's texts. Babylon fell to the Per-

sians in 538 B.C.

50, 2: Bel: originally the name of the god of Nippur in Mesopotamia, then identified with Merodach (Marduk), chief god of Babylon.

o: Jer 51, 1; Is 13, 1-14; 21, 1-10. *p:* Jer 51, 48; Is 13, 17. *q:* Jer 3, 18. Ps 126, 6. *r:* Jer 31, 31; 32, 40. *s:* Is 53, 6; 1 Pt 2, 25. *t:* Jer 31, 23. *u:* Jer 51, 6. 45; Is 48, 20. *v:* Jer 51, 27.

says the LORD.

[11] Yes, rejoice and exult,
  you that plunder my portion;
Frisk like calves on the green,
  snort like stallions!
[12] Your mother shall be sorely put to
    shame,
  she that bore you shall be abashed;
See, the last of the nations,
  a desert, dry and waste.[w]
[13] Because of the LORD's wrath she shall be
    empty,
  and become a total desert;
Everyone who passes by Babylon will be
    appalled
  and catch his breath, at all her
    wounds.[x]
[14] Take your posts encircling Babylon,
  you who bend the bow;
Shoot at her, spare not your arrows,[y]
[15] raise the war cry against her on all
    sides.
She surrenders, her bastions fall,
  her walls are torn down:[*]
Vengeance of the LORD is this! Take
    revenge on her,
  as she has done, do to her;
  for she sinned against the LORD.[z]
[16] Cut off from Babylon the sower
  and him who wields the sickle in
    harvest time!
Before the destroying sword,
  each of them turns to his own
    people,
  everyone flees to his own land.[a]
[17] A stray sheep was Israel
  that lions pursued;
Formerly the king of Assyria devoured
    her,
  now Nebuchadnezzar of Babylon
    gnaws her bones.[b]
[18]Therefore, thus says the LORD of hosts,
the God of Israel:

I will punish the king of Babylon and his
    land,
  as once I punished the king of
    Assyria;[c]
[19] But I will bring back Israel to her fold,
  to feed on Carmel and Bashan,
And on Mount Ephraim and Gilead,
  till she has her fill.[d]

[20]In those days, at that time, says the
LORD:

They shall seek Israel's guilt, but it shall
    be no more,
  and Judah's sins, but these shall no
    longer be found;
  for I will forgive the remnant I
    preserve.[e]

[21] Attack the land of Merathaim,[*]
  and those who live in Pekod;
Slaughter and doom them, says the
    LORD,
  do all I have commanded you.
[22] Battle alarm in the land,
  dire destruction!
[23] How has the hammer of the whole earth
    been broken and shattered!
What an object of horror
  Babylon has become among the
    nations.[f]
[24] You ensnared yourself, and were caught,
  O Babylon, before you knew it!
You were discovered and seized,
  because you challenged the LORD.[g]
[25] The LORD opens his armory
  and brings forth the weapons of his
    wrath;
For the Lord GOD of hosts has work to do
  in the land of the Chaldeans.[h]
[26] Come upon her from every side,
  open her granaries,
Pile up her goods in heaps and doom it,

50, 15: Her walls are torn down: the prophet is not predicting the details of Babylon's downfall, but describing such a downfall in conventional language. Actually, Babylon was surrendered peaceably, without destruction.

50, 21: Merathaim, "twice bitter," and Pekod, "punishment," are here symbolic terms for Babylonia, though probably they suggest also the names of regions in that country.

w: Jer 51, 43; Is 13, 20ff.   x: Jer 25, 12.   y: Jer 51, 11; Is 21, 2.   z: Jer 51, 11. 44. 58; Ps 137, 8.   a: Is 13, 14.   b: 2 Kgs 17, 24; 18, 14.   c: Is 10, 12; 14, 24f.   d: Jer 23, 3; Ez 34, 13f.   e: Jer 31, 34; Is 43, 25; Mi 7, 19.   f: Jer 51, 20; Is 14, 6.   g: Jer 51, 57.   h: Jer 51, 11; Is 13, 5.

leave not a remnant.

27 Slay all her oxen,
  let them go down to the slaughter;
Woe to them! their day has come,
  the time of their punishment.

28 Listen! the fugitives, the escaped
  from the land of Babylon:
They announce in Zion
  the vengeance of the LORD, our God.[i]

29 Call up against Babylon archers,
  all who bend the bow;
Encamp around her,
  let no one escape.
Repay her for her deeds;
  as she has done, do to her,
For she insulted the LORD,
  the Holy One of Israel.[j]

30 Therefore her young men shall fall in her
  streets,
  all her warriors shall perish on that
  day;
  says the LORD.[k]

31 I am against you, man of insolence,
  says the Lord GOD of hosts;
For your day has come,
  the time for me to punish you.

32 Insolence stumbles and falls;
  there is no one to raise him up.
I will kindle in his cities a fire
  that shall devour everything around
  him.

33   Thus says the LORD of hosts:
Oppressed are the men of Israel,
  and with them the men of Judah;
All their captors hold them fast
  and refuse to let them go.

34 Strong is their avenger,
  whose name is LORD of hosts;
He will defend their cause with success,
  and give rest to the earth,
  but unrest to those who live in
  Babylon.[l]

35 A sword upon the Chaldeans, says the
  LORD,
  upon Babylon's people, her princes
  and wise men!

36 A sword upon the soothsayers,
  that they may become fools!
A sword upon her warriors,
  that they may tremble;

37 A sword upon her motley throng,
  that they may become women!
A sword upon her treasures,
  that they may be plundered;[m]

38 A sword upon her waters,
  that they may dry up!
For it is a land of idols,
  and they shall be made frantic by
  fearful things.[n]

39 Hence, wildcats and desert beasts shall
  dwell there,
  and ostriches shall occupy it;
Never again shall it be peopled, or lived in,
  from age to age.[o]

40 As when God overturned Sodom
  and Gomorrah, with their neighbors,
  says the LORD,
Not a man shall dwell there,
  no human being shall tarry there.[p]

41 See! a people comes from the north.
  a great nation, and mighty kings
  roused from the ends of the earth.[q]

42 Bow and javelin they wield,
  cruel and pitiless are they;
They sound like the roaring sea,
  as they ride forth on steeds,
Each in his place for battle
  against you, daughter Babylon.

43 The king of Babylon hears news of them,
  and helpless fall his hands;
Anguish seizes him,
  throes like a mother's in childbirth.[r]

44 As when a lion comes up from the
  Jordan's thicket
  to the permanent feeding grounds,
So I, in one instant, will drive them off,
  and whom I choose I will establish
  there;
For who is like me? who calls me to
  account?
  what shepherd can stand against me?[s]

45 Therefore hear the counsel of the LORD
  which he has taken against Babylon;
Hear the plans he has made

---

i: Jer 51, 10f. j: Jer 51, 56. k: Jer 49, 26; 51, 4. l: Jer 51, 36. m: Jer 51, 30; Na 3, 13. n: Jer 51, 32. 36. o: Jer 51, 37; Is 13, 21f. p: Jer 51, 43. q: Jer 51, 27f. r: Is 13, 7. s: Jer 49, 19.

against the land of the Chaldeans:
They shall be dragged away, even the
  smallest sheep;
their own pasture shall be aghast
  because of them.*

46 At the cry "Babylon is captured!" the
  earth quakes;
the outcry is heard among the nations.*

See RG
218

CHAPTER 51

The Second Prophecy
against Babylon

1   Thus says the LORD:
See! I rouse against Babylon,
  and against those who live in Chaldea,
  a destroying wind.
2 Against Babylon I will send winnowers
  to winnow her and lay waste her land;
They shall besiege her from all sides
  on the day of affliction.*
3 Let the bowman draw his bow,
  and flaunt his coat of mail;
Spare not her young men,
  doom her entire army.*
4 The slain shall fall in the land of Chaldea,
  the transfixed, in her streets;*
5 For Israel and Judah are not widowed
  of their God, the LORD of hosts,
And the Chaldean land is full of guilt
  to be punished by the Holy One of
  Israel.

6 Flee out of Babylon;
  let each one save his life,
  perish not for her guilt;
This is a time of vengeance for the LORD,
  he pays her her due.*
7 Babylon was a golden cup in the hand of
  the LORD
which made the whole earth drunk;
The nations drank its wine,
  with this they have become mad.*
8 Babylon suddenly falls and is crushed:
  howl over her!
Bring balm for her wounds,
  in case she can be healed.*

9 "We have tried to heal Babylon,
  but she cannot be healed.
Leave her, let us go, each to his own
  land."
Her judgment reaches heaven,
  it touches the clouds.*
10 The LORD has brought to light our just
  cause;
come, let us tell in Zion
  what the LORD, our God, has done.*

11 Sharpen the arrows,
  fill the quivers;
The LORD has stirred up the spirit of
  Media's kings;*
Babylon he is resolved to destroy.
Yes, it is the vengeance of the LORD,
  vengeance for his temple.*
12 Against the walls of Babylon raise a signal,
  make strong the watch;
Post sentries,
  arrange ambushes!
For the LORD has planned and he will
  carry out
  his threat against the inhabitants of
  Babylon.
13 You who dwell by mighty waters,
  rich in treasure,
Your end has come,
  the term at which you shall be cut off!*
14 The LORD of hosts has sworn by himself:
  I will fill you with men as numerous as
  locusts,
who shall raise over you the vintage
  shout!
15 He has sworn who made the earth by his
  power,
and established the world by his
  wisdom,
and stretched out the heavens by his
  skill.*
16 When he thunders, the waters in the
  heavens roar,
and he brings up clouds from the end
  of the earth;
He makes the lightning flash in the rain,

51, 11: Media's kings: the Medes dwelt with the Persians in the land now known as Iran. At the time these words were
written the Medes were the dominant people of the two, but within a short time the Persians had gained the ascendancy.

---

t: Jer 51, 12. 29. *u:* Jer 51, 29. *v:* Jer 15, 7; Is 41, 16. *w:* Jer 50, 14. 29. *x:* Jer 50, 30. *y:* Jer 50, 8. 15. 29; Is 48, 20. *z:* Rv 14,
8; 17, 4. *a:* Rv 18, 9-18. *b:* Is 13, 14; Rv 18, 5. *c:* Jer 50, 28. *d:* 2 Kgs 17, 6; Is 13, 17. *e:* Na 2, 1. *f:* Jer 10, 12.

and releases stormwinds from their
        chambers.

17 Every man is stupid, ignorant;
        every artisan is put to shame by his idol:
He molded a fraud,
        without breath of life.
18 Nothingness are they, a ridiculous work,
        that will perish in their time of
        punishment.
19 Not like these is the portion of Jacob,
        he is the creator of all things;
Israel is his very own tribe,
        LORD of hosts is his name.

20 You are my hammer,
        my weapon for war;
With you I shatter nations,
        with you I destroy kingdoms.
21 With you I shatter horse and rider,
        with you I shatter chariot and driver.*g*
22 With you I shatter man and wife,
        with you I shatter old and young,
        with you I shatter youth and maiden.*h*
23 With you I shatter the shepherd and his
        flock,
        with you I shatter the farmer and his
        team,
        with you I shatter satraps and prefects.
24 Thus will I repay Babylon,
        and all who live in Chaldea
All the evil they did to Zion,
        as you shall see with your own eyes,
        says the LORD.*i*
25 Beware! I am against you,
        destroying mountain,
        destroyer of the entire earth, says the
        LORD;
I will stretch forth my hand against you,
        roll you down over the cliffs,
        and make you a burnt mountain:*j*
26 They will not take from you a cornerstone,
        or a foundation stone;
Ruins forever shall you be,
        say the LORD.*k*

27 Raise a signal on the earth,

blow the trumpet among the nations;
Dedicate peoples to war against her.
        summon against her the kingdoms,
        Ararat, Minni, and Ashkenaz;*
Appoint recruiting officers against her,
        send up horses like bristling locusts.*l*
28 Dedicate peoples to war against her:
        the king of Media,
Its governors and all its prefects,
        every land in his domain.
29 The earth quakes and writhes,
        the LORD's plan against Babylon is
        carried out,
Turning the land of Babylon
        into a desert where no one lives.
30 Babylon's warriors have ceased to fight,
        they remain in their strongholds;
Dried up is their strength,
        they have become women.
Burned are their homes,
        and broken their bars.
31 One runner meets another,
        herald meets herald,
Telling the king of Babylon
        that all his city is taken.*m*
32 The fords have been seized,
        and the fortresses set on fire,
        while warriors are in panic.

33 For thus says the LORD of hosts, the God
of Israel:

Daughter Babylon is like a threshing
        floor
        at the time it is trodden;
Yet a little while,
        and the harvest time will come for her.*n*
34 He has consumed me,* routed me,
        [Nebuchadnezzar, king of Babylon,]
        he has left me as an empty vessel;
He has swallowed me like a dragon:
        filled his belly with my delights, and
        cast me out.
35 My torn flesh be upon Babylon,
        says the city on Zion;
My blood upon the people of Chaldea,
        says Jerusalem.

51, 27: Ararat, Minni, and Ashkenaz: regions or people in what is now Armenia, subject at this time to Media.
51, 34: Me, my: refers to Jerusalem.

g: Dn 7, 7. 19. 23.   h: Is 13, 16. 18.   i: Jer 25, 14; 50, 29; Ps 137, 8.   j: Rv 8, 7; 18, 8f.   k: Jer 25, 12; Ps 118, 22.   l: Na 3, 17.
m: 2 Chr 30, 6; Jb 1, 14-18.   n: Rv 14, 15.

36   But now, thus says the LORD:
Surely I will defend your cause,
    I will avenge you;
I will dry up her sea,
    and drain her fountain.
37 Babylon shall become a heap of
        ruins,
    a haunt of jackals;
A place of horror and ridicule,
    where no one lives.*o*
38 They all roar like lions,
    growl like lion cubs.*p*
39 When they are parched, I will set a drink
        before them
    to make them drunk, that they may be
        overcome
    with perpetual sleep, never to
        awaken,
    says the LORD.
40 I will bring them down like lambs to the
        slaughter,
    like rams and goats.
41 How has she been seized, made
        captive,
    the glory of the whole world!
What a horror has Babylon become
    among nations:*q*
42   against Babylon the sea rises,
    she is overwhelmed by the roaring
        waves!
43 Her cities have become a desert,
    parched and arid land
Where no man lives,
    and no one passes through.
44 I will punish Bel in Babylon,
    and make him disgorge what he
        swallowed;
    peoples shall stream to him no
        more.
The wall of Babylon falls!
45   Leave her, my people, let each one
        save himself
    from the burning wrath of the LORD.

46 Be not discouraged for fear of rumors
spread in the land; this year the rumor
comes, then violence in the land, tyrant
against tyrant.*r* 47 But behold, the days are
coming when I will punish the idols of Bab-

ylon; her whole land shall be put to shame,
and all her slain shall lie fallen within her.
48 Then heaven, and earth, and everything in
them shall shout over Babylon with joy,
when the destroyers come against her from
the north, says the LORD.*s* 49 Babylon, too,
must fall, O slain of Israel, as at the hands of
Babylon have fallen the slain of all the earth.

50 You who have escaped the sword,
    go on, stand not still;
Remember the LORD from afar,
    let Jerusalem come to your
        minds.
51 We are ashamed because we have heard
        taunts,
    confusion covers our faces; strangers
        have entered
    the holy places of the house of the
        LORD.*t*
52 But behold, the days are coming, says the
        LORD,
    when I will punish her idols,
    and in her whole land the wounded
        will groan.
53 Though Babylon scale the heavens,
    and make her strong heights
        inaccessible,
    destroyers from me shall reach her,
        says the LORD.*u*
54 Hear! loud cries from Babylon,
    dire destruction from the land of the
        Chaldeans;
55 For the LORD lays Babylon waste,
    stills her loud cry,
Though her waves were roaring like
        mighty waters,
    and their clamor was heard afar.
56 For the destroyer comes upon her,
    [Babylon,]
    her heroes are captured, their bows
        broken;
The LORD is a God who requites,
    he will surely repay.*v*

57 I will make her princes and her wise
men drunk, her governors, her prefects, and
her warriors, so that they sleep an eternal
sleep, never to awaken, says the King,

o: Is 25, 2.   p: Na 2, 11f.   q: Is 13, 19.   r: Mt 24, 6f.   s: Rv 18, 20.   t: Pss 44, 16f; 78, 1-4.   u: Is 14, 13.   v: Na 1, 2.

whose name is the LORD of hosts. [58]Thus says the LORD of hosts:

The walls of spacious Babylon shall be
    leveled utterly;
    her lofty gates shall be destroyed by fire.
The toil of the nations is for nothing;
    for the flames the peoples weary
        themselves.[w]

The Prophecy Sent to Babylon. [59]This was the errand given by the prophet Jeremiah to Seraiah,* son of Neriah, son of Mahseiah, when he went to Babylon for the king in the fourth year of the reign of Zedekiah; Seraiah was chief quartermaster. [60]Jeremiah had written all the misfortune that was to befall Babylon in a single book:* all these words that were written against Babylon. [61]And Jeremiah said to Seraiah: When you reach Babylon, see that you read aloud all these words,[x] [62]and then say: O LORD, you yourself threatened to destroy this place, so that neither man nor beast should dwell in it, since it would remain an everlasting desert. [63]When you have finished reading this book, tie a stone to it and throw it in the Euphrates,[y] [64]and say: Thus shall Babylon sink. Never shall she rise, because of the evil I am bringing upon her. [To "weary themselves" are the words of Jeremiah.]*

VI: Historical Appendix*

CHAPTER 52

See RG 218 *Capture of Jerusalem.* [1]Zedakiah was twenty-one years old when he became king, and he reigned eleven years in Jerusalem.[z] His mother's name was Hamutal, daughter of Jeremiah of Libnah. [2]He did what was evil in the eyes of the LORD, just as Jehoiakim had done. [3]Indeed, what was done in Jerusalem and in Judah so angered the LORD that he cast them out from his presence.

Zedekiah rebelled against the king of Babylon. [4a]In the tenth month of the ninth year of his reign, on the tenth day of the month,* Nebuchadnezzar, king of Babylon, and his whole army advanced against Jerusalem, encamped around it, and built siege walls on every side. [5]The siege of the city continued until the eleventh year of King Zedekiah.

[6]On the ninth day of the fourth month, when famine had gripped the city and the people had no more bread, [7]the city walls were breached. Then all the soldiers took to flight and left the city by night through the gate between the two walls which was near the king's garden. With the Chaldeans surrounding the city, they went in the direction of the Arabah. [8]But the Chaldean army pursued the king and overtook Zedekiah in the desert near Jericho, while his whole army fled from him.

[9]The king, therefore, was arrested and brought to Riblah, in the land of Hamath, to the king of Babylon, who pronounced sentence on him. [10]As Zedekiah looked on, the king of Babylon slew his sons as well as all the princes of Judah at Riblah. [11]Then he blinded Zedekiah, bound him with fetters, and had him brought to Babylon and kept in prison until the day of his death.

Destruction of Jerusalem. [12]On the tenth day of the fifth month (this was in the nineteenth year* of Nebuchadnezzar, king of

---

51, 59: Seraiah: the brother of Baruch; cf Jer 32, 12. The king: Zedekiah. Perhaps Seraiah went to Babylon to explain away the presence of foreign ambassadors in Jerusalem that same year; cf Jer 27, 3.

51, 60: Jeremiah prophesied against Babylon, even as he foretold Judah's release from Babylon's power (Jer 3, 14-18; 32, 15; 33, 6-9. 12f); but his book against Babylon was thrown in the Euphrates (v 63). The preceding oracles were composed by later writers; see note on Jer 50, 1—51, 58.

51, 64: [To "weary themselves" are the words of Jeremiah]: an editorial remark concerning the end of v 58.

52, 1-34: This supplement to the Book of Jeremiah was taken by the final editor from 2 Kgs 24, 18—25, 30 and placed here in order to show the fulfillment of Jeremiah's prophecies. In part this repeats the history given in Jer 39—41; the history of Gedaliah in 2 Kgs 25, 22-26, however, has not been reproduced here.

52, 4: In the tenth month of the ninth year of his reign, on the tenth day of the month: January 15, 588 B.C. Cf Jer 39, 1.

52, 12: On the tenth day of the fifth month . . . nineteenth year: the tenth of Ab—July/August in 587 B.C.

---

w: Eb 2, 13.   x: Jer 50, 1-51.   y: Rv 18, 21.   z: 1-27: 2 Kgs 24, 18—25, 21.   a: 4-16: Jer 39, 1-10.

Babylon), Nebuzaradan, captain of the bodyguard, came to Jerusalem as the representative of the king of Babylon. [13]He burned the house of the LORD, the palace of the king, and all the houses of Jerusalem; every large building he destroyed with fire. [14]And the Chaldean troops who were with the captain of the guard tore down all the walls that surrounded Jerusalem.

[15]Then Nebuzaradan, captain of the guard, led into exile the rest of the people left in the city, and those who had deserted to the king of Babylon, and the rest of the artisans. [16]But some of the country's poor, Nebuzaradan, captain of the guard, left behind as vinedressers and farmers.

[17]The bronze pillars that belonged to the house of the LORD, and the wheeled carts and the bronze sea in the house of the LORD, the Chaldeans broke into pieces; they carried away all the bronze to Babylon. [18]They took also the pots, the shovels, the snuffers, the bowls, the pans, and all the bronze vessels used for service. [19]The basins also, the fire holders, the bowls, the pots, the lampstands, the pans, the sacrificial bowls which were of gold or silver, these too the captain of the guard carried off, [20]as well as the two pillars, the one sea, and the twelve oxen of bronze under the sea, and the wheeled carts which King Solomon had made for the house of the LORD. The bronze of all these furnishings could not be weighed.

[21]Each of the pillars was eighteen cubits high and twelve cubits in diameter; each was four fingers thick, and hollow inside. [22]A bronze capital five cubits high surmounted the one pillar, and a network with pomegranates encircled the capital, all of brass; and so for the other pillar. The pomegranates . . . , [23]there were ninety-six pomegranates. There were a hundred pomegranates, all around the network.

[24]The captain of the guard also took Seraiah, the high priest, Zephaniah, the second priest, and the three keepers of the entry. [25]And from the city he took one courtier, a commander of soldiers, and seven men in the personal service of the king who were present in the city, and the scribe of the army commander who mustered the people of the land, and sixty of the common people who were in the city. [26]The captain of the guard, Nebuzaradan, arrested these and brought them to the king of Babylon at Riblah, [27]who had them struck down and put to death in Riblah, in the land of Hamath.

Thus was Judah exiled from her land. [28]*This is the number of the people whom Nebuchadnezzar led away captive: in his seventh year, three thousand and twenty-three people of Judah; [29]in the eighteenth year of Nebuchadnezzar, eight hundred and thirty-two persons from Jerusalem; [30]in the twenty-third year of Nebuchadnezzar, Nebuzaradan, captain of the guard, exiled seven hundred and forty-five people of Judah: four thousand six hundred persons in all.

Favor Shown to Jehoiachin. [31]*b*In the thirty-seventh year of the exile of Jehoiachin, king of Judah, on the twenty-fifth day of the twelfth month, Evil-merodach, king of Babylon, in the inaugural year of his reign, took up the case of Jehoiachin, king of Judah, and released him from prison. [32]He spoke kindly to him and gave him a throne higher than that of the other kings* who were with him in Babylon. [33]Jehoiachin took off his prison garb and ate at the king's table as long as he lived. [34]The allowance given him by the king of Babylon was a perpetual allowance, in fixed daily amounts, all the days of his life until the day of his death.

52, 28-30: These verses are missing in the Greek text and have not been taken from 2 Kgs 25, but from some other source using a different system of chronology. Besides the deportations of 598 and 587 B.C., mention is made here of a final one that took place in the year 582/1, possibly as a sequel to the murder of Gedaliah; cf Jer 41, 2.

52, 31-34: In the year 561/0 B.C., Jehoiachin was released from prison by Nebuchadnezzar's successor Awel-Marduk

(Evil-merodach), who reigned only two years. Babylonian records confirm the fact that Jehoiachin and his family were supported at public expense.

52, 32: The other kings: who had also been brought as captives to Babylon.

---

b: 31-34: 2 Kgs 25, 27-30.

A Poet Laments Jerusalem

As in many prophetic books (Hosea, Jeremiah, Ezekiel), Jerusalem is personified as a woman (Lam 1, 1–11). In a striking series of contrasts, she who was great is now destitute like a widow; once a princess, she is now a slave. Political allies are called Jerusalem's dear ones or lovers (see also Hs 2, 7). Public activities (feasts and gateways, where people gather) have ceased. Priests and virgins are among the many categories of people that the book shows as suffering. All of this, the book repeatedly claims, is because the Lord has punished Israel (v. 5).

See RG 219–23

The Book of Lamentations

The sixth century B.C. was an age of crisis, a turning point in the history of Israel. With the destruction of the temple and the interruption of its ritual, the exile of the leaders and loss of national sovereignty, an era came to an end. Not long after the fall of Jerusalem (587) an eyewitness of the national humiliation composed these five laments. They combine confession of sin, grief over the suffering and humiliation of Zion, submission to merited chastisement, and strong faith in the constancy of Yahweh's love and power to restore. The union of poignant grief and unquenchable hope reflects the constant prophetic vision of the weakness of man and the strength of God's love; it also shows how Israel's faith in Yahweh could survive the shattering experience of national ruin.

As a literary work, the Book of Lamentations is carefully constructed according to a familiar structural device. The first four poems are acrostics in which the separate stanzas begin with successive letters of the Hebrew alphabet from the first to the last. Far from destroying the spontaneous pathos of the songs, this literary feature permits a symbolic and disciplined expression of the profound grief, the sinful responsibility, and the enduring hope of the suffering community. The figure of Israel as the bride of Yahweh, familiar from the prophets, appears here again; but now Zion is a desolate widow, the *Judaea Capta* of Titus' memorial coins, sustained only by the faith that God's chastisement will eventually give place to his infinite compassion.

CHAPTER 1

Jerusalem Abandoned and Disgraced*

See RG 219–23

¹ How lonely she is now,
    the once crowded city!
Widowed is she
    who was mistress over nations;
The princess among the provinces
    has been made a toiling slave.

² Bitterly she weeps at night,
    tears upon her cheeks,
With not one to console her
    of all her dear ones;
Her friends have all betrayed her
    and become her enemies.ᵃ

³ Judah has fled into exile
    from oppression and cruel
      slavery;
Yet where she lives among the
      nations
    she finds no place to rest:
All her persecutors come upon her
    where she is narrowly confined.ᵇ

⁴ The roads to Zion mourn
    for lack of pilgrims going to her
      feasts;
All her gateways are
      deserted,
    her priests groan,

1, 1-22: In this poem the poet first describes Jerusalem's miserable state after the destruction wrought by the Chaldeans (vv 1-11a); in v 11b the city itself takes up the lament.

a: Jer 30, 14; Ez 16, 37.   *b:* Dt 28, 65; Jer 45, 3.

Her virgins sigh;
    she is in bitter grief.*c*

5 Her foes are uppermost,
    her enemies are at ease;
The LORD has punished her
    for her many sins.
Her little ones have gone away,
    captive before the foe.

6 Gone from daughter Zion
    is all her glory:
Her princes, like rams
    that find no pasture,
Have gone off without strength
    before their captors.

7 Jerusalem is mindful of the days
    of her wretched homelessness,
When her people fell into enemy hands,
    and she had no one to help her;
When her foes gloated over her,
    laughed at her ruin.

8 Through the sin of which she is guilty,
    Jerusalem is defiled;
All who esteemed her think her vile
    now that they see her nakedness;
She herself groans
    and turns away.*d*

9 Her filth is on her skirt;
    she gave no thought how she would end.
Astounding is her downfall,
    with no one to console her.
Look, O LORD, upon her misery,
    for the enemy has triumphed!

10 The foe stretched out his hand
    to all her treasures;
She has seen those nations
    enter her sanctuary
Whom you forbade to come
    into your assembly.*e*

11 All her people groan,
    searching for bread;

They give their treasures for food,
    to retain the breath of life.
"Look, O LORD, and see
    how worthless I have become!*f*

12 "Come, all you who pass by the way,
    look and see
Whether there is any suffering like my
      suffering,
    which has been dealt me
When the LORD afflicted me
    on the day of his blazing wrath.

13 "From on high he sent fire
    down into my very frame;
He spread a net for my feet,
    and overthrew me.
He left me desolate,
    in pain all the day.*g*

14 "He has kept watch over my sins;
    by his hand they have been plaited:
They have settled about my neck,*
    he has brought my strength to its
      knees;
The Lord has delivered me into their
      grip,
    I am unable to rise.

15 "All the mighty ones in my midst
    the Lord has cast away;
He summoned an army against me
    to crush my young men;
The LORD has trodden in the wine press
    virgin daughter Judah.*h*

16 "At this I weep,
    my eyes run with tears:
Far from me are all who could console me,
    any who might revive me;
My sons were reduced to silence
    when the enemy prevailed."*i*

17 Zion stretched out her hands,
    but there was no one to console her;
The LORD gave orders against Jacob
    for his neighbors to be his foes;

1, 14: They have been plaited . . . my neck: the sins of the people have been bound together and laid as a yoke on their back; cf Mt 23, 4.

c: Jer 14, 2.   *d:* Is 47, 2; Jer 13, 22. 26.   *e:* Jer 51, 51.   *f:* Jer 52, 6.   *g:* Ez 12, 13.   *h:* Jer 8, 16.   *i:* Jer 13, 17; 14, 17.

Jerusalem has become in their midst
a thing unclean.*j*

18 "The LORD is just;
I had defied his command.
Listen, all you peoples,
and behold my suffering:
My maidens and my youths
have gone into captivity.*k*

19 "I cried out to my lovers,*
but they failed me.
My priests and my elders
perished in the city;
Where they sought food for themselves,
they found it not.*l*

20 "Look, O LORD, upon my distress:
all within me is in ferment,
My heart recoils within me
from my monstrous rebellion.
In the streets the sword bereaves,
at home death stalks.*m*

21 "Give heed to my groaning;
there is no one to console me.
All my enemies rejoice at my misfortune:
it is you who have wrought it.
Bring on the day you have proclaimed,
that they may be even as I.

22 "Let all their evil come before you;*
deal with them
As you have dealt with me
for all my sins;
My groans are many,
and I am sick at heart."*n*

CHAPTER 2

See RG
219-23
The Lord's Wrath against Zion

1 How the Lord in his wrath
has detested daughter Zion!
He has cast down from heaven to earth
the glory of Israel,*

Unmindful of his footstool
on the day of his wrath.

2 The Lord has consumed without pity
all the dwellings of Jacob;
He has torn down in his anger
the fortresses of daughter Judah;
He has brought to the ground in dishonor
her king and her princes.

3 He broke off, in fiery wrath,
the horn* that was Israel's whole
strength;
He withheld the support of his right hand
when the enemy approached;
He blazed up in Jacob like a flaming fire
devouring all about it.*o*

4 Like an enemy he made taut his bow;
with his arrows in his right hand
He took his stand as a foe, and slew
all on whom the eye doted;
Over the tent of daughter Zion
he poured out his wrath like fire.*p*

5 The Lord has become an enemy,
he has consumed Israel:
Consumed all her castles
and destroyed her fortresses;
For daughter Judah he has multiplied
moaning and groaning.

6 He has demolished his shelter like a
garden booth,
he has destroyed his dwelling;
In Zion the LORD has made
feast and sabbath to be forgotten;
He has scorned in fierce wrath
both king and priest.*q*

7 The Lord has disowned his altar,
rejected his sanctuary;
The walls of her towers
he has handed over to the enemy,

1, 19: My lovers: Zion's foreign allies, who failed to help her, as the prophets had warned.

1, 22: Zion fully acknowledges her guilt and the justness of divine punishment; nevertheless, she pleads that her enemies also be punished for their guilt.

2, 1: The glory of Israel: the temple. His footstool: the ark of the covenant (1 Chr 28, 2; Pss 99, 5; 132, 7); or again, the temple (Ez 43, 7).

2, 3: Horn: symbol of power and strength; cf Lam 2, 17; 1 Sm 2, 10; Lk 1, 69; etc.

---

j: Ps 74, 7.   *k:* Dt 28, 41.   *l:* Jer 30, 14.   *m:* Lam 2, 11.   *n:* Lam 3, 64.   *o:* Lam 1, 12.   *p:* Jer 30, 14.   *q:* Lam 1, 4; Is 1, 13; 5, 5.

Acrostic Poems in Hebrew

An acrostic poem is one in which the initial letters of each line of poetry follow some sort of pattern. In the Hebrew Bible, all of the acrostic poems are alphabetical acrostics: that is, the first letters of each line (or each group of lines) form the Hebrew alphabet of twenty-two letters.

The following passages in the Bible are acrostics: Psalms 9—10, 25, 34, 37, 111, 112, 119, 145; Proverbs 31, 10–31; each chapter in Lamentations except chapter 5, which nevertheless has twenty-two lines; Nahum 1, 2–8 (or perhaps 2–10; the acrostic is incomplete). The Hebrew text of Sirach 51, 13–30 is also an acrostic. Psalms 34, 37, 112, 119, Proverbs 31, and Sirach 51 are all examples of wisdom literature, and if these texts were used in schools, the acrostic feature may have been an aid to memorization.

We can compare the use of rhyme in English poetry. Rhyme is a pattern involving similar sounds at the ends of lines; it is therefore like an acrostic in combining a pattern of sound and meaning. We can admire the artistry involved in such a combination, and perhaps that will give us insight into the enjoyment that acrostic poems may have provided to their original audiences.

In the case of Lamentations, where chapters 1—4 are acrostics, and chapter 5 continues the pattern with its twenty-two lines, there may be a deeper meaning. By expressing grief in a pattern that completes the alphabet, the poet may be expressing two things: the completeness of grief—covering it "from A to Z," as we might say—and also its end. The poetical form helps the poet to channel and contain grief, as mourning rituals can do in other social settings.

Who shout in the house of the LORD
as on a feast day.[r]

[8] The LORD marked for destruction
the wall of daughter Zion:
He stretched out the measuring line;[s]
his hand brought ruin, yet he did not
relent—
He brought grief on wall and rampart
till both succumbed.[s]

[9] Sunk into the ground are her gates;
he has removed and broken her bars.
Her king and her princes are among the
pagans;
priestly instruction is wanting,
And her prophets have not received
any vision from the LORD.[t]

[10] On the ground in silence sit
the old men of daughter Zion;
They strew dust[*] on their heads

and gird themselves with
sackcloth;
The maidens of Jerusalem
bow their heads to the ground.[u]

[11] Worn out from weeping are my eyes,
within me all is in ferment;
My gall is poured out on the ground[*]
because of the downfall of the
daughter of my people,
As child and infant faint away
in the open spaces of the town.[v]

[12] They ask their mothers,
"Where is the cereal?"—in vain,
As they faint away like the wounded
in the streets of the city,
And breathe their last
in their mothers' arms.[w]

[13] To what can I liken or compare you,
O daughter Jerusalem?

2, 8: The measuring line: used not only in building, but in deciding what must be destroyed; cf Is 34, 11; 2 Kgs 21, 13.
2, 10: They strew dust: as a sign of penance; cf Jb 2, 12.
2, 11: My gall is poured out on the ground: I am afflicted with bitter sorrow; cf Jb 16, 13.

r: Ez 24, 21.   s: Jer 52, 13.   t: Dt 28, 36.   u: Is 3, 26.   v: Lam 3, 48.   w: Lam 1, 11.

What example can I show you for your
comfort,
virgin daughter Zion?
For great as the sea is your downfall;
who can heal you?[x]

[14] Your prophets had for you
false and specious visions;
They did not lay bare your guilt,
to avert your fate;
They beheld for you in vision
false and misleading portents.[y]

[15] All who pass by
clap their hands at you;
They hiss and wag their heads
over daughter Jerusalem:
"Is this the all-beautiful city,
the joy of the whole earth?"[z]

[16] All your enemies
open their mouths against you;
They hiss and gnash their teeth.
They say, "We have devoured her.
This at last is the day we hoped for;
we have lived to see it!"[a]

[17] The LORD has done as he decreed:
he has fulfilled the threat
He set forth from days of old;
he has destroyed and had no pity,
Letting the enemy gloat over you
and exalting the horn of your foes.[b]

[18] Cry out to the Lord;
moan, O daughter Zion!
Let your tears flow like a torrent
day and night;
Let there be no respite for you,
no repose for your eyes.

[19] Rise up, shrill in the night,
at the beginning of every watch;
Pour out your heart like water
in the presence of the Lord;

Lift up your hands to him
for the lives of your little ones
[Who faint from hunger
at the corner of every street].

[20] "Look, O LORD, and consider:
whom have you ever treated thus?
Must women eat their offspring,[*]
their well-formed children?
Are priest and prophet to be slain
in the sanctuary of the LORD?[c]

[21] "Dead in the dust of the streets
lie young and old;
My maidens and young men
have fallen by the sword;
You have slain on the day of your wrath,
slaughtered without pity.[d]

[22] "You summoned as for a feast day
terrors against me from all sides;
There was not, on the day of your wrath,
either fugitive or survivor;
Those whom I bore and reared
my enemy has utterly destroyed."[e]

CHAPTER 3

Sufferings of the Prophet and His People

See RG
219-23

[1] I am a man who knows affliction[*]
from the rod of his anger,[f]
[2] One whom he has led and forced to walk
in darkness, not in the light;
[3] Against me alone he brings back his
hand
again and again all the day.
[4] He has worn away my flesh and my skin,
he has broken my bones;[g]
[5] He has beset me round about
with poverty and weariness;
[6] He has left me to dwell in the dark
like those long dead.[h]
[7] He has hemmed me in with no escape
and weighed me down with chains;

2, 20: Must women eat their offspring: extreme famine in a besieged city sometimes led to this form of cannibalism; cf Lam 4, 10; 2 Kgs 6, 28f; Bar 2, 3; Ez 5, 10.
3, 1-21: The author identifies Zion's sufferings with his own.

x: Lam 1, 12.   *y:* Is 58, 1; Jer 2, 8; 23, 16.   *z:* Jer 18, 16.   *a:* Lam 3, 46   *b:* Dt 28, 15.   *c:* Lam 4, 10.   *d:* Lam 3, 43; 2 Chr 36, 17; Jer 6, 11.   *e:* Jer 42, 17.   *f:* Jer 20, 18.   *g:* Jb 30, 30; Is 38, 13.   *h:* Ps 143, 3.

A Teaching on God's Goodness

In a jarring shift at the center of the book, Lam 3, 25–41 offers beautiful statements of God's mercy, faithfulness, and compassion and teaches silence in the face of suffering. Because some passages appear to contradict material that comes before and after (v. 39: Why should anyone complain?), these verses are often considered a later addition to the book. They function, however, to balance the community's expression of suffering with the book's insistent theme that God is justifiably punishing Judah for its sins. Because God has acted justly, Judah must examine its own wrongs.

⁸ Even when I cry out for help,
    he stops my prayer;*i*
⁹ He has blocked my ways with fitted
      stones,
    and turned my paths aside.

¹⁰ A lurking bear he has been to me,
    a lion in ambush!*j*
¹¹ He deranged my ways, set me astray,
    left me desolate.*k*
¹² He bent his bow, and set me up
    as the target for his arrow.*l*

¹³ He pierces my sides
    with shafts from his quiver.*m*
¹⁴ I have become a laughingstock for all
      nations,
    their taunt all the day long;*n*
¹⁵ He has sated me with bitter food,
    made me drink my fill of wormwood.*o*

¹⁶ He has broken my teeth with gravel,
    pressed my face in the dust;
¹⁷ My soul is deprived of peace,
    I have forgotten what happiness is;
¹⁸ I tell myself my future is lost,
    all that I hoped for from the LORD.

¹⁹ The thought of my homeless poverty
    is wormwood and gall;
²⁰ Remembering it over and over
    leaves my soul downcast within me.
²¹ But I will call this to mind,
    as my reason to have hope:

²² The favors of the LORD are not
      exhausted,
    his mercies are not spent;*p*
²³ They are renewed each morning,
    so great is his faithfulness.
²⁴ My portion is the LORD, says my soul;
    therefore will I hope in him.*q*

²⁵ Good is the LORD to one who waits for
      him,
    to the soul that seeks him;*r*
²⁶ It is good to hope in silence
    for the saving help of the LORD.
²⁷ It is good for a man to bear
    the yoke* from his youth.

²⁸ Let him sit alone and in silence,
    when it is laid upon him.
²⁹ Let him put his mouth to the dust;*
    there may yet be hope.*s*
³⁰ Let him offer his cheek to be struck,
    let him be filled with disgrace.*t*

³¹ For the Lord's rejection
    does not last forever;*u*
³² Though he punishes, he takes pity,
    in the abundance of his mercies;*v*
³³ He has no joy in afflicting
    or grieving the sons of men.*w*

³⁴ When anyone tramples underfoot
    all the prisoners in the land,
³⁵ When he distorts men's rights
    in the very sight of the Most High,

3, 27: To bear the yoke: to do God's will; cf Jer 2, 20.
3, 29: Let him put his mouth to the dust: in humble submission; cf Ps 72, 9.

i: Ps 22, 2. *j:* Jb 10, 16; Hos 13, 8. *k:* Lam 1, 13. *l:* Lam 2, 4; Jb 16, 12. *m:* Jb 6, 4; Ps 38, 3. *n:* Jb 30, 9; Ps 69, 13. *o:* Jer 9, 14; 23, 15. *p:* Neh 9, 31. *q:* Pss 16, 5; 73, 26. *r:* Ps 130, 6; Is 30, 18. *s:* Jb 42, 6. *t:* Is 50, 6; Mt 5, 39. *u:* Ps 103, 9. *v:* Is 54, 8f. *w:* Heb 12, 10f.

³⁶ When he presses a crooked claim,
    the Lord does not look on unconcerned.

³⁷ Who commands, so that it comes to pass,
    except the Lord ordains it;
³⁸ Except it proceeds from the mouth of the
    Most High,
    whether the thing be good or bad!^x
³⁹ Why should any living man complain,
    any mortal, in the face of his sins?^y

⁴⁰ Let us search and examine our ways
    that we may return to the LORD!^z
⁴¹ Let us reach out our hearts
    toward God in heaven!
⁴² We have sinned and rebelled;
    you have not forgiven us.

⁴³ You veiled yourself in wrath and pursued
    us,
    you slew us and took no pity;^a
⁴⁴ You wrapped yourself in a cloud
    which prayer could not pierce.
⁴⁵ You have made us offscourings and refuse
    among the nations.^b

⁴⁶ All our enemies
    have opened their mouths against us;
⁴⁷ Terror and the pit have been our lot,
    desolation and destruction;^c
⁴⁸ My eyes run with streams of water
    over the downfall of the daughter of
    my people.^d

⁴⁹ My eyes flow without ceasing,
    there is no respite,
⁵⁰ Till the LORD from heaven
    looks down and sees.
⁵¹ My eyes torment my soul
    at the sight of all the daughters of my
    city.

⁵² Those who were my enemies without cause
    hunted me down like a bird;
⁵³ They struck me down alive in the pit,
    and sealed me in with a stone.^e
⁵⁴ The waters flowed over my head,
and I said, "I am lost!"

⁵⁵ I called upon your name, O LORD,^f
    from the bottom of the pit;
⁵⁶ You heard me call, "Let not your ear
    be deaf to my cry for help!"
⁵⁷ You came to my aid when I called to you;
    you said, "Have no fear!"

⁵⁸ You defended me in mortal danger,
    you redeemed my life.
⁵⁹ You see, O LORD, how I am wronged;
    do me justice!^g
⁶⁰ You see all their vindictiveness,
    all their plots against me.

⁶¹ You hear their insults, O LORD,
    [all their plots against me],
⁶² The whispered murmurings of my foes,
    against me all the day;
⁶³ Whether they sit or stand,
    see, I am their taunt song.

⁶⁴ Requite them as they deserve, O LORD,
    according to their deeds;
⁶⁵ Give them hardness of heart,
    as your curse upon them;^h
⁶⁶ Pursue them in wrath and destroy them
    from under your heavens!

CHAPTER 4

Miseries of the Besieged City

See RG 219–23

¹ How tarnished is the gold,
    how changed the noble metal;
How the sacred stones lie strewn
    at every street corner!

² Zion's precious sons,
    fine gold their counterpart,
Now worth no more than earthen jars
    made by the hands of a potter!ⁱ

³ Even the jackals bare their breasts
    and suckle their young;
The daughter of my people has become
    as cruel
    as the ostrich* in the desert.^j

4, 3: Cruel as the ostrich: see note on Jb 39, 14ff. Jerusalem, in her distress, had abandoned her children.

---

^{x:} Is 45, 7.   ^{y:} Prv 19, 3.   ^{z:} Jl 2, 12f.   ^{a:} Lam 2, 21.   ^{b:} 1 Cor 4, 13.   ^{c:} Is 24, 17; Jer 48, 43.   ^{d:} Ps 119, 136.   ^{e:} Jer 37, 15; 38,
6-9.   ^{f:} 55f: Ps 130, 1f.   ^{g:} Ps 35, 23.   ^{h:} Jer 11, 20; 2 Tm 4, 14.   ^{i:} Jer 19, 11.   ^{j:} Jb 39, 16.

Jerusalem's Changed Fortures

In Lam 4, 1–10, the poet portrays a world upside down, where all that is normal has vanished. The once valuable is treated as worthless. Children, once treasured, are earthen jars, and scarce food is not given to them. Ostriches, to which the people are compared, have the reputation of neglecting their young (Jb 39, 13–18). Purple, due to the costliness of its dye, was worn by royalty; thus in v. 5, the once privileged class now starves. In the most dramatic reversal, once compassionate mothers eat their children rather than feed them.

⁴ The tongue of the suckling cleaves
    to the roof of its mouth in thirst;
The babes cry for food,
    but there is no one to give it to
        them.

⁵ Those accustomed to dainty food
    perish in the streets;
Those brought up in purple
    now cling to the ash heaps.ᵏ

⁶ The punishment of the daughter of my
        people
    is greater than the penalty of
        Sodom,
Which was overthrown in an instant
    without the turning of a hand.ˡ

⁷ Brighter than snow were her princes,
    whiter than milk,
More ruddy than coral,
    more precious than sapphire.

⁸ Now their appearance is blacker than
        soot,
    they are unrecognized on the
        streets;
Their skin shrinks on their bones,
    as dry as wood.ᵐ

⁹ Better for those who perish by the
        sword
    than for those who die of hunger,
Who waste away, as though pierced
        through,
    lacking the fruits of the field!

¹⁰ The hands of compassionate women
    boiled their own children,
To serve them as mourners' food
    in the downfall of the daughter of my
        people.ⁿ

¹¹ The LORD has spent his anger,
    poured out his blazing wrath;
He has kindled a fire in Zion
    that has consumed her foundations.ᵒ

¹² The kings of the earth did not
        believe,
    nor any of the world's inhabitants,
That enemy or foe could enter
    the gates of Jerusalem.

¹³ Because of the sins of her prophets*
    and the crimes of her priests,
Who shed in her midst
    the blood of the just!—ᵖ

¹⁴ They staggered blindly in the
        streets,
    soiled with blood,
So that people could not touch
    even their garments:�q

¹⁵ "Away, you unclean!" they cried to
        them,
    "Away, away, do not draw near!"
If they left and wandered among the
        nations,
    nowhere could they remain.

¹⁶ The LORD himself has dispersed them,

4, 13ff: The priests and the false prophets lulled the people into an illusory security (Jer 2, 8; 5, 31; 6, 13; etc.), condoning and entering into their crimes so that they themselves became unclean.

---

k: Dt 28, 56.   l: Gn 19, 23-29; 2 Pt 2, 6; Jude 1, 7.   m: Lam 3, 4.   n: Lam 2, 20; Dt 28, 56f; 2 Kgs 6, 29.   o: Jer 7, 20; Ez 5, 13.
p: Jer 6, 13.   q: Is 59, 10.

he regards them no more;
He does not receive the priests with
favor,
nor show kindness to the elders.

17 Our eyes ever wasted away,
looking in vain for aid;
From our watchtower we watched
for a nation* that could not save us.

18 Men dogged our steps
so that we could not walk in our
streets;
Our end drew near, and came;
our time had expired.

19 Our pursuers were swifter
than eagles in the air,
They harassed us on the mountains
and waylaid us in the desert.r

20 The anointed one of the LORD, our breath
of life,*
was caught in their snares,
He in whose shadow we thought
we could live on among the nations.s

21 Though you rejoice and are glad, O
daughter Edom,
you who dwell in the land of Uz,*
To you also shall the cup be passed;
you shall become drunk and naked.t

22 Your chastisement is completed, O
daughter Zion,
he will not prolong your exile;
But your wickedness, O daughter Edom,
he will punish,
he will lay bare your sins.u

CHAPTER 5

The Prophet's Lament
and Supplication

See RG
219-23

1 Remember, O LORD, what has befallen
us,
look, and see our disgrace:
2 Our inherited lands have been turned
over to strangers,
our homes to foreigners.v
3 We have become orphans, fatherless;
widowed are our mothers.
4 The water we drink we must buy,
for our own wood we must pay.
5 On our necks is the yoke of those who
drive us;
we are worn out, but allowed no rest.

6 To Egypt we submitted,
and to Assyria, to fill our need of
bread.*
7 Our fathers,* who sinned, are no more;
but we bear their guilt.
8 Slaves rule over us;
there is no one to rescue us from their
hands.*
9 At the peril of our lives we bring in our
sustenance,
in the face of the desert heat;w
10 Our skin is shriveled up, as though by a
furnace,
with the searing blasts of famine.x

11 The wives in Zion were ravished by the
enemy,
the maidens in the cities of Judah;y
12 Princes were gibbeted by them,
elders shown no respect.z
13 The youths carry the millstones,

4, 17: A nation: Egypt, which failed to give effective aid against Babylon.

4, 20: Our breath of life: the king. This is a royal epithet borrowed from Egyptian usage, while the anointed one of the Lord is Israelite. After the disaster of 598 B.C. (2 Kgs 24, 1-17), Jerusalem could have hoped to live in peace amidst her neighbors; but they (vv 21f) as well as Babylon turned against her to ensure her total devastation in 587 B.C.

4, 21: Uz: see note on Jer 25, 20.

5, 6: In its state of abjection, Judah was forced to depend on its traditional enemies to the west and the east for subsistence. Mesopotamia is here called by the name it had long borne, Assyria, though in these times the power of the Assyr-

ians had been superseded by that of the Chaldeans.

5, 7: Our fathers: collective responsibility, for good and for evil, was recognized in the Old Testament; cf Jer 31, 29. But the present generation is also personally guilty of sin (v 16).

5, 8: Administrations imposed by foreign powers were notoriously corrupt and inept. The Hebrew word for "slave" is the same as that used for an official (servant of the ruler); the author doubtless intends the double meaning here.

---

r: Jer 4, 13; Hb 1, 8. s: Lam 2, 9; Ez 19, 4. 8. t: Lam 1, 21; Jer 25, 15. u: Is 40, 2. v: Ps 79, 1. w: Jer 6, 25. x: Lam 4, 8. y: Zec 14, 2. z: Lam 4, 16.

> The poem ends on a poignant note. God's power is undisputed, though God's care is questioned. The community asks that its broken relationship with God be healed but fears that God's anger may yet be too great.

boys stagger under their loads of wood;

14 The old men have abandoned the gate,*
the young men their music.

15 The joy of our hearts has ceased,
our dance has turned into mourning;a

16 The garlands have fallen from our heads:
woe to us, for we have sinned!

17 Over this our hearts are sick,
at this our eyes grow dim:

18 That Mount Zion should be desolate,
with jackals roaming there!

19 You, O LORD, are enthroned forever;
your throne stands from age to age.b

20 Why, then, should you forget us,
abandon us so long a time?c

21 Lead us back to you, O LORD, that we may be restored:
give us anew such days as we had of old.d

22 For now you have indeed rejected us,
and in full measure turned your wrath against us.e

5, 14: The gate: the place of assembly, where city decisions were made and judgment given by the elders and other notables; see note on Ru 4, 1.

a: Jer 16, 9; 25, 10; Am 8, 10.   b: Pss 9, 8; 45, 7; 102, 13. 27.   c: Pss 13, 1; 42, 10.   d: Ps 80, 19f.   e: Jer 14, 19.

See RG 223-26

The Book of Baruch

The opening verses of this book ascribe it, or at least its first part, to Baruch, the well-known secretary of the prophet Jeremiah. It contains five very different compositions, the first and the last in prose, the others in poetic form. The prose sections were certainly composed in Hebrew, though the earliest known form of the book is in Greek.

An observance of the feast of Booths with a public prayer of penitence and petition (1, 15—3, 8), such as is supposed by the introduction (1, 1-14), would not have been possible during the lifetime of Baruch after the fall of Jerusalem; this indeed is suggested in the prayer itself (2, 26). The prayer is therefore to be understood as the pious reflection of a later Jewish writer upon the circumstances of the exiles in Babylon as he knew them from the Book of Jeremiah. He expresses in their name sentiments called for by the prophet, and ascribes the wording of these sentiments to the person most intimately acquainted with Jeremiah's teaching, namely,

Baruch. The purpose of this literary device is to portray for his own and later generations the spirit of repentance which prompted God to bring the exile to an end.

The lesson thus gained is followed by a hymn in praise of Wisdom (3, 9—4, 4), exalting the law of Moses as the unique gift of God to Israel, the observance of which is the way to life and peace. The ideal city of Jerusalem is then represented (4, 5-29) as the solicitous mother of all exiles, who is assured in the name of God that all her children will be restored to her (4, 30—5, 9).

The final chapter is really a separate work, with a title of its own (6, 1). It is patterned after the earlier letter of Jeremiah (Jer 29), in the spirit of the warnings against idolatry contained in Jer 10 and Is 44. Its earnestness is impressive, but in restating previous inspired teachings at a later day, it does so with no special literary grace.

Thus the principal divisions of the book are seen to be:

The Community's Confession

The piety of the exiled community is taken as a model for the Jews of the Diaspora during the time when Baruch was written. The people wept, fasted, and prayed, and then took up a collection so that those still in Jerusalem could offer sacrifices for them in absentia. God's punishment was seen as a result of Israel's sin (cf. Neh 9; Dn 9, 4–19). The pattern of sin/punishment/repentance/salvation found in Deuteronomy 28–32 influences Baruch 1, 5—3, 8 and a number of other texts of the period (Jdt 5). The recitation of the mighty acts of God beginning in 2, 11 was a standard part of the renewal of the covenant (Ex 19, 3–6; Dt 6, 12; Jos 24), but here it is incorporated into the confession of sins instigated by Baruch's reading of the scroll. The contrast of God's gracious act and Israel's ungrateful response is sharply drawn.

I: Prayer of the Exiles (1, 1—3, 8).
II: Praise of Wisdom in the Law of Moses
(3, 9—4, 4).
III: Jerusalem Bewails and Consoles Her
Captive Children (4, 5-29).
IV: Jerusalem Consoled: The Captivity about
To End (4, 30—5, 9).
V: The Letter of Jeremiah against Idolatry
(6, 1-72).

I: Prayer of the Exiles

CHAPTER 1

See RG
224–25

Meeting in Babylon. ¹Now these are the words of the scroll which Baruch, son of Neriah, son of Mahseiah, son of Zedekiah, son of Hasadiah, son of Hilkiah, wrote in Babylon,*a* ²in the fifth year [on the seventh day of the month,* at the time when the Chaldeans took Jerusalem and burnt it with fire].*b* *³c* And Baruch read the words of this scroll for Jeconiah, son of Jehoiakim, king of Judah, to hear it, as well as all the people who came to the reading:*d* ⁴the nobles, the kings' sons, the elders, and the whole people, small and great alike— all who lived in Babylon by the river Sud.*

⁵They wept and fasted and prayed before the LORD, ⁶and collected such funds as each could furnish.*e* ⁷These they sent to Jerusalem, to Jehoiakim, son of Hilkiah, son of Shallum, the priest, and to the priests and the whole people who were with him in Jerusalem. ⁸[This was when he* received the vessels of the house of the LORD that had been removed from the temple, to restore them to the land of Judah, on the tenth of Sivan. These silver vessels Zedekiah, son of Josiah, king of Judah, had had made ⁹after Nebuchadnezzar, king of Babylon, carried off Jeconiah, and the princes, and the skilled workers, and the nobles, and the people of the land from Jerusalem, as captives, and brought them to Babylon.]

¹⁰Their message was: "We send you funds, with which you are to procure holocausts, sin offerings, and frankincense, and to prepare cereal offerings; offer these on the altar of the LORD our God,*f* ¹¹and pray for the life of Nebuchadnezzar, king of Babylon, and that of Belshazzar, his son,* that

---

1, 2: In the fifth year on the seventh day of the month: Jerusalem fell on the seventh day of the fifth month; cf 2 Kgs 25, 8; Jer 52, 12. Either the text read originally "the fifth month," or it refers to the observance of an anniversary of the fall of Jerusalem in 587 B.C.
1, 4: The river Sud: one of the Babylonian canals, not otherwise identified. In ancient non-Biblical Hebrew fragments discovered in 1952, there is reference to a river "Sur" in a similar context.
1, 8f: He: possibly Baruch; less likely Jehoiakim . . . the priest (v 7), a member of the high-priestly family not mentioned elsewhere. The silver vessels here described are distinct from the vessels referred to in 2 Kgs 25, 14 and Ezr 1,

7ff. The author of this note may have thought of the fifth year (v 1) of Zedekiah, in view of Jer 28, 1; 29, 1ff. A "fifth year," again with no month mentioned, is given in Ez 1, 2 for the inaugural vision of Ezekiel's prophetic career.
1, 11: Nebuchadnezzar . . . Belshazzar, his son: as in Dn 5, 1f. Later Jewish tradition seems to have simplified the history of the past by making the last Chaldean ruler of Babylon the son of the conqueror of Jerusalem.

a: Jer 32, 12; 36, 4; 45, 1-5.   *b:* 2 Kgs 25, 8ff.   *c:* 2 Kgs 24, 8-17; Jer 22, 24-30; 51, 59-64.   *d:* 3-4: 2 Kgs 23, 1-2.   *e:* Dt 16, 17.
f: Jer 17, 26.

their lifetimes may equal the duration of the heavens above the earth;[g] [12]and that the LORD may give us strength, and light to our eyes, that we may live under the protective shadow of Nebuchadnezzar, king of Babylon, and that of Belshazzar, his son, and serve them long, finding favor in their sight.

Confession of Guilt. [13]"Pray for us also to the LORD, our God; for we have sinned against the LORD, our God, and the wrath and anger of the LORD have not yet been withdrawn from us at the present day. [14]And read out publicly this scroll which we send you, in the house of the LORD, on the feast day and during the days of assembly:[h]

[15]"Justice is with the LORD, our God; and we today are flushed with shame, we men of Judah and citizens of Jerusalem,[i] [16]that we, with our kings and rulers and priests and prophets, and with our fathers, [17]have sinned in the LORD's sight [18]and disobeyed him. We have neither heeded the voice of the LORD, our God, nor followed the precepts which the LORD set before us. [19]From the time the LORD led our fathers out of the land of Egypt until the present day, we have been disobedient to the LORD, our God, and only too ready to disregard his voice. [20]And the evils and the curse which the LORD enjoined upon Moses, his servant, at the time he led our fathers forth from the land of Egypt to give us the land flowing with milk and honey, cling to us even today.[j] [21]For we did not heed the voice of the LORD, our God, in all the words of the prophets whom he sent us, [22]but each one of us went off after the devices of our own wicked hearts, served other gods, and did evil in the sight of the LORD, our God.

See RG
224-25

CHAPTER 2

[1]"And the LORD fulfilled the warning he had uttered against us: against our judges, who governed Israel, against our kings and princes, and against the men of Israel and Judah. [2]He brought down upon us evils so great that there has not been done anywhere under heaven what has been done in Jerusalem, as was written in the law of Moses:[k] [3]that one after another of us should eat* the flesh of his son or of his daughter. [4]He has made us subject to all the kingdoms round about us, a reproach and a horror among all the nations round about to which the LORD has scattered us.[l] [5]We are brought low, not raised up, because we sinned against the LORD, our God, not heeding his voice.

[6]"Justice is with the LORD, our God; and we, like our fathers, are flushed with shame even today.[m] [7]All the evils of which the LORD had warned us have come upon us; [8]and we did not plead before the LORD, or turn, each from the figments of his evil heart. [9]And the LORD kept watch over the evils, and brought them home to us; for the LORD is just in all the works he commanded us to do,[n] [10]but we did not heed his voice, or follow the precepts of the LORD which he set before us.

Prayer for Deliverance. [11]"And now, LORD, God of Israel, you who led your people out of the land of Egypt with your mighty hand, with signs and wonders and great might, and with your upraised arm, so that you have made for yourself a name till the present day:[o] [12]we have sinned, been impious, and violated, O LORD, our God, all your statutes.[p] [13]Let your anger be withdrawn from us, for we are left few in number among the nations to which you scattered us. [14]Hear, O LORD, our prayer of supplication, and deliver us for your own sake: grant us favor in the presence of our captors, [15]that the whole earth may know that you are the LORD, our God, and that Israel and his descendants bear your name.[q] [16]O LORD, look down from your holy dwelling and take thought of us; turn, O LORD, your ear to hear us.[r] [17]Look directly at us, and behold: it is not the dead in the nether world, whose spirits have been taken from within them, who will give glory and vindication to the LORD.[s] [18]He whose soul is deeply grieved, who

2, 3: One after another of us should eat: see note on Lam 2, 20.

g: Dt 11, 21; Jer 29, 7; Dn 5, 1-2; 1 Tm 2, 1f.   h: Ex 23, 14ff; Lv 23, 35f; Hos 9, 5; Sir 50, 6.   i: Bar 2, 6; 3, 8; Neh 9, 6-37; Ezr 9, 6-15; Dn 9, 4-19.   j: Lv 26, 14-39; Dt 28, 15-68.   k: 2f: 2 Kgs 6, 28f; Jer 19, 9; Lam 2, 20; 4, 10; Ez 5, 10.   l: Jer 29, 18.   m: Bar 1, 15.   n: Jer 1, 12; 31, 28; 44, 27.   o: Dt 6, 21-22.   p: Ps 106, 6.   q: Sir 36, 11; Jer 14, 9.   r: Dt 26, 15.   s: Ps 6, 6; Is 38, 18.

walks bowed and feeble, with failing eyes and famished soul, will declare your glory and justice, LORD!*

¹⁹"Not on the just deeds of our fathers and our kings do we base our plea for mercy in your sight, O LORD, our God. ²⁰You have brought your wrath and anger down upon us, as you had warned us through your servants the prophets: ²¹'Thus says the LORD: Bend your shoulders to the service of the king of Babylon, that you may continue in the land I gave your fathers:* ²²for if you do not hear the LORD's voice so as to serve the king of Babylon,

²³ I will make to cease from the cities of
    Judah
    and from the streets of Jerusalem
The sounds of joy and the sounds of
    gladness,
    the voice of the bridegroom
    and the voice of the bride;
And all the land shall be deserted,
    without inhabitants.'*

²⁴But we did not heed your voice, or serve the king of Babylon, and you fulfilled the threats you had made through your servants the prophets, to have the bones of our kings and the bones of our fathers brought out from their burial places.* ²⁵And indeed, they lie exposed* to the heat of day and the frost of night. They died in dire anguish, by hunger and the sword and plague.* ²⁶And you reduced the house which bears your name* to what it is today, for the wickedness of the kingdom of Israel and the kingdom of Judah.*

God's Promises Recalled. ²⁷"But with us, O Lord, our God, you have dealt in all your clemency and in all your great mercy. ²⁸This was your warning through your servant Moses, the day you ordered him to write down your law in the presence of the Israelites: ²⁹If you do not heed my voice, surely this great and numerous throng will dwindle away among the nations to which I will scatter

them. ³⁰For I know they will not heed me, because they are a stiff-necked people. But in the land of their captivity they shall have a change of heart;* ³¹they shall know that I, the LORD, am their God. I will give them hearts, and heedful ears;* ³²and they shall praise me in the land of their captivity, and shall invoke my name.* ³³Then they shall turn back from their stiff-necked stubbornness, and from their evil deeds, because they shall remember the fate of their fathers who sinned against the LORD.* ³⁴And I will bring them back to the land which with my oath I promised to their fathers, to Abraham, Isaac and Jacob; and they shall rule it. I will make them increase; they shall not then diminish. ³⁵And I will establish for them, as an eternal covenant, that I will be their God, and they shall be my people; and I will not again remove my people Israel from the land I gave them.*

CHAPTER 3

See RG 224-25

¹"LORD Almighty, God of Israel, afflicted souls and dismayed spirits call to you. ²Hear, O LORD, for you are a God of mercy; and have mercy on us, who have sinned against you: ³for you are enthroned forever, while we are perishing forever.* ⁴LORD Almighty, God of Israel, hear the prayer of Israel's few, the sons of those who sinned against you; they did not heed the voice of the LORD, their God, and the evils cling to us. ⁵Remember at this time not the misdeeds of our fathers, but your own hand and name: ⁶for you are the LORD our God; and you, O LORD, we will praise! ⁷For this, you put into our hearts the fear of you: that we may call upon your name, and praise you in our captivity, when we have removed from our hearts all the wickedness of our fathers who sinned against you.* ⁸Behold us today in our captivity, where you scattered us, a reproach, a curse, and a requital for all the misdeeds of our fathers, who withdrew from the LORD, our God."

2, 25: They lie exposed: probably an allusion to Jer 36, 30; see note on Jer 22, 19.
2, 26: The house which bears your name: the temple of Jerusalem. What it is today: during the exile it lay in ruins.

---

t: Zep 2, 3. *u:* Jer 27, 12. *v:* Jer 7, 34. *w:* Jer 8, 1f. *x:* Jer 7, 34; 14, 12; 31, 30. *y:* Jer 7, 10-15. *z:* Dt 30, 1f; 31, 27. *a:* Jer 24, 7; Ez 36, 26; Ps 40, 7. *b:* Tb 13, 7. *c:* 33ff: Dt 30, 1-10. *d:* Jer 31, 31; Lam 4, 22. *e:* Pss 29, 10; 102, 12f. *f:* Jer 31, 33.

Baruch 3, 9—4, 4 is very similar to Proverbs 8–9, Job 28, Wisdom 7, 15–22, and especially Sirach 24. However, unlike these, it lacks the role of wisdom in creation, and includes the theme of Israel's exile as punishment.

II: Praise of Wisdom in the Law of Moses

⁹ Hear, O Israel, the commandments of life:
  listen, and know prudence!ᵍ
¹⁰ How is it, Israel,
  that you are in the land of your foes,
  grown old in a foreign land,
  Defiled with the dead,
¹¹ accounted with those destined for the
    nether world?ʰ
¹² You have forsaken the fountain of
    wisdom!ⁱ
¹³ Had you walked in the way of God,
  you would have dwelt in enduring
    peace.ʲ
¹⁴ Learn where prudence is,
  where strength, where understanding;
  That you may know also
  where are length of days, and life,
  where light of the eyes, and peace.ᵏ

¹⁵ Who has found the place of wisdom,ˡ
  who has entered into her treasures?
¹⁶ Where are the rulers of the nations,
  they who lorded it over the wild beasts
    of the earth,ᵐ
¹⁷ and made sport of the birds of the
    heavens:
  They who heaped up the silver
  and the gold in which men trust;
  of whose possessions there was no
    end?
¹⁸ They schemed anxiously for money,
  but there is no trace of their work:
¹⁹ They have vanished down into the nether
    world,
  and others have risen up in their
    stead.

²⁰ Later generations have seen the light,
  have dwelt in the land,
  But the way to understanding they have
    not known,
²¹ they have not perceived her paths, or
    reached her;
  their offspring were far from the way
    to her.
²² She has not been heard of in Canaan,*
  nor seen in Teman.ⁿ
²³ The sons of Hagar who seek knowledge
    on earth,
  the merchants of Midian and Teman,
  the phrasemakers seeking
    knowledge,
  These have not known the way to wisdom,
  nor have they her paths in mind.

²⁴ O Israel, how vast is the house of God,*
  how broad the scope of his dominion:
²⁵ Vast and endless,
  high and immeasurable!
²⁶ In it were born the giants,
  renowned at the first,
  stalwarts, skilled in war.ᵒ
²⁷ Not these did God choose,
  nor did he give them the way of
    understanding;ᵖ
²⁸ They perished for lack of prudence,
  perished through their folly.�q
²⁹ Who has gone up to the heavens and
    taken her,
  or brought her down from the clouds?ʳ
³⁰ Who has crossed the sea and found her,
  bearing her away rather than choice
    gold?
³¹ None knows the way to her,
  nor has any understood her paths.
³² Yet he who knows all things knows her;

3, 22f: Despite the renown for wisdom of the peoples of Canaan or Phoenicia (Ez 28, 3f), of Teman (Jer 49, 7), of the sons of Hagar or the Arabians, they did not possess true wisdom, which is found only in the law of God.
3, 24: The house of God: here, the created universe.

g: Prv 4, 20ff. h: Ps 88, 5. i: Jer 2, 13; Jn 4, 10. 14. j: Is 48, 18. k: Prv 3, 2; 8, 14. l: 15ff: Jb 28, 1-28. m: Jer 27, 6. n: Jer 49, 7; Ez 28, 4-5; Zec 9, 2; Jb 2, 11. o: Gn 6, 4; Wis 14, 6. p: 1 Sm 16, 7-10. q: Sir 10, 8. r: Dt 30, 12f; Sir 24, 4; Rom 10, 6f.

he has probed her by his knowledge—
He who established the earth for all time,
and filled it with four-footed beasts;
33 He who dismisses the light, and it departs,
calls it, and it obeys him trembling;
34 Before whom the stars at their posts
shine and rejoice;
35 When he calls them, they answer, "Here
we are!"
shining with joy for their Maker.s
36 Such is our God;
no other is to be compared to him:
37 He has traced out all the way of
understanding,
and has given her to Jacob, his servant,
to Israel, his beloved son.t

38 Since then she has appeared on earth,
and moved among men.u

CHAPTER 4

See RG
225

1 She is the book of the precepts of
God,
the law that endures forever;
All who cling to her will live,
but those will die who forsake her.v
2 Turn, O Jacob, and receive her:
walk by her light toward splendor.w
3 Give not your glory to another,
your privileges to an alien race.
4 Blessed are we, O Israel;
for what pleases God is known to us!x

III: Jerusalem Bewails and Consoles Her Captive Children

5 Fear not, my people!
Remember, Israel,
6 You were sold to the nations
not for your destruction;
It was because you angered God
that you were handed over to your foes.y
7 For you provoked your Makerz
with sacrifices to demons, to no-gods;
8 You forsook the Eternal God who
nourished you,
and you grieved Jerusalem who
fostered you.

9 She indeed saw coming upon you
the anger of God; and she said:

"Hear, you neighbors of Zion!
God has brought great mourning upon
me,
10 For I have seen the captivity
that the Eternal God has brought
upon my sons and daughters.
11 With joy I fostered them;
but with mourning and lament I let
them go.
12 Let no one gloat over me, a widow,
bereft of many:
For the sins of my children I am left
desolate,
because they turned from the law of
God,a
13 and did not acknowledge his statutes;
In the ways of God's commandments
they did not walk,
nor did they tread the disciplined paths
of his justice.

14 "Let Zion's neighbors come,
to take note of the captivity of my sons
and daughters,
brought upon them by the Eternal
God.
15 He has brought against them a nation
from afar,
a nation ruthless and of alien speech,
That has neither reverence for age
nor tenderness for childhood:b
16 They have led away this widow's
cherished sons,
have left me solitary, without
daughters.
17 What can I do to help you?
18 He who has brought this evil upon
you
must himself deliver you from your
enemies' hands.c
19 Farewell, my children, farewell:
I am left desolate.
20 I have taken off the garment of peace,
have put on sackcloth for my prayer of
supplication,

s: Jb 38, 7; Ps 147, 4; Is 40, 26. t: Ps 147, 19; Sir 24, 8-12. u: Wis 9, 18; Jn 1, 14. v: Dt 4, 6-8; Prv 8, 35f; Sir 24, 22. w: Prv 4,
13. 19. x: Dt 4, 32-37; 33, 29. y: Jgs 2, 14; Is 50, 1; 52, 3. z: 7-8: Dt 32, 13-18; 1 Cor 10, 20. a: Lam 1, 1. 2. 7. b: Dt 23, 49f;
Jer 5, 15; 6, 22f. c: Jer 32, 42.

> Zion, representing Jerusalem, is personified as a grieving widow in 4, 9–29. This section is heavily indebted to Isaiah 51, 17–20 and Lamentations 1, 1; 2, 19–22, but it is longer and addresses the needs of a different audience and situation. Many of Baruch's earlier motifs are present here, especially the explanation of God's punishment as recompense for forsaking the law of God.

and while I live I will cry out to the
Eternal God.*d*

21 "Fear not, my children; call upon God,
who will deliver you from oppression
at enemy hands.*e*
22 I have trusted in the Eternal God for your
welfare,
and joy has come to me from the Holy
One
Because of the mercy that will swiftly
reach you
from your eternal savior.
23 With mourning and lament I sent you
forth,
but God will give you back to me
with enduring gladness and joy.*f*
24 As Zion's neighbors lately saw you taken
captive,
so shall they soon see God's salvation
come to you,
with great glory and the splendor of
the Eternal God.*g*

25 "My children, bear patiently the anger*h*
that has come from God upon you;
Your enemies have persecuted you,
and you will soon see their destruction
and trample upon their necks.*
26 My pampered children have trodden
rough roads,
carried off by their enemies like sheep
in a raid.*i*
27 Fear not, my children; call out to God!
He who brought this upon you will
remember you.*j*
28 As your hearts have been disposed to
stray from God,

turn now ten times the more to seek
him;
29 For he who has brought disaster upon you
will, in saving you, bring you back
enduring joy."*k*

IV: Jerusalem Consoled: The Captivity About to End

30 Fear not, Jerusalem!
He who gave you your name is your
encouragement.*l*
31 Fearful are those who harmed you,
who rejoiced at your downfall;
32 Fearful are the cities where your children
were enslaved,
fearful the city that took your sons.*m*
33 As that city rejoiced at your collapse,*n*
and made merry at your downfall,
so shall she grieve over her own
desolation.
34 I will take from her the joyous throngs,
and her exultation shall be turned to
mourning:
35 For fire shall come upon her*o*
from the Eternal God, for a long time,
and demons shall dwell in her from
that time on.*
36 Look to the east, Jerusalem!
behold the joy that comes to you from
God.*p*
37 Here come your sons whom you once let
go,
gathered in from the east and from the
west
By the word of the Holy One,
rejoicing in the glory of God.

4, 25: Trample upon their necks: love of enemies was not an Old Testament ideal. The Babylonians are considered here, however, to be God's enemies as well as Israel's.
4, 35: Deserts and desolate places were looked upon as the special habitations of demons; Tb 8, 3; Lk 11, 24.

d: Jdt 9, 1; Est 4, 16.   *e:* Jer 51, 5.   *f:* Jer 31, 12f.   *g:* Is 60, 1ff.   *h:* Is 51, 23.   *i:* Lam 2, 22.   *j:* Is 40, 1.   *k:* Is 35, 10.   *l:* Ps 46, 5; Is 60, 14.   *m:* Jer 51, 43.   *n:* 33f: Is 13, 20ff; 47, 1-11; Jer 50, 13.   *o:* Is 34, 9-14.   *p:* Is 60, 4f.

See RG
225

CHAPTER 5

[1]Jerusalem, take off your robe of
mourning and misery;
put on the splendor of glory from God
forever:[q]
[2] Wrapped in the cloak of justice from God,
bear on your head the mitre
that displays the glory of the eternal
name.[r]
[3] For God will show all the earth your
splendor:
[4]   you will be named by God forever
the peace of justice, the glory of God's
worship.[s]

[5] Up, Jerusalem! stand upon the heights;
look to the east and see your children
Gathered from the east and the west
at the word of the Holy One,
rejoicing that they are remembered by
God.
[6] Led away on foot by their enemies they
left you:
but God will bring them back to you
borne aloft in glory as on royal thrones.[t]
[7] For God has commanded
that every lofty mountain be made low,
And that the age-old depths and gorges
be filled to level ground,
that Israel may advance secure in the
glory of God.[u]
[8] The forests and every fragrant kind of tree
have overshadowed Israel at God's
command;[v]
[9] For God is leading Israel in joy
by the light of his glory,
with his mercy and justice for company.

V: The Letter of Jeremiah
Against Idolatry

CHAPTER 6

See RG
225

[1] A copy of the letter which Jeremiah
sent to those who were being led captive to
Babylon by the king of the Babylonians, to
convey to them what God had commanded
him:[w]

For the sins you committed before God,
you are being led captive to Babylon by Nebuchadnezzar, king of the Babylonians. [2] When
you reach Babylon you will be there many
years, a period seven generations* long; after
which I will bring you back from there in
peace. [3] And now in Babylon you will see
borne upon men's shoulders gods of silver
and gold and wood, which cast fear upon the
pagans.[x] [4] Take care that you yourselves do
not imitate their alien example and stand in
fear of them, [5] when you see the crowd before
them and behind worshiping them. Rather,
say in your hearts, "You, O LORD, are to be
worshiped!"; [6] for my angel is with you, and
he is the custodian of your lives.[y]

[7] Their tongues are smoothed by woodworkers; they are covered with gold and
silver—but they are a fraud, and cannot
speak.[z] [8] People bring gold, as to a maiden
in love with ornament, [9] and furnish crowns
for the heads of their gods. Then sometimes
the priests take the silver and gold from
their gods and spend it on themselves, [10] or
give part of it to the harlots on the terrace.*
They trick them out in garments like men,
these gods of silver and gold and wood;
[11] but though they are wrapped in purple
clothing, they are not safe from corrosion
or insects. [12] They wipe their faces clean of
the house dust which is thick upon them.
[13] Each has a scepter, like the human ruler
of a district; but none does away with those
that offend against it. [14] Each has in its right
hand an axe or dagger, but it cannot save itself from war or pillage. Thus it is known
they are not gods; do not fear them.

[15] As useless as one's broken tools [16] are
their gods, set up in their houses; their eyes
are full of dust from the feet of those who enter. [17] Their courtyards are walled in like
those of a man brought to execution for a

6, 2: Seven generations: possibly an indication of the date of this composition by an author writing for his contemporaries
for whom the conditions of the exile were still realities. He has multiplied the seventy years of Jer 29, 10 by three or four.

6, 10: Harlots on the terrace: cult prostitutes, common in the idolatrous religions of the Gentiles.

---

q: Is 52, 1.   r: Ex 39, 30; Wis 18, 24; Is 61, 10; 62, 3.   s: Is 1, 26; 32, 17; Jer 33, 16,   t: Is 49, 22.   u: Is 40, 3f.   v: Is 41, 19.   w: Jer
29, 1.   x: Is 46, 7; Jer 10, 1-16.   y: Ex 23, 20.   z: Ps 135, 16.

crime against the king; the priests reinforce their houses with gates and bars and bolts, lest they be carried off by robbers. [18]They light more lamps for them than for themselves, yet not one of these can they see. [19]They are like any beam in the house; it is said their hearts are eaten away. Though the insects out of the ground consume them and their garments, they do not feel it. [20]Their faces are blackened by the smoke of the house. [21]Bats and swallows alight on their bodies and on their heads; and cats as well as birds. [22]Know, therefore, that they are not gods, and do not fear them.

[23]Despite the gold that covers them for adornment, unless someone wipes away the corrosion, they do not shine; nor did they feel anything when they were molded. [24]They are bought at any price, and there is no spirit in them. [25]Having no feet, they are carried on men's shoulders, displaying their shame to all; and those who worship them are put to confusion[a] [26]because, if they fall to the ground, the worshipers must raise them up. They neither move of themselves if one sets them upright, nor come upright if they fall; but one puts gifts beside them as beside the dead. [27]*Their priests resell their sacrifices for their own advantage. Even their wives cure parts of the meat, but do not share it with the poor and the weak;[b] [28]the menstruous and women in childbed handle their sacrifices. Knowing from this that they are not gods, do not fear them.

[29]How can they be called gods? For women bring the offerings to these gods of silver and gold and wood; [30]and in their temples the priests squat with torn tunic and with shaven hair and beard, and with their heads uncovered.[c] [31]They shout and wail before their gods as others do at a funeral banquet. [32]The priests take some of their clothing and put it on their wives and children. [33]*Whether they are treated well or ill by

anyone, they cannot requite it; they can neither set up a king nor remove him.[d] [34]Similarly, they cannot give anyone riches or coppers; if one fails to fulfill a vow to them, they cannot exact it of him. [35]They neither save a man from death, nor deliver the weak from the strong.[e] [36]To no blind man do they restore his sight, nor do they save any man in an emergency. [37]They neither pity the widow nor benefit the orphan. [38]These gilded and silvered wooden statues are like stones from the mountains; and their worshipers will be put to shame. [39]How then can it be thought or claimed that they are gods?

[40]Even the Chaldeans themselves have no respect for them; for when they see a deaf mute, incapable of speech, they bring forward Bel* and ask the god to make noise, as though the man could understand; [41]and they are themselves unable to reflect and abandon these gods, for they have no sense. [42]*And their women, girt with cords, sit by the roads, burning chaff for incense;[f] [43]and whenever one of them is drawn aside by some passerby who lies with her, she mocks her neighbor who has not been dignified as she has, and has not had her cord broken. [44]All that takes place around these gods is a fraud: how then can it be thought or claimed that they are gods?

[45]They are produced by woodworkers and goldsmiths, and they are nothing else than what these craftsmen wish them to be. [46]Even those who produce them are not long-lived; [47]how then can what they have produced be gods? They have left frauds and opprobrium to their successors. [48]For when war or disaster comes upon them, the priests deliberate among themselves where they can hide with them. [49]How then can one not know that these are no-gods, which do not save themselves either from war or from disaster? [50]They are wooden, gilded and silvered; they will later be known for frauds.

6, 27-31: From the point of view of Jewish ritual law, the practices named here were grotesque and depraved; cf Lv 12, 2ff; 15, 19-23.

6, 33-39: All that the gods cannot do, the true God does; cf 1 Sm 2, 7; Dt 23, 22; Pss 68, 6; 146, 7-9; Is 35, 4f.

6, 40: Bel: cf note on Jer 50, 2.

6, 42f: This seems to refer to the obligation of Bab-

ylonian women to serve once in their lives as cult prostitutes. The unbroken cord was a sign that this duty had not yet been fulfilled. Chaff: burnt as an aphrodisiac or for use in erotic rites.

a: Wis 13, 16. *b:* Lv 12, 4; 15, 19f; Dt 14, 28f. *c:* Lv 10, 6; 21, 5. 10. *d:* Dn 2, 21. *e:* Pss 68, 6; 146, 7ff. *f:* 42-43: Jer 3, 2.

To all peoples and kings it will be clear that they are not gods, but human handiwork; and that God's work is not in them.

*51*Who does not know that they are not gods? *52*They set no king over the land, nor do they give men rain. *53*They neither vindicate their own rights, nor do they recover what is unjustly taken, for they are unable; *54*they are like crows between heaven and earth. For when fire breaks out in the temple of these wooden or gilded or silvered gods, though the priests flee and are safe, they themselves are burnt up in the fire like beams. *55*They cannot resist a king, or enemy forces. *56*How then can it be admitted or thought that they are gods?

They are safe from neither thieves nor bandits, these wooden and silvered and gilded gods; *57*those who seize them strip off the gold and the silver, and go away with the clothing that was on them, and they cannot help themselves. *58*How much better to be a king displaying his valor, or a handy tool in a house, the joy of its owner, than these false gods; or the door of a house, that keeps safe those who are within, rather than these false gods; or a wooden post in a palace, rather than these false gods!*g* *59*The sun and moon and stars are bright, and obedient in the service for which they are sent. *60*Likewise the lightning, when it flashes, is a goodly sight; and the same wind blows over all the land. *61*The clouds, too, when commanded by God to proceed across the whole world, fulfill the order; *62*and fire, sent from on high to burn up the mountains and the forests, does what has been commanded. But these false gods are not their equal, whether in beauty or in power; *63*so that it is unthinkable, and cannot be claimed, that they are gods. They can neither execute judgment, nor benefit man. *64*Know, therefore, that they are not gods, and do not fear them.

*65*Kings they neither curse nor bless. *66*They show the nations no signs in the heavens, nor are they brilliant like the sun, nor shining like the moon. *67*The beasts which can help themselves by fleeing to shelter are better than they are. *68*Thus in no way is it clear to us that they are gods; so do not fear them. *69*For like a scarecrow in a cucumber patch, that is no protection, are their wooden, gilded, silvered gods. *70*Just like a thornbush in a garden on which perches every kind of bird, or like a corpse hurled into darkness, are their silvered and gilded wooden gods. *71*From the rotting of the purple and the linen upon them, it can be known that they are not gods; they themselves will in the end be consumed, and be a disgrace in the land. *72*The better for the just man who has no idols: he shall be far from disgrace!

g: Wis 13, 10-15; 15, 7ff.

See RG
226–29

The Book of Ezekiel

Ezekiel's complex character makes him one of the most interesting figures in Israelite prophecy. In many ways he resembles the more primitive type of prophet represented by Elijah and Elisha; yet he clearly depends on all his predecessors in prophecy, and his teaching is a development of theirs. His unique contribution to the history of prophetism lies in his manifest interest in the temple and the liturgy, an interest paralleled in no other prophet—not even Jeremiah who, like Ezekiel, was also a priest. Particularly because of this interest, Ezekiel's influence on postexilic religion was enormous, and not without reason has he been called "the father of Judaism." This has resulted in his prophecies reaching us with the evident marks of editing and addition by the postexilic circles that shared his intense interest. However, we may be sure that in this book we have throughout what is in substance the prophet's own work.

Ezekiel became a prophet in Babylon—the first prophet to receive the call to prophesy outside the Holy Land. As one of the exiles deported by Nebuchadnezzar in 597 B.C., his first task was to prepare his fellow countrymen in Babylon for the final destruction of Jerusalem, which they believed to be inviolable. Accordingly, the first part of his book consists of reproaches for Israel's past and present sins and the confident prediction of yet a further devastation of the land of promise and a more general exile. In 587 B.C., when Nebuchadnezzar destroyed Jerusalem, Ezekiel was vindicated before his unbelieving compatriots.

After this time, Ezekiel's message changes. From now on his prophecy is characterized by the promise of salvation in a new covenant, and he is anxious to lay down the conditions necessary to obtain it. Even as Jeremiah had believed, Ezekiel thought that the exiles were the hope of Israel's restoration, once God's allotted time for the Exile had been accomplished. His final eight chapters are a utopian vision of the Israel of the future, rid of its past evils and reestablished firmly under the rule of the Lord. The famous vision of the dry bones in chapter 37 expresses his firm belief in a forthcoming restoration, Israel rising to new life from the graveyard of Babylon. But Ezekiel's new covenant, like Jeremiah's, was to see its true fulfillment only in the New Testament.

Perhaps no other prophet has stressed the absolute majesty of God as Ezekiel does. This appears not only in the tremendous vision by the river Chebar with which his prophecy opens, but throughout the book. Ultimately, says Ezekiel, whatever God does to or for man is motivated by zeal for his own holy name. The new heart and the new spirit which must exist under the new covenant cannot be the work of man; they too must be the work of God. By such teachings he helped prepare for the New Testament doctrine of salvation through grace.

The Book of Ezekiel is divided as follows:

I: Call of the Prophet (1, 1—3, 27).

II: Before the Siege of Jerusalem (4, 1—24, 27).

III: Prophecies against Foreign Nations (25, 1—32, 32).

IV: Salvation for Israel (33, 1—39, 29).

V: The New Israel (40, 1—48, 35)

I: Call of the Prophet

CHAPTER 1

See RG 230

The Vision: God on the Cherubim. [1] In the thirtieth year,* on the fifth day of the fourth month, while I was among the exiles by the river Chebar, the heavens opened, and I saw divine visions.[a] — [2] On the fifth day of the month, the fifth year,* that is, of King Jehoiachin's exile, [3] the word of the LORD came to the priest Ezekiel, the son of Buzi, in the land of the Chaldeans by the river Chebar.—There the hand of the LORD came upon me.

[4] As I looked, a stormwind came from the North,* a huge cloud with flashing fire [enveloped in brightness], from the midst of which [the midst of the fire] something gleamed like electrum. [5] Within it were figures resembling four living creatures* that looked like this: their form was human, [6] but each had four faces and four wings, [7] and their legs went straight down; the soles of their feet were round. They sparkled with a gleam like burnished bronze.

[10]*Their faces were like this:[b] each of the four had the face of a man, but on the right side was the face of a lion, and on the left side the face of an ox, and finally each had the face of an eagle. [9] Their faces [and their wings] looked out on all their four sides; they did not turn when they moved, but each went straight forward. [12] [Each went straight forward; wherever the spirit wished to go, there they went; they did not turn when they moved.]

[8] Human hands were under their wings, and the wings of one touched those of another. [11] Each had two wings spread out above so

---

1, 1: The thirtieth year, which corresponds to the fifth year of exile (v 2), has never been satisfactorily explained; possibly it refers to the prophet's age. The river Chebar: probably a canal near Nippur, southeast of Babylon, one of the sites on which the Jewish exiles were settled.

1, 2: The fifth day of the month, the fifth year: July 31, 593 B.C.; cf v 1.

1, 4: The North: the abode of God; see notes on Jb 37, 22; Ps 48, 3. Electrum: an alloy of gold and silver,

used here for some undetermined bright metal.

1, 5: Four living creatures: identified as cherubim in Ez 10, 20f.

1, 10-22: Note the changed order of the verses and the omission of the textually uncertain verses 14 and 21. Such changes also occur elsewhere in this book.

---

a: Ez 3, 23; 10, 20; 43, 3. *b:* Rv 4, 6f.

Introduction

Ezekiel presents some of the most theologically challenging and dynamic material among the prophetic books of the Hebrew Bible. It wrestles with the problem of the Babylonian exile in a manner not unlike the modern problem of the Shoah or Holocaust: Why did God allow Jerusalem and the temple to be destroyed, and why did God allow the people of Israel to be carried away into exile? In arguing that God made a deliberate decision to destroy the temple to purify Israel, Ezekiel draws upon his own priestly background in which sacrifice at the altar of the temple is an essential element in self-purification, which aids in restoring one's relationship with God. The book develops its ideas in two major sections: Chapters 1–32 focus on God's plans to punish both Israel (chs 1–24) and a select group of nations that would fall to Babylon (chs 25–32); chs 33–48 focus on God's plans to restore a purified Israel (chs 33–39) with the Jerusalem temple at the center of Israel and all creation (chs 40–48).

Ezekiel was a Zadokite priest, a descendant of Zadok, one of the priests of David. Ezekiel was exiled to Babylonia together with King Jehoiachin in 597 B.C. He began his prophetic career five years later with a vision in which "the glory of the LORD" appeared to him in the form of a divine throne chariot, from which God instructed him to speak. Ezekiel's prophetic career continued for more than 20 years and culminated in his vision of the restored Jerusalem temple. His last oracle with a specified date is from 571 B.C. (Ez 29, 17–21). The book was originally written in an effort to explain the Babylonian exile and to prepare the exiled Judahite community for its return to Jerusalem.

that they touched one another's, while the other two wings of each covered his body. [13]In among the living creatures something like burning coals of fire could be seen; they seemed like torches, moving to and fro among the living creatures. The fire gleamed, and from it came forth flashes of lightning.

[15]As I looked at the living creatures, I saw wheels on the ground, one beside each of the four living creatures. [16]The wheels had the sparkling appearance of chrysolite, and all four of them looked the same: they were constructed as though one wheel were within another. [17]They could move in any of the four directions they faced, without veering as they moved. [18c]The four of them had rims, and I saw that their rims were full of eyes all around. [19]When the living creatures moved, the wheels moved with them; and when the living creatures were raised from the ground, the wheels also were raised. [20]Wherever the spirit wished to go, there the wheels went, and they were raised together

with the living creatures; for the spirit of the living creatures was in the wheels.

[22]*Over the heads of the living creatures, something like a firmament could be seen, seeming like glittering crystal, stretched straight out above their heads. [23]Beneath the firmament their wings were stretched out, one toward the other. [Each of them had two covering his body.] [24]Then I heard the sound of their wings, like the roaring of mighty waters, like the voice of the Almighty. When they moved, the sound of the tumult was like the din of an army. [And when they stood still, they lowered their wings.]

[26]Above the firmament over their heads something like a throne could be seen, looking like sapphire. Upon it was seated, up above, one who had the appearance of a man.* [27]Upward from what resembled his waist I saw what gleamed like electrum; downward from what resembled his waist I saw what looked like fire; he was surrounded with splendor. [28]Like the bow which appears

1, 22f. 26: This symbolic description of God's throne is similar to that in Ex 24, 9f.
1, 26: One who had the appearance of a man: God appearing in human form (v 28); cf Ex 33, 18-23.

c: Ez 10, 12; Rv 4, 6. 8.

Heavenly Beasts and Beings

In ch 1 of Ezekiel, the prophet sees a vision of the throne of the LORD that moves like a chariot on wheels that are connected to four living creatures—creatures that provide the motive power for the movement. The creatures are, like many of those described in ancient Near Eastern literature, composite beings: they are human in form, but with feet like calves, and they have wings. Each one has four faces: a human face, a lion's face, an ox's face, and an eagle's face.

These creatures are probably developments of the traditional idea of the cherub, a creature with a lion's or ox's body, wings, and the head of a human being. (The Sphinx in Egypt is a sort of cherub-figure.) Cherubim were guardians of holy places (Gn 3, 24) and of palaces; in Exodus 25, 18–22, they are the guardians of the ark of the covenant. In 2 Samuel 22, 11 the LORD rides on a cherub. Ezekiel's beasts are more elaborate, because they symbolize more than speed or protection. The wings and the eagle's face symbolize the creature's ability to move swiftly through the air; the ox's face and the hoofed feet symbolize strength; the lion's face symbolizes royalty; and the human face symbolizes reason. The fact that there are four creatures symbolizes the four directions, thereby including all space, and the central throne that the creatures carry symbolizes God's presence at the center of creation.

Chapter 6 of Isaiah envisions a different sort of creature: the seraph, a fiery being that lives in the very presence of God (saraph is the Hebrew verb for "burn," and seraphim are therefore "burning ones"). As with the cherubim in Ezekiel, the seraph's physical description is symbolic, not literal: it "burns" with adoration for the LORD of hosts, and the fire also represents the purity of the heavenly beings, a purity that is transferred to the prophet when one of the seraphs touches his lips with a burning coal. The hymn that the seraphim sing in verse 3 is the basis of the Sanctus, said or sung before the Eucharistic Prayer. It is also the basis of one of the blessings in the synagogue service.

in the clouds on a rainy day was the splendor that surrounded him. Such was the vision of the likeness of the glory of the LORD.

See RG 230

CHAPTER 2

Eating of the Scroll. When I had seen it, I fell upon my face and heard a voice that said to me: *1*Son of man,* stand up! I wish to speak with you. *2*As he spoke to me, spirit* entered into me and set me on my feet, and I heard the one who was speaking *3*say to me: Son of man, I am sending you to the Israelites, rebels who have rebelled against me; they and their fathers have revolted against me to this very day. *4*Hard of face and obstinate of heart are they to whom I am sending you. But you shall say to them: Thus says the Lord GOD! *5*And whether they heed or resist—for they are a rebellious house—they shall know that a prophet has been among them. *6*But as for you, son of man, fear neither them nor their words when they contradict you and reject you, and when you sit on scorpions.* Neither fear their words nor be dismayed at their looks, for they are a rebellious house. *7*[But speak my words to them, whether they heed or resist, for they are rebellious.] *8*As for you, son of man, obey me when I speak to you: be not rebellious like this house of rebellion, but open your mouth and eat what I shall give you.

*9d*It was then I saw a hand stretched out to me, in which was a written scroll *10*which he unrolled before me. It was covered with writing front and back, and written on it was: Lamentation and wailing and woe!

2, 1: Son of man: a formal way of saying simply "man"; God's habitual way of addressing the prophet throughout this book. Probably the title is used to emphasize the separation of the divine and the human.

2, 2: Spirit: vital power, coming from God, which enables the prophet to hear the word of God; cf Ez 8, 3; 9, 24; 11, 1.

2, 6: When you sit on scorpions: the prophet must be prepared for the bitterest opposition.

d: Rv 5, 1.

CHAPTER 3

See RG 230

[1] He said to me: Son of man, eat what is before you; eat this scroll, then go, speak to the house of Israel. [2] So I opened my mouth and he gave me the scroll to eat. [3e] Son of man, he then said to me, feed your belly and fill your stomach with this scroll I am giving you. I ate it, and it was as sweet as honey* in my mouth. He said: [4] Son of man, go now to the house of Israel, and speak my words to them.

[5] Not to a people with difficult speech and barbarous language am I sending you, [6] nor to the many peoples [with difficult speech and barbarous language] whose words you cannot understand. If I were to send you to these, they would listen to you; [7] but the house of Israel will refuse to listen to you, since they will not listen to me. For the whole house of Israel is stubborn of brow and obstinate in heart. [8] But I will make your face as hard as theirs, and your brow as stubborn as theirs, [9] like diamond, harder than flint. Fear them not, nor be dismayed at their looks, for they are a rebellious house.

[10] Son of man, he said to me, take into your heart all my words that I speak to you; hear them well. [11] Now go to the exiles, to your countrymen, and say to them: Thus says the Lord GOD!—whether they heed or resist!

[12] Then spirit lifted me up, and I heard behind me the noise of a loud rumbling as the glory of the LORD* rose from its place: [13] the noise made by the wings of the living creatures striking one another, and by the wheels alongside them, a loud rumbling. [14] The spirit which had lifted me up seized me, and I went off spiritually stirred, while the hand of the LORD rested heavily upon me. [15] Thus I came to the exiles who lived at Tel-abib* by the river Chebar, and for seven days I sat among them distraught.

The Prophet as Watchman.* [17] Thus the word of the LORD came to me: Son of man, I have appointed you a watchman for the house of Israel.[f] When you hear a word from my mouth, you shall warn them for me. [18] If I say to the wicked man, You shall surely die; and you do not warn him or speak out to dissuade him from his wicked conduct so that he may live: that wicked man shall die for his sin, but I will hold you responsible for his death. [19] If, on the other hand, you have warned the wicked man, yet he has not turned away from his evil nor from his wicked conduct, then he shall die for his sin, but you shall save your life.

[20] If a virtuous man turns away from virtue and does wrong when I place a stumbling block before him, he shall die. He shall die for his sin, and his virtuous deeds shall not be remembered; but I will hold you responsible for his death if you did not warn him. [21] When, on the other hand, you have warned a virtuous man not to sin, and he has in fact not sinned, he shall surely live because of the warning, and you shall save your own life.

Ezekiel's Dumbness.* [22] The hand of the Lord came upon me, and he said to me: Get up and go out into the plain, where I will speak with you. [23g] So I got up and went out into the plain, and I saw that the glory of the LORD was in that place, like the glory I had seen by the river Chebar. I fell prone, [24] but then spirit entered into me and set me on my feet, and he spoke with me.

He said to me: Go shut yourself up in your house. [25] [As for you, son of man, they will put cords upon you and bind you with them, so that you cannot go out among them.] [26] I will make your tongue stick to your palate so that you will be dumb* and unable to rebuke them for being a rebellious house. [27] Only when I speak with you and open your mouth, shall you say to them: Thus says the Lord

---

3, 3: As sweet as honey: though the prophet must foretell terrible things the word of God is sweet to him who receives it.

3, 12: The glory of the LORD: the divine presence, manifested here in visible form.

3, 15: Tel-abib: one of the sites where the exiles were settled, probably near Nippur.

3, 17-21: This passage refers to one of the prophet's most characteristic qualities. It was placed here by an editor, though it properly belongs to a later stage in Ezekiel's minis-

try; cf chapter 33.

3, 22-27: This passage also belongs to a later period, with Ez 24, 25ff and 33, 21f, during the time of the final siege of Jerusalem, when Ezekiel's prophecies consisted mainly of symbolic actions rather than words.

3, 26: Dumb: unwilling to speak to the people in exile while Jerusalem was being besieged; cf Ez 24, 27.

e: Rv 10, 9f. f: Ez 33, 7. g: Ez 1, 3; 10, 15. 20. 22; 43, 3.

Prophets perform symbolic actions to dramatize their statements and enable them to take effect (Is 20; Jer 13; 19). Ezekiel builds a model of Jerusalem under siege. The action draws upon the imagery of Jeremiah 1, 18. The background of "three hundred and ninety" and "forty" (vv. 5–6) is not exactly certain, and the Septuagint (the Greek version of the Hebrew Bible), contains entirely different figures. If one counts backward from the destruction of the Temple in 587 B.C., the total of 430 years points to the time of the establishment of the united monarchy of Israel under Saul in 1017 B.C. Counting forward 390 years from that date takes one to 627 B.C., the twelfth year of Josiah's reign and the year in which his reforms begin (2 Chr 34, 3; cf 2 Kgs 22, 3). Josiah failed in his attempt to reunite Israel and Judah. The remaining 40 years accounts for the time between the beginning of Josiah's reform and the destruction of Jerusalem. Also see note below on 4, 5f.

GOD! Let him heed who will, and let him resist who will, for they are a rebellious house.

II: Before the Siege of Jerusalem

CHAPTER 4

See RG 230–31

Acts Symbolic of Siege and Exile. ¹⁶At the end of seven days . . . :* ¹As for you, son of man, take a clay tablet; lay it in front of you, and draw on it a city [Jerusalem]. ²Raise a siege against it: build a tower, lay out a ramp, pitch camps, and set up battering rams all around. ³Then take an iron griddle and set it up as an iron wall between you and the city. Fix your gaze on it: it shall be in the state of siege, and you shall besiege it. This shall be a sign for the house of Israel. ⁴Then you shall lie on your left side, while I place the sins of the house of Israel upon you. As many days as you lie thus, you shall bear their sins. ⁵For the years of their sins I allot you the same number of days, three hundred and ninety, during which you will bear the sins of the house of Israel. ⁶When you finish this, you are to lie down again, but on your right side, and bear the sins of the house of Judah forty days;* one day for each year I have allotted you. ⁷Fixing your gaze on the siege of Jerusalem, with bared arm* you shall prophesy against it. ⁸See, I will bind you with cords so that you cannot turn from one side to the other until you have completed the days of your siege.

⁹*Again, take wheat and barley, and beans and lentils, and millet and spelt; put them in a single vessel and make bread out of them. Eat it for as many days as you lie upon your side, three hundred and ninety. ¹⁰The food you eat shall be twenty shekels a day by weight; each day the same. ¹¹And the water you drink shall be the sixth of a hin by measure; each day the same. ¹⁶hThen he said to me: Son of man, I am breaking the staff of bread* in Jerusalem. They shall eat bread which they have weighed out anxiously, and they shall drink water which they have measured out fearfully, ¹⁷so that, owing to the scarcity of bread and water, everyone shall be filled with terror and waste away because of his sins.

¹²For your food you must bake barley loaves over human excrement in their sight, said the LORD. ¹³Thus the Israelites shall eat their food unclean among the nations where I scatter them.^i ¹⁴"Oh no, Lord GOD!" I protested. "Never have I been made unclean,

---

3, 16: At the end of seven days . . . : the incomplete sentence probably contained some such words as "the word of the Lord came to me." For seven days, see v 15. (This verse has been transposed from ch 3.)

4, 5f: Three hundred and ninety . . . forty days: symbolically representing the respective lengths of the periods of exile of northern Israelites and Judahites. Northern Israel had already fallen to Assyria in 722 B.C. The letters in the Hebrew phrase for the days of your siege (v 8), each of which has its own numerical value, add up to three hundred and ninety. Forty years represent one generation.

4, 7: Bared arm: a symbol of unrestrained power.

4, 9-17: This action represents the scarcity of food during the siege of Jerusalem, and the consequent need to eat whatever is at hand. Twenty shekels: about nine ounces. The sixth of a hin: about one quart.

4, 16: Breaking the staff of bread: reducing the supply of bread which sustains the life of man as the walking staff sustains the traveler on his journey; cf Ez 5, 16; 14, 13; Lv 26, 26; Ps 105, 16; Is 3, 1.

h: Ez 5, 16; 14, 13. *i:* Hos 9, 4.

and from my youth till now, never have I eaten carrion flesh or that torn by wild beasts: never has any unclean meat entered my mouth." [15]Very well, he replied, I allow you cow's dung in place of human excrement; bake your bread on that.

CHAPTER 5

See RG 230-31

[1]As for you, son of man, take a sharp sword and use it like a barber's razor, passing it over your head and beard. Then take a set of scales and divide the hair you have cut. [2]Burn a third in the fire, within the city,* when the days of your siege are completed; place another third around the city and strike it with the sword; the final third strew in the wind, and pursue it with the sword. [3][But of the last take a small number and tie them in the hem of your garment. [4]Then take some of these and throw them in the midst of the fire and burn them.]

Say to the whole house of Israel: [5]Thus says the Lord GOD: This is Jerusalem! In the midst of the nations I placed her, surrounded by foreign countries. [6]But she rebelled against my ordinances more wickedly than the nations, and against my statutes more than the foreign countries surrounding her; she has spurned my ordinances and has not lived by my statutes. [7]Therefore thus says the Lord GOD: Because you have been more rebellious than the nations surrounding you, not living by my statutes nor fulfilling my ordinances, but acting according to the ordinances of the surrounding nations; [8]therefore thus says the Lord GOD: see, I am coming at you!* I will inflict punishments in your midst while the nations look on. [9]Because of all your abominations I will do with you what I have never done before, the like of which I will never do again. [10]This means that fathers within you shall eat sons, and sons shall eat fathers.* I will inflict punishments upon you and scatter all that remain of your people in every direction. [11]Therefore, as I live, says the Lord GOD,

because you have defiled my sanctuary with all your detestable abominations, I swear to cut you down. I will not look upon you with pity nor have mercy. [12]A third of your people shall die of pestilence and perish of hunger within you; another third shall fall by the sword all around you; and a third I will scatter in every direction, and I will pursue them with the sword. [16j]When I loose against you the cruel, destructive arrows of hunger, I will break your staff of bread; [17]I will send famine against you, and wild beasts that shall rob you of your children. Pestilence and bloodshed shall stalk through you, and I will bring the sword upon you. I, the LORD, have spoken!

[13]Thus shall my anger spend itself, and I will wreak my fury upon them till I am appeased; they shall know that I, the LORD, have spoken in my jealousy when I spend my fury upon them. [14]I will make you a waste and a reproach among the nations that surround you, which every passer-by may see. [15]When I execute judgment upon you in anger and fury and with furious chastisements, you shall be a reproach and an object of scorn, a terrible warning to the nations that surround you. I, the LORD, have spoken!

CHAPTER 6

Against the Mountains of Israel. [1]Thus the word of the LORD came to me: [2]Son of man, turn toward the mountains of Israel, and prophesy against them: [3]Mountains of Israel, hear the word of the Lord GOD. Thus says the Lord GOD [to the mountains and hills, the ravines and valleys]:[k] See, I am bringing a sword against you, and I will destroy your high places.* [4]Your altars shall be laid waste, your incense stands shall be broken, and I will cast down your slain ones before your idols; [5]I will scatter their bones all around your altars.* [6]In all your dwelling places cities shall be made desolate and high places laid waste, so that your altars will be made desolate and laid

See RG 230-31

5, 2: The city: the one drawn on the tablet.

5, 8: I am coming at you: an expression borrowed from the language of warfare in which enemies attacked one another with the sword. You in vv 8-17 is Jerusalem.

5, 10: Fathers . . . shall eat sons, and sons . . . fathers: see note on Lam 2, 20.

6, 3: High places: the sanctuaries on the mountaintops where

illegal worship, whether of the Lord or of Canaanite deities, was performed.

6, 5: Scatter their bones . . . altars: dead men's bones defiled a place; cf 2 Kgs 23, 14.

j: Ez 4, 16; 14, 13. *k:* Ez 36, 1.

waste, your idols broken and removed, and your incense stands smashed to bits. ⁷[The slain shall fall in your midst, and you shall know that I am the LORD. ⁸I have warned you.]

When some of your people have escaped to other nations from the sword, and have been scattered over the foreign lands, ⁹then those who have escaped will remember me among the nations to which they have been exiled, after I have broken their adulterous hearts that turned away from me [and their eyes which lusted after idols]. They shall loathe themselves because of their evil deeds, all their abominations. ¹⁰Then they shall know that it was not in vain that I, the LORD, threatened to inflict this calamity upon them.

¹¹Thus says the Lord GOD: Clap your hands, stamp your feet,* and cry "Alas!" because of all the abominations of the house of Israel, for which they shall fall by the sword, by famine, and by pestilence. ¹²He that is far off shall die of pestilence, he that is near shall fall by the sword, and he that is besieged shall perish by famine; so will I spend my fury upon them. ¹³Then shall they know that I am the LORD, when their slain shall lie amid their idols, all about their altars, on every high hill and mountaintop, beneath every green tree and leafy oak,* wherever they offered appeasing odors to any of their gods. ¹⁴I will stretch out my hand against them, and wherever they live I will make the land a desolate waste, from the desert to Riblah;* thus shall they know that I am the LORD.

See RG
230-31

CHAPTER 7

The End Has Come. ¹Thus the word of the LORD came to me: ²Son of man, now say: Thus says the Lord GOD to the land of Israel: An end! The end has come upon the four corners of the land! ³Now the end is upon you; I will unleash my anger against you and judge you according to your conduct and lay upon you the consequences of all your abominations. ⁴I will not look upon you with pity

nor have mercy; I will bring your conduct down upon you, and the consequences of your abominations shall be in your midst; then shall you know that I am the LORD.

⁵Thus says the Lord GOD: Disaster upon disaster! See it coming! ⁶An end is coming, the end is coming upon you! See it coming! ⁷The climax has come for you who dwell in the land! The time has come, near is the day: a time of consternation, not of rejoicing. ⁸Soon now I will pour out my fury upon you and spend my anger upon you; I will judge you according to your conduct and lay upon you the consequences of all your abominations. ⁹I will not look upon you with pity nor have mercy; I will deal with you according to your conduct, and the consequences of your abominations shall be in your midst; then shall you know that it is I, the LORD, who strike.

¹⁰See, the day of the LORD! See, the end is coming! Lawlessness is in full bloom, insolence flourishes, ¹¹violence has risen to support wickedness. It shall not be long in coming, nor shall it delay. ¹²*The time has come, the day dawns. Let not the buyer rejoice nor the seller mourn, for wrath shall be upon all the throng. ¹³The seller shall not regain what he sold as long as he lives, for wrath shall be upon all the throng. Because of his sins, no one shall preserve his life. ¹⁴They shall sound the trumpet and make everything ready, yet no one shall go to war, for my wrath is upon all the throng.

¹⁵The sword is outside; pestilence and hunger are within. He that is in the country shall die by the sword; pestilence and famine shall devour those in the city. ¹⁶Even those who escape and flee to the mountains like the doves of the valleys—I will put them all to death, each one for his own sins. ¹⁷All their hands shall be limp, and all their knees shall run with water. ¹⁸ᶦThey shall put on sackcloth, and horror shall cover them; shame shall be on all their faces and baldness* on all their heads. ¹⁹They shall fling their silver into the streets, and their gold shall be considered refuse.ᵐ

6, 11: Clap your hands, stamp your feet: here evidently signs of mourning; in Ez 25, 6, signs of joy.

6, 13: Every green tree and leafy oak: sacred groves had a long history in Palestine as places of worship; cf Dt 12, 2; note on Gn 12, 6.

6, 14: From the desert to Riblah: the whole land, from the

far south to the far north.

7, 12f: Mundane affairs will cease to have any meaning in view of the disaster that is to come.

7, 18: Baldness: shaving the head was a sign of mourning.

l: Is 15, 2; Jer 48, 37.   *m:* Prv 11, 4; Sir 5, 10; Zep 1, 18.

Their silver and gold cannot save them on the day of the LORD's wrath. They shall not be allowed to satisfy their craving or fill their bellies, for this has been the occasion of their sin. [20]In the beauty of their ornaments they put their pride: they made of them their abominable images [their idols]. For this reason I make them refuse. [21]I will hand them over as booty to foreigners, to be spoiled and defiled by the wicked of the earth. [22]I will turn away my face from them, and my treasure* shall be profaned: robbers shall enter and profane it.

[23]They shall wreak slaughter, for the land is filled with bloodshed and the city full of violence. [24]I will bring in the worst of the nations, who shall take possession of their houses. I will put an end to their proud strength, and their sanctuaries shall be profaned. [25]When anguish comes they shall seek peace, but there will be none. [26]There shall be disaster after disaster, rumor after rumor. Prophetic vision shall fade; instruction shall be lacking to the priest, and counsel to the elders, [27]while the prince shall be enveloped in terror, and the hands of the common people shall tremble. I will deal with them according to their conduct, and according to their judgments I will judge them; thus they shall know that I am the LORD.

See RG 230-31

CHAPTER 8

Vision of Abominations in the Temple.

[3]Spirit lifted me up in the air and brought me in divine visions to Jerusalem,[n] to the entrance of the north gate, where stood the statue of jealousy which stirs up jealousy.* [5]He* said to me: Son of man, look toward the north! I looked toward the north and saw northward of the gate the altar of the statue of jealousy. [6]Son of man, he asked me, do you see what they are doing? Do you see the great abominations that the house of Israel is practicing here, so that I must depart from my sanctuary? But you shall see still greater abominations!

[7]Then he brought me to the entrance of the court, where I saw there was a hole in the wall. [8]Son of man, he ordered, dig through the wall. I dug through the wall and saw a door. [9]Enter, he said to me, and see the abominable evils which they are doing here. [10]I entered and saw that all around upon the wall were pictured the figures of all kinds of creeping things and loathsome beasts* [all the idols of the house of Israel]. [11]Before these stood seventy of the elders of the house of Israel, among whom stood Jaazaniah, son of Shaphan, each of them with his censer in his hand, and the fragrance of the incense was rising upward. [12]Then he said to me: Do you see, son of man, what each of these elders of the house of Israel is doing in his idol room? They think: "The LORD cannot see us; the LORD has forsaken the land." [13]He continued: You shall see still greater abominations that they are practicing.

[14]Then he brought me to the entrance of the north gate of the temple, and I saw sitting there the women who were weeping for Tammuz.* [15]Then he said to me: Do you see this, son of man? You shall see other abominations, greater than these!

[16]Then he brought me into the inner court of the LORD's house, and there at the door of the LORD's temple, between the vestibule and the altar, were about twenty-five men with their backs to the LORD's temple and their faces toward the east; they were bowing down to the sun.* [17]Do you see, son of man? he asked me. Is it such a trivial matter for the house of Judah to do the abominable things they have done here—for they have filled the land with violence, and again and again they

---

7, 22: My treasure: the temple of Jerusalem.

8, 3: The statue of jealousy which stirs up jealousy: the statue which provokes the Lord's jealousy for his honor. This was probably the statue of the goddess Asherah erected by the wicked King Manasseh (cf 2 Kgs 21, 7; 2 Chr 33, 7. 15). Though it had been removed by King Josiah (2 Kgs 23, 6), it had no doubt been set up again in the repaganizing of Jerusalem that followed on Josiah's death.

8, 5: He: an angel accompanies Ezekiel in these visions and represents the voice of the Lord; cf Ez 40, 3f.

8, 10: Creeping things and loathsome beasts: probably Egyptian deities, which were represented in animal form.

During the last days of Jerusalem King Zedekiah was allied with Egypt, trusting in it for protection against the Chaldeans.

8, 14: Weeping for Tammuz: the withering of trees and plants in autumn was thought to be due to the descent of Tammuz, the Babylonian god of fertility, to the nether world of the dead; this descent was bewailed by the women.

8, 16: Bowing down to the sun: sun worship had been made an important part of Judahite idolatry by the impious kings; cf 2 Kgs 23, 11.

n: Dn 14, 6.

The Slaughter of Jerusalem

S acrificial slaughter at the altar of the temple portrays the killing of the people of Jerusalem. The six men (v. 2) come from the upper gate to the north with weapons in their hands to begin the slaughter. The Babylonian army would have entered Judah from the north (see Jer 1, 13–16). The man clothed in linen (v. 3) wears the apparel of a priest who serves at the altar (Ex 28, 39; Lv 6, 10) and carries a writing case to record the sacrifices. The bronze altar had been moved to the north by Ahaz to accommodate the Assyrian altar (2 Kgs 16, 14). The mark (the ancient letter "taw," translated "mark," looks like an X) placed on the foreheads of those who groan over all the abominations would have reminded the Israelites of the mark on the doorpost that protected the Israelites from God's plague against the Egyptians (Ex 12, 23). Ezekiel attempts to intercede as Moses did (Ex 32, 1–14; Nm 14), but God states that the people believe that God lacks power.

have provoked me—that now they must also put the branch to my nose?* ¹⁸Therefore I in turn will act furiously: I will not look upon them with pity nor will I show mercy.

See RG 230-31

CHAPTER 9

Slaughter of the Idolaters. ¹Then he cried loud for me to hear: Come, you scourges of the city! ²With that I saw six men coming from the direction of the upper gate which faces the north, each with a destroying weapon in his hand. In their midst was a man dressed in linen, with a writer's case at his waist. They entered and stood beside the bronze altar. ³Then he called to the man dressed in linen with the writer's case at his waist, ⁴ᵒsaying to him:* Pass through the city [through Jerusalem] and mark an X on the foreheads of those who moan and groan over all the abominations that are practiced within it. ⁵To the others I heard him say: Pass through the city after him and strike! Do not look on them with pity nor show any mercy! ⁶Old men, youths and maidens, women and children—wipe them out! But do not touch any marked with the X; begin at my sanctuary. So they began with the men [the elders] who were in front of the temple. ⁷Defile

the temple, he said to them, and fill the courts with the slain; then go out and strike in the city.

⁸As they began to strike, I was left alone. I fell prone, crying out, "Alas, Lord GOD! Will you destroy all that is left of Israel when you pour out your fury on Jerusalem?" ⁹He answered me: The sins of the house of Israel are great beyond measure; the land is filled with bloodshed, the city with lawlessness. They think that the LORD has forsaken the land, that he does not see them. ¹⁰I, however, will not look upon them with pity, nor show any mercy. I will bring down their conduct upon their heads.

¹¹Then I saw the man dressed in linen with the writing case at his waist make his report: "I have done as you ordered."

²⁴*Spirit lifted me up and brought me back to the exiles in Chaldea [in a vision, by God's spirit]. Then the vision I had seen left me, ²⁵and I told the exiles everything the LORD had shown me.

CHAPTER 10

God's Glory Leaves Jerusalem. ⁸,¹*On the fifth day of the sixth month, in the sixth year,* as I was sitting in my house, and the

See RG 230-31

8, 17: Put the branch to my nose: the meaning is uncertain. Perhaps it refers to an Egyptian practice imported into Judah; the Egyptian sun god Re is pictured with a vine branch at his nose, signifying the transfer of creative power (divine breath) to living things. Such rites were abominable to the Lord.

9, 4: Ezekiel is preeminently the prophet of personal retribution; the innocent inhabitants of Jerusalem are to be spared when the idolatrous are punished. An X: literally, the Hebrew letter taw, which had the form of a cross.

9, 24f: These verses have been transposed from ch 11.

10, 1: In chapters 8, 1—11, 25 of the current Hebrew text, several visions involving the temple of Jerusalem were combined to form a single continuous vision. The redistribution of verses in this translation is an attempt to separate the original visions. (10, 1. 2. 4. have been transposed from ch 8)

10, 1: The fifth day of the sixth month, in the sixth year: September 17, 592 B.C.

o: Ex 12, 7; Rv 7, 3.

elders of Judah sat before me, the hand of the Lord God fell upon me there. [2]I looked up and saw a form that looked like a man. Downward from what seemed to be his waist, there was fire; from his waist upward there seemed to be a brightness like the sheen of electrum. He stretched out what appeared to be a hand and seized me by the hair of my head. . . .*

[4]I saw there the glory of the God of Israel, like the vision I had seen in the plain. The cherubim were stationed to the right of the temple; [20]these were the living creatures I had seen beneath the God of Israel by the river Chebar,[p] whom I now recognized to be cherubim. [21]Each had four faces and four wings; something like human hands were under their wings. [22]Their faces looked just like those I had seen by the river Chebar; each one went straight forward. [14q]Each had four faces: the first face was that of an ox, the second that of a man, the third that of a lion, and the fourth that of an eagle. [15]Such were the living creatures I had seen by the river Chebar.

[9r]I also saw four wheels beside them, one wheel beside each cherub; the wheels appeared to have the luster of chrysolite stone. [10]All four of them seemed to be made the same, as though there were a wheel within a wheel. [11]When they moved, they went in any one of their four directions without veering as they moved; for in whichever direction they were faced, they went straight towards it without veering as they moved. [12s]The rims of the four wheels were full of eyes all around. [13]I heard the wheels given the name "wheelwork." [16t]When the cherubim moved, the wheels went beside them; when the cherubim lifted their wings to rise from the earth, even then the wheels did not leave their sides. [17]When they stood still, the wheels stood still; when they rose, the wheels rose with them; for the living creatures' spirit was in them.

[1]I looked and saw in the firmament above the cherubim what appeared to be sapphire stone; something like a throne could be seen upon it. [2]He said to the man dressed in linen: Go within the wheelwork under the cherubim; fill both your hands with burning coals* from among the cherubim, then scatter them over the city. As I looked on, he entered.

The glory of the God of Israel had gone up from the cherubim, upon which it had been, to the threshold of the temple. [3]As the man entered, the cloud filled the inner court, [4]and the glory of the Lord rose from over the cherubim to the threshold of the temple; the temple was filled with the cloud, and all the court was bright with the glory of the Lord. [5]The noise of the wings of the cherubim could be heard as far as the outer court; it was like the voice of God the Almighty when he speaks.

[6]When he had commanded the man dressed in linen to take fire from within the wheelwork, among the cherubim, the man entered and stood by one of the wheels. [7]Thereupon its cherub stretched out his hand toward the fire that was among the cherubim. He took up some of it and put it in the hands of the one dressed in linen, who took it and came out. [8][Something like human hands could be seen under the wings of the cherubim.]

[18]Then the glory of the Lord left the threshold of the temple and rested upon the cherubim. [19]These lifted their wings, and I saw them rise from the earth, the wheels rising along with them. They stood at the entrance of the eastern gate of the Lord's house, and the glory of the God of Israel was up above them. [22]*Then the cherubim lifted their wings, and the wheels went along with them, while up above them was the glory of the God of Israel. [23]And the glory of the Lord rose from the city and took a stand on the mountain which is to the east of the city.

CHAPTER 11

Judgment of the Princes. [1]Spirit lifted me up and brought me to the east gate of the temple. At the entrance of the gate I saw twenty-five men, among whom were Jaazaniah, son of Azzur, and Pelatiah, son of Benaiah, princes of the people. [2]The Lord said

See RG 230-31

10, 2: The dots suppose the omission of some words describing the prophet's being transported in his visions to the court of the temple.

10, 2: The burning coals within the wheelwork under God's throne, a sign of the divine presence (cf Ez 28, 14;

Ps 8, 13), symbolize the judgment to be visited on the city.

10, 22f: These verses have been transposed from ch 11.

p: Ez 1, 1. 3. q: Ez 1, 10. r: Ez 1, 15f. s: Ez 1, 18. t: Ez 1, 19.

to me: Son of man, these are the men who are planning evil and giving wicked counsel in this city. *3*"Shall we not," they say, "be building houses soon? The city is the kettle, and we are the meat."* *4*Therefore prophesy against them, son of man, prophesy! *5*Then the spirit of the LORD fell upon me, and he told me to say: Thus says the LORD: This is the way you talk, house of Israel, and what you are plotting I well know. *6*You have slain many in this city and have filled its streets with your slain. *7*Therefore thus says the Lord GOD: Your slain whom you have placed within it, they are the meat, and the city is the kettle; but you I will take out of it. *8*You fear the sword, but the sword I will bring upon you, says the Lord GOD. *9*I will bring you out of the city, and hand you over to foreigners, and inflict punishments upon you. *10*By the sword you shall fall; at the boundaries of Israel I will judge you; thus you shall know that I am the LORD. *11*The city shall not be a kettle for you, nor shall you be the meat within it. At the boundaries of Israel I will judge you, *12*and you shall know that I am the LORD, by whose statutes you have not lived, and whose ordinances you have not kept; rather, you have acted according to the ordinances of the nations around you.

*13*While I was prophesying, Pelatiah, the son of Benaiah, died. I fell prone and cried out in a loud voice: "Alas, Lord GOD! will you utterly wipe out what remains of Israel?"

Restoration of the Exiles. *14*Thus the word of the LORD came to me: *15**Son of man, it is about your kinsmen, your fellow exiles, and the whole house of Israel that the inhabitants of Jerusalem say, "They are far away from the LORD; to us the land of Israel has been given as our possession." *16*Therefore say: Thus says the Lord GOD: Though I have removed them far among the nations and scattered them over foreign countries—and was for a while their only sanctuary in the countries to which they

had gone— *17*I will gather you from the nations and assemble you from the countries over which you have been scattered, and I will restore to you the land of Israel. *18*They shall return to it and remove from it all its detestable abominations. *19u*I will give them a new heart and put a new spirit within them; I will remove the stony heart from their bodies, and replace it with a natural heart, *20*so that they will live according to my statutes, and observe and carry out my ordinances; thus they shall be my people and I will be their God. *21*But as for those whose hearts are devoted to their detestable abominations, I will bring down their conduct upon their heads, says the Lord GOD.

CHAPTER 12

See RG 230-31

Acts Symbolic of the Exile. *1*Thus the word of the LORD came to me: *2*Son of man, you live in the midst of a rebellious house; they have eyes to see but do not see, and ears to hear but do not hear, for they are a rebellious house. *3*Now, son of man, during the day while they are looking on, prepare your baggage as though for exile, and again while they are looking on, migrate from where you live to another place; perhaps they will see that they are a rebellious house. *4*You shall bring out your baggage like an exile in the daytime while they are looking on; in the evening, again while they are looking on, you shall go out like one of those driven into exile; *5*while they look on, dig a hole in the wall* and pass through it; *6*while they look on, shoulder the burden and set out in the darkness; cover your face that you may not see the land, for I have made you a sign for the house of Israel.

*7*I did as I was told. During the day I brought out my baggage as though it were that of an exile, and at evening I dug a hole through the wall with my hand and, while they looked on, set out in the darkness, shouldering my burden.

*8*Then, in the morning, the word of the

11, 3: These words reflect the false confidence of the inhabitants of Jerusalem in the face of the Chaldean invasion. Jerusalem, they think, is like an iron kettle protecting the meat within it from harm; but cf Ez 24, 3-6.

11, 15-21: Like Jeremiah (cf chapter 29), Ezekiel knows that no reform is to be expected from the men of Judah who remained in Palestine; but the exiles will be the ones to form

the new Israel. The new, spiritual covenant will replace the former covenant; cf Jer 24, 7.

12, 5: Dig a hole in the wall: the exiles are to leave Jerusalem through the broken walls of the ruined city.

u: Ez 36, 26; Jer 31, 33.

LORD came to me: ⁹Son of man, did not the house of Israel, that rebellious house, ask you what you were doing? ¹⁰Tell them: Thus says the Lord GOD: This oracle concerns Jerusalem and the whole house of Israel within it. ¹¹I am a sign for you: as I have done, so shall it be done to them; as captives they shall go into exile. ¹²The prince who is among them shall shoulder his burden and set out in darkness, going through a hole that he has dug in the wall, and covering his face lest he be seen by anyone. ¹³ᵛBut I will spread my net over him, and he shall be taken in my snare. I will bring him to Babylon, into the land of the Chaldeans—but he shall not see it*—and there he shall die. ¹⁴All his retinue, his aides, and his troops I will scatter in every direction, and pursue them with the sword. ¹⁵Then shall they know that I am the LORD, when I disperse them among the nations and scatter them over foreign lands. ¹⁶Yet I will leave a few of them to escape the sword, famine and pestilence, so that they may tell of all their abominations among the nations to which they will come; thus they shall know that I am the LORD.

¹⁷Thus the word of the LORD came to me: ¹⁸Son of man, eat your bread trembling, and drink your water shaking with anxiety. ¹⁹Then say to the people of the land: Thus says the Lord GOD of the inhabitants of Jerusalem [to the land of Israel]: They shall eat their bread in anxiety and drink their water in horror, that their land may be emptied of the violence of all its inhabitants that now fills it. ²⁰Inhabited cities shall be in ruins, and the land shall be a waste; thus you shall know that I am the LORD.

Prophecy Ridiculed. ²¹Thus the word of the LORD came to me: ²²Son of man, what is this proverb that you have in the land of Israel: "The days drag on, and no vision ever comes to anything"?* ²³Say to them therefore: Thus says the Lord GOD: I will put an end to this proverb; they shall never quote it again in Israel. Rather, say to them: The days are at hand, and also the fulfillment of every vision. ²⁵Whatever I speak is final, and it shall be done without further delay. In your days, rebellious house, whatever I speak I will bring about, says the Lord GOD.

²⁴There shall no longer be any false visions or deceitful divinations within the house of Israel, because it is I, the LORD, who will speak.

²⁶Thus the word of the LORD came to me: ²⁷Son of man, listen to the house of Israel saying, "The vision he sees is a long way off; he prophesies of the distant future!" ²⁸Say to them therefore: Thus says the Lord GOD: None of my words shall be delayed any longer; whatever I speak is final, and it shall be done, says the Lord GOD.

CHAPTER 13

Against the Prophets of Peace. ¹Thus the word of the LORD came to me: ²Son of man, prophesy against the prophets of Israel, prophesy! Say to those who prophesy their own thought: Hear the word of the LORD:* ⁵You did not step into the breach, nor did you build a wall about the house of Israel that would stand firm against attack on the day of the LORD. ⁷Was not the vision you saw false, and your divination lying? ⁸Therefore thus says the Lord GOD: Because you have spoken falsehood and have seen lying visions, therefore see! I am coming at you, says the Lord GOD.

¹⁰For the very reason that they led my people astray, saying, "Peace!" when there was no peace, and that, as one built a wall, they would cover it with whitewash.* ¹¹say then to the whitewashers: I will bring down a flooding rain; hailstones shall fall, and a stormwind shall break out. ¹²And when the wall has fallen, will you not be asked: Where is the whitewash you spread on?

¹³Therefore thus says the Lord GOD: In my fury I will let loose stormwinds; because of my anger there shall be a flooding rain, and hailstones shall fall with destructive wrath. ¹⁴I will tear down the wall that you have

See RG 231

12, 13: But he shall not see it: Zedekiah was blinded by Nebuchadnezzar before being deported to Babylonia; cf 2 Kgs 25, 7.

12, 22. 27: These words used against Ezekiel because of the apparent failure of his prophecies; cf Jer 20, 7ff.

13, 3-23: These verses have been transposed according to the following order: 7-8. 10-16. 3-4. 6. 9. 17. 22-23. 18-21.

13, 10: To the confidence which the people had in their defenses against the Chaldeans, the false prophets contributed the illusion of security by predictions of peace, like men who whitewash a wall rather than allow its defects to be seen.

---

v: Ez 17, 20; 32, 3.

whitewashed and level it to the ground, laying bare its foundations. When it falls, you shall be crushed beneath it; thus you shall know that I am the LORD. *15*When I have spent my fury on the wall and its whitewashers, I tell you there shall be no wall, nor shall there be whitewashers— *16*those prophets of Israel who prophesied to Jerusalem and saw for it visions of peace when there was no peace, says the Lord GOD.

Against False Prophets in Chaldea. *3w*Thus says the Lord GOD: Woe to those prophets who are fools, who follow their own spirit and have seen no vision. *4*Like foxes among ruins are your prophets, O Israel! *6*Their visions are false and their divination lying. They say, "Thus says the LORD!" though the LORD did not send them; then they wait for him to fulfill their word! *9*But I will stretch out my hand against the prophets who have false visions and who foretell lies. They shall not belong to the community of my people, nor be recorded in the register of the house of Israel, nor enter the land of Israel; thus you shall know that I am the LORD.

Against False Prophetesses. *17*Now, son of man, turn toward the daughters of your people who prophesy their own thoughts; against these, prophesy: Thus says the Lord GOD: *22*Because you have disheartened the upright man with lies when I did not wish him grieved, and have encouraged the wicked man not to turn from his evil conduct and save his life; *23*therefore you shall no longer see false visions and practice divination, but I will rescue my people from your power. Thus you shall know that I am the LORD.

Against Sorceresses. *18*Woe to those who sew bands for everyone's wrists and make veils* for every size of head so as to entrap their owners. Do you think to entrap the lives of my people, yet keep yourselves alive? *19*You dishonor me before my people with handfuls of barley and crumbs of bread,* killing those who should not die and keeping alive those who should not live, lying to my people who willingly hear lies. *20*Therefore thus says the Lord GOD: See! I am coming at those bands of yours in which you entrap men's lives: I will tear them from their arms and set free those you have caught. *21*I will tear off your veils and rescue my people from your power, so that they shall no longer be prey to your hands. Thus you shall know that I am the LORD.

CHAPTER 14

See RG 231

Prophecy Useless for Idolaters. *1*When certain elders of Israel came and sat down before me, *2*the word of the LORD came to me: *3*Son of man, these men have the memory of their idols fresh in their hearts, and they keep the occasion of their sin before them. Why should I allow myself to be consulted by them? *4*Therefore speak with them, and say to them: Thus says the Lord GOD: If anyone of the house of Israel, holding the memory of his idols in his heart and keeping the occasion of his sin before him, has recourse to a prophet, I, the LORD, will be his answer in person because of his many idols. *5*Thus would I bring back to their senses the house of Israel, who have become estranged from me through all their idols.

*6*Therefore say to the house of Israel: Thus says the Lord GOD: Return and be converted from your idols; turn yourselves away from all your abominations. *7*For if anyone of the house of Israel or any alien resident in Israel is estranged from me, and holds the memory of his idols in his heart and keeps the occasion of his sin before him, yet asks a prophet to consult me for him, I, the LORD, will be his answer in person. *8*I will turn against that man, and make of him an example and a byword. I will cut him off from the midst of my people. Thus you shall know that I am the LORD.

*9x*As for the prophet, if he is beguiled into speaking a word, I, the LORD, shall have beguiled that prophet;* I will stretch

---

13, 18: Sew bands . . . make veils: magical practices believed to give to the sorceresses power over those on whom they placed these objects.

13, 19: Handfuls of barley and crumbs of bread: used in divination and forecasting the future.

14, 9: I, the LORD, shall have beguiled that prophet: the an-

cient Israelites attributed to God every action, good or evil; cf 1 Sm 18, 10; 2 Sm 24, 1ff. We would say, rather, that God permitted this deceit.

---

w: Ez 14, 9; 34, 2; Jer 23, 1.   x: 1 Kgs 22, 23.

Concerning Individual Righteousness

After stating that God deceives false prophets and leads them to destruction, Ezekiel claims in 14, 12–23 that the people are responsible for their own moral action and safety from punishment. Noah, Daniel, and Job (v. 14) were exemplary righteous persons who had the capacity to save others. Noah saved his family during the flood (Gn 6–9), and Job saved his three friends who spoke wrongly about God (Jb 42, 7–9). In the Canaanite legend of Aqhat, the righteous Dan-El saves his son Aqhat from death. Dan-El in Ezekiel is spelled according to the Canaanite pattern; see note below on 14, 14. In this instance, however, Noah, Job, and Daniel would have no power to save: Each individual must face the consequences of his or her breaking faith with God.

out my hand against him and root him out of my people Israel. ¹⁰Each shall receive punishment for his sin, the inquirer and the prophet shall be punished alike, ¹¹so that the house of Israel may no longer stray from me and may no longer be defiled by all their sins. Thus they shall be my people, and I will be their God, says the Lord God.

Personal Responsibility. * ¹²Thus the word of the Lord came to me: ¹³ʸSon of man, when a land sins against me by breaking faith, I stretch out my hand against it and break its staff of bread, I let famine loose upon it and cut off from it both man and beast; ¹⁴and even if these three men were in it, Noah, Daniel, and Job,* they could save only themselves by their virtue, says the Lord God. ¹⁵If I were to cause wild beasts to prowl the land, depopulating it so that it became a waste, traversed by none because of the wild beasts, ¹⁶and these three men were in it, as I live, says the Lord God, I swear they could save neither sons nor daughters; they alone would be saved, and the land would be a waste. ¹⁷Or if I brought the sword upon this country, commanding the sword to pass through the land cutting off from it man and beast, ¹⁸and these three men were in it, as I live, says the Lord God, they would be unable to save

either sons or daughters; they alone would be saved. ¹⁹Or if I were to send pestilence into this land, pouring out upon it my bloodthirsty fury, cutting off from it man and beast, ²⁰even if Noah, Daniel, and Job were in it, as I live, says the Lord God, I swear that they could save neither son nor daughter; they would save only themselves by their virtue.

²¹Thus says the Lord God: Even though I send Jerusalem my four cruel punishments, the sword, famine, wild beasts, and pestilence, to cut off from it man and beast, ²²still some survivors shall be left in it who will bring out sons and daughters; when they come out to you, you shall see their conduct and their actions and be consoled regarding the evil I have brought on Jerusalem [all that I have brought upon it]. ²³They shall console you when you see their conduct and actions, for you shall then know that it was not without reason that I did to it what I did, says the Lord God.

CHAPTER 15

See RG
231

Parable of the Vine. ¹Thus the word of the Lord came to me: ²Son of man, what makes the wood of the vine better than any other wood? That branch among the trees of the forest! ³Can you use its wood to make anything worthwhile? Can you make even a

---

14, 12-23: The doctrine of personal responsibility before God was not new (cf Ez 3, 16-21; 18; 33, 1-20); but it had not been emphasized by the prophets before the Exile, who mostly predicted national retribution and called for national repentance.

14, 14: Noah, Daniel, and Job: proverbially virtuous men.

The Daniel named here may be the traditional just judge of the ancient past, celebrated in Canaanite literature, who is possibly reflected in Dn 13, but is not the hero of Dn 1—12.

y: Ez 4, 16.

The Allegory of the Useless Vine

In ch 15, Ezekiel uses rhetorical questions to compare the inhabitants of Jerusalem to the wood of a vine, which is entirely useless except for burning (see Jgs 9, 7–21). It cannot be used to make anything, because vine branches are twisted and weak. Even when burned, the charred ends are useless. Similarly, Jerusalem will be burned.

peg from it, to hang on it any kind of vessel? ⁴If you throw it on the fire as fuel and the fire devours both ends and even the middle is scorched, is it still good for anything? ⁵Why, even when it was whole it was good for nothing; how much less, when the fire has devoured and scorched it, can it be used for anything! ⁶Therefore, thus says the Lord GOD: Like the wood of the vine among the trees of the forest, which I have destined as fuel for the fire, do I make the inhabitants of Jerusalem. ⁷I will set my face against them; they have escaped from the fire, but the fire shall devour them. Thus you shall know that I am the LORD, when I turn my face against them. ⁸I will make the land a waste, because they have broken faith, says the Lord God.

See RG 231

CHAPTER 16

The Faithless Spouse. ¹Thus the word of the LORD came to me: ²Son of man, make known to Jerusalem her abominations. ³Thus says the Lord GOD to Jerusalem: By origin and birth you are of the land of Canaan; your father was an Amorite and your mother a Hittite.* ⁴As for your birth, the day you were born your navel cord was not cut; you were neither washed with water nor anointed, nor were you rubbed with salt, nor swathed in swaddling clothes. ⁵No one looked on you with pity or compassion to do any of these things for you. Rather, you were thrown out on the ground as something loathsome, the day you were born.

⁶Then I passed by and saw you weltering in your blood. I said to you: Live in your blood ⁷and grow like a plant in the field. You grew and developed, you came to the age of puberty; your breasts were formed, your hair had grown, but you were still stark naked. ⁸Again I passed by you and saw that you were now old enough for love. So I spread the corner of my cloak over you to cover your nakedness;* I swore an oath to you and entered into a covenant with you; you became mine, says the Lord GOD. ⁹Then I bathed you with water, washed away your blood, and anointed you with oil. ¹⁰I clothed you with an embroidered gown, put sandals of fine leather on your feet; I gave you a fine linen sash and silk robes to wear. ¹¹I adorned you with jewelry: I put bracelets on your arms, a necklace about your neck, ¹²a ring in your nose, pendants in your ears, and a glorious diadem upon your head. ¹³Thus you were adorned with gold and silver; your garments were of fine linen, silk, and embroidered cloth. Fine flour, honey, and oil were your food. You were exceedingly beautiful, with the dignity of a queen. ¹⁴You were renowned among the nations for your beauty, perfect as it was, because of my splendor which I had bestowed on you, says the Lord God.

¹⁵But you were captivated by your own beauty, you used your renown to make yourself a harlot, and you lavished your harlotry on every passer-by, whose own you became. ¹⁶*You took some of your gowns and made for yourself gaudy high places, where you played the harlot. . . . ¹⁷You took the splendid gold and silver ornaments that I had given you and made for yourself male images, with which also you played the harlot.

16, 3f: By origin and birth . . . Canaan . . . Amorite . . . Hittite: the inhabitants of Jerusalem and Judah absorbed not only pre-Israelite racial strains, but also many elements of the country's pagan cult and customs.

16, 8: I spread the corner of my cloak over you to cover your nakedness: and also to signify the intention of marriage; cf Ru 3, 9.

16, 16: Fine robes were used to cover a couch for harlotry; cf Prv 7, 16f. In the allegory of this chapter the viewpoint often shifts from the figure (harlotry) to the reality (idolatry).

The Abandoned Infant

God commands the abandoned infant in 16, 6 to live but does nothing to care for her. She grows up like a plant but remains naked. Only after taking Jerusalem in marriage does God wash the blood from her and clothe her (vv. 8–9). The description of the clothing, jewelry, and food (see also Is 3, 18–23) demonstrates God's generosity to the unwanted Jerusalem.

[18]You took your embroidered gowns to cover them; my oil and my incense you set before them; [19]the food that I had given you, the fine flour, the oil, and the honey with which I fed you, you set before them as an appeasing odor, says the Lord GOD. [20]The sons and daughters you had borne me you took and offered as sacrifices* to be devoured by them! Was it not enough that you had become a harlot? [21a]You slaughtered and immolated my children to them, making them pass through fire. [22]And through all your abominations and harlotries you remembered nothing of when you were a girl, stark naked and weltering in your blood.

[23]Then after all your evildoing—woe, woe to you! says the Lord GOD— [24]you raised for yourself a platform and a dais* in every public place. [25b]At every street corner you built a dais for yourself to use your beauty obscenely, spreading your legs for every passer-by, playing the harlot countless times. [26]You played the harlot with the Egyptians, your lustful neighbors, so many times that I was provoked to anger. [27]Therefore I stretched out my hand against you, I diminished your allowance and delivered you over to the will of your enemies, the Philistines, who revolted at your lewd conduct. [28]You also played the harlot with the Assyrians, because you were not satisfied; and after playing the harlot with them, you were still not satisfied. [29]Again and again you played the harlot, now going to Chaldea, the land of the traders; but despite this, you were still not satisfied.

[30]How wild your lust! says the Lord GOD, that you did all these things, acting like a shameless prostitute, [31]building your platform at every street corner and erecting your dais in every public place! Yet you were unlike a prostitute, since you disdained payment. [32]The adulterous wife receives, instead of her husband, payment. [33]All harlots receive gifts. But you rather bestowed your gifts on all your lovers, bribing them to come to you from all sides for your harlotry. [34]Thus in your harlotry you were different from all other women. No one sought you out for prostitution. Since you gave payment instead of receiving it, how different you were!

[35]Therefore, harlot, hear the word of the LORD! [36]Thus says the Lord GOD: Because you poured out your lust and revealed your nakedness in your harlotry with your lovers and abominable idols, and because you sacrificed the life-blood of your children to them, [37c]I will now gather together all your lovers whom you tried to please, whether you loved them or loved them not; I will gather them against you from all sides and expose you naked for them to see. [38]I will inflict on you the sentence of adulteresses and murderesses; I will wreak fury and jealousy upon you. [39]I will hand you over to them to tear down your platform and demolish your dais; they shall strip you of your garments and take away your splendid ornaments, leaving you stark naked. [40]They shall lead an assembly against you to stone you and hack you with their swords. [41d]They shall burn your apartments with fire and inflict punishments on you while many women look on.

16, 20f: Human sacrifice was introduced under Judah's impious kings; cf 2 Kgs 16, 3; 17, 17; Jer 7, 31.
16, 24: A platform and a dais: associated with ritual prostitution, which the Israelites borrowed from Canaanite practice.

z: Ez 20, 26. 31; 23, 37ff; Lv 18, 21; 20, 2; Dt 12, 31; 18, 10; 2 Kgs 21, 6; 23, 10; 24, 4; Jer 7, 31; 19, 5; 32, 34; Mi 6, 7.   a: 2 Kgs 16, 3; 17, 17; 21, 6; 23, 10.   b: Ez 23, 8; Is 57, 7; Jer 2, 20; 3, 2; 5, 7; 13, 27; Hos 2, 4; 4, 13.   c: Ez 23, 10.   d: 2 Kgs 25, 9.

Thus I will put an end to your harlotry, and you shall never again give payment. [42]When I have wreaked my fury upon you I will cease to be jealous of you, I will be quiet and no longer vexed. [43]Because you did not remember what happened when you were a girl, but enraged me with all these things, therefore in return I am bringing down your conduct upon your head, says the Lord GOD. For did you not add lewdness to the rest of your abominable deeds?

[44]See, everyone who is fond of proverbs will say of you, 'Like mother, like daughter.' [45]Yes, you are the true daughter of the mother* who spurned her husband and children, and you are a true sister to those who spurned their husbands and children—your mother was a Hittite and your father an Amorite. [46]Your elder sister was Samaria* with her daughters, living to the north of you; and your younger sister, living to the south of you, was Sodom with her daughters. [47]Yet not only in their ways did you walk, and act as abominably as they did; in a very short time you became more corrupt in all your ways than they. [48]As I live, says the Lord GOD, I swear that your sister Sodom, with her daughters, has not done as you and your daughters have done! [49e]And look at the guilt of your sister Sodom: she and her daughters were proud, sated with food, complacent in their prosperity, and they gave no help to the poor and needy. [50]Rather, they became haughty and committed abominable crimes in my presence; then, as you have seen, I removed them. [51]Samaria did not commit half your sins! You have done more abominable things than they, and have even made your sisters appear just, with all the abominable deeds you have done. [52]You, then, bear your shame; you are an argument in favor of your sisters! In view of your sinful deeds, more abominable than theirs, they appear just in comparison with you. Blush for shame, and bear the shame of having made your sisters appear just.

[53]I will restore their fortunes, the fortune of Sodom and her daughters and of Samaria and her daughters [and I will restore your fortune along with them], [54]that you may bear your shame and be disgraced for all the comfort you brought them. [55]Yes, your sisters, Sodom and her daughters, Samaria and her daughters, shall return to their former state [you and your daughters shall return to your former state]. [56]Was not your sister Sodom kept in bad repute by you while you felt proud of yourself, [57]before your wickedness became evident? Now you are like her, reproached by the Edomites and all your neighbors, despised on all sides by the Philistines. [58]The penalty of your lewdness and your abominations—you must bear it all, says the LORD.

[59]For thus speaks the Lord GOD: I will deal with you according to what you have done, you who despised your oath, breaking a covenant. [60]Yet I will remember the covenant I made with you when you were a girl, and I will set up an everlasting covenant with you. [61]Then you shall remember your conduct and be ashamed when I take your sisters, those older and younger than you, and give them to you as daughters, even though I am not bound by my covenant with you. [62]For I will re-establish my covenant with you, that you may know that I am the LORD, [63]that you may remember and be covered with confusion, and that you may be utterly silenced for shame when I pardon you for all you have done, says the Lord GOD.

CHAPTER 17

The Eagles and the Vine. [1]Thus the word of the LORD came to me: [2]Son of man, propose a riddle, and speak this proverb to the house of Israel: [3]Thus speaks the Lord GOD:

See RG 231

The great eagle, with great wings, with
long pinions,

16, 45: True daughter of the mother: Jerusalem has followed in the footsteps of its heathen forebears; cf v 3.

16, 46: Your elder sister was Samaria: Samaria can be called an elder sister in view of the relatively greater importance of the northern kingdom, Israel, during most of Old Testament history. Also, the relatively insignificant Sodom of ancient history can be called your younger sister.

e: Gn 19, 24.

with thick plumage, many-hued, came
to Lebanon.

He took the crest of the cedar,

4   tearing off its topmost branch,

And brought it to a land of tradesmen,
set it in a city of merchants.

5 Then he took some seed of the land,
and planted it in a seedbed;

A shoot by plentiful waters,
like a willow he placed it,

6 To sprout and grow up a vine,
dense and low-lying,

Its branches turned toward him,
its roots lying under him.

Thus it became a vine, produced
branches

and put forth shoots.

7 But there was another great eagle,
great of wing, rich in plumage;

To him this vine bent its roots,
sent out its branches,

That he might water it more freely
than the bed where it was planted.

8 In a fertile field by plentiful waters it was
planted,

to grow branches, bear fruit,
and become a majestic vine.

9Say: Thus says the Lord GOD: Can it
prosper? Will he not rather tear it out by the
roots and strip off its fruit, so that all its
green growth will wither when he pulls it up
by the roots? [No need of a mighty arm or
many people to do this.] 10True, it is planted,
but will it prosper? Will it not rather wither,
when touched by the east wind, in the bed
where it grew?

11*Thus the word of the LORD came to me:
12Son of man, say now to the rebellious
house: Do you not understand what this
means? It is this: The king of Babylon came
to Jerusalem and took away its king and
princes with him to Babylon. 13Then he selected a man of the royal line with whom he
made a covenant, binding him under oath,
while removing the nobles of the land, 14so

that the kingdom would remain a modest one,
without aspirations, and would keep his covenant and obey him. 15But this man rebelled
against him, sending envoys to Egypt to obtain horses and a great army. Can he prosper?
Can he who does such things escape? Can he
break a covenant and still go free? 16As I live,
says the Lord GOD, in the home of the king
who set him up to rule, whose oath he
spurned, whose covenant with him he broke,
there in Babylon I swear he shall die! 17When
ramps are cast up and siege towers are built
for the destruction of many lives, he shall not
be saved in the conflict by Pharaoh with a
great army and numerous troops. 18He
spurned his oath, breaking his covenant.
Though he gave his hand in pledge, he did all
these things. He shall not escape!

19Therefore say: Thus says the Lord GOD:
As I live, my oath which he spurned, my covenant which he broke, I swear to bring down
upon his head. 20I will spread my net over
him, and he shall be taken in my snare. I will
bring him to Babylon and enter into judgment
with him there over his breaking faith with
me. 21All the crack troops among his forces
shall fall by the sword, and the survivors shall
be scattered in every direction. Thus you shall
know that I, the LORD, have spoken.

22Therefore say: Thus says the Lord GOD:

I, too, will take from the crest of the
cedar,

from its topmost branches tear off a
tender shoot,

And plant it on a high and lofty
mountain;

23 on the mountain heights of Israel I will
plant it.*

It shall put forth branches and bear fruit,
and become a majestic cedar.

Birds of every kind shall dwell beneath it,
every winged thing in the shade of its
boughs.

24 And all the trees of the field shall know
that I, the LORD,

17, 11-21: These verses explain the foregoing allegory.
In 597 B.C. Nebuchadnezzar removed King Jehoiachin and
took him into exile; in his place he set Zedekiah, Jehoiachin's uncle, on the throne and received from him the oath
of loyalty. But Zedekiah was beguiled into rebellion by
Pharaoh Hophra of Egypt, and thereby merited punish-

ment; cf 2 Kgs 24, 10—25, 7.

17, 22f: I, too, will take from the crest of the cedar . . .
plant it: the Lord will restore Israel under a messianic King
from the same Davidic dynasty.

---

f: Ez 12, 13; 32, 3.

Bring low the high tree,
    lift high the lowly tree,
Wither up the green tree,
    and make the withered tree bloom.

As I, the LORD, have spoken, so will I do.

CHAPTER 18

See RG 231

Personal Responsibility. *1*Thus the word of the LORD came to me: Son of man, *2*what is the meaning of this proverb that you recite in the land of Israel:

"Fathers have eaten green grapes,*g*
    thus their children's teeth are on
        edge"?*

*3*As I live, says the Lord GOD: I swear that there shall no longer be anyone among you who will repeat this proverb in Israel. *4*For all lives are mine; the life of the father is like the life of the son, both are mine; only the one who sins shall die.

*5*If a man is virtuous—if he does what is right and just, *6*if he does not eat on the mountains,* nor raise his eyes to the idols of the house of Israel; if he does not defile his neighbor's wife, nor have relations with a woman in her menstrual period; *7h*if he oppresses no one, gives back the pledge received for a debt, commits no robbery; if he gives food to the hungry and clothes the naked; *8*if he does not lend at interest nor exact usury; if he holds off from evildoing, judges fairly between a man and his opponent; *9*if he lives by my statutes and is careful to observe my ordinances, that man is virtuous—he shall surely live, says the Lord GOD.

*10*But if he begets a son who is a thief, a murderer, or who does any of these things *11*(though the father does none of them), a son who eats on the mountains, defiles the wife of his neighbor, *12*oppresses the poor and needy, commits robbery, does not give back a pledge, raises his eyes to idols, does abominable things, *13*lends at interest and exacts usury—this son certainly shall not

live. Because he practiced all these abominations, he shall surely die; his death shall be his own fault.

*14*On the other hand, if a man begets a son who, seeing all the sins his father commits, yet fears and does not imitate him; *15*a son who does not eat on the mountains, or raise his eyes to the idols of the house of Israel, or defile his neighbor's wife; *16*who does not oppress anyone, or exact a pledge, or commit robbery; who gives his food to the hungry and clothes the naked; *17*who holds off from evildoing, accepts no interest or usury, but keeps my ordinances and lives by my statutes—this one shall not die for the sins of his father, but shall surely live. *18*Only the father, since he violated rights, and robbed, and did what was not good among his people, shall in truth die for his sins. *19*You ask: "Why is not the son charged with the guilt of his father?" Because the son has done what is right and just, and has been careful to observe all my statutes, he shall surely live. *20i*Only the one who sins shall die. The son shall not be charged with the guilt of his father, nor shall the father be charged with the guilt of his son. The virtuous man's virtue shall be his own, as the wicked man's wickedness shall be his.

*21*But if the wicked man turns away from all the sins he committed, if he keeps all my statutes and does what is right and just, he shall surely live, he shall not die. *22*None of the crimes he committed shall be remembered against him; he shall live because of the virtue he has practiced. *23j*Do I indeed derive any pleasure from the death of the wicked? says the Lord GOD. Do I not rather rejoice when he turns from his evil way that he may live?

*24*And if the virtuous man turns from the path of virtue to do evil, the same kind of abominable things that the wicked man does, can he do this and still live? None of his virtuous deeds shall be remembered, because he has broken faith and committed sin; because of this, he shall die. *25k*You say,

---

18, 2: Fathers . . . on edge: a proverb by which the people claimed that they were being punished for their ancestors' sins rather than for their own; cf Jer 31, 29.

18, 6: Eat on the mountains: partake of ritual meals at the heathen high places.

g: Jer 13, 29.   *h:* Is 58, 7; Mt 25, 35.   *i:* Dt 24, 16; 2 Kgs 14, 6; 2 Chr 25, 4.   *j:* Ez 33, 11; 2 Pt 3, 9.   *k:* Ez 33, 20.

Guilt and Reward

The son of a righteous person who sins is responsib e and will die. The son of a sinner who does right will be spared. Ezekiel's opponents contend that the son is guilty for the sins of the father, but Ezekiel states that only the person who commits sins will be punished for them (18, 19–20). Then a new principle enters the debate. Ezekiel contends that a wicked person who repents will be saved, but a righteous person who sins will be condemned.

"The LORD's way is not fair!" Hear now, house of Israel: Is it my way that is unfair, or rather, are not your ways unfair? ²⁶When a virtuous man turns away from virtue to commit iniquity, and dies, it is because of the iniquity he committed that he must die. ²⁷But if a wicked man, turning from the wickedness he has committed, does what is right and just, he shall preserve his life; ²⁸since he has turned away from all the sins which he committed, he shall surely live, he shall not die. ²⁹And yet the house of Israel says, "The LORD's way is not fair!" Is it my way that is not fair, house of Israel, or rather, is it not that your ways are not fair?

^{30l}Therefore I will judge you, house of Israel, each one according to his ways, says the Lord GOD. Turn and be converted from all your crimes, that they may be no cause of guilt for you. ³¹Cast away from you all the crimes you have committed, and make for yourselves a new heart and a new spirit. Why should you die, O house of Israel? ^{32m}For I have no pleasure in the death of anyone who dies, says the Lord GOD. Return and live!

CHAPTER 19

See RG 231
¹As for you, son of man, raise a lamentation over the prince of Israel:

Allegory of the Lions*

² What a lioness was your mother,
   a lion of lions!
Among young lions she couched
   to rear her whelps.
³ One whelp she raised up,
   a young lion he became;

He learned to seize prey,
   men he devoured.
⁴ Then nations raised cries against him,
   in their pit he was caught;
They took him away with hooks
   to the land of Egypt.
⁵ Then she saw that in vain she had waited,
   her hope was destroyed.
She took another of her whelps,
   him she made a young lion.
⁶ He prowled among the lions,
   a young lion he became;
He learned to seize prey,
   men he devoured;
⁷ He ravaged their strongholds,
   their cities he wasted.
The land and all in it were appalled
   at the noise of his roar.
⁸ Nations laid out against him
   snares all about him;
They spread their net to take him,
   in their pit he was caught.
⁹ They put him in a cage and took him away
   to the king of Babylon,
So that his voice would not be heard
   on the mountains of Israel.

Allegory of the Vine Branch

¹⁰ Your mother was like a vine*
   planted by the water;
Fruitful and branchy was she
   because of the abundant water.
¹¹ One strong branch she put out
   as a royal scepter.
Stately was her height
   amid the dense foliage;
Notably tall was she

19, 2-9: The meaning of this allegory is uncertain. Probably the two young lions are Jehoahaz and Zedekiah, sons of the same mother, who were deported to Egypt and Babylonia respectively. Cf 2 Kgs 23, 31-34; 24, 18ff.

19, 10-14: A vine: Judah. One strong branch: the Davidic king.

l: M: 3, 2; Lk 3, 3.   *m:* Ez 18, 23; 33, 11; 2 Pt 3, 9.

with her many clusters.
12 But she was torn up in fury
    and flung to the ground;
The east wind withered her up,
    her fruit was torn off;
Then her strong branch withered up,
    fire devoured it.[n]
13 So now she is planted in the desert,
    in a land dry and parched,
14 For fire came out of the branch
    and devoured her shoots;
She is now without a strong branch,
    a ruler's scepter.

This is a lamentation and serves as a lamentation.

CHAPTER 20

See RG 231

Israel's History of Infidelity. [1]In the seventh year, on the tenth day of the fifth month,* some of the elders of Israel came to consult the LORD and sat down before me. [2]Then the word of the LORD came to me: [3]Son of man, speak with the elders of Israel and say to them: Thus says the Lord GOD: Have you come to consult me? As I live! I swear I will not allow myself to be consulted by you, says the Lord GOD.

[4]Will you judge them? Will you judge, son of man? Make known to them the abominations of their ancestors [5]in these words: Thus speaks the Lord GOD: The day I chose Israel, I swore to the decendants of the house of Jacob; in the land of Egypt I revealed myself to them and swore: I am the LORD, your God. [6]That day I swore to bring them out of the land of Egypt to the land I had scouted for them, a land flowing with milk and honey, a jewel among all lands. [7]Then I said to them: Throw away, each of you, the detestable things that have held your eyes; do not defile yourselves with the idols of Egypt: I am the LORD, your God.

[8]But they rebelled against me and refused to listen to me; none of them threw away the detestable things that had held your eyes, they did not abandon the idols of Egypt. Then I thought of pouring out my fury on them and spending my anger on them there in the land of Egypt; [9]but I acted for my name's sake, that it should not be profaned in the sight of the nations among whom they were, in whose presence I had made myself known to them, revealing that I would bring them out of the land of Egypt. [10]Therefore I led them out of the land of Egypt and brought them into the desert. [11o]Then I gave them my statutes and made known to them my ordinances, which everyone must keep, to have life through them. [12p]I also gave them my sabbaths to be a sign between me and them, to show that it was I, the LORD, who made them holy.

[13]But the house of Israel rebelled against me in the desert. They did not observe my statutes, and they despised my ordinances that bring life to those who keep them. My sabbaths, too, they desecrated grievously. Then I thought of pouring out my fury on them in the desert to put an end to them, [14]but I acted for my name's sake, that it should not be profaned in the sight of the nations in whose presence I had brought them out. [15]Nevertheless I swore to them in the desert not to bring them to the land I had given them, a land flowing with milk and honey, a jewel among all lands. [16]So much were their hearts devoted to their idols, they had not lived by my statutes, but despised my ordinances and desecrated my sabbaths. [17]But I looked on them with pity, not wanting to destroy them, so I did not put an end to them in the desert.

[18]Then I said to their children in the desert: Do not observe the statutes of your parents or keep their ordinances; do not defile yourselves with their idols. [19]I am the LORD, your God: observe my statutes and be careful to keep my ordinances; [20]keep holy my sabbaths, as a sign between me and you to show that I am the LORD, your God. [21]But their children rebelled against me: they did not observe my statutes or keep my ordinances that bring life to those who observe them, and my sabbaths they desecrated. Then I thought of pouring out my fury on them, of spending my anger on them in the desert; [22]but I stayed my

---

20, 1: The seventh year, on the tenth day of the fifth month: August 14, 591 B.C.

n: Hos 13, 15.   *o:* Lv 18, 5; Rom 10, 5.   *p:* Ex 20, 8; 31, 13; Dt 5, 12.

hand, acting for my name's sake, lest it be profaned in the sight of the nations in whose presence I brought them out. ²³Nevertheless I swore to them in the desert that I would disperse them among the nations and scatter them over foreign lands; ²⁴for they did not keep my ordinances, but despised my statutes and desecrated my sabbaths with eyes only for the idols of their fathers. ²⁵Therefore I gave them statutes that were not good,* and ordinances through which they could not live. ²⁶I let them become defiled by their gifts, by their immolation of every first-born, so as to make them an object of horror.

²⁷Therefore speak to the house of Israel, son of man, and tell them: Thus says the Lord GOD: In this way also your fathers blasphemed me, breaking faith with me: ²⁸when I had brought them to the land I had sworn to give them, and they saw all its high hills and leafy trees, there they offered their sacrifices [there they brought their offensive offerings], there they sent up appeasing odors, and there they poured out their libations. ²⁹I asked them: To what sort of high place do you betake yourselves?—and so they call it a high place even to the present day. ³⁰Therefore say to the house of Israel: Thus says the Lord GOD: Will you defile yourselves like your fathers? Will you lust after their detestable idols? ³¹By offering your gifts, by making your children pass through the fire, you defile yourselves with all your idols even to this day. Shall I let myself be consulted by you, house of Israel? As I live! says the Lord GOD: I swear I will not let myself be consulted by you.

³²What you are thinking of shall never happen: "We shall be like the nations, like the peoples of foreign lands, serving wood and stone." ³³As I live, says the Lord GOD, with a mighty hand and outstretched arm, with poured-out wrath, I swear I will be king over you! ³⁴With a mighty hand and outstretched arm, with poured-out wrath, I will bring you out from the nations and gather you from the countries over which you are scattered; ³⁵*then I will lead you to the desert of the peoples, where I will enter into judgment with you face to face. ³⁶Just as I entered into judgment with your fathers in the desert of the land of Egypt, so will I enter into judgment with you, says the Lord GOD. ³⁷I will count you with the staff and bring back but a small number. ³⁸I will separate from you those who have rebelled and transgressed against me; from the land where they sojourned as aliens I will bring them out, but they shall not return to the land of Israel. Thus you shall know that I am the LORD.

³⁹As for you, house of Israel, thus says the Lord GOD: Come, each one of you, destroy your idols! Then listen to me, and never again profane my holy name with your gifts and your idols. ⁴⁰For on my holy mountain, on the mountain height of Israel, says the Lord GOD, there the whole house of Israel without exception shall worship me; there I will accept them, and there I will claim your tributes and the first fruits of your offerings, and all that you dedicate. ⁴¹As a pleasing odor I will accept you, when I have brought you from among the nations and gathered you out of the countries over which you were scattered; and by means of you I will manifest my holiness in the sight of the nations. ⁴²Thus you shall know that I am the LORD, when I bring you back to the land of Israel, the land which I swore to give to your fathers. ⁴³There you shall recall your conduct and all the deeds by which you defiled yourselves; and you shall loathe yourselves because of all the evil things you did. ⁴⁴And you shall know that I am the LORD when I deal with you thus, for my name's sake, and not according to your evil conduct and corrupt actions, O house of Israel, says the Lord GOD.

CHAPTER 21

The Sword of the Lord. ¹Thus the word of the LORD came to me: ²*Son of man, look southward, preach toward the south,

See RG 231

20, 25f: I gave them statutes that were not good: the Lord permitted them to adopt pagan practices, including the abominable sacrifice of their newborn infants, which could only merit their destruction. See note on Ez 14, 9.

20, 35-38: Exile in the pagan lands will serve the same purpose as the desert journey after the Exodus from Egypt: the rebellious will be eliminated, and only a remnant will survive.

21, 2ff: The southern kingdom, Judah, is likened to a forest about to be burned; cf Jer 21, 14.

and prophesy against the forest of the southern land. [3]Hear the word of the LORD! you shall say to the southern forest. Thus says the Lord GOD: See! I am kindling a fire in you that shall devour all trees, the green as well as the dry. The blazing flame shall not be quenched, but from south to north every face shall be scorched by it. [4]Everyone shall see that I, the LORD, have kindled it, and it shall not be quenched.

[5]But I said, "Alas! Lord GOD, they say to me, 'Is not this the one who is forever spinning parables?' " [6]Then the word of the LORD came to me: [7]Son of man, look toward Jerusalem, preach against their sanctuary, and prophesy against the land of Israel, [8]saying to the land of Israel: Thus says the LORD: See! I am coming at you; I will draw my sword from its sheath and cut off from you the virtuous and the wicked.[*] [9]Thus my sword shall leave its sheath against everyone from south to north, [10]and everyone shall know that I, the LORD, have drawn my sword from its sheath, and it shall not be sheathed again.

Act Symbolic of the City's Fall. [11]As for you, son of man, groan! with shattered strength groan bitterly while they look on. [12]And when they ask you, "Why are you groaning?", you shall say: Because of a report;[*] when it comes every heart shall fail, every hand shall fall helpless, every spirit shall be daunted, and every knee shall run with water. See, it is coming, it is here! says the Lord GOD.

Song of the Sword. [13]Thus the word of the LORD came to me: [14]Son of man, prophesy! say: Thus says the LORD:

A sword, a sword has been sharpened,
  a sword, a sword has been burnished:
[15] To work slaughter has it been sharpened,
  to flash lightning has it been
    burnished.
Why should I now withdraw it?

You have spurned the rod and every
    judgment!
[16] I have given it over to the burnisher
  that he might hold it in his hand,
A sword sharpened and burnished
  to be put in the hand of a slayer.
[17] Cry out and wail, son of man,
  for it is destined for my people;
It is for all the princes of Israel,
  victims of the sword with my people.

Therefore, slap your thigh,[*] [18]for the sword has been tested; and why should it not be so? says the Lord GOD, since you have spurned the rod.

[19] As for you, son of man, prophesy,
  brushing one hand against the other:
While the sword is doubled and tripled,
  this sword of slaughter,
This great sword of slaughter
  which threatens all around,
[20] That every heart may tremble;
  for many will be the fallen.
At all their gates
  I have appointed the sword for
    slaughter,
Fashioned to flash lightning,
  burnished for slaughter.
[21] Cleave to the right! destroy!
  to the left! wherever your edge is turned.

[22]Then I, too, shall brush one hand against the other[*] and wreak my fury. I, the LORD, have spoken.

Nebuchadnezzar at the Crossroads. [23]Thus the word of the LORD came to me: [24]Son of man, make for yourself two roads over which the sword of the king of Babylon can come. Both roads shall lead out from the same land. Then put a signpost at the head of each road, [25]so that the sword can come to Rabbah of the Ammonites or to Judah's capital, Jerusalem. [26]For at the fork where the two roads divide stands the king of Babylon, divining;[*] he has shaken

21, 8: Cut off from you the virtuous and the wicked: a more complete devastation of Jerusalem than that described in Ez 9, 6.

21, 12: A report: the news of the fall of Jerusalem; cf Ez 33, 21f.

21, 17: Slap your thigh: a gesture signifying grief and dread.

21, 22: Brush one hand against the other: a gesture signi-

fying the rejection of responsibility; cf Ez 22, 13; Nm 24, 10.

21, 26: Three forms of divination are mentioned: arrow divination, consisting in the use of differently marked arrows extracted or shaken from a case at random; the consultation of the teraphim or household idols; and liver divination, scrutiny of the configurations of the livers of newly slaughtered animals, a common form of divination in Mesopotamia.

the arrows, inquired of the teraphim, inspected the liver. [27]In his right hand is the divining arrow marked "Jerusalem,"* bidding him to give the order for slaying, to raise his voice in the battle cry, to post battering rams at the gates, to cast up a ramp, to build a siege tower. [28]In their eyes this is but a lying oracle; yet they are bound by the oaths they have sworn, and the arrow taken in hand marks their guilt.

[29]Therefore thus says the Lord GOD: Because you have drawn attention to your guilt, with your crimes laid bare and your sinfulness in all your wicked deeds revealed (because attention has been drawn to you), you shall be taken in hand. [30]And as for you, depraved and wicked prince of Israel, whose day is coming when your life of crime will be ended, [31]thus says the Lord GOD: Off with the turban and away with the crown! Nothing shall be as it was! Up with the low and down with the high! [32]Twisted, twisted, twisted will I leave it; it shall not be the same until he comes who has the claim against the city; and to him I will hand it over.

Against the Ammonites* [33]As for you, son of man, prophesy: Thus says the Lord GOD against the Ammonites and their insults: A sword, a sword is drawn for slaughter, burnished to consume and to flash lightning, [34]because you planned with false visions and lying divinations to lay it on the necks of depraved and wicked men whose day has come when their crimes are at an end. [35]Return it to its sheath! In the place where you were created, in the land of your origin, I will judge you. [36]I will pour out my indignation upon you, breathing my fiery wrath upon you; I will hand you over to ravaging men, artisans of destruction. [37]You shall be fuel for the fire, your blood shall flow throughout the land. You shall not be remembered, for I, the LORD, have spoken.

CHAPTER 22

Crimes of Jerusalem. [1]Thus the word of the LORD came to me: [2]You, son of man, would you judge, would you judge the bloody city? Then make known all her abominations, [3]and say: Thus says the Lord GOD: Woe to the city which sheds blood within herself so that her time has come, and which has made idols for her own defilement. [4]By the blood which you shed you have been made guilty, and with the idols you made you have become defiled; you have brought on your day, so that the end of your years has come. Therefore I make you an object of scorn to the nations and a laughingstock to all foreign lands. [5]Those near you and those far off shall deride you because of your foul reputation and your great perversity. [6]See! the princes of Israel, family by family, are in you only for bloodshed. [7]Within you, father and mother are despised; in your midst, they extort from the resident alien; within you, they oppress orphans and widows. [8]What is holy to me you have spurned, and my sabbaths you have desecrated. [9]There are those in you who slander to cause bloodshed; within you are those who feast on the mountains; in your midst are those who do lewd things. [10]In you are those who uncover the nakedness of their fathers, and in you those who coerce women in their menstrual period. [11]qThere are those in you who do abominable things with the wives of their neighbors, men who defile their daughters-in-law by incest, men who coerce their sisters, the daughters of their own fathers. [12]There are those in you who take bribes to shed blood. You exact interest and usury; you despoil your neighbors violently; and me you have forgotten, says the Lord GOD.

[13]See, I am brushing one hand against the other because of the unjust profits you have made and because of the blood shed in your

---

21, 27f: An arrow marked "Jerusalem" is picked out, which marks the guilt of the city's inhabitants for having broken their oath of allegiance to Nebuchadnezzar.

21, 33-37: In the preceding section Nebuchadnezzar is represented as deciding whether to attack Jerusalem or Rabbath-Ammon. As it happened, Jerusalem was chosen for attack; later, however, the Chaldeans also invaded Ammon. The present oracle against Ammon is inserted here, rather than in chapters 25—32, in order to complement the oracle against Jerusalem.

q: Jer 5, 7f.

Purification

Just as metals are smelted to remove dross, Israel will be purified in fire to remove its sins and impurities (22, 17–31; Is 1, 21–26). The prophet names all classes of people in Jerusalem, including its princes, its priests, its officials, its prophets and the people of the land.

midst. 14Can your heart remain firm, will your hands be strong, in the days when I deal with you? I, the LORD, have spoken, and I will act. 15I will disperse you among the nations and scatter you over foreign lands, so that I may purge your uncleanness. 16In you I will allow myself to be profaned in the eyes of the nations; thus you shall know that I am the LORD.

17Thus the word of the LORD came to me: 18Son of man, the house of Israel has become dross for me. All of them are bronze and tin, iron and lead [in the midst of a furnace]: dross from silver have they become. 19Therefore thus says the Lord GOD: Because all of you have become dross, therefore I must gather you together within Jerusalem. 20Just as silver, bronze, iron, lead, and tin are gathered into a furnace and smelted in the roaring flames, so I will gather you together in my furious wrath, put you in, and smelt you. 21When I have assembled you, I will blast you with the fire of my anger and smelt you with it. 22You shall be smelted by it just as silver is smelted in a furnace. Thus you shall know that I, the Lord, have poured out my fury on you.

23Thus the word of the LORD came to me: 24Son of man, say to her: You are a land unrained on [that is, not rained on] at the time of my fury. 25Her princes are like roaring lions that tear prey; they devour people, seizing their wealth and precious things, and make widows of many within her. 26Her priests violate my law and profane what is holy to me; they do not distinguish between the sacred and the profane, nor teach the difference between the unclean and the clean; they pay no attention to my sabbaths, so that

I have been profaned in their midst. 27rHer nobles within her are like wolves that tear prey, shedding blood and destroying lives to get unjust gain. 28Her prophets cover them with whitewash, pretending to visions that are false and performing lying divinations, saying, "Thus says the Lord GOD," although the LORD has not spoken. 29The people of the land practice extortion and commit robbery; they afflict the poor and the needy, and oppress the resident alien without justice. 30Thus I have searched among them for someone who could build a wall or stand in the breach before me to keep me from destroying the land; but I found no one. 31Therefore I have poured out my fury upon them; with my fiery wrath I have consumed them; I have brought down their conduct upon their heads, says the Lord GOD.

CHAPTER 23

See RG 231

The Two Sisters. 1Thus the word of the LORD came to me: 2Son of man, there were two women, daughters of the same mother, 3who even as young girls played the harlot in Egypt. There the Egyptians caressed their bosoms and fondled their virginal breasts. 4Oholah was the name of the elder, and the name of her sister was Oholibah.* They became mine and bore sons and daughters. [As for their names: Samaria is Oholah, and Jerusalem is Oholibah.] 5Oholah became a harlot faithless to me; she lusted after her lovers, the Assyrians, warriors 6dressed in purple, governors and officers, all of them attractive young men, knights mounted on horses. 7Thus she gave herself as a harlot to them, to all the elite of the Assyrians, and she defiled herself with all those for whom she

23, 4: Oholah ... Oholibah: symbolic names. The first, standing for Samaria, may be read to mean "her own tent"; the latter, standing for Jerusalem, means "My tent is in her." The references seem to be to the schismatic temple and cult of the Lord in Samaria, as opposed to their authentic counterpart in Jerusalem.

r: Mi 3, 11; Zep 3, 3.

lusted [with all their idols]. *8*She did not give up the harlotry which she had begun in Egypt, when they had lain with her as a young girl, fondling her virginal breasts and pouring out their impurities on her. *9*Therefore I handed her over to her lovers, the Assyrians for whom she had lusted. *10s*They exposed her nakedness, her sons and daughters they took away, and herself they slew with the sword. Thus she became a byword for women, for they punished her grievously.

*11*Though her sister Oholibah saw all this, her lust was more depraved than her sister's, and she outdid her in harlotry. *12*She too lusted after the Assyrians, governors and officers, warriors impeccably clothed, knights mounted on horses, all of them attractive young men. *13*I saw that she had defiled herself. Both had gone down the same path, *14*yet she went further in her harlotry. When she saw men drawn on the wall, the images of Chaldeans drawn with vermillion, *15*with sashes girded about their waists, flowing turbans on their heads, all looking like chariot warriors, the portraits of Babylonians, natives of Chaldea, *16*she lusted for them; no sooner had she set eyes on them than she sent messengers to them in Chaldea. *17*Then the Babylonians came to her, to the love couch, and defiled her with their intercourse. As soon as she was defiled by them, she became disgusted with them. *18*Her harlotry was discovered and her shame was revealed, and I became disgusted with her as I had become disgusted with her sister. *19*But she played the harlot all the more, recalling the days of her girlhood, when she had been a harlot in the land of Egypt. *20*She lusted for the lechers of Egypt, whose members are like that of an ass, and whose heat is like those of stallions. *21*You yearned for the lewdness of your girlhood, when the Egyptians fondled your breasts, caressing your bosom. *22*Therefore, Oholibah, thus says the Lord GOD: I will now stir up your lovers against you, those with whom you are disgusted, and I will bring them against you from every side: *23*the men of Babylon and all of Chaldea, Pekod, Shoa

and Koa,* along with all those of Assyria, attractive young men, all of them governors and officers, charioteers and warriors, all of them horsemen. *24*They shall come against you from the north with chariots and wagons and many peoples. Shields, bucklers, and helmets they shall array against you everywhere. *25*I will leave it to them to judge, and they will judge you by their own ordinances. I will let loose my jealousy against you, so that they shall deal with you in fury, cutting off your nose and ears; and what is left of you shall fall by the sword. They shall take away your sons and daughters, and what is left of you shall be devoured by fire. *26*They shall strip off your clothes and seize your splendid ornaments. *27*I will put an end to your lewdness and to the harlotry you began in Egypt; you shall no longer look toward it, nor shall you remember Egypt again.

*28*For thus says the Lord GOD: I am now handing you over to those whom you hate, to those who fill you with disgust. *29*They shall deal with you in hatred, seizing all that you have worked for and leaving you stark naked, so that your indecent nakedness is exposed. Your lewdness and harlotry *30*have brought these things upon you, because you played the harlot with the nations by defiling yourself with their idols.

*31*Because you followed in the path of your sister, I will hand you her cup. *32*Thus says the Lord GOD:

The cup of your sister you shall drink,
   so wide and deep, which holds so
     much,
33 Filled with destruction and grief,
   a cup of dismay, the cup of your sister.

*34*You shall drain it dry, and gnaw at the very sherds of the cup, and you shall tear out your breasts; for I have spoken, says the Lord GOD. *35*Therefore thus says the Lord GOD: Because you have forgotten me and cast me behind your back, it is for you to bear the penalty of your lewdness and harlotry.

*36*Then the LORD said to me: Son of man, would you judge Oholah and Oholibah?

23, 23: Pekod, Shoa and Koa: peoples living about the Tigris, part of "greater Babylonia."

s: Ez 16, 37.

Then make known to them their abominations. [37]For they committed adultery, and blood is on their hands. They committed adultery with their idols; to feed them they immolated the children they had borne me. [38][This, too, they did to me: they defiled my sanctuary and desecrated my sabbaths. [39]On the very day they slew their children for their idols, they entered my sanctuary to desecrate it. Thus they acted within my house.] [40]Moreover, they sent for men who had to come from afar,* to whom messengers were sent. And so they came—and for them you bathed yourself, painted your eyes, and put on ornaments. [41]You sat on a couch prepared for them, with a table spread before it, on which you had set my incense and oil. [42]Then was heard the shout of a carefree mob in the city, and these were men brought in from the desert, who put bracelets on the women's arms and splendid diadems on their heads. [43]So I said: "Oh, this woman jaded with adulteries! Now they will commit whoredom with her, and as for her. . . ." [44]And indeed they did come to her as men come to a harlot. Thus they came to Oholah and Oholibah, the lewd women. [45]But just men shall punish them with the sentence meted out to adulteresses and murderesses, for they have committed adultery, and blood is on their hands.

[46]Thus says the Lord GOD: Summon an assembly against them, and deliver them over to terror and plunder. [47]The assembly shall stone them and hack them to pieces with their swords. They shall slay their sons and daughters, and burn their houses with fire. [48]Thus I will put an end to lewdness in the land, and all the women will be warned not to imitate your lewdness. [49]They shall inflict on you the penalty of your lewdness, and you shall pay for your sins of idolatry. Thus you shall know that I am the LORD.

CHAPTER 24

See RG 231

Allegory of the Pot. [1]On the tenth day of the tenth month, in the ninth year,* the word of the LORD came to me: [2]Son of man, write down this date today, for this very day the king of Babylon has invested Jerusalem. [3]Propose this parable to the rebellious house: Thus says the Lord GOD:

*Set up the pot, set it up,
    then pour in some water.
[4] Put in it pieces of meat,
    all good pieces: thigh and shoulder;
Fill it with the choicest joints
[5]   taken from the pick of the flock.
Then pile the wood beneath it;
    bring to a boil these pieces
    and the joints that are in it.
[6] Take out its pieces, one by one,
    without casting lots for it.

Therefore, thus says the Lord GOD: Woe to the bloody city,[t] a pot containing rust, whose rust has not been removed. [7]For the blood she shed is in her midst; she poured it on the bare rock; she did not pour it out on the earth, to be covered with dust.* [8]To work up my wrath, to excite my vengeance, she put her blood on the bare rock, not to be covered. [9]Therefore, thus says the Lord GOD:

I, too, will heap up a great bonfire,
[10]   piling on wood and kindling the fire,
Till the meat has been cooked,
    till the broth has boiled.

[11]Then I will set the pot empty on the coals till its metal glows red hot, till the impurities in it melt, and its rust disappears. [12]Yet not even with fire will its great rust be removed. [13]Because you have sullied yourself with lewdness when I would have purified you, and you refused to be purified of your uncleanness, therefore you shall not be purified until I wreak my fury on you. [14]I, the LORD,

---

23, 40: Men who had to come from afar: ambassadors from Assyria and Babylon. Alliances with these countries aided in the corruption of both Israel and Judah.

24, 1: The tenth day of the tenth month, in the ninth year: January 15, 588 B.C. The same date is given in Jer 52, 4.

24, 3ff: This present comparison of the inhabitants of Jerusalem to meat boiled in a pot symbolizes their punishment rather than their supposed protection as in Ez 11, 3.

24, 7: Blood . . . to be covered with dust: since blood was sacred to God, it had to be covered with earth (Lv 17, 13); the blood of a murdered man that was left uncovered cried to heaven for vengeance; cf Jb 16, 18; Gn 4, 10.

t: Na 3, 1; Hb 2, 12.

have spoken; it is coming, for I will bring it about without fail. I will not have pity nor repent. By your conduct and your deeds you shall be judged, says the Lord GOD.

Symbol of the Destruction of the Temple. [15]Thus the word of the LORD came to me: [16]Son of man, by a sudden blow I am taking away from you the delight of your eyes, but do not mourn or weep or shed any tears. [17]Groan in silence, make no lament for the dead, bind on your turban, put your sandals on your feet, do not cover your beard, and do not eat the customary bread.* [18]That evening my wife died, and the next morning I did as I had been commanded. [19]Then the people asked me, "Will you not tell us what all these things that you are doing mean for us?" I therefore spoke to the people that morning, [20]saying to them: Thus the word of the LORD came to me: [21]Say to the house of Israel: Thus says the Lord GOD: I will now desecrate my sanctuary, the stronghold of your pride, the delight of your eyes, the desire of your soul. The sons and daughters you left behind shall fall by the sword. [24]Ezekiel shall be a sign for you: all that he did you shall do when it happens. Thus you shall know that I am the LORD. [22]*You shall do as I have done, not covering your beards nor eating the customary bread. [23]Your turbans shall remain on your heads, your sandals on your feet. You shall not mourn or weep, but you shall rot away because of your sins and groan one to another.

End of Ezekiel's Dumbness. [25u]As for you, son of man, truly, on the day I take away from them their bulwark, their glorious joy, the delight of their eyes, the desire of their soul, and the pride of their hearts, their sons and daughters, [26]that day the fugitive will come to you, that you may hear it for yourself; [27]that day your mouth shall be opened and you shall be dumb no longer. Thus you shall be a sign to them, and they shall know that I am the LORD.

III: Prophecies Against Foreign Nations

CHAPTER 25

See RG 231

Against Ammon. [1]Thus the word of the LORD came to me: [2]Son of man, turn toward the Ammonites and prophesy against them. [3v]Say to the Ammonites: Hear the word of the LORD! Thus says the Lord GOD: Because you cried out your joy over the desecration of my sanctuary, the devastation of the land of Israel, and the exile of the house of Judah, [4]therefore I will deliver you into the possession of the Easterners.* They shall set up their encampments among you and pitch their tents; they shall eat your fruits and drink your milk. [5]I will make Rabbah a pasture for camels, and the villages of the Ammonites a resting place for flocks. Thus you shall know that I am the LORD.

[6]For thus says the Lord GOD: Because you clapped your hands and stamped your feet, rejoicing most maliciously in your heart over the land of Israel, [7]therefore I will stretch out my hand against you. I will make you plunder for the nations, I will cut you off from the peoples, and remove you from the lands. I will destroy you, and thus you shall know that I am the LORD.

Against Moab. [8w]Thus says the Lord GOD: Because Moab said, "See! the house of Judah is like all other nations," [9]therefore I will clear the shoulder of Moab* totally of its cities, the jewels of the land: Beth-jesimoth, Baalmeon, and Kiriathaim. [10]I will hand her over, along with the Ammonites, into the possession of the Easterners, that she may not be remembered among the peoples. [11]Thus I will execute judgment upon Moab, that they may know that I am the LORD.

Against Edom. [12x]Thus says the Lord GOD: Because Edom has taken vengeance on the house of Judah and has made itself

---

24, 17: The customary bread: eaten as a mourning observance; cf Jer 16, 7. The other gestures here forbidden were also popular mourning customs.

24, 22f: The fall of the city will be so sudden and final that the exiles will have no time to go into mourning.

25, 4: The Easterners: nomadic tribes to the east of Ammon and Moab.

25, 9: The shoulder of Moab: the edge of the Moabite plateau.

---

u: 25ff: Ez 3, 22-27.   *v:* Jer 40, 14; 41, 10; 49, 2; Am 1, 13ff; Zep 2, 8ff.   *w:* Sir 50, 26; Is 15, 1-9; 16, 1-14; Jer 48, 1-47; Am 2, 1ff; Zep 2, 8f.   *x:* 12ff: Ez 35, 1ff; Is 34, 5; Jer 49, 7-22; Jl 4, 19; Am 1, 11f; Ob 1-21.

Places Mentioned in the Oracles against the Nations

grievously guilty by taking vengeance on them, [13]therefore thus says the Lord GOD: I will stretch out my hand against Edom and cut off from it man and beast. I will make it a waste from Teman to Dedan; they shall fall by the sword. [14]My vengeance upon Edom I will entrust to my people Israel, who will deal with Edom in accordance with my anger and my fury; thus they shall know my vengeance, says the Lord GOD.

Against the Philistines. [15]Thus says the Lord GOD: Because the Philistines have acted revengefully, and have taken vengeance with destructive malice in their hearts, with an undying enmity, [16]therefore thus says the Lord GOD: See! I am stretching out my hand against the Philistines; I will cut off the Cherethites* and wipe out the remnant on the seacoast. [17]I will execute great acts of vengeance on them, punishing them furiously. Thus they shall know that I am the LORD, when I wreak my vengeance on them.

CHAPTER 26

See RG 231

Against the City of Tyre. [1]On the first day of the . . . month in the eleventh year, the word of the LORD came to me: [2]Son of man, because of what Tyre said of Jerusalem:

> "Aha! it is broken, the gateway to the peoples;
> now that it is ruined, its wealth reverts to me!"
> [3] therefore thus says the Lord GOD:
> See! I am coming at you, Tyre;
> I will churn up against you many nations,
> even as the sea churns up its waves;[y]
> [4] They shall destroy the walls of Tyre
> and raze her towers.
> I will scrape the ground from her
> and leave her a bare rock;*
> [5] She shall be a drying place for nets
> in the midst of the sea.

25, 16: Cherethites: a people forming part of the Philistine nation; cf Zep 2, 5.

26, 4f: A bare rock: the Tyre of Ezekiel's time was situated on a rocky island just off the Phoenician coast; it was not until the time of Alexander the Great that it was connected by a causeway to the mainland.

y: Is 26, 1-21; 47, 4; Jl 4, 4f; Zec 9, 2ff.

1176

I have spoken, says the Lord GOD: and she shall be booty for the nations. ⁶And her daughters* on the mainland shall be slaughtered by the sword; thus they shall know that I am the LORD.

⁷For thus says the Lord GOD: I am now bringing up against Tyre from the north Nebuchadnezzar the king of Babylon, the king of kings, with horses and chariots, with cavalry and a great and mighty army.

⁸ Your daughters on the mainland
  he shall slay with the sword;
He shall place a siege tower against you,
  cast up a ramp about you,
  and raise his shields against you.
⁹ He shall pound your walls with battering-
  rams
  and break down your towers with his
  weapons.
¹⁰ The surge of his horses shall cover you
  with dust,
  amid the noise of steeds, of wheels and
  of chariots.
Your walls shall shake as he enters your
  gates,
  even as one enters a city that is breached.
¹¹ With the hoofs of his horses
  he shall trample all your streets;
Your people he shall slay by the sword;
  your mighty pillars he shall pull to the
  ground.
¹² Your wealth shall be plundered,
  your merchandise pillaged;
Your walls shall be torn down,
  your precious houses demolished;
Your stones, your timber, and your clay
  shall be cast into the sea.
¹³ I will put an end to the noise of your
  songs,
  and the sound of your lyres shall be
  heard no more.
¹⁴ I will make you a bare rock;
  a drying place for nets shall you be.

Never shall you be rebuilt, for I have spoken, says the Lord GOD.

¹⁵Thus says the Lord GOD to Tyre: At the noise of your fall, at the groaning of the wounded, when the sword slays in your midst, shall not the isles quake? ¹⁶All the princes of the sea* shall step down from their thrones, lay aside their robes, and strip off their embroidered garments. They shall be clothed in mourning and, sitting on the ground, they shall tremble at every moment and be horrified at you. ¹⁷Then they shall utter a lament over you:

How have you perished, gone from the seas,
  city most prized!
Once she was mighty on the sea,
  she and her dwellers,
Who spread terror into all
  that dwelt by the sea.
¹⁸ On this, the day of your fall,
  the islands quake!

The isles in the sea are terrified at your passing.

¹⁹For thus says the Lord GOD: When I make you a city desolate like cities that are no longer inhabited, when I churn up the abyss against you, and its mighty waters cover you, ²⁰then I will thrust you down with those who descend into the pit,* those of the bygone age; and I will make you dwell in the nether lands, in the everlasting ruins, with those who go down to the pit, so that you may never return to take your place in the land of the living. ²¹I will make you a devastation, and you shall be no more; you shall be sought, but never again found, says the Lord GOD.

CHAPTER 27

The Ship Tyre. ¹Thus the word of the LORD came to me: ²As for you, son of man, utter a lament over Tyre, ³and say to Tyre that is situated at the approaches of the sea, that brought the trade of the peoples to many a coastland: Thus says the Lord GOD:

Tyre, you said, "I am a ship,

26, 6: Her daughters: tributary towns and villages on the mainland.
26, 16: The princes of the sea: the rulers of the islands and coastal cities leagued commercially with Tyre.
26, 20: Those who descend into the pit: the dead, pictured as dwelling in a place or cave of darkness.

perfect in beauty."

4 In the midst of the sea your builders
placed you,
perfected your beauty.
5 With cypress from Senir* they built for
you
all of your decks;
Cedar from Lebanon they took
to make you a mast;
6 From the highest oaks of Bashan*
they made your oars;
Your bridge they made of cypress wood
from the coasts of Kittim.
7 Fine embroidered linen from Egypt
became your sail [to serve you as a
banner].
Purple and scarlet from the coasts of
Elishah*
covered your cabin.
8 Citizens of Sidon and Arvad
served as your oarsmen;
Skilled men of Zemer were in you
to be your mariners;
9 The elders and experts of Gebal* were in
you
to caulk your seams.

Every ship and sailor on the sea came to you
to carry trade. 10Persia and Lud and Put were
in your army as warriors; shield and helmet
they hung upon you, increasing your splendor. 11The men of Arvad were all about your
walls, and the Gamadites were in your towers; they hung their bucklers all around on
your walls, and made perfect your beauty.
12Tarshish traded with you, so great was your
wealth, exchanging silver, iron, tin, and lead
for your wares. 13Javan, Tubal, and Meshech
were also traders with you, exchanging
slaves and articles of bronze for your goods.
14From Beth-togarmah horses, steeds, and
mules were exchanged for your wares. 15The
Rhodanites trafficked with you; many coastlands traded with you; ivory tusks and ebony
wood they gave you for payment. 16Edom
traded with you, so many were your products, exchanging garnets, purple, embroi-

dered cloth, fine linen, coral, and rubies for
your wares. 17Judah and the land of Israel
trafficked with you, exchanging Minnith
wheat, figs, honey, oil, and balm for your
goods. 18Damascus traded with you, so great
was your wealth, exchanging Helbon wine
and Zahar wool. 19Javan exchanged wrought
iron, cassia, and aromatic cane from Uzal for
your wares. 20Dedan traded with you for riding gear. 21The trade of Arabia and of all the
sheikhs of Kedar belonged to you; they dealt
in lambs, rams, and goats. 22The merchants
of Sheba and Raamah also traded with you,
exchanging for your wares the very choicest
spices, all kinds of precious stones, and gold.
23Haran, Canneh, and Eden, the merchants of
Sheba, Asshur, and Chilmad 24traded with
you, marketing with you rich garments, violet mantles, embroidered cloth, varicolored
carpets, and firmly woven cords. 25Ships of
Tarshish journeyed for you in your merchan-
dising.

You were full and heavily laden
in the heart of the sea.
26 Through the deep waters your oarsmen
brought you home,
But the east wind smashed you
in the heart of the sea.
27 Your wealth, your goods, your wares,
your sailors, and your crew,

[the caulkers of your seams, those who
traded for your goods, all your warriors who
were in you, and all the great crowd within
you]

Sank into the heart of the sea
on the day of your shipwreck.
28 Hearing the shouts of your mariners,
the shores begin to quake.
29 Down from their ships
come all who ply the oar;
The sailors, all the mariners of the sea,
stand on the shore,
30 Making their voice heard on your behalf,
shouting bitter cries,

27, 5: Senir: another name for Mount Hermon; cf Dt 3, 9.
27, 6: Bashan: northern Transjordan, which, like Lebanon, was noted for its great forests. Kittim: probably Cyprus.

27, 7: Elishah: probably another term for Cyprus.
27, 8f: Sidon . . . Arvad . . . Zemer . . . Gebal: Phoenician
cities in Tyre's orbit of influence; the last-named is the classical Byblos.

Strewing dust on their heads,
    rolling in the ashes.
31 For you they shave their heads
    and put on sackcloth,
For you they weep in anguish,
    with bitter lament.
32 In their mourning they utter a lament
    over you;
    thus they wail over you:
Who was ever destroyed like Tyre
    in the midst of the sea?
33 With your goods which you drew from
    the seas
    you filled many peoples;
With your great wealth and
    merchandise
    you enriched the kings of the earth.
34 Now you are wrecked in the sea,
    in the watery depths;
Your wares and all your crew
    have gone down with you.
35 All who dwell on the coastlands
    are aghast over you,
Their kings are terrified,
    their faces convulsed.
36 The traders among the peoples
    now hiss at you;
You have become a horror,
    and you shall be no more.

CHAPTER 28

See RG
231

The Prince of Tyre. 1Thus the word of
the LORD came to me: 2Son of man, say to
the prince of Tyre: Thus says the Lord GOD:

Because you are haughty of heart,
    you say, "A god am I!
I occupy a godly throne
    in the heart of the sea!"—
And yet you are a man, and not a god,
    however you may think yourself like a
    god.
3 Oh yes, you are wiser than Daniel,*
    there is no secret that is beyond you.
4 By your wisdom and your intelligence
    you have made riches for yourself;
You have put gold and silver
    into your treasuries.

5 By your great wisdom applied to your
    trading
    you have heaped up your riches;
    your heart has grown haughty from
      your riches—
6   therefore thus says the Lord GOD:
Because you have thought yourself
    to have the mind of a god,
7 Therefore I will bring against you
    foreigners, the most barbarous of
    nations.
They shall draw their swords
    against your beauteous wisdom,
    they shall run them through your
      splendid apparel.
8 They shall thrust you down to the pit,
    there to die
    a bloodied corpse, in the heart of the
      sea.
9 Will you then say, "I am a god!"
    when you face your murderers?
No, you are a man, not a god,
    handed over to those who will slay
      you.
10 You shall die the death of the
    uncircumcised
    at the hands of foreigners,
    for I have spoken,
      says the Lord GOD.

11Thus the word of the LORD came to me:
12Son of man, utter a lament over the king of
Tyre, saying to him: Thus says the Lord
GOD:

*You were stamped with the seal of
    perfection,
    of complete wisdom and perfect
      beauty.
13 In Eden, the garden of God, you were,
    and every precious stone was your
      covering

[carnelian, topaz, and beryl, chrysolite,
onyx, and jasper, sapphire, garnet, and emerald];

Of gold your pendants and jewels

28, 3: Wiser than Daniel: see note on Ez 14, 14.
28, 12-19: This picture of Tyre and its fall recalls images of the earthly paradise portraying the creation of man in perfection and his fall (Gn, chapters 2—3).

were made, on the day you were
    created.
[14] With the Cherub I placed you;
    you were on the holy mountain of God,[*]
    walking among the fiery stones.
[15] Blameless you were in your conduct
    from the day you were created,
Until evil was found in you,
[16]   the result of your far-flung trade;
    violence was your business, and you
      sinned.
Then I banned you from the mountain of
    God;
    the Cherub drove you from among the
      fiery stones.
[17] You became haughty of heart because of
    your beauty;
    for the sake of splendor you debased
      your wisdom.
I cast you to the earth, so great was your
    guilt;
    I made you a spectacle in the sight of
      kings.
[18] Because of your guilt, your sinful trade,
    I have profaned your sanctuaries,
And I have brought out fire from your
    midst
    which will devour you.
I have reduced you to dust on the earth
    in the sight of all who should see you.
[19] Among the peoples, all who knew you
    stand aghast at you;
You have become a horror,
    you shall be no more.

Against Sidon. [20][z]Thus the word of the
LORD came to me: Son of man, look toward
Sidon, [21a]and prophesy against it: [22]Thus
says the Lord GOD:[b] See! I am coming at
you, Sidon; I will be glorified in your midst.
Then they shall know that I am the LORD,
when I inflict punishments upon it and use it
to manifest my holiness.

[23] Into it I will send pestilence,
    and blood shall flow in its streets.

Within it shall fall those slain
    by the sword that comes against it
      from every side.

Thus they shall know that I am the LORD.
[24]Sidon shall no longer be a tearing thorn for
the house of Israel, a brier that scratches
them more than all the others about them
who despise them; thus they shall know that
I am the LORD.

[25]Thus says the Lord GOD: When I gather
the house of Israel from the peoples among
whom they are scattered, then I will manifest my holiness through them in the sight of
the nations. Then they shall live on their land
which I gave to my servant Jacob; [26]they
shall live on it in security, building houses
and planting vineyards. They shall dwell secure while I inflict punishments on all their
neighbors who despised them; thus they
shall know that I, the LORD, am their God.

CHAPTER 29

See RG 231

Egypt the Crocodile. [1]On the twelfth
day of the tenth month in the tenth year,[*] the
word of the LORD came to me: [2]Son of man,
set your face against Pharaoh, king of Egypt,
and prophesy against him and against all
Egypt.[*] [3]Say this to him: Thus says the Lord
GOD:

See! I am coming at you, Pharaoh,
    king of Egypt,
Great crouching monster
    amidst your Niles:[*]
Who say, "The Niles are mine;
    it is I who made them!"

[4]I will put hooks in your jaws and make the
fish of your Niles stick to your scales, then
draw you up from the midst of your Niles
along with all the fish of your Niles sticking
to your scales.

[5] I will cast you into the desert,
    you and all the fish of your Niles;

28, 14: The holy mountain of God: the residence of God
was sometimes designated as a mountain; cf Is 14, 13. The
fiery stones: associated with the divine presence; cf Ez 1, 13;
Ps 18, 13.

29, 1: The twelfth day of the tenth month in the tenth year:
January 7, 587 B.C. The siege of Jerusalem had begun a year

earlier; cf Ez 24, 1.

29, 2: Egypt was allied with Judah against the Chaldeans.
29, 3: Niles: the many rivulets of the Nile as it branches
out into the Delta.

z: Is 23, 1-18.   a: Jer 47, 4.   b: Jl 4, 4; Zec 9, 2ff.

You shall fall upon the open field,
you shall not be taken up or buried;
To the beasts of the earth and the birds of
the air
I give you as food,
6 That all who dwell in Egypt may know
that I am the LORD.
Because you have been a reed staff
for the house of Israel:c
7 When they held you in hand, you
splintered,
throwing every shoulder out of joint;
When they leaned on you, you broke,
bringing each one of them down
headlong;

8therefore thus says the Lord GOD: See! I
will bring the sword against you, and cut off
from you both man and beast. 9The land of
Egypt shall become a desolate waste; thus
they shall know that I am the LORD.

Because you said, "The Niles are mine; it
is I who made them," 10therefore see! I am
coming at you and against your Niles; I will
make the land of Egypt a waste and a desolation from Migdol to Syene,* and even to
the frontier of Ethiopia. 11No foot of man or
beast shall pass through it; they shall not
pass through it, and it will be uninhabited for
forty years. 12I will make the land of Egypt
the most desolate of lands, and its cities shall
be the most deserted of cities for forty years;
and I will scatter the Egyptians among the
nations and strew them over foreign lands.
13Yet thus says the Lord GOD: At the end of
forty years I will gather the Egyptians from
the peoples among whom they are scattered,
14and I will restore Egypt's fortune, bringing
them back to the land of Pathros, the land of
their origin,* where it will be the lowliest
15of kingdoms, never more to set itself above
the nations. I will make them few, that they
may not dominate the nations. 16No longer

shall they be for the house of Israel to trust
in, but the living reminder of its guilt for
having turned to follow after them. Thus
they shall know that I am the LORD.

The Wages of Nebuchadnezzar. 17On the
first day of the first month in the twenty-seventh year,* the word of the LORD came to
me: 18Son of man, Nebuchadnezzar, the king
of Babylon, has led his army in an exhaust-
ing campaign against Tyre.* Their heads became bald and their shoulders were galled;
but neither he nor his army received any
wages from Tyre for the campaign he led
against it. 19Therefore thus says the Lord
GOD:d I am now giving the land of Egypt to
Nebuchadnezzar, king of Babylon. He shall
carry off its riches, plundering and pillaging
it for the wages of his soldiers, who did it for
me; 20as payment for his toil I have given
him the land of Egypt, says the Lord GOD.

21On that day I will make a horn sprout for
the house of Israel, and I will cause you to
speak out in their midst; thus they shall
know that I am the LORD.

CHAPTER 30

See RG
231

The Day of the Lord against Egypt. 1Thus the word of the LORD came to me:
2Son of man, speak this prophecy: Thus says
the Lord GOD: Cry, Oh, the day! 3for near is
the day, near is the day of the Lord; a day of
clouds, doomsday for the nations shall it be.
4Then a sword shall come upon Egypt, and
anguish shall be in Ethiopia, when the slain
fall in Egypt, when her riches are seized and
her foundations are overthrown. 5Ethiopia,
Put, Lud, all Arabia, Libya, and people of
the allied territory shall fall by the sword
with them. 6Those who support Egypt shall
fall, and down shall come her proud
strength; from Migdol to Syene they shall
fall there by the sword, says the Lord GOD.
7She shall be the most devastated of lands,

29, 10: From Migdol to Syene: from the northern to the
southern extremity of Egypt. Syene is the modern Assuan.

29, 14: Pathros, the land of their origin: upper Egypt, that
is, southern Egypt, where the Egyptians were thought to have
originated; Is 11, 11; Jer 44, 1. 15.

29, 17: The first day of the first month in the twenty-seventh year: April 26, 571 B.C. This is the latest date attached
to any prophecy in Ezekiel.

29, 18f: The fulfillment of Ezekiel's prophecy against

Tyre (chapters 26—28) was a thirteen-year siege of the city
by Nebuchadnezzar (587–574 B.C.). Tyre seems to have
been taken, but its resources were exhausted and the booty
was small. Therefore Ezekiel now prophesies that Nebuchadnezzar will collect his wages as God's instrument in the punishment of Tyre, by plundering Egypt.

c: Is 36, 6. d: Jer 46, 2.

Ezekiel's Oracles Concerning the Nations

Like other prophetic books (Is 13–23; Jer 46–51), Ezekiel contains a section of oracles concerning foreign nations (Ez 25–32), which are intended to demonstrate God's power throughout the world. The nations included here, Ammon, Moab, Edom, Philistia, Tyre, and Egypt, would all be considered as targets of the Babylonian empire, although Egypt was never taken. Ezekiel identifies the projected expansion of Babylonia as an act of God.

and her cities shall be the most desolate of all. [8]Then they shall know that I am the LORD, when I set fire to Egypt and when all who help her are broken. [9]On that day messengers shall hasten forth at my command to terrify unsuspecting Ethiopia; they shall be in anguish on the day of Egypt, which is surely coming.

[10]Thus says the Lord GOD: I will put an end to the throngs of Egypt by the hand of Nebuchadnezzar, king of Babylon. [11]He and his people with him, the most ruthless of nations, shall be brought in to devastate the land. They shall draw their swords against Egypt, and fill the land with the slain. [12]I will turn the Niles into dry land and sell the land over to the power of the wicked. The land and everything in it I will hand over to foreigners to devastate. I, the LORD, have spoken.

[13e]Thus says the Lord GOD: I will put an end to the great ones of Memphis and the princes of the land of Egypt, that they may be no more. I will cast fear into the land of Egypt, and devastate Pathros. [14]I will set fire to Zoan, and inflict punishments on Thebes. [15]I will pour out my wrath on Pelusium, Egypt's stronghold, and cut down the crowds in Memphis. [16]I will set fire to Egypt; Syene shall writhe in anguish; Thebes shall be breached and its walls shall be demolished. [17]The young men of On and of Pibeseth shall fall by the sword, and the cities themselves shall go into captivity. [18]In Tehaphnehes the day shall be darkened when I break the scepter of Egypt. Her haughty pride shall cease from her, clouds shall cover her, and her daughters shall go into captivity. [19]Thus will I inflict punishments on Egypt, that they may know that I am the LORD.

Pharaoh's Broken Arm. [20]On the seventh day of the first month in the eleventh year,* the word of the LORD came to me: [21]*Son of man, I have broken the arm of Pharaoh, the king of Egypt, and see, it has not been bound up with bandages and healing remedies that it may be strong enough to hold the sword. [22]Therefore thus says the Lord GOD: See! I am coming at Pharaoh, the king of Egypt. I will break his strong arm, so that the sword drops from his hand. [23]I will scatter the Egyptians among the nations and strew them over foreign lands. [24]But I will strengthen the arms of the king of Babylon, and put my sword in his hand, which he will bring against Egypt so as to plunder and pillage it. [25][I will make the arms of the king of Babylon strong, but the arms of Pharaoh shall drop.] Then they shall know that I am the LORD, when I put my sword in the hand of the king of Babylon for him to wield against the land of Egypt. [26][I will scatter the Egyptians among the nations and strew them over foreign lands.] Thus they shall know that I am the LORD.

CHAPTER 31

See RG 231

Allegory of the Cypress. [1]On the first day of the third month in the eleventh year,* the word of the LORD came to me: [2]Son of

---

30, 20: The seventh day of the first month in the eleventh year: April 29, 587 B.C.

30, 21-26: This oracle was uttered during the siege of Jerusalem, which had now lasted more than a year (Ez 24, 1). Pharaoh Hophra went to the aid of Jerusalem, causing the Chaldeans to lift the siege temporarily; cf Jer 34, 21; 37, 6f. In the prophet's eyes, this was interfering with the divine punishment of Judah that was to be inflicted by the

Chaldeans. The Egyptians were routed by the Chaldeans, and were able to offer no more help to Jerusalem; cf chapter 31.

31, 1: The first day of the third month in the eleventh year: June 21, 587 B.C.

---

e: Zec 13, 2.

Seven Oracles Concerning Egypt and Its Rulers

The oracles against Egypt are found in chs 29–32. Egypt played a major role in instigating the revolt against its enemy Babylon. When Pharaoh Hophra attempted to relieve Jerusalem from the Babylonian siege in 588 B.C., he was repulsed (Jer 37; 44, 30; see also Jer 32).

man, say to Pharaoh, the king of Egypt, and to his hordes: What are you like in your greatness?

3 Behold, a cypress [cedar] in Lebanon,
  beautiful of branch, lofty of stature,
  amid the very clouds lifted its crest.
4 Waters made it grow, the abyss made it
    flourish,
  sending its rivers round where it was
    planted,
  turning its streams to all the trees of
    the field.
5 Thus it grew taller than every other tree
    of the field,
  and longer of branch because of the
    abundant water.
6 In its boughs nested all the birds of the
    air,
  under its branches all beasts of the
    field gave birth,
  in its shade dwelt numerous peoples of
    every race.
7 It became beautiful and stately in its
    spread of foliage,
  for its roots were turned toward
    abundant water.
8 The cedars in the garden of God were not
    its equal,
  nor could the fir trees match its boughs,
  Neither were the plane trees like it for
    branches;
  no tree in the garden of God matched
    its beauty.
9 I made it beautiful, with much foliage,
  the envy of all Eden's trees in the
    garden of God.

10Therefore thus says the Lord GOD: Because it became lofty in stature, raising its crest among the clouds, and because it became proud in heart at its height, 11I have handed it over to the mightiest of the nations, which has dealt with it in keeping with its wickedness. I humiliated it. 12Foreigners, the most ruthless of the nations, cut it down and left it on the mountains. Its foliage was brought low in all the valleys, its branches lay broken in all the ravines of the land, and all the peoples of the land withdrew from its shade, abandoning it.

13 On its fallen trunk rested all the birds of
    the air,
  and by its branches were all the beasts
    of the field.

14Thus no tree may grow lofty in stature or raise its crest among the clouds; no tree fed by water may stand by itself in its loftiness.

For all of them are destined for death,
  for the land below,
For the company of mortals,
  those who go down into the pit.

15Thus says the Lord GOD: On the day he went down to the nether world I made the abyss close up over him; I stopped its streams so that the deep waters were held back. I cast gloom over Lebanon because of him, so that all the trees in the land drooped on his account. 16At the crash of his fall I made the nations rock, when I cast him down to the nether world with those who go down into the pit. In the land below, all Eden's trees were consoled, Lebanon's choice and best, all that were fed by water. 17They too have come down with him to the nether world, to those slain by the sword; those who dwelt in his shade are dispersed among the nations. 18Which was your equal in glory or size among the trees of Eden? Yet you have been brought down with the trees of Eden to the land below. You shall lie with the uncircumcised, with those slain by the sword. Such are Pharaoh and all his hordes, says the Lord GOD.

CHAPTER 32

See RG
231

Dirge over Pharaoh. ¹On the first day of the twelfth month in the twelfth year,* the word of the LORD came to me: ²Son of man, utter a lament over Pharaoh, the king of Egypt, saying to him: Lion of the nations, you are destroyed.

You were like a monster in the sea,
    spouting in your streams,
Stirring the water with your feet
    and churning its streams.
³ Thus says the Lord GOD:
    I will spread my net over you
    [with a host of many nations],
    and draw you up in my seine.*f*
⁴ I will leave you on the land;
    on the open field I will cast you.
    I will have all the birds of the air alight
        on you,
    and all the beasts of the earth eat their
        fill of you.
⁵ I will leave your flesh on the mountains,
    and fill the valleys with your carcass.
⁶ I will water the land with what flows
        from you,
    and the river beds shall be filled with
        your blood.
⁷ When I snuff you out I will cover the
        heavens,
    and all their stars I will darken;
    The sun I will cover with clouds,
    and the moon shall not give its light.*g*
⁸ All the shining lights in the heavens
    I will darken on your account,
And I will spread darkness over your
        land,
    says the Lord GOD.

⁹I will grieve the hearts of many peoples when I lead you captive among the nations, to lands which you do not know. ¹⁰Many peoples shall be appalled at you, and their kings shall shudder over you in horror when they see me brandish my sword, and on the day of your downfall every one of them shall continuously tremble for his own life. ¹¹For

thus says the Lord GOD: The sword of the king of Babylon shall come upon you.

¹² I will cut down your horde with the
        blades of warriors,
    all of them the most ruthless of the
        nations;
    They shall lay waste the glory of Egypt,
    and all her hordes shall be destroyed.
¹³ I will have all of her animals perish
    beside her abundant waters;
    The foot of man shall stir them no longer,
    nor shall the hoof of beast disturb them.
¹⁴ Then will I make their waters clear,
    and their streams flow like oil,
    says the Lord GOD.

¹⁵When I turn Egypt into a waste, the land shall be devastated of all that is in it; when I strike all who live there, they shall know that I am the LORD. ¹⁶This is a dirge, and it shall be sung: the daughters of the nations shall chant it; over Egypt and all its hordes shall they chant it, says the Lord GOD.

Dirge over Egypt. ¹⁷On the fifteenth day of the first month in the twelfth year, the word of the LORD came to me: ¹⁸Son of man, lament over the throngs of Egypt, for the mighty nations have thrust them down to the bottom of the earth, with those who go down into the pit. ²⁰In the midst of those slain by the sword shall they fall, and place shall be made with them for all their hordes. Then from the midst of the nether world, the mighty warriors shall speak to Egypt: ¹⁹"Whom do you excel in beauty? ²¹Come down, you and your allies, lie with the uncircumcised, with those slain by the sword."

²²There is Assyria with all her company, all of them slain, ²³whose graves have been made in the recesses of the pit; her company is around Egypt's grave, all of them slain, fallen by the sword, who spread terror in the land of the living. ²⁴There is Elam with all her throng about Egypt's grave, all of them slain, fallen by the sword: they have gone down uncircumcised to the bottom of the earth, who spread their terror in the land of the living, and they

---

32, 1: The first day of the twelfth month in the twelfth year: March 3, 585 B.C.

f: Ez 12, 13; 17, 20.   *g:* Is 13, 10; Jl 2, 10; 4, 15; Mt 24, 29.

bear their disgrace with those who go down into the pit; ²⁵in the midst of the slain they are placed. ²⁶There are Meshech and Tubal and all their throng about her grave, all of them uncircumcised, slain by the sword, for they spread their terror in the land of the living.

²⁷They do not lie with the mighty men fallen of old,* who went down to the nether world with their weapons of war, whose swords were placed under their heads and whose shields were laid over their bones, though the mighty men caused terror in the land of the living. ²⁸But in the midst of the uncircumcised shall you lie, with those slain by the sword.

²⁹There are Edom, her kings, and all her princes, who despite their might have been placed with those slain by the sword; with the uncircumcised they lie, and with those who go down into the pit. ³⁰There are all the princes of the north and all the Sidonians, who have gone down with the slain, because of the terror their might inspired; they lie uncircumcised with those slain by the sword and bear their disgrace with those who go down to the pit. ³¹When Pharaoh sees these, he shall be comforted for all his hordes slain by the sword—Pharaoh and all his army, says the Lord GOD. ³²Since he spread his terror in the land of the living, therefore is he laid to rest among the uncircumcised, with those slain by the sword—Pharaoh and all his hordes, says the Lord GOD.

IV: Salvation for Israel

CHAPTER 33

See RG 231-32

The Prophet a Watchman. ¹Thus the word of the LORD came to me: ²Son of man, speak thus to your countrymen: When I bring the sword against a country, and the people of this country select one of their number to be their watchman, ³and the watchman, seeing the sword coming against the country, blows the trumpet to warn the people, ⁴anyone hearing but not heeding the warning of the trumpet and therefore slain by the sword that comes against him, shall be responsible for his own death. ⁵He heard the trumpet blast yet refused to take warning; he is responsible for his own death, for had he taken warning he would have escaped with his life. ⁶But if the watchman sees the sword coming and fails to blow the warning trumpet, so that the sword comes and takes anyone, I will hold the watchman responsible for that person's death, even though that person is taken because of his own sin.

^{7h}You, son of man, I have appointed watchman for the house of Israel; when you hear me say anything, you shall warn them for me. ⁸If I tell the wicked man that he shall surely die, and you do not speak out to dissuade the wicked man from his way, he [the wicked man] shall die for his guilt, but I will hold you responsible for his death. ⁹But if you warn the wicked man, trying to turn him from his way, and he refuses to turn from his way, he shall die for his guilt, but you shall save yourself.

Individual Retribution. ¹⁰As for you, son of man, speak to the house of Israel: You people say, "Our crimes and our sins weigh us down; we are rotting away because of them. How can we survive?" ¹¹ⁱAnswer them: As I live, says the Lord GOD, I swear I take no pleasure in the death of the wicked man, but rather in the wicked man's conversion, that he may live. Turn, turn from your evil ways! Why should you die, O house of Israel?

¹²As for you, son of man, tell your countrymen: The virtue which a man has practiced will not save him on the day that he sins; neither will the wickedness that a man has done bring about his downfall on the day that he turns from his wickedness [nor can the virtuous man, when he sins, remain alive]. ¹³Though I say to the virtuous man that he shall surely live, if he then presumes on his virtue and does wrong, none of his virtuous deeds shall be remembered; because of the wrong he has done, he shall die. ¹⁴And though I say to the wicked man that

---

32, 27: The mighty men fallen of old: the semilegendary heroes of the prehistoric past, who were thought to have once dominated the world; cf Is 14, 9.

---

h: Ez 3, 17.   *i:* Ez 18, 23-32.

he shall surely die, if he turns away from his sin and does what is right and just, [15]giving back pledges, restoring stolen goods, living by the statutes that bring life, and doing no wrong, he shall surely live, he shall not die. [16]None of the sins he committed shall be held against him; he has done what is right and just, he shall surely live.

[17]Yet your countrymen say, "The way of the LORD is not fair!"; but it is their way that is not fair. [18]When a virtuous man turns away from what is right and does wrong, he shall die for it. [19]But when a wicked man turns away from wickedness and does what is right and just, because of this he shall live. [20j]And still you say, "The way of the LORD is not fair!"? I will judge every one of you according to his ways, O house of Israel.

The Fugitive from Jerusalem. * [21]On the fifth day of the tenth month, in the twelfth year of our exile, the fugitive came to me from Jerusalem and said, "The city is taken!" [22]The hand of the LORD had come upon me the evening before the fugitive arrived, and he opened my mouth when the fugitive reached me in the morning. My mouth was opened, and I was dumb no longer.

The Survivors in Judah. * [23]Thus the word of the Lord came to me: [24]Son of man, they who live in the ruins on the land of Israel reason thus: "Abraham, though but a single individual, received possession of the land; we, therefore, being many, have as permanent possession the land that has been given to us." [25]Give them this answer: Thus says the Lord GOD: You eat on the mountains, you raise your eyes to your idols, you shed blood—yet you would keep possession of the land? [26]You rely on your sword, you do abominable things, each one of you defiles his neighbor's wife—yet you would keep possession of the land? [27]Tell them this: Thus says the Lord GOD: As I live, those who are in the ruins I

swear shall fall by the sword; those who are in the open field I have given to the wild beasts for food; and those who are in fastnesses and in caves shall die by the plague. [28]I will make the land a desolate waste, so that its proud strength will come to an end, and the mountains of Israel shall be so desolate that no one will cross them. [29]Thus they shall know that I am the LORD, when I make the land a desolate waste because of all the abominable things they have done.

The Prophet's False Popularity. [30]As for you, son of man, your countrymen are talking about you along the walls and in the doorways of houses. They say to one another, "Come and hear the latest word that comes from the LORD."* [31]My people come to you as people always do; they sit down before you and hear your words, but they will not obey them, for lies are on their lips and their desires are fixed on dishonest gain. [32]For them you are only a ballad singer, with a pleasant voice and a clever touch. They listen to your words, but they will not obey them. [33]But when it comes—and it is surely coming!—they shall know that there was a prophet among them.

CHAPTER 34

See RG 231-32

Parable of the Shepherds. [1]Thus the word of the LORD came to me: [2]Son of man, prophesy against the shepherds of Israel,* in these words prophesy to them [to the shepherds]: Thus says the Lord GOD: Woe to the shepherds of Israel who have been pasturing themselves![k] Should not shepherds, rather, pasture sheep? [3]You have fed off their milk, worn their wool, and slaughtered the fatlings, but the sheep you have not pastured. [4]You did not strengthen the weak nor heal the sick nor bind up the injured. You did not bring back the strayed nor seek the lost, but you lorded it over them harshly and bru-

---

33, 21f: January 8, 585 B.C. According to Jeremiah (39, 2), Jerusalem was taken in July, 587. Some MSS read "eleventh" for twelfth year (January, 586); even so, there was ample time between the fall of Jerusalem and the arrival of the fugitive from that city to journey to Babylon. However, this is the fugitive sent to fulfill the promise of Ez 24, 25. 27, the eyewitness who would release Ezekiel from his dumbness; cf Ez 2, 26f.

33, 23-29: News brought by the fugitive furnished the oc-

casion of this prophecy. Like Jeremiah, Ezekiel rejects the idea that the survivors in Judah have any claim to the land. The new Israel is to be formed from the exiles.

33, 30: The fulfillment of Ezekiel's prophecies about Jerusalem was responsible for this temporary enthusiasm among the unstable people.

34, 2: The shepherds of Israel: the leaders of the people.

---

j: Ez 18, 25. k: Ez 13, 3; Jer 23, 1.

tally. *5*So they were scattered for lack of a shepherd, and became food for all the wild beasts. My sheep were scattered *6*and wandered over all the mountains and high hills; my sheep were scattered over the whole earth, with no one to look after them or to search for them.

*7*Therefore, shepherds, hear the word of the LORD: *8*As I live, says the Lord GOD, because my sheep have been given over to pillage, and because my sheep have become food for every wild beast, for lack of a shepherd; because my shepherds did not look after my sheep, but pastured themselves and did not pasture my sheep; *9*because of this, shepherds, hear the word of the LORD: *10*Thus says the Lord GOD: I swear I am coming against these shepherds. I will claim my sheep from them and put a stop to their shepherding my sheep so that they may no longer pasture themselves. I will save my sheep, that they may no longer be food for their mouths.

*11*For thus says the Lord GOD: I myself will look after and tend my sheep. *12*As a shepherd tends his flock when he finds himself among his scattered sheep, so will I tend my sheep. I will rescue them from every place where they were scattered when it was cloudy and dark. *13*I will lead them out from among the peoples and gather them from the foreign lands; I will bring them back to their own country and pasture them upon the mountains of Israel [in the land's ravines and all its inhabited places]. *14*In good pastures will I pasture them, and on the mountain heights of Israel shall be their grazing ground. There they shall lie down on good grazing ground, and in rich pastures shall they be pastured on the mountains of Israel. *15*I myself will pasture my sheep; I myself will give them rest, says the Lord GOD. *16*The lost I will seek out, the strayed I will bring back, the injured I will bind up, the sick I will heal [but the sleek and the strong I will destroy], shepherding them rightly.

Separation of the Sheep. *17*As for you, my sheep, says the Lord GOD, I will judge between one sheep and another, between rams and goats. *18*Was it not enough for you to graze on the best pasture, that you had to trample the rest of your pastures with your feet? Was it not enough for you to drink the clearest water, that you had to foul the remainder with your feet? *19*Thus my sheep had to graze on what your feet had trampled and drink what your feet had fouled. *20*Therefore thus says the Lord GOD: Now will I judge between the fat and the lean sheep. *21*Because you push with side and shoulder, and butt all the weak sheep with your horns until you have driven them out, *22*I will save my sheep so that they may no longer be despoiled, and I will judge between one sheep and another. *23*I will appoint one shepherd over them to pasture them, my servant David;* he shall pasture them and be their shepherd. *24*I, the Lord, will be their God, and my servant David shall be prince among them. I, the LORD, have spoken.

*25*I will make a covenant of peace with them, and rid the country of ravenous beasts, that they may dwell securely in the desert and sleep in the forests. *26*I will place them about my hill, sending rain in due season, rains that shall be a blessing to them. *27*The trees of the field shall bear their fruits, and the land its crops, and they shall dwell securely on their own soil. Thus they shall know that I am the LORD when I break the bonds of their yoke and free them from the power of those who enslaved them. *28*They shall no longer be despoiled by the nations or devoured by beasts of the earth, but shall dwell secure, with no one to frighten them. *29*I will prepare for them peaceful fields for planting; they shall no longer be carried off by famine in the land, or bear the reproaches of the nations. *30*Thus they shall know that I, the LORD, am their God, and they are my people, the house of Israel, says the Lord GOD. *31*[You, my sheep, you are the sheep of my pasture, and I am your God, says the Lord GOD.]

34, 23: One shepherd . . . my servant David: a messianic Davidic King who will rule over the restored Israel (vv 25–31) in the name of the Lord.

l: Is 40, 21; Hos 3, 5; Jn 10, 11. 14.

CHAPTER 35

*Against Edom.** ¹Thus the word of the LORD came to me:*m* ²Son of man, set your face against Mount Seir, and prophesy against it. ³Say to it: Thus says the Lord GOD: See! I am coming at you, Mount Seir. I will stretch out my hand against you and make you a desolate waste. ⁴Your cities I will turn into ruins, and you shall be a waste; thus you shall know that I am the LORD.

⁵Because you never let die your hatred for the Israelites, whom you delivered over to the power of the sword at the time of their trouble, when their crimes came to an end, ⁶therefore, as I live, says the Lord GOD, you have been guilty of blood, and blood, I swear, shall pursue you. ⁷I will make Mount Seir a desolate waste, and cut off from it any traveler. ⁸With the slain I will fill your hills, your valleys, and all your ravines [in them the slain shall fall by the sword]: ⁹desolate will I make you forever, and leave your cities without inhabitants; thus you shall know that I am the LORD.

¹⁰Because you said: The two nations and the two lands* have become mine; we shall possess them—although the LORD was there— ¹¹therefore, as I live, says the Lord GOD, I will deal with you according to your anger and your envy which you have exercised [in your hatred] against them. I will make myself known among you when I judge you, ¹²and you shall know that I am the LORD.

I have heard all the contemptuous things you have uttered against the mountains of Israel: "They are desolate, they have been given us to devour." ¹³I have heard the insolent and wild words you have spoken against me. ¹⁴Thus says the Lord GOD: Just as you rejoiced over my land because it was desolate, so will I do to you. ¹⁵In keeping with your glee over the devastation of the inheritance of the house of Israel, so will I treat you. A waste shall you be, Mount Seir, you

and the whole of Edom. Thus they shall know that I am the LORD.

CHAPTER 36

Regeneration of the Land. ¹As for you, son of man, prophesy to the mountains of Israel: Mountains of Israel,*n* hear the word of the LORD! ²Thus says the Lord GOD: Because the enemy has said of you, "Ha! the everlasting heights have become our possession" ³[therefore prophesy in these words: Thus says the Lord GOD:]; because you have been ridiculed and despised on all sides for having become a possession for the rest of the nations, and have become a byword and a popular jeer; ⁴therefore, mountains of Israel, hear the word of the LORD: [Thus says the Lord GOD to the mountains and hills, the ravines and valleys, the desolate ruins and abandoned cities, which have been given over to the pillage and mockery of the remaining nations round about; ⁵therefore thus says the Lord GOD:] Truly, with burning jealousy I speak against the rest of the nations [and against all of Edom] who with wholehearted joy and utter contempt have considered my land their possession to be delivered over to plunder. ⁶[Therefore, prophesy concerning the land of Israel, and say to the mountains and hills, the ravines and valleys: Thus says the Lord GOD:] With jealous fury I speak, because you have borne the reproach of the nations. ⁷Therefore do I solemnly swear that your neighboring nations shall bear their own reproach.

⁸As for you, mountains of Israel, you shall grow branches and bear fruit for my people Israel, for they shall soon return. ⁹See, I come to you, it is to you that I turn; you will be tilled and sown, ¹⁰and I will settle crowds of men upon you, the whole house of Israel; cities shall be repeopled, and ruins rebuilt. ¹¹I will settle crowds of men and beasts upon you, to multiply and be fruitful. I will repeople you as in the past, and be more generous

---

35, 1-15: After the fall of Jerusalem, Edom assisted the Chaldeans in devastating the land and subduing the population, and ended by occupying part of Judah's former territory. For this reason these oracles against Edom are found in the context of the city's fall.

35, 10: The two nations and the two lands: the superseded kingdoms of Israel and Judah and their territories.

m: 1ff: Ez 25, 12ff.   *n:* Ez 6, 3.

to you than in the beginning; thus you shall know that I am the LORD.

[12][My people Israel are the ones whom I will have walk upon you; they shall take possession of you, and you shall be their heritage. Never again shall you rob them of their children.]

[13]Thus says the Lord GOD: Because they have said of you, "You are a land that devours men,* and you rob your people of their children"; [14]therefore, never again shall you devour men or rob your people of their children, says the Lord GOD. [15]No more will I permit you to hear the reproach of nations, or bear insults from peoples, or rob your people of their children, says the Lord GOD.

Regeneration of the People. [16]Thus the word of the LORD came to me: [17]Son of man, when the house of Israel lived in their land, they defiled it by their conduct and deeds. In my sight their conduct was like the defilement of a menstruous woman. [18]Therefore I poured out my fury upon them [because of the blood which they poured out on the ground, and because they defiled it with idols]. [19]I scattered them among the nations, dispersing them over foreign lands; according to their conduct and deeds I judged them. [20o]But when they came among the nations [wherever they came], they served to profane my holy name, because it was said of them: "These are the people of the LORD, yet they had to leave their land." [21]So I have relented because of my holy name which the house of Israel profaned among the nations where they came. [22]Therefore say to the house of Israel: Thus says the Lord GOD: Not for your sakes do I act, house of Israel, but for the sake of my holy name, which you profaned among the nations to which you came. [23]I will prove the holiness of my great name, profaned among the nations, in whose midst you have profaned it. Thus the nations shall know that I am the LORD, says the Lord GOD, when in their sight I prove my holiness through you. [24]For I will take you away from among the nations, gather you from all the foreign lands, and bring you back to your own land. [25p]I will sprinkle clean water upon you to cleanse you from all your impurities, and from all your idols I will cleanse you. [26q]I will give you a new heart and place a new spirit within you, taking from your bodies your stony hearts and giving you natural hearts. [27r]I will put my spirit within you and make you live by my statutes, careful to observe my decrees. [28]You shall live in the land I gave your fathers; you shall be my people, and I will be your God. [29]I will save you from all your impurities; I will order the grain to be abundant, and I will not send famine against you. [30]I will increase the fruit on your trees and the crops in your fields; thus you shall no longer bear among the nations the reproach of famine. [31]Then you shall remember your evil conduct, and that your deeds were not good; you shall loathe yourselves for your sins and your abominations. [32]Not for your sakes do I act, says the Lord GOD—let this be known to you! Be ashamed and abashed because of your conduct, O house of Israel.

[33]Thus says the Lord GOD: When I purify you from all your crimes, I will repeople the cities, and the ruins shall be rebuilt; [34]the desolate land shall be tilled, which was formerly a wasteland exposed to the gaze of every passer-by. [35]"This desolate land has been made into a garden of Eden," they shall say. "The cities that were in ruins, laid waste, and destroyed are now repeopled and fortified." [36]Thus the neighboring nations that remain shall know that I, the LORD, have rebuilt what was destroyed and replanted what was desolate. I, the LORD, have promised, and I will do it.

[37]Thus says the Lord GOD: This also I will be persuaded to do for the house of Israel: to multiply them like sheep. [38]As with sacrificial sheep, the sheep of Jerusalem on its feast days, the cities which were in ruins shall be filled with flocks of men; thus they shall know that I am the LORD.

36, 13: A land that devours men: destroys its own population, as could be seen in its disastrous political history.

---

o: Is 52, 5; Rom 2, 24.   *p:* Ps 51, 4; Zec 13, 1; Hb 10, 22; Jn 3, 5.   *q:* Jer 31, 33.   *r:* Ez 37, 14; 39, 29; Is 42, 1; 44, 3; 59, 21; Hg 2, 5; Jl 3, 1f.

The Valley of Dry Bones

Ezekiel's vision of dry bones symbolizes the restoration of the people of Israel. Many assume that it is based upon his observation of a battlefield filled with the bones of dead soldiers. The vision plays upon priestly concepts of purity, in that a priest must have no contact with the dead (Lv 21, 1–12; those who do have contact with a corpse are defiled for a period of seven days, Nm 19, 10b–22). Because such impurity is the epitome of defilement in priestly thought, this image of new life is a very powerful metaphor for the restoration and purification of Israel.

See RG 231-32

CHAPTER 37

*Vision of the Dry Bones.** [1]The hand of the LORD came upon me, and he led me out in the spirit of the LORD and set me in the center of the plain, which was now filled with bones. [2]He made me walk among them in every direction so that I saw how many they were on the surface of the plain. How dry they were! [3]He asked me: Son of man, can these bones come to life? "Lord GOD," I answered, "you alone know that." [4]Then he said to me: Prophesy over these bones, and say to them: Dry bones, hear the word of the LORD! [5]Thus says the Lord GOD to these bones: See! I will bring spirit into you, that you may come to life. [6]I will put sinews upon you, make flesh grow over you, cover you with skin, and put spirit in you so that you may come to life and know that I am the LORD. [7]I prophesied as I had been told, and even as I was prophesying I heard a noise; it was a rattling as the bones came together, bone joining bone. [8]I saw the sinews and the flesh come upon them, and the skin cover them, but there was no spirit in them. [9]Then he said to me: Prophesy to the spirit, prophesy, son of man, and say to the spirit: Thus says the Lord GOD: From the four winds come, O spirit, and breathe into these slain that they may come to life. [10]I prophesied as he told me, and the spirit came into them; they came alive and stood upright, a vast army. [11]Then he said to me: Son of man, these bones are the whole house of Israel. They have been saying, "Our bones are dried up, our hope is lost, and we are cut off." [12]Therefore, prophesy and say to them: Thus says the Lord GOD: O my people, I will open your graves and have you rise from them, and bring you back to the land of Israel. [13]Then you shall know that I am the LORD, when I open your graves and have you rise from them, O my people! [14]I will put my spirit in you that you may live, and I will settle you upon your land; thus you shall know that I am the LORD. I have promised, and I will do it, says the LORD.

The Two Sticks. [15]*Thus the word of the LORD came to me: [16]Now, son of man, take a single stick, and write on it: Judah and those Israelites who are associated with him. Then take another stick and write on it: Joseph [the stick of Ephraim] and all the house of Israel associated with him. [17]Then join the two sticks together, so that they form one stick in your hand. [18]When your countrymen ask you, "Will you not tell us what you mean by all this?", [19]answer them: Thus says the Lord GOD: [I will take the stick of Joseph, which is in the hand of Ephraim, and of the tribes of Israel associated with him, and I will join to it the stick of Judah, making them a single stick; they shall be one in my hand. [20]The sticks on which you write you shall hold up before them to see. [21]Tell them: Thus speaks the Lord GOD:] I will take the Israelites from among the nations to which they have come, and gather them from all sides to bring them back to their land. [22]I will make them one nation upon the land, in the mountains of Israel, and there shall be one prince for them all. Never again shall they be two nations, and never again shall they be divided into two kingdoms.

[23]No longer shall they defile themselves

37, 1-14: This vision is a prediction of the restoration of Israel under the figure of a resurrection from the dead; it is not concerned with the doctrine of resurrection itself.

37, 15-22: The symbolic action of joining two sticks into one signifies the future union of Israel and Judah under one messianic King.

with their idols, their abominations, and all their transgressions. I will deliver them from all their sins of apostasy, and cleanse them so that they may be my people and I may be their God. ^{24s}My servant David shall be prince over them, and there shall be one shepherd for them all; they shall live by my statutes and carefully observe my decrees. ²⁵They shall live on the land which I gave to my servant Jacob, the land where their fathers lived; they shall live on it forever, they, and their children, and their children's children, with my servant David their prince forever. ^{26t}I will make with them a covenant of peace; it shall be an everlasting covenant with them, and I will multiply them, and put my sanctuary among them forever. ²⁷My dwelling shall be with them; I will be their God, and they shall be my people. ²⁸Thus the nations shall know that it is I, the LORD, who make Israel holy, when my sanctuary shall be set up among them forever.

CHAPTER 38

See RG 232

First Prophecy against Gog. ¹Thus the word of the LORD came to me:* ²Son of man, turn toward Gog* [the land of Magog], ^u the chief prince of Meshech and Tubal, and prophesy against him: ³Thus says the Lord GOD: See! I am coming at you, Gog, chief prince of Meshech and Tubal. ⁴I will lead you forth with all your army, horses and riders all handsomely outfitted, a great horde with bucklers and shields, all of them carrying swords: ⁵Persia, Cush, and Put with them [all with shields and helmets], ⁶Gomer with all its troops, Beth-togarmah from the recesses of the north with all its troops, many peoples with you. ⁷Prepare yourself, be ready, you and all your horde assembled about you, and be at my disposal. ⁸After many days you will be mustered [in the last

years you will come] against a nation which has survived the sword, which has been assembled from many peoples [on the mountains of Israel which were long a ruin], which has been brought forth from among the peoples and all of whom now dwell in security. ⁹You shall come up like a sudden storm, advancing like a cloud to cover the earth, you and all your troops and the many peoples with you.

¹⁰Thus says the Lord GOD: At that time thoughts shall arise in your mind, and you shall devise an evil scheme: ¹¹"I will go up against a land of open villages and attack the peaceful people who are living in security, all of them living without walls, having neither bars nor gates, ¹²to plunder and pillage, turning my hand against the ruins that were repeopled and against a people gathered from the nations, a people concerned with cattle and goods, who dwell at the navel of the earth."* ¹³Sheba and Dedan, the merchants of Tarshish and all her young lions shall ask you: "Is it for plunder that you have come? Is it for pillage that you have summoned your horde, to carry off silver and gold, to take away cattle and goods, to seize much plunder?"

¹⁷Thus says the Lord GOD: It is of you that I spoke in ancient times through my servants, the prophets of Israel, who prophesied in those days that I would bring you against them. ¹⁸But on that day, the day when Gog invades the land of Israel, says the Lord GOD, my fury shall be aroused. In my anger ¹⁹and in my jealousy, in my fiery wrath, I swear: On that day there shall be a great shaking upon the land of Israel. ²⁰Before me shall tremble the fish of the sea and the birds of the air, the beasts of the field and all the reptiles that crawl upon the ground, and all men who are on the land. Mountains shall be

---

38, 1—39, 20: These three oracles against Gog may refer either to a specific foreign invasion in the future, or to the apocalyptic struggle between good and evil at the end of time. By some they are ascribed to a later author than Ezekiel, who lived after the exile and the return to Palestine.

38, 2: Gog: the name is almost certainly a symbolic one taken from that of Gyges, king of Lydia, whether or not the prophet has a specific person in mind. The gloss Magog may be an Akkadian expression, mat-Gog, "the land of Gog." Meshech and Tubal, as well as Gomer and Beth-togarmah (v 6),

were countries around the Black Sea, the northernmost countries known to the Hebrews: the north (cf also v 15) was the traditional direction from which invasion was expected; cf Jer 1, 13ff.

38, 12: Who dwell at the navel of the earth: the people of Israel (cf v 18; also Ez 5, 5). Many ancient peoples spoke of their own homelands as "the navel," that is, the center of the earth.

s: Ez 34, 23; Jer 23, 5; 33, 15.   t: Ps 110, 4.   u: Rv 20, 7f.

overturned, and cliffs shall tumble, and every wall shall fall to the ground. ²¹Against him I will summon every terror, says the Lord GOD, every man's sword against his brother. I will hold judgment with him in pestilence and bloodshed; ²²flooding rain and hailstones, fire and brimstone, I will rain upon him, upon his troops, and upon the many peoples with him. ²³I will prove my greatness and holiness and make myself known in the sight of many nations; thus they shall know that I am the LORD.

Second Prophecy against Gog. ¹⁴Therefore prophesy, son of man, and say to Gog: Thus says the Lord GOD: When my people Israel are dwelling in security, will you not bestir yourself ¹⁵and come from your home in the recesses of the north, you and many peoples with you, all mounted on horses, a great horde and a mighty army? ¹⁶You shall come up against my people Israel like a cloud covering the land. In the last days I will bring you against my land, that the nations may know of me, when in their sight I prove my holiness through you, O Gog.

CHAPTER 39

See RG 232

Third Prophecy against Gog. ¹Now, son of man, prophesy against Gog in these words: Thus says the Lord GOD: See! I am coming at you, Gog, chief prince of Meshech and Tubal. ²I will turn you about, I will urge you on, and I will make you come up from the recesses of the north; I will lead you against the mountains of Israel. ³Then I will strike the bow from your left hand, and make the arrows drop from your right. ⁴Upon the mountains of Israel you shall fall, you and all your troops and the peoples who are with you. To birds of prey of every kind and to the wild beasts I am giving you to be eaten. ⁵On the open field you shall fall, for I have decreed it, says the Lord GOD.

⁶I will send fire upon Magog and upon those who live securely in the coastlands; thus they shall know that I am the LORD. ⁷I will make my holy name known among my people Israel; I will no longer allow my holy name to be profaned. Thus the nations shall know that I am the LORD, the Holy One in Israel. ⁸Yes, it is coming and shall be fulfilled, says the Lord GOD. This is the day I have decreed.

⁹Then shall those who live in the cities of Israel go out and burn weapons: [shields and bucklers,] bows and arrows, clubs and lances; for seven years they shall make fires with them. ¹⁰They shall not have to bring in wood from the fields or cut it down in the forests, for they shall make fires with the weapons. Thus they shall plunder those who plundered them and pillage those who pillaged them, says the Lord GOD.

¹¹On that day I will give Gog for his tomb a well-known place in Israel, the Valley of Abarim* east of the sea [it is blocked to travelers]. Gog shall be buried there with all his horde, and it shall be named "Valley of Hamon-gog." ¹²To purify the land, the house of Israel shall need seven months to bury them. ¹³All the people of the land shall bury them and gain renown for it, when I reveal my glory, says the Lord GOD. ¹⁴Men shall be permanently employed to pass through the land burying those who lie unburied, so as to purify the land. For seven months they shall keep searching. ¹⁵When they pass through, should they see a human bone, let them put up a marker beside it, until others have buried it in the Valley of Hamon-gog. ¹⁶[Also the name of the city shall be Hamonah.] Thus the land shall be purified.

¹⁷As for you, son of man, says the Lord GOD, say to birds of every kind and to all the wild beasts: Come together, from all sides gather for the slaughter I am about to provide for you, a great slaughter on the mountains of Israel: you shall have flesh to eat and blood to drink. ¹⁸You shall eat the flesh of warriors and drink the blood of the princes of the land [rams, lambs, and goats, bullocks, fatlings of Bashan, all of them]. ¹⁹From the slaughter which I will provide for you, you shall eat fat until you are filled and drink blood until you are drunk. ²⁰You shall be filled at my table with horses and riders, with warriors and soldiers of every kind, says the Lord GOD.

39, 11: The Valley of Abarim: in the Abarim mountains, east of the Jordan. Hamon-gog: means "the horde of Gog."

Israel's Return. ²¹Thus I will display my glory among the nations, and all the nations shall see the judgment I have executed and the hand I have laid upon them. ²²From that day forward the house of Israel shall know that I am the LORD, their God. ²³The nations shall know that because of its sins the house of Israel went into exile; for they transgressed against me, and I hid my face from them and handed them over to their foes, so that all of them fell by the sword. ²⁴According to their uncleanness and their transgressions I dealt with them, hiding my face from them.

²⁵Therefore, thus says the Lord GOD: Now I will restore the fortunes of Jacob and have pity on the whole house of Israel, and I will be jealous for my holy name. ²⁶They shall forget their disgrace and all the times they broke faith with me, when they live in security on their land with no one to frighten them. ²⁷When I bring them back from among the peoples, I will gather them from the lands of their enemies, and will prove my holiness through them in the sight of many nations. ^{28v}Thus they shall know that I, the LORD, am their God, since I who exiled them among the nations, will gather them back on their land, not leaving any of them behind. ²⁹No longer will I hide my face from them, for I have poured out my spirit upon the house of Israel, says the Lord GOD.

V: The New Israel*

The New Temple

CHAPTER 40

See RG 232

The Man with a Measure. ¹On the tenth day of the month beginning the twenty-fifth year of our exile, fourteen years after the city was taken, that very day the hand of the LORD came upon me and brought me ²in di-vine visions to the land of Israel, where he set me down on a very high mountain. On it there seemed to be a city being built before me. ³When he had brought me there, all at once I saw a man whose appearance was that of bronze; he was standing in the gate, holding a linen cord and a measuring rod. ⁴The man said to me, "Son of man, look carefully and listen intently, and pay strict attention to all that I will show you, for you have been brought here so that I might show it to you. Tell the house of Israel all that you see." ⁵[Then I saw an outer wall that completely surrounded the temple. The man was holding a measuring rod six cubits long, each cubit being a cubit and a handbreadth;* he measured the width and the height of the structure, each of which was found to be one rod.]

*The East Gate.** ⁶Then he went to the gate which faced the east, climbed its steps, and measured the gate's threshold, which was found to be a rod wide. ⁷The cells were a rod long and a rod wide, and the pilasters between the cells measured five cubits. The threshold of the gate adjoining the vestibule of the gate toward the inside measured one rod. ⁸He measured the vestibule of the gate, ⁹which was eight cubits, and its pilasters, which were two cubits. The vestibule of the gate was toward the inside. ¹⁰The cells of the east gate were three on either side, of equal size, and the pilasters on either side were also of equal size. ¹¹He measured the gate's entrance, which was ten cubits wide, while the width of the gate's passage itself was thirteen cubits. ¹²The border before each of the cells on both sides was one cubit; the cells themselves were six cubits on either side, from opening to opening. ¹³He measured the gate from the back wall of one cell to the back wall of the cell on the opposite

40, 1—48, 35: This lengthy vision of the new Israel is dated (Ez 40, 1) April 28, 573 B.C. It is largely concerned with the new temple and the prescriptions to govern it, but other details of the restored commonwealth are included, forming a kind of program for the future. The literary form of the vision has been aptly termed "utopian": it is plain that the prophet did not expect a literal fulfillment of much of what he described. The passage doubtless underwent successive additions, both from the prophet and from later inspired writers.

40, 5: A cubit and a handbreadth: the ordinary cubit con-sisted of six handbreadths; the great cubit, of seven. In measuring the temple, a rod six great cubits long was used. The ordinary cubit was about one and a half feet, or, more exactly 17.5 inches; the large cubit, 20.4 inches.

40, 6-16: The east gate, leading into the outer court of the temple, is described more fully than the north and south gates, which, however, were of the same dimensions. On the west side of the outer court there was a large building instead of a gate (Ez 41, 12).

v: Ez 36, 23.

side: the width was twenty-five cubits. [14]He measured the vestibule, which was twenty-five cubits. The pilasters adjoining the court on either side were six cubits. [15]The length of the gate from the front entrance to the front of the vestibule on the inside was fifty cubits. [16]Within the gateway on both sides there were splayed windows let into the cells [and into their pilasters]; likewise, within the vestibule on both sides there were windows. The pilasters were decorated with palms.

The Outer Court. [17]Then he brought me to the outer court,* where there were chambers and a pavement. The pavement was laid all around the court, and the chambers, which were on the pavement, were thirty in number. [18]The pavement lay alongside the gates, as wide as the gates were long; this was the lower pavement. [19]He measured the width of the court from the front of the lower gate to the front of the inner gate; it was one hundred cubits between them.

The North Gate. Then he proceeded north, [20]where, on the outer court, there was a gate facing north, whose length and width he measured. [21]Its cells, three on either side, its pilasters, and its vestibule had the same measurements as those of the first gate; it was fifty cubits long and twenty-five cubits wide. [22]Its windows, the windows of its vestibule, and its palm decorations were of the same proportions as those of the gate facing the east. Seven steps led up to it, and its vestibule was toward the inside. [23]The inner court had a gate opposite the north gate, just as at the east gate; he measured one hundred cubits from one gate to the other.

The South Gate. [24]Then he led me south, to where there was a southern gate, whose cells, pilasters, and vestibule he measured; they were the same size as the others. [25]The gate and its vestibule had windows on both sides, like the other windows. It was fifty cubits long and twenty-five cubits wide. [26]It was ascended by seven steps; its vestibule was toward the inside; and it was decorated with palms here and there on its pilasters. [27]The inner court also had a southern gate; from gate to gate he measured one hundred cubits.

Gates of the Inner Court. * [28]Then he brought me to the inner court by the south gate, where he measured the south gate. Its dimensions were the same as the others; [29]its cells, its pilasters, and its vestibule were the same size as the others. The gate and its vestibule had windows on both sides; and it was fifty cubits long and twenty-five cubits wide. [31]But its vestibule was toward the outer court; palms were on its pilasters, and it had a stairway of eight steps. [32]Then he brought me to the gate facing the east, where he measured the gate, whose dimensions were found to be the same. [33]Its cells, its pilasters, and its vestibule were the same size as the others; the gate and its vestibule had windows on both sides; it was fifty cubits long and twenty-five cubits wide. [34]But its vestibule was toward the outer court; palms were on its pilasters here and there, and it had a stairway of eight steps. [35]Then he brought me to the north gate, where he measured the dimensions [36]of its cells, its pilasters, and its vestibule, and found them the same. The gate and its vestibule had windows on both sides; it was fifty cubits long and twenty-five cubits wide. [37]Its vestibule was toward the outer court; palms were on its pilasters here and there, and it had a stairway of eight steps.

Side Rooms. [38]There was a chamber opening off the vestibule of the gate, where the holocausts were rinsed. [39]In the vestibule of the gate there were two tables on either side, on which were slaughtered the sin offerings and guilt offerings. [40]Along the wall of the vestibule, but outside, near the entrance of the north gate, were two tables, and on the other side of the vestibule of the gate there were two tables. [41]There were four tables on either side of the gate [eight tables], on which the sacrifices were slaughtered. [42]There were four tables for holocausts, made of cut stone, one and a half cubits long, one and a half cubits wide, and one cubit

---

40, 17: The outer court: the court outside the temple area proper, which had its own inner court (vv 28-37).

40, 28-37: The gates leading into the inner court of the temple area correspond to the gates leading into the outer court, with the exception that their vestibules are on the outer rather than the inner side. (Verse 30, a dittography of v 29, is omitted.)

The Temple

Ezekiel's temple (40, 48—41, 26) is constructed according to a three-room pattern, like that of Solomon's temple (1 Kgs 6) and other examples of temples and royal palaces from Canaan and Syria. The three rooms are the vestibule (35 feet by 21 feet), an entry or reception room; the nave (71 feet by 25 feet), the main hall where the temple furnishings are placed; and the inner room (35 feet by 35 feet), also known as the holy of holies, God's throne room which houses the ark of the covenant. Ezekiel does not enter the inner room because this is restricted to the high priest on Yom Kippur or the Day of Atonement (Lv 16).

high. *43*The ledges, a handbreadth wide, were set on the inside all around, and on them were laid the instruments with which the holocausts were slaughtered. On the tables themselves the flesh was laid. *44*He then led me to the inner court where there were two chambers, one beside the north gate, facing south, and the other beside the south gate, facing north. *45*He said to me, "This chamber which faces south is for the priests who have charge of the temple, *46*and the chamber which faces north is for the priests who have charge of the altar. These are the Zadokites,* the only Levites who may come near to minister to the LORD." *47*Then he measured the court, which was a hundred cubits long and a hundred cubits wide, a perfect square. The altar stood in front of the temple.

The Temple Building.* *48*Then he brought me into the vestibule of the temple and measured the pilasters on each side, which were five cubits. The width of the doorway was fourteen cubits, and the side walls on either side of the door measured three cubits. *49**The vestibule was twenty cubits wide and twelve cubits deep; ten steps led up to it, and there were columns by the pilasters, one on either side.

See RG 232

CHAPTER 41

*1*Then he brought me to the nave and measured the pilasters, which were six cubits thick on either side. *2*The width of the entrance was ten cubits, and the walls at either side of it measured five cubits each. He measured the length of the nave, which was found to be forty cubits, while its width was twenty.

*3*Then he went in beyond and measured the pilasters flanking that entrance, which were two cubits; the width of the entrance was six cubits, and the walls at either side of it extended seven cubits each. *4*He measured the space beyond the nave, twenty cubits long and twenty cubits wide, and said to me, "This is the holy of holies."*

*5*Then he measured the wall of the temple, which was six cubits thick; the side chambers, which extended all the way around the temple, had a width of four cubits. *6*There were thirty side chambers built one above the other in three stories, and there were offsets in the outside wall of the temple that enclosed the side chambers; these served as supports, so that there were no supports in the temple wall proper. *7*There was a broad circular passageway that led upward to the side chambers, for the temple was enclosed all the way around and all the way upward; therefore the temple had a broad way running upward so that one could pass from the lowest to the middle and the highest story. *8*About the temple was a raised pavement completely enclosing it—the foundations of the side chambers—a full rod of six cubits in extent. *9*The width of the outside wall which enclosed the side chambers was five cubits. Between the side chambers of the temple *10*and the chambers of the court was an open space twenty cubits wide going all around the temple. *11*The side chambers had en-

---

40, 46: The Zadokites: descendants of the priestly line of Zadok; cf 2 Sm 15, 24-29; 1 Kgs 1, 32ff; 2, 35.

40, 48—41, 15: The description of Ezekiel's visionary temple closely follows the description of the temple of Solomon (1 Kgs 6).

40, 49—41, 4: Vestibule . . . nave . . . holy of holies: the three divisions of the temple building in progressing order of sanctity. The last is called "the inner sanctuary" in 1 Kgs 6.

trances to the open space, one entrance on the north and another on the south. The width of the wall surrounding the open space was five cubits. *12*The building* fronting the free area on the west side was seventy cubits front to back; the wall of the building was five cubits thick all around, and it measured ninety cubits from side to side. *13*He measured the temple, which was one hundred cubits long. The free area, together with the building and its walls, was a hundred cubits in length. *14*The façade of the temple, along with the free area, on the east side, was one hundred cubits wide. *15*He measured the building which lay the length of the free area and behind it, and together with its walls on both sides it was one hundred cubits.

Interior of the Temple. The inner nave and the outer vestibule *16*were paneled with precious wood all around, covered from the ground to the windows. There were splayed windows with trellises about them [facing the threshold]. *17*As high as the lintel of the door, even into the interior part of the temple as well as outside, on every wall on every side in both the inner and outer rooms were carved *18*the figures of cherubim and palmtrees: a palmtree between every two cherubim. Each cherub had two faces: *19*a man's face looking at a palmtree on one side, and a lion's face looking at a palmtree on the other; thus they were figured on every side throughout the whole temple. *20*From the ground to the lintel of the door the cherubim and palmtrees were carved on the walls. *21*The way into the nave was a square doorframe. In front of the holy place was something that looked like *22*a wooden altar,* three cubits in height, two cubits long, and two cubits wide. It had corners, and its base and sides were of wood. He said to me, "This is the table which is before the LORD." *23*The nave had a double door, and also the holy place had *24*a double door. Each door had two movable leaves; two leaves were on one doorjamb and two on the other. *25*Carved upon them [on the doors of the nave] were cherubim and palmtrees, like

those carved on the walls. Before the vestibule outside was a wooden lattice. *26*There were splayed windows [and palmtrees] on both side walls of the vestibule, and the side chambers of the temple. . . .

CHAPTER 42

See RG 232

Other Structures. *1*Then he led me north to the outer court, bringing me to some chambers on the north that lay across the free area and which were also across from the building. *2*Their length was a hundred cubits on the north side, and they were fifty cubits wide. *3*Across the twenty cubits of the inner court and the pavement of the outer court, there were three parallel rows of them on different levels. *4*In front of the chambers, to the inside, was a walk ten cubits broad and a wall of one cubit; but the entrances of the chambers were on the north. *5*The outermost chambers were the lowest, for the system of levels set them at a level lower than the closest chambers and those in between;* *6*for they were in three rows and had no foundations to conform with the foundations of the courts, therefore they were on a lower terrace of the ground than the closest and the middle chambers. *7*On the far side there was a wall running parallel to the chambers along the outer court; its length before these chambers was fifty cubits, *8*for the length of the chambers belonging to the outer court was fifty cubits, but along its entire length the wall measured one hundred cubits. *9*Below these chambers there was the way in from the east, so that one could enter from the outer court *10*where the wall of the court began.

To the south along the side of the free area and the building there were also chambers, *11*before which was a passage. These looked like the chambers to the north, just as long and just as wide, with the same exits and plan and entrances. *12*Below the chambers to the south there was an entrance at the beginning of the way which led to the back wall, by which one could enter from the east. *13*He

41, 12: The building: the function of this structure lying behind the temple is never specified.

41, 22: A wooden altar: the altar of incense, standing in the nave at the entrance to the holy of holies.

42, 5f: The three rows of identical chambers, since they rested on different ground levels, necessarily had roofs on correspondingly different levels.

said to me, "The north and south chambers which border on the free area are the sanctuary chambers; here the priests who draw near to the LORD shall eat the most sacred meals, and here they shall keep the most sacred offerings: cereal offerings, sin offerings, and guilt offerings; for it is a holy place.* ¹⁴When the priests have once entered, they shall not leave the holy place for the outer court until they have left here the clothing in which they ministered, for it is holy. They shall put on other garments, and then approach the place destined for the people."

Measuring the Outer Court. ¹⁵When he had finished measuring the inner temple area, he brought me out by way of the gate which faces east and measured all the limits of the court. ¹⁶He measured the east side: five hundred cubits by his measuring rod. Then he turned ¹⁷and measured the north side: five hundred cubits by the measuring rod. He turned ¹⁸to the south and measured five hundred cubits by the measuring rod. ¹⁹Then he turned to the west and measured five hundred cubits by the measuring rod. ²⁰Thus he measured it in the four directions, five hundred cubits long and five hundred cubits wide. It was surrounded by a wall, to separate the sacred from the profane.

Restoration of the Temple

CHAPTER 43

See RG 232

The Return of the Lord. ¹Then he led me to the gate which faces the east, ²and there I saw the glory of the God of Israel coming from the east. I heard a sound like the roaring of many waters, and the earth shone with his glory. ³ʷThe vision was like that which I had seen when he came to destroy the city, and like that which I had seen by the river Chebar. I fell prone ⁴as the glory of the LORD entered the temple by way of the gate which faces the

east, ⁵but spirit lifted me up and brought me to the inner court. And I saw that the temple was filled with the glory of the LORD. ⁶Then I heard someone speaking to me from the temple, while the man stood beside me. ⁷The voice said to me: Son of man, this is where my throne shall be, this is where I will set the soles of my feet; here I will dwell among the Israelites forever. Never again shall they and their kings profane my holy name with their harlotries and with the corpses of their kings [their high places]. ⁸When they placed their threshold against my threshold* and their doorpost next to mine, so that only a wall was between us, they profaned my holy name by their abominable deeds; therefore I consumed them in my wrath. ⁹From now on they shall put far from me their harlotry and the corpses of their kings, and I will dwell in their midst forever.

The Law of the Temple. ¹⁰As for you, son of man, describe the temple to the house of Israel [that they may be ashamed of their sins], both its measurements and its design; ¹¹[and if they are ashamed of all that they have done,] make known to them the form and design of the temple, its exits and entrances, all its statutes and laws; write these down for them to see, that they may carefully observe all its laws and statutes. ¹²This is the law of the temple: its whole surrounding area on the mountain top shall be most sacred.

The Altar. ¹³These were the measurements of the altar* in cubits of one cubit plus a handbreadth. Its base was one cubit high and one cubit deep, with a rim around its edge of one span. The height of the altar itself was as follows: ¹⁴from its base at the bottom up to the lower ledge it was two cubits high, and this ledge was one cubit deep; from the lower to the upper ledge it was four cubits high, and this ledge also was one cubit deep; ¹⁵the hearth of the altar was four cubits high, and extending from the top of the hearth

---

42, 13: The function of these chambers is explained again in Ez 46, 19f.

43, 8: They placed their threshold against my threshold: the preexilic temple and the royal palace belonged to the same complex of buildings, and this physical proximity was reflected in the use made of the temple by kings like Ahaz and Manasseh, who treated it as their pri-

vate chapel for pagan rites. In the new Israel the temple is free, even physically, from civil jurisdiction; cf Ez 45, 7f.

43, 13: The altar: of holocausts, standing in the inner court of the temple area; cf Ez 40, 47.

w: Ez 1, 1.

were the four horns of the altar. [16]The hearth was a square: twelve cubits long and twelve cubits wide. [17]The upper ledge was also a square: fourteen cubits long and fourteen cubits wide. The lower ledge, likewise a square, was sixteen cubits long and sixteen cubits wide, with a half-cubit rim surrounding it. And there was a base of one cubit all around. The steps of the altar face the east.

[18]Then he said to me: Son of man, thus says the Lord GOD: These are the statutes for the altar when it is set up for the offering of holocausts upon it and for the sprinkling of blood against it. [19]Give a young bull as a sin offering to the priests, the Levites who are of the line of Zadok, who draw near me to minister to me, says the Lord GOD. [20]Take some of its blood and put it on the four horns of the altar, and on the four corners of the ledge, and on the rim all around. Thus you shall purify it and make atonement for it. [21]Then take the bull of the sin offering, which is to be burnt in a designated part of the temple, outside the sanctuary. [22]On the second day present an unblemished he-goat as a sin offering, to purify the altar as was done with the bull. [23]When you have finished the purification, bring an unblemished young bull and an unblemished ram from the flock, [24]and present them before the LORD; the priests shall strew salt on them and offer them to the LORD as holocausts. [25]Daily for seven days you shall offer a he-goat as a sin offering, and a young bull and a ram from the flock, all unblemished, shall be offered [26]for seven days. Thus atonement shall be made for the altar, and it shall be purified and dedicated. [27]And when these days are over, from the eighth day on, the priests shall offer your holocausts and peace offerings on the altar. Then I will accept you, says the Lord GOD.

CHAPTER 44

See RG 232 **The Closed Gate.** [1]Then he brought me back to the outer gate of the sanctuary, facing the east; but it was closed. [2]He said to me: This gate is to remain closed; it is not to be opened for anyone to enter by it; since the LORD, the God of Israel, has entered by it, it shall remain closed. [3]Only the prince may sit down in it to eat his meal in the presence of the LORD. He must enter by way of the vestibule of the gate, and leave by the same way.[*]

The New Law

Admission to the Temple. [4]Then he brought me by way of the north gate to the façade of the temple, and when I looked I saw the glory of the LORD filling the LORD's temple, and I fell prone. [5]Then he said to me: Son of man, pay strict attention, look carefully, and listen intently to all that I will tell you about the statutes and laws of the LORD's temple; be attentive in regard to those who are to be admitted to the temple and all those who are to be excluded from the sanctuary. [6]Say to that rebellious house, the house of Israel: Thus says the Lord GOD: Enough of all these abominations of yours, O house of Israel! [7]You have admitted foreigners, uncircumcised both in heart and flesh, to my sanctuary to profane it when you offered me food, fat, and blood;[*] thus you have broken my covenant by all your abominations. [8]Instead of caring for the service of my temple, you have appointed such as these to serve me in my sanctuary in your stead. [9]Thus says the Lord GOD: No foreigners, uncircumcised in heart and in flesh, shall ever enter my sanctuary; none of the foreigners who live among the Israelites.

Levites.[*] [10]But as for the Levites who departed from me when Israel strayed from me to pursue their idols, they shall bear the consequences of their sin. [11]They shall serve in my sanctuary as gatekeepers and temple servants; they shall slaughter the holocausts and the sacrifices for the people, and they shall stand before the people to minister for them. [12]Because they used to minister for them before their idols, and became an occasion of sin to the house of Israel, therefore

---

44, 3: The prince stands at the eastern gate of the inner court while his sacrifice is offered up (Ez 46, 2); he then goes to the vestibule of the outer court, there to partake of his sacrificial meal. The closed outer gate on the eastern side signifies that the Lord has entered the temple permanently, not to depart again.

44, 7ff: In the preexilic temple various menial services had been performed by foreigners; cf Jos 9, 22-27. In the new temple the Levites will perform these services (vv 10-14).

44, 10-14: Levites other than the Zadokite priesthood of Jerusalem had performed priestly functions at the various

I have sworn an oath against them, says the Lord GOD: they shall bear the consequences of their sin. [13]They shall no longer draw near me to serve as my priests, nor shall they touch any of my sacred things, or the most sacred things. Thus they shall bear their disgrace because of all their abominable deeds. [14]But I will set them to the service of the temple, for all its work and for everything that is to be done in it.

Priests. [15]As for the levitical priests, however, the Zadokites who cared for my sanctuary when the Israelites strayed from me, they shall draw near me to minister to me, and they shall stand before me to offer me fat and blood, says the Lord GOD. [16]It is they who shall enter my sanctuary, they who shall approach my table to minister to me, and they who shall carry out my service. [17]Whenever they enter the gates of the inner court, they shall wear linen garments; they shall not put on anything woolen when they minister at the gates of the inner court or within the temple. [18x]They shall have linen turbans on their heads and linen drawers on their loins; they shall not gird themselves with anything that causes sweat. [19y]When they are to go out to the people in the outer court, they shall take off the garments in which they ministered and leave them in the chambers of the sanctuary, putting on other garments; thus they will not transmit holiness to the people* with their garments.

[20z]They shall not shave their heads nor let their hair hang loose, but they shall keep their hair carefully trimmed. [21a]No priest shall drink wine when he is to enter the inner court. [22b]They shall not take for their wives either widows or divorced women, but only virgins of the race of Israel; however, they may marry women who are the widows of priests. [23]They shall teach my people to distinguish between the sacred and the profane,

and make known to them the difference between the clean and the unclean. [24c]In capital cases they shall stand as judges, judging them according to my decrees. They shall observe my laws and statutes on all my festivals, and keep my sabbaths holy.

[25d]They shall not make themselves unclean by coming near any dead person, unless it be their father, mother, son, daughter, brother, or maiden sister; for these they may make themselves unclean. [26]After a priest has been cleansed, he must wait an additional seven days, [27]and on the day he enters the inner court to minister in the sanctuary, he shall present his sin offering, says the Lord GOD. [28e]They shall have no inheritance, for I am their inheritance; you shall give them no property in Israel, for I am their property. [29f]They shall eat the cereal offering, the sin offering, and the guilt offering; whatever is under the ban* in Israel shall be theirs. [30g]All the choicest first fruits of every kind, and all the best of your offerings of every kind, shall belong to the priests; likewise the best of your dough you shall give to the priests to bring a blessing down upon your house. [31h]The priests shall not eat anything, whether flesh or fowl, that has died of itself or has been killed by wild beasts.

CHAPTER 45

See RG 232

The Sacred Tract. [1]When you apportion the land into inheritances, you shall set apart a sacred tract of land for the LORD, twenty-five thousand cubits long and twenty thousand wide; its whole area shall be sacred. [2]Of this land a square plot, five hundred by five hundred cubits, surrounded by a free space of fifty cubits, shall be assigned to the sanctuary. [3]Also from this sector measure off a strip, twenty-five thousand cubits long and ten thousand wide, within which

---

sanctuaries and high places in Israel and Judah, where the worship of the Lord had often been corrupted with pagan elements. The demotion of the Levites to menial service in the temple was enforced in the actual restoration after the exile, and explains why relatively few Levites were willing to return; cf Ezr 8, 15ff.

44, 19: Thus they will not transmit holiness to the people: holiness was thought of as something physical, as though it were communicable, and therefore not to be brought in con-

tact with unconsecrated persons.

44, 29: Under the ban: dedicated to the Lord, withdrawn from profane use.

x: Ex 28, 40. 42; 29, 9; 38, 28; Lv 6, 3.   y: Ez 42, 13. 14.   z: Lv 21, 5.   a: Lv 10, 9.   b: Lv 21, 7. 14.   c: Dt 17, 9; 19, 17.   d: Lv 21, 1ff. 11.   e: Nm 18, 20; Dt 18, 1.   f: Lv 2, 3. 10; 6, 9. 22; 7, 9; 10, 12; Nm 18, 9; 18, 14.   g: Ex 34, 26; Dt 18, 4.   h: Lv 22, 8.

shall be the sanctuary, the holy of holies. [4]This shall be the sacred part of the land belonging to the priests, the ministers of the sanctuary, who draw near to minister to the LORD; it shall be a place for their homes and pasture land for their cattle. [5]Also there shall be a strip twenty-five thousand cubits long and ten thousand wide as property for the Levites, the ministers of the temple, that they may have cities to live in. [6]As property of the City you shall designate a strip five thousand cubits wide and twenty-five thousand long, parallel to the sacred tract; this shall belong to the whole house of Israel. [7]The prince shall have a section bordering on both sides of the combined sacred tract and City property, extending westward on the western side and eastward on the eastern side, corresponding in length to one of the tribal portions from the western boundary to the eastern boundary [8]of the land. This shall be his property in Israel, so that the princes of Israel will no longer oppress my people, but will leave the land to the house of Israel according to their tribes.

*Weights and Measures.** [9]Thus says the Lord GOD: Enough, you princes of Israel! Put away violence and oppression, and do what is right and just! Stop evicting my people! says the Lord GOD. [10i]You shall have honest scales, an honest ephah, and an honest liquid measure. [11]The ephah and the liquid measure shall be of the same size: the liquid measure equal to a tenth of a homer, and the ephah equal to a tenth of a homer; by the homer they shall be determined. [12j]The shekel shall be twenty gerahs. Twenty shekels, twenty-five shekels, plus fifteen shekels shall be your mina.

Offerings. [13]These are the offerings you shall make: one sixth of an ephah from each homer of wheat, and one sixth of an ephah from each homer of barley. [14]The regulation for oil: for every measure of oil, a tenth of a measure, computed by the kor* of ten liquid measures [or a homer, for ten liquid measures make a homer]. [15]One sheep from the flock for every two hundred from the pasturage of Israel, for sacrifice—holocausts and peace offerings and atonement sacrifices, says the Lord GOD. [16]All the people of the land shall be bound to this offering [for the prince in Israel]. [17]It shall be the duty of the prince to provide the holocausts, cereal offerings, and libations on the feasts, new moons, and sabbaths, on all the festivals of the house of Israel. He shall offer the sin offerings, cereal offerings, holocausts, and peace offerings, to make atonement on behalf of the house of Israel.

The Passover. [18]Thus says the Lord GOD: On the first day of the first month you shall use an unblemished young bull as a sacrifice to purify the sanctuary. [19]Then the priest shall take some of the blood from the sin offering and put it on the doorposts of the temple, on the four corners of the ledge of the altar, and on the doorposts of the gates of the inner court. [20]You shall repeat this on the first day of the seventh month for those who have sinned through inadvertence or ignorance; thus you shall make atonement for the temple. [21k]On the fourteenth day of the first month you shall observe the feast of the Passover; for seven days unleavened bread is to be eaten. [22]On that day the prince shall offer on his own behalf, and on behalf of all the people of the land, a bull as a sin offering. [23]On each of the seven days of the feast he shall offer as a holocaust to the Lord seven bulls and seven rams without blemish, and as a sin offering he shall offer one male goat each day. [24]As a cereal offering he shall offer one ephah for each bull and one ephah for each ram; and he shall offer one hin* of oil for each ephah.

The Feast of Booths. [25]On the fifteenth

45, 9-12: Besides the land monopoly fostered by royal greed and collusion with the wealthy (Mi 2, 2; Is 3, 12-15; 5, 8-10), one grave social evil of preexilic Israel was dishonesty in business; cf Hos 12, 8; Am 8, 5. Ephah: a dry measure; liquid measure: in Hebrew, a "bath," standardized according to the homer (a dry measure of about 10 bushels, or 80 gallons). In v 12 reference is made to the change in value of the mina: before the exile it was valued at 50 shekels, but afterward, in imitation of Babylonian practice, the 60-shekel mina was adopted. The shekel was a unit of weight slightly less than half an ounce. As a monetary unit, the value obviously differed greatly, depending on whether it was a gold or a silver shekel.

45, 14: Kor: both a liquid and a dry measure, corresponding to the homer.

45, 24: Hin: a sixth part of the liquid measure called a bath.

i: Lv 19, 35; Dt 25, 13-16; Hos 12, 8; Am 8, 5; Mi 6, 10f.   *j:* Ex 30, 13; Lv 27, 25; Nm 3, 47; 18, 16.   *k:* Ex 12, 6; Lv 23, 5; Nm 28, 16.

day of the seventh month, the feast day, and for seven days, he shall perform the same rites, making the same sin offerings, the same holocausts, the same cereal offerings and offerings of oil.

CHAPTER 46

See RG
232

Sabbaths. [1]Thus says the Lord GOD: The gate toward the east of the inner court shall remain closed throughout the six working days, but on the sabbath and on the day of the new moon it shall be open. [2]The prince shall enter from outside by way of the vestibule of the gate and remain standing at the doorpost of the gate; then while the priests offer his holocausts and peace offerings, he shall worship at the threshold of the gate and then leave; the gate shall not be closed until evening. [3]The people of the land shall worship before the LORD at the door of this gate on the sabbaths and new moons. [4l]The holocausts which the prince presents to the LORD on the sabbath shall consist of six unblemished lambs and an unblemished ram, [5]together with a cereal offering of one ephah for the ram, whatever he pleases for the lambs, and a hin of oil for each ephah. [6m]On the day of the new moon he shall provide an unblemished young bull, also six lambs and a ram without blemish, [7]with a cereal offering of one ephah for the bull and one for the ram, for the lambs as much as he has at hand, and for each ephah a hin of oil.

Ritual Laws. [8]The prince shall always enter and depart by the vestibule of the gate. [9n]When the people of the land enter the presence of the LORD to worship on the festivals, if they enter by the north gate they shall leave by the south gate, and if they enter by the south gate they shall leave by the north gate; no one shall return by the gate through which he has entered, but he shall leave by the opposite gate. [10]The prince shall be in their midst when they enter, and he shall also leave with them. [11]On the feasts and festivals the cereal offering shall be an ephah for a bull, an ephah for a ram, but for the lambs as much as one pleases, and a hin of oil with each ephah. [12]When the prince makes a freewill offering to the LORD, whether holocausts or peace offerings, the eastern gate shall be opened for him, and he shall offer his holocausts or his peace offerings as on the sabbath; then he shall leave, and the gate shall be closed after his departure. [13o]He shall offer as a daily holocaust to the LORD an unblemished yearling lamb; this he shall offer every morning. [14]With it every morning he shall provide as a cereal offering one sixth of an ephah, with a third of a hin of oil to moisten the fine flour. This cereal offering to the LORD is mandatory with the established holocaust. [15p]The lamb, the cereal offering, and the oil are to be offered every morning as an established holocaust.

The Prince and the Land. [16]Thus says the Lord GOD: If the prince makes a gift of part of his inheritance to any of his sons, it shall belong to his sons; that property is theirs by inheritance. [17]But if he makes a gift of part of his inheritance to one of his servants, it shall belong to the latter only until the year of release,* when it shall revert to the prince. Only the inheritance given to his sons is permanent. [18]The prince shall not seize any part of the inheritance of the people by evicting them from their property. He shall provide an inheritance for his sons from his own property, so that none of my people will be driven from their property.

The Temple Kitchens. [19]Then he brought me by the entrance which is on the side of the gate to the chambers [of the sanctuary, reserved to the priests] which face the north. There, at their west end, I saw a place, [20]concerning which he said to me, "Here the priests cook the guilt offerings and the sin offerings, and bake the cereal offerings, so that they do not have to take them into the outer court at the risk of transmitting holiness to the people." [21]Then he led me into the outer court and had me pass around the four corners of the court, and I saw that in each corner there was another court: [22]in the four corners of the court, minor courts, forty

---

46, 17: The year of release: the jubilee year; cf Lv 25, 23-55.

l: Nm 28, 9f.   m: Nm 28, 11-15.   n: Ex 23, 17; 34, 23; Dt 16, 16.   o: Ex 29, 38-42; Nm 28, 3-8.   p: Ex 29, 42.

The Role of the Temple

Once the temple is reestablished, water streams up from below the threshold of the temple (47, 1) to water the land of Israel. This indicates the role of the temple as the center of creation (the Garden of Eden, Gn 2, 10–14; Ps 46, 4). The course of the water reflects that of the Gihon spring (cf the Edenic river, Gn 2, 10. 13), and emerges east of the city of David where its waters flow south into the Siloam pool (see 1 Kgs 1, 32–40; Is 7, 3; 2 Chr 32, 4). The water flows into the Jordan Valley and eventually into the Arabah (the Jordan rift where the Dead Sea is located) to transform the waters of the Dead Sea into fresh water that supports fish and fruit trees (see Gn 2, 1–14). Everywhere it flows, the stream brings abundant life and food, a strong counterpoint to the desolation described earlier in Ezekiel and by other prophets.

cubits long and thirty wide, all four of them the same size. ²³A wall of stones surrounded each of the four, and hearths were built beneath the stones all the way around. ²⁴He said to me, "These are the kitchens where the temple ministers cook the sacrifices of the people."

CHAPTER 47

See RG 232

The Wonderful Stream.* ¹Then he brought me back to the entrance of the temple, and I saw water flowing out from beneath the threshold of the temple toward the east, for the façade of the temple was toward the east; the water flowed down from the southern side of the temple, south of the altar.*q* ²He led me outside by the north gate, and around to the outer gate facing the east, where I saw water trickling from the southern side. ³Then when he had walked off to the east with a measuring cord in his hand, he measured off a thousand cubits and had me wade through the water, which was ankle-deep. ⁴He measured off another thousand and once more had me wade through the water, which was now knee-deep. Again he measured off a thousand and had me wade; the water was up to my waist. ⁵Once more he measured off a thousand, but there was now a river through which I could not wade; for the water had risen so high it had become a river that could not be crossed except by swimming. ⁶He asked me, "Have you seen this, son of man?" Then he brought me to the bank of the river, where he had me sit. ⁷Along the bank of the river I saw very many trees on both sides. ⁸He said to me, "This water flows into the eastern district down upon the Arabah, and empties into the sea, the salt waters, which it makes fresh. ⁹Wherever the river flows, every sort of living creature that can multiply shall live, and there shall be abundant fish, for wherever this water comes the sea shall be made fresh. ¹⁰Fishermen shall be standing along it from En-gedi to En-eglaim,* spreading their nets there. Its kinds of fish shall be like those of the Great Sea, very numerous. ¹¹Only its marshes and swamps shall not be made fresh; they shall be left for salt. ¹²Along both banks of the river, fruit trees of every kind shall grow; their leaves shall not fade, nor their fruit fail. Every month they shall bear fresh fruit, for they shall be watered by the flow from the sanctuary. Their fruit shall serve for food, and their leaves for medicine."

The New Israel

Boundaries of the Land.* ¹³Thus says the Lord GOD: These are the boundaries within which you shall apportion the land among the twelve tribes of Israel [Joseph having two

47, 1-12: The wonderful and superabundant stream flowing from the temple, restoring to fertility traditionally arid ground, is symbolic of the return of the conditions of primeval paradise; cf Gn 2, 10-14. Water signifies great blessings, just as dryness signifies a curse; cf Ez 26, 5. 14.

47, 10: From En-gedi to En-eglaim: the former was about halfway down the western shore of the Dead Sea, the latter

may have been at its northern extremity.

47, 13-20: These boundaries of the restored Israel correspond to those of the Davidic kingdom at its fullest extent, the so-called "ideal boundaries" of the promised land; cf Nm 34, 3-12.

q: Sir 24, 28f; Jl 4, 18; Zec 13, 1; Rv 22, 1f.

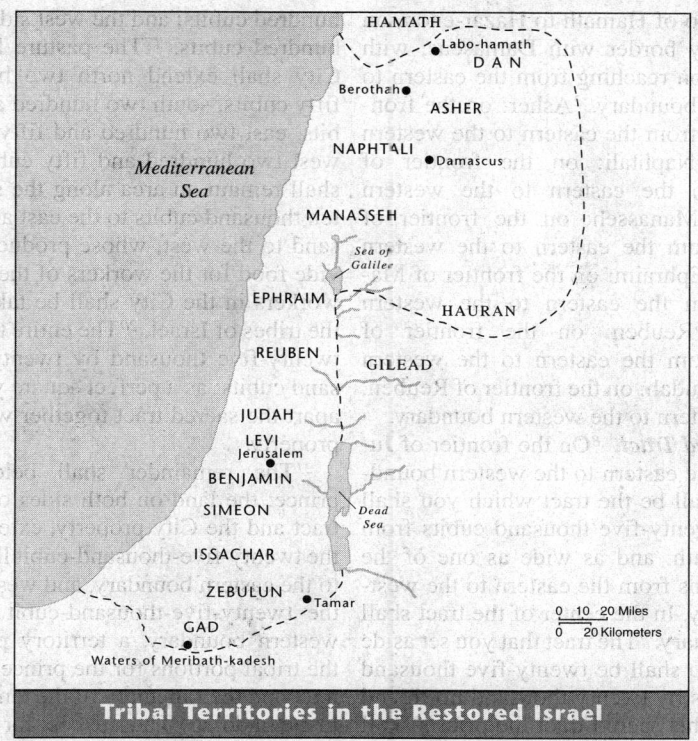

Tribal Territories in the Restored Israel

Map labels: HAMATH, Labo-hamath, DAN, Berothah, ASHER, NAPHTALI, Damascus, Mediterranean Sea, MANASSEH, Sea of Galilee, EPHRAIM, HAURAN, REUBEN, GILEAD, JUDAH, LEVI, Jerusalem, BENJAMIN, SIMEON, Dead Sea, ISSACHAR, ZEBULUN, Tamar, GAD, Waters of Meribath-kadesh

0 10 20 Miles
0 20 Kilometers

portions]. [14]All of you shall have a like portion in this land which I swore to give to your fathers, that it might fall to you as your inheritance. [15r]This is the boundary of the land on the north side: from the Great Sea in the direction of Hethlon, past Labo of Hamath, to Zedad, [16]Berothah, and Sibraim, along the frontiers of Hamath and Damascus, to Hazarenon which is on the border of the Hauran. [17]Thus the border shall extend from the sea to Hazar-enon, with the frontier of Hamath and Damascus to the north. This is the northern boundary. [18]The eastern boundary: between the Hauran—toward Damascus—and Gilead on the one side, and the land of Israel on the other side, the Jordan shall form the boundary down to the eastern sea as far as Tamar. This is the eastern boundary. [19]The southern boundary: from Tamar to the waters of Meribath-kadesh, thence to the Wadi of Egypt, and on to the Great Sea. This is the southern boundary. [20]The western boundary: the Great Sea forms the boundary up to a point parallel to Labo of Hamath. This is the western boundary.

The Northern Portions. [21]You shall distribute this land among yourselves according to the tribes of Israel. [22s]You shall allot it as inheritances for yourselves and for the aliens resident in your midst who have bred children among you. The latter shall be to you like native Israelites; along with you they shall receive inheritances among the tribes of Israel. [23]In whatever tribe the alien may be resident, there you shall assign him his inheritance, says the Lord GOD.

CHAPTER 48

See RG 232

[1]This is the list* of the tribes.[t] Dan: at the northern extremity, adjoining Hamath, all along from the approaches to Hethlon

48, 1-29: This distribution of the land among the tribes does not correspond to the geographical realities of Palestine. It is a description of the ideal order, like that in Ez 47, 1-12.

r: Nm 34, 7ff.   s: Ex 12, 48; Lv 19, 34; 24, 22; Nm 9, 14; Jos 8, 33.   t: Ez 47, 15ff.

through Labo of Hamath to Hazar-enon, on the northerly border with Damascus, with his possession reaching from the eastern to the western boundary. ²Asher: on the frontier of Dan, from the eastern to the western boundary. ³Naphtali: on the frontier of Asher, from the eastern to the western boundary. ⁴Manasseh: on the frontier of Naphtali, from the eastern to the western boundary. ⁵Ephraim: on the frontier of Manasseh, from the eastern to the western boundary. ⁶Reuben: on the frontier of Ephraim, from the eastern to the western boundary. ⁷Judah: on the frontier of Reuben, from the eastern to the western boundary.

The Sacred Tract. ⁸On the frontier of Judah, from the eastern to the western boundary there shall be the tract which you shall set apart, twenty-five thousand cubits from north to south, and as wide as one of the tribal portions from the eastern to the western boundary. In the center of the tract shall be the sanctuary. ⁹The tract that you set aside for the Lord shall be twenty-five thousand cubits across by twenty thousand north and south. ¹⁰In this sacred tract the priests shall have twenty-five thousand cubits on the north, ten thousand on the west, ten thousand on the east, and twenty-five thousand on the south; and the sanctuary of the Lord shall be in its center. ¹¹The consecrated priests, the Zadokites, who fulfilled my service and did not stray along with the Israelites as the Levites did, ¹²shall have within this tract of land their own most sacred domain, next to the territory of the Levites. ¹³The Levites shall have a territory corresponding to that of the priests, twenty-five thousand cubits by ten thousand. The whole tract shall be twenty-five thousand cubits across and twenty thousand north and south. ¹⁴They may not sell or exchange or alienate this, the best part of the land, for it is sacred to the Lord. ¹⁵The remaining five thousand cubits along the twenty-five-thousand-cubit line are profane land, assigned to the City for dwellings and pasture; the City shall be at their center. ¹⁶These are the dimensions of the City: the north side, forty-five hundred cubits; the south side, forty-five hundred cubits; the east side, forty-five

hundred cubits; and the west side, forty-five hundred cubits. ¹⁷The pasture lands of the City shall extend north two hundred and fifty cubits, south two hundred and fifty cubits, east two hundred and fifty cubits, and west two hundred and fifty cubits. ¹⁸There shall remain an area along the sacred tract, ten thousand cubits to the east and ten thousand to the west, whose produce shall provide food for the workers of the City. ¹⁹The workers in the City shall be taken from all the tribes of Israel. ²⁰The entire tract shall be twenty-five thousand by twenty-five thousand cubits; as a perfect square you shall set apart the sacred tract together with the City property.

²¹The remainder shall belong to the prince: the land on both sides of the sacred tract and the City property, extending along the twenty-five-thousand-cubit line eastward to the eastern boundary, and westward along the twenty-five-thousand-cubit line to the western boundary, a territory parallel with the tribal portions for the prince. The sacred tract and the sanctuary of the temple shall be in the middle. ²²Thus, except for the property of the Levites and the City property, which lie in the midst of the prince's property, the territory between the portions of Judah and of Benjamin shall belong to the prince.

The Southern Portions. ²³These are the remaining tribes. Benjamin: from the eastern to the western boundary. ²⁴Simeon: on the frontier of Benjamin, from the eastern to the western boundary. ²⁵Issachar: on the frontier of Simeon, from the eastern to the western boundary. ²⁶Zebulun: on the frontier of Issachar, from the eastern to the western boundary. ²⁷Gad: on the frontier of Zebulun, from the eastern to the western boundary. ²⁸Along the frontier of Gad shall be the southern boundary, which shall extend from Tamar to the waters of Meribath-kadesh, and from there to the Wadi of Egypt, and on to the Great Sea. ²⁹Such is the land which you shall apportion as inheritances among the tribes of Israel, and these are their portions, says the Lord God.

The Gates of the City. ³⁰These are the exits of the City, the gates of which are named after the tribes of Israel. On the north side, measuring forty-five hundred cubits, ³¹there shall be three gates: the gate of Reuben, the gate of Judah, and the gate of Levi. ³²On the east side, measuring forty-five hundred cubits, there shall be three gates: the gate of Joseph, the gate of Benjamin, and the gate of Dan. ³³On the south side, measuring forty-five hundred cubits, there shall be three gates: the gate of Simeon, the gate of Issachar, and the gate of Zebulun. ³⁴On the west side, measuring forty-five hundred cubits, there shall be three gates: the gate of Gad, the gate of Asher, and the gate of Naphtali. ³⁵The perimeter of the City is eighteen thousand cubits. The name of the City shall henceforth be "The LORD is here."

See RG
233–38

The Book of Daniel

This Book takes its name, not from the author, who is actually unknown, but from its hero, a young Jew taken early to Babylon, where he lived at least until 538 B.C. Strictly speaking, the book does not belong to the prophetic writings but rather to a distinctive type of literature known as "apocalyptic," of which it is an early specimen. Apocalyptic writing enjoyed its greatest popularity from 200 B.C. to 100 A.D., a time of distress and persecution for Jews, and later, for Christians. Though subsequent in time to the prophetic, apocalyptic literature has its roots in the teaching of the prophets, who often pointed ahead to the day of the Lord, the consummation of history. For both prophet and apocalyptist Yahweh was the Lord of history, and he would ultimately vindicate his people.

This work was composed during the bitter persecution carried on by Antiochus IV Epiphanes (167–164) and was written to strengthen and comfort the Jewish people in their ordeal.

The Book contains stories originating in and transmitted by popular traditions which tell of the trials and triumphs of the wise Daniel and his three companions. The moral is that men of faith can resist temptation and conquer adversity. The characters are not purely legendary but rest on older historical tradition. What is more important than the question of historicity, and closer to the intention of the author, is the fact that a persecuted Jew of the second century B.C. would quickly see the application of these stories to his own plight.

There follows a series of visions promising deliverance and glory to the Jews in the days to come. The great nations of the ancient world have risen in vain against Yahweh; his kingdom shall overthrow existing powers and last forever. Under this apocalyptic imagery are contained some of the best elements of prophetic teaching: the insistence on right conduct, the divine control over events, the certainty that the kingdom of God will ultimately triumph. The arrival of the kingdom is a central theme of the synoptic gospels, and Jesus, in calling himself the "Son of Man," reminds us that he fulfills the destiny of this mysterious figure in the seventh chapter of Daniel.

The added episodes of Susanna, Bel, and the Dragon, found only in the Greek version, are edifying short stories with a didactic purpose.

These three sections constitute the divisions of the Book of Daniel:

I: Daniel and the Kings of Babylon (1, 1—6, 29).

II: Daniel's Visions (7, 1—12, 13).

III: Appendix (13, 1—14, 42).

I: Daniel and the Kings of Babylon

CHAPTER 1

See RG
234–35

The Food Test. ¹In the third year of the reign of Jehoiakim, king of Judah, King Nebuchadnezzar of Babylon came and laid siege to Jerusalem.^{a 2b}The Lord handed over to him Jehoiakim, king of Judah, and some

a: 2 Kgs 24, 1; 2 Chr 36, 6; Jer 25, 1.   *b:* Dn 5, 2; Gn 10, 10; 2 Kgs 24, 2; 2 Chr 36, 7.

of the vessels of the temple of God, which he carried off to the land of Shinar,* and placed in the temple treasury of his god.

³The king told Ashpenaz, his chief chamberlain, to bring in some of the Israelites of royal blood and of the nobility, ⁴young men without any defect, handsome, intelligent and wise, quick to learn, and prudent in judgment, such as could take their place in the king's palace; they were to be taught the language and literature of the Chaldeans; ⁵after three years' training they were to enter the king's service. The king allotted them a daily portion of food and wine from the royal table. ⁶Among these were men of Judah: Daniel, Hananiah, Mishael, and Azariah. ⁷The chief chamberlain changed their names: Daniel to Belteshazzar, Hananiah to Shadrach, Mishael to Meshach, and Azariah to Abednego.*

⁸But Daniel was resolved not to defile himself with the king's food or wine; so he begged the chief chamberlain to spare him this defilement.* ⁹Though God had given Daniel the favor and sympathy of the chief chamberlain, ¹⁰he nevertheless said to Daniel, "I am afraid of my lord the king; it is he who allotted your food and drink. If he sees that you look wretched by comparison with the other young men of your age, you will endanger my life with the king." ¹¹Then Daniel said to the steward whom the chief chamberlain had put in charge of Daniel, Hananiah, Mishael, and Azariah, ¹²"Please test your servants for ten days. Give us vegetables to eat and water to drink. ¹³Then see how we look in comparison with the other young men who eat from the royal table, and treat your servants according to what you see." ¹⁴He acceded to this request, and tested them for ten days; ¹⁵after ten days they looked healthier and better fed than any of the young men who ate from the royal table. ¹⁶So the steward continued to take away the food and wine they were to receive, and gave them vegetables.

¹⁷To these four young men God gave knowledge and proficiency in all literature and science, and to Daniel the understanding of all visions and dreams. ¹⁸At the end of the time the king had specified for their preparation, the chief chamberlain brought them before Nebuchadnezzar. ¹⁹When the king had spoken with all of them, none was found equal to Daniel, Hananiah, Mishael, and Azariah; and so they entered the king's service. ²⁰In any question of wisdom or prudence which the king put to them, he found them ten times better than all the magicians and enchanters in his kingdom. ²¹ᶜDaniel remained there until the first year of King Cyrus.*

CHAPTER 2

See RG 234–35

*The King's Dream** ¹In the second year of his reign, King Nebuchadnezzar had a dream which left his spirit no rest and robbed him of his sleep. ²So he ordered that the magicians, enchanters, sorcerers, and Chaldeans* be summoned to interpret the dream for him. When they came and presented themselves to the king, ³he said to them, "I had a dream which will allow my spirit no rest until I know what it means." ⁴The Chaldeans answered the king [Aramaic]:* "O king, live forever! Tell your servants the dream and we will give its meaning." ⁵The king answered the Chaldeans, "This is what I have decided: unless you tell me the dream and its meaning, you shall be cut to pieces and your houses destroyed.

1, 2: Shinar: ancient name for Babylonia, a deliberate archaism in this text: cf Gn 10, 10; 11, 2.

1, 7: The young men are given Babylonian names as a sign of their adoption by the king.

1, 8: This defilement: the bread, meat, and wine of the Gentiles, which were unclean (Hos 9, 3; Tb 1, 12; Jdt 10, 5; 12, 1f) because they might have been offered to idols or prepared over firewood taken from a sacred grove. Only raw vegetables and water were safe from this danger (v 12).

1, 21: The first year of King Cyrus: the year of this Persian king's conquest of Babylon, 539/8 B.C.

2, 1-49: The chronology of v 1 is in conflict with that of

Dn 1, 5. 18, and in v 25 Daniel appears to be introduced to the king for the first time. It seems that the story of this chapter was originally entirely independent of chapter 1, and later retouched slightly to fit its present setting.

2, 2: Chaldeans: here probably astrologers, who were so associated with the Chaldeans in the Hebrew mind that in the later language they are sometimes simply called by the name of that people.

2, 4: Aramaic: from Dn 2, 4 to 7, 28 the text of Daniel is in Aramaic, not Hebrew, as indicated by this gloss.

---

c: Dn 6, 28.

⁶But if you tell me the dream and its meaning, you shall receive from me gifts and presents and great honors. Now tell me the dream and its meaning."

⁷Again they answered, "Let the king tell his servants the dream and we will give its meaning." ⁸But the king replied: "I know for certain that you are bargaining for time, since you know what I have decided. ⁹If you do not tell me the dream, there can be but one decree for you. You have framed a false and deceitful interpretation to present me with till the crisis is past. Tell me the dream, therefore, that I may be sure that you can also give its correct interpretation."

¹⁰The Chaldeans answered the king: "There is not a man on earth who can do what you ask, O king; never has any king, however great and mighty, asked such a thing of any magician, enchanter, or Chaldean. ¹¹What you demand, O king, is too difficult; there is no one who can tell it to the king except the gods who do not dwell among men." ¹²At this the king became violently angry and ordered all the wise men of Babylon to be put to death. ¹³When the decree was issued that the wise men should be slain, Daniel and his companions were also sought out.

¹⁴Then Daniel prudently took counsel with Arioch, the captain of the king's guard, who had set out to kill the wise men of Babylon: ¹⁵"O officer of the king," he asked, "what is the reason for this harsh order from the king?" When Arioch told him, ¹⁶Daniel went and asked for time from the king, that he might give him the interpretation.

¹⁷Daniel went home and informed his companions Hananiah, Mishael, and Azariah, ¹⁸that they might implore the mercy of the God of heaven in regard to this mystery, so that Daniel and his companions might not perish with the rest of the wise men of Babylon. ¹⁹During the night the mystery was revealed to Daniel in a vision, and he blessed the God of heaven:

²⁰ "Blessed be the name of God forever and
  ever,

for wisdom and power are his.
²¹ He causes the changes of the times and
  seasons,
  makes kings and unmakes them.
He gives wisdom to the wise
  and knowledge to those who understand.
²² He reveals deep and hidden things
  and knows what is in the darkness,
  for the light dwells with him.ᵈ
²³ To you, O God of my fathers,
  I give thanks and praise,
  because you have given me wisdom
    and power.
Now you have shown me what we asked
    of you,
  you have made known to us the king's
    dream."

²⁴So Daniel went to Arioch, whom the king had appointed to destroy the wise men of Babylon, and said to him, "Do not put the wise men of Babylon to death. Bring me before the king, and I will tell him the interpretation of the dream." Arioch quickly brought Daniel to the king and said, ²⁵"I have found a man among the Judean captives who can give the interpretation to the king." ²⁶The king asked Daniel, whose name was Belteshazzar, "Can you tell me the dream that I had, and its meaning?" ²⁷In the king's presence Daniel made this reply:

"The mystery about which the king has inquired, the wise men, enchanters, magicians, and astrologers could not explain to the king. ²⁸But there is a God in heaven who reveals mysteries, and he has shown King Nebuchadnezzar what is to happen in days to come; this was the dream you saw as you lay in bed. ²⁹To you in your bed there came thoughts about what should happen in the future, and he who reveals mysteries showed you what is to be. ³⁰To me also this mystery has been revealed; not that I am wiser than any other living person, but in order that its meaning may be made known to the king, that you may understand the thoughts in your own mind.

³¹"In your vision, O king, you saw a statue, very large and exceedingly bright,

d: Jn 1, 9; 8, 12; 1 Cor 4, 5; 1 Jn 1, 6.

The Neo-Babylonian Empire

terrifying in appearance as it stood before you. *32*The head of the statue was pure gold, its chest and arms were silver, its belly and thighs bronze, *33*the legs iron, its feet partly iron and partly tile.* *34*While you looked at the statue, a stone which was hewn from a mountain without a hand being put to it, struck its iron and tile feet, breaking them in pieces. *35*The iron, tile, bronze, silver, and gold all crumbled at once, fine as the chaff on the threshing floor in summer, and the wind blew them away without leaving a trace. But the stone that struck the statue became a great mountain and filled the whole earth.

36"This was the dream; the interpretation we shall also give in the king's presence. *37*You, O king, are the king of kings; to you the God of heaven has given dominion and strength, power and glory; *38*men, wild beasts, and birds of the air, wherever they may dwell, he has handed over to you, making you ruler over them all; you are the head of gold. *39*Another kingdom shall take your place, inferior to yours, then a third kingdom, of bronze, which shall rule over the whole earth. *40*There shall be a fourth kingdom, strong as iron; it shall break in pieces and subdue all these others, just as iron breaks in pieces and crushes everything else. *41*The feet and toes you saw, partly of potter's tile and partly of iron, mean that it shall be a divided kingdom, but yet have some of the hardness of iron. As you saw the iron mixed with clay tile, *42*and the toes partly iron and partly tile, the kingdom shall be partly strong and partly fragile. *43*The iron mixed with clay

---

2, 33: Partly tile: terra cotta tile was much in use among the Babylonians for decoration and for actual construction.

2, 36-45: The four successive kingdoms in this apocalyptic perspective are the Babylonian (gold), the Median (silver), the Persian (bronze), and the Hellenistic (iron). The last, after Alexander's death, was divided among his generals (vv 41f). The two resulting kingdoms, which

most affected the Jews, were the dynasty of the Ptolemies in Egypt and that of the Seleucids in Syria, who tried in vain, by war and through intermarriage, to restore the unity of Alexander's empire (v 43). The stone hewn from the mountain is the messianic kingdom awaited by the Jews (vv 44f). Our Lord made this image personal to himself; cf Lk 20, 17f.

tile means that they shall seal their alliances by intermarriage, but they shall not stay united, any more than iron mixes with clay. [44e]In the lifetime of those kings the God of heaven will set up a kingdom that shall never be destroyed or delivered up to another people; rather, it shall break in pieces all these kingdoms and put an end to them, and it shall stand forever. [45]That is the meaning of the stone you saw hewn from the mountain without a hand being put to it, which broke in pieces the tile, iron, bronze, silver, and gold. The great God has revealed to the king what shall be in the future; this is exactly what you dreamed, and its meaning is sure."

[46]Then King Nebuchadnezzar fell down and worshiped Daniel and ordered sacrifice and incense offered to him. [47]To Daniel the king said, "Truly your God is the God of gods and Lord of kings and a revealer of mysteries; that is why you were able to reveal this mystery." [48]He advanced Daniel to a high post, gave him many generous presents, made him ruler of the whole province of Babylon and chief prefect over all the wise men of Babylon. [49]At Daniel's request the king made Shadrach, Meshach, and Abednego administrators of the province of Babylon, while Daniel himself remained at the king's court.

CHAPTER 3

See RG 234–35

The Fiery Furnace. [1]King Nebuchadnezzar had a golden statue made, sixty cubits high and six cubits wide, which he set up in the plain of Dura* in the province of Babylon. [2]He then ordered the satraps,* prefects, and governors, the counselors, treasurers, judges, magistrates and all the officials of the provinces to be summoned to the dedication of the statue which he had set up. [3]The satraps, prefects, and governors, the counselors, treasurers, judges, and magistrates and all the officials of the provinces, all these came together for the dedication

and stood before the statue which King Nebuchadnezzar had set up. [4]A herald cried out: "Nations and peoples of every language, when you hear the sound of the trumpet, flute, lyre, harp, psaltery,* bagpipe, and all the other musical instruments, [5]you are ordered to fall down and worship the golden statue which King Nebuchadnezzar has set up [6]Whoever does not fall down and worship shall be instantly cast into a white-hot furnace."* [7]Therefore, as soon as they heard the sound of the trumpet, flute, lyre, harp, psaltery, bagpipe, and all the other musical instruments, the nations and peoples of every language all fell down and worshiped the golden statue which King Nebuchadnezzar had set up.

[8]At that point, some of the Chaldeans came and accused the Jews [9]to King Nebuchadnezzar: "O king, live forever! [10]O king, you issued a decree that everyone who heard the sound of the trumpet, flute, lyre, harp, psaltery, bagpipe, and all the other musical instruments should fall down and worship the golden statue; [11]whoever did not was to be cast into a white-hot furnace. [12]There are certain Jews whom you have made administrators of the province of Babylon: Shadrach, Meshach, Abednego; these men, O king, have paid no attention to you; they will not serve your god or worship the golden statue which you set up."

[13]Nebuchadnezzar flew into a rage and sent for Shadrach, Meshach, and Abednego, who were promptly brought before the king. [14]King Nebuchadnezzar questioned them: "Is it true, Shadrach, Meshach, and Abednego, that you will not serve my god, or worship the golden statue that I set up? [15]Be ready now to fall down and worship the statue I had made, whenever you hear the sound of the trumpet, flute, lyre, harp, psaltery, bagpipe, and all the other musical instruments; otherwise, you shall be instantly cast into the white-hot furnace; and who is

---

3, 1: Dura: several places in Babylonia bore this name. Probably the present reference is to one a few miles south of Babylon. Colossi of the type mentioned here were not uncommon in antiquity; a cubit was seventeen and a half inches.

3, 2: Satraps: the Persian major governors.

3, 4: Psaltery: a harplike instrument.

3, 6: Death by fire was not unknown as a punishment in Babylonia; cf Jer 29, 22.

---

e: Mt 21, 44; Lk 20, 18.

the God that can deliver you out of my hands?" [16]Shadrach, Meshach, and Abednego answered King Nebuchadnezzar, "There is no need for us to defend ourselves before you in this matter. [17]If our God, whom we serve, can save us* from the white-hot furnace and from your hands, O king, may he save us! [18]But even if he will not, know, O king, that we will not serve your god or worship the golden statue which you set up."

[19]Nebuchadnezzar's face became livid with utter rage against Shadrach, Meshach, and Abednego. He ordered the furnace to be heated seven times more than usual [20]and had some of the strongest men in his army bind Shadrach, Meshach, and Abednego and cast them into the white-hot furnace. [21]They were bound and cast into the white-hot furnace with their coats, hats, shoes and other garments, [22]for the king's order was urgent. So huge a fire was kindled in the furnace that the flames devoured the men who threw Shadrach, Meshach, and Abednego into it. [23]But these three fell, bound, into the midst of the white-hot furnace.

[24]*They walked about in the flames, singing to God and blessing the Lord. [25]In the fire Azariah stood up and prayed aloud:

[26] "Blessed are you, and praiseworthy,
    O Lord, the God of our fathers,
    and glorious forever is your name.
[27] For you are just in all you have done;
    all your deeds are faultless, all your
      ways right,
    and all your judgments proper.
[28] You have executed proper judgments
    in all that you have brought upon us
    and upon Jerusalem, the holy city of
      our fathers.
    By a proper judgment you have done all
      this
    because of our sins;
[29] For we have sinned and transgressed
    by departing from you,
    and we have done every kind of evil.

[30] Your commandments we have not
      heeded or observed,
    nor have we done as you ordered us
      for our good.
[31] Therefore all you have brought upon us,
    all you have done to us,
    you have done by a proper judgment.
[32] You have handed us over to our
      enemies,
    lawless and hateful rebels;
    to an unjust king, the worst in all the
      world.
[33] Now we cannot open our mouths;
    we, your servants, who revere you,
    have become a shame and a reproach.
[34] For your name's sake, do not deliver us
      up forever,
    or make void your covenant.
[35] Do not take away your mercy from us,
    for the sake of Abraham, your beloved,
    Isaac your servant, and Israel your
      holy one,
[36] To whom you promised to multiply their
      offspring
    like the stars of heaven,
    or the sand on the shore of the sea.
[37] For we are reduced, O Lord, beyond any
      other nation,
    brought low everywhere in the world
      this day
    because of our sins.
[38] We have in our day no prince, prophet, or
      leader,
    no holocaust, sacrifice, oblation, or
      incense,
    no place to offer first fruits, to find
      favor with you.
[39] But with contrite heart and humble
      spirit
    let us be received;
[40] As though it were holocausts of rams and
      bullocks,
    or thousands of fat lambs,
    So let our sacrifice be in your presence
      today
    as we follow you unreservedly;

3, 17: If our God . . . can save us: the youths do not question the efficacy of the divine power, but whether it will be exercised (v 18).

3, 24-90: These verses are inspired additions to the Aramaic text of Daniel, translated from the Greek form of the book. They were originally composed in Hebrew or Aramaic, which has not been preserved. The church has always regarded them as part of the canonical Scriptures.

for those who trust in you cannot be
put to shame.

41 And now we follow you with our whole
heart,
we fear you and we pray to you.
42 Do not let us be put to shame,
but deal with us in your kindness and
great mercy.
43 Deliver us by your wonders,
and bring glory to your name,
O Lord;
44 Let all those be routed
who inflict evils on your servants;
Let them be shamed and powerless,
and their strength broken;
45 Let them know that you alone are the
Lord God,
glorious over the whole world."

46Now the king's men who had thrown
them in continued to stoke the furnace with
brimstone, pitch, tow, and faggots. 47The
flames rose forty-nine cubits above the furnace, 48and spread out, burning the Chaldeans nearby. 49But the angel of the Lord
went down into the furnace with Azariah
and his companions, drove the fiery flames
out of the furnace, 50and made the inside of
the furnace as though a dew-laden breeze
were blowing through it. The fire in no
way touched them or caused them pain or
harm. 51Then these three in the furnace
with one voice sang, glorifying and blessing God:

52 "Blessed are you, O Lord, the God of our
fathers,
praiseworthy and exalted above all
forever;
And blessed is your holy and glorious
name,
praiseworthy and exalted above all for
all ages.
53 Blessed are you in the temple of your
holy glory,
praiseworthy and glorious above all
forever.
54 Blessed are you on the throne of your
kingdom,

praiseworthy and exalted above all
forever.
55 Blessed are you who look into the depths
from your throne upon the cherubim,
praiseworthy and exalted above all
forever.
56 Blessed are you in the firmament of
heaven,
praiseworthy and glorious forever.
57 Bless the Lord, all you works of the
Lord,
praise and exalt him above all forever.
58 Angels of the Lord, bless the Lord,
praise and exalt him above all forever.
59 You heavens, bless the Lord,
praise and exalt him above all forever.f
60 All you waters above the heavens, bless
the Lord,
praise and exalt him above all forever.
61 All you hosts of the Lord, bless the Lord;
praise and exalt him above all forever.
62 Sun and moon, bless the Lord;
praise and exalt him above all forever.
63 Stars of heaven, bless the Lord;
praise and exalt him above all forever.
64 Every shower and dew, bless the Lord;
praise and exalt him above all forever.
65 All you winds, bless the Lord;
praise and exalt him above all forever.
66 Fire and heat, bless the Lord;
praise and exalt him above all forever.
67 [Cold and chill, bless the Lord;
praise and exalt him above all forever.
68 Dew and rain, bless the Lord;
praise and exalt him above all forever.]
69 Frost and chill, bless the Lord;
praise and exalt him above all forever.
70 Ice and snow, bless the Lord;
praise and exalt him above all forever.
71 Nights and days, bless the Lord;
praise and exalt him above all forever.
72 Light and darkness, bless the Lord;
praise and exalt him above all forever.
73 Lightnings and clouds, bless the Lord;
praise and exalt him above all forever.
74 Let the earth bless the Lord,
praise and exalt him above all forever.
75 Mountains and hills, bless the Lord;
praise and exalt him above all forever.

f: 59f: Ps 148, 4.

⁷⁶ Everything growing from the earth, bless
    the Lord;
    praise and exalt him above all forever.
⁷⁷ You springs, bless the Lord;
    praise and exalt him above all forever.
⁷⁸ Seas and rivers, bless the Lord;
    praise and exalt him above all forever.
⁷⁹ You dolphins and all water creatures,
    bless the Lord;
    praise and exalt him above all forever.
⁸⁰ All you birds of the air, bless the Lord;
    praise and exalt him above all forever.
⁸¹ All you beasts, wild and tame, bless the
    Lord;
    praise and exalt him above all forever.
⁸² You sons of men, bless the Lord;
    praise and exalt him above all forever.
⁸³ O Israel, bless the Lord;
    praise and exalt him above all forever.
⁸⁴ Priests of the Lord, bless the Lord;
    praise and exalt him above all forever.
⁸⁵ Servants of the Lord, bless the Lord;
    praise and exalt him above all forever.
⁸⁶ Spirits and souls of the just, bless the
    Lord;
    praise and exalt him above all forever.
⁸⁷ Holy men of humble heart, bless the
    Lord;
    praise and exalt him above all forever.
⁸⁸ Hananiah, Azariah, Mishael, bless the
    Lord;
    praise and exalt him above all
    forever.
For he has delivered us from the nether
    world,
    and saved us from the power of death;
He has freed us from the raging flame
    and delivered us from the fire.
⁸⁹ Give thanks to the Lord, for he is good,
    for his mercy endures forever.
⁹⁰ Bless the God of gods, all you who fear
    the Lord;
    praise him and give him thanks,
    because his mercy endures forever."

Hearing them sing, and astonished at seeing them alive, ⁹¹King Nebuchadnezzar rose
in haste and asked his nobles, "Did we not
cast three men bound into the fire?" "Assuredly, O king," they answered. ⁹²"But," he
replied, "I see four men unfettered and unhurt, walking in the fire, and the fourth looks
like a son of God."* ⁹³Then Nebuchadnezzar
came to the opening of the white-hot furnace
and called to Shadrach, Meshach, and Abednego: "Servants of the most high God, come
out." Thereupon Shadrach, Meshach, and
Abednego came out of the fire. ⁹⁴When the
satraps, prefects, governors, and nobles of the
king came together, they saw that the fire had
had no power over the bodies of these men;
not a hair of their heads had been singed, nor
were their garments altered; there was not
even a smell of fire about them. ⁹⁵Nebuchad-
nezzar exclaimed, "Blessed be the God of
Shadrach, Meshach, and Abednego, who sent
his angel to deliver the servants that trusted in
him; they disobeyed the royal command and
yielded their bodies rather than serve or worship any god except their own God. ⁹⁶There-
fore I decree for nations and peoples of every
language that whoever blasphemes the God
of Shadrach, Meshach, and Abednego shall
be cut to pieces and his house destroyed. For
there is no other God who can rescue like
this." ⁹⁷Then the king promoted Shadrach,
Meshach, and Abednego in the province of
Babylon.

*Vision of the Great Tree.** ⁹⁸King Nebuchadnezzar to the nations and peoples of
every language, wherever they dwell on
earth: abundant peace! ⁹⁹It has seemed good
to me to publish the signs and wonders
which the most high God* has accomplished
in my regard.

¹⁰⁰How great are his signs, how mighty his
    wonders;
    his kingdom is an everlasting
      kingdom,
    and his dominion endures through all
      generations.*

3, 92: A son of God: an angel; cf Jb 1, 6.

3, 98—4, 34: This section has the form of a letter written by Nebuchadnezzar to his subjects.

3, 99: The most high God: the Jews, especially in the diaspora, used this title to distinguish their God from those of the pagans. On the lips of a polytheist (so also in v 93) it was merely the title of another god. It was an ancient divine name used in Canaan; cf Gn 14, 18.

g: Dn 4, 31; 7, 14.

CHAPTER 4

See RG
234–35

¹I, Nebuchadnezzar, was at home in my palace, content and prosperous. ²I had a terrifying dream as I lay in bed, and the images and the visions of my mind frightened me. ³So I issued a decree that all the wise men of Babylon should be brought before me to give the interpretation of the dream. ⁴When the magicians, enchanters, Chaldeans, and astrologers had come in, I related the dream before them; but none of them could tell me its meaning. ⁵ʰFinally there came before me Daniel, whose name is Belteshazzar after the name of my god,* and in whom is the spirit of the holy God. I repeated the dream to him: ⁶"Belteshazzar, chief of the magicians, I know that the spirit of the holy God is in you and no mystery is too difficult for you; tell me the meaning of the visions that I saw in my dream.

⁷"These were the visions I saw while in bed: I saw a tree of great height at the center of the world. ⁸It was large and strong, with its top touching the heavens, and it could be seen to the ends of the earth. ⁹Its leaves were beautiful and its fruit abundant, providing food for all. Under it the wild beasts found shade, in its branches the birds of the air nested; all men ate of it. ¹⁰In the vision I saw while in bed, a holy sentinel* came down from heaven, ¹¹and cried out:

*" 'Cut down the tree and lop off its
  branches,
  strip off its leaves and scatter its fruit;
  let the beasts flee its shade, and the
  birds its branches.
¹² But leave in the earth its stump and roots,
  fettered with iron and bronze, in the
  grass of the field.
Let him be bathed with the dew of
  heaven;

his lot be to eat, among beasts, the
  grass of the earth.
¹³ Let his mind be changed from the
  human;
  let him be given the sense of a beast,
  till seven years pass over him.
¹⁴ By decree of the sentinels is this decided,
  by order of the holy ones, this
  sentence;
That all who live may know
  that the Most High rules over the
  kingdom of men:
He can give it to whom he will,
  or set over it the lowliest of men.'ⁱ

¹⁵"This is the dream that I, King Nebuchadnezzar, had. Now, Belteshazzar, tell me its meaning. Although none of the wise men in my kingdom can tell me the meaning, you can, because the spirit of the holy God is in you."

¹⁵Then Daniel, whose name was Belteshazzar, was appalled for a while, terrified by his thoughts. "Belteshazzar," the king said to him, "let not the dream or its meaning terrify you." ¹⁷"My lord," Belteshazzar replied, "this dream should be for your enemies, and its meaning for your foes.* The large, strong tree that you saw, with its top touching the heavens, that could be seen by the whole earth, ¹⁸which had beautiful foliage and abundant fruit, providing food for all, under which the wild beasts lived, and in whose branches the birds of the air dwelt— ¹⁹you are that tree, O king, large and strong! Your majesty has become so great as to touch the heavens, and your rule extends over the whole earth. ²⁰As for the king's vision of a holy sentinel that came down from heaven and proclaimed: 'Cut down the tree and destroy it, but leave in the earth its stump and roots, fettered with iron and

---

4, 5: After the name of my god: Belteshazzar, the Babylonian name given to Daniel at the king's orders (Dn 1, 7), is Balatsuussur, "protect his life." In the king's intention, this would be an abbreviation for Bel-balatsu-ussur. It would thus include an appeal to the god Bel, originally the name of the city god of Nippur, and later identified with Marduk, the chief god of Babylon. Daniel's use of the name would refer the prayer rather to the true God.

4, 10: A holy sentinel: an angel. This term is found in the

Bible only in this chapter of Daniel, but it is common in later Jewish literature.

4, 11ff: As the tree is Nebuchadnezzar (v 19), the description passes from metaphor to the reality.

4, 17: "This dream . . . for your foes": Daniel speaks as a courtier.

h: Gr 41, 38. *i:* 1 Sm 2, 8; 16, 11; Is 62, 6.

bronze in the grass of the field; let him be bathed with the dew of heaven, and let his lot be among wild beasts till seven years pass over him'— ²¹this is its meaning, O king; this is the sentence which the Most High has passed upon my lord king: ²²*j*You shall be cast out from among men and dwell with wild beasts; you shall be given grass to eat like an ox and be bathed with the dew of heaven;* seven years shall pass over you, until you know that the Most High rules over the kingdom of men and gives it to whom he will. ²³The command that the stump and roots of the tree are to be left means that your kingdom shall be preserved for you, once you have learned it is heaven that rules. ²⁴*k*Therefore, O king, take my advice; atone for your sins by good deeds, and for your misdeeds by kindness to the poor; then your prosperity will be long."*

²⁵All this happened to King Nebuchadnezzar. ²⁶Twelve months later, as he was walking on the roof of the royal palace in Babylon, ²⁷the king said, "Babylon the great! Was it not I, with my great strength, who built it as a royal residence for my splendor and majesty?"* ²⁸While these words were still on the king's lips, a voice spoke from heaven, "It has been decreed for you, King Nebuchadnezzar, that your kingdom is taken from you! ²⁹You shall be cast out from among men, and shall dwell with wild beasts; you shall be given grass to eat like an ox, and seven years shall pass over you, until you learn that the Most High rules over the kingdom of men and gives it to whom he will." ³⁰*At once this was fulfilled. Nebuchadnezzar was cast out from among men, he ate grass like an ox, and his body was bathed with the dew of heaven, until his

hair grew like the feathers of an eagle, and his nails like the claws of a bird.

³¹*When this period was over, I, Nebuchadnezzar, raised my eyes to heaven; my reason was restored to me, and I blessed the Most High, I praised and glorified him who lives forever:

His dominion is an everlasting dominion,
    and his kingdom endures through all
        generations.
³² All who live on the earth are counted as
        nothing;
    he does as he pleases with the powers
        of heaven
    as well as with those who live on the
        earth.
There is no one who can stay his hand
    or say to him, "What have you done?"

³³At the same time my reason returned to me, and for the glory of my kingdom, my majesty and my splendor returned to me. My nobles and lords sought me out; I was restored to my kingdom, and became much greater than before. ³⁴Therefore, I, Nebuchadnezzar, now praise and exalt and glorify the King of heaven, because all his works are right and his ways just; and those who walk in pride he is able to humble.

CHAPTER 5

The Writing on the Wall. ¹King Belshazzar* gave a great banquet for a thousand of his lords, with whom he drank. ²Under the influence of the wine, he ordered the gold and silver vessels which Nebuchadnezzar, his father,* had taken from the temple in Jerusalem, to be brought in so that the king, his lords, his wives and his entertainers might

See RG 234-35

4, 22: The description is of a form of insanity called lycanthropy, in which the patient acts like a wolf.

4, 24: A classic Scriptural text for the efficacy of good works.

4, 27: The words attributed to the king are similar to the boastings in the royal inscriptions by which the Mesopotamian kings testified to their mighty works.

4, 30ff: There is no certainty of any such thing happening to Nebuchadnezzar as is described here. Some scholars think that the Nebuchadnezzar of this chapter is actually Nabonidus, the father of Belshazzar, who was mysteriously

absent from Babylon for a number of years. The Biblical author's chief interest was not in the historicity of this popular tale, but in the object lesson it contained for the proud "divine" kings of the Seleucid dynasty.

5, 1: King Belshazzar: Belshazzar was actually the crown prince, but he had been given royal authority in Babylon by his father Nabonidus.

5, 2: Nebuchadnezzar, his father: several kings of Babylon intervened between Nebuchadnezzar and Belshazzar. Either

j: Dn 5, 21.   *k:* Sir 3, 30; 4, 8.   *l:* Dn 3, 100; 7, 14.

drink from them. [3]When the gold and silver vessels taken from the house of God in Jerusalem had been brought in, and while the king, his lords, his wives and his entertainers were drinking [4]wine from them, they praised their gods of gold and silver, bronze and iron, wood and stone.

[5]Suddenly, opposite the lampstand, the fingers of a human hand appeared, writing on the plaster of the wall in the king's palace. When the king saw the wrist and hand that wrote, [6]his face blanched; his thoughts terrified him, his hip joints shook, and his knees knocked. [7]The king shouted for the enchanters, Chaldeans, and astrologers to be brought in. "Whoever reads this writing and tells me what it means," he said to the wise men of Babylon, "shall be clothed in purple, wear a golden collar about his neck, and be third in the government of the kingdom." [8]But though all the king's wise men came in, none of them could either read the writing or tell the king what it meant. [9]Then King Belshazzar was greatly terrified; his face went ashen, and his lords were thrown into confusion.

[10]When the queen heard of the discussion between the king and his lords, she entered the banquet hall and said, "O king, live forever! Be not troubled in mind, nor look so pale! [11]There is a man in your kingdom in whom is the spirit of the holy God; during the lifetime of your father he was seen to have brilliant knowledge and god-like wisdom. In fact, King Nebuchadnezzar, your father, made him chief of the magicians, enchanters, Chaldeans, and astrologers, [12]because of the extraordinary mind possessed by this Daniel, whom the king named Belteshazzar. He knew and understood how to interpret dreams, explain enigmas, and solve difficulties. Now therefore, summon Daniel to tell you what this means."

[13]Then Daniel was brought into the presence of the king. The king asked him, "Are you the Daniel, the Jewish exile, whom my father, the king, brought from Judah? [14]I have heard that the spirit of God is in you, that you possess brilliant knowledge and extraordinary wisdom. [15]Now, the wise men and enchanters were brought in to me to read this writing and tell me its meaning, but they could not say what the words meant. [16]But I have heard that you can interpret dreams and solve difficulties; if you are able to read the writing and tell me what it means, you shall be clothed in purple, wear a gold collar about your neck, and be third in the government of the kingdom."

[17]Daniel answered the king: "You may keep your gifts, or give your presents to someone else; but the writing I will read for you, O king, and tell you what it means. [18]The Most High God gave your father Nebuchadnezzar a great kingdom and glorious majesty. [19]Because he made him so great, the nations and peoples of every language dreaded and feared him. Whomever he wished, he killed or let live; whomever he wished, he exalted or humbled. [20]But when his heart became proud and his spirit hardened by insolence, he was put down from his royal throne and deprived of his glory; [21]*he was cast out from among men and was made insensate as a beast; he lived with wild asses, and ate grass like an ox; his body was bathed with the dew of heaven, until he learned that the Most High God rules over the kingdom of men and appoints over it whom he will. [22]You, his son, Belshazzar, have not humbled your heart, though you knew all this; [23]you have rebelled against the Lord of heaven. You had the vessels of his temple brought before you, so that you and your nobles, your wives and your entertainers, might drink wine from them; and you praised the gods of silver and gold, bronze and iron, wood and stone, that neither see nor hear nor have intelligence. But the God in whose hand is your life breath and the whole course of your life, you did not glorify. [24]By him were the wrist and hand sent, and the writing set down. [25]"This is the writing that was inscribed: MENE, TEKEL, and PERES.* These words

---

the term father is used here in the broad sense of "remote predecessor," or the name Nebuchadnezzar is used for "Nabonidus."

5, 25: MENE, TEKEL, and PERES: these seem to be the Aramaic names of weights and monetary values: the mina, the shekel (the sixtieth part of a mina), and the parsu (a half-mina).

m: Dn 4, 22.

mean: [26]*MENE, God has numbered your kingdom and put an end to it; [27]TEKEL, you have been weighed on the scales and found wanting; [28]PERES, your kingdom has been divided and given to the Medes and Persians."

[29]Then by order of Belshazzar they clothed Daniel in purple, with a gold collar about his neck, and proclaimed him third in the government of the kingdom. [30]The same night Belshazzar, the Chaldean king, was slain:

CHAPTER 6

See RG 234-35
[1]And Darius the Mede* succeeded to the kingdom at the age of sixty-two.

In the Lions' Den. [2]Darius decided to appoint over his entire kingdom one hundred and twenty satraps, to safeguard his interests; [3]these were accountable to three supervisors, one of whom was Daniel. [4]Daniel outshone all the supervisors and satraps because an extraordinary spirit was in him, and the king thought of giving him authority over the entire kingdom. [5]Therefore the supervisors and satraps tried to find grounds for accusation against Daniel as regards the administration. But they could accuse him of no wrongdoing; because he was trustworthy, no fault of neglect or misconduct was to be found in him. [6]Then these men said to themselves, "We shall find no grounds for accusation against this Daniel unless by way of the law of his God." [7]So these supervisors and satraps went thronging to the king and said to him, "King Darius, live forever! [8n]All the supervisors of the kingdom, the prefects, satraps, nobles, and governors are agreed that the following prohibition ought to be put in force by royal decree: no one is to address any petition to god or man for thirty days, except to you, O king; otherwise he shall be cast into a den of lions. [9]Now, O king, issue the prohibition over your signature, immutable and irrevocable* under Mede and Persian law." [10]So King Darius signed the prohibition and made it law.

[11]Even after Daniel heard that this law had been signed, he continued his custom of going home to kneel in prayer and give thanks to his God in the upper chamber three times a day, with the windows open toward Jerusalem. [12]So these men rushed in and found Daniel praying and pleading before his God. [13]Then they went to remind the king about the prohibition: "Did you not decree, O king, that no one is to address a petition to god or man for thirty days, except to you, O king; otherwise he shall be cast into a den of lions?" The king answered them, "The decree is absolute, irrevocable under the Mede and Persian law." [14]To this they replied, "Daniel, the Jewish exile, has paid no attention to you, O king, or to the decree you issued; three times a day he offers his prayer." [15]The king was deeply grieved at this news and he made up his mind to save Daniel; he worked till sunset to rescue him. [16]But these men insisted. "Keep in mind, O king," they said, "that under the Mede and Persian law every royal prohibition or decree is irrevocable." [17]So the king ordered Daniel to be brought and cast into the lions' den.* To Daniel he said, "May your God, whom you serve so constantly, save you." [18]To forestall any tampering, the king sealed with his own ring and the rings of the lords the stone that had been brought to block the opening of the den.

5, 26ff: Daniel interprets these three terms by a play on the words: Mene, connected with the verb meaning to number; Tekel, with the verb meaning to weigh; Peres, with the verb meaning to divide. There is also a play on the last term with the word for Persians.

6, 1: Darius the Mede: unknown in profane history. The Median kingdom had already been conquered by Cyrus the Persian, and it was Cyrus who captured Babylon. Evidently the author of Daniel has deliberately adopted an apocalyptic view of history, derived from prophecy (cf Is 13, 17ff; Jer 51, 11. 28ff), according to which the Medes formed the second of four world kingdoms preceding the messianic times; see note on Dn 2, 36-45. The character of Darius the Mede has probably been modeled on that of the Persian king Darius the Great (552–486 B.C.), the second successor of Cyrus.

6, 9: Immutable and irrevocable: the passages in Est 1, 19 and 8, 8 also refer to the immutability of Medo-Persian laws. The historian Diodorus Siculus indicates that such a concept existed in the time of Darius III (335–331 B.C.), the last of the Persian kings. Cf vv 13. 16.

6, 17: The lions' den: a pit too deep to be easily scaled; its opening was blocked with a stone (v 18).

---

n: Est 1, 19.

¹⁹Then the king returned to his palace for the night; he refused to eat and he dismissed the entertainers. Since sleep was impossible for him, ²⁰the king rose very early the next morning and hastened to the lions' den. ²¹As he drew near, he cried out to Daniel sorrowfully, "O Daniel, servant of the living God, has the God whom you serve so constantly been able to save you from the lions?" ²²ₒDaniel answered the king: "O king, live forever! ²³My God has sent his angel and closed the lions' mouths so that they have not hurt me. For I have been found innocent before him; neither to you have I done any harm, O king!" ²⁴This gave the king great joy. At his order Daniel was removed from the den, unhurt because he trusted in his God. ²⁵The king then ordered the men who had accused Daniel, along with their children and their wives, to be cast into the lions' den. Before they reached the bottom of the den, the lions overpowered them and crushed all their bones.

²⁶Then King Darius wrote to the nations and peoples of every language, wherever they dwell on the earth: "All peace to you! ²⁷I decree that throughout my royal domain the God of Daniel is to be reverenced and feared:

"For he is the living God, enduring forever;
his kingdom shall not be destroyed,
and his dominion shall be without end.
²⁸ He is a deliverer and savior,
working signs and wonders in heaven and on earth,

and he delivered Daniel from the lions' power."ᵖ

²⁹So Daniel fared well during the reign of Darius and the reign of Cyrus the Persian.

II: Daniel's Visions

CHAPTER 7

See RG 235-37

Vision of the Four Beasts.[*] ¹In the first year of King Belshazzar of Babylon, Daniel had a dream as he lay in bed, and was terrified by the visions of his mind. Then he wrote down the dream; the account began: ²In the vision I saw during the night, suddenly the four winds of heaven stirred up the great sea,[*] ³from which emerged four immense beasts, each different from the others. ⁴The first was like a lion, but with eagle's wings.[*] While I watched, the wings were plucked; it was raised from the ground to stand on two feet like a man, and given a human mind. ⁵The second was like a bear;[*] it was raised up on one side, and among the teeth in its mouth were three tusks. It was given the order, "Up, devour much flesh." ⁶After this I looked and saw another beast, like a leopard;[*] on its back were four wings like those of a bird, and it had four heads. To this beast dominion was given. ⁷After this, in the visions of the night I saw the fourth beast,[*] different from all the others, terrifying, horrible, and of extraordinary strength; it had great iron teeth with which it devoured and crushed, and what was left it trampled with its feet. ⁸I was considering the ten horns

7, 1-27: The significance of this vision is the same as that of Nebuchadnezzar's dream in chapter 2; see note on Dn 2, 36-45. To the four succeeding world kingdoms, Babylonian, Median, Persian, and Greek, is opposed the messianic kingdom of the people of God. The imagery of this chapter has been used extensively in the Revelation of St. John, where it is applied to the Roman empire, the persecutor of the church.

7, 2: The great sea: the primordial ocean beneath the earth, according to primitive cosmology (Gn 7, 11; 49, 25). This was thought to contain various monsters (Is 27, 1; Jb 7, 12), and in particular mythological monsters symbolizing the chaos which God had vanquished in ancient times (Jb 9, 13; 26, 13; etc.).

7, 4: The representation of the Babylonian empire as a winged lion, a common motif in Babylonian art, symbolizes the bestial power hostile to God. The two wings that are plucked represent Nebuchadnezzar and Belshazzar. On two

feet like a man . . . a human mind: contrasts with what is said in Dn 4, 13. 30.

7, 5: A bear: represents the Median empire, its three tusks symbolizing its destructive nature; hence, the command: "Up, devour much flesh."

7, 6: A leopard: used to symbolize the swiftness with which Cyrus the Persian established his kingdom. Four heads: corresponding to the four Persian kings of Dn 11. 2.

7, 7f: Alexander's empire was different from all the others in that it was Western rather than Oriental in inspiration. The ten horns represent the kings of the Seleucid dynasty, the only part of the Hellenistic empire that concerned the author. The little horn is Antiochus IV Epiphanes (175–163 B.C.), the worst of the Seleucid kings, who usurped the throne.

o: 1 Mc 2, 60.   p: Dn 1, 21.

it had, when suddenly another, a little horn, sprang out of their midst, and three of the previous horns were torn away to make room for it. This horn had eyes like a man, and a mouth that spoke arrogantly. 9*As I watched,

Thrones were set up
> and the Ancient One took his throne.
His clothing was snow bright,
> and the hair on his head as white as wool;
His throne was flames of fire,
> with wheels of burning fire.
10 A surging stream of fire
> flowed out from where he sat;
Thousands upon thousands were
> > ministering to him,
and myriads upon myriads attended
> > him.q

The court was convened, and the books were opened. 11I watched, then, from the first of the arrogant words which the horn spoke, until the beast was slain and its body thrown into the fire to be burnt up. 12The other beasts, which also lost their dominion, were granted a prolongation of life for a time and a season. 13As the visions during the night continued, I saw

One like a son of man* coming,
> on the clouds of heaven;
When he reached the Ancient One
> and was presented before him,
14 He received dominion, glory, and kingship;
> nations and peoples of every language
> > serve him.
His dominion is an everlasting dominion
> that shall not be taken away,
> his kingship shall not be destroyed.r

15I, Daniel, found my spirit anguished within its sheath of flesh, and I was terrified by the visions of my mind. 16I approached one of those present and asked him what all this meant in truth; in answer, he made known to me the meaning of the things: 17"These four great beasts stand for four kingdoms which shall arise on the earth. 18But the holy ones of the Most High shall receive the kingship, to possess it forever and ever."

19But I wished to make certain about the fourth beast, so very terrible and different from the others, devouring and crushing with its iron teeth and bronze claws, and trampling with its feet what was left; 20about the ten horns on its head, and the other one that sprang up, before which three horns fell; about the horn with the eyes and the mouth that spoke arrogantly, which appeared greater than its fellows. 21For, as I watched, that horn made war against the holy ones and was victorious 22until the Ancient One arrived; judgment was pronounced in favor of the holy ones of the Most High, and the time came when the holy ones possessed the kingdom. 23He answered me thus:

"The fourth beast shall be a fourth
> > kingdom on earth,
> different from all the others;
It shall devour the whole earth,
> beat it down, and crush it.
24 The ten horns shall be ten kings
> rising out of that kingdom;
> another shall rise up after them,
Different from those before him,
> who shall lay low three kings.
25 He shall speak against the Most High
> and oppress the holy ones of the Most
> > High,
> thinking to change the feast days and
> > the law.*

7, 9f: A vision of the heavenly throne of God (the Ancient One), who sits in judgment (symbolized by fire) over the nations. Some of the details of the vision, depicting the divine majesty and omnipotence, are to be found in Ez 1.

7, 13f: One like a son of man: in contrast to the worldly kingdoms opposed to God, which appear as beasts, the glorified people of God that will form his kingdom on earth is represented in human form (v 18). Just as our Lord applied the figure of the stone hewn from the mountain to himself (Dn 2, 36-45), he also made the title, "Son of Man" his most characteristic way of referring to himself, as the One in whom and through whom the salvation of God's people came to be realized.

7, 25: The reference is to the persecutions of Antiochus IV and his attempt to force the Jews to give up their customs and to adopt Hellenistic ways (1 Mc 1, 33f). A year, two years, and a half-year: an indefinite, evil period of time. As seven is the Jewish "perfect" number, half of it signifies great imperfection. Actually, this corresponds fairly accurately to the duration of Antiochus' persecution.

---

q: Rv 5, 11.   r: Dn 3, 100; 4, 31; Mi 4, 7; Lk 1, 32.

They shall be handed over to him
    for a year, two years, and a half-year.
26 But when the court is convened,
    and his power is taken away
    by final and absolute destruction,
27 Then the kingship and dominion and
       majesty
    of all the kingdoms under the
       heavens
    shall be given to the holy people of the
       Most High,
    Whose kingdom shall be everlasting:
    all dominions shall serve and obey
       him.”

28The report concluded: I, Daniel, was greatly terrified by my thoughts, and my face blanched, but I kept the matter to myself.*

CHAPTER 8

See RG
235-37
*Vision of the Ram and He-goat.** 1After this first vision, I, Daniel, had another, in the third year of the reign of King Belshazzar. 2In my vision I saw myself in the fortress of Susa* in the province of Elam; I was beside the river Ulai. 3I looked up and saw standing by the river a ram with two great horns, the one larger and newer than the other. 4I saw the ram butting toward the west, north, and south. No beast could withstand it or be rescued from its power; it did what it pleased and became very powerful.

5As I was reflecting, a he-goat with a prominent horn on its forehead suddenly came from the west across the whole earth without touching the ground. 6It approached the two-horned ram I had seen standing by the river, and rushed toward it with savage force. 7I saw it attack the ram with furious blows when they met, and break both its horns. It threw the ram, which had not the force to withstand it, to the ground, and trampled upon it; and no one could rescue it from its power.

8The he-goat became very powerful, but at the height of its power the great horn was shattered, and in its place came up four others, facing the four winds of heaven. 9Out of one of them came a little horn* which kept growing toward the south, the east, and the glorious country. 10Its power extended to the host of heaven,* so that it cast down to earth some of the host and some of the stars and trampled on them. 11It boasted even against the prince of the host, from whom it removed the daily sacrifice, and whose sanctuary it cast down, 12as well as the host, while sin replaced the daily sacrifice. It cast truth to the ground, and was succeeding in its undertaking.

13I heard a holy one speaking, and another said to whichever one it was that spoke, “How long shall the events of this vision last concerning the daily sacrifice, the desolating sin* which is placed there, the sanctuary, and the trampled host?” 14He answered him, “For two thousand three hundred evenings and mornings; then the sanctuary shall be purified.”

15While I, Daniel, sought the meaning of the vision I had seen, a manlike figure stood before me, 16and on the Ulai I heard a human voice that cried out, “Gabriel,* explain the vision to this man.” 17When he came near where I was standing, I fell prostrate in terror. But he said to me, “Understand, son of man, that the vision refers

7, 28: This verse ends the Aramaic part of the Book of Daniel.

8, 1-27: This vision repeats the major part of the preceding one, though in a more explicit fashion. As explained in vv 20ff, the two-horned ram represents the combined kingdom of the Medes and Persians, destroyed by Alexander’s Hellenistic empire originating in the west. Once again the author is interested only in the Seleucid dynasty, which emerged from the dissolution of Alexander’s empire after his death in 323 B.C.

8, 2: The fortress of Susa: the royal palace of the Persian kings in the ancient territory of Elam, east of Babylonia. The river Ulai: a canal along the northern side of Susa.

8, 9: The little horn, as in chapter 7, is Antiochus IV. The glorious country: Palestine.

8, 10ff: The host of heaven: ordinarily meaning the stars, here refers to the people of God; cf Dn 12, 3. The prince of the host: God himself, with whose holy religion Antiochus interfered (1 Mc 1, 45).

8, 13: The desolating sin: the Hebrew contains a wordplay (shomem) on the name Baal Shamem (“lord of the heavens,” the Greek Zeus Olympios), referring to the statue with which Antiochus profaned the temple of Jerusalem (2 Mc 6, 2).

8, 16: The angel Gabriel is mentioned here for the first time in the Bible. There is wordplay in the preceding verse on geber—manlike figure.

Sardis

Tarsus

Issus

Carchemish

Tigris River

Nineveh

ALEXANDER'S EMPIRE

Mediterranean Sea

Ecbatana

Zidon
Tyre

Damascus

Euphrates R.

Samaria
Jerusalem

Babylon

Shushan

Alexandria
Noph
(Memphis)

Pelusium

ARABIA

Ur

N

EGYPT

0   300   500 Mi.
0   300   500 Km.

Alexander's Empire

to the end time."* [18]As he spoke to me, I fell forward in a faint; he touched me and made me stand up. [19]"I will show you," he said, "what is to happen later in the period of wrath; for at the appointed time, there will be an end.

[20]"The two-horned ram you saw represents the kings of the Medes and Persians. [21]The he-goat is the king of the Greeks, and the great horn on its forehead is the first king. [22]The four that rose in its place when it was broken are four kingdoms that will issue from his nation, but without his strength.

[23] "After their reign,
    when sinners have reached their
       measure,
  There shall arise a king, impudent
    and skilled in intrigue.
[24] He shall be strong and powerful,
    bring about fearful ruin,
    and succeed in his undertaking.

He shall destroy powerful
    peoples;
[25] his cunning shall be against the holy
    ones,
  his treacherous conduct shall
    succeed.
He shall be proud of heart
    and destroy many by stealth.
But when he rises against the prince of
    princes,
  he shall be broken without a hand
    being raised.
[26] The vision of the evenings and the
    mornings
  is true, as spoken;
Do you, however, keep this vision
    undisclosed,
  because the days are to be many."

[27]I, Daniel, was weak and ill for some days; then I arose and took care of the king's affairs. But I was appalled at the vision, which I could not understand.

8, 17: The end time: the day of the Lord, when God sits in judgment on his enemies (v 19).

See RG
235–37

CHAPTER 9

Gabriel and the Seventy Weeks. *¹*It was the first year that Darius,* son of Ahasuerus, of the race of the Medes, reigned over the kingdom of the Chaldeans; *²ˢ*in the first year of his reign I, Daniel, tried to understand in the Scriptures the counting of the years of which the LORD spoke to the prophet Jeremiah: that for the ruins of Jerusalem seventy years* must be fulfilled.

*³*I turned to the Lord God, pleading in earnest prayer, with fasting, sackcloth, and ashes. *⁴ᵗ*I prayed to the LORD, my God, and confessed, "Ah, Lord, great and awesome God, you who keep your merciful covenant toward those who love you and observe your commandments! *⁵ᵘ*We have sinned, been wicked and done evil; we have rebelled and departed from your commandments and your laws. *⁶*We have not obeyed your servants the prophets, who spoke in your name to our kings, our princes, our fathers, and all the people of the land. *⁷*Justice, O Lord, is on your side; we are shamefaced even to this day: the men of Judah, the residents of Jerusalem, and all Israel, near and far, in all the countries to which you have scattered them because of their treachery toward you. *⁸*O LORD, we are shamefaced, like our kings, our princes, and our fathers, for having sinned against you. *⁹*But yours, O Lord, our God, are compassion and forgiveness! Yet we rebelled against you *¹⁰*and paid no heed to your command, O LORD, our God, to live by the law you gave us through your servants the prophets. *¹¹ᵛ*Because all Israel transgressed your law and went astray, not heeding your voice, the sworn malediction, recorded in the law of Moses, the servant of God, was poured out over us for our sins. *¹²*You carried out the threats you spoke against us and against those who governed us, by bringing upon us in Jerusalem the greatest calamity that has ever occurred under heaven. *¹³*As it is written* in the law of Moses, this calamity came full upon us. As we did not appease the Lord, our God, by turning back from our wickedness and recognizing his constancy, *¹⁴*so the Lord kept watch over the calamity and brought it upon us. You, O LORD, our God, are just in all that you have done, for we did not listen to your voice.

¹⁵ʷ"Now, O Lord, our God, who led your people out of the land of Egypt with a strong hand, and made a name for yourself even to this day, we have sinned, we are guilty. *¹⁶*O Lord, in keeping with all your just deeds, let your anger and your wrath be turned away from your city Jerusalem, your holy mountain. On account of our sins and the crimes of our fathers, Jerusalem and your people have become the reproach of all our neighbors. *¹⁷*Hear, therefore, O God, the prayer and petition of your servant; and for your own sake, O Lord, let your face shine upon your desolate sanctuary. *¹⁸ˣ*Give ear, O my God, and listen; open your eyes and see our ruins and the city which bears your name. When we present our petition before you, we rely not on our just deeds, but on your great mercy. *¹⁹*O Lord, hear! O Lord, pardon! O Lord, be attentive and act without delay, for your own sake, O my God, because this city and your people bear your name!"

*²⁰*I was still occupied with my prayer, confessing my sin and the sin of my people Israel, presenting my petition to the LORD, my God, on behalf of his holy mountain— *²¹ʸ*I was still occupied with this prayer, when Gabriel, the one whom I had seen before in vision, came to me in rapid flight at the time of the evening sacrifice.* *²²*He

---

9, 1: Darius: see the note on Dn 6, 1.

9, 2: Seventy years: the prophet Jeremiah (25, 11; 29, 10) prophesied a Babylonian captivity of seventy years, a round number signifying the complete passing away of the existing generation. Jeremiah's prophecy was fulfilled in the capture of Babylon by Cyrus and the subsequent return of the Jews to Palestine. However, the author of Daniel, living during the persecution of Antiochus, sees the conditions of the exile still existing; therefore in his mediation he extends Jeremiah's number to seventy weeks of years (v 24, i.e., seven times seventy years, to characterize the Jewish victory over the Seleucids as the ultimate fulfillment of the prophecy.

9, 13: As it is written: the first time that this formula of Scriptural citation is used in the Bible. The reference (v 11) is to the sanctions of Lv 26, 14ff; Dt 28, 15ff.

9, 21: At the time of the evening sacrifice: between three and four in the afternoon.

---

s: 2f: Jer 25, 11; 29, 10. *t:* Neh 1, 5. *u:* Bar 1, 17. *v:* Dt 27, 15. *w:* Bar 2, 11; Ex 14, 22. *x:* Jer 25, 29. *y:* Dn 8, 16.

instructed me in these words: "Daniel, I have now come to give you understanding. 23When you began your petition, an answer was given which I have come to announce, because you are beloved. Therefore, mark the answer and understand the vision.

24 "Seventy weeks* are decreed
for your people and for your holy city:
Then transgression will stop and sin will
end,
guilt will be expiated,
Everlasting justice will be introduced,
vision and prophecy ratified,
and a most holy will be anointed.
25   Know and understand this:
From the utterance of the word
that Jerusalem was to be rebuilt*
Until one who is anointed and a leader,
there shall be seven weeks.
During sixty-two weeks
it shall be rebuilt,
With streets and trenches,
in time of affliction.
26 After the sixty-two weeks
an anointed* shall be cut down
when he does not possess the city;

And the people of a leader who will
come
shall destroy the sanctuary.
Then the end shall come like a torrent;
until the end there shall be war,
the desolation that is decreed.
27 For one week* he shall make
a firm compact with the many;
Half the week
he shall abolish sacrifice and oblation;
On the temple wing shall be the horrible
abomination
until the ruin that is decreed
is poured out upon the horror."z

CHAPTER 10

*Vision of the Hellenistic Wars.** 1In the third year of Cyrus, king of Persia, a revelation was given to Daniel, who had been named Belteshazzar. The revelation was certain: a great war; he understood it from the vision. 2In those days, I, Daniel, mourned* three full weeks. 3I ate no savory food, I took no meat or wine, and I did not anoint myself at all until the end of the three weeks.

4On the twenty-fourth day of the first month* I was on the bank of the great river, the Tigris. 5As I looked up, I saw a man*

See RG 237

9, 24: Seventy weeks: i. e., of years. Just as Jeremiah's seventy years was an approximation (see note on v 2), the four hundred and ninety years here is not to be taken literally. Similarly, the distribution of the "weeks" in the following verses indicates only relative proportions of the total figure. A most holy: an expression used almost always of an object, the altar or the temple, but once (1 Chr 23, 13) of Aaron the high priest. The author sees the definitive establishment of the kingdom of God, realized in the reconsecration of the temple after Antiochus' desecration, or personified in the holy community (like the Son of Man of chapter 7). The Fathers of the church almost unanimously understood the reference to be to Christ, the final realization of the prophecy.

9, 25: From the utterance . . . to be rebuilt: from the time of Jeremiah's prophecy. One . . . anointed and a leader: either Cyrus, who was called the anointed of the Lord to end the exile (Is 45, 1), or the high priest Joshua, who presided over the rebuilding of the altar of sacrifice after the exile (Ezr 3, 2). Seven weeks: forty-nine years, an approximation of the time of the exile. During sixty-two weeks . . . rebuilt: a period of 434 years, roughly approximating the interval between the rebuilding of Jerusalem after the exile and the beginning of the Seleucid persecution.

9, 26: An anointed: doubtless the high priest Onias III, murdered in 171 B.C., from which the author dates the beginning of the persecution. Onias was in exile when he was killed. A leader: Antiochus IV.

9, 27: One week: the final phase of the period in view, the time of Antiochus' persecution; he is Antiochus himself. The many: the faithless Jews who allied themselves with the heathen; cf 1 Mc 1, 11ff. Half the week: three and a half years; see note on Dn 7, 25. The temple was desecrated by Antiochus from 167 to 165 B.C. The temple wing: probably the main portal. The horrible abomination: see note on Dn 8, 13. Perhaps an inscription was placed on the portal of the temple dedicating it to the Olympian Zeus. Our Lord referred to this passage in his own prediction of the destruction of Jerusalem (Mt 24, 15).

10, 1—12, 13: This final vision repeats some of the material contained in the others. It is concerned with history of the worldly kingdoms from the time of Cyrus to the defeat of the tyrant Antiochus.

10, 2: Mourned: perhaps the author intends to recall the interruption in the rebuilding of the temple, which occurred during this time (Ezr 4, 1-4).

10, 4: The first month: the month Nisan (mid-March to mid-April).

10, 5f: The heavenly person of the vision is probably the angel Gabriel, as in Dn 9, 21. Chrysolite: or topaz, a yellowish precious stone.

z: Mt 24, 15; 2 Mc 6, 2.

dressed in linen with a belt of fine gold around his waist. [6]His body was like chrysolite, his face shone like lightning, his eyes were like fiery torches, his arms and feet looked like burnished bronze, and his voice sounded like the roar of a multitude. [7]I alone, Daniel, saw the vision; but great fear seized the men who were with me; they fled and hid themselves, although they did not see the vision. [8]So I was left alone, seeing this great vision. No strength remained in me; I turned the color of death and was powerless. [9]When I heard the sound of his voice, I fell face forward in a faint.

[10]But then a hand touched me, raising me to my hands and knees. [11]"Daniel, beloved," he said to me, "understand the words which I am speaking to you; stand up, for my mission now is to you." When he said this to me, I stood up trembling. [12]"Fear not, Daniel," he continued; "from the first day you made up your mind to acquire understanding and humble yourself before God, your prayer was heard. Because of it I started out, [13]but the prince of the kingdom of Persia* stood in my way for twenty-one days, until finally Michael, one of the chief princes, came to help me. I left him there with the prince of the kings of Persia, [14]and came to make you understand what shall happen to your people in the days to come; for there is yet a vision concerning those days."

[15]While he was speaking thus to me, I fell forward and kept silent. [16]Then something like a man's hand touched my lips; I opened my mouth and said to the one facing me, "My lord, I was seized with pangs at the vision and I was powerless. [17]How can my lord's servant speak with you, my lord? For now no strength or even breath is left in me." [18]The one who looked like a man touched me again and strengthened me, saying, [19]"Fear not, beloved, you are safe; take courage and be strong." [20]When he spoke to me, I grew strong and said, "Speak, my lord, for you have strengthened me." "Do you know," he asked, "why I have come to you? Soon I must fight the prince of Persia again. When I leave, the prince of Greece will come; [21a]but I shall tell you what is written in the truthful book. No one supports me against all these except Michael, your prince, [1]standing* as a reinforcement and a bulwark for me. [2]Now I shall tell you the truth.

CHAPTER 11

See RG 237

"Three kings of Persia* are yet to come; and a fourth shall acquire the greatest riches of all. Strengthened by his riches, he shall rouse all the kingdom of Greece. [3]But a powerful king shall appear and rule with great might, doing as he pleases. [4]No sooner shall he appear than his kingdom shall be broken and divided in the four directions under heaven; but not among his descendants or in keeping with his mighty rule, for his kingdom shall be torn to pieces and belong to others than they.

[5]"The king of the south shall grow strong, but one of his princes shall grow stronger still and govern a domain greater than his. [6]After some years they shall become allies: the daughter of the king of the south shall come to the king of the north in the interest of peace. But her bid for power shall fail: and her line shall not be recognized, and she shall be given up, together with those who brought her, her son and her

---

10, 13: The prince of the kingdom of Persia: the guardian angel of Persia. The later Judaism ascribed protecting angels to various groups of human society, often as little more than personifications. Michael: the angel who is the protector of God's people (v 21).

11, 1f: Standing . . . truth: these are the first two verses of ch 11.

11, 2-4: The three kings of Persia who follow Cyrus are uncertain, since there were more than three Persian kings between Cyrus and the dissolution of the kingdom. The fourth is doubtless Xerxes I (486-465 B.C.), the great campaigner against Greece. The powerful king is Alexander the Great, who ended the Persian empire by his victory at Issus in 333 B.C.

11, 5-45: These verses describe the dynastic histories of the Ptolemies in Egypt (the king of the south) and the Seleucids in Syria (the king of the north), the two divisions of the Hellenistic empire that were of interest to the author (v 6). In vv 10-20 is described the struggle between the two kingdoms for the control of Palestine, in which the Seleucids were eventually victorious. The reference in v 20 is to Seleucus IV, who sent Heliodorus to plunder the temple treasure in Jerusalem (2 Mc 3). Finally, vv 21-45 describe the career of Antiochus IV and his persecution, in details that have been seen above.

---

a: Rv 12, 7.

husband. But later [7]a descendant of her line shall succeed to his rank, and shall come against the rampart and enter the stronghold of the king of the north, and conquer them. [8]Even their gods, with their molten images and their precious vessels of silver and gold, he shall carry away as booty into Egypt. For years he shall have nothing to do with the king of the north. [9]Then the latter shall invade the land of the king of the south, and return to his own country.

[10]"But his sons shall prepare and assemble a great armed host, which shall advance like a flood, then withdraw. When it returns and surges around the stronghold, [11]the king of the south, provoked, shall go out to fight against the king of the north, whose great host shall make a stand but shall be given into his hand [12]and be carried off. In the pride of his heart, he shall lay low tens of thousands, but he shall not triumph. [13]For the king of the north shall raise another army, greater than before; after some years he shall attack with this large army and great resources. [14b]In those times many shall resist the king of the south, and outlaws of your people shall rise up in fulfillment of vision, but they shall fail. [15]When the king of the north comes, he shall set up siegeworks and take the fortified city by storm. The power of the south shall not withstand him, and not even his picked troops shall have the strength to resist. [16]He shall attack him and do as he pleases, with no one to withstand him. He shall stop in the glorious land, dealing destruction. [17]He shall set himself to penetrate the entire strength of his kingdom. He shall conclude an agreement with him and give him a daughter in marriage in order to destroy the kingdom, but this shall not succeed in his favor. [18]He shall turn to the coastland and take many, but a leader shall put an end to his shameful conduct, so that he cannot renew it against him. [19]He shall turn to the strongholds of his own land, but shall stumble and fall, to be found no more. [20]In his stead one shall arise who will send a tax collector through the glorious kingdom, but he shall soon be destroyed, though not in conflict or in battle.

[21]"There shall rise in his place a despicable person, to whom the royal insignia shall not be given. By stealth and fraud he shall seize the kingdom. [22]Armed might shall be completely overwhelmed by him and crushed, and even the prince of the covenant. [23]After allying with him, he shall treacherously rise to power with a small party. [24]By stealth he shall enter prosperous provinces and do that which his fathers or grandfathers never did; he shall distribute spoil, booty, and riches among them and devise plots against their strongholds; but only for a time. [25]He shall call on his strength and cleverness to meet the king of the south with a great army; the king of the south shall prepare for battle with a very large and strong army, but he shall not succeed because of the plots devised against him. [26]Even his table companions shall seek to destroy him, his army shall be overwhelmed, and many shall fall slain. [27]The two kings, resolved on evil, shall sit at table together and exchange lies, but they shall have no success, because the appointed end is not yet.

[28]"He shall turn back toward his land with great riches, his mind set against the holy covenant; he shall arrange matters and return to his land. [29]At the time appointed he shall come again to the south, but this time it shall not be as before. [30]When ships of the Kittim* confront him, he shall lose heart and retreat. Then he shall direct his rage and energy against the holy covenant; those who forsake it he shall once more single out. [31]Armed forces shall move at his command and defile the sanctuary stronghold, abolishing the daily sacrifice and setting up the horrible abomination. [32]By his deceit he shall make some who were disloyal to the covenant apostatize; but those who remain loyal to their God shall take strong action. [33]The nation's wise men shall instruct the many; though for a time they will become victims

---

11, 30: Kittim: originally this word meant Cypriots or other island dwellers. Here it means the Romans, who forced Antiochus to withdraw from Egypt during his second campaign there.

b: Is 19, 1.

The Ptolemaic and Seleucid Kingdoms

of the sword, of flames, exile, and plunder. ³⁴When they fall, few people shall help them, but many shall join them out of treachery. ³⁵Of the wise men, some shall fall, so that the rest may be tested, refined, and purified, until the end time which is still appointed to come.

³⁶*"The king shall do as he pleases, exalting himself and making himself greater than any god; he shall utter dreadful blasphemies against the God of gods. He shall prosper only till divine wrath is ready, for what is determined must take place. ³⁷He shall have no regard for the gods of his ancestors or for the one in whom women delight; for no god shall he have regard, because he shall make himself greater than all. ³⁸Instead, he shall give glory to the god of strongholds; a god unknown to his fathers he shall glorify with gold, silver, precious stones, and other treasures. ³⁹To defend the strongholds he shall station a people of a foreign god. Whoever acknowledges him he shall provide with abundant honor; he shall make them rule over the many and distribute the land as a reward.

⁴⁰"At the appointed time the king of the south shall come to grips with him, but the king of the north shall overwhelm him with chariots and horsemen and a great fleet, passing through the countries like a flood. ⁴¹He shall enter the glorious land and many shall fall, except Edom, Moab, and the chief part of Ammon, which shall escape from his power. ⁴²He shall extend his power over the countries, and not even the land of Egypt shall escape. ⁴³He shall control the riches of gold and silver and all the treasures of Egypt; Libya and Ethiopia shall be in his train. ⁴⁴When news from the east and the north terrifies him, he shall set out with great fury to slay and to doom many. ⁴⁵He shall

---

11, 36-39: Instead of venerating Apollo, one of the gods of his ancestors, Antiochus venerated, and even identified himself with, Zeus Olympios, whom the Romans equated with the god of their fortress in Rome, Jupiter Capitolinus, the god of strongholds.

pitch the tents of his royal pavilion between the sea and the glorious holy mountain, but he shall come to his end with none to help him.

See RG 237

CHAPTER 12

1"At that time there shall arise
Michael, the great prince,
guardian of your people;*c*
It shall be a time unsurpassed in distress
since nations began until that time.
At that time your people shall escape,
everyone who is found written in the
book.*

2 Many of those who sleep
in the dust of the earth shall awake;*
Some shall live forever,
others shall be an everlasting horror
and disgrace.*d*

3 But the wise shall shine brightly
like the splendor of the firmament,
And those who lead the many to justice
shall be like the stars forever.*e*

4"As for you, Daniel, keep secret the message and seal the book until the end time; many shall fall away and evil shall increase."

*5*I, Daniel, looked and saw two others, one standing on either bank of the river. *6*One of them said to the man clothed in linen, who was upstream, "How long shall it be to the end of these appalling things?" *7f*The man clothed in linen, who was upstream, lifted his right and left hands to heaven; and I heard him swear by him who lives forever that it should be for a year, two years, a half-year;* and that, when the power of the destroyer of the holy people was brought to an end, all these things should end. *8*I heard, but I did not understand; so I asked, "My lord, what follows this?" *9*"Go, Daniel," he said,

"because the words are to be kept secret and sealed until the end time. *10*Many shall be refined, purified, and tested, but the wicked shall prove wicked; none of them shall have understanding, but the wise shall have it. *11*From the time that the daily sacrifice is abolished and the horrible abomination is set up, there shall be one thousand two hundred and ninety days. *12*Blessed is the man who has patience and perseveres until the one thousand three hundred and thirty-five days. *13*Go, take your rest, you shall rise for your reward at the end of days."

III: Appendix*

CHAPTER 13

See RG 237-38

Susanna's Virtue. *1*In Babylon there lived a man named Joakim, *2*who married a very beautiful and God-fearing woman, Susanna, the daughter of Hilkiah; *3*her pious parents had trained their daughter according to the law of Moses. *4*Joakim was very rich; he had a garden near his house, and the Jews had recourse to him often because he was the most respected of them all.

*5*That year, two elders of the people were appointed judges, of whom the Lord said, "Wickedness has come out of Babylon: from the elders who were to govern the people as judges." *6*These men, to whom all brought their cases, frequented the house of Joakim. *7*When the people left at noon, Susanna used to enter her husband's garden for a walk. *8*When the old men saw her enter every day for her walk, they began to lust for her. *9*They suppressed their consciences; they would not allow their eyes to look to heaven, and did not keep in mind just judgments. *10*Though both were enamored of her, they did not tell each other their trouble, *11*for they were ashamed to reveal their lustful de-

---

12, 1: Written in the book: the book of God's predestination.

12, 2: The first Israelites who have fallen (Dn 11, 33ff) shall awake, that is, rise to live forever. A resurrection of the wicked as in later, Christian teaching (Jn 5, 28f) is implied here if the others are included in the many; but cf Is 66, 24.

12, 7: A year, two years, a half-year: see note on Dn 7, 25. The author's perspective is the end of Antiochus, and beyond, the final consummation of all things.

13, 1—14, 42: The short stories in these two chapters may have originally been about some other Daniel or Daniels than the hero of the main part of the book. They exist now only in Greek, but probably were first composed in Hebrew or Aramaic. They are excluded from the Jewish canon of Scripture, but the church as always included them among the inspired writings.

c: Rv 12, 7. *d:* Mt 25, 46; Jn 5, 29. *e:* Wis 3, 7. *f:* Rv 10, 5f.

sire to have her. ¹²Day by day they watched eagerly for her. ¹³One day they said to each other, "Let us be off for home, it is time for lunch." So they went out and parted; ¹⁴but both turned back, and when they met again, they asked each other the reason. They admitted their lust, and then they agreed to look for an occasion when they could meet her alone.

¹⁵One day, while they were waiting for the right moment, she entered the garden as usual, with two maids only. She decided to bathe, for the weather was warm. ¹⁶Nobody else was there except the two elders, who had hidden themselves and were watching her. ¹⁷"Bring me oil and soap," she said to the maids, "and shut the garden doors while I bathe." ¹⁸They did as she said; they shut the garden doors and left by the side gate to fetch what she had ordered, unaware that the elders were hidden inside.

¹⁹As soon as the maids had left, the two old men got up and hurried to her. ²⁰"Look," they said, "the garden doors are shut, and no one can see us; give in to our desire, and lie with us. ²¹If you refuse, we will testify against you that you dismissed your maids because a young man was here with you."

²²"I am completely trapped," Susanna groaned. "If I yield, it will be my death; if I refuse, I cannot escape your power. ²³Yet it is better for me to fall into your power without guilt than to sin before the Lord." ²⁴Then Susanna shrieked, and the old men also shouted at her, ²⁵as one of them ran to open the garden doors. ²⁶When the people in the house heard the cries from the garden, they rushed in by the side gate to see what had happened to her. ²⁷At the accusations by the old men, the servants felt very much ashamed, for never had any such thing been said about Susanna.

²⁸When the people came to her husband Joakim the next day, the two wicked elders also came, fully determined to put Susanna to death. Before all the people they ordered: ²⁹"Send for Susanna, the daughter of Hilkiah, the wife of Joakim." When she was sent for, ³⁰she came with her parents, children and all her relatives. ³¹Susanna, very

delicate and beautiful, ³²was veiled; but those wicked men ordered her to uncover her face so as to sate themselves with her beauty. ³³All her relatives and the onlookers were weeping.

³⁴In the midst of the people the two elders rose up and laid their hands on her head. ³⁵Through her tears she looked up to heaven, for she trusted in the Lord wholeheartedly. ³⁶The elders made this accusation: "As we were walking in the garden alone, this woman entered with two girls and shut the doors of the garden, dismissing the girls. ³⁷A young man, who was hidden there, came and lay with her. ³⁸When we, in a corner of the garden, saw this crime, we ran toward them. ³⁹We saw them lying together, but the man we could not hold, because he was stronger than we; he opened the doors and ran off. ⁴⁰Then we seized this one and asked who the young man was, ⁴¹but she refused to tell us. We testify to this." The assembly believed them, since they were elders and judges of the people, and they condemned her to death.

⁴²But Susanna cried aloud: "O eternal God, you know what is hidden and are aware of all things before they come to be: ⁴³you know that they have testified falsely against me. Here I am about to die, though I have done none of the things with which these wicked men have charged me."

⁴⁴The Lord heard her prayer. ⁴⁵As she was being led to execution, God stirred up the holy spirit of a young boy named Daniel, ⁴⁶and he cried aloud: "I will have no part in the death of this woman." ⁴⁷All the people turned and asked him, "What is this you are saying?" ⁴⁸He stood in their midst and continued, "Are you such fools, O Israelites! To condemn a woman of Israel without examination and without clear evidence? ⁴⁹Return to court, for they have testified falsely against her."

⁵⁰Then all the people returned in haste. To Daniel the elders said, "Come, sit with us and inform us, since God has given you the prestige of old age." ⁵¹But he replied, "Separate these two far from one another that I may examine them."

⁵²After they were separated one from the

other, he called one of them and said: "How you have grown evil with age! Now have your past sins come to term: [53g]passing unjust sentences, condemning the innocent, and freeing the guilty, although the Lord says, 'The innocent and the just you shall not put to death.' [54]Now, then, if you were a witness, tell me under what tree you saw them together." [55]"Under a mastic tree,"[*] he answered. "Your fine lie has cost you your head," said Daniel; "for the angel of God shall receive the sentence from him and split you in two." [56]Putting him to one side, he ordered the other one to be brought. "Offspring of Canaan, not of Judah," Daniel said to him, "beauty has seduced you, lust has subverted your conscience. [57]This is how you acted with the daughters of Israel, and in their fear they yielded to you; but a daughter of Judah did not tolerate your wickedness.[*] [58]Now then, tell me under what tree you surprised them together." [59]"Under an oak," he said. "Your fine lie has cost you also your head," said Daniel; "for the angel of God waits with a sword to cut you in two so as to make an end of you both."

[60]The whole assembly cried aloud, blessing God who saves those that hope in him. [61h]They rose up against the two elders, for by their own words Daniel had convicted them of perjury. According to the law of Moses, they inflicted on them the penalty they had plotted to impose on their neighbor: [62]they put them to death. Thus was innocent blood spared that day.

[63]Hilkiah and his wife praised God for their daughter Susanna, as did Joakim her husband and all her relatives, because she was found innocent of any shameful deed. [64]And from that day onward Daniel was greatly esteemed by the people.

CHAPTER 14

See RG 237-38

Bel and the Dragon. [1]After King Astyages[*] was laid with his fathers, Cyrus the Persian succeeded to his kingdom. [2]Daniel was the king's favorite and was held in higher esteem than any of the friends of the king.[*] [3]The Babylonians had an idol called Bel,[*] and every day they provided for it six barrels of fine flour, forty sheep, and six measures of wine. [4]The king worshiped it and went every day to adore it; but Daniel adored only his God. [5]When the king asked him, "Why do you not adore Bel?" Daniel replied, "Because I worship not idols made with hands, but only the living God who made heaven and earth and has dominion over all mankind." [6]Then the king continued, "You do not think Bel is a living god? Do you not see how much he eats and drinks every day?" [7]Daniel began to laugh. "Do not be deceived, O king," he said; "it is only clay inside and bronze outside; it has never taken any food or drink." [8]Enraged, the king called his priests and said to them, "Unless you tell me who it is that consumes these provisions, you shall die. [9]But if you can show that Bel consumes them, Daniel shall die for blaspheming Bel." Daniel said to the king, "Let it be as you say!" [10]There were seventy priests of Bel, besides their wives and children.

When the king went with Daniel into the temple of Bel, [11]the priests of Bel said, "See, we are going to leave. Do you, O king, set out the food and prepare the wine; then shut the door and seal it with your ring. [12]If you do not find that Bel has eaten it all when you return in the morning, we are to die; otherwise Daniel shall die for his lies against us." [13]They were not perturbed, because under the table they had made a secret entrance

---

13, 55-59: The contrast between the mastic tree, which is small, and the majestic oak emphasizes the contradiction between the statements of the two elders. In the Greek text there is a play on words between the names of these two trees and the mortal punishment decreed by Daniel for the elders.

13, 57: Besides the evident moral intent of this story, it appears to have served the purpose of contrasting the northern and the southern kingdom, Israel and Judah, in favor of the latter.

14, 1: King Astyages: the last of the Median kings, de-

feated by Cyrus in 550 B.C. This story preserves the fiction of a successive Median and Persian rule of Babylon.

14, 2: This verse in the Septuagint Greek text reads: "There was once a priest, Daniel by name, the son of Abal, a favorite of the king of Babylon." This may represent an earlier form of the story, before it was attached to the Book of Daniel.

14, 3: Bel: see the note on Dn 4, 5.

g: Ex 23, 7.   h: 61f: Dt 19, 18. 19.

through which they always came in to consume the food. ¹⁴After they departed the king set the food before Bel, while Daniel ordered his servants to bring some ashes, which they scattered through the whole temple; the king alone was present. Then they went outside, sealed the closed door with the king's ring, and departed. ¹⁵The priests entered that night as usual, with their wives and children, and they ate and drank everything.

¹⁶Early the next morning, the king came with Daniel. ¹⁷"Are the seals unbroken, Daniel?" he asked. And Daniel answered, "They are unbroken, O king." ¹⁸As soon as he had opened the door, the king looked at the table and cried aloud, "Great you are, O Bel; there is no trickery in you." ¹⁹But Daniel laughed and kept the king from entering. "Look at the floor," he said; "whose footprints are these?" ²⁰"I see the footprints of men, women, and children!" said the king. ²¹The angry king arrested the priests, their wives, and their children. They showed him the secret door by which they used to enter to consume what was on the table. ²²He put them to death, and handed Bel over to Daniel, who destroyed it and its temple.

²³There was a great dragon which the Babylonians worshiped. ²⁴"Look!" said the king to Daniel, "you cannot deny that this is a living god, so adore it." ²⁵But Daniel answered, "I adore the Lord, my God, for he is the living God. ²⁶Give me permission, O king, and I will kill this dragon without sword or club." "I give you permission," the king said. ²⁷Then Daniel took some pitch, fat, and hair; these he boiled together and made into cakes. He put them into the mouth of the dragon, and when the dragon ate them, he burst asunder. "This," he said, "is what you worshiped."

²⁸When the Babylonians heard this, they were angry and turned against the king. "The king has become a Jew," they said; "he has destroyed Bel, killed the dragon, and put the priests to death." ²⁹They went to the king and demanded: "Hand Daniel over to us, or we will kill you and your family." ³⁰When he saw himself threatened with violence, the king was forced to hand Daniel over to them. ³¹They threw Daniel into a lions' den, where he remained six days. ³²In the den were seven lions, and two carcasses and two sheep had been given to them daily. But now they were given nothing, so that they would devour Daniel.

³³In Judea there was a prophet, Habakkuk; he mixed some bread in a bowl with the stew he had boiled, and was going to bring it to the reapers in the field, ³⁴when an angel of the Lord told him, "Take the lunch you have to Daniel in the lions' den at Babylon." ³⁵But Habakkuk answered, "Babylon, sir, I have never seen, and I do not know the den!" ³⁶The angel of the Lord seized him by the crown of his head and carried him by the hair; with the speed of the wind, he set him down in Babylon above the den. ³⁷"Daniel, Daniel," cried Habakkuk, "take the lunch God has sent you." ³⁸"You have remembered me, O God," said Daniel; "you have not forsaken those who love you." ³⁹While Daniel began to eat, the angel of the Lord at once brought Habakkuk back to his own place.

⁴⁰On the seventh day the king came to mourn for Daniel. As he came to the den and looked in, there was Daniel, sitting there! ⁴¹The king cried aloud, "You are great, O Lord, the God of Daniel, and there is no other besides you!" ⁴²Daniel he took out, but those who had tried to destroy him he threw into the den, and they were devoured in a moment before his eyes.

i: Ez 8, 3.

See RG
240–44

The Book of Hosea

Hosea belonged to the northern kingdom and began his prophetic career in the last years of Jeroboam II (786–746 B.C.). Some believe that he was a priest, others that he was a cult prophet; the prophecy, our only source of information concerning his life, gives us no certain answer in the matter. The collected oracles reveal a very sensitive, emotional man who could pass quickly from violent anger to the deepest tenderness. The prophecy pivots around his own unfortunate marriage to Gomer, a personal tragedy which profoundly influenced his teaching. In fact, his own prophetic vocation and message were immeasurably deepened by the painful experience he underwent in his married life.

Gomer, the adultress, symbolized faithless Israel. And just as Hosea could not give up his wife forever even when she played the harlot, so Yahweh could not renounce Israel, who had been betrothed to him. God would chastise, but it would be the chastisement of the jealous lover, longing to bring back the beloved to the fresh and pure joy of their first love.

Israel's infidelity took the form of idolatry and ruthless oppression of the poor. No amount of mechanically offered sacrifices could atone for her serious sins. Chastisement alone remained; God would have to strip her of the rich ornaments bestowed by her false lovers and thus bring her back to the true lover. A humiliated Israel would again seek Yahweh. The eleventh chapter of Hosea is one of the summits of Old Testament theology; God's love for his people has never been expressed more tenderly. Hosea began the tradition of describing the relation between Yahweh and Israel in terms of marriage. This symbolism appears later on in the Old Testament; and, in the New, both St. John and St. Paul express in the same imagery the union between Christ and his Church.

The Book of Hosea is divided as follows:

I: The Prophet's Marriage and Its Lesson (1, 1—3, 5).

II: Israel's Guilt and Punishment (4, 1—14, 10).

I: The Prophet's Marriage and Its Lesson[*]

CHAPTER 1

See RG
241–44

Marriage with an Unfaithful Wife. [1]The word of the LORD that came to Hosea, the son of Beeri, in the days of Uzziah, Jotham, Ahaz, Hezekiah, kings of Judah, and in the days of Jeroboam, son of Joash, king of Israel. [2]In the beginning of the LORD's speaking to Hosea, the LORD said to Hosea:

Go, take a harlot wife[*] and harlot's children,
for the land gives itself to harlotry,
turning away from the LORD.

[3]So he went and took Gomer, the daughter of Diblaim; and she conceived and bore him a son. [4]Then the LORD said to him:

Give him the name Jezreel,[*]
for in a little while
I will punish the house of Jehu
for the bloodshed at Jezreel
And bring to an end the kingdom
of the house of Israel;
[5] On that day I will break the bow of Israel
in the valley of Jezreel.

1—3: This section is ordinarily thought to be biographical, the prophet's personal tragedy figuring as the relation of God to his people Israel. Hosea's marriage to a harlot wife represents Israel's infidelity to her Lord; hence the symbolic names of the children (Hos 1, 4-9). In Hos 2, 4-25 the Lord protests this infidelity and decrees its consequences; his punishments are medicinal. In chapter 3 Hosea once more takes back his wife, but only conditionally, signifying God's long-suffering love for Israel and hope for her return.

1, 2: A harlot wife: this does not necessarily mean that Gomer was a harlot when Hosea married her; the verse describes the event in its final consequences.

1, 4: Jezreel: the strategic valley in northern Israel where Jehu brought the dynasty of Omri to an end through bloodshed (2 Kgs 9—10). Jeroboam II was the last king but one of the house of Jehu; the prophecy in this verse was fulfilled by the murder of his son, who reigned only six months (2 Kgs 15, 8-10).

⁶When she conceived again and bore a daughter, the LORD said to him:

Give her the name Lo-ruhama;*
I no longer feel pity for the house of Israel:
 rather, I abhor them utterly.
⁷ Yet for the house of Judah I feel pity;
 I will save them by the LORD, their God;
But I will not save them by war,
 by sword or bow, by horses or
  horsemen.*

⁸After she weaned Lo-ruhama, she conceived and bore a son. ⁹Then the LORD said:

Give him the name Lo-ammi,*
for you are not my people,
and I will not be your God.

CHAPTER 2

See RG 241-44

Israel's Punishment and Restoration

⁴ Protest against your mother, protest!*
 for she is not my wife,
 and I am not her husband.
Let her remove her harlotry from before
  her,
 her adultery from between her breasts,
⁵ Or I will strip her naked,*
 leaving her as on the day of her birth;
I will make her like the desert,
 reduce her to an arid land,
 and slay her with thirst.
⁶ I will have no pity on her children,
 for they are the children of harlotry.
⁷ Yes, their mother has played the harlot;
 she that conceived them has acted
  shamefully.

"I will go after my lovers,"* she said.
 "who give me my bread and my water,
 my wool and my flax, my oil and my
  drink."

¹⁰ Since she has not known
 that it was I who gave her
 the grain, the wine, and the oil,
And her abundance of silver,
 and of gold, which they used for Baal,
¹¹ Therefore I will take back my grain in its
  time,
 and my wine in its season;
I will snatch away my wool and my flax,
 with which she covers her nakedness.
¹² So now I will lay bare her shame
 before the eyes of her lovers,
 and no one can deliver her out of my
  hand.
¹³ I will bring an end to all her joy,
 her feasts, her new moons, her
  sabbaths,
 and all her solemnities.
¹⁴ I will lay waste her vines and fig trees,
 of which she said, "These are the hire
 my lovers have given me";
I will turn them into rank growth
 and wild beasts shall devour them.
¹⁵ I will punish her for the days of the Baals,*
 for whom she burnt incense
While she decked herself out with her
  rings and her jewels,
 and, in going after her lovers,
 forgot me, says the LORD.
⁸ Therefore, I will hedge in her way with
  thorns*
 and erect a wall against her,
 so that she cannot find her paths.

1, 6: Lo-ruhama: "she is not pitied." The "pity" that is here withheld from Israel is God's gratuitous love which inspires his beneficent acts.

1, 7: The terrible punishments announced by the prophets were so fully realized that later generations made a point of recalling the same prophets' messages of consolation also, even though it meant taking these from another context. Thus, an editor placed the words of Hos 2, 1ff after the repudiation of Israel in Hos 1, 9; here the more natural order has been restored. The present verse is another example of the same thing. In addition, it may be the work of a later hand, dating from a time when the prophecies of Hosea were circulated in the south, after the dissolution of the northern kingdom that he had prophesied. The second part of the verse emphasizes the power of the Lord, who needs no human agents to fulfill his will. It may refer to the deliverance of Jerusalem from the siege of Sennacherib (2 Kgs 19, 35ff).

1, 9: Lo-ammi: "not my people."

2, 4: The Lord speaks of Israel, still using the example of Hosea's wife.

2, 5: I will strip her naked: contemporary documents indicate that this was a conventional punishment for adultery.

2, 7: My lovers: the local fertility deities to whom, rather than to the Lord (v 10), the unfaithful Israelites attributed the produce of the land.

2, 15: The days of the Baals: ritual observances held in various local shrines in honor of Baal.

2, 8f: The crop failures, blight, etc., sent by the Lord (vv 11-14) have as their purpose to make Israel see the folly of her ways.

⁹ If she runs after her lovers, she shall not
    overtake them;
  if she looks for them she shall not find
    them.
Then she shall say,
  "I will go back to my first husband,
  for it was better with me then than
    now."

¹⁶ So I will allure her;*
  I will lead her into the desert
  and speak to her heart.
¹⁷ From there I will give her the vineyards
    she had,
  and the valley of Achor as a door of
    hope.
She shall respond there as in the days of
    her youth,
  when she came up from the land of
    Egypt.

¹⁸   On that day, says the LORD,
She shall call me "My husband,"
  and never again "My baal."*
¹⁹ Then will I remove from her mouth the
    names of the Baals,
  so that they shall no longer be
    invoked.
²⁰ I will make a covenant for them on that
    day,
  with the beasts of the field,
With the birds of the air,
  and with the things that crawl on the
    ground.
Bow and sword and war

  I will destroy from the land,
  and I will let them take their rest in
    security.
²¹ I will espouse you to me forever:*
  I will espouse you in right and in
    justice,
  in love and in mercy;
²² I will espouse you in fidelity,
  and you shall know the LORD.
²³ On that day I will respond, says the LORD;
  I will respond to the heavens,
  and they shall respond to the earth;
²⁴ The earth shall respond to the grain, and
    wine, and oil,
  and these shall respond to Jezreel.
²⁵ I will sow him for myself in the land,
  and I will have pity on Lo-ruhama.
I will say to Lo-ammi, "You are my
    people,"
  and he shall say, "My God!"*a*

CHAPTER 3

Triumph of Love

See RG
241-44

¹ *Again the LORD said to me:
Give your love to a woman
  beloved of a paramour, an adulteress;
Even as the LORD loves the people of
    Israel,
  though they turn to other gods
  and are fond of raisin cakes.*

²So I bought her for fifteen pieces of silver and a homer* and a lethech of barley.
³Then I said to her:

2, 16f: Israel's journey in the desert represents for Hosea
the time of Israel's fidelity, before it was corrupted by the
ways of Canaan; cf Jer 2, 2-7; Am 5, 25. Thus, he pictures a
restoration in terms of a new entry into the promised land.

2, 18: My baal: the word means "lord, master." It was
commonly used by women of their husbands, but it is to be
shunned as a title for the Lord because of its association with
the pagan god Baal. Probably it had been so used by many Israelites, who saw little if any difference between the worship
of the Lord and the worship of Baal.

2, 21f: The Lord will once more espouse Israel; the qualities ascribed to the renewed people are the bridal gift (cf Gn
24, 53) with which he will endow it. In right and in justice:
two terms dear to Hosea, used by him especially to condemn
the popular social injustice and corruption of the legal
processes. Here they mean right conduct in general. Love:
one of the most characteristic words of Hosea's prophecy. It
means a dutiful love, based on a social relation; here it refers

to the covenant between God and his people. It is a love fulfilled by the performance of mutual obligations. Mercy: from
the same root as the word translated pity in Hos 1, 6; cf v 25.
And you shall know the LORD: another characteristic expression of Hosea; cf Hos 4, 1; 5, 4; 6, 3. It means not an abstract but a practical knowledge, i.e., acknowledgment of his
will, obedience to his law.

3, 1-5: Hosea is instructed to take Gomer back, redeeming
her from her paramours. On condition of her amendment, she
will be restored to her former position of wife. This in turn
signifies God's enduring love for his people. He will put the
people through a period of trial—the dissolution of the kingdom—in order that they may return to him wholeheartedly.

3, 1: Raisin cakes: offerings to the fertility goddess
Ashera, the female counterpart of Baal; cf Jer 7, 18; 44, 19.

3, 2: Homer: about ten bushels. Lethech: a half-homer.

a: Rom 9, 25; 1 Pt 2, 10.

Hosea Marries an Adulteress

The details of the account in ch 3 are so sketchy that it is difficult to decide whether it describes 1) Hosea's first marriage to Gomer in ch 1, but from the first-person rather than third-person perspective; 2) Hosea's marriage to a second woman; or 3) Hosea's remarriage to Gomer. In any case, the point of his symbolic act is clear: Israel has been an unfaithful wife, but God desires her return.

In v. 4 Hosea predicts a coming judgment in which Israel will lose both political and religious leadership. But Israel will return to God, in the same way an unfaithful wife returns to her husband: with humility and seeking forgiveness.

"Many days you shall wait for me;
  you shall not play the harlot
Or belong to any man;
  I in turn will wait for you."
[4] For the people of Israel shall remain
    many days
  without king or prince,
Without sacrifice or sacred pillar,*
  without ephod or household idols.
[5] Then the people of Israel shall turn back
  and seek the LORD, their God,
  and David, their king;*
They shall come trembling to the LORD
  and to his bounty, in the last days.[b]
[1] *The number of the Israelites
  shall be like the sand of the sea,
  which can be neither measured nor
    counted.
Whereas they were called,
  "Lo-ammi,"
They shall be called,
  "Children of the living God."[c]
[2] Then the people of Judah and of Israel
  shall be gathered together;
They shall appoint for themselves one
    head
  and come up from other lands,
  for great shall be the day of Jezreel.

[3] Say to your brothers, "Ammi,"
  and to your sisters, "Ruhama."

II: Israel's Guilt and Punishment

CHAPTER 4

See RG
241–44

Crimes of Israel

[1] Hear the word of the LORD,
  O people of Israel,
  for the LORD has a grievance
  against the inhabitants of the land:
There is no fidelity, no mercy,
  no knowledge of God in the land.
[2] False swearing, lying, murder, stealing
    and adultery!
  in their lawlessness, bloodshed follows
    bloodshed.[d]
[3] Therefore the land mourns,
  and everything that dwells in it
    languishes:
The beasts of the field,
  the birds of the air,
  and even the fish of the sea perish.

Guilt of the Priests

[4] But let no one protest, let no one
    complain;
  with you is my grievance, O priests!*

3, 4: Sacred pillar: the stone massebah, originally perhaps a phallic symbol, representing Baal. These were also used, with another signification, in Israelite worship; see notes on Gn 28, 18; Ex 34, 13. Ephod: an instrument used in consulting the deity; cf 1 Sm 23, 6-12; 30, 7; see notes on Ex 28, 6. 15-30. Household idols: images regarded as the tutelary deities of the household; cf Gn 31, 19; Jgs 17, 5; 18, 14. 17f.

3, 5: David, their king: the messianic King of the Davidic line who will restore the kingdom of God's people; cf Jer 23, 5; Ez 34, 23f. The last days: the messianic age.

3, 1-3: These verses (The number . . . Ruhama) (transposed from ch 2) continue the conditional promise of restoration made in Hos 3, 1-5, reversing the dire predictions of chapter 1; the symbolic names now become names of honor: Jezreel, "God sows"; Ammi, "my people"; Ruhama, "she is pitied."

4, 4ff: Hosea is particularly severe with the priests in the northern kingdom, who had led the way in the general apostasy from God's law. The prophets here associated with the priests (v 5) were doubtless cult prophets, who were often unworthy of their pretended calling; cf Jer 2, 8; 4, 9f; 6, 13f; 23, 9-40

b: Ez 34, 23. c: Rom 9, 26. d: Ex 20, 13-17.

5 You shall stumble in the day,
  and the prophets shall stumble with
    you at night;
  I will destroy your mother.
6 My people perish for want of knowledge!
  Since you have rejected knowledge,
  I will reject you from my priesthood;
  Since you have ignored the law of your
    God,
  I will also ignore your sons.
7 One and all they sin against me,
  exchanging their glory for shame.
8 They feed on the sin of my people,
  and are greedy for their guilt.
9 The priests shall fare no better than the
    people:
  I will punish them for their ways,
  and repay them for their deeds.*e*
10 They shall eat but not be satisfied,
  they shall play the harlot but not
    increase,
  Because they have abandoned the LORD
11   to practice harlotry.
  Old wine and new
  deprive my people of understanding.
12 They consult their piece of wood,
  and their wand* makes
    pronouncements for them,
  For the spirit of harlotry has led them
    astray;
  they commit harlotry, forsaking their
    God.
13 On the mountaintops they offer sacrifice
  and on the hills they burn incense,
  Beneath oak and poplar and terebinth,
  because of their pleasant shade.
  That is why your daughters play the
    harlot,
  and your daughters-in-law are
    adulteresses.

14 Am I then to punish your daughters for
    their harlotry,
  your daughters-in-law for their
    adultery?
  You yourselves consort with harlots,
  and with prostitutes you offer
    sacrifice!*
  So must a people without understanding
    come to ruin.
15 Though you play the harlot, O Israel,
  let not Judah become guilty!
  Come not to Gilgal,*
  nor up to Beth-aven,
  to swear, "As the Lord lives!"
16 For Israel is as stubborn as a heifer;
  will the LORD now give them broad
    pastures
  as though they were lambs?
17 Ephraim* is an associate of idols,
  let him alone!
18 When their carousing is over,
  they give themselves to harlotry;
  in their arrogance they love shame.
19 The wind has bound them up in its
    pinions;*
  they shall have only shame from their
    altars.

CHAPTER 5

Guilt of the Leaders

See RG
241-44

1 Hear this, O priests,
  Pay attention, O house of Israel,
  O household of the king, give ear!
  It is you who are called to judgment.*f*
  For you have become a snare at Mizpah,*
  and a net spread upon Tabor.
2 In their perversity they have sunk into
    wickedness,
  and I am rejected by them all.
3 I know Ephraim,

4, 12: Wood . . . wand: an idol used in divination.
4, 14: With prostitutes you offer sacrifice: the ritual prostitution practiced at the Canaanite shrines was introduced even into sanctuaries dedicated to the Lord. In comparison, the adultery that had become common in Israel was a far less reprehensible crime.
4, 15: Gilgal: not the Gilgal of the south (Jos 4, 19f), but a sanctuary north of Bethel where there was an association of cult prophets (2 Kgs 2, 1ff; 4, 38). Beth-aven: literally, "house of iniquity," Hosea's nickname for Bethel, or a scribal substitute for Bethel, "house of god," in this context. Bethel was one of the royal shrines of Israel, where there was a schis-

matic public worship of the Lord; cf 1 Kgs 12, 26-30.
4, 17: Ephraim: the heartland of the northern kingdom. During the latter part of Hosea's prophetic career, Ephraim was all that remained of Israel after the Assyrians had overrun Transjordan and Galilee.
4, 19: The Israelites shall be carried from their country as by a whirlwind. To this their idolatry has brought them.
5, 1: Mizpah: probably the Mizpah in Transjordan is meant; cf Jos 11, 8. Tabor: the mountain that dominates the valley of Jezreel.

e: Is 24, 2.   *f:* Mi 3, 1.

and Israel is not hidden from me;
Now Ephraim has played the harlot,
  Israel is defiled.
[4] Their deeds do not allow them
  to return to their God;
For the spirit of harlotry is in them,
  and they do not recognize the LORD.

[5] The arrogance of Israel bears witness
  against him;
Ephraim stumbles in his guilt,
  and Judah stumbles with them.
[6] With their flocks and their herds they
  shall go
to seek the LORD, but they shall not
  find him:
he has withdrawn himself from them.
[7] They have been untrue to the LORD,
  for they have begotten illegitimate
  children;
Now shall the new moon devour them
  together with their fields.

Political Upheavals[*]

[8] Blow the horn in Gibeah,
  the trumpet in Ramah!
Sound the alarm in Beth-aven:
  "Look behind you, O Benjamin!"[*]
[9] Ephraim shall become a waste
  on the day of chastisement:
Against the tribes of Israel
  I announce what is sure to be.
[10] The princes of Judah have become
  like those that move a boundary line;[*]
Upon them I will pour out
  my wrath like water.[g]

[11] Is Ephraim maltreated, his rights
  violated?

No, he has willingly gone after filth![*]
[12] I am like a moth for Ephraim,
  like maggots[*] for the house of Judah.
[13] When Ephraim saw his infirmity,
  and Judah his sore,
Ephraim went to Assyria,
  and Judah sent to the great king.[*]
But he cannot heal you
  nor take away your sore.
[14] For I am like a lion to Ephraim,
  like a young lion to the house of
    Judah;
It is I who rend the prey and depart,
  I carry it away and no one can save it
    from me.

Insincere Conversion

[15] I will go back to my place
  until they pay for their guilt
  and seek my presence.[*]

CHAPTER 6

See RG
241-44

[*]In their affliction, they shall look
  for me:
[1]   "Come, let us return to the LORD,
For it is he who has rent, but he will heal
  us;
he has struck us, but he will bind our
  wounds.
[2] He will revive us after two days;[*]
  on the third day he will raise us up,
  to live in his presence.[h]
[3] Let us know, let us strive to know the
  LORD;
as certain as the dawn is his coming,
and his judgment shines forth like the
  light of day!
He will come to us like the rain,
  like spring rain that waters the earth."

5, 8-14: This passage refers to the Syro-Ephraimite war of 735–734 B.C., when a coalition of Arameans and Israelites attempted to dethrone the king of Judah. Judah repulsed the attempt with the aid of Assyria, and the latter devastated both Aram and Israel; cf 2 Kgs 16, 5-9. Hosea condemns both Israel and Judah for the war.
5, 8: A vision of invasion, from Gibeah and Ramah in northern Judah, into Israel.
5, 10: Like those that move a boundary line: comparison of the invaders to a classic case of social injustice; cf Dt 19, 14; 27, 17; Prv 23, 10f.
5, 11: Gone after filth: by allying himself with Aram.
5, 12: Moth . . . maggots: internal corruption will work the Lord's punishment on both Israel and Judah.

5. 13: Ephraim went . . . the great king: in 738 B.C. the Israelite king Menahem had to pay tribute to the Assyrian king Tiglath-pileser III, whose vassal he became (2 Kgs 15, 19f). Under the threat of the Syro-Ephraimite invasion King Ahaz of Judah also submitted himself and his country to Tiglath-pileser (2 Kgs 16, 7-9). "The great king" was the title used by the Assyrian kings.
5. 15: The Lord withdraws himself from Israel, hoping for its repentance.
6. 1: In . . . me: this is the last line of ch 5.
6. 2: After two days; on the third day: after a short lapse of time.

---

g: Dt 19, 14; 27, 17.   **h:** 1 Cor 15, 4.

⁴ What can I do with you, Ephraim?
  What can I do with you, Judah?
Your piety* is like a morning cloud,
  like the dew that early passes away.
⁵ For this reason I smote them through the
    prophets,
  I slew them by the words of my
    mouth;
⁶ For it is love that I desire, not sacrifice,
  and knowledge of God rather than
    holocausts.ⁱ
⁷ But they, in their land, violated the
    covenant;
  there they were untrue to me.
⁸ Gilead is a city of evildoers,
  tracked with blood.
⁹ As brigands ambush a man,
  a band of priests slay on the way to
    Shechem,
  committing monstrous crime.
¹⁰ In the house of Israel I have seen a
    horrible thing:
  there harlotry is found in Ephraim,
  Israel is defiled.
¹¹ For you also, O Judah,
  a harvest* has been appointed.

CHAPTER 7

**See RG
241-44** ¹When I would bring about the
    restoration of my people,
  when I would heal Israel,
The guilt of Ephraim stands out,
  the wickedness of Samaria;
They practice falsehood,
  thieves break in, bandits plunder
    abroad.
² Yet they do not remind themselves
  that I remember all their wickedness.
Even now their crimes surround them,
  present to my sight.

Failure of the Monarchy*

³ In their wickedness they regale the king,
  the princes too, with their deceits.
⁴ They are all kindled to wrath
  like a blazing oven,
Whose fire the baker desists from stirring
  once the dough is kneaded until it has
    risen.
⁵ On the day of our king,
  the princes are overcome with the heat
    of wine.
He extends his hand among dissemblers;
⁶ the plotters approach with hearts like
    ovens.
All the night their anger sleeps;
  in the morning it flares like a blazing
    fire.
⁷ They are all heated like ovens,
  and consume their rulers.
All their kings have fallen;
  none of them calls upon me.

Foreign Alliances

⁸ Ephraim mingles with the nations,
  Ephraim is a hearth cake unturned.*
⁹ Strangers have sapped his strength,
  but he takes no notice of it;
Of gray hairs, too, there is a sprinkling,
  but he takes no notice of it.
¹⁰ The arrogance of Israel bears witness
    against him;
  yet they do not return to the LORD,
    their God,
  nor seek him, for all that.
¹¹ Ephraim is like a dove,
  silly and senseless;
They call upon Egypt,
  they go to Assyria.
¹² Even as they go I will spread my net
    around them,

6, 4: Piety: the word is translated "love" in Hos 2, 21 and
in v 6 below.

6, 11: Harvest: when the land will reap the consequences
of its sins.

7, 3-7: This passage refers to the dynastic upheavals of Israel's declining days. Between the death of Jeroboam II and
the fall of Samaria to the Assyrians, a matter of some twenty-
five years, there were four separate dynasties on the throne
and as many murdered kings. The prophet compares the Israelite nobles who were inflamed with passion to an overheated
oven that consumes what it is supposed to bake; thus the land

consumes its kings. Regale: with wine (v 3). Like fire smoldering through the night and blazing up in the morning, the
sleeping anger of plotters soon breaks out in open rebellion;
the succession of night and morning suggests the short reigns
of the various kings of this troubled period.

7, 8: A hearth cake unturned: burnt on one side, half baked
on the other, and therefore useless. Israel's decline in power
is ascribed to its disastrous meddling in the power politics of
the neighboring nations.

i: 1 Sm 15, 22; Eccl 4, 17; Mt 9, 13; 12, 7.

like birds in the air I will bring them
down.
In an instant I will send them captive
from their land.

Perversity of Israel

13 Woe to them, they have strayed from
me!
Ruin to them, they have sinned against
me!
Though I wished to redeem them,
they spoke lies against me.
14 They have not cried to me from their
hearts
when they wailed upon their beds;
For wheat and wine they lacerated
themselves,*
while they rebelled against me.
15 Though I trained and strengthened their
arms,
yet they devised evil against me.
16 They have again become useless,
like a treacherous bow.
Their princes shall fall by the sword
because of the insolence of their
tongues;
thus they shall be mocked in the land
of Egypt.

CHAPTER 8

See RG
241-44 1 A trumpet to your lips,
You who watch over the house of the
LORD!
Since they have violated my covenant,
and sinned against my law,
2 While to me they cry out,
"O God of Israel, we know you!"
3 The men of Israel have thrown away
what is good;
the enemy shall pursue them.
4 *They made kings, but not by my authority;
they established princes, but without
my approval.

With their silver and gold they made
idols for themselves, to their own
destruction.
5 Cast away your calf, O Samaria!
my wrath is kindled against them;
How long will they be unable to attain
innocence in Israel?
6 The work of an artisan,
no god at all,
Destined for the flames—
such is the calf of Samaria!
7 When they sow the wind,
they shall reap the whirlwind;
The stalk of grain that forms no ear
can yield no flour;
Even if it could,
strangers would swallow it.
8 Israel is swallowed up;
he is now among the nations
a thing of no value.
9 They went up to Assyria—
a wild ass off on its own—
Ephraim bargained for lovers.
10 Even though they bargain with the
nations,
I will now gather an army;
King and princes shall shortly
succumb under the burden.

11 When Ephraim made many altars to
expiate sin,
his altars became occasions of sin.*
12 Though I write for him my many
ordinances,
they are considered as a stranger's.
13 Though they offer sacrifice,
immolate flesh and eat it,
the LORD is not pleased with them.
He shall still remember their guilt
and punish their sins;
they shall return to Egypt.
14 Israel has forgotten his maker

7, 14: They lacerated themselves: a common oriental practice in prayers of earnest impetration (1 Kgs 18, 28); the practice was forbidden in Israelite religion (Lv 19, 28; Dt 14, 1).

8, 4-6: Israel's monarchy and separate sanctuary are here associated, as in 1 Kgs 12, 20-33; both were the result of rebellion against the divinely approved Davidic dynasty and the Jerusalem temple with the ark of the covenant. The calf image set up by Jeroboam I in the royal shrines prevented Israel

from attaining innocence (vv 5f).

8, 11: The very multiplicity of sanctuaries throughout the land was a danger to the purity of worship. The local shrines were speedily assimilated to the cult places used by the Canaanites, and the Lord was identified with the god Baal worshiped there. Thus the Deuteronomic writers, influenced by prophetic ideas, ended by restricting sacrificial worship to the one temple in Jerusalem.

Prophets and Gender

Hosea's primary image for Israel's disloyalty to God is the wife who is unfaithful to her husband and has become a prostitute. One reason Hosea chose this image is the fact that his audience was primarily male—the men held the power and wealth in ancient patriarchal societies such as biblical Israel. For these men, faithless wives were a stinging shame. Hosea wanted to shock them, so they would see the seriousness of their crimes. The image of the faithless wife gave Hosea a forceful means of criticizing the abuses of Israel's male elite. The problem of the image is that it leads some readers to connect disloyalty and sin with women in particular, a connection that must be clearly rejected to keep such an image from being used to disparage and mistreat women. In fact, Hosea only refers to one specific woman who is described as unfaithful. Nowhere does Hosea imply that all women are the same; rather, it is the priests and leaders who are condemned as a group (Hos 4, 4–7).

---

and built palaces.
Judah, too, has fortified many cities;
  but I will send fire upon his cities,
  to devour their castles.[j]

See RG 241-44

CHAPTER 9

Exile without Worship

[1] Rejoice not, O Israel,
  exult not like the nations!
For you have been unfaithful to your God,
  loving a harlot's hire
  upon every threshing floor.*
[2] Threshing floor and wine press shall not nourish them,
  the new wine shall fail them.

[3] They shall not dwell in the LORD's land;
  Ephraim shall return to Egypt,
  and in Assyria they shall eat unclean food.
[4] They shall not pour libations of wine to the LORD,
  or proffer their sacrifices before him.
Theirs will be like mourners' bread,*
  that makes unclean all who eat of it;
Such food as they have shall be for themselves;
  it cannot enter the house of the LORD.

[5] What will you do on the festival day,
  the day of the LORD's feast?*
[6] When they go from the ruins,
  Egypt shall gather them in, Memphis shall bury them.
Weeds shall overgrow their silver treasures,
  and thorns invade their tents.

The Prophet Ridiculed

[7] They have come, the days of punishment!
  they have come, the days of recompense!
Let Israel know it!
  "The prophet is a fool,
  the man of the spirit is mad!"
Because your iniquity is great,
  great, too, is your hostility.
[8] A prophet is Ephraim's watchman with God,
  yet a fowler's snare is on all his ways,
  hostility in the house of his God.
[9] They have sunk to the depths of corruption,
  as in the days of Gibeah;*
He shall remember their iniquity
  and punish their sins.

9, 1f: Upon every threshing floor: an allusion to harvest festivals in honor of Baal, to whom the Israelites had attributed the fertility of the land; cf Hos 2, 7.

9, 4: Mourners' bread: bread eaten at funeral rites; cf Dt 26, 13f. Contact with a corpse made a person ritually unclean, together with everything he touched. Such bread could not be offered to the Lord.

9, 5: The LORD's feast: doubtless the autumn feast of Booths, the most important of the Israelite public celebrations; cf Lv 23, 34.

9, 9: The days of Gibeah: a reference to the outrage committed at Gibeah in the days of the Judges (Jgs 19, 22-30).

j: Am 2, 5.

Crime of Baal-peor

10 Like grapes in the desert,
    I found Israel;
Like the first fruits of the fig tree in its
    prime,
    I considered your fathers.
When they came to Baal-peor*
    and consecrated themselves to the
    Shame,
    they became as abhorrent as the thing
    they loved.
11 The glory of Ephraim flies away like a
    bird:
    no birth, no carrying in the womb, no
    conception.
Were they to bear children,
    I would slay the darlings of their
    womb.
12 Even though they bring up their
    children,
    I will make them childless, till not one
    is left.
Woe to them
    when I turn away from them!
13 Ephraim, as I saw, was like Tyre,
    planted in a beauteous spot;
But Ephraim shall bring out
    his children to the slayer.
14 Give them, O LORD!
    give them what?
Give them an unfruitful womb,*
    and dry breasts!

Crime of Gilgal

15 All their wickedness is in Gilgal;*
    yes, there they incurred my hatred.
Because of their wicked deeds
    I will drive them out of my house.
I will love them no longer;
    all their princes are rebels.[k]
16 Ephraim is stricken,
    their root is dried up;
    they shall bear no fruit.

17 My God will disown them
    because they have not listened to him;
    they shall be wanderers among the
    nations.

CHAPTER 10

See RG
241–44

Punishment of Idolatry

1 Israel is a luxuriant vine
    whose fruit matches its growth.
The more abundant his fruit,
    the more altars he built;
The more productive his land,
    the more sacred pillars* he set up.
2 Their heart is false,
    now they pay for their guilt;
God shall break down their altars
    and destroy their sacred pillars.
3 If they would say,
    "We have no king"—
Since they do not fear the LORD,
    what can the king do for them?
4 Nothing but make promises,
    swear false oaths, and make
    alliances,
While justice grows wild
    like wormwood* in a plowed field!
5 The inhabitants of Samaria fear
    for the calf of Beth-aven;*
The people mourn for it
    and its priests wail over it,
    because the glory has departed from it.
6 It too shall be carried to Assyria,
    as an offering to the great king.
Ephraim shall be taken into captivity,
    Israel be shamed by his schemes.

7 The king of Samaria shall disappear,
    like foam upon the waters.
8 The high places of Aven shall be
    destroyed,
    the sin of Israel;
    thorns and thistles shall overgrow their
    altars.

9, 10: At Baal-peor (Nm 25, 1-5) the Israelites consecrated themselves to Baal, here called the Shame.
9, 14: An unfruitful womb: this appears to be a reversal of the ancient blessing of Joseph contained in Gn 49, 25f, in which the increase, hence fruitfulness, promised to the patriarch is even signified by the name of his son Ephraim, on whose descendants the prophet now invokes the curse of extinction.
9, 15: Gilgal: see note on Hos 4, 15.

10, 1: Sacred pillars: see note on Hos 3, 4.
10, 4: Justice . . . like wormwood: the administration of justice, which should have been the mainstay of the people, has in corrupt hands become another instrument of oppression; cf Am 6, 13.
10, 5: The calf of Beth-aven: see notes on Hos 4, 15; 8, 4ff.

k: 1 Sm 8, 5.

Then they shall cry out to the mountains,
  "Cover us!"
and to the hills, "Fall upon us!"[l]

9 Since the days of Gibeah
  you have sinned, O Israel.
There they took their stand;
  war was not to reach them in Gibeah.[m]
10 Against the wanton people I came
  and I chastised them;[n]
I gathered troops against them
  when I chastised them for their two
    crimes.*

Time To Seek the Lord

11 Ephraim was a trained heifer,
  willing to thresh;
I myself laid a yoke
  upon her fair neck;
Ephraim was to be harnessed, Judah was
    to plow,
Jacob was to break his furrows:
12 "Sow for yourselves justice,
  reap the fruit of piety;
Break up for yourselves a new field,
  for it is time to seek the LORD,
till he come and rain down justice
  upon you."[o]
13 But you have cultivated wickedness,
  reaped perversity,
  and eaten the fruit of falsehood.

Because you have trusted in your
    chariots,
  and in your many warriors,
14 Turmoil shall break out among your
    tribes
  and all your fortresses shall be ravaged
As Salman ravaged Beth-arbel* in time
    of war,
  smashing mothers and their children.[p]

15 So shall it be done to you, Bethel,
  because of your utter wickedness:
At dawn the king of Israel
  shall perish utterly.

CHAPTER 11

When Israel Was a Child

See RG
241-44

1 When Israel was a child I loved him,
  out of Egypt* I called my son.[q]
2 The more I called them,
  the farther they went from me,
Sacrificing to the Baals
  and burning incense to idols.
3 Yet it was I who taught Ephraim to walk,
  who took them in my arms;
4 I drew them with human cords,
  with bands of love;*
I fostered them like one
  who raises an infant to his cheeks;
Yet, though I stooped to feed my child,
  they did not know that I was their
    healer.

5 He shall return to the land of Egypt,
  and Assyria shall be his king;
6 The sword shall begin with his cities
  and end by consuming his solitudes.
Because they refused to repent,
  their own counsels shall devour them.
7 His people are in suspense about
    returning to him;
and God, though in unison they cry out
    to him,
  shall not raise them up.

End of the Exile

8 How could I give you up, O Ephraim,
  or deliver you up, O Israel?
How could I treat you as Admah,
  or make you like Zeboiim?*
My heart is overwhelmed,

10, 10: Their two crimes: possibly the outrage described in Jgs 19 is conceived as a double crime, of adultery and murder. Or the prophet regards the proclamation of the monarchy (cf 1 Sm 10, 23f) as a crime.

10, 14: As Salman ravaged Beth-arbel: allusion to an invasion not otherwise mentioned in the Bible. Salman may have been the Moabite king of this name mentioned in an inscription of Tiglath-pileser III. There were several Beth-arbels in Palestine; this one was probably in Transjordan.

11, 1: Out of Egypt: Hosea, like most of the prophets, dates the real beginning of Israel from the time of Moses and

the Exodus. Mt 2, 15 applies this text to the return of the Christ Child from Egypt.

11, 4: I drew them . . . with bands of love: not forcing them like draft animals, but drawing them with kindness and affection.

11, 8: Admah . . . Zeboiim: cities destroyed with Sodom and Gomorrah (Dt 29, 22).

---

l: Is 2, 19; Lk 23, 30; Rv 6, 16.   *m:* Jgs 20, 1.   *n:* Jer 4, 3.   *o:* Is 45, 8.   *p:* Jgs 8, 10ff.   *q:* Mt 2, 15.

my pity is stirred.[r]

⁹ I will not give vent to my blazing anger,
  I will not destroy Ephraim again;
For I am God and not man,
  the Holy One present among you;
  I will not let the flames consume you.

¹⁰ They shall follow the LORD,
  who roars like a lion;
When he roars,
  his sons shall come frightened from
    the west,
¹¹ Out of Egypt they shall come trembling,
    like sparrows,
  from the land of Assyria, like doves;
And I will resettle them in their homes,
  says the LORD.

See RG
241-44

CHAPTER 12

Infidelity of Israel

¹ Ephraim has surrounded me with lies,
  the house of Israel, with deceit;
Judah is still rebellious against God,
  against the Holy One, who is faithful.
² Ephraim chases the wind,
  ever pursuing the gale.
His lies and falsehoods are many:
  he comes to terms with Assyria,
  and carries oil to Egypt.*
³ *The LORD has a grievance against Israel:
  he shall punish Jacob for his conduct,
  for his deeds he shall repay him.
⁴ In the womb he supplanted his brother,
  and as a man he contended with God;[s]
⁵ He contended with the angel and
    triumphed,
  entreating him with tears.
At Bethel he met God
  and there he spoke with him:
⁶ The LORD, the God of hosts,
  the LORD is his name!
⁷ You shall return by the help of your God,
  if you remain loyal and do right
  and always hope in your God.

⁸ A merchant who holds a false balance,
  who loves to defraud!
⁹ Though Ephraim says,
  "How rich I have become;
  I have made a fortune!"
All his gain shall not suffice him
  for the guilt of his sin.
¹⁰ I am the LORD, your God,
  since the land of Egypt;
I will again have you live in tents,
  as in that appointed time.
¹¹ I granted many visions
  and spoke to the prophets,
  through whom I set forth examples.
¹² In Gilead is falsehood, they have come to
    nought,
  in Gilgal they sacrifice to bullocks;
Their altars are like heaps of stones
  in the furrows of the field.

¹³ When Jacob fled to the land of Aram,
  he served for a wife;
  for a wife Israel tended sheep.[t]
¹⁴ By a prophet* the LORD brought Israel
    out of Egypt,
  and by a prophet they were protected.[u]
¹⁵ Ephraim has exasperated his lord;
  therefore he shall cast his bloodguilt
    upon him
  and repay him for his outrage.

CHAPTER 13

Furrows of the Field

See RG
241-44

¹ Ephraim's word caused fear,
  for he was exalted in Israel;
  but he sinned through Baal and died.

Punishment for Ingratitude

² Now they continue to sin,
  making for themselves molten images,
Silver idols according to their fancy,
  all of them the work of artisans.
"To these," they say, "offer sacrifice."
  Men kiss calves!

12, 2: He comes . . . Egypt: allusion to the commercial and military pacts with the great powers, consistently condemned by the prophets as derogatory of the Lord's claim on his people.
12, 3-7: Contemporary Israel and the Israel represented by its ancestor Jacob (Israel) are here alternated, a splendid example of the Hebrew concept of "corporate personality" or

easy transition from the individual to the community of which he is part. Hosea recalls the history of Jacob as it now appears in Genesis, but with some differences of detail and order.
12, 14: A prophet: Moses.

r: Gn 19, 24f.   s: Gn 25, 26; 32, 25.   t: Gn 28, 5; 29, 20.   u: Ex 14, 21f.

³ Therefore, they shall be like a morning
    cloud
  or like the dew that early passes away,
Like chaff storm-driven from the
    threshing floor
  or like smoke out of the window.

⁴ I am the LORD, your God,
  since the land of Egypt;
You know no God besides me,
  and there is no savior but me.ᵛ
⁵ I fed you in the desert,
  in the torrid land.
⁶ They ate their fill;
  when filled, they became proud of heart
  and forgot me.

⁷ Therefore, I will be like a lion to them,
  like a panther by the road I will keep
    watch.
⁸ I will attack them like a bear robbed of
    its young,
  and tear their hearts from their breasts;
I will devour them on the spot like a
    lion,
  as though a wild beast were to rend
    them.

⁹ Your destruction, O Israel!
  who is there to help you?
¹⁰ Where now is your king,
  that he may rescue you in all your
    cities?
And your rulers, of whom you said,
  "Give me a king and princes"?ʷ
¹¹ I give you a king in my anger,
  and I take him away in my wrath.*

¹² The guilt of Israel is wrapped up,
  his sin is stored away.

¹³ The birth pangs shall come for him,
  but he shall be an unwise child;

For when it is time he shall not present
    himself
  where children break forth.*
¹⁴ Shall I deliver them from the power of
    the nether world?*
  shall I redeem them from death?ˣ
Where are your plagues, O death!
  where is your sting, O nether world!
  My eyes are closed to compassion.

¹⁵ Though he be fruitful among his fellows,
  an east wind shall come, a wind from
    the LORD,
  rising from the desert,
That shall dry up his spring,
  and leave his fountain dry.
It shall loot his land
  of every precious thing.ʸ

CHAPTER 14

See RG
241-44

¹ Samaria shall expiate her guilt,
  for she has rebelled against her God.
They shall fall by the sword,
  their little ones shall be dashed to pieces,
  their expectant mothers shall be ripped
    open.

Sincere Conversion

² Return, O Israel, to the LORD, your God;
  you have collapsed through your
    guilt.
³ Take with you words,
  and return to the LORD;
Say to him, "Forgive all iniquity,
  and receive what is good, that we may
    render
  as offerings the bullocks from our stalls.
⁴ Assyria will not save us,
  nor shall we have horses to mount;
We shall say no more, 'Our god,'
  to the work of our hands;
  for in you the orphan finds
    compassion."

13, 11: I give you a king . . . in my wrath: the Lord punishes the people of the northern kingdom by giving them incompetent kings who are soon deposed.

13, 13: Israel's sin is such as to warrant its destruction (v 12), because it refuses to do penance. It will therefore perish as surely as the unborn child which dies in its mother's body because it does not properly employ the only way to safety.

13, 14: Shall . . . nether world: a vigorous affirmation of

the Lord's determination to destroy Israel. St. Paul cites these words in a different sense (1 Cor 15, 54f), that of the ultimate victory of life over death in the resurrection of the body on the last day, wrought through the merits of Christ's passion and resurrection.

v: Is 43, 11. w: 1 Sm 8, 5. x: 1 Cor 15, 54. y: Ex 19, 12.

⁵ I will heal their defection,
    I will love them freely;
    for my wrath is turned away from them.
⁶ I will be like the dew for Israel:
    he shall blossom like the lily;
    He shall strike root like the Lebanon cedar,
⁷   and put forth his shoots.
    His splendor shall be like the olive tree
      and his fragrance like the Lebanon cedar.
⁸ Again they shall dwell in his shade
    and raise grain;
    They shall blossom like the vine,
      and his fame shall be like the wine of
        Lebanon.

14, 10: A later addition in the style of the wisdom literature.

⁹ Ephraim! What more has he to do with
    idols?
    I have humbled him, but I will prosper
      him.
    "I am like a verdant cypress tree"—
      Because of me you bear fruit!

* * *

¹⁰ Let him who is wise understand these
    things;
    let him who is prudent know them.
    Straight are the paths of the LORD,
    in them the just walk,
    but sinners stumble in them.*

See RG
244–46

The Book of Joel

This prophecy is rich in apocalyptic imagery and strongly eschatological in tone. It was composed about 400 B.C. Its prevailing theme is the day of the Lord.

A terrible invasion of locusts ravaged Judah. So frightful was the scourge that the prophet visualized it as a symbol of the coming day of the Lord. In the face of this threatening catastrophe, the prophet summoned the people to repent, to turn to the Lord with fasting and weeping. They were ordered to convoke a solemn assembly in which the priests would pray for deliverance. The Lord answered their prayer and promised to drive away the locusts and bless the land with peace and prosperity. To these material blessings would be added an outpouring of the spirit on all flesh. St. Peter, in his first discourse before the people at Pentecost (Acts 2, 16-21), sees in the coming of the Holy Spirit the fulfillment of this promise (1, 1—3, 5).

The concluding poem pictures the nations gathered in the Valley of Jehoshaphat, where the Lord is about to pass judgment. Israel's enemies are summoned to hear the solemn indictment; their evil deeds are at last requited. The tumultuous throng assembled in the valley of decision is made up of the enemies of God and they face inevitable destruction. The oracle changes abruptly from the terrifying image of judgment to a vision of Israel restored and forever secure from her enemies. God is both the vindicator of his people and the source of their blessing (4, 1-21).

———

CHAPTER 1

The Land Invaded. ¹The word of the LORD which came to Joel, the son of Pethuel.

See RG
245

² Hear this, you elders!
    Pay attention, all you who dwell in the
      land!
    Has the like of this happened in your
      days,
    or in the days of your fathers?
³ Tell it to your children,
    and your children to their children,
    and their children to the next
      generation.
⁴ What the cutter left,
    the locust swarm has eaten;
    What the locust swarm left,
    the grasshopper has eaten;
    And what the grasshopper left,
    the devourer* has eaten.

1, 4: Cutter . . . locust . . . grasshopper . . . devourer: these names refer to various species of locusts: they can only be approximate.

The Desert Locust

The desert locust is a distant cousin of the American grasshopper. It lives and breeds in the great desert stretching from the Sahara in Africa to the Arabian Peninsula, including the Sinai and Judean deserts. In the right conditions, it multiplies rapidly, crowds into dense swarms, and sweeps into neighboring fertile areas, where it eats its own weight in green food each day. A swarm of desert locusts in Somaliland in 1957 was estimated to include 16 billion locusts and to weigh 50,000 tons. The desert locust's threat to Middle Eastern societies is recorded in the earliest human records and continues into the present, where it is monitored and combated by the United Nations Food and Agriculture Organization's (UNFAO) Emergency Center for Locust Operations.

5 Wake up, you drunkards, and weep;
    wail, all you drinkers of wine,
Because the juice of the grape
    will be withheld from your mouths.
6 For a people* has invaded my land,
    mighty and without number;
His teeth are the teeth of a lion,
    and his molars those of a lioness.
7 He has laid waste my vine,
    and blighted my fig tree;
He has stripped it, sheared off its bark;
    its branches are made white.
8 Lament like a virgin girt with sackcloth
    for the spouse of her youth.
9 Abolished are offering and libation
    from the house of the LORD;
In mourning are the priests,
    the ministers of the LORD.
10 The field is ravaged,
    the earth mourns,
Because the grain is ravaged,
    the must has failed,
    the oil languishes.

11 Be appalled, you husbandmen!
    wail, you vinedressers!
Over the wheat and the barley,
    because the harvest of the field has
        perished.
12 The vine has dried up,
    the fig tree is withered;
The pomegranate, the date palm also, and
    the apple,
    all the trees of the field are dried up;

Yes, joy has withered away
    from among mankind.

Call to Penance

13 Gird yourselves and weep, O priests!
    wail, O ministers of the altar!
Come, spend the night in sackcloth,
    O ministers of my God!
The house of your God is deprived
    of offering and libation.
14 Proclaim a fast,
    call an assembly;
Gather the elders,
    all who dwell in the land,
Into the house of the LORD, your
        God,
    and cry to the LORD!a

15 Alas, the day!
    for near is the day of the LORD,
    and it comes as ruin from the
        Almighty.
16 From before our very eyes
    has not the food been cut off;
And from the house of our God,
    joy and gladness?
17 The seed lies shriveled under its
        clods;
    the stores are destroyed,
The barns are broken down,
    for the grain has failed.
18 How the beasts groan!
    The herds of cattle are bewildered!
Because they have no pasturage,

1, 6: A people: the locusts compared to an invading army.

a: Jl 2, 15.

even the flocks of sheep have
    perished.

19 To you, O LORD, I cry!
    for fire has devoured the pastures of
        the plain,
    and flame has enkindled all the trees of
        the field.
20 Even the beasts of the field
    cry out to you;
For the streams of water are dried
        up,
    and fire has devoured the pastures of
        the plain.

CHAPTER 2

See RG
245

The Day of the Lord

1 Blow the trumpet in Zion,
    sound the alarm on my holy mountain!
Let all who dwell in the land tremble,
    for the day of the LORD is coming;
2 Yes, it is near, a day of darkness and of
        gloom,
    a day of clouds and somberness!
Like dawn spreading over the mountains,
    a people numerous and mighty!
Their like has not been from of old,
    nor will it be after them,
    even to the years of distant generations.
3 Before them a fire devours,
    and after them a flame enkindles;
Like the garden of Eden is the land
        before them,
    and after them a desert waste;
    from them there is no escape.

4 Their appearance is that of horses;
    like steeds they run.
5 As with the rumble of chariots
    they leap on the mountaintops;
As with the crackling of a fiery flame
    devouring stubble;
Like a mighty people
    arrayed for battle.
6 Before them peoples are in torment,
    every face blanches.

7 Like warriors they run,

like soldiers they scale the wall;
They advance, each in his own lane,
    without swerving from their paths.
8 No one crowds another,
    each advances in his own track;
Though they fall into the ditches,
    they are not checked.
9 They assault the city,
    they run upon the wall,
    they climb into the houses;
In at the windows
    they come like thieves.
10 Before them the earth trembles,
    the heavens shake;
The sun and the moon are darkened,
    and the stars withhold their
        brightness.[b]

11 The LORD raises his voice
    at the head of his army;
For immense indeed is his camp,
    yes, mighty, and it does his bidding.
For great is the day of the LORD,
    and exceedingly terrible; who can bear
        it?[c]
12 Yet even now, says the LORD,
    return to me with your whole heart,
    with fasting, and weeping, and
        mourning;
13 Rend your hearts, not your garments,
    and return to the LORD, your God.
For gracious and merciful is he,
    slow to anger, rich in kindness,
    and relenting in punishment.[d]
14 Perhaps he will again relent
    and leave behind him a blessing,
Offerings and libations
    for the LORD, your God.[e]
15 Blow the trumpet in Zion!
    proclaim a fast,
    call an assembly;[f]
16 Gather the people,
    notify the congregation;
Assemble the elders,
    gather the children
    and the infants at the breast;
Let the bridegroom quit his room,

b: Jl 4, 15; Is 13, 10; Ez 32, 7f; Mt 24, 29; Mk 13, 24; Lk 21, 25f. c: Jer 30, 7; Am 5, 18; Zep 1, 15. d: Ps 86, 5; Jon 4, 2. e: Jon 3, 9. f: Jl 1, 14.

The Day of the LORD

Appearing five times in Joel (1, 15; 2, 1; 2, 11; 3, 4; 4, 14), this expression is used in the Bible for a decisive divine act in human affairs. In its earliest occurrence, Amos uses it to describe an act of God's judgment on Israel (Am 5, 18–20). But because Amos implies that his audience believes this expression referred to an act of God's salvation, scholars think the day of the LORD originally may have had a positive meaning, describing God's victory on Israel's behalf. In some cases, in fact, this phrase is used for God's judgment on the nations and restoration of Judah (Ob 15–21; Zec 14, 1–9). Scholars disagree whether the day of the LORD is used both ways in Joel— for judgment in Joel 1, 15; 2, 1; 2, 11 and for salvation in Joel 3, 4; 4, 14—or whether all uses point toward the final salvation described in ch 3.

and the bride her chamber.
17 Between the porch and the altar*
 let the priests, the ministers of the
  LORD, weep,
And say, "Spare, O LORD, your people,
 and make not your heritage a reproach,
 with the nations ruling over them!
Why should they say among the peoples,
 'Where is their God?' "

Blessings for God's People. 18Then the LORD was stirred to concern for his land and took pity on his people. 19The LORD answered and said to his people:

See, I will send you
 grain, and wine, and oil,
 and you shall be filled with them;
No more will I make you
 a reproach among the nations.
20 No, the northerner* I will remove far
  from you,
 and drive him out into a land arid and
  waste,
With his van toward the eastern sea,
 and his rear toward the western sea;
And his foulness shall go up,
 and his stench shall go up.

21 Fear not, O land!

exult and rejoice!
 for the LORD has done great
  things.
22 Fear not, beasts of the field!
 for the pastures of the plain are
  green;
The tree bears its fruit,
 the fig tree and the vine give their
  yield.
23 And do you, O children of Zion, exult
 and rejoice in the LORD, your God!
He has given you the teacher of
  justice:*
 he has made the rain come down for
  you,
 the early and the late rain as before.g
24 The threshing floors shall be full of
  grain
 and the vats shall overflow with wine
  and oil.
25 And I will repay you for the years
 which the locust has eaten,
The grasshopper, the devourer, and the
  cutter,
 my great army which I sent among
  you.
26 You shall eat and be filled,
 and shall praise the name of the LORD,
  your God,

2, 17: The priests stood in the open space between the outdoor altar of holocausts and the temple building, facing the latter in order thereby to look toward God present in the holy of holies.

2, 20: The northerner: the locusts, that are compared to an invading army which in Palestine came from the north; cf Jer 1, 14f; 4, 6; Ez 26, 7; 38, 6. 15.

2, 23: The teacher of justice: the rain sent by God to show his fidelity to his promises, and to teach his people to be faith-

ful to his commandments; cf Dt 11, 14. There is also a play on words here between the Hebrew word moreh (teacher) and the Hebrew word yoreh (the early rain). The expression likewise has a messianic connotation; cf Is 30, 20. The founder of the Essene sect of Qumran (second century B.C.) was known as "The Teacher of Justice."

g: Hos 10, 12.

Because he has dealt wondrously with
  you;
  my people shall nevermore be put to
    shame.
27 And you shall know that I am in the
    midst of Israel;
  I am the LORD, your God, and there is
    no other;
  my people shall nevermore be put to
    shame.

See RG 245

CHAPTER 3

1Then afterward I will pour out[h]
my spirit* upon all mankind.
Your sons and daughters shall
    prophesy,
  your old men shall dream dreams,
  your young men shall see visions;
2 Even upon the servants and the
    handmaids,
  in those days, I will pour out my spirit.

3 And I will work wonders in the heavens
    and on the earth,
  blood, fire, and columns of smoke;
4 The sun will be turned to darkness,
  and the moon to blood,
  At the coming of the day of the LORD,
  the great and terrible day.[i]
5 Then everyone shall be rescued
  who calls on the name of the LORD;
  For on Mount Zion there shall be a
    remnant,
  as the LORD has said,
  And in Jerusalem survivors
  whom the LORD shall call.[j]

See RG 246

CHAPTER 4

Judgment upon the Nations

1 Yes, in those days, and at that time,
  when I would restore the fortunes
  of Judah and Jerusalem,
2 I will assemble all the nations

and bring them down to the Valley
  Jehoshaphat,*
And I will enter into judgment with them
    there
  on behalf of my people and my
    inheritance, Israel;
  Because they have scattered them among
    the nations,
  and divided my land.
2 Over my people they have cast lots;
  they gave a boy for a harlot,
  and sold a girl for the wine they drank.

4Moreover, what are you to me, Tyre and
Sidon, and all the regions of Philistia?
Would you take vengeance upon me by
some action? But if you do take action
against me, swiftly, speedily, I will return
your deed upon your own head. 5You took
my silver and my gold, and brought my precious treasures into your temples! 6You sold
the people of Judah and Jerusalem to the
Greeks, removing them far from their own
country! 7See, I will rouse them from the
place into which you have sold them, and I
will return your deed upon your own head. 8I
will sell your sons and your daughters to the
people of Judah, who shall sell them to the
Sabeans,* a nation far off. Indeed, the LORD
has spoken.

9 Declare this among the nations:
  proclaim a war,
  rouse the warriors to arms!
Let all the soldiers
  report and march!
10 Beat your plowshares into swords,
  and your pruning hooks into spears;
  let the weak man say, "I am a warrior!"*

11 Hasten and come, all you neighboring
    peoples,
  assemble there!
[Bring down, O Lord, your warriors!*]

3, 1f: I will pour out my spirit: in the Old Testament the
spirit is the gift of God bestowed on those acting as his agents.
The promise of the spirit is quoted by St. Peter in Acts 2, 17-21
as fulfilled in an eminent way by the gift of the Holy Spirit, the
Third Person of the Blessed Trinity, bestowed on the Apostles.

4, 2: Valley of Jehoshaphat: a symbolic name of
the place of final judgment (v 14). The name Jehoshaphat signifies "Yahweh judges." This place has been popularly identified with the Kidron Valley.

4, 8: Sabeans: a south Arabian people known for their
commerce.

4, 10: This imagery is used in the reverse sense in Is 2, 4;
Mi 4, 3. Here the warlike weapons are made in response to
God's summons to armies which he selected to expel forever
the unlawful invaders from the land of his chosen people.

4, 11: Warriors: the angels; cf Zec 14, 5.

h: -5: Is 44, 3; Acts 2, 17-21. i: Jl 2, 10. j: Rom 10, 13.

.. nations bestir themselves and
come up
to the Valley of Jehoshaphat;
For there will I sit in judgment
upon all the neighboring nations.

¹³ Apply the sickle,*k*
for the harvest is ripe;
Come and tread,
for the wine press is full;
The vats overflow,
for great is their malice.*
¹⁴ Crowd upon crowd
in the valley of decision;
For near is the day of the LORD
in the valley of decision.
¹⁵ Sun and moon are darkened,
and the stars withhold their
brightness.*l*
¹⁶ The LORD roars from Zion,
and from Jerusalem raises his
voice;
The heavens and the earth quake,
but the LORD is a refuge to his
people,
a stronghold to the men of Israel.*m*

Salvation for God's Elect

¹⁷ Then shall you know that I, the LORD, am
your God,
dwelling on Zion, my holy mountain;
Jerusalem shall be holy,
and strangers shall pass through her no
more.
¹⁸ And then, on that day,*n*
the mountains shall drip new wine,
and the hills shall flow with milk;
And the channels of Judah
shall flow with water:
A fountain shall issue from the house of
the LORD,
to water the Valley of Shittim.*
¹⁹ Egypt shall be a waste,
and Edom a desert waste,
Because of violence done to the people
of Judah,
because they shed innocent blood in
their land.
²⁰ But Judah shall abide forever,
and Jerusalem for all generations.
²¹ I will avenge their blood,
and not leave it unpunished.
The LORD dwells in Zion.

4, 13: Because of their numerous crimes, the nations are ripe for punishment. The use of warlike weapons against them is likened to the onslaught on the fields and vines at harvest time.

4, 18: The Valley of Shittim, or "the ravine of the acacia trees": perhaps a part of the Kidron Valley southeast of Jerusalem; the prophetic picture of a stream of water flowing from a fountain in the temple of Jerusalem is to be found in Ez 47, 1. The Shittim east of the Jordan (see note on Nm 25, 1) is hardly referred to here.

k: Rv 14, 15. *l:* Jl 2, 10; 3, 4. *m:* Jer 25, 30; Am 1, 2. *n:* Am 9, 13; Ez 47, 1-12; Zec 14, 8.

See RG
246-50

The Book of Amos

Amos was a shepherd of Tekoa in Judah, who exercised his ministry during the prosperous reign of Jeroboam II (786–746 B.C.). He prophesied in Israel at the great cult center of Bethel, from which he was finally expelled by the priest in charge of this royal sanctuary. The poetry of Amos, who denounces the hollow prosperity of the northern kingdom, is filled with imagery and language taken from his own pastoral background. The book is an anthology of his oracles and was compiled either by the prophet or by some of his disciples.

The prophecy begins with a sweeping indictment of Damascus, Philistia, Tyre, and Edom; but the forthright herdsman saves his climactic de-

nunciation for Israel, whose injustice and idolatry are sins against the light granted to her. Israel could indeed expect the day of Yahweh, but it would be a day of darkness and not light. When Amos prophesied the overthrow of the sanctuary, the fall of the royal house, and the captivity of the people, it was more than Israelite officialdom could bear. The priest of Bethel drove Amos from the shrine—but not before hearing a terrible sentence pronounced upon himself.

Amos is a prophet of divine judgment, and the sovereignty of Yahweh in nature and history dominates his thought. But he was no innovator; his conservatism was in keeping with the whole prophetic tradition calling the people back to the high moral and religious demands of Yahweh's revelation. In common with the other prophets, Amos knew that divine punishment is never completely destructive; it is part of the hidden plan of God to bring salvation to men. The perversity of the human will may retard, but it cannot totally frustrate, this design of a loving God. The last oracle opens up a perspective of restoration under a Davidic king.

The Book of Amos may be divided as follows:
I: Judgment of the Nations (1, 1—2, 16).
II: Words and Woes for Israel (3, 1—6, 14).
III: Symbolic Visions: Threats and Promises (7, 1—9, 8b).
Epilogue: Messianic Perspective (9, 8c-15).

I: Judgment of the Nations

CHAPTER 1

See RG 248–49

*1*The words of Amos, a shepherd from Tekoa,*a* which he received in vision concerning Israel, in the days of Uzziah, king of Judah, and in the days of Jeroboam, son of Joash, king of Israel, two years before the earthquake:*

2 The LORD will roar from Zion,
  and from Jerusalem raise his voice:
The pastures of the shepherds will
    languish,
  and the summit of Carmel wither.*b*

Aram

3   Thus says the LORD:
For three crimes of Damascus, and for
    four,*

1, 1: The earthquake: which according to Hebrew tradition marked the crime of Uzziah when he attempted to offer incense in the temple (2 Chr 26, 16-21). Zechariah mentions it several centuries later (Zec 14, 5).

1, 3: For three crimes . . . four: crime after crime, an indefinite number; cf Am 1, 6. The series of judgments on the foreign nations shows that the Lord demands the observance of the moral order everywhere; Israel and Judah, despite their privileged position, are no exception. I will not revoke my word: God will not withdraw his threat of punishment against each of these nations. They threshed Gilead: the people of Aram under King Hazael had devastated Gilead; cf 2 Kgs 10, 32f.

I will not revoke my word;
Because they threshed Gilead
  with sledges of iron,
4 I will send fire* upon the house of
    Hazael,
  to devour the castles of Ben-hadad.
5 I will break the bar of Damascus;*
  I will root out those who live in the
    Valley of Aven,
And the sceptered ruler of Beth-eden;
  the people of Aram shall be exiled to
    Kir,
  says the LORD.

Philistia

6   Thus says the LORD:
For three crimes of Gaza, and for four,
  I will not revoke my word;
Because they took captive whole groups
  to hand over to Edom,
7 I will send fire upon the wall of Gaza,
  to devour her castles;
8 I will root out those who live in Ashdod,
  and the sceptered ruler of Ashkelon;
I will turn my hand against Ekron,
  and the last of the Philistines shall
    perish,
  says the Lord God.

Tyre

9   Thus says the LORD:
For three crimes of Tyre, and for four,
  I will not revoke my word;
Because they delivered whole groups
    captive to Edom,
  and did not remember the pact of
    brotherhood,*
10 I will send fire upon the wall of Tyre,
  to devour her castles.

1, 4: Fire: devastation caused by the Assyrians (Am 1, 7. 10. 12. 14; 2, 2. 5); cf 1 Sm 15, 18. Hazael . . . Ben-hadad: kings of the Arameans whose capital was Damascus (v 5); they fought against Israel (2 Kgs 13, 3), and had long occupied the region of Gilead (v 3) in Transjordan.

1, 5: Bar of Damascus: the beam securing the main gate of the city against invaders, symbol of its defenses. Valley of Aven ("vale of wickedness") . . . Beth-eden ("house of pleasure"): Aramean territory from southwest to northeast.

1, 9: Pact of brotherhood: Hiram of Tyre had made a pact with Solomon and called him brother (1 Kgs 5, 12; 9, 13).

a: Zec 14, 5.   *b:* Jer 25, 30; Jl 3, 16.

Judgments on Israel's Neighbors

In typical two-part judgment speeches, containing indictments and sentences, Amos announces divine judgment on seven of Israel's closest neighbors. The indictments in each case involve acts of brutality against neighboring peoples. The phrase "says the LORD," which begins and ends these speeches, identifies them as divine oracles and the prophet as a divine spokesperson.

Edom

11   Thus says the LORD:
For three crimes of Edom, and for four,
   I will not revoke my word;
Because he pursued his brother* with the
    sword,
    choking up all pity;
Because he persisted in his anger
   and kept his wrath to the end,
12 I will send fire upon Teman,
   and it will devour the castles of
    Bozrah.*

Ammon

13   Thus says the LORD:
For three crimes of the Ammonites, and
    for four,
   I will not revoke my word;
Because they ripped open expectant
    mothers in Gilead,
   while extending their territory,
14 I will kindle a fire upon the wall of
    Rabbah,*
   and it will devour her castles
Amid clamor on the day of battle
   and stormwind in a time of tempest.
15 Their king shall go into captivity,
   he and his princes with him, says the
    LORD.

See RG 248–49

CHAPTER 2

Moab

1   Thus says the LORD:
For three crimes of Moab, and for four,

   I will not revoke my word;
Because he burned to ashes
   the bones of Edom's king,*
2 I will send fire upon Moab,
   to devour the castles of Kerioth;
Moab shall meet death amid uproar
   and shouts and trumpet blasts.
3 I will root out the judge from her midst,
   and her princes I will slay with him,
    says the LORD.

Judah

4   Thus says the LORD:
For three crimes of Judah, and for four,
   I will not revoke my word;
Because they spurned the law of the
    LORD,
   and did not keep his statutes;
Because the lies* which their fathers
    followed
   have led them astray,
5 I will send fire upon Judah,
   to devour the castles of Jerusalem.

Israel

6   Thus says the LORD:
For three crimes of Israel, and for four,*
   I will not revoke my word;
Because they sell the just man for silver,
   and the poor man for a pair of
    sandals.*
7 They trample the heads of the weak
   into the dust of the earth,
   and force the lowly out of the way.

1, 11: Pursued his brother: the Edomites were descended from Esau, the brother of Jacob (Gn 25—27); nevertheless they constantly nourished enmity against Jacob's descendants, the Israelites.

1, 12: Teman and Bozrah: two of the chief cities of Edom; cf Jer 49, 20.

1, 14: Rabbah: now called Amman, the modern capital of the Hashemite Kingdom of Jordan.

2, 1: Here the prophet stresses the gravity of Moab's violation of the Semitic custom of providing honorable burial for

the dead.

2, 4: The lies: false gods, who exist only in the minds of their worshipers. The crimes of Judah are infidelity and idolatry, in contrast to the sins for which the surrounding nations are judged.

2, 6-13: The detailed crimes of Israel are placed in strong contrast with the benefits with which the Lord favored his people.

2, 6: A pair of sandals: indicating how cheaply the rich regarded the poor.

Israel's Stubbornness

A brief historical summary in 2, 9–12 stresses Israel's stubbornness by contrasting it with Goc's acts of salvation on Israel's behalf. The judgment imposed for Israel's crimes (vv. 13–16) will bring an end to Israel's strongest defenses: its fast runners, its strongest warriors, its most skilled archers, and its best horsemen.

Son and father go to the same
    prostitute,
  profaning my holy name.
8 Upon garments taken in pledge
    they recline beside any altar;*
And the wine of those who have been
    fined
  they drink in the house of their
    god.

9 Yet it was I who destroyed the Amorites
    before them,
  who were as tall as the cedars,
    and as strong as the oak trees.
I destroyed their fruit above,
    and their roots beneath.c
10 It was I who brought you up from the
    land of Egypt,
  and who led you through the desert for
    forty years,
  to occupy the land of the Amorites:d
11 I who raised up prophets among your
    sons,
  and nazirites* among your young
    men.
Is this not so, O men of Israel?
  says the LORD.
12 But you gave the nazirites wine to
    drink,
  and commanded the prophets not to
    prophesy.

13 Beware, I will crush you into the
    ground
  as a wagon crushes when laden with
    sheaves.
14 Flight shall perish from the swift,

and the strong man shall not retain his
    strength;
The warrior shall not save his life,
15   nor the bowman stand his ground;
The swift of foot shall not escape,
  nor the horseman save his life.
16 And the most stouthearted of warriors
  shall flee naked on that day, says the
    LORD.

II: Words and Woes for Israel

CHAPTER 3

See RG. 249

First Word. 1Hear this word, O men of Israel, that the LORD pronounces over you, over the whole family that I brought up from the land of Egypt:

2 You alone have I favored,
  more than all the families of the
    earth;
Therefore I will punish you
  for all your crimes.*

3 Do two walk together
  unless they have agreed?
4 Does a lion roar in the forest
  when it has no prey?
Does a young lion cry out from its den
  unless it has seized something?
5 Is a bird brought to earth by a snare
  when there is no lure for it?
Does a snare spring up from the
    ground
  without catching anything?
6 If the trumpet sounds in a city,
  will the people not be frightened?

2, 8: Upon garments . . . any altar: usurers kept the garments taken as pledges from the poor; but instead of restoring them to their owners before nightfall (Ex 22, 25; Dt 24, 12), they used them in idolatrous worship. Wine . . . their god: under the guise of a religious ceremony they drink the wine obtained through unjust fines.

2, 11: Nazirites: see note on Nm 6, 1ff.
3, 2: God's choice of Israel brought its own responsibility.

c: Nm 21, 24; Dt 2, 24.   d: Ex 14, 21; Dt 8, 2. 14.

Judgment on Bethel

Located in the southern part of Israel, Bethel, together with Dan in the north, was one of Israel's major religious centers. The judgment against Israel's houses (3, 15) that follows the judgment on Bethel contains an implicit criticism of the rich. Israel's wealthiest citizens built winter houses in the Jordan valley to escape the cold winter climate in the mountains of Samaria, and they made furniture inlaid with ivory for their homes (6, 4).

If evil befalls a city,
    has not the LORD caused it?*
7 Indeed, the Lord GOD does nothing
    without revealing his plan
    to his servants, the prophets.

8 The lion roars—
    who will not be afraid!
The Lord GOD speaks—
    who will not prophesy!

9 Proclaim this in the castles of
    Ashdod,
    in the castles of the land of Egypt:
"Gather about the mountain of
    Samaria,
    and see the great disorders within
    her,
    the oppression in her midst."*
10 For they know not how to do what is
    right,
    says the LORD,
Storing up in their castles
    what they have extorted and
    robbed.
11   Therefore, thus says the Lord
    GOD:
An enemy shall surround the land,
    and strip you of your strength,
    and pillage your castles.
12   Thus says the LORD:
As the shepherd snatches from the mouth
    of the lion
    a pair of legs or the tip of an ear of his
    sheep,

So the Israelites who dwell in Samaria
    shall escape
    with the corner of a couch or a piece of
    a cot.

13 Hear and bear witness against the house of Jacob, says the Lord GOD, the God of hosts:

14 On the day when I punish Israel for his
    crimes,
    I will visit also the altars of Bethel:
The horns of the altar shall be broken
    off
    and fall to the ground.
15 Then will I strike the winter house
    and the summer house;
The ivory apartments* shall be ruined,
    and their many rooms shall be no
    more,
    says the LORD.

CHAPTER 4

Second Word

See RG 249

1 Hear this word, women of the mountain
    of Samaria,
    you cows of Bashan,*
You who oppress the weak
    and abuse the needy;
Who say to your lords,
    "Bring drink for us!"
2 The Lord GOD has sworn by his holiness:
    Truly the days are coming upon you
When they shall drag you away with
    hooks,
    the last of you with fishhooks;

3, 6: The sufferings which sinful man experiences through the permissive will of God are presented here, as elsewhere in the Old Testament, simply as caused by the Lord.

3, 9: Israel's southern neighbors, beyond Judah, are invited by the prophetic orator to witness the moral disorders of God's people.

3, 15: Ivory apartments: rooms containing furniture inlaid in ivory, similar to the pieces discovered in the excavations at Samaria.

4, 1: Bashan: the region east of the Sea of Galilee, famous for its rich pasture and fattened herds, to which Amos likens the indolent women of Samaria.

Judgment on Samaria's Elite Women

In this indictment of their oppression of the poor (4, 1), Amos compares Israel's leading women to cattle grazing in Israel's prime pasture land, Bashan.

[3] You shall go out through the breached
    walls
    each by the most direct way,
And you shall be cast into the mire,
    says the LORD.

[4] Come to Bethel and sin,
    to Gilgal, and sin the more;*
Each morning bring your sacrifices,
    every third day, your tithes;
[5] Burn leavened food as a thanksgiving
    sacrifice,
    proclaim publicly your freewill
      offerings,
For so you love to do, O men of Israel,
    says the Lord GOD.

[6] Though I have made your teeth
    clean of food in all your cities,
    and have made bread scarce in all your
      dwellings,
Yet you returned not to me,
    says the LORD.

[7] Though I also withheld the rain from you
    when the harvest was still three
      months away;
I sent rain upon one city
    but not upon another;
One field was watered by rain,
    but another without rain dried up;
[8] Though two or three cities staggered to
    one city
    for water that did not quench their thirst;
Yet you returned not to me,
    says the LORD.

[9] I struck you with blight and searing
    wind;
    your many gardens and vineyards,
your fig trees and olive trees the locust
    devoured;
Yet you returned not to me,
    says the LORD.[e]

[10] I sent upon you a pestilence like that of
    Egypt,*
    and with the sword I slew your young
      men;
Your horses I let be captured,
    to your nostrils I brought the stench of
      your camps;
Yet you returned not to me,
    says the LORD.

[11] I brought upon you such upheaval
    as when God overthrew Sodom and
      Gomorrah:
    you were like a brand plucked from
      the fire;
Yet you returned not to me,
    says the LORD.[f]

[12] So now I will deal with you in my own
    way, O Israel!
    and since I will deal thus with you,
    prepare to meet your God, O Israel:
[13] Him who formed the mountains, and
    created the wind,
    and declares to man his thoughts;
Who made the dawn and the darkness,
    and strides upon the heights of the
      earth:
    The LORD, the God of hosts by name.

CHAPTER 5

Third Word

See RG 249

[1] Hear this word which I utter over you,
    a lament, O house of Israel:
[2] She is fallen, to rise no more,

4, 4f: This invitation to the sanctuaries of the northern kingdom is ironical. Pilgrimages to the shrines of Bethel and Gilgal were the more displeasing to God because they were contrary to his will and ineffective toward improvement of morals.

4, 10: Pestilence like that of Egypt: plagues were well known in Egypt; cf Dt 7, 15; 28, 27. 60. Stench of your camps: caused by the unburied bodies.

e: Hg 2, 17. f: Gn 19, 24.

the virgin Israel;
She lies abandoned upon her land,
with no one to raise her up.

3   For thus says the Lord GOD:
The city that marched out with a
          thousand
     shall be left with a hundred,
Another that marched out with a
          hundred
     shall be left with ten,
     of the house of Israel.

4 For thus says the LORD
     to the house of Israel:
Seek me, that you may live,
5   but do not seek Bethel;
Do not come to Gilgal,
     and do not cross to Beer-sheba.
For Gilgal shall be led into exile,
     and Bethel shall become nought.
6 Seek the LORD, that you may live,
     lest he come upon the house of Joseph*
          like a fire
That shall consume, with none to quench it
     for the house of Israel:
8 He who made the Pleiades and Orion,
     who turns darkness into dawn,
     and darkens day into night;
Who summons the waters of the sea,
     and pours them out upon the surface of
          the earth;g
9 Who flashes destruction upon the
          strong,
     and brings ruin upon the fortress;
     whose name is LORD.

First Woe
7 Woe to those who turn judgment to
          wormwood
     and cast justice to the ground!
10 They hate him who reproves at the gate*
     and abhor him who speaks the truth.

11 Therefore, because you have trampled
          upon the weak
     and exacted of them levies of grain,
Though you have built houses of hewn
          stone,
     you shall not live in them!
Though you have planted choice
          vineyards,
     you shall not drink their wine!h

12 Yes, I know how many are your crimes,
     how grievous your sins:
Oppressing the just, accepting bribes,
     repelling the needy at the gate!
13 Therefore the prudent man is silent at
          this time,
     for it is an evil time.
14 Seek good and not evil,
     that you may live;
Then truly will the LORD, the God of hosts,
     be with you as you claim!
15 Hate evil and love good,
     and let justice prevail at the gate;
Then it may be that the LORD, the God of
          hosts,
     will have pity on the remnant of Joseph.i

16 Therefore, thus says the LORD,
     the God of hosts, the Lord:
In every square there shall be
          lamentation,
     and in every street they shall cry, Alas!
          Alas!
They shall summon the farmers to wail
     and professional mourners to lament,
17 And in every vineyard there shall be
          lamentation
     when I pass through your midst, says
          the LORD.

Second Woe
18 Woe to those who yearn for the day of
     the LORD!*

5, 6: House of Joseph: the kingdom of Israel or northern kingdom, the chief tribes of which were descended from Ephraim and Manasseh, the sons of Joseph; cf Am 5, 15; 6, 6.
5, 10: At the gate: see note on Ps 127, 5.
5, 18: Day of the LORD: a technical expression which in earliest times referred to God's special intervention in human affairs. Through it his power and justice triumphed in his people. The present passage is the first instance in which it means

a day of punishment of sinners. During the exile it assumed the meaning of a time when God would avenge Israel against her oppressors and bring about her restoration (Jer 50, 27; Ez 30, 3ff). Still later it came to mean the day of final judgment of the world when the good will be rewarded and the wicked punished (Jl 2, 1ff; Zep 1, 14ff; Mal 3, 19ff).

g: Am 9, 6.   h: Zep 1, 13.   i: Ps 97, 10; Rom 12, 9.

What will this day of the LORD mean
for you?
Darkness and not light!*j*
19 As if a man were to flee from a
lion,
and a bear should meet him;
Or as if on entering his house
he were to rest his hand against the
wall,
and a snake should bite him.
20 Will not the day of the LORD be darkness
and not light,
gloom without any brightness?

21 *I hate, I spurn your feasts,
I take no pleasure in your
solemnities;*k*
22 Your cereal offerings I will not accept,
nor consider your stall-fed peace
offerings.
23 Away with your noisy songs!
I will not listen to the melodies of your
harps.
But if you would offer me holocausts,
24 then let justice surge like water,
and goodness like an unfailing
stream.
25 Did you bring me sacrifices and
offerings*l*
for forty years in the desert, O house
of Israel?*
26 You will carry away Sakkuth, your
king,
and Kaiwan, your star god,*
the images that you have made for
yourselves;
27 For I will exile you beyond Damascus,
say I, the LORD, the God of hosts by
name.

CHAPTER 6
Third Woe

See RG
249

1 *Woe to the complacent in Zion,
To the overconfident on the mount of
Samaria,*
Leaders of a nation favored from the first,
to whom the people of Israel have
recourse!*m*
2 Pass over to Calneh and see,
go from there to Hamath the great,
and down to Gath of the Philistines!
Are you better than these kingdoms,
or is your territory wider than
theirs?
3 You would put off the evil day,
yet you hasten the reign of violence!

4 Lying upon beds of ivory,
stretched comfortably on their
couches,
They eat lambs taken from the flock,
and calves from the stall!
5 Improvising to the music of the harp,
like David, they devise their own
accompaniment.
6 They drink wine from bowls
and anoint themselves with the best
oils;
yet they are not made ill by the
collapse of Joseph!
7 Therefore, now they shall be the first to
go into exile,
and their wanton revelry shall be done
away with.

8 The Lord GOD has sworn by his very
self,
say I, the LORD, the God of hosts:

5, 21-27: The Lord condemns, not ritual worship in itself, but the cult whose exterior rites and solemnity have no relation to interior morality and justice. The Israelites falsely worshiped him as neighboring nations adored Baal or Chamos, deities which were thought to protect their respective peoples against their enemies in return for ritual observances, without any relation to right conduct.

5, 25: The meaning is not certain; according to some, the idea is that during the forty years' wandering in the desert the simple, rudimentary worship of God was accompanied by the practice of justice, in contrast to the elaborate ritual unaccompanied by works of justice in the prophet's time.

5, 26: Sakkuth . . . star god: although the text is uncertain,

it seems quite probable that reference is made to the Assyrian deities, Sakkuth, god of war and light, and Kaiwan, the planet Saturn. The people will go into exile, from which these gods have been unable to save them.

6, 1-7: The luxury of the people in Samaria will be punished by exile. They failed to learn the lesson from Calneh, Hamath and Gath at the approach of the powerful and warlike Assyrians.

6, 1: The complacent in Zion . . . the overconfident . . . of Samaria: the proud and self-interested rulers of Judah and Israel.

j: Jer 30, 7; Jl 2, 11; Zep 1, 15.   *k:* Is 1, 11; Jer 6, 20; Mal 1, 12.   *l:* Acts 7, 42.   *m:* Lk 6, 24.

I abhor the pride of Jacob,
    I hate his castles,
    and I give over the city with
        everything in it;[n]
[9] Should there remain ten men
    in a single house, these shall die.
[10] Only a few shall be left
    to carry the dead out of the houses;
If one says to a man inside a house,
    "Is anyone with you?" and he answers,
        "No one,"
Then he shall say, "Silence!"
    for no one must mention the name of
        the LORD.
[11] Indeed, the LORD has given the command
    to shatter the great house to bits,
    and reduce the small house to rubble.

[12] Can horses run across a cliff?
    or can one plow the sea with oxen?*
Yet you have turned judgment into gall,
    and the fruit of justice into
        wormwood.
[13] You rejoice in Lodebar,
    and say, "Have we not, by our own
        strength,
    seized for ourselves Karnaim?"*
[14] Beware, I am raising up against you,
    O house of Israel,
    say I, the LORD, the God of hosts,
A nation* that shall oppress you
    from Labo of Hamath even to the
        Wadi Arabah.

III: Symbolic Visions:
Threats and Promises

CHAPTER 7

See RG
249–50

Vision of Locusts. [1]This is what the
Lord GOD showed me: He was forming a locust swarm when the late growth began to
come up (the late growth after the king's

mowing*). [2]While they were eating all the
grass in the land, I said:

Forgive, O Lord GOD!
    How can Jacob stand?
    He is so small!

[3]And the LORD repented of this. "It shall
not be," said the Lord GOD.
Vision of Fire. [4]Then the Lord GOD
showed me this: he called for a judgment by
fire.* It had devoured the great abyss, and
was consuming the land, [5]when I said:

Cease, O Lord GOD!
    How can Jacob stand?
    He is so small!

[6]The LORD repented of this. "This also
shall not be," said the Lord GOD.
Vision of the Plummet. [7]Then the Lord
GOD showed me this: he was standing by a
wall, plummet in hand.* [8]The LORD asked
me, "What do you see, Amos?" And when I
answered, "A plummet," the LORD said:

See, I will lay the plummet
    in the midst of my people Israel;
    I will forgive them no longer.
[9] The high places of Isaac shall be laid
        waste,
    and the sanctuaries of Israel made
        desolate;
    I will attack the house of Jeroboam
        with the sword.

Amos and Amaziah. [10]Amaziah, the
priest of Bethel, sent word to Jeroboam, king
of Israel: "Amos has conspired against you
here within Israel; the country cannot endure
all his words. [11]For this is what Amos says:

Jeroboam shall die by the sword,
    and Israel shall surely be exiled from
        its land."

6, 12: Can horses . . . oxen?: one cannot change the course
of nature, as the Israelites attempted to do by their sins of injustice.

6, 13: Lodebar . . . Karnaim: in Transjordan; they had been
captured by the Israelites. Perhaps it is in irony that reference
is made to these two cities, for the root of the first suggests
"nothing" and that of the second, "horns" or "strength."

6, 14: A nation: Assyria.

7, 1: The king's mowing: the first mowing, a portion of
which was payable to the king as a tax.

7, 4: Fire: understood by many as a burning drought.

7, 7: Plummet in hand: signifying that God is about to
withdraw his mercy from his people and that the nation is to
be measured for destruction.

n: Jer 51, 14.

Judgment on Israel's Businessmen

In the judgment speech beginning in 8, 4, Amos indicts Israel's merchants for economic abuses (vv. 4–6) and announces a sentence of widespread devastation (vv. 7–14). The new moon and the sabbath are religious holidays (Is 1, 13; Hos 2, 11) considered an annoyance by merchants who cannot make a profit during their observance. God's judgment will turn their current condition on its head: the wealthy will starve, and joy will become mourning. Those who currently ignore their God will seek God out but be unable to find the word of the LORD.

¹²To Amos, Amaziah said: "Off with you, visionary, flee to the land of Judah! There earn your bread by prophesying, ¹³but never again prophesy in Bethel; for it is the king's sanctuary and a royal temple." ¹⁴Amos answered Amaziah, "I was no prophet, nor have I belonged to a company of prophets; I was a shepherd and a dresser of sycamores.* ¹⁵The LORD took me from following the flock, and said to me, Go, prophesy to my people Israel. ¹⁶Now hear the word of the LORD!"

You say: prophesy not against Israel,
> preach not against the house of
> > Isaac.
¹⁷   Now thus says the LORD:
Your wife shall be made a harlot in the
> > city,
> and your sons and daughters shall fall
> > by the sword;
Your land shall be divided by measuring
> > line,
> and you yourself shall die in an
> > unclean land;
Israel shall be exiled far from its
> > land.

CHAPTER 8

See RG
249-50
Vision of the Fruit Basket. ¹This is what the Lord GOD showed me: a basket of ripe fruit. ²"What do you see, Amos?" he asked. I answered, "A basket of ripe fruit." Then the LORD said to me:

The time is ripe to have done with my
> > people Israel;
> I will forgive them no longer.

³ The temple songs shall become wailings
> > on that day,
> says the Lord GOD.
Many shall be the corpses,
> strewn everywhere.—Silence!

Against Greed

⁴ Hear this, you who trample upon the
> > needy
> and destroy the poor of the land!
⁵ "When will the new moon be over," you
> > ask,
> "that we may sell our grain,
> and the sabbath, that we may display
> > the wheat?
We will diminish the ephah,*
> add to the shekel,
> and fix our scales for cheating!
⁶ We will buy the lowly man for silver,
> and the poor man for a pair of
> > sandals;
> even the refuse of the wheat we will
> > sell!"
⁷ The LORD has sworn by the pride of
> > Jacob:*
> Never will I forget a thing they have
> > done!
⁸ Shall not the land tremble because of
> > this,
> and all who dwell in it mourn,
While it rises up and tosses like the Nile,
> and settles back like the river of
> > Egypt?*

⁹ On that day, says the Lord GOD,
> I will make the sun set at midday

7, 14f: Amos denies that he belonged to the class of professional prophets; his vocation is due to the personal intervention of the Lord.

8, 5: Ephah: a standard of measure; a little more than a bushel.

8, 7: The pride of Jacob: the sinful pride detested by God (Am 6, 8), in contrast to God himself, who is the true Pride of Jacob.

8, 8: The figure is based on the annual flooding of the river Nile.

Amos's Visions Concluded

Like Amos's other visions (Am 7, 1–9; 8, 1–3), the vision in 9, 1–4 shows God's coming judgment to Amos, but the judgment predicted here is the harshest and most complete of them all.

and cover the earth with darkness in
  broad daylight.
[10] I will turn your feasts into mourning
  and all your songs into lamentations.
I will cover the loins of all with sackcloth
  and make every head bald.
I will make them mourn as for an only
    son,
  and bring their day to bitter end.[o]

[11] Yes, days are coming, says the Lord GOD,
  when I will send famine upon the land:
Not a famine of bread, or thirst for water,
  but for hearing the word of the LORD.
[12] Then shall they wander from sea to sea
  and rove from the north to the east
In search of the word of the LORD,
  but they shall not find it.

[13] On that day, fair virgins and young men
  shall faint from thirst;
[14] Those who swear by the shameful idol of
    Samaria,
  "By the life of your god, O Dan!"
"By the life of your love, O Beer-sheba!"
  those shall fall, never to rise again.*

CHAPTER 9

See RG
249-50

*Vision of the Altar.** [1] I saw the Lord
standing beside the altar, and he said:

Strike the bases, so that the doorjambs
    totter
  till you break them off on the heads of
    them all!
Those who are left I will slay with the
    sword;
  not one shall flee,
  no survivor shall escape.

[2] Though they break through to the nether
    world,
  even from there my hand shall bring
    them out;
Though they climb to the heavens,
  I will bring them down;[p]
[3] Though they hide on the summit of
    Carmel,
  there too I will hunt them out and take
    them away;
Though they hide from my gaze
  in the bottom of the sea,
  I will command the serpent* there to
    bite them;
[4] Though they are led into captivity by
    their enemies,
  there will I command the sword to slay
    them.
I will fix my gaze upon them
  for evil, and not for good.[q]
[5] I, the Lord GOD of hosts.
I melt the earth with my touch,
  so that all who dwell on it mourn,
While it all rises up like the Nile,
  and settles back like the river of
    Egypt;
[6] I have built heaven, my upper chamber,
  and established my vault over the earth;
I summon the waters of the sea
  and pour them out upon the surface of
    the earth,
  I, the LORD by name.[r]

[7] Are you not like the Ethiopians to me,
  O men of Israel, says the LORD?
Did I not bring the Israelites from the
    land of Egypt
  As I brought the Philistines from
    Caphtor

8, 14: Dan and Beer-sheba, the extreme northern and southern limits of the country, where idolatrous worship was offered.

9, 1-8: There will be no escape from God's punishment, symbolized here by the destruction of a building, probably the schismatic temple at Bethel.

9, 3: Serpent: the sea monster of familiar legend, subdued by God at the time of creation and lurking still in the ocean depths; cf Ps 89, 10f.

o: Tb 2, 6; 1 Mc 1, 41.   *p:* Ps 139, 8.   *q:* Jer 44, 11.   *r:* Am 5, 8.

Vision of Renewal

The ruined state of the hut of David (Am 9, 11), a reference to the Davidic monarchy that ruled Judah, appears to place this concluding speech after the fall of Jerusalem in 587 B.C. This image also suggests that this text was written from the perspective of Judah, the southern kingdom, rather than from the perspective of the northern kingdom, which Amos addressed. It anticipates the return of the Babylonian exiles to rebuild their ruined country.

and the Arameans* from Kir?ˢ
⁸ The eyes of the Lord GOD are on this
    sinful kingdom:
I will destroy it from off the face of
    the earth.

Epilogue: Messianic Perspective

But I will not destroy the house of Jacob
    completely,
    says the LORD.
⁹ For see, I have given the command
    to sift the house of Israel among all
      the nations,
As one sifts with a sieve,
    letting no pebble fall to the ground.
¹⁰ By the sword shall all sinners among my
    people die,
    those who say, "Evil will not reach or
      overtake us."
¹¹ *On that day I will raise up
    the fallen hut of David;
I will wall up its breaches,
    raise up its ruins,
    and rebuild it as in the days of
      old,ᵗ

¹² That they may conquer what is left of
    Edom
    and all the nations that shall bear my
      name,
say I, the LORD, who will do this.
¹³ Yes, days are coming,
    says the LORD,
When the plowman shall overtake the
    reaper,
    and the vintager, him who sows the
      seed;
The juice of grapes shall drip down the
    mountains,
    and all the hills shall run with it.ᵘ
¹⁴ I will bring about the restoration of my
    people Israel;
    they shall rebuild and inhabit their
      ruined cities,
Plant vineyards and drink the wine,
    set out gardens and eat the fruits.
¹⁵ I will plant them upon their own
    ground;
    never again shall they be plucked
From the land I have given them,
    say I, the LORD, your God.

9, 7: The Ethiopians . . . the Philistines . . . the Arameans: by nature Israel is not different from any other nation. It was not because of any merit on Israel's part that God delivered them from Egypt. Caphtor: the island of Crete.

9, 11f: In Acts 15, 15ff St. James interprets this passage in a messianic sense. Fallen hut: the kingdom. The nations that shall bear my name: the Gentile peoples who shall be converted to the Lord, that is, conquered by him, and therefore shall bear his name.

s: Dt 2, 23; Jer 47, 4.   *t:* Acts 15, 16.   *u:* Jl 3, 18.

See RG 250–51

The Book of Obadiah

The twenty-one verses of this book contain the shortest and sternest prophecy in the Old Testament. Nothing is known of the author, although his oracle against Edom, a long-standing enemy of Israel, indicates a date of composition some-time in the fifth century B.C. During this period the Edomites had been forced to abandon their ancient home near the Gulf of Aqaba and had settled in southern Judah, where they appear among the adversaries of the Jews returning from exile.

The prophecy is a bitter cry for vengeance against Edom for its heinous crimes. The mountain of Esau will be occupied and ravaged by the enemy but Zion shall remain inviolate. Judah and Israel shall again form one nation; and that triumphant refrain of Israelite eschatology will be heard once more: "The Kingdom is the Lord's!" Many of the verses in this prophecy can be paralleled in Jer 49, 7-22 but it is difficult to determine the precise relationship between these similar passages.

———

Title and Theme

1 The vision of Obadiah.
[Thus says the LORD God:]
Of Edom we have heard a message from
the LORD,
and a herald has been sent among the
nations:
"Up! let us go to war against him!"*a*

Edom Shall Perish

2 See, I make you small among the
nations;*b*
you are held in dire contempt.
3 The pride of your heart has deceived you:
you who dwell in the clefts of the rock,
whose abode is in the heights,
Who say in your heart,
"Who will bring me down to earth?"
4 Though you go as high as the eagle,
and your nest be set among the stars,
From there will I bring you down,
says the LORD.
5 If thieves came to you, if robbers by night,*c*
how could you be thus destroyed:
would they not steal merely till they
had enough?
If vintagers came to you,
would they not leave some gleanings?*
6 How they search Esau,
seek out his hiding places!

7 To the border they drive you—
all your allies;
They deceive you, they overpower you—
those at peace with you;
Those who eat your bread
lay snares beneath you:
There is no understanding in him!*
8 Shall I not, says the LORD, on that day
make the wise men* disappear from
Edom,
and understanding from the mount of
Esau?*d*
9 Your warriors, O Teman,* shall be
crushed,
till all on Mount Esau are destroyed.

The Cause

10 Because of violence to your brother
Jacob,*
disgrace shall cover you
and you shall be destroyed forever.*e*
11 On the day when you stood by,
on the day when aliens carried off his
possessions,
And strangers entered his gates
and cast lots over Jerusalem,
you too were one of them.*
12 Gaze not upon the day of your brother,
the day of his disaster;
Exult not over the children of Judah
on the day of their ruin;
Speak not haughtily
on the day of distress!
13 Enter not the gate of my people
on the day of their calamity;
Gaze not, you at least, upon his
misfortune
on the day of his calamity;
Lay not hands upon his possessions
on the day of his calamity!
14 Stand not at the crossroads
to slay his refugees;

5: Something of value may escape the robber, and the vintager always leaves something for the gleaners, but God's devastation of Edom will be complete.

7: There is no understanding in him: Edom's faithless allies assure one another that he does not have sense enough to be able to defend himself.

8: The wise men: Edom was proverbial for its wise men; cf Jer 49, 7.

9: Teman: one of the names used for the land southeast of Palestine, here synonymous with Edom. Esau: here used as

the name of the land.

10: Your brother Jacob: Esau, also called Edom, and Jacob, the father of Judah, were the sons of Isaac (Gn 25, 24ff).

11: After the devastation of Judah, Edom occupied the southern part of its territory. Edomites also joined the invading Chaldean forces (13) and assisted them in capturing the people of Judah (14).

a: Jer 49, 14. *b:* 2ff: Jer 49, 15f. *c:* Jer 49, 9. *d:* Is 29, 14; 1 Cor 1, 19. *e:* Gn 27, 41f.

Betray not his fugitives
on the day of distress!

Judgment upon the Nations

15 For near is the day of the LORD[f]
for all the nations!
As you have done, so shall it be done to you,
your deed shall come back upon your own head;
16 As you have drunk* upon my holy mountain,
so shall all the nations drink continually.
Yes, they shall drink and swallow,
and shall become as though they had not been.

Judah Shall Be Restored

17 But on Mount Zion there shall be a portion saved;*
the mountain shall be holy,
And the house of Jacob shall take possession
of those that dispossessed them.
18 The house of Jacob shall be a fire,

and the house of Joseph a flame;
The house of Esau shall be stubble,
and they shall set them ablaze and devour them;
Then none shall survive of the house of Esau,
for the LORD has spoken.
19 They shall occupy the Negeb, the mount of Esau,
and the foothills of the Philistines;
And they shall occupy the lands of Ephraim
and the lands of Samaria,
and Benjamin shall occupy Gilead.
20 The captives of this host of the children of Israel
shall occupy the Canaanite land as far as Zarephath,*
And the captives of Jerusalem who are in Sepharad
shall occupy the cities of the Negeb.
21 And saviors* shall ascend Mount Zion
to rule the mount of Esau,
and the kingship shall be the LORD's.

16: As you have drunk: the Lord addresses the people of Judah. As the people of Jerusalem have drunk the cup of retribution, so shall the nations, and especially Edom (18), suffer punishment. This metaphorical use of drinking the cup of God's wrath is common in the Bible; cf Jb 21, 20; Is 19, 14; Jer 25, 15f.

17ff: The Israelites shall be restored and shall occupy the lands of those who oppressed them. The survivors of Judah shall be rejoined by the returned exiles from northern Israel.

20: Zarephath: a town in Phoenicia, north of Tyre; cf

1 Kgs 17, 10. Ezekiel's ideal boundaries of the new Israel (Ez 47, 13ff) extend farther north. Sepharad: probably Sardis in western Asia Minor. The later rabbis thought it to be Spain.

21: Saviors: the victorious Israelites who will rule over their enemies after the fashion of the ancient Judges; cf Jgs 3, 9. 15. 31; 10, 1.

f: 15f: Ps 137, 7ff.

See RG 251–53

The Book of Jonah

Written in the postexilic era, probably in the fifth century B.C., this book is a didactic story with an important theological message. It concerns a disobedient prophet who attempted to run away from his divine commission, was cast overboard and swallowed by a great fish, rescued in a marvelous manner, and sent on his way to Nineveh, the traditional enemy of Israel. To the surprise of Jonah, the wicked city listened to his message of doom and repented immediately. All, from king to lowliest subject, humbled themselves in sackcloth and ashes. Seeing their repentance, God did not carry out the punishment he had planned for them. Whereupon Jonah complained to God about the

unexpected success of his mission; he was bitter because Yahweh, instead of destroying, had led the people to repentance and then spared them.

From this partly humorous story, a very sublime lesson may be drawn. Jonah stands for a narrow and vindictive mentality, all too common among the Jews of that period. Because they were the chosen people, a good many of them cultivated an intolerant nationalism which limited the mercy of God to their nation. It was abhorrent to their way of thinking that nations as wicked as Assyria should escape his wrath.

The prophecy, which is both instructive and entertaining, strikes directly at this viewpoint. It is a parable of mercy, showing that God's threatened punishments are but the expression of a merciful will which moves all men to repent and seek forgiveness. The universality of the story contrasts sharply with the particularistic spirit of many in the postexilic community. The book has also prepared the way for the gospel with its message of redemption for all, both Jew and Gentile.

CHAPTER 1

See RG
251-53 *The First Mission.* [1]This is the word of the LORD that came to Jonah,[a] son of Amittai:[*] [2]"Set out for the great city of Nineveh, and preach against it; their wickedness has come up before me."[b] [3]But Jonah made ready to flee to Tarshish[*] away from the LORD. He went down to Joppa, found a ship going to Tarshish, paid the fare, and went aboard to journey with them to Tarshish, away from the LORD.

[4]The LORD, however, hurled a violent wind upon the sea, and in the furious tempest that arose the ship was on the point of breaking up. [5]Then the mariners became frightened and each one cried to his god. To lighten the ship for themselves, they threw its cargo into the sea. Meanwhile, Jonah had gone down into the hold of the ship, and lay there fast asleep. [6]The captain came to him and said, "What are you doing asleep? Rise up, call upon your God! Perhaps God will be mindful of us so that we may not perish."

[7]Then they said to one another, "Come, let us cast lots to find out on whose account we have met with this misfortune." So they cast lots, and thus singled out Jonah. [8]"Tell us," they said, "what is your business? Where do you come from? What is your country, and to what people do you belong?" [9]"I am a Hebrew," Jonah answered them; "I worship the LORD, the God of heaven, who made the sea and the dry land."

[10]Now the men were seized with great fear and said to him, "How could you do such a thing!"—They knew that he was fleeing from the LORD, because he had told them.— [11]"What shall we do with you," they asked, "that the sea may quiet down for us?" For the sea was growing more and more turbulent. [12]Jonah said to them, "Pick me up and throw me into the sea, that it may quiet down for you; since I know it is because of me that this violent storm has come upon you."

[13]Still the men rowed hard to regain the land, but they could not, for the sea grew ever more turbulent. [14]Then they cried to the LORD: "We beseech you, O LORD, let us not perish for taking this man's life; do not charge us with shedding innocent blood, for you, LORD, have done as you saw fit."[*] [15]Then they took Jonah and threw him into the sea, and the sea's raging abated. [16]Struck with great fear of the LORD, the men offered sacrifice and made vows to him.

CHAPTER 2

See RG
251-53 [1]But the LORD sent a large fish, that swallowed Jonah; and he remained in the belly of the fish three days and three nights.[c] [2]From the belly of the fish Jonah said this prayer to the LORD, his God:

Psalm of Thanksgiving

[3] Out of my distress I called to the LORD,
    and he answered me;
From the midst of the nether world I
        cried for help,
    and you heard my voice.[d]
[4] For you cast me into the deep, into the
        heart of the sea,
    and the flood enveloped me;
All your breakers and your billows
        passed over me.[e]
[5] Then I said, "I am banished from your
        sight!
    yet would I again look upon your holy
        temple."[f]
[6] The waters swirled about me, threatening
        my life;

1, 1: Jonah, son of Amittai: a prophet of this name lived at the time of Jeroboam II (786–746 B.C.).

1, 3: Tarshish: identified by many with Tartessus, an ancient Phoenician colony in southwest Spain; precise identification with any particular Phoenician center in the western Mediterranean is uncertain. To the Hebrews it stood for the far west.

1, 14: Since it has pleased the Lord to punish Jonah, the mariners ask that in ridding themselves of him they be not charged with the crime of murder.

a: 2 Kgs 14, 25. *b:* Jon 3, 3; 4, 11. *c:* Mt 12, 40; 16, 4; Lk 11, 30; 1 Cor 15, 4. *d:* Pss 18, 7; 120, 1. *e:* Ps 42, 8. *f:* Ps 31, 23; Is 38, 11.

Jonah's Prayer

Jonah's prayer in ch 2, an appeal to God in poetic form, may be a traditional text taken over by the narrator to represent Jonah's petition. It is composed in the form of a lament, a common psalm type in which the worshiper pleads for God's help in a time of great distress (Pss 3; 5; 7). The lament opens with an address, in which the worshiper calls out to God. The description of distress follows the opening address. The image of deep waters swallowing the worshiper is common in such descriptions of distress (Ps 69, 1–2. 14–15). A petition to God follows the description of distress. Laments customarily end, as does this one, with the worshiper anticipating God's aid and promising to thank God by presenting a sacrifice at the temple. God answers Jonah's prayer, but when God does the same for Nineveh, Jonah responds much differently.

the abyss enveloped me;
seaweed clung about my head.*g*
⁷ Down I went to the roots of the
    mountains;
the bars of the nether world
were closing behind me forever,
But you brought up my life from the pit,
    O Lᴏʀᴅ, my God.*h*
⁸ When my soul fainted within me,
    I remembered the Lᴏʀᴅ;
My prayer reached you
    in your holy temple.*i*
⁹ Those who worship vain idols
    forsake their source of mercy.*j*
¹⁰ But I, with resounding praise,
    will sacrifice to you;
What I have vowed I will pay:
    deliverance is from the Lᴏʀᴅ.*k*

¹¹Then the Lᴏʀᴅ commanded the fish to spew Jonah upon the shore.

See RG 251–53

CHAPTER 3

Conversion of Nineveh. ¹The word of the Lᴏʀᴅ came to Jonah a second time: ²"Set out for the great city of Nineveh, and announce to it the message that I will tell you." ³So Jonah made ready and went to Nineveh, according to the Lᴏʀᴅ's bidding. Now Nineveh was an enormously large city; it took three days to go through it. ⁴Jonah began his

journey through the city, and had gone out a single day's walk announcing, "Forty days more and Nineveh shall be destroyed,"* ⁵when the people of Nineveh believed God; they proclaimed a fast and all of them, great and small, put on sackcloth.*l*

⁶When the news reached the king of Nineveh, he rose from his throne, laid aside his robe, covered himself with sackcloth, and sat in the ashes. ⁷Then he had this proclaimed throughout Nineveh, by decree of the king and his nobles: "Neither man nor beast, neither cattle nor sheep, shall taste anything; they shall not eat, nor shall they drink water. ⁸Man and beast shall be covered with sackcloth* and call loudly to God; every man shall turn from his evil way and from the violence he has in hand. ⁹Who knows, God may relent and forgive, and withhold his blazing wrath, so that we shall not perish."*m* ¹⁰When God saw by their actions how they turned from their evil way, he repented of the evil that he had threatened to do to them; he did not carry it out.

CHAPTER 4

Jonah's Anger: God's Reproof. ¹But this was greatly displeasing to Jonah, and he became angry.* ²"I beseech you, Lᴏʀᴅ," he prayed, "is not this what I said while I was

See RG 251–53

3, 4: Shall be destroyed: the Hebrew expression reminds the reader of the "overthrowing" of the wicked cities, Sodom and Gomorrah, by a special act of God.

3, 8: Beast . . . sackcloth: the animals carried the signs of this repentance, as on occasions of joy they bore garlands.

4, 1: He became angry: because of his narrowly national-

istic vindictiveness, Jonah did not wish the Lord to forgive the Ninevites.

g: Pss 18, 5; 69, 2.   *h:* Pss 16, 10; 30, 4.   *i:* Pss 5, 8; 18, 7; 88, 3.   *j:* Ps 31, 7.   *k:* Ps 50, 14.   *l:* Mt 12, 41; Lk 11, 32. *m:* Jl 2, 14.

still in my own country? This is why I fled at first to Tarshish. I knew that you are a gracious and merciful God, slow to anger, rich in clemency, loathe to punish.*n* ³And now, LORD, please take my life from me; for it is better for me to die than to live."*o* ⁴But the LORD asked, "Have you reason to be angry?"

⁵Jonah then left the city for a place to the east of it, where he built himself a hut and waited under it in the shade, to see what would happen to the city. ⁶And when the LORD God provided a gourd plant,* that grew up over Jonah's head, giving shade that relieved him of any discomfort, Jonah was very happy over the plant. ⁷But the next morning at dawn God sent a worm which attacked the plant, so that it withered. ⁸And

when the sun arose, God sent a burning east wind; and the sun beat upon Jonah's head till he became faint. Then he asked for death, saying, "I would be better off dead than alive."

⁹But God said to Jonah, "Have you reason to be angry over the plant?" "I have reason to be angry," Jonah answered, "angry enough to die." ¹⁰Then the LORD said, "You are concerned over the plant which cost you no labor and which you did not raise; it came up in one night and in one night it perished.* ¹¹And should I not be concerned over Nineveh, the great city, in which there are more than a hundred and twenty thousand persons who cannot distinguish their right hand from their left, not to mention the many cattle?"

4, 6: Gourd plant: the Hebrew word, kikayon, means here a wide-leafed plant of the cucumber or castor-bean variety.

4, 10f: Jonah is selfish in bemoaning his personal loss of a shady gourd plant without any concern over the threat of loss of life to the Ninevites through the destruction of their city. If God in his kindness provided the plant for his prophet with-

out the latter's effort or merit, how much more is he disposed to show love and mercy toward all men, Jew and Gentile, when they repent of their sins and implore his pardon! God's providence is also shown here to extend even to animals.

n: Ps 86, 5; Jl 2, 13.   *o:* 1 Kgs 19, 4.

See RG
253–55

The Book of Micah

Micah was a contemporary of Isaiah. Of his personal life and call we know nothing except that he came from the obscure village of Moresheth in the foothills. His were the broad vistas of the Judean lowland and the distant sea on the western horizon. With burning eloquence he attacked the rich exploiters of the poor, fraudulent merchants, venal judges, corrupt priests and prophets. To the man of the countryside the vices of the nation seemed centered in its capitals, for both Samaria and Jerusalem are singled out for judgment. An interesting notice in Jer 26, 17f informs us that the reform of Hezekiah was influenced by the preaching of Micah.

The prophecy may be divided into three parts: I: The impending judgment of the Lord, followed by an exposition of its causes, Israel's sins. Censure of Judah's leaders for betrayal of their responsibility (1, 1—3, 12). II: The glory of the restored Zion. A prince of David's house will rule over a reunited Israel. (St. Matthew's Nativity narrative points to Christ's birth in Bethlehem as the fulfillment of

this prophecy.) A remnant shall survive the chastisement of Judah and her adversaries shall be destroyed (4, 1—5, 14). III: The case against Israel, in which the Lord is portrayed as the plaintiff who has maintained fidelity to the covenant. The somber picture closes with a prayer for national restoration and a beautiful expression of trust in God's pardoning mercy (6, 1—7, 20).

It should be noted that each of these three divisions begins with reproach and the threat of punishment, and ends on a note of hope and promise.

I: Punishment of Israel's Sins

CHAPTER 1

See RG
254

Divine Judgment. ¹The word of the LORD which came to Micah of Moresheth in the days of Jotham, Ahaz, and Hezekiah, kings of Judah: that is, the vision he received concerning Samaria and Jerusalem.

Judgment on Samaria and Jerusalem

Micah's opening speech focuses on his primary audience: the ruling elite in the capitals of Israel and Judah. Samaria and Jerusalem (v. 5) are viewed as the centers of corruption in their respective kingdoms.

² Hear, O peoples, all of you,
　　give heed, O earth, and all that fills
　　you!ᵃ
Let the Lord GOD be witness against
　　you,
　　the Lord from his holy temple!*
³ For see, the LORD comes forth from his
　　place,ᵇ
　　he descends and treads upon the
　　heights of the earth.
⁴ The mountains melt under him
　　and the valleys split open,
Like wax before the fire,
　　like water poured down a slope.

⁵ For the crime of Jacob all this comes to
　　pass,
　　and for the sins of the house of Israel.
What is the crime of Jacob?
　　Is it not Samaria?
And what is the sin of the house of
　　Judah?
　　Is it not Jerusalem?
⁶ I will make Samaria a stone heap in the
　　field,
　　a place to plant for vineyards;
I will throw down into the valley her
　　stones,
　　and lay bare her foundations.
⁷ All her idols shall be broken to pieces,ᶜ
　　all her wages shall be burned in the
　　fire,
　　and all her statues I will destroy.
As the wages of a harlot they were
　　gathered,
　　and to the wages of a harlot shall they
　　return.*

⁸ For this reason I lament and wail,
　　I go barefoot and naked;
I utter lamentation like the jackals,
　　and mourning like the ostriches.ᵈ
⁹ There is no remedy for the blow she has
　　been struck;
　　rather, it has come even to Judah,
It reaches to the gate of my people,
　　even to Jerusalem.
¹⁰ Publish it not in Gath,*
　　weep not at all;
In Beth-leaphrah
　　roll in the dust.ᵉ
¹¹ Pass by,
　　you who dwell in Shaphir!
The inhabitants of Zaanan
　　come not forth from their city.
The lamentation of Beth-ezel
　　finds in you its grounds.
¹² How can the inhabitants of Maroth
　　hope for good?
For evil has come down from the LORD
　　to the gate of Jerusalem.
¹³ Harness steeds to the chariots,
　　O inhabitants of Lachish;
Lachish, the beginning of sin
　　for daughter Zion,
Because there were in you
　　the crimes of Israel.
¹⁴ Therefore you shall give parting gifts
　　to Moresheth-gath;
Beth-achzib is a deception
　　to the kings of Israel.
¹⁵ Yet must I bring to you the conqueror,
　　O inhabitants of Mareshah;
Even to Adullam shall go
　　the glory of Israel.

1, 2: His holy temple: God's heavenly temple; the prophet pictures a theophany (3f).

1, 7: The comparison of the unfaithful people with a prostitute, first found in Hosea, is frequent with the prophets; probably ritual prostitution is meant; cf Am 2, 7f; Hos 4, 14.

1, 10-15: The Judean cities here named were in the vicinity of Moresheth, the region with which Micah was most familiar. To protect the poor against it, a man's liar. They were to experience divine chastisement. In the Hebrew, wordplays on the names of these cities abound. The text is partly obscure.

a: Dt 32, 1; Is 1, 2.　b: 3f: Is 26, 21; Na 1, 5; Hb 3, 10.　c: Hos 9, 1.　d: Jb 30, 29.　e: 2 Sm 1, 20.

¹⁶ Make yourself bald, pluck out your
  hair,
    for the children whom you cherish;
  Let your baldness be as the eagle's,
    because they are exiled from you.*

CHAPTER 2

See RG
254

Social Evils

¹ Woe to those who plan iniquity,
    and work out evil on their couches;
  In the morning light they accomplish it
    when it lies within their power.
² They covet fields, and seize them;
    houses, and they take them;
  They cheat an owner of his house,
    a man of his inheritance.*
³   Therefore thus says the LORD:
  Behold, I am planning against this race
      an evil
    from which you shall not withdraw
      your necks;
  Nor shall you walk with head high,
    for it will be a time of evil.

⁴ On that day a satire shall be sung over
    you,
  and there shall be a plaintive chant:
  "Our ruin is complete,
    our fields are portioned out among our
      captors,
  The fields of my people are measured out,
    and no one can get them back!"
⁵ Thus you shall have no one
    to mark out boundaries by lot*
    in the assembly of the LORD.

⁶ "Preach not," they preach,
  "let them not preach of these
      things!"*
  The shame will not withdraw.
⁷ How can it be said, O house of Jacob,

"Is the LORD short of patience,
  or are such his deeds?"
Do not my words promise good
  to him who walks uprightly?

⁸ But of late my people has risen up as an
    enemy:
  you have stripped off the mantle
    covering the tunic
  Of those who go their way in confidence,
    as though it were spoils of war.
⁹ The women of my people you drive out
    from their pleasant houses;
  From their children you take away
    forever the honor I gave them.*
¹⁰ "Up! Be off,
    this is no place to rest";
  For any trifle you exact
    a crippling pledge.*

¹¹ If one, acting on impulse, should make
    the futile claim:
  "I pour you wine and strong drink as
    my prophecy,"
  then he would be the prophet of this
    people.
¹² I will gather you, O Jacob, each and
    every one,*
  I will assemble all the remnant of
    Israel;
  I will group them like a flock in the
    fold,
    like a herd in the midst of its corral;
    they shall not be thrown into panic by
      men.
¹³ With a leader to break the path
    they shall burst open the gate and go
      out through it;
  Their king shall go through before
      them,
    and the LORD at their head.

1, 16: Shaving the head was a sign of mourning; cf Is 3,
24; Am 8, 10.

2, 2: Land monopoly, also denounced by Isaiah, was a
chronic vice in Judah. To protect the poor against it, a man's
inheritance, his ancestral property, was supposed to be inviolate; cf 1 Kgs 21, 1-4; but the wealthy in their greed were enslaving men for their debts and depriving them of their land.

2, 5: To mark out boundaries by lot: an allusion to the initial distribution of the land of Palestine among the Israelites;
cf Jos 13—21. The appropriate punishment of those greedy
for land will be the loss of their land to their enemies (v 4), a

loss that will be irrevocable.

2, 6f: The words in quotation marks are the protestations
of the people against the prophet's predictions of doom.

2, 9: The honor I gave them: their dignity as free Israelites.

2, 10: A crippling pledge: Israelite law forbade exacting
pledges for loans that would work hardship on the borrower
(Ex 22, 25f; Dt 24, 6. 10-13. 17); but the law was habitually
violated.

2, 12f: This messianic passage concerning the restoration
after the Babylonian exile seems out of place here and is
probably a later addition.

Judgment on the Ruling Elite

Chapter 3 is composed of three typical judgment speeches. The first judgment speech, directed to political officials, includes an indictment (vv. 1–3), accusing them of devouring their people by their injustices, and a sentence (v. 4), according to which they are abandoned by God. The second judgment speech, directed to the false prophets, indicts them for accepting bribes to give favorable prophecies (v. 5). The sentence by which they are blocked from receiving further revelations (vv. 6–7) is contrasted with Micah's own power to preach (v. 8). The third judgment speech indicts Jerusalem's political and religious leaders alike: its political leaders, its priests, and its prophets (vv. 9–11), who are driven by greed rather than faithfulness to the LORD. Micah announces the sentence: the destruction of Jerusalem (v. 12).

See RG 254

CHAPTER 3

Downfall of Present Leaders

1 And I said:
Hear, you leaders of Jacob,
  rulers of the house of Israel!
Is it not your duty to know what is right,
2 you who hate what is good, and love
    evil?
You who tear their skin from them,
  and their flesh from their bones!*f*
3 They eat the flesh of my people,
  and flay their skin from them,
  and break their bones.
They chop them in pieces like flesh in a
    kettle,
  and like meat in a caldron.
4 When they cry to the LORD,
  he shall not answer them;
Rather shall he hide his face from them
    at that time,
  because of the evil they have done.

5 Thus says the LORD regarding the
    prophets*
who lead my people astray;
Who, when their teeth have something to
    bite,
  announce peace,
But when one fails to put something in
    their mouth,
  proclaim war against him.*g*

6 Therefore you shall have night, not
    vision,
  darkness, not divination;
The sun shall go down upon the prophets,
  and the day shall be dark for them.*h*
7 Then shall the seers be put to shame,
  and the diviners confounded;
They shall cover their lips, all of them,
  because there is no answer from God.
8 But as for me, I am filled with power,
  with the spirit of the LORD,
  with authority and with might;
To declare to Jacob his crimes
  and to Israel his sins.
9 Hear this, you leaders of the house of
    Jacob,
  you rulers of the house of Israel!
You who abhor what is just,
  and pervert all that is right;
10 Who build up Zion with bloodshed,
  and Jerusalem with wickedness!
11 Her leaders render judgment for a bribe,
  her priests give decisions for a salary,
  her prophets divine for money,
While they rely on the LORD, saying,
  "Is not the LORD in the midst of us?
  No evil can come upon us!"*i*
12 Therefore, because of you,
  Zion shall be plowed like a field,
  and Jerusalem reduced to rubble,
And the mount of the temple
  to a forest ridge.*j*

3, 5-8: Almost all the prophetic books contain oracles against the false prophets. Here Micah accuses them of prophesying for venal motives and determining the prophecy by the price that is paid them; he contrasts his own disinterested preaching of the word of God.

f: Am 2, 7. g: Ez 13, 10. h: Jer 15, 9; Am 8, 9; Zec 13, 3. i: Ez 22, 27; Zep 3, 3. j: Jer 26, 18.

God Rules from Jerusalem

Chapter 4 begins a new collection of speeches that announce salvation rather than judgment. They stress the return of the Israelite exiles and the restoration of Jerusalem to its former power and prestige. Sections of these speeches (Mi 4, 3; 5, 1) are often read during Advent as passages that point to the coming of the Messiah.

II: The New Israel

CHAPTER 4

See RG 254

The People To Be Restored

¹ In days to come*
 the mount of the LORD's house
Shall be established higher than the
  mountains;
 it shall rise high above the hills,
And peoples shall stream to it:*ᵏ*
² Many nations shall come, and say,
"Come, let us climb the mount of the
  LORD,
 to the house of the God of Jacob,
That he may instruct us in his ways,
 that we may walk in his paths."
For from Zion shall go forth
  instruction,
 and the word of the LORD from
  Jerusalem.
³ He shall judge between many peoples
 and impose terms on strong and distant
  nations;
They shall beat their swords into
  plowshares,
 and their spears into pruning hooks;
One nation shall not raise the sword
  against another,
 nor shall they train for war again.
⁴ Every man shall sit under his own vine
 or under his own fig tree, undisturbed;
 for the mouth of the LORD of hosts has
  spoken.*ˡ*
⁵ For all the peoples walk
 each in the name of its god,
But we will walk in the name of the
  LORD,

our God, forever and ever.
⁶ On that day, says the LORD,
 I will gather the lame,
And I will assemble the outcasts,
 and those whom I have afflicted.
⁷ I will make of the lame a remnant,
 and of those driven far off a strong
  nation;
And the LORD shall be king over them on
  Mount Zion,
 from now on forever.*ᵐ*
⁸ And you, O Magdal-eder,*
 hillock of daughter Zion!
Unto you shall it come:
 the former dominion shall be restored,
 the kingdom of daughter Jerusalem.

⁹ Now why do you cry out so?
 Are you without a king?
 Or has your counselor perished,
That you are seized with pains
 like a woman in travail?
¹⁰ Writhe in pain, grow faint,
 O daughter Zion,
 like a woman in travail;
For now shall you go forth from the city
 and dwell in the fields;
To Babylon shall you go,
 there shall you be rescued.
There shall the LORD redeem you
 from the hand of your enemies.*

¹¹ How many nations are gathered against
  you!
 They say, "Let her be profaned,
 let our eyes see Zion's downfall!"
¹² But they know not the thoughts of the
  LORD,

4, 1ff: See note on Is 2, 2ff.
4, 8: Magdal-eder: "tower of the flock," an ancient place name (cf Gn 35, 21), here used symbolically of Jerusalem.
4, 10: For now . . . your enemies: probably a later addition to the text, when the prediction of exile had been fulfilled in

the Babylonian captivity. The prophet sees the exile as the means whereby God will purify and restore his people.

k: 1ff: Is 2, 2ff. *l:* Hos 14, 8; Am 9, 14. *m:* Is 6, 13; Dn 7, 14; Zep 3, 19; Lk 1, 32.

A New Ruler

By associating the new ruler over a restored Israel with Bethlehem, David's home town, and with Ephrathah, David's clan (1 Sm 17, 12), the author announces in Mi 5, 1 that the coming ruler will revive the dynasty of David, which ruled in Jerusalem before it fell to the Babylonians in 587 B.C.

nor understand his counsel,
When he has gathered them
   like sheaves on the threshing floor.
[13] Arise and thresh, O daughter Zion;
   your horn I will make iron
And your hoofs bronze,
   that you may crush many peoples;
You shall devote their spoils to the LORD,
   and their riches to the Lord of the
      whole earth.[n]

Restoration through the Messiah ·
[14] Now fence yourself in, Bat-gader!*
   "They have laid siege against us!"
With the rod they strike on the cheek
   the ruler of Israel.

See RG 254

CHAPTER 5
[1] But you, Bethlehem-Ephrathah,[o]
too small to be among the clans of
      Judah,
From you shall come forth for me
   one who is to be ruler in Israel;
Whose origin is from of old,
   from ancient times.*
[2] (Therefore the Lord will give them up,
      until the time
   when she who is to give birth* has
      borne,
And the rest of his brethren shall return
   to the children of Israel.)[p]
[3] He shall stand firm and shepherd his
      flock

by the strength of the LORD,
   in the majestic name of the LORD, his
      God;
And they shall remain, for now his
      greatness
   shall reach to the ends of the earth;
[4]   he shall be peace.

If Assyria invades our country*
   and treads upon our land,
We shall raise against it seven shepherds,
   eight men of royal rank;
[5] And they shall tend the land of Assyria
      with the sword,
   and the land of Nimrod* with the
      drawn sword;
And we shall be delivered from Assyria,
   if it invades our land
   and treads upon our borders.

[6] The remnant of Jacob shall be
   in the midst of many peoples,
Like dew coming from the LORD,
   like raindrops on the grass,
Which wait for no man,
   nor tarry for the sons of men.
[7] And the remnant of Jacob shall be among
      the nations,
   in the midst of many peoples,
Like a lion among beasts of the forest,
   like a young lion among flocks of
      sheep;
When it passes through, it tramples

4, 14: Bat-gader: "fenced-in maiden," another symbolic name for Jerusalem, then under siege from the Assyrians.

5, 1: In contrast to Bat-gader (Mi 4, 14), where the ruler of Israel, the reigning king, is in peril of his life from the Assyrians, is the tiny city and clan of Bethlehem-Ephrathah, from which comes the ancient Davidic dynasty (whose origin is from of old, from ancient times) with its messianic King, one who is to be ruler in Israel.

5, 2: She who is to give birth: the mother of the Messiah: cf Is 7, 14.

5, 4f: This passage, expressing confidence in Judah's ability to deliver itself from Assyria, is in contrast with the pre-

ceding messianic oracle, which ascribes deliverance to the Lord and his agent. Some believe that here the prophet is quoting the words of the defiant men of Judah. The shepherds and men of royal rank are one and the same: warriors capable of routing Assyria. The same kind of numerical progression is used by Amos (1, 3), and elsewhere in the Bible.

5, 5: Nimrod: the legendary ancestor of the Mesopotamians; cf Gn 10, 10ff.

n: Is 41, 15; Hos 10, 11.   o: Ru 1, 2; 1 Sm 17, 12; Mt 2, 6; Jn 7, 42.   p: 2f: Is 7, 14; 11, 1f.

God Demands Justice Above All

The first half of ch 6, beginning the second collection from the eighth-century prophet Micah (Mi 6, 1—7, 7), describes God's message to Israel as a lawsuit brought against the people. A dialogue between God and the people ends, in v. 8, with God's instruction for how they can answer the LORD's complaint.

and tears, and there is none to deliver.

8 Your hand shall be lifted above your
foes,
and all your enemies shall be destroyed.

9 On that day, says the LORD,*
I will destroy the horses from your midst
and ruin your chariots;

10 I will demolish the cities of your land
and tear down all your fortresses.

11 I will abolish the means of divination
from your use,
and there shall no longer be
soothsayers among you.

12 I will abolish your carved images
and the sacred pillars from your midst;
And you shall no longer adore
the works of your hands.q

13 I will tear out the sacred poles* from your
midst,
and destroy your cities.

14 I will wreak vengeance in anger and wrath
upon the nations that have not
hearkened.

III: Admonition

CHAPTER 6

See RG
254

Accusation and Answer

1 Hear, then, what the Lord says:
Arise, present your plea before the
mountains,
and let the hills hear your voice!r

2 Hear, O mountains, the plea of the LORD,
pay attention, O foundations of the
earth!
For the LORD has a plea against his people,
and he enters into trial with Israel.

3 O my people, what have I done to you,
or how have I wearied you? Answer
me!s

4 For I brought you up from the land of
Egypt,
from the place of slavery I released you;
And I sent before you Moses,
Aaron, and Miriam.t

5 My people, remember what Moab's King
Balak planned,
and how Balaam, the son of Beor,
answered him
. . . from Shittim to Gilgal,*
that you may know the just deeds of
the LORD.u

6 With what shall I come before the LORD,*
and bow before God most high?
Shall I come before him with holocausts,
with calves a year old?v

7 Will the LORD be pleased with thousands
of rams,
with myriad streams of oil?
Shall I give my first-born* for my crime,
the fruit of my body for the sin of my
soul?

8 You have been told, O man, what is
good,

5, 9-13: Part of the messianic restoration will consist in the removal of everything that has drawn Israel away from the Lord; this includes not only the objects of false worship, but also the armaments in which the idolators had trusted.

5, 12f: Sacred pillars . . . sacred poles: see note on Ex 34, 13.

6, 5: From Shittim to Gilgal: from the east to the west side of the Jordan; the events described in Jos 3—5 are meant. The text is defective; however, it is evident that this verse continues the remembrance of God's deeds of mercy to Israel, beginning with the Exodus (v 4) and extending to the conquest, deeds which have provoked so little response from his people.

6, 6ff: The people ask how they shall worship the Lord, proposing the various forms of sacrifice. The prophet replies that sacrifice avails nothing without the true spirit of religion. This is one of the best expressions of the prophetic teaching on religion, the preparation for such New Testament passages as Jas 1, 27.

6, 7: Shall I give my first-born: through Canaanite influence the abominable practice of human sacrifice had been introduced under impious kings (cf 2 Kgs 16, 3; 21, 6).

q: Hos 3, 4; 10, 1f.   r: Is 6, 2; Ob 1.   s: Jer 2, 5.   t: Ex 15, 20.
u: Nm 22, 23.   v: 6f: Hos 6, 6; 8, 13; Am 5, 21.

Judgment on Israel's Businessmen

Micah resumes his attack on Israel's leadership, indicting its wealthy citizens for cheating the poor (6, 9–12) and imposing a sentence by which they will be unable to enjoy the profits they have earned unfairly (vv. 13–16).

and what the LORD requires of you:
Only to do the right and to love
    goodness,
and to walk humbly with your God.[w]

9 Hark! the LORD cries to the city.[*]
    [It is wisdom to fear your name!]
Hear, O tribe and city council,
12 You whose rich men are full of
    violence,
    whose inhabitants speak falsehood
with deceitful tongues in their heads!
10 Am I to bear any longer criminal
    hoarding
    and the meager ephah that is
    accursed?
11 Shall I acquit criminal balances,
    bags of false weights?

13 Rather I will begin to strike you
    with devastation because of your
    sins.
15 You shall sow, yet not reap,
    tread out the olive, yet pour no oil,
    and the grapes, yet drink no wine.[x]
14 You shall eat, without being satisfied,
    food that will leave you empty;
What you acquire, you cannot save;
    what you do save, I will deliver up to
    the sword.[y]
16 You have kept the decrees of Omri,
    and all the works of the house of
    Ahab,
    and you have walked in their
    counsels;
Therefore I will deliver you up to ruin,
    and your citizens to derision;

and you shall bear the reproach of the
    nations.[*]

CHAPTER 7

Condemnation and Prayer

See RG
254-55

1 Alas! I am as when the fruit is
    gathered,
    as when the vines have been
    gleaned;
There is no cluster to eat,
    no early fig that I crave.
2 The faithful are gone from the
    earth,
    among men the upright are no more!
They all lie in wait to shed blood,
    each one ensnares the other.[z]
3 Their hands succeed at evil;
    the prince makes demands,
The judge is had for a price,
    the great man speaks as he pleases,[a]
4 The best of them is like a brier,
    the most upright like a thorn hedge.
The day announced by your
    watchmen!
    your punishment has come;
    now is the time of your confusion.
5 Put no trust in a friend,[*]
    have no confidence in a companion;
Against her who lies in your bosom
    guard the portals of your mouth.[b]
6 For the son dishonors his father,
    the daughter rises up against her
    mother,
The daughter-in-law against her mother-
    in-law,
    and a man's enemies are those of his
    household.[c]

6, 9: The city: Jerusalem as the embodiment of the crimes of the entire land.

6, 16: Judah has followed the example of the northern kingdom epitomized in the semipaganism of Omri and his son Ahab (1 Kgs 16, 25-34), copying both the corrupted worship and the social injustice of their reigns.

7, 5f: Corresponding to the widespread civil corruption

and apostasy from religion is the breakdown of normal human and family relations.

w: Dt 26, 16; Zec 7, 9; Mt 23, 23.   x: Dt 28, 38; Am 5, 11. Hg 1,
6. y: Hos 4, 10. z: Is 1, 21; Hos 4, 2. a: Is 1, 23. b: Jer 9,
3. c: Mt 10, 35f.

Judgment on the Powerful

From the opening speech (ch 1), in which Micah singles out for criticism the capitals of Israel and Judah, to the concluding speech in 7, 1–7 (Mi 7, 8–20 is an exilic supplement), the abuse of power is a central concern in Micah's message. In this speech, Micah laments the spread of corruption from the powerful (vv. 1–4) to friends and family (vv. 5–6).

7 But as for me, I will look to the LORD,
  I will put my trust in God my savior;
  my God will hear me!ᵈ

8 Rejoice not over me, O my enemy!*
  though I have fallen, I will arise;
  though I sit in darkness, the LORD is
    my light.
9 The wrath of the LORD I will endure
  because I have sinned against him,
Until he takes up my cause,
  and establishes my right.
He will bring me forth to the light;
  I will see his justice.
10 When my enemy sees this,
  shame shall cover her:
She who said to me,
  "Where is the LORD, thy God?"
My eyes shall see her downfall;
  now shall she be trampled underfoot,
  like the mire in the streets.

11 It is the day for building your walls;*
  on that day the boundary shall be
    taken away.
12 It is the day; and they shall come to you
  from Assyria and from Egypt,
From Tyre even to the River,
  from sea to sea, and from mountain to
    mountain;ᵉ
13 And the land shall be a waste
  because of its citizens,
  as a result of their deeds.

14 Shepherd your people with your staff,*
  the flock of your inheritance,
That dwells apart in a woodland,
  in the midst of Carmel.
Let them feed in Bashan and Gilead,
  as in the days of old;
15 As in the days when you came from the
    land of Egypt,
  show us wonderful signs.

16 The nations shall behold and be put to
    shame,
  in spite of all their strength;
They shall put their hands over their mouths;
  their ears shall become deaf.
17 They shall lick the dust like the serpent,
  like reptiles on the ground;
They shall come quaking from their
    fastnesses,
  trembling in fear of you [the LORD, our
    God].

18 Who is there like you, the God who
    removes guilt
  and pardons sin for the remnant of his
    inheritance;
Who does not persist in anger forever,
  but delights rather in clemency,ᶠ
19 And will again have compassion on us,
  treading underfoot our guilt?
You will cast into the depths of the sea
  all our sins;
20 You will show faithfulness to Jacob,
  and grace to Abraham,
As you have sworn to our fathers
  from days of old.ᵍ

7, 8ff: The unnamed enemy of Judah mentioned in these verses may be Assyria or one of the neighboring countries, such as Edom, which stood by to profit at Judah's downfall.

7, 11ff: This prophecy of restoration and repopulation of the promised land by the Jews now in exile appears to be from the period after the destruction of Jerusalem by the Chaldeans (587 B.C.).

7, 14-17: This prayer appears to be from the time after the return from exile (537 B.C.), when the people few in number, possessed only a fragment of their former land, and were surrounded by hostile nations.

d: Is 8, 17. e: Zec 14, 16. f: Jer 10, 6; Acts 10, 43. g: Ps 105, 6; Is 41, 8; 63, 16.

The Book of Nahum

See RG
255-56

Shortly before the fall of Nineveh in 612 B.C., Nahum uttered his prophecy against the hated city. To understand the prophet's exultant outburst of joy over the impending destruction it is necessary to recall the savage cruelty of Assyria, which had made it the scourge of the ancient Near East for almost three centuries. The royal inscriptions of Assyria afford the best commentary on the burning denunciation of "the bloody city." In the wake of their conquests, mounds of heads, impaled bodies, enslaved citizens, and avaricious looters testified to the ruthlessness of the Assyrians. Little wonder that Judah joined in the general outburst of joy over the destruction of Nineveh!

But Nahum is not a prophet of unrestrained revenge. God's moral government of the world is asserted. Yahweh is the avenger but he is also merciful, a citadel in the day of distress. Nineveh's doom was a judgment on the wicked city. Before many years passed, Jerusalem too was to learn the meaning of such a judgment.

The book is divided as follows: The Lord's Coming in Judgment (1, 2—2, 1. 3). The Fall of Nineveh (2, 2—3, 19).

_____

See RG
255-56

CHAPTER 1

¹Oracle about Nineveh. The book of the vision of Nahum of Elkosh.

The Lord's Coming in Judgment

² *A jealous and avenging God* is the LORD,
    an avenger is the LORD, and angry;
The LORD brings vengeance on his
        adversaries,
    and lays up wrath for his enemies;
³ The LORD is slow to anger, yet great in
        power,
    and the LORD never leaves the guilty
        unpunished.

In hurricane and tempest is his path,
    and clouds are the dust at his feet;*a*
⁴ He rebukes the sea and leaves it dry,
    and all the rivers he dries up.*b*
Withered are Bashan and Carmel,
    and the bloom of Lebanon fades;*
⁵ The mountains quake before him,
    and the hills dissolve;
The earth is laid waste before him,
    the world and all who dwell in it.
⁶ Before his wrath, who can stand
        firm,*c*
    and who can face his blazing anger?
His fury is poured out like fire,
    and the rocks are rent asunder before
        him.*
⁷ The LORD is good,
    a refuge on the day of distress;
He takes care of those who have recourse
        to him,
⁸   when the flood rages;
He makes an end of his opponents,
    and his enemies he pursues with
        darkness.
⁹ What are you imputing to the LORD?*
    It is he who will make an end!
    The enemy shall not rise a second time;
¹⁰ As when a tangle of thornbushes is set
        aflame,
    like dry stubble, they shall be utterly
        consumed.
¹² For, says the LORD,
    be they* ever so many and so
        vigorous,
    still they shall be mown down and
        disappear.
Though I have humbled you,
    I will humble you no more.
¹³ Now will I break his yoke from off you,
    and burst asunder your bonds.*d*

_____

1, 2-8: A poem written in the style of the alphabetic psalms; cf Pss 9A; 25; 111; 119. Here, however, most of the verses beginning with the letters of the second half of the alphabet are not preserved.

1, 2: A jealous . . . God: see note on Ex 20, 5.

1, 4: Bashan, Carmel and Lebanon were famous for their forests.

1, 6f: The coming of God in judgment has two aspects: to those who oppose him it will be unbearable; to those who have recourse to him it will bring strength and consolation.

1, 9: What are you imputing to the LORD?: the people of Judah are asked what they think God has in mind.

1, 12f: They: the enemies of Judah. You: Judah. His yoke: the dominion of the Assyrian king over Judah.

_____

a: Ex 19, 16ff.   *b:* Is 33, 9; Hb 3, 6ff.   *c:* Zep 1, 15; 2, 3.   *d:* Is 9, 4; 10, 27.

11 From you he came
   who devised evil against the LORD,
   the scoundrel planner.*
14 The LORD has commanded regarding
         you:*
   no descendant shall come to bear your
      name;
From your temple I will abolish
   the carved and the molten image;
   I will make your grave a mockery.

See RG
255–56

CHAPTER 2

1See, upon the mountains there
      advances
   the bearer of good news, announcing
      peace!
Celebrate your feasts, O Judah,
   fulfill your vows!
For nevermore shall you be invaded
   by the scoundrel; he is completely
      destroyed.*
3 The LORD will restore the vine of Jacob,
   the pride of Israel,
Though ravagers have ravaged them
   and ruined the tendrils.

The Fall of Nineveh

2 The hammer comes up against you;*
   guard the rampart,
Keep watch on the road, gird your loins,
   marshal all your strength!
4 The shields of his warriors are
         crimsoned,
   the soldiers colored in scarlet;
Fiery steel are the chariots
   on the day of his mustering.
The horses are frenzied;
5   the chariots dash madly through the
         streets
And wheel in the squares,
   looking like firebrands,
   flashing like lightning bolts.
6 His picked troops are called,
   ranks break at their charge;

To the wall they rush,
   the mantelet* is set up.
7 The river gates are opened,
   the palace shudders,
8 Its mistress is led forth captive,
   and her handmaids,* under guard,
Moaning like doves,
   beating their breasts.
9 Nineveh is like a pool
   whose waters escape;
"Stop! Stop!"
   but none turns back.
10 "Plunder the silver, plunder the gold!"
   There is no end to the treasure,
   to their wealth in precious things of
      every kind!

11 Emptiness, desolation, waste;
   melting hearts and trembling knees,
Writhing in every frame,
   every face blanched!f
12 Where is the lions' cave,
   the young lions' den,
Where the lion* went in and out,
   and the cub, with no one to disturb them?
13 The lion snatched enough for his cubs,
   and strangled for his lionesses;
He filled his dens with prey,
   and his caves with plunder.
14 I come against you,
   says the LORD of hosts;
I will consume in smoke your chariots,
   and the sword shall devour your young
      lions;
Your preying on the land I will bring to
      an end,
   the cry of your lionesses shall be heard
      no more.

CHAPTER 3

See RG
255–56

Ruin Imminent and Inevitable

1 Woe to the bloody city, all lies,
   full of plunder, whose looting never
      stops!g

1, 11: From you . . . the scoundrel planner: addressed to Nineveh, the capital city of Sennacherib, king of Assyria, who besieged Jerusalem c. 700 B.C.

1, 14: You: the king of Assyria.

2, 2: The hammer comes up against you: the enemy is about to crush Nineveh.

2, 6: Mantelet: a movable shelter protecting the besiegers.

2, 8: Mistress . . . and her handmaids: either the queen of Nineveh with the ladies of her court, or the statue of Ishtar, Nineveh's chief goddess, with her temple prostitutes.

2, 12: The lion: the king of Assyria.

e: Is 52, 7; Rom 10, 15.   *f:* Jl 2, 6.   *g:* Hb 2, 12.

Nahum's final verse summarizes the image of Nineveh held by all who had suffered as a result of its imperial ambitions. Jonah shared this opinion, hence his resistance to God's instruction to prophesy to Nineveh and his anger when God spared the city.

2 The crack of the whip, the rumbling
        sounds of wheels;
    horses a-gallop, chariots bounding,
3 Cavalry charging,
    The flame of the sword, the flash of the
        spear,
        the many slain, the heaping corpses,
        the endless bodies to stumble upon!
4 For the many debaucheries of the harlot,
        fair and charming, a mistress of
            witchcraft,
    Who enslaved nations with her
        harlotries,
        and peoples by her witchcraft:*h*
5 I am come against you,*i*
        and I will strip your skirt from you;
    I will show your nakedness to the
            nations,
        to the kingdoms your shame!*
6 I will cast filth upon you,
        disgrace you and put you to shame;
7 Till everyone who sees you runs from
        you, saying,
        "Nineveh is destroyed; who can pity
            her?
        Where can one find any to console
            her?"

8 Are you better than No-amon*
        that was set among the streams,
    Surrounded by waters,
        with the flood for her rampart
        and water her wall?*j*
9 Ethiopia was her strength, and Egypt,
        and others without end;
        Put and the Libyans were her
            auxiliaries.
10 Yet even she went captive into exile,

even her little ones were dashed to
        pieces
    at the corner of every street;
For her nobles they cast lots,
    and all her great men were put into
        chains.
11 You, too, shall drink of this till you faint
        away;
    you, too, shall seek a refuge from the
        foe.*k*
12 All your fortresses are but fig trees,
        bearing early figs
    That fall, when shaken,
        into the hungry mouth.
13 See, the troops are women in your midst;
        to your foes the gates of your land are
            open wide,
        fire has consumed their bars.*l*
14 Draw water for the siege,*
        strengthen your fortresses;
    Go down into the mud and tread the
        clay,
        take hold of the brick mold!
15 There the fire shall consume you,
        the sword shall cut you down.
    Multiply like the grasshoppers,
        multiply like the locusts!
16 Make your couriers more numerous than
        the stars,
17   your garrisons as many as
            grasshoppers,
    And your scribes as locust swarms
        gathered on the rubble fences on a cold
            day!
    Yet when the sun warms them,
        the grasshoppers will spread their
            wings and fly,
        and vanish, no one knows where.

3, 5f: The punishment of adulteresses.

3, 8: No-amon: No was the Egyptian name of the capital of Upper Egypt, called Thebes by the Greeks; its tutelary deity was Amon. This great city was destroyed by the Assyrians in 663 B.C.

3, 14: An ironic exhortation to prepare the city for a futile

defense. Go down . . . brick mold: make bricks for the city walls.

h: Mi 1, 7; Rv 17, 1f.   *i:* Is 47, 3; Jer 13, 26; Hos 2, 12.   *j:* Jer 46, 25.   *k:* Mi 2, 11.   *l:* Jer 51, 30.

18 Alas! how your shepherds slumber, O
    king of Assyria,
    your nobles have gone to rest;
  Your people are scattered upon the
    mountains,
    with none to gather them.

19 There is no healing for your hurt,
    your wound is mortal.
  All who hear this news of you
    clap their hands over you;
  For who has not been overwhelmed,
    steadily, by your malice?

See RG
256-58

The Book of Habakkuk

This prophecy dates from the years 605–597 B.C.,
or between the great Babylonian victory at Carchemish and Nebuchadnezzar's invasion of Judah
which culminated in the capture of Jerusalem. The
situation of Judah was desperate at this time, with
political intrigue and idolatry widespread in the
small kingdom. The first two chapters consist of a
dialogue between the prophet and the Lord. For
what may be the first time in Israelite literature, a
man questions the ways of God, as Habakkuk calls
him to account for his government of the world. To
this question God replies that he has prepared a
chastising rod, Babylon, which will be the avenging instrument in his hand. There is added the divine assurance that the just Israelite will not perish
in the calamities about to be visited on the nation.

The third chapter is a magnificent religious
lyric, filled with reminiscences of Israel's past
and rich in literary borrowings from the poetry of
ancient Canaan, though still expressing authentic
Israelite faith. God appears in all his majestic
splendor and executes vengeance on Judah's enemies. The prophecy ends with a joyous profession of confidence in the Lord, the Savior.

See RG
257

CHAPTER 1

1 The oracle which Habakkuk the
prophet received in vision.

The Prophet's Complaint and Its Answer
2 How long, O LORD? I cry for help*

but you do not listen!
  I cry out to you, "Violence!"
    but you do not intervene.
3 Why do you let me see ruin;
    why must I look at misery?
  Destruction and violence are before me;
    there is strife, and clamorous discord.
4 This is why the law is benumbed,
    and judgment is never rendered:
  Because the wicked circumvent the just;
    this is why judgment comes forth
      perverted.

5 Look over the nations and see,*
    and be utterly amazed!
  For a work is being done in your days
    that you would not have believed,
      were it told.a
6 For see, I am raising up Chaldea,
    that bitter and unruly people,
  That marches the breadth of the land
    to take dwellings not his own.
7 Terrible and dreadful is he,
    from himself derive his law and his
      majesty.
8 Swifter than leopards are his horses,
    and keener than wolves at evening.*
  His horses prance,
    his horsemen come from afar:
  They fly like the eagle hastening to
      devour;
9   each comes for the rapine,

1, 2-4: Traditionally, these verses have been taken as the
prophet's complaint against the internal evils of Judah; the
language used is that employed by Amos, Isaiah, and Jeremiah to condemn the social abuses of their day. In vv 5ff the
Lord answers this complaint by indicating the Chaldean empire as his instrument for punishing his people for these sins.

1, 5: Look over the nations and see: after Nebuchadnezzar's defeat of Egypt in 605 B.C., there could be little doubt

that it was the Chaldean ambition to dominate the entire Near
East.

1, 8: Wolves at evening: the wolf is apparently thought of
as more rabid and vicious in the evening when setting out for
prey (Jer 5, 6; Zep 3, 3).

a: Acts 13, 41.

1276

Their combined onset is that of a
stormwind
that heaps up captives like sand.
[10] He scoffs at kings,
and princes are his laughingstock;
He laughs at any fortress,
heaps up a ramp, and conquers it.
[11] Then he veers like the wind* and is gone—
this culprit who makes his own
strength his god!

[12] Are you not from eternity, O LORD,*
my holy God, immortal?
O LORD, you have marked him for
judgment,
O Rock,* you have readied him for
punishment!
[13] Too pure are your eyes to look upon evil,
and the sight of misery you cannot
endure.
Why, then, do you gaze on the faithless
in silence
while the wicked man devours
one more just than himself?
[14] You have made man like the fish of the
sea,
like creeping things without a ruler.
[15] He* brings them all up with his hook,
he hauls them away with his net,
He gathers them in his seine;
and so he rejoices and exults.
[16] Therefore he sacrifices to his net,*
and burns incense to his seine;
For thanks to them his portion is generous,
and his repast sumptuous.
[17] Shall he, then, keep on brandishing his
sword

to slay peoples without mercy?

See RG
257

CHAPTER 2

[1] I will stand at my guard post,
and station myself upon the rampart,
And keep watch to see what he will say
to me,
and what answer he will give to my
complaint.[b]

[2] Then the LORD answered me and said:
Write down the vision
Clearly upon the tablets,
so that one can read it readily.
[3] For the vision still has its time,
presses on to fulfillment, and will not
disappoint;
If it delays, wait for it,
it will surely come, it will not be late.
[4] The rash man has no integrity;[c]
but the just man, because of his faith,
shall live.*
Wealth, too, is treacherous:
the proud, unstable man—
[5] He who opens wide his throat like the
nether world,
and is insatiable as death,
Who gathers to himself all the nations,
and rallies to himself all the peoples—
[6] Shall not all these take up a taunt against
him,
satire and epigrams about him, to say:

Woe to him who stores up what is not his:
how long can it last!
he loads himself down with debts.
[7] Shall not your creditors rise suddenly?

1, 11: Veers like the wind: the conquests of the ancient Near
East were mainly raiding expeditions to collect tribute. As far
as administration of conquered territories was concerned, both
the Assyrians and Chaldeans were usually content to install
friendly rulers and then depart. This culprit: though the Chaldeans were used by God as the agents of his punishment, this
did not diminish their own guilt as ruthless marauders.

1, 12—2, 1: It is generally thought that this complaint is
directed against the Chaldeans and their terrible destruction.
But it may well be a continuation of Hb 1, 2-4, against the
wicked Judahites who have merited God's punishment.

1, 12: O Rock: an ancient title celebrating the Lord's
power; cf Ps 18, 32.

1, 15: The he of this and the following verses, to whom is
attributed such extensive evil and the destruction of many peoples, may be the wicked of Judah embodied in King Jehoia-

kim, ally of the powerful Pharaoh Neco of Egypt; the devastation wrought by Jehoiakim and Neco together is condemned.

1, 16: He sacrifices to his net: in v 15 the wicked ruler in
question is represented as catching men in a net. This verse
alludes to some rite involving the sacrificial veneration of the
weapons of war.

2, 4: The just man, because of his faith, shall live: the faith
which here enables the virtuous man to survive the impending doom is both a confident belief in God's justice, and patience in awaiting its execution. St. Paul quotes these words
(Rom 1, 17; Gal 3, 11; Heb 10, 38) to confirm his teaching
that man receives justification and supernatural life through
faith in Christ.

---

b: Ps 85, 9.   c: Rom 1, 17; Gal 3, 11; Heb 10, 38.

Shall not they who make you tremble
awake?
You shall become their spoil!

8 Because you despoiled many peoples
all the rest of the nations shall despoil
you;
Because of men's blood shed,
and violence done to the land,
to the city and to all who dwell in it.

9 Woe to him who pursues evil gain for his
household,
setting his nest on high
to escape the reach of misfortune!
10 You have devised shame for your
household,
cutting off many peoples, forfeiting
your own life:
11 For the stone in the wall shall cry out,*
and the beam in the woodwork shall
answer it!

12 Woe to him who builds a city by
bloodshed,
and establishes a town by wickedness!d

13 Is not this from the LORD of hosts:
peoples toil for the flames,*
and nations grow weary for nought!e
14 But the earth shall be filled
with the knowledge of the LORD's
glory
as water covers the sea.f
15 Woe to you who give your neighbors
a flood of your wrath to drink,
and make them drunk, till their
nakedness is seen!
16 You are filled with shame instead of
glory;
drink, you too, and stagger!

On you shall revert the cup from the
LORD's right hand,
and utter shame on your glory.
17 For the violence done to Lebanon* shall
cover you,
and the destruction of the beasts shall
terrify you;
Because of men's blood shed,
and violence done to the land,
to the city and to all who dwell in it.

19 Woe to him who says to wood,
"Awake!"
to dumb stone, "Arise!"
Can such a thing give oracles?
See, it is overlaid with gold and silver,
but there is no life breath in it.
18 Of what avail is the carved image,*
that its maker should carve it?
Or the molten image and lying oracle,
that its very maker should trust in it,
and make dumb idols?
20 But the LORD is in his holy temple;
silence before him, all the earth!g

CHAPTER 3

Canticle

1 Prayer of Habakkuk,
the prophet. To a plaintive tune.*

2 O LORD, I have heard your renown,
and feared, O LORD, your work.
In the course of the years revive it,*
in the course of the years make it
known;
in your wrath remember compassion!

3 *God comes from Teman,*
the Holy One from Mount Paran.
Covered are the heavens with his glory,
and with his praise the earth is filled.

See RG 257

2, 11f: The palaces, built at the expense of gross injustice (vv 6-10), call down vengeance on their builders. This is typical prophetic language for the condemnation of social crimes within Israel and Judah.

2, 13: Peoples toil for the flames: they build only to have fire consume their work, when they build contrary to God's will.

2, 17: The violence done to Lebanon: the spoliation of the cedar forests of Lebanon, used in lavish building projects by the great conquerors; cf Is 14, 8; 37, 24. The destruction of the beasts: the killing-off of the wild animals through excessive hunting by the same conquerors; cf Bar 3, 16.

2, 18-20: Idolatrous worship is here shown to be folly by con-

trasting man-made idols with the majesty of the one true God.

3, 1: A later liturgical rubric. So also the end of v 19.

3, 2: In the course of the years revive it: renew today your wondrous deeds of the past.

3, 3-15: Cf the theophanies in Dt 33, 2f; Jgs 5, 4f; Pss 18, 8-16; 68, 8f; 77, 17-21; 97, 1-5; Na 1, 3-6, etc. Conventional language is employed to describe the appearance of the Lord, as in Ex 19, 16-19.

3, 3: Teman: a region in Edom. Mount Paran: in the territory of Edom, or the northern part of the Sinaitic peninsula.

d: Ez 24, 9; Na 3, 1. e: Jer 51, 58. f: Is 11, 9. g: Ps 11, 4.

A Hymn Praising God's Rule

The hymn in ch 3 describes a theophany, a direct appearance of God (vv. 3–15), placed in a framework describing the poet's response to it (vv. 2.16–19).

In the earlier chapters, the prophet lamented how God could allow the injustices he described. Now Habakkuk concludes with a petition to God to manifest his power, and he describes what will happen when the LORD comes into the world. Finally, he expresses a prayer of confidence in the LORD.

⁴ His splendor spreads like the light;
　rays shine forth from beside him,
　where his power is concealed.
⁵ Before him goes pestilence,
　and the plague follows in his steps.
⁶ He pauses to survey the earth;
　his look makes the nations tremble.
The eternal mountains are shattered,
　the age-old hills bow low
　along his ancient ways.
⁷ I see the tents of Cushan collapse;
　trembling are the pavilions of the land
　　of Midian.
⁸ Is your anger against the streams,
　O LORD?
Is your wrath against the streams,
　your rage against the sea,
That you drive the steeds
　of your victorious chariot?
⁹ Bared and ready is your bow,
　filled with arrows is your quiver.
Into streams you split the earth;
¹⁰ 　at sight of you the mountains
　　tremble.
A torrent of rain descends;
　the ocean gives forth its roar.
The sun forgets to rise,
¹¹ 　the moon remains in its shelter,
At the light of your flying arrows,
　at the gleam of your flashing spear.ʰ

¹² In wrath you bestride the earth,
　in fury you trample the nations.
¹³ You come forth to save your people,
　to save your anointed one.*

You crush the heads of the wicked,
　you lay bare their bases at the
　　neck.ⁱ
¹⁴ You pierce with your shafts the heads of
　　their princes
　whose boast would be of devouring
　　the wretched in their lair.
¹⁵ You tread the sea with your steeds
　amid the churning of the deep
　　waters.

¹⁶ I hear, and my body trembles;
　at the sound, my lips quiver.
Decay invades my bones,
　my legs tremble beneath me.
I await the day of distress
　that will come upon the people who
　　attack us.
¹⁷ For though the fig tree blossom not
　nor fruit be on the vines,
Though the yield of the olive fail
　and the terraces produce no
　　nourishment,
Though the flocks disappear from the
　　fold
　and there be no herd in the stalls,
¹⁸ Yet will I rejoice in the LORDʲ
　and exult in my saving God.
¹⁹ GOD, my Lord, is my strength;
　he makes my feet swift as those of
　　hinds
　and enables me to go upon the
　　heights.

For the leader; with stringed instruments.

The Lord is represented as coming from Sinai, where he had appeared to Moses and given Israel the covenant and the law.
3, 13: Your anointed one: the theocratic king, the head of God's people.

h: Jos 10, 12.　i: Is 51, 9ff.　j: 18f: Ps 18, 32f; Mi 7, 7.

The Book of Zephaniah

See RG
258–59

The title of the prophecy informs us that the ministry of Zephaniah took place during the reign of Josiah (640–609 B.C.). The protest against the worship of false gods, and the condemnation of the pro-Assyrian court ministers who served as regents during Josiah's minority, allow us to place the work in the first decade of the reign. Accordingly, the prophecy of Zephaniah comes rightly before that of Jeremiah, who was probably influenced by it in both language and ideas.

The age of Zephaniah was a time of religious degradation, when the old idolatries reappeared and men worshiped sun, moon, and stars. Rites completely alien to the pure monotheism taught by Moses flourished in Jerusalem. To the corrupt city Zephaniah announced the impending judgment, the day of the Lord. The prophecy may be divided into three sections, corresponding to the three chapters of the book:

• The Day of the Lord: A day of doom. The last few verses of this oracle give the classic description of the Day of the Lord as an overwhelming disaster. The Christian hymn *Dies Irae* is based on this passage (1, 2-18).

• The Day of the Lord: A day of judgment of the nations, traditional enemies of God's people (2, 1-15).

• Reproach and Promise for Jerusalem: Despite Judah's infidelities, the Lord in his mercy will spare a holy remnant, which will finally enjoy peace. The prophecy closes with a hymn of joy sung by the remnant restored to Zion (3, 1-20).

See RG
258

CHAPTER 1

¹The word of the LORD which came to Zephaniah, the son of Cushi, the son of Gedaliah, the son of Amariah, the son of Hezekiah, in the days of Josiah, the son of Amon, king of Judah.

The Day of the Lord: A Day of Doom

² I will completely sweep away all things
from the face of the earth, says the
LORD.
³ I will sweep away man and beast,
I will sweep away the birds of the sky,
and the fishes of the sea.
I will overthrow the wicked;
I will destroy mankind
from the face of the earth, says the
LORD.[a]
⁴ I will stretch out my hand against Judah,
and against all the inhabitants of
Jerusalem;
I will destroy from this place the last
vestige of Baal,
the very names of his priests,
⁵ And those who adore the host of heaven*
on the roofs,
with those who adore the LORD
but swear by Milcom;[b]
⁶ And those who have fallen away from
the LORD,
and those who do not seek the LORD.
⁷ Silence in the presence of the Lord GOD!
for near is the day of the LORD,
Yes, the LORD has prepared a slaughter
feast,
he has consecrated his guests.*
⁸ On the day of the LORD's
slaughter feast
I will punish the princes, and the king's
sons,
and all that dress in foreign apparel.
⁹ I will punish, on that day,
all who leap over the threshold,*
Who fill the house of their master
with violence and deceit.
¹⁰ On that day, says the LORD,
A cry will be heard from the Fish Gate,

1, 5: The host of heaven: the stars, the worship of which was introduced into Judah by the Assyrians. Milcom: the god of the Ammonites; cf 1 Kgs 11, 5. 7. 33; 2 Kgs 23, 13.

1, 7: He has consecrated his guests: God has prepared those whom he has invited to share as soldiers in the booty, or as beast and bird scavengers of carrion, on the day of slaugh-

ter. Cf Jer 46, 10; Ez 39, 17.

1, 9: Leap over the threshold: the reference is to a superstitious custom of the pagans, witnessed to at least in regard to the worship of Dagon (1 Sm 5, 5).

a: Hos 4, 3.   *b:* Jer 8, 2; 19, 13.

The Day of the LORD: Judah Is Judged

Zephaniah's speech (1, 2—2, 3) includes an indictment of Judah's sins (vv. 4–9), but, as is customary in prophetic judgment speeches, the prophet emphasizes the sentence, God's punishment on Judah and its people. Verses 2–3 give one of the most desolate images of judgment in prophetic literature (cf Jer 4, 23–26). In effect, this is a vision of "uncreation" that parallels the creation story in Genesis ch 1, insofar as it involved living things. Zephaniah describes the process of undoing God's creative act, the judgment of God on humankind's evil.

a wail from the New Quarter,*
loud crashing from the hills.
11 Wail, O inhabitants of the Mortar!*
for all the merchants will be destroyed,
all who weigh out silver, done away
with.
12 At that time I will explore Jerusalem
with lamps;
I will punish the men who thicken on
their lees,*
Who say in their hearts,
"Neither good nor evil can the LORD
do."
13 Their wealth shall be given to pillage
and their houses to devastation;
They will build houses, but shall not
dwell in them,
plant vineyards, but not drink their
wine.c
14 Near is the great day of the LORD,
near and very swiftly coming;
Hark, the day of the LORD!
bitter, then, the warrior's cry.
15 A day of wrath is that day,d
a day of anguish and distress,
A day of destruction and desolation,
a day of darkness and gloom,
A day of thick black clouds,
16 a day of trumpet blasts and battle alarm
Against fortified cities,
against battlements on high.e
17 I will hem men in
till they walk like the blind,

because they have sinned against the
LORD;
And their blood shall be poured out like
dust,
and their brains like dung.
18 Neither their silver nor their gold
shall be able to save them
on the day of the LORD's wrath,
When in the fire of his jealousy
all the earth shall be consumed.
For he shall make an end, yes, a sudden
end,
of all who live on the earth.f

CHAPTER 2

The Day of the Lord:
A Day of Judgment

See RG
258-59

1 Gather, gather yourselves together,
O nation without shame!*
2 Before you are driven away,
like chaff that passes on;
Before there comes upon you
the blazing anger of the LORD;
Before there comes upon you
the day of the LORD's anger.
3 Seek the LORD, all you humble of the
earth,
who have observed his law;
Seek justice, seek humility;
perhaps you may be sheltered
on the day of the LORD's anger.
4 For Gaza shall be forsaken,
and Ashkelon shall be a waste,

1, 10f: The New Quarter . . . the Mortar: sections of Jerusalem (cf 2 Kgs 22, 14).
1, 12: The men who thicken on their lees: those who are overconfident because, like bottles of wine in which the sediment has settled to the bottom, they have remained at peace and undisturbed for a long time.
2, 1: Nation without shame: Judah.

c: Am 5, 11. d: Jer 30, 7; Jl 2, 11; Am 5, 18. e: Am 2, 2.
f: Zep 3, 8; Ez 7, 19.

Ashdod they shall drive out at midday,
and Ekron* shall be uprooted.[g]

5 Woe to you who dwell by the seacoast,
to the Cretan folk!*
The word of the LORD is against you,
I will humble you, land of the
Philistines,
and leave you to perish without an
inhabitant!

6 The coastland of the Cretans shall
become
fields for shepherds, and folds for
flocks.

7 The coast shall belong
to the remnant of the house of Judah;
by the sea they shall pasture.
In the houses of Ashkelon at evening
they shall couch their flocks,
For the LORD their God shall visit them,
and bring about their restoration.

8 I have heard the revilings uttered by
Moab,
and the insults of the Ammonites,
When they reviled my people
and made boasts against their territory.

9 Therefore, as I live, says the LORD of
hosts,
the God of Israel,
Moab shall become like Sodom,
the land of Ammon like Gomorrah:
A field of nettles and a salt pit
and a waste forever.
The remnant of my people shall plunder
them,
the survivors of my nation dispossess
them.

10 Such shall be the requital of their pride,
because they reviled and boasted
against
the people of the LORD of hosts.

11 The LORD shall inspire them with fear
when he makes all the gods of earth to
waste away;
Then, each from its own place,

all the coastlands of the nations shall
adore him.

12 You too, O Cushites,*
shall be slain by the sword of the
LORD.

13 He will stretch out his hand against the
north,
to destroy Assyria;
He will make Nineveh a waste,
dry as the desert.

14 In her midst shall settle in droves
all the wild life of the hollows;
The screech owl and the desert owl
shall roost in her columns;
Their call shall resound from the
window,
the raven's croak from the doorway.[h]

15 Is this the exultant city*
that dwelt secure;
That told herself,
"There is no other than I!"
How has she become a waste,
a lair for wild beasts?
Whoever passes by her
hisses, and shakes his fist!

CHAPTER 3

See RG
259

Reproach and Promise
for Jerusalem

1 Woe to the city, rebellious and polluted,
to the tyrannical city!

2 She hears no voice,
accepts no correction;
In the LORD she has not trusted,
to her God she has not drawn near.[i]

3 Her princes in her midst
are roaring lions;
Her judges are wolves of the night
that have had no bones to gnaw by
morning.[j]

4 Her prophets are insolent,
treacherous men;
Her priests profane what is holy,
and do violence to the law.[k]

2, 4: Gaza . . . Ashkelon . . . Ashdod . . . Ekron: four of
the five cities of the Philistine confederation. The fifth city,
Gath, is not mentioned, perhaps because it was already destroyed.

2, 5: Cretan folk: the Philistines, who came from Crete;
see note on Dt 2, 23.

2, 12: Cushites: the Egyptians, at this time under a Cushite or Ethiopian dynasty.

2, 15: The exultant city: Nineveh.

g: Am 1, 6ff; Zec 9, 5. h: Is 34, 11. i: Jer 2, 30; 7, 28. j: Ez
22, 27; Mi 3, 11. k: Jer 23, 32.

⁵ The LORD within her is just,
    who does no wrong;
Morning after morning he renders
        judgment
    unfailingly, at dawn.

⁶ I have destroyed nations,
    their battlements are laid waste;
I have made their streets deserted,
    with no one passing through;
Their cities are devastated,
    with no man dwelling in them.ˡ
⁷ I said, "Surely now you will fear me,
    you will accept correction";
She should not fail to see
    all I have visited upon her.
Yet all the more eagerly have they done
    all their corrupt deeds.
⁸ Therefore, wait for me, says the LORD,
    against the day when I arise as
        accuser;
For it is my decision to gather together
        the nations,
    to assemble the kingdoms,
In order to pour out upon them my wrath,
    all my blazing anger;
For in the fire of my jealousy
    shall all the earth be consumed.ᵐ
⁹ For then I will change and purify
    the lips of the peoples,
That they all may call upon the name of
        the LORD,
    to serve him with one accord;
¹⁰ From beyond the rivers of Ethiopia
    and as far as the recesses of the North,
    they shall bring me offerings.

¹¹   On that day
You need not be ashamed
    of all your deeds,
    your rebellious actions against me;
For then will I remove from your midst
    the proud braggarts,
And you shall no longer exalt yourself
    on my holy mountain.
¹² But I will leave as a remnant in your
        midst

a people humble and lowly,
Who shall take refuge in the name of the
        Lord:ⁿ
¹³   the remnant of Israel.
They shall do no wrong
    and speak no lies;
Nor shall there be found in their mouths
    a deceitful tongue;
They shall pasture and couch their
        flocks
    with none to disturb them.ᵒ

¹⁴ Shout for joy, O daughter Zion!
    sing joyfully, O Israel!
Be glad and exult with all your heart,
    O daughter Jerusalem!ᵖ
¹⁵ The LORD has removed the judgment
        against you,
    he has turned away your enemies;
The King of Israel, the LORD, is in your
        midst,
    you have no further misfortune to fear.
¹⁶ On that day, it shall be said to Jerusalem:
    Fear not, O Zion, be not discouraged!�q
¹⁷ The LORD, your God, is in your midst,
    a mighty savior;
He will rejoice over you with gladness,
    and renew you in his love,
He will sing joyfully because of you,
¹⁸   as one sings at festivals.
I will remove disaster from among you,
    so that none may recount your
        disgrace.
¹⁹ Yes, at that time I will deal
    with all who oppress you:
I will save the lame,
    and assemble the outcasts;
I will give them praise and renown
    in all the earth, when I bring about
        their restoration.ʳ
²⁰ At that time I will bring you home,
    and at that time I will gather you;
For I will give you renown and praise,
    among all the peoples of the earth,
When I bring about your restoration
    before your very eyes, says the
        LORD.

l: Jer 2, 15.   m: Zep 1, 18.   n: Hos 14, 4.   o: Ml 4, 4.   p: Zec 9, 9.   q: Mt 14, 27.   r: Mi 4, 6.

The Charge to Rebuild the Temple

Haggai's first speech (Hg 1, 1–15a) directs those who have returned to Jerusalem from exile to begin reconstruction of the temple.

See RG
259–60

The Book of Haggai

Postexilic prophecy begins with Haggai, who received the word of the Lord in the second year of Darius (520 B.C.). The Jews who returned from the exile in Babylonia had encountered formidable obstacles in their efforts to re-establish Jewish life in Judah. The Samaritans had succeeded in blocking the rebuilding of the temple; but after Darius acceded to the throne (522), permission was given to resume the work. At this critical moment, when defeatism and a certain lethargy had overtaken his repatriated countrymen, Haggai came forward with his exhortations to them to complete the great task. The first oracle, an appeal to the Jews, is contained in chapter 1. To this appeal Haggai added a short oracle of encouragement (chapter 2, 1-9) for the sake of those who gloomily contrasted the former magnificence of Solomon's temple with the second temple: the Lord would be present in this new abode, and its glory, enhanced by the offerings of the Gentiles, would surpass the ancient splendor.

The prophecy may be divided into five oracles:

The call to rebuild the temple. The economic distress so apparent in Judah is due to the Jews' neglect of the Lord while they provide for their own needs (1, 1-15).

The future glory of the new temple, surpassing that of the old (2, 1-9).

Unworthiness of a people, who may be the Samaritans, to offer sacrifice at the newly restored altar. This oracle is cast in the literary form of a *torah*, an instruction given the people by a priest (2, 10-14).

A promise of immediate blessings, which follows upon the undertaking (chapter 1) to rebuild the temple (2, 15-19).

A pledge to Zerubbabel, descendant of David, repository of the messianic hopes (2, 20-23).

CHAPTER 1

See RG
260

Exhortation To Rebuild the Temple of the Lord. [1]On the first day of the sixth month in the second year* of King Darius, the word of the LORD came through the prophet Haggai to the governor of Judah, Zerubbabel, son of Shealtiel, and to the high priest Joshua, son of Jehozadak:[a]

[2]Thus says the LORD of hosts: This people says: "Not now has the time come to rebuild the house of the LORD." [3](Then this word of the LORD came through Haggai, the prophet:) [4]Is it time for you to dwell in your own paneled houses,[b] while this house lies in ruins?*

[5] Now thus says the LORD of hosts:
    Consider your ways!
[6] You have sown much, but have brought
        in little;
    you have eaten, but have not been
        satisfied;
    You have drunk, but have not been
        exhilarated;
    have clothed yourselves, but not been
        warmed;
    And he who earned wages
        earned them for a bag with holes in it.[c]

[7]   Thus says the LORD of hosts:
    Consider your ways!

1, 1: The sixth month in the second year: August/September in 520 B.C.
1, 4: The luxury of the homes of the wealthy with their paneled houses contrasts sadly with the ruined state of the Lord's house.

a: Ezr 4, 24; 5, 1; 6, 14.   *b:* 2 Sm 7, 2.   *c:* Dt 28, 38ff; Mi 6, 15.

The Glory of the Temple

To those who are disappointed with the rebuilt temple, which pales in comparison to the temple of Solomon, God has a powerful reminder in ch 2. The glory of the temple comes not from earthly riches or fine building materials, but from the LORD's residing there. For the returning exiles, there is no greater treasure than the ability to worship the LORD in the temple.

8 Go up into the hill country;
bring timber, and build the house
That I may take pleasure in it
and receive my glory, says the LORD.
9 You expected much, but it came to little;
and what you brought home, I blew
away.
For what cause? says the LORD of hosts.
Because my house lies in ruins,
while each of you hurries to his own
house.d
10 Therefore the heavens withheld from you
their dew,
and the earth her crops.e
11 And I called for a drought
upon the land and upon the mountains;
Upon the grain, and upon the wine, and
upon the oil,
and upon all that the ground brings
forth;
Upon men and upon beasts,
and upon all that is produced by hand.

12 Then Zerubbabel, son of Shealtiel, and the high priest Joshua, son of Jehozadak, and all the remnant of the people* listened to the voice of the LORD, their God, and to the words of the prophet Haggai, because the LORD, their God, had sent him, and the people feared because of the LORD. 13 And the LORD's messenger, Haggai, proclaimed to the people as the message of the LORD: I am with you, says the LORD.

14 Then the LORD stirred up the spirit of the governor of Judah, Zerubbabel, son of Shealtiel, and the spirit of the high priest Joshua, son of Jehozadak, and the spirit of all the remnant of the people, so that they came and set to work on the house of the LORD of hosts, their God, 15 on the twenty-fourth day of the sixth month.

CHAPTER 2

Future Glory of the New Temple. In the second year of King Darius, 1 on the twenty-first day of the seventh month, the word of the LORD came through the prophet Haggai: 2 Tell this to the governor of Judah, Zerubbabel, son of Shealtiel, and to the high priest Joshua, son of Jehozadak, and to the remnant of the people:

See RG 260

3 Who is left among you
that saw this house in its former
glory?
And how do you see it now?
Does it not seem like nothing in your
eyes?
4 But now take courage, Zerubbabel, says
the LORD,
and take courage, Joshua, high priest,
son of Jehozadak,
And take courage, all you people of the
land,
says the LORD, and work!
For I am with you, says the LORD of
hosts.f
5 This is the pact that I made with you
when you came out of Egypt,
And my spirit continues in your midst;
do not fear!g

6 For thus says the LORD of hosts:*
One moment yet, a little while,
and I will shake the heavens and the
earth,

1, 12: The remnant of the people: a technical term in Haggai and Zechariah for the returned exiles.
2, 6-9: From the later period of Ezekiel's preaching onward, the temple became, as here, one of the dominant messianic themes. Greater will be the future glory of this house than the former: because Christ will enter it.

d: 2 Kgs 25, 9.   e: Gn 27, 28; Am 4, 6-9.   f: Zec 8, 9.   g: Ex 29, 45; Lv 26, 45.

1285

the sea and the dry land.[h]

7 I will shake all the nations,
and the treasures of all the nations will
come in,
And I will fill this house with glory,
says the LORD of hosts.[i]

8 Mine is the silver and mine the gold,
says the LORD of hosts.

9 Greater will be the future glory of this
house
than the former, says the LORD of
hosts;
And in this place I will give peace,
says the LORD of hosts![j]

Offerings of the Unclean Rejected. 10On
the twenty-fourth day of the ninth month, in
the second year of King Darius, the word of
the LORD came to the prophet Haggai: 11Thus
says the LORD of hosts: Ask the priests for a
decision:[k] 12If a man carries sanctified flesh
in the fold of his garment and the fold
touches bread, or pottage, or wine, or oil, or
any other food, do they become sanctified?
"No," the priests answered.* 13Then Haggai
said: If a person unclean from contact with a
corpse touches any of these, do they become
unclean? The priests answered, "They become unclean."[l] 14Then Haggai continued:

So is this people, and so is this nation
in my sight, says the LORD:
And so are all the works of their hands;
and what they offer there is unclean.

Promise of Immediate Blessings.* 15But
now, consider from this day forward. Before
there was a stone laid upon a stone in the
temple of the LORD, 16how did you fare?

When one went to a heap of grain for
twenty measures,

it would yield but ten;
When another went to the vat to draw
fifty measures,
there would be but twenty.[m]

17 I struck you in all the works of your hands
with blight, searing wind, and hail,
yet you did not return to me, says the
LORD.

18[Consider from this day forward: from
the twenty-fourth day of the ninth month.*
From the day on which the temple of the
LORD was founded, consider!]

19 Indeed, the seed has not sprouted,
nor have the vine, the fig, the
pomegranate
and the olive tree yet borne.
From this day, I will bless!

Pledge to Zerubbabel. 20The message of
the LORD came a second time to Haggai on
the twenty-fourth day of the month:* 21Tell
this to Zerubbabel, the governor of Judah:

I will shake the heavens and the earth;
22 I will overthrow the thrones of
kingdoms,
destroy the power of the kingdoms of
the nations.
I will overthrow the chariots and their
riders,
and the riders with their horses
shall go down by one another's
sword.[n]
23   On that day, says the LORD of
hosts,[o]
I will take you, Zerubbabel,
son of Shealtiel, my servant, says the
LORD,
And I will set you as a signet ring;
for I have chosen you, says the LORD
of hosts. *

2, 12ff: According to the ritual concepts of the Jews, uncleanness was more contagious than sacredness. Inasmuch as
the people were unclean, their offerings became unclean (Nm
19, 22).

2, 15-19: This prophecy is intimately linked with chapter
1, and should be read with it.

2, 18: The ninth month: the ordinal ninth has been copied
incorrectly from Hg 2, 10. This note clearly concerns the
twenty-fourth day of the sixth month, on which the temple of
the Lord was founded (Hg 1, 15).

2, 20: The month: probably again the sixth month, as in
Hg 1, 15 and 2, 18; see note on the latter.

2, 23: This promise to Zerubbabel, reversing the punishment of his grandfather (Jer 22, 24), is a continuation of the
messianic hope; cf Zec 6, 11f.

h: Heb 12, 26. i: Gn 49, 10; Is 60, 5. 9. 11; Mal 3, 1; Rv 21, 26.
j: Is 2, 2ff; Zec 6, 13. k: Dt 17, 8-13; Zec 7, 3. l: Nm 19, 11;
13, 22. m: Is 5, 10. n: Ez 38, 21; Dn 2, 44; Zec 14, 13; Lk 1,
52. o: Song 8, 6; Sir 49, 11; Is 42, 1; 44, 1f.

Zechariah's Opening Speech

Zechariah's visions (Zec 1, 7—6, 8) are introduced and concluded (chs 7–8) by speeches in which Zechariah urges his listeners to embrace the social responsibilities and just behavior preached by the prophets before him.

The Book of Zechariah

See RG 261-63

Zechariah's initial prophecy is dated to 520 B.C., the same year as that in which Haggai received the prophetic call. The first eight chapters of the Book of Zechariah contain oracles which certainly belong to him while the last six (sometimes called "Deutero-Zechariah") represent the work of one or more unknown authors. In the prophecies proper to Zechariah eight symbolic visions are recorded, all meant to promote the work of rebuilding the temple and to encourage the returned exiles, especially their leaders, Joshua and Zerubbabel. In the final chapter of this first division Zechariah portrays the messianic future under the figure of a prosperous land to which the nations come in pilgrimage, eager to follow the God of Israel.

The second part of Zechariah is divided into two sections, each with its own introductory title. The first (9—11) consists of oracles whose historical background, date and authorship are extremely difficult to determine. With 9, 9 begins the messianic vision of the coming of the Prince of Peace. The verses describing the triumphant appearance of the humble king are taken up by the four Evangelists to describe the entry of Christ into Jerusalem on Palm Sunday. Chapter 12 is introduced by an oracle proclaiming the victory of God's people over the heathen. The prophecy closes by describing in apocalyptic imagery, the final assault of the enemy on Jerusalem, after which the messianic age begins.

CHAPTER 1

See RG 261-62

Necessity of Conversion. [1] In the second year of Darius, in the eighth month,* the word of the LORD came to the prophet Zechariah, son of Berechiah, son of Iddo:[a] [2] The LORD was indeed angry with your fathers. . . . [3] and say to them: Thus says the LORD of hosts: Return to me, says the LORD of hosts, and I will return to you, says the LORD of hosts. [4] Be not like your fathers whom the former prophets warned: Thus says the LORD of hosts: Turn from your evil ways and from your wicked deeds. But they would not listen or pay attention to me, says the LORD.[b] [5] Your fathers, where are they? And the prophets, can they live forever? [6] But my words and my decrees, which I entrusted to my servants the prophets, did not these overtake your fathers? Then they repented and admitted: "The LORD of hosts has treated us according to our ways and deeds, just as he had determined he would."[c]

The Four Horsemen. [7] In the second year of Darius, on the twenty-fourth day of Shebat, the eleventh month,* the word of the LORD came to the prophet Zechariah, son of Berechiah, son of Iddo, in the following way: [8] I had a vision during the night. There appeared the driver of a red horse,* standing among myrtle trees in a shady place, and behind him were red, sorrel, and white horses.[d] [9] Then I asked, "What are these, my lord?"; and the angel who spoke with me answered

---

1, 1: The second year . . . eighth month: October/November, 520 B.C.

1, 7: The second year . . . eleventh month: January/February, 519 B.C.

1, 8-11: The driver of a red horse: apparently distinct from the man, or angel of the Lord . . . standing among the myrtle

trees, who spoke with the prophet. The four horsemen are sent by God to the four corners of the earth (Zec 2, 10), to see if the whole earth is at peace.

a: Ezr 4, 24; 5, 1; 6, 14.   *b:* Jer 25, 5; 35, 15; Mal 3, 7.   *c:* Lam 2, 17; Lv 26, 14ff; Dt 28, 15.   *d:* Rv 6, 4.

me, "I will show you what these are." [10]The man who was standing among the myrtle trees spoke up and said, "These are they whom the LORD has sent to patrol the earth."[e] [11]And they answered the angel of the LORD who was standing among the myrtle trees and said, "We have patrolled the earth; see, the whole earth is tranquil and at rest!"

[12][f]Then the angel of the Lord spoke out and said, "O LORD of hosts, how long will you be without mercy for Jerusalem and the cities of Judah that have felt your anger these seventy years?"* [13]To the angel who spoke with me, the LORD replied with comforting words.[g]

[14]And the angel who spoke with me said to me, Proclaim: Thus says the LORD of hosts: I am deeply moved for the sake of Jerusalem and Zion,[h] [15]and I am exceedingly angry with the complacent nations;* whereas I was but a little angry, they added to the harm.[i] [16]Therefore, says the LORD: I will turn to Jerusalem in mercy; my house shall be built in it, says the LORD of hosts, and a measuring line* shall be stretched over Jerusalem.[j] [17]Proclaim further: Thus says the LORD of hosts: My cities shall again overflow with prosperity; the LORD will again comfort Zion, and again choose Jerusalem.[k]

See RG 261-62

CHAPTER 2

Four Horns and Four Blacksmiths. [1]I raised my eyes and looked: there were four horns.* [2]Then I asked the angel who spoke with me what these were. He answered me, "These are the horns that scattered Judah and Israel and Jerusalem."

[3]Then the LORD showed me four blacksmiths. And I asked, "What are these coming to do?" [4]And he said, "Here are the horns that scattered Judah, so that no man raised his head any more; but these have come to terrify them: to cast down the horns of the nations that raised their horns to scatter the land of Judah."

The New Jerusalem. [5]Again I raised my eyes and looked: there was a man with a measuring line in his hand.[l] [6]"Where are you going?" I asked. "To measure Jerusalem," he answered; "to see how great is its width and how great its length."[m]

[7]Then the angel who spoke with me advanced, and another angel came out to meet him [8]and said to him, "Run, tell this to that young man:* People will live in Jerusalem as though in open country, because of the multitude of men and beasts in her midst.[n] [9]But I will be for her an encircling wall of fire, says the LORD, and I will be the glory in her midst."

[10]Up, up! Flee from the land of the north,* says the LORD; for I scatter you to the four winds of heaven, says the LORD. [11]Up, escape to Zion! you who dwell in daughter Babylon. [12]For thus said the LORD of hosts (after he had already sent me) concerning the nations that have plundered you: Whoever touches you touches the apple of my eye.[o] [13]See, I wave my hand over them; they become plunder for their slaves. Thus you shall know that the LORD of hosts has sent me.

[14]Sing and rejoice, O daughter Zion! See, I am coming to dwell among you, says the LORD.[p] [15]Many nations shall join themselves to the LORD on that day, and they shall be his people, and he will dwell among you, and you shall know that the LORD of hosts has sent me to you. [16]The LORD will possess Judah as his portion in the holy land, and he will again choose Jerusalem. [17]Silence, all mankind, in the presence of the LORD! for he stirs forth from his holy dwelling.

CHAPTER 3

See RG 261-62

Joshua the High Priest. [1]Then he showed me Joshua the high priest standing before the angel of the LORD, while Satan

---

1, 12: These seventy years: see note on Jer 25, 1-14.

1, 15: The complacent nations: the neighbors of Judah, especially Edom, which enjoyed their present prosperity and security at Judah's expense.

1, 16: Measuring line: not for devastation, as in Is 34, 11, but for reconstruction.

2, 1-4: Four horns: symbolic of the hostile forces which, from the four corners of the earth, invaded and devastated the land of Judah. Four blacksmiths: the powers used by God to

destroy these enemies of his people.

2, 8: That young man: the angel or man with a measuring line of v 5.

2, 10: The land of the north: Babylonia (v 11).

---

e: Zec 6, 7. *f:* Zec 7, 5; Jer 25, 11; Dn 9, 2. *g:* Jer 29, 10. *h:* Zec 8, 2; Jl 2, 18. *i:* Is 47, 6; Ob 10-14. *j:* Zec 8, 3; Ezr 6, 14. *k:* Is 51, 3. *l:* Rv 11, 1. *m:* Dt 28, 64. *n:* Ez 36, 11. *o:* Dt 32, 10; Ps 17, 8. *p:* Ez 37, 26.

stood at his right hand to accuse him.*q* *2*And the angel of the LORD said to Satan, "May the LORD rebuke you, Satan; may the LORD who has chosen Jerusalem rebuke you! Is not this man a brand snatched from the fire?"*r*

*3*Now Joshua was standing before the angel, clad in filthy garments.* *4*He spoke and said to those who were standing before him, "Take off his filthy garments, and clothe him in festal garments."*s* *5*He also said, "Put a clean miter on his head." And they put a clean miter on his head and clothed him with the garments. Then the angel of the LORD, standing, said, "See, I have taken away your guilt."

*6*The angel of the LORD then gave Joshua this assurance: *7*"Thus says the LORD of hosts: If you walk in my ways and heed my charge, you shall judge my house and keep my courts, and I will give you access among these standing here. *8*Listen, O Joshua, high priest! You and your associates who sit before you are men of good omen.* Yes, I will bring my servant the Shoot.*t* *9*Look at the stone that I have placed before Joshua, one stone with seven facets.* I will engrave its inscription, says the LORD of hosts, and I will take away the guilt of the land in one day.*u* *10*On that day, says the LORD of hosts, you will invite one another under your vines and fig trees."*v*

CHAPTER 4

See RG 261-62
*4*Then I said to the angel who spoke with me, "What are these things, my lord?" *5*And the angel who spoke with me replied, "Do you not know what these things are?" "No, my lord," I answered. *6*Then he said to me, "This is the LORD's message to Zerubba-

bel: Not by an army, nor by might, but by my spirit, says the LORD of hosts. *7*What are you, O great mountain?* Before Zerubbabel you are but a plain. He shall bring out the capstone amid exclamations of 'Hail, Hail' to it."*w*

*8*This word of the LORD then came to me: *9*The hands of Zerubbabel have laid the foundations of this house,*x* and his hands shall finish it; then you shall know that the LORD of hosts has sent me to you. *10y*For even they who were scornful on that day of small beginnings shall rejoice to see the select stone in the hands of Zerubbabel. These seven facets are the eyes of the LORD that range over the whole earth.

The Lampstand. *1*Then the angel who spoke with me returned and awakened me, like a man awakened from his sleep. *2*"What do you see?" he asked me. "I see a lampstand all of gold, with a bowl at the top," I replied; "on it are seven lamps with their tubes,*z* *3*and beside it are two olive trees, one on the right and the other on the left."*a* *11*I then asked him, "What are these two olive trees at each side of the lampstand?" *12*And again I asked, "What are the two olive tufts which freely pour out fresh oil through the two golden channels?" *13*"Do you not know what these are?" he said to me. "No, my lord," I answered him. *14*He said, "These are the two anointed* who stand by the LORD of the whole earth."

CHAPTER 5

*The Flying Scroll.** *1*Then I raised my eyes again and saw a scroll flying.*b* *2*"What do you see?" he asked me. I answered, "I see

See RG 261-62

3, 3: Filthy garments: symbolic of mourning for the dead, or of national catastrophe, and implying acknowledgment of guilt (v 5).

3, 8: Men of good omen: the restoration of the priesthood is a sign of the coming of the messianic times. My servant the Shoot: identified, in the earliest form of Zec 6, 11f as the prophet composed it, with Zerubbabel, direct descendant of King David and rebuilder of the temple; and, as such, a type of the Messiah; cf Jer 23, 5.

3, 9: One stone with seven facets: apparently the same as the select stone of Zec 4, 10, which seems to be a precious gem. The seven facets are explained in Zec 4, 10 as signifying the Lord's vigilance over the world. I will engrave its inscription: the same Hebrew verb for engrave is used in Ex 28, 9. 11 in regard to the inscriptions on the twelve precious stones of the priestly breastpiece.

4, 7: Great mountain: figure of the obstacles confronting Zerubbabel in building the temple. A plain: figure of the ease with which he will overcome these obstacles.

4, 1ff. 11-14: The two anointed: literally, "the two sons of oil," Joshua, the anointed high priest, and Zerubbabel, the anointed prince. Just as the two olive trees in this imagery supply the sacred seven-branched lampstand (Ex 25, 31-40) with oil (v 12), so these two men, in ministering to the community, stand by (serve) the Lord.

5, 1-4: The enormous scroll, thirty feet by fifteen (the dimensions in length and breadth of the portico of Solomon's

q: Hg 1, 1; 1 Chr 21, 1.   *r:* Rom 8, 33; Jude 9.   *s:* Lk 15, 22.   *t:* Is 4, 2; 11, 1; Jer 23, 5; 33, 15.   *u:* Zec 4, 10.   *v:* 1 Kgs 4, 25.   *w:* Ezr 3, 11f; Ps 118, 22.   *x:* Ezr 6, 14ff.   *y:* Zec 3, 9.   *z:* Rv 1, 12.   *a:* Rv 11, 4.   *b:* Ez 2, 9.

a scroll flying; it is twenty cubits long and ten cubits wide." [3]Then he said to me: "This is the curse which is to go forth over the whole earth; in accordance with it shall every thief be swept away, and in accordance with it shall every perjurer be expelled from here. [4]I will send it forth, says the LORD of hosts, and it shall come into the house of the thief, or into the house of him who perjures himself with my name; it shall lodge within his house, consuming it, timber and stones."[c]

The Flying Bushel.[*] [5]Then the angel who spoke with me came forward and said to me, "Raise your eyes and see what this is that comes forth." [6]"What is it?" I asked. And he answered, "This is a bushel container coming. This is their guilt in all the land." [7]Then a leaden cover was lifted, and there was a woman sitting inside the bushel. [8]"This is Wickedness," he said; and he thrust her inside the bushel, pushing the leaden cover into the opening. [9]Then I raised my eyes and saw two women coming forth with a wind ruffling their wings, for they had wings like the wings of a stork. As they lifted up the bushel into the air, [10]I said to the angel who spoke with me, "Where are they taking the bushel?" [11]He replied, "To build a temple for it in the land of Shinar; when the temple is ready, they will deposit it there in its place."[d]

CHAPTER 6

See RG 261–62 **Four Chariots.**[*] [1]Again I raised my eyes and saw four chariots coming out from between two mountains; and the mountains were of bronze. [2]The first chariot had red horses, the second chariot black horses,[e] [3]the third chariot white horses, and the fourth chariot spotted horses—all of them strong horses. [4]I asked the angel who spoke with me, "What are these, my lord?" [5]The angel said to me in reply, "These are the four winds of the heavens, which are coming forth after being reviewed by the LORD of all the earth."[f] [6]The chariot with the black horses was turning toward the land of the north, the red and the white horses went after them, and the spotted ones went toward the land of the south. [7]As these strong horses emerged, eager to set about patrolling the earth, he said, "Go, patrol the earth!" Then, as they patrolled the earth, [8]he called out to me and said, "See, they that go forth to the land of the north will make my spirit rest in the land of the north."

The Coronation. [9]This word of the LORD then came to me: [10]Take from the returned captives Heldai, Tobijah, Jedaiah; and go the same day to the house of Josiah, son of Zephaniah (these had come from Babylon). [11]Silver and gold you shall take, and make a crown; place it on the head of [Joshua, son of Jehozadak, the high priest] Zerubbabel.[*] [12]And say to him: Thus says the LORD of hosts: Here is a man whose name is Shoot, and where he is he shall sprout, and he shall build the temple of the LORD.[g] [13]Yes, he shall build the temple of the LORD, and taking up the royal insignia, he shall sit as ruler upon his throne. The priest shall be at his right hand, and between the two of them there shall be friendly understanding.[h] [14]The crown itself shall be a memorial offering in the temple of the LORD in favor of Heldai, Tobijah, Jedaiah, and the son of Zephaniah. [15]And they who are from afar shall come and build the temple of the LORD, and you shall know that the LORD

---

temple, 1 Kgs 6, 3), contains a list of maledictions on sinners, similar to that in Dt 27, 15-26. The thief and the perjurer represent all sinners, who are expelled from the holy community.

5, 5-11: The woman sealed in the bushel container is a figure of the general corruption of the people of Judah. She is removed from the Holy Land and transported to Shinar, that is, Babylonia, where a dwelling is being prepared for her; that is a symbol of the reign of Wickedness in pagan lands, contrasted with the reign of holiness in the Lord's dwelling on Mount Zion.

6, 1-8: The four chariots represent the angelic hosts sent by the Lord to the four ends of the earth. The chariot with the black horses brings the spirit, i.e., anger of the Lord against

the land of the north, Babylonia.

6, 11: Make a crown; place it on the head of [Joshua, son of Jehozadak, the high priest] Zerubbabel: according to the current Hebrew text, Joshua the high priest is to be crowned. However, since the crown is a sign of royalty, the original text must have had the name of Zerubbabel here, not that of Joshua. In Zec 3, 8 Joshua is a different man from the one called the Shoot, and in v 12 it is upon the Shoot that the crown is to be placed.

c: Lv 19, 12.   *d:* Gn 11, 2ff.   *e:* Zec 1, 8; Rv 6, 4.   *f:* Ps 104, 4.   *g:* Zec 3, 8; Eph 2, 20; Heb 3, 3.   *h:* Ps 110, 4; Heb 3, 1.

Rituals of Practice

By responding to a question about mourning rituals (7, 3) with a charge to create a just society, Zechariah appears to side with his predecessors, the former prophets, who claimed that religious rituals were meaningless apart from the practice of justice in all areas of life (Am 5, 21–24).

---

of hosts has sent me to you.[i] And if you heed carefully the voice of the LORD your God. . . .

See RG
261–62

CHAPTER 7

True Fasting. [1]In the fourth year of Darius the king [the word of the LORD came to Zechariah], on the fourth day of Chislev, the ninth month,* [2]Bethel-sarezer sent Regemmelech and his men to implore favor of the LORD [3]and to ask the priests of the house of the LORD of hosts, and the prophets, "Must I mourn and abstain in the fifth month as I have been doing these many years?"[j] [4]Thereupon this word of the LORD of hosts came to me: [5]Say to all the people of the land and to the priests: When you fasted and mourned in the fifth and in the seventh month these seventy years, was it really for me that you fasted?[k] [6]And when you were eating and drinking, was it not for yourselves that you ate, and for yourselves that you drank? [7]Were not these the words which the LORD spoke through the former prophets, when Jerusalem and the surrounding cities were inhabited and at peace, when the Negeb and the foothills were inhabited?[l] [8][This word of the LORD came to Zechariah: [9]Thus says the LORD of hosts:] Render true judgment, and show kindness and compassion toward each other.[m] [10]Do not oppress the widow or the orphan, the alien or the poor; do not plot evil against one another in your hearts.[n] [11]But they refused to listen; they stubbornly turned their backs and stopped their ears so as not to hear.[o] [12]And they made their hearts diamond-hard so as not to hear the teaching and the message that the LORD of hosts had sent by his spirit

through the former prophets.[p] [13]Then the LORD of hosts in his great anger said that, as they had not listened when he called, so he would not listen when they called,[q] [14]but would scatter them with a whirlwind among all the nations that they did not know. Thus the land was left desolate after them with no one traveling to and fro; they made the pleasant land into a desert.[r]

CHAPTER 8

See RG
261–62

In the Days of the Messiah. [1]This word of the LORD of hosts came: Thus says the LORD of hosts:

[2] I am intensely jealous for Zion,
 stirred to jealous wrath for her.[s]
[3]   Thus says the LORD:
I will return to Zion,
 and I will dwell within Jerusalem;
Jerusalem shall be called the faithful city,
 and the mountain of the LORD of hosts,
 the holy mountain.[t]

[4]Thus says the LORD of hosts: Old men and old women, each with staff in hand because of old age, shall again sit in the streets of Jerusalem. [5]The city shall be filled with boys and girls playing in her streets. [6]Thus says the LORD of hosts: Even if this should seem impossible in the eyes of the remnant of this people, shall it in those days be impossible in my eyes also, says the LORD of hosts? [7]Thus says the LORD of hosts: Lo, I will rescue my people from the land of the rising sun, and from the land of the setting sun,[u] [8]I will bring them back to dwell within Jerusalem. They

---

7, 1: The fourth year of Darius . . . the fourth day of Chislev, the ninth month: November, 518 B.C.

---

i: Eph 2, 19f. *j:* Zec 8, 19. *k:* Is 58, 5; Rom 14, 6. *l:* Jer 17, 26. *m:* Is 58, 6. *n:* Ex 22, 21-24; Dt 24, 17; Is 1, 17; Jer 5, 28. *o:* Neh 9, 29; Hos 4, 16. *p:* Ez 11, 19; 36, 26; Neh 9, 29. *q:* Is 1, 15; Mi 3, 4. *r:* Dt 4, 27. *s:* Na 1, 2. *t:* Is 2, 2; Jer 31, 23. *u:* Is 11, 11; Jer 30, 18.

shall be my people, and I will be their God, with faithfulness and justice.[v]

[9]Thus says the LORD of hosts: Let your hands be strong, you who in these days hear these words spoken by the prophets on the day when the foundation of the house of the LORD of hosts was laid for the building of the temple.[w] [10]For before those days there were no wages for men, or hire for beasts; those who came and went had no security from the enemy, for I set every man against his neighbor. [11]But now I will not deal with the remnant of this people as in former days, says the LORD of hosts, [12]for it is the seedtime of peace: the vine shall yield its fruit, the land shall bear its crops, and the heavens shall give their dew; all these things I will have the remnant of the people possess. [13]Just as you were a curse among the nations, O house of Judah and house of Israel, so will I save you that you may be a blessing; do not fear, but let your hands be strong.[x]

[14]Thus says the LORD of hosts: As I determined to harm you when your fathers provoked me to wrath, says the LORD of hosts, and I did not relent,[y] [15]so again in these days I have determined to favor Jerusalem and the house of Judah; do not fear! [16]These then are the things you should do: Speak the truth to one another; let there be honesty and peace in the judgments at your gates,[z] [17]and let none of you plot evil against another in his heart, nor love a false oath. For all these things I hate, says the LORD.[a]

[18]This word of the LORD of hosts came to me: [19]Thus says the LORD of hosts: The fast days of the fourth, the fifth, the seventh, and the tenth months shall become occasions of joy and gladness, cheerful festivals for the house of Judah; only love faithfulness and peace.* [20]Thus says the LORD of hosts: There shall yet come peoples, the inhabitants of many cities; [21]and the inhabitants of one city shall approach those of another, and say, "Come! let us go to implore the favor of the LORD"; and, "I too will go to seek the LORD."[b] [22]Many peoples and strong nations shall come to seek the LORD of hosts in Jerusalem and to implore the favor of the LORD.[c] [23]Thus says the LORD of hosts: In those days ten men of every nationality, speaking different tongues, shall take hold, yes, take hold of every Jew by the edge of his garment and say, "Let us go with you, for we have heard that God is with you."[d]

CHAPTER 9

Invasion by the Lord*

See RG 262-63

[1] An oracle:
The word of the LORD is upon the land of Hadrach,
and Damascus is its resting place,
For the cities of Aram are the LORD's,
as are all the tribes of Israel,
[2] Hamath also, on its border,
Tyre, too, and Sidon, however wise they be.[e]
[3] Tyre built herself a stronghold,
and heaped up silver like dust,
and gold like the mire of the streets.
[4] Lo, the LORD will strip her of her possessions,
and smite her power on the sea,
and she shall be devoured by fire.[f]
[5] Ashkelon shall see it and be afraid;
Gaza also: she shall be in great anguish;
Ekron, too, for her hope shall come to nought.
The king shall disappear from Gaza,
and Ashkelon shall not be inhabited,
[6] and the baseborn* shall occupy Ashdod.
I will destroy the pride of the Philistine[g]

8, 19: The fast day of the fourth month recalled the fall of Jerusalem in June, 587 B.C. (2 Kgs 25, 3f); that of the fifth month, the burning of the temple by Nebuzaradan in July of the same year (2 Kgs 25, 8f); that of the seventh month, the murder of Gedaliah in September of the same year (Jer 41, 1f); that of the tenth month, the beginning of the final siege of Jerusalem in January, 588 B.C. (2 Kgs 25, 1).

9, 1-8: Divine judgment is about to fall on the surrounding hostile peoples: Aram (Syria), including the cities of Hadrach and Damascus; Phoenicia, with its cities of Tyre and Sidon; Philistia, with its cities of Ashkelon, Gaza, Ekron, and Ashdod.

9, 6: The baseborn: people of mixed ancestry.

[v]: Jer 4, 2. [w]: Ezr 5, 1; Hg 2, 18. [x]: Is 19, 24; Jer 42, 18; Hg 2, 19; Zep 3, 20. [y]: Jer 31, 28. [z]: Zec 7, 9. [a]: Zec 7, 10. [b]: Is 2, 3. [c]: Is 60, 3. [d]: Is 66, 23. [e]: Jer 49, 23. [f]: Is 23, 1-18; Ez 26, 1—28, 26. [g]: Am 1, 8.

7 and take from his mouth his bloody
    meat,
and his abominations from between
    his teeth:
He also shall become a remnant* for our
    God,
and shall be like a family in Judah,
and Ekron shall be like the Jebusites.
8 I will encamp by my house* as a guard
    that none may pass to and fro;
No oppressor shall pass over them again,
    for now I have regard for their
    affliction.

Restoration under the Messiah
9 Rejoice heartily, O daughter Zion,[h]
    shout for joy, O daughter Jerusalem!
See, your king shall come to you;
    a just savior is he,
Meek, and riding on an ass,
    on a colt, the foal of an ass.*
10 He shall banish the chariot from
    Ephraim,
and the horse from Jerusalem;
The warrior's bow shall be banished,
    and he shall proclaim peace to the
    nations.
His dominion shall be from sea to sea,
    and from the River* to the ends of the
    earth.[i]
11 As for you, for the blood of your
    covenant with me,*
I will bring forth your prisoners from
    the dungeon.[j]
12 In the return to the fortress
    of the waiting prisoners,*
This very day, I will return you
    double for your exile.[k]
13 For I will bend Judah as my bow,

I will arm myself with Ephraim;
I will arouse your sons, O Zion,
    [against your sons, O Yavan,]
and I will use you as a warrior's sword.
14 The LORD shall appear over them,
    and his arrow shall shoot forth as
    lightning;
The LORD God shall sound the trumpet,
    and come in a storm from the south.
15 The LORD of hosts shall be a shield over
    them,
they shall overcome sling stones
    and trample them underfoot;
They shall drink blood like wine,
    till they are filled with it like libation
    bowls,
like the corners of the altar.
16 And the LORD, their God, shall save them
    on that day,
his people, like a flock.
For they are the jewels in a crown
    raised aloft over his land.[l]
17 For what wealth is theirs, and what
    beauty!
grain that makes the youths flourish,
    and new wine, the maidens!

CHAPTER 10
The New Order of Things
1 Ask of the LORD rain in the spring
    season!
It is the LORD who makes the storm
    clouds,
And sends men the pouring rain;
    for everyone, grassy fields.[m]
2 For the teraphim* speak nonsense,
    the diviners have false visions:
Deceitful dreams they tell,
    empty comfort they offer.

See RG
262–63

9, 7: Remnant: see note on Hg 1, 12. The Jebusites: the pre-Israelite inhabitants of Jerusalem, conquered by David and incorporated into Israel.

9, 8: My house: the Holy Land; cf Hos 8, 1; 9, 15; Jer 12, 7.

9, 9: The Messiah will come, not as a conquering warrior, but in lowliness and peace. Not like the last kings of Judah, who rode in chariots and on horses (Jer 17, 25; 22, 4), but like the princes of old (Gn 49, 11; Jgs 5, 10; 10, 4), the Messiah will ride on an ass. The Evangelists see a literal fulfillment of this prophecy in the Savior's triumphal entry into Jerusalem (Mt 21, 4f; Jn 12, 14f).

9, 10: The River: the Euphrates; see note on Ps 72, 8.

9, 11: The blood of your covenant with me: the covenant between the Lord and Israel sealed with sacrificial blood (Ex 24, 8).

9, 12: The waiting prisoners: the exiles awaiting the return to their country, where they will receive a double compensation for the double punishment they had suffered; cf Is 40, 2; 61, 7.

10, 2: Teraphim: household idols, used for divination; cf Gn 31, 19. 34f; Jgs 17, 5; 18, 17f. 20; Ez 21, 26; Hos 3, 4.

h: Is 62, 11; Jer 23, 5; Mt 21, 5; Jn 12, 15.   *i:* Hos 1, 7.   *j:* Is 42, 7; Ez 24, 8.   *k:* Is 61, 7.   *l:* Is 62, 3.   *m:* Dt 11, 14; Jer 14, 22.

Land of Israel

In the vision in 10, 6–12, God will gather all the people of Israel together, recalling them from exile and rebuilding Israel to be greater than ever, taking over neighboring territories, and bringing low Israel's traditional enemies. The house of Joseph and Ephraim are references to the northern kingdom of Israel. Egypt and Assyria are two of the countries to which Israelites were exiled (2 Kgs 17, 5–6; 25, 26). Gilead and Lebanon are territories to the north of Israel.

This is why they wander like sheep,
   wretched: they have no shepherd.[n]
3 My wrath is kindled against the
      shepherds,
   and I will punish the leaders;
For the LORD of hosts will visit his flock,
   the house of Judah,
   and make them his stately war horse.

4 From him shall come leader and chief,
   from him warrior's bow and every
      officer.
5 They shall all be warriors,
   trampling the mire of the streets in
      battle;
They shall wage war because the LORD is
   with them,
   and shall put the horsemen to rout.
6 I will strengthen the house of Judah,
   the house of Joseph I will save;
I will bring them back, because I have
   mercy on them,
   they shall be as though I had never
      cast them off,
   for I am the LORD, their God, and I
      will hear them.
7 Then Ephraim shall be valiant men,
   and their hearts shall be cheered as by
      wine.
Their children shall see it and be glad,
   their hearts shall rejoice in the LORD.

8 I will whistle for them to come together,
   and when I redeem them
   they will be as numerous as before.[o]

9 I sowed them among the nations,
   yet in distant lands they remember me;
   they shall rear their children and return.
10 I will bring them back from the land of
      Egypt,
   and gather them from Assyria.
I will bring them into Gilead and into
      Lebanon,
   but these shall not suffice them;[p]
11 I will cross over to Egypt
   and smite the waves of the sea
   and all the depths of the Nile shall be
      dried up.
The pride of Assyria shall be cast down,
   and the scepter of Egypt taken away.[q]
12 I will strengthen them in the LORD,
   and they shall walk in his name, says
      the LORD.[r]

CHAPTER 11

See RG 262–63

1 Open your doors, O Lebanon,
   that the fire may devour your cedars!
2 Wail, you cypress trees,
   for the cedars are fallen,
   the mighty have been despoiled.
Wail, you oaks of Bashan,
   for the impenetrable forest is cut
      down!
3 Hark! the wailing of the shepherds,
   their glory has been ruined.
Hark! the roaring of the young lions,
   the jungle of the Jordan is laid waste.

Allegory of the Shepherds.* 4Thus said the LORD, my God: Shepherd the flock to be

---

11, 4-17: In this allegory the prophet becomes the good shepherd of God's flock, which is being slaughtered; he is the defender of the people exploited by bad rulers. The three shepherds, rulers in general, are to destroy one another in a short time (a single month). The service of the good shepherd is contemptuously valued at thirty pieces of silver, the legal indemnity (Ex 21, 32) for a gored slave. The prophet is thus a type of Christ whose mission of salvation to his people was appraised by the Sanhedrists, the false shepherds, at the same base price (Mt 26, 14ff). In the case of the prophet as well as of Christ (Mt 27, 5), the money is thrown into the temple

n: Jer 10, 8; Ez 34, 5.   o: Ez 36, 37.   p: Is 11, 11; 49, 20; Hos 11, 11.   q: Is 11, 15; Ez 30, 13.   r: Mi 4, 5.

slaughtered. [5]For they who buy them slay them with impunity; while those who sell them say, "Blessed be the LORD, I have become rich!" Even their own shepherds do not feel for them.[s] [6](Nor shall I spare the inhabitants of the earth any more, says the LORD. Yes, I will deliver each of them into the power of his neighbor, or into the power of his king; they shall crush the earth, and I will not deliver it out of their power.)

[7]So I became the shepherd of the flock to be slaughtered for the sheep merchants. I took two staffs, one of which I called "Favor," and the other, "Bonds," and I fed the flock.[t] [8]In a single month I did away with the three shepherds. I wearied of them, and they behaved badly toward me. [9]"I will not feed you," I said. "What is to die, let it die; what is to perish, let it perish, and let those that are left devour one another's flesh."[u]

[10]Then I took my staff "Favor" and snapped it asunder, breaking off the covenant which I had made with all peoples; [11]that day it was broken off. The sheep merchants who were watching me understood that this was the word of the LORD. [12]I said to them, "If it seems good to you, give me my wages; but if not, let it go." And they counted out my wages, thirty pieces of silver.[v] [13]But the LORD said to me, "Throw it in the treasury, the handsome price at which they valued me." So I took the thirty pieces of silver and threw them into the treasury in the house of the LORD.[w]

[14]Then I snapped asunder my other staff, "Bonds," breaking off the brotherhood between Judah and Israel. [15]The LORD said to me: This time take the gear of a foolish shepherd. [16]For I will raise up a shepherd in the land who will take no note of those that perish, nor seek the strays, nor heal the injured, nor feed what survives—he will eat the flesh of the fat ones and tear off their hoofs![x]

[17] Woe to my foolish shepherd
  who forsakes the flock!

May the sword fall upon his arm
  and upon his right eye;
Let his arm wither away entirely,
  and his right eye be blind forever![y]

CHAPTER 12

See RG 263

Jerusalem God's Instrument.[*] [1]An oracle: the word of the LORD concerning Israel. Thus says the LORD, who spreads out the heavens, lays the foundations of the earth, and forms the spirit of man within him:[z] [2]See, I will make Jerusalem a bowl to stupefy all peoples round about. [Judah will be besieged, even Jerusalem.][a] [3]On that day I will make Jerusalem a weighty stone for all peoples. All who attempt to lift it shall injure themselves badly, and all the nations of the earth shall be gathered against her.[b] [4]On that day, says the LORD, I will strike every horse with fright, and its rider with madness. I will strike blind all the horses of the peoples, but upon the house of Judah I will open my eyes, [5]and the princes of Judah shall say to themselves, "The inhabitants of Jerusalem have their strength in the LORD of hosts, their God." [6]On that day I will make the princes of Judah like a brazier of fire in the woodland, and like a burning torch among sheaves, and they shall devour right and left all the surrounding peoples; but Jerusalem shall still abide on its own site.[c] [7]The LORD shall save the tents of Judah first, that the glory of the house of David and the glory of the inhabitants of Jerusalem may not be exalted over Judah. [8]On that day, the LORD will shield the inhabitants of Jerusalem, and the weakling among them shall be like David on that day, and the house of David godlike, like an angel of the LORD before them.[d] [9]On that day I will seek the destruction of all nations that come against Jerusalem.

Messianic Jerusalem. [10]I will pour out on the house of David and on the inhabitants of Jerusalem a spirit of grace and petition;[e] and they shall look on him whom they have thrust through, and they shall mourn for him as one

---

treasury, i.e., paid to God, showing thereby how shamefully his divine love and care are requited.

12, 1-9: Under the image of the deliverance of Judah and Jerusalem from invading enemies, the prophet foretells the ultimate victory of God's people in the messianic age.

---

s: Jer 50, 7.　*t:* Hos 5, 6.　*u:* Jer 15, 2.　*v:* Ex 21, 32; Mt 26, 15.　*w:* Mt 27, 9f.　*x:* Ez 34, 2ff.　*y:* Jn 10, 12.　*z:* Is 42, 5.　*a:* Is 51, 17; Jer 51, 7.　*b:* Mt 21, 44.　*c:* Ob 18.　*d:* Ex 32, 34.　*e:* Jer 6, 26; Jn 19, 34; Rv 1, 7.

mourns for an only son, and they shall grieve over him as one grieves over a firstborn.*

*11*On that day the mourning in Jerusalem shall be as great as the mourning of Hadadrimmon in the plain of Megiddo.*f* *12*And the land shall mourn, each family apart: the family of the house of David, and their wives; the family of the house of Nathan, and their wives; *13*the family of the house of Levi, and their wives; the family of Shemei, and their wives; *14*and all the rest of the families, each family apart, and the wives apart.

CHAPTER 13

See RG 263

The End of Falsehood. *1*On that day there shall be open to the house of David and to the inhabitants of Jerusalem, a fountain to purify from sin* and uncleanness.*g* *2*On that day, says the LORD of hosts, I will destroy the names of the idols from the land, so that they shall be mentioned no more; I will also take away the prophets and the spirit of uncleanness from the land.*h* *3*If a man still prophesies, his parents, father and mother, shall say to him, "You shall not live, because you have spoken a lie in the name of the LORD." When he prophesies, his parents, father and mother, shall thrust him through.*i*

*4*On that day, every prophet shall be ashamed to prophesy his vision, neither shall he assume the hairy mantle* to mislead, *5*but he shall say, "I am no prophet, I am a tiller of the soil, for I have owned land since my youth."*j* *6*And if anyone asks him, "What are these wounds on your chest?"* he shall answer, "With these I was wounded in the house of my dear ones."

The Song of the Sword

7 Awake, O sword, against my shepherd,
    against the man who is my associate,
    says the LORD of hosts.

Strike the shepherd
    that the sheep may be dispersed,*
    and I will turn my hand against the
        little ones.*k*

8 In all the land, says the LORD,
    two thirds of them shall be cut off and
        perish,
    and one third shall be left.

9 I will bring the one third through fire,
    and I will refine them as silver is
        refined,
    and I will test them as gold is tested.*l*
    They shall call upon my name, and I
        will hear them.

I will say, "They are my people,"
    and they shall say, "The LORD is my
        God."

CHAPTER 14

See RG 263

The Fight for Jerusalem.* *1*Lo, a day shall come for the LORD when the spoils shall be divided in your midst. *2*And I will gather all the nations against Jerusalem for

---

12, 10: The divine blessings (a spirit of grace and petition) will be poured out on God's people through the intervention of an unnamed sufferer (him whom they have thrust through), similar to the Servant of the Lord in Is 52, 13—53, 12. In Jn 19, 37 the Evangelist sees in this passage a prophecy fulfilled in the piercing of Christ's side.

12, 11: The mourning for the pierced victim in Jerusalem is compared to a lamentation in the plain of Megiddo apparently over a certain personage called Hadadrimmon. The reference is no longer clear. Both Hadad and Rimmon were names of the Semitic storm god, often identified with the god Baal. Some see here a reference to the annual mourning by the pagans over the death of the fertility god. According to others, Hadadrimmon is the name of a place near Megiddo, and the reference would then be to the mourning over the death of King Josiah, who was killed in battle there; cf 2 Chr 35, 22-25.

13, 1: A fountain to purify from sin: in contrast to the lustral water used in ritual purification; cf Nm 19, 9. 13. 20; 31, 23. The Lord himself is the fountain of living water (Jer 2, 13); cf Is 12, 2ff.

13, 4: Hairy mantle: worn by prophets as a mark of their

calling; cf 2 Kgs 1, 8; Mt 3, 4.

13, 6: Wounds on your chest: literally "wounds between your hands." The false prophets, like the prophet of Baal (1 Kgs 13, 28), apparently inflicted wounds on themselves; to defend himself against the accusation of being a false prophet, a man will deny having inflicted wounds on himself and say instead that he received them at home, "in the house of my dear ones." In the liturgy this text is applied to Christ in an accommodated sense.

13, 7: When the shepherd is killed, the sheep are scattered. In Mt 26, 31 the Evangelist quotes from this verse, in somewhat different form, the words, I will smite the shepherd, and the sheep of the flock will be scattered, as said by Christ shortly before his arrest in the Garden of Olives and the flight of the Apostles.

14, 1-21: An apocalyptic description of the day of the Lord, in which Jerusalem, the figure of God's elect, after much

---

f: 2 Chr 35, 22-25. *g:* Heb 9, 14; 1 Pt 1, 18f; Rv 1, 5. *h:* Mi 5, 12; 2 Pt 2, 1. *i:* Dt 18, 20; Mi 3, 5ff. *j:* Am 7, 14. *k:* Mt 26, 31. *l:* Jer 30, 22; Ps 66, 10.

battle: the city shall be taken, houses plundered, women ravished; half of the city shall go into exile, but the rest of the people shall not be removed from the city. ³Then the LORD shall go forth and fight against those nations, fighting as on a day of battle. ⁴That day his feet shall rest upon the Mount of Olives, which is opposite Jerusalem to the east. The Mount of Olives shall be cleft in two from east to west by a very deep valley, and half of the mountain shall move to the north and half of it to the south. ⁵And the valley of the LORD's mountain shall be filled up when the valley of those two mountains reaches its edge; it shall be filled up as it was filled up by the earthquake in the days of King Uzziah of Judah. Then the LORD, my God, shall come, and all his holy ones with him.

⁶On that day there shall no longer be cold or frost. ⁷There shall be one continuous day, known to the LORD, not day and night, for in the evening time there shall be light.ᵐ

⁸On that day, living waters shall flow from Jerusalem, half to the eastern sea, and half to the western sea, and it shall be so in summer and in winter.ⁿ ⁹The LORD shall become king over the whole earth; on that day the LORD shall be the only one, and his name the only one.ᵒ

¹⁰And from Geba to Rimmon in the Negeb, all the land shall turn into a plain; but Jerusalem shall remain exalted in its place. From the Gate of Benjamin to the place of the First Gate, to the Corner Gate; and from the Tower of Hananel to the king's wine presses,ᵖ ¹¹they shall occupy her. Never again shall she be doomed; Jerusalem shall abide in security.�q

¹²And this shall be the plague with which the LORD shall strike all the nations that have fought against Jerusalem: their flesh shall rot while they stand upon their feet, and their eyes shall rot in their sockets, and their tongues shall rot in their mouths.

¹³On that day there shall be among them a great tumult from the LORD: every man shall seize the hand of his neighbor, and the hand of each shall be raised against that of his neighbor. ¹⁴Judah also shall fight against Jerusalem. The riches of all the surrounding nations shall be gathered together, gold, silver, and garments, in great abundance.

¹⁵Similar to this plague shall be the plague upon the horses, mules, camels, asses, and upon all the beasts that are in those camps.

¹⁶All who are left of all the nations that came against Jerusalem shall come up year after year to worship the King, the LORD of hosts, and to celebrate the feast of Booths.ʳ ¹⁷If any of the families of the earth does not come up to Jerusalem to worship the King, the LORD of hosts, no rain shall fall upon them. ¹⁸And if the family of Egypt does not come up, or enter, upon them shall fall the plague which the LORD will inflict upon all the nations that do not come up to celebrate the feast of Booths. ¹⁹This shall be the punishment of Egypt, and the punishment of all the nations that do not come up to celebrate the feast of Booths.

²⁰On that day there shall be upon the bells of the horses, "Holy to the LORD." The pots in the house of the LORD shall be as the libation bowls before the altar. ²¹And every pot in Jerusalem and in Judah shall be holy to the LORD of hosts; and all who come to sacrifice shall take them and cook in them. On that day there shall no longer be any merchant in the house of the LORD of hosts.ˢ

suffering (siege: vv 1ff; riot: v 13; plague: vv 12, 15), is rescued by the Lord (vv 4f) and given great blessings (vv 6-11. 14. 16-21).

m: Rv 21, 23.   *n:* Zec 13, 1; Ez 47, 1-8; Jl 3, 18.   *o:* Dt 6, 4; Eph 4, 5f; Rv 11, 15.   *p:* Zec 12, 6; Neh 3, 6; 12, 38.   *q:* Jer 31, 40; Rv 22, 3.   *r:* Lv 23, 34. 43; Neh 8, 14; Is 60, 6. 9.   *s:* Mt 21, 12; Jn 2, 13-16.

See RG
263–65

The Book of Malachi

This work was composed by an anonymous writer shortly before Nehemiah's arrival in Jerusalem (445 B.C.). Because of the sharp reproaches he was leveling against the priests and rulers of the people, the author probably wished to conceal his identity. To do this he made a proper name out of the Hebrew expression for "My Messenger" (Malachi), which occurs in 1, 1 and 3, 1. The historical value of the prophecy is considerable in that it gives us a picture of life in the Jewish community returned from Babylon, between the period of Haggai and the reform measures of Ezra and Nehemiah. It is likely that the author's trenchant criticism of abuses and religious indifference in the community prepared the way for these necessary reforms.

The chosen people had made a sorry return for divine love. The priests, who should have been leaders, had dishonored God by their blemished sacrifices. In his first chapter, the writer foresees the time when all nations will offer a pure oblation (1, 11)—a prophecy whose fulfillment the church sees in the Sacrifice of the Mass. The author then turns from priests to people, denouncing their marriages with pagans and their callous repudiation of Israelite wives. Imbued with the rationalist and critical spirit of the times, many had wearied God with the question, "Where is the God of justice?" To this question the prophet replies that the day of the Lord is coming. But first the forerunner must come, who will prepare the soil for repentance and true worship. The Gospel writers point to John the Baptizer, as the forerunner ushering in the messianic age, the true day of the Lord. When the ground is prepared God will appear, measuring out rewards and punishments and purifying the nation in the furnace of judgment. He will create a new order in which the ultimate triumph of good is inevitable.

CHAPTER 1

See RG
264

[1] An oracle. The word of the LORD to Israel through Malachi.

Israel Preferred to Edom

[2] I have loved you, says the LORD;
　but you say, "How have you loved
　　us?"[a]
[3] Was not Esau Jacob's brother? says the
　　LORD:*
　yet I loved Jacob, but hated Esau;
I made his mountains a waste,
　his heritage a desert for jackals.[b]
[4] If Edom says, "We have been crushed
　but we will rebuild the ruins,"
Thus says the LORD of hosts:
　They indeed may build, but I will tear
　　down,
And they shall be called the land of
　　guilt,[c]
　the people with whom the LORD is
　　angry forever.
[5] Your own eyes shall see it, and you will
　　say,
　"Great is the LORD, even beyond the
　　land of Israel."[d]

Sins of the Priests and Levites

[6] A son honors his father,
　and a servant fears his master;
If then I am a father,
　where is the honor due to me?
And if I am a master,
　where is the reverence due to me?—
So says the LORD of hosts to you,
　O priests,
who despise his name.
But you ask, "How have we despised
　　your name?"
[7]　By offering polluted food on my altar!

1, 3ff: The thought passes from the person Esau to his descendants, Edom, and from the person Jacob to his descendants, Israel. Loved: preferred; hated: rejected; cf Gn 25, 21ff. St. Paul uses this passage as an example of God's freedom of choice in calling the Gentiles to the faith (Rom 9, 13).

---

a: Dt 7, 6ff; Ez 16; Am 1, 11.　*b:* Gn 25, 23; Rom 9, 13.　*c:* Is 34, 5f; 63, 1-6; Jer 49, 7-22; Ob 21.　*d:* Is 60.

The Priests' Sins

Making up one-third of the entire book of Malachi, the accusation in 1, 6 to 2, 9 singles out two priestly sins: making improper offerings (1, 6—2, 3) and giving improper instruction (2, 4–9). The importance of proper sacrifice and truthful, relevant teaching of the Torah were central to Jewish priesthood. Just as Judah's priests are not following their obligations for proper worship at the temple, so Judah's people are not fulfilling theirs. They are not bringing to the temple the full tithes of their produce required by Israelite law (Lv 27, 30–33; Dt 14, 22–29).

Then you ask, "How have we polluted
it?"
By saying the table of the LORD may
be slighted!
[8] When you offer a blind animal for
sacrifice,[e]
is this not evil?
When you offer the lame or the sick,
is it not evil?
Present it to your governor; see if he will
accept it,
or welcome you, says the LORD of
hosts.*
[9] So now if you implore God for mercy on
us,
when you have done the like
Will he welcome any of you?
says the LORD of hosts.

[10] Oh, that one among you would shut the
temple gates*
to keep you from kindling fire on my
altar in vain!
I have no pleasure in you, says the LORD
of hosts;
neither will I accept any sacrifice from
your hands,
[11] For from the rising of the sun, even to its
setting,
my name is great among the nations;
And everywhere they bring sacrifice to
my name,
and a pure offering;
For great is my name among the
nations,

says the LORD of hosts.[f]
[12] But you behave profanely toward me by
thinking
the LORD's table and its offering may
be polluted,
and its food slighted.
[13] You also say, "What a burden!"
and you scorn it, says the LORD of
hosts;
You bring in what you seize, or the lame,
or the sick;
yes, you bring it as a sacrifice.
Shall I accept it from your hands?
says the LORD.
[14] Cursed is the deceiver, who has in his
flock a male,
but under his vow sacrifices to the
LORD a gelding;
For a great King am I, says the LORD of
hosts,
and my name will be feared among the
nations.

CHAPTER 2

See RG
264

[1] And now, O priests, this
commandment is for you:
If you do not listen,
[2] And if you do not lay it to heart,
to give glory to my name, says the
LORD of hosts,
I will send a curse upon you
and of your blessing I will make a
curse.
Yes, I have already cursed it,
because you do not lay it to heart.[g]

1, 8: The offering in sacrifice of a lame, sick or blind animal was forbidden in the law (Lv 22, 17-25; Dt 17, 1).

1, 10f: The imperfect sacrifices offered without sincerity by the people of Judah are displeasing to the Lord. He will rather be pleased with the offerings of the Gentile nations throughout the world (from the rising of the sun, even to its setting), which anticipate the pure offering to be sacrificed in messianic times, the universal Sacrifice of the Mass, as we are told by the Council of Trent.

e: Lv 22, 19-25; Dt 15, 21. f: Ps 113, 3; Is 59, 19. g: Lv 26, 14-45; D: 28, 15-68.

3 Lo, I will deprive you of the shoulder*
   and I will strew dung in your faces,
The dung of your feasts,
   and you will be carried off with it.
4 Then you will know that I sent you this
      commandment
   because I have a covenant with Levi,
   says the LORD of hosts.[h]
5 My covenant with him was one of life
      and peace;
   fear I put in him, and he feared me,
   and stood in awe of my name.[i]
6 True doctrine was in his mouth,
   and no dishonesty was found upon his
      lips;
He walked with me in integrity and
      uprightness,
   and turned many away from evil.[j]
7 For the lips of the priest are to keep
      knowledge,
   and instruction is to be sought from his
      mouth,
   because he is the messenger of the
      LORD of hosts.[k]
8 But you have turned aside from the way,
   and have caused many to falter by
      your instruction;
You have made void the covenant of
      Levi,
   says the LORD of hosts.
9 I, therefore, have made you
      contemptible
   and base before all the people,
Since you do not keep my ways,
   but show partiality in your decisions.

Sins of the People

10 Have we not all the one Father?*
   Has not the one God created us?
Why then do we break faith with each
      other,
   violating the covenant of our fathers?[l]

11 Judah has broken faith; an abominable
      thing
   has been done in Israel and in
      Jerusalem.
Judah has profaned the temple which the
      LORD loves,
   and has married an idolatrous
      woman.[m]
12 May the LORD cut off from the man who
      does this
   both witness and advocate out of the
      tents of Jacob,
   and anyone to offer sacrifice to the
      LORD of hosts!

13 This also you do: the altar of the LORD
      you cover
   with tears, weeping and groaning,
Because he no longer regards your
      sacrifice
   nor accepts it favorably from your
      hand;
14 And you say, "Why is it?"—
   Because the LORD is witness
   between you and the wife of your
      youth,
With whom you have broken faith
   though she is your companion, your
      betrothed wife.[n]
15 Did he not make one being, with flesh
      and spirit:
   and what does that one require but
      godly offspring?
You must then safeguard life that is your
      own,
   and not break faith with the wife of
      your youth.[o]
16 For I hate divorce,
   says the LORD, the God of Israel,
And covering one's garment with
      injustice,
   says the LORD of hosts;

2, 3: I will deprive you of the shoulder: this part of a sac-rificial animal, allotted by the law (Dt 18, 3) to the priests, will be withheld from them.

2, 10-16: Intermarriage of Israelites with foreigners was forbidden according to Dt 7, 1-4. After the exile this law was strictly enforced (Ezr 9—10). Foreign marriages are here portrayed as a violation of the covenant (v 10), which made the sacrifices offered by the offenders unacceptable to God (v 13). They were all the more reprehensible when accompanied by the divorce of Israelite wives (vv 14ff). This gradual return to the primitive ideal of the indissolubility of marriage was fully realized in New Testament times through the teaching of Christ; cf Mt 19, 3-12.

h: Nm 25, 12f.   i: Nm 25, 12; Ez 37, 26ff.   j: Dt 33, 8-11.
k: Lv 10, 10f; Dt 17, 9f; Jer 18, 18; Hg 2, 12.   l: Mt 23, 9; Jb 31, 15; Eph 4, 6.   m: Ezr 9, 2; Neh 13, 25.   n: Gn 31, 49f; Prv 5, 18ff.   o: Gn 2, 7. 22ff.

You must then safeguard life that is your
own,
and not break faith.

[17] You have wearied the LORD with your
words,
yet you say, "How have we wearied
him?"
By your saying, "Every evildoer
is good in the sight of the LORD,
And he is pleased with him";
or else, "Where is the just God?"

CHAPTER 3

See RG
264-65

The Messenger of
the Covenant

[1] Lo, I am sending my messenger
to prepare the way before me;*
And suddenly there will come to the
temple
the LORD whom you seek,
And the messenger of the covenant
whom you desire.
Yes, he is coming, says the LORD of
hosts.[p]
[2] But who will endure the day of his
coming?
And who can stand when he appears?
For he is like the refiner's fire,
or like the fuller's lye.
[3] He will sit refining and purifying
[silver],
and he will purify the sons of Levi,
Refining them like gold or like silver
that they may offer due sacrifice to
the LORD.[q]
[4] Then the sacrifice of Judah and
Jerusalem
will please the LORD,
as in the days of old, as in years gone
by.
[5] I will draw near to you for judgment,
and I will be swift to bear witness
Against the sorcerers, adulterers, and
perjurers,

those who defraud the hired man of
his wages,
Against those who defraud widows and
orphans;
those who turn aside the stranger,
and those who do not fear me, says
the LORD of hosts.

[6] Surely I, the LORD, do not change,*
nor do you cease to be sons of Jacob.
[7] Since the days of your fathers you have
turned aside
from my statutes, and have not kept
them.
Return to me, and I will return to you,
says the LORD of hosts.
Yet you say, "How must we return?"[r]
[8] Dare a man rob God? Yet you are
robbing me!
And you say, "How do we rob you?"
In tithes and in offerings![s]
[9] You are indeed accursed,
for you, the whole nation, rob me.
[10] Bring the whole tithe
into the storehouse,*
That there may be food in my house,
and try me in this, says the LORD of
hosts:
Shall I not open for you the floodgates of
heaven,
to pour down blessing upon you
without measure?[t]
[11] For your sake I will forbid the locust
to destroy your crops;
And the vine in the field will not be
barren,
says the LORD of hosts.
[12] Then all nations will call you blessed,
for you will be a delightful land,
says the LORD of hosts.

[13] You have defied me in word, says the
LORD,
yet you ask, "What have we spoken
against you?"

3, 1: My messenger . . . before me: in v 23 this messenger
is called Elijah. In Mt 11, 10 these words are quoted by Christ
as referring to John the Baptizer, who prepared the way for
the coming of the Savior; cf Mt 3, 1ff. 11f; 17, 11ff; Mk 1, 2-
8; Lk 3, 2-18; Jn 1, 31-34.

3, 6f: God is faithful to his promises. He will not abandon

the Israelites, who are still his people.
3, 10: Storehouse: the temple treasury.

p: Is 40, 3; Mt 11, 10; Mk 1, 2; Lk 1, 17; 7, 27.   q: Is 1, 25; Zec
13, 9.   r: Zec 1, 3f; Acts 7, 51.   s: Neh 13, 10-14.   t: 2 Chr 31,
10f; Neh 10, 38; 13, 12; Prv 3, 9f.

14 You have said, "It is vain to serve God,
  and what do we profit by keeping his
      command,
And going about in penitential dress
  in awe of the LORD of hosts?*u*
15 Rather must we call the proud blessed;
  for indeed evildoers prosper,
  and even tempt God with impunity."
16 Then they who fear the LORD spoke with
      one another,
  and the LORD listened attentively;
And a record book* was written before
      him
  of those who fear the LORD and trust in
      his name.*v*
17 And they shall be mine, says the LORD of
      hosts,
  my own special possession, on the day
      I take action.
And I will have compassion on them,
  as a man has compassion on his son
      who serves him.*w*
18 Then you will again see the distinction
  between the just and the wicked;
Between him who serves God,
  and him who does not serve him.
19 For lo, the day is coming, blazing like an
      oven,
  when all the proud and all evildoers
      will be stubble,
And the day that is coming will set them
      on fire,

leaving them neither root nor branch,
  says the LORD of hosts.*x*
20 But for you who fear my name, there will
      arise
  the sun of justice with its healing rays;
And you will gambol like calves out of
      the stall
21   and tread down the wicked;*y*
They will become ashes under the soles
      of your feet,
  on the day I take action, says the LORD
      of hosts.

22 Remember the law of Moses my servant,
  which I enjoined upon him on Horeb,
The statutes and ordinances
  for all Israel.*z*
23 Lo, I will send you
  Elijah,* the prophet,
Before the day of the LORD comes,
  the great and terrible day,
24 To turn the hearts of the fathers to their
      children,
  and the hearts of the children to their
      fathers,*a*
Lest I come and strike
  the land with doom.

Lo, I will send you
  Elijah, the prophet,
Before the day of the LORD comes,
  the great and terrible day.*

3, 16: Record book: see note on Ex 32, 32.
3, 23: Elijah: described in 2 Kgs 2, 11 as taken heavenward in a fiery chariot. Here his return to earth seems to be foretold. Jewish tradition has interpreted this literally; Christ declares it to be fulfilled in the coming of John the Baptizer (Mt 17, 10-13).
3, 24: The words in fine print, a repetition of v 23a-d, have

been added by the scribes so that the collection of the twelve minor prophets will not end with the threat of doom.

---

u: Jb 21, 14f; 22, 17; Ps 73, 11f.   *v:* Rv 20, 12.   *w:* Ex 19, 5; Dt 7, 6; Pss 103, 13; 135, 4.   *x:* Is 13, 9; 34, 8; Jl 3, 3; Zep 1, 18; 2 Pt 3, 7.   *y:* Lk 1, 78f.   *z:* Ex 20; Lv 26; Dt 4, 1. 5f.   *a:* Mt 11, 14; 17, 10; Mk 9, 10ff; Lk 1, 17.

THE NEW TESTAMENT

NEW AMERICAN BIBLE

PREFACE TO THE *NEW AMERICAN BIBLE*

First Edition of the New Testament

The New Testament translation has been approached with essentially the same fidelity to the thought and individual style of the biblical writers as was applied in the Old Testament. In some cases, however, the problem of marked literary peculiarities had to be met. What by any Western standard are the limited vocabularies and stylistic infelicities of the evangelists cannot be retained in the exact form in which they appear in the originals without displeasing the modern ear. A compromise is here attempted whereby some measure of the poverty of the evangelists' expression is kept and placed at the service of their message in its richness. Similarly, the syntactical shortcomings of Paul, his frequent lapses into anacoluthon, and the like, are rendered as they occur in his epistles rather than "smoothed out." Only thus, the translators suppose, will contemporary readers have some adequate idea of the kind of writing they have before them. When the prose of the original flows more smoothly, as in Luke, Acts, and Hebrews, it is reflected in the translation.

The Gospel according to John comprises a special case. Absolute fidelity to his technique of reiterated phrasing would result in an assault on the English ear, yet the softening of the vocal effect by substitution of other words and phrases would destroy the effectiveness of his poetry. Again, resort is had to compromise. This is not an easy matter when the very repetitiousness which the author deliberately employed is at the same time regarded by those who read and speak English to be a serious stylistic defect. Only those familiar with the Greek originals can know what a relentless tattoo Johannine poetry can produce. A similar observation could be made regarding other New Testament books as well. Matthew and Mark are given to identical phrasing twice and three times in the same sentence. As for the rhetorical overgrowth and mixed figures of speech in the letters of Peter, James, and Jude, the translator must resist a powerful compulsion to tidy them up if only to render these letters intelligibly.

Without seeking refuge in complaints against the inspired authors, however, the translators of *The New American Bible* here state that what they have attempted is a translation rather than a paraphrase. To be sure, all translation can be called paraphrase by definition. Any striving for complete fidelity will shortly end in infidelity. Nonetheless, it must be pointed out that the temptation to improve overladen sentences by the consolidation or elimination of multiplied adjectives, or the simplification of clumsy hendiadys, has been resisted here. For the most part, rhetorically ineffective words and phrases are retained in this translation in some form, even when it is clear that a Western contemporary writer would never have employed them.

The spelling of proper names in *The New American Bible* follows the customary forms found in most English Bibles since the Authorized Version.

Despite the arbitrary character of the divisions into numbered verses (a scheme which in its present form is only four centuries old), the translators have made a constant effort to keep within an English verse the whole verbal content of the Greek verse. At times the effort has not seemed worth the result since it often does violence to the original author's flow of expression, which preceded it by so many centuries. If this translation had been prepared for purposes of public reading only, the editors would have foregone the effort at an early stage. But since they never departed from the threefold objective of preparing a translation suitable for liturgical use, private reading, and the purposes of students, the last-named consideration prevailed. Those familiar with Greek should be able to discover how the translators of the New Testament have rendered any given original verse of scripture, if their exegetical or theological tasks require them to know this. At the same time, the fact should be set down here that the editors did not commit themselves in the synoptic gospels to rendering repeated words or phrases identically.

This leads to a final consideration: the Greek text used for the New Testament. Here, punctuation and verse division are at least as important as variant readings. In general, Nestle-Aland's *Novum Testamentum Graece* (25th edition, 1963) was followed. Additional help was derived from *The Greek New Testament* (Aland, Black, Metzger, Wikgren), produced for the use of translators by the United Bible Societies in 1966. However, the editors did not confine themselves strictly to these texts; at times, they inclined toward readings otherwise attested. The omission of alternative translations does not mean that the translators think them without merit, but only that in every case they had to make a choice.

Poorly attested readings do not occur in this translation. Doubtful readings of some merit appear within brackets; public readers may include such words or phrases, or omit them entirely without any damage to sense. Parentheses are used, as ordinarily in English, as a punctuation device. Material they enclose is in no sense textually doubtful. It is simply thought to be parenthetical in the intention of the biblical author, even though there is no such punctuation mark in Greek. The difficulty in dealing with quotation marks is well known. Since they do not appear in any form in the original text, wherever they occur here they constitute an editorial decision.

PREFACE TO THE REVISED EDITION

The New Testament of *The New American Bible,* a fresh translation from the Greek text, was first published in complete form in 1970, together with the Old Testament translation that had been completed the previous year. Portions of the New Testament had appeared earlier, in somewhat different form, in the provisional Mass lectionary of 1964 and in the *Lectionary for Mass* of 1970.

Since 1970 many different printings of the New Testament have been issued by a number of publishers, both separately and in complete Bibles, and the text has become widely known both in the United States and in other English-speaking countries. Most American Catholics have been influenced by it because of its widespread use in the liturgy, and it has received a generally favorable reception from many other Christians as well. It has taken its place among the standard contemporary translations of the New Testament, respected for its fidelity to the original and its attempt to render this into current American English.

Although the scriptures themselves are timeless, translations and explanations of them quickly become dated in an era marked by rapid cultural change to a degree never previously experienced. The explosion of biblical studies that has taken place in our century and the changing nature of our language itself require periodic adjustment both in translations and in the accompanying explanatory materials. The experience of actual use of the New Testament of *The New American Bible*, especially in oral proclamation, has provided a basis for further improvement. Accordingly, it was decided in 1978 to proceed with a thorough revision of the New Testament to reflect advances in scholarship and to satisfy needs identified through pastoral experience.

For this purpose a steering committee was formed to plan, organize, and direct the work of revision, to engage collaborators, and to serve as an editorial board to coordinate the work of the various revisers and to determine the final form of the text and the explanatory materials. Guidelines were drawn up and collaborators selected in 1978 and early 1979, and November of 1980 was established as the deadline for manuscripts. From December 1980 through September 1986 the editorial board met a total of fifty times and carefully reviewed and revised all the material in order to ensure accuracy and consistency of approach. The editors also worked together with the bishops' ad hoc committee that was appointed by the National Conference of Catholic Bishops in 1982 to oversee the revision.

The threefold purpose of the translation that was expressed in the preface to the first edition has been maintained in the revision: to provide a version suitable for liturgical proclamation, for private reading, and for purposes of study. Special attention has been given to the first of these purposes, since oral proclamation demands special qualities in a translation, and experience had provided insights and suggestions that could lead to improvement in this area. Efforts have also been made, however, to facilitate devotional reading by providing suitable notes and introductory materials, and to assist the student by achieving greater accuracy and consistency in the translation and supplying more abundant information in the introductions and notes.

The primary aim of the revision is to produce a version as accurate and faithful to the meaning of the Greek original as is possible for a translation. The editors have consequently moved in the direction of a formal-equivalence approach to translation, matching the vocabulary, structure, and even word order of the original as closely as possible in the receptor language. Some other contemporary biblical versions have adopted, in varying degrees, a dynamic-equivalence approach, which attempts to respect the individuality of each language by expressing the meaning of the original in a linguistic structure suited to English, even though this may be very different from the corresponding Greek structure. While this approach often results in fresh and brilliant renderings, it has the disadvantages of more or less radically abandoning traditional biblical and liturgical terminology and phraseology, of expanding the text to include what more properly belongs in notes, commentaries, or preaching, and of tending toward paraphrase. A more formal approach seems better suited to the specific purposes intended for this translation.

At the same time, the editors have wished to produce a version in English that reflects contemporary American usage and is readily understandable to ordinary educated people, but one that will be recognized as dignified speech, on the level of formal rather than colloquial usage. These aims are not in fact contradictory, for there are different levels of language in current use: the language of formal situations is not that of colloquial conversation, though people understand both and may pass from one to the other without adverting to the transition. The liturgy is a formal situation that requires a level of discourse more dignified, formal, and hieratic than the world of business, sport, or informal communication. People readily understand this more formal level even though they may not often use it; our passive vocabulary is much larger than our active vocabulary. Hence this revision, while avoiding archaisms, does not shrink from traditional biblical terms that are easily understood even though not in common use in everyday speech. The level of language consciously aimed

at is one appropriate for liturgical proclamation; this may also permit the translation to serve the purposes of devotional reading and serious study.

A particular effort has been made to insure consistency of vocabulary. Always to translate a given Greek word by the same English equivalent would lead to ludicrous results and to infidelity to the meaning of the text. But in passages where a particular Greek term retains the same meaning, it has been rendered in the same way insofar as this has been feasible; this is particularly significant in the case of terms that have a specific theological meaning. The synoptic gospels have been carefully translated so as to reveal both the similarities and the differences of the Greek.

An especially sensitive problem today is the question of discrimination in language. In recent years there has been much discussion about allegations of anti-Jewish expressions in the New Testament and of language that discriminates against various minorities. Above all, however, the question of discrimination against women affects the largest number of people and arouses the greatest degree of interest and concern. At present there is little agreement about these problems or about the best way to deal with them. In all these areas the present translation attempts to display a sensitivity appropriate to the present state of the questions under discussion, which are not yet resolved and in regard to which it is impossible to please everyone, since intelligent and sincere participants in the debate hold mutually contradictory views.

The primary concern in this revision is fidelity to what the text says. When the meaning of the Greek is inclusive of both sexes, the translation seeks to reproduce such inclusivity insofar as this is possible in normal English usage, without resort to inelegant circumlocutions or neologisms that would offend against the dignity of the language. Although the generic sense of *man* is traditional in English, many today reject it; its use has therefore generally been avoided, though it is retained in cases where no fully satisfactory equivalent could be found. English does not possess a gender-inclusive third personal pronoun in the singular, and this translation continues to use the masculine resumptive pronoun after *everyone* or *anyone,* in the traditional way, where this cannot be avoided without infidelity to the meaning.

The translation of the Greek word *adelphos,* particularly in the plural form *adelphoi,* poses an especially delicate problem. While the term literally means *brothers* or other male blood relatives, even in profane Greek the plural can designate two persons, one of either sex, who were born of the same parents. It was adopted by the early Christians to designate, in a figurative sense, the members of the Christian community, who were conscious of a new familial relationship to one another by reason of their adoption as children of God. They are consequently addressed as *adelphoi.* This has traditionally been rendered into English by *brothers* or, more archaically, *brethren.* There has never been any doubt that this designation includes *all* the members of the Christian community, both male and female. Given the absence in English of a corresponding term that explicitly includes both sexes, this translation retains the usage of *brothers,* with the inclusive meaning that has been traditionally attached to it in this biblical context.

Since the New Testament is the product of a particular time and culture, the views expressed in it and the language in which they are expressed reflect a particular cultural conditioning, which sometimes makes them quite different from contemporary ideas and concerns. Discriminatory language should be eliminated insofar as possible whenever it is unfaithful to the meaning of the New Testament, but the text should not be altered in order to adjust it to contemporary concerns. This translation does not introduce any changes, expansions, additions to, or subtractions from the text of scripture. It further retains the traditional biblical ways of speaking about God and about Christ, including the use of masculine nouns and pronouns.

The Greek text followed in this translation is that of the third edition of *The Greek New Testament,* edited by Kurt Aland, Matthew Black, Carlo Martini, Bruce Metzger, and Allen Wikgren, and published by the United Bible Societies in 1975. The same text, with a different critical apparatus and variations in punctuation and typography, was published as the twenty-sixth edition of the Nestle-Aland *Novum Testamentum Graece* in 1979 by the Deutsche Bibelstiftung, Stuttgart. This edition has also been consulted.

When variant readings occur, the translation, with few exceptions, follows the reading that was placed in the text of these Greek editions, though the occurrence of the principal variants is pointed out in the notes.

The editors of the Greek text placed square brackets around words or portions of words of which the authenticity is questionable because the evidence of textual witnesses is inconclusive. The same has been done in the translation insofar as it is possible to reproduce this convention in English. It should be possible to read the text either with or without the disputed words, but in English it is not always feasible to provide this alternative, and in some passages the bracketed words must be included to make sense. As in the first edition, parentheses do not indicate textual uncertainty, but are simply a punctuation device to indicate a passage that in the editors' judgment appears parenthetical to the thought of the author.

Citations from the Old Testament are placed within quotation marks; longer citations are set off as block quotations in a separate indented paragraph. The sources of such citations, as well as those of many more or less subtle allusions to the Old Testament, are identified in the biblical cross-reference section at the bottom of each page. Insofar as possible, the translation of such Old Testament citations agrees with that of *The New American Bible* Old Testament whenever the underlying Greek agrees with the Hebrew (or, in some cases, the Aramaic or Greek) text from which the Old Testament translation was made. But citations in the New Testament frequently follow the Septuagint or some other version, or were made from memory; hence, in many cases the translation in the New Testament passage will not agree with what appears in the Old Testament. Some of these cases are explained in the notes.

It is a further aim of the revised edition to supply explanatory materials more abundantly than in the first edition. In most cases the introductions and notes have been entirely rewritten and expanded, and the cross-references checked and revised. It is intended that these materials should reflect the present state of sound biblical scholarship and should be presented in such a form that they can be assimilated by the ordinary intelligent reader without specialized biblical training. While they have been written with the ordinary educated Christian in mind, not all technical vocabulary can be entirely dispensed with in approaching the Bible, any more than in any other field. It is the hope of the editors that these materials, even if they sometimes demand an effort, will help the reader to a fuller and more intelligent understanding of the New Testament and a fruitful appropriation of its meaning for personal spiritual growth.

The New American Bible is a Roman Catholic translation. This revision, however, like the first edition, has been accomplished with the collaboration of scholars from other Christian churches, both among the revisers and on the editorial board, in response to the encouragement of Vatican Council II (*Dei Verbum,* 22). The editorial board expresses gratitude to all who have collaborated in the revision: to all the revisers, consultants, and bishops who contributed to it, to reviewers of the first edition, and to those who voluntarily submitted suggestions. May this translation fulfill its threefold purpose, "so that the word of the Lord may speed forward and be glorified" (2 Thes 3, 1).

September 30, 1986
The Feast of St. Jerome

THE GOSPELS

See RG
266-75

The collection of writings that constitutes the New Testament begins with four gospels. Next comes the Acts of the Apostles, followed by twenty-one letters that are attributed to Paul, James, Peter, John, and Jude. Finally, at the end of the early church's scriptures stands the Revelation to John. Virtually all Christians agree that these twenty-seven books constitute the "canon," a term that means "rule" and designates the list of writings that are regarded as authoritative for Christian faith and life.

It is the purpose of this Introduction to describe those features that are common to the four gospels. A similar treatment of the letters of the New Testament is provided in the two Introductions that appear before the Letter to the Romans and before the Letter of James, respectively. The Acts of the Apostles, a work that is both historical and theological, and Revelation, an apocalyptic work, have no counterparts in the New Testament; the special Introductions prefixed to these books treat of the literary characteristics proper to each of them.

While the New Testament contains four writings called "gospels," there is in reality only one gospel running through all of the Christian scriptures, the gospel of and about Jesus Christ. Our English word "gospel" translates the Greek term *euangelion*, meaning "good news." This noun was used in the plural by the Greek translators of the Old Testament to render the Hebrew term for "good news" (2 Sm 4, 10; possibly also 18, 20.25). But it is the corresponding verb *euangelizomai*, "to proclaim good news," that was especially significant in preparing for the New Testament idea of "gospel," since this term is used by Deutero-Isaiah of announcing the great victory of God that was to establish his universal kingship and inaugurate the new age (Is 40, 9; 52, 7; 61, 1).

Paul used the word *euangelion* to designate the message that he and the other apostles proclaimed, the "gospel of God" (Rom 1, 1; 15, 16; 2 Cor 11, 7; 1 Thes 2, 2.8.9). He often referred to it simply as "the gospel" (Rom 1, 16; 10, 16; 11, 28; etc.) or, because of its content and origin, as "the gospel of Christ" (Rom 15, 19; 1 Cor 9, 12; 1 Thes 3, 2; etc.). Because of its personal meaning for him and his own particular manner of telling the story about Jesus Christ and of explaining the significance of his cross and resurrection, Paul also referred to this message as "my gospel" (Rom 2, 16; cf Gal 1, 11; 2, 2) or "our gospel" (2 Cor 4, 3; 1 Thes 1, 5; 2 Thes 2, 14).

It was Mark, as far as we know, who first applied the term "gospel" to a book telling the story of Jesus; see Mk 1, 1 and the note there. This form of presenting Jesus' life, works, teachings, passion, and resurrection was developed further by the other evangelists; see the Introduction to each gospel. The first three of the canonical gospels, Matthew, Mark, and Luke, are so similar at many points when viewed together, particularly when arranged in parallel columns or lines, that they are called "synoptic" gospels, from the Greek word for such a general view. The fourth gospel, John, often differs significantly from the synoptics in outline and approach. This work never uses the word "gospel" or its corresponding verb; nevertheless, its message concerns the same Jesus, and the reader is urged to believe in him as the Messiah, "that through this belief you may have life in his name" (20, 31).

From the second century onward, the practice arose of designating each of these four books as a "gospel," understood as a title, and of adding a phrase with a name that identified the traditional author, e.g., "The Gospel according to Matthew." The arrangement of the canon that was adopted, with the four gospels grouped together at the beginning followed by Acts, provides a massive focus upon Jesus and allows Acts to serve as a framework for the letters of the New Testament. This order, however, conceals the fact that Luke's two volumes, a gospel and Acts, were intended by their author to go together. It further obscures the point that Paul's letters were written before any of our gospels, though the sayings and deeds of Jesus stand behind all the New Testament writings.

See RG
275-91

The Gospel According to Matthew

The position of the Gospel according to Matthew as the first of the four gospels in the New Testament reflects both the view that it was the first to be written, a view that goes back to the late second century A.D., and the esteem in which it was held by the church; no other was so frequently quoted in the noncanonical literature of earliest Christianity. Although the majority of scholars now reject the opinion about the time of its composition, the high estimation of this work remains. The reason for that becomes clear upon study of the way in which Matthew presents his story of Jesus, the demands of Christian discipleship, and the breaking-in of the new and final age through the ministry but particularly through the death and resurrection of Jesus.

The gospel begins with a narrative prologue (1, 1—2, 23), the first part of which is a genealogy of Jesus starting with Abraham, the father of Israel (1, 1–17). Yet at the beginning of that genealogy Jesus is designated as "the son of David, the son of Abraham" (1, 1). The kingly ancestor who lived about a thousand years after Abraham is named first, for this is the genealogy of Jesus Christ, the Messiah, the royal anointed one (1, 16). In the first of the episodes of the infancy narrative that follow the genealogy, the mystery of Jesus' person is declared. He is conceived of a virgin by the power of the Spirit of God (1, 18–25). The first of the gospel's fulfillment citations, whose purpose it is to show that he was the one to whom the prophecies of Israel were pointing, occurs here (1, 23): he shall be named Emmanuel, for in him God is with us.

The announcement of the birth of this newborn king of the Jews greatly troubles not only King Herod but all Jerusalem (2, 1–3), yet the Gentile magi are overjoyed to find him and offer him their homage and their gifts (2, 10–11). Thus his ultimate rejection by the mass of his own people and his acceptance by the Gentile nations is foreshadowed. He must be taken to Egypt to escape the murderous plan of Herod. By his sojourn there and his subsequent return after the king's death he relives the Exodus experience of Israel. The words of the Lord spoken through the prophet Hosea, "Out of Egypt I called my son," are fulfilled in him (2, 15); if Israel was God's son, Jesus is so in a way far surpassing the dignity of that nation, as his marvelous birth and the unfolding of his story show (see 3, 17; 4, 1–11; 11, 27; 14, 33; 16, 16; 27, 54). Back in the land of Israel, he must be taken to Nazareth in Galilee because of the danger to his life in Judea, where Herod's son Archelaus is now ruling (2, 22–23). The sufferings of Jesus in the infancy narrative anticipate those of his passion, and if his life is spared in spite of the dangers, it is because his destiny is finally to give it on the cross as "a ransom for many" (20, 28). Thus the word of the angel will be fulfilled, ". . . he will save his people from their sins" (1, 21; cf 26, 28).

In 4, 12 Matthew begins his account of the ministry of Jesus, introducing it by the preparatory preaching of John the Baptist (3, 1–12), the baptism of Jesus that culminates in God's proclaiming him his "beloved Son" (3, 13–17), and the temptation in which he proves his true sonship by his victory over the devil's attempt to deflect him from the way of obedience to the Father (4, 1–11). The central message of Jesus' preaching is the coming of the kingdom of heaven and the need for repentance, a complete change of heart and conduct, on the part of those who are to receive this great gift of God (4, 17). Galilee is the setting for most of his ministry; he leaves there for Judea only in 19, 1, and his ministry in Jerusalem, the goal of his journey, is limited to a few days (21, 1—25, 46).

In this extensive material there are five great discourses of Jesus, each concluding with the formula "When Jesus finished these words" or one closely similar (7, 28; 11, 1; 13, 53; 19, 1; 26, 1). These are an important structure of the gospel. In every case the discourse is preceded by a narrative section, each narrative and discourse together constituting a "book" of the gospel. The discourses are, respectively, the "Sermon on the Mount" (5, 3–7, 27), the missionary discourse (10, 5–42), the parable discourse (13, 3–52), the "church order" discourse (18, 3–35), and the eschatological discourse (24, 4—25, 46). In large measure the material of these discourses came to Matthew from his tradition, but his work in modifying and adding to what he had received is abundantly evident. No other evangelist gives the teaching of Jesus with such elegance and order as he.

In the "Sermon on the Mount" the theme of righteousness is prominent, and even at this early stage of the ministry the note of opposition is struck between Jesus and the Pharisees, who are designated as "the hypocrites" (6, 2.5.16). The righteousness of his disciples must surpass that of the scribes and Pharisees; otherwise, in spite of their alleged following of Jesus, they will not enter into the kingdom of heaven (5, 20). Righteousness means doing the will of the heavenly Father (7, 21), and his will is proclaimed in a manner that is startling to all who have identified it with the law of Moses. The antitheses of the Sermon (5, 21–48) both accept (5, 21–30.43–48) and reject (5, 31–42) elements of that law, and in the former case the understanding of the law's demands is deepened and extended. The antitheses are the best commentary on the meaning of Jesus' claim that he has come not to abolish but to fulfill the law (5, 17). What is meant by fulfillment of the law is not the demand to keep it exactly as it stood before the coming of Jesus, but rather his bringing the law to be a lasting expression of the will of God, and in that fulfillment there is much that will pass away. Should this appear contradictory to his saying that "until heaven and earth pass away" not even the smallest part of the law will pass (5, 18), that time of fulfillment is not the dissolution of the universe but the coming of the new age, which will occur with Jesus' death and resurrection. While righteousness in the new age will continue to mean conduct that is in accordance with the law, it will be conduct in accordance with the law as expounded and interpreted by Jesus (cf 28, 20, ". . . all that I have commanded you").

Though Jesus speaks harshly about the Pharisees in the Sermon, his judgment is not solely a condemnation of them. The Pharisees are portrayed as a negative example for his disciples, and his condemnation of those who claim to belong to him while disobeying his word is no less severe (7, 21–23.26–27).

In 4, 23 a summary statement of Jesus' activity speaks not only of his teaching and proclaiming the gospel but of his "curing every disease and illness among the people"; this is repeated almost verbatim in 9, 35. The narrative section that follows the Sermon on the Mount (8, 1—9, 38) is composed principally of accounts of those merciful deeds of Jesus, but it is far from being simply a collection of stories about miraculous cures. The nature of the community that Jesus will establish is shown; it will always be under the protection of him whose power can deal with all dangers (8, 23–27), but it is only for those who are prepared to follow him at whatever cost (8, 16–22), not only believing Israelites but Gentiles who have come to faith in him (8, 10–12). The disciples begin to have some insight, however imperfect, into the mystery of Jesus' person. They wonder about him whom "the winds and the sea obey" (8, 27), and they witness his bold declaration of the forgiveness of the paralytic's sins (9, 2). That episode of the narrative moves on two levels. When the crowd sees the cure that testifies to the authority of Jesus, the Son of Man, to forgive sins (9, 6), they glorify God "who had given such authority to human beings" (9, 8). The forgiveness of sins is now not the prerogative of Jesus alone but of "human beings," that is, of the disciples who constitute the community of Jesus, the church. The ecclesial character of this narrative section could hardly be more plainly indicated.

The end of the section prepares for the discourse on the church's mission (10, 5–42). Jesus is moved to pity at the sight of the crowds who are like sheep without a shepherd (9, 36), and he sends out the twelve disciples to make the proclamation with which his own ministry began, "The kingdom of heaven is at hand" (10, 7; cf 4, 17), and to drive out demons and cure the sick as he has done (10, 1). Their mission is limited to Israel (10, 5–6) as Jesus' own was (15, 24), yet in 15, 16 that perspective broadens and the discourse begins to speak of the mission that the disciples will have after the resurrection and of the severe persecution that will attend it (10, 18). Again, the discourse moves on two levels: that of the time of Jesus and that of the time of the church.

The narrative section of the third book (11, 2—12, 50) deals with the growing opposition to Jesus. Hostility toward him has already been manifested (8, 10; 9, 3.10–13.34), but here it becomes more intense. The rejection of Jesus comes, as before, from Pharisees, who take "counsel against him to put him to death" (12, 14) and repeat their earlier accusation that he drives out demons because he is in league with demonic power (12, 22–24). But they are not alone in their rejection. Jesus complains of the lack of faith of "this generation" of Israelites (11, 16–19) and reproaches the towns "where most of his mighty deeds had been done" for not heeding his call to repentance (11, 20–24). This dark picture is relieved by Jesus' praise of the Father who has enabled "the childlike" to accept him (11, 25–27), but on the whole the story is one of opposition to his word and blindness to the meaning of his deeds. The whole section ends with his declaring that not even the most intimate blood relationship with him counts for anything; his only true relatives are those who do the will of his heavenly Father (12, 48–50).

The narrative of rejection leads up to the parable discourse (13, 3–52). The reason given for Jesus' speaking to the crowds in parables is that they have hardened themselves against his clear teaching, unlike the disciples to whom knowledge of "the mysteries of the kingdom has been granted" (13, 10–16). In 13, 36 he dismisses the crowds and continues the discourse to his disciples alone, who claim, at the end, to have understood all that he has said (13, 51). But, lest the impression be given that the church of Jesus is made up only of true disciples, the explanation of the parable of the weeds among the wheat (13, 37–43), as well as the parable of the net thrown into the sea "which collects fish of every kind" (13, 47–49), shows that it is composed of both the righteous and the wicked, and that separation between the two will be made only at the time of the final judgment.

In the narrative that constitutes the first part of the fourth book of the gospel (13, 54—17, 27),

Jesus is shown preparing for the establishment of his church with its teaching authority that will supplant the blind guidance of the Pharisees (15, 13–14), whose teaching, curiously said to be that of the Sadducees also, is repudiated by Jesus as the norm for his disciples (16, 6.11–12). The church of Jesus will be built on Peter (16, 18), who will be given authority to bind and loose on earth, an authority whose exercise will be confirmed in heaven (16, 19). The metaphor of binding and loosing has a variety of meanings, among them that of giving authoritative teaching. This promise is made to Peter directly after he has confessed Jesus to be the Messiah, the Son of the living God (16, 16), a confession that he has made as the result of revelation given to him by the heavenly Father (16, 17); Matthew's ecclesiology is based on his high christology.

Directly after that confession Jesus begins to instruct his disciples about how he must go the way of suffering and death (16, 21). Peter, who has been praised for his confession, protests against this and receives from Jesus the sharpest of rebukes for attempting to deflect Jesus from his God-appointed destiny. The future rock upon whom the church will be built is still a man of "little faith" (see 14, 31). Both he and the other disciples must know not only that Jesus will have to suffer and die but that they too will have to follow him on the way of the cross if they are truly to be his disciples (16, 24–25).

The discourse following this narrative (18, 1–35) is often called the "church order" discourse, although that title is perhaps misleading since the emphasis is not on the structure of the church but on the care that the disciples must have for one another in respect to guarding each other's faith in Jesus (18, 6–7), to seeking out those who have wandered from the fold (18, 10–14), and to repeated forgiving of their fellow disciples who have offended them (18, 21–35). But there is also the obligation to correct the sinful fellow Christian and, should one refuse to be corrected, separation from the community is demanded (18, 15–18).

The narrative of the fifth book (19, 1—23, 39) begins with the departure of Jesus and his disciples from Galilee for Jerusalem. In the course of their journey Jesus for the third time predicts the passion that awaits him at Jerusalem and also his resurrection (20, 17–19). At his entrance into the city he is hailed as the Son of David by the crowds accompanying him (21, 9). He cleanses the temple (21, 12–17), and in the few days of his Jerusalem ministry he engages in a series of controversies with the Jewish religious leaders (21, 23–27; 22, 15–22.23–33.34–40.41–46), meanwhile speaking parables against them (21, 28–32.33–46), against all those Israelites who have rejected God's invitation to the messianic banquet (22, 1–10), and against all, Jew and Gentile, who have accepted but have shown themselves unworthy of it (22, 11–14). Once again, the perspective of the evangelist includes not only the time of Jesus' ministry but that of the preaching of the gospel after his resurrection. The narrative culminates in Jesus' denunciation of the scribes and Pharisees, reflecting not only his own opposition to them but that of Matthew's church (23, 1–36), and in Jesus' lament over Jerusalem (23, 37–39).

In the discourse of the fifth book (24, 1—25, 46), the last of the great structural discourses of the gospel, Jesus predicts the destruction of the temple and his own final coming. The time of the latter is unknown (24, 36.44), and the disciples are exhorted in various parables to live in readiness for it, a readiness that entails faithful attention to the duties of the interim period (24, 45—25, 30). The coming of Jesus will bring with it the great judgment by which the everlasting destiny of all will be determined (25, 31–46).

The story of Jesus' passion and resurrection (26, 1—28, 20), the climax of the gospel, throws light on all that has preceded. In Mt "righteousness" means both the faithful response to the will of God demanded of all to whom that will is announced and also the saving activity of God for his people (see 3, 15; 5, 6; 6, 33). The passion supremely exemplifies both meanings of that central Matthean word. In Jesus' absolute faithfulness to the Father's will that he drink the cup of suffering (26, 39), the incomparable model for Christian obedience is given; in his death "for the forgiveness of sins" (26, 28), the saving power of God is manifested as never before.

Matthew's portrayal of Jesus in his passion combines both the majestic serenity of the obedient Son who goes his destined way in fulfillment of the scriptures (26, 52–54), confident of his ultimate vindication by God, and the depths of fear and abandonment that he feels in face of death (26, 38–39; 27, 46). These two aspects are ex-pressed by an Old Testament theme that occurs often in the narrative, i.e., the portrait of the suffering Righteous One who complains to God in his misery, but is certain of eventual deliverance from his terrible ordeal.

The passion-resurrection of God's Son means nothing less than the turn of the ages, a new stage of history, the coming of the Son of Man in his kingdom (28, 18; cf 16, 28). That is the sense of the apocalyptic signs that accompany Jesus' death (27, 51–53) and resurrection (28, 2). Although the old age continues, as it will until the manifestation of Jesus' triumph at his parousia, the final age has now begun. This is known only to those who have seen the Risen One and to those, both Jews and Gentiles, who have believed in their announcement of Jesus' triumph and have themselves become his disciples (cf 28, 19). To them he is constantly, though invisibly, present (28, 20), verifying the name Emmanuel, "God is with us" (cf 1, 23).

The questions of authorship, sources, and the time of composition of this gospel have received many answers, none of which can claim more than a greater or lesser degree of probability. The one now favored by the majority of scholars is the following.

The ancient tradition that the author was the disciple and apostle of Jesus named Matthew (see 10, 3) is untenable because the gospel is based, in large part, on the Gospel according to Mark (almost all the verses of that gospel have been utilized in this), and it is hardly likely that a companion of Jesus would have followed so extensively an account that came from one who admittedly never had such an association rather than rely on his own memories. The attribution of the gospel to the disciple Matthew may have been due to his having been responsible for some of the traditions found in it, but that is far from certain.

The unknown author, whom we shall continue to call Matthew for the sake of convenience, drew not only upon the Gospel according to Mark but upon a large body of material (principally, sayings of Jesus) not found in Mk that corresponds, sometimes exactly, to material found also in the Gospel according to Luke. This material, called "Q" (probably from the first letter of the German word *Quelle,* meaning "source"), represents traditions, written and oral, used by both Matthew and Luke. Mark and Q are sources common to the two other synoptic gospels; hence the name the "Two-Source Theory" given to this explanation of the relation among the synoptics.

In addition to what Matthew drew from Mk and Q, his gospel contains material that is found only there. This is often designated "M," written or oral tradition that was available to the author. Since Mk was written shortly before or shortly after A.D. 70 (see Introduction to Mk), Mt was composed certainly after that date, which marks the fall of Jerusalem to the Romans at the time of the First Jewish Revolt (A.D. 66–70), and probably at least a decade later since Matthew's use of Mk presupposes a wide diffusion of that gospel. The post-A.D. 70 date is confirmed within the text by 22, 7, which refers to the destruction of Jerusalem.

As for the place where the gospel was composed, a plausible suggestion is that it was Antioch, the capital of the Roman province of Syria. That large and important city had a mixed population of Greek-speaking Gentiles and Jews. The tensions between Jewish and Gentile Christians there in the time of Paul (see Gal 2, 1–14) in respect to Christian obligation to observe Mosaic law are partially similar to tensions that can be seen between the two groups in Matthew's gospel. The church of Matthew, originally strongly Jewish Christian, had become one in which Gentile Christians were predominant. His gospel answers the question how obedience to the will of God is to be expressed by those who live after the "turn of the ages," the death and resurrection of Jesus.

1, 1—2, 23: The infancy narrative forms the prologue of the gospel. Consisting of a genealogy and five stories, it presents the coming of Jesus as the climax of Israel's history, and the events of his conception, birth, and early childhood as the fulfillment of Old Testament prophecy. The genealogy is probably traditional material that Matthew edited. In its first two sections (1, 2–11) it was drawn from Ru 4, 18–22 and 1 Chr 1–3. Except for Jechoniah, Shealtiel, and Zerubbabel, none of the names in the third section (1, 12–16) is found in any Old Testament genealogy. While the genealogy shows the continuity of God's providential plan from Abraham on, discontinuity is also present. The women Tamar (1, 3), Rahab and Ruth (1, 5), and the wife of Uriah, Bathsheba (1, 6), bore their sons through unions that were in varying degrees strange and unexpected. These "irregularities" culminate in the supreme "irregularity" of the Messiah's birth of a virgin mother; the age of fulfillment is inaugurated by a creative act of God.

Drawing upon both biblical tradition and Jewish stories, Matthew portrays Jesus as reliving the Exodus experience of Israel and the persecutions of Moses. His rejection by his own

The principal divisions of the Gospel according to Matthew are the following:

I: The Infancy Narrative (1, 1—2, 23)
II: The Proclamation of the Kingdom (3, 1—7, 29)
III: Ministry and Mission in Galilee (8, 1—11, 1)
IV: Opposition from Israel (11, 2—13, 53)
V: Jesus, the Kingdom, and the Church (13, 54—18, 35)
VI: Ministry in Judea and Jerusalem (19, 1—25, 46)
VII: The Passion and Resurrection (26, 1—28, 20)

I: The Infancy Narrative

CHAPTER 1

See RG 279–80

The Genealogy of Jesus. ¹ᵃ*The book of the genealogy of Jesus Christ, the son of David, the son of Abraham.

²ᵇᶜAbraham became the father of Isaac, Isaac the father of Jacob, Jacob the father of Judah and his brothers. ³ᵈJudah became the father of Perez and Zerah, whose mother was Tamar. Perez became the father of Hezron, Hezron the father of Ram, ⁴ᵉRam the father of Amminadab. Amminadab became the father of Nahshon, Nahshon the father of Salmon, ⁵ᶠSalmon the father of Boaz, whose mother was Rahab. Boaz became the father

people and his passion are foreshadowed by the troubled reaction of "all Jerusalem" to the question of the magi who are seeking the "newborn king of the Jews" (2, 2–3), and by Herod's attempt to have him killed. The magi who do him homage prefigure the Gentiles who will accept the preaching of the gospel. The infancy narrative proclaims who Jesus is, the savior of his people from their sins (1, 21), Emmanuel in whom "God is with us" (1, 23), and the Son of God (2, 15).

1, 1: The son of David, the son of Abraham: two links of the genealogical chain are singled out. Although the later, David is placed first in order to emphasize that Jesus is the royal Messiah. The mention of Abraham may be due not only to his being the father of the nation Israel but to Matthew's interest in the universal scope of Jesus' mission; cf Gn 22, 18, ". . . in your descendants all the nations of the earth shall find blessing."

a: Gn 5, 1 / 1 Chr 17, 11 / Gn 22, 18.   *b:* Lk 3, 23-38.   *c:* Gn 21, 3; 25, 26; 29, 35; 1 Chr 2, 1.   *d:* Gn 38, 29-30; Ru 4, 18; 1 Chr 2, 4-9.   *e:* Ru 4, 19-20; 1 Chr 2, 10-11.   *f:* Ru 4, 21-22; 1 Chr 2, 11-12.

of Obed, whose mother was Ruth. Obed became the father of Jesse, *6g*Jesse the father of David the king.

David became the father of Solomon, whose mother had been the wife of Uriah. *7h**Solomon became the father of Rehoboam, Rehoboam the father of Abijah, Abijah the father of Asaph. *8*Asaph became the father of Jehoshaphat, Jehoshaphat the father of Joram, Joram the father of Uzziah. *9*Uzziah became the father of Jotham, Jotham the father of Ahaz, Ahaz the father of Hezekiah. *10**Hezekiah became the father of Manasseh, Manasseh the father of Amos, Amos the father of Josiah. *11*Josiah became the father of Jechoniah and his brothers at the time of the Babylonian exile.

*12i*After the Babylonian exile, Jechoniah became the father of Shealtiel, Shealtiel the father of Zerubbabel, *13*Zerubbabel the father of Abiud. Abiud became the father of Eliakim, Eliakim the father of Azor, *14*Azor the father of Zadok. Zadok became the father of Achim, Achim the father of Eliud, *15*Eliud the father of Eleazar. Eleazar became the father of Matthan, Matthan the father of Jacob, *16*Jacob the father of Joseph, the husband of Mary. Of her was born Jesus who is called the Messiah.

17*Thus the total number of generations from Abraham to David is fourteen generations; from David to the Babylonian exile, fourteen generations; from the Babylonian exile to the Messiah, fourteen generations.

The Birth of Jesus. *18**Now this is how the birth of Jesus Christ came about. When his mother Mary was betrothed to Joseph, but before they lived together, she was found with child through the holy Spirit. *19**Joseph her husband, since he was a righteous man, yet unwilling to expose her to shame, decided to divorce her quietly. *20j**Such was his intention when, behold, the angel of the Lord appeared to him in a dream and said, "Joseph, son of David, do not be afraid to take Mary your wife into your home. For it is through the holy Spirit that this child has been conceived in her. *21**She will bear a son and you are to name him Jesus, because he will save his people from their sins." *22*All this took place to fulfill what the Lord had said through the prophet:

1, 7: The successor of Abijah was not Asaph but Asa (see 1 Chr 3, 10). Some textual witnesses read the latter name; however, **Asaph** is better attested. Matthew may have deliberately introduced the psalmist Asaph into the genealogy (and in v 10 the prophet Amos) in order to show that Jesus is the fulfillment not only of the promises made to David (see 2 Sm 7) but of all the Old Testament.

1, 10: Amos: some textual witnesses read **Amon,** who was the actual successor of Manasseh (see 1 Chr 3, 14).

1, 17: Matthew is concerned with fourteen generations, probably because fourteen is the numerical value of the Hebrew letters forming the name of David. In the second section of the genealogy (6b-11), three kings of Judah, Ahaziah, Joash, and Amaziah, have been omitted (see 1 Chr 3, 11–12), so that there are fourteen generations in that section. Yet the third (12–16) apparently has only thirteen. Since Matthew here emphasizes that each section has fourteen, it is unlikely that the thirteen of the last was due to his oversight. Some scholars suggest that **Jesus who is called the Messiah** (16b) doubles the final member of the chain: **Jesus,** born within the family of David, opens up the new age as **Messiah,** so that in fact there are fourteen generations in the third section. This is perhaps too subtle, and the hypothesis of a slip not on the part of Matthew but of a later scribe seems likely. On **Messiah,** see the note on Lk 2, 11.

1, 18–25: This first story of the infancy narrative spells out what is summarily indicated in v 16. The virginal conception of Jesus is the work of the Spirit of God. Joseph's decision to divorce Mary is overcome by the heavenly command that he take her into his home and accept the child as his own. The natural genealogical line is broken but the promises to David are fulfilled; through Joseph's adoption the child belongs to the family of David. Matthew sees the virginal conception as the fulfillment of Is 7, 14.

1, 18: Betrothed to Joseph: betrothal was the first part of the marriage, constituting a man and woman as husband and wife. Subsequent infidelity was considered adultery. The betrothal was followed some months later by the husband's taking his wife into his home, at which time normal married life began.

1, 19: A righteous man: as a devout observer of the Mosaic law, Joseph wished to break his union with someone whom he suspected of gross violation of the law. It is commonly said that the law required him to do so, but the texts usually given in support of that view, e.g., Dt 22, 20–21, do not clearly pertain to Joseph's situation. **Unwilling to expose her to shame:** the penalty for proved adultery was death by stoning; cf Dt 22, 21–23.

1, 20: The angel of the Lord: in the Old Testament a common designation of God in communication with a human being. **In a dream:** see 2, 13.19.22. These dreams may be meant to recall the dreams of Joseph, son of Jacob the patriarch (Gn 37, 5–11.19). A closer parallel is the dream of Amram, father of Moses, related by Josephus (**Antiquities** 2, 9, 3 §§212, 215–16).

1, 21: Jesus: in first-century Judaism the Hebrew name Joshua (Greek **Iēsous**) meaning "Yahweh helps" was interpreted as "Yahweh saves."

g: 2 Sm 12, 24; 1 Chr 2, 15; 3, 5.   h: 2 Kgs 25, 1-21; 1 Chr 3, 10-15.   i: 1 Chr 3, 16-19.   j: Mt 2, 13.19; Lk 1, 35.

23 k *"Behold, the virgin shall be with child
      and bear a son,
      and they shall name him Emmanuel,"

which means "God is with us." 24When Joseph awoke, he did as the angel of the Lord had commanded him and took his wife into his home. 25l*He had no relations with her until she bore a son, and he named him Jesus.

CHAPTER 2

See RG 279–80

The Visit of the Magi. 1*When Jesus was born in Bethlehem of Judea, in the days of King Herod, behold, magi from the east arrived in Jerusalem, 2m*saying, "Where is the newborn king of the Jews? We saw his star at its rising and have come to do him homage." 3When King Herod heard this, he was greatly troubled, and all Jerusalem with him. 4*Assembling all the chief priests and the scribes of the people, he inquired of them where the Messiah was to be born. 5nThey said to him, "In Bethlehem of Judea, for thus it has been written through the prophet:

6 'And you, Bethlehem, land of Judah,
    are by no means least among the rulers
        of Judah;
  since from you shall come a ruler,
    who is to shepherd my people
        Israel.' "

7Then Herod called the magi secretly and ascertained from them the time of the star's appearance. 8He sent them to Bethlehem and said, "Go and search diligently for the child. When you have found him, bring me word, that I too may go and do him homage." 9After their audience with the king they set out. And behold, the star that they had seen at its rising preceded them, until it came and stopped over the place where the child was. 10They were overjoyed at seeing the star, 11o*and on entering the house they saw the child with Mary his mother. They prostrated themselves and did him homage. Then they opened their treasures and offered him gifts of gold, frankincense, and myrrh. 12And having been warned in a dream not to return to Herod, they departed for their country by another way.

The Flight to Egypt. 13*When they had departed, behold, the angel of the Lord appeared to Joseph in a dream and said, "Rise, take the child and his mother, flee to Egypt, and stay there until I tell you. Herod is going to search for the child to destroy him." 14Joseph rose and took the child and his mother by night and departed for Egypt. 15p*He stayed there until the death of Herod, that what the Lord had said through the prophet might be fulfilled, "Out of Egypt I called my son."

1, 23: God is with us: God's promise of deliverance to Judah in Isaiah's time is seen by Matthew as fulfilled in the birth of Jesus, in whom God is with his people. The name Emmanuel is alluded to at the end of the gospel where the risen Jesus assures his disciples of his continued presence, ". . . I am with you always, until the end of the age" (28, 20).

1, 25: Until she bore a son: the evangelist is concerned to emphasize that Joseph was not responsible for the conception of Jesus. The Greek word translated "until" does not imply normal marital conduct after Jesus' birth, nor does it exclude it.

2, 1–12: The future rejection of Jesus by Israel and his acceptance by the Gentiles are retrojected into this scene of the narrative.

2, 1: In the days of King Herod: Herod reigned from 37 to 4 B.C. **Magi:** originally a designation of the Persian priestly caste, the word became used of those who were regarded as having more than human knowledge. Matthew's magi are astrologers.

2, 2: We saw his star: it was a common ancient belief that a new star appeared at the time of a ruler's birth. Matthew also draws upon the Old Testament story of Balaam, who had prophesied that "A star shall advance from Jacob" (Nm 24, 17), though there the star means not an astral phenomenon but the king himself.

2, 4: Herod's consultation with the chief priests and

scribes has some similarity to a Jewish legend about the child Moses in which the "sacred scribes" warn Pharaoh about the imminent birth of one who will deliver Israel from Egypt and the king makes plans to destroy him.

2, 11: Cf Ps 72, 10.15; Is 60, 6. These Old Testament texts led to the interpretation of the magi as kings.

2, 13–23: Biblical and nonbiblical traditions about Moses are here applied to the child Jesus, though the dominant Old Testament type is not Moses but Israel (see v 15).

2, 13: Flee to Egypt: Egypt was a traditional place of refuge for those fleeing from danger in Palestine (see 1 Kgs 11, 40; Jer 26, 21), but the main reason why the child is to be taken to Egypt is that he may relive the Exodus experience of Israel.

2, 15: The fulfillment citation is taken from Hos 11, 1. Israel, God's son, was called out of Egypt at the time of the Exodus; Jesus, the Son of God, will similarly be called out of that land in a new exodus. The father-son relationship between God and the nation is set in a higher key. Here the son is not a group adopted as "son of God," but the child who, as conceived by the holy Spirit, stands in unique relation to God. He is son of David and of Abraham, of Mary and of Joseph, but, above all, of God.

k: Is 7, 14 LXX. *l:* Lk 2, 7. *m:* Nm 24, 17. *n:* Mi 5, 1 / 2 Sm 5, 2. *o:* Ps 72, 10-11.15; Is 60, 6. *p:* Hos 11, 1.

The Massacre of the Infants. [16]When Herod realized that he had been deceived by the magi, he became furious. He ordered the massacre of all the boys in Bethlehem and its vicinity two years old and under, in accordance with the time he had ascertained from the magi. [17]Then was fulfilled what had been said through Jeremiah the prophet:

[18] q *"A voice was heard in Ramah,
    sobbing and loud lamentation;
Rachel weeping for her children,
    and she would not be consoled,
    since they were no more."

The Return from Egypt. [19]When Herod had died, behold, the angel of the Lord appeared in a dream to Joseph in Egypt [20]r*and said, "Rise, take the child and his mother and go to the land of Israel, for those who sought the child's life are dead." [21]He rose, took the child and his mother, and went to the land of Israel. [22]*But when he heard that Archelaus was ruling over Judea in place of his father Herod, he was afraid to go back there. And because he had been warned in a dream, he departed for the region of Galilee. [23]s*He went and dwelt in a town called Nazareth, so that what had been spoken through the prophets might be fulfilled, "He shall be called a Nazorean."

II: The Proclamation of the Kingdom

CHAPTER 3

See RG 280-81

The Preaching of John the Baptist. [1]*In those days John the Baptist appeared, preaching in the desert of Judea [2]u*[and] saying, "Repent, for the kingdom of heaven is at hand!" [3]v*It was of him that the prophet Isaiah had spoken when he said:

"A voice of one crying out in the desert,
    'Prepare the way of the Lord,
    make straight his paths.' "

[4]w*John wore clothing made of camel's hair and had a leather belt around his waist. His

---

2, 18: Jer 31, 15 portrays Rachel, wife of the patriarch Jacob, weeping for her children taken into exile at the time of the Assyrian invasion of the northern kingdom (722–21 B.C.). Bethlehem was traditionally identified with Ephrath, the place near which Rachel was buried (see Gn 35, 19; 48, 7), and the mourning of Rachel is here applied to her lost children of a later age. **Ramah:** about six miles north of Jerusalem. The lamentation of Rachel is so great as to be heard at a far distance.

2, 20: For those who sought the child's life are dead: Moses, who had fled from Egypt because the Pharaoh sought to kill him (see Ex 2, 15), was told to return there, "for all the men who sought your life are dead" (Ex 4, 19).

2, 22: With the agreement of the emperor Augustus, Archelaus received half of his father's kingdom, including Judea, after Herod's death. He had the title "ethnarch" (i.e., "ruler of a nation") and reigned from 4 B.C. to A.D. 6.

2, 23: Nazareth ... he shall be called a Nazorean: the tradition of Jesus' residence in Nazareth was firmly established, and Matthew sees it as being in accordance with the foreannounced plan of God. The town of Nazareth is not mentioned in the Old Testament, and no such prophecy can be found there. The vague expression "through the prophets" may be due to Matthew's seeing a connection between Nazareth and certain texts in which there are words with a remote similarity to the name of that town. Some such Old Testament texts are Is 11, 1 where the Davidic king of the future is called "a bud" (ne⁻ ser) that shall blossom from the roots of Jesse, and Jgs 13, 5.7 where Samson, the future deliverer of Israel from the Philistines, is called one who shall be consecrate (a na⁻ zîr) to God.

3, 1–12: Here Matthew takes up the order of Jesus' ministry found in the gospel of Mark, beginning with the prepara-

tory preaching of John the Baptist.

3, 1: Unlike Luke, Matthew says nothing of the Baptist's origins and does not make him a relative of Jesus. **The desert of Judea:** the barren region west of the Dead Sea extending up the Jordan valley.

3, 2: Repent: the Baptist calls for a change of heart and conduct, a turning of one's life from rebellion to obedience toward God. **The kingdom of heaven is at hand:** "heaven" (literally, "the heavens") is a substitute for the name "God" that was avoided by devout Jews of the time out of reverence. The expression "the kingdom of heaven" occurs only in the gospel of Matthew. It means the effective rule of God over his people. In its fullness it includes not only human obedience to God's word, but the triumph of God over physical evils, supremely over death. In the expectation found in Jewish apocalyptic, the kingdom was to be ushered in by a judgment in which sinners would be condemned and perish, an expectation shared by the Baptist. This was modified in Christian understanding where the kingdom was seen as being established in stages, culminating with the parousia of Jesus.

3, 3: See the note on Jn 1, 23.

3, 4: The clothing of John recalls the austere dress of the prophet Elijah (2 Kgs 1, 8). The expectation of the return of Elijah from heaven to prepare Israel for the final manifestation of God's kingdom was widespread, and according to Matthew this expectation was fulfilled in the Baptist's ministry (11, 14; 17, 11–13).

---

q: Jer 31, 15.   r: Ex 4, 19.   s: 13, 54; Mk 1, 9; Lk 2, 39; 4, 34; Jn 19, 19.   t: Mk 1, 2-8; Lk 3, 2-17.   u: 4, 17; 10, 7.   v: Is 40, 3.   w: 11, 7-8; 2 Kgs 1, 8; Zec 13, 4.

food was locusts and wild honey. *5*At that time Jerusalem, all Judea, and the whole region around the Jordan were going out to him *6**and were being baptized by him in the Jordan River as they acknowledged their sins.

*7x**When he saw many of the Pharisees and Sadducees coming to his baptism, he said to them, "You brood of vipers! Who warned you to flee from the coming wrath? *8*Produce good fruit as evidence of your repentance. *9y*And do not presume to say to yourselves, 'We have Abraham as our father.' For I tell you, God can raise up children to Abraham from these stones. *10*Even now the ax lies at the root of the trees. Therefore every tree that does not bear good fruit will be cut down and thrown into the fire. *11z**I am baptizing you with water, for repentance, but the one who is coming after me is mightier than I. I am not worthy to carry his sandals. He will baptize you with the holy Spirit and fire. *12a**His winnowing fan is in his hand. He will clear his threshing floor and gather his wheat into his barn, but the chaff he will burn with unquenchable fire."

The Baptism of Jesus. *13b**Then Jesus came from Galilee to John at the Jordan to be baptized by him. *14**John tried to prevent him, saying, "I need to be baptized by you, and yet you are coming to me?" *15*Jesus said to him in reply, "Allow it now, for thus it is fitting for us to fulfill all righteousness." Then he allowed him. *16c**After Jesus was baptized, he came up from the water and behold, the heavens were opened [for him], and he saw the Spirit of God descending like a dove [and] coming upon him. *17d**And a voice came from the heavens, saying, "This is my beloved Son, with whom I am well pleased."

CHAPTER 4

See RG 280–81

The Temptation of Jesus. *1e**Then Jesus was led by the Spirit into the desert to

---

3, 6: Ritual washing was practiced by various groups in Palestine between 150 B.C. and A.D. 250. John's baptism may have been related to the purificatory washings of the Essenes at Qumran.

3, 7: Pharisees and Sadducees: the former were marked by devotion to the law, written and oral, and the scribes, experts in the law, belonged predominantly to this group. The Sadducees were the priestly aristocratic party, centered in Jerusalem. They accepted as scripture only the first five books of the Old Testament, followed only the letter of the law, rejected the oral legal traditions, and were opposed to teachings not found in the Pentateuch, such as the resurrection of the dead. Matthew links both of these groups together as enemies of Jesus (16, 1.6.11.12; cf Mk 8, 11–13.15). The threatening words that follow are addressed to them rather than to "the crowds" as in Lk 3, 7. **The coming wrath:** the judgment that will bring about the destruction of unrepentant sinners.

3, 11: Baptize you with the holy Spirit and fire: the water baptism of John will be followed by an "immersion" of the repentant in the cleansing power of the Spirit of God, and of the unrepentant in the destroying power of God's judgment. However, some see **the holy Spirit** and **fire** as synonymous, and the effect of this "baptism" as either purification or destruction. See the note on Lk 3, 16.

3, 12: The discrimination between the good and the bad is compared to the procedure by which a farmer separates wheat and chaff. The **winnowing fan** was a forklike shovel with which the threshed wheat was thrown into the air. The kernels fell to the ground; the light chaff, blown off by the wind, was gathered and burned up.

3, 13–17: The baptism of Jesus is the occasion on which he is equipped for his ministry by the holy Spirit and proclaimed to be the Son of God.

3, 14–15: This dialogue, peculiar to Matthew, reveals John's awareness of Jesus' superiority to him as the mightier one who is coming and who will baptize with the holy Spirit (11). His reluctance to admit Jesus among the sinners whom he is baptizing with water is overcome by Jesus' response. **To fulfill all righteousness:** in this gospel to **fulfill** usually refers to fulfillment of prophecy, and **righteousness** to moral conduct in conformity with God's will. Here, however, as in 5, 6 and 6, 33, **righteousness** seems to mean the saving activity of God. **To fulfill all righteousness** is to submit to the plan of God for the salvation of the human race. This involves Jesus' identification with sinners; hence the propriety of his accepting John's baptism.

3, 16: The Spirit . . . coming upon him: cf Is 42, 1.

3, 17: This is my beloved Son: the Marcan address to Jesus (Mk 1, 11) is changed into a proclamation. The Father's voice speaks in terms that reflect Is 42, 1, Ps 2, 7, and Gn 22, 2.

4, 1–11: Jesus, proclaimed Son of God at his baptism, is subjected to a triple temptation. Obedience to the Father is a characteristic of true sonship, and Jesus is tempted by the devil to rebel against God, overtly in the third case, more subtly in the first two. Each refusal of Jesus is expressed in language taken from the Book of Deuteronomy (Dt 8, 3; 6, 13.16). The testings of Jesus resemble those of Israel during the wandering in the desert and later in Canaan, and the victory of Jesus, the true Israel and the true Son, contrasts with the failure of the ancient and disobedient "son," the old Israel. In the temptation account Matthew is almost identical with Luke; both seem to have drawn upon the same source.

x: 12, 34; 23, 33; Is 59, 5. *y:* Jn 8, 33.39; Rom 9, 7-8; Gal 4, 21-31. *z:* Jn 1, 26-27.33; Acts 1, 5. *a:* 13, 30; Is 41, 16; Jer 15, 7. *b:* Mk 1, 9-11; Lk 3, 21-22; Jn 1, 31-34. *c:* Is 42, 1. *d:* 12, 18; 17, 5; Gn 22, 2; Ps 2, 7; Is 42, 1. *e:* Mk 1, 12-13; Lk 4, 1-13.

be tempted by the devil. [2f]*He fasted for forty days and forty nights, and afterwards he was hungry. [3]The tempter approached and said to him, "If you are the Son of God, command that these stones become loaves of bread." [4g]*He said in reply, "It is written:

> 'One does not live by bread alone,
> but by every word that comes forth
> from the mouth of God.' "

[5]*Then the devil took him to the holy city, and made him stand on the parapet of the temple, [6h]and said to him, "If you are the Son of God, throw yourself down. For it is written:

> 'He will command his angels concerning
> you'
> and 'with their hands they will support
> you,
> lest you dash your foot against a stone.' "

[7i]Jesus answered him, "Again it is written, 'You shall not put the Lord, your God, to the test.' " [8]Then the devil took him up to a very high mountain, and showed him all the kingdoms of the world in their magnificence, [9]*and he said to him, "All these I shall give to you, if you will prostrate yourself and worship me." [10j]At this, Jesus said to him, "Get away, Satan! It is written:

> 'The Lord, your God, shall you worship
> and him alone shall you serve.' "

[11]Then the devil left him and, behold, angels came and ministered to him.

The Beginning of the Galilean Ministry. [12k]*When he heard that John had been arrested, he withdrew to Galilee. [13l]He left Nazareth and went to live in Capernaum by the sea, in the region of Zebulun and Naphtali, [14]that what had been said through Isaiah the prophet might be fulfilled:

> [15m] "Land of Zebulun and land of Naphtali,
> the way to the sea, beyond the Jordan,
> Galilee of the Gentiles,
> [16n] the people who sit in darkness
> have seen a great light,
> on those dwelling in a land
> overshadowed by death
> light has arisen."

[17o]*From that time on, Jesus began to preach and say, "Repent, for the kingdom of heaven is at hand."

The Call of the First Disciples. [18p]*As he was walking by the Sea of Galilee, he saw two brothers, Simon who is called Peter, and his brother Andrew, casting a net into the sea; they were fishermen. [19]He said to them, "Come after me, and I will make you fishers of men." [20]*At once they left their nets and followed him. [21]He walked along from there and saw two other brothers, James, the son of Zebedee, and his brother John. They were in a boat, with their father Zebedee, mending their nets. He called them, [22]and immedi-

---

4, 2: Forty days and forty nights: the same time as that during which Moses remained on Sinai (Ex 24, 18). The time reference, however, seems primarily intended to recall the forty years during which Israel was tempted in the desert (Dt 8, 2).

4, 4: Cf Dt 8, 3. Jesus refuses to use his power for his own benefit and accepts whatever God wills.

4, 5–7: The devil supports his proposal by an appeal to the scriptures, Ps 91, 11a.12. Unlike Israel (Dt 6, 16), Jesus refuses to "test" God by demanding from him an extraordinary show of power.

4, 9: The worship of Satan to which Jesus is tempted is probably intended to recall Israel's worship of false gods. His refusal is expressed in the words of Dt 6, 13.

4, 12–17: Isaiah's prophecy of the light rising upon Zebulun and Naphtali (Is 8, 23—9, 1) is fulfilled in Jesus' residence at Capernaum. The territory of these two tribes was the first to be devastated (733–32 B.C.) at the time of the Assyrian invasion. In order to accommodate Jesus' move to Capernaum to the prophecy, Matthew speaks of that town as being "in the region of Zebulun and Naphtali" (13), whereas it was

only in the territory of the latter, and he understands the sea of the prophecy, the Mediterranean, as the sea of Galilee.

4, 17: At the beginning of his preaching Jesus takes up the words of John the Baptist (3, 2) although with a different meaning; in his ministry the kingdom of heaven has already begun to be present (12, 28).

4, 18–22: The call of the first disciples promises them a share in Jesus' work and entails abandonment of family and former way of life. Three of the four, Simon, James, and John, are distinguished among the disciples by a closer relation with Jesus (17, 1; 26, 37).

4, 20: Here and in v 22, as in Mark (1, 16–20) and unlike the Lucan account (5, 1–11), the disciples' response is motivated only by Jesus' invitation, an element that emphasizes his mysterious power.

f: Ex 24, 18; Dt 8, 2. g: Dt 8, 3. h: Ps 91, 11-12. i: Dt 6, 16. j: 16, 23; Dt 6, 13. k: Mk 1, 14-15; Lk 4, 14.31. l: Jn 2, 12. m: Is 8, 23 LXX; 9, 1. n: Lk 1, 79. o: 3, 2. p: Mk 1, 16-20; Lk 5, 1-11.

ately they left their boat and their father and followed him.

Ministering to a Great Multitude. [23]*He went around all of Galilee, teaching in their synagogues, proclaiming the gospel of the kingdom, and curing every disease and illness among the people. [24]*His fame spread to all of Syria, and they brought to him all who were sick with various diseases and racked with pain, those who were possessed, lunatics, and paralytics, and he cured them. [25]r*And great crowds from Galilee, the Decapolis, Jerusalem, and Judea, and from beyond the Jordan followed him.

See RG 281-82

CHAPTER 5

The Sermon on the Mount. [1]*When he saw the crowds, he went up the mountain, and after he had sat down, his disciples came to him. [2]He began to teach them, saying:

The Beatitudes

[3] s *"Blessed are the poor in spirit,
    for theirs is the kingdom of heaven.
[4] t *Blessed are they who mourn,
    for they will be comforted.
[5] u *Blessed are the meek,
    for they will inherit the land.
[6] *Blessed are they who hunger and thirst
    for righteousness,
    for they will be satisfied.
[7] v Blessed are the merciful,
    for they will be shown mercy.
[8] w *Blessed are the clean of heart,
    for they will see God.
[9] Blessed are the peacemakers,
    for they will be called children of God.
[10] x *Blessed are they who are persecuted
    for the sake of righteousness,
    for theirs is the kingdom of heaven.

[11]yBlessed are you when they insult you and

4, 23–25: This summary of Jesus' ministry concludes the narrative part of the first book of Matthew's gospel (chs 3–4). The activities of his ministry are teaching, proclaiming the gospel, and healing; cf 9, 35.

4, 23: Their synagogues: Matthew usually designates the Jewish synagogues as **their synagogue(s)** (9, 35; 10, 17; 12, 9; 13, 54) or, in address to Jews, **your synagogues** (23, 34), an indication that he wrote after the break between church and synagogue.

4, 24: Syria: the Roman province to which Palestine belonged.

4, 25: The Decapolis: a federation of Greek cities in Palestine, originally ten in number, all but one east of the Jordan.

5, 1—7, 29: The first of the five discourses that are a central part of the structure of this gospel. It is the discourse section of the first book and contains sayings of Jesus derived from Q and from M. The Lucan parallel is in that gospel's "Sermon on the Plain" (Lk 6, 20–49), although some of the sayings in Matthew's "Sermon on the Mount" have their parallels in other parts of Luke. The careful topical arrangement of the sermon is probably not due only to Matthew's editing; he seems to have had a structured discourse of Jesus as one of his sources. The form of that source may have been as follows: four beatitudes (5, 3–4.6.11–12), a section on the new righteousness with illustrations (5, 17.20–24.27–28.33–48), a section on good works (6, 1–6.16–18), and three warnings (7, 1–2.15–21.24–27).

5, 1–2: Unlike Luke's sermon, this is addressed not only to the disciples but to the crowds (see 7, 28).

5, 3–12: The form **Blessed are (is)** occurs frequently in the Old Testament in the Wisdom literature and in the psalms. Although modified by Matthew, the first, second, fourth, and ninth beatitudes have Lucan parallels (5, 3 // Lk 6, 20; 5, 4 // Lk 6, 21b; 5, 6 // Lk 6, 21a; 5, 11–12 // Lk 5, 22–23). The oth-

ers were added by the evangelist and are probably his own composition. A few manuscripts, Western and Alexandrian, and many versions and patristic quotations give the second and third beatitudes in inverted order.

5, 3: The poor in spirit: in the Old Testament, the **poor** (ănāwîm) are those who are without material possessions and whose confidence is in God (see Is 61, 1; Zep 2, 3; in the NAB the word is translated **lowly** and **humble,** respectively, in those texts). Matthew added **in spirit** in order either to indicate that only the devout poor were meant or to extend the beatitude to all, of whatever social rank, who recognized their complete dependence on God. The same phrase **poor in spirit** is found in the Qumran literature (1QM 14, 7).

5, 4: Cf Is 61, 2, "(The Lord has sent me) . . . to comfort all who mourn." **They will be comforted:** here the passive is a "theological passive" equivalent to the active "God will comfort them"; so also in vv 6 and 7.

5, 5: Cf Ps 37, 11, ". . . the meek shall possess the land." In the psalm "the land" means the land of Palestine; here it means the kingdom.

5, 6: For righteousness: a Matthean addition. For the meaning of **righteousness** here, see the note on 3, 14–15.

5, 8: Cf Ps 24, 4. Only one "whose heart is clean" can take part in the temple worship. To be with God in the temple is described in Ps 42, 3 as "beholding his face," but here the promise to **the clean of heart** is that they will **see God** not in the temple but in the coming kingdom.

5, 10: Righteousness here, as usually in Matthew, means conduct in conformity with God's will.

q: 9, 35; Mk 1, 39; Lk 4, 15.44. r: Mk 3, 7-8; Lk 6, 17-19. s: Lk 6, 20-23. t: Is 61, 2-3; Rv 21, 4. u: Gn 13, 15; Ps 37, 11. v: 18, 33; Jas 2, 13. w: Pss 24, 4-5; 73, 1. x: 1 Pt 2, 20; 3, 14; 4, 14. y: 10, 22; Acts 5, 41.

persecute you and utter every kind of evil against you [falsely] because of me. *12z*Rejoice and be glad, for your reward will be great in heaven. Thus they persecuted the prophets who were before you.

The Similes of Salt and Light. *13a**"You are the salt of the earth. But if salt loses its taste, with what can it be seasoned? It is no longer good for anything but to be thrown out and trampled underfoot. *14b*You are the light of the world. A city set on a mountain cannot be hidden. *15c*Nor do they light a lamp and then put it under a bushel basket; it is set on a lampstand, where it gives light to all in the house. *16d*Just so, your light must shine before others, that they may see your good deeds and glorify your heavenly Father.

Teaching about the Law. *17**"Do not think that I have come to abolish the law or the prophets. I have come not to abolish but to fulfill. *18e*Amen, I say to you, until heaven and earth pass away, not the smallest letter or the smallest part of a letter will pass from the law, until all things have taken place. *19**Therefore, whoever breaks one of the least of these commandments and teaches others to do so will be called least in the kingdom of heaven. But whoever obeys and teaches these commandments will be called greatest in the kingdom of heaven. *20*I tell you, unless your righteousness surpasses that of the scribes and Pharisees, you will not enter into the kingdom of heaven.

Teaching about Anger. *21f**"You have heard that it was said to your ancestors, 'You shall not kill; and whoever kills will be liable to judgment.' *22g**But I say to you, whoever is angry with his brother will be liable to judgment, and whoever says to his brother, 'Raqa,' will be answerable to the Sanhedrin, and whoever says, 'You fool,' will be liable to

5, 12: The prophets who were before you: the disciples of Jesus stand in the line of the persecuted prophets of Israel. Some would see the expression as indicating also that Matthew considered all Christian disciples as prophets.

5, 13–16: By their deeds the disciples are to influence the world for good. They can no more escape notice than **a city set on a mountain.** If they fail in good works, they are as useless as flavorless salt or as a lamp whose light is concealed.

5, 13: The unusual supposition of salt losing its flavor has led some to suppose that the saying refers to the salt of the Dead Sea that, because chemically impure, could lose its taste.

5, 17–20: This statement of Jesus' position concerning the Mosaic law is composed of traditional material from Matthew's sermon documentation (see the note on 5, 1—7, 29), other Q material (cf 18 and Lk 16, 17), and the evangelist's own editorial touches. **To fulfill** the law appears at first to mean a literal enforcement of the law in the least detail: **until heaven and earth pass away** nothing of the law **will pass** (18). Yet the "passing away" of heaven and earth is not necessarily the end of the world understood, as in much apocalyptic literature, as the dissolution of the existing universe. The "turning of the ages" comes with the apocalyptic event of Jesus' death and resurrection, and those to whom this gospel is addressed are living in the new and final age, prophesied by Isaiah as the time of "new heavens and a new earth" (Is 65, 17; 66, 22). Meanwhile, during Jesus' ministry when the kingdom is already breaking in, his mission remains within the framework of the law, though with significant anticipation of the age to come, as the following antitheses (vv 21–48) show.

5, 19: Probably **these commandments** means those of the Mosaic law. But this is an interim ethic "until heaven and earth pass away."

5, 21–48: Six examples of the conduct demanded of the Christian disciple. Each deals with a commandment of the law, introduced by **You have heard that it was said to your ancestors** or an equivalent formula, followed by Jesus' teach-ing in respect to that commandment, **But I say to you;** thus their designation as "antitheses." Three of them accept the Mosaic law but extend or deepen it (21–22; 27–28; 43–44); three reject it as a standard of conduct for the disciples (31–32; 33–37; 38–39).

5, 21: Cf Ex 20, 13; Dt 5, 17. The second part of the verse is not an exact quotation from the Old Testament, but cf Ex 21, 12.

5, 22: Anger is the motive behind murder, as the insulting epithets are steps that may lead to it. They, as well as the deed, are all forbidden. **Raqa:** an Aramaic word **rēqā'** or **rēqâ** probably meaning "imbecile," "blockhead," a term of abuse. The ascending order of punishment, **judgment** (by a local council?), trial before **the Sanhedrin,** condemnation to **Gehenna,** points to a higher degree of seriousness in each of the offenses. **Sanhedrin:** the highest judicial body of Judaism. **Gehenna:** in Hebrew **gê-hinnōm,** "Valley of Hinnom," or **gê ben-hinnōm,** "Valley of the son of Hinnom," southwest of Jerusalem, the center of an idolatrous cult during the monarchy in which children were offered in sacrifice (see 2 Kgs 23, 10; Jer 7, 31). In Jos 18, 16 (Septuagint, Codex Vaticanus) the Hebrew is transliterated into Greek as **gaienna,** which appears in the New Testament as **geenna.** The concept of punishment of sinners by fire either after death or after the final judgment is found in Jewish apocalyptic literature (e.g., Enoch 90, 26) but the name **geenna** is first given to the place of punishment in the New Testament.

5, 22–26: Reconciliation with an offended brother is urged in the admonition of vv 23–24 and the parable of vv 25–26 (// Lk 12, 58–59). The severity of the judge in the parable is a warning of the fate of unrepentant sinners in the coming judgment by God.

z: 2 Chr 36, 16; Heb 11, 32-38; Jas 5, 10. a: Mk 9, 50; Lk 14, 34-35. b: Jn 8, 12. c: Mk 4, 21; Lk 8, 16; 11, 33. d: Jn 3, 21. e: Lk 16, 17. f: Ex 20, 13; Dt 5, 17. g: Jas 1, 19-20.

fiery Gehenna. [23h]Therefore, if you bring your gift to the altar, and there recall that your brother has anything against you, [24]leave your gift there at the altar, go first and be reconciled with your brother, and then come and offer your gift. [25i]Settle with your opponent quickly while on the way to court with him. Otherwise your opponent will hand you over to the judge, and the judge will hand you over to the guard, and you will be thrown into prison. [26]Amen, I say to you, you will not be released until you have paid the last penny.

Teaching about Adultery. [27j]*"You have heard that it was said, 'You shall not commit adultery.' [28]But I say to you, everyone who looks at a woman with lust has already committed adultery with her in his heart. [29k]*If your right eye causes you to sin, tear it out and throw it away. It is better for you to lose one of your members than to have your whole body thrown into Gehenna. [30]And if your right hand causes you to sin, cut it off and throw it away. It is better for you to lose one of your members than to have your whole body go into Gehenna.

Teaching about Divorce. [31l]*"It was also said, 'Whoever divorces his wife must give her a bill of divorce.' [32m]But I say to you,

whoever divorces his wife (unless the marriage is unlawful) causes her to commit adultery, and whoever marries a divorced woman commits adultery.

Teaching about Oaths. [33n]*"Again you have heard that it was said to your ancestors, 'Do not take a false oath, but make good to the Lord all that you vow.' [34o]*But I say to you, do not swear at all; not by heaven, for it is God's throne; [35]nor by the earth, for it is his footstool; nor by Jerusalem, for it is the city of the great King. [36]Do not swear by your head, for you cannot make a single hair white or black. [37]*Let your 'Yes' mean 'Yes,' and your 'No' mean 'No.' Anything more is from the evil one.

Teaching about Retaliation. [38p]*"You have heard that it was said, 'An eye for an eye and a tooth for a tooth.' [39q]But I say to you, offer no resistance to one who is evil. When someone strikes you on [your] right cheek, turn the other one to him as well. [40]If anyone wants to go to law with you over your tunic, hand him your cloak as well. [41r]*Should anyone press you into service for one mile, go with him for two miles. [42s]Give to the one who asks of you, and do not turn your back on one who wants to borrow.

5, 27: See Ex 20, 14; Dt 5, 18.

5, 29–30: No sacrifice is too great to avoid total destruction in **Gehenna.**

5, 31–32: See Dt 24, 1–5. The Old Testament commandment that a bill of divorce be given to the woman assumes the legitimacy of divorce itself. It is this that Jesus denies. (**Unless the marriage is unlawful**): this "exceptive clause," as it is often called, occurs also in 19, 9, where the Greek is slightly different. There are other sayings of Jesus about divorce that prohibit it absolutely (see Mk 10, 11–12; Lk 16, 18; cf 1 Cor 7, 10.11b), and most scholars agree that they represent the stand of Jesus. Matthew's "exceptive clauses" are understood by some as a modification of the absolute prohibition. It seems, however, that the unlawfulness that Matthew gives as a reason why a marriage must be broken refers to a situation peculiar to his community: the violation of Mosaic law forbidding marriage between persons of certain blood and/or legal relationship (Lv 18, 6–18). Marriages of that sort were regarded as incest (**porneia**), but some rabbis allowed Gentile converts to Judaism who had contracted such marriages to remain in them. Matthew's "exceptive clause" is against such permissiveness for Gentile converts to Christianity; cf the similar prohibition of **porneia** in Acts 15, 20.29. In this interpretation, the clause constitutes no exception to the absolute prohibition of divorce when the marriage is lawful.

5, 33: This is not an exact quotation of any Old Testament text, but see Ex 20, 7; Dt 5, 11, and Lv 19, 12. The purpose of

an oath was to guarantee truthfulness by one's calling on God as witness.

5, 34–36: The use of these oath formularies that avoid the divine name is in fact equivalent to swearing by it, for all the things sworn by are related to God.

5, 37: Let your 'Yes' mean 'Yes,' and your 'No' mean 'No': literally, "let your speech be 'Yes, yes,' 'No, no.' " Some have understood this as a milder form of oath, permitted by Jesus. In view of v 34, "Do not swear at all," that is unlikely. **From the evil one:** i.e., from the devil. Oath-taking presupposes a sinful weakness of the human race, namely, the tendency to lie. Jesus demands of his disciples a truthfulness that makes oaths unnecessary.

5, 38–42: See Lv 24, 20. The Old Testament commandment was meant to moderate vengeance; the punishment should not exceed the injury done. Jesus forbids even this proportionate retaliation. Of the five examples that follow, only the first deals directly with retaliation for evil; the others speak of liberality.

5, 41: Roman garrisons in Palestine had the right to requisition the property and services of the native population.

h: Mk 11, 25.　*i:* 18, 34-35; Lk 12, 58-59.　*j:* Ex 20, 14; Dt 5, 18. *k:* 18, 8-9; Mk 9, 43-47.　*l:* 19, 3-9; Dt 24, 1.　*m:* Lk 16, 18; 1 Cor 7, 10-11.　*n:* Lv 19, 12; Nm 30, 3.　*o:* Ps 48, 3; Sir 23, 9; Is 66, 1; Jas 5, 12.　*p:* Ex 21, 24; Lv 24, 19-20.　*q:* Lk 6, 29-30. *r:* Lam 3, 30.　*s:* Dt 15, 7-8.

Love of Enemies. [43]*t[u]*"You have heard that it was said, 'You shall love your neighbor and hate your enemy.' [44]But I say to you, love your enemies, and pray for those who persecute you, [45]that you may be children of your heavenly Father, for he makes his sun rise on the bad and the good, and causes rain to fall on the just and the unjust. [46]*For if you love those who love you, what recompense will you have? Do not the tax collectors do the same? [47]*And if you greet your brothers only, what is unusual about that? Do not the pagans do the same? [48]*[v]*So be perfect, just as your heavenly Father is perfect.

CHAPTER 6

See RG
281–82

Teaching about Almsgiving. [1]*[w]*"[But] take care not to perform righteous deeds in order that people may see them; otherwise, you will have no recompense from your heavenly Father. [2]*[x]*When you give alms, do not blow a trumpet before you, as the hypocrites do in the synagogues and in the streets to win the praise of others. Amen, I say to you, they have received their reward. [3]But when you give alms, do not let your left hand know what your right is doing, [4]so that your almsgiving may be secret. And your Father who sees in secret will repay you.

Teaching about Prayer. [5]"When you pray, do not be like the hypocrites, who love to stand and pray in the synagogues and on street corners so that others may see them. Amen, I say to you, they have received their reward. [6]But when you pray, go to your inner room, close the door, and pray to your Father in secret. And your Father who sees in secret will repay you. [7]*In praying, do not babble like the pagans, who think that they will be heard because of their many words. [8]Do not be like them. Your Father knows what you need before you ask him.

The Lord's Prayer. [9]*[y]*"This is how you are to pray:

Our Father in heaven,
hallowed be your name,

5, 43–48: See Lv 19, 18. There is no Old Testament commandment demanding hatred of one's enemy, but the "neighbor" of the love commandment was understood as one's fellow countryman. Both in the Old Testament (Ps 139, 19–22) and at Qumran (1QS 9, 21) hatred of evil persons is assumed to be right. Jesus extends the love commandment to the enemy and the persecutor. His disciples, as children of God, must imitate the example of their Father, who grants his gifts of sun and rain to both the good and the bad.

5, 46: Tax collectors: Jews who were engaged in the collection of indirect taxes such as tolls and customs. See the note on Mk 2, 14.

5, 47: Jesus' disciples must not be content with merely usual standards of conduct; see v 20 where the verb "surpass" (Greek perisseuō) is cognate with the unusual (perisson) of this verse.

5, 48: Perfect: in the gospels this word occurs only in Matthew, here and in 19, 21. The Lucan parallel (6, 36) demands that the disciples be merciful.

6, 1–18: The sermon continues with a warning against doing good in order to be seen and gives three examples, almsgiving (2–4), prayer (5, 15), and fasting (16–18). In each, the conduct of the hypocrites (2) is contrasted with that demanded of the disciples. The sayings about reward found here and elsewhere (5, 12.46; 10, 41–42) show that this is a genuine element of Christian moral exhortation. Possibly to underline the difference between the Christian idea of reward and that of the hypocrites, the evangelist uses two different Greek verbs to express the rewarding of the disciples and that of the hypocrites; in the latter case it is the verb apechō, a commercial term for giving a receipt for what has been paid in full (2.5.16).

6, 2: The hypocrites: the scribes and Pharisees, see 23, 13.15.23.25.27.29. The designation reflects an attitude resulting not only from the controversies at the time of Jesus' ministry but from the opposition between Pharisaic Judaism and the church of Matthew. They have received their reward: they desire praise and have received what they were looking for.

6, 7–15: Matthew inserts into this basic traditional material an expansion of the material on prayer that includes the model prayer, the "Our Father." That prayer is found in Lk 11, 2–4 in a different context and in a different form.

6, 7: The example of what Christian prayer should be like contrasts it now not with the prayer of the hypocrites but with that of the pagans. Their babbling probably means their reciting a long list of divine names, hoping that one of them will force a response from the deity.

6, 9–13: Matthew's form of the "Our Father" follows the liturgical tradition of his church. Luke's less developed form also represents the liturgical tradition known to him, but it is probably closer than Matthew's to the original words of Jesus.

6, 9: Our Father in heaven: this invocation is found in many rabbinic prayers of the post-New Testament period. Hallowed be your name: though the "hallowing" of the divine name could be understood as reverence done to God by human praise and by obedience to his will, this is more probably a petition that God hallow his own name, i.e., that he manifest his glory by an act of power (cf Ez 36, 23), in this case, by the establishment of his kingdom in its fullness.

t: Lk 6, 27.32-36.   u: Lv 19, 18.   v: Lv 11, 44; 19, 2; Dt 18, 13; Jas 1. 4; 1 Pt 1, 16; 1 Jn 3, 3.   w: 23, 5.   x: Jn 12, 43.   y: Lk 11, 2-4.

10 *z* *your kingdom come,
 your will be done,
  on earth as in heaven.
11 *a* *Give us today our daily bread;
12 *b* *and forgive us our debts,
  as we forgive our debtors;
13 *c* *and do not subject us to the final
   test,
  but deliver us from the evil one.

14*d**If you forgive others their transgressions, your heavenly Father will forgive you. 15*e*But if you do not forgive others, neither will your Father forgive your transgressions.

Teaching about Fasting. 16*"When you fast, do not look gloomy like the hypocrites. They neglect their appearance, so that they may appear to others to be fasting. Amen, I say to you, they have received their reward. 17But when you fast, anoint your head and wash your face, 18so that you may not appear to others to be fasting, except to your Father who is hidden. And your Father who sees what is hidden will repay you.

Treasure in Heaven. 19*f**"Do not store up for yourselves treasures on earth, where moth and decay destroy, and thieves break in and steal. 20*g*But store up treasures in

heaven, where neither moth nor decay destroy, nor thieves break in and steal. 21For where your treasure is, there also will your heart be.

The Light of the Body. 22*h**"The lamp of the body is the eye. If your eye is sound, your whole body will be filled with light; 23but if your eye is bad, your whole body will be in darkness. And if the light in you is darkness, how great will the darkness be.

God and Money. 24*i**"No one can serve two masters. He will either hate one and love the other, or be devoted to one and despise the other. You cannot serve God and mammon.

Dependence on God. 25*j**"Therefore I tell you, do not worry about your life, what you will eat [or drink], or about your body, what you will wear. Is not life more than food and the body more than clothing? 26*k*Look at the birds in the sky; they do not sow or reap, they gather nothing into barns, yet your heavenly Father feeds them. Are not you more important than they? 27*Can any of you by worrying add a single moment to your life-span? 28Why are you anxious about clothes? Learn from the way the wild flowers grow. They do not work or spin. 29But I tell you that not even Solomon in all his

---

6, 10: **Your kingdom come:** this petition sets the tone of the prayer, and inclines the balance toward divine rather than human action in the petitions that immediately precede and follow it. **Your will be done, on earth as in heaven:** a petition that the divine purpose to establish the kingdom, a purpose present now **in heaven,** be executed **on earth.**

6, 11: **Give us today our daily bread:** the rare Greek word **epiousios,** here **daily,** occurs in the New Testament only here and in Lk 11, 3. A single occurrence of the word outside of these texts and of literature dependent on them has been claimed, but the claim is highly doubtful. The word may mean **daily** or "future" (other meanings have also been proposed). The latter would conform better to the eschatological tone of the whole prayer. So understood, the petition would be for a speedy coming of the kingdom (**today**), which is often portrayed in both the Old Testament and the New under the image of a feast (Is 25, 6; Mt 8, 11; 22, 1–10; Lk 13, 29; 14, 15–24).

6, 12: **Forgive us our debts:** the word **debts** is used metaphorically of sins, "debts" owed to God (see Lk 11, 4). The request is probably for forgiveness at the final judgment.

6, 13: Jewish apocalyptic writings speak of a period of severe trial before the end of the age, sometimes called the "messianic woes." This petition asks that the disciples be spared that **final test.**

6, 14–15: These verses reflect a set pattern called "Principles of Holy Law." Human action now will be met by a corresponding action of God at the final judgment.

6, 16: The only fast prescribed in the Mosaic law was that of the Day of Atonement (Lv 16, 31), but the practice of regular fasting was common in later Judaism; cf **Didache** 9, 1.

6, 19–34: The remaining material of this chapter is taken almost entirely from Q. It deals principally with worldly possessions, and the controlling thought is summed up in v 24: the disciple can serve only one master and must choose between God and wealth (**mammon**). See further the note on Lk 16, 9.

6, 22–23: In this context the parable probably points to the need for the disciple to be enlightened by Jesus' teaching on the transitory nature of earthly riches.

6, 24: **Mammon:** an Aramaic word meaning wealth or property.

6, 25–34: Jesus does not deny the reality of human needs (32), but forbids making them the object of anxious care and, in effect, becoming their slave.

6, 27: **Life-span:** the Greek word can also mean "stature." If it is taken in that sense, the word here translated **moment** (literally, "cubit") must be translated literally as a unit not of time but of spatial measure. The cubit is about eighteen inches.

---

z: 26, 42.   a: Prv 30, 8-9.   b: 18, 21-22; Sir 28, 2.   c: Jn 17, 15;
2 Thes 3, 3.   d: 18, 35; Sir 28, 1-5; Mk 11, 25.   e: Jas 2, 13.
f: Jas 5, 2-3.   g: Lk 12, 33-34.   h: Lk 11, 34-36.   i: Lk 16, 13.
j: Lk 12, 22-31.   k: Pss 145, 15-16; 147, 9.

splendor was clothed like one of them. ³⁰*If God so clothes the grass of the field, which grows today and is thrown into the oven to-morrow, will he not much more provide for you, O you of little faith? ³¹So do not worry and say, 'What are we to eat?' or 'What are we to drink?' or 'What are we to wear?' ³²All these things the pagans seek. Your heavenly Father knows that you need them all. ³³*But seek first the kingdom [of God] and his righ-teousness, and all these things will be given you besides. ³⁴Do not worry about tomor-row; tomorrow will take care of itself. Suffi-cient for a day is its own evil.

CHAPTER 7

See RG 281-82 *Judging Others.* ¹¹ᵐ*"Stop judging, that you may not be judged. ²ⁿFor as you judge, so will you be judged, and the meas-ure with which you measure will be meas-ured out to you. ³Why do you notice the splinter in your brother's eye, but do not per-ceive the wooden beam in your own eye? ⁴How can you say to your brother, 'Let me remove that splinter from your eye,' while the wooden beam is in your eye? ⁵*You hyp-ocrite, remove the wooden beam from your eye first; then you will see clearly to remove the splinter from your brother's eye.

Pearls before Swine. ⁶ᵒ*"Do not give what is holy to dogs, or throw your pearls before swine, lest they trample them under-foot, and turn and tear you to pieces.

The Answer to Prayers. ⁷ᵖᵍ"Ask and it will be given to you; seek and you will find; knock and the door will be opened to you. ⁸ʳFor everyone who asks, receives; and the one who seeks, finds; and to the one who knocks, the door will be opened. ⁹*Which one of you would hand his son a stone when he asks for a loaf of bread, ¹⁰or a snake when he asks for a fish? ¹¹ˢIf you then, who are wicked, know how to give good gifts to your children, how much more will your heavenly Father give good things to those who ask him.

The Golden Rule. ¹²ᵗ*"Do to others what-ever you would have them do to you. This is the law and the prophets.

The Narrow Gate. ¹³ᵘ*"Enter through the narrow gate; for the gate is wide and the road broad that leads to destruction, and those who enter through it are many. ¹⁴How nar-row the gate and constricted the road that leads to life. And those who find it are few.

False Prophets. ¹⁵ᵛ*"Beware of false prophets, who come to you in sheep's cloth-ing, but underneath are ravenous wolves. ¹⁶ʷBy their fruits you will know them. Do

6, 30: Of little faith: except for the parallel in Lk 12, 28, the word translated **of little faith** is found in the New Testament only in Matthew. It is used by him of those who are disciples of Jesus but whose faith in him is not as deep as it should be (see Mt 8, 26; 14, 31; 16, 8 and the cognate noun in 17, 20).

6, 33: Righteousness: see the note on 3, 14–15.

7, 1–12: In v 1 Matthew returns to the basic traditional material of the sermon (Lk 6, 37–38.41–42). The governing thought is the correspondence between conduct toward one's fellows and God's conduct toward the one so acting.

7, 1: This is not a prohibition against recognizing the faults of others, which would be hardly compatible with vv 5 and 6, but against passing judgment in a spirit of arrogance, forgetful of one's own faults.

7, 5: Hypocrite: the designation previously given to the scribes and Pharisees is here given to the Christian disciple who is concerned with the faults of another and ignores his own more serious offenses.

7, 6: Dogs and **swine** were Jewish terms of contempt for Gentiles. This saying may originally have derived from a Jewish Christian community opposed to preaching the gospel (**what is holy, pearls**) to Gentiles. In the light of 28, 19 that can hardly be Matthew's meaning. He may have taken the saying as applying to a Christian dealing with an obstinately impenitent fellow Christian (18, 17).

7, 9–10: There is a resemblance between a stone and a

round loaf of bread and between a serpent and the scaleless fish called **barbut.**

7, 12: See Lk 6, 31. This saying, known since the eigh-teenth century as the "Golden Rule," is found in both positive and negative form in pagan and Jewish sources, both earlier and later than the gospel. **This is the law and the prophets** is an addition probably due to the evangelist.

7, 13–28: The final section of the discourse is composed of a series of antitheses, contrasting two kinds of life within the Christian community, that of those who obey the words of Jesus and that of those who do not. Most of the sayings are from Q and are found also in Luke.

7, 13–14: The metaphor of the "two ways" was common in pagan philosophy and in the Old Testament. In Christian literature it is found also in the **Didache** (1–6) and the **Epis-tle of Barnabas** (18–20).

7, 15–20: Christian disciples who claimed to speak in the name of God are called **prophets** (15) in 10, 41 and in 23, 34. They were presumably an important group within the church of Matthew. As in the case of the Old Testament prophets, there were both true and false ones, and for Matthew the dif-

l: Lk 6, 37-38.41-42. *m:* Rom 2, 1-2; 1 Cor 4, 5. *n:* Wis 12, 22; Mk 4, 24. *o:* Prv 23, 9. *p:* Mk 11, 24; Lk 11, 9-13. *q:* 18, 19. *r:* Lk 18, 1-8; Jn 14, 13. *s:* 1 Jn 5, 14-15. *t:* Lk 6, 31. *u:* Lk 13, 24. *v:* 2 Pt 2, 1. *w:* 12, 33; Lk 6, 43-44.

people pick grapes from thornbushes, or figs from thistles? *17*Just so, every good tree bears good fruit, and a rotten tree bears bad fruit. *18*A good tree cannot bear bad fruit, nor can a rotten tree bear good fruit. *19x*Every tree that does not bear good fruit will be cut down and thrown into the fire. *20*So by their fruits you will know them.

The True Disciple. *21y**"Not everyone who says to me, 'Lord, Lord,' will enter the kingdom of heaven, but only the one who does the will of my Father in heaven. *22za*Many will say to me on that day, 'Lord, Lord, did we not prophesy in your name? Did we not drive out demons in your name? Did we not do mighty deeds in your name?' *23b**Then I will declare to them solemnly, 'I never knew you. Depart from me, you evildoers.'

The Two Foundations. *24c**"Everyone who listens to these words of mine and acts on them will be like a wise man who built his house on rock. *25d*The rain fell, the floods came, and the winds blew and buffeted the house. But it did not collapse; it had been set solidly on rock. *26*And everyone who listens to these words of mine but does not act on them will be like a fool who built his house on sand. *27*The rain fell, the floods came, and the winds blew and buffeted the house. And it collapsed and was completely ruined."

28*When Jesus finished these words, the crowds were astonished at his teaching, *29e**for he taught them as one having authority, and not as their scribes.

III: Ministry and Mission in Galilee

CHAPTER 8

See RG 282-83

The Cleansing of a Leper. *1f**When Jesus came down from the mountain, great crowds followed him. *2**And then a leper approached, did him homage, and said, "Lord, if you wish, you can make me clean." *3*He stretched out his hand, touched him, and said, "I will do it. Be made clean." His leprosy was cleansed immediately. *4g**Then Jesus said to him, "See that you tell no one, but go show yourself to the priest, and offer the gift that Moses prescribed; that will be proof for them."

The Healing of a Centurion's Servant. *5h**When he entered Capernaum, a centurion

---

ference could be recognized by the quality of their deeds, the **fruits** (16). The mention of **fruits** leads to the comparison with trees, some producing good fruit, others bad.

7, 21–23: The attack on the false prophets is continued, but is broadened to include those disciples who perform works of healing and exorcism in the name of Jesus (**Lord**) but live evil lives. Entrance into the kingdom is only for those who do the will of the Father. On the day of judgment (**on that day**) the morally corrupt prophets and miracle workers will be rejected by Jesus.

7, 23: I never knew you: cf 10, 33. **Depart from me, you evildoers:** cf Ps 6, 9.

7, 24–27: The conclusion of the discourse (cf Lk 6, 47–49). Here the relation is not between saying and doing as in vv 15–23 but between hearing and doing, and the words of Jesus are applied to every Christian (**everyone who listens**).

7, 28–29: When Jesus finished these words: this or a similar formula is used by Matthew to conclude each of the five great discourses of Jesus (cf 11, 1; 13, 53; 19, 1; 26, 1).

7, 29: Not as their scribes: scribal instruction was a faithful handing down of the traditions of earlier teachers; Jesus' teaching is based on his own authority. **Their scribes:** for the implications of **their,** see the note on 4, 23.

8, 1—9, 38: This narrative section of the second book of the gospel is composed of nine miracle stories, most of which are found in Mark, although Matthew does not follow the Marcan order and abbreviates the stories radically. The stories are arranged in three groups of three, each group followed by a section composed principally of sayings of Jesus about discipleship. Verse 9, 35 is an almost verbatim repetition of 4, 23. Each speaks of Jesus' teaching, preaching, and healing. The teaching and preaching form the content of chs 5–7; the healing, that of chs 8–9. Some scholars speak of a portrayal of Jesus as "Messiah of the Word" in 5–7 and "Messiah of the Deed" in 8–9. That is accurate so far as it goes, but there is also a strong emphasis on discipleship in 8–9; these chapters have not only christological but ecclesiological import.

8, 2: A leper: see the note on Mk 1, 40.

8, 4: Cf Lv 14, 2–9. **That will be proof for them:** the Greek can also mean "that will be proof against them." It is not clear whether **them** refers to the priests or the people.

8, 5–13: This story comes from Q (see Lk 7, 1–10) and is also reflected in Jn 4, 46–54. The similarity between the Q story and the Johannine is due to a common oral tradition, not to a common literary source. As in the later story of the daughter of the Canaanite woman (15, 21–28) Jesus here breaks with his usual procedure of ministering only to Israelites and anticipates the mission to the Gentiles.

8, 5: A centurion: a military officer commanding a hundred men. He was probably in the service of Herod Antipas, tetrarch of Galilee; see the note on 14, 1.

x: 3, 10. *y:* Is 29, 13; Lk 6, 46. *z:* Lk 13, 26-27. *a:* 25, 11-12. *b:* Pss 5, 5; 6, 9. *c:* Lk 6, 47-49. *d:* Prv 10, 25. *e:* Mk 1, 22; Lk 4, 32. *f:* Mk 1, 40-44; Lk 5, 12-14. *g:* Lv 14, 2-32; Lk 17, 14. *h:* Lk 7, 1-10; Jn 4, 46-53.

approached him and appealed to him, ⁶saying, "Lord, my servant is lying at home paralyzed, suffering dreadfully." ⁷He said to him, "I will come and cure him." ⁸*The centurion said in reply, "Lord, I am not worthy to have you enter under my roof; only say the word and my servant will be healed. ⁹For I too am a person subject to authority, with soldiers subject to me. And I say to one, 'Go,' and he goes; and to another, 'Come here,' and he comes; and to my slave, 'Do this,' and he does it." ¹⁰*When Jesus heard this, he was amazed and said to those following him, "Amen, I say to you, in no one in Israel have I found such faith. ¹¹*I say to you, many will come from the east and the west, and will recline with Abraham, Isaac, and Jacob at the banquet in the kingdom of heaven, ¹²but the children of the kingdom will be driven out into the outer darkness, where there will be wailing and grinding of teeth." ¹³And Jesus said to the centurion, "You may go; as you have believed, let it be done for you." And at that very hour [his] servant was healed.

The Cure of Peter's Mother-in-Law. ¹⁴*Jesus entered the house of Peter, and saw his mother-in-law lying in bed with a fever. ¹⁵*He touched her hand, the fever left her, and she rose and waited on him.

Other Healings ¹⁶*When it was evening, they brought him many who were possessed by demons, and he drove out the spirits by a word and cured all the sick, ¹⁷*to fulfill what had been said by Isaiah the prophet:

> "He took away our infirmities
>   and bore our diseases."

The Would-be Followers of Jesus. ¹⁸*When Jesus saw a crowd around him, he gave orders to cross to the other side. ¹⁹*A scribe approached and said to him, "Teacher, I will follow you wherever you go." ²⁰*Jesus answered him, "Foxes have dens and birds of the sky have nests, but the Son of Man has nowhere to rest his head." ²¹Another of [his] disciples said to him, "Lord, let me go first and bury my father." ²²*But Jesus answered him, "Follow me, and let the dead bury their dead."

The Calming of the Storm at Sea. ²³*He got into a boat and his disciples followed him. ²⁴*Suddenly a violent storm came up on

---

8, 8–9: Acquainted by his position with the force of a command, the centurion expresses faith in the power of Jesus' mere word.

8, 10: In no one in Israel: there is good textual attestation (e.g., Codex Sinaiticus) for a reading identical with that of Lk 7, 9, "not even in Israel." But that seems to be due to a harmonization of Matthew with Luke.

8, 11–12: Matthew inserts into the story a Q saying (see Lk 13, 28–29) about the entrance of Gentiles into the kingdom and the exclusion of those Israelites who, though descended from the patriarchs and members of the chosen nation (**the children of the kingdom**), refused to believe in Jesus. **There will be wailing and grinding of teeth:** the first occurrence of a phrase used frequently in this gospel to describe final condemnation (13, 42.50; 22, 13; 24, 51; 25, 30). It is found elsewhere in the New Testament only in Lk 13, 28.

8, 14–15: Cf Mk 1, 29–31. Unlike Mark, Matthew has no implied request by others for the woman's cure. Jesus acts on his own initiative, and the cured woman rises and waits not on "them" (Mk 1, 31) but on **him.**

8, 16: By a word: a Matthean addition to Mk 1, 34; cf 8, 8.

8, 17: This fulfillment citation from Is 53, 4 follows the MT, not the LXX. The prophet speaks of the Servant of the Lord who suffers vicariously for the sins ("infirmities") of others; Matthew takes the **infirmities** as physical afflictions.

8, 18–22: This passage between the first and second series of miracles about following Jesus is taken from Q (see Lk 9, 57–62). The third of the three sayings found in the source is absent from Matthew.

8, 18: The other side: i.e., of the Sea of Galilee.

8, 19: Teacher: for Matthew, this designation of Jesus is true, for he has Jesus using it of himself (10, 24.25; 23, 8; 26, 18), yet when it is used of him by others they are either his opponents (9, 11; 12, 38; 17, 24; 22, 16.24.36) or, as here and in 19, 15, well-disposed persons who cannot see more deeply. Thus it reveals an inadequate recognition of who Jesus is.

8, 20: Son of Man: see the note on Mk 8, 31. This is the first occurrence in Mt of a term that appears in the New Testament only in sayings of Jesus, except for Acts 7, 56 and possibly 9, 6 (// Mk 2, 10; Lk 5, 24). In Mt it refers to Jesus in his ministry (seven times, as here), in his passion and resurrection (nine times, e.g., 17, 22), and in his glorious coming at the end of the age (thirteen times, e.g., 24, 30).

8, 22: Let the dead bury their dead: the demand of Jesus overrides what both the Jewish and the Hellenistic world regarded as a filial obligation of the highest importance. See the note on Lk 9, 60.

8, 23: His disciples followed him: the first miracle in the second group (8, 23—9, 8) is introduced by a verse that links it with the preceding sayings by the catchword "follow." In Mk the initiative in entering the boat is taken by the disciples (Mk 4, 35–41); here, Jesus enters first and the disciples follow.

8, 24: Storm: literally, "earthquake," a word commonly used in apocalyptic literature for the shaking of the old world

i: 13, 42.50; 22, 13; 24, 51; 25, 30; Lk 13, 28–29. *j:* Mk 1, 29–34; Lk 4, 38–41. *k:* 9, 25. *l:* Is 53, 4. *m:* Mk 4, 35. *n:* Lk 9, 57–60. *o:* Mk 4, 35–40; Lk 8, 22–25.

the sea, so that the boat was being swamped by waves; but he was asleep. 25p*They came and woke him, saying, "Lord, save us! We are perishing!" 26*He said to them, "Why are you terrified, O you of little faith?" Then he got up, rebuked the winds and the sea, and there was great calm. 27The men were amazed and said, "What sort of man is this, whom even the winds and the sea obey?"

The Healing of the Gadarene Demoniacs. 28q*When he came to the other side, to the territory of the Gadarenes, two demoniacs who were coming from the tombs met him. They were so savage that no one could travel by that road. 29*They cried out, "What have you to do with us, Son of God? Have you come here to torment us before the appointed time?" 30*Some distance away a herd of many swine was feeding. 31rThe demons pleaded with him, "If you drive us out, send us into the herd of swine." 32And he said to them, "Go then!" They came out and entered the swine, and the whole herd rushed down the steep bank into the sea where they drowned. 33The swineherds ran away, and when they came to the town they reported

everything, including what had happened to the demoniacs. 34Thereupon the whole town came out to meet Jesus, and when they saw him they begged him to leave their district.

CHAPTER 9

See RG 283

The Healing of a Paralytic. 1s*He entered a boat, made the crossing, and came into his own town. 2tAnd there people brought to him a paralytic lying on a stretcher. When Jesus saw their faith, he said to the paralytic, "Courage, child, your sins are forgiven." 3*At that, some of the scribes said to themselves, "This man is blaspheming." 4Jesus knew what they were thinking, and said, "Why do you harbor evil thoughts? 5Which is easier, to say, 'Your sins are forgiven,' or to say, 'Rise and walk'? 6u*But that you may know that the Son of Man has authority on earth to forgive sins"—he then said to the paralytic, "Rise, pick up your stretcher, and go home." 7He rose and went home. 8*When the crowds saw this they were struck with awe and glorified God who had given such authority to human beings.

The Call of Matthew. 9v*As Jesus passed

---

when God brings in his kingdom. All the synoptics use it in depicting the events preceding the parousia of the Son of Man (24, 7; Mk 13, 8; Lk 21, 11). Matthew has introduced it here and in his account of the death and resurrection of Jesus (27, 51–54; 28, 2).

8, 25: The reverent plea of the disciples contrasts sharply with their reproach of Jesus in Mk 4, 38.

8, 26: You of little faith: see the note on 6, 30. **Great calm:** Jesus' calming the sea may be meant to recall the Old Testament theme of God's control over the chaotic waters (Pss 65, 8; 89, 10; 93, 3–4; 107, 29).

8, 28: Gadarenes: this is the reading of Codex Vaticanus, supported by other important textual witnesses. The original reading of Codex Sinaiticus was Gazarenes, later changed to Gergesenes, and a few versions have Gerasenes. Each of these readings points to a different territory connected, respectively, with the cities Gadara, Gergesa, and Gerasa (modern Jerash). There is the same confusion of readings in the parallel texts, Mk 5, 1 and Lk 8, 26; there the best reading seems to be "Gerasenes," whereas "Gadarenes" is probably the original reading in Mt. The town of Gadara was about five miles southeast of the Sea of Galilee, and Josephus (*Life* 9 §42) refers to it as possessing territory that lay on that sea. **Two demoniacs:** Mark (5, 1–20) has one.

8, 29: What have you to do with us?: see the note on Jn 2, 4. **Before the appointed time:** the notion that evil spirits were allowed by God to afflict human beings until the time of the final judgment is found in Enoch 16, 1 and Jubilees 10, 7–10.

8, 30: The tending of pigs, animals considered unclean by

Mosaic law (Lv 11, 6–7), indicates that the population was Gentile.

9, 1: His own town: Capernaum; see 4, 13.

9, 3: Scribes: see the note on Mk 2, 6. Matthew omits the reason given in the Marcan story for the charge of blasphemy: "Who but God alone can forgive sins?" (Mk 2, 7).

9, 6: It is not clear whether "But that you may know . . . to forgive sins" is intended to be a continuation of the words of Jesus or a parenthetical comment of the evangelist to those who would hear or read this gospel. In any case, Matthew here follows the Marcan text.

9, 8: Who had given such authority to human beings: a significant difference from Mk 2, 12 ("They . . . glorified God saying, 'We have never seen anything like this.'"). Matthew's extension to **human beings** of the authority to forgive sins points to the belief that such authority was being claimed by Matthew's church.

9, 9–17: In this section the order is the same as that of Mk 2, 13–22.

9, 9: A man named Matthew: Mark names this tax collector Levi (2, 14). No such name appears in the four lists of the twelve who were the closest companions of Jesus (10, 2–4; Mk 3, 16–19; Lk 6, 14–16; Acts 1, 13 [eleven, because of the defection of Judas Iscariot]), whereas all four list a Matthew, designated in 10, 3 as "the tax collector." The evan-

p: Ps 107, 28-29.   q: Mk 5, 1-17; Lk 8, 26-37.   r: Lk 4, 34.41.   s: Mk 2, 3-12; Lk 5, 18-26.   t: Lk 7, 48.   u: Jn 5, 27.   v: Mk 2, 14-17; Lk 5, 27-32.

on from there, he saw a man named Matthew sitting at the customs post. He said to him, "Follow me." And he got up and followed him. [10w]*While he was at table in his house, many tax collectors and sinners came and sat with Jesus and his disciples. [11]*The Pharisees saw this and said to his disciples, "Why does your teacher eat with tax collectors and sinners?" [12]*He heard this and said, "Those who are well do not need a physician, but the sick do. [13x]*Go and learn the meaning of the words, 'I desire mercy, not sacrifice.' I did not come to call the righteous but sinners."

The Question about Fasting. [14y]Then the disciples of John approached him and said, "Why do we and the Pharisees fast [much], but your disciples do not fast?" [15]*Jesus answered them, "Can the wedding guests mourn as long as the bridegroom is with them? The days will come when the bridegroom is taken away from them, and then they will fast. [16]*No one patches an old cloak with a piece of unshrunken cloth, for its fullness pulls away from the cloak and the tear gets worse. [17]People do not put new wine into old wineskins. Otherwise the skins burst, the wine spills out, and the skins are ruined. Rather, they pour new wine into fresh wineskins, and both are preserved."

The Official's Daughter and the Woman with a Hemorrhage. [18z]*While he was saying these things to them, an official came forward, knelt down before him, and said, "My daughter has just died. But come, lay your hand on her, and she will live." [19]Jesus rose and followed him, and so did his disciples. [20]*A woman suffering hemorrhages for twelve years came up behind him and touched the tassel on his cloak. [21a]She said to herself, "If only I can touch his cloak, I shall be cured." [22]Jesus turned around and saw her, and said, "Courage, daughter! Your faith has saved you." And from that hour the woman was cured.

[23]When Jesus arrived at the official's house and saw the flute players and the crowd who were making a commotion, [24]*he said, "Go away! The girl is not dead but sleeping." And they ridiculed him. [25]When the crowd was put out, he came and took her by the hand, and the little girl arose. [26]And news of this spread throughout all that land.

The Healing of Two Blind Men. [27bc]*And

---

gelist may have changed the "Levi" of his source to **Matthew** so that this man, whose call is given special notice, like that of the first four disciples (4, 18–22), might be included among the twelve. Another reason for the change may be that the disciple Matthew was the source of traditions peculiar to the church for which the evangelist was writing.

9, 10: His house: it is not clear whether **his** refers to Jesus or Matthew. **Tax collectors:** see the note on 5, 46. Table association with such persons would cause ritual impurity.

9, 11: Teacher: see the note on 8, 19.

9, 12: See the note on Mk 2, 17.

9, 13: Go and learn . . . not sacrifice: Matthew adds the prophetic statement of Hos 6, 6 to the Marcan account (see also 12, 7). If mercy is superior to the temple sacrifices, how much more to the laws of ritual impurity.

9, 15: Fasting is a sign of mourning and would be as inappropriate at this time of joy, when Jesus is proclaiming the kingdom, as it would be at a marriage feast. Yet the saying looks forward to the time when Jesus will no longer be with the disciples visibly, the time of Matthew's church. **Then they will fast:** see **Didache** 8, 1.

9, 16–17: Each of these parables speaks of the unsuitability of attempting to combine the old and the new. Jesus' teaching is not a patching up of Judaism, nor can the gospel be contained within the limits of Mosaic law.

9, 18–34: In this third group of miracles, the first (18–26) is clearly dependent on Mark (Mk 5, 21–43). Though it tells of two miracles, the cure of the woman had already been included within the story of the raising of the official's daughter, so that the two were probably regarded as a single unit. The other miracles seem to have been derived from Mark and Q respectively, though there Matthew's own editing is much more evident.

9, 18: Official: literally, "ruler." Mark calls him "one of the synagogue officials" (Mk 5, 22). **My daughter has just died:** Matthew heightens the Marcan "my daughter is at the point of death" (Mk 5, 23).

9, 20: Tassel: possibly "fringe." The Mosaic law prescribed that tassels be worn on the corners of one's garment as a reminder to keep the commandments (see Nm 15, 37–39; Dt 22, 12).

9, 24: Sleeping: sleep is a biblical metaphor for death (see Ps 87, 6 LXX; Dn 12, 2; 1 Thes 5, 10). Jesus' statement is not a denial of the child's real death, but an assurance that she will be roused from her sleep of death.

9, 27–31: This story was probably composed by Matthew out of Mark's story of the healing of a blind man named Bartimaeus (Mk 10, 46–52). Mark places the event late in Jesus' ministry, just before his entrance into Jerusalem, and Matthew has followed his Marcan source at that point in his gospel also (see 20, 29–34). In each of the Matthean stories the single blind man of Mark becomes two. The reason why

w: 11, 19; Lk 15, 1-2. x: 12, 7; Hos 6, 6. y: Mk 2, 18-22; Lk 5, 33-39. z: Mk 5, 22-43; Lk 8, 41-56. a: 14, 36; Nm 15, 37. b: 20, 29-34. c: 15, 22.

as Jesus passed on from there, two blind men followed [him], crying out, "Son of David, have pity on us!" ²⁸When he entered the house, the blind men approached him and Jesus said to them, "Do you believe that I can do this?" "Yes, Lord," they said to him. ²⁹Then he touched their eyes and said, "Let it be done for you according to your faith." ³⁰And their eyes were opened. Jesus warned them sternly, "See that no one knows about this." ³¹But they went out and spread word of him through all that land.

The Healing of a Mute Person. ^{32d}*As they were going out, a demoniac who could not speak was brought to him, ^{33e}and when the demon was driven out the mute person spoke. The crowds were amazed and said, "Nothing like this has ever been seen in Israel." ^{34f}*But the Pharisees said, "He drives out demons by the prince of demons."

The Compassion of Jesus. ^{35g}*Jesus went around to all the towns and villages, teaching in their synagogues, proclaiming the gospel of the kingdom, and curing every disease and illness. ^{36h}*At the sight of the crowds, his heart was moved with pity for them because they were troubled and abandoned, like sheep without a shepherd. ³⁷ⁱ*Then he said to his disciples, "The harvest is abundant but the laborers are few; ³⁸so ask the master of the harvest to send out laborers for his harvest."

CHAPTER 10

See RG 283

The Mission of the Twelve. ^{1j}*Then he summoned his twelve disciples and gave them authority over unclean spirits to drive them out and to cure every disease and every illness. ²*The names of the twelve apostles are these: first, Simon called Peter, and his brother Andrew; James, the son of Zebedee, and his brother John; ³Philip and Bartholomew, Thomas and Matthew the tax collector; James, the son of Alphaeus, and Thaddeus; ⁴Simon the Cananean, and Judas Iscariot who betrayed him.

The Commissioning of the Twelve. ^{5k}*Jesus sent out these twelve after instructing them

Matthew would have given a double version of the Marcan story and placed the earlier one here may be that he wished to add a story of Jesus' curing the blind at this point in order to prepare for Jesus' answer to the emissaries of the Baptist (11, 4–6) in which Jesus, recounting his works, begins with his giving sight to the blind.

9, 27: Son of David: this messianic title is connected once with the healing power of Jesus in Mark (10, 47–48) and Luke (18, 38–39) but more frequently in Matthew (see also 12, 23; 15, 22; 20, 30–31).

9, 32–34: The source of this story seems to be Q (see Lk 11, 14–15). As in the preceding healing of the blind, Matthew has two versions of this healing, the later in 12, 22–24 and the earlier here.

9, 34: This spiteful accusation foreshadows the growing opposition to Jesus in chs 11 and 12.

9, 35: See the notes on 4, 23–25 and 8, 1—9, 38.

9, 36: See Mk 6, 34; Nm 27, 17; 1 Kgs 22, 17.

9, 37–38: This Q saying (see Lk 10, 2) is only imperfectly related to this context. It presupposes that only God (**the master of the harvest**) can take the initiative in sending out preachers of the gospel, whereas in Matthew's setting it leads into ch 10, where Jesus does so.

10, 1—11, 1: After an introductory narrative (10, 1–4), the second of the discourses of the gospel. It deals with the mission now to be undertaken by the disciples (5–15), but the perspective broadens and includes the missionary activity of the church between the time of the resurrection and the parousia.

10, 1: His twelve disciples: although, unlike Mark (3, 13–14) and Luke (6, 12–16), Matthew has no story of Jesus' choosing the Twelve, he assumes that the group is known to the reader. The earliest New Testament text to speak of it is

1 Cor 15, 5. The number probably is meant to recall the twelve tribes of Israel and implies Jesus' authority to call all Israel into the kingdom. While Luke (6, 13) and probably Mark (4, 10.34) distinguish between the Twelve and a larger group also termed disciples, Matthew tends to identify the disciples and the Twelve. **Authority . . . every illness:** activities the same as those of Jesus; see 4, 23; 9, 35; 10, 8. The Twelve also share in his proclamation of the kingdom (10, 7). But although he teaches (4, 23; 7, 28; 9, 35), they do not. Their commission to teach comes only after Jesus' resurrection, after they have been fully instructed by him (28, 20).

10, 2–4: Here, for the only time in Matthew, the Twelve are designated **apostles.** The word "apostle" means "one who is sent," and therefore fits the situation here described. In the Pauline letters, the place where the term occurs most frequently in the New Testament, it means primarily one who has seen the risen Lord and has been commissioned to proclaim the resurrection. With slight variants in Luke and Acts, the names of those who belong to this group are the same in the four lists given in the New Testament (see the note on 9, 9). **Cananean:** this represents an Aramaic word meaning "zealot." The meaning of that designation is unclear (see the note on Lk 6, 15).

10, 5–6: Like Jesus (15, 24), the Twelve are sent only to Israel. This saying may reflect an original Jewish Christian refusal of the mission to the Gentiles, but for Matthew it expresses rather the limitation that Jesus himself observed during his ministry.

d: 12, 22-24; Lk 11, 14-15. *e:* Mk 2, 12; 7, 37. *f:* 10, 25; Mk 3, 22. *g:* 4, 23; Lk 8, 1. *h:* Nm 27, 17; 1 Kgs 22, 17; Jer 50, 6; Ez 34, 5; Mk 6, 34. *i:* Lk 10, 2; Jn 4, 35. *j:* Mk 3, 14-19; Lk 6, 13-16; Acts 1, 13. *k:* Mk 6, 7-13; Lk 9, 1-6.

thus, "Do not go into pagan territory or enter a Samaritan town. [6]Go rather to the lost sheep of the house of Israel. [7m]As you go, make this proclamation: 'The kingdom of heaven is at hand.' [8]*Cure the sick, raise the dead, cleanse lepers, drive out demons. Without cost you have received; without cost you are to give. [9n]Do not take gold or silver or copper for your belts; [10o]no sack for the journey, or a second tunic, or sandals, or walking stick. The laborer deserves his keep. [11p]Whatever town or village you enter, look for a worthy person in it, and stay there until you leave. [12]As you enter a house, wish it peace. [13]*If the house is worthy, let your peace come upon it; if not, let your peace return to you. [14q]*Whoever will not receive you or listen to your words—go outside that house or town and shake the dust from your feet. [15r]Amen, I say to you, it will be more tolerable for the land of Sodom and Gomorrah on the day of judgment than for that town.

Coming Persecutions. [16s]"Behold, I am sending you like sheep in the midst of wolves; so be shrewd as serpents and simple as doves. [17tu]*But beware of people, for they will hand you over to courts and scourge you in their synagogues, [18]and you will be led before governors and kings for my sake as a witness before them and the pagans. [19v]When they hand you over, do not worry about how you are to speak or what you are to say. You will be given at that moment what you are to say. [20]For it will not be you who speak but the Spirit of your Father speaking through you. [21w]*Brother will hand over brother to death, and the father his child; children will rise up against parents and have them put to death. [22]*You will be hated by all because of my name, but whoever endures to the end will be saved. [23]*When they persecute you in one town, flee to another. Amen, I say to you, you will not finish the towns of Israel before the Son of Man comes. [24x]No disciple is above his teacher, no slave above his master. [25]*It is enough for the disciple that he become like his teacher, for the slave that he become like his master. If they have called the master of the house Beelzebul, how much more those of his household!

Courage under Persecution. [26yz]*"Therefore do not be afraid of them. Nothing is concealed that will not be revealed, nor secret that will not be known. [27]What I say to you in the darkness, speak in the light; what you hear whispered, proclaim on the housetops. [28a]And do not be afraid of those who kill the body but cannot kill the soul; rather, be afraid of the one who can destroy both soul and body in Gehenna. [29]Are not two sparrows sold for a small coin? Yet not one of them falls to the ground without your Father's knowledge. [30]Even all the hairs of your head are counted. [31]So do not be afraid;

10, 8–11: The Twelve have received their own call and mission through God's gift, and the benefits they confer are likewise to be given freely. They are not to take with them money, provisions, or unnecessary clothing; their lodging and food will be provided by those who receive them.

10, 13: The greeting of peace is conceived of not merely as a salutation but as an effective word. If it finds no worthy recipient, it will return to the speaker.

10, 14: Shake the dust from your feet: this gesture indicates a complete disassociation from such unbelievers.

10, 17: The persecutions attendant upon the post-resurrection mission now begin to be spoken of. Here Matthew brings into the discourse sayings found in Mk 13, which deals with events preceding the parousia.

10, 21: See Mi 7, 6, which is cited in vv 35.36.

10, 22: To the end: the original meaning was probably "until the parousia." But it is not likely that Matthew expected no missionary disciples to suffer death before then, since he envisages the martyrdom of other Christians (21). For him, **the end** is probably that of the individual's life (see 28).

10, 23: Before the Son of Man comes: since the coming of the Son of Man at the end of the age had not taken place when this gospel was written, much less during the mission of the Twelve during Jesus' ministry, Matthew cannot have meant the coming to refer to the parousia. It is difficult to know what he understood it to be: perhaps the "proleptic parousia" of 28, 16–20, or the destruction of the temple in A.D. 70, viewed as a coming of Jesus in judgment on unbelieving Israel.

10, 25: Beelzebul: see 9, 34 for the charge linking Jesus with "the prince of demons," who is named **Beelzebul** in 12, 24. The meaning of the name is uncertain; possibly, "lord of the house."

10, 26: The **concealed** and **secret** coming of the kingdom is to be proclaimed by them, and no fear must be allowed to deter them from that proclamation.

l: 15, 24. *m:* 3, 2; 4, 17. *n:* Mk 6, 8-9; Lk 9, 3; 10, 4. *o:* Lk 10, 7; 1 Cor 9, 14; 2 Tm 5, 18. *p:* Mk 6, 10-11; Lk 9, 4-5; 10, 5-12. *q:* Acts 13, 51; 18, 6. *r:* 11, 24; Gn 19, 1-29; Jude 7. *s:* Lk 10, 3. *t:* Mk 13, 9-13; Lk 21, 12-19. *u:* Acts 5, 40. *v:* Ex 4, 11-12; Jer 1, 6-10; Lk 12, 11-12. *w:* 24, 9.13. *x:* Lk 6, 40; Jn 13, 16; 15, 20. *y:* Lk 12, 2-9. *z:* Mk 4, 22; Lk 8, 17; 1 Tm 5, 25. *a:* Jas 4, 12.

you are worth more than many sparrows. [32]*Everyone who acknowledges me before others I will acknowledge before my heavenly Father. [33b]But whoever denies me before others, I will deny before my heavenly Father.

Jesus: A Cause of Division. [34c]"Do not think that I have come to bring peace upon the earth. I have come to bring not peace but the sword. [35]For I have come to set

a man 'against his father,
    a daughter against her mother,
and a daughter-in-law against her
      mother-in-law;
[36]   and one's enemies will be those of his
      household.'

The Conditions of Discipleship. [37d]"Whoever loves father or mother more than me is not worthy of me, and whoever loves son or daughter more than me is not worthy of me; [38]*and whoever does not take up his cross and follow after me is not worthy of me. [39e]*Whoever finds his life will lose it, and whoever loses his life for my sake will find it.

Rewards. [40f]*"Whoever receives you receives me, and whoever receives me receives the one who sent me. [41]*Whoever receives a prophet because he is a prophet will receive a prophet's reward, and whoever receives a righteous man because he is righteous will receive a righteous man's reward. [42g]And whoever gives only a cup of cold water to one of these little ones to drink because he is a disciple—amen, I say to you, he will surely not lose his reward."

CHAPTER 11

See RG 283–84

[1]*When Jesus finished giving these commands to his twelve disciples, he went away from that place to teach and to preach in their towns.

IV: Opposition from Israel

The Messengers from John the Baptist. [2h]*When John heard in prison of the works of the Messiah, he sent his disciples to him [3]*with this question, "Are you the one who is to come, or should we look for another?" [4]Jesus said to them in reply, "Go and tell John what you hear and see: [5i]*the blind regain their sight, the lame walk, lepers are cleansed, the deaf hear, the dead are raised, and the poor have the good news proclaimed to them. [6]And blessed is the one who takes no offense at me."

Jesus' Testimony to John. [7j]*As they were going off, Jesus began to speak to the crowds

10, 32–33: In the Q parallel (Lk 12, 8–9), the Son of Man will acknowledge those who have acknowledged Jesus, and those who deny him will be denied (by the Son of Man) before the angels of God at the judgment. Here Jesus and the Son of Man are identified, and the acknowledgment or denial will be before his heavenly Father.

10, 38: The first mention of the cross in Matthew, explicitly that of the disciple, but implicitly that of Jesus (**and follow after me**). Crucifixion was a form of capital punishment used by the Romans for offenders who were not Roman citizens.

10, 39: One who denies Jesus in order to save one's earthly life will be condemned to everlasting destruction; loss of earthly life for Jesus' sake will be rewarded by everlasting life in the kingdom.

10, 40–42: All who receive the disciples of Jesus receive him, and God who sent him, and will be rewarded accordingly.

10, 41: **A prophet:** one who speaks in the name of God; here, the Christian prophets who proclaim the gospel. **Righteous man:** since righteousness is demanded of all the disciples, it is difficult to take the **righteous man** of this verse and **one of these little ones** (42) as indicating different groups within the followers of Jesus. Probably all three designations are used here of Christian missionaries as such.

11, 1: The closing formula of the discourse refers back to the original addressees, the Twelve.

11, 2—12, 50: The narrative section of the third book deals with the growing opposition to Jesus. It is largely devoted to disputes and attacks relating to faith and discipleship and thus contains much sayings-material, drawn in large part from Q.

11, 2: **In prison:** see 4, 12; 14, 1–12. **The works of the Messiah:** the deeds of chs 8–9.

11, 3: The question probably expresses a doubt of the Baptist that Jesus is **the one who is to come** (cf Mal 3, 1) because his mission has not been one of fiery judgment as John had expected (3, 2).

11, 5–6: Jesus' response is taken from passages of Isaiah (26, 19; 29, 18–19; 35, 5–6; 61, 1) that picture the time of salvation as marked by deeds such as those that Jesus is doing. The beatitude is a warning to the Baptist not to disbelieve because his expectations have not been met.

11, 7–19: Jesus' rebuke of John is counterbalanced by a reminder of the greatness of the Baptist's function (7–15) that is followed by a complaint about those who have heeded neither John nor Jesus (16–19).

b: Mk 8, 38; Lk 9, 26; 2 Tm 2, 12; Rv 3, 5.   c: Lk 12, 51-53. d: 16, 24-25; Lk 14, 26-27.   e: Mk 8, 35; Lk 9, 24; Jn 12, 25. f: Lk 10, 16; Jn 12, 44; 13, 20.   g: 25, 40; Mk 9, 41.   h: Lk 7, 18-28.   i: Is 26, 19; 29, 18-19; 35, 5-6; 61, 1.   j: 3, 3.5.

about John, "What did you go out to the desert to see? A reed swayed by the wind? ⁸Then what did you go out to see? Someone dressed in fine clothing? Those who wear fine clothing are in royal palaces. ⁹*Then why did you go out? To see a prophet? Yes, I tell you, and more than a prophet. ¹⁰ᵏThis is the one about whom it is written:

'Behold, I am sending my messenger
    ahead of you;
he will prepare your way before you.'

¹¹*Amen, I say to you, among those born of women there has been none greater than John the Baptist; yet the least in the kingdom of heaven is greater than he. ¹²ᶩ*From the days of John the Baptist until now, the kingdom of heaven suffers violence, and the violent are taking it by force. ¹³*All the prophets and the law prophesied up to the time of John. ¹⁴ᵐAnd if you are willing to accept it, he is Elijah, the one who is to come. ¹⁵Whoever has ears ought to hear.

¹⁶ⁿ*"To what shall I compare this generation? It is like children who sit in marketplaces and call to one another, ¹⁷'We played the flute for you, but you did not dance, we sang a dirge but you did not mourn.' ¹⁸ᵒFor John came neither eating nor drinking, and they said, 'He is possessed by a demon.'

¹⁹ᵖThe Son of Man came eating and drinking and they said, 'Look, he is a glutton and a drunkard, a friend of tax collectors and sinners.' But wisdom is vindicated by her works."

Reproaches to Unrepentant Towns. ²⁰�q Then he began to reproach the towns where most of his mighty deeds had been done, since they had not repented. ²¹ʳ*"Woe to you, Chorazin! Woe to you, Bethsaida! For if the mighty deeds done in your midst had been done in Tyre and Sidon, they would long ago have repented in sackcloth and ashes. ²²But I tell you, it will be more tolerable for Tyre and Sidon on the day of judgment than for you. ²³ˢ*And as for you, Capernaum:

'Will you be exalted to heaven?
    You will go down to the netherworld.'

For if the mighty deeds done in your midst had been done in Sodom, it would have remained until this day. ²⁴ᵗBut I tell you, it will be more tolerable for the land of Sodom on the day of judgment than for you."

The Praise of the Father. ²⁵ᵘ*At that time Jesus said in reply, "I give praise to you, Father, Lord of heaven and earth, for although you have hidden these things from the wise and the learned you have revealed them to the childlike. ²⁶Yes, Father, such has been

11, 9–10: In common Jewish belief there had been no prophecy in Israel since the last of the Old Testament prophets, Malachi. The coming of a new prophet was eagerly awaited, and Jesus agrees that John was such. Yet he was **more than a prophet,** for he was the precursor of the one who would bring in the new and final age. The Old Testament quotation is a combination of Mal 3, 1 and Ex 23, 20, with the significant change that the **before me** of Malachi becomes **before you.** The messenger now precedes not God, as in the original, but Jesus.

11, 11: John's preeminent greatness lies in his function of announcing the imminence of the kingdom (3, 1). But to be in the kingdom is so great a privilege that the least who has it is greater than the Baptist.

11, 12: The meaning of this difficult saying is probably that the opponents of Jesus are trying to prevent people from accepting the kingdom and to snatch it away from those who have received it.

11, 13: **All the prophets and the law:** Matthew inverts the usual order, "law and prophets," and says that both have **prophesied.** This emphasis on the prophetic character of the law points to its fulfillment in the teaching of Jesus and to the transitory nature of some of its commandments (see the note on 5, 17–20).

11, 16–19: See Lk 7, 31–35. The meaning of the parable

(16–17) and its explanation (18–19b) is much disputed. A plausible view is that the **children** of the parable are two groups, one of which proposes different entertainments to the other that will not agree with either proposal. The first represents John, Jesus, and their disciples; the second those who reject John for his asceticism and Jesus for his table association with those despised by the religiously observant. Verse 19c (**her works**) forms an inclusion with v 2 ("the works of the Messiah"). The original form of the saying is better preserved in Lk 7, 35, ". . . wisdom is vindicated by all her children." There John and Jesus are the children of Wisdom; here the works of Jesus the Messiah are those of divine Wisdom, of which he is the embodiment. Some important textual witnesses, however, have essentially the same reading as in Luke.

11, 21: Tyre and Sidon were pagan cities denounced for their wickedness in the Old Testament; cf Jl 4, 4–7.

11, 23: Capernaum's pride and punishment are described in language taken from the taunt song against the king of Babylon (Is 14, 13–15).

11, 25–27: This Q saying, identical with Lk 10, 21–22 ex-

k: Ex 23, 20; Mal 3, 1; Mk 1, 2; Lk 1, 76. l: Lk 16, 16. m: 17, 10-13; Mal 3, 23; Lk 1, 17. n: Lk 7, 31-35. o: Lk 1, 15. p: 9, 10-11. q: Lk 10, 12-15. r: Jl 4, 4-7. s: Is 14, 13-15. t: 10, 15. u: Lk 10, 21-22.

your gracious will. *27v*All things have been handed over to me by my Father. No one knows the Son except the Father, and no one knows the Father except the Son and anyone to whom the Son wishes to reveal him.

The Gentle Mastery of Christ. *28**"Come to me, all you who labor and are burdened, and I will give you rest. *29w**Take my yoke upon you and learn from me, for I am meek and humble of heart; and you will find rest for yourselves. *30*For my yoke is easy, and my burden light."

See RG
283–84

CHAPTER 12

Picking Grain on the Sabbath. *1xy**At that time Jesus was going through a field of grain on the sabbath. His disciples were hungry and began to pick the heads of grain and eat them. *2*When the Pharisees saw this, they said to him, "See, your disciples are doing what is unlawful to do on the sabbath." *3z**He said to them, "Have you not read what David did when he and his companions were hungry, *4a*how he went into the house of God and ate the bread of offering, which neither

he nor his companions but only the priests could lawfully eat? *5b**Or have you not read in the law that on the sabbath the priests serving in the temple violate the sabbath and are innocent? *6*I say to you, something greater than the temple is here. *7c**If you knew what this meant, 'I desire mercy, not sacrifice,' you would not have condemned these innocent men. *8d**For the Son of Man is Lord of the sabbath."

The Man with a Withered Hand. *9e*Moving on from there, he went into their synagogue. *10**And behold, there was a man there who had a withered hand. They questioned him, "Is it lawful to cure on the sabbath?" so that they might accuse him. *11**He said to them, "Which one of you who has a sheep that falls into a pit on the sabbath will not take hold of it and lift it out? *12*How much more valuable a person is than a sheep. So it is lawful to do good on the sabbath." *13*Then he said to the man, "Stretch out your hand." He stretched it out, and it was restored as sound as the other. *14f**But the Pharisees went out and took counsel against him to put him to death.

cept for minor variations, introduces a joyous note into this section, so dominated by the theme of unbelief. While the **wise and the learned,** the scribes and Pharisees, have rejected Jesus' preaching and the significance of his mighty deeds, **the childlike** have accepted them. Acceptance depends upon the Father's revelation, but this is granted to those who are open to receive it and refused to the arrogant. Jesus can speak of all mysteries because he is **the Son** and there is perfect reciprocity of knowledge between him and the Father; what has been **handed over** to him is revealed only to those whom he wishes.

11, 28–29: These verses are peculiar to Matthew and are similar to Ben Sirach's invitation to learn wisdom and submit to her yoke (Sir 51, 23.26).

11, 28: Who labor and are burdened: burdened by the law as expounded by the scribes and Pharisees (23, 4).

11, 29: In place of the yoke of the law, complicated by scribal interpretation, Jesus invites the burdened to take the yoke of obedience to his word, under which they **will find rest;** cf Jer 6, 16.

12, 1–14: Matthew here returns to the Marcan order that he left in 9, 18. The two stories depend on Mk 2, 23–28 and 3, 1–6, respectively, and are the only places in either gospel that deal explicitly with Jesus' attitude toward sabbath observance.

12, 1–2: The picking of the heads of grain is here equated with reaping, which was forbidden on the sabbath (Ex 34, 21).

12, 3–4: See 1 Sm 21, 2–7. In the Marcan parallel (2, 25–26) the high priest is mistakenly called Abiathar, although in 1 Sm this action is attributed to Ahimelech. The Old Testament story is not about a violation of the sabbath rest; its pertinence to this dispute is that a violation of the law was permissible because of David's men being without food.

12, 5–6: This and the following argument (7) are peculiar to Matthew. The temple service seems to be the changing of the showbread on the sabbath (Lv 24, 8) and the doubling on the sabbath of the usual daily holocausts (Nm 28, 9–10). The argument is that the law itself requires work that breaks the sabbath rest, because of the higher duty of temple service. If temple duties outweigh the sabbath law, how much more does the presence of Jesus, with his proclamation of the kingdom (**something greater than the temple**), justify the conduct of his disciples.

12, 7: See the note on 9, 13.

12, 8: The ultimate justification for the disciples' violation of the sabbath rest is that Jesus, the Son of Man, has supreme authority over the law.

12, 10: Rabbinic tradition later than the gospels allowed relief to be given to a sufferer on the sabbath if life was in danger. This may also have been the view of Jesus' Pharisaic contemporaries. But the case here is not about one in danger of death.

12, 11: Matthew omits the question posed by Jesus in Mk 3, 4 and substitutes one about rescuing a sheep on the sabbath, similar to that in Lk 14, 5.

12, 14: See Mk 3, 6. Here the plan to bring about Jesus' death is attributed to the Pharisees only. This is probably due to the situation of Matthew's church, when the sole opponents were the Pharisees.

v: Jn 3, 35; 6, 46; 7, 28; 10, 15. *w:* Sir 51, 26; Jer 6, 16. *x:* Mk 2, 23-28; Lk 6, 1-5. *y:* Dt 23, 26. *z:* 1 Sm 21, 2-7. *a:* Lv 24, 5-9. *b:* Lv 24, 8; Nm 28, 9-10. *c:* Hos 6, 6. *d:* Jn 5, 16-17. *e:* Mk 3, 1-6; Lk 6, 6-11. *f:* Jn 5, 18.

The Chosen Servant. [15]*When Jesus realized this, he withdrew from that place. Many [people] followed him, and he cured them all, [16]but he warned them not to make him known. [17]This was to fulfill what had been spoken through Isaiah the prophet:

[18] g "Behold, my servant whom I have chosen,
my beloved in whom I delight;
I shall place my spirit upon him,
and he will proclaim justice to the Gentiles.
[19] *He will not contend or cry out,
nor will anyone hear his voice in the streets.
[20] A bruised reed he will not break,
a smoldering wick he will not quench,
until he brings justice to victory.
[21] *And in his name the Gentiles will hope."

Jesus and Beelzebul. [22h]*Then they brought to him a demoniac who was blind and mute. He cured the mute person so that he could speak and see. [23i]*All the crowd was astounded, and said, "Could this perhaps be the Son of David?" [24j]*But when the Pharisees heard this, they said, "This man drives out demons only by the power of Beelzebul, the prince of demons." [25k]*But he knew what they were thinking and said to them, "Every kingdom divided against itself will be laid waste, and no town or house divided against itself will stand. [26]And if Satan drives out Satan, he is divided against himself; how, then, will his kingdom stand? [27]*And if I drive out demons by Beelzebul, by whom do your own people drive them out? Therefore they will be your judges. [28l]*But if it is by the Spirit of God that I drive out demons, then the kingdom of God has come upon you. [29]*How can anyone enter a strong man's house and steal his property, unless he first ties up the strong man? Then he can plunder his house. [30m]*Whoever is not with me is against me, and whoever does not gather with me scatters. [31n]*Therefore, I say to you, every sin and blasphemy will be forgiven people, but blasphemy against the Spirit will not be forgiven. [32]And whoever speaks a word against the Son of Man will be forgiven; but whoever speaks against the holy Spirit will not be forgiven, either in this age or in the age to come.

12, 15–21: Matthew follows Mk 3, 7–12 but summarizes his source in two verses (15.16) that pick up the withdrawal, the healings, and the command for silence. To this he adds a fulfillment citation from the first Servant Song (Is 42, 1–4) that does not correspond exactly to either the Hebrew or the LXX of that passage. It is the longest Old Testament citation in this gospel, emphasizing the meekness of Jesus, the Servant of the Lord, and foretelling the extension of his mission to the Gentiles.

12, 15: Jesus' knowledge of the Pharisees' plot and his healing **all** are peculiar to Matthew.

12, 19: The servant's not contending is seen as fulfilled in Jesus' withdrawal from the disputes narrated in 1–14.

12, 21: Except for a minor detail, Matthew here follows the LXX, although the meaning of the Hebrew ("the coastlands will wait for his teaching") is similar.

12, 22–32: For the exorcism, see the note on 9, 32–34. The long discussion combines Marcan and Q material (Mk 3, 22–30; Lk 11, 19–20.23; 12, 10). Mk 3, 20–21 is omitted, with a consequent lessening of the sharpness of 12, 48.

12, 23: See the note on 9, 27.

12, 24: See the note on 10, 25.

12, 25–26: Jesus' first response to the Pharisees' charge is that if it were true, Satan would be destroying his own kingdom.

12, 27: Besides pointing out the absurdity of the charge, Jesus asks how the work of Jewish exorcists (**your own people**) is to be interpreted. Are they, too, to be charged with collusion with Beelzebul? For an example of Jewish exorcism see Josephus, Antiquities 8, 2, 5 §§42–49.

12, 28: The Q parallel (Lk 11, 20) speaks of the "finger" rather than of the "spirit" of God. While the difference is probably due to Matthew's editing, he retains **the kingdom of God** rather than changing it to his usual "kingdom of heaven." **Has come upon you:** see 4, 17.

12, 29: A short parable illustrates what Jesus is doing. The **strong man** is Satan, whom Jesus has tied up and whose **house** he is plundering. Jewish expectation was that Satan would be chained up in the last days (Rv 20, 2); Jesus' exorcisms indicate that those days have begun.

12, 30: This saying, already attached to the preceding verses in Q (see Lk 11, 23), warns that there can be no neutrality where Jesus is concerned. Its pertinence in a context where Jesus is addressing not the neutral but the bitterly opposed is not clear. The accusation of scattering, however, does fit the situation. Jesus is the shepherd of God's people (2, 6), his mission is to the lost sheep of Israel (15, 24); the Pharisees, who oppose him, are guilty of scattering the sheep.

12, 31: Blasphemy against the Spirit: the sin of attributing to Satan (24) what is the work of the Spirit of God (28).

g: Is 42, 1-4.   h: 9, 32-34; Lk 11, 14-15.   i: 9, 27.   j: 10, 25; Mk 3, 22.   k: Mk 3, 23-27; Lk 11, 17-22.   l: Lk 11, 20.   m: Lk 11, 23.   n: Mk 3, 28-30; Lk 12, 10.

A Tree and Its Fruits. [33o]*"Either declare the tree good and its fruit is good, or declare the tree rotten and its fruit is rotten, for a tree is known by its fruit. [34p]*You brood of vipers, how can you say good things when you are evil? For from the fullness of the heart the mouth speaks. [35]A good person brings forth good out of a store of goodness, but an evil person brings forth evil out of a store of evil. [36q]*I tell you, on the day of judgment people will render an account for every careless word they speak. [37]By your words you will be acquitted, and by your words you will be condemned."

The Demand for a Sign. [38r]*Then some of the scribes and Pharisees said to him, "Teacher, we wish to see a sign from you." [39]*He said to them in reply, "An evil and unfaithful generation seeks a sign, but no sign will be given it except the sign of Jonah the prophet. [40]*Just as Jonah was in the belly of the whale three days and three nights, so will the Son of Man be in the heart of the earth three days and three nights. [41]*At the judgment, the men of Nineveh will arise with this generation and condemn it, because they repented at the preaching of Jonah; and there is something greater than Jonah here. [42s]At the judgment the queen of the south will arise with this generation and condemn it, because she came from the ends of the earth to hear the wisdom of Solomon; and there is something greater than Solomon here.

The Return of the Unclean Spirit. [43t]*"When an unclean spirit goes out of a person it roams through arid regions searching for rest but finds none. [44]Then it says, 'I will return to my home from which I came.' But upon returning, it finds it empty, swept clean, and put in order. [45]Then it goes and brings back with itself seven other spirits more evil than itself, and they move in and dwell there; and the last condition of that person is worse than the first. Thus it will be with this evil generation."

The True Family of Jesus. [46u]*While he was still speaking to the crowds, his mother and his brothers appeared outside, wishing to speak with him. [[47]*Someone told him, "Your mother and your brothers are standing outside, asking to speak with you."] [48]But he said in reply to the one who told him, "Who is my mother? Who are my brothers?" [49]And stretching out his hand toward his disciples, he said, "Here are my mother and my brothers. [50]For whoever does the will of my heavenly Father is my brother, and sister, and mother."

12, 33: Declare: literally, "make." The meaning of this verse is obscure. Possibly it is a challenge to the Pharisees either to declare Jesus and his exorcisms good or both of them bad. A tree is known by its fruit; if the fruit is good, so must the tree be. If the driving out of demons is good, so must its source be.

12, 34: The admission of Jesus' goodness cannot be made by the Pharisees, for they are evil, and the words that proceed from their evil hearts cannot be good.

12, 36–37: If on the day of judgment people will be held accountable for even their **careless** words, the vicious accusations of the Pharisees will surely lead to their condemnation.

12, 38–42: This section is mainly from Q (see Lk 11, 29–32). Mk 8, 11–12, which Matthew has followed in 16, 1–4, has a similar demand for a sign. The scribes and Pharisees refuse to accept the exorcisms of Jesus as authentication of his claims and demand a sign that will end all possibility of doubt. Jesus' response is that no such sign will be given. Because his opponents are evil and see him as an agent of Satan, nothing will convince them.

12, 38: Teacher: see the note on 8, 19. In 16, 1 the request is for a sign "from heaven" (Mk 8, 11).

12, 39: Unfaithful: literally, "adulterous." The covenant between God and Israel was portrayed as a marriage bond, and unfaithfulness to the covenant as adultery; cf Hos 2, 4–15; Jer 3, 6–10.

12, 40: See Jon 2, 1. While in Q the sign was simply Jo-

nah's preaching to the Ninevites (Lk 11, 30.32), Matthew here adds Jonah's sojourn **in the belly of the whale** for **three days and three nights,** a prefigurement of Jesus' sojourn in the abode of the dead and, implicitly, of his resurrection.

12, 41–42: The Ninevites who **repented** (see Jon 3, 1–10) **and the queen of the south** (i.e., of Sheba; see 1 Kgs 10, 1–13) were pagans who responded to lesser opportunities than have been offered to Israel in the ministry of Jesus, **something greater than Jonah** or **Solomon.** At the final judgment they will condemn the faithless **generation** that has rejected him.

12, 43–45: Another Q passage; cf 11, 24–26. Jesus' ministry has broken Satan's hold over Israel, but the refusal of **this evil generation** to accept him will lead to a worse situation than what preceded his coming.

12, 46–50: See Mk 3, 31–35. Matthew has omitted Mk 3, 20–21, which is taken up in Mk 3, 31 (see the note on 12, 22–32), yet the point of the story is the same in both gospels: natural kinship with Jesus counts for nothing; only one who **does the will** of his **heavenly Father** belongs to his true family.

12, 47: This verse is omitted in some important textual witnesses, including Codex Sinaiticus (original reading) and Codex Vaticanus.

o: Lk 6, 43-45. *p:* 3, 7; 23, 33; 15, 11-12; Lk 3, 7. *q:* Jas 3, 1-2. *r:* 16, 1-4; Jon 2, 1; 3, 1-10; Mk 8, 11-12; Lk 11, 29-32. *s:* 1 Kgs 10, 1-10. *t:* Lk 11, 24-26. *u:* Mk 3, 31-35; Lk 8, 19-21.

See RG
284–85

CHAPTER 13

The Parable of the Sower. [1v]*On that day, Jesus went out of the house and sat down by the sea. [2]Such large crowds gathered around him that he got into a boat and sat down, and the whole crowd stood along the shore. [3]*And he spoke to them at length in parables, saying: "A sower went out to sow. [4]And as he sowed, some seed fell on the path, and birds came and ate it up. [5]Some fell on rocky ground, where it had little soil. It sprang up at once because the soil was not deep, [6]and when the sun rose it was scorched, and it withered for lack of roots. [7]Some seed fell among thorns, and the thorns grew up and choked it. [8]But some seed fell on rich soil, and produced fruit, a hundred or sixty or thirtyfold. [9]Whoever has ears ought to hear."

The Purpose of Parables. [10]The disciples approached him and said, "Why do you speak to them in parables?" [11]*He said to them in reply, "Because knowledge of the mysteries of the kingdom of heaven has been granted to you, but to them it has not been granted. [12w]*To anyone who has, more will be given and he will grow rich; from anyone who has not, even what he has will be taken away. [13x]*This is why I speak to them in parables, because 'they look but do not see and hear but do not listen or understand.' [14y]Isaiah's prophecy is fulfilled in them, which says:

'You shall indeed hear but not understand,
    you shall indeed look but never see.
[15] Gross is the heart of this people,
    they will hardly hear with their ears,
    they have closed their eyes,
lest they see with their eyes
    and hear with their ears
and understand with their heart and be
    converted,
    and I heal them.'

13, 1–53: The discourse in parables is the third great discourse of Jesus in Mt and constitutes the second part of the third book of the gospel. Matthew follows the Marcan outline (Mk 4, 1–35) but has only two of Mark's parables, the five others being from Q and M. In addition to the seven parables, the discourse gives the reason why Jesus uses this type of speech (10–15), declares the blessedness of those who understand his teaching (16–17), explains the parable of the sower (18–23) and of the weeds (36–43), and ends with a concluding statement to the disciples (51–52).

13, 3: In parables: the word "parable" (Greek **parabolē**) is used in the LXX to translate the Hebrew **māshāl,** a designation covering a wide variety of literary forms such as axioms, proverbs, similitudes, and allegories. In the New Testament the same breadth of meaning of the word is found, but there it primarily designates stories that are illustrative comparisons between Christian truths and events of everyday life. Sometimes the event has a strange element that is quite different from usual experience (e.g., in v 33, the enormous amount of dough in the parable of the yeast); this is meant to sharpen the curiosity of the hearer. If each detail of such a story is given a figurative meaning, the story is an allegory. Those who maintain a sharp distinction between parable and allegory insist that a parable has only one point of comparison, and that while parables were characteristic of Jesus' teaching, to see allegorical details in them is to introduce meanings that go beyond their original intention and even falsify it. However, to exclude any allegorical elements from a parable is an excessively rigid mode of interpretation, now abandoned by many scholars.

13, 3–8: Since in Palestine sowing often preceded plowing, much of the seed is scattered on ground that is unsuitable. Yet while much is wasted, the seed that falls on good ground bears fruit in extraordinarily large measure. The point of the parable is that, in spite of some failure because of opposition and indifference, the message of Jesus about the coming of the kingdom will have enormous success.

13, 11: Since a parable is figurative speech that demands reflection for understanding, only those who are prepared to explore its meaning can come to know it. To understand is a gift of God, granted to the disciples but not to the crowds. In Semitic fashion, both the disciples' understanding and the crowd's obtuseness are attributed to God. The question of human responsibility for the obtuseness is not dealt with, although it is asserted in v 13. **The mysteries:** as in Lk 8, 10; Mk 4, 11 has "the mystery." The word is used in Dn 2, 18.19.27 and in the Qumran literature (1QpHab 7, 8; 1QS 3, 23; 1QM 3, 9) to designate a divine plan or decree affecting the course of history that can be known only when revealed. **Knowledge of the mysteries of the kingdom of heaven** means recognition that the kingdom has become present in the ministry of Jesus.

13, 12: In the New Testament use of this axiom of practical "wisdom" (see 25, 29; Mk 4, 25; Lk 8, 18; 19, 26), the reference transcends the original level. God gives further understanding to one who accepts the revealed mystery; from the one who does not, he will take it away (note the "theological passive," **more will be given, what he has will be taken away**).

13, 13: Because 'they look . . . or understand': Matthew softens his Marcan source, which states that Jesus speaks in parables so that the crowds may not understand (Mk 4, 12), and makes such speaking a punishment given **because** they have not accepted his previous clear teaching. However, his citation of Is 6, 9–10 in v 14 supports the harsher Marcan view.

v: Mk 4, 1-12; Lk 8, 4-10. *w:* 25, 29; Mk 4, 25; Lk 8, 18; 19, 26.
x: Jn 9, 39. *y:* Is 6, 9-10; Jn 12, 40; Acts 28, 26-27; Rom 11, 8.

The Privilege of Discipleship. [16z]*"But blessed are your eyes, because they see, and your ears, because they hear. [17]Amen, I say to you, many prophets and righteous people longed to see what you see but did not see it, and to hear what you hear but did not hear it.

The Explanation of the Parable of the Sower. [18a]*"Hear then the parable of the sower. [19]The seed sown on the path is the one who hears the word of the kingdom without understanding it, and the evil one comes and steals away what was sown in his heart. [20]The seed sown on rocky ground is the one who hears the word and receives it at once with joy. [21]But he has no root and lasts only for a time. When some tribulation or persecution comes because of the word, he immediately falls away. [22]The seed sown among thorns is the one who hears the word, but then worldly anxiety and the lure of riches choke the word and it bears no fruit. [23]But the seed sown on rich soil is the one who hears the word and understands it, who indeed bears fruit and yields a hundred or sixty or thirtyfold."

The Parable of the Weeds among the Wheat. [24]*He proposed another parable to them. "The kingdom of heaven may be likened to a man who sowed good seed in his field. [25]*While everyone was asleep his enemy came and sowed weeds all through the wheat, and then went off. [26]When the crop grew and bore fruit, the weeds appeared as well. [27]The slaves of the householder came to him and said, 'Master, did you not sow good seed in your field? Where have the weeds come from?' [28]He answered, 'An enemy has done this.' His slaves said to him, 'Do you want us to go and pull them up?' [29]He replied, 'No, if you pull up the weeds you might uproot the wheat along with them. [30b]*Let them grow together until harvest; then at harvest time I will say to the harvesters, "First collect the weeds and tie them in bundles for burning; but gather the wheat into my barn." ' "

The Parable of the Mustard Seed. [31c]*He proposed another parable to them: "The kingdom of heaven is like a mustard seed that a person took and sowed in a field. [32d]*It is the smallest of all the seeds, yet when full-grown it is the largest of plants. It becomes a large bush, and the 'birds of the sky come and dwell in its branches.' "

The Parable of the Yeast. [33e]*He spoke to them another parable. "The kingdom of

---

13, 16–17: Unlike the unbelieving crowds, the disciples have seen that which the **prophets** and the **righteous** of the Old Testament **longed to see** without having their longing fulfilled.

13, 18–23: See Mk 4, 14–20; Lk 8, 11–15. In this explanation of the parable the emphasis is on the various types of soil on which the seed falls, i.e., on the dispositions with which the preaching of Jesus is received. The second and third types particularly are explained in such a way as to support the view held by many scholars that the explanation derives not from Jesus but from early Christian reflection upon apostasy from the faith that was the consequence of persecution and worldliness respectively. Others, however, hold that the explanation may come basically from Jesus even though it was developed in the light of later Christian experience. The four types of persons envisaged are (1) those who never accept **the word of the kingdom** (19); (2) those who believe for a while but fall away because of **persecution** (20–21); (3) those who believe, but in whom **the word** is choked by **worldly anxiety** and the seduction of **riches** (22); (4) those who respond to **the word** and produce **fruit** abundantly (23).

13, 24–30: This parable is peculiar to Matthew. The comparison in v 24 does not mean that **the kingdom of heaven may be likened** simply to the person in question but to the situation narrated in the whole story. The refusal of the **householder** to allow his **slaves** to separate **the wheat** from

the weeds while they are still growing is a warning to the disciples not to attempt to anticipate the final judgment of God by a definitive exclusion of sinners from the kingdom. In its present stage it is composed of the good and the bad. The judgment of God alone will eliminate the sinful. Until then there must be patience and the preaching of repentance.

13, 25: Weeds: darnel, a poisonous weed that in its first stage of growth resembles wheat.

13, 30: Harvest: a common biblical metaphor for the time of God's judgment; cf Jer 51, 33; Jl 4, 13; Hos 6, 11.

13, 31–33: See Mk 4, 30–32; Lk 13, 18–21. The parables of the mustard seed and the yeast illustrate the same point: the amazing contrast between the small beginnings of the kingdom and its marvelous expansion.

13, 32: See Dn 4, 7–9.17–19, where the birds nesting in the tree represent the people of Nebuchadnezzar's kingdom. See also Ez 17, 23 and 31, 6.

13, 33: Except in this Q parable and in 16, 12, **yeast** (or "leaven") is, in New Testament usage, a symbol of corruption (see 16, 6.11–12; Mk 8, 15; Lk 12, 1; 1 Cor 5, 6–8; Gal 5, 9). **Three measures:** an enormous amount, enough to feed a hundred people. The exaggeration of this element of the parable points to the greatness of the kingdom's effect.

z: Lk 10, 23-24; 1 Pt 1, 10-12. a: Mk 4, 13-20; Lk 8, 11-15. b: 3, 12. c: Mk 4, 30-32; Lk 13, 18-19. d: Ez 17, 23; 31, 6; Dn 4, 7-9.17-19. e: Lk 13, 20-21.

heaven is like yeast that a woman took and mixed with three measures of wheat flour until the whole batch was leavened."

The Use of Parables. [34f]*All these things Jesus spoke to the crowds in parables. He spoke to them only in parables, [35g]*to fulfill what had been said through the prophet:

"I will open my mouth in parables,
I will announce what has lain hidden
    from the foundation [of the
    world]."

The Explanation of the Parable of the Weeds. [36]*Then, dismissing the crowds, he went into the house. His disciples approached him and said, "Explain to us the parable of the weeds in the field." [37]*He said in reply, "He who sows good seed is the Son of Man, [38]*the field is the world, the good seed the children of the kingdom. The weeds are the children of the evil one, [39]*and the enemy who sows them is the devil. The harvest is the end of the age, and the harvesters are angels. [40]*Just as weeds are collected and burned [up] with fire, so will it be at the end of the age. [41]*The Son of Man will send his angels, and they will collect out of his king-

dom all who cause others to sin and all evildoers. [42h]*They will throw them into the fiery furnace, where there will be wailing and grinding of teeth. [43i]*Then the righteous will shine like the sun in the kingdom of their Father. Whoever has ears ought to hear.

More Parables. [44j]*"The kingdom of heaven is like a treasure buried in a field, which a person finds and hides again, and out of joy goes and sells all that he has and buys that field. [45]Again, the kingdom of heaven is like a merchant searching for fine pearls. [46]When he finds a pearl of great price, he goes and sells all that he has and buys it. [47]Again, the kingdom of heaven is like a net thrown into the sea, which collects fish of every kind. [48]When it is full they haul it ashore and sit down to put what is good into buckets. What is bad they throw away. [49]Thus it will be at the end of the age. The angels will go out and separate the wicked from the righteous [50]and throw them into the fiery furnace, where there will be wailing and grinding of teeth.

Treasures New and Old. [51]*"Do you understand all these things?" They answered, "Yes." [52]*And he replied, "Then every scribe

---

13, 34: Only in parables: see vv 10–15.

13, 35: The prophet: some textual witnesses read "Isaiah the prophet." The quotation is actually from Ps 78, 2; the first line corresponds to the LXX text of the psalm. The psalm's title ascribes it to Asaph, the founder of one of the guilds of temple musicians. He is called "the prophet" (NAB "the seer") in 2 Chr 29, 30, but it is doubtful that Matthew averted to that; for him, any Old Testament text that could be seen as fulfilled in Jesus was prophetic.

13, 36: Dismissing the crowds: the return of Jesus to the house marks a break with the crowds, who represent unbelieving Israel. From now on his attention is directed more and more to his disciples and to their instruction. The rest of the discourse is addressed to them alone.

13, 37–43: In the explanation of the parable of the weeds emphasis lies on the fearful end of the wicked, whereas the parable itself concentrates on patience with them until judgment time.

13, 38: The field is the world: this presupposes the resurrection of Jesus and the granting to him of "all power in heaven and on earth" (28, 18).

13, 39: The end of the age: this phrase is found only in Mt (13, 40.49; 24, 3; 28, 20).

13, 41: His kingdom: the **kingdom** of the **Son of Man** is distinguished from that of the Father (43); see 1 Cor 15, 24–25. The church is the place where Jesus' kingdom is manifested, but his royal authority embraces the entire world; see the note on 13, 38.

13, 43: See Dn 12, 3.

13, 44–50: The first two of the last three parables of the discourse have the same point. The **person** who **finds** a buried **treasure** and the **merchant** who finds a **pearl of great price** sell **all** that they have to acquire these finds; similarly, the one who understands the supreme value of the kingdom gives up whatever he must to obtain it. The **joy** with which this is done is made explicit in the first parable, but it may be presumed in the second also. The concluding parable of the fishnet resembles the explanation of the parable of the weeds with its stress upon the final exclusion of evil persons from the kingdom.

13, 44: In the unsettled conditions of Palestine in Jesus' time, it was not unusual to guard valuables by burying them in the ground.

13, 51: Matthew typically speaks of the understanding of the disciples.

13, 52: Since Matthew tends to identify the disciples and the Twelve (see the note on 10, 1), this saying about the Christian **scribe** cannot be taken as applicable to all who accept the message of Jesus. While the Twelve are in many ways representative of all who believe in him, they are also distinguished from them in certain respects. The church of Matthew has leaders among whom are a group designated as "scribes" (23, 34). Like the scribes of Israel, they are teachers. It is the Twelve and these their later counterparts to whom

f: Mk 4, 33-34.   *g:* Ps 78, 2.   *h:* 8, 12; Rv 21, 8.   *i:* Dn 12, 3.   *j:* Prv 2, 4; 4, 7.

who has been instructed in the kingdom of heaven is like the head of a household who brings from his storeroom both the new and the old." [53] When Jesus finished these parables, he went away from there.

V: Jesus, the Kingdom, and the Church

The Rejection at Nazareth. [54k]*He came to his native place and taught the people in their synagogue. They were astonished and said, "Where did this man get such wisdom and mighty deeds? [55m] Is he not the carpenter's son? Is not his mother named Mary and his brothers James, Joseph, Simon, and Judas? [56] Are not his sisters all with us? Where did this man get all this?" [57n] And they took offense at him. But Jesus said to them, "A prophet is not without honor except in his native place and in his own house." [58] And he did not work many mighty deeds there because of their lack of faith.

CHAPTER 14

See RG 284–85

Herod's Opinion of Jesus. [1opq]*At that time Herod the tetrarch heard of the reputation of Jesus [2] and said to his servants, "This man is John the Baptist. He has been raised from the dead; that is why mighty powers are at work in him."

The Death of John the Baptist. [3r]*Now Herod had arrested John, bound [him], and put him in prison on account of Herodias, the wife of his brother Philip, [4s] for John had said to him, "It is not lawful for you to have her." [5t] Although he wanted to kill him, he feared the people, for they regarded him as a prophet. [6] But at a birthday celebration for Herod, the daughter of Herodias performed a dance before the guests and delighted Herod [7] so much that he swore to give her whatever she might ask for. [8] Prompted by her mother, she said, "Give me here on a platter the head of John the Baptist." [9] The king was distressed, but because of his oaths and the guests who were present, he ordered that it be given, [10] and he had John beheaded in the prison. [11] His head was brought in on a platter and given to the girl, who took it to her mother. [12] His disciples came and took away the corpse and buried him; and they went and told Jesus.

The Return of the Twelve and the Feeding of the Five Thousand. [13u]*When Jesus heard

---

this verse applies. The **scribe . . . instructed in the kingdom of heaven** knows both the teaching of Jesus (**the new**) and the law and prophets (**the old**) and provides in his own teaching **both the new and the old** as interpreted and fulfilled by the new. On the translation **head of a household** (for the same Greek word translated **householder** in v 27), see the note on 24, 45–51.

13, 54—17, 27: This section is the narrative part of the fourth book of the gospel.

13, 54–58: After the Sermon on the Mount the crowds are in admiring astonishment at Jesus' teaching (7, 28); here the astonishment is of those who take **offense at him.** Familiarity with his background and family leads them to regard him as pretentious. Matthew modifies his Marcan source (6, 1–6). Jesus is not the carpenter but **the carpenter's son** (55), "and among his own kin" is omitted (57), **he did not work many mighty deeds** in face of such unbelief (58) rather than the Marcan ". . . he was not able to perform any mighty deed there" (6, 5), and there is no mention of his amazement at his townspeople's lack of faith.

14, 1–12: The murder of the Baptist by Herod Antipas prefigures the death of Jesus (see 17, 12). The Marcan source (6, 14–29) is much reduced and in some points changed. In Mk Herod reveres John as a holy man and the desire to kill him is attributed to Herodias (6, 19.20), whereas here that desire is Herod's from the beginning (5).

14, 1: Herod the tetrarch: Herod Antipas, son of Herod the Great. When the latter died, his territory was divided among three of his surviving sons, Archelaus who received half of it (2, 23), Herod Antipas who became ruler of Galilee and Perea, and Philip who became ruler of northern Transjordan. Since he received a quarter of his father's domain, Antipas is accurately designated **tetrarch** ("ruler of a fourth [part]"), although in v 9 Matthew repeats the "king" of his Marcan source (6, 26).

14, 3: Herodias was not the wife of Herod's half-brother Philip but of another half-brother, Herod Boethus. The union was prohibited by Lv 18, 16; 20, 21. According to Josephus (**Antiquities** 18, 5, 2 §§116–19), Herod imprisoned and then executed John because he feared that the Baptist's influence over the people might enable him to lead a rebellion.

14, 13–21: The feeding of the five thousand is the only miracle of Jesus that is recounted in all four gospels. The principal reason for that may be that it was seen as anticipating the Eucharist and the final banquet in the kingdom (8, 11; 26, 29), but it looks not only forward but backward, to the feeding of Israel with manna in the desert at the time of the Exodus (Ex 16), a miracle that in some contemporary Jewish expectation would be repeated in the messianic age (2 Baruch 29, 8). It may also be meant to recall Elisha's feeding a hundred men with small provisions (2 Kgs 4, 42–44).

k: Mk 6, 1-6; Lk 4, 16-30. l: 2, 23; Jn 1, 46; 7, 15. m: 12, 46; 27, 56; Jn 6, 42. n: Jn 4, 44. o: Mk 6, 14-29. p: Lk 3, 1. q: Lk 9, 7-9. r: Lk 3, 19-20. s: Lv 18, 16; 20, 21. t: 21, 26. u: 15, 32-38; Mk 6, 32-44; Lk 9, 10-17; Jn 6, 1-13.

of it, he withdrew in a boat to a deserted place by himself. The crowds heard of this and followed him on foot from their towns. [14]When he disembarked and saw the vast crowd, his heart was moved with pity for them, and he cured their sick. [15]When it was evening, the disciples approached him and said, "This is a deserted place and it is already late; dismiss the crowds so that they can go to the villages and buy food for themselves." [16][Jesus] said to them, "There is no need for them to go away; give them some food yourselves." [17]But they said to him, "Five loaves and two fish are all we have here." [18]Then he said, "Bring them here to me," [19]*and he ordered the crowds to sit down on the grass. Taking the five loaves and the two fish, and looking up to heaven, he said the blessing, broke the loaves, and gave them to the disciples, who in turn gave them to the crowds. [20]*They all ate and were satisfied, and they picked up the fragments left over—twelve wicker baskets full. [21]Those who ate were about five thousand men, not counting women and children.

The Walking on the Water. [22v]*Then he made the disciples get into the boat and precede him to the other side, while he dismissed the crowds. [23w]After doing so, he went up on the mountain by himself to pray. When it was evening he was there alone. [24]Meanwhile the boat, already a few miles offshore, was being tossed about by the waves, for the wind was against it. [25]*During the fourth watch of the night, he came toward them, walking on the sea. [26]When the disciples saw him walking on the sea they were terrified. "It is a ghost," they said, and they cried out in fear. [27]*At once [Jesus] spoke to them, "Take courage, it is I; do not be afraid." [28]Peter said to him in reply, "Lord, if it is you, command me to come to you on the water." [29]He said, "Come." Peter got out of the boat and began to walk on the water toward Jesus. [30x]But when he saw how [strong] the wind was he became frightened; and, beginning to sink, he cried out, "Lord, save me!" [31]*Immediately Jesus stretched out his hand and caught him, and said to him, "O you of little faith, why did you doubt?" [32]After they got into the boat, the wind died down. [33y]*Those who were in the boat did him homage, saying, "Truly, you are the Son of God."

The Healings at Gennesaret. [34z]After making the crossing, they came to land at Gennesaret. [35]When the men of that place recognized him, they sent word to all the surrounding country. People brought to him all those who were sick [36a]and begged him that they might touch only the tassel on his cloak, and as many as touched it were healed.

CHAPTER 15

The Tradition of the Elders. [1b]*Then Pharisees and scribes came to Jesus from

See RG 284-85

14, 19: The **taking,** saying the blessing, breaking, and giving to the disciples correspond to the actions of Jesus over the bread at the Last Supper (26, 26). Since they were usual at any Jewish meal, that correspondence does not necessarily indicate a eucharistic reference here. Matthew's silence about Jesus' dividing the fish among the people (Mk 6, 41) is perhaps more significant in that regard.

14, 20: The fragments left over: as in Elisha's miracle, food was **left over** after all had been fed. The word **fragments** (Greek **klasmata**) is used, in the singular, of the broken bread of the Eucharist in **Didache** 9, 3–4.

14, 22–33: The disciples, laboring against the turbulent sea, are saved by Jesus. For his power over the waters, see the note on 8, 26. Here that power is expressed also by his **walking on the sea** (25; cf Ps 77, 20; Jb 9, 8). Matthew has inserted into the Marcan story (Mk 6, 45–52) material that belongs to his special traditions on Peter (28–31).

14, 25: The fourth watch of the night: between 3 a.m. and 6 a.m. The Romans divided the twelve hours between 6 p.m. and 6 a.m. into four equal parts called "watches."

14, 27: It is I: see the note on Mk 6, 50.

14, 31: You of little faith: see the note on 6, 30. **Why did you doubt?:** the verb is peculiar to Matthew and occurs elsewhere only in 28, 17.

14, 33: This confession is in striking contrast to the Marcan parallel (6, 51) where the disciples are "completely astounded."

15, 1–20: This dispute begins with the question of the Pharisees and scribes why Jesus' disciples are breaking **the tradition of the elders** about washing one's hands before eating (2). Jesus' counterquestion accuses his opponents of breaking **the commandment of God for the sake of** their **tradition** (3) and illustrates this by their interpretation of the commandment of the Decalogue concerning parents (4–6). Denouncing them as hypocrites, he applies to them a derogatory prophecy of Isaiah (7–8). Then with a wider audience (**the crowd,** 10) he goes beyond the violation of tradition with which the dispute has started. The parable (11) is an attack on the Mosaic law concerning clean and unclean foods, similar

v: Mk 6, 45-52; Jn 6, 16-21. w: Mk 1, 35; Lk 5, 16; 6, 12. x: 8, 25-26. y: 16, 16. z: Mk 6, 53-56. a: 9, 20-22. b: Mk 7, 1-23.

Jerusalem and said, [2c]*"Why do your disciples break the tradition of the elders? They do not wash [their] hands when they eat a meal." [3]*He said to them in reply, "And why do you break the commandment of God for the sake of your tradition? [4d]For God said, 'Honor your father and your mother,' and 'Whoever curses father or mother shall die.' [5]*But you say, 'Whoever says to father or mother, "Any support you might have had from me is dedicated to God," [6]need not honor his father.' You have nullified the word of God for the sake of your tradition. [7]Hypocrites, well did Isaiah prophesy about you when he said:

[8e]*"This people honors me with their lips,
  but their hearts are far from me;
[9f]in vain do they worship me,
  teaching as doctrines human
    precepts.' "

[10g]He summoned the crowd and said to them, "Hear and understand. [11]It is not what enters one's mouth that defiles that person; but what comes out of the mouth is what defiles one." [12]Then his disciples approached and said to him, "Do you know that the Pharisees took offense when they heard what you said?" [13]*He said in reply, "Every plant that my heavenly Father has not planted will be uprooted. [14h]Let them alone; they are blind guides [of the blind]. If a blind person leads a blind person, both will fall into a pit." [15]*Then Peter said to him in reply, "Explain [this] parable to us." [16]He said to them, "Are even you still without understanding? [17]Do you not realize that everything that enters the mouth passes into the stomach and is expelled into the latrine? [18i]But the things that come out of the mouth come from the heart, and they defile. [19]*For from the heart come evil thoughts, murder, adultery, unchastity, theft, false witness, blasphemy. [20]These are what defile a person, but to eat with unwashed hands does not defile."

The Canaanite Woman's Faith. [21j]*Then Jesus went from that place and withdrew to the region of Tyre and Sidon. [22]And behold, a Canaanite woman of that district came and called out, "Have pity on me, Lord, Son of David! My daughter is tormented by a demon." [23]But he did not say a word in answer to her. His disciples came and asked him, "Send her away, for she keeps calling out after us." [24]*He said in reply, "I was sent only to the lost sheep of the house of Israel." [25k]But the woman came and did him homage, saying, "Lord, help me." [26]*He said in reply, "It is not right to take the food of the children and throw it to the dogs." [27]She said, "Please, Lord, for even the dogs eat the scraps that fall from the table of their masters." [28l]*Then Jesus said to her in reply, "O woman, great is your

---

to those antitheses that abrogate the law (5, 31–32.33–34.38–39). After a warning to his disciples not to follow the moral guidance of the Pharisees (13–14), he explains the **parable (15)** to them, saying that defilement comes not from what **enters the mouth** (17) but from the evil thoughts and deeds that rise from within, **from the heart** (18–20). The last verse returns to the starting point of the dispute (eating **with unwashed hands**). Because of Matthew's omission of Mk 7, 19b, some scholars think that Matthew has weakened the Marcan repudiation of the Mosaic food laws. But that half verse is ambiguous in the Greek, which may be the reason for its omission here.

15, 2: **The tradition of the elders:** see the note on Mk 7, 5. The purpose of the handwashing was to remove defilement caused by contact with what was ritually unclean.

15, 3–4: For the commandment see Ex 20, 12 (// Dt 5, 16); 21, 17. The honoring of one's parents had to do with supporting them in their needs.

15, 5: See the note on Mk 7, 11.

15, 8: The text of Is 29, 13 is quoted approximately according to the Septuagint.

15, 13–14: Jesus leads his disciples away from the teaching authority of the Pharisees.

15, 15: Matthew specifies **Peter** as the questioner, unlike Mk 7, 17. Given his tendency to present the disciples as more understanding than in his Marcan source, it is noteworthy that here he retains the Marcan rebuke, although in a slightly milder form. This may be due to his wish to correct the Jewish Christians within his church who still held to the food laws and thus separated themselves from Gentile Christians who did not observe them.

15, 19: The Marcan list of thirteen things that defile (7, 21–22) is here reduced to seven that partially cover the content of the Decalogue.

15, 21–28: See the note on 8, 5–13.

15, 24: See the note on 10, 5–6.

15, 26: **The children:** the people of Israel. **Dogs:** see note on 7, 6.

15, 28: As in the case of the cure of the centurion's servant (8, 10), Matthew ascribes Jesus' granting the request to the woman's **great faith,** a point not made equally explicit in the Marcan parallel (7, 24–30).

c: Lk 11, 38. d: Ex 20, 12; 21, 17; Lv 20, 9; Dt 5, 16; Prv 20, 20. e: Is 29, 13 LXX. f: Col 2, 23. g: Mk 7, 14. h: 23, 16.19.24; Lk 6, 39; Jn 9, 40. i: 12, 34. j: Mk 7, 24-30. k: 10, 6. l: 8, 10.

faith! Let it be done for you as you wish." And her daughter was healed from that hour.

The Healing of Many People. [29]Moving on from there Jesus walked by the Sea of Galilee, went up on the mountain, and sat down there. [30m]Great crowds came to him, having with them the lame, the blind, the deformed, the mute, and many others. They placed them at his feet, and he cured them. [31]The crowds were amazed when they saw the mute speaking, the deformed made whole, the lame walking, and the blind able to see, and they glorified the God of Israel.

The Feeding of the Four Thousand. [32n]Jesus summoned his disciples and said, "My heart is moved with pity for the crowd, for they have been with me now for three days and have nothing to eat. I do not want to send them away hungry, for fear they may collapse on the way." [33]The disciples said to him, "Where could we ever get enough bread in this deserted place to satisfy such a crowd?" [34]Jesus said to them, "How many loaves do you have?" "Seven," they replied, "and a few fish." [35]He ordered the crowd to sit down on the ground. [36]Then he took the seven loaves and the fish, gave thanks, broke the loaves, and gave them to the disciples, who in turn gave them to the crowds. [37o]They all ate and were satisfied. They picked up the fragments left over—seven baskets full. [38]Those who ate were four thousand men, not counting women and children. [39]And when he had dismissed the

crowds, he got into the boat and came to the district of Magadan.

CHAPTER 16

See RG 284–87

The Demand for a Sign. [1p]*The Pharisees and Sadducees came and, to test him, asked him to show them a sign from heaven. [2]*He said to them in reply, "[In the evening you say, 'Tomorrow will be fair, for the sky is red'; [3q]and, in the morning, 'Today will be stormy, for the sky is red and threatening.' You know how to judge the appearance of the sky, but you cannot judge the signs of the times.] [4r]*An evil and unfaithful generation seeks a sign, but no sign will be given it except the sign of Jonah." Then he left them and went away.

The Leaven of the Pharisees and Sadducees. [5s]*In coming to the other side of the sea, the disciples had forgotten to bring bread. [6t]*Jesus said to them, "Look out, and beware of the leaven of the Pharisees and Sadducees." [7]*They concluded among themselves, saying, "It is because we have brought no bread." [8]When Jesus became aware of this he said, "You of little faith, why do you conclude among yourselves that it is because you have no bread? [9u]Do you not yet understand, and do you not remember the five loaves for the five thousand, and how many wicker baskets you took up? [10v]Or the seven loaves for the four thousand, and how many baskets you took up? [11]How do you not comprehend that I was not speaking to you about bread? Beware of the

---

15, 32–39: Most probably this story is a doublet of that of the feeding of the five thousand (14, 13–21). It differs from it notably only in that Jesus takes the initiative, not the disciples (32), and in the numbers: the crowd has been with Jesus **three days** (32), **seven loaves** are multiplied (36), **seven baskets** of **fragments** remain after the feeding (37), and **four thousand** men are fed (38).

15, 36: Gave thanks: see 14, 19, "said the blessing." There is no difference in meaning. The thanksgiving was a blessing of God for his benefits.

16, 1: A sign from heaven: see the note on 12, 38–42.

16, 2–3: The answer of Jesus in these verses is omitted in many important textual witnesses, and it is very uncertain that it is an original part of this gospel. It resembles Lk 12, 54–56 and may have been inserted from there. It rebukes the Pharisees and Sadducees who are able to read indications of coming weather but not the indications of the coming kingdom in the signs that Jesus does offer, his mighty deeds and teaching.

16, 4: See the notes on 12, 39.40.

16, 5–12: Jesus' warning his disciples against **the teaching of the Pharisees and Sadducees** comes immediately before his promise to confer on Peter the authority to bind and to loose on earth (19), an authority that will be confirmed in heaven. Such authority most probably has to do, at least in part, with teaching. The rejection of the teaching authority of the Pharisees (see also 12, 12–14) prepares for a new one derived from Jesus.

16, 6: Leaven: see the note on 13, 33. **Sadducees:** Matthew's Marcan source speaks rather of "the leaven of Herod" (8, 15).

16, 7–11: The disciples, men **of little faith,** misunderstand Jesus' metaphorical use of **leaven,** forgetting that, as the feeding of the crowds shows, he is not at a loss to provide them with bread.

m: Is 35, 5-6. *n:* Mk 8, 1-10. *o:* 16, 10. *p:* Mk 8, 11-21. *q:* Lk 12, 54-56. *r:* 12, 39; Jon 2, 1. *s:* Mk 8, 14-21. *t:* Lk 12, 1. *u:* 14, 17-21; Jn 6, 9. *v:* 15, 34-38.

leaven of the Pharisees and Sadducees." [12]*Then they understood that he was not telling them to beware of the leaven of bread, but of the teaching of the Pharisees and Sadducees.

Peter's Confession about Jesus. [13w]*When Jesus went into the region of Caesarea Philippi he asked his disciples, "Who do people say that the Son of Man is?" [14x]*They replied, "Some say John the Baptist, others Elijah, still others Jeremiah or one of the prophets." [15]He said to them, "But who do you say that I am?" [16y]*Simon Peter said in reply, "You are the Messiah, the Son of the living God." [17]*Jesus said to him in reply, "Blessed are you, Simon son of Jonah. For flesh and blood has not revealed this to you, but my heavenly Father. [18z]*And so I say to you, you are Peter, and upon this rock I will build my church, and the gates of the netherworld shall not prevail against it. [19a]*I will give you the keys to the kingdom of heaven.

16, 12: After his rebuke, the disciples understand that by **leaven** he meant the corrupting influence of the **teaching of the Pharisees and Sadducees.** The evangelist probably understands this **teaching** as common to both groups. Since at the time of Jesus' ministry the two differed widely on points of teaching, e.g., the resurrection of the dead, and at the time of the evangelist the Sadducee party was no longer a force in Judaism, the supposed common **teaching** fits neither period. The disciples' eventual understanding of Jesus' warning contrasts with their continuing obtuseness in the Marcan parallel (8, 14–21).

16, 13–20: The Marcan confession of Jesus as Messiah, made by Peter as spokesman for the other disciples (8, 27–29; cf also Lk 9, 18–20), is modified significantly here. The confession is of Jesus both as **Messiah** and as **Son of the living God** (16). Jesus' response, drawn principally from material peculiar to Matthew, attributes the confession to a divine revelation granted to Peter alone (17) and makes him the **rock** on which Jesus **will build** his **church** (18) and the church whose authority in the church **on earth** will be confirmed in **heaven,** i.e., by God (19).

16, 13: Caesarea Philippi: situated about twenty miles north of the Sea of Galilee in the territory ruled by Philip, a son of Herod the Great, tetrarch from 4 B.C. until his death in A.D. 34 (see the note on 14, 1). He rebuilt the town of Paneas, naming it **Caesarea** in honor of the emperor, and **Philippi** ("of Philip") to distinguish it from the seaport in Samaria that was also called Caesarea. **Who do people say that the Son of Man is?:** although the question differs from the Marcan parallel (8, 27: "Who . . . that I am?"), the meaning is the same, for Jesus here refers to himself as the **Son of Man** (cf 15).

16, 14: John the Baptist: see 14, 2. Elijah: cf Mal 3, 23–24; Sir 48, 10; and see the note on 3, 4. Jeremiah: an addition of Matthew to the Marcan source.

16, 16: The Son of the living God: see 2, 15; 3, 17. The addition of this exalted title to the Marcan confession eliminates whatever ambiguity was attached to the title Messiah. This, among other things, supports the view proposed by many scholars that Matthew has here combined his source's confession with a post-resurrectional confession of faith in Jesus as **Son of the living God** that belonged to the appearance of the risen Jesus to Peter; cf 1 Cor 15, 5; Lk 24, 34.

16, 17: Flesh and blood: a Semitic expression for human beings, especially in their weakness. **Has not revealed this . . . but my heavenly Father:** that Peter's faith is spoken of as coming not through human means but through a revelation from God is similar to Paul's description of his recognition of who Jesus was; see Gal 1, 15–16, ". . . when he [God] . . . was pleased to reveal his Son to me. . . ."

16, 18: You are Peter, and upon this rock I will build my church: the Aramaic word kēpā'* meaning **rock** and transliterated into Greek as **Kēphas** is the name by which Peter is called in the Pauline letters (1 Cor 1, 12; 3, 22; 9, 5; 15, 4; Gal 1, 18; 2, 9.11.14) except in Gal 2, 7–8 ("Peter"). It is translated as **Petros** ("Peter") in Jn 1, 42. The presumed original Aramaic of Jesus' statement would have been, in English, "You are the Rock (**Kēpā'***) and upon this rock (**kēpā'***) I will build my church." The Greek text probably means the same, for the difference in gender between the masculine noun **petros**, the disciple's new name, and the feminine noun **petra** (rock) may be due simply to the unsuitability of using a feminine noun as the proper name of a male. Although the two words were generally used with slightly different nuances, they were also used interchangeably with the same meaning, "rock." **Church:** this word (Greek **ekklēsia**) occurs in the gospels only here and in 18, 17 (twice). There are several possibilities for an Aramaic original. Jesus' **church** means the community that he **will** gather and that, like a building, will have Peter as its solid foundation. That function of Peter consists in his being witness to Jesus as **the Messiah, the Son of the living God. The gates of the netherworld shall not prevail against it:** the netherworld (Greek **Hadēs**, the abode of the dead) is conceived of as a walled city whose **gates** will not close in upon the church of Jesus, i.e., it will not be overcome by the power of death.

16, 19: The keys to the kingdom of heaven: the image of the **keys** is probably drawn from Is 22, 15–25, where Eliakim, who succeeds Shebna as master of the palace, is given "the key of the House of David," which he authoritatively "opens" and "shuts" (22, 22). **Whatever you bind . . . loosed in heaven:** there are many instances in rabbinic literature of the binding-loosing imagery. Of the several meanings given there to the metaphor, two are of special importance here: the giving of authoritative teaching, and the lifting or imposing of the ban of excommunication. It is disputed whether the image of **the keys** and that of binding and loosing are different metaphors meaning the same thing. In any case, the promise of the keys is given to Peter alone. In 18, 18 all the disciples are given the power of binding and loosing, but the context of that verse suggests that there the power of excommunication alone is intended. That **the keys** are those to the **kingdom of heaven** and that Peter's exercise of authority in the church **on earth** will be confirmed **in heaven** show an intimate connection between, but not an identification of, the church and the **kingdom of heaven.**

w: Mk 8, 27-29; Lk 9, 18-20.　x: 14, 2.　y: Jn 6, 69.　z: Jn 1, 42.
a: Is 22, 22; Rv 3, 7.

Whatever you bind on earth shall be bound in heaven; and whatever you loose on earth shall be loosed in heaven." [20b]*Then he strictly ordered his disciples to tell no one that he was the Messiah.

The First Prediction of the Passion. [21cd]*From that time on, Jesus began to show his disciples that he must go to Jerusalem and suffer greatly from the elders, the chief priests, and the scribes, and be killed and on the third day be raised. [22]*Then Peter took him aside and began to rebuke him, "God forbid, Lord! No such thing shall ever happen to you." [23e]He turned and said to Peter, "Get behind me, Satan! You are an obstacle to me. You are thinking not as God does, but as human beings do."

The Conditions of Discipleship. [24f]*Then

Jesus said to his disciples, "Whoever wishes to come after me must deny himself, take up his cross, and follow me. [25g]*For whoever wishes to save his life will lose it, but whoever loses his life for my sake will find it. [26]What profit would there be for one to gain the whole world and forfeit his life? Or what can one give in exchange for his life? [27h]*For the Son of Man will come with his angels in his Father's glory, and then he will repay everyone according to his conduct. [28]*Amen, I say to you, there are some standing here who will not taste death until they see the Son of Man coming in his kingdom."

CHAPTER 17

The Transfiguration of Jesus. [1i]*After six days Jesus took Peter, James, and John

See RG 235-87

16, 20: Cf Mk 8, 30. Matthew makes explicit that the prohibition has to do with speaking of Jesus as **the Messiah;** see the note on Mk 8, 27–30.

16, 21–23: This first prediction of the passion follows Mk 8, 31–33 in the main and serves as a corrective to an understanding of Jesus' messiahship as solely one of glory and triumph. By his addition of **from that time on** (21) Matthew has emphasized that Jesus' revelation of his coming suffering and death marks a new phase of the gospel. Neither this nor the two later passion predictions (17, 22–23; 20, 17–19) can be taken as sayings that, as they stand, go back to Jesus himself. However, it is probable that he foresaw that his mission would entail suffering and perhaps death, but was confident that he would ultimately be vindicated by God (see 26, 29).

16, 21: He: the Marcan parallel (8, 31) has "the Son of Man." Since Matthew has already designated Jesus by that title (13), its omission here is not significant. The Matthean prediction is equally about the sufferings of the Son of Man. **Must:** this necessity is part of the tradition of all the synoptics; cf Mk 8, 31; Lk 9, 21. **The elders, the chief priests, and the scribes:** see the note on Mk 8, 31. **On the third day:** so also Lk 9, 22, against the Marcan "after three days" (8, 31). Matthew's formulation is, in the Greek, almost identical with the pre-Pauline fragment of the kerygma in 1 Cor 15, 4, and also with Hos 6, 2, which many take to be the Old Testament background to the confession that Jesus was raised **on the third day.** Josephus uses "after three days" and "on the third day" interchangeably (**Antiquities** 7, 11, 6 §§280–81; 8, 8, 1–2 §§214, 218) and there is probably no difference in meaning between the two phrases.

16, 22–23: Peter's refusal to accept Jesus' predicted suffering and death is seen as a satanic attempt to deflect Jesus from his God-appointed course, and the disciple is addressed in terms that recall Jesus' dismissal of the devil in the temptation account (4, 10: "Get away, Satan!"). Peter's satanic purpose is emphasized by Matthew's addition to the Marcan source of the words **You are an obstacle to me.**

16, 24–28: A readiness to follow Jesus even to giving up

one's life for him is the condition for true discipleship; this will be repaid by him at the final judgment.

16, 24: Deny himself: to deny someone is to disown him (see 10, 33; 26, 34–35) and to deny oneself is to disown oneself as the center of one's existence.

16, 25: See the notes on 10, 38.39.

16, 27: The parousia and final judgment are described in 25, 31 in terms almost identical with these.

16, 28: Coming in his kingdom: since the **kingdom** of **the Son of Man** has been described as "the world" and Jesus' sovereignty precedes his final coming in glory (13, 38.41), the **coming** in this verse is not the parousia as in the preceding but the manifestation of Jesus' rule after his resurrection; see the notes on 13, 38.41.

17, 1–8: The account of the transfiguration confirms that Jesus is the **Son** of God (5) and points to fulfillment of the prediction that he will come **in his Father's glory** at the end of the age (16, 27). It has been explained by some as a resurrection appearance retrojected into the time of Jesus' ministry, but that is not probable since the account lacks many of the usual elements of the resurrection-appearance narratives. It draws upon motifs from the Old Testament and noncanonical Jewish apocalyptic literature that express the presence of the heavenly and the divine, e.g., brilliant light, white garments, and the overshadowing cloud.

17, 1: These three disciples are also taken apart from the others by Jesus in Gethsemane (26, 37). **A high mountain:** this has been identified with Tabor or Hermon, but probably no specific mountain was intended by the evangelist or by his Marcan source (9, 2). Its meaning is theological rather than geographical, possibly recalling the revelation to Moses on Mount Sinai (Ex 24, 12–18) and to Elijah at the same place (1 Kgs 19, 8–18; Horeb Sinai).

b: Mk 8, 30; Lk 9, 21. c: Mk 8, 31—9, 1; Lk 9, 22-27. d: 17, 22-23; 20, 17-19. e: 4, 10. f: Lk 14, 27. g: Lk 17, 33; Jn 12, 25. h: 25, 31-33; Jb 34, 11; Ps 62, 13; Jer 17, 10; 2 Thes 1, 7-8. i: Mk 9, 2-8; Lk 9, 28-36.

his brother, and led them up a high mountain by themselves. [2]j*And he was transfigured before them; his face shone like the sun and his clothes became white as light. [3]*And behold, Moses and Elijah appeared to them, conversing with him. [4]*Then Peter said to Jesus in reply, "Lord, it is good that we are here. If you wish, I will make three tents here, one for you, one for Moses, and one for Elijah." [5]k*While he was still speaking, behold, a bright cloud cast a shadow over them, then from the cloud came a voice that said, "This is my beloved Son, with whom I am well pleased; listen to him." [6]*When the disciples heard this, they fell prostrate and were very much afraid. [7]But Jesus came and touched them, saying, "Rise, and do not be afraid." [8]And when the disciples raised their eyes, they saw no one else but Jesus alone.

The Coming of Elijah. [9]l*As they were coming down from the mountain, Jesus charged them, "Do not tell the vision to anyone until the Son of Man has been raised from the dead." [10]m*Then the disciples asked him, "Why do the scribes say that Elijah must come first?" [11]n*He said in reply, "Elijah will indeed come and restore all things; [12]obut I tell you that Elijah has already come, and they did not recognize him but did to him whatever they pleased. So also will the Son of Man suffer at their hands." [13]*Then the disciples understood that he was speaking to them of John the Baptist.

The Healing of a Boy with a Demon. [14]p*When they came to the crowd a man approached, knelt down before him, [15]*and said, "Lord, have pity on my son, for he is a lunatic and suffers severely; often he falls into fire, and often into water. [16]I brought him to your disciples, but they could not cure him." [17]q*Jesus said in reply, "O faithless and perverse generation, how long will

---

17, 2: His face shone like the sun: this is a Matthean addition; cf Dn 10, 6. **His clothes became white as light:** cf Dn 7, 9, where the clothing of God appears "snow bright." For the **white** garments of other heavenly beings, see Rv 4, 4; 7, 9; 19, 14.

17, 3: See the note on Mk 9, 5.

17, 4: Three tents: the booths in which the Israelites lived during the feast of Tabernacles (cf Jn 7, 2) were meant to recall their ancestors' dwelling in booths during the journey from Egypt to the promised land (Lv 23, 39–42). The same Greek word, **skēnē,** here translated **tents,** is used in the LXX for the booths of that feast, and some scholars have suggested that there is an allusion here to that liturgical custom.

17, 5: Cloud cast a shadow over them: see the note on Mk 9, 7. **This is my beloved Son . . . listen to him:** cf 3, 17. The voice repeats the baptismal proclamation about Jesus, with the addition of the command **listen to him.** The latter is a reference to Dt 18, 15 in which the Israelites are commanded to **listen to** the prophet like Moses whom God will raise up for them. The command to **listen to** Jesus is general, but in this context it probably applies particularly to the preceding predictions of his passion and resurrection (16, 21) and of his coming (16, 27.28).

17, 6–7: A Matthean addition; cf Dn 10, 9–10.18–19.

17, 9–13: In response to the disciples' question about the expected return of Elijah, Jesus interprets the mission of the Baptist as the fulfillment of that expectation. But that was not suspected by those who opposed and finally killed him, and Jesus predicts a similar fate for himself.

17, 9: The vision: Matthew alone uses this word to describe the transfiguration. **Until the Son of Man has been raised from the dead:** only in the light of Jesus' resurrection can the meaning of his life and mission be truly understood; until then no testimony to **the vision** will lead people to faith.

17, 10: See the notes on 3, 4; 16, 14.

17, 11–12: The preceding question and this answer may reflect later controversy with Jews who objected to the Christian claims for Jesus that Elijah had not yet come.

17, 13: See 11, 14.

17, 14–20: Matthew has greatly shortened the Marcan story (9, 14–29). Leaving aside several details of the boy's illness, he concentrates on the need for faith, not so much on the part of the boy's father (as does Mark, for Matthew omits Mk 9, 22b-24) but on that of his own disciples whose inability to drive out the demon is ascribed to their **little faith** (20).

17, 15: A lunatic: this description of the boy is peculiar to Matthew. The word occurs in the New Testament only here and in 4, 24 and means one affected or struck by the moon. The symptoms of the boy's illness point to epilepsy, and attacks of this were thought to be caused by phases of the moon.

17, 17: Faithless and perverse: so Matthew and Luke (9, 41) against Mark's **faithless** (9, 19). The Greek word here translated **perverse** is the same as that in Dt 32, 5 LXX, where Moses speaks to his people. There is a problem in knowing to whom the reproach is addressed. Since the Matthean Jesus normally chides his disciples for their **little faith** (as in 20), it would appear that the charge of lack of faith could not be made against them and that the reproach is addressed to unbelievers among the Jews. However in v 20b (**if you have faith the size of a mustard seed**), which is certainly addressed to the disciples, they appear to have not even the smallest faith; if they had, they would have been able to cure the boy. In the light of v 20b the reproach of v 17 could have applied to the disciples. There seems to be an inconsistency between the charge of **little faith** in v 20a and that of not even a little in v 20b.

---

j: 28, 3; Dn 7, 9; 10, 6; Rv 4, 4; 7, 9; 19, 14. *k:* 3, 17; Dt 18, 15; 2 Pt 1, 17. *l:* Mk 9, 9-13. *m:* Mal 3, 23-24. *n:* Lk 1, 17. *o:* 11, 14. *p:* Mk 9, 14-29; Lk 9, 37-43. *q:* Dt 32, 5 LXX.

I be with you? How long will I endure you? Bring him here to me." [18]*Jesus rebuked him and the demon came out of him, and from that hour the boy was cured. [19]Then the disciples approached Jesus in private and said, "Why could we not drive it out?" [20]r*He said to them, "Because of your little faith. Amen, I say to you, if you have faith the size of a mustard seed, you will say to this mountain, 'Move from here to there,' and it will move. Nothing will be impossible for you." [[21]]*

The Second Prediction of the Passion. [22]s*As they were gathering in Galilee, Jesus said to them, "The Son of Man is to be handed over to men, [23]and they will kill him, and he will be raised on the third day." And they were overwhelmed with grief.

Payment of the Temple Tax. [24]t*When they came to Capernaum, the collectors of the tem-

ple tax approached Peter and said, "Doesn't your teacher pay the temple tax?" [25]*"Yes," he said. When he came into the house, before he had time to speak, Jesus asked him, "What is your opinion, Simon? From whom do the kings of the earth take tolls or census tax? From their subjects or from foreigners?" [26]*When he said, "From foreigners," Jesus said to him, "Then the subjects are exempt. [27]*But that we may not offend them, go to the sea, drop in a hook, and take the first fish that comes up. Open its mouth and you will find a coin worth twice the temple tax. Give that to them for me and for you."

CHAPTER 18

The Greatest in the Kingdom. [1]u*At that time the disciples approached Jesus and said, "Who is the greatest in the kingdom of

See RG 285–87

17, 18: The demon came out of him: not until this verse does Matthew indicate that the boy's illness is a case of demoniacal possession.

17, 20: The entire verse is an addition of Matthew who (according to the better attested text) omits the reason given for the disciples' inability in Mk 9, 29. **Little faith:** see the note on 6, 30. **Faith the size of a mustard seed . . . and it will move:** a combination of a Q saying (cf Lk 17, 6) with a Marcan saying (cf Mk 11, 23).

17, 21: Some manuscripts add, "But this kind does not come out except by prayer and fasting"; this is a variant of the better reading of Mk 9, 29.

17, 22–23: The second passion prediction (cf 16, 21–23) is the least detailed of the three and may be the earliest. In the Marcan parallel the disciples do not understand (9, 32); here they understand and are **overwhelmed with grief** at the prospect of Jesus' death (23).

17, 24–27: Like 14, 28–31 and 16, 16b-19, this episode comes from Matthew's special material on Peter. Although the question of **the collectors** concerns Jesus' payment of **the temple tax,** it is put to **Peter.** It is he who receives instruction from Jesus about freedom from the obligation of payment and yet why it should be made. The means of doing so is provided miraculously. The pericope deals with a problem of Matthew's church, whether its members should pay the temple tax, and the answer is given through a word of Jesus conveyed to Peter. Some scholars see here an example of the teaching authority of Peter exercised in the name of Jesus (see 16, 19). The specific problem was a Jewish Christian one and may have arisen when the Matthean church was composed largely of that group.

17, 24: The temple tax: before the destruction of the Jerusalem temple in A.D. 70 every male Jew above nineteen years of age was obliged to make an annual contribution to its upkeep (cf Ex 30, 11–16; Neh 10, 33). After the destruction the Romans imposed upon Jews the obligation of paying that tax for the temple of Jupiter Capitolinus. There is disagreement about which period the story deals with.

17, 25: From their subjects or from foreigners?: the

Greek word here translated **subjects** literally means "sons."

17, 26: Then the subjects are exempt: just as **subjects** are not bound by laws applying to **foreigners,** neither are Jesus and his disciples, who belong to the kingdom of heaven, bound by the duty of paying the temple tax imposed on those who are not of the kingdom. If the Greek is translated "sons," the freedom of Jesus, the Son of God, and of his disciples, children ("sons") of the kingdom (cf 13, 38), is even more clear.

17, 27: That we may not offend them: though they are **exempt** (26), Jesus and his disciples are to avoid giving offense; therefore the tax is to be paid. **A coin worth twice the temple tax:** literally, "a stater," a Greek coin worth two double drachmas. Two double drachmas were equal to the Jewish shekel and the tax was a half-shekel. **For me and for you:** not only Jesus but Peter pays the tax, and this example serves as a standard for the conduct of all the disciples.

18, 1–35: This discourse of the fourth book of the gospel is often called the "church order" discourse, but it lacks most of the considerations usually connected with church order, such as various offices in the church and the duties of each, and deals principally with the relations that must obtain among the members of the church. Beginning with the warning that greatness in **the kingdom of heaven** is measured not by rank or power but by childlikeness (1–5), it deals with the care that the disciples must take not to cause the **little ones to sin** or to neglect them if they stray from the community (6–14), the correction of members who sin (15–18), the efficacy of the prayer of the disciples because of the presence of Jesus (19–20), and the forgiveness that must be repeatedly extended to sinful members who repent (21–35).

18, 1: The initiative is taken not by Jesus as in the Marcan parallel (9, 33–34) but by the disciples. **Kingdom of heaven:** this may mean **the kingdom** in its fullness, i.e., after the parousia and the final judgment. But what follows about causes of sin, church discipline, and forgiveness, all dealing

r: 21, 21; Lk 17, 6; 1 Cor 13, 2. *s:* 16, 21; 20, 18-19. *t:* Ex 30, 11-16; Neh 10, 33. *u:* Mk 9, 36-37; Lk 9, 46-48.

heaven?" [2]He called a child over, placed it in their midst, [3v*]and said, "Amen, I say to you, unless you turn and become like children, you will not enter the kingdom of heaven. [4w]Whoever humbles himself like this child is the greatest in the kingdom of heaven. [5*]And whoever receives one child such as this in my name receives me.

Temptations to Sin. [6x*]"Whoever causes one of these little ones who believe in me to sin, it would be better for him to have a great millstone hung around his neck and to be drowned in the depths of the sea. [7*]Woe to the world because of things that cause sin! Such things must come, but woe to the one through whom they come! [8y*]If your hand or foot causes you to sin, cut it off and throw it away. It is better for you to enter into life maimed or crippled than with two hands or

two feet to be thrown into eternal fire. [9]And if your eye causes you to sin, tear it out and throw it away. It is better for you to enter into life with one eye than with two eyes to be thrown into fiery Gehenna.

The Parable of the Lost Sheep. [10z*]"See that you do not despise one of these little ones, for I say to you that their angels in heaven always look upon the face of my heavenly Father.[*] [11]*a [12]What is your opinion? If a man has a hundred sheep and one of them goes astray, will he not leave the ninety-nine in the hills and go in search of the stray? [13]And if he finds it, amen, I say to you, he rejoices more over it than over the ninety-nine that did not stray. [14]In just the same way, it is not the will of your heavenly Father that one of these little ones be lost.

A Brother Who Sins. [15b*]"If your brother

with the present age, suggests that the question has to do with rank also in the church, where **the kingdom** is manifested here and now, although only partially and by anticipation; see the notes on 3, 2; 4, 17.

18, 3: Become like children: the child is held up as a model for the disciples not because of any supposed innocence of children but because of their complete dependence on, and trust in, their parents. So must the disciples be, in respect to God.

18, 5: Cf 10, 40.

18, 6: One of these little ones: the thought passes from the child of vv 2–4 to the disciples, **little ones** because of their becoming **like children.** It is difficult to know whether this is a designation of all who are disciples or of those who are insignificant in contrast to others, e.g., the leaders of the community. Since apart from this chapter the designation **little ones** occurs in Mt only in 10, 42 where it means disciples as such, that is its more likely meaning here. **Who believe in me:** since discipleship is impossible without at least some degree of faith, this further specification seems superfluous. However, it serves to indicate that the warning against causing a **little one** to sin is principally directed against whatever would lead such a one to a weakening or loss of faith. The Greek verb **skandalizein,** here translated **causes . . . to sin,** means literally "causes to stumble"; what the stumbling is depends on the context. It is used of falling away from faith in 13, 21. According to the better reading of Mk 9, 42, **in me** is a Matthean addition to the Marcan source. **It would be better . . . depths of the sea:** cf Mk 9, 42.

18, 7: This is a Q saying; cf Lk 17, 1. The inevitability of **things that cause sin** (literally, "scandals") does not take away the responsibility of **the one through whom they come.**

18, 8–9: These verses are a doublet of 5, 29–30. In that context they have to do with causes of sexual sin. As in the Marcan source from which they have been drawn (Mk 9, 42–48), they differ from the first warning about scandal, which deals with causing another person to sin, for they concern what **causes** oneself **to sin** and they do not seem to be re-

lated to another's loss of faith, as the first warning is. It is difficult to know how Matthew understood the logical connection between these verses and vv 6–7.

18, 10–14: The first and last verses are peculiar to Mt. The parable itself comes from Q; see Lk 15, 3–7. In Lk it serves as justification for Jesus' table-companionship with sinners; here, it is an exhortation for the disciples to seek out fellow disciples who have gone **astray.** Not only must no one cause a fellow disciple to sin, but those who have strayed must be sought out and, if possible, brought back to the community. The joy of the shepherd on finding the sheep, though not absent in Mt (13), is more emphasized in Lk. By his addition of vv 10 and 14, Matthew has drawn out explicitly the application of the parable to the care of the **little ones.**

18, 10: Their angels in heaven . . . my heavenly Father: for the Jewish belief in angels as guardians of nations and individuals, see Dn 10, 13.20–21; Tb 5, 4–7; 1QH 5, 20–22; as intercessors who present the prayers of human beings to God, see Tb 13, 12.15. The high worth of the **little ones** is indicated by their being represented before God by these heavenly beings.

18, 11: Some manuscripts add, "For the Son of Man has come to save what was lost"; cf 9, 13. This is practically identical with Lk 19, 10 and is probably a copyist's addition from that source.

18, 15–20: Passing from the duty of Christian disciples toward those who have strayed from their number, the discourse now turns to how they are to deal with one who sins and yet remains within the community. First there is to be private correction (15); if this is unsuccessful, further correction before **two or three witnesses** (16); if this fails, the matter is to be brought before the assembled community (**the church**), and if the sinner refuses to attend to the correction of **the church,** he is to be expelled (17). The church's judgment will be ratified **in heaven,** i.e., by God (18). This three-step

v: 19, 14; Mk 10, 15; Lk 18, 17.   w: 23, 12.   x: Mk 9, 42; Lk 17, 1-2.   y: 5, 29-30; Mk 9, 43-47.   z: Ez 34, 1-3.16; Lk 15, 3-7. a: Lk 19, 10.   b: Lv 19, 17; Sir 19, 13; Gal 6, 1.

sins [against you], go and tell him his fault between you and him alone. If he listens to you, you have won over your brother. [16c]*If he does not listen, take one or two others along with you, so that 'every fact may be established on the testimony of two or three witnesses.' [17d]*If he refuses to listen to them, tell the church. If he refuses to listen even to the church, then treat him as you would a Gentile or a tax collector. [18e]*Amen, I say to you, whatever you bind on earth shall be bound in heaven, and whatever you loose on earth shall be loosed in heaven. [19f]*Again, [amen,] I say to you, if two of you agree on earth about anything for which they are to pray, it shall be granted to them by my heavenly Father. [20g]*For where two or three are gathered together in my name, there am I in the midst of them."

The Parable of the Unforgiving Servant. [21h]*Then Peter approaching asked him, "Lord, if my brother sins against me, how often must I forgive him? As many as seven times?" [22]*Jesus answered, "I say to you, not seven times but seventy-seven times. [23i]That is why the kingdom of heaven may be likened to a king who decided to settle accounts with his servants. [24]*When he began the accounting, a debtor was brought before him who owed him a huge amount. [25]Since he had no way of paying it back, his master ordered him to be sold, along with his wife, his children, and all his property, in payment of the debt. [26]*At that, the servant fell down, did him homage, and said, 'Be patient with me, and I will pay you back in full.' [27]Moved with compassion the master of that servant let him go and forgave him the loan.

process of correction corresponds, though not exactly, to the procedure of the Qumran community; see 1QS 5, 25—6, 1; 6, 24—7, 25; CD 9, 2–8. The section ends with a saying about the favorable response of God to prayer, even to that of a very small number, for Jesus is in the midst of any gathering of his disciples, however small (19–20). Whether this prayer has anything to do with the preceding judgment is uncertain.

18, 15: Your brother: a fellow disciple; see 23, 8. The bracketed words, **against you,** are widely attested but they are not in the important codices Sinaiticus and Vaticanus or in some other textual witnesses. Their omission broadens the type of sin in question. **Won over:** literally, "gained."

18, 16: Cf Dt 19, 15.

18, 17: The church: the second of the only two instances of this word in the gospels; see the note on 16, 18. Here it refers not to the entire **church** of Jesus, as in 16, 18, but to the local congregation. **Treat him . . . a Gentile or a tax collector:** just as the observant Jew avoided the company of Gentiles and tax collectors, so must the congregation of Christian disciples separate itself from the arrogantly sinful member who refuses to repent even when convicted of his sin by the whole **church.** Such a one is to be set outside the fellowship of the community. The harsh language about **Gentile** and **tax collector** probably reflects a stage of the Matthean **church** when it was principally composed of Jewish Christians. That time had long since passed, but the principle of exclusion for such a sinner remained. Paul makes a similar demand for excommunication in 1 Cor 5, 1–13.

18, 18: Except for the plural of the verbs **bind** and **loose,** this verse is practically identical with 16, 19b, and many scholars understand it as granting to all the disciples what was previously given to Peter alone. For a different view, based on the different contexts of the two verses, see the note on 16, 19.

18, 19–20: Some take these verses as applying to prayer on the occasion of the church's gathering to deal with the sinner of v 17. Unless an **a fortiori** argument is supposed, this seems unlikely. God's answer to the prayer of **two or three** envisages a different situation from one that involves the en-

tire congregation. In addition, the object of this prayer is expressed in most general terms as **anything for which they are to pray.**

18, 20: For where two or three . . . midst of them: the presence of Jesus guarantees the efficacy of the prayer. This saying is similar to one attributed to a rabbi executed in A.D. 135 at the time of the second Jewish revolt: ". . . When two sit and there are between them the words of the Torah, the divine presence (Shekinah) rests upon them" **(Pirqê 'Abôt** 3, 3).

18, 21–35: The final section of the discourse deals with the forgiveness that the disciples are to give to their fellow disciples who sin against them. To the question of Peter how often forgiveness is to be granted (21), Jesus answers that it is to be given without limit (22) and illustrates this with the parable of the unmerciful servant (23–34), warning that his **heavenly Father** will give those who do not forgive the same treatment as that given to the unmerciful servant (35). Verses 21–22 correspond to Lk 17, 4; the parable and the final warning are peculiar to Mt. That the parable did not originally belong to this context is suggested by the fact that it really does not deal with repeated forgiveness, which is the point of Peter's question and Jesus' reply.

18, 22: Seventy-seven times: the Greek corresponds exactly to the LXX of Gn 4, 24. There is probably an allusion, by contrast, to the limitless vengeance of Lamech in the Gn text In any case, what is demanded of the disciples is limitless forgiveness.

18, 24: A huge amount: literally, "ten thousand talents." The talent was a unit of coinage of high but varying value depending on its metal (gold, silver, copper) and its place of origin. It is mentioned in the New Testament only here and in 25, 14–30.

18, 26: Pay you back in full: an empty promise, given the size of the debt.

c: Dt 19, 15; Jn 8, 17; 1 Tm 5, 19. d: 1 Cor 5, 1-13. e: 16, 19; Jn 20, 23. f: 7, 7-8; Jn 15, 7. g: 1 Cor 5, 4. h: 6, 12. Lk 17, 4. i: 25, 19.

28*When that servant had left, he found one of his fellow servants who owed him a much smaller amount. He seized him and started to choke him, demanding, 'Pay back what you owe.' 29Falling to his knees, his fellow servant begged him, 'Be patient with me, and I will pay you back.' 30But he refused. Instead, he had him put in prison until he paid back the debt. 31Now when his fellow servants saw what had happened, they were deeply disturbed, and went to their master and reported the whole affair. 32His master summoned him and said to him, 'You wicked servant! I forgave you your entire debt because you begged me to. 33jShould you not have had pity on your fellow servant, as I had pity on you?' 34*Then in anger his master handed him over to the torturers until he should pay back the whole debt. 35k*So will my heavenly Father do to you, unless each of you forgives his brother from his heart."

VI: Ministry in Judea and Jerusalem

CHAPTER 19

See RG 285–87

Marriage and Divorce. 1*When Jesus finished these words, he left Galilee and went to the district of Judea across the Jordan. 2Great crowds followed him, and he cured them there. 31*Some Pharisees approached him, and tested him, saying, "Is it lawful for a man to divorce his wife for any cause whatever?" 4m*He said in reply, "Have you not read that from the beginning the Creator 'made them male and female' 5nand said, 'For this reason a man shall leave his father and mother and be joined to his wife, and the two shall become one flesh'? 6So they are no longer two, but one flesh. Therefore, what God has joined together, no human being must separate." 7o*They said to

18, 28: **A much smaller amount:** literally, "a hundred denarii." A denarius was the normal daily wage of a laborer. The difference between the two debts is enormous and brings out the absurdity of the conduct of the Christian who has received the great forgiveness of God and yet refuses to forgive the relatively minor offenses done to him.

18, 34: Since the debt is so great as to be unpayable, the punishment will be endless.

18, 35: The Father's forgiveness, already given, will be withdrawn at the final judgment for those who have not imitated his forgiveness by their own.

19, 1—23, 39: The narrative section of the fifth book of the gospel. The first part (19, 1—20, 34) has for its setting the journey of Jesus from Galilee to Jerusalem; the second (21, 1—23, 39) deals with Jesus' ministry in Jerusalem up to the final great discourse of the gospel (chs 24–25). Matthew follows the Marcan sequence of events, though adding material both special to this gospel and drawn from Q. The second part ends with the denunciation of the scribes and Pharisees (23, 1–36) followed by Jesus' lament over Jerusalem (37–39). This long and important speech raises a problem for the view that Mt is structured around five other discourses of Jesus (see Introduction) and that this one has no such function in the gospel. However, it is to be noted that this speech lacks the customary concluding formula that follows the five discourses (see the note on 7, 28), and that those discourses are all addressed either exclusively (chs 10, 18, 24–25) or primarily (chs 5–7, 13) to the disciples, whereas this is addressed primarily to the scribes and Pharisees (13–36). Consequently, it seems plausible to maintain that the evangelist did not intend to give it the structural importance of the five other discourses, and that, in spite of its being composed of sayings-material, it belongs to the narrative section of this book. In that regard, it is similar to the sayings-material of 11, 7–30. Some have proposed that Matthew wished to regard it as part of the final discourse of chs 24–25, but the intervening material (24, 1–4) and the change in matter and style of those chapters do not support that view.

19, 1–12: In giving Jesus' teaching on divorce (3–9), Matthew here follows his Marcan source (10, 2–12) as he does Q in 5, 31–32 (cf Lk 16, 18). Verses 10–12 are peculiar to Mt.

19, 1: **When Jesus finished these words:** see the note on 7, 28–29. **The district of Judea across the Jordan:** an inexact designation of the territory. Judea did not extend **across the Jordan;** the territory east of the river was Perea. The route to Jerusalem by way of Perea avoided passage through Samaria.

19, 3: **Tested him:** the verb is used of attempts of Jesus' opponents to embarrass him by challenging him to do something they think impossible (16, 1; Mk 8, 11; Lk 11, 16) or by having him say something that they can use against him (22, 18.35; Mk 10, 2; 12, 15). **For any cause whatever:** this is peculiar to Mt and has been interpreted by some as meaning that Jesus was being asked to take sides in the dispute between the schools of Hillel and Shammai on the reasons for divorce, the latter holding a stricter position than the former. It is unlikely, however, that to ask Jesus' opinion about the differing views of two Jewish schools, both highly respected, could be described as "testing" him, for the reason indicated above.

19, 4–6: Matthew recasts his Marcan source, omitting Jesus' question about Moses' command (Mk 10, 3) and having him recall at once two Genesis texts that show the will and purpose of **the Creator** in making human beings **male and female** (Gn 1, 27), namely, that **a man** may **be joined to his wife** in marriage in the intimacy of **one flesh** (Gn 2, 24). **What God has** thus **joined** must not be separated by any **human being.** (The NAB translation of the Hebrew bāśār of Gn 2, 24 as "body" rather than "flesh" obscures the reference of Mt to that text.)

19, 7: See Dt 24, 1–4.

j: Sir 28, 4.　k: 6, 15; Jas 2, 13.　l: Mk 10, 2-12.　m: Gn 1, 27. n: Gn 2, 24; 1 Cor 6, 16; Eph 5, 31.　o: Dt 24, 1-4.

him, "Then why did Moses command that the man give the woman a bill of divorce and dismiss [her]?" [8]He said to them, "Because of the hardness of your hearts Moses allowed you to divorce your wives, but from the beginning it was not so. [9][p]*I say to you, whoever divorces his wife (unless the marriage is unlawful) and marries another commits adultery." [10][His] disciples said to him, "If that is the case of a man with his wife, it is better not to marry." [11]*He answered, "Not all can accept [this] word, but only those to whom that is granted. [12]*Some are incapable of marriage because they were born so; some, because they were made so by others; some, because they have renounced marriage for the sake of the kingdom of heaven. Whoever can accept this ought to accept it."

Blessing of the Children. [13][q]*Then children were brought to him that he might lay his hands on them and pray. The disciples rebuked them, [14][r]but Jesus said, "Let the children come to me, and do not prevent them; for the kingdom of heaven belongs to such as these." [15]After he placed his hands on them, he went away.

The Rich Young Man. [16][s]*Now someone approached him and said, "Teacher, what good must I do to gain eternal life?" [17]*He answered him, "Why do you ask me about the good? There is only One who is good. If you wish to enter into life, keep the commandments." [18][t]*He asked him, "Which ones?" And Jesus replied, " 'You shall not kill; you shall not commit adultery; you shall not steal; you shall not bear false witness; [19]honor your father and your mother'; and 'you shall love your neighbor as yourself.' " [20]*The young man said to him, "All of these I have observed. What do I still

19, 9: Moses' concession to human sinfulness (**the hardness of your hearts,** 8) is repudiated by Jesus, and the original will of the Creator is reaffirmed against that concession. (**Unless the marriage is unlawful**): see the note on 5, 31–32. There is some evidence suggesting that Jesus' absolute prohibition of divorce was paralleled in the Qumran community (see 11QTemple 57, 17–19; CD 4, 12b—5, 14). Matthew removes Mark's setting of this verse as spoken to the disciples alone "in the house" (Mk 10, 10) and also his extension of the divorce prohibition to the case of a woman's divorcing her husband (10, 12), probably because in Palestine, unlike the places where Roman and Greek law prevailed, the woman was not allowed to initiate the divorce.

19, 11: [**This**] **word:** probably the disciples' **it is better not to marry** (10). Jesus agrees but says that celibacy is not for all but only for those **to whom that is granted** by God.

19, 12: Incapable of marriage: literally, "eunuchs." Three classes are mentioned, eunuchs from birth, eunuchs by castration, and those who have voluntarily **renounced marriage** (literally, "have made themselves eunuchs") **for the sake of the kingdom,** i.e., to devote themselves entirely to its service. Some scholars take the last class to be those who have been divorced by their spouses and have refused to enter another marriage. But it is more likely that it is rather those who have chosen never to marry, since that suits better the optional nature of the decision: **whoever can . . . ought to accept it.**

19, 13–15: This account is understood by some as intended to justify the practice of infant baptism. That interpretation is based principally on the command not to **prevent** the children from coming, since that word sometimes has a baptismal connotation in the New Testament; see Acts 8, 36.

19, 16–30: Cf Mk 10, 17–31. This story does not set up a "two-tier" morality, that of those who seek (only) **eternal life** (16) and that of those who **wish to be perfect** (21). It speaks rather of the obstacle that riches constitute for the

following of Jesus and of the impossibility, humanly speaking, for one who has **many possessions** (22) **to enter the kingdom** (24). Actual renunciation of riches is not demanded of all; Matthew counts the rich Joseph of Arimathea as a disciple of Jesus (27, 57). But only the poor in spirit (5, 3) can **enter the kingdom** and, as here, such poverty may entail the sacrifice of one's **possessions.** The Twelve, who **have given up everything** (27) to follow Jesus, will have as their reward a share in Jesus' (the Son of Man's) **judging the twelve tribes of Israel** (28), and all who have similarly sacrificed family or property for his sake **will inherit eternal life** (29).

19, 16: Gain eternal life: this is equivalent to "entering into life" (17) and "being saved" (25); the **life** is that of the new age after the final judgment (see 25, 46). It probably is also equivalent here to "entering the kingdom of heaven" (23) or "the kingdom of God" (24), but see the notes on 3, 2; 4, 17; 18, 1 for the wider reference of **the kingdom** in Mt.

19, 17: By Matthew's reformulation of the Marcan question and reply (Mk 10, 17–18) Jesus' repudiation of the term "good" for himself has been softened. Yet the Marcan assertion that "no one is good but God alone" stands, with only unimportant verbal modification.

19, 18–19: The first five commandments cited are from the Decalogue (see Ex 20, 12–16; Dt 5, 16–20). Matthew omits Mark's "you shall not defraud" (10, 19; see Dt 24, 14) and adds Lv 19, 18. This combination of commandments of the Decalogue with Lv 19, 18 is partially the same as Paul's enumeration of the demands of Christian morality in Rom 13, 9.

19, 20: Young man: in Mt alone of the synoptics the questioner is said to be a **young man;** thus the Marcan "from my youth" (10, 20) is omitted.

p: 5, 32; Lk 16, 18; 1 Cor 7, 10-11.   *q:* Mk 10, 13-16; Lk 18, 15-17.   *r:* 18, 3; Acts 8, 36.   *s:* Mk 10, 17-31; Lk 18, 18-30.   *t:* Ex 20, 12-16; Dt 5, 16-20 / Lv 19, 18; Rom 13, 9.

lack?" [21u*]Jesus said to him, "If you wish to be perfect, go, sell what you have and give to [the] poor, and you will have treasure in heaven. Then come, follow me." [22]When the young man heard this statement, he went away sad, for he had many possessions. [23*]Then Jesus said to his disciples, "Amen, I say to you, it will be hard for one who is rich to enter the kingdom of heaven. [24v]Again I say to you, it is easier for a camel to pass through the eye of a needle than for one who is rich to enter the kingdom of God." [25*]When the disciples heard this, they were greatly astonished and said, "Who then can be saved?" [26w]Jesus looked at them and said, "For human beings this is impossible, but for God all things are possible." [27x]Then Peter said to him in reply, "We have given up everything and followed you. What will there be for us?" [28y*]Jesus said to them, "Amen, I say to you that you who have followed me, in the new age, when the Son of Man is seated on his throne of glory, will yourselves sit on twelve thrones, judging the twelve tribes of Israel. [29]And everyone who has given up houses or brothers or sisters or father or mother or children or lands for the sake of my name will receive a hundred times more, and will inherit eternal

life. [30z*]But many who are first will be last, and the last will be first.

CHAPTER 20

See RG
285-87

The Workers in the Vineyard. [1*]"The kingdom of heaven is like a landowner who went out at dawn to hire laborers for his vineyard. [2]After agreeing with them for the usual daily wage, he sent them into his vineyard. [3]Going out about nine o'clock, he saw others standing idle in the marketplace, [4*]and he said to them, 'You too go into my vineyard, and I will give you what is just.' [5]So they went off. [And] he went out again around noon, and around three o'clock, and did likewise. [6]Going out about five o'clock, he found others standing around, and said to them, 'Why do you stand here idle all day?' [7]They answered, 'Because no one has hired us.' He said to them, 'You too go into my vineyard.' [8a*]When it was evening the owner of the vineyard said to his foreman, 'Summon the laborers and give them their pay, beginning with the last and ending with the first.' [9]When those who had started about five o'clock came, each received the usual daily wage. [10]So when the first came, they thought that they would receive more, but each of them also got the usual wage. [11]And

19, 21: If you wish to be perfect: to be perfect is demanded of all Christians; see 5, 48. In the case of this man, it involves selling his possessions and giving to the poor; only so can he follow Jesus.

19, 23–24: Riches are an obstacle to entering the kingdom that cannot be overcome by human power. The comparison with the impossibility of a camel's passing through the eye of a needle should not be mitigated by such suppositions as that the eye of a needle means a low or narrow gate. The kingdom of God: as in 12, 28; 21, 31.43, instead of Mt's usual kingdom of heaven.

19, 25–26: See the note on Mk 10, 23–27.

19, 28: This saying, directed to the Twelve, is from Q; see Lk 22, 29–30. The new age: the Greek word here translated "new age" occurs in the New Testament only here and in Ti 3, 5. Literally, it means "rebirth" or "regeneration," and is used in Ti of spiritual rebirth through baptism. Here it means the "rebirth" effected by the coming of the kingdom. Since that coming has various stages (see the notes on 3, 2; 4, 17), the new age could be taken as referring to the time after the resurrection when the Twelve will govern the true Israel, i.e., the church of Jesus. (For "judge" in the sense of "govern," cf Jgs 12, 8.9.11; 15, 20; 16, 31; Ps 2, 10). But since it is connected here with the time when the Son of Man will be seated on his throne of glory, language that Matthew uses in 25, 31 for the time of final judgment, it is more likely that

what the Twelve are promised is that they will be joined with Jesus then in judging the people of Israel.

19, 30: Different interpretations have been given to this saying, which comes from Mk 10, 31. In view of Matthew's associating it with the following parable (20, 1–15) and substantially repeating it (in reverse order) at the end of that parable (20, 16), it may be that his meaning is that all who respond to the call of Jesus, at whatever time (first or last), will be the same in respect to inheriting the benefits of the kingdom, which is the gift of God.

20, 1–16: This parable is peculiar to Mt. It is difficult to know whether the evangelist composed it or received it as part of his traditional material and, if the latter is the case, what its original reference was. In its present context its close association with 19, 30 suggests that its teaching is the equality of all the disciples in the reward of inheriting eternal life.

20, 4: What is just: although the wage is not stipulated as in the case of those first hired, it will be fair.

20, 8: Beginning with the last . . . the first: this element of the parable has no other purpose than to show how the first knew what the last were given (12).

u: 5, 48; 6, 20.   v: 7, 14.   w: Gn 18, 14; Jb 42, 2; Lk 1, 37.   x: 4, 20.22.   y: 25, 31; Dn 7, 9.22; Lk 22, 30; Rv 3, 21; 20, 4.   z: 20, 16.   a: Lv 19, 13; Dt 24, 15.

on receiving it they grumbled against the landowner, [12] saying, 'These last ones worked only one hour, and you have made them equal to us, who bore the day's burden and the heat.' [13]*He said to one of them in reply, 'My friend, I am not cheating you. Did you not agree with me for the usual daily wage? [14]*Take what is yours and go. What if I wish to give this last one the same as you? [15][Or] am I not free to do as I wish with my own money? Are you envious because I am generous?' [16]*Thus, the last will be first, and the first will be last."

The Third Prediction of the Passion. [17b]*As Jesus was going up to Jerusalem, he took the twelve [disciples] aside by themselves, and said to them on the way, [18]"Behold, we are going up to Jerusalem, and the Son of Man will be handed over to the chief priests and the scribes, and they will condemn him to death, [19]and hand him over to the Gentiles to be mocked and scourged and crucified, and he will be raised on the third day."

The Request of James and John. [20c]*Then the mother of the sons of Zebedee approached him with her sons and did him homage, wishing to ask him for something. [21]He said to her, "What do you wish?" She answered him, "Command that these two sons of mine sit, one at your right and the other at your left, in your kingdom." [22]*Jesus said in reply, "You do not know what you are asking. Can you drink the cup that I am going to drink?" They said to him, "We can." [23]He replied, "My cup you will indeed drink, but to sit at my right and at my left [, this] is not mine to give but is for those for whom it has been prepared by my Father." [24d]When the ten heard this, they became indignant at the two brothers. [25]But Jesus summoned them and said, "You know that the rulers of the Gentiles lord it over them, and the great ones make their authority over them felt. [26]But it shall not be so among you. Rather, whoever wishes to be great among you shall be your servant; [27e]whoever wishes to be first among you shall be your slave. [28f]*Just so, the Son of Man did not come to be served but to serve and to give his life as a ransom for many."

The Healing of Two Blind Men. [29g]*As

20, 13: I am not cheating you: literally, "I am not treating you unjustly."

20, 14–15: The owner's conduct involves no violation of justice (4.13), and that all the workers receive the same wage is due only to his generosity to the latest arrivals; the resentment of the first comes from envy.

20, 16: See the note on 19, 30.

20, 17–19: Cf Mk 10, 32–34. This is the third and the most detailed of the passion predictions (16, 21–23; 17, 22–23). It speaks of Jesus' **being handed over to the Gentiles** (27, 2), his being **mocked** (27, 27–30), **scourged** (27, 26), and **crucified** (27, 31.35). In all but the last of these points Matthew agrees with his Marcan source, but whereas Mk speaks of Jesus' being killed (10, 34), Mt has the specific **to be . . . crucified.**

20, 20–28: Cf Mk 10, 35–45. The request of the sons of Zebedee, made through their mother, for the highest places of honor in the **kingdom,** and the indignation of **the** other **ten** disciples at this request, show that neither **the two brothers** nor the others have understood that what makes for greatness in the kingdom is not lordly power but humble service. Jesus gives the example, and his ministry of service will reach its highest point when he gives his life for the deliverance of the human race from sin.

20, 20–21: The reason for Matthew's making **the mother** the petitioner (cf Mk 10, 35) is not clear. Possibly he intends an allusion to Bathsheba's seeking the kingdom for Solomon; see 1 Kgs 1, 11–21. **Your kingdom:** see the note on 16, 28.

20, 22: You do not know what you are asking: the Greek verbs are plural and, with the rest of the verse, indicate that

the answer is addressed not to the woman but to her sons. **Drink the cup:** see the note on Mk 10, 38–40. Matthew omits the Marcan "or be baptized with the baptism with which I am baptized" (10, 38).

20, 28: Ransom: this noun, which occurs in the New Testament only here and in the Marcan parallel (10, 45), does not necessarily express the idea of liberation by payment of some price. The cognate verb is used frequently in the LXX of God's liberating Israel from Egypt or from Babylonia after the Exile; see Ex 6, 6; 15, 13; Ps 77 (76 LXX), 16; Is 43, 1; 44, 22. The liberation brought by Jesus' death will be **for many;** cf Is 53, 12. **Many** does not mean that some are excluded, but is a Semitism designating the collectivity who benefit from the service of the one, and is equivalent to "all." While there are few verbal contacts between this saying and the fourth Servant Song (Is 52, 13—53, 12), the ideas of that passage are reflected here.

20, 29–34: The cure of the blind men is probably symbolic of what will happen to the disciples, now blind to the meaning of Jesus' passion and to the necessity of their sharing his suffering. As the men are given sight, so, after the resurrection, will the disciples come to see that to which they are now blind. Matthew has abbreviated his Marcan source (10, 46–52) and has made Mk's one man two. Such doubling is characteristic of this gospel; see 8, 28–34 (// Mk 5, 1–20) and the note on 9, 27–31.

b: 16, 21; 17, 22-23; Mk 10, 32-34; Lk 18, 31-33. c: Mk 10, 35-45. d: Lk 22, 25-27. e: Mk 9, 35. f: 26, 28; Is 53, 12; Rom 5, 6; 1 Tm 2, 6. g: Mk 10, 46-52; Lk 18, 35-43.

they left Jericho, a great crowd followed him. *30h**Two blind men were sitting by the roadside, and when they heard that Jesus was passing by, they cried out, "[Lord,] Son of David, have pity on us!" *31*The crowd warned them to be silent, but they called out all the more, "Lord, Son of David, have pity on us!" *32*Jesus stopped and called them and said, "What do you want me to do for you?" *33*They answered him, "Lord, let our eyes be opened." *34*Moved with pity, Jesus touched their eyes. Immediately they received their sight, and followed him.

See RG 287–88

CHAPTER 21

The Entry into Jerusalem. *1i**When they drew near Jerusalem and came to Bethphage on the Mount of Olives, Jesus sent two disciples, *2**saying to them, "Go into the village opposite you, and immediately you will find an ass tethered, and a colt with her. Untie them and bring them here to me. *3*And if anyone should say anything to you, reply, 'The master has need of them.' Then he will send them at once." *4**This happened so that

what had been spoken through the prophet might be fulfilled:

5 j "Say to daughter Zion,
'Behold, your king comes to you,
   meek and riding on an ass,
      and on a colt, the foal of a beast of
         burden.' "

*6*The disciples went and did as Jesus had ordered them. *7**They brought the ass and the colt and laid their cloaks over them, and he sat upon them. *8k**The very large crowd spread their cloaks on the road, while others cut branches from the trees and strewed them on the road. *9l**The crowds preceding him and those following kept crying out and saying:

"Hosanna to the Son of David;
   blessed is he who comes in the name
      of the Lord;
hosanna in the highest."

10*And when he entered Jerusalem the whole city was shaken and asked, "Who is this?" *11**And the crowds replied, "This is

---

20, 30: [**Lord**]: some important textual witnesses omit this, but that may be because copyists assimilated this verse to 9, 27. **Son of David:** see the note on 9, 27.

21, 1–11: Jesus' coming to Jerusalem is in accordance with the divine will that he must go there (cf 16, 21) to suffer, die, and be raised. He prepares for his entry into the city in such a way as to make it a fulfillment of the prophecy of Zec 9, 9 (2) that emphasizes the humility of the **king** who **comes** (5). That prophecy, absent from the Marcan parallel account (11, 1–11) although found also in the Johannine account of the entry (12, 15), is the center of the Matthean story. During the procession from Bethphage to Jerusalem, Jesus is acclaimed as the Davidic messianic king by the crowds who accompany him (9). On his arrival **the whole city was shaken,** and to the inquiry of the amazed populace about Jesus' identity the crowds with him reply that he is **the prophet, from Nazareth in Galilee** (10.11).

21, 1: Bethphage: a village that can no longer be certainly identified. Mk mentions it before Bethany (11, 1), which suggests that it lay to the east of the latter. **The Mount of Olives:** the hill east of Jerusalem that is spoken of in Zec 14, 4 as the place where the Lord will come to rescue Jerusalem from the enemy nations.

21, 2: An ass tethered, and a colt with her: instead of the one animal of Mk 11, 2, Mt has two, as demanded by his understanding of Zec 9, 9.

21, 4–5: The prophet: this fulfillment citation is actually composed of two distinct Old Testament texts, Is 62, 11 (**Say to daughter Zion**) and Zec 9, 9. The ass and the colt are the same animal in the prophecy, mentioned twice in different

ways, the common Hebrew literary device of poetic parallelism. That Matthew takes them as two is one of the reasons why some scholars think that he was a Gentile rather than a Jewish Christian who would presumably not make that mistake (see Introduction).

21, 7: Upon them: upon the two animals; an awkward picture resulting from Matthew's misunderstanding of the prophecy.

21, 8: Spread . . . on the road: cf 2 Kgs 9, 13. There is a similarity between the cutting and strewing of the **branches** and the festivities of Tabernacles (Lv 23, 39–40); see also 2 Mc 10, 5–8 where the celebration of the rededication of the temple is compared to that of Tabernacles.

21, 9: Hosanna: the Hebrew means "(O LORD) grant salvation"; see Ps 118, 25, but that invocation had become an acclamation of jubilation and welcome. **Blessed is he . . . in the name of the Lord:** see Ps 118, 26 and the note on Jn 12, 13. **In the highest:** probably only an intensification of the acclamation, although **Hosanna in the highest** could be taken as a prayer, "May God save (him)."

21, 10: Was shaken: in the gospels this verb is peculiar to Mt where it is used also of the earthquake at the time of the crucifixion (27, 51) and of the terror of the guards of Jesus' tomb at the appearance of the angel (28, 4). For Matthew's use of the cognate noun, see the note on 8, 24.

21, 11: The prophet: see 16, 14 ("one of the prophets") and 21, 46.

h: 9, 27. *i:* Mk 11, 1-11; Lk 19, 28-38; Jn 12, 12-15. *j:* Is 62, 11; Zec 9, 9. *k:* 2 Kgs 9, 13. *l:* Ps 118, 25-26.

Jerusalem in the Time of Jesus

Jesus the prophet, from Nazareth in Galilee."

The Cleansing of the Temple. [12mn*]Jesus entered the temple area and drove out all those engaged in selling and buying there. He overturned the tables of the money changers and the seats of those who were selling doves. [13o*]And he said to them, "It is written:

'My house shall be a house of prayer,'
　but you are making it a den of thieves.'"

21, 12–17: Matthew changes the order of Mk (11, 11.12.15) and places the cleansing of the temple on the same day as the entry into Jerusalem, immediately after it. The activities going on in **the temple area** were not secular but connected with the temple worship. Thus Jesus' attack on those so engaged and his charge that they were **making** God's **house of prayer a den of thieves** (12–13) constituted a claim to authority over the religious practices of Israel and were a challenge to the priestly authorities. Verses 14–17 are peculiar to Mt. Jesus' healings and his countenancing the children's cries of praise rouse the indignation of **the chief priests and the scribes** (15). These two groups appear in the infancy narrative (2, 4) and have been mentioned in the first and third passion predictions (16, 21; 20, 18). Now, as the passion approaches, they come on the scene again, exhibiting their hostility to Jesus.

21, 12: These activities were carried on in the court of the Gentiles, the outermost court of **the temple area.** Animals for sacrifice were sold; the **doves** were for those who could not afford a more expensive offering; see Lv 5, 7. **Tables of the money changers:** only the coinage of Tyre could be used for the purchases; other money had to be exchanged for that.

21, 13: 'My house . . . prayer': cf Is 56, 7. Matthew omits

m: Mk 11, 15-19; Lk 19, 45-48; Jn 2, 14-22.　*n:* Lv 5, 7.　*o:* Is 56, 7; Jer 7, 11.

[14p]*The blind and the lame approached him in the temple area, and he cured them. [15]*When the chief priests and the scribes saw the wondrous things he was doing, and the children crying out in the temple area, "Hosanna to the Son of David," they were indignant [16q]*and said to him, "Do you hear what they are saying?" Jesus said to them, "Yes; and have you never read the text, 'Out of the mouths of infants and nurslings you have brought forth praise'?" [17]And leaving them, he went out of the city to Bethany, and there he spent the night.

The Cursing of the Fig Tree. [18r]*When he was going back to the city in the morning, he was hungry. [19s]Seeing a fig tree by the road, he went over to it, but found nothing on it except leaves. And he said to it, "May no fruit ever come from you again." And immediately the fig tree withered. [20]When the disciples saw this, they were amazed and said, "How was it that the fig tree withered immediately?" [21t]*Jesus said to them in reply, "Amen, I say to you, if you have faith and do not waver, not only will you do what has been done to the fig tree, but even if you say to this mountain, 'Be lifted up and thrown into the sea,' it will be done. [22u]Whatever you ask for in prayer with faith, you will receive."

The Authority of Jesus Questioned. [23vw]*When he had come into the temple area, the chief priests and the elders of the people approached him as he was teaching and said, "By what authority are you doing these things? And who gave you this authority?" [24]*Jesus said to them in reply, "I shall ask you one question, and if you answer it for me, then I shall tell you by what authority I do these things. [25]Where was John's baptism from? Was it of heavenly or of human origin?" They discussed this among themselves and said, "If we say 'Of heavenly origin,' he will say to us, 'Then why did you not believe him?' [26x]*But if we say, 'Of human origin,' we fear the crowd, for they all regard John as a prophet." [27]*So they said to Jesus in reply, "We do not know." He himself said to them, "Neither shall I tell you by what authority I do these things.

The Parable of the Two Sons. [28]*"What is your opinion? A man had two sons. He came

---

the final words of the quotation, "for all peoples" ("all nations"), possibly because for him the worship of the God of Israel by all nations belongs to the time after the resurrection; see 28, 19. **A den of thieves:** the phrase is taken from Jer 7, 11.

21, 14: The blind and the lame: according to 2 Sm 5, 8 (LXX) **the blind and the lame** were forbidden to enter "the house of the Lord," the temple. These are the last of Jesus' healings in Mt.

21, 15: The wondrous things: the healings.

21, 16: 'Out of the mouths ... praise': cf Ps 8, 3 (LXX).

21, 18–22: In Mk the effect of Jesus' cursing the fig tree is not immediate; see 11, 14.20. By making it so, Matthew has heightened the miracle. Jesus' act seems arbitrary and ill-tempered, but it is a prophetic action similar to those of Old Testament prophets that vividly symbolize some part of their preaching; see, e.g., Ez 12, 1–20. It is a sign of the judgment that is to come upon the Israel that with all its apparent piety lacks the fruit of good deeds (3, 10) and will soon bear the punishment of its fruitlessness (43). Some scholars propose that this story is the development in tradition of a parable of Jesus about the destiny of a fruitless tree, such as Lk 13, 6–9. Jesus' answer to the question of the amazed disciples (20) makes the miracle an example of the power of prayer made with unwavering **faith** (21–22).

21, 21: See 17, 20.

21, 23–27: Cf Mk 11, 27–33. This is the first of five controversies between Jesus and the religious authorities of Judaism in 21, 23—22, 46, presented in the form of questions and answers.

21, 23: These things: probably his entry into the city, his cleansing of the temple, and his healings there.

21, 24: To reply by counterquestion was common in rabbinical debate.

21, 26: We fear ... as a prophet: cf 14, 5.

21, 27: Since through embarrassment on the one hand and fear on the other the religious authorities claim ignorance of the origin of John's baptism, they show themselves incapable of speaking with authority; hence Jesus refuses to discuss with them the grounds of his authority.

21, 28–32: The series of controversies is interrupted by three parables on the judgment of Israel (21, 28—22, 14) of which this, peculiar to Mt, is the first. The second (21, 33–46) comes from Mk (12, 1–12), and the third (22, 1–14) from Q; see Lk 14, 15–24. This interruption of the controversies is similar to that in Mk, although Mk has only one parable between the first and second controversy. As regards Mt's first parable, vv 28–30 if taken by themselves could point simply to the difference between saying and doing, a theme of much importance in this gospel (cf 7, 21; 12, 50); that may have been the parable's original reference. However, it is given a more specific application by the addition of vv 31–32. The two sons represent, respectively, the religious leaders and the religious outcasts who followed John's call to repentance. By the answer they give to Jesus' question (31) the leaders con-

p: 2 Sm 5, 8 LXX.   q: Ps 8, 2 LXX; Wis 10, 21.   r: Mk 11, 12-14.20-24.   s: Jer 8, 13; Lk 13, 6-9.   t: 17, 20; Lk 17, 6.   u: 7, 7; 1 Jn 3, 22.   v: Mk 11, 27-33; Lk 20, 1-8.   w: Jn 2, 18.   x: 14, 5.

to the first and said, 'Son, go out and work in the vineyard today.' [29]He said in reply, 'I will not,' but afterwards he changed his mind and went. [30]The man came to the other son and gave the same order. He said in reply, 'Yes, sir,' but did not go. [31]*Which of the two did his father's will?" They answered, "The first." Jesus said to them, "Amen, I say to you, tax collectors and prostitutes are entering the kingdom of God before you. [32]y*When John came to you in the way of righteousness, you did not believe him; but tax collectors and prostitutes did. Yet even when you saw that, you did not later change your minds and believe him.

The Parable of the Tenants. [33]za*"Hear another parable. There was a landowner who planted a vineyard, put a hedge around it, dug a wine press in it, and built a tower. Then he leased it to tenants and went on a journey. [34]*When vintage time drew near, he sent his servants to the tenants to obtain his produce. [35]But the tenants seized the servants and one they beat, another they killed,

and a third they stoned. [36]Again he sent other servants, more numerous than the first ones, but they treated them in the same way. [37]Finally, he sent his son to them, thinking, 'They will respect my son.' [38]*But when the tenants saw the son, they said to one another, 'This is the heir. Come, let us kill him and acquire his inheritance.' [39b]b*They seized him, threw him out of the vineyard, and killed him. [40]What will the owner of the vineyard do to those tenants when he comes?" [41]*They answered him, "He will put those wretched men to a wretched death and lease his vineyard to other tenants who will give him the produce at the proper times." [42]c*Jesus said to them, "Did you never read in the scriptures:

'The stone that the builders rejected
    has become the cornerstone;
by the Lord has this been done,
    and it is wonderful in our eyes'?

[43]*Therefore, I say to you, the kingdom of

demn themselves. There is much confusion in the textual tradition of the parable. Of the three different forms of the text given by important textual witnesses, one has the leaders answer that the son who agreed to go but did not was the one who did the father's will. Although some scholars accept that as the original reading, their arguments in favor of it seem unconvincing. The choice probably lies only between a reading that puts the son who agrees and then disobeys before the son who at first refuses and then obeys, and the reading followed in the present translation. The witnesses to the latter reading are slightly better than those that support the other.

21, 31: Entering . . . before you: this probably means "they enter; you do not."

21, 32: Cf Lk 7, 29–30. Although the thought is similar to that of the Lucan text, the formulation is so different that it is improbable that the saying comes from Q. **Came to you . . . way of righteousness:** several meanings are possible: that John himself was righteous, that he taught righteousness to others, or that he had an important place in God's plan of salvation. For the last, see the note on 3, 14–15.

21, 33–46: Cf Mk 12, 1–12. In this parable there is a close correspondence between most of the details of the story and the situation that it illustrates, the dealings of God with his people. Because of that heavy allegorizing, some scholars think that it does not in any way go back to Jesus, but represents the theology of the later church. That judgment applies to the Marcan parallel as well, although the allegorizing has gone farther in Mt. There are others who believe that while many of the allegorical elements are due to church sources, they have been added to a basic parable spoken by Jesus. This view is now supported by the Gospel of Thomas, 65, where a less allegorized and probably more primitive form of the parable is found.

21, 33: Planted a vineyard . . . a tower: cf Is 5, 1–2. The **vineyard** is defined in Is 5, 7 as "the house of Israel."

21, 34–35: His servants: Mt has two sendings of **servants** as against Mk's three sendings of a single servant (11, 2–5a) followed by a statement about the sending of "many others" (11, 2.5b). That these **servants** stand for the prophets sent by God to Israel is clearly implied but not made explicit here, but see 23, 37. **His produce:** cf Mk 12, 2, "some of the produce." The **produce** is the good works demanded by God, and his claim to them is total.

21, 38: Acquire his inheritance: if a Jewish proselyte died without heir, the tenants of his land would have final claim on it.

21, 39: Threw him out . . . and killed him: the change in the Marcan order where the son is killed and his corpse then thrown out (12, 8) was probably made because of the tradition that Jesus died outside the city of Jerusalem; see Jn 19, 17; Heb 13, 12.

21, 41: They answered: in Mk 12, 9 the question is answered by Jesus himself; here the leaders answer and so condemn themselves; cf v 31. Matthew adds that the new **tenants** to whom the vineyard will be transferred **will give** the owner **the produce at the proper times.**

21, 42: Cf Ps 118, 22–23. The psalm was used in the early church as a prophecy of Jesus' resurrection; see Acts 4, 11; 1 Pt 2, 7. If, as some think, the original parable ended at v 39, it was thought necessary to complete it by a reference to Jesus' vindication by God.

21, 43: Peculiar to Mt. **Kingdom of God:** see the note on

y: Lk 7, 29-30.   z: Mk 12, 1-12; Lk 20, 9-19.   a: Is 5, 1-2.7.
b: Heb 13, 12.   c: Ps 118, 22-23; Is 28, 16; Acts 4, 11; 1 Pt 2, 7.

God will be taken away from you and given to a people that will produce its fruit. [44] *The one who falls on this stone will be dashed to pieces; and it will crush anyone on whom it falls.]" [45]*When the chief priests and the Pharisees heard his parables, they knew that he was speaking about them. [46]And although they were attempting to arrest him, they feared the crowds, for they regarded him as a prophet.

CHAPTER 22

See RG 287–88

The Parable of the Wedding Feast. [1]d*Jesus again in reply spoke to them in parables, saying, [2]*"The kingdom of heaven may be likened to a king who gave a wedding feast for his son. [3]*He dispatched his servants to summon the invited guests to the feast, but they refused to come. [4]A second time he sent other servants, saying, 'Tell those invited: "Behold, I have prepared my banquet, my calves and fattened cattle are killed, and everything is ready; come to the feast."' [5]Some ignored the invitation and went away, one to his farm, another to his business. [6]eThe rest laid hold of his servants, mistreated them, and killed them. [7]*The king was enraged and sent his troops, destroyed those murderers, and burned their city. [8]Then he said to his servants, 'The feast is ready, but those who were invited were not worthy to come. [9]Go out, therefore, into the main roads and invite to the feast whomever you find.' [10]*The servants went out into the streets and gathered all they found, bad and good alike, and the hall was filled with guests. [11]*But when the king came in to meet the guests he saw a man there not dressed in a wedding garment. [12]He said to him, 'My friend, how is it that you came in here without a wedding garment?' But he was reduced to silence. [13]f*Then the king said to his attendants, 'Bind his hands and feet, and cast him into the darkness outside, where there will be wailing and grinding of teeth.' [14]Many are invited, but few are chosen."

Paying Taxes to the Emperor. [15]g*Then the Pharisees went off and plotted how they might entrap him in speech. [16]*They sent their disciples to him, with the Herodians, saying,

---

19, 23–24. Its presence here instead of Mt's usual "kingdom of heaven" may indicate that the saying came from Matthew's own traditional material. **A people that will produce its fruit:** believing Israelites and Gentiles, the church of Jesus.

21, 44: The majority of textual witnesses omit this verse. It is probably an early addition to Mt from Lk 20, 18 with which it is practically identical.

21, 45: The Pharisees: Matthew inserts into the group of Jewish leaders (23) those who represented the Judaism of his own time.

22, 1–14: This parable is from Q; see Lk 14, 15–24. It has been given many allegorical traits by Matthew, e.g., the burning of the **city** of the guests who refused the invitation (7), which corresponds to the destruction of Jerusalem by the Romans in A.D. 70. It has similarities with the preceding parable of the tenants: the sending of two groups of **servants** (3.4), the murder of the **servants** (6), the punishment of the **murderers** (7), and the entrance of a new group into a privileged situation of which the others had proved themselves unworthy (8–10). The parable ends with a section that is peculiar to Mt (11–14), which some take as a distinct parable. Mt presents the **kingdom** in its double aspect, already present and something that can be entered here and now (1–10), and something that will be possessed only by those present members who can stand the scrutiny of the final judgment (11–14). The parable is not only a statement of God's judgment on Israel but a warning to Matthew's church.

22, 2: Wedding feast: the Old Testament's portrayal of final salvation under the image of a banquet (Is 25, 6) is taken up also in 8, 11; cf Lk 13, 15.

22, 3–4: Servants . . . other servants: probably Christian missionaries in both instances; cf 23, 34.

22, 7: See the note on vv 1–14.

22, 10: Bad and good alike: cf 13, 47.

22, 11: A wedding garment: the repentance, change of heart and mind, that is the condition for entrance into the kingdom (3, 2; 4, 17) must be continued in a life of good deeds (7, 21–23).

22, 13: Wailing and grinding of teeth: the Christian who lacks the wedding garment of good deeds will suffer the same fate as those Jews who have rejected Jesus; see the note on 8, 11–12.

22, 15–22: The series of controversies between Jesus and the representatives of Judaism (see the note on 21, 23–27) is resumed. As in the first (21, 23–27), here and in the following disputes Matthew follows his Marcan source with few modifications.

22, 15: The Pharisees: while Matthew retains the Marcan union of Pharisees and Herodians in this account, he clearly emphasizes the Pharisees' part. They alone are mentioned here, and the Herodians are joined with them only in a prepositional phrase of v 16. **Entrap him in speech:** the question that they will pose is intended to force Jesus to take either a position contrary to that held by the majority of the people or one that will bring him into conflict with the Roman authorities.

22, 16: Herodians: see the note on Mk 3, 6. They would favor payment of the tax; the Pharisees did not.

---

d: Lk 14, 15-24.   e: 21, 35.   f: 8, 12; 25, 30.   g: Mk 12, 13-17; Lk 20, 20-26.

"Teacher, we know that you are a truthful man and that you teach the way of God in accordance with the truth. And you are not concerned with anyone's opinion, for you do not regard a person's status. [17]*Tell us, then, what is your opinion: Is it lawful to pay the census tax to Caesar or not?" [18]Knowing their malice, Jesus said, "Why are you testing me, you hypocrites? [19]*Show me the coin that pays the census tax." Then they handed him the Roman coin. [20]He said to them, "Whose image is this and whose inscription?" [21h]*They replied, "Caesar's." At that he said to them, "Then repay to Caesar what belongs to Caesar and to God what belongs to God." [22]When they heard this they were amazed, and leaving him they went away.

The Question about the Resurrection. [23i]*On that day Sadducees approached him, saying that there is no resurrection. They put this question to him, [24j]*saying, "Teacher, Moses said, 'If a man dies without children,

his brother shall marry his wife and raise up descendants for his brother.' [25]Now there were seven brothers among us. The first married and died and, having no descendants, left his wife to his brother. [26]The same happened with the second and the third, through all seven. [27]Finally the woman died. [28]Now at the resurrection, of the seven, whose wife will she be? For they all had been married to her." [29]*Jesus said to them in reply, "You are misled because you do not know the scriptures or the power of God. [30]At the resurrection they neither marry nor are given in marriage but are like the angels in heaven. [31]*And concerning the resurrection of the dead, have you not read what was said to you by God, [32k]'I am the God of Abraham, the God of Isaac, and the God of Jacob'? He is not the God of the dead but of the living." [33]When the crowds heard this, they were astonished at his teaching.

The Greatest Commandment. [34l]*When

22, 17: Is it lawful: the law to which they refer is the law of God.

22, 19: They handed him the Roman coin: their readiness in producing the money implies their use of it and their acceptance of the financial advantages of the Roman administration in Palestine.

22, 21: Caesar's: the emperor Tiberius (A.D. 14–37). **Repay to Caesar what belongs to Caesar:** those who willingly use the coin that is Caesar's should **repay** him in kind. The answer avoids taking sides in the question of the lawfulness of the tax. **To God what belongs to God:** Jesus raises the debate to a new level. Those who have hypocritically asked about tax in respect to its relation to the law of God should be concerned rather with repaying **God** with the good deeds that are his due; cf 21, 41.43.

22, 23–33: Here Jesus' opponents are the **Sadducees**, members of the powerful priestly party of his time; see the note on 3, 7. Denying the resurrection of the dead, a teaching of relatively late origin in Judaism (cf Dn 12, 2), they appeal to a law of the Pentateuch (Dt 25, 5–10) and present a case based on it that would make resurrection from the dead ridiculous (24–28). Jesus chides them for knowing neither **the scriptures** nor **the power of God** (29). His argument in respect to God's **power** contradicts the notion, held even by many proponents as well as by opponents of the teaching, that the life of those raised from the dead would be essentially a continuation of the type of life they had had before death (30). His argument based on the scriptures (31–32) is of a sort that was accepted as valid among Jews of the time.

22, 23: Saying that there is no resurrection: in the Marcan parallel (12, 18) the Sadducees are correctly defined as those "who say there is no resurrection"; see also Lk 20, 27. Matthew's rewording of Mk can mean that these particular Sadducees deny the resurrection, which would imply that he

was not aware that the denial was characteristic of the party. For some scholars this is an indication of his being a Gentile Christian; see the note on 21, 4–5.

22, 24: 'If a man dies . . . his brother': this is known as the "law of the levirate," from the Latin **levir**, "brother-in-law." Its purpose was to continue the family line of the deceased **brother** (Dt 25, 6).

22, 29: The sexual relationships of this world will be transcended; the risen body will be the work of the creative **power of God.**

22, 31–32: Cf Ex 3, 6. In the Pentateuch, which the Sadducees accepted as normative for Jewish belief and practice, God speaks even now (**to you**) of himself as the God of the patriarchs who died centuries ago. He identifies himself in relation to them, and because of their relation to him, the living God, they too are alive. This might appear no argument for the resurrection, but simply for life after death as conceived in Wis 3, 1–3. But the general thought of early first-century Judaism was not influenced by that conception; for it human immortality was connected with the existence of the body.

22, 34–40: The Marcan parallel (12, 28–34) is an exchange between Jesus and a scribe who is impressed by the way in which Jesus has conducted himself in the previous controversy (12, 28), who compliments him for the answer he gives him (12, 32), and who is said by Jesus to be "not far from the kingdom of God" (12, 34). Matthew has sharpened that scene. The questioner, as the representative of other Pharisees, tests Jesus by his question (34–35), and both his reaction to Jesus' reply and Jesus' commendation of him are lacking.

h: Rom 13, 7. i: Mk 12, 18-27; Lk 20, 27-40. j: Gn 38, 8; Dt 25, 5-6. k: Ex 3, 6. l: Mk 12, 28-34; Lk 10, 25-28.

the Pharisees heard that he had silenced the Sadducees, they gathered together, ³⁵*and one of them [a scholar of the law] tested him by asking, ³⁶*"Teacher, which commandment in the law is the greatest?" ³⁷ᵐ*He said to him, "You shall love the Lord, your God, with all your heart, with all your soul, and with all your mind. ³⁸This is the greatest and the first commandment. ³⁹ⁿ*The second is like it: You shall love your neighbor as yourself. ⁴⁰ᵒ*The whole law and the prophets depend on these two commandments."

The Question about David's Son. ⁴¹ᵖ*While the Pharisees were gathered together, Jesus questioned them, ⁴²*saying, "What is your opinion about the Messiah? Whose son is he?" They replied, "David's."

⁴³He said to them, "How, then, does David, inspired by the Spirit, call him 'lord,' saying:

⁴⁴ �q 'The Lord said to my lord,
   "Sit at my right hand
      until I place your enemies under your
         feet" '?

⁴⁵*If David calls him 'lord,' how can he be his son?" ⁴⁶ʳNo one was able to answer him a word, nor from that day on did anyone dare to ask him any more questions.

CHAPTER 23

See RG 287–88

Denunciation of the Scribes and Pharisees. ¹ˢ*Then Jesus spoke to the crowds and to his disciples, ²*saying, "The scribes and the Pharisees have taken their

---

22, 35: [A scholar of the law]: meaning "scribe." Although this reading is supported by the vast majority of textual witnesses, it is the only time that the Greek word so translated occurs in Mt. It is relatively frequent in Lk, and there is reason to think that it may have been added here by a copyist since it occurs in the Lucan parallel (10, 25–28). **Tested:** see the note on 19, 3.

22, 36: For the devout Jew all the commandments were to be kept with equal care, but there is evidence of preoccupation in Jewish sources with the question put to Jesus.

22, 37–38: Cf Dt 6, 5. Matthew omits the first part of Mk's fuller quotation (12, 29; Dt 6, 4–5), probably because he considered its monotheistic emphasis needless for his church. The love of God must engage the total person (**heart, soul, mind**).

22, 39: Jesus goes beyond the extent of the question put to him and joins **to the greatest and the first commandment** a **second,** that of **love** of **neighbor,** Lv 19, 18; see the note on 19, 18–19. This combination of the two commandments may already have been made in Judaism.

22, 40: The double commandment is the source from which **the whole law and the prophets** are derived.

22, 41–46: Having answered the questions of his opponents in the preceding three controversies, Jesus now puts a question to them about the sonship of the Messiah. Their easy response (43a) is countered by his quoting a verse of Ps 110 that raises a problem for their response (43b–45). They are unable to solve it and **from that day on** their questioning of him is ended.

22, 41: The Pharisees . . . questioned them: Mk is not specific about who are questioned (12, 35).

22, 42–44: David's: this view of the Pharisees was based on such Old Testament texts as Is 11, 1–9; Jer 23, 5; and Ez 34, 23; see also the extrabiblical Psalms of Solomon 17, 21. **How, then . . . saying:** Jesus cites Ps 110, 1, accepting the Davidic authorship of the psalm, a common view of his time. The psalm was probably composed for the enthronement of a Davidic king of Judah. Matthew assumes that the Pharisees interpret it as referring to the Messiah, although there is no clear evidence that it was so interpreted in the Judaism of Jesus' time. It was widely used in the early church as referring to the exaltation of the risen Jesus. **My lord:** understood as the Messiah.

22, 45: Since Matthew presents Jesus both as Messiah (16, 16) and as Son of David (1, 1; see also the note on 9, 27), the question is not meant to imply Jesus' denial of Davidic sonship. It probably means that although he is the Son of David, he is someone greater, Son of Man and Son of God, and recognized as greater by David who calls him my **'lord.'**

23, 1–39: The final section of the narrative part of the fifth book of the gospel is a denunciation by Jesus of the scribes and the Pharisees (see the note on 3, 7). It depends in part on Mk and Q (cf Mk 12, 38–39; Lk 11, 37–52; 13, 34–35), but in the main it is peculiar to Mt. (For the reasons against considering this extensive body of sayings-material either as one of the structural discourses of this gospel or as part of the one that follows in chs 24–25, see the note on 19, 1—23, 39.) While the tradition of a deep opposition between Jesus and the Pharisees is well founded, this speech reflects an opposition that goes beyond that of Jesus' ministry and must be seen as expressing the bitter conflict between Pharisaic Judaism and the church of Matthew at the time when the gospel was composed. The complaint often made that the speech ignores the positive qualities of Pharisaism and of its better representatives is true, but the complaint overlooks the circumstances that gave rise to the invective. Nor is the speech purely anti-Pharisaic. The evangelist discerns in his church many of the same faults that he finds in its opponents and warns his fellow Christians to look to their own conduct and attitudes.

23, 2–3: Have taken their seat . . . Moses: it is uncertain whether this is simply a metaphor for Mosaic teaching authority or refers to an actual **chair** on which the teacher sat. It has been proved that there was a seat so designated in synagogues of a later period than that of this gospel. **Do and observe . . . they tell you:** since the Matthean Jesus abrogates Mosaic law (5, 31–42), warns his disciples against the teaching of the Pharisees (14, 1–12), and, in this speech, denounces the Pharisees as blind guides in respect to their teaching on oaths (16–22), this commandment **to observe all things**

m: Dt 6, 5.   n: Lv 19, 18; Jas 2, 8.   o: Rom 13, 8-10; Gal 5, 14.   p: Mk 12, 35-37; Lk 20, 41-44.   q: Ps 110, 1; Acts 2, 35; Heb 1, 13.   r: Lk 20, 40.   s: Mk 12, 38-39; Lk 11, 37-52; 13, 34-35.

seat on the chair of Moses. ³Therefore, do and observe all things whatsoever they tell you, but do not follow their example. For they preach but they do not practice. ⁴ᵗ*They tie up heavy burdens [hard to carry] and lay them on people's shoulders, but they will not lift a finger to move them. ⁵ᵘ*All their works are performed to be seen. They widen their phylacteries and lengthen their tassels. ⁶ᵛ*They love places of honor at banquets, seats of honor in synagogues, ⁷greetings in marketplaces, and the salutation 'Rabbi.' ⁸*As for you, do not be called 'Rabbi.' You have but one teacher, and you are all brothers. ⁹Call no one on earth your father; you have but one Father in heaven. ¹⁰Do not be called 'Master'; you have but one master, the Messiah. ¹¹ʷThe greatest among you must be your servant. ¹²ˣWhoever exalts himself will be humbled; but whoever humbles himself will be exalted.

¹³ʸ*"Woe to you, scribes and Pharisees, you hypocrites. You lock the kingdom of heaven before human beings. You do not enter yourselves, nor do you allow entrance to those trying to enter. [¹⁴]*

¹⁵*"Woe to you, scribes and Pharisees, you hypocrites. You traverse sea and land to make one convert, and when that happens you make him a child of Gehenna twice as much as yourselves.

¹⁶ᶻ*"Woe to you, blind guides, who say, 'If

whatsoever they (the scribes and Pharisees) **tell you** cannot be taken as the evangelist's understanding of the proper standard of conduct for his church. The saying may reflect a period when the Matthean community was largely Jewish Christian and was still seeking to avoid a complete break with the synagogue. Matthew has incorporated this traditional material into the speech in accordance with his view of the course of salvation history, in which he portrays the time of Jesus' ministry as marked by the fidelity to the law, although with significant pointers to the new situation that would exist after his death and resurrection (see the note on 5, 17–20). The crowds and the disciples (1) are exhorted not to **follow** the **example** of the Jewish leaders, whose deeds do not conform to their teaching (3).

23, 4: Tie up heavy burdens: see the note on 11, 28.

23, 5: To the charge of preaching but not practicing (3), Jesus adds that of acting in order to earn praise. The disciples have already been warned against this same fault (see the note on 6, 1–18). **Phylacteries:** the Mosaic law required that during prayer small boxes containing parchments on which verses of scripture were written be worn on the left forearm and the forehead (see Ex 13, 9.16; Dt 6, 8; 11, 18). **Tassels:** see the note on 9, 20. The widening of **phylacteries** and the lengthening of **tassels** were for the purpose of making these evidences of piety more noticeable.

23, 6–7: Cf Mk 12, 38–39. **'Rabbi':** literally, "my great one," a title of respect for teachers and leaders.

23, 8–12: These verses, warning against the use of various titles, are addressed to the disciples alone. While only the title **'Rabbi'** has been said to be used in addressing the scribes and Pharisees (7), the implication is that **Father** and **'Master'** also were. The prohibition of these titles to the disciples suggests that their use was present in Matthew's church. The Matthean Jesus forbids not only the titles but the spirit of superiority and pride that is shown by their acceptance. **Whoever exalts . . . will be exalted:** cf Lk 14, 11.

23, 13–36: This series of seven "woes," directed against the **scribes and Pharisees** and addressed to them, is the heart of the speech. The phrase **woe to** occurs often in the prophetic and apocalyptic literature, expressing horror of a sin and punishment for those who commit it. **Hypocrites:** see the note on 6, 2. The hypocrisy of the **scribes and Pharisees** consists in the difference between their speech and action (3) and in demonstrations of piety that have no other purpose than to enhance their reputation as religious persons (5).

23, 13: You lock the kingdom of heaven: cf 16, 19 where Jesus tells Peter that he will give him the keys to **the kingdom of heaven.** The purpose of the authority expressed by that metaphor is to give entrance into the kingdom (the kingdom is closed only to those who reject the authority); here the charge is made that the authority of the **scribes and Pharisees** is exercised in such a way as to be an obstacle to entrance. Cf Lk 11, 52 where the accusation against the "scholars of the law" (Mt's **scribes**) is that they "have taken away the key of knowledge."

23, 14: Some manuscripts add a verse here or after v 12, "Woe to you, scribes and Pharisees, you hypocrites. You devour the houses of widows and, as a pretext, recite lengthy prayers. Because of this, you will receive a very severe condemnation." Cf Mk 12, 40; Lk 20, 47. This "woe" is almost identical with Mk 12, 40 and seems to be an interpolation derived from that text.

23, 15: In the first century A.D. until the First Jewish Revolt against Rome (A.D. 66–70), many Pharisees conducted a vigorous missionary campaign among Gentiles. **Convert:** literally, "proselyte," a Gentile who accepted Judaism fully by submitting to circumcision and all other requirements of Mosaic law. **Child of Gehenna:** worthy of everlasting punishment; for **Gehenna,** see the note on 5, 22. **Twice as much as yourselves:** possibly this refers simply to the zeal of the **convert,** surpassing that of the one who converted him.

23, 16–22: An attack on the casuistry that declared some oaths binding (**one is obligated**) and others not (**it means nothing**) and held the binding oath to be the one made by something of lesser value (**the gold; the gift on the altar**). Such teaching, which inverts the order of values, reveals the teachers to be **blind guides;** cf 15, 14. Since the Matthean Jesus forbids all oaths to his disciples (5, 33–37), this **woe** does not set up a standard for Christian moral conduct, but ridicules the Pharisees on their own terms.

t: Lk 11, 46.   *u:* 6, 1-6; Ex 13, 9.16; Nm 15, 38-39; Dt 6, 8; 11, 18.   *v:* Mk 12, 38-39; Lk 11, 43; 20, 46.   *w:* 20, 26.   *x:* Lk 14, 11; 18, 14.   *y:* Lk 11, 52.   *z:* 15, 14.

one swears by the temple, it means nothing, but if one swears by the gold of the temple, one is obligated.' ¹⁷Blind fools, which is greater, the gold, or the temple that made the gold sacred? ¹⁸And you say, 'If one swears by the altar, it means nothing, but if one swears by the gift on the altar, one is obligated.' ¹⁹You blind ones, which is greater, the gift, or the altar that makes the gift sacred? ^{20a}One who swears by the altar swears by it and all that is upon it; ²¹one who swears by the temple swears by it and by him who dwells in it; ²²one who swears by heaven swears by the throne of God and by him who is seated on it.

^{23b}*"Woe to you, scribes and Pharisees, you hypocrites. You pay tithes of mint and dill and cummin, and have neglected the weightier things of the law: judgment and mercy and fidelity. [But] these you should have done, without neglecting the others. ^{24c}*Blind guides, who strain out the gnat and swallow the camel!

^{25d}*"Woe to you, scribes and Pharisees, you hypocrites. You cleanse the outside of cup and dish, but inside they are full of plunder and self-indulgence. ²⁶Blind Pharisee, cleanse first the inside of the cup, so that the outside also may be clean.

²⁷*"Woe to you, scribes and Pharisees, you hypocrites. You are like whitewashed tombs, which appear beautiful on the outside, but inside are full of dead men's bones and every kind of filth. ^{28e}Even so, on the outside you appear righteous, but inside you are filled with hypocrisy and evildoing.

²⁹*"Woe to you, scribes and Pharisees, you hypocrites. You build the tombs of the prophets and adorn the memorials of the righteous, ^{30f}and you say, 'If we had lived in the days of our ancestors, we would not have joined them in shedding the prophets' blood.' ^{31g}Thus you bear witness against yourselves that you are the children of those who murdered the prophets; ³²now fill up what your ancestors measured out! ^{33h}You serpents, you brood of vipers, how can you flee from the judgment of Gehenna? ³⁴ⁱ*Therefore, behold, I send to you prophets

---

23, 23: The Mosaic law ordered tithing of the produce of the land (Lv 27, 30; Dt 14, 22–23), and the scribal tradition is said here to have extended this law to even the smallest herbs. The practice is criticized not in itself but because it shows the Pharisees' preoccupation with matters of less importance while they neglect **the weightier things of the law.**

23, 24: Cf Lv 11, 41–45 that forbids the eating of any "swarming creature." The Pharisees' scrupulosity about minor matters and neglect of greater ones (23) is further brought out by this contrast between straining liquids that might contain a tiny "swarming creature" and yet swallowing **the camel.** The latter was one of the unclean animals forbidden by the law (Lv 11, 4), but it is hardly possible that the scribes and Pharisees are being denounced as guilty of so gross a violation of the food laws. To **swallow the camel** is only a hyperbolic way of speaking of their neglect of what is important.

23, 25–26: The ritual washing of utensils for dining (cf Mk 7, 4) is turned into a metaphor illustrating a concern for appearances while inner purity is ignored. The **scribes and Pharisees** are compared to cups carefully washed on the outside but filthy within. **Self-indulgence:** the Greek word here translated means lack of self-control, whether in drinking or in sexual conduct.

23, 27–28: The sixth **woe,** like the preceding one, deals with concern for externals and neglect of what is **inside.** Since contact with dead bodies, even when one was unaware of it, caused ritual impurity (Nm 19, 11–22), tombs were whitewashed so that no one would contract such impurity inadvertently.

23, 29–36: The final **woe** is the most serious indictment of all. It portrays the **scribes and Pharisees** as standing in the same line as their **ancestors** who murdered **the prophets** and **the righteous.**

23, 29–32: In spite of honoring the slain dead by building their **tombs** and adorning their **memorials,** and claiming that they would not have joined in their ancestors' crimes if they **had lived in** their **days,** the **scribes and Pharisees** are true **children** of their ancestors and are defiantly ordered by Jesus to **fill up** what those **ancestors measured out.** This order reflects the Jewish notion that there was an allotted measure of suffering that had to be completed before God's final judgment would take place.

23, 34–36: There are important differences between the Matthean and the Lucan form of this Q material; cf Lk 11, 49–51. In Lk the one who sends the emissaries is the "wisdom of God." If, as many scholars think, that is the original wording of Q, Matthew, by making Jesus the sender, has presented him as the personified divine wisdom. In Lk, wisdom's emissaries are the Old Testament "prophets" and the Christian "apostles." Mt's **prophets and wise men and scribes** are probably Christian disciples alone; cf 10, 41 and see the note on 13, 52. **You will kill:** see 24, 9. **Scourge in your synagogues . . . town to town:** see 10, 17.23 and the note on 10, 17. **All the righteous blood shed upon the earth:** the slaying of the disciples is in continuity with all the shedding of **righteous blood** beginning with that of **Abel.** The persecution of Jesus' disciples by **this generation** involves the persecutors in the guilt of their murderous ancestors. **The blood of Zechariah:** see the note on Lk 11, 51. By identifying him as **the son of Barachiah** Matthew understands him to be Zechariah the Old Testament minor prophet; see Zec 1, 1.

---

a: 5, 34-35.   b: Lv 27, 30; Dt 14, 22; Lk 11, 42.   c: Lv 11, 41-45.   d: Mk 7, 4; Lk 11, 39.   e: Lk 16, 15; 18, 9.   f: Lk 11, 47.
g: Acts 7, 52.   h: 3, 7; 12, 34.   i: 5, 12; Gn 4, 8; 2 Chr 24, 20-22; Zec 1, 1; Lk 11, 49-51; Rv 18, 24.

and wise men and scribes; some of them you will kill and crucify, some of them you will scourge in your synagogues and pursue from town to town, [35] so that there may come upon you all the righteous blood shed upon earth, from the righteous blood of Abel to the blood of Zechariah, the son of Barachiah, whom you murdered between the sanctuary and the altar. [36] Amen, I say to you, all these things will come upon this generation.

The Lament over Jerusalem. [37jk]*"Jerusalem, Jerusalem, you who kill the prophets and stone those sent to you, how many times I yearned to gather your children together, as a hen gathers her young under her wings, but you were unwilling! [38l] Behold, your house will be abandoned, desolate. [39m] I tell you, you will not see me again until you say, 'Blessed is he who comes in the name of the Lord.' "

CHAPTER 24

See RG 287–88

The Destruction of the Temple Foretold. [1n]*Jesus left the temple area and was going away, when his disciples approached him to point out the temple buildings. [2]*He said to them in reply, "You see all these things, do you not? Amen, I say to you, there will not be left here a stone upon another stone that will not be thrown down."

The Beginning of Calamities. [3]*As he was sitting on the Mount of Olives, the disciples approached him privately and said, "Tell us, when will this happen, and what sign will there be of your coming, and of the end of the age?" [4]*Jesus said to them in reply, "See that no one deceives you. [5] For many will come in my name, saying, 'I am the Messiah,' and they will deceive many. [6o]*You will hear of wars and reports of wars;

23, 37–39: Cf Lk 13, 34–35. The denunciation of Pharisaic Judaism ends with this lament over **Jerusalem,** which has repeatedly rejected and murdered those whom God has **sent to** her. **How many times:** this may refer to various visits of Jesus to the city, an aspect of his ministry found in Jn but otherwise not in the synoptics. **As a hen . . . under her wings:** for imagery similar to this, see Pss 17, 8; 91, 4. **Your house . . . desolate:** probably an allusion to the destruction of the temple in A.D. 70. **You will not see me . . . in the name of the Lord:** Israel will not see Jesus again until he comes in glory for the final judgment. The acclamation has been interpreted in contrasting ways, as an indication that Israel will at last accept Jesus at that time, and as its troubled recognition of him as its dreaded judge who will pronounce its condemnation; in support of the latter view see 24, 30.

24, 1–25, 46: The discourse of the fifth book, the last of the five around which the gospel is structured. It is called the "eschatological" discourse since it deals with the coming of the new age (the **eschaton**) in its fullness, with events that will precede it, and with how the disciples are to conduct themselves while awaiting an event that is as certain as its exact time is unknown to all but the Father (24, 36). The discourse may be divided into two parts, 24, 1–44 and 24, 45–25, 46. In the first, Matthew follows his Marcan source (13, 1–37) closely. The second is drawn from Q and from the evangelist's own traditional material. Both parts show Matthew's editing of his sources by deletions, additions, and modifications. The vigilant waiting that is emphasized in the second part does not mean a cessation of ordinary activity and concentration only on what is to come, but a faithful accomplishment of duties at hand, with awareness that the end, for which the disciples must always be ready, will entail the great judgment by which the everlasting destiny of all will be determined.

24, 2: As in Mk, Jesus predicts the destruction of the temple. By omitting the Marcan story of the widow's contribution (12, 41–44) that immediately precedes the prediction in that gospel, Matthew has established a close connection between it

and 23, 38, ". . . your house will be abandoned desolate."

24, 3: The Mount of Olives: see the note on 21, 1. **The disciples:** cf Mk 13, 3–4 where only Peter, James, John, and Andrew put the question that is answered by the discourse. In both gospels, however, the question is put **privately:** the ensuing discourse is only for those who are **disciples** of Jesus. **When will this happen . . . end of the age?:** Matthew distinguishes carefully between the destruction of the temple [this] and the **coming** of Jesus that will bring **the end of the age.** In Mk the two events are more closely connected, a fact that may be explained by Mark's believing that the one would immediately succeed the other. **Coming:** this translates the Greek word **parousia,** which is used in the gospels only here and in vv 27, 37, and 39. It designated the official visit of a ruler to a city or the manifestation of a saving deity, and it was used by Christians to refer to the final coming of Jesus in glory, a term first found in the New Testament with that meaning in 1 Thes 2, 19. **The end of the age:** see the note on 13, 39.

24, 4–14: This section of the discourse deals with calamities in the world (6–7) and in the church (9–12). The former **must happen** before **the end** comes (6), but they are only **the beginning of the labor pains** (8). (It may be noted that the Greek word translated **the end** in v 6 and in vv 13–14 is not the same as the phrase "the end of the age" in v 3, although the meaning is the same.) The latter are sufferings of the church, both from within and without, that will last until the **gospel** is **preached . . . to all nations. Then the end will come** and those who have endured the sufferings with fidelity **will be saved** (13–14).

24, 6–7: The disturbances mentioned here are a commonplace of apocalyptic language, as is the assurance that they **must happen** (see Dn 2, 28 LXX), for that is the plan of God. **Kingdom against kingdom:** see Is 19, 2.

j: Lk 13, 34-35; 19, 41-44. k: 21, 35. l: Jer 12, 7. m: Ps 118, 26. n: Mk 13, 1-37; Lk 21, 5-36. o: Dn 2, 28 LXX.

see that you are not alarmed, for these things must happen, but it will not yet be the end. [7p]Nation will rise against nation, and kingdom against kingdom; there will be famines and earthquakes from place to place. [8*]All these are the beginning of the labor pains. [9q*]Then they will hand you over to persecution, and they will kill you. You will be hated by all nations because of my name. [10]And then many will be led into sin; they will betray and hate one another. [11]Many false prophets will arise and deceive many; [12]and because of the increase of evildoing, the love of many will grow cold. [13r]But the one who perseveres to the end will be saved. [14s*]And this gospel of the kingdom will be preached throughout the world as a witness to all nations, and then the end will come.

The Great Tribulation. [15t*]"When you see the desolating abomination spoken of through Daniel the prophet standing in the holy place (let the reader understand), [16*]then those in Judea must flee to the mountains, [17u*]a person on the housetop must not go down to get things out of his house, [18]a person in the field must not return to get his cloak. [19]Woe to pregnant women and nursing mothers in those days. [20*]Pray that your flight not be in winter or on the sabbath, [21v*]for at that time there will be great tribulation, such as has not been since the beginning of the world until now, nor ever will be. [22]And if those days had not been

24, 8: The labor pains: the tribulations leading up to the end of the age are compared to the pains of a woman about to give birth. There is much attestation for rabbinic use of the phrase "the woes (or birth pains) of the Messiah" after the New Testament period, but in at least one instance it is attributed to a rabbi who lived in the late first century A.D. In this Jewish usage it meant the distress of the time preceding the coming of the Messiah; here, the **labor pains** precede the coming of the Son of Man in glory.

24, 9–12: Matthew has used Mk 13, 9–12 in his missionary discourse (10, 17–21) and omits it here. Besides the sufferings, including death, and the hatred of **all nations** that the disciples will have to endure, there will be worse affliction within the church itself. This is described in vv 10–12, which are peculiar to Mt. **Will be led into sin:** literally, "will be scandalized," probably meaning that they will become apostates; see 13, 21 where "fall away" translates the same Greek word as here. **Betray:** in the Greek this is the same word as the **hand over** of v 9. The handing over to persecution and hatred from outside will have their counterpart within the church. **False prophets:** these are Christians; see the note on 7, 15–20. **Evildoing:** see 7, 23. Because of the apocalyptic nature of much of this discourse, the literal meaning of this description of the church should not be pressed too hard. However, there is reason to think that Mt's addition of these verses reflects in some measure the condition of his community.

24, 14: Except for the last part (**and then the end will come**), this verse substantially repeats Mk 13, 10. The Matthean addition raises a problem since what follows in vv 15–23 refers to the horrors of the First Jewish Revolt including the destruction of the temple, and Matthew, writing after that time, knew that the parousia of Jesus was still in the future. A solution may be that the evangelist saw the events of those verses as foreshadowing the cosmic disturbances that he associates with the parousia (29) so that the period in which the former took place could be understood as belonging to **the end.**

24, 15–28: Cf Mk 13, 14–23; Lk 17, 23–24.37. A further stage in the tribulations that will precede the coming of the Son of Man, and an answer to the question of v 3a, "when will this (the destruction of the temple) happen?"

24, 15: The desolating abomination: in 167 B.C. the Syrian king Antiochus IV Epiphanes desecrated the temple by setting up in it a statue of Zeus Olympios (see 1 Mc 1, 54). That event is referred to in Dn 12, 11 LXX as the "desolating abomination" (NAB "horrible abomination") and the same Greek term is used here; cf also Dn 9, 27; 11, 31. Although the desecration had taken place before Dn was written, it is presented there as a future event, and Matthew sees that "prophecy" fulfilled in the desecration of the temple by the Romans. **In the holy place:** the temple; more precise than Mk's **where he should not** (13, 14). **Let the reader understand:** this parenthetical remark, taken from Mk 13, 14, invites **the reader** to realize the meaning of Dn's "prophecy."

24, 16: The tradition that the Christians of Jerusalem fled from that city to Pella, a city of Transjordan, at the time of the First Jewish Revolt is found in Eusebius (**Ecclesiastical History,** 3, 5, 3), who attributes the flight to "a certain oracle given by revelation before the war." The tradition is not improbable but the Matthean command, derived from its Marcan source, is vague in respect to the place of flight (**to the mountains**), although some scholars see it as applicable to the flight to Pella.

24, 17–19: Haste is essential, and the journey will be particularly difficult for women who are burdened with unborn or infant children.

24, 20: On the sabbath: this addition to **in winter** (cf Mk 13, 18) has been understood as an indication that Mt was addressed to a church still observing the Mosaic law of sabbath rest and the scribal limitations upon the length of journeys that might lawfully be made on that day. That interpretation conflicts with Mt's view on sabbath observance (cf 12, 1–14). The meaning of the addition may be that those undertaking on the sabbath a journey such as the one here ordered would be offending the sensibilities of law-observant Jews and would incur their hostility.

24, 21: For the unparalleled distress of that time, see Dn 12, 1.

p: Is 19, 2.　*q:* 10, 17.　*r:* 10, 22.　*s:* 28, 19; Rom 10, 18.　*t:* Dn 9, 27; 11, 31; 12, 11; Mk 13, 14.　*u:* Lk 17, 31.　*v:* Dn 12, 1.

shortened, no one would be saved; but for the sake of the elect they will be shortened. ²³ʷIf anyone says to you then, 'Look, here is the Messiah!' or, 'There he is!' do not believe it. ²⁴False messiahs and false prophets will arise, and they will perform signs and wonders so great as to deceive, if that were possible, even the elect. ²⁵Behold, I have told it to you beforehand. ²⁶*So if they say to you, 'He is in the desert,' do not go out there; if they say, 'He is in the inner rooms,' do not believe it. ²⁷ˣFor just as lightning comes from the east and is seen as far as the west, so will the coming of the Son of Man be. ²⁸Wherever the corpse is, there the vultures will gather.

The Coming of the Son of Man. ²⁹ʸ*"Immediately after the tribulation of those days,

the sun will be darkened,
and the moon will not give its light,
and the stars will fall from the sky,
and the powers of the heavens will be shaken.

³⁰ᶻ*And then the sign of the Son of Man will appear in heaven, and all the tribes of the earth will mourn, and they will see the Son of

Man coming upon the clouds of heaven with power and great glory. ³¹ᵃ*And he will send out his angels with a trumpet blast, and they will gather his elect from the four winds, from one end of the heavens to the other.

The Lesson of the Fig Tree. ³²*"Learn a lesson from the fig tree. When its branch becomes tender and sprouts leaves, you know that summer is near. ³³In the same way, when you see all these things, know that he is near, at the gates. ³⁴*Amen, I say to you, this generation will not pass away until all these things have taken place. ³⁵ᵇHeaven and earth will pass away, but my words will not pass away.

The Unknown Day and Hour. ³⁶ᶜ*"But of that day and hour no one knows, neither the angels of heaven, nor the Son, but the Father alone. ³⁷ᵈ*For as it was in the days of Noah, so it will be at the coming of the Son of Man. ³⁸In [those] days before the flood, they were eating and drinking, marrying and giving in marriage, up to the day that Noah entered the ark. ³⁹They did not know until the flood came and carried them all away. So will it be [also] at the coming of the Son of Man. ⁴⁰ᵉ*Two men will be out in the field; one will

---

24, 26–28: Claims that the Messiah is to be found in some distant or secret place must be ignored. **The coming of the Son of Man** will be as clear as **lightning** is to all and as **the corpse** of an animal is to **vultures;** cf Lk 17, 24.37. Here there is clear identification of **the Son of Man** and the Messiah; cf v 23.

24, 29: The answer to the question of v 3b, "What will be the sign of your coming?" **Immediately after . . . those days:** the shortening of time between the preceding **tribulation** and the parousia has been explained as Matthew's use of a supposed device of Old Testament prophecy whereby certainty that a predicted event will occur is expressed by depicting it as imminent. While it is questionable that that is an acceptable understanding of the Old Testament predictions, it may be applicable here, for Matthew knew that the parousia had not come **immediately after** the fall of Jerusalem, and it is unlikely that he is attributing a mistaken calculation of time to Jesus. **The sun . . . be shaken:** cf Is 13, 10.13.

24, 30: The sign of the Son of Man: perhaps this means **the sign** that is the glorious appearance **of the Son of Man;** cf 12, 39–40 where "the sign of Jonah" is Jonah's being in the "belly of the whale." **Tribes of the earth will mourn:** peculiar to Mt; cf Zec 12, 12–14. **Coming upon the clouds . . . glory:** cf Dn 7, 13, although there the "one like a son of man" comes to God to receive kingship; here **the Son of Man** comes from heaven for judgment.

24, 31: Send out his angels: cf 13, 41 where they are sent out to collect the wicked for punishment. **Trumpet blast:** cf Is 27, 13; 1 Thes 4, 16.

24, 32–35: Cf Mk 13, 28–31.

24, 34: The difficulty raised by this verse cannot be satisfactorily removed by the supposition that **this generation** means the Jewish people throughout the course of their history, much less the entire human race. Perhaps for Matthew it means the **generation** to which he and his community belonged.

24, 36–44: The statement of v 34 is now counterbalanced by one that declares that the exact time of the parousia is known only to **the Father** (36), and the disciples are warned to be always ready for it. This section is drawn from Mk and Q (cf Lk 17, 26–27.34–35; 12, 39–40).

24, 36: Many textual witnesses omit **nor the Son,** which follows Mk 13, 32. Since its omission can be explained by reluctance to attribute this ignorance to **the Son,** the reading that includes it is probably original.

24, 37–39: Cf Lk 17, 26–27. **In the days of Noah:** the Old Testament account of the flood lays no emphasis upon what is central for Matthew, i.e., the unexpected coming of the flood upon those who were unprepared for it.

24, 40–41: Cf Lk 17, 34–35. **Taken . . . left:** the former probably means **taken** into the kingdom; the latter, **left** for destruction. People in the same situation will be dealt with in opposite ways. In this context, the discrimination between them will be based on their readiness for the coming of the Son of Man.

w: Lk 17, 23.   *x:* Lk 17, 24.37.   *y:* Is 13, 10.13; Ez 32, 7; Am 8, 9.   *z:* Dn 7, 13; Zec 12, 12-14; Rv 1, 7.   *a:* Is 27, 13; 1 Cor 15, 52; 1 Thes 4, 16.   *b:* Is 40, 8.   *c:* Acts 1, 7.   *d:* Gn 6, 5—7, 23; Lk 17, 26-27; 2 Pt 3, 6.   *e:* Lk 17, 34-35.

be taken, and one will be left. *41*Two women will be grinding at the mill; one will be taken, and one will be left. *42f**Therefore, stay awake! For you do not know on which day your Lord will come. *43g*Be sure of this: if the master of the house had known the hour of night when the thief was coming, he would have stayed awake and not let his house be broken into. *44*So too, you also must be prepared, for at an hour you do not expect, the Son of Man will come.

The Faithful or the Unfaithful Servant.
45h*"Who, then, is the faithful and prudent servant, whom the master has put in charge of his household to distribute to them their food at the proper time? *46*Blessed is that servant whom his master on his arrival finds doing so. *47*Amen, I say to you, he will put him in charge of all his property. *48**But if that wicked servant says to himself, 'My master is long delayed,' *49*and begins to beat his fellow servants, and eat and drink with drunkards, *50*the servant's master will come on an unexpected day and at an unknown hour *51i**and will punish him severely and assign him a place with the hypocrites, where there will be wailing and grinding of teeth.

CHAPTER 25

See RG 287-88

The Parable of the Ten Virgins.
1*"Then the kingdom of heaven will be like ten virgins who took their lamps and went out to meet the bridegroom. *2**Five of them were foolish and five were wise. *3*The foolish ones, when taking their lamps, brought no oil with them, *4*but the wise brought flasks of oil with their lamps. *5*Since the bridegroom was long delayed, they all became drowsy and fell asleep. *6*At midnight, there was a cry, 'Behold, the bridegroom! Come out to meet him!' *7*Then all those virgins got up and trimmed their lamps. *8*The foolish ones said to the wise, 'Give us some of your oil, for our lamps are going out.' *9*But the wise ones replied, 'No, for there may not be enough for us and you. Go instead to the merchants and buy some for yourselves.' *10*While they went off to buy it, the bridegroom came and those who were ready went into the wedding feast with him. Then the door was locked. *11j**Afterwards the other virgins came and said, 'Lord, Lord, open the door for us!' *12*But he said in reply, 'Amen, I say to you, I do not know you.' *13k**Therefore, stay awake, for you know neither the day nor the hour.

The Parable of the Talents. *14L**"It will be as when a man who was going on a journey called in his servants and entrusted his possessions to them. *15**To one he gave five talents; to another, two; to a third, one—to each according to his ability. Then he went away.

24, 42–44: Cf Lk 12, 39–40. The theme of vigilance and readiness is continued with the bold comparison of the Son of Man to a thief who comes to break into a house.

24, 45–51: The second part of the discourse (see the note on 24, 1—25, 46) begins with this parable of **the faithful** or unfaithful **servant;** cf Lk 12, 41–46. It is addressed to the leaders of Matthew's church; **the servant has** been **put in charge** of his master's **household** (45) even though that **household** is composed of those who are his **fellow servants** (49).

24, 45: To distribute . . . proper time: readiness for the master's return means a vigilance that is accompanied by faithful performance of the duty assigned.

24, 48: My master . . . delayed: the note of delay is found also in the other parables of this section; cf 25, 5.19.

24, 51: Punish him severely: the Greek verb, found in the New Testament only here and in the Lucan parallel (12, 46), means, literally, "cut in two." **With the hypocrites:** see the note on 6, 2. Matthew classes the unfaithful Christian leader with the unbelieving leaders of Judaism. **Wailing and grinding of teeth:** see the note on 8, 11–12.

25, 1–13: Peculiar to Mt.

25, 1: Then: at the time of the parousia. **Kingdom . . . will be like:** see the note on 13, 24–30.

25, 2–4: Foolish . . . wise: cf the contrasted "wise man" and "fool" of 7, 24.26, where the two are distinguished by good deeds and lack of them, and such deeds may be signified by the **oil** of this parable.

25, 11–12: Lord, Lord: cf 7, 21. **I do not know you:** cf 7, 23, where the Greek verb is different but synonymous.

25, 13: Stay awake: some scholars see this command as an addition to the original parable of Matthew's traditional material, since in v 5 all the virgins, wise and foolish, fall asleep. But the wise virgins are adequately equipped for their task, and **stay awake** may mean no more than to be prepared; cf 24, 42.44.

25, 14–30: Cf Lk 19, 12–27.

25, 14: It will be as when . . . journey: literally, "For just as a man who was going on a journey." Although the comparison is not completed, the sense is clear; the kingdom of heaven is like the situation here described. Faithful use of one's gifts will lead to participation in the fullness of the kingdom, lazy inactivity to exclusion from it.

25, 15: Talents: see the note on 18, 24.

f: 25, 13; Lk 12, 39-40. *g:* 1 Thes 5, 2. *h:* Lk 12, 41-46. *i:* 13, 42; 25, 30. *j:* 7, 21.23; Lk 13, 25.27. *k:* 24, 42; Mk 13, 33. *l:* Lk 19, 12-27.

Immediately [16]the one who received five talents went and traded with them, and made another five. [17]Likewise, the one who received two made another two. [18]*But the man who received one went off and dug a hole in the ground and buried his master's money. [19]After a long time the master of those servants came back and settled accounts with them. [20]*The one who had received five talents came forward bringing the additional five. He said, 'Master, you gave me five talents. See, I have made five more.' [21m]His master said to him, 'Well done, my good and faithful servant. Since you were faithful in small matters, I will give you great responsibilities. Come, share your master's joy.' [22][Then] the one who had received two talents also came forward and said, 'Master, you gave me two talents. See, I have made two more.' [23]His master said to him, 'Well done, my good and faithful servant. Since you were faithful in small matters, I will give you great responsibilities. Come, share your master's joy.' [24]Then the one who had received the one talent came forward and said, 'Master, I knew you were a demanding person, harvesting where you did not plant and gathering where you did not scatter; [25]so out of fear I went off and buried your talent in the ground. Here it is back.' [26]*His master said to him in reply, 'You wicked, lazy servant! So you knew that I harvest where I did not plant and gather where I did not scatter? [27]Should you not then have put my money in the bank so that I could have got it back with interest on my return? [28]Now then! Take the talent from him and give it to the one with ten. [29n]*For to everyone who has, more will be given and he will grow rich; but from the one who has not, even what he has will be taken away. [30]*And throw this useless servant into the darkness outside, where there will be wailing and grinding of teeth.'

The Judgment of the Nations. [31o]*"When the Son of Man comes in his glory, and all the angels with him, he will sit upon his glorious throne, [32p]*and all the nations will be assembled before him. And he will separate them one from another, as a shepherd separates the sheep from the goats. [33]He will place the sheep on his right and the goats on his left. [34]Then the king will say to those on his right, 'Come, you who are blessed by my Father. Inherit the kingdom prepared for you from the foundation of the world. [35q]For I was hungry and you gave me food, I was thirsty and you gave me drink, a stranger and you welcomed me, [36]naked and you clothed me, ill and you cared for me, in prison and you visited me.' [37]*Then the righteous will answer him and say, 'Lord, when did we see

25, 18: Buried his master's money: see the note on 13, 44.

25, 20–23: Although the first two servants have received and doubled large sums, their faithful trading is regarded by the master as fidelity **in small matters** only, compared with the **great responsibilities** now to be given to them. The latter are unspecified. **Share your master's joy:** probably the joy of the banquet of the kingdom; cf 8, 11.

25, 26–28: Wicked, lazy servant: this man's inactivity is not negligible but seriously culpable. As punishment, he loses the gift he had received, that is now given to the first servant, whose possessions are already great.

25, 29: See the note on 13, 12 where there is a similar application of this maxim.

25, 30: See the note on 8, 11–12.

25, 31–46: The conclusion of the discourse, which is peculiar to Mt, portrays the final judgment that will accompany the parousia. Although often called a "parable," it is not really such, for the only parabolic elements are the depiction of **the Son of Man** as **a shepherd** and of **the righteous** and the wicked as **sheep** and **goats** respectively (32–33). The criterion of judgment will be the deeds of mercy that have been done for the **least** of Jesus' **brothers** (40). A difficult and important question is the identification of these **least brothers.** Are they all people who have suffered hunger, thirst, etc. (35.36) or a particular group of such sufferers? Scholars are divided in their response and arguments can be made for either side. But leaving aside the problem of what the traditional material that Matthew edited may have meant, it seems that a stronger case can be made for the view that in the evangelist's sense the sufferers are Christians, probably Christian missionaries whose sufferings were brought upon them by their preaching of the gospel. The criterion of judgment for **all the nations** is their treatment of those who have borne to the world the message of Jesus, and this means ultimately their acceptance or rejection of Jesus himself; cf 10, 40, "Whoever receives you, receives me."

25, 31: See the note on 16, 27.

25, 32: All the nations: before the end the gospel will have been preached throughout the world (24, 14); thus the Gentiles will be judged on their response to it. But the phrase **all the nations** includes the Jews also, for at the judgment "the Son of Man . . . will repay everyone according to his conduct' (16, 27).

25, 37–40: The righteous will be astonished that in caring for the needs of the sufferers they were ministering to the **Lord** himself. **One of these least brothers of mine:** cf 10, 42.

m: Lk 16, 10.   n: 13, 12; Mk 4, 25; Lk 8, 18; 19, 26.   o: 16, 27; Dt 33 2 LXX.   p: Ez 34, 17.   q: Is 58, 7; Ez 18, 7.

you hungry and feed you, or thirsty and give you drink? *38*When did we see you a stranger and welcome you, or naked and clothe you? *39*When did we see you ill or in prison, and visit you?' *40r*And the king will say to them in reply, 'Amen, I say to you, whatever you did for one of these least brothers of mine, you did for me.' *41s*Then he will say to those on his left, 'Depart from me, you accursed, into the eternal fire prepared for the devil and his angels. *42t*For I was hungry and you gave me no food, I was thirsty and you gave me no drink, *43*a stranger and you gave me no welcome, naked and you gave me no clothing, ill and in prison, and you did not care for me.' *44*Then they will answer and say, 'Lord, when did we see you hungry or thirsty or a stranger or naked or ill or in prison, and not minister to your needs?' *45*He will answer them, 'Amen, I say to you, what you did not do for one of these least ones, you did not do for me.' *46u*And these will go off to eternal punishment, but the righteous to eternal life."

VII: The Passion and Resurrection

CHAPTER 26

See RG 288–89

The Conspiracy against Jesus. *1*When Jesus finished all these words, he said to his disciples, *2v*"You know that in two days' time it will be Passover, and the Son of Man will be handed over to be crucified." *3*Then the chief priests and the elders of the people assembled in the palace of the high priest, who was called Caiaphas, *4w*and they consulted together to arrest Jesus by treachery and put him to death. *5*But they said, "Not during the festival, that there may not be a riot among the people."

The Anointing at Bethany. *6x*Now when Jesus was in Bethany in the house of Simon the leper, *7*a woman came up to him with an alabaster jar of costly perfumed oil, and poured it on his head while he was reclining at table. *8*When the disciples saw this, they were indignant and said, "Why this waste? *9*It could have been sold for much, and the money given to the poor." *10*Since Jesus knew this, he said to them, "Why do you make trouble for the woman? She has done a good thing for me. *11y*The poor you will always have with you; but you will not always have me. *12*In pouring this perfumed oil upon my body, she did it to prepare me for burial. *13*Amen, I say to you, wherever this gospel is proclaimed in the whole world, what she has done will be spoken of, in memory of her."

The Betrayal by Judas. *14z*Then one of the Twelve, who was called Judas Iscariot, went to the chief priests *15a*and said, "What

---

25, 41: Fire prepared . . . his angels: cf 1 Enoch 10, 13 where it is said of the evil angels and Semyaza, their leader, "In those days they will lead them into the bottom of the fire—and in torment—in the prison (where) they will be locked up forever."

25, 44–45: The **accursed** (41) will be likewise astonished that their neglect of the sufferers was neglect of the **Lord** and will receive from him a similar answer.

26, 1–28, 20: The five books with alternating narrative and discourse (3, 1—25, 46) that give this gospel its distinctive structure lead up to the climactic events that are the center of Christian belief and the origin of the Christian church, the passion and resurrection of Jesus. In his passion narrative (chs 26–27) Matthew follows his Marcan source closely but with omissions (e.g., Mk 14, 51–52) and additions (e.g., 27, 3–10.19). Some of the additions indicate that he utilized traditions that he had received from elsewhere; others are due to his own theological insight (e.g., 26, 28, ". . . for the forgiveness of sins"; 27, 52). In his editing Matthew also altered Mk in some minor details. But there is no need to suppose that he knew any passion narrative other than Mark's.

26, 1–2: When Jesus finished all these words: see the note on 7, 28–29. **"You know . . . crucified":** Matthew turns

Mk's statement of the time (14, 1) into Jesus' final prediction of his passion. **Passover:** see the note on Mk 14, 1.

26, 3: Caiaphas was high priest from A.D. 18 to 36.

26, 5: Not during the festival: the plan to delay Jesus' arrest and execution until after **the festival** was not carried out, for according to the synoptics he was arrested on the night of Nisan 14 and put to death the following day. No reason is given why the plan was changed.

26, 6–13: See the notes on Mk 14, 3–9 and Jn 12, 1–8.

26, 12: To prepare me for burial: cf Mk 14, 8. In accordance with the interpretation of this act as Jesus' **burial** anointing, Matthew, more consistent than Mark, changes the purpose of the visit of the women to Jesus' tomb; they do not go to anoint him (Mk 16, 1) but "to see the tomb" (28, 1).

26, 14: Iscariot: see the note on Lk 6, 16.

26, 15: The motive of avarice is introduced by Judas's question about the price for betrayal, which is absent in the Marcan source (14, 10–11). **Hand him over:** the same Greek

r: 10, 40.42. *s*: 7, 23; Lk 13, 27. *t*: Jb 22, 7; Jas 2, 15-16. *u*: Dn 12, 2. *v*: Mk 14, 1-2; Lk 22, 1-2. *w*: Jn 11, 47-53. *x*: Mk 14, 3-9; Jn 12, 1-8. *y*: Dt 15, 11. *z*: Mk 14, 10-11; Lk 22, 3-6. *a*: Zec 11, 12.

are you willing to give me if I hand him over to you?" They paid him thirty pieces of silver, *16*and from that time on he looked for an opportunity to hand him over.

Preparations for the Passover. *17bc**On the first day of the Feast of Unleavened Bread, the disciples approached Jesus and said, "Where do you want us to prepare for you to eat the Passover?" *18**He said, "Go into the city to a certain man and tell him, 'The teacher says, "My appointed time draws near; in your house I shall celebrate the Passover with my disciples." ' " *19*The disciples then did as Jesus had ordered, and prepared the Passover.

The Betrayer. *20*When it was evening, he reclined at table with the Twelve. *21**And while they were eating, he said, "Amen, I say to you, one of you will betray me." *22*Deeply distressed at this, they began to say to him one after another, "Surely it is not I, Lord?" *23*He said in reply, "He who has dipped his hand into the dish with me is the one who will betray me. *24d**The Son of Man indeed goes, as it is written of him, but woe to that man by whom the Son of Man is betrayed. It would be better for that man if he had never been born." *25**Then Judas, his betrayer, said in reply, "Surely it is not I, Rabbi?" He answered, "You have said so."

The Lord's Supper. *26ef**While they were eating, Jesus took bread, said the blessing, broke it, and giving it to his disciples said, "Take and eat; this is my body." *27**Then he took a cup, gave thanks, and gave it to them, saying, "Drink from it, all of you, *28g*for this is my blood of the covenant, which will be shed on behalf of many for the forgiveness of sins. *29**I tell you, from now on I shall not drink this fruit of the vine until the day when I drink it with you new in the kingdom of my Father." *30**Then, after singing a hymn, they went out to the Mount of Olives.

verb is used to express the saving purpose of God by which Jesus is handed over to death (cf 17, 22; 20, 18; 26, 2) and the human malice that hands him over. **Thirty pieces of silver:** the price of the betrayal is found only in Mt. It is derived from Zec 11, 12 where it is the wages paid to the rejected shepherd, a cheap price (Zec 11, 13). That amount is also the compensation paid to one whose slave has been gored by an ox (Ex 21, 12).

26, 17: The first day of the Feast of Unleavened Bread: see the note on Mk 14, 1. Matthew omits Mk's "when they sacrificed the Passover lamb."

26, 18: By omitting much of Mk 14, 13–15, adding **My appointed time draws near,** and turning the question into a statement, **in your house I shall celebrate the Passover,** Matthew has given this passage a solemnity and majesty greater than that of his source.

26, 21: Given Matthew's interest in the fulfillment of the Old Testament, it is curious that he omits the Marcan designation of Jesus' betrayer as "one who is eating with me" (14, 18), since that is probably an allusion to Ps 41, 10. However, the shocking fact that the betrayer is one who shares table fellowship with Jesus is emphasized in v 23.

26, 24: It would be better . . . born: the enormity of the deed is such that it would be better not to exist than to do it.

26, 25: Peculiar to Mt. **You have said so:** cf 26, 64; 27, 11. This is a half-affirmative. Emphasis is laid on the pronoun and the answer implies that the statement would not have been made if the question had not been asked.

26, 26–29: See the note on Mk 14, 22–24. The Marcan-Matthean is one of the two major New Testament traditions of the words of Jesus when instituting the Eucharist. The other (and earlier) is the Pauline-Lucan (1 Cor 11, 23–25; Lk 22, 19–20). Each shows the influence of Christian liturgical usage, but the Marcan-Matthean is more developed in that regard than the Pauline-Lucan. The words over the

bread and cup succeed each other without the intervening meal mentioned in 1 Cor 11, 25; Lk 22, 20; and there is parallelism between the consecratory words (**this is my body . . . this is my blood**). Matthew follows Mk closely but with some changes.

26, 26: See the note on 14, 19. **Said the blessing:** a prayer blessing God. **Take and eat:** literally, **Take, eat. Eat** is an addition to Mk's "take it" (literally, "take": 14, 22). **This is my body:** the bread is identified with Jesus himself.

26, 27–28: **Gave thanks:** see the note on 15, 36. **Gave it to them . . . all of you:** cf Mk 14, 23–24. In the Marcan sequence the disciples drink and then Jesus says the interpretative words. Matthew has changed this into a command to **drink** followed by those words. **My blood:** see Lv 17, 11 for the concept that the **blood** is "the seat of life" and that when placed on the altar it "makes atonement." **Which will be shed:** the present participle, "being shed" or "going to be shed," is future in relation to the Last Supper. **On behalf of:** Greek **peri;** see the note on Mk 14, 24. **Many:** see the note on 20, 28. **For the forgiveness of sins:** a Matthean addition. The same phrase occurs in Mk 1, 4 in connection with John's baptism but Matthew avoids it there (3, 11). He places it here probably because he wishes to emphasize that it is the sacrificial death of Jesus that brings **forgiveness of sins.**

26, 29: Although his death will interrupt the table fellowship he has had with the disciples, Jesus confidently predicts his vindication by God and a new table fellowship with them at the banquet of the kingdom.

26, 30: See the note on Mk 14, 26.

b: Mk 14, 12–21; Lk 22, 7–23. *c:* Ex 12, 14–20. *d:* Is 53, 8–10. *e:* Mk 14, 22–26; Lk 22, 14–23; 1 Cor 11, 23–25. *f:* 1 Cor 10, 16. *g:* Ex 24, 8; Is 53, 12.

Peter's Denial Foretold. [31][hi]*Then Jesus said to them, "This night all of you will have your faith in me shaken, for it is written:

'I will strike the shepherd,
    and the sheep of the flock will be
        dispersed';

[32]but after I have been raised up, I shall go before you to Galilee." [33]Peter said to him in reply, "Though all may have their faith in you shaken, mine will never be." [34][jk]*Jesus said to him, "Amen, I say to you, this very night before the cock crows, you will deny me three times." [35]Peter said to him, "Even though I should have to die with you, I will not deny you." And all the disciples spoke likewise.

The Agony in the Garden. [36][lm]*Then Jesus came with them to a place called Gethsemane, and he said to his disciples, "Sit here while I go over there and pray." [37][n]*He took along Peter and the two sons of Zebedee, and began to feel sorrow and distress. [38][o]*Then he said to them, "My soul is sorrowful even to death. Remain here and keep watch with me." [39][p]*He advanced a lit-tle and fell prostrate in prayer, saying, "My Father, if it is possible, let this cup pass from me; yet, not as I will, but as you will." [40]When he returned to his disciples he found them asleep. He said to Peter, "So you could not keep watch with me for one hour? [41]*Watch and pray that you may not undergo the test. The spirit is willing, but the flesh is weak." [42][q]*Withdrawing a second time, he prayed again, "My Father, if it is not possi-ble that this cup pass without my drinking it, your will be done!" [43]Then he returned once more and found them asleep, for they could not keep their eyes open. [44]He left them and withdrew again and prayed a third time, say-ing the same thing again. [45][r]Then he re-turned to his disciples and said to them, "Are you still sleeping and taking your rest? Be-hold, the hour is at hand when the Son of Man is to be handed over to sinners. [46]Get up, let us go. Look, my betrayer is at hand."

The Betrayal and Arrest of Jesus. [47][s]While he was still speaking, Judas, one of the Twelve, arrived, accompanied by a large crowd, with swords and clubs, who had come from the chief priests and the eld-

---

26, 31: Will have . . . shaken: literally, "will be scandal-ized in me"; see the note on 24, 9–12. **I will strike . . . dis-persed:** cf Zec 13, 7.

26, 34: Before the cock crows: see the note on 14, 25. The third watch of the night was called "cockcrow." **Deny me:** see the note on 16, 24.

26, 36–56: Cf Mk 14, 32–52. The account of Jesus in Gethsemane is divided between that of his agony (36–46) and that of his betrayal and arrest (47–56). Jesus' **sorrow and dis-tress** (37) in face of death is unrelieved by the presence of his three disciples who, though urged to **watch with** him (38.41), fall asleep (40.43). He prays that **if . . . possible** his death may be avoided (39) but that his Father's will be done (39.42.44). Knowing then that his death must take place, he announces to his companions that **the hour** for his being **handed over** has come (45). Judas arrives with an armed band provided by the Sanhedrin and greets Jesus with a kiss, the prearranged sign for his identification (47–49). After his arrest, he rebukes a disciple who has attacked the **high priest's servant** with a **sword** (51–54), and chides those who have come out to seize him with **swords and clubs** as if he were a **robber** (55–56). In both rebukes Jesus declares that the treatment he is now re-ceiving is the fulfillment of the scriptures (55.56). The subse-quent flight of **all the disciples** is itself the fulfillment of his own prediction (cf 31). In this episode, Matthew follows Mk with a few alterations.

26, 36: Gethsemane: the Hebrew name means "oil press" and designates an olive orchard on the western slope of the Mount of Olives; see the note on 21, 1. The name appears only in Mt and Mk. The place is called a "garden" in Jn 18, 1.

26, 37: Peter and the two sons of Zebedee: cf 17, 1.

26, 38: Cf Ps 42, 6.12. In the Septuagint (Ps 41, 5.12) the same Greek word for **sorrowful** is used as here. **To death:** i.e., "enough to die"; cf Jon 4, 9.

26, 39: My Father: see the note on Mk 14, 36. Matthew omits the Aramaic **'abbā'** and adds the qualifier **my. This cup:** see the note on Mk 10, 38–40.

26, 41: Undergo the test: see the note on 6, 13. In that verse "the final test" translates the same Greek word as is here translated **the test,** and these are the only instances of the use of that word in Mt. It is possible that the passion of Jesus is seen here as an anticipation of the great tribulation that will precede the parousia (see the notes on 24, 8; 24, 21) to which 6, 13 refers, and that just as Jesus prays to be delivered from death (39), so he exhorts the disciples to pray that they will not have to **undergo the** great **test** that his passion would be for them. Some scholars, however, understand **not undergo** (literally, "not enter") **the test** as meaning not that the disci-ples may be spared **the test** but that they may not yield to the temptation of falling away from Jesus because of his passion even though they will have to endure it.

26, 42: Your will be done: cf 6, 10.

h: Mk 14, 7-31. *i:* Zec 13, 7; Jn 16, 32. *j:* Lk 22, 33-34; Jn 13, 37-38. *k:* 26, 69-75. *l:* Mk 14, 32-42; Lk 22, 39-46. *m:* Jn 18, 1. *n:* Heb 5, 7. *o:* Ps 42, 6.12; Jon 4, 9. *p:* Jn 4, 34; 6, 38; Phil 2, 8. *q:* 6, 10; Heb 10, 9. *r:* Jn 12, 23; 13, 1; 17, 1. *s:* Mk 14, 43-50; Lk 22, 47-53; Jn 18, 3-11.

ers of the people. [48]His betrayer had arranged a sign with them, saying, "The man I shall kiss is the one; arrest him." [49]*Immediately he went over to Jesus and said, "Hail, Rabbi!" and he kissed him. [50]Jesus answered him, "Friend, do what you have come for." Then stepping forward they laid hands on Jesus and arrested him. [51]And behold, one of those who accompanied Jesus put his hand to his sword, drew it, and struck the high priest's servant, cutting off his ear. [52]Then Jesus said to him, "Put your sword back into its sheath, for all who take the sword will perish by the sword. [53]Do you think that I cannot call upon my Father and he will not provide me at this moment with more than twelve legions of angels? [54]But then how would the scriptures be fulfilled which say that it must come to pass in this way?" [55]*At that hour Jesus said to the crowds, "Have you come out as against a robber, with swords and clubs to seize me? Day after day I sat teaching in the temple area, yet you did not arrest me. [56]*But all this has come to pass that the writings of the prophets may be fulfilled." Then all the disciples left him and fled.

Jesus before the Sanhedrin. [57]*u*Those who had arrested Jesus led him away to Caiaphas the high priest, where the scribes and the elders were assembled. [58]Peter was following him at a distance as far as the high priest's courtyard, and going inside he sat down with the servants to see the outcome. [59]*The chief priests and the entire Sanhedrin kept trying to obtain false testimony against Jesus in order to put him to death, [60]v*but they found none, though many false witnesses came forward. Finally two came forward [61]who stated, "This man said, 'I can destroy the temple of God and within three days rebuild it.' " [62]The high priest rose and addressed him, "Have you no answer? What are these men testifying against you?" [63]w*But Jesus was silent. Then the high priest said to him, "I order you to tell us under oath before the living God whether you are the Messiah, the Son of God." [64]x*Jesus said to him in reply, "You have said so. But I tell you:

26, 49: Rabbi: see the note on 23, 6–7. Jesus is so addressed twice in Mt (cf 25), both times by Judas. For the significance of the closely related address "teacher" in Mt, see the note on 8, 19.

26, 55: Day after day . . . arrest me: cf Mk 14, 49. This suggests that Jesus had taught for a relatively long period in Jerusalem, whereas 21, 1–11 puts his coming to the city for the first time only a few days before.

26, 57–68: Following Mk 14, 53–65, Matthew presents the nighttime appearance of Jesus before **the Sanhedrin** as a real trial. After **many false witnesses** bring charges against him that do not suffice for the death sentence (60), **two came forward** who charge him with claiming to be able to **destroy the temple . . . and within three days** to rebuild it (60–61). Jesus makes no answer even when challenged to do so by **the high priest**, who then orders him to declare **under oath . . . whether** he is **the Messiah, the Son of God** (62–63). Matthew changes Mk's clear affirmative response (14, 62) to the same one as that given to Judas (cf 25), but follows Mk almost verbatim in Jesus' predicting that his judges will see him (**the Son of Man**) seated at the right hand of God and coming on the clouds of heaven (64). The high priest then charges him with blasphemy (65), a charge with which the other members of **the Sanhedrin** agree by declaring that **he deserves to die** (66). They then attack him (67) and mockingly demand that he **prophesy** (68). This account contains elements that are contrary to the judicial procedures prescribed in the Mishnah, the Jewish code of law that dates in written form from ca. A.D. 200, e.g., trial on a feast day, a night session of the court, pronouncement of a verdict of condemnation at the same session at which testimony was re-

ceived. Consequently, some scholars regard the account entirely as a creation of the early Christians without historical value. However, it is disputable whether the norms found in the Mishnah were in force at the time of Jesus. More to the point is the question whether the Matthean-Marcan night trial derives from a combination of two separate incidents, a nighttime preliminary investigation (cf Jn 18, 13.19–24) and a formal trial on the following morning (cf Lk 22, 66–71).

26, 57: Caiaphas: see the note on 26, 3.

26, 59: Sanhedrin: see the note on Lk 22, 66.

26, 60–61: Two: cf Dt 19, 15. **I can destroy . . . rebuild it:** there are significant differences from the Marcan parallel (14, 58). Matthew omits "made with hands" and "not made with hands" and changes Mk's "will destroy" and "will build another" to **can destroy** and (can) **rebuild.** The charge is probably based on Jesus' prediction of the temple's destruction; see the notes on 23, 37–39; 24, 2; and Jn 2, 19. A similar prediction by Jeremiah was considered as deserving death; cf Jer 7, 1–15; 26, 1–8.

26, 63: Silent: possibly an allusion to Is 53, 7. **I order you . . . living God:** peculiar to Mt; cf Mk 14, 61.

26, 64: You have said so: see the note on 26, 25. **From now on . . . heaven:** the Son of Man who is to be crucified (cf 20, 19) will be seen in glorious majesty (cf Ps 110, 1) and **coming on the clouds of heaven** (cf Dn 7, 13). **The Power:** see the note on Mk 14, 61–62.

t: 26, 31. u: Mk 14, 53–65; Lk 22, 54–55.63–71; Jn 18, 12–14.19–24. v: Dt 19, 15; Jn 2, 19; Acts 6, 14. w: Is 53, 7. x: Ps 110, 1; Dn 7, 13.

From now on you will see 'the Son of Man

seated at the right hand of the Power'

and 'coming on the clouds of heaven.' "

65*Then the high priest tore his robes and said, "He has blasphemed! What further need have we of witnesses? You have now heard the blasphemy; 66what is your opinion?" They said in reply, "He deserves to die!" 67y*Then they spat in his face and struck him, while some slapped him, 68saying, "Prophesy for us, Messiah: who is it that struck you?"

Peter's Denial of Jesus. 69z Now Peter was sitting outside in the courtyard. One of the maids came over to him and said, "You too were with Jesus the Galilean." 70*But he denied it in front of everyone, saying, "I do not know what you are talking about!" 71As he went out to the gate, another girl saw him and said to those who were there, "This man was with Jesus the Nazorean." 72Again he denied it with an oath, "I do not know the man!" 73*A little later the bystanders came over and said to Peter, "Surely you too are one of them; even your speech gives you away."

74At that he began to curse and to swear, "I do not know the man." And immediately a cock crowed. 75aThen Peter remembered the word that Jesus had spoken: "Before the cock crows you will deny me three times." He went out and began to weep bitterly.

CHAPTER 27

See RG 288-89

Jesus before Pilate. 1b*When it was morning, all the chief priests and the elders of the people took counsel against Jesus to put him to death. 2They bound him, led him away, and handed him over to Pilate, the governor.

The Death of Judas. 3cd*Then Judas, his betrayer, seeing that Jesus had been condemned, deeply regretted what he had done. He returned the thirty pieces of silver to the chief priests and elders, 4saying, "I have sinned in betraying innocent blood." They said, "What is that to us? Look to it yourself." 5*Flinging the money into the temple, he departed and went off and hanged himself. 6The chief priests gathered up the money, but said, "It is not lawful to deposit this in the temple treasury, for it is the price of blood." 7After consultation, they used it to buy the potter's field as a burial place for foreigners. 8That is why that field even today is called

26, 65: **Blasphemed:** the punishment for **blasphemy** was death by stoning (see Lv 24, 10–16). According to the Mishnah, to be guilty of **blasphemy** one had to pronounce "the Name itself," i.e. Yahweh; cf **Sanhedrin** 7, 4.5. Those who judge the gospel accounts of Jesus' trial by the later Mishnah standards point out that Jesus uses the surrogate "the Power," and hence no Jewish court would have regarded him as guilty of **blasphemy;** others hold that the Mishnah's narrow understanding of **blasphemy** was a later development.

26, 67–68: The physical abuse, apparently done to Jesus by the members of the Sanhedrin themselves, recalls the sufferings of the Isaian Servant of the Lord; cf Is 50, 6. The mocking challenge to **prophesy** is probably motivated by Jesus' prediction of his future glory (64).

26, 70: **Denied it in front of everyone:** see 10, 33. Peter's repentance (75) saves him from the fearful destiny of which Jesus speaks there.

26, 73: **Your speech . . . away:** Matthew explicates Mk's "you too are a Galilean" (14, 70).

27, 1–31: Cf Mk 15, 1–20. Matthew's account of the Roman trial before **Pilate** is introduced by a consultation of the Sanhedrin after which Jesus is **handed over to . . . the governor** (1–2). Matthew follows his Marcan source closely but adds some material that is peculiar to him, the death of **Judas** (3–10), possibly Jesus as the name **Jesus** as the name of **Barabbas** also (16–17), the intervention of Pilate's **wife** (19), Pilate's washing **his hands** in token of his disclaiming responsibility

for Jesus' death (24), and the assuming of that responsibility by **the whole people** (25).

27, 1–2: There is scholarly disagreement about the meaning of the Sanhedrin's taking **counsel** (**symboulion elabon;** cf 12, 14; 22, 15; 27, 7; 28, 12); see the note on Mk 15, 1. Some understand it as a discussion about the strategy for putting their death sentence against **Jesus** into effect since they lacked the right to do so themselves. Others see it as the occasion for their passing that sentence, holding that Matthew, unlike Mark (14, 64), does not consider that it had been passed in the night session (26, 66). Even in the latter interpretation, their handing **him over to Pilate** is best explained on the hypothesis that they did not have competence to put their sentence into effect, as is stated in Jn 18, 31.

27, 3: **The thirty pieces of silver:** see 26, 15.

27, 5–8: For another tradition about the death of Judas, cf Acts 1, 18–19. The two traditions agree only in the purchase of a field with **the money** paid to Judas for his betrayal of Jesus and the name given to the **field, the Field of Blood.** In Acts Judas himself buys the field and its name comes from his own blood shed in his fatal accident on it. **The potter's field:** this designation of the field is based on the fulfillment citation in v 10.

y: Wis 2, 19; Is 50, 6. z: Mk 14, 66-72; Lk 22, 56-62; Jn 18, 17-18.25-27. a: 26, 34. b: Mk 15, 1; Lk 23, 1; Jn 18, 28. c: Acts 1, 18-19. d: 26, 15.

the Field of Blood. [9]*Then was fulfilled what had been said through Jeremiah the prophet, "And they took the thirty pieces of silver, the value of a man with a price on his head, a price set by some of the Israelites, [10e]and they paid it out for the potter's field just as the Lord had commanded me."

Jesus Questioned by Pilate. [11f]*Now Jesus stood before the governor, and he questioned him, "Are you the king of the Jews?" Jesus said, "You say so." [12g]*And when he was accused by the chief priests and elders, he made no answer. [13]Then Pilate said to him, "Do you not hear how many things they are testifying against you?" [14]But he did not answer him one word, so that the governor was greatly amazed.

The Sentence of Death. [15h]*Now on the occasion of the feast the governor was accustomed to release to the crowd one prisoner whom they wished. [16]*And at that time they had a notorious prisoner called [Jesus] Barabbas. [17]So when they had assembled, Pilate said to them, "Which one do you want me to release to you, [Jesus] Barabbas, or Jesus called Messiah?" [18]*For he knew that it was out of envy that they had handed him over. [19]*While he was still seated on the bench, his wife sent him a message, "Have nothing to do with that righteous man. I suffered much in a dream today because of him." [20i]The chief priests and the elders persuaded the crowds to ask for Barabbas but to destroy Jesus. [21]The governor said to them in reply, "Which of the two do you want me to release to you?" They answered, "Barabbas!" [22]*Pilate said to them, "Then what shall I do with Jesus called Messiah?" They all said, "Let him be crucified!" [23]But he said, "Why? What evil has he done?" They only shouted the louder, "Let him be crucified!" [24j]*When Pilate saw that he was not

---

27, 9–10: Cf 26, 15. Matthew's attributing this text to Jeremiah is puzzling, for there is no such text in that book, and **the thirty pieces of silver** thrown by Judas "into the temple" (5) recall rather Zec 11, 12–13. It is usually said that the attribution of the text to Jeremiah is due to Matthew's combining the Zechariah text with texts from Jeremiah that speak of a **potter** (18, 2–3), the buying of a **field** (32, 6–9), or the breaking of a potter's flask at Topheth in the valley of Ben-Hinnom with the prediction that it will become a burial place (19, 1–13).

27, 11: King of the Jews: this title is used of Jesus only by pagans. The Matthean instances are, besides this verse, 2, 2; 27, 29.37. Matthew equates it with "Messiah"; cf 2, 2.4 and 27, 17.22 where he has changed "the king of the Jews" of his Marcan source (15, 9.12) to "(Jesus) called Messiah." The normal political connotation of both titles would be of concern to the Roman **governor. You say so:** see the note on 26, 25. An unqualified affirmative response is not made because Jesus' kingship is not what Pilate would understand it to be.

27, 12–14: Cf 26, 62–63. As in the trial before the Sanhedrin, Jesus' silence may be meant to recall Is 53, 7. **Greatly amazed:** possibly an allusion to Is 52, 14–15.

27, 15–26: The choice that Pilate offers **the crowd** between **Barabbas** and **Jesus** is said to be in accordance with a custom of releasing at the Passover feast **one prisoner** chosen by **the crowd** (15). This custom is mentioned also in Mk 15, 6 and Jn 18, 39 but not in Lk; see the note on Lk 23, 17. Outside of the gospels there is no direct attestation of it, and scholars are divided in their judgment of the historical reliability of the claim that there was such a practice.

27, 16–17: [Jesus] Barabbas: it is possible that the double name is the original reading; **Jesus** was a common Jewish name; see the note on 1, 21. This reading is found in only a few textual witnesses, although its absence in the majority can be explained as an omission of **Jesus** made for reverential reasons. That name is bracketed because of its uncertain textual attestation. The Aramaic name **Barabbas** means "son

of the father"; the irony of the choice offered between him and Jesus, the true son of the Father, would be evident to those addressees of Mt who knew that.

27, 18: Cf Mk 14, 10. This is an example of the tendency, found in varying degree in all the gospels, to present Pilate in a relatively favorable light and emphasize the hostility of the Jewish authorities and eventually of the people.

27, 19: Jesus' innocence is declared by a Gentile woman. **In a dream:** in Mt's infancy narrative, dreams are the means of divine communication; cf 1, 20; 2, 12.13.19.22.

27, 22: Let him be crucified: incited by the chief priests and elders (20), the crowds demand that Jesus be executed by crucifixion, a peculiarly horrible form of Roman capital punishment. The Marcan parallel, "Crucify him" (15, 3), addressed to Pilate, is changed by Matthew to the passive, probably to emphasize the responsibility of the crowds.

27, 24–25: Peculiar to Mt. **Took water . . . blood:** cf Dt 21, 1–8, the handwashing prescribed in the case of a murder when the killer is unknown. The elders of the city nearest to where the corpse is found must wash their hands, declaring, "Our hands did not shed this blood." **Look to it yourselves:** cf v 4. **The whole people:** Matthew sees in those who speak these words **the** entire **people** (Greek laos) of Israel **His blood . . . and upon our children:** cf Jer 26, 15. The responsibility for Jesus' death is accepted by the nation that was God's special possession (Ex 19, 5), his own **people** (Hos 2, 25), and they thereby lose that high privilege; see 21, 43 and the note on that verse. The controversy between Matthew's church and Pharisaic Judaism about which was the true people of God is reflected here. As the Second Vatican Council has pointed out, guilt for Jesus' death is not attributable to all the Jews of his time or to any Jews of later times.

e: Zec 11, 12-13. f: Mk 15, 2-5; Lk 23, 2-3; Jn 18, 29-38. g: Is 53, 7. h: Mk 15, 6-15; Lk 23, 17-25; Jn 18, 39—19, 16. i: Acts 3, 14. j: Dt 21, 1-8.

succeeding at all, but that a riot was breaking out instead, he took water and washed his hands in the sight of the crowd, saying, "I am innocent of this man's blood. Look to it yourselves." [25] And the whole people said in reply, "His blood be upon us and upon our children." [26]*Then he released Barabbas to them, but after he had Jesus scourged, he handed him over to be crucified.

Mockery by the Soldiers. [27k]*Then the soldiers of the governor took Jesus inside the praetorium and gathered the whole cohort around him. [28]*They stripped off his clothes and threw a scarlet military cloak about him. [29l]*Weaving a crown out of thorns, they placed it on his head, and a reed in his right hand. And kneeling before him, they mocked him, saying, "Hail, King of the Jews!" [30m]*They spat upon him and took the reed and kept striking him on the head. [31] And when they had mocked him, they stripped him of the cloak, dressed him in his own clothes, and led him off to crucify him.

The Way of the Cross. [32n]*As they were going out, they met a Cyrenian named Simon; this man they pressed into service to carry his cross.

The Crucifixion. [33o] And when they came to a place called Golgotha (which means Place of the Skull), [34p]*they gave Jesus wine to drink mixed with gall. But when he had tasted it, he refused to drink. [35q]*After they had crucified him, they divided his garments by casting lots; [36] then they sat down and kept watch over him there. [37]*And they placed over his head the written charge against him: This is Jesus, the King of the Jews. [38]*Two revolutionaries were crucified with him, one on his right and the other on his left. [39r]*Those passing by reviled him, shaking their heads [40s] and saying, "You who would destroy the temple and rebuild it in three days, save yourself, if you are the Son of God, [and] come down from the cross!" [41] Likewise the chief priests with the scribes and elders mocked him and said, [42]*"He saved others; he cannot save himself. So he is the king of Israel! Let him come down from the cross now, and we will believe in him. [43t]*He trusted in God; let him deliver him now if he wants him. For he said, 'I am

---

27, 26: He had Jesus scourged: the usual preliminary to crucifixion.

27, 27: The praetorium: the residence of the Roman governor. His usual place of residence was at Caesarea Maritima on the Mediterranean coast, but he went to Jerusalem during the great feasts, when the influx of pilgrims posed the danger of a nationalistic riot. It is disputed whether **the praetorium** in Jerusalem was the old palace of Herod in the west of the city or the fortress of Antonia northwest of the temple area. **The whole cohort:** normally six hundred soldiers.

27, 28: Scarlet military cloak: so Mt as against the royal purple of Mk 15, 17 and Jn 19, 2.

27, 29: Crown out of thorns: probably of long **thorns** that stood upright so that it resembled the "radiant" **crown,** a diadem with spikes worn by Hellenistic kings. The soldiers' purpose was mockery, not torture. **A reed:** peculiar to Mt; a mock scepter.

27, 30: Spat upon him: cf 26, 67 where there also is a possible allusion to Is 50, 6.

27, 32: See the note on Mk 15, 21. **Cyrenian named Simon:** Cyrenaica was a Roman province on the north coast of Africa and Cyrene was its capital city. The city had a large population of Greek-speaking Jews. **Simon** may have been living in Palestine or have come there for the Passover as a pilgrim. **Pressed into service:** see the note on 5, 41.

27, 34: Wine ... mixed with gall: cf Mk 15, 23 where the drink is "wine drugged with myrrh," a narcotic. Mt's text is probably an inexact allusion to Ps 69, 22. That psalm belongs to the class called the individual lament, in which a persecuted just man prays for deliverance in the midst of great suf-

fering and also expresses confidence that his prayer will be heard. That theme of the suffering Just One is frequently applied to the sufferings of Jesus in the passion narratives.

27, 35: The clothing of an executed criminal went to his executioner(s), but the description of that procedure in the case of Jesus, found in all the gospels, is plainly inspired by Ps 22, 19. However, that psalm verse is quoted only in Jn 19, 24.

27, 37: The offense of a person condemned to death by crucifixion was written on a tablet that was displayed on his cross. The **charge** against **Jesus** was that he had claimed to be the **King of the Jews** (cf 11), i.e., the Messiah (cf 17.22).

27, 38: Revolutionaries: see the note on Jn 18, 40 where the same Greek word as that found here is used for Barabbas.

27, 39–40: Reviled him . . . heads: cf Ps 22, 8. **You who would destroy . . . three days:** cf 26, 61. **If you are the Son of God:** the same words as those of the devil in the temptation of Jesus; cf 4, 3.6.

27, 42: King of Israel: in their mocking of Jesus the members of the Sanhedrin call themselves and their people not "the Jews" but **Israel.**

27, 43: Peculiar to Mt. **He trusted in God . . . wants him:** cf Ps 22, 9. **He said . . . of God:** probably an allusion to Wis 2, 12–20 where the theme of the suffering just one appears.

k: Mk 15, 16-20; Jn 19, 2-3. *l:* 27, 11. *m:* Is 50, 6. *n:* Mk 15, 21; Lk 23, 26. *o:* Mk 15, 22-32; Lk 23, 32-38; Jn 19, 17-19.23-24. *p:* Ps 69, 21. *q:* Ps 22, 19. *r:* Ps 22, 8. *s:* 4, 3.6; 26, 61. *t:* Ps 22, 9; Wis 2, 12-20.

the Son of God.' " [44]The revolutionaries who were crucified with him also kept abusing him in the same way.

The Death of Jesus. [45uv]*From noon onward, darkness came over the whole land until three in the afternoon. [46w]*And about three o'clock Jesus cried out in a loud voice, "*Eli, Eli, lema sabachthani?*" which means, "My God, my God, why have you forsaken me?" [47]*Some of the bystanders who heard it said, "This one is calling for Elijah." [48x]Immediately one of them ran to get a sponge; he soaked it in wine, and putting it on a reed, gave it to him to drink. [49]But the rest said, "Wait, let us see if Elijah comes to save him." [50]*But Jesus cried out again in a loud voice, and gave up his spirit. [51y]*And behold, the veil of the sanctuary was torn in two from top to bottom. The earth quaked, rocks were split, [52z]tombs were opened, and the bodies of many saints who had fallen asleep were raised. [53]And coming forth from their tombs after his resurrection, they entered the holy city and appeared to many. [54]*The centurion and the men with him who were keeping watch over Jesus feared greatly when they saw the earthquake and all that was happening, and they said, "Truly, this was the Son of God!" [55]*There were many women there, looking on from a distance, who had followed Jesus from Galilee, ministering to him. [56a]Among them were Mary Magdalene and Mary the mother of James and Joseph, and the mother of the sons of Zebedee.

The Burial of Jesus. [57bc]*When it was evening, there came a rich man from Arimathea named Joseph, who was himself a disciple of Jesus. [58]He went to Pilate and asked for the body of Jesus; then Pilate ordered it to be handed over. [59]Taking the body, Joseph wrapped it [in] clean linen [60]and laid it in his

27, 45: Cf Amos 8, 9 where on the day of the Lord "the sun will set at midday."

27, 46: Eli, Eli, lema sabachthani?: Jesus cries out in the words of Ps 22, 2a, a psalm of lament that is the Old Testament passage most frequently drawn upon in this narrative. In Mk the verse is cited entirely in Aramaic, which Matthew partially retains but changes the invocation of God to the Hebrew **Eli,** possibly because that is more easily related to the statement of the following verse about Jesus' calling for Elijah.

27, 47: Elijah: see the note on 3, 4. This prophet, taken up into heaven (2 Kgs 2, 11), was believed to come to the help of those in distress, but the evidences of that belief are all later than the gospels.

27, 50: Gave up his spirit: cf the Marcan parallel (15, 37), "breathed his last." Matthew's alteration expresses both Jesus' control over his destiny and his obedient giving up of his life to God.

27, 51–53: Veil of the sanctuary . . . bottom: cf Mk 15, 38; Lk 23, 45. Lk puts this event immediately before the death of Jesus. There were two veils in the Mosaic tabernacle on the model of which the temple was constructed, the outer one before the entrance of the Holy Place and the inner one before the Holy of Holies (see Ex 26, 31–36). Only the high priest could pass through the latter and that only on the Day of Atonement (see Lv 16, 1–18). Probably the **torn veil** of the gospels is the inner one. The meaning of the scene may be that now, because of Jesus' death, all people have access to the presence of God, or that the temple, its holiest part standing exposed, is now profaned and will soon be destroyed. **The earth quaked . . . appeared to many:** peculiar to Mt. The earthquake, the splitting of the **rocks,** and especially the resurrection of the dead **saints** indicate the coming of the final age. In the Old Testament the coming of God is frequently portrayed with the imagery of an earthquake (see Pss 68, 9; 77, 19), and Jesus speaks of the earthquakes that will accompany the "labor pains" that signify the beginning of the dissolution of the old world (24, 7–8). For the expectation of the resurrection of the dead at the coming of the new and final age, see Dn 12, 1–3. Matthew knows that the end of the old age has not yet come (28, 20), but the new age has broken in with the death (and resurrection; cf the earthquake in 28, 2) of Jesus; see the note on 16, 28. **After his resurrection:** this qualification seems to be due to Matthew's wish to assert the primacy of Jesus' **resurrection** even though he has placed the resurrection of the dead **saints** immediately after Jesus' death.

27, 54: Cf Mk 15, 39. The Christian confession of faith is made by Gentiles, not only **the centurion,** as in Mk, but the other soldiers **who were keeping watch over Jesus** (cf 36).

27, 55–56: Looking on from a distance: cf Ps 38, 12. **Mary Magdalene . . . Joseph:** these two women are mentioned again in v 61 and 28, 1 and are important as witnesses of the reality of the empty tomb. A **James** and **Joseph** are referred to in 13, 55 as brothers of Jesus.

27, 57–61: Cf Mk 15, 42–47. Matthew drops Mk's designation of **Joseph** of **Arimathea** as "a distinguished member of the council" (the Sanhedrin), and makes him **a rich man** and **a disciple** of Jesus. The former may be an allusion to Is 53, 9 (the Hebrew reading of that text is disputed and the one followed in the NAB OT has nothing about the rich, but they are mentioned in the LXX version). That the tomb was the **new tomb** of a **rich man** and that it was seen by the women are indications of an apologetic intent of Matthew; there could be no question about the identity of Jesus' burial place. **The other Mary:** the mother of James and Joseph (56).

u: Mk 15, 33–41; Lk 23, 44–49; Jn 19, 28–30.　*v:* Am 8, 9.　*w:* Ps 22, 2.　*x:* Ps 69, 21.　*y:* Ex 26, 31–36; Ps 68, 9; 77, 19.　*z:* Dn 12, 1–3.　*a:* 13, 55.　*b:* Mk 15, 42–47; Lk 23, 50–56; Jn 19, 38–42.　*c:* Is 53, 9.

new tomb that he had hewn in the rock. Then he rolled a huge stone across the entrance to the tomb and departed. *61*But Mary Magdalene and the other Mary remained sitting there, facing the tomb.

The Guard at the Tomb. *62**The next day, the one following the day of preparation, the chief priests and the Pharisees gathered before Pilate *63d*and said, "Sir, we remember that this impostor while still alive said, 'After three days I will be raised up.' *64**Give orders, then, that the grave be secured until the third day, lest his disciples come and steal him and say to the people, 'He has been raised from the dead.' This last imposture would be worse than the first." *65**Pilate said to them, "The guard is yours; go secure it as best you can." *66*So they went and secured

the tomb by fixing a seal to the stone and setting the guard.

CHAPTER 28

The Resurrection of Jesus. *1e**After the sabbath, as the first day of the week was dawning, Mary Magdalene and the other Mary came to see the tomb. *2f**And behold, there was a great earthquake; for an angel of the Lord descended from heaven, approached, rolled back the stone, and sat upon it. *3g*His appearance was like lightning and his clothing was white as snow. *4*The guards were shaken with fear of him and became like dead men. *5*Then the angel said to the women in reply, "Do not be afraid! I know that you are seeking Jesus the crucified. *6**He is not here, for he has been raised just

See RG
289–90

27, 62–66: Peculiar to Mt. The story prepares for 28, 11–15 and the Jewish charge that the tomb was empty because the **disciples** had stolen the body of Jesus (28, 13.15).

27, 62: The next day . . . preparation: the sabbath. According to the synoptic chronology, in that year **the day of preparation** (for the sabbath) was the Passover; cf Mk 15, 42. **The Pharisees:** the principal opponents of Jesus during his ministry and, in Matthew's time, of the Christian church, join with the **chief priests** to guarantee against a possible attempt of Jesus' **disciples** to steal his body.

27, 64: This last imposture . . . the first: the claim that Jesus **has been raised from the dead** is clearly the **last imposture; the first** may be either his claim that he would be **raised up** (63) or his claim that he was the one with whom the ministry of the kingdom of God had come (see 12, 28).

27, 65: The guard is yours: literally, "have a guard" or "you have a guard." Either the imperative or the indicative could mean that Pilate granted the petitioners some Roman soldiers as guards, which is the sense of the present translation. However, if the verb is taken as an indicative it could also mean that Pilate told them to use their own Jewish guards.

28, 1–20: Except for vv 1–8, based on Mk 16, 1–8, the material of this final chapter is peculiar to Mt. Even where he follows Mk, Matthew has altered his source so greatly that a very different impression is given from that of the Marcan account. The two points that are common to the resurrection testimony of all the gospels are that the tomb of Jesus had been found empty and that the risen Jesus had appeared to certain persons, or, in the original form of Mk, that such an appearance was promised as soon to take place (see Mk 16, 7). On this central and all-important basis, Matthew has constructed an account that interprets the resurrection as the turning of the ages (2–4), shows the Jewish opposition to Jesus as continuing **to the present** in the claim that the resurrection is a deception perpetrated by the **disciples** who stole his body from the tomb (11–15), and marks a new stage in the mission of the **disciples** once limited to Israel (10, 5–6); now they are to **make disciples of all nations.** In this work they will be strengthened by the presence of the exalted Son of Man, who

will be with them **until** the kingdom comes in fullness at **the end of the age** (16–20).

28, 1: After the sabbath . . . dawning: since the sabbath ended at sunset, this could mean in the early evening, for **dawning** can refer to the appearance of the evening star; cf Lk 23, 54. However, it is probable that Matthew means the morning dawn of the day after the sabbath, as in the similar though slightly different text of Mk, "when the sun had risen" (16, 2). **Mary Magdalene and the other Mary:** see the notes on 27, 55–56; 57–61. **To see the tomb:** cf Mk 16, 1–2 where the purpose of the women's visit is to anoint Jesus' body.

28, 2–4: Peculiar to Mt. **A great earthquake:** see the note on 27, 51–53. **Descended from heaven:** this trait is peculiar to Mt, although his interpretation of the "young man" of his Marcan source (16, 5) as an **angel** is probably true to Mk's intention; cf Lk 24, 23 where the "two men" of 24, 4 are said to be "angels." **Rolled back the stone . . . upon it:** not to allow the risen Jesus to leave the tomb but to make evident that the tomb is empty (see 6). Unlike the apocryphal Gospel of Peter (9, 35—11, 44), the New Testament does not describe the resurrection of Jesus, nor is there anyone who sees it. **His appearance was like lightning . . . snow:** see the note on 17, 2.

28, 6–7: Cf Mk 16, 6–7. **Just as he said:** a Matthean addition referring to Jesus' predictions of his resurrection, e.g., 16, 21; 17, 23; 20, 19. **Tell his disciples:** like the angel of the Lord of the infancy narrative, the angel interprets a fact and gives a commandment about what is to be done; cf 1, 20–21. Matthew omits Mk's "and Peter" (16, 7); considering his interest in Peter, this omission is curious. Perhaps the reason is that the Marcan text may allude to a first appearance of Jesus to Peter alone (cf 1 Cor 15, 5; Lk 24, 34) which Matthew has already incorporated into his account of Peter's confession at Caesarea Philippi; see the note on 16, 16. **He is going . . . Galilee:** like Mk 16, 7, a reference to Jesus' prediction at the Last Supper (26, 32; Mk 14, 28). Matthew changes Mk's "as he told you" to a declaration of the angel.

d: 12, 40; 16, 21; 17, 23; 20, 19. *e:* Mk 16, 1-8; Lk 24, 1-12; Jn 20, 1-10. *f:* 25, 51. *g:* 17, 2.

as he said. Come and see the place where he lay. *7h*Then go quickly and tell his disciples, 'He has been raised from the dead, and he is going before you to Galilee; there you will see him.' Behold, I have told you." *8**Then they went away quickly from the tomb, fearful yet overjoyed, and ran to announce this to his disciples. *9i**And behold, Jesus met them on their way and greeted them. They approached, embraced his feet, and did him homage. *10*Then Jesus said to them, "Do not be afraid. Go tell my brothers to go to Galilee, and there they will see me."

The Report of the Guard. *11**While they were going, some of the guard went into the city and told the chief priests all that had happened. *12*They assembled with the elders and took counsel; then they gave a large sum of money to the soldiers, *13*telling them, "You are to say, 'His disciples came by night and stole him while we were asleep.' *14*And if this gets to the ears of the governor, we will satisfy [him] and keep you out of trouble." *15*The soldiers took the money and did as they were instructed. And this story has circulated among the Jews to the present [day].

The Commissioning of the Disciples. *16j**The eleven disciples went to Galilee, to the mountain to which Jesus had ordered them. *17**When they saw him, they worshiped, but they doubted. *18k**Then Jesus approached and said to them, "All power in heaven and on earth has been given to me. *19l**Go, therefore, and make disciples of all nations, baptizing them in the name of the Father, and of the Son, and of the holy Spirit, *20m**teaching them to observe all that I have commanded you. And behold, I am with you always, until the end of the age."

28, 8: Contrast Mk 16, 8 where the women in their fear "said nothing to anyone."

28, 9–10: Although these verses are peculiar to Mt, there are similarities between them and Jn's account of the appearance of Jesus to Mary Magdalene (20, 17). In both there is a touching of Jesus' body, and a command of Jesus to bear a message to his disciples, designated as his **brothers.** Matthew may have drawn upon a tradition that appears in a different form in Jn. Jesus' words to the women are mainly a repetition of those of the angel (5a; 7b).

28, 11–15: This account indicates that the dispute between Christians and Jews about the empty tomb was not whether the tomb was empty but why.

28, 16–20: This climactic scene has been called a "proleptic parousia," for it gives a foretaste of the final glorious coming of the Son of Man (26, 64). Then his triumph will be manifest to all; now it is revealed only to **the disciples,** who are commissioned to announce it to **all nations** and bring them to belief in Jesus and obedience to his commandments.

28, 16: **The eleven:** the number recalls the tragic defection of Judas Iscariot. **To the mountain . . . ordered them:** since the message to **the disciples** was simply that they were to go to Galilee (10), some think that **the mountain** comes from a tradition of the message known to Matthew and alluded to here. For the significance of **the mountain,** see the note on 17, 1.

28, 17: **But they doubted:** the Greek can also be translated, "but some doubted." The verb occurs elsewhere in the New Testament only in 14, 31 where it is associated with Peter's being of "little faith." For the meaning of that designation, see the note on 6, 30.

28, 18: **All power . . . me:** the Greek word here translated **power** is the same as that found in the LXX translation of Dn 7, 13–14 where one "like a son of man" is given **power** and an everlasting kingdom by God. The risen Jesus here claims universal power, i.e., **in heaven and on earth.**

28, 19: **Therefore:** since universal power belongs to the risen Jesus (18), he gives the eleven a mission that is universal. They are to **make disciples of all nations.** While **all nations** is understood by some scholars as referring only to all Gentiles, it is probable that it included the Jews as well. **Baptizing them:** baptism is the means of entrance into the community of the risen one, the Church. **In the name of the Father . . . holy Spirit:** this is perhaps the clearest expression in the New Testament of trinitarian belief. It may have been the baptismal formula of Matthew's church, but primarily it designates the effect of baptism, the union of the one baptized with the Father, Son, and holy Spirit.

28, 20: **All that I have commanded you:** the moral teaching found in this gospel, preeminently that of the Sermon on the Mount (chs 5–7). The commandments of Jesus are the standard of Christian conduct, not the Mosaic law as such, even though some of the Mosaic commandments have now been invested with the authority of Jesus. **Behold, I am with you always:** the promise of Jesus' real though invisible presence echoes the name Emmanuel given to him in the infancy narrative; see the note on 1, 23. End of the age: see the notes on 13, 39 and 24, 3.

h: 26 32. *i:* Jn 20, 17. *j:* Mk 16, 14-16; Lk 24, 36-49; Jn 20, 19-23. *k:* Dn 7, 14 LXX. *l:* Acts 1, 8. *m:* 1, 23; 13, 39; 24, 3.

See RG
291–300

The Gospel According to Mark

This shortest of all New Testament gospels is likely the first to have been written, yet it often tells of Jesus' ministry in more detail than either Matthew or Luke (for example, the miracle stories at 5, 1–20 or 9, 14–29). It recounts what Jesus did in a vivid style, where one incident follows directly upon another. In this almost breathless narrative, Mark stresses Jesus' message about the kingdom of God now breaking into human life as good news (1, 14–15) and Jesus himself as the gospel of God (1, 1; 8, 35; 10, 29). Jesus is the Son whom God has sent to rescue humanity by serving and by sacrificing his life (10, 45).

The opening verse about good news in Mark (1, 1) serves as a title for the entire book. The action begins with the appearance of John the Baptist, a messenger of God attested by scripture. But John points to a mightier one, Jesus, at whose baptism God speaks from heaven, declaring Jesus his Son. The Spirit descends upon Jesus, who eventually, it is promised, will baptize "with the holy Spirit." This presentation of who Jesus really is (1, 1–13) is rounded out with a brief reference to the temptation of Jesus and how Satan's attack fails. Jesus as Son of God will be victorious, a point to be remembered as one reads of Jesus' death and the enigmatic ending to Mark's Gospel.

The key verses at 1, 14–15, which are programmatic, summarize what Jesus proclaims as gospel: fulfillment, the nearness of the kingdom, and therefore the need for repentance and for faith. After the call of the first four disciples, all fishermen (1, 16–20), we see Jesus engaged in teaching (1, 21.22.27), preaching (1, 38.39), and healing (1, 29–31.34.40–45), and exorcising demons (1, 22–27.34.39). The content of Jesus' teaching is only rarely stated, and then chiefly in parables (ch 4) about the kingdom. His cures, especially on the sabbath (3, 1–5); his claim, like God, to forgive sins (2, 3–12); his table fellowship with tax collectors and sinners (2, 14–17); and the statement that his followers need not now fast but should rejoice while Jesus is present (2, 18–22), all stir up opposition that will lead to Jesus' death (3, 6).

In Mark, Jesus is portrayed as immensely pop-ular with the people in Galilee during his ministry (2, 2; 3, 7; 4, 1). He appoints twelve disciples to help preach and drive out demons, just as he does (3, 13–19). He continues to work many miracles; the blocks 4, 35—6, 44 and 6, 45—7, 10 are cycles of stories about healings, miracles at the Sea of Galilee, and marvelous feedings of the crowds. Jesus' teaching in ch 7 exalts the word of God over "the tradition of the elders" and sees defilement as a matter of the heart, not of unclean foods. Yet opposition mounts. Scribes charge that Jesus is possessed by Beelzebul (3, 22). His relatives think him "out of his mind" (3, 21). Jesus' kinship is with those who do the will of God, in a new eschatological family, not even with mother, brothers, or sisters by blood ties (3, 31–35; cf 6, 1–6). But all too often his own disciples do not understand Jesus (4, 13.40; 6, 52; 8, 17–21). The fate of John the Baptist (6, 17–29) hints ominously at Jesus' own passion (9, 13; cf 8, 31).

A breakthrough seemingly comes with Peter's confession that Jesus is the Christ (Messiah; 8, 27–30). But Jesus himself emphasizes his passion (8, 31; 9, 31; 10, 33–34), not glory in the kingdom (10, 35–45). Momentarily he is glimpsed in his true identity when he is transfigured before three of the disciples (9, 2–8), but by and large Jesus is depicted in Mark as moving obediently along the way to his cross in Jerusalem. Occasionally there are miracles (9, 17–27; 10, 46–52; 11, 12–14.20–21, the only such account in Jerusalem), sometimes teachings (10, 2–11.23–31), but the greatest concern is with discipleship (8, 34—9, 1; 9, 33–50). For the disciples do not grasp the mystery being revealed (9, 32; 10, 32.38). One of them will betray him, Judas (14, 10–11.43–45); one will deny him, Peter (14, 27.31.54.66–72); all eleven men will desert Jesus (14, 27.50).

The passion account, with its condemnation of Jesus by the Sanhedrin (14, 53.55–65; 15, 1a) and sentencing by Pilate (15, 1), is prefaced with the entry into Jerusalem (11, 1–11), ministry and controversies there (11, 15—12, 44), Jesus' Last Supper with the disciples (14, 1–26), and his arrest at Gethsemane (14, 32–52). A chapter of apocalyptic tone about the destruction of the temple (13, 1–2.14–23) and the coming of the Son of Man (13, 24–27), a discourse filled with promises (13, 11.31) and admonitions to be watchful (13, 2.23.37), is significant for Mark's Gospel, for it helps one see that God, in Jesus, will be victorious after the cross and at the end of history.

The Gospel of Mark ends in the most ancient manuscripts with an abrupt scene at Jesus' tomb, which the women find empty (16, 1–8). His own prophecy of 14, 28 is reiterated, that Jesus goes before the disciples into Galilee; "there you will see him." These words may imply resurrection appearances there, or Jesus' parousia there, or the start of Christian mission, or a return to the roots depicted in 1, 9.14–15 in Galilee. Other hands have attached additional endings after 16, 8; see the note on 16, 9–20.

The framework of Mark's Gospel is partly geographical: Galilee (1, 14—9, 49), through the area "across the Jordan" (10, 1) and through Jericho (10, 46–52), to Jerusalem (11, 1—16, 8). Only rarely does Jesus go into Gentile territory (5, 1–20; 7, 24–37), but those who acknowledge him there and the centurion who confesses Jesus at the cross (15, 39) presage the gospel's expansion into the world beyond Palestine.

Mark's Gospel is even more oriented to christology. Jesus is the Son of God (1, 11; 9, 7; 15, 39; cf 1, 1; 14, 61). He is the Messiah, the anointed king of Davidic descent (12, 35; 15, 32), the Greek for which, *Christos,* has, by the time Mark wrote, become in effect a proper name (1, 1; 9, 41). Jesus is also seen as Son of Man, a term used in Mark not simply as a substitute for "I" or for humanity in general (cf 2, 10.27–28; 14, 21) or with reference to a mighty figure who is to come (13, 26; 14, 62), but also in connection with Jesus' predestined, necessary path of suffering and vindication (8, 31; 10, 45).

The unfolding of Mark's story about Jesus is sometimes viewed by interpreters as centered around the term "mystery." The word is employed just once, at 4, 11, in the singular, and its content there is the kingdom, the open secret that God's reign is now breaking into human life with its reversal of human values. There is a related sense in which Jesus' real identity remained a secret during his lifetime, according to Mark, although demons and demoniacs knew it (1, 24; 3, 11; 5, 7); Jesus warned against telling of his mighty deeds and revealing his identity (1, 44;

3, 12; 5, 43; 7, 36; 8, 26.30), an injunction sometimes broken (1, 45; cf 5, 19–20). Further, Jesus teaches by parables, according to Mark, in such a way that those "outside" the kingdom do not understand, but only those to whom the mystery has been granted by God.

Mark thus shares with Paul, as well as with other parts of the New Testament, an emphasis on election (13, 20.22) and upon the gospel as Christ and his cross (cf 1 Cor 1, 23). Yet in Mark the person of Jesus is also depicted with an unaffected naturalness. He reacts to events with authentic human emotion: pity (1, 44), anger (3, 5), triumph (4, 40), sympathy (5, 36; 6, 34), surprise (6, 9), admiration (7, 29; 10, 21), sadness (14, 33–34), and indignation (14, 48–49).

Although the book is anonymous, apart from the ancient heading "According to Mark" in manuscripts, it has traditionally been assigned to John Mark, in whose mother's house (at Jerusalem) Christians assembled (Acts 12, 12). This Mark was a cousin of Barnabas (Col 4, 10) and accompanied Barnabas and Paul on a missionary journey (Acts 12, 25; 13, 3; 15, 36–39). He appears in Pauline letters (2 Tm 4, 11; Phlm 1, 24) and with Peter (1 Pt 5, 13). Papias (ca. A.D. 135) described Mark as Peter's "interpreter," a view found in other patristic writers. Petrine influence should not, however, be exaggerated. The evangelist has put together various oral and possibly written sources—miracle stories, parables, sayings, stories of controversies, and the passion—so as to speak of the crucified Messiah for Mark's own day

Traditionally, the gospel is said to have been written shortly before A.D. 70 in Rome, at a time of impending persecution and when destruction loomed over Jerusalem. Its audience seems to have been Gentile, unfamiliar with Jewish customs (hence 7, 3–4.11). The book aimed to equip such Christians to stand faithful in the face of persecution (13, 9–13), while going on with the proclamation of the gospel begun in Galilee (13, 10; 14, 9). Modern research often proposes as the author an unknown Hellenistic Jewish Christian, possibly in Syria, and perhaps shortly after the year 70.

The principal divisions of the Gospel according to Mark are the following:

I. The Preparation for the Public Ministry of Jesus (1, 1–13)

————

I: The Preparation
for the Public Ministry
of Jesus

CHAPTER 1

See RG
294-95 *1**The beginning of the gospel of
Jesus Christ [the Son of God].

The Preaching of John the Baptist. *2ab**As
it is written in Isaiah the prophet:

> "Behold, I am sending my messenger
>   ahead of you;
>   he will prepare your way.
> *3* *c*A voice of one crying out in the desert:
>   'Prepare the way of the Lord,
>   make straight his paths.' "

*4*John [the] Baptist appeared in the desert
proclaiming a baptism of repentance for the
forgiveness of sins. *5*People of the whole Judean countryside and all the inhabitants of
Jerusalem were going out to him and were
being baptized by him in the Jordan River as
they acknowledged their sins. *6**John was
clothed in camel's hair, with a leather belt
around his waist. He fed on locusts and wild
honey. *7*And this is what he proclaimed:
"One mightier than I is coming after me. I am
not worthy to stoop and loosen the thongs of
his sandals. *8d**I have baptized you with water; he will baptize you with the holy Spirit."

The Baptism of Jesus. *9e*It happened in
those days that Jesus came from Nazareth of
Galilee and was baptized in the Jordan by
John. *10**On coming up out of the water he
saw the heavens being torn open and the
Spirit, like a dove, descending upon him.
*11f*And a voice came from the heavens, "You
are my beloved Son; with you I am well
pleased."

The Temptation of Jesus. *12g**At once the
Spirit drove him out into the desert, *13*and he
remained in the desert for forty days,
tempted by Satan. He was among wild
beasts, and the angels ministered to him.

1, 1–13: The prologue of the Gospel according to Mark
begins with the title (1) followed by three events preparatory
to Jesus' preaching: (1) the appearance in the Judean wilderness of John, baptizer, preacher of repentance, and precursor
of Jesus (2–8); (2) the baptism of Jesus, at which a voice from
heaven acknowledges Jesus to be God's Son, and the holy
Spirit descends on him (9–11); (3) the temptation of Jesus by
Satan (12–13).
1, 1: The gospel of Jesus Christ [the Son of God]: the
"good news" of salvation in and through Jesus, crucified and
risen, acknowledged by the Christian community as Messiah
(8, 29; 14, 61–62) and Son of God (11; 9, 7; 15, 39), although
some important manuscripts here omit **the Son of God.**
1, 2–3: Although Mark attributes the prophecy to Isaiah,
the text is a combination of Mal 3, 1; Is 40, 3; and Ex 23, 20;
cf Mt 11, 10; Lk 7, 27. John's ministry is seen as God's prelude to the saving mission of his Son. **The way of the Lord:**
this prophecy of Deutero-Isaiah concerning the end of the
Babylonian exile is here applied to the coming of Jesus; John
the Baptist is to prepare the way for him.
1, 6: Clothed in camel's hair . . . waist: the Baptist's garb
recalls that of Elijah in 2 Kgs 1, 8. Jesus speaks of the Baptist
as Elijah who has already come (9, 11–13; Mt 17, 10–12; cf
Mal 3, 23–24; Lk 1, 17).
1, 8–9: Through the life-giving baptism with the holy
Spirit (8), Jesus will create a new people of God. But first he
identifies himself with the people of Israel in submitting to

John's baptism of repentance and in bearing on their behalf
the burden of God's decisive judgment (9; cf 4). As in the
desert of Sinai, so here in the wilderness of Judea, Israel's
sonship with God is to be renewed.
**1, 10–11: He saw the heavens . . . and the Spirit . . .
upon him:** indicating divine intervention in fulfillment of
promise. Here the descent of the Spirit on Jesus is meant,
anointing him for his ministry; cf Is 11, 2; 42, 1; 61, 1; 63, 9.
A voice . . . with you I am well pleased: God's acknowledgment of Jesus as his unique Son, the object of his love. His approval of Jesus is the assurance that Jesus will fulfill his messianic mission of salvation.
1, 12–13: The same Spirit who descended on Jesus in his
baptism now drives him into the desert for forty days. The result is radical confrontation and temptation by Satan who attempts to frustrate the work of God. The presence of wild
beasts may indicate the horror and danger of the desert regarded as the abode of demons or may reflect the paradise
motif of harmony among all creatures; cf Is 11, 6–9. The presence of ministering angels to sustain Jesus recalls the angel
who guided the Israelites in the desert in the first Exodus (14,
19; 23, 20) and the angel who supplied nourishment to Elijah
in the wilderness (1 Kgs 19, 5–7). The combined forces of

a: Mt 3, 1-11; Lk 3, 2-16. *b:* Mal 3, 1. *c:* Is 40, 3; Jn 1, 23.
d: Jn 1, 27; Acts 1, 5; 11, 16. *e:* Mt 3, 13-17; Lk 3, 21-23; Jn 1,
32-33. *f:* Ps 2, 7. *g:* Mt 4, 1-11; Lk 4, 1-13.

II: The Mystery of Jesus

The Beginning of the Galilean Ministry.
14h *After John had been arrested, Jesus came to Galilee proclaiming the gospel of God: *15i* "This is the time of fulfillment. The kingdom of God is at hand. Repent, and believe in the gospel."

The Call of the First Disciples. *16j* *As he passed by the Sea of Galilee, he saw Simon and his brother Andrew casting their nets into the sea; they were fishermen. *17* Jesus said to them, "Come after me, and I will make you fishers of men." *18* Then they abandoned their nets and followed him. *19* He walked along a little farther and saw James, the son of Zebedee, and his brother John. They too were in a boat mending their nets. *20* Then he called them. So they left their father Zebedee in the boat along with the hired men and followed him.

The Cure of a Demoniac. *21k* *Then they came to Capernaum, and on the sabbath he entered the synagogue and taught. *22l* The people were astonished at his teaching, for he taught them as one having authority and not as the scribes. *23* *In their synagogue was a man with an unclean spirit; *24* *he cried out, "What have you to do with us, Jesus of Nazareth? Have you come to destroy us? I know who you are—the Holy One of God!" *25* Jesus rebuked him and said, "Quiet! Come out of him!" *26* The unclean spirit convulsed him and with a loud cry came out of him. *27* All were amazed and asked one another, "What is this? A new teaching with authority. He commands even the unclean spirits and they obey him." *28* His fame spread everywhere throughout the whole region of Galilee.

The Cure of Simon's Mother-in-Law.
29m On leaving the synagogue he entered the house of Simon and Andrew with James and John. *30* Simon's mother-in-law lay sick with a fever. They immediately told him about her. *31* He approached, grasped her hand, and helped her up. Then the fever left her and she waited on them.

Other Healings. *32* When it was evening, after sunset, they brought to him all who were ill or possessed by demons. *33* The whole town was gathered at the door. *34* He cured many who were sick with various diseases, and he drove out many demons, not permitting them to speak because they knew him.

Jesus Leaves Capernaum. *35n* Rising very early before dawn, he left and went off to a deserted place, where he prayed. *36* Simon and those who were with him pursued him *37* and on finding him said, "Everyone is looking for you." *38* He told them, "Let us go on to the nearby villages that I may preach there also. For this purpose have I come." *39* So he went into their synagogues, preaching and driving out demons throughout the whole of Galilee.

The Cleansing of a Leper. *40o* *A leper came to him [and kneeling down] begged

---

good and evil were present to Jesus in the desert. His sustained obedience brings forth the new Israel of God there where Israel's rebellion had brought death and alienation.

1, 14–15: After John had been arrested: in the plan of God, Jesus was not to proclaim the good news of salvation prior to the termination of the Baptist's active mission. **Galilee:** in the Marcan account, scene of the major part of Jesus' public ministry before his arrest and condemnation. **The gospel of God:** not only the good news from God but about God at work in Jesus Christ. **This is the time of fulfillment:** i.e., of God's promises. **The kingdom of God . . . Repent:** see the note on Mt 3, 2.

1, 16–20: These verses narrate the call of the first disciples. See the notes on Mt 4, 18–22 and 4, 20.

1, 21–45: The account of a single day's ministry of Jesus on a sabbath in and outside the synagogue of Capernaum (21–31) combines teaching and miracles of exorcism and healing. Mention is not made of the content of the teaching but of the effect of astonishment and alarm on the people. Jesus' teaching with authority, making an absolute claim on the hearer, was in the best tradition of the ancient prophets, not of

the scribes. The narrative continues with events that evening (32–34; see the notes on Mt 8, 14–17) and the next day (35–39). The cleansing in vv 40–45 stands as an isolated story.

1, 23: An unclean spirit: so called because of the spirit's resistance to the holiness of God. The spirit knows and fears the power of Jesus to destroy his influence; cf 32.34; 3, 11; 6, 13.

1, 24: What have you to do with us?: see the note on Jn 2, 4.

1, 24–25: The Holy One of God: not a confession but an attempt to ward off Jesus' power, reflecting the notion that use of the precise name of an opposing spirit would guarantee mastery over him. Jesus silenced the cry of the unclean spirit and drove him out of the man.

1, 40: A leper: for the various forms of skin disease, see Lv 13, 1–50 and the note on Lv 13, 2–4. There are only two instances in the Old Testament in which God is shown to have cured a leper (Nm 12, 10–15 and 2 Kgs 5, 1–14). The law of

h: Mt 4, 12-17; Lk 4, 14-15. *i:* Mt 3, 2. *j:* Mt 4, 18-22; Lk 5, 2-11. *k:* Lk 4, 31-37. *l:* Mt 7, 28-29. *m:* Mt 8, 14-16; Lk 4, 38-41. *n:* Lk 4, 42-44. *o:* Mt 8, 2-4; Lk 5, 12-14.

Tax Collectors and Sinners

Levi (called Matthew in Mt 9, 9) was a customs officer at the border village of Capernaum. Such tax collectors were despised as Roman collaborators and extortionists. "Sinners" are those who deliberately place themselves apart from the observance of Torah. The Pharisees, a branch of Judaism that was dedicated to interpreting biblical law, likely including the extension of the sanctity of the temple to the home (including the table), regarded eating with them (Mk 2, 16) as contact with impure people and social outcasts.

him and said, "If you wish, you can make me clean." *41p* Moved with pity, he stretched out his hand, touched him, and said to him, "I do will it. Be made clean." *42q* The leprosy left him immediately, and he was made clean. *43* Then, warning him sternly, he dismissed him at once. *44r* Then he said to him, "See that you tell no one anything, but go, show yourself to the priest and offer for your cleansing what Moses prescribed; that will be proof for them." *45* The man went away and began to publicize the whole matter. He spread the report abroad so that it was impossible for Jesus to enter a town openly. He remained outside in deserted places, and people kept coming to him from everywhere.

CHAPTER 2

See RG
295-96
The Healing of a Paralytic. *1s* When Jesus returned to Capernaum after some days, it became known that he was at home. *2* Many gathered together so that there was no longer room for them, not even around the door, and he preached the word to them. *3* They came bringing to him a paralytic carried by four men. *4* Unable to get near Jesus because of the crowd, they opened up the roof above him. After they had broken through, they let down the mat on which the paralytic was lying. *5* When Jesus saw their faith, he said to the paralytic, "Child, your sins are forgiven." *6* Now some of the scribes were sitting there asking themselves, *7t* "Why does this man speak that way? He is blaspheming. Who but God alone can forgive sins?" *8* Jesus immediately knew in his mind what they were thinking to themselves, so he said, "Why are you thinking such things in your hearts? *9* Which is easier, to say to the paralytic, 'Your sins are forgiven,' or to say, 'Rise, pick up your mat and walk'? *10* But that you may know that the Son of Man has authority to forgive sins on earth"— *11* he said to the paralytic, "I say to you, rise, pick up your mat, and go home." *12* He rose, picked up his mat at once, and went away in the sight of everyone. They were all astounded and glorified God, saying, "We have never seen anything like this."

The Call of Levi. *13u* Once again he went out along the sea. All the crowd came to him

Moses provided for the ritual purification of a leper. In curing the leper, Jesus assumes that the priests will reinstate the cured man into the religious community. See also the note on Lk 5, 14.

2, 1–3, 6: This section relates a series of conflicts between Jesus and the scribes and Pharisees in which the growing opposition of the latter leads to their plot to put Jesus to death (3, 6).

2, 1–2: He was at home: to the crowds that gathered in and outside the house Jesus **preached the word,** i.e., the gospel concerning the nearness of the kingdom and the necessity of repentance and faith (1, 14).

2, 5: It was the faith of the paralytic and those who carried him that moved Jesus to heal the sick man. Accounts of other miracles of Jesus reveal more and more his emphasis on faith as the requisite for exercising his healing powers (5, 34; 9, 23–24; 10, 52).

2, 6: Scribes: trained in oral interpretation of the written

law; in Mark's gospel, adversaries of Jesus, with one exception (12, 28.34).

2, 7: He is blaspheming: an accusation made here and repeated during the trial of Jesus (14, 60–64).

2, 10: But that you may know that the Son of Man . . . on earth: although vv 8–9 are addressed to the scribes, the sudden interruption of thought and structure in v 10 seems not addressed to them nor to the paralytic. Moreover, the early public use of the designation "Son of Man" to unbelieving scribes is most unlikely. The most probable explanation is that Mark's insertion of v 10 is a commentary addressed to Christians for whom he recalls this miracle and who already accept in faith that Jesus is Messiah and Son of God.

2, 13: He taught them: see the note on 1, 21–45.

p: 5, 30. *q:* Lk 17, 14. *r:* Lv 14, 2-32. *s:* Mt 9, 2-8; Lk 5, 18-26. *t:* Is 43, 25. *u:* 4, 1.

and he taught them. *14v**As he passed by, he saw Levi, son of Alphaeus, sitting at the customs post. He said to him, "Follow me." And he got up and followed him. *15**While he was at table in his house, many tax collectors and sinners sat with Jesus and his disciples; for there were many who followed him. *16**Some scribes who were Pharisees saw that he was eating with sinners and tax collectors and said to his disciples, "Why does he eat with tax collectors and sinners?" *17**Jesus heard this and said to them [that], "Those who are well do not need a physician, but the sick do. I did not come to call the righteous but sinners."

The Question about Fasting. *18w**The disciples of John and of the Pharisees were accustomed to fast. People came to him and objected, "Why do the disciples of John and the disciples of the Pharisees fast, but your disciples do not fast?" *19**Jesus answered them, "Can the wedding guests fast while the bridegroom is with them? As long as they have the bridegroom with them they cannot fast. *20*But the days will come when the bridegroom is taken away from them, and then they will fast on that day. *21*No one sews a piece of un-

shrunken cloth on an old cloak. If he does, its fullness pulls away, the new from the old, and the tear gets worse. *22*Likewise, no one pours new wine into old wineskins. Otherwise, the wine will burst the skins, and both the wine and the skins are ruined. Rather, new wine is poured into fresh wineskins."

The Disciples and the Sabbath. *23x**As he was passing through a field of grain on the sabbath, his disciples began to make a path while picking the heads of grain. *24y*At this the Pharisees said to him, "Look, why are they doing what is unlawful on the sabbath?" *25**He said to them, "Have you never read what David did when he was in need and he and his companions were hungry? *26z*How he went into the house of God when Abiathar was high priest and ate the bread of offering that only the priests could lawfully eat, and shared it with his companions?" *27a**Then he said to them, "The sabbath was made for man, not man for the sabbath. *28**That is why the Son of Man is lord even of the sabbath."

CHAPTER 3

A Man with a Withered Hand. *1b**Again he entered the synagogue. There

See RG 295-96

2, 14: As he passed by: see the note on 1, 16–20. **Levi, son of Alphaeus:** see the note on Mt 9, 9. **Customs post:** such tax collectors paid a fixed sum for the right to collect customs duties within their districts. Since whatever they could collect above this amount constituted their profit, the abuse of extortion was widespread among them. Hence, Jewish customs officials were regarded as sinners (16), outcasts of society, and disgraced along with their families. **He got up and followed him:** i.e., became a disciple of Jesus.

2, 15: In his house: cf v 1; Mt 9, 10. Luke 5, 29 clearly calls it Levi's house.

2, 16–17: This and the following conflict stories reflect a similar pattern: a statement of fact, a question of protest, and a reply by Jesus.

2, 17: Do not need a physician: this maxim of Jesus with its implied irony was uttered to silence his adversaries who objected that he ate with **tax collectors and sinners** (16). Because the scribes and Pharisees were self-righteous, they were not capable of responding to Jesus' call to repentance and faith in the gospel.

2, 18–22: This conflict over the question of fasting has the same pattern as vv 16–17; see the notes on Mt 9, 15 and 9, 16–17.

2, 19: Can the wedding guests fast?: the bridal metaphor expresses a new relationship of love between God and his people in the person and mission of Jesus to his disciples. It is the inauguration of the new and joyful messianic time of fulfillment and the passing of the old. Any attempt at assimi-

lating the Pharisaic practice of fasting, or of extending the preparatory discipline of John's disciples beyond the arrival of the bridegroom, would be as futile as sewing **a piece of unshrunken cloth on an old cloak** or pouring **new wine into old wineskins** with the resulting destruction of both cloth and wine (21–22). Fasting is rendered superfluous during the earthly ministry of Jesus; cf v 20.

2, 23–28: This conflict regarding the sabbath follows the same pattern as in vv 18–22.

2, 25–26: Have you never read what David did?: Jesus defends the action of his disciples on the basis of 1 Sm 21, 2–7 in which an exception is made to the regulation of Lv 24, 9 because of the extreme hunger of David and his men. According to 1 Sm, the priest who gave the bread to David was Ahimelech, father of Abiathar.

2, 27: The sabbath was made for man: a reaffirmation of the divine intent of the sabbath to benefit Israel as contrasted with the restrictive Pharisaic tradition added to the law.

2, 28: The Son of Man is lord even of the sabbath: Mark's comment on the theological meaning of the incident is to benefit his Christian readers; see the note on 2, 10.

3, 1–5: Here Jesus is again depicted in conflict with his adversaries over the question of sabbath-day observance. His opponents were already ill disposed toward him because they

v: Mt 9, 9-13; Lk 5, 27-32.   w: Mt 9, 14-17; Lk 5, 33-39.   x: Mt 12, 1-8; Lk 6, 1-5.   y: Dt 23, 25.   z: 1 Sm 21, 2-7 / Lv 24, 5-9.   a: 2 Mc 5, 19.   b: Mt 12, 9-14; Lk 6, 6-11.

was a man there who had a withered hand. [2]They watched him closely to see if he would cure him on the sabbath so that they might accuse him. [3]He said to the man with the withered hand, "Come up here before us." [4]Then he said to them, "Is it lawful to do good on the sabbath rather than to do evil, to save life rather than to destroy it?" But they remained silent. [5c]Looking around at them with anger and grieved at their hardness of heart, he said to the man, "Stretch out your hand." He stretched it out and his hand was restored. [6*]The Pharisees went out and immediately took counsel with the Herodians against him to put him to death.

The Mercy of Jesus. [7d*]Jesus withdrew toward the sea with his disciples. A large number of people [followed] from Galilee and from Judea. [8]Hearing what he was doing, a large number of people came to him also from Jerusalem, from Idumea, from beyond the Jordan, and from the neighborhood of Tyre and Sidon. [9]He told his disciples to have a boat ready for him because of the crowd, so that they would not crush him. [10e]He had cured many and, as a result, those who had diseases were pressing upon him to touch him. [11f*]And whenever unclean spirits saw

him they would fall down before him and shout, "You are the Son of God." [12]He warned them sternly not to make him known.

The Mission of the Twelve. [13g*]He went up the mountain and summoned those whom he wanted and they came to him. [14h*]He appointed twelve [whom he also named apostles] that they might be with him and he might send them forth to preach [15]and to have authority to drive out demons: [16*][he appointed the twelve:] Simon, whom he named Peter; [17i]James, son of Zebedee, and John the brother of James, whom he named Boanerges, that is, sons of thunder; [18]Andrew, Philip, Bartholomew, Matthew, Thomas, James the son of Alphaeus; Thaddeus, Simon the Cananean, [19]and Judas Iscariot who betrayed him.

Blasphemy of the Scribes. [20j*]He came home. Again [the] crowd gathered, making it impossible for them even to eat. [21k]When his relatives heard of this they set out to seize him, for they said, "He is out of his mind." [22l*]The scribes who had come from Jerusalem said, "He is possessed by Beelzebul," and "By the prince of demons he drives out demons."

Jesus and Beelzebul. [23]Summoning them,

regarded Jesus as a violator of the sabbath. Jesus' question **Is it lawful to do good on the sabbath rather than to do evil?** places the matter in the broader theological context outside the casuistry of the scribes. The answer is obvious. Jesus heals the man with the withered hand in the sight of all and reduces his opponents to silence; cf Jn 5, 17–18.

3, 6: In reporting the plot of the Pharisees and Herodians to put Jesus to death after this series of conflicts in Galilee, Mark uses a pattern that recurs in his account of later controversies in Jerusalem (11, 17–18; 12, 13–17). The help of the Herodians, supporters of Herod Antipas, tetrarch of Galilee and Perea, is needed to take action against Jesus. Both series of conflicts point to their gravity and to the impending passion of Jesus.

3, 7–19: This overview of the Galilean ministry manifests the power of Jesus to draw people to himself through his teaching and deeds of power. The crowds of Jews from many regions surround Jesus (7–12). This phenomenon prepares the way for creating a new people of Israel. The choice and mission of the Twelve is the prelude (13–19).

3, 11–12: See the note on 1, 24–25.

3, 13: He went up the mountain: here and elsewhere the mountain is associated with solemn moments and acts in the mission and self-revelation of Jesus (6, 46; 9, 2–8; 13, 3). Jesus acts with authority as he **summoned those whom he wanted and they came to him.**

3, 14–15: He appointed twelve [whom he also named apostles] that they might be with him: literally "he made,"

i.e., instituted them as apostles to extend his messianic mission through them (6, 7–13). See the notes on Mt 10, 1 and 10, 2–4.

3, 16: Simon, **whom he named Peter:** Mark indicates that Simon's name was changed on this occasion. Peter is first in all lists of the apostles (Mt 10, 2; Lk 6, 14; Acts 1, 13; cf 1 Cor 15, 5–8).

3, 20–35: Within the narrative of the coming of Jesus' relatives (20–21) is inserted the account of the unbelieving scribes from Jerusalem who attributed Jesus' power over demons to Beelzebul (22–30); see the note on 5, 21–43. There were those even among the relatives of Jesus who disbelieved and regarded Jesus as **out of his mind** (21). Against this background, Jesus is informed of the arrival of his mother and brothers [and sisters] (32). He responds by showing that not family ties but doing God's will (35) is decisive in the kingdom; cf the note on Mt 12, 46–50.

3, 20: He came home: cf 2, 1–2 and see the note on 2, 15.

3, 22: By Beelzebul: see the note on Mt 10, 25. Two accusations are leveled against Jesus: (1) that **he is possessed** by an unclean spirit, and (2) **by the prince of demons he drives out demons.** Jesus answers the second charge by a parable (24–27) and responds to the first charge in vv 28–29.

c: Lk 14, 4. d: Mt 4, 23-25; 12, 15; Lk 6, 17-19. e: 5, 30. f: 1, 34; Lk 4, 41. g: Mt 10, 1-4; Lk 6, 12-16. h: 6, 7. i: Mt 16, 18; Jn 1, 42. j: 2, 2. k: Jn 10, 20. l: Mt 12, 24-32; Lk 11, 15-22; 12, 10.

Rejections

Jesus' family doubts his sanity (3, 21), and he replaces the biological family with the family of faith. The scribes accept Jesus' power but question the source of his authority; they ironically charge Jesus the exorcist with being possessed by Beelzebul, a false god (2 Kgs 1, 2) or demon.

he began to speak to them in parables, "How can Satan drive out Satan? ²⁴If a kingdom is divided against itself, that kingdom cannot stand. ²⁵And if a house is divided against itself, that house will not be able to stand. ²⁶And if Satan has risen up against himself and is divided, he cannot stand; that is the end of him. ²⁷But no one can enter a strong man's house to plunder his property unless he first ties up the strong man. Then he can plunder his house. ^{28m}Amen, I say to you, all sins and all blasphemies that people utter will be forgiven them. ²⁹*But whoever blasphemes against the holy Spirit will never have forgiveness, but is guilty of an everlasting sin." ³⁰For they had said, "He has an unclean spirit."

Jesus and His Family. ³¹ⁿHis mother and his brothers arrived. Standing outside they sent word to him and called him. ³²*A crowd seated around him told him, "Your mother and your brothers [and your sisters] are outside asking for you." ³³But he said to them in reply, "Who are my mother and [my] brothers?" ³⁴And looking around at those seated in the circle he said, "Here are my mother and my brothers. ³⁵[For] whoever does the will of God is my brother and sister and mother."

CHAPTER 4

See RG 296-97

The Parable of the Sower. ¹*^o*^p*On another occasion he began to teach by the sea. A very large crowd gathered around him so that he got into a boat on the sea and sat down. And the whole crowd was beside the sea on land. ²And he taught them at length in parables, and in the course of his instruction he said to them, ³*"Hear this! A sower went out to sow. ⁴And as he sowed, some seed fell on the path, and the birds came and ate it up. ⁵Other seed fell on rocky ground where it had little soil. It sprang up at once because the soil was not deep. ⁶And when the sun rose, it was scorched and it withered for lack of roots. ⁷Some seed fell among thorns, and the thorns grew up and choked it and it produced no grain. ⁸And some seed fell on rich soil and produced fruit. It came up and grew and yielded thirty, sixty, and a hundredfold." ⁹He added, "Whoever has ears to hear ought to hear."

The Purpose of the Parables. ¹⁰And when he was alone, those present along with the Twelve questioned him about the parables. ¹¹*He answered them, "The mystery of the kingdom of God has been granted to you. But to those outside everything comes in parables, ^{12q}so that

---

3, 29: Whoever blasphemes against the holy Spirit: this sin is called **an everlasting sin** because it attributes to Satan, who is the power of evil, what is actually the work of the holy Spirit, namely, victory over the demons.

3, 32: Your brothers: see the note on 6, 3.

4, 1–34: In parables (2): see the note on Mt 13, 3. The use of parables is typical of Jesus' enigmatic method of teaching the crowds (2–9.12) as compared with the interpretation of the parables he gives to his disciples (10–25.33–34), to each group according to its capacity to understand (9–11). The key feature of the parable at hand is the sowing of the seed (3), representing the breakthrough of the kingdom of God into the world. The various types of soil refer to the diversity of response accorded the word of God (4–7). The climax of the parable is the harvest of thirty, sixty, and a hundredfold, indicating the consummation of the kingdom (8). Thus both the present and the future action of God, from the initiation to the fulfillment of the kingdom, is

presented through this and other parables (26–29.30–32).

4, 1: By the sea: the shore of the Sea of Galilee or a boat near the shore (2, 13; 3, 7–8) is the place where Mark depicts Jesus teaching the crowds. By contrast the mountain is the scene of Jesus at prayer (6, 46) or in the process of forming his disciples (3, 13; 9, 2).

4, 3–8: See the note on Mt 13, 3–8.

4, 11–12: These verses are to be viewed against their background in 3, 6.22 concerning the unbelief and opposition Jesus encountered in his ministry. It is against this background that the distinction in Jesus' method becomes clear of presenting the kingdom to the disbelieving crowd in one manner and to the disciples in another. To the former it is pre-

---

m: Lk 12, 10. *n:* Mt 12, 46-50; Lk 8, 19-21. *o:* Mt 13, 1-13. Lk 8, 4-1C. *p:* 2, 13; Lk 5, 1. *q:* Is 6, 9; Jn 12, 40; Acts 28, 26; Rom 11, 8.

'they may look and see but not perceive,
and hear and listen but not understand,
in order that they may not be converted
and be forgiven.' "

[13r]*Jesus said to them, "Do you not understand this parable? Then how will you understand any of the parables? [14]The sower sows the word. [15]These are the ones on the path where the word is sown. As soon as they hear, Satan comes at once and takes away the word sown in them. [16]And these are the ones sown on rocky ground who, when they hear the word, receive it at once with joy. [17]But they have no root; they last only for a time. Then when tribulation or persecution comes because of the word, they quickly fall away. [18]Those sown among thorns are another sort. They are the people who hear the word, [19]but worldly anxiety, the lure of riches, and the craving for other things intrude and choke the word, and it bears no fruit. [20]But those sown on rich soil are the ones who hear the word and accept it and bear fruit thirty and sixty and a hundredfold."

Parable of the Lamp. [21s]*He said to them, "Is a lamp brought in to be placed under a bushel basket or under a bed, and not to be placed on a lampstand? [22u]For there is nothing hidden except to be made visible; nothing is secret except to come to light. [23]Anyone who has ears to hear ought to hear." [24v]He also told them, "Take care what you hear. The measure with which you measure will be measured out to you, and still more will be given to you. [25w]To the one who has, more will be given; from the one who has not, even what he has will be taken away."

Seed Grows of Itself. [26x]*He said, "This is how it is with the kingdom of God; it is as if a man were to scatter seed on the land [27]and would sleep and rise night and day and the seed would sprout and grow, he knows not how. [28]Of its own accord the land yields fruit, first the blade, then the ear, then the full grain in the ear. [29]And when the grain is ripe, he wields the sickle at once, for the harvest has come."

The Mustard Seed. [30y]He said, "To what shall we compare the kingdom of God, or what parable can we use for it? [31]It is like a mustard seed that, when it is sown in the ground, is the smallest of all the seeds on the earth. [32]*But once it is sown, it springs up and becomes the largest of plants and puts forth large branches, so that the birds of the sky can dwell in its shade." [33z]With many such parables he spoke the word to them as they were able to understand it. [34]Without parables he did not speak to them, but to his own disciples he explained everything in private.

The Calming of a Storm at Sea. [35a]*On that day, as evening drew on, he said to them, "Let us cross to the other side." [36]Leaving the crowd, they took him with them in the boat just as he was. And other boats were with him. [37]A violent squall came up and waves were breaking over the boat, so that it was already filling up. [38]Jesus was in the stern, asleep on a cushion. They woke him and said to him, "Teacher, do you not care that we are perishing?" [39]*He woke up, rebuked the wind, and said to the sea, "Quiet! Be still!" The wind ceased and there was great calm. [40]Then he asked them, "Why are you terrified? Do you not yet have faith?" [41b]*They

sented in parables and the truth remains hidden; for the latter the parable is interpreted and the mystery is partially revealed because of their faith; see the notes on Mt 13, 11 and 13, 13.

4, 13–20: See the note on Mt 13, 18–23.

4, 26–29: Only Mark records the parable of the seed's growth. Sower and harvester are the same. The emphasis is on the power of the seed to grow of itself without human intervention (27). Mysteriously it produces **blade** and **ear** and **full grain** (28). Thus the kingdom of God initiated by Jesus in proclaiming the word develops quietly yet powerfully until it is fully established by him at the final judgment (29); cf Rv 14, 15.

4, 32: The universality of the kingdom of God is indicated here; cf Ez 17, 23; 31, 6; Dn 4, 17–19.

4, 35—5, 43: After the chapter on parables, Mark narrates

four miracle stories: 4, 35–41; 5, 1–20; and two joined together in 5, 21–43. See also the notes on Mt 8, 23–34 and 9, 8–26.

4, 39: Quiet! Be still!: as in the case of silencing a demon (1, 25), Jesus rebukes the wind and subdues the turbulence of the sea by a mere word; see the note on Mt 8, 26.

4, 41: Jesus is here depicted as exercising power over wind and sea. In the Christian community this event was seen as a sign of Jesus' saving presence amid persecutions that threatened its existence.

r: Mt 13, 18-23; Lk 8, 11-15.   s: Lk 8, 16-18.   t: Mt 5, 15; Lk 11, 33.   u: Mt 10, 26; Lk 12, 2.   v: Mt 7, 2; Lk 6, 38.   w: Mt 13, 12; Lk 19, 26.   x: Jas 5, 7.   y: Mt 13, 31-32; Lk 13, 18-19.   z: Mt 13, 34.   a: Mt 8, 18.23-37; Lk 8, 22-25.   b: 1, 27.

were filled with great awe and said to one another, "Who then is this whom even wind and sea obey?"

See RG 296–97

CHAPTER 5

The Healing of the Gerasene Demoniac. [1c]*They came to the other side of the sea, to the territory of the Gerasenes. [2]*When he got out of the boat, at once a man from the tombs who had an unclean spirit met him. [3]The man had been dwelling among the tombs, and no one could restrain him any longer, even with a chain. [4]In fact, he had frequently been bound with shackles and chains, but the chains had been pulled apart by him and the shackles smashed, and no one was strong enough to subdue him. [5]Night and day among the tombs and on the hillsides he was always crying out and bruising himself with stones. [6]Catching sight of Jesus from a distance, he ran up and prostrated himself before him, [7]*crying out in a loud voice, "What have you to do with me, Jesus, Son of the Most High God? I adjure you by God, do not torment me!" [8](He had been saying to him, "Unclean spirit, come out of the man!") [9d]*He asked him, "What is your name?" He replied, "Legion is my name. There are many of us." [10]And he pleaded earnestly with him not to drive them away from that territory.

[11]*Now a large herd of swine was feeding there on the hillside. [12]And they pleaded with him, "Send us into the swine. Let us enter them." [13]And he let them, and the unclean spirits came out and entered the swine. The herd of about two thousand rushed down a steep bank into the sea, where they were drowned. [14]The swineherds ran away and reported the incident in the town and throughout the countryside. And people came out to see what had happened. [15]As they approached Jesus, they caught sight of the man who had been possessed by Legion, sitting there clothed and in his right mind. And they were seized with fear. [16]Those who witnessed the incident explained to them what had happened to the possessed man and to the swine. [17]Then they began to beg him to leave their district. [18]As he was getting into the boat, the man who had been possessed pleaded to remain with him. [19]*But he would not permit him but told him instead, "Go home to your family and announce to them all that the Lord in his pity has done for you." [20]Then the man went off and began to proclaim in the Decapolis what Jesus had done for him; and all were amazed.

Jairus's Daughter and the Woman with a Hemorrhage. [21e]*When Jesus had crossed again [in the boat] to the other side, a large crowd gathered around him, and he stayed close to the sea. [22f]One of the synagogue officials, named Jairus, came forward. Seeing him he fell at his feet [23]*and pleaded earnestly with him, saying, "My daughter is at the point of death. Please, come lay your hands on her that she may get well and live." [24]He went off with him, and a large crowd followed him and pressed upon him.

[25]There was a woman afflicted with hemorrhages for twelve years. [26]She had suffered greatly at the hands of many doctors and had spent all that she had. Yet she was not helped

---

5, 1: The territory of the Gerasenes: the reference is to pagan territory; cf Is 65, 1. Another reading is "Gadarenes"; see the note on Mt 8, 28.

5, 2–6: The man was an outcast from society, dominated by unclean spirits (8.13), living among the tombs. The prostration before Jesus (6) indicates Jesus' power over evil spirits.

5, 7: What have you to do with me?: cf 1, 24 and see the note on Jn 2, 4.

5, 9: Legion is my name: the demons were numerous and the condition of the possessed man was extremely serious; cf Mt 12, 45.

5, 11: Herd of swine: see the note on Mt 8, 30.

5, 19: Go home: Jesus did not accept the man's request **to remain with him** as a disciple (18), yet invited him to announce to his own people what the Lord had done for him,

i.e., proclaim the gospel message to his pagan family; cf 1, 14.39; 3, 14; 13, 10.

5, 21–43: The story of the raising to life of Jairus's daughter is divided into two parts: vv 21–24 and 35–43. Between these two separated parts the account of the cure of the hemorrhage victim (25–34) is interposed. This technique of intercalating or sandwiching one story within another occurs several times in Mk: 3, 19b-21 (22–30) 31–35; 6, 6b-13 (14–29) 30; 11, 12–14 (15–19) 20–25; 14, 53 (54) 55–65 (66–73).

5, 23: Lay your hands on her: this act for the purpose of healing is frequent in Mk (6, 5; 7, 32–35; 8, 23–25; 16, 18) and is also found in Mt 9, 18; Lk 4, 40; 13, 13; Acts 9, 17; 28, 8.

c: Mt 8, 28-34; Lk 8, 26-39. *d:* Mt 12, 45; Lk 8, 2; 11, 26. *e:* 2, 13. *f:* Mt 9, 18-26; Lk 8, 41-56.

but only grew worse. ²⁷She had heard about Jesus and came up behind him in the crowd and touched his cloak. ²⁸*She said, "If I but touch his clothes, I shall be cured." ²⁹Immediately her flow of blood dried up. She felt in her body that she was healed of her affliction. ³⁰Jesus, aware at once that power had gone out from him, turned around in the crowd and asked, "Who has touched my clothes?" ³¹But his disciples said to him, "You see how the crowd is pressing upon you, and yet you ask, 'Who touched me?' " ³²And he looked around to see who had done it. ³³The woman, realizing what had happened to her, approached in fear and trembling. She fell down before Jesus and told him the whole truth. ³⁴ᵍHe said to her, "Daughter, your faith has saved you. Go in peace and be cured of your affliction."

³⁵*While he was still speaking, people from the synagogue official's house arrived and said, "Your daughter has died; why trouble the teacher any longer?" ³⁶Disregarding the message that was reported, Jesus said to the synagogue official, "Do not be afraid; just have faith." ³⁷He did not allow anyone to accompany him inside except Peter, James, and John, the brother of James. ³⁸When they arrived at the house of the synagogue official, he caught sight of a commotion, people weeping and wailing loudly. ³⁹ʰ*So he went in and said to them, "Why this commotion and weeping? The child is not dead but asleep." ⁴⁰And they ridiculed him. Then he put them all out. He took along the child's father and mother and those who were with him and entered the room where the child was. ⁴¹*He took the child by the hand and said to her, "Talitha koum," which means, "Little girl, I say to you, arise!" ⁴²The girl, a child of twelve, arose immediately and walked around. [At that] they were utterly astounded. ⁴³He gave strict orders that no one should know this and said that she should be given something to eat.

CHAPTER 6

See RG 296-97

The Rejection at Nazareth. ¹ⁱ*He departed from there and came to his native place, accompanied by his disciples. ²*When the sabbath came he began to teach in the synagogue, and many who heard him were astonished. They said, "Where did this man get all this? What kind of wisdom has been given him? What mighty deeds are wrought by his hands! ³ʲ*Is he not the carpenter, the son of Mary, and the brother of James and Joses and Judas and Simon? And are not his sisters here with us?" And they took offense at him. ⁴ᵏ*Jesus said to them, "A prophet is not without honor except in his native place and among his own kin and in

5, 28: Both in the case of Jairus and his daughter (23) and in the case of the hemorrhage victim, the inner conviction that physical contact (30) accompanied by faith in Jesus' saving power could effect a cure was rewarded.

5, 35: The faith of Jairus was put to a twofold test: (1) that his daughter might be cured and, now that she had died, (2) that she might be restored to life. His faith contrasts with the lack of faith of the crowd.

5, 39: Not dead but asleep: the New Testament often refers to death as sleep (Mt 27, 52; Jn 11, 11; 1 Cor 15, 6; 1 Thes 4, 13–15); see the note on Mt 9, 24.

5, 41: Arise: the Greek verb egeirein is the verb generally used to express resurrection from death (6, 14.16; Mt 11, 5; Lk 7, 14) and Jesus' own resurrection (16, 6; Mt 28, 6; Lk 24, 6).

6, 1: His native place: the Greek word **patris** here refers to Nazareth (cf 1, 9; Lk 4, 16.23–24), though it can also mean native land.

6, 2–6: See the note on Mt 13, 54–58.

6, 3: Is he not the carpenter?: no other gospel calls Jesus a carpenter. Some witnesses have "the carpenter's son," as in Mt 13, 55. **Son of Mary:** contrary to Jewish custom, which calls a man the son of his father, this expression may reflect Mark's own faith that God is the Father of Jesus (1, 1.11; 8, 38; 13, 32; 14, 36). **The brother of James . . . Simon:** in Semitic usage, the terms 'brother,' 'sister' are applied not only

to children of the same parents, but to nephews, nieces, cousins, half-brothers, and half-sisters; cf Gn 14, 16; 29, 15; Lv 10, 4. While one cannot suppose that the meaning of a Greek word should be sought in the first place from Semitic usage, the Septuagint often translates the Hebrew 'āh by the Greek word **adelphos**, "brother," as in the cited passages, a fact that may argue for a similar breadth of meaning in some New Testament passages. For instance, there is no doubt that in v 17, "brother" is used of Philip, who was actually the half-brother of Herod Antipas. On the other hand, Mark may have understood the terms literally; see also Mt 3, 31–32; 12, 46; 13, 55–56; Lk 8, 19; Jn 7, 3.5. The question of meaning here would not have arisen but for the faith of the church in Mary's perpetual virginity.

6, 4: A prophet is not without honor except . . . in his own house: a saying that finds parallels in other literatures, especially Jewish and Greek, but without reference to a prophet. Comparing himself to previous Hebrew prophets whom the people rejected, Jesus intimates his own eventual rejection by the nation especially in view of the dishonor his own relatives had shown him (3, 21) and now his townspeople as well.

g: Lk 7, 30.　h: Acts 9, 40.　i: Mt 13, 54-58; Lk 4, 16-30.　j: 15, 40; Mt 12, 46; Jn 6, 42.　k: Jn 4, 44.

his own house." [5]*So he was not able to perform any mighty deed there, apart from curing a few sick people by laying his hands on them. [6]He was amazed at their lack of faith.

The Mission of the Twelve. He went around to the villages in the vicinity teaching. [7]*He summoned the Twelve and began to send them out two by two and gave them authority over unclean spirits. [8]*He instructed them to take nothing for the journey but a walking stick—no food, no sack, no money in their belts. [9]They were, however, to wear sandals but not a second tunic. [10]*He said to them, "Wherever you enter a house, stay there until you leave from there. [11]Whatever place does not welcome you or listen to you, leave there and shake the dust off your feet in testimony against them." [12]So they went off and preached repentance. [13m]*They drove out many demons, and they anointed with oil many who were sick and cured them.

Herod's Opinion of Jesus. [14no]*King Herod heard about it, for his fame had become widespread, and people were saying, "John the Baptist has been raised from the dead; that is why mighty powers are at work in him." [15p]Others were saying, "He is Elijah"; still others, "He is a prophet like any of the prophets." [16]But when Herod learned of it, he said, "It is John whom I beheaded. He has been raised up."

The Death of John the Baptist. [17q]*Herod was the one who had John arrested and bound in prison on account of Herodias, the wife of his brother Philip, whom he had married. [18r]John had said to Herod, "It is not lawful for you to have your brother's wife." [19]*Herodias harbored a grudge against him and wanted to kill him but was unable to do so. [20]Herod feared John, knowing him to be a righteous and holy man, and kept him in custody. When he heard him speak he was very much perplexed, yet he liked to listen to him. [21]She had an opportunity one day when Herod, on his birthday, gave a banquet for his courtiers, his military officers, and the leading men of Galilee. [22]Herodias's own daughter came in and performed a dance that delighted Herod and his guests. The king said to the girl, "Ask of me whatever you wish and I will grant it to you." [23s]He even swore [many things] to her, "I will grant you whatever you ask of me, even to half of my kingdom." [24]She went out and said to her mother, "What shall I ask for?" She replied, "The head of John the Baptist." [25]The girl hurried back to the king's presence and made her request, "I want you to give me at once on a platter the head of John the Baptist." [26]The king was deeply distressed, but because of his oaths and the guests he did not wish to break his word to her. [27t]So he

---

6, 5: He was not able to perform any mighty deed there: according to Mark, Jesus' power could not take effect because of a person's lack of faith.

6, 7–13: The preparation for the mission of the Twelve is seen in the call (1) of first disciples to be fishers of men (1, 16–20), (2) then of the Twelve set apart to be with Jesus and to receive authority to preach and expel demons (3, 13–19). Now they are given the specific mission to exercise that authority in word and power as representatives of Jesus during the time of their formation.

6, 8–9: In Mk the use of a **walking stick** (8) and **sandals** (9) is permitted, but not in Mt 10, 10 nor in Lk 10, 4. Mark does not mention any prohibition to visit pagan territory and to enter Samaritan towns. These differences indicate a certain adaptation to conditions in and outside of Palestine and suggest in Mark's account a later activity in the church. For the rest, Jesus required of his apostles a total dependence on God for food and shelter; cf vv 35–44; 8, 1–9.

6, 10–11: Remaining in the same house as a guest (10) rather than moving to another offering greater comfort avoided any impression of seeking advantage for oneself and prevented dishonor to one's host. Shaking the dust off one's feet served as testimony against those who rejected the call

to repentance.

6, 13: Anointed with oil . . . cured them: a common medicinal remedy, but seen here as a vehicle of divine power for healing.

6, 14–16: The various opinions about Jesus anticipate the theme of his identity that reaches its climax in 8, 27–30.

6, 14: King Herod: see the note on Mt 14, 1.

6, 17–29: Similarities are to be noted between Mark's account of the imprisonment and death of John the Baptist in this pericope, and that of the passion of Jesus (15, –47). Herod and Pilate, each in turn, acknowledges the holiness of life of one over whom he unjustly exercises the power of condemnation and death (26–27; 15, 9–10.14–15). The hatred of Herodias toward John parallels that of the Jewish leaders toward Jesus. After the deaths of John and of Jesus, well-disposed persons request the bodies of the victims of Herod and of Pilate in turn to give them respectful burial (29; 15, 45–46).

6, 19: Herodias: see the note on Mt 14, 3.

l: Mt 10, 1.9-14; Lk 9, 15; 10, 4-11. *m:* Jas 5, 14. *n:* Lk 9, 7-8. *o:* Mt 14, 1-12. *p:* Mt 16, 14. *q:* Lk 3, 19-20. *r:* Lv 18, 16. *s:* Est 5, 3. *t:* Lk 9, 9.

The Problem of the Disciples

Mark's portrait of the twelve is highly problematic. On the one hand, they come when Jesus calls them; they do not hesitate to leave their boats, their property, and their families (1, 16–20; 2, 14; 10, 28). They successfully complete their first mission, during which they perform exorcisms, anoint the sick with oil, and heal (6, 12–30).

On the other hand, they consistently fail to understand Jesus' teachings, exhortations, and desires. As early as Mark 1, 37, they interrupt Jesus, who has withdrawn from the crowds for prayer and solitude. Mark 4, 13 recounts Jesus' impatience with their lack of understanding of the parables. In Mark 4, 40, following the calming of the storm, Jesus asks, "Why are you terrified? Do you not yet have faith?" Upon the healing of the woman with the hemorrhages, they chide Jesus: "You see how the crowd is pressing upon you, and yet you ask, 'Who touched me?'" (5, 31). The disciples are unable to recognize Jesus' power; as Mark states, "They were completely astounded. They had not understood the incident of the loaves. On the contrary, their hearts were hardened" (6, 51–52). In Mark 7, 17–18, confused by Jesus' discussion of dietary regulations, the twelve ask Jesus about his parable. Jesus responds, "Do you not yet understand or comprehend?" Following the miraculous feedings of first 5,000 and then 4,000, the disciples worry in Mark 8, 16 that they have no bread.

In the latter half of the Gospel, the failure of the twelve intensifies. They are unable to accept the passion predictions; they have insufficient faith to heal the child with a mute spirit (9, 18–19, 28–29); without warrant they reprove the exorcist who heals in Jesus' name (9, 38–41); they attempt to prevent children from approaching Jesus (10, 13–16); they yearn for positions of honor rather than service (10, 35–40); and they display anger with each other (10, 41–44). Judas betrays Jesus, Peter denies him, and the last collective action of the disciples in the Gospel is to forsake Jesus by fleeing from Gethsemane (14, 50). Even the women who follow him from Galilee come to anoint the body: Had they known of, or believed in, the resurrection, this would not have been necessary. The last sentence of the original Gospel ends with the women fleeing from the tomb: "They said nothing to anyone, for they were afraid" (16, 8).

Scholars debate the meaning of Mark's depiction of Jesus' followers. Perhaps Mark wanted the twelve to represent the range of believers; members of Mark's community may have doubted, denied Jesus under pressure of persecution, or failed to grasp the need for service. Perhaps Mark wanted readers to first to identify with the disciples and then, finally, to reject their misconceptions of Jesus' nature and mission.

promptly dispatched an executioner with orders to bring back his head. He went off and beheaded him in the prison. [28]He brought in the head on a platter and gave it to the girl. The girl in turn gave it to her mother. [29]When his disciples heard about it, they came and took his body and laid it in a tomb.

The Return of the Twelve. [30u]*The apostles gathered together with Jesus and reported all they had done and taught. [31v]*He

---

6, 30: Apostles: here, and in some manuscripts at 3, 14, Mark calls apostles (i.e., those sent forth) the Twelve whom Jesus sends as his emissaries, empowering them to preach, to expel demons, and to cure the sick (13). Only after Pentecost is the title used in the technical sense.

6, 31–34: The withdrawal of Jesus with his disciples to a desert place to rest attracts a great number of people to follow

them. Toward this people of the new exodus Jesus is moved with pity; he satisfies their spiritual hunger by teaching them many things, thus gradually showing himself the faithful shepherd of a new Israel; cf Nm 27, 17; Ez 34, 15.

u: Lk 9, 10.   v: 3, 20; Mt 14, 13; Lk 9, 10.

said to them, "Come away by yourselves to a deserted place and rest a while." People were coming and going in great numbers, and they had no opportunity even to eat. [32w]So they went off in the boat by themselves to a deserted place. [33]People saw them leaving and many came to know about it. They hastened there on foot from all the towns and arrived at the place before them.

The Feeding of the Five Thousand. [34]When he disembarked and saw the vast crowd, his heart was moved with pity for them, for they were like sheep without a shepherd; and he began to teach them many things. [35*]By now it was already late and his disciples approached him and said, "This is a deserted place and it is already very late. [36]Dismiss them so that they can go to the surrounding farms and villages and buy themselves something to eat." [37]He said to them in reply, "Give them some food yourselves." But they said to him, "Are we to buy two hundred days' wages worth of food and give it to them to eat?" [38]He asked them, "How many loaves do you have? Go and see." And when they had found out they said, "Five loaves and two fish." [39]So he gave orders to have them sit down in groups on the green grass. [40*]The people took their places in rows by hundreds and by fifties. [41*]Then, taking the five loaves and the two fish and looking up to heaven, he said the blessing, broke the loaves, and gave them to [his] disciples to set before the people; he also divided the two fish among them all. [42]They all ate and were satisfied. [43]And they picked up twelve wicker baskets full of fragments and what was left of the fish. [44]Those who ate [of the loaves] were five thousand men.

The Walking on the Water. [45x*]Then he made his disciples get into the boat and precede him to the other side toward Bethsaida, while he dismissed the crowd. [46*]And when he had taken leave of them, he went off to the mountain to pray. [47]When it was evening, the boat was far out on the sea and he was alone on shore. [48*]Then he saw that they were tossed about while rowing, for the wind was against them. About the fourth watch of the night, he came towards them walking on the sea. He meant to pass by them. [49]But when they saw him walking on the sea, they thought it was a ghost and cried out. [50*]They had all seen him and were terrified. But at once he spoke with them, "Take courage, it is I, do not be afraid!" [51]He got into the boat with them and the wind died down. They were [completely] astounded. [52y*]They had not understood the incident of the loaves. On the contrary, their hearts were hardened.

The Healings at Gennesaret. [53z]After making the crossing, they came to land at Gennesaret and tied up there. [54]As they were leaving the boat, people immediately recognized him. [55]They scurried about the surrounding country and began to bring in the sick on mats to wherever they heard he

6, 35–44: See the note on Mt 14, 13–21. Compare this section with 8, 1–9. The various accounts of the multiplication of loaves and fishes, two each in Mark and in Matthew and one each in Luke and in John, indicate the wide interest of the early church in their eucharistic gatherings; see, e.g., v 41; 8, 6; 14, 22; and recall also the sign of bread in Ex 16; Dt 8, 3–16; Pss 78, 24–25; 105, 40; Wis 16, 20–21.

6, 40: The people . . . in rows by hundreds and by fifties: reminiscent of the groupings of Israelites encamped in the desert (Ex 18, 21–25) and of the wilderness tradition of the prophets depicting the transformation of the wasteland into pastures where the true shepherd feeds his flock (Ez 34, 25–26) and makes his people beneficiaries of messianic grace.

6, 41: On the language of this verse as eucharistic (cf 14, 22), see the notes on Mt 14, 19.20. Jesus observed the Jewish table ritual of blessing God before partaking of food.

6, 45–52: See the note on Mt 14, 22–33.

6, 45: To the other side toward Bethsaida: a village at the northeastern shore of the Sea of Galilee.

6, 46: He went off to the mountain to pray: see 1, 35–38. In Jn 6, 15 Jesus withdrew to evade any involvement in the false messianic hopes of the multitude.

6, 48: Walking on the sea: see the notes on Mt 14, 22–33 and on Jn 6, 19.

6, 50: It is I, do not be afraid!: literally, "I am." This may reflect the divine revelatory formula of Ex 3, 14; Is 41, 4.10.14; 43, 1.3.10.13. Mark implies the hidden identity of Jesus as Son of God.

6, 52: They had not understood . . . the loaves: the revelatory character of this sign and that of the walking on the sea completely escaped the disciples. **Their hearts were hardened:** in 3, 5–6 hardness of heart was attributed to those who did not accept Jesus and plotted his death. Here the same disposition prevents the disciples from comprehending Jesus' self-revelation through signs; cf 8, 17.

w: Mt 14, 13-21; Lk 9, 10-17; Jn 6, 1-13.   x: Mt 14, 22-32; Jn 6, 15-21.   y: 4, 13.   z: Mt 14, 34-36.

was. 56aWhatever villages or towns or countryside he entered, they laid the sick in the marketplaces and begged him that they might touch only the tassel on his cloak; and as many as touched it were healed.

CHAPTER 7

See RG
296–97

The Tradition of the Elders. 1b*Now when the Pharisees with some scribes who had come from Jerusalem gathered around him, 2they observed that some of his disciples ate their meals with unclean, that is, unwashed, hands. 3*(For the Pharisees and, in fact, all Jews, do not eat without carefully washing their hands, keeping the tradition of the elders. 4And on coming from the marketplace they do not eat without purifying themselves. And there are many other things that they have traditionally observed, the purification of cups and jugs and kettles [and beds].) 5*So the Pharisees and scribes questioned him, "Why do your disciples not follow the tradition of the elders but instead eat a meal with unclean hands?" 6cHe responded, "Well did Isaiah prophesy about you hypocrites, as it is written:

'This people honors me with their lips,
    but their hearts are far from me;
7 In vain do they worship me,
    teaching as doctrines human precepts.'

8You disregard God's commandment but cling to human tradition." 9He went on to say, "How well you have set aside the commandment of God in order to uphold your tradition! 10dFor Moses said, 'Honor your father and your mother,' and 'Whoever curses father or mother shall die.' 11*Yet you say, 'If a person says to father or mother, "Any support you might have had from me is *qorban*" ' (meaning, dedicated to God), 12you allow him to do nothing more for his father or mother. 13You nullify the word of God in favor of your tradition that you have handed on. And you do many such things." 14eHe summoned the crowd again and said to them, "Hear me, all of you, and understand. 15Nothing that enters one from outside can defile that person; but the things that come out from within are what defile." [16]*

17f*When he got home away from the crowd his disciples questioned him about the parable. 18He said to them, "Are even you likewise without understanding? Do you not realize that everything that goes into a person from outside cannot defile, 19g*since it enters not the heart but the stomach and passes out into the latrine?" (Thus he declared all foods clean.) 20"But what comes out of a person, that is what defiles. 21hFrom within people, from their hearts, come evil thoughts, unchastity, theft, murder, 22adultery, greed, malice, deceit, licentiousness, envy, blasphemy, arrogance, folly. 23All these evils come from within and they defile."

7, 1–23: See the note on Mt 15, 1–20. Against the Pharisees' narrow, legalistic, and external practices of piety in matters of purification (2–5), external worship (6–7), and observance of commandments, Jesus sets in opposition the true moral intent of the divine law (8–13). But he goes beyond contrasting the law and Pharisaic interpretation of it. The parable of vv 14–15 in effect sets aside the law itself in respect to clean and unclean food. He thereby opens the way for unity between Jew and Gentile in the kingdom of God, intimated by Jesus' departure for pagan territory beyond Galilee. For similar contrast see 2, 1–3. 6; 3, 20–35; 6, 1–6.

7, 3: Carefully washing their hands: refers to ritual purification.

7, 5: Tradition of the elders: the body of detailed, unwritten, human laws regarded by the scribes and Pharisees to have the same binding force as that of the Mosaic law; cf Gal 1, 14.

7, 11: Qorban: a formula for a gift to God, dedicating the offering to the temple, so that the giver might continue to use it for himself but not give it to others, even needy parents.

7, 16: Verse 16, "Anyone who has ears to hear ought to hear," is omitted because it is lacking in some of the best Greek manuscripts and was probably transferred here by scribes from 4, (9).23.

7, 17: Away from the crowd . . . the parable: in this context of privacy the term **parable** refers to something hidden, about to be revealed to the disciples; cf 4, 10–11.34. Jesus sets the Mosaic food laws in the context of the kingdom of God where they are abrogated, and he declares moral defilement the only cause of uncleanness.

7, 19: (Thus he declared all foods clean): if this bold declaration goes back to Jesus, its force was not realized among Jewish Christians in the early church; cf Acts 10, 1–11, 18.

a: 5, 27-28; Acts 5, 15. *b:* Mt 15, 1-20. *c:* Is 29, 13. *d:* Ex 21, 17; Lv 20, 9; Dt 5, 16; Eph 6, 2. *e:* Mt 15, 10-20. *f:* 4, 10.13. *g:* Acts 10, 15. *h:* Jer 17, 9.

The Syrophoenician Woman's Faith. [24i]*From that place he went off to the district of Tyre. He entered a house and wanted no one to know about it, but he could not escape notice. [25]Soon a woman whose daughter had an unclean spirit heard about him. She came and fell at his feet. [26j]The woman was a Greek, a Syrophoenician by birth, and she begged him to drive the demon out of her daughter. [27]*He said to her, "Let the children be fed first. For it is not right to take the food of the children and throw it to the dogs." [28]She replied and said to him, "Lord, even the dogs under the table eat the children's scraps." [29]Then he said to her, "For saying this, you may go. The demon has gone out of your daughter." [30]When the woman went home, she found the child lying in bed and the demon gone.

The Healing of a Deaf Man. [31k]Again he left the district of Tyre and went by way of Sidon to the Sea of Galilee, into the district of the Decapolis. [32]And people brought to him a deaf man who had a speech impediment and begged him to lay his hand on him. [33]He took him off by himself away from the crowd. He put his finger into the man's ears and, spitting, touched his tongue; [34]then he looked up to heaven and groaned, and said to him, "*Ephphatha!*" (that is, "Be opened!") [35]And [immediately] the man's ears were opened, his speech impediment was removed, and he spoke plainly. [36]*He ordered them not to tell anyone. But the more he ordered them not to, the more they proclaimed

it. [37l]They were exceedingly astonished and they said, "He has done all things well. He makes the deaf hear and [the] mute speak."

CHAPTER 8

See RG 297-98

The Feeding of the Four Thousand. [1]*In those days when there again was a great crowd without anything to eat, he summoned the disciples and said, [2]"My heart is moved with pity for the crowd, because they have been with me now for three days and have nothing to eat. [3]If I send them away hungry to their homes, they will collapse on the way, and some of them have come a great distance." [4]His disciples answered him, "Where can anyone get enough bread to satisfy them here in this deserted place?" [5]Still he asked them, "How many loaves do you have?" "Seven," they replied. [6]*He ordered the crowd to sit down on the ground. Then, taking the seven loaves he gave thanks, broke them, and gave them to his disciples to distribute, and they distributed them to the crowd. [7]They also had a few fish. He said the blessing over them and ordered them distributed also. [8]They ate and were satisfied. They picked up the fragments left over—seven baskets. [9]There were about four thousand people.

He dismissed them [10]and got into the boat with his disciples and came to the region of Dalmanutha.

The Demand for a Sign. [11no]*The Pharisees came forward and began to argue with him, seeking from him a sign from heaven to test him. [12]He sighed from the depth of his

7, 24–37: The withdrawal of Jesus to the district of Tyre may have been for a respite (24), but he soon moved onward to Sidon and, by way of the Sea of Galilee, to the Decapolis. These districts provided a Gentile setting for the extension of his ministry of healing because the people there acknowledged his power (29.37). The actions attributed to Jesus (33–35) were also used by healers of the time.

7, 27–28: The figure of a household in which children at table are fed first and then their leftover food is given to the dogs under the table is used effectively to acknowledge the prior claim of the Jews to the ministry of Jesus; however, Jesus accedes to the Gentile woman's plea for the cure of her afflicted daughter because of her faith.

7, 36: The more they proclaimed it: the same verb **proclaim** attributed here to the crowd in relation to the miracles of Jesus is elsewhere used in Mark for the preaching of the gospel on the part of Jesus, of his disciples, and of the Christian community (1, 14; 13, 10; 14, 9). Implied in the action of

the crowd is a recognition of the salvific mission of Jesus; see the note on Mt 11, 5–6.

8, 1–10: The two accounts of the multiplication of loaves and fishes (8, 1–10 and 6, 31–44) have eucharistic significance. Their similarity of structure and themes but dissimilarity of detail are considered by many to refer to a single event that, however, developed in two distinct traditions, one Jewish Christian and the other Gentile Christian, since Jesus in Mark's presentation (7, 24–37) has extended his saving mission to the Gentiles.

8, 6: See the note on 6, 41.

8, 11–12: The objection of the Pharisees that Jesus' miracles are unsatisfactory for proving the arrival of God's kingdom is comparable to the request of the crowd for a sign in Jn 6, 30–31. Jesus' response shows that a sign originating in human demand will not be provided; cf Nm 14, 11.22.

i: Mt 15, 21-28.   *j:* Mt 8, 29.   *k:* Mt 15, 29-31.   *l:* Mt 15, 31.   *m:* 5, 34-44; Mt 15, 32-39.   *n:* Mt 12, 38-39; 16, 1-4.   *o:* Lk 11, 16.

Mediterranean
Sea

• Sidon

• Damascus

• Tyre

• Caesarea Philippi

GALILEE   TETRARCHY
OF PHILIP

Capernaum • Bethsaida
•
Sea of
Galilee

Nazareth

(Tetrarchy of Herod Antipas)

River Jordan

DECAPOLIS

• Gerasa

SAMARIA

PEREA

• Gadara

• Jericho

Jerusalem •• Bethphage
JUDEA   • Bethany

Dead
Sea

IDUMEA

33°

32°

31°

| 0 | 10 | 20 Miles |
| 0 | 10 | 20 Kilometers |

35°

36°

Sites of Jesus' Travels in Galilee and Vicinity

spirit and said, "Why does this generation seek a sign? Amen, I say to you, no sign will be given to this generation." [13]Then he left them, got into the boat again, and went off to the other shore.

The Leaven of the Pharisees. [14p]They had forgotten to bring bread, and they had only one loaf with them in the boat. [15]*He enjoined them, "Watch out, guard against the leaven of the Pharisees and the leaven of Herod." [16]They concluded among themselves that it was because they had no bread. [17q]When he became aware of this he said to them, "Why do you conclude that it is because you have no bread? Do you not yet understand or comprehend? Are your hearts hardened? [18r]Do you have eyes and not see, ears and not hear? And do you not remember, [19]when I broke the five loaves for the five thousand, how many wicker baskets full of fragments you picked up?" They answered him, "Twelve." [20]"When I broke the seven loaves for the four thousand, how many full baskets of fragments did you pick up?" They answered [him], "Seven." [21]He said to them, "Do you still not understand?"

The Blind Man of Bethsaida. [22]*When they arrived at Bethsaida, they brought to him a blind man and begged him to touch him. [23s]He took the blind man by the hand and led him outside the village. Putting spittle on his eyes he laid his hands on him and asked, "Do you see anything?" [24]Looking up he replied, "I see people looking like trees and walking." [25]Then he laid hands on his eyes a second time and he saw clearly; his sight was restored and he could see everything distinctly. [26]Then he sent him home and said, "Do not even go into the village."

III: The Mystery Begins to Be Revealed

Peter's Confession about Jesus. [27t]*Now Jesus and his disciples set out for the villages of Caesarea Philippi. Along the way he asked his disciples, "Who do people say that I am?" [28]They said in reply, "John the Baptist, others Elijah, still others one of the prophets." [29]And he asked them, "But who do you say that I am?" Peter said to him in reply, "You are the Messiah." [30]Then he warned them not to tell anyone about him.

The First Prediction of the Passion. [31u]*He began to teach them that the Son of Man must suffer greatly and be rejected by the elders, the chief priests, and the scribes, and be killed, and rise after three days. [32]He spoke this openly. Then Peter took him aside and began to rebuke him. [33]At this he turned

---

8, 15: The leaven of the Pharisees . . . of Herod: the corruptive action of leaven (1 Cor 5, 6–8; Gal 5, 9) was an apt symbol of the evil dispositions both of the Pharisees (11–13; 7, 5–13) and of Herod (6, 14–29) toward Jesus. The disciples of Jesus are warned against sharing such rebellious attitudes toward Jesus; cf vv 17, 21.

8, 22–26: Jesus' actions and the gradual cure of the blind man probably have the same purpose as in the case of the deaf man (7, 31–37). Some commentators regard the cure as an intended symbol of the gradual enlightenment of the disciples concerning Jesus' messiahship.

8, 27–30: This episode is the turning point in Mark's account of Jesus in his public ministry. Popular opinions concur in regarding him as a prophet. The disciples by contrast believe him to be the Messiah. Jesus acknowledges this identification but prohibits them from making his messianic office known to avoid confusing it with ambiguous contemporary ideas on the nature of that office. See further the notes on Mt 16, 13–20.

8, 31: Son of Man: an enigmatic title. It is used in Dn 7, 13–14 as a symbol of "the saints of the Most High," the faithful Israelites who receive the everlasting kingdom from the Ancient One (God). They are represented by a human figure that contrasts with the various beasts who represent the pre-

vious kingdoms of the earth. In the Jewish apocryphal books of 1 Enoch and 4 Ezra the "Son of Man" is not, as in Dn, a group, but a unique figure of extraordinary spiritual endowments, who will be revealed as the one through whom the everlasting kingdom decreed by God will be established. It is possible though doubtful that this individualization of the Son of Man figure had been made in Jesus' time, and therefore his use of the title in that sense is questionable. Of itself, this expression means simply a human being, or, indefinitely, someone, and there are evidences of this use in pre-Christian times. Its use in the New Testament is probably due to Jesus' speaking of himself in that way, "a human being," and the later church's taking this in the sense of the Jewish apocrypha and applying it to him with that meaning. **Rejected by the elders, the chief priests, and the scribes:** the supreme council called the Sanhedrin was made up of seventy-one members of these three groups and presided over by the high priest. It exercised authority over the Jews in religious matters. See the note on Mt 8, 20.

p: Mt 16, 5-12; Lk 12, 1.   q: 4, 13.   r: Jer 5, 21; Ez 12, 2.   s: 7, 33; Jn 9, 6.   t: Mt 16, 13-20; Lk 9, 18-21.   u: Mt 16, 21-27; Lk 9, 22-26.

around and, looking at his disciples, rebuked Peter and said, "Get behind me, Satan. You are thinking not as God does, but as human beings do."

The Conditions of Discipleship. [34v]*He summoned the crowd with his disciples and said to them, "Whoever wishes to come after me must deny himself, take up his cross, and follow me. [35w]*For whoever wishes to save his life will lose it, but whoever loses his life for my sake and that of the gospel will save it. [36]What profit is there for one to gain the whole world and forfeit his life? [37]What could one give in exchange for his life? [38x]Whoever is ashamed of me and of my words in this faithless and sinful generation, the Son of Man will be ashamed of when he comes in his Father's glory with the holy angels."

See RG 297–98

CHAPTER 9

[1y]*He also said to them, "Amen, I say to you, there are some standing here who will not taste death until they see that the kingdom of God has come in power."

The Transfiguration of Jesus. [2z]*After six days Jesus took Peter, James, and John and led them up a high mountain apart by themselves. And he was transfigured before them, [3]and his clothes became dazzling white, such as no fuller on earth could bleach them. [4]Then Elijah appeared to them along with Moses, and they were conversing with Jesus. [5]*Then Peter said to Jesus in reply, "Rabbi, it is good that we are here! Let us make three tents: one for you, one for Moses, and one for Elijah." [6]He hardly knew what to say, they were so terrified. [7]*Then a cloud came, casting a shadow over them; then from the cloud came a voice, "This is my beloved Son. Listen to him." [8]Suddenly, looking around, they no longer saw anyone but Jesus alone with them.

The Coming of Elijah. [9a]*As they were coming down from the mountain, he charged them not to relate what they had seen to anyone, except when the Son of Man had risen from the dead. [10]So they kept the matter to themselves, questioning what rising from the dead meant. [11b]Then they asked him, "Why do the scribes say that Elijah must come first?" [12]He told them, "Elijah will indeed come first and restore all things, yet how is it written regarding the Son of Man that he must suffer greatly and be treated with contempt? [13c]But I tell you that Elijah has come and they did to him whatever they pleased, as it is written of him."

The Healing of a Boy with a Demon.

8, 34–35: This utterance of Jesus challenges all believers to authentic discipleship and total commitment to himself through self-renunciation and acceptance of the cross of suffering, even to the sacrifice of life itself. **Whoever wishes to save his life will lose it . . . will save it:** an expression of the ambivalence of life and its contrasting destiny. Life seen as mere self-centered earthly existence and lived in denial of Christ ends in destruction, but when lived in loyalty to Christ, despite earthly death, it arrives at fullness of life.

8, 35: For my sake and that of the gospel: Mark here, as at 10, 29, equates Jesus with the gospel.

9, 1: There are some standing . . . come in power: understood by some to refer to the establishment by God's power of his kingdom on earth in and through the church; more likely, as understood by others, a reference to the imminent parousia.

9, 2–8: Mk and Mt 17, 1 place the transfiguration of Jesus six days after the first prediction of his passion and death and his instruction to the disciples on the doctrine of the cross; Lk 9, 28 has "about eight days." Thus the transfiguration counterbalances the prediction of the passion by affording certain of the disciples insight into the divine glory that Jesus possessed. His glory will overcome his death and that of his disciples; cf 2 Cor 3, 18; 2 Pt 1, 16–19. The heavenly voice (7) prepares the disciples to understand that in the divine plan Jesus must die ig-

nominiously before his messianic glory is made manifest; cf Lk 24, 25–27. See further the note on Mt 17, 1–8.

9, 5: Moses and Elijah represent respectively law and prophecy in the Old Testament and are linked to Mt. Sinai; cf Ex 19, 16—20, 17; 1 Kgs 19, 2.8–14. They now appear with Jesus as witnesses to the fulfillment of the law and the prophets taking place in the person of Jesus as he appears in glory.

9, 7: A cloud came, casting a shadow over them: even the disciples enter into the mystery of his glorification. In the Old Testament the cloud covered the meeting tent, indicating the Lord's presence in the midst of his people (Ex 40, 34–35) and came to rest upon the temple in Jerusalem at the time of its dedication (1 Kgs 8, 10).

9, 9–13: At the transfiguration of Jesus his disciples had seen Elijah. They were perplexed because, according to the rabbinical interpretation of Mal 3, 23–24, Elijah was to come first. Jesus' response shows that Elijah has come, in the person of John the Baptist, to prepare for the day of the Lord. Jesus **must suffer greatly and be treated with contempt** (12) like the Baptist (13); cf 6, 17–29.

v: Mt 10, 38-39; 16, 24-27; Lk 14, 26-27.   w: Jn 12, 25.   x: Mt 10, 33; Lk 12, 8.   y: Mt 16, 28; Lk 9, 27.   z: Mt 17, 1-13; Lk 9, 28-36.   a: 8, 31.   b: Is 53, 3; Mal 3, 23.   c: 1 Kgs 19, 2-10.

14d*When they came to the disciples, they saw a large crowd around them and scribes arguing with them. 15Immediately on seeing him, the whole crowd was utterly amazed. They ran up to him and greeted him. 16He asked them, "What are you arguing about with them?" 17Someone from the crowd answered him, "Teacher, I have brought to you my son possessed by a mute spirit. 18Wherever it seizes him, it throws him down; he foams at the mouth, grinds his teeth, and becomes rigid. I asked your disciples to drive it out, but they were unable to do so." 19He said to them in reply, "O faithless generation, how long will I be with you? How long will I endure you? Bring him to me." 20They brought the boy to him. And when he saw him, the spirit immediately threw the boy into convulsions. As he fell to the ground, he began to roll around and foam at the mouth. 21Then he questioned his father, "How long has this been happening to him?" He replied, "Since childhood. 22It has often thrown him into fire and into water to kill him. But if you can do anything, have compassion on us and help us." 23Jesus said to him, " 'If you can!' Everything is possible to one who has faith." 24Then the boy's father cried out, "I do believe, help my unbelief!" 25Jesus, on seeing a crowd rapidly gathering, rebuked the unclean spirit and said to it, "Mute and deaf spirit, I command you: come out of him and never enter him again!" 26Shouting and throwing the boy into convulsions, it came out. He became like a corpse, which caused many to say, "He is dead!" 27But Jesus took him by the hand, raised him, and he stood up. 28When he entered the house, his disciples asked him in private, "Why could we not drive it out?" 29*He said to them, "This kind can only come out through prayer."

The Second Prediction of the Passion. 30ef They left from there and began a journey through Galilee, but he did not wish anyone to know about it. 31He was teaching his disciples and telling them, "The Son of Man is to be handed over to men and they will kill him, and three days after his death he will rise." 32But they did not understand the saying, and they were afraid to question him.

IV: The Full Revelation of the Mystery

The Greatest in the Kingdom. 33g*They came to Capernaum and, once inside the house, he began to ask them, "What were you arguing about on the way?" 34But they remained silent. They had been discussing among themselves on the way who was the greatest. 35hThen he sat down, called the Twelve, and said to them, "If anyone wishes to be first, he shall be the last of all and the servant of all." 36Taking a child he placed it in their midst, and putting his arms around it he said to them, 37i"Whoever receives one child such as this in my name, receives me; and whoever receives me, receives not me but the One who sent me."

Another Exorcist. 38j*John said to him, "Teacher, we saw someone driving out demons in your name, and we tried to prevent him because he does not follow us." 39Jesus replied, "Do not prevent him. There is no one who performs a mighty deed in my name who can at the same time speak ill of me. 40kFor whoever is not against us is for us. 41l Anyone who gives you a cup of water to drink because you belong to Christ, amen, I say to you, will surely not lose his reward.

Temptations to Sin. 42m"Whoever causes

9, 14–29: The disciples' failure to effect a cure seems to reflect unfavorably on Jesus (14–18.22). In response Jesus exposes their lack of trust in God (19) and scores their lack of prayer (29), i.e., of conscious reliance on God's power when acting in Jesus' name. For Mt, see the note on 17, 14–20. Luke 9, 37–43 centers attention on Jesus' sovereign power.

9, 29: **This kind can only come out through prayer:** a variant reading adds "and through fasting."

9, 33–37: Mark probably intends this incident and the sayings that follow as commentary on the disciples' lack of understanding (32). Their role in Jesus' work is one of service, especially to the poor and lowly. Children were the symbol

Jesus used for the **anawim**, the poor in spirit, the lowly in the Christian community.

9, 38–41: Jesus warns against jealousy and intolerance toward others, such as exorcists who do **not follow us.** The saying in v 40 is a broad principle of the divine tolerance. Even the smallest courtesies shown to those who teach in Jesus' name do not go unrewarded.

d: Mt 17, 14-21; Lk 9, 37-43.   e: Jn 7, 1.   f: 8, 31; Mt 17, 22-23; Lk 9, 43-45.   g: Mt 18, 1-5; Lk 9, 46-48.   h: Mt 20, 27.   i: Mt 10, 40; 18, 5; Jn 13, 20.   j: Nm 11, 28; Lk 9, 49-50; 1 Cor 12, 3.   k: Mt 12, 30.   l: Mt 10, 42; 1 Cor 3, 23.   m: Mt 5, 29-30; 18, 6-9; Lk 17, 1-2.

one of these little ones who believe [in me] to sin, it would be better for him if a great millstone were put around his neck and he were thrown into the sea. *43* *If your hand causes you to sin, cut it off. It is better for you to enter into life maimed than with two hands to go into Gehenna, into the unquenchable fire. [*44*]* *45* And if your foot causes you to sin, cut if off. It is better for you to enter into life crippled than with two feet to be thrown into Gehenna. [*46*]* *47* And if your eye causes you to sin, pluck it out. Better for you to enter into the kingdom of God with one eye than with two eyes to be thrown into Gehenna, *48n* where 'their worm does not die, and the fire is not quenched.'

The Simile of Salt. *49**"Everyone will be salted with fire. *50o* Salt is good, but if salt becomes insipid, with what will you restore its flavor? Keep salt in yourselves and you will have peace with one another."

CHAPTER 10

See RG 297-98

Marriage and Divorce. *1* He set out from there and went into the district of Judea [and] across the Jordan. Again crowds gathered around him and, as was his custom, he again taught them. *2p* *The Pharisees approached and asked, "Is it lawful for a husband to divorce his wife?" They were testing him. *3* He said to them in reply, "What did Moses command you?" *4q* They replied, "Moses permitted him to write a bill of divorce and dismiss her." *5* But Jesus told them, "Because of the hardness of your hearts he wrote you this commandment. *6r* But from the beginning of creation, 'God made them male and female. *7s* For this rea-

son a man shall leave his father and mother [and be joined to his wife], *8* and the two shall become one flesh.' So they are no longer two but one flesh. *9* Therefore what God has joined together, no human being must separate." *10* In the house the disciples again questioned him about this. *11t* He said to them, "Whoever divorces his wife and marries another commits adultery against her; *12* and if she divorces her husband and marries another, she commits adultery."

Blessing of the Children. *13uv* And people were bringing children to him that he might touch them, but the disciples rebuked them. *14* When Jesus saw this he became indignant and said to them, "Let the children come to me; do not prevent them, for the kingdom of God belongs to such as these. *15w* *Amen, I say to you, whoever does not accept the kingdom of God like a child will not enter it." *16* Then he embraced them and blessed them, placing his hands on them.

The Rich Man. *17x* As he was setting out on a journey, a man ran up, knelt down before him, and asked him, "Good teacher, what must I do to inherit eternal life?" *18* *Jesus answered him, "Why do you call me good? No one is good but God alone. *19y* You know the commandments: 'You shall not kill; you shall not commit adultery; you shall not steal; you shall not bear false witness; you shall not defraud; honor your father and your mother.' " *20* He replied and said to him, "Teacher, all of these I have observed from my youth." *21* Jesus, looking at him, loved him and said to him, "You are lacking in one thing. Go, sell what you have,

---

9, 43.45.47: Gehenna: see the note on Mt 5, 22.

9, 44.46: These verses, lacking in some important early manuscripts, are here omitted as scribal additions. They simply repeat v 48, itself a modified citation of Is 66, 24.

9, 49: Everyone will be salted with fire: so the better manuscripts. Some add "every sacrifice will be salted with salt." The purifying and preservative use of salt in food (Lv 2, 13) and the refinement effected through fire refer here to comparable effects in the spiritual life of the disciples of Jesus.

10, 2–9: In the dialogue between Jesus and the Pharisees on the subject of divorce, Jesus declares that the law of Moses permitted divorce (Dt 24, 1) only **because of the hardness of your hearts** (4–5). In citing Gn 1, 27 and 2, 24, Jesus proclaims permanence to be the divine intent from the beginning concerning human marriage (6–8). He reaffirms this with the declaration that **what God has joined together, no**

human being must separate (9). See further the notes on Mt 5, 31–32 and 19, 3–9.

10, 15: Whoever does not accept the kingdom of God like a child: i.e., in total dependence upon and obedience to the gospel; cf Mt 18, 3–4.

10, 18: Why do you call me good?: Jesus repudiates the term "good" for himself and directs it to God, the source of all goodness who alone can grant the gift of eternal life; cf Mt 19, 16–17.

n: Is 66, 24.   *o:* Lv 2, 13; Mt 5, 13; Lk 14, 34-35; Col 4, 6.   *p:* Mt 19, 3-9.   *q:* Dt 24, 1-4.   *r:* Gn 1, 27.   *s:* Gn 2, 24; 1 Cor 6, 16; Eph 5, 31.   *t:* Mt 5, 32; Lk 16, 18; 1 Cor 7, 10-11.   *u:* Mt 19, 13-15; Lk 18, 15-17.   *v:* Lk 9, 47.   *w:* Mt 18, 3.   *x:* Mt 19, 16-30; Lk 18, 18-30.   *y:* Ex 20, 12-16; Dt 5, 16-21.

and give to [the] poor and you will have treasure in heaven; then come, follow me." ²²At that statement his face fell, and he went away sad, for he had many possessions.

²³ᶻ*Jesus looked around and said to his disciples, "How hard it is for those who have wealth to enter the kingdom of God!" ²⁴The disciples were amazed at his words. So Jesus again said to them in reply, "Children, how hard it is to enter the kingdom of God! ²⁵It is easier for a camel to pass through [the] eye of [a] needle than for one who is rich to enter the kingdom of God." ²⁶They were exceedingly astonished and said among themselves, "Then who can be saved?" ²⁷Jesus looked at them and said, "For human beings it is impossible, but not for God. All things are possible for God." ²⁸Peter began to say to him, "We have given up everything and followed you." ²⁹Jesus said, "Amen, I say to you, there is no one who has given up house or brothers or sisters or mother or father or children or lands for my sake and for the sake of the gospel ³⁰who will not receive a hundred times more now in this present age: houses and brothers and sisters and mothers and children and lands, with persecutions, and eternal life in the age to come. ³¹ᵃBut many that are first will be last, and [the] last will be first."

The Third Prediction of the Passion. ³²ᵇThey were on the way, going up to Jerusalem, and Jesus went ahead of them. They were amazed, and those who followed were afraid. Taking the Twelve aside again, he began to tell them what was going to happen to him. ³³"Behold, we are going up to Jerusalem, and the Son of Man will be handed over to the chief priests and the scribes, and they will condemn him to death and hand him over to the Gentiles ³⁴who will mock him, spit upon him, scourge him, and put him to death, but after three days he will rise."

Ambition of James and John. ³⁵ᶜThen James and John, the sons of Zebedee, came to him and said to him, "Teacher, we want you to do for us whatever we ask of you." ³⁶He replied, "What do you wish [me] to do for you?" ³⁷They answered him, "Grant that in your glory we may sit one at your right and the other at your left." ³⁸ᵈ*Jesus said to them, "You do not know what you are asking. Can you drink the cup that I drink or be baptized with the baptism with which I am baptized?" ³⁹They said to him, "We can." Jesus said to them, "The cup that I drink, you will drink, and with the baptism with which I am baptized, you will be baptized; ⁴⁰but to sit at my right or at my left is not mine to give but is for those for whom it has been prepared." ⁴¹When the ten heard this, they became indignant at James and John. ⁴²ᵉ*Jesus summoned them and said to them, "You know that those who are recognized as rulers over the Gentiles lord it over them, and their great ones make their authority over them felt. ⁴³But it shall not be so among you. Rather, whoever wishes to be great among you will be your servant; ⁴⁴whoever wishes to be first among you will be the slave of all. ⁴⁵For the Son of Man did not come to be served but to serve and to give his life as a ransom for many."

The Blind Bartimaeus. ⁴⁶ᶠ*They came to Jericho. And as he was leaving Jericho with

---

10, 23–27: In the Old Testament wealth and material goods are considered a sign of God's favor (Jb 1, 10; Ps 128, 1–2; Is 3, 10). The words of Jesus in 23–25 provoke astonishment among the disciples because of their apparent contradiction of the Old Testament concept (24.26). Since wealth, power, and merit generate false security, Jesus rejects them utterly as a claim to enter the kingdom. Achievement of salvation is beyond human capability and depends solely on the goodness of God who offers it as a gift (27).

10, 38–40: Can you drink the cup . . . I am baptized?: the metaphor of drinking the cup is used in the Old Testament to refer to acceptance of the destiny assigned by God; see the note on Ps 11, 6. In Jesus' case, this involves divine judgment on sin that Jesus the innocent one is to expiate on behalf of the guilty (14, 24; Is 53, 5). His baptism is to be his crucifixion and death for the salvation of the human race; cf Lk 12, 50.

The request of James and John for a share in the glory (35–37) must of necessity involve a share in Jesus' sufferings, the endurance of tribulation and suffering for the gospel (39). The authority of assigning places of honor in the kingdom is reserved to God (40).

10, 42–45: Whatever authority is to be exercised by the disciples must, like that of Jesus, be rendered as service to others (45) rather than for personal aggrandizement (42–44). The service of Jesus is his passion and death for the sins of the human race (45); cf 14, 24; Is 53, 11–12; Mt 26, 28; Lk 22, 19–20.

10, 46–52: See the notes on Mt 9, 27–31 and 20, 29–34.

z: Prv 11, 28.   a: Mt 19, 30; Lk 13, 30.   b: 8, 31; Mt 20, 17-19; Lk 18, 31-33.   c: Mt 20, 20-28.   d: Lk 12, 50.   e: Lk 22, 25-27. f: Mt 20, 29-34; Lk 18, 35-43.

his disciples and a sizable crowd, Bartimaeus, a blind man, the son of Timaeus, sat by the roadside begging. [47]On hearing that it was Jesus of Nazareth, he began to cry out and say, "Jesus, son of David, have pity on me." [48]And many rebuked him, telling him to be silent. But he kept calling out all the more, "Son of David, have pity on me." [49]Jesus stopped and said, "Call him." So they called the blind man, saying to him, "Take courage; get up, he is calling you." [50]He threw aside his cloak, sprang up, and came to Jesus. [51]Jesus said to him in reply, "What do you want me to do for you?" The blind man replied to him, "Master, I want to see." [52]Jesus told him, "Go your way; your faith has saved you." Immediately he received his sight and followed him on the way.

See RG 298

The Entry into Jerusalem.

[1g]*When they drew near to Jerusalem, to Bethphage and Bethany at the Mount of Olives, he sent two of his disciples [2]and said to them, "Go into the village opposite you, and immediately on entering it, you will find a colt tethered on which no one has ever sat. Untie it and bring it here. [3]If anyone should say to you, 'Why are you doing this?' reply, 'The Master has need of it and will send it back here at once.' " [4]So they went off and found a colt tethered at a gate outside on the street, and they untied it. [5]Some of the bystanders said to them, "What are you doing, untying the colt?" [6]They answered them just as Jesus had told them to, and they permitted them to do it. [7]So they brought the colt to Jesus and put their cloaks over it. And he sat on it. [8]Many people spread their cloaks on the road, and others spread leafy branches that they had cut from the fields. [9h]Those preceding him as well as those following kept crying out:

"Hosanna!
Blessed is he who comes in the name of the Lord!
[10] Blessed is the kingdom of our father David that is to come!
Hosanna in the highest!"

[11i]He entered Jerusalem and went into the temple area. He looked around at everything and, since it was already late, went out to Bethany with the Twelve.

Jesus Curses a Fig Tree.

[12j]*The next day as they were leaving Bethany he was hungry. [13]Seeing from a distance a fig tree in leaf, he went over to see if he could find anything on it. When he reached it he found nothing but leaves; it was not the time for figs. [14]And he said to it in reply, "May no one ever eat of your fruit again!" And his disciples heard it.

Cleansing of the Temple.

[15k]*They came to Jerusalem, and on entering the temple area he began to drive out those selling and buying there. He overturned the tables of the money changers and the seats of those who were selling doves. [16]He did not permit anyone to carry anything through the temple area. [17l]Then he taught them saying, "Is it not written:

'My house shall be called a house of prayer for all peoples'?
But you have made it a den of thieves."

[18]The chief priests and the scribes came to hear of it and were seeking a way to put him to death, yet they feared him because the whole crowd was astonished at his teaching. [19m]When evening came, they went out of the city.

The Withered Fig Tree.

[20n]Early in the morning, as they were walking along, they saw the fig tree withered to its roots. [21]Peter

---

11, 1–11: In Mark's account Jesus takes the initiative in ordering the preparation for his entry into Jerusalem (1–6) even as he later orders the preparation of his last Passover Supper (14, 12–16). In vv 9–10 the greeting Jesus receives stops short of proclaiming him Messiah. He is greeted rather as the prophet of the coming messianic kingdom. Contrast Mt 21, 9.

11, 12–14: Jesus' search for fruit on the fig tree recalls the prophets' earlier use of this image to designate Israel; cf Jer 8, 13; 29, 17; Jl 1, 7; Hos 9, 10.16. Cursing the fig tree is a

parable in action representing Jesus' judgment (20) on barren Israel and the fate of Jerusalem for failing to receive his teaching; cf Is 34, 4; Hos 2, 14; Lk 13, 6–9.

11, 15–19: See the note on Mt 21, 12–17.

g: Mt 21, 1-9; Lk 19, 29-38; Jn 12, 12-15.　h: 2 Sm 7, 16; Ps 118, 26.　i: Mt 21, 10.17.　j: Mt 21, 18-20; Lk 13, 6-9.　k: Mt 21, 12-13; Lk 19, 45-46; Jn 2, 14-16.　l: Is 56, 7; Jer 7, 11.　m: Lk 21, 37.　n: Mt 21, 20-22.

remembered and said to him, "Rabbi, look! The fig tree that you cursed has withered." [22]Jesus said to them in reply, "Have faith in God. [23]o Amen, I say to you, whoever says to this mountain, 'Be lifted up and thrown into the sea,' and does not doubt in his heart but believes that what he says will happen, it shall be done for him. [24]p Therefore I tell you, all that you ask for in prayer, believe that you will receive it and it shall be yours. [25]q When you stand to pray, forgive anyone against whom you have a grievance, so that your heavenly Father may in turn forgive you your transgressions. [[26]]"*

The Authority of Jesus Questioned.
[27]r*They returned once more to Jerusalem. As he was walking in the temple area, the chief priests, the scribes, and the elders approached him [28]and said to him, "By what authority are you doing these things? Or who gave you this authority to do them?" [29]Jesus said to them, "I shall ask you one question. Answer me, and I will tell you by what authority I do these things. [30]Was John's baptism of heavenly or of human origin? Answer me." [31]They discussed this among themselves and said, "If we say, 'Of heavenly origin,' he will say, '[Then] why did you not believe him?' [32]But shall we say, 'Of human origin'?"—they feared the crowd, for they all thought John really was a prophet. [33]So they said to Jesus in reply, "We do not know." Then Jesus said to them, "Neither shall I tell you by what authority I do these things."

CHAPTER 12

See RG 298

Parable of the Tenants.
[1]s1*He began to speak to them in parables. "A man planted a vineyard, put a hedge around it, dug a wine press, and built a tower. Then he leased it to tenant farmers and left on a journey. [2]At the proper time he sent a servant to the tenants to obtain from them some of the produce of the vineyard. [3]But they seized him, beat him, and sent him away empty-handed. [4]Again he sent them another servant. And that one they beat over the head and treated shamefully. [5]He sent yet another whom they killed. So, too, many others; some they beat, others they killed. [6]He had one other to send, a beloved son. He sent him to them last of all, thinking, 'They will respect my son.' [7]But those tenants said to one another, 'This is the heir. Come, let us kill him, and the inheritance will be ours.' [8]So they seized him and killed him, and threw him out of the vineyard. [9]What [then] will the owner of the vineyard do? He will come, put the tenants to death, and give the vineyard to others. [10]u Have you not read this scripture passage:

'The stone that the builders rejected
　has become the cornerstone;
[11] by the Lord has this been done,
　and it is wonderful in our
　　eyes'?"

[12]They were seeking to arrest him, but they feared the crowd, for they realized that he had addressed the parable to them. So they left him and went away.

Paying Taxes to the Emperor.
[13]vw*They sent some Pharisees and Herodians to him to ensnare him in his speech. [14]They came and said to him, "Teacher, we know that you are a truthful man and that you are not concerned with anyone's opinion. You do not regard a person's status but teach the way of God in accordance with the truth. Is it lawful

---

11, 26: This verse, which reads, "But if you do not forgive, neither will your heavenly Father forgive your transgressions," is omitted in the best manuscripts. It was probably added by copyists under the influence of Mt 6, 15.

11, 27–33: The mounting hostility toward Jesus came from the chief priests, the scribes, and the elders (27); the Herodians and the Pharisees (12, 13); and the Sadducees (12, 18). By their rejection of God's messengers, John the Baptist and Jesus, they incurred the divine judgment implied in vv 27–33 and confirmed in the parable of the vineyard tenants (12, 1–12).

12, 1–12: The vineyard denotes Israel (Is 5, 1–7). The tenant farmers are the religious leaders of Israel. God is the owner of the vineyard. His servants are his messengers, the

prophets. The beloved son is Jesus (1, 11; 9, 7; Mt 3, 17; 17, 5; Lk 3, 22; 9, 35). The punishment of the tenants refers to the religious leaders, and the transfer of the vineyard to others refers to the people of the new Israel.

12, 13–34: In the ensuing conflicts (cf also 2, 1—3, 6) Jesus vanquishes his adversaries by his responses to their questions and reduces them to silence (34).

12, 13–17: See the note on Mt 22, 15–22.

---

o: Mt 17, 20-21; Lk 17, 6.　p: Mt 7, 7; Jn 11, 22; 14, 13.　q: Mt 6, 14; 18, 35.　r: Mt 21, 23-27; Lk 20, 1-8.　s: Mt 21, 33-46; Lk 20, 9-19.　t: Is 5, 1-7; Jer 2, 21.　u: Ps 118, 22-23; Is 28, 16. v: Mt 22, 15-33; Lk 20, 20-39.　w: 3, 6.

to pay the census tax to Caesar or not? Should we pay or should we not pay?" ¹⁵Knowing their hypocrisy he said to them, "Why are you testing me? Bring me a denarius to look at." ¹⁶They brought one to him and he said to them, "Whose image and inscription is this?" They replied to him, "Caesar's." ¹⁷ˣSo Jesus said to them, "Repay to Caesar what belongs to Caesar and to God what belongs to God." They were utterly amazed at him.

The Question about the Resurrection. ¹⁸*Some Sadducees, who say there is no resurrection, came to him and put this question to him, ¹⁹ʸsaying, "Teacher, Moses wrote for us, 'If someone's brother dies, leaving a wife but no child, his brother must take the wife and raise up descendants for his brother.' ²⁰Now there were seven brothers. The first married a woman and died, leaving no descendants. ²¹So the second married her and died, leaving no descendants, and the third likewise. ²²And the seven left no descendants. Last of all the woman also died. ²³At the resurrection [when they arise] whose wife will she be? For all seven had been married to her." ²⁴Jesus said to them, "Are you not misled because you do not know the scriptures or the power of God? ²⁵When they rise from the dead, they neither marry nor are given in marriage, but they are like the angels in heaven. ²⁶ᶻAs for the dead being raised, have you not read in the Book of Moses, in the passage about the bush, how God told him, 'I am the God of Abraham, [the] God of Isaac, and [the] God of Jacob'? ²⁷He is not God of the dead but of the living. You are greatly misled."

The Greatest Commandment. ²⁸ᵃ*One of the scribes, when he came forward and heard them disputing and saw how well he had answered them, asked him, "Which is the first of all the commandments?" ²⁹Jesus replied, "The first is this: 'Hear, O Israel! The Lord our God is Lord alone! ³⁰ᵇYou shall love the Lord your God with all your heart, with all your soul, with all your mind, and with all your strength.' ³¹ᶜThe second is this: 'You shall love your neighbor as yourself.' There is no other commandment greater than these." ³²The scribe said to him, "Well said, teacher. You are right in saying, 'He is One and there is no other than he.' ³³ᵈAnd 'to love him with all your heart, with all your understanding, with all your strength, and to love your neighbor as yourself' is worth more than all burnt offerings and sacrifices." ³⁴ᵉAnd when Jesus saw that [he] answered with understanding, he said to him, "You are not far from the kingdom of God." And no one dared to ask him any more questions.

The Question about David's Son. ³⁵ᶠ*As Jesus was teaching in the temple area he said, "How do the scribes claim that the Messiah is the son of David? ³⁶ᵍDavid himself, inspired by the holy Spirit, said:

'The Lord said to my lord,
"Sit at my right hand
   until I place your enemies under your feet."'

³⁷David himself calls him 'lord'; so how is he his son?" [The] great crowd heard this with delight.

Denunciation of the Scribes. ³⁸ʰ*In the course of his teaching he said, "Beware of the scribes, who like to go around in long robes and accept greetings in the marketplaces, ³⁹seats of honor in synagogues, and places of honor at banquets. ⁴⁰They devour the houses of widows and, as a pretext, recite lengthy prayers. They will receive a very severe condemnation."

The Poor Widow's Contribution. ⁴¹ⁱ*He

12, 18–27: See the note on Mt 22, 23–33.

12, 28–34: See the note on Mt 22, 34–40.

12, 35–37: Jesus questions the claim of the scribes about the Davidic descent of the Messiah, not to deny it (Mt 1, 1; Acts 2, 20.34; Rom 1, 3; 2 Tm 2, 8) but to imply that he is more than this. His superiority derives from his transcendent origin, to which David himself attested when he spoke of the Messiah with the name "Lord" (Ps 110, 1). See also the note on Mt 22, 41–46.

12, 38–40: See the notes on 7, 1–23 and Mt 23, 1–39.

12, 41–44: See the note on Lk 21, 1–4.

x: Rom 13, 7.   y: Dt 25, 5.   z: Ex 3, 6.   a: Mt 22, 34-40; Lk 10, 25-28.   b: Dt 6, 4-5.   c: Lv 19, 18; Rom 13, 9; Gal 5, 14; Jas 2, 8.   d: Dt 6, 4; Ps 40, 7-9.   e: Mt 22, 46; Lk 20, 40.   f: Mt 22, 41-45; Lk 20, 41-44.   g: Ps 110, 1.   h: Mt 23, 1-7; Lk 11, 43; 20, 45-47.   i: Lk 21, 1-4.

sat down opposite the treasury and observed how the crowd put money into the treasury. Many rich people put in large sums. [42]A poor widow also came and put in two small coins worth a few cents. [43]Calling his disciples to himself, he said to them, "Amen, I say to you, this poor widow put in more than all the other contributors to the treasury. [44]For they have all contributed from their surplus wealth, but she, from her poverty, has contributed all she had, her whole livelihood."

See RG 298

CHAPTER 13

The Destruction of the Temple Foretold. [1j]*As he was making his way out of the temple area one of his disciples said to him, "Look, teacher, what stones and what buildings!" [2]Jesus said to him, "Do you see these great buildings? There will not be one stone left upon another that will not be thrown down."

The Signs of the End. [3k]*As he was sitting on the Mount of Olives opposite the temple area, Peter, James, John, and Andrew asked him privately, [4]"Tell us, when will this happen, and what sign will there be when all these things are about to come to an end?" [51]Jesus began to say to them, "See that no one deceives you. [6]Many will come in my name saying, 'I am he,' and they will deceive many. [7]When you hear of wars and reports of wars do not be alarmed; such things must happen, but it will not yet be the end. [8]Nation will rise against nation and kingdom against kingdom. There will be earthquakes from place to place and there will be famines. These are the beginnings of the labor pains.

The Coming Persecution. [9m]"Watch out for yourselves. They will hand you over to the courts. You will be beaten in synagogues. You will be arraigned before governors and kings because of me, as a witness before them. [10]*But the gospel must first be preached to all nations. [11n]When they lead you away and hand you over, do not worry beforehand about what you are to say. But say whatever will be given to you at that hour. For it will not be you who are speaking but the holy Spirit. [12]Brother will hand over brother to death, and the father his child; children will rise up against parents and have them put to death. [13]You will be hated by all because of my name. But the one who perseveres to the end will be saved.

The Great Tribulation. [14o p]*"When you see the desolating abomination standing where he should not (let the reader understand), then those in Judea must flee to the mountains, [15q][and] a person on a housetop must not go down or enter to get anything out of his house, [16]and a person in a field must not return to get his cloak. [17]Woe to pregnant women and nursing mothers in those days. [18]Pray that this does not happen in winter. [19r]For those times will have tribulation such as has not been since the beginning of God's creation until now, nor ever will be. [20]If the Lord had not shortened those days, no one would be saved; but for the sake of the elect whom he chose, he did shorten the days. [21]If anyone says to you then, 'Look, here is the Messiah!

13, 1–2: The reconstructed temple with its precincts, begun under Herod the Great ca. 20 B.C., was completed only some seven years before it was destroyed by fire in A.D. 70 at the hands of the Romans; cf Jer 26, 18; Mt 24, 1–2. For the dating of the reconstruction of the temple, see further the note on Jn 2, 20.

13, 3–37: Jesus' prediction of the destruction of the temple (2) provoked questions that the four named disciples put to him in private regarding the time and the sign when all **these things are about to come to an end** (3–4). The response to their questions was Jesus' eschatological discourse prior to his imminent death. It contained instruction and consolation exhorting the disciples and the church to faith and obedience through the trials that would confront them (5–13). The sign is the presence of **the desolating abomination** (14; see Dn 9, 27), i.e., of the Roman power profaning the temple. Flight from Jerusalem is urged rather than defense of the city through misguided messianic hope (14–23). Intervention will occur only after destruction (24–27), which will happen before the end of the first Christian generation (28–31). No one but the Father knows the precise time, or that of the parousia (32); hence the necessity of constant vigilance (33–37). Luke sets the parousia at a later date, after "the time of the Gentiles" (Lk 21, 24). See also the notes on Mt 24, 1—25, 46.

13, 10: The gospel . . . to all nations: the period of the Christian mission.

13, 14: The participle **standing** is masculine, in contrast to the neuter at Mt 24, 15.

---

j: Mt 24, 1-2; Lk 21, 5-6.   k: Mt 24, 3-8; Lk 21, 7-11.   l: Eph 5, 6; 2 Thes 2, 3.   m: Mt 24, 9-14; Lk 21, 12-19.   n: Mt 10, 19-22; Lk 12, 11-12.   o: Mt 24, 15-22; Lk 21, 20-24.   p: Dn 9, 27; Mt 24, 15.   q: Lk 17, 31.   r: Dn 12, 1.

Apocalyptic

The term "apocalyptic" derives from a Greek word meaning "to uncover, to reveal." It gives its name to the last book of the Christian canon, the Book of Revelation, which is also known as the Apocalypse of John (see Rv 1, 1). The name also extends to the type of literature associated with the Book of Revelation: Apocalyptic materials contain elements such as a pessimistic view of the present world, a dualistic outlook that divides people into the few to be saved and the many damned, tours of heaven and hell, descriptions of future cataclysms, cryptic signs in need of interpretation, and angels to provide such interpretation.

Within the Gospel tradition, Mark 13—often called the Little Apocalypse to distinguish it from the Book of Revelation—contains several hallmarks of the genre: predictions of destruction, heavenly portents, the gathering of the elect, and so forth. Matthew uses much of this material but takes it out of its end-of-the-world context. What for Mark are signs of the end (persecution, family disintegration) are for Matthew indications that one is living according to Jesus' teaching.

Although the literature can be frightening, apocalyptic writing serves to encourage the group to which it is addressed. It urges steadfastness in the face of persecution, assures the reader of heavenly control of what appears to be a chaotic world, and offers the promise that, with the momentous entry of the divine into human history, the righteous will be rewarded and the wicked punished. Likely, not all early readers took the signs literally; rather, they recognized the conventional aspects of the genre.

Apocalyptic literature is found, cross-culturally, among both groups that are persecuted and groups that perceive themselves to be fully disenfranchised, with no hope of affecting their future. Scholars debate whether Jesus was an apocalyptic prophet or whether his early followers added apocalyptic statements to the collection of his sayings. On the one hand, the parables are not typically apocalyptic; they use quite mundane images to convey their points. On the other, Mark 13 and its parallels in Matthew and Luke, the writings of Paul (especially 1 Thessalonians), and quite likely the preaching of John the Baptist all suggest that apocalyptic thinking was part of Jesus' legacy.

Look, there he is!' do not believe it. ²²False messiahs and false prophets will arise and will perform signs and wonders in order to mislead, if that were possible, the elect. ²³Be watchful! I have told it all to you beforehand.

The Coming of the Son of Man. ²⁴ˢᵗ"But in those days after that tribulation

> the sun will be darkened,
>   and the moon will not give its light,
> ²⁵ and the stars will be falling from the sky,
>   and the powers in the heavens will be
>   shaken.

²⁶ᵘ"And then they will see 'the Son of Man coming in the clouds' with great power and glory, ²⁷and then he will send out the angels and gather [his] elect from the four winds, from the end of the earth to the end of the sky.

The Lesson of the Fig Tree. ²⁸ᵛ"Learn a lesson from the fig tree. When its branch becomes tender and sprouts leaves, you know that summer is near. ²⁹In the same way, when you see these things happening, know that he is near, at the gates. ³⁰Amen, I say to you, this generation will not pass away until all these things have taken place. ³¹Heaven

13, 26: Son of Man . . . with great power and glory: Jesus cites this text from Dn 7, 13 in his response to the high priest, **Are you the Messiah?** (14, 61). In Ex 34, 5; Lv 16, 2; and Nm 11, 25 the clouds indicate the presence of the divinity. Thus in his role of Son of Man, Jesus is a heavenly being who will come in power and glory.

s: Mt 24, 29-31; Lk 21, 25-27.   t: Is 13, 10; Ez 32, 7; Jl 2, 10.   u: 14, 62: Dn 7, 13-14.   v: Mt 24, 32-36; Lk 21, 29-33.

and earth will pass away, but my words will not pass away.

Need for Watchfulness. [32]"But of that day or hour, no one knows, neither the angels in heaven, nor the Son, but only the Father. [33]wBe watchful! Be alert! You do not know when the time will come. [34]xIt is like a man traveling abroad. He leaves home and places his servants in charge, each with his work, and orders the gatekeeper to be on the watch. [35]Watch, therefore; you do not know when the lord of the house is coming, whether in the evening, or at midnight, or at cockcrow, or in the morning. [36]May he not come suddenly and find you sleeping. [37]What I say to you, I say to all: 'Watch!' "

See RG 298–99

CHAPTER 14

The Conspiracy against Jesus. [1]y*The Passover and the Feast of Unleavened Bread were to take place in two days' time. So the chief priests and the scribes were seeking a way to arrest him by treachery and put him to death. [2]They said, "Not during the festival, for fear that there may be a riot among the people."

The Anointing at Bethany. [3]z*When he was in Bethany reclining at table in the house of Simon the leper, a woman came with an alabaster jar of perfumed oil, costly genuine spikenard. She broke the alabaster jar and poured it on his head. [4]There were some who were indignant. "Why has there been this waste of perfumed oil? [5]It could have been sold for more than three hundred days' wages and the money given to the poor." They were infuriated with her. [6]Jesus said, "Let her alone. Why do you make trouble for her? She has done a good thing for me. [7]The poor you will always have with you, and whenever you wish you can do good to them, but you will not always have me. [8]She has done what she could. She has anticipated anointing my body for burial. [9]Amen, I say to you, wherever the gospel is proclaimed to the whole world, what she has done will be told in memory of her."

The Betrayal by Judas. [10]aThen Judas Iscariot, one of the Twelve, went off to the chief priests to hand him over to them. [11]When they heard him they were pleased and promised to pay him money. Then he looked for an opportunity to hand him over.

Preparations for the Passover. [12]b*On the first day of the Feast of Unleavened Bread, when they sacrificed the Passover lamb, his disciples said to him, "Where do you want us to go and prepare for you to eat the Passover?" [13]*He sent two of his disciples and said to them, "Go into the city and a man will meet you, carrying a jar of water. Follow him. [14]Wherever he enters, say to the master of the house, 'The Teacher says, "Where is my guest room where I may eat the Passover with my disciples?" ' [15]Then he will show you a large upper room furnished and ready. Make the preparations for us there." [16]The disciples then went off, entered

---

14, 1—16, 8: In the movement of Mark's gospel the cross is depicted as Jesus' way to glory in accordance with the divine will. Thus the passion narrative is seen as the climax of Jesus' ministry.

14, 1: The Passover and the Feast of Unleavened Bread: the connection between the two festivals is reflected in Ex 12, 3–20; 34, 18; Lv 23, 4–8; Nm 9, 2–14; 28, 16–17; Dt 16, 1–8. The Passover commemorated the redemption from slavery and the departure of the Israelites from Egypt by night. It began at sundown after the Passover lamb was sacrificed in the temple in the afternoon of the fourteenth day of the month of Nisan. With the Passover Supper on the same evening was associated the eating of unleavened bread. The latter was continued through Nisan 21, a reminder of the affliction of the Israelites and of the haste surrounding their departure. Praise and thanks to God for his goodness in the past were combined at this dual festival with the hope of future salvation. **The chief priests . . . to death:** the intent to put Jesus to death was plotted for a long time but delayed for fear of the crowd (3, 6; 11, 18; 12, 12).

14, 3–9: At Bethany on the Mount of Olives, a few miles from Jerusalem, **in the house of Simon the leper,** Jesus defends a woman's loving action of anointing his head with perfumed oil in view of his impending death and burial as a criminal, in which case his body would not be anointed. See further the note on Jn 12, 7. He assures the woman of the remembrance of her deed in the worldwide preaching of the good news.

14, 12: The first day of the Feast of Unleavened Bread . . . the Passover lamb: a less precise designation of the day for sacrificing the Passover lamb as evidenced by some rabbinical literature. For a more exact designation, see the note on 14, 1. It was actually Nisan 14.

14, 13: A man . . . carrying a jar of water: perhaps a prearranged signal, for only women ordinarily carried water in jars. The Greek word used here, however, implies simply a person and not necessarily a male.

w: Mt 24, 42; 25, 13-15.   x: Mt 25, 14-30; Lk 19, 12-27.   y: Mt 26, 2-5; Lk 22, 1-2; Jn 11, 45-53.   z: Mt 26, 6-13; Jn 12, 1-8.   a: Mt 26, 14-16; Lk 22, 3-6.   b: Mt 26, 17-19; Lk 22, 7-13.

the city, and found it just as he had told them; and they prepared the Passover.

The Betrayer. *17c*When it was evening, he came with the Twelve. *18**And as they reclined at table and were eating, Jesus said, "Amen, I say to you, one of you will betray me, one who is eating with me." *19*They began to be distressed and to say to him, one by one, "Surely it is not I?" *20*He said to them, "One of the Twelve, the one who dips with me into the dish. *21**For the Son of Man indeed goes, as it is written of him, but woe to that man by whom the Son of Man is betrayed. It would be better for that man if he had never been born."

The Lord's Supper. *22d**While they were eating, he took bread, said the blessing, broke it, and gave it to them, and said, "Take it; this is my body." *23*Then he took a cup, gave thanks, and gave it to them, and they all drank from it. *24**He said to them, "This is my blood of the covenant, which will be shed for many. *25*Amen, I say to you, I shall not drink again the fruit of the vine until the day when I drink it new in the kingdom of God." *26e**Then, after singing a hymn, they went out to the Mount of Olives.

Peter's Denial Foretold. *27f**Then Jesus said to them, "All of you will have your faith shaken, for it is written:

'I will strike the shepherd,
and the sheep will be dispersed.'

*28*But after I have been raised up, I shall go before you to Galilee." *29*Peter said to him, "Even though all should have their faith shaken, mine will not be." *30*Then Jesus said to him, "Amen, I say to you, this very night before the cock crows twice you will deny me three times." *31*But he vehemently replied, "Even though I should have to die with you, I will not deny you." And they all spoke similarly.

The Agony in the Garden. *32gh**Then they came to a place named Gethsemane, and he said to his disciples, "Sit here while I pray." *33*He took with him Peter, James, and John, and began to be troubled and distressed. *34*Then he said to them, "My soul is sorrowful even to death. Remain here and keep watch." *35*He advanced a little and fell to the ground and prayed that if it were possible the hour might pass by him; *36**he said, "Abba, Father, all things are possible to you. Take this cup away from me, but not what I will but what you will." *37*When he returned he found them asleep. He said to Peter, "Simon, are you asleep? Could you not keep watch for one hour? *38i**Watch and pray that

14, 18: One of you will betray me, one who is eating with me: contrasts the intimacy of table fellowship at the Passover meal with the treachery of the traitor; cf Ps 41, 10.

14, 21: The Son of Man indeed goes, as it is written of him: a reference to Ps 41, 10 cited by Jesus concerning Judas at the Last Supper; cf Jn 13, 18–19.

14, 22–24: The actions and words of Jesus express within the framework of the Passover meal and the transition to a new covenant the sacrifice of himself through the offering of his body and blood in anticipation of his passion and death. His **blood of the covenant** both alludes to the ancient rite of Ex 24, 4–8 and indicates the new community that the sacrifice of Jesus will bring into being (Mt 26, 26–28; Lk 22, 19–20; 1 Cor 11, 23–25).

14, 24: Which will be shed: see the note on Mt 26, 27–28. **For many:** the Greek preposition **hyper** is a different one from that at Mt 26, 28 but the same as that found at Lk 22, 19.20 and 1 Cor 11, 24. The sense of both words is vicarious, and it is difficult in Hellenistic Greek to distinguish between them. For **many** in the sense of "all," see the note on Mt 20, 28.

14, 26: After singing a hymn: Pss 114–118, thanksgiving songs concluding the Passover meal.

14, 27–31: Jesus predicted that the Twelve would waver in their faith, even abandon him, despite their protestations to the contrary. Yet he reassured them that after his resurrection he would regather them in Galilee (16, 7; cf Mt 26, 32; 28,

7.16; Jn 21), where he first summoned them to be his followers as he began to preach the good news (1, 14–20)

14, 32–34: The disciples who had witnessed the raising to life of the daughter of Jairus (5, 37) and the transfiguration of their Master (9, 2) were now invited to witness his degradation and agony and to watch and pray with him.

14, 36: Abba, Father: an Aramaic term, here also translated by Mark, Jesus' special way of addressing God with filial intimacy. The word **'abba** seems not to have been used in earlier or contemporaneous Jewish sources to address God without some qualifier. Cf Rom 8, 15; Gal 4, 6 for other occurrences of the Aramaic word in the Greek New Testament. **Not what I will but what you will:** note the complete obedient surrender of the human will of Jesus to the divine will of the Father; cf Jn 4, 34; 8, 29; Rom 5, 19; Phil 2, 8; Heb 5, 8.

14, 38: The spirit is willing but the flesh is weak: the spirit is drawn to what is good yet found in conflict with the flesh, inclined to sin; cf Ps 51, 7.12. Everyone is faced with this struggle, the full force of which Jesus accepted on our behalf and, through his bitter passion and death, achieved the victory.

c: Mt 26, 20–24; Lk 22, 21–23; Jn 13, 21–26. *d:* Mt 26, 26–30; Lk 22, 19–20; 1 Cor 11, 23–25. *e:* Mt 26, 30–35; Lk 22, 34.39; Jn 13, 36–38. *f:* Zec 13, 7; Jn 16, 32. *g:* Mt 26, 36–46; Lk 22, 40–46. *h:* Jn 18, 1. *i:* Rom 7, 5.

you may not undergo the test. The spirit is willing but the flesh is weak." [39]Withdrawing again, he prayed, saying the same thing. [40]Then he returned once more and found them asleep, for they could not keep their eyes open and did not know what to answer him. [41]He returned a third time and said to them, "Are you still sleeping and taking your rest? It is enough. The hour has come. Behold, the Son of Man is to be handed over to sinners. [42]Get up, let us go. See, my betrayer is at hand."

The Betrayal and Arrest of Jesus. [43j]Then, while he was still speaking, Judas, one of the Twelve, arrived, accompanied by a crowd with swords and clubs who had come from the chief priests, the scribes, and the elders. [44]His betrayer had arranged a signal with them, saying, "The man I shall kiss is the one; arrest him and lead him away securely." [45]He came and immediately went over to him and said, "Rabbi." And he kissed him. [46]At this they laid hands on him and arrested him. [47]One of the bystanders drew his sword, struck the high priest's servant, and cut off his ear. [48]Jesus said to them in reply, "Have you come out as against a robber, with swords and clubs, to seize me? [49]Day after day I was with you teaching in the temple area, yet you did not arrest me; but that the scriptures may be fulfilled." [50]And they all left him and fled. [51]Now a young man followed him wearing nothing but a linen cloth about his body. They seized him, [52]but he left the cloth behind and ran off naked.

Jesus before the Sanhedrin. [53k]*They led Jesus away to the high priest, and all the chief priests and the elders and the scribes came together. [54]Peter followed him at a distance into the high priest's courtyard and was seated with the guards, warming himself at the fire. [55]The chief priests and the entire Sanhedrin kept trying to obtain testimony against Jesus in order to put him to death, but they found none. [56]Many gave false witness against him, but their testimony did not agree. [57]*Some took the stand and testified falsely against him, alleging, [58]l"We heard him say, 'I will destroy this temple made with hands and within three days I will build another not made with hands.'" [59]Even so their testimony did not agree. [60]The high priest rose before the assembly and questioned Jesus, saying, "Have you no answer? What are these men testifying against you?" [61]*But he was silent and answered nothing. Again the high priest asked him and said to him, "Are you the Messiah, the son of the Blessed One?" [62m]Then Jesus answered, "I am;

and 'you will see the Son of Man
    seated at the right hand of the Power
    and coming with the clouds of
        heaven.'"

[63]At that the high priest tore his garments and said, "What further need have we of witnesses? [64]You have heard the blasphemy. What do you think?" They all condemned him as deserving to die. [65n]Some began to spit on him. They blindfolded him and struck him and said to him, "Prophesy!" And the guards greeted him with blows.

Peter's Denial of Jesus. [66o]While Peter was below in the courtyard, one of the high priest's maids came along. [67]Seeing Peter warming himself, she looked intently at him and said, "You too were with the Nazarene, Jesus." [68]*But he denied it saying, "I neither know nor understand what you are talking

14, 53: **They led Jesus away . . . came together:** Mark presents a formal assembly of the whole Sanhedrin (chief priests, elders, and scribes) at night, leading to the condemnation of Jesus (64), in contrast to Lk 22, 66.71, where Jesus is condemned in a daytime meeting of the council; see also Jn 18, 13.19–24.

14, 57–58: See the notes on Mt 26, 60–61 and Jn 2, 19.

14, 61–62: **The Blessed One:** a surrogate for the divine name, which Jews did not pronounce. **I am:** indicates Jesus' acknowledgment that he is the Messiah and Son of God; cf 1, 1. Contrast Mt 26, 64 and Lk 22, 67–70, in which Jesus leaves his interrogators to answer their own question. **You will see**

the Son of Man . . . with the clouds of heaven: an allusion to Dn 7, 13 and Ps 110, 1, portending the enthronement of Jesus as judge in the transcendent glory of God's kingdom. **The Power:** another surrogate for the name of God.

14, 68: [Then the cock crowed]: found in most manuscripts, perhaps in view of vv 30 and 72, but omitted in others.

j: Mt 26, 47-56; Lk 22, 47-53; Jn 18, 3-11. k: Mt 26, 57-68; Lk 22, 54-55.63-65.67-71; Jn 18, 12-13. l: 15, 29; 2 Cor 5, 1. m: 13, 26; Ps 110, 1; Dn 7, 13; Mt 24, 30. n: Lk 22, 63-65. o: Mt 26, 69-75; Lk 22, 56-62; Jn 18, 16-18.25-27.

about." So he went out into the outer court. [Then the cock crowed.] [69]The maid saw him and began again to say to the bystanders, "This man is one of them." [70]Once again he denied it. A little later the bystanders said to Peter once more, "Surely you are one of them; for you too are a Galilean." [71]He began to curse and to swear, "I do not know this man about whom you are talking." [72p]And immediately a cock crowed a second time. Then Peter remembered the word that Jesus had said to him, "Before the cock crows twice you will deny me three times." He broke down and wept.

CHAPTER 15

See RG 298-99

Jesus before Pilate. [1qr]*As soon as morning came, the chief priests with the elders and the scribes, that is, the whole Sanhedrin, held a council. They bound Jesus, led him away, and handed him over to Pilate. [2]*Pilate questioned him, "Are you the king of the Jews?" He said to him in reply, "You say so." [3]The chief priests accused him of many things. [4]Again Pilate questioned him, "Have you no answer? See how many things they accuse you of." [5]Jesus gave him no further answer, so that Pilate was amazed.

The Sentence of Death. [6s]*Now on the occasion of the feast he used to release to them one prisoner whom they requested. [7]*A man called Barabbas was then in prison along with the rebels who had committed murder in a rebellion. [8]The crowd came forward and began to ask him to do for them as he was accustomed. [9]Pilate answered, "Do you want me to release to you the king of the Jews?" [10]For he knew that it was out of envy that the chief priests had handed him over. [11]But the chief priests stirred up the crowd to have him release Barabbas for them instead. [12]Pilate again said to them in reply, "Then what [do you want] me to do with [the man you call] the king of the Jews?" [13]*They shouted again, "Crucify him." [14]Pilate said to them, "Why? What evil has he done?" They only shouted the louder, "Crucify him." [15]*So Pilate, wishing to satisfy the crowd, released Barabbas to them and, after he had Jesus scourged, handed him over to be crucified.

Mockery by the Soldiers. [16t]*The soldiers led him away inside the palace, that is, the praetorium, and assembled the whole cohort. [17]They clothed him in purple and, weaving a crown of thorns, placed it on him. [18]They began to salute him with, "Hail, King of the Jews!" [19]and kept striking his head with a reed and spitting upon him. They knelt before him in homage. [20]And when they had mocked him, they stripped him of the purple cloak, dressed him in his own clothes, and led him out to crucify him.

The Way of the Cross. [21u]*They pressed into service a passer-by, Simon, a Cyrenian, who was coming in from the country, the father of Alexander and Rufus, to carry his cross.

The Crucifixion. [22v]They brought him to the place of Golgotha (which is translated Place of the Skull). [23]They gave him wine drugged with myrrh, but he did not take it. [24w]*Then they crucified him and divided

---

15, 1: Held a council: the verb here, **poieō**, can mean either "convene a council" or "take counsel." This reading is preferred to a variant "reached a decision" (cf 3, 6), which 14, 64 describes as having happened at the night trial; see the note on Mt 27, 1–2. **Handed him over to Pilate:** lacking authority to execute their sentence of condemnation (14, 64), the Sanhedrin had recourse to Pilate to have Jesus tried and put to death (15); cf Jn 18, 31.

15, 2: The king of the Jews: in the accounts of the evangelists a certain irony surrounds the use of this title as an accusation against Jesus (see the note on 15, 26). While Pilate uses this term (2.9.12), he is aware of the evil motivation of the chief priests who handed Jesus over for trial and condemnation (10; Lk 23, 14–16.20; Mt 27, 18.24; Jn 18, 38; 19, 4.6.12).

15, 6–15: See the note on Mt 27, 15–26.

15, 7: Barabbas: see the note on Mt 27, 16–17.

15, 13: Crucify him: see the note on Mt 27, 22.

15, 15: See the note on Mt 27, 26.

15, 16: Praetorium: see the note on Mt 27, 27.

15, 21: They pressed into service . . . Simon, a Cyrenian: a condemned person was constrained to bear his own instrument of torture, at least the crossbeam. The precise naming of Simon and his sons is probably due to their being known among early Christian believers to whom Mark addressed his gospel. See also the notes on Mt 27, 32 and Lk 23, 26–32.

15, 24: See the notes on Mt 27, 35 and Jn 19, 23–25a.

p: Jn 13, 38.   q: Mt 27, 1-2.11-14; Lk 23, 1-3.   r: Jn 18, 28. s: Mt 27, 15-26; Lk 23, 17-25; Jn 18, 39-40.   t: Mt 27, 27-31; Jn 19, 2-3.   u: Mt 27, 32; Lk 23, 26.   v: Mt 27, 33-51; Lk 23, 32-46; Jr 19, 17-30.   w: Ps 22, 18.

his garments by casting lots for them to see what each should take. ²⁵*It was nine o'clock in the morning when they crucified him. ²⁶*The inscription of the charge against him read, "The King of the Jews." ^{27x}With him they crucified two revolutionaries, one on his right and one on his left. [²⁸]* ^{29y}*Those passing by reviled him, shaking their heads and saying, "Aha! You who would destroy the temple and rebuild it in three days, ³⁰save yourself by coming down from the cross." ³¹Likewise the chief priests, with the scribes, mocked him among themselves and said, "He saved others; he cannot save himself. ^{32z}Let the Messiah, the King of Israel, come down now from the cross that we may see and believe." Those who were crucified with him also kept abusing him.

The Death of Jesus. ³³At noon darkness came over the whole land until three in the afternoon. ^{34a}*And at three o'clock Jesus cried out in a loud voice, "*Eloi, Eloi, lema sabachthani?*" which is translated, "My God, my God, why have you forsaken me?" ³⁵*Some of the bystanders who heard it said, "Look, he is calling Elijah." ³⁶One of them ran, soaked a sponge with wine, put it on a reed, and gave it to him to drink, saying, "Wait, let us see if Elijah comes to take him down." ³⁷Jesus gave a loud cry and breathed his last. ³⁸*The veil of the sanctuary was torn in two from top to bottom. ^{39b}*When the

centurion who stood facing him saw how he breathed his last he said, "Truly this man was the Son of God!" ^{40c}*There were also women looking on from a distance. Among them were Mary Magdalene, Mary the mother of the younger James and of Joses, and Salome. ⁴¹These women had followed him when he was in Galilee and ministered to him. There were also many other women who had come up with him to Jerusalem.

The Burial of Jesus. ^{42d}When it was already evening, since it was the day of preparation, the day before the sabbath, ⁴³*Joseph of Arimathea, a distinguished member of the council, who was himself awaiting the kingdom of God, came and courageously went to Pilate and asked for the body of Jesus. ⁴⁴Pilate was amazed that he was already dead. He summoned the centurion and asked him if Jesus had already died. ⁴⁵And when he learned of it from the centurion, he gave the body to Joseph. ⁴⁶Having bought a linen cloth, he took him down, wrapped him in the linen cloth and laid him in a tomb that had been hewn out of the rock. Then he rolled a stone against the entrance to the tomb. ⁴⁷Mary Magdalene and Mary the mother of Joses watched where he was laid.

CHAPTER 16

See RG 299–300

The Resurrection of Jesus. ^{1ef}*When the sabbath was over, Mary Magdalene,

15, 25: It was nine o'clock in the morning: literally, "the third hour," thus between 9 a.m. and 12 noon. Cf vv 33.34.42 for Mark's chronological sequence, which may reflect liturgical or catechetical considerations rather than the precise historical sequence of events; contrast the different chronologies in the other gospels, especially Jn 19, 14.

15, 26: The inscription . . . the King of the Jews: the political reason for the death penalty falsely charged by the enemies of Jesus. See further the notes on Mt 27, 37 and Jn 19, 19.

15, 28: This verse, "And the scripture was fulfilled that says, 'And he was counted among the wicked,' " is omitted in the earliest and best manuscripts. It contains a citation from Is 53, 12, and was probably introduced from Lk 22, 37.

15, 29: See the note on Mt 27, 39–40.

15, 34: An Aramaic rendering of Ps 22, 2. See also the note on Mt 27, 46.

15, 35: Elijah: a verbal link with Eloi (34). See the note on 9, 9–13; cf Mal 3, 23–24. See also the note on Mt 27, 47.

15, 38: See the note on Mt 27, 51–53.

15, 39: The closing portion of Mark's gospel returns to the theme of its beginning in the Gentile centurion's climactic declaration of belief that Jesus **was the Son of God.** It indi-

cates the fulfillment of the good news announced in the prologue (1, 1) and may be regarded as the firstfruit of the passion and death of Jesus.

15, 40–41: See the note on Mt 27, 55–56.

15, 43: Joseph of Arimathea: see the note on Mt 27, 57–61.

16, 1–8: The purpose of this narrative is to show that the tomb is empty and that Jesus **has been raised** (6) and **is going before you to Galilee** (7) in fulfillment of 14, 28. The women find the tomb empty, and an angel stationed there announces to them what has happened. They are told to proclaim the news to Peter and the disciples in order to prepare them for a reunion with him. Mark's composition of the gospel ends at v 8 with the women telling no one, because they were afraid. This abrupt termination causes some to believe that the original ending of this gospel may have been lost. See the following note.

x: Lk 23, 33. y: Jn 2, 19. z: Lk 23, 39. a: Ps 22, 2. b: Mt 27, 54-56; Lk 23, 47-49. c: 6, 3; Lk 8, 2-3. d: Mt 27, 57-61; Lk 23, 50-56; Jn 19, 38-42. e: Mt 28, 1-8; Lk 24, 1-10; Jn 20, 1-10. f: Mt 28, 1; Lk 23, 56.

Mary, the mother of James, and Salome bought spices so that they might go and anoint him. ²Very early when the sun had risen, on the first day of the week, they came to the tomb. ³They were saying to one another, "Who will roll back the stone for us from the entrance to the tomb?" ⁴When they looked up, they saw that the stone had been rolled back; it was very large. ⁵ᵍOn entering the tomb they saw a young man sitting on the right side, clothed in a white robe, and they were utterly amazed. ⁶He said to them, "Do not be amazed! You seek Jesus of Nazareth, the crucified. He has been raised; he is not here. Behold, the place where they laid him. ⁷ʰBut go and tell his disciples and Peter, 'He is going before you to Galilee; there you will see him, as he told you.' " ⁸Then they went out and fled from the tomb, seized with trembling and bewilderment. They said nothing to anyone, for they were afraid.

The Longer Ending

The Appearance to Mary Magdalene. [⁹ⁱ*When he had risen, early on the first day of the week, he appeared first to Mary Magdalene, out of whom he had driven seven demons. ¹⁰ʲShe went and told his companions who were mourning and weeping. ¹¹When they heard that he was alive and had been seen by her, they did not believe.

The Appearance to Two Disciples. ¹²ᵏAfter this he appeared in another form to two of them walking along on their way to the country. ¹³They returned and told the others; but they did not believe them either.

The Commissioning of the Eleven. ¹⁴ˡ[But] later, as the eleven were at table, he appeared to them and rebuked them for their unbelief and hardness of heart because they had not believed those who saw him after he had been raised. ¹⁵ᵐHe said to them, "Go into the whole world and proclaim the gospel to every creature. ¹⁶Whoever believes and is baptized will be saved; whoever does not believe will be condemned. ¹⁷These signs will accompany those who believe: in my name they will drive out demons, they will speak new languages. ¹⁸ⁿThey will pick up serpents [with their hands], and if they drink any deadly thing, it will not harm them. They will lay hands on the sick, and they will recover."

The Ascension of Jesus. ¹⁹ᵒSo then the Lord Jesus, after he spoke to them, was taken up into heaven and took his seat at the right hand of God. ²⁰ᵖBut they went forth and preached everywhere, while the Lord worked with them and confirmed the word through accompanying signs.]

The Shorter Ending

[And they reported all the instructions briefly to Peter's companions. Afterwards Jesus himself, through them, sent forth from east to west the sacred and imperishable proclamation of eternal salvation. Amen.]

16, 9–20: This passage, termed the Longer Ending to the Marcan gospel by comparison with a much briefer conclusion found in some less important manuscripts, has traditionally been accepted as a canonical part of the gospel and was defined as such by the Council of Trent. Early citations of it by the Fathers indicate that it was composed by the second century, although vocabulary and style indicate that it was written by someone other than Mark. It is a general resume of the material concerning the appearances of the risen Jesus, reflecting, in particular, traditions found in Luke (24) and John (20).

The Shorter Ending: Found after v 8 before the Longer Ending in four seventh-to-ninth-century Greek manuscripts as well as in one Old Latin version, where it appears alone without the Longer Ending.

The Freer Logion: Found after v 14 in a fourth-fifth century manuscript preserved in the Freer Gallery of Art, Washington, DC, this ending was known to Jerome in the fourth century. It reads: "And they excused themselves, saying, 'This age of lawlessness and unbelief is under Satan, who does not allow the truth and power of God to prevail over the unclean things dominated by the spirits [or, does not allow the unclean things dominated by the spirits to grasp the truth and power of God]. Therefore reveal your righteousness now.' They spoke to Christ. And Christ responded to them, 'The limit of the years of Satan's power is completed, but other terrible things draw near. And for those who sinned I was handed over to death, that they might return to the truth and no longer sin, in order that they might inherit the spiritual and incorruptible heavenly glory of righteousness. But . . . .' "

g: Jn 20, 12.   *h:* 14, 28.   *i:* Mt 28, 1-10; Jn 20, 11-18.   *j:* Lk 24, 10-11; Jn 20, 18.   *k:* Lk 24, 13-35.   *l:* Lk 24, 36-49; 1 Cor 15, 5.   *m:* 13, 10; Mt 28, 18-20; Lk 24, 47; Jn 20, 21.   *n:* Mt 10, 1; Lk 10, 19; Acts 28, 3-6.   *o:* Lk 24, 50-53.   *p:* 1 Tm 3, 16.

See RG
300-19

The Gospel According to Luke

The Gospel according to Luke is the first part of a two-volume work that continues the biblical history of God's dealings with humanity found in the Old Testament, showing how God's promises to Israel have been fulfilled in Jesus and how the salvation promised to Israel and accomplished by Jesus has been extended to the Gentiles. The stated purpose of the two volumes is to provide Theophilus and others like him with certainty—assurance—about earlier instruction they have received (1, 4). To accomplish his purpose, Luke shows that the preaching and teaching of the representatives of the early church are grounded in the preaching and teaching of Jesus, who during his historical ministry (Acts 1, 21–22) prepared his specially chosen followers and commissioned them to be witnesses to his resurrection and to all else that he did (Acts 10, 37–42). This continuity between the historical ministry of Jesus and the ministry of the apostles is Luke's way of guaranteeing the fidelity of the church's teaching to the teaching of Jesus.

Luke's story of Jesus and the church is dominated by a historical perspective. This history is first of all salvation history. God's divine plan for human salvation was accomplished during the period of Jesus, who through the events of his life (22, 22) fulfilled the Old Testament prophecies (4, 21; 18, 31; 22, 37; 24, 26–27.44), and this salvation is now extended to all humanity in the period of the church (Acts 4, 12). This salvation history, moreover, is a part of human history. Luke relates the story of Jesus and the church to events in contemporary Palestinian (1, 5; 3, 1–2; Acts 4, 6) and Roman (2, 1–2; 3, 1; Acts 11, 28; 18, 2.12) history for, as Paul says in Acts 26, 26, "this was not done in a corner." Finally, Luke relates the story of Jesus and the church to contemporaneous church history. Luke is concerned with presenting Christianity as a legitimate form of worship in the Roman world, a religion that is capable of meeting the spiritual needs of a world empire like that of Rome. To this end, Luke depicts the Roman governor Pilate declaring Jesus innocent of any wrongdoing three times (Luke 23, 4.14.22). At the same time

Luke argues in Acts that Christianity is the logical development and proper fulfillment of Judaism and is therefore deserving of the same toleration and freedom traditionally accorded Judaism by Rome (Acts 13, 16–41; 23, 6–9; 24, 10–21; 26, 2–23).

The prominence given to the period of the church in the story has important consequences for Luke's interpretation of the teachings of Jesus. By presenting the time of the church as a distinct phase of salvation history, Luke accordingly shifts the early Christian emphasis away from the expectation of an imminent parousia to the day-to-day concerns of the Christian community in the world. He does this in the gospel by regularly emphasizing the words "each day" (9, 23; cf Mk 8, 34; 11, 3; 16, 19; 19, 47) in the sayings of Jesus. Although Luke still believes the parousia to be a reality that will come unexpectedly (12, 38.45–46), he is more concerned with presenting the words and deeds of Jesus as guides for the conduct of Christian disciples in the interim period between the ascension and the parousia and with presenting Jesus himself as the model of Christian life and piety.

Throughout the gospel, Luke calls upon the Christian disciple to identify with the master Jesus, who is caring and tender toward the poor and lowly, the outcast, the sinner, and the afflicted, toward all those who recognize their dependence on God (4, 18; 6, 20–23; 7, 36–50; 14, 12–14; 15, 1–32; 16, 19–31; 18, 9–14; 19, 1–10; 21, 1–4), but who is severe toward the proud and self-righteous, and particularly toward those who place their material wealth before the service of God and his people (6, 24–26; 12, 13–21; 16, 13–15.19–31; 18, 9–14.15–25; cf 1, 50–53). No gospel writer is more concerned than Luke with the mercy and compassion of Jesus (7, 41–43; 10, 29–37; 13, 6–9; 15, 11–32). No gospel writer is more concerned with the role of the Spirit in the life of Jesus and the Christian disciple (1, 35.41; 2, 25–27; 4, 1.14.18; 10, 21; 11, 13; 24, 49), with the importance of prayer (3, 21; 5, 16; 6, 12; 9, 28; 11, 1–13; 18, 1–8), or with Jesus' concern for women (7, 11–17.36–50; 8, 2–3; 10, 38–42). While Jesus calls all humanity to repent (5, 32; 10, 13; 11, 32; 13, 1–5; 15, 7–10; 16, 30; 17, 3–4; 24, 47), he is particularly demanding of those who would be his disciples. Of them he demands absolute and total detachment from family and material possessions (9, 57–62; 12, 32–34; 14, 25–35). To all who respond in faith and repentance to the word Jesus preaches, he brings salvation (2, 30–32; 3, 6; 7, 50; 8, 48.50; 17, 19; 19, 9) and peace (2, 14; 7, 50; 8, 48; 19, 38.42) and life (10, 25–28; 18, 26–30).

Early Christian tradition, from the late second century on, identifies the author of this gospel and of the Acts of the Apostles as Luke, a Syrian from Antioch, who is mentioned in the New Testament in Col 4, 14, Phlm 24 and 2 Tim 4, 11. The prologue of the gospel makes it clear that Luke is not part of the first generation of Christian disciples but is himself dependent upon the traditions he received from those who were eyewitnesses and ministers of the word (1, 2). His two-volume work marks him as someone who was highly literate both in the Old Testament traditions according to the Greek versions and in Hellenistic Greek writings.

Among the likely sources for the composition of this gospel (1, 3) were the Gospel of Mark, a written collection of sayings of Jesus known also to the author of the Gospel of Matthew (Q; see Introduction to Matthew), and other special traditions that were used by Luke alone among the gospel writers. Some hold that Luke used Mark only as a complementary source for rounding out the material he took from other traditions. Because of its dependence on the Gospel of Mark and because details in Luke's Gospel (13, 35a; 19, 43–44; 21, 20; 23, 28–31) imply that the author was acquainted with the destruction of the city of Jerusalem by the Romans in A.D. 70, the Gospel of Luke is dated by most scholars after that date; many propose A.D. 80–90 as the time of composition.

Luke's consistent substitution of Greek names

for the Aramaic or Hebrew names occurring in his sources (e.g., 23, 33 // Mk 15, 22 // 18, 41; Mk 10, 51), his omission from the gospel of specifically Jewish Christian concerns found in his sources (e.g., Mk 7, 1–23), his interest in Gentile Christians (2, 30–32; 3, 6.38; 4, 16–30; 13, 28–30; 14, 15–24; 17, 11–19; 24, 47–48), and his incomplete knowledge of Palestinian geography, customs, and practices are among the characteristics of this gospel that suggest that Luke was a non-Palestinian writing to a non-Palestinian audience that was largely made up of Gentile Christians.

The principal divisions of the Gospel according to Luke are the following:

I: The Prologue (1, 1–4)
II: The Infancy Narrative (1, 5—2, 52)
III: The Preparation for the Public Ministry (3, 1—4, 13)
IV: The Ministry in Galilee (4, 14—9, 50)
V: The Journey to Jerusalem: Luke's Travel Narrative (9, 51—19, 27)
VI: The Teaching Ministry in Jerusalem (19, 28—21, 38)
VII: The Passion Narrative (22, 1—23, 56)
VIII: The Resurrection Narrative (24, 1–53)

I: The Prologue

CHAPTER 1

See RG 307-309

1a *Since many have undertaken to compile a narrative of the events that have been fulfilled among us, *2b* just as those who were eyewitnesses from the beginning and ministers of the word have handed them down to us, *3* I too have decided, after investigating everything accurately anew, to write it down in an orderly sequence for you, most excellent Theophilus, *4* so that you may realize the certainty of the teachings you have received.

1, 1–4: The Gospel according to Luke is the only one of the synoptic gospels to begin with a literary prologue. Making use of a formal, literary construction and vocabulary, the author writes the prologue in imitation of Hellenistic Greek writers and, in so doing, relates his story about Jesus to contemporaneous Greek and Roman literature. Luke is not only interested in the words and deeds of Jesus, but also in the larger context of the birth, ministry, death, and resurrection of Jesus as the fulfillment of the promises of God in the Old Tes-

tament. As a second- or third-generation Christian, Luke acknowledges his debt to earlier **eyewitnesses** and **ministers of the word,** but claims that his contribution to this developing tradition is a complete and accurate account, told in an orderly manner, and intended to provide **Theophilus** ("friend of God," literally) and other readers with certainty about earlier teachings they have received.

a: Acts 1, 1; 1 Cor 15, 3.   *b:* 24, 48; Jn 15, 27; Acts 1, 21-22.

II: The Infancy Narrative

Announcement of the Birth of John. *5c**In the days of Herod, King of Judea,* there was a priest named Zechariah of the priestly division of Abijah; his wife was from the daughters of Aaron, and her name was Elizabeth. *6*Both were righteous in the eyes of God, observing all the commandments and ordinances of the Lord blamelessly. *7d**But they had no child, because Elizabeth was barren and both were advanced in years. *8*Once when he was serving as priest in his division's turn before God, *9e*according to the practice of the priestly service, he was chosen by lot to enter the sanctuary of the Lord to burn incense. *10*Then, when the whole assembly of the people was praying outside at the hour of the incense offering, *11*the angel of the Lord appeared to him, standing at the right of the altar of incense. *12*Zechariah was troubled by what he saw, and fear came upon him. *13f**But the angel said to him, "Do not be afraid, Zechariah, because your prayer has been heard. Your wife Elizabeth will bear you a son, and you shall name him John. *14*And you will have joy and gladness, and many will rejoice at his birth, *15g**for he will be great in the sight of [the] Lord. He will drink neither wine nor strong drink. He will be filled with the holy Spirit even from his mother's womb, *16*and he will turn many of the children of Israel to the Lord their God. *17h**He will go before him in the spirit and power of Elijah to turn the hearts of fathers toward children and the disobedient to the understanding of the righteous, to prepare a people fit for the Lord." *18*Then Zechariah said to the angel, "How shall I know this? For I am an old man, and my wife is advanced in years." *19i**And

1, 5—2, 52: Like the Gospel according to Matthew, this gospel opens with an infancy narrative, a collection of stories about the birth and childhood of Jesus. The narrative uses early Christian traditions about the birth of Jesus, traditions about the birth and circumcision of John the Baptist, and canticles such as the Magnificat (1, 46–55) and Benedictus (1, 67–79), composed of phrases drawn from the Greek Old Testament. It is largely, however, the composition of Luke who writes in imitation of Old Testament birth stories, combining historical and legendary details, literary ornamentation and interpretation of scripture, to answer in advance the question, "Who is Jesus Christ?" The focus of the narrative, therefore, is primarily christological. In this section Luke announces many of the themes that will become prominent in the rest of the gospel: the centrality of Jerusalem and the temple, the journey motif, the universality of salvation, joy and peace, concern for the lowly, the importance of women, the presentation of Jesus as savior, Spirit-guided revelation and prophecy, and the fulfillment of Old Testament promises. The account presents parallel scenes (diptychs) of angelic announcements of the birth of John the Baptist and of Jesus, and of the birth, circumcision, and presentation of John and Jesus. In this parallelism, the ascendency of Jesus over John is stressed: John is prophet of the Most High (1, 76); Jesus is Son of the Most High (1, 32). John is great in the sight of the Lord (1, 15); Jesus will be Great (a LXX attribute, used absolutely, of God) (1, 32). John will go before the Lord (1, 16–17); Jesus will be Lord (1, 43; 2, 11).

1, 5: In the days of Herod, King of Judea: Luke relates the story of salvation history to events in contemporary world history. Here and in 3, 1–2, he connects his narrative with events in Palestinian history; in 2, 1–2 and 3, 1, he casts the Jesus story in the light of events of Roman history. Herod the Great, the son of the Idumean Antipater, was declared "King of Judea" by the Roman Senate in 40 B.C., but became the undisputed ruler of Palestine only in 37 B.C. He continued as king until his death in 4 B.C. **Priestly division of Abijah:** a reference to the eighth of the twenty-four divisions of priests who, for a week at a time, twice a year, served in the Jerusalem temple.

1, 7: They had no child: though childlessness was looked upon in contemporary Judaism as a curse or punishment for sin, it is intended here to present Elizabeth in a situation similar to that of some of the great mothers of important Old Testament figures: Sarah (Gn 15, 3; 16, 1); Rebekah (Gn 25, 21); Rachel (Gn 29, 31; 30, 1); the mother of Samson and wife of Manoah (Jgs 13, 2–3); Hannah (1 Sm 1, 2).

1, 13: Do not be afraid: a stereotyped Old Testament phrase spoken to reassure the recipient of a heavenly vision (Gn 15, 1; Jos 1, 9; Dn 10, 12.19 and elsewhere in 1, 30; 2, 10). **You shall name him John:** the name means "Yahweh has shown favor," an indication of John's role in salvation history.

1, 15: He will drink neither wine nor strong drink: like Samson (Jgs 13, 4–5) and Samuel (1 Sm 1, 11 LXX and 4QSamᵃ), John is to be consecrated by Nazirite vow and set apart for the Lord's service.

1, 17: He will go before him in the spirit and power of Elijah: John is to be the messenger sent before Yahweh, as described in Mal 3, 1–2. He is cast, moreover, in the role of the Old Testament fiery reformer, the prophet Elijah, who according to Mal 3, 23 (4, 5) is sent before "the great and terrible day of the Lord comes."

1, 19: I am Gabriel: "the angel of the Lord" is identified as Gabriel, the angel who in Dn 9, 20–25 announces the seventy weeks of years and the coming of an anointed one, a prince. By alluding to Old Testament themes in vv 17 and 19, such as the coming of the day of the Lord and the dawning of the messianic era, Luke is presenting his interpretation of the significance of the births of John and Jesus.

c: 1 Chr 24, 10.   *d:* Gn 18, 11; Jgs 13, 2-5; 1 Sm 1, 5-6.   *e:* Ex 30, 7.   *f:* 1, 57.60.63; Mt 1, 20-21.   *g:* 7, 33; Nm 6, 1-21; Jgs 13, 4; 1 Sm 1, 11 LXX.   *h:* Sir 48, 10; Mal 3, 1; 3, 23-24; Mt 11, 14; 17, 11-13.   *i:* Dn 8, 16; 9, 21.

the angel said to him in reply, "I am Gabriel, who stand before God. I was sent to speak to you and to announce to you this good news. [20]j*But now you will be speechless and unable to talk until the day these things take place, because you did not believe my words, which will be fulfilled at their proper time."

[21]Meanwhile the people were waiting for Zechariah and were amazed that he stayed so long in the sanctuary. [22]But when he came out, he was unable to speak to them, and they realized that he had seen a vision in the sanctuary. He was gesturing to them but remained mute. [23]Then, when his days of ministry were completed, he went home. [24]After this time his wife Elizabeth conceived, and she went into seclusion for five months, saying, [25]k"So has the Lord done for me at a time when he has seen fit to take away my disgrace before others."

Announcement of the Birth of Jesus. [26]*In the sixth month, the angel Gabriel was sent from God to a town of Galilee called Nazareth, [27]l to a virgin betrothed to a man named Joseph, of the house of David, and the virgin's name was Mary. [28]m And coming to her, he said, "Hail, favored one! The Lord is with you." [29]But she was greatly troubled at what was said and pondered what sort of greeting this might be. [30]Then the angel said to her, "Do not be afraid, Mary, for you have found favor with God. [31]nBehold, you will conceive in your womb and bear a son, and you shall name him Jesus. [32]o*He will be great and will be called Son of the Most High, and the Lord God will give him the throne of David his father, [33]p and he will rule over the house of Jacob forever, and of his kingdom there will be no end." [34]*But Mary said to the angel, "How can this be, since I have no relations with a man?" [35]q And the angel said to her in reply, "The holy Spirit will come upon you, and the power of the Most High will overshadow you. Therefore the child to be born will be called holy, the Son of God. [36]*And behold, Elizabeth, your relative, has also conceived a son in her old age, and this is the sixth month for her who was called barren; [37]rfor nothing will be impossible for God." [38]Mary said, "Behold, I am the handmaid of the Lord. May it be done to me according to your word." Then the angel departed from her.

Mary Visits Elizabeth. [39]During those days Mary set out and traveled to the hill country in haste to a town of Judah, [40]where she entered the house of Zechariah and greeted Elizabeth. [41]sWhen Elizabeth heard Mary's greeting, the infant leaped in her womb, and Elizabeth, filled with the holy Spirit, [42]tcried out in a loud voice and said, "Most blessed are you among women, and blessed is the fruit of your womb. [43]*And how does this happen to me, that the mother of my Lord should come to me? [44]For at the moment the sound of your greeting reached my ears, the infant in my womb leaped for joy. [45]u*Blessed are you who be-

1, 20: You will be speechless and unable to talk: Zechariah's becoming mute is the sign given in response to his question in v 18. When Mary asks a similar question in 1, 34, unlike Zechariah who was punished for his doubt, she, in spite of her doubt, is praised and reassured (35–37).

1, 26–38: The announcement to Mary of the birth of Jesus is parallel to the announcement to Zechariah of the birth of John. In both the angel Gabriel appears to the parent who is troubled by the vision (11–12.26–29) and then told by the angel not to fear (13.30). After the announcement is made (14–17.31–33) the parent objects (18.34) and a sign is given to confirm the announcement (20.36). The particular focus of the announcement of the birth of Jesus is on his identity as Son of David (32–33) and Son of God (32.35).

1, 32: Son of the Most High: cf 1, 76 where John is described as "prophet of the Most High." "Most High" is a title for God commonly used by Luke (35.76; 6, 35; 8, 28; Acts 7, 48; 16, 17).

1, 34: Mary's questioning response is a denial of sexual relations and is used by Luke to lead to the angel's declaration about the Spirit's role in the conception of this child (35). According to Luke, the virginal conception of Jesus takes place through the holy Spirit, the power of God, and therefore Jesus has a unique relationship to Yahweh: he is Son of God.

1, 36–37: The sign given to Mary in confirmation of the angel's announcement to her is the pregnancy of her aged relative Elizabeth. If a woman past the childbearing age could become pregnant, why, the angel implies, should there be doubt about Mary's pregnancy, for **nothing will be impossible for God.**

1, 43: Even before his birth, Jesus is identified in Lk as the Lord.

1, 45: Blessed are you who believed: Luke portrays Mary as a believer whose faith stands in contrast to the disbelief of Zechariah (20). Mary's role as believer in the infancy narrative should be seen in connection with the explicit mention of her presence among "those who believed" after the resurrection at the beginning of the Acts of the Apostles (14).

j: 1, 45.   k: Gn 30, 23.   l: 2, 5; Mt 1, 16.18.   m: Jgs 6, 12; Ru 2, 4; Jdt 13, 18.   n: Gn 16, 11; Jgs 13, 3; Is 7, 14; Mt 1, 21-23.   o: 2 Sm 7, 12.13.16; Is 9, 7.   p: Dn 2, 44; 7, 14; Mi 4, 7; Mt 28, 18.   q: Mt 1, 20.   r: Gn 18, 14; Jer 32, 27; Mt 19, 26.   s: 1, 15; Gn 25, 22 LXX.   t: 11, 27-28; Jgs 5, 24; Jdt 13, 18; Dt 28, 4.   u: 1, 20.

lieved that what was spoken to you by the Lord would be fulfilled."

The Canticle of Mary. [46 v w *]And Mary said:

"My soul proclaims the greatness of the
Lord;
[47] [x]my spirit rejoices in God my savior.
[48] [y]For he has looked upon his handmaid's
lowliness;
behold, from now on will all ages call
me blessed.
[49] [z]The Mighty One has done great things
for me,
and holy is his name.
[50] [a]His mercy is from age to age
to those who fear him.
[51] [b]He has shown might with his arm,
dispersed the arrogant of mind and
heart.
[52] [c]He has thrown down the rulers from
their thrones
but lifted up the lowly.
[53] [d]The hungry he has filled with good
things;
the rich he has sent away empty.
[54] [e]He has helped Israel his servant,
remembering his mercy,
[55] [f]according to his promise to our fathers,
to Abraham and to his descendants
forever."

[56]Mary remained with her about three months and then returned to her home.

The Birth of John. [57 *]When the time arrived for Elizabeth to have her child she gave birth to a son. [58 g]Her neighbors and relatives heard that the Lord had shown his great mercy toward her, and they rejoiced with her. [59 h *]When they came on the eighth day to circumcise the child, they were going to call him Zechariah after his father, [60 i]but his mother said in reply, "No. He will be called John." [61]But they answered her, "There is no one among your relatives who has this name." [62]So they made signs, asking his father what he wished him to be called. [63]He asked for a tablet and wrote, "John is his name," and all were amazed. [64 j]Immediately his mouth was opened, his tongue freed, and he spoke blessing God. [65]Then fear came upon all their neighbors, and all these matters were discussed throughout the hill country of Judea. [66]All who heard these things took them to heart, saying, "What, then, will this child be?" For surely the hand of the Lord was with him.

The Canticle of Zechariah. [67]Then Zechariah his father, filled with the holy Spirit, prophesied, saying:

[68 k *]"Blessed be the Lord, the God of Israel,
for he has visited and brought
redemption to his people.

1, 46–55: Although Mary is praised for being the mother of the Lord and because of her belief, she reacts as the servant in a psalm of praise, the Magnificat. Because there is no specific connection of the canticle to the context of Mary's pregnancy and her visit to Elizabeth, the Magnificat (with the possible exception of v 48) may have been a Jewish Christian hymn that Luke found appropriate at this point in his story. Even if not composed by Luke, it fits in well with themes found elsewhere in Lk: joy and exultation in the Lord; the lowly being singled out for God's favor; the reversal of human fortunes; the fulfillment of Old Testament promises. The loose connection between the hymn and the context is further seen in the fact that a few Old Latin manuscripts identify the speaker of the hymn as Elizabeth, even though the overwhelming textual evidence makes Mary the speaker.

1, 57–66: The birth and circumcision of John above all emphasize John's incorporation into the people of Israel by the sign of the covenant (Gn 17, 1–12). The narrative of John's circumcision also prepares the way for the subsequent description of the circumcision of Jesus in 2, 21. At the beginning of his two-volume work Luke shows those who play crucial roles in the inauguration of Christianity to be wholly a part of the people of Israel. At the end of the Acts of the Apostles (21, 20; 22, 3; 23, 6–9; 24, 14–16; 26, 2–8.22–23)

he will argue that Christianity is the direct descendant of Pharisaic Judaism.

1, 59: The practice of Palestinian Judaism at this time was to name the child at birth; moreover, though naming a male child after the father is not completely unknown, the usual practice was to name the child after the grandfather (see 61). The naming of the child John and Zechariah's recovery from his loss of speech should be understood as fulfilling the angel's announcement to Zechariah in 1, 13 and 20.

1, 68–79: Like the canticle of Mary (46–55) the canticle of Zechariah is only loosely connected with its context. Apart from vv 76–77, the hymn in speaking of **a horn for our salvation** (69) and **the daybreak from on high** (78) applies more closely to Jesus and his work than to John. Again like

---

v: 1 Sm 2, 1-10. *w:* Ps 35, 9; Is 61, 10; Hb 3, 18. *x:* Ti 3, 4; Jude 25. *y:* 11, 27; 1 Sm 1, 11; 2 Sm 16, 12; 2 Kgs 14, 26; Ps 113, 7. *z:* Dt 10, 21; Pss 71, 19; 111, 9; 126, 2-3. *a:* Pss 89, 2; 103, 13.17. *b:* Pss 89, 10; 118, 15; Jer 32, 17 (39, 17 LXX). *c:* 1 Sm 2, 7; 2 Sm 22, 28; Jb 5, 11; 12, 19; Ps 147, 6; Sir 10, 14; Jas 4, 6; 1 Pt 5, 5. *d:* 1 Sm 2, 5; Ps 107, 9. *e:* Ps 98, 3; Is 41, 8-9. *f:* Gn 13, 15; 17, 7; 18, 18; 22, 17-18; Mi 7, 20. *g:* 1, 14. *h:* 2, 21; Gn 17, 10.12; Lv 12, 3. *i:* 1, 13. *j:* 1, 20. *k:* 7, 16; Pss 41, 13; 72, 18; 106, 48; 111, 9.

69 1*He has raised up a horn for our
    salvation
  within the house of David his servant,
70 even as he promised through the mouth
    of his holy prophets from of old:
71 m salvation from our enemies and from
    the hand of all who hate us,
72 n to show mercy to our fathers
    and to be mindful of his holy covenant
73 p and of the oath he swore to Abraham
    our father,
  and to grant us that, 74 rescued from the
    hand of enemies,
  without fear we might worship him 75 q in
    holiness and righteousness
  before him all our days.
76 r *And you, child, will be called prophet
    of the Most High,
  for you will go before the Lord to
    prepare his ways,
77 to give his people knowledge of salvation
    through the forgiveness of their sins,
78 s t *because of the tender mercy of our God

by which the daybreak from on high
    will visit us
79 to shine on those who sit in darkness and
    death's shadow,
  to guide our feet into the path of
    peace."

80 u *The child grew and became strong in
spirit, and he was in the desert until the day
of his manifestation to Israel.

CHAPTER 2

The Birth of Jesus. 1 *In those days a
decree went out from Caesar Augustus that
the whole world should be enrolled. 2 This
was the first enrollment, when Quirinius was
governor of Syria. 3 So all went to be enrolled,
each to his own town. 4 v And Joseph too went
up from Galilee from the town of Nazareth to
Judea, to the city of David that is called Bethlehem, because he was of the house and family of David, 5 w to be enrolled with Mary, his
betrothed, who was with child. 6 While they

Mary's canticle, it is largely composed of phrases taken from
the Greek Old Testament and may have been a Jewish Christian hymn of praise that Luke adapted to fit the present context by inserting vv 76–77 to give Zechariah's reply to the
question asked in v 66.
    1, 69: A horn for our salvation: the horn is a common
Old Testament figure for strength (Pss 18, 3; 75, 5–6; 89, 18;
112, 9; 148, 14). This description is applied to God in Ps 18,
3 and is here transferred to Jesus. The connection of the
phrase with **the house of David** gives the title messianic
overtones and may indicate an allusion to a phrase in Hannah's song of praise (1 Sm 2, 10), "the horn of his
anointed."
    1, 76: You will go before the Lord: here **the Lord** is most
likely a reference to Jesus (contrast 15–17 where Yahweh is
meant) and John is presented as the precursor of Jesus.
    1, 78: The daybreak from on high: three times in the
LXX (Jer 23, 5; Zec 3, 8; 6, 12), the Greek word used here for
daybreak translates the Hebrew word for "scion, branch," an
Old Testament messianic title.
    2, 1–2: Although universal registrations of Roman citi-
zens are attested in 28 B.C., 8 B.C., and A.D. 14 and en-
rollments in individual provinces of those who are not Roman citizens are also attested, such a universal census of
the Roman world under Caesar Augustus is unknown outside the New Testament. Moreover, there are notorious
historical problems connected with Luke's dating the census **when Quirinius was governor of Syria,** and the various attempts to resolve the difficulties have proved unsuccessful. P. Sulpicius Quirinius became legate of the
province of Syria in A.D. 6–7 when Judea was annexed to
the province of Syria. At that time, a provincial census of
Judea was taken up. If Quirinius had been legate of Syria

previously, it would have to have been before 10 B.C. because the various legates of Syria from 10 B.C. to 4 B.C.
(the death of Herod) are known, and such a dating for an
earlier census under Quirinius would create additional
problems for dating the beginning of Jesus' ministry (3,
1.23). A previous legateship after 4 B.C. (and before A.D.
6) would not fit with the dating of Jesus' birth in the days
of Herod (1, 5; Mt 2, 1). Luke may simply be combining
Jesus' birth in Bethlehem with his vague recollection of a
census under Quirinius (see also Acts 5, 37) to underline
the significance of this birth for the whole Roman world:
through this child born in Bethlehem peace and salvation
come to the empire.
    2, 1: Caesar Augustus: the reign of the Roman emperor
Caesar Augustus is usually dated from 27 B.C. to his death
in A.D. 14. According to Greek inscriptions, Augustus was
regarded in the Roman Empire as "savior" and "god," and
he was credited with establishing a time of peace, the **pax
Augusta,** throughout the Roman world during his long
reign. It is not by chance that Luke relates the birth of Jesus
to the time of Caesar Augustus: the real savior (11) and
peace-bearer (14; see also 19, 38) is the child born in Bethlehem. The great emperor is simply God's agent (like the
Persian king Cyrus in Is 44, 28—45, 1) who provides the occasion for God's purposes to be accomplished. **The whole
world:** that is, the whole Roman world: Rome, Italy, and the
Roman provinces.

l: Ps 18, 3.   m: Ps 106, 10.   n: Ps 106, 45-46.   o: Gn 17, 7; Lv
26, 42; Ps 105, 8-9; Mi 7, 20.   p: Gn 22, 16-17.   q: Ti 2, 12.
r: Is 40, 3; Mal 3, 1; Mt 3, 3; 11, 10.   s: Mal 3, 20.   t: Is 60, 1-
2.   u: 2, 40; Mt 3, 1.   v: Mi 5, 2; Mt 2, 6.   w: 1, 27; Mt 1, 18.

were there, the time came for her to have her child, [7x*]and she gave birth to her firstborn son. She wrapped him in swaddling clothes and laid him in a manger, because there was no room for them in the inn.

[8*]Now there were shepherds in that region living in the fields and keeping the night watch over their flock. [9y]The angel of the Lord appeared to them and the glory of the Lord shone around them, and they were struck with great fear. [10]The angel said to them, "Do not be afraid; for behold, I proclaim to you good news of great joy that will be for all the people. [11z*]For today in the city of David a savior has been born for you who is Messiah and Lord. [12]And this will be a sign for you: you will find an infant wrapped in swaddling clothes and lying in a manger." [13]And suddenly there was a multitude of the heavenly host with the angel, praising God and saying:

[14 a*]"Glory to God in the highest
    and on earth peace to those on whom
        his favor rests."

The Visit of the Shepherds. [15]When the angels went away from them to heaven, the shepherds said to one another, "Let us go, then, to Bethlehem to see this thing that has taken place, which the Lord has made known to us." [16]So they went in haste and found Mary and Joseph, and the infant lying in the manger. [17]When they saw this, they made known the message that had been told them about this child. [18]All who heard it were amazed by what had been told them by the shepherds. [19]And Mary kept all these things, reflecting on them in her heart. [20]Then the shepherds returned, glorifying and praising God for all they had heard and seen, just as it had been told to them.

The Circumcision and Naming of Jesus. [21b*]When eight days were completed for his circumcision, he was named Jesus, the name given him by the angel before he was conceived in the womb.

The Presentation in the Temple. [22c*]When the days were completed for their purification according to the law of Moses, they took him up to Jerusalem to present him to

2, 7: Firstborn son: the description of Jesus as **firstborn son** does not necessarily mean that Mary had other sons. It is a legal description indicating that Jesus possessed the rights and privileges of the firstborn son (Gn 27; Ex 13, 2; Nm 3, 12–13; 18, 15–16; Dt 21, 15–17). See the notes on Mt 1, 25 and Mk 6, 3. **Wrapped him in swaddling clothes:** there may be an allusion here to the birth of another descendant of David, his son Solomon, who though a great king was wrapped in swaddling clothes like any other infant (Wis 7, 4–6). **Laid him in a manger:** a feeding trough for animals. A possible allusion to Is 1, 3 LXX.

2, 8–20: The annoucement of Jesus' birth to the shepherds is in keeping with Luke's theme that the lowly are singled out as the recipients of God's favors and blessings (see also 1, 48.52).

2, 11: The basic message of the infancy narrative is contained in the angel's announcement: this child is **savior, Messiah,** and **Lord.** Luke is the only synoptic gospel writer to use the title **savior** for Jesus (11; Acts 5, 31; 13, 23; see also 1, 69; 19, 9; Acts 4, 12). As savior, Jesus is looked upon by Luke as the one who rescues humanity from sin and delivers humanity from the condition of alienation from God. The title **christos,** "Christ," is the Greek equivalent of the Hebrew **mãšîah,** "Messiah," "anointed one." Among certain groups in first-century Palestinian Judaism, the title was applied to an expected royal leader from the line of David who would restore the kingdom to Israel (see Acts 1, 6). The political overtones of the title are played down in Lk and instead the Messiah of the Lord (26) or the Lord's anointed is the one who now brings salvation to all humanity, Jew and Gentile (29–32). **Lord** is the most frequently used title for Jesus in Lk and Acts. In the New Testament it is also applied to Yahweh, as it is in the Old Testament. When used of Jesus it points to his transcendence and dominion over humanity.

2, 14: On earth peace to those on whom his favor rests: the peace that results from the Christ event is for those whom God has favored with his grace. This reading is found in the oldest representatives of the Western and Alexandrian text traditions and is the preferred one; the Byzantine text tradition, on the other hand, reads: "on earth peace, good will toward men." The peace of which Luke's gospel speaks (14; 7, 50; 8, 48; 10, 5–6; 19, 38.42; 24, 36) is more than the absence of war of the **pax Augusta;** it also includes the security and well-being characteristic of peace in the Old Testament.

2, 21: Just as John before him had been incorporated into the people of Israel through his circumcision, so too this child (see the note on 1, 57–66).

2, 22–40: The presentation of Jesus in the temple depicts the parents of Jesus as devout Jews, faithful observers of the law of the Lord (23.24.39), i.e., the law of Moses. In this respect, they are described in a fashion similar to the parents of John (1, 6) and Simeon (25) and Anna (36–37).

2, 22: Their purification: syntactically, **their** must refer to Mary and Joseph, even though the Mosaic law never mentions the purification of the husband. Recognizing the problem, some Western scribes have altered the text to read "his purification," understanding the presentation of Jesus in the temple as a form of purification; the Vulgate version has a Latin form that could be either "his" or "her." According to

x: Mt 1, 25. y: 1, 11.26. z: Mt 1, 21; 16, 16; Jn 4, 42; Acts 2, 36; 5, 31; Phil 2, 11. a: 19, 38. b: 1, 31; Gn 17, 12; Mt 1, 21. c: Lv 12, 2-8.

the Lord, [23d]just as it is written in the law of the Lord, "Every male that opens the womb shall be consecrated to the Lord," [24]and to offer the sacrifice of "a pair of turtledoves or two young pigeons," in accordance with the dictate in the law of the Lord.

[25]*Now there was a man in Jerusalem whose name was Simeon. This man was righteous and devout, awaiting the consolation of Israel, and the holy Spirit was upon him. [26]It had been revealed to him by the holy Spirit that he should not see death before he had seen the Messiah of the Lord. [27]He came in the Spirit into the temple; and when the parents brought in the child Jesus to perform the custom of the law in regard to him, [28]he took him into his arms and blessed God, saying:

[29] "Now, Master, you may let your servant
    go
in peace, according to your word,
[30] [e]for my eyes have seen your salvation,
[31]   which you prepared in sight of all the
    peoples,
[32] [f]a light for revelation to the Gentiles,
    and glory for your people Israel."

[33]The child's father and mother were amazed at what was said about him; [34g]and Simeon blessed them and said to Mary his mother, "Behold, this child is destined for the fall and rise of many in Israel, and to be a sign that will be contradicted [35]*(and you yourself a sword will pierce) so that the thoughts of many hearts may be revealed."

[36]There was also a prophetess, Anna, the daughter of Phanuel, of the tribe of Asher. She was advanced in years, having lived seven years with her husband after her marriage, [37]and then as a widow until she was eighty-four. She never left the temple, but worshiped night and day with fasting and prayer. [38h]And coming forward at that very time, she gave thanks to God and spoke about the child to all who were awaiting the redemption of Jerusalem.

The Return to Nazareth. [39i]When they had fulfilled all the prescriptions of the law of the Lord, they returned to Galilee, to their own town of Nazareth. [40j]The child grew and became strong, filled with wisdom; and the favor of God was upon him.

The Boy Jesus in the Temple. [41k]*Each year his parents went to Jerusalem for the feast of Passover, [42]and when he was twelve years old, they went up according to festival custom. [43]After they had completed its days, as they were returning, the boy Jesus remained behind in Jerusalem, but his parents did not know it. [44]Thinking that he was in the caravan, they journeyed for a day and looked for him among their relatives and acquaintances, [45]but not finding him, they returned to Jerusalem to look for him. [46]After three days they found him in the temple, sitting in the midst of the teachers, listening to them and asking them questions, [47]and all who heard him were astounded at his understand-

the Mosaic law (Lv 12, 2–8), the woman who gives birth to a boy is unable for forty days to touch anything sacred or to enter the temple area by reason of her legal impurity. At the end of this period she is required to offer a year-old lamb as a burnt offering and a turtledove or young pigeon as an expiation of sin. The woman who could not afford a lamb offered instead two turtledoves or two young pigeons, as Mary does here. **They took him up to Jerusalem to present him to the Lord:** as the firstborn son (7) Jesus was consecrated to the Lord as the law required (Ex 13, 2.12), but there was no requirement that this be done at the temple. The concept of a presentation at the temple is probably derived from 1 Sm 1, 24–28, where Hannah offers the child Samuel for sanctuary services. The law further stipulated (Nm 3, 47–48) that the firstborn son should be redeemed by the parents through their payment of five shekels to a member of a priestly family. About this legal requirement Luke is silent.

2, 25: Awaiting the consolation of Israel: Simeon here and later Anna who speak about the child to all who were awaiting the redemption of Jerusalem represent the hopes and expectations of faithful and devout Jews who at this time were looking forward to the restoration of God's rule in Israel. The birth of Jesus brings these hopes to fulfillment.

2, 35: (And you yourself a sword will pierce): Mary herself will not be untouched by the various reactions to the role of Jesus (34). Her blessedness as mother of the Lord will be challenged by her son who describes true blessedness as "hearing the word of God and observing it" (11, 27–28 and 8, 20–21).

2, 41–52: This story's concern with an incident from Jesus' youth is unique in the canonical gospel tradition. It presents Jesus in the role of the faithful Jewish boy, raised in the traditions of Israel, and fulfilling all that the law requires. With this episode, the infancy narrative ends just as it began, in the setting of the Jerusalem temple.

d: Ex 13, 2.12.   e: 3, 6; Is 40, 5 LXX; 52, 10.   f: Is 42, 6; 46, 13; 49, 6; Acts 13, 47; 26, 23.   g: 12, 51; Is 8, 14; Jn 9, 39; Rom 9, 33; 1 Cor 1, 23; 1 Pt 2, 7-8.   h: Is 52, 9.   i: Mt 2, 23.   j. 1, 80; 2, 52.   k: Ex 12, 24-27; 23, 15; Dt 16, 1-8.

ing and his answers. [48]When his parents saw him, they were astonished, and his mother said to him, "Son, why have you done this to us? Your father and I have been looking for you with great anxiety." [49]*And he said to them, "Why were you looking for me? Did you not know that I must be in my Father's house?" [50]But they did not understand what he said to them. [51]*He went down with them and came to Nazareth, and was obedient to them; and his mother kept all these things in her heart. [52]*m And Jesus advanced [in] wisdom and age and favor before God and man.

III: The Preparation for the Public Ministry

CHAPTER 3

See RG 309

The Preaching of John the Baptist. [1]*n*In the fifteenth year of the reign of Tiberius Caesar, when Pontius Pilate was governor of Judea, and Herod was tetrarch of Galilee, and his brother Philip tetrarch of the region of Ituraea and Trachonitis, and Lysanias was tetrarch of Abilene, [2]*during the high priesthood of Annas and Caiaphas, the word of God came to John the son of Zechariah in the desert. [3]*p*He went throughout [the] whole region of the Jordan, proclaiming a baptism of repentance for the forgiveness of sins, [4]*q*r*as it is written in the book of the words of the prophet Isaiah:

"A voice of one crying out in the desert:
'Prepare the way of the Lord,
   make straight his paths.
[5] Every valley shall be filled
   and every mountain and hill shall be
      made low.
The winding roads shall be made straight,
   and the rough ways made smooth,
[6] *and all flesh shall see the salvation of
     God.' "

2, 49: I must be in my Father's house: this phrase can also be translated, "I must be about my Father's work." In either translation, Jesus refers to God as his Father. His divine sonship, and his obedience to his heavenly Father's will, take precedence over his ties to his family.

3, 1–20: Although Luke is indebted in this section to his sources, the Gospel of Mark and a collection of sayings of John the Baptist, he has clearly marked this introduction to the ministry of Jesus with his own individual style. Just as the gospel began with a long periodic sentence (1, 1–4), so too this section (1–2). He casts the call of John the Baptist in the form of an Old Testament prophetic call (2) and extends the quotation from Isaiah found in Mk 1, 3 (Is 40, 3) by the addition of Is 40, 4–5 in vv 5–6. In doing so, he presents his theme of the universality of salvation, which he has announced earlier in the words of Simeon (2, 30–32). Moreover, in describing the expectation of the people (15), Luke is characterizing the time of John's preaching in the same way as he had earlier described the situation of other devout Israelites in the infancy narrative (2, 25–26.37–38). In vv 7–18 Luke presents the preaching of John the Baptist who urges the crowds to reform in view of **the coming wrath** (7.9: eschatological preaching), and who offers the crowds certain standards for reforming social conduct (10–14: ethical preaching), and who announces to the crowds the coming of **one mightier than** he (15–18: messianic preaching).

3, 1: Tiberius Caesar: Tiberius succeeded Augustus as emperor in A.D. 14 and reigned until A.D. 37. The fifteenth year of his reign, depending on the method of calculating his first regnal year, would have fallen between A.D. 27 and 29. **Pontius Pilate:** prefect of Judea from A.D. 26 to 36. The Jewish historian Josephus describes him as a greedy and ruthless prefect who had little regard for the local Jewish population and their religious practices (see 13, 1). **Herod:** i.e., Herod Antipas, the son of Herod the Great. He ruled over Galilee and Perea from 4 B.C. to A.D. 39. His official title **tetrarch** means literally, "ruler of a quarter," but came to designate any subordinate prince. **Philip:** also a son of Herod the Great, tetrarch of the territory to the north and east of the Sea of Galilee from 4 B.C. to A.D. 34. Only two small areas of this territory are mentioned by Luke. **Lysanias:** nothing is known about this Lysanias who is said here to have been tetrarch of Abilene, a territory northwest of Damascus.

3, 2: During the high priesthood of Annas and Caiaphas: after situating the call of John the Baptist in terms of the civil rulers of the period, Luke now mentions the religious leadership of Palestine (see the note on 1, 5). Annas had been high priest A.D. 6–15. After being deposed by the Romans in A.D. 15 he was succeeded by various members of his family and eventually by his son-in-law, Caiaphas, who was high priest A.D. 18–36. Luke refers to Annas as high priest at this time (but see Jn 18, 13.19), possibly because of the continuing influence of Annas or because the title continued to be used for the ex-high priest. **The word of God came to John:** Luke is alone among the New Testament writers in associating the preaching of John with a call from God. Luke is thereby identifying John with the prophets whose ministries began with similar calls. In 7, 26 John will be described as "more than a prophet"; he is also the precursor of Jesus (7, 27), a transitional figure inaugurating the period of the fulfillment of prophecy and promise.

3, 3: See the note on Mt 3, 2.

3, 4: The Essenes from Qumran used the same passage to explain why their community was in the desert studying and observing the law and the prophets (1QS 8, 12–15).

l: 2, 19. *m:* 1, 80; 2, 40; 1 Sm 2, 26. *n:* Mt 3, 1-12; Mk 1, 1-8; Jn 1, 19-28. *o:* 1, 80. *p:* Acts 13, 24; 19, 4. *q:* Is 40, 3-5. *r:* Jn 1, 23. *s:* 2, 30-31.

[7t]He said to the crowds who came out to be baptized by him, "You brood of vipers! Who warned you to flee from the coming wrath? [8u]Produce good fruits as evidence of your repentance; and do not begin to say to yourselves, 'We have Abraham as our father,' for I tell you, God can raise up children to Abraham from these stones. [9v]Even now the ax lies at the root of the trees. Therefore every tree that does not produce good fruit will be cut down and thrown into the fire."

[10]And the crowds asked him, "What then should we do?" [11]He said to them in reply, "Whoever has two cloaks should share with the person who has none. And whoever has food should do likewise." [12w]Even tax collectors came to be baptized and they said to him, "Teacher, what should we do?" [13]He answered them, "Stop collecting more than what is prescribed." [14]Soldiers also asked him, "And what is it that we should do?" He told them, "Do not practice extortion, do not falsely accuse anyone, and be satisfied with your wages."

[15x]Now the people were filled with expectation, and all were asking in their hearts whether John might be the Messiah. [16y]*John answered them all, saying, "I am baptizing you with water, but one mightier than I is coming. I am not worthy to loosen the thongs of his sandals. He will baptize you with the holy Spirit and fire. [17z]*His winnowing fan is in his hand to clear his threshing floor and to gather the wheat into his barn, but the chaff he will burn with unquenchable fire." [18]Exhorting them in many other ways, he preached good news to the people. [19a]*Now Herod the tetrarch, who had been censured by him because of Herodias, his brother's wife, and because of all the evil deeds Herod had committed, [20]added still another to these by [also] putting John in prison.

The Baptism of Jesus. [21b]*After all the people had been baptized and Jesus also had been baptized and was praying, heaven was opened [22c]*and the holy Spirit descended upon him in bodily form like a dove. And a voice came from heaven, "You are my beloved Son; with you I am well pleased."

The Genealogy of Jesus. [23de]*When Jesus began his ministry he was about thirty years of age. He was the son, as was thought, of Joseph, the son of Heli, [24]the son of Matthat, the son of Levi, the son of Melchi, the son of Jannai, the son of Joseph, [25]the son of Mattathias, the son of Amos, the son of Nahum, the son of Esli, the son of Naggai, [26]the son of Maath, the son of Mattathias, the son of Semein, the son of Josech, the son of Joda,

3, 16: He will baptize you with the holy Spirit and fire: in contrast to John's baptism with water, Jesus is said to baptize with the holy Spirit and with fire. From the point of view of the early Christian community, the Spirit and fire must have been understood in the light of the fire symbolism of the pouring out of the Spirit at Pentecost (Acts 2, 1–4); but as part of John's preaching, the Spirit and fire should be related to their purifying and refining characteristics (Ez 36, 25–27; Mal 3, 2–3). See the note on Mt 3, 11.

3, 16: Winnowing fan: see the note on Mt 3, 12.

3, 19–20: Luke separates the ministry of John the Baptist from that of Jesus by reporting the imprisonment of John before the baptism of Jesus (21–22). Luke uses this literary device to serve his understanding of the periods of salvation history. With John the Baptist, the time of promise, the period of Israel, comes to an end; with the baptism of Jesus and the descent of the Spirit upon him, the time of fulfillment, the period of Jesus, begins. In his second volume, the Acts of the Apostles, Luke will introduce the third epoch in salvation history, the period of the church.

3, 21–22: This episode in Luke focuses on the heavenly message identifying Jesus as **Son** and, through the allusion to Is 42, 1, as Servant of Yahweh. The relationship of Jesus to the Father has already been announced in the infancy narrative (1, 32.35; 2, 49); it occurs here at the beginning of Jesus'

Galilean ministry and will reappear in 9, 35 before another major section of Luke's gospel, the travel narrative (9, 51— 19, 27). Elsewhere in Luke's writings (4, 18; Acts 10, 38), this incident will be interpreted as a type of anointing of Jesus.

3, 21: Was praying: Luke regularly presents Jesus at prayer at important points in his ministry: here at his baptism; at the choice of the Twelve (6, 12); before Peter's confession (9, 18); at the transfiguration (9, 28); when he teaches his disciples to pray (11, 1); at the Last Supper (22, 32); on the Mount of Olives (22, 41); on the cross (23, 46).

3, 22: You are my beloved Son; with you I am well pleased: this is the best attested reading in the Greek manuscripts. The Western reading, "You are my Son, this day I have begotten you," is derived from Ps 2, 7.

3, 23–38: Whereas Mt 1, 2 begins the genealogy of Jesus with Abraham to emphasize Jesus' bonds with the people of Israel, Luke's universalism leads him to trace the descent of Jesus beyond Israel to Adam and beyond that to God (38) to stress again Jesus' divine sonship.

t: Mt 12, 34.   *u:* Jn 8, 39.   *v:* Mt 7, 19; Jn 15, 6.   *w:* 7, 29.   *x:* Acts 13, 25.   *y:* 7, 19-20; Jn 1, 27; Acts 1, 5; 11, 16.   *z:* Mt 3, 12.   *a:* Mt 14, 3-4; Mk 6, 17-18.   *b:* Mt 3, 13-17; Mk 1, 9-11.   *c:* 9, 35; Ps 2, 7; Is 42, 1; Mt 12, 18; 17, 5; Mk 9, 7; Jn 1, 32; 2 Pt 1, 17.   *d:* Mt 1, 1-17.   *e:* 4, 22; Jn 6, 42.

[27f]the son of Joanan, the son of Rhesa, the son of Zerubbabel, the son of Shealtiel, the son of Neri, [28]the son of Melchi, the son of Addi, the son of Cosam, the son of Elmadam, the son of Er, [29]the son of Joshua, the son of Eliezer, the son of Jorim, the son of Matthat, the son of Levi, [30]the son of Simeon, the son of Judah, the son of Joseph, the son of Jonam, the son of Eliakim, [31ghi*]the son of Melea, the son of Menna, the son of Mattatha, the son of Nathan, the son of David, [32]the son of Jesse, the son of Obed, the son of Boaz, the son of Sala, the son of Nahshon, [33j]the son of Amminadab, the son of Admin, the son of Arni, the son of Hezron, the son of Perez, the son of Judah, [34kl]the son of Jacob, the son of Isaac, the son of Abraham, the son of Terah, the son of Nahor, [35]the son of Serug, the son of Reu, the son of Peleg, the son of Eber, the son of Shelah, [36m]the son of Cainan, the son of Arphaxad, the son of Shem, the son of Noah, the son of Lamech, [37]the son of Methuselah, the son of Enoch, the son of Jared, the son of Mahalaleel, the son of Cainan, [38]the son of Enos, the son of Seth, the son of Adam, the son of God.

CHAPTER 4

See RG
309–10

The Temptation of Jesus. [1n*]Filled with the holy Spirit, Jesus returned from the Jordan and was led by the Spirit into the desert [2o*]for forty days, to be tempted by the devil. He ate nothing during those days, and when they were over he was hungry. [3]The devil said to him, "If you are the Son of God, command this stone to become bread." [4p]Jesus answered him, "It is written, 'One

does not live by bread alone.' " [5]Then he took him up and showed him all the kingdoms of the world in a single instant. [6q]The devil said to him, "I shall give to you all this power and their glory; for it has been handed over to me, and I may give it to whomever I wish. [7]All this will be yours, if you worship me." [8r]Jesus said to him in reply, "It is written:

'You shall worship the Lord, your God,
    and him alone shall you serve.' "

[9*]Then he led him to Jerusalem, made him stand on the parapet of the temple, and said to him, "If you are the Son of God, throw yourself down from here, [10s]for it is written:

'He will command his angels concerning
    you,
        to guard you,'

[11]and:

'With their hands they will support you,
    lest you dash your foot against a
        stone.' "

[12u]Jesus said to him in reply, "It also says, 'You shall not put the Lord, your God, to the test.' " [13v*]When the devil had finished every temptation, he departed from him for a time.

IV: The Ministry in Galilee

The Beginning of the Galilean Ministry. [14wx*]Jesus returned to Galilee in the power of the Spirit, and news of him spread throughout the whole region. [15]He taught in their synagogues and was praised by all.

3, 31: The son of Nathan, the son of David: in keeping with Jesus' prophetic role in Lk and Acts (e.g., 7, 16.39; 9, 8; 13, 33; 24, 19; Acts 3, 22–23; 7, 37) Luke traces Jesus' Davidic ancestry through the prophet Nathan (see 2 Sm 7, 2) rather than through King Solomon, as Mt 1, 6–7.

4, 1–13: See the note on Mt 4, 1–11.

4, 1: Filled with the holy Spirit: as a result of the descent of the Spirit upon him at his baptism (3, 21–22), Jesus is now equipped to overcome the devil. Just as the Spirit is prominent at this early stage of Jesus' ministry (1.14.18), so too it will be at the beginning of the period of the church in Acts (Acts 1, 4; 2, 4.17).

4, 2: For forty days: the mention of forty days recalls the forty years of the wilderness wanderings of the Israelites during the Exodus (Dt 8, 2).

4, 9: To Jerusalem: the Lucan order of the temptations

concludes on the parapet of the temple in Jerusalem, the city of destiny in Luke-Acts. It is in Jerusalem that Jesus will ultimately face his destiny (9, 51; 13, 33).

4, 13: For a time: the devil's opportune time will occur before the passion and death of Jesus (Lk 22, 3.31–32.53).

4, 14: News of him spread: a Lucan theme; see v 37; 5, 15; 7, 17.

f: 1 Chr 3, 17; Ez 3, 2. g: 2 Sm 5, 14. h: 1 Sm 16, 1.18. i: Ru 4, 17-22; 1 Chr 2, 1-15. j: Gn 29, 35; 38, 29. k: Gn 21, 3; 25, 26; 1 Chr 1, 34; 28, 34. l: Gn 11, 10-26; 1 Chr 1, 24-27. m: Gn 4, 25—5, 32; 1 Chr 1, 1-4. n: Mt 4, 1-11; Mk 1, 12-13. o: Heb 4, 15. p: Dt 8, 3. q: Jer 27, 5; Mt 28, 18. r: Dt 6, 13. s: Ps 91, 11. t: Ps 91, 12. u: Dt 6, 16; 1 Cor 10, 9. v: 22, 3; Jn 13, 2.27; Heb 4, 15. w: Mt 4, 12-17; Mk 1, 14-15. x: 5, 15; Mt 3, 16.

The Rejection at Nazareth. *16y**He came to Nazareth, where he had grown up, and went according to his custom into the synagogue on the sabbath day. He stood up to read *17*and was handed a scroll of the prophet Isaiah. He unrolled the scroll and found the passage where it was written:

18 z*"The Spirit of the Lord is upon me,
  because he has anointed me
    to bring glad tidings to the poor.
He has sent me to proclaim liberty to
    captives
  and recovery of sight to the blind,
    to let the oppressed go free,
19 and to proclaim a year acceptable to the
    Lord."

*20*Rolling up the scroll, he handed it back to the attendant and sat down, and the eyes of all in the synagogue looked intently at him. *21**He said to them, "Today this scripture passage is fulfilled in your hearing." *22a*And all spoke highly of him and were amazed at the gracious words that came from his mouth. They also asked, "Isn't this the son of Joseph?" *23**He said to them, "Surely you will quote me this proverb, 'Physician, cure yourself,' and say, 'Do here in your native place the things that we heard were done in Capernaum.' " *24*And he said, "Amen, I say to you, no prophet is accepted in his own native place. *25b**Indeed, I tell you, there were many widows in Israel in the days of Elijah when the sky was closed for three and a half years and a severe famine spread over the entire land. *26c**It was to none of these that Elijah was sent, but only to a widow in Zarephath in the land of Sidon. *27d*Again, there were many lepers in Israel during the time of Elisha the prophet; yet not one of them was cleansed, but only Naaman the Syrian." *28*When the people in the synagogue heard this, they were all filled with fury. *29*They rose up, drove him out of the town, and led him to the brow of the hill on which their town had been built, to hurl him down headlong. *30*But he passed through the midst of them and went away.

The Cure of a Demoniac. *31ef**Jesus then went down to Capernaum, a town of Galilee. He taught them on the sabbath, *32g*and they were astonished at his teaching because he

---

4, 16–30: Luke has transposed to the beginning of Jesus' ministry an incident from his Marcan source, which situated it near the end of the Galilean ministry (Mk 6, 1–6a). In doing so, Luke turns the initial admiration (22) and subsequent rejection of Jesus (28–29) into a foreshadowing of the whole future ministry of Jesus. Moreover, the rejection of Jesus in his own hometown hints at the greater rejection of him by Israel (Acts 13, 46).

4, 16: According to his custom: Jesus' practice of regularly attending synagogue is carried on by the early Christians' practice of meeting in the temple (Acts 2, 46; 3, 1; 5, 12).

4, 18: The Spirit of the Lord is upon me, because he has anointed me: see the note on 3, 21–22. As this incident develops, Jesus is portrayed as a prophet whose ministry is compared to that of the prophets Elijah and Elisha. Prophetic anointings are known in first-century Palestinian Judaism from the Qumran literature that speaks of prophets as God's anointed ones. **To bring glad tidings to the poor:** more than any other gospel writer Luke is concerned with Jesus' attitude toward the economically and socially poor (see 6, 20.24; 12, 16–21; 14, 12–14; 16, 19–26; 19, 8). At times, the poor in Luke's gospel are associated with the downtrodden, the oppressed and afflicted, the forgotten and the neglected (18; 6, 20–22; 7, 22; 14, 12–14), and it is they who accept Jesus' message of salvation.

4, 21: Today this scripture passage is fulfilled in your hearing: this sermon inaugurates the time of fulfillment of Old Testament prophecy. Luke presents the ministry of Jesus as fulfilling Old Testament hopes and expectations (7, 22); for

Luke, even Jesus' suffering, death, and resurrection are done in fulfillment of the scriptures (24, 25–27.44–46; Acts 3, 18).

4, 23: The things that we heard were done in Capernaum: Luke's source for this incident reveals an awareness of an earlier ministry of Jesus in Capernaum that Luke has not yet made use of because of his transposition of this Nazareth episode to the beginning of Jesus' Galilean ministry. It is possible that by use of the future tense **you** will quote me. . . , Jesus is being portrayed as a prophet.

4, 25–26: The references to Elijah and Elisha serve several purposes in this episode: they emphasize Luke's portrait of Jesus as a prophet like Elijah and Elisha; they help to explain why the initial admiration of the people turns to rejection; and they provide the scriptural justification for the future Christian mission to the Gentiles.

4, 26: A widow in Zarephath in the land of Sidon: like Naaman the Syrian in v 27, a non-Israelite becomes the object of the prophet's ministry.

4, 31–44: The next several incidents in Jesus' ministry take place in Capernaum and are based on Luke's source, Mk 1, 21–39. To the previous portrait of Jesus as prophet (16–30) they now add a presentation of him as teacher (31–32), exorcist (32–37.41), healer (38–40), and proclaimer of God's kingdom (43).

y: Mt 13, 53-58; Mk 6, 1-6. *z:* Is 61, 1-2; 58, 6. *a:* 3, 23; Jn 6, 42. *b:* 1 Kgs 17, 1-7; 18, 1; Jas 5, 17. *c:* 1 Kgs 17, 9. *d:* 2 Kgs 5, 1-14. *e:* Mk 1, 21-28. *f:* Mt 4, 13; Jn 2, 12. *g:* Mt 7, 23-29.

spoke with authority. [33h]In the synagogue there was a man with the spirit of an unclean demon, and he cried out in a loud voice, [34i]*"Ha! What have you to do with us, Jesus of Nazareth? Have you come to destroy us? I know who you are—the Holy One of God!" [35]Jesus rebuked him and said, "Be quiet! Come out of him!" Then the demon threw the man down in front of them and came out of him without doing him any harm. [36]They were all amazed and said to one another, "What is there about his word? For with authority and power he commands the unclean spirits, and they come out." [37]And news of him spread everywhere in the surrounding region.

The Cure of Simon's Mother-in-Law. [38j]*After he left the synagogue, he entered the house of Simon. Simon's mother-in-law was afflicted with a severe fever, and they interceded with him about her. [39]He stood over her, rebuked the fever, and it left her. She got up immediately and waited on them.

Other Healings. [40k]At sunset, all who had people sick with various diseases brought them to him. He laid his hands on each of them and cured them. [41l]*And demons also came out from many, shouting, "You are the Son of God." But he rebuked them and did not allow them to speak because they knew that he was the Messiah.

Jesus Leaves Capernaum. [42m]*At daybreak, Jesus left and went to a deserted place. The crowds went looking for him, and when they came to him, they tried to prevent him from leaving them. [43n]But he said to them, "To the other towns also I must proclaim the good news of the kingdom of God, because for this purpose I have been sent." [44]*And he was preaching in the synagogues of Judea.

CHAPTER 5

See RG 310-11

The Call of Simon the Fisherman. [1o p]*While the crowd was pressing in on Jesus and listening to the word of God, he was standing by the Lake of Gennesaret. [2]He saw two boats there alongside the lake; the fishermen had disembarked and were washing their nets. [3]Getting into one of the boats, the one belonging to Simon, he asked him to put out a short distance from the shore. Then he sat down and taught the crowds from the boat. [4q]After he had finished speaking, he said to Simon, "Put out into deep water and lower your nets for a catch." [5]Simon said in reply, "Master, we have worked hard all night and have caught nothing, but at your command I will lower the nets." [6]When they

4, 34: What have you to do with us?: see the note on Jn 2, 4. **Have you come to destroy us?:** the question reflects the current belief that before the day of the Lord control over humanity would be wrested from the evil spirits, evil destroyed, and God's authority over humanity reestablished. The synoptic gospel tradition presents Jesus carrying out this task.

4, 38: The house of Simon: because of Luke's arrangement of material, the reader has not yet been introduced to Simon (cf Mk 1, 16–18.29–31). Situated as it is before the call of Simon (5, 1–11), it helps the reader to understand Simon's eagerness to do what Jesus says (5, 5) and to follow him (5, 11).

4, 41: They knew that he was the Messiah: that is, the Christ (see the note on 2, 11).

4, 42: They tried to prevent him from leaving them: the reaction of these strangers in Capernaum is presented in contrast to the reactions of those in his hometown who rejected him (28–30).

4, 44: In the synagogues of Judea: instead of **Judea,** which is the best reading of the manuscript tradition, the Byzantine text tradition and other manuscripts read "Galilee," a reading that harmonizes Lk with Mt 4, 23 and Mk 1, 39. Up to this point Luke has spoken only of a ministry of Jesus in Galilee. Luke may be using **Judea** to refer to the land of Israel, the territory of the Jews, and not to a specific portion of it.

5, 1–11: This incident has been transposed from his source, Mk 1, 16–20, which places it immediately after Jesus makes his appearance in Galilee. By this transposition Luke uses this example of Simon's acceptance of Jesus to counter the earlier rejection of him by his hometown people, and since several incidents dealing with Jesus' power and authority have already been narrated, Luke creates a plausible context for the acceptance of Jesus by Simon and his partners. Many commentators have noted the similarity between the wondrous catch of fish reported here (4–9) and the post-resurrectional appearance of Jesus in Jn 21, 1–11. There are traces in Luke's story that the post-resurrectional context is the original one: in v 8 Simon addresses Jesus as **Lord** (a post-resurrectional title for Jesus—see 24, 34; Acts 2, 36—that has been read back into the historical ministry of Jesus) and recognizes himself as a sinner (an appropriate recognition for one who has denied knowing Jesus—22, 54–62). As used by Luke, the incident looks forward to Peter's leadership in Luke-Acts (6, 14; 9, 20; 22, 31–32; 24, 34; Acts 1, 15; 2, 14–40; 10, 11–18; 15, 7–12) and symbolizes the future success of Peter as fisherman (Acts 2, 41).

h: 8, 28; Mt 8, 29; Mk 1, 23-24; 5, 7. i: 4, 41; Jn 6, 69. j: Mt 8, 14-15; Mk 1, 29-31. k: Mt 8, 16; Mk 1, 32-34. l: 4, 34; Mt 8, 29; Mk 3, 11-12. m: Mk 1, 35-39. n: 8, 1; Mk 1, 14-15. o: Mt 4, 18-22; Mk 1, 16-20. p: Mt 13, 1-2; Mk 2, 13; 3, 9-10; 4, 1-2. q: Jn 21, 1-11.

had done this, they caught a great number of fish and their nets were tearing. ⁷They signaled to their partners in the other boat to come to help them. They came and filled both boats so that they were in danger of sinking. ⁸When Simon Peter saw this, he fell at the knees of Jesus and said, "Depart from me, Lord, for I am a sinful man." ⁹For astonishment at the catch of fish they had made seized him and all those with him, ¹⁰ʳand likewise James and John, the sons of Zebedee, who were partners of Simon. Jesus said to Simon, "Do not be afraid; from now on you will be catching men." ¹¹ˢ*When they brought their boats to the shore, they left everything and followed him.

The Cleansing of a Leper. ¹²ᵗ*Now there was a man full of leprosy in one of the towns where he was; and when he saw Jesus, he fell prostrate, pleaded with him, and said, "Lord, if you wish, you can make me clean." ¹³Jesus stretched out his hand, touched him, and said, "I do will it. Be made clean." And the leprosy left him immediately. ¹⁴ᵘ*Then he ordered him not to tell anyone, but "Go, show yourself to the priest and offer for your cleansing what Moses prescribed; that will be proof for them." ¹⁵The report about him spread all the more, and great crowds assembled to listen to him and to be cured of their ailments, ¹⁶ᵛbut he would withdraw to deserted places to pray.

The Healing of a Paralytic. ¹⁷ʷ*One day as Jesus was teaching, Pharisees and teachers of the law were sitting there who had come from every village of Galilee and Judea and Jerusalem, and the power of the Lord was with him for healing. ¹⁸And some men brought on a stretcher a man who was paralyzed; they were trying to bring him in and set [him] in his presence. ¹⁹*But not finding a way to bring him in because of the crowd, they went up on the roof and lowered him on the stretcher through the tiles into the middle in front of Jesus. ²⁰*When he saw their faith, he said, "As for you, your sins are forgiven." ²¹ˣ*Then the scribes and Pharisees began to ask themselves, "Who is this who speaks blasphemies? Who but God alone can forgive sins?" ²²ʸJesus knew their thoughts and said to them in reply, "What are you thinking in your hearts? ²³Which is easier, to say, 'Your sins are forgiven,' or to say, 'Rise and walk'? ²⁴ᶻ*But that you may know that the Son of Man has authority on earth to forgive sins"—he said to the man who was paralyzed, "I say to you, rise, pick up your stretcher, and go home." ²⁵He stood up immediately before them, picked up what he had been lying on, and went home, glorifying God. ²⁶Then astonishment seized them all and they glorified God, and, struck with awe, they said, "We have seen incredible things today."

The Call of Levi. ²⁷ᵃAfter this he went out and saw a tax collector named Levi sitting at the customs post. He said to him, "Follow me." ²⁸*And leaving everything behind, he

---

5, 11: They left everything: in Mk 1, 16-20 and Mt 4, 18-22 the fishermen who follow Jesus leave their nets and their father; in Luke, they leave **everything** (see also 28; 12, 33; 14, 33; 18, 22), an indication of Luke's theme of complete detachment from material possessions.

5, 12: Full of leprosy: see the note on Mk 1, 40.

5, 14: Show yourself to the priest . . . what Moses prescribed: this is a reference to Lv 14, 2-9 that gives detailed instructions for the purification of one who had been a victim of leprosy and thereby excluded from contact with others (see Lv 13, 45-46.49; Nm 5, 2-3). **That will be proof for them:** see the note on Mt 8, 4.

5, 17—6, 11: From his Marcan source, Luke now introduces a series of controversies with Pharisees: controversy over Jesus' power to forgive sins (17-26); controversy over his eating and drinking with tax collectors and sinners (27-32); controversy over not fasting (33-36); and finally two episodes narrating controversies over observance of the sabbath (1-11).

5, 17: Pharisees: see the note on Mt 3, 7.

5, 19: Through the tiles: Luke has adapted the story found in Mk to his non-Palestinian audience by changing "opened up the roof" (Mk 2, 4, a reference to Palestinian straw and clay roofs) to **through the tiles,** a detail that reflects the Hellenistic Greco-Roman house with tiled roof.

5, 20: As for you, your sins are forgiven: literally, "O man, your sins are forgiven you." The connection between the forgiveness of sins and the cure of the paralytic reflects the belief of first-century Palestine (based on the Old Testament: Ex 20, 5; Dt 5, 9) that sickness and infirmity are the result of sin, one's own or that of one's ancestors (see also 13, 2; Jn 5, 14; 9, 2).

5, 21: The scribes: see the note on Mk 2, 6.

5, 24: See the notes on Mt 9, 6 and Mk 2, 10.

5, 28: Leaving everything behind: see the note on 5, 11.

r: Jer 16, 16. s: Mt 19, 27. t: Mt 8, 2-4; Mk 1, 40-45. u: 8, 56; Lv 14, 2-32; Mk 7, 36. v: Mk 1, 35. w: Mt 9, 1-8; Mk 2, 1-12. x: 7, 49; Is 43, 25. y: 6, 8; 9, 47. z: Jn 5, 8-9.27. a: Mt 9, 9-13; Mk 2, 13-17.

got up and followed him. *29b*Then Levi gave a great banquet for him in his house, and a large crowd of tax collectors and others were at table with them. *30*The Pharisees and their scribes complained to his disciples, saying, "Why do you eat and drink with tax collectors and sinners?" *31*Jesus said to them in reply, "Those who are healthy do not need a physician, but the sick do. *32*I have not come to call the righteous to repentance but sinners."

The Question about Fasting. *33c*And they said to him, "The disciples of John fast often and offer prayers, and the disciples of the Pharisees do the same; but yours eat and drink." *34**Jesus answered them, "Can you make the wedding guests fast while the bridegroom is with them? *35*But the days will come, and when the bridegroom is taken away from them, then they will fast in those days." *36**And he also told them a parable. "No one tears a piece from a new cloak to patch an old one. Otherwise, he will tear the new and the piece from it will not match the old cloak. *37*Likewise, no one pours new wine into old wineskins. Otherwise, the new wine will burst the skins, and it will be spilled, and the skins will be ruined. *38*Rather, new wine must be poured into fresh wineskins. *39**[And] no one who has been drinking old wine desires new, for he says, 'The old is good.' "

CHAPTER 6

See RG 311

Debates about the Sabbath. *1de**While he was going through a field of grain on a sabbath, his disciples were picking the heads of grain, rubbing them in their hands, and eating them. *2*Some Pharisees said, "Why are you doing what is unlawful on the sabbath?" *3f*Jesus said to them in reply, "Have you not read what David did when he and those [who were] with him were hungry? *4g**[How] he went into the house of God, took the bread of offering, which only the priests could lawfully eat, ate of it, and shared it with his companions." *5*Then he said to them, "The Son of Man is lord of the sabbath."

*6h*On another sabbath he went into the synagogue and taught, and there was a man there whose right hand was withered. *7i*The scribes and the Pharisees watched him closely to see if he would cure on the sabbath so that they might discover a reason to accuse him. *8j*But he realized their intentions and said to the man with the withered hand, "Come up and stand before us." And he rose and stood there. *9*Then Jesus said to them, "I ask you, is it lawful to do good on the sabbath rather than to do evil, to save life rather than to destroy it?" *10*Looking around at them all, he then said to him, "Stretch out your hand." He did so and his hand was restored. *11*But they became enraged and discussed together what they might do to Jesus.

The Mission of the Twelve. *12k**In those days he departed to the mountain to pray, and he spent the night in prayer to God. *13**When day came, he called his disciples to himself, and from them he chose Twelve,

5, 34–35: See the notes on Mt 9, 15 and Mk 2, 19.

5, 34: Wedding guests: literally, "sons of the bridal chamber."

5, 36–39: See the notes on Mt 9, 16–17 and Mk 2, 19.

5, 39: The old is good: this saying is meant to be ironic and offers an explanation for the rejection by some of the new wine that Jesus offers: satisfaction with old forms will prevent one from sampling the new.

6, 1–11: The two episodes recounted here deal with gathering grain and healing, both of which were forbidden on the sabbath. In his defense of his disciples' conduct and his own charitable deed, Jesus argues that satisfying human needs such as hunger and performing works of mercy take precedence even over the sacred sabbath rest. See also the notes on Mt 12, 1–14 and Mk 2, 25–26.

6, 4: The bread of offering: see the note on Mt 12, 5–6.

6, 12–16: See the notes on Mt 10, 1—11, 1 and Mk 3, 14–15.

6, 12: Spent the night in prayer: see the note on 3, 21.

6, 13: He chose Twelve: the identification of this group as

the **Twelve** is a part of early Christian tradition (see 1 Cor 15, 5), and in Mt and Lk, the Twelve are associated with the twelve tribes of Israel (22, 29–30; Mt 19, 28). After the fall of Judas from his position among the Twelve, the need is felt on the part of the early community to reconstitute this group before the Christian mission begins at Pentecost (Acts 1, 15–26). From Luke's perspective, they are an important group who because of their association with Jesus from the time of his baptism to his ascension (Acts 1, 21–22) provide the continuity between the historical Jesus and the church of Luke's day and who as the original eyewitnesses guarantee the fidelity of the church's beliefs and practices to the teachings of Jesus (1, 1–4). **Whom he also named apostles:** only Luke among the gospel writers attributes to Jesus the bestowal of the name apostles upon the Twelve. See the note on

b: 15, 1-2. *c:* Mt 9, 14-17; Mk 2, 18-22. *d:* Mt 12, 1-8; Mk 2, 23-28. *e:* Dt 23, 26. *f:* 1 Sm 21, 1-6. *g:* Lv 24, 5-9. *h:* Mt 12, 9-14; Mk 3, 1-6. *i:* 14, 1. *j:* 5, 22; 9, 47. *k:* Mt 10, 1-4; Mk 3, 13-19.

whom he also named apostles: [14]*Simon, whom he named Peter, and his brother Andrew, James, John, Philip, Bartholomew, [15]*Matthew, Thomas, James the son of Alphaeus, Simon who was called a Zealot, [16]*and Judas the son of James, and Judas Iscariot, who became a traitor.

Ministering to a Great Multitude. [17m]*And he came down with them and stood on a stretch of level ground. A great crowd of his disciples and a large number of the people from all Judea and Jerusalem and the coastal region of Tyre and Sidon [18]came to hear him and to be healed of their diseases; and even those who were tormented by unclean spirits were cured. [19]Everyone in the crowd sought to touch him because power came forth from him and healed them all.

Sermon on the Plain. [20n]*And raising his eyes toward his disciples he said:

"Blessed are you who are poor,
for the kingdom of God is yours.
[21] oBlessed are you who are now hungry,
for you will be satisfied.

Blessed are you who are now weeping,
for you will laugh.
[22] pBlessed are you when people hate you,
and when they exclude and insult you,
and denounce your name as evil
on account of the Son of Man.

[23q]Rejoice and leap for joy on that day! Behold, your reward will be great in heaven. For their ancestors treated the prophets in the same way.

[24] rBut woe to you who are rich,
for you have received your
consolation.
[25] sBut woe to you who are filled now,
for you will be hungry.
Woe to you who laugh now,
for you will grieve and weep.
[26] tWoe to you when all speak well of you,
for their ancestors treated the false
prophets in this way.

Love of Enemies. [27uv]*"But to you who hear I say, love your enemies, do good to those who hate you, [28w]bless those who curse you, pray for those who mistreat you.

Mt 10, 2–4. "Apostle" becomes a technical term in early Christianity for a missionary sent out to preach the word of God. Although Luke seems to want to restrict the title to the Twelve (only in Acts 4, 4.14 are Paul and Barnabas termed apostles), other places in the New Testament show an awareness that the term was more widely applied (1 Cor 15, 5–7; Gal 1, 19; 1 Cor 1, 1; 9, 1; Rom 16, 7).

6, 14: Simon, whom he named Peter: see the note on Mk 3, 16.

6, 15: Simon who was called a Zealot: the Zealots were the instigators of the First Revolt of Palestinian Jews against Rome in A.D. 66–70. Because the existence of the Zealots as a distinct group during the lifetime of Jesus is the subject of debate, the meaning of the identification of Simon as a Zealot is unclear.

6, 16: Judas Iscariot: the name **Iscariot** may mean "man from Kerioth."

6, 17: The coastal region of Tyre and Sidon: not only Jews from Judea and Jerusalem, but even Gentiles from outside Palestine come to hear Jesus (see 2, 31–32; 3, 6; 4, 24–27).

6, 20–49: Luke's "Sermon on the Plain" is the counterpart to Mt's "Sermon on the Mount" (Mt 5, 1—7, 27). It is addressed to the disciples of Jesus, and, like the sermon in Mt, it begins with beatitudes (20–22) and ends with the parable of the two houses (46–49). Almost all the words of Jesus reported by Lk are found in Mt's version, but because Mt includes sayings that were related to specifically Jewish Christian problems (e.g., Mt 5, 17–20; 6, 1–8.16–18) that Luke did not find appropriate for his predominantly Gentile Christian audience, the "Sermon on the Mount" is considerably longer. Lk's sermon may be outlined as follows: an introduction con-

sisting of blessings and woes (20–26); the love of one's enemies (27–36); the demands of loving one's neighbor (37–42); good deeds as proof of one's goodness (43–45); a parable illustrating the result of listening to and acting on the words of Jesus (46–49). At the core of the sermon is Jesus' teaching on the love of one's enemies (27–36) that has as its source of motivation God's graciousness and compassion for all humanity (35–36) and Jesus' teaching on the love of one's neighbor (37–42) that is characterized by forgiveness and generosity.

6, 20–26: The introductory portion of the sermon consists of blessings and woes that address the real economic and social conditions of humanity (the poor—the rich; the hungry—the satisfied; those grieving—those laughing; the outcast—the socially acceptable). By contrast, Matthew emphasizes the religious and spiritual values of disciples in the kingdom inaugurated by Jesus ("poor in spirit," 5, 5; "hunger and thirst for righteousness" 5, 6). In the sermon, **blessed** extols the fortunate condition of persons who are favored with the blessings of God; the woes, addressed as they are to the disciples of Jesus, threaten God's profound displeasure on those so blinded by their present fortunate situation that they do not recognize and appreciate the real values of God's kingdom. In all the blessings and woes, the present condition of the persons addressed will be reversed in the future.

6, 27–36: See the notes on Mt 5, 43–48 and 5, 48.

l: Acts 1, 13.   m: Mt 4, 23–25; Mk 3, 7–10.   n: Mt 5, 1–12. o: Ps 126, 5–6; Is 61, 3; Jer 31, 25; Rv 7, 16–17.   p: Jn 15, 19; 16, 2; 1 Pt 4, 14.   q: 11, 47–48; 2 Chr 36, 16; Mt 23, 30–31.   r: Jas 5, 1.   s: Is 65, 13–14.   t: Jas 4, 4.   u: Mt 5, 38–48.   v: Prv 25, 21; Rom 12, 20–21.   w: Rom 12, 14; 1 Pt 3, 9.

²⁹To the person who strikes you on one cheek, offer the other one as well, and from the person who takes your cloak, do not withhold even your tunic. ³⁰Give to everyone who asks of you, and from the one who takes what is yours do not demand it back. ³¹ˣDo to others as you would have them do to you. ³²For if you love those who love you, what credit is that to you? Even sinners love those who love them. ³³And if you do good to those who do good to you, what credit is that to you? Even sinners do the same. ³⁴ʸIf you lend money to those from whom you expect repayment, what credit [is] that to you? Even sinners lend to sinners, and get back the same amount. ³⁵ᶻBut rather, love your enemies and do good to them, and lend expecting nothing back; then your reward will be great and you will be children of the Most High, for he himself is kind to the ungrateful and the wicked. ³⁶Be merciful, just as [also] your Father is merciful.

Judging Others. ³⁷ᵃᵇ*"Stop judging and you will not be judged. Stop condemning and you will not be condemned. Forgive and you will be forgiven. ³⁸ᶜGive and gifts will be given to you; a good measure, packed together, shaken down, and overflowing, will be poured into your lap. For the measure with which you measure will in return be measured out to you." ³⁹ᵈAnd he told them a parable, "Can a blind person guide a blind person? Will not both fall into a pit? ⁴⁰ᵉNo disciple is superior to the teacher; but when fully trained, every disciple will be like his teacher. ⁴¹Why do you notice the splinter in your brother's eye, but do not perceive the wooden beam in your own? ⁴²How can you say to your brother, 'Brother, let me remove that splinter in your

eye,' when you do not even notice the wooden beam in your own eye? You hypocrite! Remove the wooden beam from your eye first; then you will see clearly to remove the splinter in your brother's eye.

A Tree Known by Its Fruit. ⁴³ᶠ*"A good tree does not bear rotten fruit, nor does a rotten tree bear good fruit. ⁴⁴For every tree is known by its own fruit. For people do not pick figs from thornbushes, nor do they gather grapes from brambles. ⁴⁵A good person out of the store of goodness in his heart produces good, but an evil person out of a store of evil produces evil; for from the fullness of the heart the mouth speaks.

The Two Foundations. ⁴⁶ᵍ"Why do you call me, 'Lord, Lord,' but not do what I command? ⁴⁷ʰ*I will show you what someone is like who comes to me, listens to my words, and acts on them. ⁴⁸That one is like a person building a house, who dug deeply and laid the foundation on rock; when the flood came, the river burst against that house but could not shake it because it had been well built. ⁴⁹But the one who listens and does not act is like a person who built a house on the ground without a foundation. When the river burst against it, it collapsed at once and was completely destroyed."

CHAPTER 7

See RG 311-12

The Healing of a Centurion's Slave. ¹ⁱ*When he had finished all his words to the people, he entered Capernaum. ²*A centurion there had a slave who was ill and about to die, and he was valuable to him. ³When he heard about Jesus, he sent elders of the Jews to him, asking him to come and save the life of his slave. ⁴They approached Jesus and

6, 37–42: See the notes on Mt 7, 1–12; 7, 1; 7, 5.

6, 43–46: See the notes on Mt 7, 15–20 and 12, 33.

6, 47–49: See the note on Mt 7, 24–27.

7, 1—8, 3: The episodes in this section present a series of reactions to the Galilean ministry of Jesus and reflect some of Luke's particular interests: the faith of a Gentile (1–10); the prophet Jesus' concern for a widowed mother (11–17); the ministry of Jesus directed to the afflicted and unfortunate of Is 61, 1 (18–23); the relation between John and Jesus and their role in God's plan for salvation (24–35); a forgiven sinner's manifestation of love (36–50); the association of women with the ministry of Jesus (8, 1–3).

7, 1–10: This story about the faith of the centurion, a Gentile who cherishes the Jewish nation (5), prepares for the story

in Acts of the conversion by Peter of the Roman centurion Cornelius who is similarly described as one who is generous to the Jewish nation (Acts 10, 2). See also Acts 10, 34–35 in the speech of Peter: "God shows no partiality . . . the person who fears him and acts righteously is acceptable to him." See also the notes on Mt 8, 5–13 and Jn 4, 43–54.

7, 2: A centurion: see the note on Mt 8, 5.

x: Mt 7, 12. y: Dt 15, 7-8. z: Lv 25, 35-36. a: Mt 7, 1-5. b: Mt 6, 14; Jas 2, 13. c: Mk 4, 24. d: Mt 15, 14; 23, 16-17.24. e: Mt 10, 24-25; Jn 13, 16; 15, 20. f: Mt 7, 16-20; 12, 33.35. g: Mt 7, 21; Rom 2, 13; Jas 1, 22. h: Mt 7, 24-27. i: Mt 8, 5-13; Jn 4, 43-54.

strongly urged him to come, saying, "He deserves to have you do this for him, [5]for he loves our nation and he built the synagogue for us." [6]*And Jesus went with them, but when he was only a short distance from the house, the centurion sent friends to tell him, "Lord, do not trouble yourself, for I am not worthy to have you enter under my roof. [7]Therefore, I did not consider myself worthy to come to you; but say the word and let my servant be healed. [8]For I too am a person subject to authority, with soldiers subject to me. And I say to one, 'Go,' and he goes; and to another, 'Come here,' and he comes; and to my slave, 'Do this,' and he does it." [9]When Jesus heard this he was amazed at him and, turning, said to the crowd following him, "I tell you, not even in Israel have I found such faith." [10]When the messengers returned to the house, they found the slave in good health.

Raising of the Widow's Son. [11j]*Soon afterward he journeyed to a city called Nain, and his disciples and a large crowd accompanied him. [12k]As he drew near to the gate of the city, a man who had died was being carried out, the only son of his mother, and she was a widow. A large crowd from the city was with her. [13]When the Lord saw her, he was moved with pity for her and said to her, "Do not weep." [14]He stepped forward and touched the coffin; at this the bearers halted, and he said, "Young man, I tell you, arise!" [15l]The dead man sat up and began to speak, and Jesus gave him to his mother. [16m]Fear seized them all, and they glorified God, ex-

claiming, "A great prophet has arisen in our midst," and "God has visited his people." [17]This report about him spread through the whole of Judea and in all the surrounding region.

The Messengers from John the Baptist. [18n]*The disciples of John told him about all these things. John summoned two of his disciples [19o]and sent them to the Lord to ask, "Are you the one who is to come, or should we look for another?" [20]When the men came to him, they said, "John the Baptist has sent us to you to ask, 'Are you the one who is to come, or should we look for another?'" [21]At that time he cured many of their diseases, sufferings, and evil spirits; he also granted sight to many who were blind. [22p]And he said to them in reply, "Go and tell John what you have seen and heard: the blind regain their sight, the lame walk, lepers are cleansed, the deaf hear, the dead are raised, the poor have the good news proclaimed to them. [23]*And blessed is the one who takes no offense at me."

Jesus' Testimony to John. [24q]*When the messengers of John had left, Jesus began to speak to the crowds about John. "What did you go out to the desert to see—a reed swayed by the wind? [25]Then what did you go out to see? Someone dressed in fine garments? Those who dress luxuriously and live sumptuously are found in royal palaces. [26r]Then what did you go out to see? A prophet? Yes, I tell you, and more than a prophet. [27s]This is the one about whom scripture says:

7, 6: **I am not worthy to have you enter under my roof:** to enter the house of a Gentile was considered unclean for a Jew; cf Acts 10, 28.

7, 11–17: In the previous incident Jesus' power was displayed for a Gentile whose servant was dying; in this episode it is displayed toward a widowed mother whose only son has already died. Jesus' power over death prepares for his reply to John's disciples in v 22: "the dead are raised." This resuscitation in alluding to the prophet Elijah's resurrection of the only son of a widow of Zarephath (1 Kgs 7, 18–24) leads to the reaction of the crowd: "A great prophet has arisen in our midst" (16).

7, 18–23: In answer to John's question, **Are you the one who is to come?**—a probable reference to the return of the fiery prophet of reform, Elijah, "before the day of the Lord comes, the great and terrible day" (Mal 3, 23)—Jesus responds that his role is rather to bring the blessings spoken of in Is 61,

to the oppressed and neglected of society (22; cf 4, 18).

7, 23: **Blessed is the one who takes no offense at me:** this beatitude is pronounced on the person who recognizes Jesus' true identity in spite of previous expectations of what "the one who is to come" would be like.

7, 24–30: In his testimony to John, Jesus reveals his understanding of the relationship between them: John is the precursor of Jesus (27); John is the messenger spoken of in Mal 3, 1 who in Mal 3, 23 is identified as Elijah. Taken with the previous episode, it can be seen that Jesus identifies John as precisely the person John envisioned Jesus to be: the Elijah who prepares the way for the coming of the day of the Lord.

j: 4, 25-26; 1 Kgs 17, 17-24. k: 8, 42; 1 Kgs 17, 17. l: 2 Kgs 17, 23; 2 Kgs 4, 36. m: 1, 68; 19, 44. n: Mt 11, 2-6. o: Mal 3, 1; Rv 1, 4.8; 4, 8. p: 4, 18; Is 35, 5-6; 61, 1. q: Mt 11, 7-15. r: 1, 76. s: Mal 3, 1 / Is 40, 3.

'Behold, I am sending my messenger
ahead of you,
he will prepare your way before you.'

[28]I tell you, among those born of women, no one is greater than John; yet the least in the kingdom of God is greater than he." [29]t(All the people who listened, including the tax collectors, and who were baptized with the baptism of John, acknowledged the righteousness of God; [30]but the Pharisees and scholars of the law, who were not baptized by him, rejected the plan of God for themselves.) [31]u*"Then to what shall I compare the people of this generation? What are they like? [32]They are like children who sit in the marketplace and call to one another,

'We played the flute for you, but you did
not dance.
We sang a dirge, but you did not
weep.'

[33]For John the Baptist came neither eating food nor drinking wine, and you said, 'He is possessed by a demon.' [34]vThe Son of Man came eating and drinking and you said, 'Look, he is a glutton and a drunkard, a friend of tax collectors and sinners.' [35]But wisdom is vindicated by all her children."

The Pardon of the Sinful Woman. [36]w*A Pharisee invited him to dine with him, and he entered the Pharisee's house and reclined at table. [37]x yNow there was a sinful woman in the city who learned that he was at table in the house of the Pharisee. Bringing an alabaster flask of ointment, [38]she stood behind him at his feet weeping and began to bathe his feet with her tears. Then she wiped them with her hair, kissed them, and anointed them with the ointment. [39]When the Pharisee who had invited him saw this he said to himself, "If this man were a prophet, he would know who and what sort of woman this is who is touching him, that she is a sinner." [40]Jesus said to him in reply, "Simon, I have something to say to you." "Tell me, teacher," he said. [41]*"Two people were in debt to a certain creditor; one owed five hundred days' wages and the other owed fifty. [42]Since they were unable to repay the debt, he forgave it for both. Which of them will love him more?" [43]Simon said in reply, "The one, I suppose, whose larger debt was forgiven." He said to him, "You have judged rightly." [44]Then he turned to the woman and said to Simon, "Do you see this woman? When I entered your house, you did not give me water for my feet, but she has bathed them with her tears and wiped them with her hair. [45]You did not give me a kiss, but she has not ceased kissing my feet since the time I entered. [46]You did not anoint my head with oil, but she anointed my feet with ointment. [47]*So I tell you, her many sins have been forgiven; hence, she has shown great love. But the one to whom little is forgiven, loves little." [48]zHe said to her, "Your sins are forgiven." [49]aThe others at table said to themselves, "Who is this who even forgives sins?" [50]But he said to the woman, "Your faith has saved you; go in peace."

7, 31–35: See the note on Mt 11, 16–19.

7, 36–50: In this story of the pardoning of the sinful woman Luke presents two different reactions to the ministry of Jesus. A Pharisee, suspecting Jesus to be a prophet, invites Jesus to a festive banquet in his house, but the Pharisee's self-righteousness leads to little forgiveness by God and consequently little love shown toward Jesus. The sinful woman, on the other hand, manifests a faith in God (50) that has led her to seek forgiveness for her sins, and because so much was forgiven, she now overwhelms Jesus with her display of love; cf the similar contrast in attitudes in 18, 9–14. The whole episode is a powerful lesson on the relation between forgiveness and love.

7, 36: **Reclined at table:** the normal posture of guests at a banquet. Other oriental banquet customs alluded to in this story include the reception by the host with a kiss (45), washing the feet of the guests (44), and the anointing of the guests' heads (46).

7, 41: **Days' wages:** one denarius is the normal daily wage of a laborer.

7, 47: **Her many sins have been forgiven; hence, she has shown great love:** literally, "her many sins have been forgiven, seeing that she has loved much." That the woman's sins have been forgiven is attested by the great love she shows toward Jesus. Her love is the consequence of her forgiveness. This is also the meaning demanded by the parable in vv 41–43.

t: 3, 7.12; Mt 21, 32.   u: Mt 11, 16–19.   v: 15, 2.   w: 11, 37; 14, 1.   x: Mt 26, 7; Mk 14, 3.   y: Jn 12, 3.   z: 5, 20; Mt 9, 20; Mk 2, 5.   a: 5, 21.

See RG
311–12

CHAPTER 8

Galilean Women Follow Jesus.
¹ᵇ*Afterward he journeyed from one town and village to another, preaching and proclaiming the good news of the kingdom of God. Accompanying him were the Twelve ²ᶜand some women who had been cured of evil spirits and infirmities, Mary, called Magdalene, from whom seven demons had gone out, ³Joanna, the wife of Herod's steward Chuza, Susanna, and many others who provided for them out of their resources.

The Parable of the Sower. ⁴ᵈ*When a large crowd gathered, with people from one town after another journeying to him, he spoke in a parable. ⁵"A sower went out to sow his seed. And as he sowed, some seed fell on the path and was trampled, and the birds of the sky ate it up. ⁶Some seed fell on rocky ground, and when it grew, it withered for lack of moisture. ⁷Some seed fell among thorns, and the thorns grew with it and choked it. ⁸ᵉAnd some seed fell on good soil, and when it grew, it produced fruit a hundredfold." After saying this, he called out, "Whoever has ears to hear ought to hear."

The Purpose of the Parables. ⁹ᶠThen his disciples asked him what the meaning of this parable might be. ¹⁰ᵍHe answered, "Knowledge of the mysteries of the kingdom of God has been granted to you; but to the rest, they are made known through parables so that 'they may look but not see, and hear but not understand.'

The Parable of the Sower Explained. ¹¹ʰⁱ*"This is the meaning of the parable. The seed is the word of God. ¹²Those on the path are the ones who have heard, but the devil comes and takes away the word from their hearts that they may not believe and be saved. ¹³Those on rocky ground are the ones who, when they hear, receive the word with joy, but they have no root; they believe only for a time and fall away in time of trial. ¹⁴As for the seed that fell among thorns, they are the ones who have heard, but as they go along, they are choked by the anxieties and riches and pleasures of life, and they fail to produce mature fruit. ¹⁵But as for the seed that fell on rich soil, they are the ones who, when they have heard the word, embrace it with a generous and good heart, and bear fruit through perseverance.

The Parable of the Lamp. ¹⁶ʲᵏ*"No one who lights a lamp conceals it with a vessel or sets it under a bed; rather, he places it on a lampstand so that those who enter may see the light. ¹⁷ˡFor there is nothing hidden that will not become visible, and nothing secret that will not be known and come to light. ¹⁸ᵐTake care, then, how you hear. To anyone who has, more will be given, and from the one who has not, even what he seems to have will be taken away."

Jesus and His Family. ¹⁹ⁿ*Then his mother and his brothers came to him but were unable to join him because of the crowd. ²⁰ᵒHe was told, "Your mother and your brothers are standing outside and they

8, 1–3: Luke presents Jesus as an itinerant preacher traveling in the company of the Twelve and of the Galilean women who are sustaining them out of their means. These Galilean women will later accompany Jesus on his journey to Jerusalem and become witnesses to his death (23, 49) and resurrection (24, 9–11, where Mary Magdalene and Joanna are specifically mentioned; cf also Acts 1, 14). The association of women with the ministry of Jesus is most unusual in the light of the attitude of first-century Palestinian Judaism toward women. The more common attitude is expressed in Jn 4, 27, and early rabbinic documents caution against speaking with women in public.

8, 4–21: The focus in this section is on how one should hear the word of God and act on it. It includes the parable of the sower and its explanation (4–15), a collection of sayings on how one should act on the word that is heard (16–18), and the identification of the mother and brothers of Jesus as the ones who hear the word and act on it (19–

21). See also the notes on Mt 13, 1–53 and Mk 4, 1–34.

8, 4–8: See the note on Mt 13, 3–8.

8, 11–15: On the interpretation of the parable of the sower, see the note on Mt 13, 18–23.

8, 16–18: These sayings continue the theme of responding to the word of God. Those who hear the word must become a light to others (16); even the mysteries of the kingdom that have been made known to the disciples (9–10) must come to light (17); a generous and persevering response to the word of God leads to a still more perfect response to the word.

8, 19: His brothers: see the note on Mk 6, 3.

b: 4, 43.   c: 23, 49; 24, 10; Mt 27, 55-56; Mk 15, 40-41; Jn 19, 5.
d: Mt 13, 1-9; Mk 4, 1-9.   e: 14, 35; Mt 11, 15; 13, 43; Mk 4, 23.
f: Mt 13, 10-13; Mk 4, 10-12.   g: Is 6, 9.   h: Mt 13, 18-23; Mk 4, 13-20.   i: 1 Pt 1, 23.   j: Mk 4, 21-25.   k: 11, 33; Mt 5, 15.
l: 12, 2; Mt 10, 26.   m: 19, 26; Mt 13, 12; 25, 29.   n: Mt 12, 46-50; Mk 3, 31-35.   o: 11, 27-28.

wish to see you." [21]*He said to them in reply, "My mother and my brothers are those who hear the word of God and act on it."

The Calming of a Storm at Sea. [22]p*One day he got into a boat with his disciples and said to them, "Let us cross to the other side of the lake." So they set sail, [23]and while they were sailing he fell asleep. A squall blew over the lake, and they were taking in water and were in danger. [24]They came and woke him saying, "Master, master, we are perishing!" He awakened, rebuked the wind and the waves, and they subsided and there was a calm. [25]Then he asked them, "Where is your faith?" But they were filled with awe and amazed and said to one another, "Who then is this, who commands even the winds and the sea, and they obey him?"

The Healing of the Gerasene Demoniac. [26]q*Then they sailed to the territory of the Gerasenes, which is opposite Galilee. [27]When he came ashore a man from the town who was possessed by demons met him. For a long time he had not worn clothes; he did not live in a house, but lived among the tombs. [28]r When he saw Jesus, he cried out and fell down before him; in a loud voice he shouted, "What have you to do with me, Jesus, son of the Most High God? I beg you, do not torment me!" [29]For he had ordered the unclean spirit to come out of the man. (It had taken hold of him many times, and he used to be bound with chains and shackles as a restraint, but he would break his bonds and

be driven by the demon into deserted places.) [30]*Then Jesus asked him, "What is your name?" He replied, "Legion," because many demons had entered him. [31]*And they pleaded with him not to order them to depart to the abyss.

[32]A herd of many swine was feeding there on the hillside, and they pleaded with him to allow them to enter those swine; and he let them. [33]The demons came out of the man and entered the swine, and the herd rushed down the steep bank into the lake and was drowned. [34]When the swineherds saw what had happened, they ran away and reported the incident in the town and throughout the countryside. [35]*People came out to see what had happened and, when they approached Jesus, they discovered the man from whom the demons had come out sitting at his feet. He was clothed and in his right mind, and they were seized with fear. [36]Those who witnessed it told them how the possessed man had been saved. [37]The entire population of the region of the Gerasenes asked Jesus to leave them because they were seized with great fear. So he got into a boat and returned. [38]The man from whom the demons had come out begged to remain with him, but he sent him away, saying, [39]"Return home and recount what God has done for you." The man went off and proclaimed throughout the whole town what Jesus had done for him.

Jairus's Daughter and the Woman with a Hemorrhage. [40]s*When Jesus returned, the

---

8, 21: The family of Jesus is not constituted by physical relationship with him but by obedience to the word of God. In this, Luke agrees with the Marcan parallel (3, 31–35), although by omitting Mk 3, 33 and especially Mk 3, 20–21 Luke has softened the Marcan picture of Jesus' natural family. Probably he did this because Mary has already been presented in 1, 38 as the obedient handmaid of the Lord who fulfills the requirement for belonging to the eschatological family of Jesus; cf also 11, 27–28.

8, 22–56: This section records four miracles of Jesus that manifest his power and authority: (1) the calming of a storm on the lake (22–25); (2) the exorcism of a demoniac (26–39); (3) the cure of a hemorrhaging woman (40–48); (4) the raising of Jairus's daughter to life (49–56). They parallel the same sequence of stories at Mk 4, 35–5, 43.

8, 26: Gerasenes: other manuscripts read Gadarenes or Gergesenes. See also the note on Mt 8, 28. **Opposite Galilee:** probably Gentile territory (note the presence in the area of pigs—unclean animals to Jews) and an indication that the person who receives salvation (36) is a Gentile.

8, 30: What is your name?: the question reflects the popular belief that knowledge of the spirit's name brought control over the spirit. **Legion:** to Jesus' question the demon replies with a Latin word transliterated into Greek. The Roman legion at this period consisted of 5,000 to 6,000 foot soldiers; hence the name implies a very large number of demons.

8, 31: Abyss: the place of the dead (Rom 10, 7) or the prison of Satan (Rv 20, 3) or the subterranean "watery deep" that symbolizes the chaos before the order imposed by creation (Gn 1, 2).

8, 35: Sitting at his feet: the former demoniac takes the position of a disciple before the master (10, 39; Acts 22, 3).

8, 40–56: Two interwoven miracle stories, one a healing and the other a resuscitation, present Jesus as master over sickness and death. In the Lucan account, faith in Jesus is responsible for the cure (48) and for the raising to life (50).

p: Mt 8, 18.23-27; Mk 4, 35-41.   q: Mt 8, 28-34; Mk 5, 1-20.
r: 4, 33-35; Mt 8, 29; Mk 1, 23-24.   s: Mt 9, 18-26; Mk 5, 21-43.

crowd welcomed him, for they were all waiting for him. *41*And a man named Jairus, an official of the synagogue, came forward. He fell at the feet of Jesus and begged him to come to his house, *42**because he had an only daughter, about twelve years old, and she was dying. As he went, the crowds almost crushed him. *43**And a woman afflicted with hemorrhages for twelve years, who [had spent her whole livelihood on doctors and] was unable to be cured by anyone, *44*came up behind him and touched the tassel on his cloak. Immediately her bleeding stopped. *45*Jesus then asked, "Who touched me?" While all were denying it, Peter said, "Master, the crowds are pushing and pressing in upon you." *46t*But Jesus said, "Someone has touched me; for I know that power has gone out from me." *47*When the woman realized that she had not escaped notice, she came forward trembling. Falling down before him, she explained in the presence of all the people why she had touched him and how she had been healed immediately. *48u*He said to her, "Daughter, your faith has saved you; go in peace."

*49*While he was still speaking, someone from the synagogue official's house arrived and said, "Your daughter is dead; do not trouble the teacher any longer." *50*On hearing this, Jesus answered him, "Do not be afraid; just have faith and she will be saved." *51*When he arrived at the house he allowed no one to enter with him except Peter and John and James, and the child's father and mother. *52v*All were weeping and mourning for her, when he said, "Do not weep any longer, for she is not dead, but sleeping." *53*And they ridiculed him, because they knew that she was dead. *54*But he took her by the hand and called to her, "Child, arise!" *55*Her breath returned and she immediately arose. He then directed that she should be given something to eat. *56*Her parents were astounded, and he instructed them to tell no one what had happened.

CHAPTER 9

The Mission of the Twelve. *1w**He summoned the Twelve and gave them power and authority over all demons and to cure diseases, *2*and he sent them to proclaim the kingdom of God and to heal [the sick]. *3**He said to them, "Take nothing for the journey, neither walking stick, nor sack, nor food, nor money, and let no one take a second tunic. *4x*Whatever house you enter, stay there and leave from there. *5y**And as for those who do not welcome you, when you leave that town, shake the dust from your feet in testimony against them." *6*Then they set out and went from village to village proclaiming the good news and curing diseases everywhere.

Herod's Opinion of Jesus. *7za**Herod the tetrarch heard about all that was happening, and he was greatly perplexed because some were saying, "John has been raised from the dead"; *8*others were saying, "Elijah has appeared"; still others, "One of the ancient prophets has arisen." *9b**But Herod said,

---

8, 42: An only daughter: cf the son of the widow of Nain whom Luke describes as an "only" son (7, 12; see also 9, 38).

8, 43: Afflicted with hemorrhages for twelve years: according to the Mosaic law (Lv 15, 25–30) this condition would render the woman unclean and unfit for contact with other people.

8, 52: Sleeping: her death is a temporary condition; cf Jn 11, 11–14.

9, 1–6: Armed with the power and authority that Jesus himself has been displaying in the previous episodes, the Twelve are now sent out to continue the work that Jesus has been performing throughout his Galilean ministry: (1) proclaiming the kingdom (4, 43; 8, 1); (2) exorcising demons (4, 33–37.41; 8, 26–39) and (3) healing the sick (4, 38–40; 5, 12–16.17–26; 6, 6–10; 7, 1–10.17.22; 8, 40–56).

9, 3: Take nothing for the journey: the absolute detachment required of the disciple (14, 33) leads to complete reliance on God (12, 22–31).

9, 5: Shake the dust from your feet: see the note on Mt 10, 14.

9, 7–56: This section in which Luke gathers together incidents that focus on the identity of Jesus is introduced by a question that Herod is made to ask in this gospel: "Who then is this about whom I hear such things?" (9). In subsequent episodes, Luke reveals to the reader various answers to Herod's question: Jesus is one in whom God's power is present and who provides for the needs of God's people (10–17); Peter declares Jesus to be "the Messiah of God" (18–21); Jesus says he is the suffering Son of Man (22.43–45); Jesus is the Master to be followed, even to death (23–27); Jesus is God's Son, his Chosen One (28–36).

9, 7: Herod the tetrarch: see the note on 3, 1.

9, 9: And he kept trying to see him: this indication of Herod's interest in Jesus prepares for 13, 31–33 and for 23, 8–12 where Herod's curiosity about Jesus' power to perform miracles remains unsatisfied.

---

t: 6, 19.   *u:* 7, 50; 17, 19; 18, 42.   *v:* 7, 13.   *w:* Mt 10, 1.5–15; Mk 6, 7–13.   *x:* 10, 5–7.   *y:* 10, 10–11; Acts 13, 51.   *z:* Mt 14, 1–12; Mk 6, 14–29.   *a:* 9, 19; Mt 16, 14; Mk 8, 28.   *b:* 23, 8.

"John I beheaded. Who then is this about whom I hear such things?" And he kept trying to see him.

The Return of the Twelve and the Feeding of the Five Thousand. *10c*When the apostles returned, they explained to him what they had done. He took them and withdrew in private to a town called Bethsaida. *11*The crowds, meanwhile, learned of this and followed him. He received them and spoke to them about the kingdom of God, and he healed those who needed to be cured. *12*As the day was drawing to a close, the Twelve approached him and said, "Dismiss the crowd so that they can go to the surrounding villages and farms and find lodging and provisions; for we are in a deserted place here." *13d*He said to them, "Give them some food yourselves." They replied, "Five loaves and two fish are all we have, unless we ourselves go and buy food for all these people." *14*Now the men there numbered about five thousand. Then he said to his disciples, "Have them sit down in groups of [about] fifty." *15*They did so and made them all sit down. *16e**Then taking the five loaves and the two fish, and looking up to heaven, he said the blessing over them, broke them, and gave them to the disciples to set before the crowd. *17*They all ate and were satisfied. And when the leftover fragments were picked up, they filled twelve wicker baskets.

Peter's Confession about Jesus. *18f**Once when Jesus was praying in solitude, and the disciples were with him, he asked them,

"Who do the crowds say that I am?" *19g*They said in reply, "John the Baptist; others, Elijah; still others, 'One of the ancient prophets has arisen.' " *20**Then he said to them, "But who do you say that I am?" Peter said in reply, "The Messiah of God." *21*He rebuked them and directed them not to tell this to anyone.

The First Prediction of the Passion. *22h*He said, "The Son of Man must suffer greatly and be rejected by the elders, the chief priests, and the scribes, and be killed and on the third day be raised."

The Conditions of Discipleship. *23i j**Then he said to all, "If anyone wishes to come after me, he must deny himself and take up his cross daily and follow me. *24k*For whoever wishes to save his life will lose it, but whoever loses his life for my sake will save it. *25*What profit is there for one to gain the whole world yet lose or forfeit himself? *26l*Whoever is ashamed of me and of my words, the Son of Man will be ashamed of when he comes in his glory and in the glory of the Father and of the holy angels. *27*Truly I say to you, there are some standing here who will not taste death until they see the kingdom of God."

The Transfiguration of Jesus. *28m**About eight days after he said this, he took Peter, John, and James and went up the mountain to pray. *29*While he was praying his face changed in appearance and his clothing became dazzling white. *30**And behold, two men were conversing with him, Moses and

---

9, 16: Then taking . . . : the actions of Jesus recall the institution of the Eucharist in 22, 19; see also the note on Mt 14, 19.

9, 18–22: This incident is based on Mk 8, 27–33, but Luke has eliminated Peter's refusal to accept Jesus as suffering Son of Man (Mk 8, 32) and the rebuke of Peter by Jesus (Mk 8, 33). Elsewhere in the gospel, Luke softens the harsh portrait of Peter and the other apostles found in his Marcan source (cf 22, 39–46, which similarly lacks a rebuke of Peter that occurs in the source, Mk 14, 37–38).

9, 18: When Jesus was praying in solitude: see the note on 3, 21.

9, 20: The Messiah of God: on the meaning of this title in first-century Palestinian Judaism, see the notes on 2, 11 and on Mt 16, 13–20 and Mk 8, 27–30.

9, 23: Daily: this is a Lucan addition to a saying of Jesus, removing the saying from a context that envisioned the imminent suffering and death of the disciple of Jesus (as does the saying in Mk 8, 34–35) to one that focuses on the de-

mands of daily Christian existence.

9, 28–36: Situated shortly after the first announcement of the passion, death, and resurrection, this scene of Jesus' transfiguration provides the heavenly confirmation to Jesus' declaration that his suffering will end in glory (32); see also the notes on Mt 17, 1–8 and Mk 9, 2–8.

9, 28: Up the mountain to pray: the "mountain" is the regular place of prayer in Lk (see 6, 12; 22, 39–41).

9, 30: Moses and Elijah: the two figures represent the Old Testament law and the prophets. At the end of this episode, the heavenly voice will identify Jesus as the one to be listened to now (35). See also the note on Mk 9, 5.

c: Mt 14, 13-21; Mk 6, 30-44; Jn 6, 1-14. *d:* 2 Kgs 4, 42-44. *e:* 22, 19; 24, 30-31; Acts 2, 42; 20, 11; 27, 35. *f:* Mt 16, 13-20; Mk 8, 27-30. *g:* 9, 7-8. *h:* 24, 7.26; Mt 16, 21; 20, 18-19; Mk 8, 31; 10, 33-34. *i:* Mt 16, 24-28; Mk 8, 34—9, 1. *j:* 14, 27; Mt 10, 38. *k:* 17, 33; Mt 10, 39; Jn 12, 25. *l:* 12, 9; Mt 10, 33; 2 Tm 2, 12. *m:* Mt 17, 1-8; Mk 9, 2-8.

Elijah, [31n]*who appeared in glory and spoke of his exodus that he was going to accomplish in Jerusalem. [32o]*Peter and his companions had been overcome by sleep, but becoming fully awake, they saw his glory and the two men standing with him. [33]*As they were about to part from him, Peter said to Jesus, "Master, it is good that we are here; let us make three tents, one for you, one for Moses, and one for Elijah." But he did not know what he was saying. [34]*While he was still speaking, a cloud came and cast a shadow over them, and they became frightened when they entered the cloud. [35p]*Then from the cloud came a voice that said, "This is my chosen Son; listen to him." [36]*After the voice had spoken, Jesus was found alone. They fell silent and did not at that time tell anyone what they had seen.

The Healing of a Boy with a Demon. [37q]*On the next day, when they came down from the mountain, a large crowd met him. [38]There was a man in the crowd who cried out, "Teacher, I beg you, look at my son; he is my only child. [39]For a spirit seizes him and he suddenly screams and it convulses him until he foams at the mouth; it releases him only with difficulty, wearing him out. [40]I begged your disciples to cast it out but they could not." [41]Jesus said in reply, "O faithless and perverse generation, how long will I be with you and endure you? Bring your son here." [42]As he was coming forward, the demon threw him to the ground in a convulsion; but Jesus rebuked the unclean spirit, healed the boy, and returned him to his father. [43r]And all were astonished by the majesty of God.

The Second Prediction of the Passion. While they were all amazed at his every deed, he said to his disciples, [44]"Pay attention to what I am telling you. The Son of Man is to be handed over to men." [45]But they did not understand this saying; its meaning was hidden from them so that they should not understand it, and they were afraid to ask him about this saying.

The Greatest in the Kingdom. [46s1]*An argument arose among the disciples about which of them was the greatest. [47]Jesus realized the intention of their hearts and took a child and placed it by his side [48u]and said to them, "Whoever receives this child in my name receives me, and whoever receives me receives the one who sent me. For the one who is least among all of you is the one who is the greatest."

Another Exorcist. [49v]Then John said in reply, "Master, we saw someone casting out demons in your name and we tried to prevent him because he does not follow in our company." [50]Jesus said to him, "Do not prevent him, for whoever is not against you is for you."

V: The Journey to Jerusalem: Luke's Travel Narrative

Departure for Jerusalem; Samaritan Inhospitality. [51w]*When the days for his being taken

---

9, 31: His exodus that he was going to accomplish in Jerusalem: Luke identifies the subject of the conversation as the exodus of Jesus, a reference to the death, resurrection, and ascension of Jesus that will take place in Jerusalem, the city of destiny (see 9, 51). The mention of exodus, however, also calls to mind the Israelite Exodus from Egypt to the promised land.

9, 32: They saw his glory: the glory that is proper to God is here attributed to Jesus (see 24, 26).

9, 33: Let us make three tents: in a possible allusion to the feast of Tabernacles, Peter may be likening his joy on the occasion of the transfiguration to the joyful celebration of this harvest festival.

9, 34: Over them: it is not clear whether them refers to Jesus, Moses, and Elijah, or to the disciples. For the cloud casting its shadow, see the note on Mk 9, 7.

9, 35: Like the heavenly voice that identified Jesus at his baptism prior to his undertaking the Galilean ministry (3, 22), so too here before the journey to the city of destiny is begun

(51) the heavenly voice again identifies Jesus as Son. **Listen to him:** the two representatives of Israel of old depart (33) and Jesus is left alone (36) as the teacher whose words must be heeded (see also Acts 3, 22).

9, 36: At that time: i.e., before the resurrection.

9, 37–43a: See the note on Mk 9, 14–29.

9, 46–50: These two incidents focus on attitudes that are opposed to Christian discipleship: rivalry and intolerance of outsiders.

9, 51—18, 14: The Galilean ministry of Jesus finishes with the previous episode and a new section of Luke's gospel

n: 9, 22; 13, 33. o: Jn 1, 14; 2 Pt 1, 16. p: 3, 22; Dt 18, 15; Ps 2, 7; Is 42, 1; Mt 3, 17; 12, 18; Mk 1, 11; 2 Pt 1, 17-18. q: Mt 17, 14-18; Mk 9, 14-27. r: 18, 32-34; Mt 17, 22-23; Mk 9, 30-32. s: Mt 18, 1-5; Mk 9, 33-37. t: 22, 24. u: 10, 16; Mt 10, 40; Jn 13, 20. v: Mk 9, 38-40. w: 9, 53; 13, 22.33; 17, 11; 18, 31; 19, 28; 24, 51; Acts 1, 2.9-11.22.

up* were fulfilled, he resolutely determined to journey to Jerusalem, *52x*and he sent messengers ahead of him. On the way they entered a Samaritan village to prepare for his reception there, *53*but they would not welcome him because the destination of his journey was Jerusalem. *54y*When the disciples James and John saw this they asked, "Lord, do you want us to call down fire from heaven to consume them?" *55*Jesus turned and rebuked them, *56*and they journeyed to another village.

The Would-be Followers of Jesus. *57z*As they were proceeding on their journey someone said to him, "I will follow you wherever you go." *58*Jesus answered him, "Foxes have dens and birds of the sky have nests, but the Son of Man has nowhere to rest his head." *59*And to another he said, "Follow me." But he replied, "[Lord,] let me go first and bury my father." *60*But he answered him, "Let the dead bury their dead. But you, go and proclaim the kingdom of God." *61a*And another said, "I will follow you, Lord, but first let me say farewell to my family at home." *62*[To him] Jesus said, "No one who sets a hand to the plow and looks to what was left behind is fit for the kingdom of God."

CHAPTER 10

See RG 312–13

The Mission of the Seventy-two. *1b*After this the Lord appointed seventy [-two] others whom he sent ahead of him in pairs to every town and place he intended to visit. *2c*He said to them, "The harvest is abundant but the laborers are few; so ask the master of the harvest to send out laborers for his harvest. *3d*Go on your way; behold, I am sending you like lambs among wolves. *4ef*Carry no money bag, no sack, no sandals; and greet no one along the way. *5*Into whatever house you enter, first say, 'Peace to this household.' *6*If a peaceful person lives

---

begins, the journey to Jerusalem. This journey is based on Mk 10, 1–52, but Luke uses his Marcan source only in 18, 15—19, 27. Before that point he has inserted into his gospel a distinctive collection of sayings of Jesus and stories about him that he has drawn from Q, a collection of sayings of Jesus used also by Matthew, and from his own special traditions. All of the material collected in this section is loosely organized within the framework of a journey of Jesus to Jerusalem, the city of destiny, where his exodus (suffering, death, resurrection, ascension) is to take place (9, 31), where salvation is accomplished, and from where the proclamation of God's saving word is to go forth (24, 47; Acts 1, 8). Much of the material in the Lucan travel narrative is teaching for the disciples. During the course of this journey Jesus is preparing his chosen Galilean witnesses for the role they will play after his exodus (9, 31): they are to be his witnesses to the people (Acts 10, 39; 13, 31) and thereby provide certainty to the readers of Luke's gospel that the teachings they have received are rooted in the teachings of Jesus (1, 1–4).

9, 51–55: Just as the Galilean ministry began with a rejection of Jesus in his hometown, so too the travel narrative begins with the rejection of him by Samaritans. In this episode Jesus disassociates himself from the attitude expressed by his disciples that those who reject him are to be punished severely. The story alludes to 2 Kgs 1, 10.12, where the prophet Elijah takes the course of action Jesus rejects, and Jesus thereby rejects the identification of himself with Elijah.

9, 51: Days for his being taken up: like the reference to his exodus in v 31, this is probably a reference to all the events (suffering, death, resurrection, ascension) of his last days in Jerusalem. He resolutely determined: literally, "he set his face."

9, 52: Samaritan: Samaria was the territory between Judea and Galilee west of the Jordan river. For ethnic and religious reasons, the Samaritans and the Jews were bitterly opposed to one another (see Jn 4, 9).

9, 57–62: In these sayings Jesus speaks of the severity and

the unconditional nature of Christian discipleship. Even family ties and filial obligations, such as burying one's parents, cannot distract one no matter how briefly from proclaiming the kingdom of God. The first two sayings are paralleled in Mt 8, 19–22; see also the notes there.

9, 60: Let the dead bury their dead: i.e., let the spiritually dead (those who do not follow) bury their physically dead. See also the note on Mt 8, 22.

10, 1–12: Only the Gospel of Luke contains two episodes in which Jesus sends out his followers on a mission: the first (9, 1–6) is based on the mission in Mk 6, 6b-13 and recounts the sending out of the Twelve; here in vv 1–12 a similar report based on Q becomes the sending out of seventy-two in this gospel. The episode continues the theme of Jesus preparing witnesses to himself and his ministry. These witnesses include not only the Twelve but also the seventy-two who may represent the Christian mission in Luke's own day. Note that the instructions given to the Twelve and to the seventy-two are similar and that what is said to the seventy-two in v 4 is directed to the Twelve in 22, 35.

10, 1: Seventy[-two]: important representatives of the Alexandrian and Caesarean text types read "seventy," while other important Alexandrian texts and Western readings have "seventy-two."

10, 4: Carry no money bag . . . greet no one along the way: because of the urgency of the mission and the single-mindedness required of missionaries, attachment to material possessions should be avoided and even customary greetings should not distract from the fulfillment of the task.

10, 5: First say, 'Peace to this household': see the notes on 2, 14 and Mt 10, 13.

10, 6: A peaceful person: literally, "a son of peace."

---

x: Mal 3, 1. y: 2 Kgs 1, 10.12. z: Mt 8, 19-22. a: 1 Kgs 19, 20. b: Mk 6, 7. c: Mt 9, 37-38; Jn 4, 35. d: Mt 10, 16. e: 9, 3; 2 Kgs 4, 29. f: Mt 10, 7-14.

there, your peace will rest on him; but if not, it will return to you. [7g]Stay in the same house and eat and drink what is offered to you, for the laborer deserves his payment. Do not move about from one house to another. [8h]Whatever town you enter and they welcome you, eat what is set before you, [9i]cure the sick in it and say to them, 'The kingdom of God is at hand for you.' [10j]Whatever town you enter and they do not receive you, go out into the streets and say, [11k]'The dust of your town that clings to our feet, even that we shake off against you.' Yet know this: the kingdom of God is at hand. [12l]I tell you, it will be more tolerable for Sodom on that day than for that town.

Reproaches to Unrepentant Towns. [13mn]*"Woe to you, Chorazin! Woe to you, Bethsaida! For if the mighty deeds done in your midst had been done in Tyre and Sidon, they would long ago have repented, sitting in sackcloth and ashes. [14]But it will be more tolerable for Tyre and Sidon at the judgment than for you. [15o]*And as for you, Capernaum, 'Will you be exalted to heaven? You will go down to the netherworld.' " [16p]Whoever listens to you listens to me. Whoever rejects you rejects me. And whoever rejects me rejects the one who sent me."

Return of the Seventy-two. [17]The seventy [-two] returned rejoicing, and said, "Lord, even the demons are subject to us because of your name." [18q]*Jesus said, "I have observed Satan fall like lightning from the sky. [19r]Behold, I have given you the power 'to tread upon serpents' and scorpions and upon the full force of the enemy and nothing will harm you. [20s]Nevertheless, do not rejoice because the spirits are subject to you, but rejoice because your names are written in heaven."

Praise of the Father. [21tu]*At that very moment he rejoiced [in] the holy Spirit and said, "I give you praise, Father, Lord of heaven and earth, for although you have hidden these things from the wise and the learned you have revealed them to the childlike. Yes, Father, such has been your gracious will. [22v]All things have been handed over to me by my Father. No one knows who the Son is except the Father, and who the Father is except the Son and anyone to whom the Son wishes to reveal him."

The Privileges of Discipleship. [23w]Turning to the disciples in private he said, "Blessed are the eyes that see what you see. [24]For I say to you, many prophets and kings desired to see what you see, but did not see it, and to hear what you hear, but did not hear it."

The Greatest Commandment. [25xy]*There was a scholar of the law who stood up to test him and said, "Teacher, what must I do to inherit eternal life?" [26]Jesus said to him, "What is written in the law? How do you read it?" [27z]He said in reply, "You shall love the Lord, your God, with all your heart, with all your being, with all your strength, and with all your mind, and your neighbor as yourself." [28a]He replied to him, "You have

---

10, 13–16: The call to repentance that is a part of the proclamation of the kingdom brings with it a severe judgment for those who hear it and reject it.

10, 15: The netherworld: the underworld, the place of the dead (Acts 2, 27.31), here contrasted with heaven; see also the note on Mt 11, 23.

10, 18: I have observed Satan fall like lightning: the effect of the mission of the seventy-two is characterized by the Lucan Jesus as a symbolic fall of Satan. As the kingdom of God is gradually being established, evil in all its forms is being defeated; the dominion of Satan over humanity is at an end.

10, 21: Revealed them to the childlike: a restatement of the theme announced in 8, 10: the mysteries of the kingdom are revealed to the disciples. See also the note on Mt 11, 25–27.

10, 25–37: In response to a question from a Jewish legal expert about inheriting eternal life, Jesus illustrates the superiority of love over legalism through the story of the good Samaritan. The law of love proclaimed in the "Sermon on the Plain" (6, 27–36) is exemplified by one whom the legal ex-

pert would have considered ritually impure (see Jn 4, 9). Moreover, the identity of the "neighbor" requested by the legal expert (29) turns out to be a Samaritan, the enemy of the Jew (see the note on 9, 52).

10, 25: Scholar of the law: an expert in the Mosaic law, and probably a member of the group elsewhere identified as the scribes (5, 21).

g: 9, 4; Mt 10, 10; 1 Cor 9, 6-14; 1 Tm 5, 18. h: 1 Cor 10, 27. i: Mt 3, 2; 4, 17; Mk 1, 15. j: 9, 5. k: Acts 13, 51; 18, 6. l: Mt 10, 15; 11, 24. m: Mt 11, 20-24. n: Is 23; Ez 26-28; Jl 3 4-8; Am 1, 1-10; Zec 9, 2-4. o: Is 14, 13-15. p: Mt 10, 40; Jn 5, 23; 13, 20; 15, 23. q: Is 14, 12; Jn 12, 31; Rv 12, 7-12. r: Ps 19, 13; Mk 16, 18. s: Ex 32, 32; Dn 12, 1; Mt 7, 22; Phil 4, 3; Heb 12, 23; Rv 3, 5; 21, 27. t: Mt 11, 25-27. u: 1 Cor 1, 26-28. v: Jn 3, 35; 10, 15. w: Mt 13, 16-17. x: Mt 22, 34-40; Mk 12, 28-34. y: 18, 18; Mt 19, 16; Mk 10, 17. z: Lv 19, 18; Dt 6, 5; 10, 12; Jos 22, 5; Mt 19, 19; 22, 37-39; Rom 13, 9; Gal 5, 14; Jas 2, 8. a: Lv 18, 5; Prv 19, 16; Rom 10, 5; Gal 3, 12.

answered correctly; do this and you will live."

The Parable of the Good Samaritan. *29*But because he wished to justify himself, he said to Jesus, "And who is my neighbor?" *30*Jesus replied, "A man fell victim to robbers as he went down from Jerusalem to Jericho. They stripped and beat him and went off leaving him half-dead. *31**A priest happened to be going down that road, but when he saw him, he passed by on the opposite side. *32*Likewise a Levite came to the place, and when he saw him, he passed by on the opposite side. *33*But a Samaritan traveler who came upon him was moved with compassion at the sight. *34*He approached the victim, poured oil and wine over his wounds and bandaged them. Then he lifted him up on his own animal, took him to an inn and cared for him. *35*The next day he took out two silver coins and gave them to the innkeeper with the instruction, 'Take care of him. If you spend more than what I have given you, I shall repay you on my way back.' *36*Which of these three, in your opinion, was neighbor to the robbers' victim?" *37*He answered, "The one who treated him with mercy." Jesus said to him, "Go and do likewise."

Martha and Mary. *38b**As they continued their journey he entered a village where a woman whose name was Martha welcomed him. *39**She had a sister named Mary [who] sat beside the Lord at his feet listening to him speak. *40*Martha, burdened with much serving, came to him and said, "Lord, do you not care that my sister has left me by myself to do the serving? Tell her to help me." *41*The Lord said to her in reply, "Martha, Martha, you are anxious and worried about many things. *42**There is need of only one thing. Mary has chosen the better part and it will not be taken from her."

CHAPTER 11

See RG 312-13

The Lord's Prayer. *1c**He was praying in a certain place, and when he had finished, one of his disciples said to him, "Lord, teach us to pray just as John taught his disciples." *2**He said to them, "When you pray, say:

Father, hallowed be your name,
   your kingdom come.
3 *Give us each day our daily bread
4 and forgive us our sins
   for we ourselves forgive everyone in
      debt to us,
   and do not subject us to the final test."

Further Teachings on Prayer. *5d*And he said to them, "Suppose one of you has a friend to whom he goes at midnight and says, 'Friend, lend me three loaves of bread, *6*for a friend of mine has arrived at my house from a journey and I have nothing to offer him,' *7*and he says in reply from within, 'Do not bother me; the door has already been locked and my children and I are already in bed. I cannot get up to give you anything.' *8*I tell you, if he does not get up to give him the loaves because of their friendship, he will get up to give him whatever he needs because of his persistence.

10, 31–32: Priest . . . Levite: those religious representatives of Judaism who would have been expected to be models of "neighbor" to the victim pass him by.

10, 38–42: The story of Martha and Mary further illustrates the importance of hearing the words of the teacher and the concern with women in Lk.

10, 39: Sat beside the Lord at his feet: it is remarkable for first-century Palestinian Judaism that a woman would assume the posture of a disciple at the master's feet (see also 8, 35; Acts 22, 3), and it reveals a characteristic attitude of Jesus toward women in this gospel (see 8, 2–3).

10, 42: There is need of only one thing: some ancient versions read, "there is need of few things"; another important, although probably inferior, reading found in some manuscripts is, "there is need of few things, or of one."

11, 1–13: Luke presents three episodes concerned with prayer. The first (1–4) recounts Jesus teaching his disciples the Christian communal prayer, the "Our Father"; the second (5–8), the importance of persistence in prayer; the third

(9–13), the effectiveness of prayer.

11, 1–4: The Matthean form of the "Our Father" occurs in the "Sermon on the Mount" (Mt 6, 9–15); the shorter Lucan version is presented while Jesus is at prayer (see the note on 3, 21) and his disciples ask him to teach them to pray just as John taught his disciples to pray. In answer to their question, Jesus presents them with an example of a Christian communal prayer that stresses the fatherhood of God and acknowledges him as the one to whom the Christian disciple owes daily sustenance (3), forgiveness (4), and deliverance from the final trial (4). See also the notes on Mt 6, 9–13.

11, 2: Your kingdom come: in place of this petition, some early church Fathers record: "May your holy Spirit come upon us and cleanse us," a petition that may reflect the use of the "Our Father" in a baptismal liturgy.

11, 3–4: Daily bread: see the note on Mt 6, 11. **The final test:** see the note on Mt 6, 13.

b: Jn 11, 1; 12, 2-3.   *c:* Mt 6, 9-15.   *d:* 18, 1-5.

The Answer to Prayer. [9e f]"And I tell you, ask and you will receive; seek and you will find; knock and the door will be opened to you. [10]For everyone who asks, receives; and the one who seeks, finds; and to the one who knocks, the door will be opened. [11]What father among you would hand his son a snake when he asks for a fish? [12]Or hand him a scorpion when he asks for an egg? [13]*If you then, who are wicked, know how to give good gifts to your children, how much more will the Father in heaven give the holy Spirit to those who ask him?"

Jesus and Beelzebul. [14g]He was driving out a demon [that was] mute, and when the demon had gone out, the mute person spoke and the crowds were amazed. [15h]Some of them said, "By the power of Beelzebul, the prince of demons, he drives out demons." [16i]Others, to test him, asked him for a sign from heaven. [17]But he knew their thoughts and said to them, "Every kingdom divided against itself will be laid waste and house will fall against house. [18]And if Satan is divided against himself, how will his kingdom stand? For you say that it is by Beelzebul that I drive out demons. [19]*If I, then, drive out demons by Beelzebul, by whom do your own people drive them out? Therefore they will be your judges. [20j]But if it is by the finger of God that [I] drive out demons, then the kingdom of God has come upon you. [21]When a strong man fully armed guards his palace, his possessions are safe. [22]*But when one stronger than he attacks and overcomes him, he takes away the armor on which he relied and distributes the spoils. [23k]Whoever is not with me is against me, and whoever does not gather with me scatters.

The Return of the Unclean Spirit. [24l]"When an unclean spirit goes out of someone, it roams through arid regions searching for rest but, finding none, it says, 'I shall return to my home from which I came.' [25]But upon returning, it finds it swept clean and put in order. [26m]Then it goes and brings back seven other spirits more wicked than itself who move in and dwell there, and the last condition of that person is worse than the first."

True Blessedness. [27n]*While he was speaking, a woman from the crowd called out and said to him, "Blessed is the womb that carried you and the breasts at which you nursed." [28]He replied, "Rather, blessed are those who hear the word of God and observe it."

The Demand for a Sign. [29o p]*While still more people gathered in the crowd, he said to them, "This generation is an evil generation; it seeks a sign, but no sign will be given it, except the sign of Jonah. [30]Just as Jonah became a sign to the Ninevites, so will the Son of Man be to this generation. [31q]At the judgment the queen of the south will rise with the men of this generation and she will condemn them, because she came from the ends of the earth to hear the wisdom of Solomon, and there is something greater than Solomon here. [32r]At the judgment the men of Nineveh will arise with this generation and condemn it, because at the preaching of Jonah they repented, and there is something greater than Jonah here.

The Simile of Light. [33s]"No one who lights a lamp hides it away or places it [under a bushel basket], but on a lampstand so that those who enter might see the light. [34t]The lamp of the body is your eye. When your eye is sound, then your whole body is filled with

---

11, 13: The holy Spirit: this is a Lucan editorial alteration of a traditional saying of Jesus (see Mt 7, 11). Luke presents the gift of the holy Spirit as the response of the Father to the prayer of the Christian disciple.

11, 19: Your own people: the Greek reads "your sons." Other Jewish exorcists (see Acts 19, 13–20), who recognize that the power of God is active in the exorcism, would themselves convict the accusers of Jesus. See also the note on Mt 12, 27.

11, 22: One stronger: i.e., Jesus. Cf 3, 16 where John the Baptist identifies Jesus as "more powerful than I."

11, 27–28: The beatitude in v 28 should not be interpreted as a rebuke of the mother of Jesus; see the note on 8, 21. Rather, it emphasizes (like 2, 35) that attentiveness to God's

word is more important than biological relationship to Jesus.

11, 29–32: The "sign of Jonah" in Lk is the preaching of the need for repentance by a prophet who comes from afar. Cf Mt 12, 38–42 (and see the notes there) where the "sign of Jonah" is interpreted by Jesus as his death and resurrection.

e: Mt 7, 7-11. f: Mt 21, 22; Mk 11, 24; Jn 14, 13; 15, 7; 1 Jn 5, 14-15. g: Mt 12, 22-30; Mk 3, 20-27. h: Mt 9, 34. i: Mt 12, 38; 16, 1; Mk 8, 11; 1 Cor 1, 22. j: Ex 8, 19. k: 9, 50; Mk 9, 40. l: Mt 12, 43-45. m: Jn 5, 14. n: 1, 28.42.48. o: Mt 12, 38-42; Mk 8, 12. p: Mt 16, 1.4; Jn 6, 30; 1 Cor 1, 22. q: 1 Kgs 10, 1-10; 2 Chr 9, 1-12. r: Jon 3, 8.10. s: 8, 16; Mt 5, 15; Mk 4, 21. t: Mt 6, 22-23.

light, but when it is bad, then your body is in darkness. [35]Take care, then, that the light in you not become darkness. [36]If your whole body is full of light, and no part of it is in darkness, then it will be as full of light as a lamp illuminating you with its brightness."

Denunciation of the Pharisees and Scholars of the Law. [37uv]*After he had spoken, a Pharisee invited him to dine at his home. He entered and reclined at table to eat. [38w]The Pharisee was amazed to see that he did not observe the prescribed washing before the meal. [39x]The Lord said to him, "Oh you Pharisees! Although you cleanse the outside of the cup and the dish, inside you are filled with plunder and evil. [40]You fools! Did not the maker of the outside also make the inside? [41]But as to what is within, give alms, and behold, everything will be clean for you. [42y]Woe to you Pharisees! You pay tithes of mint and of rue and of every garden herb, but you pay no attention to judgment and to love for God. These you should have done, without overlooking the others. [43z]Woe to you Pharisees! You love the seat of honor in synagogues and greetings in marketplaces. [44a]*Woe to you! You are like unseen graves over which people unknowingly walk."

[45b]*Then one of the scholars of the law said to him in reply, "Teacher, by saying this you are insulting us too." [46]And he said, "Woe also to you scholars of the law! You impose on people burdens hard to carry, but you yourselves do not lift one finger to touch them. [47c]Woe to you! You build the memorials of the prophets whom your ancestors killed. [48]Consequently, you bear witness and give consent to the deeds of your ancestors, for they killed them and you do the building. [49d]*Therefore, the wisdom of God said, 'I will send to them prophets and apostles; some of them they will kill and persecute' [50]in order that this generation might be charged with the blood of all the prophets shed since the foundation of the world, [51e]*from the blood of Abel to the blood of Zechariah who died between the altar and the temple building. Yes, I tell you, this generation will be charged with their blood! [52f]Woe to you, scholars of the law! You have taken away the key of knowledge. You yourselves did not enter and you stopped those trying to enter." [53g]When he left, the scribes and Pharisees began to act with hostility toward him and to interrogate him about many things, [54h]for they were plotting to catch him at something he might say.

CHAPTER 12

See RG 312-13

The Leaven of the Pharisees. [1i]*Meanwhile, so many people were crowding together that they were trampling one another underfoot. He began to speak, first to his disciples, "Beware of the leaven—that is, the hypocrisy—of the Pharisees.

Courage under Persecution. [2jk]*"There is nothing concealed that will not be revealed, nor secret that will not be known. [3]Therefore whatever you have said in the darkness will be heard in the light, and what you have whispered behind closed doors will be proclaimed on the housetops. [4]I tell you, my friends, do

---

11, 37–54: This denunciation of the Pharisees (39–44) and the scholars of the law (45–52) is set by Luke in the context of Jesus' dining at the home of a Pharisee. Controversies with or reprimands of Pharisees are regularly set by Luke within the context of Jesus' eating with Pharisees (see 5, 29–39; 7, 36–50; 14, 1–24). A different compilation of similar sayings is found in Mt 23 (see also the notes there).

11, 44: Unseen graves: contact with the dead or with human bones or graves (see Nm 19, 16) brought ritual impurity. Jesus presents the Pharisees as those who insidiously lead others astray through their seeming attention to the law.

11, 45: Scholars of the law: see the note on 10, 25.

11, 49: I will send to them prophets and apostles: Jesus connects the mission of the church (apostles) with the mission of the Old Testament prophets who often suffered the rebuke of their contemporaries.

11, 51: From the blood of Abel to the blood of Zecha-

riah: the murder of Abel is the first murder recounted in the Old Testament (Gn 4, 8). The Zechariah mentioned here may be the Zechariah whose murder is recounted in 2 Chr 24, 20–22, the last murder presented in the Hebrew canon of the Old Testament.

12, 1: See the notes on Mk 8, 15 and Mt 16, 5–12.

12, 2–9: Luke presents a collection of sayings of Jesus exhorting his followers to acknowledge him and his mission fearlessly and assuring them of God's protection even in times of persecution. They are paralleled in Mt 10, 26–33.

u: 20, 45-47; Mt 23, 1-36; Mk 12, 38-40. v: 7, 36; 14, 1. w: Mt 15, 2; Mk 7, 2-5. x: Mt 23, 25-26. y: Lv 27, 30; Mt 23, 23. z: 20, 46; Mt 23, 6; Mk 12, 38-39. a: Mt 23, 27. b: Mt 23, 4. c: Mt 23, 29-32. d: Mt 23, 34-36. e: Gn 4, 8; 2 Chr 24, 20-22. f: Mt 23, 13. g: 6, 11; Mt 22, 15-22. h: 20, 20. i: Mt 16, 6; Mk 8, 15. j: Mt 10, 26-33. k: 8, 17; Mk 4, 22.

not be afraid of those who kill the body but after that can do no more. [5]*I shall show you whom to fear. Be afraid of the one who after killing has the power to cast into Gehenna; yes, I tell you, be afraid of that one. [6]*Are not five sparrows sold for two small coins? Yet not one of them has escaped the notice of God. [7]lEven the hairs of your head have all been counted. Do not be afraid. You are worth more than many sparrows. [8]I tell you, everyone who acknowledges me before others the Son of Man will acknowledge before the angels of God. [9]mBut whoever denies me before others will be denied before the angels of God.

Sayings about the holy Spirit. [10]n*"Everyone who speaks a word against the Son of Man will be forgiven, but the one who blasphemes against the holy Spirit will not be forgiven. [11]oWhen they take you before synagogues and before rulers and authorities, do not worry about how or what your defense will be or about what you are to say. [12]For the holy Spirit will teach you at that moment what you should say."

Saying against Greed. [13]*Someone in the crowd said to him, "Teacher, tell my brother to share the inheritance with me." [14]pHe replied to him, "Friend, who appointed me as your judge and arbitrator?" [15]qThen he said to the crowd, "Take care to guard against all greed, for though one may be rich, one's life does not consist of possessions."

Parable of the Rich Fool. [16]Then he told them a parable. "There was a rich man whose land produced a bountiful harvest. [17]He asked himself, 'What shall I do, for I do not have space to store my harvest?' [18]And he said, 'This is what I shall do: I shall tear down my barns and build larger ones. There

I shall store all my grain and other goods [19]r,sand I shall say to myself, "Now as for you, you have so many good things stored up for many years, rest, eat, drink, be merry!" ' [20]But God said to him, 'You fool, this night your life will be demanded of you; and the things you have prepared, to whom will they belong?' [21]*Thus will it be for the one who stores up treasure for himself but is not rich in what matters to God."

Dependence on God. [22]tHe said to [his] disciples, "Therefore I tell you, do not worry about your life and what you will eat, or about your body and what you will wear. [23]For life is more than food and the body more than clothing. [24]uNotice the ravens: they do not sow or reap; they have neither storehouse nor barn, yet God feeds them. How much more important are you than birds! [25]Can any of you by worrying add a moment to your life-span? [26]If even the smallest things are beyond your control, why are you anxious about the rest? [27]vNotice how the flowers grow. They do not toil or spin. But I tell you, not even Solomon in all his splendor was dressed like one of them. [28]If God so clothes the grass in the field that grows today and is thrown into the oven tomorrow, will he not much more provide for you, O you of little faith? [29]As for you, do not seek what you are to eat and what you are to drink, and do not worry anymore. [30]All the nations of the world seek for these things, and your Father knows that you need them. [31]Instead, seek his kingdom, and these other things will be given you besides. [32]wDo not be afraid any longer, little flock, for your Father is pleased to give you the kingdom. [33]xSell your belongings and give

---

12, 5: **Gehenna:** see the note on Mt 5, 22.

12, 6: **Two small coins:** the Roman copper coin, the assarion (Latin *as*), was worth about one-sixteenth of a denarius (see the note on 7, 41).

12, 10–12: The sayings about the holy Spirit are set in the context of fearlessness in the face of persecution (2–9; cf Mt 12, 31–32). The holy Spirit will be presented in Luke's second volume, the Acts of the Apostles, as the power responsible for the guidance of the Christian mission and the source of courage in the face of persecution.

12, 13–34: Luke has joined together sayings contrasting those whose focus and trust in life is on material possessions, symbolized here by the rich fool of the parable (16–21), with

those who recognize their complete dependence on God (21), those whose radical detachment from material possessions symbolizes their heavenly treasure (33–34).

12, 21: **Rich in what matters to God:** literally, "rich for God."

l: 12, 24; 21, 18; Acts 27, 34. *m:* 9, 26; Mk 8, 38; 2 Tm 2, 12. *n:* Mt 12, 31-32; Mk 3, 28-29. *o:* 21, 12-15; Mt 10, 17-20; Mk 13, 11. *p:* Ex 2, 14; Acts 7, 27. *q:* 1 Tm 6, 9-10. *r:* Mt 6, 19-21; 1 Tm 6, 17. *s:* Sir 11, 19. *t:* Mt 6, 25-34. *u:* 12, 7. *v:* 1 Kgs 10, 4-7; 2 Chr 9, 3-6. *w:* 22, 29; Rv 1, 6. *x:* 18, 22; Mt 6, 20-21; Mk 10, 21.

alms. Provide money bags for yourselves that do not wear out, an inexhaustible treasure in heaven that no thief can reach nor moth destroy. *34*For where your treasure is, there also will your heart be.

Vigilant and Faithful Servants. *35y**"Gird your loins and light your lamps *36z*and be like servants who await their master's return from a wedding, ready to open immediately when he comes and knocks. *37*Blessed are those servants whom the master finds vigilant on his arrival. Amen, I say to you, he will gird himself, have them recline at table, and proceed to wait on them. *38*And should he come in the second or third watch and find them prepared in this way, blessed are those servants. *39a*Be sure of this: if the master of the house had known the hour when the thief was coming, he would not have let his house be broken into. *40*You also must be prepared, for at an hour you do not expect, the Son of Man will come."

*41*Then Peter said, "Lord, is this parable meant for us or for everyone?" *42*And the Lord replied, "Who, then, is the faithful and prudent steward whom the master will put in charge of his servants to distribute [the] food allowance at the proper time? *43*Blessed is that servant whom his master on arrival finds doing so. *44*Truly, I say to you, he will put him in charge of all his property. *45**But if that servant says to himself, 'My master is delayed in coming,' and begins to beat the menservants and the maidservants, to eat and drink and get drunk, *46*then that servant's master will come on an unexpected day and at an unknown hour and will punish him severely and assign him a place with the unfaithful. *47b*That servant who knew his master's will but did not make preparations nor act in accord with his will shall be beaten se-

verely; *48*and the servant who was ignorant of his master's will but acted in a way deserving of a severe beating shall be beaten only lightly. Much will be required of the person entrusted with much, and still more will be demanded of the person entrusted with more.

Jesus: A Cause of Division. *49**"I have come to set the earth on fire, and how I wish it were already blazing! *50c**There is a baptism with which I must be baptized, and how great is my anguish until it is accomplished! *51de*Do you think that I have come to establish peace on the earth? No, I tell you, but rather division. *52*From now on a household of five will be divided, three against two and two against three; *53f*a father will be divided against his son and a son against his father, a mother against her daughter and a daughter against her mother, a mother-in-law against her daughter-in-law and a daughter-in-law against her mother-in-law."

Signs of the Times. *54g*He also said to the crowds, "When you see [a] cloud rising in the west you say immediately that it is going to rain—and so it does; *55*and when you notice that the wind is blowing from the south you say that it is going to be hot—and so it is. *56*You hypocrites! You know how to interpret the appearance of the earth and the sky; why do you not know how to interpret the present time?

Settlement with an Opponent. *57h*"Why do you not judge for yourselves what is right? *58*If you are to go with your opponent before a magistrate, make an effort to settle the matter on the way; otherwise your opponent will turn you over to the judge, and the judge hand you over to the constable, and the constable throw you into prison. *59**I say to you, you will not be released until you have paid the last penny."

12, 35–48: This collection of sayings relates to Luke's understanding of the end time and the return of Jesus. Luke emphasizes for his readers the importance of being faithful to the instructions of Jesus in the period before the parousia.

12, 45: My master is delayed in coming: this statement indicates that early Christian expectations for the imminent return of Jesus had undergone some modification. Luke cautions his readers against counting on such a delay and acting irresponsibly. Cf the similar warning in Mt 24, 48.

12, 49–53: Jesus' proclamation of the kingdom is a refining and purifying fire. His message that meets with accept-

ance or rejection will be a source of conflict and dissension even within families.

12, 50: Baptism: i.e., his death.

12, 59: The last penny: Greek, **lepton,** a very small amount. Mt 5, 26 has for "the last penny" the Greek word **kodrantēs** (Latin **quadrans,** "farthing").

---

y: Mt 24, 45-51.   z: Mt 25, 1-13; Mk 13, 35-37.   a: Mt 24, 43-44; 1 Thes 5, 2.   b: Jas 4, 17.   c: Mk 10, 38-39.   d: Mt 10, 34-35.   e: 2, 14.   f: Mi 7, 6.   g: Mt 16, 2-3.   h: Mt 5, 25-26.

See RG 312–13

CHAPTER 13

A Call to Repentance. [1]*At that time some people who were present there told him about the Galileans whose blood Pilate had mingled with the blood of their sacrifices. [2][i]He said to them in reply, "Do you think that because these Galileans suffered in this way they were greater sinners than all other Galileans? [3][j]By no means! But I tell you, if you do not repent, you will all perish as they did! [4]*Or those eighteen people who were killed when the tower at Siloam fell on them—do you think they were more guilty than everyone else who lived in Jerusalem? [5]By no means! But I tell you, if you do not repent, you will all perish as they did!"

The Parable of the Barren Fig Tree. [6][k]*And he told them this parable: "There once was a person who had a fig tree planted in his orchard, and when he came in search of fruit on it but found none, [7]he said to the gardener, 'For three years now I have come in search of fruit on this fig tree but have found none. [So] cut it down. Why should it exhaust the soil?' [8]He said to him in reply, 'Sir, leave it for this year also, and I shall cultivate the ground around it and fertilize it; [9]it may bear fruit in the future. If not you can cut it down.' "

Cure of a Crippled Woman on the Sabbath. [10]*He was teaching in a synagogue on the sabbath. [11]And a woman was there who for eighteen years had been crippled by a spirit; she was bent over, completely incapable of standing erect. [12]When Jesus saw her, he called to her and said, "Woman, you are set free of your infirmity." [13]He laid his hands on her, and she at once stood up straight and glorified God. [14][l]But the leader of the synagogue, indignant that Jesus had cured on the sabbath, said to the crowd in reply, "There are six days when work should be done. Come on those days to be cured, not on the sabbath day." [15][m]*The Lord said to him in reply, "Hypocrites! Does not each one of you on the sabbath untie his ox or his ass from the manger and lead it out for watering? [16][n]*This daughter of Abraham, whom Satan has bound for eighteen years now, ought she not to have been set free on the sabbath day from this bondage?" [17]When he said this, all his adversaries were humiliated; and the whole crowd rejoiced at all the splendid deeds done by him.

The Parable of the Mustard Seed. [18][o]*Then he said, "What is the kingdom of God like? To what can I compare it? [19][p]It is like a mustard seed that a person took and

---

13, 1–5: The death of the Galileans at the hands of Pilate (1) and the accidental death of those on whom the tower fell (4) are presented by the Lucan Jesus as timely reminders of the need for all to repent, for the victims of these tragedies should not be considered outstanding sinners who were singled out for punishment.

13, 1: The slaughter of the Galileans by Pilate is unknown outside Lk; but from what is known about Pilate from the Jewish historian Josephus, such a slaughter would be in keeping with the character of Pilate. Josephus reports that Pilate had disrupted a religious gathering of the Samaritans on Mt. Gerizim with a slaughter of the participants (**Antiquities** 18, 4, 1 §§86–87), and that on another occasion Pilate had killed many Jews who had opposed him when he appropriated money from the temple treasury to build an aqueduct in Jerusalem (**Jewish War** 2, 9, 4 §§175–77; **Antiquities** 18, 3, 2 §§60–62).

13, 4: Like the incident mentioned in v 1, nothing of this accident in Jerusalem is known outside Lk and the New Testament.

13, 6–9: Following on the call to repentance in vv 1–5, the parable of the barren fig tree presents a story about the continuing patience of God with those who have not yet given evidence of their repentance (see 3, 8). The parable may also be alluding to the delay of the end time, when punishment will be meted out, and the importance of preparing for the end of the age because the delay will not be permanent (8–9).

13, 10–17: The cure of the crippled woman on the sabbath and the controversy that results furnishes a parallel to an incident that will be reported by Lk in 14, 1–6, the cure of the man with dropsy on the sabbath. A characteristic of Luke's style is the juxtaposition of an incident that reveals Jesus' concern for a man with an incident that reveals his concern for a woman; cf, e.g., 7, 11–17 and 8, 49–56.

13, 15–16: If the law as interpreted by Jewish tradition allowed for the untying of bound animals on the sabbath, how much more should this woman who has been bound by Satan's power be freed on the sabbath from her affliction.

13, 16: Whom Satan has bound: affliction and infirmity are taken as evidence of Satan's hold on humanity. The healing ministry of Jesus reveals the gradual wresting from Satan of control over humanity and the establishment of God's kingdom.

13, 18–21: Two parables are used to illustrate the future proportions of the kingdom of God that will result from its deceptively small beginning in the preaching and healing ministry of Jesus. They are paralleled in Mt 13, 31–33 and Mk 4, 30–32.

i: Jn 9, 2. *j:* Jn 8, 24. *k:* Jer 8, 13; Hb 3, 17; Mt 21, 19; Mk 11, 13. *l:* 6, 7; 14, 3; Ex 20, 8-11; Dt 5, 12-15; Mt 12, 10; Mk 3, 2-4; Jn 5, 16; 7, 23; 9, 14.16. *m:* 14, 5; Dt 22, 4; Mt 12, 11. *n:* 19, 9. *o.* Mt 13, 31-32; Mk 4, 30-32. *p:* Ez 17, 23-24; 31, 6.

planted in the garden. When it was fully grown, it became a large bush and 'the birds of the sky dwelt in its branches.' "

The Parable of the Yeast. [20q]Again he said, "To what shall I compare the kingdom of God? [21]It is like yeast that a woman took and mixed [in] with three measures of wheat flour until the whole batch of dough was leavened."

The Narrow Door; Salvation and Rejection. [22]*He passed through towns and villages, teaching as he went and making his way to Jerusalem. [23]Someone asked him, "Lord, will only a few people be saved?" He answered them, [24rs]"Strive to enter through the narrow gate, for many, I tell you, will attempt to enter but will not be strong enough. [25t]After the master of the house has arisen and locked the door, then will you stand outside knocking and saying, 'Lord, open the door for us.' He will say to you in reply, 'I do not know where you are from.' [26]And you will say, 'We ate and drank in your company and you taught in our streets.' [27u]Then he will say to you, 'I do not know where [you] are from. Depart from me, all you evildoers!' [28v]And there will be wailing and grinding of teeth when you see Abraham, Isaac, and Jacob and all the prophets in the kingdom of God and you yourselves cast out. [29w]And people will come from the east and the west and from the north and the south and will recline at table in the kingdom of God. [30x]For behold, some are last who will be first, and some are first who will be last."

Herod's Desire to Kill Jesus. [31]At that time some Pharisees came to him and said, "Go away, leave this area because Herod wants to kill you." [32]*He replied, "Go and tell that fox, 'Behold, I cast out demons and I perform healings today and tomorrow, and on the third day I accomplish my purpose. [33y]*Yet I must continue on my way today, tomorrow, and the following day, for it is impossible that a prophet should die outside of Jerusalem.'

The Lament over Jerusalem. [34z]"Jerusalem, Jerusalem, you who kill the prophets and stone those sent to you, how many times I yearned to gather your children together as a hen gathers her brood under her wings, but you were unwilling! [35a]Behold, your house will be abandoned. [But] I tell you, you will not see me until [the time comes when] you say, 'Blessed is he who comes in the name of the Lord.' "

CHAPTER 14

See RG 312–13

Healing of the Man with Dropsy on the Sabbath. [1bc]*On a sabbath he went to dine at the home of one of the leading Pharisees, and the people there were observing him carefully. [2]*In front of him there was a man suffering from dropsy. [3d]Jesus spoke to the scholars of the law and Pharisees in reply, asking, "Is it lawful to cure on the sabbath or not?" [4]But they kept silent; so he took the man and, after he had healed him, dismissed him. [5e]*Then he said to them, "Who among you, if your son or ox falls into a cistern, would not immediately pull him out on the sabbath day?" [6f]But they were unable to answer his question.

13, 22–30: These sayings of Jesus follow in Lk upon the parables of the kingdom (18–21) and stress that great effort is required for entrance into the kingdom (24) and that there is an urgency to accept the present opportunity to enter because the narrow door will not remain open indefinitely (25). Lying behind the sayings is the rejection of Jesus and his message by his Jewish contemporaries (26) whose places at table in the kingdom will be taken by Gentiles from the four corners of the world (29). Those called last (the Gentiles) will precede those to whom the invitation to enter was first extended (the Jews). See also 14, 15–24.

13, 32: Nothing, not even Herod's desire to kill Jesus, stands in the way of Jesus' role in fulfilling God's will and in establishing the kingdom through his exorcisms and healings.

13, 33: It is impossible that a prophet should die outside of Jerusalem: Jerusalem is the city of destiny and the goal of the journey of the prophet Jesus. Only when he reaches the holy city will his work be accomplished.

14, 1–6: See the note on 13, 10–17.

14, 2: Dropsy: an abnormal swelling of the body because of the retention and accumulation of fluid.

14, 5: Your son or ox: this is the reading of many of the oldest and most important New Testament manuscripts. Because of the strange collocation of **son** and **ox,** some copyists have altered it to "your ass or ox," on the model of the saying in 13, 15.

q: Mt 13, 33. r: Mt 7, 13-14.21-23. s: Mk 10, 25. t: Mt 25, 10-12. u: Ps 6, 9; Mt 7, 23; 25, 41. v: Mt 8, 11-12. w: Ps 107, 2-3. x: Mt 19, 20; 20, 16; Mk 10, 31. y: 2, 38; Jn 6, 30; 8, 20. z: 19, 41-44; Mt 23, 37-39. a: 19, 38; 1 Kgs 9, 7-8; Ps 118, 26; Jer 7, 4-7.13-15; 12, 7; 22, 5. b: 6, 6-11; 13, 10-17. c: 11, 37. d: 6, 9; Mk 3, 4. e: 13, 15; Dt 22, 4; Mt 12, 11. f: Mt 22, 46.

Conduct of Invited Guests and Hosts.
[7g]*He told a parable to those who had been invited, noticing how they were choosing the places of honor at the table. [8h]"When you are invited by someone to a wedding banquet, do not recline at table in the place of honor. A more distinguished guest than you may have been invited by him, [9]and the host who invited both of you may approach you and say, 'Give your place to this man,' and then you would proceed with embarrassment to take the lowest place. [10]Rather, when you are invited, go and take the lowest place so that when the host comes to you he may say, 'My friend, move up to a higher position.' Then you will enjoy the esteem of your companions at the table. [11i]For everyone who exalts himself will be humbled, but the one who humbles himself will be exalted." [12j]Then he said to the host who invited him, "When you hold a lunch or a dinner, do not invite your friends or your brothers or your relatives or your wealthy neighbors, in case they may invite you back and you have repayment. [13]Rather, when you hold a banquet, invite the poor, the crippled, the lame, the blind; [14k]blessed indeed will you be because of their inability to repay you. For you will be repaid at the resurrection of the righteous."

The Parable of the Great Feast. [15]*One of his fellow guests on hearing this said to him, "Blessed is the one who will dine in the kingdom of God." [16l]He replied to him, "A man gave a great dinner to which he invited many. [17]When the time for the dinner came, he dispatched his servant to say to those invited, 'Come, everything is now ready.' [18]But one by one, they all began to excuse themselves.

The first said to him, 'I have purchased a field and must go to examine it; I ask you, consider me excused.' [19]And another said, 'I have purchased five yoke of oxen and am on my way to evaluate them; I ask you, consider me excused.' [20]And another said, 'I have just married a woman, and therefore I cannot come.' [21]The servant went and reported this to his master. Then the master of the house in a rage commanded his servant, 'Go out quickly into the streets and alleys of the town and bring in here the poor and the crippled, the blind and the lame.' [22]The servant reported, 'Sir, your orders have been carried out and still there is room.' [23]The master then ordered the servant, 'Go out to the highways and hedgerows and make people come in that my home may be filled. [24]For, I tell you, none of those men who were invited will taste my dinner.' "

Sayings on Discipleship. [25]*Great crowds were traveling with him, and he turned and addressed them, [26mn]*"If anyone comes to me without hating his father and mother, wife and children, brothers and sisters, and even his own life, he cannot be my disciple. [27o]Whoever does not carry his own cross and come after me cannot be my disciple. [28]Which of you wishing to construct a tower does not first sit down and calculate the cost to see if there is enough for its completion? [29]Otherwise, after laying the foundation and finding himself unable to finish the work the onlookers should laugh at him [30]and say, 'This one began to build but did not have the resources to finish.' [31]Or what king marching into battle would not first sit down and decide whether with ten thousand troops he can successfully oppose another king ad-

---

14, 7–14: The banquet scene found only in Luke provides the opportunity for these teachings of Jesus on humility and presents a setting to display Luke's interest in Jesus' attitude toward the rich and the poor (see the notes on 4, 18; 6, 20–26; 12, 13–34).

14, 15–24: The parable of the great dinner is a further illustration of the rejection by Israel, God's chosen people, of Jesus' invitation to share in the banquet in the kingdom and the extension of the invitation to other Jews whose identification as the poor, crippled, blind, and lame (21) classifies them among those who recognize their need for salvation, and to Gentiles (23). A similar parable is found in Mt 22, 1–10.

14, 25–33: This collection of sayings, most of which are peculiar to Lk, focuses on the total dedication necessary for the disciple of Jesus. No attachment to family (26) or possessions (33) can stand in the way of the total commitment demanded of the disciple. Also, acceptance of the call to be a disciple demands readiness to accept persecution and suffering (27) and a realistic assessment of the hardships and costs (28–32).

14, 26: Hating his father . . . : cf the similar saying in Mt 10, 37. The disciple's family must take second place to the absolute dedication involved in following Jesus (see also 9, 59–62).

g: 11, 43; Mt 23, 6; Mk 12, 38-39.   h: Prv 25, 6-7.   i: 18, 14.   j: 6, 32-35.   k: Jn 5, 29.   l: Mt 22, 2-10.   m: Mt 10, 37-38.   n: 9, 57-62; 18, 29; Jn 12, 25.   o: 9, 23; Mt 16, 24; Mk 8, 34.

vancing upon him with twenty thousand troops? [32]But if not, while he is still far away, he will send a delegation to ask for peace terms. [33p]In the same way, everyone of you who does not renounce all his possessions cannot be my disciple.

The Simile of Salt. [34q]*"Salt is good, but if salt itself loses its taste, with what can its flavor be restored? [35r]It is fit neither for the soil nor for the manure pile; it is thrown out. Whoever has ears to hear ought to hear."

See RG 312–13

CHAPTER 15

The Parable of the Lost Sheep. [1s]*The tax collectors and sinners were all drawing near to listen to him, [2t]but the Pharisees and scribes began to complain, saying, "This man welcomes sinners and eats with them." [3]So to them he addressed this parable. [4uvw]"What man among you having a hundred sheep and losing one of them would not leave the ninety-nine in the desert and go after the lost one until he finds it? [5]And when he does find it, he sets it on his shoulders with great joy [6]and, upon his arrival home, he calls together his friends and neighbors and says to them, 'Rejoice with me because I have found my lost sheep.' [7x]I tell you, in just the same way there will be more joy in heaven over one sinner who repents than over ninety-nine righteous people who have no need of repentance.

The Parable of the Lost Coin. [8]*"Or what woman having ten coins and losing one would not light a lamp and sweep the house, searching carefully until she finds it? [9]And when she does find it, she calls together her friends and neighbors and says to them, 'Rejoice with me because I have found the coin that I lost.' [10]In just the same way, I tell you, there will be rejoicing among the angels of God over one sinner who repents."

The Parable of the Lost Son. [11]Then he said, "A man had two sons, [12]and the younger son said to his father, 'Father, give me the share of your estate that should come to me.' So the father divided the property between them. [13y]After a few days, the younger son collected all his belongings and set off to a distant country where he squandered his inheritance on a life of dissipation. [14]When he had freely spent everything, a severe famine struck that country, and he found himself in dire need. [15]So he hired himself out to one of the local citizens who sent him to his farm to tend the swine. [16]And he longed to eat his fill of the pods on which the swine fed, but nobody gave him any. [17]Coming to his senses he thought, 'How many of my father's hired workers have more than enough food to eat, but here am I, dying from hunger. [18]I shall get up and go to my father and I shall say to him, "Father, I have sinned against heaven and against you. [19]I no longer deserve to be called your son; treat me as you would treat one of your hired workers." ' [20]So he got up and went back to his father. While he was still a long way off, his father caught sight of him, and was filled with compassion. He ran to his son, embraced him and kissed him. [21]His son said to him, 'Father, I have sinned against heaven and against you; I no longer deserve to be called your son.' [22]But his father ordered his servants, 'Quickly bring the finest robe and put it on him; put a ring on his finger and sandals on his feet. [23]Take the fattened calf and slaughter it. Then let us celebrate with a feast, [24]because this son of mine was dead, and has come to life again; he was lost, and has been found.' Then the celebration began. [25]Now the older son had been out in the field and, on his way back, as he neared the house, he heard the sound of music and dancing. [26]He called one of the servants and asked what this might mean. [27]The servant said to him, 'Your brother has returned and

---

14, 34–35: The simile of salt follows the sayings of Jesus that demanded of the disciple total dedication and detachment from family and possessions and illustrates the condition of one who does not display this total commitment. The half-hearted disciple is like salt that cannot serve its intended purpose. See the simile of salt in Mt 5, 13 and the note there.

15, 1–32: To the parable of the lost sheep (1–7) that Luke shares with Matthew (Mt 18, 12–14), Luke adds two parables (the lost coin, 8–10; the prodigal son, 11–32) from his own

special tradition to illustrate Jesus' particular concern for the lost and God's love for the repentant sinner.

15, 8: Ten coins: literally, "ten drachmas." A drachma was a Greek silver coin.

p: 5, 11.   q: Mt 5, 13; Mk 9, 50.   r: 8, 8; Mt 11, 15; 13, 9; Mk 4, 9.23.   s: Mt 9, 10-13.   t: 5, 30; 19, 7.   u: Mt 18, 12-14.   v: 19, 10.   w: Ez 34, 11-12.16.   x: Ez 18, 23.   y: Prv 29, 3.

your father has slaughtered the fattened calf because he has him back safe and sound.' ²⁸He became angry, and when he refused to enter the house, his father came out and pleaded with him. ²⁹He said to his father in reply, 'Look, all these years I served you and not once did I disobey your orders; yet you never gave me even a young goat to feast on with my friends. ³⁰But when your son returns who swallowed up your property with prostitutes, for him you slaughter the fattened calf.' ³¹He said to him, 'My son, you are here with me always; everything I have is yours. ³²But now we must celebrate and rejoice, because your brother was dead and has come to life again; he was lost and has been found.' "

See RG 312–13

CHAPTER 16

The Parable of the Dishonest Steward. ¹*Then he also said to his disciples, "A rich man had a steward who was reported to him for squandering his property. ²He summoned him and said, 'What is this I hear about you? Prepare a full account of your stewardship, because you can no longer be my steward.' ³The steward said to himself, 'What shall I do, now that my master is taking the position of steward away from me? I am not strong enough to dig and I am ashamed to beg. ⁴I know what I shall do so that, when I am removed from the stewardship, they may welcome me into their homes.' ⁵He called in his master's debtors one by one. To the first he said, 'How much do you owe my master?' ⁶*He replied, 'One hundred measures of olive oil.' He said to him, 'Here is your promissory note. Sit down and quickly write one for fifty.' ⁷*Then to another he said, 'And you, how much do you owe?' He replied, 'One hundred kors of wheat.' He said to him, 'Here is your promissory note; write one for eighty.' ⁸ᶻ*And the master commended that dishonest steward for acting prudently.

Application of the Parable. "For the children of this world are more prudent in dealing with their own generation than are the children of light. ⁹ᵃ*I tell you, make friends for yourselves with dishonest wealth, so that when it fails, you will be welcomed into eternal dwellings. ¹⁰ᵇ*The person who is trustworthy in very small matters is also trustworthy in great ones; and the person who is dishonest in very small matters is also dishonest in great ones. ¹¹If, therefore, you are not trustworthy with dishonest wealth, who will trust you with true wealth? ¹²If you are not trustworthy with what belongs to another, who will give you what is yours? ¹³ᶜ*No servant can serve two masters. He will either hate one and love the other, or be devoted to one and despise the other. You cannot serve God and mammon."

16, 1–8a: The parable of the dishonest steward has to be understood in the light of the Palestinian custom of agents acting on behalf of their masters and the usurious practices common to such agents. The dishonesty of the steward consisted in the squandering of his master's property (1) and not in any subsequent graft. The master commends the dishonest steward who has forgone his own usurious commission on the business transaction by having the debtors write new notes that reflected only the real amount owed the master (i.e., minus the steward's profit). The dishonest steward acts in this way in order to ingratiate himself with the debtors because he knows he is being dismissed from his position (3). The parable, then, teaches the prudent use of one's material goods in light of an imminent crisis.

16, 6: **One hundred measures:** literally, "one hundred baths." A bath is a Hebrew unit of liquid measurement equivalent to eight or nine gallons.

16, 7: **One hundred kors:** a **kor** is a Hebrew unit of dry measure for grain or wheat equivalent to ten or twelve bushels.

16, 8b–13: Several originally independent sayings of Jesus are gathered here by Luke to form the concluding application of the parable by the dishonest steward.

16, 8b-9: The first conclusion recommends the prudent use of one's wealth (in the light of the coming of the end of the age) after the manner of the children of this world, represented in the parable by the dishonest steward.

16, 9: **Dishonest wealth:** literally, "mammon of iniquity." Mammon is the Greek transliteration of a Hebrew or Aramaic word that is usually explained as meaning "that in which one trusts." The characterization of this wealth as **dishonest** expresses a tendency of wealth to lead one to dishonesty. **Eternal dwellings:** or, "eternal tents," i.e., heaven.

16, 10–12: The second conclusion recommends constant fidelity to those in positions of responsibility.

16, 13: The third conclusion is a general statement about the incompatibility of serving God and being a slave to riches. To be dependent upon wealth is opposed to the teachings of Jesus who counseled complete dependence on the Father as one of the characteristics of the Christian disciple (12, 22–39). **God and mammon:** see the note on 16, 9. Mammon is used here as if it were itself a god.

z: Eph 5, 8; 1 Thes 5, 5. a: 12, 33. b: 19, 17; Mt 25, 20-23. c: Mt 6, 24.

A Saying against the Pharisees. [14]*The Pharisees, who loved money, heard all these things and sneered at him. [15d]And he said to them, "You justify yourselves in the sight of others, but God knows your hearts; for what is of human esteem is an abomination in the sight of God.

Sayings about the Law. [16e]*"The law and the prophets lasted until John; but from then on the kingdom of God is proclaimed, and everyone who enters does so with violence. [17f]It is easier for heaven and earth to pass away than for the smallest part of a letter of the law to become invalid.

Sayings about Divorce. [18g]"Everyone who divorces his wife and marries another commits adultery, and the one who marries a woman divorced from her husband commits adultery.

The Parable of the Rich Man and Lazarus. [19]*"There was a rich man who dressed in purple garments and fine linen and dined sumptuously each day. [20]And lying at his door was a poor man named Lazarus, covered with sores, [21h]who would gladly have eaten his fill of the scraps that fell from the rich man's table. Dogs even used to come and lick his sores. [22]When the poor man died, he was carried away by angels to the bosom of Abraham. The rich man also died and was buried, [23]*and from the netherworld, where he was in torment, he raised his eyes and saw Abraham far off and Lazarus at his side. [24]And he cried out, 'Father Abraham, have pity on me. Send Lazarus to dip the tip of his finger in water and cool my tongue, for I am suffering torment in these flames.' [25i]Abraham replied, 'My child, remember that you received what was good during your lifetime while Lazarus likewise received what was bad; but now he is comforted here, whereas you are tormented. [26]Moreover, between us and you a great chasm is established to prevent anyone from crossing who might wish to go from our side to yours or from your side to ours.' [27]He said, 'Then I beg you, father, send him to my father's house, [28]for I have five brothers, so that he may warn them, lest they too come to this place of torment.' [29]But Abraham replied, 'They have Moses and the prophets. Let them listen to them.' [30]*He said, 'Oh no, father Abraham, but if someone from the dead goes to them, they will repent.' [31j]Then Abraham said, 'If they will not listen to Moses and the prophets, neither will they be persuaded if someone should rise from the dead.' "

CHAPTER 17

See RG 312–13

Temptations to Sin. [1k]He said to his disciples, "Things that cause sin will inevitably occur, but woe to the person through whom they occur. [2]It would be better for him if a millstone were put around his neck and he be thrown into the sea than for him to cause one of these little ones to sin. [3]*Be on your guard! If your brother sins, rebuke him; and if he repents, forgive him. [4m]And if he wrongs you seven times in one day and returns to you seven times saying, 'I am sorry,' you should forgive him."

Saying of Faith. [5]And the apostles said to

16, 14–18: The two parables about the use of riches in ch 16 are separated by several isolated sayings of Jesus on the hypocrisy of the Pharisees (14–15), on the law (16–17), and on divorce (18).

16, 14–15: The Pharisees are here presented as examples of those who are slaves to wealth (see 16, 13) and, consequently, they are unable to serve God.

16, 16: John the Baptist is presented in Luke's gospel as a transitional figure between the period of Israel, the time of promise, and the period of Jesus, the time of fulfillment. With John, the fulfillment of the Old Testament promises has begun.

16, 19–31: The parable of the rich man and Lazarus again illustrates Luke's concern with Jesus' attitude toward the rich and the poor. The reversal of the fates of the rich man and Lazarus (22–23) illustrates the teachings of Jesus in Luke's "Sermon on the Plain" (6, 20–21.24–25).

16, 19: The oldest Greek manuscript of Lk dating from ca. A.D. 175–225 records the name of the rich man as an abbreviated form of "Nineveh," but there is very little textual support in other manuscripts for this reading. "Dives" of popular tradition is the Latin Vulgate's translation for "rich man."

16, 23: The netherworld: see the note on 10, 15.

16, 30–31: A foreshadowing in Luke's gospel of the rejection of the call to repentance even after Jesus' resurrection.

17, 3a: Be on your guard: the translation takes v 3a as the conclusion to the saying on scandal in vv 1–2. It is not impossible that it should be taken as the beginning of the saying on forgiveness in vv 3b–4.

---

d: 18, 9-14.   e: Mt 11, 12-13.   f: Mt 5, 18.   g: Mt 5, 32; 19, 9; Mk 10, 11-12; 1 Cor 7, 10-11.   h: Mt 15, 27; Mk 7, 28.   i: 6, 24-25.   j: Jn 5, 46-47; 11, 44-48.   k: Mt 18, 6-7.   l: Mt 18, 15.   m: Mt 6, 14; 18, 21-22.35; Mk 11, 25.

TEMPLE

Courts of
Priests   Women
Israel

Court
of
Gentiles

Beautiful
Gate

Solomon's Portico

Royal Portico

Golgotha

Royal
Palace
Praetorium

Gethsemane

Mount of Olives

GALILEE

Mediterranean Sea

Sea of
Galilee

SAMARIA

River Jordan

Jericho
Bethphage
Jerusalem
Bethany

Dead
Sea

33°

32°

35°   36°

0   5   10 Miles

0   5   10 Kilometers

0   300 Meters

0   300 Yards

Sites of Jesus' Journey to Jerusalem and within It

the Lord, "Increase our faith." [6n]The Lord replied, "If you have faith the size of a mustard seed, you would say to [this] mulberry tree, 'Be uprooted and planted in the sea,' and it would obey you.

Attitude of a Servant. [7]*"Who among you would say to your servant who has just come in from plowing or tending sheep in the field, 'Come here immediately and take your place at table'? [8]Would he not rather say to him, 'Prepare something for me to eat. Put on your apron and wait on me while I eat and drink. You may eat and drink when I am finished'? [9]Is he grateful to that servant because he did what was commanded? [10]So should it be with you. When you have done all you have been commanded, say, 'We are unprofitable servants; we have done what we were obliged to do.' "

The Cleansing of Ten Lepers. [11o]*As he continued his journey to Jerusalem, he traveled through Samaria and Galilee. [12]As he was entering a village, ten lepers met [him]. They stood at a distance from him [13p]and raised their voice, saying, "Jesus, Master! Have pity on us!" [14q]*And when he saw them, he said, "Go show yourselves to the priests." As they were going they were cleansed. [15]And one of them, realizing he had been healed, returned, glorifying God in a loud voice; [16]and he fell at the feet of Jesus and thanked him. He was a Samaritan. [17]Jesus said in reply, "Ten were cleansed, were they not? Where are the other nine? [18]Has none but this foreigner returned to give thanks to God?" [19r]Then he said to him, "Stand up and go; your faith has saved you."

The Coming of the Kingdom of God. [20s]*Asked by the Pharisees when the kingdom of God would come, he said in reply, "The coming of the kingdom of God cannot be observed, [21t]*and no one will announce, 'Look, here it is,' or, 'There it is.' For behold, the kingdom of God is among you."

The Day of the Son of Man. [22]Then he said to his disciples, "The days will come when you will long to see one of the days of the Son of Man, but you will not see it. [23u]There will be those who will say to you, 'Look, there he is,' [or] 'Look, here he is.' Do not go off, do not run in pursuit. [24v]For just as lightning flashes and lights up the sky from one side to the other, so will the Son of Man be [in his day]. [25w]But first he must suffer greatly and be rejected by this generation. [26x]As it was in the days of Noah, so it will be in the days of the Son of Man; [27]they were eating and drinking, marrying and giving in marriage up to the day that Noah entered the ark, and the flood came and destroyed them all. [28y]Similarly, as it was in the days of Lot: they were eating, drinking, buying, selling, planting, building; [29]on the day when Lot left Sodom, fire and brimstone rained from the sky to destroy them all. [30]So it will be on the day the Son of Man is revealed. [31za]On that day, a person who is on the housetop and whose belongings are in the house must not go down to get them, and likewise a person in the field must not return to what was left

---

17, 7–10: These sayings of Jesus, peculiar to Luke, which continue his response to the apostles' request to increase their faith (5–6), remind them that Christian disciples can make no claim on God's graciousness; in fulfilling the exacting demands of discipleship, they are only doing their duty.

17, 11–19: This incident recounting the thankfulness of the cleansed Samaritan leper is narrated only in Luke's gospel and provides an instance of Jesus holding up a non-Jew (18) as an example to his Jewish contemporaries (cf 10, 33 where a similar purpose is achieved in the story of the good Samaritan). Moreover, it is the faith in Jesus manifested by the foreigner that has brought him salvation (19; cf the similar relationship between faith and salvation in 7, 50; 8, 48.50).

17, 11: Through Samaria and Galilee: or, "between Samaria and Galilee."

17, 14: See the note on 5, 14.

17, 20–37: To the question of the Pharisees about the time of the coming of God's kingdom, Jesus replies that the kingdom is **among you** (20–21). The emphasis has thus been shifted from an imminent observable coming of the kingdom to something that is already present in Jesus' preaching and healing ministry. Luke has also appended further traditional sayings of Jesus about the unpredictable suddenness of the day of the Son of Man, and assures his readers that in spite of the delay of that day (12, 45), it will bring judgment unexpectedly on those who do not continue to be vigilant.

17, 21: Among you: the Greek preposition translated as **among** can also be translated as "within." In the light of other statements in Luke's gospel about the presence of the kingdom (see 10, 9.11; 11, 20) "among" is to be preferred.

n: Mt 17, 20; 21, 21; Mk 11, 23. o: 9, 51-53; 13, 22.33; 18, 31; 19, 28; Jn 4, 4. p: 18, 38; Mt 9, 27; 15, 22. q: 5, 14; Lv 14, 2-32; Mt 8, 4; Mk 1, 44. r: 7, 50; 18, 42. s: Jn 3, 3. t: 17, 23; Mt 24, 23; Mk 13, 21. u: 17, 21; Mt 24, 23.26; Mk 13, 21. v: Mt 24, 27. w: 9, 22; 18, 32-33; Mt 16, 21; 17, 22-23; 20, 18-19; Mk 8, 31; 9, 31; 10, 33-34. x: Gn 6-8; Mt 24, 37-39. y: Gn 18, 20-21; 19, 1-29. z: Mt 24, 17-18; Mk 13, 15-16. a: Gn 19, 17.26.

behind. [32]Remember the wife of Lot. [33b]Whoever seeks to preserve his life will lose it, but whoever loses it will save it. [34]I tell you, on that night there will be two people in one bed; one will be taken, the other left. [35c]And there will be two women grinding meal together; one will be taken, the other left." [[36]]* [37d]They said to him in reply, "Where, Lord?" He said to them, "Where the body is, there also the vultures will gather."

CHAPTER 18

See RG 312–13

The Parable of the Persistent Widow.

[1e]*Then he told them a parable about the necessity for them to pray always without becoming weary. He said, [2]"There was a judge in a certain town who neither feared God nor respected any human being. [3]And a widow in that town used to come to him and say, 'Render a just decision for me against my adversary.' [4]For a long time the judge was unwilling, but eventually he thought, 'While it is true that I neither fear God nor respect any human being, [5f]*because this widow keeps bothering me I shall deliver a just decision for her lest she finally come and strike me.' " [6]The Lord said, "Pay attention to what the dishonest judge says. [7]Will not God then secure the rights of his chosen ones who call out to him day and night? Will he be slow to answer them? [8]I tell you, he will see to it that justice is done for them speedily. But when the Son of Man comes, will he find faith on earth?"

The Parable of the Pharisee and the Tax Collector.

[9g]He then addressed this parable to those who were convinced of their own righteousness and despised everyone else. [10]"Two people went up to the temple area to pray, one was a Pharisee and the other was a tax collector. [11]The Pharisee took up his position and spoke this prayer to himself, 'O God, I thank you that I am not like the rest of humanity—greedy, dishonest, adulterous—or even like this tax collector. [12h]I fast twice a week, and I pay tithes on my whole income.' [13i]But the tax collector stood off at a distance and would not even raise his eyes to heaven but beat his breast and prayed, 'O God, be merciful to me a sinner.' [14j]I tell you, the latter went home justified, not the former; for everyone who exalts himself will be humbled, and the one who humbles himself will be exalted."

Saying on Children and the Kingdom.

[15k]*People were bringing even infants to him that he might touch them, and when the disciples saw this, they rebuked them. [15]Jesus, however, called the children to himself and said, "Let the children come to me and do not prevent them; for the kingdom of God belongs to such as these. [17l]Amen, I say to you, whoever does not accept the kingdom of God like a child will not enter it."

The Rich Official.

[18mn]An official asked him this question, "Good teacher, what must I do to inherit eternal life?" [19]Jesus answered him, "Why do you call me good? No one is good but God alone. [20o]You know the com-

---

17, 36: The inclusion of v 36, "There will be two men in the field; one will be taken, the other left behind," in some Western manuscripts appears to be a scribal assimilation to Mt 24, 40.

18, 1–14: The particularly Lucan material in the travel narrative concludes with two parables on prayer. The first (1–8) teaches the disciples the need of persistent prayer so that they not fall victims to apostasy (8). The second (9–14) condemns the self-righteous, critical attitude of the Pharisee and teaches that the fundamental attitude of the Christian disciple must be the recognition of sinfulness and complete dependence on God's graciousness. The second parable recalls the story of the pardoning of the sinful woman (7, 36–50) where a similar contrast is presented between the critical attitude of the Pharisee Simon and the love shown by the pardoned sinner.

18, 5: Strike me: the Greek verb translated as strike means "to strike under the eye" and suggests the extreme situation to which the persistence of the widow might lead. It may, however, be used here in the much weaker sense of "to wear one out."

18, 15—19, 27: Luke here includes much of the material about the journey to Jerusalem found in his Marcan source (10, 1–52) and adds to it the story of Zacchaeus (19, 1–10) from his own particular tradition and the parable of the gold coins (minas) (19, 11–27) from Q, the source common to Lk and Mt.

18, 15–17: The sayings on children furnish a contrast to the attitude of the Pharisee in the preceding episode (9–14) and that of the wealthy official in the following one (18–23) who think that they can lay claim to God's favor by their own merit. The attitude of the disciple should be marked by the receptivity and trustful dependence characteristic of the child.

b: 9, 24; Mt 10, 39; 16, 25; Mk 8, 35; Jn 12, 25.   *c:* Mt 24, 40-41.
d: Jt 39, 30; Mt 24, 28.   *e:* Rom 12, 12; Col 4, 2; 1 Thes 5, 17.
f: 11, 8.   *g:* 16, 5; Mt 23, 25-28.   *h:* Mt 23, 23.   *i:* Ps 51, 3.
j: 14, 11; Mt 23, 12.   *k:* Mt 19, 13-15; Mk 10, 13-16.   *l:* Mt 18,
3.   *m:* Mt 19, 16-30; Mk 10, 17-31.   *n:* 10, 25.   *o:* Ex 20, 12-
16; Dt 5, 16-20.

mandments, 'You shall not commit adultery; you shall not kill; you shall not steal; you shall not bear false witness; honor your father and your mother.' " *21*And he replied, "All of these I have observed from my youth." *22 p**When Jesus heard this he said to him, "There is still one thing left for you: sell all that you have and distribute it to the poor, and you will have a treasure in heaven. Then come, follow me." *23*But when he heard this he became quite sad, for he was very rich.

On Riches and Renunciation. *24*Jesus looked at him [now sad] and said, "How hard it is for those who have wealth to enter the kingdom of God! *25*For it is easier for a camel to pass through the eye of a needle than for a rich person to enter the kingdom of God." *26*Those who heard this said, "Then who can be saved?" *27q*And he said, "What is impossible for human beings is possible for God." *28*Then Peter said, "We have given up our possessions and followed you." *29r*He said to them, "Amen, I say to you, there is no one who has given up house or wife or brothers or parents or children for the sake of the kingdom of God *30*who will not receive [back] an overabundant return in this present age and eternal life in the age to come."

The Third Prediction of the Passion. *31s**Then he took the Twelve aside and said to them, "Behold, we are going up to Jerusalem and everything written by the prophets about the Son of Man will be fulfilled. *32t*He will be handed over to the Gentiles and he will be mocked and insulted and spat upon;

*33*and after they have scourged him they will kill him, but on the third day he will rise." *34u*But they understood nothing of this; the word remained hidden from them and they failed to comprehend what he said.

The Healing of the Blind Beggar. *35v*Now as he approached Jericho a blind man was sitting by the roadside begging, *36*and hearing a crowd going by, he inquired what was happening. *37*They told him, "Jesus of Nazareth is passing by." *38w**He shouted, "Jesus, Son of David, have pity on me!" *39*The people walking in front rebuked him, telling him to be silent, but he kept calling out all the more, "Son of David, have pity on me!" *40*Then Jesus stopped and ordered that he be brought to him; and when he came near, Jesus asked him, *41x*"What do you want me to do for you?" He replied, "Lord, please let me see." *42y*Jesus told him, "Have sight; your faith has saved you." *43*He immediately received his sight and followed him, giving glory to God. When they saw this, all the people gave praise to God.

CHAPTER 19

See RG 312-14

Zacchaeus the Tax Collector. *1**He came to Jericho and intended to pass through the town. *2*Now a man there named Zacchaeus, who was a chief tax collector and also a wealthy man, *3*was seeking to see who Jesus was; but he could not see him because of the crowd, for he was short in stature. *4*So he ran ahead and climbed a sycamore tree in order to see Jesus, who was about to pass that way.

18, 22: Detachment from material possessions results in the total dependence on God demanded of one who would inherit eternal life. **Sell all that you have:** the original saying (cf Mk 10, 21) has characteristically been made more demanding by Luke's addition of "all."

18, 31–33: The details included in this third announcement of Jesus' suffering and death suggest that the literary formulation of the announcement has been directed by the knowledge of the historical passion and death of Jesus.

18, 31: Everything written by the prophets . . . will be fulfilled: this is a Lucan addition to the words of Jesus found in the Marcan source (Mk 10, 32–34). Luke understands the events of Jesus' last days in Jerusalem to be the fulfillment of Old Testament prophecy, but, as is usually the case in Luke-Acts, the author does not specify which Old Testament prophets he has in mind; cf 24, 25.27.44; Acts 3, 8; 13, 27; 26, 22–23.

18, 38: Son of David: the blind beggar identifies Jesus

with a title that is related to Jesus' role as Messiah (see the note on 2, 11). Through this Son of David, salvation comes to the blind man. Note the connection between salvation and house of David mentioned earlier in Zechariah's canticle (1, 69). See also the note on Mt 9, 27.

19, 1–10: The story of the tax collector Zacchaeus is unique to this gospel. While a rich man (2), Zacchaeus provides a contrast to the rich man of 18, 18–23 who cannot detach himself from his material possessions to become a follower of Jesus. Zacchaeus, according to Luke, exemplifies the proper attitude toward wealth: he promises to give half of his possessions to the poor (8) and consequently is the recipient of salvation (9–10).

p: 12, 33; Sir 29, 11; Mt 6, 20. *q:* Mk 14, 36. *r:* 14, 26. *s:* 24, 25-27.44; Mt 20, 17-19; Mk 10, 32-34; Acts 3, 18. *t:* 9, 22.44. *u:* Mk 9, 32. *v:* Mt 20, 29-34; Mk 10, 46-52. *w:* 17, 13; Mt 9, 27; 15, 22. *x:* Mk 10, 36. *y:* 7, 50; 17, 19.

5When he reached the place, Jesus looked up and said to him, "Zacchaeus, come down quickly, for today I must stay at your house." 6And he came down quickly and received him with joy. 7zWhen they all saw this, they began to grumble, saying, "He has gone to stay at the house of a sinner." 8aBut Zacchaeus stood there and said to the Lord, "Behold, half of my possessions, Lord, I shall give to the poor, and if I have extorted anything from anyone I shall repay it four times over." 9b*And Jesus said to him, "Today salvation has come to this house because this man too is a descendant of Abraham. 10c*For the Son of Man has come to seek and to save what was lost."

The Parable of the Ten Gold Coins. 11d*While they were listening to him speak, he proceeded to tell a parable because he was near Jerusalem and they thought that the kingdom of God would appear there immediately. 12eSo he said, "A nobleman went off to a distant country to obtain the kingship for himself and then to return. 13*He called ten of his servants and gave them ten gold coins and told them, 'Engage in trade with these until I return.' 14His fellow citizens, however, despised him and sent a delegation after him to announce, 'We do not want this man to be our king.' 15But when he returned after obtaining the kingship, he had the servants called, to whom he had given the money, to learn what they had gained by trading. 16The first came forward and said, 'Sir, your gold coin has earned ten additional ones.' 17fHe replied, 'Well done, good servant! You have been faithful in this very small matter; take charge of ten cities.' 18Then the second came and reported, 'Your gold coin, sir, has earned five more.' 19And to this servant too he said, 'You, take charge of five cities.' 20Then the other servant came and said, 'Sir, here is your gold coin; I kept it stored away in a handkerchief, 21for I was afraid of you, because you are a demanding person; you take up what you did not lay down and you harvest what you did not plant.' 22He said to him, 'With your own words I shall condemn you, you wicked servant. You knew I was a demanding person, taking up what I did not lay down and harvesting what I did not plant; 23why did you not put my money in a bank? Then on my return I would have collected it with interest.' 24And to those standing by he said, 'Take the gold coin from him and give it to the servant who has ten.' 25But they said to him, 'Sir, he has ten gold coins.' 26g'I tell you, to everyone who has, more will be given, but from the one who has not, even what he has will be taken away. 27Now as for those enemies of mine who did not want me as their king, bring them here and slay them before me.' "

VI: The Teaching Ministry in Jerusalem

The Entry into Jerusalem. 28h*After he had said this, he proceeded on his journey up to

19, 9: A descendant of Abraham: literally, "a son of Abraham." The tax collector Zacchaeus, whose repentance is attested by his determination to amend his former ways, shows himself to be a true descendant of Abraham, the true heir to the promises of God in the Old Testament. Underlying Luke's depiction of Zacchaeus as a descendant of Abraham, the father of the Jews (1, 73; 16, 22–31), is his recognition of the central place occupied by Israel in the plan of salvation.

19, 10: This verse sums up for Luke his depiction of the role of Jesus as savior in this gospel.

19, 11–27: In this parable Luke has combined two originally distinct parables: (1) a parable about the conduct of faithful and productive servants (13,15b–26) and (2) a parable about a rejected king (12.14–15a.27). The story about the conduct of servants occurs in another form in Mt 25, 14–20. The story about the rejected king may have originated in a contemporary historical event. After the death of Herod the Great, his son Archelaus traveled to Rome to receive the title of king. A delegation of Jews appeared in Rome before Caesar Augustus to oppose the request of Archelaus. Although

not given the title of king, Archelaus was made ruler over Judea and Samaria. As the story is used by Luke, however, it furnishes a correction to the expectation of the imminent end of the age and of the establishment of the kingdom in Jerusalem (11). Jesus is not on his way to Jerusalem to receive the kingly power; for that, he must go away and only after returning from the distant country (a reference to the parousia) will reward and judgment take place.

19, 13: Ten gold coins: literally, "ten minas." A mina was a monetary unit that in ancient Greece was the equivalent of one hundred drachmas.

19, 28—21, 38: With the royal entry of Jesus into Jerusalem, a new section of Luke's gospel begins, the ministry of Jesus in Jerusalem before his death and resurrection. Luke suggests that this was a lengthy ministry in Jerusalem (19, 47;

z: 5, 30; 15, 2. a: Ex 21, 37; Nm 5, 6-7; 2 Sm 12, 6. b: 13, 16; Mt 21, 31. c: 15, 4-10; Ez 34, 16. d: Mt 25, 14-30. e: Mk 13, 34. f: 16, 10. g: 8, 18; Mt 13, 12; Mk 4, 25. h: Mt 21, 1-11; Mk 1, 1-11; Jn 12, 12-19.

Jerusalem. [29i]As he drew near to Bethphage and Bethany at the place called the Mount of Olives, he sent two of his disciples. [30j]He said, "Go into the village opposite you, and as you enter it you will find a colt tethered on which no one has ever sat. Untie it and bring it here. [31]And if anyone should ask you, 'Why are you untying it?' you will answer, 'The Master has need of it.' " [32k]So those who had been sent off and found everything just as he had told them. [33]And as they were untying the colt, its owners said to them, "Why are you untying this colt?" [34]They answered, "The Master has need of it." [35l]So they brought it to Jesus, threw their cloaks over the colt, and helped Jesus to mount. [36]As he rode along, the people were spreading their cloaks on the road; [37]and now as he was approaching the slope of the Mount of Olives, the whole multitude of his disciples began to praise God aloud with joy for all the mighty deeds they had seen. [38m]*They proclaimed:

"Blessed is the king who comes
    in the name of the Lord.
Peace in heaven
    and glory in the highest."

[39]*Some of the Pharisees in the crowd said to him, "Teacher, rebuke your disciples." [40]He said in reply, "I tell you, if they keep silent, the stones will cry out!"

The Lament for Jerusalem. [41no]*As he drew near, he saw the city and wept over it, [42p]saying, "If this day you only knew what makes for peace—but now it is hidden from your eyes. [43q]*For the days are coming upon you when your enemies will raise a palisade against you; they will encircle you and hem you in on all sides. [44r]They will smash you to the ground and your children within you, and they will not leave one stone upon another within you because you did not recognize the time of your visitation."

The Cleansing of the Temple. [45st]*Then Jesus entered the temple area and proceeded to drive out those who were selling things, [46u]saying to them, "It is written, 'My house shall be a house of prayer, but you have made it a den of thieves.' " [47vw]And every day he was teaching in the temple area. The chief priests, the scribes, and the leaders of the people, meanwhile, were seeking to put him to death, [48]but they could find no way to accomplish their purpose because all the people were hanging on his words.

CHAPTER 20

The Authority of Jesus Questioned.
See RG 314–15

[1x]*One day as he was teaching the people in the temple area and proclaiming the good news, the chief priests and scribes, together with the elders, approached him [2y]and said

20, 1; 21, 37–38; 22, 53) and it is characterized by Jesus' daily teaching in the temple (21, 37–38). For the story of the entry of Jesus into Jerusalem, see also Mt 21, 1–11; Mk 11, 1–10; Jn 12, 12–19 and the notes there.

19, 38: Blessed is the king who comes in the name of the Lord: only in Lk is Jesus explicitly given the title **king** when he enters Jerusalem in triumph. Luke has inserted this title into the words of Ps 118, 26 that heralded the arrival of the pilgrims coming to the holy city and to the temple. Jesus is thereby acclaimed as **king** (see 1, 32) and as the one **who comes** (see Mal 3, 1; Lk 7, 19). **Peace in heaven . . . :** the acclamation of the disciples of Jesus in Lk echoes the announcement of the angels at the birth of Jesus (2, 14). The peace Jesus brings is associated with the salvation to be accomplished here in Jerusalem.

19, 39: Rebuke your disciples: this command, found only in Lk, was given so that the Roman authorities would not interpret the acclamation of Jesus as king as an uprising against them; cf 23, 2–3.

19, 41–44: The lament for Jerusalem is found only in Lk. By not accepting Jesus (the one who mediates peace), Jerusalem will not find peace but will become the victim of devastation.

19, 43–44: Luke may be describing the actual disaster that

befell Jerusalem in A.D. 70 when it was destroyed by the Romans during the First Revolt.

19, 45–46: Immediately upon entering the holy city, Jesus in a display of his authority enters the temple (see Mal 3, 1–3) and lays claim to it after cleansing it that it might become a proper place for his teaching ministry in Jerusalem (19, 47; 20, 1; 21, 37; 22, 53). See Mt 21, 12–17; Mk 11, 15–19; Jn 2, 13–17 and the notes there.

20, 1–47: The Jerusalem religious leaders or their representatives, in an attempt to incriminate Jesus with the Romans and to discredit him with the people, pose a number of questions to him (about his authority, 2; about payment of taxes, 22; about the resurrection, 28–33).

i: Zec 14, 4. *j:* Nm 19, 2; Dt 21, 3; 1 Sm 6, 7; Zec 9, 9. *k:* 22, 13. *l:* 2 Kgs 9, 13. *m:* 2, 14; Ps 118, 26. *n:* 13, 34-35. *o:* 2 Kgs 8, 11-12; Jer 14, 17; 15, 5. *p:* 8, 10; Is 6, 9-10; Mt 13, 14; Mk 4, 12; Acts 28, 26-27; Rom 11, 8.10. *q:* Is 29, 3. *r:* 1, 68; 21, 6; Ps 137, 9; Mt 24, 2; Mk 13, 2. *s:* Mt 21, 12-13; Mk 11, 15-17; Jn 2, 13-17. *t:* 3, 1 / Hos 9, 15. *u:* Is 56, 7; Jer 7, 11. *v:* 20, 19; 22, 2; Mt 21, 46; Mk 11, 18; 12, 12; 14, 1-2; Jn 5, 18; 7, 30. *w:* 21, 37; 22, 53; Jn 18, 20. *x:* Mt 21, 23-27; Mk 11, 27-33. *y:* Acts 4, 7.

to him, "Tell us, by what authority are you doing these things? Or who is the one who gave you this authority?" [3]He said to them in reply, "I shall ask you a question. Tell me, [4z]was John's baptism of heavenly or of human origin?" [5a]They discussed this among themselves, and said, "If we say, 'Of heavenly origin,' he will say, 'Why did you not believe him?' [6]But if we say, 'Of human origin,' then all the people will stone us, for they are convinced that John was a prophet." [7]So they answered that they did not know from where it came. [8]Then Jesus said to them, "Neither shall I tell you by what authority I do these things."

The Parable of the Tenant Farmers. [9bc]*Then he proceeded to tell the people this parable. "[A] man planted a vineyard, leased it to tenant farmers, and then went on a journey for a long time. [10d]At harvest time he sent a servant to the tenant farmers to receive some of the produce of the vineyard. But they beat the servant and sent him away empty-handed. [11]So he proceeded to send another servant, but him also they beat and insulted and sent away empty-handed. [12]Then he proceeded to send a third, but this one too they wounded and threw out. [13e]The owner of the vineyard said, 'What shall I do? I shall send my beloved son; maybe they will respect him.' [14]But when the tenant farmers saw him they said to one another, 'This is the heir. Let us kill him that the inheritance may become ours.' [15]*So they threw him out of the vineyard and killed him. What will the owner of the vineyard do to them? [16]He will come and put those tenant farmers to death and turn over the vineyard to others." When the people heard this, they exclaimed, "Let it not be so!" [17f]But he looked at them and asked, "What then does this scripture passage mean:

'The stone which the builders rejected
has become the cornerstone'?

[18]Everyone who falls on that stone will be dashed to pieces; and it will crush anyone on whom it falls." [19g]The scribes and chief priests sought to lay their hands on him at that very hour, but they feared the people, for they knew that he had addressed this parable to them.

Paying Taxes to the Emperor. [20hi]*They watched him closely and sent agents pretending to be righteous who were to trap him in speech, in order to hand him over to the authority and power of the governor. [21j]They posed this question to him, "Teacher, we know that what you say and teach is correct, and you show no partiality, but teach the way of God in accordance with the truth. [22]*Is it lawful for us to pay tribute to Caesar or not?" [23]Recognizing their craftiness he said to them, [24]*"Show me a denarius; whose image and name does it bear?" They replied, "Caesar's." [25k]So he said to them, "Then repay to Caesar what belongs to Caesar and to God what belongs to God." [26]They were unable to trap him by something he might say before the people, and so amazed were they at his reply that they fell silent.

The Question about the Resurrection. [27lm]*Some Sadducees, those who deny that there is a resurrection, came forward and put

---

20, 9–19: This parable about an absentee landlord and a tenant farmers' revolt reflects the social and economic conditions of rural Palestine in the first century. The synoptic gospel writers use the parable to describe how the rejection of the landlord's son becomes the occasion for the vineyard to be taken away from those to whom it was entrusted (the religious leadership of Judaism that rejects the teaching and preaching of Jesus; 19).

20, 15: **They threw him out of the vineyard and killed him:** cf Mk 12, 8. Luke has altered his Marcan source and reports that the murder of the son takes place outside the vineyard to reflect the tradition of Jesus' death outside the walls of the city of Jerusalem (see Heb 13, 12).

20, 20: **The governor:** i.e., Pontius Pilate, the Roman administrator responsible for the collection of taxes and maintenance of order in Palestine.

20, 22: Through their question the agents of the Jerusalem religious leadership hope to force Jesus to take sides on one of the sensitive political issues of first-century Palestine. The issue of nonpayment of taxes to Rome becomes one of the focal points of the First Jewish Revolt (A.D. 66–70) that resulted in the Roman destruction of Jerusalem and the temple. See also the note on Mt 22, 15–22.

20, 24: **Denarius:** a Roman silver coin (see the note on 7, 41)

20, 27: **Sadducees:** see the note on Mt 3, 7.

z: 3, 3.16.   a: Mt 21, 32.   b: Mt 21, 33-46; Mk 12, 1-12.   c: Is 5, 1-7.   d: 2 Chr 36, 15-16.   e: 3, 22.   f: Ps 118, 22; Is 28, 16.   g: 19, 47-48; 22, 2; Mt 21, 46; Mk 11, 18; 12, 12; 14, 1-2; Jr 5, 18; 7, 30.   h: Mt 22, 15-22; Mk 12, 13-17.   i: 11, 54.   j: Jn 3, 2.   k: Rom 13, 6-7.   l: Mt 22, 23-33; Mk 12, 18-27.   m: Acts 23, 8.

this question to him, [28n]*saying, "Teacher, Moses wrote for us, 'If someone's brother dies leaving a wife but no child, his brother must take the wife and raise up descendants for his brother.' [29]Now there were seven brothers; the first married a woman but died childless. [30]Then the second [31]and the third married her, and likewise all the seven died childless. [32]Finally the woman also died. [33]Now at the resurrection whose wife will that woman be? For all seven had been married to her." [34]Jesus said to them, "The children of this age marry and remarry; [35]but those who are deemed worthy to attain to the coming age and to the resurrection of the dead neither marry nor are given in marriage. [36]*They can no longer die, for they are like angels; and they are the children of God because they are the ones who will rise. [37o]That the dead will rise even Moses made known in the passage about the bush, when he called 'Lord' the God of Abraham, the God of Isaac, and the God of Jacob; [38p]and he is not God of the dead, but of the living, for to him all are alive." [39]Some of the scribes said in reply, "Teacher, you have answered well." [40q]And they no longer dared to ask him anything.

The Question about David's Son. [41r]*Then he said to them, "How do they claim that the Messiah is the Son of David? [42s]For David himself in the Book of Psalms says:

'The Lord said to my lord,
   "Sit at my right hand
[43]   till I make your enemies your
         footstool." '

[44]Now if David calls him 'lord,' how can he be his son?"

Denunciation of the Scribes. [45t]Then, within the hearing of all the people, he said to [his] disciples, [46u]"Be on guard against the scribes, who like to go around in long robes and love greetings in marketplaces, seats of honor in synagogues, and places of honor at banquets. [47]They devour the houses of widows and, as a pretext, recite lengthy prayers. They will receive a very severe condemnation."

CHAPTER 21

The Poor Widow's Contribution. See RG 314–15 [1v]*When he looked up he saw some wealthy people putting their offerings into the treasury [2]and he noticed a poor widow putting in two small coins. [3]He said, "I tell you truly, this poor widow put in more than all the rest; [4]for those others have all made offerings from their surplus wealth, but she, from her poverty, has offered her whole livelihood."

The Destruction of the Temple Foretold. [5w]*While some people were speaking about how the temple was adorned with costly stones and votive offerings, he said, [6x]"All

---

20, 28–33: The Sadducees' question, based on the law of levirate marriage recorded in Dt 25, 5–10, ridicules the idea of the resurrection. Jesus rejects their naive understanding of the resurrection (35–36) and then argues on behalf of the resurrection of the dead on the basis of the written law (37–38) that the Sadducees accept. See also the notes on Mt 22, 23–33.

20, 36: Because they are the ones who will rise: literally, "being sons of the resurrection."

20, 41–44: After successfully answering the three questions of his opponents, Jesus now asks them a question. Their inability to respond implies that they have forfeited their position and authority as the religious leaders of the people because they do not understand the scriptures. This series of controversies between the religious leadership of Jerusalem and Jesus reveals Jesus as the authoritative teacher whose words are to be listened to (see 9, 35). See also the notes on Mt 22, 41–46.

21, 1–4: The widow is another example of the poor ones in this gospel whose detachment from material possessions and dependence on God leads to their blessedness (6, 20). Her simple offering provides a striking contrast to the pride and pretentiousness of the scribes denounced in the preceding section (20, 45–47). The story is taken from Mk 12, 41–44.

21, 5–36: Jesus' eschatological discourse in Lk is inspired by Mk 13, but Luke has made some significant alterations to the words of Jesus found there. Luke maintains, though in a modified form, the belief in the early expectation of the end of the age (see 27.28.31.32.36), but, by focusing attention throughout the gospel on the importance of the day-to-day following of Jesus and by reinterpreting the meaning of some of the signs of the end from Mk 13, he has come to terms with what seemed to the early Christian community to be a delay of the parousia. Mark, for example, described the desecration of the Jerusalem temple by the Romans (Mk 13, 14) as the apocalyptic symbol (see Dn 9, 27; 12, 11) accompanying the end of the age and the coming of the Son of Man. Luke (21, 20–24), however, removes the apocalyptic setting and separates the historical destruction of Jerusalem from the signs of the coming of the Son of Man by a period that he refers to as "the times of the Gentiles" (21, 24). See also the notes on Mt 24, 1–36 and Mk 13, 1–37.

n: Gn 38, 8; Dt 25, 5.   o: Ex 3, 2.6.15-16.   p: Rom 14, 8-9.
q: Mt 22, 46; Mk 12, 34.   r: Mt 22, 41-45; Mk 12, 35-37.   s: Ps 110, 1.   t: 11, 37-54; Mt 23, 1-36; Mk 12, 38-40.   u: 14, 7-11.
v: Mk 12, 41-44.   w: Mt 24, 1-2; Mk 13, 1-2.   x: 19, 44.

that you see here—the days will come when there will not be left a stone upon another stone that will not be thrown down."

The Signs of the End. [7y]Then they asked him, "Teacher, when will this happen? And what sign will there be when all these things are about to happen?" [8z]*He answered, "See that you not be deceived, for many will come in my name, saying, 'I am he,' and 'The time has come.' Do not follow them! [9]When you hear of wars and insurrections, do not be terrified; for such things must happen first, but it will not immediately be the end." [10a]Then he said to them, "Nation will rise against nation, and kingdom against kingdom. [11]There will be powerful earthquakes, famines, and plagues from place to place; and awesome sights and mighty signs will come from the sky.

The Coming Persecution. [12bc]*"Before all this happens, however, they will seize and persecute you, they will hand you over to the synagogues and to prisons, and they will have you led before kings and governors because of my name. [13]It will lead to your giving testimony. [14]Remember, you are not to prepare your defense beforehand, [15d]*for I myself shall give you a wisdom in speaking that all your adversaries will be powerless to resist or refute. [16ef]You will even be handed over by parents, brothers, relatives, and friends, and they will put some of you to death. [17]You will be hated by all because of my name, [18g]but not a hair on your head will be destroyed. [19h]By your perseverance you will secure your lives.

The Great Tribulation. [20ij]*"When you see Jerusalem surrounded by armies, know that its desolation is at hand. [21k]Then those in Judea must flee to the mountains. Let those within the city escape from it, and let those in the countryside not enter the city, [22]for these days are the time of punishment when all the scriptures are fulfilled. [23l]Woe to pregnant women and nursing mothers in those days, for a terrible calamity will come upon the earth and a wrathful judgment upon this people. [24m]*They will fall by the edge of the sword and be taken as captives to all the Gentiles; and Jerusalem will be trampled underfoot by the Gentiles until the times of the Gentiles are fulfilled.

The Coming of the Son of Man. [25no]"There will be signs in the sun, the moon, and the stars, and on earth nations will be in dismay, perplexed by the roaring of the sea and the waves. [26p]*People will die of fright in anticipation of what is coming upon the world, for the powers of the heavens will be shaken. [27q]And then they will see the Son of Man coming in a cloud with power and great glory. [28r]But when these signs begin to happen, stand erect and raise your heads because your redemption is at hand."

The Lesson of the Fig Tree. [29s]He taught them a lesson. "Consider the fig tree and all the other trees. [30]When their buds burst open, you see for yourselves and know that summer is now near; [31]in the same way, when you see these things happening, know that the kingdom of God is near. [32t]Amen, I say to you, this generation will not pass away until all these things have taken place. [33u]Heaven and earth will pass away, but my words will not pass away.

21, 8: The time has come: in Lk, the proclamation of the imminent end of the age has itself become a false teaching.

21, 12: Before all this happens . . . : to Luke and his community, some of the signs of the end just described (10–11) still lie in the future. Now in dealing with the persecution of the disciples (12–19) and the destruction of Jerusalem (20–24) Luke is pointing to eschatological signs that have already been fulfilled.

21, 15: A wisdom in speaking: literally, "a mouth and wisdom."

21, 20–24: The actual destruction of Jerusalem by Rome in A.D. 70 upon which Luke and his community look back provides the assurance that, just as Jesus' prediction of Jerusalem's destruction was fulfilled, so too will be his announcement of their final redemption (27–28).

21, 24: The times of the Gentiles: a period of indeterminate length separating the destruction of Jerusalem from the cosmic signs accompanying the coming of the Son of Man.

21, 26: The powers of the heavens: the heavenly bodies mentioned in v 25 and thought of as cosmic armies.

y: Mt 24, 3-14; Mk 13, 3-13.   z: 17, 23; Mk 13, 5.6.21; 1 Jn 2, 18.
a: 2 Chr 15, 6; Is 19, 2.   b: 12, 11-12; Mt 10, 17-20; Mk 13, 9-11.   c: Jn 16, 2; Acts 25, 24.   d: Acts 6, 10.   e: Mt 10, 21-22.
f: 12, 52-53.   g: 12, 7; 1 Sm 14, 45; Mt 10, 30; Acts 27, 34.
h: 8, 15.   i: Mt 24, 15-21; Mk 13, 14-19.   j: 19, 41-44.   k: 17, 31.   l: 1 Cor 7, 26.   m: Tb 14, 5; Ps 79, 1; Is 63, 18; Jer 21, 7; Rom 11, 25; Rv 11, 2.   n: Mt 24, 29-31; Mk 13, 24-27.   o: Wis 5, 22; Is 13, 10; Ez 32, 7; Jl 2, 10; 3, 3-4; 4, 15; Rv 6, 12-14.
p: Hg 2, 6.21.   q: Dn 7, 13-14; Mt 26, 64; Rv 1, 7.   r: 2, 38.
s: Mt 24, 32-35; Mk 13, 28-31.   t: 9, 27; Mt 16, 28.   u: 16, 17.

Exhortation to be Vigilant. [34v]"Beware that your hearts do not become drowsy from carousing and drunkenness and the anxieties of daily life, and that day catch you by surprise [35]like a trap. For that day will assault everyone who lives on the face of the earth. [36w]Be vigilant at all times and pray that you have the strength to escape the tribulations that are imminent and to stand before the Son of Man."

Ministry in Jerusalem. [37x]During the day, Jesus was teaching in the temple area, but at night he would leave and stay at the place called the Mount of Olives. [38]And all the people would get up early each morning to listen to him in the temple area.

VII: The Passion Narrative

CHAPTER 22

See RG 315–16

The Conspiracy against Jesus. [1y]*Now the feast of Unleavened Bread, called the Passover, was drawing near, [2z]and the chief priests and the scribes were seeking a way to put him to death, for they were afraid of the people. [3ab]*Then Satan entered into Judas, the one surnamed Iscariot, who was counted among the Twelve, [4]and he went to the chief priests and temple guards to discuss a plan for handing him over to them. [5]They were pleased and agreed to pay him money. [6]He accepted their offer and sought a favorable opportunity to hand him over to them in the absence of a crowd.

Preparations for the Passover. [7cd]When the day of the feast of Unleavened Bread arrived, the day for sacrificing the Passover lamb, [8]he sent out Peter and John, instructing them, "Go and make preparations for us to eat the Passover." [9]They asked him, "Where do you want us to make the preparations?" [10]*And he answered them, "When you go into the city, a man will meet you carrying a jar of water. Follow him into the house that he enters [11]and say to the master of the house, 'The teacher says to you, "Where is the guest room where I may eat the Passover with my disciples?" ' [12]He will show you a large upper room that is furnished. Make the preparations there." [13e]Then they went off and found everything exactly as he had told them, and there they prepared the Passover.

The Last Supper. [14f]When the hour came, he took his place at table with the apostles. [15]*He said to them, "I have eagerly desired to eat this Passover with you before I suffer, [16g]for, I tell you, I shall not eat it [again] until there is fulfillment in the kingdom of God." [17]*Then he took a cup, gave thanks, and said, "Take this and share it among yourselves; [18]for I tell you [that] from this time on I shall not drink of the fruit of the vine until the kingdom of God comes."

22, 1–23, 56a: The passion narrative. Luke is still dependent upon Mk for the composition of the passion narrative but has incorporated much of his own special tradition into the narrative. Among the distinctive sections in Lk are: (1) the tradition of the institution of the Eucharist (22, 15–20); (2) Jesus' farewell discourse (22, 21–38); (3) the mistreatment and interrogation of Jesus (22, 63–71); (4) Jesus before Herod and his second appearance before Pilate (23, 6–16); (5) words addressed to the women followers on the way to the crucifixion (23, 27–32); (6) words to the penitent thief (23, 39–41); (7) the death of Jesus (23, 46.47b-49). Luke stresses the innocence of Jesus (23, 4.14–15.22) who is the victim of the powers of evil (22, 3.31.53) and who goes to his death in fulfillment of his Father's will (22, 42.46). Throughout the narrative Luke emphasizes the mercy, compassion, and healing power of Jesus (22, 51; 23, 43) who does not go to death lonely and deserted, but is accompanied by others who follow him on the way of the cross (23, 26–31.49).

22, 1: Feast of Unleavened Bread, called the Passover: see the note on Mk 14, 1.

22, 3: Satan entered into Judas: see the note on 4, 13.

22, 10: A man will meet you carrying a jar of water: see the note on Mk 14, 13.

22, 15: This Passover: Luke clearly identifies this last supper of Jesus with the apostles as a Passover meal that commemorated the deliverance of the Israelites from slavery in Egypt. Jesus reinterprets the significance of the Passover by setting it in the context of the kingdom of God (16). The "deliverance" associated with the Passover finds its new meaning in the blood that will be shed (20).

22, 17: Because of a textual problem in vv 19 and 20, some commentators interpret this cup as the eucharistic cup.

v: 12, 45-46; Mt 24, 48-50; 1 Thes 5, 3.6-7. *w:* Mk 13, 33. *x:* 19, 47; 22, 39. *y:* Mt 26, 1-5; Mk 14, 1-2; Jn 11, 47-53. *z:* 19, 47-48; 20, 19; Mt 21, 46; Mk 12, 12; Jn 5, 18; 7, 30. *a:* Mt 26, 14-16; Mk 14, 10-11; Jn 13, 2.27. *b:* Acts 1, 17. *c:* Mt 26, 17-19; Mk 14, 12-16. *d:* Ex 12, 6.14-20. *e:* 19, 32. *f:* Mt 26, 20.26-30; Mk 14, 17.22-26; 1 Cor 11, 23-25. *g:* 13, 29.

19h *Then he took the bread, said the blessing, broke it, and gave it to them, saying, "This is my body, which will be given for you; do this in memory of me." 20i And likewise the cup after they had eaten, saying, "This cup is the new covenant in my blood, which will be shed for you.

The Betrayal Foretold. 21j "And yet behold, the hand of the one who is to betray me is with me on the table; 22 for the Son of Man indeed goes as it has been determined; but woe to that man by whom he is betrayed." 23 And they began to debate among themselves who among them would do such a deed.

The Role of the Disciples. 24k *Then an argument broke out among them about which of them should be regarded as the greatest. 25l *He said to them, "The kings of the Gentiles lord it over them and those in authority over them are addressed as 'Benefactors'; 26m but among you it shall not be so. Rather, let the greatest among you be as the youngest, and the leader as the servant. 27 For who is greater: the one seated at table or the one who serves? Is it not the one seated at table? I am among you as the one who serves. 28 It is you who have stood by me in my trials; 29n and I confer a kingdom on you, just as my Father has conferred one on me, 30o that you may eat and drink at my table in my kingdom; and you will sit on thrones judging the twelve tribes of Israel.

Peter's Denial Foretold. 31pq *"Simon, Si-

mon, behold Satan has demanded to sift all of you like wheat, 32 but I have prayed that your own faith may not fail; and once you have turned back, you must strengthen your brothers." 33r He said to him, "Lord, I am prepared to go to prison and to die with you." 34s But he replied, "I tell you, Peter, before the cock crows this day, you will deny three times that you know me."

Instructions for the Time of Crisis. 25t He said to them, "When I sent you forth without a money bag or a sack or sandals, were you in need of anything?" "No, nothing," they replied. 36u He said to them, "But now one who has a money bag should take it, and likewise a sack, and one who does not have a sword should sell his cloak and buy one. 37v For I tell you that this scripture must be fulfilled in me, namely, 'He was counted among the wicked'; and indeed what is written about me is coming to fulfillment." 38 Then they said, "Lord, look, there are two swords here." But he replied, "It is enough!"

The Agony in the Garden. 39w Then going out he went, as was his custom, to the Mount of Olives, and the disciples followed him. 40x When he arrived at the place he said to them, "Pray that you may not undergo the test." 41y After withdrawing about a stone's throw from them and kneeling, he prayed, 42 saying, "Father, if you are willing, take this cup away from me; still, not my will but yours be done." [43 *And to strengthen him

22, 19c-20: Which will be given . . . do this in memory of me: these words are omitted in some important Western text manuscripts and a few Syriac manuscripts. Other ancient text types, including the oldest papyrus manuscript of Lk dating from the late second or early third century, contain the longer reading presented here. The Lucan account of the words of institution of the Eucharist bears a close resemblance to the words of institution in the Pauline tradition (see 1 Cor 11, 23–26). See also the notes on Mt 26, 26–29; 26, 27–28; and Mk 14, 22–24.

22, 24–38: The Gospel of Luke presents a brief farewell discourse of Jesus; compare the lengthy farewell discourses and prayer in Jn, chs 13–17.

22, 25: 'Benefactors': this word occurs as a title of rulers in the Hellenistic world.

22, 31: All of you: literally, "you." The translation reflects the meaning of the Greek text that uses a second person plural pronoun here.

22, 31–32: Jesus' prayer for Simon's faith and the commission to strengthen his brothers anticipates the post-resurrectional prominence of Peter in the first half of Acts, where

he appears as the spokesman for the Christian community and the one who begins the mission to the Gentiles (Acts 10–11).

22, 36: In contrast to the ministry of the Twelve and of the seventy-two during the period of Jesus (9, 3; 10, 4), in the future period of the church the missionaries must be prepared for the opposition they will face in a world hostile to their preaching.

22, 38: It is enough!: the farewell discourse ends abruptly with these words of Jesus spoken to the disciples when they take literally what was intended as figurative language about being prepared to face the world's hostility.

22, 43–44: These verses, though very ancient, were probably not part of the original text of Lk. They are absent from

h: 24, 30; Acts 27, 35.   i: Ex 24, 8; Jer 31, 31; 32, 40; Zec 9, 11.   j: Ps 41, 10; Mt 26, 21-25; Mk 14, 18-21; Jn 13, 21-30.   k: 9, 46; Mt 18, 1; Mk 9, 34.   l: Mt 20, 25-27; Mk 10, 42-44; Jn 13, 3-16.   m: Mt 23, 11; Mk 9, 35.   n: 12, 32.   o: Mt 19, 28.   p: Mt 26, 33-35; Mk 14, 29-31; Jn 13, 37-38.   q: Jb 1, 6-12; Am 9, 9.   r: 22, 54.   s: 22, 54-62.   t: 9, 3; 10, 4; Mt 10, 9-10; Mk 6, 7-9.   u: 22, 49.   v: Is 53, 12.   w: Mt 26, 30.36-46; Mk 14, 26.32-42; Jn 18, 1-2.   x: 22, 46.   y: Heb 5, 7-8.   z: Mt 6, 10.

an angel from heaven appeared to him. [44]He was in such agony and he prayed so fervently that his sweat became like drops of blood falling on the ground.] [45]When he rose from prayer and returned to his disciples, he found them sleeping from grief. [46a]He said to them, "Why are you sleeping? Get up and pray that you may not undergo the test."

The Betrayal and Arrest of Jesus. [47b]While he was still speaking, a crowd approached and in front was one of the Twelve, a man named Judas. He went up to Jesus to kiss him. [48]Jesus said to him, "Judas, are you betraying the Son of Man with a kiss?" [49c]His disciples realized what was about to happen, and they asked, "Lord, shall we strike with a sword?" [50d]And one of them struck the high priest's servant and cut off his right ear. [51*]But Jesus said in reply, "Stop, no more of this!" Then he touched the servant's ear and healed him. [52e]And Jesus said to the chief priests and temple guards and elders who had come for him, "Have you come out as against a robber, with swords and clubs? [53f]Day after day I was with you in the temple area, and you did not seize me; but this is your hour, the time for the power of darkness."

Peter's Denial of Jesus. [54gh]After arresting him they led him away and took him into the house of the high priest; Peter was following at a distance. [55]They lit a fire in the middle of the courtyard and sat around it, and Peter sat down with them. [56]When a maid saw him seated in the light, she looked intently at him and said, "This man too was with him." [57]But he denied it saying,

"Woman, I do not know him." [58]A short while later someone else saw him and said, "You too are one of them"; but Peter answered, "My friend, I am not." [59]About an hour later, still another insisted, "Assuredly, this man too was with him, for he also is a Galilean." [60]But Peter said, "My friend, I do not know what you are talking about." Just as he was saying this, the cock crowed, [61i*]and the Lord turned and looked at Peter; and Peter remembered the word of the Lord, how he had said to him, "Before the cock crows today, you will deny me three times." [62]He went out and began to weep bitterly. [63j]The men who held Jesus in custody were ridiculing and beating him. [64]They blindfolded him and questioned him, saying, "Prophesy! Who is it that struck you?" [65]And they reviled him in saying many other things against him.

Jesus before the Sanhedrin. [66kl*]When day came the council of elders of the people met, both chief priests and scribes, and they brought him before their Sanhedrin. [67m]They said, "If you are the Messiah, tell us," but he replied to them, "If I tell you, you will not believe, [68]and if I question, you will not respond. [69n]But from this time on the Son of Man will be seated at the right hand of the power of God." [70]They all asked, "Are you then the Son of God?" He replied to them, "You say that I am." [71]Then they said, "What further need have we for testimony? We have heard it from his own mouth."

CHAPTER 23

See RG 316

Jesus before Pilate. [1o*]Then the whole assembly of them arose and brought

---

the oldest papyrus manuscripts of Lk and from manuscripts of wide geographical distribution.

22, 51: And healed him: only Luke recounts this healing of the injured servant.

22, 61: Only Luke recounts that **the Lord turned and looked at Peter.** This look of Jesus leads to Peter's weeping bitterly over his denial (62).

22, 66–71: Luke recounts one daytime trial of Jesus (66–71) and hints at some type of preliminary nighttime investigation (54–65). Mark (and Matthew who follows Mk) has transferred incidents of this day into the nighttime interrogation with the result that there appear to be two Sanhedrin trials of Jesus in Mk (and Mt); see the note on Mk 14, 53.

22, 66: Sanhedrin: the word is a Hebraized form of a Greek word meaning a "council," and refers to the elders, chief priests, and scribes who met under the high priest's

leadership to decide religious and legal questions that did not pertain to Rome's interests. Jewish sources are not clear on the competence of the Sanhedrin to sentence and to execute during this period.

23, 1–5.13–25: Twice Jesus is brought before Pilate in Luke's account, and each time Pilate explicitly declares Jesus innocent of any wrongdoing (4.14.22). This stress on the innocence of Jesus before the Roman authorities is also charac-

a: 22, 40. b: Mt 26, 47-56; Mk 14, 43-50; Jn 18, 3-4. c: 22, 36. d: Jn 18, 26. e: 22, 37. f: 19, 47; 21, 37; Jn 7, 30; 8, 20; Col 1, 13. g: Mt 26, 57-58.69-75; Mk 14, 53-54.66-72; Jn 18, 12-18.25-27. h: 22, 33. i: 22, 34. j: Mt 26, 67-68; Mk 14, 65. k: Mt 26, 59-66; Mk 14, 55-64. l: Mt 27, 1; Mk 15, 1. m: Jn 3, 12; 8, 45; 10, 24. n: Ps 110, 1; Dn 7, 13-14; Acts 7, 56. o: Mt 27, 1-2.11-14; Mk 15, 1-5; Jn 18, 28-38.

him before Pilate. [2p]They brought charges against him, saying, "We found this man misleading our people; he opposes the payment of taxes to Caesar and maintains that he is the Messiah, a king." [3q]Pilate asked him, "Are you the king of the Jews?" He said to him in reply, "You say so." [4r]Pilate then addressed the chief priests and the crowds, "I find this man not guilty." [5]But they were adamant and said, "He is inciting the people with his teaching throughout all Judea, from Galilee where he began even to here."

Jesus before Herod. [6]*On hearing this Pilate asked if the man was a Galilean; [7s]and upon learning that he was under Herod's jurisdiction, he sent him to Herod who was in Jerusalem at that time. [8t]Herod was very glad to see Jesus; he had been wanting to see him for a long time, for he had heard about him and had been hoping to see him perform some sign. [9u]He questioned him at length, but he gave him no answer. [10v]The chief priests and scribes, meanwhile, stood by accusing him harshly. [11w][Even] Herod and his soldiers treated him contemptuously and mocked him, and after clothing him in resplendent garb, he sent him back to Pilate. [12]Herod and Pilate became friends that very day, even though they had been enemies formerly. [13]Pilate then summoned the chief priests, the rulers, and the people [14x]and said to them, "You brought this man to me and accused him of inciting the people to revolt. I have conducted my investigation in your presence and have not found this man guilty of the charges you have brought against him, [15]nor did Herod, for he sent him back to us. So no capital crime has been committed by

him. [16y]Therefore I shall have him flogged and then release him." [[17]]*

The Sentence of Death. [18z]But all together they shouted out, "Away with this man! Release Barabbas to us." [19](Now Barabbas had been imprisoned for a rebellion that had taken place in the city and for murder.) [20]Again Pilate addressed them, still wishing to release Jesus, [21]but they continued their shouting, "Crucify him! Crucify him!" [22]Pilate addressed them a third time, "What evil has this man done? I found him guilty of no capital crime. Therefore I shall have him flogged and then release him." [23]With loud shouts, however, they persisted in calling for his crucifixion, and their voices prevailed. [24]The verdict of Pilate was that their demand should be granted. [25]So he released the man who had been imprisoned for rebellion and murder, for whom they asked, and he handed Jesus over to them to deal with as they wished.

The Way of the Cross. [26a]*As they led him away they took hold of a certain Simon, a Cyrenian, who was coming in from the country; and after laying the cross on him, they made him carry it behind Jesus. [27]A large crowd of people followed Jesus, including many women who mourned and lamented him. [28b]Jesus turned to them and said, "Daughters of Jerusalem, do not weep for me; weep instead for yourselves and for your children, [29]for indeed, the days are coming when people will say, 'Blessed are the barren, the wombs that never bore and the breasts that never nursed.' [30c]At that time people will say to the mountains, 'Fall upon us!' and to the hills, 'Cover us!' [31]for if these things are done when the wood is green what

---

teristic of John's gospel (Jn 18, 38; 19, 4.6). Luke presents the Jerusalem Jewish leaders as the ones who force the hand of the Roman authorities (1–2.5.10.13.18.21.23–25).

23, 6–12: The appearance of Jesus before Herod is found only in this gospel. Herod has been an important figure in Lk (9, 7–9; 13, 31–33) and has been presented as someone who has been curious about Jesus for a long time. His curiosity goes unrewarded. It is faith in Jesus, not curiosity, that is rewarded (7, 50; 8, 48.50; 17, 19).

23, 17: This verse, "He was obliged to release one prisoner for them at the festival," is not part of the original text of Lk. It is an explanatory gloss from Mk 15, 6 (also Mt 27, 15) and is not found in many early and important Greek manuscripts. On its historical background, see the notes on Mt 27, 15–26.

23, 26–32: An important Lucan theme throughout the

gospel has been the need for the Christian disciple to follow in the footsteps of Jesus. Here this theme comes to the fore with the story of Simon of Cyrene who takes up the cross and follows Jesus (see 9, 23; 14, 27) and with the large crowd who likewise follow Jesus on the way of the cross. See also the note on Mk 15, 21.

p: 20, 22-25; Acts 17, 7; 24, 5. *q:* 22, 70; 1 Tm 6, 13. *r:* 23, 14.22.41; Mt 27, 24; Jn 19, 4.6; Acts 13, 28. *s:* 3, 1; 9, 7. *t:* 9, 9; Acts 4, 27-28. *u:* Mk 15, 5. *v:* Mt 27, 12; Mk 15, 3. *w:* Mt 27, 28-30; Mk 15, 17-19; Jn 19, 2-3. *x:* 23, 4.22.41. *y:* 23, 22; Jn 19, 12-14. *z:* Mt 27, 20-26; Mk 15, 6-7.11-15; Jn 18, 38b-40; 19, 14-16; Acts 3, 13-14. *a:* Mt 27, 32.38; Mk 15, 21.27; Jn 19, 17. *b:* 19, 41-44; 21, 23-24. *c:* Hos 10, 8; Rv 6, 16.

will happen when it is dry?" [32]Now two others, both criminals, were led away with him to be executed.

The Crucifixion. [33de]When they came to the place called the Skull, they crucified him and the criminals there, one on his right, the other on his left. [34f]*[Then Jesus said, "Father, forgive them, they know not what they do."] They divided his garments by casting lots. [35gh]The people stood by and watched; the rulers, meanwhile, sneered at him and said, "He saved others, let him save himself if he is the chosen one, the Messiah of God." [36i]Even the soldiers jeered at him. As they approached to offer him wine [37]they called out, "If you are King of the Jews, save yourself." [38]Above him there was an inscription that read, "This is the King of the Jews."

[39]*Now one of the criminals hanging there reviled Jesus, saying, "Are you not the Messiah? Save yourself and us." [40]The other, however, rebuking him, said in reply, "Have you no fear of God, for you are subject to the same condemnation? [41j]And indeed, we have been condemned justly, for the sentence we received corresponds to our crimes, but this man has done nothing criminal." [42k]Then he said, "Jesus, remember me when you come into your kingdom." [43l]He replied to him, "Amen, I say to you, today you will be with me in Paradise."

The Death of Jesus. [44mn]*It was now about noon and darkness came over the whole land until three in the afternoon [45o]because of an eclipse of the sun. Then the veil of the temple was torn down the middle. [46p]Jesus cried out in a loud voice, "Father, into your hands I commend my spirit"; and when he had said this he breathed his last. [47]*The centurion who witnessed what had happened glorified God and said, "This man was innocent beyond doubt." [48q]When all the people who had gathered for this spectacle saw what had happened, they returned home beating their breasts; [49r]but all his acquaintances stood at a distance, including the women who had followed him from Galilee and saw these events.

The Burial of Jesus. [50s]Now there was a virtuous and righteous man named Joseph who, though he was a member of the council, [51t]had not consented to their plan of action. He came from the Jewish town of Arimathea and was awaiting the kingdom of God. [52]He went to Pilate and asked for the body of Jesus. [53u]After he had taken the body down, he wrapped it in a linen cloth and laid him in a rock-hewn tomb in which no one had yet been buried. [54]It was the day of preparation, and the sabbath was about to begin. [55v]The women who had come from Galilee with him followed behind, and when they had seen the tomb and the way in which his body was laid in it, [56w]they returned and prepared spices and perfumed oils. Then they rested on the sabbath according to the commandment.

VIII: The Resurrection Narrative

CHAPTER 24

See RG 316-18

The Resurrection of Jesus. [1x]*But at daybreak on the first day of the week they

---

23, 34a: [Then Jesus said, "Father, forgive them, they know not what they do."]: this portion of v 34 does not occur in the oldest papyrus manuscript of Lk and in other early Greek manuscripts and ancient versions of wide geographical distribution.

23, 39–43: This episode is recounted only in this gospel. The penitent sinner receives salvation through the crucified Jesus. Jesus' words to the penitent thief reveal Luke's understanding that the destiny of the Christian is "to be with Jesus."

23, 44: Noon . . . three in the afternoon: literally, the sixth and ninth hours. See the note on Mk 15, 25.

23, 47: This man was innocent: or, "This man was righteous."

24, 1–53: The resurrection narrative in Lk consists of five sections: (1) the women at the empty tomb (23, 56b—24, 12); (2) the appearance to the two disciples on the way to Emmaus (24, 13–35); (3) the appearance to the disciples in Jerusalem (24, 36–43); (4) Jesus' final instructions (24, 44–49); (5) the ascension (24, 50–53). In Lk, all the resurrection appearances take place in and around Jerusalem; moreover, they are all recounted as having taken place on Easter Sunday. A consistent

---

d: Mt 27, 33-44; Mk 15, 22-32; Jn 19, 17-24.   e: 22, 37; Is 53, 12.   f: Nm 15, 27-31; Ps 22, 19; Mt 5, 44; Acts 7, 60.   g: Ps 22, 8-9.   h: 4, 23.   i: Ps 69, 22; Mt 27, 48; Mk 15, 36.   j: 23, 4.14.22.   k: 9, 27; 23, 2.3.38.   l: 2 Cor 12, 3; Rv 2, 7.   m: Mt 27, 45-56; Mk 15, 33-41; Jn 19, 25-30.   n: Am 8, 9.   o: Ex 26, 31-33; 36, 35.   p: Ps 31, 6; Acts 7, 59.   q: 18, 13; Zec 12, 10.   r: 8, 1-3; 23, 55-56; 24, 10; Ps 38, 12.   s: Mt 27, 57-61; Mk 15, 42-47; Jn 19, 38-42; Acts 13, 29.   t: 2, 25.38.   u: 19, 30; Acts 13, 29.   v: 8, 2; 23, 49; 24, 10.   w: Ex 12, 16; 20, 10; Dt 5, 14.   x: Mt 28, 1-8; Mk 16, 1-8; Jn 20, 1-17.

took the spices they had prepared and went to the tomb. ²They found the stone rolled away from the tomb; ³but when they entered, they did not find the body of the Lord Jesus. ⁴ʸWhile they were puzzling over this, behold, two men in dazzling garments appeared to them. ⁵ᶻThey were terrified and bowed their faces to the ground. They said to them, "Why do you seek the living one among the dead? ⁶*He is not here, but he has been raised. Remember what he said to you while he was still in Galilee, ⁷ᵃthat the Son of Man must be handed over to sinners and be crucified, and rise on the third day." ⁸ᵇAnd they remembered his words. ⁹ᶜ*Then they returned from the tomb and announced all these things to the eleven and to all the others. ¹⁰ᵈThe women were Mary Magdalene, Joanna, and Mary the mother of James; the others who accompanied them also told this to the apostles, ¹¹but their story seemed like nonsense and they did not believe them. ¹²ᵉ*But Peter got up and ran to the tomb, bent down, and saw the burial cloths alone; then he went home amazed at what had happened.

The Appearance on the Road to Emmaus.
¹³ᶠ*Now that very day two of them were going to a village seven miles from Jerusalem called Emmaus, ¹⁴and they were conversing about all the things that had occurred. ¹⁵And

it happened that while they were conversing and debating, Jesus himself drew near and walked with them, ¹⁶ᵍ*but their eyes were prevented from recognizing him. ¹⁷He asked them, "What are you discussing as you walk along?" They stopped, looking downcast. ¹⁸One of them, named Cleopas, said to him in reply, "Are you the only visitor to Jerusalem who does not know of the things that have taken place there in these days?" ¹⁹ʰAnd he replied to them, "What sort of things?" They said to him, "The things that happened to Jesus the Nazarene, who was a prophet mighty in deed and word before God and all the people, ²⁰how our chief priests and rulers both handed him over to a sentence of death and crucified him. ²¹ⁱBut we were hoping that he would be the one to redeem Israel; and besides all this, it is now the third day since this took place. ²²ʲSome women from our group, however, have astounded us: they were at the tomb early in the morning ²³and did not find his body; they came back and reported that they had indeed seen a vision of angels who announced that he was alive. ²⁴ᵏThen some of those with us went to the tomb and found things just as the women had described, but him they did not see." ²⁵ˡAnd he said to them, "Oh, how foolish you are! How slow of heart to believe all that the prophets spoke! ²⁶*Was it not neces-

---

theme throughout the narrative is that the suffering, death, and resurrection of Jesus were accomplished in fulfillment of Old Testament promises and of Jewish hopes (19a.21.26–27.44.46). In his second volume, Acts, Luke will argue that Christianity is the fulfillment of the hopes of Pharisaic Judaism and its logical development (see Acts 24, 10–21).

24, 6a: He is not here, but he has been raised: this part of the verse is omitted in important representatives of the Western text tradition, but its presence in other text types and the slight difference in wording from Mt 28, 6 and Mk 16, 6 argue for its retention.

24, 9: The women in this gospel do not flee from the tomb and tell no one, as in Mk 16, 8, but return and tell the disciples about their experience. The initial reaction to the testimony of the women is disbelief (11).

24, 12: This verse is missing from the Western textual tradition but is found in the best and oldest manuscripts of other text types.

24, 13–35: This episode focuses on the interpretation of scripture by the risen Jesus and the recognition of him in the breaking of the bread. The references to the quotations of scripture and explanation of it (25–27), the kerygmatic proclamation (34), and the liturgical gesture (30) suggest that

the episode is primarily catechetical and liturgical rather than apologetic.

24, 13: Seven miles: literally, "sixty stades." A stade was 607 feet. Some manuscripts read "160 stades" or more than eighteen miles. The exact location of Emmaus is disputed.

24, 16: A consistent feature of the resurrection stories is that the risen Jesus was different and initially unrecognizable (37; Mk 16, 12; Jn 20, 14; 21, 4).

24, 26: That the Messiah should suffer . . . : Luke is the only New Testament writer to speak explicitly of a suffering Messiah (26.46; Acts 3, 18; 17, 3; 26, 23). The idea of a suffering Messiah is not found in the Old Testament or in other Jewish literature prior to the New Testament period, although the idea is hinted at in Mk 8, 31–33. See the notes on Mt 26, 63 and 26, 67–68.

---

y: 2 Mc 3, 26; Acts 1, 10. *z:* Acts 2, 9. *a:* 9, 22.44; 17, 25; 18, 32-33; Mt 16, 21; 17, 22-23; Mk 9, 31; Acts 17, 3. *b:* Jn 2, 22. *c:* Mk 16, 10-11; Jn 20, 18. *d:* 8, 2-3; Mk 16, 9. *e:* Jn 20, 3-7. *f:* Mk 16, 12-13. *g:* Jn 20, 14; 21, 4. *h:* Mt 2, 23; 21, 11; Acts 2, 22. *i:* 1, 54.68; 2, 38. *j:* 24, 1-11; Mt 28, 1-8; Mk 16, 1-8. *k:* Jn 20, 3-10. *l:* 9, 22; 18, 31; 24, 44; Acts 3, 24; 17, 3.

sary that the Messiah should suffer these things and enter into his glory?" [27m]Then beginning with Moses and all the prophets, he interpreted to them what referred to him in all the scriptures. [28]As they approached the village to which they were going, he gave the impression that he was going on farther. [29]But they urged him, "Stay with us, for it is nearly evening and the day is almost over." So he went in to stay with them. [30]And it happened that, while he was with them at table, he took bread, said the blessing, broke it, and gave it to them. [31]With that their eyes were opened and they recognized him, but he vanished from their sight. [32]Then they said to each other, "Were not our hearts burning [within us] while he spoke to us on the way and opened the scriptures to us?" [33]So they set out at once and returned to Jerusalem where they found gathered together the eleven and those with them [34n]who were saying, "The Lord has truly been raised and has appeared to Simon!" [35]Then the two recounted what had taken place on the way and how he was made known to them in the breaking of the bread.

The Appearance to the Disciples in Jerusalem. [36 o p]*While they were still speaking about this, he stood in their midst and said to them, "Peace be with you." [37q]But they were startled and terrified and thought that they were seeing a ghost. [38]Then he said to them, "Why are you troubled? And why do ques- tions arise in your hearts? [39]*Look at my hands and my feet, that it is I myself. Touch me and see, because a ghost does not have flesh and bones as you can see I have." [40r]And as he said this, he showed them his hands and his feet. [41]While they were still incredulous for joy and were amazed, he asked them, "Have you anything here to eat?" [42s]They gave him a piece of baked fish; [43]he took it and ate it in front of them.

[44t]He said to them, "These are my words that I spoke to you while I was still with you, that everything written about me in the law of Moses and in the prophets and psalms must be fulfilled." [45u]Then he opened their minds to understand the scriptures. [46v]*And he said to them, "Thus it is written that the Messiah would suffer and rise from the dead on the third day [47w]and that repentance, for the forgiveness of sins, would be preached in his name to all the nations, beginning from Jerusalem. [48x]You are witnesses of these things. [49y]*And [behold] I am sending the promise of my Father upon you; but stay in the city until you are clothed with power from on high."

The Ascension. [50z]*Then he led them [out] as far as Bethany, raised his hands, and blessed them. [51]As he blessed them he parted from them and was taken up to heaven. [52a]They did him homage and then returned to Jerusalem with great joy, [53]*and they were continually in the temple praising God.

24, 36–43.44–49: The Gospel of Luke, like each of the other gospels (Mt 28, 16–20; Mk 16, 14–15; Jn 20, 19–23), focuses on an important appearance of Jesus to the Twelve in which they are commissioned for their future ministry. As in vv 6 and 12, so in vv 36 and 40 there are omissions in the Western text.

24, 39–42: The apologetic purpose of this story is evident in the concern with the physical details and the report that Jesus ate food.

24, 46: See the note on 24, 26.

24, 49: The promise of my Father: i.e., the gift of the holy Spirit.

24, 50–53: Luke brings his story about the time of Jesus to a close with the report of the ascension. He will also begin the story of the time of the church with a recounting of the ascension. In the gospel, Luke recounts the ascension of Jesus on Easter Sunday night, thereby closely associating it with the resurrection. In Acts (1, 3.9–11; 13, 31) he historicizes the ascension by speaking of a forty-day period between the resurrection and the ascension. The Western text omits some phrases in vv 51 and 52, perhaps to avoid any chronological conflict with Acts 1 about the time of the ascension.

24, 53: The Gospel of Luke ends as it began (1, 9), in the Jerusalem temple.

m: 24, 44; Dt 18, 25; Ps 22, 1-18; Is 53; 1 Pt 1, 10-11.   *n:* 1 Cor 15, 4-5.   *o:* Mk 16, 14-19; Jn 20, 19-20.   *p:* 1 Cor 15, 5.   *q:* Mt 14, 26.   *r:* Jn 21, 5.9-10.13.   *s:* Acts 10, 41.   *t:* 18, 31; 24, 27; Mt 16, 21; Jn 5, 39.46.   *u:* Jn 20, 9.   *v:* 9, 22; Is 53; Hos 6, 2.   *w:* Mt 3, 2; 28, 19-20; Mk 16, 15-16; Acts 10, 41.   *x:* Acts 1, 8.   *y:* Jn 14, 26; Acts 1, 4; 2, 3-4.   *z:* Mk 16, 19; Acts 1, 9-11.   *a:* Acts 1, 12.

See RG
319–34

The Gospel According to John

The Gospel according to John is quite different in character from the three synoptic gospels. It is highly literary and symbolic. It does not follow the same order or reproduce the same stories as the synoptic gospels. To a much greater degree, it is the product of a developed theological reflection and grows out of a different circle and tradition. It was probably written in the 90s of the first century.

The Gospel of John begins with a magnificent prologue, which states many of the major themes and motifs of the gospel, much as an overture does for a musical work. The prologue proclaims Jesus as the preexistent and incarnate Word of God who has revealed the Father to us. The rest of the first chapter forms the introduction to the gospel proper and consists of the Baptist's testimony about Jesus (there is no baptism of Jesus in this gospel—John simply points him out as the Lamb of God), followed by stories of the call of the first disciples, in which various titles predicated of Jesus in the early church are presented.

The gospel narrative contains a series of "signs"—the gospel's word for the wondrous deeds of Jesus. The author is primarily interested in the significance of these deeds, and so interprets them for the reader by various reflections, narratives, and discourses. The first sign is the transformation of water into wine at Cana (2, 1–11); this represents the replacement of the Jewish ceremonial washings and symbolizes the entire creative and transforming work of Jesus. The second sign, the cure of the royal official's son (4, 46–54) simply by the word of Jesus at a distance, signifies the power of Jesus' life-giving word. The same theme is further developed by other signs, probably for a total of seven. The third sign, the cure of the paralytic at the pool with five porticoes in ch 5, continues the theme of water offering newness of life. In the preceding chapter, to the woman at the well in Samaria Jesus had offered living water springing up to eternal life, a symbol of the revelation that Jesus brings; here Jesus' life-giving word replaces the water of the pool that failed to bring life. Chapter 6 contains two signs, the multiplication of loaves and the walking on the waters of the Sea of Galilee. These signs are connected much as the manna and the crossing of the Red Sea are in the Passover narrative and symbolize a new exodus. The multiplication of the loaves is interpreted for the reader by the discourse that follows, where the bread of life is used first as a figure for the revelation of God in Jesus and then for the Eucharist. After a series of dialogues reflecting Jesus' debates with the Jewish authorities at the Feast of Tabernacles in chapters 7 and 8, the sixth sign is presented in ch 9, the sign of the young man born blind. This is a narrative illustration of the theme of conflict in the preceding two chapters; it proclaims the triumph of light over darkness, as Jesus is presented as the Light of the world. This is interpreted by a narrative of controversy between the Pharisees and the young man who had been given his sight by Jesus, ending with a discussion of spiritual blindness and spelling out the symbolic meaning of the cure. And finally, the seventh sign, the raising of Lazarus in ch 11, is the climax of signs. Lazarus is presented as a token of the real life that Jesus, the Resurrection and the Life, who will now ironically be put to death because of his gift of life to Lazarus, will give to all who believe in him once he has been raised from the dead.

After the account of the seven signs, the "hour" of Jesus arrives, and the author passes from sign to reality, as he moves into the discourses in the upper room that interpret the meaning of the passion, death, and resurrection narratives that follow. The whole gospel of John is a progressive revelation of the glory of God's only Son, who comes to reveal the Father and then returns in glory to the Father. The author's purpose is clearly expressed in what must have been the original ending of the gospel at the end of ch 20: "Now Jesus did many other signs in the presence of [his] disciples that are not written in this book. But these are written that you may [come to] believe that Jesus is the Messiah, the Son of God, and that through this belief you may have life in his name."

Critical analysis makes it difficult to accept the idea that the gospel as it now stands was written by one person. Chapter 21 seems to have been added after the gospel was completed; it exhibits a Greek style somewhat different from that of the rest of the work. The prologue (1, 1–18) apparently contains an independent hymn, subsequently adapted to serve as a preface to the gospel. Within the gospel itself there are also some inconsistencies, e.g., there are two endings of Jesus' discourse in the upper room (14, 31; 18, 1). To solve these problems, scholars have proposed various rearrangements that would produce a smoother order. However, most have come to the conclusion that the inconsistencies were probably produced by subsequent editing in which homogeneous materials were added to a shorter original.

Other difficulties for any theory of eyewitness authorship of the gospel in its present form are presented by its highly developed theology and by certain elements of its literary style. For instance, some of the wondrous deeds of Jesus have been worked into highly effective dramatic scenes (ch 9); there has been a careful attempt to have these followed by discourses that explain them (chs 5 and 6); and the sayings of Jesus have been woven into long discourses of a quasi-poetic form resembling the speeches of personified Wisdom in the Old Testament.

The polemic between synagogue and church produced bitter and harsh invective, especially regarding the hostility toward Jesus of the authorities—Pharisees and Sadducees—who are combined and referred to frequently as "the Jews" (see the note on 1, 19). These opponents are even described in 8, 44 as springing from their father the devil, whose conduct they imitate in opposing God by rejecting Jesus, whom God has sent. On the other hand, the author of this gospel seems to take pains to show that women are not inferior to

men in the Christian community: the woman at the well in Samaria (4) is presented as a prototype of a missionary (4, 4–42), and the first witness of the resurrection is a woman (20, 11–18).

The final editing of the gospel and arrangement in its present form probably dates from between A.D. 90 and 100. Traditionally, Ephesus has been favored as the place of composition, though many support a location in Syria, perhaps the city of Antioch, while some have suggested other places, including Alexandria.

The principal divisions of the Gospel according to John are the following:

I: Prologue (1, 1–18)

II: The Book of Signs (1, 19—12, 50)

III: The Book of Glory (13, 1—20, 31)

IV: Epilogue: The Resurrection Appearance in Galilee (21, 1–25)

I: Prologue

CHAPTER 1

See RG 324-25

^{1} ^{a}*In the beginning was the Word,

and the Word was with God,

and the Word was God.

^{2} He was in the beginning with God.

^{3} ^{b}*All things came to be through him,

and without him nothing came to be.

What came to be ^{4c}through him was life,

and this life was the light of the human race;

^{5} ^{d}*the light shines in the darkness,

and the darkness has not overcome it.

1, 1–18: The prologue states the main themes of the gospel: life, light, truth, the world, testimony, and the preexistence of Jesus Christ, the incarnate **Logos,** who reveals God the Father. In origin, it was probably an early Christian hymn. Its closest parallel is in other christological hymns, Col 1, 15–20 and Phil 2, 6–11. Its core (1–5.10–11.14) is poetic in structure, with short phrases linked by "staircase parallelism," in which the last word of one phrase becomes the first word of the next. Prose inserts (at least 6–8 and 15) deal with John the Baptist.

1, 1: In the beginning: also the first words of the Old Testament (Gn 1, 1). **Was:** this verb is used three times with different meanings in this verse: existence, relationship, and predication. **The Word** (Greek **logos**): this term combines God's dynamic, creative word (Genesis), personified preexistent Wisdom as the instrument of God's creative activity (Proverbs), and the ultimate intelligibility of reality (Hellenistic philosophy). **With God:** the Greek preposition here

connotes communication with another. **Was God:** lack of a definite article with "God" in Greek signifies predication rather than identification.

1, 3: What came to be: while the oldest manuscripts have no punctuation here, the corrector of Bodmer Papyrus P^{75}, some manuscripts, and the Ante-Nicene Fathers take this phrase with what follows, as staircase parallelism. Connection with v 3 reflects fourth-century anti-Arianism.

1, 5: The ethical dualism of light and darkness is paralleled in intertestamental literature and in the Dead Sea Scrolls. **Overcome:** "comprehend" is another possible translation, but cf 12, 35; Wis 7, 29–30.

a: 10, 30; Gn 1, 1-5; Jb 28, 12-27; Prv 8, 22-25; Wis 9, 1-2; 1 Jn 1, 1-2; Col 1, 1.15; Rv 3, 14; 19, 13.   *b:* Ps 33, 9; Wis 9, 1; Sir 42, 15; 1 Cor 8, 6; Col 1, 16; Heb 1, 2; Rv 3, 14.   *c:* 5, 26; 8, 12; 1 Jn 1, 2.   *d:* 3, 19; 8, 12; 9, 5; 12, 35.46; Wis 7, 29-30; 1 Thes 5, 4; 1 Jn 2, 8.

6e *A man named John was sent from God. *7f* *He came for testimony, to testify to the light, so that all might believe through him. *8g* He was not the light, but came to testify to the light. *9h* The true light, which enlightens everyone, was coming into the world.

10 He was in the world,
  and the world came to be through him,
  but the world did not know him.
11 *He came to what was his own,
  but his own people did not accept him.

12i But to those who did accept him he gave power to become children of God, to those who believe in his name, *13j* *who were born not by natural generation nor by human choice nor by a man's decision but of God.

14 k *And the Word became flesh
  and made his dwelling among us,

and we saw his glory,
  the glory as of the Father's only Son,
  full of grace and truth.

15l *John testified to him and cried out, saying, "This was he of whom I said, 'The one who is coming after me ranks ahead of me because he existed before me.' " *16* *From his fullness we have all received, grace in place of grace, *17m* because while the law was given through Moses, grace and truth came through Jesus Christ. *18n* *No one has ever seen God. The only Son, God, who is at the Father's side, has revealed him.

II: The Book of Signs

John the Baptist's Testimony to Himself. *19* *And this is the testimony of John. When the Jews from Jerusalem sent priests and Levites [to him] to ask him, "Who are

1, 6: John was **sent** just as Jesus was "sent" (4, 34) in divine mission. Other references to John the Baptist in this gospel emphasize the differences between them and John's subordinate role.

1, 7: Testimony: the testimony theme of Jn is introduced, which portrays Jesus as if on trial throughout his ministry. All testify to Jesus: John the Baptist, the Samaritan woman, scripture, his works, the crowds, the Spirit, and his disciples.

1, 11: What was his own . . . his own people: first a neuter, literally, "his own property/possession" (probably = Israel), then a masculine, "his own people" (the Israelites).

1, 13: Believers in Jesus become children of God not through any of the three natural causes mentioned but through God who is the immediate cause of the new spiritual life. **Were born:** the Greek verb can mean "begotten" (by a male) or "born" (from a female or of parents). The variant "he who was begotten," asserting Jesus' virginal conception, is weakly attested in Old Latin and Syriac versions.

1, 14: Flesh: the whole person, used probably against docetic tendencies (cf 1 Jn 4, 2; 2 Jn 7). **Made his dwelling:** literally, "pitched his tent/tabernacle." Cf the tabernacle or tent of meeting that was the place of God's presence among his people (Ex 25, 8–9). The incarnate Word is the new mode of God's presence among his people. The Greek verb has the same consonants as the Aramaic word for God's presence (Shekinah). **Glory:** God's visible manifestation of majesty in power, which once filled the tabernacle (Ex 40, 34) and the temple (1 Kgs 8, 10–11.27), is now centered in Jesus. **Only Son:** Greek, **monogenēs,** but see the note on 1, 18. **Grace and truth:** these words may represent two Old Testament terms describing Yahweh in covenant relationship with Israel (cf Ex 34, 6), thus God's "love" and "fidelity." The Word shares Yahweh's covenant qualities.

1, 15: This verse, interrupting vv 14 and 16, seems drawn from v 30.

1, 16: Grace in place of grace: replacement of the Old Covenant with the New (cf 17). Other possible translations are 'grace upon grace" (accumulation) and "grace for grace" (correspondence).

1, 18: The only Son, God: while the vast majority of later textual witnesses have another reading, "the Son, the only one" or "the only Son," the translation above follows the best and earliest manuscripts, **monogenēs theos,** but takes the first term to mean not just "Only One" but to include a filial relationship with the Father, as at Lk 9, 38 ("only child") or Heb 11, 17 ("only son") and as translated at Jn 1, 14. The Logos is thus "only Son" and God but not Father/God.

1, 19–51: The testimony of John the Baptist about the Messiah and Jesus' self-revelation to the first disciples. This section constitutes the introduction to the gospel proper and is connected with the prose inserts in the prologue. It develops the major theme of testimony in four scenes: John's negative testimony about himself; his positive testimony about Jesus; the revelation of Jesus to Andrew and Peter; the revelation of Jesus to Philip and Nathanael.

1, 19: The Jews: throughout most of the gospel, the "Jews" does not refer to the Jewish people as such but to the hostile authorities, both Pharisees and Sadducees, particularly in Jerusalem, who refuse to believe in Jesus The usage reflects the atmosphere, at the end of the first century, of polemics between church and synagogue, or possibly it refers to Jews as representative of a hostile world (10–11).

e: Mt 3, 1; Mk 1, 4; Lk 3, 2-3. *f:* 1, 19-34; 5, 33. *g:* 5, 35. *h:* 3, 19; 8, 12; 9, 39; 12, 46. *i:* 3, 11-12; 5, 43-44; 12, 46-50; Gal 3, 26; 4, 6-7; Eph 1, 5; 1 Jn 3, 2. *j:* 3, 5-6. *k:* Ex 16, 10; 24, 17; 25, 8-9; 33, 22; 34, 6; Sir 24, 4.8; Is 60,1; Ez 43, 7; Jl 4, 17; Hb 2, 14; 1 Jn 1, 2; 4, 2; 2 Jn 7. *l:* 1, 30; 3, 27-30. *m:* 7, 19; Ex 31, 18; 34, 28. *n:* 5, 37; 6, 46; Ex 33, 20; Jgs 13, 21-22; 1 Tm 6, 16; 1 Jn 4, 12.

you?" [20o]*he admitted and did not deny it, but admitted, "I am not the Messiah." [21p]*So they asked him, "What are you then? Are you Elijah?" And he said, "I am not." "Are you the Prophet?" He answered, "No." [22]So they said to him, "Who are you, so we can give an answer to those who sent us? What do you have to say for yourself?" [23q]*He said:

"I am 'the voice of one crying out in the
desert,
"Make straight the way of the Lord,'"'

as Isaiah the prophet said." [24]*Some Pharisees were also sent. [25r]They asked him, "Why then do you baptize if you are not the Messiah or Elijah or the Prophet?" [26s]*John answered them, "I baptize with water; but there is one among you whom you do not recognize, [27]the one who is coming after me, whose sandal strap I am not worthy to untie." [28]*This happened in Bethany across the Jordan, where John was baptizing.

John the Baptist's Testimony to Jesus. [29t]*The next day he saw Jesus coming toward him and said, "Behold, the Lamb of God, who takes away the sin of the world. [30u]*He is the one of whom I said, 'A man is coming after me who ranks ahead of me because he existed before me.' [31]*I did not know him, but the reason why I came baptizing with water was that he might be made known to Israel." [32v]*John testified further, saying, "I saw the Spirit come down like a dove from the sky and remain upon him. [33w]I did not know him, but the one who sent me to baptize with water told me, 'On whomever you see the Spirit come down and remain, he is the one who will baptize with the holy Spirit.' [34x]*Now I have seen and testified that he is the Son of God."

The First Disciples. [35y]The next day John was there again with two of his disciples, [36]*and as he watched Jesus walk by, he said, "Behold, the Lamb of God." [37]*The two disciples heard what he said and followed Jesus. [38]Jesus turned and saw them following him and said to them, "What are you looking for?" They said to him, "Rabbi" (which translated means Teacher), "where

1, 20: Messiah: the anointed agent of Yahweh, usually considered to be of Davidic descent. See further the note on 1, 41.

1, 21: Elijah: the Baptist did not claim to be Elijah returned to earth (cf Mal 3, 23; Mt 11, 14). **The Prophet:** probably the prophet like Moses (Dt 18, 15; cf Acts 3, 22).

1, 23: This is a repunctuation and reinterpretation (as in the synoptic gospels and Septuagint) of the Hebrew text of Is 40, 3, which reads, "A voice cries out: In the desert prepare the way of the LORD."

1, 24: Some Pharisees: other translations, such as "Now they had been sent from the Pharisees," misunderstand the grammatical construction. This is a different group from that in v 19; the priests and Levites would have been Sadducees, not Pharisees.

1, 26: I baptize with water: the synoptics add "but he will baptize you with the holy Spirit" (Mk 1, 8) or ". . . holy Spirit and fire" (Mt 3, 11; Lk 3, 16). John's emphasis is on purification and preparation for a better baptism.

1, 28: Bethany across the Jordan: site unknown. Another reading is "Bethabara."

1, 29: The Lamb of God: the background for this title may be the victorious apocalyptic lamb who would destroy evil in the world (Rv 5–7; 17, 14); the paschal lamb, whose blood saved Israel (Ex 12); and/or the suffering servant led like a lamb to the slaughter as a sin-offering (Is 53, 7.10).

1, 30: He existed before me: possibly as Elijah (to come, 27); for the evangelist and his audience, Jesus' preexistence would be implied (see the note on 1, 1).

1, 31: I did not know him: this gospel shows no knowledge of the tradition (Lk 1) about the kinship of Jesus and

John the Baptist. **The reason why I came baptizing with water:** in this gospel, John's baptism is not connected with forgiveness of sins; its purpose is revelatory, that Jesus may be made known to Israel.

1, 32: Like a dove: a symbol of the new creation (Gn 8, 8) or the community of Israel (Hos 11, 11). **Remain:** the first use of a favorite verb in Jn, emphasizing the permanency of the relationship between Father and Son (as here) and between the Son and the Christian. Jesus is the permanent bearer of the Spirit.

1, 34: The Son of God: this reading is supported by good Greek manuscripts, including the Chester Beatty and Bodmer Papyri and the Vatican Codex, but is suspect because it harmonizes this passage with the synoptic version: "This is my beloved Son" (Mt 3, 17; Mk 1, 11; Lk 3, 22). The poorly attested alternate reading, "God's chosen One," is probably a reference to the Servant of Yahweh (Is 42, 1).

1, 36: John the Baptist's testimony makes his disciples' following of Jesus plausible.

1, 37: The two disciples: Andrew (40) and, traditionally, John, son of Zebedee (see the note on 13, 23).

o: 3, 28; Lk 3, 15; Acts 13, 25.   *p*: Dt 18, 15.18; 2 Kgs 2, 11; Sir 48, 10; Mal 3, 1.23; Mt 11, 14; 17, 11-13; Mk 9, 13; Acts 3, 22. *q*: Is 40, 3; Mt 3, 3; Mk 1, 2; Lk 3, 4.   *r*: Ez 36, 25; Zec 13, 1; Mt 16, 14.   *s*: Mt 3, 11; Mk 1, 7-8; Lk 3, 16; Acts 13, 25.   *t*: 1, 36; Ex 12; Is 53, 7; Rv 5-7; 17, 14.   *u*: 1, 15; Mt 3, 11; Mk 1, 7; Lk 3, 16.   *v*: Sg 5, 2; Is 11, 2; Hos 11, 11; Mt 3, 16; Mk 1, 10; Lk 3, 21-22.   *w*: Is 42, 1; Mt 3, 11; Mk 1, 8; Lk 3, 16.   *x*: Is 42, 1; Mt 3, 17; Mk 1, 11; Lk 9, 35.   *y*: Mt 4, 18-22; Mk 1, 16-20; Lk 5, 1-11.

"Behold, the Lamb of God, who takes away the sin of the world."

This phrase appears only in the Gospel of John (Jn 1, 29.36), where John the Baptist applies it to Jesus. The Gospel writer provides no guidance, however, to help us understand what it means. For that, we need to look within the biblical text itself.

Although various animals and birds, as well as flour and oil, could be sacrificed (see "Holiness and Sacrifice," p. 129), the lamb gradually came to stand for sacrifice in general. This may have been because, as a relatively small animal, it was more commonly sacrificed than the larger ones like oxen. It may also have come more readily to mind because it was the main part of the Passover meal (Ex 12, 3–10). The blood of the Passover lamb marked the doorposts of the Jewish people, signaling that the LORD should not kill any of those within (Ex 12, 21–23). In subsequent celebrations of the Passover, the people were told to recall this (Ex 12, 24–27). Later (Lv 14, 12), the lamb was used for the guilt offering (or "offering of reparation").

The prophets Isaiah and Jeremiah developed another part of the imagery of the sacrificial lamb. The fourth "Servant Song" (Is 52, 13—53, 12) compares the servant to "a lamb led to the slaughter . . . [who] was silent and opened not his mouth" (53, 7), and Jeremiah compares himself to "a trusting lamb led to slaughter" (11, 19). On the natural level this is no doubt based on the fact that a lamb is a very docile animal, and it will often allow itself to be brought somewhere with little or no resistance. In the imagery of the prophets, however, it is transformed into the one who was betrayed (Jeremiah) and the one who went willingly to death (the servant of the Isaiah passage).

When the Gospel of John has John the Baptist call Jesus "the Lamb of God," therefore, it may be referring to this background of meaning. The Lamb is the willing sacrificial victim who makes reparation for sin. At the end of the Gospel of John, there is a subtle echo of this passage. According to John's chronology, the Last Supper takes place before Passover (Jn 13, 1); the day of the crucifixion of Jesus was "preparation day" (Jn 19, 31), the day during which the Passover meal was prepared before the supper that evening (Ex 12, 16). Thus, as Jesus is dying on the cross, the lambs for the Passover meal are being slaughtered.

The image of the sacrificial lamb makes one other significant appearance in the Bible, in Revelation 5, 6–12. There the scroll that contains the divine plan of salvation must be opened, and the only one able to open it is "the lion of the tribe of Judah" (Rv 5, 5) who in fact is the "Lamb that seemed to have been slain" (Rv 5, 6). That Lamb (Christ) is "worthy" of honor and worship (Rv 5, 12–14) because of his willing self-sacrifice.

This acclamation in the Gospel formed the basis of a portion of the *Gloria in excelsis*—"Lord God, Lamb of God, you take away the sin of the world"—and of the *Agnus Dei*, now recited at the Fraction—"Lamb of God, you take away the sins of the world: have mercy on us/grant us peace."

are you staying?" [39]*He said to them, "Come, and you will see." So they went and saw where he was staying, and they stayed with him that day. It was about four in the afternoon. [40]Andrew, the brother of Simon Peter, was one of the two who heard John and followed Jesus. [41z]*He first found his own brother Simon and told him, "We have found the Messiah" (which is translated Anointed). [42a]*Then he brought him to Jesus. Jesus looked at him and said, "You are Simon the son of John; you will be called Cephas" (which is translated Peter).

[43]*The next day he decided to go to Galilee, and he found Philip. And Jesus said to him, "Follow me." [44]Now Philip was from Bethsaida, the town of Andrew and Peter. [45b]Philip found Nathanael and told him, "We have found the one about whom Moses wrote in the law, and also the prophets, Jesus son of Joseph, from Nazareth." [46]But Nathanael said to him, "Can anything good come from Nazareth?" Philip said to him, "Come and see." [47]*Jesus saw Nathanael coming toward him and said of him, "Here is a true Israelite. There is no duplicity in him." [48c]*Nathanael said to him, "How do you know me?" Jesus answered and said to him, "Before Philip called you, I saw you under the fig tree." [49d]*Nathanael answered him, "Rabbi, you are the Son of God; you are the King of Israel." [50]*Jesus answered and said to him, "Do you believe because I told you that I saw you under the fig tree? You will see greater things than this." [51e]*And he said to him, "Amen, amen, I say to you, you will see the sky opened and the angels of God ascending and descending on the Son of Man."

CHAPTER 2

See RG 325-26

The Wedding at Cana. [1f]*On the third day there was a wedding in Cana in Galilee, and the mother of Jesus was there. [2]Jesus and his disciples were also invited to the wedding. [3]When the wine ran short, the mother of Jesus said to him, "They have no wine." [4g]*[And] Jesus said to her, "Woman, how does your concern affect me? My hour

---

1, 39: Four in the afternoon: literally, the tenth hour, from sunrise, in the Roman calculation of time. Some suggest that the next day, beginning at sunset, was the sabbath; they would have stayed with Jesus to avoid travel on it.

1, 41: Messiah: the Hebrew word **māšiaḥ,** "anointed one" (see the note on Lk 2, 11), appears in Greek as the transliterated **messias** only here and in 4, 25. Elsewhere the Greek translation **christos** is used.

1, 42: Simon the son of John: in Mt 16, 17, Simon is called **Barïōna,** "son of Jonah," a different tradition for the name of Simon's father. **Cephas:** in Aramaic = the Rock; cf Mt 16, 18. Neither the Greek equivalent **Petros** nor, with one isolated exception, **Cephas** is attested as a personal name before Christian times.

1, 43: He: grammatically, could be Peter, but logically is probably Jesus.

1, 47: A true Israelite. There is no duplicity in him: Jacob was the first to bear the name "Israel" (Gn 32, 29), but Jacob was a man of duplicity (Gn 27, 35–36).

1, 48: Under the fig tree: a symbol of messianic peace (cf Mi 4, 4; Zec 3, 10).

1, 49: Son of God: this title is used in the Old Testament, among other ways, as a title of adoption for the Davidic king (2 Sm 7, 14; Pss 2, 7; 89, 27), and thus here, with **King of Israel,** in a messianic sense. For the evangelist, Son of God also points to Jesus' divinity (cf 20, 28).

1, 50: Possibly a statement: "You [singular] believe because I saw you under the fig tree."

1, 51: The double "Amen" is characteristic of John. **You** is plural in Greek. The allusion is to Jacob's ladder (Gn 28, 12).

2, 1—6, 71: Signs revealing Jesus as the Messiah to all Israel. "Sign" (**sēmeion**) is John's symbolic term for Jesus'

wondrous deeds (see Introduction). The Old Testament background lies in the Exodus story (cf Dt 11, 3; 29, 2). John is interested primarily in what the **sēmeia** signify: God's intervention in human history in a new way through Jesus.

2, 1–11: The first sign. This story of replacement of Jewish ceremonial washings (6) presents the initial revelation about Jesus at the outset of his ministry. He manifests his glory; the disciples believe. There is no synoptic parallel.

2, 1: The mother of Jesus: she is never named in John. **Cana:** unknown from the Old Testament.

2, 4: This verse may seek to show that Jesus did not work miracles to help his family and friends, as in the apocryphal gospels. **Woman:** a normal, polite form of address, but unattested in reference to one's mother. Cf also 19, 26. **How does your concern affect me?:** literally, "What is this to me and to you?"—a Hebrew expression of either hostility (Jgs 11, 12; 2 Chr 35, 21; 1 Kgs 17, 18) or denial of common interest (Hos 14, 9; 2 Kgs 3, 13). Cf Mk 1, 24; 5, 7, used by demons to Jesus. **My hour has not yet come:** the translation as a question ("Has not my hour now come?"), while preferable grammatically and supported by Greek Fathers, seems unlikely from a comparison with 7, 6.30. The "hour" is that of Jesus' passion, death, resurrection, and ascension (13, 1).

---

z: 4, 25. *a:* Mt 16, 18; Mk 3, 16. *b:* 21, 2. *c:* Mi 4, 4; Zec 3, 10. *d:* 12, 13; Ex 4, 22; Dt 14, 1; 2 Sm 7, 14; Jb 1, 6; 2, 1; 38, 7; Pss 2, 7; 29, 1; 89, 27; Wis 2, 18; Sir 4, 10; Dn 3, 25; Hos 11, 1; Mt 14, 33; 16, 16; Mk 13, 32. *e:* Gn 28, 10-17; Dn 7, 13. *f:* 4, 46; Jgs 14, 12; Tb 11, 8. *g:* 7, 30; 8, 20; 12, 23; 13, 1; Jgs 11, 12; 1 Kgs 17, 18; 2 Kgs 3, 13; 2 Chr 35, 21; Hos 14, 9; Mk 1, 24; 5, 7; 7, 30; 8, 20; 12, 23; 13, 1.

Geography of the Gospel of John

has not yet come." [5h]His mother said to the servers, "Do whatever he tells you." [6i]*Now there were six stone water jars there for Jewish ceremonial washings, each holding twenty to thirty gallons. [7]Jesus told them, "Fill the jars with water." So they filled them to the brim. [8]*Then he told them, "Draw some out now and take it to the headwaiter." So they took it. [9]And when the headwaiter tasted the water that had become wine, without knowing where it came from (although the servers who had drawn the water knew), the headwaiter called the bridegroom [10]and said to him, "Everyone serves good wine first, and then when people have drunk freely, an inferior one; but you have kept the good wine until now." [11j]*Jesus did this as the beginning of his signs in Cana in Galilee and so revealed his glory, and his disciples began to believe in him.

[12]*After this, he and his mother, [his] brothers, and his disciples went down to Capernaum and stayed there only a few days.

Cleansing of the Temple. [13k]*Since the Passover of the Jews was near, Jesus went up to Jerusalem. [14l]*He found in the temple area those who sold oxen, sheep, and doves, as well as the money-changers seated there.

[15]He made a whip out of cords and drove them all out of the temple area, with the sheep and oxen, and spilled the coins of the money-changers and overturned their tables, [16m]and to those who sold doves he said, "Take these out of here, and stop making my Father's house a marketplace." [17n]*His disciples recalled the words of scripture, "Zeal for your house will consume me." [18o]At this the Jews answered and said to him, "What sign can you show us for doing this?" [19p]*Jesus answered and said to them, "Destroy this temple and in three days I will raise it up." [20]*The Jews said, "This temple has been under construction for forty-six years, and you will raise it up in three days?" [21]But he was speaking about the temple of his body. [22q]Therefore, when he was raised from the dead, his disciples remembered that he had said this, and they came to believe the scripture and the word Jesus had spoken.

[23r]While he was in Jerusalem for the feast of Passover, many began to believe in his name when they saw the signs he was doing. [24]But Jesus would not trust himself to them because he knew them all, [25s]and did not need anyone to testify about human nature. He himself understood it well.

2, 6: Twenty to thirty gallons: literally, "two or three measures"; the Attic liquid measure contained 39.39 liters. The vast quantity recalls prophecies of abundance in the last days; cf Am 9, 13–14; Hos 14, 7; Jer 31, 12.

2, 8: Headwaiter: used of the official who managed a banquet, but there is no evidence of such a functionary in Palestine. Perhaps here a friend of the family acted as master of ceremonies; cf Sir 32, 1.

2, 11: The beginning of his signs: the first of seven (see Introduction).

2, 12—3, 21: The next three episodes take place in Jerusalem. Only the first is paralleled in the synoptic gospels.

2, 12: This transitional verse may be a harmonization with the synoptic tradition in Lk 4, 31 and Mt 4, 13. There are many textual variants. John depicts no extended ministry in Capernaum as do the synoptics.

2, 13–22: This episode indicates the post-resurrectional replacement of the temple by the person of Jesus.

2, 13: Passover: this is the first Passover mentioned in John; a second is mentioned in 6, 4, a third in 13, 1. Taken literally, they point to a ministry of at least two years.

2, 14–22: The other gospels place the cleansing of the temple in the last days of Jesus' life (Mt, on the day Jesus entered Jerusalem; Mk, on the next day). The order of events in the gospel narratives is often determined by theological motives rather than by chronological data.

2, 14: Oxen, sheep, and doves: intended for sacrifice.

The doves were the offerings of the poor (Lv 5, 7). **Money-changers:** for a temple tax paid by every male Jew more than nineteen years of age, with a half-shekel coin (Ex 30, 11–16), in Tyrian currency. See the note on Mt 17, 24.

2, 17: Ps 69, 10, changed to future tense to apply to Jesus.

2, 19: This saying about the destruction of the temple occurs in various forms (Mt 24, 2; 27, 40; Mk 13, 2; 15, 29; Lk 21, 6; cf Acts 6, 14). Mt 26, 61 has: "I can destroy the temple of God . . ."; see the note there. In Mk 14, 58, there is a metaphorical contrast with a new temple: "I will destroy this temple **made with hands** and within three days I will build another **not made with hands**." Here it is symbolic of Jesus' resurrection and the resulting community (see 21 and Rv 21, 2). **In three days:** an Old Testament expression for a short, indefinite period of time; cf Hos 6, 2.

2, 20: Forty-six years: based on references in Josephus (**Jewish Wars** 1, 21, 1 §§401; **Antiquities** 15, 11, 1 §380), possibly the spring of A.D. 28. Cf the note on Lk 3, 1.

---

h: Gn 41, 55. i: 3, 25; Lv 11, 33; Am 9, 13-14; Mt 15, 2; 23, 25-26; Mk 7, 2-4; Lk 11, 38. j: 4, 54. k: Mt 21, 12-13; Mk 11, 15-17; Lk 19, 45-46. l: Ex 30, 11-16; Lv 5, 7. m: Zec 14, 21. n: Ps 69, 9. o: 6, 30. p: Mt 24, 2; 26, 61; 27, 40; Mk 13, 2; 14, 58; 15, 29; Lk 21, 6; Acts 6, 14. q: 5, 39; 12, 16; 14, 26; 20, 9; Mt 12, 6; Lk 24, 6-8; Rv 21, 22. r: 4, 45. s: 1 Kgs 8, 39; Pss 33, 15; 94, 11; Sir 42, 18; Jer 17, 10; 20, 12.

CHAPTER 3

See RG
326–27

Nicodemus. ^{1t}*Now there was a Phari-see named Nicodemus, a ruler of the Jews. ^{2u}He came to Jesus at night and said to him, "Rabbi, we know that you are a teacher who has come from God, for no one can do these signs that you are doing unless God is with him." ³*Jesus answered and said to him, "Amen, amen, I say to you, no one can see the kingdom of God without being born from above." ^{4v}Nicodemus said to him, "How can a person once grown old be born again? Surely he cannot reenter his mother's womb and be born again, can he?" ^{5w}Jesus an-swered, "Amen, amen, I say to you, no one can enter the kingdom of God without being born of water and Spirit. ^{6x}What is born of flesh is flesh and what is born of spirit is spirit. ⁷Do not be amazed that I told you, 'You must be born from above.' ^{8y}*The wind blows where it wills, and you can hear the sound it makes, but you do not know where it comes from or where it goes; so it is with everyone who is born of the Spirit." ⁹Nicodemus an-swered and said to him, "How can this hap-pen?" ¹⁰Jesus answered and said to him, "You are the teacher of Israel and you do not under-stand this? ^{11z}Amen, amen, I say to you, we speak of what we know and we testify to what we have seen, but you people do not accept our testimony. ^{12a}If I tell you about earthly things and you do not believe, how will you believe if I tell you about heavenly things? ^{13b}No one has gone up to heaven except the one who has come down from heaven, the Son of Man. ^{14c}*And just as Moses lifted up the serpent in the desert, so must the Son of Man be lifted up, ¹⁵*so that everyone who be-lieves in him may have eternal life."

^{16d}*For God so loved the world that he gave his only Son, so that everyone who believes in him might not perish but might have eternal life. ^{17e}*For God did not send his Son into the world to condemn the world, but that the world might be saved through him. ^{18f}Who-ever believes in him will not be condemned, but whoever does not believe has already been condemned, because he has not believed in the name of the only Son of God. ^{19g}*And this is the verdict, that the light came into the world, but people preferred darkness to light, because their works were evil. ^{20h}For every-one who does wicked things hates the light and does not come toward the light, so that his works might not be exposed. ²¹ⁱBut whoever lives the truth comes to the light, so that his works may be clearly seen as done in God.

Final Witness of the Baptist. ^{22j}*After this, Jesus and his disciples went into the region of

---

3, 1–21: Jesus instructs Nicodemus on the necessity of a new birth from above. This scene in Jerusalem at Passover exemplifies the faith engendered by signs (2, 23). It continues the self-manifestation of Jesus in Jerusalem begun in ch 2. This is the first of the Johannine discourses, shifting from di-alogue to monologue (11–15) to reflection of the evangelist (16–21). The shift from singular through v 10 to plural in v 11 may reflect the early church's controversy with the Jews.

3, 1: A ruler of the Jews: most likely a member of the Jewish council, the Sanhedrin; see the note on Mk 8, 31.

3, 3: Born: see the note on 1, 13. **From above:** the Greek adverb **anōthen** means both "from above" and "again." Jesus means "from above" (see 31), but Nicodemus misunder-stands it as "again." This misunderstanding serves as a springboard for further instruction.

3, 8: Wind: the Greek word **pneuma** (as well as the He-brew **rûah**) means both "wind" and "spirit." In the play on the double meaning, "wind" is primary.

3, 14: Lifted up: in Nm 21, 9, Moses simply "mounted" a serpent upon a pole. John here substitutes a verb implying glorification. Jesus, exalted to glory at his cross and resurrec-tion, represents healing for all.

3, 15: Eternal life: used here for the first time in John, this term stresses quality of life rather than duration.

3, 16: Gave: as a gift in the incarnation, and also "over to death" in the crucifixion; cf Rom 8, 32.

3, 17–19: Condemn: the Greek root means both judg-ment and condemnation. Jesus' purpose is to save, but his coming provokes judgment; some condemn themselves by turning from the light.

3, 19: Judgment is not only future but is partially realized here and now.

3, 22–26: Jesus' ministry in Judea is only loosely connected with 2, 13—3, 21; cf 1, 19–36. Perhaps John the Baptist's fur-ther testimony was transposed here to give meaning to "water" in v 5. Jesus is depicted as baptizing (22); contrast 4, 2.

---

t: 7, 50-51; 19, 39.   *u:* 9, 4.16.33; 10, 21; 11, 10; 13, 30; Mt 22, 16; Mk 12, 14; Lk 20, 21.   *v:* 1, 13.   *w:* 1, 32; 7, 39; 19, 30.34-35; Is 32, 15; 44, 3; Ez 36, 25-27; Jl 3, 1-2.   *x:* 6, 63; 1 Cor 15, 44-50.   *y:* Eccl 11, 4-5; Acts 2, 2-4.   *z:* 3, 32.34; 8, 14; Mt 11, 27.   *a:* 6, 62-65; Wis 9, 16-17; 1 Cor 15, 40; 2 Cor 5, 1; Phil 2, 10; 3, 19-20.   *b:* 1, 18; 6, 62; Dn 7, 13; Rom 10, 6; Eph 4, 9.   *c:* 8, 28; 12, 32.34; Nm 21, 4-9; Wis 16, 5-7.   *d:* 1 Jn 4, 9.   *e:* 5, 22.30; 8, 15-18; 12, 47.   *f:* 5, 24; Mk 16, 16.   *g:* 1, 5.9-11; 3, 12; 9, 5.   *h:* Jb 24, 13-17.   *i:* Gn 47, 29 LXX; Jos 2, 14 LXX; 2 Sm 2, 6 LXX; 15, 20 LXX; Tb 4, 6 LXX; 13, 6; Is 26, 10 LXX; Mt 5, 14-15.   *j:* 4, 1-2.

Judea, where he spent some time with them baptizing. [23]*John was also baptizing in Aenon near Salim, because there was an abundance of water there, and people came to be baptized, [24k]*for John had not yet been imprisoned. [25]*Now a dispute arose between the disciples of John and a Jew about ceremonial washings. [26l]So they came to John and said to him, "Rabbi, the one who was with you across the Jordan, to whom you testified, here he is baptizing and everyone is coming to him." [27m]John answered and said, "No one can receive anything except what has been given him from heaven. [28n]You yourselves can testify that I said [that] I am not the Messiah, but that I was sent before him. [29o]*The one who has the bride is the bridegroom; the best man, who stands and listens to him, rejoices greatly at the bridegroom's voice. So this joy of mine has been made complete. [30p]He must increase; I must decrease."

The One from Heaven. [31q]*The one who comes from above is above all. The one who is of the earth is earthly and speaks of earthly things. But the one who comes from heaven [is above all]. [32r]He testifies to what he has seen and heard, but no one accepts his testimony. [33s]Whoever does accept his testimony certifies that God is trustworthy. [34]*For the one whom God sent speaks the words of God. He does not ration his gift of the Spirit.

[35t]The Father loves the Son and has given everything over to him. [36u]Whoever believes in the Son has eternal life, but whoever disobeys the Son will not see life, but the wrath of God remains upon him.

CHAPTER 4

See RG 326–27

[1]*Now when Jesus learned that the Pharisees had heard that Jesus was making and baptizing more disciples than John [2]*(although Jesus himself was not baptizing, just his disciples), [3]he left Judea and returned to Galilee.

The Samaritan Woman. [4]*He had to pass through Samaria. [5v]*So he came to a town of Samaria called Sychar, near the plot of land that Jacob had given to his son Joseph. [6]Jacob's well was there. Jesus, tired from his journey, sat down there at the well. It was about noon.

[7]A woman of Samaria came to draw water. Jesus said to her, "Give me a drink." [8]His disciples had gone into the town to buy food. [9w]*The Samaritan woman said to him, "How can you, a Jew, ask me, a Samaritan woman, for a drink?" (For Jews use nothing in common with Samaritans.) [10x]*Jesus answered and said to her, "If you knew the gift of God and who is saying to you, 'Give me a drink,' you would have asked him and he would have given you living water." [11]*[The

---

3, 23: Aenon near Salim: site uncertain, either in the upper Jordan valley or in Samaria.

3, 24: A remark probably intended to avoid objections based on a chronology like that of the synoptics (Mt 4, 12; Mk 1, 14).

3, 25: A Jew: some think Jesus is meant. Many manuscripts read "Jews."

3, 29: The best man: literally, "the friend of the groom," the **shoshben** of Jewish tradition, who arranged the wedding. Competition between him and the groom would be unthinkable.

3, 31–36: It is uncertain whether these are words by the Baptist, Jesus, or the evangelist. They are reflections on the two preceding scenes.

3, 34: His gift: of God or to Jesus, perhaps both. This verse echoes vv 5 and 8.

4, 1–42: Jesus in Samaria. The self-revelation of Jesus continues with his second discourse, on his mission to "half-Jews." It continues the theme of replacement, here with regard to cult (21). Water (7–15) serves as a symbol (as at Cana and in the Nicodemus episode).

4, 2: An editorial refinement of 3, 22, perhaps directed against followers of John the Baptist who claimed that Jesus imitated him.

4, 4: He had to: a theological necessity; geographically, Jews often bypassed Samaria by taking a route across the Jordan.

4, 5: Sychar: Jerome identifies this with Shechem, a reading found in Syriac manuscripts.

4, 9: Samaritan women were regarded by Jews as ritually impure, and therefore Jews were forbidden to drink from any vessel they had handled.

4, 10: Living water: the water of life, i.e., the revelation that Jesus brings; the woman thinks of "flowing water," so much more desirable than stagnant cistern water. On John's device of such misunderstanding, cf the note on 3, 3.

4, 11: Sir: the Greek **kyrios** means "master" or "lord," as a respectful mode of address for a human being or a deity; cf 4, 19. It is also the word used in the Septuagint for the Hebrew **'ădônai**, substituted for the tetragrammaton YHWH.

k: Mt 4, 12; 14, 3; Mk 1, 14; 6, 17; Lk 3, 20.   l: 1, 26.32-34.36.   m: 19, 11; 1 Cor 4, 7; 2 Cor 3, 5; Heb 5, 4.   n: 1, 20-23; Lk 3, 15.   o: 15, 11; 17, 13; Mt 9, 15.   p: 2 Sm 3, 1.   q: 8, 23.   r: 3, 11.   s: 8, 26; 12, 44-50; 1 Jn 5, 10.   t: 13, 3; Mt 11, 27; 28, 18; Lk 10, 22.   u: 3, 16; 1 Jn 5, 13.   v: Gn 33, 18-19; 48, 22; Jos 24, 32.   w: Sir 50, 25-26; Mt 10, 5.   x: Sir 24, 20-21; Is 55, 1; Jer 2, 13.

woman] said to him, "Sir, you do not even have a bucket and the cistern is deep; where then can you get this living water? *12y* Are you greater than our father Jacob, who gave us this cistern and drank from it himself with his children and his flocks?" *13* Jesus answered and said to her, "Everyone who drinks this water will be thirsty again; *14z* but whoever drinks the water I shall give will never thirst; the water I shall give will become in him a spring of water welling up to eternal life." *15* The woman said to him, "Sir, give me this water, so that I may not be thirsty or have to keep coming here to draw water."

16 Jesus said to her, "Go call your husband and come back." *17* The woman answered and said to him, "I do not have a husband." Jesus answered her, "You are right in saying, 'I do not have a husband.' *18a* For you have had five husbands, and the one you have now is not your husband. What you have said is true." *19b* The woman said to him, "Sir, I can see that you are a prophet. *20c* *Our ancestors worshiped on this mountain; but you people say that the place to worship is in Jerusalem." *21* Jesus said to her, "Believe me, woman, the hour is coming when you will worship the Father neither on this mountain nor in Jerusalem. *22d* You people worship what you do not understand; we worship what we understand, because salvation is from the Jews. *23* *But the hour is coming, and is now here, when true worshipers will worship the Father in Spirit and truth; and indeed the Father seeks such people to worship him. *24e* God is Spirit, and those who worship him must worship in Spirit and truth." *25f* *The woman said to him, "I know

that the Messiah is coming, the one called the Anointed; when he comes, he will tell us everything." *26* *Jesus said to her, "I am he, the one who is speaking with you."

27 *At that moment his disciples returned, and were amazed that he was talking with a woman, but still no one said, "What are you looking for?" or "Why are you talking with her?" *28* The woman left her water jar and went into the town and said to the people, *29* "Come see a man who told me everything I have done. Could he possibly be the Messiah?" *30* They went out of the town and came to him. *31* Meanwhile, the disciples urged him, "Rabbi, eat." *32* But he said to them, "I have food to eat of which you do not know." *33* So the disciples said to one another, "Could someone have brought him something to eat?" *34h* Jesus said to them, "My food is to do the will of the one who sent me and to finish his work. *35i* *Do you not say, 'In four months the harvest will be here'? I tell you, look up and see the fields ripe for the harvest. *36j* *The reaper is already receiving his payment and gathering crops for eternal life, so that the sower and reaper can rejoice together. *37k* For here the saying is verified that 'One sows and another reaps.' *38* I sent you to reap what you have not worked for; others have done the work, and you are sharing the fruits of their work."

39 *Many of the Samaritans of that town began to believe in him because of the word of the woman who testified, "He told me everything I have done." *40* When the Samaritans came to him, they invited him to stay with them; and he stayed there two days. *41* Many more began to believe in him be-

---

4, 20: This mountain: Gerizim, on which a temple was erected in the fourth century B.C. by Samaritans to rival Mt. Zion in Jerusalem; cf Dt 27, 4 (Mt. Ebal = the Jews' term for Gerizim).

4, 23: In Spirit and truth: not a reference to an interior worship within one's own spirit. The Spirit is the spirit given by God that reveals truth and enables one to worship God appropriately (14, 16–17). Cf "born of water and Spirit" (3, 5).

4, 25: The expectations of the Samaritans are expressed here in Jewish terminology. They did not expect a messianic king of the house of David but a prophet like Moses (Dt 18, 15).

4, 26: I am he: it could also be translated "I am," an Old Testament self-designation of Yahweh (Is 43, 3, etc.); cf 6, 20; 8, 24.28.58; 13, 19; 18, 5.6.8. See the note on Mk 6, 50.

4, 27: Talking with a woman: a religious and social re-

striction that Jesus is pictured treating as unimportant.

4, 35: 'In four months . . .': probably a proverb; cf Mt 9, 37–38.

4, 36: Already: this word may go with the preceding verse rather than with 36.

4, 39: The woman is presented as a missionary, described in virtually the same words as the disciples are in Jesus' prayer (17, 20).

y: 8, 53; Mt 12, 41. *z:* 6, 35.58; 7, 37-39; Is 44, 3; 49, 10; Jl 4, 18; Rv 7, 16; 21, 6. *a:* 2 Kgs 17, 24-34. *b:* 9, 17; Hos 1, 3. *c:* Dt 11, 29; 27, 4; Jos 8, 33; Ps 122, 1-5. *d:* 2 Kgs 17, 27; Ps 76, 2-3. *e:* 2 Cor 3, 17. *f:* 1, 41. *g:* 9, 37. *h:* 5, 30.36; 6, 38; 9, 4; 17, 4. *i:* Mt 9, 37-38; Lk 10, 2; Rv 14, 15. *j:* Ps 126, 5-6; Am 9, 13-14. *k:* Dt 20, 6; 28, 30; Jb 31, 8; Mi 6, 15.

cause of his word, [42l]and they said to the woman, "We no longer believe because of your word; for we have heard for ourselves, and we know that this is truly the savior of the world."

Return to Galilee. [43]*After the two days, he left there for Galilee. [44m]*For Jesus himself testified that a prophet has no honor in his native place. [45]When he came into Galilee, the Galileans welcomed him, since they had seen all he had done in Jerusalem at the feast; for they themselves had gone to the feast.

Second Sign at Cana. [46n]*Then he returned to Cana in Galilee, where he had made the water wine. Now there was a royal official whose son was ill in Capernaum. [47]When he heard that Jesus had arrived in Galilee from Judea, he went to him and asked him to come down and heal his son, who was near death. [48o]Jesus said to him, "Unless you people see signs and wonders, you will not believe." [49]The royal official said to him, "Sir, come down before my child dies." [50p]Jesus said to him, "You may go; your son will live." The man believed what Jesus said to him and left. [51]While he was on his way back, his slaves met him and told him that his boy would live. [52]He asked them when he began to recover. They told him, "The fever left him yesterday, about

one in the afternoon." [53]The father realized that just at that time Jesus had said to him, "Your son will live," and he and his whole household came to believe. [54q][Now] this was the second sign Jesus did when he came to Galilee from Judea.

CHAPTER 5

See RG 327

Cure on a Sabbath. [1r]*After this, there was a feast of the Jews, and Jesus went up to Jerusalem. [2s]*Now there is in Jerusalem at the Sheep [Gate] a pool called in Hebrew Bethesda, with five porticoes. [3]*In these lay a large number of ill, blind, lame, and crippled. [4]* [5]One man was there who had been ill for thirty-eight years. [6]When Jesus saw him lying there and knew that he had been ill for a long time, he said to him, "Do you want to be well?" [7]The sick man answered him, "Sir, I have no one to put me into the pool when the water is stirred up; while I am on my way, someone else gets down there before me." [8t]Jesus said to him, "Rise, take up your mat, and walk." [9u]Immediately the man became well, took up his mat, and walked.

Now that day was a sabbath. [10v]So the Jews said to the man who was cured, "It is the sabbath, and it is not lawful for you to carry your mat." [11]He answered them, "The man who made me well told me, 'Take up

4, 43–54: Jesus' arrival in Cana in Galilee; the second sign. This section introduces another theme, that of the life-giving word of Jesus. It is explicitly linked to the first sign (2, 11). The royal official believes (50). The natural life given his son is a sign of eternal life.

4, 44: Probably a reminiscence of a tradition as in Mk 6, 4. Cf Gospel of Thomas 31: "No prophet is acceptable in his village, no physician heals those who know him."

4, 46–54: The story of the cure of the royal official's son may be a third version of the cure of the centurion's son (Mt 8, 5–13) or servant (Lk 7, 1–10). Cf also Mt 15, 21–28 // Mk 7, 24–30.

5, 1–47: The self-revelation of Jesus continues in Jerusalem at a feast. The third sign (cf 2, 11; 4, 54) is performed, the cure of a paralytic by Jesus' life-giving word. The water of the pool fails to bring life; Jesus' word does.

5, 1: The reference in vv 45–46 to Moses suggests that the feast was Pentecost. The connection of that feast with the giving of the law to Moses on Sinai, attested in later Judaism, may already have been made in the first century. The feast could also be Passover (cf 6, 4). John stresses that the day was a sabbath (9).

5, 2: There is no noun with **Sheep.** "Gate" is supplied on the grounds that there must have been a gate in the NE wall of the temple area where animals for sacrifice were brought

in; cf Neh 3, 1.32; 12, 39. **Hebrew:** more precisely, Aramaic. **Bethesda:** preferred to variants "Be(th)zatha" and "Bethsaida"; **bêt-'ešdatayīn** is given as the name of a double pool northeast of the temple area in the Qumran Copper Roll. **Five porticoes:** a pool excavated in Jerusalem actually has five porticoes.

5, 3: The Caesarean and Western recensions, followed by the Vulgate, add "waiting for the movement of the water." Apparently an intermittent spring in the pool bubbled up occasionally (see 7). This turbulence was believed to cure.

5, 4: Toward the end of the second century in the West and among the fourth-century Greek Fathers, an additional verse was known: "For [from time to time] an angel of the Lord used to come down into the pool; and the water was stirred up, so the first one to get in [after the stirring of the water] was healed of whatever disease afflicted him." The angel was a popular explanation of the turbulence and the healing powers attributed to it. This verse is missing from all early Greek

l: 1 Jn 4, 14. *m:* Mt 13, 57; Mk 6, 4; Lk 4, 24. *n:* 2, 1–11; Mt 8, 5-13; 15, 21-28; Mk 7, 24-30; Lk 7, 1-10. *o:* 2, 18.23; Wis 8, 8; Mt 12, 38; 1 Cor 1, 22. *p:* 1 Kgs 17, 23. *q:* 2, 11. *r:* 6, 4. *s:* Neh 3, 1.32; 12, 39. *t:* Mt 9, 6; Mk 2, 11; Lk 5, 24; Acts 3, 6. *u:* Mk 2, 12; Lk 5, 25 / 9, 14. *v:* Ex 20, 8; Jer 17, 21-27; Mk 3, 2; Lk 13, 10; 14, 1.

your mat and walk.' " [12]They asked him, "Who is the man who told you, 'Take it up and walk'?" [13w]The man who was healed did not know who it was, for Jesus had slipped away, since there was a crowd there. [14x*]After this Jesus found him in the temple area and said to him, "Look, you are well; do not sin any more, so that nothing worse may happen to you." [15]The man went and told the Jews that Jesus was the one who had made him well. [16y]Therefore, the Jews began to persecute Jesus because he did this on a sabbath. [17z*]But Jesus answered them, "My Father is at work until now, so I am at work." [18a]For this reason the Jews tried all the more to kill him, because he not only broke the sabbath but he also called God his own father, making himself equal to God.

The Work of the Son. [19b*]Jesus answered and said to them, "Amen, amen, I say to you, a son cannot do anything on his own, but only what he sees his father doing; for what he does, his son will do also. [20c]For the Father loves his Son and shows him everything that he himself does, and he will show him greater works than these, so that you may be amazed. [21d*]For just as the Father raises the dead and gives life, so also does the Son give life to whomever he wishes. [22e*]Nor does the Father judge anyone, but he has given all judgment to his Son, [23]so that all may honor the Son just as they honor the Father. Whoever does not honor the Son does not honor the Father who sent him. [24f]Amen, amen, I say to you, whoever hears my word and believes in the one who sent me has eternal life and will not come to condemnation, but has passed from death to life. [25g]Amen, amen, I say to you, the hour is coming and is now here when the dead will hear the voice of the Son of God, and those who hear will live. [26h]For just as the Father has life in himself, so also he gave to his Son the possession of life in himself. [27i]And he gave him power to exercise judgment, because he is the Son of Man. [28j*]Do not be amazed at this, because the hour is coming in which all who are in the tombs will hear his voice [29k]and will come out, those who have done good deeds to the resurrection of life, but those who have done wicked deeds to the resurrection of condemnation.

[30l]"I cannot do anything on my own; I judge as I hear, and my judgment is just, because I do not seek my own will but the will of the one who sent me.

Witnesses to Jesus. [31m]"If I testify on my own behalf, my testimony cannot be verified. [32*]But there is another who testifies on my behalf, and I know that the testimony he gives on my behalf is true. [33n]You sent emissaries to John, and he testified to the truth. [34o]I do not accept testimony from a human being, but I say this so that you may

---

manuscripts and the earliest versions, including the original Vulgate. Its vocabulary is markedly non-Johannine.

5, 14: While the cure of the paralytic in Mk 2, 1–12 is associated with the forgiveness of sins, Jesus never drew a one-to-one connection between sin and suffering (cf 9, 3; Lk 12, 1–5), as did Ez 18, 20.

5, 17: Sabbath observance (10) was based on God's resting on the seventh day (cf Gn 2, 2–3; Ex 20, 11). Philo and some rabbis insisted that God's providence remains active on the sabbath, keeping all things in existence, giving life in birth and taking it away in death. Other rabbis taught that God rested from creating, but not from judging (= ruling, governing). Jesus here claims the same authority to work as the Father, and, in the discourse that follows, the same divine prerogatives: power over life and death (21.24–26) and judgment (22.27).

5, 19: This proverb or parable is taken from apprenticeship in a trade: the activity of a son is modeled on that of his father. Jesus' dependence on the Father is justification for doing what the Father does.

5, 21: Gives life: in the Old Testament, a divine preroga-tive (Dt 32, 39; 1 Sm 2, 6; 2 Kgs 5, 7; Tob 13, 2; Is 26, 19; Dan 12, 2).

5, 22: Judgment: another divine prerogative, often expressed as acquittal or condemnation (Dt 32, 36; Ps 43, 1).

5, 28–29: While vv 19–27 present realized eschatology, vv 28–29 are future eschatology; cf Dn 12, 2.

5, 32: Another: likely the Father, who in four different ways gives testimony to Jesus, as indicated in the verse groupings 33–34, 36, 37–38, 39–40.

w: Mt 8, 18; 13, 36; Mk 4, 36; 7, 17. x: 8, 11; 9, 2; Ez 18, 20. y: 7, 23; Mt 12, 8. z: Ex 20, 11. a: 7, 1.25; 8, 37.40; 10, 33.36; 14, 28; Gn 3, 5-6; Wis 2, 16; Mt 26, 4; 2 Thes 2, 4. b: 3, 34; 8, 26; 12, 49; 9, 4; 10, 30. c: 3, 35. d: 11, 25; Dt 32, 39; 1 Sm 2, 6; 2 Kgs 5, 7; Tb 13, 2; Wis 16, 13; Is 26, 19; Dn 7, 10.13; 12, 2; Rom 4, 17; 2 Cor 1, 9. e: Acts 10, 42; 17, 31. f: 3, 18; 8, 51; 1 Jn 3, 14. g: 5, 28; 8, 51; 11, 25-26; Eph 2, 1; 5, 14; Rv 3, 1. h: 1, 4; 1 Jn 5, 11. i: 5, 22; Dn 7, 13.22; Mt 25, 31; Lk 21, 36. j: 11, 43. k: Dn 12, 2; Mt 16, 27; 25, 46; Acts 24, 15; 2 Cor 5, 10. l: 6, 38. m: 8, 13-14.18. n: 1, 19-27; Mt 11, 10-11. o: 1 Jn 5, 9.

be saved. 35p*He was a burning and shining lamp, and for a while you were content to rejoice in his light. 36qBut I have testimony greater than John's. The works that the Father gave me to accomplish, these works that I perform testify on my behalf that the Father has sent me. 37rMoreover, the Father who sent me has testified on my behalf. But you have never heard his voice nor seen his form, 38sand you do not have his word remaining in you, because you do not believe in the one whom he has sent. 39t*You search the scriptures, because you think you have eternal life through them; even they testify on my behalf. 40But you do not want to come to me to have life.

Unbelief of Jesus' Hearers. 41*"I do not accept human praise; 42umoreover, I know that you do not have the love of God in you. 43vI came in the name of my Father, but you do not accept me; yet if another comes in his own name, you will accept him. 44wHow can you believe, when you accept praise from one another and do not seek the praise that comes from the only God? 45xDo not think that I will accuse you before the Father: the one who will accuse you is Moses, in whom you have placed your hope. 46yFor if you had believed Moses, you would have believed me, because he wrote about me. 47But if you do not believe his writings, how will you believe my words?"

CHAPTER 6

See RG 327–28

Multiplication of the Loaves. 1z*After this, Jesus went across the Sea of Galilee [of Tiberias]. 2A large crowd followed him, because they saw the signs he was performing on the sick. 3Jesus went up on the mountain, and there he sat down with his disciples. 4aThe Jewish feast of Passover was near. 5b*When Jesus raised his eyes and saw that a large crowd was coming to him, he said to Philip, "Where can we buy enough food for them to eat?" 6*He said this to test him, because he himself knew what he was going to do. 7c*Philip answered him, "Two hundred days' wages worth of food would not be enough for each of them to have a little [bit]." 8One of his disciples, Andrew, the brother of Simon Peter, said to him, 9d*"There is a boy here who has five barley loaves and two fish; but what good are these for so many?" 10e*Jesus said, "Have the people recline." Now there was a great deal of grass in that place. So the men reclined, about five thousand in number. 11fThen Jesus took the loaves, gave thanks, and distributed them to those who were reclining, and also as much of the fish as they wanted. 12When they had had their fill, he said to his disciples, "Gather the fragments left over, so that nothing will be wasted." 13*So they collected them, and filled twelve wicker baskets with fragments from the five barley

---

5, 35: Lamp: cf Ps 132, 17: "I will place a lamp for my Anointed (= David)," and possibly the description of Elijah in Sir 48, 1. But only **for a while,** indicating the temporary and subordinate nature of John's mission.

5, 39: You search: this may be an imperative: "Search the scriptures, because you think that you have eternal life through them."

5, 41: Praise: the same Greek word means "praise" or "honor" (from others) and "glory" (from God). There is a play on this in v 44.

6, 1–15: This story of the multiplication of the loaves is the fourth sign (cf the note on 5, 1–47). It is the only miracle story found in all four gospels (occurring twice in Mk and Mt). See the notes on Mt 14, 13–21 and 15, 32–39. John differs on the roles of Philip and Andrew, the proximity of Passover (4), and the allusion to Elisha (see 9). The story here symbolizes the food that is really available through Jesus. It connotes a new exodus and has eucharistic overtones.

6, 1: [Of Tiberias]: the awkward apposition represents a later name of the Sea of Galilee. It was probably originally a marginal gloss.

6, 5: Jesus takes the initiative (in the synoptics, the disciples do), possibly pictured as (cf 14) the new Moses (cf Nm 11, 13).

6, 6: Probably the evangelist's comment; in this gospel Jesus is never portrayed as ignorant of anything.

6, 7: Days' wages: literally, "denarii"; a Roman denarius is a day's wage in Mt 20, 2.

6, 9: Barley loaves: the food of the poor. There seems an allusion to the story of Elisha multiplying the barley bread in 2 Kgs 4, 42–44.

6, 10: Grass: implies springtime, and therefore Passover. **Five thousand:** so Mk 6, 39.44 and parallels.

6, 13: Baskets: the word describes the typically Palestinian wicker basket, as in Mk 6, 43 and parallels.

p: 1, 8; Ps 132, 17; Sir 48, 1. q: 10, 25. r: 8, 18; Dt 4, 12.15; 1 Jn 5, 9. s: 1 Jn 2, 14. t: 12, 16; 19, 28; 20, 9; Lk 24, 27.44; 1 Pt 1, 10. u: 1 Jn 2, 15. v: Mt 24, 5.24. w: 12, 43. x: Dt 31, 26. y: 5, 39; Dt 18, 15; Lk 16, 31; 24, 44. z: Mt 14, 13-21; Mk 6, 32-44; Lk 9, 10-17. a: 2, 13; 11, 55. b: Nm 11, 13. c: Mt 20, 2. d: 2 Kgs 4, 42-44. e: Mt 14, 21; Mk 6, 44. f: 21, 13.

loaves that had been more than they could eat. [14g]*When the people saw the sign he had done, they said, "This is truly the Prophet, the one who is to come into the world." [15h]Since Jesus knew that they were going to come and carry him off to make him king, he withdrew again to the mountain alone.

Walking on the Water. [16i]*When it was evening, his disciples went down to the sea, [17]embarked in a boat, and went across the sea to Capernaum. It had already grown dark, and Jesus had not yet come to them. [18]The sea was stirred up because a strong wind was blowing. [19j]*When they had rowed about three or four miles, they saw Jesus walking on the sea and coming near the boat, and they began to be afraid. [20]*But he said to them, "It is I. Do not be afraid." [21]They wanted to take him into the boat, but the boat immediately arrived at the shore to which they were heading.

The Bread of Life Discourse. [22]*The next day, the crowd that remained across the sea saw that there had been only one boat there, and that Jesus had not gone along with his disciples in the boat, but only his disciples had left. [23]*Other boats came from Tiberias near the place where they had eaten the bread when the Lord gave thanks. [24]When the crowd saw that neither Jesus nor his disciples were there, they themselves got into boats and came to Capernaum looking for Jesus. [25]And when they found him across the sea they said to him, "Rabbi, when did you get here?" [26]Jesus answered them and said,

"Amen, amen, I say to you, you are looking for me not because you saw signs but because you ate the loaves and were filled. [27k]*Do not work for food that perishes but for the food that endures for eternal life, which the Son of Man will give you. For on him the Father, God, has set his seal." [28]So they said to him, "What can we do to accomplish the works of God?" [29]Jesus answered and said to them, "This is the work of God, that you believe in the one he sent." [30l]So they said to him, "What sign can you do, that we may see and believe in you? What can you do? [31m]*Our ancestors ate manna in the desert, as it is written:

'He gave them bread from heaven to eat.' "

[32n]So Jesus said to them, "Amen, amen, I say to you, it was not Moses who gave the bread from heaven; my Father gives you the true bread from heaven. [33]For the bread of God is that which comes down from heaven and gives life to the world."

[34o]So they said to him, "Sir, give us this bread always." [35p]*Jesus said to them, "I am the bread of life; whoever comes to me will never hunger, and whoever believes in me will never thirst. [36q]But I told you that although you have seen [me], you do not believe. [37]Everything that the Father gives me will come to me, and I will not reject anyone who comes to me, [38r]because I came down from heaven not to do my own will but the will of the one who sent me. [39s]And this is the will of the one who sent me, that I should not

---

6, 14: The Prophet: probably the prophet like Moses (see the note on 1, 21). **The one who is to come into the world:** probably Elijah; cf Mal 3, 1.23.

6, 16–21: The fifth sign is a nature miracle, portraying Jesus sharing Yahweh's power. Cf the parallel stories following the multiplication of the loaves in Mk 6, 45–52 and Mt 14, 22–33.

6, 19: Walking on the sea: although the Greek (cf 16) could mean "on the seashore" or "by the sea" (cf 21, 1), the parallels, especially Mt 14, 25, make clear that Jesus walked upon the water. John may allude to Job 9, 8: God "treads upon the crests of the sea."

6, 20: It is I: literally, "I am." See also the notes on 4, 26 and Mk 6, 50.

6, 22–71: Discourse on the bread of life; replacement of the manna. Verses 22–34 serve as an introduction, vv 35–59 constitute the discourse proper, vv 60–71 portray the reaction of the disciples and Peter's confession.

6, 23: Possibly a later interpolation, to explain how the crowd got to Capernaum.

6, 27: The food that endures for eternal life: cf 4, 14, on water "springing up to eternal life."

6, 31: Bread from heaven: cf Ex 16, 4.15.32–34 and the notes there; Ps 78, 24. The manna, thought to have been hidden by Jeremiah (2 Mc 2, 5–8), was expected to reappear miraculously at Passover, in the last days.

6, 35–59: Up to v 50, "bread of life" is a figure for God's revelation in Jesus; in vv 51–58, the eucharistic theme comes to the fore. There may thus be a break between vv 50 and 51.

g: Dt 18, 15.18; Mal 3, 1.23; Acts 3, 22.   h: 18, 36.   i: Mt 14, 22-27; Mk 6, 45-52.   j: Jb 9, 8; Pss 29, 3-4; 77, 20; Is 43, 16.   k: 6, 50.51.54.58.   l: Mt 16, 1-4; Lk 11, 29-30.   m: Ex 16, 4-5; Nm 11, 7-9; Ps 78, 24.   n: Mt 6, 11.   o: 4, 15.   p: Is 55, 1-3; Am 8, 11-13.   q: 20, 29.   r: 4, 34; Mt 26, 39; Heb 10, 9.   s: 10, 28-29; 17, 12; 18, 9.

lose anything of what he gave me, but that I should raise it [on] the last day. *40t*For this is the will of my Father, that everyone who sees the Son and believes in him may have eternal life, and I shall raise him [on] the last day."

*41*The Jews murmured about him because he said, "I am the bread that came down from heaven," *42u*and they said, "Is this not Jesus, the son of Joseph? Do we not know his father and mother? Then how can he say, 'I have come down from heaven'?" *43v*Jesus answered and said to them, "Stop murmuring among yourselves. *44*No one can come to me unless the Father who sent me draw him, and I will raise him on the last day. *45w*It is written in the prophets:

'They shall all be taught by God.'

Everyone who listens to my Father and learns from him comes to me. *46x*Not that anyone has seen the Father except the one who is from God; he has seen the Father. *47*Amen, amen, I say to you, whoever believes has eternal life. *48*I am the bread of life. *49y*Your ancestors ate the manna in the desert, but they died; *50*this is the bread that comes down from heaven so that one may eat it and not die. *51z*I am the living bread that came down from heaven; whoever eats this bread will live forever; and the bread that I will give is my flesh for the life of the world."

*52*The Jews quarreled among themselves, saying, "How can this man give us [his] flesh to eat?" *53*Jesus said to them, "Amen, amen, I say to you, unless you eat the flesh of the Son of Man and drink his blood, you do not have life within you. *54**Whoever eats my flesh and drinks my blood has eternal life, and I will raise him on the last day. *55*For my flesh is true food, and my blood is true drink. *56*Whoever eats my flesh and drinks my blood remains in me and I in him. *57a*Just as the living Father sent me and I have life because of the Father, so also the one who feeds on me will have life because of me. *58*This is the bread that came down from heaven. Unlike your ancestors who ate and still died, whoever eats this bread will live forever." *59*These things he said while teaching in the synagogue in Capernaum.

The Words of Eternal Life. *60**Then many of his disciples who were listening said, "This saying is hard; who can accept it?" *61*Since Jesus knew that his disciples were murmuring about this, he said to them, "Does this shock you? *62**What if you were to see the Son of Man ascending to where he was before? *63**It is the spirit that gives life, while the flesh is of no avail. The words I have spoken to you are spirit and life. *64b*But there are some of you who do not believe." Jesus knew from the beginning the ones who would not believe and the one who would betray him. *65*And he said, "For this reason I have told you that no one can come to me unless it is granted him by my Father."

*66*As a result of this, many [of] his disciples returned to their former way of life and no longer accompanied him. *67*Jesus then said to the Twelve, "Do you also want to leave?" *68*Simon Peter answered him, "Master, to whom shall we go? You have the words of eternal life. *69c*We have come to believe and are convinced that you are the Holy One of God." *70*Jesus answered them, "Did I not choose you twelve? Yet is not one of you a devil?" *71d*He was referring to Judas, son of Simon the Iscariot; it was he who would betray him, one of the Twelve.

6, 43: Murmuring: the word may reflect the Greek of Ex 16, 2.7.8.

6, 54–58: Eats: the verb used in these verses is not the classical Greek verb used of human eating, but that of animal eating: "munch," "gnaw." This may be part of John's emphasis on the reality of the flesh and blood of Jesus (cf 55), but the same verb eventually became the ordinary verb in Greek meaning "eat."

6, 60–71: These verses refer more to themes of vv 35–50 than to those of 51–58 and seem to be addressed to members of the Johannine community who found it difficult to accept the high christology reflected in the bread of life discourse.

6, 62: This unfinished conditional sentence is obscure.

Probably there is a reference to vv 49–51. Jesus claims to be **the bread that comes down from heaven** (50); this claim provokes incredulity (60); and so Jesus is pictured as asking what his disciples will say when he goes up to heaven.

6, 63: Spirit . . . flesh: probably not a reference to the eucharistic body of Jesus but to the supernatural and the natural, as in 3, 6. **Spirit and life:** all Jesus said about the bread of life is the revelation of the Spirit.

t: 1 Jn 2, 25. *u:* Mt 13, 54-57; Mk 6, 1-4; Lk 4, 22. *v:* Ex 16, 2.7.8; Lk 4, 22. *w:* Is 54, 13; Jer 31, 33-34. *x:* 1, 18; 7, 29; Ex 33, 20. *y:* 1 Cor 10, 3.5. *z:* Mt 26, 26-27; Lk 22, 19. *a:* 5, 26. *b:* 13, 11. *c:* 11, 27; Mt 16, 16; Mk 1, 24; Lk 4, 34. *d:* 12, 4; 13, 2.27.

See RG
328–29

CHAPTER 7[*]

The Feast of Tabernacles. [1e]After this, Jesus moved about within Galilee; but he did not wish to travel in Judea, because the Jews were trying to kill him. [2f]But the Jewish feast of Tabernacles was near. [3*]So his brothers said to him, "Leave here and go to Judea, so that your disciples also may see the works you are doing. [4g]No one works in secret if he wants to be known publicly. If you do these things, manifest yourself to the world." [5]For his brothers did not believe in him. [6*]So Jesus said to them, "My time is not yet here, but the time is always right for you. [7h]The world cannot hate you, but it hates me, because I testify to it that its works are evil. [8*]You go up to the feast. I am not going up to this feast, because my time has not yet been fulfilled." [9]After he had said this, he stayed on in Galilee.

[10]But when his brothers had gone up to the feast, he himself also went up, not openly but [as it were] in secret. [11]The Jews were looking for him at the feast and saying, "Where is he?" [12]And there was considerable murmuring about him in the crowds. Some said, "He is a good man," [while] others said, "No; on the contrary, he misleads the crowd." [13i]Still, no one spoke openly about him because they were afraid of the Jews.

The First Dialogue. [14*]When the feast was already half over, Jesus went up into the temple area and began to teach. [15j*]The Jews were amazed and said, "How does he know scripture without having studied?" [16]Jesus answered them and said, "My teaching is not my own but is from the one who sent me. [17k*]Whoever chooses to do his will shall know whether my teaching is from God or whether I speak on my own. [18]Whoever speaks on his own seeks his own glory, but whoever seeks the glory of the one who sent him is truthful, and there is no wrong in him. [19l]Did not Moses give you the law? Yet none of you keeps the law. Why are you trying to kill me?" [20m*]The crowd answered, "You are possessed! Who is trying to kill you?" [21n*]Jesus answered and said to them, "I performed one work and all of you are amazed [22o]because of it. Moses gave you circumcision—not that it came from Moses but rather from the patriarchs—and you circumcise a man on the sabbath. [23p]If a man can receive circumcision on a sabbath so that the law of Moses may not be broken, are you angry with me because I made a whole person well on a sabbath? [24q]Stop judging by appearances, but judge justly."

[25]So some of the inhabitants of Jerusalem said, "Is he not the one they are trying to

---

7—8: These chapters contain events about the feast of Tabernacles (Sukkoth, Ingathering: Ex 23, 16; Tents, Booths: Dt 16, 13–16), with its symbols of booths (originally built to shelter harvesters), rain (water from Siloam poured on the temple altar), and lights (illumination of the four torches in the Court of the Women). They continue the theme of the replacement of feasts (Passover, 2, 13; 6, 4; Hanukkah, 10, 22; Pentecost, 5, 1), here accomplished by Jesus as the Living Water. These chapters comprise seven miscellaneous controversies and dialogues. There is a literary inclusion with Jesus in hiding in 7, 4.10 and 8, 59. There are frequent references to attempts on his life: 7, 1.13.19.25.30.32.44; 8, 37.40.59.

7, 3: **Brothers:** these relatives (cf 2, 12 and see the note on Mk 6, 3) are never portrayed as disciples until after the resurrection (Acts 1, 14). Mt 13, 55 and Mk 6, 3 give the names of four of them. Jesus has already performed works/signs in Judea; cf 2, 23; 3, 2; 4, 45; 5, 8.

7, 6: **Time:** the Greek word means "opportune time," here a synonym for Jesus' "hour" (see the note on 2, 4), his death and resurrection. In the wordplay, any time is suitable for Jesus' brothers, because they are not dependent on God's will.

7, 8: **I am not going up:** an early attested reading "not yet" seems a correction, since Jesus in the story does go up to

the feast. "Go up," in a play on words, refers not only to going up to Jerusalem but also to exaltation at the cross, resurrection, and ascension; cf 3, 14; 6, 62; 20, 17.

7, 14–31: Jesus teaches in the temple; debate with the Jews.

7, 15: **Without having studied:** literally, "How does he know letters without having learned?" Children were taught to read and write by means of the scriptures. But here more than Jesus' literacy is being discussed; the people are wondering how he can teach like a rabbi. Rabbis were trained by other rabbis and traditionally quoted their teachers.

7, 17: **To do his will:** presumably a reference back to the "work" of 6, 29: belief in the one whom God has sent.

7, 20: **You are possessed:** literally, "You have a demon." The insane were thought to be possessed by a demoniacal spirit.

7, 21: **One work:** the cure of the paralytic (5, 1–9) because of the reference to the sabbath (22; 5, 9–10).

e: 5, 18; 8, 37.40.   *f:* Ex 23, 16; Lv 23, 34; Nm 29, 12; Dt 16, 13-16; Zec 14, 16-19.   *g:* 14, 22.   *h:* 15, 18.   *i:* 9, 22; 19, 38; 20, 19.   *j:* Lk 2, 47.   *k:* 6, 29.   *l:* Acts 7, 53.   *m:* 8, 48-49; 10, 20.   *n:* 5 1-9.   *o:* Gn 17, 10; Lv 12, 3.   *p:* 5, 2-9.16; Mt 12, 1-12; Lk 14, 5.   *q:* 8, 15; Lv 19, 15; Is 11, 3-4.

kill? [26]*And look, he is speaking openly and they say nothing to him. Could the authorities have realized that he is the Messiah? [27r]But we know where he is from. When the Messiah comes, no one will know where he is from." [28s]So Jesus cried out in the temple area as he was teaching and said, "You know me and also know where I am from. Yet I did not come on my own, but the one who sent me, whom you do not know, is true. [29t]I know him, because I am from him, and he sent me." [30u]So they tried to arrest him, but no one laid a hand upon him, because his hour had not yet come. [31v]But many of the crowd began to believe in him, and said, "When the Messiah comes, will he perform more signs than this man has done?"

Officers Sent to Arrest Jesus. [32]*The Pharisees heard the crowd murmuring about him to this effect, and the chief priests and the Pharisees sent guards to arrest him. [33w]So Jesus said, "I will be with you only a little while longer, and then I will go to the one who sent me. [34x]You will look for me but not find [me], and where I am you cannot come." [35]*So the Jews said to one another, "Where is he going that we will not find him? Surely he is not going to the dispersion among the Greeks to teach the Greeks, is he? [36]What is the meaning of his saying, 'You will look for me and not find [me], and where I am you cannot come'?"

Rivers of Living Water. [37y]*On the last and greatest day of the feast, Jesus stood up and exclaimed, "Let anyone who thirsts come to me and drink. [38z]*Whoever believes in me, as scripture says:

'Rivers of living water will flow from within him.' "

[39a]*He said this in reference to the Spirit that those who came to believe in him were to receive. There was, of course, no Spirit yet, because Jesus had not yet been glorified.

Discussion about the Origins of the Messiah. [40b]*Some in the crowd who heard these words said, "This is truly the Prophet." [41]Others said, "This is the Messiah." But others said, "The Messiah will not come from Galilee, will he? [42c]Does not scripture say that the Messiah will be of David's family and come from Bethlehem, the village where David lived?" [43]So a division occurred in the crowd because of him. [44]Some of them even wanted to arrest him, but no one laid hands on him.

[45]So the guards went to the chief priests and Pharisees, who asked them, "Why did you not bring him?" [46]The guards answered, "Never before has anyone spoken like this one." [47]So the Pharisees answered them, "Have you also been deceived? [48d]Have any of the authorities or the Pharisees believed in him? [49]But this crowd, which does not know the law, is accursed." [50e]Nicodemus, one of their members who had come to him earlier, said to them, [51f]"Does our law condemn a person before it first hears him and finds out what he is doing?" [52]They answered and said to him, "You are not from Galilee also, are you? Look and see that no prophet arises from Galilee."

CHAPTER 8

See RG 328–29

A Woman Caught in Adultery. [53]*Then each went to his own house,

---

7, 26: The authorities: the members of the Sanhedrin (same term as 3, 1).

7, 32–36: Jesus announces his approaching departure (cf also 8, 21; 12, 36; 13, 33) and complete control over his destiny.

7, 35: Dispersion: or "diaspora": Jews living outside Palestine. **Greeks:** probably refers to the Gentiles in the Mediterranean area; cf 12, 20.

7, 37–39: Promise of living water through the Spirit.

7, 38: Living water: not an exact quotation from any Old Testament passage; in the gospel context the gift of the Spirit is meant; cf 3, 5. **From within him:** either Jesus or the believer; if Jesus, it continues the Jesus-Moses motif (water from the rock, Ex 17, 6; Nm 20, 11) as well as Jesus as the new temple (cf Ez 47, 1). Grammatically, it goes better with the believer.

7, 39: No Spirit yet: Codex Vaticanus and early Latin,

Syriac, and Coptic versions add "given." In this gospel, the sending of the Spirit cannot take place until Jesus' glorification through his death, resurrection, and ascension; cf 20, 22.

7, 40–53: Discussion of the Davidic lineage of the Messiah.

7, 53—8, 11: The story of the woman caught in adultery is a later insertion here, missing from all early Greek manuscripts. A Western text-type insertion, attested mainly in Old Latin translations, it is found in different places in different

r: Heb 7, 3. *s:* 8, 19. *t:* 6, 46; 8, 55. *u:* 7, 44; 8, 20; Lk 4, 29-30. *v:* 2, 11; 10, 42; 11, 45. *w:* 13, 33; 16, 16. *x:* 8, 21; 12, 36; 13, 33.36; 16, 5; Dt 4, 29; Prv 1, 28; Is 55, 6; Hos 5, 6. *y:* Rv 21, 6. *z:* 4, 10.14; 19, 34; Is 12, 3; Ez 47, 1. *a:* 16, 7. *b:* Dt 18, 15.18. *c:* 2 Sm 7, 12-14; Pss 89, 3-4; 132, 11; Mi 5, 1; Mt 2, 5-6. *d:* 12, 42. *e:* 3, 1; 19, 39. *f:* Dt 1, 16-17.

¹ᵍ*while Jesus went to the Mount of Olives. ²But early in the morning he arrived again in the temple area, and all the people started coming to him, and he sat down and taught them. ³Then the scribes and the Pharisees brought a woman who had been caught in adultery and made her stand in the middle. ⁴They said to him, "Teacher, this woman was caught in the very act of committing adultery. ⁵ʰ*Now in the law, Moses commanded us to stone such women. So what do you say?" ⁵*They said this to test him, so that they could have some charge to bring against him. Jesus bent down and began to write on the ground with his finger. ⁷ⁱ*But when they continued asking him, he straightened up and said to them, "Let the one among you who is without sin be the first to throw a stone at her." ⁸Again he bent down and wrote on the ground. ⁹And in response, they went away one by one, beginning with the elders. So he was left alone with the woman before him. ¹⁰ʲThen Jesus straightened up and said to her, "Woman, where are they? Has no one condemned you?" ¹¹ᵏShe replied, "No one, sir." Then Jesus said, "Neither do I condemn you. Go, [and] from now on do not sin any more."]

The Light of the World. ¹²ˡ*Jesus spoke to them again, saying, "I am the light of the world. Whoever follows me will not walk in darkness, but will have the light of life." ¹³So the Pharisees said to him, "You testify on your own behalf, so your testimony cannot be verified." ¹⁴ᵐ*Jesus answered and said to them, "Even if I do testify on my own behalf, my testimony can be verified, because I know where I came from and where I am going. But you do not know where I come from or where I am going. ¹⁵ⁿ*You judge by appearances, but I do not judge anyone. ¹⁶ᵒAnd even if I should judge, my judgment is valid, because I am not alone, but it is I and the Father who sent me. ¹⁷ᵖ*Even in your law it is written that the testimony of two men can be verified. ¹⁸�q I testify on my behalf and so does the Father who sent me." ¹⁹ʳSo they said to him, "Where is your father?" Jesus answered, "You know neither me nor my Father. If you knew me, you would know my Father also." ²⁰ˢHe spoke these words while teaching in the treasury in the temple area. But no one arrested him, because his hour had not yet come.

Jesus, the Father's Ambassador. ²¹ᵗ*He said to them again, "I am going away and you will look for me, but you will die in your sin. Where I am going you cannot come." ²²*So the Jews said, "He is not going to kill himself, is he, because he said, 'Where I am going you cannot come'?" ²³ᵘHe said to them, "You belong to what is below, I belong

manuscripts: here, or after 7, 36, or at the end of this gospel, or after Lk 21, 38, or at the end of that gospel. There are many non-Johannine features in the language, and there are also many doubtful readings within the passage. The style and motifs are similar to those of Luke, and it fits better with the general situation at the end of Lk 21, but it was probably inserted here because of the allusion to Jer 17, 13 (cf the note on 8, 6) and the statement, "I do not judge anyone," in 8, 15. The Catholic Church accepts this passage as canonical scripture.

8, 1: Mount of Olives: not mentioned elsewhere in the gospel tradition outside of passion week.

8, 5: Lv 20, 10 and Dt 22, 22 mention only death, but Dt 22, 23–24 prescribes stoning for a betrothed virgin.

8, 6: Cf Jer 17, 13 (RSV): "Those who turn away from thee shall be written in the earth, for they have forsaken the LORD, the fountain of living water"; cf 7, 38.

8, 7: The first stones were to be thrown by the witnesses (Dt 17, 7).

8, 12–20: Jesus the light of the world. Jesus replaces the four torches of the illumination of the temple as the light of joy.

8, 14: My testimony can be verified: this seems to contradict 5, 31, but the emphasis here is on Jesus' origin from the Father and his divine destiny. **Where I am going:** indicates Jesus' passion and glorification.

8, 15: By appearances: literally, "according to the flesh." **I do not judge anyone:** superficial contradiction of 5, 22.27.30; here the emphasis is that the judgment is not by material standards.

8, 17: Your law: a reflection of later controversy between church and synagogue.

8, 21–30: I whose ambassador I am is with me. Jesus' origin is from God; he can reveal God.

8, 21: You will die in your sin: i.e., of disbelief, cf v 24. **Where I am going you cannot come:** except through faith in Jesus' passion-resurrection.

8, 22: The Jews suspect that he is referring to his death. Johannine irony is apparent here; Jesus' death will not be self-inflicted but destined by God.

g: Lk 21, 37-38. h: Lv 20, 10; Dt 22, 22-29. i: Dt 17, 7. j: Ez 33, 11. k: 5, 14. l: 1, 4-5.9; 12, 46; Ex 13, 22; Is 42, 6; Zec 14, 8. m: 5, 31. n: 12, 47; 1 Sm 16, 7. o: 5, 30. p: Dt 17, 6; 19, 15; Nm 35, 30. q: 5, 23.37. r: 7, 28; 14, 7; 15, 21. s: 7, 30. t: 7, 34; 13, 33. u: 3, 31; 17, 14; 18, 36.

to what is above. You belong to this world, but I do not belong to this world. [24v]*That is why I told you that you will die in your sins. For if you do not believe that I AM, you will die in your sins." [25w]*So they said to him, "Who are you?" Jesus said to them, "What I told you from the beginning. [26x]I have much to say about you in condemnation. But the one who sent me is true, and what I heard from him I tell the world." [27]They did not realize that he was speaking to them of the Father. [28y]So Jesus said [to them], "When you lift up the Son of Man, then you will realize that I AM, and that I do nothing on my own, but I say only what the Father taught me. [29]The one who sent me is with me. He has not left me alone, because I always do what is pleasing to him." [30]Because he spoke this way, many came to believe in him.

Jesus and Abraham. [31]*Jesus then said to those Jews who believed in him, "If you remain in my word, you will truly be my disciples, [32z]and you will know the truth, and the truth will set you free." [33a]*They answered him, "We are descendants of Abraham and have never been enslaved to anyone. How can you say, 'You will become free'?" [34b]Jesus answered them, "Amen, amen, I say to you, everyone who commits sin is a slave of sin. [35c]*A slave does not remain in a household forever, but a son always remains. [36]So if a son frees you, then you will truly be free. [37]I know that you are descendants of Abraham. But you are trying to kill me, because my word has no room

among you. [38]*I tell you what I have seen in the Father's presence; then do what you have heard from the Father."

[39d]*They answered and said to him, "Our father is Abraham." Jesus said to them, "If you were Abraham's children, you would be doing the works of Abraham. [40]But now you are trying to kill me, a man who has told you the truth that I heard from God; Abraham did not do this. [41e]You are doing the works of your father!" [So] they said to him, "We are not illegitimate. We have one Father, God." [42f]Jesus said to them, "If God were your Father, you would love me, for I came from God and am here; I did not come on my own, but he sent me. [43]Why do you not understand what I am saying? Because you cannot bear to hear my word. [44g]You belong to your father the devil and you willingly carry out your father's desires. He was a murderer from the beginning and does not stand in truth, because there is no truth in him. When he tells a lie, he speaks in character, because he is a liar and the father of lies. [45]But because I speak the truth, you do not believe me. [46h]Can any of you charge me with sin? If I am telling the truth, why do you not believe me? [47i]Whoever belongs to God hears the words of God; for this reason you do not listen, because you do not belong to God."

[48]*The Jews answered and said to him, "Are we not right in saying that you are a Samaritan and are possessed?" [49]Jesus answered, "I am not possessed; I honor my Father, but you dishonor me. [50j]I do not seek my

---

8, 24.28: I AM: an expression that late Jewish tradition understood as Yahweh's own self-designation (Is 43, 10); see the note on 4, 26. Jesus is here placed on a par with Yahweh.

8, 25: What I told you from the beginning: this verse seems textually corrupt, with several other possible translations: "(I am) what I say to you"; "Why do I speak to you at all?" The earliest attested reading (Bodmer Papyrus P[66]) has (in a second hand), "I told you at the beginning what I am also telling you (now)." The answer here (cf Prv 8, 22) seems to hinge on a misunderstanding of v 24 "that I AM" as "what I am."

8, 31–59: Jesus' origin ("before Abraham") and destiny are developed; the truth will free them from sin (34) and death (51).

8, 31: Those Jews who believed in him: a rough editorial suture, since in v 37 they are described as trying to kill Jesus.

8, 33: Have never been enslaved to anyone: since, historically, the Jews were enslaved almost continuously, this verse is probably Johannine irony, about slavery to sin.

8, 35: A slave . . . a son: an allusion to Ishmael and Isaac (Gn 16 and 21), or to the release of a slave after six years (Ex 21, 2; Dt 15, 12).

8, 38: The Father: i.e., God. It is also possible, however, to understand the second part of the verse as a sarcastic reference to descent of the Jews from the devil (44), "You do what you have heard from [your] father."

8, 39: The works of Abraham: Abraham believed; cf Rom 4, 11–17; Jas 2, 21–23.

8, 48: Samaritan: therefore interested in magical powers; cf Acts 7, 14–24.

v: Ex 3, 14; Dt 32, 39; Is 43, 10. w: 10, 24. x: 12, 44-50. y: 3, 14; 12, 32.34. z: Is 42, 7; Gal 4, 31. a: Mt 3, 9. b: Rom 6, 16-17. c: Gn 21, 10; Gal 4, 30; Heb 3, 5-6. d: Gn 26, 5; Rom 4, 11-17; Jas 2, 21-23. e: Mal 2, 10. f: 1 Jn 5, 1. g: Gn 3, 4; Wis 1, 13; 2, 24; Acts 13, 10; 1 Jn 3, 8-15. h: Heb 4, 15; 1 Pt 2, 22; 1 Jn 3, 5. i: 10, 26; 1 Jn 4, 6. j: 7, 18.

own glory; there is one who seeks it and he is the one who judges. [51k]Amen, amen, I say to you, whoever keeps my word will never see death." [52][So] the Jews said to him, "Now we are sure that you are possessed. Abraham died, as did the prophets, yet you say, 'Whoever keeps my word will never taste death.' [53l]*Are you greater than our father Abraham, who died? Or the prophets, who died? Who do you make yourself out to be?" [54]Jesus answered, "If I glorify myself, my glory is worth nothing; but it is my Father who glorifies me, of whom you say, 'He is our God.' [55m]You do not know him, but I know him. And if I should say that I do not know him, I would be like you a liar. But I do know him and I keep his word. [56n]*Abraham your father rejoiced to see my day; he saw it and was glad. [57]*So the Jews said to him, "You are not yet fifty years old and you have seen Abraham?" [58o]*Jesus said to them, "Amen, amen, I say to you, before Abraham came to be, I AM." [59p]So they picked up stones to throw at him; but Jesus hid and went out of the temple area.

CHAPTER 9

See RG 329

The Man Born Blind. [1q]*As he passed by he saw a man blind from birth. [2r]*His disciples asked him, "Rabbi, who sinned, this man or his parents, that he was born blind?" [3s]Jesus answered, "Neither he nor his parents sinned; it is so that the works of God might be made visible through him. [4t]We have to do the works of the one who sent me while it is day. Night is coming when no one can work. [5u]While I am in the world, I am the light of the world." [6v]When he had said this, he spat on the ground and made clay with the saliva, and smeared the clay on his eyes, [7w]*and said to him, "Go wash in the Pool of Siloam" (which means Sent). So he went and washed, and came back able to see.

[8]His neighbors and those who had seen him earlier as a beggar said, "Isn't this the one who used to sit and beg?" [9]Some said, "It is," but others said, "No, he just looks like him." He said, "I am." [10]So they said to him, "[So] how were your eyes opened?" [11]He replied, "The man called Jesus made clay and anointed my eyes and told me, 'Go to Siloam and wash.' So I went there and washed and was able to see." [12]And they said to him, "Where is he?" He said, "I don't know."

[13]They brought the one who was once blind to the Pharisees. [14x]*Now Jesus had made clay and opened his eyes on a sabbath. [15]So then the Pharisees also asked him how he was able to see. He said to them, "He put clay on my eyes, and I washed, and now I can see." [16y]So some of the Pharisees said, "This man is not from God, because he does not keep the sabbath." [But] others said, "How can a sinful man do such signs?" And there was a division among them. [17z]So they said to the blind man again, "What do you have to say about him, since he opened your eyes?" He said, "He is a prophet."

[18]Now the Jews did not believe that he had been blind and gained his sight until they summoned the parents of the one who had gained his sight. [19]They asked them, "Is this your son, who you say was born blind? How does he

---

8, 53: Are you greater than our father Abraham?: cf 4, 12.

8, 56: He saw it: this seems a reference to the birth of Isaac (Gn 17, 7; 21, 6), the beginning of the fulfillment of promises about Abraham's seed.

8, 57: The evidence of the third-century Bodmer Papyrus P[75] and the first hand of Codex Sinaiticus indicates that the text originally read: "How can Abraham have seen you?"

8, 58: Came to be, I AM: the Greek word used for "came to be" is the one used of all creation in the prologue, while the word used for "am" is the one reserved for the Logos.

9, 1—10, 21: Sabbath healing of the man born blind. This sixth sign is introduced to illustrate the saying, "I am the light of the world" (8, 12; 9, 5). The narrative of conflict about Jesus contrasts Jesus (light) with the Jews (blindness, 39–41). The theme of water is reintroduced in the reference to the pool of Siloam. Ironically, Jesus is being judged by

the Jews, yet the Jews are judged by the Light of the world; cf 3, 19–21.

9, 2: See the note on 5, 14, and Ex 20, 5, that parents' sins were visited upon their children. Jesus denies such a cause and emphasizes the purpose: the infirmity was providential.

9, 7: Go wash: perhaps a test of faith; cf 2 Kgs 5, 10–14. The water tunnel Siloam (= Sent) is used as a symbol of Jesus, sent by his Father.

9, 14: In using spittle, kneading clay, and healing, Jesus had broken the sabbath rules laid down by Jewish tradition.

k: 5, 24-29; 6, 40.47; 11, 25-26. *l:* 4, 12. *m:* 7, 28-29. *n:* Gn 17, 17; Mt 13, 17; Lk 17, 22. *o:* 1, 30; 17, 5. *p:* 10, 31.39; 11, 8; Lk 4, 29-30. *q:* Is 42, 7. *r:* Ex 20, 5; Ez 18, 20; Lk 13, 2. *s:* 5, 14; 11, 4. *t:* 11, 9-10; 12, 35-36. *u:* 8, 12. *v:* 5, 11; Mk 7, 33; 8, 23. *w:* 2 Kgs 5, 10-14. *x:* 5, 9. *y:* 3, 2; Mt 12, 10-11; Lk 13, 10-11; 14, 1-4. *z:* 4, 19.

now see?" [20]His parents answered and said, "We know that this is our son and that he was born blind. [21]We do not know how he sees now, nor do we know who opened his eyes. Ask him, he is of age; he can speak for himself." [22a]*His parents said this because they were afraid of the Jews, for the Jews had already agreed that if anyone acknowledged him as the Messiah, he would be expelled from the synagogue. [23b]For this reason his parents said, "He is of age; question him."

[24c]*So a second time they called the man who had been blind and said to him, "Give God the praise! We know that this man is a sinner." [25]He replied, "If he is a sinner, I do not know. One thing I do know is that I was blind and now I see." [26]So they said to him, "What did he do to you? How did he open your eyes?" [27]He answered them, "I told you already and you did not listen. Why do you want to hear it again? Do you want to become his disciples, too?" [28]They ridiculed him and said, "You are that man's disciple; we are disciples of Moses! [29d]We know that God spoke to Moses, but we do not know where this one is from." [30]The man answered and said to them, "This is what is so amazing, that you do not know where he is from, yet he opened my eyes. [31e]We know that God does not listen to sinners, but if one is devout and does his will, he listens to him. [32]*It is unheard of that anyone ever opened the eyes of a person born blind. [33f]If this man were not from God, he would not be able to do anything." [34]They answered and said to him, "You were born totally in sin, and are you trying to teach us?" Then they threw him out.

[35]When Jesus heard that they had thrown him out, he found him and said, "Do you believe in the Son of Man?" [36]He answered and said, "Who is he, sir, that I may believe in him?" [37g]Jesus said to him, "You have seen him and the one speaking with you is he." [38]He said, "I do believe, Lord," and he worshiped him. [39h]*Then Jesus said, "I came into this world for judgment, so that those who do not see might see, and those who do see might become blind."

[40i]Some of the Pharisees who were with him heard this and said to him, "Surely we are not also blind, are we?" [41j]Jesus said to them, "If you were blind, you would have no sin; but now you are saying, 'We see,' so your sin remains.

CHAPTER 10

See RG 329

The Good Shepherd. [1k]*"Amen, amen, I say to you, whoever does not enter a sheepfold through the gate but climbs over elsewhere is a thief and a robber. [2]But whoever enters through the gate is the shepherd of the sheep. [3]The gatekeeper opens it for him, and the sheep hear his voice, as he calls his own sheep by name and leads them out. [4l]*When he has driven out all his own, he walks ahead of them, and the sheep follow him, because they recognize his voice. [5]But they will not follow a stranger; they will run away from him, because they do not recognize the voice of strangers." [6]*Although Jesus used this figure of speech, they did not realize what he was trying to tell them.

9, 22: This comment of the evangelist (in terms used again in 12, 42 and 16, 2) envisages a situation after Jesus' ministry. Rejection/excommunication from the synagogue of Jews who confessed Jesus as Messiah seems to have begun ca. A.D. 85, when the curse against the mînîm or heretics was introduced into the "Eighteen Benedictions."

9, 24: Give God the praise!: an Old Testament formula of adjuration to tell the truth; cf Jos 7, 19; 1 Sm 6, 5 LXX. Cf 5, 41.

9, 32: A person born blind: the only Old Testament cure from blindness is found in Tobit (cf Tb 7, 7; 11, 7–13; 14, 1–2), but Tobit was not born blind.

9, 39–41: These verses spell out the symbolic meaning of the cure; the Pharisees are not the innocent blind, willing to accept the testimony of others.

10, 1–21: The good shepherd discourse continues the theme of attack on the Pharisees that ends ch 9. The figure is allegorical: the hired hands are the Pharisees who excommunicated the cured blind man. It serves as a commentary on ch 9. For the shepherd motif, used of Yahweh in the Old Testament, cf Ex 34; Gn 48, 15; 49, 24; Mi 7, 14; Pss 23, 1–4; 80, 1.

10, 1: Sheepfold: a low stone wall open to the sky.

10, 4: Recognize his voice: the Pharisees do not recognize Jesus, but the people of God, symbolized by the blind man, do.

10, 6: Figure of speech: John uses a different word for illustrative speech than the "parable" of the synoptics, but the idea is similar.

a: 7, 13; 12, 42; 16, 2; 19, 38. b: 12, 42. c: Jos 7, 19; 1 Sm 6, 5 LXX. d: Ex 33, 11. e: 10, 21; Pss 34, 16; 66, 18; Prv 15, 29; Is 1, 15. f: 3, 2. g: 4, 26; Dn 7, 13. h: Mt 13, 33-35. i: Mt 15, 14; 23, 26; Rom 2, 19. j: 15, 22. k: Gn 48, 15; 49, 24; Pss 23, 1-4; 80, 2; Jer 23, 1-4; Ez 34, 1-31; Mi 7, 14. l: Mi 2, 12-13.

[7]*So Jesus said again, "Amen, amen, I say to you, I am the gate for the sheep. [8]*All who came [before me] are thieves and robbers, but the sheep did not listen to them. [9]I am the gate. Whoever enters through me will be saved, and will come in and go out and find pasture. [10]A thief comes only to steal and slaughter and destroy; I came so that they might have life and have it more abundantly. [11m]I am the good shepherd. A good shepherd lays down his life for the sheep. [12n]A hired man, who is not a shepherd and whose sheep are not his own, sees a wolf coming and leaves the sheep and runs away, and the wolf catches and scatters them. [13]This is because he works for pay and has no concern for the sheep. [14]I am the good shepherd, and I know mine and mine know me, [15o]just as the Father knows me and I know the Father; and I will lay down my life for the sheep. [16p]*I have other sheep that do not belong to this fold. These also I must lead, and they will hear my voice, and there will be one flock, one shepherd. [17q]This is why the Father loves me, because I lay down my life in order to take it up again. [18r]*No one takes it from me, but I lay it down on my own. I have power to lay it down, and power to take it up again. This command I have received from my Father."

[19s]Again there was a division among the Jews because of these words. [20t]Many of them said, "He is possessed and out of his mind; why listen to him?" [21u]Others said, "These are not the words of one possessed; surely a demon cannot open the eyes of the blind, can he?"

Feast of the Dedication. [22v]*The feast of the Dedication was then taking place in Jerusalem. It was winter. [23]*And Jesus walked about in the temple area on the Portico of Solomon. [24w]*So the Jews gathered around him and said to him, "How long are you going to keep us in suspense? If you are the Messiah, tell us plainly." [25x]*Jesus answered them, "I told you and you do not believe. The works I do in my Father's name testify to me. [26y]But you do not believe, because you are not among my sheep. [27]My sheep hear my voice; I know them, and they follow me. [28z]I give them eternal life, and they shall never perish. No one can take them out of my hand. [29a]*My Father, who has given them to me, is greater than all, and no one can take them out of the Father's hand. [30b]*The Father and I are one."

[31c]The Jews again picked up rocks to stone him. [32]Jesus answered them, "I have shown you many good works from my Father. For which of these are you trying to stone me?" [33d]The Jews answered him, "We are not stoning you for a good work but for blasphemy. You, a man, are making yourself God." [34e]*Jesus answered them, "Is it not written in

---

10, 7–10: In vv 7–8, the figure is of a gate for the shepherd to come to the sheep; in vv 9–10, the figure is of a gate for the sheep to **come in and go out.**

10, 8: **[Before me]:** these words are omitted in many good early manuscripts and versions.

10, 16: **Other sheep:** the Gentiles, possibly a reference to "God's dispersed children" of 11, 52 destined to be gathered into one, or "apostolic Christians" at odds with the community of the beloved disciple.

10, 18: **Power to take it up again:** contrast the role of the Father as the efficient cause of the resurrection in Acts 2, 24; 4, 10; etc.; Rom 1, 4; 4, 24. Yet even here is added: **This command I have received from my Father.**

10, 22: **Feast of the Dedication:** an eight-day festival of lights (Hebrew, Hanukkah) held in December, three months after the feast of Tabernacles (7, 2), to celebrate the Maccabees' rededication of the altar and reconsecration of the temple in 164 B.C., after their desecration by Antiochus IV Epiphanes (Dn 8, 13; 9, 27; cf 1 Mc 4, 36–59; 2 Mc 1, 18—2, 19; 10, 1–8).

10, 23: **Portico of Solomon:** on the east side of the temple area, offering protection against the cold winds from the desert.

10, 24: **Keep us in suspense:** literally, "How long will

you take away our life?" Cf 11, 48–50. **If you are the Messiah, tell us plainly:** cf Lk 22, 67. This is the climax of Jesus' encounters with the Jewish authorities. There has never yet been an open confession before them.

10, 25: **I told you:** probably at 8, 25, which was an evasive answer.

10, 29: The textual evidence for the first clause is very divided; it may also be translated: "As for the Father, what he has given me is greater than all," or "My Father is greater than all, in what he has given me."

10, 30: This is justification for v 29; it asserts unity of power and reveals that the words and deeds of Jesus are the words and deeds of God.

10, 34: This is a reference to the judges of Israel who, since they exercised the divine prerogative to judge (Dt 1,

---

m: Ps 23, 1-4; Is 40, 11; 49, 9-10; Heb 13, 20; Rv 7, 17. *n:* Zec 11, 17. *o:* 15, 13; 1 Jn 3, 16. *p:* 11, 52; Is 56, 8; Jer 23, 3; Ez 34, 23; 37, 24; Mi 2, 12. *q:* Heb 10, 10. *r:* 19, 11. *s:* 7, 43; 9, 16. *t:* 7, 20; 8, 48. *u:* 3, 2. *v:* 1 Mc 4, 54.59. *w:* Lk 22, 67. *x:* 8, 25 / 5, 36; 10, 38. *y:* 8, 45.47. *z:* Dt 32, 39. *a:* Ws 3, 1; Is 43, 13. *b:* 1, 1; 12, 45; 14, 9; 17, 21. *c:* 8, 59. *d:* 5, 18; 19, 7; Lv 24, 16. *e:* Ps 82, 6.

your law, 'I said, "You are gods" '? [35]If it calls them gods to whom the word of God came, and scripture cannot be set aside, [36f]*can you say that the one whom the Father has consecrated and sent into the world blasphemes because I said, 'I am the Son of God'? [37]If I do not perform my Father's works, do not believe me; [38g]but if I perform them, even if you do not believe me, believe the works, so that you may realize [and understand] that the Father is in me and I am in the Father." [39][Then] they tried again to arrest him; but he escaped from their power.

[40h]He went back across the Jordan to the place where John first baptized, and there he remained. [41]*Many came to him and said, "John performed no sign, but everything John said about this man was true." [42i]And many there began to believe in him.

See RG 329

CHAPTER 11

The Raising of Lazarus. [1j]*Now a man was ill, Lazarus from Bethany, the village of Mary and her sister Martha. [2]Mary was the one who had anointed the Lord with perfumed oil and dried his feet with her hair; it was her brother Lazarus who was ill. [3]So the sisters sent word to him, saying, "Master, the one you love is ill." [4k]*When Jesus heard this he said, "This illness is not to end in death, but is for the glory of God, that the Son of God may be glorified through it." [5]Now Jesus loved Martha and her sister and Lazarus. [6]So when he heard that he was ill,

he remained for two days in the place where he was. [7]Then after this he said to his disciples, "Let us go back to Judea." [8l]The disciples said to him, "Rabbi, the Jews were just trying to stone you, and you want to go back there?" [9mn]Jesus answered, "Are there not twelve hours in a day? If one walks during the day, he does not stumble, because he sees the light of this world. [10]*But if one walks at night, he stumbles, because the light is not in him." [11]He said this, and then told them, "Our friend Lazarus is asleep, but I am going to awaken him." [12]So the disciples said to him, "Master, if he is asleep, he will be saved." [13o]But Jesus was talking about his death, while they thought that he meant ordinary sleep. [14]So then Jesus said to them clearly, "Lazarus has died. [15]And I am glad for you that I was not there, that you may believe. Let us go to him." [16p]*So Thomas, called Didymus, said to his fellow disciples, "Let us also go to die with him."

[17]When Jesus arrived, he found that Lazarus had already been in the tomb for four days. [18]*Now Bethany was near Jerusalem, only about two miles away. [19q]And many of the Jews had come to Martha and Mary to comfort them about their brother. [20]When Martha heard that Jesus was coming, she went to meet him; but Mary sat at home. [21r]Martha said to Jesus, "Lord, if you had been here, my brother would not have died. [22][But] even now I know that whatever you ask of God, God will give you." [23]Jesus said

---

17), were called "gods"; cf Ex 21, 6, besides Ps 82, 6, from which the quotation comes.

10, 36: Consecrated: this may be a reference to the rededicated altar at the Hanukkah feast; see the note on 10, 22.

10, 41: Performed no sign: this is to stress the inferior role of John the Baptist. The Transjordan topography recalls the great witness of John the Baptist to Jesus, as opposed to the hostility of the authorities in Jerusalem.

11, 1–44: The raising of Lazarus, the longest continuous narrative in John outside of the Passion account, is the climax of the signs. It leads directly to the decision of the Sanhedrin to kill Jesus. The theme of life predominates. Lazarus is a token of the real life that Jesus dead and raised will give to all who believe in him. Johannine irony is found in the fact that Jesus' gift of life leads to his own death. The story is not found in the synoptics, but cf Mk 5, 21 and parallels; Lk 7, 11–17. There are also parallels between this story and Luke's parable of the rich man and poor Lazarus (Lk 16, 19–31). In both a man named Lazarus dies; in Luke, there is a request that he return to convince his contemporaries of the need for

faith and repentance, while in John, Lazarus does return and some believe but others do not.

11, 4: Not to end in death: this is misunderstood by the disciples as referring to physical death, but it is meant as spiritual death.

11, 10: The light is not in him: the ancients apparently did not grasp clearly the entry of light **through** the eye; they seem to have thought of it as being **in** the eye; cf Lk 11, 34; Mt 6, 23.

11, 16: Called Didymus: Didymus is the Greek word for twin. Thomas is derived from the Aramaic word for twin; in an ancient Syriac version and in the Gospel of Thomas (80, 11–12) his given name, Judas, is supplied.

11, 18: About two miles: literally, "about fifteen stades"; a stade was 607 feet.

f: 5, 18. *g:* 14, 10-11.20. *h:* 1, 28. *i:* 2, 23; 7, 31; 8, 30. *j:* 12, 1-8; Lk 10, 38-42; 16, 19-31. *k:* 9, 3.24. *l:* 8, 59; 10, 31. *m:* 8, 12; 9, 4. *n:* 12, 35; 1 Jn 2, 10. *o:* Mt 9, 24. *p:* 14, 5.22. *q:* 12, 9.17-18. *r:* 11, 32.

to her, "Your brother will rise." [24s]Martha said to him, "I know he will rise, in the resurrection on the last day." [25t]Jesus told her, "I am the resurrection and the life; whoever believes in me, even if he dies, will live, [26]and everyone who lives and believes in me will never die. Do you believe this?" [27u]*She said to him, "Yes, Lord. I have come to believe that you are the Messiah, the Son of God, the one who is coming into the world."

[28]When she had said this, she went and called her sister Mary secretly, saying, "The teacher is here and is asking for you." [29]As soon as she heard this, she rose quickly and went to him. [30]For Jesus had not yet come into the village, but was still where Martha had met him. [31]So when the Jews who were with her in the house comforting her saw Mary get up quickly and go out, they followed her, presuming that she was going to the tomb to weep there. [32]When Mary came to where Jesus was and saw him, she fell at his feet and said to him, "Lord, if you had been here, my brother would not have died." [33]*When Jesus saw her weeping and the Jews who had come with her weeping, he became perturbed and deeply troubled, [34]and said, "Where have you laid him?" They said to him, "Sir, come and see." [35v]And Jesus wept. [36]So the Jews said, "See how he loved him." [37]But some of them said, "Could not the one who opened the eyes of the blind man have done something so that this man would not have died?"

[38]So Jesus, perturbed again, came to the tomb. It was a cave, and a stone lay across it. [39]Jesus said, "Take away the stone." Martha, the dead man's sister, said to him, "Lord, by now there will be a stench; he has been dead for four days." [40]Jesus said to her, "Did I not tell you that if you believe you will see the glory of God?" [41]*So they took away the stone. And Jesus raised his eyes and said, "Father, I thank you for hearing me. [42w]I know that you always hear me; but because of the crowd here I have said this, that they may believe that you sent me." [43]*And when he had said this, he cried out in a loud voice, "Lazarus, come out!" [44]The dead man came out, tied hand and foot with burial bands, and his face was wrapped in a cloth. So Jesus said to them, "Untie him and let him go."

Session of the Sanhedrin. [45x]Now many of the Jews who had come to Mary and seen what he had done began to believe in him. [46]But some of them went to the Pharisees and told them what Jesus had done. [47y]So the chief priests and the Pharisees convened the Sanhedrin and said, "What are we going to do? This man is performing many signs. [48]*If we leave him alone, all will believe in him, and the Romans will come and take away both our land and our nation." [49z]*But one of them, Caiaphas, who was high priest that year, said to them, "You know nothing, [50]nor do you consider that it is better for you that one man should die instead of the people, so that the whole nation may not perish." [51]He did not say this on his own, but since he was high priest for that year, he prophesied that Jesus was going to die for the nation, [52]*and not only for the nation, but also to gather into one the dispersed children of God. [53a]So from that day on they planned to kill him.

[54]*So Jesus no longer walked about in public among the Jews, but he left for the region near the desert, to a town called Ephraim, and there he remained with his disciples.

11, 27: The titles here are a summary of titles given to Jesus earlier in the gospel.

11, 33: Became perturbed: a startling phrase in Greek, literally, "He snorted in spirit," perhaps in anger at the presence of evil (death).

11, 41: Father: in Aramaic, 'abbā'. See the note on Mk 14, 36.

11, 43: Cried out in a loud voice: a dramatization of 5, 28: "the hour is coming when all who are in the tombs will hear his voice."

11, 48: The Romans will come: Johannine irony; this is precisely what happened after Jesus' death.

11, 49: That year: emphasizes the conjunction of the office and the year. Actually, Caiaphas was high priest A.D. 18–36. The Jews attributed a gift of prophecy, sometimes unconscious, to the high priest.

11, 52: Dispersed children of God: perhaps the "other sheep" of 10, 16.

11, 54: Ephraim is usually located about twelve miles northeast of Jerusalem, where the mountains descend into the Jordan valley.

s: 5 29; 6, 39-40.44.54; 12, 48; Is 2, 2; Mi 4, 1; Acts 23. 8; 24, 15. t: 5 24; 8, 51; 14, 6; Dn 12, 2. u: 1, 9; 6, 69. v: Lk 19, 41. w: 12, 30. x: Lk 16, 31. y: 12, 19; Mt 26, 3-5; Lk 22, 2; Acts 4, 15. z: 18, 13-14. a: 5, 18; 7, 1; Mt 12, 14.

The Last Passover. [55b]*Now the Passover of the Jews was near, and many went up from the country to Jerusalem before Passover to purify themselves. [56]They looked for Jesus and said to one another as they were in the temple area, "What do you think? That he will not come to the feast?" [57]For the chief priests and the Pharisees had given orders that if anyone knew where he was, he should inform them, so that they might arrest him.

CHAPTER 12

See RG 329

The Anointing at Bethany. [1cd]*Six days before Passover Jesus came to Bethany, where Lazarus was, whom Jesus had raised from the dead. [2e]They gave a dinner for him there, and Martha served, while Lazarus was one of those reclining at table with him. [3f]*Mary took a liter of costly perfumed oil made from genuine aromatic nard and anointed the feet of Jesus and dried them with her hair; the house was filled with the fragrance of the oil. [4]Then Judas the Iscariot, one [of] his disciples, and the one who would betray him, said, [5]*"Why was this oil not sold for three hundred days' wages and given to the poor?" [6g]He said this not because he cared about the poor but because he was a thief and held the money bag and used to steal the contributions. [7]*So Jesus said, "Leave her alone. Let her keep this for the day of my burial. [8h]You always have the poor with you, but you do not always have me."

[9i][The] large crowd of the Jews found out that he was there and came, not only because of Jesus, but also to see Lazarus, whom he had raised from the dead. [10]And the chief priests plotted to kill Lazarus too, [11j]because many of the Jews were turning away and believing in Jesus because of him.

The Entry into Jerusalem. [12k]*On the next day, when the great crowd that had come to the feast heard that Jesus was coming to Jerusalem, [13l]*they took palm branches and went out to meet him, and cried out:

"Hosanna!
Blessed is he who comes in the name of the Lord,
[even] the king of Israel."

[14]Jesus found an ass and sat upon it, as is written:

[15m]*"Fear no more, O daughter Zion;
see, your king comes, seated upon an ass's colt."

[16n]*His disciples did not understand this at first, but when Jesus had been glorified they remembered that these things were written about him and that they had done this for him. [17]*So the crowd that was with him when he called Lazarus from the tomb and raised him from death continued to testify. [18]This

---

11, 55: Purify: prescriptions for purity were based on Ex 19, 10–11.15; Nm 9, 6–14; 2 Chr 30, 1–3.15–18.

12, 1–8: This is probably the same scene of anointing found in Mk 14, 3–9 (see the note there) and Mt 26, 6–13. The anointing by a penitent woman in Lk 7, 36–38 is different. Details from these various episodes have become interchanged.

12, 3: The feet of Jesus: so Mk 14, 3; but in Mt 26, 6, Mary anoints Jesus' head as a sign of regal, messianic anointing.

12, 5: Days' wages: literally, "denarii." A denarius is a day's wage in Mt 20, 2; see the note on 6, 7.

12, 7: Jesus' response reflects the rabbinical discussion of what was the greatest act of mercy, almsgiving or burying the dead. Those who favored proper burial of the dead thought it an essential condition for sharing in the resurrection.

12, 12–19: In Jn, the entry into Jerusalem follows the anointing whereas in the synoptics it precedes. In John, the crowd, not the disciples, are responsible for the triumphal procession.

12, 13: Palm branches: used to welcome great conquerors; cf 1 Mc 13, 51; 2 Mc 10, 7. They may be related to the lûlāb, the twig bundles used at the feast of Tabernacles.

Hosanna: see Ps 118, 25–26. The Hebrew word means: "(O Lord), grant salvation." **He who comes in the name of the Lord:** referred in Ps 118, 26 to a pilgrim entering the temple gates, but here a title for Jesus (see the notes on Mt 11, 3 and Jn 6, 14; 11, 27). **The king of Israel:** perhaps from Zep 3, 14–15, in connection with the next quotation from Zec 9, 9.

12, 15: Daughter Zion: Jerusalem. **Ass's colt:** symbol of peace, as opposed to the war-horse.

12, 16: They had done this: the antecedent of **they** is ambiguous.

12, 17–18: There seem to be two different crowds in these verses. There are some good witnesses to the text that have another reading for v 17: "Then the crowd that was with him began to testify that he had called Lazarus out of the tomb and raised him from the dead."

---

b: 2, 13; 5, 1; 6, 4; 18, 28; Ex 19, 10-11.15; Nm 9, 6-14; 19, 12; Dt 16, 6; 2 Chr 30, 1-3.15-18. *c:* Mt 26, 6-13; Mk 14, 3-9. *d:* 11, 1. *e:* Lk 10, 38-42. *f:* 11, 2. *g:* 13, 29. *h:* Dt 15, 11. *i:* 11, 19. *j:* 11, 45. *k:* Mt 21, 1-16; Mk 11, 1-10; Lk 19, 28-40. *l:* 1, 49; Lv 23, 40; 1 Mc 13, 51; 2 Mc 10, 7; Rv 7, 9. *m:* Is 40, 9; Zec 9, 9. *n:* 2, 22.

was [also] why the crowd went to meet him, because they heard that he had done this sign. [19o]*So the Pharisees said to one another, "You see that you are gaining nothing. Look, the whole world has gone after him."

The Coming of Jesus' Hour. [20p]*Now there were some Greeks among those who had come up to worship at the feast. [21q]*They came to Philip, who was from Bethsaida in Galilee, and asked him, "Sir, we would like to see Jesus." [22r]Philip went and told Andrew; then Andrew and Philip went and told Jesus. [23s]*Jesus answered them, "The hour has come for the Son of Man to be glorified. [24t]*Amen, amen, I say to you, unless a grain of wheat falls to the ground and dies, it remains just a grain of wheat; but if it dies, it produces much fruit. [25u]*Whoever loves his life loses it, and whoever hates his life in this world will preserve it for eternal life. [26v]Whoever serves me must follow me, and where I am, there also will my servant be. The Father will honor whoever serves me.

[27w]*"I am troubled now. Yet what should I say? 'Father, save me from this hour'? But it was for this purpose that I came to this hour. [28x]Father, glorify your name." Then a voice came from heaven, "I have glorified it and will glorify it again." [29y]The crowd there heard it and said it was thunder; but others said, "An angel has spoken to him." [39z]Jesus answered and said, "This voice did not come for my sake but for yours. [31a]*Now is the time of judgment on this world; now the ruler of this world will be driven out. [32b]And when I am lifted up from the earth, I will draw everyone to myself." [33]He said this indicating the kind of death he would die. [34c]*So the crowd answered him, "We have heard from the law that the Messiah remains forever. Then how can you say that the Son of Man must be lifted up? Who is this Son of Man?" [35d]Jesus said to them, "The light will be among you only a little while. Walk while you have the light, so that darkness may not overcome you. Whoever walks in the dark does not know where he is going. [36e]While you have the light, believe in the light, so that you may become children of the light."

Unbelief and Belief among the Jews. After he had said this, Jesus left and hid from them. [37f]*Although he had performed so many signs in their presence they did not believe in him, [38g]*in order that the word which Isaiah the prophet spoke might be fulfilled:

"Lord, who has believed our preaching,
to whom has the might of the Lord
been revealed?"

12, 19: The whole world: the sense is that everyone is following Jesus, but John has an ironic play on **world;** he alludes to the universality of salvation (3, 17; 4, 42).

12, 20–36: This announcement of glorification by death is an illustration of "the whole world" (19) going after him.

12, 20: Greeks: not used here in a nationalistic sense. These are probably Gentile proselytes to Judaism; cf 7, 35.

12, 21–22: Philip . . . Andrew: the approach is made through disciples who have distinctly Greek names, suggesting that access to Jesus was mediated to the Greek world through his disciples. Philip and Andrew were from Bethsaida (1, 44); Galileans were mostly bilingual. **See:** here seems to mean "have an interview with."

12, 23: Jesus' response suggests that only after the crucifixion could the gospel encompass both Jew and Gentile.

12, 24: This verse implies that through his death Jesus will be accessible to all. **It remains just a grain of wheat:** this saying is found in the synoptic triple and double traditions (Mk 8, 35 // Mt 16, 25 // Lk 9, 24; Mt 10, 39 // Lk 17, 33). John adds the phrases (25) **in this world** and **for eternal life.**

12, 25: His life: the Greek word **psyche** refers to a person's natural life. It does not mean "soul," for Hebrew anthropology did not postulate body/soul dualism in the way that is familiar to us.

12, 27: I am troubled: perhaps an allusion to the Gethsemane agony scene of the synoptics.

12, 31: Ruler of this world: Satan.

12, 34: There is no passage in the Old Testament that states precisely that **the Messiah remains forever.** Perhaps the closest is Ps 89, 37.

12, 37–50: These verses, on unbelief of the Jews, provide an epilogue to the Book of Signs.

12, 38–41: John gives a historical explanation of the disbelief of the Jewish people, not a psychological one. The Old Testament had to be fulfilled; the disbelief that met Isaiah's message was a foreshadowing of the disbelief that Jesus encountered. In v 42 and also in 3, 20, we see that there is no negation of freedom.

o: 11, 47-48. p: Acts 10, 2. q: 1, 44. r: 1, 40. s: 2, 4. t: Is 53, 10-12; 1 Cor 15, 36. u: Mt 10, 39; 16, 25; Mk 8, 35. Lk 9, 24; 17, 33. v: 14, 3; 17, 24; Mt 16, 24; Mk 8, 34; Lk 9, 23. w: 6, 38; 18, 11; Mt 26, 38-39; Mk 14, 34-36; Lk 22, 42; Heb 5, 7-8 x: 2, 11; 17, 5; Dn 4, 31.34. y: Ex 9, 28; 2 Sm 22, 14; Jb 37, 4; Ps 29, 3; Lk 22, 43; Acts 23, 9. z: 11, 42. a: 16, 11; Lk 10, 18; Rv 12, 9. b: 3, 14; 8, 28; Is 52, 13. c: Pss 89, 5; 110, 4; Is 9, 7; Dn 7, 13-14; Rv 20, 1-6. d: 9, 4; 11, 10; Jb 5, 14. e: Eph 5, 8. f: Dt 29, 2-4; Mk 4, 11-12; Rom 9-11. g: Is 53, 1; Rom 10, 16.

[39]For this reason they could not believe, because again Isaiah said:

[40] h"He blinded their eyes
and hardened their heart,
so that they might not see with their eyes
and understand with their heart and be
converted,
and I would heal them."

[41] i*Isaiah said this because he saw his glory and spoke about him. [42] jNevertheless, many, even among the authorities, believed in him, but because of the Pharisees they did not acknowledge it openly in order not to be expelled from the synagogue. [43] kFor they preferred human praise to the glory of God.

Recapitulation. [44] lJesus cried out and said, "Whoever believes in me believes not only in me but also in the one who sent me, [45] mand whoever sees me sees the one who sent me. [46] nI came into the world as light, so that everyone who believes in me might not remain in darkness. [47] oAnd if anyone hears my words and does not observe them, I do not condemn him, for I did not come to condemn the world but to save the world. [48] pWhoever rejects me and does not accept my words has something to judge him: the word that I spoke, it will condemn him on the last day, [49] qbecause I did not speak on my own, but the Father who sent me commanded me what to say and speak. [50] And I know that his commandment is eternal life. So what I say, I say as the Father told me."

III: The Book Of Glory *

CHAPTER 13

See RG 329-31

The Washing of the Disciples' Feet.
[1] r*Before the feast of Passover, Jesus knew that his hour had come to pass from this world to the Father. He loved his own in the world and he loved them to the end. [2] s*The devil had already induced Judas, son of Simon the Iscariot, to hand him over. So, during supper, [3] tfully aware that the Father had put everything into his power and that he had come from God and was returning to God, [4]he rose from supper and took off his outer garments. He took a towel and tied it around his waist. [5] u*Then he poured water into a basin and began to wash the disciples' feet and dry them with the towel around his waist. [6]He came to Simon Peter, who said to him, "Master, are you going to wash my feet?" [7]Jesus answered and said to him, "What I am doing, you do not understand now, but you will understand later." [8] vPeter said to him, "You will never wash my feet." Jesus answered him, "Unless I wash you, you will have no inheritance with me." [9]Simon Peter said to him, "Master, then not only my feet, but my hands and head as well." [10] w*Jesus said to him, "Whoever has bathed has no need except to have his feet washed, for he is clean all over; so you are clean, but not all." [11] xFor he knew who would betray him; for this reason, he said, "Not all of you are clean."

12, 41: His glory: Isaiah saw the glory of Yahweh enthroned in the heavenly temple, but in John the antecedent of **his** is Jesus.

13, 1—19, 42: The Book of Glory. There is a major break here; the word "sign" is used again only in 20, 30. In this phase of Jesus' return to the Father, the discourses (chs 13–17) precede the traditional narrative of the passion (chs 18–20) to interpret them for the Christian reader. This is the only extended example of esoteric teaching of disciples in John.

13, 1–20: Washing of the disciples' feet. This episode occurs in John at the place of the narration of the institution of the Eucharist in the synoptics. It may be a dramatization of Lk 22, 27: "I am your servant." It is presented as a "model" ("pattern") of the crucifixion. It symbolizes cleansing from sin by sacrificial death.

13, 1: Before the feast of Passover: this would be Thursday evening, before the day of preparation; in the synoptics, the Last Supper is a Passover meal taking place, in John's chronology, on Friday evening. **To the end:** or, "completely."

13, 2: Induced: literally, "The devil put into the heart that Judas should hand him over."

13, 5: The act of washing another's feet was one that could not be required of the lowliest Jewish slave. It is an allusion to the humiliating death of the crucifixion.

13, 10: Bathed: many have suggested that this passage is a symbolic reference to baptism. The Greek root involved is used in baptismal contexts in 1 Cor 6, 11; Eph 5, 26; Ti 3, 5; Heb 10, 22.

---

h: Is 6, 9-10; Mt 13, 13-15; Mk 4, 12.   *i:* 5, 39; Is 6, 1.4.   *j:* 9, 22.   *k:* 5, 44.   *l:* 13, 20; 14, 1.   *m:* 14, 7-9.   *n:* 1, 9; 8, 12. *o:* 3, 17.   *p:* Lk 10, 16; Heb 4, 12.   *q:* 14, 10.31; Dt 18, 18-19. *r:* 2, 4; 7, 30; 8, 20; Mt 26, 17.45; Mk 14, 12.41; Lk 22, 7.   *s:* 6, 71; 17, 12; Mt 26, 20-21; Mk 14, 17-18; Lk 22, 3.   *t:* 3, 35. *u:* 1 Sm 25, 41.   *v:* 2 Sm 20, 1.   *w:* 15, 3.   *x:* 6, 70.

¹²So when he had washed their feet [and] put his garments back on and reclined at table again, he said to them, "Do you realize what I have done for you? ¹³ʸYou call me 'teacher' and 'master,' and rightly so, for indeed I am. ¹⁴If I, therefore, the master and teacher, have washed your feet, you ought to wash one another's feet. ¹⁵ᶻI have given you a model to follow, so that as I have done for you, you should also do. ¹⁶ᵃ*Amen, amen, I say to you, no slave is greater than his master nor any messenger greater than the one who sent him. ¹⁷If you understand this, blessed are you if you do it. ¹⁸ᵇI am not speaking of all of you. I know those whom I have chosen. But so that the scripture might be fulfilled, 'The one who ate my food has raised his heel against me.' ¹⁹From now on I am telling you before it happens, so that when it happens you may believe that I AM. ²⁰ᶜAmen, amen, I say to you, whoever receives the one I send receives me, and whoever receives me receives the one who sent me."

Announcement of Judas's Betrayal. ²¹ᵈWhen he had said this, Jesus was deeply troubled and testified, "Amen, amen, I say to you, one of you will betray me." ²²The disciples looked at one another, at a loss as to whom he meant. ²³ᵉ*One of his disciples, the one whom Jesus loved, was reclining at Jesus' side. ²⁴So Simon Peter nodded to him to find out whom he meant. ²⁵ᶠHe leaned back against Jesus' chest and said to him, "Master, who is it?" ²⁶*Jesus answered, "It is the one to whom I hand the morsel after I have dipped it." So he dipped the morsel and [took it and] handed it to Judas, son of Simon the Iscariot. ²⁷ᵍAfter he took the morsel, Satan entered him. So Jesus said to him, "What you are going to do, do quickly." ²⁸[Now] none of those reclining at table realized why he said this to him. ²⁹ʰSome thought that since Judas kept the money bag, Jesus had told him, "Buy what we need for the feast," or to give something to the poor. ³⁰So he took the morsel and left at once. And it was night.

The New Commandment. ³¹*When he had left, Jesus said, "Now is the Son of Man glorified, and God is glorified in him. ³²ⁱ[If God is glorified in him,] God will also glorify him in himself, and he will glorify him at once. ³³ʲMy children, I will be with you only a little while longer. You will look for me, and as I told the Jews, 'Where I go you cannot come,' so now I say it to you. ³⁴ᵏ*I give you a new commandment: love one another. As I have loved you, so you also should love one another. ³⁵This is how all will know that you are my disciples, if you have love for one another."

Peter's Denial Predicted. ³⁶ˡSimon Peter said to him, "Master, where are you going?" Jesus answered [him], "Where I am going, you cannot follow me now, though you will follow later." ³⁷Peter said to him, "Master, why can't I follow you now? I will lay down my life for you." ³⁸ᵐJesus answered, "Will you lay down your life for me? Amen, amen, I say to you, the cock will not crow before you deny me three times."

13, 16: Messenger: the Greek has **apostolos,** the only occurrence of the term in John. It is not used in the technical sense here.

13, 23: The one whom Jesus loved: also mentioned in 19, 26; 20, 2; 21, 7. A disciple, called "another disciple" or "the other disciple," is mentioned in 18, 15 and 20, 2; in the latter reference he is identified with the disciple whom Jesus loved. There is also an unnamed disciple in 1, 35–40; see the note on 1, 37.

13, 26: Morsel: probably the bitter herb dipped in salt water.

13, 31—17, 26: Two farewell discourses and a prayer. These seem to be Johannine compositions, including sayings of Jesus at the Last Supper and on other occasions, modeled on similar farewell discourses in Greek literature and the Old Testament (of Moses, Joshua, David).

13, 31–38: Introduction: departure and return. Terms of coming and going predominate. These verses form an introduction to the last discourse of Jesus, which extends through chs 14 to 17. In it John has collected Jesus' words to **his own** (13, 1). There are indications that several speeches have been fused together, e.g., in 14, 31 and 17, 1.

13, 34: I give you a new commandment: this puts Jesus on a par with Yahweh. The commandment itself is not new; cf Lv 19, 18 and the note there.

---

y: Mt 23, 8.10.   z: Lk 22, 27; 1 Pt 2, 21.   a: 15, 20; Mt 10, 24; Lk 6, 40.   b: Ps 41, 10.   c: Mt 10, 40; Mk 9, 37; Lk 9, 48. d: Mt 26, 21-25; Mk 14, 18-21; Lk 22, 21-23.   e: 19, 26; 20, 2; 21, 7.20; Mt 10, 37.   f: 21, 20.   g: 13, 2; Lk 22, 3.   h: 12, 5-6. i: 17, 1-5.   j: 7, 33; 8, 21.   k: 15, 12-13.17; Lv 19, 18; 1 Thes 4, 9; 1 Jn 2, 7-10; 3, 23; 2 Jn 5.   l: Mk 14, 27; Lk 22, 23.   m: 18, 27; Mt 26, 33-35; Mk 14, 29-31; Lk 22, 33-34.

See RG
330–31

CHAPTER 14

Last Supper Discourses. [1]*"Do not let your hearts be troubled. You have faith in God; have faith also in me. [2]In my Father's house there are many dwelling places. If there were not, would I have told you that I am going to prepare a place for you? [3n]*And if I go and prepare a place for you, I will come back again and take you to myself, so that where I am you also may be. [4]*Where [I] am going you know the way." [5]Thomas said to him, "Master, we do not know where you are going; how can we know the way?" [6o]*Jesus said to him, "I am the way and the truth and the life. No one comes to the Father except through me. [7p]*If you know me, then you will also know my Father. From now on you do know him and have seen him." [8q]*Philip said to him, "Master, show us the Father, and that will be enough for us." [9r]Jesus said to him, "Have I been with you for so long a time and you still do not know me, Philip? Whoever has seen me has seen the Father. How can you say, 'Show us the Father'? [10s]Do you not believe that I am in the Father and the Father is in me? The words that I speak to you I do not speak on my own. The Father who dwells in me is doing his works. [11t]Believe me that I am in the Father and the Father is in me, or else, believe because of the works themselves. [12u]Amen, amen, I say to you, whoever believes in me will do the works that I do, and will do greater ones than these, because I am going to the Father. [13v]And whatever you ask in my name, I will do, so that the Father may be glorified in the Son. [14]If you ask anything of me in my name, I will do it.

The Advocate. [15w]"If you love me, you will keep my commandments. [16x]*And I will ask the Father, and he will give you another Advocate to be with you always, [17y]*the Spirit of truth, which the world cannot accept, because it neither sees nor knows it. But you know it, because it remains with you, and will be in you. [18]*I will not leave you orphans; I will come to you. [19z]In a little while the world will no longer see me, but you will see me, because I live and you will live. [20a]On that day you will realize that I am in my Father and you are in me and I in you. [21b]Whoever has my commandments and observes them is the one who loves me. And whoever loves me will be loved by my Father, and I will love him and reveal myself to him." [22c]*Judas, not the Iscariot, said to him, "Master, [then] what happened that you will reveal yourself to us and not to the world?" [23d]Jesus answered and said to him, "Whoever loves me will keep my

---

14, 1–31: Jesus' departure and return. This section is a dialogue marked off by a literary inclusion in vv 1 and 27: "Do not let your hearts be troubled."

14, 1: You have faith: could also be imperative: "Have faith."

14, 3: Come back again: a rare Johannine reference to the parousia; cf 1 Jn 2, 28.

14, 4: The way: here, of Jesus himself; also a designation of Christianity in Acts 9, 2; 19, 9.23; 22, 4; 24, 14.22.

14, 6: The truth: in John, the divinely revealed reality of the Father manifested in the person and works of Jesus. The possession of truth confers knowledge and liberation from sin (8, 32).

14, 7: An alternative reading, "If you knew me, then you would have known my Father also," would be a rebuke, as in 8, 19.

14, 8: Show us the Father: Philip is pictured asking for a theophany like Ex 24, 9–10; 33, 18.

14, 16: Another Advocate: Jesus is the first advocate (paraclete); see 1 Jn 2, 1, where Jesus is an advocate in the sense of intercessor in heaven. The Greek term derives from legal terminology for an advocate or defense attorney, and can mean spokesman, mediator, intercessor, comforter, consoler, although no one of these terms encompasses the meaning in John. The Paraclete in John is a teacher, a witness to

Jesus, and a prosecutor of the world, who represents the continued presence on earth of the Jesus who has returned to the Father.

14, 17: The Spirit of truth: this term is also used at Qumran, where it is a moral force put into a person by God, as opposed to the spirit of perversity. It is more personal in John; it will teach the realities of the new order (26), and testify to the truth (6). While it has been customary to use masculine personal pronouns in English for the Advocate, the Greek word for "spirit" is neuter, and the Greek text and manuscript variants fluctuate between masculine and neuter pronouns.

14, 18: I will come to you: indwelling, not parousia.

14, 22: Judas, not the Iscariot: probably not the brother of Jesus in Mk 6, 3 // Mt 13, 55 or the apostle named Jude in Lk 6, 16, but Thomas (see the note on 11, 16), although other readings have "Judas the Cananean."

---

n: 12, 26; 17, 24; 1 Jn 2, 28. *o:* 8, 31-47. *p:* 8, 19; 12, 45. *q:* Ex 24, 9-10; 33, 18. *r:* 1, 18; 10, 30; 12, 45; 2 Cor 4, 4; Col 1, 15; Heb 1, 3. *s:* 1, 1; 10, 37-38; 12, 49. *t:* 10, 38. *u:* 1, 50; 5, 20. *v:* 15, 7.16; 16, 23-24; Mt 7, 7-11. *w:* 15, 10; Dt 6, 4-9; Ps 119; Wis 6, 18; 1 Jn 5, 3; 2 Jn 6. *x:* 15, 26; Lk 24, 49; 1 Jn 2, 1. *y:* 16, 13; Mt 28, 20; 2 Jn 1-2. *z:* 16, 16. *a:* 10, 38; 17, 21; Is 2, 17; 4, 2-3. *b:* 16, 27; 1 Jn 2, 5; 3, 24. *c:* 7, 4; Acts 10, 40-41. *d:* Rv 3, 20.

word, and my Father will love him, and we will come to him and make our dwelling with him. *24*Whoever does not love me does not keep my words; yet the word you hear is not mine but that of the Father who sent me.

25"I have told you this while I am with you. *26e*The Advocate, the holy Spirit that the Father will send in my name—he will teach you everything and remind you of all that [I] told you. *27f**Peace I leave with you; my peace I give to you. Not as the world gives do I give it to you. Do not let your hearts be troubled or afraid. *28g**You heard me tell you, 'I am going away and I will come back to you.' If you loved me, you would rejoice that I am going to the Father; for the Father is greater than I. *29h*And now I have told you this before it happens, so that when it happens you may believe. *30**I will no longer speak much with you, for the ruler of the world is coming. He has no power over me, *31i*but the world must know that I love the Father and that I do just as the Father has commanded me. Get up, let us go.

CHAPTER 15

See RG
330-31

The Vine and the Branches. *1j**"I am the true vine, and my Father is the vine grower. *2**He takes away every branch in me that does not bear fruit, and every one that does he prunes so that it bears more fruit. *3k*You are already pruned because of the word that I spoke to you. *4*Remain in me, as I remain in you. Just as a branch cannot bear fruit on its own unless it remains on the vine, so neither can you unless you remain in me. *5*I am the vine, you are the branches. Whoever remains in me and I in him will bear much fruit, because without me you can do nothing. *6l**Anyone who does not remain in me will be thrown out like a branch and wither; people will gather them and throw them into a fire and they will be burned. *7m*If you remain in me and my words remain in you, ask for whatever you want and it will be done for you. *8n*By this is my Father glorified, that you bear much fruit and become my disciples. *9o*As the Father loves me, so I also love you. Remain in my love. *10p*If you keep my commandments, you will remain in my love, just as I have kept my Father's commandments and remain in his love.

11q"I have told you this so that my joy may be in you and your joy may be complete. *12r*This is my commandment: love one another as I love you. *13s**No one has greater love than this, to lay down one's life for one's friends. *14*You are my friends if you do what I command you. *15t**I no longer call you slaves, because a slave does not know what his master is doing. I have called you friends, because I have told you everything I have heard from my Father. *16u*It was not you who chose me, but I who chose you and appointed you to go and bear fruit that will remain, so that whatever you ask the Father in my name he may give you. *17v*This I command you: love one another.

14, 27: Peace: the traditional Hebrew salutation **šālôm**; but Jesus' "Shalom" is a gift of salvation, connoting the bounty of messianic blessing.

14, 28: The Father is greater than I: because he **sent, gave,** etc., and Jesus is "a man who has told you the truth that I heard from God" (8, 40).

14, 30: The ruler of the world: Satan; cf 12, 31; 16, 11.

15, 1—16, 4: Discourse on the union of Jesus with his disciples. His words become a monologue and go beyond the immediate crisis of the departure of Jesus.

15, 1–17: Like 10, 1–5, this passage resembles a parable. Israel is spoken of as a vineyard at Is 5, 1–7; Mt 21, 33–46 and as a vine at Ps 80, 9–17; Jer 2, 21; Ez 15, 2; 17, 5–10; 19, 10; Hos 10, 1. The identification of the vine as the Son of Man in Ps 80, 16, and Wisdom's description of herself as a vine in Sir 24, 17, are further background for portrayal of Jesus by this figure. There may be secondary eucharistic symbolism here; cf Mk 14, 25, "the fruit of the vine."

15, 2: Takes away ... prunes: in Greek there is a play on two related verbs.

15, 6: Branches were cut off and dried on the wall of the vineyard for later use as fuel.

15, 13: For one's friends: or: "those whom one loves." In 9–13a, the words for love are related to the Greek **agapaō.** In 13b-15, the words for love are related to the Greek **phileō.** For John, the two roots seem synonymous and mean "to love"; cf also 21, 15–17. The word **philos** is used here.

15, 15: Slaves ... friends: in the Old Testament, Moses (Dt 34, 5), Joshua (Jos 24, 29), and David (Ps 89, 21) were called "servants" or "slaves of Yahweh"; only Abraham (Is 41, 8; 2 Chr 20, 7; cf Jas 2, 23) was called a "friend of God."

e: 15, 26; 16, 7.13-14; Ps 51, 13; Is 63, 10. *f:* 16, 33; Eph 2, 14-18. *g:* 8, 40. *h:* 13, 19; 16, 4. *i:* 6, 38. *j:* Ps 80, 9-17; Is 5, 1-7; Jer 2, 21; Ez 15, 2; 17, 5-10; 19, 10. *k:* 13, 10. *l:* Ez 15, 6-7; 19, 10-14. *m:* 14, 13; Mt 7, 7; Mk 11, 24; 1 Jn 5, 14. *n:* Mt 5, 16. *o:* 17, 23. *p:* 8, 29; 14, 15. *q:* 16, 22; 17, 13. *r:* 13, 34. *s:* Rom 5, 6-8; 1 Jn 3, 16. *t:* Dt 34, 5; Jos 24, 29; 2 Chr 20, 7; Ps 89, 21; Is 41, 8; Rom 8, 15; Gal 4, 7; Jas 2, 23. *u:* 14, 13; Dt 7, 6. *v:* 13, 34; 1 Jn 3, 23; 4, 21.

The World's Hatred. [18w]*"If the world hates you, realize that it hated me first. [19x]If you belonged to the world, the world would love its own; but because you do not belong to the world, and I have chosen you out of the world, the world hates you. [20y]*Remember the word I spoke to you, 'No slave is greater than his master.' If they persecuted me, they will also persecute you. If they kept my word, they will also keep yours. [21z]*And they will do all these things to you on account of my name, because they do not know the one who sent me. [22a]*If I had not come and spoken to them, they would have no sin; but as it is they have no excuse for their sin. [23b]Whoever hates me also hates my Father. [24c]If I had not done works among them that no one else ever did, they would not have sin; but as it is, they have seen and hated both me and my Father. [25d]*But in order that the word written in their law might be fulfilled, 'They hated me without cause.'

[26e]*"When the Advocate comes whom I will send you from the Father, the Spirit of truth that proceeds from the Father, he will testify to me. [27f]And you also testify, because you have been with me from the beginning.

See RG 330–31

CHAPTER 16

[1]"I have told you this so that you may not fall away. [2g]*They will expel you from the synagogues; in fact, the hour is coming when everyone who kills you will think he is offering worship to God. [3h]They will do this because they have not known either the Father or me. [4i]*I have told you this so that when their hour comes you may remember that I told you.

Jesus' Departure; Coming of the Advocate. "I did not tell you this from the beginning, because I was with you. [5j]*But now I am going to the one who sent me, and not one of you asks me, 'Where are you going?' [6]But because I told you this, grief has filled your hearts. [7k]But I tell you the truth, it is better for you that I go. For if I do not go, the Advocate will not come to you. But if I go, I will send him to you. [8]*And when he comes he will convict the world in regard to sin and righteousness and condemnation: [9i]sin, because they do not believe in me; [10]righteousness, because I am going to the Father and you will no longer see me; [11m]condemnation, because the ruler of this world has been condemned.

[12]"I have much more to tell you, but you cannot bear it now. [13n]*But when he comes, the Spirit of truth, he will guide you to all truth. He will not speak on his own, but he will speak what he hears, and will declare to you the things that are coming. [14]He will glorify me, because he will take from what is

---

15, 18—16, 4: The hostile reaction of the world. There are synoptic parallels, predicting persecution, especially at Mt 10, 17–25; 24, 9–10.

15, 20: The word I spoke to you: a reference to 13, 16.

15, 21: On account of my name: the idea of persecution for Jesus' name is frequent in the New Testament (Mt 10, 22; 24, 9; Acts 9, 14). For John, association with Jesus' name implies union with Jesus.

15, 22.24: Jesus' words (**spoken**) and deeds (**works**) are the great motives of credibility. **They have seen and hated:** probably means that they have seen his works and still have hated; but the Greek can be read: "have seen both me and my Father and still have hated both me and my Father." **Works . . . that no one else ever did:** so Yahweh in Dt 4, 32–33.

15, 25: In their law: law is here used as a larger concept than the Pentateuch, for the reference is to Ps 35, 19 or 69, 5. See the notes on 10, 34; 12, 34. **Their** law reflects the argument of the church with the synagogue.

15, 26: Whom I will send: in 14, 16.26, the Paraclete is to be sent by the Father, at the request of Jesus. Here the Spirit comes from both Jesus and the Father in mission; there is no reference to the eternal procession of the Spirit.

16, 2: Hour: of persecution, not Jesus' "hour" (see the note on 2, 4).

16, 4b–33: A duplicate of 14, 1–31 on departure and return.

16, 5: Not one of you asks me: the difficulty of reconciling this with Simon Peter's question in 13, 36 and Thomas' words in 14, 5 strengthens the supposition that the last discourse has been made up of several collections of Johannine material.

16, 8–11: These verses illustrate the forensic character of the Paraclete's role: in the forum of the disciples' conscience he prosecutes the world. He leads believers to see (a) that the basic sin was and is refusal to believe in Jesus; (b) that, although Jesus was found guilty and apparently died in disgrace, in reality righteousness has triumphed, for Jesus has returned to his Father; (c) finally, that it is **the ruler of this world,** Satan, who has been condemned through Jesus' death (12, 32).

16, 13: Declare to you the things that are coming: not a reference to new predictions about the future, but interpretation of what has already occurred or been said.

---

w: 7, 7; 14, 17; Mt 10, 22; 24, 9; Mk 13, 13; Lk 6, 22; 1 Jn 3, 13. x: 17, 14-16; 1 Jn 4, 5. y: 13, 16; Mt 10, 24. z: 8, 19; 16, 3. a: 8, 21.24; 9, 41. b: 5, 23; Lk 10, 16; 1 Jn 2, 23. c: 3, 2; 9, 32; Dt 4, 32-33. d: Ps 35, 19; 69, 4. e: 14, 16.26; Mt 10, 19-20. f: Lk 1, 2; Acts 1, 8. g: 9, 22; 12, 42; Mt 10, 17; Lk 21, 12; Acts 26, 11. h: 15, 21. i: 13, 19; 14, 29. j: 7, 33; 13, 36; 14, 5. k: 7, 39; 14, 16-17.26; 15, 26. l: 8, 21-24; 15, 22. m: 12, 31. n: 14, 17.26; 15, 26; Pss 25, 5; 143, 10; 1 Jn 2, 27; Rv 7, 17.

mine and declare it to you. [15]Everything that the Father has is mine; for this reason I told you that he will take from what is mine and declare it to you.

[16o]"A little while and you will no longer see me, and again a little while later and you will see me." [17]So some of his disciples said to one another, "What does this mean that he is saying to us, 'A little while and you will not see me, and again a little while and you will see me,' and 'Because I am going to the Father'?" [18]So they said, "What is this 'little while' [of which he speaks]? We do not know what he means." [19]Jesus knew that they wanted to ask him, so he said to them, "Are you discussing with one another what I said, 'A little while and you will not see me, and again a little while and you will see me'? [20p]Amen, amen, I say to you, you will weep and mourn, while the world rejoices; you will grieve, but your grief will become joy. [21q]When a woman is in labor, she is in anguish because her hour has arrived; but when she has given birth to a child, she no longer remembers the pain because of her joy that a child has been born into the world. [22r]So you also are now in anguish. But I will see you again, and your hearts will rejoice, and no one will take your joy away from you. [23s]On that day you will not question me about anything. Amen, amen, I say to you, whatever you ask the Father in my name he will give you. [24]Until now you have not asked anything in my name; ask and you will receive, so that your joy may be complete.

[25t*]"I have told you this in figures of speech. The hour is coming when I will no longer speak to you in figures but I will tell you clearly about the Father. [26u]On that day you will ask in my name, and I do not tell you that I will ask the Father for you. [27]For the Father himself loves you, because you have loved me and have come to believe that I came from God. [28v]I came from the Father and have come into the world. Now I am leaving the world and going back to the Father." [29]His disciples said, "Now you are talking plainly, and not in any figure of speech. [30*]Now we realize that you know everything and that you do not need to have anyone question you. Because of this we believe that you came from God." [31]Jesus answered them, "Do you believe now? [32w*]Behold, the hour is coming and has arrived when each of you will be scattered to his own home and you will leave me alone. But I am not alone, because the Father is with me. [33x]I have told you this so that you might have peace in me. In the world you will have trouble, but take courage, I have conquered the world."

CHAPTER 17

See RG 330-31

The Prayer of Jesus. [1y*]When Jesus had said this, he raised his eyes to heaven and said, "Father, the hour has come. Give glory to your son, so that your son may glorify you, [2z*]just as you gave him authority over all people, so that he may give eternal life to all you gave him. [3a*]Now this is eternal life, that they should know you, the only true God,

---

16, 25: See the note on 10, 6. Here, possibly a reference to 15, 1–16 or 16, 21.

16, 30: The reference is seemingly to the fact that Jesus could anticipate their question in v 19. The disciples naively think they have the full understanding that is the climax of "the hour" of Jesus' death, resurrection, and ascension (25), but the only part of the hour that is at hand for them is their share in the passion (32).

16, 32: You will be scattered: cf Mk 14, 27 and Mt 26, 31, where both cite Zec 13, 7 about the sheep being dispersed.

17, 1–26: Climax of the last discourse(s). Since the sixteenth century, this chapter has been called the "high priestly prayer" of Jesus. He speaks as intercessor, with words addressed directly to the Father and not to the disciples, who supposedly only overhear. Yet the prayer is one of petition, for immediate (6–19) and future (20–21) disciples. Many phrases reminiscent of the Lord's Prayer occur. Although still in the world (13), Jesus looks on his earthly ministry as a

thing of the past (4.12). Whereas Jesus has up to this time stated that the disciples could follow him (13, 33.36), now he wishes them to be with him in union with the Father (12–14).

17, 1: The action of looking up to heaven and the address **Father** are typical of Jesus at prayer; cf 11, 41 and Lk 11, 2.

17, 2: Another possible interpretation is to treat the first line of the verse as parenthetical and the second as an appositive to the clause that ends v 1: **so that your son may glorify you (just as . . . all people), so that he may give eternal life. . . .**

17, 3: This verse was clearly added in the editing of the gospel as a reflection on the preceding verse; Jesus nowhere else refers to himself as Jesus Christ.

o: 7, 33; 14, 19.   *p:* Ps 126, 6.   *q:* Is 26, 17-18; Jer 31, 13; Mic 4, 9.   *r:* 14, 19; 15, 11; 20, 20.   *s:* 14, 13.   *t:* Mt 13, 34-35. *u:* 14, 13.   *v:* 1, 1.   *w:* 8, 29; Zec 13, 7; Mt 26, 31; Mk 14, 27. *x:* 14, 27.   *y:* 13, 31.   *z:* 3, 35; Mt 28, 18.   *a:* 1, 17; Wis 14, 7; 15, 3; 1 Jn 5, 20.

and the one whom you sent, Jesus Christ. [4]I glorified you on earth by accomplishing the work that you gave me to do. [5b]Now glorify me, Father, with you, with the glory that I had with you before the world began.

[6]*"I revealed your name to those whom you gave me out of the world. They belonged to you, and you gave them to me, and they have kept your word. [7]Now they know that everything you gave me is from you, [8]because the words you gave to me I have given to them, and they accepted them and truly understood that I came from you, and they have believed that you sent me. [9c]I pray for them. I do not pray for the world but for the ones you have given me, because they are yours, [10d]and everything of mine is yours and everything of yours is mine, and I have been glorified in them. [11]And now I will no longer be in the world, but they are in the world, while I am coming to you. Holy Father, keep them in your name that you have given me, so that they may be one just as we are. [12e]When I was with them I protected them in your name that you gave me, and I guarded them, and none of them was lost except the son of destruction, in order that the scripture might be fulfilled. [13f]But now I am coming to you. I speak this in the world so that they may share my joy completely. [14g]I gave them your word, and the world hated them, because they do not belong to the world any more than I belong to the world. [15h]*I do not ask that you take them out of the world but that you keep them from the evil one. [16]They do not belong to the world any more than I belong to the world. [17i]Consecrate them in the truth. Your word is truth. [18j]As you sent me into the world, so I sent them into the world. [19]And I consecrate myself for them, so that they also may be consecrated in truth.

[20]"I pray not only for them, but also for those who will believe in me through their word, [21k]so that they may all be one, as you, Father, are in me and I in you, that they also may be in us, that the world may believe that you sent me. [22]And I have given them the glory you gave me, so that they may be one, as we are one, [23]I in them and you in me, that they may be brought to perfection as one, that the world may know that you sent me, and that you loved them even as you loved me. [24l]*Father, they are your gift to me. I wish that where I am they also may be with me, that they may see my glory that you gave me, because you loved me before the foundation of the world. [25m]Righteous Father, the world also does not know you, but I know you, and they know that you sent me. [26]*I made known to them your name and I will make it known, that the love with which you loved me may be in them and I in them."

CHAPTER 18

See RG 331-32

Jesus Arrested. [1n]*When he had said this, Jesus went out with his disciples across the Kidron valley to where there was a garden, into which he and his disciples entered. [2]Judas his betrayer also knew the place, because Jesus had often met there with his disciples. [3o]*So Judas got a band of soldiers and guards from the chief priests and the Pharisees and went there with lanterns, torches, and weapons. [4]Jesus, knowing everything that was going to happen to him, went out and said to them, "Whom are you looking for?"

17, 6: I revealed your name: perhaps the name **I AM;** cf 8, 24. 28.58; 13, 19.

17, 15: Note the resemblance to the petition of the Lord's Prayer, "deliver us from the evil one." Both probably refer to the devil rather than to abstract evil.

17, 24: Where I am: Jesus prays for the believers ultimately to join him in heaven. Then they will not see his glory as in a mirror but clearly (2 Cor 3, 18; 1 Jn 3, 2).

17, 26: I will make it known: through the Advocate.

18, 1–14: John does not mention the agony in the garden and the kiss of Judas, nor does he identify the place as Gethsemane or the Mount of Olives.

18, 1: Jesus went out: see 14, 31, where it seems he is leaving the supper room. **Kidron valley:** literally, "the winter-flowing Kidron"; this wadi has water only during

the winter rains.

18, 3: Band of soldiers: seems to refer to Roman troops, either the full cohort of 600 men (1/10 of a legion), or more likely the maniple of 200 under their tribune (12). In this case, John is hinting at Roman collusion in the action against Jesus before he was brought to Pilate. The lanterns and torches may be symbolic of the hour of darkness.

b: 1, 1.2; 12, 28; Phil 2, 6.9-11. *c:* 17, 20. *d:* 16, 15; 2 Thes 1, 10.12. *e:* 13, 18; 18, 9; Ps 41, 10; Mt 26, 24; Acts 1, 16. *f:* 15, 11. *g:* 15, 19. *h:* Mt 6, 13; 2 Thes 3, 3; 1 Jn 5, 18. *i:* 1 Pt 1, 22. *j:* 20, 21-22. *k:* 10, 30; 14, 10-11.20. *l:* 14, 3; 1 Thes 4, 17. *m:* 1, 10. *n:* 2 Sm 15, 23; Mt 26, 30.36; Mk 14, 26.32; Lk 22, 39. *o:* Mt 26, 47-51; Mk 14, 43-44; Lk 22, 47.

⁵*They answered him, "Jesus the Nazorean." He said to them, "I AM." Judas his betrayer was also with them. ⁶When he said to them, "I AM," they turned away and fell to the ground. ⁷So he again asked them, "Whom are you looking for?" They said, "Jesus the Nazorean." ⁸Jesus answered, "I told you that I AM. So if you are looking for me, let these men go." ⁹ᵖ*This was to fulfill what he had said, "I have not lost any of those you gave me." ¹⁰*Then Simon Peter, who had a sword, drew it, struck the high priest's slave, and cut off his right ear. The slave's name was Malchus. ¹¹�q*Jesus said to Peter, "Put your sword into its scabbard. Shall I not drink the cup that the Father gave me?"

¹²ʳSo the band of soldiers, the tribune, and the Jewish guards seized Jesus, bound him, ¹³ˢ*and brought him to Annas first. He was the father-in-law of Caiaphas, who was high priest that year. ¹⁴ᵗIt was Caiaphas who had counseled the Jews that it was better that one man should die rather than the people.

Peter's First Denial. ¹⁵ᵘ*Simon Peter and another disciple followed Jesus. Now the other disciple was known to the high priest, and he entered the courtyard of the high priest with Jesus. ¹⁶But Peter stood at the gate outside. So the other disciple, the acquaintance of the high priest, went out and spoke to the gatekeeper and brought Peter in. ¹⁷Then the maid who was the gatekeeper said to Peter, "You are not one of this man's disciples, are you?" He said, "I am not."

¹⁸Now the slaves and the guards were standing around a charcoal fire that they had made, because it was cold, and were warming themselves. Peter was also standing there keeping warm.

The Inquiry before Annas. ¹⁹ᵛThe high priest questioned Jesus about his disciples and about his doctrine. ²⁰ʷ*Jesus answered him, "I have spoken publicly to the world. I have always taught in a synagogue or in the temple area where all the Jews gather, and in secret I have said nothing. ²¹Why ask me? Ask those who heard me what I said to them. They know what I said." ²²ˣWhen he had said this, one of the temple guards standing there struck Jesus and said, "Is this the way you answer the high priest?" ²³Jesus answered him, "If I have spoken wrongly, testify to the wrong; but if I have spoken rightly, why do you strike me?" ²⁴ʸ*Then Annas sent him bound to Caiaphas the high priest.

Peter Denies Jesus Again. ²⁵ᶻNow Simon Peter was standing there keeping warm. And they said to him, "You are not one of his disciples, are you?" He denied it and said, "I am not." ²⁶One of the slaves of the high priest, a relative of the one whose ear Peter had cut off, said, "Didn't I see you in the garden with him?" ²⁷*Again Peter denied it. And immediately the cock crowed.

The Trial before Pilate. ²⁸ᵃ*Then they brought Jesus from Caiaphas to the praetorium. It was morning. And they themselves did not enter the praetorium, in order not to

---

18, 5: Nazorean: the form found in Mt 26, 71 (see the note on Mt 2, 23) is here used, not **Nazarene** of Mark. **I AM:** or "I am he," but probably intended by the evangelist as an expression of divinity (cf their appropriate response in 6); see the note on 8, 24. John sets the confusion of the arresting party against the background of Jesus' divine majesty.

18, 9: The citation may refer to 6, 39; 10, 28; or 17, 12.

18, 10: Only John gives the names of the two antagonists; both John and Luke mention the right ear.

18, 11: The theme of the cup is found in the synoptic account of the agony (Mk 14, 36 and parallels).

18, 13: **Annas:** only John mentions an inquiry before Annas; cf 16.19–24; see the note on Lk 3, 2. It is unlikely that this nighttime interrogation before Annas is the same as the trial before Caiaphas placed by Matthew and Mark at night and by Luke in the morning.

18, 15–16: Another disciple . . . the other disciple: see the note on 13, 23.

18, 20: I have always taught . . . in the temple area: cf Mk 14, 49 for a similar statement.

18, 24: Caiaphas: see Mt 26, 3.57; Lk 3, 2; and the notes there. John may leave room here for the trial before Caiaphas described in the synoptic gospels.

18, 27: Cockcrow was the third Roman division of the night, lasting from midnight to 3 a.m.

18, 28: Praetorium: see the note on Mt 27, 27. **Morning:** literally, "the early hour," or fourth Roman division of the night, 3 to 6 a.m. **The Passover:** the synoptic gospels give the impression that the Thursday night supper was the Passover meal (Mk 14, 12); for John that meal is still to be eaten Friday night.

p: 6, 39; 10, 28; 17, 12. *q:* Mt 20, 22; 26, 39; Mk 10, 38; Lk 22, 42. *r:* Mt 26, 57-58; Mk 14, 53-55; Lk 22, 54-55. *s:* Lk 3, 2. *t:* 11, 49-50. *u:* Mt 26, 58.69-70; Mk 14, 54.66-68; Lk 22, 54-57. *v:* Mt 26, 59-66; Mk 14, 55-64; Lk 22, 66-71. *w:* 6, 59; 7, 14.26; Is 48, 16; Mt 26, 55; Mk 4, 23; Lk 19, 47; 22, 53. *x:* Acts 23, 2. *y:* Mt 26, 57. *z:* Mt 26, 71-75; Mk 14, 69-72; Lk 22, 58-62. *a:* Mt 27, 1-2.11-25; Mk 15, 1-5; Lk 23, 1-5.

be defiled so that they could eat the Passover. ²⁹So Pilate came out to them and said, "What charge do you bring [against] this man?" ³⁰They answered and said to him, "If he were not a criminal, we would not have handed him over to you." ³¹*At this, Pilate said to them, "Take him yourselves, and judge him according to your law." The Jews answered him, "We do not have the right to execute anyone," ^{32b}*in order that the word of Jesus might be fulfilled that he said indicating the kind of death he would die. ³³So Pilate went back into the praetorium and summoned Jesus and said to him, "Are you the King of the Jews?" ³⁴Jesus answered, "Do you say this on your own or have others told you about me?" ^{35c}Pilate answered, "I am not a Jew, am I? Your own nation and the chief priests handed you over to me. What have you done?" ^{36d}Jesus answered, "My kingdom does not belong to this world. If my kingdom did belong to this world, my attendants [would] be fighting to keep me from being handed over to the Jews. But as it is, my kingdom is not here." ^{37e}*So Pilate said to him, "Then you are a king?" Jesus answered, "You say I am a king. For this I was born and for this I came into the world, to testify to the truth. Everyone who belongs to the truth listens to my voice." ^{38f}Pilate said to him, "What is truth?"

When he had said this, he again went out to the Jews and said to them, "I find no guilt in him. ³⁹*But you have a custom that I release one prisoner to you at Passover. Do you want me to release to you the King of the Jews?" ⁴⁰*They cried out again, "Not this one but Barabbas!" Now Barabbas was a revolutionary.

CHAPTER 19

^{1g}*Then Pilate took Jesus and had him See RG
331-32 scourged. ²And the soldiers wove a crown out of thorns and placed it on his head, and clothed him in a purple cloak, ³and they came to him and said, "Hail, King of the Jews!" And they struck him repeatedly. ^{4h}Once more Pilate went out and said to them, "Look, I am bringing him out to you, so that you may know that I find no guilt in him." ⁵ⁱSo Jesus came out, wearing the crown of thorns and the purple cloak. And he said to them, "Behold, the man!" ^{6j}When the chief priests and the guards saw him they cried out, "Crucify him, crucify him!" Pilate said to them, "Take him yourselves and crucify him. I find no guilt in him." ^{7k}*The Jews answered, "We have a law, and according to that law he ought to die, because he made himself the Son of God." ⁸Now when Pilate heard this statement, he became even more afraid, ^{9l}and went back into the praetorium and said to Jesus, "Where are you from?" Jesus did not answer him. ¹⁰So Pilate said to him, "Do you not speak to me? Do you not know that I have power to release you and I have power to crucify you?" ^{11m}Jesus answered [him], "You would have no power over me if it had not been given to you from above. For this reason the one who handed me over to you has the greater sin." ¹²ⁿ*Consequently, Pilate tried to release him; but the

---

18, 31: We do not have the right to execute anyone: only John gives this reason for their bringing Jesus to Pilate. Jewish sources are not clear on the competence of the Sanhedrin at this period to sentence and to execute for political crimes.

18, 32: The Jewish punishment for blasphemy was stoning (Lv 24, 16). In coming to the Romans to ensure that Jesus would be crucified, the Jewish authorities fulfilled his prophecy that he would be **exalted** (3, 14; 12, 32–33). There is some historical evidence, however, for Jews crucifying Jews.

18, 37: You say I am a king: see Mt 26, 64 for a similar response to the high priest. It is at best a reluctant affirmative.

18, 39: See the note on Mt 27, 15.

18, 40: Barabbas: see the note on Mt 27, 16–17. **Revolutionary:** a guerrilla warrior fighting for nationalist aims, though the term can also denote a robber. See the note on Mt 27, 38.

19, 1: Luke places the mockery of Jesus at the midpoint in the trial when Jesus was sent to Herod. Mark and Matthew place the scourging and mockery at the end of the trial after the sentence of death. Scourging was an integral part of the crucifixion penalty.

19, 7: Made himself the Son of God: this question was not raised in John's account of the Jewish interrogations of Jesus as it was in the synoptic account. Nevertheless, see 5, 18; 8, 53; 10, 36.

19, 12: Friend of Caesar: a Roman honorific title bestowed upon high-ranking officials for merit.

b: 3, 14; 8, 28; 12, 32-33. *c:* 1, 11. *d:* 1, 10; 8, 23. *e:* 8, 47; 1 Tm 6, 13. *f:* Mt 27, 15-26; Mk 15, 6-15; Lk 23, 18-25; Acts 3, 14. *g:* Mt 27, 27-31; Mk 15, 16-20; Lk 23, 13-25. *h:* 18, 38. *i:* Is 52, 14. *j:* 18, 31; 19, 15. *k:* 10, 33-36; Lv 24, 16. *l:* 7, 28. *m:* 3, 27; 10, 18; Rom 13, 1. *n:* Acts 17, 7.

Jews cried out, "If you release him, you are not a Friend of Caesar. Everyone who makes himself a king opposes Caesar."

13*When Pilate heard these words he brought Jesus out and seated him on the judge's bench in the place called Stone Pavement, in Hebrew, Gabbatha. *14**It was preparation day for Passover, and it was about noon. And he said to the Jews, "Behold, your king!" *15*They cried out, "Take him away, take him away! Crucify him!" Pilate said to them, "Shall I crucify your king?" The chief priests answered, "We have no king but Caesar." *16**Then he handed him over to them to be crucified.

The Crucifixion of Jesus. So they took Jesus, *17o**and carrying the cross himself he went out to what is called the Place of the Skull, in Hebrew, Golgotha. *18*There they crucified him, and with him two others, one on either side, with Jesus in the middle. *19**Pilate also had an inscription written and put on the cross. It read, "Jesus the Nazorean, the King of the Jews." *20*Now many of the Jews read this inscription, because the place where Jesus was crucified was near the city; and it was written in Hebrew, Latin, and Greek. *21p*So the chief priests of the Jews said to Pilate, "Do not write 'The King of the Jews,' but that he said, 'I am the King of the Jews.' " *22*Pilate answered, "What I have written, I have written."

23qr*When the soldiers had crucified Jesus, they took his clothes and divided them into four shares, a share for each soldier. They also took his tunic, but the tunic was seamless, woven in one piece from the top down. *24*So they said to one another, "Let's not tear it, but cast lots for it to see whose it will be," in order that the passage of scripture might be fulfilled [that says]:

"They divided my garments among them,
and for my vesture they cast lots."

This is what the soldiers did. *25s**Standing by the cross of Jesus were his mother and his mother's sister, Mary the wife of Clopas, and Mary of Magdala. *26t**When Jesus saw his mother and the disciple there whom he loved, he said to his mother, "Woman,

---

19, 13: Seated him: others translate "(Pilate) sat down." In John's thought, Jesus is the real judge of the world, and John may here be portraying him seated on the judgment bench. **Stone Pavement:** in Greek **lithostrotos**; under the fortress Antonia, one of the conjectured locations of the praetorium, a massive stone pavement has been excavated. **Gabbatha** (Aramaic rather than Hebrew) probably means "ridge, elevation."

19, 14: Noon: Mk 15, 25 has Jesus crucified "at the third hour," which means either 9 a.m. or the period from 9 to 12. Noon, the time when, according to John, Jesus was sentenced to death, was the hour at which the priests began to slaughter Passover lambs in the temple; see Jn 1, 29.

19, 16: He handed him over to them to be crucified: in context this would seem to mean "handed him over to the chief priests." Lk 23, 25 has a similar ambiguity. There is a polemic tendency in the gospels to place the guilt of the crucifixion on the Jewish authorities and to exonerate the Romans from blame. But John later mentions the Roman soldiers (23), and it was to these soldiers that Pilate handed Jesus over.

19, 17: Carrying the cross himself: a different picture from that of the synoptics, especially Lk 23, 26, where Simon of Cyrene is made to carry the cross, walking behind Jesus. In John's theology, Jesus remained in complete control and master of his destiny (cf 10, 18). **Place of the Skull:** the Latin word for skull is **Calvaria;** hence "Calvary." **Golgotha** is actually an Aramaic rather than a Hebrew word.

19, 19: The inscription differs with slightly different words in each of the four gospels. John's form is fullest and gives the equivalent of the Latin **INRI = Iesus Nazarenus Rex Iudaeorum.** Only John mentions its polyglot character

(20) and Pilate's role in keeping the title unchanged (21–22).

19, 23–25a: While all four gospels describe the soldiers casting lots to divide Jesus' garments (see the note on Mt 27, 35), only John quotes the underlying passage from Ps 22, 19, and only John sees each line of the poetic parallelism literally carried out in two separate actions (23a; 23b-24).

19, 25: It is not clear whether four women are meant, or three (i.e., **Mary the wife of Cl[e]opas** [cf Lk 24, 18] is in apposition with **his mother's sister**) or two (his mother and his mother's sister, i.e., Mary of Cl[e]opas and Mary of Magdala). Only John mentions the mother of Jesus here. The synoptics have a group of women looking on from a distance at the cross (Mk 15, 40).

19, 26–27: This scene has been interpreted literally, of Jesus' concern for his mother; and symbolically, e.g., in the light of the Cana story in ch 2 (the presence of the mother of Jesus, the address **woman,** and the mention of the **hour**) and of the upper room in ch 13 (the presence of the beloved disciple; the **hour**). Now that the hour has come (28), Mary (a symbol of the church?) is given a role as the mother of Christians (personified by the beloved disciple); or, as a representative of those seeking salvation, she is supported by the disciple who interprets Jesus' revelation; or Jewish and Gentile Christianity (or Israel and the Christian community) are reconciled.

---

o: Mt 27, 32-37; Mk 15, 21-26; Lk 23, 26-35. *p:* 18, 33; Lk 19, 14. *q:* Mt 27, 38-44; Mk 15, 27-32; Lk 23, 36-43. *r:* Ps 22, 19; Mt 27, 35; Mk 15, 24; Lk 23, 34. *s:* Mt 27, 55; Mk 15, 40-41; Lk 8, 2 23, 49. *t:* 13, 23.

behold, your son." [27]Then he said to the disciple, "Behold, your mother." And from that hour the disciple took her into his home.

[28uv]*After this, aware that everything was now finished, in order that the scripture might be fulfilled, Jesus said, "I thirst." [29]*There was a vessel filled with common wine. So they put a sponge soaked in wine on a sprig of hyssop and put it up to his mouth. [30w]*When Jesus had taken the wine, he said, "It is finished." And bowing his head, he handed over the spirit.

The Blood and Water. [31x]Now since it was preparation day, in order that the bodies might not remain on the cross on the sabbath, for the sabbath day of that week was a solemn one, the Jews asked Pilate that their legs be broken and they be taken down. [32]So the soldiers came and broke the legs of the first and then of the other one who was crucified with Jesus. [33]But when they came to Jesus and saw that he was already dead, they did not break his legs, [34y]*but one soldier thrust his lance into his side, and immediately blood and water flowed out. [35z]*An eyewitness has testified, and his testimony is true; he knows that he is speaking the truth, so that you also may [come to] believe. [36a]For this happened so that the scripture passage might be fulfilled:

"Not a bone of it will be broken."

[37b]And again another passage says:

"They will look upon him whom they
	have pierced."

The Burial of Jesus. [38c]*After this, Joseph of Arimathea, secretly a disciple of Jesus for fear of the Jews, asked Pilate if he could remove the body of Jesus. And Pilate permitted it. So he came and took his body. [39d]Nicodemus, the one who had first come to him at night, also came bringing a mixture of myrrh and aloes weighing about one hundred pounds. [40]They took the body of Jesus and bound it with burial cloths along with the spices, according to the Jewish burial custom. [41]Now in the place where he had been crucified there was a garden, and in the garden a new tomb, in which no one had yet been buried. [42]So they laid Jesus there because of the Jewish preparation day; for the tomb was close by.

CHAPTER 20

See RG 331–32

The Empty Tomb. [1ef]*On the first day of the week, Mary of Magdala came to the tomb early in the morning, while it was still dark, and saw the stone removed from the tomb. [2]*So she ran and went to Simon Peter and to the other disciple whom Jesus loved, and told them, "They have taken the Lord

---

19, 28: The scripture . . . fulfilled: either in the scene of vv 25–27, or in the **I thirst** of v 28. If the latter, Pss 22, 16 and 69, 22 deserve consideration.

19, 29: Wine: John does not mention the drugged wine, a narcotic that Jesus refused as the crucifixion began (Mk 15, 23), but only this final gesture of kindness at the end (Mk 15, 36). **Hyssop,** a small plant, is scarcely suitable for carrying a sponge (Mark mentions a reed) and may be a symbolic reference to the hyssop used to daub the blood of the paschal lamb on the doorpost of the Hebrews (Ex 12, 22).

19, 30: Handed over the spirit: there is a double nuance of dying (giving up the last breath or spirit) and that of passing on the holy Spirit; see 7, 39, which connects the giving of the Spirit with Jesus' glorious return to the Father, and 20, 22, where the author portrays the conferral of the Spirit.

19, 34–35: John probably emphasizes these verses to show the reality of Jesus' death, against the docetic heretics. In the blood and water there may also be a symbolic reference to the Eucharist and baptism.

19, 35: He knows: it is not certain from the Greek that this **he** is the **eyewitness** of the first part of the sentence. **May [come to] believe:** see the note on 20, 31.

19, 38–42: In the first three gospels there is no anointing

on Friday. In Mt and Lk, the women come to the tomb on Sunday morning precisely to anoint Jesus.

20, 1–31: The risen Jesus reveals his glory and confers the Spirit. This story fulfills the basic need for testimony to the resurrection. What we have here is not a record but a series of single stories.

20, 1–10: The story of the empty tomb is found in both the Matthean and the Lucan traditions; John's version seems to be a fusion of the two.

20, 1: Still dark: according to Mark the sun had risen, Matthew describes it as "dawning," and Luke refers to early dawn. Mary sees the stone removed, not the empty tomb.

20, 2: Mary runs away, not directed by an angel/young man as in the synoptic accounts. The plural "we" in the second part of her statement might reflect a tradition of more women going to the tomb.

u: Mt 27, 45-56; Mk 15, 33-41; Lk 23, 44-49.   *v:* Pss 22, 16; 69, 22.   *w:* 4, 34; 10, 18; 17, 4; Lk 23, 46.   *x:* Ex 12, 16; Dt 21, 23.   *y:* Nm 20, 11; 1 Jn 5, 6.   *z:* 7, 37-39; 21, 24.   *a:* Ex 12, 46; Nm 9, 12; Ps 34, 21.   *b:* Nm 21, 9; Zec 12, 10; Rv 1, 7.   *c:* Mt 27, 57-60; Mk 15, 42-46; Lk 34, 50-54.   *d:* 3, 1-2; 7, 50; Ps 45, 9.   *e:* Mt 28, 1-10; Mk 16, 1-11; Lk 24, 1-12.   *f:* 19, 25.

from the tomb, and we don't know where they put him." ³*So Peter and the other disciple went out and came to the tomb. ⁴They both ran, but the other disciple ran faster than Peter and arrived at the tomb first; ⁵he bent down and saw the burial cloths there, but did not go in. ^{6g}*When Simon Peter arrived after him, he went into the tomb and saw the burial cloths there, ^{7h}and the cloth that had covered his head, not with the burial cloths but rolled up in a separate place. ⁸Then the other disciple also went in, the one who had arrived at the tomb first, and he saw and believed. ⁹ⁱ*For they did not yet understand the scripture that he had to rise from the dead. ¹⁰Then the disciples returned home.

The Appearance to Mary of Magdala. ^{11j}*But Mary stayed outside the tomb weeping. And as she wept, she bent over into the tomb ¹²and saw two angels in white sitting there, one at the head and one at the feet where the body of Jesus had been. ¹³And they said to her, "Woman, why are you weeping?" She said to them, "They have taken my Lord, and I don't know where they laid him." ^{14k}When she had said this, she turned around and saw Jesus there, but did not know it was Jesus. ^{15l}Jesus said to her, "Woman, why are you weeping? Whom are you looking for?" She thought it was the gardener and said to him, "Sir, if you carried him away, tell me where you laid him, and I will take him." ¹⁶*Jesus said to her, "Mary!" She turned and said to him in Hebrew, "Rabbouni," which means Teacher. ^{17m}*Jesus said to her, "Stop holding on to me, for I have not yet ascended to the Father. But go to my brothers and tell them, 'I am going to my Father and your Father, to my God and your God.'" ¹⁸Mary of Magdala went and announced to the disciples, "I have seen the Lord," and what he told her.

Appearance to the Disciples. ¹⁹ⁿ*On the evening of that first day of the week, when the doors were locked, where the disciples were, for fear of the Jews, Jesus came and stood in their midst and said to them, "Peace be with you." ^{20o}*When he had said this, he showed them his hands and his side. The disciples rejoiced when they saw the Lord. ^{21p}*[Jesus] said to them again, "Peace be

20, 3–10: The basic narrative is told of Peter alone in Lk 24, 12, a verse missing in important manuscripts and which may be borrowed from tradition similar to John. Cf also Lk 24, 24.

20, 6–8: Some special feature about the state of the burial cloths caused the beloved disciple to believe. Perhaps the details emphasized that the grave had not been robbed.

20, 9: Probably a general reference to the scriptures is intended, as in Lk 24, 26 and 1 Cor 15, 4. Some individual Old Testament passages suggested are Ps 16, 10; Hos 6, 2; Jon 2, 1.2.11.

20, 11–18: This appearance to Mary is found only in Jn, but cf Mt 28, 8–10 and Mk 16, 9–11.

20, 16: Rabbouni: Hebrew or Aramaic for "my master."

20, 17: Stop holding on to me: see Mt 28, 9, where the women take hold of his feet. **I have not yet ascended:** for John and many of the New Testament writers, the ascension in the theological sense of going to the Father to be glorified took place with the resurrection as one action. This scene in John dramatizes such an understanding, for by Easter night Jesus is glorified and can give the Spirit. Therefore his ascension takes place immediately after he has talked to Mary. In such a view, the ascension after forty days described in Acts 1, 1–11 would be simply a termination of earthly appearances or, perhaps better, an introduction to the conferral of the Spirit upon the early church, modeled on Elisha's being able to have a (double) share in the spirit of Elijah if he saw him being taken up (same verb as ascending) into heaven (2 Kgs 2, 9–12). **To my Father and your Father, to my God and your God:** this echoes Ru 1, 16: "Your people shall be my people, and your God my God." The Father of Jesus will now become the Father of the disciples because, once ascended, Jesus can give them the Spirit that comes from the Father and they can be reborn as God's children (3, 5). That is why he calls them **my brothers.**

20, 19–29: The appearances to the disciples, without or with Thomas (cf 11, 16; 14, 5), have rough parallels in the other gospels only for vv 19–23; cf Lk 24, 36–39; Mk 16, 14–18.

20, 19: The disciples: by implication from v 24, this means ten of the Twelve, presumably in Jerusalem. **Peace be with you:** although this could be an ordinary greeting, John intends here to echo 14, 27. The theme of rejoicing in v 20 echoes 16, 22.

20, 20: Hands and . . . side: Lk 24, 39–40 mentions "hands and feet," based on Ps 22, 17.

20, 21: By means of this sending, the Eleven were made apostles, that is, "those sent" (cf 17, 18), though John does not use the noun in reference to them (see the note on 13, 16). A solemn mission or "sending" is also the subject of the post-resurrection appearances to the Eleven in Mt 28, 19; Lk 24, 47; Mk 16, 15.

g: Lk 24, 12.　h: 11, 44; 19, 40.　i: Acts 2, 26-27; 1 Cor 15, 4.　j: Mk 16, 9-11.　k: 21, 4; Mk 16, 12; Lk 24, 16; 1 Cor 15, 43-44.　l: Mt 28, 9-10.　m: Acts 1, 9.　n: Mt 28, 16-20; Mk 16, 14-18; Lk 24, 36-44.　o: 14, 27.　p: 17, 18; Mt 28, 19; Mk 16, 15; Lk 24, 47-48.

with you. As the Father has sent me, so I send you." [22q]*And when he had said this, he breathed on them and said to them, "Receive the holy Spirit. [23r]*Whose sins you forgive are forgiven them, and whose sins you retain are retained."

Thomas. [24]Thomas, called Didymus, one of the Twelve, was not with them when Jesus came. [25s]So the other disciples said to him, "We have seen the Lord." But he said to them, "Unless I see the mark of the nails in his hands and put my finger into the nail-marks and put my hand into his side, I will not believe." [26t]Now a week later his disciples were again inside and Thomas was with them. Jesus came, although the doors were locked, and stood in their midst and said, "Peace be with you." [27]Then he said to Thomas, "Put your finger here and see my hands, and bring your hand and put it into my side, and do not be unbelieving, but believe." [28u]*Thomas answered and said to him, "My Lord and my God!" [29v]*Jesus said to him, "Have you come to believe because you have seen me? Blessed are those who have not seen and have believed."

Conclusion. [30w]*Now Jesus did many other signs in the presence of [his] disciples that are not written in this book. [31x]But these are written that you may [come to] believe that Jesus is the Messiah, the Son of God, and that through this belief you may have life in his name.

IV: Epilogue: The Resurrection Appearance in Galilee

CHAPTER 21

See RG 332

The Appearance to the Seven Disciples.
[1y]*After this, Jesus revealed himself again to his disciples at the Sea of Tiberias. He revealed himself in this way. [2]*Together were Simon Peter, Thomas called Didymus, Nathanael from Cana in Galilee, Zebedee's sons, and two others of his disciples. [3z]*Simon Peter said to them, "I am going fishing." They said to him, "We also will come with you." So they went out and got into the boat, but that night they caught nothing. [4a]When it was already dawn, Jesus was standing on the shore; but the disciples did not realize that it was Jesus. [5b]Jesus said to them, "Children, have you caught anything to eat?" They answered him, "No." [6]So he said to them, "Cast the net over the right side of the boat and you will find something." So they cast it, and were not able to pull it in because of the number of fish. [7]So the disciple whom Jesus loved said to Peter, "It is the Lord." When Simon Peter heard that it was the Lord, he tucked in his garment, for he was lightly clad, and jumped into the sea. [8]The other disciples came in the boat, for they were not far from shore, only about a hundred yards, dragging

20, 22: This action recalls Gn 2, 7, where God breathed on the first man and gave him life; just as Adam's life came from God, so now the disciples' new spiritual life comes from Jesus. Cf also the revivification of the dry bones in Ez 37. This is the author's version of Pentecost. Cf also the note on 19, 30.

20, 23: The Council of Trent defined that this power to forgive sins is exercised in the sacrament of penance. See Mt 16, 19 and 18, 18.

20, 28: My Lord and my God: this forms a literary inclusion with the first verse of the gospel: "and the Word was God."

20, 29: This verse is a beatitude on future generations; faith, not sight, matters.

20, 30–31: These verses are clearly a conclusion to the gospel and express its purpose. While many manuscripts read **come to believe,** possibly implying a missionary purpose for John's gospel, a small number of quite early ones read "continue to believe," suggesting that the audience consists of Christians whose faith is to be deepened by the book; cf 19, 35.

21, 1–23: There are many non-Johannine peculiarities in this chapter, some suggesting Lucan Greek style; yet this passage is closer to John than 7, 53—8, 11. There are many Jo-

hannine features as well. Its closest parallels in the synoptic gospels are found in Lk 5, 1–11 and Mt 14, 28–31. Perhaps the tradition was ultimately derived from John but preserved by some disciple other than the writer of the rest of the gospel. The appearances narrated seem to be independent of those in ch 20. Even if a later addition, the chapter was added before publication of the gospel, for it appears in all manuscripts.

21, 2: Zebedee's sons: the only reference to James and John in this gospel (but see the note on 1, 37). Perhaps the phrase was originally a gloss to identify, among the five, the **two others of his disciples.** The anonymity of the latter phrase is more Johannine (1, 35). The total of seven may suggest the community of the disciples in its fullness.

21, 3–6: This may be a variant of Luke's account of the catch of fish; see the note on Lk 5, 1–11.

q: Gn 2, 7; Ez 37, 9; 1 Cor 15, 45. *r:* Mt 16, 19; 18, 18. *s:* 1 Jn 1, 1. *t:* 21, 14. *u:* 1, 1. *v:* 4, 48; Lk 1, 45; 1 Pt 1, 8. *w:* 21, 25. *x:* 3, 14.15; 1 Jn 5, 13. *y:* Mt 26, 32; 28, 7. *z:* Mt 4, 18; Lk 5, 4-10. *a:* 20, 14; Mt 28, 17; Lk 24, 16. *b:* Lk 24, 41.

the net with the fish. [9c]*When they climbed out on shore, they saw a charcoal fire with fish on it and bread. [10]Jesus said to them, "Bring some of the fish you just caught." [11d]*So Simon Peter went over and dragged the net ashore full of one hundred fifty-three large fish. Even though there were so many, the net was not torn. [12]*Jesus said to them, "Come, have breakfast." And none of the disciples dared to ask him, "Who are you?" because they realized it was the Lord. [13e]Jesus came over and took the bread and gave it to them, and in like manner the fish. [14f]*This was now the third time Jesus was revealed to his disciples after being raised from the dead.

Jesus and Peter. [15]*When they had finished breakfast, Jesus said to Simon Peter, "Simon, son of John, do you love me more than these?" He said to him, "Yes, Lord, you know that I love you." He said to him, "Feed my lambs." [16]He then said to him a second time, "Simon, son of John, do you love me?" He said to him, "Yes, Lord, you know that I love you." He said to him, "Tend my sheep." [17g]He said to him the third time, "Simon, son of John, do you love me?" Peter was distressed that he had said to him a third time, "Do you love me?" and he said to him, "Lord, you know everything; you know that I love you." [Jesus] said to him, "Feed my sheep. [18h]*Amen, amen, I say to you, when you were younger, you used to dress yourself and go where you wanted; but when you grow old, you will stretch out your hands, and someone else will dress you and lead you where you do not want to go." [19i]He said this signifying by what kind of death he would glorify God. And when he had said this, he said to him, "Follow me."

The Beloved Disciple. [20j]Peter turned and saw the disciple following whom Jesus loved, the one who had also reclined upon his chest during the supper and had said, "Master, who is the one who will betray you?" [21]When Peter saw him, he said to Jesus, "Lord, what about him?" [22k]*Jesus said to him, "What if I want him to remain until I come? What concern is it of yours? You follow me." [23]*So the word spread among the brothers that that disciple would not die. But Jesus had not told him that he would not die, just "What if I want him to remain until I come? [What concern is it of yours?]"

Conclusion. [24l]*It is this disciple who testifies to these things and has written them, and we know that his testimony is true. [25m]There are also many other things that Jesus did, but if these were to be described individually, I do not think the whole world would contain the books that would be written.

21, 9.12–13: It is strange that Jesus already has fish since none have yet been brought ashore. This meal may have had eucharistic significance for early Christians since v 13 recalls Jn 6, 11, which uses the vocabulary of Jesus' action at the Last Supper; but see also the note on Mt 14, 19.

21, 11: The exact number 153 is probably meant to have a symbolic meaning in relation to the apostles' universal mission; Jerome claims that Greek zoologists catalogued 153 species of fish. Or 153 is the sum of the numbers from 1 to 17. Others invoke Ez 47, 10.

21, 12: None . . . dared to ask him: is Jesus' appearance strange to them? Cf Lk 24, 16; Mk 16, 12; Jn 20, 14. The disciples do, however, recognize Jesus **before** the breaking of the bread (opposed to Lk 24, 35).

21, 14: This verse connects chs 20 and 21; cf 20, 19.26.

21, 15–23: This section constitutes Peter's rehabilitation and emphasizes his role in the church.

21, 15–17: In these three verses there is a remarkable variety of synonyms: two different Greek verbs for **love** (see the note on 15, 13); two verbs for **feed/tend;** two nouns for **sheep;** two verbs for **know.** But apparently there is no difference of meaning. The threefold confession of Peter is meant to counteract his earlier threefold denial (18, 17.25.27). The First Vatican Council cited these verses in defining that Jesus after his resurrection gave Peter the jurisdiction of supreme shepherd and ruler over the whole flock.

21, 15: More than these: probably "more than these disciples do" rather than "more than you love them" or "more than you love these things [fishing, etc.]."

21, 18: Originally probably a proverb about old age, now used as a figurative reference to the crucifixion of Peter.

21, 22: Until I come: a reference to the parousia.

21, 23: This whole scene takes on more significance if the disciple is already dead. The death of the apostolic generation caused problems in the church because of a belief that Jesus was to have returned first. Loss of faith sometimes resulted; cf 2 Pt 3, 4.

21, 24: Who . . . has written them: this does not necessarily mean he wrote them with his own hand. The same expression is used in 19, 22 of Pilate, who certainly would not have written the inscription himself. **We know:** i.e., the Christian community; cf 1, 14.16.

c: Lk 24, 41-43. d: 2 Chr 2, 16. e: Lk 24, 42. f: 20, 19.26. g: 13, 37-38; 18, 15-18.25-27; Mt 26, 69-75; Mk 14, 66-72: Lk 22, 55-62. h: Acts 21, 11.14; 2 Pt 1, 14. i: 13, 36. j: 13, 25. k: Mt 16, 28. l: 19, 35. m: 20, 30.

See RG
334–50

The Acts of the Apostles

The Acts of the Apostles, the second volume of Luke's two-volume work, continues Luke's presentation of biblical history, describing how the salvation promised to Israel in the Old Testament and accomplished by Jesus has now under the guidance of the holy Spirit been extended to the Gentiles. This was accomplished through the divinely chosen representatives (10, 41) whom Jesus prepared during his historical ministry (1, 21–22) and commissioned after his resurrection as witnesses to all that he taught (1, 8; 10, 37–43; Lk 24, 48). Luke's preoccupation with the Christian community as the Spirit-guided bearer of the word of salvation rules out of his book detailed histories of the activity of most of the preachers. Only the main lines of the roles of Peter and Paul serve Luke's interest.

Peter was the leading member of the Twelve (1, 13.15), a miracle worker like Jesus in the gospel (3, 1–10; 5, 1–11.15; 9, 32–35.36–42), the object of divine care (5, 17–21; 12, 6–11), and the spokesman for the Christian community (2, 14–36; 3, 12–26; 4, 8–12; 5, 29–32; 10, 34–43; 15, 7–11), who, according to Luke, was largely responsible for the growth of the community in the early days (2, 4; 4, 4). Paul eventually joined the community at Antioch (11, 25–26), which subsequently commissioned him and Barnabas to undertake the spread of the gospel to Asia Minor. This missionary venture generally failed to win the Jews of the diaspora to the gospel but enjoyed success among the Gentiles (13, 14—14, 27).

Paul's refusal to impose the Mosaic law upon his Gentile converts provoked very strong objection among the Jewish Christians of Jerusalem (15, 1), but both Peter and James supported his position (15, 6–21). Paul's second and third missionary journeys (16, 36—21, 16) resulted in the same pattern of failure among the Jews generally but of some success among the Gentiles. Paul, like Peter, is presented as a miracle worker (14, 8–18; 19, 12; 20, 7–12; 28, 7–10) and the object of divine care (16, 25–31).

In Acts, Luke has provided a broad survey of the church's development from the resurrection of Jesus to Paul's first Roman imprisonment, the point at which the book ends. In telling this story, Luke describes the emergence of Christianity from its origins in Judaism to its position as a religion of worldwide status and appeal. Originally a Jewish Christian community in Jerusalem, the church was placed in circumstances impelling it to include within its membership people of other cultures: the Samaritans (8, 4–25), at first an occasional Gentile (8, 26–30; 10, 1–48), and finally the Gentiles on principle (11, 20–21). Fear on the part of the Jewish people that Christianity, particularly as preached to the Gentiles, threatened their own cultural heritage caused them to be suspicious of Paul's gospel (13, 42–45; 15, 1–5; 28, 17–24). The inability of Christian missionaries to allay this apprehension inevitably created a situation in which the gospel was preached more and more to the Gentiles. Toward the end of Paul's career, the Christian communities, with the exception of those in Palestine itself (9, 31), were mainly of Gentile membership. In tracing the emergence of Christianity from Judaism, Luke is insistent upon the prominence of Israel in the divine plan of salvation (see the note on 1, 26; see also 2, 5–6; 3, 13–15; 10, 36; 13, 16–41; 24, 14–15) and that the extension of salvation to the Gentiles has been a part of the divine plan from the beginning (see 15, 13–18; 26, 22–23).

In the development of the church from a Jewish Christian origin in Jerusalem, with its roots in Jewish religious tradition, to a series of Christian communities among the Gentiles of the Roman empire, Luke perceives the action of God in history laying open the heart of all humanity to the divine message of salvation. His approach to the history of the church is motivated by his theological interests. His history of the apostolic church is the story of a Spirit-guided community and a Spirit-guided spread of the Word of God (1, 8). The travels of Peter and Paul are in reality the travels of the Word of God as it spreads from Jerusalem, the city of destiny for Jesus, to Rome, the capital of the civilized world of Luke's day. Nonetheless, the historical data he utilizes are of value for the understanding of the church's early life and development and as general background to the Pauline epistles. In the interpretation of Acts, care must be exercised to determine Luke's theological aims and interests and to evaluate his historical data without either exaggerating their literal accuracy or underestimating their factual worth.

Finally, an apologetic concern is evident throughout Acts. By stressing the continuity between Judaism and Christianity (13, 16–41; 23, 6–9; 24, 10–21; 26, 2–23), Luke argues that Christianity is deserving of the same toleration accorded Judaism by Rome. Part of Paul's defense before Roman authorities is to show that Christianity is not a disturber of the peace of the Roman Empire (24, 5.12–13; 25, 7–8). Moreover, when he stands before Roman authorities, he is declared innocent of any crime against the empire (18, 13–15; 23, 29; 25, 25–27; 26, 31–32). Luke tells his story with the hope that Christianity will be treated as fairly.

Concerning the date of Acts, see the Introduction to the Gospel according to Luke.

The principal divisions of the Acts of the Apostles are the following:

I: The Preparation for the Christian Mission (1, 1—2, 13)

II: The Mission in Jerusalem (2, 14—8, 3)

III: The Mission in Judea and Samaria (8, 4—9, 43)

IV: The Inauguration of the Gentile Mission (10, 1—15, 35)

V: The Mission of Paul to the Ends of the Earth (15, 36—28, 31)

I: The Preparation For The Christian Mission

CHAPTER 1

See RG 337–38

The Promise of the Spirit. [1a]*In the first book, Theophilus, I dealt with all that Jesus did and taught [2b]until the day he was taken up, after giving instructions through the holy Spirit to the apostles whom he had chosen. [3c]*He presented himself alive to them by many proofs after he had suffered, appearing to them during forty days and speaking about the kingdom of God. [4d]*While meeting with them, he enjoined them not to depart from Jerusalem, but to wait for "the promise of the Father about which you have heard me speak; [5e]for John baptized with water, but in a few days you will be baptized with the holy Spirit."

The Ascension of Jesus. [6]*When they had gathered together they asked him, "Lord, are you at this time going to restore the kingdom to Israel?" [7f]*He answered them, "It is not for you to know the times or seasons that the Father has established by his own authority. [8g]*But you will receive power when the holy Spirit comes upon you, and you will be my witnesses in Jerusalem, throughout Judea and Samaria, and to the ends of the earth."

1, 1–26: This introductory material (1–2) connects Acts with the Gospel of Luke, shows that the apostles were instructed by the risen Jesus (3–5), points out that the parousia or second coming in glory of Jesus will occur as certainly as his ascension occurred (6–11), and lists the members of the Twelve, stressing their role as a body of divinely mandated witnesses to his life, teaching, and resurrection (12–26).

1, 3: Appearing to them during forty days: Luke considered especially sacred the interval in which the appearances and instructions of the risen Jesus occurred and expressed it therefore in terms of the sacred number forty (cf Dt 8, 2). In his gospel, however, Luke connects the ascension of Jesus with the resurrection by describing the ascension on Easter Sunday evening (Lk 24, 50–53). What should probably be understood as one event (resurrection, glorification, ascension, sending of the Spirit—the paschal mystery) has been historicized by Luke when he writes of a visible ascension of Jesus after forty days and the descent of the Spirit at Pentecost. For Luke, the ascension marks the end of the appearances of Jesus except for the extraordinary appearance to Paul. With regard to Luke's understanding of salvation history, the ascension also marks the end of the time of Jesus (Lk 24, 50–53) and signals the beginning of the time of the church.

1, 4: The promise of the Father: the holy Spirit, as is clear from the next verse. This gift of the Spirit was first promised in Jesus' final instructions to his chosen witnesses in Luke's gospel (Lk 24, 49) and formed part of the continuing instructions of the risen Jesus on the kingdom of God, of which Luke speaks in v 3.

1, 6: The question of the disciples implies that in believing Jesus to be the Christ (see the note on Lk 2, 11) they had expected him to be a political leader who would restore self-rule to Israel during his historical ministry. When this had not taken place, they ask if it is to take place at this time, the period of the church.

1, 7: This verse echoes the tradition that the precise time of the parousia is not revealed to human beings; cf Mk 13, 32; 1 Thes 5, 1–3.

1, 8: Just as Jerusalem was the city of destiny in the Gospel of Luke (the place where salvation was accomplished), so here at the beginning of Acts, Jerusalem occupies a central position. It is the starting point for the mission of the Christian disciples to "the ends of the earth," the place where the apostles were situated and the doctrinal focal point in the early days of the community (15, 2.6). **The ends of the earth:** for Luke, this means Rome.

a: Lk 1, 1-4. b: Mt 28, 19-20; Lk 24, 44-49; Jn 20, 22; 1 Tm 3, 16 c: 10, 41; 13, 31. d: Jn 14, 16.17.26. e: 11, 15; Mt 3, 11; Mk 1, 8; Lk 3, 16; Jn 1, 26; Eph 1, 13. f: Mt 24, 36; 1 Thes 5, 1-2. g: 2, 1-13; 10, 39; Is 43, 10; Mt 28, 19; Lk 24, 47-48.

⁹ʰWhen he had said this, as they were looking on, he was lifted up, and a cloud took him from their sight. ¹⁰ⁱWhile they were looking intently at the sky as he was going, suddenly two men dressed in white garments stood beside them. ¹¹ʲThey said, "Men of Galilee, why are you standing there looking at the sky? This Jesus who has been taken up from you into heaven will return in the same way as you have seen him going into heaven." ¹²ᵏThen they returned to Jerusalem from the mount called Olivet, which is near Jerusalem, a sabbath day's journey away.

The First Community in Jerusalem. ¹³When they entered the city they went to the upper room where they were staying, Peter and John and James and Andrew, Philip and Thomas, Bartholomew and Matthew, James son of Alphaeus, Simon the Zealot, and Judas son of James. ¹⁴ˡAll these devoted themselves with one accord to prayer, together with some women, and Mary the mother of Jesus, and his brothers.

The Choice of Judas's Successor. ¹⁵During those days Peter stood up in the midst of the brothers (there was a group of about one hundred and twenty persons in the one place). He said, ¹⁶ᵐ"My brothers, the scripture had to be fulfilled which the holy Spirit spoke beforehand through the mouth of David, concerning Judas, who was the guide for those who arrested Jesus. ¹⁷He was numbered among us and was allotted a share in this ministry. ¹⁸ⁿ*He bought a parcel of land with the wages of his iniquity, and falling headlong, he burst open in the middle, and all

his insides spilled out. ¹⁹This became known to everyone who lived in Jerusalem, so that the parcel of land was called in their language 'Akeldama,' that is, Field of Blood. ²⁰ᵒFor it is written in the Book of Psalms:

'Let his encampment become desolate,
    and may no one dwell in it.'

And:

'May another take his office.'

²¹Therefore, it is necessary that one of the men who accompanied us the whole time the Lord Jesus came and went among us, ²²ᵖbeginning from the baptism of John until the day on which he was taken up from us, become with us a witness to his resurrection." ²³So they proposed two, Joseph called Barsabbas, who was also known as Justus, and Matthias. ²⁴Then they prayed, "You, Lord, who know the hearts of all, show which one of these two you have chosen ²⁵to take the place in this apostolic ministry from which Judas turned away to go to his own place." ²⁶ᑫ*Then they gave lots to them, and the lot fell upon Matthias, and he was counted with the eleven apostles.

CHAPTER 2

See RG 338–39

The Coming of the Spirit. ¹ʳ*When the time for Pentecost was fulfilled, they were all in one place together. ²ˢ*And suddenly there came from the sky a noise like a strong driving wind, and it filled the entire house in which they were. ³ᵗ*Then there appeared to them tongues as of fire, which parted and

---

1, 18: Luke records a popular tradition about the death of Judas that differs from the one in Mt 27, 5, according to which Judas hanged himself. Here, although the text is not certain, Judas is depicted as purchasing a piece of property with the betrayal money and being killed on it in a fall.

1, 26: The need to replace Judas was probably dictated by the symbolism of the number twelve, recalling the twelve tribes of Israel. This symbolism also indicates that for Luke (see Lk 22, 30) the Christian church is a reconstituted Israel.

2, 1–41: Luke's pentecostal narrative consists of an introduction (1–13), a speech ascribed to Peter declaring the resurrection of Jesus and its messianic significance (14–36), and a favorable response from the audience (37–41). It is likely that the narrative telescopes events that took place over a period of time and on a less dramatic scale. The Twelve were not originally in a position to proclaim publicly the messianic office of Jesus without incurring immediate reprisal from those

religious authorities in Jerusalem who had brought about Jesus' death precisely to stem the rising tide in his favor.

2, 2: There came from the sky a noise like a strong driving wind: wind and spirit are associated in Jn 3, 8. The sound of a great rush of wind would herald a new action of God in the history of salvation.

2, 3: Tongues of fire: see Ex 19, 18 where fire symbolizes the presence of God to initiate the covenant on Sinai. Here the holy Spirit acts upon the apostles, preparing them to proclaim the new covenant with its unique gift of the Spirit (38).

h: 2 Kgs 2, 11; Mk 16, 19; Lk 24, 51. i: Jn 20, 17. j: Lk 24, 51; Eph 4, 8-10; 1 Pt 3, 22; Rv 1, 7. k: Lk 6, 14-16. l: Lk 23, 49. m: Ps 41, 10; Lk 22, 47. n: Mt 27, 3-10. o: Pss 69, 26; 109, 8; Jn 17, 12. p: 1, 8-9; 10, 39. q: Prv 16, 33. r: Lv 23, 15-21; Dt 16, 9-11. s: Jn 3, 8. t: Lk 3, 16.

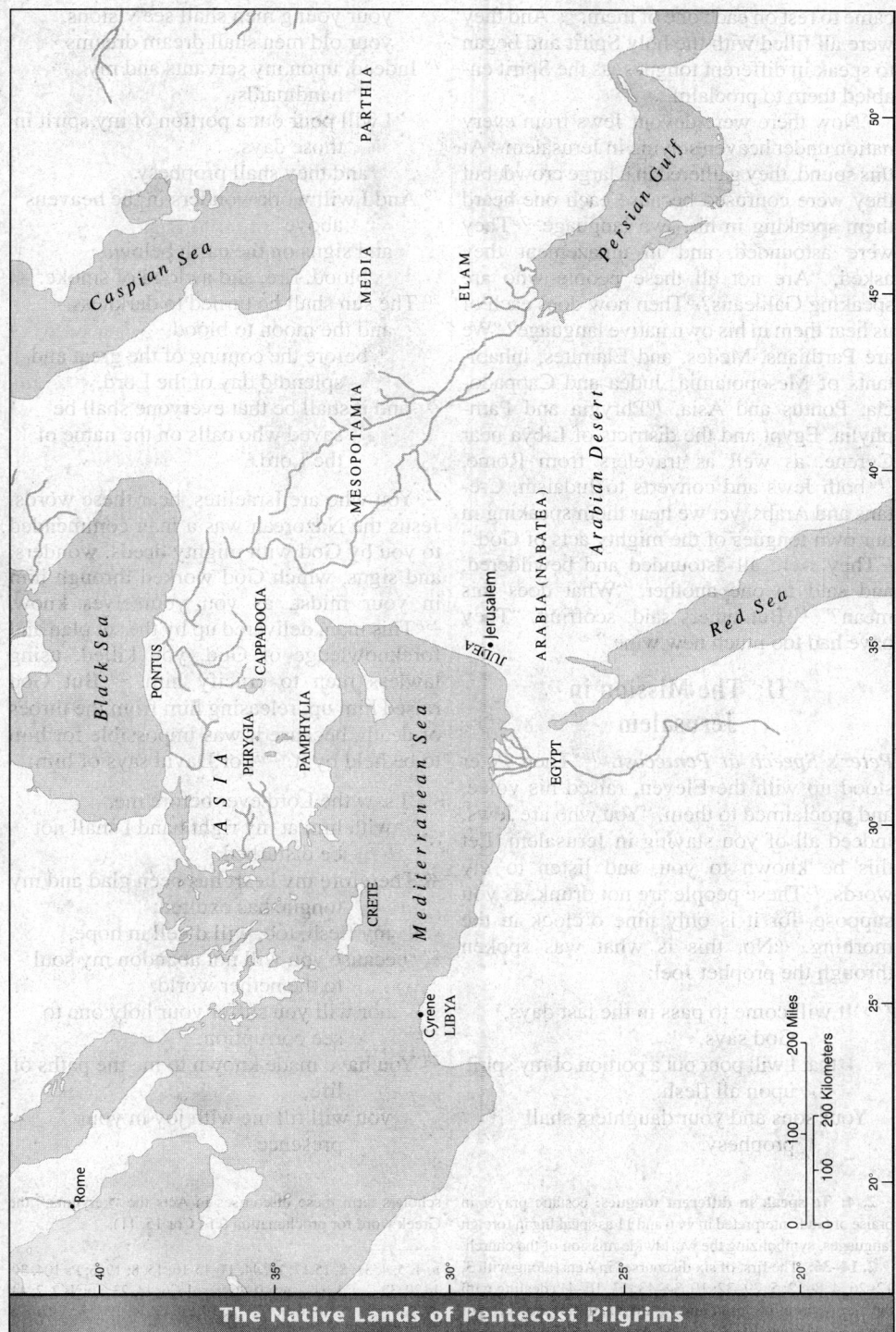

The Native Lands of Pentecost Pilgrims

came to rest on each one of them. [4u]*And they were all filled with the holy Spirit and began to speak in different tongues, as the Spirit enabled them to proclaim.

[5]Now there were devout Jews from every nation under heaven staying in Jerusalem. [6]At this sound, they gathered in a large crowd, but they were confused because each one heard them speaking in his own language. [7v]They were astounded, and in amazement they asked, "Are not all these people who are speaking Galileans? [8]Then how does each of us hear them in his own native language? [9]We are Parthians, Medes, and Elamites, inhabitants of Mesopotamia, Judea and Cappadocia, Pontus and Asia, [10]Phrygia and Pamphylia, Egypt and the districts of Libya near Cyrene, as well as travelers from Rome, [11w]both Jews and converts to Judaism, Cretans and Arabs, yet we hear them speaking in our own tongues of the mighty acts of God." [12]They were all astounded and bewildered, and said to one another, "What does this mean?" [13x]But others said, scoffing, "They have had too much new wine."

II: The Mission in Jerusalem

Peter's Speech at Pentecost. [14]*Then Peter stood up with the Eleven, raised his voice, and proclaimed to them, "You who are Jews, indeed all of you staying in Jerusalem. Let this be known to you, and listen to my words. [15]These people are not drunk, as you suppose, for it is only nine o'clock in the morning. [16]No, this is what was spoken through the prophet Joel:

[17y]'It will come to pass in the last days,'
God says,
'that I will pour out a portion of my spirit
upon all flesh.
Your sons and your daughters shall
prophesy,

your young men shall see visions,
your old men shall dream dreams.
[18] Indeed, upon my servants and my
handmaids
I will pour out a portion of my spirit in
those days,
and they shall prophesy.
[19] And I will work wonders in the heavens
above
and signs on the earth below:
blood, fire, and a cloud of smoke.
[20] The sun shall be turned to darkness,
and the moon to blood,
before the coming of the great and
splendid day of the Lord,
[21z]and it shall be that everyone shall be
saved who calls on the name of
the Lord.'

[22a]You who are Israelites, hear these words. Jesus the Nazorean was a man commended to you by God with mighty deeds, wonders, and signs, which God worked through him in your midst, as you yourselves know. [23b]This man, delivered up by the set plan and foreknowledge of God, you killed, using lawless men to crucify him. [24c]But God raised him up, releasing him from the throes of death, because it was impossible for him to be held by it. [25d]For David says of him:

'I saw the Lord ever before me,
with him at my right hand I shall not
be disturbed.
[26] Therefore my heart has been glad and my
tongue has exulted;
my flesh, too, will dwell in hope,
[27e]because you will not abandon my soul
to the nether world,
nor will you suffer your holy one to
see corruption.
[28] You have made known to me the paths of
life;
you will fill me with joy in your
presence.'

2, 4: To speak in different tongues: ecstatic prayer in praise of God, interpreted in vv 6 and 11 as speaking in foreign languages, symbolizing the worldwide mission of the church.

2, 14–36: The first of six discourses in Acts (along with 3, 12–26; 4, 8–12; 5, 29–32; 10, 34–43; 13, 16–41) dealing with the resurrection of Jesus and its messianic import. Five of these are attributed to Peter, the final one to Paul. Modern

scholars term these discourses in Acts the "kerygma," the Greek word for proclamation (cf 1 Cor 15, 11).

---

u: 1, 5; 4, 31; 8, 15.17; 10, 44; 11, 15-16; 15, 8; 19, 6; Ps 104, 30; Jn 20, 33. *v:* 1, 11. *w:* 10, 46. *x:* 1 Cor 14, 23. *y:* Is 2, 2; 44, 3; Jl 3, 1-5. *z:* Rom 10, 13. *a:* 10, 38; Lk 24, 19. *b:* 1 Thes 2, 15. *c:* 13, 34. *d:* Ps 16, 8-11. *e:* 13, 35.

²⁹My brothers, one can confidently say to you about the patriarch David that he died and was buried, and his tomb is in our midst to this day. ³⁰ᶠBut since he was a prophet and knew that God had sworn an oath to him that he would set one of his descendants upon his throne, ³¹ᵍhe foresaw and spoke of the resurrection of the Messiah, that neither was he abandoned to the netherworld nor did his flesh see corruption. ³²God raised this Jesus; of this we are all witnesses. ³³ʰ*Exalted at the right hand of God, he received the promise of the holy Spirit from the Father and poured it forth, as you [both] see and hear. ³⁴ⁱFor David did not go up into heaven, but he himself said:

'The Lord said to my Lord,
"Sit at my right hand
³⁵   until I make your enemies your
        footstool." '

³⁶ʲTherefore let the whole house of Israel know for certain that God has made him both Lord and Messiah, this Jesus whom you crucified."

³⁷ᵏNow when they heard this, they were cut to the heart, and they asked Peter and the other apostles, "What are we to do, my brothers?" ³⁸ˡ*Peter [said] to them, "Repent and be baptized, every one of you, in the name of Jesus Christ for the forgiveness of your sins;

and you will receive the gift of the holy Spirit. ³⁹ᵐFor the promise is made to you and to your children and to all those far off, whomever the Lord our God will call." ⁴⁰ⁿHe testified with many other arguments, and was exhorting them, "Save yourselves from this corrupt generation." ⁴¹ᵒThose who accepted his message were baptized, and about three thousand persons were added that day.

Communal Life. ⁴²ᵖᑫ*They devoted themselves to the teaching of the apostles and to the communal life, to the breaking of the bread and to the prayers. ⁴³ʳAwe came upon everyone, and many wonders and signs were done through the apostles. ⁴⁴ˢAll who believed were together and had all things in common; ⁴⁵they would sell their property and possessions and divide them among all according to each one's need. ⁴⁶Every day they devoted themselves to meeting together in the temple area and to breaking bread in their homes. They ate their meals with exultation and sincerity of heart, ⁴⁷praising God and enjoying favor with all the people And every day the Lord added to their number those who were being saved.

CHAPTER 3

See RG 338-39

Cure of a Crippled Beggar. ¹*Now Peter and John were going up to the temple

2, 33: **At the right hand of God:** or "by the right hand of God."

2, 38: **Repent and be baptized:** repentance is a positive concept, a change of mind and heart toward God reflected in the actual goodness of one's life. It is in accord with the apostolic teaching derived from Jesus (42) and ultimately recorded in the four gospels. Luke presents baptism in Acts as the expected response to the apostolic preaching about Jesus and associates it with the conferring of the Spirit (1, 5; 10, 44–48; 11, 16).

2, 42–47: The first of three summary passages (along with 4, 32–37 and 5, 12–16) that outline, somewhat idyllically, the chief characteristics of the Jerusalem community: adherence to the teachings of the Twelve and the centering of its religious life in the eucharistic liturgy (42); a system of distribution of goods that led wealthier Christians to sell their possessions when the needs of the community's poor required it (44 and the note on 4, 32–37); and continued attendance at the temple, since in this initial stage there was little or no thought of any dividing line between Christianity and Judaism (46).

3, 1—4, 31: This section presents a series of related events: the dramatic cure of a lame beggar (3, 1–10) produces a large audience for the kerygmatic discourse of Peter (3, 11–26). The Sadducees, taking exception to the doctrine of

resurrection, have Peter, John, and apparently the beggar as well, arrested (4, 1–4) and brought to trial before the Sanhedrin. The issue concerns the authority by which Peter and John publicly teach religious doctrine in the temple (4, 5–7). Peter replies with a brief summary of the kerygma, implying that his authority is prophetic (4, 8–12). The court warns the apostles to abandon their practice of invoking prophetic authority in the name of Jesus (4, 13–18). When Peter and John reply that the prophetic role cannot be abandoned to satisfy human objections, the court nevertheless releases them, afraid to do otherwise since the beggar, lame from birth and over forty years old, is a well-known figure in Jerusalem and the facts of his cure are common property (4, 19–22). The narrative concludes with a prayer of the Christian community imploring divine aid against threats of persecution (4, 23–31).

3, 1: **For the three o'clock hour of prayer:** literally, "at the ninth hour of prayer." With the day beginning at 6 a.m., the ninth hour would be 3 p.m.

f: 2 Sm 7, 12; Ps 132, 11.   g: 13, 35; Ps 16, 10.   h: 1, 4-5.   i: Ps 110, 1.   j: 9, 22; Rom 10, 9; Phil 2, 11.   k: Lk 3, 10.   l: 5, 19; 16, 31; Lk 3, 3.   m: Is 57, 19; Jl 3, 5; Eph 2, 17.   n: Dt 32, 5; Ps 78, 8; Lk 9, 41; Phil 2, 15.   o: 2, 47; 4, 4; 5, 14; 6, 7; 11, 21.24; 21, 20.   p: 4, 32-35.   q: 1, 14; 6, 4.   r: 5, 12-16.   s: 4, 32.34-35.

area for the three o'clock hour of prayer. [2t]And a man crippled from birth was carried and placed at the gate of the temple called "the Beautiful Gate" every day to beg for alms from the people who entered the temple. [3]When he saw Peter and John about to go into the temple, he asked for alms. [4]But Peter looked intently at him, as did John, and said, "Look at us." [5]He paid attention to them, expecting to receive something from them. [6u]*Peter said, "I have neither silver nor gold, but what I do have I give you: in the name of Jesus Christ the Nazorean, [rise and] walk." [7]Then Peter took him by the right hand and raised him up, and immediately his feet and ankles grew strong. [8v]He leaped up, stood, and walked around, and went into the temple with them, walking and jumping and praising God. [9]When all the people saw him walking and praising God, [10]they recognized him as the one who used to sit begging at the Beautiful Gate of the temple, and they were filled with amazement and astonishment at what had happened to him.

Peter's Speech. [11w]As he clung to Peter and John, all the people hurried in amazement toward them in the portico called "Solomon's Portico." [12x]When Peter saw

this, he addressed the people, "You Israelites, why are you amazed at this, and why do you look so intently at us as if we had made him walk by our own power or piety? [13y]*The God of Abraham, [the God] of Isaac, and [the God] of Jacob, the God of our ancestors, has glorified his servant Jesus whom you handed over and denied in Pilate's presence, when he had decided to release him. [14z]*You denied the Holy and Righteous One and asked that a murderer be released to you. [15a]*The author of life you put to death, but God raised him from the dead; of this we are witnesses. [16]And by faith in his name, this man, whom you see and know, his name has made strong, and the faith that comes through it has given him this perfect health, in the presence of all of you. [17b]*Now I know, brothers, that you acted out of ignorance, just as your leaders did; [18c]*but God has thus brought to fulfillment what he had announced beforehand through the mouth of all the prophets, that his Messiah would suffer. [19d]Repent, therefore, and be converted, that your sins may be wiped away, [20]*and that the Lord may grant you times of refreshment and send you the Messiah already appointed for you, Jesus, [21]*whom heaven must receive until the times of universal

3, 6–10: The miracle has a dramatic cast; it symbolizes the saving power of Christ and leads the beggar to enter the temple, where he hears Peter's proclamation of salvation through Jesus.

3, 13: Has glorified: through the resurrection and ascension of Jesus, God reversed the judgment against him on the occasion of his trial. **Servant:** the Greek word can also be rendered as "son" or even "child" here and also in 3, 26; 4, 25 (applied to David); 4, 27; and 4, 30. Scholars are of the opinion, however, that the original concept reflected in the words identified Jesus with the suffering Servant of the Lord of Is 52, 13—53, 12.

3, 14: The Holy and Righteous One: so designating Jesus emphasizes his special relationship to the Father (see Lk 1, 35; 4, 34) and emphasizes his sinlessness and religious dignity that are placed in sharp contrast with the guilt of those who rejected him in favor of Barabbas.

3, 15: The author of life: other possible translations of the Greek title are "leader of life" or "pioneer of life." The title clearly points to Jesus as the source and originator of salvation.

3, 17: Ignorance: a Lucan motif, explaining away the actions not only of the people but also of their leaders in crucifying Jesus. On this basis the presbyters in Acts could continue to appeal to the Jews in Jerusalem to believe in Jesus, even while affirming their involvement in his death because they were unaware of his messianic dignity. See also 13, 27 and Lk 23, 34.

3, 18: Through the mouth of all the prophets: Christian

prophetic insight into the Old Testament saw the crucifixion and death of Jesus as the main import of messianic prophecy. The Jews themselves did not anticipate a suffering Messiah; they usually understood the Servant Song in Is 52, 13—53, 12 to signify their own suffering as a people. In his typical fashion (cf Lk 18, 31; 24, 25.27.44), Luke does not specify the particular Old Testament prophecies that were fulfilled by Jesus. See also the note on Lk 24, 26.

3, 20: The Lord . . . and send you the Messiah already appointed for you, Jesus: an allusion to the parousia or second coming of Christ, judged to be imminent in the apostolic age. This reference to its nearness is the only explicit one in Acts. Some scholars believe that this verse preserves a very early christology, in which the title "Messiah" (Greek "Christ") is applied to him as of his parousia, his second coming (contrast 2, 36). This view of a future messiahship of Jesus is not found elsewhere in the New Testament.

3, 21: The times of universal restoration: like "the times of refreshment" (20), an apocalyptic designation of the messianic age, fitting in with the christology of v 20 that associates the messiahship of Jesus with his future coming.

t: 14, 8-10.   u: 4, 10.   v: Is 35, 6; Lk 7, 22.   w: 5, 12; Jn 10, 23. x: 14, 15.   y: Ex 3, 6.15; Is 52, 13; Lk 23, 14-25.   z: Mt 27, 20-21; Mk 15, 11; Lk 23, 18; Jn 18, 40.   a: 4, 10; 5, 31 / 1, 8; 2, 32.   b: 13, 27; Lk 23, 34; 1 Cor 2, 8; 1 Tm 1, 13.   c: Lk 18, 31.   d: 2, 38.

restoration of which God spoke through the mouth of his holy prophets from of old. [22e]*For Moses said:

'A prophet like me will the Lord, your God, raise up for you
from among your own kinsmen;
to him you shall listen in all that he may say to you.
[23] [f]Everyone who does not listen to that prophet
will be cut off from the people.'

[24]Moreover, all the prophets who spoke, from Samuel and those afterwards, also announced these days. [25g]You are the children of the prophets and of the covenant that God made with your ancestors when he said to Abraham, 'In your offspring all the families of the earth shall be blessed.' [26h]For you first, God raised up his servant and sent him to bless you by turning each of you from your evil ways."

See RG 339

CHAPTER 4

[1]*While they were still speaking to the people, the priests, the captain of the temple guard, and the Sadducees confronted them, [2i]disturbed that they were teaching the people and proclaiming in Jesus the resurrection of the dead. [3]They laid hands on them and put them in custody until the next day, since it was already evening. [4]But many of those who heard the word came to believe and [the] number of men grew to [about] five thousand.

Before the Sanhedrin. [5]On the next day, their leaders, elders, and scribes were assembled in Jerusalem, [6]with Annas the high priest, Caiaphas, John, Alexander, and all who were of the high-priestly class. [7]They brought them into their presence and questioned them, "By what power or by what name have you done this?" [8j]Then Peter, filled with the holy Spirit, answered them, "Leaders of the people and elders: [9]If we are being examined today about a good deed done to a cripple, namely, by what means he was saved, [10]then all of you and all the people of Israel should know that it was in the name of Jesus Christ the Nazorean whom you crucified, whom God raised from the dead; in his name this man stands before you healed. [11k]*He is 'the stone rejected by you, the builders, which has become the cornerstone.' [12l]*There is no salvation through anyone else, nor is there any other name under heaven given to the human race by which we are to be saved."

[13]Observing the boldness of Peter and John and perceiving them to be uneducated, ordinary men, they were amazed, and they recognized them as the companions of Jesus. [14]Then when they saw the man who had been cured standing there with them, they could say nothing in reply. [15]So they ordered them to leave the Sanhedrin, and conferred with one another, saying, [16]"What are we to do with these men? Everyone living in Jerusalem knows that a remarkable sign was done through them, and we cannot deny it. [17m]But so that it may not be spread any further among the people, let us give them a stern warning never again to speak to anyone in this name."

[18]So they called them back and ordered them not to speak or teach at all in the name of Jesus. [19n]Peter and John, however, said to them in reply, "Whether it is right in the sight of God for us to obey you rather than

---

3, 22: A loose citation of Dt 18, 15, which teaches that the Israelites are to learn the will of Yahweh from no one but their prophets. At the time of Jesus, some Jews expected a unique prophet to come in fulfillment of this text. Early Christianity applied this tradition and text to Jesus and used them especially in defense of the divergence of Christian teaching from traditional Judaism.

4, 1: **The priests, the captain of the temple guard, and the Sadducees:** the priests performed the temple liturgy; the temple guard was composed of Levites, whose captain ranked next after the high priest. The Sadducees, a party within Judaism at this time, rejected those doctrines, including bodily resurrection, which they believed alien to the ancient Mosaic religion. The Sadducees were drawn from

priestly families and from the lay aristocracy.

4, 11: Early Christianity applied this citation from Ps 118, 22 to Jesus; cf Mk 12, 10; 1 Pt 2, 7.

4, 12: In the Roman world of Luke's day, salvation was often attributed to the emperor who was hailed as "savior" and "god." Luke, in the words of Peter, denies that deliverance comes through anyone other than Jesus.

---

e: 7, 37; Dt 18, 15.18. *f:* Lv 23, 29; Dt 18, 19. *g:* Gn 12, 3; 18, 18; 22, 18; Sir 44, 19-21; Gal 3, 8-9. *h:* 13, 46; Rom 1, 16. *i:* 23, 6-8; 24, 21. *j:* Mt 10, 20. *k:* Ps 118, 22; Is 28, 16; Mt 21, 42; Mk 12, 10; Lk 20, 17; Rom 9, 33; 1 Pt 2, 7. *l:* Mt 1, 21; 1 Cor 3, 11. *m:* 5, 28. *n:* 5, 29-32.

God, you be the judges. 20It is impossible for us not to speak about what we have seen and heard." 21After threatening them further, they released them, finding no way to punish them, on account of the people who were all praising God for what had happened. 22For the man on whom this sign of healing had been done was over forty years old.

Prayer of the Community. 23After their release they went back to their own people and reported what the chief priests and elders had told them. 24And when they heard it, they raised their voices to God with one accord and said, "Sovereign Lord, maker of heaven and earth and the sea and all that is in them, 25ayou said by the holy Spirit through the mouth of our father David, your servant:

'Why did the Gentiles rage
        and the peoples entertain folly?
26 The kings of the earth took their stand
        and the princes gathered together
            against the Lord and against his
            anointed.'

27p*Indeed they gathered in this city against your holy servant Jesus whom you anointed, Herod and Pontius Pilate, together with the Gentiles and the peoples of Israel, 28to do what your hand and [your] will had long ago planned to take place. 29And now, Lord, take note of their threats, and enable your servants to speak your word with all boldness, 30as you stretch forth [your] hand to heal, and signs and wonders are done through the name of your holy servant Jesus." 31q*As they prayed, the place where they were gathered shook, and they were all filled with the holy Spirit and continued to speak the word of God with boldness.

Life in the Christian Community. 32*The community of believers was of one heart and mind, and no one claimed that any of his possessions was his own, but they had everything in common. 33With great power the apostles bore witness to the resurrection of the Lord Jesus, and great favor was accorded them all. 34rThere was no needy person among them, for those who owned property or houses would sell them, bring the proceeds of the sale, 35and put them at the feet of the apostles, and they were distributed to each according to need.

36sThus Joseph, also named by the apostles Barnabas (which is translated "son of encouragement"), a Levite, a Cypriot by birth, 37sold a piece of property that he owned, then brought the money and put it at the feet of the apostles.

CHAPTER 5

See RG 339

Ananias and Sapphira. 1*A man named Ananias, however, with his wife Sapphira, sold a piece of property. 2He retained for himself, with his wife's knowledge, some of the purchase price, took the remainder, and put it at the feet of the apostles. 3tBut Peter said, "Ananias, why has Satan filled your heart so that you lied to the holy Spirit and retained part of the price of the land? 4While it remained unsold, did it not remain yours? And when it was sold, was it not still under your control? Why did you contrive this deed? You have lied not to human beings, but to God." 5When Ananias heard these words, he fell down and breathed his last,

---

4, 27: Herod: Herod Antipas, ruler of Galilee and Perea from 4 B.C. to A.D. 39, who executed John the Baptist and before whom Jesus was arraigned; cf Lk 23, 6–12.

4, 31: The place . . . shook: the earthquake is used as a sign of the divine presence in Ex 19, 18; Is 6, 4. Here the shaking of the building symbolizes God's favorable response to the prayer. Luke may have had as an additional reason for using the symbol the fact that it was familiar in the Hellenistic world. Ovid and Virgil also employ it.

4, 32–37: This is the second summary characterizing the Jerusalem community (see the note on 2, 42–47). It emphasizes the system of the distribution of goods and introduces Barnabas, who appears later in Acts as the friend and companion of Paul, and who, as noted here (37), endeared himself to the community by a donation of money through the sale of property. This sharing of material possessions continues a practice that Luke describes during the historical ministry of Jesus (Lk 8, 3) and is in accord with the sayings of Jesus in Luke's gospel (Lk 12, 33; 16, 9.11.13).

5, 1–11: The sin of Ananias and Sapphira did not consist in the withholding of part of the money but in their deception of the community. Their deaths are ascribed to a lie to the holy Spirit (3.9), i.e., they accepted the honor accorded them by the community for their generosity, but in reality they were not deserving of it.

---

o: Ps 2, 1-2.   p: Lk 23, 12-13.   q: 2, 4.   r: 2, 44-45.   s: 9, 27; 11, 22.30; 12, 25; 13, 15; 1 Cor 9, 6; Gal 2, 1.9.13; Col 4, 10.   t: Lk 22, 3; Jn 13, 2.

1516

and great fear came upon all who heard of it. [6]The young men came and wrapped him up, then carried him out and buried him.

[7]After an interval of about three hours, his wife came in, unaware of what had happened. [8]Peter said to her, "Tell me, did you sell the land for this amount?" She answered, "Yes, for that amount." [9]Then Peter said to her, "Why did you agree to test the Spirit of the Lord? Listen, the footsteps of those who have buried your husband are at the door, and they will carry you out." [10]At once, she fell down at his feet and breathed her last. When the young men entered they found her dead, so they carried her out and buried her beside her husband. [11u]And great fear came upon the whole church and upon all who heard of these things.

Signs and Wonders of the Apostles. [12v]*Many signs and wonders were done among the people at the hands of the apostles. They were all together in Solomon's portico. [13]None of the others dared to join them, but the people esteemed them. [14]Yet more than ever, believers in the Lord, great numbers of men and women, were added to them. [15w]Thus they even carried the sick out into the streets and laid them on cots and mats so that when Peter came by, at least his shadow might fall on one or another of them. [16]A large number of people from the towns in the vicinity of Jerusalem also gathered, bringing the sick and those disturbed by unclean spirits, and they were all cured.

Trial before the Sanhedrin. [17x]*Then the high priest rose up and all his companions, that is, the party of the Sadducees, and, filled with jealousy, [18]laid hands upon the apostles and put them in the public jail. [19y]But during the night, the angel of the Lord opened the doors of the prison, led them out, and said, [20]"Go and take your place in the temple area, and tell the people everything about this life." [21]When they heard this, they went to the temple early in the morning and taught. When the high priest and his companions arrived, they convened the Sanhedrin, the full senate of the Israelites, and sent to the jail to have them brought in. [22]But the court officers who went did not find them in the prison, so they came back and reported, [23]"We found the jail securely locked and the guards stationed outside the doors, but when we opened them, we found no one inside." [24]When they heard this report, the captain of the temple guard and the chief priests were at a loss about them, as to what this would come to. [25]Then someone came in and reported to them, "The men whom you put in prison are in the temple area and are teaching the people." [26z]Then the captain and the court officers went and brought them in, but without force, because they were afraid of being stoned by the people.

[27]When they had brought them in and made them stand before the Sanhedrin, the high priest questioned them, [28a]"We gave you strict orders [did we not?] to stop teaching in that name. Yet you have filled Jerusalem with your teaching and want to bring this man's blood upon us." [29b]But Peter and the apostles said in reply, "We must obey God rather than men. [30c]*The God of our ancestors raised Jesus, though you had him killed by hanging him on a tree. [31d]*God exalted him at his right hand as leader and savior to grant Israel repentance and forgive-

---

5, 12–16: This, the third summary portraying the Jerusalem community, underscores the Twelve as its bulwark, especially because of their charismatic power to heal the sick; cf 2, 42–47; 4, 32–37.

5, 17–42: A second action against the community is taken by the Sanhedrin in the arrest and trial of the Twelve; cf 4, 1–3. The motive is the jealousy of the religious authorities over the popularity of the apostles (17) who are now charged with the defiance of the Sanhedrin's previous order to them to abandon their prophetic role (28; cf 4, 18). In this crisis the apostles are favored by a miraculous release from prison (18–24). (For similar incidents involving Peter and Paul, see 12, 6–11; 16, 25–29.) The real significance of such an event, however, would be manifest only to people of faith, not to unbelievers; since the Sanhedrin already judged

the Twelve to be inauthentic prophets, it could disregard reports of their miracles. When the Twelve immediately resumed public teaching, the Sanhedrin determined to invoke upon them the penalty of death (33) prescribed in Dt 13, 6–10. Gamaliel's advice against this course finally prevailed, but it did not save the Twelve from the punishment of scourging (40) in a last endeavor to shake their conviction of their prophetic mission.

5, 30: Hanging him on a tree: that is, crucifying him (cf also Gal 3, 13).

5, 31: At his right hand: see the note on 2, 33.

u: 2, 43; 5, 5; 19, 17.   v: 2, 43; 6, 8; 14, 3; 15, 12.   w: 19, 11-12; Mk 6, 56.   x: 4, 1-3.6.   y: 12, 7-10; 16, 25-26.   z: Lk 20, 19. a: Mt 27, 25.   b: 4, 19.   c: 2, 23-24.   d: 2, 38.

ness of sins. *32e*We are witnesses of these things, as is the holy Spirit that God has given to those who obey him."

*33*When they heard this, they became infuriated and wanted to put them to death. *34f*But a Pharisee in the Sanhedrin named Gamaliel, a teacher of the law, respected by all the people, stood up, ordered the men to be put outside for a short time, *35*and said to them, "Fellow Israelites, be careful what you are about to do to these men. *36*Some time ago, Theudas appeared, claiming to be someone important, and about four hundred men joined him, but he was killed, and all those who were loyal to him were disbanded and came to nothing. *37*After him came Judas the Galilean at the time of the census. He also drew people after him, but he too perished and all who were loyal to him were scattered. *38*So now I tell you, have nothing to do with these men, and let them go. For if this endeavor or this activity is of human origin, it will destroy itself. *39*But if it comes from God, you will not be able to destroy them; you may even find yourselves fighting against God." They were persuaded by him. *40g*After recalling the apostles, they had them flogged, ordered them to stop speaking in the name of Jesus, and dismissed them. *41h*So they left the presence of the Sanhedrin, rejoicing that they had been found worthy to suffer dishonor for the sake of the name. *42i*And all day long, both at the temple and in their homes, they did not stop teaching and proclaiming the Messiah, Jesus.

CHAPTER 6

See RG 339-41

The Need for Assistants. *1j*At that time, as the number of disciples continued to grow, the Hellenists complained against the Hebrews because their widows were being neglected in the daily distribution. *2*So the Twelve called together the community of the disciples and said, "It is not right for us to neglect the word of God to serve at table. *3*Brothers, select from among you seven reputable men, filled with the Spirit and wisdom, whom we shall appoint to this task, *4*whereas we shall devote ourselves to prayer and to the ministry of the word." *5*The proposal was acceptable to the whole community, so they chose Stephen, a man filled with faith and the holy Spirit, also Philip, Prochorus, Nicanor, Timon, Parmenas, and Nicholas of Antioch, a convert to Judaism. *6k*They presented these men to the apostles who prayed and laid hands on them. *7l*The word of God continued to spread, and the number of the disciples in Jerusalem increased greatly; even a large group of priests were becoming obedient to the faith.

Accusation against Stephen. *8*Now Ste-

5, 34: Gamaliel: in 22, 3, Paul identifies himself as a disciple of this Rabbi Gamaliel I who flourished in Jerusalem between A.D. 25 and 50.

5, 36–37: Gamaliel offers examples of unsuccessful contemporary movements to argue that if God is not the origin of this movement preached by the apostles it will perish by itself. The movement initiated by Theudas actually occurred when C. Cuspius Fadus was governor, A.D. 44–46. Luke's placing of Judas the Galilean after Theudas and at the time of the census (see the note on Lk 2, 1–2) is an indication of the vagueness of his knowledge of these events.

6, 1–7: The Hellenists . . . the Hebrews: the Hellenists were not necessarily Jews from the diaspora, but were more probably Palestinian Jews who spoke only Greek. The Hebrews were Palestinian Jews who spoke Hebrew or Aramaic and who may also have spoken Greek. Both groups belong to the Jerusalem Jewish Christian community. The conflict between them leads to a restructuring of the community that will better serve the community's needs. The real purpose of the whole episode, however, is to introduce Stephen as a prominent figure in the community whose long speech and martyrdom will be recounted in ch 7.

6, 2–4: The essential function of the Twelve is the "service

of the word," including development of the kerygma by formulation of the teachings of Jesus.

6, 2: To serve at table: some commentators think that it is not the serving of food that is described here but rather the keeping of the accounts that recorded the distribution of food to the needy members of the community. In any case, after Stephen and the others are chosen, they are never presented carrying out the task for which they were appointed (2–3). Rather, two of their number, Stephen and Philip, are presented as preachers of the Christian message. They, the Hellenist counterpart of the Twelve, are active in the ministry of the word.

6, 6: They . . . laid hands on them: the customary Jewish way of designating persons for a task and invoking upon them the divine blessing and power to perform it.

6, 8—8, 1: The summary (6, 7) on the progress of the Jerusalem community, illustrated by the conversion of the priests, is followed by a lengthy narrative regarding Stephen. Stephen's defense is not a response to the charges made

e: Lk 24, 48; Jn 15, 26. *f:* 22, 3. *g:* Mt 10, 17; Acts 4, 17-18. *h:* Mt 5, 10-11; 1 Pt 4, 13. *i:* 2, 46; 5, 20-21.25; 8, 35; 17, 3; 18, 5.28; 19, 4-5. *j:* 2, 45; 4, 34-35. *k:* 1, 24; 13, 3; 14, 23. *l:* 9, 31; 12, 24; 16, 5; 19, 20; 28, 30-31.

phen, filled with grace and power, was working great wonders and signs among the people. [9]Certain members of the so-called Synagogue of Freedmen, Cyrenians, and Alexandrians, and people from Cilicia and Asia, came forward and debated with Stephen, [10m]but they could not withstand the wisdom and the spirit with which he spoke. [11n]Then they instigated some men to say, "We have heard him speaking blasphemous words against Moses and God." [12]They stirred up the people, the elders, and the scribes, accosted him, seized him, and brought him before the Sanhedrin. [13*]They presented false witnesses who testified, "This man never stops saying things against [this] holy place and the law. [14o]For we have heard him claim that this Jesus the Nazorean will destroy this place and change the customs that Moses handed down to us." [15]All those who sat in the Sanhedrin looked intently at him and saw that his face was like the face of an angel.

CHAPTER 7

See RG 340-41

Stephen's Discourses. [1]Then the high priest asked, "Is this so?" [2p*]And he replied, "My brothers and fathers, listen. The God of glory appeared to our father Abraham while he was in Mesopotamia, before he had settled in Haran, [3q]and said to him, 'Go forth from your land and [from] your kinsfolk to the land that I will show you.' [4r]So he went forth from the land of the Chaldeans and set-

tled in Haran. And from there, after his father died, he made him migrate to this land where you now dwell. [5s]Yet he gave him no inheritance in it, not even a foot's length, but he did promise to give it to him and his descendants as a possession, even though he was childless. [6t]And God spoke thus, 'His descendants shall be aliens in a land not their own, where they shall be enslaved and oppressed for four hundred years; [7u]but I will bring judgment on the nation they serve,' God said, 'and after that they will come out and worship me in this place.' [8v]Then he gave him the covenant of circumcision, and so he became the father of Isaac, and circumcised him on the eighth day, as Isaac did Jacob, and Jacob the twelve patriarchs.

[9w]"And the patriarchs, jealous of Joseph, sold him into slavery in Egypt; but God was with him [10x]and rescued him from all his afflictions. He granted him favor and wisdom before Pharaoh, the king of Egypt, who put him in charge of Egypt and [of] his entire household. [11y]Then a famine and great affliction struck all Egypt and Canaan, and our ancestors could find no food; [12z]but when Jacob heard that there was grain in Egypt, he sent our ancestors there a first time. [13a]The second time, Joseph made himself known to his brothers, and Joseph's family became known to Pharaoh. [14b]Then Joseph sent for his father Jacob, inviting him and his whole clan, seventy-five persons; [15c]and Jacob

---

against him but takes the form of a discourse that reviews the fortunes of God's word to Israel and leads to a prophetic declaration: a plea for the hearing of that word as announced by Christ and now possessed by the Christian community.

The charges that Stephen depreciated the importance of the temple and the Mosaic law and elevated Jesus to a stature above Moses (6, 13–14) were in fact true. Before the Sanhedrin, no defense against them was possible. With Stephen, who thus perceived the fuller implications of the teachings of Jesus, the differences between Judaism and Christianity began to appear. Luke's account of Stephen's martyrdom and its aftermath shows how the major impetus behind the Christian movement passed from Jerusalem, where the temple and law prevailed, to Antioch in Syria, where these influences were less pressing.

6, 13: False witnesses: here, and in his account of Stephen's execution (7, 54–60), Luke parallels the martyrdom of Stephen with the death of Jesus.

7, 2–53: Stephen's speech represents Luke's description of Christianity's break from its Jewish matrix. Two motifs become prominent in the speech: (1) Israel's reaction to God's chosen

leaders in the past reveals that the people have consistently rejected them; and (2) Israel has misunderstood God's choice of the Jerusalem temple as the place where he is to be worshiped.

7, 2: God . . . appeared to our father Abraham . . . in Mesopotamia: the first of a number of minor discrepancies between the data of the Old Testament and the data of Stephen's discourse. According to Gn 12, 1, God first spoke to Abraham in Haran. The main discrepancies are these: in v 16 it is said that Jacob was buried in Shechem, whereas Gn 50, 13 says he was buried at Hebron; in the same verse it is said that the tomb was purchased by Abraham, but in Gn 33, 19 and Jos 24, 32 the purchase is attributed to Jacob himself.

---

m: Lk 21, 15. **n:** Mt 26, 59-61; Mk 14, 55-58; Acts 21, 21. **o:** Mt 26, 59-61; 27, 40; Jn 2, 19. **p:** Gn 11, 31; 12, 1; Ps 29, 3. **q:** Gn 12, 1. **r:** Gn 12, 5; 15, 7. **s:** Gn 12, 7; 13, 15; 15 2; 16, 1; Dt 2, 5. **t:** Gn 15, 13-14. **u:** Ex 3, 12. **v:** Gn 17, 10-14; 21, 2-4. **w:** Gn 37, 11.28; 39, 2.3.21.23. **x:** Gn 41, 37-43; Ps 105, 21; Wis 10, 13-14. **y:** Gn 41, 54-57; 42, 5. **z:** Gn 42, 1-2. **a:** Gn 45, 3-4.16. **b:** Gn 45, 9-11.18-19; 46, 27; Ex 1, 5 LXX; Dt 10, 22. **c:** Gn 46, 5-6; 49, 33.

went down to Egypt. And he and our ancestors died [16d] and were brought back to Shechem and placed in the tomb that Abraham had purchased for a sum of money from the sons of Hamor at Shechem.

[17e]"When the time drew near for the fulfillment of the promise that God pledged to Abraham, the people had increased and become very numerous in Egypt, [18f]until another king who knew nothing of Joseph came to power [in Egypt]. [19]He dealt shrewdly with our people and oppressed [our] ancestors by forcing them to expose their infants, that they might not survive. [20g]At this time Moses was born, and he was extremely beautiful. For three months he was nursed in his father's house; [21h]but when he was exposed, Pharaoh's daughter adopted him and brought him up as her own son. [22]Moses was educated [in] all the wisdom of the Egyptians and was powerful in his words and deeds.

[23i]"When he was forty years old, he decided to visit his kinsfolk, the Israelites. [24]When he saw one of them treated unjustly, he defended and avenged the oppressed man by striking down the Egyptian. [25]He assumed [his] kinsfolk would understand that God was offering them deliverance through him, but they did not understand. [26j]The next day he appeared to them as they were fighting and tried to reconcile them peacefully, saying, 'Men, you are brothers. Why are you harming one another?' [27]Then the one who was harming his neighbor pushed him aside, saying, 'Who appointed you ruler and judge over us? [28]Are you thinking of killing me as you killed the Egyptian yesterday?' [29k]Moses fled when he heard this and settled as an alien in the land of Midian, where he became the father of two sons.

[30l]"Forty years later, an angel appeared to him in the desert near Mount Sinai in the flame of a burning bush. [31]When Moses saw it, he was amazed at the sight, and as he drew near to look at it, the voice of the Lord came, [32]'I am the God of your fathers, the God of Abraham, of Isaac, and of Jacob.' Then Moses, trembling, did not dare to look at it. [33]But the Lord said to him, 'Remove the sandals from your feet, for the place where you stand is holy ground. [34]I have witnessed the affliction of my people in Egypt and have heard their groaning, and I have come down to rescue them. Come now, I will send you to Egypt.' [35m]This Moses, whom they had rejected with the words, 'Who appointed you ruler and judge?' God sent as [both] ruler and deliverer, through the angel who appeared to him in the bush. [36n]This man led them out, performing wonders and signs in the land of Egypt, at the Red Sea, and in the desert for forty years. [37o]It was this Moses who said to the Israelites, 'God will raise up for you, from among your own kinsfolk, a prophet like me.' [38p]It was he who, in the assembly in the desert, was with the angel who spoke to him on Mount Sinai and with our ancestors, and he received living utterances to hand on to us.

[39q]"Our ancestors were unwilling to obey him; instead, they pushed him aside and in their hearts turned back to Egypt, [40r]saying to Aaron, 'Make us gods who will be our leaders. As for that Moses who led us out of the land of Egypt, we do not know what has happened to him.' [41s]So they made a calf in those days, offered sacrifice to the idol, and reveled in the works of their hands. [42tu]Then God turned and handed them over to worship the host of heaven, as it is written in the book of the prophets:

'Did you bring me sacrifices and
 offerings
 for forty years in the desert, O house
  of Israel?
[43] No, you took up the tent of Moloch
 and the star of [your] god Rephan,
 the images that you made to
  worship.
So I shall take you into exile beyond
  Babylon.'

[44v]Our ancestors had the tent of testimony in the desert just as the One who spoke to Moses directed him to make it according to the

d: Gn 23, 3-20; 33, 19; 49, 29-30; 50, 13; Jos 24, 32. e: Ex 1, 7. f: Ex 1, 8. g: Ex 2, 2; Heb 11, 23. h: Ex 2, 3-10. i: Ex 2, 11-12. j: Ex 2, 13-14. k: Ex 2, 15.21-22; 18, 3-4. l: Ex 3, 2-3. m: Ex 2, 14. n: Ex 7, 3.10; 14, 21; Nm 14, 33. o: Dt 18, 15; Acts 3, 22. p: Ex 19, 3; 20, 1-17; Dt 5, 4-22; 6, 4-25. q: Nm 14, 3. r: Ex 32, 1.23. s: Ex 32, 4-6. t: Am 5, 25-27. u: Jer 7, 18; 8, 2; 19, 13. v: Ex 25, 9.40.

pattern he had seen. [45w]Our ancestors who inherited it brought it with Joshua when they dispossessed the nations that God drove out from before our ancestors, up to the time of David, [46x]who found favor in the sight of God and asked that he might find a dwelling place for the house of Jacob. [47y]But Solomon built a house for him. [48z]Yet the Most High does not dwell in houses made by human hands. As the prophet says:

[49] [a]'The heavens are my throne,
    the earth is my footstool.
What kind of house can you build for me?
    says the Lord,
    or what is to be my resting place?
[50] Did not my hand make all these things?'

Conclusion. [51]"You stiff-necked people, uncircumcised in heart and ears, you always oppose the holy Spirit; you are just like your ancestors. [52b]Which of the prophets did your ancestors not persecute? They put to death those who foretold the coming of the righteous one, whose betrayers and murderers you have now become. [53c]You received the law as transmitted by angels, but you did not observe it."

Stephen's Martyrdom. [54]When they heard this, they were infuriated, and they ground their teeth at him. [55d]*But he, filled with the holy Spirit, looked up intently to heaven and saw the glory of God and Jesus standing at the right hand of God, [56]and he said, "Behold, I

see the heavens opened and the Son of Man standing at the right hand of God." [57]*But they cried out in a loud voice, covered their ears, and rushed upon him together. [58e]They threw him out of the city, and began to stone him. The witnesses laid down their cloaks at the feet of a young man named Saul. [59]ƒ*As they were stoning Stephen, he called out, "Lord Jesus, receive my spirit." [60g]Then he fell to his knees and cried out in a loud voice, "Lord, do not hold this sin against them"; and when he said this, he fell asleep.

CHAPTER 8

See RG 340-41

[1h]*Now Saul was consenting to his execution.

Persecution of the Church. On that day, there broke out a severe persecution of the church in Jerusalem, and all were scattered throughout the countryside of Judea and Samaria, except the apostles. [2]Devout men buried Stephen and made a loud lament over him. [3i]*Saul, meanwhile, was trying to destroy the church; entering house after house and dragging out men and women, he handed them over for imprisonment.

III: The Mission in Judea and Samaria

Philip in Samaria. [4j]Now those who had been scattered went about preaching the word. [5k]Thus Philip went down to [the] city

---

7, 55: He . . . saw . . . **Jesus standing at the right hand of God:** Stephen affirms to the Sanhedrin that the prophecy Jesus made before them has been fulfilled (Mk 14, 62).

7, 57: Covered their ears: Stephen's declaration, like that of Jesus, is a scandal to the court, which regards it as blasphemy.

7, 59: Compare Lk 23, [34].46.

8, 1–40: Some idea of the severity of the persecution that now breaks out against the Jerusalem community can be gathered from 22, 4 and 26, 9–11. Luke, however, concentrates on the fortunes of the word of God among people, indicating how the dispersal of the Jewish community resulted in the conversion of the Samaritans (4–17.25). His narrative is further expanded to include the account of Philip's acceptance of an Ethiopian (26–39).

8, 1: All were scattered . . . except the apostles: this observation leads some modern scholars to conclude that the persecution was limited to the Hellenist Christians and that the Hebrew Christians were not molested, perhaps because their attitude toward the law and temple was still more in line with that of their fellow Jews (see the charge leveled against the

Hellenist Stephen in 6, 13–14). Whatever the facts, it appears that the Twelve took no public stand regarding Stephen's position, choosing, instead, to await the development of events.

8, 3: Saul . . . was trying to destroy the church: like Stephen, Saul was able to perceive that the Christian movement contained the seeds of doctrinal divergence from Judaism. A pupil of Gamaliel, according to 22, 3, and totally dedicated to the law as the way of salvation (Gal 1, 13–14), Saul accepted the task of crushing the Christian movement, at least insofar as it detracted from the importance of the temple and the law. His vehement opposition to Christianity reveals how difficult it was for a Jew of his time to accept a messianism that differed so greatly from the general expectation.

---

w: Jos 3, 14-17; 18, 1; 2 Sm 7, 5-7. x: 2 Sm 7, 1-2; 1 Kgs 8, 17; Ps 132, 1-5. y: 1 Kgs 6, 1; 1 Chr 17, 12. z: 17, 24. a: Is 66, 1-2. b: 2 Chr 36, 16; Mt 23, 31.34. c: Gal 3, 19; Heb 2, 2. d: Mt 26, 64; Mk 14, 62; Lk 22, 69; Acts 2, 34. e: 22, 20. f: Ps 31, 6. Lk 23, 46. g: Mt 27, 46.50; Mk 15, 34; Lk 23, 46. h: 22, 20. i: 9, 1.13; 22, 4; 26, 9-11; 1 Cor 5, 9; Gal 1, 13. j: 11, 19. k: 6, 5; 21, 8-9.

Sites of Early Christian Missionary Activities

Inset map labels:
Tarsus
Antioch
CYPRUS
MEDITERRANEAN SEA
Cyrene
Damascus
EGYPT
Red Sea
0 100 200 Miles
0 100 200 Kilometers

Main map labels:
Caesarea Philippi
PHOENICIA
GALILEE
Sea of Galilee
33°
Caesarea
Plain of Sharon
SAMARIA
River Jordan
Mediterranean Sea
32°
Joppa
Lydda
Jerusalem
Azotus
JUDEA
Dead Sea
Gaza
35°
36°
0 10 20 Miles
0 10 20 Kilometers

of Samaria and proclaimed the Messiah to them. ⁶With one accord, the crowds paid attention to what was said by Philip when they heard it and saw the signs he was doing. ⁷ᶦFor unclean spirits, crying out in a loud voice, came out of many possessed people, and many paralyzed and crippled people were cured. ⁸There was great joy in that city.

Simon the Magician. ⁹*A man named Simon used to practice magic in the city and astounded the people of Samaria, claiming to be someone great. ¹⁰All of them, from the least to the greatest, paid attention to him, saying, "This man is the 'Power of God' that is called 'Great.' " ¹¹They paid attention to him because he had astounded them by his magic for a long time, ¹²ᵐbut once they began to believe Philip as he preached the good news about the kingdom of God and the name of Jesus Christ, men and women alike were baptized. ¹³Even Simon himself believed and, after being baptized, became devoted to Philip; and when he saw the signs and mighty deeds that were occurring, he was astounded.

¹⁴Now when the apostles in Jerusalem heard that Samaria had accepted the word of God, they sent them Peter and John, ¹⁵who went down and prayed for them, that they might receive the holy Spirit, ¹⁶*for it had not yet fallen upon any of them; they had only been baptized in the name of the Lord Jesus. ¹⁷ⁿThen they laid hands on them and they received the holy Spirit.

¹⁸*When Simon saw that the Spirit was conferred by the laying on of the apostles' hands, he offered them money ¹⁹and said, "Give me this power too, so that anyone upon whom I lay my hands may receive the holy Spirit." ²⁰But Peter said to him, "May your money perish with you, because you thought that you could buy the gift of God with money. ²¹You have no share or lot in this matter, for your heart is not upright before God. ²²Repent of this wickedness of yours and pray to the Lord that, if possible, your intention may be forgiven. ²³For I see that you are filled with bitter gall and are in the bonds of iniquity." ²⁴Simon said in reply, "Pray for me to the Lord, that nothing of what you have said may come upon me." ²⁵So when they had testified and proclaimed the word of the Lord, they returned to Jerusalem and preached the good news to many Samaritan villages.

Philip and the Ethiopian. ²⁶*Then the angel of the Lord spoke to Philip, "Get up and head south on the road that goes down from Jerusalem to Gaza, the desert route." ²⁷ᵒ*So he got up and set out. Now there was an Ethiopian eunuch, a court official of the Candace, that is, the queen of the Ethiopians, in charge of her entire treasury, who had come to Jerusalem to worship, ²⁸and was returning home. Seated in his chariot, he was reading the prophet Isaiah. ²⁹The Spirit said to Philip, "Go and join up with that chariot." ³⁰*Philip ran up and heard him reading Isaiah the prophet and said, "Do you understand what you are reading?" ³¹ᵖHe replied, "How can I, unless someone instructs me?" So he invited

8, 9–13.18–24: Sorcerers were well known in the ancient world. Probably the incident involving Simon and his altercation with Peter is introduced to show that the miraculous charisms possessed by members of the Christian community (6–7) were not to be confused with the magic of sorcerers.

8, 16: Here and in 10, 44–48 and 19, 1–6, Luke distinguishes between baptism in the name of the Lord Jesus and the reception of the Spirit. In each case, the Spirit is conferred through members of the Twelve (Peter and John) or their representative (Paul). This may be Luke's way of describing the role of the church in the bestowal of the Spirit. Elsewhere in Acts, baptism and the Spirit are more closely related (1, 5; 11, 16).

8, 18–20: Simon attempts to buy the gift of God (20) with money. Peter's cursing of Simon's attempt so to use his money expresses a typically Lucan attitude toward material wealth (cf Lk 6, 24; 12, 16–21; 16, 13).

8, 26–40: In the account of the conversion of the Ethiopian eunuch, Luke adduces additional evidence to show that the spread of Christianity outside the confines of Judaism it-

self was in accord with the plan of God. He does not make clear whether the Ethiopian was originally a convert to Judaism or, as is more probable, a "God-fearer" (10, 1), i.e., one who accepted Jewish monotheism and ethic and attended the synagogue but did not consider himself bound by other regulations such as circumcision and observance of the dietary laws. The story of his conversion to Christianity is given a strong supernatural cast by the introduction of an angel (26), instruction from the holy Spirit (29), and the strange removal of Philip from the scene (39).

8, 27: The Candace: Candace is not a proper name here but the title of a Nubian queen.

8, 30–34: Philip is brought alongside the carriage at the very moment when the Ethiopian is pondering the meaning of Is 53 7–8, a passage that Christianity, from its earliest origins, has applied to Jesus; cf the note on 3, 13.

l: Mk 16, 17. *m:* 1, 3; 19, 8; 28, 23.31. *n:* 2, 4; 4, 31; 10 44-47; 15, 8-9; 19, 2.6. *o:* Is 56, 3-5. *p:* Jn 16, 13.

Philip to get in and sit with him. 32q This was the scripture passage he was reading:

"Like a sheep he was led to the slaughter,
    and as a lamb before its shearer is
        silent,
    so he opened not his mouth.
33 In [his] humiliation justice was denied
        him.
    Who will tell of his posterity?
    For his life is taken from the earth."

34 Then the eunuch said to Philip in reply, "I beg you, about whom is the prophet saying this? About himself, or about someone else?" 35 Then Philip opened his mouth and, beginning with this scripture passage, he proclaimed Jesus to him. 36r As they traveled along the road they came to some water, and the eunuch said, "Look, there is water. What is to prevent my being baptized?" [37]* 38 Then he ordered the chariot to stop, and Philip and the eunuch both went down into the water, and he baptized him. 39s When they came out of the water, the Spirit of the Lord snatched Philip away, and the eunuch saw him no more, but continued on his way rejoicing. 40t Philip came to Azotus, and went about proclaiming the good news to all the towns until he reached Caesarea.

CHAPTER 9

See RG 341–42 **Saul's Conversion.** 1uv*Now Saul, still breathing murderous threats against the disciples of the Lord, went to the high priest 2*and asked him for letters to the syna-gogues in Damascus, that, if he should find any men or women who belonged to the Way, he might bring them back to Jerusalem in chains. 3w On his journey, as he was near-ing Damascus, a light from the sky suddenly flashed around him. 4x He fell to the ground and heard a voice saying to him, "Saul, Saul, why are you persecuting me?" 5y He said, "Who are you, sir?" The reply came, "I am Jesus, whom you are persecuting. 6z Now get up and go into the city and you will be told what you must do." 7a The men who were traveling with him stood speechless, for they heard the voice but could see no one. 8b*Saul got up from the ground, but when he opened his eyes he could see nothing; so they led him by the hand and brought him to Damas-cus. 9 For three days he was unable to see, and he neither ate nor drank.

Saul's Baptism. 10c There was a disciple in Damascus named Ananias, and the Lord said to him in a vision, "Ananias." He answered, "Here I am, Lord." 11d The Lord said to him, "Get up and go to the street called Straight and ask at the house of Judas for a man from Tarsus named Saul. He is there praying, 12 and [in a vision] he has seen a man named Ananias come in and lay [his] hands on him, that he may regain his sight." 13e*But Ana-nias replied, "Lord, I have heard from many sources about this man, what evil things he has done to your holy ones in Jerusalem. 14f And here he has authority from the chief priests to imprison all who call upon your name." 15g But the Lord said to him, "Go, for

---

8, 37: The oldest and best manuscripts of Acts omit this verse, which is a Western text reading: "And Philip said, 'If you believe with all your heart, you may.' And he said in re-ply, 'I believe that Jesus Christ is the Son of God.' "

9, 1–19: This is the first of three accounts of Paul's con-version (with 22, 3–16 and 26, 2–18) with some differences of detail owing to Luke's use of different sources. Paul's experi-ence was not visionary but was precipitated by the appearance of Jesus, as he insists in 1 Cor 15, 8. The words of Jesus, "Saul, Saul, why are you persecuting me?" related by Luke with no variation in all three accounts, exerted a profound and lasting influence on the thought of Paul. Under the influence of this experience he gradually developed his understanding of justi-fication by faith (see the letters to the Galatians and Romans) and of the identification of the Christian community with Jesus Christ (see 1 Cor 12, 27). That Luke would narrate this conversion three times is testimony to the importance he at-taches to it. This first account occurs when the word is first

spread to the Gentiles. At this point, the conversion of the hero of the Gentile mission is recounted. The emphasis in the ac-count is on Paul as a divinely chosen instrument (15).

9, 2: The Way: a name used by the early Christian com-munity for itself (18, 26; 19, 9.23; 22, 4; 24, 14.22). The Es-sene community at Qumran used the same designation to de-scribe its mode of life.

9, 8: He could see nothing: a temporary blindness (18) symbolizing the religious blindness of Saul as persecutor (cf 26, 18).

9, 13: Your holy ones: literally, "your saints."

q: Is 53, 7-8 LXX.   r: 10, 47.   s: 1 Kgs 18, 12.   t: 21, 8.   u: 8, 3; 9, 13; 22, 4; 1 Cor 15, 9; Gal 1, 13-14.   v: 9, 14; 26, 10. w: 1 Cor 9, 1; 15, 8; Gal 1, 16.   x: 22, 6; 26, 14.   y: 22, 8; 26, 15; Mt 25, 40.   z: 22, 10; 26, 16.   a: 22, 9; 26, 13-14.   b: 22, 11.   c: 22, 12-16.   d: 21, 39.   e: 8, 3; 9, 1.   f: 9, 1-2; 26, 10; 1 Cor 1, 2; 2 Tm 2, 22.   g: 22, 15; 26, 1; 27, 24.

this man is a chosen instrument of mine to carry my name before Gentiles, kings, and Israelites, ¹⁶and I will show him what he will have to suffer for my name." ¹⁷So Ananias went and entered the house; laying his hands on him, he said, "Saul, my brother, the Lord has sent me, Jesus who appeared to you on the way by which you came, that you may regain your sight and be filled with the holy Spirit." ¹⁸Immediately things like scales fell from his eyes and he regained his sight. He got up and was baptized, ¹⁹*and when he had eaten, he recovered his strength.

Saul Preaches in Damascus. He stayed some days with the disciples in Damascus, ²⁰*and he began at once to proclaim Jesus in the synagogues, that he is the Son of God. ²¹All who heard him were astounded and said, "Is not this the man who in Jerusalem ravaged those who call upon this name, and came here expressly to take them back in chains to the chief priests?" ²²But Saul grew all the stronger and confounded [the] Jews who lived in Damascus, proving that this is the Messiah.

Saul Visits Jerusalem. ²³After a long time had passed, the Jews conspired to kill him, ^{24h}but their plot became known to Saul. Now they were keeping watch on the gates day and night so as to kill him, ²⁵but his disciples took him one night and let him down through an opening in the wall, lowering him in a basket.

²⁶ⁱ*When he arrived in Jerusalem he tried to join the disciples, but they were all afraid of him, not believing that he was a disciple. ²⁷Then Barnabas took charge of him and brought him to the apostles, and he reported to them how on the way he had seen the Lord

and that he had spoken to him, and how in Damascus he had spoken out boldly in the name of Jesus. ²⁸He moved about freely with them in Jerusalem, and spoke out boldly in the name of the Lord. ²⁹*He also spoke and debated with the Hellenists, but they tried to kill him. ^{30j}And when the brothers learned of this, they took him down to Caesarea and sent him on his way to Tarsus.

The Church at Peace. ³¹*The church throughout all Judea, Galilee, and Samaria was at peace. It was being built up and walked in the fear of the Lord, and with the consolation of the holy Spirit it grew in numbers.

Peter Heals Aeneas at Lydda. ³²As Peter was passing through every region, he went down to the holy ones living in Lydda. ³³There he found a man named Aeneas, who had been confined to bed for eight years, for he was paralyzed. ³⁴Peter said to him, "Aeneas, Jesus Christ heals you. Get up and make your bed." He got up at once. ³⁵And all the inhabitants of Lydda and Sharon saw him, and they turned to the Lord.

Peter Restores Tabitha to Life. ³⁶*Now in Joppa there was a disciple named Tabitha (which translated means Dorcas). She was completely occupied with good deeds and almsgiving. ³⁷Now during those days she fell sick and died, so after washing her, they laid [her] out in a room upstairs. ³⁸Since Lydda was near Joppa, the disciples, hearing that Peter was there, sent two men to him with the request, "Please come to us without delay." ³⁹So Peter got up and went with them. When he arrived, they took him to the room upstairs where all the widows came to him weeping and showing him the tunics and cloaks that Dorcas had made while she

---

9, 19–30: This is a brief resume of Paul's initial experience as an apostolic preacher. At first he found himself in the position of being regarded as an apostate by the Jews and suspect by the Christian community of Jerusalem. His acceptance by the latter was finally brought about through his friendship with Barnabas (27).

9, 20: Son of God: the title "Son of God" occurs in Acts only here, but cf the citation of Ps 2, 7 in Paul's speech at Antioch in Pisidia (13, 33).

9, 26: This visit of Paul to Jerusalem is mentioned by Paul in Gal 1, 18.

9, 29: Hellenists: see the note on 6, 1–7.

9, 31–43: In the context of the period of peace enjoyed by

the community through the cessation of Paul's activities against it, Luke introduces two traditions concerning the miraculous power exercised by Peter as he was making a tour of places where the Christian message had already been preached. The towns of Lydda, Sharon, and Joppa were populated by both Jews and Gentiles and their Christian communities may well have been mixed.

9, 36: Tabitha (Dorcas), respectively the Aramaic and Greek words for "gazelle," exemplifies the right attitude toward material possessions expressed by Jesus in the Lucan Gospel (Lk 6, 30; 11, 41; 12, 33; 18, 22; 19, 8).

h: 2 Cor 11, 32-33.   *i:* Gal 1, 18.   *j:* 11, 25.

was with them. [40k]Peter sent them all out and knelt down and prayed. Then he turned to her body and said, "Tabitha, rise up." She opened her eyes, saw Peter, and sat up. [41]He gave her his hand and raised her up, and when he had called the holy ones and the widows, he presented her alive. [42]This became known all over Joppa, and many came to believe in the Lord. [43]*And he stayed a long time in Joppa with Simon, a tanner.

IV: The Inauguration of the Gentile Mission

CHAPTER 10

See RG 342-43

The Vision of Cornelius. [1m]*Now in Caesarea there was a man named Cornelius, a centurion of the Cohort called the Italica, [2]*devout and God-fearing along with his whole household, who used to give alms generously to the Jewish people and pray to God constantly. [3]*One afternoon about three o'clock, he saw plainly in a vision an angel of God come in to him and say to him, "Cornelius." [4]He looked intently at him and, seized with fear, said, "What is it, sir?" He said to him, "Your prayers and almsgiving have ascended as a memorial offering before God. [5]Now send some men to Joppa and summon one Simon who is called Peter. [6n]He is staying with another Simon, a tanner, who has a house by the sea." [7]*When the an-

gel who spoke to him had left, he called two of his servants and a devout soldier from his staff, [8]explained everything to them, and sent them to Joppa.

The Vision of Peter. [9]*The next day, while they were on their way and nearing the city, Peter went up to the roof terrace to pray at about noontime. [10]He was hungry and wished to eat, and while they were making preparations he fell into a trance. [11o]He saw heaven opened and something resembling a large sheet coming down, lowered to the ground by its four corners. [12]In it were all the earth's four-legged animals and reptiles and the birds of the sky. [13]A voice said to him, "Get up, Peter. Slaughter and eat." [14p]But Peter said, "Certainly not, sir. For never have I eaten anything profane and unclean." [15q]The voice spoke to him again, a second time, "What God has made clean, you are not to call profane." [16]This happened three times, and then the object was taken up into the sky.

[17]*While Peter was in doubt about the meaning of the vision he had seen, the men sent by Cornelius asked for Simon's house and arrived at the entrance. [18]They called out inquiring whether Simon, who is called Peter, was staying there. [19r]As Peter was pondering the vision, the Spirit said [to him], "There are three men here looking for you. [20]So get up, go downstairs, and accompany them without hesitation, because I have sent them." [21]Then Peter went down to the men

---

9, 43: The fact that Peter lodged with a tanner would have been significant to both the Gentile and Jewish Christians, for Judaism considered the tanning occupation unclean.

10, 1–48: The narrative centers on the conversion of Cornelius, a Gentile and a "God-fearer" (see the note on 8, 26–40). Luke considers the event of great importance, as is evident from his long treatment of it. The incident is again related in 11, 1-18 where Peter is forced to justify his actions before the Jerusalem community and alluded to in 15, 7–11 where at the Jerusalem "Council" Peter supports Paul's missionary activity among the Gentiles. The narrative divides itself into a series of distinct episodes, concluding with Peter's presentation of the Christian kerygma (34–43) and a pentecostal experience undergone by Cornelius' household preceding their reception of baptism (44–48).

10, 1: The Cohort called the Italica: this battalion was an auxiliary unit of archers formed originally in Italy but transferred to Syria shortly before A.D. 69.

10, 2: Used to give alms generously: like Tabitha (9, 36), Cornelius exemplifies the proper attitude toward wealth (see the note on 9, 36).

10, 3: About three o'clock: literally, "about the ninth hour." See the note on 3, 1.

10, 7: A devout soldier: by using this adjective, Luke probably intends to classify him as a "God-fearer" (see note on 8, 26–40).

10, 9–16: The vision is intended to prepare Peter to share the food of Cornelius' household without qualms of conscience (48). The necessity of such instructions to Peter reveals that at first not even the apostles fully grasped the implications of Jesus' teaching on the law. In Acts, the initial insight belongs to Stephen.

10, 9: At about noontime: literally, "about the sixth hour."

10, 17–23: The arrival of the Gentile emissaries with their account of the angelic apparition illuminates Peter's vision: he is to be prepared to admit Gentiles, who were considered unclean like the animals of his vision, into the Christian community.

k: Mk 5, 40-41. l: 10, 6. m: 10, 30-33. n: 9, 43. o: 11, 5-12.
p: Lv 11, 1-47; Ez 4, 14. q: Mk 7, 15-19; Gal 2, 12. r: 13, 2.

and said, "I am the one you are looking for. What is the reason for your being here?" [22s]They answered, "Cornelius, a centurion, an upright and God-fearing man, respected by the whole Jewish nation, was directed by a holy angel to summon you to his house and to hear what you have to say." [23]So he invited them in and showed them hospitality.

The next day he got up and went with them, and some of the brothers from Joppa went with him. [24*]On the following day he entered Caesarea. Cornelius was expecting them and had called together his relatives and close friends. [25t]When Peter entered, Cornelius met him and, falling at his feet, paid him homage. [26]Peter, however, raised him up, saying, "Get up. I myself am also a human being." [27]While he conversed with him, he went in and found many people gathered together [28u*]and said to them, "You know that it is unlawful for a Jewish man to associate with, or visit, a Gentile, but God has shown me that I should not call any person profane or unclean. [29]And that is why I came without objection when sent for. May I ask, then, why you summoned me?"

[30*]Cornelius replied, "Four days ago at this hour, three o'clock in the afternoon, I was at prayer in my house when suddenly a man in dazzling robes stood before me and said,

[31]'Cornelius, your prayer has been heard and your almsgiving remembered before God. [32]Send therefore to Joppa and summon Simon, who is called Peter. He is a guest in the house of Simon, a tanner, by the sea.' [33]So I sent for you immediately, and you were kind enough to come. Now therefore we are all here in the presence of God to listen to all that you have been commanded by the Lord."

Peter's Speech. [34v*]Then Peter proceeded to speak and said, "In truth, I see that God shows no partiality. [35]Rather, in every nation whoever fears him and acts uprightly is acceptable to him. [36w*]You know the word [that] he sent to the Israelites as he proclaimed peace through Jesus Christ, who is Lord of all, [37x]what has happened all over Judea, beginning in Galilee after the baptism that John preached, [38y*]how God anointed Jesus of Nazareth with the holy Spirit and power. He went about doing good and healing all those oppressed by the devil, for God was with him. [39*]We are witnesses of all that he did both in the country of the Jews and [in] Jerusalem. They put him to death by hanging him on a tree. [40]This man God raised [on] the third day and granted that he be visible, [41z]not to all the people, but to us, the witnesses chosen by God in advance, who ate and drank with him after he rose from the

10, 24–27: So impressed is Cornelius with the apparition that he invites close personal friends to join him in his meeting with Peter. But his understanding of the person he is about to meet is not devoid of superstition, suggested by his falling down before him. For a similar experience of Paul and Barnabas, see 14, 11–18.

10, 28: Peter now fully understands the meaning of his vision; see the note on 10, 17–23.

10, 30: Four days ago: literally, "from the fourth day up to this hour."

10, 34–43: Peter's speech to the household of Cornelius typifies early Christian preaching to Gentiles.

10, 34–35: The revelation of God's choice of Israel to be the people of God did not mean he withheld the divine favor from other people.

10, 36–43: These words are more directed to Luke's Christian readers than to the household of Cornelius, as indicated by the opening words, "You know." They trace the continuity between the preaching and teaching of Jesus of Nazareth and the proclamation of Jesus by the early community. The emphasis on this divinely ordained continuity (41) is meant to assure Luke's readers of the fidelity of Christian tradition to the words and deeds of Jesus.

10, 36: To the Israelites: Luke, in the words of Peter,

speaks of the prominent position occupied by Israel in the history of salvation.

10, 38: Jesus of Nazareth: God's revelation of his plan for the destiny of humanity through Israel culminated in Jesus of Nazareth. Consequently, the ministry of Jesus is an integral part of God's revelation. This viewpoint explains why the early Christian communities were interested in conserving the historical substance of the ministry of Jesus, a tradition leading to the production of the four gospels.

10, 39: We are witnesses: the apostolic testimony was not restricted to the resurrection of Jesus but also included his historical ministry. This witness, however, was theological in character; the Twelve, divinely mandated as prophets, were empowered to interpret his sayings and deeds in the light of his redemptive death and resurrection. The meaning of these words and deeds was to be made clear to the developing Christian community as the bearer of the word of salvation (cf 1, 21–26). **Hanging him on a tree:** see the note on 5, 30.

s: Lk 7, 4-5. t: 14, 13-15; Rv 19, 10. u: Gal 2, 11-16. v: Dt 17, 2. 2 Chr 19, 7; Jb 34, 19; Wis 6, 7; Rom 2, 11; Gal 2, 6; Eph 6, 9; 1 Pt 1, 17. w: Is 52, 7; Na 2, 1. x: Mt 4, 12; Mk 1, 14; Lk 4, 14. y: Is 61, 1; Lk 4, 18. z: Lk 24, 41-43.

dead. *42a**He commissioned us to preach to the people and testify that he is the one appointed by God as judge of the living and the dead. *43*To him all the prophets bear witness, that everyone who believes in him will receive forgiveness of sins through his name."

The Baptism of Cornelius. *44b**While Peter was still speaking these things, the holy Spirit fell upon all who were listening to the word. *45*The circumcised believers who had accompanied Peter were astounded that the gift of the holy Spirit should have been poured out on the Gentiles also, *46*for they could hear them speaking in tongues and glorifying God. Then Peter responded, *47c*"Can anyone withhold the water for baptizing these people, who have received the holy Spirit even as we have?" *48*He ordered them to be baptized in the name of Jesus Christ. *49*Then they invited him to stay for a few days.

See RG
342–43

CHAPTER 11

The Baptism of the Gentiles Explained. *1**Now the apostles and the brothers who were in Judea heard that the Gentiles too had accepted the word of God. *2*So when Peter went up to Jerusalem the circumcised believers confronted him, *3**saying, "You entered the house of uncircumcised people and ate with them." *4*Peter began and explained it to them step by step, saying, *5d*"I was at prayer in the city of Joppa when in a trance I had a vision, something resembling a large sheet coming down, lowered from the sky by its four corners, and it came to me. *6*Looking intently into it, I observed and saw the four-legged animals of the earth, the wild beasts,

the reptiles, and the birds of the sky. *7*I also heard a voice say to me, 'Get up, Peter. Slaughter and eat.' *8*But I said, 'Certainly not, sir, because nothing profane or unclean has ever entered my mouth.' *9*But a second time a voice from heaven answered, 'What God has made clean, you are not to call profane.' *10*This happened three times, and then everything was drawn up again into the sky. *11*Just then three men appeared at the house where we were, who had been sent to me from Caesarea. *12**The Spirit told me to accompany them without discriminating. These six brothers also went with me, and we entered the man's house. *13e*He related to us how he had seen [the] angel standing in his house, saying, 'Send someone to Joppa and summon Simon, who is called Peter, *14*who will speak words to you by which you and all your household will be saved.' *15f*As I began to speak, the holy Spirit fell upon them as it had upon us at the beginning, *16g*and I remembered the word of the Lord, how he had said, 'John baptized with water but you will be baptized with the holy Spirit.' *17h*If then God gave them the same gift he gave to us when we came to believe in the Lord Jesus Christ, who was I to be able to hinder God?" *18*When they heard this, they stopped objecting and glorified God, saying, "God has then granted life-giving repentance to the Gentiles too."

The Church at Antioch. *19i**Now those who had been scattered by the persecution that arose because of Stephen went as far as Phoenicia, Cyprus, and Antioch, preaching the word to no one but Jews. *20*There were

---

10, 42: **As judge of the living and the dead:** the apostolic preaching to the Jews appealed to their messianic hope, while the preaching to Gentiles stressed the coming divine judgment; cf 1 Thes 1, 10.

10, 44: Just as the Jewish Christians received the gift of the Spirit, so too do the Gentiles.

11, 1–18: The Jewish Christians of Jerusalem were scandalized to learn of Peter's sojourn in the house of the Gentile Cornelius. Nonetheless, they had to accept the divine directions given to both Peter and Cornelius. They concluded that the setting aside of the legal barriers between Jew and Gentile was an exceptional ordinance of God to indicate that the apostolic kerygma was also to be directed to the Gentiles. Only in ch 15 at the "Council" in Jerusalem does the evangelization of the Gentiles become the official position of the church leadership in Jerusalem.

11, 3: **You entered . . . :** alternatively, this could be punctuated as a question.

11, 12: **These six brothers:** companions from the Christian community of Joppa (see 10, 23).

11, 19–26: The Jewish Christian antipathy to the mixed community was reflected by the early missionaries generally. The few among them who entertained a different view succeeded in introducing Gentiles into the community at Antioch (in Syria). When the disconcerted Jerusalem community sent Barnabas to investigate, he was so favorably impressed by what he observed that he persuaded his friend Saul to participate in the Antioch mission.

a: 1, 8; 3, 15; 17, 31; Lk 24, 48; Rom 14, 9; 2 Tm 4, 1.   *b:* 11, 15; 15, 8.   *c:* 8, 36.   *d:* 10, 11-20.   *e:* 10, 3-5.22.30-32.   *f:* 10, 44.   *g:* 1, 5; 19, 4; Lk 3, 16.   *h:* 15, 8-9.   *i:* 8, 1-4.

some Cypriots and Cyrenians among them, however, who came to Antioch and began to speak to the Greeks as well, proclaiming the Lord Jesus. 21The hand of the Lord was with them and a great number who believed turned to the Lord. 22The news about them reached the ears of the church in Jerusalem, and they sent Barnabas [to go] to Antioch. 23When he arrived and saw the grace of God, he rejoiced and encouraged them all to remain faithful to the Lord in firmness of heart, 24for he was a good man, filled with the holy Spirit and faith. And a large number of people was added to the Lord. 25Then he went to Tarsus to look for Saul, 26*and when he had found him he brought him to Antioch. For a whole year they met with the church and taught a large number of people, and it was in Antioch that the disciples were first called Christians.

The Prediction of Agabus. 27*At that time some prophets came down from Jerusalem to Antioch, 28jand one of them named Agabus stood up and predicted by the Spirit that there would be a severe famine all over the world, and it happened under Claudius. 29kSo the disciples determined that, according to ability, each should send relief to the brothers who lived in Judea. 30*This they did, sending it to the presbyters in care of Barnabas and Saul.

See RG 343

CHAPTER 12

Herod's Persecution of the Christians. 1*About that time King Herod laid hands upon some members of the church to harm them. 2*He had James, the brother of John, killed by the sword, 3*and when he saw that this was pleasing to the Jews he proceeded to arrest Peter also. (It was [the] feast of Un-

leavened Bread.) 4He had him taken into custody and put in prison under the guard of four squads of four soldiers each. He intended to bring him before the people after Passover. 51Peter thus was being kept in prison, but prayer by the church was fervently being made to God on his behalf.

6On the very night before Herod was to bring him to trial, Peter, secured by double chains, was sleeping between two soldiers, while outside the door guards kept watch on the prison. 7Suddenly the angel of the Lord stood by him and a light shone in the cell. He tapped Peter on the side and awakened him, saying, "Get up quickly." The chains fell from his wrists. 8The angel said to him, "Put on your belt and your sandals." He did so. Then he said to him, "Put on your cloak and follow me." 9So he followed him out, not realizing that what was happening through the angel was real; he thought he was seeing a vision. 10They passed the first guard, then the second, and came to the iron gate leading out to the city, which opened for them by itself. They emerged and made their way down an alley, and suddenly the angel left him. 11Then Peter recovered his senses and said, "Now I know for certain that [the] Lord sent his angel and rescued me from the hand of Herod and from all that the Jewish people had been expecting." 12mWhen he realized this, he went to the house of Mary, the mother of John who is called Mark, where there were many people gathered in prayer. 13When he knocked on the gateway door, a maid named Rhoda came to answer it. 14She was so overjoyed when she recognized Peter's voice that, in-

11, 26: **Christians:** "Christians" is first applied to the members of the community at Antioch because the Gentile members of the community enable it to stand out clearly from Judaism.

11, 27–30: It is not clear whether the prophets from Jerusalem came to Antioch to request help in view of the coming famine or whether they received this insight during their visit there. The former supposition seems more likely. Suetonius and Tacitus speak of famines during the reign of Claudius (A.D. 41–54), while the Jewish historian Josephus mentions a famine in Judea in A.D. 46–48. Luke is interested, rather, in showing the charity of the Antiochene community toward the Jewish Christians of Jerusalem despite their differences on mixed communities.

11, 30: **Presbyters:** this is the same Greek word that else-

where is translated "elders," primarily in reference to the Jewish community.

12, 1–19: Herod Agrippa ruled Judea A.D. 41–44. While Luke does not assign a motive for his execution of James and his intended execution of Peter, the broad background lies in Herod's support of Pharisaic Judaism. The Jewish Christians had lost the popularity they had had in Jerusalem (2, 47), perhaps because of suspicions against them traceable to the teaching of Stephen.

12, 2: **James, the brother of John:** this James, the son of Zebedee, was beheaded by Herod Agrippa ca. A.D. 44.

12, 3.4: **Feast of Unleavened Bread . . . Passover:** see the note on Lk 22, 1.

j: 21, 10.   k: 12, 25.   l: Jas 5, 16.   m: 12, 25; 15, 37.

stead of opening the gate, she ran in and announced that Peter was standing at the gate. [15]They told her, "You are out of your mind," but she insisted that it was so. But they kept saying, "It is his angel." [16]But Peter continued to knock, and when they opened it, they saw him and were astounded. [17]*He motioned to them with his hand to be quiet and explained [to them] how the Lord had led him out of the prison, and said, "Report this to James and the brothers." Then he left and went to another place. [18n]At daybreak there was no small commotion among the soldiers over what had become of Peter. [19]Herod, after instituting a search but not finding him, ordered the guards tried and executed. Then he left Judea to spend some time in Caesarea.

Herod's Death. [20]*He had long been very angry with the people of Tyre and Sidon, who now came to him in a body. After winning over Blastus, the king's chamberlain, they sued for peace because their country was supplied with food from the king's territory. [21]On an appointed day, Herod, attired in royal robes, [and] seated on the rostrum, addressed them publicly. [22]The assembled crowd cried out, "This is the voice of a god, not of a man." [23]At once the angel of the Lord struck him down because he did not ascribe the honor to God, and he was eaten by worms and breathed

his last. [24o]But the word of God continued to spread and grow.

Mission of Barnabas and Saul. [25p]*After Barnabas and Saul completed their relief mission, they returned to Jerusalem, taking with them John, who is called Mark.

CHAPTER 13

See RG 343

[1]*Now there were in the church at Antioch prophets and teachers: Barnabas, Symeon who was called Niger, Lucius of Cyrene, Manaen who was a close friend of Herod the tetrarch, and Saul. [2]While they were worshiping the Lord and fasting, the holy Spirit said, "Set apart for me Barnabas and Saul for the work to which I have called them." [3]Then, completing their fasting and prayer, they laid hands on them and sent them off.

First Mission Begins in Cyprus. [4]*So they, sent forth by the holy Spirit, went down to Seleucia and from there sailed to Cyprus. [5]*When they arrived in Salamis, they proclaimed the word of God in the Jewish synagogues. They had John also as their assistant. [6]*When they had traveled through the whole island as far as Paphos, they met a magician named Bar-Jesus who was a Jewish false prophet. [7]He was with the proconsul Sergius Paulus, a man of intelligence, who had summoned Barnabas and Saul and wanted to hear the word of God. [8]But Elymas the magician (for that is what his name

---

12, 17: To James: this James is not the son of Zebedee mentioned in v 2, but is James, the "brother of the Lord" (Gal 1, 19), who in chs 15 and 21 is presented as leader of the Jerusalem Christian community. **He left and went to another place:** the conjecture that Peter left for Rome at this time has nothing to recommend it. His chief responsibility was still the leadership of the Jewish Christian community in Palestine (see Gal 2, 7). The concept of the great missionary effort of the church was yet to come (see 13, 1–3).

12, 20–23: Josephus gives a similar account of Herod's death that occurred in A.D. 44. Early Christian tradition considered the manner of it to be a divine punishment upon his evil life. See 2 Kgs 19, 35 for the figure of the angel of the Lord in such a context.

12, 25: They returned to Jerusalem: many manuscripts read "from Jerusalem," since 11, 30 implies that Paul and Barnabas are already in Jerusalem. This present verse could refer to a return visit or subsequent relief mission.

13, 1–3: The impulse for the first missionary effort in Asia Minor is ascribed to the prophets of the Antiochene community, under the inspiration of the holy Spirit. Just as the Jerusalem community had earlier been the center of missionary

activity, so too Antioch becomes the center from which the missionaries Barnabas and Saul are sent out.

13, 4—14, 27: The key event in Luke's account of the first missionary journey is the experience of Paul and Barnabas at Pisidian Antioch (13, 14–52). The Christian kerygma proclaimed by Paul in the synagogue was favorably received. Some Jews and "God-fearers" (see the note on 8, 26–40) became interested and invited the missionaries to speak again on the following sabbath (13, 42). By that time, however, the appearance of a large number of Gentiles from the city had so disconcerted the Jews that they became hostile toward the apostles (13, 44–50). This hostility of theirs appears in all three accounts of Paul's missionary journeys in Acts, the Jews of Iconium (14, 1–2) and Beroea (17, 11) being notable exceptions.

13, 5: John: that is, John Mark (see 12, 12.25).

13, 6: A magician named Bar-Jesus who was a Jewish false prophet: that is, he posed as a prophet. Again Luke takes the opportunity to dissociate Christianity from the magical acts of the time (7–11); see also 8, 18–24.

---

n: 5, 22-24.   o: 6, 7.   p: 11, 29-30.

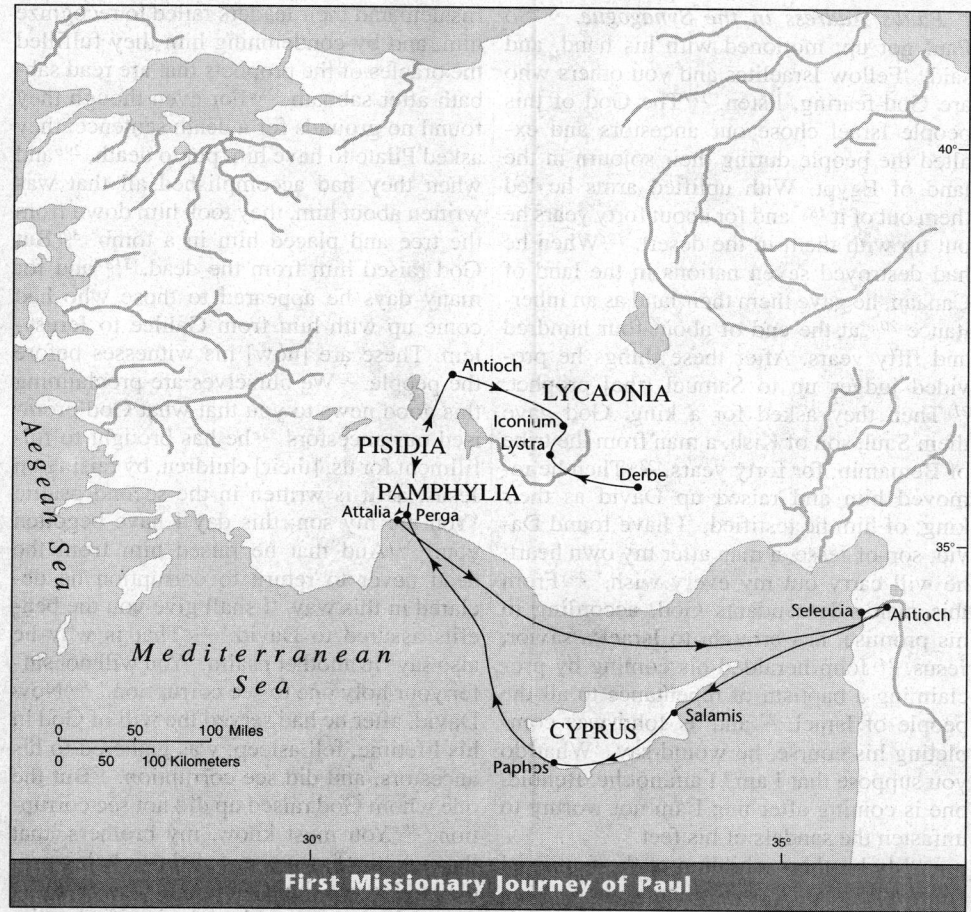

First Missionary Journey of Paul

means) opposed them in an attempt to turn the proconsul away from the faith. ⁹*But Saul, also known as Paul, filled with the holy Spirit, looked intently at him ¹⁰and said, "You son of the devil, you enemy of all that is right, full of every sort of deceit and fraud. Will you not stop twisting the straight paths of [the] Lord? ¹¹Even now the hand of the Lord is upon you. You will be blind, and unable to see the sun for a time." Immediately a dark mist fell upon him, and he went about seeking people to lead him by the hand. ¹²When the proconsul saw what had happened, he came to believe, for he was astonished by the teaching about the Lord.

Paul's Arrival at Antioch in Pisidia. ¹³�qFrom Paphos, Paul and his companions set sail and arrived at Perga in Pamphylia. But John left them and returned to Jerusalem. ¹⁴They continued on from Perga and reached Antioch in Pisidia. On the sabbath they entered [into] the synagogue and took their seats. ¹⁵After the reading of the law and the prophets, the synagogue officials sent word to them, "My brothers, if one of you has a word of exhortation for the people, please speak."

13, 9: Saul, also known as Paul: there is no reason to believe that his name was changed from Saul to Paul upon his conversion. The use of a double name, one Semitic (Saul), the other Greco-Roman (Paul), is well attested (cf 1, 23, Joseph Justus; 12, 12.25, John Mark).

q: 15, 38.

Paul's Address in the Synagogue. [16]*So Paul got up, motioned with his hand, and said, "Fellow Israelites and you others who are God-fearing, listen. [17r]The God of this people Israel chose our ancestors and exalted the people during their sojourn in the land of Egypt. With uplifted arms he led them out of it [18s]*and for about forty years he put up with them in the desert. [19t]When he had destroyed seven nations in the land of Canaan, he gave them their land as an inheritance [20u]*at the end of about four hundred and fifty years. After these things he provided judges up to Samuel [the] prophet. [21v]Then they asked for a king. God gave them Saul, son of Kish, a man from the tribe of Benjamin, for forty years. [22w]Then he removed him and raised up David as their king; of him he testified, 'I have found David, son of Jesse, a man after my own heart; he will carry out my every wish.' [23x]From this man's descendants God, according to his promise, has brought to Israel a savior, Jesus. [24y]John heralded his coming by proclaiming a baptism of repentance to all the people of Israel; [25z]and as John was completing his course, he would say, 'What do you suppose that I am? I am not he. Behold, one is coming after me; I am not worthy to unfasten the sandals of his feet.'

[26]"My brothers, children of the family of Abraham, and those others among you who are God-fearing, to us this word of salvation has been sent. [27]The inhabitants of Jerusalem and their leaders failed to recognize him, and by condemning him they fulfilled the oracles of the prophets that are read sabbath after sabbath. [28a]For even though they found no grounds for a death sentence, they asked Pilate to have him put to death, [29b]and when they had accomplished all that was written about him, they took him down from the tree and placed him in a tomb. [30c]But God raised him from the dead, [31d]*and for many days he appeared to those who had come up with him from Galilee to Jerusalem. These are [now] his witnesses before the people. [32]We ourselves are proclaiming this good news to you that what God promised our ancestors [33e]he has brought to fulfillment for us, [their] children, by raising up Jesus, as it is written in the second psalm, 'You are my son; this day I have begotten you.' [34f]And that he raised him from the dead never to return to corruption he declared in this way, 'I shall give you the benefits assured to David.' [35g]That is why he also says in another psalm, 'You will not suffer your holy one to see corruption.' [36h]Now David, after he had served the will of God in his lifetime, fell asleep, was gathered to his ancestors, and did see corruption. [37]But the one whom God raised up did not see corruption. [38]*You must know, my brothers, that through him forgiveness of sins is being proclaimed to you, [and] in regard to everything from which you could not be justified under the law of Moses, [39i]in him every believer is

---

13, 16–41: This is the first of several speeches of Paul to Jews proclaiming that the Christian church is the logical development of Pharisaic Judaism (see also 24, 10–21; 26, 2–23).

13, 16: Who are God-fearing: see the note on 8, 26–40.

13, 18: Put up with: some manuscripts read "sustained."

13, 20: At the end of about four hundred and fifty years: the manuscript tradition makes it uncertain whether the mention of four hundred and fifty years refers to the sojourn in Egypt before the Exodus, the wilderness period and the time of the conquest (see Ex 12, 40–41), as the translation here suggests, or to the time between the conquest and the time of Samuel, the period of the judges, if the text is read, "After these things, for about four hundred and fifty years, he provided judges."

13, 31: The theme of the Galilean witnesses is a major one in the Gospel of Luke and in Acts and is used to signify the continuity between the teachings of Jesus and the teachings of the church and to guarantee the fidelity of the church's teachings to the words of Jesus.

13, 38–39: Justified: the verb is the same as that used in Paul's letters to speak of the experience of justification and, as in Paul, is here connected with the term "to have faith" ("every believer"). But this seems the only passage about Paul in Acts where justification is mentioned. In Lucan fashion it is paralleled with "forgiveness of sins" (a theme at 2, 38; 3, 19; 5, 31; 10, 43) based on Jesus' resurrection (37) rather than his cross, and is put negatively (38). Therefore, some would translate, "in regard to everything from which you could not be acquitted . . . every believer is acquitted."

r: Ex 6, 1.6; 12, 51. *s:* Ex 16, 1.35; Nm 14, 34. *t:* Dt 7, 1; Jos 14, 1-2. *u:* Jgs 2, 16; 1 Sm 3, 20. *v:* 1 Sm 8, 5.19; 9, 16; 10, 1.20-21.24; 11, 15. *w:* 1 Sm 13, 14; 16, 12-13; Ps 89, 20-21. *x:* Is 11, 1. *y:* Mt 3, 1-2; Mk 1, 4-5; Lk 3, 2-3. *z:* Mt 3, 11; Mk 1, 7; Lk 3, 16; Jn 1, 20.27. *a:* Mt 27, 20.22-23; Mk 15, 13-14; Lk 23, 4.14-15.21-23; Jn 19, 4-6.15. *b:* Mt 27, 59-60; Mk 15, 46; Lk 23, 53; Jn 19, 38.41-42. *c:* 2, 24.32; 3, 15; 4, 10; 17, 31. *d:* 1, 3.8; 10, 39.41; Mt 28, 8-10.16-20; Mk 16, 9.12-20; Lk 24, 13-53; Jn 20, 11-29; 21, 1-23. *e:* Ps 2, 7. *f:* Is 55, 3. *g:* Ps 16, 10. *h:* 2, 29; 1 Kgs 2, 10. *i:* Rom 3, 20.

justified. [40]Be careful, then, that what was said in the prophets not come about:

[41] [j]'Look on, you scoffers,
be amazed and disappear.
For I am doing a work in your days,
a work that you will never believe
even if someone tells you.' "

[42]As they were leaving, they invited them to speak on these subjects the following sabbath. [43]After the congregation had dispersed, many Jews and worshipers who were converts to Judaism followed Paul and Barnabas, who spoke to them and urged them to remain faithful to the grace of God.

Address to the Gentiles. [44]On the following sabbath almost the whole city gathered to hear the word of the Lord. [45]When the Jews saw the crowds, they were filled with jealousy and with violent abuse contradicted what Paul said. [46][k]*Both Paul and Barnabas spoke out boldly and said, "It was necessary that the word of God be spoken to you first, but since you reject it and condemn yourselves as unworthy of eternal life, we now turn to the Gentiles. [47][l]For so the Lord has commanded us, 'I have made you a light to the Gentiles, that you may be an instrument of salvation to the ends of the earth.' "

[48]The Gentiles were delighted when they heard this and glorified the word of the Lord. All who were destined for eternal life came to believe, [49]and the word of the Lord continued to spread through the whole region. [50]The Jews, however, incited the women of prominence who were worshipers and the leading men of the city, stirred up a persecution against Paul and Barnabas, and expelled them from their territory. [51][m]*So they shook the dust from their feet in protest against

them and went to Iconium. [52]The disciples were filled with joy and the holy Spirit.

CHAPTER 14

See RG 343

Paul and Barnabas at Iconium. [1]In Iconium they entered the Jewish synagogue together and spoke in such a way that a great number of both Jews and Greeks came to believe, [2]although the disbelieving Jews stirred up and poisoned the minds of the Gentiles against the brothers. [3][n]So they stayed for a considerable period, speaking out boldly for the Lord, who confirmed the word about his grace by granting signs and wonders to occur through their hands. [4]The people of the city were divided: some were with the Jews; others, with the apostles. [5][o]When there was an attempt by both the Gentiles and the Jews, together with their leaders, to attack and stone them, [6]they realized it and fled to the Lycaonian cities of Lystra and Derbe and to the surrounding countryside, [7]where they continued to proclaim the good news.

Paul and Barnabas at Lystra. [8]*At Lystra there was a crippled man, lame from birth, who had never walked. [9]He listened to Paul speaking, who looked intently at him, saw that he had the faith to be healed, [10]and called out in a loud voice, "Stand up straight on your feet." He jumped up and began to walk about. [11][p]When the crowds saw what Paul had done, they cried out in Lycaonian, "The gods have come down to us in human form." [12]*They called Barnabas "Zeus" and Paul "Hermes," because he was the chief speaker. [13]And the priest of Zeus, whose temple was at the entrance to the city, brought oxen and garlands to the gates, for he together with the people intended to offer sacrifice.

[14]*The apostles Barnabas and Paul tore their garments when they heard this and

---

13, 46: The refusal to believe frustrates God's plan for his chosen people; however, no adverse judgment is made here concerning their ultimate destiny. Again, Luke, in the words of Paul, speaks of the priority of Israel in the plan for salvation (see 10, 36).

13, 51: See the note on Lk 9, 5.

14, 8–18: In an effort to convince his hearers that the divine power works through his word, Paul cures the cripple. However, the pagan tradition of the occasional appearance of gods among human beings leads the people astray in interpreting the miracle. The incident reveals the cultural difficul-

ties with which the church had to cope. Note the similarity of the miracle worked here by Paul to the one performed by Peter in 3, 2–10.

14, 12: Zeus . . . Hermes: in Greek religion, Zeus was the chief of the Olympian gods, the "father of gods and men"; Hermes was a son of Zeus and was usually identified as the herald and messenger of the gods.

14, 14: Tore their garments: a gesture of protest.

---

j: Hb 1, 5.   *k*: 3, 26; Rom 1, 16.   *l*: Is 49, 6.   *m*: Mt 10, 14; Mk 6, 11; Lk 9, 5; 10, 11.   *n*: Mk 16, 17-20.   *o*: 2 Tm 3, 11.   *p*: 28, 6.

rushed out into the crowd, shouting, [15q]*"Men, why are you doing this? We are of the same nature as you, human beings. We proclaim to you good news that you should turn from these idols to the living God, 'who made heaven and earth and sea and all that is in them.' [16r]In past generations he allowed all Gentiles to go their own ways; [17s]yet, in bestowing his goodness, he did not leave himself without witness, for he gave you rains from heaven and fruitful seasons, and filled you with nourishment and gladness for your hearts." [18]Even with these words, they scarcely restrained the crowds from offering sacrifice to them.

[19t]However, some Jews from Antioch and Iconium arrived and won over the crowds. They stoned Paul and dragged him out of the city, supposing that he was dead. [20]But when the disciples gathered around him, he got up and entered the city. On the following day he left with Barnabas for Derbe.

End of the First Mission. [21]After they had proclaimed the good news to that city and made a considerable number of disciples, they returned to Lystra and to Iconium and to Antioch. [22u]They strengthened the spirits of the disciples and exhorted them to persevere in the faith, saying, "It is necessary for us to undergo many hardships to enter the kingdom of God." [23]*They appointed presbyters for them in each church and, with prayer and fasting, commended them to the Lord in whom they had put their faith. [24]Then they traveled through Pisidia and reached Pam-

phylia. [25]After proclaiming the word at Perga they went down to Attalia. [26v]From there they sailed to Antioch, where they had been commended to the grace of God for the work they had now accomplished. [27]And when they arrived, they called the church together and reported what God had done with them and how he had opened the door of faith to the Gentiles. [28]Then they spent no little time with the disciples.

CHAPTER 15

See RG 343-46

Council of Jerusalem. [1wx]*Some who had come down from Judea were instructing the brothers, "Unless you are circumcised according to the Mosaic practice, you cannot be saved." [2]Because there arose no little dissension and debate by Paul and Barnabas with them, it was decided that Paul, Barnabas, and some of the others should go up to Jerusalem to the apostles and presbyters about this question. [3]They were sent on their journey by the church, and passed through Phoenicia and Samaria telling of the conversion of the Gentiles, and brought great joy to all the brothers. [4]When they arrived in Jerusalem, they were welcomed by the church, as well as by the apostles and the presbyters, and they reported what God had done with them. [5]But some from the party of the Pharisees who had become believers stood up and said, "It is necessary to circumcise them and direct them to observe the Mosaic law."

[6]*The apostles and the presbyters met together to see about this matter. [7y]*After

---

14, 15–17: This is the first speech of Paul to Gentiles recorded by Luke in Acts (cf 17, 22–31). Rather than showing how Christianity is the logical outgrowth of Judaism, as he does in speeches before Jews, Luke says that God excuses past Gentile ignorance and then presents a natural theology arguing for the recognition of God's existence and presence through his activity in natural phenomena.

14, 23: They appointed presbyters: the communities are given their own religious leaders by the traveling missionaries. The structure in these churches is patterned on the model of the Jerusalem community (11, 30; 15, 2.5.22; 21, 18).

15, 1–35: The Jerusalem "Council" marks the official rejection of the rigid view that Gentile converts were obliged to observe the Mosaic law completely. From here to the end of Acts, Paul and the Gentile mission become the focus of Luke's writing.

15, 1–5: When some of the converted Pharisees of Jerusalem discover the results of the first missionary journey of

Paul, they urge that the Gentiles be taught to follow the Mosaic law. Recognizing the authority of the Jerusalem church, Paul and Barnabas go there to settle the question of whether Gentiles can embrace a form of Christianity that does not include this obligation.

15, 6–12: The gathering is possibly the same as that recalled by Paul in Gal 2, 1–10. Note that in v 2 it is only the apostles and presbyters, a small group, with whom Paul and Barnabas are to meet. Here Luke gives the meeting a public character because he wishes to emphasize its doctrinal significance (see 22).

15, 7–11: Paul's refusal to impose the Mosaic law on the Gentile Christians is supported by Peter on the ground that within his own experience God bestowed the holy Spirit upon

q: 3, 12; 10, 26; Ex 20, 11; Ps 146, 6. *r:* 17, 30. *s:* Wis 13, 1. *t:* 2 Cor 11, 25; 2 Tm 3, 11. *u:* 1 Thes 3, 3. *v:* 13, 1-3. *w:* Gal 2, 1-9. *x:* Lv 12, 3; Gal 5, 2. *y:* 10, 27-43.

much debate had taken place, Peter got up and said to them, "My brothers, you are well aware that from early days God made his choice among you that through my mouth the Gentiles would hear the word of the gospel and believe. [8z]And God, who knows the heart, bore witness by granting them the holy Spirit just as he did us. [9a]He made no distinction between us and them, for by faith he purified their hearts. [10b]Why, then, are you now putting God to the test by placing on the shoulders of the disciples a yoke that neither our ancestors nor we have been able to bear? [11c]*On the contrary, we believe that we are saved through the grace of the Lord Jesus, in the same way as they." [12]The whole assembly fell silent, and they listened while Paul and Barnabas described the signs and wonders God had worked among the Gentiles through them.

James on Dietary Law. [13]*After they had fallen silent, James responded, "My brothers, listen to me. [14]*Symeon has described how God first concerned himself with acquiring from among the Gentiles a people for his name. [15]The words of the prophets agree with this, as is written:

[16 d]'After this I shall return
    and rebuild the fallen hut of
        David;
from its ruins I shall rebuild it
    and raise it up again,
[17] so that the rest of humanity may seek out
        the Lord,
    even all the Gentiles on whom my
        name is invoked.

Thus says the Lord who accomplishes
        these things,
[18]   known from of old.'

[19e]It is my judgment, therefore, that we ought to stop troubling the Gentiles who turn to God, [20f]but tell them by letter to avoid pollution from idols, unlawful marriage, the meat of strangled animals, and blood. [21]For Moses, for generations now, has had those who proclaim him in every town, as he has been read in the synagogues every sabbath."

Letter of the Apostles. [22]Then the apostles and presbyters, in agreement with the whole church, decided to choose representatives and to send them to Antioch with Paul and Barnabas. The ones chosen were Judas, who was called Barsabbas, and Silas, leaders among the brothers. [23]This is the letter delivered by them: "The apostles and the presbyters, your brothers, to the brothers in Antioch, Syria, and Cilicia of Gentile origin: greetings. [24]Since we have heard that some of our number [who went out] without any mandate from us have upset you with their teachings and disturbed your peace of mind, [25]we have with one accord decided to choose representatives and to send them to you along with our beloved Barnabas and Paul, [26]who have dedicated their lives to the name of our Lord Jesus Christ. [27]So we are sending Judas and Silas who will also convey this same message by word of mouth: [28g]'It is the decision of the holy Spirit and of us not to place on you any burden beyond these necessities, [29h]namely, to abstain from meat sacrificed to idols, from blood, from

---

Cornelius and his household without preconditions concerning the adoption of the Mosaic law (see 10, 44–47).

15, 11: In support of Paul, Peter formulates the fundamental meaning of the gospel: that all are invited to be saved through faith in the power of Christ.

15, 13–35: Some scholars think that this apostolic decree suggested by James, the immediate leader of the Jerusalem community, derives from another historical occasion than the meeting in question. This seems to be the case if the meeting is the same as the one related in Gal 2, 1–10. According to that account, nothing was imposed upon Gentile Christians in respect to Mosaic law; whereas the decree instructs Gentile Christians of mixed communities to abstain from meats sacrificed to idols and from blood-meats, and to avoid marriage within forbidden degrees of consanguinity and affinity (Lv 18), all of which practices were especially abhorrent to Jews. Luke seems to have telescoped two originally independent in-

cidents here: the first a Jerusalem "Council" that dealt with the question of circumcision, and the second a Jerusalem decree dealing mainly with Gentile observance of dietary laws (see 21, 25 where Paul seems to be learning of the decree for the first time).

15, 14: Symeon: elsewhere in Acts he is called either Peter or Simon. The presence of the name Symeon here suggests that, in the source Luke is using for this part of the Jerusalem "Council" incident, the name may have originally referred to someone other than Peter (see 13, 1 where the Antiochene Symeon Niger is mentioned). As the text now stands, however, it is undoubtedly a reference to Simon Peter (7).

---

z: 10, 44-48.   a: 10, 34-35.   b: Mt 23, 4; Gal 5, 1.   c: Gal 2, 16; 3, 11; Eph 2, 5-8.   d: Am 9, 11-12.   e: 15, 28-29; 21, 25.   f: Gn 9, 4; Lv 3, 17; 17, 10-14.   g: 15, 19-20.   h: Gn 9, 4; Lv 3, 17; 17, 10-14.

Second Missionary Journey of Paul

meats of strangled animals, and from unlawful marriage. If you keep free of these, you will be doing what is right. Farewell.' "

Delegates at Antioch. [30]And so they were sent on their journey. Upon their arrival in Antioch they called the assembly together and delivered the letter. [31]When the people read it, they were delighted with the exhortation. [32]Judas and Silas, who were themselves prophets, exhorted and strengthened the brothers with many words. [33]After they had spent some time there, they were sent off with greetings of peace from the brothers to those who had commissioned them. [[34]]* [35]But Paul and Barnabas remained in Antioch, teaching and proclaiming with many others the word of the Lord.

V: The Mission of Paul to the Ends of the Earth

Paul and Barnabas Separate. [36]*After some time, Paul said to Barnabas, "Come, let us make a return visit to see how the brothers are getting on in all the cities where we proclaimed the word of the Lord." [37]Barnabas wanted to take with them also John, who was called Mark, [38]ibut Paul insisted that they should not take with them someone who had deserted them at Pamphylia and who had not continued with them in their work. [39]So sharp was their disagreement that they separated. Barnabas took Mark and sailed to Cyprus. [40]But Paul chose Silas and departed after being commended by the

brothers to the grace of the Lord. [41]He traveled through Syria and Cilicia bringing strength to the churches.

CHAPTER 16

Paul in Lycaonia: Timothy. [1]jHe reached [also] Derbe and Lystra where there was a disciple named Timothy, the son of a Jewish woman who was a believer, but his father was a Greek. [2]kThe brothers in Lystra and Iconium spoke highly of him, [3]*and Paul wanted him to come along with him. On account of the Jews of that region, Paul had him circumcised, for they all knew that his father was a Greek. [4]As they traveled from city to city, they handed on to the people for observance the decisions reached by the apostles and presbyters in Jerusalem. [5]Day after day the churches grew stronger in faith and increased in number.

Through Asia Minor. [6]They traveled through the Phrygian and Galatian territory because they had been prevented by the holy Spirit from preaching the message in the province of Asia. [7]*When they came to Mysia, they tried to go on into Bithynia, but the Spirit of Jesus did not allow them, [8]so they crossed through Mysia and came down to Troas. [9]During [the] night Paul had a vision. A Macedonian stood before him and implored him with these words, "Come over to Macedonia and help us." [10]*When he had seen the vision, we sought passage to Macedonia at once, concluding that God had called us to proclaim the good news to them.

See RG 344-46

15, 34: Some manuscripts add, in various wordings, "But Silas decided to remain there."

15, 36—18, 22: This continuous narrative recounts Paul's second missionary journey. On the internal evidence of the Lucan account, it lasted about three years. Paul first visited the communities he had established on his first journey (16, 1–5), then pushed on into Macedonia, where he established communities at Philippi, Thessalonica, and Beroea (16, 7—17, 5). To escape the hostility of the Jews of Thessalonica, he left for Greece and while resident in Athens attempted, without success, to establish an effective Christian community there. From Athens he proceeded to Corinth and, after a stay of a year and a half, returned to Antioch by way of Ephesus and Jerusalem (17, 16—18, 22). Luke does not concern himself with the structure or statistics of the communities but aims to show the general progress of the gospel in the Gentile world as well as its continued failure to take root in the Jewish community.

16, 3: Paul had him circumcised: he did this in order that

Timothy might be able to associate with the Jews and so perform a ministry among them. Paul did not object to the Jewish Christians' adherence to the law. But he insisted that the law could not be imposed on the Gentiles. Paul himself lived in accordance with the law, or as exempt from the law, according to particular circumstances (see 1 Cor 9, 19–23).

16, 7: The Spirit of Jesus: this is an unusual formulation in Luke's writings. The parallelism with v 6 indicates its meaning, the holy Spirit.

16, 10–17: This is the first of the so-called "we-sections" in Acts, where Luke writes as one of Paul's companions. The other passages are 20, 5–15; 21, 1–18; 27, 1—28, 16. Scholars debate whether Luke may not have used the first person plural simply as a literary device to lend color to the narrative. The realism of the narrative, however, lends weight to the argument that the "we" includes Luke or another companion of Paul whose data Luke used as a source.

i: 13, 13.   j: 1 Tm 1, 2; 2 Tm 1, 5.   k: Phil 2, 20.

Into Europe. [11]*We set sail from Troas, making a straight run for Samothrace, and on the next day to Neapolis, [12]and from there to Philippi, a leading city in that district of Macedonia and a Roman colony. We spent some time in that city. [13]On the sabbath we went outside the city gate along the river where we thought there would be a place of prayer. We sat and spoke with the women who had gathered there. [14]*One of them, a woman named Lydia, a dealer in purple cloth, from the city of Thyatira, a worshiper of God, listened, and the Lord opened her heart to pay attention to what Paul was saying. [15]After she and her household had been baptized, she offered us an invitation, "If you consider me a believer in the Lord, come and stay at my home," and she prevailed on us.

Imprisonment at Philippi. [16]*As we were going to the place of prayer, we met a slave girl with an oracular spirit, who used to bring a large profit to her owners through her fortune-telling. [17]She began to follow Paul and us, shouting, "These people are slaves of the Most High God, who proclaim to you a way of salvation." [18]She did this for many days. Paul became annoyed, turned, and said to the spirit, "I command you in the name of Jesus Christ to come out of her." Then it came out at that moment.

[19]When her owners saw that their hope of profit was gone, they seized Paul and Silas and dragged them to the public square before the local authorities. [20]*They brought them before the magistrates and said, "These people are Jews and are disturbing our city [21]and are advocating customs that are not lawful for us Romans to adopt or practice." [22]The crowd joined in the attack on them, and the magistrates had them stripped and ordered them to be beaten with rods. [23]After

inflicting many blows on them, they threw them into prison and instructed the jailer to guard them securely. [24]When he received these instructions, he put them in the innermost cell and secured their feet to a stake.

Deliverance from Prison. [25]About midnight, while Paul and Silas were praying and singing hymns to God as the prisoners listened, [26]there was suddenly such a severe earthquake that the foundations of the jail shook; all the doors flew open, and the chains of all were pulled loose. [27]When the jailer woke up and saw the prison doors wide open, he drew [his] sword and was about to kill himself, thinking that the prisoners had escaped. [28]But Paul shouted out in a loud voice, "Do no harm to yourself; we are all here." [29]He asked for a light and rushed in and, trembling with fear, he fell down before Paul and Silas. [30]Then he brought them out and said, "Sirs, what must I do to be saved?" [31]And they said, "Believe in the Lord Jesus and you and your household will be saved." [32]So they spoke the word of the Lord to him and to everyone in his house. [33]He took them in at that hour of the night and bathed their wounds; then he and all his family were baptized at once. [34]He brought them up into his house and provided a meal and with his household rejoiced at having come to faith in God.

[35]*But when it was day, the magistrates sent the lictors with the order, "Release those men." [36]The jailer reported the[se] words to Paul, "The magistrates have sent orders that you be released. Now, then, come out and go in peace." [37]m*But Paul said to them, "They have beaten us publicly, even though we are Roman citizens and have not been tried, and have thrown us into prison. And now, are they going to release us

---

16, 11–40: The church at Philippi became a flourishing community to which Paul addressed one of his letters (see Introduction to the Letter to the Philippians).

16, 14: **A worshiper of God:** a "God-fearer." See the note on 8, 26–40.

16, 16: **With an oracular spirit:** literally, "with a Python spirit." The Python was the serpent or dragon that guarded the Delphic oracle. It later came to designate a "spirit that pronounced oracles" and also a ventriloquist who, it was thought, had such a spirit in the belly.

16, 20: **Magistrates:** in Greek, **stratēgoi,** the popular des-

ignation of the **duoviri,** the highest officials of the Roman colony of Philippi.

16, 35: **The lictors:** the equivalent of police officers, among whose duties were the apprehension and punishment of criminals.

16, 37: Paul's Roman citizenship granted him special privileges in regard to criminal process. Roman law forbade under severe penalty the beating of Roman citizens (see also 22, 25).

---

l: 2 Cor 11, 25; Phil 1, 30; 1 Thes 2, 2.   *m:* 22, 25.

secretly? By no means. Let them come themselves and lead us out." ³⁸ⁿThe lictors reported these words to the magistrates, and they became alarmed when they heard that they were Roman citizens. ³⁹So they came and placated them, and led them out and asked that they leave the city. ⁴⁰When they had come out of the prison, they went to Lydia's house where they saw and encouraged the brothers, and then they left.

See RG 344–46

CHAPTER 17

Paul in Thessalonica. ¹ᵒWhen they took the road through Amphipolis and Apollonia, they reached Thessalonica, where there was a synagogue of the Jews. ²Following his usual custom, Paul joined them, and for three sabbaths he entered into discussions with them from the scriptures, ³ᵖexpounding and demonstrating that the Messiah had to suffer and rise from the dead, and that "This is the Messiah, Jesus, whom I proclaim to you." ⁴Some of them were convinced and joined Paul and Silas; so, too, a great number of Greeks who were worshipers, and not a few of the prominent women. ⁵�q But the Jews became jealous and recruited some worthless men loitering in the public square, formed a mob, and set the city in turmoil. They marched on the house of Jason, intending to bring them before the people's assembly. ⁶*When they could not find them, they dragged Jason and some of the brothers before the city magistrates, shouting, "These people who have been creating a disturbance all over the world have now come here,

⁷ʳ*and Jason has welcomed them. They all act in opposition to the decrees of Caesar and claim instead that there is another king, Jesus." ⁸They stirred up the crowd and the city magistrates who, upon hearing these charges, ⁹took a surety payment from Jason and the others before releasing them.

Paul in Beroea. ¹⁰The brothers immediately sent Paul and Silas to Beroea during the night. Upon arrival they went to the synagogue of the Jews. ¹¹ˢThese Jews were more fair-minded than those in Thessalonica, for they received the word with all willingness and examined the scriptures daily to determine whether these things were so. ¹²Many of them became believers, as did not a few of the influential Greek women and men. ¹³But when the Jews of Thessalonica learned that the word of God had now been proclaimed by Paul in Beroea also, they came there too to cause a commotion and stir up the crowds. ¹⁴ᵗSo the brothers at once sent Paul on his way to the seacoast, while Silas and Timothy remained behind. ¹⁵After Paul's escorts had taken him to Athens, they came away with instructions for Silas and Timothy to join him as soon as possible.

Paul in Athens. ¹⁶*While Paul was waiting for them in Athens, he grew exasperated at the sight of the city full of idols. ¹⁷So he debated in the synagogue with the Jews and with the worshipers, and daily in the public square with whoever happened to be there. ¹⁸*Even some of the Epicurean and Stoic philosophers engaged him in discussion. Some asked, "What is this scavenger trying

17, 6–7: The accusations against Paul and his companions echo the charges brought against Jesus in Lk 23, 2.

17, 7: There is another king, Jesus: a distortion into a political sense of the apostolic proclamation of Jesus and the kingdom of God (see 8, 12).

17, 16–21: Paul's presence in Athens sets the stage for the great discourse before a Gentile audience in vv 22–31. Although Athens was a politically insignificant city at this period, it still lived on the glories of its past and represented the center of Greek culture. The setting describes the conflict between Christian preaching and Hellenistic philosophy.

17, 18: Epicurean and Stoic philosophers: for the followers of Epicurus (342–271 B.C.), the goal of life was happiness attained through sober reasoning and the searching out of motives for all choice and avoidance. The Stoics were followers of Zeno, a younger contemporary of Alexander the Great. Zeno and his followers believed in a type of pan-

theism that held that the spark of divinity was present in all reality and that, in order to be free, each person must live "according to nature." **This scavenger:** literally, "seedpicker," as of a bird that picks up grain. The word is later used of scrap collectors and of people who take other people's ideas and propagate them as if they were their own. **Promoter of foreign deities:** according to Xenophon, Socrates was accused of promoting new deities. The accusation against Paul echoes the charge against Socrates. **'Jesus' and 'Resurrection':** the Athenians are presented as misunderstanding Paul from the outset; they think he is preaching about Jesus and a goddess named **Anastasis,** i.e., Resurrection.

n: 22, 29. *o:* 1 Thes 2, 1-2. *p:* 3, 18; Lk 24, 25-26.46. *q:* Rom 16, 21. *r:* Lk 23, 2; Jn 19, 12-15. *s:* Jn 5, 39. *t:* 1 Thes 3, 1-2.

to say?" Others said, "He sounds like a promoter of foreign deities," because he was preaching about 'Jesus' and 'Resurrection.' [19u]*They took him and led him to the Areopagus and said, "May we learn what this new teaching is that you speak of? [20]For you bring some strange notions to our ears; we should like to know what these things mean." [21]Now all the Athenians as well as the foreigners residing there used their time for nothing else but telling or hearing something new.

Paul's Speech at the Areopagus. [22]*Then Paul stood up at the Areopagus and said:

"You Athenians, I see that in every respect you are very religious. [23]*For as I walked around looking carefully at your shrines, I even discovered an altar inscribed, 'To an Unknown God.' What therefore you unknowingly worship, I proclaim to you. [24v]The God who made the world and all that is in it, the Lord of heaven and earth, does not dwell in sanctuaries made by human hands, [25]nor is he served by human hands because he needs anything. Rather it is he who gives to everyone life and breath and everything. [26]*He made from one the whole human race to dwell on the entire surface of the earth, and he fixed the ordered seasons and the boundaries of their regions, [27w]so that people might seek God, even perhaps grope for him and find him, though indeed he is not far from any one of us. [28]*For 'In him we live and

move and have our being,' as even some of your poets have said, 'For we too are his offspring.' [29x]Since therefore we are the offspring of God, we ought not to think that the divinity is like an image fashioned from gold, silver, or stone by human art and imagination. [30]God has overlooked the times of ignorance, but now he demands that all people everywhere repent [31y]because he has established a day on which he will 'judge the world with justice' through a man he has appointed, and he has provided confirmation for all by raising him from the dead."

[32]When they heard about resurrection of the dead, some began to scoff, but others said, "We should like to hear you on this some other time." [33]And so Paul left them. [34]But some did join him, and became believers. Among them were Dionysius, a member of the Court of the Areopagus, a woman named Damaris, and others with them.

CHAPTER 18

See RG 344-48

Paul in Corinth. [1]After this he left Athens and went to Corinth. [2z]*There he met a Jew named Aquila, a native of Pontus, who had recently come from Italy with his wife Priscilla because Claudius had ordered all the Jews to leave Rome. He went to visit them [3]and, because he practiced the same trade, stayed with them and worked, for they were tentmakers by trade. [4]Every sabbath, he

---

17, 19: To the Areopagus: the "Areopagus" refers either to the Hill of Ares west of the Acropolis or to the Council of Athens, which at one time met on the hill but which at this time assembled in the Royal Colonnade (**Stoa Basileios**).

17, 22–31: In Paul's appearance at the Areopagus he preaches his climactic speech to Gentiles in the cultural center of the ancient world. The speech is more theological than christological. Paul's discourse appeals to the Greek world's belief in divinity as responsible for the origin and existence of the universe. It contests the common belief in a multiplicity of gods supposedly exerting their powers through their images. It acknowledges that the attempt to find God is a constant human endeavor. It declares, further, that God is the judge of the human race, that the time of the judgment has been determined, and that it will be executed through a man whom God raised from the dead. The speech reflects sympathy with pagan religiosity, handles the subject of idol worship gently, and appeals for a new examination of divinity, not from the standpoint of creation but from the standpoint of judgment.

17, 23: 'To an Unknown God': ancient authors such as Pausanias, Philostratus, and Tertullian speak of Athenian altars with no specific dedication as altars of "unknown gods" or "nameless altars."

17, 26: From one: many manuscripts read "from one blood." **Fixed . . . seasons:** or "fixed limits to the epochs."

17, 28: 'In him we live and move and have our being': some scholars understand this saying to be based on an earlier saying of Epimenides of Knossos (6th century B.C.). **'For we too are his offspring':** here Paul is quoting Aratus of Soli, a third-century B.C. poet from Cilicia.

18, 2: Aquila . . . Priscilla: both may already have been Christians at the time of their arrival in Corinth (see 26). According to 1 Cor 16, 19, their home became a meeting place for Christians. **Claudius:** the Emperor Claudius expelled the Jews from Rome ca. A.D. 49. The Roman historian Suetonius gives as reason for the expulsion disturbances among the Jews "at the instigation of Chrestos," probably meaning disputes about the messiahship of Jesus.

---

u: 1 Cor 1, 22. *v:* 7, 48-50; Gn 1, 1; 1 Kgs 8, 27; Is 42, 5. *w:* Jer 23, 23; Wis 13, 6; Rom 1, 19. *x:* 19, 26; Is 40, 18-20; 44, 10-17; Rom 1, 22-23. *y:* 10, 42. *z:* Rom 16, 3.

entered into discussions in the synagogue, attempting to convince both Jews and Greeks.

[5]When Silas and Timothy came down from Macedonia, Paul began to occupy himself totally with preaching the word, testifying to the Jews that the Messiah was Jesus. [6a]*When they opposed him and reviled him, he shook out his garments and said to them, "Your blood be on your heads! I am clear of responsibility. From now on I will go to the Gentiles." [7b]*So he left there and went to a house belonging to a man named Titus Justus, a worshiper of God; his house was next to a synagogue. [8c]*Crispus, the synagogue official, came to believe in the Lord along with his entire household, and many of the Corinthians who heard believed and were baptized. [9d]One night in a vision the Lord said to Paul, "Do not be afraid. Go on speaking, and do not be silent, [10]for I am with you. No one will attack and harm you, for I have many people in this city." [11]He settled there for a year and a half and taught the word of God among them.

Accusations before Gallio. [12]*But when Gallio was proconsul of Achaia, the Jews rose up together against Paul and brought him to the tribunal, [13]*saying, "This man is inducing people to worship God contrary to the law." [14]When Paul was about to reply, Gallio spoke to the Jews, "If it were a matter of some crime or malicious fraud, I should with reason hear the complaint of you Jews; [15]but since it is a question of arguments over doctrine and titles and your own law, see to it yourselves. I do not wish to be a judge of such matters." [16]And he drove them away from the tribunal. [17]They all seized Sosthenes, the synagogue official, and beat him in full view of the tribunal. But none of this was of concern to Gallio.

Return to Syrian Antioch. [18e]*Paul remained for quite some time, and after saying farewell to the brothers he sailed for Syria, together with Priscilla and Aquila. At Cenchreae he had his hair cut because he had taken a vow. [19]When they reached Ephesus, he left them there, while he entered the synagogue and held discussions with the Jews. [20]Although they asked him to stay for a longer time, he did not consent, [21]but as he said farewell he promised, "I shall come back to you again, God willing." Then he set sail from Ephesus. [22]*Upon landing at Caesarea, he went up and greeted the church and then went down to Antioch. [23]*After staying there some time, he left and traveled in orderly sequence through the Galatian country and Phrygia, bringing strength to all the disciples.

Apollos. [24f]*A Jew named Apollos, a native of Alexandria, an eloquent speaker, arrived in Ephesus. He was an authority on the scriptures. [25]He had been instructed in the Way of the Lord and, with ardent spirit, spoke and taught accurately about Jesus, although he knew only the baptism of John. [26]*He began to speak boldly in the synagogue; but when Priscilla and Aquila heard him, they took him aside and explained to him the Way [of God] more accurately. [27]And when he wanted to cross to Achaia, the brothers encouraged him and wrote to the disciples there to welcome him. After his arrival he gave great assistance

---

18, 6: Shook out his garments: a gesture indicating Paul's repudiation of his mission to the Jews there; cf 28, 17–31.

18, 7: A worshiper of God: see the note on 8, 26–40.

18, 8: Crispus: in 1 Cor 1, 14, Paul mentions that Crispus was one of the few he himself baptized at Corinth.

18, 12: When Gallio was proconsul of Achaia: Gallio's proconsulship in Achaia is dated to A.D. 51–52 from an inscription discovered at Delphi. This has become an important date in establishing a chronology of the life and missionary work of Paul.

18, 13: Contrary to the law: Gallio (15) understands this to be a problem of Jewish, not Roman, law.

18, 18: He had his hair cut because he had taken a vow: a reference to a Nazirite vow (see Nm 6, 1–21, especially, 6, 18) taken by Paul (see also 21, 23–27).

18, 22: He went up and greeted the church: "going up" suggests a visit to the church in Jerusalem.

18, 23—21, 16: Luke's account of Paul's third missionary journey devotes itself mainly to his work at Ephesus (19, 1—20, 1). There is a certain restiveness on Paul's part and a growing conviction that the Spirit bids him return to Jerusalem and prepare to go to Rome (19, 21).

18, 24–25: Apollos appears as a preacher who knows the teaching of Jesus in the context of John's baptism of repentance. Aquila and Priscilla instruct him more fully. He is referred to in 1 Cor 1, 12; 3, 5–6.22.

18, 26: The Way [of God]: for the Way, see the note on 9, 2. Other manuscripts here read "the Way of the Lord." "the word of the Lord," or simply "the Way."

---

a: 13, 51; Mt 10, 14; 27, 24-25; Mk 6, 11; Lk 9, 5; 10, 10-11. *b:* 13, 46-47; 28, 28. *c:* 1 Cor 1, 14. *d:* Jer 1, 8. *e:* 21, 24; Nm 6, 18. *f:* 1 Cor 1, 12.

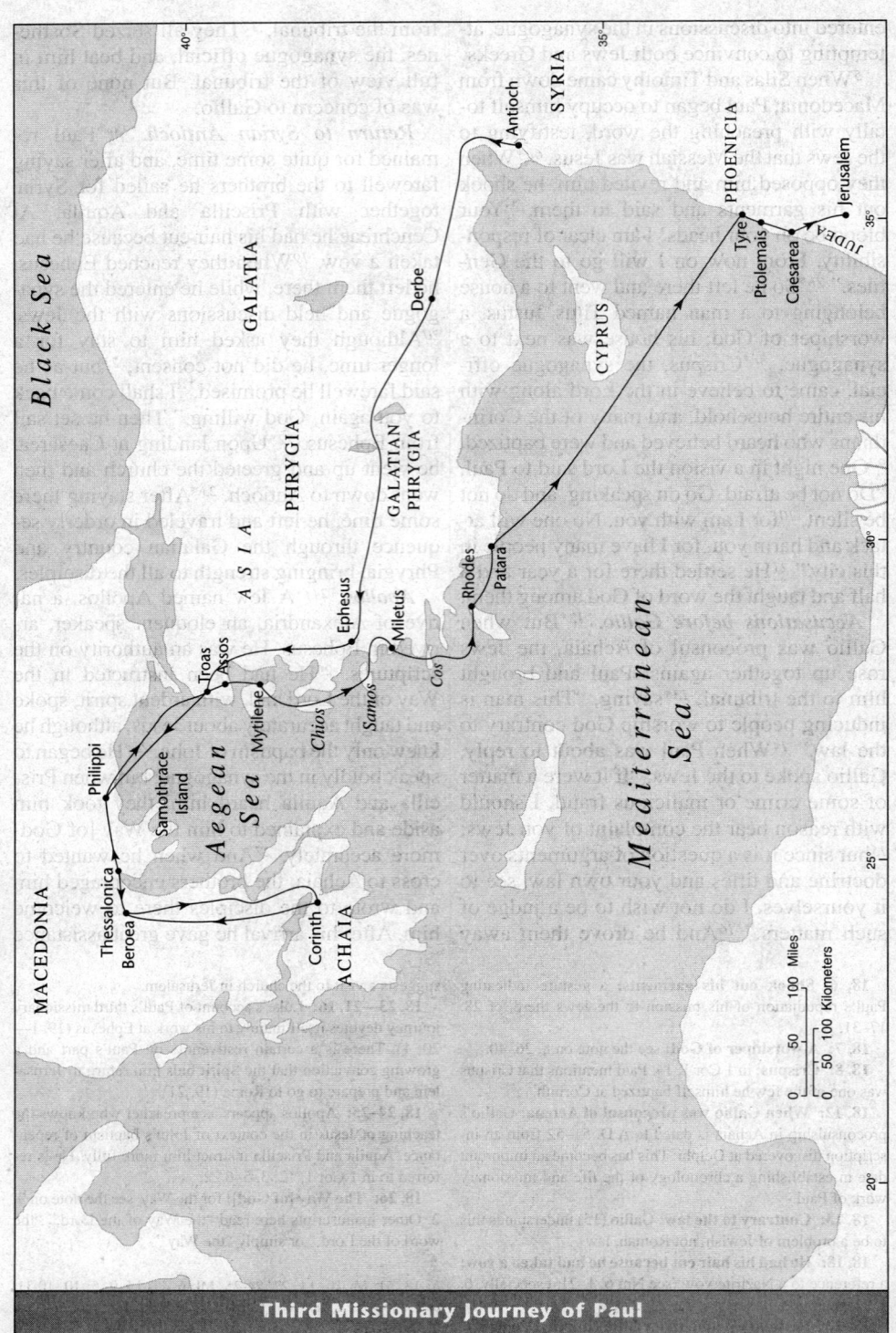

Third Missionary Journey of Paul

to those who had come to believe through grace. [28]He vigorously refuted the Jews in public, establishing from the scriptures that the Messiah is Jesus.

See RG 346–48

CHAPTER 19

Paul in Ephesus. [1]*While Apollos was in Corinth, Paul traveled through the interior of the country and came [down] to Ephesus where he found some disciples. [2]He said to them, "Did you receive the holy Spirit when you became believers?" They answered him, "We have never even heard that there is a holy Spirit." [3]He said, "How were you baptized?" They replied, "With the baptism of John." [4]gPaul then said, "John baptized with a baptism of repentance, telling the people to believe in the one who was to come after him, that is, in Jesus." [5]When they heard this, they were baptized in the name of the Lord Jesus. [6]hAnd when Paul laid [his] hands on them, the holy Spirit came upon them, and they spoke in tongues and prophesied. [7]Altogether there were about twelve men.

[8]He entered the synagogue, and for three months debated boldly with persuasive arguments about the kingdom of God. [9]But when some in their obstinacy and disbelief disparaged the Way before the assembly, he withdrew and took his disciples with him and began to hold daily discussions in the lecture hall of Tyrannus. [10]This continued for two years with the result that all the inhabitants of the province of Asia heard the word of the Lord, Jews and Greeks alike. [11]So extraordinary were the mighty deeds God accomplished at the hands of Paul [12]ithat when face cloths or aprons that touched his skin were applied to the sick, their diseases left them and the evil spirits came out of them.

The Jewish Exorcists. [13]Then some itinerant Jewish exorcists tried to invoke the name of the Lord Jesus over those with evil spirits, saying, "I adjure you by the Jesus whom Paul preaches." [14]When the seven sons of Sceva, a Jewish high priest, tried to do this, [15]the evil spirit said to them in reply, "Jesus I recognize, Paul I know, but who are you?" [16]The person with the evil spirit then sprang at them and subdued them all. He so overpowered them that they fled naked and wounded from that house. [17]When this became known to all the Jews and Greeks who lived in Ephesus, fear fell upon them all, and the name of the Lord Jesus was held in great esteem. [18]Many of those who had become believers came forward and openly acknowledged their former practices. [19]Moreover, a large number of those who had practiced magic collected their books and burned them in public. They calculated their value and found it to be fifty thousand silver pieces. [20]Thus did the word of the Lord continue to spread with influence and power.

Paul's Plans. [21]jWhen this was concluded, Paul made up his mind to travel through Macedonia and Achaia, and then to go on to Jerusalem, saying, "After I have been there, I must visit Rome also." [22]Then he sent to Macedonia two of his assistants, Timothy and Erastus, while he himself stayed for a while in the province of Asia.

The Riot of the Silversmiths. [23]About that time a serious disturbance broke out concerning the Way. [24]*There was a silversmith named Demetrius who made miniature silver shrines of Artemis and provided no little work for the craftsmen. [25]He called a meeting of these and other workers in related crafts and said, "Men, you know well that our prosperity derives from this work. [26]kAs you can now see and hear, not only in Ephesus but throughout most of the province of Asia this Paul has persuaded and misled a great number of people by saying that gods made by hands are not gods at all. [27]The dan-

19, 1–6: Upon his arrival in Ephesus, Paul discovers other people at the same religious stage as Apollos, though they seem to have considered themselves followers of Christ, not of the Baptist. On the relation between baptism and the reception of the Spirit, see the note on 8, 16.

19, 24: Miniature silver shrines of Artemis: the temple of Artemis at Ephesus was one of the seven wonders of the ancient world. Artemis, originally the Olympian virgin hunter, moon goddess, and goddess of wild nature, was worshiped at Ephesus as an Asian mother goddess and goddess of fertility. She was one of the most widely worshiped female deities in the Hellenistic world (see 18, 27).

g: 1, 5; 11, 16; 13, 24-25; Mt 3, 11; Mk 1, 8; Lk 3, 16. *h.* 8, 15-17; 10, 44.46. *i:* 5, 15-16; Lk 8, 44-47. *j:* 23, 11; Rom 1, 13; 15, 22-32. *k:* 17, 29.

ger grows, not only that our business will be discredited, but also that the temple of the great goddess Artemis will be of no account, and that she whom the whole province of Asia and all the world worship will be stripped of her magnificence."

[28]When they heard this, they were filled with fury and began to shout, "Great is Artemis of the Ephesians!" [29]*l*The city was filled with confusion, and the people rushed with one accord into the theater, seizing Gaius and Aristarchus, the Macedonians, Paul's traveling companions. [30]Paul wanted to go before the crowd, but the disciples would not let him, [31]*and even some of the Asiarchs who were friends of his sent word to him advising him not to venture into the theater. [32]Meanwhile, some were shouting one thing, others something else; the assembly was in chaos, and most of the people had no idea why they had come together. [33]Some of the crowd prompted Alexander, as the Jews pushed him forward, and Alexander signaled with his hand that he wished to explain something to the gathering. [34]But when they recognized that he was a Jew, they all shouted in unison, for about two hours, "Great is Artemis of the Ephesians!" [35]*Finally the town clerk restrained the crowd and said, "You Ephesians, what person is there who does not know that the city of the Ephesians is the guardian of the temple of the great Artemis and of her image that fell from the sky? [36]Since these things are undeniable, you must calm yourselves and not do anything rash. [37]The men you brought here are not temple robbers, nor have they insulted our goddess. [38]If Demetrius and his fellow craftsmen have a complaint against

anyone, courts are in session, and there are proconsuls. Let them bring charges against one another. [39]If you have anything further to investigate, let the matter be settled in the lawful assembly, [40]*for, as it is, we are in danger of being charged with rioting because of today's conduct. There is no cause for it. We shall [not] be able to give a reason for this demonstration." With these words he dismissed the assembly.

CHAPTER 20

See RG 346–48

Journey to Macedonia and Greece. [1]*m*When the disturbance was over, Paul had the disciples summoned and, after encouraging them, he bade them farewell and set out on his journey to Macedonia. [2]As he traveled throughout those regions, he provided many words of encouragement for them. Then he arrived in Greece, [3]where he stayed for three months. But when a plot was made against him by the Jews as he was about to set sail for Syria, he decided to return by way of Macedonia.

Return to Troas. [4]*n*Sopater, the son of Pyrrhus, from Beroea, accompanied him, as did Aristarchus and Secundus from Thessalonica, Gaius from Derbe, Timothy, and Tychicus and Trophimus from Asia [5]*o*who went on ahead and waited for us at Troas. [6]*We sailed from Philippi after the feast of Unleavened Bread, and rejoined them five days later in Troas, where we spent a week.

Eutychus Restored to Life. [7]*On the first day of the week when we gathered to break bread, Paul spoke to them because he was going to leave on the next day, and he kept on speaking until midnight. [8]There were many lamps in the upstairs room where we

---

19, 31: Asiarchs: the precise status and role of the Asiarchs is disputed. They appear to have been people of wealth and influence who promoted the Roman imperial cult and who may also have been political representatives in a league of cities in the Roman province of Asia.

19, 35: Guardian of the temple: this title was accorded by Rome to cities that provided a temple for the imperial cult. Inscriptional evidence indicates that Ephesus was acknowledged as the temple keeper of Artemis and of the imperial cult. **That fell from the sky:** many scholars think that this refers to a meteorite that was worshiped as an image of the goddess.

19, 40: Some manuscripts omit the negative in [not] be

able, making the meaning, "There is no cause for which we shall be able to give a reason for this demonstration."

20, 5: The second "we-section" of Acts begins here. See the note on 16, 10–17.

20, 6: Feast of Unleavened Bread: see the note on Lk 22, 1.

20, 7: The first day of the week: the day after the sabbath and the first day of the Jewish week, apparently chosen originally by the Jerusalem community for the celebration of the liturgy of the Eucharist in order to relate it to the resurrection of Christ.

l: Col 4, 10. *m*: 1 Cor 16, 1. *n*: Rom 16, 21. *o*: 21, 29; 2 Tm 4, 20.

were gathered, [9]and a young man named Eutychus who was sitting on the window sill was sinking into a deep sleep as Paul talked on and on. Once overcome by sleep, he fell down from the third story and when he was picked up, he was dead. [10p]*Paul went down, threw himself upon him, and said as he embraced him, "Don't be alarmed; there is life in him." [11]Then he returned upstairs, broke the bread, and ate; after a long conversation that lasted until daybreak, he departed. [12]And they took the boy away alive and were immeasurably comforted.

Journey to Miletus. [13]We went ahead to the ship and set sail for Assos where we were to take Paul on board, as he had arranged, since he was going overland. [14]When he met us in Assos, we took him aboard and went on to Mitylene. [15]We sailed away from there on the next day and reached a point off Chios, and a day later we reached Samos, and on the following day we arrived at Miletus. [16]*Paul had decided to sail past Ephesus in order not to lose time in the province of Asia, for he was hurrying to be in Jerusalem, if at all possible, for the day of Pentecost.

Paul's Farewell Speech at Miletus. [17]From Miletus he had the presbyters of the church at Ephesus summoned. [18]When they came to him, he addressed them, "You know how I lived among you the whole time from the day I first came to the province of Asia. [19]I served the Lord with all humility and with the tears and trials that came to me because of the plots of the Jews, [20]and I did not at all shrink from telling you what was for your benefit, or from teaching you in public or in your homes. [21]I earnestly bore witness for both Jews and Greeks to repentance before God

and to faith in our Lord Jesus. [22]But now, compelled by the Spirit, I am going to Jerusalem. What will happen to me there I do not know, [23q]except that in one city after another the holy Spirit has been warning me that imprisonment and hardships await me. [24r]Yet I consider life of no importance to me, if only I may finish my course and the ministry that I received from the Lord Jesus, to bear witness to the gospel of God's grace.

[25]"But now I know that none of you to whom I preached the kingdom during my travels will ever see my face again. [26]And so I solemnly declare to you this day that I am not responsible for the blood of any of you, [27]for I did not shrink from proclaiming to you the entire plan of God. [28s]*Keep watch over yourselves and over the whole flock of which the holy Spirit has appointed you overseers, in which you tend the church of God that he acquired with his own blood. [29]I know that after my departure savage wolves will come among you, and they will not spare the flock. [30u]And from your own group, men will come forward perverting the truth to draw the disciples away after them. [31v]So be vigilant and remember that for three years, night and day, I unceasingly admonished each of you with tears. [32]And now I commend you to God and to that gracious word of his that can build you up and give you the inheritance among all who are consecrated. [33]I have never wanted anyone's silver or gold or clothing. [34w]You know well that these very hands have served my needs and my companions. [35x]In every way I have shown you that by hard work of that sort we must help the weak, and keep in mind the words of the Lord Jesus who himself said, 'It is more blessed to give than to receive.' "

20, 10: The action of Paul in throwing himself upon the dead boy recalls that of Elijah in 1 Kgs 17, 21 where the son of the widow of Zarephath is revived and that of Elisha in 2 Kgs 4, 34 where the Shunamite woman's son is restored to life.

20, 16–35: Apparently aware of difficulties at Ephesus and neighboring areas, Paul calls the presbyters together at Miletus, about thirty miles from Ephesus. He reminds them of his dedication to the gospel (18–21), speaks of what he is about to suffer for the gospel (22–27), and admonishes them to guard the community against false prophets, sure to arise upon his departure (28–31). He concludes by citing a saying of Jesus (35) not recorded in the gospel tradition. Luke pre-

sents this farewell to the Ephesian presbyters as Paul's last will and testament.

20, 28: **Overseers:** see the note on Phil 1, 1. **The church of God:** because the clause "that he acquired with his own blood" following "the church of God" suggests that "his own blood" refers to God's blood, some early copyists changed "the church of Goc" to "the church of the Lord." Some prefer the translation "acquired with the blood of his own," i.e., Christ.

p: 1 Kgs 17, 17-24; 2 Kgs 4, 30-37; Mt 9, 24; Mk 5, 39; Lk 8, 52. q: 9, 16. r: 2 Tm 4, 7. s: Jn 21, 15-17; 1 Pt 5, 2. t: Jn 10, 12. u: Mt 7, 15; 2 Pt 2, 1-3; 1 Jn 2, 18-19. v: 1 Thes 2, 11. w: 1 Cor 4, 12; 1 Thes 2, 9; 2 Thes 3, 8. x: Sir 4, 31.

[36]When he had finished speaking he knelt down and prayed with them all. [37]They were all weeping loudly as they threw their arms around Paul and kissed him, [38]for they were deeply distressed that he had said that they would never see his face again. Then they escorted him to the ship.

CHAPTER 21

See RG
346–48

Arrival at Tyre. [1]*When we had taken leave of them we set sail, made a straight run for Cos, and on the next day for Rhodes, and from there to Patara. [2]Finding a ship crossing to Phoenicia, we went on board and put out to sea. [3]We caught sight of Cyprus but passed by it on our left and sailed on toward Syria and put in at Tyre where the ship was to unload cargo. [4]There we sought out the disciples and stayed for a week. They kept telling Paul through the Spirit not to embark for Jerusalem. [5]At the end of our stay we left and resumed our journey. All of them, women and children included, escorted us out of the city, and after kneeling on the beach to pray, [6]we bade farewell to one another. Then we boarded the ship, and they returned home.

Arrival at Ptolemais and Caesarea. [7]We continued the voyage and came from Tyre to Ptolemais, where we greeted the brothers and stayed a day with them. [8]y*On the next day we resumed the trip and came to Caesarea, where we went to the house of Philip the evangelist, who was one of the Seven, and stayed with him. [9]He had four virgin daughters gifted with prophecy. [10]*We had been there several days when a prophet named Agabus came down from Judea. [11]z*He came up to us, took Paul's belt, bound his own feet and hands

with it, and said, "Thus says the holy Spirit: This is the way the Jews will bind the owner of this belt in Jerusalem, and they will hand him over to the Gentiles." [12]When we heard this, we and the local residents begged him not to go up to Jerusalem. [13]aThen Paul replied, "What are you doing, weeping and breaking my heart? I am prepared not only to be bound but even to die in Jerusalem for the name of the Lord Jesus." [14]b*Since he would not be dissuaded we let the matter rest, saying, "The Lord's will be done."

Paul and James in Jerusalem. [15]After these days we made preparations for our journey, then went up to Jerusalem. [16]Some of the disciples from Caesarea came along to lead us to the house of Mnason, a Cypriot, a disciple of long standing, with whom we were to stay. [17]*When we reached Jerusalem the brothers welcomed us warmly. [18]The next day, Paul accompanied us on a visit to James, and all the presbyters were present. [19]He greeted them, then proceeded to tell them in detail what God had accomplished among the Gentiles through his ministry. [20]They praised God when they heard it but said to him, "Brother, you see how many thousands of believers there are from among the Jews, and they are all zealous observers of the law. [21]They have been informed that you are teaching all the Jews who live among the Gentiles to abandon Moses and that you are telling them not to circumcise their children or to observe their customary practices. [22]What is to be done? They will surely hear that you have arrived. [23]c*So do what we tell you. We have four men who have taken a vow. [24]*Take these men and purify yourself

---

21, 1–18: The third "we-section" of Acts (see the note on 16, 10–17).

21, 8: One of the Seven: see the note on 6, 2–4.

21, 10: Agabus: mentioned in 11, 28 as the prophet who predicted the famine that occurred when Claudius was emperor.

21, 11: The symbolic act of Agabus recalls those of Old Testament prophets. Compare Is 20, 2; Ez 4, 1; Jer 13, 1.

21, 14: The Christian disciples' attitude reflects that of Jesus (see Lk 22, 42).

21, 17–26: The leaders of the Jewish Christians of Jerusalem inform Paul that the Jews there believe he has encouraged the Jews of the diaspora to abandon the Mosaic law. According to Acts, Paul had no objection to the retention of the law by the Jewish Christians of Jerusalem and left the Jews of the diaspora who accepted Christianity free to follow the same practice.

21, 23–26: The leaders of the community suggest that Paul, on behalf of four members of the Jerusalem community, make the customary payment for the sacrifices offered at the termination of the Nazirite vow (see Nm 6, 1–24) in order to impress favorably the Jewish Christians in Jerusalem with his high regard for the Mosaic law. Since Paul himself had once made this vow (18, 18), his respect for the law would be on public record.

21, 24: Pay their expenses: according to Nm 6, 14–15 the Nazirite had to present a yearling lamb for a holocaust, a yearling ewe lamb for a sin offering, and a ram for a peace offering, along with food and drink offerings, upon completion of the period of the vow.

y: 6, 5; 8, 5-6. *z:* 11, 28; 20, 23. *a:* 19, 15-16. *b:* Mt 6, 10; 26, 39; Mk 14, 36; Lk 22, 42. *c:* 18, 18; Nm 6, 1-21.

with them, and pay their expenses that they may have their heads shaved. In this way everyone will know that there is nothing to the reports they have been given about you but that you yourself live in observance of the law. 25d*As for the Gentiles who have come to believe, we sent them our decision that they abstain from meat sacrificed to idols, from blood, from the meat of strangled animals, and from unlawful marriage." 26eSo Paul took the men, and on the next day after purifying himself together with them entered the temple to give notice of the day when the purification would be completed and the offering made for each of them.

Paul's Arrest. 27When the seven days were nearly completed, the Jews from the province of Asia noticed him in the temple, stirred up the whole crowd, and laid hands on him, 28f*shouting, "Fellow Israelites, help us. This is the man who is teaching everyone everywhere against the people and the law and this place, and what is more, he has even brought Greeks into the temple and defiled this sacred place." 29For they had previously seen Trophimus the Ephesian in the city with him and supposed that Paul had brought him into the temple. 30The whole city was in turmoil with people rushing together. They seized Paul and dragged him out of the temple, and immediately the gates were closed. 31*While they were trying to kill him, a report reached the cohort commander that all Jerusalem was rioting. 32He immediately took soldiers and centurions and charged down on them. When

they saw the commander and the soldiers they stopped beating Paul. 33The cohort commander came forward, arrested him, and ordered him to be secured with two chains; he tried to find out who he might be and what he had done. 34Some in the mob shouted one thing, others something else; so, since he was unable to ascertain the truth because of the uproar, he ordered Paul to be brought into the compound. 35When he reached the steps, he was carried by the soldiers because of the violence of the mob, 36g*for a crowd of people followed and shouted, "Away with him!" 27Just as Paul was about to be taken into the compound, he said to the cohort commander, "May I say something to you?" He replied, "Do you speak Greek? 38h*So then you are not the Egyptian who started a revolt some time ago and led the four thousand assassins into the desert?" 39Paul answered, "I am a Jew, of Tarsus in Cilicia, a citizen of no mean city; I request you to permit me to speak to the people." 40*When he had given his permission, Paul stood on the steps and motioned with his hand to the people; and when all was quiet he addressed them in Hebrew.

CHAPTER 22

See RG 348

Paul's Defense before the Jerusalem Jews. 1*"My brothers and fathers, listen to what I am about to say to you in my defense." 2When they heard him addressing them in Hebrew they became all the more quiet. And he continued, 3i"I am a Jew, born in Tarsus in Cilicia, but brought up in this

21, 25: Paul is informed about the apostolic decree, seemingly for the first time (see the note on 15, 13–35). The allusion to the decree was probably introduced here by Luke to remind his readers that the Gentile Christians themselves were asked to respect certain Jewish practices deriving from the law.

21, 28: The charges against Paul by the diaspora Jews are identical to the charges brought against Stephen by diaspora Jews in 6, 13. **Brought Greeks into the temple:** non-Jews were forbidden, under penalty of death, to go beyond the Court of the Gentiles. Inscriptions in Greek and Latin on a stone ballustrade marked off the prohibited area.

21, 31: **Cohort commander:** literally, "the leader of a thousand in a cohort." At this period the Roman cohort commander usually led six hundred soldiers, a tenth of a legion; but the number in a cohort varied.

21, 36: **Away with him:** at the trial of Jesus before Pilate in Lk 23, 18, the people similarly shout, "Away with this man."

21, 38: **The Egyptian:** according to the Jewish historian

Josephus, an Egyptian gathered a large crowd on the Mount of Olives to witness the destruction of the walls of Jerusalem that would fall at the Egyptian "prophet's" word. The commotion was put down by the Roman authorities and the Egyptian escaped, but only after thousands had been killed. **Four thousand assassins:** literally, **sicarii.** According to Josephus, these were political nationalists who removed their opponents by assassination with a short dagger, called in Latin a sica.

22, 40: **In Hebrew:** meaning, perhaps, in Aramaic, which at this time was the Semitic tongue in common use.

22, 1–21: Paul's first defense speech is presented to the Jerusalem crowds. Luke here presents Paul as a devout Jew (3) and zealous persecutor of the Christian community (4–5), and then recounts the conversion of Paul for the second time in Acts (see the note on 9, 1–19).

d: 15, 19-20.28-29.   e: 1 Cor 9, 20.   f: Rom 15, 31.   g: 22, 22; Lk 23, 18; Jn 19, 15.   h: 5, 36-37.   i: 5, 34; 26, 4-5; 2 Cor 11, 22; Gal 1, 13-14; Phil 3, 5-6.

city. At the feet of Gamaliel I was educated strictly in our ancestral law and was zealous for God, just as all of you are today. [4j]I persecuted this Way to death, binding both men and women and delivering them to prison. [5]Even the high priest and the whole council of elders can testify on my behalf. For from them I even received letters to the brothers and set out for Damascus to bring back to Jerusalem in chains for punishment those there as well.

[6k]"On that journey as I drew near to Damascus, about noon a great light from the sky suddenly shone around me. [7l]I fell to the ground and heard a voice saying to me, 'Saul, Saul, why are you persecuting me?' [8m]I replied, 'Who are you, sir?' And he said to me, 'I am Jesus the Nazorean whom you are persecuting.' [9n]My companions saw the light but did not hear the voice of the one who spoke to me. [10o]I asked, 'What shall I do, sir?' The Lord answered me, 'Get up and go into Damascus, and there you will be told about everything appointed for you to do.' [11p]Since I could see nothing because of the brightness of that light, I was led by hand by my companions and entered Damascus.

[12q]"A certain Ananias, a devout observer of the law, and highly spoken of by all the Jews who lived there, [13]came to me and stood there and said, 'Saul, my brother, regain your sight.' And at that very moment I regained my sight and saw him. [14]Then he said, 'The God of our ancestors designated you to know his will, to see the Righteous One, and to hear the sound of his voice; [15]*for you will be his witness before all to what you have seen and heard. [16]Now, why delay? Get up and have yourself baptized and your sins washed away, calling upon his name.'

[17]"After I had returned to Jerusalem and while I was praying in the temple, I fell into a trance [18]and saw the Lord saying to me, 'Hurry, leave Jerusalem at once, because they will not accept your testimony about me.' [19r]But I replied, 'Lord, they themselves know that from synagogue to synagogue I used to imprison and beat those who believed in you. [20s]And when the blood of your witness Stephen was being shed, I myself stood by giving my approval and keeping guard over the cloaks of his murderers.' [21t]*Then he said to me, 'Go, I shall send you far away to the Gentiles.' "

Paul Imprisoned. [22u]*They listened to him until he said this, but then they raised their voices and shouted, "Take such a one as this away from the earth. It is not right that he should live." [23]And as they were yelling and throwing off their cloaks and flinging dust into the air, [24]the cohort commander ordered him to be brought into the compound and gave instruction that he be interrogated under the lash to determine the reason why they were making such an outcry against him. [25v]*But when they had stretched him out for the whips, Paul said to the centurion on duty, "Is it lawful for you to scourge a man who is a Roman citizen and has not been tried?" [26]When the centurion heard this, he went to the cohort commander and reported it, saying, "What are you going to do? This man is a Roman citizen." [27]Then the commander came and said to him, "Tell me, are you a Roman citizen?" "Yes," he answered. [28]The commander replied, "I acquired this citizenship for a large sum of money." Paul said, "But I was born one." [29]At once those who were going to interrogate him backed away from him, and the commander became alarmed when he realized that he was a Roman citizen and that he had had him bound.

22, 15: **His witness:** like the Galilean followers during the historical ministry of Jesus, Paul too, through his experience of the risen Christ, is to be a witness to the resurrection (compare 1, 8; 10, 39–41; Lk 24, 48).

22, 21: Paul endeavors to explain that his position on the law has not been identical with that of his audience because it has been his prophetic mission to preach to the Gentiles to whom the law was not addressed and who had no faith in it as a way of salvation.

22, 22: Paul's suggestion that his prophetic mission to the Gentiles did not involve his imposing the law on them pro-

vokes the same opposition as occurred in Pisidian Antioch (13, 45).

22, 25: **Is it lawful for you to scourge a man who is a Roman citizen and has not been tried?:** see the note on 16, 37.

j: 8, 3; 9, 1-2; 22, 19; 26, 9-11; Phil 3, 6.   k: 9, 3; 26, 13; 1 Cor 15, 8.   l: 9, 4; 26, 14.   m: 9, 5; 26, 15; Mt 25, 40.   n: 9, 7; 26, 13-14.   o: 9, 6; 26, 16.   p: 9, 8.   q: 9, 10-19.   r: 8, 3; 9, 1-2; 22, 4-5; 26, 9-11.   s: 7, 58; 8, 1.   t: 9, 15; Gal 2, 7-9.   u: 21, 36; Lk 23, 18; Jn 19, 15.   v: 16, 37.

Paul before the Sanhedrin. [30]The next day, wishing to determine the truth about why he was being accused by the Jews, he freed him and ordered the chief priests and the whole Sanhedrin to convene. Then he brought Paul down and made him stand before them.

See RG 348

CHAPTER 23

[1w]Paul looked intently at the Sanhedrin and said, "My brothers, I have conducted myself with a perfectly clear conscience before God to this day." [2*]The high priest Ananias ordered his attendants to strike his mouth. [3x*]Then Paul said to him, "God will strike you, you whitewashed wall. Do you indeed sit in judgment upon me according to the law and yet in violation of the law order me to be struck?" [4]The attendants said, "Would you revile God's high priest?" [5y*]Paul answered, "Brothers, I did not realize he was the high priest. For it is written, 'You shall not curse a ruler of your people.' "

[6z]Paul was aware that some were Sadducees and some Pharisees, so he called out before the Sanhedrin, "My brothers, I am a Pharisee, the son of Pharisees; [I] am on trial for hope in the resurrection of the dead." [7]When he said this, a dispute broke out between the Pharisees and Sadducees, and the group became divided. [8a]For the Sadducees say that there is no resurrection or angels or spirits, while the Pharisees acknowledge all three. [9]A great uproar occurred, and some scribes belonging to the Pharisee party stood up and sharply argued, "We find nothing wrong with this man. Suppose a spirit or an angel has spoken to him?" [10]The dispute was so serious that the commander, afraid that Paul would be torn to pieces by them, ordered his troops to go down and rescue him from their midst and take him into the compound.

[11b*]The following night the Lord stood by him and said, "Take courage. For just as you have borne witness to my cause in Jerusalem, so you must also bear witness in Rome."

Transfer to Caesarea. [12]When day came, the Jews made a plot and bound themselves by oath not to eat or drink until they had killed Paul. [13]There were more than forty who formed this conspiracy. [14]They went to the chief priests and elders and said, "We have bound ourselves by a solemn oath to taste nothing until we have killed Paul. [15]You, together with the Sanhedrin, must now make an official request to the commander to have him bring him down to you, as though you meant to investigate his case more thoroughly. We on our part are prepared to kill him before he arrives." [16]The son of Paul's sister, however, heard about the ambush; so he went and entered the compound and reported it to Paul. [17*]Paul then called one of the centurions and requested, "Take this young man to the commander; he has something to report to him." [18]So he took him and brought him to the commander and explained, "The prisoner Paul called me and asked that I bring this young man to you; he has something to say to you." [19]The commander took him by the hand, drew him aside, and asked him privately, "What is it you have to report to me?" [20]He replied, "The Jews have conspired to ask you to bring Paul down to the Sanhedrin tomorrow, as though they meant to inquire about him more thoroughly, [21]but do not believe them. More than forty of them are lying in wait for him; they have bound themselves by oath not to eat or drink until they have killed him. They are now ready and only wait for your consent." [22]As the commander dismissed the young man he directed him, "Tell no one that you gave me this information."

23, 2: The high priest Ananias: Ananias, son of Nedebaeus, was high priest from A.D. 47 to 59.

23, 3: God will strike you: Josephus reports that Ananias was later assassinated in A.D. 66 at the beginning of the First Revolt.

23, 5: Luke portrays Paul as a model of one who is obedient to the Mosaic law. Paul, because of his reverence for the law (Ex 22, 27), withdraws his accusation of hypocrisy, "whitewashed wall" (cf Mt 23, 27), when he is told Ananias is the high priest.

23, 11: The occurrence of the vision of Christ consoling Paul and assuring him that he will be his witness in Rome prepares the reader for the final section of Acts: the journey of Paul and the word he preaches to Rome under the protection of the Romans.

23, 17: Centurions: a centurion was a military officer in charge of one hundred soldiers.

w: 24, 16.   x: Ez 13, 10-15; Mt 23, 27.   y: Ex 22, 27.   z: 24, 15.21; 26, 5; Phil 3, 5.   a: Mt 22, 23; Lk 20, 27.   b: 19, 21.

23*Then he summoned two of the centurions and said, "Get two hundred soldiers ready to go to Caesarea by nine o'clock tonight, along with seventy horsemen and two hundred auxiliaries. 24Provide mounts for Paul to ride and give him safe conduct to Felix the governor." 25Then he wrote a letter with this content: 26*"Claudius Lysias to his excellency the governor Felix, greetings. 27cThis man, seized by the Jews and about to be murdered by them, I rescued after intervening with my troops when I learned that he was a Roman citizen. 28I wanted to learn the reason for their accusations against him so I brought him down to their Sanhedrin. 29dI discovered that he was accused in matters of controversial questions of their law and not of any charge deserving death or imprisonment. 30Since it was brought to my attention that there will be a plot against the man, I am sending him to you at once, and have also notified his accusers to state [their case] against him before you."

31So the soldiers, according to their orders, took Paul and escorted him by night to Antipatris. 32The next day they returned to the compound, leaving the horsemen to complete the journey with him. 33When they arrived in Caesarea they delivered the letter to the governor and presented Paul to him. 34When he had read it and asked to what province he belonged, and learned that he was from Cilicia, 35he said, "I shall hear your case when your accusers arrive." Then he ordered that he be held in custody in Herod's praetorium.

CHAPTER 24

See RG 348

Trial before Felix. 1Five days later the high priest Ananias came down with some elders and an advocate, a certain Tertullus, and they presented formal charges against Paul to the governor. 2When he was called, Tertullus began to accuse him, saying, "Since we have attained much peace through you, and reforms have been accomplished in this nation through your provident care, 3we acknowledge this in every way and everywhere, most excellent Felix, with all gratitude. 4But in order not to detain you further, I ask you to give us a brief hearing with your customary graciousness. 5e*We found this man to be a pest; he creates dissension among Jews all over the world and is a ringleader of the sect of the Nazoreans. 6fHe even tried to desecrate our temple, but we arrested him. [7]* 8If you examine him you will be able to learn from him for yourself about everything of which we are accusing him." 9The Jews also joined in the attack and asserted that these things were so.

10*Then the governor motioned to him to speak and Paul replied, "I know that you have been a judge over this nation for many years and so I am pleased to make my defense before you. 11As you can verify, not more than twelve days have passed since I went up to Jerusalem to worship. 12Neither in the temple, nor in the synagogues, nor anywhere in the city did they find me arguing with anyone or instigating a riot among the people. 13Nor can they prove to you the accusations they are now making against me. 14gBut this I do admit to you, that according to the Way, which they call a sect, I worship the God of our ancestors and I believe everything that is in accordance with the law and written in the prophets. 15hI have

23, 23: **By nine o'clock tonight:** literally, "by the third hour of the night." The night hours began at 6 p.m. **Two hundred auxiliaries:** the meaning of the Greek is not certain. It seems to refer to spearmen from the local police force and not from the cohort of soldiers, which would have numbered only 500–1000 men.

23, 26–30: The letter emphasizes the fact that Paul is a Roman citizen and asserts the lack of evidence that he is guilty of a crime against the empire. The tone of the letter implies that the commander became initially involved in Paul's case because of his Roman citizenship, but this is not an exact description of what really happened (see 21, 31–33; 22, 25–29).

23, 26: M. Antonius Felix was procurator of Judea from A.D. 52 to 60. His procuratorship was marked by cruelty toward and oppression of his Jewish subjects.

24, 5: **Nazoreans:** that is, followers of Jesus of Nazareth.

24, 7: The Western text has added here a verse (really 6b-8a) that is not found in the best Greek manuscripts. It reads, "and would have judged him according to our own law, but the cohort commander Lysias came and violently took him out of our hands and ordered his accusers to come before you."

24, 10–21: Whereas the advocate Tertullus referred to Paul's activities on his missionary journeys, the apostle narrowed the charges down to the riot connected with the incident in the temple (see 21, 27–30; 24, 17–20). In his defense, Paul stresses the continuity between Christianity and Judaism.

c: 21, 30-34; 22, 27.   d: 18, 14-15; 25, 18-19.   e: 24, 14; Lk 23, 2.   f: 21, 28.   g: 24, 5.   h: Dn 12, 2; Jn 5, 28-29.

the same hope in God as they themselves have that there will be a resurrection of the righteous and the unrighteous. [16i]Because of this, I always strive to keep my conscience clear before God and man. [17j]After many years, I came to bring alms for my nation and offerings. [18k]While I was so engaged, they found me, after my purification, in the temple without a crowd or disturbance. [19]But some Jews from the province of Asia, who should be here before you to make whatever accusation they might have against me— [20]or let these men themselves state what crime they discovered when I stood before the Sanhedrin, [21l]unless it was my one outcry as I stood among them, that 'I am on trial before you today for the resurrection of the dead.' "

[22]Then Felix, who was accurately informed about the Way, postponed the trial, saying, "When Lysias the commander comes down, I shall decide your case." [23]He gave orders to the centurion that he should be kept in custody but have some liberty, and that he should not prevent any of his friends from caring for his needs.

Captivity in Caesarea. [24*]Several days later Felix came with his wife Drusilla, who was Jewish. He had Paul summoned and listened to him speak about faith in Christ Jesus. [25]But as he spoke about righteousness and self-restraint and the coming judgment, Felix became frightened and said, "You may go for now; when I find an opportunity I shall summon you again." [26]At the same time he hoped that a bribe would be offered him by Paul, and so he sent for him very often and conversed with him.

[27*]Two years passed and Felix was succeeded by Porcius Festus. Wishing to ingratiate himself with the Jews, Felix left Paul in prison.

CHAPTER 25

See RG 348

Appeal to Caesar. [1]Three days after his arrival in the province, Festus went up from Caesarea to Jerusalem [2*]where the chief priests and Jewish leaders presented him their formal charges against Paul. They asked him [3]as a favor to have him sent to Jerusalem, for they were plotting to kill him along the way. [4]Festus replied that Paul was being held in custody in Caesarea and that he himself would be returning there shortly. [5]He said, "Let your authorities come down with me, and if this man has done something improper, let them accuse him."

[6]After spending no more than eight or ten days with them, he went down to Caesarea, and on the following day took his seat on the tribunal and ordered that Paul be brought in. [7]When he appeared, the Jews who had come down from Jerusalem surrounded him and brought many serious charges against him, which they were unable to prove. [8]In defending himself Paul said, "I have committed no crime either against the Jewish law or against the temple or against Caesar." [9*]Then Festus, wishing to ingratiate himself with the Jews, said to Paul in reply, "Are you willing to go up to Jerusalem and there stand trial before me on these charges?" [10]Paul answered, "I am standing before the tribunal of Caesar; this is where I should be tried. I have committed no crime against the Jews, as you very well know. [11]If I have committed a crime or done anything deserving death, I do not seek to escape the death penalty; but if there is no substance to the charges they are bringing against me, then no one has the right to hand me over to them. I appeal to Caesar." [12]Then Festus, after conferring with his council, replied, "You have appealed to Caesar. To Caesar you will go."

24, 24–25: The way of Christian discipleship greatly disquiets Felix, who has entered into an adulterous marriage with Drusilla, daughter of Herod Agrippa I. This marriage provides the background for the topics Paul speaks about and about which Felix does not want to hear.

24, 27: Very little is known of Porcius Festus who was a procurator of Judea from A.D. 60 to 62.

25, 2: Even after two years the animosity toward Paul in Jerusalem had not subsided (see 24, 27).

25, 9–12: Paul refuses to acknowledge that the Sanhedrin in Jerusalem has any jurisdiction over him now (11). Paul uses his right as a Roman citizen to appeal his case to the jurisdiction of the Emperor (Nero, ca. A.D. 60) (12). This move broke the deadlock between Roman protective custody of Paul and the plan of his enemies to kill him (3).

i: 23, 1. *j:* Rom 15, 25-26; Gal 2, 10. *k:* 21, 26-30. *l:* 23, 6; 24, 15.

Paul before King Agrippa. ¹³*When a few days had passed, King Agrippa and Bernice arrived in Caesarea on a visit to Festus. ^{14m}Since they spent several days there, Festus referred Paul's case to the king, saying, "There is a man here left in custody by Felix. ¹⁵When I was in Jerusalem the chief priests and the elders of the Jews brought charges against him and demanded his condemnation. ¹⁶I answered them that it was not Roman practice to hand over an accused person before he has faced his accusers and had the opportunity to defend himself against their charge. ¹⁷So when [they] came together here, I made no delay; the next day I took my seat on the tribunal and ordered the man to be brought in. ¹⁸ⁿHis accusers stood around him, but did not charge him with any of the crimes I suspected. ¹⁹Instead they had some issues with him about their own religion and about a certain Jesus who had died but who Paul claimed was alive. ²⁰Since I was at a loss how to investigate this controversy, I asked if he were willing to go to Jerusalem and there stand trial on these charges. ²¹And when Paul appealed that he be held in custody for the Emperor's decision, I ordered him held until I could send him to Caesar." ²²Agrippa said to Festus, "I too should like to hear this man." He replied, "Tomorrow you will hear him."

²³The next day Agrippa and Bernice came with great ceremony and entered the audience hall in the company of cohort commanders and the prominent men of the city and, by command of Festus, Paul was brought in. ²⁴And Festus said, "King Agrippa and all you here present with us, look at this man about whom the whole Jewish populace petitioned me here and in Jerusalem, clamoring that he should live no longer. ²⁵I found, however, that he had done nothing deserving death, and so when he appealed to the Emperor, I decided to send him. ²⁶But I have nothing definite to write about him to our

sovereign; therefore I have brought him before all of you, and particularly before you, King Agrippa, so that I may have something to write as a result of this investigation. ²⁷For it seems senseless to me to send up a prisoner without indicating the charges against him."

CHAPTER 26

See RG
348

King Agrippa Hears Paul. ¹Then Agrippa said to Paul, "You may now speak on your own behalf." So Paul stretched out his hand and began his defense. ²*"I count myself fortunate, King Agrippa, that I am to defend myself before you today against all the charges made against me by the Jews, ³especially since you are an expert in all the Jewish customs and controversies. And therefore I beg you to listen patiently. ⁴*My manner of living from my youth, a life spent from the beginning among my people and in Jerusalem, all [the] Jews know. ^{5o}They have known about me from the start, if they are willing to testify, that I have lived my life as a Pharisee, the strictest party of our religion. ^{6p}But now I am standing trial because of my hope in the promise made by God to our ancestors. ⁷Our twelve tribes hope to attain to that promise as they fervently worship God day and night; and on account of this hope I am accused by Jews, O king. ⁸Why is it thought unbelievable among you that God raises the dead? ^{9q}I myself once thought that I had to do many things against the name of Jesus the Nazorean, ^{10r}and I did so in Jerusalem. I imprisoned many of the holy ones with the authorization I received from the chief priests, and when they were to be put to death I cast my vote against them. ¹¹Many times, in synagogue after synagogue, I punished them in an attempt to force them to blaspheme; I was so enraged against them that I pursued them even to foreign cities.

¹²"On one such occasion I was traveling to Damascus with the authorization and com-

25, 13: King Agrippa and Bernice: brother and sister, children of Herod Agrippa I whose activities against the Jerusalem community are mentioned in 12, 1–19. Agrippa II was a petty ruler over small areas in northern Palestine and some villages in Perea. His influence on the Jewish population of Palestine was insignificant.

26, 2–23: Paul's final defense speech in Acts is now made before a king (see 9, 15). In the speech Paul presents himself as

a zealous Pharisee and Christianity as the logical development of Pharisaic Judaism. The story of his conversion is recounted for the third time in Acts in this speech (see the note on 9, 1–19).

26, 4: Among my people: that is, among the Jews.

m: 24, 27.　*n:* 18, 14-15; 23, 29.　*o:* Phil 3, 5-6; Gal 1, 13-14; 2 Cor 11, 22.　*p:* 23, 6; 24, 15.21; 28, 20.　*q:* 8, 3; 9, 1-2; 22, 19; Phil 3, 6.　*r:* 9, 14.

mission of the chief priests. *13st*At midday, along the way, O king, I saw a light from the sky, brighter than the sun, shining around me and my traveling companions. *14u**We all fell to the ground and I heard a voice saying to me in Hebrew, 'Saul, Saul, why are you persecuting me? It is hard for you to kick against the goad.' *15v*And I said, 'Who are you, sir?' And the Lord replied, 'I am Jesus whom you are persecuting. *16w**Get up now, and stand on your feet. I have appeared to you for this purpose, to appoint you as a servant and witness of what you have seen [of me] and what you will be shown. *17x*I shall deliver you from this people and from the Gentiles to whom I send you, *18y**to open their eyes that they may turn from darkness to light and from the power of Satan to God, so that they may obtain forgiveness of sins and an inheritance among those who have been consecrated by faith in me.'

19"And so, King Agrippa, I was not disobedient to the heavenly vision. *20*On the contrary, first to those in Damascus and in Jerusalem and throughout the whole country of Judea, and then to the Gentiles, I preached the need to repent and turn to God, and to do works giving evidence of repentance. *21z*That is why the Jews seized me [when I was] in the temple and tried to kill me. *22a**But I have enjoyed God's help to this very day, and so I stand here testifying to small and great alike, saying nothing different from what the prophets and Moses fore-

told, *23b**that the Messiah must suffer and that, as the first to rise from the dead, he would proclaim light both to our people and to the Gentiles."

Reactions to Paul's Speech. *24*While Paul was so speaking in his defense, Festus said in a loud voice, "You are mad, Paul; much learning is driving you mad." *25*But Paul replied, "I am not mad, most excellent Festus; I am speaking words of truth and reason. *26**The king knows about these matters and to him I speak boldly, for I cannot believe that [any] of this has escaped his notice; this was not done in a corner. *27**King Agrippa, do you believe the prophets? I know you believe." *28*Then Agrippa said to Paul, "You will soon persuade me to play the Christian." *29*Paul replied, "I would pray to God that sooner or later not only you but all who listen to me today might become as I am except for these chains."

*30*Then the king rose, and with him the governor and Bernice and the others who sat with them. *31**And after they had withdrawn they said to one another, "This man is doing nothing [at all] that deserves death or imprisonment." *32c*And Agrippa said to Festus, "This man could have been set free if he had not appealed to Caesar."

CHAPTER 27

See RG 348–49

Departure for Rome. *1**When it was decided that we should sail to Italy, they handed Paul and some other prisoners over

---

26, 14: In Hebrew: see the note on 21, 40. **It is hard for you to kick against the goad:** this proverb is commonly found in Greek literature and in this context signifies the senselessness and ineffectiveness of any opposition to the divine influence in his life.

26, 16: The words of Jesus directed to Paul here reflect the dialogues between Christ and Ananias (9, 15) and between Ananias and Paul (22, 14–15) in the two previous accounts of Paul's conversion.

26, 18: To open their eyes: though no mention is made of Paul's blindness in this account (cf 9, 8–9.12.18; 22, 11–13), the task he is commissioned to perform is the removal of other people's spiritual blindness.

26, 22: Saying nothing different from what the prophets and Moses foretold: see the note on Lk 18, 31.

26, 23: That the Messiah must suffer: see the note on Lk 24, 26.

26, 26: Not done in a corner: for Luke, this Greek proverb expresses his belief that he is presenting a story about Jesus and the church that is already well known. As such, the

entire history of Christianity is public knowledge and incontestable. Luke presents his story in this way to provide "certainty" to his readers about the instructions they have received (Lk 1, 4).

26, 27–28: If the Christian missionaries proclaim nothing different from what the Old Testament prophets had proclaimed (22–23), then the logical outcome for the believing Jew, according to Luke, is to become a Christian.

26, 31–32: In recording the episode of Paul's appearance before Agrippa, Luke wishes to show that, when Paul's case was judged impartially, no grounds for legal action against him were found (see 23, 29; 25, 25).

27, 1—28, 16: Here Luke has written a stirring account of adventure on the high seas, incidental to his main purpose of showing how well Paul got along with his captors and how

s: 9, 7.   t: 9, 3; 22, 6.   u: 9, 4; 22, 7.   v: 9, 5; 22, 8; Mt 25, 40. w: 9, 6; 22, 10; Ez 2, 1.   x: Jer 1, 7.   y: Is 42, 7.16; 61, 1 LXX; Col 1, 13.   z: 21, 31.   a: 3, 18; Lk 24, 26-27.44-47.   b: Is 42, 6; 49, 6; Lk 2, 32; 1 Cor 15, 20-23.   c: 25, 11-12.

to a centurion named Julius of the Cohort Augusta. [2d]We went on board a ship from Adramyttium bound for ports in the province of Asia and set sail. Aristarchus, a Macedonian from Thessalonica, was with us. [3]On the following day we put in at Sidon where Julius was kind enough to allow Paul to visit his friends who took care of him. [4]From there we put out to sea and sailed around the sheltered side of Cyprus because of the headwinds, [5]and crossing the open sea off the coast of Cilicia and Pamphylia we came to Myra in Lycia.

Storm and Shipwreck. [6]There the centurion found an Alexandrian ship that was sailing to Italy and put us on board. [7]For many days we made little headway, arriving at Cnidus only with difficulty, and because the wind would not permit us to continue our course we sailed for the sheltered side of Crete off Salmone. [8]We sailed past it with difficulty and reached a place called Fair Havens, near which was the city of Lasea.

[9e*]Much time had now passed and sailing had become hazardous because the time of the fast had already gone by, so Paul warned them, [10]"Men, I can see that this voyage will result in severe damage and heavy loss not only to the cargo and the ship, but also to our lives." [11]The centurion, however, paid more attention to the pilot and to the owner of the ship than to what Paul said. [12]Since the harbor was unfavorably situated for spending the winter, the majority planned to put out to sea from there in the hope of reaching Phoenix, a port in Crete facing west-northwest, there to spend the winter.

[13]A south wind blew gently, and thinking they had attained their objective, they weighed anchor and sailed along close to the coast of Crete. [14]Before long an offshore wind of hurricane force called a "Northeaster" struck. [15]Since the ship was caught up in it and could not head into the wind we

gave way and let ourselves be driven. [16]We passed along the sheltered side of an island named Cauda and managed only with difficulty to get the dinghy under control. [17]They hoisted it aboard, then used cables to undergird the ship. Because of their fear that they would run aground on the shoal of Syrtis, they lowered the drift anchor and were carried along in this way. [18]We were being pounded by the storm so violently that the next day they jettisoned some cargo, [19]and on the third day with their own hands they threw even the ship's tackle overboard. [20]Neither the sun nor the stars were visible for many days, and no small storm raged. Finally, all hope of our surviving was taken away.

[21]When many would no longer eat, Paul stood among them and said, "Men, you should have taken my advice and not have set sail from Crete and you would have avoided this disastrous loss. [22]I urge you now to keep up your courage; not one of you will be lost, only the ship. [23]For last night an angel of the God to whom [I] belong and whom I serve stood by me [24f]and said, 'Do not be afraid, Paul. You are destined to stand before Caesar; and behold, for your sake, God has granted safety to all who are sailing with you.' [25]Therefore, keep up your courage, men; I trust in God that it will turn out as I have been told. [26]We are destined to run aground on some island."

[27]On the fourteenth night, as we were still being driven about on the Adriatic Sea, toward midnight the sailors began to suspect that they were nearing land. [28]They took soundings and found twenty fathoms; a little farther on, they again took soundings and found fifteen fathoms. [29]Fearing that we would run aground on a rocky coast, they dropped four anchors from the stern and prayed for day to come. [30]The sailors then tried to abandon ship; they lowered the dinghy to the sea on the pretext of going to lay out anchors from the bow. [31]But

his prophetic influence saved the lives of all on board. The recital also establishes the existence of Christian communities in Puteoli and Rome. This account of the voyage and shipwreck also constitutes the final "we-section" in Acts (see the note on 16, 10–17).

27, 1: Cohort Augusta: the presence of a Cohort Augusta in Syria during the first century A.D. is attested in inscriptions. Whatever the historical background to this information

given by Luke may be, the name Augusta serves to increase the prominence and prestige of the prisoner Paul whose custodians bear so important a Roman name.

27, 9: The time of the fast: the fast kept on the occasion of the Day of Atonement (Lv 16, 29–31), which occurred in late September or early October.

d: 19, 29; 20, 4.   e: Lv 16, 29-31.   f: 23, 11.

Paul's Journey to Rome

Paul said to the centurion and the soldiers, "Unless these men stay with the ship, you cannot be saved." [32]So the soldiers cut the ropes of the dinghy and set it adrift.

[33]Until the day began to dawn, Paul kept urging all to take some food. He said, "Today is the fourteenth day that you have been waiting, going hungry and eating nothing. [34]I urge you, therefore, to take some food; it will help you survive. Not a hair of the head of anyone of you will be lost." [35]g*When he said this, he took bread, gave thanks to God in front of them all, broke it, and began to eat. [36]They were all encouraged, and took some food themselves. [37]In all, there were two hundred seventy-six of us on the ship. [38]After they had eaten enough, they lightened the ship by throwing the wheat into the sea.

[39]When day came they did not recognize the land, but made out a bay with a beach. They planned to run the ship ashore on it, if they could. [40]So they cast off the anchors and abandoned them to the sea, and at the same time they unfastened the lines of the rudders, and hoisting the foresail into the wind, they made for the beach. [41]But they struck a sandbar and ran the ship aground. The bow was wedged in and could not be moved, but the stern began to break up under the pounding [of the waves]. [42]The soldiers planned to kill the prisoners so that none might swim away and escape, [43]but the centurion wanted to save Paul and so kept them from carrying out their plan. He ordered those who could swim to jump overboard first and get to the shore, [44]and then the rest, some on planks, others on debris from the ship. In this way, all reached shore safely.

CHAPTER 28

See RG 348-49

Winter in Malta. [1]Once we had reached safety we learned that the island was called Malta. [2]The natives showed us extraordinary hospitality; they lit a fire and welcomed all of us because it had begun to rain

and was cold. [3]Paul had gathered a bundle of brushwood and was putting it on the fire when a viper, escaping from the heat, fastened on his hand. [4]*When the natives saw the snake hanging from his hand, they said to one another, "This man must certainly be a murderer; though he escaped the sea, Justice has not let him remain alive." [5]But he shook the snake off into the fire and suffered no harm. [6]hThey were expecting him to swell up or suddenly to fall down dead but, after waiting a long time and seeing nothing unusual happen to him, they changed their minds and began to say that he was a god. [7]In the vicinity of that place were lands belonging to a man named Publius, the chief of the island. He welcomed us and received us cordially as his guests for three days. [8]It so happened that the father of Publius was sick with a fever and dysentery. Paul visited him and, after praying, laid his hands on him and healed him. [9]After this had taken place, the rest of the sick on the island came to Paul and were cured. [10]They paid us great honor and when we eventually set sail they brought us the provisions we needed.

Arrival in Rome. [11]*Three months later we set sail on a ship that had wintered at the island. It was an Alexandrian ship with the Dioscuri as its figurehead. [12]We put in at Syracuse and stayed there three days, [13]and from there we sailed round the coast and arrived at Rhegium. After a day, a south wind came up and in two days we reached Puteoli. [14]There we found some brothers and were urged to stay with them for seven days. And thus we came to Rome. [15]The brothers from there heard about us and came as far as the Forum of Appius and Three Taverns to meet us. On seeing them, Paul gave thanks to God and took courage. [16]*When he entered Rome, Paul was allowed to live by himself, with the soldier who was guarding him.

Testimony to Jews in Rome. [17]i*Three days later he called together the leaders of

---

27, 35: **He took bread . . . :** the words recall the traditional language of the celebration of the Eucharist (see Lk 22, 19).

28, 4: **Justice:** in Greek mythology, the pursuing goddess of vengeance and justice.

28, 11: **Dioscuri:** that is, the Twin Brothers, Castor and Pollux, the sons of Zeus and the patrons of the sailors.

28, 16: With Paul's arrival in Rome, the programmatic spread of the word of the Lord to "the ends of the earth" (1,

8) is accomplished. In Rome, Paul is placed under house arrest, and under this mild form of custody he is allowed to proclaim the word in the capital of the civilized world of his day.

28, 17–22: Paul's first act in Rome is to learn from the leaders of the Jewish community whether the Jews of Jeru-

g: Mt 15, 36; Mk 6, 41; 8, 6; Lk 22, 19; 1 Cor 11, 23-24.   h: 14, 11.   i: 24, 12-13; 25, 8.

the Jews. When they had gathered he said to them, "My brothers, although I had done nothing against our people or our ancestral customs, I was handed over to the Romans as a prisoner from Jerusalem. ¹⁸^jAfter trying my case the Romans wanted to release me, because they found nothing against me deserving the death penalty. ¹⁹^kBut when the Jews objected, I was obliged to appeal to Caesar, even though I had no accusation to make against my own nation. ²⁰^l*This is the reason, then, I have requested to see you and to speak with you, for it is on account of the hope of Israel that I wear these chains." ²¹They answered him, "We have received no letters from Judea about you, nor has any of the brothers arrived with a damaging report or rumor about you. ²²^mBut we should like to hear you present your views, for we know that this sect is denounced everywhere."

²³So they arranged a day with him and came to his lodgings in great numbers. From early morning until evening, he expounded his position to them, bearing witness to the kingdom of God and trying to convince them about Jesus from the law of Moses and the prophets. ²⁴Some were convinced by what he had said, while others did not believe. ²⁵*Without reaching any agreement among themselves they began to leave; then Paul made one final statement. "Well did the holy Spirit speak to your ancestors through the prophet Isaiah, saying:

²⁶ ⁿ'Go to this people and say:
You shall indeed hear but not understand.
   You shall indeed look but never see.
²⁷ Gross is the heart of this people;
   they will not hear with their ears;
      they have closed their eyes,
so they may not see with their eyes
   and hear with their ears
and understand with their heart and be
      converted,
   and I heal them.'

²⁸^oLet it be known to you that this salvation of God has been sent to the Gentiles; they will listen." [²⁹]*

³⁰*He remained for two full years in his lodgings. He received all who came to him, ³¹and with complete assurance and without hindrance he proclaimed the kingdom of God and taught about the Lord Jesus Christ.

---

salem plan to pursue their case against him before the Roman jurisdiction. He is informed that no such plan is afoot, but that the Jews of Rome have heard the Christian teaching denounced. Paul's offer to explain it to them is readily accepted.

28, 20: The hope of Israel: in the words of Paul (23, 6), Luke has identified this hope as hope in the resurrection of the dead.

28, 25–28: Paul's final words in Acts reflect a major concern of Luke's writings: how the salvation promised in the Old Testament, accomplished by Jesus, and offered first to Israel (13, 26), has now been offered to and accepted by the Gentiles. Quoting Is 6, 9–10, Paul presents the scriptural support for his indictment of his fellow Jews who refuse to accept the message he proclaims. Their rejection leads to its proclamation among the Gentiles.

28, 29: The Western text has added here a verse that is not found in the best Greek manuscripts: "And when he had said this, the Jews left, seriously arguing among themselves."

28, 30–31: Although the ending of Acts may seem to be abrupt, Luke has now completed his story with the establishment of Paul and the proclamation of Christianity in Rome. Paul's confident and unhindered proclamation of the gospel in Rome forms the climax to the story whose outline was provided in 1, 8: "You will be my witnesses in Jerusalem . . . and to the ends of the earth."

j: 23, 29; 25, 25; 26, 31-32. *k:* 25, 11. *l:* 23, 6; 24, 15.21; 26, 6-8. *m:* 24, 5.14. *n:* Is 6, 9-10; Mt 13, 14-15; Mk 4, 12; Lk 8, 10; Jn 12, 40; Rom 11, 8. *o:* 13, 46; 18, 6; Ps 67, 2; Is 40, 5 LXX; Lk 3, 6.

NEW TESTAMENT LETTERS

In the New Testament canon, between the Acts of the Apostles and Revelation, there are twenty-one documents that take the form of letters or epistles. Most of these are actual letters, but some are more like treatises in the guise of letters. In a few cases even some of the more obvious elements of the letter form are absent; see the Introductions to Hebrews and to 1 John.

The virtually standard form found in these documents, though with some variation, is dependent upon the conventions of letter writing common in the ancient world, but these were modified to suit the purposes of Christian writers. The New Testament letters usually begin with a greeting including an identification of the sender or senders and of the recipients. Next comes a prayer, usually in the form of a thanksgiving. The body of the letter provides an exposition of Christian teaching, usually provoked by concrete circumstances, and generally also draws conclusions regarding ethical behavior. There often follows a discussion of practical matters, such as the writer's travel plans, and the letter concludes with further advice and a formula of farewell.

Fourteen of the twenty-one letters have been traditionally attributed to Paul. One of these, the Letter to the Hebrews, does not itself claim to be the work of Paul; when it was accepted into the canon after much discussion, it was attached at the very end of the Pauline corpus. The other thirteen identify Paul as their author, but most scholars believe that some of them were actually written by his disciples; see the Introductions to

Ephesians, Colossians, 2 Thessalonians, and 1 Timothy.

Four of the letters in the Pauline corpus (Ephesians, Philippians, Colossians, and Philemon) are called the "Captivity Epistles" because in each of them the author speaks of being in prison at the time of writing. Three others (1–2 Timothy and Titus) are known as the "Pastoral Epistles" because, addressed to individuals rather than communities, they give advice to disciples about caring for the flock. The letters of the Pauline corpus are arranged in roughly descending order of length from Romans to Philemon, with Hebrews added at the end.

The other seven letters of the New Testament that follow the Pauline corpus are collectively referred to as the "Catholic Epistles." This term, which means "universal," refers to the fact that most of them are directed not to a single Christian community, as are most of the Pauline letters, but to a wider audience; see the Introduction to the catholic letters. Three of them (1–2–3 John) are closely related to the fourth gospel and thus belong to the Johannine corpus. The catholic letters, like those of the Pauline corpus, are also arranged in roughly descending order of length, but the three Johannine letters are kept together and Jude is placed at the end.

The genuine letters of Paul are earlier in date than any of our written gospels. The dates of the other New Testament letters are more difficult to determine, but for the most part they belong to the second and third Christian generations rather than to the first.

See RG
353-63

The Letter to the Romans

Of all the letters of Paul, that to the Christians at Rome has long held pride of place. It is the longest and most systematic unfolding of the apostle's thought, expounding the gospel of God's righteousness that saves all who believe (1, 16–17); it reflects a universal outlook, with special implications for Israel's relation to the church (chs 9—11). Yet, like all Paul's letters, Romans too arose out of a specific situation, when the apostle wrote from Greece, likely Corinth, between A.D. 56 and 58 (cf Acts 20, 2–3).

Paul at that time was about to leave for Jerusalem with a collection of funds for the impoverished Jewish Christian believers there, taken up from his predominantly Gentile congregations (15, 25–27). He planned then to travel on to Rome and to enlist support there for a mission to Spain (15, 24.28). Such a journey had long been on his mind (1, 9–13; 15, 23). Now, with much missionary preaching successfully accomplished in the East (15, 19), he sought new opportunities in the West (15, 20–21), in order to complete the divine plan of evangelization in the Roman world. Yet he recognized that the visit to Jerusalem would be hazardous (15, 30–32), and we know from Acts that Paul was arrested there and came to Rome only in chains, as a prisoner (Acts 21–28, especially 21, 30–33 and 28, 14.30–31).

The existence of a Christian community in Rome antedates Paul's letter there. When it arose, likely within the sizable Jewish population at Rome, and how, we do not know. The Roman historian Suetonius mentions an edict of the Emperor Claudius about A.D. 49 ordering the expulsion of Jews from Rome in connection with a certain "Chrestus," probably involving a dispute in the Jewish community over Jesus as the Messiah ("Christus"). According to Acts 18, 2, Aquila and Priscilla (or Prisca, as in 16, 3) were among those driven out; from them, in Corinth, Paul may have learned about conditions in the church at Rome.

Opinions vary as to whether Jewish or Gentile Christians predominated in the house churches (cf 16, 5) in the capital city of the empire at the time Paul wrote. Perhaps already by then Gentile Christians were in the majority. Paul speaks in Romans of both Jews and Gentiles (3, 9.29; see the note on 1, 14). The letter also refers to those "weak in faith" (14, 1) and those "who are strong" (15, 1); this terminology may reflect not so much differences between believers of Jewish and of Gentile background, respectively, as an ascetic tendency in some converts (14, 2) combined with Jewish laws about clean and unclean foods (14, 14.20). The issues were similar to problems that Paul had faced in Corinth (1 Cor 8). If Romans 16 is part of the Letter to Rome (see the note on 16, 1–23), then Paul had considerable information about conditions in Rome through all these people there whom he knew, and our letter does not just reflect a generalized picture of an earlier situation in Corinth.

In any case, Paul writes to introduce himself and his message to the Christians at Rome, seeking to enlist their support for the proposed mission to Spain. He therefore employs formulations likely familiar to the Christians at Rome; see the note on the confessional material at 1, 3–4 and compare 3, 25–26; and 4, 25. He cites the Old Testament frequently (1, 17; 3, 10–18; ch 4; 9, 7.12–13.15.17.25–29.33; 10, 5–13.15–21; 15, 9–12). The gospel Paul presents is meant to be a familiar one to those in Rome, even though they heard it first from other preachers.

As the outline below shows, this gospel of Paul (see 16, 25) finds its center in salvation and justification through faith in Christ (1, 16–17). While God's wrath is revealed against all sin and wickedness of Gentile and Jew alike (1, 18—3, 20), God's power to save by divine righteous or justifying action in Christ is also revealed (1, 16–17; 3, 21–5, 21). The consequences and implications for those who believe are set forth (6, 1—8, 39), as are results for those in Israel (ch 9—11) who, to Paul's great sorrow (9, 1–5), disbelieve. The apostle's hope is that, just as rejection of the gospel by some in Israel has led to a ministry of salvation for non-Jews, so one day, in God's mercy, "all Israel" will be saved (11, 11–15.25–29.30–32). The fuller ethical response of believers is also drawn out, both with reference to life in Christ's body (12) and with regard to the world (ch 13, 1–7), on the basis of the eschatological situation (13, 11–14) and conditions in the community (14, 1—15, 13).

Others have viewed Romans more in the light of Paul's earlier, quite polemical Letter to the Galatians and so see the theme as the relationship between Judaism and Christianity, a topic judged to be much in the minds of the Roman Christians. Each of these religious faiths claimed to be the way of salvation based upon a covenant between God and a people chosen and made the beneficiary of divine gifts. But Christianity regarded itself as the prophetic development and fulfillment of the faith of the Old Testament, declaring that the preparatory Mosaic covenant must now give way to the new and more perfect covenant in Jesus Christ. Paul himself had been the implacable advocate of freedom of Gentiles from the laws of the Mosaic covenant and, especially in Galatia, had refused to allow attempts to impose them on Gentile converts to the gospel. He had witnessed the personal hostilities that developed between the adherents of the two faiths and had written his strongly worded Letter to the Galatians against those Jewish Christians who were seeking to persuade Gentile Christians to adopt the religious practices of Judaism. For him, the purity of the religious understanding of Jesus as the source of salvation would be seriously impaired if Gentile Christians were obligated to amalgamate the two religious faiths.

Still others find the theme of Israel and the church as expressed in Romans 9—11 to be the heart of Romans. Then the implication of Paul's exposition of justification by faith rather than by means of law is that the divine plan of salvation works itself out on a broad theological plane to include the whole of humanity, despite the differences in the content of the given religious system to which a human culture is heir. Romans pre-

sents a plan of salvation stretching from Adam through Abraham and Moses to Christ (chs 4 and 5) and on to the future revelation at Christ's parousia (8, 18–25). Its outlook is universal.

Paul's Letter to the Romans is a powerful exposition of the doctrine of the supremacy of Christ and of faith in Christ as the source of salvation. It is an implicit plea to the Christians at Rome, and to all Christians, to hold fast to that faith. They are to resist any pressure put on them to accept a doctrine of salvation through works of the law (see the note on 10, 4). At the same time they are not to exaggerate Christian freedom as an abdication of responsibility for others (12, 1–2) or as a repudiation of God's law and will (see the notes on 3, 9–26; 3, 31; 7, 7–12.13–25).

The principal divisions of the Letter to the Romans are the following:

I: Address (1, 1–15)
II: Humanity Lost without the Gospel (1, 16—3, 20)
III: Justification through Faith in Christ (3, 21—5, 21)
IV: Justification and the Christian Life (6, 1—8, 39)
V: Jews and Gentiles in God's Plan (9, 1—11, 36)
VI: The Duties of Christians (12, 1—15, 13)
VII: Conclusion (15, 14—16, 27)

I: Address

CHAPTER 1

See RG 355–58

Greeting. 1a*Paul, a slave of Christ Jesus, called to be an apostle and set apart for the gospel of God, 2bwhich he promised previously through his prophets in the holy

---

1, 1–7: In Paul's letters the greeting or **praescriptio** follows a standard form, though with variations. It is based upon the common Greco-Roman epistolary practice, but with the addition of Semitic and specifically Christian elements. The three basic components are: name of sender; name of addressee; greeting. In identifying himself, Paul often adds phrases to describe his apostolic mission; this element is more developed in Rom than in any other letter. Elsewhere he associates co-workers with himself in the greeting: Sosthenes (1 Cor), Timothy (2 Cor; Phil; Phlm), Silvanus (1–2 Thes). The standard secular greeting was the infinitive **chairein,** "greetings." Paul uses instead the similar-sounding **charis,** "grace," together with the Semitic greeting **šālôm** (Greek **eirēnē**), "peace." These gifts, foreshadowed in God's deal-

ings with Israel (see Nm 6, 24–26), have been poured out abundantly in Christ, and Paul wishes them to his readers. In Rom the Pauline **praescriptio** is expanded and expressed in a formal tone; it emphasizes Paul's office as apostle to the Gentiles. Verses 3–4 stress the gospel or kerygma, v 2 the fulfillment of God's promise, and vv 1 and 5 Paul's office. On his call, see Gal 1, 15–16; 1 Cor 9, 1; 15, 8–10; Acts 9, 1–22; 22, 3–16; 26, 4–18.

1, 1: Slave of Christ Jesus: Paul applies the term slave to himself in order to express his undivided allegiance to the Lord of the church, the Master of all, including slaves and

a: Gal 1, 10; Phil 1, 1; Jas 1, 1 / Acts 9, 15; 13, 2; 1 Cor 1, 1; Gal 1, 15; Ti 1, 1. *b:* 16, 25–26; Ti 1, 2.

scriptures, *3c**the gospel about his Son, descended from David according to the flesh, *4d*but established as Son of God in power according to the spirit of holiness through resurrection from the dead, Jesus Christ our Lord. *5e**Through him we have received the grace of apostleship, to bring about the obedience of faith, for the sake of his name, among all the Gentiles, *6f*among whom are you also, who are called to belong to Jesus Christ; *7g**to all the beloved of God in Rome, called to be holy. Grace to you and peace from God our Father and the Lord Jesus Christ.

Thanksgiving. *8h**First, I give thanks to my God through Jesus Christ for all of you, because your faith is heralded throughout the world. *9i*God is my witness, whom I serve with my spirit in proclaiming the gospel of his Son, that I remember you constantly, *10j**always asking in my prayers that some-

how by God's will I may at last find my way clear to come to you. *11k*For I long to see you, that I may share with you some spiritual gift so that you may be strengthened, *12*that is, that you and I may be mutually encouraged by one another's faith, yours and mine. *13l**I do not want you to be unaware, brothers, that I often planned to come to you, though I was prevented until now, that I might harvest some fruit among you, too, as among the rest of the Gentiles. *14**To Greeks and non-Greeks alike, to the wise and the ignorant, I am under obligation; *15m*that is why I am eager to preach the gospel also to you in Rome.

II: Humanity Lost without the Gospel

God's Power for Salvation. *16n**For I am not ashamed of the gospel. It is the power of God for the salvation of everyone who be-

---

masters. "No one can serve (i.e., be a slave to) two masters," said Jesus (Mt 6, 24). It is this aspect of the slave-master relationship rather than its degrading implications that Paul emphasizes when he discusses Christian commitment.

1, 3–4: Paul here cites an early confession that proclaims Jesus' sonship as messianic descendant of David (cf Mt 22, 42; 2 Tm 2, 8; Rv 22, 16) and as Son of God by the resurrection. As "life-giving spirit" (1 Cor 15, 45), Jesus Christ is able to communicate the Spirit to those who believe in him.

1, 5: Paul recalls his apostolic office, implying that the Romans know something of his history. **The obedience of faith:** as Paul will show at length in chs 6–8 and 12–15, faith in God's justifying action in Jesus Christ relates one to God's gift of the new life that is made possible through the death and resurrection of Jesus Christ and the activity of the holy Spirit (see especially 8, 1–11).

1, 7: Called to be holy: Paul often refers to Christians as "the holy ones" or "the saints." The Israelite community was called a "holy assembly" because they had been separated for the worship and service of the Lord (see Lv 11, 44; 23, 1–44). The Christian community regarded its members as sanctified by baptism (6, 22; 15, 16; 1 Cor 6, 11; Eph 5, 26–27). Christians are called to holiness (1 Cor 1, 2; 1 Thes 4, 7), that is, they are called to make their lives conform to the gift they have already received.

1, 8: In Greco-Roman letters, the greeting was customarily followed by a prayer. The Pauline letters usually include this element (except Gal and Ti), expressed in Christian thanksgiving formulas and usually stating the principal theme of the letter. In 2 Cor the thanksgiving becomes a blessing, and in Eph it is preceded by a lengthy blessing. Sometimes the thanksgiving is blended into the body of the letter, especially in 1 Thes. In Rom it is stated briefly.

1, 10–12: Paul lays the groundwork for his more detailed statement in 15, 22–24 about his projected visit to Rome.

1, 13: Brothers is idiomatic for all Paul's "kin in Christ," all those who believe in the gospel; it includes women as well as men (cf 4, 3).

1, 14: Greeks and non-Greeks: literally, "Greeks and barbarians." As a result of Alexander's conquests, Greek became the standard international language of the Mediterranean world. **Greeks** in Paul's statement therefore means people who know Greek or who have been influenced by Greek culture. **Non-Greeks** were people whose cultures remained substantially unaffected by Greek influences. Greeks called such people "barbarians" (cf Acts 28, 2), meaning people whose speech was foreign. Roman citizens would scarcely classify themselves as such, and Nero, who was reigning when Paul wrote this letter, prided himself on his admiration for Greek culture. **Under obligation:** Paul will expand on the theme of obligation in 13; 15, 1.27.

1, 16–17: The principal theme of the letter is salvation through faith. **I am not ashamed of the gospel:** Paul is not ashamed to proclaim the gospel, despite the criticism that Jews and Gentiles leveled against the proclamation of the crucified savior; cf 1 Cor 1, 23–24. Paul affirms, however, that it is precisely through the crucifixion and resurrection of Jesus that God's saving will and power become manifest. **Jew first** (cf 2, 9–10) means that Jews especially, in view of the example of Abraham (ch 4), ought to be the leaders in the response of faith.

---

c: 9, 5; 2 Sm 7, 12; Mt 1, 1; Mk 12, 35; Jn 7, 42; Acts 13, 22-23; 2 Tm 2, 8; Rv 22, 16. *d:* 10, 9; Acts 13, 33; Phil 3, 10. *e:* 15, 15; Gal 2, 7.9 / 15, 18; Acts 9, 15; 26, 16-18; Gal 1, 16; 2 7.9. *f:* 1 Cor 1, 9. *g:* Nm 6, 25-26; 1 Cor 1, 2-3; 2 Cor 1, 1-2. *h:* 16, 19; 1 Thes 1, 8. *i:* 2 Cor 1, 23; Eph 1, 16; Phil 1, 8; 1 Thes 1, 2; 2, 5.10; 2 Tm 1, 3. *j:* 15, 23.32; Acts 18, 21; 1 Cor 4, 19; 1 Thes 2, 17. *k:* 1 Thes 2, 17; 3, 10. *l:* 15, 22; Jn 15, 16; Acts 19, 21. *m:* Acts 28, 30-31. *n:* Ps 119, 46; 1 Cor 1, 18.24 / 2, 9. Acts 3, 26; 13, 46.

lieves: for Jew first, and then Greek. [17o]*For in it is revealed the righteousness of God from faith to faith; as it is written, "The one who is righteous by faith will live."

Punishment of Idolators. [18p]*The wrath of God is indeed being revealed from heaven against every impiety and wickedness of those who suppress the truth by their wickedness. [19q]For what can be known about God is evident to them, because God made it evident to them. [20r]Ever since the creation of the world, his invisible attributes of eternal power and divinity have been able to be understood and perceived in what he has made. As a result, they have no excuse; [21s]for although they knew God they did not accord him glory as God or give him thanks. Instead, they became vain in their reasoning, and their senseless minds were darkened. [22t]While claiming to be wise, they became fools [23u]and exchanged the glory of the immortal God for the likeness of an image of mortal man or of birds or of four-legged animals or of snakes.

[24v]*Therefore, God handed them over to impurity through the lusts of their hearts for the mutual degradation of their bodies.

[25w]They exchanged the truth of God for a lie and revered and worshiped the creature rather than the creator, who is blessed forever. Amen. [26]Therefore, God handed them over to degrading passions. Their females exchanged natural relations for unnatural, [27x]and the males likewise gave up natural relations with females and burned with lust for one another. Males did shameful things with males and thus received in their own persons the due penalty for their perversity. [28]And since they did not see fit to acknowledge God, God handed them over to their undiscerning mind to do what is improper. [29y]They are filled with every form of wickedness, evil, greed, and malice; full of envy, murder, rivalry, treachery, and spite. They are gossips [30]and scandalmongers and they hate God. They are insolent, haughty, boastful, ingenious in their wickedness, and rebellious toward their parents. [31]They are senseless, faithless, heartless, ruthless. [32z]Although they know the just decree of God that all who practice such things deserve death, they not only do them but give approval to those who practice them.

1, 17: In it is revealed the righteousness of God from faith to faith: the gospel centers in Jesus Christ, in whom God's saving presence and righteousness in history have been made known. Faith is affirmation of the basic purpose and meaning of the Old Testament as proclamation of divine promise (2; 4, 13) and exposure of the inability of humanity to effect its salvation even through covenant law. Faith is the gift of the holy Spirit and denotes acceptance of salvation as God's righteousness, that is, God's gift of a renewed relationship in forgiveness and power for a new life. Faith is response to God's total claim on people and their destiny. **The one who is righteous by faith will live:** see the note on Hb 2, 4.

1, 18—3, 20: Paul aims to show that all humanity is in a desperate plight and requires God's special intervention if it is to be saved.

1, 18–32: In this passage Paul uses themes and rhetoric common in Jewish-Hellenistic mission proclamation (cf Wis 13, 1—14, 31) to indict especially the non-Jewish world. The close association of idolatry and immorality is basic, but the generalization needs in all fairness to be balanced against the fact that non-Jewish Christian society on many levels displayed moral attitudes and performance whose quality would challenge much of contemporary Christian culture. Romans themselves expressed abhorrence over devotion accorded to animals in Egypt. Paul's main point is that the wrath of God does not await the end of the world but goes into action at each present moment in humanity's history when misdirected piety serves as a facade for self-interest.

1, 18: The wrath of God: God's reaction to human sinfulness, an Old Testament phrase that expresses the irreconcilable opposition between God and evil (see Is 9, 11.16.18.20; 10, 4; 30, 27). It is not contrary to God's universal love for his creatures, but condemns Israel's turning aside from the covenant obligations. Hosea depicts Yahweh as suffering intensely at the thought of having to punish Israel (Hos 11, 8–9). God's wrath was to be poured forth especially on the "Day of Yahweh" and thus took on an eschatological connotation (see Zep 1, 15).

1, 24: In order to expose the depth of humanity's rebellion against the Creator, **God handed them over to impurity through the lusts of their hearts.** Instead of curbing people's evil interests, God abandoned them to self-indulgence, thereby removing the facade of apparent conformity to the divine will. Subsequently Paul will show that the Mosaic law produces the same effect; cf 5, 20; 7, 13–24. The divine judgment expressed here is related to the theme of hardness of heart described in 9, 17–18.

o: 3, 21-22; Hb 2, 4; Gal 3, 11; Heb 10, 38.   p: 2, 5.8-9; Is 66, 15; Eph 5, 6; Col 3, 6.   q: Wis 13-19; Acts 14, 15-17; 17, 23-29.   r: Jb 12, 7-9; Ps 8, 4; 19, 2; Sir 17, 7-9; Is 40, 26; Acts 14, 17;17, 25-28.   s: Eph 4, 17-18.   t: Wis 13, 1-9; Is 5, 21; Jer 10, 14; Acts 17, 29-30;1 Cor 1, 19-21.   u: Dt 4, 15-19; Ps 106, 20; Wis 11, 15; 12, 24; 13, 10-19; Jer 2, 11.   v: Wis 12, 25; 14, 22-31; Acts 7, 41-42; Eph 4, 19.   w: 9, 5; Jer 13, 25-27.   x: Lv 18, 22; 20, 13; Wis 14, 26; 1 Cor 6, 9; 1 Tm 1, 10.   y: 13, 13; Mt 15, 19; Mk 7, 21-22; Gal 5, 19-21; 2 Tm 3, 2-4.   z: Acts 8, 1; 2 Thes 2, 12.

CHAPTER 2

See RG
357-58

God's Just Judgment. [1a]*Therefore, you are without excuse, every one of you who passes judgment. For by the standard by which you judge another you condemn yourself, since you, the judge, do the very same things. [2]We know that the judgment of God on those who do such things is true. [3b]Do you suppose, then, you who judge those who engage in such things and yet do them yourself, that you will escape the judgment of God? [4c]Or do you hold his priceless kindness, forbearance, and patience in low esteem, unaware that the kindness of God would lead you to repentance? [5d]By your stubbornness and impenitent heart, you are storing up wrath for yourself for the day of wrath and revelation of the just judgment of God, [6e]*who will repay everyone according to his works: [7]eternal life to those who seek glory, honor, and immortality through perseverance in good works, [8f]but wrath and fury to those who selfishly disobey the truth and obey wickedness. [9]Yes, affliction and distress will come upon every human being who does evil, Jew first and then Greek. [10g]But there will be glory, honor, and peace for everyone who does good, Jew first and then Greek. [11h]*There is no partiality with God.

Judgment by the Interior Law. [12i]*All who sin outside the law will also perish without reference to it, and all who sin under der the law will be judged in accordance with it. [13j]For it is not those who hear the law who are just in the sight of God; rather, those who observe the law will be justified. [14k]For when the Gentiles who do not have the law by nature observe the prescriptions of the law, they are a law for themselves even though they do not have the law. [15]*They show that the demands of the law are written in their hearts, while their conscience also bears witness and their conflicting thoughts accuse or even defend them [16l]on the day when, according to my gospel, God will judge people's hidden works through Christ Jesus.

Judgment by the Mosaic Law. [17m]*Now if you call yourself a Jew and rely on the law and boast of God [18n]and know his will and are able to discern what is important since you are instructed from the law, [19o]and if you are confident that you are a guide for the blind and a light for those in darkness, [20p]that you are a trainer of the foolish and teacher of the simple, because in the law you have the formulation of knowledge and truth— [21q]then you who teach another, are you failing to teach yourself? You who preach against stealing, do you steal? [22]You who forbid adultery, do you commit adultery? You who detest idols, do you rob temples? [23]You who boast of the law, do you dis-

2, 1—3, 20: After his general indictment of the Gentile, Paul shows that in spite of special revelation Jews enjoy no advantage in moral status before God (3, 1–8). With the entire human race now declared guilty before God (3, 9–20), Paul will then be able to display the solution for the total problem: salvation through God's redemptive work that is revealed in Christ Jesus for all who believe (3, 21–31).

2, 1–11: As a first step in his demonstration that Jews enjoy no real moral supremacy over Gentiles, Paul explains that the final judgment will be a review of performance, not of privilege. From this perspective Gentiles stand on an equal footing with Jews, and Jews cannot condemn the sins of Gentiles without condemning themselves.

2, 6: Will repay everyone according to his works: Paul reproduces the Septuagint text of Ps 62, 12 and Prv 24, 12.

2, 11: No partiality with God: this sentence is not at variance with the statements in vv 9–10. Since Jews are the first to go under indictment, it is only fair that they be given first consideration in the distribution of blessings. Basic, of course, is the understanding that God accepts no bribes (Dt 10, 17).

2, 12–16: Jews cannot reasonably demand from Gentiles the standard of conduct inculcated in the Old Testament since

God did not address its revelation to them. Rather, God made it possible for Gentiles to know instinctively the difference between right and wrong. But, as Paul explained in 1, 18–32, humanity misread the evidence of God's existence, power, and divinity, and "while claiming to be wise, they became fools" (1, 22).

2, 15: Paul expands on the thought of Jer 31, 33; Wis 17, 11.

2, 17–29: Mere possession of laws is no evidence of virtue. By eliminating circumcision as an elitist moral sign, Paul clears away the last obstacle to his presentation of justification through faith without claims based on the receipt of circumcision and its attendant legal obligations.

a: Mt 7, 1-2. *b:* Wis 16, 15-16. *c:* 3, 25-26; 9, 22; Wis 11, 23; 15, 1; 2 Pt 3, 9.15. *d:* Ex 33, 3; Acts 7, 51; Rv 6, 17; 11, 18. *e:* Ps 62, 12; Prv 24, 12; Sir 16, 14; Mt 16, 27; Jn 5, 29; 2 Cor 5, 10. *f:* 2 Thes 1, 8. *g:* 1, 16; 3, 9. *h:* Dt 10, 17; 2 Chr 19, 7; Sir 35, 12-13; Acts 10, 34; Gal 2, 6; Eph 6, 9; Col 3, 25; 1 Pt 1, 17. *i:* 3, 19. *j:* Mt 7, 21; Lk 6, 46-49; 8, 21; Jas 1, 22-25; 1 Jn 3, 7. *k:* Acts 10, 35. *l:* Acts 10, 42; 17, 31. *m:* Is 48, 1-2; Mi 3, 11; Phil 3, 4-6. *n:* Phil 1, 10. *o:* Mt 15, 14; Lk 6, 39. *p:* 2 Tm 3, 15. *q:* Ps 50, 16-21; Mt 23, 3-4.

honor God by breaking the law? [24r]*For, as it is written, "Because of you the name of God is reviled among the Gentiles."

[25s t]Circumcision, to be sure, has value if you observe the law; but if you break the law, your circumcision has become uncircumcision. [26u]Again, if an uncircumcised man keeps the precepts of the law, will he not be considered circumcised? [27]Indeed, those who are physically uncircumcised but carry out the law will pass judgment on you, with your written law and circumcision, who break the law. [28v]One is not a Jew outwardly. True circumcision is not outward, in the flesh. [29w]Rather, one is a Jew inwardly, and circumcision is of the heart, in the spirit, not the letter; his praise is not from human beings but from God.

See RG 357-58

CHAPTER 3

Answers to Objections. [1]*What advantage is there then in being a Jew? Or what is the value of circumcision? [2x]Much, in every respect. [For] in the first place, they were entrusted with the utterances of God. [3y]What if some were unfaithful? Will their infidelity nullify the fidelity of God? [4z]*Of course not! God must be true, though every human being is a liar, as it is written:

"That you may be justified in your
 words,
 and conquer when you are judged."

[5a]But if our wickedness provides proof of God's righteousness, what can we say? Is God unjust, humanly speaking, to inflict his wrath? [6]Of course not! For how else is God to judge the world? [7]But if God's truth redounds to his glory through my falsehood, why am I still being condemned as a sinner? [8b]And why not say—as we are accused and as some claim we say—that we should do evil that good may come of it? Their penalty is what they deserve.

Universal Bondage to Sin. [9c]*Well, then, are we better off? Not entirely, for we have already brought the charge against Jews and Greeks alike that they are all under the domination of sin, [10d]as it is written:

"There is no one just, not one,
[11] there is no one who understands,
    there is no one who seeks God.
[12] All have gone astray; all alike are
    worthless;
    there is not one who does good,
    [there is not] even one.
[13] [e]Their throats are open graves;
    they deceive with their tongues;
    the venom of asps is on their lips;
[14] [f]their mouths are full of bitter cursing.
[15] [g]Their feet are quick to shed blood;
[16]   ruin and misery are in their ways,
[17] and the way of peace they know not.
[18]   [h]There is no fear of God before their
        eyes."

[19i]*Now we know that what the law says is addressed to those under the law, so that every mouth may be silenced and the whole world stand accountable to God, [20j]*since no

---

2, 24: According to Is 52, 5 the suffering of Israel prompts her enemies to revile God. Paul uses the passage in support of his point that the present immorality of Israelites is the cause of such defamation.

3, 1–4: In keeping with the popular style of diatribe, Paul responds to the objection that his teaching on the sinfulness of all humanity detracts from the religious prerogatives of Israel. He stresses that Jews have remained the vehicle of God's revelation despite their sins, though this depends on the fidelity of God.

3, 4: Though every human being is a liar: these words reproduce the Greek text of Ps 116, 11. The rest of the verse is from Ps 51, 6.

3, 9–20: Well, then, are we better off?: this phrase can also be translated "Are we at a disadvantage?" but the latter version does not substantially change the overall meaning of the passage. Having explained that Israel's privileged status is guaranteed by God's fidelity, Paul now demonstrates the infidelity of the Jews by a catena of citations from scripture, possibly derived from an existing collection of **testimonia.**

These texts show that all human beings share the common burden of sin. They are linked together by mention of organs of the body: throat, tongue, lips, mouth, feet, eyes.

3, 19: The law: Paul here uses the term in its broadest sense to mean all of the scriptures; none of the preceding texts is from the Torah or Pentateuch.

3, 20: No human being will be justified in his sight: these words are freely cited from Ps 143, 2. In place of the psalmist's "no living person," Paul substitutes "no human being" (literally "no flesh," a Hebraism), and he adds "by observing the law."

r: Is 52, 5; Ez 36, 20; 2 Pt 2, 2. s: Jer 4, 4; 9, 24-25. t: 1 Cor 7, 19; Gal 5, 3. u: Gal 5, 6. v: Jn 7, 24; 8, 15.39. w: Dt 30, 6; Jer 4, 4; 9, 25; Col 2, 11 / 1 Cor 4, 5; 2 Cor 10, 18. x: 9, 4; Dt 4, 7-8; Pss 103, 7; 147, 19-20. y: 9, 6; 11, 1.29; Ps 89, 30-37; 2 Tm 2, 13. z: Ps 116, 11 / Ps 51, 6. a: 9, 14; Jb 34, 12-17. b: 6, 1. c: 1, 18—2, 25; 3, 23; Sir 8, 5. d: Pss 14, 1-3; 53, 2-4; Eccl 7, 20. e: Pss 5, 10; 140, 4. f: Ps 10, 7. g: Prv 1, 16; Is 59, 7-8. h: Ps 36, 2. i: 7, 7. j: Ps 143, 2; Gal 2, 16 / 7, 7.

human being will be justified in his sight by observing the law; for through the law comes consciousness of sin.

III: Justification through Faith in Christ

Justification apart from the Law. [21k]*But now the righteousness of God has been manifested apart from the law, though testified to by the law and the prophets, [22l]the righteousness of God through faith in Jesus Christ for all who believe. For there is no distinction; [23m]all have sinned and are deprived of the glory of God. [24n]They are justified freely by his grace through the redemption in Christ Jesus, [25o]*whom God set forth as an expiation, through faith, by his blood, to prove his righteousness because of the forgiveness of sins previously committed, [26]through the forbearance of God—to prove his righteousness in the present time, that he might be righteous and justify the one who has faith in Jesus.

[27p]*What occasion is there then for boasting? It is ruled out. On what principle, that of works? No, rather on the principle of faith. [28q]For we consider that a person is justified by faith apart from works of the law. [29r]Does God belong to Jews alone? Does he not belong to Gentiles, too? Yes, also to Gentiles, [30s]for God is one and will justify the circumcised on the basis of faith and the uncircumcised through faith. [31t]*Are we then annulling the law by this faith? Of course not! On the contrary, we are supporting the law.

CHAPTER 4

See RG 358

Abraham Justified by Faith. [1u]*What then can we say that Abraham found, our ancestor according to the flesh? [2]*Indeed, if Abraham was justified on the basis of his works, he has reason to boast; but this was not so in the sight of God. [3v]*For what does

---

3, 21–31: These verses provide a clear statement of Paul's "gospel," i.e., the principle of justification by faith in Christ. God has found a means of rescuing humanity from its desperate plight: Paul's general term for this divine initiative is the righteousness of God (21). Divine mercy declares the guilty innocent and makes them so. God does this not as a result of the law but apart from it (21), and not because of any merit in human beings but through forgiveness of their sins (24), in virtue of the redemption wrought in Christ Jesus for all who believe (22.24–25). God has manifested his righteousness in the coming of Jesus Christ, whose saving activity inaugurates a new era in human history.

3, 21: But now: Paul adopts a common phrase used by Greek authors to describe movement from disaster to prosperity. The expressions indicate that vv 21–26 are the consolatory answer to vv 9–20.

3, 25: Expiation: this rendering is preferable to "propitiation," which suggests hostility on the part of God toward sinners. As Paul will be at pains to point out (5, 8–10), it is humanity that is hostile to God.

3, 27–31: People cannot boast of their own holiness, since it is God's free gift (27), both to the Jew who practices circumcision out of faith and to the Gentile who accepts faith without the Old Testament religious culture symbolized by circumcision (29–30).

3, 27: Principle of faith: literally, "law of faith." Paul is fond of wordplay involving the term "law"; cf 7, 21.23; 8, 2. Since "law" in Greek may also connote "custom" or "principle," his readers and hearers would have sensed no contradiction in the use of the term after the negative statement concerning law in v 20.

3, 31: We are supporting the law: giving priority to God's intentions. God is the ultimate source of law, and the essence of law is fairness. On the basis of the Mosaic cov-

enant, God's justice is in question if those who sinned against the law are permitted to go free (see 23–26). In order to rescue all humanity rather than condemn it, God thinks of an alternative: the law or "principle" of faith (27). What can be more fair than to admit everyone into the divine presence on the basis of forgiveness grasped by faith? Indeed, this principle of faith antedates the Mosaic law, as Paul will demonstrate in ch 4, and does not therefore mark a change in divine policy.

4, 1–25: This is an expanded treatment of the significance of Abraham's faith, which Paul discusses in Gal 3, 6–18; see the notes there.

4, 2–5: Verse 2 corresponds to v 4, and v 3 to v 5. The Greek term here rendered **credited** means "made an entry." The context determines whether it is credit or debit. Verse 8 speaks of "recording sin" as a debit. Paul's repeated use of accountants' terminology in this and other passages can be traced both to the Old Testament texts he quotes and to his business activity as a tentmaker. The commercial term in Gn 15, 6, "credited it to him," reminds Paul in vv 7–8 of Ps 32, 2, in which the same term is used and applied to forgiveness of sins. Thus Paul is able to argue that Abraham's faith involved receipt of forgiveness of sins and that all believers benefit as he did through faith.

4, 3: Jas 2, 24 appears to conflict with Paul's statement. However, James combats the error of extremists who used the doctrine of justification through faith as a screen for moral self-determination. Paul discusses the subject of holiness in greater detail than does James and beginning with ch 6 shows

k: Is 51, 6-8; Acts 10, 43. *l:* 1, 17; Gal 2, 16; Phil 3, 9. *m:* 3, 9; 5, 12. *n:* Eph 2, 8; Ti 3, 7 / 5, 1-2; Eph 1, 7. *o:* Lv 16, 12-15; Acts 17, 31; 1 Jn 4, 10. *p:* 8, 2; 1 Cor 1, 29-31. *q:* 5, 1; Gal 2 16. *r:* 10, 12. *s:* Dt 6, 4; Gal 3, 20; Jas 2, 19 / 4, 11-12. *t:* 8, 4; Mt 5, 17. *u:* Gal 3, 6-9. *v:* Gn 15, 6; Gal 3, 6; Jas 2, 14.20-24.

the scripture say? "Abraham believed God, and it was credited to him as righteousness." [4w]A worker's wage is credited not as a gift, but as something due. [5]But when one does not work, yet believes in the one who justifies the ungodly, his faith is credited as righteousness. [6]So also David declares the blessedness of the person to whom God credits righteousness apart from works:

[7] [x]"Blessed are they whose iniquities are forgiven
and whose sins are covered.
[8] Blessed is the man whose sin the Lord does not record."

[9y]*Does this blessedness apply only to the circumcised, or to the uncircumcised as well? Now we assert that "faith was credited to Abraham as righteousness." [10]Under what circumstances was it credited? Was he circumcised or not? He was not circumcised, but uncircumcised. [11z]And he received the sign of circumcision as a seal on the righteousness received through faith while he was uncircumcised. Thus he was to be the father of all the uncircumcised who believe, so that to them [also] righteousness might be credited, [12]as well as the father of the circumcised who not only are circumcised but also follow the path of faith that our father Abraham walked while still uncircumcised.

Inheritance through Faith. [13a]It was not through the law that the promise was made to Abraham and his descendants that he would inherit the world, but through the righteousness that comes from faith. [14b]For if those who adhere to the law are the heirs, faith is null and the promise is void. [15c]*For the law produces wrath; but where there is no law, neither is there violation. [16d]For this reason, it depends on faith, so that it may be a gift, and the promise may be guaranteed to all his descendants, not to those who only adhere to the law but to those who follow the faith of Abraham, who is the father of all of us, [17e]as it is written, "I have made you father of many nations." He is our father in the sight of God, in whom he believed, who gives life to the dead and calls into being what does not exist. [18f]He believed, hoping against hope, that he would become "the father of many nations," according to what was said, "Thus shall your descendants be." [19g]He did not weaken in faith when he considered his own body as [already] dead (for he was almost a hundred years old) and the dead womb of Sarah. [20]*He did not doubt God's promise in unbelief; rather, he was empowered by faith and gave glory to God [21h]and was fully convinced that what he had promised he was also able to do. [22i]That is why "it was credited to him as righteousness." [23]But it was not for him alone that it was written that "it was credited to him"; [24j]it was also for us, to whom it will be credited, who believe in the one who raised Jesus our Lord from the dead, [25k]who was handed over for our transgressions and was raised for our justification.

how justification through faith introduces one to the gift of a new life in Christ through the power of the holy Spirit.

4, 9: Blessedness: evidence of divine favor.

4, 15: Law has the negative function of bringing the deep-seated rebellion against God to the surface in specific sins; see the note on 1, 18–32.

4, 20: He did not doubt God's promise in unbelief: any doubts Abraham might have had were resolved in commitment to God's promise. Heb 11, 8–12 emphasizes the faith of Abraham and Sarah.

5, 1–11: Popular piety frequently construed reverses and troubles as punishment for sin; cf Jn 9, 2. Paul therefore assures believers that God's justifying action in Jesus Christ is a declaration of peace. The crucifixion of Jesus Christ displays God's initiative in certifying humanity for unimpeded access into the divine presence. Reconciliation is God's gift of pardon to the entire human race. Through faith one benefits personally from this pardon or, in Paul's term, is justified. The ultimate aim of God is to liberate believers from the pre-Christian self as described in chs 1–3. Since this libera-

tion will first find completion in the believer's resurrection, salvation is described as future in 5, 10. Because this fullness of salvation belongs to the future it is called the Christian hope. Paul's Greek term for hope does not, however, suggest a note of uncertainty, to the effect: "I wonder whether God really means it." Rather, God's promise in the gospel fills believers with expectation and anticipation for the climactic gift of unalloyed commitment in the holy Spirit to the performance of the will of God. The persecutions that attend Christian commitment are to teach believers patience and to strengthen this hope, which will not disappoint them because the holy Spirit dwells in their hearts and imbues them with God's love (5).

w: 11, 6.   *x*: Ps 32, 1-2.   *y*: 4, 3.   *z*: Gn 17, 10-11; Gal 3, 6-8. *a*: Gn 12, 7; 18, 18; 22, 17-18; Sir 44, 21; Gal 3, 16-18.29. *b*: Gal 3, 18.   *c*: 3, 20; 5, 13; 7, 8; Gal 3, 19.   *d*: Sir 44, 19; Gal 3, 7-9.   *e*: Gn 17, 5; Heb 11, 19 / Is 48, 13.   *f*: Gn 15, 5.   *g*: Gn 17, 17; Heb 11, 11.   *h*: Gn 18, 14; Lk 1, 37.   *i*: Gn 15, 6.   *j*: 10, 9; 1 Pt 1, 21.   *k*: Is 53, 4-5.12; 1 Cor 15, 17; 1 Pt 1, 3 / 8, 11.

See RG
358–59

CHAPTER 5

Faith, Hope, and Love. [1]*Therefore, since we have been justified by faith, we have peace with God through our Lord Jesus Christ, [2m]through whom we have gained access [by faith] to this grace in which we stand, and we boast in hope of the glory of God. [3]Not only that, but we even boast of our afflictions, knowing that affliction produces endurance, [4n]and endurance, proven character, and proven character, hope, [5o]and hope does not disappoint, because the love of God has been poured out into our hearts through the holy Spirit that has been given to us. [6]For Christ, while we were still helpless, yet died at the appointed time for the ungodly. [7]*Indeed, only with difficulty does one die for a just person, though perhaps for a good person one might even find courage to die. [8p]But God proves his love for us in that while we were still sinners Christ died for us. [9q]How much more then, since we are now justified by his blood, will we be saved through him from the wrath. [10r]Indeed, if, while we were enemies, we were reconciled to God through the death of his Son, how much more, once reconciled, will we be saved by his life. [11]Not only that, but we also boast of God through our Lord Jesus Christ, through whom we have now received reconciliation.

Humanity's Sin through Adam. [12s]*Therefore, just as through one person sin entered the world, and through sin, death, and thus death came to all, inasmuch as all sinned—

[13t]for up to the time of the law, sin was in the world, though sin is not accounted when there is no law. [14u]But death reigned from Adam to Moses, even over those who did not sin after the pattern of the trespass of Adam, who is the type of the one who was to come.

Grace and Life through Christ. [15]But the gift is not like the transgression. For if by that one person's transgression the many died, how much more did the grace of God and the gracious gift of the one person Jesus Christ overflow for the many. [16]And the gift is not like the result of the one person's sinning. For after one sin there was the judgment that brought condemnation; but the gift, after many transgressions, brought acquittal. [17]For if, by the transgression of one person, death came to reign through that one, how much more will those who receive the abundance of grace and of the gift of justification come to reign in life through the one person Jesus Christ. [18v]In conclusion, just as through one transgression condemnation came upon all, so through one righteous act acquittal and life came to all. [19w]For just as through the disobedience of one person the many were made sinners, so through the obedience of one the many will be made righteous. [20x]*The law entered in so that transgression might increase but, where sin increased, grace overflowed all the more, [21y]so that, as sin reigned in death, grace also might reign through justification for eternal life through Jesus Christ our Lord.

5, 1: **We have peace:** a number of manuscripts, versions, and church Fathers read "Let us have peace"; cf 14, 19.

5, 7: In the world of Paul's time the **good person** is especially one who is magnanimous to others.

5, 12–21: Paul reflects on the sin of Adam (Gn 3, 1–13) in the light of the redemptive mystery of Christ. Sin, as used in the singular by Paul, refers to the dreadful power that has gripped humanity, which is now in revolt against the Creator and engaged in the exaltation of its own desires and interests. But no one has a right to say, "Adam made me do it," for all are culpable (12): Gentiles under the demands of the law written in their hearts (2, 14–15), and Jews under the Mosaic covenant. Through the Old Testament law, the sinfulness of humanity that was operative from the beginning (13) found further stimulation, with the result that sins were generated in even greater abundance. According to vv 15–21, God's act in Christ is in total contrast to the disastrous effects of the virus of sin that invaded humanity through Adam's crime.

5, 12: **Inasmuch as all sinned:** others translate "because all sinned," and understand v 13 as a parenthetical remark. Unlike Wis 2, 24, Paul does not ascribe the entry of death to the devil.

5, 20: **The law entered in:** sin had made its entrance (12); now the law comes in alongside sin. See the notes on 1, 18–32; 5, 12–21. **Where sin increased, grace overflowed all the more:** Paul declares that grace outmatches the productivity of sin.

l: 3, 24-28; Gal 2, 16.   m: Eph 2, 18; 3, 12.   n: 2 Cor 12, 9-10; Jas 1, 2-4; 1 Pt 1, 5-7; 4, 12-14.   o: 8, 14-16; Pss 22, 5-6; 25, 20.   p: Jn 3, 16; 1 Jn 4, 10.19.   q: 1, 18; 1 Thes 1, 10.   r: 8, 7-8; 2 Cor 5, 18; Col 1, 21-22.   s: Gn 2, 17; 3, 1-19; Wis 2, 24 / 3, 19.23.   t: 4, 15.   u: 1 Cor 15, 21.   v: 1 Cor 15, 21-22.   w: Is 53, 11; Phil 2, 8-9.   x: 4, 15; 7, 7-8; Gal 3, 19.   y: 6, 23.

IV: Justification and the Christian Life

CHAPTER 6

See RG 358–59

Freedom from Sin; Life in God. [1z]*What then shall we say? Shall we persist in sin that grace may abound? Of course not! [2a]How can we who died to sin yet live in it? [3b]Or are you unaware that we who were baptized into Christ Jesus were baptized into his death? [4c]We were indeed buried with him through baptism into death, so that, just as Christ was raised from the dead by the glory of the Father, we too might live in newness of life.

[5d]For if we have grown into union with him through a death like his, we shall also be united with him in the resurrection. [6e]We know that our old self was crucified with him, so that our sinful body might be done away with, that we might no longer be in slavery to sin. [7]For a dead person has been absolved from sin. [8f]If, then, we have died with Christ, we believe that we shall also live with him. [9g]We know that Christ, raised from the dead, dies no more; death no longer has power over him. [10h]As to his death, he died to sin once and for all; as to his life, he lives for God. [11i]Consequently, you too must think of yourselves as [being] dead to sin and living for God in Christ Jesus.

[12j]*Therefore, sin must not reign over your mortal bodies so that you obey their desires. [13k]And do not present the parts of your bodies to sin as weapons for wickedness, but present yourselves to God as raised from the dead to life and the parts of your bodies to God as weapons for righteousness. [14l]For sin is not to have any power over you, since you are not under the law but under grace.

[15m]What then? Shall we sin because we are not under the law but under grace? Of course not! [16n]Do you not know that if you present yourselves to someone as obedient slaves, you are slaves of the one you obey, either of sin, which leads to death, or of obedience, which leads to righteousness? [17]*But thanks be to God that, although you were once slaves of sin, you have become obedient from the heart to the pattern of teaching to which you were entrusted. [18]Freed from sin, you have become slaves of righteousness. [19]I am speaking in human terms because of the weakness of your nature. For just as you presented the parts of your bodies as slaves to impurity and to lawlessness for lawlessness, so now present them as slaves to righteousness for sanctification. [20p]*For when you were slaves of sin, you were free from righteousness. [21q]But what profit did you get then from the things of which you are now ashamed? For the end of those things is death. [22r]*But now that you have been freed from sin and have become slaves of God, the benefit that you have leads to sanctification,

---

6, 1–11: To defend the gospel against the charge that it promotes moral laxity (cf 3, 5–8), Paul expresses himself in the typical style of spirited diatribe. God's display of generosity or grace is not evoked by sin but, as stated in 5, 8, is the expression of God's love, and this love pledges eternal life to all believers (5, 21). Paul views the present conduct of the believers from the perspective of God's completed salvation when the body is resurrected and directed totally by the holy Spirit. Through baptism believers share the death of Christ and thereby escape from the grip of sin. Through the resurrection of Christ the power to live anew becomes reality for them, but the fullness of participation in Christ's resurrection still lies in the future. But life that is lived in dedication to God now is part and parcel of that future. Hence anyone who sincerely claims to be interested in that future will scarcely be able to say, "Let us sin so that grace may prosper" (cf 1).

6, 12–19: Christians have been released from the grip of sin, but sin endeavors to reclaim its victims. The antidote is constant remembrance that divine grace has claimed them and identifies them as people who are alive only for God's interests.

6, 17: In contrast to humanity, which was handed over to self-indulgence (1, 24–32), believers are **entrusted** ("handed over") to God's **pattern of teaching,** that is, the new life God aims to develop in Christians through the productivity of the holy Spirit. Throughout this passage Paul uses the slave-master model in order to emphasize the fact that one cannot give allegiance to both God and sin.

6, 20: You were free from righteousness: expressed ironically, for such freedom is really tyranny. The commercial metaphors in vv 21–23 add up only one way: sin is a bad bargain.

6, 22: Sanctification: or holiness.

---

z: 3, 5-8. a: 1 Pt 4, 1. b: Gal 3, 27. c: Col 2, 12; 1 Pt 3, 21-22. d: Phil 3, 10-11; 2 Tm 2, 11. e: Gal 5, 24; 6, 14; Eph 4, 22-23. f: 1 Thes 4, 17. g: Acts 13, 34; 1 Cor 15, 26; 2 Tm 1, 10; Rv 1, 18. h: Heb 9, 26-28; 1 Pt 3, 18. i: 2 Cor 5, 15; 1 Pt 2, 24. j: Gn 4, 7. k: 12, 1; Eph 2, 5; 5, 14 / Col 3, 5. l: Gal 5, 18; 1 Jn 3, 6. m: 5, 17.21. n: Jn 8, 31-34; 2 Pt 2, 19. o: Jn 8, 32-36. p: Jn 8, 34. q: 8, 6.13; Prv 12, 28; Ez 16, 61.63. r: 1 Pt 1, 9.

and its end is eternal life. [23s]For the wages of sin is death, but the gift of God is eternal life in Christ Jesus our Lord.

CHAPTER 7

See RG 359

Freedom from the Law. [1]*Are you unaware, brothers (for I am speaking to people who know the law), that the law has jurisdiction over one as long as one lives? [2t]Thus a married woman is bound by law to her living husband; but if her husband dies, she is released from the law in respect to her husband. [3]Consequently, while her husband is alive she will be called an adulteress if she consorts with another man. But if her husband dies she is free from that law, and she is not an adulteress if she consorts with another man.

[4]In the same way, my brothers, you also were put to death to the law through the body of Christ, so that you might belong to another, to the one who was raised from the dead in order that we might bear fruit for God. [5u]For when we were in the flesh, our sinful passions, awakened by the law, worked in our members to bear fruit for death. [6v]But now we are released from the law, dead to what held us captive, so that we may serve in the newness of the spirit and not under the obsolete letter.

Acquaintance with Sin through the Law. [7w]*What then can we say? That the law is sin? Of course not! Yet I did not know sin except through the law, and I did not know what it is to covet except that the law said, "You shall not covet." [8x]But sin, finding an opportunity in the commandment, produced in me every kind of covetousness. Apart from the law sin is dead. [9]I once lived outside the law, but when the commandment came, sin became alive; [10y]then I died, and the commandment that was for life turned out to be death for me. [11z]For sin, seizing an opportunity in the commandment, deceived me and through it put me to death. [12a]So then the law is holy, and the commandment is holy and righteous and good.

Sin and Death. [13b]*Did the good, then, become death for me? Of course not! Sin, in order that it might be shown to be sin, worked death in me through the good, so that sin might become sinful beyond measure through the commandment. [14c]We know that the law is spiritual; but I am carnal, sold into slavery to sin. [15]What I do, I do not understand. For I do not do what I want, but I do what I hate. [16]Now if I do what I do not want, I concur that the law is good. [17]So now it is no longer I who do it, but sin that dwells in me. [18d]For I know that good does not dwell in me, that is, in my flesh. The willing is ready at hand, but doing the good is not. [19]For I do not do the good I want, but I do the evil I do not want. [20]Now if [I] do what I do not want, it is no longer I who do it, but sin that dwells in me. [21]So, then, I discover the principle that when I want to do right, evil is at hand. [22]For I take delight in the law of God, in my inner self, [23e]*but I see in my members another principle at war with the law of my mind, taking me captive to the

---

7, 1–6: Paul reflects on the fact that Christians have a different understanding of the law because of their faith in Christ. Law binds the living, not the dead, as exemplified in marriage, which binds in life but is dissolved through death. Similarly, Christians who through baptism have died with Christ to sin (cf 6, 2–4) are freed from the law that occasioned transgressions, which in turn were productive of death. Now that Christians are joined to Christ, the power of Christ's resurrection makes it possible for them to bear the fruit of newness of life for God.

7, 7–25: In this passage Paul uses the first person singular in the style of diatribe for the sake of argument. He aims to depict the disastrous consequences when a Christian reintroduces the law as a means to attain the objective of holiness pronounced in 6, 22.

7, 7–12: The apostle defends himself against the charge of identifying the law with sin. Sin does not exist in law but in human beings, whose sinful inclinations are not overcome by the proclamation of law.

7, 13–25: Far from improving the sinner, law encourages sin to expose itself in transgressions or violations of specific commandments (see 1, 24; 5, 20). Thus persons who do not experience the justifying grace of God, and Christians who revert to dependence on law as the criterion for their relationship with God, will recognize a rift between their reasoned desire for the goodness of the law and their actual performance that is contrary to the law. Unable to free themselves from the slavery of sin and the power of death, they can only be rescued from defeat in the conflict by the power of God's grace working through Jesus Christ.

7, 23: As in 3, 27, Paul plays on the term **law,** which in Greek can connote custom, system, or **principle.**

s: Gn 2, 17; Gal 6, 7-9; Jas 1, 15.   t: 1 Cor 7, 39.   u: 6, 21; 8, 6.13.   v: 8, 2; 2 Cor 3, 6.   w: 3, 20; Ex 20, 17; Dt 5, 21.   x: 5, 13.20; 1 Cor 15, 56 / 4, 15.   y: Lv 18, 5.   z: Gn 3, 13; Heb 3, 13.   a: 1 Tm 1, 8.   b: 4, 15; 5, 20.   c: 8, 7-8; Ps 51, 7.   d: Gn 6, 5; 8, 21; Phil 2, 13.   e: Gal 5, 17; 1 Pt 2, 11.

law of sin that dwells in my members.
[24]Miserable one that I am! Who will deliver
me from this mortal body? [25f]Thanks be to
God through Jesus Christ our Lord. Therefore, I myself, with my mind, serve the law
of God but, with my flesh, the law of sin.

CHAPTER 8

See RG
359–60
The Flesh and the Spirit. [1]*Hence,
now there is no condemnation for those who
are in Christ Jesus. [2g]For the law of the spirit
of life in Christ Jesus has freed you from the
law of sin and death. [3h]For what the law,
weakened by the flesh, was powerless to do,
this God has done: by sending his own Son
in the likeness of sinful flesh and for the sake
of sin, he condemned sin in the flesh, [4i]so
that the righteous decree of the law might be
fulfilled in us, who live not according to the
flesh but according to the spirit. [5]For those
who live according to the flesh are concerned with the things of the flesh, but those
who live according to the spirit with the
things of the spirit. [6j]The concern of the
flesh is death, but the concern of the spirit is
life and peace. [7k]For the concern of the flesh
is hostility toward God; it does not submit to
the law of God, nor can it; [8l]and those who
are in the flesh cannot please God. [9m]But
you are not in the flesh; on the contrary, you
are in the spirit, if only the Spirit of God
dwells in you. Whoever does not have the
Spirit of Christ does not belong to him.
[10n]But if Christ is in you, although the body
is dead because of sin, the spirit is alive because of righteousness. [11]If the Spirit of the
one who raised Jesus from the dead dwells
in you, the one who raised Christ from the
dead will give life to your mortal bodies
also, through his Spirit that dwells in you.
[12]Consequently, brothers, we are not debtors
to the flesh, to live according to the flesh.
[13o]For if you live according to the flesh, you
will die, but if by the spirit you put to death
the deeds of the body, you will live.

Children of God through Adoption.
[14p]*For those who are led by the Spirit of
God are children of God. [15q]*For you did not
receive a spirit of slavery to fall back into
fear, but you received a spirit of adoption,
through which we cry, "*Abba,* Father!"
[16r]The Spirit itself bears witness with our
spirit that we are children of God, [17s]and if
children, then heirs, heirs of God and joint
heirs with Christ, if only we suffer with him
so that we may also be glorified with him.

Destiny of Glory. [18t]*I consider that the
sufferings of this present time are as nothing
compared with the glory to be revealed for
us. [19]For creation awaits with eager expectation the revelation of the children of God;
[20u]for creation was made subject to futility,
not of its own accord but because of the one
who subjected it, in hope [21v]that creation it-

8, 1–13: After his warning in ch 7 against the wrong route
to fulfillment of the objective of holiness expressed in 6, 22,
Paul points his addressees to the correct way. Through the redemptive work of Christ, Christians have been liberated from
the terrible forces of sin and death. Holiness was impossible
so long as the **flesh** (or our "old self"), that is, self-interested
hostility toward God (7), frustrated the divine objectives expressed in the law. What is worse, sin used the law to break
forth into all manner of lawlessness (8). All this is now
changed. At the cross God broke the power of sin and pronounced sentence on it (3). Christians still retain the flesh, but
it is alien to their new being, which is life in the spirit, namely
the new self, governed by the holy Spirit. Under the direction
of the holy Spirit Christians are able to fulfill the divine will
that formerly found expression in the law (4). The same Spirit
who enlivens Christians for holiness will also resurrect their
bodies at the last day (11). Christian life is therefore the experience of a constant challenge to put to death the evil deeds
of the body through life of the spirit (13).

8, 14–17: Christians, by reason of the Spirit's presence
within them, enjoy not only new life but also a new relationship to God, that of adopted children and heirs

through Christ, whose sufferings and glory they share.
8, 15: Abba: see the note on Mk 14, 36.
8, 18–27: The glory that believers are destined to share
with Christ far exceeds the sufferings of the present life. Paul
considers the destiny of the created world to be linked with the
future that belongs to the believers. As it shares in the penalty
of corruption brought about by sin, so also will it share in the
benefits of redemption and future glory that comprise the ultimate liberation of God's people (19–22). After patient endurance in steadfast expectation, the full harvest of the Spirit's
presence will be realized. On earth believers enjoy the firstfruits, i.e., the Spirit, as a guarantee of the total liberation of
their bodies from the influence of the rebellious old self (23).

f: 1 Cor 15, 57.   *g:* 7, 23-24; 2 Cor 3, 17.   *h:* Acts 13, 38; 15, 10
/ Jn 3, 16-17; 2 Cor 5, 21; Gal 3, 13; 4, 4; Phil 2, 7; Col 1, 22; Heb
2, 17; 4, 15; 1 Jn 4, 9.   *i:* Gal 5, 16-25.   *j:* 6, 21; 7, 5; 8, 13; Gal
6, 8.   *k:* 5, 10; Jas 4, 4.   *l:* 1 Jn 2, 16.   *m:* 1 Cor 3, 16.   *n:* Gal
2, 20; 1 Pt 4, 6.   *o:* Gal 5, 24; 6, 8; Eph 4, 22-24.   *p:* Gal 5, 18.
q: Mk 14, 36; Gal 4, 5-6; 2 Tm 1, 7.   *r:* Jn 1, 12; Gal 3, 26-29.
s: Gal 4, 7; 1 Pt 4, 13; 5, 1.   *t:* 2 Cor 4, 17.   *u:* Gn 3, 17-19.
v: 2 Pt 3, 12-13; Rv 21, 1.

self would be set free from slavery to corruption and share in the glorious freedom of the children of God. [22w]We know that all creation is groaning in labor pains even until now; [23x]and not only that, but we ourselves, who have the firstfruits of the Spirit, we also groan within ourselves as we wait for adoption, the redemption of our bodies. [24y]For in hope we were saved. Now hope that sees for itself is not hope. For who hopes for what one sees? [25]But if we hope for what we do not see, we wait with endurance.

[26]In the same way, the Spirit too comes to the aid of our weakness; for we do not know how to pray as we ought, but the Spirit itself intercedes with inexpressible groanings. [27z]And the one who searches hearts knows what is the intention of the Spirit, because it intercedes for the holy ones according to God's will.

God's Indomitable Love in Christ. [28a]*We know that all things work for good for those who love God, who are called according to his purpose. [29b]*For those he foreknew he also predestined to be conformed to the image of his Son, so that he might be the firstborn among many brothers. [30c]And those he predestined he also called; and those he called he also justified; and those he justified he also glorified.

[31d]*What then shall we say to this? If God is for us, who can be against us? [32e]He who did not spare his own Son but handed him

over for us all, how will he not also give us everything else along with him? [33f]Who will bring a charge against God's chosen ones? It is God who acquits us. [34g]Who will condemn? It is Christ [Jesus] who died, rather, was raised, who also is at the right hand of God, who indeed intercedes for us. [35]What will separate us from the love of Christ? Will anguish, or distress, or persecution, or famine, or nakedness, or peril, or the sword? [36h]As it is written:

> "For your sake we are being slain all the day;
> we are looked upon as sheep to be slaughtered."

[37i]No, in all these things we conquer overwhelmingly through him who loved us. [38j]*For I am convinced that neither death, nor life, nor angels, nor principalities, nor present things, nor future things, nor powers, [39]*nor height, nor depth, nor any other creature will be able to separate us from the love of God in Christ Jesus our Lord.

V: Jews And Gentiles in God's Plan

CHAPTER 9

See RG 360-61

Paul's Love for Israel. [1k]*I speak the truth in Christ, I do not lie; my conscience joins with the holy Spirit in bearing me wit-

---

8, 28–30: These verses outline the Christian vocation as it was designed by God: **to be conformed to the image of his Son,** who is to **be the firstborn among many brothers** (29). God's redemptive action on behalf of the believers has been in process before the beginning of the world. Those whom God chooses are **those he foreknew** (29) or elected. Those who are **called** (30) are **predestined** or predetermined. These expressions do not mean that God is arbitrary. Rather, Paul uses them to emphasize the thought and care that God has taken for the Christian's salvation.

8, 28: We know that all things work for good for those who love God: a few ancient authorities have God as the subject of the verb, and some translators render: "We know that God makes everything work for good for those who love God . . . ."

8, 29: Image: while man and woman were originally created in God's image (Gn 1, 26–27), it is through baptism into Christ, the image of God (2 Cor 4, 4; Col 1, 15), that we are renewed according to the image of the Creator (Col 3, 10).

8, 31–39: The all-conquering power of God's love has overcome every obstacle to Christians' salvation and every

threat to separate them from God. That power manifested itself fully when God's own Son was delivered up to death for their salvation. Through him Christians can overcome all their afflictions and trials.

8, 38: Present things and **future things** may refer to astrological data. Paul appears to be saying that the gospel liberates believers from dependence on astrologers.

8, 39: Height, depth may refer to positions in the zodiac, positions of heavenly bodies relative to the horizon. In astrological documents the term for "height" means "exaltation" or the position of greatest influence exerted by a planet. Since hostile spirits were associated with the planets and stars, Paul includes **powers** (38) in his list of malevolent forces.

9, 1—11, 36: Israel's unbelief and its rejection of Jesus as

w: 2 Cor 5, 2-5. *x:* 2 Cor 1, 22; Gal 5, 5. *y:* 2 Cor 5, 7. Heb 11, 1. *z:* Ps 139, 1; 1 Cor 4, 5. *a:* Eph 1, 4-14; 3, 11. *b:* Eph. 1, 5; 1 Pt 1, 2. *c:* Is 45, 25; 2 Thes 2, 13-14. *d:* Ps 118, 6; Heb 13, 6. *e:* Jn 3, 16. *f:* Is 50, 8. *g:* Ps 110, 1; Heb 7, 25; 1 Jn 2, 1. *h:* Ps 44, 23; 1 Cor 4, 9; 15, 30; 2 Cor 4, 11; 2 Tm 3, 12. *i:* 1 Jn 5, 4. *j:* 1 Cor 3, 22; Eph 1, 21; 1 Pt 3, 22. *k:* 2 Cor 11, 31; 1 Tm 2, 7.

ness [2]that I have great sorrow and constant anguish in my heart. [3l]For I could wish that I myself were accursed and separated from Christ for the sake of my brothers, my kin according to the flesh. [4m]They are Israelites; theirs the adoption, the glory, the covenants, the giving of the law, the worship, and the promises; [5n]*theirs the patriarchs, and from them, according to the flesh, is the Messiah. God who is over all be blessed forever. Amen.

God's Free Choice. [6o]But it is not that the word of God has failed. For not all who are of Israel are Israel, [7p]nor are they all children of Abraham because they are his descendants; but "It is through Isaac that descendants shall bear your name." [8q]This means that it is not the children of the flesh who are the children of God, but the children of the promise are counted as descendants. [9r]For this is the wording of the promise, "About this time I shall return and Sarah will have a son." [10s]*And not only that, but also when Rebecca had conceived children by one husband, our father Isaac— [11]before they had yet been born or had done anything,

good or bad, in order that God's elective plan might continue, [12t]not by works but by his call—she was told, "The older shall serve the younger." [13u]*As it is written:

"I loved Jacob
   but hated Esau."

[14v]*What then are we to say? Is there injustice on the part of God? Of course not! [15w]For he says to Moses:

"I will show mercy to whom I will,
   I will take pity on whom I will."

[16x]So it depends not upon a person's will or exertion, but upon God, who shows mercy. [17y]For the scripture says to Pharaoh, "This is why I have raised you up, to show my power through you that my name may be proclaimed throughout the earth." [18z]*Consequently, he has mercy upon whom he wills, and he hardens whom he wills.

[19a]*You will say to me then, "Why [then] does he still find fault? For who can oppose his will?" [20b]But who indeed are you, a human being, to talk back to God? Will what

savior astonished and puzzled Christians. It constituted a serious problem for them in view of God's specific preparation of Israel for the advent of the Messiah. Paul addresses himself here to the essential question of how the divine plan could be frustrated by Israel's unbelief. At the same time, he discourages both complacency and anxiety on the part of Gentiles. To those who might boast of their superior advantage over Jews, he warns that their enjoyment of the blessings assigned to Israel can be terminated. To those who might anxiously ask, "How can we be sure that Israel's fate will not be ours?" he replies that only unbelief can deprive one of salvation.

9, 1–5: The apostle speaks in strong terms of the depth of his grief over the unbelief of his own people. He would willingly undergo a curse himself for the sake of their coming to the knowledge of Christ (3; cf Lv 27, 28–29). His love for them derives from God's continuing choice of them and from the spiritual benefits that God bestows on them and through them on all of humanity (4–5).

9, 5: Some editors punctuate this verse differently and prefer the translation, "Of whom is Christ according to the flesh, who is God over all." However, Paul's point is that **God who is over all** aimed to use Israel, which had been entrusted with every privilege, in outreach to the entire world through the Messiah.

9, 10: Children by one husband, our father Isaac: Abraham had two children, Ishmael and Isaac, by two wives, Hagar and Sarah, respectively. In that instance Isaac, although born later than Ishmael, became the bearer of the messianic promise. In the case of twins born to Rebecca, God's elective procedure is seen even more dramatically, and again the younger, contrary to Semitic custom, is given the preference.

9, 13: The literal rendering, **"Jacob I loved, but Esau I hated,"** suggests an attitude of divine hostility that is not implied in Paul's statement. In Semitic usage "hate" means to love less; cf Lk 14, 26 with Mt 10, 37. Israel's unbelief reflects the mystery of the divine election that is always operative within it. Mere natural descent from Abraham does not ensure the full possession of the divine gifts; it is God's sovereign prerogative to bestow this fullness upon, or to withhold it from, whomsoever he wishes; cf Mt 3, 9; Jn 8, 39. The choice of Jacob over Esau is a case in point.

9, 14–18: The principle of divine election does not invite Christians to theoretical inquiry concerning the nonelected, nor does this principle mean that God is unfair in his dealings with humanity. The instruction concerning divine election is a part of the gospel and reveals that the gift of faith is the enactment of God's mercy (16). God raised up Moses to display that mercy, and Pharaoh to display divine severity in punishing those who obstinately oppose their Creator.

9, 18: The basic biblical principle is: those who will not see or hear **shall** not see or hear. On the other hand, the same God who thus makes stubborn or hardens the heart can reconstruct it through the work of the holy Spirit.

9, 19–29: The apostle responds to the objection that if God rules over faith through the principle of divine election, God

l: Ex 32, 32.   m: 3, 2; Ex 4, 22; Dt 7, 6; 14, 1-2.   n: Mt 1, 1-16; Lk 3, 23-38 / 1, 25; Ps 41, 14.   o: Nm 23, 19 / Mt 3, 9.   p: Gn 21, 12; Gal 3, 29.   q: Gal 4, 23.28.   r: Gn 18, 10.14.   s: Gn 25, 21. t: 11, 5-6 / Gn 25, 23-24.   u: Mal 1, 3.   v: Dt 32, 4.   w: Ex 33, 19.   x: Eph 2, 8; Ti 3, 5.   y: Ex 9, 16.   z: 11, 30-32; Ex 4, 21; 7, 3.   a: 3, 7; Wis 12, 12.   b: Wis 15, 7; Is 29, 16; 45, 9; Jer 18, 6.

is made say to its maker, "Why have you created me so?" [21]Or does not the potter have a right over the clay, to make out of the same lump one vessel for a noble purpose and another for an ignoble one? [22c]What if God, wishing to show his wrath and make known his power, has endured with much patience the vessels of wrath made for destruction? [23]This was to make known the riches of his glory to the vessels of mercy, which he has prepared previously for glory, [24]namely, us whom he has called, not only from the Jews but also from the Gentiles.

Witness of the Prophets. [25d*]As indeed he says in Hosea:

"Those who were not my people I will
    call 'my people,'
and her who was not beloved I will
    call 'beloved.'
[26 e]And in the very place where it was said
        to them, 'You are not my people,'
    there they shall be called children of
        the living God."

[27f]And Isaiah cries out concerning Israel, "Though the number of the Israelites were like the sand of the sea, only a remnant will be saved; [28]for decisively and quickly will the Lord execute sentence upon the earth." [29g]And as Isaiah predicted:

"Unless the Lord of hosts had left us
    descendants,
we would have become like Sodom
    and have been made like Gomorrah."

Righteousness Based on Faith. [30h*]What then shall we say? That Gentiles, who did not pursue righteousness, have achieved it, that is, righteousness that comes from faith; [31i]but that Israel, who pursued the law of righteousness, did not attain to that law? [32j*]Why not? Because they did it not by faith, but as if it could be done by works. They stumbled over the stone that causes stumbling, [33k]as it is written:

"Behold, I am laying a stone in Zion
    that will make people stumble
    and a rock that will make them fall,
and whoever believes in him shall not be
        put to shame."

CHAPTER 10

See RG 360-61

[1]*Brothers, my heart's desire and prayer to God on their behalf is for salvation. [2m]I testify with regard to them that they have zeal for God, but it is not discerning. [3n]For, in their unawareness of the righteousness that comes from God and their attempt to establish their own [righteousness], they did not submit to the righteousness of God. [4o*]For Christ is the end of the law for the justification of everyone who has faith.

---

cannot then accuse unbelievers of sin (19). For Paul, this objection is in the last analysis a manifestation of human insolence, and his "answer" is less an explanation of God's ways than the rejection of an argument that places humanity on a level with God. At the same time, Paul shows that God is far less arbitrary than appearances suggest, for God endures **with much patience** (22) a person like the Pharaoh of the Exodus.

9, 25: Beloved: in Semitic discourse means "preferred" or "favorite" (cf 13). See Hos 2, 1, which is transposed after Hos 3, 5 in the NAB.

9, 30–33: In the conversion of the Gentiles and, by contrast, of relatively few Jews, the Old Testament prophecies are seen to be fulfilled; cf 25–29. Israel feared that the doctrine of justification through faith would jeopardize the validity of the Mosaic law, and so they never reached their goal of righteousness that they sought to attain through meticulous observance of the law (31). Since Gentiles, including especially Greeks and Romans, had a great regard for righteousness, Paul's statement concerning Gentiles in v 30 is to be understood from a Jewish perspective: quite evidently they had not been interested in "God's" righteousness, for it had not been revealed to them; but now in response to the proclamation of the gospel they respond in faith.

9, 32: Paul discusses Israel as a whole from the perspective of contemporary Jewish rejection of Jesus as Messiah. The Old Testament and much of Jewish noncanonical literature in fact reflect a fervent faith in divine mercy.

10, 1–13: Despite Israel's lack of faith in God's act in Christ, Paul does not abandon hope for her salvation (1). However, Israel must recognize that the Messiah's arrival in the person of Jesus Christ means the termination of the Mosaic law as the criterion for understanding oneself in a valid relationship to God. Faith in God's saving action in Jesus Christ takes precedence over any such legal claim (6).

10, 4: The Mosaic legislation has been superseded by God's action in Jesus Christ. Others understand **end** here in the sense that Christ is the goal of the law, i.e., the true meaning of the Mosaic law, which cannot be correctly understood apart from him. Still others believe that both meanings are intended.

c: 2, 4; Wis 12, 20-21; Jer 50, 25. d: Hos 2, 25. e: Hos 2, 1. f: Is 10, 22-23; Hos 2, 1 / 11, 5 / Is 28, 22. g: Is 1, 9; Mt 10, 15. h: 10, 4.20. i: 10, 3. j: Is 8, 14. k: Is 28, 16; 1 Pt 2, 6-8. l: 9, 1.3. m: Acts 22, 3. n: 9, 31-32; Phil 3, 9. o: Acts 13, 38-39; 2 Cor 3, 14; Heb 8, 13.

5p*Moses writes about the righteousness that comes from [the] law, "The one who does these things will live by them." 6q But the righteousness that comes from faith says, "Do not say in your heart, 'Who will go up into heaven?' (that is, to bring Christ down) 7r*or 'Who will go down into the abyss?' (that is, to bring Christ up from the dead)." 8s But what does it say?

"The word is near you,
   in your mouth and in your heart"

(that is, the word of faith that we preach), 9t*for, if you confess with your mouth that Jesus is Lord and believe in your heart that God raised him from the dead, you will be saved. 10 For one believes with the heart and so is justified, and one confesses with the mouth and so is saved. 11u For the scripture says, "No one who believes in him will be put to shame." 12v For there is no distinction between Jew and Greek; the same Lord is Lord of all, enriching all who call upon him. 13w For "everyone who calls on the name of the Lord will be saved."

14x*But how can they call on him in whom they have not believed? And how can they believe in him of whom they have not heard? And how can they hear without someone to preach? 15y*And how can people preach unless they are sent? As it is written, "How beautiful are the feet of those who bring [the] good news!" 16z But not everyone has heeded the good news; for Isaiah says, "Lord, who has believed what was heard from us?" 17a Thus faith comes from what is heard, and what is heard comes through the word of Christ. 18b But I ask, did they not hear? Certainly they did; for

"Their voice has gone forth to all the
      earth,
   and their words to the ends of the
      world."

19c But I ask, did not Israel understand? First Moses says:

"I will make you jealous of those who
      are not a nation;
   with a senseless nation I will make
      you angry."

20d Then Isaiah speaks boldly and says:

"I was found [by] those who were not
      seeking me;
   I revealed myself to those who were
      not asking for me."

21 But regarding Israel he says, "All day long I stretched out my hands to a disobedient and contentious people."

CHAPTER 11

The Remnant of Israel. 1ef*I ask, then, has God rejected his people? Of course not! For I too am an Israelite, a descendant of Abraham, of the tribe of Benjamin. 2 God has not rejected his people whom he foreknew. Do you not know what the scripture says about Elijah, how he pleads with God against Israel? 3g"Lord, they have

See RG 360–61

10, 5–6: The subject of the verb **says** (6) is **righteousness** personified. Both of the statements in vv 5 and 6 derive from Moses, but Paul wishes to contrast the language of law and the language of faith.

10, 7: Here Paul blends Dt 30, 13 and Ps 107, 26.

10, 9–11: To confess Jesus as Lord was frequently quite hazardous in the first century (cf Mt 10, 18; 1 Thes 2, 2; 1 Pt 2, 18–21; 3, 14). For a Jew it could mean disruption of normal familial and other social relationships, including great economic sacrifice. In the face of penalties imposed by the secular world, Christians are assured that **no one who believes** in Jesus **will be put to shame** (11).

10, 14–21: The gospel has been sufficiently proclaimed to Israel, and Israel has adequately understood God's plan for the messianic age, which would see the gospel brought to the uttermost parts of the earth. As often in the past, Israel has not accepted the prophetic message; cf Acts 7, 51–53.

10, 15: How beautiful are the feet of those who bring

[the] good news: in Semitic fashion, the parts of the body that bring the messenger with welcome news are praised; cf Lk 11, 27.

11, 1–10: Although Israel has been unfaithful to the prophetic message of the gospel (10, 14–21), God remains faithful to Israel. Proof of the divine fidelity lies in the existence of Jewish Christians like Paul himself. The unbelieving Jews, says Paul, have been blinded by the Christian teaching concerning the Messiah.

p: Lv 18, 5; Gal 3, 12.   q: Dt 9, 4; 30, 12.   r: Dt 30, 13; 1 Pt 3, 19.   s: Dt 30, 14.   t: 1 Cor 12, 3.   u: 9, 33; Is 28, 16.   v: 1, 16; 3, 22.29; Acts 10, 34; 15, 9.11; Gal 3, 28; Eph 2, 14.   w: Jl 3, 5; Acts 2, 21.   x: Acts 8, 31.   y: Is 52, 7; Na 2, 1; Eph 6, 15.   z: Is 53, 1; Jn 12, 38.   a: Jn 17, 20.   b: Ps 19, 5; Mt 24, 14.   c: 11, 11.14; Dt 32, 21.   d: 9, 30; Is 65, 1-2.   e: 2 Cor 11, 22; Phil 3, 5.   f: 1 Sm 12, 22; Ps 94, 14.   g: 1 Kgs 19, 10.14.

killed your prophets, they have torn down your altars, and I alone am left, and they are seeking my life." [4h]But what is God's response to him? "I have left for myself seven thousand men who have not knelt to Baal." [5i]So also at the present time there is a remnant, chosen by grace. [6j]But if by grace, it is no longer because of works; otherwise grace would no longer be grace. [7k]What then? What Israel was seeking it did not attain, but the elect attained it; the rest were hardened, [8l]as it is written:

"God gave them a spirit of deep sleep,
  eyes that should not see
  and ears that should not hear,
down to this very day."

[9m]And David says:

"Let their table become a snare and a
    trap,
  a stumbling block and a retribution for
    them;
[10] let their eyes grow dim so that they may
    not see,
  and keep their backs bent forever."

The Gentiles' Salvation. [11n]*Hence I ask, did they stumble so as to fall? Of course not! But through their transgression salvation has come to the Gentiles, so as to make them jealous. [12]Now if their transgression is enrichment for the world, and if their diminished number is enrichment for the Gentiles, how much more their full number.

[13o]Now I am speaking to you Gentiles. Inasmuch then as I am the apostle to the Gentiles, I glory in my ministry [14]in order to make my race jealous and thus save some of them. [15]For if their rejection is the reconciliation of the world, what will their acceptance be but life from the dead? [16p]*If the firstfruits are holy, so is the whole batch of dough; and if the root is holy, so are the branches.

[17q]But if some of the branches were broken off, and you, a wild olive shoot, were grafted in their place and have come to share in the rich root of the olive tree, [18r]do not boast against the branches. If you do boast, consider that you do not support the root; the root supports you. [19]Indeed you will say, "Branches were broken off so that I might be grafted in." [20s]That is so. They were broken off because of unbelief, but you are there because of faith. So do not become haughty, but stand in awe. [21t]For if God did not spare the natural branches, [perhaps] he will not spare you either. [22u]See, then, the kindness and severity of God: severity toward those who fell, but God's kindness to you, provided you remain in his kindness; otherwise you too will be cut off. [23v]And they also, if they do not remain in unbelief, will be grafted in, for God is able to graft them in again. [24]For if you were cut from what is by nature a wild olive tree, and grafted, contrary to nature, into a cultivated one, how much more will they who belong to it by nature be grafted back into their own olive tree.

God's Irrevocable Call. [25w]*I do not want you to be unaware of this mystery, brothers, so that you will not become wise [in] your own estimation: a hardening has come upon Israel in part, until the full number of the Gentiles comes in, [26xy]and thus all Israel will be saved, as it is written:

11, 11–15: The unbelief of the Jews has paved the way for the preaching of the gospel to the Gentiles and for their easier acceptance of it outside the context of Jewish culture. Through his mission to the Gentiles Paul also hopes to fill his fellow Jews with jealousy. Hence he hastens to fill the entire Mediterranean world with the gospel. Once all the Gentile nations have heard the gospel, Israel as a whole is expected to embrace it. This will be tantamount to resurrection of the dead, that is, the reappearance of Jesus Christ with all the believers at the end of time.

11, 16–24: Israel remains holy in the eyes of God and stands as a witness to the faith described in the Old Testament because of **the firstfruits** (or the first piece baked) (16), that is, the converted remnant, and **the root** that **is holy,** that is, the patriarchs (16). The Jews' failure to believe in Christ is a

warning to Gentile Christians to be on guard against any semblance of anti-Jewish arrogance, that is, failure to recognize their total dependence on divine grace.

11, 25–29: In God's design, Israel's unbelief is being used to grant the light of faith to the Gentiles. Meanwhile, Israel remains dear to God (cf 9, 13), still the object of special providence, the mystery of which will one day be revealed.

h: 1 Kgs 19, 18. i: 9, 27. j: 4, 4; Gal 3, 18. k: 9, 31. l: Dt 29, 3; Is 29, 10; Mt 13, 13-15; Acts 28, 26-27. m: Pss 69, 23-24; 35, 8. n: Acts 13, 46; 18, 6; 28, 28 / 10, 19; Dt 32, 21. o: 1, 5. p: Nm 15, 17-21; Ez 44, 30; Neh 10, 36-38. q: Eph 2, 11-19. r: 1 Cor 1, 31. s: 12, 16. t: 1 Cor 10, 12. u: Jn 15, 2.4; Heb 3, 14. v: 2 Cor 3, 16. w: Prv 3, 7 / 12, 16; Mk 13, 10; Lk 21, 24; Jn 10, 16. x: Mt 23, 39. y: Ps 14, 7; Is 59, 20-21.

"The deliverer will come out of Zion,
    he will turn away godlessness from
        Jacob;
27 *z*and this is my covenant with them
    when I take away their sins."

28*a*In respect to the gospel, they are enemies on your account; but in respect to election, they are beloved because of the patriarchs. 29*b*For the gifts and the call of God are irrevocable.

Triumph of God's Mercy. 30*Just as you once disobeyed God but have now received mercy because of their disobedience, 31so they have now disobeyed in order that, by virtue of the mercy shown to you, they too may [now] receive mercy. 32*c*For God delivered all to disobedience, that he might have mercy upon all.

33*d*Oh, the depth of the riches and wisdom and knowledge of God! How inscrutable are his judgments and how unsearchable his ways!

34 *e**"For who has known the mind of the
        Lord
    or who has been his counselor?"
35 *f**"Or who has given him anything
    that he may be repaid?"

36*g*For from him and through him and for him are all things. To him be glory forever. Amen.

VI: The Duties of Christians

CHAPTER 12

Sacrifice of Body and Mind. 1*h*I urge you therefore, brothers, by the mercies of God, to offer your bodies as a living sacrifice, holy and pleasing to God, your spiritual worship. 2*i*Do not conform yourselves to this age but be transformed by the renewal of your mind, that you may discern what is the will of God, what is good and pleasing and perfect.

Many Parts in One Body. 3*j*For by the grace given to me I tell everyone among you not to think of himself more highly than one ought to think, but to think soberly, each according to the measure of faith that God has apportioned. 4*k*For as in one body we have many parts, and all the parts do not have the same function, 5*so we, though many, are one body in Christ and individually parts of one another. 6*l*Since we have gifts that differ according to the grace given to us, let us exercise

---

11, 30–32: Israel, together with the Gentiles who have been handed over to all manner of vices (ch 1), has been **delivered . . . to disobedience.** The conclusion of v 32 repeats the thought of 5, 20, "Where sin increased, grace overflowed all the more."

11, 33–36: This final reflection celebrates the wisdom of God's plan of salvation. As Paul has indicated throughout these chapters, both Jew and Gentile, despite the religious recalcitrance of each, have received the gift of faith. The methods used by God in making this outreach to the world stagger human comprehension but are at the same time a dazzling invitation to abiding faith.

11, 34: The citation is from the Greek text of Is 40, 13. Paul does not explicitly mention Isaiah in this verse, nor Job in v 35.

11, 35: Paul quotes from an old Greek version of Jb 41, 3a, which differs from the Hebrew text (Jb 41, 11a).

12, 1—13, 14: Since Christ marks the termination of the Mosaic law as the primary source of guidance for God's people (10, 4), the apostle explains how Christians can function, in the light of the gift of justification through faith, in their relation to one another and the state.

12, 1–8: The Mosaic code included elaborate directions on sacrifices and other cultic observances. The gospel, however, invites believers to present their **bodies as a living sacrifice** (1). Instead of being limited by specific legal maxims, Christians are liberated for the exercise of good judgment as they are confronted with the many and varied decisions required in

the course of daily life. To assist them, God distributes a variety of gifts to the fellowship of believers, including those of prophecy, teaching, and exhortation (6–8). Prophets assist the community to understand the will of God as it applies to the present situation (6). Teachers help people to understand themselves and their responsibilities in relation to others (7). One who **exhorts** offers encouragement to the community to exercise their faith in the performance of all that is pleasing to God (8). Indeed, this very section, beginning with v 1, is a specimen of Paul's own style of exhortation.

12, 5: One body in Christ: on the church as the body of Christ, see 1 Cor 12, 12–27.

12, 6: Everyone has some gift that can be used for the benefit of the community. When the instruction on justification through faith is correctly grasped, the possessor of a gift will understand that it is not an instrument of self-aggrandizement. Possession of a gift is not an index to quality of faith. Rather, the gift is a challenge to faithful use.

z: Is 27, 9; Jer 31, 33-34. *a:* 15, 8; 1 Thes 2, 15-16. *b:* 9, 6; Nm 23, 19; Is 54, 10. *c:* Gal 3, 22; 1 Tm 2, 4. *d:* Jb 11, 7-8; Ps 139, 6.17-18; Wis 17, 1; Is 55, 8-9. *e:* Jb 15, 8; Wis 9, 13; Is 40, 13; Jer 23, 18; 1 Cor 2, 11-16. *f:* Jb 41, 3; Is 40, 14. *g:* 1 Cor 8, 6; Col 1, 16-17. *h:* 2 Cor 1, 3 / 6, 13; 1 Pt 2, 5. *i:* Eph 4, 17.22-23; 1 Pt 1, 14 / Eph 5, 10.17; Phil 1, 10. *j:* 15, 15 / Phil 2, 3 / 1 Cor 12, 11; Eph 4, 7. *k:* 1 Cor 12, 12.27; Eph 4, 25. *l:* 1 Cor 12, 4-11.28-31; Eph 4, 7-12; 1 Pt 4, 10-11 / 2 Cor 9, 7.

them: if prophecy, in proportion to the faith; [7]if ministry, in ministering; if one is a teacher, in teaching; [8]*if one exhorts, in exhortation; if one contributes, in generosity; if one is over others, with diligence; if one does acts of mercy, with cheerfulness.

Mutual Love. [9m]Let love be sincere; hate what is evil, hold on to what is good; [10n]love one another with mutual affection; anticipate one another in showing honor. [11o]Do not grow slack in zeal, be fervent in spirit, serve the Lord. [12p]Rejoice in hope, endure in affliction, persevere in prayer. [13q]Contribute to the needs of the holy ones, exercise hospitality. [14rs]*Bless those who persecute [you], bless and do not curse them. [15t]Rejoice with those who rejoice, weep with those who weep. [16u]Have the same regard for one another; do not be haughty but associate with the lowly; do not be wise in your own estimation. [17v]Do not repay anyone evil for evil; be concerned for what is noble in the sight of all. [18w]If possible, on your part, live at peace with all. [19x]Beloved, do not look for revenge but leave room for the wrath; for it is written, "Vengeance is mine, I will repay, says the Lord." [20y]Rather, "if your enemy is hungry, feed him; if he is thirsty, give him something to drink; for by so doing you will heap burning coals upon his head." [21]Do not be conquered by evil but conquer evil with good.

CHAPTER 13

See RG 361

Obedience to Authority. [1z]*Let every person be subordinate to the higher authorities, for there is no authority except from God, and those that exist have been established by God. [2]Therefore, whoever resists authority opposes what God has appointed, and those who oppose it will bring judgment upon themselves. [3a]For rulers are not a cause of fear to good conduct, but to evil. Do you wish to have no fear of authority? Then do what is good and you will receive approval from it, [4b]for it is a servant of God for your good. But if you do evil, be afraid, for it does not bear the sword without purpose; it is the servant of God to inflict wrath on the evildoer. [5c]Therefore, it is necessary to be subject not only because of the wrath but also because of conscience. [6]This is why you also pay taxes, for the authorities are ministers of God, devoting themselves to this very thing. [7d]Pay to all their dues, taxes to whom taxes are due, toll to whom toll is due, respect to whom respect is due, honor to whom honor is due.

Love Fulfills the Law. [8e]*Owe nothing to anyone, except to love one another; for the

12, 8: Over others: usually taken to mean "rule over" but possibly "serve as a patron." Wealthier members in Greco-Roman communities were frequently asked to assist in public service projects. In view of the references to contributing **in generosity** and to **acts of mercy,** Paul may have in mind people like Phoebe (16, 1–2), who is called a **benefactor** (or "patron") because of the services she rendered to many Christians, including Paul.

12, 14–21: Since God has justified the believers, it is not necessary for them to take justice into their own hands by taking vengeance. God will ultimately deal justly with all, including those who inflict injury on the believers. This question of personal rights as a matter of justice prepares the way for more detailed consideration of the state as adjudicator.

13, 1–7: Paul must come to grips with the problem raised by a message that declares people free from the law. How are they to relate to Roman authority? The problem was exacerbated by the fact that imperial protocol was interwoven with devotion to various deities. Paul builds on the traditional instruction exhibited in Wis 6, 1–3, according to which kings and magistrates rule by consent of God. From this perspective, then, believers who render obedience to the governing authorities are obeying the one who is highest in command. At the same time, it is recognized that Caesar has the responsibility to make just ordinances and to commend uprightness;

cf Wis 6, 4–21. That Caesar is not entitled to obedience when such obedience would nullify God's prior claim to the believers' moral decision becomes clear in the light of the following verses.

13, 8–10: When love directs the Christian's moral decisions, the interest of law in basic concerns, such as familial relationships, sanctity of life, and security of property, is safeguarded (9). Indeed, says Paul, the same applies to any **other commandment** (9), whether one in the Mosaic code or one drawn up by local magistrates under imperial authority. Love anticipates the purpose of public legislation, namely, to secure the best interests of the citizenry. Since Caesar's obligation is to punish the wrongdoer (4), the Christian who acts in love is free from all legitimate indictment.

m: 2 Cor 6, 6; 1 Tm 1, 5; 1 Pt 1, 22 / Am 5, 15. n: Jr 13, 34; 1 Thes 4, 9; 1 Pt 2, 17; 2 Pt 1, 7 / Phil 2, 3. o: Acts 18, 25. p: 5, 2-3; Col 4, 2; 1 Thes 5, 17. q: Heb 13, 2; 1 Pt 4, 9. r: Mt 5, 38-48; 1 Cor 4, 12; 1 Pt 3, 9. s: Lk 6, 27-28. t: Ps 35, 13; Sir 7, 34; 1 Cor 12, 26. u: 15, 5; Phil 2, 2-3 / 11, 20; Prv 3, 7; Is 5, 21. v: Prv 3, 4; 1 Thes 5, 15; 1 Pt 3, 9. w: Heb 12, 14. x: Lv 19, 18; Dt 32, 35.41; Mt 5, 39; 1 Cor 6, 6-7; Heb 10, 30. y: Prv 25, 21-22; Mt 5, 44. z: Prv 8, 15-16; Wis 6, 3; Jn 19, 11; 1 Pt 2, 13-17; Ti 3, 1. a: 1 Pt 2, 13-14; 3, 13. b: 12, 19. c: 1 Pt 2, 19. d: Mt 22, 21; Mk 12, 17; Lk 20, 25. e: Jn 13, 34; Gal 5, 14.

one who loves another has fulfilled the law. [9f]The commandments, "You shall not commit adultery; you shall not kill; you shall not steal; you shall not covet," and whatever other commandment there may be, are summed up in this saying, [namely] "You shall love your neighbor as yourself." [10g]Love does no evil to the neighbor; hence, love is the fulfillment of the law.

Awareness of the End of Time. [11h]*And do this because you know the time; it is the hour now for you to awake from sleep. For our salvation is nearer now than when we first believed; [12i]the night is advanced, the day is at hand. Let us then throw off the works of darkness [and] put on the armor of light; [13j]*let us conduct ourselves properly as in the day, not in orgies and drunkenness, not in promiscuity and licentiousness, not in rivalry and jealousy. [14k]But put on the Lord Jesus Christ, and make no provision for the desires of the flesh.

CHAPTER 14

See RG 361–62

To Live and Die for Christ. [11m]*Welcome anyone who is weak in faith, but not for disputes over opinions. [2n]One person believes that one may eat anything, while the weak person eats only vegetables. [3o]The one who eats must not despise the one who abstains, and the one who abstains must not pass judgment on the one who eats; for God has welcomed him. [4p]Who are you to pass judgment on someone else's servant? Before his own master he stands or falls. And he will be upheld, for the Lord is able to make him stand. [5q]*[For] one person considers one day more important than another, while another person considers all days alike. Let everyone be fully persuaded in his own mind. [6]Whoever observes the day, observes it for the Lord. Also whoever eats, eats for the Lord, since he gives thanks to God; while whoever abstains, abstains for the Lord and gives thanks to God. [7]None of us lives for oneself, and no one dies for oneself. [8r]*For if we live, we live for the Lord, and if we die, we die for the Lord; so then, whether we live or die, we are the Lord's. [9s]For this is why Christ died and came to life, that he might be Lord of both the dead and the living. [10t]Why then do you judge your brother? Or you, why do you look down on your brother? For we shall all stand before the judgment seat of God; [11u]for it is written:

> "As I live, says the Lord, every knee
>   shall bend before me,
>   and every tongue shall give praise to
>   God."

[12v]So [then] each of us shall give an account of himself [to God].

Consideration for the Weak Conscience. [13w]Then let us no longer judge one another, but rather resolve never to put a stumbling block or hindrance in the way of a brother. [14x]I know and am convinced in the Lord

---

13, 11–14: These verses provide the motivation for the love that is encouraged in vv 8–10.

13, 13: Let us conduct ourselves properly as in the day: the behavior described in 1, 29–30 is now to be reversed. Secular moralists were fond of making references to people who could not wait for nightfall to do their carousing. Paul says that Christians claim to be people of the new day that will dawn with the return of Christ. Instead of planning for nighttime behavior they should be concentrating on conduct that is consonant with avowed interest in the Lord's return.

14, 1—15, 6: Since Christ spells termination of the law, which included observance of specific days and festivals as well as dietary instruction, the jettisoning of long-practiced customs was traumatic for many Christians brought up under the Mosaic code. Although Paul acknowledges that in principle no food is a source of moral contamination (14), he recommends that the consciences of Christians who are scrupulous in this regard be respected by other Christians (21). On the other hand, those who have scruples are not to sit in judgment on those who know that the gospel has liberated them from such ordinances (10). See 1 Cor 8 and 10.

14, 5: Since the problem to be overcome was humanity's perverted mind or judgment (1, 28), Paul indicates that the **mind** of the Christian is now able to function with appropriate discrimination (cf 12, 2).

14, 8: The Lord: Jesus, our Master. The same Greek word, **kyrios**, was applied to both rulers and holders of slaves. Throughout the Letter to the Romans Paul emphasizes God's total claim on the believer; see the note on 1, 1.

f: Ex 20, 13-17 / Lv 19, 18; Dt 5, 17-21; Mt 5, 43-44; 19, 18-19; 22, 39; Mk 12, 31; Lk 10, 27; Gal 5, 14; Jas 2, 8. g: Mt 22, 40; 1 Cor 13, 4-7. h: Eph 5, 8-16; 1 Thes 5, 5-7. i: Jn 8, 12; 1 Thes 5, 4-8; 1 Jn 2, 8 / 2 Cor 6, 7; 10, 4; Eph 5, 11; 6, 13-17. j: Lk 21, 34; Eph 5, 18. k: Gal 3, 27; 5, 16; Eph 4, 24; 6, 11. l: 1 Cor 8, 1-13. m: 15, 1.7; 1 Cor 9, 22. n: Gn 1, 29; 9, 3; 1 Cor 8, 1-13; 10, 14-33. o: Col 2, 16. p: 2, 1; Mt 7, 11; Jas 4, 11-12. q: Gal 4, 10. r: Lk 20, 38; 2 Cor 5, 15; Gal 2, 20; 1 Thes 5, 10. s: Acts 10, 42. t: Acts 17, 31; 2 Cor 5, 10. u: Is 49, 18 / Is 45, 23; Phil 2, 10-11. v: Gal 6, 5. w: 1 Cor 8, 9.13. x: Mk 7, 5.20; Acts 10, 15; 1 Cor 10, 25-27; 1 Tm 4, 4.

Jesus that nothing is unclean in itself; still, it is unclean for someone who thinks it unclean. ¹⁵ʸIf your brother is being hurt by what you eat, your conduct is no longer in accord with love. Do not because of your food destroy him for whom Christ died. ¹⁶ᶻSo do not let your good be reviled. ¹⁷ᵃFor the kingdom of God is not a matter of food and drink, but of righteousness, peace, and joy in the holy Spirit; ¹⁸whoever serves Christ in this way is pleasing to God and approved by others. ¹⁹ᵇ*Let us then pursue what leads to peace and to building up one another. ²⁰ᶜFor the sake of food, do not destroy the work of God. Everything is indeed clean, but it is wrong for anyone to become a stumbling block by eating; ²¹it is good not to eat meat or drink wine or do anything that causes your brother to stumble. ²²Keep the faith [that] you have to yourself in the presence of God; blessed is the one who does not condemn himself for what he approves. ²³ᵈ*But whoever has doubts is condemned if he eats, because this is not from faith; for whatever is not from faith is sin.

See RG 361-62

CHAPTER 15

Patience and Self-Denial. ¹ᵉWe who are strong ought to put up with the failings of the weak and not to please ourselves; ²ᶠlet each of us please our neighbor for the good, for building up. ³ᵍ*For Christ did not please himself; but, as it is written, "The insults of those who insult you fall upon me." ⁴ʰFor whatever was written previously was written for our instruction, that by endurance and by the encouragement of the scriptures we

might have hope. ⁵ⁱ*May the God of endurance and encouragement grant you to think in harmony with one another, in keeping with Christ Jesus, ⁶that with one accord you may with one voice glorify the God and Father of our Lord Jesus Christ.

God's Fidelity and Mercy. ⁷ʲ*Welcome one another, then, as Christ welcomed you, for the glory of God. ⁸ᵏFor I say that Christ became a minister of the circumcised to show God's truthfulness, to confirm the promises to the patriarchs, ⁹ˡbut so that the Gentiles might glorify God for his mercy. As it is written:

"Therefore, I will praise you among the
      Gentiles
   and sing praises to your name."

¹⁰ᵐ*And again it says:

"Rejoice, O Gentiles, with his people."

¹¹ⁿAnd again:

"Praise the Lord, all you Gentiles,
   and let all the peoples praise him."

¹²ᵒAnd again Isaiah says:

"The root of Jesse shall come,
   raised up to rule the Gentiles;
in him shall the Gentiles hope."

¹³ᵖMay the God of hope fill you with all joy and peace in believing, so that you may abound in hope by the power of the holy Spirit.

VII: Conclusion

Apostle to the Gentiles. ¹⁴*I myself am convinced about you, my brothers, that you your-

---

14, 19: Some manuscripts, versions, and church Fathers read, "We then pursue . . ."; cf 5, 1.

14, 23: Whatever is not from faith is sin: Paul does not mean that all the actions of unbelievers are sinful. He addresses himself to the question of intracommunity living. **Sin** in the singular is the dreadful power described in 5, 12–14.

15, 3: Liberation from the law of Moses does not make the scriptures of the old covenant irrelevant. Much consolation and motivation for Christian living can be derived from the Old Testament, as in the citation from Ps 69, 10. Because this psalm is quoted several times in the New Testament, it has been called indirectly messianic.

15, 5: Think in harmony: a Greco-Roman ideal. Not rigid uniformity of thought and expression but thoughtful consideration of other people's views finds expression here.

15, 7–13: True oneness of mind is found in pondering the

ultimate mission of the church: to bring it about that God's name be glorified throughout the world and that Jesus Christ be universally recognized as God's gift to all humanity. Paul here prepares his addressees for the climactic appeal he is about to make.

15, 10: Paul's citation of Dt 32, 43 follows the Greek version.

15, 14–33: Paul sees himself as apostle and benefactor in

---

y: 1 Cor 8, 11-13. z: 2, 24; Ti 2, 5. a: 1 Cor 8, 8. b: 12, 18 / 15, 2. c: 1 Cor 8, 11-13; 10, 28-29; Ti 1, 15. d: Ti 1, 15; Jas 4, 17. e: 14, 1-2. f: 14, 1.19; 1 Cor 9, 19; 10, 24.33. g: Ps 69, 10. h: 4, 23-24; 1 Mc 12, 9; 1 Cor 10, 11; 2 Tm 3, 16. i. 12, 16; Phil 2, 2; 4, 2. j: 14, 1. k: Mt 15, 24 / Mi 7, 20; Acts 3. 25. l: 11, 30 / 2 Sm 22, 50; Ps 18, 50. m: Dt 32, 43. n: Ps 117, 1. o: Is 11, 10; Rv 5, 5; 22, 16. p: 5, 1-2.

selves are full of goodness, filled with all knowledge, and able to admonish one another. [15q]But I have written to you rather boldly in some respects to remind you, because of the grace given me by God [16r]to be a minister of Christ Jesus to the Gentiles in performing the priestly service of the gospel of God, so that the offering up of the Gentiles may be acceptable, sanctified by the holy Spirit. [17]In Christ Jesus, then, I have reason to boast in what pertains to God. [18s]For I will not dare to speak of anything except what Christ has accomplished through me to lead the Gentiles to obedience by word and deed, [19*]by the power of signs and wonders, by the power of the Spirit [of God], so that from Jerusalem all the way around to Illyricum I have finished preaching the gospel of Christ. [20t*]Thus I aspire to proclaim the gospel not where Christ has already been named, so that I do not build on another's foundation, [21u*]but as it is written:

> "Those who have never been told of him
>   shall see,
> and those who have never heard of
>   him shall understand."

Paul's Plans; Need for Prayers. [22]That is why I have so often been prevented from coming to you. [23v]But now, since I no longer have any opportunity in these regions and since I have desired to come to you for many years, [24w]I hope to see you in passing as I go to Spain and to be sent on my way there by you, after I have enjoyed being with you for a time. [25x*]Now, however, I am going to Jerusalem to minister to the holy ones. [26y*]For Macedonia and Achaia have decided to make some contribution for the poor among the holy ones in Jerusalem; [27z]they decided to do it, and in fact they are indebted to them, for if the Gentiles have come to share in their spiritual blessings, they ought also to serve them in material blessings. [28]So when I have completed this and safely handed over this contribution to them, I shall set out by way of you to Spain; [29]and I know that in coming to you I shall come in the fullness of Christ's blessing.

[30a]I urge you, [brothers,] by our Lord Jesus Christ and by the love of the Spirit, to join me in the struggle by your prayers to God on my behalf, [31]that I may be delivered from the disobedient in Judea, and that my ministry for Jerusalem may be acceptable to the holy ones, [32]so that I may come to you with joy by the will of God and be refreshed together with you. [33b]The God of peace be with all of you. Amen.

CHAPTER 16

See RG 362

Phoebe Commended. [1c*]I commend to you Phoebe our sister, who is [also] a minister of the church at Cenchreae, [2]that you may receive her in the Lord in a manner wor-

---

the priestly service of the gospel and so sketches plans for a mission in Spain, supported by those in Rome.

15, 14: Full of goodness: the opposite of what humanity was filled with according to 1, 29–30.

15, 19: Illyricum: Roman province northwest of Greece on the eastern shore of the Adriatic.

15, 20: I aspire: Paul uses terminology customarily applied to philanthropists. Unlike some philanthropists of his time, Paul does not engage in cheap competition for public acclaim. This explanation of his missionary policy is to assure the Christians in Rome that he is also not planning to remain in that city and build on other people's foundations (cf 2 Cor 10, 12–18). However, he does solicit their help in sending him on his way to Spain, which was considered the limit of the western world. Thus Paul's addressees realize that evangelization may be understood in the broader sense of mission or, as in Rom 1, 15, of instruction within the Christian community that derives from the gospel.

15, 21: The citation from Is 52, 15 concerns the Servant of the Lord. According to Isaiah, the Servant is first of all Israel, which was to bring the knowledge of Yahweh to the nations. In chs 9–11 Paul showed how Israel failed in this mission. Therefore, he himself undertakes almost singlehandedly Is-

rael's responsibility as the Servant and moves as quickly as possible with the gospel through the Roman empire.

15, 25–27: Paul may have viewed the contribution he was gathering from Gentile Christians for the poor in Jerusalem (cf 2 Cor 8 and 9) as a fulfillment of the vision of Is 60, 5–6. In confidence that the messianic fulfillment was taking place, Paul stresses in chs 14–16 the importance of harmonious relationships between Jews and Gentiles.

15, 26: Achaia: the Roman province of southern Greece.

16, 1–23: Some authorities regard these verses as a later addition to the letter, but in general the evidence favors the view that they were included in the original. Paul endeavors through the long list of greetings (3–16; 21–23) to establish strong personal contact with congregations that he has not personally encountered before. The combination of Jewish and Gentile names dramatically attests the unity in the gospel

q: 1, 5; 12, 3.   r: 11, 13; Phil 2, 17.   s: Acts 15, 12; 2 Cor 12, 12. t: 2 Cor 10, 13-18.   u: Is 52, 15.   v: 1, 10-13; Acts 19, 21-22. w: 1 Cor 16, 6.   x: Acts 19, 21; 20, 22.   y: 1 Cor 16, 1; 2 Cor 8, 1-4; 9, 2.12.   z: 9, 4 / 1 Cor 9, 11.   a: 2 Cor 1, 11; Phil 1, 27; Col 4, 3; 2 Thes 3, 1.   b: 16, 20; 2 Cor 13, 11; Phil 4, 9; 1 Thes 5, 23; 2 Thes 3, 16; Heb 13, 20.   c: Acts 18, 18.

thy of the holy ones, and help her in whatever she may need from you, for she has been a benefactor to many and to me as well.

Paul's Greetings. *3d**Greet Prisca and Aquila, my co-workers in Christ Jesus, *4*who risked their necks for my life, to whom not only I am grateful but also all the churches of the Gentiles; *5e**greet also the church at their house. Greet my beloved Epaenetus, who was the firstfruits in Asia for Christ. *6*Greet Mary, who has worked hard for you. *7**Greet Andronicus and Junia, my relatives and my fellow prisoners; they are prominent among the apostles and they were in Christ before me. *8*Greet Ampliatus, my beloved in the Lord. *9*Greet Urbanus, our co-worker in Christ, and my beloved Stachys. *10*Greet Apelles, who is approved in Christ. Greet those who belong to the family of Aristobulus. *11*Greet my relative Herodion. Greet those in the Lord who belong to the family of Narcissus. *12*Greet those workers in the Lord, Tryphaena and Tryphosa. Greet the beloved Persis, who has worked hard in the Lord. *13f**Greet Rufus, chosen in the Lord, and his mother and mine. *14*Greet Asyncritus, Phlegon, Hermes, Patrobas, Hermas, and the brothers who are with them. *15*Greet Philologus, Julia, Nereus and his sister, and Olympas, and all the holy ones who are with them. *16g*Greet one another with a holy kiss. All the churches of Christ greet you.

Against Factions. *17h**I urge you, brothers, to watch out for those who create dissensions and obstacles, in opposition to the teaching that you learned; avoid them. *18i*For such people do not serve our Lord Christ but their own appetites, and by fair and flattering speech they deceive the hearts of the innocent. *19j*For while your obedience is known to all, so that I rejoice over you, I want you to be wise as to what is good, and simple as to what is evil; *20k**then the God of peace will quickly crush Satan under your feet. The grace of our Lord Jesus be with you.

Greetings from Corinth. *21l*Timothy, my co-worker, greets you; so do Lucius and Jason and Sosipater, my relatives. *22*I, Tertius, the writer of this letter, greet you in the Lord. *23m**Gaius, who is host to me and to the whole church, greets you. Erastus, the city treasurer, and our brother Quartus greet you. [*24*]*

Doxology. [*25n**Now to him who can strengthen you, according to my gospel and the proclamation of Jesus Christ, according to the revelation of the mystery kept secret for long ages *26o*but now manifested through the prophetic writings and, according to the command of the eternal God, made known to all nations to bring about the obedience of faith, *27p*to the only wise God, through Jesus Christ be glory forever and ever. Amen.]

that transcends previous barriers of nationality, religious ceremony, or racial status.

16, 1: Minister: in Greek, **diakonos;** see the note on Phil 1, 1.

16, 3: Prisca and Aquila: presumably the couple mentioned at Acts 18, 2; 1 Cor 16, 19; 2 Tm 4, 19.

16, 5: The church at their house: i.e., that meets there. Such local assemblies (cf 1 Cor 16, 19; Col 4, 15; Phlm 2) might consist of only one or two dozen Christians each. It is understandable, therefore, that such smaller groups might experience difficulty in relating to one another on certain issues. **Firstfruits:** cf 8, 23; 11, 16; 1 Cor 16, 15.

16, 7: The name Junia is a woman's name. One ancient Greek manuscript and a number of ancient versions read the name "Julia." Most editors have interpreted it as a man's name, Junias.

16, 13: This Rufus cannot be identified to any degree of certainty with the Rufus of Mk 15, 21.

16, 17–18: Paul displays genuine concern for the congregations in Rome by warning them against self-seeking teachers. It would be a great loss, he intimates, if their obedience, which is known to all (cf 1, 8), would be diluted.

16, 20: This verse contains the only mention of Satan in Romans.

16, 23: This Erastus is not necessarily to be identified with the Erastus of Acts 19, 22 or of 2 Tm 4, 20.

16, 24: Some manuscripts add, similarly to v 20, 'The grace of our Lord Jesus Christ be with you all. Amen."

16, 25–27: This doxology is assigned variously to the end of chs 14, 15, and 16 in the manuscript tradition. Some manuscripts omit it entirely. Whether written by Paul or not, it forms an admirable conclusion to the letter at this point.

16, 25: Paul's gospel reveals **the mystery kept secret for long ages:** justification and salvation through faith, with all the implications for Jews and Gentiles that Paul has developed in the letter.

d: Acts 18, 2.18-26; 1 Cor 16, 19; 2 Tm 4, 19. *e:* 1 Cor 16, 19; Col 4, 15; Phlm 2 / 1 Cor 16, 15. *f:* Mk 15, 21. *g:* 1 Cor 16, 20; 2 Cor 13, 12; 1 Thes 5, 26; 1 Pt 5, 14. *h:* Mt 7, 15; Ti 3, 10. *i:* Phil 3, 18-19 / Col 2, 4; 2 Pt 2, 3. *j:* 1, 8; Mt 10, 16; 1 Cor 14, 20. *k:* 15, 33; Gn 3, 15; Lk 10, 19 / 1 Cor 16, 23; 1 Thes 5, 28; 2 Thes 3, 18. *l:* Acts 16, 1-2; 19, 22; 20, 4; 1 Cor 4, 17; 16, 10; Phil 2, 19-22; Heb 13, 23. *m:* Acts 19, 29; 1 Cor 1, 14 / 2 Tm 4, 20. *n:* 1 Cor 2, 7; Eph 1, 9; 3, 3-9; Col 1, 26. *o:* 2 Tm 1, 10 / 1, 5; Eph 3, 4-5.9; 1 Pt 1, 20. *p:* 11, 36; Gal 1, 5; Eph 3, 20-21; Phil 4, 20; 1 Tm 1, 17; 2 Tm 4, 18; Heb 13, 21; 1 Pt 4, 11; 2 Pt 3, 18; Jude 25; Rev 1, 6.

See RG
364-74

The First Letter to the Corinthians

Paul's first letter to the church of Corinth provides us with a fuller insight into the life of an early Christian community of the first generation than any other book of the New Testament. Through it we can glimpse both the strengths and the weaknesses of this small group in a great city of the ancient world, men and women who had accepted the good news of Christ and were now trying to realize in their lives the implications of their baptism. Paul, who had founded the community and continued to look after it as a father, responds both to questions addressed to him and to situations of which he had been informed. In doing so, he reveals much about himself, his teaching, and the way in which he conducted his work of apostleship. Some things are puzzling because we have the correspondence only in one direction. For the person studying this letter, it seems to raise as many questions as it answers, but without it our knowledge of church life in the middle of the first century would be much poorer.

Paul established a Christian community in Corinth about the year 51, on his second missionary journey. The city, a commercial crossroads, was a melting pot full of devotees of various pagan cults and marked by a measure of moral depravity not unusual in a great seaport. The Acts of the Apostles suggests that moderate success attended Paul's efforts among the Jews in Corinth at first, but that they soon turned against him (Acts 18, 1–8). More fruitful was his year and a half spent among the Gentiles (Acts 18, 11), which won to the faith many of the city's poor and underprivileged (1, 26). After his departure the eloquent Apollos, an Alexandrian Jewish Christian, rendered great service to the community, expounding "from the scriptures that the Messiah is Jesus" (Acts 18, 24–28).

While Paul was in Ephesus on his third journey (16, 8; Acts 19, 1–20), he received disquieting news about Corinth. The community there was displaying open factionalism, as certain members were identifying themselves exclusively with individual Christian leaders and interpreting Christian teaching as a superior wisdom for the initiated few (1, 10—4, 21). The community lacked the decisiveness to take appropriate action

against one of its members who was living publicly in an incestuous union (5, 1–13). Other members engaged in legal conflicts in pagan courts of law (6, 1–11); still others may have participated in religious prostitution (6, 12–20) or temple sacrifices (10, 14–22).

The community's ills were reflected in its liturgy. In the celebration of the Eucharist certain members discriminated against others, drank too freely at the agape, or fellowship meal, and denied Christian social courtesies to the poor among the membership (11, 17–22). Charisms such as ecstatic prayer, attributed freely to the impulse of the holy Spirit, were more highly prized than works of charity (13, 1–2.8), and were used at times in a disorderly way (14, 1–40). Women appeared at the assembly without the customary head-covering (11, 3–16), and perhaps were quarreling over their right to address the assembly (14, 34–35).

Still other problems with which Paul had to deal concerned matters of conscience discussed among the faithful members of the community: the eating of meat that had been sacrificed to idols (8, 1–13), the use of sex in marriage (7, 1–7), and the attitude to be taken by the unmarried toward marriage in view of the possible proximity of Christ's second coming (7, 25–40). There was also a doctrinal matter that called for Paul's attention, for some members of the community, despite their belief in the resurrection of Christ, were denying the possibility of general bodily resurrection.

To treat this wide spectrum of questions, Paul wrote this letter from Ephesus about the year 56. The majority of the Corinthian Christians may well have been quite faithful. Paul writes on their behalf to guard against the threats posed to the community by the views and conduct of various minorities. He writes with confidence in the authority of his apostolic mission, and he presumes that the Corinthians, despite their deficiencies, will recognize and accept it. On the other hand, he does not hesitate to exercise his authority as his judgment dictates in each situation, even going so far as to promise a direct confrontation with recalcitrants, should the abuses he scores remain uncorrected (4, 18–21).

The letter illustrates well the mind and character of Paul. Although he is impelled to insist on his office as founder of the community, he recognizes that he is only one servant of God among many and generously acknowledges the labors of Apollos (3, 5–8). He provides us in this letter with many valuable examples of his method of theological reflection and exposition. He always treats the questions at issue on the level of the purity of Christian teaching and conduct. Certain passages of the letter are of the greatest importance for the understanding of early Christian teaching on the Eucharist (10, 14–22; 11, 17–34) and on the resurrection of the body (15, 1–58).

Paul's authorship of 1 Corinthians, apart from a few verses that some regard as later interpolations, has never been seriously questioned. Some scholars have proposed, however, that the letter as we have it contains portions of more than one original Pauline letter. We know that Paul wrote at least two other letters to Corinth (see 5, 9; 2 Cor 2, 3–4) in addition to the two that we now have; this theory holds that the additional letters are actually contained within the two canonical ones. Most commentators, however, find 1 Corinthians quite understandable as a single coherent work.

The principal divisions of the First Letter to the Corinthians are the following:

I: Address

CHAPTER 1

See RG 366–67

Greeting. ¹ᵃ*Paul, called to be an apostle of Christ Jesus by the will of God, and Sosthenes our brother, ²ᵇto the church of God that is in Corinth, to you who have been sanctified in Christ Jesus, called to be holy, with all those everywhere who call upon the name of our Lord Jesus Christ, their Lord and ours. ³Grace to you and peace from God our Father and the Lord Jesus Christ.

Thanksgiving. ⁴I give thanks to my God always on your account for the grace of God bestowed on you in Christ Jesus, ⁵that in him you were enriched in every way, with all discourse and all knowledge, ⁶*as the testimony to Christ was confirmed among you, ⁷ᶜso that you are not lacking in any spiritual gift as you wait for the revelation of our Lord Jesus Christ. ⁸ᵈHe will keep you firm to the end, irreproachable on the day of our Lord Jesus [Christ]. ⁹ᵉGod is faithful, and by him you were called to fellowship with his Son, Jesus Christ our Lord.

II: Disorders in the Corinthian Community

A. Divisions in the Church

Groups and Slogans. ¹⁰ᶠ*I urge you, brothers, in the name of our Lord Jesus Christ,

---

1, 1–9: Paul follows the conventional form for the opening of a Hellenistic letter (cf Rom 1, 1–7), but expands the opening with details carefully chosen to remind the readers of their situation and to suggest some of the issues the letter will discuss.

1, 1: Called . . . by the will of God: Paul's mission and the church's existence are grounded in God's initiative. God's call, grace, and fidelity are central ideas in this introduction, emphasized by repetition and wordplays in the Greek.

1, 6: The testimony: this defines the purpose of Paul's mission (see also 15, 15 and the note on 2, 1). The forms of his testimony include oral preaching and instruction, his letters, and the life he leads as an apostle.

1, 10—4, 21: The first problem Paul addresses is that of divisions within the community. Although we are unable to

---

a: Rom 1, 1. *b:* Acts 18, 1-11. *c:* Ti 2, 13. *d:* Phil 1, 6. *e:* 1 Jn 1, 3. *f:* Phil 2, 2.

that all of you agree in what you say, and that there be no divisions among you, but that you be united in the same mind and in the same purpose. [11]For it has been reported to me about you, my brothers, by Chloe's people, that there are rivalries among you. [12g]*I mean that each of you is saying, "I belong to Paul," or "I belong to Apollos," or "I belong to Cephas," or "I belong to Christ." [13]*Is Christ divided? Was Paul crucified for you? Or were you baptized in the name of Paul? [14h]I give thanks [to God] that I baptized none of you except Crispus and Gaius, [15]so that no one can say you were baptized in my name. [16i](I baptized the household of Stephanas also; beyond that I do not know whether I baptized anyone else.) [17j]*For Christ did not send me to baptize but to preach the gospel, and not with the wisdom of human eloquence, so that the cross of Christ might not be emptied of its meaning.

Paradox of the Cross. [18k]The message of the cross is foolishness to those who are perishing, but to us who are being saved it is the power of God. [19l]For it is written:

"I will destroy the wisdom of the wise,
and the learning of the learned I will set aside."

[20m]Where is the wise one? Where is the scribe? Where is the debater of this age? Has not God made the wisdom of the world foolish? [21]*For since in the wisdom of God the world did not come to know God through wisdom, it was the will of God through the foolishness of the proclamation to save those who have faith. [22n]For Jews demand signs and Greeks look for wisdom, [23o]but we proclaim Christ crucified, a stumbling block to Jews and foolishness to Gentiles, [24]but to those who are called, Jews and Greeks alike, Christ the power of God and the wisdom of God. [25]For the foolishness of God is wiser than human wisdom, and the weakness of God is stronger than human strength.

The Corinthians and Paul. [26]*Consider your own calling, brothers. Not many of you were wise by human standards, not many were powerful, not many were of noble birth. [27p]Rather, God chose the foolish of the world to shame the wise, and God chose the weak

reconstruct the situation in Corinth completely, Paul clearly traces the divisions back to a false self-image on the part of the Corinthians, coupled with a false understanding of the apostles who preached to them (cf 4, 6.9; 9, 1–5) and of the Christian message itself. In these chapters he attempts to deal with those underlying factors and to bring the Corinthians back to a more correct perspective.

1, 12: I belong to: the activities of Paul and Apollos in Corinth are described in Acts 18. **Cephas** (i.e., "the Rock," a name by which Paul designates Peter also in 3, 22; 9, 5; 15, 5 and in Gal 1, 18; 2, 9.11.14) may well have passed through Corinth; he could have baptized some members of the community either there or elsewhere. The reference to **Christ** may be intended ironically here.

1, 13–17: The reference to baptism and the contrast with preaching the gospel in v 17a suggest that some Corinthians were paying special allegiance to the individuals who initiated them into the community.

1, 17b-18: The basic theme of chs 1–4 is announced. Adherence to individual leaders has something to do with differences in rhetorical ability and also with certain presuppositions regarding wisdom, eloquence, and effectiveness (power), which Paul judges to be in conflict with the gospel and the cross.

1, 17b: Not with the wisdom of human eloquence: both of the nouns employed here involve several levels of meaning, on which Paul deliberately plays as his thought unfolds. **Wisdom (sophia)** may be philosophical and speculative, but in biblical usage the term primarily denotes practical knowledge such as is demonstrated in the choice and effective application of means to achieve an end. The same term can designate the arts of building (cf 3, 10) or of persuasive speaking (cf 2, 4) or effectiveness in achieving salvation. **Eloquence (logos):** this translation emphasizes one possible meaning of the term **logos** (cf the references to rhetorical style and persuasiveness in 2, 1.4). But the term itself may denote an internal reasoning process, plan, or intention, as well as an external word, speech, or message. So by his expression **ouk en sophia logou** in the context of gospel preaching, Paul may intend to exclude both human ways of reasoning or thinking about things and human rhetorical technique. **Human:** this adjective does not stand in the Greek text but is supplied from the context. Paul will begin immediately to distinguish between **sophia** and **logos** from their divine counterparts and play them off against each other.

1, 21–25: True wisdom and power are to be found paradoxically where one would least expect them, in the place of their apparent negation. To human eyes the crucified Christ symbolizes impotence and absurdity.

1, 26—2, 5: The pattern of God's wisdom and power is exemplified in their own experience, if they interpret it rightly (1, 26–31), and can also be read in their experience of Paul as he first appeared among them preaching the gospel (2, 1–5).

g: 3, 4.22; 16, 12; Acts 18, 24-28. h: Acts 18, 8 / Rom 16, 23. i: 16, 15-17. j: 2, 1.4. k: 2, 14 / Rom 1, 16. l: Is 29, 14. m: Is 19, 12. n: Mt 12, 38; 16, 1 / Acts 17, 18-21. o: 2, 2; Gal 3, 1 / Gal 5, 11. p: Jas 2, 5.

of the world to shame the strong, [28]and God chose the lowly and despised of the world, those who count for nothing, to reduce to nothing those who are something, [29]q*so that no human being might boast before God. [30]rIt is due to him that you are in Christ Jesus, who became for us wisdom from God, as well as righteousness, sanctification, and redemption, [31]sso that, as it is written, "Whoever boasts, should boast in the Lord."

CHAPTER 2

See RG
366–67 [1]t*When I came to you, brothers, proclaiming the mystery of God, I did not come with sublimity of words or of wisdom. [2]uFor I resolved to know nothing while I was with you except Jesus Christ, and him crucified. [3]*I came to you in weakness and fear and much trembling, [4]v*and my message and my proclamation were not with persuasive [words of] wisdom, but with a demonstration of spirit and power, [5]wso that your faith might rest not on human wisdom but on the power of God.

The True Wisdom. [6]*Yet we do speak a wisdom to those who are mature, but not a wisdom of this age, nor of the rulers of this age who are passing away. [7]*Rather, we speak God's wisdom, mysterious, hidden, which God predetermined before the ages for our glory, [8]*and which none of the rulers of this age knew; for, if they had known it, they would not have crucified the Lord of glory. [9]xBut as it is written:

"What eye has not seen, and ear has not heard,
   and what has not entered the human heart,
   what God has prepared for those who love him,"

[10]ythis God has revealed to us through the Spirit.

For the Spirit scrutinizes everything, even the depths of God. [11]Among human beings, who knows what pertains to a person except the spirit of the person that is within? Similarly, no one knows what pertains to God except the Spirit of God. [12]We have not received the spirit of the world but the Spirit that is from God, so that we may understand the things freely given us by God. [13]*And we speak about them not with words taught by

---

1, 29–31: "Boasting (about oneself)" is a Pauline expression for the radical sin, the claim to autonomy on the part of a creature, the illusion that we live and are saved by our own resources. "Boasting in the Lord" (31), on the other hand, is the acknowledgment that we live only from God and for God.

2, 1: The mystery of God: God's secret, known only to himself, is his plan for the salvation of his people; it is clear from 1, 18–25; 2, 2.8–10 that this secret involves Jesus and the cross. In place of **mystery,** other good manuscripts read "testimony" (cf 1, 6).

2, 3: The **weakness** of the crucified Jesus is reflected in Paul's own bearing (cf 2 Cor 10–13). **Fear and much trembling:** reverential fear based on a sense of God's transcendence permeates Paul's existence and preaching. Compare his advice to the Philippians to work out their salvation with "fear and trembling" (Phil 2, 12), because God is at work in them just as his exalting power was paradoxically at work in the emptying, humiliation, and obedience of Jesus to death on the cross (Phil 2, 6–11).

2, 4: Among many manuscript readings here the best is either "not with the persuasion of wisdom" or "not with persuasive words of wisdom," which differ only by a nuance. Whichever reading is accepted, the inefficacy of human wisdom for salvation is contrasted with the power of the cross.

2, 6—3, 4: Paul now asserts paradoxically what he has previously been denying. To the Greeks who "are looking for wisdom" (1, 22), he does indeed bring a wisdom, but of a higher order and an entirely different quality, the only wisdom really worthy of the name. The Corinthians would be

able to grasp Paul's preaching as wisdom and enter into a wisdom-conversation with him if they were more open to the Spirit and receptive to the new insight and language that the Spirit teaches.

2, 7–10a: God's wisdom: his plan for our salvation. This was his own eternal secret that no one else could fathom, but in this new age of salvation he has graciously revealed it to us. For the pattern of God's secret, hidden to others and now revealed to the Church, cf also Rom 11, 25–36; 16, 25–27; Eph 1, 3–10; 3, 3–11; Col 1, 25–28.

2, 8: The rulers of this age: this suggests not only the political leaders of the Jews and Romans under whom Jesus was crucified (cf Acts 4, 25–28) but also the cosmic powers behind them (cf Eph 1, 20–23; 3, 10). **They would not have crucified the Lord of glory:** they became the unwitting executors of God's plan, which will paradoxically bring about their own conquest and submission (15, 24–28).

2, 13: In spiritual terms: the Spirit teaches spiritual people a new mode of perception (12) and an appropriate language by which they can share their self-understanding, their knowledge about what God has done in them. The final phrase in v 13 can also be translated "describing spiritual realities to spiritual people," in which case it prepares for vv 14–16.

q: Eph 2, 9.   r: Rom 4, 17 / 6, 11; Rom 3, 24-26; 2 Cor 5, 21 / Eph 1, 7; Col 1, 14; 1 Thes 5, 23.   s: Jer 9, 23; 2 Cor 10, 17.   t: 1, 17.   u: 1, 23; Gal 6, 14.   v: 4, 20; Rom 15, 19; 1 Thes 1, 5.   w: 2 Cor 4, 7.   x: Is 64, 3.   y: Mt 11, 25; 13, 11; 16, 17.

human wisdom, but with words taught by the Spirit, describing spiritual realities in spiritual terms. [14]*Now the natural person does not accept what pertains to the Spirit of God, for to him it is foolishness, and he cannot understand it, because it is judged spiritually. [15]*The spiritual person, however, can judge everything but is not subject to judgment by anyone. [16z]For "who has known the mind of the Lord, so as to counsel him?" But we have the mind of Christ.

CHAPTER 3

See RG 366–67

[1]*Brothers, I could not talk to you as spiritual people, but as fleshly people, as infants in Christ. [2a]I fed you milk, not solid food, because you were unable to take it. Indeed, you are still not able, even now, [3b]*for you are still of the flesh. While there is jealousy and rivalry among you, are you not of the flesh and behaving in an ordinary human way? [4c]Whenever someone says, "I belong to Paul," and another, "I belong to Apollos," are you not merely human?

The Role of God's Ministers. [5]*What is Apollos, after all, and what is Paul? Ministers through whom you became believers, just as the Lord assigned each one. [6d]I planted, Apollos watered, but God caused the growth. [7]Therefore, neither the one who plants nor the one who waters is anything, but only God, who causes the growth. [8]The one who plants and the one who waters are equal, and each will receive wages in proportion to his labor. [9e]For we are God's co-workers; you are God's field, God's building.

[10]*According to the grace of God given to me, like a wise master builder I laid a foundation, and another is building upon it. But each one must be careful how he builds upon it, [11]for no one can lay a foundation other than the one that is there, namely, Jesus Christ. [12]If anyone builds on this foundation with gold, silver, precious stones, wood, hay, or straw, [13f]*the work of each will come to light, for the Day will disclose it. It will be revealed with fire, and the fire [itself] will test the quality of each one's work. [14]If the work stands that someone built upon the foundation, that person will receive a wage. [15]*But if someone's work is burned up, that

2, 14: The natural person: see the note on 3, 1.

2, 15: The spiritual person . . . is not subject to judgment: since spiritual persons have been given knowledge of what pertains to God (11–12), they share in God's own capacity to judge. One to whom the mind of the Lord (and of Christ) is revealed (16) can be said to share in some sense in God's exemption from counseling and criticism.

3, 1–4: The Corinthians desire a sort of wisdom dialogue or colloquy with Paul; they are looking for solid, adult food, and he appears to disappoint their expectations. Paul counters: if such a dialogue has not yet taken place, the reason is that they are still at an immature stage of development (cf 2, 6).

3, 1: Spiritual people . . . fleshly people: Paul employs two clusters of concepts and terms to distinguish what later theology will call the "natural" and the "supernatural." (1) The natural person (2, 14) is one whose existence, perceptions, and behavior are determined by purely natural principles, the **psychē** (2, 14) and the **sarx** (flesh, a biblical term that connotes creatureliness, 1.3). Such persons are only infants (1); they remain on a purely human level (**anthrōpoi,** 4). (2) On the other hand, they are called to be animated by a higher principle, the **pneuma,** God's spirit. They are to become spiritual (**pneumatikoi,** 1) and mature (2, 6) in their perceptions and behavior (cf Gal 5, 16–26). The culmination of existence in the Spirit is described in 15, 44–49.

3, 3–4: Jealousy, rivalry, and divisions in the community are symptoms of their arrested development; they reveal the immaturity both of their self-understanding (4) and of the judgments about their apostles (21).

3, 5—4, 5: The Corinthians tend to evaluate their leaders by the criteria of human wisdom and to exaggerate their importance. Paul views the role of the apostles in the light of his theology of spiritual gifts (cf chs 12–14, where the charism of the apostle heads the lists). The essential aspects of all spiritual gifts (12, 4–6 presents them as gifts of grace, as services, and as modes of activity) are exemplified by the apostolate, which is a gift of grace (3, 10) through which God works (3, 9) and a form of service (3, 5) for the common good (elsewhere expressed by the verb "build up," suggested here by the image of the building, 3, 9). The apostles serve the church, but their accountability is to God and to Christ (4, 1–5).

3, 5: Ministers: for other expressions of Paul's understanding of himself as minister or steward to the church, cf 4, 1; 9, 17.19–27; 2 Cor 3, 6–9; 4, 1; 5, 18; 6, 3–4; and 11, 23 (the climax of Paul's defense).

3, 10–11: There are diverse functions in the service of the community, but each individual's task is serious, and each will stand accountable for the quality of his contribution.

3, 13: The Day: the great day of Yahweh, the day of judgment, which can be a time of either gloom or joy. **Fire** both destroys and purifies.

3, 15: Will be saved: although Paul can envision very harsh divine punishment (cf 17), he appears optimistic about the success of divine corrective means both here and elsewhere (cf 5, 5; 11, 32 [discipline]). The text of v 15 has sometimes been used to support the notion of purgatory, though it does not envisage this.

z: Wis 9, 13; Is 40, 13; Rom 11, 34. a: Heb 5, 12-14. b: Jas 3, 13-16. c: 1, 12. d: Acts 18, 1-11.24-28. e: Eph 2, 20-22; 1 Pt 2, 5. f: Mt 3, 11-12; 2 Thes 1, 7-10.

one will suffer loss; the person will be saved, but only as through fire. *16g*Do you not know that you are the temple of God, and that the Spirit of God dwells in you? *17**If anyone destroys God's temple, God will destroy that person; for the temple of God, which you are, is holy.

*18h*Let no one deceive himself. If anyone among you considers himself wise in this age, let him become a fool so as to become wise. *19i*For the wisdom of this world is foolishness in the eyes of God, for it is written:

"He catches the wise in their own ruses,"

*20j*and again:

"The Lord knows the thoughts of the wise, that they are vain."

21k*So let no one boast about human beings, for everything belongs to you, *22*Paul or Apollos or Cephas, or the world or life or death, or the present or the future: all belong to you, *23*and you to Christ, and Christ to God.

CHAPTER 4

See RG 366–67

*1l*Thus should one regard us: as servants of Christ and stewards of the mysteries of God. *2*Now it is of course required of stewards that they be found trustworthy. *3*It does not concern me in the least that I be judged by you or any human tribunal; I do not even pass judgment on myself; *4m*I am not conscious of anything against me, but I do not thereby stand acquitted; the one who judges me is the Lord. *5*Therefore, do not make any judgment before the appointed time, until the Lord comes, for he will bring to light what is hidden in darkness and will manifest the motives of our hearts, and then everyone will receive praise from God.

Paul's Life as Pattern. *6**I have applied these things to myself and Apollos for your benefit, brothers, so that you may learn from us not to go beyond what is written, so that none of you will be inflated with pride in favor of one person over against another. *7*Who confers distinction upon you? What do you possess that you have not received? But if you have received it, why are you boasting as if you did not receive it? *8**You are already satisfied; you have already grown rich; you have become kings without us! Indeed, I wish that you had become kings, so that we also might become kings with you.

9n*For as I see it, God has exhibited us apostles as the last of all, like people sen-

---

3, 17: Holy: i.e., "belonging to God." The cultic sanctity of the community is a fundamental theological reality to which Paul frequently alludes (cf 1, 2.30; 6, 11; 7, 14).

3, 21–23: These verses pick up the line of thought of 1, 10–13. If the Corinthians were genuinely wise (18–20), their perceptions would be reversed, and they would see everything in the world and all those with whom they exist in the church in their true relations with one another. Paul assigns all the persons involved in the theological universe a position on a scale: God, Christ, church members, church leaders. Read from top to bottom, the scale expresses ownership; read from bottom to top, the obligation to serve. This picture should be complemented by similar statements such as those in 8, 6 and 15, 20–28.

4, 6–21: This is an emotionally charged peroration to the discussion about divisions. It contains several exhortations and statements of Paul's purpose in writing (cf 6.14–17.21) that counterbalance the initial exhortation at 1, 10.

4, 6: That you may learn from us not to go beyond what is written: the words "to go" are not in the Greek, but have here been added as the minimum necessary to elicit sense from this difficult passage. It probably means that the Corinthians should avoid the false wisdom of vain speculation, contenting themselves with Paul's proclamation of the cross, which is the fulfillment of God's promises in the Old Testament (what is written). **Inflated with pride:** literally, "puffed up," i.e., arrogant, filled with a sense of self-importance. The

term is particularly Pauline, found in the New Testament only in 1 Cor 4, 6.18–19; 5, 2; 8, 1; 13, 4; Col 2, 18 (cf the related noun at 2 Cor 12, 20). It sometimes occurs in conjunction with the theme of "boasting," as in vv 6–7 here.

4, 8: Satisfied . . . rich . . . kings: these three statements could also be punctuated as questions continuing the series begun in v 7. In any case these expressions reflect a tendency at Corinth toward an overrealized eschatology, a form of self-deception that draws Paul's irony. The underlying attitude has implications for the Corinthians' thinking about other issues, notably morality and the resurrection, that Paul will address later in the letter.

4, 9–13: A rhetorically effective catalogue of the circumstances of apostolic existence, in the course of which Paul ironically contrasts his own sufferings with the Corinthians' illusion that they have passed beyond the folly of the passion and have already reached the condition of glory. His language echoes that of the beatitudes and woes, which assert a future reversal of present conditions. Their present sufferings ("to this very hour," 11) place the apostles in the class of those to whom the beatitudes promise future relief (Mt 5, 3–11; Lk 6, 20–23); whereas the Corinthians' image of themselves as "al-

g: 6, 19; 2 Cor 6, 16; Eph 2, 20-22. *h:* 8, 2; Is 5, 21; Gal 6, 3. *i:* 1, 20 / Jb 5, 13. *j:* Ps 94, 11. *k:* 4, 6 / Rom 8, 32. *l:* Ti 1, 7; 1 Pt 4, 10. *m:* 2 Cor 1, 12 / Rom 2, 16; 2 Cor 5, 10. *n:* 15, 31; Rom 8, 36; 2 Cor 4, 8-12; 11, 23 / Heb 10, 33.

tenced to death, since we have become a spectacle to the world, to angels and human beings alike. [10o]We are fools on Christ's account, but you are wise in Christ; we are weak, but you are strong; you are held in honor, but we in disrepute. [11p]To this very hour we go hungry and thirsty, we are poorly clad and roughly treated, we wander about homeless [12q]and we toil, working with our own hands. When ridiculed, we bless; when persecuted, we endure; [13]when slandered, we respond gently. We have become like the world's rubbish, the scum of all, to this very moment.

[14*]I am writing you this not to shame you, but to admonish you as my beloved children. [15r]Even if you should have countless guides to Christ, yet you do not have many fathers, for I became your father in Christ Jesus through the gospel. [16s]Therefore, I urge you, be imitators of me. [17t]For this reason I am sending you Timothy, who is my beloved and faithful son in the Lord; he will remind you of my ways in Christ [Jesus], just as I teach them everywhere in every church.

[18*]Some have become inflated with pride, as if I were not coming to you. [19]But I will come to you soon, if the Lord is willing, and I shall ascertain not the talk of these inflated people but their power. [20u]For the kingdom of God is not a matter of talk but of power. [21v]Which do you prefer? Shall I come to you with a rod, or with love and a gentle spirit?

B. Moral Disorders

CHAPTER 5

See RG 366-68

A Case of Incest. [1w*]It is widely reported that there is immorality among you, and immorality of a kind not found even among pagans—a man living with his father's wife. [2*]And you are inflated with pride. Should you not rather have been sorrowful? The one who did this deed should be expelled from your midst. [3x]I, for my part, although absent in body but present in spirit, have already, as if present, pronounced judgment on the one who has committed this deed, [4]in the name of [our] Lord Jesus: when you have gathered together and I am with you in spirit with the power of the Lord Jesus, [5y*]you are to deliver this man to Satan for the destruction of his flesh, so that his spirit may be saved on the day of the Lord.

[6z*]Your boasting is not appropriate. Do you not know that a little yeast leavens all

---

ready" filled, rich, ruling (8), as wise, strong, and honored (10) places them paradoxically in the position of those whom the woes threaten with future undoing (Lk 6, 24–26). They have lost sight of the fact that the reversal is predicted for the future.

4, 14–17: My beloved children: the close of the argument is dominated by the tender metaphor of the father who not only gives his children life but also educates them. Once he has begotten them through his preaching, Paul continues to present the gospel to them existentially, by his life as well as by his word, and they are to learn, as children do, by imitating their parents (16). The reference to the **rod** in v 21 belongs to the same image-complex. So does the image of the **ways** in v 17: the ways that Paul teaches everywhere, "his ways in Christ Jesus," mean a behavior pattern quite different from the human ways along which the Corinthians are walking (3, 3).

4, 18–21: Verse 20 picks up the contrast between a certain kind of talk (**logos**) and true power (**dynamis**) from 1, 17–18 and 2, 4–5. The kingdom, which many of them imagine to be fully present in their lives (8), will be rather unexpectedly disclosed in the strength of Paul's encounter with them, if they make a powerful intervention on his part necessary. Compare the similar ending to an argument in 2 Cor 13, 1–4.10.

5, 1—6, 20: Paul now takes up a number of other matters that require regulation. These have come to his attention by hearsay (5, 1), probably in reports brought by "Chloe's people" (1, 11).

5, 1–13: Paul first deals with the incestuous union of a man with his stepmother (1–8) and then attempts to clarify general admonitions he has given about associating with fellow Christians guilty of immorality (9–13). Each of these three brief paragraphs expresses the same idea: the need of separation between the holy and the unholy.

5, 2: Inflated with pride: this remark and the reference to **boasting** in v 6 suggest that they are proud of themselves despite the infection in their midst, tolerating and possibly even approving the situation. The attitude expressed in 6, 2.13 may be influencing their thinking in this case.

5, 5: Deliver this man to Satan: once the sinner is expelled from the church, the sphere of Jesus' lordship and victory over sin, he will be in the region outside over which Satan is still master. **For the destruction of his flesh:** the purpose of the penalty is medicinal: through affliction, sin's grip over him may be destroyed and the path to repentance and reunion laid open. With Paul's instructions for an excommunication ceremony here, contrast his recommendations for the reconciliation of a sinner in 2 Cor 2, 5–11.

5, 6: A little yeast: yeast, which induces fermentation, is

---

o: 1, 18; 3, 18; 2 Cor 11, 19 / 2, 3; 2 Cor 13, 9. *p:* Rom 8, 35; 2 Cor 11, 23-27. *q:* Acts 9, 6-14; 18, 3; 20, 34; 1 Thes 2, 9 / 1 Pt 3, 9. *r:* Gal 4, 19; Phlm 10. *s:* 11, 1; Phil 3, 17; 4, 9; 1 Thes 1, 6; 2 Thes 3, 7.9. *t:* 16, 10; Acts 19, 22. *u:* 2, 4; 1 Thes 1, 5. *v:* 2 Cor 1, 23; 10, 2. *w:* Lv 18, 7-8; 20, 11; Dt 27, 20. *x:* Col 2, 5. *y:* 1 Tm 1, 20. *z:* Gal 5, 9.

the dough? *7a**Clear out the old yeast, so that you may become a fresh batch of dough, inasmuch as you are unleavened. For our paschal lamb, Christ, has been sacrificed. *8b*Therefore, let us celebrate the feast, not with the old yeast, the yeast of malice and wickedness, but with the unleavened bread of sincerity and truth.

9*I wrote you in my letter not to associate with immoral people, *10c*not at all referring to the immoral of this world or the greedy and robbers or idolaters; for you would then have to leave the world. *11d*But I now write to you not to associate with anyone named a brother, if he is immoral, greedy, an idolater, a slanderer, a drunkard, or a robber, not even to eat with such a person. *12*For why should I be judging outsiders? Is it not your business to judge those within? *13e*God will judge those outside. "Purge the evil person from your midst."

CHAPTER 6

See RG
367–68

Lawsuits before Unbelievers. *1**How can any one of you with a case against another dare to bring it to the unjust for judgment instead of to the holy ones? *2f**Do you not know that the holy ones will judge the

world? If the world is to be judged by you, are you unqualified for the lowest law courts? *3*Do you not know that we will judge angels? Then why not everyday matters? *4*If, therefore, you have courts for everyday matters, do you seat as judges people of no standing in the church? *5*I say this to shame you. Can it be that there is not one among you wise enough to be able to settle a case between brothers? *6*But rather brother goes to court against brother, and that before unbelievers?

*7g*Now indeed [then] it is, in any case, a failure on your part that you have lawsuits against one another. Why not rather put up with injustice? Why not rather let yourselves be cheated? *8*Instead, you inflict injustice and cheat, and this to brothers. *9h**Do you not know that the unjust will not inherit the kingdom of God? Do not be deceived; neither fornicators nor idolaters nor adulterers nor boy prostitutes nor sodomites *10*nor thieves nor the greedy nor drunkards nor slanderers nor robbers will inherit the kingdom of God. *11i*That is what some of you used to be; but now you have had yourselves washed, you were sanctified, you were justified in the name of the Lord Jesus Christ and in the Spirit of our God.

Sexual Immorality. *12j**"Everything is

a natural symbol for a source of corruption that becomes all-pervasive. The expression is proverbial.

5, 7–8: In the Jewish calendar, Passover was followed immediately by the festival of Unleavened Bread. In preparation for this feast all traces of old bread were removed from the house, and during the festival only unleavened bread was eaten. The sequence of these two feasts provides Paul with an image of Christian existence: Christ's death (the true Passover celebration) is followed by the life of the Christian community, marked by newness, purity, and integrity (a perpetual feast of unleavened bread). Paul may have been writing around Passover time (cf 16, 5); this is a little Easter homily, the earliest in Christian literature.

5, 9–13: Paul here corrects a misunderstanding of his earlier directives against associating with immoral fellow Christians. He concedes the impossibility of avoiding contact with sinners in society at large but urges the Corinthians to maintain the inner purity of their own community.

6, 1–11: Christians at Corinth are suing one another before pagan judges in Roman courts. A barrage of rhetorical questions (1–9) betrays Paul's indignation over this practice, which he sees as an infringement upon the holiness of the Christian community.

6, 2–3: The principle to which Paul appeals is an eschatological prerogative promised to Christians: they are to share with Christ the judgment of the world (cf Dn 7, 22.27). Hence they ought to be able to settle minor disputes within the community.

6, 9–10: A catalogue of typical vices that exclude from the kingdom of God and that should be excluded from God's church. Such lists (cf 5, 10) reflect the common moral sensibility of the New Testament period.

6, 9: The Greek word translated as **boy prostitutes** may refer to catamites, i.e., boys or young men who were kept for purposes of prostitution, a practice not uncommon in the Greco-Roman world. In Greek mythology this was the function of Ganymede, the "cupbearer of the gods," whose Latin name was Catamitus. The term translated **sodomites** would then refer to adult males who indulged in homosexual practices with such boys. See similar condemnations of such practices in Rom 1, 26–27; 1 Tm 1, 10.

6, 12–20: Paul now turns to the opinion of some Corinthians that sexuality is a morally indifferent area (12–13). This leads him to explain the mutual relation between the Lord Jesus and our bodies (13b) in a densely packed paragraph that contains elements of a profound theology of sexuality (15–20).

6, 12–13: Everything is lawful for me: the Corinthians may have derived this slogan from Paul's preaching about Christian freedom, but they mean something different by it:

a: Ex 12, 1-13; Dt 16, 1-2; 1 Pt 1, 19. *b:* Ex 12, 15-20; 13, 7; Dt 16, 3. *c:* 10, 27; Jn 17, 15. *d:* Mt 18, 17; 2 Thes 3, 6.14; 2 Jn 10. *e:* Dt 13, 6; 17, 7; 22, 24. *f:* Wis 3, 8; Mt 19, 28; Rv 20, 4. *g:* Mt 5, 38-42; Rom 12, 17-21; 1 Thes 5, 15. *h:* 15, 50; Gal 5, 19-21; Eph 5, 5. *i:* Ti 3, 3-7. *j:* 10, 23.

lawful for me," but not everything is beneficial. "Everything is lawful for me," but I will not let myself be dominated by anything. [13]"Food for the stomach and the stomach for food," but God will do away with both the one and the other. The body, however, is not for immorality, but for the Lord, and the Lord is for the body; [14k]God raised the Lord and will also raise us by his power.

[15l]*Do you not know that your bodies are members of Christ? Shall I then take Christ's members and make them the members of a prostitute? Of course not! [16m][Or] do you not know that anyone who joins himself to a prostitute becomes one body with her? For "the two," it says, "will become one flesh." [17n]But whoever is joined to the Lord becomes one spirit with him. [18]*Avoid immorality. Every other sin a person commits is outside the body, but the immoral person sins against his own body. [19o]*Do you not know that your body is a temple of the holy Spirit within you, whom you have from God, and that you are not your own? [20p]For you have been purchased at a price. Therefore glorify God in your body.

III: Answers to the Corinthians' Questions

A. Marriage and Virginity

CHAPTER 7

See RG 368

Advice to the Married. [1]*Now in regard to the matters about which you wrote: "It is a good thing for a man not to touch a woman," [2]but because of cases of immorality every man should have his own wife, and every woman her own husband. [3]The husband should fulfill his duty toward his wife, and likewise the wife toward her husband. [4]A wife does not have authority over her own body, but rather her husband, and similarly a husband does not have authority over his own body, but rather his wife. [5]Do not deprive each other, except perhaps by mutual consent for a time, to be free for prayer, but then return to one another, so that Satan may not tempt you through your lack of self-control. [6]*This I say by way of concession, however, not as a command. [7q]*Indeed, I wish everyone to be as I am, but each has a partic-

they consider sexual satisfaction a matter as indifferent as food, and they attribute no lasting significance to bodily functions (13a). Paul begins to deal with the slogan by two qualifications, which suggest principles for judging sexual activity. **Not everything is beneficial:** cf 10, 23, and the whole argument of chs 8–10 on the finality of freedom and moral activity. **Not let myself be dominated:** certain apparently free actions may involve in fact a secret servitude in conflict with the lordship of Jesus.

6, 15b-16: **A prostitute:** the reference may be specifically to religious prostitution, an accepted part of pagan culture at Corinth and elsewhere; but the prostitute also serves as a symbol for any sexual relationship that conflicts with Christ's claim over us individually. **The two . . . will become one flesh:** the text of Gn 2, 24 is applied positively to human marriage in Mt and Mk, and in Eph 5, 29–32: love of husband and wife reflect the love of Christ for his church. The application of the text to union with a prostitute is jarring, for such a union is a parody, an antitype of marriage, which does conflict with Christ's claim over us. This explains the horror expressed in 15b.

6, 18: **Against his own body:** expresses the intimacy and depth of sexual disorder, which violates the very orientation of our bodies.

6, 19–20: Paul's vision becomes trinitarian. **A temple:** sacred by reason of God's gift, his indwelling Spirit. **Not your own:** but "for the Lord," who acquires ownership by the act of redemption. **Glorify God in your body:** the argument concludes with a positive imperative to supplement the negative "avoid immorality" of v 18. Far from being a terrain that is morally indifferent, the area of sexuality is one in which our relationship with God (and his Christ and his Spirit) is very intimately expressed:

he is either highly glorified or deeply offended.

7, 1–40: Paul now begins to answer questions addressed to him by the Corinthians (7, 1—11, 1). The first of these concerns marriage. This chapter contains advice both to the married (1–16) and to the unmarried (25–38) or widowed (39–40); these two parts are separated by vv 17–24, which enunciate a principle applicable to both.

7, 1–16: It seems that some Christians in Corinth were advocating asceticism in sexual matters. The pattern **it is a good thing . . . , but** occurs twice (1–2.8–9; cf 26), suggesting that in this matter as in others the Corinthians have seized upon a genuine value but are exaggerating or distorting it in some way. Once again Paul calls them to a more correct perspective and a better sense of their own limitations. The phrase **it is a good thing** (1) may have been the slogan of the ascetic party at Corinth.

7, 1–7: References to Paul's own behavior (7–8) suggest that his celibate way of life and his preaching to the unmarried (cf 25–35) have given some the impression that asceticism within marriage, i.e., suspension of normal sexual relations, would be a laudable ideal. Paul points to their experience of widespread immorality to caution them against overestimating their own strength (2); as individuals they may not have the particular gift that makes such asceticism feasible (7) and hence are to abide by the principle to be explained in vv 17–24.

7, 6: **By way of concession:** this refers most likely to the

k: Rom 8, 11; 2 Cor 4, 14. l: 12, 27; Rom 6, 12-13; 12, 5; Eph 5, 30. m: Gn 2, 24; Mt 19, 5; Mk 10, 8; Eph 5, 31. n: Rom 8, 9-10; 2 Cor 3, 17. o: 3, 16-17; Rom 5, 5. p: 3, 23; 7, 23; Acts 20, 28 / Rom 12, 1; Phil 1, 20. q: Mt 19, 11-12.

ular gift from God, one of one kind and one of another.

⁸ʳ*Now to the unmarried and to widows I say: It is a good thing for them to remain as they are, as I do, ⁹but if they cannot exercise self-control they should marry, for it is better to marry than to be on fire. ¹⁰ˢ*To the married, however, I give this instruction (not I, but the Lord): A wife should not separate from her husband ¹¹—and if she does separate she must either remain single or become reconciled to her husband—and a husband should not divorce his wife.

¹²*To the rest I say (not the Lord): If any brother has a wife who is an unbeliever, and she is willing to go on living with him, he should not divorce her; ¹³and if any woman has a husband who is an unbeliever, and he is willing to go on living with her, she should not divorce her husband. ¹⁴ᵗFor the unbelieving husband is made holy through his wife, and the unbelieving wife is made holy through the brother. Otherwise your children would be unclean, whereas in fact they are holy.

¹⁵*If the unbeliever separates, however, let him separate. The brother or sister is not bound in such cases; God has called you to peace. ¹⁶For how do you know, wife, whether you will save your husband; or how do you know, husband, whether you will save your wife?

The Life That the Lord Has Assigned. ¹⁷*Only, everyone should live as the Lord has assigned, just as God called each one. I give this order in all the churches. ¹⁸ᵘWas someone called after he had been circumcised? He should not try to undo his circumcision. Was an uncircumcised person called? He should not be circumcised. ¹⁹ᵛCircumcision means nothing, and uncircumcision means nothing; what matters is keeping God's commandments. ²⁰Everyone should remain in the state in which he was called.

²¹Were you a slave when you were called? Do not be concerned but, even if you can gain your freedom, make the most of it. ²²ʷFor the slave called in the Lord is a freed person in the Lord, just as the free person who has been called is a slave of Christ. ²³ˣYou have been purchased at a price. Do not become slaves to human beings. ²⁴Brothers, everyone should continue before God in the state in which he was called.

Advice to Virgins and Widows. ²⁵*Now in regard to virgins I have no commandment from the Lord, but I give my opinion as one who by the Lord's mercy is trustworthy. ²⁶ʸSo this is what I think best because of the present distress: that it is a good thing for a person to remain as he is. ²⁷Are you bound to a wife? Do not seek a separation. Are you free of a wife? Then do not look for a wife. ²⁸If you marry, however, you do not sin, nor does an unmarried woman sin if she marries; but such people will experience affliction in their earthly life, and I would like to spare you that.

²⁹ᶻ*I tell you, brothers, the time is running out. From now on, let those having wives act

---

concession mentioned in v 5a: temporary interruption of relations for a legitimate purpose.

7, 7: A particular gift from God: use of the term **charisma** suggests that marriage and celibacy may be viewed in the light of Paul's theology of spiritual gifts (chs 12–14).

7, 8: Paul was obviously unmarried when he wrote this verse. Some interpreters believe that he had previously been married and widowed; there is no clear evidence either for or against this view, which was expressed already at the end of the second century by Clement of Alexandria.

7, 10–11: (Not I, but the Lord): Paul reminds the married of Jesus' principle of nonseparation (Mk 10, 9). This is one of his rare specific references to the teaching of Jesus.

7, 12–14: To the rest: marriages in which only one partner is a baptized Christian. Jesus' prohibition against divorce is not addressed to them, but Paul extends the principle of nonseparation to such unions, provided they are marked by peacefulness and shared sanctification.

7, 15–16: If the unbeliever separates: the basis of the "Pauline privilege" in Catholic marriage legislation.

7, 17–24: On the ground that distinct human conditions are less significant than the whole new existence opened up by God's call, Paul urges them to be less concerned with changing their states of life than with answering God's call where it finds them. The principle applies both to the married state (1–16) and to the unmarried (25–38).

7, 25–28: Paul is careful to explain that the principle of v 17 does not bind under sin but that present earthly conditions make it advantageous for the unmarried to remain as they are (28). These remarks must be complemented by the statement about "particular gifts" from v 7.

7, 29–31: The world . . . is passing away: Paul advises Christians to go about the ordinary activities of life in a manner different from those who are totally immersed in them and unaware of their transitoriness.

r: 1 Tm 5, 11-16 / 9, 5; s: Mt 5, 32; 19, 9. t: Rom 11, 16. u: 1 Mc 1, 15 / Acts 15, 1-2. v: Rom 2, 25.29; Gal 5, 6; 6, 15. w: Eph 6, 5-9; Col 3, 11; Phlm 16. x: 6, 20. y: 1 Cor 7, 8. z: Rom 13, 11.

as not having them, [30]those weeping as not weeping, those rejoicing as not rejoicing, those buying as not owning, [31]those using the world as not using it fully. For the world in its present form is passing away.

[32]I should like you to be free of anxieties. An unmarried man is anxious about the things of the Lord, how he may please the Lord. [33a]But a married man is anxious about the things of the world, how he may please his wife, [34b]and he is divided. An unmarried woman or a virgin is anxious about the things of the Lord, so that she may be holy in both body and spirit. A married woman, on the other hand, is anxious about the things of the world, how she may please her husband. [35c]I am telling you this for your own benefit, not to impose a restraint upon you, but for the sake of propriety and adherence to the Lord without distraction.

[36]*If anyone thinks he is behaving improperly toward his virgin, and if a critical moment has come and so it has to be, let him do as he wishes. He is committing no sin; let them get married. [37]The one who stands firm in his resolve, however, who is not under compulsion but has power over his own will, and has made up his mind to keep his virgin, will be doing well. [38]So then, the one who marries his virgin does well; the one who does not marry her will do better.

[39d]*A wife is bound to her husband as long as he lives. But if her husband dies, she is free to be married to whomever she wishes, provided that it be in the Lord. [40e]She is more blessed, though, in my opinion, if she remains as she is, and I think that I too have the Spirit of God.

B. Offerings to Idols

CHAPTER 8

See RG 368–69

Knowledge Insufficient. [1f]*Now in regard to meat sacrificed to idols: we realize that "all of us have knowledge"; knowledge inflates with pride, but love builds up. [2]If anyone supposes he knows something, he does not yet know as he ought to know. [3g]But if one loves God, one is known by him.

[4h]So about the eating of meat sacrificed to idols: we know that "there is no idol in the world," and that "there is no God but one." [5]Indeed, even though there are so-called gods in heaven and on earth (there are, to be sure, many "gods" and many "lords"), [6i]*yet for us there is

---

7, 36–38: The passage is difficult to interpret, because it is unclear whether Paul is thinking of a father and his unmarried daughter (or slave), or of a couple engaged in a betrothal or spiritual marriage. The general principles already enunciated apply: there is no question of sin, even if they should marry, but staying as they are is "better" (for the reasons mentioned in 28–35). Once again the **charisma** of v 7, which applies also to the unmarried (8–9), is to be presupposed.

7, 36: A critical moment has come: either because the woman will soon be beyond marriageable age, or because their passions are becoming uncontrollable (cf 9).

7, 39–40: Application of the principles to the case of widows. If they do choose to remarry, they ought to prefer Christian husbands.

8, 1—11, 1: The Corinthians' second question concerns meat that has been sacrificed to idols; in this area they were exhibiting a disordered sense of liberation that Paul here tries to rectify. These chapters contain a sustained and unified argument that illustrates Paul's method of theological reflection on a moral dilemma. Although the problem with which he is dealing is dated, the guidelines for moral decisions that he offers are of lasting validity.

Essentially Paul urges them to take a communitarian rather than an individualistic view of their Christian freedom. Many decisions that they consider pertinent only to their private relationship with God have, in fact, social consequences. Nor can moral decisions be determined by merely theoretical consider-

ations; they must be based on concrete circumstances, specifically on the value and needs of other individuals and on mutual responsibility within the community. Paul here introduces the theme of "building up" (**oikodomē**), i.e., of contributing by individual action to the welfare and growth of the community. This theme will be further developed in ch 14; see the note on 14, 3b-5. Several years later Paul would again deal with the problem of meat sacrificed to idols in Rom 14, 1—15, 6.

8, 1a: Meat sacrificed to idols: much of the food consumed in the city could have passed through pagan religious ceremonies before finding its way into markets and homes. **"All of us have knowledge":** a slogan, similar to 6, 12, which reveals the self-image of the Corinthians. Verse 4 will specify the content of this knowledge.

8, 6: This verse rephrases the monotheistic confession of v 4 in such a way as to contrast it with polytheism (5) and to express our relationship with the one God in concrete, i.e., in personal and Christian terms. **And for whom we exist:** since the Greek contains no verb here and the action intended must be inferred from the preposition **eis,** another translation is equally possible: "toward whom we return." **Through whom all things:** the earliest reference in the New Testament to Jesus' role in creation.

a: Lk 14, 20. *b:* 1 Tm 5, 5. *c:* Lk 10, 39-42. *d:* Rom 7, 2. *e:* 1 Cor 7, 25. *f:* Rom 15, 14 / 13, 1-13; Rom 14, 15.19. *g:* Rom 8, 29; Gal 4, 9. *h:* 10, 19; Dt 6, 4. *i:* Mal 2, 10 / Rom 11, 36; Eph 4, 5-6 / 1, 2-3 / Jn 1, 3; Col 1, 16.

one God, the Father,
　from whom all things are and for
　　whom we exist,
and one Lord, Jesus Christ,
　through whom all things are and
　　through whom we exist.

Practical Rules. ⁷^jBut not all have this knowledge. There are some who have been so used to idolatry up until now that, when they eat meat sacrificed to idols, their conscience, which is weak, is defiled. ^{8k}*Now food will not bring us closer to God. We are no worse off if we do not eat, nor are we better off if we do. ^{9l}But make sure that this liberty of yours in no way becomes a stumbling block to the weak. ¹⁰If someone sees you, with your knowledge, reclining at table in the temple of an idol, may not his conscience too, weak as it is, be "built up" to eat the meat sacrificed to idols? ^{11m}Thus through your knowledge, the weak person is brought to destruction, the brother for whom Christ died. ¹²When you sin in this way against your brothers and wound their consciences, weak as they are, you are sinning against Christ. ¹³ⁿ*Therefore if food causes my brother to sin, I will never eat meat again, so that I may not cause my brother to sin.

CHAPTER 9

See RG 369–70

Paul's Rights as an Apostle. ¹^o*Am I not free? Am I not an apostle? Have I not seen Jesus our Lord? Are you not my work in the Lord? ²Although I may not be an apostle for others, certainly I am for you, for you are the seal of my apostleship in the Lord.

³*My defense against those who would pass judgment on me is this. ⁴*Do we not have the right to eat and drink? ⁵Do we not have the right to take along a Christian wife, as do the rest of the apostles, and the brothers of the Lord, and Cephas? ^{6p}Or is it only myself and Barnabas who do not have the right not to work? ^{7q}Who ever serves as a soldier at his own expense? Who plants a vineyard without eating its produce? Or who shepherds a flock without using some of the milk from the flock? ⁸Am I saying this on human authority, or does not the law also speak of these things? ^{9r}It is written in the law of Moses, "You shall not muzzle an ox while it is treading out the grain." Is God concerned about oxen, ^{10s}or is he not really speaking for our sake? It was written for our sake, because the plowman should plow in hope, and the thresher in hope of receiving a share. ^{11t}If we have sown spiritual seed for you, is it a great thing that we reap a material harvest from you? ^{12u}*If

---

8, 8–9: Although the food in itself is morally neutral, extrinsic circumstances may make the eating of it harmful. A **stumbling block:** the image is that of tripping or causing someone to fall (cf 13; 9, 12; 10, 12.32; 2 Cor 6, 3; Rom 14, 13.20–21). This is a basic moral imperative for Paul, a counterpart to the positive imperative to "build one another up"; compare the expression "giving offense" as opposed to "pleasing" in 10, 32–33.

8, 13: His own course is clear: he will avoid any action that might harm another Christian. This statement prepares for the paradigmatic development in ch 9.

9, 1–27: This chapter is an emotionally charged expansion of Paul's appeal to his own example in 8, 13; its purpose is to reinforce the exhortation of 8, 9. The two opening questions introduce the themes of Paul's freedom and his apostleship (1), themes that the chapter will develop in reverse order, vv 1–18 treating the question of his apostleship and the rights that flow from it, and vv 19–27 exploring dialectically the nature of Paul's freedom. The language is highly rhetorical, abounding in questions, wordplays, paradoxes, images, and appeals to authority and experience. The argument is unified by repetitions; its articulations are highlighted by inclusions and transitional verses.

9, 3: **My defense against those who would pass judgment on me:** the reference to a defense (**apologia**) is surprising, and suggests that Paul is incorporating some material here that he has previously used in another context. The defense will touch on two points: the fact of Paul's rights as an apostle (4–12a and 13–14) and his nonuse of those rights (12b and 15–18).

9, 4–12a: Apparently some believe that Paul is not equal to the other apostles and therefore does not enjoy equal privileges. His defense on this point (here and in 13–14) reinforces the assertion of his apostolic character in v 2. It consists of a series of analogies from natural equity (7) and religious custom (13) designed to establish his equal right to support from the churches (4–6.11–12a); these analogies are confirmed by the authority of the law (8–10) and of Jesus himself (14).

9, 12b: It appears, too, that suspicion or misunderstanding has been created by Paul's practice of not living from his

j: 10, 28; Rom 14, 23 / Rom 14, 1; 15, 1. *k:* Rom 14, 17. *l:* Rom 14, 13.20–21. *m:* Rom 14, 15.20. *n:* Mt 18, 6; Rom 14, 20–21. *o:* 1 Cor 9, 19 / 2 Cor 12, 12 / 15, 8-9; Acts 9, 17; 26, 16. *p:* Acts 4, 36-37; 13, 1-2; Gal 2, 1.9.13; Col 4, 10. *q:* 2 Tm 2, 3-4. *r:* Dt 25, 4; 1 Tm 5, 18. *s:* 2 Tm 2, 6. *t:* Rom 15, 27. *u:* 2 Cor 11, 7-12; 12, 13-18; 2 Thes 3, 6-12.

others share this rightful claim on you, do not we still more?

Reason for Not Using His Rights. Yet we have not used this right. On the contrary, we endure everything so as not to place an obstacle to the gospel of Christ. [13v]*Do you not know that those who perform the temple services eat [what] belongs to the temple, and those who minister at the altar share in the sacrificial offerings? [14w]In the same way, the Lord ordered that those who preach the gospel should live by the gospel.

[15x]*I have not used any of these rights, however, nor do I write this that it be done so in my case. I would rather die. Certainly no one is going to nullify my boast. [16y]If I preach the gospel, this is no reason for me to boast, for an obligation has been imposed on me, and woe to me if I do not preach it! [17z]If I do so willingly, I have a recompense, but if unwillingly, then I have been entrusted with a stewardship. [18a]What then is my recompense? That, when I preach, I offer the gospel free of charge so as not to make full use of my right in the gospel.

All Things to All. [19b]*Although I am free in regard to all, I have made myself a slave to all so as to win over as many as possible. [20]To the Jews I became like a Jew to win over Jews; to those under the law I became like one under the law—though I myself am not under the law—to win over those under the law. [21]To those outside the law I became like one outside the law—though I am not outside God's law but within the law of Christ—to win over those outside the law. [22c]To the weak I became weak, to win over the weak. I have become all things to all, to save at least some. [23]All this I do for the sake of the gospel, so that I too may have a share in it.

[24d]*Do you not know that the runners in the stadium all run in the race, but only one wins the prize? Run so as to win. [25e]Every athlete exercises discipline in every way. They do it to win a perishable crown, but we an imperishable one. [26]Thus I do not run aimlessly; I do not fight as if I were shadowboxing. [27]*No, I drive my body and train it, for fear that, after having preached to others, I myself should be disqualified.

CHAPTER 10

See RG 369

Warning against Overconfidence. [1f]*I do not want you to be unaware, brothers, that our ancestors were all under the cloud and all passed through the sea, [2g]and all of them were baptized into Moses in the cloud and in the sea. [3]All ate the same spiritual food,

preaching. The first reason he asserts in defense of this practice is an entirely apostolic one; it anticipates the developments to follow in vv 19–22. He will give a second reason in vv 15–18.

9, 13–14: The position of these verses produces an interlocking of the two points of Paul's defense. These arguments by analogy (13) and from authority (14) belong with those of vv 7–10 and ground the first point. But Paul defers them until he has had a chance to mention "the gospel of Christ" (12b), after which it is more appropriate to mention Jesus' injunction to his preachers and to argue by analogy from the sacred temple service to his own liturgical service, the preaching of the gospel (cf Rom 1, 9; 15, 16).

9, 15–18: Paul now assigns a more personal motive to his nonuse of his right to support. His preaching is not a service spontaneously undertaken on his part but a stewardship imposed by a sort of divine compulsion. Yet to merit any reward he must bring some spontaneous quality to his service, and this he does by freely renouncing his right to support. The material here is quite similar to that contained in Paul's "defense" at 2 Cor 11, 5–12; 12, 11–18.

9, 19–23: In a rhetorically balanced series of statements Paul expands and generalizes the picture of his behavior and explores the paradox of apostolic freedom. It is not essentially freedom **from** restraint but freedom **for** service—a possibility of constructive activity.

9, 24–27: A series of miniparables from sports, appealing to readers familiar with Greek gymnasia and the nearby Isthmian games.

9, 27: For fear that . . . I myself should be disqualified: a final paradoxical turn to the argument: what appears at first a free, spontaneous renunciation of rights (12–18) seems subsequently to be required for fulfillment of Paul's stewardship (to preach effectively he must reach his hearers wherever they are, 19–22), and finally is seen to be necessary for his own salvation (23–27). Mention of the possibility of disqualification provides a transition to ch 10.

10, 1–5: Paul embarks unexpectedly upon a panoramic survey of the events of the Exodus period. The privileges of Israel in the wilderness are described in terms that apply strictly only to the realities of the new covenant ("baptism," "spiritual food and drink"); interpreted in this way they point forward to the Christian experience (1–4). But those privileges did not guarantee God's permanent pleasure (5).

v: Nm 18, 8.31; Dt 18, 1-5. *w:* Mt 10, 10; Lk 10, 7-8. *x:* 2 Cor 11, 9-10. *y:* Acts 26, 14-18. *z:* 4, 1; Gal 2, 7. *a:* 2 Cor 11, 7-12. *b:* Mt 20, 26-27. *c:* 10, 33; Rom 15, 1; 2 Cor 11, 29. *d:* Heb 12, 1. *e:* 2 Tm 2, 5 / 2 Tm 4, 7-8; Jas 1, 12; 1 Pt 5, 4. *f:* Ex 13, 21-22; 14, 19-20 / Ex 14, 21-22.26-30. *g:* Rom 6, 3; Gal 3, 27 / Ex 16, 4-35.

4h*and all drank the same spiritual drink, for they drank from a spiritual rock that followed them, and the rock was the Christ. 5i Yet God was not pleased with most of them, for they were struck down in the desert.

6j*These things happened as examples for us, so that we might not desire evil things, as they did. 7k And do not become idolaters, as some of them did, as it is written, "The people sat down to eat and drink, and rose up to revel." 8l Let us not indulge in immorality as some of them did, and twenty-three thousand fell within a single day. 9m*Let us not test Christ as some of them did, and suffered death by serpents. 10n Do not grumble as some of them did, and suffered death by the destroyer. 11*These things happened to them as an example, and they have been written down as a warning to us, upon whom the end of the ages has come. 12*Therefore whoever thinks he is standing secure should take care not to fall. 13o No trial has come to you but what is human. God is faithful and will not let you be tried beyond your strength; but with the trial he will also provide a way out, so that you may be able to bear it.

Warning against Idolatry. 14p*Therefore, my beloved, avoid idolatry. 15I am speaking as to sensible people; judge for yourselves what I am saying. 16q The cup of blessing that we bless, is it not a participation in the blood of Christ? The bread that we break, is it not a participation in the body of Christ? 17r Because the loaf of bread is one, we, though many, are one body, for we all partake of the one loaf.

18s Look at Israel according to the flesh; are not those who eat the sacrifices participants in the altar? 19So what am I saying? That meat sacrificed to idols is anything? Or that an idol is anything? 20t*No, I mean that what they sacrifice, [they sacrifice] to demons, not to God, and I do not want you to become participants with demons. 21u You cannot drink the cup of the Lord and also the cup of demons. You cannot partake of the table of the Lord and of the table of demons. 22v Or are we provoking the Lord to jealous anger? Are we stronger than he?

Seek the Good of Others. 23w*"Everything is lawful," but not everything is beneficial. "Everything is lawful," but not everything builds up. 24x No one should seek his own advantage, but that of his neighbor. 25*Eat any-

---

10, 4: A spiritual rock that followed them: the Torah speaks only about a rock from which water issued, but rabbinic legend amplified this into a spring that followed the Israelites throughout their migration. Paul uses this legend as a literary type: he makes the rock itself accompany the Israelites, and he gives it a spiritual sense. **The rock was the Christ:** in the Old Testament, Yahweh is the Rock of his people (cf Dt 32, Moses's song to Yahweh the Rock). Paul now applies this image to the Christ, the source of the living water, the true Rock that accompanied Israel, guiding their experiences in the desert.

10, 6–13: This section explicitates the typological value of these Old Testament events: the desert experiences of the Israelites are examples, meant as warnings, to deter us from similar sins (idolatry, immorality, etc.) and from a similar fate.

10, 9: Christ: to avoid Paul's concept of Christ present in the wilderness events, some manuscripts read "the Lord."

10, 11: Upon whom the end of the ages has come: it is our period in time toward which past ages have been moving and in which they arrive at their goal.

10, 12–13: Take care not to fall: the point of the whole comparison with Israel is to caution against overconfidence, a sense of complete security (12). This warning is immediately balanced by a reassurance, based, however, on God (13).

10, 14–22: The warning against idolatry from v 7 is now repeated (14) and explained in terms of the effect of sacrifices: all sacrifices, Christian (16–17), Jewish (18), or pagan (20), establish communion. But communion with Christ is exclusive, incompatible with any other such communion (21). Compare the line of reasoning at 6, 15.

10, 20: To demons: although Jews denied divinity to pagan gods, they often believed that there was some noncivine reality behind the idols, such as the dead, or angels, or demons. The explanation Paul offers in v 20 is drawn from Dt 32, 7: the power behind the idols, with which the pagans commune, consists of demonic powers hostile to God.

10, 23—11, 1: By way of peroration Paul returns to the opening situation (ch 8) and draws conclusions based on the intervening considerations (chs 9–10).

10, 23–24: He repeats in the context of this new problem the slogans of liberty from 6, 12, with similar qualifications. Liberty is not merely an individual perfection, nor an end in itself, but is to be used for the common good. The language of v 24 recalls the descriptions of Jesus' self-emptying in Phil 2.

10, 25–30: A summary of specific situations in which the eating of meat sacrificed to idols could present problems of conscience. Three cases are considered. In the first (the marketplace, 25–26) and the second (at table, 27), there is no need to be concerned with whether food has passed through a pagan

h: Ex 17, 1-7; Nm 20, 7-11; Dt 8, 15. i: Nm 14, 28-38; Jude 5. j: Nm 11, 4.34. k: Ex 32, 6. l: Nm 25, 1-9. m: Nm 21, 5-9. n: Nm 14, 2-37; 16, 1-35. o: Mt 6, 13; Jas 1, 13-14 / 1, 9. p: 1 Jn 5, 21. q: Mt 26, 26-29; Acts 2, 42. r: Rom 12, 5; Eph 4, 4. s: Lv 7, 6. t: Dt 32, 17. u: 2 Cor 6, 14-18. v: Dt 32, 21 / Eccl 6, 10. w: 6, 12. x: Rom 15, 2; Phil 2, 4.21.

thing sold in the market, without raising questions on grounds of conscience, [26y]for "the earth and its fullness are the Lord's." [27]If an unbeliever invites you and you want to go, eat whatever is placed before you, without raising questions on grounds of conscience. [28]But if someone says to you, "This was offered in sacrifice," do not eat it on account of the one who called attention to it and on account of conscience; [29]I mean not your own conscience, but the other's. For why should my freedom be determined by someone else's conscience? [30z]If I partake thankfully, why am I reviled for that over which I give thanks?

[31]So whether you eat or drink, or whatever you do, do everything for the glory of God. [32]*Avoid giving offense, whether to Jews or Greeks or the church of God, [33a]just as I try to please everyone in every way, not seeking my own benefit but that of the many, that they may be saved.

CHAPTER 11

See RG 370-71 [1b]Be imitators of me, as I am of Christ.

IV: Problems In Liturgical Assemblies

[2c]*I praise you because you remember me in everything and hold fast to the traditions, just as I handed them on to you.

A. Women's Headdresses

Man and Woman. [3d]*But I want you to know that Christ is the head of every man, and a husband the head of his wife, and God the head of Christ. [4]*Any man who prays or prophesies with his head covered brings shame upon his head. [5]But any woman who prays or prophesies with her head unveiled brings shame upon her head, for it is one and the same thing as if she had had her head shaved. [6]For if a woman does not have her head veiled, she may as well have her hair cut off. But if it is shameful for a woman to have her hair cut off or her head shaved, then she should wear a veil.

[7e]*A man, on the other hand, should not cover his head, because he is the image and glory of God, but woman is the glory of

sacrifice or not, for the principle of 8, 4–6 still stands, and the whole creation belongs to the one God. But in the third case (28), the situation changes if someone present explicitly raises the question of the sacrificial origin of the food; eating in such circumstances may be subject to various interpretations, some of which could be harmful to individuals. Paul is at pains to insist that the enlightened Christian conscience need not change its judgment about the neutrality, even the goodness, of the food in itself (29–30); yet the total situation is altered to the extent that others are potentially endangered, and this calls for a different response, for the sake of others.

10, 32—11, 1: In summary, the general rule of mutually responsible use of their Christian freedom is enjoined first negatively (32), then positively, as exemplified in Paul (33), and finally grounded in Christ, the pattern for Paul's behavior and theirs (11, 1; cf Rom 15, 1–3).

11, 2—14, 40: This section of the letter is devoted to regulation of conduct at the liturgy. The problems Paul handles have to do with the dress of women in the assembly (11, 3–16), improprieties in the celebration of community meals (11, 17–34), and the use of charisms or spiritual gifts (12, 1—14, 40). The statement in 11, 2 introduces all of these discussions, but applies more appropriately to the second (cf the mention of praise in 11, 17 and of tradition in 11, 23).

11, 3–16: Women have been participating in worship at Corinth without the head-covering normal in Greek society of the period. Paul's stated goal is to bring them back into conformity with contemporary practice and propriety. In his desire to convince, he reaches for arguments from a variety of sources, though he has space to develop them only sketchily and is perhaps aware that they differ greatly in persuasiveness.

11, 3: A husband the head of his wife: the specific problem suggests to Paul the model of the head as a device for clarifying relations within a hierarchical structure. The model is similar to that developed later in greater detail and nuance in Eph 5, 21–33. It is a hybrid model, for it grafts onto a strictly theological scale of existence (cf 3, 21–23) the hierarchy of sociosexual relations prevalent in the ancient world: men, dominant, reflect the active function of Christ in relation to his church; women, submissive, reflect the passive role of the church with respect to its savior. This gives us the functional scale: God, Christ, man, woman.

11, 4–6: From man's direct relation to Christ, Paul infers that his head should not be covered. But woman, related not directly to Christ on the scale but to her husband, requires a covering as a sign of that relationship. **Shameful . . . to have her hair cut off:** certain less honored classes in society, such as lesbians and prostitutes, are thought to have worn their hair close-cropped.

11, 7–9: The hierarchy of v 3 is now expressed in other metaphors: the image (**eikōn**) and the reflected glory (**doxa**). Paul is alluding basically to the text of Gn 1, 27, in which mankind as a whole, the male-female couple, is created in God's image and given the command to multiply and together dominate the lower creation. But Gn 1, 24 is interpreted here in the light of the second creation narrative in Gn 2, in which each of the sexes is created separately (first the man and then the woman **from** man and **for** him, to be his helpmate, Gn 2,

y: Pss 24, 1; 50, 12. z: Rom 14, 6; 1 Tm 4, 3-4. a: 9, 22; Rom 15, 2. b: 4, 16; Phil 3, 17. c: 15, 3; 2 Thes 2, 15. d: Eph 5, 23. e: Gn 1, 26-27; 5, 1.

man. [8]*For man did not come from woman, but woman from man; [9]*nor was man created for woman, but woman for man; [10]*for this reason a woman should have a sign of authority on her head, because of the angels. [11h]*Woman is not independent of man or man of woman in the Lord. [12i]For just as woman came from man, so man is born of woman; but all things are from God.

[13]*Judge for yourselves: is it proper for a woman to pray to God with her head unveiled? [14]Does not nature itself teach you that if a man wears his hair long it is a disgrace to him, [15]whereas if a woman has long hair it is her glory, because long hair has been given [her] for a covering? [16]But if anyone is inclined to be argumentative, we do not have such a custom, nor do the churches of God.

B. The Lord's Supper

An Abuse at Corinth. [17]*In giving this instruction, I do not praise the fact that your meetings are doing more harm than good. [18j]First of all, I hear that when you meet as a church there are divisions among you, and to a degree I believe it; [19]*there have to be factions among you in order that [also] those who are approved among you may become known. [20]When you meet in one place, then, it is not to eat the Lord's supper, [21]for in eating, each one goes ahead with his own supper, and one goes hungry while another gets drunk. [22k]Do you not have houses in which you can eat and drink? Or do you show contempt for the church of God and make those who have nothing feel ashamed? What can I say to you? Shall I praise you? In this matter I do not praise you.

Tradition of the Institution. [23l]*For I received from the Lord what I also handed on to you, that the Lord Jesus, on the night he was handed over, took bread, [24]and, after he had given thanks, broke it and said, "This is my body that is for you. Do this in remembrance of me." [25m]In the same way also the cup, after supper, saying, "This cup is the new covenant in my blood. Do this, as often as you drink it, in remembrance of me." [26]For as often as you eat this bread and drink the cup, you proclaim the death of the Lord until he comes.

[27]*Therefore whoever eats the bread or drinks the cup of the Lord unworthily will have to answer for the body and blood of the

20–23), and under the influence of the story of the fall, as a result of which the husband rules over the woman (Gn 3, 16). This interpretation splits the single image of God into two, at different degrees of closeness.

11, 10: A sign of authority: "authority" (**exousia**) may possibly be due to mistranslation of an Aramaic word for "veil"; in any case, the connection with v 9 indicates that the covering is a sign of woman's subordination. **Because of the angels:** a surprising additional reason, which the context does not clarify. Presumably the reference is to cosmic powers who might inflict harm on women or whose function is to watch over women or the cult.

11, 11–12: These parenthetical remarks relativize the argument from Gn 2–3. **In the Lord:** in the Christian economy the relation between the sexes is characterized by a mutual dependence, which is not further specified. And even in the natural order conditions have changed: the mode of origin described in Gn 2 has been reversed (12a). But the ultimately significant fact is the origin that all things have in common (12b).

11, 13–16: The argument for conformity to common church practice is summed up and pressed home. Verses 14–15 contain a final appeal to the sense of propriety that contemporary Greek society would consider "natural" (cf 5–6).

11, 17–34: Paul turns to another abuse connected with the liturgy, and a more serious one, for it involves neglect of ba-

sic Christian tradition concerning the meaning of the Lord's Supper. Paul recalls that tradition for them and reminds them of its implications.

11, 19: That . . . those who are approved among you may become known: Paul situates their divisions within the context of the eschatological separation of the authentic from the inauthentic and the final revelation of the difference. The notion of authenticity-testing recurs in the injunction to self-examination in view of present and future judgment (28–32).

11, 23–25: This is the earliest written account of the institution of the Lord's Supper in the New Testament. The narrative emphasizes Jesus' action of self-giving (expressed in the words over the bread and the cup) and his double command to repeat his own action.

11, 27: It follows that the only proper way to celebrate the Eucharist is one that corresponds to Jesus' intention, which fits with the meaning of his command to reproduce his action in the proper spirit. If the Corinthians eat and drink unworthily, i.e., without having grasped and internalized the meaning of his death for them, they **will have to answer for the body and blood,** i.e., will be guilty of a sin against the Lord himself (cf 8, 12).

---

f: Gn 2, 21-23. g: Gn 2, 18. h: Gal 3, 27-28. i: 8, 6; Rcm 11, 36. j: 1, 10-12; Gal 5, 20. k: Jas 2, 1-7. l: 2; 15, 3 / 13, 16-17; Mt 26, 26-29; Mk 14, 22-25; Lk 22, 14-20. m: Ex 24, 8; 2 Cor 3, 6; Heb 8, 6-13.

Lord. [28]*A person should examine himself, and so eat the bread and drink the cup. [29]*For anyone who eats and drinks without discerning the body, eats and drinks judgment on himself. [30]That is why many among you are ill and infirm, and a considerable number are dying. [31]If we discerned ourselves, we would not be under judgment; [32n]but since we are judged by [the] Lord, we are being disciplined so that we may not be condemned along with the world.

[33]Therefore, my brothers, when you come together to eat, wait for one another. [34]If anyone is hungry, he should eat at home, so that your meetings may not result in judgment. The other matters I shall set in order when I come.

C. Spiritual Gifts

CHAPTER 12

See RG 371

Unity and Variety. [1]*Now in regard to spiritual gifts, brothers, I do not want you to be unaware. [2o]*You know how, when you were pagans, you were constantly attracted and led away to mute idols. [3p]Therefore, I tell you that nobody speaking by the spirit of God says, "Jesus be accursed." And no one can say, "Jesus is Lord," except by the holy Spirit.

[4q]*There are different kinds of spiritual gifts but the same Spirit; [5]there are different forms of service but the same Lord; [6]there are different workings but the same God who produces all of them in everyone. [7]To each individual the manifestation of the Spirit is given for some benefit. [8r]To one is given through the Spirit the expression of wisdom; to another the expression of knowledge according to the same Spirit; [9]to another faith by the same Spirit; to another gifts of healing by the one Spirit; [10s]to another mighty deeds; to another prophecy; to another discernment of spirits; to another varieties of tongues; to another interpretation of tongues. [11]But one and the same Spirit produces all of these, distributing them individually to each person as he wishes.

One Body, Many Parts. [12u]*As a body is one though it has many parts, and all the parts of the body, though many, are one body, so also Christ. [13v]For in one Spirit we were all baptized into one body, whether Jews or Greeks, slaves or free persons, and we were all given to drink of one Spirit.

[14]Now the body is not a single part, but many. [15]If a foot should say, "Because I am not a hand I do not belong to the body," it does not for this reason belong any less to

---

11, 28: Examine himself: the Greek word is similar to that for "approved" in v 19, which means "having been tested and found true." The self-testing required for proper eating involves **discerning the body** (29), which, from the context, must mean understanding the sense of Jesus' death (26), perceiving the imperative to unity that follows from the fact that Jesus gives himself to all and requires us to repeat his sacrifice in the same spirit (18–25).

11, 29–32: Judgment: there is a series of wordplays in these verses that would be awkward to translate literally into English; it includes all the references to judgment (**krima,** 29.34; **krinō,** 31.32), discernment (**diakrinō,** 29.31), and condemnation (**katakrinō,** 32). The judgment is concretely described as the illness, infirmity, and death that have visited the community. These are signs that the power of Jesus' death is not yet completely recognized and experienced. Yet even the judgment incurred is an expression of God's concern; it is a medicinal measure meant to rescue us from condemnation with God's enemies.

12, 1—14, 40: Ecstatic and charismatic activity were common in early Christian experience, as they were in other ancient religions. But the Corinthians seem to have developed a disproportionate esteem for certain phenomena, especially tongues, to the detriment of order in the liturgy. Paul's response to this development provides us with the fullest exposition we have of his theology of the charisms.

12, 2–3: There is an experience of the Spirit and an understanding of ecstatic phenomena that are specifically Christian and that differ, despite apparent similarities, from those of the pagans. It is necessary to discern which spirit is leading one; ecstatic phenomena must be judged by their effect (2). Verse 3 illustrates this by an example: power to confess Jesus as Lord can come only from the Spirit, and it is inconceivable that the Spirit would move anyone to curse the Lord.

12, 4–6: There are some features common to all charisms, despite their diversity: all are **gifts** (**charismata**), grace from outside ourselves; all are **forms of service** (**diakoniai**), an expression of their purpose and effect; and all are **workings** (**energēmata**), in which God is at work. Paul associates each of these aspects with what later theology will call one of the persons of the Trinity, an early example of "appropriation."

12, 12–26: The image of **a body** is introduced to explain Christ's relationship with believers (12). Verse 13 applies this model to the church: by baptism all, despite diversity of ethnic or social origins, are integrated into one organism. Verses 14–26 then develop the need for diversity of function among the parts of a body without threat to its unity.

---

n: Dt 8, 5; Heb 12, 5-11. *o:* Eph 2, 11-18. *p:* Rom 10, 9; 1 Jn 4, 2-3. *q:* Rom 12, 6; Eph 4, 7.11. *r:* 2, 6-13. *s:* 14, 5.26.39; Acts 2, 4. *t:* 7, 7; Eph 4, 7. *u:* 10, 17; Rom 12, 4-5; Eph 2, 16; Col 3, 15. *v:* Gal 3, 28; Eph 2, 13-18; Col 3, 11 / Jn 7, 37-39.

the body. [16]Or if an ear should say, "Because I am not an eye I do not belong to the body," it does not for this reason belong any less to the body. [17]If the whole body were an eye, where would the hearing be? If the whole body were hearing, where would the sense of smell be? [18]But as it is, God placed the parts, each one of them, in the body as he intended. [19]If they were all one part, where would the body be? [20]But as it is, there are many parts, yet one body. [21]The eye cannot say to the hand, "I do not need you," nor again the head to the feet, "I do not need you." [22]Indeed, the parts of the body that seem to be weaker are all the more necessary, [23]and those parts of the body that we consider less honorable we surround with greater honor, and our less presentable parts are treated with greater propriety, [24]whereas our more presentable parts do not need this. But God has so constructed the body as to give greater honor to a part that is without it, [25]so that there may be no division in the body, but that the parts may have the same concern for one another. [26]If [one] part suffers, all the parts suffer with it; if one part is honored, all the parts share its joy.

Application to Christ. [27w]*Now you are Christ's body, and individually parts of it. [28x]*Some people God has designated in the church to be, first, apostles; second, prophets; third, teachers; then, mighty deeds; then gifts of healing, assistance, administration,

and varieties of tongues. [29]Are all apostles? Are all prophets? Are all teachers? Do all work mighty deeds? [30]Do all have gifts of healing? Do all speak in tongues? Do all interpret? [31]Strive eagerly for the greatest spiritual gifts.

The Way of Love. But I shall show you a still more excellent way.

CHAPTER 13

See RG 371

[1y]*If I speak in human and angelic tongues, but do not have love, I am a resounding gong or a clashing cymbal. [2z]And if I have the gift of prophecy and comprehend all mysteries and all knowledge; if I have all faith so as to move mountains, but do not have love, I am nothing. [3a]If I give away everything I own, and if I hand my body over so that I may boast but do not have love, I gain nothing.

[4b]*Love is patient, love is kind. It is not jealous, [love] is not pompous, it is not inflated, [5c]it is not rude, it does not seek its own interests, it is not quick-tempered, it does not brood over injury, [6]it does not rejoice over wrongdoing but rejoices with the truth. [7d]It bears all things, believes all things, hopes all things, endures all things.

[8]*Love never fails. If there are prophecies, they will be brought to nothing; if tongues, they will cease; if knowledge, it will be brought to nothing. [9]For we know partially and we prophesy partially, [10]but when the

---

12, 27–30: Paul now applies the image again to the church as a whole and its members (27). The lists in vv 28–30 spell out the parallelism by specifying the diversity of functions found in the church (cf Rom 12, 6–8; Eph 4, 11).

12, 28: First, apostles: apostleship was not mentioned in vv 8–10, nor is it at issue in these chapters, but Paul gives it pride of place in his listing. It is not just one gift among others but a prior and fuller gift that includes the others. They are all demonstrated in Paul's apostolate, but he may have developed his theology of charisms by reflecting first of all on his own grace of apostleship (cf 3, 5—4, 14; 9, 1–27; 2 Cor 2, 14—6, 13; 10, 1—13, 30, esp. 11, 23 and 12, 12).

13, 1–13: This chapter involves a shift of perspective and a new point. All or part of the material may once have been an independent piece in the style of Hellenistic eulogies of virtues, but it is now integrated, by editing, into the context of chs 12–14 (cf the reference to tongues and prophecy) and into the letter as a whole (cf the references to knowledge and to behavior). The function of ch 13 within the discussion of spiritual gifts is to relativize all the charisms by contrasting them with the more basic, pervasive, and enduring value that gives

them their purpose and their effectiveness. The rhetoric of this chapter is striking.

13, 1–3: An inventory of gifts, arranged in careful gradation: neither tongues (on the lowest rung), nor prophecy, knowledge, or faith, nor even self-sacrifice has value unless informed by love.

13, 4–7: This paragraph is developed by personification and enumeration, defining love by what it does or does not do. The Greek contains fifteen verbs; it is natural to translate many of them by adjectives in English.

13, 8–13: The final paragraph announces its topic, **Love never fails** (8), then develops the permanence of love in contrast to the charisms (9–12), and finally asserts love's superiority even over the other "theological virtues" (13).

w: Rom 12, 5-8; Eph 1, 23; 4, 12; 5, 30; Col 1, 18.24.   x: Eph 2, 20; 3, 5; 4, 11.   y: 8, 1; 16, 14; Rom 12, 9-10; 13, 8-10.   z: 4, 1; 14, 2 / 1, 5; 8, 1-3; 12, 8 / Mt 17, 20; 21, 21; Col 2, 3.   a: Mt 6, 2.   b: Eph 4, 2 / 4, 6.18; 5, 2; 8, 1.   c: 10, 24.33; Phil 2, 4.21; 1 Thes 5, 15.   d: Prv 10, 12; 1 Pt 4, 8.

perfect comes, the partial will pass away. *11*When I was a child, I used to talk as a child, think as a child, reason as a child; when I became a man, I put aside childish things. *12e*At present we see indistinctly, as in a mirror, but then face to face. At present I know partially; then I shall know fully, as I am fully known. *13f**So faith, hope, love remain, these three; but the greatest of these is love.

See RG 371

CHAPTER 14

Prophecy Greater than Tongues. *1g**Pursue love, but strive eagerly for the spiritual gifts, above all that you may prophesy. *2**For one who speaks in a tongue does not speak to human beings but to God, for no one listens; he utters mysteries in spirit. *3h**On the other hand, one who prophesies does speak to human beings, for their building up, encouragement, and solace. *4*Whoever speaks in a tongue builds himself up, but whoever prophesies builds up the church. *5*Now I should like all of you to speak in tongues, but even more to prophesy. One who prophesies is greater than one who speaks in tongues, unless he interprets, so that the church may be built up.

6*Now, brothers, if I should come to you speaking in tongues, what good will I do you if I do not speak to you by way of revelation, or knowledge, or prophecy, or instruction? *7*Likewise, if inanimate things that produce sound, such as flute or harp, do not give out the tones distinctly, how will what is being played on flute or harp be recognized? *8*And if the bugle gives an indistinct sound, who will get ready for battle? *9*Similarly, if you, because of speaking in tongues, do not utter intelligible speech, how will anyone know what is being said? For you will be talking to the air. *10*It happens that there are many different languages in the world, and none is meaningless; *11*but if I do not know the meaning of a language, I shall be a foreigner to one who speaks it, and one who speaks it a foreigner to me. *12*So with yourselves: since you strive eagerly for spirits, seek to have an abundance of them for building up the church.

Need for Interpretation. *13**Therefore, one who speaks in a tongue should pray to be able to interpret. *14**[For] if I pray in a tongue, my spirit is at prayer but my mind is unproductive. *15i*So what is to be done? I will pray with the spirit, but I will also pray with the mind. I will sing praise with the

13, 13: In speaking of love, Paul is led by spontaneous association to mention faith and hope as well. They are already a well-known triad (cf 1 Thes 1, 3), three interrelated (cf 7) features of Christian life, more fundamental than any particular charism. **The greatest . . . is love:** love is operative even within the other members of the triad (7), so that it has a certain primacy among them. Or, if the perspective is temporal, love will remain (cf "never fails," 8) even when faith has yielded to sight and hope to possession.

14, 1–5: Verse 1b returns to the thought of 12, 31a and reveals Paul's primary concern. The series of contrasts in vv 2–5 discloses the problem at Corinth: a disproportionate interest in tongues, with a corresponding failure to appreciate the worth of prophecy. Paul attempts to clarify the relative values of those gifts by indicating the kind of communication achieved in each and the kind of effect each produces.

14, 2–3a: They involve two kinds of communication: tongues, private speech toward God in inarticulate terms that need interpretation to be intelligible to others (see 27–28); prophecy, communication with others in the community.

14, 3b-5: They produce two kinds of effect. One who speaks in tongues **builds himself up;** it is a matter of individual experience and personal perfection, which inevitably recalls Paul's previous remarks about being inflated, seeking one's own good, pleasing oneself. But a prophet **builds up the church:** the theme of "building up" or "edifying" others, the main theme of the letter, comes to clearest expression in

this chapter (3.4.5.12.17). It has been anticipated at 8, 1 and 10, 23, and by the related concept of "the beneficial" in 6, 12; 10, 23; 12, 7; etc.

14, 6–12: Sound, in order to be useful, must be intelligible. This principle is illustrated by a series of analogies from music (7–8) and from ordinary human speech (10–11); it is applied to the case at hand in v 9 and v 12.

14, 13–19: The charism of interpretation lifts tongues to the level of intelligibility, enabling them to produce the same effect as prophecy (cf 5.26–28).

14, 14–15: My spirit: Paul emphasizes the exclusively ecstatic, nonrational quality of tongues. The tongues at Pentecost are also described as an ecstatic experience (Acts 2, 4.12–13), though Luke superimposes further interpretations of his own. **My mind:** the ecstatic element, dominant in earliest Old Testament prophecy as depicted in 1 Sam 10, 5–13; 19, 20–24, seems entirely absent from Paul's notion of prophecy and completely relegated to tongues. He emphasizes the role of reason when he specifies instruction as a function of prophecy (6.19.31). But he does not exclude intuition and emotion; cf references to encouragement and consolation (3.31) and the scene describing the ideal exercise of prophecy (24–25).

e: 2 Cor 5, 7; Heb 11, 1 / 2 Tm 2, 19; 1 Jn 3, 2.   *f:* Col 1, 4; 1 Thes 1, 3; 5, 8.   *g:* 1 Cor 14, 5.12.39.   *h:* 1 Cor 14, 4–5.12.17.26; 3, 9; 8, 1.10; 10, 23.   *i:* Eph 5, 19; Col 3, 16.

spirit, but I will also sing praise with the mind. ¹⁶Otherwise, if you pronounce a blessing [with] the spirit, how shall one who holds the place of the uninstructed say the "Amen" to your thanksgiving, since he does not know what you are saying? ¹⁷For you may be giving thanks very well, but the other is not built up. ¹⁸I give thanks to God that I speak in tongues more than any of you, ¹⁹but in the church I would rather speak five words with my mind, so as to instruct others also, than ten thousand words in a tongue.

Functions of These Gifts. ²⁰ʲ*Brothers, stop being childish in your thinking. In respect to evil be like infants, but in your thinking be mature. ²¹ᵏIt is written in the law:

"By people speaking strange tongues
    and by the lips of foreigners
I will speak to this people,
    and even so they will not listen to me,

says the Lord." ²²Thus, tongues are a sign not for those who believe but for unbelievers, whereas prophecy is not for unbelievers but for those who believe.

²³ˡ*So if the whole church meets in one place and everyone speaks in tongues, and then uninstructed people or unbelievers should come in, will they not say that you are out of your minds? ²⁴But if everyone is prophesying, and an unbeliever or uninstructed person should come in, he will be convinced by everyone and judged by everyone, ²⁵ᵐand the secrets of his heart will be disclosed, and so he will fall down and worship God, declaring, "God is really in your midst."

Rules of Order. ²⁶ⁿ*So what is to be done, brothers? When you assemble, one has a psalm, another an instruction, a revelation, a tongue, or an interpretation. Everything should be done for building up. ²⁷If anyone speaks in a tongue, let it be two or at most three, and each in turn, and one should interpret. ²⁸But if there is no interpreter, the person should keep silent in the church and speak to himself and to God.

²⁹Two or three prophets should speak, and the others discern. ³⁰But if a revelation is given to another person sitting there, the first one should be silent. ³¹For you can all prophesy one by one, so that all may learn and all be encouraged. ³²Indeed, the spirits of prophets are under the prophets' control, ³³*since he is not the God of disorder but of peace.

As in all the churches of the holy ones, ³⁴ᵒwomen should keep silent in the churches, for they are not allowed to speak, but should be subordinate, as even the law says. ³⁵But if they want to learn anything,

---

14, 20–22: The Corinthians pride themselves on tongues as a sign of God's favor, a means of direct communication with him (2.28). To challenge them to a more mature appraisal, Paul draws from scripture a less flattering explanation of what speaking in tongues may signify. Isaiah threatened the people that if they failed to listen to their prophets, the Lord would speak to them (in punishment) through the lips of Assyrian conquerors (Is 28, 11–12). Paul compresses Isaiah's text and makes God address his people directly. Equating tongues with foreign languages (cf 10–11), Paul concludes from Isaiah that **tongues are a sign not for those who believe,** i.e., not a mark of God's pleasure for those who listen to him but a mark of his displeasure with those in the community who are faithless, who have not heeded the message that he has sent through the prophets.

14, 23–25: Paul projects the possible missionary effect of two hypothetical liturgical experiences, one consisting wholly of tongues, the other entirely of prophecy. **Uninstructed (idiōtai):** the term may simply mean people who do not speak or understand tongues, as in v 16, where it seems to designate Christians. But coupled with the term "unbelievers" it may be another way of designating those who have not been initiated into the community of faith; some believe it denotes a special class of non-Christians who are close to the

community, such as catechumens. **Unbelievers (apistoi):** he has shifted from the inner-community perspective of v 22; the term here designates non-Christians (cf 6, 6; 7, 15; 10, 27).

14, 26–33a: Paul concludes with specific directives regarding exercise of the gifts in their assemblies. Verse 26 enunciates the basic criterion in the use of any gift: it must contribute to "building up."

14, 33b–36: Verse 33b may belong with what precedes, so that the new paragraph would begin only with v 34. Verses 34–35 change the subject. These two verses have the theme of submission in common with ch 11, despite differences in vocabulary, and a concern with what is or is not becoming; but it is difficult to harmonize the injunction to silence here with ch 11, which appears to take it for granted that women do pray and prophesy aloud in the assembly (cf 11, 5.13). Hence the verses are often considered an interpolation, reflecting the discipline of later churches; such an interpolation would have to have antedated our manuscripts, all of which contain them, though some transpose them to the very end of the chapter.

j: Mt 10, 16; Rom 16, 19; Eph 4, 14.   *k:* Is 28, 11-12; Dt 28. 49.   *l:* Acts 2, 6.13.   *m:* 4, 5 / Is 45, 14; Zec 8, 23.   *n:* Eph 4, 12.   *o:* 1 Tm 2, 11-15; 1 Pt 3, 1.

they should ask their husbands at home. For it is improper for a woman to speak in the church. *36*Did the word of God go forth from you? Or has it come to you alone?

*37*If anyone thinks that he is a prophet or a spiritual person, he should recognize that what I am writing to you is a commandment of the Lord. *38*If anyone does not acknowledge this, he is not acknowledged. *39*So, [my] brothers, strive eagerly to prophesy, and do not forbid speaking in tongues, *40*but everything must be done properly and in order.

V: The Resurrection
A. The Resurrection of Christ

CHAPTER 15

See RG 371-72

The Gospel Teaching. *1**Now I am reminding you, brothers, of the gospel I preached to you, which you indeed received and in which you also stand. *2*Through it you are also being saved, if you hold fast to the word I preached to you, unless you believed in vain. *3 p**For I handed on to you as of first importance what I also received: that Christ died for our sins in accordance with the scriptures; *4 q*that he was buried; that he was raised on the third day in accordance with the scriptures; *5 r*that he appeared to Cephas, then to the Twelve. *6*After that, he appeared to more than five hundred brothers at once, most of whom are still living, though some have fallen asleep. *7*After that he appeared to James, then to all the apostles. *8 s*Last of all, as to one born abnormally, he appeared to me. *9 t**For I am the least of the apostles, not fit to be called an apostle, because I persecuted the church of God. *10*But by the grace of God I am what I am, and his grace to me has not been ineffective. Indeed, I have toiled harder than all of them; not I, however, but the grace of God [that is] with me. *11*Therefore, whether it be I or they, so we preach and so you believed.

B. The Resurrection of the Dead

Results of Denial. *12**But if Christ is preached as raised from the dead, how can some among you say there is no resurrection of the dead? *13 u*If there is no resurrection of the dead, then neither has Christ been raised. *14*And if Christ has not been raised, then empty [too] is our preaching; empty, too, your faith. *15 v*Then we are also false witnesses to God, because we testified against God that he raised Christ, whom he did not raise if in fact the dead are not raised. *16*For if the dead are not raised, nei-

15, 1–58: Some consider this chapter an earlier Pauline composition inserted into the present letter. The problem that Paul treats is clear to a degree: some of the Corinthians are denying the resurrection of the dead (12), apparently because of their inability to imagine how any kind of bodily existence could be possible after death (35). It is plausibly supposed that their attitude stems from Greek anthropology, which looks with contempt upon matter and would be content with the survival of the soul, and perhaps also from an overrealized eschatology of gnostic coloration, such as that reflected in 2 Tm 2, 18, which considers the resurrection a purely spiritual experience already achieved in baptism and in the forgiveness of sins. Paul, on the other hand, will affirm both the essential corporeity of the resurrection and its futurity.

His response moves through three steps: a recall of the basic kerygma about Jesus' resurrection (1–11), an assertion of the logical inconsistencies involved in denial of the resurrection (12–34), and an attempt to perceive theologically what the properties of the resurrected body must be (35–58).

15, 1–11: Paul recalls the tradition (3–7), which he can presuppose as common ground and which provides a starting point for his argument. This is the fundamental content of all Christian preaching and belief (1–2.11).

15, 3–7: The language by which Paul expresses the essence of the "gospel" (1) is not his own but is drawn from older credal formulas. This credo highlights Jesus' death for

our sins (confirmed by his burial) and Jesus' resurrection (confirmed by his appearances) and presents both of them as fulfillment of prophecy. **In accordance with the scriptures:** conformity of Jesus' passion with the scriptures is asserted in Mt 16, 1; Lk 24, 25–27.32.44–46. Application of some Old Testament texts (Pss 2, 7; 16, 8–11) to his resurrection is illustrated by Acts 2, 27–31; 13, 29–39; and Is 52, 13—53, 12 and Hos 6, 2 may also have been envisaged.

15, 9–11: A persecutor may have appeared disqualified (**ouk . . . hikanos**) from apostleship, but in fact God's grace has qualified him. Cf the remarks in 2 Cor about his qualifications (2, 16; 3, 5) and his greater labors (11, 23). These verses are parenthetical, but a nerve has been touched (the references to his abnormal birth and his activity as a persecutor may echo taunts from Paul's opponents), and he is instinctively moved to self-defense.

15, 12–19: Denial of the resurrection (12) involves logical inconsistencies. The basic one, stated twice (13.16), is that if there is no such thing as (bodily) resurrection, then it has not taken place even in Christ's case.

p: 11, 23 / 1 Pt 2, 24; 3, 18 / Is 53, 4-12. *q:* Acts 2, 23-24 / Ps 16, 8-11; Hos 6, 1-2; Jon 2, 1. *r:* Mk 16, 14; Mt 28, 16-17; Lk 24, 36; Jn 20, 19. *s:* 9, 1; Acts 9, 3-6; Gal 1, 16. *t:* Acts 8, 3; 9, 1-2; Gal 1, 23; Eph 3, 8; 1 Tm 1, 15. *u:* 1 Thes 4, 14. *v:* Acts 5, 32.

ther has Christ been raised, [17]*and if Christ has not been raised, your faith is vain; you are still in your sins. [18]Then those who have fallen asleep in Christ have perished. [19]If for this life only we have hoped in Christ, we are the most pitiable people of all.

Christ the Firstfruits. [20w]*But now Christ has been raised from the dead, the firstfruits of those who have fallen asleep. [21]*For since death came through a human being, the resurrection of the dead came also through a human being. [22x]For just as in Adam all die, so too in Christ shall all be brought to life, [23y]but each one in proper order: Christ the firstfruits; then, at his coming, those who belong to Christ; [24z]*then comes the end, when he hands over the kingdom to his God and Father, when he has destroyed every sovereignty and every authority and power. [25a]For he must reign until he has put all his enemies under his feet. [26b]*The last enemy to be destroyed is death, [27c]*for "he subjected everything under his feet." But when it says that everything has been subjected, it is clear that it excludes the one who subjected everything to him. [28d]When everything is subjected to him, then the Son himself will [also] be subjected to the one who subjected everything to him, so that God may be all in all.

Practical Arguments. [29]*Otherwise, what will people accomplish by having themselves baptized for the dead? If the dead are not raised at all, then why are they having themselves baptized for them?

[30e]*Moreover, why are we endangering ourselves all the time? [31f]Every day I face death; I swear it by the pride in you [brothers] that I have in Christ Jesus our Lord. [32g]If at Ephesus I fought with beasts, so to speak, what benefit was it to me? If the dead are not raised:

"Let us eat and drink,
for tomorrow we die."

[33]Do not be led astray:

"Bad company corrupts good morals."

15, 17–18: The consequences for the Corinthians are grave: both forgiveness of sins and salvation are an illusion, despite their strong convictions about both. Unless Christ is risen, their faith does not save.

15, 20–28: After a triumphant assertion of the reality of Christ's resurrection (20a), Paul explains its positive implications and consequences. As a soteriological event of both human (20–23) and cosmic (24–28) dimensions, Jesus' resurrection logically and necessarily involves ours as well.

15, 20: The firstfruits: the portion of the harvest offered in thanksgiving to God implies the consecration of the entire harvest to come. Christ's resurrection is not an end in itself; its finality lies in the whole harvest, ourselves.

15, 21–22: Our human existence, both natural and supernatural, is corporate, involves solidarity. **In Adam . . . in Christ:** the Hebrew word 'ādām in Genesis is both a common noun for mankind and a proper noun for the first man. Paul here presents Adam as at least a literary type of Christ; the parallelism and contrast between them will be developed further in vv 45–49 and in Rom 5, 12–21.

15, 24–28: Paul's perspective expands to cosmic dimensions, as he describes the climax of history, **the end.** His viewpoint is still christological, as in vv 20–23. Verses 24 and 28 describe Christ's final relations to his enemies and his Father in language that is both royal and military; vv 25–28 insert a proof from scripture (Pss 110, 1; 8, 7) into this description. But the viewpoint is also theological, for God is the ultimate agent and end, and likewise soteriological, for we are the beneficiaries of all the action.

15, 26: The last enemy . . . is death: a parenthesis that specifies the final fulfillment of the two Old Testament texts just referred to, Ps 110, 1 and Ps 8, 7. Death is not just one cosmic power among many, but the ultimate effect of sin in the universe (cf 56; Rom 5, 12). Christ defeats death where it prevails, in our bodies. The destruction of the last enemy is concretely the "coming to life" (22) of "those who belong to Christ" (23).

15, 27b–28: The one who subjected everything to him: the Father is the ultimate agent in the drama, and the final end of the process, to whom the Son and everything else is ordered (24.28). **That God may be all in all:** his reign is a dynamic exercise of creative power, an outpouring of life and energy through the universe, with no further resistance. This is the supremely positive meaning of "subjection": that God may fully be God.

15, 29–34: Paul concludes his treatment of logical inconsistencies with a listing of miscellaneous Christian practices that would be meaningless if the resurrection were not a fact.

15, 29: Baptized for the dead: this practice is not further explained here, nor is it necessarily mentioned with approval, but Paul cites it as something in their experience that attests in one more way to belief in the resurrection.

15, 30–34: A life of sacrifice, such as Paul describes in 4, 9–13 and 2 Cor, would be pointless without the prospect of resurrection; a life of pleasure, such as that expressed in the Epicurean slogan of v 32, would be far more consistent. **I fought with beasts:** since Paul does not elsewhere mention a combat with beasts at Ephesus, he may be speaking figuratively about struggles with adversaries.

---

w: Rom 8, 11; Col 1, 18; 1 Thes 4, 14.   x: Gn 3, 17-19; Rom 5, 12-19.   y: 1 Thes 4, 15-17.   z: Eph 1, 22.   a: Ps 110, 1.
b: Rom 6, 9; 2 Tm 1, 10; Rv 20, 14; 21, 4.   c: Ps 8, 7; Eph , 22; Phil 3, 21.   d: Eph 4, 6; Col 3, 11.   e: 2 Cor 4, 8-12; 11, 23-27.
f: Ps 44, 23; Rom 8, 36.   g: 4, 9; 2 Cor 4, 10-11 / Wis 2, 5-7; Is 22, 13.

34h Become sober as you ought and stop sinning. For some have no knowledge of God; I say this to your shame.

C. The Manner of the Resurrection

35*But someone may say, "How are the dead raised? With what kind of body will they come back?"

The Resurrection Body. 36i*You fool! What you sow is not brought to life unless it dies. 37And what you sow is not the body that is to be but a bare kernel of wheat, perhaps, or of some other kind; 38jbut God gives it a body as he chooses, and to each of the seeds its own body. 39*Not all flesh is the same, but there is one kind for human beings, another kind of flesh for animals, another kind of flesh for birds, and another for fish. 40There are both heavenly bodies and earthly bodies, but the brightness of the heavenly is one kind and that of the earthly another. 41The brightness of the sun is one kind, the brightness of the moon another, and the brightness of the stars another. For star differs from star in brightness.

42*So also is the resurrection of the dead. It is sown corruptible; it is raised incorruptible. 43kIt is sown dishonorable; it is raised glorious. It is sown weak; it is raised powerful. 44It is sown a natural body; it is raised a spiritual body. If there is a natural body, there is also a spiritual one.

45l*So, too, it is written, "The first man, Adam, became a living being," the last Adam a life-giving spirit. 46But the spiritual was not first; rather the natural and then the spiritual. 47The first man was from the earth, earthly; the second man, from heaven. 48As was the earthly one, so also are the earthly, and as is the heavenly one, so also are the heavenly. 49m*Just as we have borne the image of the earthly one, we shall also bear the image of the heavenly one.

The Resurrection Event. 50n*This I declare, brothers: flesh and blood cannot inherit the kingdom of God, nor does corruption inherit incorruption. 51o*Behold, I tell you a mystery. We shall not all fall asleep,

15, 35–58: Paul imagines two objections that the Corinthians could raise: one concerning the manner of the resurrection (**how?**), the other pertaining to the qualities of the risen body (**what kind?**). These questions probably lie behind their denial of the resurrection (12), and seem to reflect the presumption that no kind of body other than the one we now possess would be possible. Paul deals with these objections in inverse order, in vv 36–49 and vv 50–58. His argument is fundamentally theological and its appeal is to the understanding.

15, 35–49: Paul approaches the question of the nature of the risen body (**what kind of body?**) by means of two analogies: the seed (36–44) and the first man, Adam (45–49).

15, 36–38: The analogy of the seed: there is a change of attributes from seed to plant; the old life-form must be lost for the new to emerge. By speaking about the seed as a **body** that dies and comes to life, Paul keeps the point of the analogy before the reader's mind.

15, 39–41: The expression "its own body" (38) leads to a development on the marvelous diversity evident in bodily life.

15, 42–44: The principles of qualitative difference before and after death (36–38) and of diversity on different levels of creation (39–41) are now applied to the human body. Before: a body animated by a lower, natural life-principle (**psyche**) and endowed with the properties of natural existence (corruptibility, lack of glory, weakness). After: a body animated by a higher life-principle (**pneuma**; cf 45) and endowed with other qualities (incorruptibility, glory, power, spirituality), which are properties of God himself.

15, 45: The analogy of **the first man, Adam,** is introduced by a citation from Gn 2, 7. Paul alters the text slightly, adding the adjective **first,** and translating the Hebrew

'adam twice, so as to give it its value both as a common noun (**man**) and as a proper name (**Adam**). Verse 45b then specifies similarities and differences between the two Adams. **The last Adam,** Christ (cf 21–22) has become **a . . . spirit** (**pneuma**), a life-principle transcendent with respect to the natural soul (**psyche**) of the first Adam (on the terminology here, cf the note on 3, 1). Further, he is not just alive, but **life-giving,** a source of life for others.

15, 49: We shall also bear the image: although it has less manuscript support, this reading better fits the context's emphasis on futurity and the transforming action of God; on future transformation as conformity to the image of the Son, cf Rom 8, 29; Phil 3, 21. The majority reading, "let us bear the image," suggests that the image of the heavenly man is already present and exhorts us to conform to it.

15, 50–57: These verses, an answer to the first question of v 35, explain theologically how the change of properties from one image to another will take place: God has the power to transform, and he will exercise it.

15, 50–53: Flesh and blood . . . corruption: living persons and the corpses of the dead, respectively. In both cases, the gulf between creatures and God is too wide to be bridged unless God himself transforms us.

15, 51–52: A mystery: the last moment in God's plan is disclosed; cf the notes on 2, 1.7–10a. The final trumpet and the awakening of the dead are stock details of the apocalyptic scenario. **We shall not all fall asleep:** Paul expected that some of

h: Mt 22, 29; Mk 12, 24. i: Jn 12, 24. j: Gn 1, 11. k: Phil 3, 20-21; Col 3, 4. l: Gn 2, 7 / Jn 5, 21-29; 2 Cor 3, 6.17. m: Gn 5, 3 / Rom 8, 29; Phil 3, 21. n: Jn 3, 3-6. o: 1 Thes 4, 14-17.

but we will all be changed, [52p]in an instant, in the blink of an eye, at the last trumpet. For the trumpet will sound, the dead will be raised incorruptible, and we shall be changed. [53q]For that which is corruptible must clothe itself with incorruptibility, and that which is mortal must clothe itself with immortality. [54r*]And when this which is corruptible clothes itself with incorruptibility and this which is mortal clothes itself with immortality, then the word that is written shall come about:

"Death is swallowed up in victory.
[55] [s]Where, O death, is your victory?
Where, O death, is your sting?"

[56t*]The sting of death is sin, and the power of sin is the law. [57u]But thanks be to God who gives us the victory through our Lord Jesus Christ.

[58]Therefore, my beloved brothers, be firm, steadfast, always fully devoted to the work of the Lord, knowing that in the Lord your labor is not in vain.

VI: Conclusion

CHAPTER 16

See RG 372

The Collection. [1v*]Now in regard to the collection for the holy ones, you also should do as I ordered the churches of Galatia. [2]On the first day of the week each of you should set aside and save whatever he can afford, so that collections will not be going on when I come. [3]And when I arrive, I shall send those whom you have approved with letters of recommendation to take your gracious gift to Jerusalem. [4*]If it seems fitting that I should go also, they will go with me.

Paul's Travel Plans. [5w*]I shall come to you after I pass through Macedonia (for I am going to pass through Macedonia), [6]and perhaps I shall stay or even spend the winter with you, so that you may send me on my way wherever I may go. [7x]For I do not wish to see you now just in passing, but I hope to spend some time with you, if the Lord permits. [8y*]I shall stay in Ephesus until Pentecost, [9z]because a door has opened for me wide and productive for work, but there are many opponents.

[10a]If Timothy comes, see that he is without fear in your company, for he is doing the work of the Lord just as I am. [11]Therefore, no one should disdain him. Rather, send him on his way in peace that he may come to me, for I am expecting him with the brothers. [12b]Now in regard to our brother Apollos, I urged him strongly to go to you with the brothers, but it was not at all his will that he go now. He will go when he has an opportunity.

Exhortation and Greetings. [13]Be on your guard, stand firm in the faith, be courageous, be strong. [14]Your every act should be done with love.

[15c]I urge you, brothers—you know that the household of Stephanas is the firstfruits of Achaia and that they have devoted them-

---

his contemporaries might still be alive at Christ's return; after the death of Paul and his whole generation, copyists altered this statement in various ways. **We will all be changed:** the statement extends to all Christians, for Paul is not directly speaking about anyone else. Whether they have died before the end or happen still to be alive, all must be transformed.

15, 54–55: Death is swallowed up in victory: scripture itself predicts death's overthrow. **O death:** in his prophetic vision Paul may be making Hosea's words his own, or imagining this cry of triumph on the lips of the risen church.

15, 56: The sting of death is sin: an explanation of Hosea's metaphor. Death, scorpion-like, is equipped with a sting, sin, by which it injects its poison. Christ defeats sin, the cause of death (Gn 3, 19; Rom 5, 12).

16, 1–4: This paragraph contains our earliest evidence for a project that became a major undertaking of Paul's ministry. The collection for the church at Jerusalem was a symbol in his mind for the unity of Jewish and Gentile Christianity. Cf Gal 2, 10; Rom 15, 25–29; 2 Cor 8–9 and the notes to this last passage.

16, 1: In regard to the collection: it has already begun in Galatia and Macedonia (cf 2 Cor 8), and presumably he has already instructed the Corinthians about its purpose.

16, 4: That I should go also: presumably Paul delivered the collection on his final visit to Jerusalem; cf Rom 15, 25–32; Acts 24, 14.

16, 5–12: The travel plans outlined here may not have materialized precisely as Paul intended; cf 2 Cor 1, 8–2, 13; 7, 4–16.

16, 8: In Ephesus until Pentecost: this tells us the place from which he wrote the letter and suggests he may have composed it about Easter time (cf 5, 7–8).

p: Jl 2, 1; Zec 9, 14; Mt 24, 31; Rv 11, 15-18.   *q:* 2 Cor 5, 2-4.   *r:* Is 25, 8; 2 Cor 5, 4; 2 Tm 1, 10; Heb 2, 14-15.   *s:* Hos 13, 14.   *t:* Rom 4, 15; 7, 7.13.   *u:* Jn 16, 33; 1 Jn 5, 4.   *v:* Acts 24, 17; Rom 15, 25-32; 2 Cor 8-9; Gal 2, 10.   *w:* Acts 19, 21; Rom 15, 26; 2 Cor 1, 15-16.   *x:* Acts 18, 21.   *y:* 15, 32; Acts 18, 19; 19, 1-10.   *z:* Acts 14, 27; 2 Cor 2, 12.   *a:* 4, 17; Acts 16, 1; 19, 22; Phil 2, 19-23.   *b:* 1, 12; 3, 4-6.22; Acts 18, 24-28.   *c:* 1, 16.

selves to the service of the holy ones— [16]be subordinate to such people and to everyone who works and toils with them. [17]I rejoice in the arrival of Stephanas, Fortunatus, and Achaicus, because they made up for your absence, [18d]for they refreshed my spirit as well as yours. So give recognition to such people.

[19e]*The churches of Asia send you greetings. Aquila and Prisca together with the church at their house send you many greetings in the Lord. [20f]All the brothers greet you. Greet one another with a holy kiss.

[21g]I, Paul, write you this greeting in my own hand. [22h]*If anyone does not love the Lord, let him be accursed. *Marana tha.* [23i]The grace of the Lord Jesus be with you. [24]My love to all of you in Christ Jesus.

16, 19–24: These paragraphs conform to the normal epistolary conclusion, but their language is overlaid with liturgical coloration as well. The **greetings** of the Asian churches are probably to be read, along with the letter, in the liturgy at Corinth, and the union of the church is to be expressed by a **holy kiss** (19–20). Paul adds to this his own greeting (21) and blessings (23–24).

16, 22: *Accursed:* literally, "anathema." This expression (cf 12, 3) is a formula for exclusion from the community; it may imply here a call to self-examination before celebration of the Eucharist, in preparation for the Lord's coming and judgment (cf 11, 17–34). **Marana tha:** an Aramaic expression, probably used in the early Christian liturgy. As understood here ("O Lord, come!"), it is a prayer for the early return of Christ. If the Aramaic words are divided differently (**Maran atha,** "Our Lord has come"), it becomes a credal declaration. The former interpretation is supported by what appears to be a Greek equivalent of this acclamation in Rv 22, 20: "Amen. Come, Lord Jesus!"

---

d: 1 Thes 5, 12-13. *e:* Acts 18, 2.18.26; Rom 16, 3-5. *f:* Rom 16, 16; 2 Cor 13, 12; 1 Thes 5, 26; 1 Pt 5, 14. *g:* Gal 6, 11; Col 4, 18; 2 Thes 3, 17. *h:* 12, 3; Rom 9, 3; Gal 1, 8-9; Rv 22, 20. *i:* Rom 16, 20.

See RG 375–82

The Second Letter to the Corinthians

The Second Letter to the Corinthians is the most personal of all of Paul's extant writings, and it reveals much about his character. In it he deals with one or more crises that have arisen in the Corinthian church. The confrontation with these problems caused him to reflect deeply on his relationship with the community and to speak about it frankly. One moment he is venting his feelings of frustration and uncertainty, the next he is pouring out his relief and affection. The importance of the issues at stake between them calls forth from him an enormous effort of personal persuasion, as well as doctrinal considerations that are of great value for us. Paul's ability to produce profound theological foundations for what may at first sight appear to be rather commonplace circumstances is perhaps nowhere better exemplified than in Second Corinthians. The emotional tone of the letter, its lack of order, and our ignorance of some of its background do not make it easy to follow, but it amply repays the effort required of the reader.

Second Corinthians is rich and varied in content. The interpretation of Exodus in chapter 3, for instance, offers a striking example of early apologetic use of the Old Testament. Paul's discussion of the collection in chs 8–9 contains a theology of sharing of possessions, of community of goods among Christian churches, which is both balanced and sensitive. Furthermore, the closing chapters provide an illustration of early Christian invective and polemic, because the conflict with intruders forces Paul to assert his authority. But in those same chapters Paul articulates the vision and sense of values that animate his own apostolate, revealing his faith that Jesus' passion and resurrection are the pattern for all Christian life and expressing a spirituality of ministry unsurpassed in the New Testament.

The letter is remarkable for its rhetoric. Paul falls naturally into the style and argumentation of contemporary philosophic preachers, employing with ease the stock devices of the "diatribe." By a barrage of questions, by challenges both serious and ironic, by paradox heaped upon paradox, even by insults hurled at his opponents, he strives to awaken in his hearers a true sense of values and an appropriate response. All his argument centers on the destiny of Jesus, in which a paradoxical reversal of values is revealed. But Paul appeals to his own personal experience as well. In passages of great rhetorical power (4, 7–15; 6, 3–10; 11, 21–29; 12, 5–10; 13, 3–4) he enumerates the circumstances of his ministry and the tribulations he has had to endure for Jesus and the gospel, in the hope of illustrating the pattern of Jesus' existence in his own and of drawing the Corinthians into a reappraisal of the values they cherish. Similar passages in the same style in his other letters (cf especially Rom 8, 31–39; 1 Cor 1, 26–31; 4, 6–21; 9, 1–27; 13, 1–13; Phil 4, 10–19) confirm Paul's familiarity with contemporary rhetoric and demonstrate how effectively it served to express his vision of Christian life and ministry.

Second Corinthians was occasioned by events and problems that developed after Paul's first letter reached Corinth. We have no information about these circumstances except what is contained in the letter itself, which of course supposes that they are known to the readers. Consequently the reconstruction of the letter's background is an uncertain enterprise about which there is not complete agreement.

The letter deals principally with these three topics: (1) a crisis between Paul and the Corinthians, occasioned at least partially by changes in his travel plans (1, 12—2, 13), and the successful resolution of that crisis (7, 5–16); (2) further directives and encouragement in regard to the collection for the church in Jerusalem (8, 1—9, 15); (3) the definition and defense of Paul's ministry as an apostle. Paul's reflections on this matter are occasioned by visitors from other churches who passed through Corinth, missionaries who differed from Paul in a variety of ways, both in theory and in practice. Those differences led to comparisons. Either the visitors themselves or some of the local church members appear to have sown confusion among the Corinthians with regard to Paul's authority or his style, or both. Paul deals at length with aspects of this situation in 2, 14—7, 4 and again in 10, 1—13, 10, though the manner of treatment and the thrust of the argument differ in each of these sections.

Scholars have noticed a lack of continuity in this document. For example, the long section of 2, 14—7, 4 seems abruptly spliced into the narrative of a crisis and its resolution. Identical or similar topics, moreover, seem to be treated several times during the letter (compare 2, 14—7, 4 with 10, 1—13, 10, and 8, 1–24 with 9, 1–15). Many judge, therefore, that this letter as it stands incorporates several briefer letters sent to Corinth over a certain span of time. If this is so, then Paul himself or, more likely, some other editor clearly took care to gather those letters together and impose some literary unity upon the collection, thus producing the document that has come down to us as the Second Letter to the Corinthians. Others continue to regard it as a single letter, attributing its inconsistencies to changes of perspective in Paul that may have been occasioned by the arrival of fresh news from Corinth during its composition. The letter, or at least some sections of it, appears to have been composed in Macedonia (2, 12–13; 7, 5–6; 8, 1–4; 9, 2–4). It is generally dated about the autumn of A.D. 57; if it is a compilation, of course, the various parts may have been separated by intervals of at least some months.

The principal divisions of the Second Letter to the Corinthians are the following:

I: Address (1, 1–11)
II: The Crisis between Paul and the Corinthians (1, 12—7, 16)
  A: Past Relationships (1, 12—2, 13)
  B: Paul's Ministry (2, 14—7, 4)
  C: Resolution of the Crisis (7, 5–16)
III: The Collection for Jerusalem (8, 1—9, 15)
IV: Paul's Defense of His Ministry (10, 1—13, 10)
V: Conclusion (13, 11–13)

I: Address

CHAPTER 1

See RG 376–77

Greeting. [1a]*Paul, an apostle of Christ Jesus by the will of God, and Timothy our brother, to the church of God that is in Corinth, with all the holy ones throughout Achaia: [2]grace to you and peace from God our Father and the Lord Jesus Christ.

1, 1–11: The opening follows the usual Pauline form, except that the thanksgiving takes the form of a doxology or glorification of God (3). This introduces a meditation on the experience of suffering and encouragement shared by Paul and the Corinthians (4–7), drawn, at least in part, from Paul's reflections on a recent affliction (8–10). The section ends with a modified and delayed allusion to thanksgiving (11).

---

a: Eph 1, 1; Col 1, 1 / 1, 19; Acts 16 / Rom 1, 7; 1 Cor 1, 2.

Thanksgiving. *3b**Blessed be the God and Father of our Lord Jesus Christ, the Father of compassion and God of all encouragement, *4c*who encourages us in our every affliction, so that we may be able to encourage those who are in any affliction with the encouragement with which we ourselves are encouraged by God. *5**For as Christ's sufferings overflow to us, so through Christ does our encouragement also overflow. *6*If we are afflicted, it is for your encouragement and salvation; if we are encouraged, it is for your encouragement, which enables you to endure the same sufferings that we suffer. *7**Our hope for you is firm, for we know that as you share in the sufferings, you also share in the encouragement.

8d*We do not want you to be unaware, brothers, of the affliction that came to us in the province of Asia; we were utterly weighed down beyond our strength, so that we despaired even of life. *9e**Indeed, we had accepted within ourselves the sentence of death, that we might trust not in ourselves but in God who raises the dead. *10f*He rescued us from such great danger of death, and he will continue to rescue us; in him we have put our hope [that] he will also rescue us again, *11g*as you help us with prayer, so that thanks may be given by many on our behalf for the gift granted us through the prayers of many.

II: The Crisis Between Paul and the Corinthians
A. Past Relationships

Paul's Sincerity and Constancy. *12**For our boast is this, the testimony of our conscience that we have conducted ourselves in the world, and especially toward you, with the simplicity and sincerity of God, [and] not by human wisdom but by the grace of God. *13*For we write you nothing but what you can read and understand, and I hope that you will understand completely, *14h*as you have come to understand us partially, that we are your boast as you also are ours, on the day of [our] Lord Jesus.

15*With this confidence I formerly intended to come to you so that you might receive a double favor, *16*namely, to go by way of you to Macedonia, and then to come to you again on my return from Macedonia, and have you send me on my way to Judea. *17j**So when I intended this, did I act lightly?

1, 3: God of all encouragement: Paul expands a standard Jewish blessing so as to state the theme of the paragraph. The theme of "encouragement" or "consolation" (**paraklēsis**) occurs ten times in this opening, against a background formed by multiple references to "affliction" and "suffering."

1, 5: Through Christ: the Father of compassion is the Father of our Lord Jesus (3); Paul's sufferings and encouragement (or "consolation") are experienced in union with Christ. Cf Lk 2, 25: the "consolation of Israel" is Jesus himself.

1, 7: You also share in the encouragement: the eschatological reversal of affliction and encouragement that Christians expect (cf Mt 5, 4; Lk 6, 24) permits some present experience of reversal in the Corinthians' case, as in Paul's.

1, 8: Asia: a Roman province in western Asia Minor, the capital of which was Ephesus.

1, 9–10: The sentence of death: it is unclear whether Paul is alluding to a physical illness or to an external threat to life. The result of the situation was to produce an attitude of faith in God alone. **God who raises the dead:** rescue is the constant pattern of God's activity; his final act of encouragement is the resurrection.

1, 12–2, 13: The autobiographical remarks about the crisis in Asia Minor lead into consideration of a crisis that has arisen between Paul and the Corinthians. Paul will return to this question, after a long digression, in 7, 5–16. Both of these sections deal with travel plans Paul had made, changes in the plans, alternative measures adopted, a breach that opened between him and the community, and finally a reconciliation between them.

1, 12–14: Since Paul's own conduct will be under discussion here, he prefaces the section with a statement about his habitual behavior and attitude toward the community. He protests his openness, single-mindedness, and conformity to God's grace; he hopes that his relationship with them will be marked by mutual understanding and pride, which will constantly increase until it reaches its climax at the judgment. Two references to boasting frame this paragraph (12.14), the first appearances of a theme that will be important in the letter, especially in chs 10–13; the term is used in a positive sense (cf the note on 1 Cor 1, 29–31).

1, 15: I formerly intended to come: this plan reads like a revision of the one mentioned in 1 Cor 16, 5. Not until 1, 23–2, 1 will Paul tell us something his original readers already knew, that he has canceled one or the other of these projected visits.

1, 17: Did I act lightly?: the subsequent change of plans casts suspicion on the original intention, creating the impression that Paul is vacillating and inconsistent or that **human**

b: 1 Cor 15, 24; Eph 1, 3; 1 Pt 1, 3 / Rom 15, 5. *c*: 7, 6-7.13; 1 Thes 3, 6-8; 2 Thes 2, 16. *d*: Acts 20, 18-19; 1 Cor 15, 32. *e*: 4, 7-11; Rom 4, 17. *f*: 2 Tm 4, 18. *g*: 4, 15; 9, 12. *h*: Phil 2, 16; 1 Thes 2, 19-20. *i*: 1 Cor 16, 5-9; Acts 19, 21. *j*: Mt 5, 37; Jas 5, 12.

Or do I make my plans according to human considerations, so that with me it is "yes, yes" and "no, no"? *18**As God is faithful, our word to you is not "yes" and "no." *19k*For the Son of God, Jesus Christ, who was proclaimed to you by us, Silvanus and Timothy and me, was not "yes" and "no," but "yes" has been in him. *20l*For however many are the promises of God, their Yes is in him; therefore, the Amen from us also goes through him to God for glory. *21m**But the one who gives us security with you in Christ and who anointed us is God; *22n*he has also put his seal upon us and given the Spirit in our hearts as a first installment.

Paul's Change of Plan. *23o**But I call upon God as witness, on my life, that it is to spare you that I have not yet gone to Corinth. *24*Not that we lord it over your faith; rather, we work together for your joy, for you stand firm in the faith.

See RG 377–78

CHAPTER 2

*1*For I decided not to come to you again in painful circumstances. *2*For if I inflict pain upon you, then who is there to cheer me except the one pained by me? *3**And I wrote as I did so that when I came I might not be pained by those in whom I should have rejoiced, confident about all of you that my joy is that of all of you. *4*For out of much affliction and anguish of heart I wrote to you with many tears, not that you might be pained but that you might know the abundant love I have for you.

The Offender. *5**If anyone has caused pain, he has caused it not to me, but in some measure (not to exaggerate) to all of you. *6*This punishment by the majority is enough for such a person, *7p*so that on the contrary you should forgive and encourage him instead, or else the person may be overwhelmed by excessive pain. *8*Therefore, I urge you to reaffirm your love for him. *9q*For this is why I wrote, to know your proven character, whether you were obedient in everything. *10*Whomever you forgive anything, so do I. For indeed what I have forgiven, if I have forgiven anything, has been for you in the presence of Christ, *11r*so that

---

considerations keep dictating shifts in his goals and projects (cf the counterclaim of 12). **"Yes, yes" and "no, no":** stating something and denying it in the same or the next breath; being of two minds at once, or from one moment to the next.

1, 18–22: As God is faithful: unable to deny the change in plans, Paul nonetheless asserts the firmness of the original plan and claims a profound constancy in his life and work. He grounds his defense in God himself, who is firm and reliable; this quality can also be predicated in various ways of those who are associated with him. Christ, Paul, and the Corinthians all participate in analogous ways in the constancy of God. A number of the terms here, which appear related only conceptually in Greek or English, would be variations of the same root, 'mn, in a Semitic language, and thus naturally associated in a Semitic mind, such as Paul's. These include the words **yes** (17–20), **faithful** (18), **Amen** (20), **gives us security** (21), **faith, stand firm** (24).

1, 21–22: The commercial terms **gives us security, seal, first installment** are here used analogously to refer to the process of initiation into the Christian life, perhaps specifically to baptism. The passage is clearly trinitarian. The Spirit is the **first installment** or "down payment" of the full messianic benefits that God guarantees to Christians. Cf Eph 1, 13–14.

1, 23–24: I have not yet gone to Corinth: some suppose that Paul received word of some affair in Corinth, which he decided to regulate by letter even before the first of his projected visits (cf 16). Others conjecture that he did pay the first visit, was offended there (cf 2, 5), returned to Ephesus, and sent a letter (2, 3–9) in place of the second visit. The expressions **to spare you** (23) and **work together for your joy** (24)

introduce the major themes of the next two paragraphs, which are remarkable for insistent repetition of key words and ideas. These form two clusters of terms in the English translation: (1) cheer, rejoice, encourage, joy; (2) pain, affliction, anguish. These clusters reappear when Paul resumes treatment of this subject in 7, 5–16.

2, 3–4: I wrote as I did: we learn for the first time about the sending of a letter in place of the proposed visit. Paul mentions the letter in passing, but emphasizes his motivation in sending it: to avoid being saddened by them (cf 1), and to help them realize the depth of his love. Another motive will be added in 7, 12: to bring to light their own concern for him. **With many tears:** it has been suggested that we may have all or part of this "tearful letter" somewhere in the Corinthian correspondence, either in 1 Cor 5 (the case of the incestuous man), or in 1 Cor as a whole, or in 2 Cor 10–13. None of these hypotheses is entirely convincing. See the note on 13, 1.

2, 5–11: The nature of the **pain** (5) is unclear, though some believe an individual at Corinth rejected Paul's authority, thereby scandalizing many in the community. In any case, action has been taken, and Paul judges the measures adequate to right the situation (6). The follow-up directives he now gives are entirely positive: forgive, encourage, love. **Overwhelmed** (7): a vivid metaphor (literally "swallowed") that Paul employs positively at 5, 4 and in 1 Cor 15, 54 (7). It is often used to describe satanic activity (cf 1 Pt 5, 8); note the reference to Satan here in v 11.

---

k: Acts 16, 1-3; 1 Thes 1, 1; 2 Thes 1, 1. *l:* 1 Cor 14, 16; Rv 3, 14. *m:* 1 Jn 2, 20.27. *n:* Eph 1, 13-14; 4, 30 / 5, 5; Rom 5, 5; 8, 16.23. *o:* 13, 2. *p:* Col 3, 13. *q:* 7, 15. *r:* Eph 4, 27.

we might not be taken advantage of by Satan, for we are not unaware of his purposes.

Paul's Anxiety. [12s*]When I went to Troas for the gospel of Christ, although a door was opened for me in the Lord, [13t*]I had no relief in my spirit because I did not find my brother Titus. So I took leave of them and went on to Macedonia.

B. Paul's Ministry

Ministers of a New Covenant. [14*]But thanks be to God, who always leads us in triumph in Christ and manifests through us the odor of the knowledge of him in every place. [15u]For we are the aroma of Christ for God among those who are being saved and among those who are perishing, [16*]to the latter an odor of death that leads to death, to the former an odor of life that leads to life. Who is qualified for this? [17v]For we are not like the many who trade on the word of God; but as out of sincerity, indeed as from God and in the presence of God, we speak in Christ.

CHAPTER 3

See RG
378

[1w*]Are we beginning to commend ourselves again? Or do we need, as some do, letters of recommendation to you or from you? [2*]You are our letter, written on our hearts, known and read by all, [3x*]shown to

---

2, 12–13: I had no relief: Paul does not explain the reason for his anxiety until he resumes the thread of his narrative at 7, 5: he was waiting to hear how the Corinthians would respond to his letter. Since 7, 5–16 describes their response in entirely positive terms, we never learn in detail why he found it necessary to defend and justify his change of plans, as in 1, 15–24. Was this portion of the letter written before the arrival of Titus with his good news (7, 6–7)?

2, 13: Macedonia: a Roman province in northern Greece.

2, 14—7, 4: This section constitutes a digression within the narrative of the crisis and its resolution (1, 12—2, 13 and 7, 5–16). The main component (2, 14—6, 10) treats the nature of Paul's ministry and his qualifications for it; this material bears some similarity to the defense of his ministry in chs 10–13, but it may well come from a period close to the crisis. This is followed by a supplementary block of material quite different in character and tone (6, 14—7, 1). These materials may have been brought together into their present position during final editing of the letter; appeals to the Corinthians link them to one another (6, 11–13) and lead back to the interrupted narrative (7, 2–4).

2, 14—6, 10: The question of Paul's adequacy (16; cf 3, 5) and his credentials (3, 1–2) has been raised. Paul responds by an extended treatment of the nature of his ministry. It is a ministry of glory (3, 7—4, 6), of life (4, 7—5, 10), of reconciliation (5, 11—6, 10).

2, 14–16a: The initial statement plunges us abruptly into another train of thought. Paul describes his personal existence and his function as a preacher in two powerful images (14) that constitute a prelude to the development to follow.

2, 14a: Leads us in triumph in Christ: this metaphor of a festive parade in honor of a conquering military hero can suggest either a positive sharing in Christ's triumph or an experience of defeat, being led in captivity and submission (cf 4, 8–11; 1 Cor 4, 9). Paul is probably aware of the ambiguity, as he is in the case of the next metaphor.

2, 14b-16a: The odor of the knowledge of him: incense was commonly used in triumphal processions. The metaphor suggests the gradual diffusion of the knowledge of God through the apostolic preaching. **The aroma of Christ:** the image shifts from the fragrance Paul diffuses to the aroma that he is. Paul is probably thinking of the "sweet odor" of the sacrifices in the Old Testament (e.g., Gn 8, 21; Ex 29, 18) and per-

haps of the metaphor of wisdom as a sweet odor (Sir 24, 15). **Death . . . life:** the aroma of Christ that comes to them through Paul is perceived differently by various classes of people. To some his preaching and his life (cf 1 Cor 1, 17—2, 6) are perceived as **death,** and the effect is death for them; others perceive him, despite appearances, as **life,** and the effect is life for them. This fragrance thus produces a separation and a judgment (cf the function of the "light" in John's gospel).

2, 16b-17: Qualified: Paul may be echoing either the self-satisfied claims of other preachers or their charges about Paul's deficiencies. No one is really qualified, but the apostle contrasts himself with those who dilute or falsify the preaching for personal advantage and insists on his totally good conscience: his ministry is from God, and he has exercised it with fidelity and integrity (cf 3, 5–6).

3, 1: Paul seems to allude to certain preachers who pride themselves on their written credentials. Presumably they reproach him for not possessing similar credentials and compel him to spell out his own qualifications (4, 2; 5, 12; 6, 4). The Corinthians themselves should have performed this function for Paul (5, 12; cf 12, 11). Since he is forced to find something that can recommend him, he points to them: their very existence constitutes his **letter** of recommendation (1–2). Others who engage in self-commendation will also be mentioned in 10, 12–18.

3, 2–3: Mention of "letters of recommendation" generates a series of metaphors in which Paul plays on the word "letter": (1) the community is Paul's letter of recommendation (2a); (2) they are a letter engraved on his affections for all to see and read (2b); (3) they are a letter from Christ that Paul merely delivers (3a); (4) they are a letter written by the Spirit on the tablets of human hearts (3b). One image dissolves into another.

3, 3b: This verse contrasts Paul's letter with those **written . . . in ink** (like the credentials of other preachers) and those **written . . . on tablets of stone** (like the law of Moses). These contrasts suggest that the other preachers may have claimed special relationship with Moses. If they were Judaizers zealous for the Mosaic law, that would explain the detailed contrast between the old and the new covenants (6; 4, 7—6, 10). If they were charismatics who claimed Moses as their model,

s: Acts 16, 8. t: 7, 6; 1 Tm 1, 3. u: 4, 3; 1 Cor 1, 18. v: 4, 2; 1 Cor 5, 8. w: Acts 18, 27; Rom 16, 1; 1 Cor 16, 3. x: Ex 24, 12; 31, 18; 32, 15-19 / Jer 31, 33; Ez 11, 19; 36, 26-27.

be a letter of Christ administered by us, written not in ink but by the Spirit of the living God, not on tablets of stone but on tablets that are hearts of flesh. [4]*Such confidence we have through Christ toward God. [5y]Not that of ourselves we are qualified to take credit for anything as coming from us; rather, our qualification comes from God, [6z]*who has indeed qualified us as ministers of a new covenant, not of letter but of spirit; for the letter brings death, but the Spirit gives life.

Contrast with the Old Covenant. [7a]*Now if the ministry of death, carved in letters on stone, was so glorious that the Israelites could not look intently at the face of Moses because of its glory that was going to fade, [8]*how much more will the ministry of the Spirit be glorious? [9]For if the ministry of condemnation was glorious, the ministry of righteousness will abound much more in glory. [10]Indeed, what was endowed with glory has come to have no glory in this respect because of the glory that surpasses it. [11]For if what was going to fade was glorious, how much more will what endures be glorious.

[12]*Therefore, since we have such hope, we act very boldly [13]*and not like Moses, who put a veil over his face so that the Israelites could not look intently at the cessation of what was fading. [14]*Rather, their thoughts were rendered dull, for to this present day the same veil remains unlifted when they read the old covenant, because through Christ it is taken away. [15b]To this day, in fact, whenever Moses is read, a veil lies over their hearts, [16c]but whenever a person turns to the Lord the veil is removed. [17]*Now the Lord is the Spirit, and where the Spirit of the Lord is, there is

that would explain the extended treatment of Moses himself and his glory (3, 7—4, 6). **Hearts of flesh:** cf Ezekiel's contrast between the heart of flesh that the Spirit gives and the heart of stone that it replaces (Ez 36, 26); the context is covenant renewal and purification that makes observance of the law possible.

3, 4–6: These verses resume 2, 1—3, 3. Paul's confidence (4) is grounded in his sense of God-given mission (2, 17), the specifics of which are described in vv 1–3. Verses 5–6 return to the question of his qualifications (2, 16), attributing them entirely to God. Verse 6 further spells out the situation described in v 3b and "names" it: Paul is living within a **new covenant,** characterized by the Spirit, which **gives life.** The usage of a **new covenant** is derived from Jer 31, 31–33, a passage that also speaks of writing on the heart; cf 2.

3, 6b: This verse serves as a topic sentence for 3, 7—6, 10. For the contrast between **letter** and **spirit,** cf Rom 2, 29; 7, 5–6.

3, 7—4, 6: Paul now develops the contrast enunciated in 3, 6b in terms of the relative glory of the two covenants, insisting on the greater glory of the new. His polemic seems directed against individuals who appeal to the glorious Moses and fail to perceive any comparable glory either in Paul's life as an apostle or in the gospel he preaches. He asserts in response that Christians have a glory of their own that far surpasses that of Moses.

3, 7: The **ministry of death:** from his very first words, Paul describes the Mosaic covenant and ministry from the viewpoint of their limitations. They lead to **death** rather than life (6–7; cf 4, 7—5, 10), to **condemnation** rather than reconciliation (9; cf 5, 11—6, 10). **Was so glorious:** the basic text to which Paul alludes is Ex 34, 29–35, to which his opponents have undoubtedly laid claim. **Going to fade:** Paul concedes the glory of Moses' covenant and ministry, but grants them only temporary significance.

3, 8–11: How much more: the argument "from the less to the greater" is repeated three times (8.9.11). Verse 10 expresses another point of view: the difference in glory is so great that only the new covenant and ministry can properly be called "glorious" at all.

3, 12: Such hope: the glory is not yet an object of experience, but that does not lessen Paul's confidence. **Boldly:** the term **parrēsia** expresses outspoken declaration of Christian conviction (cf 4, 1–2). Paul has nothing to hide and no reason for timidity.

3, 13–14a: Not like Moses: in Exodus Moses veiled his face to protect the Israelites from God's reflected glory. Without impugning Moses' sincerity, Paul attributes another effect to the veil. Since it lies between God's glory and the Israelites, it explains how they could fail to notice the glory disappearing. **Their thoughts were rendered dull:** the problem lay with their understanding. This will be expressed in vv 14b-16 by a shift in the place of the veil: it is no longer over Moses' face but over their perception.

3, 14b-16: The parallelism in these verses makes it necessary to interpret corresponding parts in relation to one another. **To this present day:** this signals the shift of Paul's attention to his contemporaries; his argument is typological, as in 1 Cor 10. The Israelites of Moses' time typify the Jews of Paul's time, and perhaps also Christians of Jewish origin or mentality who may not recognize the temporary character of Moses' glory. **When they read the old covenant:** the lasting dullness prevents proper appraisal of Moses' person and covenant. When his writings are read in the synagogue, a veil still impedes their understanding. **Through Christ:** i.e., in the new covenant. **Whenever a person turns to the Lord:** Moses in Exodus appeared before God without the veil and gazed on his face unprotected. Paul applies that passage to converts to Christianity: when they turn to the Lord fully and authentically, the impediment to their understanding is removed.

3, 17: The Lord is the Spirit: the "Lord" to whom the Christian turns (16) is the Spirit of whom Paul has been

y: Jn 3, 27. z: Eph 3, 7 / Jer 31, 31-34. a: Ex 34, 29-35. b: Rom 11, 7-10. c: Ex 34, 34.

freedom. [18d]*All of us, gazing with unveiled face on the glory of the Lord, are being transformed into the same image from glory to glory, as from the Lord who is the Spirit.

See RG 378–79

CHAPTER 4

Integrity in the Ministry. [1]*Therefore, since we have this ministry through the mercy shown us, we are not discouraged. [2e]Rather, we have renounced shameful, hidden things; not acting deceitfully or falsifying the word of God, but by the open declaration of the truth we commend ourselves to everyone's conscience in the sight of God. [3f]*And even though our gospel is veiled, it is veiled for those who are perishing, [4g]in whose case the god of this age has blinded the minds of the unbelievers, so that they may not see the light of the gospel of the glory of Christ, who is the image of God. [5]*For we do not preach our-selves but Jesus Christ as Lord, and ourselves as your slaves for the sake of Jesus. [6h]*For God who said, "Let light shine out of darkness," has shone in our hearts to bring to light the knowledge of the glory of God on the face of [Jesus] Christ.

The Paradox of the Ministry. [7]*But we hold this treasure in earthen vessels, that the surpassing power may be of God and not from us. [8i]*We are afflicted in every way, but not constrained; perplexed, but not driven to despair; [9]persecuted, but not abandoned; struck down, but not destroyed; [10j]*always carrying about in the body the dying of Jesus, so that the life of Jesus may also be manifested in our body. [11k]For we who live are constantly being given up to death for the sake of Jesus, so that the life of Jesus may be manifested in our mortal flesh. [12]So death is at work in us, but life in

speaking, the life-giving Spirit of the living God (6.8), the inaugurator of the new covenant and ministry, who is also the Spirit of Christ. **The Spirit of the Lord:** the Lord here is the living God (3), but there may also be an allusion to Christ as Lord (14.16). **Freedom:** i.e., from the ministry of death (7) and the covenant that condemned (9).

3, 18: Another application of the veil image. **All of us . . . with unveiled face:** Christians (Israelites from whom the veil has been removed) are like Moses, standing in God's presence, beholding and reflecting his glory. **Gazing:** the verb may also be translated "contemplating as in a mirror"; 4, 6 would suggest that the mirror is Christ himself. **Are being transformed:** elsewhere Paul speaks of transformation, conformity to Jesus, God's image, as a reality of the end time, and even v 12 speaks of the glory as an object of hope. But the life-giving Spirit, the distinctive gift of the new covenant, is already present in the community (cf 1, 22, the "first installment"), and the process of transformation has already begun. **Into the same image:** into the image of God, which is Christ (4, 4).

4, 1–2: A ministry of this sort generates confidence and forthrightness; cf 1, 12–14; 2, 17.

4, 3–4: Though our gospel is veiled: the final application of the image. Paul has been reproached either for obscurity in his preaching or for his manner of presenting the gospel. But he confidently asserts that there is no veil over his gospel. If some fail to perceive its light, that is because of unbelief. The veil lies over their eyes (3, 14), a blindness induced by Satan, and a sign that they are headed for destruction (cf 2, 15).

4, 5: We do not preach ourselves: the light seen in his gospel is the glory of Christ (4). Far from preaching himself, the preacher should be a transparent medium through whom Jesus is perceived (cf 10–11). **Your slaves:** Paul draws attention away from individuals as such and toward their role in relation to God, Christ, and the community; cf 1 Cor 3, 5; 4, 1.

4, 6: Autobiographical allusion to the episode at Damascus clarifies the origin and nature of Paul's service; cf Acts 9, 1–19;

22, 3–16; 26, 2–18. **"Let light shine out of darkness":** Paul seems to be thinking of Gn 1, 3 and presenting his apostolic ministry as a new creation. There may also be an allusion to Is 9, 1, suggesting his prophetic calling as servant of the Lord and light to the nations; cf Is 42, 6.16; 49, 6; 60, 1–2, and the use of light imagery in Acts 26, 13–23. **To bring to light the knowledge:** Paul's role in the process of revelation, expressed at the beginning under the image of the odor and aroma (2, 14–15), is restated now, at the end of this first moment of the development, in the imagery of light and glory (3–6).

4, 7—5, 10: Paul now confronts the difficulty that his present existence does not appear glorious at all; it is marked instead by suffering and death. He deals with this by developing the topic already announced in 3, 3.6, asserting his faith in the presence and ultimate triumph of life, in his own and every Christian existence, despite the experience of death.

4, 7: This treasure: the glory that he preaches and into which they are being transformed. **In earthen vessels:** the instruments God uses are human and fragile; some imagine small terracotta lamps in which light is carried.

4, 8–9: A catalogue of his apostolic trials and afflictions. Yet in these the negative never completely prevails; there is always some experience of rescue, of salvation.

4, 10–11: Both the negative and the positive sides of the experience are grounded christologically. The logic is similar to that of 1, 3–11. His sufferings are connected with Christ's, and his deliverance is a sign that he is to share in Jesus' resurrection.

4, 12–15: His experience does not terminate in himself, but in others (12.15; cf 1, 4–5). Ultimately, everything is ordered even beyond the community, toward God (15; cf 1, 11).

d: Rom 8, 29-30; 12, 2; Gal 4, 19; Phil 3, 10.20-21 / 4, 4-6;1 Cor 15, 49; Col 1, 15; 3, 9-11; 1 Jn 3, 2. *e:* 2, 17; 1 Thes 2, 4-7. *f:* 2, 15-16; 2 Thes 2, 10. *g:* Jn 12, 31-36 / 1 Tm 1, 11. *h:* Gn 1, 3; Is 9, 1; Acts 26, 13-23; Gal 1, 15-16 / Jn 8, 12; Heb 1, 3. *i:* 6, 4-10; 1 Cor 4, 9-13. *j:* Col 1, 24. *k:* Rom 8, 36; 1 Cor 15, 31.

you. *13 l* *Since, then, we have the same spirit of faith, according to what is written, "I believed, therefore I spoke," we too believe and therefore speak, *14m* knowing that the one who raised the Lord Jesus will raise us also with Jesus and place us with you in his presence. *15n* Everything indeed is for you, so that the grace bestowed in abundance on more and more people may cause the thanksgiving to overflow for the glory of God.

16o *Therefore, we are not discouraged; rather, although our outer self is wasting away, our inner self is being renewed day by day. *17p* For this momentary light affliction is producing for us an eternal weight of glory beyond all comparison, *18q* as we look not to what is seen but to what is unseen; for what is seen is transitory, but what is unseen is eternal.

CHAPTER 5

See RG 379

Our Future Destiny. *1r* *For we know that if our earthly dwelling, a tent, should be destroyed, we have a building from God, a dwelling not made with hands, eternal in heaven. *2s* *For in this tent we groan, longing to be further clothed with our heavenly habitation *3* *if indeed, when we have taken it off, we shall not be found naked. *4t* *For while we are in this tent we groan and are weighed down, because we do not wish to be unclothed but to be further clothed, so that what is mortal may be swallowed up by life. *5u* *Now the one who has prepared us for this very thing is God, who has given us the Spirit as a first installment.

6 *So we are always courageous, although we know that while we are at home in the body we are away from the Lord, *7* for we

---

4, 13–14: Like the Psalmist, Paul clearly proclaims his faith, affirming life within himself despite death (10–11) and the life-giving effect of his experience upon the church (12.14–15). **And place us with you in his presence:** Paul imagines God presenting him and them to Jesus at the parousia and the judgment; cf 11, 2; Rom 14, 10.

4, 16–18: In a series of contrasts Paul explains the extent of his faith in life. Life is not only already present and revealing itself (8–11.16) but will outlast his experience of affliction and dying: it is eternal (17–18).

4, 16: Not discouraged: i.e., despite the experience of death. Paul is still speaking of himself personally, but he assumes his faith and attitude will be shared by all Christians. **Our outer self:** the individual subject of ordinary perception and observation, in contrast to the interior and hidden self, which undergoes renewal. **Is being renewed day by day:** this suggests a process that has already begun; cf 3, 18. The renewal already taking place even in Paul's dying is a share in the life of Jesus, but this is recognized only by faith (13.18; 5, 7).

5, 1: Our earthly dwelling: the same contrast is restated in the imagery of a dwelling. The language recalls Jesus' saying about the destruction of the temple and the construction of another building **not made with hands** (Mk 14, 58), a prediction later applied to Jesus' own body (Jn 2, 20).

5, 2–5: Verses 2–3 and 4 are largely parallel in structure. **We groan, longing:** see the note on 5, 5. **Clothed with our heavenly habitation:** Paul mixes his metaphors, adding the image of the garment to that of the building. **Further clothed:** the verb means strictly "to put one garment on over another." Paul may desire to put the resurrection body on over his mortal body, without dying; vv 2 and 4 permit this meaning but do not impose it. Or perhaps he imagines the resurrection body as a garment put on over the Christ-garment first received in baptism (Gal 3, 27) and preserved by moral behavior (Rom 13, 12–14; Col 3, 12; cf Mt 22, 11–13). Some support for this interpretation may be found in the context; cf the references to baptism (5), to judgment according to works (10), and to present renewal (4, 16), an idea elsewhere com-

bined with the image of "putting on" a new nature (Eph 4, 22–24; Col 3, 1–5.9–10).

5, 3: When we have taken it off: the majority of witnesses read "when we have put it on," i.e., when we have been clothed (in the resurrection body), then we shall not be without a body (naked). This seems mere tautology, though some understand it to mean: whether we are "found" (by God at the judgment) clothed or naked depends upon whether we have preserved or lost our original investiture in Christ (cf the previous note). In this case to "put it on" does not refer to the resurrection body, but to keeping intact the Christ-garment of baptism. The translation follows the western reading (Codex Bezae, Tertullian), the sense of which is clear: to "take it off" is to shed our mortal body in death, after which we shall be clothed in the resurrection body and hence not "naked" (cf 1 Cor 15, 51–53).

5, 4: We do not wish to be unclothed: a clear allusion to physical death (4, 16; 5, 1). Unlike the Greeks, who found dissolution of the body desirable (cf Socrates), Paul has a Jewish horror of it. He seems to be thinking of the "intermediate period," an interval between death and resurrection. **Swallowed up by life:** cf 1 Cor 15, 54.

5, 5: God has created us for resurrected bodily life and already prepares us for it by the gift of the Spirit in baptism. **The Spirit as a first installment:** the striking parallel to 5, 1–5 in Rom 8, 17–30 describes Christians who have received the "firstfruits" (cf "first installment" here) of the Spirit as "groaning" (cf 2.4 here) for the resurrection, the complete redemption of their bodies. In place of clothing and building, Rom 8 uses other images for the resurrection: adoption and conformity to the image of the Son.

5, 6–9: Tension between present and future is expressed

---

l: Ps 116, 10.   *m:* Rom 4, 24-25; 8, 11; 1 Cor 6, 14; 1 Thes 4, 14.
n: 1, 11.   *o:* 2 Cor 4, 11.   *p:* Mt 5, 11-12; Rom 8, 18.   *q:* Rom 8, 24-25; Heb 11, 1.   *r:* Is 38, 12 / Col 3, 1-4 / Mk 14, 58; Col 2, 11; Heb 9, 11.24.   *s:* Rom 8, 23 / 1 Cor 15, 51-54.   *t:* Is 25, 8; 1 Cor 15, 54.   *u:* 1, 22.

walk by faith, not by sight. [8v]Yet we are courageous, and we would rather leave the body and go home to the Lord. [9]Therefore, we aspire to please him, whether we are at home or away. [10w]*For we must all appear before the judgment seat of Christ, so that each one may receive recompense, according to what he did in the body, whether good or evil.

The Ministry of Reconciliation. [11x]*Therefore, since we know the fear of the Lord, we try to persuade others; but we are clearly apparent to God, and I hope we are also apparent to your consciousness. [12y]We are not commending ourselves to you again but giving you an opportunity to boast of us, so that you may have something to say to those who boast of external appearance rather than of the heart. [13]*For if we are out of our minds, it is for God; if we are rational, it is for you. [14z]*For the love of Christ impels us, once we have come to the conviction that one died for all; therefore, all have died. [15a]He indeed died for all, so that those who live might no longer live for themselves but for him who for their sake died and was raised.

[16]*Consequently, from now on we regard no one according to the flesh; even if we once knew Christ according to the flesh, yet now we know him so no longer. [17b]So whoever is in Christ is a new creation: the old things have passed away; behold, new things have come. [18]*And all this is from God, who has reconciled us to himself through Christ and given us the ministry of reconciliation, [19c]namely, God was reconciling the world to himself in Christ, not counting their trespasses against them and entrusting to us the message of reconciliation. [20d]So we are ambassadors for Christ, as if God were appealing through us. We implore you on behalf of Christ, be reconciled to God. [21e]*For our sake he made him to be sin who did not know sin, so that we might become the righteousness of God in him.

CHAPTER 6

See RG 377-78

The Experience of the Ministry. [1f]*Working together, then, we appeal to you not to receive the grace of God in vain. [2g]*For he says:

---

by another spatial image, the metaphor of the country and its citizens. At present we are like citizens in exile or far away from home. The Lord is the distant homeland, believed in but unseen (7).

5, 10: We must all appear: the verb is ambiguous: we are scheduled to "appear" for judgment, at which we will be "revealed" as we are (cf 11; 2, 14; 4, 10–11).

5, 11–15: This paragraph is transitional. Paul sums up much that has gone before. Still playing on the term "appearance," he reasserts his transparency before God and the Corinthians, in contrast to the self-commendation, boasting, and preoccupation with externals that characterize some others (cf 1, 12–14; 2, 14; 3, 1; 3, 7—4, 6). Verse 14 recalls 3, 7—4, 6, and sums up 4, 7—5, 10.

5, 13: Out of our minds: this verse confirms that a concern for ecstasy and charismatic experience may lie behind the discussion about "glory" in 3, 7—4, 6. Paul also enjoys such experiences but, unlike others, does not make a public display of them or consider them ends in themselves. **Rational:** the Greek virtue sōphrosynē, to which Paul alludes, implies reasonableness, moderation, good judgment, self-control.

5, 14–15: These verses echo 4, 14 and resume the treatment of "life despite death" from 4, 7—5, 10.

5, 16–17: Consequently: the death of Christ described in vv 14–15 produces a whole new order (17) and a new mode of perception (16). **According to the flesh:** the natural mode of perception, characterized as "fleshly," is replaced by a mode of perception proper to the Spirit. Elsewhere Paul contrasts what Christ looks like according to the old criteria (weakness, powerlessness, folly, death) and according to the new (wisdom, power, life); cf vv 15.21; 1 Cor 1, 17—3, 3. Similarly, he de-

scribes the paradoxical nature of Christian existence, e.g., in 4, 10–11.14. **A new creation:** rabbis used this expression to describe the effect of the entrance of a proselyte or convert into Judaism or of the remission of sins on the Day of Atonement. The new order created **in Christ** is the new covenant (3, 6).

5, 18–21: Paul attempts to explain the meaning of God's action by a variety of different categories; his attention keeps moving rapidly back and forth from God's act to his own ministry as well. **Who has reconciled us to himself:** i.e., he has brought all into oneness. **Not counting their trespasses:** the reconciliation is described as an act of justification (cf "righteousness," 21); this contrasts with the covenant that condemned (3, 8). **The ministry of reconciliation:** Paul's role in the wider picture is described: entrusted with the message of reconciliation (19), he is Christ's ambassador, through whom God appeals (20a). In v 20b Paul acts in the capacity just described.

5, 21: This is a statement of God's purpose, expressed paradoxically in terms of sharing and exchange of attributes. As Christ became our righteousness (1 Cor 1, 30), we become God's righteousness (cf vv 14–15).

6, 1–10: This paragraph is a single long sentence in the Greek, interrupted by the parenthesis of v 2. The one main verb is "we appeal." In this paragraph Paul both exercises his

v: Phil 1, 21-23. w: Mt 16, 27; 25, 31-46; Rom 2, 16; 14, 10-11.
x: 1, 12-14. y: 3, 1 / 1, 14; Phil 1, 26. z: Rom 6, 1-6. a: Rom 4, 25; 6, 4-11; 14, 9; Col 3, 3-4. b: Gal 6, 15; Eph 2, 15 / Is 43, 18-21; Rv 21, 5. c: Rom 5, 10-11; Col 1, 20. d: Eph 6, 20; Phlm 9. e: Is 53, 6-9; Gal 3, 13 / Rom 3, 24-26; 1 Cor 1, 30; 1 Pt 2, 24; 1 Jn 3, 5-8. f: 1 Cor 3, 9; 1 Thes 3, 2. g: Is 49, 8.

"In an acceptable time I heard you,
and on the day of salvation I helped
you."

Behold, now is a very acceptable time; behold, now is the day of salvation. *3h*We
cause no one to stumble in anything, in order
that no fault may be found with our ministry;
*4i*on the contrary, in everything we commend ourselves as ministers of God, through
much endurance, in afflictions, hardships,
constraints, *5j*beatings, imprisonments, riots, labors, vigils, fasts; *6k*by purity, knowledge, patience, kindness, in a holy spirit, in
unfeigned love, *7l*in truthful speech, in the
power of God; with weapons of righteousness at the right and at the left; *8*through
glory and dishonor, insult and praise. We are
treated as deceivers and yet are truthful; *9m*as
unrecognized and yet acknowledged; as dying and behold we live; as chastised and yet
not put to death; *10n*as sorrowful yet always
rejoicing; as poor yet enriching many; as
having nothing and yet possessing all things.
*11*We have spoken frankly to you, Corinthians; our heart is open wide. *12o*You are not
constrained by us; you are constrained by
your own affections. *13p*As recompense in
kind (I speak as to my children), be open
yourselves.

Call to Holiness. *14*Do not be yoked with
those who are different, with unbelievers.
For what partnership do righteousness and
lawlessness have? Or what fellowship does
light have with darkness? *15*What accord has
Christ with Beliar? Or what has a believer in
common with an unbeliever? *16q*What
agreement has the temple of God with idols?
For we are the temple of the living God; as
God said:

ministry of reconciliation (cf 5, 20) and describes how his
ministry is exercised: the "message of reconciliation" (5, 19)
is lived existentially in his apostolic experience.

6, 1: Not to receive . . . in vain: i.e., conform to the gift of
justification and new creation. The context indicates how this
can be done concretely: become God's righteousness (5, 21),
not live for oneself (5, 15), be reconciled with Paul (6, 11–13;
7, 2–3).

6, 2: In an acceptable time: Paul cites the Septuagint text
of Is 49, 8; the Hebrew reads "in a time of favor"; it is parallel to "on the day of salvation." **Now:** God is bestowing favor
and salvation at this very moment, as Paul is addressing his
letter to them.

6, 3: Cause no one to stumble: the language echoes that
of 1 Cor 8–10, as does the expression "no longer live for
themselves" in 5, 15. **That no fault may be found:** i.e., at the
eschatological judgment (cf 1 Cor 4, 2–5).

6, 4a: This is the central assertion, the topic statement for
the catalogue that follows. **We commend ourselves:** Paul's
self-commendation is ironical (with an eye on the charges
mentioned in 3, 1–3) and paradoxical (pointing mostly to experiences that would not normally be considered points of
pride but are perceived as such by faith). Cf also the self-commendation in 11, 23–29. **As ministers of God:** the same
Greek word, **diakonos,** means "minister" and "servant"; cf 11,
23, the central assertion in a similar context, and 1 Cor 3, 5.

6, 4b–5: Through much endurance: this phrase functions as a subtitle; it is followed by an enumeration of nine
specific types of trials endured.

6, 6–7a: A list of virtuous qualities in two groups of four,
the second fuller than the first.

6, 8b–10: A series of seven rhetorically effective antitheses, contrasting negative external impressions with positive
inner reality. Paul perceives his existence as a reflection of
Jesus' own and affirms an inner reversal that escapes outward observation. The final two members illustrate two distinct kinds of paradox or apparent contradiction that are
characteristic of apostolic experience.

6, 11–13: Paul's tone becomes quieter, but his appeal for
acceptance and affection is emotionally charged. References
to the heart and their mutual relations bring the development
begun in 2, 14—3, 3 to an effective conclusion.

6, 14—7, 1: Language and thought shift noticeably here.
Suddenly we are in a different atmosphere, dealing with a
quite different problem. Both the vocabulary and the thought,
with their contrast between good and evil, are more characteristic of Qumran documents or the Book of Revelation than
they are of Paul. Hence, critics suspect that this section was
inserted by another hand.

6, 14–16a: The opening injunction to separate from unbelievers is reinforced by five rhetorical questions to make the
point that Christianity is not compatible with paganism. Their
opposition is emphasized also by the accumulation of five distinct designations for each group. These verses are a powerful
statement of God's holiness and the exclusiveness of his claims.

6, 16c–18: This is a chain of scriptural citations carefully woven together. God's covenant relation to his people and his presence among them (16) is seen as conditioned on cultic separation from the profane and cultically impure (17); that relation is
translated into the personal language of the parent-child relationship, an extension to the community of the language of
2 Sm 7, 14 (18). Some remarkable parallels to this chain are
found in the final chapters of Revelation. God's presence among
his people (21, 22) is expressed there, too, by applying 2 Sm 7,
14 to the community (21, 7). There is a call to separation (18, 4)
and exclusion of the unclean from the community and its liturgy
(21, 27). The title "Lord Almighty" (**Pantokratōr**) occurs in the
New Testament only here in 18 and nine times in Rv.

h: 1 Cor 9, 12; 10, 32 / 8, 20-21. *i:* 4, 8-11; 11, 23-27; 1 Cor 4,
9-13. *j:* Acts 16, 23. *k:* Gal 5, 22-23. *l:* 10, 4; Rom 13, 12;
Eph 6, 11-17. *m:* 4, 10-11; Rom 8, 36. *n:* Rom 8, 32; 1 Cor 3,
21. *o:* 7, 3. *p:* Gal 4, 19. *q:* 1 Cor 10, 20-21 / 1 Cor 3, 16-17;
6, 19 / Ex 25, 8; 29, 45; Lv 26, 12; Jer 31, 1; 32, 38; Ez 37, 27.

"I will live with them and move among
    them,
  and I will be their God
  and they shall be my people.
[17] [r]Therefore, come forth from them
  and be separate," says the Lord,
"and touch nothing unclean;
  then I will receive you
[18] [s]and I will be a father to you,
  and you shall be sons and daughters to
    me,
says the Lord Almighty."

CHAPTER 7

See RG
379 [1]Since we have these promises,
beloved, let us cleanse ourselves from every
defilement of flesh and spirit, making holiness perfect in the fear of God.

[2]*Make room for us; we have not wronged
anyone, or ruined anyone, or taken advantage of anyone. [3][t]I do not say this in condemnation, for I have already said that you
are in our hearts, that we may die together
and live together. [4]I have great confidence in
you, I have great pride in you; I am filled
with encouragement, I am overflowing with
joy all the more because of all our affliction.

C. Resolution of the Crisis

Paul's Joy in Macedonia. [5][u]*For even when
we came into Macedonia, our flesh had no
rest, but we were afflicted in every way—
external conflicts, internal fears. [6][v]But God,
who encourages the downcast, encouraged
us by the arrival of Titus, [7]and not only by

his arrival but also by the encouragement
with which he was encouraged in regard to
you, as he told us of your yearning, your
lament, your zeal for me, so that I rejoiced
even more. [8][w]*For even if I saddened you by
my letter, I do not regret it; and if I did regret it ([for] I see that that letter saddened
you, if only for a while), [9]I rejoice now, not
because you were saddened, but because
you were saddened into repentance; for you
were saddened in a godly way, so that you
did not suffer loss in anything because of us.
[10]For godly sorrow produces a salutary repentance without regret, but worldly sorrow
produces death. [11]For behold what earnestness this godly sorrow has produced for
you, as well as readiness for a defense, and
indignation, and fear, and yearning, and
zeal, and punishment. In every way you
have shown yourselves to be innocent in the
matter. [12][x]So then even though I wrote to
you, it was not on account of the one who
did the wrong, or on account of the one who
suffered the wrong, but in order that your
concern for us might be made plain to you
in the sight of God. [13]*For this reason we are
encouraged.

And besides our encouragement, we rejoice even more because of the joy of Titus,
since his spirit has been refreshed by all of
you. [14]For if I have boasted to him about
you, I was not put to shame. No, just as
everything we said to you was true, so our
boasting before Titus proved to be the truth.
[15][y]And his heart goes out to you all the more,

7, 2–4: These verses continue the thought of 6, 11–13, before the interruption of 6, 14—7, 1. Verse 4 serves as a transition to the next section: the four themes it introduces (confidence; pride or "boasting"; encouragement; joy in affliction) are developed in vv 5–16. All have appeared previously in the letter.

7, 5–16: This section functions as a peroration or formal summing up of the whole first part of the letter, chs 1–7. It deals with the restoration of right relations between Paul and the Corinthians, and it is marked by fullness and intensity of emotion.

7, 5–7: Paul picks up the thread of the narrative interrupted at 2, 13 (5) and describes the resolution of the tense situation there depicted (6–7). Finally Titus arrives and his coming puts an end to Paul's restlessness (2, 13; 7, 5), casts out his fears, and reverses his mood. The theme of encouragement and affliction is reintroduced (cf 1, 3–11); here, too, encouragement is traced back to God and is described as contagious (6). The language of joy and sorrow also reappears in v

7 (cf 1, 23—2, 1 and the note on 1, 23–24).

7, 5: Macedonia: see the note on 2, 13.

7, 8–12: Paul looks back on the episode from the viewpoint of its ending. The goal of their common activity, promotion of their joy (1, 24), has been achieved, despite and because of the sorrow they felt. That sorrow was God-given. Its salutary effects are enumerated fully and impressively in vv 10–11; not the least important of these is that it has revealed to them the attachment they have to Paul.

7, 13–16: Paul summarizes the effect of the experience on Titus: encouragement, joy, love, relief. Finally, he describes its effects on himself: encouragement, joy, confidence, pride or "boasting" (i.e., the satisfaction resulting from a boast that proves well-founded; cf 4; 1, 12.14).

r: Is 52, 11; Ez 20, 34.41; Rv 18, 4; 21, 27. s: 2 Sm 7, 14; Ps 2, 7; Is 43, 6; Jer 31, 9; Rv 21, 7 / Rv 4, 8; 11, 17; 15, 3; 21, 22. t: 6, 11-13. u: 2, 13. v: 7, 13-14; 1 Thes 3, 6-8. w: 2, 2-4; Heb 12, 11. x: 2, 3.9; 7, 8. y: 2, 9.

as he remembers the obedience of all of you, when you received him with fear and trembling. [16]I rejoice, because I have confidence in you in every respect.

III: The Collection for Jerusalem

CHAPTER 8

See RG 379–80

Generosity in Giving. [1z]*We want you to know, brothers, of the grace of God that has been given to the churches of Macedonia, [2]*for in a severe test of affliction, the abundance of their joy and their profound poverty overflowed in a wealth of generosity on their part. [3]*For according to their means, I can testify, and beyond their means,

spontaneously, [4a]they begged us insistently for the favor of taking part in the service to the holy ones, [5]*and this, not as we expected, but they gave themselves first to the Lord and to us through the will of God, [6b]*so that we urged Titus that, as he had already begun, he should also complete for you this gracious act also. [7c]*Now as you excel in every respect, in faith, discourse, knowledge, all earnestness, and in the love we have for you, may you excel in this gracious act also.

[8]I say this not by way of command, but to test the genuineness of your love by your concern for others. [9d]*For you know the gracious act of our Lord Jesus Christ, that for your sake he became poor although he was

---

8, 1–9, 15: Paul turns to a new topic, the collection for the church in Jerusalem. There is an early precedent for this project in the agreement mentioned in Gal 2, 6–10. According to Acts, the church at Antioch had sent Saul and Barnabas to Jerusalem with relief (Acts 11, 27–30). Subsequently Paul organized a project of relief for Jerusalem among his own churches. Our earliest evidence for it comes in 1 Cor 16, 1–4, after it had already begun (see the notes there); by the time Paul wrote Rom 15, 25–28 the collection was completed and ready for delivery. Chapters 8 and 9 contain what appear to be two letters on the subject. In them Paul gives us his fullest exposition of the meaning he sees in the enterprise, presenting it as an act of Christian charity and as an expression of the unity of the church, both present and eschatological. These chapters are especially rich in the recurrence of key words, on which Paul plays; it is usually impossible to do justice to these wordplays in the translation.

8, 1–24: This is a letter of recommendation for Titus and two unnamed companions, written from Macedonia probably at least a year later than 1 Cor 16. The recommendation proper is prefaced by remarks about the ideals of sharing and equality within the Christian community (1–15). Phil 4, 10–20 shows that Paul has reflected on his personal experience of need and relief in his relations with the community at Philippi; he now develops his reflections on the larger scale of relations between his Gentile churches and the mother church in Jerusalem.

8, 1–5: The example of the Macedonians, a model of what ought to be happening at Corinth, provides Paul with the occasion for expounding his theology of "giving."

8, 1: The grace of God: the fundamental theme is expressed by the Greek noun **charis**, which will be variously translated throughout these chapters as "grace" (8, 1; 9, 8.14), "favor" (8, 4), "gracious act" (8, 6.7.9) or "gracious work" (8, 19), to be compared to "gracious gift" (1 Cor 16, 3). The related term, **eucharistia**, "thanksgiving," also occurs at 9, 11.12. The wordplay is not superficial; various mutations of the same root signal inner connection between aspects of a single reality, and Paul consciously exploits the similarities in vocabulary to highlight that connection.

8, 2: Three more terms are now introduced. **Test (dokimē):**

the same root is translated as "to test" (8) and "evidence" (9, 13); it means to be tried and found genuine. **Abundance:** variations on the same root lie behind "overflow" (8, 2; 9, 12), "excel" (8, 7), "surplus" (8, 14), "superfluous" (9, 1), "make abundant" and "have an abundance" (9, 8). These expressions of fullness contrast with references to need (8, 14; 9, 12). **Generosity:** the word **haplotēs** has nuances of both simplicity and sincerity; here and in 9, 11.13 it designates the singleness of purpose that manifests itself in generous giving.

8, 3–4: Paul emphasizes the spontaneity of the Macedonians and the nature of their action. **They begged us insistently:** the same root is translated as "urge," "appeal," "encourage" (8, 6.17; 9, 5). **Taking part:** the same word is translated "contribution" in 9, 13 and a related term as "partner" in 8, 23. **Service (diakonia):** this word occurs also in 9, 1.13 as "service"; in 9, 12 it is translated "administration," and in 8, 19.20 the corresponding verb is rendered "administer."

8, 5: They gave themselves . . . to the Lord and to us: on its deepest level their attitude is one of self-giving.

8, 6: Titus: 1 Cor 16 seemed to leave the organization up to the Corinthians, but apparently Paul has sent Titus to initiate the collection as well; 8, 16–17 will describe Titus' attitude as one of shared concern and cooperation.

8, 7: The charitable service Paul is promoting is seen briefly and in passing within the perspective of Paul's theology of the charisms. **Earnestness (spoudē):** this or related terms occur also in v 22 ("earnest") and 8, 8.16.17 ("concern").

8, 9: The dialectic of Jesus' experience, expressed earlier in terms of life and death (5, 15), sin and righteousness (5, 21), is now rephrased in terms of poverty and wealth. Many scholars think this is a reference to Jesus' preexistence with God (his "wealth") and to his incarnation and death (his "poverty"), and they point to the similarity between this verse and Phil 2, 6–8. Others interpret the wealth and poverty as succeeding phases of Jesus' earthly existence, e.g., his sense of intimacy with God and then the desolation and the feeling of abandonment by God in his death (cf Mk 15, 34).

---

z: 11, 9; Rom 15, 26.   *a:* Acts 24, 17; Rom 15, 31.   *b:* 2, 13; 7, 6–7.13–14; 8, 16.23; 12, 18.   *c:* 1 Cor 1, 5.   *d:* 6, 10; Phil 2, 6–8.

rich, so that by his poverty you might become rich. [10e]And I am giving counsel in this matter, for it is appropriate for you who began not only to act but to act willingly last year: [11*]complete it now, so that your eager willingness may be matched by your completion of it out of what you have. [12*]For if the eagerness is there, it is acceptable according to what one has, not according to what one does not have; [13]not that others should have relief while you are burdened, but that as a matter of equality [14]your surplus at the present time should supply their needs, so that their surplus may also supply your needs, that there may be equality. [15f]As it is written:

"Whoever had much did not have more,
    and whoever had little did not have
    less."

Titus and His Collaborators. [16*]But thanks be to God who put the same concern for you into the heart of Titus, [17]for he not only welcomed our appeal but, since he is very concerned, he has gone to you of his own accord. [18g*]With him we have sent the brother who is praised in all the churches for his preaching of the gospel. [19h]And not only that, but he has also been appointed our traveling companion by the churches in this gracious work administered by us for the glory of the Lord [himself] and for the expression of our eagerness. [20*]This we desire to avoid, that anyone blame us about this lavish gift administered by us, [21i]for we are concerned for what is honorable not only in the sight of the Lord but also in the sight of others. [22]And with them we have sent our brother whom we often tested in many ways and found earnest, but who is now much more earnest because of his great confidence in you. [23]As for Titus, he is my partner and co-worker for you; as for our brothers, they are apostles of the churches, the glory of Christ. [24*]So give proof before the churches of your love and of our boasting about you to them.

CHAPTER 9

See RG 379–80

God's Indescribable Gift. [1*]Now about the service to the holy ones, it is superfluous for me to write to you, [2j*]for I know your eagerness, about which I boast of you to the Macedonians, that Achaia has been ready since last year; and your zeal has stirred up most of them. [3*]Nonetheless, I sent the brothers so that our boast about you might not prove empty in this case, so that you might be ready, as I said, [4]for fear that if any Macedonians come with me and find you not ready we might be put to shame (to say nothing of you) in this conviction. [5]So I thought it necessary to encourage the brothers to go on ahead to you and arrange in advance for your promised gift, so that in this

8, 11: **Eager:** the word **prothymia** also occurs in 8, 12.19; 9, 2.

8, 12–15: Paul introduces the principle of **equality** into the discussion. The goal is not impoverishment but sharing of resources; balance is achieved at least over the course of time. In v 15 Paul grounds his argument unexpectedly in the experience of Israel gathering manna in the desert: equality was achieved, independently of personal exertion, by God, who gave with an even hand according to need. Paul touches briefly here on the theme of "living from God."

8, 16–24: In recommending Titus and his companions, Paul stresses their personal and apostolic qualities, their good dispositions toward the Corinthians, and their authority as messengers of the churches and representatives of Christ.

8, 18: **The brother:** we do not know the identity of this co-worker of Paul, nor of the third companion mentioned below in v 22.

8, 20–22: **That anyone blame us:** 12, 16–18 suggests that misunderstandings may indeed have arisen concerning Paul's management of the collection through the messengers mentioned here, but those same verses seem to imply that the Corinthians by and large would recognize the honesty of Paul's

conduct in this area as in others (cf 6, 3).

8, 24: As Paul began by holding up the Macedonians as examples to be imitated, he closes by exhorting the Corinthians to show their love (by accepting the envoys and by cooperating as the Macedonians do), thus justifying the pride Paul demonstrates because of them before other churches.

9, 1–15: Quite possibly this was originally an independent letter, though it deals with the same subject and continues many of the same themes. In that case, it may have been written a few weeks later than ch 8, while the delegation there mentioned was still on its way.

9, 2: **Achaia:** see the note on Rom 15, 26.

9, 3: **I sent the brothers:** the Greek aorist tense here could be epistolary, referring to the present; in that case Paul would be sending them now, and ch 9 would merely conclude the letter of recommendation begun in ch 8. But the aorist may also refer to a sending that is past as Paul writes; then ch 9, with its apparently fresh beginning, is a follow-up message entrusted to another carrier.

e: 9, 2; 1 Cor 16, 1-4. f: Ex 16, 18. g: 12, 18. h: 1 Cor 16, 3-4. i: Rom 12, 17. j: 8, 10; Rom 15, 26.

way it might be ready as a bountiful gift and not as an exaction.

⁶ᵏConsider this: whoever sows sparingly will also reap sparingly, and whoever sows bountifully will also reap bountifully. ⁷ᵀEach must do as already determined, without sadness or compulsion, for God loves a cheerful giver. ⁸*Moreover, God is able to make every grace abundant for you, so that in all things, always having all you need, you may have an abundance for every good work. ⁹ᵐAs it is written:

> "He scatters abroad, he gives to the poor;
> his righteousness endures forever."

¹⁰ⁿThe one who supplies seed to the sower and bread for food will supply and multiply your seed and increase the harvest of your righteousness.

¹¹*You are being enriched in every way for all generosity, which through us produces thanksgiving to God, ¹²for the administration of this public service is not only supplying the needs of the holy ones but is also overflowing in many acts of thanksgiving to God. ¹³ᵒThrough the evidence of this service, you are glorifying God for your obedient confession of the gospel of Christ and the generosity of your contribution to them and to all others, ¹⁴while in prayer on your behalf they long for you, because of the surpassing grace of God upon you. ¹⁵ᵖThanks be to God for his indescribable gift!

IV: Paul's Defense of His Ministry

CHAPTER 10

See RG 380–81

Accusation of Weakness. ¹*Now I myself, Paul, urge you through the gentleness and clemency of Christ, I who am humble when face to face with you, but brave toward you when absent, ²�q*I beg you that, when present, I may not have to be brave with that confidence with which I intend to act boldly

---

9, 8–10: The behavior to which he exhorts them is grounded in God's own pattern of behavior. God is capable of overwhelming generosity, as scripture itself attests (9), so that they need not fear being short. He will provide in abundance, both supplying their natural needs and increasing their righteousness. Paul challenges them to godlike generosity and reminds them of the fundamental motive for encouragement: God himself cannot be outdone.

9, 11–15: Paul's vision broadens to take in all the interested parties in one dynamic picture. His language becomes liturgically colored and conveys a sense of fullness. With a final play on the words **charis** and **eucharistia** (see the note on 8, 1), he describes a circle that closes on itself: the movement of grace overflowing from God to them and handed on from them through Paul to others is completed by the prayer of praise and thanksgiving raised on their behalf to God.

10, 1—13, 10: These final chapters have their own unity of structure and theme and could well have formed the body of a separate letter. They constitute an **apologia** on Paul's part, i.e., a legal defense of his behavior and his ministry; the writing is emotionally charged and highly rhetorical. In the central section (11, 16—12, 10), the **apologia** takes the form of a boast. This section is prepared for by a prologue (11, 1–15) and followed by an epilogue (12, 11–18), which are similar in content and structure. These sections, in turn, are framed by an introduction (10, 1–18) and a conclusion (12, 19—13, 10), both of which assert Paul's apostolic authority and confidence and define the purpose of the letter. The structure that results from this disposition of the material is chiastic, i.e., the first element corresponds to the last, the second to the second last, etc., following the pattern **a b c b¹ a¹**.

10, 1–18: Paul asserts his apostolic authority and ex-

presses the confidence this generates in him. He writes in response to certain opinions that have arisen in the community and certain charges raised against him and in preparation for a forthcoming visit in which he intends to set things in order. This section gives us an initial glimpse of the situation in Corinth that Paul must address; much of its thematic material will be taken up again in the finale (12, 19—13, 10).

10, 1–2: A strong opening plunges us straight into the conflict. Contrasts dominate here: presence versus absence, gentleness-clemency-humility versus boldness-confidence-bravery. **Through the gentleness and clemency of Christ:** the figure of the gentle Christ, presented in a significant position before any specifics of the situation are suggested. forms a striking contrast to the picture of the bold and militant Paul (2–6); this tension is finally resolved in 13, 3–4. **Absent . . . present:** this same contrast, with a restatement of the purpose of the letter, recurs in 13, 10, which forms an inclusion with 10, 1–2.

10, 2b-4a: Flesh: the Greek word **sarx** can express both the physical life of the body without any pejorative overtones (as in "we are in the flesh," 3) and also our natural life insofar as it is marked by limitation and weakness (as in the other expressions) in contrast to the higher life and power conferred by the Spirit; cf the note on 1 Cor 3, 1. The wordplay is intended to express the paradoxical situation of a life already taken over by the Spirit but not yet seen as such except by faith. Lack of empirical evidence of the Spirit permits misunderstanding and misjudgment, but Paul resolutely denies that his behavior and effectiveness are as limited as some suppose.

---

k: Prv 11, 24-25.　l: Prv 22, 8 LXX.　m: Ps 112, 9.　n: Is 55, 10.　o: 8, 4; Rom 15, 31.　p: Rom 5, 15-16.　q: 13, 2.10; 1 Cor 4, 21.

against some who consider us as acting according to the flesh. *3*For, although we are in the flesh, we do not battle according to the flesh, *4r*for the weapons of our battle are not of flesh but are enormously powerful, capable of destroying fortresses. We destroy arguments *5*and every pretension raising itself against the knowledge of God, and take every thought captive in obedience to Christ, *6s*and we are ready to punish every disobedience, once your obedience is complete.

*7t*Look at what confronts you. Whoever is confident of belonging to Christ should consider that as he belongs to Christ, so do we. *8u*And even if I should boast a little too much of our authority, which the Lord gave for building you up and not for tearing you down, I shall not be put to shame. *9*May I not seem as one frightening you through letters. *10v*For someone will say, "His letters are severe and forceful, but his bodily presence is weak, and his speech contemptible." *11w*Such a person must understand that what we are in word through letters when absent, that we also are in action when present.

10, 3b-6: Paul is involved in combat. The strong military language and imagery are both an assertion of his confidence in the divine power at his disposal and a declaration of war against those who underestimate his resources. The threat is echoed in 13, 2–3.

10, 7–8: Belonging to Christ . . . so do we: these phrases already announce the pattern of Paul's boast in 11, 21b-29, especially 11, 22–23. **For building you up and not for tearing you down:** Paul draws on the language by which Jeremiah described the purpose of the prophetic power the Lord gave to him (Jer 1, 9–10; 12, 16–17; 24, 6). Though Paul's power may have destructive effects on others (2–6), its intended effect on the community is entirely constructive (cf 13, 10). **I shall not be put to shame:** his assertions will not be refuted; they will be revealed as true at the judgment.

10, 9–10: Paul cites the complaints of some who find him lacking in personal forcefulness and holds out the threat of a personal **parousia** (both "return" and "presence") that will be forceful, indeed will be a demonstration of Christ's own power (cf 13, 2–4).

10, 12–18: Paul now qualifies his claim to boldness, indicating its limits. He distinguishes his own behavior from that of others, revealing those "others" as they appear to him: as self-recommending, immoderately boastful, encroaching on territory not assigned to them, and claiming credit not due to them.

10, 13: Will keep to the limits: the notion of proper limits is expressed here by two terms with overlapping meanings, **metron** and **kanōn**, which are played off against several expressions denoting overreaching or expansion beyond a legitimate sphere.

*12x*Not that we dare to class or compare ourselves with some of those who recommend themselves. But when they measure themselves by one another and compare themselves with one another, they are without understanding. *13*But we will not boast beyond measure but will keep to the limits God has apportioned us, namely, to reach even to you. *14*For we are not overreaching ourselves, as though we did not reach you; we indeed first came to you with the gospel of Christ. *15*We are not boasting beyond measure, in other people's labors; yet our hope is that, as your faith increases, our influence among you may be greatly enlarged, within our proper limits, *16y*so that we may preach the gospel even beyond you, not boasting of work already done in another's sphere. *17z*"Whoever boasts, should boast in the Lord." *18a*For it is not the one who recommends himself who is approved, but the one whom the Lord recommends.

CHAPTER 11

See RG 381

Preaching without Charge. *1b*If only you would put up with a little foolishness

10, 17: Boast in the Lord: there is a legitimate boasting, in contrast to the immoderate boasting to which vv 13 and 15 allude. God's work through Paul in the community is the object of his boast (13–16; 1, 12–14) and constitutes his recommendation (3, 1–3). Cf the notes on 1, 12–14 and 1 Cor 1, 29–31.

10, 18: Approved: to be approved is to come successfully through the process of testing for authenticity (cf 13, 3–7 and the note on 8, 2). **Whom the Lord recommends:** self-commendation is a premature and unwarranted anticipation of the final judgment, which the Lord alone will pass (cf 1 Cor 4, 3–5). Paul alludes to this judgment throughout chs 10–13, frequently in final or transitional positions; cf 11, 15; 12, 19a; 13, 3–7.

11, 1–15: Although these verses continue to reveal information about Paul's opponents and the differences he perceives between them and himself, 11, 1 signals a turn in Paul's thought. This section constitutes a prologue to the boasting that he will undertake in 11, 16—12, 10, and it bears remarkable similarities to the section that follows the central boast, 12, 11–18.

11, 1: Put up with a little foolishness from me: this verse indicates more clearly than the general statement of intent in 10, 13 the nature of the project Paul is about to undertake. He alludes ironically to the Corinthians' toleration for others. **Foolishness:** Paul qualifies his project as folly from beginning to end; see the note on 11, 16—12, 10.

r: 6, 7; 13, 2-3; 1 Cor 1, 25; Eph 6, 10-14.   s: 2, 9.   t: 1 Cor 1, 12.   u: 13, 10.   v: 1 Cor 2, 3.   w: 13, 1-2.   x: 3, 1-2; 4, 2; 5, 12; 6, 4; 10, 18; 12, 11.   y: Rom 15, 20-21.   z: Jer 9, 22-23; 1 Cor 1, 31.   a: 13, 3-9.   b: 11, 21; 12, 11.

from me! Please put up with me. [2c]*For I am jealous of you with the jealousy of God, since I betrothed you to one husband to present you as a chaste virgin to Christ. [3d]*But I am afraid that, as the serpent deceived Eve by his cunning, your thoughts may be corrupted from a sincere [and pure] commitment to Christ. [4e]*For if someone comes and preaches another Jesus than the one we preached, or if you receive a different spirit from the one you received or a different gospel from the one you accepted, you put up with it well enough. [5f]*For I think that I am not in any way inferior to these "superapostles." [6g]*Even if I am untrained in speaking, I am not so in knowledge; in every way we have made this plain to you in all things.

[7h]*Did I make a mistake when I humbled myself so that you might be exalted, because I preached the gospel of God to you without charge? [8]I plundered other churches by accepting from them in order to minister to you. [9i]And when I was with you and in need, I did not burden anyone, for the brothers who came from Macedonia supplied my needs. So I refrained and will refrain from burdening you in any way. [10j]By the truth of Christ in me, this boast of mine shall not be silenced in the regions of Achaia. [11k]*And why? Because I do not love you? God knows I do!

[12]And what I do I will continue to do, in order to end this pretext of those who seek a pretext for being regarded as we are in the mission of which they boast. [13]*For such people are false apostles, deceitful workers, who masquerade as apostles of Christ. [14]And no wonder, for even Satan masquerades as an angel of light. [15]So it is not strange that his ministers also masquerade as ministers of righteousness. Their end will correspond to their deeds.

11, 2: Paul gives us a sudden glimpse of the theological values that are at stake. **The jealousy of God:** the perspective is that of the covenant, described in imagery of love and marriage, as in the prophets; cf 1 Cor 10, 22. **I betrothed you:** Paul, like a father (cf 12, 14), betroths the community to Christ as his bride (cf Eph 5, 21–33) and will present her to him at his second coming. Cf Mt 25, 1–13 and the nuptial imagery in Rv 21.

11, 3: **As the serpent deceived Eve:** before Christ can return for the community Paul fears a repetition of the primal drama of seduction. Corruption of minds is satanic activity (see 2, 11; 4, 4). Satanic imagery recurs in 11, 13–15.20; 12, 7b.16–17; see the notes on these passages.

11, 4: **Preaches another Jesus:** the danger is specified, and Paul's opponents are identified with the cunning serpent. The battle for minds has to do with the understanding of Jesus, the Spirit, the gospel; the Corinthians have flirted with another understanding than the one that Paul handed on to them as traditional and normative.

11, 5: **These "superapostles":** this term, employed again in 12, 11b, designates the opponents of whom Paul has spoken in ch 10 and again in 11, 4. They appear to be intruders at Corinth. Their preaching is marked at least by a different emphasis and style, and they do not hesitate to accept support from the community. Perhaps these itinerants appeal to the authority of church leaders in Jerusalem and even carry letters of recommendation from them. But it is not those distant leaders whom Paul is attacking here. The intruders are "superapostles" not in the sense of the "pillars" at Jerusalem (Gal 2), but in their own estimation. They consider themselves superior to Paul as apostles and ministers of Christ, and they are obviously enjoying some success among the Corinthians. Paul rejects their claim to be apostles in any superlative sense (**hyperlian**), judging them bluntly as "false apostles," ministers of Satan masquerading as apostles of Christ (13–15). On the contrary, he himself will claim to be a superminister of Christ (**hyper egō**, 23).

11, 6: Apparently found deficient in both rhetorical ability (cf 10, 10) and knowledge (cf 10, 5), Paul concedes the former charge but not the latter. **In every way:** in all their contacts with him revelation has been taking place. Paul, through whom God reveals the knowledge of himself (2, 14), and in whom the death and life of Jesus are revealed (4, 10–11; cf 6, 4), also demonstrates his own role as the bearer of true knowledge. Cf 1 Cor 1, 18—2, 16.

11, 7–10: Abruptly Paul passes to another reason for complaints: his practice of preaching without remuneration (cf 1 Cor 9, 3–18). He deftly defends his practice by situating it from the start within the pattern of Christ's own self-humiliation (cf 10, 1) and reduces objections to absurdity by rhetorical questions (cf 12, 13).

11, 11–12: Paul rejects lack of affection as his motive (possibly imputed to him by his opponents) and states his real motive, a desire to emphasize the disparity between himself and the others (cf 19–21). The topic of his gratuitous service will be taken up once more in 12, 13–18. 1 Cor 9, 15–18 gives a different but complementary explanation of his motivation.

11, 13–15: Paul picks up again the imagery of v 3 and applies it to the opponents: they are false apostles of Christ, really serving another master. **Deceitful . . . masquerade:** deception and simulation, like cunning (3), are marks of the satanic. **Angel of light:** recalls the contrast between light and darkness, Christ and Beliar at 6, 14–15. **Ministers of righteousness:** recalls the earlier contrast between the ministry of condemnation and that of righteousness (3, 9). **Their end:** the section closes with another allusion to the judgment, when all participants in the final conflict will be revealed or unmasked and dealt with as they deserve.

c: Hos 2, 21-22; Eph 5, 26-27. d: Gn 3, 1-6. e: Gal 1, 6-9. f: 12, 11. g: 1 Cor 1, 5.17; 2, 1-5. h: 12, 13-18; Acts 18, 3; 1 Cor 9, 6-18. i: Phil 4, 15.18. j: 1 Cor 9, 15. k: 12, 15.

Paul's Boast: His Labors. [16]*I repeat, no one should consider me foolish; but if you do, accept me as a fool, so that I too may boast a little. [17]What I am saying I am not saying according to the Lord but as in foolishness, in this boastful state. [18]Since many boast according to the flesh, I too will boast. [19]For you gladly put up with fools, since you are wise yourselves. [20]*For you put up with it if someone enslaves you, or devours you, or gets the better of you, or puts on airs, or slaps you in the face. [21]*To my shame I say that we were too weak!

But what anyone dares to boast of (I am speaking in foolishness) I also dare. [21]*Are they Hebrews? So am I. Are they Israelites? So am I. Are they descendants of Abraham? So am I. [23m]*Are they ministers of Christ? (I am talking like an insane person.) I am still more, with far greater labors, far more imprisonments, far worse beatings, and numerous brushes with death. [24n]Five times at the hands of the Jews I received forty lashes minus one. [25o]Three times I was beaten with rods, once I was stoned, three times I was shipwrecked, I passed a night and a day on the deep; [26]on frequent journeys, in dangers from rivers, dangers from robbers, dangers from my own race, dangers from Gentiles, dangers in the city, dangers in the wilderness, dangers at sea, dangers among false brothers; [27p]in toil and hardship, through many sleepless nights, through hunger and thirst, through frequent fastings, through cold and exposure. [28]And apart from these things, there is the daily pressure upon me of my anxiety for all the churches. [29q]Who is weak, and I am not weak? Who is led to sin, and I am not indignant?

Paul's Boast: His Weakness. [30]*If I must boast, I will boast of the things that show my weakness. [31]*The God and Father of the Lord Jesus knows, he who is blessed forever, that I do not lie. [32]At Damascus, the governor under King Aretas guarded the city of Damascus, in order to seize me, [33r]but I was lowered in a basket through a window in the wall and escaped his hands.

CHAPTER 12

See RG 380–81

[1]*I must boast; not that it is profitable, but I will go on to visions and revelations of

11, 16—12, 10: Paul now accepts the challenge of his opponents and indulges in boasting similar to theirs, but with differences that he has already signaled in 10, 12–18 and that become clearer as he proceeds. He defines the nature of his project and unmistakably labels it as folly at the beginning and the end (11, 16–23; 12, 11). Yet his boast does not spring from ignorance (11, 21; 12, 6) nor is it concerned merely with human distinctions (11, 18). Paul boasts "in moderation" (10, 13.15) and "in the Lord" (10, 17).

11, 16–29: The first part of Paul's boast focuses on labors and afflictions, in which authentic service of Christ consists.

11, 16–21: These verses recapitulate remarks already made about the foolishness of boasting and the excessive toleration of the Corinthians. They form a prelude to the boast proper.

11, 20: Paul describes the activities of the "others" in terms that fill out the picture drawn in vv 3–4.13–15. Much of the vocabulary suggests fleshly or even satanic activity. **Enslaves:** cf Gal 2, 4. **Devours:** cf 1 Pt 5, 8. **Gets the better:** the verb **lambanō** means "to take," but is used in a variety of senses; here it may imply financial advantage, as in the English colloquialism "to take someone." It is similarly used at 12, 16 and is there connected with cunning and deceit. **Puts on airs:** the same verb is rendered "raise oneself" (10, 5) and "be too elated" (12, 7).

11, 21: Paul ironically concedes the charge of personal weakness from 10, 1–18 but will refute the other charge there mentioned, that of lack of boldness, accepting the challenge to demonstrate it by his boast.

11, 22: The opponents apparently pride themselves on their "Jewishness." Paul, too, can claim to be a Jew by race, religion, and promise. **Descendants of Abraham:** elsewhere Paul distinguishes authentic from inauthentic heirs of Abraham and the promise (Rom 4, 13–18; 9, 7–13; 11, 1; Gal 3, 9.27–29; cf Jn 8, 33–47). Here he grants his opponents this title in order to concentrate on the principal claim that follows.

11, 23a: Ministers of Christ . . . I am still more: the central point of the boast (cf the note on 11, 5). **Like an insane person:** the climax of his folly.

11, 23b-29: Service of the humiliated and crucified Christ is demonstrated by trials endured for him. This rhetorically impressive catalogue enumerates many of the labors and perils Paul encountered on his missionary journeys.

11, 30—12, 10: The second part of Paul's boast, marked by a change of style and a shift in focus. After recalling the project in which he is engaged, he states a new topic: his weaknesses as matter for boasting. Everything in this section, even the discussion of privileges and distinctions, will be integrated into this perspective.

11, 31–32: The episode at Damascus is symbolic. It aptly illustrates Paul's weakness but ends in deliverance (cf 4, 7–11).

12, 1–4: In the body or out of the body: he seemed no longer confined to bodily conditions, but he does not claim to understand the mechanics of the experience. **Caught up:** i.e., in ecstasy. **The third heaven . . . Paradise:** ancient cosmolo-

l: Acts 22, 3 / Rom 11, 1; Phil 3, 5-6. *m:* 6, 5; Acts 16, 22-24; 1 Cor 15, 31-32. *n:* Dt 25, 2-3. *o:* Acts 14, 19; 27, 43-44. *p:* 1 Cor 4, 11. *q:* 1 Cor 9, 22. *r:* Acts 9, 23-25.

the Lord. ²I know someone in Christ who, fourteen years ago (whether in the body or out of the body I do not know, God knows), was caught up to the third heaven. ³And I know that this person (whether in the body or out of the body I do not know, God knows) ⁴ˢwas caught up into Paradise and heard ineffable things, which no one may utter. ⁵*About this person I will boast, but about myself I will not boast, except about my weaknesses. ⁶Although if I should wish to boast, I would not be foolish, for I would be telling the truth. But I refrain, so that no one may think more of me than what he sees in me or hears from me ⁷ᵗ*because of the abundance of the revelations. Therefore, that I might not become too elated, a thorn in the flesh was given to me, an angel of Satan, to beat me, to keep me from being too elated. ⁸ᵘ*Three times I begged the Lord about this, that it might leave me, ⁹ᵛ*but he said to me, "My grace is sufficient for you, for power is made perfect in weakness." I will rather boast most gladly of my weaknesses, in order that the power of Christ may dwell with me. ¹⁰ʷ*Therefore, I am content with weaknesses, insults, hardships, persecutions, and constraints, for the sake of Christ; for when I am weak, then I am strong.

Selfless Concern for the Church. ¹¹ˣ*I have been foolish. You compelled me, for I ought to have been commended by you. For I am in no way inferior to these "superapostles," even though I am nothing. ¹²ʸ*The

---

gies depicted a multitiered universe. Jewish intertestamental literature contains much speculation about the number of heavens. Seven is the number usually mentioned, but the Testament of Levi (2, 7–10; 3, 1–4) speaks of three; God himself dwelt in the third of these. Without giving us any clear picture of the cosmos, Paul indicates a mental journey to a nonearthly space, set apart by God, in which secrets were revealed to him. **Ineffable things:** i.e., privileged knowledge, which it was not possible or permitted to divulge.

12, 5–7: This person: the indirect way of referring to himself has the effect of emphasizing the distance between that experience and his everyday life, just as the indirect **someone in Christ** (2) and all the passive verbs emphasize his passivity and receptivity in the experience. The revelations were not a personal achievement, nor were they meant to draw attention to any quality of his own.

12, 7b: That I might not become too elated: God assures that there is a negative component to his experience, so that he cannot lose proper perspective; cf 1, 9; 4, 7–11. **A thorn in the flesh:** variously interpreted as a sickness or physical disability, a temptation, or a handicap connected with his apostolic activity. But since Hebrew "thorn in the flesh," like English "thorn in my side," refers to persons (cf Nm 33, 55; Ez 28, 24), Paul may be referring to some especially persistent and obnoxious opponent. The language of vv 7–8 permits this interpretation. If this is correct, the frequent appearance of singular pronouns in depicting the opposition may not be merely a stylistic variation; the singular may be provoked and accompanied by the image of one individual in whom criticism of Paul's preaching, way of life, and apostolic consciousness is concentrated, and who embodies all the qualities Paul attributes to the group. **An angel of Satan:** a personal messenger from Satan; cf the satanic language already applied to the opponents in 11, 3.13–15.20.

12, 8: Three times: his prayer was insistent, like that of Jesus in Gethsemane, a sign of how intolerable he felt the thorn to be.

12, 9: But he said to me: Paul's petition is denied; release and healing are withheld for a higher purpose. The Greek perfect tense indicates that Jesus' earlier response still holds at the time of writing. **My grace is sufficient for you:** this is not a statement about the sufficiency of grace in general. Jesus speaks directly to Paul's situation. **Is made perfect:** i.e., is given most fully and manifests itself fully.

12, 9b-10a: Paul draws the conclusion from the autobiographical anecdote and integrates it into the subject of this part of the boast. **Weaknesses:** the apostolic hardships he must endure, including active personal hostility, as specified in a final catalogue (10a). **That the power of Christ may dwell with me:** Paul pinpoints the ground for the paradoxical strategy he has adopted in his self-defense.

12, 10b: When I am weak, then I am strong: Paul recognizes a twofold pattern in the resolution of the weakness-power (and death-life) dialectic, each of which looks to Jesus as the model and is experienced in him. The first is personal, involving a reversal in oneself (Jesus, 13, 4a; Paul, 1, 9–10; 4, 10–11; 6, 9). The second is apostolic, involving an effect on others (Jesus, 5, 14–15; Paul, 1, 6; 4, 12; 13, 9). The specific kind of "effectiveness in ministry" that Paul promises to demonstrate on his arrival (13, 4b; cf 10, 1–11) involves elements of both; this, too, will be modeled on Jesus' experience and a participation in that experience (9; 13, 3b).

12, 11–18: This brief section forms an epilogue or concluding observation to Paul's boast, corresponding to the prologue in 11, 1–15. A four-step sequence of ideas is common to these two sections: Paul qualifies his boast as folly (11, 1; 12, 11a), asserts his noninferiority to the "superapostles" (11, 5; 12, 11b), exemplifies this by allusion to charismatic endowments (11, 6; 12, 12), and finally denies that he has been a financial burden to the community (11, 7–12; 12, 13–18).

12, 12: Despite weakness and affliction (suggested by the mention of endurance), his ministry has been accompanied by demonstrations of power (cf 1 Cor 2, 3–4). **Signs of an apostle:** visible proof of belonging to Christ and of mediating Christ's power, which the opponents require as touchstones of apostleship (11; cf 13, 3).

---

s: Lk 23, 43; Rv 2, 7. t: Nm 33, 55; Jos 23, 13; Ez 28, 24. u: Mt 26, 39-44. v: 4, 7. w: 6, 4-5; Rom 5, 3 / Phil 4, 13. x: 11, 5. y: Rom 15, 19; 1 Thes 1, 5.

signs of an apostle were performed among you with all endurance, signs and wonders, and mighty deeds. 13z*In what way were you less privileged than the rest of the churches, except that on my part I did not burden you? Forgive me this wrong!

14Now I am ready to come to you this third time. And I will not be a burden, for I want not what is yours, but you. Children ought not to save for their parents, but parents for their children. 15I will most gladly spend and be utterly spent for your sakes. If I love you more, am I to be loved less? 16aBut granted that I myself did not burden you, yet I was crafty and got the better of you by deceit. 17Did I take advantage of you through any of those I sent to you? 18bI urged Titus to go and sent the brother with him. Did Titus take advantage of you? Did we not walk in the same spirit? And in the same steps?

Final Warnings and Appeals. 19*Have you been thinking all along that we are defending ourselves before you? In the sight of God we are speaking in Christ, and all for building you up, beloved. 20c*For I fear that when I come I may find you not such as I wish, and that you may find me not as you wish; that there may be rivalry, jealousy, fury, selfishness, slander, gossip, conceit, and disorder. 21*I fear that when I come again my God may humiliate me before you, and I may have to mourn over many of those who sinned earlier and have not repented of the impurity, immorality, and licentiousness they practiced.

CHAPTER 13

See RG 380-81

1d*This third time I am coming to you. "On the testimony of two or three witnesses a fact shall be established." 2*I warned those who sinned earlier and all the others, and I warn them now while absent, as I did when present on my second visit, that if I come again I will not be lenient, 3*since you are looking for proof of Christ speaking in me. He is not weak toward you but powerful in you. 4For indeed he was crucified out of

12, 13–18: Paul insists on his intention to continue refusing support from the community (cf 11, 8–12). In defending his practice and his motivation, he once more protests his love (cf 11, 11) and rejects the suggestion of secret self-enrichment. He has recourse here again to language applied to his opponents earlier: "cunning" (11, 3), "deceit" (11, 13), "got the better of you" (see the note on 11, 20), "take advantage" (2, 11).

12, 19—13, 10: This concludes the development begun in ch 10. In the chiastic arrangement of the material (see the note on 10, 1—13, 10), this final part corresponds to the opening; there are important similarities of content between the two sections as well.

12, 19: This verse looks back at the previous chapters and calls them by their proper name, a defense, an **apologia** (cf 1 Cor 9, 3). Yet Paul insists on an important distinction: he has indeed been speaking for their benefit, but the ultimate judgment to which he submits is God's (cf 1 Cor 4, 3–5). This verse also leads into the final section, announcing two of its themes: judgment and building up.

12, 20: I fear that . . . : earlier Paul expressed fear that the Corinthians were being victimized, exploited, seduced from right thinking by his opponents (11, 3–4.19–21). Here he alludes unexpectedly to moral disorders among the Corinthians themselves. The catalogue suggests the effects of factions that have grown up around rival apostles.

12, 21: Again: one can also translate, "I fear that when I come my God may again humiliate me." Paul's allusion to the humiliation and mourning that may await him recall the mood he described in 2, 1–4, but there is no reference here to any individual such as there is in 2, 5–11. The crisis of ch 2 has happily been resolved by integration of the offender and repentance (7, 4–16), whereas 12, 21 is preoccupied with still

unrepentant sinners. The sexual sins recall 1 Cor 5–7.

13, 1: This third time I am coming: designation of the forthcoming visit as the "third" (cf 12, 14) may indicate that, in addition to his founding sojourn in Corinth, Paul had already made the first of two visits mentioned as planned in 1, 15, and the next visit will be the long-postponed second of these. If so, the materials in 1, 12—2, 13 plus 7, 4–16 and chs 10–13 may date from the same period of time, presumably of some duration, between Paul's second and third visit, though it is not clear that they are addressing the same crisis. The chronology is too unsure and the relations between sections of 2 Cor too unclear to yield any certainty. The hypothesis that chs 10–13 are themselves the "tearful letter" mentioned at 2, 3–4 creates more problems than it solves.

13, 2: I warned those who sinned earlier: mention of unrepentant sinners (12, 21 and here) and of an oral admonition given them on an earlier visit complicates the picture at the very end of Paul's development. It provides, in fact, a second explanation for the show of power that has been threatened from the beginning (10, 1–6), but a different reason for it, quite unsuspected until now. It is not clear whether Paul is merely alluding to a dimension of the situation that he has not previously had occasion to mention, or whether some other community crisis, not directly connected with that behind chs 10–13, has influenced the final editing. **I will not be lenient:** contrast Paul's hesitation and reluctance to inflict pain in 1, 23 and 2, 1–4. The next visit will bring the showdown.

13, 3–4: Paul now gives another motive for severity when he comes, the charge of weakness leveled against him as an apostle. The motive echoes more closely the opening section

z: 11, 9-12.   a: 11, 3.13.   b: 2, 13; 8, 16.23.   c: 1 Cor 1, 11; 3, 3.   d: Dt 19, 15; Mt 18, 16; Jn 8, 17; Heb 10, 28.

weakness, but he lives by the power of God. So also we are weak in him, but toward you we shall live with him by the power of God.

⁵*Examine yourselves to see whether you are living in faith. Test yourselves. Do you not realize that Jesus Christ is in you?—unless, of course, you fail the test. ⁶I hope you will discover that we have not failed. ⁷But we pray to God that you may not do evil, not that we may appear to have passed the test but that you may do what is right, even though we may seem to have failed. ⁸For we cannot do anything against the truth, but only for the truth. ⁹For we rejoice when we are weak but you are strong. What we pray for is your improvement.

¹⁰ᵉ*I am writing this while I am away, so that when I come I may not have to be severe in virtue of the authority that the Lord has given me to build up and not to tear down.

V: Conclusion

¹¹*Finally, brothers, rejoice. Mend your ways, encourage one another, agree with one another, live in peace, and the God of love and peace will be with you. ¹²ᶠGreet one another with a holy kiss. All the holy ones greet you.

¹³ᵍThe grace of the Lord Jesus Christ and the love of God and the fellowship of the holy Spirit be with all of you.

(10, 1–18) and the intervening development (especially 11, 30—12, 10). **Proof of Christ speaking in me:** the threat of 10, 1–2 is reworded to recall Paul's conformity with the pattern of Christ, his insertion into the interplay of death and life, weakness and power (cf the note on 12, 10b).

13, 5–9: Paul turns the challenge mentioned in v 3 on them: they are to put themselves to the test to demonstrate whether Christ is in them. These verses involve a complicated series of plays on the theme of **dokimē** (testing, proof, passing and failing a test). Behind this stands the familiar distinction between present human judgment and final divine judgment. This is the final appearance of the theme (cf 10, 18; 11, 15; 12, 19).

13, 10: Authority . . . to build up and not to tear down: Paul restates the purpose of his letter in language that echoes 10, 2.8, emphasizing the positive purpose of his authority in

their regard. This verse forms an inclusion with the topic sentence of the section (12, 19), as well as with the opening of this entire portion of the letter (10, 1–2).

13, 11–13: These verses may have originally concluded chs 10–13, but they have nothing specifically to do with the material of that section. It is also possible to consider them a conclusion to the whole of 2 Cor in its present edited form. The exhortations are general, including a final appeal for peace in the community. The letter ends calmly, after its many storms, with the prospect of ecclesial unity and divine blessing. The final verse is one of the clearest trinitarian passages in the New Testament.

─────────────

e: 10, 8. *f*: Rom 16, 16; 1 Cor 16, 20 / Phil 4, 22; 1 Thes 5, 26; 1 Pt 5, 14. *g*: Rom 16, 20; 1 Cor 16, 23.

See RG 382–90

The Letter to the Galatians

The Galatians to whom the letter is addressed were Paul's converts, most likely among the descendants of Celts who had invaded western and central Asia Minor in the third century B.C. and had settled in the territory around Ancyra (modern Ankara, Turkey). Paul had passed through this area on his second missionary journey (Acts 16, 6) and again on his third (Acts 18, 23). It is less likely that the recipients of this letter were Paul's churches in the southern regions of Pisidia, Lycaonia, and Pamphylia where he had preached earlier in the Hellenized cities of Perge, Iconium, Pisidian Antioch, Lystra, and Derbe (Acts 13, 13—14, 27); this area was part of the Roman province of Galatia, and some scholars think that South Galatia was the destination of this letter.

If it is addressed to the Galatians in the north, the letter was probably written around A.D. 54 or 55, most likely from Ephesus after Paul's arrival there for a stay of several years on his third missionary journey (Acts 19; 20, 31). On the South Galatian theory, the date would be earlier, perhaps A.D. 48–50. Involved is the question of how one relates the events of 2, 1–10 to the "Council of Jerusalem" described in Acts 15 (see the notes on each passage).

In any case, the new Christians whom Paul is addressing were converts from paganism (4, 8–9) who were now being enticed by other missionaries to add the observances of the Jewish law, including the rite of circumcision, to the cross of Christ as a means of salvation. For, since Paul's visit, some other interpretation of Christianity had been brought to these neophytes, probably by converts from Judaism (the name "Judaizers" is sometimes applied to them); it has specifically been suggested that they were Jewish Christians who had come from the austere Essene sect.

These interlopers insisted on the necessity of following certain precepts of the Mosaic law along with faith in Christ. They were undermining Paul's authority also, asserting that he had not been trained by Jesus himself, that his gospel did not agree with that of the original and true apostles in Jerusalem, that he had kept from his converts in Galatia the necessity of accepting circumcision and other key obligations of the Jewish law, in order more easily to win them to Christ, and that his gospel was thus not the full and authentic one held by "those of repute" in Jerusalem (2, 2). Some scholars also see in chapters 5 and 6 another set of opponents against whom Paul writes, people who in their emphasis on the Spirit set aside all norms for conduct and became libertines in practice.

When Paul learned of the situation, he wrote this defense of his apostolic authority and of the correct understanding of the faith. He set forth the unique importance of Christ and his redemptive sacrifice on the cross, the freedom that Christians enjoy from the old burdens of the law, the total sufficiency of Christ and of faith in Christ as the way to God and to eternal life, and the beauty of the new life of the Spirit. Galatians is thus a summary of basic Pauline theology. Its themes were more fully and less polemically developed in the Letter to the Romans.

Autobiographically, the letter gives us Paul's own accounts of how he came to faith (1, 15–24), the agreement in "the truth of the gospel" (2, 5.14) that he shared with the Jewish Christian leaders in Jerusalem, James, Cephas, and John (2, 1–10), and the rebuke he had to deliver to Cephas in Antioch for inconsistency, contrary to the gospel, on the issue of table fellowship in the racially mixed church of Jewish and Gentile

Christians in Antioch (2, 11–14; cf 2, 15–21). At the conclusion of the letter (6, 11–18), Paul wrote in his own hand (cf 2 Thes 3, 17–18) a vivid summary of the message to the Galatians.

In his vigorous emphasis on the absolute preeminence of Christ and his cross as God's way to salvation and holiness, Paul stresses Christian freedom and the ineffectiveness of the Mosaic law for gaining divine favor and blessings (3, 19–29). The pious Jew saw in the law a way established by God to win divine approval by a life of meticulous observance of ritual, social, and moral regulations. But Paul's profound insight into the higher designs of God in Christ led him to understand and welcome the priority of promise and faith (shown in the experience of Abraham, 3, 6–18) and the supernatural gifts of the Spirit (3, 2–5; 5, 16—6, 10). His enthusiasm for this new vision of the life of grace in Christ and of the uniquely salvific role of Christ's redemptive death on the cross shines through this whole letter.

The principal divisions of the Letter to the Galatians are the following:

I: Address (1, 1–5)
II: Loyalty to the Gospel (1, 6–10)
III: Paul's Defense of His Gospel and His Authority (1, 11—2, 21)
IV: Faith and Liberty (3, 1—4, 31)
V: Exhortation to Christian Living (5, 1—6, 10)
VI: Conclusion (6, 11–18)

I: Address

CHAPTER 1

See RG 385–86

Greeting. [1ab]*Paul, an apostle not from human beings nor through a human being but through Jesus Christ and God the Father who raised him from the dead, [2]*and all the brothers who are with me, to the churches of Galatia: [3]grace to you and peace from God our Father and the Lord Jesus Christ, [4c]*who

---

1, 1–5: See the note on Rom 1, 1–7, concerning the greeting.

1, 1: **Apostle:** because of attacks on his authority in Galatia, Paul defends his apostleship. He is not an apostle commissioned by a congregation (Phil 2, 25; 2 Cor 8, 23) or even by prophets (1 Tm 1, 18 and 4, 14) but **through Jesus Christ and God the Father.**

1, 2: **All the brothers:** fellow believers in Christ, male and female; cf 3, 27–28. Paul usually mentions the co-

sender(s) at the start of a letter, but the use of all is unique, adding weight to the letter. **Galatia:** central Turkey more likely than the Roman province of Galatia; see Introduction.

1, 4: The greeting in v 3 is expanded by a christological

a: Rom 1, 1-7; 1 Cor 1, 1-3. *b:* 1, 11-12. *c:* 2, 20; Eph 5, 2; 1 Tm 2, 6 / 1 Jn 5, 19 / Rom 12, 2; Eph 5, 16; Heb 10, 10.

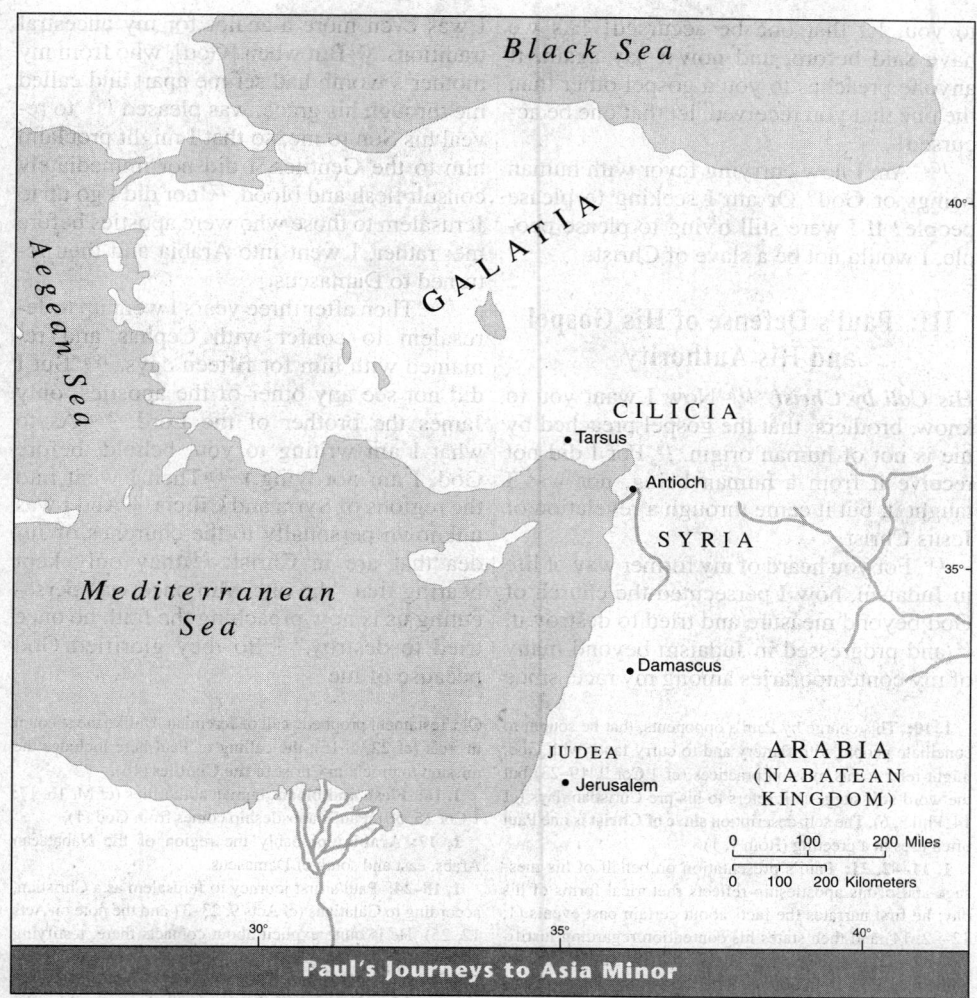

Paul's Journeys to Asia Minor

gave himself for our sins that he might rescue us from the present evil age in accord with the will of our God and Father, ^{5d}to whom be glory forever and ever. Amen.

II: Loyalty To The Gospel

^{6e}*I am amazed that you are so quickly for-saking the one who called you by [the] grace [of Christ] for a different gospel ⁷(not that there is another). But there are some who are disturbing you and wish to pervert the gospel of Christ. ^{8f}*But even if we or an angel from heaven should preach [to you] a gospel other than the one that we preached

formula that stresses deliverance through the Lord Jesus from a world dominated by Satan; cf 2 Cor 4, 4; Eph 2, 2; 6, 12.

1, 6–10: In place of the usual thanksgiving (see the note on Rom 1, 8), Paul, with little to be thankful for in the Galatian situation, expresses amazement at the way his converts are deserting the gospel of Christ for a perverted message. He reasserts the one gospel he has preached (7–9) and begins to defend himself (10).

1, 6: **The one who called you:** God or Christ, though in actuality Paul was the divine instrument to call the Galatians.

1, 8: **Accursed:** in Greek, **anathema;** cf Rom 9, 3; 1 Cor 12, 3; 16, 22.

d: Rom 16, 27; 2 Tm 4, 18. e: 5, 8.10; Acts 15, 1.24; 2 Cor 11, 4. f: 1 Cor 16, 22 / 5, 3.21; 2 Cor 13, 2.

to you, let that one be accursed! ⁹As we have said before, and now I say again, if anyone preaches to you a gospel other than the one that you received, let that one be accursed!

¹⁰ᵍ*Am I now currying favor with human beings or God? Or am I seeking to please people? If I were still trying to please people, I would not be a slave of Christ.

III: Paul's Defense of His Gospel and His Authority

His Call by Christ. ¹¹ʰ*Now I want you to know, brothers, that the gospel preached by me is not of human origin. ¹²*For I did not receive it from a human being, nor was I taught it, but it came through a revelation of Jesus Christ.

¹³ⁱ*For you heard of my former way of life in Judaism, how I persecuted the church of God beyond measure and tried to destroy it, ¹⁴ʲand progressed in Judaism beyond many of my contemporaries among my race, since

I was even more a zealot for my ancestral traditions. ¹⁵ᵏBut when [God], who from my mother's womb had set me apart and called me through his grace, was pleased ¹⁶ˡ*to reveal his Son to me, so that I might proclaim him to the Gentiles, I did not immediately consult flesh and blood, ¹⁷*nor did I go up to Jerusalem to those who were apostles before me; rather, I went into Arabia and then returned to Damascus.

¹⁸ᵐ*Then after three years I went up to Jerusalem to confer with Cephas and remained with him for fifteen days. ¹⁹ⁿ*But I did not see any other of the apostles, only James the brother of the Lord. ²⁰ᵒ(As to what I am writing to you, behold, before God, I am not lying.) ²¹ᵖThen I went into the regions of Syria and Cilicia. ²²And I was unknown personally to the churches of Judea that are in Christ; ²³ᵠthey only kept hearing that "the one who once was persecuting us is now preaching the faith he once tried to destroy." ²⁴So they glorified God because of me.

1, 10: This charge by Paul's opponents, that he sought to conciliate people with flattery and to curry favor with God, might refer to his mission practices (cf 1 Cor 9, 19–23) but the word **still** suggests it refers to his pre-Christian days (cf 14; Phil 3, 6). The self-description **slave of Christ** is one Paul often uses in a greeting (Rom 1, 1).

1, 11—2, 21: Paul's presentation on behalf of his message and of his apostleship reflects rhetorical forms of his day: he first narrates the facts about certain past events (1, 12—2, 14) and then states his contention regarding justification by faith as the gospel message (2, 15–21). Further arguments follow from both experience and scripture in chs 3 and 4, before he draws out the ethical consequences (5, 1—6, 10). The specific facts that he takes up here to show that his gospel is not a human invention (1, 11) but **came through a revelation of Jesus Christ** (1, 12) deal with his own calling as a Christian missionary (1, 13–17), his initial relations with the apostles in Jerusalem (1, 18–24), a later journey to Jerusalem (2, 1–10), and an incident in Antioch involving Cephas and persons from James (2, 11–14). The content of Paul's revealed gospel is then set forth in the heart of the letter (2, 15–21).

1, 12: Although Paul received his gospel **through a revelation** from Christ, this did not exclude his use of early Christian confessional formulations. See the note on 1, 4.

1, 13–17: Along with Phil 3, 4–11, which also moves from autobiography to its climax in a discussion on justification by faith (cf Gal 2, 15–21), this passage is Paul's chief account of the change from his **former way of life** (13) to service as a Christian missionary (16); cf Acts 9, 1–22; 22, 4–16; 26, 9–18. Paul himself does not use the term "conversion" but stresses revelation (12.16). In v 15 his language echoes the

Old Testament prophetic call of Jeremiah. Unlike the account in Acts (cf 22, 4–16), the calling of Paul here includes the mission to proclaim Christ **to the Gentiles** (16).

1, 16: Flesh and blood: human authorities (cf Mt 16, 17; 1 Cor 15, 50). Paul's apostleship comes from God (1).

1, 17: Arabia: probably the region of the Nabataean Arabs, east and south of Damascus.

1, 18–24: Paul's first journey to Jerusalem as a Christian, according to Galatians (cf Acts 9, 23–31 and the note on Acts 12, 25). He is quite explicit about contacts there, testifying under oath (20). On returning to **Syria** (perhaps specifically Damascus, cf v 17) and **Cilicia** (including his home town Tarsus, cf Acts 9, 30; 22, 3), Paul most likely engaged in missionary work. He underscores the fact that Christians in Judea knew of him only by reputation.

1, 18: After three years: two years and more, since Paul's call. To **confer with** Cephas may mean simply "pay a visit" or more specifically "get information from" him about Jesus, over a two-week period. **Cephas:** Aramaic name of Simon (Peter); cf Mt 16, 16–18 and the notes there.

1, 19: James the brother of the Lord: not one of the Twelve, but a brother of Jesus (see the note on Mk 6, 3). He played an important role in the Jerusalem church (see the note on Gal 2, 9), the leadership of which he took over from Peter (Acts 12, 17). Paul may have regarded James as an apostle.

g: 2 Cor 5, 11 / 1 Thes 2, 4. h: 1 Cor 15, 1 / 1, 1; Eph 3, 3. i: Acts 8, 1-3; 9, 1-2; 1 Cor 15, 9. j: Acts 26, 4-5. k: Is 49, 1; Jer 1, 4. l: 1, 11-12; Rom 1, 5; 1 Cor 15, 10; Acts 9, 3-9 / 2, 2.7 /Mt 16, 17. m: Acts 9, 26-30 / Jn 1, 42. n: 2, 9; Mt 13, 55; Acts 12, 17. o: Rom 9, 1; 2 Cor 11, 31. p: Acts 9, 30. q: 1, 13.

See RG
386–87

CHAPTER 2

The Council of Jerusalem. ¹ʳ*Then after fourteen years I again went up to Jerusalem with Barnabas, taking Titus along also. ²ˢ*I went up in accord with a revelation, and I presented to them the gospel that I preach to the Gentiles—but privately to those of repute—so that I might not be running, or have run, in vain. ³ᵗ*Moreover, not even Titus, who was with me, although he was a Greek, was compelled to be circumcised, ⁴ᵘ*but because of the false brothers secretly brought in, who slipped in to spy on our freedom that we have in Christ Jesus, that they might enslave us— ⁵ᵛ*to them we did not submit even for a moment, so that the truth of the gospel might remain intact for you. ⁶ʷBut from those who were reputed to be important (what they once were makes no difference to me; God shows no partiality)—those of repute made me add nothing. ⁷ˣ*On the contrary, when they saw that I had been entrusted with the gospel to the uncircumcised, just as Peter to the circumcised, ⁸for the one who worked in Peter for an apostolate to the circumcised worked also in me for the Gentiles, ⁹ʸ*and when they recognized the grace bestowed upon me, James and Cephas and John, who were reputed to be pillars, gave me and Barnabas their right hands in partnership, that we should go to the Gentiles and they to the circumcised. ¹⁰ᶻ*Only, we were to be mindful of the poor, which is the very thing I was eager to do.

Peter's Inconsistency at Antioch. ¹¹ᵃ*And when Cephas came to Antioch, I opposed him to his face because he clearly was wrong.

2, 1–10: Paul's second journey to Jerusalem, according to Galatians, involved a private meeting with **those of repute** (2). At issue was a Gentile, Titus, and the question of circumcision, which **false brothers** (4) evidently demanded for him. Paul insists that the gospel he preaches (2; cf 1, 9.11) remained intact with no addition by those of repute (6); that **Titus** was not **compelled** to accept circumcision (3); and that he and the reputed **pillars** in Jerusalem agreed on how each would advance the missionary task (7–10). Usually, 1–10 is equated with the "Council of Jerusalem," as it is called, described in Acts 15. See the notes on Acts 15, 6–12 and 15, 13–35, the latter concerning the "decree" that Paul does not mention.

2, 1: After fourteen years: thirteen or more years, probably reckoned from the return to Syria and Cilicia (1, 21), though possibly from Paul's calling as a Christian (1, 15). **Barnabas:** cf 9.13; 1 Cor 9, 6. A Jewish Christian missionary, with whom Paul worked (Acts 4, 36–37; 11, 22.25.30; 12, 25; 13, 1–3; 15, 2). **Titus:** a missionary companion of Paul (2 Cor 2, 13; 7, 6.13–15; 8, 6.16.23; 12, 18), non-Jewish (Gal 2, 3), never mentioned in Acts.

2, 2: A revelation: cf 1, 1.12. Paul emphasizes it was God's will, not Jerusalem authority, that led to the journey. Acts 15, 2 states that the church in Antioch appointed Paul and Barnabas for the task. **Those of repute:** leaders of the Jerusalem church; the term, while positive, may be slightly ironic (cf 6.9). **Run, in vain:** while Paul presents a positive picture in what follows, his missionary work in Galatia would have been to no purpose if his opponents were correct that circumcision is needed for complete faith in Christ.

2, 3: Not even a Gentile Christian like Titus was compelled to receive the rite of circumcision. The Greek text could be interpreted that he voluntarily accepted circumcision, but this is unlikely in the overall argument.

2, 4: False brothers: Jewish Christians who took the position that Gentile Christians must first become Jews through circumcision and observance of the Mosaic law in order to become Christians; cf Acts 15, 1.

2, 5: The truth of the gospel: the true gospel, in contrast to the false one of the opponents (1, 6–9); the gospel of grace, used as a norm (14).

2, 7–9: Some think that actual "minutes" of the meeting are here quoted. Paul's apostleship to the Gentiles (1, 16) is recognized alongside that of Peter to the Jews. Moreover, the right to proclaim the gospel without requiring circumcision and the Jewish law is sealed by a handshake. That Paul and colleagues **should go to the Gentiles** did not exclude his preaching to the Jews as well (Rom 1, 13–16) or Cephas to Gentile areas.

2, 9: James and Cephas and John: see the notes on 1, 18 and 19; on Peter and John as leaders in the Jerusalem church, cf Acts 3, 1 and 8, 14. The order here, with James first, may reflect his prominence in Jerusalem after Peter (Cephas) departed (Acts 12, 17).

2, 10: The poor: Jerusalem Christians or a group within the church there (cf Rom 15, 26). The collection for them was extremely important in Paul's thought and labor (cf Rom 15, 25–28; 1 Cor 16, 1–4; 2 Cor 8 and 9).

2, 11–14: The decision reached in Jerusalem (3–7) recognized the freedom of Gentile Christians from the Jewish law. But the problem of table fellowship between Jewish Christians who possibly still kept kosher food regulations, and Gentile believers was not yet settled. When Cephas first came to the racially mixed community of Jewish and Gentile Christians in Antioch (12), he ate with non-Jews. Pressure from persons arriving later from Jerusalem caused him and Barnabas to draw back. Paul therefore publicly rebuked Peter's inconsistency toward the gospel (14). Some think that what Paul said on that occasion extends through v 16 or v 21.

2, 11: Clearly was wrong: literally, "stood condemned," by himself and also by Paul. His action in breaking table fel-

r: Acts 15, 2. *s:* 1, 11-12.16 / 1, 16 / Phil 2, 16. *t:* 2 Cor 2, 13; 7, 6-7; 8, 16-17; 12, 18; Ti 1, 4 / 2, 14; 6, 12. *u:* 5, 1; Acts 15, 1.24. *v:* 2, 14; 4, 16. *w:* Dt 10, 17; Rom 2, 11. *x:* 1, 15-16; Acts 9, 15; 15, 12; 22, 21; Rom 1, 5. *y:* Rom 15, 15 / 1, 18-19; Jn 1, 42; Acts 12, 17 / 2, 1. *z:* Acts 11, 29-30; Rom 15, 25-28; 1 Cor 16, 1-4; 2 Cor 8, 9. *a:* 1, 18 / Acts 11, 19-30; 15, 1-2.

12b*For, until some people came from James, he used to eat with the Gentiles; but when they came, he began to draw back and separated himself, because he was afraid of the circumcised. *13c**And the rest of the Jews [also] acted hypocritically along with him, with the result that even Barnabas was carried away by their hypocrisy. *14d**But when I saw that they were not on the right road in line with the truth of the gospel, I said to Cephas in front of all, "If you, though a Jew, are living like a Gentile and not like a Jew, how can you compel the Gentiles to live like Jews?"

Faith and Works. *15**We, who are Jews by nature and not sinners from among the Gentiles, *16e**[yet] who know that a person is not justified by works of the law but through faith in Jesus Christ, even we have believed in Christ Jesus that we may be justified by faith in Christ and not by works of the law, because by works of the law no one will be justified. *17**But if, in seeking to be justified in Christ, we ourselves are found to be sinners, is Christ then a minister of sin? Of course not! *18**But if I am building up again those things that I tore down, then I show myself to be a transgressor. *19f**For through the law I died to the law, that I might live for God. I have been crucified with Christ; *20g*yet I live, no longer I, but Christ lives in me; insofar as I now live in the flesh, I live by faith in the Son of God who has loved me and given himself up for me. *21h*I do not nullify the grace of God; for if justification comes through the law, then Christ died for nothing.

IV: Faith and Liberty

CHAPTER 3

See RG 387–88

Justification by Faith. *1i**O stupid Galatians! Who has bewitched you, before whose eyes Jesus Christ was publicly portrayed as crucified? *2j**I want to learn only this from you: did you receive the Spirit from works of the law, or from faith in what you heard? *3k**Are you so stupid? After beginning with the Spirit, are you now ending with the flesh? *4**Did you experience so many things

---

lowship was especially grievous if the eating involved the meal at the Lord's supper (cf 1 Cor 11, 17–25).

2, 12: Some people came from James: strict Jewish Christians (cf Acts 15, 1.5; 21, 20–21), either sent by James (1, 19; 2, 9) or claiming to be from the leader of the Jerusalem church. **The circumcised:** presumably Jewish Christians, not Jews.

2, 13: The Jews: Jewish Christians, like Barnabas. **Hypocrisy:** literally, "pretense," "play-acting"; moral insincerity.

2, 14: Compel the Gentiles to live like Jews: that is, conform to Jewish practices, such as circumcision (3–5) or regulations about food (12).

2, 15–21: Following on the series of incidents cited above, Paul's argument, whether spoken to Cephas at Antioch or only now articulated, is pertinent to the Galatian situation, where believers were having themselves circumcised (6, 12–13) and obeying other aspects of Jewish law (4, 9–10; 5, 1–4). He insists that salvation is by faith in Christ, not by works of the law. His teaching on the gospel concerns justification by faith (16) in relation to sin (17), law (19), life in Christ (19–20), and grace (21).

2, 16: No one will be justified: Ps 143, 2 is reflected.

2, 17: A minister of sin: literally, "a servant of sin" (cf Rom 15, 8), an agent of sin, one who promotes it. This is possibly a claim by opponents that justification on the basis of faith in Christ makes Christ an abettor of sin when Christians are found to be sinners. Paul denies the conclusion (cf Rom 6, 1–4).

2, 18: To return to observance of the law as the means to salvation would entangle one not only in inevitable transgressions of it but also in the admission that it was wrong to have abandoned the law in the first place.

2, 19: Through the law I died to the law: this is vari-

ously explained: the law revealed sin (Rom 7, 7–9) and led to death and then to belief in Christ; or, the law itself brought the insight that law cannot justify (16; Ps 143, 2); or, the "law of Christ" (6, 2) led to abandoning the Mosaic law; or, the law put Christ to death (cf 3, 13) and so provided a way to our salvation, through baptism into Christ, through which we die (**crucified with Christ;** see Rom 6, 6). Cf also 3, 19–25 on the role of the law in reference to salvation.

3, 1–14: Paul's contention that justification comes not through the law or the works of the law but by faith in Christ and in his death (2, 16.21) is supported by appeals to Christian experience (1–5) and to scripture (6–14). The gift of God's Spirit to the Galatians came from the gospel received in faith, not from doing what the law enjoins. The story of Abraham shows that faith in God brings **righteousness** (6; Gn 15, 6). The promise to Abraham (8; Gn 12, 3) extends to the Gentiles (14).

3, 1: Stupid: not just senseless, for they were in danger of deserting their salvation.

3, 2: Faith in what you heard: Paul's message received with faith. The Greek can also mean "the proclamation of the faith" or "a hearing that comes from faith."

3, 3: On the contrast of **Spirit** and **flesh,** cf Rom 8, 1–11. Having received the Spirit, they need not be circumcised now.

3, 4: Experience so many things: probably the **mighty deeds** of v 5 but possibly the experience of sufferings.

---

b: Acts 10, 15.28; 11, 3. *c:* 2, 1.9. *d:* 2, 5 / 1, 18; 2, 9 / 2, 3. *e:* 3, 2.11; Ps 143, 1-2; Rom 3, 20.28; 4, 5; 11, 6; Eph 2, 8-9; Phil 3, 9. *f:* 6, 14; Rom 6, 6.8.10; 7, 6. *g:* 1, 4; Rom 8, 10-11; Col 3, 3-4. *h:* 5, 2. *i:* 5, 7; 1 Cor 1, 23. *j:* 2, 16 / 3, 14; Rom 10, 17. *k:* 5, 16-18.

in vain?—if indeed it was in vain. [5]Does, then, the one who supplies the Spirit to you and works mighty deeds among you do so from works of the law or from faith in what you heard? [6m]*Thus Abraham "believed God, and it was credited to him as righteousness."

[7n]*Realize then that it is those who have faith who are children of Abraham. [8o]Scripture, which saw in advance that God would justify the Gentiles by faith, foretold the good news to Abraham, saying, "Through you shall all the nations be blessed." [9p]Consequently, those who have faith are blessed along with Abraham who had faith. [10q]*For all who depend on works of the law are under a curse; for it is written, "Cursed be everyone who does not persevere in doing all the things written in the book of the law." [11r]And that no one is justified before God by the law is clear, for "the one who is righteous by faith will live." [12s]But the law does not depend on faith; rather, "the one who does these things will live by them." [13t]Christ ransomed us from the curse of the law by becoming a curse for us, for it is written, "Cursed be everyone who hangs on a tree," [14u]that the blessing of Abraham might be extended to the Gentiles through Christ Jesus, so that we might receive the promise of the Spirit through faith.

The Law Did Not Nullify the Promise.
[15v]*Brothers, in human terms I say that no one can annul or amend even a human will once ratified. [16w]*Now the promises were made to Abraham and to his descendant. It does not say, "And to descendants," as referring to many, but as referring to one, "And to your descendant," who is Christ. [17x]*This is what I mean: the law, which came four hundred and thirty years afterward, does not annul a covenant previously ratified by God, so as to cancel the promise. [18y]*For if the inheritance comes from the law, it is no longer from a promise; but God bestowed it on Abraham through a promise.

[19z]*Why, then, the law? It was added for

3, 6: Abraham . . . righteousness: see Gn 15, 6; Rom 4, 3. The Galatians like Abraham heard with faith and experienced justification. This first argument forms the basis for the further scriptural evidence that follows.

3, 7–9: Faith is what matters, for **Abraham** and the **children of Abraham,** in contrast to the claims of the opponents that circumcision and observance of the law are needed to bring the promised blessing of Gn 12, 3; cf Gn 18, 18; Sir 44, 21; Acts 3, 25.

3, 10–14: Those **who depend** not on promise and faith but **on works of the law are under a curse** because they do **not persevere in doing all the things written in the book of the law** (10; Dt 27, 26) in order to gain life (12; Lv 18, 5; cf Rom 10, 5). But scripture teaches that **no one is justified before God by the law** (11; Hb 2, 4, adapted from the Greek version of Habakkuk; cf Rom 1, 17; Heb 10, 38). Salvation, then, depends on faith in Christ who died on the cross (13), taking upon himself a curse found in Dt 21, 23 (about executed criminals hanged in public view), to free us from **the curse of the law** (13). That the Gentile Galatians have received the promised Spirit (14) by faith and in no other way returns the argument to the experience cited in vv 1–5.

3, 15–18: A third argument to support Paul's position that salvation is not through the law but by promise (1–14) comes from legal practice and scriptural history. A legal agreement or **human will,** duly **ratified,** is unalterable (15). God's **covenant** with **Abraham** and its repeated promises (Gn 12, 2–3.7; 13, 15; 17, 7–8; 22, 16–18; 24, 7) is not superseded by **the law,** which came much later, in the time of Moses. **The inheritance** (of the Spirit and the blessings) is by promise, not by law (18). Paul's argument hinges on the fact that the same Greek word, **diathēkē,** can be rendered as **will** or testament (15) and as **covenant** (17).

3, 16: Descendant: literally, "and to his seed." The Hebrew, as in Gn 12, 7; 15, 18; 22, 17–18, is a collective singular, traditionally rendered as a plural, **descendants,** but taken by Paul in its literal number to refer to **Christ** as descendant of Abraham.

3, 17: Four hundred and thirty years afterward: follows Ex 12, 40 in the Greek (Septuagint) version, in contrast to Gn 15, 13 and Acts 7, 6, for chronology.

3, 18: This refutes the opponents' contention that the promises of God are fulfilled only as a reward for human observance of the law.

3, 19–22: A digression: if the Mosaic law, then, does not save or **bring life,** why was it given? Elsewhere, Paul says the law served to show what sin is (Rom 3, 20; 7, 7–8). Here the further implication is that the law in effect served to produce transgressions. Moreover, it was received at second hand **by angels,** through a **mediator,** not directly from God (19). The law does not, however, oppose God's purposes, for it carries out its function (22), so that **righteousness** comes by **faith** and **promise,** not by human works of the law.

3, 19: The descendant: Christ (16). **By angels:** Dt 33, 2–4 stressed their presence as enhancing the importance of the law; Paul uses their role to diminish its significance (cf Acts 7, 38.53). **A mediator:** Moses. But in a covenant of

l: 2, 16. *m:* Gn 15, 6; Rom 4, 3; Jas 2, 23. *n:* 3, 29; Rom 4, 11-12 / Sir 44, 19-21. *o:* Gn 12, 3; 18, 17-19; Acts 3, 25. *p:* Rom 4, 16. *q:* Dt 27, 26; Jas 2, 10. *r:* 2, 16; Hb 2, 4; Rom 1, 17. *s:* Lv 18, 5; Rom 10, 5. *t:* Dt 21, 23; Rom 8, 3; 2 Cor 5, 21. *u:* 3, 2-3.5; Is 44, 3; Jl 3, 1-2; Acts 2, 33. *v:* Rom 3, 5 / Heb 9, 16-17. *w:* Gn 12, 7; 13, 15; 17, 8; 22, 17; 24, 7; Mt 1, 1. *x:* Ex 12, 40. *y:* Rom 4, 16; 11, 6. *z:* Rom 4, 15; 5, 20; 7, 7.13 / Acts 7, 38.53.

transgressions, until the descendant came to whom the promise had been made; it was promulgated by angels at the hand of a mediator. 20aNow there is no mediator when only one party is involved, and God is one. 21bIs the law then opposed to the promises [of God]? Of course not! For if a law had been given that could bring life, then righteousness would in reality come from the law. 22cBut scripture confined all things under the power of sin, that through faith in Jesus Christ the promise might be given to those who believe.

What Faith Has Brought Us. 23d*Before faith came, we were held in custody under law, confined for the faith that was to be revealed. 24e*Consequently, the law was our disciplinarian for Christ, that we might be justified by faith. 25fBut now that faith has come, we are no longer under a disciplinarian. 26g*For through faith you are all children of God in Christ Jesus. 27h*For all of you who were baptized into Christ have clothed yourselves with Christ. 28iThere is neither Jew nor Greek, there is neither slave nor free person, there is not male and fe-male; for you are all one in Christ Jesus. 29jAnd if you belong to Christ, then you are Abraham's descendant, heirs according to the promise.

CHAPTER 4

See RG 388

God's Free Children in Christ. 1*I mean that as long as the heir is not of age, he is no different from a slave, although he is the owner of everything, 2but he is under the supervision of guardians and administrators until the date set by his father. 3k*In the same way we also, when we were not of age, were enslaved to the elemental powers of the world. 4lBut when the fullness of time had come, God sent his Son, born of a woman, born under the law, 5mto ransom those under the law, so that we might receive adoption. 6n*As proof that you are children, God sent the spirit of his Son into our hearts, crying out, "Abba, Father!" 7oSo you are no longer a slave but a child, and if a child then also an heir, through God.

Do Not Throw This Freedom Away. 8p*At a time when you did not know God, you became slaves to things that by nature are not

promise, where all depends on the one God, no mediator is needed (20).

3, 23–29: Paul adds a further argument in support of righteousness or justification by faith and through God's promise rather than by works of the law (2, 16; 3, 22): as **children of God . . . baptized into Christ,** the Galatians are all **Abraham's descendant** and **heirs** of **the promise** to Abraham (8.14.16–18.29). The teaching in 23–25, that since **faith** (Christianity) **has come, we are no longer under** the law, could be taken with the previous paragraph on the role of the Mosaic law, but it also fits here as a contrast between the situation **before faith** (23) and the results after faith has come (25–29).

3, 24–25: Disciplinarian: the Greek **paidagōgos** referred to a slave who escorted a child to school but did not teach or tutor; hence, a guardian or monitor. Applying this to the law fits the role of the law described in vv 19–25.

3, 26: Children of God: literally "sons," in contrast to the young child under the disciplinarian in vv 24–25. The term includes males and females (28).

3, 27–28: Likely a formula used at baptism that expresses racial, social-economic, and sexual equality in Christ (cf Col 3, 11).

3, 27: Clothed yourselves with Christ: literally "have put on Christ"; cf Rom 13, 14; Eph 4, 24; Col 3, 10. Baptismal imagery, traceable to the Old Testament (Jb 29, 14; Is 59, 17) but also found in pagan mystery cults.

4, 1–7: What Paul has argued in 3, 26–29 is now elaborated in terms of the Christian as **the heir** (1.7; cf 3, 18.29) freed from control by others. Again, as in 3, 2–5, the proof

that Christians are children of God is the gift of the Spirit of Christ relating them intimately to God.

4, 1.3: Not of age: an infant or minor.

4, 3: The elemental powers of the world: while the term can refer to the "elements" like earth, air, fire, and water or to elementary forms of religion, the sense here is more likely that of celestial beings that were thought in pagan circles to control the world; cf 8; Col 2, 8.20.

4, 6: Children: see the note on 3, 26; here in contrast to the infant or young person **not of age** (1.3). **Abba:** cf Mk 14, 36 and the note; Rom 8, 15.

4, 8–11: On the basis of the arguments advanced from 3, 1 through 4, 7, Paul now launches his appeal to the Galatians with the question, **how can you turn back** to the slavery of the law (9)? The question is posed with reference to bondage to the **elemental powers** (see the note on 4, 3) because the Galatians had originally been converted to Christianity from paganism, not Judaism (8). The use of the direct question is like 3, 3–5.

4, 8: Things that by nature are not gods: or "gods that by nature do not exist."

---

a: Dt 6, 4. *b:* Rom 7, 10; 8, 2-4. *c:* Rom 3, 9-20.23; 11, 32. *d:* 4, 3-5; 5, 18. *e:* 2, 16. *f:* Rom 10, 4. *g:* 4, 5-7; Jn 1, 12; Rom 8, 14-17. *h:* Rom 6, 3; 13, 14; Eph 4, 24. *i:* Rom 10, 12; 1 Cor 12, 13; Col 3, 11. *j:* 3, 7.14.16.18; Rom 4, 16-17; 9, 7 / 4, 1.7; Rom 4, 13-14; 8, 17; Heb 6, 12; Jas 2, 5. *k:* 3, 23 / 4, 9; Col 2, 20. *l:* Mk 1, 15. *m:* 3, 13.26. *n:* 3, 26; Rom 8, 15. *o:* 3, 29; Rom 8, 16-17. *p:* 1 Cor 12, 2.

gods; [9q]but now that you have come to know God, or rather to be known by God, how can you turn back again to the weak and destitute elemental powers? Do you want to be slaves to them all over again? [10r]*You are observing days, months, seasons, and years. [11]*I am afraid on your account that perhaps I have labored for you in vain.

Appeal to Former Loyalty. [12s]*I implore you, brothers, be as I am, because I have also become as you are. You did me no wrong; [13]*you know that it was because of a physical illness that I originally preached the gospel to you, [14]and you did not show disdain or contempt because of the trial caused you by my physical condition, but rather you received me as an angel of God, as Christ Jesus. [15]*Where now is that blessedness of yours? Indeed, I can testify to you that, if it had been possible, you would have torn out your eyes and given them to me. [16]So now have I become your enemy by telling you the truth? [17t]*They show interest in you, but not in a good way; they want to isolate you, so that you may show interest in them. [18]Now it is good to be shown interest for good reason at all times, and not only when I am with you. [19u]My children, for whom I

am again in labor until Christ be formed in you! [20]I would like to be with you now and to change my tone, for I am perplexed because of you.

An Allegory on Christian Freedom. [21]*Tell me, you who want to be under the law, do you not listen to the law? [22v]For it is written that Abraham had two sons, one by the slave woman and the other by the freeborn woman. [23w]The son of the slave woman was born naturally, the son of the freeborn through a promise. [24x]Now this is an allegory. These women represent two covenants. One was from Mount Sinai, bearing children for slavery; this is Hagar. [25]*Hagar represents Sinai, a mountain in Arabia; it corresponds to the present Jerusalem, for she is in slavery along with her children. [26y]But the Jerusalem above is freeborn, and she is our mother. [27z]*For it is written:

"Rejoice, you barren one who bore no children;
break forth and shout, you who were not in labor;
for more numerous are the children of the deserted one
than of her who has a husband."

4, 10: This is likely a reference to ritual observances from the Old Testament, promoted by opponents: sabbaths or Yom Kippur, new moon, Passover or Pentecost, sabbatical years.

4, 11: Cf 2, 2. If the Galatians become **slaves . . . all over again** to the law (9), Paul will have worked in vain among them.

4, 12–20: A strongly personal section. Paul appeals to past ties between the Galatians and himself. He speaks sharply of the opponents (17–18) and pastorally to the Galatians (19–20).

4, 12: **Because I have also become as you are:** a terse phrase in Greek, meaning "Be as I, Paul, am," i.e., living by faith, independent of the law, for, in spite of my background in Judaism (1, 13), I have become as you Galatians are now, a brother in Christ.

4, 13: **Physical illness:** because its nature is not described, some assume an eye disease (15); others, epilepsy; some relate it to 2 Cor 12, 7–9. **Originally:** this may also be translated "formerly" or "on the first (of two) visit(s)"; cf Acts 16, 6; 18, 23.

4, 15: **That blessedness of yours:** possibly a reference to the Galatians' initial happy reception of Paul (14) and of his gospel (1, 6; 3, 1–4) and their felicitation at such blessedness, but the phrase could also refer ironically to earlier praise by Paul of the Galatians, no longer possible when they turn from the gospel to the claims of the opponents (17–18; 1, 7). If the word is a more literal reference to a beatitude, Gal 3, 26–28 may be in view.

4, 17: **Isolate you:** that is, from the blessings of the gospel and/or from Paul.

4, 21–31: Paul supports his appeal for the gospel (9; 1, 6–9; 2, 16; 3, 2) by a further argument from scripture (cf 3, 6–18). It involves the relationship of **Abraham** (3, 6–16) to his wife, Sarah, the **freeborn woman,** and to Hagar, **the slave woman,** and the contrast between the sons born to each, **Isaac,** child of promise, and Ishmael, son of Hagar (Gn 16 and 21). Only through Isaac is the promise of God preserved. This **allegory** (24), with its equation of the Sinai covenant and Mosaic law with slavery and of the promise of God with freedom, Paul uses only in light of previous arguments. His quotation of Gn 21, 10 at v 30 suggests on a scriptural basis that the Galatians should expel those who are troubling them (1, 7).

4, 25: **Hagar represents Sinai . . . :** some manuscripts have what seems a geographical note, "For Sinai is a mountain in Arabia."

4, 27: Is 54, 1 in the Septuagint translation is applied to Sarah as the **barren one** (in Gn 15) who ultimately becomes the mother not only of Isaac but now of numerous children, i.e., of all those who believe, the **children of the promise** (28).

---

q: 4, 3; Col 2, 20.   r: Col 2, 16-20.   s: 1 Cor 11, 1.   t: 1, 7; 6, 12; Acts 20, 30.   u: 1 Cor 4, 14-15; 2 Cor 6, 13; 1 Thes 2, 7-8. v: Gn 16, 15; 21, 2-3.   w: Gn 17, 16; Rom 4, 19-20; 9, 7-9.   x: 3, 17 / Ex 19, 20 / Gn 16, 1.   y: Heb 12, 22; Rv 21, 2.   z: Is 54, 1.

28a Now you, brothers, like Isaac, are children of the promise. 29But just as then the child of the flesh persecuted the child of the spirit, it is the same now. 30bBut what does the scripture say?

"Drive out the slave woman and her son! For the son of the slave woman shall not share the inheritance with the son"

of the freeborn. 31cTherefore, brothers, we are children not of the slave woman but of the freeborn woman.

V: Exhortation to Christian Living

CHAPTER 5

See RG 389

The Importance of Faith. 1d*For freedom Christ set us free; so stand firm and do not submit again to the yoke of slavery. 2eIt is I, Paul, who am telling you that if you have yourselves circumcised, Christ will be of no benefit to you. 3f*Once again I declare to every man who has himself circumcised that he is bound to observe the entire law. 4You are separated from Christ, you who are trying to be justified by law; you have fallen from grace. 5gFor through the Spirit, by faith, we await the hope of righteousness. 6h*For in Christ Jesus, neither circumcision nor uncircumcision counts for anything, but only faith working through love.

Be Not Misled. 7*You were running well; who hindered you from following [the] truth? 8i*That enticement does not come from the one who called you. 9jA little yeast leavens the whole batch of dough. 10kI am confident of you in the Lord that you will not take a different view, and that the one who is troubling you will bear the condemnation, whoever he may be. 111*As for me, brothers, if I am still preaching circumcision, why am I still being persecuted? In that case, the stumbling block of the cross has been abolished. 12*Would that those who are upsetting you might also castrate themselves!

Freedom for Service. 13m*For you were called for freedom, brothers. But do not use this freedom as an opportunity for the flesh; rather, serve one another through love. 14n*For the whole law is fulfilled in one statement, namely, "You shall love your neighbor as yourself." 15But if you go on biting and devouring one another, beware that you are not consumed by one another.

16o*I say, then: live by the Spirit and you will certainly not gratify the desire of the

---

5, 1–6: Paul begins the exhortations, continuing through 6, 10, with an appeal to the Galatians to side with freedom instead of slavery (1). He reiterates his message of justification or righteousness by faith instead of law and circumcision (2–5); cf 2, 16; 3, 3. Faith, not circumcision, is what counts (6).

5, 1: Freedom: Paul stresses as the conclusion from the allegory in 4, 21–31 this result of Christ's work for us. It is a principle previously mentioned (2, 4), the responsible use of which v 13 will emphasize.

5, 3: Cf 3, 10–12. Just as those who seek to live by the law must carry out all its contents, so those who have faith and live by promise must stand firm in their freedom (1.13).

5, 6: Cf Rom 2, 25–26; 1 Cor 7, 19; Gal 6, 15. The Greek for **faith working through love** or "faith expressing itself through love" can also be rendered as "faith energized by (God's) love."

5, 7–12: Paul addresses the Galatians directly: with questions (7.11), a proverb (9), a statement (8), and biting sarcasm (12), seeking to persuade the Galatians to break with those trying to add law and circumcision to Christ as a basis for salvation.

5, 7: Running well: as in an athletic contest; cf 2, 2; 1 Cor 9, 24–26; Phil 2, 16; 3, 14.

5, 8: The one who called you: see the note on 1, 6.

5, 11: Preaching circumcision: this could refer to Paul's

pre-Christian period (possibly as a missionary for Judaism); more probably it arose as a charge from opponents, based perhaps on the story in Acts 16, 1–3 that Paul had circumcised Timothy "on account of the Jews." Unlike the Gentile Titus in Gal 2, 3, Timothy was the son of a Jewish mother. **The stumbling block of the cross:** cf 1 Cor 1, 23.

5, 12: A sarcastic half-wish that their knife would go beyond mere circumcision; cf Phil 3, 2 and the note there.

5, 13–26: In light of another reminder of the freedom of the gospel (13; cf 1), Paul elaborates on what believers are called to do and be: they fulfill the law by love of neighbor (14–15), walking in the Spirit (16–26), as is illustrated by concrete **fruit of the Spirit** (22–23).

5, 13: Serve . . . through love: cf v 6.

5, 14: Lv 19, 18, emphasized by Jesus (Mt 22, 39; Lk 10, 27); cf Rom 13, 8–10.

5, 16–25: Spirit . . . flesh: cf 3, 3 and the note on Rom 8, 1–13.

---

a: Rom 9, 8. b: Gn 21, 10. c: 3, 29; Jn 8, 35. d: 2, 4; 4, 5.9; Jn 8, 32.36. e: 2, 21; Acts 15, 1-29. f: 3, 10; Rom 2, 25; Jas 2, 10. g: Rom 8, 23.25. h: 3, 28; 6, 15; 1 Cor 7, 19. i: 1, 6. j: 1 Cor 5, 6. k: 1, 7. l: 6, 12.14; 1 Cor 1, 23. m: 5, 1 / Rom 6, 18; 1 Cor 8, 9; 1 Pt 2, 16. n: Lv 19, 18; Mt 22, 39; Rom 13, 8-10. o: 5, 24-25; Rom 8, 5.

flesh. [17p]For the flesh has desires against the Spirit, and the Spirit against the flesh; these are opposed to each other, so that you may not do what you want. [18q]But if you are guided by the Spirit, you are not under the law. [19r*]Now the works of the flesh are obvious: immorality, impurity, licentiousness, [20s]idolatry, sorcery, hatreds, rivalry, jealousy, outbursts of fury, acts of selfishness, dissensions, factions, [21*]occasions of envy, drinking bouts, orgies, and the like. I warn you, as I warned you before, that those who do such things will not inherit the kingdom of God. [22t]In contrast, the fruit of the Spirit is love, joy, peace, patience, kindness, generosity, faithfulness, [23u]gentleness, self-control. Against such there is no law. [24v]Now those who belong to Christ [Jesus] have crucified their flesh with its passions and desires. [25w]If we live in the Spirit, let us also follow the Spirit. [26x]Let us not be conceited, provoking one another, envious of one another.

See RG
389

CHAPTER 6

Life in the Community of Christ. [1y*]Brothers, even if a person is caught in some transgression, you who are spiritual should correct that one in a gentle spirit, looking to yourself, so that you also may not be tempted. [2z*]Bear one another's burdens, and so you will fulfill the law of Christ. [3a]For if anyone thinks he is something when he is nothing, he is deluding himself. [4*]Each one must examine his own work, and then he will have reason to boast with regard to himself alone, and not with regard to someone else; [5b]for each will bear his own load.

[6c*]One who is being instructed in the word should share all good things with his instructor. [7]Make no mistake: God is not mocked, for a person will reap only what he sows, [8d]because the one who sows for his flesh will reap corruption from the flesh, but the one who sows for the spirit will reap eternal life from the spirit. [9e]Let us not grow tired of doing good, for in due time we shall reap our harvest, if we do not give up. [10f*]So then, while we have the opportunity, let us do good to all, but especially to those who belong to the family of the faith.

VI: Conclusion

Final Appeal. [11g*]See with what large letters I am writing to you in my own hand! [12h*]It is those who want to make a good appearance in the flesh who are trying to compel you to

---

5, 19–23: Such lists of vices and virtues (cf Rom 1, 29–31; 1 Cor 6, 9–10) were common in the ancient world. Paul contrasts **works of the flesh** (19) with **fruit** (not "works") **of the Spirit** (22). Not law, but the Spirit, leads to such traits.

5, 21: Occasions of envy: after the Greek word **phthonoi,** "envies," some manuscripts add a similar sounding one, **phonoi,** "murders."

6, 1–10: The ethical exhortations begun at 5, 1 continue with a variety of admonitions to the community (**brothers:** see the note on 1, 2). Nearly every sentence contains a separate item of practical advice; the faith and freedom of the gospel underlie each maxim. Tensions and temptation within communal life have previously been addressed in 5, 15.26, and v 1 continues with a case in which **a person is caught in some transgression** such as those in 5, 19–21; cf 2, 17.

6, 2: The law of Christ: cf Rom 8, 2; 1 Cor 9, 21; Gal 5, 14. The principle of love for others is meant. To **bear one another's burdens** is to "serve one another through love" (5, 13).

6, 4–5: Self-examination is the cure for self-deception. Compare what you are with what you were before, and give the glory to God; cf Rom 6, 19–22. **Load:** used elsewhere of a soldier's pack. Correcting one's own conduct avoids burdening others with it.

6, 6: Implies oral instruction in the faith by catechists; these are to be remunerated for their service; cf Rom 15, 27.

6, 10: The family of the faith: the Christian household or church. Doing good has a universal object (**to all**), but the lo-cal community makes specific the reality of those to be served.

6, 11–18: A postscript in Paul's own hand, as was his practice (see 1 Cor 16, 21; 2 Thes 3, 17). Paul summarizes his appeal against his opponents (12–13), then returns to his message of glorying in the cross, not in circumcision, as the means of salvation (14–15; cf 5, 11). A benediction follows at v 16. In the polemical spirit that the attack on his apostleship called forth (1, 11—2, 21), Paul reasserts his missionary credentials (17) before giving a final benediction (18).

6, 11: Large letters: in contrast to the finer hand of the scribe who wrote the letter up to this point. The larger Greek letters make Paul's message even more emphatic. Some find a hint of poor eyesight on Paul's part. See the note on 4, 13.

6, 12–15: The Jewish Christian opponents wished **not** to **be persecuted,** possibly by Jews. But since Judaism seems to

p: Rcm 7, 15.23; 8, 6. *q:* Rom 6, 14; 8, 14. *r:* Rom 1, 29-31; 1 Cor 6, 9-10; Col 3, 5-6.8. *s:* Rv 22, 15. *t:* Eph 5, 9 / 1 Ccr 13, 4-7; 2 Cor 6, 6; 1 Tm 4, 12; 2 Pt 1, 6. *u:* 1 Tm 1, 9. *v:* 2, 19; Rom 5, 6; 8, 13. *w:* 5, 16. *x:* Phil 2, 3. *y:* Mt 18, 15; Jas 5, 19 / 1 Cor 10, 12-13. *z:* Col 3, 13 / 1 Cor 9, 21. *a:* 1 Cor 3, 18; 8, 2; 2 Cor 12, 11. *b:* Rom 14, 12. *c:* 1 Cor 9, 14. *d:* Prv 11, 18; Rom 8, 6.13. *e:* 2 Thes 3, 13; Heb 12, 1-3. *f:* 1 Thes 5, 15. *g:* 1 Cor 16, 21. *h:* 5, 2.11.

have yourselves circumcised, only that they may not be persecuted for the cross of Christ. *13* *Not even those having themselves circumcised observe the law themselves; they only want you to be circumcised so that they may boast of your flesh. *14i* *But may I never boast except in the cross of our Lord Jesus Christ, through which the world has been crucified to me, and I to the world. *15j* *For neither does

circumcision mean anything, nor does uncircumcision, but only a new creation. *16k* *Peace and mercy be to all who follow this rule and to the Israel of God.

17l *From now on, let no one make troubles for me; for I bear the marks of Jesus on my body.

18m The grace of our Lord Jesus Christ be with your spirit, brothers. Amen.

have had a privileged status as a religion in the Roman empire, circumcised Christians might, if taken as Jews, thereby avoid persecution from the Romans. In any case, Paul instead stresses conformity with **the cross of our Lord Jesus Christ;** cf 2, 19–21; 5, 11.

6, 13: Those having themselves circumcised: other manuscripts read, "those who have had themselves circumcised."

6, 14: Through which: or "through whom."

6, 15: New creation: or "new creature"; cf 2 Cor 5, 17.

6, 16: This rule: the principle in vv 14 and 15. **The Israel of God:** while the church may be meant (the phrase can be translated "to all who follow this rule, even the Israel of God"; cf 10; 1 Cor 10, 18), the reference may also be to God's

ancient people, Israel; cf Pss 125, 5; 128, 6.

6, 17: The marks of Jesus: slaves were often branded by marks (**stigmata**) burned into their flesh to show to whom they belonged; so also were devotees of pagan gods. Paul implies that instead of outdated circumcision, his body bears the scars of his apostolic labors (2 Cor 11, 22–31), such as floggings (Acts 16, 22; 2 Cor 11, 25) and stonings (Acts 14, 19), that mark him as belonging to the Christ who suffered (cf Rom 6, 3; 2 Cor 4, 10; Col 1, 24) and will protect his own.

i: 2, 20; 1 Cor 2, 2.   *j*: 5, 6; 1 Cor 7, 19 / 2 Cor 5, 17.   *k*: Pss 125, 5; 128, 6.   *l*: 2 Cor 4, 10.   *m*: Phil 4, 23; 2 Tm 4, 22; Phlm 25.

See RG 390–95

The Letter to the Ephesians

Ephesians is the great Pauline letter about the church. It deals, however, not so much with a congregation in the city of Ephesus in Asia Minor as with the worldwide church, the head of which is Christ (4, 15), the purpose of which is to be the instrument for making God's plan of salvation known throughout the universe (3, 9–10). Yet this ecclesiology is anchored in God's saving love, shown in Jesus Christ (2, 4–10), and the whole of redemption is rooted in the plan and accomplishment of the triune God (1, 3–14). The language is often that of doxology (1, 3–14) and prayer (cf 1, 15–23; 3, 14–19), indeed of liturgy and hymns (3, 20–21; 5, 14).

The majestic chapters of Ephesians emphasize the unity in the church of Christ that has come about for both Jews and Gentiles within God's household (1, 15—2, 22, especially 2, 11–22) and indeed the "seven unities" of church, Spirit, hope, one Lord, faith, baptism, and the one God (4, 4–6). Yet the concern is not with the church for its own sake but rather as the means for mission in the world (3, 1—4, 24). The gifts Christ gives its members are to lead to growth and renewal (4, 7–24). Ethical admonition is not lacking either; all aspects of human life and relationships are illumined by the light of Christ (4, 25—6, 20).

The letter is seemingly addressed by Paul to Christians in Ephesus (1, 1), a place where the apostle labored for well over two years (Acts 19, 10). Yet there is a curiously impersonal tone to the writing for a community with which Paul was so intimately acquainted (cf 3, 2 and 4, 21). There are no personal greetings (cf 6, 23). More significantly, important early manuscripts omit the words "in Ephesus" (see the note on 1, 1). Many therefore regard the letter as an encyclical or "circular letter" sent to a number of churches in Asia Minor, the addressees to be designated in each place by its bearer, Tychicus (6, 21–22). Others think that Ephesians is the letter referred to in Colossians 4, 16 as "to the Laodiceans."

Paul, who is designated as the sole author at 1, 1, is described in almost unparalleled terms with regard to the significant role he has in God's plan for bringing the Gentiles to faith in Christ (3, 1–12). Yet at the time of writing he is clearly in prison (3, 1; 4, 1; 6, 20), suffering afflictions (3, 13). Traditionally this "Captivity Epistle" has, along with Colossians, Philippians, and Philemon, been dated to an imprisonment in Rome, likely in A.D. 61–63. Others appeal to an earlier imprisonment, perhaps in Caesarea (Acts 23, 27—27, 2). Since the early nineteenth century, however, much of critical scholarship has considered the letter's style and use of words (especially when compared with Colossians), its concept of the church, and other points of doctrine put forward by the writer as grounds for serious doubt about authorship by Paul. The letter may then be the work of a secretary writing at the apostle's direction or of a later disciple who sought to develop Paul's ideas for a new situation around A.D. 80–100.

The principal divisions of the Letter to the Ephesians are the following:

I: Address (1, 1–14)

II: Unity of the Church in Christ (1, 15—2, 22)

III: World Mission of the Church (3, 1—4, 24)

IV: Daily Conduct, an Expression of Unity (4, 25—6, 20)

V: Conclusion (6, 21–24).

I: Address

CHAPTER 1

See RG 391–92

Greeting. *1a**Paul, an apostle of Christ Jesus by the will of God, to the holy ones who are [in Ephesus] faithful in Christ

Jesus: *2b*grace to you and peace from God our Father and the Lord Jesus Christ.

The Father's Plan of Salvation. *3c**Blessed be the God and Father of our Lord Jesus Christ, who has blessed us in Christ with every spiritual blessing in the heavens, *4d*as he chose us in him, before the foundation of the world, to be holy and without blemish before him. In love *5e*he destined us for adoption to himself through Jesus Christ, in accord with the favor of his will, *6f*for the praise of the glory of his grace that he granted us in the beloved.

Fulfillment through Christ. *7g*In him we have redemption by his blood, the forgiveness of transgressions, in accord with the riches of his grace *8h*that he lavished upon us. In all wisdom and insight, *9i**he has made known to us the mystery of his will in accord with his favor that he set forth in him *10j*as a plan for the fullness of times, to sum up all things in Christ, in heaven and on earth.

Inheritance through the Spirit. *11k*In him we were also chosen, destined in accord with the purpose of the One who accomplishes all things according to the intention of his will, *12**so that we might exist for the

1, 1–2: For the epistolary form used at the beginning of letters, see the note on Rom 1, 1–7. Twenty-two of the thirty Greek words in vv 1–2 also occur in Col 1, 1–2.

1, 1: [In Ephesus]: the phrase is lacking in important early witnesses such as P46 (3rd cent.), and Sinaiticus and Vaticanus (4th cent.), appearing in the latter two as a fifth-century addition. Basil and Origen mention its absence from manuscripts. See Introduction. Without the phrase, the Greek can be rendered, as in Col 1, 2, "to the holy ones and faithful brothers in Christ."

1, 3–14: While a Pauline letter usually continues after the greeting with a prayer of thanksgiving, as in 15–23 below, Ephesians first inserts a blessing of God for the blessings Christians have experienced, as in 2 Cor 1, 3–4 and 1 Pt 1, 3–12. The blessing here, akin to a Jewish **berakah**, is rich in images almost certainly drawn from hymns and liturgy. Many ideas here are also found in Col 1, 3–23. Certain phrases are frequently repeated, such as **in Christ** (3.10.12) or **in him** (4.7.9.11.13) or **in the beloved** (6) and **(for) the praise of (his) glory** (6.12.14). Some terms like **chose** (4) and **destined** (5) reflect Old Testament theology (Dt 7, 7; 9, 4–6; 23, 5) or Pauline themes (**redemption,** 7.14; **grace,** 6.7) or specific emphases in Col (**forgiveness,** Col 1, 14).

A triadic structure is discernible in vv 3–14: **God the Father** (3–6.8.11), **Christ** (3.5.7–10.12), and the **Spirit** (13–14). The spiritual blessings Christians have received through Christ (3) are gratefully enumerated: the call to holiness (4; cf Col 1, 22); the gift of divine **adoption** establishing a unique spiritual relationship with God the Father through Christ (5; cf Gal 4, 5); liberation from sin through Christ's sacrificial death (7); revelation of God's plan of salvation in Christ (9; cf 3, 3–4; Rom 16, 25); the gift of election and faith in Christ bestowed upon Jewish Christians (see the note on 12, **we who first hoped in Christ**); and finally, the same gift granted to Gentiles (13, **you also**). In the Christ-centered faith and existence of the Christian communities the apostle sees the predetermined **plan** of God to bring all creation under the final rule of Christ (4–5.9–10) being **made known** (9) and carried through, to God's glory (6.12.14).

1, 3: In the heavens: literally, "in the heavenlies" or "in the heavenly places," a term in Eph for the divine realm.

1, 9: Mystery: as in Rom 16, 25; Col 1, 26.27 and elsewhere, a secret of God now revealed in the **plan** to save and **sum up all things in Christ** (10); cf 3, 3–6.

1, 12: We who first hoped: probably Jewish Christians (contrast 13, **you,** the Gentiles); possibly the people of Israel, "we who already enjoyed the hope of Christ," or perhaps present hope in contrast to future redemption (cf 14).

a: Rom 1, 7; 1 Cor 1, 1-2; Col 1, 1. b: Col 1, 2. c: 2, 6; 2 Cor 1, 3. d: 5, 27; Jn 15, 16; 17, 24; Rom 8, 29; 2 Thes 2, 13. e: Jn 1, 12; 1 Jn 3, 1. f: Mt 3, 17; Col 1, 13. g: 2, 7-13; Rom 3, 24; Col 1, 14.20. h: Col 1, 9. i: 3, 9; Rom 16, 25. j: Gal 4, 4; Col 1, 16.20. k: Is 46, 10; Rom 8, 28; Col 1, 12; Rv 4, 11.

praise of his glory, we who first hoped in Christ. [131]*In him you also, who have heard the word of truth, the gospel of your salvation, and have believed in him, were sealed with the promised holy Spirit, [14m]*which is the first installment of our inheritance toward redemption as God's possession, to the praise of his glory.

II: Unity of the Church in Christ

The Church as Christ's Body. [15n]*Therefore, I, too, hearing of your faith in the Lord Jesus and of your love for all the holy ones, [16o]do not cease giving thanks for you, remembering you in my prayers, [17p]that the God of our Lord Jesus Christ, the Father of glory, may give you a spirit of wisdom and revelation resulting in knowledge of him. [18q]May the eyes of [your] hearts be enlightened, that you may know what is the hope that belongs to his call, what are the riches of glory in his inheritance among the holy ones, [19r]and what is the surpassing greatness of his power for us who believe, in accord with the exercise of his great might, [20s]which he worked in Christ, raising him from the dead and seating him at his right hand in the heavens, [21t]far above every principality, authority, power, and dominion, and every name that is named not only in this age but also in the one to come. [22u]And he put all things beneath his feet and gave him as head over all things to the church, [23v]*which is his body, the fullness of the one who fills all things in every way.

CHAPTER 2

Generosity of God's Plan. [1w]*You were dead in your transgressions and sins [2x]*in which you once lived following the

See RG 392

1, 13: Sealed: by God, in baptism; cf 4, 30; 2 Cor 1, 22.

1, 14: First installment: down payment by God on full salvation, as at 2 Cor 1, 22.

1, 15–23: See the note on Rom 1, 8 for the thanksgiving form in a letter. Much of the content parallels thoughts in Col 1, 3–20. The prayer moves from God and Christ (17.20–21) to the Ephesians (17–19) and the church (22–23). Paul asks that the blessing imparted by God the Father (3) to the Ephesians will be strengthened in them through the message of the gospel (13.17–19). Those blessings are seen in the context of God's **might** in establishing the sovereignty of Christ over all other creatures (19–21) and in appointing him **head** of the church (22–23). For the allusion to angelic spirits in v 21, see Rom 8, 38 and Col 1, 16. Here, as in 1 Cor 15, 24–25 and Col 2, 15, every such **principality** and **power** is made subject to Christ.

1, 15: Your faith . . . your love: some manuscripts omit the latter phrase, but cf Col 1, 4.

1, 23: His body: the church (22); cf the note on Col 1, 18. Only in Eph and Col is Christ the **head** of the **body,** in contrast to the view in 1 Cor 12 and Rom 12, 4–8 where Christ is equated with the entire body or community. **Fullness:** see the note on Col 1, 19. Some take **the one who fills** as God, others as Christ (cf 4, 10). If in Christ "dwells the fullness of the deity bodily" (Col 2, 9), then, as God "fills" Christ, Christ in turn fills the church and the believer (3, 19; 5, 18). But the difficult phrases here may also allow the church to be viewed as the "complement" of Christ who is "being filled" as God's plan for the universe is carried out through the church (cf 3, 9–10).

2, 1–22: The gospel of **salvation** (1, 13) that God **worked in Christ** (1, 20) is reiterated in terms of what God's **great love** (4), expressed in Christ, means for us. The passage sometimes addresses **you,** Gentiles (1–2.8.11–13.19.22), but other times speaks of **all of us** who believe (3–7.10.14.18). In urging people to **remember** their grim past when they were **dead** in sins (1–3.11–12) and what they are **now in Christ** (4–10.13), the author sees both Jew and Gentile reconciled

with God, now **one new person,** a new humanity, **one body, the household of God, a temple** and **dwelling place** of God's Spirit (15–16.19–22). The presentation falls into two parts, the second stressing more the meaning for the church.

2, 1–10: The recipients of Paul's letter have experienced, in their redemption from **transgressions and sins,** the effect of Christ's supremacy over the power of the devil (1–2; cf 6, 11–12), who rules not from the netherworld but from the **air** between God in heaven and human beings on earth. Both Jew and Gentile have experienced, through Christ, God's free gift of salvation that already marks them for a future heavenly destiny (3–7). The language **dead, raised us up,** and **seated us . . . in the heavens** closely parallels Jesus' own passion and Easter experience. The terms in vv 8–9 describe salvation in the way Paul elsewhere speaks of justification: **by grace, through faith, the gift of God, not from works;** cf Gal 2, 16–21; Rom 3, 24–28. Christians are a newly created people in Christ, fashioned by God for a life of goodness (10).

2, 1–7: These verses comprise one long sentence in Greek, the main verb coming in v 5, God **brought us to life,** the object you/us **dead in . . . transgressions** being repeated in 1 and 5; cf Col 2, 13.

2, 2: Age of this world: or "aeon," a term found in gnostic thought, possibly synonymous with the **rulers of this world,** but also reflecting the Jewish idea of "two ages," this present evil age and "the age to come"; cf 1 Cor 3, 19; 5, 10; 7, 31; Gal 1, 4; Ti 2, 12. **The disobedient:** literally, "the sons of disobedience," a Semitism as at Is 30, 9.

---

l: 4, 30; Acts 2, 33; Col 1, 5-6.   *m:* 2 Cor 1, 22; 5, 5.   *n:* Col 1, 3-4; Phlm 4-5.   *o:* Col 1, 3.9.   *p:* 3, 14.16; Col 1, 9-10; 1 Jn 5, 20.   *q:* 4, 4; Col 1, 12.27.   *r:* 2 Cor 13, 4; Col 1, 11; 2, 12.   *s:* Ps 110, 1; Heb 1, 3.   *t:* Phil 2, 9; Col 1, 16; 1 Pt 3, 22.   *u:* 4, 15; Ps 8, 7; Mt 28, 18; Col 1, 18.   *v:* 4, 10.12; Rom 12, 5; 1 Cor 12, 27; Col 1, 19.   *w:* Col 1, 21; 2, 13.   *x:* 6, 12; Jn 12, 31; Col 1, 13.

age of this world, following the ruler of the power of the air, the spirit that is now at work in the disobedient. [3y] All of us once lived among them in the desires of our flesh, following the wishes of the flesh and the impulses, and we were by nature children of wrath, like the rest. [4] But God, who is rich in mercy, because of the great love he had for us, [5z*] even when we were dead in our transgressions, brought us to life with Christ (by grace you have been saved), [6a] raised us up with him, and seated us with him in the heavens in Christ Jesus, [7b] that in the ages to come he might show the immeasurable riches of his grace in his kindness to us in Christ Jesus. [8c] For by grace you have been saved through faith, and this is not from you; it is the gift of God; [9d] it is not from works, so no one may boast. [10e] For we are his handiwork, created in Christ Jesus for the good works that God has prepared in advance, that we should live in them.

One in Christ. [11*] Therefore, remember that at one time you, Gentiles in the flesh, called the uncircumcision by those called the circumcision, which is done in the flesh by human hands, [12f*] were at that time without Christ, alienated from the community of Israel and strangers to the covenants of promise, without hope and without God in the world. [13g] But now in Christ Jesus you

who once were far off have become near by the blood of Christ. [14h*] For he is our peace, he who made both one and broke down the dividing wall of enmity, through his flesh, [15i*] abolishing the law with its commandments and legal claims, that he might create in himself one new person in place of the two, thus establishing peace, [16j] and might reconcile both with God, in one body, through the cross, putting that enmity to death by it. [17k] He came and preached peace to you who were far off and peace to those who were near, [18l] for through him we both have access in one Spirit to the Father.

[19m] So then you are no longer strangers and sojourners, but you are fellow citizens with the holy ones and members of the household of God, [20n*] built upon the foundation of the apostles and prophets, with Christ Jesus himself as the capstone. [21o] Through him the whole structure is held together and grows into a temple sacred in the Lord; [22p] in him you also are being built together into a dwelling place of God in the Spirit.

III: World Mission of the Church

CHAPTER 3

Commission to Preach God's Plan. [1q*] Because of this, I, Paul, a prisoner of

See RG 392-93

2, 5: Our relation through baptism **with Christ**, the risen Lord, is depicted in terms of realized eschatology, as already exaltation, though v 7 brings in the future aspect too.

2, 11–22: The Gentiles lacked Israel's messianic expectation, lacked the various **covenants** God made with **Israel**, lacked **hope** of salvation and knowledge of the true **God** (11–12); but through Christ all these religious barriers between Jew and Gentile have been transcended (13–14) by the abolition of the Mosaic covenant-law (15) for the sake of uniting Jew and Gentile into a single religious community (15–16), imbued with the same holy **Spirit** and worshiping the same **Father** (18). The Gentiles are now included in God's **household** (19) as it arises upon the **foundation** of **apostles** assisted by those endowed with the prophetic gift (3, 5), the preachers of Christ (20; cf 1 Cor 12, 28). With Christ as the **capstone** (20; cf Is 28, 16; Mt 21, 42), they are being built into the holy **temple** of God's people where the divine presence dwells (21–22).

2, 12: **The community of Israel:** or "commonwealth"; cf 4, 18. **The covenants:** cf Rom 9, 4: with Abraham, with Moses, with David.

2, 14–16: The elaborate imagery here combines pictures

of Christ as **our peace** (Is 9, 5), his crucifixion, the ending of the Mosaic law (cf Col 2, 14), reconciliation (2 Cor 5, 18–21), and the destruction of **the dividing wall** such as kept people from God in the temple or a barrier in the heavens.

2, 15: **One new person:** a corporate body, the Christian community, made up of Jews and Gentiles, replacing ancient divisions; cf Rom 1, 16.

2, 20: **Capstone:** the Greek can also mean cornerstone or keystone.

3, 1–13: Paul reflects on his mission to the Gentiles. He alludes to his call and appointment to the apostolic office (2–3) and how his **insight** through revelation, as well as that of the other apostles and charismatic prophets in the church (4–5),

---

y: Col 3, 6-7.   z: Rom 5, 8; 6, 13; Col 2, 13.   a: Rom 8, 10-11; Phil 3, 20; Col 2, 12.   b: 1, 7.   c: Rom 3, 24; Gal 2, 16.   d: 1 Cor 1, 29.   e: 4, 24; Ti 2, 14.   f: Rom 9, 4; Col 1, 21.27.   g: 2, 17; Is 57, 19; Col 1, 20.   h: Gal 3, 28.   i: 2 Cor 5, 17; Col 2, 14.   j: Col 1, 20.22.   k: Is 57, 19; Zec 9, 10.   l: 3, 12.   m: Heb 12, 22-23.   n: Is 28, 16; Rv 21, 14.   o: 1 Cor 3, 16; Col 2, 19.   p: 1 Pt 2, 5.   q: Phil 1, 7.13; Col 1, 24-29; 4, 18; Phlm 1, 9; 2 Tm 2, 9.

Christ [Jesus] for you Gentiles— [2r*]if, as I suppose, you have heard of the stewardship of God's grace that was given to me for your benefit, [3s*][namely, that] the mystery was made known to me by revelation, as I have written briefly earlier. [4]When you read this you can understand my insight into the mystery of Christ, [5t]which was not made known to human beings in other generations as it has now been revealed to his holy apostles and prophets by the Spirit, [6u]that the Gentiles are coheirs, members of the same body, and copartners in the promise in Christ Jesus through the gospel.

[7v]Of this I became a minister by the gift of God's grace that was granted me in accord with the exercise of his power. [8w]To me, the very least of all the holy ones, this grace was given, to preach to the Gentiles the inscrutable riches of Christ, [9x*]and to bring to light [for all] what is the plan of the mystery hidden from ages past in God who created all things, [10y*]so that the manifold wisdom of God might now be made known through the church to the principalities and authorities in the heavens. [11]This was according to the eternal purpose that he accomplished in Christ Jesus our Lord, [12z]in whom we have boldness of speech and confidence of access through faith in him. [13a]So I ask you not to lose heart over my afflictions for you; this is your glory.

Prayer for the Readers. [14*]For this reason I kneel before the Father, [15]from whom every family in heaven and on earth is named, [16b]that he may grant you in accord with the riches of his glory to be strengthened with power through his Spirit in the inner self, [17c]and that Christ may dwell in your hearts through faith; that you, rooted and grounded in love, [18d]may have strength to comprehend with all the holy ones what is the breadth and length and height and depth, [19e]and to know the love of Christ that surpasses knowledge, so that you may be filled with all the fullness of God.

[20f]Now to him who is able to accomplish far more than all we ask or imagine, by the power at work within us, [21]to him be glory in the church and in Christ Jesus to all generations, forever and ever. Amen.

CHAPTER 4

Unity in the Body. [1g*]I, then, a prisoner for the Lord, urge you to live in a manner worthy of the call you have received, [2h]with all humility and gentleness, with pa-

See RG
392-93

---

has deepened understanding of God's plan of salvation in Christ. Paul is the special herald (7) of a new **promise** to the **Gentiles** (6): that the divine plan includes them in the spiritual benefits promised to Israel. Not only is this unique apostolic role his; Paul also has been given the task of explaining to all the divine **plan** of salvation (8–9), once **hidden.** Through **the church,** God's plan to save through Christ is becoming manifest to angelic beings (10; cf 1, 21), in accord with God's **purpose** (11). The fulfillment of the plan in Christ gives the whole church more **confidence** through **faith** in God (12). The readers of this letter are also thereby encouraged to greater confidence despite Paul's imprisonment (13).

3, 1: A **prisoner of Christ:** see Introduction. Paul abruptly departs from his train of thought at the end of v 1, leaving an incomplete sentence.

3, 2: Stewardship: the Greek is the same term employed at 1, 10 for the **plan** that God administers (Col 1, 25) and in which Paul plays a key role.

3, 3–4: The mystery: God's resolve to deliver Gentiles along with Israel through Christ; cf the notes on 1, 10; 3, 9.

3, 9: [For all]: while some think this phrase was added so as to yield the sense "to enlighten all about the plan . . . ," it is more likely that some manuscripts and Fathers omitted it accidentally or to avoid the idea that **all** conflicted with Paul's assignment to preach to **the Gentiles** (8) specifically.

3, 10: Principalities and authorities: see the note on 1, 15–23 regarding v 21.

3, 14–21: The apostle prays that those he is addressing may, like the rest of the church, deepen their understanding of God's plan of salvation in Christ. It is a plan that affects the whole universe (15) with **the breadth and length and height and depth** of God's love in Christ (18) or possibly the universe in all its dimensions. The apostle prays that they may perceive the redemptive love of Christ for them and be completely immersed in the fullness of God (19). The prayer concludes with a doxology to God (20–21).

3, 14–15: Every family: in the Greek there is wordplay on the word for **the Father (patria, patēr).** The phrase could also mean "God's whole family" (cf 2, 21).

4, 1–16: A general plea for unity in the church. Christians have been fashioned through the **Spirit** into a single harmonious religious community (one **body,** 4.12; cf 16), belonging to a single **Lord** (in contrast to the many gods of the pagan world), and by one way of salvation through **faith,** brought out especially by the significance of **baptism** (1–6; cf Rom 6, 1–11). But Christian unity is more than adherence to a com-

---

r: Col 1, 25. *s:* 1, 9-10; Col 1, 26. *t:* Col 1, 26. *u:* 2, 13.18-19. *v:* Rom 15, 15; Col 1, 25.29. *w:* 1 Cor 15, 8-10; Gal 1, 16; 2, 7-9. *x:* Rom 16, 25; Col 1, 26-27. *y:* 1 Pt 1, 12. *z:* Rom 5, 1-2; Heb 4, 16. *a:* Col 1, 22.24; 2 Tm 2, 10. *b:* 6, 10; Rom 7, 22; 2 Cor 4, 16; Col 1, 11. *c:* Jn 14, 23; Col 1, 23; 2, 7. *d:* Col 2, 2. *e:* Col 2, 3.9. *f:* Rom 16, 25-27; Col 1, 29. *g:* 3, 1; Col 1, 10. *h:* Col 3, 12-13.

tience, bearing with one another through love, ³¹striving to preserve the unity of the spirit through the bond of peace: ⁴ʲ*one body and one Spirit, as you were also called to the one hope of your call; ⁵ᵏone Lord, one faith, one baptism; ⁶ˡone God and Father of all, who is over all and through all and in all.

Diversity of Gifts. ⁷ᵐBut grace was given to each of us according to the measure of Christ's gift. ⁸ⁿ*Therefore, it says:

"He ascended on high and took prisoners captive;
he gave gifts to men."

⁹What does "he ascended" mean except that he also descended into the lower [regions] of the earth? ¹⁰The one who descended is also the one who ascended far above all the heavens, that he might fill all things.

¹¹ᵒ*And he gave some as apostles, others as prophets, others as evangelists, others as pastors and teachers, ¹²*to equip the holy ones for the work of ministry, for building up the body of Christ, ¹³ᵖ*until we all attain to the unity of faith and knowledge of the Son of God, to mature manhood, to the extent of the full stature of Christ, ¹⁴�q so that we may no longer be infants, tossed by waves

and swept along by every wind of teaching arising from human trickery, from their cunning in the interests of deceitful scheming. ¹⁵ʳ*Rather, living the truth in love, we should grow in every way into him who is the head, Christ, ¹⁶ˢfrom whom the whole body, joined and held together by every supporting ligament, with the proper functioning of each part, brings about the body's growth and builds itself up in love.

Renewal in Christ. ¹⁷ᵗ*So I declare and testify in the Lord that you must no longer live as the Gentiles do, in the futility of their minds; ¹⁸ᵘdarkened in understanding, alienated from the life of God because of their ignorance, because of their hardness of heart, ¹⁹ᵛthey have become callous and have handed themselves over to licentiousness for the practice of every kind of impurity to excess. ²⁰That is not how you learned Christ, ²¹assuming that you have heard of him and were taught in him, as truth is in Jesus, ²²ʷthat you should put away the old self of your former way of life, corrupted through deceitful desires, ²³ˣand be renewed in the spirit of your minds, ²⁴ʸ*and put on the new self, created in God's way in righteousness and holiness of truth.

mon belief. It is manifested in the exalted Christ's gifts to individuals to serve so as to make the community more Christlike (11–16). This teaching on Christ as the source of the gifts is introduced in v 8 by a citation of Ps 68, 18, which depicts Yahweh triumphantly leading Israel to salvation in Jerusalem. It is here understood of Christ, ascending **above all the heavens,** the **head** of the church; through his redemptive death, resurrection, and ascension he has become the source of the church's spiritual gifts. The "descent" of Christ (9–10) refers more probably to the incarnation (cf Phil 2, 6–8) than to Christ's presence after his death in the world of the dead (cf 1 Pt 3, 19).

4, 4–6: The "seven unities" (church, **Spirit, hope; Lord, faith** in Christ [1, 13], **baptism; one God**) reflect the triune structure of later creeds in reverse.

4, 8–10: While the emphasis is on an ascension and gift-giving by Christ, there is also a reference in taking **prisoners captive** to the aeons and powers mentioned at 1, 21; 2, 2; 3, 10; and 6, 12.

4, 11: Concerning this list of ministers, cf 1 Cor 12, 28 and Rom 12, 6–8. **Evangelists:** missionary preachers (cf Acts 21, 8 and 2 Tm 4, 5), not those who wrote gospels. **Pastors and teachers:** a single group in the Greek, shepherding congregations.

4, 12: The ministerial leaders in v 11 are to equip the whole people of God for their **work of ministry.**

4, 13: Mature manhood: literally, "a perfect man" (cf

Col 1, 28), possibly the "one new person" of 2, 15, though there **anthrōpos** suggests humanity, while here **anēr** is the term for male. This personage becomes visible in the church's growing to its fullness in the unity of those who believe in Christ.

4, 15–16: The head, Christ: cf Col 1, 18 and contrast 1 Cor 12, 12–27 and Rom 12, 4–5 where Christ is identified with the whole body, including the head. The imagery may derive from ancient views in medicine, the **head** coordinating and caring for the body, each **ligament** (perhaps the ministers of v 11) supporting the whole. But as at 2, 19–22, where the temple is depicted as a growing organism, there may also be the idea here of growing toward the capstone, Christ.

4, 17–24: Paul begins to indicate how the new life in Christ contrasts with the Gentiles' old way of existence. Literally, **the old self** (22) and **the new self** (24) are "the old man" and "the new man" (**anthrōpos,** person), as at 2, 15; cf the note on 4, 13.

4, 24: Put on: in baptism. See the note on Gal 3, 27.

i: Col 3, 14-15.   *j:* Rom 12, 5; 1 Cor 10, 17; 12, 12-13.   *k:* 1 Cor 8, 6.   *l:* 1 Cor 12, 6.   *m:* Rom 12, 3.6; 1 Cor 12, 28.   *n:* Ps 68, 19; Col 2, 15.   *o:* 1 Cor 12, 28.   *p:* Col 1, 28.   *q:* 1 Cor 14, 20; Col 2, 4.8; Heb 13, 9; Jas 1, 6.   *r:* 1 Cor 11, 3; Col 1, 18; 2, 19.   *s:* Col 2, 19.   *t:* Rom 1, 21.   *u:* Col 1, 21; 1 Pt 1, 14.   *v:* Col 3, 5.   *w:* Rom 8, 13; Gal 6, 8; Col 3, 9.   *x:* Rom 12, 2.   *y:* Gn 1, 26-27; Col 3, 10.

IV: Daily Conduct, an Expression of Unity

Rules for the New Life. 25z*Therefore, putting away falsehood, speak the truth, each one to his neighbor, for we are members one of another. 26a*Be angry but do not sin; do not let the sun set on your anger, 27band do not leave room for the devil. 28c*The thief must no longer steal, but rather labor, doing honest work with his [own] hands, so that he may have something to share with one in need. 29dNo foul language should come out of your mouths, but only such as is good for needed edification, that it may impart grace to those who hear. 30*And do not grieve the holy Spirit of God, with which you were sealed for the day of redemption. 31eAll bitterness, fury, anger, shouting, and reviling must be removed from you, along with all malice. 32f[And] be kind to one another, compassionate, forgiving one another as God has forgiven you in Christ.

CHAPTER 5

See RG
393

1g*So be imitators of God, as beloved children, 2hand live in love, as Christ loved us and handed himself over for us as a sacrificial offering to God for a fragrant aroma. 3iImmorality or any impurity or greed must not even be mentioned among you, as is fitting among holy ones, 4jno obscenity or silly or suggestive talk, which is out of place, but instead, thanksgiving. 5kBe sure of this, that no immoral or impure or greedy person, that is, an idolater, has any inheritance in the kingdom of Christ and of God.

Duty to Live in the Light. 6l*Let no one deceive you with empty arguments, for because of these things the wrath of God is coming upon the disobedient. 7So do not be associated with them. 8mFor you were once darkness, but now you are light in the Lord. Live as children of light, 9nfor light produces every kind of goodness and righteousness and truth. 10oTry to learn what is pleasing to the Lord. 11pTake no part in the fruitless works of darkness; rather expose them, 12for it is shameful even to mention the things done by them in secret; 13qbut everything exposed by the light becomes visible, 14r*for everything that becomes visible is light. Therefore, it says:

"Awake, O sleeper,
    and arise from the dead,
    and Christ will give you light."

15s*Watch carefully then how you live, not as foolish persons but as wise, 16making the most of the opportunity, because the days are evil. 17Therefore, do not continue in ignorance, but try to understand what is the will of the Lord. 18tAnd do not get drunk on wine, in which lies debauchery, but be filled with the Spirit, 19uaddressing one another [in] psalms and hymns and spiritual songs, singing and playing to the Lord in your hearts, 20vgiving thanks always and for everything in the name of our Lord Jesus Christ to God the Father.

Wives and Husbands. 21w*Be subordinate

4, 25—6, 20: For similar exhortations to a morally good life in response to God's gift of faith, see the notes on Rom 12, 1—13, 14 and Gal 5, 13—26.
4, 26: If angry, seek reconciliation that day, not giving the devil (6, 11) opportunity to lead into sin.
4, 28: Honest work: literally, "the good." **His [own] hands:** some manuscripts have the full phrase as in 1 Cor 4, 12.
4, 30: See the note on 1, 13.
5, 1: Imitators of God: in forgiving (4, 32) and in loving (as exhibited in how **Christ loved us**).
5, 6: See the note on 2, 2.
5, 14: An early Christian hymn, possibly from a baptismal liturgy. For the content compare 2, 5–6; 3, 9 and Is 60, 1.
5, 15–16.19–20: The wording is similar to Col 4, 5 and 3, 16–17.
5, 21—6, 9: Cf the notes on Col 3, 18—4, 1 and 1 Pt 2, 18—3, 7 for a similar listing of household duties where the inferior is admonished first (**wives,** 5, 22; **children,** 6, 1; **slaves,** 6, 5),

then the superior (**husbands,** 5, 25; **fathers,** 6, 4; **masters,** 6, 9). Paul varies this pattern by an emphasis on mutuality (see 5, 20); use of Old Testament material about **father and mother** in 6, 2; the judgment to come for slave-owners (**you have a Master in heaven,** 6, 9); and above all the initial principle of subordination **to one another** under **Christ,** thus effectively undermining exclusive claims to domination by one party. Into the section on **wives** and **husbands** an elaborate teaching on

---

z: Zec 8, 16. a: Ps 4, 5 LXX; Mt 5, 22. b: 2 Cor 2, 11. c: 1 Thes 4, 11. d: 5, 4; Col 3, 16; 4, 6. e: Col 3, 8. f: Mt 6, 14; Col 3, 12-13. g: Mt 5, 45.48. h: Ex 29, 18; Ps 40, 7; Gal 2, 20; 1 Jn 3, 16. i: Gal 5, 19; Col 3, 5. j: 4, 29; Col 3, 8. k: 1 Cor 6, 9-10; Gal 5, 21; Col 3, 5. l: Rom 1, 18; Col 2, 4.8. m: 2, 11-13; Jn 12, 36; Col 1, 12-13. n: Gal 5, 22. o: Rom 12, 2. p: Rom 13, 12. q: Jn 3, 20-21. r: Is 26, 19; 60, 1. s: Col 4, 5. t: Prv 23, 31 LXX; Lk 21, 34. u: Ps 33, 2-3; Col 3, 16. v: Col 3, 17. w: 1 Pt 5, 5.

to one another out of reverence for Christ. ^{22x}Wives should be subordinate to their husbands as to the Lord. ^{23y}For the husband is head of his wife just as Christ is head of the church, he himself the savior of the body. ^{24}As the church is subordinate to Christ, so wives should be subordinate to their husbands in everything. ^{25z}Husbands, love your wives, even as Christ loved the church and handed himself over for her ^{26a}to sanctify her, cleansing her by the bath of water with the word, ^{27b}that he might present to himself the church in splendor, without spot or wrinkle or any such thing, that she might be holy and without blemish. ^{28}So [also] husbands should love their wives as their own bodies. He who loves his wife loves himself. ^{29}For no one hates his own flesh but rather nourishes and cherishes it, even as Christ does the church, ^{30c}because we are members of his body.

^{31} ^{d}"For this reason a man shall leave [his]
father and [his] mother
and be joined to his wife,
and the two shall become one flesh."

^{32e}This is a great mystery, but I speak in reference to Christ and the church. ^{33}In any case, each one of you should love his wife as himself, and the wife should respect her husband.

See RG
393-94

CHAPTER 6

Children and Parents. ^{1f}Children, obey your parents [in the Lord], for this is right. ^{2g}"Honor your father and mother." This is the first commandment with a promise, ^{3}"that it may go well with you and that

you may have a long life on earth." ^{4h}Fathers, do not provoke your children to anger, but bring them up with the training and instruction of the Lord.

Slaves and Masters. ^{5i}Slaves, be obedient to your human masters with fear and trembling, in sincerity of heart, as to Christ, ^{6j}not only when being watched, as currying favor, but as slaves of Christ, doing the will of God from the heart, ^{7}willingly serving the Lord and not human beings, ^{8}knowing that each will be requited from the Lord for whatever good he does, whether he is slave or free. ^{9k}Masters, act in the same way toward them, and stop bullying, knowing that both they and you have a Master in heaven and that with him there is no partiality.

Battle against Evil. ^{10}*Finally, draw your strength from the Lord and from his mighty power. ^{11l}Put on the armor of God so that you may be able to stand firm against the tactics of the devil. ^{12m}For our struggle is not with flesh and blood but with the principalities, with the powers, with the world rulers of this present darkness, with the evil spirits in the heavens. ^{13n}Therefore, put on the armor of God, that you may be able to resist on the evil day and, having done everything, to hold your ground. ^{14o}So stand fast with your loins girded in truth, clothed with righteousness as a breastplate, ^{15p}and your feet shod in readiness for the gospel of peace. ^{16q}In all circumstances, hold faith as a shield, to quench all [the] flaming arrows of the evil one. ^{17r}And take the helmet of salvation and the sword of the Spirit, which is the word of God.

Constant Prayer. ^{18s}With all prayer and supplication, pray at every opportunity in

Christ and the church has been woven (5, 22–33).

5, 21–33: The apostle exhorts married Christians to a strong mutual love. Holding with Gn 2, 24 that marriage is a divine institution (31), Paul sees Christian marriage as taking on a new meaning symbolic of the intimate relationship of love between Christ and the church. The wife should serve her husband in the same spirit as that of the church's service to Christ (22.24), and the husband should care for his wife with the devotion of Christ to the church (25–30). Paul gives to the Genesis passage its highest meaning in the light of the union of Christ and the church, of which Christlike loyalty and devotion in Christian marriage are a clear reflection (31–33).

6, 10–20: A general exhortation to courage and prayer. Drawing upon the imagery and ideas of Is 11, 5; 59, 16–17; and Wis 5, 17–23, Paul describes the Christian in terms of the

dress and equipment of Roman soldiers. He observes, however, that the Christian's readiness for combat is not directed against human beings but against the spiritual powers of evil (10–17; cf 1, 21; 2, 2; 3, 10). Unique importance is placed upon prayer (18–20).

x: Col 3, 18—4, 1; 1 Pt 3, 1-7. y: 1 Cor 11, 3; Col 1, 18. z: Col 3, 19; 1 Tm 2, 6. a: Rom 6, 4; Ti 3, 5-7. b: 2 Cor 11, 2; Col 1, 22. c: Rom 12, 5; 1 Cor 6, 15. d: Gn 2, 24; Mt 19, 5; Mk 10, 7-8. e: Rv 19, 7. f: Prv 6, 20; Sir 3, 1-6; Col 3, 20. g: Ex 20, 12; Dt 5, 16. h: Col 3, 21-22. i: Col 3, 22-25; 1 Tm 6, 1-2; Ti 2, 9-10. j: 1 Pt 2, 18. k: Col 4, 1. l: Rom 13, 12; 2 Cor 6, 7; 10, 4; Jas 4, 7. m: 1, 21; 2, 2; Col 1, 13. n: Rom 13, 12. o: Wis 5, 17-20; Is 11, 5; Lk 12, 35; 1 Thes 5, 8. p: Is 52, 7. q: 1 Pt 5, 9. r: Is 59, 17; 1 Thes 5, 8. s: Mt 26, 41; Col 4, 2-3.

the Spirit. To that end, be watchful with all perseverance and supplication for all the holy ones [19t]and also for me, that speech may be given me to open my mouth, to make known with boldness the mystery of the gospel [20u]for which I am an ambassador in chains, so that I may have the courage to speak as I must.

V: Conclusion

A Final Message. [21v]*So that you also may have news of me and of what I am doing, Tychicus, my beloved brother and trustworthy minister in the Lord, will tell you everything. [22w]I am sending him to you for this very purpose, so that you may know about us and that he may encourage your hearts.

[23]Peace be to the brothers, and love with faith, from God the Father and the Lord Jesus Christ. [24x]Grace be with all who love our Lord Jesus Christ in immortality.

6, 21–24: Tychicus: the bearer of the letter; see the note on Col 4, 7. Verses 21–22 parallel Col 4, 7–8, often word for word. If Ephesians is addressed to several Christian communities (see Introduction), it is understandable that no greetings to individual members of these communities should have been included in it.

t: Acts 4, 29; Col 4, 3; 2 Thes 3, 1. *u:* 2 Cor 5, 20; Col 4, 4. *v:* Acts 20, 4; Col 4, 7; 2 Tm 4, 12. *w:* Col 4, 8. *x:* 1 Pt 1, 8.

See RG 395–99

The Letter to the Philippians

Philippi, in northeastern Greece, was a city of some importance in the Roman province of Macedonia. Lying on the great road from the Adriatic coast to Byzantium, the Via Egnatia, and in the midst of rich agricultural plains near the gold deposits of Mt. Pangaeus, it was in Paul's day a Roman town (Acts 16, 21), with a Greek-Macedonian population and a small group of Jews (see Acts 16, 13). Originally founded in the sixth century B.C. as Krenides by the Thracians, the town was taken over after 360 B.C. by Philip II of Macedon, the father of Alexander the Great, and was renamed for himself, "Philip's City." The area became Roman in the second century B.C. On the plains near Philippi in October 42 B.C., Antony and Octavian decisively defeated the forces of Brutus and Cassius, the slayers of Julius Caesar. Octavian (Augustus) later made Philippi a Roman colony and settled many veterans of the Roman armies there.

Paul, according to Acts (16, 9–40), established at Philippi the first Christian community in Europe. He came to Philippi, via its harbor town of Neapolis (modern Kavalla), on his second missionary journey, probably in A.D. 49 or 50, accompanied by Silas and Timothy (Acts 15, 40; 16, 3; cf Phil 1, 1) and Luke, if he is to be included in the "we" references of Acts 16, 10–17. The Acts account tells of the conversion of a business woman, Lydia; the exorcism of a slave girl; and, after an earthquake, while Paul and Silas were imprisoned in Philippi, the faith and baptism of a jailer and his family. None of these persons, however, is directly mentioned in Philippians (cf the notes on 4, 2 and 4, 3). Acts 16 concludes its account by describing how Paul (and Silas), asked by the magistrates to leave Philippi, went on to Thessalonica (Acts 17, 1–10), where several times his loyal Philippians continued to support him with financial aid (Phil 4, 16). Later, Paul may have passed through Philippi on his way from Ephesus to Greece (Acts 20, 1–2), and he definitely stopped there on his fateful trip to Jerusalem (Acts 20, 6).

Paul's letter to the Christians at Philippi was written while he was in a prison somewhere (1, 7.13.14.17), indeed in danger of death (1, 20–23). Although under guard for preaching Christ, Paul rejoices at the continuing progress of the gospel (1, 12–26) and expresses gratitude for the Philippians' renewed concern and help in an expression of thanks most clearly found at 4, 10–20. Much of the letter is devoted to instruction about unity and humility within the Christian community at Philippi (1, 27—2, 18) and exhortations to growth, joy, and peace in their life together (4, 1–9). The letter seems to be drawing to a close at the end of what we number as ch 2, as Paul reports the plans of his helper Timothy and of Epaphroditus (whom the Philippians had sent to aid Paul) to come to Philippi (2, 19—3, 1), and even Paul's own expectation that he will go free and come to Philippi (1, 25–26; 2, 24). Yet quite abruptly at 3, 2, Paul erupts into warnings against false teachers who threaten to impose on the Philippians the burdens of the Mosaic law, including circumcision. The section that follows, 3, 2–21, is a vigorous attack on these Judaizers (cf Gal 2, 11—3, 29) or Jewish Christian teachers (cf 2 Cor 11, 12–23), giving us insights into Paul's own life story (3, 4–6) and into the doctrine of justification, the Christian life, and ultimate hope (3, 7–21).

The location of Paul's imprisonment when he wrote to the Philippians, and thus the date of the letter, are uncertain. The traditional view has been that it stems from Paul's confinement in Rome, between A.D. 59 and 63 (cf Acts 28, 14–31). One modern view suggests the period when he was imprisoned at Caesarea, on the coast of Palestine, A.D. 57 or 58 (Acts 23, 23—26, 32); another suggests Corinth (cf 2 Cor 11, 9). Much recent scholarship favors Ephesus, around A.D. 55, a situation referred to in 2 Cor 1, 8 concerning "the affliction that came to us" in Asia Minor (cf also 1 Cor 15, 32). The reference at 1, 13 to the "praetorium" (cf also 4, 22) can be understood to mean the imperial guard or government house at Ephesus (or Caesarea), or the praetorian camp in Rome. Involved in a decision are the several journeys back and forth between Philippi and wherever Paul is imprisoned, mentioned in the letter (2, 25–28; 4, 14); this factor causes many to prefer Ephesus because of its proximity to Philippi. The Ephesian hypothesis dates the composition of Philippians to the mid-50s when most of Paul's major letters were written.

There is also a likelihood, according to some scholars, that the letter as we have it is a composite from parts of three letters by Paul to the Philippians. Seemingly 4, 10–20 is a brief note of appreciation for help sent through Epaphroditus. The long section from 1, 3 to 3, 1 is then another letter, with news of Paul's imprisonment and reports on Timothy and Epaphroditus (who has fallen ill while with Paul), along with exhortations to the Philippians about Christian conduct; and 3, 2–21 a third communication warning about threats to Philippian Christianity. The other verses in ch 4 and 1, 1–2, are variously assigned by critics to these three underlying letters, which an editor presumably put together to produce a picture of Paul writing earnestly from prison (1–2), facing opponents of the faith (ch 3), and with serene joy advising and thanking his Philippians (ch 4). If all four chapters were originally a unity, then one must assume that a break occurred between the writing of 3, 1 and 3, 2, possibly involving the receipt of bad news from Philippi, and that Paul had some reasons for delaying his words of thanks for the aid brought by Epaphroditus till the end of his letter.

This beautiful letter is rich in insights into Paul's theology and his apostolic love and concern for the gospel and his converts. In Philippians, Paul reveals his human sensitivity and tenderness, his enthusiasm for Christ as the key to life and death (1, 21), and his deep feeling for those in Christ who dwell in Philippi. With them he shares his hopes and convictions, his anxieties and fears, revealing the total confidence in Christ that constitutes faith (3, 8–10). The letter incorporates a hymn about the salvation that God has brought about through Christ (2, 6–11), applied by Paul to the relations of Christians with one another (2, 1–5). Philippians has been termed "the letter of joy" (4, 4.10). It is the rejoicing of faith, based on true understanding of Christ's unique role in the salvation of all who profess his lordship (2, 11; 3, 8–12.14.20–21).

The principal divisions of the Letter to the Philippians are the following:

I: Address (1, 1–11)
II: Progress of the Gospel (1, 12–26)
III: Instructions for the Community (1, 27—2, 18)
IV: Travel Plans of Paul and His Assistants (2, 19–3, 1)
V: Polemic: Righteousness and the Goal in Christ (3, 2–21)
VI: Instructions for the Community (4, 1–9)
VII: Gratitude for the Philippians' Generosity (4, 10–20)
VIII: Farewell (4, 21–23)

I: Address

CHAPTER 1

See RG
396–97

Greeting. *1a**Paul and Timothy, slaves of Christ Jesus, to all the holy ones in Christ Jesus who are in Philippi, with the overseers and ministers: *2b**grace to you and peace from God our Father and the Lord Jesus Christ.

Thanksgiving. *3c**I give thanks to my God at every remembrance of you, *4*praying always with joy in my every prayer for all of you, *5*because of your partnership for the gospel from the first day until now. *6d**I am confident of this, that the one who began a good work in you will continue to complete it until the day of Christ Jesus. *7*It is right that I should think this way about all of you, because I hold you in my heart, you who are all partners with me in grace, both in my imprisonment and in the defense and confirmation of the gospel. *8e*For God is my witness, how I long for all of you with the affection of Christ Jesus. *9f*And this is my prayer: that your love may increase ever more and more in knowledge and every kind of perception, *10g*to discern what is of value, so that you may be pure and blameless for the day of Christ, *11h*filled with the fruit of righteousness that comes through Jesus Christ for the glory and praise of God.

II: Progress of the Gospel

12i*I want you to know, brothers, that my situation has turned out rather to advance the gospel, *13j**so that my imprisonment has become well known in Christ throughout the whole praetorium and to all the rest, *14**and so that the majority of the brothers, having taken encouragement in the Lord from my

---

1, 1–2: See the note on Rom 1, 1–7, concerning the greeting.

1, 1: Slaves: Paul usually refers to himself at the start of a letter as an apostle. Here he substitutes a term suggesting the unconditional obligation of himself and Timothy to the service of Christ, probably because, in view of the good relationship with the Philippians, he wishes to stress his status as a co-servant rather than emphasize his apostolic authority. Reference to Timothy is a courtesy: Paul alone writes the letter, as the singular verb throughout shows (3–26), and the reference (2, 19–24) to Timothy in the third person. **Overseers:** the Greek term **episkopos** literally means "one who oversees" or "one who supervises," but since the second century it has come to designate the "bishop," the official who heads a local church. In New Testament times this office had not yet developed into the form that it later assumed, though it seems to be well on the way to such development in the Pastorals; see 1 Tm 3, 2 and Ti 1, 7, where it is translated **bishop.** At Philippi, however (and at Ephesus, according to Acts 20, 28), there was more than one **episkopos,** and the precise function of these officials is uncertain. In order to distinguish this office from the later stages into which it developed, the term is here translated as **overseers. Ministers:** the Greek term **diakonoi** is used frequently in the New Testament to designate "servants," "attendants," or "ministers." Paul refers to himself and to other apostles as "ministers of God" (2 Cor 6, 4) or "ministers of Christ" (2 Cor 11, 23). In the Pastorals (1 Tm 3, 8.12) the **diakonos** has become an established official in the local church; hence the term is there translated as **deacon.** The **diakonoi** at Philippi seem to represent an earlier stage of development of the office; we are uncertain about their precise functions. Hence the term is here translated as **ministers.** See Rom 16, 1, where Phoebe is described as a **diakonos (minister)** of the church of Cenchreae.

1, 2: The gifts come **from** Christ the Lord, not simply through him from the Father; compare the christology in 2, 6–11.

1, 3–11: As in Rom 1, 8–15 and all the Pauline letters except Galatians, a thanksgiving follows, including a direct prayer for the Philippians (9–11); see the note on Rom 1, 8. On their **partnership for the gospel** (5), cf 29–30; 4, 10–20. Their devotion to the faith and to Paul made them his pride and joy (4, 1). The characteristics thus manifested are evidence of the community's continuing preparation for the Lord's parousia (6.10). Paul's especially warm relationship with the Philippians is suggested here (7.8) as elsewhere in the letter. The eschatology serves to underscore a concern for ethical growth (9–11), which appears throughout the letter.

1, 6: The day of Christ Jesus: the parousia or triumphant return of Christ, when those loyal to him will be with him and share in his eternal glory; cf 10; 2, 16; 3, 20–21; 1 Thes 4, 17; 5, 10; 2 Thes 1, 10; 1 Cor 1, 8.

1, 12–26: The body of the letter begins with an account of Paul's present **situation,** i.e., his **imprisonment** (12–13; see Introduction), and then goes on with advice for the Philippians (1, 27—2, 18). The **advance** of **the gospel** (12) and the **progress** of the Philippians **in the faith** (25) frame what is said.

1, 13: Praetorium: either the praetorian guard in the city where Paul was imprisoned or the governor's official residence in a Roman province (cf Mk 15, 16; Acts 23, 35). See Introduction on possible sites.

1, 14–18: Although Paul is imprisoned, Christians there nonetheless go on preaching Christ. But they do so with varied motives, **some** with personal hostility toward Paul, others out of personal ambition.

a: Rom 1, 1; 2 Cor 1, 1; 1 Thes 1, 1; Phlm 1 / 1 Tm 3, 1-13. *b:* Rom 1, 7; Gal 1, 3; Phlm 3. *c:* Rom 1, 8; 1 Cor 1, 4; 1 Thes 1, 2. *d:* 2, 13 / 1, 10; 2, 16; 1 Cor 1, 8. *e:* Rom 1, 9; 2 Cor 1, 23; 1 Thes 2, 5. *f:* Eph 3, 14-19; Col 1, 9-10; Phlm 6. *g:* Rom 2, 18; 12, 2 / 1, 6. *h:* Jn 15, 8. *i:* Eph 3, 1; 6, 20; 2 Tm 2, 9; Phlm 9. *j:* 4, 22.

imprisonment, dare more than ever to proclaim the word fearlessly.

¹⁵Of course, some preach Christ from envy and rivalry, others from good will. ¹⁶The latter act out of love, aware that I am here for the defense of the gospel; ¹⁷the former proclaim Christ out of selfish ambition, not from pure motives, thinking that they will cause me trouble in my imprisonment. ¹⁸ᵏ*What difference does it make, as long as in every way, whether in pretense or in truth, Christ is being proclaimed? And in that I rejoice.

Indeed I shall continue to rejoice, ¹⁹*for I know that this will result in deliverance for me through your prayers and support from the Spirit of Jesus Christ. ²⁰ᵐMy eager expectation and hope is that I shall not be put to shame in any way, but that with all boldness, now as always, Christ will be magnified in my body, whether by life or by death. ²¹ⁿFor to me life is Christ, and death is gain. ²²ᵒIf I go on living in the flesh, that means fruitful labor for me. And I do not know which I shall choose. ²³ᵖI am caught between the two. I long to depart this life and be with Christ, [for] that is far better. ²⁴Yet that I remain [in] the flesh is more necessary for your benefit. ²⁵And this I know with confidence, that I shall remain and continue in the service of all of you for your progress and joy in the faith, ²⁶so that your boasting in Christ Jesus may abound on account of me when I come to you again.

III: Instructions for the Communtiy

Steadfastness in Faith. ²⁷ᵍ*Only, conduct yourselves in a way worthy of the gospel of Christ, so that, whether I come and see you or am absent, I may hear news of you, that you are standing firm in one spirit, with one mind struggling together for the faith of the gospel, ²⁸not intimidated in any way by your opponents. This is proof to them of destruction, but of your salvation. And this is God's doing. ²⁹ʳFor to you has been granted, for the sake of Christ, not only to believe in him but also to suffer for him. ³⁰ˢ*Yours is the same struggle as you saw in me and now hear about me.

CHAPTER 2

Plea for Unity and Humility. ¹*If there is any encouragement in Christ, any solace in love, any participation in the Spirit, any compassion and mercy, ²ᵗcomplete my joy by being of the same mind, with the same love, united in heart, thinking one thing. ³ᵘDo nothing out of selfishness or out of vainglory; rather, humbly regard others as more important than yourselves, ⁴ᵛeach looking out not for his own interests, but [also] everyone for those of others.

⁵*Have among yourselves the same attitude that is also yours in Christ Jesus,

See RG 397

1, 18: **Rejoice:** a major theme in the letter; see Introduction.

1, 19–25: Paul earnestly debates his prospects of martyrdom or continued missionary labor. While he may **long to depart this life** and thus **be with Christ** (23), his overall and final expectation is that he will be delivered from this imprisonment and **continue in the service** of the Philippians and of others (19.25; 2, 24). In either case, Christ is central (20.21); if to live means Christ for Paul, death means to be united with Christ in a deeper sense.

1, 19: **Result in deliverance for me:** an echo of Jb 13, 16, hoping that God will turn suffering to ultimate good and deliverance from evil.

1, 27–30: Ethical admonition begins at this early point in the letter, emphasizing steadfastness and congregational unity in the face of possible suffering. The **opponents** (28) are those in Philippi, probably pagans, who oppose the gospel cause. **This is proof . . .** (28) may refer to the whole outlook and conduct of the Philippians, turning out for their salvation but to the judgment of the opponents (cf 2 Cor 2, 15–16), or possibly the sentence refers to the opinion of the opponents,

who hold that the obstinacy of the Christians points to the destruction of such people as defy Roman authority (though in reality, Paul holds, such faithfulness leads to salvation)

1, 30: A reference to Paul's earlier imprisonment in Philippi (Acts 16, 19–24; 1 Thes 2, 2) and to his present confinement.

2, 1–11: The admonition to likemindedness and unity (2–5) is based on the believers' threefold experience with Christ, God's love, and the Spirit. The appeal to humility (3) and to obedience (12) is rooted in christology, specifically in a statement about Christ Jesus (6–11) and his humbling of self and obedience to the point of death (8).

2, 5: **Have . . . the same attitude that is also yours in Christ Jesus:** or, "that also Christ Jesus had." While it is often held that Christ here functions as a model for moral imi-

k: 4, 10. l: Jb 13, 16 / 2 Cor 1, 11. m: 1 Cor 6, 20; 1 Pt 4, 16. n: Gal 2, 20. o: Rom 1, 13. p: 2 Cor 5, 8. q: Eph 4, 1; Col 1, 10; 1 Thes 2, 12 / 4, 3. r: Mt 5, 10; 10, 38; Mk 8, 34; Acts 5, 41. s: 1, 13; Acts 16, 22-24. t: Rom 15, 5; 1 Cor 1, 10. u: Rom 12, 3.10; Gal 5, 26. v: 1 Cor 10, 24.33; 13, 5.

6 *w**Who, though he was in the form of God,
  did not regard equality with God
      something to be grasped.

7   *x**Rather, he emptied himself,
  taking the form of a slave,
  coming in human likeness;
  and found human in appearance,

8   *y**he humbled himself,
  becoming obedient to death,
      even death on a cross.

9 *z**Because of this, God greatly exalted him
  and bestowed on him the name
  that is above every name,

10   *a**that at the name of Jesus
  every knee should bend,
  of those in heaven and on earth and
      under the earth,

11   *b**and every tongue confess that
  Jesus Christ is Lord,
  to the glory of God the Father.

Obedience and Service in the World. *12c**So
then, my beloved, obedient as you have always been, not only when I am present but

all the more now when I am absent, work out
your salvation with fear and trembling.
*13d*For God is the one who, for his good purpose, works in you both to desire and to
work. *14e*Do everything without grumbling
or questioning, *15f**that you may be blameless and innocent, children of God without
blemish in the midst of a crooked and perverse generation, among whom you shine
like lights in the world, *16g*as you hold on to
the word of life, so that my boast for the day
of Christ may be that I did not run in vain or
labor in vain. *17h**But, even if I am poured out
as a libation upon the sacrificial service of
your faith, I rejoice and share my joy with all
of you. *18i*In the same way you also should
rejoice and share your joy with me.

IV: Travel Plans of Paul
and His Assistants

Timothy and Paul. *19j**I hope, in the Lord
Jesus, to send Timothy to you soon, so that I
too may be heartened by hearing news of

tation, it is not the historical Jesus but the entire Christ event
that vv 6–11 depict. Therefore, the appeal is to have in relations among yourselves that same relationship you have in
Jesus Christ, i.e., serving one another as you serve Christ (4).

2, 6–11: Perhaps an early Christian hymn quoted here by
Paul. The short rhythmic lines fall into two parts, vv 6–8
where the subject of every verb is Christ, and vv 9–11 where
the subject is God. The general pattern is thus of Christ's humiliation and then exaltation. More precise analyses propose
a division into six three-line stanzas (6; 7abc; 7d-8; 9; 10; 11)
or into three stanzas (6–7ab; 7cd-8; 9–11). Phrases such as
even death on a cross (8c) are considered by some to be additions (by Paul) to the hymn, as are vv 10c and 11c.

2, 6: Either a reference to Christ's preexistence and those
aspects of divinity that he was willing to give up in order to
serve in human form, or to what the man Jesus refused to
grasp at to attain divinity. Many see an allusion to the Genesis story: unlike Adam, Jesus, **though . . . in the form of God**
(Gn 1, 26–27), did not reach out for **equality with God,** in
contrast with the first Adam in Gn 3, 5–6.

**2, 7: Taking the form of a slave, coming in human like-
ness:** or ". . . taking the form of a slave. // Coming in human
likeness, and found human in appearance." While it is common to take vv 6 and 7 as dealing with Christ's preexistence
and v 8 with his incarnate life, so that lines 7b and c are parallel, it is also possible to interpret so as to exclude any reference
to preexistence (see the note on 2, 6) and to take vv 6–8 as presenting two parallel stanzas about Jesus' human state (6–7b;
7cd-8); in the latter alternative, **coming in human likeness**
begins the second stanza and parallels 6a to some extent.

2, 8: There may be reflected here language about the servant of the Lord, Is 52, 13—53, 12, especially 53, 12.

2, 9: The name: "Lord" (11), revealing the true nature of

the one who is named.

**2, 10–11: Every knee should bend . . . every tongue con-
fess:** into this language of Is 45, 23 there has been inserted a
reference to the three levels in the universe, according to ancient thought, **heaven, earth, under the earth.**

2, 11: Jesus Christ is Lord: a common early Christian acclamation; cf 1 Cor 12, 3; Rom 10, 9. But doxology to God
the Father is not overlooked here (11c) in the final version of
the hymn.

2, 12–18: Paul goes on to draw out further ethical implications for daily life (14–18) from the salvation God works in
Christ.

2, 12: Fear and trembling: a common Old Testament expression indicating awe and seriousness in the service of God
(cf Ex 15, 16; Jdt 2, 28; Ps 2, 11; Is 19, 16).

2, 15–16: Generation . . . as you hold on to . . . : or
". . . generation. Among them shine like lights in the world
because you hold the word of life . . . ."

2, 17: Libation: in ancient religious ritual, the pouring out
on the ground of a liquid offering as a sacrifice. Paul means
that he may be facing death.

2, 19—3, 1: The plans of Paul and his assistants for future

w: Jn 1, 1-2; 17, 5; Col 2, 9; Heb 1, 3.   *x:* Is 53, 3.11; Jn 1, 14;
Rom 8, 3; 2 Cor 8, 9; Gal 4, 4; Heb 2, 14.17.   *y:* Mt 26, 39; Jn 10,
17; Heb 5, 8; 12, 2.   *z:* Acts 2, 33; Mt 23, 12; Eph 1, 20-21; Heb
1, 3-4.   *a:* Is 45, 23; Jn 5, 23; Rom 14, 11; Rv 5, 13.   *b:* Acts 2,
36; Rom 10, 9; 1 Cor 12, 3.   *c:* Ps 2, 11; 1 Cor 2, 3; 2 Cor 7, 15.
d: 1, 6; 1 Cor 12, 6; 15, 10; 2 Cor 3, 5.   *e:* 1 Cor 10, 10; 1 Pt 4, 9.
f: 1 Thes 3, 13 / Dt 32, 5; Mt 10, 16; Acts 2, 40 / Dn 12, 3; Mt 5,
14.16; Eph 5, 8.   *g:* 1 Thes 2, 19 / Is 49, 4; 65, 23; Gal 2, 2.
h: Rom 15, 16; 2 Tm 4, 6.   *i:* 3, 1; 4, 4.   *j:* Acts 16, 1-3; 17, 14-
15; 1 Cor 4, 17; 16, 10.

you. [20]For I have no one comparable to him for genuine interest in whatever concerns you. [21][k]For they all seek their own interests, not those of Jesus Christ. [22]But you know his worth, how as a child with a father he served along with me in the cause of the gospel. [23]He it is, then, whom I hope to send as soon as I see how things go with me, [24]*but I am confident in the Lord that I myself will also come soon.

Epaphroditus. [25][l]*With regard to Epaphroditus, my brother and co-worker and fellow soldier, your messenger and minister in my need, I consider it necessary to send him to you. [26]For he has been longing for all of you and was distressed because you heard that he was ill. [27]He was indeed ill, close to death; but God had mercy on him, not just on him but also on me, so that I might not have sorrow upon sorrow. [28]I send him therefore with the greater eagerness, so that, on seeing him, you may rejoice again, and I may have less anxiety. [29][m]Welcome him then in the Lord with all joy and hold such people in esteem, [30]because for the sake of the work of Christ he came close to death,

risking his life to make up for those services to me that you could not perform.

CHAPTER 3

See RG 397–98

Concluding Admonitions. [1][n]*Finally, my brothers, rejoice in the Lord. Writing the same things to you is no burden for me but is a safeguard for you.

V: Polemic: Righteousness and the Goal in Christ

Against Legalistic Teachers. [2][o]*Beware of the dogs! Beware of the evil-workers! Beware of the mutilation! [3][p]*For we are the circumcision, we who worship through the Spirit of God, who boast in Christ Jesus and do not put our confidence in flesh, [4][q]although I myself have grounds for confidence even in the flesh.

Paul's Autobiography. If anyone else thinks he can be confident in flesh, all the more can I. [5][r]*Circumcised on the eighth day, of the race of Israel, of the tribe of Benjamin, a Hebrew of Hebrew parentage, in observance of the law a Pharisee, [6][s]in zeal I

travel are regularly a part of a Pauline letter near its conclusion; cf Rom 15, 22–29; 1 Cor 16, 5–12.

2, 19: Timothy: already known to the Philippians (Acts 16, 1–15; cf 1 Cor 4, 17; 16, 10).

2, 24: I myself will also come soon: cf 1, 19–25 for the significance of this statement.

2, 25: Epaphroditus: sent by the Philippians as their **messenger** (literally, "apostle") to aid Paul in his imprisonment, he had fallen seriously ill; Paul commends him as he sends him back to Philippi.

3, 1: Finally . . . rejoice: the adverb often signals the close of a letter; cf 4, 8; 2 Cor 13, 11. While the verb could also be translated "good-bye" or "farewell," although it is never so used in Greek epistolography, the theme of joy has been frequent in the letter (1, 18; 2, 2.18); note also 4, 4 and the addition of "always" there as evidence for the meaning "rejoice." To write **the same things** may refer to what Paul has previously taught in Philippi or to what he has just written or to what follows.

3, 2–21: An abrupt change in content and tone, either because Paul at this point responds to disturbing news he has just heard about a threat to the faith of the Philippians in the form of false teachers, or because part of another Pauline letter was inserted here; see Introduction. The chapter describes these teachers in strong terms as **dogs**. The persons meant are evidently different from the rival preachers of 1, 14–18 and the opponents of 1, 28. Since vv 2–4 emphasize Jewish terms like **circumcision** (2–3.5), some relate them to the "Judaizers" of the Letter to the Galatians. Other phrases make them

appear more like the false teachers of 2 Cor 11, 12–15, the **evil-workers.** The latter part of the chapter depicts the **many** who are **enemies** of Christ's cross in terms that may sound more Gentile or even "gnostic" than Jewish (18–19). Accordingly, some see two groups of false teachers in ch 3, others one group characterized by a claim of having attained "perfect maturity" (12–15).

3, 2–11: Paul sets forth the Christian claim, especially using personal, autobiographical terms that are appropriate to the situation. He presents his own experience in coming to know Christ Jesus in terms of **righteousness** or justification (cf Rom 1, 16–17; 3, 21—5, 11; Gal 2, 5–11), contrasting **the righteousness from God** through faith and that of one's own **based on the law** as two exclusive ways of pleasing God.

3, 2: Beware of the mutilation: literally, "incision," an ironic wordplay on "circumcision"; cf Gal 5, 12. There may be an association with the self-inflicted mutilations of the prophets of Baal (1 Kgs 18, 28) and of devotees of Cybele who slashed themselves in religious frenzy.

3, 3: We are the circumcision: the true people of God, seed and offspring of Abraham (Gal 3, 7.29; 6, 15). **Spirit of God:** some manuscripts read "worship God by the Spirit."

3, 5: Circumcised on the eighth day: as the law required (Gn 17, 12; Lv 12, 3).

k: 1 Cor 13, 5; 2 Tm 4, 10.   l: 4, 10-11.15-16.18.   m: 1 Cor 16, 18.
n: 2, 18; 4, 4.   o: Ps 22, 17.21; Rv 22, 15 / 2 Cor 11, 13 / Gal 5, 6.12.
p: Rom 2, 28-29; Col 2, 11.   q: 2 Cor 11, 18.21-23.   r: Lk 1, 59;
2, 21 / Acts 22, 3; 23, 6; 26, 5.   s: Acts 8, 3; 22, 4; 26, 9-11.

persecuted the church, in righteousness based on the law I was blameless.

Righteousness from God. *7t**[But] whatever gains I had, these I have come to consider a loss because of Christ. *8*More than that, I even consider everything as a loss because of the supreme good of knowing Christ Jesus my Lord. For his sake I have accepted the loss of all things and I consider them so much rubbish, that I may gain Christ *9u*and be found in him, not having any righteousness of my own based on the law but that which comes through faith in Christ, the righteousness from God, depending on faith *10v*to know him and the power of his resurrection and [the] sharing of his sufferings by being conformed to his death, *11w*if somehow I may attain the resurrection from the dead.

Forward in Christ. *12x**It is not that I have already taken hold of it or have already attained perfect maturity, but I continue my pursuit in hope that I may possess it, since I have indeed been taken possession of by Christ [Jesus]. *13*Brothers, I for my part do not consider myself to have taken possession. Just one thing: forgetting what lies behind but straining forward to what lies ahead, *14y*I continue my pursuit toward the goal, the prize of God's upward calling, in Christ Jesus. *15*Let us, then, who are "perfectly mature" adopt this attitude. And if you have a

different attitude, this too God will reveal to you. *16**Only, with regard to what we have attained, continue on the same course.

Wrong Conduct and Our Goal. *17z**Join with others in being imitators of me, brothers, and observe those who thus conduct themselves according to the model you have in us. *18a*For many, as I have often told you and now tell you even in tears, conduct themselves as enemies of the cross of Christ. *19b*Their end is destruction. Their God is their stomach; their glory is in their "shame." Their minds are occupied with earthly things. *20c**But our citizenship is in heaven, and from it we also await a savior, the Lord Jesus Christ. *21d*He will change our lowly body to conform with his glorified body by the power that enables him also to bring all things into subjection to himself.

VI: Instructions for the Community

CHAPTER 4

See RG 398

Live in Concord. *1e**Therefore, my brothers, whom I love and long for, my joy and crown, in this way stand firm in the Lord, beloved.

2*I urge Euodia and I urge Syntyche to come to a mutual understanding in the Lord. *3f**Yes, and I ask you also, my true yoke-

---

3, 7: Loss: his knowledge of Christ led Paul to reassess the ways of truly pleasing and serving God. His reevaluation indicates the profound and lasting effect of his experience of the meaning of Christ on the way to Damascus some twenty years before (Gal 1, 15–16; Acts 9, 1–22).

3, 12–16: To be **taken possession of by Christ** does not mean that one has already arrived at perfect spiritual maturity. Paul and the Philippians instead press on, trusting in God.

3, 12: Attained perfect maturity: possibly an echo of the concept in the mystery religions of being an initiate, admitted to divine secrets.

3, 16: Some manuscripts add, probably to explain Paul's cryptic phrase, "thinking alike."

3, 17–21: Paul and those who live a life centered in Christ, envisaging both his suffering and resurrection, provide a model that is the opposite of opponents who reject Christ's cross (cf 1 Cor 1, 23).

3, 17: Being imitators of me: not arrogance, but humble simplicity, since all his converts know that Paul is wholly dedicated to imitating Christ (1 Cor 11, 1; cf also Phil 4, 9; 1 Thes 1, 6; 2 Thes 3, 7.9; 1 Cor 4, 6).

3, 20: Citizenship: Christians constitute a colony of

heaven, as Philippi was a **colonia** of Rome (Acts 16, 12). The hope Paul expresses involves the final coming of Christ, not a status already attained, such as the opponents claim.

4, 1–9: This series of ethical admonitions rests especially on the view of Christ and his coming (cf 5) in 3, 20–21. Paul's instructions touch on unity within the congregation, joy, prayer, and the Christian outlook on life.

4, 2: Euodia . . . Syntyche: two otherwise unknown women in the Philippian congregation; on the advice to them, cf 2, 2–4.

4, 3: Yokemate: or "comrade," although the Greek **syzygos** could also be a proper name. **Clement:** otherwise unknown, although later writers sought to identify him with Clement, bishop of Rome (Eusebius, **Ecclesiastical History** 3.15.1).

t: Mt 13, 44.46; Lk 14, 33. *u:* Rom 3, 21-22. *v:* Rom 6, 3-5; 8, 17; Gal 6, 17. *w:* Jn 11, 23-26; Acts 4, 2; Rv 20, 5-6. *x:* 1 Tm 6, 12.19. *y:* 1 Cor 9, 24-25; 2 Tm 4, 7. *z:* 1 Cor 4, 16; 11, 1; 1 Thes 1, 7; 1 Pt 5, 3. *a:* 1 Cor 1, 17.23; Gal 6, 12. *b:* Rom 8, 5-6; 16, 18. *c:* Eph 2, 6.19; Col 3, 1-3; Heb 12, 22. *d:* Rom 8, 23.29; 1 Cor 15, 42-57; 2 Cor 3, 18; 5, 1-5 / 1 Cor 15, 27-28. *e:* 1 Thes 2, 19-20. *f:* Ex 32, 32-33; Ps 69, 29; Dn 12, 1; Lk 10, 20; Rv 3, 5; 13, 8; 17, 8; 20, 12.15; 21, 27.

mate, to help them, for they have struggled at my side in promoting the gospel, along with Clement and my other co-workers, whose names are in the book of life.

Joy and Peace. [4g]*Rejoice in the Lord always. I shall say it again: rejoice! [5h]*Your kindness should be known to all. The Lord is near. [6i]Have no anxiety at all, but in everything, by prayer and petition, with thanksgiving, make your requests known to God. [7j]Then the peace of God that surpasses all understanding will guard your hearts and minds in Christ Jesus.

[8k]*Finally, brothers, whatever is true, whatever is honorable, whatever is just, whatever is pure, whatever is lovely, whatever is gracious, if there is any excellence and if there is anything worthy of praise, think about these things. [9l]*Keep on doing what you have learned and received and heard and seen in me. Then the God of peace will be with you.

VII: Gratitude for the Philippians' Generosity

[10m]*I rejoice greatly in the Lord that now at last you revived your concern for me. You were, of course, concerned about me but lacked an opportunity. [11n]Not that I say this because of need, for I have learned, in whatever situation I find myself, to be self-sufficient. [12]I know indeed how to live in humble circumstances; I know also how to live with abundance. In every circumstance and in all things I have learned the secret of being well fed and of going hungry, of living in abundance and of being in need. [13o]I have the strength for everything through him who empowers me. [14]Still, it was kind of you to share in my distress.

[15]*You Philippians indeed know that at the beginning of the gospel, when I left Macedonia, not a single church shared with me in an account of giving and receiving, except you alone. [16]For even when I was at Thessalonica you sent me something for my needs, not only once but more than once. [17]It is not that I am eager for the gift; rather, I am eager for the profit that accrues to your account. [18p]*I have received full payment and I abound. I am very well supplied because of what I received from you through Epaphroditus, "a fragrant aroma," an acceptable sacrifice, pleasing to God. [19q]My God will fully supply whatever you need, in accord with his glorious riches in Christ Jesus. [20r]To our God and Father, glory forever and ever. Amen.

VIII: Farewell

[21]*Give my greetings to every holy one in Christ Jesus. The brothers who are with me send you their greetings; [22s]*all the holy ones send you their greetings, especially those of Caesar's household. [23]The grace of the Lord Jesus Christ be with your spirit.

4, 4: Rejoice: see the note on 3, 1.

4, 5: Kindness: considerateness, forbearance, fairness. **The Lord is near:** most likely a reference to Christ's parousia (1, 6.10; 3, 20–21; 1 Cor 16, 22), although some sense an echo of Ps 119, 151 and the perpetual presence of the Lord.

4, 8: The language employs terms from Roman Stoic thought.

4, 9: Cf the note on 3, 17.

4, 10–20: Paul, more directly than anywhere else in the letter (cf 1, 3–5), here thanks the Philippians for their gift of money sent through Epaphroditus (2, 25). Paul's own policy was **to be self-sufficient** as a missionary, supporting himself by his own labor (1 Thes 2, 5–9; 1 Cor 9, 15–18; cf Acts 18, 2–3). In spite of this reliance on self and on God to provide (11–13), Paul accepted gifts from the Philippians **not only once but more than once** (16) when he was in Thessalonica (Acts 17, 1–9), as he does now, in prison (**my distress,** 14). While commercial terms appear in the passage, like **an account of giving and receiving** (15) and **received full payment** (18), Paul is most concerned about the spiritual growth of the Philippians (10.17.19); he emphasizes that God will care for their needs, through Christ.

4, 15: The beginning of the gospel: it was at Philippi that Paul first preached Christ in Europe, going on from there to Thessalonica and Beroea (Acts 16, 9—17, 14).

4, 18: Aroma . . . sacrifice: Old Testament cultic language (cf Gn 8, 21; Ex 29, 18.25.41; Lv 1, 9.13; Ez 20, 41) applied to the Philippians' gift; cf Eph 5, 2; 2 Cor 2, 14–16.

4, 21–23: On the usual greetings at the conclusion of a letter, see the note on 1 Cor 16, 19–24. Inclusion of greetings from **all the holy ones** in the place from which Paul writes would involve even the Christians of 1, 14–18 who had their differences with Paul.

4, 22: Those of Caesar's household: minor officials or even slaves and freedmen, found in Ephesus or Rome, among other places.

g: 2, 18; 3, 1. *h:* Ti 3, 2 / Ps 145, 18; Heb 10, 37; Jas 5, 8-9. *i:* Mt 6, 25-34; 1 Pt 5, 7 / Col 4, 2. *j:* Jn 14, 27; Col 3, 15. *k:* Rom 12, 17. *l:* 1 Thes 4, 1 / Rom 15, 33; 16, 20; 1 Cor 14, 33; 1 Thes 5, 23. *m:* 1, 18; 2, 25; 1 Cor 9, 11; 2 Cor 11, 9. *n:* 1 Cor 4, 11; 2 Cor 6, 10; 11, 27 / 2 Cor 12, 9-10. *o:* Col 1, 29; 2 Tm 4, 17. *p:* Gn 8, 21; Ex 29, 18; Eph 5, 2; Heb 13, 16. *q:* 1 Thes 3, 11.13. *r:* Rom 16, 27; Eph 5, 20. *s:* 1, 13.

See RG
399–403

The Letter to the Colossians

This letter is addressed to a congregation at Colossae in the Lycus Valley in Asia Minor, east of Ephesus. At the time of writing, Paul had not visited there, the letter says (1, 4; 2, 1). The community had apparently been established by Epaphras of Colossae (1, 7; 4, 12; Phlm 23). Problems, however, had arisen, brought on by teachers who emphasized Christ's relation to the universe (cosmos). Their teachings stressed angels (2, 18; "principalities and powers," 2, 15), which were connected with astral powers and cultic practices (see the note on 2, 16) and rules about food and drink and ascetical disciplines (2, 16.18). These teachings, Paul insists, detract from the person and work of Christ for salvation as set forth magnificently in a hymnic passage at Col 1, 15–20 and reiterated throughout the letter. Such teachings are but "shadows"; Christ is "reality" (2, 17).

For help in dealing with these problems that the new teachers posed at Colossae, Epaphras sought out Paul, who was then imprisoned (4, 10.18) at a place that the letter does not mention. Paul, without entering into debate over the existence of angelic spirits or their function, simply affirms that Christ possesses the sum total of redemptive power (1, 19) and that the spiritual renewal of the human person occurs through contact in baptism with the person of Christ, who died and rose again (2, 9–14). It is unnecessary for the Christian to be concerned about placating spirits (2, 15) or avoiding imagined defilement through ascetical practices in regard to food and drink (2, 20–23). True Christian asceticism consists in the conquering of personal sins (3, 5–10) and the practice of love of neighbor in accordance with the standard set by Christ (3, 12–16).

Paul commends the community as a whole (1, 3–8); this seems to indicate that, though the Colossians have been under pressure to adopt the false doctrines, they have not yet succumbed. The apostle expresses his prayerful concern for them (1, 9–14). His preaching has cost him persecution, suffering, and imprisonment, but he regards these as reflective of the sufferings of Christ, a required discipline for the sake of the gospel (see the note on 1, 24; cf 1, 29; 2, 1). His instructions to the Christian family and to slaves and masters

require a new spirit of reflection and action. Love, obedience, and service are to be rendered "in the Lord" (3, 18—4, 1).

Colossians follows the outline of a typical Pauline letter. It is distinguished by the poetic lines in 1, 15–20 concerning who Christ is and what Christ means in creation and redemption. This hymn may be compared with similar passages in Philippians 2, 6–11; 1 Timothy 3, 16; and Jn 1, 1–18. It was apparently familiar liturgical material to the author, the audience, and the false teachers. In 1, 21—2, 7, however, Paul interprets the relation between the body of Christ, which he insists is the church (1, 18), and the world or cosmos to be one not simply of Christ's preexistence and rule but one of missionary advance into the world by the spreading of the word (1, 25.28). In this labor of the missionary body of Christ, Paul as a minister plays a prime part in bringing Christ and the gospel as hope to the Gentiles (1, 23.25.27). To "every creature under heaven" the word is to be proclaimed, so that everyone receives Christ, is established in faith, and walks in Christ (1, 28; 2, 6.7).

Paul wrote the Letter to the Colossians while in prison, but his several imprisonments leave the specific place and date of composition uncertain. On this point the same problem exists as with Ephesians and Philippians (see the Introductions to these letters). Traditionally the house arrest at Rome, in which Paul enjoyed a certain restricted freedom in preaching (see Acts 28, 16–28), or a second Roman imprisonment has been claimed as the setting. Others suggest a still earlier imprisonment at Caesarea (see Acts 23, 12—27, 1) or in Ephesus (see Acts 19). Still others regard the letter as the work of some pupil or follower of Paul, writing in his name. In any case, the contents are often closely paralleled by thoughts in Ephesians.

The principal divisions of the Letter to the Colossians are the following:

I: Address (1, 1–14)

II: The Preeminence of Christ (1, 15—2, 3)

III: Warnings against False Teachers (2, 4–23)

IV: The Ideal Christian Life in the World
(3, 1—4, 6)

V: Conclusion (4, 7–18)

I: Address

CHAPTER 1

See RG 400–401

Greeting. *1a**Paul, an apostle of Christ Jesus by the will of God, and Timothy our brother, ²to the holy ones and faithful brothers in Christ in Colossae: grace to you and peace from God our Father.

Thanksgiving. *3b**We always give thanks to God, the Father of our Lord Jesus Christ, when we pray for you, ⁴for we have heard of your faith in Christ Jesus and the love that you have for all the holy ones *5c*because of the hope reserved for you in heaven. Of this you have already heard through the word of truth, the gospel, ⁶that has come to you. Just as in the whole world it is bearing fruit and growing, so also among you, from the day you heard it and came to know the grace of God in truth, *7d**as you learned it from Epaphras our beloved fellow slave, who is a trustworthy minister of Christ on your behalf ⁸and who also told us of your love in the Spirit.

Prayer for Continued Progress. *9e**There-fore, from the day we heard this, we do not cease praying for you and asking that you may be filled with the knowledge of his will through all spiritual wisdom and understanding ¹⁰to live in a manner worthy of the Lord, so as to be fully pleasing, in every good work bearing fruit and growing in the knowledge of God, ¹¹strengthened with every power, in accord with his glorious might, for all endurance and patience, with joy *12f**giving thanks to the Father, who has made you fit to share in the inheritance of the holy ones in light. ¹³He delivered us from the power of darkness and transferred us to the kingdom of his beloved Son, *14g*in whom we have redemption, the forgiveness of sins.

II: The Preeminence of Christ— His Person and Work

¹⁵ *h**He is the image of the invisible God,
    the firstborn of all creation.
¹⁶ *i**For in him were created all things in
    heaven and on earth,
    the visible and the invisible,

1, 1–2: For the epistolary form used by Paul at the beginning of his letters, see the note on Rom 1, 1–7. On **holy ones** or "God's people," see the note on Rom 1, 7. Awareness of their calling helps this group to be **faithful brothers** and sisters **in Christ,** i.e., dedicated to the tasks implied in their calling.

1, 3–8: On thanksgiving at the start of a letter, see the note on Rom 1, 8. The apostle, recalling his own prayers for them and the good report about them he has received (3–4), congratulates the Colossians upon their acceptance of Christ and their faithful efforts to live the gospel (3, 6–8). To encourage them he mentions the success of the gospel elsewhere (6) and assures them that his knowledge of their community is accurate, since he has been in personal contact with Epaphras (7–8), who likely had evangelized Colossae and other cities in the Lycus Valley of Asia Minor (cf 4, 12.13; Phlm 23). On **faith, love,** and **hope** (4.5.8), see the note on 1 Cor 13, 13; cf 1 Thes 1, 3; 5, 8.

1, 7: Epaphras: now with Paul but a Colossian, founder of the church there.

1, 9–14: Moved by Epaphras' account, the apostle has prayed and continues to pray fervently for the Colossians that, in their response to the gospel, they **may be filled with the knowledge of** God's **will** (9; cf 3, 10). Paul expects a mutual interaction between their life according to the gospel and this knowledge (10), yielding results (**fruit;** 10; cf 6) **in every good work:** growth, strength, **endurance, patience, with joy** (11), and the further giving of thanks (12).

1, 12–14: A summary about **redemption** by **the Father** precedes the statement in vv 15–20 about the **beloved Son** who is God's love in person (13). Christians share **the inher-itance . . . in light** with **the holy ones,** here probably the angels (12). The imagery reflects the Exodus (**delivered . . . transferred**) and Jesus' theme of the **kingdom. Redemption** is explained as **forgiveness of sins** (cf Acts 2, 38; Rom 3, 24–25; Eph 1, 7).

1, 15–20: As the poetic arrangement indicates, these lines are probably an early Christian hymn, known to the Colossians and taken up into the letter from liturgical use (cf Phil 2, 6–11; 1 Tm 3, 16). They present Christ as the mediator of creation (15–18a) and of redemption (18b-20). There is a parallelism between **firstborn of all creation** (15) and firstborn from the dead (18). While many of the phrases were at home in Greek philosophical use and even in gnosticism, the basic ideas also reflect Old Testament themes about Wisdom found in Prv 8, 22–31; Wis 7, 22—8, 1; and Sir 1, 4. See also the notes on what is possibly a hymn in Jn 1, 1–18.

1, 15: Image: cf Gn 1, 27. Whereas the man and the woman were originally created in the image and likeness of God (see also Gn 1, 26), Christ as image (2 Cor 4, 4) of **the invisible God** (Jn 1, 18) now shares this new nature in baptism with those redeemed (cf 3, 10–11).

1, 16–17: Christ (though not mentioned by name) is preeminent and supreme as God's agent in the creation of **all things** (cf Jn 1, 3), as prior to **all things** (17; cf Heb 1, 3).

---

a: Eph 1, 1.   *b:* Eph 1, 15-16; Phlm 4-5.   *c:* Eph 1, 13 18; 1 Pt 1, 4.   *d:* Phlm 23.   *e:* Eph 1, 15-17; 5, 17; Phil 1, 9.   *f:* 3, 17; Jn 8, 12; Acts 26, 18; 1 Tm 6, 16; 1 Pt 2, 9.   *g:* Eph 1, 7.   *h:* Ps 89, 28; Jn 1, 3.18; 2 Cor 4, 4.   *i:* 1 Cor 8, 6; Eph 1, 10.21.

whether thrones or dominions or
    principalities or powers;
all things were created through him
    and for him.
[17] He is before all things,
    and in him all things hold together.
[18] j*He is the head of the body, the
    church.
He is the beginning, the firstborn from
    the dead,
    that in all things he himself might be
    preeminent.
[19] *For in him all the fullness was pleased
    to dwell,
[20]   k*and through him to reconcile all
    things for him,
    making peace by the blood of his cross
    [through him], whether those on earth
    or those in heaven.

[21] l*And you who once were alienated and
hostile in mind because of evil deeds [22] he
has now reconciled in his fleshly body
through his death, to present you holy, without
blemish, and irreproachable before him,

[23] provided that you persevere in the faith,
firmly grounded, stable, and not shifting
from the hope of the gospel that you heard,
which has been preached to every creature
under heaven, of which I, Paul, am a minister.

Christ in Us. [24] *Now I rejoice in my sufferings for your sake, and in my flesh I am
filling up what is lacking in the afflictions of
Christ on behalf of his body, which is the
church, [25] of which I am a minister in accordance with God's stewardship given to me to
bring to completion for you the word of
God, [26] m the mystery hidden from ages and
from generations past. But now it has been
manifested to his holy ones, [27] n to whom God
chose to make known the riches of the glory
of this mystery among the Gentiles; it is
Christ in you, the hope for glory. [28] o It is he
whom we proclaim, admonishing everyone
and teaching everyone with all wisdom, that
we may present everyone perfect in Christ.
[29] p For this I labor and struggle, in accord
with the exercise of his power working
within me.

1, 18: Church: such a reference seemingly belongs under
"redemption" in the following lines, not under the "creation"
section of the hymn. Stoic thought sometimes referred to the
world as "the body of Zeus." Pauline usage is to speak of the
church as the body of Christ (1 Cor 12, 12–27; Rom 12, 4–5).
Some think that the author of Colossians has inserted the reference to the church here so as to define "head of the body"
in Paul's customary way. See v 24. **Preeminent:** when Christ
was raised by God as **firstborn from the dead** (cf Acts 26,
23; Rv 1, 5), he was placed over the community, the church,
that he had brought into being, but he is also indicated as
crown of the whole new creation, over **all things.** His further
role is to **reconcile all things** (20) for God or possibly "to
himself."

1, 19: Fullness: in gnostic usage this term referred to a
spiritual world of beings above, between God and the world;
many later interpreters take it to refer to **the fullness of the
deity** (2, 9); the reference could also be to the fullness of
grace (cf Jn 1, 16).

1, 20: The blood of his cross: the most specific reference
in the hymn to redemption through Christ's death, a central
theme in Paul; cf 2, 14–15; 1 Cor 1, 17.18.23. **[Through
him]:** the phrase, lacking in some manuscripts, seems superfluous but parallels the reference to reconciliation through
Christ earlier in the verse.

1, 21–23: Paul, in applying this hymn to the Colossians,
reminds them that they have experienced the reconciling effect of Christ's death. He sees the effects of the cross in the
redemption of human beings, not of cosmic powers such as
those referred to in vv 16 and 20 (**all things**). Paul also urges
adherence to Christ in faith and begins to point to his own

role as minister (23), sufferer (24), and proclaimer (27–28)
of this gospel.

1, 24—2, 3: As the community at Colossae was not personally known to Paul (see Introduction), he here invests
his teaching with greater authority by presenting a brief
sketch of his apostolic ministry and sufferings as they reflect those of Christ on behalf of the church (24). The
preaching of God's word (25) carries out the divine plan
(**the mystery,** 26) to make Christ known to the Gentiles
(27). It teaches the God-given wisdom about Christ (28),
whose power works mightily in the apostle (29). Even in
those communities that do not know him personally (2, 1),
he can increase the perception of God in Christ, unite the
faithful more firmly in love, and so bring encouragement to
them (2). He hopes that his apostolic authority will make
the Colossians perceive more readily the defects in the
teaching of others who have sought to delude them, the
next concern in the letter.

1, 24: What is lacking: although variously interpreted,
this phrase does not imply that Christ's atoning death on the
cross was defective. It may refer to the apocalyptic concept
of a quota of "messianic woes" to be endured before the end
comes; cf Mk 13, 8.19–20.24 and the note on Mt 23, 29–32.
Others suggest that Paul's mystical unity with Christ allowed him to call his own **sufferings the afflictions of
Christ.**

j: 1 Cor 11, 3; 12, 12.27; 15, 20; Eph 1, 22-23; Rv 1, 5.   k: 2 Cor
5, 18-19; Eph 1, 10.   l: Eph 2, 14-16.   m: Rom 16, 25-26; 1 Cor
2, 7; Eph 3, 3.9.   n: 3, 4; Rom 8, 10.   o: Eph 4, 13.   p: 2, 1; 4,
12; Phil 4, 13.

See RG
401

CHAPTER 2

1*For I want you to know how great a struggle I am having for you and for those in Laodicea and all who have not seen me face to face, *2q*that their hearts may be encouraged as they are brought together in love, to have all the richness of fully assured understanding, for the knowledge of the mystery of God, Christ, *3r*in whom are hidden all the treasures of wisdom and knowledge.

III: Warnings against
False Teachers

A General Admonition. *4s**I say this so that no one may deceive you by specious arguments. *5t*For even if I am absent in the flesh, yet I am with you in spirit, rejoicing as I observe your good order and the firmness of your faith in Christ. *6*So, as you received Christ Jesus the Lord, walk in him, *7u*rooted in him and built upon him and established in the faith as you were taught, abounding in thanksgiving. *8v**See to it that no one captivate you with an empty, seductive philosophy according to human tradition, according to the elemental powers of the world and not according to Christ.

Sovereign Role of Christ. *9w**For in him dwells the whole fullness of the deity bodily, *10*and you share in this fullness in him, who is the head of every principality and power. *11x**In him you were also circumcised with a circumcision not administered by hand, by stripping off the carnal body, with the circumcision of Christ. *12y*You were buried with him in baptism, in which you were also raised with him through faith in the power of God, who raised him from the dead. *13z*And even when you were dead [in] transgressions and the uncircumcision of your flesh, he brought you to life along with him, having forgiven us all our transgressions; *14a**obliterating the bond against us, with its legal claims, which was opposed to us, he also removed it from our midst, nailing it to the cross; *15b**despoiling the principalities and the powers, he made a public spectacle of them, leading them away in triumph by it.

Practices Contrary to Faith. *16c**Let no one, then, pass judgment on you in matters of food and drink or with regard to a festival or new moon or sabbath. *17d*These are shad-

2, 1: Laodicea: chief city in Phrygia, northwest of Colossae; cf 4, 13.16; Rv 3, 14–22.

2, 4–23: In face of the threat posed by false teachers (4), the Colossians are admonished to adhere to the gospel as it was first preached to them (6), steeping themselves in it with grateful hearts (7). They must reject religious teachings originating in any source except the gospel (8) because in Christ alone will they have access to God, **the deity** (9). So fully has Christ enlightened them that they need no other source of religious knowledge or virtue (10). They do not require **circumcision** (11), for **in baptism** their whole being has been affected by Christ (12) through forgiveness of sin and resurrection to a new life (13; cf 3, 1 and Rom 6, 1–11).

On the cross Christ canceled the record of the debt that stood against us with all its claims (14), i.e., he eliminated the law (cf Eph 2, 15) that human beings could not observe—and that could not save them. He forgave sins against the law (14) and exposed as false and misleading (15) all other powers (cf 1, 16) that purport to offer salvation. Therefore, the Colossians are not to accept judgments from such teachers on **food and drink** or to keep certain religious festivals or engage in certain cultic practices (16), for the Colossians would thereby risk severing themselves from Christ (19). If, when they accepted the gospel, they believed in Christ as their savior, they must be convinced that their salvation cannot be achieved by appeasing ruling spirits through dietary practices or through a wisdom gained simply by means of harsh asceticism (20–23).

2, 8: Elemental powers of the world: see the note on Gal 4, 3.

2, 9: Fullness of the deity: the divine nature, not just attributes; see the note on 1, 19.

2, 11: A description of baptism (12) in symbolic terms of the Old Testament rite for entry into the community. The false teachers may have demanded physical circumcision of the Colossians.

2, 14: The elaborate metaphor here about how God canceled the legal claims against us through Christ's cross depicts not Christ being nailed to the cross by men but **the bond . . . with its legal claims** being nailed to the cross by God.

2, 15: The picture derives from the **public spectacle** and **triumph** of a Roman emperor's victory parade, where captives marched in subjection. **The principalities and the powers** are here conquered, not reconciled (cf 1, 16.20). An alternate rendering for **by it** (the cross) is "by him" (Christ).

2, 16: Festival or new moon or sabbath: yearly, monthly, and weekly observances determined by religious powers associated with a calendar set by the heavenly bodies, sun, moon, and stars (cf 8).

q: 1, 26-27; Eph 3, 18-19.   *r*: Prv 2, 4-5; Is 45, 3; Rom 11, 33; 1 Cor 1, 30.   *s*: Eph 4, 14.   *t*: 1 Cor 5, 3; Phil 1, 27.   *u*: Eph 2, 20-22; 3, 17.   *v*: Gal 4, 3; Eph 5, 6.   *w*: 1, 19; Eph 3, 19.   *x*: 1, 22; Jer 4, 4; Rom 2, 25-29; Phil 3, 3.   *y*: Rom 6, 3-4.   *z*: Eph 2, 1.5.   *a*: Eph 2, 14-15.   *b*: 1, 16.20; 2 Cor 2, 14; Eph 1, 21.   *c*: Rom 14, 3-4; 1 Tm 4, 3.   *d*: Heb 8, 5; 10, 1.

ows of things to come; the reality belongs to Christ. *18e**Let no one disqualify you, delighting in self-abasement and worship of angels, taking his stand on visions, inflated without reason by his fleshly mind, *19f*and not holding closely to the head, from whom the whole body, supported and held together by its ligaments and bonds, achieves the growth that comes from God.

*20*If you died with Christ to the elemental powers of the world, why do you submit to regulations as if you were still living in the world? *21*"Do not handle! Do not taste! Do not touch!" *22g*These are all things destined to perish with use; they accord with human precepts and teachings. *23*While they have a semblance of wisdom in rigor of devotion and self-abasement [and] severity to the body, they are of no value against gratification of the flesh.

IV: The Ideal Christian Life in the World

CHAPTER 3

See RG
401-402 *Mystical Death and Resurrection.* *1h**If then you were raised with Christ, seek what is above, where Christ is seated at the right hand of God. *2*Think of what is above, not of what is on earth. *3i*For you have died, and your life is hidden with Christ in God. *4*When Christ your life appears, then you too will appear with him in glory.

Renunciation of Vice. *5j**Put to death, then, the parts of you that are earthly: immorality, impurity, passion, evil desire, and the greed that is idolatry. *6k**Because of these the wrath of God is coming [upon the disobedient]. *7*By these you too once conducted yourselves, when you lived in that way. *8l**But now you must put them all away: anger, fury, malice, slander, and obscene language out of your mouths. *9m*Stop lying to one another, since you have taken off the old self with its practices *10n**and have put on the new self, which is being renewed, for knowledge, in the image of its creator. *11o**Here there is not Greek and Jew, circumcision and uncircumcision, barbarian, Scythian, slave, free; but Christ is all and in all.

*12p*Put on then, as God's chosen ones, holy and beloved, heartfelt compassion, kindness, humility, gentleness, and patience, *13q*bearing with one another and forgiving one another, if one has a grievance against another; as the Lord has forgiven you, so must you also do. *14r*And over all these put on love, that is, the bond of perfection. *15s*And let the peace of Christ control your hearts, the peace into which you were also called in one body. And be thankful. *16t*Let the word of Christ dwell in you richly, as in all wisdom you teach and admonish one another, singing psalms, hymns, and spiritual songs with gratitude in your hearts to God. *17u*And whatever you do, in word or in deed, do everything in the name of the Lord Jesus, giving thanks to God the Father through him.

The Christian Family. *18v**Wives, be

2, 18: Ascetic practices encouraged by the false teachers included subjection of self humbly to their rules, worship of angels, and cultivation of visions, though exact details are unclear.

3, 1–4: By retaining the message of the gospel that the risen, living Christ is the source of their salvation, the Colossians will be free from false religious evaluations of the things of the world (1–2). They have died to these; but one day **when Christ . . . appears,** they will live with Christ in the presence of God (3–4).

3, 5–17: In lieu of false asceticism and superstitious festivals, the apostle reminds the Colossians of the moral life that is to characterize their response to God through Christ. He urges their participation in the liturgical hymns and prayers that center upon God's plan of salvation in Christ (16).

3, 5.8: The two lists of five vices each are similar to enumerations at Rom 1, 29–31 and Gal 5, 19–21.

3, 6: **The wrath of God:** see the note on Rom 1, 18. Many manuscripts add, as at Eph 5, 6, "upon the disobedient."

3, 8–10: **Put . . . away; have taken off; have put on:** the

terms may reflect baptismal practice, taking off garments and putting on new ones after being united with Christ, here translated into ethical terms.

3, 10: **Image:** see the note on 1, 15.

3, 11: **Scythian:** a barbarous people from north of the Black Sea.

3, 18—4, 6: After general recommendations that connect family life and the social condition of slavery with the service of Christ (3, 18—4, 1), Paul requests prayers for himself, especially in view of his imprisonment (2–3), and recommends

e: 2, 23; Mt 24, 4. *f:* Eph 2, 21-22; 4, 16. *g:* Is 29, 13. *h:* 2, 12; Ps 110, 1; Phil 3, 20; Eph 2, 6. *i:* Rom 6, 2-5. *j:* Mt 15, 19; Rom 1, 29-30; Gal 5, 19-21; Eph 5, 3.5. *k:* Rom 1, 18. *l:* Eph 4, 22.25.31. *m:* Rom 6, 4.6; Eph 4, 22-25; Heb 12, 1; 1 Pt 2, 1; 4, 2. *n:* Gn 1, 26-27. *o:* 1 Cor 12, 13; Gal 3, 27-28. *p:* Eph 4, 1-2.32; 1 Thes 5, 15. *q:* Mt 6, 14; 18, 21-35; Eph 4, 32. *r:* Rom 13, 8-10. *s:* Rom 12, 5; 1 Cor 12, 12; Eph 2, 16; 4, 3-4; Phil 4, 7. *t:* Eph 5, 19-20. *u:* 1 Cor 10, 31. *v:* Eph 5, 22; Ti 2, 5; 1 Pt 3, 1.

subordinate to your husbands, as is proper in the Lord. [19]Husbands, love your wives, and avoid any bitterness toward them. [20w]Children, obey your parents in everything, for this is pleasing to the Lord. [21x]Fathers, do not provoke your children, so they may not become discouraged.

Slaves and Masters. [22y]*Slaves, obey your human masters in everything, not only when being watched, as currying favor, but in simplicity of heart, fearing the Lord. [23]Whatever you do, do from the heart, as for the Lord and not for others, [24]knowing that you will receive from the Lord the due payment of the inheritance; be slaves of the Lord Christ. [25z]For the wrongdoer will receive recompense for the wrong he committed, and there is no partiality.

See RG
401-402

CHAPTER 4

[1]Masters, treat your slaves justly and fairly, realizing that you too have a Master in heaven.

Prayer and Apostolic Spirit. [2a]Persevere in prayer, being watchful in it with thanksgiving; [3b]at the same time, pray for us, too, that God may open a door to us for the word, to speak of the mystery of Christ, for which I am in prison, [4]that I may make it clear, as I must speak. [5c]Conduct yourselves wisely toward outsiders, making the most of the opportunity. [6]Let your speech always be gracious, seasoned with salt, so that you know how you should respond to each one.

V: Conclusion

Tychicus and Onesimus. [7d]*Tychicus, my beloved brother, trustworthy minister, and fellow slave in the Lord, will tell you all the news of me. [8]I am sending him to you for this very purpose, so that you may know about us and that he may encourage your hearts, [9e]together with Onesimus, a trustworthy and beloved brother, who is one of you. They will tell you about everything here.

From Paul's Co-Workers. [10f]*Aristarchus, my fellow prisoner, sends you greetings, as does Mark the cousin of Barnabas (concerning whom you have received instructions; if he comes to you, receive him), [11]*and Jesus, who is called Justus, who are of the circumcision; these alone are my co-workers for the kingdom of God, and they have been a comfort to me. [12g]*Epaphras sends you greetings; he is one of you, a slave of Christ [Jesus], always striving for you in his prayers so that you may be perfect and fully assured in all the will of God. [13]*For I can testify that he works very hard for you and for those in Laodicea and those in Hierapolis. [14h]*Luke the beloved physician sends greetings, as does Demas.

A Message for the Laodiceans. [15]*Give greetings to the brothers in Laodicea and to Nympha and to the church in her house. [16]*And when this letter is read before you, have it read also in the church of the Laodiceans, and you yourselves read the one from

friendly relations and meaningful discussions of Christian teaching with **outsiders**, i.e., non-Christians (4, 5–6). See the note on Eph 5, 21—6, 9.

3, 22–25: Slaves: within this table of duties in family and societal relations, involving wives and husbands, children and parents (18–21), such as also appears in Eph 5, 22—6, 9, slaves here receive special attention because of the case of Onesimus the slave returning to his master (4, 9; Phlm 10–12).

4, 7–18: Paul concludes with greetings and information concerning various Christians known to the Colossians.

4, 7: Tychicus: Acts 20, 4 mentions his role in the collection for Jerusalem; Eph 6, 21 repeats what is said here; see also 2 Tm 4, 12; Ti 3, 12.

4, 10: Aristarchus: a Thessalonian who was with Paul at Ephesus and Caesarea and on the voyage to Rome (Acts 19, 29; 20, 4; 27, 2). **Mark:** also referred to at Phlm 24 and 2 Tm 4, 11 and, as "John Mark," in Acts (12, 12.25; 13, 13; 15, 37–40). See also 1 Pt 5, 13 and the note there. Traditionally the author of the second gospel.

4, 11: Jesus: a then common Jewish name, the Greek form of Joshua.

4, 12: Epaphras: see the notes on 1, 3–8 and 1, 7.

4, 13: Laodicea: see the note on 2, 1. **Hierapolis:** a city northeast of Laodicea and northwest of Colossae.

4, 14: Luke: only here described as a medical doctor; cf Phlm 24 and 2 Tm 4, 11. Traditionally the author of the third gospel. **Demas:** cf Phlm 24; he later deserted Paul (2 Tm 4, 10).

4, 15: Nympha and . . . her house: some manuscripts read a masculine for the house-church leader, "Nymphas and . . . his house."

4, 16: The one from Laodicea: either a letter by Paul that

w: Eph 6, 1.   x: Eph 6, 4.   y: Eph 6, 5; 1 Tm 6, 1; Ti 2, 9-10; 1 Pt 2, 18.   z: Rom 2, 11.   a: Lk 18, 1; Rom 12, 12; Eph 6. 18-20; 1 Thes 5, 17.   b: Rom 15, 30; 1 Cor 16, 9; Eph 6, 19; 2 Thes 3, 1.   c: Eph 5, 15-16.   d: Acts 20, 4; Eph 6, 21-22; Phil 1, 12. e: Phlm 10-11.   f: Acts 19, 29; 20, 4; 27, 2 / Acts 12, 12.25; 13, 13; 15, 37.40; 2 Tm 4, 11; Phlm 24; 1 Pt 5, 13.   g: 1, 7; Rom 15, 30.   h: Phlm 24; 2 Tm 4, 10-11.

Laodicea. [17i]*And tell Archippus, "See that you fulfill the ministry that you received in the Lord."

[18j]*The greeting is in my own hand, Paul's. Remember my chains. Grace be with you.

has been lost or the Letter to the Ephesians (cf the note on Eph 1, 1, in Ephesus).

4, 17: Fulfill the ministry: usually taken to mean that **Archippus,** the son of Philemon and Apphia (Phlm 1–2), is "pastor" at Colossae. An alternate interpretation is that Archippus, not Philemon, is the owner of the slave Onesimus and that Paul is asking Archippus to complete the service he

has received in the Lord by sending Onesimus back to minister to Paul in his captivity (cf Phlm 20).

4, 18: **My own hand:** a postscript in Paul's own hand was his custom; cf Gal 6, 11–18 and 2 Thes 3, 17–18.

i: Phlm 2. *j:* 1 Cor 16, 21; Gal 6, 11; Eph 3, 1; 2 Thes 3, 17.

See RG
403–406

The First Letter to the Thessalonians

When Paul parted from Barnabas (Acts 15, 36–41) at the beginning of what is called his second missionary journey, he chose Silvanus (Silas) as his traveling companion. Soon afterwards he took Timothy along with him (Acts 16, 1–3). Paul was now clearly at the head of his own missionary band. About A.D. 50, he arrived in Greece for the first time. In making converts in Philippi and, soon afterwards, in Thessalonica, he was beset by persecution from Jews and Gentiles alike. Moving on to Beroea, he was again harassed by enemies from Thessalonica and hurriedly left for Athens (Acts 16, 11—17, 15). Silvanus and Timothy remained behind for a while. Paul soon sent Timothy back to Thessalonica to strengthen that community in its trials (3, 1–5). Timothy and Silvanus finally returned to Paul when he reached Corinth (Acts 18, 1–18), probably in the early summer of A.D. 51. Timothy's return with a report on conditions at Thessalonica served as the occasion for Paul's first letter (3, 6–8).

The letter begins with a brief address (1, 1) and concludes with a greeting (5, 26–28). The body of the letter consists of two major parts. The first (1, 2—3, 13) is a set of three sections of thanksgiving connected by two *apologiae* (defenses) dealing, respectively, with the missionaries' previous conduct and their current concerns. Paul's thankful optimism regarding the Thessalonians' spiritual welfare is tempered by his insistence on their recognition of the selfless love shown by the missionaries. In an age of itinerant peddlers of new religions, Paul found it necessary to emphasize not only the content of his gospel but also his

manner of presenting it, for both attested to God's grace as freely bestowed and powerfully effected.

The second part of the letter (4, 1—5, 25) is specifically hortatory or parenetic. The superabundant love for which Paul has just prayed (3, 12–13) is to be shown practically by living out the norms of conduct that he has communicated to them. Specific "imperatives" of Christian life, principles for acting morally, stem from the "indicative" of one's relationship to God through Christ by the sending of the holy Spirit. Thus, moral conduct is the practical, personal expression of one's Christian faith, love, and hope.

The principal divisions of the First Letter to the Thessalonians are the following:

I: Address (1, 1–10)

II: Previous Relations with the Thessalonians (2, 1—3, 13)

III: Specific Exhortations (4, 1—5, 25)

IV: Final Greeting (5, 26–28)

I: Address

CHAPTER 1

See RG
404

Greeting. [1a]*Paul, Silvanus, and Timothy to the church of the Thessalonians in God the Father and the Lord Jesus Christ: grace to you and peace.

Thanksgiving for Their Faith. [2b]We give thanks to God always for all of you, remembering you in our prayers, unceasingly [3]*calling to mind your work of faith and labor of

1, 1: On the address, see the note on Rom 1, 1–7.

1, 3: Faith ... love ... hope: this, along with 5, 8, is the earliest mention in Christian literature of the three "theological virtues" (see 1 Cor 13, 13). The order here stresses escha-

tological hope, in line with the letter's emphasis on the Lord's second, triumphal coming, or parousia (10; 2, 12.19; 3, 13; 4, ——————

a: Acts 15, 40; 16, 1-3.19; 17, 14-15; 2 Thes 1, 1-2. *b:* 2 Thes 1, 3.

love and endurance in hope of our Lord Jesus Christ, before our God and Father, *4c*knowing, brothers loved by God, how you were chosen. *5d*For our gospel did not come to you in word alone, but also in power and in the holy Spirit and [with] much conviction. You know what sort of people we were [among] you for your sake. *6**And you became imitators of us and of the Lord, receiving the word in great affliction, with joy from the holy Spirit, *7e*so that you became a model for all the believers in Macedonia and in Achaia. *8f*For from you the word of the Lord has sounded forth not only in Macedonia and [in] Achaia, but in every place your faith in God has gone forth, so that we have no need to say anything. *9g*For they themselves openly declare about us what sort of reception we had among you, and how you turned to God from idols to serve the living and true God *10h*and to await his Son from heaven, whom he raised from [the] dead, Jesus, who delivers us from the coming wrath.

II: Previous Relations with the Thessalonians

See RG
404–405

CHAPTER 2

Paul's Ministry Among Them. *1*For you yourselves know, brothers, that our reception among you was not without effect. *2i*Rather, after we had suffered and been insolently treated, as you know, in Philippi, we drew courage through our God to speak to you the gospel of God with much struggle. *3*Our exhortation was not from delusion or impure motives, nor did it work through de-

ception. *4j**But as we were judged worthy by God to be entrusted with the gospel, that is how we speak, not as trying to please human beings, but rather God, who judges our hearts. *5*Nor, indeed, did we ever appear with flattering speech, as you know, or with a pretext for greed—God is witness— *6k*nor did we seek praise from human beings, either from you or from others, *7**although we were able to impose our weight as apostles of Christ. Rather, we were gentle among you, as a nursing mother cares for her children. *8*With such affection for you, we were determined to share with you not only the gospel of God, but our very selves as well, so dearly beloved had you become to us. *9l*You recall, brothers, our toil and drudgery. Working night and day in order not to burden any of you, we proclaimed to you the gospel of God. *10*You are witnesses, and so is God, how devoutly and justly and blamelessly we behaved toward you believers. *11m*As you know, we treated each one of you as a father treats his children, *12n*exhorting and encouraging you and insisting that you conduct yourselves as worthy of the God who calls you into his kingdom and glory.

Further Thanksgiving. *13*And for this reason we too give thanks to God unceasingly, that, in receiving the word of God from hearing us, you received not a human word but, as it truly is, the word of God, which is now at work in you who believe. *14**For you, brothers, have become imitators of the churches of God that are in Judea in Christ Jesus. For you suffer the same things from your compatriots as they did from the Jews, *15c**who killed both the Lord Jesus and the

13—5, 11; 5, 23).

1, 6: Imitators: the Pauline theme of "imitation" (see 2, 14; 1 Cor 4, 16; 11, 1; 2 Thes 3, 9) is rooted in Paul's view of solidarity in Christ through sharing in Jesus' cross and in the Spirit of the risen Lord.

2, 4: Judged worthy: Paul regards "worthiness" not as grounded in one's own talent or moral self-righteousness but in God's discernment of genuinely selfless attitudes and actions (see 2 Cor 10, 17–18).

2, 7: Gentle: many excellent manuscripts read "infants" (nēpioi), but "gentle" (ēpioi) better suits the context here.

2, 14: Luke's picture of the persecutions at Philippi (by Gentiles) and in Thessalonica and Beroea (by Jews) seems to be considerably schematized (Acts 16, 11–40; 17, 1–15). Paul pictures the Thessalonian community as composed of con-

verts from paganism (1, 9) and speaks here of persecution by their (pagan) compatriots rather than by Jews.

2, 15–16: Paul is speaking of historical opposition on the part of Palestinian Jews in particular and does so only some twenty years after Jesus' crucifixion. Even so, he quickly proceeds to depict the persecutors typologically, in apocalyptic terms. His remarks give no grounds for anti-Semitism to those willing to understand him, especially in view of

c: 2 Thes 2, 13. *d:* Acts 13, 52; 17, 1-9. *e:* 2 Thes 1, 4; 1 Cor 4, 16; 11, 1 / 2, 14; Phil 3, 17. *f:* Rom 1, 8. *g:* Acts 14, 15; Gal 4, 8 / 4, 5. *h:* Rom 2, 1-16; 5, 9; 13, 4 / 5, 9. *i:* Acts 16, 19— 17, 10. *j:* Gal 1, 10. *k:* Jn 5, 41.44; 1 Cor 10, 31; 2 Cor 4, 17. *l:* Acts 20, 34; 1 Cor 4, 12; 9, 3-18; 2 Thes 3, 7-9. *m:* Acts 20, 31. *n:* 1 Pt 5, 10 / 4, 7; 2 Thes 2, 14. *o:* Acts 2, 23; 7, 52.

prophets and persecuted us; they do not please God, and are opposed to everyone, [16p]trying to prevent us from speaking to the Gentiles that they may be saved, thus constantly filling up the measure of their sins. But the wrath of God has finally begun to come upon them.

Paul's Recent Travel Plans. [17q]Brothers, when we were bereft of you for a short time, in person, not in heart, we were all the more eager in our great desire to see you in person. [18r]We decided to go to you—I, Paul, not only once but more than once—yet Satan thwarted us. [19s]For what is our hope or joy or crown to boast of in the presence of our Lord Jesus at his coming if not you yourselves? [20]For you are our glory and joy.

See RG 404-405

CHAPTER 3

[1t]That is why, when we could bear it no longer, we decided to remain alone in Athens [2u]and sent Timothy, our brother and co-worker for God in the gospel of Christ, to strengthen and encourage you in your faith, [3*]so that no one be disturbed in these afflictions. For you yourselves know that we are destined for this. [4v]For even when we were among you, we used to warn you in advance that we would undergo affliction, just as has happened, as you know. [5]For this reason, when I too could bear it no longer, I sent to learn about your faith, for fear that somehow the tempter had put you to the test and our toil might come to nothing.

[6]But just now Timothy has returned to us from you, bringing us the good news of your faith and love, and that you always think kindly of us and long to see us as we long to see you. [7]Because of this, we have been reassured about you, brothers, in our every distress and affliction, through your faith. [8]For we now live, if you stand firm in the Lord.

Concluding Thanksgiving and Prayer. [9*]What thanksgiving, then, can we render to God for you, for all the joy we feel on your account before our God? [10]Night and day we pray beyond measure to see you in person and to remedy the deficiencies of your faith. [11]Now may God himself, our Father, and our Lord Jesus direct our way to you, [12w]and may the Lord make you increase and abound in love for one another and for all, just as we have for you, [13x]so as to strengthen your hearts, to be blameless in holiness before our God and Father at the coming of our Lord Jesus with all his holy ones. [Amen.]

III: Specific Exhortations

CHAPTER 4

See RG 405-406

General Exhortations. [1]Finally, brothers, we earnestly ask and exhort you in the Lord Jesus that, as you received from us how you should conduct yourselves to please God—and as you are conducting yourselves—you do so even more. [2*]For you know what instructions we gave you through the Lord Jesus.

Holiness in Sexual Conduct. [3*]This is the

Paul's pride in his own ethnic and religious background (Rom 9, 1–5; 10, 1; 11, 1–3; Phil 3, 4–6). Sinful conduct (16) is itself an anticipation of the ultimate wrath or judgment of God (Rom 1, 18—2, 5), whether or not it is perceived as such.

3, 3: We are destined: the Greek phraseology and the context suggest Paul's concern to alert his readers to difficulties he knew they would necessarily face and to enable them to see their present experience in the light of what he warned them would happen in the future. This line of thought is followed in 2 Thes 2, 1–15.

3, 9–10: The tension between Paul's optimism concerning the Thessalonians' faith and his worries about their perseverance remains unresolved. Perhaps this is accounted for not only by the continuing harassment but also by the shortness of his own stay in Thessalonica (even if that were over twice as long as the conventional three weeks that Luke assigns to it, Acts 17, 2).

4, 2: Instructions: these include specific guidelines on the basis of the Lord's authority, not necessarily sayings Jesus

actually uttered. More profoundly, as v 8 implies, the instructions are practical principles that Paul worked out in accordance with his understanding of the role of the Spirit.

4, 3–8: Many think that this passage deals with a variety of moral regulations (fornication, adultery, sharp business practices). It can be more specifically interpreted as bringing general norms to bear on a specific problem, namely, marriage within degrees of consanguinity (as between uncle and niece) forbidden in Jewish law but allowed according to a Greek heiress law, which would insure retention of an inheritance within the family and perhaps thereby occasion divorce. In that case, "immorality" (3) should be rendered as "unlawful marriage" and "this matter" (6) as "a lawsuit." The phrase in v 4, "acquire a wife for himself," has often been interpreted to mean "control one's body."

p: Gn 15, 16; 2 Mc 6, 14 / Rom 1, 18; 2, 5-6.   q: 3, 10; Rom 1, 10-11.   r: Rom 15, 22.   s: 2 Cor 1, 14; Phil 2, 16; 4, 1.   t: Acts 17, 14.   u: Acts 16, 1-2; 1 Cor 3, 5-9.   v: Acts 14, 22; 2 Thes 2, 5-7; 2 Tm 3, 12.   w: 4, 9-10; 2 Thes 1, 3.   x: 5, 23; 1 Cor 1, 8.

will of God, your holiness: that you refrain from immorality, ⁴that each of you know how to acquire a wife for himself in holiness and honor, ^{5y}not in lustful passion as do the Gentiles who do not know God; ⁶not to take advantage of or exploit a brother in this matter, for the Lord is an avenger in all these things, as we told you before and solemnly affirmed. ⁷For God did not call us to impurity but to holiness. ^{8z}Therefore, whoever disregards this, disregards not a human being but God, who [also] gives his holy Spirit to you.

Mutual Charity. ^{9a}On the subject of mutual charity you have no need for anyone to write you, for you yourselves have been taught by God to love one another. ^{10b}Indeed, you do this for all the brothers throughout Macedonia. Nevertheless we urge you, brothers, to progress even more, ¹¹and to aspire to live a tranquil life, to mind your own affairs, and to work with your [own] hands, as we instructed you, ¹²that you may conduct yourselves properly toward outsiders and not depend on anyone.

Hope for the Christian Dead. ¹³We do not want you to be unaware, brothers, about those who have fallen asleep, so that you may not grieve like the rest, who have no hope. ^{14c}For if we believe that Jesus died and rose, so too will God, through Jesus, bring with him those who have fallen asleep. ^{15d}*Indeed, we tell you this, on the word of the Lord, that we who are alive, who are left until the coming of the Lord, will surely not precede those who have fallen asleep. ^{16e}For the Lord himself, with a word of command, with the voice of an archangel and with the

trumpet of God, will come down from heaven, and the dead in Christ will rise first. ¹⁷*Then we who are alive, who are left, will be caught up together with them in the clouds to meet the Lord in the air. Thus we shall always be with the Lord. ¹⁸Therefore, console one another with these words.

CHAPTER 5

See RG 405–406

Vigilance. ^{1f}Concerning times and seasons, brothers, you have no need for anything to be written to you. ^{2g}For you yourselves know very well that the day of the Lord will come like a thief at night. ³When people are saying, "Peace and security," then sudden disaster comes upon them, like labor pains upon a pregnant woman, and they will not escape.

^{4h}But you, brothers, are not in darkness, for that day to overtake you like a thief. ⁵*For all of you are children of the light and children of the day. We are not of the night or of darkness. ⁶ⁱTherefore, let us not sleep as the rest do, but let us stay alert and sober. ⁷Those who sleep go to sleep at night, and those who are drunk get drunk at night. ^{8j}But since we are of the day, let us be sober, putting on the breastplate of faith and love and the helmet that is hope for salvation. ⁹For God did not destine us for wrath, but to gain salvation through our Lord Jesus Christ, ¹⁰*who died for us, so that whether we are awake or asleep we may live together with him. ^{11k}Therefore, encourage one another and build one another up, as indeed you do.

Church Order. ¹²We ask you, brothers, to respect those who are laboring among you and who are over you in the Lord and who

---

4, 15: Coming of the Lord: Paul here assumes that the second coming, or parousia, will occur within his own lifetime but insists that the time or season is unknown (5, 1–2). Nevertheless, the most important aspect of the parousia for him was the fulfillment of union with Christ. His pastoral exhortation focuses first on hope for the departed faithful, then (5, 1–3) on the need of preparedness for those who have to achieve their goal.

4, 17: Will be caught up together: literally, snatched up, carried off; cf 2 Cor 12, 2; Rv 12, 5. From the Latin verb here used, **rapiemur,** has come the idea of "the rapture," when believers will be transported away from the woes of the world; this construction combines this verse with Mt 24, 40–41 (see the note there) // Lk 17, 34–35 and passages from Rv in a scheme of millennial dispensationalism.

5, 5: Children of the light: that is, belonging to the daylight

of God's personal revelation and expected to achieve it (an analogous development of imagery that appears in Jn 12, 36).

5, 10: Characteristically, Paul plays on words suggesting ultimate and anticipated death and life. Union with the crucified and risen Lord at his parousia is anticipated in some measure in contrasted states of our temporal life. The essential element he urges is our indestructible personal union in Christ's own life (see Rom 5, 1–10).

y: Ps 79, 6; Jer 10, 25; 2 Thes 1, 8; 1 Pt 3, 7. *z:* Lk 10, 16. *a:* Jn 6, 45; 13, 34; 1 Jn 2, 20-21.27; 4, 7. *b:* 2 Thes 3, 6-12. *c:* 1 Cor 15, 3-4.12.20. *d:* 1 Cor 15, 51; Rv 14, 13; 20, 4-6. *e:* Mt 24, 31; 1 Cor 15, 23.52. *f:* Mt 24, 36-45. *g:* 2 Pt 3, 10. *h:* Eph 5, 8-9. *i:* Mt 24, 42; Rom 13, 12-13; 1 Pt 5, 8. *j:* Is 59, 17; Rom 13, 11-14; Eph 6, 11.14-17. *k:* Rom 15, 2; 1 Cor 8, 1; 14, 12.26; Eph 4, 29.

admonish you, [13]and to show esteem for them with special love on account of their work. Be at peace among yourselves.

[14]We urge you, brothers, admonish the idle, cheer the fainthearted, support the weak, be patient with all. [15l]See that no one returns evil for evil; rather, always seek what is good [both] for each other and for all. [16]Rejoice always. [17]Pray without ceasing. [18m]In all circumstances give thanks, for this is the will of God for you in Christ Jesus. [19]*Do not quench the Spirit. [20]Do not despise prophetic utterances. [21]Test everything; retain what is good. [22]Refrain from every kind of evil.

Concluding Prayer. [23n]*May the God of peace himself make you perfectly holy and may you entirely, spirit, soul, and body, be preserved blameless for the coming of our Lord Jesus Christ. [24]The one who calls you is faithful, and he will also accomplish it. [25]Brothers, pray for us [too].

IV: Final Greeting

[26]*Greet all the brothers with a holy kiss. [27]I adjure you by the Lord that this letter be read to all the brothers. [28]The grace of our Lord Jesus Christ be with you.

5, 19–21: Paul's buoyant encouragement of charismatic freedom sometimes occasioned excesses that he or others had to remedy (see 1 Cor 14; 2 Thes 2, 1–15; 2 Pt 3, 1–16).

5, 23: Another possible translation is, "May the God of peace himself make you perfectly holy and sanctify your spirit fully, and may both soul and body be preserved blameless for the coming of our Lord Jesus Christ." In either case, Paul is not offering an anthropological or philosophical analysis of human nature. Rather, he looks to the wholeness of what may be called the supernatural and natural aspects of a person's service of God.

5, 26: Kiss: the holy embrace (see Rom 16, 16; 1 Cor 16, 20; 2 Cor 13, 12; 1 Pt 5, 14) was a greeting of respect and affection, perhaps given during a liturgy at which Paul's letter would have been read.

l: Prv 20, 22; Mt 5, 38-42; Rom 12, 17. *m:* Eph 5, 20. *n:* 2 Thes 3, 16.

See RG 407–409

The Second Letter to the Thessalonians

This letter is addressed to the same church as the letter that precedes it in the canon and contains many expressions parallel to those in the First Letter to the Thessalonians, indeed verbatim with them. Yet other aspects of the contents of the Second Letter to the Thessalonians suggest a more impersonal tone and changed circumstances in the situation at Thessalonica.

The letter begins with an address (1, 1–2) that expands only slightly on that of 1 Thes 1, 1. It ends with a greeting insisting on its Pauline authority in the face of false claims made in Paul's name (see the note on 2, 2). The body of the letter falls into three short parts, of which the second is notoriously difficult (ch 2).

The opening thanksgiving and prayer (1, 3–12) speak of the Thessalonians' increasing faith and love in the face of outside persecution. God's eventual judgment against persecutors and his salvation for the faithful are already evidenced by the very fact of persecution. The second part (2, 1–17), the heart of the letter, deals with a problem threatening the faith of the community. A message involving a prophetic oracle and apparently a forged letter, possibly presented at a liturgical gathering (cf 2, 2 and 1 Cor 14, 26–33), to the effect that the day of the Lord and all that it means have already come, has upset the life of the Thessalonian church.

The writer counters their preoccupation with the date of the parousia (or coming again of the Lord Jesus from heaven, 2, 1) by recalling Paul's teaching concerning what must happen first and by going on to describe what will happen at the Lord's coming (2, 8); he indicates the twofold process by which the "activity of Satan" and God's actions (2, 9–11) are working out, namely, a growing division between believers and those who succumb to false prophecy and "the lie." He concludes by insisting on Pauline traditions and by praying for divine strength (2, 13–17). The closing part of the letter (3, 1–16) deals in particular with the apostle's directives and model style of life and with correction of disorderly elements within the community.

Traditional opinion holds that this letter was written shortly after 1 Thessalonians. Occasionally it has been argued that 2 Thessalonians was written first or that the two letters are addressed to different segments within the church at Thessalonica (2 Thessalonians being directed to the Jewish Christians there) or even that 2 Thessalonians was originally written to some other nearby place where Paul carried out mission work, such as Philippi or Beroea. Increasingly in recent times, however, the opinion has been advanced that 2 Thessalonians is a pseudepigraph, that is, a letter written authoritatively in Paul's name, to maintain apostolic traditions in a later period, perhaps during the last two decades of the first century.

In any case, the presumed audience of Second Thessalonians and certain features of its style and content require that it be read and studied in a Pauline context, particularly that provided by 1 Thessalonians. At the same time, and especially if the letter is regarded as not by Paul himself, its apocalyptic presentation of preconditions for the parousia (2, 1–12) may profit from and require recourse to a wider biblical basis for interpretation, namely Old Testament books such as Daniel and Isaiah and especially, in the New Testament, the synoptic apocalyptic discourse (Mk 13; Mt 24–25; Lk 21, 5–36) and the Book of Revelation.

The principal divisions of the Second Letter to the Thessalonians are the following:

I: Address (1, 1–12)
II: Warning against Deception Concerning the Parousia (2, 1–17)
III: Concluding Exhortations (3, 1–16)
IV: Final Greetings (3, 17–18)

I: Address

CHAPTER 1

See RG 408

Greeting. *1a**Paul, Silvanus, and Timothy to the church of the Thessalonians in God our Father and the Lord Jesus Christ: *2*grace to you and peace from God [our] Father and the Lord Jesus Christ.

Thanksgiving. *3b**We ought to thank God always for you, brothers, as is fitting, because your faith flourishes ever more, and the love of every one of you for one another grows ever greater. *4*Accordingly, we ourselves boast of you in the churches of God regarding your endurance and faith in all your persecutions and the afflictions you endure.

*5c*This is evidence of the just judgment of God, so that you may be considered worthy of the kingdom of God for which you are suffering. *6*For it is surely just on God's part to repay with afflictions those who are afflicting you, *7*and to grant rest along with us to you who are undergoing afflictions, at the revelation of the Lord Jesus from heaven with his mighty angels, *8d*in blazing fire, inflicting punishment on those who do not acknowledge God and on those who do not obey the gospel of our Lord Jesus. *9e*These will pay the penalty of eternal ruin, separated from the presence of the Lord and from the glory of his power, *10f**when he comes to be glorified among his holy ones and to be marveled at on that day among all who have believed, for our testimony to you was believed.

Prayer. *11g*To this end, we always pray for you, that our God may make you worthy of his calling and powerfully bring to fulfillment every good purpose and every effort of faith, *12h**that the name of our Lord Jesus may be glorified in you, and you in him, in accord with the grace of our God and Lord Jesus Christ.

1, 1–2: On the address, see the note on Rom 1, 1–7 and cf 1 Thes 1, 1.

1, 3–12: On the thanksgiving, see the note on Rom 1, 8 and cf 1 Thes 1, 2–10. Paul's gratitude to God for the faith and love of the Thessalonians (3) and his Christian pride in their faithful endurance (4–5) contrast with the condemnation announced for those who afflict them, a judgment to be carried out at the parousia (6–10), which is described in vivid language drawn from Old Testament apocalyptic. A prayer for the fulfillment of God's purpose in the Thessalonians (11–12) completes the section, as is customary in a Pauline letter (cf 1 Thes 1, 2–3).

1, 10: **Among his holy ones:** in the Old Testament, this term can refer to an angelic throng (cf also Jude 14), but here, in parallel with **among all who have believed,** it can refer to the triumphant people of God.

1, 12: **The grace of our God and Lord Jesus Christ:** the Greek can also be translated, "the grace of our God and of the Lord Jesus Christ."

---

a: 1 Thes 1, 1.   *b:* 1 Cor 1, 4; 1 Thes 1, 2; 3, 12.   *c:* Phil 1, 28; 1 Thes 2, 12.   *d:* Ps 79, 5-6; Is 66, 15; Jer 10, 25.   *e:* Is 2, 10.19.21.   *f:* Ps 89, 8; Dn 7, 18-22.27; 1 Thes 3, 13.   *g:* 1 Thes 1, 2-3.   *h:* Is 66, 5.

II: Warning against Deception Concerning the Parousia

CHAPTER 2

See RG 408

Christic and the Lawless One. [1i]*We ask you, brothers, with regard to the coming of our Lord Jesus Christ and our assembling with him, [2j]*not to be shaken out of your minds suddenly, or to be alarmed either by a "spirit," or by an oral statement, or by a let-ter allegedly from us to the effect that the day of the Lord is at hand. [3]*Let no one de-ceive you in any way. For unless the apos-tasy comes first and the lawless one is re-vealed, the one doomed to perdition, [4k]*who opposes and exalts himself above every so-called god and object of worship, so as to seat himself in the temple of God, claiming that he is a god— [5]do you not recall that while I was still with you I told you these things? [6]*And now you know what is re-straining, that he may be revealed in his time. [7l]*For the mystery of lawlessness is

2, 1–17: The Thessalonians have been **shaken** by a mes-sage purporting to come from Paul himself that **the day of the Lord** is already present. He warns against this deception in eschatology by citing a scenario of events that must first occur (3–12) before the end will come. The overall point Paul makes is the need to reject such lies as Satan sends; he also reaffirms the Thessalonians in their calling (13–14). They are to uphold what Paul himself has taught (15). As in 1, 8–10, the Old Testament provides a good deal of coloring; cf espe-cially Is 14, 13–14; 66, 15.18–21; Ez 28, 2–9; Dn 11, 36–37. The contents of 2, 3b–8 may come from a previously existing apocalypse. The details have been variously interpreted.

An alternative to the possibilities noted below understands that an oracular utterance, supposedly coming from a pro-phetic spirit (2–3a), has so disrupted the community's think-ing that its effects may be compared to those of the mania connected with the worship of the Greek god Dionysus. On this view, the writer seems to allude in vv 6–8 to Dionysiac "seizure," although, of course, ironically, somewhat as Paul alludes to witchcraft ("an evil eye") in Gal 3, 1 in speaking of the threat to faith posed by those disturbing the Galatians (Gal 1, 6–7; 5, 10b). On this view of 2 Thes 2, the Greek partici-ples **katechon** (rendered above as **what is restraining**) and **katechōn** (**the one who restrains**) are to be translated "the seizing power" in v 6 and "the seizer" in v 7. They then allude to a pseudocharismatic force or spirit of Dionysiac character that has suddenly taken hold of the Thessalonian community (see 2). The addressees **know** (6) this force or spirit because of the problem it is causing. This pseudocharismatic force or spirit is a kind of anticipation and advance proof of the ulti-mate, climactic figure (**the lawless one** or the rebel, 3), of which the community has been warned (see the note on 1 Thes 3, 3). It is, however, only the beginning of the end that the latter's manifestation entails; the end is not yet. For in the course of **the mystery of lawlessness** (7), false prophetism, after it ceases in the Thessalonian community, will be mani-fested in the world at large (8–12), where it will also be elim-inated in turn by the Lord Jesus.

2, 2: "**Spirit**": a Spirit-inspired utterance or ecstatic revela-tion. **An oral statement:** literally, a "word" or pronouncement, not necessarily of ecstatic origin. **A letter allegedly from us:** possibly a forged letter, so that Paul calls attention in 3, 17 to his practice of concluding a genuine letter with a summary note or greeting in his own hand, as at Gal 6, 11–18 and elsewhere.

2, 3b–5: This incomplete sentence (anacoluthon, 4) recalls what the Thessalonians had already been taught, an apoca-lyptic scenario depicting, in terms borrowed especially from Dn 11, 36–37 and related verses, human self-assertiveness against God in **the temple of God** itself. **The lawless one** represents the climax of such activity in this account.

2, 4: Seat himself in the temple of God: a reflection of the language in Dn 7, 23–25; 8, 9–12; 9, 27; 11, 36–37; and 12, 11 about the attempt of Antiochus IV Epiphanes to set up a statue of Zeus in the Jerusalem temple and possibly of the Roman emperor Caligula to do a similar thing (Mk 13, 14). Here the imagery suggests an attempt to install someone in the place of God, **claiming that he is a god** (cf Ez 28, 2). Usually, it is the Jerusalem temple that is assumed to be meant; on the alternative view sketched above (see the note on 2, 1–17), **the temple** refers to the Christian community.

2, 6–7: What is restraining . . . the one who restrains: neuter and masculine, respectively, of a force and person holding back the lawless one. The Thessalonians know what is meant (6), but the terms, seemingly found only in this pas-sage and in writings dependent on it, have been variously in-terpreted. Traditionally, v 6 has been applied to the Roman empire and v 7 to the Roman emperor (in Paul's day, Nero) as bulwarks holding back chaos (cf Rom 13, 1–7). A second in-terpretation suggests that cosmic or angelic powers are bind-ing Satan (9) and so restraining him; some relate this to an anti-Christ figure (1 Jn 2, 18) or to Michael the archangel (Rv 12, 7–9; 20, 1–3). A more recent view suggests that it is the preaching of the Christian gospel that restrains the end, for in God's plan the end cannot come until the gospel is preached to all nations (Mk 13, 10); in that case, Paul as missionary preacher par excellence is "the one who restrains," whose re-moval (death) will bring the end (7). On the alternative view (see the note on 2, 1–17), the phrases should be referred to that which and to him who seizes (a prophet) in ecstasy so as to have him speak pseudo-oracles.

2, 7–12: The lawless one and **the one who restrains** are involved in an activity or process, **the mystery of lawless-ness,** behind which **Satan** stands (9). The action of the **Lord [Jesus]** in overcoming the lawless one is described in Old Testament language (**with the breath of his mouth;** cf Is 11,

i: 1 Thes 4, 13–17. *j:* Mt 24, 6; 1 Cor 14, 26.32–33; 1 Thes 5, 1-2. *k:* Dn 11, 36–37; Ez 28, 2. *l:* Mt 13, 36–43; Acts 20, 29; Gal 5, 10; 2 Pt 2, 1; Rv 22, 11.

already at work. But the one who restrains is to do so only for the present, until he is removed from the scene. [8m]And then the lawless one will be revealed, whom the Lord [Jesus] will kill with the breath of his mouth and render powerless by the manifestation of his coming, [9n]the one whose coming springs from the power of Satan in every mighty deed and in signs and wonders that lie, [10]and in every wicked deceit for those who are perishing because they have not accepted the love of truth so that they may be saved. [11]Therefore, God is sending them a deceiving power so that they may believe the lie, [12]that all who have not believed the truth but have approved wrongdoing may be condemned.

[13o]*But we ought to give thanks to God for you always, brothers loved by the Lord, because God chose you as the firstfruits for salvation through sanctification by the Spirit and belief in truth. [14p]To this end he has [also] called you through our gospel to possess the glory of our Lord Jesus Christ. [15]*Therefore, brothers, stand firm and hold fast to the traditions that you were taught, either by an oral statement or by a letter of ours.

[16]May our Lord Jesus Christ himself and God our Father, who has loved us and given us everlasting encouragement and good hope through his grace, [17]encourage your hearts and strengthen them in every good deed and word.

III: Concluding Exhortations

CHAPTER 3

See RG 408–409

Request for Prayers. [1q]*Finally, brothers, pray for us, so that the word of the Lord may speed forward and be glorified, as it did among you, [2]and that we may be delivered from perverse and wicked people, for not all have faith. [3r]But the Lord is faithful; he will strengthen you and guard you from the evil one. [4s]We are confident of you in the Lord that what we instruct you, you [both] are doing and will continue to do. [5]May the Lord direct your hearts to the love of God and to the endurance of Christ.

Neglect of Work. [6]*We instruct you, brothers, in the name of [our] Lord Jesus Christ, to shun any brother who conducts himself in a disorderly way and not according to the tradition they received from us. [7]For you know how one must imitate us. For we did not act in a disorderly way among you, [8t]nor did we eat food received free from anyone. On the contrary, in toil and drudgery, night and day we worked, so as not to burden any of you. [9u]Not that we do not have the right. Rather, we wanted to present ourselves as a model for you, so that you might imitate us. [10v]In fact, when we were with you, we instructed you that if anyone was unwilling to work, neither should that one eat. [11w]We hear that some are conducting themselves among you in a

---

4; Jb 4, 9; Rv 19, 15). His **coming** is literally the Lord's "parousia." The biblical concept of the "holy war," eschatologically conceived, may underlie the imagery.

2, 13: As the **firstfruits**: there is also strong manuscript evidence for the reading, "God chose you from the beginning," thus providing a focus on God's activity from beginning to end; **firstfruits** is a Pauline term, however; cf Rom 8, 23; 11, 16; 16, 5, among other references.

2, 15: Reference to an **oral statement** and **a letter** (2) and the content here, including a formula of conclusion (cf 1 Cor 16, 13; Gal 5, 1), suggest that vv 1–15 or even 1–17 are to be taken as a literary unit, notwithstanding the incidental thanksgiving formula in v 13.

3, 1–18: The final chapter urges the Thessalonians to pray for Paul and his colleagues (1–2) and reiterates confidence in the Thessalonians (3–5), while admonishing them about a specific problem in their community that has grown out of the intense eschatological speculation, namely, not to work but to become instead disorderly busybodies (6–15). A benediction

(16) and postscript in Paul's own hand round out the letter. On vv 17–18, cf the note on 2, 2.

3, 6: Some members of the community, probably because they regarded the parousia as imminent or the new age of the Lord to be already here (2, 2), had apparently ceased to work for a living. The disciplinary problem they posed could be rooted in distorted thinking about Paul's own teaching (cf 1 Thes 2, 16; 3, 3–4; 5, 4–5) or, more likely, in a forged letter (2, 2) and the type of teaching dealt with in 2, 1–15. The apostle's own moral teaching, reflected in his selfless labors for others, was rooted in a deep doctrinal concern for the gospel message (cf 1 Thes 2, 3–10).

m: Is 11, 4; Rv 19, 15. *n:* Mt 24, 24; Rv 13, 13. *o:* 1 Thes 2, 13; 5, 9. *p:* Rom 5, 1-10; 8, 29-30; 1 Thes 4, 7; 5, 9. *q:* Eph 6, 19; Col 4, 3. *r:* 1 Thes 5, 24 / 1 Cor 16, 13 / Mt 6, 13. *s:* 2 Cor 7, 16; 1 Thes 4, 1-2. *t:* 1 Thes 2, 9. *u:* Mt 10, 10; Phil 3, 17. *v:* 1 Thes 4, 11. *w:* 1 Thes 5, 14.

disorderly way, by not keeping busy but minding the business of others. *12*Such people we instruct and urge in the Lord Jesus Christ to work quietly and to eat their own food. *13*But you, brothers, do not be remiss in doing good. *14*If anyone does not obey our word as expressed in this letter, take note of this person not to associate with him, that he may be put to shame. *15x*Do not regard him as an enemy but ad-

monish him as a brother. *16y*May the Lord of peace himself give you peace at all times and in every way. The Lord be with all of you.

IV: Final Greetings

*17z*This greeting is in my own hand, Paul's. This is the sign in every letter; this is how I write. *18*The grace of our Lord Jesus Christ be with all of you.

x: 2 Cor 2, 7; Gal 6, 1.   y: Jn 14, 27; Rom 15, 33.   z: 1 Cor 16, 21; Gal 6, 11.

See RG
410–14

The First Letter to Timothy

The three letters, First and Second Timothy and Titus, form a distinct group within the Pauline corpus. In the collection of letters by the Apostle to the Gentiles, they differ from the others in form and contents. All three suggest they were written late in Paul's career. The opponents are not "Judaizers" as in Galatians but false teachers stressing "knowledge" (*gnosis;* see the note on 1 Tm 6, 20–21). Attention is given especially to correct doctrine and church organization. Jesus' second coming recedes into the background compared to references in Paul's earlier letters (though not Colossians and Ephesians). The three letters are addressed not to congregations but to those who shepherd congregations (Latin, *pastores*). These letters were first named "Pastoral Epistles" in the eighteenth century because they all are concerned with the work of a pastor in caring for the community or communities under his charge.

The first of the Pastorals, 1 Timothy, is presented as having been written from Macedonia. Timothy, whom Paul converted, was of mixed Jewish and Gentile parentage (Acts 16, 1–3). He was the apostle's companion on both the second and the third missionary journeys (Acts 16, 3; 19, 22) and was often sent by him on special missions (Acts 19, 22; 1 Cor 4, 17; 1 Thes 3, 2). In 1 Timothy (1, 3), he is described as the administrator of the entire Ephesian community.

The letter instructs Timothy on his duty to restrain false and useless teaching (1, 3–11; 4, 1–5; 6, 3–16) and proposes principles pertaining to his relationship with the older members of the community (5, 1–2) and with the presbyters (5, 17–22). It gives rules for aid to widows

(5, 3–8) and their selection for charitable ministrations (5, 9–16) and also deals with liturgical celebrations (2, 1–15), selections for the offices of bishop and deacon (3, 1–13), relation of slaves with their masters (6, 1–2), and obligations of the wealthier members of the community (6, 17–19). This letter also reminds Timothy of the prophetic character of his office (1, 12–20) and encourages him in his exercise of it (4, 6–16). The central passage of the letter (3, 14–16) expresses the principal motive that should guide the conduct of Timothy—preservation of the purity of the church's doctrine against false teaching. On this same note the letter concludes (6, 20–21).

From the late second century to the nineteenth, Pauline authorship of the three Pastoral Epistles went unchallenged. Since then, the attribution of these letters to Paul has been questioned. Most scholars are convinced that Paul could not have been responsible for the vocabulary and style, the concept of church organization, or the theological expressions found in these letters. A second group believes, on the basis of statistical evidence, that the vocabulary and style are Pauline, even if at first sight the contrary seems to be the case. They state that the concept of church organization in the letters is not as advanced as the questioners of Pauline authorship hold since the notion of hierarchical order in a religious community existed in Israel before the time of Christ, as evidenced in the Dead Sea Scrolls. Finally, this group sees affinities between the theological thought of the Pastorals and that of the unquestionably genuine letters of Paul. Other scholars, while conceding a degree of validity to the positions mentioned above, suggest that the apostle made use of a secretary who was responsible for the composition of the letters. A fourth group of scholars believes that these letters are the work of a compiler, that they are based on traditions about Paul in his later years, and that they include, in varying amounts, actual fragments of genuine Pauline correspondence.

If Paul is considered the more immediate author, the Pastorals are to be dated between the end of his first Roman imprisonment (Acts 28, 16) and his execution under Nero (A.D. 63–67); if they are regarded as only more remotely Pauline, their date may be as late as the early second century. In spite of these problems of authorship and dating, the Pastorals are illustrative of early Christian life and remain an important element of canonical scripture.

The principal divisions of the First Letter to Timothy are the following:

   I: Address (1, 1–2)
  II: Sound Teaching (1, 3–20)
 III: Problems of Discipline (2, 1—4, 16)
 IV: Duties toward Others (5, 1—6, 2a)
  V: False Teaching and True Wealth (6, 2)
 VI: Final Recommendation and Warning
     (6, 20–21)

I: Address

CHAPTER 1

See RG 411-12 **Greeting.** *1a**Paul, an apostle of Christ Jesus by command of God our savior and of Christ Jesus our hope, *2b*to Timothy, my true child in faith: grace, mercy, and peace from God the Father and Christ Jesus our Lord.

II: Sound Teaching

Warning against False Doctrine. *3c**I repeat the request I made of you when I was on my way to Macedonia, that you stay in Ephesus to instruct certain people not to teach false doctrines *4d**or to concern themselves with myths and endless genealogies, which promote speculations rather than the plan of God that is to be received by faith. *5e*The aim of this instruction is love from a pure heart, a good conscience, and a sincere faith. *6f*Some people have deviated from these and turned to meaningless talk, *7*wanting to be teachers of the law, but without understanding either what they are saying or what they assert with such assurance.

8g*We know that the law is good, provided that one uses it as law, *9*with the understanding that law is meant not for a righteous person but for the lawless and unruly, the godless and sinful, the unholy and profane, those who kill their fathers or mothers, murderers, *10h**the unchaste, sodomites, kidnappers, liars, perjurers, and whatever else is opposed to sound teaching, *11i*according to the glorious gospel of the blessed God, with which I have been entrusted.

Gratitude for God's Mercy. *12j**I am grateful to him who has strengthened me, Christ Jesus our Lord, because he considered me trustworthy in appointing me to the ministry.

1, 1–2: For the Pauline use of the conventional epistolary form, see the note on Rom 1, 1–7.

1, 3–7: Here Timothy's initial task **in Ephesus** (cf Acts 20, 17–35) is outlined: to suppress the idle religious speculations, probably about Old Testament figures (3–4, but see the note on 6, 20–21), which do not contribute to the development of love within the community (5) but rather encourage similar useless conjectures (6–7).

1, 4: The **plan of God that is to be received by faith:** the Greek may also possibly mean "God's trustworthy plan" or "the training in faith that God requires."

1, 8–11: Those responsible for the speculations that are to be suppressed by Timothy do not present the Old Testament from the Christian viewpoint. The Christian values the Old Testament not as a system of law but as the first stage in God's revelation of his saving plan, which is brought to fulfillment in the good news of salvation through faith in Jesus Christ.

1, 10: Sodomites: see 1 Cor 6, 9 and the note there.

1, 12–17: Present gratitude for the Christian apostleship leads Paul to recall an earlier time when he had been a fierce persecutor of the Christian communities (cf Acts 26, 9–11) until his conversion by intervention of divine mercy through the appearance of Jesus. This and his subsequent apostolic experience testify to the saving purpose of Jesus' incarnation. The fact of his former ignorance of the truth has not kept the apostle from regarding himself as having been the worst of sinners (15). Yet he was chosen to be an apostle, that God might manifest his firm will to save sinful humanity through Jesus Christ (16). The recounting of so great a mystery leads to a spontaneous outpouring of adoration (17).

a: 2, 3; Lk 1, 47; Ti 1, 3; 2, 10 / Col 1, 27. *b:* 2 Tm 1, 2; Ti 1, 4. *c:* Acts 20, 1. *d:* 4, 7; Ti 1, 14; 3, 9; 2 Pt 1, 16. *e:* Rom 13, 10. *f:* 6, 4.20; Ti 1, 10. *g:* Rom 7, 12.16. *h:* 4, 6; 6, 3; 2 Tm 4, 3; Ti 1, 9; 2, 1. *i:* Ti 1, 3. *j:* Phil 4, 13 / Acts 9, 15; Gal 1, 15-16.

13k I was once a blasphemer and a persecutor and an arrogant man, but I have been mercifully treated because I acted out of ignorance in my unbelief. 14l Indeed, the grace of our Lord has been abundant, along with the faith and love that are in Christ Jesus. 15m *This saying is trustworthy and deserves full acceptance: Christ Jesus came into the world to save sinners. Of these I am the foremost. 16 But for that reason I was mercifully treated, so that in me, as the foremost, Christ Jesus might display all his patience as an example for those who would come to believe in him for everlasting life. 17n *To the king of ages, incorruptible, invisible, the only God, honor and glory forever and ever. Amen.

Responsibility of Timothy. 18o *I entrust this charge to you, Timothy, my child, in accordance with the prophetic words once spoken about you. Through them may you fight a good fight 19p by having faith and a good conscience. Some, by rejecting conscience, have made a shipwreck of their faith, 20q *among them Hymenaeus and Alexander, whom I have handed over to Satan to be taught not to blaspheme.

III: Problems of Discipline

CHAPTER 2

See RG 412-13

Prayer and Conduct. 1r *First of all, then, I ask that supplications, prayers, petitions, and thanksgivings be offered for everyone, 2 for kings and for all in authority, that we may lead a quiet and tranquil life in all devotion and dignity. 3s This is good and pleasing to God our savior, 4t who wills everyone to be saved and to come to knowledge of the truth.

5 u For there is one God.
There is also one mediator between God
      and the human race,
Christ Jesus, himself human,
6 v *who gave himself as ransom for all.

This was the testimony at the proper time. 7w For this I was appointed preacher and apostle (I am speaking the truth, I am not lying), teacher of the Gentiles in faith and truth.

8 *It is my wish, then, that in every place the men should pray, lifting up holy hands,

---

1, 15: This saying is trustworthy: this phrase regularly introduces in the Pastorals a basic truth of early Christian faith; cf 3, 1; 4, 9; 2 Tm 2, 11; Ti 3, 8.

1, 17: King of ages: through Semitic influence, the Greek expression could mean "everlasting king"; it could also mean "king of the universe."

1, 18–20: Timothy is to be mindful of his calling, which is here compared to the way Barnabas and Saul were designated by Christ as prophets for missionary service; cf Acts 13, 1–3. Such is probably the sense of the allusion to the prophetic words (18). His task is not to yield, whether in doctrine or in conduct, to erroneous opinions, taking warning from what has already happened at Ephesus in the case of Hymenaeus and Alexander (19–20).

1, 18: The prophetic words once spoken about you: the Greek may also be translated, "the prophecies that led (me) to you." It probably refers to testimonies given by charismatic figures in the Christian communities. **Fight a good fight:** this translation preserves the play on words in Greek. The Greek terms imply a lengthy engagement in battle and might well be translated "wage a good campaign."

1, 20: Hymenaeus: mentioned in 2 Tm 2, 17 as saying that the resurrection has already taken place (in baptism). **Alexander:** probably the Alexander mentioned in 2 Tm 4, 14 as the coppersmith who "did me a great deal of harm." **Whom I have handed over to Satan:** the same terms are used in the condemnation of the incestuous man in 1 Cor 5, 5.

2, 1–7: This marked insistence that the liturgical prayer of the community concern itself with the needs of all, whether Christian or not, and especially of those in authority, may imply that a disposition existed at Ephesus to refuse prayer for pagans. In actuality, such prayer aids the community to achieve peaceful relationships with non-Christians (2) and contributes to salvation, since it derives its value from the presence within the community of Christ, who is the one and only savior of all (3–6). The vital apostolic mission to the Gentiles (7) reflects Christ's purpose of universal salvation.

Verse 5 contains what may well have been a very primitive creed. Some interpreters have called it a Christian version of the Jewish **shema:** "Hear, O Israel, the LORD is our God, the LORD alone . . ." (Dt 6, 4–5). The assertion in v 7, "I am speaking the truth, I am not lying," reminds one of similar affirmations in Rom 9, 1; 2 Cor 11, 31; and Gal 1, 20.

2, 6: The testimony: to make sense of this overly concise phrase, many manuscripts supply "to which" (or "to whom"); two others add "was given." The translation has supplied "this was."

2, 8–15: The prayer of the community should be unmarred by internal dissension (8); cf Mt 5, 21–26; 6, 14; Mk 11, 25. At the liturgical assembly the dress of women should be ap-

---

k: Acts 8, 3; 9, 1-2; 1 Cor 15, 9; Gal 1, 13.   l: Rom 5, 20; 2 Tm 1, 13.   m: Lk 15, 2; 19, 10.   n: Rom 16, 27.   o: 4, 14 / 6, 12; 2 Tm 4, 7; Jude 3.   p: 3, 9.   q: 2 Tm 2, 17; 4, 14 / 1 Cor 5, 5.   r: Eph 6, 18; Phil 4, 6.   s: 1, 1; 4, 10.   t: 2 Tm 3, 7; 2 Pt 3, 9.   u: 1 Cor 8, 6; Heb 8, 6; 9, 15; 12, 24 / Rom 5, 15.   v: Mk 10, 45; Gal 1, 4; 2, 20; Eph 5, 25; Ti 2, 14.   w: Acts 9, 15; 1 Cor 9, 1; Gal 2, 7-8.

without anger or argument. ⁹ˣSimilarly, [too,] women should adorn themselves with proper conduct, with modesty and self-control, not with braided hairstyles and gold ornaments, or pearls, or expensive clothes, ¹⁰ʸbut rather, as befits women who profess reverence for God, with good deeds. ¹¹ᶻA woman must receive instruction silently and under complete control. ¹²*I do not permit a woman to teach or to have authority over a man. She must be quiet. ¹³ᵃFor Adam was formed first, then Eve. ¹⁴ᵇFurther, Adam was not deceived, but the woman was deceived and transgressed. ¹⁵ᶜBut she will be saved through motherhood, provided women persevere in faith and love and holiness, with self-control.

See RG
412–13

CHAPTER 3

Qualifications of Various Ministers.

¹ᵈ*This saying is trustworthy: whoever aspires to the office of bishop desires a noble task. ²Therefore, a bishop must be irreproachable, married only once, temperate, self-controlled, decent, hospitable, able to teach, ³ᵉnot a drunkard, not aggressive, but gentle, not contentious, not a lover of money.

⁴He must manage his own household well, keeping his children under control with perfect dignity; ⁵for if a man does not know how to manage his own household, how can he take care of the church of God? ⁶*He should not be a recent convert, so that he may not become conceited and thus incur the devil's punishment. ⁷ᶠHe must also have a good reputation among outsiders, so that he may not fall into disgrace, the devil's trap.

⁸*Similarly, deacons must be dignified, not deceitful, not addicted to drink, not greedy for sordid gain, ⁹holding fast to the mystery of the faith with a clear conscience. ¹⁰Moreover, they should be tested first; then, if there is nothing against them, let them serve as deacons. ¹¹ᵍ*Women, similarly, should be dignified, not slanderers, but temperate and faithful in everything. ¹²Deacons may be married only once and must manage their children and their households well. ¹³Thus those who serve well as deacons gain good standing and much confidence in their faith in Christ Jesus.

The Mystery of Our Religion. ¹⁴*I am writing you about these matters, although I hope to visit you soon. ¹⁵ʰBut if I should be delayed, you should know how to behave in the house-

---

propriate to the occasion (9); their chief adornment is to be reputation for good works (10). Women are not to take part in the charismatic activity of the assembly (11–12; cf 1 Cor 14, 34) or exercise authority; their conduct there should reflect the role of man's helpmate (13; cf Gn 2, 18) and not the later relationship of Eve to Adam (14; cf Gn 3, 6–7). As long as women perform their role as wives and mothers in faith and love, their salvation is assured (15).

2, 12: A man: this could also mean "her husband."

3, 1–7: The passage begins by commending those who aspire to the office of bishop (**episkopos;** see the note on Phil 1, 1) within the community, but this first sentence (1) may also imply a warning about the great responsibilities involved. The writer proceeds to list the qualifications required: personal stability and graciousness; talent for teaching (2); moderation in habits and temperament (3); managerial ability (4); and experience in Christian living (5–6). Moreover, the candidate's previous life should provide no grounds for the charge that he did not previously practice what he now preaches. No list of qualifications for presbyters appears in 1 Tm. The presbyter-bishops here and in Ti (see the note on Ti 1, 5–9) lack certain functions reserved here for Paul and Timothy.

3, 1: This saying is trustworthy: the saying introduced is so unlike others after this phrase that some later Western manuscripts read, "This saying is popular." It is understood by some interpreters as concluding the preceding section (2, 8–15). **Bishop:** literally, "overseer"; see the note on Phil 1, 1.

3, 6: The devil's punishment: this phrase could mean the

punishment once incurred by the devil (objective genitive) or a punishment brought about by the devil (subjective genitive).

3, 8–13: Deacons, besides possessing the virtue of moderation (8), are to be outstanding for their faith (9) and well respected within the community (10). Women in the same role, although some interpreters take them to mean wives of deacons, must be dignified, temperate, dedicated, and not given to malicious talebearing (11). Deacons must have shown stability in marriage and have a good record with their families (12), for such experience prepares them well for the exercise of their ministry on behalf of the community (13). See further the note on Phil 1, 1.

3, 11: Women: this seems to refer to women deacons but may possibly mean wives of deacons. The former is preferred because the word is used absolutely; if deacons' wives were meant, a possessive "their" would be expected. Moreover, they are also introduced by the word "similarly," as in v 8; this parallel suggests that they too exercised ecclesiastical functions.

3, 14–16: In case there is some delay in the visit to Timothy at Ephesus planned for the near future, the present letter is being sent on ahead to arm and enlighten him in his task of preserving sound Christian conduct in the Ephesian church. The care he must exercise over this community is required by

x: 1 Pt 3, 3-5. y: 5, 10; 1 Pt 3, 1. z: 1 Cor 14, 34-35. a: Gn 1, 27; 2, 7.22; 1 Cor 11, 8-9. b: Gn 3, 6.13; 2 Cor 11, 3. c: 5, 14. d: Ti 1, 6-9. e: Heb 13, 5. f: 2 Cor 8, 21; 2 Tm 2, 26. g: Ti 2, 3. h: Eph 2, 19-22.

hold of God, which is the church of the living God, the pillar and foundation of truth. [16i]*Undeniably great is the mystery of devotion,

Who was manifested in the flesh,
vindicated in the spirit,
seen by angels,
proclaimed to the Gentiles,
believed in throughout the world,
taken up in glory.

CHAPTER 4

See RG
412-13

False Asceticism. [1j]*Now the Spirit explicitly says that in the last times some will turn away from the faith by paying attention to deceitful spirits and demonic instructions [2]through the hypocrisy of liars with branded consciences. [3k]They forbid marriage and require abstinence from foods that God created to be received with thanksgiving by those who believe and know the truth. [4l]For everything created by God is good, and nothing is to be rejected when received with thanksgiving, [5]*for it is made holy by the invocation of God in prayer.

Counsel to Timothy. [6]*If you will give these instructions to the brothers, you will be a good minister of Christ Jesus, nourished on the words of the faith and of the sound teaching you have followed. [7m]Avoid profane and silly myths. Train yourself for devotion, [8n]for, while physical training is of limited value, devotion is valuable in every respect, since it holds a promise of life both for the present and for the future. [9o]This saying is trustworthy and deserves full acceptance. [10p]*For this we toil and struggle, because we have set our hope on the living God, who is the savior of all, especially of those who believe.

[11]*Command and teach these things. [12q]*Let no one have contempt for your youth, but set an example for those who believe, in speech, conduct, love, faith, and purity. [13]*Until I arrive, attend to the reading, exhortation, and teaching. [14r]*Do not neglect the gift you have, which was conferred on you through the prophetic word with the imposition of hands of the presbyterate. [15]Be diligent in these matters, be absorbed in them, so that your progress may be evident

the profound nature of Christianity. It centers in Christ, appearing in human flesh, vindicated by the holy Spirit; the mystery of his person was revealed to the angels, announced to the Gentiles, and accepted by them in faith. He himself was taken up (through his resurrection and ascension) to the divine glory (16). This passage apparently includes part of a liturgical hymn used among the Christian communities in and around Ephesus. It consists of three couplets in typical Hebrew balance: flesh-spirit (contrast), seen-proclaimed (complementary), world-glory (contrast).

3, 16: Who: the reference is to Christ, who is himself "the mystery of our devotion." Some predominantly Western manuscripts read "which," harmonizing the gender of the pronoun with that of the Greek word for mystery; many later (eighth/ninth century on), predominantly Byzantine manuscripts read "God," possibly for theological reasons.

4, 1–5: Doctrinal deviations from the true Christian message within the church have been prophesied, though the origin of the prophecy is not specified (1–2); cf Acts 20, 29–30. The letter warns against a false asceticism that prohibits marriage and regards certain foods as forbidden, though they are part of God's good creation (3).

4, 5: The invocation of God in prayer: literally, "the word of God and petition." The use of "word of God" without an article in Greek suggests that it refers to the name of God being invoked in blessing rather than to the "word of God" proclaimed to the community.

4, 6–10: Timothy is urged to be faithful, both in his teaching and in his own life, as he looks only to God for salvation.

4, 10: Struggle: other manuscripts and patristic witnesses read "suffer reproach."

4, 11–16: Timothy is urged to preach and teach with confidence, relying on the gifts and the mission that God has bestowed on him.

4, 12: Youth: some commentators find this reference a sign of pseudepigraphy. Timothy had joined Paul as a missionary already in A.D. 49, some fifteen years before the earliest supposed date of composition.

4, 13: Reading: the Greek word refers to private or public reading. Here, it probably designates the public reading of scripture in the Christian assembly.

4, 14: Prophetic word: this may mean the utterance of a Christian prophet designating the candidate or a prayer of blessing accompanying the rite. **Imposition of hands:** this gesture was used in the Old Testament to signify the transmission of authority from Moses to Joshua (Nm 27, 18–23; Dt 34, 9). The early Christian community used it as a symbol of installation into an office: the Seven (Acts 6, 6) and Paul and Barnabas (Acts 13, 3). **Of the presbyterate:** this would mean that each member of the college of presbyters imposed hands and appears to contradict 2 Tm 1, 6, in which Paul says that he imposed hands on Timothy. This latter text, however, does not exclude participation by others in the rite. Some prefer to translate "for the presbyterate," and thus understand it to designate the office into which Timothy was installed rather than the agents who installed him.

i: Jn 1, 14; Rom 1, 3-4. *j:* 2 Tm 3, 1; 4, 3; 2 Pt 3, 3; Jude 18. *k:* Gn 9, 3; Rom 14, 6; 1 Cor 10, 30-31. *l:* Gn 1, 31; Acts 10, 15. *m:* 1, 4; 2 Tm 2, 16; Ti 1, 14. *n:* 6, 6. *o:* 1, 15; 2 Tm 2, 11; Ti 3, 8. *p:* 2, 4; Ti 2, 11. *q:* 1 Cor 16, 11; Ti 2, 15 / Phil 3, 17. *r:* 5, 22; Acts 6, 6; 8, 17; 2 Tm 1, 6.

to everyone. [16]Attend to yourself and to your teaching; persevere in both tasks, for by doing so you will save both yourself and those who listen to you.

IV: Duties toward Others

CHAPTER 5

See RG 413 [1s]*Do not rebuke an older man, but appeal to him as a father. Treat younger men as brothers, [2]older women as mothers, and younger women as sisters with complete purity.

Rules for Widows. [3]Honor widows who are truly widows. [4]But if a widow has children or grandchildren, let these first learn to perform their religious duty to their own family and to make recompense to their parents, for this is pleasing to God. [5t]The real widow, who is all alone, has set her hope on God and continues in supplications and prayers night and day. [6]But the one who is self-indulgent is dead while she lives. [7]Command this, so that they may be irreproachable. [8]And whoever does not provide for relatives and especially family members has denied the faith and is worse than an unbeliever.

[9]Let a widow be enrolled if she is not less than sixty years old, married only once, [10u]with a reputation for good works, namely, that she has raised children, practiced hospitality, washed the feet of the holy ones, helped those in distress, involved herself in every good work. [11]But exclude younger widows, for when their sensuality estranges them from Christ, they want to marry [12]and will incur condemnation for breaking their first pledge. [13v]And furthermore, they learn to be idlers, going about from house to house, and not only idlers but gossips and busybodies as well, talking about things that ought not to be mentioned. [14w]So I would like younger widows to marry, have children, and manage a home, so as to give the adversary no pretext for maligning us. [15]For some have already turned away to follow Satan. [16]*If any woman believer has widowed relatives, she must assist them; the church is not to be burdened, so that it will be able to help those who are truly widows.

Rules for Presbyters. [17x]*Presbyters who preside well deserve double honor, especially those who toil in preaching and teaching. [18y]For the scripture says, "You shall not muzzle an ox when it is threshing," and, "A worker deserves his pay." [19z]Do not accept an accusation against a presbyter unless it is supported by two or three witnesses. [20a]Reprimand publicly those who do sin, so that the rest also will be afraid. [21]I charge you before God and Christ Jesus and the elect angels to keep these rules without prejudice, doing nothing out of favoritism. [22b]Do not lay hands too readily on anyone, and do not share in another's sins.

5, 1–16: After a few words of general advice based on common sense (1–2), the letter takes up, in its several aspects, the subject of widows. The first responsibility for their care belongs to the family circle, not to the Christian community as such (3–4.16). The widow left without the aid of relatives may benefit the community by her prayer, and the community should consider her material sustenance its responsibility (5–8). Widows who wish to work directly for the Christian community should not be accepted unless they are well beyond the probability of marriage, i.e., sixty years of age, married only once, and with a reputation for good works (9–10). Younger widows are apt to be troublesome and should be encouraged to remarry (11–15).

5, 16: Woman believer: some early Latin manuscripts and Fathers have a masculine here, while most later manuscripts and patristic quotations conflate the two readings, perhaps to avoid unfair restriction to women.

5, 17–25: The function of presbyters is not exactly the same as that of the **episkopos**, "bishop" (3, 1); in fact, the relation of the two at the time of this letter is obscure (but cf the note on Ti 1, 5–9). The Pastorals seem to reflect a transitional stage that developed in many regions of the church into the monarchical episcopate of the second and third centuries. The presbyters possess the responsibility of preaching and teaching, for which functions they are supported by the community (17–18). The realization that their position subjects them to adverse criticism is implied in the direction to Timothy (19–20) to make sure of the truth of any accusation against them before public reproof is given. He must be as objective as possible in weighing charges against presbyters (21), learning from his experience to take care in selecting them (22). Some scholars take v 22 as a reference not to ordination of presbyters but to reconciliation of public sinners. The letter now sounds an informal note of personal concern in its advice to Timothy not to be so ascetic that he even avoids wine (23). Judgment concerning the fitness of candidates to serve as presbyters is easy with persons of open conduct, more difficult and prolonged with those of greater reserve (24–25).

s: Lv 19, 32; Ti 2, 2.　t: Jer 49, 11; Lk 2, 37; 18, 7.　u: Jn 13, 14; Heb 13, 2.　v: 2 Thes 3, 11.　w: 1 Cor 7, 9.　x: 1 Cor 16, 18; Phil 2, 29.　y: Dt 25, 4; 1 Cor 9, 8 / Mt 10, 10; Lk 10, 7.　z: Dt 17, 6; 19, 15; Mt 18, 16; 2 Cor 13, 1.　a: Gal 2, 14; Eph 5, 11; 2 Tm 4, 2; Ti 1, 9.13.　b: 4, 14; 2 Tm 1, 6.

Keep yourself pure. [23]Stop drinking only water, but have a little wine for the sake of your stomach and your frequent illnesses.

[24]Some people's sins are public, preceding them to judgment; but other people are followed by their sins. [25]Similarly, good works are also public; and even those that are not cannot remain hidden.

See RG 413

CHAPTER 6

Rules for Slaves. [1c]*Those who are under the yoke of slavery must regard their masters as worthy of full respect, so that the name of God and our teaching may not suffer abuse. [2d]*Those whose masters are believers must not take advantage of them because they are brothers but must give better service because those who will profit from their work are believers and are beloved.

V: False Teaching and True Wealth

Teach and urge these things. [3e]Whoever teaches something different and does not agree with the sound words of our Lord Jesus Christ and the religious teaching [4]is conceited, understanding nothing, and has a morbid disposition for arguments and verbal disputes. From these come envy, rivalry, insults, evil suspicions, [5f]and mutual friction among people with corrupted minds, who are deprived of the truth, supposing religion to be a means of gain. [6g]*Indeed, religion with contentment is a great gain. [7h]For we brought nothing into the world, just as we shall not be able to take anything out of it.

[8i]If we have food and clothing, we shall be content with that. [9j]Those who want to be rich are falling into temptation and into a trap and into many foolish and harmful desires, which plunge them into ruin and destruction. [10]For the love of money is the root of all evils, and some people in their desire for it have strayed from the faith and have pierced themselves with many pains.

Exhortations to Timothy. [11k]*But you, man of God, avoid all this. Instead, pursue righteousness, devotion, faith, love, patience, and gentleness. [12l]Compete well for the faith. Lay hold of eternal life, to which you were called when you made the noble confession in the presence of many witnesses. [13m]I charge [you] before God, who gives life to all things, and before Christ Jesus, who gave testimony under Pontius Pilate for the noble confession, [14]to keep the commandment without stain or reproach until the appearance of our Lord Jesus Christ [15n]that the blessed and only ruler will make manifest at the proper time, the King of kings and Lord of lords, [16o]who alone has immortality, who dwells in unapproachable light, and whom no human being has seen or can see. To him be honor and eternal power. Amen.

Right Use of Wealth. [17p]*Tell the rich in the present age not to be proud and not to rely on so uncertain a thing as wealth but rather on God, who richly provides us with all things for our enjoyment. [18]Tell them to do good, to be rich in good works, to be generous, ready to share, [19q]thus accumulating as treasure a good foundation for the future, so as to win the life that is true life.

6, 1–2: Compare the tables for household duties, such as that of Col 3, 18—4, 1. Domestic relationships derive new meaning from the Christian faith.

6, 1: Our teaching: this refers to the teaching of the Christian community.

6, 2b-10: Timothy is exhorted to maintain steadfastly the position outlined in this letter, not allowing himself to be pressured into any other course. He must realize that false teachers can be discerned by their pride, envy, quarrelsomeness, and greed for material gain. Verse 6 is rather obscure and is interpreted, and therefore translated, variously. The suggestion seems to be that the important gain that religion brings is spiritual, but that there is material gain, too, up to the point of what is needed for physical sustenance (cf 17–19).

6, 6: Contentment: the word **autarkeia** is a technical Greek philosophical term for the virtue of independence from

material goods (Aristotle, Cynics, Stoics).

6, 11–16: Timothy's position demands total dedication to God and faultless witness to Christ (11–14) operating from an awareness, through faith, of the coming revelation in Jesus of the invisible God (15–16).

6, 11: Man of God: a title applied to Moses and the prophets (Dt 33, 1; 1 Sm 2, 27; 1 Kgs 12, 22; 13, 1; etc.).

6, 17–19: Timothy is directed to instruct the rich, advising them to make good use of their wealth by aiding the poor.

c: Eph 6, 5; Ti 2, 9-10.   *d:* Phlm 16.   *e:* Gal 1, 6-9; 2 Tm 1, 13; Ti 1, 1.   *f:* 2 Tm 3, 8; 4, 4; Ti 1, 14.   *g:* 4, 8; Phil 4, 11-12; Heb 13, 5.   *h:* Jb 1, 21; Eccl 5, 14.   *i:* Prv 30, 8.   *j:* Prv 23, 4; 28, 22.   *k:* 2 Tm 2, 22.   *l:* 1 Cor 9, 26; 2 Tm 4, 7.   *m:* Jn 18, 36-37; 19, 11.   *n:* 2 Mc 13, 4; Rv 17, 14.   *o:* Ex 33, 20; Ps 104, 2.   *p:* Ps 62, 11; Lk 12, 20.   *q:* Mt 6, 20.

VI: Final Recommendation and Warning

²⁰ʳ*O Timothy, guard what has been entrusted to you. Avoid profane babbling and the absurdities of so-called knowledge. ²¹ˢBy professing it, some people have deviated from the faith.

Grace be with all of you.

6, 20–21: A final solemn warning against the heretical teachers, with what seems to be a specific reference to gnosticism, the great rival and enemy of the church for two centuries and more (the Greek word for "knowledge" is **gnōsis**). If gnosticism is being referred to here, it is probable that the warnings against "speculations" and "myths and genealogies" (cf especially 1, 4; Ti 3, 9) involve allusions to that same kind of heresy. Characteristic of the various gnostic systems of speculation was an elaborate mythology of innumerable superhuman intermediaries, on a descending scale ("genealogies"), between God and the world. Thus would be explained the emphasis upon Christ's being the one mediator (as in 2, 5). Although fully developed gnosticism belonged to the second and later centuries, there are signs that incipient forms of it belonged to Paul's own period.

r: 2 Tm 1, 14 / 4, 7.   s: 1, 6; 2 Tm 2, 18.

See RG
414–17

The Second Letter to Timothy

The authorship and date of this letter, as one of the Pastoral Epistles, are discussed in the Introduction to the First Letter to Timothy.

The tone here is more personal than in First Timothy, for this letter addresses Timothy in vivid terms (1, 6–14; 2, 1–13) and depicts Paul's courage and hope in the face of discouragements late in the course of his apostolic ministry (1, 15–18; 3, 10–17; 4, 9–18). Indeed, the letter takes on the character of a final exhortation and testament from Paul to the younger Timothy (4, 1–8). Paul is portrayed as a prisoner (1, 8,16; 2, 9) in Rome (1, 17), and there is a hint that Timothy may be in Ephesus (2, 17). The letter reveals that, with rare exceptions, Christians have not rallied to Paul's support (1, 15–18) and takes a pessimistic view of the outcome of his case (4, 6). It describes Paul as fully aware of what impends, looking to God, not to human beings, for his deliverance (4, 3—8,18). It recalls his mission days with Timothy (1, 3–5; cf Acts 16, 1–4). It points to his preaching of the gospel as the reason for his imprisonment and offers Timothy, as a motive for steadfastness, his own example of firmness in faith despite adverse circumstances (1, 6–14). The letter suggests that Timothy should prepare others to replace himself as Paul has prepared Timothy to replace him (2, 1–2). Paul urges him not to desist out of fear from preserving and spreading the Christian message (2, 3–7). It presents the resurrection of Jesus and his messianic role as the heart of the gospel for which Paul has been ready to lay down his life (2, 8–9) and thus not only to express his own conviction fully but to support the conviction of others (2, 10–13).

This letter, like the preceding one, urges Timothy to protect the community from the inevitable impact of false teaching (2, 14—3, 9), without fear of the personal attacks that may result (3, 10–13). It recommends that he rely on the power of the scriptures, on proclamation of the word, and on sound doctrine (3, 14—4, 2), without being troubled by those who do not accept him (4, 3–5). The letter poignantly observes in passing that Paul has need of his reading materials and his cloak (4, 13) and, what will be best of all, a visit from Timothy.

On the theory of authorship by Paul himself, Second Timothy appears to be the last of the three Pastoral Epistles. The many scholars who argue that the Pastorals are products of the Pauline school often incline toward Second Timothy as the earliest of the three and the one most likely to have actual fragments of material from Paul himself.

The principal divisions of the Second Letter to Timothy are the following:

  I: Address (1, 1–5)
 II: Exhortations to Timothy (1, 6—2, 13)
III: Instructions Concerning False Teaching (2, 14—4, 8)
 IV: Personal Requests and Final Greetings (4, 9–22)

I: Address

CHAPTER 1

See RG
415

Greeting. [1a]*Paul, an apostle of Christ Jesus by the will of God for the promise of life in Christ Jesus, [2]to Timothy, my dear child: grace, mercy, and peace from God the Father and Christ Jesus our Lord.

Thanksgiving. [3b]*I am grateful to God, whom I worship with a clear conscience as my ancestors did, as I remember you constantly in my prayers, night and day. [4]*I yearn to see you again, recalling your tears, so that I may be filled with joy, [5c]as I recall your sincere faith that first lived in your grandmother Lois and in your mother Eunice and that I am confident lives also in you.

II: Exhortations to Timothy

The Gifts Timothy Has Received. [6d]*For this reason, I remind you to stir into flame the gift of God that you have through the imposition of my hands. [7e]For God did not give us a spirit of cowardice but rather of power and love and self-control. [8f]*So do not be ashamed of your testimony to our Lord, nor of me, a prisoner for his sake; but bear your share of hardship for the gospel with the strength that comes from God.

[9g]*He saved us and called us to a holy life, not according to our works but according to his own design and the grace bestowed on us in Christ Jesus before time began, [10h]but now made manifest through the appearance of our savior Christ Jesus, who destroyed death and brought life and immortality to light through the gospel, [11i]*for which I was appointed preacher and apostle and teacher. [12j]*On this account I am suffering these things; but I am not ashamed, for I know him in whom I have believed and am confident that he is able to guard what has been entrusted to me until that day. [13k]Take as your norm the sound words that you heard from me, in the faith and love that are in Christ Jesus. [14l]Guard this rich trust with the help of the holy Spirit that dwells within us.

Paul's Suffering. [15m]*You know that everyone in Asia deserted me, including Phygelus and Hermogenes. [16n]*May the Lord grant mercy to the family of Onesiphorus because he often gave me new heart and was not ashamed of my chains. [17]But when he came to Rome, he promptly searched for me and found me. [18o]*May the

---

1, 1–2: For the formula of address and greeting, see the note on Rom 1, 1–7.

1, 1: The promise of life in Christ Jesus: that God grants through union with Christ in faith and love; cf Col 3, 4; 1 Tm 4, 8.

1, 3: As my ancestors did: this emphasizes the continuity of Judaism and Christianity; for a similar view, see Rom 9, 3–5; Phil 3, 4–6.

1, 4–5: Purportedly written from prison in Rome (8.17; 4, 6–8) shortly before the writer's death, the letter recalls the earlier sorrowful parting from Timothy, commending him for his faith and expressing the longing to see him again.

1, 6: The gift of God: the grace resulting from the conferral of an ecclesiastical office. **The imposition of my hands:** see the note on 1 Tm 4, 14.

1, 8: Do not be ashamed of your testimony to our Lord: i.e., of preaching and suffering for the sake of the gospel.

1, 9–10: Redemption from sin and the call to holiness of life are not won by personal deeds but are freely and graciously bestowed according to God's eternal plan; cf Eph 1, 4.

1, 11: Teacher: the overwhelming majority of manuscripts and Fathers read "teacher of the nations," undoubtedly a harmonization with 1 Tm 2, 7.

1, 12: He is able to guard . . . until that day: the intervening words can also be translated "what I have entrusted to him" (i.e., the fruit of his ministry) as well as "what has been

entrusted to me" (i.e., the faith). The same difficult term occurs in v 14, where it is modified by the adjective "rich" and used without a possessive.

1, 15: Keen disappointment is expressed, here and later (4, 16), that the Christians of the province of Asia, especially Phygelus and Hermogenes, should have abandoned the writer and done nothing to defend his case in court.

1, 16–18: The family of Onesiphorus because he . . . of my chains: Onesiphorus seems to have died before this letter was written. His family is mentioned twice (here and in 4, 19), though it was Onesiphorus himself who was helpful to Paul in prison and rendered much service to the community of Ephesus. Because the apostle complains of abandonment by all in Asia during his second imprisonment and trial, the assistance of Onesiphorus seems to have been given to Paul during his first Roman imprisonment (A.D. 61–63).

1, 18: Lord . . . Lord: the first "Lord" here seems to refer to Christ, the second "Lord" to the Father.

---

a: 1 Tm 4, 8. b: 1 Tm 3, 9 / Phil 3, 5. c: 1 Tm 1, 5 / Acts 16, 1. d: 1 Tm 4, 14; 5, 22 / Acts 6, 6; 8, 17. e: Rom 5, 5; 8, 15; 1 Cor 2, 4. f: 2, 3.15; Rom 1, 16. g: Eph 2, 8-9; Ti 3, 5 / Eph 1, 4; Ti 1, 2. h: Rom 16, 26; 1 Pt 1, 20 / 1 Tm 6, 14 / Phil 3, 20; Ti 1, 4; 2, 13; 2 Pt 1, 11 / 1 Cor 15, 54-55; Heb 2, 14 / 1 Cor 15, 53-54. i: 1 Tm 2, 7. j: 1 Pt 4, 16 / 1 Tm 1, 10-11. k: 1 Tm 1, 14. l: 1 Tm 6, 20 / Rom 8, 11. m: 4, 16. n: 4, 19. o: Jude 21.

Lord grant him to find mercy from the Lord on that day. And you know very well the services he rendered in Ephesus.

See RG
415-16

CHAPTER 2

Timothy's Conduct. ¹*So you, my child, be strong in the grace that is in Christ Jesus. ²And what you heard from me through many witnesses entrust to faithful people who will have the ability to teach others as well. ³ᵖBear your share of hardship along with me like a good soldier of Christ Jesus. ⁴ᑫTo satisfy the one who recruited him, a soldier does not become entangled in the business affairs of life. ⁵ʳSimilarly, an athlete cannot receive the winner's crown except by competing according to the rules. ⁶ˢThe hardworking farmer ought to have the first share of the crop. ⁷ᵗReflect on what I am saying, for the Lord will give you understanding in everything.

⁸ᵘ*Remember Jesus Christ, raised from the dead, a descendant of David: such is my gospel, ⁹ᵛfor which I am suffering, even to the point of chains, like a criminal. But the word of God is not chained. ¹⁰ʷTherefore, I bear with everything for the sake of those who are chosen, so that they too may obtain the salvation that is in Christ Jesus, together with eternal glory. ¹¹ˣThis saying is trustworthy:

If we have died with him
  we shall also live with him;

¹² ʸif we persevere
  we shall also reign with him.
But if we deny him
  he will deny us.
¹³ ᶻIf we are unfaithful
  he remains faithful,
  for he cannot deny himself.

III: Instructions Concerning False Teaching

Warning against Useless Disputes. ¹⁴ᵃ*Remind people of these things and charge them before God to stop disputing about words. This serves no useful purpose since it harms those who listen. ¹⁵ᵇBe eager to present yourself as acceptable to God, a workman who causes no disgrace, imparting the word of truth without deviation. ¹⁶ᶜAvoid profane, idle talk, for such people will become more and more godless, ¹⁷ᵈand their teaching will spread like gangrene. Among them are Hymenaeus and Philetus, ¹⁸ᵉwho have deviated from the truth by saying that [the] resurrection has already taken place and are upsetting the faith of some. ¹⁹ᶠNevertheless, God's solid foundation stands, bearing this inscription, "The Lord knows those who are his"; and, "Let everyone who calls upon the name of the Lord avoid evil."

²⁰In a large household there are vessels not only of gold and silver but also of wood

---

2, 1–7: This passage manifests a characteristic deep concern for safeguarding the faith and faithfully transmitting it through trustworthy people (1–2; cf 1, 14; 1 Tm 6, 20; Ti 1, 9). Comparisons to the soldier's detachment, the athlete's sportsmanship, and the farmer's arduous work as the price of recompense (4–6) emphasize the need of singleness of purpose in preaching the word, even at the cost of hardship, for the sake of Christ (3).

2, 8–13: The section begins with a sloganlike summary of Paul's gospel about Christ (8) and concludes with what may be part of an early Christian hymn (11b-12a; most exegetes include the rest of v 12 and all of v 13 as part of the quotation). The poetic lines suggest that through baptism Christians die spiritually with Christ and hope to live with him and reign with him forever, but the Christian life includes endurance, witness, and even suffering, as the final judgment will show and as Paul's own case makes clear; while he is imprisoned for preaching the gospel (9), his sufferings are helpful to the elect for obtaining the salvation and glory available in Christ (10), who will be true to those who are faithful and will disown those who deny him (12–13).

2, 14–19: For those who dispute about mere words (cf 23–24) and indulge in irreligious talk to the detriment of their listeners (16–19), see the notes on 1 Tm 1, 3–7; 6, 20–21 Hymenaeus and Philetus (17), while accepting the Christian's mystical death and resurrection in Christ through baptism, claimed that baptized Christians are already risen with Christ in this life and thus that there is no future bodily resurrection or eternal glory to come. The first quotation in v 19 is from Nm 16, 5; the other quotation is from some unidentified Jewish or Christian writing.

2, 14: Before God: many ancient manuscripts read "before the Lord."

---

p: 1, 8; 4, 5; Phlm 2. q: 1 Cor 9, 6. r: 1 Cor 9, 25. s: 1 Cor 9, 7-10. t: Prv 2, 6. u: Rom 1, 3; 1 Cor 15, 4.20 / Rom 2, 16; Gal 1, 11; 2, 2. v: Phil 1, 12-14. w: Col 1, 24; 1 Tm 1, 15. x: Rom 6, 8. y: Mt 10, 22.33; Lk 12, 9. z: Nm 23, 19; Rom 3. 3-4; 1 Cor 10, 13; Ti 1, 2. a: 1 Tm 6, 4. b: 1, 8; 2 Cor 6, 7; Eph 1, 13; Col 1, 5. c: 1 Tm 4, 7. d: 1 Tm 1, 20. e: 2 Thes 2, 2. f: Is 28, 16; 1 Cor 3, 10-15 / Nm 16, 5; Jn 10, 14.

and clay, some for lofty and others for humble use. 21gIf anyone cleanses himself of these things, he will be a vessel for lofty use, dedicated, beneficial to the master of the house, ready for every good work. 22h*So turn from youthful desires and pursue righteousness, faith, love, and peace, along with those who call on the Lord with purity of heart. 23iAvoid foolish and ignorant debates, for you know that they breed quarrels. 24jA slave of the Lord should not quarrel, but should be gentle with everyone, able to teach, tolerant, 25kcorrecting opponents with kindness. It may be that God will grant them repentance that leads to knowledge of the truth, 26l*and that they may return to their senses out of the devil's snare, where they are entrapped by him, for his will.

CHAPTER 3

See RG
415-16

The Dangers of the Last Days. 1m*But understand this: there will be terrifying times in the last days. 2nPeople will be self-centered and lovers of money, proud, haughty, abusive, disobedient to their parents, ungrateful, irreligious, 3callous, implacable, slanderous, licentious, brutal, hating what is good, 4traitors, reckless, conceited, lovers of pleasure rather than lovers of God, 5oas they make a pretense of religion but deny its power. Reject them. 6pFor some of these slip into homes and make captives of women weighed down by sins, led by various desires, 7qalways trying to

learn but never able to reach a knowledge of the truth. 8rJust as Jannes and Jambres opposed Moses, so they also oppose the truth—people of depraved mind, unqualified in the faith. 9But they will not make further progress, for their foolishness will be plain to all, as it was with those two.

Paul's Example and Teaching. 10*You have followed my teaching, way of life, purpose, faith, patience, love, endurance, 11spersecutions, and sufferings, such as happened to me in Antioch, Iconium, and Lystra, persecutions that I endured. Yet from all these things the Lord delivered me. 12tIn fact, all who want to live religiously in Christ Jesus will be persecuted. 13But wicked people and charlatans will go from bad to worse, deceivers and deceived. 14uBut you, remain faithful to what you have learned and believed, because you know from whom you learned it, 15vand that from infancy you have known [the] sacred scriptures, which are capable of giving you wisdom for salvation through faith in Christ Jesus. 16w*All scripture is inspired by God and is useful for teaching, for refutation, for correction, and for training in righteousness, 17xso that one who belongs to God may be competent, equipped for every good work.

CHAPTER 4

See RG
416

Solemn Charge. 1y*I charge you in the presence of God and of Christ Jesus, who will

---

2, 22: Those who call on the Lord: those who believe in Christ and worship him as Lord, i.e., Christians (Acts 9, 14–16.20–21; Rom 10, 12–13; cf 19, literally, "Everyone who names the name of the Lord").

2, 26: Some interpreters would render this passage, "Thus they may come to their senses and, forced to do his (i.e., God's) will, may escape the devil's trap." This interpretation of the Greek is possible, but the one accepted in the text seems more likely.

3, 1–9: The moral depravity and false teaching that will be rampant in the last days are already at work (1–5). The frivolous and superficial, too, devoid of the true spirit of religion, will be easy victims of those who pervert them by falsifying the truth (6–8), just as Jannes and Jambres, Pharaoh's magicians of Egypt (Ex 7, 11–12.22), discredited the truth in Moses' time. Exodus does not name the magicians, but the two names are widely found in much later Jewish, Christian, and even pagan writings. Their origins are legendary.

3, 10–17: Paul's example for Timothy includes persecution, a frequent emphasis in the Pastorals. Timothy is to be steadfast to what he has been taught and to scripture. The scriptures are the source of wisdom, i.e., of belief in and lov-

ing fulfillment of God's word revealed in Christ, through whom salvation is given.

3, 16: All scripture is inspired by God: this could possibly also be translated, "All scripture inspired by God is useful for . . . ." In this classic reference to inspiration, God is its principal author, with the writer as the human collaborator. Thus the scriptures are the word of God in human language. See also 2 Pt 1, 20–21.

3, 16–17: Useful for teaching . . . every good work: because as God's word the scriptures share his divine authority. It is exercised through those who are ministers of the word.

4, 1–5: The gravity of the obligation incumbent on Timo-

g: 3, 17. h: Gal 5, 22; 1 Tm 6, 11 / Rom 10, 13; 1 Cor 1, 2. i: 1 Tm 1, 4; 4, 7; 6, 4; Ti 3, 9. j: 1 Tm 3, 2-3. k: 3, 7; 1 Tm 2, 4. l: 1 Tm 3, 7. m: 1 Tm 4, 1; 2 Pt 3, 3; Jude 18. n: Rom 1, 29-31. o: Rom 2, 20-22; Ti 1, 16. p: Ti 1, 11. q: 2, 25. r: Ex 7, 11.22; 1 Tm 6, 5. s: Acts 13, 50; 14, 5.19 / Ps 34, 20. t: Jn 15, 20; Acts 14, 22. u: 2, 2. v: Jn 5, 39. w: Rom 15, 4; 2 Pt 1, 19-21. x: 2, 21. y: 1 Tm 5, 21; 6, 14 / Acts 10, 42; Rom 14, 9-10; 1 Pt 4, 5.

judge the living and the dead, and by his appearing and his kingly power: [2]proclaim the word; be persistent whether it is convenient or inconvenient; convince, reprimand, encourage through all patience and teaching. [3a]*For the time will come when people will not tolerate sound doctrine but, following their own desires and insatiable curiosity, will accumulate teachers [4b]and will stop listening to the truth and will be diverted to myths. [5]But you, be self-possessed in all circumstances; put up with hardship; perform the work of an evangelist; fulfill your ministry.

Reward for Fidelity. [6c]*For I am already being poured out like a libation, and the time of my departure is at hand. [7d]*I have competed well; I have finished the race; I have kept the faith. [8e]*From now on the crown of righteousness awaits me, which the Lord, the just judge, will award to me on that day, and not only to me, but to all who have longed for his appearance.

IV: Personal Requests and Final Greetings

Paul's Loneliness. [9]*Try to join me soon, [10f]*for Demas, enamored of the present world, deserted me and went to Thessalonica, Crescens to Galatia, and Titus to Dalmatia. [11g]Luke is the only one with me. Get Mark and bring him with you, for he is helpful to me in the ministry. [12h]I have sent Tychicus to Ephesus. [13i]When you come, bring the cloak I left with Carpus in Troas, the papyrus rolls, and especially the parchments.

[14j]*Alexander the coppersmith did me a great deal of harm; the Lord will repay him according to his deeds. [15]You too be on guard against him, for he has strongly resisted our preaching.

[16k]At my first defense no one appeared on my behalf, but everyone deserted me. May it not be held against them! [17l]But the Lord stood by me and gave me strength, so that through me the proclamation might be completed and all the Gentiles might hear it. And I was rescued from the lion's mouth. [18m]The Lord will rescue me from every evil threat and will bring me safe to his heavenly kingdom. To him be glory forever and ever. Amen.

Final Greeting. [19n]*Greet Prisca and Aq-

thy to preach the word can be gauged from the solemn adjuration: in the presence of God, and of Christ coming as universal judge, and by his appearance and his kingly power (1). Patience, courage, constancy, and endurance are required despite the opposition, hostility, indifference, and defection of many to whom the truth has been preached (2–5).

4, 3: Insatiable curiosity: literally, "with itching ears."

4, 6: The apostle recognizes his death through martyrdom to be imminent. He regards it as an act of worship in which his blood will be poured out in sacrifice; cf Ex 29, 38–40; Phil 2, 17.

4, 7: At the close of his life Paul could testify to the accomplishment of what Christ himself foretold concerning him at the time of his conversion, "I will show him what he will have to suffer for my name" (Acts 9, 16).

4, 8: When the world is judged at the parousia, all who have eagerly looked for the Lord's appearing and have sought to live according to his teachings will be rewarded. The crown is a reference to the laurel wreath placed on the heads of victorious athletes and conquerors in war; cf 2, 5; 1 Cor 9, 25.

4, 9–13: Demas either abandoned the work of the ministry for worldly affairs or, perhaps, gave up the faith itself (10). Luke (11) may have accompanied Paul on parts of his second and third missionary journeys (Acts 16, 10–12; 20, 5–7). Notice the presence of the first personal pronoun "we" in these Acts passages, suggesting to some that Luke (or at least some

traveling companion of Paul's) was the author of Acts. Mark, once rejected by Paul (Acts 13, 13; 15, 39), is now to render him a great service (11); cf Col 4, 10; Phlm 24. For Tychicus, see Eph 6, 21; cf also Acts 20, 4; Col 4, 7.

4, 10: Galatia: some manuscripts read "Gaul" or "Gallia."

4, 14–18: Alexander: an opponent of Paul's preaching (14–15), perhaps the one who is mentioned in 1 Tm 1, 20. Despite Paul's abandonment by his friends in the province of Asia (cf 1, 15–16), the divine assistance brought this first trial to a successful issue, even to the point of making the gospel message known to those who participated in or witnessed the tria. (16–17).

4, 19: Prisca and Aquila: they assisted Paul in his ministry in Corinth (Acts 18, 2–3) and Ephesus (Acts 18, 19.26; 1 Cor 16, 19). They risked death to save his life, and all the Gentile communities are indebted to them (Rom 16, 3–5).

z: Acts 20, 20.31; 1 Tm 5, 20. a: 1 Tm 4, 1. b: 1 Tm 1, 4; 4, 7; Ti 1, 14. c: Phil 2, 17. d: 1 Tm 1, 18; 6, 12; Jude 3 / Acts 20, 24; 1 Cor 9, 24; Heb 12, 1. e: 2, 5; Wis 5, 16; 1 Cor 9, 25; Phil 3, 14; Jas 1, 12; 1 Pt 5, 4; Rv 2, 10. f: Col 4, 14; Phlm 24 / 2 Cor 2, 13; 7, 6-7; 8, 23; Gal 2, 3; Ti 1, 4. g: Col 4, 14; Phlm 24 / Col 4, 10; Phlm 24. h: Acts 20, 4; Eph 6, 21; Col 4, 7. i: Acts 16, 8; 20, 6. j: 1 Tm 1, 20 / 2 Sm 3, 39; Pss 28, 4; 62, 12; Prv 24, 12; Rom 2, 6. k: 1, 15. l: Acts 23, 11; 27, 23; Phil 4, 13 / 1 Mc 2, 60; Ps 22, 22; Dn 6, 23. m: 2 Cor 1, 10 / Rom 16, 27. n: Acts 18, 2; Rom 16, 3; 1 Cor 16, 19 / 1, 16.

uila and the family of Onesiphorus. ²⁰ₒ*Erastus remained in Corinth, while I left Trophimus sick at Miletus. ²¹*Try to get here before winter. Eubulus, Pudens, Linus,

Claudia, and all the brothers send greetings.

²² ₚThe Lord be with your spirit. Grace be with all of you.

4, 20: **Erastus:** he was the treasurer of the city of Corinth (Rom 16, 24); cf also Acts 19, 22. **Trophimus:** from the province of Asia, he accompanied Paul from Greece to Troas (Acts 20, 4–5).

4, 21: **Linus:** Western tradition sometimes identified this Linus with the supposed successor of Peter as bishop of Rome, and Claudia as the mother of Linus (**Apostolic Constitutions,** fourth century).

o: Acts 19, 22; Rom 16, 24 / Acts 20, 4; 21, 29.   p: Gal 6, 18; Phil 4, 23; Col 4, 18; 1 Tm 6, 21; Ti 3, 15.

See RG
417–19

The Letter to Titus

The third of the Pastoral Epistles in the New Testament is addressed to a different co-worker of Paul than are First and Second Timothy. The situation is different, too, for Titus is addressed as the person in charge of developing the church on the large Mediterranean island of Crete (1, 5), a place Paul had never, according to the New Testament, visited. The tone is closer to that of First Timothy as three topics of church life and structure are discussed: presbyter-bishops (see the note on 1, 5–9), groups with which one must work in the church (2, 1–10), and admonitions for conduct based on the grace and love of God that appeared in Jesus Christ (2, 11—3, 10). The warmer personal tone of Second Timothy is replaced by emphasis on church office and on living in the society of the day, in which deceivers and heretics abound (1, 10–16; 3, 9–10).

The Pauline assistant who is addressed, Titus, was a Gentile Christian, but we are nowhere informed of his place of birth or residence. He went from Antioch with Paul and Barnabas to Jerusalem (Gal 2, 1; cf Acts 15, 2). According to 2 Corinthians (2, 13; 7, 6.13–14), he was with Paul on his third missionary journey; his name, however, does not appear in Acts. Besides being the bearer of Paul's severe letter to the Corinthians (2 Cor 7, 6–8), he had the responsibility of taking up the collection in Corinth for the Christian community of Jerusalem (2 Cor 8, 6.16–19.23). In the present letter (1, 5), he is mentioned as the administrator of the Christian community in Crete, charged with the task of organizing it through the appointment of presbyters

and bishops (1, 5–9; here the two terms refer to the same personages).

The letter instructs Titus about the character of the assistants he is to choose in view of the pastoral difficulties peculiar to Crete (1, 5–16). It suggests the special individual and social virtues that the various age groups and classes in the Christian community should be encouraged to acquire (2, 1–10). The motivation for transformation of their lives comes from christology, especially the redemptive sacrifice of Christ and his future coming, as applied through baptism and justification (2, 11–14; 3, 4–8). The community is to serve as a leaven for Christianizing the social world about it (3, 1–3). Good works are to be the evidence of their faith in God (3, 8); those who engage in religious controversy are, after suitable warning, to be ignored (3, 9–11).

The authorship and date of the Letter to Titus are discussed in the Introduction to 1 Timothy. Those who assume authorship by Paul himself usually place Titus after 1 Timothy and before 2 Timothy. Others see it as closely related to 1 Timothy, in a growing emphasis on church structure and opposition to heresy, later than the letters of Paul himself and 2 Timothy. It has also been suggested that, if the three Pastorals once circulated as a literary unit, Titus was meant to be read ahead of 1 and 2 Timothy.

The principal divisions of the Letter to Titus are the following:

I: Address (1, 1–4)

II: Pastoral Charge (1, 5–16)

III: Teaching the Christian Life (2, 1—3, 15)

I: Address

CHAPTER 1

See RG
418

Greeting. ¹ᵃ*Paul, a slave of God and apostle of Jesus Christ for the sake of the faith of God's chosen ones and the recognition of religious truth, ²ᵇin the hope of eternal life that God, who does not lie, promised before time began, ³ᶜwho indeed at the proper time revealed his word in the proclamation with which I was entrusted by the command of God our savior, ⁴ᵈto Titus, my true child in our common faith: grace and peace from God the Father and Christ Jesus our savior.

II: Pastoral Charge

Titus in Crete. ⁵*For this reason I left you in Crete so that you might set right what remains to be done and appoint presbyters in every town, as I directed you, ⁶ᵉon condition that a man be blameless, married only once, with believing children who are not accused of licentiousness or rebellious. ⁷For a bishop as God's steward must be blameless, not arrogant, not irritable, not a drunkard, not aggressive, not greedy for sordid gain, ⁸but hospitable, a lover of goodness, temperate, just, holy, and self-controlled, ⁹ᶠholding fast to the true message as taught so that he will be able both to exhort with sound doctrine and to refute opponents. ¹⁰*For there are also many rebels, idle talkers and deceivers, especially the Jewish Christians. ¹¹It is imperative to silence them, as they are upsetting whole families by teaching for sordid gain what they should not. ¹²*One of them, a prophet of their own, once said, "Cretans have always been liars, vicious beasts, and lazy gluttons." ¹³ᵍThat testimony is true. Therefore, admonish them sharply, so that they may be sound in the faith, ¹⁴ʰinstead of paying attention to Jewish myths and regulations of people who have repudiated the truth. ¹⁵ⁱTo the clean all things are clean, but to those who are defiled and unbelieving nothing is clean; in fact, both their minds and their consciences are tainted. ¹⁶They claim to know God, but by their deeds they deny him. They are vile and disobedient and unqualified for any good deed.

III: Teaching the Christian Life

CHAPTER 2

See RG
418-19

Christian Behavior. ¹ʲ*As for yourself, you must say what is consistent with sound doctrine, namely, ²that older men should be temperate, dignified, self-controlled, sound in faith, love, and endurance. ³Similarly, older women should be reverent in their behavior, not slanderers, not addicted to drink, teaching what is good, ⁴so that they may train younger women to love their husbands and children, ⁵ᵏto be self-controlled, chaste, good homemakers, under the control of their husbands, so that the word of God may not be discredited.

1, 1–4: On the epistolary form, see the note on Rom 1, 1–7. The apostolate is the divinely appointed mission to lead others to the true faith and through it to eternal salvation (1–3).

1, 5–9: This instruction on the selection and appointment of presbyters, substantially identical with that in 1 Tm 3, 1–7 on a bishop (see the note there), was aimed at strengthening the authority of Titus by apostolic mandate; cf 2, 15. In vv 5.7 and Acts 20, 17.28, the terms **episkopos** and **presbyteros** ("bishop" and "presbyter") refer to the same persons. Deacons are not mentioned in Titus. See also the note on Phil 1, 1.

1, 10–16: This adverse criticism of the defects within the community is directed especially against certain Jewish Christians, who busy themselves with useless speculations over persons mentioned in the Old Testament, insist on the observance of Jewish ritual purity regulations, and thus upset whole families by teaching things they have no right to teach; cf 3, 9; 1 Tm 1, 3–10.

1, 10: Jewish Christians: literally, "those of the circumcision."

1, 12: Cretans . . . gluttons: quoted from Epimenides, a Cretan poet of the sixth century B.C.

2, 1–10: One of Titus' main tasks in Crete is to become acquainted with the character of the Cretans and thereby learn to cope with its deficiencies (see 1, 12). The counsel is not only for Titus himself but for various classes of people with whom he must deal: older men and women (2–4), younger women and men (4–7), and slaves (9–10); cf Eph 6, 1–9; Col 3, 18—4, 1.

a: 1 Tm 2, 4; 4, 3; 2 Tm 2, 25; 3, 7; Heb 10, 26. *b:* 3, 7; 2 Tm 1, 1; 1 Jn 2, 25. *c:* 2, 10; 3, 4; Ps 24, 5; 1 Tm 1, 1; 2, 3; 4, 10; Jude 25. *d:* 2, 13; 3, 6; Phil 3, 20; 2 Tm 1, 10; 2 Pt 1, 1.11; 2, 20; 3, 2.18. *e:* 1 Tm 3, 2-7; 2 Tm 2, 24-26. *f:* 1, 13; 2, 1-2.8; 1 Tm 1, 10; 6, 3; 2 Tm 1, 13; 4, 3. *g:* 1, 9. *h:* 3, 9; 1 Tm 1, 4; 4, 7; 2 Tm 4, 4; 2 Pt 1, 16. *i:* Mk 7, 18-23; Acts 10, 15; Rom 14, 14-23. *j:* 1, 9.13; 2, 8; 1 Tm 1, 10; 6, 3; 2 Tm 1, 13; 4, 3. *k:* 1 Cor 11, 3; 14, 34; Eph 5, 22-24; Col 3, 18; 1 Tm 2, 11-15; 1 Pt 3, 1-6.

⁶Urge the younger men, similarly, to control themselves, ⁷showing yourself as a model of good deeds in every respect, with integrity in your teaching, dignity, ⁸and sound speech that cannot be criticized, so that the opponent will be put to shame without anything bad to say about us.

⁹ˡSlaves are to be under the control of their masters in all respects, giving them satisfaction, not talking back to them ¹⁰ᵐor stealing from them, but exhibiting complete good faith, so as to adorn the doctrine of God our savior in every way.

Transformation of Life. ¹¹ⁿ*For the grace of God has appeared, saving all ¹²and training us to reject godless ways and worldly desires and to live temperately, justly, and devoutly in this age, ¹³ᵒ*as we await the blessed hope, the appearance of the glory of the great God and of our savior Jesus Christ, ¹⁴ᵖwho gave himself for us to deliver us from all lawlessness and to cleanse for himself a people as his own, eager to do what is good.

¹⁵�q Say these things. Exhort and correct with all authority. Let no one look down on you.

CHAPTER 3

See RG 418–19

¹ʳ*Remind them to be under the control of magistrates and authorities, to be obedient, to be open to every good enterprise. ²They are to slander no one, to be peaceable, considerate, exercising all graciousness toward everyone. ³ˢFor we ourselves were once foolish, disobedient, deluded, slaves to various desires and pleasures, living in malice and envy, hateful ourselves and hating one another.

⁴ ᵗBut when the kindness and generous love
   of God our savior appeared,
⁵ ᵘnot because of any righteous deeds we had done
   but because of his mercy,
he saved us through the bath of rebirth
   and renewal by the holy Spirit,
⁶ ᵛwhom he richly poured out on us
   through Jesus Christ our savior,
⁷ ʷso that we might be justified by his grace
   and become heirs in hope of eternal life.

⁸ˣ*This saying is trustworthy.

Advice to Titus. I want you to insist on these points, that those who have believed in God be careful to devote themselves to good works; these are excellent and beneficial to others. ⁹ʸ*Avoid foolish arguments, genealogies, rivalries, and quarrels about the law, for they are useless and futile. ¹⁰ᶻAfter a first and second warning, break off contact with a heretic, ¹¹realizing that such a person is perverted and sinful and stands self-condemned.

Directives, Greetings, and Blessing. ¹²ᵃ*When I send Artemas to you, or Tychicus,

2, 11–15: Underlying the admonitions for moral improvement in 1–10 as the moving force is the constant appeal to God's revelation of salvation in Christ, with its demand for transformation of life.

2, 13: The blessed hope, the appearance: literally, "the blessed hope and appearance," but the use of a single article in Greek strongly suggests an epexegetical, i.e., explanatory sense. **Of the great God and of our savior Jesus Christ:** another possible translation is "of our great God and savior Jesus Christ."

3, 1–8: The list of Christian duties continues from 2, 9–10, undergirded again as in 2, 11–13 by appeal to what God in Christ has done (4–7; cf 2, 11–14). The spiritual renewal of the Cretans, signified in God's merciful gift of baptism (4–7), should be reflected in their improved attitude toward civil authority and in their Christian relationship with all (1–3).

3, 1: Magistrates and authorities: some interpreters understand these terms as referring to the principalities and powers of the heavenly hierarchy. **To be open to every good enterprise:** this implies being good citizens. It could also be

translated "ready to do every sort of good work" (as Christians); cf 14.

3, 8–11: In matters of good conduct and religious doctrine, Titus is to stand firm.

3, 9: See the note on 1 Tm 6, 20–21.

3, 12–15: Artemas or Tychicus (2 Tm 4, 12) is to replace

l: 1 Cor 7, 21-22; Eph 6, 5-8; Col 3, 22-25; 1 Tm 6, 1-2; 1 Pt 2, 18. *m*: 1, 3; 3, 4; Ps 24, 5; 1 Tm 1, 1; 2, 3; 4, 10; Jude 25. *n*: 1 Tm 2, 4; 4, 10. *o*: 1 Cor 1, 7; Phil 3, 20; 1 Thes 1, 10 / 2 Tm 1, 10 / 1, 4; 3, 6; 2 Pt 1, 1.11; 2, 20; 3, 2.18. *p*: Gal 1, 4; 2, 20; Eph 5, 2.25; 1 Tm 2, 6; 1 Pt 1, 18-19 / Ps 130, 8. *q*: 1 Tm 4, 12. *r*: Rom 13, 1-7; 1 Tm 2, 1-2; 1 Pt 2, 13-14. *s*: 1 Cor 6, 9-11; Eph 2, 1-3; 5, 8; Col 3, 5-7; 1 Pt 4, 3. *t*: 1, 3; 2, 10; Ps 24, 5; 1 Tm 1, 1; 2, 3; 4, 10; Jude 25. *u*: Dt 9, 5; Eph 2, 4-5.8-9; 2 Tm 1, 9. *v*: 1, 4; 2, 13; Phil 3, 20; 2 Tm 1, 10; 2 Pt 1, 1.11; 2, 20; 3, 2.18. *w*: 1, 2; 2 Tm 1, 1; 1 Jn 2, 25. *x*: 1 Tm 1, 15; 3, 1; 4, 9; 2 Tm 2, 11. *y*: 1 Tm 1, 4; 4, 7; 2 Tm 2, 23. *z*: Mt 18, 15-18; Rom 16, 17; 1 Cor 5, 11; 2 Thes 3, 6.14-15. *a*: Acts 20, 4; Eph 6, 21; Col 4, 7; 2 Tm 4, 12.

try to join me at Nicopolis, where I have decided to spend the winter. *13b*Send Zenas the lawyer and Apollos on their journey soon, and see to it that they have everything they need. *14c*But let our people, too, learn to devote themselves to good works to supply urgent needs, so that they may not be unproductive.

*15d*All who are with me send you greetings. Greet those who love us in the faith. Grace be with all of you.

Titus, who will join Paul in his winter sojourn at Nicopolis in Epirus, on the western coast of Greece.

b: Acts 18, 24-26; 1 Cor 1, 12; 3, 4-6.22; 4, 6; 16, 12.   *c:* 2, 14; 3, 8; Heb 10, 24; 1 Pt 3, 13.   *d:* Heb 13, 25.

See RG 420–22

The Letter to Philemon

This short letter addressed to three specific individuals was written by Paul during an imprisonment, perhaps in Rome between A.D. 61 and 63 (see the Introduction to Colossians for other possible sites). It concerns Onesimus, a slave from Colossae (Col 4, 9), who had run away from his master, perhaps guilty of theft in the process (18). Onesimus was converted to Christ by Paul (10). Paul sends him back to his master (12) with this letter asking that he be welcomed willingly by his old master (8–10.14.17) not just as a slave but as a brother in Christ (16). Paul uses very strong arguments (especially 19) in his touching appeal on behalf of Onesimus. It is unlikely that Paul is subtly hinting that he would like to retain Onesimus as his own slave, lent to Paul by his master. Rather, he suggests he would like to have Onesimus work with him for the gospel (13.20–21). There is, however, little evidence connecting this Onesimus with a bishop of Ephesus of the same name mentioned by Ignatius of Antioch (ca. A.D. 110).

Paul's letter deals with an accepted institution of antiquity, human slavery. But Paul breathes into this letter the spirit of Christ and of equality within the Christian community. He does not attack slavery directly, for this is something the Christian communities of the first century were in no position to do, and the expectation that Christ would soon come again militated against social reforms. Yet Paul, by presenting Onesimus as "brother, beloved . . . to me, but even more so to you" (16), voiced an idea revolutionary in that day and destined to break down worldly barriers of division "in the Lord."

See RG 420–21

Address and Greeting. *1a**Paul, a prisoner for Christ Jesus, and Timothy our brother, to Philemon, our beloved and our co-worker, *2b**to Apphia our sister, to Archippus our fellow soldier, and to the church at your house. *3c**Grace to you and peace from God our Father and the Lord Jesus Christ.

Thanksgiving. *4d**I give thanks to my God always, remembering you in my prayers, *5**as I hear of the love and the faith you have in the Lord Jesus and for all the holy ones, *6e**so that your partnership in the faith may become effective in recognizing every good there is in us that leads to Christ.

Plea for Onesimus. *7f**For I have experi-

1: Prisoner: as often elsewhere (cf Rom, 1 Cor, Gal especially), the second word in Greek enunciates the theme and sets the tone of the letter. Here it is the prisoner appealing rather than the apostle commanding.

2: Apphia our sister: sister is here used (like brother) to indicate a fellow Christian. **The church at your house: your** here is singular. It more likely refers to Philemon than to the last one named, Archippus; Philemon is then the owner of the slave Onesimus (10). An alternate view is that the actual master of the slave is Archippus and that the one to whom the letter is addressed, Philemon, is the most prominent Christian there; see the note on Col 4, 17.

3: Grace . . . and peace: for this greeting, which may be a combination of Greek and Aramaic epistolary formulae, see the note on Rom 1, 1–7.

4: In my prayers: literally, "at the time of my prayers."

5: Holy ones: a common term for members of the Christian community (so also 7).

6: In us: some good ancient manuscripts have in you (plural). **That leads to Christ: leads to** translates the Greek preposition **eis,** indicating direction or purpose.

7: Encouragement: the Greek word **paraklēsis** is cognate with the verb translated "urge" in vv 9.10, and serves as an introduction to Paul's plea. **Hearts:** literally, "bowels," expressing in Semitic fashion the seat of the emotions, one's "inmost self." The same Greek word is used in v 12 and again

a: 9; Eph 3, 1; 4, 1; Phil 1, 7.13.   *b:* Col 4, 17.   *c:* Rom 1, 7; Gal 1, 3; Phil 1, 2.   *d:* Rom 1, 8-9; Eph 1, 15-16.   *e:* Phil 1, 9; Col 1, 9.   *f:* 2 Cor 7, 4.

enced much joy and encouragement from your love, because the hearts of the holy ones have been refreshed by you, brother. [8]*Therefore, although I have the full right in Christ to order you to do what is proper, [9g]*I rather urge you out of love, being as I am, Paul, an old man, and now also a prisoner for Christ Jesus. [10h]I urge you on behalf of my child Onesimus, whose father I have become in my imprisonment, [11]*who was once useless to you but is now useful to [both] you and me. [12]I am sending him, that is, my own heart, back to you. [13i]*I should have liked to retain him for myself, so that he might serve me on your behalf in my imprisonment for the gospel, [14j]but I did not want to do anything without your consent, so that the good you do might not be forced but voluntary. [15]*Perhaps this is why he was away from you for a while, that you might have him back forever, [16k]*no longer as a

slave but more than a slave, a brother, beloved especially to me, but even more so to you, as a man and in the Lord. [17]So if you regard me as a partner, welcome him as you would me. [18]*And if he has done you any injustice or owes you anything, charge it to me. [19l]I, Paul, write this in my own hand: I will pay. May I not tell you that you owe me your very self. [20]Yes, brother, may I profit from you in the Lord. Refresh my heart in Christ.

[21]With trust in your compliance I write to you, knowing that you will do even more than I say. [22m]At the same time prepare a guest room for me, for I hope to be granted to you through your prayers.

Final Greetings. [23n]*Epaphras, my fellow prisoner in Christ Jesus, greets you, [24o]as well as Mark, Aristarchus, Demas, and Luke, my co-workers. [25]The grace of the Lord Jesus Christ be with your spirit.

in v 20, where it forms a literary inclusion marking off the body of the letter.

8: Full right: often translated "boldness," the Greek word **parrēsia** connotes the full franchise of speech, as the right of a citizen to speak before the body politic, claimed by the Athenians as their privilege (Euripides).

9: Old man: some editors conjecture that Paul here used a similar Greek word meaning "ambassador" (cf Eph 6, 20). This conjecture heightens the contrast with "prisoner" but is totally without manuscript support.

11: Useless . . . useful: here Paul plays on the name Onesimus, which means "useful" or "beneficial." The verb translated "profit" in v 20 is cognate.

13: Serve: the Greek **diakoneō** could connote a ministry.

15: Was away from: literally, "was separated from," but the same verb means simply "left" in Acts 18, 1. It is a euphemism for his running away.

16: As a man: literally, "in the flesh." With this and the following phrase, Paul describes the natural and spiritual orders.

18–19: Charge it to me . . . I will pay: technical legal and commercial terms in account keeping and acknowledgment of indebtedness.

23–24: Epaphras: a Colossian who founded the church there (Col 1, 7) and perhaps also in Laodicea and Hierapolis (Col 2, 1; 4, 12–13). **Aristarchus:** a native of Thessalonica and fellow worker of Paul (Acts 19, 29; 20, 4; 27, 2). For Mark, Demas, and Luke, see 2 Tm 4, 9–13 and the note there.

g: 1; Eph 3, 1; 4, 1; Phil 1, 7.13.   h: 1 Cor 4, 14-15; Gal 4, 19; Col 4, 9.   i: Phil 2, 30.   j: 2 Cor 9, 7; 1 Pt 5, 2.   k: 1 Tm 6, 2. l: Gal 6, 11; 2 Thes 3, 17.   m: Heb 13, 19.   n: Col 1, 7; 4, 12-13. o: Acts 12, 12.15; 13, 13; 15, 37-39; 19, 29; 20, 4; 27, 2; Col 4, 10.14; 2 Tm 4, 10-13.

See RG
422-28

The Letter to the Hebrews

As early as the second century, this treatise, which is of great rhetorical power and force in its admonition to faithful pilgrimage under Christ's leadership, bore the title "To the Hebrews." It was assumed to be directed to Jewish Christians. Usually Hebrews was attached in Greek manuscripts to the collection of letters by Paul. Although no author is mentioned (for there is no address), a reference to Timothy (13, 23) suggested connections to the circle of Paul and his assistants. Yet the exact audience, the author, and

even whether Hebrews is a letter have long been disputed.

The author saw the addressees in danger of apostasy from their Christian faith. This danger was due not to any persecution from outsiders but to a weariness with the demands of Christian life and a growing indifference to their calling (2, 1; 4, 14; 6, 1–12; 10, 23–32). The author's main theme, the priesthood and sacrifice of Jesus (ch 3–10), is not developed for its own sake but as a means of restoring their lost fervor and strengthening them in their faith. Another important theme of the letter is that of the pilgrimage of the people of God to the heavenly Jerusalem (11, 10; 12, 1–3. 18–29; 13, 14). This theme is intimately connected with that of Jesus' ministry in the heavenly sanctuary (9, 11—10, 22).

The author calls this work a "message of encouragement" (13, 22), a designation that is given to a synagogue sermon in Acts 13, 15. Hebrews is probably therefore a written homily, to which the author gave an epistolary ending (13, 22–25).

The author begins with a reminder of the preexistence, incarnation, and exaltation of Jesus (1, 3) that proclaimed him the climax of God's word to humanity (1, 1–3). He dwells upon the dignity of the person of Christ, superior to the angels (1, 4—2, 2). Christ is God's final word of salvation communicated (in association with accredited witnesses to his teaching: cf 2, 3–4) not merely by word but through his suffering in the humanity common to him and to all others (2, 5–16). This enactment of salvation went beyond the pattern known to Moses, faithful prophet of God's word though he was, for Jesus as high priest expiated sin and was faithful to God with the faithfulness of God's own Son (2, 17—3, 6).

Just as the infidelity of the people thwarted Moses' efforts to save them, so the infidelity of any Christian may thwart God's plan in Christ (3, 6—4, 13). Christians are to reflect that it is their humanity that Jesus took upon himself, with all its defects save sinfulness, and that he bore the burden of it until death out of obedience to God. God declared this work of his Son to be the cause of salvation for all (4, 14—5, 10). Although Christians recognize this fundamental teaching, they may grow weary of it and of its implications, and therefore require other reflections to stimulate their faith (5, 11—6, 20).

Therefore, the author presents to the readers for their reflection the everlasting priesthood of Christ (7, 1–28), a priesthood that fulfills the promise of the Old Testament (8, 1–13). It also provides the meaning God ultimately intended in the sacrifices of the Old Testament (9, 1–28): these pointed to the unique sacrifice of Christ, which alone obtains forgiveness of sins (10, 1–18). The trial of faith experienced by the readers should resolve itself through their consideration of Christ's ministry in the heavenly sanctuary and his perpetual intercession there on their

behalf (7, 25; 8, 1–13). They should also be strengthened by the assurance of his foreordained parousia, and by the fruits of faith that they have already enjoyed (10, 19–39).

It is in the nature of faith to recognize the reality of what is not yet seen and is the object of hope, and the saints of the Old Testament give striking example of that faith (11, 1–40). The perseverance to which the author exhorts the readers is shown forth in the early life of Jesus. Despite the afflictions of his ministry and the supreme trial of his suffering and death, he remained confident of the triumph that God would bring him (12, 1–3). The difficulties of human life have meaning when they are accepted as God's discipline (12, 4–13), and if Christians persevere in fidelity to the word in which they have believed, they are assured of possessing forever the unshakable kingdom of God (12, 14–29).

The letter concludes with specific moral commandments (13, 1–17), in the course of which the author recalls again his central theme of the sacrifice of Jesus and the courage needed to associate oneself with it in faith (13, 9–16).

As early as the end of the second century, the church of Alexandria in Egypt accepted Hebrews as a letter of Paul, and that became the view commonly held in the East. Pauline authorship was contested in the West into the fourth century, but then accepted. In the sixteenth century, doubts about that position were again raised, and the modern consensus is that the letter was not written by Paul. There is, however, no widespread agreement on any of the other suggested authors, e.g., Barnabas, Apollos, or Prisc(ill)a and Aquila. The document itself has no statement about its author.

Among the reasons why Pauline authorship has been abandoned are the great difference of vocabulary and style between Hebrews and Paul's letters, the alternation of doctrinal teaching with moral exhortation, the different manner of citing the Old Testament, and the resemblance between the thought of Hebrews and that of Alexandrian Judaism. The Greek of the letter is in many ways the best in the New Testament.

Since the letter of Clement of Rome to the Corinthians, written about A.D. 96, most probably cites Hebrews, the upper limit for the date of composition is reasonably certain. While the letter's references in the present tense to the Old

Testament sacrificial worship do not necessarily show that temple worship was still going on, many older commentators and a growing number of recent ones favor the view that it was and that the author wrote before the destruction of the temple of Jerusalem in A.D. 70. In that case, the argument of the letter is more easily explained as directed toward Jewish Christians rather than those of Gentile origin, and the persecutions they have suffered in the past (cf 10, 32–34) may have been connected with the disturbances that preceded the expulsion of the Jews from Rome in A.D. 49 under the emperor Claudius. These were probably caused by disputes between Jews who accepted Jesus as the Messiah and those who did not.

The principal divisions of the Letter to the Hebrews are the following:

I: Introduction (1, 1–4)
II: The Son Higher than the Angels (1, 5—2, 18)
III: Jesus, Faithful and Compassionate High Priest (3, 1—5, 10)
IV: Jesus' Eternal Priesthood and Eternal Sacrifice (5, 11—10, 39)
V: Examples, Discipline, Disobedience (11, 1—12, 29)
VI: Final Exhortation, Blessing, Greetings (13, 1–25)

I: Introduction

CHAPTER 1

See RG 424-25

[1]*In times past, God spoke in partial and various ways to our ancestors through the prophets; [2a]in these last days, he spoke to us through a son, whom he made heir of all things and through whom he created the universe,

[3] [b]who is the refulgence of his glory,
  the very imprint of his being,
and who sustains all things by his mighty word.
When he had accomplished purification from sins,
he took his seat at the right hand of the Majesty on high,
[4] [c]as far superior to the angels
as the name he has inherited is more excellent than theirs.

II: The Son Higher than the Angels

Messianic Enthronement. [5d]*For to which of the angels did God ever say:

"You are my son; this day I have begotten you"?

Or again:

"I will be a father to him, and he shall be a son to me"?

1, 1–4: The letter opens with an introduction consisting of a reflection on the climax of God's revelation to the human race in his Son. The divine communication was initiated and maintained during Old Testament times in fragmentary and varied ways through **the prophets** (1), including Abraham, Moses, and all through whom God spoke. But now **in these last days** (2), the final age, God's revelation of his saving purpose is achieved **through a son,** i.e., one who is Son, whose role is redeemer and mediator of creation. He was made **heir of all things** through his death and exaltation to glory, yet he existed before he appeared as man; through him God **created the universe.** Verses 3–4, which may be based upon a liturgical hymn, assimilate the Son to the personified Wisdom of the Old Testament as **refulgence of** God's **glory** and **imprint of his being** (3; cf Wis 7, 26). These same terms are used of the Logos in Philo. The author now turns from the cosmological role of the preexistent Son to the redemptive work of Jesus: he brought about purification from sins and has been exalted to the right hand of God (see Ps 110, 1). The once-humiliated and crucified Jesus has been declared God's Son, and this name shows his superiority to the angels. The reason for the author's insistence on that superiority is,

among other things, that in some Jewish traditions angels were mediators of the old covenant (see Acts 7, 53; Gal 3, 19). Finally, Jesus' superiority to the angels emphasizes the superiority of the new covenant to the old because of the heavenly priesthood of Jesus.

1, 5–14: Jesus' superiority to the angels is now demonstrated by a series of seven Old Testament texts. Some scholars see in the stages of Jesus' exaltation an order corresponding to that of enthronement ceremonies in the ancient Near East, especially in Egypt, namely, elevation to divine status (5–6); presentation to the angels and proclamation of everlasting lordship (7–12); enthronement and conferral of royal power (13). The citations from the Psalms in vv 5 and 13 were traditionally used of Jesus' messianic sonship (cf Acts 13, 33) through his resurrection and exaltation (cf Acts 2, 33–35); those in vv 8 and 10–12 are concerned with his divine king-

---

a: Is 2, 2; Jer 23, 20; Ez 38, 16; Dn 10, 14 / Jn 3, 17; Rom 8, 3; Gal 4, 4 / Prv 8, 30; Wis 7, 22; Jn 1, 3; 1 Cor 8, 6; Col 1, 16. *b:* Wis 7, 26; 2 Cor 4, 4; Col 1, 15 / 8, 1; 10, 12; 12, 2; Mk 16, 19; Acts 2, 33; 7, 55-56; Rom 8, 34; Eph 1, 20; Col 3, 1; 1 Pt 3, 22. *c:* Eph 1, 21; Phil 2, 9-11. *d:* Ps 2, 7 / 2 Sm 7, 14.

[6e]*And again, when he leads the first-born into the world, he says:

"Let all the angels of God worship him."

[7f]Of the angels he says:

"He makes his angels winds
　　and his ministers a fiery flame";

[8g]*but of the Son:

"Your throne, O God, stands forever and
　　ever;
　and a righteous scepter is the scepter
　　of your kingdom.
[9] You loved justice and hated wickedness;
　　therefore God, your God, anointed you
　　with the oil of gladness above your
　　companions";

[10h]and:

"At the beginning, O Lord, you
　　established the earth,
　and the heavens are the works of your
　　hands.
[11] They will perish, but you remain;
　　and they will all grow old like a
　　garment.
[12] You will roll them up like a cloak,
　　and like a garment they will be changed.
But you are the same, and your years will
　　have no end."

[13i]But to which of the angels has he ever said:

"Sit at my right hand
　　until I make your enemies your
　　　footstool"?

[14j]Are they not all ministering spirits sent to serve, for the sake of those who are to inherit salvation?

CHAPTER 2

Exhortation to Faithfulness. [1]*Therefore, we must attend all the more to what we have heard, so that we may not be carried away. [2k]For if the word announced through angels proved firm, and every transgression and disobedience received its just recompense, [3l]how shall we escape if we ignore so great a salvation? Announced originally through the Lord, it was confirmed for us by those who had heard. [4m]God added his testimony by signs, wonders, various acts of power, and distribution of the gifts of the holy Spirit according to his will.

Exaltation through Abasement. [5]*For it was not to angels that he subjected the world to come, of which we are speaking. [6n]Instead, someone has testified somewhere:

"What is man that you are mindful of
　　him,

See RG 424-25

---

ship and his creative function. The central quotation in v 7 serves to contrast the angels with the Son. The author quotes it according to the Septuagint translation, which is quite different in meaning from that of the Hebrew ("You make the winds your messengers, and flaming fire your ministers"). The angels are only **sent to serve . . . those who are to inherit salvation** (14).

1, 6: And again, when he leads: the Greek could also be translated "And when he again leads" in reference to the parousia.

1, 8–12: O God: the application of the name "God" to the Son derives from the preexistence mentioned in vv 2–3; the psalmist had already used it of the Hebrew king in the court style of the original. See the note on Ps 45, 7. It is also important for the author's christology that in vv 10–12 an Old Testament passage addressed to God is redirected to Jesus.

2, 1–4: The author now makes a transition into exhortation, using an a fortiori argument (as at 7, 21–22; 9, 13–14; 10, 28–29; 12, 25). The **word announced through angels** (2), the Mosaic law, is contrasted with the more powerful word that Christians have received (3–4). Christ's supremacy strengthens Christians against being **carried away** from their faith.

2, 5–18: The humanity and the suffering of Jesus do not constitute a valid reason for relinquishing the Christian faith.

Ps 8 (6–7) is also applied to Jesus in 1 Cor 15, 27; Eph 1, 22; and probably 1 Pt 3, 22. This christological interpretation, therefore, probably reflects a common early Christian tradition, which may have originated in the expression **the son of man** (6). The psalm contrasts God's greatness with man's relative insignificance but also stresses the superiority of man to the rest of creation, of which he is lord. Heb applies this christologically: Jesus lived a truly human existence, **lower than the angels,** in the days of his earthly life, particularly in his suffering and death; now, **crowned with glory and honor,** he is raised above all creation. The author considers all things as already **subject to him** because of his exaltation (8–9), though **we do not see** this yet. The reference to Jesus as **leader** (10) sounds the first note of an important leitmotif in Heb: the journey of the people of God to the sabbath rest (4, 9), the heavenly sanctuary, following Jesus, their "forerunner" (6, 20). It was fitting that God should make him **perfect through suffering,** consecrated by obedient suffering. Because he is perfected as high priest, Jesus is then able to consecrate his peo-

e: Dt 32, 43 LXX; Ps 97, 7.　f: Ps 104, 4 LXX.　g: Ps 45, 7-8.　h: Ps 102, 26-28.　i: Ps 110, 1.　j: Ps 91, 11; Dn 7, 10.　k: Acts 7, 38.53; Gal 3, 19.　l: 10, 29; 12, 25.　m: Mk 16, 20; Acts 14, 3; 19, 11.　n: Ps 8, 5-7.

or the son of man that you care for
him?

7 You made him for a little while lower
than the angels;

you crowned him with glory and honor,

8 °subjecting all things under his feet."

In "subjecting" all things [to him], he left
nothing not "subject to him." Yet at present
we do not see "all things subject to him,"
9pbut we do see Jesus "crowned with glory
and honor" because he suffered death, he
who "for a little while" was made "lower
than the angels," that by the grace of God he
might taste death for everyone.

10qFor it was fitting that he, for whom and
through whom all things exist, in bringing
many children to glory, should make the
leader to their salvation perfect through suffering. 11He who consecrates and those who
are being consecrated all have one origin.
Therefore, he is not ashamed to call them
"brothers," 12rsaying:

"I will proclaim your name to my
brothers,
in the midst of the assembly I will
praise you";

13sand again:

"I will put my trust in him";

and again:

"Behold, I and the children God has
given me."

14tNow since the children share in blood and
flesh, he likewise shared in them, that
through death he might destroy the one who
has the power of death, that is, the devil,
15and free those who through fear of death
had been subject to slavery all their life.
16Surely he did not help angels but rather the
descendants of Abraham; 17utherefore, he
had to become like his brothers in every
way, that he might be a merciful and faithful
high priest before God to expiate the sins of
the people. 18Because he himself was tested
through what he suffered, he is able to help
those who are being tested.

III: Jesus, Faithful and Compassionate High Priest

CHAPTER 3

See RG 425-26

Jesus, Superior to Moses. 1*Therefore, holy "brothers," sharing in a heavenly
calling, reflect on Jesus, the apostle and high
priest of our confession, 2vwho was faithful
to the one who appointed him, just as Moses
was "faithful in [all] his house." 3wBut he is
worthy of more "glory" than Moses, as the

---

ple (11); access to God is made possible by each of these two
consecrations. If Jesus is able to help human beings, it is because he has become one of us; we are his "brothers." The author then cites three Old Testament texts as proofs of this unity
between ourselves and the Son. Psalm 22, 23 is interpreted so
as to make Jesus the singer of this lament, which ends with
joyful praise of the Lord in the assembly of "brothers." The
other two texts are from Is 8, 17.18. The first of these seems
intended to display in Jesus an example of the trust in God that
his followers should emulate. The second curiously calls these
followers "children"; probably this is to be understood to
mean children of Adam, but the point is our solidarity with
Jesus. By sharing human nature, including the ban of death,
Jesus broke the power of the devil over death (14); the author
shares the view of Hellenistic Judaism that death was not intended by God and that it had been introduced into the world
by the devil. The **fear of death** (15) is a religious fear based
on the false conception that death marks the end of a person's
relations with God (cf Ps 115, 17–18; Is 38, 18). Jesus deliberately allied himself with the **descendants of Abraham** (16)
in order to be a **merciful and faithful high priest.** This is the
first appearance of the central theme of Heb, Jesus the great
high priest expiating the **sins of the people** (17), as one who
experienced the same tests as they (18).

3, 1–6: The author now takes up the two qualities of Jesus
mentioned in 2, 17, but in inverse order: faithfulness (3, 1—4,
13) and mercy (4, 14—5, 10). Christians are called **holy
"brothers"** because of their common relation to him (2, 11),
the **apostle,** a designation for Jesus used only here in the New
Testament (cf Jn 13, 16; 17, 3), meaning one sent as God's final word to us (1, 2). He is compared with Moses probably because he is seen as mediator of the new covenant (9, 15) just
as Moses was of the old (9, 19–22, including his sacrifice). But
when the author of Heb speaks of Jesus' sacrifice, he does not
consider Moses as the Old Testament antitype, but rather the
high priest on the Day of Atonement (9, 6–15). Moses' faithfulness **"in [all] his house"** refers back to Nm 12, 7, on which
this section is a midrashic commentary. In vv 3–6, the author
does not indicate that he thinks of either Moses or Christ as the
founder of the household. **His house** (2.5.6) means God's
house, not that of Moses or Christ; in the case of Christ, compare v 6 with 10, 21. The **house** of v 6 is the Christian com-

o: Mt 28, 18; 1 Cor 15, 25-28; Eph 1, 20-23; Phil 3, 21; 1 Pt 3, 22.
p: Phil 2, 6-11. *q:* 12, 2; Is 53, 4 / Rom 11, 36; 1 Cor 8, 6. *r:* Ps
22, 23. *s:* Is 8, 17.18. *t:* Is 25, 8; Hos 13, 14; Jn 12, 31; Rom 6,
9; 1 Cor 15, 54-55; 2 Tm 1, 10; Rv 12, 10. *u:* 4, 15; 5, 1-3.
v: Nm 12, 7. *w:* 2 Cor 3, 7-8.

founder of a house has more "honor" than the house itself. *4*Every house is founded by someone, but the founder of all is God. *5*Moses was "faithful in all his house" as a "servant" to testify to what would be spoken, *6x**but Christ was faithful as a son placed over his house. We are his house, if [only] we hold fast to our confidence and pride in our hope.

Israel's Infidelity a Warning. *7y**Therefore, as the holy Spirit says:

"Oh, that today you would hear his
          voice,
8   'Harden not your hearts as at the
          rebellion
       in the day of testing in the desert,
9   *z*where your ancestors tested and tried
          me
       and saw my works *10*for forty
          years.
       Because of this I was provoked with
          that generation
       and I said, "They have always been
          of erring heart,
       and they do not know my ways."
11   As I swore in my wrath,
       "They shall not enter into my
          rest." ' "

*12*Take care, brothers, that none of you may have an evil and unfaithful heart, so as to forsake the living God. *13*Encourage yourselves daily while it is still "today," so that none of you may grow hardened by the deceit of sin. *14a*We have become partners of Christ if only we hold the beginning of the reality firm until the end, *15b*for it is said:

"Oh, that today you would hear his
          voice:
'Harden not your hearts as at the
          rebellion.' "

*16c*Who were those who rebelled when they heard? Was it not all those who came out of Egypt under Moses? *17d*With whom was he "provoked for forty years"? Was it not those who had sinned, whose corpses fell in the desert? *18e*And to whom did he "swear that they should not enter into his rest," if not to those who were disobedient? *19*And we see that they could not enter for lack of faith.

CHAPTER 4

See RG 425-26

The Sabbath Rest. *1*Therefore, let us be on our guard while the promise of entering into his rest remains, that none of you seem to have failed. *2*For in fact we have received the good news just as they did. But the word that they heard did not profit them, for they were not united in faith with those who listened. *3f*For we who believed enter into [that] rest, just as he has said:

"As I swore in my wrath,
   'They shall not enter into my rest,' "

---

munity; the author suggests its continuity with Israel by speaking not of two houses but of only one. Verse 6 brings out the reason why Jesus is superior to Moses: the latter was the faithful **servant** laboring in the house founded by God, but Jesus is God's **son,** placed **over** the house.

3, 6: The majority of manuscripts add "firm to the end," but these words are not found in the three earliest and best witnesses and are probably an interpolation derived from v 14.

3, 7—4, 13: The author appeals for steadfastness of faith in Jesus, basing his warning on the experience of Israel during the Exodus. In the Old Testament the Exodus had been invoked as a symbol of the return of Israel from the Babylonian exile (Is 42, 9; 43, 16–21; 51, 9–11). In the New Testament the redemption was similarly understood as a new exodus, both in the experience of Jesus himself (Lk 9, 31) and in that of his followers (1 Cor 10, 1–4). The author cites Ps 95, 7–11, a salutary example of hardness of heart, as a warning against the danger of growing weary and giving up the journey. To call God **living** (12) means that he reveals himself in his works (cf Jos 3, 10; Jer 10, 10). The **rest** (11) into which Israel was to enter was only a foreshadowing of that rest to which Christians are called. They are to remember the exam-

ple of Israel's revolt in the desert that cost a whole generation the loss of the promised land (15–19; cf Nm 14, 20–29). In 4, 1–11, the symbol of **rest** is seen in deeper dimension because the promise to the ancient Hebrews foreshadowed that given to Christians, it is **good news;** and because the promised land was the place of rest that God provided for his people, it was a share in his own rest, which he enjoyed after he had finished his creative work (3–4; cf Gn 2, 2). The author attempts to read this meaning of God's rest into Ps 95, 7–11 (6–9). The Greek form of the name of Joshua, who led Israel into the promised land, is Jesus (8). The author plays upon the name but stresses the superiority of Jesus, who leads his followers into heavenly rest. Verses 12 and 13 are meant as a continuation of the warning, for the word of God brings judgment as well as salvation. Some would capitalize **the word of God** and see it as a personal title of Jesus, comparable to that of Jn 1, 1–18.

x: 10, 21; Eph 2, 19; 1 Tm 3, 15; 1 Pt 4, 17.   *y:* Ps 95, 7-11.   *z:* Ex 17, 7; Nm 20, 2-5.   *a:* Rom 8, 17.   *b:* Ps 95, 7-8.   *c:* Nm 14, 1-38; Dt 1, 19-40.   *d:* Nm 14, 29.   *e:* Nm 14, 22-23; Dt 1, 35.   *f:* 3, 11; Ps 95, 11.

and yet his works were accomplished at the foundation of the world. [4g]For he has spoken somewhere about the seventh day in this manner, "And God rested on the seventh day from all his works"; [5h]and again, in the previously mentioned place, "They shall not enter into my rest." [6]Therefore, since it remains that some will enter into it, and those who formerly received the good news did not enter because of disobedience, [7i]he once more set a day, "today," when long afterwards he spoke through David, as already quoted:

"Oh, that today you would hear his voice:
    'Harden not your hearts.' "

[8j]Now if Joshua had given them rest, he would not have spoken afterwards of another day. [9]Therefore, a sabbath rest still remains for the people of God. [10]And whoever enters into God's rest, rests from his own works as God did from his. [11]Therefore, let us strive to enter into that rest, so that no one may fall after the same example of disobedience.

[12k]Indeed, the word of God is living and effective, sharper than any two-edged sword, penetrating even between soul and spirit, joints and marrow, and able to discern reflections and thoughts of the heart. [13l]No creature is concealed from him, but everything is naked and exposed to the eyes of him to whom we must render an account.

Jesus, Compassionate High Priest. [14m]*Therefore, since we have a great high priest who has passed through the heavens, Jesus, the Son of God, let us hold fast to our confession. [15n]For we do not have a high priest who is unable to sympathize with our weaknesses, but one who has similarly been tested in every way, yet without sin. [16o]So let us confidently approach the throne of grace to receive mercy and to find grace for timely help.

CHAPTER 5

See RG
425–27

[1]*Every high priest is taken from among men and made their representative before God, to offer gifts and sacrifices for sins. [2]*He is able to deal patiently with the ignorant and erring, for he himself is beset by weakness [3p]and so, for this reason, must make sin offerings for himself as well as for the people. [4q]No one takes this honor upon himself but only when called by God, just as Aaron was. [5r]In the same way, it was not Christ who glorified himself in becoming high priest, but rather the one who said to him:

"You are my son;
    this day I have begotten you";

[6s]*just as he says in another place:

"You are a priest forever
    according to the order of Melchizedek."

4, 14–16: These verses, which return to the theme first sounded in 2, 16—3, 1, serve as an introduction to the section that follows. The author here alone calls Jesus **a great high priest** (14), a designation used by Philo for the Logos; perhaps he does so in order to emphasize Jesus' superiority over the Jewish high priest. He has **been tested in every way, yet without sin** (15); this indicates an acquaintance with the tradition of Jesus' temptations, not only at the beginning (as in Mk 1, 13) but throughout his public life (cf Lk 22, 28). Although the reign of the exalted Jesus is a theme that occurs elsewhere in Heb, and Jesus' throne is mentioned in 1, 8, **the throne of grace** (16) refers to the throne of God. The similarity of v 16 to 10, 19–22 indicates that the author is thinking of our confident access to God, made possible by the priestly work of Jesus.

5, 1–10: The true humanity of Jesus (see the note on 2, 5–18) makes him a more rather than a less effective high priest to the Christian community. In Old Testament tradition, the high priest was identified with the people, guilty of personal sin just as they were (1–3). Even so, the office was of divine appointment (4), as was also the case with the sinless Christ (5). For v 6, see the note on Ps 110, 4. Although Jesus was Son of God, he was destined as a human being to learn obedience by accepting the suffering he had to endure (8).

Because of his perfection through this experience of human suffering, he is the cause of salvation for all (9), a **high priest according to the order of Melchizedek** (10; cf 6 and 7, 3).

5, 1: **To offer gifts and sacrifices for sins:** the author is thinking principally of the Day of Atonement rite, as is clear from 9, 7. This ritual was celebrated to atone for "all the sins of the Israelites" (Lv 16, 34).

5, 2: **Deal patiently:** the Greek word **metriopathein** occurs only here in the Bible; this term was used by the Stoics to designate the golden mean between excess and defect of passion. Here it means rather the ability to sympathize.

5, 6–8: The author of Heb is the only New Testament writer to cite v 4 of Ps 110, here and in 7, 17.21, to show that Jesus has been called by God to his role as priest. Verses 7–8 deal with his ability to sympathize with sinners, because of his own experience of the trials and weakness of human nature, especially fear of death. In his present exalted state,

g: Gn 2, 2. h: Ps 95, 11. i: 3, 7-8.15; Ps 95, 7-8. j: Dt 31, 7; Jos 22, 4. k: Wis 18, 15-16; Is 49, 2; Eph 6, 17; Rv 1, 16; 2, 12. l: Jb 34, 21-22; Pss 90, 8; 139, 2-4. m: 9, 11.24. n: 2, 17-18; 5, 2. o: 8, 1; 10, 19.22.35; 12, 2; Eph 3, 12. p: Lv 9, 7; 16, 15-17.30.34. q: Ex 28, 1. r: Ps 2, 7. s: Ps 110, 4.

[7t]*In the days when he was in the flesh, he offered prayers and supplications with loud cries and tears to the one who was able to save him from death, and he was heard because of his reverence. [8u]*Son though he was, he learned obedience from what he suffered; [9v]and when he was made perfect, he became the source of eternal salvation for all who obey him, [10w]declared by God high priest according to the order of Melchizedek.

IV: Jesus' Eternal Priesthood and Eternal Sacrifice

Exhortation to Spiritual Renewal. [11]*About this we have much to say, and it is difficult to explain, for you have become sluggish in hearing. [12x]Although you should be teachers by this time, you need to have someone teach you again the basic elements of the utterances of God. You need milk, [and] not solid food. [13]Everyone who lives on milk lacks experience of the word of righteousness, for he is a child. [14]But solid food is for the mature, for those

whose faculties are trained by practice to discern good and evil.

CHAPTER 6

See RG
426-27

[1y]Therefore, let us leave behind the basic teaching about Christ and advance to maturity, without laying the foundation all over again: repentance from dead works and faith in God, [2z]*instruction about baptisms and laying on of hands, resurrection of the dead and eternal judgment. [3]And we shall do this, if only God permits. [4a]*For it is impossible in the case of those who have once been enlightened and tasted the heavenly gift and shared in the holy Spirit [5]*and tasted the good word of God and the powers of the age to come, [6b]*and then have fallen away, to bring them to repentance again, since they are recrucifying the Son of God for themselves and holding him up to contempt. [7c]Ground that has absorbed the rain falling upon it repeatedly and brings forth crops useful to those for whom it is cultivated receives a blessing from God. [8d]But if it produces thorns and thistles, it is rejected; it will soon be cursed and finally burned.

weakness is foreign to him, but he understands what we suffer because of his previous earthly experience.

5, 7: **He offered prayers . . . to the one who was able to save him from death:** at Gethsemane (cf Mk 14, 35), though some see a broader reference (see the note on Jn 12, 27).

5, 8: **Son though he was:** two different though not incompatible views of Jesus' sonship coexist in Heb, one associating it with his exaltation, the other with his preexistence. The former view is the older one (cf Rom 1, 4).

5, 11—6, 20: The central section of Heb (5, 11—10, 39) opens with a reprimand and an appeal. Those to whom the author directs his teaching about Jesus' priesthood, which is **difficult to explain,** have become **sluggish in hearing** and forgetful of even **the basic elements** (5, 12). But rather than treating of basic teachings, the author apparently believes that the challenge of more advanced ones may shake them out of their inertia (**therefore,** 6, 1). The six examples of **basic teaching** in 6, 1–3 are probably derived from a traditional catechetical list. No effort is made to address apostates, for their very hostility to the Christian message cuts them off completely from Christ (6, 4–8). This harsh statement seems to rule out repentance after apostasy, but perhaps the author deliberately uses hyperbole in order to stress the seriousness of abandoning Christ. With 6, 9 a milder tone is introduced, and the criticism of the community (6, 1–3.9) is now balanced by an expression of confidence that its members are living truly Christian lives, and that God will justly reward their efforts (10). The author is concerned especially about their persevering (11–12), citing in this regard the achievement of Abraham, who relied on God's

promise and on God's oath (13–18; cf Gn 22, 16), and proposes to them as a firm anchor of Christian hope the high priesthood of Christ, who is now living with God (19–20).

6, 2: Instruction about baptisms: not simply about Christian baptism but about the difference between it and similar Jewish rites, such as proselyte baptism, John's baptism, and the washings of the Qumran sectaries. **Laying on of hands:** in Acts 8, 17; 19, 6 this rite effects the infusion of the holy Spirit; in Acts 6, 6; 13, 3; 1 Tm 4, 14; 5, 22; 2 Tm 1, 6 it is a means of conferring some ministry or mission in the early Christian community.

6, 4: Enlightened and tasted the heavenly gift: this may refer to baptism and the Eucharist, respectively, but more probably means the neophytes' enlightenment by faith and their experience of salvation.

6, 5: Tasted the good word of God and the powers of the age to come: the proclamation of the **word of God** was accompanied by signs of the Spirit's power (1 Thes 1, 5; 1 Cor 2, 4).

6, 6: They are recrucifying the Son of God for themselves: a colorful description of the malice of apostasy, which is portrayed as again crucifying and deriding the Son of God.

t: Mt 26, 38-44; Mk 14, 34-40; Lk 22, 41-46; Jn 12, 27. *u:* Rom 5, 19; Phil 2, 8. *v:* 7, 24-25.28. *w:* 6, 20; Ps 110, 4. *x:* 1 Cor 3, 1-3. *y:* 9, 14. *z:* 9, 10; Mk 7, 4 / Acts 6, 6; 8, 17; 13, 3; 19, 6; 1 Tm 4, 14; 5, 22; 2 Tm 1, 6. *a:* 10, 26.32; Ps 34, 6; 2 Cor 4, 6. *b:* 2 Pt 2, 21. *c:* Gn 1, 11-12; Dt 11, 11. *d:* Gn 3, 17-18; Mt 7, 16; 13, 7; Mk 4, 7; Lk 8, 7.

[9]But we are sure in your regard, beloved, of better things related to salvation, even though we speak in this way. [10]For God is not unjust so as to overlook your work and the love you have demonstrated for his name by having served and continuing to serve the holy ones. [11e]We earnestly desire each of you to demonstrate the same eagerness for the fulfillment of hope until the end, [12f*]so that you may not become sluggish, but imitators of those who, through faith and patience, are inheriting the promises.

God's Promise Immutable. [13g*]When God made the promise to Abraham, since he had no one greater by whom to swear, "he swore by himself," [14h]and said, "I will indeed bless you and multiply" you. [15i*]And so, after patient waiting, he obtained the promise. [16]Human beings swear by someone greater than themselves; for them an oath serves as a guarantee and puts an end to all argument. [17j]So when God wanted to give the heirs of his promise an even clearer demonstration of the immutability of his purpose, he intervened with an oath, [18k*]so that by two immutable things, in which it was impossible

for God to lie, we who have taken refuge might be strongly encouraged to hold fast to the hope that lies before us. [19l*]This we have as an anchor of the soul, sure and firm, which reaches into the interior behind the veil, [20m]where Jesus has entered on our behalf as forerunner, becoming high priest forever according to the order of Melchizedek.

CHAPTER 7

See RG 426–27

Melchizedek, a Type of Christ. [1n*]This "Melchizedek, king of Salem and priest of God Most High," "met Abraham as he returned from his defeat of the kings" and "blessed him." [2*]And Abraham apportioned to him "a tenth of everything." His name first means righteous king, and he was also "king of Salem," that is, king of peace. [3o*]Without father, mother, or ancestry, without beginning of days or end of life, thus made to resemble the Son of God, he remains a priest forever.

[4p*]See how great he is to whom the patriarch "Abraham [indeed] gave a tenth" of his spoils. [5q]The descendants of Levi who receive the office of priesthood have a com-

6, 12: Imitators of those . . . inheriting the promises: the author urges the addressees to imitate the faith of the holy people of the Old Testament, who now possess the promised goods of which they lived in hope. This theme will be treated fully in ch 11.

6, 13: He swore by himself: God's promise to Abraham, which he confirmed by an oath ("I swear by myself," Gen 22, 16) was the basis for the hope of all Abraham's descendants.

6, 15: He obtained the promise: this probably refers not to Abraham's temporary possession of the land but to the eschatological blessings that Abraham and the other patriarchs have now come to possess.

6, 18: Two immutable things: the promise and the oath, both made by God.

6, 19: Anchor . . . into the interior behind the veil: a mixed metaphor. The Holy of Holies, beyond the veil that separates it from the Holy Place (Ex 26, 31–33), is seen as the earthly counterpart of the heavenly abode of God. This theme will be developed in ch 9.

7, 1–3: Recalling the meeting between Melchizedek and Abraham described in Gn 14, 17–20, the author enhances the significance of this priest by providing the popular etymological meaning of his name and that of the city over which he ruled (2). Since Genesis gives no information on the parentage or the death of Melchizedek, he is seen here as a type of Christ, representing a priesthood that is unique and eternal (3).

7, 1: The author here assumes that Melchizedek was a priest of the God of Israel (cf Gn 14, 22 and the note there).

7, 2: In Gn 14, the Hebrew text does not state explicitly who gave tithes to whom. The author of Heb supplies Abra-

ham as the subject, according to a contemporary interpretation of the passage. This supports the argument of the midrash and makes it possible to see in Melchizedek a type of Jesus. The messianic blessings of righteousness and peace are foreshadowed in the names "Melchizedek" and "Salem."

7, 3: Without father, mother, or ancestry, without beginning of days or end of life: this is perhaps a quotation from a hymn about Melchizedek. The rabbis maintained that anything not mentioned in the Torah does not exist. Consequently, since the Old Testament nowhere mentions Melchizedek's ancestry, birth, or death, the conclusion can be drawn that he **remains . . . forever.**

7, 4–10: The tithe that Abraham gave to Melchizedek (4), a practice later followed by the levitical priesthood (5), was a gift (6) acknowledging a certain superiority in Melchizedek, the foreign priest (7). This is further indicated by the fact that the institution of the levitical priesthood was sustained by hereditary succession in the tribe of Levi, whereas the absence of any mention of Melchizedek's death in Gn implies that his personal priesthood is permanent (8). The levitical priesthood itself, through Abraham, its ancestor, paid tithes to Melchizedek, thus acknowledging the superiority of his priesthood over its own (9–10).

e: 3, 14. *f:* 5, 11; Gal 3, 14; Eph 1, 13-14. *g:* Gn 22, 16. *h:* Gn 22, 17. *i:* Heb 6, 12; Rom 4, 20. *j:* Heb 6, 12. *k:* Nm 23, 19; 1 Sm 15, 29; Jn 8, 17; 2 Tm 2, 13. *l:* 10, 20; Ex 26, 31-33; Lv 16, 2. *m:* 5, 10; Ps 110, 4. *n:* Gn 14, 17-20. *o:* 4, 14; 6, 6; 10, 29. *p:* Gn 14, 20. *q:* Nm 18, 21 / Gn 35, 11.

mandment according to the law to exact tithes from the people, that is, from their brothers, although they also have come from the loins of Abraham. ⁶But he who was not of their ancestry received tithes from Abraham and blessed him who had received the promises. ⁷*Unquestionably, a lesser person is blessed by a greater. ⁸In the one case, mortal men receive tithes; in the other, a man of whom it is testified that he lives on. ⁹*One might even say that Levi himself, who receives tithes, was tithed through Abraham, ¹⁰for he was still in his father's loins when Melchizedek met him.

¹¹*If, then, perfection came through the levitical priesthood, on the basis of which the people received the law, what need would there still have been for another priest to arise according to the order of Melchizedek, and not reckoned according to the order of Aaron? ¹²When there is a change of priesthood, there is necessarily a change of law as well. ¹³*Now he of whom these things are said belonged to a different tribe, of which no member ever officiated at the altar. ¹⁴*It is clear that our Lord arose from Judah, and in regard to that tribe Moses said nothing about priests. ¹⁵*It is even more obvious if another priest is raised up after the likeness of Melchizedek, ¹⁶*who has become so, not by a law expressed in a commandment concerning physical descent but by the power of a life that cannot be destroyed. ¹⁷For it is testified:

"You are a priest forever
   according to the order of
     Melchizedek."

¹⁸On the one hand, a former commandment is annulled because of its weakness and uselessness, ¹⁹*for the law brought nothing to perfection; on the other hand, a better hope is introduced, through which we draw near to God. ²⁰*And to the degree that this happened not without the taking of an oath—for others became priests without an oath, ²¹but he with an oath, through the one who said to him:

"The Lord has sworn, and he will not
    repent:
  'You are a priest forever' "—

7, 7: A lesser person is blessed by a greater: though this sounds like a principle, there are some examples in the Old Testament that do not support it (cf 2 Sm 14, 22; Jb 31, 20). The author may intend it as a statement of a liturgical rule.

7, 9: Levi: for the author this name designates not only the son of Jacob mentioned in Genesis but the priestly tribe that was thought to be descended from him.

7, 11–14: The levitical priesthood was not typified by the priesthood of Melchizedek, for Ps 110, 4 spoke of a priesthood of a new order, the order of Melchizedek, to arise in messianic times (11). Since the levitical priesthood served the Mosaic law, a new priesthood (12) would not come into being without a change in the law itself. Thus Jesus was not associated with the Old Testament priesthood, for he was a descendant of the tribe of Judah, which had never exercised the priesthood (13–14).

7, 13: He of whom these things are said: Jesus, the priest "according to the order of Melchizedek." According to the author's interpretation, Ps 110 spoke prophetically of Jesus.

7, 14: Judah: the author accepts the early Christian tradition that Jesus was descended from the family of David (cf Mt 1, 1–2.16.20; Lk 1, 27; 2, 4; Rom 1, 3). The Qumran community expected two Messiahs, one descended from Aaron and one from David; Heb shows no awareness of this view or at least does not accept it. Our author's view is not attested in contemporaneous Judaism.

7, 15–19: Jesus does not exercise a priesthood through family lineage but through his immortal existence (15–16),

fulfilling Ps 110, 4 (17; cf 3). Thus he abolishes forever both the levitical priesthood and the law it serves, because neither could effectively sanctify people (18) by leading them into direct communication with God (19).

7, 16: A life that cannot be destroyed: the life to which Jesus has attained by virtue of his resurrection; it is his exaltation rather than his divine nature that makes him priest. The Old Testament speaks of the Aaronic priesthood as eternal (see Ex 40, 15); our author does not explicitly consider this possible objection to his argument but implicitly refutes it in vv 23–24.

7, 19: A better hope: this hope depends upon the sacrifice of the Son of God; through it we "approach the throne of grace" (4, 16); cf 6, 19.20.

7, 20–25: As was the case with the promise to Abraham (6, 13), though not with the levitical priesthood, the eternal priesthood of the order of Melchizedek was confirmed by God's oath (20–21); cf Ps 110, 4. Thus Jesus becomes the guarantee of a permanent covenant (22) that does not require a succession of priests as did the levitical priesthood (23) because his high priesthood is eternal and unchangeable (24). Consequently, Jesus is able to save all who draw near to God through him since he is their ever-living intercessor (25).

7, 20: An oath: God's oath in Ps 110, 4.

r: 5, 6; Ps 110, 4. s: Gn 49, 10; Is 11, 1; Mt 1, 1-2.16.20; 2, 6; Lk 1, 27; 2, 4; Rom 1, 3; Rv 5, 5. t: 5, 6; Ps 110, 4. u: 10, 1. v: Ps 110, 4.

[22w]*to that same degree has Jesus [also] become the guarantee of an [even] better covenant. [23]Those priests were many because they were prevented by death from remaining in office, [24x]but he, because he remains forever, has a priesthood that does not pass away. [25y]*Therefore, he is always able to save those who approach God through him, since he lives forever to make intercession for them.

[26z]*It was fitting that we should have such a high priest: holy, innocent, undefiled, separated from sinners, higher than the heavens. [27a]*He has no need, as did the high priests, to offer sacrifice day after day, first for his own sins and then for those of the people; he did that once for all when he offered himself. [28b]For the law appoints men subject to weakness to be high priests, but the word of the oath, which was taken after the law, appoints a son, who has been made perfect forever.

CHAPTER 8

See RG
426–27

Heavenly Priesthood of Jesus. [1c]*The main point of what has been said is this: we have such a high priest, who has taken his seat at the right hand of the throne of the Majesty in heaven, [2d]*a minister of the sanctuary and of the true tabernacle that the Lord, not man, set up. [3e]Now every high priest is appointed to offer gifts and sacrifices; thus the necessity for this one also to have something to offer. [4f]If then he were on earth, he would not be a priest, since there are those who offer gifts according to the law. [5g]They worship in a copy and shadow of the heavenly sanctuary, as Moses was warned when he was about to erect the tabernacle. For he says, "See that you make everything according to the pattern shown you on the mountain." [6h]Now he has obtained so much more excellent a ministry as he is mediator of a better covenant, enacted on better promises.

Old and New Covenants. [7]*For if that first covenant had been faultless, no place would have been sought for a second one. [8i]*But he finds fault with them and says:

7, 22: **An [even] better covenant:** better than the Mosaic covenant because it will be eternal, like the priesthood of Jesus upon which it is based. Verse 12 argued that a change of priesthood involves a change of law; since "law" and "covenant" are used correlatively, a new covenant is likewise instituted.

7, 25: **To make intercession:** the intercession of the exalted Jesus, not the sequel to his completed sacrifice but its eternal presence in heaven; cf Rom 8, 34.

7, 26–28: Jesus is precisely the high priest whom the human race requires, holy and sinless, installed far above humanity (26); one having no need to offer sacrifice daily for sins but making a single offering of himself (27) once for all. The law could only appoint high priests with human limitations, but the fulfillment of God's oath regarding the priesthood of Melchizedek (Ps 110, 4) makes the Son of God the perfect priest forever (28).

7, 26: This verse with its list of attributes is reminiscent of v 3 and is perhaps a hymnic counterpart to it, contrasting the exalted Jesus with Melchizedek.

7, 27: Such daily sacrifice is nowhere mentioned in the Mosaic law; only on the Day of Atonement is it prescribed that the high priest must **offer sacrifice . . . for his own sins and then for those of the people** (Lv 16, 11–19). **Once for all:** this translates the Greek words **ephapax/hapax** that occur eleven times in Heb.

8, 1–6: The Christian community has in Jesus the kind of high priest described in 7, 26–28. In virtue of his ascension Jesus has taken his place at God's right hand in accordance with Ps 110, 1 (1), where he presides over the heavenly sanctuary established by God himself (2). Like every high priest, he has his offering to make (3; cf 9, 12.14), but it differs from that of the levitical priesthood in which he had no share (4) and which was in any case but a shadowy reflection of the true offering in the heavenly sanctuary (5). But Jesus' ministry in the heavenly sanctuary is that of mediator of a superior covenant that accomplishes what it signifies (6).

8, 2: **The sanctuary:** the Greek term could also mean "holy things" but bears the meaning "sanctuary" elsewhere in Heb (9, 8.12.24.25; 10, 19; 13, 11). **The true tabernacle:** the heavenly tabernacle **that the Lord . . . set up** is contrasted with the earthly tabernacle that Moses set up in the desert. **True** means "real" in contradistinction to a mere "copy and shadow" (5); compare the Johannine usage (e.g., Jn 1, 9; 6, 32; 15, 1). The idea that the earthly sanctuary is a reflection of a heavenly model may be based upon Ex 25, 9, but probably also derives from the Platonic concept of a real world of which our observable world is merely a shadow.

8, 7–13: Since the first covenant was deficient in accomplishing what it signified, it had to be replaced (7), as Jeremiah (31, 31–34) had prophesied (8–12). Even in the time of Jeremiah, the first covenant was antiquated (13). In 7, 22–24, the superiority of the new covenant was seen in the permanence of its priesthood; here the superiority is based on better promises, made explicit in the citation of Jer 31 (LXX: 38), 31–34, namely, in the immediacy of the people's knowledge of God (11) and in the forgiveness of sin (12).

w: 8, 6-10; 9, 15-20; 10, 29; 12, 24; 13, 20.   x: 5, 6; 13, 8.   y: Rom 8, 34; 1 Jn 2, 1; Rv 1, 18.   z: 4, 14.15.   a: 5, 3; 9, 12.25-28; 10, 11-14; Ex 29, 38-39; Lv 16, 6.11.15-17; Nm 28, 3-4; Is 53, 10; Rom 6, 10.   b: 5, 1.2.9.   c: 1, 3; 4, 14; 7, 26-28.   d: 9, 11; Ex 33, 7; Nm 24, 6 LXX.   e: 5, 1.   f: 7, 13.   g: 9, 23; Ex 25, 40; Acts 7, 44; Col 2, 17.   h: 7, 22; 9, 15.   i: Jer 31, 31-34.

"Behold, the days are coming, says the
    Lord,
    when I will conclude a new covenant
        with the house of Israel and the
        house of Judah.
9 It will not be like the covenant I made
        with their fathers
    the day I took them by the hand to lead
        them forth from the land of
        Egypt;
    for they did not stand by my covenant
        and I ignored them, says the Lord.
10 *j*But this is the covenant I will establish
        with the house of Israel
    after those days, says the Lord:
    I will put my laws in their minds
        and I will write them upon their hearts.
    I will be their God,
        and they shall be my people.
11 And they shall not teach, each one his
        fellow citizen
    and kinsman, saying, 'Know the
        Lord,'
    for all shall know me,
        from least to greatest.
12 For I will forgive their evildoing
    and remember their sins no more."

*13k**When he speaks of a "new" covenant, he declares the first one obsolete. And what has become obsolete and has grown old is close to disappearing.

CHAPTER 9

The Worship of the First Covenant. See RG 426-27 *1**Now [even] the first covenant had regulations for worship and an earthly sanctuary. *2l**For a tabernacle was constructed, the outer one, in which were the lampstand, the table, and the bread of offering; this is called the Holy Place. *3m**Behind the second veil was the tabernacle called the Holy of Holies, *4n**in which were the gold altar of incense and the ark of the covenant entirely covered with gold. In it were the gold jar containing the manna, the staff of Aaron that had sprouted, and the tablets of the covenant. *5o**Above it were the cherubim of glory overshadowing the place of expiation. Now is not the time to speak of these in detail.

*5p**With these arrangements for worship, the priests, in performing their service, go into the outer tabernacle repeatedly, *7q**but the high priest alone goes into the inner one once a year, not without blood that he offers

8, 8–12: In citing Jer the author follows the Septuagint; some apparent departures from it may be the result of a different Septuagintal text rather than changes deliberately introduced.

8, 13: Close to disappearing: from the prophet's perspective, not that of the author of Heb.

9, 1–10: The regulations for worship under the old covenant permitted all the priests to enter the Holy Place (2, 6), but only the high priest to enter the Holy of Holies and then only once a year (3–5.7). The description of the sanctuary and its furnishings is taken essentially from Ex 25–26. This exclusion of the people from the Holy of Holies signified that they were not allowed to stand in God's presence (8) because their offerings and sacrifices, which were merely symbols of their need of spiritual renewal (10), could not obtain forgiveness of sins (9).

9, 2: The outer one: the author speaks of the **outer tabernacle** (6) and **the inner one** (7) rather than of one Mosaic tabernacle divided into two parts or sections.

9, 3: The second veil: what is meant is the veil that divided the Holy Place from the Holy of Holies. It is here called **the second,** because there was another veil at the entrance to the Holy Place, or "outer tabernacle" (Ex 26, 36).

9, 4: The gold altar of incense: Ex 30, 6 locates this altar in the Holy Place, i.e., the first tabernacle, rather than in the Holy of Holies. Neither is there any Old Testament support for the assertion that the jar of manna and the staff of Aaron were in the ark of the covenant. For the tablets of the

covenant, see Ex 25, 16.

9, 5: The place of expiation: the gold "mercy seat" (Greek **hilastērion,** as in Rom 3, 25), where the blood of the sacrificial animals was sprinkled on the Day of Atonement (Lv 16, 14–15). This rite achieved "expiation" or atonement for the sins of the preceding year.

9, 6: In performing their service: the priestly services that had to be performed regularly in the Holy Place or **outer tabernacle** included burning incense on the incense altar twice each day (Ex 30, 7), replacing the loaves on the table of the bread of offering once each week (Lv 24, 8), and constantly caring for the lamps on the lampstand (Ex 27, 21).

9, 7: Not without blood: blood was essential to Old Testament sacrifice because it was believed that life was located in the blood. Hence blood was especially sacred, and its outpouring functioned as a meaningful symbol of cleansing from sin and reconciliation with God. Unlike Heb, the Old Testament never says that the blood is "offered." The author is perhaps retrojecting into his description of Mosaic ritual a concept that belongs to the New Testament antitype, as Paul does when he speaks of the Israelites' passage through the sea as a "baptism" (1 Cor 10, 2).

j: 10, 16-17.   *k:* Rom 10, 4.   *l:* Ex 25, 23-30.   *m:* Ex 26, 31-34. *n:* Ex 16, 32-34; 25, 10.16.21; 30, 1-10; Lv 16, 12-13; Nm 17, 2-7.16-26.   *o:* Ex 25, 16-22; 26, 34; Lv 16, 14-15.   *p:* Ex 27, 21; 30, 7; Lv 24, 8.   *q:* Ex 30, 10; Lv 16, 1-14.

for himself and for the sins of the people. [8]In this way the holy Spirit shows that the way into the sanctuary had not yet been revealed while the outer tabernacle still had its place. [9]*This is a symbol of the present time, in which gifts and sacrifices are offered that cannot perfect the worshiper in conscience [10r]but only in matters of food and drink and various ritual washings: regulations concerning the flesh, imposed until the time of the new order.

Sacrifice of Jesus. [11s]*But when Christ came as high priest of the good things that have come to be, passing through the greater and more perfect tabernacle not made by hands, that is, not belonging to this creation, [12t]he entered once for all into the sanctuary, not with the blood of goats and calves but with his own blood, thus obtaining eternal redemption. [13u]*For if the blood of goats and bulls and the sprinkling of a heifer's ashes can sanctify those who are defiled so that their flesh is cleansed, [14v]*how much more

will the blood of Christ, who through the eternal spirit offered himself unblemished to God, cleanse our consciences from dead works to worship the living God.

[15w]*For this reason he is mediator of a new covenant: since a death has taken place for deliverance from transgressions under the first covenant, those who are called may receive the promised eternal inheritance. [16]*Now where there is a will, the death of the testator must be established. [17]For a will takes effect only at death; it has no force while the testator is alive. [18]Thus not even the first covenant was inaugurated without blood. [19x]*When every commandment had been proclaimed by Moses to all the people according to the law, he took the blood of calves [and goats], together with water and crimson wool and hyssop, and sprinkled both the book itself and all the people, [20y]saying, "This is 'the blood of the covenant which God has enjoined upon you.'" [21z]*In the same way, he sprinkled also the taberna-

---

9, 9: The present time: this expression is equivalent to the "present age," used in contradistinction to the "age to come."

9, 11–14: Christ, the high priest of the spiritual blessings foreshadowed in the Old Testament sanctuary, has actually entered the true sanctuary of heaven that is not of human making (11). His place there is permanent, and his offering is his own blood that won eternal redemption (12). If the sacrifice of animals could bestow legal purification (13), how much more effective is the blood of the sinless, divine Christ who spontaneously offered himself to purge the human race of sin and render it fit for the service of God (14).

9, 11: The good things that have come to be: the majority of later manuscripts here read "the good things to come"; cf 10, 1.

9, 13: A heifer's ashes: ashes from a red heifer that had been burned were mixed with water and used for the cleansing of those who had become ritually defiled by touching a corpse; see Nm 19, 9.14–21.

9, 14: Through the eternal spirit: this expression does not refer either to the holy Spirit or to the divine nature of Jesus but to the life of the risen Christ, "a life that cannot be destroyed" (7, 16).

9, 15–22: Jesus' role as **mediator of a new covenant** is based upon his sacrificial **death** (cf 8, 6). His death has effected **deliverance from transgressions,** i.e., deliverance from sins committed under the old covenant, which the Mosaic sacrifices were incapable of effacing. Until this happened, the **eternal inheritance** promised by God could not be obtained (15). This effect of his work follows the human pattern by which a last will and testament becomes effective only with the death of the testator (16–17). The Mosaic covenant was also associated with death, for Moses made use of

blood to seal the pact between God and the people (18–21). In Old Testament tradition, guilt could normally not be remitted without the use of blood (22; cf Lv 17, 11).

9, 16–17: A will . . . death of the testator: the same Greek word **diathēkē,** meaning "covenant" in vv 15 and 18, is used here with the meaning **will.** The new covenant, unlike the old, is at the same time a will that requires the **death of the testator.** Jesus as eternal Son is the one who established the new covenant together with his Father, author of both covenants; at the same time he is the testator whose death puts his **will** into effect.

9, 19–20: A number of details here are different from the description of this covenant rite in Ex 24, 5–8. Exodus mentions only calves ("young bulls," NAB), not goats (but this addition in Heb is of doubtful authenticity), says nothing of the use of **water and crimson wool and hyssop** (these features probably came from a different rite; cf Lv 14, 3–7; Nm 19, 6–18), and describes Moses as splashing blood on the altar, whereas Heb says he sprinkled it on the book (but both book and altar are meant to symbolize the agreement of God). The words of Moses are also slightly different from those in Exodus and are closer to the words of Jesus at the Last Supper in Mk 14, 24 // Mt 26, 28.

9, 21: According to Ex, the tabernacle did not yet exist at the time of the covenant rite. Moreover, nothing is said of sprinkling it with blood at its subsequent dedication (Ex 40, 9–11).

---

r: 13, 9; Lv 11; 14, 8; Nm 19, 11-21; Col 2, 16.   s: 4, 14; 10, 1.20. t: 7, 27; Mt 26, 28.   u: 10, 4; Lv 16, 6-16; Nm, 19, 9.14-21. v: 10, 10; Rom 5, 9; 1 Tm 3, 9; Ti 2, 14; 1 Pt 1, 18-19; 1 Jn 1, 7; Rv 1, 5.   w: 1 Tm 2, 5.   x: Heb 9, 12-13.   y: Ex 24, 3-8; Mt 26, 28; Mk 14, 24.   z: Ex 40, 9; Lv 8, 15.19.

cle and all the vessels of worship with blood. [22a*]According to the law almost everything is purified by blood, and without the shedding of blood there is no forgiveness.

[23b*]Therefore, it was necessary for the copies of the heavenly things to be purified by these rites, but the heavenly things themselves by better sacrifices than these. [24c]For Christ did not enter into a sanctuary made by hands, a copy of the true one, but heaven itself, that he might now appear before God on our behalf. [25]Not that he might offer himself repeatedly, as the high priest enters each year into the sanctuary with blood that is not his own; [26d*]if that were so, he would have had to suffer repeatedly from the foundation of the world. But now once for all he has appeared at the end of the ages to take away sin by his sacrifice. [27e]Just as it is appointed that human beings die once, and after this the judgment, [28f*]so also Christ, offered once to take away the sins of many, will appear a second time, not to take away sin but to bring salvation to those who eagerly await him.

CHAPTER 10

One Sacrifice instead of Many. [1g*]Since the law has only a shadow of the good things to come, and not the very image of them, it can never make perfect those who come to worship by the same sacrifices that they offer continually each year. [2]Otherwise, would not the sacrifices have ceased to be offered, since the worshipers, once cleansed, would no longer have had any consciousness of sins? [3h]But in those sacrifices there is only a yearly remembrance of sins, [4i]for it is impossible that the blood of bulls and goats take away sins. [5j*]For this reason, when he came into the world, he said:

"Sacrifice and offering you did not
        desire,
    but a body you prepared for me;

9, 22: Without the shedding of blood there is no forgiveness: in fact, ancient Israel did envisage other means of obtaining forgiveness; the Old Testament mentions contrition of heart (Ps 51, 19), fasting (Jl 2, 12), and almsgiving (Sir 3, 29). The author is limiting his horizon to the sacrificial cult, which did always involve the shedding of blood for its expiatory and unitive value.

9, 23–28: Since the blood of animals became a cleansing symbol among Old Testament prefigurements, it was necessary that the realities foreshadowed be brought into being by a shedding of blood that was infinitely more effective by reason of its worth (23). Christ did not simply prefigure the heavenly realities (24) by performing an annual sacrifice with a blood not his own (25); he offered the single sacrifice of himself as the final annulment of sin (26). Just as death is the unrepeatable act that ends a person's life, so Christ's offering of himself for all is the unrepeatable sacrifice that has once for all achieved redemption (27–28).

9, 26: At the end of the ages: the use of expressions such as this shows that the author of Heb, despite his interest in the Platonic concept of an eternal world above superior to temporal reality here below, nevertheless still clings to the Jewish Christian eschatology with its sequence of "the present age" and "the age to come."

9, 28: To take away the sins of many: the reference is to Is 53, 12. Since the Greek verb **anapherō** can mean both "to take away" and "to bear," the author no doubt intended to play upon both senses: Jesus took away sin by bearing it himself. See the similar wordplay in Jn 1, 29. **Many** is used in the Semitic meaning of "all" in the inclusive sense, as in Mk 14, 24. **To those who eagerly await him:** Jesus will appear a second time at the parousia, as the high priest reappeared on the Day of Atonement, emerging from the Holy of Holies, which

he had entered **to take away sin.** This dramatic scene is described in Sir 50, 5–11.

10, 1–10: Christian faith now realizes that the Old Testament sacrifices did not effect the spiritual benefits to come but only prefigured them (1). For if the sacrifices had actually effected the forgiveness of sin, there would have been no reason for their constant repetition (2). They were rather a continual reminder of the people's sins (3). It is not reasonable to suppose that human sins could be removed by the blood of animal sacrifices (4). Christ, therefore, is here shown to understand his mission in terms of Ps 40, 6–8, cited according to the Septuagint (5–7). Jesus acknowledged that the Old Testament sacrifices did not remit the sins of the people and so, perceiving the will of God, offered his own body for this purpose (8–10).

10, 1: A shadow of the good things to come: the term **shadow** was used in 8, 5 to signify the earthly counterpart of the Platonic heavenly reality. But here it means a prefiguration of what is to come in Christ, as it is used in the Pauline literature; cf Col 2, 17.

10, 5–7: A passage from Ps 40, 7–9a is placed in the mouth of the Son at his incarnation. As usual, the author follows the Septuagint text. There is a notable difference in v 5 (Ps 40, 7b), where the Masoretic text reads "ears you have dug for me" ("ears open to obedience you gave me," NAB), but most Septuagint manuscripts have "a body you prepared for me," a reading obviously more suited to the interpretation of Heb.

a: Lv 17, 11.   *b:* Jb 15, 15.   *c:* 7, 25; Rom 8, 34; 1 Jn 2, 1-2.
d: 7, 27; Jn 1, 29; Gal 4, 4.   *e:* Gn 3, 19.   *f:* 10, 10; Is 53, 12.
g: 8, 5; Col 2, 17.   *h:* Lv 16, 21; Nm 5, 15 LXX.   *i:* Is 1, 11; Mi 6, 6-8.   *j:* Ps 40, 7-9.

6 holocausts and sin offerings you took no
delight in.
7 Then I said, 'As is written of me in the
scroll,
Behold, I come to do your will,
O God.' "

8k*First he says, "Sacrifices and offerings,
holocausts and sin offerings, you neither desired nor delighted in." These are offered according to the law. 9l*Then he says, "Behold, I
come to do your will." He takes away the first
to establish the second. 10m By this "will," we
have been consecrated through the offering of
the body of Jesus Christ once for all.

11n*Every priest stands daily at his ministry, offering frequently those same sacrifices
that can never take away sins. 12o But this one
offered one sacrifice for sins, and took his
seat forever at the right hand of God; 13*now
he waits until his enemies are made his footstool. 14p For by one offering he has made
perfect forever those who are being consecrated. 15*The holy Spirit also testifies to us,
for after saying:

16 q"This is the covenant I will establish
with them after those days, says
the Lord:
'I will put my laws in their hearts,
and I will write them upon their
minds,' "

17r*he also says:

"Their sins and their evildoing
I will remember no more."

18Where there is forgiveness of these, there
is no longer offering for sin.

Recalling the Past. 19s*Therefore, brothers, since through the blood of Jesus we
have confidence of entrance into the sanctuary
20t*by the new and living way he opened for us
through the veil, that is, his flesh, 21u*and

**10, 8: Sacrifices and offerings, holocausts and sin of-
ferings:** these four terms taken from the preceding passage of
Ps 40 (with the first two changed to plural forms) are probably intended as equivalents to the four principal types of Old
Testament sacrifices: peace offerings (Lv 3, here called **sacrifices**); cereal offerings (Lv 2, here called **offerings**); **holocausts** (Lv 1); and **sin offerings** (Lv 4–5). This last category
includes the guilt offerings of Lv 5, 14–26.

10, 11–18: Whereas the levitical priesthood offered daily
sacrifices that were ineffectual in remitting sin (11), Jesus offered a single sacrifice that won him a permanent place at
God's right hand. There he has only to await the final outcome of his work (12–13; cf Ps 110, 1). Thus he has brought
into being in his own person the new covenant prophesied by
Jeremiah (31, 33–34) that has rendered meaningless all other
offerings for sin (14–18).

10, 13: Until his enemies are made his footstool: Ps 110,
1 is again used; the reference here is to the period of time between the enthronement of Jesus and his second coming. The
identity of the **enemies** is not specified; cf 1 Cor 15, 25–27.

10, 15–17: The testimony of the scriptures is now invoked
to support what has just preceded. The passage cited is a portion of the new covenant prophecy of Jer 31, 31–34, which
the author previously used in 8, 8–12.

10, 17: He also says: these words are not in the Greek
text, which has only **kai,** "also," but the expression **after saying** in v 15 seems to require such a phrase to divide the Jeremiah text into two sayings. Others understand "the Lord
says" of v 16 (here rendered **says the Lord**) as outside the
quotation and consider v 16b as part of the second saying.
Two ancient versions and a number of minuscules introduce
the words "then he said" or a similar expression at the beginning of v 17.

10, 19–39: Practical consequences from these reflections
on the priesthood and the sacrifice of Christ should make it
clear that Christians may now have direct and confident access
to God through the person of Jesus (19–20), who rules God's
house as high priest (21). They should approach God with sincerity and faith, in the knowledge that through baptism their
sins have been remitted (22), reminding themselves of the hope
they expressed in Christ at that event (23). They are to encourage one another to Christian love and activity (24), not refusing, no matter what the reason, to participate in the community's assembly, especially in view of the parousia (25; cf
1 Thes 4, 13–18). If refusal to participate in the assembly indicates rejection of Christ, no sacrifice exists to obtain forgiveness for so great a sin (26); only the dreadful judgment of God
remains (27). For if violation of the Mosaic law could be punished by death, how much worse will be the punishment of
those who have turned their backs on Christ by despising his
sacrifice and disregarding the gifts of the holy Spirit (28–29).
Judgment belongs to the Lord, and he enacts it by his living
presence (30–31). There was a time when the spirit of their
community caused them to welcome and share their sufferings
(32–34). To revitalize that spirit is to share in the courage of the
Old Testament prophets (cf Is 26, 20; Hb 2, 3–4), the kind of
courage that must distinguish the faith of the Christian (35–39).

10, 20: Through the veil, that is, his flesh: the term **flesh**
is used pejoratively. As the temple veil kept people from entering the Holy of Holies (it was rent at Christ's death, Mk 15,
38), so the flesh of Jesus constituted an obstacle to approaching God.

10, 21: The house of God: this refers back to 3, 6, "we are
his house."

k: 5-6; Ps 40, 7. l: Heb 10, 7; Ps 40, 8; Mt 26, 39; Mk 14, 36; Lk
22, 42; Jn 6, 38. m: 9, 12.14. n: 7, 27; Dt 10, 8; 18, 7. o: Ps
110, 1. p: 9, 28. q: 8, 10; Jer 31, 33. r: 8, 12; Jer 31, 34.
s: 3, 6; 4, 16; 6, 19-20; Eph 1, 7; 3, 12. t: Jn 14, 6 / 6, 19-20; 9,
8.11-12; Mt 27, 51; Mk 15, 38; Lk 23, 45. u: 3, 6.

since we have "a great priest over the house of God," 22v*let us approach with a sincere heart and in absolute trust, with our hearts sprinkled clean from an evil conscience and our bodies washed in pure water. 23wLet us hold unwaveringly to our confession that gives us hope, for he who made the promise is trustworthy. 24We must consider how to rouse one another to love and good works. 25x*We should not stay away from our assembly, as is the custom of some, but encourage one another, and this all the more as you see the day drawing near.

26y*If we sin deliberately after receiving knowledge of the truth, there no longer remains sacrifice for sins 27zbut a fearful prospect of judgment and a flaming fire that is going to consume the adversaries. 28a*Anyone who rejects the law of Moses is put to death without pity on the testimony of two or three witnesses. 29bDo you not think that a much worse punishment is due the one who has contempt for the Son of God, considers unclean the covenant-blood by which he was consecrated, and insults the spirit of grace? 30cWe know the one who said:

"Vengeance is mine; I will repay,"

and again:

"The Lord will judge his people."

31dIt is a fearful thing to fall into the hands of the living God.

32e*Remember the days past when, after you had been enlightened, you endured a great contest of suffering. 33fAt times you were publicly exposed to abuse and affliction; at other times you associated yourselves with those so treated. 34gYou even joined in the sufferings of those in prison and joyfully accepted the confiscation of your property, knowing that you had a better and lasting possession. 35hTherefore, do not throw away your confidence; it will have great recompense. 36iYou need endurance to do the will of God and receive what he has promised.

37 j*"For, after just a brief moment,
he who is to come shall come;
he shall not delay.
38 kBut my just one shall live by faith,
and if he draws back I take no pleasure
in him."

39We are not among those who draw back and perish, but among those who have faith and will possess life.

V: Examples, Discipline, Disobedience

CHAPTER 11

Faith of the Ancients. 11*Faith is the realization of what is hoped for and evidence

See RG 427

10, 22: With our hearts sprinkled clean from an evil conscience: as in 9, 13 (see the note there), the sprinkling motif refers to the Mosaic rite of cleansing from ritual impurity. This could produce only an external purification, whereas sprinkling with the blood of Christ (9, 14) cleanses the **conscience. Washed in pure water:** baptism is elsewhere referred to as a washing; cf 1 Cor 6, 11; Eph 5, 26.

10, 25: Our assembly: the liturgical **assembly** of the Christian community, probably for the celebration of the Eucharist. **The day:** this designation for the parousia also occurs in the Pauline letters, e.g., Rom 2, 16; 1 Cor 3, 13; 1 Thes 5, 2.

10, 26: If we sin deliberately: verse 29 indicates that the author is here thinking of apostasy; cf 3, 12; 6, 4–8.

10, 28: Rejects the law of Moses: evidently not any sin against the law, but idolatry. Dt 17, 2–7 prescribed capital punishment for idolaters who were convicted on the testimony of two or three witnesses.

10, 32: After you had been enlightened: "enlightenment" is an ancient metaphor for baptism (cf Eph 5, 14; Jn 9, 11), but see 6, 4 and the note there.

10, 37–38: In support of his argument, the author uses Hb

2, 3–4 in a wording almost identical with the text of the Codex Alexandrinus of the Septuagint but with the first and second lines of v 4 inverted. He introduces it with a few words from Is 26, 20: **after just a brief moment.** Note the Pauline usage of Hb 2, 4 in Rom 1, 17; Gal 3, 11.

11, 1–40: This chapter draws upon the people and events of the Old Testament to paint an inspiring portrait of religious faith, firm and unyielding in the face of any obstacles that confront it. These pages rank among the most eloquent and lofty to be found in the Bible. They expand the theme announced in 6, 12, to which the author now returns (10, 39). The material of this chapter is developed chronologically. Verses 3–7 draw upon the first nine chapters of Gn; vv 8–22,

v: 9, 13-14; Ez 36, 25; 1 Cor 6, 11; Ti 3, 5; 1 Pt 3, 21. w: 3, 1.6; 4, 14; 1 Cor 10, 13. x: Rom 13, 12; 1 Cor 3, 13. y: 3, 12; 6, 4-8. z: Heb 10, 31; 9, 27; Is 26, 11 LXX; Zep 1, 18. a: Dt 17, 6. b: 6, 6. c: Dt 32, 35.36; Rom 12, 19. d: Heb 10, 27; Mt 10, 28; Lk 12, 4-5. e: 6, 4. f: 1 Cor 4, 9. g: 13, 3; Mt 6, 19-20; Lk 12, 33-34. h: 4, 16. i: Lk 21, 19. j: Is 26, 20; Hb 2, 3. k: Hb 2, 4; Rom 1, 17; Gal 3, 11. l: 1, 3; 3, 14; Rom 8, 24; 2 Cor 4, 18.

of things not seen. [2]Because of it the ancients were well attested. [3m]*By faith we understand that the universe was ordered by the word of God, so that what is visible came into being through the invisible. [4n]*By faith Abel offered to God a sacrifice greater than Cain's. Through this he was attested to be righteous, God bearing witness to his gifts, and through this, though dead, he still speaks. [5o]By faith Enoch was taken up so that he should not see death, and "he was found no more because God had taken him." Before he was taken up, he was attested to have pleased God. [6p]*But without faith it is impossible to please him, for anyone who approaches God must believe that he exists and that he rewards those who seek him. [7q]By faith Noah, warned about what was not yet seen, with reverence built an ark for the salvation of his household. Through this he condemned the world and inherited the righteousness that comes through faith.

[8r]By faith Abraham obeyed when he was called to go out to a place that he was to receive as an inheritance; he went out, not knowing where he was to go. [9s]By faith he sojourned in the promised land as in a foreign country, dwelling in tents with Isaac and Jacob, heirs of the same promise; [10t]for he was looking forward to the city with foundations, whose architect and maker is God. [11u]By faith he received power to generate, even though he was past the normal age—and Sarah herself was sterile—for he thought that the one who had made the promise was trustworthy. [12v]So it was that there came forth from one man, himself as good as dead, descendants as numerous as the stars in the sky and as countless as the sands on the seashore.

[13w]All these died in faith. They did not receive what had been promised but saw it and greeted it from afar and acknowledged themselves to be strangers and aliens on earth, [14]for those who speak thus show that they are seeking a homeland. [15]If they had been thinking of the land from which they had come, they would have had opportunity to return. [16x]But now they desire a better homeland, a heavenly one. Therefore, God is not ashamed to be called their God, for he has prepared a city for them.

[17y]By faith Abraham, when put to the test, offered up Isaac, and he who had received the promises was ready to offer his only son, [18z]of whom it was said, "Through Isaac descendants shall bear your name." [19a]*He reasoned that God was able to raise even from

upon the period of the patriarchs; vv 23–31, upon the time of Moses; vv 32–38, upon the history of the judges, the prophets, and the Maccabean martyrs. The author gives the most extensive description of faith provided in the New Testament, though his interest does not lie in a technical, theological definition. In view of the needs of his audience he describes what authentic faith does, not what it is in itself. Through faith God guarantees the blessings to be hoped for from him, providing evidence in the gift of faith that what he promises will eventually come to pass (1). Because they accepted in faith God's guarantee of the future, the biblical personages discussed in vv 3–38 were themselves commended by God (2). Christians have even greater reason to remain firm in faith since they, unlike the Old Testament men and women of faith, have perceived the beginning of God's fulfillment of his messianic promises (39–40).

11, 1: **Faith is the realization . . . evidence:** the author is not attempting a precise definition. There is dispute about the meaning of the Greek words **hypostasis** and **elenchos,** here translated **realization** and **evidence,** respectively. **Hypostasis** usually means "substance," "being" (as translated in 1, 3), or "reality" (as translated in 3, 14); here it connotes something more subjective, and so **realization** has been chosen rather than "assurance" (RSV). **Elenchos,** usually "proof," is used here in an objective sense and so translated **evidence** rather than the transferred sense of "(inner) conviction" (RSV).

11, 3: **By faith . . . God:** this verse does not speak of the faith of the Old Testament men and women but is in the first person plural. Hence it seems out of place in the sequence of thought.

11, 4: The "Praise of the Ancestors" in Sir 44, 1—50, 21 gives a similar list of heroes. The Cain and Abel narrative in Gn 4, 1–16 does not mention Abel's faith. It says, however, that God "looked with favor on Abel and his offering" (Gn 4, 4); in view of v 6 the author probably understood God's favor to have been activated by Abel's faith. **Though dead, he still speaks:** possibly because his blood "cries out to me from the soil" (Gn 4, 10), but more probably a way of saying that the repeated story of Abel provides ongoing witness to faith.

11, 6: One must believe not only that God exists but that he is concerned about human conduct; the Old Testament defines folly as the denial of this truth; cf Ps 52, 2.

11, 19: **As a symbol:** Isaac's "return from death" is seen

m: Gn 1, 3; Ps 33, 6; Wis 9, 1; Jn 1, 3. n: 12, 24; Gn 4, 4.10. o: Gn 5, 24; Sir 44, 16. p: Wis 4, 10. q: Gn 6, 8-22; Sir 44, 17-18; Mt 24, 37-39; Lk 17, 26-27; 1 Pt 3, 20; 2 Pt 2, 5. r: Gn 12, 1-4; 15, 7-21; Sir 44, 19-22; Acts 7, 2-8; Rom 4, 16-22. s: Gn 12, 8; 13, 12; 23, 4; 26, 3; 35, 27. t: 12, 22; 13, 14; Rv 21, 10-22. u: Gn 17, 19; 21, 2; Rom 4, 19-21 / 1 Cor 10, 13. v: Gn 15, 5; 22, 17; 32, 13; Ex 32, 13; Dt 10, 22; Dn 3, 36 LXX. w: Gn 23, 4; Ps 39, 13. x: 13, 14; Ex 3, 6. y: Gn 22, 1-10; Sir 44, 20; 1 Mc 2, 52; Jas 2, 21. z: Gn 21, 12 LXX; Rom 9, 7. a: Rom 4, 16-22.

the dead, and he received Isaac back as a symbol. [20b]*By faith regarding things still to come Isaac blessed Jacob and Esau. [21c]By faith Jacob, when dying, blessed each of the sons of Joseph and "bowed in worship, leaning on the top of his staff." [22d]By faith Joseph, near the end of his life, spoke of the Exodus of the Israelites and gave instructions about his bones.

[23e]By faith Moses was hidden by his parents for three months after his birth, because they saw that he was a beautiful child, and they were not afraid of the king's edict. [24f]*By faith Moses, when he had grown up, refused to be known as the son of Pharaoh's daughter; [25]he chose to be ill-treated along with the people of God rather than enjoy the fleeting pleasure of sin. [26]He considered the reproach of the Anointed greater wealth than the treasures of Egypt, for he was looking to the recompense. [27g]By faith he left Egypt, not fearing the king's fury, for he persevered as if seeing the one who is invisible. [28h]By faith he kept the Passover and sprinkled the blood, that the Destroyer of the firstborn might not touch them. [29i]By faith they crossed the Red Sea as if it were dry land, but when the Egyptians attempted it they were drowned. [30j]By faith the walls of Jericho fell after being encircled for seven days. [31k]By faith Rahab the harlot did not perish with the disobedient, for she had received the spies in peace.

[32l]What more shall I say? I have not time to tell of Gideon, Barak, Samson, Jephthah, of David and Samuel and the prophets, [33m]who by faith conquered kingdoms, did what was righteous, obtained the promises; they closed the mouths of lions, [34n]put out raging fires, escaped the devouring sword; out of weakness they were made powerful, became strong in battle, and turned back foreign invaders. [35o]Women received back their dead through resurrection. Some were tortured and would not accept deliverance, in order to obtain a better resurrection. [36p]Others endured mockery, scourging, even chains and imprisonment. [37q]They were stoned, sawed in two, put to death at sword's point; they went about in skins of sheep or goats, needy, afflicted, tormented. [38r]The world was not worthy of them. They wandered about in deserts and on mountains, in caves and in crevices in the earth.

[39]Yet all these, though approved because of their faith, did not receive what had been promised. [40]*God had foreseen something better for us, so that without us they should not be made perfect.

CHAPTER 12

See RG 427

God our Father. [1]*Therefore, since we are surrounded by so great a cloud of witnesses, let us rid ourselves of every burden and sin that clings to us and persevere in running the race that lies before us [2]while keeping our eyes fixed on Jesus, the leader and perfecter of faith. For the sake of the joy

---

as a **symbol** of Christ's resurrection. Others understand the words **en parabolē** to mean "in figure," i.e., the word **dead** is used figuratively of Isaac, since he did not really die. But in the one other place that **parabolē** occurs in Heb, it means symbol (9, 9).

11, 20–22: Each of these three patriarchs, Isaac, Jacob, and Joseph, had faith in the future fulfillment of God's promise and renewed this faith when near death.

11, 24–27: The reason given for Moses' departure from Egypt differs from the account in Ex 2, 11–15. The author also gives a christological interpretation of his decision to share the trials of his people.

11, 40: So that without us they should not be made perfect: the heroes of the Old Testament obtained their recompense only after the saving work of Christ had been accomplished. Thus they already enjoy what Christians who are still struggling do not yet possess in its fullness.

12, 1–13: Christian life is to be inspired not only by the Old Testament men and women of faith (1) but above all by Jesus. As the architect of Christian faith, he had himself to en-

dure the cross before receiving the glory of his triumph (2). Reflection on his sufferings should give his followers courage to continue the struggle, if necessary even to the shedding of blood (3–4). Christians should regard their own sufferings as the affectionate correction of the Lord, who loves them as a father loves his children.

12, 1: That clings to us: the meaning is uncertain, since the Greek word **euperistatos,** translated **cling,** occurs only here. The papyrus P46 and one minuscule read **euperispastos,** "easily distracting," which also makes good sense.

---

b: Gn 27, 27-40. *c:* Gn 27, 38-40; 47, 31 LXX; 48, 15-16. *d:* Gn 50, 24-25. *e:* Ex 2, 2; Acts 7, 20. *f:* Ex 2, 10-15; Acts 7, 23-29. *g:* Ex 2, 15; Acts 7, 29. *h:* Ex 12, 21-23; Wis 18, 25; 1 Cor 10, 10. *i:* Ex 14, 22-28. *j:* Jos 6, 12-21. *k:* Jos 2, 1-21; 6, 22-25; Jas 2, 25. *l:* Jgs 4, 6-22; 6, 11—8, 32; 11, 1—12, 7. *m:* Dn 6, 23. *n:* Dn 3, 22-25.49-50. *o:* 1 Kgs 17, 17-24; 2 Kgs 4, 18-37; 2 Mc 7, 1—8, 7, 42. *p:* 2 Chr 36, 16; Jer 20, 2; 37, 15. *q:* 2 Chr 24, 21. *r:* 1 Mc 2, 28-30. *s:* 2, 10; Ps 110, 1; Phil 2, 6-8.

that lay before him he endured the cross, despising its shame, and has taken his seat at the right of the throne of God. ³Consider how he endured such opposition from sinners, in order that you may not grow weary and lose heart. ⁴In your struggle against sin you have not yet resisted to the point of shedding blood. ⁵ᵗYou have also forgotten the exhortation addressed to you as sons:

"My son, do not disdain the discipline of
    the Lord
    or lose heart when reproved by him;
⁶ for whom the Lord loves, he disciplines;
    he scourges every son he
        acknowledges."

⁷ᵘEndure your trials as "discipline"; God treats you as sons. For what "son" is there whom his father does not discipline? ⁸If you are without discipline, in which all have shared, you are not sons but bastards. ⁹ᵛBesides this, we have had our earthly fathers to discipline us, and we respected them. Should we not [then] submit all the more to the Father of spirits and live? ¹⁰They disciplined us for a short time as seemed right to them, but he does so for our benefit, in order that we may share his holiness. ¹¹ʷAt the time, all discipline seems a cause not for joy but for pain, yet later it brings the peaceful fruit of righteousness to those who are trained by it.

¹²ˣSo strengthen your drooping hands and your weak knees. ¹³ʸMake straight paths for your feet, that what is lame may not be dislocated but healed.

Penalties of Disobedience. ¹⁴ᶻStrive for peace with everyone, and for that holiness without which no one will see the Lord. ¹⁵ᵃ*See to it that no one be deprived of the grace of God, that no bitter root spring up and cause trouble, through which many may become defiled, ¹⁶ᵇthat no one be an immoral or profane person like Esau, who sold his birthright for a single meal. ¹⁷ᶜFor you know that later, when he wanted to inherit his father's blessing, he was rejected because he found no opportunity to change his mind, even though he sought the blessing with tears.

¹⁸ᵈ*You have not approached that which could be touched and a blazing fire and gloomy darkness and storm ¹⁹ᵉand a trumpet blast and a voice speaking words such that those who heard begged that no message be further addressed to them, ²⁰ᶠfor they could not bear to hear the command: "If even an animal touches the mountain, it shall be stoned." ²¹ᵍIndeed, so fearful was the spectacle that Moses said, "I am terrified and trembling." ²²ʰNo, you have approached Mount Zion and the city of the living God, the heavenly Jerusalem, and countless angels in festal gathering, ²³ⁱ*and the assembly of the firstborn enrolled in heaven, and God the judge of all, and the spirits of the just made perfect, ²⁴ʲ*and Jesus, the mediator of

12, 15–17: Esau serves as an example in two ways: his **profane** attitude illustrates the danger of apostasy, and his inability to secure a blessing afterward illustrates the impossibility of repenting after falling away (see 6, 4–6).

12, 18–29: As a final appeal for adherence to Christian teaching, the two covenants, of Moses and of Christ, are compared. The Mosaic covenant, the author argues, is shown to have originated in fear of God and threats of divine punishment (18–21). The covenant in Christ gives us direct access to God (22), makes us members of the Christian community, God's children, a sanctified people (23), who have Jesus as mediator to speak for us (24). Not to heed the voice of the risen Christ is a graver sin than the rejection of the word of Moses (25–26). Though Christians fall away, God's kingdom in Christ will remain and his justice will punish those guilty of deserting it (28–29).

12, 18–24: This remarkably beautiful passage contrasts two great assemblies of people: that of the Israelites gathered at Mount Sinai for the sealing of the old covenant and the promulgation of the Mosaic law, and that of the followers of Jesus gathered at **Mount Zion, the heavenly Jerusalem,** the

assembly of the **new covenant.** This latter scene, marked by the presence of **countless angels** and of **Jesus** with his redeeming **blood,** is reminiscent of the celestial liturgies of the Book of Revelation.

12, 23: The assembly of the firstborn enrolled in heaven: this expression may refer to the angels of v 22, or to the heroes of the Old Testament (see ch 11), or to the entire assembly of the new covenant.

12, 24: Speaks more eloquently: the blood of Abel, the first human blood to be shed, is contrasted with that of Jesus. Abel's blood cried out from the earth for vengeance, but the blood of Jesus has opened the way for everyone, providing cleansing and access to God (10, 19).

t: Prv 3, 11-12 / Dt 8, 5; 1 Cor 11, 32.   *u:* Prv 13, 24; Sir 30, 1.
v: Nm 16, 22; 27, 16 LXX.   *w:* 2 Cor 4, 17; Phil 1, 11; Jas 3, 18.
x: Is 35, 3; Sir 25, 23; Jb 4, 3-4.   *y:* Prv 4, 26 LXX.   *z:* Rom 12,
18; 14, 19.   *a:* Dt 29, 18 (17 LXX).   *b:* Gn 25, 33.   *c:* Gn 27,
34-38.   *d:* Ex 19, 12-14; Dt 4, 11; 5, 22-23.   *e:* Ex 19, 16.19; 20,
18-19.   *f:* Ex 19, 12-13.   *g:* Dt 9, 19.   *h:* Gal 4, 26; Rv 21, 2.
i: Lk 10, 20; Rv 5, 11.   *j:* 7, 22; 8, 6; 9, 15 / 11, 4; Gn 4, 10.

a new covenant, and the sprinkled blood that speaks more eloquently than that of Abel.

25k See that you do not reject the one who speaks. For if they did not escape when they refused the one who warned them on earth, how much more in our case if we turn away from the one who warns from heaven. 26l His voice shook the earth at that time, but now he has promised, "I will once more shake not only earth but heaven." 27m That phrase, "once more," points to [the] removal of shaken, created things, so that what is unshaken may remain. 28n Therefore, we who are receiving the unshakable kingdom should have gratitude, with which we should offer worship pleasing to God in reverence and awe. 29o For our God is a consuming fire.

VI: Final Exhortation, Blessing, Greetings

CHAPTER 13

See RG 427–28 1*Let mutual love continue. 2p Do not neglect hospitality, for through it some have unknowingly entertained angels. 3q Be mindful of prisoners as if sharing their imprisonment, and of the ill-treated as of yourselves, for you also are in the body. 4r Let marriage be honored among all and the marriage bed be kept undefiled, for God will judge the immoral and adulterers. 5s Let your life be free from love of money but be content with what you have, for he has said, "I will never forsake you or abandon you." 6t Thus we may say with confidence:

"The Lord is my helper,
[and] I will not be afraid.
What can anyone do to me?"

7Remember your leaders who spoke the word of God to you. Consider the outcome of their way of life and imitate their faith. 8u Jesus Christ is the same yesterday, today, and forever.

9v*Do not be carried away by all kinds of strange teaching. It is good to have our hearts strengthened by grace and not by foods, which do not benefit those who live by them. 10*We have an altar from which those who serve the tabernacle have no right to eat. 11w The bodies of the animals whose blood the high priest brings into the sanctuary as a sin offering are burned outside the camp. 12x Therefore, Jesus also suffered outside the gate, to consecrate the people by his own blood. 13Let us then go to him outside the camp, bearing the reproach that he bore. 14y For here we have no lasting city, but we seek the one that is to come. 15z Through him [then] let us continually offer God a sacrifice of praise, that is, the fruit of lips that confess his name. 16a Do not neglect to do good and to share what you have; God is pleased by sacrifices of that kind.

17*Obey your leaders and defer to them, for they keep watch over you and will have to give an account, that they may fulfill their task with joy and not with sorrow, for that would be of no advantage to you.

18Pray for us, for we are confident that we have a clear conscience, wishing to act rightly in every respect. 19I especially ask for

---

13, 1–16: After recommendations on social and moral matters (1–6), the letter turns to doctrinal issues. The fact that the original leaders are dead should not cause the recipients of this letter to lose their faith (7), for Christ still lives and he remains always the same (8). They must not rely for their personal sanctification on regulations concerning foods (9), nor should they entertain the notion that Judaism and Christianity can be intermingled (10; cf the notes on Gal 2, 11–14 and 2, 15–21). As Jesus died separated from his own people, so must the Christian community remain apart from the religious doctrines of Judaism (11–14). Christ must be the heart and center of the community (15–16).

13, 9: **Strange teaching**: this doctrine about **foods** probably refers to the Jewish food laws; in view of v 10, however, the author may be thinking of the Mosaic sacrificial banquets.

13, 10: **We have an altar**: this does not refer to the Eu-

charist, which is never clearly mentioned in Heb, but to the sacrifice of Christ.

13, 17–25: Recommending obedience to the leaders of the community, the author asks for prayers (17–19). The letter concludes with a blessing (20–21), a final request for the acceptance of its message (22), information regarding Timothy (23) and general greetings (24–25).

---

k: Ex 20, 19.   l: Ex 19, 18; Jgs 5, 4-5; Ps 68, 9; Hg 2, 6.   m: Is 66, 22; Mt 24, 35; Mk 13, 31; Lk 21, 33.   n: Dn 7, 14.18 / Rom 1, 9.   o: Dt 4, 24; Is 33, 14.   p: Gn 18, 3; 19, 2-3; Jgs 6, 11-22; Tb 5. 4.   q: Mt 25, 36.   r: 1 Cor 5, 13; Eph 5, 5.   s: Dt 31, 6.8; Jos 1, 5.   t: Pss 27, 1-3; 118, 6.   u: 1, 12; 7, 24; Rv 1, 17.   v: Rom 14, 17; 1 Cor 8, 8; Eph 4, 14; Col 2, 16.   w: Ex 29, 14; Lv 16, 27.   x: Mt 21, 39; Mk 12, 8; Lk 20, 15; Jn 19, 17.   y: 11, 10.14.   z: Hos 14, 3.   a: Phil 4, 18.

your prayers that I may be restored to you very soon.

20b*May the God of peace, who brought up from the dead the great shepherd of the sheep by the blood of the eternal covenant, Jesus our Lord, 21furnish you with all that is good, that you may do his will. May he carry out in you what is pleasing to him through Jesus Christ, to whom be glory forever [and ever]. Amen.

22Brothers, I ask you to bear with this message of encouragement, for I have written to you rather briefly. 23cI must let you know that our brother Timothy has been set free. If he comes soon, I shall see you together with him. 24Greetings to all your leaders and to all the holy ones. Those from Italy send you greetings. 25dGrace be with all of you.

13, 20–21: These verses constitute one of the most beautiful blessings in the New Testament. The resurrection of Jesus is presupposed throughout Heb, since it is included in the author's frequently expressed idea of his exaltation, but this is the only place where it is explicitly mentioned.

b: Is 63, 11; Zec 9, 11; Jn 10, 11; Acts 2, 24; Rom 15, 33.   c: Acts 16, 1.   d: Ti 3, 15.

THE CATHOLIC LETTERS

See RG
429–55

In addition to the thirteen letters attributed to Paul and the Letter to the Hebrews, the New Testament contains seven other letters. Three of these are attributed to John, two to Peter, and one each to James and Jude, all personages of the apostolic age. The term "catholic letter" first appears, with reference only to 1 John, in the writings of Apollonius of Ephesus, a second-century apologist, known only from a citation in Eusebius's *Ecclesiastical History*. Eusebius himself (A.D. 260–340) used the term to refer to all seven letters.

The reason for the term "catholic," which means "universal," was the perception that these letters, unlike those of Paul, which were directed to a particular local church, were apparently addressed more generally to the universal church. This designation is not entirely accurate, however. On the one hand, Hebrews has no specifically identified addressees, and originally this was probably true of Ephesians as well. On the other hand, 3 John is addressed to a named individual, 2 John to a specific, though unnamed, community, and 1 Peter to a number of churches that are specified as being located in Asia Minor.

While all seven of these writings begin with an epistolary formula, several of them do not appear to be real letters in the modern sense of the term. In the ancient world it was not unusual to cast an exhortation in the form of a letter for literary effect, a phenomenon comparable to the "open letter" that is sometimes used today.

With the exception of 1 Peter and 1 John, the ancient church showed reluctance to include the catholic letters in the New Testament canon. The reason for this was widespread doubt whether they had actually been written by the apostolic figures to whom they are attributed. The early Christians saw the New Testament as the depository of apostolic faith; therefore, they wished to include only the testimony of apostles. Today we distinguish more clearly between the authorship of a work and its canonicity: even though written by other, later witnesses than those whose names they bear, these writings nevertheless testify to the apostolic faith and constitute canonical scripture. By the late fourth or early fifth centuries, most objections had been overcome in both the Greek and Latin churches (though not in the Syriac), and all seven of the catholic letters have since been acknowledged as canonical.

The Letter of James

See RG
429–34

The person to whom this letter is ascribed can scarcely be one of the two members of the Twelve who bore the name James (see Mt 10, 2–3; Mk 3, 17–18; Lk 6, 14–15), for he is not identified as an apostle but only as "slave of God and of the Lord Jesus Christ" (1, 1). This designation most probably refers to the third New Testament personage named James, a relative of Jesus who is usually called "brother of the Lord" (see Mt 13, 55; Mk 6, 3). He was the leader of the Jewish Christian community in Jerusalem whom Paul acknowledged as one of the "pillars" (Gal 2, 9). In Acts he appears as the authorized spokesman for the Jewish Christian

1703

position in the early Church (Acts 12, 17; 15, 13–21). According to the Jewish historian Josephus (Antiquities 20, 9, 1 § 200–203), he was stoned to death by the Jews under the high priest Ananus II in A.D. 62.

The letter is addressed to "the twelve tribes in the dispersion." In Old Testament terminology the term "twelve tribes" designates the people of Israel; the "dispersion" or "diaspora" refers to the non-Palestinian Jews who had settled throughout the Greco-Roman world (see Jn 7, 35). Since in Christian thought the church is the new Israel, the address probably designates the Jewish Christian churches located in Palestine, Syria, and elsewhere. Or perhaps the letter is meant more generally for all Christian communities, and the "dispersion" has the symbolic meaning of exile from our true home, as it has in the address of 1 Peter (1, 1). The letter is so markedly Jewish in character that some scholars have regarded it as a Jewish document subsequently "baptized" by a few Christian insertions, but such an origin is scarcely tenable in view of the numerous contacts discernible between the Letter of James and other New Testament literature.

From the viewpoint of its literary form, James is a letter only in the most conventional sense; it has none of the characteristic features of a real letter except the address. It belongs rather to the genre of *parenesis* or exhortation and is concerned almost exclusively with ethical conduct. It therefore falls within the tradition of Jewish wisdom literature, such as can be found in the Old Testament (Proverbs, Sirach) and in the extracanonical Jewish literature (*Testaments of the Twelve Patriarchs,* the *Books of Enoch,* the *Manual of Discipline* found at Qumran). More specifically, it consists of sequences of didactic proverbs, comparable to Tob 4, 5–19, to many passages in Sirach, and to sequences of sayings in the synoptic gospels. Numerous passages in James treat of subjects that also appear in the synoptic sayings of Jesus, especially in Matthew's Sermon on the Mount, but the correspondences are too general to establish any literary dependence. James represents a type of early Christianity that emphasized sound teaching and responsible moral behavior. Ethical norms are derived not primarily from christology, as in Paul, but from a concept of salvation that involves conversion, baptism, forgiveness of sin, and expectation of judgment (1, 17; 4, 12).

Paradoxically, this very Jewish work is written in an excellent Greek style, which ranks among the best in the New Testament and appears to be the work of a trained Hellenistic writer. Those who continue to regard James of Jerusalem as its author are therefore obliged to suppose that a secretary must have put the letter into its present literary form. This assumption is not implausible in the light of ancient practice. Some regard the letter as one of the earliest writings in the New Testament and feel that its content accurately reflects what we would expect of the leader of Jewish Christianity. Moreover, they argue that the type of Jewish Christianity reflected in the letter cannot be situated historically after the fall of Jerusalem in A.D. 70.

Others, however, believe it more likely that James is a pseudonymous work of a later period. In addition to its Greek style, they observe further that (a) the prestige that the writer is assumed to enjoy points to the later legendary reputation of James; (b) the discussion of the importance of good works seems to presuppose a debate subsequent to that in Paul's own day; (c) the author does not rely upon prescriptions of the Mosaic law, as we would expect from the historical James; (d) the letter contains no allusions to James's own history and to his relationship with Jesus or to the early Christian community of Jerusalem. For these reasons, many recent interpreters assign James to the period A.D. 90–100.

The principal divisions of the Letter of James are the following:

I: Address (1, 1)

II: The Value of Trials and Temptation (1, 2–18)

III: Exhortations and Warnings (1, 19—5, 12)

IV: The Power of Prayer (5, 13–20)

I: Address

CHAPTER 1

See RG
430-31

1a *James, a slave of God and of the Lord Jesus Christ, to the twelve tribes in the dispersion, greetings.

II: The Value of Trials and Temptation

Perseverance in Trial. *2b* *Consider it all joy, my brothers, when you encounter various trials, *3* *for you know that the testing of your faith produces perseverance. *4* And let perseverance be perfect, so that you may be perfect and complete, lacking in nothing. *5c* *But if any of you lacks wisdom, he should ask God who gives to all generously and ungrudgingly, and he will be given it. *6d* But he should ask in faith, not doubting, for the one who doubts is like a wave of the sea that is driven and tossed about by the wind. *7* For that person must not suppose that he will receive anything from the Lord, *8* since he is a man of two minds, unstable in all his ways. *9e* *The brother in lowly circumstances should take pride in his high standing, *10f* and the rich one in his lowliness, for he will pass away "like the flower of the field." *11* For the sun comes up with its scorching heat and dries up the grass, its flower droops, and the beauty of its appearance vanishes. So will the rich person fade away in the midst of his pursuits.

Temptation. *12g* *Blessed is the man who perseveres in temptation, for when he has been proved he will receive the crown of life that he promised to those who love him. *13h* *No one experiencing temptation should say, "I am being tempted by God"; for God is not subject to temptation to evil, and he himself tempts no one. *14* Rather, each person is tempted when he is lured and enticed by his own desire. *15* Then desire conceives and brings forth sin, and when sin reaches maturity it gives birth to death.

16 *Do not be deceived, my beloved brothers: *17* *all good giving and every perfect gift is from above, coming down from the Father of lights, with whom there is no alteration or shadow caused by change. *18i* *He willed to give us birth by the word of truth that we may be a kind of firstfruits of his creatures.

1, 1: James, a slave of God and of the Lord Jesus Christ: a declaration of the writer's authority for instructing the Christian communities; cf Rom 1, 1. Regarding the identity of the author, see Introduction. **Dispersion:** see Introduction.

1, 2: Consider it all joy . . . various trials: a frequent teaching of the New Testament derived from the words and sufferings of Jesus (Mt 5, 10–12; Jn 10, 11; Acts 5, 41).

1, 3–8: The sequence of testing, perseverance, and being perfect and complete indicates the manner of attaining spiritual maturity and full preparedness for the coming of Christ (5, 7–12; cf 1 Pt 1, 6–7; Rom 5, 3–5). These steps require wisdom (5).

1, 5: Wisdom: a gift that God readily grants to all who ask in faith and that sustains the Christian in times of trial. It is a kind of knowledge or understanding not accessible to the unbeliever or those who doubt, which gives the recipient an understanding of the real importance of events. In this way a Christian can deal with adversity with great calm and hope (cf 1 Cor 2, 6–12).

1, 9–11: Throughout his letter (see 2, 5; 4, 10.13–16; 5, 1–6), the author reaffirms the teaching of Jesus that worldly prosperity is not necessarily a sign of God's favor but can even be a hindrance to proper humility before God (cf Lk 6, 20–25; 12, 16–21; 16, 19–31).

1, 12: Temptation: the Greek word used here is the same one used for "trials" in v 2. **The crown of life:** in ancient Palestine, crowns or wreaths of flowers were worn at festive occasions as signs of joy and honor. In the Hellenistic world, wreaths were given as a reward to great statesmen, soldiers, athletes. **Life:** here means eternal life. **He promised:** some manuscripts read "God" or "the Lord," while the best witnesses do not specify the subject of "promised."

1, 13–15: It is contrary to what we know of God for God to be the author of human temptation (13). In the commission of a sinful act, one is first beguiled by passion (14), then consent is given, which in turn causes the sinful act. When sin permeates the entire person, it incurs the ultimate penalty of death (15).

1, 16–18: The author here stresses that God is the source of all good and of good alone, and the evil of temptation does not come from him.

1, 17: All good giving and every perfect gift may be a proverb written in hexameter. **Father of lights:** God is here called the Father of the heavenly luminaries, i.e., the stars, sun, and moon that he created (Gn 1, 14–18). Unlike orbs moving from nadir to zenith, he never changes or diminishes in brightness.

1, 18: Acceptance of the gospel message, **the word of truth,** constitutes new birth (Jn 3, 5–6) and makes the recipient the **firstfruits** (i.e., the cultic offering of the earliest grains, symbolizing the beginning of an abundant harvest) of a new creation; cf 1 Cor 15, 20; Rom 8, 23.

a: Jn 7, 35; 1 Pt 1, 1.   *b:* Rom 5, 3-5; 1 Pt 1, 6; 4, 13-16.   *c:* Prv 2, 2-6; Wis 9, 4.9-12.   *d:* Mt 7, 7; Mk 11, 24.   *e:* 2, 5.   *f:* Is 40, 6-7.   *g:* 1 Cor 9, 25; 2 Tm 4, 8; 1 Pt 5, 4; Rv 2, 10.   *h:* Sir 15, 11-20; 1 Cor 10, 13.   *i:* Jn 1, 12-13; 1 Pt 1, 23.

III: Exhortations and Warnings

Doers of the Word. [19]j*Know this, my dear brothers: everyone should be quick to hear, slow to speak, slow to wrath, [20]kfor the wrath of a man does not accomplish the righteousness of God. [21]lTherefore, put away all filth and evil excess and humbly welcome the word that has been planted in you and is able to save your souls.

[22]mBe doers of the word and not hearers only, deluding yourselves. [23]For if anyone is a hearer of the word and not a doer, he is like a man who looks at his own face in a mirror. [24]He sees himself, then goes off and promptly forgets what he looked like. [25]n*But the one who peers into the perfect law of freedom and perseveres, and is not a hearer who forgets but a doer who acts, such a one shall be blessed in what he does.

[26]o*If anyone thinks he is religious and does not bridle his tongue but deceives his heart, his religion is vain. [27]p*Religion that is pure and undefiled before God and the Father is this: to care for orphans and widows in their affliction and to keep oneself unstained by the world.

See RG 431-32

CHAPTER 2

Sin of Partiality. [1]*My brothers, show no partiality as you adhere to the faith in our glorious Lord Jesus Christ. [2]For if a man with gold rings on his fingers and in fine clothes comes into your assembly, and a poor person in shabby clothes also comes in, [3]and you pay attention to the one wearing the fine clothes and say, "Sit here, please," while you say to the poor one, "Stand there," or "Sit at my feet," [4]*have you not made distinctions among yourselves and become judges with evil designs?

[5]q*Listen, my beloved brothers. Did not God choose those who are poor in the world to be rich in faith and heirs of the kingdom that he promised to those who love him? [6]But you dishonored the poor person. Are not the rich oppressing you? And do they themselves not haul you off to court? [7]rIs it not they who blaspheme the noble name that was invoked over you? [8]s*However, if you fulfill the royal law according to the scripture, "You shall love your neighbor as yourself," you are doing well. [9]tBut if you show partiality, you commit sin, and are convicted by the law as transgressors. [10]uFor whoever keeps the whole law, but falls short in one particular, has become guilty in respect to all of it. [11]vFor he who said, "You shall not commit adultery," also said, "You shall not kill." Even if you do not commit adultery but kill, you have become a transgressor of the law. [12]w*So speak and so act as people who will be judged by the

---

1, 19–25: To **be quick to hear** the gospel is to accept it readily and to act in conformity with it, removing from one's soul whatever is opposed to it, so that it may take root and effect salvation (19–21). To listen to the gospel message but not practice it is failure to improve oneself (22–24). Only conformity of life to the perfect law of true freedom brings happiness (25).

1, 25: Peers into the perfect law: the image of a person doing this is paralleled to that of hearing God's word. The **perfect law** applies the Old Testament description of the Mosaic law to the gospel of Jesus Christ that brings freedom.

1, 26–27: A practical application of v 22 is now made.

1, 26: For control of the tongue, see the note on 3, 1–12.

1, 27: In the Old Testament, orphans and widows are classical examples of the defenseless and oppressed.

2, 1–13: In the Christian community there must be no discrimination or favoritism based on status or wealth (2–4; cf Mt 5, 3; 11, 5; 23, 6; 1 Cor 1, 27–29). Divine favor rather consists in God's election and promises (5). The rich who oppress the poor blaspheme the name of Christ (6–7). By violating one law of love of neighbor, they offend against the whole law (8–11). On the other hand, conscious awareness of the final judgment helps the faithful to fulfill the whole law (12).

2, 4: When Christians show favoritism to the rich they are guilty of the worst kind of prejudice and discrimination. The author says that such Christians set themselves up as judges who judge not by divine law but by the basest, self-serving motives.

2, 5: The poor, "God's poor" of the Old Testament, were seen by Jesus as particularly open to God for belief in and reliance on him alone (Lk 6, 20). God's law cannot tolerate their oppression in any way (9).

2, 8: Royal: literally, "kingly"; because the Mosaic law came from God, the universal king. There may be an allusion to Jesus' uses of this commandment in his preaching of the kingdom of God (Mt 22, 39; Mk 12, 31; Lk 10, 27).

2, 12–13: The law upon which the last judgment will be based is the law of freedom. As Jesus taught, mercy (which participates in God's own loving mercy) includes forgiveness of those who wrong us (see Mt 6, 12.14–15).

j: Prv 14, 17; Sir 5, 11.   k: Eph 4, 26.   l: Col 3, 8.   m: Mt 7, 26; Rom 2, 13.   n: 2, 12; Ps 19, 8; Rom 8, 2.   o: 3, 2; Ps 34, 14.   p: Ex 22, 21.   q: 1 Cor 1, 26-28; Rv 2, 9.   r: 1 Pt 4, 4.   s: Lv 19, 18; Mt 22, 39; Rom 13, 9.   t: Dt 1, 17.   u: Gal 3, 10.   v: Ex 20, 13-14; Dt 5, 17-18.   w: 1, 25; Rom 8, 2.

law of freedom. [13x]For the judgment is merciless to one who has not shown mercy; mercy triumphs over judgment.

Faith and Works. [14y]*What good is it, my brothers, if someone says he has faith but does not have works? Can that faith save him? [15]If a brother or sister has nothing to wear and has no food for the day, [16z]and one of you says to them, "Go in peace, keep warm, and eat well," but you do not give them the necessities of the body, what good is it? [17]So also faith of itself, if it does not have works, is dead.

[18]Indeed someone may say, "You have faith and I have works." Demonstrate your faith to me without works, and I will demonstrate my faith to you from my works. [19]You believe that God is one. You do well. Even the demons believe that and tremble. [20]Do you want proof, you ignoramus, that faith without works is useless? [21a]Was not Abraham our father justified by works when he offered his son Isaac upon the altar? [22]You see that faith was active along with his works, and faith was completed by the works. [23b]Thus the scripture was fulfilled that says, "Abraham believed God, and it was credited to him as righteousness," and he was called "the friend of God." [24]See how a person is justified by works and not by faith alone. [25c]And in the same way, was not Rahab the harlot also justified by works when she welcomed the messengers and sent them out by a different route? [26]For just as a body without a spirit is dead, so also faith without works is dead.

CHAPTER 3

See RG
432-33

Power of the Tongue. [1]*Not many of you should become teachers, my brothers, for you realize that we will be judged more strictly, [2d]for we all fall short in many respects. If anyone does not fall short in speech, he is a perfect man, able to bridle his whole body also. [3]If we put bits into the mouths of horses to make them obey us, we also guide their whole bodies. [4]It is the same with ships: even though they are so large and driven by fierce winds, they are steered by a very small rudder wherever the pilot's inclination wishes. [5]In the same way the tongue is a small member and yet has great pretensions.

Consider how small a fire can set a huge forest ablaze. [6]The tongue is also a fire. It exists among our members as a world of malice, defiling the whole body and setting the entire course of our lives on fire, itself set on fire by Gehenna. [7]For every kind of beast and bird, of reptile and sea creature, can be tamed and has been tamed by the human species, [8e]but no human being can tame the tongue. It is a restless evil, full of deadly poison. [9]With it we bless the Lord and Father, and with it we curse human beings who are made in the likeness of God. [10]From the same mouth come blessing and cursing. This need not be so, my brothers. [11]Does a spring gush forth from the same opening both pure and brackish water? [12f]Can a fig tree, my brothers, produce olives, or a grapevine figs? Neither can salt water yield fresh.

True Wisdom. [13g]*Who among you is wise and understanding? Let him show his works by a good life in the humility that comes from wisdom. [14]But if you have bitter jealousy and selfish ambition in your hearts, do not boast and be false to the truth. [15]Wisdom of this kind does not come down from above but is earthly, unspiritual, demonic. [16]For where

---

2, 14–26: The theme of these verses is the relationship of faith and works (deeds). It has been argued that the teaching here contradicts that of Paul (see especially Rom 4, 5–6). The problem can only be understood if the different viewpoints of the two authors are seen. Paul argues against those who claim to participate in God's salvation because of their good deeds as well as because they have committed themselves to trust in God through Jesus Christ (Paul's concept of faith). Paul certainly understands, however, the implications of true faith for a life of love and generosity (see Gal 5, 6.13–15). The author of James is well aware that proper conduct can only come about with an authentic commitment to God in faith (18.26). Many think he was seeking to correct a misunderstanding of Paul's view.

3, 1–12: The use and abuse of the important role of teaching in the church (1) are here related to the good and bad use of the tongue (9–12), the instrument through which teaching was chiefly conveyed (see Sir 5, 11—6, 1; 28, 12–26).

3, 13–18: This discussion of true wisdom is related to the previous reflection on the role of the teacher as one who is in control of his speech. The qualities of the wise man endowed from above are detailed (17–18; cf Gal 5, 22–23), in contrast to the qualities of earthbound wisdom (14–16; cf 2 Cor 12, 20).

x: Mt 5, 7; 6, 14-15; 18, 32-33. y: Mt 25, 31-46; Gal 5, 6. z: 1 Jn 3, 17. a: Gn 22, 9-12; Heb 11, 17. b: Gn 15, 6; Rom 4, 3; Gal 3, 6/2 Chr 20, 7; Is 41, 8. c: Jos 2, 1-21. d: 1, 26; Prv 13, 3; Sir 28, 12-26. e: Ps 140, 4. f: Mt 7, 16-17. g: Eph 4, 1-2.

jealousy and selfish ambition exist, there is disorder and every foul practice. [17h]But the wisdom from above is first of all pure, then peaceable, gentle, compliant, full of mercy and good fruits, without inconstancy or insincerity. [18i]And the fruit of righteousness is sown in peace for those who cultivate peace.

See RG 432–34

CHAPTER 4

Causes of Division. [1j]*Where do the wars and where do the conflicts among you come from? Is it not from your passions that make war within your members? [2]You covet but do not possess. You kill and envy but you cannot obtain; you fight and wage war. You do not possess because you do not ask. [3]You ask but do not receive, because you ask wrongly, to spend it on your passions. [4k]*Adulterers! Do you not know that to be a lover of the world means enmity with God? Therefore, whoever wants to be a lover of the world makes himself an enemy of God. [5]*Or do you suppose that the scripture speaks without meaning when it says, "The spirit that he has made to dwell in us tends toward jealousy"? [6l]*But he bestows a greater grace; therefore, it says:

"God resists the proud,
  but gives grace to the humble."

[7m]So submit yourselves to God. Resist the devil, and he will flee from you. [8n]Draw near to God, and he will draw near to you. Cleanse your hands, you sinners, and purify your hearts, you of two minds. [9]Begin to lament, to mourn, to weep. Let your laughter be turned into mourning and your joy into dejection. [10o]Humble yourselves before the Lord and he will exalt you.

[11]*Do not speak evil of one another, brothers. Whoever speaks evil of a brother or judges his brother speaks evil of the law and judges the law. If you judge the law, you are not a doer of the law but a judge. [12p]There is one lawgiver and judge who is able to save or to destroy. Who then are you to judge your neighbor?

Warning against Presumption. [13]*Come now, you who say, "Today or tomorrow we shall go into such and such a town, spend a year there doing business, and make a profit"— [14q]*you have no idea what your life will be like tomorrow. You are a puff of smoke that appears briefly and then disappears. [15]*Instead you should say, "If the Lord wills it, we shall live to do this or that." [16]But

---

4, 1–12: The concern here is with the origin of conflicts in the Christian community. These are occasioned by love **of the world,** which **means enmity with God** (4). Further, the conflicts are bound up with failure to pray properly (cf Mt 7, 7–11; Jn 14, 13; 15, 7; 16, 23), that is, not asking God at all or using God's kindness only for one's pleasure (2–3). In contrast, the proper dispositions are submission to God, repentance, humility, and resistance to evil (7–10).

4, 1: Passions: the Greek word here (literally, "pleasures") does not indicate that pleasure is evil. Rather, as the text points out (2–3), it is the manner in which one deals with needs and desires that determines good or bad. The motivation for any action can be wrong, especially if one does not pray properly but seeks only selfish enjoyment (3).

4, 4: Adulterers: a common biblical image for the covenant between God and his people is the marriage bond. In this image, breaking the covenant with God is likened to the unfaithfulness of adultery.

4, 5: The meaning of this saying is difficult because the author of Jas cites, probably from memory, a passage that is not in any extant manuscript of the Bible. Other translations of the text with a completely different meaning are possible: "The Spirit that he (God) made to dwell in us yearns (for us) jealously," or, "He (God) yearns jealously for the spirit that he has made to dwell in us." If this last translation is correct, the author perhaps had in mind an apocryphal religious text that

echoes the idea that God is zealous for his creatures; cf Ex 20, 5; Dt 4, 24; Zec 8, 2.

4, 6: The point of this whole argument is that God wants the happiness of all, but that selfishness and pride can make that impossible. We must work with him in humility (10).

4, 11: Slander of a fellow Christian does not break just one commandment but makes mockery of the authority of law in general and therefore of God.

4, 13–17: The uncertainty of life (14), its complete dependence on God, and the necessity of submitting to God's will (15) all help one know and do what is right (17). To disregard this is to live in pride and arrogance (16); failure to do what is right is a sin (17).

4, 14: Some important Greek manuscripts here have, "You who have no idea what tomorrow will bring. Why, what is your life?"

4, 15: If the Lord wills it: often in piety referred to as the **"conditio Jacobaea,"** the condition James says we should employ to qualify all our plans.

---

h: 1, 17; Wis 7, 22-23. *i:* Mt 5, 9. *j:* Rom 7, 23; 1 Pt 2, 11. *k:* Mt 6, 24; Lk 16, 13; Rom 8, 7; 1 Jn 2, 15-16. *l:* Jb 22, 29; Prv 3, 34; Mt 23, 12; 1 Pt 5, 5. *m:* 1 Pt 5, 8-9. *n:* Zec 1, 3; Mal 3, 7. *o:* Jb 5, 11; Mt 23, 12; Lk 14, 11; 18, 14; 1 Pt 5, 6. *p:* Mt 7, 1; Rom 2, 1; 14, 4. *q:* Prv 27, 1 / Ps 39, 6-7.

now you are boasting in your arrogance. All such boasting is evil. [17r]*So for one who knows the right thing to do and does not do it, it is a sin.

See RG 433-34

CHAPTER 5

Warning to the Rich. [1s]*Come now, you rich, weep and wail over your impending miseries. [2t]Your wealth has rotted away, your clothes have become moth-eaten, [3u]your gold and silver have corroded, and that corrosion will be a testimony against you; it will devour your flesh like a fire. You have stored up treasure for the last days. [4v]Behold, the wages you withheld from the workers who harvested your fields are crying aloud, and the cries of the harvesters have reached the ears of the Lord of hosts. [5w]You have lived on earth in luxury and pleasure; you have fattened your hearts for the day of slaughter. [6x]*You have condemned; you have murdered the righteous one; he offers you no resistance.

Patience and Oaths. [7]*Be patient, therefore, brothers, until the coming of the Lord. See how the farmer waits for the precious fruit of the earth, being patient with it until it receives the early and the late rains. [8y]You too must be patient. Make your hearts firm, because the coming of the Lord is at hand. [9]Do not complain, brothers, about one another, that you may not be judged. Behold, the Judge is standing before the gates. [10]Take as an example of hardship and patience, brothers, the prophets who spoke in the name of the Lord. [11z]Indeed we call blessed those who have persevered. You have heard of the perseverance of Job, and you have seen the purpose of the Lord, because "the Lord is compassionate and merciful."

[12a]*But above all, my brothers, do not swear, either by heaven or by earth or with any other oath, but let your "Yes" mean "Yes" and your "No" mean "No," that you may not incur condemnation.

IV: The Power of Prayer

Anointing of the Sick. [13]Is anyone among you suffering? He should pray. Is anyone in good spirits? He should sing praise. [14b]*Is anyone among you sick? He should summon the presbyters of the church, and they should pray over him and anoint [him] with oil in the name of the Lord, [15]*and the prayer of faith will save the sick person, and the Lord will raise him up. If he has committed any sins, he will be forgiven.

Confession and Intercession. [16]Therefore, confess your sins to one another and pray for one another, that you may be healed. The fervent prayer of a righteous person is very

---

4, 17: It is a sin: those who live arrogantly, forgetting the contingency of life and our dependence on God (13–16), are guilty of sin.

5, 1–6: Continuing with the theme of the transitory character of life on earth, the author points out the impending ruin of the godless. He denounces the unjust rich, whose victims cry to heaven for judgment on their exploiters (4–6). The decay and corrosion of the costly garments and metals, which symbolize wealth, prove them worthless and portend the destruction of their possessors (2–3).

5, 6: The author does not have in mind any specific crime in his readers' communities but rather echoes the Old Testament theme of the harsh oppression of the righteous poor (see Prv 1, 11; Wis 2, 10.12.20).

5, 7–11: Those oppressed by the unjust rich are reminded of the need for patience, both in bearing the sufferings of human life (9) and in their expectation of the coming of the Lord. It is then that they will receive their reward (7–8.10–11; cf Heb 10, 25; 1 Jn 2, 18).

5, 7: The early and the late rains: an expression related to the agricultural season in ancient Palestine (see Dt 11, 14; Jer 5, 24; Jl 2, 23).

5, 12: This is the threat of condemnation for the abuse of swearing oaths (cf Mt 5, 33–37). **By heaven or by earth:** these words were substitutes for the original form of an oath, to circumvent its binding force and to avoid pronouncing the holy name of God (see Ex 22, 10).

5, 14: In case of sickness a Christian should ask for the presbyters of the church, i.e., those who have authority in the church (cf Acts 15, 2.22–23; 1 Tm 5, 17; Ti 1, 5). They are to pray over the person and anoint with oil; oil was used for medicinal purposes in the ancient world (see Is 1, 6; Lk 10, 34). In Mk 6, 13, the Twelve anoint the sick with oil on their missionary journey. **In the name of the Lord:** by the power of Jesus Christ.

5, 15: The results of the prayer and anointing are physical health and forgiveness of sins. The Roman Catholic Church (Council of Trent, Session 14) declared that this anointing of the sick is a sacrament "instituted by Christ and promulgated by blessed James the apostle."

---

r: Lk 12, 47.   s: Lk 6, 24.   t: Mt 6, 19.   u: Ps 21, 10; Prv 11, 4; Jdt 16, 17.   v: Lv 19, 13; Dt 24, 14-15; Mal 3, 5.   w: Jer 12, 3; Lk 16, 19-25.   x: Wis 2, 10-20.   y: Lk 21, 19; Heb 10, 36 [1] Heb 10, 25; 1 Pt 4, 7.   z: Ex 34, 6; Ps 103, 8.   a: Mt 5, 34-37.   b: Mk 6, 13.

powerful. [17c]Elijah was a human being like us; yet he prayed earnestly that it might not rain, and for three years and six months it did not rain upon the land. [18d]Then he prayed again, and the sky gave rain and the earth produced its fruit.

Conversion of Sinners. [19e]My brothers, if anyone among you should stray from the truth and someone bring him back, [20f]*he should know that whoever brings back a sinner from the error of his way will save his soul from death and will cover a multitude of sins.

5, 20: When a Christian is instrumental in the conversion of a sinner, the result is forgiveness of sins and a reinstatement of the sinner to the life of grace.

c: 1 Kgs 17, 1; Lk 4, 25.   *d:* 1 Kgs 18, 45.   *e:* Mt 18, 15; Gal 6, 1.   *f:* Prv 10, 12; 1 Pt 4, 8.

See RG
435–40

The First Letter of Peter

This letter begins with an address by Peter to Christian communities located in five provinces of Asia Minor (1, 1), including areas evangelized by Paul (Acts 16, 6–7; 18, 23). Christians there are encouraged to remain faithful to their standards of belief and conduct in spite of threats of persecution. Numerous allusions in the letter suggest that the churches addressed were largely of Gentile composition (1, 14.18; 2, 9–10; 4, 3–4), though considerable use is made of the Old Testament (1, 24; 2, 6–7, 9–10.22; 3, 10–12).

The contents following the address both inspire and admonish these "chosen sojourners" (1, 1) who, in seeking to live as God's people, feel an alienation from their previous religious roots and the society around them. Appeal is made to Christ's resurrection and the future hope it provides (1, 3–5) and to the experience of baptism as new birth (1, 3.23–25; 3, 21). The suffering and death of Christ serve as both source of salvation and example (1, 19; 2, 21–25; 3, 18). What Christians are in Christ, as a people who have received mercy and are to proclaim and live according to God's call (2, 9–10), is repeatedly spelled out for all sorts of situations in society (2, 11–17), work (even as slaves, 2, 18–20), the home (3, 1–7), and general conduct (3, 8–12; 4, 1–11). But over all hangs the possibility of suffering as a Christian (3, 13–17). In 4, 12–19 persecution is described as already occurring, so that some have supposed the letter was addressed both to places where such a "trial by fire" was already present and to places where it might break out.

The letter constantly mingles moral exhortation (*paraklēsis*) with its catechetical summaries of mercies in Christ. Encouragement to fidelity in spite of suffering is based upon a vision of the meaning of Christian existence. The emphasis on baptism and allusions to various features of the baptismal liturgy suggest that the author has incorporated into his exposition numerous homiletic, credal, hymnic, and sacramental elements of the baptismal rite that had become traditional at an early date.

From Irenaeus in the late second century until modern times, Christian tradition regarded Peter the apostle as author of this document. Since he was martyred at Rome during the persecution of Nero between A.D. 64 and 67, it was supposed that the letter was written from Rome shortly before his death. This is supported by its reference to "Babylon" (5, 13), a code name for Rome in the early church.

Some modern scholars, however, on the basis of a number of features that they consider incompatible with Petrine authenticity, regard the letter as the work of a later Christian writer. Such features include the cultivated Greek in which it is written, difficult to attribute to a Galilean fisherman, together with its use of the Greek Septuagint translation when citing the Old Testament; the similarity in both thought and expression to the Pauline literature; and the allusions to widespread persecution of Christians, which did not occur until at least the reign of Domitian (A.D. 81–96). In this view the letter would date from the end of the first century or even the beginning of the second, when there is evidence for persecution of Christians in Asia Minor (the letter of Pliny the Younger to Trajan, A.D. 111–12).

Other scholars believe, however, that these objections can be met by appeal to use of a secretary, Silvanus, mentioned in 5, 12. Such secretaries often gave literary expression to the author's thoughts in their own style and language. The persecutions may refer to local harassment rather than to systematic repression by the state. Hence there is nothing in the document incompatible with Petrine authorship in the 60s.

Still other scholars take a middle position. The many literary contacts with the Pauline literature, James, and 1 John suggest a common fund of traditional formulations rather than direct dependence upon Paul. Such liturgical and catechetical traditions must have been very ancient and in some cases of Palestinian origin.

Yet it is unlikely that Peter addressed a letter to the Gentile churches of Asia Minor while Paul was still alive. This suggests a period after the death of the two apostles, perhaps A.D. 70–90. The author would be a disciple of Peter in Rome, representing a Petrine group that served as a bridge between the Palestinian origins of Christianity and its flowering in the Gentile world. The problem addressed would not be official persecution but the difficulty of living the Christian life in a hostile, secular environment that espoused different values and subjected the Christian minority to ridicule and oppression.

The principal divisions of the First Letter of Peter are the following:

I: Address (1, 1–2)
II: The Gift and Call of God in Baptism (1, 3—2, 10)
III: The Christian in a Hostile World (2, 11—4, 11)
IV: Advice to the Persecuted (4, 12—5, 11)
V: Conclusion (5, 12–14)

I: Address

CHAPTER 1

See RG 436-38

Greeting. 1a*Peter, an apostle of Jesus Christ, to the chosen sojourners of the dispersion in Pontus, Galatia, Cappadocia, Asia, and Bithynia, 2bin the foreknowledge of God the Father, through sanctification by the Spirit, for obedience and sprinkling with the blood of Jesus Christ: may grace and peace be yours in abundance.

II: The Gift and Call of God in Baptism

Blessing. 3c*Blessed be the God and Father of our Lord Jesus Christ, who in his great mercy gave us a new birth to a living hope through the resurrection of Jesus Christ from the dead, 4dto an inheritance that is imperishable, undefiled, and unfading, kept in heaven for you 5who by the power of God are safeguarded through faith, to a salvation that is ready to be revealed in the final time. 6e*In this you rejoice, although now for a little while you may have to suffer through various trials, 7fso that the genuineness of your faith, more precious than gold that is perishable even though tested by fire, may prove to be for praise, glory, and honor at the revelation of Jesus Christ. 8gAlthough you have not seen him you love him; even though you do not see him now yet believe in him, you rejoice with an indescribable and glorious joy, 9as you attain the goal of [your] faith, the salvation of your souls.

10*Concerning this salvation, prophets

1, 1–2: The introductory formula names **Peter** as the writer (but see Introduction). In his comments to the presbyters (5, 1), the author calls himself a "fellow presbyter." He addresses himself to the Gentile converts of Asia Minor. Their privileged status as a **chosen** and sanctified people makes them worthy of God's **grace** and **peace.** In contrast is their actual existence as aliens and **sojourners,** scattered among pagans, far from their true country.

1, 1: Dispersion: literally, diaspora; see Jas 1, 1 and Introduction to that letter. **Pontus . . . Bithynia:** five provinces in Asia Minor, listed in clockwise order from the north, perhaps in the sequence in which a messenger might deliver the letter.

1, 3–5: A prayer of praise and thanksgiving to God who bestows the gift of new life and hope in baptism (**new birth,** 3) **through the resurrection of Jesus Christ from the dead.** The new birth is a sign of an **imperishable inheritance** (4),

of **salvation** that is still in the future (**to be revealed in the final time,** 5).

1, 6–9: As the glory of Christ's resurrection was preceded by his sufferings and death, the new life of faith that it bestows is to be subjected to many **trials** (6) while achieving its goal: the glory of the fullness of **salvation** (9) at the coming of Christ (7).

1, 10–12: The **Spirit of Christ** (11) is here shown to have been present in the prophets, moving them to search, investigate, and prophesy about the **grace** of **salvation** that was to come (10), and in the apostles impelling them to preach the fulfillment of salvation in the message of Christ's sufferings and glory (12).

a: Jas 1, 1. *b:* Rom 8, 29. *c:* Ti 3, 5. *d:* Mt 6, 19-20. *e:* Jas 1, 2-3. *f:* 1 Cor 3, 13. *g:* 2 Cor 5, 6-7.

who prophesied about the grace that was to be yours searched and investigated it, [11h]investigating the time and circumstances that the Spirit of Christ within them indicated when it testified in advance to the sufferings destined for Christ and the glories to follow them. [12]It was revealed to them that they were serving not themselves but you with regard to the things that have now been announced to you by those who preached the good news to you [through] the holy Spirit sent from heaven, things into which angels longed to look.

Obedience. [13]*Therefore, gird up the loins of your mind, live soberly, and set your hopes completely on the grace to be brought to you at the revelation of Jesus Christ. [14]*Like obedient children, do not act in compliance with the desires of your former ignorance [15i]but, as he who called you is holy, be holy yourselves in every aspect of your conduct, [16j]for it is written, "Be holy because I [am] holy."

Reverence. [17k]Now if you invoke as Father him who judges impartially according to each one's works, conduct yourselves with reverence during the time of your sojourning, [18l]realizing that you were ransomed from your futile conduct, handed on by your ancestors, not with perishable things like silver or gold [19m]*but with the precious blood of Christ as of a spotless unblemished lamb. [20]He was known before the foundation of the world but revealed in the final

time for you, [21]who through him believe in God who raised him from the dead and gave him glory, so that your faith and hope are in God.

Mutual Love. [22n]*Since you have purified yourselves by obedience to the truth for sincere mutual love, love one another intensely from a [pure] heart. [23o]*You have been born anew, not from perishable but from imperishable seed, through the living and abiding word of God, [24p]for:

"All flesh is like grass,
    and all its glory like the flower of the
        field;
the grass withers,
    and the flower wilts;
[25] but the word of the Lord remains
        forever."

This is the word that has been proclaimed to you.

CHAPTER 2

See RG 437–38

God's House and People. [1q]*Rid yourselves of all malice and all deceit, insincerity, envy, and all slander; [2]like newborn infants, long for pure spiritual milk so that through it you may grow into salvation, [3r]*for you have tasted that the Lord is good. [4s]*Come to him, a living stone, rejected by human beings but chosen and precious in the sight of God, [5t]*and, like living stones, let yourselves be built into a spiritual house to be a holy priesthood to offer spiritual sacri-

---

1, 13–25: These verses are concerned with the call of God's people to holiness and to mutual love by reason of their redemption through the blood of Christ (18–21).

1, 13: Gird up the loins of your mind: a figure reminiscent of the rite of Passover when the Israelites were in flight from their oppressors (Ex 12, 11), and also suggesting the vigilance of the Christian people in expectation of the parousia of Christ (Lk 12, 35).

1, 14–16: The **ignorance** here referred to (14) was their former lack of knowledge of God, leading inevitably to godless conduct. Holiness (15–16), on the contrary, is the result of their call to the knowledge and love of God.

1, 19: Christians have received the redemption prophesied by Isaiah (52, 3), through the blood (Jewish symbol of life) of the spotless lamb (Is 53, 7.10; Jn 1, 29; Rom 3, 24–25; cf 1 Cor 6, 20).

1, 22–25: The new birth of Christians (23) derives from Christ, the **imperishable seed** or sowing that produces a new and lasting existence in those who accept the gospel (24–25), with the consequent duty of loving **one another** (22).

1, 23: The living and abiding word of God: or, "the word of the living and abiding God."

2, 1–3: Growth toward salvation is seen here as two steps: first, stripping away all that is contrary to the new life in Christ; second, the nourishment (**pure spiritual milk**) that the newly baptized have received.

2, 3: Tasted that the Lord is good: cf Ps 34, 9.

2, 4–8: Christ is the cornerstone (cf Is 28, 16) that is the foundation of the spiritual edifice of the Christian community (5). To unbelievers, Christ is an obstacle and a stumbling block on which they are destined to fall (8); cf Rom 11, 11.

2, 5: Let yourselves be built: the form of the Greek word could also be indicative passive, "you are being built" (cf 9).

h: Is 52, 13—53, 12; Dn 9, 24. i: Mt 5, 48; 1 Jn 3, 3. j: Lv 11, 44; 19, 2. k: 2, 11. l: Is 52, 3; 1 Cor 6, 20. m: Ex 12, 5; Jn 1, 29; Heb 9, 14. n: Rom 12, 10. o: 1 Jn 3, 9. p: Is 40, 6-8. q: Jas 1, 21. r: Ps 34, 9. s: Ps 118, 22; Mt 21, 42; Acts 4, 11. t: Eph 2, 21-22.

fices acceptable to God through Jesus Christ. [6u]For it says in scripture:

"Behold, I am laying a stone in Zion,
a cornerstone, chosen and precious,
and whoever believes in it shall not be
put to shame."

[7v]Therefore, its value is for you who have faith, but for those without faith:

"The stone which the builders rejected
has become the cornerstone,"

[8w]and

"A stone that will make people
stumble,
and a rock that will make them fall."

They stumble by disobeying the word, as is their destiny.

[9x]*But you are "a chosen race, a royal priesthood, a holy nation, a people of his own, so that you may announce the praises" of him who called you out of darkness into his wonderful light.

[10 y]Once you were "no people"
but now you are God's people;
you "had not received mercy"
but now you have received mercy.

2, 9–10: The prerogatives of ancient Israel mentioned here are now more fully and fittingly applied to the Christian people: "a chosen race" (cf Is 43, 20–21) indicates their divine election (Eph 1, 4–6); "a royal priesthood" (cf Ex 19, 6) to serve and worship God in Christ, thus continuing the priestly functions of his life, passion, and resurrection; "a holy nation" (Ex 19, 6) reserved for God, a people he claims for his own (cf Mal 3, 17) in virtue of their baptism into his death and resurrection. This transcends all natural and national divisions and unites the people into one community to glorify the one who led them from the darkness of paganism to the light of faith in Christ. From being "no people" deprived of all mercy, they have become the very people of God, the chosen recipients of his mercy (cf Hos 1, 9; 2, 25).

2, 11—3, 12: After explaining the doctrinal basis for the Christian community, the author makes practical applications in terms of the virtues that should prevail in all the social relationships of the members of the community: good example to Gentile neighbors (2, 11–12); respect for human authority (2, 13–17); obedience, patience, and endurance of hardship in domestic relations (2, 18–25); Christian behavior of husbands and wives (3, 1–7); mutual charity (3, 8–12).

2, 11: Aliens and sojourners: no longer signifying absence from one's native land (Gn 23, 4), this image denotes

III: The Christian in a Hostile World

Christian Examples. [11z]*Beloved, I urge you as aliens and sojourners to keep away from worldly desires that wage war against the soul. [12]Maintain good conduct among the Gentiles, so that if they speak of you as evildoers, they may observe your good works and glorify God on the day of visitation.

Christian Citizens. [13a]*Be subject to every human institution for the Lord's sake, whether it be to the king as supreme [14]or to governors as sent by him for the punishment of evildoers and the approval of those who do good. [15]For it is the will of God that by doing good you may silence the ignorance of foolish people. [16b]Be free, yet without using freedom as a pretext for evil, but as slaves of God. [17c]Give honor to all, love the community, fear God, honor the king.

Christian Slaves. [18d]*Slaves, be subject to your masters with all reverence, not only to those who are good and equitable but also to those who are perverse. [19]For whenever anyone bears the pain of unjust suffering because of consciousness of God, that is a grace. [20]But

rather their estrangement from the world during their earthly pilgrimage (see also 1, 1.17).

2, 13–17: True Christian freedom is the result of being servants of God (16; see the note on 2, 18–23). It includes reverence for God, esteem for every individual, and committed love for fellow Christians (17). Although persecution may threaten, subjection to human government is urged (13.17) and concern for the impact of Christians' conduct on those who are not Christians (12.15).

2, 18–21: Most of the labor in the commercial cities of first-century Asia Minor was performed by a working class of slaves. The sense of freedom contained in the gospel undoubtedly caused great tension among Christian slaves: witness the special advice given concerning them here and in 1 Cor 7, 21–24; Eph 6, 5–8; Col 3, 22–25; Phlm. The point made here does not have so much to do with the institution of slavery, which the author does not challenge, but with the nonviolent reaction (20) of slaves to unjust treatment. Their patient suffering is compared to that of Jesus (21), which won righteousness for all humanity.

---

u: Is 28, 16. *v:* Ps 118, 22; Mt 21, 42; Lk 20, 17; Acts 4, 11. *w:* Is 8, 14; Rom 9, 33. *x:* Ex 19, 6; Is 61, 6; Rv 1, 6; 20, 6. *y:* Hos 1, 9; 2, 25 / Hos 1, 6. *z:* Gal 5, 24. *a:* Rom 13, 1-7. *b:* Gal 5, 13. *c:* Prv 24, 21; Mt 22, 21. *d:* Eph 6, 5.

what credit is there if you are patient when beaten for doing wrong? But if you are patient when you suffer for doing what is good, this is a grace before God. [21e]*For to this you have been called, because Christ also suffered for you, leaving you an example that you should follow in his footsteps.

[22] [f]*"He committed no sin,
and no deceit was found in his mouth."

[23g]When he was insulted, he returned no insult; when he suffered, he did not threaten; instead, he handed himself over to the one who judges justly. [24h]He himself bore our sins in his body upon the cross, so that, free from sin, we might live for righteousness. By his wounds you have been healed. [25i]*For you had gone astray like sheep, but you have now returned to the shepherd and guardian of your souls.

CHAPTER 3

See RG 438–39

Christian Spouses. [1]*Likewise, you wives should be subordinate to your husbands so that, even if some disobey the word, they may be won over without a word by their wives' conduct [2j]when they observe your reverent and chaste behavior. [3k]Your adornment should not be an external one: braiding the hair, wearing gold jewelry, or dressing in fine clothes, [4]but rather the hidden character of the heart, expressed in the imperishable beauty of a gentle and calm

disposition, which is precious in the sight of God. [5]For this is also how the holy women who hoped in God once used to adorn themselves and were subordinate to their husbands; [6]thus Sarah obeyed Abraham, calling him "lord." You are her children when you do what is good and fear no intimidation.

[7]*Likewise, you husbands should live with your wives in understanding, showing honor to the weaker female sex, since we are joint heirs of the gift of life, so that your prayers may not be hindered.

Christian Conduct. [8]*Finally, all of you, be of one mind, sympathetic, loving toward one another, compassionate, humble. [9m]Do not return evil for evil, or insult for insult; but, on the contrary, a blessing, because to this you were called, that you might inherit a blessing. [10n]For:

"Whoever would love life
and see good days
must keep the tongue from evil
and the lips from speaking deceit,
[11] must turn from evil and do good,
seek peace and follow after it.
[12] For the eyes of the Lord are on the
righteous
and his ears turned to their prayer,
but the face of the Lord is against
evildoers."

Christian Suffering. [13]*Now who is going to harm you if you are enthusiastic for what

---

2, 21: Suffered: some ancient manuscripts and versions read "died" (cf 3, 18).

2, 22–25: After the quotation of Is 53, 9b, the passage describes Jesus' passion with phrases concerning the Suffering Servant from Is 53, 4–12, perhaps as employed in an early Christian confession of faith; cf 1, 18–21 and 3, 18–22.

2, 25: The shepherd and guardian of your souls: the familiar shepherd and flock figures express the care, vigilance, and love of God for his people in the Old Testament (Ps 23; Is 40, 11; Jer 23, 4–5; Ez 34, 11–16) and of Jesus for all humanity in the New Testament (Mt 18, 10–14; Lk 15, 4–7; Jn 10, 1–16; Heb 13, 20).

3, 1–6: The typical marital virtues of women of the ancient world, obedience, reverence, and chastity (1–2), are outlined here by the author, who gives them an entirely new motivation: Christian wives are to be virtuous so that they may be instrumental in the conversion of their husbands. In imitation of **holy women** in the past (5) they are to cultivate the interior life (4) instead of excessive concern with their appearance (3).

3, 7: Husbands who do not respect their wives will have as little success in prayer as those who, according to Paul, have

no love: their prayers will be "a resounding gong or a clashing cymbal" (1 Cor 13, 1). Consideration for others is shown as a prerequisite for effective prayer also in Mt 5, 23–24; 1 Cor 11, 20–22; Jas 4, 3. After all, whatever the social position of women in the world and in the family, they are equal recipients of the gift of God's salvation. Paul is very clear on this point, too (see 1 Cor 11, 11–12; Gal 3, 28).

3, 8–12: For the proper ordering of Christian life in its various aspects as described in 2, 11—3, 9, there is promised the blessing expressed in Ps 34, 13–17. In the Old Testament this refers to longevity and prosperity; here, it also refers to eternal life.

3, 13–22: This exposition, centering on v 17, runs as follows: by his suffering and death Christ the righteous one saved the unrighteous (18); by his resurrection he received new life in the spirit, which he communicates to believers

e: Mt 16, 24. **f:** Is 53, 9. **g:** Mt 5, 39. **h:** Is 53, 4.12 / Is 53, 5. **i:** Is 53, 6. **j:** 1 Cor 7, 12-16; Eph 5, 22-24; Col 3, 18; 1 Tm 2, 9-15. **k:** 1 Tm 2, 9-10. **l:** Eph 5, 25-33; Col 3, 19. **m:** Mt 5, 44; Lk 6, 28; Rom 12, 14. **n:** Ps 34, 13-17.

is good? [14]But even if you should suffer because of righteousness, blessed are you. Do not be afraid or terrified with fear of them, [15o]but sanctify Christ as Lord in your hearts. Always be ready to give an explanation to anyone who asks you for a reason for your hope, [16]but do it with gentleness and reverence, keeping your conscience clear, so that, when you are maligned, those who defame your good conduct in Christ may themselves be put to shame. [17]For it is better to suffer for doing good, if that be the will of God, than for doing evil.

[18p]*For Christ also suffered for sins once, the righteous for the sake of the unrighteous, that he might lead you to God. Put to death in the flesh, he was brought to life in the spirit. [19]*In it he also went to preach to the spirits in prison, [20q]who had once been disobedient while God patiently waited in the days of Noah during the building of the ark, in which a few persons, eight in all, were saved through water. [21r]*This prefigured baptism, which saves you now. It is not a removal of dirt from the body but an appeal to God for a clear conscience, through the resurrection of Jesus Christ, [22s]who has gone into heaven and is at the right hand of God, with angels, authorities, and powers subject to him.

CHAPTER 4

See RG 438–39

Christian Restraint. [1]*Therefore, since Christ suffered in the flesh, arm yourselves also with the same attitude (for whoever suffers in the flesh has broken with sin), [2]so as not to spend what remains of one's life in the flesh on human desires, but on the will of God. [3t]For the time that has passed is sufficient for doing what the Gentiles like to do: living in debauchery, evil desires, drunkenness, orgies, carousing, and wanton idolatry. [4]They are surprised that you do not plunge into the same swamp of profligacy, and they vilify you; [5u]but they will give an account to him who stands ready to judge the living and the dead. [6]*For this is why the gospel was preached even to the dead that, though condemned in the flesh in human estimation, they might live in the spirit in the estimation of God.

Christian Charity. [7]*The end of all things is at hand. Therefore, be serious and sober for prayers. [8v]*Above all, let your love for one another be intense, because love covers a multitude of sins. [9w]Be hospitable to one another without complaining. [10x]As each one has received a gift, use it to serve one another as good stewards of God's varied grace. [11y]*Whoever preaches, let it be with the words of God; whoever serves, let it be

---

through the baptismal bath that cleanses their consciences from sin. As Noah's family was saved **through water,** so Christians are saved through the waters of baptism (19–22). Hence they need not share the fear of sinners; they should rather rejoice in suffering because of their hope in Christ. Thus their innocence disappoints their accusers (13–16; cf Mt 10, 28; Rom 8, 35–39).

3, 18: Suffered: very many ancient manuscripts and versions read "died." **Put to death in the flesh:** affirms that Jesus truly died as a human being. **Brought to life in the spirit:** that is, in the new and transformed existence freed from the limitations and weaknesses of natural human life (cf 1 Cor 15, 45).

3, 19: The spirits in prison: it is not clear just who these spirits are. They may be the spirits of the sinners who died in the flood, or angelic powers, hostile to God, who have been overcome by Christ (cf 22; Gn 6, 4; Enoch 6–36, especially 21, 6; 2 Enoch 7, 1–5).

3, 21: Appeal to God: this could also be translated "pledge," that is, a promise on the part of Christians to live with a good conscience before God, or a pledge from God of forgiveness and therefore a good conscience for us.

4, 1–6: Willingness to suffer with Christ equips the Christian with the power to conquer sin (1). Christ is here por-

trayed as the judge to whom those guilty of pagan vices must render an account (5; cf Jn 5, 22–27; Acts 10, 42; 2 Tm 4, 1).

4, 6: The dead: these may be the sinners of the flood generation who are possibly referred to in 3, 19. But many scholars think that there is no connection between these two verses, and that **the dead** here are Christians who have died since hearing the preaching of the gospel.

4, 7–11: The inner life of the eschatological community is outlined as **the end** (the parousia of Christ) and the judgment draws near in terms of seriousness, sobriety, prayer, and love expressed through hospitality and the use of one's gifts for the glory of God and of Christ.

4, 8: Love covers a multitude of sins: a maxim based on Prv 10, 12; see also Ps 32, 1; Jas 5, 20.

4, 11: Some scholars feel that this doxology concludes the part of the homily addressed specifically to the newly baptized, begun in 1, 3; others that it concludes a baptismal liturgy. Such doxologies do occur within a New Testament letter, e.g., Rom 9, 5. Some propose that v 11 was an alternate

---

o: Is 8, 12.   p: 1 Cor 15, 45.   q: Gn 7, 7.17; 2 Pt 2, 5.   r: Eph 5, 26; Heb 10, 22.   s: Eph 1, 20-21.   t: Eph 2, 2-3; 4, 17-19; Col 3, 7; Ti 3, 3.   u: Acts 10, 42; 2 Tm 4, 1.   v: Prv 10, 12; Jas 5, 20.   w: Heb 13, 2.   x: Rom 12, 6-8; 1 Cor 12, 4-11.   y: 1 Cor 10, 31.

with the strength that God supplies, so that in all things God may be glorified through Jesus Christ, to whom belong glory and dominion forever and ever. Amen.

IV: Advice to the Persecuted

Trial of Persecution. [12z]*Beloved, do not be surprised that a trial by fire is occurring among you, as if something strange were happening to you. [13a]But rejoice to the extent that you share in the sufferings of Christ, so that when his glory is revealed you may also rejoice exultantly. [14b]If you are insulted for the name of Christ, blessed are you, for the Spirit of glory and of God rests upon you. [15]But let no one among you be made to suffer as a murderer, a thief, an evildoer, or as an intriguer. [16]But whoever is made to suffer as a Christian should not be ashamed but glorify God because of the name. [17c]For it is time for the judgment to begin with the household of God; if it begins with us, how will it end for those who fail to obey the gospel of God?

[18] [d]"And if the righteous one is barely saved,
where will the godless and the sinner appear?"

[19]As a result, those who suffer in accord with God's will hand their souls over to a faithful creator as they do good.

See RG 439

CHAPTER 5

Advice to Presbyters. [1]*So I exhort the presbyters among you, as a fellow presbyter and witness to the sufferings of Christ and one who has a share in the glory to be revealed. [2e]Tend the flock of God in your midst, [overseeing] not by constraint but willingly, as God would have it, not for shameful profit but eagerly. [3]Do not lord it over those assigned to you, but be examples to the flock. [4f]*And when the chief Shepherd is revealed, you will receive the unfading crown of glory.

Advice to the Community. [5g]*Likewise, you younger members, be subject to the presbyters. And all of you, clothe yourselves with humility in your dealings with one another, for:

"God opposes the proud
    but bestows favor on the humble."

[6h]So humble yourselves under the mighty hand of God, that he may exalt you in due time. [7i]Cast all your worries upon him because he cares for you.

[8j]Be sober and vigilant. Your opponent the devil is prowling around like a roaring lion looking for [someone] to devour. [9]Resist him, steadfast in faith, knowing that your fellow believers throughout the world undergo the same sufferings. [10k]The God of all grace who called you to his eternal glory through Christ [Jesus] will himself restore, confirm, strengthen, and establish you after you have suffered a little. [11]To him be dominion forever. Amen.

---

ending, with 4, 12—5, 14 being read in places where persecution was more pressing. But such doxologies usually do not occur at the end of letters (the only examples are 2 Pt 3, 18, Jude 25, and Rom 16, 27, the last probably a liturgical insertion).

4, 12–19: The suffering to which the author has already frequently referred is presented in more severe terms. This has led some scholars to see these verses as referring to an actual persecution. Others see the heightening of the language as only a rhetorical device used at the end of the letter to emphasize the suffering motif.

5, 1–4: In imitation of Christ, the chief shepherd, those entrusted with a pastoral office are to tend the flock by their care and example.

5, 1: Presbyters: the officially appointed leaders and teachers of the Christian community (cf 1 Tm 5, 17–18; Ti 1, 5–8; Jas 5, 14).

5, 4: See the note on 2, 25.

5, 5–11: The community is to be subject to the presbyters and to show humility toward one another and trust in God's love and care (5–7). With sobriety, alertness, and steadfast faith they must resist the evil one; their sufferings are shared with Christians everywhere (8–9). They will be strengthened and called to eternal glory (10–11).

5, 5: Younger members: this may be a designation for office-holders of lesser rank.

---

z: 1, 6-7; 3, 14.17. a: Rom 5, 3-5; 8, 17; 2 Tm 2, 12. b: Acts 5, 41 / Is 11, 2. c: Lk 23, 31; 2 Thes 1, 8. d: Prv 11, 31 LXX. e: Acts 20, 28; Ti 1, 7. f: Wis 5, 15-16; 1 Cor 9, 25; 2 Tm 4, 8; Jas 1, 12. g: Prv 3, 34. h: Jb 22, 29; Jas 4, 10. i: Ps 55, 23; Mt 6, 25-33; Lk 12, 22-31; Phil 4, 6. j: 1 Thes 5, 6. k: Rom 8, 18; 2 Cor 4, 17.

V: Conclusion

12 *I write you this briefly through Silvanus, whom I consider a faithful brother, exhorting you and testifying that this is the true grace of God. Remain firm in it. *13* *The chosen one at Babylon sends you greeting, as does Mark, my son. *14l* Greet one another with a loving kiss. Peace to all of you who are in Christ.

5, 12: Silvanus: the companion of Paul (see 2 Cor 1, 19; 1 Thes 1, 1; 2 Thes 1, 1). Jews and Jewish Christians, like Paul, often had a Hebrew name (Saoul, Silas) and a Greek or Latin name (Paul, Silvanus). On Silvanus's possible role as amanuensis, see Introduction.
5, 13: The chosen one: feminine, referring to the Christian community (**ekklēsia**) at **Babylon,** the code name for Rome in Rv 14, 8; 17, 5; 18, 2. **Mark, my son:** traditionally a prominent disciple of Peter and co-worker at the church in Rome, perhaps the John Mark referred to in Acts 12, 12.25; 13, 5.13; and in 15, 37–39, a companion of Barnabas. Perhaps this is the same Mark mentioned as Barnabas's cousin in Col 4, 10, a co-worker with Paul in Phlm 24 (see also 2 Tm 4, 11).

l: Rom 16, 16; 1 Cor 16, 20; 2 Cor 13, 12.

See RG 440–44

The Second Letter of Peter

This letter can be appreciated both for its positive teachings and for its earnest warnings. It seeks to strengthen readers in faith (1, 1), hope for the future (3, 1–10), knowledge (1, 2.6.8), love (1, 7), and other virtues (1, 5–6). This aim is carried out especially by warning against false teachers, the condemnation of whom occupies the long central section of the letter (2, 1–22). A particular crisis is the claim by "scoffers" that there will be no second coming of Jesus, a doctrine that the author vigorously affirms (3, 1–10). The concept of God's "promises" is particularly precious in the theology of 2 Peter (1, 4; 3, 4.9.13). Closing comments at 3, 17–18 well sum up the twin concerns: that you not "be led into" error and "fall" but instead "grow in grace" and "knowledge" of Jesus Christ.

Second Peter is clearly structured in its presentation of these points. It reminds its readers of the divine authenticity of Christ's teaching (1, 3–4), continues with reflections on Christian conduct (1, 5–15), then returns to the exalted dignity of Jesus by incorporating into the text the apostolic witness to his transfiguration (1, 16–18). It takes up the question of the interpretation of scripture by pointing out that it is possible to misunderstand the sacred writings (1, 19–21) and that divine punishment will overtake false teachers (2, 1–22). It proclaims that the parousia is the teaching of the Lord and of the apostles and is therefore an eventual certainty (3, 1–13). At the same time, it warns that the meaning of Paul's writings on this question should not be distorted (3, 14–18).

In both content and style this letter is very different from 1 Peter, which immediately precedes it in the canon. The opening verse attributes it to "Symeon Peter, a slave and apostle of Jesus Christ." Moreover, the author in 3, 1 calls his work a "second letter," referring probably to 1 Peter as his first, and in 1, 18 counts himself among those present at the transfiguration of Jesus.

Nevertheless, acceptance of 2 Peter into the New Testament canon met with great resistance in the early church. The oldest certain reference to it comes from Origen in the early third century. While he himself accepted both Petrine letters as canonical, he testifies that others rejected 2 Peter. As late as the fifth century some local churches still excluded it from the canon, but eventually it was universally adopted. The principal reason for the long delay was the persistent doubt that the letter stemmed from the apostle Peter.

Among modern scholars there is wide agreement that 2 Peter is a pseudonymous work, i.e., one written by a later author who attributed it to Peter according to a literary convention popular at the time. It gives the impression of being more remote in time from the apostolic period than 1 Peter; indeed, many think it is the latest work in the New Testament and assign it to the first or even the second quarter of the second century.

The principal reasons for this view are the following. The author refers to the apostles and "our ancestors" as belonging to a previous generation, now dead (3, 2–4). A collection of Paul's letters exists and appears to be well known, but disputes have arisen about the interpretation of them (3, 14–16). The passage about false teachers

(2, 1–18) contains a number of literary contacts with Jude 4–16, and it is generally agreed that 2 Peter depends upon Jude, not vice versa. Finally, the principal problem exercising the author is the false teaching of "scoffers" who have concluded from the delay of the parousia that the Lord is not going to return. This could scarcely have been an issue during the lifetime of Simon Peter.

The Christians to whom the letter is addressed are not identified, though it may be the intent of 3, 1 to identify them with the churches of Asia Minor to which 1 Peter was sent. Except for the epistolary greeting in 1, 1–2, 2 Peter does not have the features of a genuine letter at all, but is rather a general exhortation cast in the form of a letter. The author must have been a Jewish Christian of the dispersion for, while his Jewish heritage is evident in various features of his thought and style, he writes in the rather stilted literary Greek of the Hellenistic period. He appeals to tradition against the twin threat of doctrinal error and moral laxity, which appear to reflect an early stage of what later developed into full-blown gnosticism. Thus he forms a link between the apostolic period and the church of subsequent ages.

The principal divisions of the Second Letter of Peter are the following:

I: Address (1, 1–2)

II: Exhortation to Christian Virtue (1, 3–21)

III: Condemnation of the False Teachers (2, 1–22)

IV: The Delay of the Second Coming (3, 1–16)

V: Final Exhortation and Doxology (3, 17–18)

I: Address

CHAPTER 1

See RG 441–42

Greeting. *1**Symeon Peter, a slave and apostle of Jesus Christ, to those who have received a faith of equal value to ours through the righteousness of our God and savior Jesus Christ: *2**may grace and peace be yours in abundance through knowledge of God and of Jesus our Lord.

II: Exhortation to Christian Virtue

The Power of God's Promise. *3a**His divine power has bestowed on us everything that makes for life and devotion, through the knowledge of him who called us by his own glory and power. *4b*Through these, he has bestowed on us the precious and very great promises, so that through them you may come to share in the divine nature, after escaping from the corruption that is in the world because of evil desire. *5c**For this very reason, make every effort to supplement your faith with virtue, virtue with knowledge, *6*knowledge with self-control, self-control with endurance, endurance with devotion, *7*devotion with mutual affection, mutual affection with love. *8*If these are yours and increase in abundance, they will keep you from being idle or unfruitful in the knowledge of our Lord Jesus Christ. *9d*Anyone who lacks them is blind and shortsighted, forgetful of the cleansing of his past sins. *10**Therefore, brothers, be all the

---

1, 1: Symeon Peter: on the authorship of 2 Peter, see Introduction; on the spelling here of the Hebrew name **Šim'ôn**, cf Acts 15, 14. The greeting is especially similar to those in 1 Peter and Jude. The words translated **our God and savior Jesus Christ** could also be rendered "our God and the savior Jesus Christ"; cf 11; 2, 20; 3, 2.18.

1, 2: Knowledge: a key term in the letter (3.8; 2, 20; 3, 18), perhaps used as a Christian emphasis against gnostic claims.

1, 3–4: Christian life in its fullness is a gift of divine power effecting a knowledge of Christ and the bestowal of divine promises (3, 4.9). **To share in the divine nature,** escaping from a corrupt world, is a thought found elsewhere in the Bible but expressed only here in such Hellenistic terms, since it is said to be accomplished through knowledge (3); cf 2; 2, 20; but see also Jn 15, 4; 17, 22–23; Rom 8, 14–17; Heb 3, 14; 1 Jn 1, 3; 3, 2.

1, 3: By his own glory and power: the most ancient papyrus and the best codex read "through glory and power."

1, 5–9: Note the climactic gradation of qualities (5–7), beginning with faith and leading to the fullness of Christian life, which is love; cf Rom 5, 3–4; Gal 5, 6.22 for a similar series of "virtues," though the program and sense here are different than in Paul. The fruit of these is knowledge of Christ (8) referred to in v 3; their absence is spiritual blindness (9).

1, 10–11: Perseverance in the Christian vocation is the best preventative against losing it and the safest provision for attaining its goal, the kingdom. **Kingdom of . . . Christ,** instead of "God," is unusual; cf Col 1, 13 and Mt 13, 41, as well as the **righteousness of . . . Christ** (1).

a: 2 Cor 4, 6; 1 Pt 2, 9.   *b:* 2 Cor 7, 1; 1 Jn 2, 15.   *c:* Gal 5, 22–23.   *d:* 1 Jn 2, 9.11.

more eager to make your call and election firm, for, in doing so, you will never stumble. [11]For, in this way, entry into the eternal kingdom of our Lord and savior Jesus Christ will be richly provided for you.

Apostolic Witness. [12]*Therefore, I will always remind you of these things, even though you already know them and are established in the truth you have. [13]*I think it right, as long as I am in this "tent," to stir you up by a reminder, [14e]since I know that I will soon have to put it aside, as indeed our Lord Jesus Christ has shown me. [15]I shall also make every effort to enable you always to remember these things after my departure.

[16f]*We did not follow cleverly devised myths when we made known to you the power and coming of our Lord Jesus Christ, but we had been eyewitnesses of his majesty. [17g]*For he received honor and glory from God the Father when that unique declaration came to him from the majestic glory, "This is my Son, my beloved, with whom I am well pleased." [18]*We ourselves heard this voice come from heaven while we were with him on the holy mountain. [19h]Moreover, we possess the prophetic message that is altogether reliable. You will do well to be attentive to it, as to a lamp shining in a dark place, until day dawns and the morning star rises in your hearts. [20]*Know this first of all, that there is no prophecy of scripture that is a matter of personal interpretation, [21]for no prophecy ever came through human will; but rather human beings moved by the holy Spirit spoke under the influence of God.

III: Condemnation of the False Teachers

CHAPTER 2

See RG 442

False Teachers. [1i]*There were also false prophets among the people, just as there will be false teachers among you, who will introduce destructive heresies and even deny the Master who ransomed them, bringing swift destruction on themselves. [2j]Many will follow their licentious ways, and because of them the way of truth will be reviled. [3k]In their greed they will exploit you with fabrications, but from of old their condemnation has not been idle and their destruction does not sleep.

Lessons from the Past. [41]*For if God did

1, 12–19: The purpose in writing is to call to mind the apostle's witness to the truth, even as he faces the end of his life (12–15), his eyewitness testimony to Christ (16–18), and the true prophetic message (19) through the Spirit in scripture (20–21), in contrast to what false teachers are setting forth (ch 2).

1, 13: **Tent:** a biblical image for transitory human life (Is 38, 12), here combined with a verb that suggests not folding or packing up a tent but its being discarded in death (cf 2 Cor 5, 1–4).

1, 16: **Coming:** in Greek **parousia,** used at 3, 4.12 of the second coming of Christ. The word was used in the extrabiblical writings for the visitation of someone in authority; in Greek cult and Hellenistic Judaism it was used for the manifestation of the divine presence. What the apostles **made known** has been interpreted to refer to Jesus' transfiguration (17) or to his entire first coming or to his future coming in power (ch 3).

1, 17: The author assures the readers of the reliability of the apostolic message (including Jesus' power, glory, and coming) by appeal to the transfiguration of Jesus in glory (cf Mt 17, 1–8 and parallels) and by appeal to the prophetic message (19; perhaps Nm 24, 17). Here, as elsewhere, the New Testament insists on continued reminders as necessary to preserve the historical facts about Jesus and the truths of the faith; cf 3, 1–2; 1 Cor 11, 2; 15, 1–3. **My Son, my beloved:** or, "my beloved Son."

1, 18: **We:** at Jesus' transfiguration, referring to Peter, James, and John (Mt 17, 1).

1, 20–21: Often cited, along with 2 Tm 3, 16, on the "inspiration" of scripture or against private interpretation, these verses in context are directed against the false teachers of ch 2 and clever tales (16). The prophetic word in scripture comes admittedly through **human beings** (21), but **moved by the holy Spirit,** not from their own interpretation, and is a matter of what the author and Spirit intended, not the **personal interpretation** of false teachers. Instead of under the **influence of God,** some manuscripts read "holy ones of God."

2, 1–3: The pattern of **false prophets** among the Old Testament people of God will recur through **false teachers** in the church. Such destructive opinions of heretical sects bring loss of faith in Christ, contempt for the way of salvation (cf 21), and immorality.

2, 4–6: The false teachers will be punished just as surely and as severely as were the fallen **angels** (4; cf Jude 6; Gn 6, 1–4), the sinners of Noah's day (5; Gn 7, 21–23), and the inhabitants of the cities of the Plain (6; Jude 7; Gn 19, 25). Whereas there are three examples in Jude 5–7 (Exodus and wilderness; rebellious angels; Sodom and Gomorrah), 2 Peter omitted the first of these, has inserted a new illustration about Noah (5) between Jude's second and third examples, and listed the resulting three examples in their Old Testament order (Gn 6; 7; 19).

2, 4: **Chains of Tartarus:** cf Jude 6; other manuscripts in

e: Is 38, 12; Jn 21, 18-19.   f: Lk 9, 28-36; Jn 1, 14.   g: Ps 2, 7; Mt 17, 4-6.   h: Lk 1, 78-79; Rv 2, 28.   i: Mt 24, 11.24; 1 Tm 4, 1; Jude 4.   j: Is 52, 5.   k: Rom 16, 18.   l: Jude 6.

not spare the angels when they sinned, but condemned them to the chains of Tartarus and handed them over to be kept for judgment; [5m]*and if he did not spare the ancient world, even though he preserved Noah, a herald of righteousness, together with seven others, when he brought a flood upon the godless world; [6n]and if he condemned the cities of Sodom and Gommorah [to destruction], reducing them to ashes, making them an example for the godless [people] of what is coming; [7]and if he rescued Lot, a righteous man oppressed by the licentious conduct of unprincipled people [8](for day after day that righteous man living among them was tormented in his righteous soul at the lawless deeds that he saw and heard), [9o]then the Lord knows how to rescue the devout from trial and to keep the unrighteous under punishment for the day of judgment, [10p]*and especially those who follow the flesh with its depraved desire and show contempt for lordship.

False Teachers Denounced. Bold and arrogant, they are not afraid to revile glorious beings, [11q]*whereas angels, despite their superior strength and power, do not bring a reviling judgment against them from the Lord. [12r]But these people, like irrational animals born by nature for capture and destruction, revile things that they do not understand, and in their destruction they will also be destroyed, [13s]*suffering wrong as payment for wrongdoing. Thinking daytime revelry a delight, they are stains and defilements as they revel in their deceits while carousing with you. [14]Their eyes are full of adultery and insatiable for sin. They seduce unstable people, and their hearts are trained in greed. Accursed children! [15t]*Abandoning the straight road, they have gone astray, following the road of Balaam, the son of Bosor, who loved payment for wrongdoing, [16u]but he received a rebuke for his own crime: a mute beast spoke with a human voice and restrained the prophet's madness.

[17v]These people are waterless springs and mists driven by a gale; for them the gloom of darkness has been reserved. [18w]*For, talking empty bombast, they seduce with licentious desires of the flesh those who have barely escaped from people who live in error. [19x]They promise them freedom, though they themselves are slaves of corruption, for a person is a slave of whatever overcomes him. [20y]For if they, having escaped the defilements of the world through the knowledge of [our] Lord and savior Jesus Christ, again become entangled and overcome by them, their last condition is worse than their first. [21z]*For it would have been better for them not to have known the way of righteousness than after knowing it to turn back from the holy commandment handed down to them. [22a]*What

---

2 Peter read "pits of Tartarus." **Tartarus:** a term borrowed from Greek mythology to indicate the infernal regions.

2, 5–10a: Although God did not spare the sinful, he kept and saved the righteous, such as **Noah** (5) and **Lot** (7), and he **knows how to rescue the devout** (9), who are contrasted with the false teachers of the author's day. On Noah, cf Gn 5, 32—9, 29, especially 7, 1. On Lot, cf Gn 13 and 19.

2, 10b-22: Some take 10b and 11 with the preceding paragraph. Others begin the new paragraph with 10a, supplying from v 9 **The Lord knows how . . . to keep . . . under punishment,** with reference to God and probably specifically Christ (1). The conduct of the false teachers is described and condemned in language similar to that of Jude 8–16. This arrogance knows no bounds; animal-like, they are due to be caught and destroyed. They seduce even those who have knowledge of Christ (20).

2, 10b: Glorious beings: literally, "glories"; cf Jude 8. While some think that illustrious personages are meant or even political officials behind whom (fallen) angels stand, it is more likely that the reference is to glorious angelic beings (cf Jude 9).

2, 11: From the Lord: some manuscripts read "before the Lord"; cf Jude 9.

2, 13: Suffering wrong: some manuscripts read "receiving a reward." **In their deceits:** some manuscripts read "in their love feasts" (Jude 12).

2, 15: Balaam, the son of Bosor: in Nm 22, 5, Balaam is said to be the son of Beor, and it is this name that turns up in a few ancient Greek manuscripts by way of "correction" of the text. Balaam is not portrayed in such a bad light in Nm 22. His evil reputation and his **madness** (16), and possibly his surname Bosor, may have come from a Jewish tradition about him in the first/second century, of which we no longer have any knowledge.

2, 18: Barely escaped: some manuscripts read "really escaped."

2, 21: Commandment handed down: cf 3, 2 and Jude 3.

2, 22: The second proverb is of unknown origin, while the first appears in Prv 26, 11.

m: Gn 8, 15-19; Heb 11, 7. n: Gn 19, 24-25; Jude 7. o: 1 Cor 10, 13; Rv 3, 10. p: Jude 8. q: Jude 9. r: Ps 49, 13-15; Jude 10. s: Jude 12. t: Nm 31, 16; Jude 11. u: Nm 22, 28-33. v: Jude 12-13. w: Jude 16. x: Jn 8, 34; Rom 6, 16-17. y: Mt 12, 45. z: Ez 3, 20. a: Prv 26, 11.

is expressed in the true proverb has happened to them, "The dog returns to its own vomit," and "A bathed sow returns to wallowing in the mire."

IV: The Delay of the Second Coming

CHAPTER 3

See RG 442-44

Denial of the Parousia. *1**This is now, beloved, the second letter I am writing to you; through them by way of reminder I am trying to stir up your sincere disposition, *2b*to recall the words previously spoken by the holy prophets and the commandment of the Lord and savior through your apostles. *3c**Know this first of all, that in the last days scoffers will come [to] scoff, living according to their own desires *4d**and saying, "Where is the promise of his coming? From the time when our ancestors fell asleep, everything has remained as it was from the beginning of creation." *5e**They deliberately ignore the fact that the heavens existed of old and earth was formed out of water and

through water by the word of God; *6f**through these the world that then existed was destroyed, deluged with water. *7g*The present heavens and earth have been reserved by the same word for fire, kept for the day of judgment and of destruction of the godless.

8h*But do not ignore this one fact, beloved, that with the Lord one day is like a thousand years and a thousand years like one day. *9i*The Lord does not delay his promise, as some regard "delay," but he is patient with you, not wishing that any should perish but that all should come to repentance. *10j**But the day of the Lord will come like a thief, and then the heavens will pass away with a mighty roar and the elements will be dissolved by fire, and the earth and everything done on it will be found out.

Exhortation to Preparedness. *11k**Since everything is to be dissolved in this way, what sort of persons ought [you] to be, conducting yourselves in holiness and devotion, *12l**waiting for and hastening the coming of the day of God, because of which the heavens will be dissolved in

3, 1–4: The false teachers not only flout Christian morality (cf Jude 8–19); they also deny the second coming of Christ and the judgment (4; cf 7). They seek to justify their licentiousness by arguing that the promised return of Christ has not been realized and the world is the same, no better than it was before (3–4). The author wishes to strengthen the faithful against such errors by reminding them in this **second letter** of the instruction in 1 Pt and of the teaching of the **prophets** and of Christ, conveyed through the **apostles** (1–2; cf Jude 17); cf 1 Pt 1, 10–12.16–21, especially 16–21; Eph 2, 20.

3, 3: Scoffers: cf Jude 18, where, however, only the passions of the scoffers are mentioned, not a denial on their part of Jesus' parousia.

3, 4–7: The false teachers tried to justify their immorality by pointing out that the promised **coming (parousia)** of the Lord has not yet occurred, even though early Christians expected it in their day. They thus insinuate that God is not guiding the world's history anymore, since nothing has changed and the first generation of Christians, **our ancestors** (4) has all died by this time. The author replies that, just as God destroyed the earth by water in the flood (5–6, cf 2, 5), so he will destroy it along with the false teachers on judgment day (7). **The word of God,** which called the world into being (Gn 1; Ps 33, 6) and **destroyed** it by the waters of a flood, will destroy it again by fire on **the day of judgment** (5–7).

3, 5: Formed out of water and through water: Gn 1, 2.6–8 is reflected as well as Greek views that water was the basic element from which all is derived.

3, 6: Destroyed, deluged with water: cf 2, 5; Gn 7, 11—8, 2.

3, 8–10: The scoffers' objection (4) is refuted also by showing that **delay** of the Lord's second coming is not a failure to fulfill his word but rather a sign of his patience: God is giving time for repentance before the final judgment (cf Wis 11, 23–26; Ez 18, 23; 33, 11).

3, 8: Cf Ps 90, 4.

3, 10: Like a thief: Mt 24, 43; 1 Thes 5, 2; Rv 3, 3. **Will be found out:** cf 1 Cor 3, 13–15. Some few versions read, as the sense may demand, "will not be found out"; many manuscripts read "will be burned up"; there are further variants in other manuscripts, versions, and Fathers. Total destruction is assumed (11).

3, 11–16: The second coming of Christ and the judgment of the world are the doctrinal bases for the moral exhortation to readiness through vigilance and a virtuous life; cf Mt 24, 42.50–51; Lk 12, 40; 1 Thes 5, 1–11; Jude 20–21.

3, 12: Flames . . . fire: although this is the only New Testament passage about a final conflagration, the idea was common in apocalyptic and Greco-Roman thought. **Hastening:** eschatology is here used to motivate ethics (11), as elsewhere in the New Testament. Jewish sources and Acts 3, 19–20 assume that proper ethical conduct can help bring the promised day of the Lord; cf 9. Some render the phrase, however, "desiring it earnestly."

b: Jude 17.   *c:* 1 Tm 4, 1; 2 Tm 3, 1; Jude 18.   *d:* Is 5, 19.
e: Gn 1, 2.6.8; Ps 24, 2.   *f:* Gn 7, 21.   *g:* Is 51, 6; Mt 3, 12.
h: Ps 90, 4.   *i:* Ez 18, 23; 1 Tm 2, 4.   *j:* Is 66, 15-16; Mt 24, 29.
k: Acts 3, 19-21.   *l:* Is 34, 4; Heb 10, 27.

flames and the elements melted by fire. [13m]*But according to his promise we await new heavens and a new earth in which righteousness dwells.

[14]Therefore, beloved, since you await these things, be eager to be found without spot or blemish before him, at peace. [15n]And consider the patience of our Lord as salvation, as our beloved brother Paul, according to the wisdom given to him, also wrote to you, [16]*speaking of these things as he does in all his letters. In them there are some things hard to understand that the ignorant and un-

stable distort to their own destruction, just as they do the other scriptures.

V: Final Exhortation and Doxology

[17o]*Therefore, beloved, since you are forewarned, be on your guard not to be led into the error of the unprincipled and to fall from your own stability. [18p]But grow in grace and in the knowledge of our Lord and savior Jesus Christ. To him be glory now and to the day of eternity. [Amen.]

3, 13: New heavens and a new earth: cf Is 65, 17; 66, 22. The divine promises will be fulfilled after the day of judgment will have passed. The universe will be transformed by the reign of God's **righteousness** or justice; cf Is 65, 17–18; Acts 3, 21; Rom 8, 18–25; Rv 21, 1.

3, 16: These things: the teachings of this letter find parallels in Paul, e.g., God's will to save (Rom 2, 4; 9, 22–23; 1 Cor 1, 7–8), the coming of Christ (1 Thes 4, 16–17; 1 Cor 15, 23–52), and preparedness for the judgment (Col 1, 22–23; Eph 1, 4–14; 4, 30; 5, 5–14). **Other scriptures:** used to guide the faith and life of the Christian community. The letters of

Paul are thus here placed on the same level as books of the Old Testament. Possibly other New Testament writings could also be included.

3, 17–18: To avoid the dangers **of error** and loss of **stability,** Christians are **forewarned** to be **on guard** and to **grow in grace and knowledge** (1, 2) of Christ. The doxology (18) recalls 1 Pt 4, 11. Some manuscripts add **Amen.**

m: Is 65, 17; 66, 22; Rom 8, 21; Rv 21, 1.27.   *n:* Rom 8, 19; Jude 24.   *o:* Mk 13, 5; Heb 2, 1.   *p:* Rom 16, 27.

See RG 444–49

The First Letter of John

Early Christian tradition identified this work as a letter of John the apostle. Because of its resemblance to the fourth gospel in style, vocabulary, and ideas, it is generally agreed that both works are the product of the same school of Johannine Christianity. The terminology and the presence or absence of certain theological ideas in 1 John suggest that it was written after the gospel; it may have been composed as a short treatise on ideas that were developed more fully in the fourth gospel. To others, the evidence suggests that 1 John was written after the fourth gospel as part of a debate on the proper interpretation of that gospel. Whatever its relation to the gospel, 1 John may be dated toward the end of the first century. Unlike 2 and 3 John, it lacks in form the salutation and epistolary conclusion of a letter. These features, its prologue, and its emphasis on doctrinal teaching make it more akin to a theological treatise than to most other New Testament letters.

The purpose of the letter is to combat certain false ideas, especially about Jesus, and to deepen the spiritual and social awareness of the Christian

community (3, 17). Some former members (2, 19) of the community refused to acknowledge Jesus as the Christ (2, 22) and denied that he was a true man (4, 2). The specific heresy described in this letter cannot be identified exactly, but it is a form of docetism or gnosticism; the former doctrine denied the humanity of Christ to insure that his divinity was untainted, and the latter viewed the appearance of Christ as a mere stepping-stone to higher knowledge of God. These theological errors are rejected by an appeal to the reality and continuity of the apostolic witness to Jesus. The author affirms that authentic Christian love, ethics, and faith take place only within the historical revelation and sacrifice of Jesus Christ. The fullness of Christian life as fellowship with the Father must be based on true belief and result in charitable living; knowledge of God and love for one another are inseparable, and error in one area inevitably affects the other. Although the author recognizes that Christian doctrine presents intangible mysteries of faith about Christ, he insists that the concrete Christian life brings to light the deeper realities of the gospel.

The structure and language of the letter are straightforward yet repetitious. The author sets forth the striking contrasts between light and darkness, Christians and the world, and truth and error to illustrate the threats and responsibilities of Christian life. The result is not one of theological argument but one of intense religious conviction expressed in simple truths. The letter is of particular value for its declaration of the humanity and divinity of Christ as an apostolic teaching and for its development of the intrinsic connection between Christian moral conduct and Christian doctrine.

The principal divisions of the First Letter of John are the following:

I: Prologue (1, 1–4)
II: God as Light (1, 5—3, 10)
III: Love for One Another (3, 11—5, 12)
IV: Epilogue (5, 13–21)

I: Prologue

CHAPTER 1

See RG
446

The Word of Life

1a*What was from the beginning,
what we have heard,
what we have seen with our eyes,
what we looked upon
and touched with our hands
concerns the Word of life—
2 bfor the life was made visible;
we have seen it and testify to it
and proclaim to you the eternal life
that was with the Father and was made
visible to us—

3 cwhat we have seen and heard
we proclaim now to you,
so that you too may have fellowship with
us;
for our fellowship is with the Father
and with his Son, Jesus Christ.
4 dWe are writing this so that our joy may
be complete.

II: God as Light

God is Light. 5*Now this is the message that we have heard from him and proclaim to you: God is light, and in him there is no darkness at all. 6eIf we say, "We have fellowship with him," while we continue to walk in darkness, we lie and do not act in truth. 7fBut if we walk in the light as he is in the light, then we have fellowship with one another, and the blood of his Son Jesus cleanses us from all sin. 8g*If we say, "We are without sin," we deceive ourselves, and the truth is not in us. 9hIf we acknowledge our sins, he is faithful and just and will forgive our sins and cleanse us from every wrongdoing. 10iIf we say, "We have not sinned," we make him a liar, and his word is not in us.

CHAPTER 2

Christel and His Commandments. See RG
446–47 1j*My children, I am writing this to you so that you may not commit sin. But if anyone does sin, we have an Advocate with the Father, Jesus Christ the righteous one. 2kHe is expiation for our sins, and not for our sins only but for those of the whole world.

1, 1–4: There is a striking parallel to the prologue of the gospel of John (Jn 1, 1–18), but the emphasis here is not on the preexistent Word but rather on the apostles' witness to the incarnation of life by their experience of the historical Jesus. He is the **Word of life** (1; cf Jn 1, 4), **the eternal life that was with the Father and was made visible** (2; cf Jn 1, 14), and was **heard, seen, looked upon,** and **touched** by the apostles. The purpose of their teaching is to share that **life,** called **fellowship . . . with the Father and with his Son, Jesus Christ,** with those who receive their witness (3; Jn 1, 14.16).

1, 5–7: Light is to be understood here as truth and goodness; **darkness** here is error and depravity (cf Jn 3, 19–21; 17, 17; Eph 5, 8). To **walk** in light or darkness is to live according to truth or error, not merely intellectual but moral as well. Fellowship with God and with one another consists in a life according to the truth as found in God and in Christ.

1, 8–10: Denial of the condition of sin is self-deception and even contradictory of divine revelation; there is also the continual possibility of sin's recurrence. Forgiveness and deliverance from sin through Christ are assured through acknowledgment of them and repentance.

2, 1: Children: like the term "beloved," this is an expression of pastoral love (cf Jn 13, 33; 21, 5; 1 Cor 4, 14). **Advocate:** for the use of the term, see Jn 14, 16. Forgiveness of sin is assured through Christ's intercession and expiation or "offering"; the death of Christ effected the removal of sin.

a: 2, 13; Jn 1, 1.14; 20, 20.25.27.   *b:* Jn 15, 27; 17, 5.   *c:* Jn 17, 21; Acts 4, 20.   *d:* Jn 15, 11; 2 Jn 12.   *e:* Jn 12, 35.   *f:* Mt 26, 28; Rom 3, 24-25; Heb 9, 14; 1 Pt 1, 19; Rv 1, 5.   *g:* 2 Chr 6, 36; Prv 20, 9.   *h:* Prv 28, 13; Jas 5, 16.   *i:* 5, 10.   *j:* Jn 14, 16; Heb 7, 25.   *k:* 4, 10.

3l*The way we may be sure that we know him is to keep his commandments. *4m*Whoever says, "I know him," but does not keep his commandments is a liar, and the truth is not in him. *5n*But whoever keeps his word, the love of God is truly perfected in him. This is the way we may know that we are in union with him: *6*whoever claims to abide in him ought to live [just] as he lived.

The New Commandment. *7o**Beloved, I am writing no new commandment to you but an old commandment that you had from the beginning. The old commandment is the word that you have heard. *8p**And yet I do write a new commandment to you, which holds true in him and among you, for the darkness is passing away, and the true light is already shining. *9q*Whoever says he is in the light, yet hates his brother, is still in the darkness. *10r*Whoever loves his brother remains in the light, and there is nothing in him to cause a fall. *11*Whoever hates his brother is in darkness; he walks in darkness and does not know where he is going because the darkness has blinded his eyes.

Members of the Community. *12s**I am writing to you, children, because your sins have been forgiven for his name's sake.

*13t*I am writing to you, fathers, because you know him who is from the beginning.

I am writing to you, young men, because you have conquered the evil one.

*14*I write to you, children, because you know the Father.

I write to you, fathers, because you know him who is from the beginning.

I write to you, young men, because you are strong and the word of God remains in you, and you have conquered the evil one.

15u*Do not love the world or the things of the world. If anyone loves the world, the love of the Father is not in him. *16**For all that is in the world, sensual lust, enticement for the eyes, and a pretentious life, is not from the Father but is from the world. *17v*Yet the world and its enticement are passing away. But whoever does the will of God remains forever.

Antichrists. *18w**Children, it is the last hour; and just as you heard that the antichrist was coming, so now many antichrists have appeared. Thus we know this is the last hour. *19**They went out from us, but they were not really of our number; if they had been, they would have remained with us. Their desertion shows that none of them was of our number. *20x**But you have the anointing that comes

2, 3–6: The way we may be sure: to those who claim, "I have known Christ and therefore I know him," our author insists on not mere intellectual knowledge but obedience to God's commandments in a life conformed to the example of Christ; this confirms our knowledge of him and is **the love of God . . . perfected.** Disparity between moral life and the commandments proves improper belief.

2, 7–11: The author expresses the continuity and freshness of mutual charity in Christian experience. Through Christ the commandment of love has become the **light** defeating the **darkness** of evil in a new age. All hatred as darkness is incompatible with the light and Christian life. Note also the characteristic Johannine polemic in which a positive assertion is emphasized by the negative statement of its opposite.

2, 8: Which holds true in him and among you: literally, "a thing that holds true in him and in you."

2, 12–17: The Christian community that has experienced the grace of God through forgiveness of sin and knowledge of Christ is armed against the evil one.

2, 12: For his name's sake: because of Christ our sins are forgiven.

2, 15: The world: all that is hostile toward God and alienated from him. Love of the **world** and love of God are thus mutually exclusive; cf Jas 4, 4.

2, 16: Sensual lust: literally, "the lust of the flesh," inordinate desire for physical gratification. **Enticement for the eyes:** literally, "the lust of the eyes," avarice or covetousness; the eyes are regarded as the windows of the soul. **Pretentious life:** literally, "pride of life," arrogance or ostentation in one's earthly style of life that reflects a willful independence from God and others.

2, 18: It is the last hour: literally, "a last hour," the period between the death and resurrection of Christ and his second coming. **The antichrist:** opponent or adversary of Christ; the term appears only in 1–2 John, but "pseudochrists" (translated "false messiahs") in Mt 24, 24 and Mk 13, 22, and Paul's "lawless one" in 2 Thes 2, 3, are similar figures. **Many antichrists:** Mt, Mk, and Rv seem to indicate a collectivity of persons, here related to the false teachers.

2, 19: Not really of our number: the apostate teachers only proved their lack of faith by leaving the community.

2, 20: The anointing that comes from the holy one: this anointing is in the Old Testament sense of receiving the Spirit of God. The **holy one** probably refers to Christ. True knowledge is the gift of the Spirit (cf Is 11, 2), and the function of the Spirit is to lead Christians to the truth (Jn 14, 17.26; 16, 13).

l: Jn 14, 15; 15, 10. *m:* 4, 20. *n:* Jn 14, 23. *o:* 3, 11; Dt 6, 5; Mt 22, 37-40. *p:* Jn 13, 34 / Jn 1, 5; Rom 13, 12. *q:* Jn 8, 12. *r:* Eccl 2, 14; Jn 11, 10. *s:* 1 Cor 6, 11. *t:* 1, 1; Jn 1, 1. *u:* Rom 8, 7-8; Jas 4, 4; 2 Pt 1, 4. *v:* Is 40, 8; Mt 7, 21; 1 Cor 7, 31; 1 Pt 4, 2. *w:* 1 Tim 4, 1. *x:* Jn 14, 26.

from the holy one, and you all have knowledge. ^{21y}I write to you not because you do not know the truth but because you do, and because every lie is alien to the truth. ^{22z}*Who is the liar? Whoever denies that Jesus is the Christ. Whoever denies the Father and the Son, this is the antichrist. ^{23a}No one who denies the Son has the Father, but whoever confesses the Son has the Father as well.

Life from God's Anointing. ^{24b}*Let what you heard from the beginning remain in you. If what you heard from the beginning remains in you, then you will remain in the Son and in the Father. ^{25c}And this is the promise that he made us: eternal life. ²⁶I write you these things about those who would deceive you. ²⁷As for you, the anointing that you received from him remains in you, so that you do not need anyone to teach you. But his anointing teaches you about everything and is true and not false; just as it taught you, remain in him.

Children of God. ²⁸*And now, children, remain in him, so that when he appears we may have confidence and not be put to shame by him at his coming. ²⁹If you consider that he is righteous, you also know that everyone who acts in righteousness is begotten by him.

CHAPTER 3

See RG
446–47 ^{1d}*See what love the Father has bestowed on us that we may be called the children of God. Yet so we are. The reason the world does not know us is that it did not know him. ^{2e}*Beloved, we are God's children now; what we shall be has not yet been revealed. We do know that when it is revealed we shall be like him, for we shall see him as he is. ^{3f}Everyone who has this hope based on him makes himself pure, as he is pure.

Avoiding Sin. ⁴*Everyone who commits sin commits lawlessness, for sin is lawlessness. ^{5g}You know that he was revealed to take away sins, and in him there is no sin. ⁶No one who remains in him sins; no one who sins has seen him or known him. ⁷Children, let no one deceive you. The person who acts in righteousness is righteous, just as he is righteous. ^{8h}Whoever sins belongs to the devil, because the devil has sinned from the beginning. Indeed, the Son of God was revealed to destroy the works of the devil. ⁹*No one who is begotten by God commits sin, because God's seed remains in him; he cannot sin because he is begotten by God. ¹⁰In this way, the children of God and the children of the devil are made plain; no one who fails to act in righteousness belongs to God, nor anyone who does not love his brother.

III: Love for One Another

¹¹ⁱ*For this is the message you have heard from the beginning: we should love one another, ^{12j}unlike Cain who belonged to the evil one and slaughtered his brother. Why

2, 22–23: Certain gnostics denied that the earthly Jesus was the Christ; to deny knowledge of the Son is to deny the Father, since only through the Son has God been fully revealed (Jn 1, 18; 14, 8–9).

2, 24: Continuity with the apostolic witness as proclaimed in the prologue is the safeguard of right belief.

2, 28–29: Our confidence at his judgment is based on the daily assurance of salvation. Our actions reflect our true relation to him.

3, 1–3: The greatest sign of God's love is the gift of his Son (Jn 3, 16) that has made Christians true children of God. This relationship is a present reality and also part of the life to come; true knowledge of God will ultimately be gained, and Christians prepare themselves now by virtuous lives in imitation of the Son.

3, 2: When it is revealed: or "when he is revealed" (the subject of the verb could be Christ).

3, 4: Lawlessness: a reference to the activity of the antichrist, so it is expressed as hostility toward God and a rejection of Christ. The author goes on to contrast the states of sin and righteousness. Christians do not escape sin but realize

that when they sin they cease to have fellowship with God. Virtue and sin distinguish the children of God from the children of the devil.

3, 9: A habitual sinner is a child of the devil, while a child of God, who by definition is in fellowship with God, cannot sin. **Seed:** Christ or the Spirit who shares the nature of God with the Christian.

3, 11–18: Love, even to the point of self-sacrifice, is the point of the commandment. The story of Cain and Abel (12–15; Gn 4, 1–16) presents the rivalry of two brothers, in a contrast of evil and righteousness, where envy led to murder. For Christians, proof of deliverance is love toward others, after the example of Christ. This includes concrete acts of charity, out of our material abundance.

y: 3, 19; 2 Pt 1, 12. *z:* 2 Thes 2, 4. *a:* Jn 14, 7-9. *b:* Jn 14, 23. *c:* Jn 5, 24; 10, 28; 17, 2. *d:* Jn 1, 12; Eph 1, 5 / Jn 15, 21; 17, 25. *e:* Phil 3, 21. *f:* 2, 6. *g:* Is 53, 9; Jn 1, 29; 8, 46; 1 Pt 2, 22. *h:* Jn 8, 44; 12, 31-32. *i:* 2, 7; Jn 13, 34; 15, 12.17. *j:* Gn 4, 8; Jude 11.

did he slaughter him? Because his own works were evil, and those of his brother righteous. [13k]Do not be amazed, [then,] brothers, if the world hates you. [14l]We know that we have passed from death to life because we love our brothers. Whoever does not love remains in death. [15m]Everyone who hates his brother is a murderer, and you know that no murderer has eternal life remaining in him. [16n]The way we came to know love was that he laid down his life for us; so we ought to lay down our lives for our brothers. [17o]If someone who has worldly means sees a brother in need and refuses him compassion, how can the love of God remain in him? [18p]Children, let us love not in word or speech but in deed and truth.

Confidence before God. [19]*[Now] this is how we shall know that we belong to the truth and reassure our hearts before him [20]in whatever our hearts condemn, for God is greater than our hearts and knows everything. [21]Beloved, if [our] hearts do not condemn us, we have confidence in God [22q]and receive from him whatever we ask, because we keep his commandments and do what pleases him. [23r]And his commandment is this: we should believe in the name of his Son, Jesus Christ, and love one another just as he commanded us. [24s]Those who keep his commandments remain in him, and he in them, and the way we know that he remains in us is from the Spirit that he gave us.

CHAPTER 4

See RG
447-48

Testing the Spirits. [1]*Beloved, do not trust every spirit but test the spirits to see whether they belong to God, because many false prophets have gone out into the world. [2u]This is how you can know the Spirit of God: every spirit that acknowledges Jesus Christ come in the flesh belongs to God, [3v]*and every spirit that does not acknowledge Jesus does not belong to God. This is the spirit of the antichrist that, as you heard, is to come, but in fact is already in the world. [4]You belong to God, children, and you have conquered them, for the one who is in you is greater than the one who is in the world. [5w]They belong to the world; accordingly, their teaching belongs to the world, and the world listens to them. [6x]We belong to God, and anyone who knows God listens to us, while anyone who does not belong to God refuses to hear us. This is how we know the spirit of truth and the spirit of deceit.

God's Love and Christian Life. [7]*Beloved, let us love one another, because love is of God; everyone who loves is begotten by God and knows God. [8]Whoever is without love does not know God, for God is love. [9y]In this way the love of God was revealed to us: God sent his only Son into the world so that we might have life through him. [10z]In this is love: not that we have loved God, but that he loved us and sent his Son as expiation for our sins. [11]Beloved, if God so loved us, we also must love one another. [12a]No one has ever

---

3, 19–24: Living a life of faith in Jesus and of Christian love assures us of abiding in God no matter what our feelings may at times tell us. Our obedience gives us confidence in prayer and trust in God's judgment. This obedience includes our belief in Christ and love for one another.

3, 19b-20: This difficult passage may also be translated "we shall be at peace before him in whatever our hearts condemn, for . . ." or "and before God we shall convince our hearts, if our hearts condemn us, that God is greater than our hearts."

4, 1–6: Deception is possible in spiritual phenomena and may be tested by its relation to Christian doctrine (cf 1 Cor 12, 3): those who fail to acknowledge Jesus Christ in the flesh are false prophets and belong to the antichrist. Even though these false prophets are well received in the world, the Christian who belongs to God has a greater power in the truth.

4, 3: **Does not acknowledge Jesus:** some ancient manuscripts add "Christ" and/or "to have come in the flesh" (cf 2),

and others read "every spirit that annuls (or severs) Jesus."

4, 7–12: Love as we share in it testifies to the nature of God and to his presence in our lives. One who loves shows that one is a child of God and knows God, for God's very being is love; one without love is without God. The revelation of the nature of God's love is found in the free gift of his Son to us, so that we may share life with God and be delivered from our sins. The love we have for one another must be of the same sort: authentic, merciful; this unique Christian love is our proof that we know God and can "see" the invisible God.

k: Mt 24, 9; Jn 15, 18; 17, 14. l: Lv 19, 17; Jn 5, 24. m: Jn 8, 44. n: Mt 20, 28; Jn 10, 11; 15, 13. o: Dt 15, 7.11; Jas 2, 15-16. p: Jas 1, 22. q: 5, 15; Mt 7, 7-11; 21, 22; Jn 14, 13-14. r: Jn 13, 34; 15, 17. s: 4, 13; Jn 14, 21-23. t: 2, 18; Mt 24, 24. u: 1 Cor 12, 3; 1 Thes 5, 21. v: 1, 22. w: Jn 15, 19. x: Jn 8, 47; 10, 16. y: Jn 3, 16. z: Rom 5, 8. a: Jn 1, 18; 1 Tm 6, 16.

seen God. Yet, if we love one another, God remains in us, and his love is brought to perfection in us.

[13]*This is how we know that we remain in him and he in us, that he has given us of his Spirit. [14]Moreover, we have seen and testify that the Father sent his Son as savior of the world. [15]Whoever acknowledges that Jesus is the Son of God, God remains in him and he in God. [16]We have come to know and to believe in the love God has for us.

God is love, and whoever remains in love remains in God and God in him. [17b]In this is love brought to perfection among us, that we have confidence on the day of judgment because as he is, so are we in this world. [18]There is no fear in love, but perfect love drives out fear because fear has to do with punishment, and so one who fears is not yet perfect in love. [19]We love because he first loved us. [20c]*If anyone says, "I love God," but hates his brother, he is a liar; for whoever does not love a brother whom he has seen cannot love God whom he has not seen. [21d]This is the commandment we have from him: whoever loves God must also love his brother.

CHAPTER 5

See RG 447-48
Faith is Victory over the World.
[1e]*Everyone who believes that Jesus is the Christ is begotten by God, and everyone who loves the father loves [also] the one begotten by him. [2]In this way we know that we love the children of God when we love God and obey his commandments. [3f]For the love of God is this, that we keep his commandments. And his commandments are not burdensome, [4g]for whoever is begotten by God conquers the world. And the victory that conquers the world is our faith. [5h]Who [indeed] is the victor over the world but the one who believes that Jesus is the Son of God?

[6i]*This is the one who came through water and blood, Jesus Christ, not by water alone, but by water and blood. The Spirit is the one that testifies, and the Spirit is truth. [7]So there are three that testify, [8j]the Spirit, the water, and the blood, and the three are of one accord. [9k]If we accept human testimony, the testimony of God is surely greater. Now the testimony of God is this, that he has testified on behalf of his Son. [10l]Whoever believes in the Son of God has this testimony within himself. Whoever does not believe God has made him a liar by not believing the testimony God has given about his Son. [11m]And this is the testimony: God gave us eternal life, and this life is in his Son. [12]Whoever possesses the Son has life; whoever does not possess the Son of God does not have life.

IV: Epilogue

Prayer for Sinners. [13n]*I write these things to you so that you may know that you have

4, 13–21: The testimony of the Spirit and that of faith join the testimony of love to confirm our knowledge of God. Our love is grounded in the confession of Jesus as the Son of God and the example of God's love for us. Christian life is founded on the knowledge of God as love and on his continuing presence that relieves us from fear of judgment (16–18). What Christ is gives us confidence, even as we live and love in this world. Yet Christian love is not abstract but lived in the concrete manner of love for one another.

4, 20: **Cannot love God:** some ancient manuscripts read "how can he love . . . ?"

5, 1–5: Children of God are identified not only by their love for others (4, 7–9) and for God (5, 1–2) but by their belief in the divine sonship of Jesus Christ. Faith, the acceptance of Jesus in his true character and the obedience in love to God's commands (3), is the source of the Christian's power in the world and conquers the world of evil (4–5), even as Christ overcame the world (Jn 16, 33).

5, 6–12: **Water and blood** (6) refers to Christ's baptism (Mt 3, 16–17) and to the shedding of his blood on the cross (Jn 19, 34). **The Spirit** was present at the baptism (Mt 3, 16; Mk 1, 10; Lk 3, 22; Jn 1, 32.34). **The testimony** to Christ as

the Son of God is confirmed by divine witness (7–9), greater by far than the two legally required human witnesses (Dt 17, 6). To deny this is to deny God's truth; cf Jn 8, 17–18. The gist of the divine witness or **testimony** is that **eternal life** (11–12) is given in Christ and nowhere else. To **possess the Son** is not acceptance of a doctrine but of a person who lives now and provides life.

5, 13–21: As children of God we have confidence in prayer because of our intimate relationship with him (14–15). In love, we pray (16–17) for those who are in **sin,** but not in **deadly sin** (literally, "sin unto death"), probably referring to apostasy or activities brought on under the antichrist; cf Mk 3, 29; Heb 6, 4–6; 10, 26–31. Even in the latter case, however, prayer, while not enjoined, is not forbidden. The letter concludes with a summary of the themes of the letter (18–20). There is a sharp antithesis between the children of God and those belonging to the world and to the evil one. The Son re-

b: 2, 28. c: 2, 4. d: Jn 13, 34; 14, 15.21; 15, 17. e: Jn 8, 42; 1 Pt 1, 23. f: Jn 14, 15. g: Jn 16, 33. h: 1 Cor 15, 57. i: Jn 15, 26; 19, 34. j: Jn 5, 32.36; 15, 26. k: Jn 5, 32.37. l: 3, 33. m: 1, 2; Jn 1, 4; 5, 21.26; 17, 3. n: Jn 1, 12; 20, 31.

eternal life, you who believe in the name of the Son of God. [14o]And we have this confidence in him, that if we ask anything according to his will, he hears us. [15]And if we know that he hears us in regard to whatever we ask, we know that what we have asked him for is ours. [16p]If anyone sees his brother sinning, if the sin is not deadly, he should pray to God and he will give him life. This is only for those whose sin is not deadly. There is such a thing as deadly sin, about which I do not say that you should pray. [17]All

wrongdoing is sin, but there is sin that is not deadly.

[18]We know that no one begotten by God sins; but the one begotten by God he protects, and the evil one cannot touch him. [19]We know that we belong to God, and the whole world is under the power of the evil one. [20q]We also know that the Son of God has come and has given us discernment to know the one who is true. And we are in the one who is true, in his Son Jesus Christ. He is the true God and eternal life. [21]Children, be on your guard against idols.

veals the God of truth; Christians dwell in the true God, **in his Son,** and have eternal life. The final verse (21) voices a perennial warning about **idols,** any type of rival to God.

o: 3, 21-22; Mt 7, 7; Jn 14, 13-14.　*p:* Mt 12, 31.　*q:* Jer 24, 7; Jn 17, 3; Eph 1, 17.

See RG
449–51

The Second Letter of John

Written in response to similar problems, the Second and Third Letters of John are of the same length, perhaps determined by the practical consideration of the writing space on one piece of papyrus. In each letter the writer calls himself "the Presbyter," and their common authorship is further evidenced by internal similarities in style and wording, especially in the introductions and conclusions. The literary considerations that link 2 John and 3 John also link them with the First Letter and the Gospel of John. The concern with "truth," christology, mutual love, the new commandment, antichrist, and the integrity of witness to the earthly Jesus mark these works as products of the Johannine school. The identity of the Presbyter is problematic. The use of the title implies more than age, and refers to his position of leadership in the early church. The absence of a proper name indicates that he was well known and acknowledged in authority by the communities to which he writes. Although traditionally attributed to John the apostle, these letters were probably written by a disciple or scribe of an apostle. The traditional place and date of composition, Ephesus at the end of the first century, are plausible for both letters.

The Second Letter is addressed to "the chosen Lady" and "to her children." This literary image of a particular Christian community reflects the specific destination and purpose of the letter. Unlike 1 John, this brief letter is not a theological treatise but a reply to problems within the church. The Johannine themes of love and truth are used to support practical advice on Christian living. The Presbyter encourages community members to show their Christianity by adhering to the great commandment of mutual love and to the historical truth about Jesus. The false teaching present among them is a spiritualizing christology that may tempt some members to discount teachings about the incarnation and death of Jesus the Christ; cf 1 Jn 4, 2. For their protection the Presbyter forbids hospitality toward unknown or "progressive" Christians to prevent their infiltration of the community. The Second Letter preserves the Johannine concerns of doctrinal purity and active love in the form of pastoral advice to a threatened community.

[1a]*The Presbyter to the chosen Lady and to her children whom I love in

See RG
449–51

1: The chosen Lady: literally "elected"; this could also be translated "Kyria (a woman's name) chosen (by God)" or "the lady Electa" or "Electa Kyria." The adjective "chosen" is applied to all Christians at the beginning of other New Testament letters (1 Pt 1, 1; Ti 1, 1). The description is of a spe-

cific community with "children" who are its members. **The truth:** the affirmation of Jesus in the flesh and in contrast to false teaching (7).

a: Jn 8, 32; 3 Jn 1.

truth—and not only I but also all who know the truth— ²because of the truth that dwells in us and will be with us forever. ³*Grace, mercy, and peace will be with us from God the Father and from Jesus Christ the Father's Son in truth and love.

⁴ᵇ*I rejoiced greatly to find some of your children walking in the truth just as we were commanded by the Father. ⁵ᶜBut now, Lady, I ask you, not as though I were writing a new commandment but the one we have had from the beginning: let us love one another. ⁶ᵈ*For this is love, that we walk according to his commandments; this is the commandment, as you heard from the beginning, in which you should walk.

⁷ᵉ*Many deceivers have gone out into the world, those who do not acknowledge Jesus Christ as coming in the flesh; such is the deceitful one and the antichrist. ⁸*Look to yourselves that you do not lose what we worked for but may receive a full recompense. ⁹ᶠ*Anyone who is so "progressive" as not to remain in the teaching of the Christ does not have God; whoever remains in the teaching has the Father and the Son. ¹⁰ᵍ*If anyone comes to you and does not bring this doctrine, do not receive him in your house or even greet him; ¹¹for whoever greets him shares in his evil works.

¹²ʰ*Although I have much to write to you, I do not intend to use paper and ink. Instead, I hope to visit you and to speak face to face so that our joy may be complete. ¹³*The children of your chosen sister send you greetings.

3: **Grace, mercy, and peace:** like 1 and 2 Tm this letter adds **mercy** to the terms used frequently in a salutation to describe Christian blessing; it appears only here in the Johannine writings. The author also puts the blessing in relation to **truth** and **love,** the watchwords of the Johannine teaching. **The Father's Son:** the title that affirms the close relationship of Christ to God; similar variations of this title occur elsewhere (Jn 1, 14; 3, 35), but the precise wording is not found elsewhere in the New Testament.

4: **Some of your children:** this refers to those whom the Presbyter has recently encountered, but it may also indicate the presence of false doctrine in the community: the Presbyter encourages those who have remained faithful. **Walking in the truth:** an expression used in the Johannine writings to describe a way of living in which the Christian faith is visibly expressed; cf 1 Jn 1, 6–7; 2, 6.11, 3 Jn 3.

6: **His commandments:** cf 1 Jn 2, 7–8; 3, 23; 4, 21; obedience to the commandment of faith and love includes all others.

7: **The antichrist:** see 1 Jn 2, 18–19.22; 4, 3.

8: **You** (plural): it is not certain whether this means the Christians addressed or includes the Presbyter, since some of the ancient Greek manuscripts and Greek Fathers have "we."

9: **Anyone who is so "progressive":** literally, "Anyone who goes ahead." Some gnostic groups held the doctrine of the Christ come in the flesh to be a first step in belief, which the more advanced and spiritual believer surpassed and abandoned in his knowledge of the spiritual Christ. The author affirms that fellowship with God may be gained only by holding to the complete doctrine of Jesus Christ (1 Jn 2, 22–23; 4, 2; 5, 5–6).

10–11: At this time false teachers were considered so dangerous and divisive as to be shunned completely. From this description they seem to be wandering preachers. We see here a natural suspicion of early Christians concerning such itinerants and can envisage the problems faced by missionaries such as those mentioned in 3 Jn 10.

12: **Our joy:** a number of other Greek manuscripts read "your joy."

13: **Chosen sister:** the community of which the Presbyter is now a part greets you (singular), the community of the Lady.

b: 3 Jn 3.   *c:* Jn 13, 34; 15, 12; 1 Jn 4, 7.   *d:* Jn 13, 34; 14, 15; 1 Jn 5, 3.   *e:* 1 Jn 2, 22; 4, 2.   *f:* Jn 8, 31; 1 Jn 2, 23; 4, 15. *g:* Rom 16, 17; 2 Thes 3, 6.   *h:* Jn 15, 11; 1 Jn 1, 4; 3 Jn 13.

See RG 451–52

The Third Letter of John

The Third Letter of John preserves a brief glimpse into the problems of missionary activity and local autonomy in the early church. In contrast to the other two letters of John, this work was addressed to a specific individual, Gaius. This letter is less theological in content and purpose. The author's goal was to secure hospitality and material support for his missionaries, and the Presbyter is writing to another member of the church who has welcomed missionaries in the past. The Presbyter commends Gaius for his hospitality and encourages his future help. He indicates he may come to challenge the policy of Diotrephes that is based on evil gossip.

The problems of the Presbyter in this short letter provide us with valuable evidence of the flexible and personal nature of authority in the early church. The Presbyter writes to Gaius, whom perhaps he had converted or instructed, on the basis of their personal links. The brothers have also confirmed him as a loyal Christian in action and belief. Gaius accepted the missionaries from the Presbyter and presumably will accept Demetrius on the Presbyter's recommendation. In contrast, Diotrephes refuses to receive either letters or friends of the Presbyter. Although he is portrayed as ambitious and hostile, he perhaps exemplifies the cautious and sectarian nature of early Christianity; for its own protection the local community mistrusted missionaries as false teachers. Most interestingly, Diotrephes seems comfortable in ignoring the requests of the Presbyter. The Presbyter seems to acknowledge that only a personal confrontation with Diotrephes will remedy the situation (10). The division, however, may also rest on doctrinal disagreement in which Gaius and the other "friends" accept the teaching of the Presbyter, and Diotrephes does not; the missionaries are not received for suspicion of theological error. Diotrephes has thus been viewed by some as an overly ambitious local upstart trying to thwart the advance of orthodox Christianity, by others as an orthodox church official suspicious of the teachings of the Presbyter and those in the Johannine school who think as he does, or by still others as a local leader anxious to keep the debates in the Johannine community out of his own congregation.

This brief letter and the situation that it mirrors show us how little we know about some details of early development in the church: schools of opinion existed around which questions of faith and life were discussed, and personal ties as well as doctrine and authority played a role in what happened amid divisions and unity.

1a*The Presbyter to the beloved Gaius whom I love in truth.

*2*Beloved, I hope you are prospering in every respect and are in good health, just as your soul is prospering. *3b**I rejoiced greatly when some of the brothers came and testified to how truly you walk in the truth. *4c*Nothing gives me greater joy than to hear that my children are walking in the truth.

5d*Beloved, you are faithful in all you do for the brothers, especially for strangers; *6e**they have testified to your love before the church. Please help them in a way worthy of God to continue their journey. *7**For they have set out for the sake of the Name and are accepting nothing from the pagans. *8*Therefore, we ought to support such persons, so that we may be co-workers in the truth.

9*I wrote to the church, but Diotrephes, who loves to dominate, does not acknowledge us. *10**Therefore, if I come, I will draw attention to what he is doing, spreading evil nonsense about us. And not content with that, he will not receive the brothers, hindering those who wish to do so and expelling them from the church.

11f*Beloved, do not imitate evil but imitate good. Whoever does what is good is of God; whoever does what is evil has never seen God. *12g**Demetrius receives a good report from all, even from the truth itself. We give our testimonial as well, and you know our testimony is true.

1: Beloved Gaius: a frequent form of address for fellow Christians in New Testament epistolary literature.

3: The brothers: in this letter, the term may refer to Christians who have been missionaries and received hospitality from Gaius (5–6). **Walk in the truth:** the common Johannine term to describe Christian living; this description presents Gaius as following the teachings of the Presbyter in contrast to Diotrephes.

5: You are faithful in all you do: Gaius's aid to the missionaries is a manifestation of his true Christian faith.

6: Help them . . . to continue their journey: the Presbyter asks Gaius not only to continue to welcome the missionaries to his community but also to equip them for further travels.

7: The Name: of Jesus Christ (cf Acts 5, 41; 1 Jn 2, 12; 3, 23; 5, 13). **Accepting nothing:** not expecting support from the pagans to whom they preach the gospel, so that they will not be considered as beggars; they required support from

other Christians; cf Paul's complaints to the Corinthians (1 Cor 9, 3–12).

9: Who loves to dominate: the Presbyter does not deny Diotrephes' place as leader but indicates that his ambition may have caused him to disregard his letter and his influence.

10: If I come: the Presbyter may visit the community to challenge the actions of Diotrephes toward himself and the missionaries. **Will not receive the brothers:** Diotrephes may have been critical of the teachings of the Presbyter and sought to maintain doctrinal purity; cf 1 Jn 2, 19 and 2 Jn 10–11.

11: Do not imitate evil: Gaius should not be influenced by the behavior of Diotrephes.

12: Demetrius: because of the fear of false teachers,

a: 2 Jn 1. *b:* 3 Jn 5; Gal 6, 10; 2 Jn 4. *c:* 1 Thes 2, 11-12; 1 Tm 1, 2; 2 Tm 1, 2; 1 Jn 2, 1; 2 Jn 4. *d:* Rom 12, 13; Gal 6, 10; Heb 13, 2. *e:* Acts 15, 3; Col 1, 10; 1 Thes 2, 12. *f:* 1 Jn 2, 29; 3, 6.10. *g:* Jn 19, 35; 21, 24; 1 Tm 3, 7.

*13h*I have much to write to you, but I do not wish to write with pen and ink. *14*Instead, I hope to see you soon, when we can talk face to face. *15i**Peace be with you. The friends greet you; greet the friends there each by name.

Demetrius, perhaps the bearer of the letter, is provided with a recommendation from the Presbyter; cf 2 Cor 3, 1; Rom 16, 1. **Even from the truth itself:** this refers probably to the manner of Demetrius's life that testifies to his true belief; cf Gaius above (v 3).

15: Friends: although a Johannine term for Christians (Jn 15, 15), the word here may refer to those in the community loyal to the Presbyter and to Gaius.

h: 2 Jn 12.   *i:* Jn 20, 19.21.26; Eph 6, 23; 1 Pt 5, 14.

See RG
452-55

The Letter of Jude

This letter is by its address attributed to "Jude, a slave of Jesus Christ and brother of James" (1). Since he is not identified as an apostle, this designation can hardly be meant to refer to the Jude or Judas who is listed as one of the Twelve (Lk 6, 16; Acts 1, 13; cf Jn 14, 22). The person intended is almost certainly the other Jude, named in the gospels among the relatives of Jesus (Mt 13, 55; Mk 6, 3), and the James who is listed there as his brother is the one to whom the Letter of James is attributed (see the Introduction to James). Nothing else is known of this Jude, and the apparent need to identify him by reference to his better-known brother indicates that he was a rather obscure personage in the early church.

The letter is addressed in the most general terms to "those who are called, beloved in God the Father and kept safe for Jesus Christ" (1), hence apparently to all Christians. But since its purpose is to warn the addressees against false teachers, the author must have had in mind one or more specific Christian communities located in the unidentified region where the errors in question constituted a danger. While the letter contains some Semitic features, there is nothing to identify the addressees specifically as Jewish Christians; indeed, the errors envisaged seem to reflect an early form of gnosticism, opposed to law, that points rather to the cultural context of the Gentile world. Like James and 2 Peter, the Letter of Jude manifests none of the typical features of the letter form except the address.

There is so much similarity between Jude and 2 Peter, especially Jude 4–16 and 2 Peter 2, 1–18, that there must be a literary relationship between them. Since there is no evidence for the view that both authors borrowed from the same source, it is usually supposed that one of them borrowed from the other. Most scholars believe that Jude is the earlier of the two, principally because he quotes two apocryphal Jewish works, the Assumption of Moses (9) and the Book of Enoch (14–15) as part of his structured argument, whereas 2 Peter omits both references. Since there was controversy in the early church about the propriety of citing non-canonical literature that included legendary material, it is more probable that a later writer would omit such references than that he would add them.

Many interpreters today consider Jude a pseudonymous work dating from the end of the first century or even later. In support of this view they adduce the following arguments: (a) the apostles are referred to as belonging to an age that has receded into the past (17–18); (b) faith is understood as a body of doctrine handed down by a process of tradition (3); (c) the author's competent Greek style shows that he must have had a Hellenistic cultural formation; (d) the gnostic character of the errors envisaged fits better into the early second century than into a period several decades earlier. While impressive, these arguments are not entirely compelling and do not completely rule out the possibility of composition around the year A.D. 80, when the historical Jude may still have been alive.

This little letter is an urgent note by an author who intended to write more fully about salvation to an unknown group of readers, but who was forced by dangers from false teachers worming their way into the community (3–4) to dash off a warning against them (5–16) and to deliver some pressing Christian admonitions (17–23). The letter is justly famous for its majestic closing doxology (24–25).

See RG 452–55 **Address and Greeting.** [1a]*Jude, a slave of Jesus Christ and brother of James, to those who are called, beloved in God the Father and kept safe for Jesus Christ: [2b]may mercy, peace, and love be yours in abundance.

Occasion for Writing. [3c]*Beloved, although I was making every effort to write to you about our common salvation, I now feel a need to write to encourage you to contend for the faith that was once for all handed down to the holy ones. [4d]For there have been some intruders, who long ago were designated for this condemnation, godless persons, who pervert the grace of our God into licentiousness and who deny our only Master and Lord, Jesus Christ.

The False Teachers. [5e]*I wish to remind you, although you know all things, that [the] Lord who once saved a people from the land of Egypt later destroyed those who did not believe. [6f]*The angels too, who did not keep to their own domain but deserted their proper dwelling, he has kept in eternal chains, in gloom, for the judgment of the great day. [7g]*Likewise, Sodom, Gomorrah, and the surrounding towns, which, in the same manner as they, indulged in sexual promiscuity and practiced unnatural vice, serve as an example by undergoing a punishment of eternal fire.

[8]*Similarly, these dreamers nevertheless also defile the flesh, scorn lordship, and revile glorious beings. [9h]*Yet the archangel Michael, when he argued with the devil in a dispute over the body of Moses, did not venture to pronounce a reviling judgment upon him but said, "May the Lord rebuke you!" [10i]But these people revile what they do not understand and are destroyed by what they know by nature like irrational animals. [11j]*Woe to them! They followed the way of Cain, abandoned themselves to Balaam's error for the sake of gain, and perished in the rebellion of Korah. [12k]*These are blemishes on your love feasts, as they carouse fearlessly and look after themselves. They are

1: Jude ... brother of James: for the identity of the author of this letter, see Introduction. **To those who are called:** the vocation to the Christian faith is God's free gift to those whom he loves and whom he safely protects in Christ until the Lord's second coming.

3–4: Our common salvation: the teachings of the Christian faith derived from the apostolic preaching and to be kept by the Christian community.

5: For this first example of divine punishment on those who had been saved but did not then keep faith, see Nm 14, 28–29 and the note there. Some manuscripts have the word "once" (**hapax** as at 3) after "you know"; some commentators have suggested that it means "knowing one thing" or "you know all things once for all." Instead of "[the] Lord" manuscripts vary, having "Jesus," "God," or no subject stated.

6: This second example draws on Gn 6, 1–4 as elaborated in the apocryphal Book of Enoch (cf 14): heavenly beings came to earth and had sexual intercourse with women. God punished them by casting them out of heaven into darkness and bondage.

7: Practiced unnatural vice: literally, "went after alien flesh." This example derives from Gn 19, 1–25, especially 4–11, when the townsmen of Sodom violated both hospitality and morality by demanding that Lot's two visitors (really messengers of Yahweh) be handed over to them so that they could abuse them sexually. **Unnatural vice:** this refers to the desire for intimacies by human beings with angels (the reverse of the example in 6). Sodom (whence "sodomy") and Gomorrah became proverbial as object lessons for God's punishment on sin (Is 1, 9; Jer 50, 40; Am 4, 11; Mt 10, 15; 2 Pt 2, 6).

8: Dreamers: the writer returns to the false teachers of v

4, applying charges from the three examples in vv 5, 6, 7. This may apply to claims they make for revelations they have received by night (to the author, hallucinations). **Defile the flesh:** this may mean bodily pollutions from the erotic dreams of sexual license (7). **Lordship ... glorious beings:** these may reflect the Lord (5; Jesus, 4) whom they spurn and the angels (6; cf the note on 2 Pt 2, 10, here, as there, literally, "glories").

9: The archangel Michael ... judgment: a reference to an incident in the apocryphal Assumption of Moses. Dt 34, 6 had said of Moses, literally in Greek, "they buried him" or "he (God?) buried him" (taken to mean "he was buried"). The later account tells how Michael, who was sent to bury him, was challenged by the devil's interest in the body. Our author draws out the point that if an archangel refrained from reviling even the devil, how wrong it is for mere human beings to revile glorious beings (angels).

11: Cain ... Balaam ... Korah: examples of rebellious men and of the punishment their conduct incurred; cf Gn 4, 8–16; Nm 16, 1–35; 31, 16. See the note on 2 Pt 2, 15.

12: Blemishes on your love feasts: or "hidden rocks" or "submerged reefs" (cf 13). The opponents engaged in scandalous conduct in connection with community gatherings called **love feasts** (agape meals), which were associated with eucharistic celebrations at certain stages of early Christian practice; cf 1 Cor 11, 18–34 and the note on 2 Pt 2, 13.

a: Mt 13, 55; Mk 6, 3; Acts 12, 17; Rom 1, 7. b: Gal 6, 16; 1 Tm 1, 2; 2 Pt 1, 2. c: Jude 17.20; 1 Tm 6, 12. d: Gal 2, 4; 2 Tm 3, 6; 2 Pt 2, 1. e: Nm 14, 35; 1 Cor 10, 5; Heb 3, 16.17. f: 2 Pt 2, 4.9. g: Dt 29, 22-24; Mt 25, 41; 2 Thes 1, 8-9; 2 Pt 2, 6; 3, 7. h: Dn 10, 21; 12, 1. i: 2 Pt 2, 12. j: Gn 4, 8-16; 1 Jn 3, 12 / Nm 31, 15-16; 2 Pt 2, 15; Rv 2, 14 / Nm 16, 19-35. k: 2 Pt 2, 13.17.

waterless clouds blown about by winds, fruitless trees in late autumn, twice dead and uprooted. *13*They are like wild waves of the sea, foaming up their shameless deeds, wandering stars for whom the gloom of darkness has been reserved forever.

14l*Enoch, of the seventh generation from Adam, prophesied also about them when he said, "Behold, the Lord has come with his countless holy ones *15*to execute judgment on all and to convict everyone for all the godless deeds that they committed and for all the harsh words godless sinners have uttered against him." *16m*These people are complainers, disgruntled ones who live by their desires; their mouths utter bombast as they fawn over people to gain advantage.

Exhortations. *17n*But you, beloved, remember the words spoken beforehand by the apostles of our Lord Jesus Christ, *18o**for they

told you, "In [the] last time there will be scoffers who will live according to their own godless desires." *19p*These are the ones who cause divisions; they live on the natural plane, devoid of the Spirit. *20q*But you, beloved, build yourselves up in your most holy faith; pray in the holy Spirit. *21r*Keep yourselves in the love of God and wait for the mercy of our Lord Jesus Christ that leads to eternal life. *22**On those who waver, have mercy; *23**save others by snatching them out of the fire; on others have mercy with fear, abhorring even the outer garment stained by the flesh.

Doxology. *24s**To the one who is able to keep you from stumbling and to present you unblemished and exultant, in the presence of his glory, *25t*to the only God, our savior, through Jesus Christ our Lord be glory, majesty, power, and authority from ages past, now, and for ages to come. Amen.

14–15: Cited from the apocryphal Book of Enoch 1, 9.

18: This is the substance of much early Christian preaching rather than a direct quotation of any of the various New Testament passages on this theme (see Mk 13, 22; Acts 20, 30; 1 Tm 4, 1–3; 2 Pt 3, 3).

22: Have mercy: some manuscripts read "convince," "confute," or reprove." Others have "even though you waver" or "doubt" instead of **who waver.**

23: With fear: some manuscripts connect the phrase "with fear" with the imperative "save" or with the participle "snatching." Other manuscripts omit the phrase "on others have mercy," so that only two groups are envisioned. Rescue of those led astray and caution in the endeavor are both en-

joined. **Outer garment stained by the flesh:** the imagery may come from Zec 3, 3–5, just as that of **snatching . . . out of the fire** comes from Zec 3, 2; the very garments of the godless are to be abhorred because of their contagion.

24–25: With this liturgical statement about the power of God to keep the faithful from stumbling, and praise to him through Jesus Christ, the letter reaches its conclusion by returning to the themes with which it began (1–2).

l: Mt 16, 27; Heb 12, 22–23. *m:* Jude 18; 1 Cor 10, 10; 2 Pt 2, 10.18. *n:* Heb 2, 3; 2 Pt 3, 2. *o:* 1 Tm 4, 1; 2 Tm 3, 1–5; 2 Pt 3, 3. *p:* 1 Cor 2, 14; Jas 3, 15. *q:* Jude 2; Eph 3, 15; Co 2, 7. *r:* Ti 2, 13. *s:* 2 Cor 4, 14; 1 Pt 4, 13. *t:* Rom 11, 36; 1 Tm 1, 17.

See RG 455–62

The Revelation to John

The Apocalypse, or Revelation to John, the last book of the Bible, is one of the most difficult to understand because it abounds in unfamiliar and extravagant symbolism, which at best appears unusual to the modern reader. Symbolic language, however, is one of the chief characteristics of apocalyptic literature, of which this book is an outstanding example. Such literature enjoyed wide popularity in both Jewish and Christian circles from ca. 200 B.C. to A.D. 200.

This book contains an account of visions in symbolic and allegorical language borrowed extensively from the Old Testament, especially Ezekiel, Zechariah, and Daniel. Whether or not these visions were real experiences of the author

or simply literary conventions employed by him is an open question.

This much, however, is certain: symbolic descriptions are not to be taken as literal descriptions, nor is the symbolism meant to be pictured realistically. One would find it difficult and repulsive to visualize a lamb with seven horns and seven eyes; yet Jesus Christ is described in precisely such words (5, 6). The author used these images to suggest Christ's universal (seven) power (horns) and knowledge (eyes). A significant feature of apocalyptic writing is the use of symbolic colors, metals, garments (1, 13–16; 3, 18; 4, 4; 6, 1–8; 17, 4; 19, 8), and numbers (*four* signifies the world, *six* imperfection, *seven* totality or perfection, *twelve* Israel's tribes or the apostles, *one thousand* immensity). Finally the vindictive language in the book (6, 9–10; 18, 1–19, 4) is also to be understood symbolically and not literally. The cries for vengeance on the lips of Christian martyrs that sound so harsh are in fact literary devices the author employed to evoke in the reader and hearer a feeling of horror for apostasy and rebellion that will be severely punished by God.

The lurid descriptions of the punishment of Jezebel (2, 22) and of the destruction of the great harlot, Babylon (16, 9—19, 2), are likewise literary devices. The metaphor of Babylon as harlot would be wrongly construed if interpreted literally. On the other hand, the stylized figure of the woman clothed with the sun (12, 1–6), depicting the New Israel, may seem to be a negative stereotype. It is necessary to look beyond the literal meaning to see that these images mean to convey a sense of God's wrath at sin in the former case and trust in God's providential care over the church in the latter.

The Book of Revelation cannot be adequately understood except against the historical background that occasioned its writing. Like Daniel and other apocalypses, it was composed as resistance literature to meet a crisis. The book itself suggests that the crisis was ruthless persecution of the early church by the Roman authorities; the harlot Babylon symbolizes pagan Rome, the city on seven hills (17, 9). The book is, then, an exhortation and admonition to Christians of the first century to stand firm in the faith and to avoid compromise with paganism, despite the threat of adversity and martyrdom; they are to await patiently the fulfillment of God's mighty promises. The triumph of God in the world of men and women remains a mystery, to be accepted in faith and longed for in hope. It is a triumph that unfolded in the history of Jesus of Nazareth and continues to unfold in the history of the individual Christian who follows the way of the cross, even, if necessary, to a martyr's death.

Though the perspective is eschatological—ultimate salvation and victory are said to take place at the end of the present age when Christ will come in glory at the parousia—the book presents the decisive struggle of Christ and his followers against Satan and his cohorts as already over. Christ's overwhelming defeat of the kingdom of Satan ushered in the everlasting reign of God

(11, 15; 12, 10). Even the forces of evil unwittingly carry out the divine plan (17, 17), for God is the sovereign Lord of history.

The Book of Revelation had its origin in a time of crisis, but it remains valid and meaningful for Christians of all time. In the face of apparently insuperable evil, either from within or from without, all Christians are called to trust in Jesus' promise, "Behold, I am with you always, until the end of the age" (Mt 28, 20). Those who remain steadfast in their faith and confidence in the risen Lord need have no fear. Suffering, persecution, even death by martyrdom, though remaining impenetrable mysteries of evil, do not comprise an absurd dead end. No matter what adversity or sacrifice Christians may endure, they will in the end triumph over Satan and his forces because of their fidelity to Christ the victor. This is the enduring message of the book; it is a message of hope and consolation and challenge for all who dare to believe.

The author of the book calls himself John (1, 1.4.9; 22, 8), who because of his Christian faith has been exiled to the rocky island of Patmos, a Roman penal colony. Although he never claims to be John the apostle, whose name is attached to the fourth gospel, he was so identified by several of the early church Fathers, including Justin, Irenaeus, Clement of Alexandria, Tertullian, Cyprian, and Hippolytus. This identification, however, was denied by other Fathers, including Denis of Alexandria, Eusebius of Caesarea, Cyril of Jerusalem, Gregory Nazianzen, and John Chrysostom. Indeed, vocabulary, grammar, and style make it doubtful that the book could have been put into its present form by the same person(s) responsible for the fourth gospel. Nevertheless, there are definite linguistic and theological affinities between the two books. The tone of the letters to the seven churches (1, 4—3, 22) is indicative of the great authority the author enjoyed over the Christian communities in Asia. It is possible, therefore, that he was a disciple of John the apostle, who is traditionally associated with that part of the world. The date of the book in its present form is probably near the end of the reign of Domitian (A.D. 81–96), a fierce persecutor of the Christians.

The principal divisions of the Book of Revelation are the following:

I: Prologue (1, 1–3)

I: Prologue

See RG 457–58

CHAPTER 1

1a*The revelation of Jesus Christ, which God gave to him, to show his servants what must happen soon. He made it known by sending his angel to his servant John, *2*who gives witness to the word of God and to the testimony of Jesus Christ by reporting what he saw. *3b**Blessed is the one who reads aloud and blessed are those who listen to this prophetic message and heed what is written in it, for the appointed time is near.

II: Letters to the Churches of Asia

Greeting. *4c**John, to the seven churches in Asia: grace to you and peace from him who is and who was and who is to come, and from the seven spirits before his throne, *5d**and from Jesus Christ, the faithful witness, the firstborn of the dead and ruler of the kings of the earth. To him who loves us and has freed us from our sins by his blood, *6e*who has made us into a kingdom, priests for his God and Father, to him be glory and power forever [and ever]. Amen.

7 *f*Behold, he is coming amid the clouds,
and every eye will see him,
even those who pierced him.
All the peoples of the earth will lament him.
Yes. Amen.

8g*"I am the Alpha and the Omega," says the Lord God, "the one who is and who was and who is to come, the almighty."

The First Vision. *9**I, John, your brother, who share with you the distress, the kingdom, and the endurance we have in Jesus, found myself on the island called Patmos because I proclaimed God's word and gave testimony to Jesus. *10**I was caught up in spirit on the Lord's day and heard behind me a voice as loud as a trumpet, *11**which said, "Write on a scroll what you see and send it to the seven churches: to Ephesus, Smyrna, Pergamum, Thyatira, Sardis, Philadelphia,

1, 1–3: This prologue describes the source, contents, and audience of the book and forms an inclusion with the epilogue (22, 6–21), with its similar themes and expressions.

1, 3: Blessed is the one: this is the first of seven beatitudes in this book; the others are in 14, 13; 16, 15; 19, 9; 20, 6; 22, 7.14. **This prophetic message:** literally, "the words of the prophecy"; so 22, 7.10.18.19 by inclusion. **The appointed time:** when Jesus will return in glory; cf 1, 7; 3, 11; 22, 7.10.12.20.

1, 4–8: Although Revelation begins and ends (22, 21) with Christian epistolary formulae, there is nothing between chs 4 and 22 resembling a letter. The author here employs the standard word order for greetings in Greek letter writing: "N. to N., greetings . . ."; see the note on Rom 1, 1.

1, 4: Seven churches in Asia: Asia refers to the Roman province of that name in western Asia Minor (modern Turkey); these representative churches are mentioned by name in v 11, and each is the recipient of a message (2, 1–3, 22). **Seven** is the biblical number suggesting fullness and completeness; thus the seer is writing for the whole church.

1, 5: Freed us: the majority of Greek manuscripts and several early versions read "washed us"; but "freed us" is supported by the best manuscripts and fits well with Old Testament imagery, e.g., Is 40, 2.

1, 8: The Alpha and the Omega: the first and last letters of the Greek alphabet. In 22, 13 the same words occur together with the expressions "the First and the Last, the Beginning and the End"; cf 1; 2, 8; 21, 6; Is 41, 4; 44, 6.

1, 9–20: In this first vision, the seer is commanded to write what he sees to the seven churches (9–11). He sees Christ in glory, whom he depicts in stock apocalyptic imagery (12–16), and hears him describe himself in terms meant to encourage Christians by emphasizing his victory over death (17–20).

1, 9: Island called Patmos: one of the Sporades islands in the Aegean Sea, some fifty miles south of Ephesus, used by the Romans as a penal colony. **Because I proclaimed God's word:** literally, "on account of God's word."

1, 10: The Lord's day: Sunday. **As loud as a trumpet:** the imagery is derived from the theophany at Sinai (Ex 19, 16.19; cf Heb 12, 19 and the trumpet in other eschatological settings in Is 27, 13; Jl 2, 1; Mt 24, 31; 1 Cor 15, 52; 1 Thes 4, 16).

1, 11: Scroll: a papyrus roll.

a: 22, 6-8.20; Dn 2, 28 / 19, 10. *b:* 22, 7 / Lk 11, 28. *c:* Rv 1, 8; 4, 3; 11, 17; 16, 5; Ex 3, 14. *d:* 3, 14; 1 Cor 15, 20; Col 1, 18 / Heb 9, 14; 1 Pt 1, 19; 1 Jn 1, 7. *e:* Ex 19, 6; 1 Pt 2, 9. *f:* Dn 7, 13 / Zec 12, 10; Mt 24, 30; Jn 19, 37. *g:* Rv 1, 17; 21, 6; 22, 13; Is 41, 4; 44, 6; 48, 12.

and Laodicea." [12]*Then I turned to see whose voice it was that spoke to me, and when I turned, I saw seven gold lampstands [13h]*and in the midst of the lampstands one like a son of man, wearing an ankle-length robe, with a gold sash around his chest. [14]*The hair of his head was as white as white wool or as snow, and his eyes were like a fiery flame. [15]*His feet were like polished brass refined in a furnace, and his voice was like the sound of rushing water. [16i]*In his right hand he held seven stars. A sharp two-edged sword came out of his mouth, and his face shone like the sun at its brightest.

[17j]*When I caught sight of him, I fell down at his feet as though dead. He touched me with his right hand and said, "Do not be afraid. I am the first and the last, [18]*the one who lives. Once I was dead, but now I am alive forever and ever. I hold the keys to death and the netherworld. [19]*Write down, therefore, what you have seen, and what is happening, and what will happen after-

wards. [20]*This is the secret meaning of the seven stars you saw in my right hand, and of the seven gold lampstands: the seven stars are the angels of the seven churches, and the seven lampstands are the seven churches.

CHAPTER 2

See RG 458–59

To Ephesus. [1]*"To the angel of the church in Ephesus, write this:

" 'The one who holds the seven stars in his right hand and walks in the midst of the seven gold lampstands says this: [2]*"I know your works, your labor, and your endurance, and that you cannot tolerate the wicked; you have tested those who call themselves apostles but are not, and discovered that they are impostors. [3]Moreover, you have endurance and have suffered for my name, and you have not grown weary. [4]Yet I hold this against you: you have lost the love you had at first. [5]Realize how far you have fallen. Repent, and do the works you did at first. Otherwise, I will come to you and remove

1, 12–16: A symbolic description of Christ in glory. The metaphorical language is not to be understood literally; cf Introduction.

1, 13: Son of man: see the note on Mk 8, 31. Ankle-length robe: Christ is priest; cf Ex 28, 4; 29, 5; Wis 18, 24; Zec 3, 4. Gold sash: Christ is king; cf Ex 28, 4; 1 Mc 10, 89; 11, 58; Dn 10, 5.

1, 14: Hair . . . as white as white wool or as snow: Christ is eternal, clothed with the dignity that belonged to the "Ancient of Days"; cf 18; Dn 7, 9. His eyes were like a fiery flame: Christ is portrayed as all-knowing; cf 2, 23; Ps 7, 10; Jer 17, 10; and similar expressions in 2, 18; 19, 12; cf Dn 10, 6.

1, 15: His feet . . . furnace: Christ is depicted as unchangeable; cf Ez 1, 27; Dn 10, 6. The Greek word translated "refined" is unconnected grammatically with any other word in the sentence. His voice . . . water: Christ speaks with divine authority; cf Ez 1, 24.

1, 16: Seven stars: in the pagan world, Mithras and the Caesars were represented with seven stars in their right hand, symbolizing their universal dominion. A sharp two-edged sword: this refers to the word of God (cf Eph 6, 17; Heb 4, 12) that will destroy unrepentant sinners; cf 2, 16; 19, 15; Wis 18, 15; Is 11, 4; 49, 2. His face . . . brightest: this symbolizes the divine majesty of Christ; cf 10, 1; 21, 23; Jgs 5, 31; Is 60, 19; Mt 17, 2.

1, 17: It was an Old Testament belief that for sinful human beings to see God was to die; cf Ex 19, 21; 33, 20; Jgs 6, 22–23; Is 6, 5.

1, 18: Netherworld: Greek Hades, Hebrew Sheol, the abode of the dead; cf 20, 13–14; Nm 16, 33.

1, 19: What you have seen, and what is happening, and what will happen afterwards: the three parts of the Book of Revelation, the vision (10–20), the situation in the seven

churches (chs 2–3), and the events of chs 6–22.

1, 20: Secret meaning: literally, "mystery." Angels: these are the presiding spirits of the seven churches. Angels were thought to be in charge of the physical world (cf 7, 1; 14, 18; 16, 5) and of nations (Dn 10, 13; 12, 1), communities (the seven churches), and individuals (Mt 18, 10; Acts 12, 15). Some have seen in the "angel" of each of the seven churches its pastor or a personification of the spirit of the congregation.

2, 1—3, 22: Each of the seven letters follows the same pattern: address; description of the exalted Christ; blame and/or praise for the church addressed; threat and/or admonition; final exhortation and promise to all Christians.

2, 1–7: The letter to Ephesus praises the members of the church there for their works and virtues, including discerning false teachers (2–3), but admonishes them to repent and return to their former devotion (4–5). It concludes with a reference to the Nicolaitans (see the note on 6) and a promise that the victor will have access to eternal life (7).

2, 1: Ephesus: this great ancient city had a population of ca. 250,000; it was the capital of the Roman province of Asia and the commercial, cultural, and religious center of Asia. The other six churches were located in the same province, situated roughly in a circle; they were selected for geographical reasons rather than for the size of their Christian communities. Walks in the midst of the seven gold lampstands: this signifies that Christ is always present in the church; see the note on 1, 4.

2, 2: Who call themselves . . . impostors: this refers to unauthorized and perverse missionaries; cf Acts 20, 29–30.

h: Dn 7, 13; 10, 5.   i: Heb 4, 12.   j: Dn 8, 18 / 1, 8.

your lampstand from its place, unless you repent. *6**But you have this in your favor: you hate the works of the Nicolaitans, which I also hate.

7k** ' "Whoever has ears ought to hear what the Spirit says to the churches. To the victor I will give the right to eat from the tree of life that is in the garden of God." '

To Smyrna. *8**"To the angel of the church in Smyrna, write this:

" 'The first and the last, who once died but came to life, says this: *9l**"I know your tribulation and poverty, but you are rich. I know the slander of those who claim to be Jews and are not, but rather are members of the assembly of Satan. *10*Do not be afraid of anything that you are going to suffer. Indeed, the devil will throw some of you into prison, that you may be tested, and you will face an ordeal for ten days. Remain faithful until death, and I will give you the crown of life.

11m** ' "Whoever has ears ought to hear what the Spirit says to the churches. The victor shall not be harmed by the second death." '

To Pergamum. *12**"To the angel of the church in Pergamum, write this:

" 'The one with the sharp two-edged sword says this: *13**"I know that you live where Satan's throne is, and yet you hold fast to my name and have not denied your faith in me, not even in the days of Antipas, my faithful witness, who was martyred among you, where Satan lives. *14n**Yet I have a few things against you. You have some people there who hold to the teaching of Balaam, who instructed Balak to put a stumbling block before the Israelites: to eat food sacrificed to idols and to play the harlot. *15*Likewise, you also have some people who hold to the teaching of [the] Nicolaitans. *16*Therefore, repent. Otherwise, I will come to you quickly and wage war against them with the sword of my mouth.

17o** ' "Whoever has ears ought to hear what the Spirit says to the churches. To the victor I shall give some of the hidden manna; I shall also give a white amulet upon which is inscribed a new name, which no one knows except the one who receives it." '

2, 6: Nicolaitans: these are perhaps the impostors of v 2; see the note on vv 14–15. There is little evidence for connecting this group with Nicolaus, the proselyte from Antioch, mentioned in Acts 6, 5.

2, 7: Victor: referring to any Christian individual who holds fast to the faith and does God's will in the face of persecution. **The tree of life that is in the garden of God:** this is a reference to the tree in the primeval paradise (Gn 2, 9); cf 22, 2.14.19. The decree excluding humanity from the tree of life has been revoked by Christ.

2, 8–11: The letter to Smyrna encourages the Christians in this important commercial center by telling them that although they are impoverished, they are nevertheless rich, and calls those Jews who are slandering them members of the assembly of Satan (9). There is no admonition; rather, the Christians are told that they will suffer much, even death, but the time of tribulation will be short compared to their eternal reward (10), and they will thus escape final damnation (11).

2, 8: Smyrna: modern Izmir, ca. thirty miles north of Ephesus, and the chief city of Lydia, with a temple to the goddess Roma. It was renowned for its loyalty to Rome, and it also had a large Jewish community very hostile toward Christians.

2, 9–10: The church in Smyrna was materially poor but spiritually rich. Accusations made by Jewish brethren there occasioned the persecution of Christians; cf Acts 14, 2.19; 17, 5.13.

2, 11: The second death: this refers to the eternal death, when sinners will receive their final punishment; cf 20, 6.14–15; 21, 8.

2, 12–17: The letter to Pergamum praises the members of the church for persevering in their faith in Christ even in the midst of a pagan setting and in face of persecution and martyrdom (13). But it admonishes them about members who advocate an unprincipled morality (14; cf 2 Pt 2, 15; Jude 11) and others who follow the teaching of the Nicolaitans (15; see the note there). It urges them to repent (16) and promises them the hidden manna and Christ's amulet (17).

2, 12: Pergamum: modern Bergama, ca. forty-five miles northeast of Smyrna, a center for various kinds of pagan worship. It also had an outstanding library (the word **parchment** is derived from its name).

2, 13: Satan's throne: the reference is to emperor worship and other pagan practices that flourished in Pergamum, perhaps specifically to the white marble altar erected and dedicated to Zeus by Eumenes II (197–160 B.C.).

2, 14–15: Like Balaam, the biblical prototype of the religious compromiser (cf Nm 25, 1–3; 31, 16; 2 Pt 2, 15; Jude 11), the Nicolaitans in Pergamum and Ephesus (6) accommodated their Christian faith to paganism. They abused the principle of liberty enunciated by Paul (1 Cor 9, 19–23).

2, 17: The hidden manna: this is the food of life; cf Ps 78, 24–25. **White amulet:** literally, "white stone," on which was written a magical name, whose power could be tapped by one who knew the secret name. It is used here as a symbol of victory and joy; cf 3, 4–5. **New name:** this is a reference to the Christian's rebirth in Christ; cf 3, 12; 19, 12; Is 62, 2; 65, 15.

---

k: Rv 2, 11.17.29; 3, 6.13.22; 13, 9; Mt 11, 15. *l:* Jas 2, 5. *m:* 20, 6.14; 21, 8. *n:* Nm 22-24; 25, 1-3; 31, 16; 2 Pt 2, 15; Jude 11. *o:* Is 62, 2; 65, 15.

The Seven Churches

To Thyatira. *18**"To the angel of the church in Thyatira, write this:

" 'The Son of God, whose eyes are like a fiery flame and whose feet are like polished brass, says this: *19*"I know your works, your love, faith, service, and endurance, and that your last works are greater than the first. *20**Yet I hold this against you, that you tolerate the woman Jezebel, who calls herself a prophetess, who teaches and misleads my servants to play the harlot and to eat food sacrificed to idols. *21*I have given her time to repent, but she refuses to repent of her harlotry. *22*So I will cast her on a sickbed and plunge those who commit adultery with her into intense suffering unless they repent of her works. *23 p**I will also put her children to death. Thus shall all the churches come to know that I am the searcher of hearts and minds and that I will give each of you what your works deserve. *24**But I say to the rest of you in Thyatira, who do not uphold this teaching and know nothing of the so-called deep secrets of Satan: on you I will place no further burden, *25*except that you must hold fast to what you have until I come.

26 q*" "To the victor, who keeps to my
　　　　ways until the end,

2, 18–29: The letter to Thyatira praises the progress in virtue of this small Christian community (19) but admonishes them for tolerating a false prophet who leads them astray (20). Her fate is sealed, but there is hope of repentance for her followers (21–22). Otherwise, they too shall die (23). They are warned against Satanic power or knowledge (24–25). Those who remain faithful will share in the messianic reign, having authority over nations (26–27), and will in fact possess Christ himself (28).

2, 18: **Thyatira:** modern Akhisar, ca. forty miles southeast of Pergamum, a frontier town famous for its workers' guilds (cf Acts 16, 14), membership in which may have involved festal meals in pagan temples.

2, 20: The scheming and treacherous Jezebel of old (cf 1 Kgs 19, 1–2; 21, 1–14; 2 Kgs 9, 22.30–34) introduced pagan customs into the religion of Israel; this new Jezebel was doing the same to Christianity.

2, 23: **Children:** spiritual descendants.

2, 24: **The so-called deep secrets of Satan:** literally, "the deep things of Satan," a scathing reference to the perverse teaching of the Nicolaitans (15).

2, 26–28: The Christian who perseveres in faith will share

─────────
p: 1 Sm 16, 7; Jer 11, 20; 17, 10. 　*q:* 12, 5; Ps 2, 8-9.

I will give authority over the nations. [27] He will rule them with an iron rod.
Like clay vessels will they be smashed,

[28]just as I received authority from my Father. And to him I will give the morning star. [29] ' "Whoever has ears ought to hear what the Spirit says to the churches." '

See RG 458–59

CHAPTER 3

To Sardis. [1]*"To the angel of the church in Sardis, write this:

" 'The one who has the seven spirits of God and the seven stars says this: "I know your works, that you have the reputation of being alive, but you are dead. [2]Be watchful and strengthen what is left, which is going to die, for I have not found your works complete in the sight of my God. [3]rRemember then how you accepted and heard; keep it, and repent. If you are not watchful, I will come like a thief, and you will never know at what hour I will come upon you. [4]sHowever, you have a few people in Sardis who have not soiled their garments; they will walk with me dressed in white, because they are worthy.

[5]t*" ' "The victor will thus be dressed in white, and I will never erase his name from the book of life but will acknowledge his name in the presence of my Father and of his angels. [6]" ' "Whoever has ears ought to hear what the Spirit says to the churches." '

To Philadelphia. [7]u*"To the angel of the church in Philadelphia, write this:

" 'The holy one, the true,
who holds the key of David,
who opens and no one shall close,
who closes and no one shall open,

says this: [8]*" ' "I know your works (behold, I have left an open door before you, which no one can close). You have limited strength, and yet you have kept my word and have not denied my name. [9]vBehold, I will make those of the assembly of Satan who claim to be Jews and are not, but are lying, behold I will make them come and fall prostrate at your feet, and they will realize that I love you. [10]*Because you have kept my message of endurance, I will keep you safe in the time of trial that is going to come to the whole world to test the inhabitants of the earth. [11]wI am coming quickly. Hold fast to what you have, so that no one may take your crown.

[12]x*" ' "The victor I will make into a pillar in the temple of my God, and he will never

---

in Christ's messianic authority (cf Ps 2, 8–9) and resurrection victory over death, symbolized by the morning star; cf 22, 16.

2, 26: Who keeps to my ways: literally, "who keeps my works."

3, 1–6: The letter to Sardis does not praise the community but admonishes its members to watchfulness, mutual support, and repentance (2–3). The few who have remained pure and faithful will share Christ's victory and will be inscribed in the book of life (4–5).

3, 1: Sardis: this city, located ca. thirty miles southeast of Thyatira, was once the capital of Lydia, known for its wealth at the time of Croesus (6th century B.C.). Its citadel, reputed to be unassailable, was captured by surprise, first by Cyrus and later by Antiochus. The church is therefore warned to be on guard.

3, 5: In white: white is a sign of victory and joy as well as resurrection; see the note on 2, 17. **The book of life:** the roll in which the names of the redeemed are kept; cf 13, 8; 17, 8; 20, 12.15; 21, 27; Phil 4, 3; Dn 12, 1. They will be acknowledged by Christ in heaven; cf Mt 10, 32.

3, 7–13: The letter to Philadelphia praises the Christians there for remaining faithful even with their limited strength (8). Members of the assembly of Satan are again singled out (9; see 2, 9 above). There is no admonition; rather, the letter promises that they will be kept safe at the great trial (10–11) and that the victors will become pillars of the heavenly temple, upon which three names will be inscribed: God, Jerusalem, and Christ (12).

3, 7: Philadelphia: modern Alasehir, ca. thirty miles southeast of Sardis, founded by Attalus II Philadelphus of Pergamum to be an "open door" (8) for Greek culture; it was destroyed by an earthquake in A.D. 17. Rebuilt by money from the Emperor Tiberius, the city was renamed Neo-Caesarea; this may explain the allusions to "name" in v 12. **Key of David:** to the heavenly city of David (cf Is 22, 22), "the new Jerusalem" (12), over which Christ has supreme authority.

3, 8: An open door: opportunities for sharing and proclaiming the faith; cf Acts 14, 27; 1 Cor 16, 9; 2 Cor 2, 12.

3, 10: My message of endurance: this does not refer to a saying of Jesus about patience but to the example of Christ's patient endurance. **The inhabitants of the earth:** literally, "those who live on the earth." This expression, which also occurs in 6, 10; 8, 13; 11, 10; 13, 8.12.14; 17, 2.8, always refers to the pagan world.

3, 12: Pillar: this may be an allusion to the rebuilding of the city; see the note on v 7. **New Jerusalem:** it is described in 21, 10—22, 5.

r: Mt 24, 42-44; Mk 13, 33; 1 Thes 5, 2; 2 Pt 3, 10. *s:* 7, 13-14. *t:* Ps 69, 29; Dn 12, 1 / Mt 10, 32. *u:* Is 22, 22; Mt 16, 19. *v:* 2, 9 / Is 45, 14; 60, 14. *w:* 2, 25; 22, 7.20. *x:* 21, 2-3; Ez 48, 35 / 19, 13.

leave it again. On him I will inscribe the name of my God and the name of the city of my God, the new Jerusalem, which comes down out of heaven from my God, as well as my new name.

13" ' "Whoever has ears ought to hear what the Spirit says to the churches." '

To Laodicea. *14y**"To the angel of the church in Laodicea, write this:

" 'The Amen, the faithful and true witness, the source of God's creation, says this: *15**"I know your works; I know that you are neither cold nor hot. I wish you were either cold or hot. *16**So, because you are lukewarm, neither hot nor cold, I will spit you out of my mouth. *17z**For you say, 'I am rich and affluent and have no need of anything,' and yet do not realize that you are wretched, pitiable, poor, blind, and naked. *18**I advise you to buy from me gold refined by fire so that you may be rich, and white garments to put on so that your shameful nakedness may not be exposed, and buy ointment to smear on your eyes so that you may see. *19a*Those whom I love, I reprove and chastise. Be earnest, therefore, and repent. *20**" ' "Behold, I stand at the door and knock. If anyone hears my voice and opens

the door, [then] I will enter his house and dine with him, and he with me. *21b*I will give the victor the right to sit with me on my throne, as I myself first won the victory and sit with my Father on his throne.

22" ' "Whoever has ears ought to hear what the Spirit says to the churches." ' "

III: God and the Lamb in Heaven

CHAPTER 4

See RG
459

Vision of Heavenly Worship. *1**After this I had a vision of an open door to heaven, and I heard the trumpetlike voice that had spoken to me before, saying, "Come up here and I will show you what must happen afterwards." *2c**At once I was caught up in spirit. A throne was there in heaven, and on the throne sat *3*one whose appearance sparkled like jasper and carnelian. Around the throne was a halo as brilliant as an emerald. *4d**Surrounding the throne I saw twenty-four other thrones on which twenty-four elders sat, dressed in white garments and with gold crowns on their heads. *5**From the throne came flashes of lightning,

---

3, 14–22: The letter to Laodicea reprimands the community for being lukewarm (15–16), but no particular faults are singled out. Their material prosperity is contrasted with their spiritual poverty, the violet tunics that were the source of their wealth with the white robe of baptism, and their famous eye ointment with true spiritual perception (17–18). But Christ's chastisement is inspired by love and a desire to be allowed to share the messianic banquet with his followers in the heavenly kingdom (19–21).

3, 14: Laodicea: ca. forty miles southeast of Philadelphia and ca. eighty miles east of Ephesus, a wealthy industrial and commercial center, with a renowned medical school. It exported fine woolen garments and was famous for its eye salves. It was so wealthy that it was proudly rebuilt without outside aid after the devastating earthquake of A.D. 60/61. **The Amen:** this is a divine title (cf Hebrew text of Is 65, 16) applied to Christ; cf 2 Cor 1, 20. **Source of God's creation:** literally, "the beginning of God's creation," a concept found also in Jn 1, 3; Col 1, 16–17; Heb 1, 2; cf Prv 8, 22–31; Wis 9, 1–2.

3, 15–16: Halfhearted commitment to the faith is nauseating to Christ; cf Rom 12, 11.

3, 16: Spit: literally, "vomit." The image is that of a beverage that should be either hot or cold. Perhaps there is an allusion to the hot springs of Hierapolis across the Lycus river from Laodicea, which would have been lukewarm by the time they reached Laodicea.

3, 17: Economic prosperity occasioned spiritual bankruptcy.

3, 18: Gold . . . fire: God's grace. **White garments:** sym-

bol of an upright life; the city was noted for its violet/purple cloth. **Ointment . . . eyes:** to remove spiritual blindness; one of the city's exports was eye ointment (see the note on 3, 14).

3, 20: Christ invites all to the messianic banquet in heaven; cf Is 25, 6; Lk 14, 15; 22, 30.

4, 1–11: The seer now describes a vision of the heavenly court in worship of God enthroned. He reverently avoids naming or describing God but pictures twenty-four elders in priestly and regal attire (4) and God's throne and its surroundings made of precious gems and other symbols that traditionally express the majesty of God (5–6). Universal creation is represented by the four living creatures (6–7). Along with the twenty-four elders, they praise God unceasingly in humble adoration (8–11).

4, 1: The ancients viewed heaven as a solid vault, entered by way of actual doors.

4, 2–8: Much of the imagery here is taken from Ez 1 and 10.

4, 4: Twenty-four elders: these represent the twelve tribes of Israel and the twelve apostles; cf 21, 12–14.

4, 5: Flashes of lightning, rumblings, and peals of thunder: as in other descriptions of God's appearance or activity; cf 8, 5; 11, 19; 16, 18; Ex 19, 16; Ez 1, 4.13. **The seven spirits of God:** the seven "angels of the presence" as in 8, 2 and Tb 12, 15.

---

y: 1, 5. z: Prv 13, 7; Lk 12, 21. a: Prv 3, 11-12; 1 Cor 11, 32; Heb 12, 5-11. b: Lk 22, 28-30; Mt 19, 28. c: Is 6, 1 / Ez 1, 26-28. d: Is 24, 23.

rumblings, and peals of thunder. Seven flaming torches burned in front of the throne, which are the seven spirits of God. *6e**In front of the throne was something that resembled a sea of glass like crystal.

In the center and around the throne, there were four living creatures covered with eyes in front and in back. *7**The first creature resembled a lion, the second was like a calf, the third had a face like that of a human being, and the fourth looked like an eagle in flight. *8f**The four living creatures, each of them with six wings, were covered with eyes inside and out. Day and night they do not stop exclaiming:

"Holy, holy, holy is the Lord God
        almighty,
    who was, and who is, and who is to
        come."

*9*Whenever the living creatures give glory and honor and thanks to the one who sits on the throne, who lives forever and ever, *10*the twenty-four elders fall down before the one who sits on the throne and worship him, who lives forever and ever. They throw down their crowns before the throne, exclaiming:

11 g"Worthy are you, Lord our God,
    to receive glory and honor and power,
for you created all things;
    because of your will they came to be
        and were created."

CHAPTER 5

See RG 459

The Scroll and the Lamb. *1h**I saw a scroll in the right hand of the one who sat on the throne. It had writing on both sides and was sealed with seven seals. *2*Then I saw a mighty angel who proclaimed in a loud voice, "Who is worthy to open the scroll and break its seals?" *3*But no one in heaven or on earth or under the earth was able to open the scroll or to examine it. *4*I shed many tears because no one was found worthy to open the scroll or to examine it. *5i**One of the elders said to me, "Do not weep. The lion of the tribe of Judah, the root of David, has triumphed, enabling him to open the scroll with its seven seals."

6j*Then I saw standing in the midst of the throne and the four living creatures and the elders a Lamb that seemed to have been slain. He had seven horns and seven eyes; these are the [seven] spirits of God sent out into the whole world. *7*He came and received the scroll from the right hand of the one who sat on the throne. *8*When he took it, the four living creatures and the twenty-four elders fell down before the Lamb. Each of the elders held a harp and gold bowls filled with incense, which are the prayers of the holy ones. *9*They sang a new hymn:

"Worthy are you to receive the scroll
    and to break open its seals,

4, 6: A sea of glass like crystal: an image adapted from Ez 1, 22–26. **Four living creatures:** these are symbols taken from Ez 1, 5–21; they are identified as cherubim in Ez 10, 20. **Covered with eyes:** these suggest God's knowledge and concern.

4, 7: Lion . . . calf . . . human being . . . eagle: these symbolize, respectively, what is noblest, strongest, wisest, and swiftest in creation. **Calf:** traditionally translated "ox," the Greek word refers to a heifer or young bull. Since the second century, these four creatures have been used as symbols of the evangelists Mark, Luke, Matthew, and John, respectively.

4, 8: Six wings: like the seraphim of Is 6, 2.

5, 1–14: The seer now describes a papyrus roll in God's right hand (1) with seven seals indicating the importance of the message. A mighty angel asks who is worthy to open the scroll, i.e., who can accomplish God's salvific plan (2). There is despair at first when no one in creation can do it (3–4). But the seer is comforted by an elder who tells him that Christ, called the lion of the tribe of Judah, has won the right to open it (5). Christ then appears as a Lamb, coming to receive the scroll from God (6–7), for which he is acclaimed as at a coronation (8–10). This is followed by a doxology of the angels

(11–12) and then finally by the heavenly church united with all of creation (13–14).

5, 1: A scroll: a papyrus roll possibly containing a list of afflictions for sinners (cf Ez 2, 9–10) or God's plan for the world. **Sealed with seven seals:** it is totally hidden from all but God. Only the Lamb (7–9) has the right to carry out the divine plan.

5, 5: The lion of the tribe of Judah, the root of David: these are the messianic titles applied to Christ to symbolize his victory; cf 22, 16; Gn 49, 9; Is 11, 1.10; Mt 1, 1.

5, 6: Christ is the Paschal Lamb without blemish, whose blood saved the new Israel from sin and death; cf Ex 12; Is 53, 7; Jn 1, 29.36; Acts 8, 32; 1 Pt 1, 18–19. This is the main title for Christ in Rv, used twenty-eight times. **Seven horns and seven eyes:** Christ has the fullness (see the note on 1, 4) of power (horns) and knowledge (eyes); cf Zec 4, 10. **[Seven] spirits:** as in 1, 4; 3, 1; and 4, 5.

e: Ex 24, 10.   *f:* Is 6, 2-3 / 1, 4.8; 11, 17; 16, 5.   *g:* Rom 4, 17; 16, 27.   *h:* Is 29, 11.   *i:* Is 11, 1.10; Rom 15, 12.   *j:* Jn 1, 29.

for you were slain and with your blood
    you purchased for God
those from every tribe and tongue,
    people and nation.
[10] [k]You made them a kingdom and priests
    for our God,
    and they will reign on earth."

[11] [l]*I looked again and heard the voices of many angels who surrounded the throne and the living creatures and the elders. They were countless in number, [12]and they cried out in a loud voice:

"Worthy is the Lamb that was slain
    to receive power and riches, wisdom
        and strength,
    honor and glory and blessing."

[13]Then I heard every creature in heaven and on earth and under the earth and in the sea, everything in the universe, cry out:

"To the one who sits on the throne and to
        the Lamb
    be blessing and honor, glory and
        might,
    forever and ever."

[14]The four living creatures answered, "Amen," and the elders fell down and worshiped.

IV: The Seven Seals, Trumpets, and Plagues, with Interludes

CHAPTER 6

See RG
459–60

The First Six Seals. [1]*Then I watched while the Lamb broke open the first of seven seals, and I heard one of the four living creatures cry out in a voice like thunder, "Come forward." [2][m]*I looked, and there was a white horse, and its rider had a bow. He was given a crown, and he rode forth victorious to further his victories.

[3]When he broke open the second seal, I heard the second living creature cry out, "Come forward." [4][n]*Another horse came out, a red one. Its rider was given power to take peace away from the earth, so that people would slaughter one another. And he was given a huge sword.

[5]*When he broke open the third seal, I heard the third living creature cry out, "Come forward." I looked, and there was a black horse, and its rider held a scale in his hand. [6][o]*I heard what seemed to be a voice in the midst of the four living creatures. It said, "A ration of wheat costs a day's pay, and three rations of barley cost a day's pay. But do not damage the olive oil or the wine."

[7]When he broke open the fourth seal, I

5, 11: Countless: literally, "100,000,000 plus 1,000,000," used by the author to express infinity.

6, 1—16, 21: A series of seven disasters now begins as each seal is broken (6, 1—8, 1), followed by a similar series as seven trumpets sound (8, 2—11, 19) and as seven angels pour bowls on the earth causing plagues (15, 1—16, 21). These gloomy sequences are interrupted by longer or shorter scenes suggesting the triumph of God and his witnesses (e.g., chs 7, 10, 11, 12, 13, 14).

6, 1–17: This chapter provides a symbolic description of the contents of the sealed scroll. The breaking of the first four seals reveals four riders. The first rider (of a white horse) is a conquering power (1–2), the second (red horse) a symbol of bloody war (3–4), the third (black horse) a symbol of famine (5–6), the fourth (pale green horse) a symbol of Death himself, accompanied by Hades (the netherworld) as his page (7–8). Verse 8b summarizes the role of all four riders. The breaking of the fifth seal reveals Christian martyrs in an attitude of sacrifice as blood poured out at the foot of an altar begging God for vindication, which will come only when their quota is filled; but they are given a white robe symbolic of victory (9–11). The breaking of the sixth seal reveals typical apocalyptic signs in the sky and the sheer terror of all people at the imminent divine judgment (12–17).

6, 1–8: The imagery is adapted from Zec 1, 8–10; 6, 1–8.

6, 2: White horse . . . bow: this may perhaps allude specifically to the Parthians on the eastern border of the Roman empire. Expert in the use of the bow, they constantly harassed the Romans and won a major victory in A.D. 62; see the note on 9, 13–21. But the Old Testament imagery typifies the history of oppression of God's people at all times.

6, 4: Huge sword: this is a symbol of war and violence; cf Ez 21, 14–17.

6, 5: Black horse: this is a symbol of famine, the usual accompaniment of war in antiquity; cf Lv 26, 26; Ez 4, 16–17. The **scale** is a symbol of shortage of food with a corresponding rise in price.

6, 6: A day's pay: literally, "a denarius," a Roman silver coin that constitutes a day's wage in Mt 20, 2. Because of the famine, food was rationed and sold at an exorbitant price. A liter of flour was considered a day's ration in the Greek historians Herodotus and Diogenes Laertius. **Barley:** food of the poor (Jn 6, 9.13; cf 2 Kgs 7, 1.16.18); it was also used to feed animals; cf 1 Kgs 5, 8. **Do not damage:** the olive and the vine are to be used more sparingly in time of famine.

[k]: 1, 6; Ex 19, 6; Is 61, 6.   [l]: Dn 7, 10; Jude 14-15.   [m]: Zec 1, 8-10; 6, 1-3.   [n]: Ez 21, 14-16.   [o]: Lv 26, 26; Ez 4, 16-17.

heard the voice of the fourth living creature cry out, "Come forward." *8p*"I looked, and there was a pale green horse. Its rider was named Death, and Hades accompanied him. They were given authority over a quarter of the earth, to kill with sword, famine, and plague, and by means of the beasts of the earth.

9"When he broke open the fifth seal, I saw underneath the altar the souls of those who had been slaughtered because of the witness they bore to the word of God. *10*"They cried out in a loud voice, "How long will it be, holy and true master, before you sit in judgment and avenge our blood on the inhabitants of the earth?" *11*Each of them was given a white robe, and they were told to be patient a little while longer until the number was filled of their fellow servants and brothers who were going to be killed as they had been.

12q"Then I watched while he broke open the sixth seal, and there was a great earthquake; the sun turned as black as dark sackcloth and the whole moon became like blood. *13*"The stars in the sky fell to the earth like unripe figs shaken loose from the tree in a strong wind. *14r*"Then the sky was divided like a torn scroll curling up, and every mountain and is-

land was moved from its place. *15*"The kings of the earth, the nobles, the military officers, the rich, the powerful, and every slave and free person hid themselves in caves and among mountain crags. *16s*They cried out to the mountains and the rocks, "Fall on us and hide us from the face of the one who sits on the throne and from the wrath of the Lamb, *17*"because the great day of their wrath has come and who can withstand it?"

CHAPTER 7

See RG 459–60

The 144,000 Sealed. 1t"After this I saw four angels standing at the four corners of the earth, holding back the four winds of the earth so that no wind could blow on land or sea or against any tree. *2*"Then I saw another angel come up from the East, holding the seal of the living God. He cried out in a loud voice to the four angels who were given power to damage the land and the sea, *3u*"Do not damage the land or the sea or the trees until we put the seal on the foreheads of the servants of our God." *4v*"I heard the number of those who had been marked with the seal, one hundred and forty-four thousand marked from every tribe of the Israelites: *5*"twelve thousand were marked from the

---

6, 8: Pale green: symbol of death and decay; cf Ez 14, 21.

6, 9: The altar: this altar corresponds to the altar of holocausts in the temple in Jerusalem; see also 11, 1. **Because of the witness . . . word of God:** literally, "because of the word of God and the witness they had borne."

6, 10: Holy and true master: Old Testament usage as well as the context indicates that this is addressed to God rather than to Christ.

6, 12–14: Symbolic rather than literal description of the cosmic upheavals attending the day of the Lord when the martyrs' prayer for vindication (10) would be answered; cf Am 8, 8–9; Is 34, 4; 50, 3; Jl 2, 10; 3, 3–4; Mt 24, 4–36; Mk 13, 5–37; Lk 21, 8–36.

6, 12: Dark sackcloth: for mourning, sackcloth was made from the skin of a black goat.

6, 13: Unripe figs: literally, "summer (or winter) fruit."

6, 14: Was divided: literally, "was split," like a broken papyrus roll torn in two, each half then curling up to form a roll on either side.

6, 15: Nobles: literally, "courtiers," "grandees." **Military officers:** literally, "commanders of 1,000 men," used in Josephus and other Greek authors as the equivalent of the Roman **tribunus militum.** The listing of various ranks of society represents the universality of terror at the impending doom.

6, 17: Their: this reading is attested in the best manuscripts, but the vast majority read "his" in reference to the wrath of the Lamb in the preceding verse.

7, 1–17: An interlude of two visions precedes the breaking of the seventh seal, just as two more will separate the sixth and seventh trumpets (ch 10). In the first vision (1–8), the elect receive the seal of the living God as protection against the coming cataclysm; cf 14, 1; Ez 9, 4–6; 2 Cor 1, 22; Eph 1, 13; 4, 30. The second vision (9–17) portrays the faithful Christians before God's throne to encourage those on earth to persevere to the end, even to death.

7, 1: The four corners of the earth: the earth is seen as a table or rectangular surface.

7, 2: East: literally, "rising of the sun." The east was considered the source of light and the place of paradise (Gn 2, 8). **Seal:** whatever was marked by the impression of one's signet ring belonged to that person and was under his protection.

7, 4–9: One hundred and forty-four thousand: the square of twelve (the number of Israel's tribes) multiplied by a thousand, symbolic of the new Israel (cf 14, 1–5; Gal 6, 16; Jas 1, 1) that embraces people **from every nation, race, people, and tongue** (9).

7, 5–8: Judah is placed first because of Christ; cf "the Lion of the tribe of Judah" (5, 5). Dan is omitted because of a later tradition that the antichrist would arise from it.

p: Ez 14, 21. *q:* Jl 3, 4; Mt 24, 29. *r:* Is 34, 4 / 16, 20. *s:* Is 2, 19; Hos 10, 8; Lk 23, 30. *t:* Jer 49, 36; Zec 6, 5. *u.* Ex 12, 7-14; Ez 9, 4; 2 Cor 1, 22; Eph 1, 13; 4, 30. *v:* 14, 1.

tribe of Judah, twelve thousand from the tribe of Reuben, twelve thousand from the tribe of Gad, 6twelve thousand from the tribe of Asher, twelve thousand from the tribe of Naphtali, twelve thousand from the tribe of Manasseh, 7twelve thousand from the tribe of Simeon, twelve thousand from the tribe of Levi, twelve thousand from the tribe of Issachar, 8twelve thousand from the tribe of Zebulun, twelve thousand from the tribe of Joseph, and twelve thousand were marked from the tribe of Benjamin.

Triumph of the Elect. 9*After this I had a vision of a great multitude, which no one could count, from every nation, race, people, and tongue. They stood before the throne and before the Lamb, wearing white robes and holding palm branches in their hands. 10*They cried out in a loud voice:

"Salvation comes from our God, who is
　　seated on the throne,
　and from the Lamb."

11All the angels stood around the throne and around the elders and the four living creatures. They prostrated themselves before the throne, worshiped God, 12and exclaimed:

"Amen. Blessing and glory, wisdom and
　　thanksgiving,
　honor, power, and might
　be to our God forever and ever.
　　Amen."

13Then one of the elders spoke up and said to me, "Who are these wearing white robes, and where did they come from?" 14w*I said to him, "My lord, you are the one who knows." He said to me, "These are the ones who have survived the time of great distress; they have washed their robes and made them white in the blood of the Lamb.

15 "For this reason they stand before God's
　　throne
　and worship him day and night in his
　　temple.
　The one who sits on the throne will
　　shelter them.
16 xThey will not hunger or thirst anymore,
　nor will the sun or any heat strike them.
17 y*For the Lamb who is in the center of
　　the throne will shepherd them
　and lead them to springs of life-giving
　　water,
　and God will wipe away every tear
　　from their eyes."

CHAPTER 8

See RG 459-60

The Seven Trumpets. 1z*When he broke open the seventh seal, there was silence in heaven for about half an hour. 2aAnd I saw that the seven angels who stood before God were given seven trumpets.

The Gold Censer. 3b*Another angel came and stood at the altar, holding a gold censer. He was given a great quantity of incense to offer, along with the prayers of all the holy ones, on the gold altar that was before the throne. 4The smoke of the incense along with the prayers of the holy ones went up before God from the hand of the angel. 5cThen the angel took the censer, filled it with burning coals from the altar, and hurled it down to the earth. There were peals of thunder, rumblings, flashes of lightning, and an earthquake.

The First Four Trumpets. 6dThe seven an-

7, 9: **White robes . . . palm branches:** symbols of joy and victory; see the note on 3, 5.

7, 10: **Salvation comes from:** literally, "(let) salvation (be ascribed) to." A similar hymn of praise is found at the fall of the dragon (12, 10) and of Babylon (19, 1).

7, 14: **Time of great distress:** fierce persecution by the Romans; cf Introduction.

7, 17: **Life-giving water:** literally, "the water of life," God's grace, which flows from Christ; cf 21, 6; 22, 1.17; Jn 4, 10.14.

8, 1–13: The breaking of the seventh seal produces at first silence and then seven symbolic disasters, each announced by a trumpet blast, of which the first four form a unit as did the first four seals. A minor liturgy (3–5) is enclosed by a vision of seven angels (2.6). Then follow the first four trumpet blasts, each heralding catastrophes modeled on the plagues of Egypt affecting the traditional prophetic third (cf Ez 5, 12) of the earth, sea, fresh water, and stars (7–12). Finally, there is a vision of an eagle warning of the last three trumpet blasts (13).

8, 1: **Silence in heaven:** as in Zep 1, 7, a prelude to the eschatological woes that are to follow; cf Introduction.

8, 3: **Altar:** there seems to be only one altar in the heavenly temple, corresponding to the altar of holocausts in 6, 9, and here to the altar of incense in Jerusalem; cf also 9, 13; 11, 1; 14, 18; 16, 7.

w: Mt 24, 21.　x: Is 49, 10.　y: 21, 4; Is 25, 8.　z: Hb 2, 20; Zep 1, 7; Zec 2, 17.　a: 4, 5; Tb 12, 15.　b: Ps 141, 2; Tb 12, 12.　c: Ez 10, 2; Ps 11, 6 / 4, 5; 11, 19; 16, 18.　d: 16, 1-21.

gels who were holding the seven trumpets prepared to blow them.

⁷*When the first one blew his trumpet, there came hail and fire mixed with blood, which was hurled down to the earth. A third of the land was burned up, along with a third of the trees and all green grass.

⁸ᵉ*When the second angel blew his trumpet, something like a large burning mountain was hurled into the sea. A third of the sea turned to blood, ⁹*a third of the creatures living in the sea died, and a third of the ships were wrecked.

¹⁰ᶠWhen the third angel blew his trumpet, a large star burning like a torch fell from the sky. It fell on a third of the rivers and on the springs of water. ¹¹ᵍ*The star was called "Wormwood," and a third of all the water turned to wormwood. Many people died from this water, because it was made bitter.

¹²ʰWhen the fourth angel blew his trumpet, a third of the sun, a third of the moon, and a third of the stars were struck, so that a third of them became dark. The day lost its light for a third of the time, as did the night.

¹³*Then I looked again and heard an eagle flying high overhead cry out in a loud voice, "Woe! Woe! Woe to the inhabitants of the earth from the rest of the trumpet blasts that the three angels are about to blow!"

CHAPTER 9

See RG
459-60 *The Fifth Trumpet.* ¹ⁱ*Then the fifth angel blew his trumpet, and I saw a star that had fallen from the sky to the earth. It was

given the key for the passage to the abyss. ²ʲIt opened the passage to the abyss, and smoke came up out of the passage like smoke from a huge furnace. The sun and the air were darkened by the smoke from the passage. ³ᵏ*Locusts came out of the smoke onto the land, and they were given the same power as scorpions of the earth. ⁴They were told not to harm the grass of the earth or any plant or any tree, but only those people who did not have the seal of God on their foreheads. ⁵*They were not allowed to kill them but only to torment them for five months; the torment they inflicted was like that of a scorpion when it stings a person. ⁶ˡDuring that time these people will seek death but will not find it, and they will long to die but death will escape them.

⁷ᵐ*The appearance of the locusts was like that of horses ready for battle. On their heads they wore what looked like crowns of gold; their faces were like human faces, ⁸ⁿand they had hair like women's hair. Their teeth were like lions' teeth, ⁹and they had chests like iron breastplates. The sound of their wings was like the sound of many horse-drawn chariots racing into battle. ¹⁰They had tails like scorpions, with stingers; with their tails they had power to harm people for five months. ¹¹*They had as their king the angel of the abyss, whose name in Hebrew is Abaddon and in Greek Apollyon.

¹²The first woe has passed, but there are two more to come.

8, 7: This woe resembles the seventh plague of Egypt (Ex 9, 23–24); cf Jl 3, 3.

8, 8–11: The background of these two woes is the first plague of Egypt (Ex 7, 20–21).

8, 9: Creatures living in the sea: literally, "creatures in the sea that had souls."

8, 11: Wormwood: an extremely bitter and malignant plant symbolizing the punishment God inflicts on the ungodly; cf Jer 9, 12–14; 23, 15.

8, 13: Woe! Woe! Woe: each of the three woes pronounced by the angel represents a separate disaster; cf 9, 12; 11, 14. The final woe, released by the seventh trumpet blast, includes the plagues of ch 16.

9, 1–12: The fifth trumpet heralds a woe containing elements from the eighth and ninth plagues of Egypt (Ex 10, 12–15.21–23) but specifically reminiscent of the invasion of locusts in Jl 1, 4—2, 10.

9, 1: A star: late Judaism represented fallen powers as stars (Is 14, 12–15; Lk 10, 18; Jude 13), but a comparison

with 1, 20 and 20, 1 suggests that here it means an angel. **The passage to the abyss:** referring to Sheol, the netherworld, where Satan and the fallen angels are kept for a thousand years, to be cast afterwards into the pool of fire; cf 20, 7–10. The abyss was conceived of as a vast subterranean cavern full of fire. Its only link with the earth was a kind of passage or mine shaft, which was kept locked.

9, 3: Scorpions: their poisonous sting was proverbial; Ez 2, 6; Lk 11, 12.

9, 5: For five months: more or less corresponding to the life-span of locusts.

9, 7–10: Eight characteristics are listed to show the eschatological and diabolical nature of these locusts.

9, 11: Abaddon: Hebrew (more precisely, Aramaic) for destruction or ruin. **Apollyon:** Greek for the "Destroyer."

e: Ex 7, 20. *f:* Is 14, 12. *g:* Jer 9, 14. *h:* Ex 10, 21-23. *i:* 20, 1. *j:* Gn 19, 28. *k:* Ex 10, 12-15; Wis 16, 9. *l:* Jb 3, 21. *m:* Jl 2, 4. *n:* Jl 1, 6.

The Sixth Trumpet. [13]*Then the sixth angel blew his trumpet, and I heard a voice coming from the [four] horns of the gold altar before God, [14]*telling the sixth angel who held the trumpet, "Release the four angels who are bound at the banks of the great river Euphrates." [15]So the four angels were released, who were prepared for this hour, day, month, and year to kill a third of the human race. [16]The number of cavalry troops was two hundred million; I heard their number. [17][p]*Now in my vision this is how I saw the horses and their riders. They wore red, blue, and yellow breastplates, and the horses' heads were like heads of lions, and out of their mouths came fire, smoke, and sulfur. [18]By these three plagues of fire, smoke, and sulfur that came out of their mouths a third of the human race was killed. [19]For the power of the horses is in their mouths and in their tails; for their tails are like snakes, with heads that inflict harm.

[20][q]*The rest of the human race, who were not killed by these plagues, did not repent of the works of their hands, to give up the worship of demons and idols made from gold, silver, bronze, stone, and wood, which cannot see or hear or walk. [21]Nor did they repent of their murders, their magic potions, their unchastity, or their robberies.

See RG
459-60

CHAPTER 10

The Angel with the Small Scroll.
[1]*Then I saw another mighty angel come down from heaven wrapped in a cloud, with a halo around his head; his face was like the sun and his feet were like pillars of fire. [2]*In his hand he held a small scroll that had been opened. He placed his right foot on the sea and his left foot on the land, [3][r]and then he cried out in a loud voice as a lion roars. When he cried out, the seven thunders raised their voices, too. [4]When the seven thunders had spoken, I was about to write it down; but I heard a voice from heaven say, "Seal up what the seven thunders have spoken, but do not write it down." [5]Then the angel I saw standing on the sea and on the land raised his right hand to heaven [6][s]*and swore by the one who lives forever and ever, who created heaven and earth and sea and all that is in them, "There shall be no more delay. [7][t]*At the time when you hear the seventh angel blow his trumpet, the mysterious plan of God shall be fulfilled, as he promised to his servants the prophets."

[8]Then the voice that I had heard from heaven spoke to me again and said, "Go, take the scroll that lies open in the hand of the angel who is standing on the sea and on the land." [9]*So I went up to the angel and told him to give me the small scroll. He said to me, "Take and swallow it. It will turn your stomach sour, but in your mouth it will taste as sweet as honey." [10][u]I took the small scroll

---

9, 13–21: The sixth trumpet heralds a woe representing another diabolical attack symbolized by an invasion by the Parthians living east of the Euphrates; see the note on 6, 2. At the appointed time (15), the frightful horses act as God's agents of judgment. The imaginative details are not to be taken literally; see Introduction and the note on 6, 12–14.

9, 13: [Four]: many Greek manuscripts and versions omit the word. The horns were situated at the four corners of the altar (Ex 27, 2; 30, 2–3); see the note on 8, 3.

9, 14–15: The four angels: they are symbolic of the destructive activity that will be extended throughout the universe.

9, 17: Blue: literally, "hyacinth-colored." Yellow: literally, "sulfurous."

9, 20: The works of their hands: i.e., the gods their hands had made.

10, 1—11, 14: An interlude in two scenes (10, 1–11 and 11, 1–14) precedes the sounding of the seventh trumpet; cf 7, 1–17. The first vision describes an angel astride sea and land like a colossus, with a small scroll open, the contents of which indicate that the end is imminent (ch 10). The second vision is of the measuring of the temple and of two witnesses, whose martyr-

dom means that the kingdom of God is about to be inaugurated.

10, 1–4: The seven thunders: God's voice announcing judgment and doom; cf Ps 29, 3–9, where thunder, as the voice of Yahweh, is praised seven times.

10, 2: He placed . . . on the land: this symbolizes the universality of the angel's message, as does the figure of the small scroll open to be read.

10, 6: Heaven and earth and sea: the three parts of the universe. No more delay: cf Dn 12, 7; Hb 2, 3.

10, 7: The mysterious plan of God: literally, "the mystery of God," the end of the present age when the forces of evil will be put down (17, 1—19, 4.11–21; 20, 7–10; cf 2 Thes 2, 6–12; Rom 16, 25–26), and the establishment of the reign of God when all creation will be made new (21, 1—22, 5).

10, 9–10: The small scroll was sweet because it predicted the final victory of God's people; it was sour because it also announced their sufferings. Cf Ez 3, 1–3.

o: Ex 30, 1-3. p: Jb 41, 10-13. q: Ps 135, 15-17; Is 17, 8; Dn 5, 4. r: Ps 29, 3-9; Jer 25, 30; Am 3, 8. s: Dt 32, 40; Dn 12, 7 / Ez 12, 28. t: Am 3, 7. u: Ez 3, 1-3.

from the angel's hand and swallowed it. In my mouth it was like sweet honey, but when I had eaten it, my stomach turned sour. *11**Then someone said to me, "You must prophesy again about many peoples, nations, tongues, and kings."

See RG 459–60

CHAPTER 11

The Two Witnesses. *1v**Then I was given a measuring rod like a staff and I was told, "Come and measure the temple of God and the altar, and count those who are worshiping in it. *2**But exclude the outer court of the temple; do not measure it, for it has been handed over to the Gentiles, who will trample the holy city for forty-two months. *3**I will commission my two witnesses to prophesy for those twelve hundred and sixty days, wearing sackcloth." *4w**These are the two olive trees and the two lampstands that stand before the Lord of the earth. *5**If anyone wants to harm them, fire comes out of their mouths and devours their enemies. In this way, anyone wanting to harm them is sure to be slain. *6x*They have the power to close up the sky so that no rain can fall during the time of their prophesying. They also have power to turn water into blood and to afflict the earth with any plague as often as they wish.

*7y**When they have finished their testimony, the beast that comes up from the abyss will wage war against them and conquer them and kill them. *8**Their corpses will lie in the main street of the great city, which has the symbolic names "Sodom" and "Egypt," where indeed their Lord was crucified. *9**Those from every people, tribe, tongue, and nation will gaze on their corpses for three and a half days, and they will not allow their corpses to be buried. *10*The inhabitants of the earth will gloat over them and be glad and exchange gifts because these two prophets tormented the inhabitants of the earth. *11z*But after the three and a half days, a breath of life from God entered them. When they stood on their feet, great fear fell on those who saw them. *12a*Then they heard a loud voice from heaven say to them, "Come up here." So they went up to heaven in a cloud as their enemies looked on. *13**At that moment there was a great earthquake, and a tenth of the city fell in ruins. Seven thousand people were killed during the earthquake; the rest were terrified and gave glory to the God of heaven.

*14*The second woe has passed, but the third is coming soon.

The Seventh Trumpet. *15**Then the sev-

10, 11: This further prophecy is contained in chs 12–22.

11, 1: The temple and altar symbolize the new Israel; see the note on 7, 4–9. The worshipers represent Christians. The measuring of the temple (cf Ez 40, 3—42, 20; 47, 1–12; Zec 2, 5–6) suggests that God will preserve the faithful remnant (cf Is 4, 2–3) who remain true to Christ (14, 1–5).

11, 2: The outer court: the Court of the Gentiles. Trample . . . forty-two months: the duration of the vicious persecution of the Jews by Antiochus IV Epiphanes (Dn 7, 25; 12, 7); this persecution of three and a half years (half of seven, counted as 1260 days in 3; 12, 6) became the prototype of periods of trial for God's people; cf Lk 4, 25; Jas 5, 17. The reference here is to the persecution by the Romans; cf Introduction.

11, 3: The two witnesses, wearing sackcloth symbolizing lamentation and repentance, cannot readily be identified. Do they represent Moses and Elijah, or the Law and the Prophets, or Peter and Paul? Most probably they refer to the universal church, especially the Christian martyrs, fulfilling the office of witness (two because of Dt 19, 15; cf Mk 6, 7; Jn 8, 17).

11, 4: The two olive trees and the two lampstands: the martyrs who stand in the presence of the Lord; the imagery is taken from Zec 4, 1–3.11–14, where the olive trees refer to Zerubbabel and Joshua.

11, 5–6: These details are derived from stories of Moses, who turned water into blood (Ex 7, 17–20), and of Elijah, who called down fire from heaven (1 Kgs 18, 36–40; 2 Kgs 1, 10)

and closed up the sky for three years (1 Kgs 17, 1; cf 18, 1).

11, 7: The beast . . . from the abyss: the Roman emperor Nero, who symbolizes the forces of evil, or the antichrist (13, 1.8; 17, 8); cf Dn 7, 2–8.11–12.19–22 and Introduction.

11, 8: The great city: this expression is used constantly in Rv for Babylon, i.e., Rome; cf 14, 8; 16, 19; 17, 18; 18, 2.10.21. **"Sodom" and "Egypt":** symbols of immorality (cf Is 1, 10) and oppression of God's people (cf Ex 1, 11–14). **Where indeed their Lord was crucified:** not the geographical but the symbolic Jerusalem that rejects God and his witnesses, i.e., Rome, called Babylon in chs 16–18; see the note on 17, 9 and Introduction.

11, 9–12: Over the martyrdom (7) of the two witnesses, now called prophets, the ungodly rejoice **for three and a half days,** a symbolic period of time; see the note on v 2. Afterwards they go in triumph to heaven, as did Elijah (2 Kgs 2, 11).

11, 13: Seven thousand people: a symbolic sum to represent all social classes (seven) and large numbers (thousands); cf Introduction.

11, 15–19: The seventh trumpet proclaims the coming of God's reign after the victory over diabolical powers; see the note on 10, 7.

v: Ez 40, 3-5 / Zec 2, 5-9.   *w:* Zec 4, 3.14.   *x:* Ex 7, 17.   *y:* Dn 7, 21.   *z:* Ez 37, 5.10.   *a:* 2 Kgs 2, 11.

enth angel blew his trumpet. There were loud voices in heaven, saying, "The kingdom of the world now belongs to our Lord and to his Anointed, and he will reign forever and ever." ¹⁶The twenty-four elders who sat on their thrones before God prostrated themselves and worshiped God ¹⁷and said:

"We give thanks to you, Lord God
        almighty,
    who are and who were.
For you have assumed your great power
        and have established your reign.
¹⁸ ᵇThe nations raged,
    but your wrath has come,
    and the time for the dead to be judged,
    and to recompense your servants, the
            prophets,
    and the holy ones and those who fear
            your name,
    the small and the great alike,
    and to destroy those who destroy the
            earth."

¹⁹Then God's temple in heaven was opened, and the ark of his covenant could be seen in the temple. There were flashes of lightning, rumblings, and peals of thunder, an earthquake, and a violent hailstorm.

CHAPTER 12

The Woman and the Dragon. ¹ᶜ*A great sign appeared in the sky, a woman clothed with the sun, with the moon under her feet, and on her head a crown of twelve stars. ²*She was with child and wailed aloud in pain as she labored to give birth. ³ᵈ*Then another sign appeared in the sky; it was a huge red dragon, with seven heads and ten horns, and on its heads were seven diadems. ⁴ᵉIts tail swept away a third of the stars in the sky and hurled them down to the earth. Then the dragon stood before the woman about to give birth, to devour her child when she gave birth. ⁵ᶠ*She gave birth to a son, a male child, destined to rule all the nations with an iron rod. Her child was caught up to God and his throne. ⁶*The woman herself fled into the desert where she had a place prepared by God, that there she might be taken care of for twelve hundred and sixty days.

⁷*Then war broke out in heaven; Michael and his angels battled against the dragon. The dragon and its angels fought back, ⁸but they did not prevail and there was no longer any place for them in heaven. ⁹ᵍ*The huge dragon, the ancient serpent, who is called the Devil and Satan, who deceived the whole

See RG 459–60

12, 1—14, 20: This central section of Rv portrays the power of evil, represented by a dragon, in opposition to God and his people. First, the dragon pursues the woman about to give birth, but her son is saved and "caught up to God and his throne" (12, 5). Then Michael and his angels cast the dragon and his angels out of heaven (12, 7–9). After this, the dragon tries to attack the boy indirectly by attacking members of his church (12, 13–18). A beast, symbolizing the Roman empire, then becomes the dragon's agent, mortally wounded but restored to life and worshiped by all the world (13, 1–10). A second beast arises from the land, symbolizing the antichrist, which leads people astray by its prodigies to idolize the first beast (13, 11–18). This is followed by a vision of the Lamb and his faithful ones, and the proclamation of imminent judgment upon the world in terms of the wine of God's wrath (14, 1–20).

12, 1–6: The woman adorned with the sun, the moon, and the stars (images taken from Gn 37, 9–10) symbolizes God's people in the Old and the New Testament. The Israel of old gave birth to the Messiah (5) and then became the new Israel, the church, which suffers persecution by the dragon (6, 13–17); cf Is 50, 1; 66, 7; Jer 50, 12. This corresponds to a widespread myth throughout the ancient world that a goddess pregnant with a savior was pursued by a horrible monster; by miraculous intervention, she bore a son who then killed the monster.

12, 2: Because of Eve's sin, the woman gives birth in distress and pain (Gn 3, 16; cf Is 66, 7–14).

12, 3: Huge red dragon: the Devil or Satan (cf 9; 20, 2), symbol of the forces of evil, a mythical monster known also as Leviathan (Ps 74, 13–14) or Rahab (Jb 26, 12–13; Ps 89, 11). **Seven diadems:** these are symbolic of the fullness of the dragon's sovereignty over the kingdoms of this world; cf Christ with many diadems (19, 12).

12, 5: Rule . . . iron rod: fulfilled in 19, 15; cf Ps 2, 9. **Was caught up to God:** reference to Christ's ascension.

12, 6: God protects the persecuted church in the desert, the traditional Old Testament place of refuge for the afflicted, according to the typology of the Exodus; see the note on 11, 2.

12, 7–12: Michael, mentioned only here in Rv, wins a victory over the dragon. A hymn of praise follows.

12, 7: Michael: the archangel, guardian and champion of Israel; cf Dn 10, 13.21; 12, 1; Jude 9. In Hebrew, the name Michael means "Who can compare with God?"; cf 13, 4.

12, 9: The ancient serpent: who seduced Eve (Gn 3, 1–6), mother of the human race; cf 20, 2; Eph 6, 11–12. **Was thrown down:** allusion to the expulsion of Satan from heaven; cf Lk 10, 18.

b: Ps 2, 1.5 / Am 3, 7.   *c:* Gn 37, 9.   *d:* Dn 7, 7.   *e:* Dn 8, 10. *f:* Is 66, 7 / Ps 2, 9.   *g:* Gn 3, 1-4 / Lk 10, 18.

world, was thrown down to earth, and its angels were thrown down with it. [10]*Then I heard a loud voice in heaven say:

"Now have salvation and power come,
   and the kingdom of our God
   and the authority of his Anointed.
For the accuser of our brothers is cast out,
   who accuses them before our God day
      and night.
[11] They conquered him by the blood of the
      Lamb
   and by the word of their testimony;
   love for life did not deter them from
      death.
[12] Therefore, rejoice, you heavens,
   and you who dwell in them.
But woe to you, earth and sea,
   for the Devil has come down to you in
      great fury,
   for he knows he has but a short time."

[13h]When the dragon saw that it had been thrown down to the earth, it pursued the woman who had given birth to the male child. [14i]*But the woman was given the two wings of the great eagle, so that she could fly to her place in the desert, where, far from the serpent, she was taken care of for a year, two years, and a half-year. [15]*The serpent, however, spewed a torrent of water out of his mouth after the woman to sweep her away with the current. [16]But the earth helped the woman and opened its mouth and swallowed the flood that the dragon spewed out of its mouth. [17j]*Then the dragon became angry with the woman and went off to wage war against the rest of her offspring, those who keep God's commandments and bear witness to Jesus. [18]*It took its position on the sand of the sea.

CHAPTER 13

See RG 459–60

The First Beast. [1k]*Then I saw a beast come out of the sea with ten horns and seven heads; on its horns were ten diadems, and on its heads blasphemous name[s]. [2l]*The beast I saw was like a leopard, but it had feet like a bear's, and its mouth was like the mouth of a lion. To it the dragon gave its own power and throne, along with great authority. [3]*I saw that one of its heads seemed to have been mortally wounded, but this mortal wound was healed. Fascinated, the whole world followed after the beast. [4]*They worshiped the dragon because it gave its authority to the beast; they also worshiped the beast and said, "Who can compare with the beast or who can fight against it?"

[5m]*The beast was given a mouth uttering proud boasts and blasphemies, and it was given authority to act for forty-two months. [6]It opened its mouth to utter blasphemies against God, blaspheming his name and his dwelling and those who dwell in heaven. [7n]It was also allowed to wage war against the holy ones and conquer them, and it was granted authority over every tribe, people, tongue, and nation. [8o]All the inhabitants of

---

12, 10: The accuser: the meaning of the Hebrew word "Satan," found in v 9; Jb 1—2; Zec 3, 1; 1 Chr 21, 1; he continues to accuse Christ's disciples.

12, 14: Great eagle: symbol of the power and swiftness of divine help; cf Ex 19, 4; Dt 32, 11; Is 40, 31.

12, 15: The serpent is depicted as the sea monster; cf 13, 1; Is 27, 1; Ez 32, 2; Ps 74, 13–14.

12, 17: Although the church is protected by God's special providence (16), the individual Christian is to expect persecution and suffering.

12, 18: It took its position: many later manuscripts and versions read "I took my position," thus connecting the sentence to the following paragraph.

13, 1–10: This wild beast, combining features of the four beasts in Dn 7, 2–28, symbolizes the Roman empire; the seven heads represent the emperors; see the notes on 17, 10 and 17, 12–14. The blasphemous names are the divine titles assumed by the emperors.

13, 2: Satan (12, 9), the prince of this world (Jn 12, 31), commissioned the beast to persecute the church (5–7).

13, 3: This may be a reference to the popular legend that Nero would come back to life and rule again after his death (which occurred in A.D. 68 from a self-inflicted stab wound in the throat); cf v 14; 17, 8. Domitian (A.D. 81–96) embodied all the cruelty and impiety of Nero. Cf Introduction.

13, 4: Worshiped the beast: allusion to emperor worship, which Domitian insisted upon and ruthlessly enforced. **Who can compare with the beast:** perhaps a deliberate parody of the name Michael; see the note on 12, 7.

13, 5–6: Domitian, like Antiochus IV Epiphanes (Dn 7, 8.11.25), demanded that he be called by divine titles such as "our lord and god" and "Jupiter." See the note on 11, 2.

13, 5: Forty-two months: this is the same duration as the profanation of the holy city (11, 2), the prophetic mission of the two witnesses (11, 3), and the retreat of the woman into the desert (12, 6.14).

---

h: Gn 3, 15. *i:* Ex 19, 4; Dn 7, 25; 12, 7. *j:* Gn 3, 15. *k:* 2 Thes 2, 3-12. *l:* Dn 7, 3-6. *m:* Dn 7, 8.11.25; 8, 14; 9, 27; 11, 36; 12, 7. *n:* Dn 7, 21. *o:* 3, 5; 17, 8; 20, 12.

the earth will worship it, all whose names were not written from the foundation of the world in the book of life, which belongs to the Lamb who was slain.

9 *p*Whoever has ears ought to hear these words.
10 *q*Anyone destined for captivity goes into captivity.
Anyone destined to be slain by the sword shall be slain by the sword.

Such is the faithful endurance of the holy ones.

The Second Beast. *11**Then I saw another beast come up out of the earth; it had two horns like a lamb's but spoke like a dragon. *12*It wielded all the authority of the first beast in its sight and made the earth and its inhabitants worship the first beast, whose mortal wound had been healed. *13r*It performed great signs, even making fire come down from heaven to earth in the sight of everyone. *14*It deceived the inhabitants of the earth with the signs it was allowed to perform in the sight of the first beast, telling them to make an image for the beast who had been wounded by the sword and revived. *15s*It was then permitted to breathe life into the beast's image, so that the beast's image could speak and [could] have anyone who did not worship it put to death. *16t*It forced all the people, small and great, rich and poor, free and slave, to be given a stamped image on their right hands or their foreheads, *17*so that no one could buy or sell except one who had the stamped image of the beast's name or the number that stood for its name.

18u*Wisdom is needed here; one who understands can calculate the number of the beast, for it is a number that stands for a person. His number is six hundred and sixty-six.

CHAPTER 14

See RG 459–60

The Lamb's Companions. *1v**Then I looked and there was the Lamb standing on Mount Zion, and with him a hundred and forty-four thousand who had his name and his Father's name written on their foreheads. *2*I heard a sound from heaven like the sound of rushing water or a loud peal of thunder. The sound I heard was like that of harpists playing their harps. *3w*They were singing [what seemed to be] a new hymn before the throne, before the four living creatures and the elders. No one could learn this hymn except the hundred and forty-four thousand who had been ransomed from the earth. *4x**These are they who were not defiled with women; they are virgins and these are the ones who follow the Lamb wherever he goes. They have been ransomed as the firstfruits of the human race for God and the Lamb. *5y**On their lips no deceit has been found; they are unblemished.

The Three Angels. *6**Then I saw another

13, 11–18: The second beast is described in terms of the false prophets (cf 16, 13; 19, 20; 20, 10) who accompany the false messiahs (the first beast); cf Mt 24, 24; Mk 13, 22; 2 Thes 2, 9; cf also Dt 13, 2–4. Christians had either to worship the emperor and his image or to suffer martyrdom.

13, 18: Each of the letters of the alphabet in Hebrew as well as in Greek has a numerical value. Many possible combinations of letters will add up to 666, and many candidates have been nominated for this infamous number. The most likely is the emperor Caesar Nero (see the note on 13, 3), the Greek form of whose name in Hebrew letters gives the required sum. (The Latin form of this name equals 616, which is the reading of a few manuscripts.) Nero personifies the emperors who viciously persecuted the church. It has also been observed that "6" represents imperfection, falling short of the perfect number "7," and is represented here in a triple or superlative form.

14, 1–5: Now follows a tender and consoling vision of the Lamb and his companions.

14, 1: Mount Zion: in Jerusalem, the traditional place where the true remnant, the Israel of faith, is to be gathered in the messianic reign; cf 2 Kgs 19, 30–31; Jl 3, 5; Ob 17; Mi 4,

6–8; Zep 3, 12–20. **A hundred and forty-four thousand:** see the note on 7, 4–9. **His Father's name . . . foreheads:** in contrast to the pagans who were marked with the name or number of the beast (13, 16–17).

14, 4: **Virgins:** metaphorically, because they never indulged in any idolatrous practices, which are considered in the Old Testament to be adultery and fornication (2, 14–15.20–22; 17, 1–6; cf Ez 16, 1–58; 23, 1–49). The parallel passages (7, 3; 22, 4) indicate that the 144,000 whose foreheads are sealed represent all Christian people.

14, 5: **No deceit:** because they did not deny Christ or do homage to the beast. Lying is characteristic of the opponents of Christ (Jn 8, 44), but the Suffering Servant spoke no falsehood (Is 53, 9; 1 Pt 2, 22). **Unblemished:** a cultic term taken from the vocabulary of sacrificial ritual.

14, 6–13: Three angels proclaim imminent judgment on the pagan world, calling all peoples to worship God the cre-

---

p: Mt 13, 9. *q:* Jer 15, 2. *r:* Dt 13, 2-4; Mt 24, 24; 2 Thes 2, 9-10. *s:* Dn 3, 5-7.15. *t:* 14, 9; 16, 2; 19, 20; 20, 4. *u:* 17, 9. *v:* Jl 3, 5; Ob 17; Acts 2, 21. *w:* Pss 33, 3; 96, 1; 98, 1; Is 42, 10. *x:* Jer 2, 2; Jas 1, 18. *y:* Zep 3, 13.

angel flying high overhead, with everlasting good news to announce to those who dwell on earth, to every nation, tribe, tongue, and people. [7z]He said in a loud voice, "Fear God and give him glory, for his time has come to sit in judgment. Worship him who made heaven and earth and sea and springs of water."

[8a*]A second angel followed, saying:

"Fallen, fallen is Babylon the great,
that made all the nations drink
the wine of her licentious passion."

[9]A third angel followed them and said in a loud voice, "Anyone who worships the beast or its image, or accepts its mark on forehead or hand, [10*]will also drink the wine of God's fury, poured full strength into the cup of his wrath, and will be tormented in burning sulfur before the holy angels and before the Lamb. [11b]The smoke of the fire that torments them will rise forever and ever, and there will be no relief day or night for those who worship the beast or its image or accept the mark of its name." [12c*]Here is what sustains the holy ones who keep God's commandments and their faith in Jesus.

[13d*]I heard a voice from heaven say, "Write this: Blessed are the dead who die in the Lord from now on." "Yes," said the Spirit, "let them find rest from their labors, for their works accompany them."

The Harvest of the Earth. [14e*]Then I looked and there was a white cloud, and sit-

ting on the cloud one who looked like a son of man, with a gold crown on his head and a sharp sickle in his hand. [15f]Another angel came out of the temple, crying out in a loud voice to the one sitting on the cloud, "Use your sickle and reap the harvest, for the time to reap has come, because the earth's harvest is fully ripe." [16]So the one who was sitting on the cloud swung his sickle over the earth, and the earth was harvested.

[17]Then another angel came out of the temple in heaven who also had a sharp sickle. [18*]Then another angel [came] from the altar, [who] was in charge of the fire, and cried out in a loud voice to the one who had the sharp sickle, "Use your sharp sickle and cut the clusters from the earth's vines, for its grapes are ripe." [19g]So the angel swung his sickle over the earth and cut the earth's vintage. He threw it into the great wine press of God's fury. [20*]The wine press was trodden outside the city and blood poured out of the wine press to the height of a horse's bridle for two hundred miles.

CHAPTER 15

See RG 459-60

The Seven Last Plagues. [1*]Then I saw in heaven another sign, great and awe-inspiring: seven angels with the seven last plagues, for through them God's fury is accomplished.

[2h*]Then I saw something like a sea of glass mingled with fire. On the sea of glass

---

ator. Babylon (Rome) will fall, and its supporters will be tormented forever.

14, 6: Everlasting good news: that God's eternal reign is about to begin; see the note on 10, 7.

14, 8: This verse anticipates the lengthy dirge over Babylon (Rome) in 18, 1—19, 4. The oracle of Is 21, 9 to Babylon is applied here.

14, 10–11: The wine of God's fury: image taken from Is 51, 17; Jer 25, 15–16; 49, 12; 51, 7; Ez 23, 31–34. Eternal punishment in the fiery pool of burning sulfur (or "fire and brimstone"; cf Gn 19, 24) is also reserved for the Devil, the beast, and the false prophet (19, 20; 20, 10; 21, 8).

14, 12: In addition to **faith in Jesus,** the seer insists upon the necessity and value of works, as in 2, 23; 20, 12–13; 22, 12; cf Mt 16, 27; Rom 2, 6.

14, 13: See the note on 1, 3. According to Jewish thought, people's actions followed them as witnesses before the court of God.

14, 14–20: The reaping of the harvest symbolizes the gathering of the elect in the final judgment, while the reaping and treading of the grapes symbolizes the doom of the un-

godly (cf Jl 4, 12–13; Is 63, 1–6) that will come in 19, 11–21.

14, 18: Altar: there was only one altar in the heavenly temple; see the notes above on 6, 9; 8, 3; 11, 1.

14, 20: Two hundred miles: literally sixteen hundred stades. The **stadion,** a Greek unit of measurement, was about 607 feet in length, approximately the length of a furlong.

15, 1—16, 21: The seven bowls, the third and last group of seven after the seven seals and the seven trumpets, foreshadow the final cataclysm. Again, the series is introduced by a heavenly prelude, in which the victors over the beast sing the canticle of Moses (15, 2–4).

15, 1–4: A vision of the victorious martyrs precedes the vision of woe in 15, 5—16, 21; cf 7, 9–12.

15, 2: Mingled with fire: fire symbolizes the sanctity involved in facing God, reflected in the trials that have prepared the victorious Christians or in God's wrath.

---

z: 2, 10; Mt 10, 28.　a: 18, 2-3; Is 21, 9; Jer 51, 8 / Is 51, 17; Jer 25, 15-17.　b: 19, 3.　c: 12, 17.　d: Mt 11, 28-29; 2 Thes 1, 7; Heb 4, 10.　e: 1, 7; Dn 7, 13.　f: Jl 4, 13; Mt 13, 36-43.　g: 19, 15; Is 63, 1-6.　h: 7, 9.14; 13, 15-18.

were standing those who had won the victory over the beast and its image and the number that signified its name. They were holding God's harps, [3i]*and they sang the song of Moses, the servant of God, and the song of the Lamb:

"Great and wonderful are your works,
Lord God almighty.
Just and true are your ways,
O king of the nations.
[4] [j]Who will not fear you, Lord,
or glorify your name?
For you alone are holy.
All the nations will come
and worship before you,
for your righteous acts have been
revealed."

[5]*After this I had another vision. The temple that is the heavenly tent of testimony opened, [6k]and the seven angels with the seven plagues came out of the temple. They were dressed in clean white linen, with a gold sash around their chests. [7]One of the four living creatures gave the seven angels seven gold bowls filled with the fury of God, who lives forever and ever. [8l]Then the temple became so filled with the smoke from God's glory and might that no one could enter it until the seven plagues of the seven angels had been accomplished.

CHAPTER 16

See RG 459–60

The Seven Bowls. [1]*I heard a loud voice speaking from the temple to the seven angels, "Go and pour out the seven bowls of God's fury upon the earth."

[2]*The first angel went and poured out his bowl on the earth. Festering and ugly sores broke out on those who had the mark of the beast or worshiped its image.

[3]*The second angel poured out his bowl on the sea. The sea turned to blood like that from a corpse; every creature living in the sea died.

[4m]The third angel poured out his bowl on the rivers and springs of water. These also turned to blood. [5n]Then I heard the angel in charge of the waters say:

"You are just, O Holy One,
who are and who were,
in passing this sentence.
[6] [o]For they have shed the blood of the holy
ones and the prophets,
and you [have] given them blood to
drink;
it is what they deserve."

[7p]Then I heard the altar cry out,

"Yes, Lord God almighty,
your judgments are true and just."

[8]The fourth angel poured out his bowl on the sun. It was given the power to burn people with fire. [9q]People were burned by the scorching heat and blasphemed the name of God who had power over these plagues, but they did not repent or give him glory.

[10r]*The fifth angel poured out his bowl on the throne of the beast. Its kingdom was plunged into darkness, and people bit their tongues in pain [11s]and blasphemed the God of heaven because of their pains and sores. But they did not repent of their works.

[12]*The sixth angel emptied his bowl on the great river Euphrates. Its water was dried up to prepare the way for the kings of the East. [13t]*I saw three unclean spirits like frogs come from the mouth of the dragon, from

---

15, 3: **The song of Moses:** the song that Moses and the Israelites sang after their escape from the oppression of Egypt (Ex 15, 1–18). The martyrs have escaped from the oppression of the Devil. **Nations:** many other Greek manuscripts and versions read "ages."

15, 5–8: Seven angels receive the bowls of God's wrath.

15, 5: **Tent of testimony:** the name of the meeting tent in the Greek text of Ex 40. Cf 2 Mc 2, 4–7.

16, 1–21: These seven bowls, like the seven seals (6, 1–17; 8, 1) and the seven trumpets (8, 2—9, 21; 11, 15–19), bring on a succession of disasters modeled in part on the plagues of Egypt (Ex 7—12). See the note on 6, 12–14.

16, 2: Like the sixth Egyptian plague (Ex 9, 8–11).

16, 3–4: Like the first Egyptian plague (Ex 7, 20–21). The same woe followed the blowing of the second trumpet (8, 8–9).

16, 10: **The throne of the beast:** symbol of the forces of evil. **Darkness:** like the ninth Egyptian plague (Ex 10, 21–23); cf 9, 2.

16, 12: **The kings of the East:** Parthians; see the notes on 6, 2 and 17, 12–13. **East:** literally, "rising of the sun," as in 7, 2.

16, 13: **Frogs:** possibly an allusion to the second Egyptian

i: Pss 92, 6; 98, 1 / Dt 32, 4; Ps 145, 17.   *j:* Ps 86, 9-10; Jer 10, 7.
k: 19, 8.   *l:* 1 Kgs 8, 10; Is 6, 4.   *m:* Ex 7, 14-24.   *n:* 1, 4.
o: Ez 35, 6; Mt 23, 34-35.   *p:* Dn 3, 27; Tb 3, 2.   *q:* Am 4, 6.
r: Ex 10, 21-23.   *s:* Ex 9, 8-11 / Jer 5, 3.   *t:* Ex 8, 2-3.

the mouth of the beast, and from the mouth of the false prophet. [14u]These were demonic spirits who performed signs. They went out to the kings of the whole world to assemble them for the battle on the great day of God the almighty. [15v]*("Behold, I am coming like a thief." Blessed is the one who watches and keeps his clothes ready, so that he may not go naked and people see him exposed.) [16]*They then assembled the kings in the place that is named Armageddon in Hebrew.

[17w]The seventh angel poured out his bowl into the air. A loud voice came out of the temple from the throne, saying, "It is done." [18x]Then there were lightning flashes, rumblings, and peals of thunder, and a great earthquake. It was such a violent earthquake that there has never been one like it since the human race began on earth. [19]*The great city was split into three parts, and the gentile cities fell. But God remembered great Babylon, giving it the cup filled with the wine of his fury and wrath. [20]*Every island fled, and mountains disappeared. [21y]Large hailstones like huge weights came down from the sky on people, and they blasphemed God for the plague of hail because this plague was so severe.

V: The Punishment of Babylon and the Destruction of Pagan Nations

CHAPTER 17

See RG
460-61

Babylon the Great. [1z]*Then one of

the seven angels who were holding the seven bowls came and said to me, "Come here. I will show you the judgment on the great harlot who lives near the many waters. [2a]*The kings of the earth have had intercourse with her, and the inhabitants of the earth became drunk on the wine of her harlotry." [3b]*Then he carried me away in spirit to a deserted place where I saw a woman seated on a scarlet beast that was covered with blasphemous names, with seven heads and ten horns. [4c]*The woman was wearing purple and scarlet and adorned with gold, precious stones, and pearls. She held in her hand a gold cup that was filled with the abominable and sordid deeds of her harlotry. [5]On her forehead was written a name, which is a mystery, "Babylon the great, the mother of harlots and of the abominations of the earth." [6]*I saw that the woman was drunk on the blood of the holy ones and on the blood of the witnesses to Jesus.

Meaning of the Beast and Harlot When I saw her I was greatly amazed. [7]The angel said to me, "Why are you amazed? I will explain to you the mystery of the woman and of the beast that carries her, the beast with the seven heads and the ten horns. [8d]*The beast that you saw existed once but now exists no longer. It will come up from the abyss and is headed for destruction. The inhabitants of the earth whose names have not been written in the book of life from the foundation of the world shall be amazed when they see the beast, because it existed once but exists no longer, and yet it will

---

plague (Ex 7, 26—8, 11). **The false prophet:** identified with the two-horned second beast (13, 11–18 and the note there).

16, 15: Like a thief: as in 3, 3 (cf Mt 24, 42–44; 1 Thes 5, 2). **Blessed:** see the note on 1, 3.

16, 16: Armageddon: in Hebrew, this means "Mountain of Megiddo." Since Megiddo was the scene of many decisive battles in antiquity (Jgs 5, 19–20; 2 Kgs 9, 27; 2 Chr 35, 20–24), the town became the symbol of the final disastrous rout of the forces of evil.

16, 19: The great city: Rome and the empire.

16, 20–21: See the note on 6, 12–14. **Hailstones:** as in the seventh Egyptian plague (Ex 9, 23–24); cf 8, 7. **Like huge weights:** literally, "weighing a talent," about one hundred pounds.

17, 1—19, 10: The punishment of Babylon is now described as a past event and, metaphorically, under the image of the great harlot who leads people astray into idolatry.

17, 1–6: Babylon, the symbolic name (5) of Rome, is graphically described as "the great harlot."

17, 2: Intercourse . . . harlotry: see the note on 14, 4. The pagan kings subject to Rome adopted the cult of the emperor.

17, 3: Scarlet beast: see the note on 13, 1–10. **Blasphemous names:** divine titles assumed by the Roman emperors; see the note on 13, 5–6.

17, 4: Reference to the great wealth and idolatrous cults of Rome.

17, 6b-18: An interpretation of the vision is here given.

17, 8: Allusion to the belief that the dead Nero would return to power (11); see the note on 13, 3.

u: 1 Cor 1, 8.   v: Mt 24, 42-44 / 3, 17.   w: Is 66, 6.   x: Mk 13, 19.   y: Ex 9, 22-26.   z: Jer 50, 38; 51, 13.   a: Jer 51, 7.   b: 13, 1.   c: 18, 16.   d: 13, 3-4 / 3, 5; 13, 8; 20, 12.

come again. [9e]*Here is a clue for one who has wisdom. The seven heads represent seven hills upon which the woman sits. They also represent seven kings: [10]*five have already fallen, one still lives, and the last has not yet come, and when he comes he must remain only a short while. [11]*The beast that existed once but exists no longer is an eighth king, but really belongs to the seven and is headed for destruction. [12f]*The ten horns that you saw represent ten kings who have not yet been crowned; they will receive royal authority along with the beast for one hour. [13]They are of one mind and will give their power and authority to the beast. [14g]They will fight with the Lamb, but the Lamb will conquer them, for he is Lord of lords and king of kings, and those with him are called, chosen, and faithful."

[15]Then he said to me, "The waters that you saw where the harlot lives represent large numbers of peoples, nations, and tongues. [16h]*The ten horns that you saw and the beast will hate the harlot; they will leave her desolate and naked; they will eat her flesh and consume her with fire. [17]For God has put it into their minds to carry out his purpose and to make them come to an agreement to give their kingdom to the beast until the words of God are accomplished. [18]The woman whom you saw represents the great city that has sovereignty over the kings of the earth."

CHAPTER 18

See RG 460–61

The Fall of Babylon. [1i]*After this I saw another angel coming down from heaven, having great authority, and the earth became illumined by his splendor. [2j]*He cried out in a mighty voice:

"Fallen, fallen is Babylon the great.
    She has become a haunt for demons.
She is a cage for every unclean spirit,
    a cage for every unclean bird,
    [a cage for every unclean] and
        disgusting [beast].
[3k]*For all the nations have drunk
    the wine of her licentious passion.
The kings of the earth had intercourse
    with her,
    and the merchants of the earth grew
        rich from her drive for luxury."

[4]*Then I heard another voice from heaven say:

"Depart from her, my people,
    so as not to take part in her sins
    and receive a share in her plagues,
[5m]for her sins are piled up to the sky,
    and God remembers her crimes.
[6n]Pay her back as she has paid others.
    Pay her back double for her deeds.
    Into her cup pour double what she
        poured.
[7o]To the measure of her boasting and
        wantonness

17, 9: Here is a clue: literally, "Here a mind that has wisdom." **Seven hills:** of Rome.

17, 10: There is little agreement as to the identity of the Roman emperors alluded to here. The number seven (9) suggests that all the emperors are meant; see the note on 1, 4.

17, 11: The beast: Nero; see the note on v 8.

17, 12–13: Ten kings who have not yet been crowned: perhaps Parthian satraps who are to accompany the revived Nero (the beast) in his march on Rome to regain power; see the note on 13, 3. In 19, 11–21, the Lamb and his companions will conquer them.

17, 16–18: The ten horns: the ten pagan kings (12) who unwittingly fulfill God's will against harlot Rome, the great city; cf Ez 16, 37.

18, 1—19, 4: A stirring dirge over the fall of Babylon-Rome. The perspective is prophetic, as if the fall of Rome had already taken place. The imagery here, as elsewhere in this book, is not to be taken literally. The vindictiveness of some of the language, borrowed from the scathing Old Tes-

tament prophecies against Babylon, Tyre, and Nineveh (Is 23; 24; 27; Jer 50–51; Ez 26–27), is meant to portray symbolically the inexorable demands of God's holiness and justice; cf Introduction. The section concludes with a joyous canticle on the future glory of heaven.

18, 2: Many Greek manuscripts and versions omit **a cage for every unclean . . . beast.**

18, 3–24: Rome is condemned for her immorality, symbol of idolatry (see the note on 14, 4), and for persecuting the church; cf 19, 2.

18, 4: Depart from her: not evacuation of the city but separation from sinners, as always in apocalyptic literature.

e: 13, 18.   f: Dn 7, 24.   g: 19, 11-21; 2 Mc 13, 4; 1 Tm 6, 15 / Rom 1, 6; 1 Pt 2, 9; Jude 1.   h: Ez 16, 37-41; 23, 25-29.   i: Ez 43, 2.   j: 14, 8; Is 21, 9; Jer 50, 2-3; 51, 8.   k: 17, 2; Jer 51, 7.   l: Is 48, 20; Jer 50, 8.   m: Jer 51, 9.   n: Jer 50, 15 / Jer 16, 18.   o: Is 47, 8-9.

repay her in torment and grief;
for she said to herself,
  'I sit enthroned as queen;
  I am no widow,
  and I will never know grief.'
8 Therefore, her plagues will come in one
    day,
  pestilence, grief, and famine;
  she will be consumed by fire.
For mighty is the Lord God who judges
  her."

9The kings of the earth who had intercourse with her in their wantonness will weep and mourn over her when they see the smoke of her pyre. 10They will keep their distance for fear of the torment inflicted on her, and they will say:

  "Alas, alas, great city,
  Babylon, mighty city.
  In one hour your judgment has
    come."

11*The merchants of the earth will weep and mourn for her, because there will be no more markets for their cargo: 12their cargo of gold, silver, precious stones, and pearls; fine linen, purple silk, and scarlet cloth; fragrant wood of every kind, all articles of ivory and all articles of the most expensive wood, bronze, iron, and marble; 13*cinnamon, spice, incense, myrrh, and frankincense; wine, olive oil, fine flour, and wheat; cattle and sheep, horses and chariots, and slaves, that is, human beings.

14 p"The fruit you craved
  has left you.
All your luxury and splendor are gone,
  never again will one find them."

15The merchants who deal in these goods, who grew rich from her, will keep their distance for fear of the torment inflicted on her. Weeping and mourning, 16qthey cry out:

  "Alas, alas, great city,
  wearing fine linen, purple and scarlet,
  adorned [in] gold, precious stones, and
    pearls.
17 In one hour this great wealth has been
  ruined."

Every captain of a ship, every traveler at sea, sailors, and seafaring merchants stood at a distance 18and cried out when they saw the smoke of her pyre, "What city could compare with the great city?" 19rThey threw dust on their heads and cried out, weeping and mourning:

  "Alas, alas, great city,
  in which all who had ships at sea
  grew rich from her wealth.
In one hour she has been ruined.
20 sRejoice over her, heaven,
  you holy ones, apostles, and prophets.
For God has judged your case against
  her."

21A mighty angel picked up a stone like a huge millstone and threw it into the sea and said:

  "With such force will Babylon the great
    city be thrown down,
  and will never be found again.
22 uNo melodies of harpists and musicians,
  flutists and trumpeters,
  will ever be heard in you again.
No craftsmen in any trade
  will ever be found in you again.
No sound of the millstone
  will ever be heard in you again.
23 vNo light from a lamp
  will ever be seen in you again.
No voices of bride and groom
  will ever be heard in you again.
Because your merchants were the great
    ones of the world,
  all nations were led astray by your
    magic potion.
24 wIn her was found the blood of prophets
    and holy ones
  and all who have been slain on the
    earth."

18, 11: Ironically, the merchants weep not so much for Babylon-Rome, but for their lost markets; cf Ez 27, 36.
18, 13: Spice: an unidentified spice plant called in Greek amōmon.

p: Hos 10, 5 / Am 6, 7.   q: 17, 4.   r: Ez 27, 27-32.   s: 19, 1-2; Dt 32, 43.   t: Jer 51, 63-64; Ez 26, 21.   u: Is 24, 8; Ez 26, 13.   v: Jer 7, 34; 16, 9; 25, 10.   w: 16, 6.

CHAPTER 19

See RG
460–61 *1**After this I heard what sounded like the loud voice of a great multitude in heaven, saying:

"Alleluia!
Salvation, glory, and might belong to our God,
2 ˣfor true and just are his judgments.
He has condemned the great harlot
who corrupted the earth with her harlotry.
He has avenged on her the blood of his servants."

*3ʸ*They said a second time:

"Alleluia! Smoke will rise from her forever and ever."

*4*The twenty-four elders and the four living creatures fell down and worshiped God who sat on the throne, saying, "Amen. Alleluia."

The Victory Song. *5ᶻ**A voice coming from the throne said:

"Praise our God, all you his servants,
[and] you who revere him, small and great."

*6*Then I heard something like the sound of a great multitude or the sound of rushing water or mighty peals of thunder, as they said:

"Alleluia!
The Lord has established his reign,
[our] God, the almighty.

7 ᵃ*Let us rejoice and be glad
and give him glory.
For the wedding day of the Lamb has come,
his bride has made herself ready."
8 ᵇ*She was allowed to wear
a bright, clean linen garment."

(The linen represents the righteous deeds of the holy ones.)

9ᶜ*Then the angel said to me, "Write this: Blessed are those who have been called to the wedding feast of the Lamb." And he said to me, "These words are true; they come from God." *10ᵈ**I fell at his feet to worship him. But he said to me, "Don't! I am a fellow servant of yours and of your brothers who bear witness to Jesus. Worship God. Witness to Jesus is the spirit of prophecy."

The King of Kings. *11ᵉ**Then I saw the heavens opened, and there was a white horse; its rider was [called] "Faithful and True." He judges and wages war in righteousness. *12ᶠ**His eyes were [like] a fiery flame, and on his head were many diadems. He had a name inscribed that no one knows except himself. *13ᵍ**He wore a cloak that had been dipped in blood, and his name was called the Word of God. *14ʰ*The armies of heaven followed him, mounted on white horses and wearing clean white linen. *15ⁱ**Out of his mouth came a sharp sword to strike the nations. He will rule them with an iron rod, and he himself will tread out in the wine press the wine of the fury and wrath of

---

19, 1.3.4.6: Alleluia: found only here in the New Testament, this frequent exclamation of praise in the Hebrew psalms was important in Jewish liturgy.

19, 5–10: A victory song follows, sung by the entire church, celebrating the marriage of the Lamb, the union of the Messiah with the community of the elect.

19, 7: The wedding day of the Lamb: symbol of God's reign about to begin (21, 1—22, 5); see the note on 10, 7. **His bride:** the church; cf 2 Cor 11, 2; Eph 5, 22–27. Marriage is one of the biblical metaphors used to describe the covenant relationship between God and his people; cf Hos 2, 16–22; Is 54, 5–6; 62, 5; Ez 16, 6–14. Hence, idolatry and apostasy are viewed as adultery and harlotry (Hos 2, 4–15; Ez 16, 15–63); see the note on 14, 4.

19, 8: See the note on 14, 12.

19, 9: Blessed: see the note on 1, 3.

19, 10: The spirit of prophecy: as the prophets were inspired to proclaim God's word, so the Christian is called to give witness to the Word of God (13) made flesh; cf 1, 2; 6, 9; 12, 17.

19, 11–16: Symbolic description of the exalted Christ (cf 1, 13–16) who together with the armies of heaven overcomes the beast and its followers; cf 17, 14.

19, 12: A name: in Semitic thought, the name conveyed the reality of the person; cf Mt 11, 27; Lk 10, 22.

19, 13: Had been dipped in: other Greek manuscripts and versions read "had been sprinkled with"; cf v 15. **The Word of God:** Christ is the revelation of the Father; cf Jn 1, 1.14; 1 Jn 2, 14.

19, 15: The treading of the wine press is a prophetic symbol used to describe the destruction of God's enemies; cf Is 63, 1–6; Jl 4, 13.

ˣ: Dn 3, 27 / Jer 51, 48-49. ʸ: 14, 11; Is 34, 10. ᶻ: 11, 18; Ps 115, 13. ᵃ: Mt 22, 9; Eph 5, 27. ᵇ: 15, 6; Is 61, 10; Mt 22, 11-12. ᶜ: Mt 8, 11; Lk 14, 15. ᵈ: 22, 8-9. ᵉ: Is 11, 4. ᶠ: 1, 14-16; 2, 18 / Lk 10, 22. ᵍ: Is 63, 1 / Jn 1, 1. ʰ: 15, 6; 19, 8. ⁱ: 14, 20; Is 63, 3.

God the almighty. *16j*He has a name written on his cloak and on his thigh, "King of kings and Lord of lords."

17*Then I saw an angel standing on the sun. He cried out [in] a loud voice to all the birds flying high overhead, "Come here. Gather for God's great feast, *18k*to eat the flesh of kings, the flesh of military officers, and the flesh of warriors, the flesh of horses and of their riders, and the flesh of all, free and slave, small and great." *19*Then I saw the beast and the kings of the earth and their armies gathered to fight against the one riding the horse and against his army. *20l**The beast was caught and with it the false prophet who had performed in its sight the signs by which he led astray those who had accepted the mark of the beast and those who had worshiped its image. The two were thrown alive into the fiery pool burning with sulfur. *21*The rest were killed by the sword that came out of the mouth of the one riding the horse, and all the birds gorged themselves on their flesh.

See RG 460-61

CHAPTER 20

The Thousand-year Reign. *1m**Then I saw an angel come down from heaven, holding in his hand the key to the abyss and a heavy chain. *2n**He seized the dragon, the ancient serpent, which is the Devil or Satan, and tied it up for a thousand years *3*and threw it into the abyss, which he locked over it and sealed, so that it could no longer lead the nations astray until the thousand years

are completed. After this, it is to be released for a short time.

4o*Then I saw thrones; those who sat on them were entrusted with judgment. I also saw the souls of those who had been beheaded for their witness to Jesus and for the word of God, and who had not worshiped the beast or its image nor had accepted its mark on their foreheads or hands. They came to life and they reigned with Christ for a thousand years. *5*The rest of the dead did not come to life until the thousand years were over. This is the first resurrection. *6**Blessed and holy is the one who shares in the first resurrection. The second death has no power over these; they will be priests of God and of Christ, and they will reign with him for [the] thousand years.

7*When the thousand years are completed, Satan will be released from his prison. *8p**He will go out to deceive the nations at the four corners of the earth, Gog and Magog, to gather them for battle; their number is like the sand of the sea. *9q**They invaded the breadth of the earth and surrounded the camp of the holy ones and the beloved city. But fire came down from heaven and consumed them. *10*The Devil who had led them astray was thrown into the pool of fire and sulfur, where the beast and the false prophet were. There they will be tormented day and night forever and ever.

The Large White Throne. *11r**Next I saw a large white throne and the one who was sitting on it. The earth and the sky fled from his

---

19, 17–21: The certainty of Christ's victory is proclaimed by an angel, followed by a reference to the mustering of enemy forces and a fearsome description of their annihilation. The gruesome imagery is borrowed from Ez 39, 4.17–20.

19, 20: Beast . . . false prophet: see the notes on ch 13. **The fiery pool . . . sulfur:** symbol of God's punishment (14, 10; 20, 10.14–15), different from the abyss; see the note on 9, 1.

20, 1–6: Like the other numerical values in this book, the thousand years are not to be taken literally; they symbolize the long period of time between the chaining up of Satan (a symbol for Christ's resurrection-victory over death and the forces of evil) and the end of the world. During this time God's people share in the glorious reign of God that is present to them by virtue of their baptismal victory over death and sin; cf Rom 6, 1–8; Jn 5, 24–25; 16, 33; 1 Jn 3, 14; Eph 2, 1.

20, 1: Abyss: see the note on 9, 1.

20, 2: Dragon . . . serpent . . . Satan: see the notes on 12, 3.9.10.15.

20, 4: Beast . . . mark: see ch 13 and its notes.

20, 6: Blessed: see the note on 1, 3. **Second death:** see the note on 2, 11. **Priests:** as in 1, 6; 5, 10; cf 1 Pt 2, 9.

20, 7–10: A description of the symbolic battle to take place when Satan is released at the end of time, when the thousand years are over; see the note on vv 1–6.

20, 8: Gog and Magog: symbols of all pagan nations; the names are taken from Ez 38, 1—39, 20.

20, 9: The breadth of the earth: Palestine. **The beloved city:** Jerusalem; see the note on 14, 1.

20, 11–15: A description of the final judgment. After the intermediate reign of Christ, all the dead are raised and judged, thus inaugurating the new age.

---

j: 17, 14; 2 Mc 13, 4.   *k:* Ez 39, 17-20.   *l:* 14, 10.   *m:* 9, 1.   *n:* Gn 3, 1.   *o:* Mt 19, 28.   *p:* Ez 38, 2.9.16.   *q:* Ez 38, 22.   *r:* 2 Pt 3, 7.10.12.

presence and there was no place for them. [12s]*I saw the dead, the great and the lowly, standing before the throne, and scrolls were opened. Then another scroll was opened, the book of life. The dead were judged according to their deeds, by what was written in the scrolls. [13]*The sea gave up its dead; then Death and Hades gave up their dead. All the dead were judged according to their deeds. [14t]*Then Death and Hades were thrown into the pool of fire. (This pool of fire is the second death.) [15]Anyone whose name was not found written in the book of life was thrown into the pool of fire.

VI: The New Creation

CHAPTER 21

See RG 461

The New Heaven and the New Earth.

[1u]*Then I saw a new heaven and a new earth. The former heaven and the former earth had passed away, and the sea was no more. [2v]*I also saw the holy city, a new Jerusalem, coming down out of heaven from God, prepared as a bride adorned for her husband. [3w]*I heard a loud voice from the throne saying, "Behold, God's dwelling is with the human race. He will dwell with them and they will be his people and God himself will always be with them [as their God]. [4x]He will wipe every tear from their eyes, and there shall be no more death or mourning, wailing or pain, [for] the old order has passed away."

[5y]*The one who sat on the throne said,

"Behold, I make all things new." Then he said, "Write these words down, for they are trustworthy and true." [6z]*He said to me, "They are accomplished. I [am] the Alpha and the Omega, the beginning and the end. To the thirsty I will give a gift from the spring of life-giving water. [7a]*The victor will inherit these gifts, and I shall be his God, and he will be my son. [8b]*But as for cowards, the unfaithful, the depraved, murderers, the unchaste, sorcerers, idol-worshipers, and deceivers of every sort, their lot is in the burning pool of fire and sulfur, which is the second death."

The New Jerusalem.

[9]*One of the seven angels who held the seven bowls filled with the seven last plagues came and said to me, "Come here. I will show you the bride, the wife of the Lamb." [10c]He took me in spirit to a great, high mountain and showed me the holy city Jerusalem coming down out of heaven from God. [11d]It gleamed with the splendor of God. Its radiance was like that of a precious stone, like jasper, clear as crystal. [12]It had a massive, high wall, with twelve gates where twelve angels were stationed and on which names were inscribed, [the names] of the twelve tribes of the Israelites. [13e]There were three gates facing east, three north, three south, and three west. [14f]*The wall of the city had twelve courses of stones as its foundation, on which were inscribed the twelve names of the twelve apostles of the Lamb.

20, 12: **The book of life:** see the note on 3, 5. **Judged . . . scrolls:** see the note on 14, 12.

20, 13: **Hades:** the netherworld; see the note on 1, 18.

20, 14: **Second death:** see the note on 2, 11.

21, 1—22, 5: A description of God's eternal kingdom in heaven under the symbols of a new heaven and a new earth; cf Is 65, 17–25; 66, 22; Mt 19, 28.

21, 1: **Sea . . . no more:** because as home of the dragon it was doomed to disappear; cf Jb 7, 12.

21, 2: **New Jerusalem . . . bride:** symbol of the church (Gal 4, 26); see the note on 19, 7.

21, 3: **People:** other ancient manuscripts read a plural, "peoples."

21, 3–4: Language taken from Ez 37, 27; Is 25, 8; 35, 10; cf 7, 17.

21, 5: **The one . . . on the throne:** God himself; cf 4, 1–11.

21, 6: **They are accomplished:** God's reign has already begun; see the note on 20, 1–6. **Alpha . . . Omega:** see the note on 1, 8. **Life-giving water:** see the note on 7, 17.

21, 7: **The victor:** over the forces of evil; see the conclu-

sions of the seven letters (2, 7.11.17.26; 3, 5.12.21). **He will be my son:** the victorious Christian enjoys divine affiliation by adoption (Gal 4, 4–7; Rom 8, 14–17); see the note on 2, 26–28.

21, 8: **Cowards:** their conviction is so weak that they deny Christ in time of trial and become traitors. **Second death:** see the note on 2, 11.

21, 9—22, 5: Symbolic descriptions of the new Jerusalem, the church. Most of the images are borrowed from Ez 40—48.

21, 9: **The bride, the wife of the Lamb:** the church (2), the new Jerusalem (10); cf 2 Cor 11, 2.

21, 14: **Courses of stones . . . apostles:** literally, "twelve foundations"; cf Eph 2, 19–20.

---

s: Rom 2, 6. *t:* 1 Cor 15, 26.54-55. *u:* Is 65, 17; 66, 22; Rom 8, 19-23; 2 Pt 3, 13. *v:* 19, 7-9. *w:* Ez 37, 27. *x:* 7, 17; Is 25, 8; 35, 10. *y:* Is 43, 19; 2 Cor 5, 17. *z:* 22, 17; Ps 36, 8-9; Is 55, 1. *a:* 2 Sm 7, 14. *b:* 22, 15; Rom 1, 29-32. *c:* Ez 40, 2. *d:* Heb 11, 10. *e:* Ez 48, 31-35. *f:* Eph 2, 20.

15 The one who spoke to me held a gold measuring rod to measure the city, its gates, and its wall. *16* The city was square, its length the same as [also] its width. He measured the city with the rod and found it fifteen hundred miles in length and width and height. *17* He also measured its wall: one hundred and forty-four cubits according to the standard unit of measurement the angel used. *18* The wall was constructed of jasper, while the city was pure gold, clear as glass. *19g* The foundations of the city wall were decorated with every precious stone; the first course of stones was jasper, the second sapphire, the third chalcedony, the fourth emerald, *20* the fifth sardonyx, the sixth carnelian, the seventh chrysolite, the eighth beryl, the ninth topaz, the tenth chrysoprase, the eleventh hyacinth, and the twelfth amethyst. *21* The twelve gates were twelve pearls, each of the gates made from a single pearl; and the street of the city was of pure gold, transparent as glass.

22h I saw no temple in the city, for its temple is the Lord God almighty and the Lamb. *23i* The city had no need of sun or moon to shine on it, for the glory of God gave it light, and its lamp was the Lamb. *24j* The nations will walk by its light, and to it the kings of the earth will bring their treasure. *25* During the day its gates will never be shut, and there will be no night there. *26* The treasure and wealth of the nations will be brought there, *27k* but nothing unclean will enter it, nor any[one] who does abominable things or tells lies. Only those will enter whose names are written in the Lamb's book of life.

CHAPTER 22

See RG 461

1 Then the angel showed me the river of life-giving water, sparkling like crystal, flowing from the throne of God and of the Lamb *2* down the middle of its street. On either side of the river grew the tree of life that produces fruit twelve times a year, once each month; the leaves of the trees serve as medicine for the nations. *3* Nothing accursed will be found there anymore. The throne of God and of the Lamb will be in it, and his servants will worship him. *4* They will look upon his face, and his name will be on their foreheads. *5m* Night will be no more, nor will they need light from lamp or sun, for the Lord God shall give them light, and they shall reign forever and ever.

VII: Epilogue

6n And he said to me, "These words are trustworthy and true, and the Lord, the God of prophetic spirits, sent his angel to show his servants what must happen soon." *7o* "Behold, I am coming soon." Blessed is the one who keeps the prophetic message of this book.

8 It is I, John, who heard and saw these things, and when I heard and saw them I fell down to worship at the feet of the angel who showed them to me. *9p* But he said to me,

21, 15–17: The city is shaped like a gigantic cube, a symbol of perfection (cf 1 Kgs 6, 19–20). The measurements of the city and its wall are multiples of the symbolic number twelve; see the note on 7, 4–9.

21, 16: **Fifteen hundred miles:** literally, twelve thousand stades, about 12,000 furlongs (see the note on 14, 20); the number is symbolic: twelve (the apostles as leaders of the new Israel) multiplied by 1,000 (the immensity of Christians); cf Introduction. **In length and width and height:** literally, "its length and width and height are the same."

21, 17: **One hundred and forty-four cubits:** the cubit was about eighteen inches in length. **Standard unit of measurement the angel used:** literally, "by a human measure, i.e., an angel's."

21, 18–21: The gold and precious gems symbolize the beauty and excellence of the church; cf Ex 28, 15–21; Tb 13, 16–17; Is 54, 11–12.

21, 22: Christ is present throughout the church; hence, no temple is needed as an earthly dwelling for God; cf Mt 18, 20; 28, 20; Jn 4, 21.

21, 23: **Lamp . . . Lamb:** cf Jn 8, 12.

21, 24–27: All men and women of good will are welcome in the church; cf Is 60, 1.3.5.11. **The . . . book of life:** see the note on 3, 5.

22, 1.17: **Life-giving water:** see the note on 7, 17.

22, 2: **The tree of life:** cf v 14; see the note on 2, 7. **Fruit . . . medicine:** cf Ez 47, 12.

22, 4: **Look upon his face:** cf Mt 5, 8; 1 Cor 13, 12; 1 Jn 3, 2.

22, 6–21: The book ends with an epilogue consisting of a series of warnings and exhortations and forming an inclusion with the prologue by resuming its themes and expressions; see the note on 1, 1–3.

22, 7.12.20: **I am coming soon:** Christ is the speaker; see the note on 1, 3.

22, 7.14: **Blessed:** see the note on 1, 3.

g: Is 54, 11-12.   h: Jn 2, 19-20.   i: Is 60, 1-2.19-20.   j: Is 60, 11.   k: Is 35, 8; 52, 1; Zec 13, 2 / Rv 3, 5; 20, 12.   l: Ez 47, 1-12.   m: Is 60, 20.   n: 1, 1.   o: Rv 22, 12.20 / 1, 3.   p: 19, 10.

"Don't! I am a fellow servant of yours and of your brothers the prophets and of those who keep the message of this book. Worship God."

[10]*Then he said to me, "Do not seal up the prophetic words of this book, for the appointed time is near. [11]Let the wicked still act wickedly, and the filthy still be filthy. The righteous must still do right, and the holy still be holy."

[12q]"Behold, I am coming soon. I bring with me the recompense I will give to each according to his deeds. [13r]*I am the Alpha and the Omega, the first and the last, the beginning and the end."

[14s]*Blessed are they who wash their robes so as to have the right to the tree of life and enter the city through its gates. [15t]Outside are the dogs, the sorcerers, the unchaste, the murderers, the idol-worshipers, and all who love and practice deceit.

[16u]*"I, Jesus, sent my angel to give you this testimony for the churches. I am the root and offspring of David, the bright morning star."

[17v]*The Spirit and the bride say, "Come." Let the hearer say, "Come." Let the one who thirsts come forward, and the one who wants it receive the gift of life-giving water.

[18]I warn everyone who hears the prophetic words in this book: if anyone adds to them, God will add to him the plagues described in this book, [19w]and if anyone takes away from the words in this prophetic book, God will take away his share in the tree of life and in the holy city described in this book.

[20x]*The one who gives this testimony says, "Yes, I am coming soon." Amen! Come, Lord Jesus!

[21]The grace of the Lord Jesus be with all.

22, 10: **The appointed time:** see the note on 1, 3.

22, 13: Christ applies to himself words used by God in 1, 8.

22, 14: **The city:** heavenly Jerusalem; see the note on 21, 2.

22, 16: **The root . . . of David:** see the note on 5, 5. **Morning star:** see the note on 2, 26–28.

22, 17: **Bride:** the church; see the note on 21, 2.

22, 20: **Come, Lord Jesus:** a liturgical refrain, similar to the Aramaic expression **Marana tha**—"Our Lord, come!"—in 1 Cor 16, 22; cf the note there. It was a prayer for the coming of Christ in glory at the parousia; see the note on 1, 3.

q: Rv 22, 7.20 / Ps 62, 12; 2 Tm 4, 14. r: 1, 8; 21, 6; Is 41, 4; 44, 6. s: 7, 14-15; 22, 2. t: 21, 8; Rom 1, 29-32. u: 1, 1.11-12; 22, 6 / 2, 28. v: 21, 6; Is 55, 1. w: Dt 4, 2. x: Rv 22, 7.12 / Acts 3, 20-21; 1 Cor 15, 23; 16, 22.

ESSAYS
TABLES
GLOSSARY
CONCORDANCE

THE CATECHISM OF THE CATHOLIC CHURCH

What are some of the things *The Catechism of the Catholic Church* (CCC) teaches about the Bible?

How We Read and Understand Inspiration

The CCC teaches that because the books of the Bible are written in a human way, we must pay attention to what the authors intended and to what God wanted to reveal through them. To do this, we are attentive to what culture the writers lived in and how their culture influenced their writing. We also take into consideration the historical times and setting that influenced the writers, to how literature of their times was written, as well as how people at that time and place spoke and felt. We know that the various writers used many forms of expression in the Bible such as poetry, and the books must be read with that in mind (CCC#109–110).

The Catechism also reminds us to look at the unity of the whole of Scriptures and the message they teach together. We are told to keep in mind that the Holy Spirit helps the Church interpret Scriptures within its own tradition (CCC#111–114).

Meanings or Senses of Scripture

The Catechism teaches that there are two "senses" to Scripture: the *literal* sense and the *spiritual* sense. The literal sense is based on scholars' study and exegesis based on sound interpretation. In the spiritual sense of Scripture, there are three traditional senses: allegorical, moral, and anagogical.

The first, the allegorical sense, shows a correspondence between the Scripture's image and a deeper meaning within it. We may, for example, see a sacramental significance in the scriptural uses of water and blood in the Old and New Testaments. They may represent Baptism or Eucharist to us as we read it.

The moral sense of Scripture, obviously, instructs us to live in a just manner, to behave ethically.

Then the anagogical sense, which comes from the Greek word that means "leading," is the sense in which all of what we read in and learn from Scripture has an eternal meaning, leading us to our final home in heaven (CCC#115–117).

Books of the Bible

The list of books in the Catholic tradition is called the "canon" of the Scriptures. The Catholic canon has 46 Old Testament and 27 New Testament books. When Jeremiah and Lamentations are counted as one, it is obviously 45 books.

The Old Testament books are essential and have a permanent value. The Church has always opposed those who want to reject the Old Testament as unnecessary in light of the New Testament for both shed light on each other.

Within the New Testament the gospels are the heart, and Christ is their center. They tell the life of Jesus, they record what his first followers handed on orally after his ascension, and when they were written down, the truth of Jesus Christ was recorded (CCC#122–126; 139).

CATHOLIC BELIEFS IN SCRIPTURE

It can be helpful to see the basis in Scripture for many Catholic beliefs. This list, showing where certain beliefs are found in Scripture, is useful for both individual and group study. Candidates and catechumens going through the process of preparation for the Rite of Christian Initiation will find this information especially helpful. Groups may use the index as the basis for their study and reflection. These references can also be helpful in private prayer and meditation. Choose one of the topics for reflection, slowly read through one or more of the Scripture citations, and quietly think over that passage after asking the Holy Spirit to be present. This can be an effective method of self-evangelization or spiritual formation.

Abraham
   Gn 12, 1–5; 15, 1–8; 17, 1–8; 22, 1–8;
      Mt 8, 11; Lk 16, 15–31; Jn 15, 23; Jn 8,
      51–59; Heb 11, 8–16; Gal 3, 1–29.
Anointing of the Sick (see Sacraments)
Apostles
   Mk 3, 13–19; Jn 6, 10; 13, 1; Lk 8, 1; 9, 12;
      18, 31–34; Mk 4, 10–11; 11, 11; 14, 17.
      22–30;
   Mt 19, 28; Acts 1, 12–26; Eph 2, 20.
Authority
   Mk 1, 14–45; Mt 3, 13–17; 16, 19; 17, 5;
      18, 18; 28, 18; Gal 1, 1. 11–12;
      1 Cor 4, 1–3; Lk 10, 6; Jn 17, 6–7;
      Eph 4, 11–13.
Baptism (see Sacraments)
Beatitudes
   Mt 5, 1–12; Lk 6, 20–26.
Bishops/presbyters
   Acts 11, 29–30; 14, 23; 15, 2–6. 22–23;

20, 17; 1 Pt 5, 1–4; 1 Tm 2, 8–10; 3, 2;
4, 1–8; 6, 20; 2 Tm 1, 6.
Charism
   1 Cor 12, 8–10. 28–30; 14, 4–5;
      Acts 20, 35; Rom 12, 8.
Charity (see Virtues)
Chosen People
   Gn 17, 1–14; Ex 34, 10–27; Mt 12, 38–50.
Christ: God reveals himself in Christ
   1 Tm 6, 16; Eph 1, 4–5; Lk 24, 45.
Church
   Jn 21, 15–19; Col 3, 18—4, 1; Rv 12.
Communion (see Eucharist)
Communion of Saints
   Acts 2, 42; 1 Cor 12, 7; Rom 14, 7;
      1 Cor 12, 26–27; 13, 5; 10, 24.
Confirmation (see Sacraments)
Conscience
   1 Tm 1, 18–19.
Conversion
   Acts 9, 1–19.
Creation
   Gn 1, 1; Rom 1, 19–20; 8, 18–23; Jn 1, 1–3;
      Acts 17, 24–29; Eph 1, 5–6; Rv 4, 11.
Creed
   Acts 4, 5–12.
Death
   Lk 10, 25–28; Mt 7, 13–14; 25, 46;
      Mk 9, 43–48; Rom 6, 20–23; 8, 1–2;
      Gal 2, 19–20; Col 3, 1–5; 2 Tm 1, 9–10.
Desire of God
   Acts 17, 26–28; Lk 12, 31–34.
Devil; Satan
   1 Thes 2, 18; Lk 23, 3; 1 Cor 7, 5.
Disciple
   Jn 12, 24–26; 13, 13–17; 15, 12–17;

1 Jn 3, 16; Lk 6, 40; 9, 57–62; 14, 25–33; Mt 8, 19–22; 18, 18–22; 19, 17–21; Lk 5, 10–11. 27–28; 18, 22–30; 1 Pt 2, 21–25; Eph 5, 1–9.

Equality
Gal 3, 28.

Eucharist (*see* Sacraments)

Extreme Unction (Anointing of the Sick; *see* Sacraments)

Faith
Mk 9, 14–29; Lk 17, 5; 22, 32; 1 Cor 13, 12; 2 Cor 5, 7; Jn 3, 16; Rom 1, 5; 11, 1–17; 15, 13; 16, 26.

Faith and works
Mt 25, 31–46; 1 Jn 1, 3–10; Jas 2, 14–26.

Forgiveness
Lk 3, 8–11; 6, 27–36; 15, 4–32; Jn 8, 2–11; 20, 21–23; Acts 2, 32–36; Mt 18, 21–35.

Freedom
Gal 2, 19–20; 5, 11–16; Rom 5, 12–17; 6, 14–15.

Fruits of the Holy Spirit
Gal 5, 22–23.

God (*see* Trinity)

Grace
Gen 6, 8; 18, 3; 2 Kgs 15, 25; Lk 1, 28–30; 2, 40. 52; 3, 22; Jn 1,14. 16–17; Rom 5, 12–17; 6, 14–15; 16, 20; Eph 1, 6–12; 2, 5–7; 4, 7; 2 Cor 13, 13; Col 4, 8; 1 Tm 6, 21; Heb 13, 25.

Healing
Mt 8, 1—9, 6; 11, 2–6; Jas 5, 14–16.

Holy Spirit (*see* Trinity)

Hope (*see* Virtues)

Image of God
Lk 15, 11–32; Col 1, 15–20; 3, 1–11; Jn 1, 1–18; Lk 11, 1–4; Gen 1, 26—3, 24; Ps 12, 5; Ps 23; Wis 6, 12–20.

Incarnation
Jn 1, 1–5. 14–16; 3, 13; 6, 33; 13, 3; Gal 4, 4–5; 1 Jn 4, 2; Phil 3, 8–11.

Inspiration
Lk 10, 16. 2 Pt 1, 12–21.

Jesus Christ (cf p. 1902 for subheads)

Joseph
Mt 2, 13–23.

Justice
Ps 32, 1–5; 35, 6–11; 39, 10–12; Is 12, 4–6; Jgs 5, 9–11; 1 Jn 1, 8—10, 2; 2 Pt 1, 1–2.

Kingdom of God
Mt 5, 3–11; 6, 4–13; 7, 21; 11, 12; 20, 1–15;

23, 13; Mk 1, 14; 9, 35; Lk 9, 2. 60–62; 11, 20–22; 1 Thes 2, 12.

Law
Ex 20, 1–17; Jer 31, 31–34; Heb 8, 8–12.
Commandments: Mt 5, 17–48; Gal 2, 19–20; Rom 5, 12–17.
Two Great Commandments: Mk 12, 28–34; Rom 13, 8–10; Jn 13, 34–35; 1 Jn 2, 7–11.

Love (*see* Virtues, Charity)

Mary
Lk 1, 38; Jn 2, 1–11; Jn 19, 26–28.

Matrimony (*see* Sacraments)

Messiah
Ps 2; 71; 109; Is 45, 1–8; Lev 8; Is 61, 1; 42, 1; Mt 3, 16; Mk 1, 10; Lk 3, 22; Heb 1, 1–12.

Ministry
2 Cor 3, 1–11; Jn 10, 11–17; 13, 1–8; Lk 9, 51—19, 17.

Mission
Is 41, 8–16; Lk 9, 2; 10, 1–9; 24, 46–48; Acts 1, 8; 2, 22–24; 8, 4; 10, 42; 18, 10; 20, 24; 2 Cor 5, 18.

New Covenant
Mt 26, 14–27; Jer 24, 7

Old Covenant
Dt 11, 22–25; Ex 20, 1–17; Jer 31, 33; Ez 11, 19–20.

Orders (*see* Sacraments)

Paschal mystery
Jn 12, 24–26; Mk 14, 22–25; Mt 26, 26–29; Lk 22, 7–20; 1 Cor 11, 23–25.

Plan of God
Jn 6, 37–40; Mt 26, 36–46; Eph 1, 3–14.

Penance (*see* Sacraments, Reconciliation)

Peter
Mt 16, 13–20; Mk 8, 27–30; Lk 9, 18–20; Jn 21, 15–22.

Poverty
Lk 6, 20; Mk 10, 23–25; Mt 6, 25–34; Lk 4, 16–20; 6, 20–26; Mt 8, 18–20; 11, 2–6; Mt 11, 25–29; 18, 5; 25, 31–46; Jn 19, 36 (cf Ps 33, 21); Jn 13, 10 (cf Ps 40, 10); Mt 27, 34. 48 (cf Ps 68, 22); Phil 2, 6–11; 2 Cor 8, 9; Mt 5, 42; 2 Cor 8, 1–15.

Presence of God
Gn 15, 7; Ex 3, 1–6; Mt 18, 20.

Prayer
Lk 11, 1–13; 2, 39–56; 5, 33; Eph 6, 10–18; Jn 17; Ps 62; 96; 103.

Priest
Gn 14, 17–20; Heb 7, 1–10.
Priesthood of the Faithful
Heb 7, 23–28; 1 Pt 2, 4–9.
Providence
Jer 1, 5–10; Is 46, 9–12; Eccl 42, 15–25;
Ps 22, 77; Mt 6, 25–34.
Redemption
Is 19, 20–22; 43, 3–5; Mt 11, 2–6; 20, 28;
Jn 10, 17–18; 1 Tm 2, 6;
Rom 5, 6–8; 8, 1–4; Gal 3, 13; Ti 2, 13–14;
Acts 2, 32–36; 3, 17–26;
1 Pt 2, 19–25; 2 Cor 5, 18–20;
1 Cor 6, 19–20; 7, 23; Lk 1, 46–54. 77;
3, 6; 4, 16–21; Eph 1, 7.
Resurrection
Lk 24, 36–49; Jn 20–21; Mt 28, 1–7;
Mk 16, 1–7; Acts 2, 24–32;
Jn 20, 1; Rom 4, 24–26; 2 Cor 5, 14–16;
Eph 1, 19–20; Rom 6, 7–10; 1 Thes 4, 13–18.
Sacraments
Anointing of the sick: Mk 6, 7–13;
Lk 13, 10–13; 2 Tm 2, 11–12; Jas 5,
14–16.
Baptism: Mt 3, 13–17; 28, 19–20;
Mk 1, 9–11; Lk 3, 21–22; Jn 1, 29–34; 3, 5;
Acts 2, 37–41; Rom 6, 3–4.
Confirmation: Mt 3, 13–17; Jn 1, 33–34;
14, 15–31; 16, 5–15; Acts 2, 1–4; 8,
14–17; 2 Cor 1, 21–22; Gal 5, 22–23.
Eucharist: Mk 6, 30–44; 14, 12–25;
Jn 6, 1–13. 35–59;
Holy Orders: Rom 12, 1–8; 1 Tm 3, 1–13;
Mt 10, 1–4; Mk 3, 14–19; Lk 6, 12–16;
Jn 13, 1–14; Heb 4, 14—5, 10; Ti 1, 5–9.
Matrimony: Jn 2, 1–11; Mt 19, 1–12;
Mk 2, 2–12; 1 Jn 4, 4–16; 1 Cor 13;
Eph 5, 21–33.
Reconciliation: Mt 5, 21–26. 38–48;
18, 23–35; Mk 2, 1–12; Lk 15, 11–32;
Jn 20, 19–23; Rom 6.
Sacrifice
Ex 24, 1–8. 11; Heb 2, 17–18; 10, 5–7;
Lk 18, 9–14; Rom 1, 9.
Salvation
Ps 68; 69; 97; Is 33, 2–6; Ex 12–15;
Lk 1, 31. 78–79; 2, 21. 30–32; 4, 18–19;
Mt 1, 21; Rom 10, 9–17;11, 25–32;
Heb 2, 10–18; 5, 7–10; Mk 5, 34;
10, 52; 16 , 12; Lk 7, 50; Acts 3, 23–26;
Jn 11, 25.

Sacred Scripture
Dt 4, 32–39; Jn 5, 39; 7, 22; Rom 9, 4–5;
Mt 5, 17; 22, 53; Acts 1, 16; 28, 25;
1 Pt 1, 11; 2 Pt 1, 21; Heb 3, 9; 10, 15;
2 Tm 3, 14–16; 2 Cor 3, 24–28;
Mt 26, 54–56; Lk 4, 21; 11, 37–53;
Mk 7, 1–23; 1 Cor 11, 23; Gal 1, 9–12;
Col 2, 6.
Sin
Mt 12, 33–37; 15, 19–20; 1 Jn 16–17;
Mk 3, 5–6; 10, 19; Lk 5, 30–32; 12, 1–2;
16, 19–31; 18, 9–14; 19, 1–10; Mk 3. 29;
Gal 4, 3; 6, 7–8; 1 Cor 8, 12;
1 Jn 2, 3–11; Rom 5, 12–21; 6, 20–23;
Col 2, 13–14.
Social doctrine
Mt 5, 42; 6, 24; 10, 8; 11, 5; 25, 31–36;
Lk 4, 18; 6, 20–22; 16, 13; 2 Thes 3, 10;
4, 11; Jas 5, 1–6; Mk 12, 41–44; Eph 4. 28.
Stewardship
Lk 21, 1–4; Acts 4, 32–37; 2 Cor 8–9.
Suffering
Mk 15, 21–41.
Temptation
Mt 4, 1–11; Mk 1, 12–13; 7, 14–23;
Lk 4, 1–13.
Tradition
Lk 1, 2; 2 Pt 2, 21; Jude 3; 1 Thes 2, 13;
2 Thes 2, 15; 3, 6; Rom 6, 17; Col 2, 6f;
2 Tm 1, 13; 1 Cor 9, 14; 7, 10—12, 40;
11, 2–6. 23. 26; Mt 28, 20.
Trinity
Jn 6, 40–57; 8, 12–19; 12, 20–28; 14, 9–26;
17, 4–26; Mt 28, 19; 3, 13–17;
Rom 6, 3–11; 2 Cor 1, 21; 13, 12–13.
Father
Jer 3, 4. 19–22; Mt 2, 13–15; 5, 45;
6, 9–13; Jn 5, 30–47; 6, 44–47;
Lk 6, 35–36; Eph 3, 14.
Son
1 Jn 5, 20; Jn 1, 1; 5, 1–20; 8, 24. 28. 58;
10, 22–38; Heb 1, 8–9; Col 2, 2; Ti 2,
13; 2 Pt 1, 1.
Spirit
Mt 3, 13–17; Acts 1, 5; 2, 1–21; 4, 31;
8, 29–30; Jn 3, 1–15; 4, 21–24;
1 Jn 1, 5–7; 1 Cor 3, 16–17.
Truth
Jn 8, 26–50; 6, 32–40; 8, 13–28; 10, 22–30;
16, 12–15; 14, 16; 1 Jn 1, 6;
2, 4; 5, 6–10; Mt 18, 16.

Catholic Beliefs in Scripture

Virtues
 Cardinal
 Fortitude Ps 118, 14; Jn 16, 33.
 Justice Lev 19, 15; Col 4, 1.
 Prudence Prov 14, 15; 1 Pt 4, 7.
 Temperance Sir 5, 2; 18, 30; 37, 27–31;
  Ti 2, 12.
 Theological

Faith Rom 1, 17; Gal 5, 6; Jas 2, 26;
 Mt 10, 32–33.
Hope Heb 10, 23; Ti 3, 6–7; Rom 4, 18;
 Gen 17, 4–8; 22, 1–18.
Charity Jn 13, 1; 15, 9–12;
 Mt 5, 44; 22, 40; 25, 40;
 Rom 13, 8–10; 1 Cor 13, 1–13;
 Col 3, 14.

THE BIBLE IN THE LECTIONARY

Eileen Schuller

One of the enduring results of the Second Vatican Council has been a renewed emphasis on the place of the Bible within Catholic life, and greater attention to its use in worship, study, and devotion. As a Church and as individuals, we are discovering anew the truth of St. Jerome's insight that "ignorance of the Scriptures is ignorance of Christ." Still, for most Catholics, their main exposure to the Bible comes at those times when the Church gathers for liturgy, to offer together praise and worship to God through Jesus. Each time the Mass is celebrated there are two or three readings from the Bible, always one from the Gospel and others from the book of Acts, the Epistles, or the Old Testament. Whenever the sacraments are celebrated, readings from the Word of God are an integral part of the ritual. The first reading from Scripture is regularly followed by a psalm so that we might give our response in the words of Scripture. The Gospel Acclamation, the Entrance and Communion antiphons are usually taken directly from Scripture, and other prayers and texts of the Mass reflect or are based on scriptural sources (for instance, the Glory to God in the Highest, the Lamb of God, the Lord's Prayer).

Why is the Church so insistent that we read the Word of God whenever we gather to pray as Church? The *Constitution on the Sacred Liturgy (CSL),* one of the foundational documents of the Second Vatican Council, puts it this way: "Christ is present in His Word since it is He Himself who speaks when the holy Scriptures are read in the church" *(Constitution on the Sacred Liturgy,* 7). The *Eucharistic Instruction* of 1967 elaborates at greater length

"the principal modes by which the Lord is present to his Church in liturgical celebrations. First of all, Christ is present in the assembly of the faithful gathered in his name; He is also present in his word for it is He who is speaking as the sacred Scriptures are read in the Church; in the eucharistic sacrifice, He is present both in the person of the minister . . . and above all under the eucharistic elements" (9).

Roman Catholicism has traditionally placed primary emphasis (at times, almost the sole emphasis) on the eucharistic presence of Christ under the appearances of bread and wine. More recent theological reflection has emphasized that Christ is present from the moment when the people gather together in the Christian Assembly, and that He is present especially during the proclamation of the Word of God, both in the reading of Scripture and in its unfolding in the homily. The *Eucharistic Instruction* brings this all together with the beautiful imagery of food: "The Church is nourished by the bread of life, which she finds at the table both of the Word of God and the Body of Christ" (10).

The Revision of the Lectionary

Very early on in the Second Vatican Council, the Bishops of the Church said there should be "more reading from holy Scripture," and it should be "more varied and suitable" (*CSL*, 35); or, to put it in more poetic fashion, "the treasures of the Bible are to be opened up more lavishly, so that richer fare may be provided for the faithful at the table of God's Word" (*CSL*, 51). The reforms envisaged by the Council meant not only that the readings would be in English, but that new and previously unheard sections of the Bible would be introduced both on Sundays and at weekday Masses.

The revision of the Lectionary has been one of the most extensive and significant reforms of the Council. Unfortunately, it has not always been given the attention it deserves, nor are some of its fundamental principles always well understood, either by the clergy who preach on these readings or by the laity who hear them. Our appreciation of the Scriptures in the liturgy can be greatly enriched by a more careful examination of the Lectionary.

Why a Lectionary at All?

The decision to use a lectionary means that the readings for a given Sunday or weekday are predetermined, and therefore they are the starting point for the planning of the liturgy as a whole as well as the homily. On certain other occasions (for instance, celebrations of marriages, funerals), there are more options given for Scripture readings, and a choice is to be made of what is most appropriate to the pastoral needs of a given congregation. When a special group gathers for a one-time occasion (a Retreat Day, a meeting), it is recognized that the given readings for the day may not be appropriate, and provision is made for using readings "that are more suited to the particular celebration, provided that they are chosen from the texts of an approved lectionary" (*Masses with Special Groups,* 6e). Interestingly, the greatest flexibility is allowed in choosing readings for Masses with children, although a reading from the Gospels is always to be included (*Directory for Masses with Children,* 43).

The norm in the Roman Catholic tradition is that the Scripture readings are set; they are not the choice of the priest or anyone else in the congregation. Certainly a case can be made (and has been made in the Reform and Free Church traditions) for the freedom and spontaneity to choose readings suitable to a specific community on this occasion. But the Catholic tradition has opted for a structured and planned system of readings that "provides the faithful with a knowledge of the whole of God's Word, in a pattern suited to the purpose" (*CSL: Introduction,* 60).

Foundational Principles of the Lectionary

On a first examination of the Lectionary, it is easy to get bogged down in a mass of details about different cycles and lists of what is read when, so that the whole thing can seem somewhat intimidating. Rather than trying to determine why certain texts are read on a certain day, it is more important to get an overall sense of the arrangement and rationale of the whole. The general principles and foundational decisions that have determined the basic shape and ordering of the Roman Lectionary will then be clear.

The Paschal Mystery

The focal point of the whole Lectionary is Jesus Christ, especially "the paschal mystery of his blessed passion, resurrection from the dead and glorious ascension" (*CSL,* 5). Throughout the cycle of the Church's Year, the Lectionary sets before us the totality of this central mystery of the Christian life, a mystery that was not only accomplished in Jesus, but a mystery in which we now share through Baptism and faith.

Thus, primacy is given to readings from the Gospels, which speak most directly of the person of Jesus. Furthermore, we read these texts not as individuals, but as a people gathered for praise and thanksgiving. "Within the Christian assembly the proclamation of the word inevitably has a Christian aura . . . the God whom we worship in our liturgy is not, first of all, the God of the Book (which is why we freely interpret the Book by arranging it in a lectionary). Our God is the God of the Gathering" (R. Keifer, *To Hear and To Proclaim,* p. 115). At Mass, every passage of Scripture, whether from the Old or New Testament, is set in relationship to the passion and resurrection of Jesus as made present to us in the Eucharist.

The Church Year

Not everything in the Lectionary is of equal importance. The Lectionary is divided into six parts: the major section (and the one that will be the main focus of our attention) is the Temporal Cycle, that is, the readings for Sundays and weekdays throughout the Church Year; the rest of the Lectionary contains the readings for special occasions (Proper of the Saints, Commons, Ritual Masses [e.g., readings for sacraments, funerals], Masses for Various Occasions, and Votive Masses).

Within the Temporal Cycle, not all days of the year are of equal importance. Sundays have special importance because they are the weekly celebration of the Lord's resurrection and the occasion for the gathering of the whole community; thus, "the more important biblical passages" (*CSL: Introduction*, 65) are assigned to Sundays and the Solemnities of the Lord. The Sunday cycle is set up independent from the weekday cycle which, in a sense, complements it.

The Church Year as a whole has its own rhythm. "The solemnity of Easter has the same kind of preeminence [in the year] . . . that Sunday has in the week" (*Norms for the Liturgical Year*, 18); there are six Sundays in Easter season, followed by Pentecost and Trinity Sundays. Then, next to Easter, the Church "holds most sacred the memorial of Christ's birth and early manifestation" (*Norms*, 32). There are two Sundays after Christmas, followed by Epiphany and the Sunday after it. These two major feasts, each with their preparatory period (Lent, with six Sundays, before Easter, and Advent, with four Sundays, before Christmas) are the primary seasons of the Church Year; the other thirty-four Sundays, which celebrate "the mystery of Christ in all its aspects" (*Norms*, 43), form what is called simply "Ordinary Time." (The Lectionary provides for more than fifty-two Sundays to allow for variations in the length of time after Easter, because Easter can fall anywhere from March 22 to April 25.)

Continuous or Chosen Readings

There are many different ways in which we could go about reading the Bible in a systematic fashion. We could start with the story of Creation and work through the events of the Old Testament chronologically, then move on to the New Testament and conclude with the book of Revelation; this would be a kind of salvation–history approach. Another option would be to organize the Scripture readings around certain great themes (grace, salvation, forgiveness, creation) or moral principles; the traditional name for this approach is *lectio electa*, "readings chosen" to suit a predetermined theme. Or, we could adopt *lectio continua*, a "continuous reading" of the Bible from beginning to end. This is the system of the Jewish synagogue in which the Torah, the first five books, are read continuously through a year; on the day that the last chapter of Deuteronomy is finished, on that same day the first chapter of Genesis is begun so that the reading of the Torah is unceasing.

The Roman Lectionary has opted for a combination of *lectio electa* (particularly in the major seasons of the Church Year) and *lectio continua* (particularly during Ordinary Time and in the weekday cycle); in fact, it is really more correct to talk of *lectio semicontinua* because no biblical book is read through in its entirety.

Basic Arrangement of the Sunday Lectionary

The planners of the Sunday Lectionary decided on a three-year cycle. That is, there are different readings for each Sunday in Years A, B, and C (as they are commonly designated), and then the cycle starts over again. (The year begins on the First Sunday of Advent.)

For each Sunday there are three readings: one from the Old Testament (with a few exceptions, as we will note in the Sundays after Easter), one from the Epistles or the book of Revelation, and one from the Gospels. Although provision is made for an individual Conference of Bishops to allow only two readings "for pastoral reasons" (*General Instruction*, 318), three is clearly the norm.

Because there is considerable difference in the Lectionary during the major seasons of Advent–Christmas and Lent–Easter as compared with the Sundays of Ordinary Time, it is easier and less confusing to look at each separately, beginning with Ordinary Time.

The Gospels in Ordinary Time

One of the three Synoptic Gospels forms the central focus of each of the thirty-three (occasionally thirty-four) Sundays of each year of Ordinary Time.

Year A is always the Gospel of Matthew;

Year B, the Gospel of Mark; and

Year C, the Gospel of Luke.

The Gospel of John is not neglected, even though it does not form the core of a specific year. In accord with an ancient tradition of the Church, John has always been read during the Lent and Easter seasons "because it is the 'spiritual' Gospel in which the mystery of Christ is

The Bible in the Lectionary

sounded out to greater depths" (*CSL: Introduction*, 1969, 7); in addition, because of the shortness of the Gospel of Mark, chapter 6 of John (the Bread of Life discourse) is taken up on five Sundays during Year B.

This particular arrangement of the Lectionary allows us to hear each of the Gospels in its own right; over the course of a year, we come to know the distinctive picture of Jesus presented by Matthew or Mark or Luke.

The Epistles in Ordinary Time

Over the Sundays of Ordinary Time, passages are selected from the Epistles for the second reading, according to the following outline:

Year A	1 Corinthians 1–4	(Sundays 2–8)
	Romans	(Sundays 9–24)
	Philippians	(Sundays 25–28)
	1 Thessalonians	(Sundays 29–33)
Year B	1 Corinthians 6–11	(Sundays 2–6)
	2 Corinthians	(Sundays 7–14)
	Ephesians	(Sundays 15–21)
	James	(Sundays 22–26)
	Hebrews 2–10	(Sundays 27–33)
Year C	1 Corinthians 12–15	(Sundays 2–8)
	Galatians	(Sundays 9–14)
	Colossians	(Sundays 15–18)
	Hebrews 11–12	(Sundays 19–22)
	Philemon	(Sunday 23)
	1 Timothy	(Sundays 24–26)
	2 Timothy	(Sundays 27–30)
	2 Thessalonians	(Sundays 31–33)

Though individual passages are quite short, and there is no attempt to read the Epistles in their entirety, over the three years the Lectionary gives a "rich and varied" exposure to the main themes and emphases of this part of Scripture. As already noted, in the Sundays in Ordinary Time, there is no direct correlation between the Gospel reading and the Epistle reading; although at times they may touch on similar aspects of the Christian mystery, they have not been picked to provide a common theme.

The Old Testament Reading in Ordinary Time

In contrast to the selection of the Epistle, the first reading from the Old Testament has been carefully chosen to correlate with the Gospel text of the day. Sometimes it is a common theme that binds the two readings together; at other times the Old Testament will foreshadow or suggest something that is more fully developed in the Gospel (e.g., on Sunday 16, Year C, the story of Martha and Mary giving hospitality to Jesus is paired with the story from Genesis of Abraham receiving his three guests). Often, if the Gospel quotes a verse from the Old Testament or refers to a specific incident, this passage will be the first reading (e.g., on the Third Sunday, Year A, Matthew quotes Is 8, 23—9, 1, and that Isaianic text serves as the first reading). At times, the single lines given before the readings in the Lectionary are most helpful (though they are not meant to be read publicly) to indicate the point of correspondence that led to the choice of a particular reading.

While the desirability of a weekly Old Testament reading is undisputed, it is probably fair to say that the selection of Old Testament passages has been the single most controversial aspect of the Lectionary. The decision to link the first reading so closely with the Gospel imposes certain limitations. Many of the most important Old Testament passages simply do not readily lend themselves to correlation with a particular Gospel passage and so are never heard in the Sunday assembly; often, such a brief or peripheral section of a major Old Testament story is read that it is difficult to get a sense of the whole picture. Furthermore, relatively little ever appears from the Wisdom literature (only three selections from Proverbs and two, both truncated, from the book of Job). The passages selected from the prophets are those that are readily seen to be fulfilled in Jesus, or which at least have christological implications, but other aspects of the prophetic message are given less prominence (e.g., the relatively few "social justice" passages read over the three years).

The Lent–Easter Season

As noted above, the seasons of Lent–Easter and Advent–Christmas form independent units; both cycles (the Advent even more so than the Lent) are carefully crafted so that through the Scripture readings we may be more closely initiated into the Church's understanding of these great feasts.

Easter, especially the Easter Triduum (Holy Thursday, Good Friday, and Easter Vigil on

Saturday), is "the culmination of the entire liturgical year" (*Norms for the Liturgical Year*, 18); Lent serves as a time of preparation, especially as a period of "closer attention to the Word of God" (*CSL*, 109). During Lent, "those important passages from the Gospels which were read to catechumens in the early centuries to prepare them for Baptism are proclaimed. These readings are directed to *all* the faithful because during Lent the whole Church, along with those about to be baptized, calls to mind the mystery of its initiation into Christ." Though it is not possible to examine closely all the readings for the Lent–Easter season, a few examples will illustrate the care and theological insight that finds expression in the arrangement of the Lectionary for this season.

The baptismal thrust is seen most clearly in Year A on the final three Sundays of Lent, where the great themes of water, light, and life are proclaimed through the reading from John's Gospel of the Samaritan woman at the well (Third Sunday), the curing of the man born blind (Fourth), and the raising of Lazarus from the dead (Fifth); so pivotal are these particular texts to the process of Christian initiation that they can be used in any of the three years, especially when there are candidates preparing for Baptism.

The readings for the first two Sundays of Lent are always the account of the Temptation and the Transfiguration respectively, read according to the Gospel being followed in a given year. In Year B, the Gospels for the rest of Lent focus on the cross and Resurrection; in Year C, on the process of conversion.

At first glance, the choice of Old Testament readings for the Sundays of Lent might look entirely diverse and random; certainly they are not specifically linked to the Gospel. Rather, each year, they are meant to lead us through the Old Testament, presenting "the main elements of salvation history from its beginning until the promise of the New Covenant" (*CSL: Introduction*, 97):

Year A	First Sunday:	Creation and fall
	Second Sunday:	The call of Abraham
	Third Sunday:	Water from the rock in the desert
	Fourth Sunday:	The anointing of David as king
	Fifth Sunday:	Promise of the restoration

Year B	First Sunday:	Flood and covenant
	Second Sunday:	Abraham's sacrifice of his son
	Third Sunday:	The ten commandments
	Fourth Sunday:	Exile and destruction of the Temple
	Fifth Sunday:	Promise of the new covenant

Year C	First Sunday:	Retelling the deliverance from Egypt
	Second Sunday:	The covenant with Abraham
	Third Sunday:	The call of Moses
	Fourth Sunday:	The Passover celebrated in the Promised Land
	Fifth Sunday:	Promise of a new exodus

The Epistle readings during Lent highlight themes such as faith, repentance, baptismal motifs, and often are related to the first reading (e.g., on the First Sunday of Lent, A, the passage from Romans about Christ as the Second Adam corresponds to the reading about the sin of Adam in Gn 2).

The reading of the Gospel of John continues on most of the Sundays after Easter in all three years with texts about the Good Shepherd (Fourth Sunday) and from John's presentation of the Farewell Discourse and Prayer of Jesus (the Fifth to Seventh Sundays). This is the only time when there are no Old Testament readings; in keeping with a very ancient tradition, the Church turns to the Acts of the Apostles in all three years so that we ponder the work of the Spirit in the early Church. For the second reading, semi-continuous selections are taken from 1 Peter in Year A, 1 John in Year B (both rich in baptismal allusions), and from the book of Revelation (with its emphasis on heavenly worship) in Year C.

Advent–Christmas Season

The Lectionary for Advent is very carefully planned, with a definite movement toward the celebration of Christmas. The First Sunday emphasizes the Second Coming of Christ, picking up on a theme already sounded in the final Sunday of the Church Year (the feast of Christ the King). On the Second and Third Sundays, the Gospel is always about John the Baptist, so that the focus of attention moves more to the historical coming of a Messiah. On the Fourth Sunday, we turn to the first chapters of Matthew and Luke for events immediately prior to the birth of Jesus (the Annunciation to Mary and Joseph, and the Visitation).

In keeping with a long tradition in the Church, the book of Isaiah with its messianic prophecies has a special place in both the Advent and Christmas readings. The Epistle readings are more general, offering exhortations and reflections; often, as the Advent focus moves to the birth of Jesus in time, the second reading serves to remind us of the Coming that still awaits us in the future.

Throughout the Christmas season, the Lectionary preserves many of the readings that have been traditional in the Roman Church. On the Octave of Christmas, the Solemnity of Mary, Mother of God (New Year's Day), the first reading is the priestly blessing from Numbers 6, and the other two speak more specifically of Mary.

The Lectionary for Weekdays

The readings for weekdays throughout the year form a separate cycle, independent of the Sunday cycle. Even with only two readings, obviously more of the Bible can be covered on weekdays, although still only portions of many of the longer Old Testament books are included. The seasons of Advent–Christmas, Lent–Easter follow an annual cycle, that is, the readings are repeated every year; in Ordinary Time, the same Gospel passages are read every year, while the first reading follows a two-year cycle (designated as Year I and Year II).

The following will give a brief outline of the weekday cycle.

Advent–Christmas Season

During the first nine days of Advent, the Lectionary follows a very ancient custom of the Church and reads (in sequence) selected passages from the prophet Isaiah; on these days, contrary to usual practice, the Gospel is chosen to relate to this first reading. After the Thursday of the Second Week of Advent, the Gospel consistently speaks of John the Baptist, while the first reading is still from Isaiah or chosen to relate to the Gospel. From December 17–24, passages are selected from the first chapters of

Matthew and Luke of events leading up to the birth of Christ; the first reading presents some of the major Old Testament messianic prophecies. From December 27 on throughout the Epiphany season, there is a virtually continuous reading of 1 John. The Gospels relate various manifestations of Jesus; the whole of the first chapter of John's Gospel is read between December 31 and January 5.

Lent–Easter Season

Throughout Lent, the Gospel and Old Testament are rather closely related to each other and present to us different aspects of the major Lenten themes of Baptism and penance. In accord with an ancient custom in the Church, the Gospel of John is read from the fourth week on; in Holy Week the focus is more specifically on Christ's passion.

During the Easter season, on weekdays as on Sundays, the Lectionary maintains the ancient custom of reading semi-continuously from the Acts of the Apostles. During the Octave of Easter, the Gospel selections recount the different occasions on which Christ appeared; over the next weeks there is semi-continuous reading of the teaching and prayer of Jesus at the Last Supper from John 13–17.

Ordinary Time

Over the course of the year, the Gospels are read on a semi-continuous basis: Mark 1–12 in Weeks 1–12, Matthew 5–25 in Weeks 10–21, and Luke 4–21 in Weeks 22–34. The Church Year ends with those passages from Luke that talk specifically of the Second Coming.

The first reading is completely independent from the Gospel and provides the opportunity to read selections from the majority of the Old Testament books and Epistles. Longer books are sometimes divided (e.g., Genesis 1–11 is read in Weeks 5–6 of Year I, Genesis 12–50 in Weeks 12–14). At the very end of the Church Year, we read from Daniel in Year I and the book of Revelation in Year II with their eschatological themes.

The Responsorial Psalm

The Lectionary also introduces us to the psalms in the Bible; in fact, more than 80 psalms (or verses thereof) are used in the Sunday Lectionary, and some 130 of the 150 psalms appear somewhere in the complete Lectionary. The psalm comes between the first and second reading and is considered "an integral part of the Liturgy of the Word" (*General Instruction,* 36).

The psalms are poetry, the majority of them certainly originally composed to be sung with musical accompaniment. The *Introduction* to the Lectionary strongly encourages singing the psalm at Mass, preferably by a soloist (cantor) with the congregation joining in with a refrain; if the psalm is spoken, it is "to be recited in a manner conducive to meditation on the Word" (*CSL: Introduction,* 22).

Although the psalm always serves in some way as a response to the Word of God, there is considerable diversity in terms of its precise relationship to other readings. If the first reading or the epistle or even the Gospel quotes a particular psalm verse, that psalm is usually taken up as an echo or anticipated response (e.g., the use of Psalm 91 on the First Sunday of Lent, C, when a verse from this psalm, "He has put his angels in charge of you," is quoted during the temptation story in the Gospel). Often a psalm simply picks up and carries on the mood of the first reading, whether lamentation, thanksgiving, or praise. Some psalms have a long tradition of usage on particular feasts (Psalm 47, "God goes up with shouts of joy" for the Ascension; Psalm 72, ". . . the kings of Arabia and Seba shall bring tribute. All Kings shall pay him homage, all nations shall serve him" for Epiphany). According to Lucien Deiss (a member of the committee involved in the choice of psalms when the Lectionary was compiled), some psalms that would not otherwise be used were introduced primarily so that the Christian community could become more familiar with the entire psalter (*Spirit and Song of the New Liturgy,* pp. 110–11).

Ecumenical Importance of the Lectionary

One of the unexpected and unforeseen results of the revision of the Roman Lectionary has been its adoption (with some modifications) by many Protestant churches, including Anglican/ Episcopalian, Methodist, Presbyterian, Lutheran, and United Church of Canada. James White, a Methodist minister, in a much-quoted statement remarked that the Lectionary has become "Catholicism's greatest gift to Protestant preaching, just as Protestant biblical scholarship has given so much impetus to Catholic preaching" (*Christian Worship in Transition,* 1976, p. 139).

In recent years, many of these Churches came together under the auspices of the Consultation on Common Texts and developed the *Common Lectionary,* an order of readings for use on Sundays and a few special days of the Christian year. The *Common Lectionary* basically follows the Roman Lectionary, with some significant changes in the choice of Old Testament passages to deal with some of the problem areas noted above.

Although Catholics and Protestants do not share exactly the same Lectionary, tremendous progress has been made toward common reading of Scripture. The ecumenical import, even on a practical level, is significant already; in many places ministers of different churches gather together to reflect and prepare their Sunday sermons. And, although we are still not at the point of being able to be united at the table of the Lord's banquet, we can be united and nourished at the common table of his Word.

Using the Lectionary for Prayer and Study

Many people, both clergy and laity, now use the Lectionary as a basic resource for daily prayer, whether or not they are able to celebrate liturgy with the Christian community every day. Consistent use of the Lectionary over a period of years will necessarily expose us to a broad expanse of Scripture and protect us against the subjective reading of the Bible spoken about earlier. The Lectionary puts us in touch with the Church's understanding of the mysteries of our faith as presented through the Church year, helping us to recover dimensions that may have been lost in popular piety (e.g., the baptismal dimension of the season of Lent as opposed to a solely ascetic focus).

Many religious educators use the Lectionary as a valuable resource in catechetics; reflection on the readings as appropriate to various age groups provides a common focus when the whole community gathers in prayer. Parish study groups or Bible studies often take the Gospel of a given year as their text for study. Often the Lectionary is used as the core of the RCIA program to introduce the new catechumens to the life of faith and community.

Though the Lectionary contains the Word of God, the particular selection of material is a human endeavor and thus only more or less perfect. It is recognized that some choices of specific readings could have been more auspicious, and certainly revisions will probably be made in time.

Conclusion

The revision of the Lectionary stands as one of the most tangible and permanent implementations of the vision and challenge of the Second Vatican Council. In the Lectionary, "the treasures of the Bible are . . . opened up more lavishly so that a richer share in God's Word may be provided for the faithful" (*CSL*, 51). The Lectionary has the potential to shape the life of the Christian community, not only as the Word of God is proclaimed in the celebration of the liturgy, but also as it is broken open for us in the homily, in catechetics, and in private and group study and prayer that is rooted in Scripture. As the Lectionary is used over the cycle of years, and even generations, "there is reason to hope for a new awakening of the spiritual life deriving from an increased dedication to God's word which 'abides forever' [Is 40, 8]" (*Dei Verbum*, 26).

BIBLIOGRAPHY

The text of the *Constitution on the Sacred Liturgy: Introduction to the Lectionary (CSL)* has been published by the United States Catholic Conference, Lectionary for Mass: Introduction, Liturgy Documentation Series 1, 1982.

National Bulletin on Liturgy, Canadian Conference of Bishops, Number 50, 1975.

Proclaim the Word: The Lectionary for Mass, Liturgy Study Text Series 8. Washington, DC: U.S. Catholic Conference, 1982.

Fitzsimmons, John H. *Guide to the Lectionary.* London: Mayhew-McCrimmon, 1981.

Keifer, Ralph. "To Hear and To Proclaim: Introduction." *Lectionary for Mass with Commentary for Musicians and Priests.* Washington, DC: National Association of Pastoral Musicians, 1983.

Pawlikowski, John J. and James A. Wilde, *When Catholics Speak About Jews.* Chicago: Liturgy Training Program, 1987. A discussion of some of the issues around the Bible and our relationship to the Jewish people.

Skudlarek, William. *The Word in Worship: Preaching in a Liturgical Context,* Abingdon's Preacher's Library. Nashville: Abingdon, 1981.

LECTIONARY

THE NEW 3-YEAR CYCLE OF READINGS FOR SUNDAY MASS

See pp. 1782–1783 for Readings of Feasts that displace the Sunday Readings.
Guide: 1 refers to Reading I; 2 refers to Reading II; 3 refers to Gospel reading.

YEAR A
2005 2008 2011 2014 2017 2020 2023

Advent Season

1st Sunday of Advent
1 Is 2, 1–5
2 Rom 13, 11–14
3 Mt 24, 37–44

2nd Sunday of Advent
1 Is 11, 1–10
2 Rom 15, 4–9
3 Mt 3, 1–12

3rd Sunday of Advent
1 Is 35, 1–6a. 10
2 Jas 5, 7–10
3 Mt 11, 2–11

4th Sunday of Advent
1 Is 7, 10–14
2 Rom 1, 1–7
3 Mt 1, 18–24

Christmas Season

Christmas Vigil
1 Is 62, 1–5
2 Acts 13, 16–17. 22–25
3 Mt 1, 1–25

Christmas (At Midnight)
1 Is 9, 1–6

2 Ti 2, 11–14
3 Lk 2, 1–14

Christmas (At Dawn)
1 Is 62, 11–12
2 Ti 3, 4–7
3 Lk 2, 15–20

Christmas (During the Day)
1 Is 52, 7–10
2 Heb 1, 1–6
3 Jn 1, 1–18

Sunday After Christmas (Holy Family)
1 Sir 3, 3–7. 14–17a
2 Col 3, 12–21
3 Mt 2, 13–15. 19–23

January 1 (Solemnity of Mary, Mother of God)
1 Nm 6, 22–27
2 Gal 4, 4–7
3 Lk 2, 16–21

2nd Sunday After Christmas
1 Sir 24, 1–4. 12–16
2 Eph 1, 3–6. 15–18
3 Jn 1, 1–18

Epiphany
1 Is 60, 1–6
2 Eph 3, 2–3a. 5–6
3 Mt 2, 1–12

Sunday After Epiphany (Baptism of the Lord)
1 Is 42, 1–4. 6–7
2 Acts 10, 34–38
3 Mt 3, 13–17

Lenten Season

Ash Wednesday
1 Jl 2, 12–18
2 2 Cor 5, 20—6, 2
3 Mt 6, 1–6. 16–18

1st Sunday of Lent
1 Gn 2, 7–9; 3, 1–7
2 Rom 5, 12–19
3 Mt 4, 1–11

2nd Sunday of Lent
1 Gn 12, 1–4a
2 2 Tm 1, 8b–10
3 Mt 17, 1–9

3rd Sunday of Lent
1 Ex 17, 3–7
2 Rom 5, 1–2. 5–8
3 Jn 4, 5–42

4th Sunday of Lent
1 1 Sm 16, 1b. 6–7. 10–13a
2 Eph 5, 8–14
3 Jn 9, 1–41

5th Sunday of Lent
1 Ez 37, 12–14
2 Rom 8, 8–11
3 Jn 11, 1–45

Passion Sunday (Palm Sunday)
Procession: Mt 21, 1–11
1 Is 50, 4–7
2 Phil 2, 6–11
3 Mt 26, 14—27, 66

Easter Triduum and Easter Season

Mass of Lord's Supper
1 Ex 12, 1–8. 11–14
2 1 Cor 11, 23–26
3 Jn 13, 1–15

Good Friday
1 Is 52, 13—53, 12
2 Heb 4, 14–16; 5, 7–9
3 Jn 18, 1—19, 42

Easter Vigil
1 Gn 1, 1—2, 2
  Gn 22, 1–18
  Ex 14, 15—15, 1

Is 54, 5–14
Is 55, 1–11
Bar 3, 9–15. 32—
  4, 4
Ez 36, 16–17a.
  18–28
2 Rom 6, 3–11
3 Mt 28, 1–10

Easter Sunday
1 Acts 10, 34a. 37–
    43
2 Col 3, 1–4
    or 1 Cor 5, 6b–8
3 Jn 20, 1–9
    or Mt 28, 1–10
Evening: 3 Lk 24,
  13–35

2nd Sunday of Easter
1 Acts 2, 42–47
2 1 Pt 1, 3–9
3 Jn 20, 19–31

3rd Sunday of Easter
1 Acts 2, 14. 22–33
2 1 Pt 1, 17–21
3 Lk 24, 13–35

4th Sunday of Easter
1 Acts 2, 14a. 36–41
2 1 Pt 2, 20b–25
3 Jn 10, 1–10

5th Sunday of Easter
1 Acts 6, 1–7
2 1 Pt 2, 4–9
3 Jn 14, 1–12

6th Sunday of Easter
1 Acts 8, 5–8. 14–17
2 1 Pt 3, 15–18
3 Jn 14, 15–21

Ascension of Our Lord
1 Acts 1, 1–11
2 Eph 1, 17–23
3 Mt 28, 16–20

7th Sunday of Easter
1 Acts 1, 12–14
2 1 Pt 4, 13–16
3 Jn 17, 1–11a

Pentecost Vigil
1 Gn 11, 1–9
    or Ex 19, 3–8a.
    16–20b
    or Ez 37, 1–14
    or Jl 3, 1–5

2 Rom 8, 22–27
3 Jn 7, 37–39

Mass of the Day
1 Acts 2, 1–11
2 1 Cor 12, 3b–7.
    12–13
3 Jn 20, 19–23

Solemnities of the Lord During Ordinary Time

Trinity Sunday (Sunday after Pentecost)
1 Ex 34, 4b–6. 8–9
2 2 Cor 13, 11–13
3 Jn 3, 16–18

Corpus Christi
1 Dt 8, 2–3. 14b–16a
2 1 Cor 10, 16–17
3 Jn 6, 51–58

Sacred Heart of Jesus
1 Dt 7, 6–11
2 1 Jn 4, 7–16
3 Mt 11, 25–30

Ordinary Time

1st Sunday
(See Baptism of the Lord, above)

2nd Sunday
1 Is 49, 3. 5–6
2 1 Cor 1, 1–3
3 Jn 1, 29–34

3rd Sunday
1 Is 8, 23b—9, 3
2 1 Cor 1, 10–13. 17
3 Mt 4, 12–23

4th Sunday
1 Zep 2, 3; 3, 12–13
2 1 Cor 1, 26–31
3 Mt 5, 1–12a

5th Sunday
1 Is 58, 7–10
2 1 Cor 2, 1–5
3 Mt 5, 13–16

6th Sunday
1 Sir 15, 16–21
2 1 Cor 2, 6–10
3 Mt 5, 17–37

7th Sunday
1 Lv 19, 1–2. 17–18

2 1 Cor 3, 16–23
3 Mt 5, 38–48

8th Sunday
1 Is 49, 14–15
2 1 Cor 4, 1–5
3 Mt 6, 24–34

9th Sunday
1 Dt 11, 18. 26–28.
    32
2 Rom 3, 21–25a.
    28
3 Mt 7, 21–27

10th Sunday
1 Hos 6, 3–6
2 Rom 4, 18–25
3 Mt 9, 9–13

11th Sunday
1 Ex 19, 2–6a
2 Rom 5, 6–11
3 Mt 9, 36—10, 8

12th Sunday
1 Jer 20, 10–13
2 Rom 5, 12–15
3 Mt 10, 26–33

13th Sunday
1 2 Kgs 4, 8–11.
    14–16a
2 Rom 6, 3–4. 8–11
3 Mt 10, 37–42

14th Sunday
1 Zec 9, 9–10
2 Rom 8, 9. 11–13
3 Mt 11, 25–30

15th Sunday
1 Is 55, 10–11
2 Rom 8, 18–23
3 Mt 13, 1–23

16th Sunday
1 Wis 12, 13. 16–
    19
2 Rom 8, 26–27
3 Mt 13, 24–43

17th Sunday
1 1 Kgs 3, 5. 7–12
2 Rom 8, 28–30
3 Mt 13, 44–52

18th Sunday
1 Is 55, 1–3
2 Rom 8, 35. 37–39
3 Mt 14, 13–21

19th Sunday
1 1 Kgs 19, 9a.
    11–13a
2 Rom 9, 1–5
3 Mt 14, 22–33

20th Sunday
1 Is 56, 1. 6–7
2 Rom 11, 13–15.
    29–32
3 Mt 15, 21–28

21st Sunday
1 Is 22, 19–23
2 Rom 11, 33–36
3 Mt 16, 13–20

22nd Sunday
1 Jer 20, 7–9
2 Rom 12, 1–2
3 Mt 16, 21–27

23rd Sunday
1 Ez 33, 7–9
2 Rom 13, 8–10
3 Mt 18, 15–20

24th Sunday
1 Sir 27, 30—28, 7
2 Rom 14, 7–9
3 Mt 18, 21–35

25th Sunday
1 Is 55, 6–9
2 Phil 1, 20c–24. 27a
3 Mt 20, 1–16a

26th Sunday
1 Ez 18, 25–28
2 Phil 2, 1–11
3 Mt 21, 28–32

27th Sunday
1 Is 5, 1–7
2 Phil 4, 6–9
3 Mt 21, 33–43

28th Sunday
1 Is 25, 6–10a
2 Phil 4, 12–14.
    19–20
3 Mt 22, 1–14

29th Sunday
1 Is 45, 1. 4–6
2 1 Thes 1, 1–5b
3 Mt 22, 15–21

30th Sunday
1 Ex 22, 20–26
2 1 Thes 1, 5c–10
3 Mt 22, 34–40

31st Sunday
1   Mal 1, 14b—2, 2b. 8–10
2   1 Thes 2, 7b–9. 13
3   Mt 23, 1–12

32nd Sunday
1   Wis 6, 12–16
2   1 Thes 4, 13–18
3   Mt 25, 1–13

33rd Sunday
1   Prv 31, 10–13. 19–20. 30–31
2   1 Thes 5, 1–6
3   Mt 25, 14–30

34th Sunday
(Christ the King)
1   Ez 34, 11–12. 15–17
2   1 Cor 15, 20–26. 28
3   Mt 25, 31–46

YEAR B
2006 2009 2012 2015
2018 2021 2024

Advent Season

1st Sunday of Advent
1   Is 63, 16b–17. 19b; 64, 2b–7
2   1 Cor 1, 3–9
3   Mk 13, 33–37

2nd Sunday of Advent
1   Is 40, 1–5. 9–11
2   2 Pt 3, 8–14
3   Mk 1, 1–8

3rd Sunday of Advent
1   Is 61, 1–2a. 10–11
2   1 Thes 5, 16–24
3   Jn 1, 6–8. 19–28

4th Sunday of Advent
1   2 Sm 7, 1–5. 8b–12. 14a. 16
2   Rom 16, 25–27
3   Lk 1, 26–38

Christmas Season

Christmas Vigil
1   Is 62, 1–5
2   Acts 13, 16–17. 22–25
3   Mt 1, 1–25

Christmas (At Midnight)
1   Is 9, 1–6
2   Ti 2, 11–14
3   Lk 2, 1–14

Christmas (At Dawn)
1   Is 62, 11–12
2   Ti 3, 4–7
3   Lk 2, 15–20

Christmas (During the Day)
1   Is 52, 7–10
2   Heb 1, 1–6
3   Jn 1, 1–18

Sunday After Christmas (Holy Family)
1   Gn 15, 1–6; 21, 1–3
2   Heb 11, 8. 11–12. 17–19
3   Lk 2, 22–40 or 22. 39–40

January 1 (Solemnity of Mary, Mother of God)
1   Nm 6, 22–27
2   Gal 4, 4–7
3   Lk 2, 16–21

2nd Sunday After Christmas
1   Sir 24, 1–2. 8–12
2   Eph 1, 3–6. 15–18
3   Jn 1, 1–18

Epiphany
1   Is 60, 1–6
2   Eph 3, 2–3a. 5–6
3   Mt 2, 1–12

Sunday After Epiphany (Baptism of the Lord)
1   Is 55, 1–11
2   1 Jn 5, 1–9
3   Mk 1, 7–11

Lenten Season

Ash Wednesday
1   Jl 2, 12–18
2   2 Cor 5, 20—6, 2
3   Mt 6, 1–6. 16–18

1st Sunday of Lent
1   Gn 9, 8–15
2   1 Pt 3, 18–22
3   Mk 1, 12–15

2nd Sunday of Lent
1   Gn 22, 1–2. 9a. 10–13. 15–18
2   Rom 8, 31b–34
3   Mk 9, 2–10

3rd Sunday of Lent
1   Ex 20, 1–17
2   1 Cor 1, 22–25
3   Jn 2, 13–25

4th Sunday of Lent
1   2 Chr 36, 14–16. 19–23
2   Eph 2, 4–10
3   Jn 3, 14–21

5th Sunday of Lent
1   Jer 31, 31–34
2   Heb 5, 7–9
3   Jn 12, 20–33

Passion Sunday (Palm Sunday)
Procession: Mk 11, 1–10 or Jn 12, 12–16
1   Is 50, 4–7
2   Phil 2, 6–11
3   Mk 14, 1—15,47

Easter Triduum and Easter Season

Mass of Lord's Supper
1   Ex 12, 1–8. 11–14
2   1 Cor 11, 23–26
3   Jn 13, 1–15

Good Friday
1   Is 52, 13—53, 12
2   Heb 4, 14—16. 5. 7–9
3   Jn 18, 1—19, 42

Easter Vigil
1   Gn 1, 1—2, 2
    Gn 22, 1–18
    Ex 14, 15—15, 1
    Is 54, 5–14
    Is 55, 1–11
    Bar 3, 9–15. 32—4, 4
    Ez 36, 16–28
2   Rom 6, 3–11
3   Mk 16, 1–7

Easter Sunday
1   Acts 10, 34a. 37–43
2   Col 3, 1–4
    or 1 Cor 5, 6b–8

3   Jn 20, 1–9
    or Mk 16, 1–8
Evening: 3 Lk 24, 13–35

2nd Sunday of Easter
1   Acts 4, 32–35
2   1 Jn 5, 1–6
3   Jn 20, 19–31

3rd Sunday of Easter
1   Acts 3, 13–15. 17–19
2   1 Jn 2, 1–5a
3   Lk 24, 35–48

4th Sunday of Easter
1   Acts 4, 8–12
2   1 Jn 3, 1–2
3   Jn 10, 11–18

5th Sunday of Easter
1   Acts 9, 26–31
2   1 Jn 3, 18–24
3   Jn 15, 1–8

6th Sunday of Easter
1   Acts 10, 25–26. 34–35. 44–48
2   1 Jn 4, 7–10
3   Jn 15, 9–17

Ascension of Our Lord
1   Acts 1, 1–11
2   Eph 1, 17–23 or 4, 1–13
3   Mk 16, 15–20

7th Sunday of Easter
1   Acts 1, 15–17. 20a. 20c–26
2   1 Jn 4, 11–16
3   Jn 17, 11b–19

Pentecost Vigil
1   Gn 11, 1–9
    or Ex 19, 3–8a. 16–20b
    or Ez 37, 1–14
    or Jl 3, 1–5
2   Rom 8, 22–27
3   Jn 7, 37–39

Mass of the Day
1   Acts 2, 1–11
2   1 Cor 12, 3b–7. 12–13
3   Jn 20, 19–23
Pentecost-Optional
2   Gal 5, 16–25

3   Jn 15, 26–27; 16,
    12–15

**Solemnities of the Lord
During Ordinary Time**

**Trinity Sunday
(Sunday after
Pentecost)**
1   Dt 4, 32–34. 39–40
2   Rom 8, 14–17
3   Mt 28, 16–20

Corpus Christi
1   Ex 24, 3–8
2   Heb 9, 11–15
3   Mk 14, 12–16.
    22–26

Sacred Heart of Jesus
1   Hos 11, 1. 3–4.
    8c–9
2   Eph 3, 8–12. 14–19
3   Jn 19, 31–37

Ordinary Time

1st Sunday
*(See Baptism of the Lord,
above)*

2nd Sunday
1   1 Sm 3, 3b–10. 19
2   1 Cor 6, 13c–15a.
    17–20
3   Jn 1, 35–42

3rd Sunday
1   Jon 3, 1–5. 10
2   1 Cor 7, 29–31
3   Mk 1, 14–20

4th Sunday
1   Dt 18, 15–20
2   1 Cor 7, 32–35
3   Mk 1, 21–28

5th Sunday
1   Jb 7, 1–4. 6–7
2   1 Cor 9, 16–19.
    22–23
3   Mk 1, 29–39

6th Sunday
1   Lv 13, 1–2. 45–46
2   1 Cor 10, 31—11, 1
3   Mk 1, 40–45

7th Sunday
1   Is 43, 18–19.
    21–22. 24b–25
2   2 Cor 1, 18–22
3   Mk 2, 1–12

8th Sunday
1   Hos 2, 16b. 17b.
    21–22
2   2 Cor 3, 1b–6
3   Mk 2, 18–22

9th Sunday
1   Dt 5, 12–15
2   2 Cor 4, 6–11
3   Mk 2, 23—3, 6

10th Sunday
1   Gn 3, 9–15
2   2 Cor 4, 13—5, 1
3   Mk 3, 20–35

11th Sunday
1   Ez 17, 22–24
2   2 Cor 5, 6–10
3   Mk 4, 26–34

12th Sunday
1   Jb 38, 1. 8–11
2   2 Cor 5, 14–17
3   Mk 4, 35–41

13th Sunday
1   Wis 1, 13–15; 2,
    23–24
2   2 Cor 8, 7. 9. 13–15
3   Mk 5, 21–43

14th Sunday
1   Ez 2, 2–5
2   2 Cor 12, 7–10
3   Mk 6, 1–6

15th Sunday
1   Am 7, 12–15
2   Eph 1, 3–14
3   Mk 6, 7–13

16th Sunday
1   Jer 23, 1–6
2   Eph 2, 13–18
3   Mk 6, 30–34

17th Sunday
1   2 Kgs 4, 42–44
2   Eph 4, 1–6
3   Jn 6, 1–15

18th Sunday
1   Ex 16, 2–4. 12–15
2   Eph 4, 17. 20–24
3   Jn 6, 24–35

19th Sunday
1   1 Kgs 19, 4–8
2   Eph 4, 30—5, 2
3   Jn 6, 41–51

20th Sunday
1   Prv 9, 1–6
2   Eph 5, 15–20
3   Jn 6, 51–58

21st Sunday
1   Jos 24, 1–2a.
    15–17. 18b
2   Eph 5, 21–32
3   Jn 6, 60–69

22nd Sunday
1   Dt 4, 1–2. 6–8
2   Jas 1, 17–18.
    21b–22. 27
3   Mk 7, 1–8. 14–15.
    21–23

23rd Sunday
1   Is 35, 4–7a
2   Jas 2, 1–5
3   Mk 7, 31–37

24th Sunday
1   Is 50, 5–9a
2   Jas 2, 14–18
3   Mk 8, 27–35

25th Sunday
1   Wis 2, 12. 17–20
2   Jas 3, 16—4, 3
3   Mk 9, 30–37

26th Sunday
1   Nm 11, 25–29
2   Jas 5, 1–6
3   Mk 9, 38–43. 45.
    47–48

27th Sunday
1   Gn 2, 18–24
2   Heb 2, 9–11
3   Mk 10, 2–16

28th Sunday
1   Wis 7, 7–11
2   Heb 4, 12–13
3   Mk 10, 17–30

29th Sunday
1   Is 53, 10–11
2   Heb 4, 14–16
3   Mk 10, 35–45

30th Sunday
1   Jer 31, 7–9
2   Heb 5, 1–6
3   Mk 10, 46–52

31st Sunday
1   Dt 6, 2–6

2   Heb 7, 23–28
3   Mk 12, 28b–34

32nd Sunday
1   1 Kgs 17, 10–16
2   Heb 9, 24–28
3   Mk 12, 38–44

33rd Sunday
1   Dn 12, 1–3
2   Heb 10, 11–14. 18
3   Mk 13, 24–32

**34th Sunday
(Christ the King)**
1   Dn 7, 13–14
2   Rv 1, 5–8
3   Jn 18, 33b–37

YEAR C
**2007 2010 2013 2016
2019 2022 2025**

Advent Season

1st Sunday of Advent
1   Jer 33, 14–16
2   1 Thes 3, 12—4, 2
3   Lk 21, 25–28.
    34–36

2nd Sunday of Advent
1   Bar 5, 1–9
2   Phil 1, 4–6. 8–11
3   Lk 3, 1–6

3rd Sunday of Advent
1   Zep 3, 14–18a
2   Phil 4, 4–7
3   Lk 3, 10–18

4th Sunday of Advent
1   Mi 5, 1–4a
2   Heb 10, 5–10
3   Lk 1, 39–45

Christmas Season

Christmas Vigil
1   Is 62, 1–6
2   Acts 13, 16–17.
    22–25
3   Mt 1, 1–25

**Christmas
(At Midnight)**
1   Is 9, 1–6
2   Ti 2, 11–14
3   Lk 2, 1–14

Christmas (At Dawn)
1   Is 62, 11–12

2 Ti 3, 4–7
3 Lk 2, 15–20

**Christmas
(During the Day)**
1 Is 57, 7–10
2 Heb 1, 1–6
3 Jn 1, 1–18

**Sunday After
Christmas
(Holy Family)**
1 1 Sm 1, 20–22.
    24–28
2 1 Jn 3, 1–2. 21–24
3 Lk 2, 41–52

**January 1
(Solemnity of Mary,
Mother of God)**
1 Nm 6, 22–27
2 Gal 4, 4–7
3 Lk 2, 16–21

**2nd Sunday After
Christmas**
1 Sir 24, 1–2. 8–12
2 Eph 1, 3–6. 15–18
3 Jn 1, 1–18

Epiphany
1 Is 60, 1–6
2 Eph 3, 2–3a. 5–6
3 Mt 2, 1–12

**Sunday After Epiphany
(Baptism of the Lord)**
1 Is 40, 1–5. 9–11
2 Ti 2, 11–14; 3, 4–7
3 Lk 3, 15–16. 21–
    22

Lenten Season

Ash Wednesday
1 Jl 2, 12–18
2 2 Cor 5, 20—6, 2
3 Mt 6, 1–6. 16–18

1st Sunday of Lent
1 Dt 26, 4–10
2 Rom 10, 8–13
3 Lk 4, 1–13

2nd Sunday of Lent
1 Gn 15, 5–12. 17–18
2 Phil 3, 17—4, 1
3 Lk 9, 28b–36

3rd Sunday of Lent
1 Ex 3, 1–8a. 13–15

2 1 Cor 10, 1–6.
    10–12
3 Lk 13, 1–9

4th Sunday of Lent
1 Jos 5, 9a. 10–12
2 2 Cor 5, 17–21
3 Lk 15, 1–3. 11–32

5th Sunday of Lent
1 Is 43, 16–21
2 Phil 3, 8–14
3 Jn 8, 1–11

**Passion Sunday
(Palm Sunday)**
Procession: Lk 19,
    28–40
1 Is 50, 4–7
2 Phil 2, 6–11
3 Lk 22, 14—23, 56

**Easter Triduum and
Easter Season**

Mass of Lord's Supper
1 Ex 12, 1–8. 11–14
2 1 Cor 11, 23–26
3 Jn 13, 1–15

Good Friday
1 Is 52, 13—53, 12
2 Heb 4, 14–16; 5,
    7–9
3 Jn 18, 1—19, 42

Easter Vigil
1 Gn 1, 1–2, 2
    Gn 22, 1–18
    Ex 14, 15—15, 1
    Is 54, 5–14
    Is 55, 1–11
    Bar 3, 9–15. 32—
    4, 4
    Ez 36, 16–28
2 Rom 6, 3–11
3 Lk 24, 1–12

Easter Sunday
1 Acts 10, 34a. 37–
    43
2 Col 3, 1–4
    or 1 Cor 5, 6b–8
3 Jn 20, 1–9
    or Lk 24, 1–12
Evening: 3 Lk 24,
    13–35

2nd Sunday of Easter
1 Acts 5, 12–16

2 Rv 1, 9–11a. 12–13.
    17–19
3 Jn 20, 19–31

3rd Sunday of Easter
1 Acts 5, 27b–32.
    40b–41
2 Rv 5, 11–14
3 Jn 21, 1–19 or
    1–14

4th Sunday of Easter
1 Acts 13, 14.
    43–52
2 Rv 7, 9. 14b–17
3 Jn 10, 27–30

5th Sunday of Easter
1 Acts 14, 21b–27
2 Rv 21, 1–5a
3 Jn 13, 31–33a.
    34–35

6th Sunday of Easter
1 Acts 15, 1–2.
    22–29
2 Rv 21, 10–14.
    22–23
3 Jn 14, 23–29

Ascension of the Lord
1 Acts 1, 1–11
2 Eph 1, 17–23 or
    Heb 9, 24–28;
    10, 19–23
3 Lk 24, 46–53

7th Sunday of Easter
1 Acts 7, 55–60
2 Rv 22, 12–14.
    16–17. 20
3 Jn 17, 20–26

Pentecost Vigil
1 Gn 11, 1–9
    or Ex 19, 3–8a.
    16–20b
    or Ez 37, 1–14
    or Jl 3, 1–5
2 Rom 8, 22–27
3 Jn 7, 37–39

Mass of the Day
1 Acts 2, 1–11
2 1 Cor 12, 3b–7.
    12–13
    or Rom 8, 8–27
3 Jn 20, 19–23
    or Jn 14, 15–16.
    23b–26

**Solemnities of the Lord
During Ordinary Time**

**Trinity Sunday
(Sunday After
Pentecost)**
1 Prv 8, 22–31
2 Rom 5, 1–5
3 Jn 16, 12–15

Corpus Christi
1 Gn 14, 18–20
2 1 Cor 11, 23–26
3 Lk 9, 11b–17

Sacred Heart of Jesus
1 Ez 34, 11–16
2 Rom 5, 5b–11
3 Lk 15, 3–7

Ordinary Time

1st Sunday
*(See Baptism of the Lord,
above)*

2nd Sunday
1 Is 62, 1–5
2 1 Cor 12, 4–11
3 Jn 2, 1–12

3rd Sunday
1 Neh 8, 2–4a. 5–6.
    8–10
2 1 Cor 12, 12–30
3 Lk 1, 1–4; 4, 14–21

4th Sunday
1 Jer 1, 4–5. 17–19
2 1 Cor 12, 31—13,
    13
3 Lk 4, 21–30

5th Sunday
1 Is 6, 1–2a. 3–8
2 1 Cor 15, 1–11
3 Lk 5, 1–11

6th Sunday
1 Jer 17, 5–8
2 1 Cor 15, 12. 16–20
3 Lk 6, 17. 20–26

7th Sunday
1 1 Sm 26, 2. 7–9
    12–13. 22–23
2 1 Cor 15, 45–49
3 Lk 6, 27–38

8th Sunday
1 Sir 27, 5–8
2 1 Cor 15, 54–58
3 Lk 6, 39–45

9th Sunday
1 1 Kgs 8, 41–43
2 Gal 1, 1–2. 6–10
3 Lk 7, 1–10

10th Sunday
1 1 Kgs 17, 17–24
2 Gal 1, 11–19
3 Lk 7, 11–17

11th Sunday
1 2 Sm 12, 7–10.
   13
2 Gal 2, 16. 19–21
3 Lk 7, 36—8, 3

12th Sunday
1 Zec 12, 10–11
2 Gal 3, 26–29
3 Lk 9, 18–24

13th Sunday
1 1 Kgs 19, 16b.
   19–21
2 Gal 5, 1. 13–18
3 Lk 9, 51–62

14th Sunday
1 Is 66, 10–14c
2 Gal 6, 14–18
3 Lk 10, 1–12. 17–
   20

15th Sunday
1 Dt 30, 10–14

2 Col 1, 15–20
3 Lk 10, 25–37

16th Sunday
1 Gn 18, 1–10a
2 Col 1, 24–28
3 Lk 10, 38–42

17th Sunday
1 Gn 18, 20–32
2 Col 2, 12–14
3 Lk 11, 1–13

18th Sunday
1 Eccl 1, 2; 2, 21–23
2 Col 3, 1–5. 9–11
3 Lk 12, 13–31

19th Sunday
1 Wis 18, 6–9
2 Heb 11, 1–2. 8–19
3 Lk 12, 32–48

20th Sunday
1 Jer 38, 4–6. 8–10
2 Heb 12, 1–4
3 Lk 12, 49–53

21st Sunday
1 Is 66, 18–21
2 Heb 12, 5–7. 11–
   13
3 Lk 13, 22–30

22nd Sunday
1 Sir 3, 19–21. 30–31

2 Heb 12, 18–19.
   22–24a
3 Lk 14, 1. 7–14

23rd Sunday
1 Wis 9, 13–19
2 Phlm 9b–10. 12–
   17
3 Lk 14, 25–33

24th Sunday
1 Ex 32, 7–11. 13–
   14
2 1 Tm 1, 12–17
3 Lk 15, 1–32

25th Sunday
1 Am 8, 4–7
2 1 Tm 2, 1–8
3 Lk 16, 1–13

26th Sunday
1 Am 6, 1a. 4–7
2 1 Tm 6, 11–16
3 Lk 16, 19–31

27th Sunday
1 Hb 1, 2–3; 2,
   2–4
2 2 Tm 1, 6–8. 13–
   14
3 Lk 17, 5–10

28th Sunday
1 2 Kgs 5, 14–17

2 2 Tm 2, 8–13
3 Lk 17, 11–19

29th Sunday
1 Ex 17, 8–13
2 2 Tm 3, 14—4, 2
3 Lk 18, 1–8

30th Sunday
1 Sir 35, 15b–17.
   20–22a
2 2 Tm 4, 6–8. 16–
   18
3 Lk 18, 9–14

31st Sunday
1 Wis 11, 23—12, 2
2 2 Thes 1, 11—2, 2
3 Lk 19, 1–10

32nd Sunday
1 2 Mc 7, 1–2. 9–14
2 2 Thes 2, 16—3, 5
3 Lk 20, 27–38

33rd Sunday
1 Mal 3, 19–20a
2 2 Thes 3, 7–12
3 Lk 21, 5–19

34th Sunday
(Christ the King)
1 2 Sm 5, 1–3
2 Col 1, 12–20
3 Lk 23, 35–43

READINGS FOR THE MAJOR FEASTS OF THE YEAR

Feb. 2: Presentation of the Lord
1 Mal 3, 1–4
2 Heb 2, 14–18
3 Lk 2, 22–40

Mar. 19: Joseph, Husband of Mary
1 2 Sm 7, 4–5a.
   12–14a. 16
2 Rom 4, 13. 16–18.
   22
3 Mt 1, 16. 18–21.
   24a
   or Lk 2, 41–51a

Mar. 25: Annunciation
1 Is 7, 10–14
2 Heb 10, 4–10
3 Lk 1, 26–28

June 24: John the Baptist Vigil
1 Jer 1, 4–10
2 1 Pt 1, 8–12
3 Lk 1, 5–17

Mass of the Day
1 Is 49, 1–6
2 Acts 13, 22–26
3 Lk 1, 57–66. 80

June 29: Peter and Paul Vigil
1 Acts 3, 1–10
2 Gal 1, 11–20
3 Jn 21, 15–19

Mass of the Day
1 Acts 12, 1–11
2 2 Tm 4, 6–8. 17–18
3 Mt 16, 13–19

Aug. 6: Transfiguration
1 Dn 7, 9–10. 13–
   14
2 2 Pt 1, 16–19
3 (A) Mt 7, 1–9
   (B) Mk 9, 2–10
   (C) Lk 9, 28b–36

Aug. 15: Assumption Vigil
1 1 Chr 15, 3–4. 15;
   16, 1–2
2 1 Cor 15, 54–57
3 Lk 11, 27–28

Mass of the Day
1 Rv 11, 19a; 12,
   1–6a. 10ab
2 1 Cor 15, 20–26
3 Lk 1, 39–56

Sept. 14: Triumph of the Cross
1 Nm 21, 4–9
2 Phil 2, 6–11
3 Jn 3, 13–17

Nov. 1: All Saints
1 Rv 7, 2–4. 9–14
2 1 Jn 3, 1–3
3 Mt 5, 1–12a

Nov. 2: All Souls
First Mass
1 Jb 19, 1. 23–27
2 1 Cor 15, 51–57
3 Jn 6, 37–40

Second Mass
1 Wis 3, 1–9
2 Phil 3, 20–21
3 Jn 11, 17–27

Third Mass
1   2 Mc 12, 43–46
2   Rv 14, 13
3   Jn 14, 1–6
(Other Readings may be chosen)

Nov. 9: Dedication of St. John Lateran
1   2 Chr 5, 6–10. 13—6, 2

2   1 Cor 3, 9–13. 16–17
3   Lk 19, 1–10
(Other Readings may be chosen)

Dec. 8: Immaculate Conception
1   Gn 3, 9–15. 20
2   Eph 1, 3–6. 11–12
3   Lk 1, 26–38

WEEKDAY READINGS

Advent Season

First Week of Advent

Monday: Is 2, 1–5 (Year A Is 4, 2–6); Mt 8, 5–11
Tuesday: Is 11, 1–10; Lk 10, 21–24
Wednesday: Is 25, 6–10a; Mt 15, 29–37
Thursday: Is 26, 1–6; Mt 7, 21. 24–27
Friday: Is 29, 17–24; Mt 9, 27–31
Saturday: Is 30, 19–21. 23–26; Mt 9, 35—10, 1. 6–8

Second Week of Advent

Monday: Is 35, 1–10; Lk 5, 17–26
Tuesday: Is 40, 1–11; Mt 18, 12–14
Wednesday: Is 40, 25–31; Mt 11, 28–30
Thursday: Is 41, 13–20; Mt 11, 11–15
Friday: Is 48, 17–19; Mt 11, 16–19
Saturday: Sir 48, 1–4. 9–11; Mt 17, 10–13

Third Week of Advent

Monday: Num 24, 2–7. 15–17a; Mt 21, 23–27
Tuesday: Zep 3, 1–2. 9–13; Mt 21, 28–32
Wednesday: Is 45, 6b–8. 18. 21b–25; Lk 7, 18b–23
Thursday: Is 54, 1–10; Lk 7, 24–30
Friday: Is 56, 1–3a. 6–8; Jn 5, 33–36
Dec. 17: Gn 49, 2. 8–10; Mt 1, 1–17
Dec. 18: Jer 23, 5–8; Mt 1, 18–24
Dec. 19: Jgs 13, 2–7. 24–25a; Lk 1, 5–25
Dec. 20: Is 7, 10–14; Lk 1, 26–38
Dec. 21: Sg 2, 8–14 or Zep 3, 14–18a; Lk 1, 39–45

Dec. 22: 1 Sm 1, 24–28; Lk 1, 46–56
Dec. 23: Mal 3, 1–4. 23–24; Lk 1, 57–66
Dec. 24: 2 Sm 7, 1–5. 8b–11. 16; Lk 1, 67–79

Christmas Season

Octave of Christmas

Second day (St. Stephen): Acts 6, 8–10; 7, 54–59; Mt 10, 17–22
Third day (St. John): 1 Jn 1, 1–4; Jn 20, 2–8
Fourth day (Holy Innocents): 1 Jn 1, 5—2, 2; Mt 2, 13–18
Fifth day: 1 Jn 2, 3–11; Lk 2, 22–35
Sixth day: 1 Jn 2, 12–17; Lk 2, 36–40
Seventh day: 1 Jn 2, 18–21; Jn 1, 1–18
January 2: 1 Jn 2, 22–28; Jn 1, 19–28
January 3: 1 Jn 2, 29—3, 6; Jn 1, 29–34
January 4: 1 Jn 3, 7–10; Jn 1, 35–42
January 5: 1 Jn 3, 11–21; Jn 1, 43–51
January 6 (if Epiphany not celebrated): 1 Jn 5, 5–13; Mk 1, 6b–11
Readings may vary slightly depending on when Epiphany is celebrated

Week After Epiphany

Monday after Epiphany: 1 Jn 3, 22—4, 6; Mt 4, 12–17. 23–25
Tuesday after Epiphany: 1 Jn 4, 7–10; Mk 6, 34–44
Wednesday after Epiphany: 1 Jn 4, 11–18; Mk 6, 45–52
Thursday after Epiphany: 1 Jn 4, 19—5, 4; Lk 4, 14–22a

Friday after Epiphany: 1 Jn 5, 5–13; Lk 5, 12–16
Saturday after Epiphany: 1 Jn 5, 14–21; Jn 3, 22–30

Lenten Season

Ash Wednesday: Jl 2, 12–18; 2 Cor 5, 20—6, 2; Mt 6, 1–6. 16–18
Thursday after Ash Wednesday: Dt 30, 15–20; Lk 9, 22–25
Friday after Ash Wednesday: Is 58, 1–9a; Mt 9, 14–15
Saturday after Ash Wednesday: Is 58, 9b–14; Lk 5, 27–32

First Week of Lent

Monday: Lv 19, 1–2. 11–18; Mt 25, 31–46
Tuesday: Is 55, 10–11; Mt 6, 7–15
Wednesday: Jon 3, 1–10; Lk 11, 29–32
Thursday: Est C, 12. 14–16. 23–25; Mt 7, 7–12
Friday: Ez 18, 21–28; Mt 5, 20–26
Saturday: Dt 26, 16–19; Mt 5, 43–48

Second Week of Lent

Monday: Dn 9, 4b–10; Lk 6, 36–38
Tuesday: Is 1, 10. 16–20; Mt 23, 1–12
Wednesday: Jer 18, 18–20; Mt 20, 17–28
Thursday: Jer 17, 5–10; Lk 16, 19–31
Friday: Gn 37, 3–4. 12–13a. 17b–28; Mt 21, 33–43. 45–46
Saturday: Mi 7, 14–15. 18–20; Lk 15, 1–3. 11–32

Third Week of Lent

Monday: 2 Kgs 5, 1–15a; Lk 4, 24–30
Tuesday: Dn 3, 25. 34–43; Mt 18, 21–35

Wednesday: Dt 4, 1. 5–9; Mt 5,
　17–19
Thursday: Jer 7, 23–28; Lk 11,
　14–23
Friday: Hos 14, 2–10; Mk 12,
　28b–34
Saturday: Hos 6, 1–6; Lk 18,
　19–24

Fourth Week of Lent
Monday: Is 65, 17–21; Jn 4,
　43–54
Tuesday: Ez 47, 1–9. 12; Jn 5,
　1–3a. 5–16
Wednesday: Is 49, 8–15; Jn 5,
　17–30
Thursday: Ex 32, 7–14; Jn 5,
　31–47
Friday: Wis 2, 1a. 12–22; Jn 7,
　1–2. 10. 25–30
Saturday: Jer 11, 18–20; Jn 7,
　40–53

Fifth Week of Lent
Monday: Dn 13, 1–9. 15–17.
　19–30. 33–62; Jn 8, 1–11
　(Year C: Jn 8, 12–20)
Tuesday: Nm 21, 4–9; Jn 8, 21–30
Wednesday: Dn 3, 14–20. 91–92.
　95; Jn 8, 31–42
Thursday: Gn 17, 3–9; Jn 8, 51–59
Friday: Jer 20, 10–13; Jn 10,
　31–42
Saturday: Ez 37, 21–28; Jn 11,
　45–56

Holy Week
Monday: Is 42, 1–7; Jn 12, 1–11
Tuesday: Is 49, 1–6; Jn 13, 21–33.
　36–38
Wednesday: Is 50, 4–9a; Mt 26,
　14–25
Thursday Chrism Mass: Is 61,
　1–3a. 6a. 8b–9; Rv 1, 5–8;
　Lk 4, 16–21

Easter Season

Octave of Easter
Monday: Acts 2, 14. 22–32;
　Mt 28, 8–15
Tuesday: Acts 2, 36–41; Jn 20,
　11–18
Wednesday: Acts 3, 1–10; Lk 24,
　13–35
Thursday: Acts 3, 11–26; Lk 24,
　35–48
Friday: Acts 4, 1–12; Jn 21, 1–14

Saturday: Acts 4, 13–21; Mk 16,
　9–15

Second Week of Easter
Monday: Acts 4, 23–31; Jn 3, 1–8
Tuesday: Acts 4, 32–37; Jn 3, 7–15
Wednesday: Acts 5, 17–26; Jn 3,
　16–21
Thursday: Acts 5, 27–33; Jn 3,
　31–36
Friday: Acts 5, 34–42; Jn 6, 1–15
Saturday: Acts 6, 1–7; Jn 6, 16–21

Third Week of Easter
Monday: Acts 6, 8–15; Jn 6, 22–29
Tuesday: Acts 7, 51—8, 1a; Jn 6,
　30–35
Wednesday: Acts 8, 1–8; Jn 6,
　35–40
Thursday: Acts 8, 26–40; Jn 6,
　44–51
Friday: Acts 9, 1–20; Jn 6, 52–59
Saturday: Acts 9, 31–42; Jn 6,
　60–69

Fourth Week of Easter
Monday: Acts 11, 1–18; Jn 10,
　1–10 (Year A: Jn 10, 11–18)
Tuesday: Acts 11, 19–26; Jn 10,
　22–30
Wednesday: Acts 12, 24—13, 5a;
　Jn 12, 44–50
Thursday: Acts 13, 13–25; Jn 13,
　16–20
Friday: Acts 13, 26–33; Jn 14,
　1–6
Saturday: Acts 13, 44–52; Jn 14,
　7–14

Fifth Week of Easter
Monday: Acts 14, 5–18; Jn 14,
　21–26
Tuesday: Acts 14, 19–28; Jn 14,
　27–31a
Wednesday: Acts 15, 1–6; Jn 15,
　1–8
Thursday: Acts 15, 7–21; Jn 15,
　9–11
Friday: Acts 15, 22–31; Jn 15,
　12–17
Saturday: Acts 16, 1–10; Jn 15,
　18–21

Sixth Week of Easter
Monday: Acts 16, 11–15; John 15,
　26—16, 4a
Tuesday: Acts 16, 22–34; Jn 16,
　5–11

Wednesday: Acts 17, 15. 22—18,
　1; Jn 16, 12–15
Thursday: Acts 18, 1–8; Jn 16,
　16–20
Friday: Acts 18, 9–18; Jn 16,
　20–23a
Saturday: Acts 18, 23–28; Jn 16,
　23b–28

Seventh Week of Easter
Monday: Acts 19, 1–8; Jn 16,
　29–33
Tuesday: Acts 20, 17–27; Jn 17,
　1–11a
Wednesday: Acts 20, 28–38; Jn 17,
　11b–19
Thursday: Acts 22, 30; 23, 6–11;
　Jn 17, 20–26
Friday: Acts 25, 13–21; Jn 21,
　15–19
Saturday: Acts 28, 16–20. 30–31;
　Jn 21, 20–25

SEASON OF THE YEAR
*(I is the reading for Year 1; II
is the reading for Year II; the
Gospel is the same each year)*

Week One
Monday: I – Heb 1, 1–6; II –
　1 Sm 1, 1–8; Mk 1, 14–20
Tuesday: I – Heb 2, 5–12; II –
　1 Sm 1, 9–20; Mk 1, 21–28
Wednesday: I – Heb 2, 14–18;
　II – 1 Sm 3, 1–10. 19–20; Mk
　1, 29–39
Thursday: I – Heb 3, 7–14; II –
　1 Sm 4, 1–11; Mk 1, 40–45
Friday: I – Heb 4, 1–5. 11; II –
　1 Sm 8, 4–7. 10–22a; Mk 2,
　1–12
Saturday: I – Heb 4, 12–16; II –
　1 Sm 9, 1–14. 17–19; 10, 1a;
　Mk 2, 13–17

Week Two
Monday: I – Heb 5, 1–10; II –
　1 Sm 15, 16–23; Mk 2, 18–22
Tuesday: I – Heb 6, 10–20; II –
　1 Sm 16, 1–13; Mk 2, 23–28
Wednesday: I – Heb 7, 1–3.
　15–17; II – 1 Sm 17, 32–33.
　37. 40–51; Mk 3, 1–6
Thursday: I – Heb 7, 25—8, 6; II –
　1 Sm 18, 6–9; 19, 1–7; Mk 3,
　7–12
Friday: I – Heb 8, 6–13; II – 1 Sm
　24, 3–21; Mk 3, 13–19

Saturday: I – Heb 9, 2–3. 11–14;
II – 2 Sm 1, 1–4. 11–12. 19.
23–27; Mk 3, 20–21

Week Three
Monday: I – Heb 9, 15. 24–28; II –
2 Sm 5, 1–7. 10; Mk 3, 22–30
Tuesday: I – Heb 10, 1–10; II –
2 Sm 6, 12b–15. 17–19;
Mk 3, 31–35
Wednesday: I – Heb 10, 11–18;
II – 2 Sm 7, 4–17; Mk 4,
1–20
Thursday: I – Heb 10, 19–25; II –
2 Sm 7, 18–19. 24–29; Mk 4,
21–25
Friday: I – Heb 10, 32–39; II –
2 Sm 11, 1–4a. 5–10a. 13–17;
Mk 4, 26–34
Saturday: I – Heb 11, 1–2. 8–9;
II – 2 Sm 12, 1–7a. 10–17;
Mk 4, 35–41

Week Four
Monday: I – Heb 11, 32–40; II –
2 Sm 15, 13–14. 30; 16,
5–13a; Mk 5, 1–20
Tuesday: I – Heb 12, 1–4; II –
2 Sm 18, 9–10. 14b. 24–25a.
30—19, 3; Mk 5, 21–43
Wednesday: I – Heb 12, 4–7.
11–15; II – 2 Sm 24, 2. 9–17;
Mk 6, 1–6
Thursday: I – Heb 12, 18–19.
21–24; II – 1 Kgs 2, 1–4.
10–12; Mk 6, 7–13
Friday: I – Heb 13, 1–8; II – Sir
47, 2–11; Mk 6, 14–29
Saturday: 1 – Heb 13, 15–17.
20–21; II – 1 Kgs 3, 4–13;
Mk 6, 30–34

Week Five
Monday: I – Gn 1, 1–19; II –
1 Kgs 8, 1–7. 9–13; Mk 6,
53–56
Tuesday: I – Gn 1, 20—2, 4a; II –
1 Kgs 8, 22–23. 27–30; Mk 7,
1–13
Wednesday: I – Gn 2, 4b–9.
15–17; II – 1 Kgs 10, 1–10;
Mk 7, 14–23
Thursday: I – Gn 2, 18–25; II –
1 Kgs 11, 4–13; Mk 7, 24–30
Friday: I – Gn 3, 1–8; II – 1 Kgs
11, 29–32; 12, 19; Mk 7,
31–37

Saturday: I – Gn 3, 9–24; II –
1 Kgs 12, 26–32; 13, 33–34;
Mk 8, 1–10

Week Six
Monday: I – Gn 4, 1–15. 25; II –
Jas 1, 1–11; Mk 8, 11–13
Tuesday: I – Gn 6, 5–8; 7, 1–5. 10;
II – Jas 1, 12–18; Mk 8,
14–21
Wednesday: I – Gn 8, 6–13.
20–22; II – Jas 1, 19–27;
Mk 8, 22–26
Thursday: I – Gn 9, 1–13; II –
Jas 2, 1–9; Mk 8, 27–33
Friday: I – Gn 11, 1–9; II –
Jas 2, 14–24. 26; Mk 8, 34—
9, 1
Saturday: I – Heb 11, 1–7; II –
Jas 3, 1–10; Mk 9, 2–13

Week Seven
Monday: I – Sir 1, 1–10; II – Jas 3,
13–18; Mk 9, 14–29
Tuesday: I – Sir 2, 1–11; II – Jas 4,
1–10; Mk 9, 30–37
Wednesday: I – Sir 4, 11–19; II –
Jas 4, 13–17; Mk 9, 38–40
Thursday: I – Sir 5, 1–8; II – Jas 5,
1–6; Mk 9, 41–50
Friday: I – Sir 6, 5–17; II – Jas 5,
9–12; Mk 10, 1–12
Saturday: I – Sir 17, 1–15; II –
Jas 5, 13–20; Mk 10, 13–16

Week Eight
Monday: I – Sir 17, 19–27; II –
1 Pt 1, 3–9; Mk 10, 17–27
Tuesday: I – Sir 35, 1–12; II – 1 Pt
1, 10–16; Mk 10, 28–31
Wednesday: I – Sir 36, 1. 5–6.
10–17; II – 1 Pt 1, 18–25; Mk
10, 32–45
Thursday: I – Sir 42, 15–25; II –
1 Pt 2, 2–5. 9–12; Mk 10,
46–52
Friday: I – Sir 44, 1. 9–13; II –
1 Pt 4, 7–13; Mk 11, 11–26
Saturday: I – Sir 51, 12b–20; II –
Jude 17, 20b–25; Mk 11,
27–33

Week Nine
Monday: I – Tb 1, 1a–2; 2, 1–9;
II – 2 Pt 1, 2–7; Mk 12, 1–12
Tuesday: I – Tb 2, 9–14; II – 2 Pt
3, 12–15a. 17–18; Mk 12,
13–17

Wednesday: I – Tb 3, 1–11. 16;
II – 2 Tm 1, 1–3. 6–12; Mk
12, 18–27
Thursday: I – Tb 6, 10–11; 7, 1.
9–17; 8, 4–7; II – 2 Tm 2,
8–15; Mk 12, 28b–34
Friday: I – Tb 11, 5–17; II – 2 Tm
3, 10–17; Mk 12, 35–37
Saturday: I – Tb 12, 1. 5–15. 20;
II – 2 Tm 4, 1–8; Mk 12,
38–44

Week Ten
Monday: I – 2 Cor 1, 1–7; II –
1 Kgs 17, 1–6; Mt 5, 1–12
Tuesday: I – 2 Cor 1, 18–22; II –
1 Kgs 17, 7–16; Mt 5, 13–16
Wednesday: I – 2 Cor 3, 4–11; II –
1 Kgs 18, 20–39; Mt 5, 17–19
Thursday: I – 2 Cor 3, 15—4, 1.
3–6; II – 1 Kgs 18, 41–46; Mt
5, 20–26
Friday: I – 2 Cor 4, 7–15; II –
1 Kgs 19, 9a. 11–16; Mt 5,
27–32
Saturday: I – 2 Cor 5, 14–21; II –
1 Kgs 19, 19–21; Mt 5, 33–37

Week Eleven
Monday: I – 2 Cor 6, 1–10; II –
1 Kgs 21, 1–16; Mt 5, 38–42
Tuesday: I – 2 Cor 8, 1–9; II – 1
Kgs 21, 17–29; Mt 5, 43–48
Wednesday: I – 2 Cor 9, 6–11; II –
1 Kgs 2, 1. 6–14; Mt 6, 1–6.
16–18
Thursday: I – 2 Cor 11, 1–11; II –
Sir 48, 1–15; Mt 6, 7–15
Friday: I – 2 Cor 11, 18. 21b–30;
II – 2 Kgs 11, 1–4. 9–18. 20;
Mt 6, 19–23
Saturday: I – 2 Cor 12, 1–10; II –
2 Chr 24, 17–25; Mt 6, 24–34

Week Twelve
Monday: I – Gn 12, 1–9; II –
2 Kgs 17, 5–8. 13–15a. 18;
Mt 7, 1–5
Tuesday: I – Gn 13, 2. 5–8; II –
2 Kgs 19, 9b–11. 14–21.
31–35a. 36; Mt 7, 6. 12–14
Wednesday: I – Gn 15, 1–12.
17–18; II – 2 Kgs 22, 8–13;
23, 1–3; Mt 7, 15–20
Thursday: I – Gn 16, 1–12. 15–16;
II – 2 Kgs 24, 8–17; Mt 7,
21–29

Friday: I – Gn 17, 1. 9–10. 15–22;
II – 2 Kgs 25, 1–12; Mt 8,
1–4
Saturday: I – Gn 18, 1–15; II –
Lam 2, 2. 10–14. 18–19; Mt
8, 5–17

Week Thirteen
Monday: I – Gn 18, 16–33; II –
Am 2, 6–10. 13–16; Mt 8,
18–22
Tuesday: I – Gn 19, 15–29; II –
Am 3, 1–8; 4, 11–12; Mt 8,
23–27
Wednesday: I – Gn 21, 5. 8–20;
II – Am 5, 14–15. 21–24; Mt
8, 28–34
Thursday: I – Gn 22, 1–19; II –
Am 7, 10–17; Mt 9, 1–8
Friday: I – Gn 23, 1–4. 19; 24,
1–8. 62–67; II – Am 8, 4–6.
9–12; Mt 9, 9–13
Saturday: I – Gn 27, 1–5. 15–29;
II – Am 9, 11–15; Mt 9,
14–17

Week Fourteen
Monday: I – Gn 28, 10–22a; II –
Hos 2, 16. 17b–18. 21–22; Mt
9, 18–26
Tuesday: I – Gn 32, 22–33; II –
Hos 8, 4–7. 11–13; Mt 9,
32–38
Wednesday: I – Gn 41, 51–57; 42,
5–7a. 17–24a; II – Hos 10,
1–3. 7–8. 12; Mt 10, 1–7
Thursday: I – Gn 44, 18–21.
23b–29; 45, 1–5; II – Hos 11,
1. 3–4. 8c–9; Mt 10, 7–15
Friday: I – Gn 46, 1–7. 28–30; II –
Hos 14, 2–10; Mt 10, 16–23
Saturday: I – Gn 49, 29–33; 50,
15–24; II – Is 6, 1–8; Mt 10,
24–33

Week Fifteen
Monday: I – Ex 1, 8–14. 22; II –
Is 1, 10–17; Mt 10, 34—
11, 1
Tuesday: I – Ex 2, 1–15a; II – Is 7,
1–9; Mt 11, 20–24
Wednesday: I – Ex 3, 1–6. 9–12;
II – Is 10, 5–7. 13–16; Mt 11,
25–27
Thursday: I – Ex 3, 13–20; II – Is
26, 7–9. 12. 16–19; Mt 11,
28–30

Friday: I – Ex 11, 10–12. 14;
II – Is 38, 1–6. 21–22. 7–8;
Mt 12, 1–8
Saturday: I – Ex 12, 37–42; II –
Mi 2, 1–5; Mt 12, 14–21

Week Sixteen
Monday: I – Ex 14, 5–18; II –
Mi 6, 1–4. 6–8; Mt 12,
38–42
Tuesday: I – Ex 14, 21—15, 1;
II – Mi 7, 14–15. 18–20; Mt
12, 46–50
Wednesday: I – Ex 16, 1–5. 9–15;
II – Jer 1, 1. 4–10; Mt 13, 1–9
Thursday: I – Ex 19, 1–2. 9–11.
16–20b; II – Jer 2, 1–3. 7–8.
12–13; Mt 13, 10–17
Friday: I – Ex 20, 1–17; II – Jer 3,
14–17; Mt 13, 18–23
Saturday: I – Ex 24, 3–8; II – Jer
7, 1–11; Mt 13, 24–30

Week Seventeen
Monday: I – Ex 32, 15–24. 30–34;
II – Jer 13, 1–11; Mt 13,
31–35
Tuesday: I – Ex 33, 7–11; 34,
5b–9. 28; II – Jer 14, 17–22;
Mt 13, 36–43
Wednesday: I – Ex 34, 29–34; II –
Jer 15, 10. 16–21; Mt 13,
44–46
Thursday: I – Ex 40, 16–21.
34–38; II – Jer 18, 1–6; Mt
13, 47–53
Friday: I – Lv 23, 1. 4–11. 15–16.
27. 34b–37; II – Jer 26, 1–9;
Mt 13, 54–58
Saturday: I – Lv 25, 1. 8–17; II –
Jer 26, 11–16. 24; Mt 14,
1–12

Week Eighteen
Monday: I – Nm 11, 4b–15; II –
Jer 28, 1–17; Mt 14, 13–21 or
Mt 14, 22–36
Tuesday: I – Nm 12, 1–13; II – Jer
30, 1–2. 12–15. 18–22; Mt
14, 22–36 or Mt 15, 1–2.
10–14
Wednesday: I – Nm 13, 1–2a.
25—14, 1. 26–29. 34–35;
II – Jer 31, 1–7; Mt 15, 21–28
Thursday: I – Nm 20, 1–13; II –
Jer 31, 31–34; Mt 16,
13–23

Friday: I – Dt 4, 32–40; II – Na 2,
1. 3; 3, 1–3. 6–7; Mt 16,
24–28
Saturday: I – Dt 6, 4–13; II – Hb 1,
12—2, 4; Mt 17, 14–20

Week Nineteen
Monday: I – Dt 10, 12–22; II –
Ez 1, 2–5. 24–28c; Mt 17,
22–27
Tuesday: I – Dt 31, 1–8; II – Ez 2,
8—3, 4; Mt 18, 1–5. 10.
12–14
Wednesday: I – Dt 34, 1–12; II –
Ez 9, 1–7; 10, 18–22; Mt 18,
15–20
Thursday: I – Jos 3, 7–10a. 11.
13–17; II – Ez 12, 1–12; Mt
18, 21—19, 1
Friday: I – Jos 24, 1–13; II – Ez
16, 1–15. 60. 63; Mt 19, 3–12
Saturday: I – Jos 24, 14–29; II –
Ez 18, 1–10. 13b. 30–32; Mt
19, 13–15

Week Twenty
Monday: I – Jgs 2, 11–19; II –
Ez 24, 15–24; Mt 19, 16–22
Tuesday: I – Jgs 6, 11–24a; II –
Ez 28, 1–10; Mt 19, 23–30
Wednesday: I – Jgs 9, 6–15; II –
Ez 34, 1–11; Mt 20, 1–16a
Thursday: I – Jgs 11, 29–39a; II –
Ez 36, 23–28; Mt 22, 1–14
Friday: I – Ru 1, 1. 3–6. 14b–16.
22; II – Ez 37, 1–14; Mt 22,
34–40
Saturday: I – Ru 2, 1–3. 8–11; 4,
13–17; II – Ez 43, 1–7a; Mt
23, 1–12

Week Twenty-one
Monday: I – 1 Thes 1, 2b–5. 8b–10;
II – 2 Thes 1, 1–5. 11b–12;
Mt 23, 13–22
Tuesday: I – 1 Thes 2, 1–8; II –
2 Thes 2, 1–3a. 13–17; Mt 23,
23–26
Wednesday: I – 1 Thes 2, 9–13;
II – 2 Thes 3, 6–10. 16–18;
Mt 23, 27–32
Thursday: I – 1 Thes 3, 7–13; II –
1 Cor 1, 1–9; Mt 24, 42–51
Friday: I – 1 Thes 4, 1–8; II –
1 Cor 1, 17–25; Mt 25, 1–13
Saturday: I – 1 Thes 4, 9–12; II –
1 Cor 1, 26–31; Mt 25, 14–30

Week Twenty-two

Monday: I – 1 Thes 4, 13–18; II –
1 Cor 2, 1–5; Lk 4, 16–30
Tuesday: I – 1 Thes 5, 1–6. 9–11;
II – 1 Cor 2, 10b–16; Lk 4,
31–37
Wednesday: I – Col 1, 1–8; II –
1 Cor 3, 1–9; Lk 4, 38–44
Thursday: I – Col 1, 9–14; II –
1 Cor 3, 18–23; Lk 5, 1–11
Friday: I – Col 1, 15–20; II – 1 Cor
4, 1–5; Lk 5, 33–39
Saturday: I – Col 1, 21–23; II –
1 Cor 4, 9–15; Lk 6, 1–5

Week Twenty-three

Monday: I – Col 1, 24—2, 3; II –
1 Cor 5, 1–8; Lk 6, 6–11
Tuesday: I – Col 2, 6–15; II –
1 Cor 6, 1–11; Lk 6, 12–19
Wednesday: I – Col 3, 1–11; II –
1 Cor 7, 25–31; Lk 6, 20–26
Thursday: I – Col 3, 12–17; II –
1 Cor 8, 1b–7. 11–13; Lk 6,
27–38
Friday: I – 1 Tm 1, 1–2. 12–14;
II – 1 Cor 9, 16–19. 22b–27;
Lk 6, 39–42
Saturday: I – 1 Tm 1, 15–17; II –
1 Cor 10, 14–22a; Lk 6,
43–49

Week Twenty-four

Monday: I – 1 Tm 2, 1–8; II –
1 Cor 11, 17–26. 33; Lk 7,
1–10
Tuesday: I – 1 Tm 3, 1–13; II –
1 Cor 12, 12–14. 27–31a; Lk
7, 11–17
Wednesday: I – 1 Tm 3, 14–16;
II – 1 Cor 12, 31—13, 13;
Lk 7, 31–35
Thursday: I – 1 Tm 4, 12–16;
II – 1 Cor 15, 1–11; Lk 7,
36–50
Friday: I – 1 Tm 6, 2c–12; II –
1 Cor 15, 12–20; Lk 8, 1–3
Saturday: I – 1 Tm 6, 13–16; II –
1 Cor 15, 36–37. 42–49; Lk
8, 4–15

Week Twenty-five

Monday: I – Ezr 1, 1–6; II – Prv 3,
27–34; Lk 8, 16–18
Tuesday: I – Ezr 6, 7–8. 12b.
14–20; II – Prv 21, 1–6.
10–13; Lk 8, 19–21

Wednesday: I – Ezr 9, 5–9; II –
Prv 30, 5–9; Lk 9, 1–6
Thursday: I – Hg 1, 1–8; II – Eccl
1, 2–11; Lk 9, 7–9
Friday: I – Hg 1, 15b—2, 9; II –
Eccl 3, 1–11; Lk 9, 18–22
Saturday: I – Zec 2, 5–9a. 14–15a;
II – Eccl 11, 9—12, 8; Lk 9,
43b–45

Week Twenty-six

Monday: I – Zec 8, 1–8; II – Jb 1,
6–22; Lk 9, 46–50
Tuesday: I – Zec 8, 20–23; II – Jb
3, 1–3. 11–17. 20–23; Lk 9,
51–56
Wednesday: I – Neh 2, 1–8; II –
Jb 9, 1–12. 14–16; Lk 9,
57–62
Thursday: I – Neh 8, 1–4a. 5–6.
7b–12; II – Jb 19, 12–27; Lk
10, 1–12
Friday: I – Bar 1, 15–22; II – Jb
38, 1. 12–21; 40, 3–5; Lk 10,
13–16
Saturday: I – Bar 4, 5–12. 27–29;
II – Jb 42, 1–3. 5–6. 12–17;
Lk 10, 17–24

Week Twenty-seven

Monday: I – Jon 1, 1—2, 1. 11;
II – Gal 1, 6–12; Lk 10,
25–37
Tuesday: I – Jon 3, 1–10; II – Gal
1, 13–24; Lk 10, 38–42
Wednesday: I – Jon 4, 1–11; II –
Gal 2, 1–2. 7–14; Lk 11, 1–4
Thursday: I – Mal 3, 13–20a;
II – Gal 3, 1–5; Lk 11, 5–13
Friday: I – Jl 1, 13–15; 2, 1–2;
II – Gal 3, 7–14; Lk 11,
15–26
Saturday: I – Jl 4, 12–21; II – Gal
3, 22–29; Lk 11, 27–28

Week Twenty-eight

Monday: I – Rom 1, 1–7; II – Gal
4, 22–24. 26–27; Lk 11,
29–32
Tuesday: I – Rom 1, 16–25; II –
Gal 5, 1–6; Lk 11, 37–41
Wednesday: I – Rom 2, 1–11; II –
Gal 5, 18–25; Lk 11, 42–46
Thursday: I – Rom 3, 21–29; II –
Eph 1, 3–10; Lk 11, 47–54
Friday: I – Rom 4, 1–8; II – Eph 1,
11–14; Lk 12, 1–7

Saturday: I – Rom 4, 13. 16–18;
II – Eph 1, 15–23; Lk 12,
8–12

Week Twenty-nine

Monday: I – Rom 4, 20–25; II –
Eph 2, 1–10; Lk 12, 13–21
Tuesday: I – Rom 5, 12. 15b.
17–19. 20b–21; II – Eph 2,
12–22; Lk 12, 35. 38
Wednesday: I – Rom 6, 12–18;
II – Eph 3, 2–12; Lk 12,
39–48
Thursday: I – Rom 6, 19–23; II –
Eph 3, 14–21; Lk 12, 49–53
Friday: I – Rom 7, 18–25a; II –
Eph 4, 1–6; Lk 12, 54–59
Saturday: I – Rom 8, 1–11; II –
Eph 4, 7–16; Lk 13, 1–9

Week Thirty

Monday: I – Rom 8, 12–17; II –
Eph 4, 32—5, 8; Lk 13,
10–17
Tuesday: I – Rom 8, 18–25; II –
Eph 5, 21–33; Lk 13, 18–21
Wednesday: I – Rom 8, 26–30; II –
Eph 6, 1–9; Lk 13, 22–30
Thursday: I – Rom 3, 31b–39; II –
Eph 6, 10–20; Lk 13, 31–35
Friday: I – Rom 9, 1–5; II – Phil 1,
1–11; Lk 14, 1–6
Saturday: I – Rom 11, 1–2a.
11–12. 25–29; II – Phil 1,
18b–26; Lk 14, 1. 7–11

Week Thirty-one

Monday: I – Rom 11, 29–36; II –
Phil 2, 1–4; Lk 14, 12–14
Tuesday: I – Rom 12, 5–16a; II –
Phil 2, 5–11; Lk 14, 15–24
Wednesday: I – Rom 13, 8–10; II –
Phil 2, 12–18; Lk 14, 25–33
Thursday: I – Rom 14, 7–12; II –
Phil 3, 3–8a; Lk 15, 1–10
Friday: I – Rom 15, 14–21; II –
Phil 3, 17—4, 1; Lk 16, 1–8
Saturday: I – Rom 16, 3–9. 16.
22–27; II – Phil 4, 10–19; Lk
16, 9–15

Week Thirty-two

Monday: I – Wis 1, 1–7; II – Ti 1,
1–9; Lk 17, 1–6
Tuesday: I – Wis 2, 23—3, 9; II –
Ti 2, 1–8. 11–14; Lk 17, 7–10
Wednesday: I – Wis 6, 1–11; II –
Ti 3, 1–7; Lk 17, 11–19

Thursday: I – Wis 7, 22—8, 1; II – Phlm 7–20; Lk 17, 20–25

Friday: I – Wis 13, 1–9; II – 2 Jn 4–9; Lk 17, 26–37

Saturday: I – Wis 18, 14–16; 19, 6–9; II – 3 Jn 5–8; Lk 18, 1–8

Week Thirty-three

Monday: I – 1 Mc 1, 10–15. 41–43. 54. 57. 62. 64; II – Rv 1, 1–4; 2, 1–5a; Lk 18, 35–43

Tuesday: I – 2 Mc 6, 18–31; II – Rv 3, 1–6. 14–22; Lk 19, 1–10

Wednesday: I – 2 Mc 7, 1. 20–31; II – Rv 4, 1–11; Lk 19, 11–28

Thursday: I – 1 Mc 2, 15–29; II – Rv 5, 1–10; Lk 19, 41–44

Friday: I – 1 Mc 4, 36–37. 52–59; II – Rv 10, 8–11; Lk 19, 45–48

Saturday: I – 1 Mc 6, 1–13; II – Rv 11, 4–12; Lk 20, 27–40

Week Thirty-four

Monday: I – Dn 1, 1–6. 8–20; II – Rv 14, 1–3. 4b–5; Lk 21, 1–4

Tuesday: I – Dn 2, 31–45; II – Rv 14, 14–19; Lk 21, 5–11

Wednesday: I – Dn 5, 1–6. 13–14. 16–17. 23–28; II – Rv 15, 1–4; Lk 21, 12–19

Thursday: I – Dn 6, 11–28; II – Rv 18, 1–2. 21–23; 19, 1–3. 9a; Lk 21, 20–28

Friday: I – Dn 7, 2–14; II – Rv 20, 1–4; 20, 11—21, 2; Lk 21, 29–33

Saturday: I – Dn 7, 15–27; II – Rv 22, 1–7; Lk 21, 34–36

CHART OF OLD TESTAMENT CANONS

Jewish Canon	Protestant Canon	Roman Catholic/ Orthodox Canon
Torah (LAW)	PENTATEUCH	PENTATEUCH
Genesis	Genesis	Genesis
Exodus	Exodus	Exodus
Leviticus	Leviticus	Leviticus
Numbers	Numbers	Numbers
Deuteronomy	Deuteronomy	Deuteronomy
Nevi'im (PROPHETS)	HISTORIES	HISTORIES
FORMER PROPHETS	Joshua	Joshua
Joshua	Judges	Judges
Judges	Ruth	Ruth
Samuel (1 & 2)	1 & 2 Samuel	1 & 2 Samuel
Kings (1 & 2)	1 & 2 Kings	1 & 2 Kings
	1 & 2 Chronicles	1 & 2 Chronicles
LATTER PROPHETS	Ezra	Ezra
Isaiah	Nehemiah	Nehemiah
Jeremiah	Esther	Tobit
Ezekiel		Judith
The Twelve	POETICAL/WISDOM BOOKS	Esther
Hosea	Job	1 & 2 Maccabees
Joel	Psalms	
Amos	Proverbs	POETICAL/WISDOM BOOKS
Obadiah	Ecclesiastes	Job
Jonah	Song of Solomon	Psalms
Micah		Proverbs
Nahum	PROPHETS	Ecclesiastes
Habakkuk	Isaiah	Song of Solomon
Zephaniah	Jeremiah	Wisdom of Solomon
Haggai	Lamentations	Sirach
Zechariah	Ezekiel	
Malachi	Daniel	PROPHETS
	Hosea	Isaiah
Ketubim (WRITINGS)	Joel	Jeremiah
Psalms	Amos	Lamentations
Proverbs	Obadiah	Baruch
Job	Jonah	Ezekiel
	Micah	Daniel
	Nahum	Hosea

Chart of Old Testament Canons

Jewish Canon	Protestant Canon	Roman Catholic/ Orthodox Canon
(Five Scrolls):	Habakkuk	Joel
Song of Solomon	Zephaniah	Amos
Ruth	Haggai	Obadiah
Lamentations	Zechariah	Jonah
Ecclesiastes	Malachi	Micah
Esther		Nahum
Daniel	THE APOCRYPHA	Habakkuk
Ezra-Nehemiah	1 & 2 Esdras	Zephaniah
Chronicles (1 & 2)	Tobit	Haggai
	Judith	Zechariah
There is no Apocrypha	Esther	Malachi
in the Hebrew Bible	(with additions)	
	Wisdom of Solomon	Orthodox Canons generally
	Ecclesiasticus (Sirach)	include
	Baruch	1 & 2 Esdras
	Letter of Jeremiah	Prayer of Manasseh
	(Baruch ch 6)	Psalm 151
	Prayer of Azariah and Song of	3 Maccabees
	Three	4 Maccabees (as an Appendix)
	Daniel and Susanna	
	Daniel, Bel, & Snake	
	Prayer of Manasseh	
	1 & 2 Maccabees	

TIMELINE OF BIBLICAL TIMES

DATE	PERIOD	
C. 3200–2000 B.C.	**EARLY BRONZE AGE**	
3300–3100	Early Bronze I	Earliest forms of writing
3100–2700	Early Bronze II	Political unification; Early Dynastic period
2700–2600	Early Bronze III	Old Kingdom, Dynasties 3–6
2300–2000	Early Bronze IV	First Intermediate Period
c. 2000–1550 B.C.	**MIDDLE BRONZE AGE**	
2000–1650	Middle Bronze I–II	Middle Kingdom Dynasties 11–12
1650–1550	Middle Bronze III	Second Intermediate (Hyksos) Period
Ca. 1550–1200 B.C.	**LATE BRONZE AGE**	New Kingdom, Dynasties 18–19; Thutmoses III (1479–1425), Akhenaton (1352–1336), Seti I (1294–1279), Ramesses II (1279–1213), Merneptah (1213–1203); Sea Peoples (groups including Philistines) invasions begin
Ca. 1200–586 B.C.	**IRON AGE**	
C. 1200–1025	Iron I	Ramesses III (1184–1153)
Ca. 1025–586	Iron II	
Ca. 1025–928	Iron IIA	
Ca. 928–722	Iron IIB	Shishak I invades Palestine (925)

TIMELINE OF BIBLICAL TIMES

DATE	PERIOD	EGYPT
Ca. 3300–2000 B.C.	**EARLY BRONZE AGE**	
3300–3100	Early Bronze I	Earliest forms of writing
3100–2700	Early Bronze II	Political unification; Early Dynastic period
2700–2300	Early Bronze III	Old Kingdom; Dynasties 3–5
2300–2000	Early Bronze IV	First Intermediate Period
Ca. 2000–1550 B.C.	**MIDDLE BRONZE AGE**	
2000–1650	Middle Bronze I–II	Middle Kingdom; Dynasties 11–12
1650–1550	Middle Bronze III	Second Intermediate/ Hyksos Period
Ca. 1550–1200 B.C.	**LATE BRONZE AGE**	New Kingdom; Dynasties 18–19: Thutmose III (1479–1425), Akenhaten (1352–1336), Seti I (1294–1279), Rameses II (1279–1213), Merneptah (1213–1203); Sea Peoples (groups including Philistines) invasions begin
Ca. 1200–586 B.C.	**IRON AGE**	
Ca. 1200–1025	Iron I	Rameses III (1184–1153)
Ca. 1025–586	Iron II	
Ca. 1025–928	Iron IIA	
Ca. 928–722	Iron IIB	Shishak I invades Palestine (925)

SYRIA-PALESTINE	MESOPOTAMIA, ASIA MINOR
	Earliest forms of writing; Full urbanization; Sumerian culture develops
In Egyptian sphere	High point of Sumerian culture
Flourishing city-states	Sargon of Akkad; Naram-Sin of Akkad; Gudea of Lagash
Decline/abandonment of city-states	Third Dynasty of Ur
Revival of urbanism; Invention of alphabet	Amorite kingdoms: Shamshi-Adad of Assyria (ca. 1813–1781); Hammurapi of Babylon (ca. 1792–1750); Rise of Hittites
In Egyptian sphere; Rise of Mitanni in north; Ugarit flourishes;	
Exodus of the Hebrews from Egypt;	Hittites challenge Egypt for control of Syria;
Collapse of city-states	Hittite empire collapses; Trojan War
Israel emerges in Canaan; Philistines settle on SW coast; Small city-states develop in Phoenicia, Syria, Transjordan	Resurgence of Assyria: Tiglath-pileser I (1114–1076)
United Monarchy in Israel: Saul (1025–1005); David (1005–965); Solomon (968–928)	

Divided Monarchy:
JUDAH: ISRAEL:
Rehoboam (928–911) Jeroboam I (928–907)
                  Omri (882–871); Capital at
                  Samaria
	Rise of Neo-Assyrian Empire
	Shalmaneser III (858–824);
	Battle of Qarqar (853)

DATE	PERIOD	EGYPT
Ca. 722–586	Iron IIC	
		Egypt conquered by Assyria (671) Psammetichus I (664–610)
		Neco II (610–595)
Ca. 586–539	NEO-BABYLONIAN	

		GREECE AND ROME
539–332	PERSIAN	
		Greeks repel Persian invasions
		Peloponnesian War (431–404)
332–63	HELLENISTIC	Alexander the Great (336–323); Defeats Persians at Issus (332); Occupies the Levant and Egypt
		Rome gains control over Greece (ca. 188–146);

SYRIA-PALESTINE		MESOPOTAMIA, ASIA MINOR
	Ahab (873–852)	
	Prophet Elijah (mid-ninth	
Jehoshaphat	century)	
(867–846)	Prophet Elisha (mid-	
	to late ninth century)	
	Jehu (842–814)	
Athaliah (842–836)	Jehoash (800–788)	
Jehoash (836–798)	Jeroboam II (788–747)	Adad-nirari III (811–783)
	Prophet Amos (mid-	
	eighth century)	
	Prophet Hosea (mid-	
	eighth century)	Tiglath-pileser III (745–727);
	Hoshea (732–722)	Assyrian conquest of the Levant
Ahaz (743/735–		Shalmaneser V (727–722)
727/715)		Samaria captured (722)

JUDAH:

Prophet Isaiah (late eighth to early seventh centuries)	Sargon II (722–705)
Prophet Micah (late eighth century)	Sennacherib (705–681); Attack on Judah and
Hezekiah (727/715–698/687)	seige of Jerusalem (701)
Manasseh (698/687–642)	Esar-haddon (681–669)
Josiah (639–609)	Ashurbanipal (669–627)
Prophet Zephaniah (late seventh century)	
Prophet Jeremiah (late seventh to early sixth centuries)	Rise of Babylon
Jehoahaz (609)	Assyrian capital of Nineveh captured (612)
Jehoiakim (608–598)	
Jehoiachin (597)	Nebuchadrezzar II (604–562) of Babylon
Prophet Ezekiel (early sixth century)	
Zedekiah (597–586); Capture of Jerusalem (586)	
	Nabonidus (556–539)

EASTERN MEDITERRANEAN

	Cyrus II (the Great) (559–530);
	Capture of Babylon
Some exiles return from Babylon (538)	Cambyses (530–522); Capture of Egypt (525)
Second Temple built (520–515)	Darius I (522–486)
Prophet Haggai (520); Prophet Zechariah (520–518)	Xerxes I (486–465)
Nehemiah governor of Judah (ca. 445–430)	Artaxerxes I (465–424)
Mission of Ezra the scribe (mid-fifth [or early	Artaxerxes II (405–359)
fourth] century)	

Seleucus I (312/311–281) controls Syria and
  Mesopotamia
Ptolemy I (323–282) controls Egypt, Palestine,
  Phoenicia
Antiochus III (223–187) gains control of southern
  Syria, Phoenicia, and Judea from Ptolemy IV
  (202–198)
Ben Sira (Sirach) (early second century)

DATE	PERIOD	GREECE AND ROME
		Sack of Carthage and Corinth (146)
63 B.C.–330 A.D.	ROMAN	Julius Caesar named dictator (49); assassinated (44)
		Octavian (Augustus) defeats Antony at Actium (31); (Emperor 27 B.C.–14 A.D.)
		Tiberius (14–37 CE)
		Gaius (Caligula) (37–41)
		Claudius (41–54)
		Nero (54–68)
		Vespasian (69–79)
		Titus (79–81)
		Domitian (81–96)
		Nerva (96–98)
		Trajan (98–117)
		Hadrian (117–138)

EASTERN MEDITERRANEAN	MESOPOTAMIA, ASIA MINOR
Antiochus IV Epiphanes (175–164) Revolt of the Maccabees (167–164) HASMONEAN RULE OF JUDEA (165–37): John Hyrcanus (135–104); Alexander Janneus (103–76); Salome Alexandra (76–67)	

Pompey conquers the Levant (66–62); Enters
  Jerusalem (63)
Herod the Great king of Judea (37–4); Rebuilds
  Second Temple
(Herod) Antipas (4 B.C.–39 A.D.)
Life of Jesus of Nazareth (ca. 4 B.C.–30 A.D.)
Pontius Pilate governor of Judea (26–36)
(Herod) Agrippa I (39–44)
Missionary activity of Paul (mid-first century)
(Herod) Agrippa II (53–93)
First Jewish Revolt in Judea against Rome (66–73);
  Jerusalem is captured (70)
 	
Jewish revolts in Egypt, Libya, Cyprus (115–118)
Second Jewish Revolt in Judea against Rome
  (132–135)	

MEASURES AND WEIGHTS

The modern equivalents for biblical measures and weights are presented in the following tables.

Hebrew Measures of Capacity: Liquid Measures

HEBREW	NAB	EQUIVALENCE	U.S. MEASURES	METRIC UNITS
kor	kor	10 baths	60.738 gallons	230 liters
bat	bath	6 hins	6.073 gallons	23 liters
hin	hin	3 kabs	1.012 gallons	3.829 liters
qab	kab	4 logs	1.4349 quarts	1.276 liters
log	log		.674 pint	.32 liter

Hebrew Measures of Capacity: Dry Measures

HEBREW	NAB	EQUIVALENCE	U.S. MEASURES	METRIC UNITS
homer	homer	2 lethechs	6.524 bushels	229.7 liters
kor	measure, cor	2 lethechs	6.524 bushels	229.7 liters
letek	lethech, measure	5 ephahs	3.262 bushels	114.8 liters
'epah	ephah, measure	3 seahs	20.878 quarts	22.9 liters
tse'ah	measure	3.33 omers	6.959 quarts	7.7 liters
'omer	omer	1.8 kabs	2.087 quarts	2.3 liters
'issaron	tenth part (of ephah)			
qab	kab		1.159 quarts	1.3 liters

Measures of Capacity in the New Testament

GREEK	NAB	EQUIVALENCE	U.S. MEASURES	METRIC UNITS
batos	measure	(Hebrew) bat	6.073 gallons	23 liters
koros	kor	(Hebrew) kor	60.738 gallons or 6.524 bushels	230 liters
saton	measure	(Hebrew) tse'ah	6.959 dry quarts	7.71 liters
metretes	measure		10.3 gallons	39 liters
choinix	ration		.98 dry quart	1.079 liters
modios	bushel	(Latin) modius	7.68 dry quarts	8.458 liters

Measures and Weights

Hebrew Measures of Length

HEBREW	NAB	EQUIVALENCE	U.S. MEASURES	METRIC UNITS
'ammaḥ	cubit	2 spans	17.49 inches	.443 meter
zeret	span	3 handbreadths	8.745 inches	.221 meter
topaḥ, tepaḥ	handbreadth	4 fingers	2.915 inches	.074 meter
'etsbaʿ	finger		.728 inch	.019 meter

The cubit described in Ezekiel 40, 5; 43, 13 is equal to seven (not six) handbreadths, namely 20.405 inches.

Measures of Length in the New Testament

GREEK	NAB	U.S. MEASURES	METRIC UNITS
pechus	cubit	about 1.5 feet	.456 meter
orguia	fathom	about 72.44 inches	1.839 meters
stadion	stade	about 606 feet	184.7 meters
milion	mile	about 4,854 feet	1.482 kilometers

Hebrew Weights

HEBREW	NAB	EQUIVALENCE	U.S. UNITS	METRIC UNITS
kikkar	talent	60 minas	75.558 pounds	34.3 kilograms
maneh	mina	50 shekels	20.148 ounces	571.2 grams
sheqel	shekel	2 bekas	176.29 grains	11.42 grams
beqaʿ	bekah, half a shekel	10 gerahs	88.14 grains	5.71 grams
gerah	gerah		8.81 grains	.57 gram

The practice of weighing unmarked ingots of metal used in commercial transactions prior to the invention of money explains that the names of the units of weight were used later as indications of value, and as names for monetary standards. There is, however, no direct relation between the shekel-weight and the weight of a shekel piece.

Weights in the New Testament

GREEK	NAB	EQUIVALENCE	U.S. UNITS	METRIC UNITS
talenton	talent	(Hebrew) talent	75.558 pounds	34.3 kilograms
mna	gold coin	(Hebrew) mina	20.148 ounces	571.2 grams
litra	pound	(Latin) libra	.719 pound	326.4 grams

1800

GLOSSARY

A

Abba (Aram. "father"), the word Jesus (Mk 14, 36 and many other places) and, following him, the early church (Rom 8, 15) used to address God.

Abaddon (Heb. "place of destruction"), the realm of the dead (Jb 26, 6; Prv 15, 11; Ps 88, 10–12; Rv 9, 11).

accession the act of taking one's place as a ruler.

acrostic a literary device in which the first letter of each line of poetry occurs according to a pre-determined pattern. In the poetry of the Hebrew Bible all acrostics are alphabetical: the individual lines of a poem (or occasionally small groups of lines) begin with the twenty-two letters of the Hebrew alphabet in order. (This would be equivalent to the first line of an English poem beginning with A, the second with B, etc.) The acrostic form, besides giving the esthetic pleasure of a pattern, may have been intended to make memorization easier. It may also have been intended as a way of expressing completeness: in Lamentations, for instance, the acrostic format of the individual chapters might have been used to express both the completeness of the outpouring of grief and its finality. The following poems in the Bible are acrostics: Psalms 9–10, 25, 34, 37, 111, 112, 119, 145; Proverbs 31, 10–31; Lamentations 1, 2, 3, 4 (ch 5 is not an acrostic, but preserves part of the form by having 22 lines, the number of letters in the Hebrew alphabet); Nahum 1, 2–8 (or 9) (incomplete). In the Hebrew text of Sirach, 51, 13–30 is acrostic.

Adonai (Heb. "my Lord") a divine title and the word generally substituted for the

tetragrammaton, **YHWH,** when the Bible is read aloud.

allegorical a method of reading a text as an allegory; explaining or interpreting elements in a narrative as if they stood for something else. Paul uses an allegorical method in Galatians 4, 22–26. "Allegorical interpretation," such as that used by **Philo Judaeus** to draw out the meaning of the Bible, is an effort to make an allegory out of a writing that was not originally intended to be one, but that is, in the view of the interpreter, presenting a hidden meaning that the allegorical interpretation will reveal.

allegory an extended comparison which directly describes one reality while indirectly describing something entirely different. An allegory as a narrative uses action, setting, and characters to point symbolically to something else. Biblical allegories include the "Song of the Vineyard" in Isaiah 5, in which the story of the vineyard is also the story of Judah, and the parable of the sower in Matthew 13, 1–8 and 18–23. Allegory is infrequent in present-day literature, but allegorical treatments or uses of art still occur: The statue of Justice in courthouses uses allegorical elements: a beautiful woman (justice attracts us), blindfolded (justice is indifferent to external appearance), holding balancing scales (justice weighs the merits of a case in a publicly observable way) and a sword (justice can punish), all of which express our ideals of justice.

alleluia a Greek and Latin form of a Hebrew verb, meaning "Praise the Lord." See **hallelujah.**

Amorites according to the Bible, one of the native nations of Canaan. Amorites are attested

1801

in other ancient Near Eastern documents from the third millennium and onwards as residents of Syria who migrated to Mesopotamia and other areas. They spoke a language related to Hebrew.

anachronism an element in a story that is out of place because it did not exist at the time of the story. Anachronisms can be valuable clues to when a particular narrative was written.

anawim the Hebrew word for "the poor," "the afflicted," "the meek or humble." Often used in Psalms for the group to which the Psalmist belongs.

anoint touch or rub with oil. Both things and people can be anointed. Anointing was a sign that the person or thing was dedicated to God: kings (1 Kgs 1, 39) and priests (Lv 8, 30) were anointed, as were the bodies of those who had died (Lk 23, 56).

anthropomorphic (Gr. "human form") language that presents God in human or human-like terms. "Your right hand, O LORD, magnificent in power, your right hand, O LORD, has shattered the enemy" (Ex 15, 6).

antithesis the contrast of ideas through closely contrasted words: "A mild answer calms wrath, but a harsh word stirs up anger" (Prv 15, 1).

antithetic parallelism two parallel lines related to one another by opposition (e.g., Prv 10, 4, "The slack hand impoverishes, but the hand of the diligent enriches").

aphorism a short, memorable saying. Many of the Proverbs are aphorisms, as are many of Jesus' statements.

apocalypse (Gr. *apokalypsis,* "removal of the veil, revelation") a narrative literary genre in which an angel or other heavenly being communicates to a human being the divine plan for history and the arrangement of the supernatural order. Many apocalypses are a series of visions of heaven and earth that are then explained. Apocalypses are a feature of late biblical religion.

apocalyptic having the character of an apocalypse; assuming the existence of a supernatural realm closely related to the natural; maintaining the imminence of a final judgment.

Apocrypha (Gr. "hidden things") a group of about 20 mostly Jewish works, many of which were included in the **Septuagint,** but which were not accepted into the Jewish canon of the Bible. All of these works are extra-canonical for Protestants; some are canonical for Roman Catholics; a few more are canonical for Orthodox Christians. See **deuterocanonical.**

apodictic law law stated absolutely, as in the Decalogue's "you shall not," rather than casuistically, "if a person . . . " See **casuistic law.**

apologia (Gr. "explanation") a defense of one's actions or beliefs, usually in a formal speech or written document.

apostasy abandoning a set of beliefs, or the position of having abandoned them.

apostle (Gr. "one who is sent"), a delegate or representative. In the New Testament, an apostle was one who had known Jesus and could witness to the resurrection (Acts 1, 21–22) or a preacher of the gospel who had been called by God (1 Cor 12, 28; Rom 16, 7).

apostrophe an address to an absent person or personified object. There is an apostrophe to Assyria in Isaiah 10, 5.

Aramaic a Semitic language used widely in Mesopotamia and the Land of Israel during the Persian period, though it developed earlier. In the mid-first millennium, it eventually replaced Akkadian as the lingua franca of the ancient near eastern world. It became the ordinary language of Jews and is the language of much rabbinic commentary. The Aramaic translation of the Bible is the Targum.

Arameans a Semitic people living in the area of Syria from the second millennium onwards. Some biblical texts suggest particular kinship between Israel and the Arameans (see esp. Dt 26, 5). Damascus was their main city.

Ark (for the Torah) a box or cabinet, typically of wood, in which the Torah scrolls are stored at the front of the synagogue. It is often finely decorated, reflecting the centrality of the Torah scrolls to Judaism.

Ark of the Covenant the chest (Heb. *'aron*) in the Tabernacle or Temple that contained the Pact (Heb. *'edut*) (Ex 40, 20), or the tablets (Dt 10, 2), or that served as the throne of the LORD (1 Sm 4, 4).

Armageddon the traditional site of the final battle between good and evil (Rv 16, 16), possibly derived from Megiddo, a battle site in Israel's history (Jgs 5, 19; 2 Kgs 9, 27).

Asherah (pl. Asherim) Canaanite goddess, wife or consort of El; her sacred symbol, a pole or tree, was the object of prophetic condemnation.

Assyria a Mesopotamian world power, in addition to Egypt and Babylonia. Its capital cities included Asshur and Nineveh. The Assyrian empire conquered the northern kingdom of Israel in 722 and exiled its people. The Assyrians were well-known for their massive building projects, and for their cruelty in war.

'atbash a form of cipher in which a word is transformed into a code by letter substitution, in which the last letter of the alphabet is substituted for the first, the next-to-last for the second, and so on: *alef* becomes *tav,* *bet* becomes *shin, gimel* becomes *resh,* and so on. (In English, A would become Z, B would become Y, etc.) Using this method, Jeremiah transforms Babylon into Sheshach (Jer 25, 26; 51, 41): "b–b–l" or *bet-bet-lamed* becomes "sh-sh-k" or *shin-shin-kaf.*

atonement the expiation for sin, or reparation for an injury committed against another. The Hebrew *kapparah* (with possible root meaning "to cover") refers to ritual cleansing of the Temple precincts.

B

baal (Heb. "master," "lord," "husband") the chief god of the Canaanite religion; the storm god.

Babylonia a Mesopotamian world power. It often competed against Assyria, which it conquered in 612 B.C. Its major city was Babylon, Akkadian for "gate of the gods." Its main god became Marduk, and its religion and literature were extremely influential, even on its arch-rival Assyria. Babylonia destroyed the First Temple in 586, and was conquered by Cyrus the Great in 539.

Babylonian Exile the forced relocation of some of the population of Judah, perhaps the ruling portion of it, after the conquest by Babylonia in 595–586 B.C. The exile ended with the permitted return to the land under Cyrus (beginning ca. 538 B.C.).

Babylonian Talmud see **Talmud.**

ban (Heb. *herem*) the devotion of war booty (including people) in its entirety to the deity (see esp. Dt 20, 17), or the forfeiture of goods (e.g., idols) from which no benefit is permissible. See *herem.*

baptism ritual purification by immersion in water, a practice in use throughout the ancient Mediterranean world. New Testament baptism, based on the reported practice of John the Baptist (Mk 1, 4) may have been derived from Jewish purification ritual (Lv 15, 18), but Paul's connection of baptism with the death and resurrection of Christ (Rom 6, 1–14) changed its meaning from purification to initiation into a new community and new identity.

basilica a church built according to an ancient Roman plan, with a rectangular nave and a semicircular apse at one end; also, a Catholic church with certain ceremonial or liturgical privileges.

B.C.E. before the Common Era, an alternative to B.C.

Bedouin an Arab nomad; in general, a member of a nomadic desert tribe.

Beelzebul (also Baalzebul, Baalzebub, Beelzebub) the ruler of the demons (Mt 12, 24–27). It is based on the Hebrew *Baalzebul,* "lord of heaven," a title of the Phoenician god at Ekron (2 Kgs 1, 2–18), transformed (probably as a derogatory name) into Baalzebub, "lord of the flies."

behemoth a mythical beast, sometimes identified with the hippopotamus (Jb 40, 15–24) who represents violent forces in the world.

berit (Heb. "treaty") a term that may be used of a treaty between two individuals, groups, or nations, or between God and Israel. See **covenant.**

bicolon: unit of Hebrew poetry composed of two *cola,* or lines (sometimes called a *distich*).

Book of the Covenant see **Covenant Collection.**

Booths, Feast of the final harvest festival of grapes and olives, falling usually within our month of October. It was called "Booths" because the harvesters lived in the fields in makeshift tents or booths. Also called Tabernacles, Sukkoth.

C

Canaan a designation for the area roughly equivalent to the land of Israel in pre-biblical Mesopotamian and Egyptian documents. In the Bible, it most often refers to the pre-Israelite land of Israel.

canon (Gr. "measuring rod") the rule by which something is determined to belong or not to a category. Christian tradition uses the word for the official list of the individual books that make up the Scriptures. The canon of the Catholic church is more extensive than that of the Protestant churches, but less extensive than that of the Orthodox churches.

canonical criticism the interpretation of a biblical text based upon its final form, rather than interpretation built up from viewing it as an assemblage of smaller, pre-existing units.

casemate two parallel walls, joined by short cross-walls. The small rooms, like closets, that result were sometimes used for storage and sometimes filled with rubble or earth to strengthen them.

casuistic law (also called "case law") the form of law dealing with the treatment of specific cases. It is frequently in the form of "if/when . . . then" formulae. Most ancient near eastern law collections are formulated this way.

C.E. common era; equivalent to the christological term A.D.

ceramic typology dating different levels of an archeological site by classifying the pieces of pottery found in them according to the approximate eras in which they were made.

chaos complete lack of order. In ancient Near Eastern mythology, chaos was sometimes personified as divine beings who had to be conquered by other gods to establish an orderly, habitable universe.

charisma a gift of spiritual grace, particularly a gift of one of the manifestations of the Holy Spirit in the New Testament church.

charismatic (Gr. "gifted, graced") characterized by the ability to influence or lead others; personally magnetic; talented.

cherubim mythical, composite creatures with body parts from various animals; they often had wings and human heads. They were commonly guardians of temples and palaces in the ancient near east.

chiasm, chiasmus (from Gr. "chi," the letter that resembles an "X") inverting the second pair of terms in a parallel structure, so that the corresponding terms, if laid out in a square, would form an X. The resultant pattern is ABBA, ABCBA, ABCCBA, etc. "The king takes delight (A) in honest lips (B), and the man who speaks what is right (B) he loves (A)" (Prv 16, 13). Chiasmus can also describe the structure of an entire passage, and it can involve several terms or parts of a passage, each of which has an analog that occurs in the reverse order of the original list of terms or sequence of parts.

Christ (Gr. "anointed"), the translation of the Hebrew *mashshiach,* "messiah." In the New Testament and in general usage, Christ always refers to Jesus of Nazareth, though in contrast to New Testament usage (where it is always a title, "the anointed one"), in general use today "Christ" is simply an alternative name for Jesus.

Christian Hebraists Christian scholars, inspired by the examples of Origen and Jerome, who taught the importance of returning to the Hebrew text of the Christian Old Testament, and who therefore studied Hebrew with rabbinic scholars and influenced Christian Bible translation and commentary to rely on the Hebrew and not on the Latin Vulgate text. The beginnings of Christian Hebraism are generally traced to Andrew of St. Victor (d. 1175), a monk at the Abbey of St. Victor in Paris, where Hugh of St. Victor (d. 1141) had established a school specializing in biblical exposition. There was a significant renaissance of Christian Hebraism during the Renaissance.

Christology the theological doctrines covering the nature of Christ.

chronicle an account of events in the order in which they occurred.

Chronicler the name for the unknown author of the books of Chronicles; sometimes also applied to the author of Ezra and Nehemiah.

church fathers see **patristic writers**.

circumcision the removal of the foreskin of the penis. In the Bible it is a sign of entry into the covenant community, whether the circumcision is meant literally (Jos 5, 5–7) or metaphorically ("uncircumcised hearts," Lv 26, 41). In the writings of Paul, "the circumcised" and "the uncircumcised" (Gal 2, 7) refer to Jews and Gentiles, respectively.

citadel a stronghold or fortress, whether standing alone or serving as the inner fortification of a city.

clan a social unit of those considered to be descended from one common ancestor; several clans constitute a tribe.

climax (Gr. "ladder"), a series of clauses in which each succeeding clause repeats the important term from the previous clause, each clause in turn making a more important point: ". . . affliction produces endurance, and endurance, proven character, and proven character, hope . . ." (Rom 5, 3–4).

codex a manuscript of separate leaves of writing, bound into a unit along one edge. Modern books are a development of the codex.

colon (pl. *cola*) a single line of poetry (also known as a *stich*).

colophon (Gr. "summit," by extension "finishing touch") a notice, usually printed at the end of a book, giving information about authorship: Sirach 50, 27.

Community Rule (or "Rule of the Community") a scroll from the Dead Sea community, 1QS, that sets out the communal arrangements under which the community functioned, or at least those that they held up as an ideal: holding property in common; eating, blessing, and advising one another in unity; preparing for the eschaton; and training new members of the community in their responsibilities.

concordance a word index to a given text, listing each occurrence of a given word along with a context line so that scholars may better see how a particular word is used.

concubine a woman who is the sexual partner of a man, and is legally recognized as such, but who does not have the full status of a wife.

cosmology any account (mythical or otherwise) of the origin of the world.

cosmos (Gr. "order, regularity") the created world of order, stability, relative permanence; the opposite of chaos.

Council of Trent the twenty-ninth ecumenical council of the Catholic Church (1545–1563), held after the Protestant Reformation had begun. Among other decisions, it defined the books that are included in the Catholic canon of Scripture.

covenant (Heb. *berit*) a treaty between God and Israel. Some covenants have specific conditions or treaty stipulations, while others are covenants of grant. The biblical notion of covenant between God and Israel, especially as it appears in Deuteronomy, may reflect a theologized reworking of treaties between Assyrian kings and their vassals.

Covenant Code another term for **Covenant Collection**.

Covenant Collection Exodus 20, 19—23, 33, which details the terms of the covenant between God and Israel.

cult rituals and religious practices at a place of worship. The cult of the Jerusalem Temple means the religious practices carried out there, with no judgment about their value.

cult prostitute one available for sexual intercourse with worshipers at the temple of a god. The biblical accusation (Dt 23, 17–18; 1 Kgs 14, 24) that non-Israelite religions have cult prostitutes may be a polemical exaggeration.

Cyrus king of Persia (559–530 B.C.). He defeated Media in 550 and conquered most of the ancient Near East, including Babylonia, allowing the Jewish exiles in Babylonia to return to the land beginning about 538.

D

D the Deuteronomic source, which covers almost the entire book of Deuteronomy (except for sections of the last few chapters).

Davidic dynasty the direct descendants of King David, who reigned in Jerusalem from the tenth century through the sixth. An attempt to reinstitute this dynasty after the return from exile was not successful.

Day of Atonement (Heb. **Yom Kippur**) commemorated on the tenth day of the seventh month in the fall. It was a day of fasting and abstinence, as well as performance of certain key Temple rituals (see Lv. 16).

Day of the LORD the time mentioned in many prophetic books where God appears as a warrior, sometimes fighting against Israel, sometimes against Israel's enemies. The earliest text to mention this Day is Amos 5, 18.

Dead Sea Scrolls a group of manuscripts found in 1947 in caves near the Dead Sea, at wadi Qumran. The scrolls were probably the library of an Essene settlement that flourished at the site from the second century B.C. until it was destroyed by the Romans in A.D. 68. The library included Hebrew manuscripts of biblical books older than those previously known, and other scrolls regulating the life of the community that shed light on the variety of Jewish belief and practice in the time of Jesus.

decalogue (Gr. "ten words") the traditional name for the list of commandments in Exodus 20, 1–17 and Deuteronomy 5, 6–21.

defilement a state of ritual impurity caused by contact with a corpse or other impure object. Priestly literature in the Torah is especially concerned with defilement and removing defilement.

demon (Gr. *daimon*, "spirit") a spiritual or non-physical being, generally hostile to human beings, but in most Old Testament passages still under God's control (see Jb 1 and 2). A common Hebrew name was *satan*, meaning "adversary." By the time of the New Testament demons were generally regarded as hostile to God as well, and therefore evil, or the cause of bad influences—disease, mental distress—on human beings.

demonic marked by spiritual evil, like a demon.

deuterocanon, deuterocanonical (Gr. "second canon") those books or portions of books not included in the Hebrew canon but accepted as canonical by some Christian churches (Roman Catholic and Orthodox) because they were included in the Septuagint.

Deutero-Isaiah the general term for the portion

of Isaiah beginning with chapter 40. Most scholars consider Deutero-Isaiah to consist of chapters 40–55 (or 40–54). These chapters are primarily concerned with the promise of return from exile and the events leading up to the decree of Cyrus (538 B.C.) permitting the exiles to return to Judah and rebuild their city and Temple. See **Trito-Isaiah.**

deuteronomistic pertaining to the editor(s) of the history comprised in the books of Joshua, Judges, Samuel, and Kings, as prefaced by the book of Deuteronomy. The term is also applied to the style of these books, reflecting concern for such matters as obedience to the laws given in Deuteronomy, centralized worship in Jerusalem, and support for the Davidic dynasty.

Deuteronomistic History the account in the books Deuteronomy, Joshua, Judges, Samuel, and Kings, that portrays the history of Israel as a partial failure to keep the covenant faithfully, and the consequences of that failure in the subsequent history of the people. These books show significant theological and linguistic similarities, suggesting that they have a common editor or editors.

deuteronomistic having the qualities or the theology of the **Deuteronomistic History.**

diaspora (Gr. "dispersal") the scattering of Jews outside the land of Israel.

diatribe an argument against a position, or one critical of a person or group. Diatribe often includes an imagined dialogue between opposing viewpoints, as in the book of Job.

Didache (Gr. "teaching") an early Christian writing, dating from around A.D. 150 but including earlier materials. It consists of moral exhortation, a manual of church order, and guidance for community life. It is valuable for providing insight into the concerns of early Christian communities. It contains material similar to that in the Pastoral Letters (1 and 2 Tm and Ti).

discernment the ability to distinguish between what is valuable and what is not, especially in the spiritual or moral realms.

disciple a follower, an adherent of a particular teaching.

divination the effort to learn about the future or the current situation, particularly such an effort undertaken by occult means, such as consulting mediums.

divine warrior God in the role of leader of the heavenly armies, usually seen as fighting for Israel.

doctrine (Lat. *doctrina,* "teaching") the beliefs or tenets held by a particular group; Christian doctrines are rooted in the person of Christ.

documentary hypothesis a theory about the formation of the first five books of the Bible, Genesis through Deuteronomy. The hypothesis holds that there are four traditions underlying these books, naming them after a chief characteristic of each: "J" or the "Yahwist" ("J" from the German spelling "Jahveh") uses the divine name "YHWH" (the LORD) consistently and contains much of the oldest material; "E" or the "Elohist" uses the divine name "Elohim" (God) fairly consistently and contains traditions from the northern kingdom of Israel; "P" or the "Priestly" writer is concerned largely with legal codes and matters of religious practice; and "D" or the "Deuteronomist" represents the traditions gathered mostly in Deuteronomy and continued through the deuteronomistic history in Joshua, Judges, Samuel, and Kings. There have been many modifications in the documentary hypothesis, and most scholars now agree that these "documents" are much more like streams of tradition, at least partly oral, than they are like fully-conceived, written texts that could be combined in a cut-and-paste process.

doxology (Gr. "word of glory") a prayer of praise to God, or one glorifying God.

dualism the religious view that reality consists of two basic elements, often seen as "good" and "evil." Some dualistic thought is primarily ethical, arguing that human actions ultimately fall into one category or the other; other dualistic philosophies see good and evil as the basic constituents of the nature of the universe.

dynasty a ruling family; when a leader dies, the next leader is always chosen from among the family members.

E

E one of the four sources or traditions in the Torah, which characteristically refers to God as *elohim.* More recently, as scholars have exam-

ined the texts more closely, they speak of a JE tradition, since E as a separate source is difficult to isolate entirely. It may represent the traditions and practices of the inhabitants of the northern areas of Israel.

early Christian writings besides the books contained in the New Testament, many other writings from the first century or so of the Christian church are known to have survived, or are quoted or referred to by later writers. These writings include letters, gospels, narrative books like the Acts of the Apostles, apocalypses, and collections of teachings. In some cases these works provide direct evidence of teachings that were later rejected by the main body of Christians. In other cases they contain similar material, or parallel arguments, to those in parts of the New Testament, such as the instructions to local churches in the Pastoral Letters. In still other cases, they provide further examples of kinds of literature found in the New Testament.

ecclesiology the theological study of the church; the doctrines that concern the nature of the Christian community.

ecumenism (from the Greek *oikoumene,* "the whole inhabited world") any attempts to deal with the relations between different Christian groups, or to think about ways in which divisions among them might be overcome. Since the Second Vatican Council (1963–65), ecumenical activity has become a major goal of the Catholic Church.

ecumenical (from **ecumenism**) aimed at fostering ecumenism, or characterized by aims supporting ecumenism; having the character of ecumenism.

edom/Edomites the territory and people to the south of Judah, first attested in late second millennium texts. Edom is identified in Genesis 36 with Esau, Jacob's brother. The enmity between these brothers and that between Judah and Edom mirror each other.

eisegesis (Gr. "lead into"; opposed to **exegesis,** "lead out of") the practice of reading into the text what one desires to find there, rather than reading out of the text to determine what it actually says.

El a Canaanite deity popular in the second millennium. In the texts from Ugarit, he is a significant deity, but is often depicted as old and is largely supplanted by Baal.

Elohim the Hebrew word usually translated "God," though its plural form is sometimes translated "gods" (e.g., Gn 6, 2, "sons of elohim," NAB note: "sons of the gods"). It is originally a common noun (a god), though it is often used as a proper noun for The God of Israel, even though it is a plural form.

Elohist the putative author of the E source (see **E**).

ephod two different objects are called an ephod: (1) the linen apron worn by priests in the Temple; (2) a device used to divine the will of God. The second kind of ephod was carried in priestly garments, which may explain why the same word was used for both (1 Sm 2, 18). "Ephod" in Judges 8, 27 seems to be an idol rather than a priestly garment.

Ephraim the most important tribe of the **Northern Kingdom.**

Epicureans a Greek philosophical school, founded by Epicurus, who taught that human beings naturally seek pleasure, and that the best way to achieve this pursuit was in moderation, since moderation permits the longest possible life of pleasure-seeking.

epigraph an inscription, usually carved or etched in stone.

Epiphanes a title, "[God] made manifest," adopted by Antiochus IV, the ruler of the part of the Greek empire that included Israel during the second century B.C. He was the king who forced pagan worship to occur in the Jerusalem Temple, thus provoking the revolt of the Maccabees.

epiphany (Gr. "manifestation, appearance") usually the appearance of a god or divine being in a form that can be seen by human beings.

epistle a letter, sometimes intended for public reading and therefore written according to a particular literary form.

epithet a word or phrase that characterizes a person or thing, and that can often be used by itself to refer to the person. The name "Maccabeus," or "Hammer," is an epithet of Judas, the

son of Mattathias and leader of the Jewish revolt against Antiochus IV in 167 B.C.

eschatological, eschatology (Gr. *eschata,* "last things") a concern with the end time, or the end of the world as we know it, whether that involves a new historical era radically discontinuous from this one, or an entirely new cosmos after the destruction of the current one.

Essenes a communal society in Judaism around the first century B.C. to the first century A.D. that kept the law with utmost rigor and lived apart in communities that were similar in some respects to later monastic groups. It is generally agreed that the Dead Sea Scrolls of Qumran were collected and preserved by an Essene community.

etiology (Gr. *aition,* "cause") an explanation for a word, an event, or a natural phenomenon. An etiological story is one that posits a particular cause (not necessarily the right cause) for some event. For example, the story at the end of Genesis 32 explains why Israelites do not eat the thigh muscle.

Eucharist a ritual or service of thanksgiving, centering on the sharing of bread and wine, based on the final meal Jesus shared with his followers before his trial and crucifixion; also called Communion, the Lord's Supper, and the Mass.

euphemism the substitution of an inoffensive word for one that is too explicit or impolite. The word "feet" in Isaiah 6, 2; 7, 20 (NAB: "between the legs") and possibly Ruth 3, 4. 7. 8. 14 is a euphemism for "genitals."

evangelist (from Greek *euangelion,* "good news") the author of a gospel.

exegesis (Gr. "lead out of") the explanation or interpretation of the meaning of a written text.

exhortation urging a particular course of action or behavior by argument or advice.

Exile the forced removal of a people from its land, and the community in which they lived in the foreign land. The Israelites of the northern kingdom were exiled by the Assyrians in the late eighth century, and the Judeans were exiled by the Babylonians in the early sixth century. Specifically, "the Exile" is the period from 586 to approximately 539 B.C. During this time the ruling classes of Judah were forced to leave Judah and live in Babylonia. See **Babylonian Exile.**

F

fable an illustrative story in which animals or plants have speaking parts. Judges 9, 8–15 is a fable about the dangers of kingship in which plants speak.

Fertile Crescent the agriculturally fertile areas of Egypt, Israel, and Mesopotamia, forming a rough arc from the Nile through the coastal regions of Israel to the Tigris-Euphrates basin.

Festival of Weeks see **Shavuot.**

festival scrolls the five short books that are read on five holy days in the Jewish calendar: Song of Songs on Passover, Ruth on Pentecost (Weeks or Shavuoth), Lamentations on 9 Ab (the date of the Temple's destruction), Ecclesiastes on Booths (Sukkoth), and Esther on Purim.

First Temple the Temple in Jerusalem from Solomon's time (tenth century) until the destruction of Jerusalem by the Babylonians in 586 B.C. The First Temple period extends from the tenth to sixth centuries B.C.

form criticism the interpretation of a text—a parable, a psalm, a proverb—with particular attention to the structure of the text and to the original setting of that form out of which it arose. Form criticism attempts to recover the original context, audience, or situation of a particular kind of literature, before the unit was made a part of a larger narrative such as a gospel or a historical book with its own context, audience, and situation.

Former Prophets the name in the Hebrew Bible for the first part of the longer section called "the Prophets." The Former Prophets are Joshua, Judges, Samuel, and Kings.

fundamentalist in its narrow meaning, a conservative Protestant who holds to the five fundamentals: the sole authority of Scripture; the Virgin Birth of Jesus Christ; the doctrine of the substitutionary atonement of the death of Christ; the physical, bodily resurrection of Christ; and the literal Second Coming of Christ to judge the world. In a wider sense, a fundamentalist is any rigidly conservative adherent to a belief system who regards all those outside the belief system as without hope of salvation and who treats the sacred text of the tradition as an infallible guide to belief and action.

G

Galilee the northernmost geographical area of Israel.

Gehenna the place of punishment after death (e.g., see Mt 5, 22). The name means "valley of Hinnom," a place south of Jerusalem that had been thought to be the area where children were burnt as sacrificial offerings: Josiah (2 Kgs 23, 10) destroyed the site, but its associations with burning and evil remained and developed into the image of burning punishment that is found in the New Testament.

genealogy a list or history of the ancestors of an individual or group.

genre a form of literature with particular characteristics. The detective story is a genre. Once a genre is established, the audience for it knows what to expect and can respond more easily to any given work. Biblical genres include oracles, laments, proverbs, hymns, parables, letters, gospels, and apocalypses.

gentile a non-Jew.

Gilgamesh the Babylonian and Assyrian epic, whose hero, Gilgamesh, travels the world in search of immortality. Among the characters he encounters is Utnapishtim, whose tale of the flood has parallels with the biblical account of Noah (Gn chs 6–9). This epic explores the tension between nature and culture and addresses the mortality of human beings.

glean to gather or collect, usually by hand, grain that is left behind by reapers. People too poor to own their own fields were permitted to glean in the fields of those better off (Lv 19, 9–10; Dt 24, 19–24).

gnosticism (from Gk. *gnosis,* "knowledge") a philosophy that regards spirit and matter as opposites. According to gnostic teaching, human beings are spirits trapped or imprisoned in matter; the material world is an illusion or the work of an inferior, even demonic, divine being; and the purpose of life is to learn how to free oneself from material things (including the body) and attain eternal life in the spiritual realm. This is accomplished by learning specialized or secret knowledge about the nature of reality; it is from this emphasis on knowledge that gnosticism gets its name. Gnostic teachings were often in the form of secret doctrines or mysteries, and many mystery religions were gnostic. Gnosticism, though influential during the first few centuries of the Christian church's existence, was ultimately rejected by what became the main body of Christians, and most of the gnostic writings were lost or suppressed. Because gnosticism itself did not continue as an established form of Christianity, it did not develop an "orthodox" or systematic body of thought, and most of what is attributed to it as a philosophy has had to be assembled from disparate sources that do not always agree with each other in every particular.

God, names for see **Adonai, Elohim, YHWH.**

Greek Bible a general term for the variety of ancient translations of the Bible into Greek in antiquity, including the Septuagint and the translations of Aquila, Symmachus, and Theodotion.

H

Hades the abode of the dead in Greek religion, used in the New Testament as the general name for the place where souls go after death (e.g., see Mt 11, 23; Acts 2, 27).

haggadah (poss. from Heb. *huggad,* "things said" or "what is told") the nonlegal portions of the Talmud and Midrash (see *halakhah*). Haggadah is concerned with explicating the meaning of Scripture in the moral sense, and with elaborating on the stories in the Bible. As such, it is more akin to preaching than to legal analysis, and many haggadic collections are homiletical in character. The legal sections, called *halakhah,* are concerned with understanding the obligations placed on the believer by the biblical text; *haggadah,* by contrast, contains ethical teaching as well as illustrative narrative, prayers, legends, and folklore.

Haggadah of Pesah ("telling of Passover") the liturgical recitation, used at the Passover **seder;** also the book that contains the recitation and instructions of the seder.

halakhah (Heb. "way," from *halakh* "go"; pl. *halakhot*) the legal portions of the Talmud, or any legal ruling according to Jewish law.

Hallel (Heb. "praise") Psalms 113–118, which are recited on major Jewish festivals.

hallelujah a Hebrew acclamation, "Praise Yah!" It is frequent in the Psalms.

Hammurabi Babylonian monarch (ruled 1792–1750 B.C.), responsible for the formulation of a legal collection (the Code [or Laws] of Hammurabi) that is one of the earliest collections of case law on various subjects.

Hasidic, Hasidim (Heb. *Hasid,* "pious one") (1) a Jewish group in the Maccabean period, concerned with re-establishing Jewish practices in ritual and purity laws. The Hasidim supported the Maccabees for a time; they may have been the precursors of the Sadducees. (2) a renewal movement that began in the mid-eighteenth century in eastern Europe under the influence of the Baal Shem Tov ("master of the good Name"), R. Yisrael ben Eliezer (ca. 1700–1760).

Hasmonean the dynasty descended from the Maccabee brothers. It ruled Israel from 135 to 36 B.C.; the last Hasmonean was overthrown by Herod the Great.

Hasmonean Revolt the uprising led by the family of Mattathias Heshmon against the Seleucid ruler Antiochus IV Epiphanes beginning in 166 B.C., particularly by Mattathias' son Judah (or Judas) Maccabeus ("the hammer"), which succeeded in liberating Jerusalem and the surrounding territory from Seleucid rule in 164. When the Temple, which had been desecrated by Antiochus, was retaken by the Jews, it was rededicated, an event commemorated in the festival of Hanukkah ("dedication").

Hebrew Bible a term used to refer to what Christians call the (Protestant) Old Testament. Though the two terms refer to basically the same body of writings, the order of books in the Hebrew Bible (i.e., the Jewish Bible) differs from that found in the Old Testament.

Hellenism a general term for the spread of Greek culture, politics, and language around the Mediterranean in the period after the conquests of Alexander the Great (d. 323 B.C.).

Hellenistic Greek-speaking or influenced by Greek culture after the time of Alexander.

Hellenize bring under the influence of Greek language and culture.

herem (Heb. "ban") the total dedication of conquest to God; later, the exile or suspension of someone from the community ("excommunication").

heresy (Gr. *hairesis,* "choice") an opinion or belief contrary to the accepted doctrine of the Catholic Church; an unorthodox position.

hermeneutics (Gr. "interpretation") the theory and practice of interpretation.

Herodian followers and members of the court of Herod the Great and his sons (36 B.C. to A.D. 40).

Hexateuch (Gr. "six scrolls") a grouping of the first six books in the Bible—Genesis through Joshua—to complete the narrative with the conquest of the Land that is in Joshua. See **Pentateuch, Tetrateuch.**

high places shrines, usually on a hill or a raised platform, where worship, especially sacrifices, took place. Because they were outside of Jerusalem and sometimes, though not always, used for other gods, they were regularly condemned in the Deuteronomistic History, though in earlier writings, and even in the narratives in Kings, there are clear indications that sacrifice and worship took place in numerous locations throughout Israel.

higher criticism the effort to distinguish among the sources of biblical documents, and to trace them back to their origins, so far as that is possible; distinguished from textual criticism ("lower criticism"), which is concerned with establishing the most accurate text in its final form. See **documentary hypothesis.**

historical-critical method interpreting a text by trying to understand its original setting and audience, and what it would have meant when it was originally written or spoken. This method uses the tools of historical research to understand the conditions of the past, and critical tools to understand the traditions and developments that lie behind the surface of the text. It is also an umbrella term that includes such methods as form criticism and redaction criticism.

holocaust a sacrifice entirely consumed by fire, a whole burnt offering.

holy war battles conducted under divine guidance in which the LORD fought for Israel in the role of divine warrior (Jgs 6).

homiletical having the character or function of a sermon.

hortatory characteristic of writing or speech that aims at changing the behavior of the hearers or inspiring them to a particular course of action.

hosanna a Hebrew word, meaning "Save!" that was used as a cry of acclamation (Ps 118, 26; Mt 21, 9).

household code a list of rules or prescribed behaviors for the members of an extended family and their servants living under one roof. There are household codes in some of the New Testament letters, for instance Ephesians 5, 22—6, 9.

Hyksos the mostly Semitic rulers of Egypt during the period 1665–1560 B.C. (approximately).

hyperbole exaggeration for effect. "Will the LORD be pleased with thousands of rams, with myriad streams of oil?" (Mi 6, 7).

hypostasis (Gr. "that which stands under," i.e., the real nature or essence of anything; pl. *hypostases*) a Greek philosophical term, meaning both "essential being" or what defines a thing as a member of a class of things and "individual being" or what a thing is in itself. It was used by, among others, the neo-Platonist mystics. It refers to the three constitutive orders of reality, the One, Mind, and Soul, each of which is an hypostasis.

hyssop a shrub related to mint. It was used as a medicine and, because of its leafy branches, for ritual sprinkling of water or blood (Ex 12, 22).

I

idolatry the worship of anything other than what the worshiper defines as the true God.

Idumea the Greek form of the name Edom; province in the Land during Persian, Hellenistic, and Roman times, located south of Judah (Yehud), between the Dead Sea and the Mediterranean.

Ignatius, Letters of early Christian writings of instruction. The author, Ignatius, bishop of Antioch, wrote them (seven are known to have survived) on his way to martyrdom in Rome. They are largely concerned with overcoming divisions in local churches, combating false teaching, and conducting one's life properly. They therefore are very similar to some of the canonical New Testament letters, particularly 1 and 2 Timothy and Titus. The letters of Ignatius are addressed to the Ephesians, the Magnesians, the Trallians, the Romans, the Philadelphians, and the Smyrnians, as well as one to Polycarp, bishop of Smyrna.

impurity a ritual state which forbade the impure individual to partake in Temple rituals. See **defilement**.

incarnation (Lat., "enfleshment") the belief that a divine being has become human in some form.

incubation the practice of sleeping in a particular place, or in contact with particular things (animal skins, the ground) to induce dreams that might provide divine guidance.

inerrancy the doctrine that the biblical materials are without error. In its most expansive form, as held for instance by Protestant fundamentalists, inerrancy includes the assertion that in the original manuscripts of the biblical books, there are no errors of fact, whether theological, historical, or scientific. A more restrained version of the doctrine would claim that the Bible is an inerrant guide in matters of faith but that it may contain historical errors or assertions that cannot be reconciled with present-day science. Vatican II expressed it this way: "Therefore, since everything asserted by the inspired authors or sacred writers must be held to be asserted by the Holy Spirit, it follows that the books of Scriptures must be acknowledged as teaching firmly, faithfully, and without error that truth which God wanted put into the sacred writings for the sake of our salvation" (Document on Revelation, *Dei Verbum*, n. 11). The final phrase, "for the sake of our salvation"—that is, not for the sake of giving us historical or scientific information—establishes the limits of inerrancy.

inspiration the belief that the words uttered by a human being are really the words of a divine be-

ing. In the ancient world, prophets and oracles were thought to be inspired. In Christian tradition, the notion of inspiration was eventually applied to the whole Bible. Inspiration in a more expanded sense speaks of an inspired tradition, in which numerous authors, anonymous contributors, editors, and others all worked together more or less consciously to create the biblical materials; in this view, God used all these people and their human traditions to express the Bible's teachings. The Second Vatican Council affirms the inspiration of Scripture, but warns that God speaks "through men in human fashion" so that careful attention must be given "to what the sacred writers really intended" (*Dogmatic Constitution on Divine Revelation*, III.12).

interpolation an insertion of material into a previously existent text. In the absence of textual evidence, e.g. differing forms of a manuscript for a given text, interpolation must be inferred and is often the subject of scholarly disagreement.

interpretation There are a number of different methods of interpreting the Bible, each meant to answer different questions. In general, the purpose of interpretation is to help make the meaning of the text clear, but this sometimes means not only understanding the sentences and paragraphs that we read today, but also understanding the possible ways by which they came to be written, trying to determine the original context of the story or saying, and looking at the different stages through which a biblical text does on its way to its final form. So interpreters are interested in examining the meanings of words used in the Bible, the historical religious, or social background of a particular story or saying, the process by which a story was written down, how groups of stories were combined into a longer narrative, how different biblical writers treated the same materials, what the original audience would have gotten out of a story, how a saying was adapted to address the concerns of later readers, and many similar paths of investigation. Terms used by biblical interpreters include: canonical criticism, documentary hypothesis, form criticism, redaction criticism, source criticism, synoptic problem, tradition criticism, textual criticism.

interregnum an interruption or gap between the end of one reign or dynasty and the beginning of the next.

intertextuality the interrelationship between

one part of a text (or collection of texts) and other parts. Intertextuality can take the form of recurrent images (the vineyard in Is 5, 1–10 and 27, 2–4), quotation and/or inner biblical interpretation (Jer 25, 11–12 is partly quoted in Dn 9, 2 before it is reinterpreted; 1 Cor 3, 20 quotes Ps 94, 11), or allusion (Is 54, 8 alludes to the promise made to Noah in Gn 9, 11).

irony, ironic a characteristic of literature in which the reader or listener knows more than the characters about the situation in the story. A character in an ironic situation is missing a vital piece of information that is known to the audience. By extension, an ironic aspect of a story, situation, or fact is one that from the outside looks very different than it does from the inside. Irony thus becomes a rhetorical technique in which the author's plain or literal meaning (what the words mean in the dictionary sense) is different from, even in conflict with, the author's intended meaning (what the words mean in their context, with particular emphasis, etc.). Saying "My! Don't you look lovely!" to someone dressed in old work clothes who has just finished a strenuous and messy task is an example of irony in this sense.

Isis the Egyptian mother-goddess, wife of Osiris, the god of vegetation and hence of regeneration.

Israel the name for both the kingdom of twelve tribal groups, of which David and Solomon were kings, and for the northern section of this kingdom, which split off after the death of Solomon and began a separate political existence under Jeroboam (1 Kgs 12). See **Northern Kingdom, Southern Kingdom.**

J

J the posited document or narrative tradition that is one of the constituent parts of the Torah (Pentateuch), according to a scholarly hypothesis codified by J. Wellhausen and subsequently developed by numerous biblical researchers. J is usually understood to be the earliest source, and is Judean; it frequently depicts God, for whom it uses the tetragrammaton (YHWH, misvocalized Jehovah, thus J), in very anthropomorphic terms.

Jerome (ca. 340–420) Christian theologian and translator. Beginning in 382, he produced a Latin version of the Bible, the Old Testament of which was based not on a previous Latin version nor on the Greek text (Septuagint) but on the Hebrew. To do this, Jerome studied Hebrew with rabbis of

the time, an unusual step for a Christian. His version, which became known as the **Vulgate** ("common") because it was the translation into commonly used Latin in the Western world, was completed in 405.

Jerusalem Talmud also called the Palestinian Talmud or the Talmud of the Land of Israel—none of these titles is fully accurate. This Talmud, mostly reflecting traditions of the Galilean rabbis of the third and fourth centuries A.D., is a commentary on several tractates of the Mishnah. It was ultimately seen as less authoritative than the longer, more comprehensive, and more carefully edited **Babylonian Talmud**. See **Talmud.**

Joseph and Aseneth an ancient Greek novel about Joseph's life in Egypt, his marriage to the haughty daughter of an Egyptian priest, and her conversion to faith in Joseph's God, and their triumph over a plot to kill them.

Josephus a Hellenistic Jewish historian who lived from about A.D. 37 to about A.D. 100. Four of his writings have survived: *The Jewish War,* an account of the rebellion against Rome in A.D. 66–70, with background information starting at about 200 B.C.; *The Antiquities of the Jews,* a complete history from the creation up to the point where *The Jewish War* begins; *Against Apion,* a defense of Judaism; and an autobiography, the *Life.* Josephus provides invaluable historical information about Judaism and its background from 200 B.C. to A.D. 100; his account of the rebellion, in which he was involved, is in part that of an eyewitness. He also provides first-hand information about the Essenes and the Pharisees, because at one time or another he was associated with both groups, as well as giving information about the Sadducees. Josephus is important to scholars in trying to understand the religious context in which Jesus lived and from which early Christianity and rabbinic Judaism developed.

Jubilee (Heb. *yovel,* perhaps "ram" from the sounding of the ram's horn to mark the beginning of the observance) the year of release for slaves and return of ancestral lands to their original owners (or descendants of the owners), to occur every 50 years (after seven sabbaths of years) (Lv ch 25). It is a cornerstone of Priestly ideology, but it is uncertain if it was ever practiced.

Judah the major tribal group of the southern kingdom. According to the biblical text, after the death of Solomon, the kingdom was divided into two, with Judah in the south and Israel in the north. The capital of Judah was Jerusalem.

Judea the Roman name for the area of Judah.

K

kabbalah "what is received," that is, matter handed to one. In the twelfth century and later, however, *kabbalah* came to mean esoteric or in some sense mystical teaching. *Kabbalah* taught that God was inaccessible by direct experience and could only be apprehended through emanations of the Godhead; Torah in kabbalistic teaching had a hidden meaning, and meditation on texts was a method of ascent to a mystical vision.

kaddish (Aram. "holiness, sanctification") prayer in praise of God that is recited at the conclusion of a principal section of the synagogue service; a special type of kaddish is also recited in memory of the deceased.

Kiddush short for *kiddush ha-yom,* "sanctification of the day," both the ceremony and the prayer that proclaims the holiness of the Sabbath (or festival), recited over wine before the Sabbath (or festival) meal.

kohen (Heb. "priest") a member of the hereditary group within the Levites, traditionally supposed to be descended from Aaron or Zadok, who alone were allowed to serve as Temple priests.

kosher (Heb. "fit" or "proper") a general term used in post-biblical texts for dietary laws; usually applied to food, but also to other ritual objects and practices. Most dietary laws apply to meat: It may not be consumed with blood in it, certain kinds of internal fat are not to be eaten, it may not be consumed along with dairy products, and some meats (e.g., pork), sea creatures (e.g., shellfish), and "creeping things" (e.g., snails) are not permitted.

L

lament a poem of grief or mourning. See **qinah meter.**

Latter Prophets the canonical division of Nevi'im that includes the books of Isaiah, Jeremiah, Ezekiel, and the Twelve.

law the usual English translation of Hebrew *torah,* which more generally means "teaching,

instruction." *Torah* is also the name for the first five books of the Hebrew Bible, Genesis through Deuteronomy.

lectionary a list of readings of Scripture passages for Sabbaths and holy days (in Judaism) or Sundays and holy days (in Christianity). Christian lectionaries also sometimes include readings for weekdays. Lectionaries are partly designed to read certain portions of the Bible—for instance, the Torah, in Jewish lectionaries, or the first three Gospels, in Christian lectionaries—completely through, in order, over a lectionary cycle of a year or several years. In addition, in Christian lectionaries important seasons (e.g., Christmas or Easter) have their own specific readings outside the continuous readings. In the synagogue, the Torah reading is followed by what is called a Haftarah reading (*haphtarah* is Hebrew for "conclusion, completion") from one of the prophets; in addition, the five **festival scrolls** are read on five holy days. In many Christian churches, the Gospel reading is preceded by a reading from the Hebrew Scriptures, a psalm, and a reading from elsewhere in the New Testament, usually a letter. The Gospel of John is read during Easter season.

legate an official representative.

legend, legendary a popular story, sometimes exaggerated or romanticized, about a holy or righteous person or a special place. The characters in legends can themselves be legendary, like Paul Bunyan, or they can be real historical personages about whom stories are told, like George Washington and the cherry tree. Characters that are legendary are those who are famous enough to have legends told about their exploits. Many of the stories told about Elijah and especially Elisha have legendary elements.

leviathan the monster of the sea in Canaanite mythology, who is defeated by Baal. It is sometimes identified with the crocodile (Jb 41, 1) and represents the forces of watery chaos that must be overcome at creation (Ps 74, 1–17) and that will be finally defeated at the end of time (Is 27, 1). In the book of Revelation, the dragon, the enemy of God, is identified with the sea (17, 1. 3), and in the new creation there is no more sea (21, 1).

levirate marriage (from Lat. *levir,* "husband's brother") the provision that if a man died without an heir to carry on his name, his brother would marry the widow and the first son she bore would be regarded as the dead brother's heir. This practice is dealt with in Deuteronomy 25, 5–10, but it is unclear whether it was actually carried out to any extent; by rabbinic times *halitzah,* the ceremony that released the levir from this obligation, was preferred.

Levite (from Heb. "descendant of Levi") originally the tribe or group from which priests were chosen; later, after the establishment of the Zadokites as priests (1 Kgs 1), a subordinate Temple servant who assisted the priests in their duties (see Ex 32, 28; Nm 3, 18; Ez 4, 10–14).

lex talionis (Lat. "law [of retribution] in kind") punishment fitting the crime. See **talion.**

liminal (Lat. *limina,* "threshhold") the term for rites or practices that governed life passages, such as entry into puberty or marriage.

literal meaning the "plain sense" of a text, as opposed to an allegorical, homiletical, or spiritual interpretation.

literary criticism the older name for **source criticism.**

liturgy the form or rite for communal, public worship.

LXX the roman numeral 70, the standard abbreviation for the **Septuagint.**

M

Ma'at Egyptian goddess of reason and order; her name literally means "truth."

malediction curse; opposite of benediction, "blessing."

martyr (Gr. "witness") a person who demonstrates loyalty by remaining faithful even when being threatened with death or being killed.

Martyrdom of Isaiah a Greco-Roman, Jewish work that is the origin of the legend that Isaiah died by being sawn in two. It is alluded to in Hebrews 11, 37.

Masoretic text the text of the Hebrew Bible, established by Jewish scholars (called Masoretes). (*Masorah* means "tradition.") The text consists of the Hebrew consonants, vowel signs, accent markings, and other notes. Texts derived from

this effort date from circa A.D. 900 to 1000. The Masoretic text is the only complete form of the Hebrew Bible that has come down to us, though individual manuscripts of books are among the Dead Sea Scrolls.

matrilineal tracing descent through female ancestors. See **patrilineal.**

matzah unleavened bread, associated with Passover, but also used with certain sacrifices.

Mesopotamia (Gr. "between the rivers") the area between the Tigris and Euphrates rivers.

messiah the Hebrew word for "anointed." A king could be referred to as "the LORD's anointed" (1 Sm 24, 6); even a foreign king could be so called (Is 45, 1). Later the term came to be used of the expected savior of the Jewish people and was taken over by Christians to refer to Jesus, whom they believed to be the messiah (Gr. *christos,* "anointed").

Messiah (Heb. *mashshiach,* "anointed [one]") a title for the king or other servant or agent of God (priest, prophet, or even non-Israelite Cyrus in Is 45, 1).

metaphor a direct comparison between two things: "The LORD is my shepherd" (Ps 23, 1). See **simile.**

metonymy a figure of speech in which a word is used in place of another word to which it is closely related. "The coastlands have seen and are afraid" (Is 41, 5) means "the inhabitants of the coastlands," that is, foreigners.

mezuzah (Heb. "doorpost") a parchment on which are written the paragraphs of the Shema (Dt 6, 4–9; 11, 13–21), and on the back of which *sh-d-y* ("Shaddai," "Almighty") is written so as to be visible through a small opening in the case. *Sh-d-y* is interpreted as an acronym for *shomer delatot Yisrael,* "guardian of the doors of Israel."

midrash, midrashic (Heb. *derash* "inquire") interpretation to draw out meanings from a text that are other than, or go beyond, the "plain sense."

Minor Prophets (so-called because compared to the Major Prophets, Isaiah, Jeremiah, and Ezekiel, they are much shorter) the books from Hosea through Malachi; in the Hebrew Bible they are treated as one collection, "The Book of the Twelve."

mitzvah (Heb. "commandment") a religious obligation; by extension, any good deed.

Moab/Moabites the territory and inhabitants south and east of the Dead Sea.

Molech the title—"king"—of the Ammonite god. The worshipers of this god were accused of child sacrifice.

motif an image or character type that recurs throughout a literary work. The Servant motif occurs in Isaiah at 42, 1–4; 49, 1–6; 50, 4–11; 52, 13—53, 12.

mystery in the New Testament, a divine truth that is kept hidden or secret by God until the right moment for it to be revealed (see Rom 16, 25–26). A "mystery" in this sense is a revelation about God's plan (Eph 1, 9–10). The later, theological meaning of "mystery," a religious teaching that is based on a revelation from God or other divine messenger, rather than on conclusions from reasoning, and that therefore can never be fully understood by reason alone, is not present in the New Testament.

mystery religion any one of various religious groups in the Greek and Roman empires that practiced secret rites of initiation. These rites often involved rituals enacting the myth of creation of other underlying teaching about the meaning of the universe according to the particular group. Mystery religions taught that the real meaning of life could not be learned without divine guidance and that such guidance was available in their secret teachings and practices. These secret rites were themselves known as "mysteries" and had the sense of a revelation from the divine realm that is similar to some of the New Testament uses of "mystery."

myth a story that expresses a spiritual truth or basic conviction of a culture through narrative. In particular myths give explanations of origins, often through the struggles of divine beings or superhuman creatures. Because the Bible firmly maintains the teaching that there is only one God, in biblical myths the presence of multiple deities has faded out, but the titanic struggle between good and evil is still maintained, as in the story of Paradise in Genesis 2–3, or the Tower of Babel story in Genesis

11, 1–9. Such stories, for example, express the impossibility of human efforts to attain the level of God. Myths are not meant to be taken literally.

N

narrative a connected, orderly account of an incident, or a longer account including many incidents. Narratives can be historical, fictional, legendary, mythical, or a combination of types.

Negev the high plateau south of the central hill country of Israel.

Neoplatonism a development of **Platonism**. It originated with Plotinus (ca. 204–270) and saw the universe as a series of emanations flowing out from the One, the unknowable source of all. The emanations, Mind, the realm of knowledge, and Soul, the realm of thought and activity, are called hypostases. All of existence is a balance between emanation, or movement outward, and contemplation or return, movement back toward the One. The individual's task is to return to the One by contemplation, involving a progressive detachment from the world of matter and sense and ultimately from all categories of thought until the One can be grasped in an indescribable void of thought. There may be early neoplatonic influences in the Wisdom of Solomon 7, 25.

Nevi'im the Prophets, the second division of the Hebrew Scriptures.

new moon the beginning of any month in the Jewish calendar.

Northern Kingdom the political assembly of tribal groups that split off from the kingdom of Israel after Solomon's death (1 Kgs 12). This newly-formed kingdom was itself called Israel, and in some of the prophets (e.g., Hos 8, 11), Ephraim, after its largest tribe.

novel a fictional work in prose. Ancient novels were often **romances**.

O

obelisk a four-sided stone shaft, usually tapered and topped with a pyramid, characteristic of ancient Egypt.

Old Latin the Latin translation of the Bible based on the Greek text, the Septuagint. The Old Latin version was replaced by Jerome's Latin translation, the **Vulgate.**

oracle a statement uttered by a prophet or other sacred person, purporting to be the words of a deity.

oracular having the qualities of an oracle or sacred speech.

Oral Torah a synonym for the **Mishnah** and **Talmud.** According to traditional rabbinic belief, the Oral Law was given to Moses on Mount Sinai along with the written law, the Torah. The Oral Law was, however, as its name suggests, originally transmitted orally alongside the Torah, as the authoritative interpretation of the Torah. As a result of historical exigencies, it was committed to writing by the rabbis, in stages, in the first millennium A.D.

ordination a formal ceremony and process by which certain members of the community are set apart for religious service, for instance as priests (Lv 8, 1–46).

oxymoron (Gr. "swift-slow") combining two terms that appear contradictory. "For the foolishness of God is wiser than human wisdom, and the weakness of God is stronger than human strength" (1 Cor 1, 25).

P

P the Priestly document in the Torah, comprised of both narratives and laws. It is concerned, among other things, with laws and regulations, ritual practices, the proper conduct of the Temple worship, holiness and purity, and genealogies. P may also have had a hand in the shaping or redaction of the Torah.

paleography the study of ancient writing, used to date manuscripts.

Palestine a name derived from the Roman designation *Provincia Syria Palaestina,* "Syro-Palestinian Province," which replaced *Provincia Judaea* after the revolt of A.D. 135; *Palaestina* was the Roman spelling of "Philistine," and the designation was probably intended as a derogation of Jewish claims to the territory.

Palestinian Talmud the **Jerusalem Talmud** or Talmud Yerushalmi; see **Talmud.**

parable a statement or story that uses figurative or imaginative language to evoke a reality that lies beyond the literal level of the story or statement. A parable makes its point by analogy, or the comparison of a known fact, situation, or experience with one that is less familiar. The analogy is usually not made explicit; for instance, in the parable of the Prodigal Son (Lk 15, 11–32) the father is meant to represent, by analogy, the merciful action of God's forgiveness, but this is not stated. Sometimes an interpretation is added, however, as with the parable of the Sower (Mk 4, 1–8, interpreted in vv. 14–20).

paraenesis moral exhortation.

parallelism a characteristic feature of biblical Hebrew poetry in which the second line of a unit in some way echoes the meaning or grammatical structure of the first line. This can take the form of a repetition of the meaning, or of a statement of opposites, or of a further statement that serves to extend or modify the first line in some way. Psalms and Proverbs are largely composed in parallelistic form and demonstrate the great degree of variation that the form permits.

parousia (Gr. "coming") the second coming of Christ; the expected return of the messiah at the end of the age or the end of the world.

Paschal pertaining to the Passover (ultimately from the Gr. *pascha,* derived from Heb. *pesah*).

Passover (Heb. *pesach,* prob. "protection"; others "pass over") the name of the festival commemorating the Exodus from Egypt. The first day involves the sacrifice of the lamb, which took place on the eve of the Exodus (14 Nisan); the rest of the festival, the "festival of unleavened bread," was probably originally a festival marking the beginning of the spring barley harvest.

Passover Haggadah, Haggadah of Pesah the "telling" of the Passover story in the context of the household liturgy of Pesah, which accompanies the ritual meal, the **seder.**

patriarchs the founding fathers of Israel: Abraham, Isaac, and Jacob.

patrilineal tracing one's descent through male ancestors. See **matrilineal.**

patristic writers the theologians of the early Christian centuries, from the time of the close of the New Testament period (sometime after A.D. 100) to about the fifth century. Clement, Irenaeus, Origen, and Jerome are patristic figures of importance to biblical studies.

penitential psalms Psalms 6, 32, 38, 51, 102, 130, and 143, used in Christian services of repentance from the earliest times, and by the Middle Ages in regular use during Lent.

Pentapolis the five cities of the **Philistines:** Ashdod, Ashkelon, Ekron, Gath, Gaza.

Pentateuch (Gr. "five scrolls") the first five books of the Bible—Genesis through Deuteronomy—regarded as a unit after its final editing during or after the Exile. The traditional term in Judaism for this collection of books is **Torah,** "teaching." Although these five books are traditionally grouped together, they contain markedly different kinds of writing—prehistory, narrative, law, ritual instruction, and so on—and scholars have investigated the materials of which they are composed. Deuteronomy is largely a separate work that was probably attached to the first four books at a later stage, leading some scholars to speak of a **Tetrateuch** consisting of Genesis through Numbers; and it is also the case that the actual narrative climax of the story, the conquest of the Land, is given in the book of Joshua, leading other scholars to speak of a **Hexateuch** consisting of Genesis through Joshua.

Pentecost (Gr. "fiftieth [day]") the Greek name for the Jewish festival of Weeks (Shavuoth), which occurs 50 days after Passover. On the Pentecost after Jesus' crucifixion, according to Acts chapter 2, the Holy Spirit descended on his followers and inspired them to speak in different languages.

Persian era the period of domination of the Persian empire over the Near East, beginning at around 550 B.C. when Cyrus the Great, King of Persia, defeated the Medes, and lasting until about 330 B.C., when Alexander the Great of Macedon conquered the lands surrounding the Mediterranean and brought them under Greek rule. It was during the Persian era that the Israelites were allowed to return to their land from exile (537 B.C.) and rebuild the Temple (515 B.C. or thereafter).

Persian period the era from approximately 539–333 B.C., from the time of Cyrus the Great until the Greek conquest under Alexander.

personification representing an idea, a value, or other abstract thought as a person. Wisdom is personified as a woman in Proverbs 8.

Pesach the Hebrew word usually translated "Passover."

Pharisees a movement among Jews in the first century A.D., according to Josephus and the writings in the New Testament. The Pharisees were concerned to extend Jewish practice into all areas of life, and followed the tradition of interpretation (**Oral Law**) associated with the schools of Hillel and Shammai. They were thus proponents of a Jewish identity separate from the larger non-Jewish culture that surrounded Judea, but were also opponents of the more conservative Sadducees, who did not accept their traditions of oral law. See **Sadducees.**

Philistines a group from the "Sea Peoples," who invaded and settled on the coastal region of Canaan. They had been repulsed from an invasion of Egypt (ca. 1190 B.C.). The five major Philistine cities (the **Pentapolis**) were Ashkelon, Ashdod, Ekron, Gath, and Gaza.

Philo Judaeus Hellenistic Jewish philosopher (ca. 20 B.C.–A.D. 50) of Alexandria, Egypt. Philo worked out a system that tried to interpret biblical concepts and beliefs in terms of the philosophy of Plato and his followers. In this system, God cannot be known directly, but only through intermediate beings; the soul, the higher element in the human person, is always attempting to return to God, its origin, although if this task is not far enough along at the time of the individual's death, the soul may have to transmigrate into another body and try again. In Philo's view, the best insights of Greek philosophy were compatible with the religion of the Hebrew Scriptures and could be found in the Bible by means of allegorical interpretation, which he used in his own interpretive works. He influenced Jewish writers like the author of the Wisdom of Solomon and Christian theologians such as Clement, Origen, and Ambrose.

Phoenicians the people who lived in the area north of Israel, in part of what is present-day

Lebanon. Their chief cities were Tyre and Sidon. The Phoenicians were known throughout the eastern Mediterranean region as merchants, and for producing a reddish-purple dye, from which they apparently got their name (*phoinix* is the Greek word for the color of the dye).

phylacteries (Gr. *phulakterion,* "amulet," from *phulax,* "guard") see **tefillin.**

Platonism a particular philosophy derived from the teaching of Plato, saying that there is a profound difference, even an opposition, between the realm of matter and the realm of spirit, and that the world of sense experience is essentially an illusion, deriving what reality it has from a correspondence with a true, ultimately real world of Forms. The influence of Platonism on religious thought can be seen in the Wisdom of Solomon; it is also apparent in the thought of **Philo Judaeus** and Christian thinkers like Clement, Origen, and Augustine.

pogrom an officially encouraged, organized massacre of a minority group.

polemic, polemical (Gr. *polemos,* "war") an argument or debate in the form of an attack on one's opponent or on the opposing position. Polemical speech is characterized by verbal attacks, exaggerated language, and sometimes violent imagery.

Polycarp, Letter of an early Christian letter of instruction. it was written by Polycarp, bishop of Smyrna, and addressed to the church of Philippi. It gives advice about dealing with problems in the congregation, exhorts readers to behave in a moral fashion, and combats false teachings. It is therefore similar to many canonical New Testament writings, some of which (like the Gospels and Paul's letters) Polycarp seems to know.

potsherd a broken piece of pottery. Examination of such pieces allows archeologists to date the different levels of a site according to the type of pottery represented at a given level.

primogeniture the social arrangement by which the eldest son inherits a father's title or the bulk of the father's property.

proem a short introduction or preface to a literary text.

prophet (Gr. *prophetes,* "speak out" or "speak forth") the LXX translation of *nabi'* ("one who is called"), the standard Hebrew term for prophet. Synonyms include "seer," "man of God," and "visionary." Besides the authors of the prophetic books, Moses, Samuel, and others are called prophets. Prophets do not so much predict the future, as the current use would imply, as they speak about the situation of their own time and what it will result in if nothing changes.

Prophets, The the second division of the Hebrew Scriptures.

proverb (Heb. *mashal,* "comparison") a short statement of traditional wisdom, supported by long experience and expressed in memorable form. In Hebrew proverbs, generally the second line repeats or develops, sometimes by contrast, the thought of the first line. This feature is called parallelism and is common in Hebrew poetry. Proverbs are quoted in many books of the Bible, but the major collection is in the book of Proverbs. There are also proverbs in the Wisdom of Solomon and, in a longer "essay" form, in Sirach (Ecclesiasticus).

psalm (from Gr. *psalmos*) a song accompanied by musical instruments. In the Bible these songs cover a wide variety of styles and greatly differing content; psalms appear in many places (e.g., 1 Sm 2, 1–10; Jon 2, 1–9), but the principal collection of them is found in the book of Psalms. The Hebrew name for this book is *Tehillim,* meaning "praises," even though the majority of the psalms are not hymns of praise but spread over many other categories such as laments, prayers of thanksgiving and confidence, wisdom, and psalms of royalty.

pseudonymous written or published under a false name (e.g., Testaments of the Twelve Patriarchs). Most pseudonymous writing is attributed to someone much better known than the actual writer, to give the text the benefit of the presumed authority of the famous person.

Ptolemies the rulers of Egypt and its surrounding areas after the breakup of the Greek empire of Alexander the Great, following his death.

Purim the festival that commemorates the delivery of the Jews in Persia from destruction, as recounted in the book of Esther. It is celebrated on 14 or 15 Adar.

Q

Q see **synoptic problem.**

qinah meter a metrical pattern consisting of a line with three stresses followed by a line with two stresses; it is primarily used in psalms of lament or complaint, and in the book of Lamentations, though it can also express joy (Ps 65).

Qumran Community the settlement near Wadi Qumran at the Dead Sea, most likely composed of Essenes. The Qumran group was a sectarian Jewish community that kept its own practices in opposition to the established community in Jerusalem and Judea; the library of this group was discovered in 1948 and is known as the Dead Sea Scrolls.

R

rabbi (Aram. "teacher") a Jewish religious leader who studied Torah and its associated commentaries, particularly the Talmud, and offered his own teaching based on that study.

reader-response criticism analyzing a text by looking at the relationship between the text and its reader, including the clues within the text that guide the reader in drawing meaning from it.

redaction criticism the study of how already existing textual units—narratives of incidents, laws, proverbs, or other isolatable pieces that can be disentangled by **source criticism**—were combined into larger texts by the activities of editors called "redactors." Redaction criticism concentrates on the perspective of the editor, trying to deduce what editorial intentions can be understood from the way smaller units are arranged, expanded, and combined.

redactor an editor who works with already existing units to combine them into larger wholes.

resident alien a foreigner with legal rights living in Israel or an Israelite residing in the territory of another tribe.

revelation (Lat. "remove the veil," translating Gr. *apokalypsis*) belief or insight granted to a human being by a deity or heavenly being.

rhetoric (Gr. *rhetor*, "speaker, orator") the art or study of persuasive speech or writing.

Roman Period the period from 63 B.C. onwards, marking the beginning of Roman rule of Judea.

romance a popular storytelling technique in the ancient Mediterranean world that recounted the situation of young lovers and how they overcome obstacles to their marriage. Tobit is the purest romance in biblical literature. In early Christianity the form was modified to tell the stories of early converts and martyrs and the obstacles to their faith.

Rosh ha-Shanah (Heb. "head [i.e., beginning] of the year") the fall New Year in the Jewish calendar, 1 Tishri. (Rosh Ha-Shanah is now observed for two days.) The beginning of the religious calendar is 1 Nisan.

S

sackcloth rough cloth, often made from animal hair. A garment made of sackcloth is uncomfortable and is worn to indicate penitence or grief.

sacrifice (Lat. "make holy") the practice of giving something of value to God to show one's devotion or commitment. In Israelite religion, sacrifice, usually of an animal or bird (though grain and wine were also offered), was carried out by the ritual destruction of part or all of it by fire on an altar; by chasing it off into the wilderness; by letting it fly away; or by pouring it out on the ground or against the side of the altar. By giving to God something of value, the offerer symbolized the bonding of self with God or the reunion with God after a sinful or unclean person received forgiveness and purification. Christianity took over this idea of sacrifice and applied it to the death of Jesus Christ, teaching that Christ's sacrifice was an atonement for human sin. In modern-day Christianity, sacrifice usually entails doing without things of value (money, material possessions, or time) by giving them away, to the church to promote its work of worship and service, to any organization engaged in the service of others, or directly to those in need.

Sadducees a movement among Jews in the first century A.D., according to Josephus and the New Testament. They held to a strict application of Torah and to maintaining Temple worship according to its mandate; to continue the Temple practices without interference, the Sadducees were apparently willing to collaborate with the occupying Roman power to some extent, including accepting Roman interference in the choice of high priest. They were opposed to the Pharisees in not accepting the traditions of oral law as a guide to Torah practices, and they were also opposed to the political activists who wished to rebel against Roman rule, fearing that any rebellion would bring an end to the limited autonomy under which they could maintain Temple worship. See **Pharisees**.

Samaritan Pentateuch a text of the Torah in Hebrew used by the **Samaritans**. This text disagrees with the Masoretic text at many points. Some of these disagreements reflect Samaritan beliefs (e.g., in the religious importance of Mt. Gerizim), but others are supported by the **Dead Sea Scrolls** and reflect an alternate textual tradition.

Samaritans the descendants of the population of Samaria (northern kingdom) after the invasion of that kingdom and the deportation of the inhabitants in 722 B.C. The Samaritans regard themselves as descended from the Jewish remnant after the deportation, but the returning exiles from the southern kingdom (after the Babylonian Exile) did not regard them as Jews, seeing them rather as descendants of foreigners who had been settled there after the Jewish population had been removed. Therefore, beginning with Ezra and Nehemiah, the leadership forbade intermarriage between Samaritans and Jews. The Samaritans maintained worship (with a Temple on Mt. Gerizim) and the Torah (but not the rest of the Bible), although their calendar is not the same as the Jewish calendar.

Sanhedrin (ultimately from Gr. *synedria* from *syn-* and *hedra,* "with seat," i.e., "council") the religious court, whose membership was drawn from the Jewish ruling classes, that held ruling authority over the territory of Palestine under the Roman empire. The Sanhedrin was responsible for census-taking and taxation, as well as for acting as a court that would decide cases on its own and also, after preliminary determination, send cases on to the Roman governors.

scribe in general, one who could write, especially official documents, and take down dictation for letters, legal proceedings, etc. In the New Testament, a scribe was a lawyer, one who was expert in the requirements and meaning of Jewish law.

scroll a long strip of parchment (treated leather) or papyrus (reeds split, moistened, and pressed together), on which a text was written in columns. The scroll was read by unrolling one side while rolling up the other, to expose successive columns of text.

Second Isaiah see **Deutero-Isaiah**.

Second Temple the Temple constructed ca. 515 B.C. by the returning exiles, and continued and expanded over the course of time, until its destruction by the Romans in A.D. 70.

sect a religious grouping that emphasizes strict adherence to particular teachings and excludes those who do not conform.

seder (Heb. "order") the ritual meal and recitation of Passover eve. Also, the major divisions of the Mishnah (pl. *sedarim*).

Seleucid Empire the political entity that ruled over Syria and (at times) Judea after the death of Alexander the Great. The Seleucid ruler Antiochus IV "Epiphanes" desecrated the Temple in 167 B.C., leading to the Maccabean revolt and the rededication of the Temple in 164 B.C., an event commemorated in the festival of Hanukkah.

Seleucids (after Seleucus, the general who was the first of this ruling group) the rulers of Syria and its surrounding areas after the breakup of the Greek empire of Alexander the Great, following his death.

Septuagint the ancient Greek translation of the Hebrew Scriptures. The Septuagint was translated over a lengthy period beginning probably in the third century B.C. Traditionally there were 72 translators, a number that is rounded off to 70 and, in roman numerals, used as the abbreviation for this translation (LXX). The Septuagint was prepared for the use of Jews who lived outside the land of Israel and whose main language was Greek. It is important for several reasons: it translated a version of the Hebrew text that is older than the currently available Hebrew (Masoretic) text (see **Masoretic text**); it contains additional works, the Apocryphal/Deuterocanonical Books, most of which were originally written in Greek; and it was the Bible of early Christians and therefore represents what they thought of as Scripture.

Shabbat (Heb. "cessation") the Sabbath day.

Shavuot the festival of "Weeks," (also "Pentecost," Gr. for "fiftieth" [day]) the spring harvest, occurring, according to Priestly texts, 50 days (seven full weeks) after Passover.

Shekhinah a post-biblical term for the "dwelling" or "presence" of God with Israel; by extension, the divine manifestation in the community's life, or the sense of divine immanence within the world.

Shema the first word, used as a title, of the exhortation (Dt 6, 4), "Hear, O Israel, the LORD our God is one LORD" (or, "the LORD our God, the LORD is one"); also the name of perhaps the most important and best-known prayer in Judaism, comprised of Deuteronomy 6, 4–9; 11, 13–21 and Numbers 15, 37–41.

Sheol the underworld or abode of the dead. In the Hebrew Bible (Old Testament), all deceased descended to Sheol; there is no concept of a separate heaven and hell.

shofar the ram's horn for ceremonial use. In ancient Israel it was sounded to announce the anointing of a king or as a summons to war or to sound an alarm; today, in the synagogue, it is sounded on the High Holy Days.

simile a comparison, using "like" or "as" rather than, as in metaphor, linking two things directly. "[He] made my feet swift as a deer's" (Ps 18, 34).

source criticism the effort to discover the sources or documents behind a text and to explore how the sources were combined into larger units. See **documentary hypothesis.**

Southern Kingdom the remaining part of the undivided kingdom of Israel, after the northern tribes withdrew from Israel at Solomon's death (1 Kgs 12). It is also called Judah.

Stoics Greek philosophers in the Hellenistic and Roman periods, who taught that emotions should be strictly controlled by reason.

Sukkot (Heb. "booths") the autumn harvest festival ("festival of ingathering"), during which it is customary, following Leviticus 23, 42–43, to dwell in temporary booths. See **Tabernacles, feast of.**

suzerain the lord or ruler to whom loyalty is due in a covenant relationship. (Although the term is actually Old French for "sovereign," and originally applied to the feudal relationship of lord to peasant or subsidiary, it has been adapted for the ancient Near Eastern covenant system.)

synagogue (Gr. "coming together with") an assembly; a congregation. For Jews who were too distant from the Temple to worship at it, and for all Jews after the final destruction of the Temple by the Romans in A.D. 70, the synagogue became the only form of worship. Services consisted of prayer, song, and study of the sacred text.

syncretism the incorporation into one religion of practices and teachings derived from another, or the effort to combine two different religious traditions into a third, composite religion.

synonymous parallelism an imprecise term used for the type of **parallelism** where the second line or *colon* of a *bicolon* echoes the meaning of the first in different terms, for example, Isaiah 1, 3, "An ox knows its owner, and an ass its master's manger: But Israel does not know, my people has not understood."

Synoptic Gospels Matthew, Mark, and Luke. "Synoptic" means "view together" and is applied to these writings because they, unlike John, can be readily compared.

synoptic problem the observation that in many passages Matthew and Luke repeat with only minor changes what Mark says, yet in other passages they do not follow Mark, or include stories or sayings that Mark does not have, yet match each other very closely. (They also each include material that none of the others have, but that is not a characteristic that needs to be explained.) Many commentators, from the earliest years of Christianity, have tried to understand the relationship among the Synoptic Gospels. According to the most widely held theory, Matthew and Luke relied on Mark and on another document (now lost) that contained mostly sayings of Jesus; this second document is referred to as "Q" from the German word "Quelle," meaning "source." In addition, Matthew and Luke each had their own sources.

T

tabernacle the portable sanctuary used by the Israelites during their wanderings in the wilderness. Exodus chapters 25–30 contain instructions for building it; the construction is narrated in Exodus chapters 35–40. It was eventually replaced by the Temple.

Tabernacles, Feast of the final harvest festival of grapes and olives, falling within our month of October. It was also called the "Feast of Booths" because the harvesters lived in the field in makeshift tents or booths. See **Sukkot.**

tablet a slab, typically of clay, with a smoothed surface that can be inscribed with a text.

talion (Lat. *talio,* "in kind" from *talis,* "like," "such like") a punishment that is of the same kind as the crime: exacting an equivalent penalty, such as an equal economic loss for theft, or death for murder, or "an eye for an eye." Talion is well-attested in Mesopotamian law, and in some biblical legal collections.

Talmud (Heb. "teaching") the title of the two great collections of rabbinic teaching, the Jerusalem Talmud or Talmud Yerushalmi and the Babylonian Talmud or Talmud Bavli. The Talmuds were compiled beginning after A.D. 200, as an extensive commentary on the Mishnah; they consist of comments on, and extensions of, the Mishnah sections to work out the application of Jewish teaching to everyday life, but they also include much other material, and information and teaching on a wide range of topics. The form of the Talmuds is that passages of the Mishnah are commented on by rabbinic teachings (called *gemara*). The Mishnah is not treated in its entirety. At the beginning of the Talmud's formation, the two centers of rabbinic study (the land of Israel and Babylonia) were in contact with each other and the commentary therefore reflected a common effort; later, especially with the completion of the Talmud in Israel (ca. A.D. 400), the Babylonian effort continued to refine and extend the applications, and it was the Talmud developed in Babylonia (completion after A.D. 500) that was distributed worldwide, under the auspices of the academies that continued to work in Babylon until the beginning of the second millennium A.D.

tefillin small black leather boxes containing biblical passages from Exodus 13, 1–10; 13, 11–16 and Deuteronomy 6, 4–9; 11, 13–21. Two are worn during weekday morning prayer: one on the head (above the space between the eyes, just below the hairline) and one on the (left) arm (see e.g., Dt 6, 8). Also called "phylacteries."

tel a mound formed by repeated construction, occupation, and destruction of buildings on a particular site.

Temple the central place of worship for Israelite religion in Jerusalem, referring either to the first Temple built by Solomon or the Second Temple of Zerubbabel that was enlarged and rebuilt by Herod the Great.

testament (Lat. *testamentum,* "will, covenant"; translating Gr. *diatheke,* "covenant") an agreement, especially between God and human beings; also, the collections of books detailing various covenants between God and human beings: the "Old Testament" or "first covenant," that between God and Noah, Abraham, Moses, and the Israelites in general; and the "New Testament" or "new covenant" established by Jesus Christ.

Tetrateuch the first four books of the Bible, Genesis through Numbers, regarded as an edited collection to which Deuteronomy was then attached. See **Pentateuch.**

Text any fixed, written form of words; particularly, any writing that is subject to historical investigation, interpretation, exegesis, or homiletics.

textual criticism the effort to establish, by scholarly assessment of manuscript copies and other sources, an accurate version of a text according to what the original author had written.

theodicy the theological effort to justify the goodness of God in the face of suffering.

theophany (Gr. "appearance of god") the temporary appearance or manifestation of a divine being in a form that can be apprehended by the human senses.

Third Isaiah see **Trito-Isaiah.**

Thomas, Gospel of an early collection of sayings attributed to Jesus. It contains no miracle stories and no account of Jesus' deeds, his birth, his death, or the resurrection. Some of the sayings resemble those in the canonical Gospels, but others reflect a philosophy that regards spirit and matter as radically different and opposed to each other; in this view, life on earth is one of spirits trapped in matter, and the purpose of life is to free oneself from matter and attain eternal life in the spiritual realm. This philosophy, called **gnosticism,** was rejected by the main body of early Christians, and this may explain why the Gospel of Thomas was never accepted as canonical.

thresh to beat gathered stalks of grain to separate the grain from the stems and husks. See **winnow.** A threshing floor, a flat area used for threshing grain, was often built on a hilltop to catch the breeze necessary for winnowing. This hilltop location made a threshing floor an ideal location for holding sacrifices (1 Chr 21, 18–27).

threshing floor a location where the usable portion of grain is separated from its outer covering. Grain is threshed by being beaten to crack the husks and separate the grain from the stems. It is then winnowed by being tossed in a flat basket in a breeze, allowing the husks (chaff), which are lighter, to blow away. A good location for this process is a flat area on a hilltop; this was also an ideal spot for offering sacrifice (see 1 Chr 21, 18–27).

toledoth (Heb. "generations") lists of descendants; also, histories of ancestors and their descendants.

Torah (Heb. "teaching, instruction") the first division of the Hebrew Scriptures, consisting of Genesis through Deuteronomy. The word (and hence the title) is sometimes translated "law," but this translation can be misleading since the full collection of books contains much more than law codes and regulations.

tradition (Lat. *traditio,* "what is handed on") the means by which beliefs, customs, stories, laws, religious practices, and other cultural phenomena are handed down from one generation to the next. The Bible is in part a record of traditions, first among the Hebrew people and then among the Christians. The Bible itself was first represented in tradition: in traditional stories and beliefs, in religious practices, and so on; only later was it written down and handed on in that form. The study of tradition—of how things are handed on, and how they change or stay the same during the process—is of great importance for understanding the Bible and the beliefs that are based on it.

tradition criticism the interpretation of the history of a tradition, including stages such as oral transmission, the alteration of a tradition to address a changed situation, and the examination of particular kinds of traditions, such as the explanation of place names, the development of religious practices, or the growth or disuse of social practices.

Transjordan the area to the east of the Jordan River.

transmission history an account, usually inferred, of how a text came down to the present from its originator. Steps in transmission history

can include oral transmission, redaction, manuscript copying, and scribal emendation.

Trito-Isaiah the scholarly term for chs 56–66 (or 55–66) of Isaiah. These chapters are primarily concerned with the life of the returned exiles in the province of Yehud (the Persian name for Judah) after 538 B.C. Some scholars doubt the separate existence of Trito-Isaiah; others maintain that it is not the product of one author, but a collection of diverse oracles by different members of a "school of Isaiah" collected during the Persian period.

Twelve, Book of the the Hebrew Bible's designation for the **Minor Prophets.**

typology (Gr. *typos,* the raised design on a seal for imprinting in wax, then by extension a pattern or model) understanding persons or events, especially in the New Testament, by referring them to Old Testament "types," such as the Exodus (1 Cor 10, 1–6); Solomon (Lk 11, 31); or narratives like that of Jonah (Lk 11, 29–30).

U

uncircumcised, the Gentiles (Rom 4, 9; Gal 2, 7).

unleavened bread (Heb. *matzah, matzot*) bread made without yeast; also the festival that follows **Passover.**

V

vassal the underlord in a covenant relationship, who is granted power and control over people in a particular area in return for loyalty to the suzerain.

Vatican II the Council of Catholic bishops under the leadership of Popes John XXIII and Paul VI, held 1962–1965 in the Vatican. It undertook numerous reforms, including establishing vernacular liturgies and issuing decrees on ecumenism, relations with Judaism and other religions, and the Church and the modern world. The Council also promoted the study and reading of the Scriptures and encouraged new Catholic translations and commentaries to help the understanding of nonexperts.

Vulgate (Lat., "common") the Latin translation of the Bible begun by St. Jerome in the fourth century A.D., completed 405. Jerome translated his version directly from the Hebrew (unlike that of the previous Latin version [the "Old Latin" or "Vetus Latina"], which was translated from the Septuagint) and Greek texts and also separated the Old Testament text that was not part of the Hebrew Bible, but included in the Septuagint, into a separate section of "deuterocanonical" books. In the Middle Ages the Vulgate became the standard translation of the Bible for Western Christians. With the Protestant Reformation, its authority was questioned, but was reaffirmed by the Roman Catholic Church at the Council of Trent (1546).

W

wadi (Arabic) a stream bed or valley that is dry for part of the year; an arroyo or gulch.

Weeks, Feast of Shavuoth or Pentecost.

winnow to separate grain from its husks (called chaff) after it has been threshed. The threshed grain is placed in a wide, flat basket and tossed repeatedly into the air, allowing a breeze to blow away the lighter chaff while the grain drops back down into the basket.

wisdom literature Job, Proverbs, and Ecclesiastes in the Hebrew Bible; Sirach and Wisdom in the Septuagint; and some Psalms, for example, 37. Wisdom literature is concerned with insight, instruction, meditation of the meaning of life, and moral exhortation. It does not generally concern itself with key events in Israel's history, such as the Exodus; central teachings, such as the covenant; or focal institutions, such as the Davidic monarchy, prophecy, or the Temple.

Writings the third division of the Hebrew Scriptures.

X

xenophobia fear of, or contempt for, foreigners; racial exclusiveness.

Y

Yehud designation of the province of Judea during Persian times.

YHWH the name of God, which conventionally remains unpronounced and is represented in the text by the Hebrew letters *yod-he-vav-he* and the vowels for the title *Adonai,* "my Lord." In standard English translations, YHWH is represented by the word LORD written in capital and small capital letters. The original vocalization and meaning of this name is unknown, though it is connected to the verb *h-y-h,* "be" or "become," most likely in a causitive sense, "he who causes to be."

Yom Kippur (Heb. "day of atonement") the solemn fast observed each year on 10 Tishri, according to the command recorded in Leviticus 23, 26–32. The observance involves abstention of various kinds and focuses on personal and communal repentance (teshuvah). The prayer services begin with the evening service and continue through the next day, with a morning service, an additional service, an afternoon service, and a concluding service.

Z

Zealot a member of the Jewish revolutionary movement during the Roman occupation of Palestine; an advocate of armed resistance in Roman rule.

ziggurat a temple-tower in ancient Mesopotamia. Ziggurats are presumed to represent a mount, on the top of which the earthly and divine realms merged.

Zion the name of the fortified hill within Jerusalem and thus, by extension, an alternative name for Jerusalem itself.

INDEX TO READING GUIDE

INDEX TO READING GUIDE

COLLABORATORS
on the Old Testament of the *New American Bible*

BISHOPS' COMMITTEE OF THE CONFRATERNITY OF CHRISTIAN DOCTRINE

Most Rev. Charles P. Greco, D.D., *Chairman* Most Rev. Joseph T. McGucken, S.T.D. Most Rev. Vincent S. Waters, D.D.
Most Rev. Romeo Blanchette, D.D. Most Rev. Christopher J. Weldon, D.D.

EDITORS IN CHIEF

Rev. Louis F. Hartman, C.SS.R., S.S.L., LING. OR. L., *Chairman* Rev. Msgr. Patrick W. Skehan, S.T.D., LL.D., *Vice-Chairman*
Rev. Stephen J. Hartdegen, O.F.M., S.S.L., *Secretary*

ASSOCIATE EDITORS AND TRANSLATORS

Rev. Edward P. Arbez, S.S., S.T.D. Rev. Msgr. Edward J. Byrne, PH.D., S.T.D. Rev. Edward A. Cerny, S.S., S.T.D.
Rev. James E. Coleran, S.J., S.T.L., S.S.L. Rev. John J. Collins, S.J., M.A., S.S.L.
Sr. M. Emmanuel Collins, O.S.F., PH.D. Prof. Frank M. Cross, Jr., PH.D. Rev. Patrick Cummins, O.S.B., S.T.D.
Rev. Antonine A. DeGuglielmo, O.F.M., S.T.D., S.S.L., S.S. LECT. GEN. Rev. Alexander A. DiLella, O.F.M., S.T.L., S.S.L., PH.D.
Most Rev. John J. Dougherty, S.T.L., S.S.D. William A. Dowd, S.J., S.T.D., S.S.L. Prof. David Noel Freedman, PH.D.
Rev. Michael J. Gruenthaner, S.J., S.T.D., S.S.D. Rev. Msgr. Maurice A. Hofer, S.S.L. Rev. Justin Krellner, O.S.B., S.T.D.
Rev. Joseph L. Lilly, C.M., S.T.D., S.S.L. Rev. Roderick F. MacKenzie, S.J., M.A., S.S.D.
Rev. Edward A. Mangan, C.SS.R., S.S.L. Rev. Daniel W. Martin, C.M., S.T.L., S.S.L. Rev. William H. McClellan, S.J.
Rev. James McGlinchey, C.M., S.T.D. Rev. Frederick Moriarty, S.J., S.S.L., S.T.D. Rev. Richard T. Murphy, O.P., S.T.D., S S.D.
Rev. Roland E. Murphy, O. CARM., M.A., S.T.D., S.S.L. Rev. Msgr. William R. Newton, M.S., S.S.D.
Rev. Eberhard Olinger, O.S.B. Rev. Charles H. Pickar, O.S.A., S.T.L., S.S.L.
Rev. Christopher Rehwinkel, O.F.M., S.T.D., S.S. LECT. GEN. Rev. Msgr. John R. Rowan, S.T.D., S.S.L.
Prof. J. A. Sanders, PH.D. Rev. Edward F. Siegman, C.PP.S., S.T.D., S.S.L. Rev. Msgr. Matthew P. Stapleton, S.T.D., S.S.L.
Rev. Msgr. John E. Steinmueller, S.T.D., S.S.L. Rev. John Ujlaki, O.S.B., LITT.D.
Rev. Bruce Vawter, C.M., S.T.L., S.S.D. Rev. John B. Weisengoff, S.T.D., S.S.L.

COLLABORATORS
on the Revised New Testament of the *New American Bible*

BISHOPS' AD HOC COMMITTEE

Most Rev. Theodore E. McCarrick, D.D.   Most Rev. Richard J. Sklba, D.D.   Most Rev. J. Francis Stafford, D.D.
Most Rev. John F. Whealon, D.D., *Chairman*

BOARD OF EDITORS

Rev. Msgr. Myles M. Bourke   Rev. Francis T. Gignac, S.J., *Chairman*   Rev. Stephen J. Hartdegen, O.F.M., *Secretary*
Rev. Claude J. Peifer, O.S.B.   Rev. John H. Reumann

REVISERS

Rev. Msgr. Myles M. Bourke   Rev. Frederick W. Danker   Rev. Alexander A. Di Lella, O.F.M.   Rev. Charles H. Giblin, S.J.
Rev. Francis T. Gignac, S.J.   Rev. Stephen J. Hartdegen, O.F.M.   Dr. Maurya P. Horgan   Rev. John R. Keating, S.J.
Rev. John Knox   Dr. Paul J. Kobelski   Dr. J. Rebecca Lyman   Bro. Elliott C. Maloney, O.S.B.   Dr. Janet A. Timbie

CONSULTANTS

Rev. Joseph Jensen, O.S.D.   Rev. Aidan Kavanagh, O.S.D.   Dr. Marianne Sawicki

BUSINESS MANAGER

Charles A. Buggé

WORD PROCESSOR

Suzanna Jordan

COLLABORATORS
on the Revised Psalms of the *New American Bible*

BISHOPS' AD HOC COMMITTEE

Most Rev. Enrique San Pedro, s.j.   Most Rev. Richard Sklba, d.d.   Most Rev. Donald W. Trautman, s.t.d., s.s.l.
Most Rev. Emil A. Wcela   Most Rev. John F. Whealon, s.s.l., *Chairman*

BOARD OF EDITORS

Rev. Richard Clifford, s.j.   Bro. Aloysius Fitzgerald, f.s.c.   Rev. Joseph Jensen, o.s.b.   Rev. Roland Murphy, o. carm.
Sr. Irene Nowell, o.s.b.   Dr. Judith Sanderson

REVISERS

Prof. Gary Anderson   Rev. Michael L. Barré   Rev. Christopher T. Begg   Dr. Joseph Blenkinsopp
Rev. Anthony R. Ceresko, o.s.f.s.   Rev. Richard J. Clifford, s.j.   Rev. Aelred Cody, o.s.b.   Prof. Michael D. Coogan
Rev. Alexander A. Di Leila, o.f.m.   Dr. Robert A. Di Vito   Bro. Aloysius Fitzgerald, f.s.c.   Rev. Michael D. Guinan, o.f.m.
Rev. William L. Holladay   Rev. William Irwin, c.s.b.   Rev. Joseph Jensen, o.s.b.   Rev. John S. Kselman
Dr. Conrad E. L'Heureux   Rev. Leo Laberge, o.m.i.   Dr. Paul G. Mosca   Rev. Dr. Roland E. Murphy, o. carm.
Dr. Michael Patrick O'Connor   Rev. Brian J. Peckham, s.j.   Prof. Jimmy J. Roberts   Sr. Eileen M. Schuller, o.s.u.
Dr. Byron E. Shafer   Prof. Mark S. Smith

ENGLISH CONSULTANTS

Dr. Catherine Dunn   Bro. Daniel Burke, f.s.c.

BUSINESS MANAGER

Charles A. Buggé

1851

A CONCORDANCE
TO THE *NEW AMERICAN BIBLE*

SPECIAL SYMBOLS

* *GOD, *LORD and *LORD'S index the proper name of God *(Yahweh)* typeset in small capital letters (GOD, LORD, LORD'S) in the NAB.

→ An arrow following an entry heading points to related words for additional study

= An equals sign marks an alternate proper name for additional study (e.g., ISRAEL = JACOB)

John R. Kohlenberger III

TABLE OF ABBREVIATIONS

Ac . . . . Acts	Jer . . . . Jeremiah	2Pe . . . . 2 Peter
Am . . . . Amos	Jn . . . . John	Phm . . . . Philemon
Bar . . . . Baruch	1Jn . . . . 1 John	Php . . . . Philippians
1Ch . . . . 1 Chronicles	2Jn . . . . 2 John	Pr . . . . Proverbs
2Ch . . . . 2 Chronicles	3Jn . . . . 3 John	Ps . . . . Psalms
1Co . . . . 1 Corinthians	Jnh . . . . Jonah	Rev . . . . Revelation
2Co . . . . 2 Corinthians	Job . . . . Job	Ro . . . . Romans
Col . . . . Colossians	Joel . . . . Joel	Ru . . . . Ruth
Da . . . . Daniel	Jos . . . . Joshua	1Sa . . . . 1 Samuel
Dt . . . . Deuteronomy	Jude . . . . Jude	2Sa . . . . 2 Samuel
Ecc . . . . Ecclesiastes	1Ki . . . . 1 Kings	Sir . . . . Sirach
Eph . . . . Ephesians	2Ki . . . . 2 Kings	SS . . . . Song of Songs
Est . . . . Esther	La . . . . Lamentations	1Th . . . . 1 Thessalonians
Ex . . . . Exodus	Lev . . . . Leviticus	2Th . . . . 2 Thessalonians
Eze . . . . Ezekiel	Lk . . . . Luke	1Ti . . . . 1 Timothy
Ezr . . . . Ezra	Mal . . . . Malachi	2Ti . . . . 2 Timothy
Gal . . . . Galatians	1Mc . . . . 1 Maccabees	Tit . . . . Titus
Ge . . . . Genesis	2Mc . . . . 2 Maccabees	Tob . . . . Tobit
Hab . . . . Habakkuk	Mic . . . . Micah	Wis . . . . Wisdom
Hag . . . . Haggai	Mk . . . . Mark	Zec . . . . Zechariah
Heb . . . . Hebrews	Mt . . . . Matthew	Zep . . . . Zephaniah
Hos . . . . Hosea	Na . . . . Nahum	
Isa . . . . Isaiah	Ne . . . . Nehemiah	
Jas . . . . James	Nu . . . . Numbers	**OTHER**
Jdg . . . . Judges	Ob . . . . Obadiah	S . . . . Shorter Ending of Mark
Jdt . . . . Judith	1Pe . . . . 1 Peter	Pr: . . . . Sirach Prologue

A

AARON

Genealogy (Ex 6:16-20; Jos 21:4, 10; 1Ch 6:3-15). Priesthood of (Ex 28:1; Nu 17; Heb 5:1-4; 7), vestments of (Ex 28; 39), consecration of (Ex 29), ordination of (Lev 8).

Spokesman for Moses (Ex 4:14-16, 27-31; 7:1-2). Supported Moses' hands in battle (Ex 17:8-13). Built golden calf (Ex 32; Dt 9:20). Spoke against Moses (Nu 12). Priesthood opposed (Nu 16); staff budded (Nu 17). Forbidden to enter the promised land (Nu 20:1-12). Death of (Nu 20:22-29; 33:38-39). Praise of (Sir 45:6-22).

ABANDON → ABANDONED

Dt   4:31   God, he will not **a** and destroy you,
2Ch 15: 2   you; but if you **a** him, he will **a** you.
Ac   2:27   because you will not **a** my soul

ABANDONED → ABANDON

Jdg   2:13   Because they had thus **a** him
2Ch 12: 5   'You have **a** me, and therefore I have
    12: 5   therefore I have **a** you to the power
Sir   49: 4   They **a** the law of the Most High,
Isa 54: 7   For a brief moment I **a** you,

ABBA

Mk 14:36   he said, "**A**, Father, all things are
Ro   8:15   through which we cry, "**A**, Father!"
Gal   4: 6   our hearts, crying out, "**A**, Father!"

ABEDNEGO → = AZARIAH

Deported to Babylon with Daniel (Da 1:1-6). Name changed from Azariah (Da 1:7). Refused defilement by food (Da 1:8-20). Refused idol worship (Da 3:1-12); saved from furnace (Da 3:13-30).

ABEL

Second son of Adam (Ge 4:2). Offered acceptable sacrifice (Ge 4:4; Heb 11:4; 12:24). Murdered by Cain (Ge 4:8; Mt 23:35; Lk 11:51; 1Jn 3:12).

ABIATHAR

High priest in days of Saul and David (1Sa 22; 2Sa 15; 1Ki 1-2; Mk 2:26). Escaped Saul's slaughter of priests (1Sa 22:18-23). Supported David in Absalom's revolt (2Sa 15:24-29). Supported Adonijah (1Ki 1:7-42); deposed by Solomon (1Ki 2:22-35; cf. 1Sa 2:31-35).

ABIDE

Ps   15: 1   LORD, who may **a** in your tent?
    91: 1   High, who **a** in the shadow
Wis   3: 9   the faithful shall **a** with him in love:

ABIGAIL

1. Sister of David (1Ch 2:16-17).
2. Wife of Nabal (1Sa 25:30); pled for his life with David (1Sa 25:14-35). Became David's wife after Nabal's death (1Sa 25:36-42).

ABIHU

Son of Aaron (Ex 6:23; 24:1, 9); killed for offering illicit fire (Lev 10; Nu 3:2-4; 1Ch 24:1-2).

ABIJAH

1. Second son of Samuel (1Ch 6:28); a corrupt judge (1Sa 8:1-5).
2. An Aaronic priest (1Ch 24:10; Lk 1:5).
3. Son of Jeroboam I; died as prophesied by Ahijah (1Ki 14:1-18).
4. Son of Rehoboam, also called Abijam; king of Judah who fought Jeroboam I attempting to reunite Israel (1Ki 14:31-15:8; 2Ch 12:16-14:1).

ABILITY → ABLE

Mt 25:15   third, one—to each according to his **a**.

ABIMELECH

1. King of Gerar who took Abraham's wife Sarah, believing her to be his sister (Ge 20). Covenanted with Abraham (Ge 21:22-33).
2. King of Gerar who took Isaac's wife Rebekah, believing her to be his sister (Ge 26:1-11). Covenanted with Isaac (Ge 26:12-31).
3. Son of Gideon (Jdg 8:31). Attempted to become king (Jdg 9).

ABIRAM

Sided with Dathan in rebellion against Moses and Aaron (Nu 16; 26:9; Dt 11:6; Sir 45:18).

ABISHAI

Son of Zeruiah, David's sister (1Sa 26:6; 1Ch 2:16). One of David's chief warriors (1Ch 11:15-21): against Edom (1Ch 18:12-13), Ammon (2Sa 10), Absalom (2Sa 18), Sheba (2Sa 20). Wanted to kill Saul (1Sa 26), killed Abner (2Sa 2:18-27; 3:22-39).

ABLE → ABILITY

Ex   18:25   He picked out **a** men from all Israel
Jdt   11:18   of them will be a to withstand you.
Ro   14: 4   for the Lord is **a** to make him stand.
2Co   9: 8   God is **a** to make every grace
Eph   6:11   you may be **a** to stand firm against
2Ti   1:12   that he is **a** to guard what has been
Heb   2:18   he is **a** to help those who are being
    5: 2   He is **a** to deal patiently
    7:25   he is always **a** to save those who
Rev   5: 3   or under the earth was **a** to open

ABNER

Cousin of Saul and commander of his army (1Sa 14:50; 17:55-57; 26). Made Ish-Bosheth king after Saul (2Sa 2:8-10), but later defected to David (2Sa 3:6-21). Killed Asahel (2Sa 2:18-32), for which he was killed by Joab and Abishai (2Sa 3:22-39).

ABOLISH → ABOLISHING

Mt   5:17   think that I have come to **a** the law

ABOLISHING → ABOLISH

Da   11:31   **a** the daily sacrifice and setting

ABOMINABLE → ABOMINATION

2Ch 28: 3   by fire according to the **a** practice
Eze   7:20   of them their **a** images [their idols].

ABOMINATION → ABOMINABLE, ABOMINATIONS

1Ma   6: 7   they had pulled down the **A**
Pr   6:16   hates, yes, seven are an **a** to him;
Da   9:27   temple wing shall be the horrible **a**

ABOMINATIONS → ABOMINATION

Eze 44: 7   broken my covenant by all your **a**.
Rev 17: 5   of harlots and of the **a** of the earth."

ABOUND

Ro   6: 1   we persist in sin that grace may **a**?

ABOVE

Dt   4:39   the LORD is God in the heavens **a**
Jn   3: 7   told you, 'You must be born from **a**.'
Php   2: 9   him the name that is **a** every name,
Col   3: 2   Think of what is **a**, not of what is

ABRAHAM

Abram, son of Terah (Ge 11:26-27), husband of Sarah (Ge 11:29).

Covenant relation with the LORD (Ge 12:1-3; 13:14-17; 15; 17; 22:15-18; Ex 2:24; Ne 9:8; Ps 105; Mic 7:20; Lk 1:68-75; Ro 4; Heb 6:13-15).

Called from Ur, via Haran, to Canaan (Ge 12:1; Ac 7:2-4; Heb 11:8-10). Moved to Egypt, nearly lost Sarah to Pharoah (Ge 12:10-20). Divided the land with Lot; settled in Hebron (Ge 13). Saved Lot from four kings (Ge 14:1-16); blessed by Melchizedek (Ge 14:17-20; Heb 7:1-20). Declared righteous by faith (Ge 15:6; Ro 4:3; Gal 3:6-9; 1Ma 2:52). Fathered Ishmael by Hagar (Ge 16).

Name changed from Abram (Ge 17:5; Ne 9:7). Circumcised (Ge 17; Ro 4:9-12). Entertained three visitors (Ge 18); promised a son by Sarah (Ge 18:9-15; 17:16). Questioned destruction of Sodom and Gomorrah (Ge 18:16-33). Moved to Gerar; nearly lost Sarah to Abimelech (Ge 20). Fathered Isaac by Sarah (Ge 21:1-7; Ac 7:8; Heb 11:11-12); sent away Hagar and Ishmael (Ge 21:8-21; Gal 4:22-30). Covenant with Abimelech (Ge 21:22-32). Tested by offering Isaac (Ge 22; Heb 11:17-19; Jas 2:21-24). Sarah died; bought field of Ephron for burial (Ge 23). Secured wife for Isaac (Ge 24). Fathered children by Keturah (Ge 25:1-6; 1Ch 1:32-33). Death (Ge 25:7-11).

Called servant of God (Ge 26:24), friend of God (2Ch 20:7; Isa 41:8; Jas 2:23), prophet (Ge 20:7), father of Israel (Ex 3:15; Isa 51:2; Mt 3:9; Jn 8:39-58). Praised (Sir 44:19-45:1).

ABSALOM
Son of David by Maacah (2Sa 3:3; 1Ch 3:2). Killed Amnon for rape of his sister Tamar; banished by David (2Sa 13). Returned to Jerusalem; received by David (2Sa 14). Rebelled against David (2Sa 15-17). Killed (2Sa 18).

ABSENT
1Co	5: 3	although a in body but present
Col	2: 5	For even if I am a in the flesh, yet I

ABUNDANCE → ABUNDANTLY
2Co	9: 8	you may have an a for every good

ABUNDANTLY → ABUNDANCE
Jn	10:10	might have life and have it more a.

ABYSS
Lk	8:31	not to order them to depart to the a.
Ro	10: 7	or "Who will go down into the a?"

ACCEPT → ACCEPTED
Mt	19:11	"Not all can a [this] word, but only
Jn	1:11	but his own people did not a him.

ACCEPTED → ACCEPT
Lk	4:24	no prophet is a in his own native

ACCESS
Ro	5: 2	through whom we have gained a
Eph	2:18	through him we both have a in one

ACCORDING
Sir	16:12	he judges men, each a to his deeds.
Mt	9:29	it be done for you a to your faith."
Ro	8: 4	who live not a to the flesh but a
Heb	2: 4	gifts of the holy Spirit a to his will.
1Jn	5:14	that if we ask anything a to his will,
Rev	20:12	life. The dead were judged a to their

ACCOUNT
Mt	12:36	of judgment people will render an a
Heb	4:13	him to whom we must render an a.

ACCURSED → CURSE
Ro	9: 3	I could wish that I myself were a
Rev	22: 3	Nothing a will be found there

ACCUSE → ACCUSER
Zec	3: 1	stood at his right hand to a him.
Mt	12:10	sabbath?" so that they might a him.

ACCUSER → ACCUSE
Rev	12:10	For the a of our brothers is cast out,

ACHAN
Sinned at Jericho; stoned (Jos 7; 22:20; 1Ch 2:7).

ACHISH
King of Gath before whom David feigned insanity (1Sa 21:10-15). Later "ally" of David (2Sa 27-29).

ACKNOWLEDGE
Mt	10:32	others I will a before my heavenly
Ro	1:28	since they did not see fit to a God,

ACT → ACTED, ACTIVE, ACTS
Ps	37: 5	to the LORD; trust that God will a

ACTED → ACT
Eze	20: 9	but I a for my name's sake, that it
Ac	3:17	that you a out of ignorance, just as
1Ti	1:13	been mercifully treated because I a

ACTIVE → ACT
Jas	2:22	faith was a along with his works,

ACTS → ACT
Ex	6: 6	arm and with mighty a of judgment.
Ps	71:15	day after day your a of deliverance,
Mt	7:24	a on them will be like a wise man
Jas	1:25	who forgets but a doer who a,

ADAM
First man (Tob 8:6; Ge 1:26-2:25; Ro 5:14; 1Ti 2:13). Sin of (Ge 3; Hos 6:7 [note]; Ro 5:12-21). Children of (Ge 4:1-5:5). Death of (Ge 5:5; Ro 5:12-21; 1Co 15:22).

ADD
Dt	4: 2	you shall not a to what I command
Pr	30: 6	A nothing to his words, lest he
Lk	12:25	of you by worrying a a moment

ADMONISH → ADMONITION
Col	3:16	you teach and a one another,

ADMONITION → ADMONISH
Pr	15: 5	The fool spurns his father's a,

ADONIJAH
1. Son of David by Haggith (2Sa 3:4; 1Ch 3:2). Attempted to be king after David; killed at Solomon's order (1Ki 1-2).
2. Levite; teacher of the Law (2Ch 17:8).

ADOPTION
Ro	8:15	fear, but you received a spirit of a,
	8:23	within ourselves as we wait for a,
Gal	4: 5	the law, so that we might receive a.

ADORNED → ADORNMENT
Lk	21: 5	how the temple was a with costly
Rev	17: 4	purple and scarlet and a with gold,
	21: 2	God, prepared as a bride a for her

ADORNMENT → ADORNED
Pr	3:22	to your soul, and an a for your neck.

ADULTERERS → ADULTERY
Jer	23:10	With a the land is filled; on their
1Co	6: 9	nor idolaters nor a nor boy

ADULTERESS → ADULTERY
Lev	20:10	and the a shall be put to death.
Pr	2:16	from the a with her smooth words,

ADULTERY → ADULTERERS, ADULTERESS
Ex	20:14	"You shall not commit a
Jer	3: 9	committing a with stone and wood.
Mt	5:28	lust has already committed a
Lk	16:18	and marries another commits a,
	16:18	from her husband commits a.
Jn	8: 3	a woman who had been caught in a

ADVANTAGE
Ecc	7:12	the a of knowledge is that wisdom
Ro	3: 1	What a is there then in being a Jew?
1Co	10:24	No one should seek his own a,

ADVERSARIES → ADVERSARY
2Sa	22:49	Above my a you exalt me

ADVERSARY
1Ti	5:14	so as to give the a no pretext

ADVICE
2Ch	10:13	Ignoring the a the elders had given
Tob	4:18	lightly of any a that can be useful.
Pr	8:14	Mine are counsel and a; Mine is
Sir	37:11	pay no attention to any a they give.

ADVOCATE
Jn	14:26	The A, the holy Spirit
	15:26	the A comes whom I will send you
1Jn	2: 1	sin, we have an A with the Father,

AFFLICT → AFFLICTED, AFFLICTION
2Sa	7:10	continue to a them as they did

AFFLICTED → AFFLICT
2Co	4: 8	We are a in every way, but not

AFFLICTION → AFFLICT
Dt	16: 3	bread, the bread of a, that you may
Ps	25:18	Put an end to my a and suffering;
2Co	4:17	this momentary light a is producing

AFRAID → FEAR

Ge 3:10 but I was **a**, because I was naked,

Ex 3: 6 face, for he was **a** to look at God.

Dt 20: 3 Be not weakhearted or **a**; be neither

Mt 10:31 So do not be **a**; you are worth more

28:10 Jesus said to them, "Do not be **a**.

Lk 12:32 Do not be **a** any longer, little flock,

Heb 13: 6 [and] I will not be **a**. What can

AGABUS

A Christian prophet (Ac 11:28; 21:10).

AGAG

King of Amalekites; not killed by Saul (1Sa 15).

AGAIN

Job 14:14 a man has died, were he to live **a**,

Jn 14: 3 I will come back **a** and take you

Heb 6: 6 to bring them to repentance **a**,

AGE → AGES

Ge 21: 2 bore Abraham a son in his old **a**,

Mt 28:20 you always, until the end of the **a**."

Gal 1: 4 us from the present evil **a** in accord

AGES → AGE

1Co 2: 7 God predetermined before the **a**

Col 1:26 the mystery hidden from **a**

1Ti 1:17 To the king of **a**, incorruptible,

AGREE

Mt 18:19 you, if two of you **a** on earth

Mk 14:56 him, but their testimony did not **a**.

AGRIPPA

Descendant of Herod; king before whom Paul argued his case in Caesarea (Ac 25:13-26:32).

AHAB

1. Son of Omri; king of Israel (1Ki 16:28-22:40), husband of Jezebel (1Ki 16:31. Promoted Baal worship (1Ki 16:31-33); opposed by Elijah (1Ki 17:1; 18; 21), a prophet (1Ki 20:35-43), Micaiah (1Ki 22:1-28). Defeated Ben-Hadad (1Ki 20). Killed for failing to kill Ben-Hadad and for murder of Naboth (1Ki 20:35-21:40).

2. A false prophet (Jer 29:21-22).

AHASUERUS → = ARTAXERXES

King of Persia (Ezr 4:6), husband of Esther (called Artaxerxes in Est 11:1; 12:2; 13:1; 16:1). Deposed Vashti; replaced her with Esther (Est 1-2). Sealed Haman's edict to annihilate the Jews (Est 3). Received Esther without having called her (Est 5:1-8). Honored Mordecai (Est 6). Hanged Haman (Est 7). Issued edict allowing Jews to defend themselves (Est 8). Promoted Mordecai (Est 8:1-2, 15; 9:4; 10).

AHAZ

Son of Jotham; king of Judah, (2Ki 16; 2Ch 28; Mt 1:9). Idolatry of (2Ki 16:3-4, 10-18; 2Ch 28:1-4, 22-25). Defeated by Aram and Israel (2Ki 16:5-6; 2Ch 28:5-15). Sought help from Assyria rather than the LORD (2Ki 16:7-9; 2Ch 28:16-21; Isa 7).

AHAZIAH → = JEHOAHAZ

1. Son of Ahab; king of Israel (1Ki 22:51-2Ki 1:18; 2Ch 20:35-37). Made an unsuccessful alliance with Jehoshaphat (2Ch 20:35-37). Died for seeking Baal rather than the LORD (2Ki 1).

2. Son of Jehoram; king of Judah (2Ki 8:25-29; 9:14-29), also called Jehoahaz (2Ch 21:17-22:9; 25:23). Killed by Jehu while visiting Joram (2Ki 9:14-29; 2Ch 22:1-9).

AHEAD

Mt 11:10 I am sending my messenger **a**

Php 3:13 but straining forward to what lies **a**,

AHIJAH

1. Priest during Saul's reign (1Sa 14:3,18).

2. Prophet of Shiloh (1Ki 11:29-39; 14:1-18).

AHIKAM

Father of Gedaliah (2Ki 25:22), protector of Jeremiah (Jer 26:24).

AHIMAAZ

1. Father-in-law of Saul (1Sa 14:50).

2. Son of Zadok, the high priest, loyal to David (2Sa 15:27,36; 17:17-20; 18:19-33).

AHIMELECH

1. Priest who helped David in his flight from Saul (1Sa 21-22).

2. One of David's warriors (1Sa 26:6).

AHITHOPHEL

One of David's counselors who sided with Absalom (2Sa 15:12, 31-37; 1Ch 27:33-34); committed suicide when his advice was ignored (2Sa 16:15-17:23).

AI

Jos 7: 4 they were defeated by those at **A**,

AIR

Eph 2: 2 the ruler of the power of the **a**,

1Th 4:17 the clouds to meet the Lord in the **a**.

Rev 16:17 poured out his bowl into the **a**.

ALARMED

Mk 13: 7 and reports of wars do not be **a**;

2Th 2: 2 or to be **a** either by a "spirit,"

ALEXANDER

1Ma 1: 1 After **A** the Macedonian,

ALIEN → ALIENS

Lev 19:34 You shall treat the **a** who resides

Dt 24:17 shall not violate the rights of the **a**

ALIENS → ALIEN

Ge 15:13 that your descendants shall be **a**

1Pe 2:11 I urge you as **a** and sojourners

ALIVE → LIVE

Ge 6:19 that you may keep them **a** with you.

Ac 1: 3 He presented himself **a** to them

1Th 4:17 Then we who are **a**, who are left,

Rev 1:18 but now I am **a** forever and ever.

19:20 The two were thrown **a**

ALL

Ge 6:13 to put an end to **a** mortals on earth;

6:13 destroy them and **a** life on earth.

Dt 6: 5 with **a** your heart, and with **a** your

6: 5 your soul, and with **a** your strength.

Sir 7:29 With **a** your soul, fear God,

Jer 29:13 you seek me with **a** your heart,

Lk 10:27 God, with **a** your heart, with **a** your

10:27 with **a** your strength, and with **a**

Ro 3:23 **a** have sinned and are deprived

6:10 death, he died to sin once and for **a**;

1Co 15:51 We shall not **a** fall asleep, but we will **a** be changed,

2Co 5:15 He indeed died for **a**, so that those

Eph 1:23 the one who fills **a** things in every

Col 3:11 slave, free; but Christ is **a** and in **a**.

2Ti 3:16 **A** scripture is inspired by God and is

2Pe 3: 9 that **a** should come to repentance.

Rev 21: 5 said, "Behold, I make **a** things new."

ALMIGHTY → MIGHT

Ge 17: 1 to him and said: "I am God the **A**.

Ex 6: 3 As God the **A** I appeared

Ps 91: 1 who abide in the shadow of the **A**,

Bar 3: 1 "LORD **A**, God of Israel,

Rev 1: 8 who was and who is to come, the **a**."

21:22 for its temple is the Lord God **a**

ALMS

Tob 12: 8 It is better to give **a** than to store

Sir 7:10 and neglect not the giving of **a**.

Mt 6: 2 When you give **a**, do not blow

ALONE → LONELY

Ge 2:18 "It is not good for the man to be **a**.

Dt 6: 4 The LORD is our God, the LORD **a**!

Isa 2:11 and the LORD **a** will be exalted,

Mk 2: 7 Who but God **a** can forgive sins?"

10:18 good? No one is good but God **a**.

Jas 2:24 by works and not by faith **a**.

ALPHA

Rev 1: 8 "I am the **A** and the Omega,"
22:13 I am the **A** and the Omega, the first

ALTAR → ALTARS

Ge 22: 9 him, Abraham built an **a** there
22: 9 put him on top of the wood on the **a**.
Ex 27: 1 "You shall make an **a** of acacia
30: 1 burning incense you shall make an **a**
Ezr 3: 2 about rebuilding the **a** of the God
Jdt 4:12 The **a**, too, they draped in sackcloth;
1Ma 1:54 upon the **a** of holocausts,
4:47 built a new **a** like the former one.
Mt 5:24 leave your gift there at the **a**,
Heb 13:10 We have an **a** from which those
Jas 2:21 he offered his son Isaac upon the **a**?
Rev 6: 9 I saw underneath the **a** the souls

ALTARS → ALTAR

Ex 34:13 Tear down their **a**; smash their
Nu 3:31 the **a**, the utensils
1Ma 2:45 about and tore down the pagan **a**;

ALWAYS

Mt 28:20 I am with you **a**, until the end
Lk 18: 1 to pray **a** without becoming weary.
Php 4: 4 Rejoice in the Lord **a**. I shall say it

AMALEK

Ex 17: 8 **A** came and waged war against
1Sa 15: 3 attack **A**, and deal with him and all

AMASA

Nephew of David (1Ch 2:17). Commander of Absalom's forces (2Sa 17:24-27). Returned to David (2Sa 19:13). Killed by Joab (2Sa 20:4-13).

AMAZED

Mt 8:27 The men were **a** and said, "What sort
Mk 6: 6 He was **a** at their lack of faith.

AMAZIAH

1. Son of Joash; king of Judah (2Ki 14; 2Ch 25). Defeated Edom (2Ki 14:7; 2Ch 25:5-13); defeated by Israel for worshiping Edom's gods (2Ki 14:8-14; 2Ch 25:14-24).
2. Idolatrous priest; opposed Amos (Am 7:10-17).

AMBASSADOR → AMBASSADORS

Eph 6:20 for which I am an **a** in chains,

AMBASSADORS → AMBASSADOR

2Co 5:20 So we are **a** for Christ, as if God

AMBITION

Jas 3:14 and selfish **a** in your hearts, do not

AMEN

Dt 27:15 And all the people shall answer, '**A**!'

2Co 1:20 the **A** from us also goes through him
Rev 3:14 " 'The **A**, the faithful and true witness,

AMMONITES

Ge 19:38 He is the ancestor of the **A** of today.
Jer 49: 6 the lot of the **A**, says the LORD.

AMNON

Firstborn of David (2Sa 3:2; 1Ch 3:1). Killed by Absalom for raping his sister Tamar (2Sa 13).

AMON

1. Son of Manasseh; king of Judah (2Ki 21:18-26; 1Ch 3:14; 2Ch 33:21-25).
2. Ruler of Samaria (1Ki 22:26; 2Ch 18:25).

AMORITES

Ge 15:16 the **A** will not have reached its full
Nu 21:31 had settled in the land of the **A**,

AMOS

Prophet from Tekoa (Am 1:1; 7:10-17; Tob 2:6).

ANANIAS

1. Early disciple; died for lying to God (Ac 5:1-11).
2. Disciple who baptized Saul (Ac 9:10-19).
3. High priest at Paul's arrest (Ac 22:30-24:1).

ANCESTORS

Ac 5:30 The God of our **a** raised Jesus,
Heb 1: 1 ways to our **a** through the prophets;

ANCHOR

Heb 6:19 This we have as an **a** of the soul,

ANCIENT

Ps 24: 7 rise up, you **a** portals, that the king
Da 7: 9 and the **A** One took his throne.
Rev 20: 2 He seized the dragon, the **a** serpent,

ANDREW

Apostle; brother of Simon Peter (Mt 4:18; 10:2; Mk 1:16-18, 29; 3:18; 13:3; Lk 6:14; Jn 1:35-44; 6:8-9; 12:22; Ac 1:13).

ANGEL → ANGELS, ARCHANGEL

Ex 3: 2 There an **a** of the LORD appeared
23:20 I am sending an **a** before you,
Nu 22:22 the **a** of the LORD stationed himself
1Ch 21:15 also sent an **a** to destroy Jerusalem;
21:15 and said to the destroying **a**,
21:15 The **a** of the LORD was then standing
Tob 5: 4 he found the **a** Raphael standing
5: 4 not know that this was an **a** of God.
1Ma 7:41 your **a** went out and killed
Ps 34: 8 The **a** of the LORD, who encamps

Isa 37:36 The **a** of the LORD went forth
Da 3:49 the **a** of the Lord went down
3:95 who sent his **a** to deliver
13:59 "for the **a** of God waits with a sword
14:34 when an **a** of the Lord told him,
Mt 1:20 the **a** of the Lord appeared to him
Lk 1:26 the **a** Gabriel was sent from God
Ac 5:19 the **a** of the Lord opened the doors
2Co 11:14 even Satan masquerades as an **a**
Gal 1: 8 an **a** from heaven should preach

ANGELS → ANGEL

Ge 19: 1 The two **a** reached Sodom
Tob 11:14 and blessed be all his holy **a**.
Ps 103:20 Bless the LORD, all you **a**,
Mk 12:25 but they are like the **a** in heaven.
Lk 4:10 will command his **a** concerning you,
Jn 1:51 opened and the **a** of God ascending
Ac 23: 8 say that there is no resurrection or **a**
Ro 8:38 nor life, nor **a**, nor principalities,
1Co 6: 3 you not know that we will judge **a**?
Col 2:18 in self-abasement and worship of **a**,
Heb 2: 7 for a little while lower than the **a**;
1Pe 1:12 things into which **a** longed to look.
2Pe 2: 4 if God did not spare the **a** when they
Rev 1:20 the seven stars are the **a** of the seven
7: 1 this I saw four **a** standing at the four
21:12 gates where twelve **a** were stationed

ANGER → ANGRY

Ex 34: 6 slow to **a** and rich in kindness,
1Ki 16:13 the God of Israel, to **a** by their idols.
Ps 30: 6 For divine **a** lasts but a moment;
Pr 12:16 The fool immediately shows his **a**,
Isa 48: 9 sake of my name I restrain my **a**,
Joel 2:13 is he, slow to **a**, rich in kindness,
Jnh 4: 2 God, slow to **a**, rich in clemency,
Mk 3: 5 Looking around at them with **a**
Eph 4:26 sin; do not let the sun set on your **a**,

ANGRY → ANGER

Jer 3:12 LORD, I will not remain **a** with you;
Mt 5:22 whoever is **a** with his brother will

ANGUISH
Zep 1:15 is that day, a day of **a** and distress,

ANIMAL → ANIMALS
Ps 50:10 For every **a** of the forest is mine,

ANIMALS → ANIMAL
Ge 2:19 out of the ground various wild **a**
3:14 from all the **a** and from all the wild
9: 2 come upon all the **a** of the earth

ANNA
1. Prophetess; spoke of the child Jesus (Lk 2:36-38).
2. Wife of Tobit (Tob 1:20; 2:1, 11).

ANNAS
High priest A.D. 6-15 (Lk 3:2; Jn 18:13, 24; Ac 4:6).

ANOINT → ANOINTED, ANOINTING
Ex 30:30 and his sons you shall also **a**
1Sa 15: 1 to **a** you king over his people Israel.
Ps 23: 5 watch; You **a** my head with oil;

ANOINTED → ANOINT
1Sa 2:10 his king and exalt the horn of his **a**"
26: 9 who can lay hands on the LORD's **a**
1Ch 16:22 "Touch not my **a**, and to my prophets
Ps 2: 2 together against the LORD and his **a**:
Isa 61: 1 because the LORD has **a** me; He has
Da 9:24 ratified, and a most holy will be **a**.
9:26 weeks an **a** shall be cut down
Zec 4:14 "These are the two **a** who stand
Lk 4:18 because he has **a** me to bring glad
Jn 1:41 the Messiah" (which is translated **A**).
12: 3 nard and **a** the feet of Jesus

ANOINTING → ANOINT
Ex 30:25 and blend them into sacred **a** oil,
1Jn 2:27 the **a** that you received from him
2:27 his **a** teaches you about everything

ANOTHER
Pr 27: 2 Let **a** praise you—not your own
Isa 48:11 My glory I will not give to **a**.
Jn 14:16 he will give you **a** Advocate to be
Gal 1: 7 (not that there is **a**). But there are

ANSWER → ANSWERED
1Ki 18:37 **A** me, LORD! **A** me, that this people
Job 30:20 I cry to you, but you do not **a** me;
Pr 15: 1 A mild **a** calms wrath, but a harsh

Isa 65:24 Before they call, I will **a**; while they
Lk 23: 9 him at length, but he gave him no **a**.

ANSWERED → ANSWER
1Ch 21:26 he **a** him by sending down fire
Ps 118:21 I thank you for you **a** me; you have

ANT
Pr 6: 6 Go to the **a**, O sluggard, study her

ANTICHRIST
1Jn 2:18 as you heard that the **a** was coming,
2:22 the Father and the Son, this is the **a**.
4: 3 This is the spirit of the **a** that, as you
2Jn 1: 7 such is the deceitful one and the **a**.

ANTIOCH
Ac 11:26 had found him he brought him to **A**.
11:26 it was in **A** that the disciples were
13: 1 were in the church at **A** prophets
Gal 2:11 And when Kephas came to **A**,

ANTIOCHUS
Antiochus IV Epiphanes, king of the Syrian Greeks B.C. 175-164 (1Ma 1:10-19). Plundered the temple in Jerusalem (1Ma 1:20-28). Attempted to force the Hellenization of the Jewish people (1Ma 1:41-53), including defiling the altar and holy place (1Ma 1:54-64). His policies sparked the Maccabean revolt.

ANXIETIES
1Co 7:32 I should like you to be free of **a**.

ANYTHING
Ge 18:14 Is **a** too marvelous for the LORD
Jer 32:27 all mankind! Is **a** impossible to me?
Mt 18:19 of you agree on earth about **a**
Jn 16:23 you will not question me about **a**.

APART
Ro 3:21 God has been manifested **a**

APOLLOS
Christian from Alexandria, learned in the Scriptures; instructed by Aquila and Priscilla (Ac 18:24-28). At Corinth (Ac 19:1; 1Co 1:12; 3; Tit 3:13).

APOSTASY
1Ma 2:15 of enforcing the **a** came to the city

APOSTLE → APOSTLES
Ro 11:13 then as I am the **a** to the Gentiles,
1Co 9: 1 Am I not an **a**? Have I not seen
2Co 12:12 of an **a** were performed among you
Heb 3: 1 Jesus, the **a** and high priest of our

APOSTLES → APOSTLE
See also Andrew, Bartholomew, Barnabas, James, John, Judas, Matthew, Matthias, Nathanael, Paul, Peter, Philip, Simon, Thaddaeus, Thomas.
Mt 10: 2 names of the twelve **a** are these:
Lk 6:13 Twelve, whom he also named **a**:
Ac 2:43 and signs were done through the **a**.
1Co 12:28 in the church to be, first, **a**; second,
Eph 2:20 built upon the foundation of the **a**
4:11 And he gave some as **a**, others as
Rev 21:14 names of the twelve **a** of the Lamb.

APPEAL
Ac 25:11 hand me over to them. I **a** to Caesar."
1Pe 3:21 an **a** to God for a clear conscience,

APPEAR → APPEARANCE, APPEARANCES, APPEARED, APPEARING
Mt 24:30 of the Son of Man will **a** in heaven,
2Co 5:10 we must all **a** before the judgment
Heb 9:28 sins of many, will **a** a second time,

APPEARANCE → APPEAR
1Sa 16: 7 "Do not judge from his **a** or from his
16: 7 because man sees the **a** but the LORD
2Co 5:12 who boast of external **a** rather than

APPEARANCES → APPEAR
Jn 7:24 Stop judging by **a**, but judge justly."

APPEARED → APPEAR
1Co 15: 5 that he **a** to Kephas,
Heb 9:26 now once for all he has **a** at the end

APPEARING → APPEAR
Ac 1: 3 **a** to them during forty days

APPETITES
Ro 16:18 our Lord Christ but their own **a**,

APPLE
Dt 32:10 guarding them as the **a** of his eye.

APPOINT → APPOINTED
1Sa 8: 5 your example, **a** a king over us,
Isa 60:17 iron; I will **a** peace your governor,

APPOINTED → APPOINT
Mk 3:16 [he **a** the twelve:] Simon, whom he
Ac 3:20 send you the Messiah already **a**
Heb 9:27 Just as it is **a** that human beings die

APPROACH
Heb 4:16 So let us confidently **a** the throne

AQUILA

Husband of Priscilla; co-worker with Paul, instructor of Apollos (Ac 18; Ro 16:3; 1Co 16:19; 2Ti 4:19).

ARABS

1Ma 5:39 they have also hired **A** to help them,

ARAM → ARAMAIC, ARAMEAN

Jdg 10: 6 the gods of **A**, the gods of Sidon,

2Ch 16: 7 "Because you relied on the king of **A**

16: 7 king of **A** has escaped your hand.

ARAMAIC → ARAM

2Ki 18:26 "Please speak to your servants in **A**;

Ezr 4: 7 The document was written in **A**

4: 7 accompanied by a translation. [**A**:]

Da 2: 4 Chaldeans answered the king [**A**]:

ARAMEAN → ARAM

Dt 26: 5 was a wandering **A** who went down

ARARAT

Ge 8: 4 came to rest on the mountains of **A**.

ARAUNAH → = ORNAN

2Sa 24:16 the threshing floor of **A** the Jebusite.

ARCHANGEL → ANGEL

Jude 1: 9 Yet the **a** Michael, when he argued

ARCHITECT

Heb 11:10 whose **a** and maker is God.

AREOPAGUS

Ac 17:22 Paul stood up at the **A** and said:

ARGUMENT → ARGUMENTS

Lk 9:46 An **a** arose among the disciples

1Ti 2: 8 up holy hands, without anger or **a**.

ARGUMENTS → ARGUMENT

2Co 10: 4 destroying fortresses. We destroy **a**

Col 2: 4 one may deceive you by specious **a**.

ARIMATHEA

Jn 19:38 Joseph of **A**, secretly a disciple

ARISE → ARISES, RISE

SS 2:10 "**A**, my beloved, my beautiful one,

Mt 24:11 Many false prophets will **a**

ARISES → ARISE, RISE

1Ma 14:41 high priest until a true prophet **a**.

ARK

Ge 6:14 "Make yourself an **a** of gopherwood,

Ex 25:10 "You shall make an **a** of acacia

1Sa 4:11 The **a** of God was captured, and Eli's

1Ki 8: 9 There was nothing in the **a**

2Ma 2: 4 and the **a** should accompany him

1Pe 3:20 Noah during the building of the **a**,

Rev 11:19 the **a** of his covenant could be seen

ARM → ARMIES, ARMOR, ARMS, ARMY

Ex 6: 6 rescue you by my outstretched **a**

Dt 7:19 outstretched **a** with which the LORD,

2Ch 32: 8 For he has only an **a** of flesh, but we

Job 40: 9 Have you an **a** like that of God,

Isa 53: 1 To whom has the **a** of the LORD been

ARMIES → ARM

1Sa 17:36 because he has insulted the **a**

Lk 21:20 you see Jerusalem surrounded by **a**,

Rev 19:14 The **a** of heaven followed him,

ARMOR → ARM

Wis 5:17 He shall take his zeal for **a** and he

Ro 13:12 darkness [and] put on the **a** of light;

Eph 6:11 Put on the **a** of God so that you may

ARMS → ARM

Pr 31:17 with strength, and sturdy are her **a**.

Hos 11: 3 to walk, who took them in my **a**;

ARMY → ARM

Ex 15: 4 and **a** he hurled into the sea;

Ps 27: 3 Though an **a** encamp against me,

33:16 A king is not saved by a mighty **a**,

Rev 19:19 riding the horse and against his **a**.

AROMA

2Co 2:15 For we are the **a** of Christ for God

ARRESTED

Mt 14: 3 Now Herod had **a** John,

26:50 they laid hands on Jesus and **a** him.

ARROGANCE → ARROGANT

1Ma 1:24 after he had spoken with great **a**

Pr 8:13 to hate evil;] Pride, **a**, the evil way,

Sir 10: 7 Odious to the LORD and to men is **a**,

ARROGANT → ARROGANCE

Ps 73: 3 Because I was envious of the **a**

Da 7:11 the first of the **a** words

ARROW → ARROWS

Isa 49: 2 He made me a polished **a**, in his

ARROWS → ARROW

1Sa 20:20 day of the month I will shoot **a**,

Ps 64: 8 But God will shoot **a** at them

Eph 6:16 to quench all [the] flaming **a**

ARTAXERXES → = AHASUERUS

1. King of Persia; allowed rebuilding of temple under Ezra (Ezr 4; 7), and of walls of Jerusalem under his cupbearer Nehemiah (Ne 2; 5:14; 13:6).

2. See Ahasuerus.

ARTEMIS

Ac 19:27 of the great goddess **A** will be of no

ASA

King of Judah (1Ki 15:8-24; 1Ch 3:10; 2Ch 14-16). Godly reformer (2Ch 15); in later years defeated Israel with help of Aram, not the LORD (1Ki 15:16-22; 2Ch 16).

ASAHEL

Nephew of David, one of his warriors (2Sa 23:24; 1Ch 2:16; 11:26; 27:7). Killed by Abner (2Sa 2); avenged by Joab (2Sa 3:22-39).

ASAPH

1. Recorder to Hezekiah (2Ki 18:18, 37; Isa 36:3, 22).

2. Levitical musician (1Ch 6:39; 15:17-19; 16:4-7, 37), seer (2Ch 29:30). Sons of (1Ch 25; 2Ch 5:12; 20:14; 29:13; 35:15; Ezr 2:41; 3:10; Ne 7:44; 11:17; 12:27-47). Psalms of (2Ch 29:30; Ps 50; 73-83).

ASCEND → ASCENDING, ASCENTS

Ps 139: 8 If I **a** to the heavens, you are there;

ASCENDING → ASCEND

Jn 1:51 the angels of God **a** and descending

ASCENTS → ASCEND

Songs of ascents (Ps 120-134).

ASHAMED → SHAME

Isa 29:22 Jacob shall have nothing to be **a** of,

Mk 8:38 Whoever is **a** of me and of my

8:38 the Son of Man will be **a**

Ro 1:16 For I am not **a** of the gospel. It is

Heb 2:11 he is not **a** to call them "brothers,"

11:16 God is not **a** to be called their God,

ASHER

Son of Jacob by Zilpah (Ge 30:13; 35:26; 46:17; Ex 1:4; 1Ch 2:2). Tribe of blessed (Ge 49:20; Dt 33:24-25), numbered (Nu 1:40-41; 26:44-47), allotted land (Jos 10:24-31; Eze 48:2), failed to fully possess (Jdg 1:31-32), failed to support Deborah (Jdg 5:17), supported Gideon (Jdg 6:35; 7:23) and David (1Ch 12:36), 12,000 from (Rev 7:6).

ASHERAH → ASHERAHS, ASTARTE

1Ki 18:19 four hundred prophets of **A** who eat

2Ch 15:16 made an outrageous object for **A**;

ASHERAHS → ASHERAH

Jdg 3: 7 and serving the Baals and the **A**,

ASHES

Ge 18:27 Lord, though I am but dust and **a**!

1859

ASHES (cont.)
Jdt 4:11 with a strewn on their heads,
Est 4: 1 put on sackcloth and a, and walked
Job 42: 6 have said, and repent in dust and a.
Jnh 3: 6 with sackcloth, and sat in the a.
Mt 11:21 have repented in sackcloth and a.

ASIA
Ac 16: 6 the message in the province of A.
Rev 1: 4 John, to the seven churches in A:

ASIDE → SIDE
Ex 32: 8 They have soon turned a
Dt 28:14 not turning a to the right

ASK
Ps 2: 8 Only a it of me, and I will make
Mt 6: 8 what you need before you a him.
    7: 7 "A and it will be given to you;
Jn 16:24 a and you will receive, so that your
Jas 4: 3 You a but do not receive,
    4: 3 because you a wrongly, to spend it
1Jn 5:14 if we a anything according to his

ASLEEP → SLEEP
Jnh 1: 5 hold of the ship, and lay there fast a.
Mt 8:24 swamped by waves; but he was a.

ASSEMBLE → ASSEMBLY
Zep 3: 8 to a the kingdoms, In order to pour
Rev 16:14 of the whole world to a them

ASSEMBLY → ASSEMBLE
Ne 8: 2 priest brought the law before the a,
Ps 149: 1 song, a hymn in the a of the faithful.
Heb 12:23 and the a of the firstborn enrolled

ASSIGNED
1Co 3: 5 just as the Lord a each one.
    7:17 should live as the Lord has a, just as

ASSYRIA
2Ki 18:11 The king of A then deported
   18:11 then deported the Israelites to A
Jer 50:18 as once I punished the king of A;

ASTARTE → ASHERAH
1Ki 11: 5 By adoring A, the goddess

ASTONISHED
Lk 2:48 they were a, and his mother said

ASTRAY → STRAY
Dt 30:17 but are led a and adore and serve
Isa 53: 6 We had all gone a like sheep,
Mt 18:12 sheep and one of them goes a,
1Pe 2:25 For you had gone a like sheep,

ATE → EAT
Ge 3: 6 she took some of its fruit and a it;
    3: 6 who was with her, and he a it.
Ex 16:35 The Israelites a this manna for forty
  16:35 they a manna until they reached
Ps 78:25 All a a meal fit for heroes; food he
Eze 3: 3 I a it, and it was as sweet as honey
Mt 14:20 They all a and were satisfied,
  15:37 They all a and were satisfied.

ATHALIAH
    Granddaughter of Omri; wife of Jehoram and mother of Ahaziah; encouraged their evil ways (2Ki 8:18, 27; 2Ch 22:2). At death of Ahaziah she made herself queen, killing all his sons but Joash (2Ki 11:1-3; 2Ch 22:10-12); killed six years later when Joash revealed (2Ki 11:4-16; 2Ch 23:1-15).

ATHLETE
2Ti 2: 5 an a cannot receive the winner's

ATONEMENT → ATONES
Ex 29:36 day as a sin offering, to make a.
  29:36 purge the altar in making a for it;
  30:10 a year Aaron shall perform the a rite
  30:10 your generations this a is to be
  32:30 may be able to make a for your sin."
Lev 23:28 because it is the Day of A, when a is

ATONES → ATONEMENT
Sir 3: 3 He who honors his father a for sins;

ATTAIN → ATTAINED
Pr 8:12 and judicious knowledge I a.
Php 3:11 if somehow I may a the resurrection

ATTAINED → ATTAIN
Php 3:16 with regard to what we have a,

AUTHOR
Ac 3:15 The a of life you put to death,

AUTHORITIES → AUTHORITY
Ro 13: 1 be subordinate to the higher a,

AUTHORITY → AUTHORITIES
Mk 1:27 is this? A new teaching with a.
Lk 5:24 the Son of Man has a on earth
Ro 13: 1 for there is no a except from God,
1Co 11:10 a woman should have a sign of a
1Ti 2:12 to teach or to have a over a man.
Rev 12:10 and the a of his Anointed.

AVENGE → VENGEANCE
1Ma 2:67 and you shall a the wrongs of your
Rev 6:10 a our blood on the inhabitants

AVENGER → VENGEANCE
Nu 35:12 of asylum from the a of blood,
Ps 8: 3 your foes, to silence enemy and a.
1Th 4: 6 the Lord is an a in all these things,

AVENGES → VENGEANCE
Dt 32:43 For he a the blood of his servants

AVENGING → VENGEANCE
Na 1: 2 A jealous and a God is the LORD,

AVOID → AVOIDS
2Ti 2:16 A profane, idle talk, for such people
Tit 3: 9 A foolish arguments, genealogies,

AVOIDS → AVOID
Pr 16: 6 by the fear of the LORD man a evil.

AWAKE
Ps 44:24 A! Why do you sleep, O Lord?
  57: 9 A, my soul; a, lyre and harp! I will
Isa 51: 9 A, a, put on strength, O arm
  51: 9 of the LORD! A as in the days of old,
Da 12: 2 sleep in the dust of the earth shall a;
Eph 5:14 Therefore, it says: "A, O sleeper,

AWE → AWESOME
Isa 29:23 and be in a of the God of Israel.
Mt 9: 8 saw this they were struck with a
Ac 2:43 A came upon everyone, and many
Ro 11:20 not become haughty, but stand in a.

AWESOME → AWE
Dt 10:17 mighty and a, who has no favorites,
Ne 1: 5 great and a God, you who preserve
Ps 65: 6 You answer us with a deeds
  68:36 A is God in his holy place, the God
Da 9: 4 great and a God, you who keep your

AX
Mt 3:10 Even now the a lies at the root

AZARIAH → = ABEDNEGO, = UZZIAH
    1. King of Judah; see Uzziah (2Ki 15:1-7).
    2. Prophet (2Ch 15:1-8).
    3. Opponent of Jeremiah (Jer 43:2).
    4. Jewish exile; see Abednego (Da 1:6-19).

AZAZEL
Lev 16: 8 one is for the LORD and which for A.

B

BAAL → BAALS
Nu 25: 3 submitted to the rites of B of Peor,

Jdg 2:13 him and served **B** and the Ashtaroth,

1Ki 18:25 Elijah then said to the prophets of **B**,

    19:18 those who have not knelt to **B**

Jer   2: 8 The prophets prophesied by **B**,

Ro 11: 4 men who have not knelt to **B**."

BAALS → BAAL

Jdg 3: 7 and serving the **B** and the Asherahs,

1Sa 7: 4 So the Israelites put away their **B**

BAASHA

King of Israel (1Ki 15:16-16:7; 2Ch 16:1-6).

BABEL → BABYLON

Ge 11: 9 That is why it was called **B**,

BABES

Ps   8: 3 Out of the mouths of **b** and infants

BABYLON → BABEL

2Ki 24:15 He deported Jehoiachin to **B**,

    24:15 Jerusalem to **B** the king's mother

Ps 137: 1 By the rivers of **B** we sat mourning

Isa 14: 4 taunt-song against the king of **B**:

    21: 9 says, 'Fallen, fallen is **B**, And all

Jer 25:11 shall be enslaved to the king of **B**:

Da 14:36 he set him down in **B** above the den.

1Pe 5:13 chosen one at **B** sends you greeting,

Rev 14: 8 "Fallen, fallen is **B** the great,

BACK

Ge 19:26 But Lot's wife looked **b**, and she was

BAD

Pr 20:14 "**B, b**!" says the buyer; but once he

Mt   7:17 fruit, and a rotten tree bears **b** fruit.

1Co 15:33 "**B** company corrupts good morals."

BALAAM

Prophet who attempted to curse Israel (Nu 22-24; Dt 23:4-5; 2Pe 2:15; Jude 11; Rev 2:14). Killed in Israel's vengeance on Midianites (Nu 31:8; Jos 13:22).

BALAK

Moabite king who hired Balaam to curse Israel (Nu 22-24; Jos 24:9; Mic 6:5).

BALANCE

Isa 40:12 in scales and the hills in a **b**?

BALM

Jer   8:22 Is there no **b** in Gilead, no physician

BAPTISM → BAPTIZE

Mk   1: 4 in the desert proclaiming a **b**

    10:38 be baptized with the **b** with which I

Lk 20: 4 was John's **b** of heavenly

Ac 18:25 although he knew only the **b**

Ac 19: 3 They replied, "With the **b** of John."

Ro   6: 4 with him through **b** into death,

Eph 4: 5 one Lord, one faith, one **b**;

Col 2:12 You were buried with him in **b**,

1Pe 3:21 This prefigured **b**, which saves you

BAPTISMS → BAPTIZE

Heb 6: 2 instruction about **b** and laying

BAPTIST → BAPTIZE

Mt   3: 1 In those days John the **B** appeared,

    11:11 been none greater than John the **B**;

    14: 8 on a platter the head of John the **B**."

    16:14 "Some say John the **B**, others Elijah,

BAPTIZE → BAPTISM, BAPTISMS, BAPTIST, BAPTIZED, BAPTIZING

Mt   3:11 He will **b** you with the holy Spirit

Lk   3:16 He will **b** you with the holy Spirit

1Co 1:17 For Christ did not send me to **b**

BAPTIZED → BAPTIZE

Mt   3:13 to John at the Jordan to be **b** by him.

Ac   1: 5 for John **b** with water, but in a few

    1: 5 in a few days you will be **b**

    2:38 "Repent and be **b**, every one of you,

Ro   6: 3 we who were **b** into Christ Jesus

    6: 3 Christ Jesus were **b** into his death?

1Co 10: 2 all of them were **b** into Moses

    12:13 in one Spirit we were all **b** into one

BAPTIZING → BAPTIZE

Mt 28:19 **b** them in the name of the Father,

Jn   4: 1 and **b** more disciples than John

BARABBAS

Prisoner released by Pilate instead of Jesus (Mt 27:16-26; Mk 15:7-15; Lk 23:18-19; Jn 18:40).

BARAK

Judge who fought with Deborah against Canaanites (Jdg 4-5; 1Sa 12:11; Heb 11:32).

BARBARIAN

Col   3:11 circumcision and uncircumcision, **b**,

BARBS

Nu 33:55 to remain will become as **b** in your

BARE → BARED

Ps 18:16 the world's foundations lay **b**,

BARED → BARE

Isa 52:10 The Lord has **b** his holy arm

BARN → BARNS

Lk 12:24 they have neither storehouse nor **b**,

BARNABAS → = JOSEPH

Disciple, originally Joseph (Ac 4:36), prophet (Ac 13:1), apostle (Ac 14:14). Brought Paul to apostles (Ac 9:27), Antioch (Ac 11:22-29; Gal 2:1-13), on the first missionary journey (Ac 13-14). Together at Jerusalem Council, they separated over John Mark (Ac 15). Later co-workers (1Co 9:6; Col 4:10).

BARNS → BARN

Dt 28: 8 upon you, on your **b** and on all your

Ps 144:13 May our **b** be full with every kind

Lk 12:18 do: I shall tear down my **b** and build

BARREN

Ge 11:30 Sarai was **b**; she had no child.

Ex 23:26 no woman in your land will be **b**

1Sa 2: 5 spoil. The **b** wife bears seven sons,

Isa 54: 1 cry, you **b** one who did not bear,

Lk   1: 7 because Elizabeth was **b** and both

BARTHOLOMEW → = NATHANAEL?

Apostle (Mt 10:3; Mk 3:18; Lk 6:14; Ac 1:13). Possibly also called Nathanael (Jn 1:45-49; 21:2).

BARUCH

Jeremiah's secretary (Jer 32:12-16; 36; 43:1-6; 45:1-2). Deuterocanonical book ascribed to (Bar 1:1, 3, 8).

BARZILLAI

1. Gileadite who aided David during Absalom's revolt (2Sa 17:27; 19:31-39).

2. Son-in-law of 1. (Ezr 2:61; Ne 7:63).

BASHAN

Nu 21:33 and went up along the road to **B**.

    21:33 king of **B**, advanced against them

Ps 22:13 me; fierce bulls of **B** encircle me.

Mic 7:14 Let them feed in **B** and Gilead,

BASIN

Jn 13: 5 he poured water into a **b** and began

BASKET

Ex   2: 3 she took a papyrus **b**, daubed it

Mt   5:15 and then put it under a bushel **b**; it is

Ac   9:25 in the wall, lowering him in a **b**.

BATHING

2Sa 11: 2 From the roof he saw a woman **b**,

BATHSHEBA

Wife of Uriah; committed adultery with and married David (2Sa 11; Ps 51), mother of Solomon (2Sa 12:24; 1Ki 1-2; 1Ch 3:5).

BATTLE

1Sa 17:47 For the **b** is the Lord's, and he shall

2Ch 20:15 for the **b** is not yours but God's.

BATTLE (*cont.*)
Ps 24: 8 warrior, the LORD, mighty in **b**.
Ecc 9:11 the swift, nor the **b** by the valiant,
Rev 16:14 them for the **b** on the great day
20: 8 and Magog, to gather them for **b**;

BEAR → BEARS, BIRTH, BIRTHRIGHT, BORE, BORN, CHILDBEARING, FIRSTBORN
Ge 4:13 "My punishment is too great t o **b**.
17:19 your wife Sarah is to **b** you a son,
Isa 7:14 and **b** a son, and shall name him
Mt 1:23 shall be with child and **b** a son,
7:18 A good tree cannot **b** bad fruit,
7:18 nor can a rotten tree **b** good fruit.
Jn 15: 2 branch in me that does not **b** fruit,
Gal 6: 2 **B** one another's burdens, and so you

BEARS → BEAR
1Co 13: 7 It **b** all things, believes all things,

BEAST → BEASTS
Rev 11: 7 the **b** that comes up from the abyss
13:18 can calculate the number of the **b**,
16: 2 on those who had the mark of the **b**
19:20 The **b** was caught and with it
19:20 who had accepted the mark of the **b**

BEASTS → BEAST
Da 7: 3 which emerged four immense **b**,
Mk 1:13 He was among wild **b**,

BEAT → BEATEN, BEATING
Isa 2: 4 They shall **b** their swords

BEATEN → BEAT
2Co 11:25 Three times I was **b** with rods,
1Pe 2:20 if you are patient when **b** for doing

BEATING → BEAT
Lk 22:63 custody were ridiculing and **b** him.

BEAUTIFUL → BEAUTY
Ge 12:11 "I know well how **b** a woman you
Tob 6:12 is sensible, courageous, and very **b**;
Job 42:15 women were as **b** as the daughters
Isa 52: 7 How **b** upon the mountains
Da 13: 2 who married a very **b**
Ac 3: 2 temple called "the **B** Gate" every day
Ro 10:15 "How **b** are the feet of those who

BEAUTY → BEAUTIFUL
2Sa 14:25 so be praised for his **b** as Absalom,
Jdt 16: 9 and her **b** captivated his mind.

1Ma 2:12 We see our sanctuary and our **b**
Ps 27: 4 To gaze on the LORD's **b**, to visit his
Pr 6:25 Lust not in your heart after her **b**,
31:30 Charm is deceptive and **b** fleeting;
Wis 13: 3 in their **b** they thought them gods,
13: 3 original source of **b** fashioned them.
Sir 9: 8 gaze not upon the **b** of an-other's wife—
9: 8 Through woman's **b** many perish,
Da 13:56 said to him, "**b** has seduced you,
1Pe 3: 4 in the imperishable of a gentle

BED → BEDS
Ge 47:31 Israel bowed at the head of the **b**.
Heb 13: 4 the marriage **b** be kept unde-filed,

BEDS → BED
Ps 36: 5 In their **b** they hatch plots; they set

BEE → BEES
Sir 11: 3 Least is the **b** among winged things,
Isa 7:18 and for the **b** in the land of Assyria.

BEER-SHEBA
Ge 21:31 This is why the place is called **B**;
1Sa 3:20 Israel from Dan to **B** came to know

BEES → BEE
Jdg 14: 8 found a swarm of **b** and honey

BEFORE
Ex 33: 2 Jebusites, I will send an angel **b** you
Isa 43:10 that it is I. **B** me no god was formed,
65:24 **B** they call, I will answer;
Mal 3: 1 to prepare the way **b** me;
Mt 6: 8 what you need **b** you ask him.
Lk 22:61 said to him, "**B** the cock crows today,
Heb 12: 2 that lay **b** him he endured the cross,

BEGGAR
Jn 9: 8 had seen him earlier as a **b** said,

BEGINNING
Ge 1: 1 In the **b**, when God created
Ps 111:10 fear of the LORD is the **b** of wisdom;
Pr 1: 7 of the LORD is the **b** of knowl-edge;
Ecc 7: 8 is the end of speech than its **b**;
Isa 40:21 Was it not foretold you from the **b**?
Mt 24: 8 All these are the **b** of the labor
Jn 1: 1 In the **b** was the Word,
1Jn 1: 1 What was from the **b**, what we have
2Jn 1: 6 as you heard from the **b**,

Rev 21: 6 and the Omega, the **b** and the end.

BEGOTTEN
Ac 13:33 are my son; this day I have **b** you.'
Heb 1: 5 are my son; this day I have **b** you"?

BEHEADED → HEAD
Lk 9: 9 But Herod said, "John I **b**.
Rev 20: 4 of those who had been **b** for their

BEHEMOTH
Job 40:15 See, besides you I made **B**,

BEHIND
Isa 38:17 When you cast **b** your back all my
Mt 16:23 turned and said to Peter, "Get **b** me,
Php 3:13 forgetting what lies **b** but straining

BEING
Ge 2: 7 life, and so man became a liv-ing **b**.
1Co 15:45 became a living **b**," the last Adam
Heb 1: 3 the very imprint of his **b**, and who

BEL
Babylonian deity (Isa 46:1; Jer 50:2; 51:44; Bar 6:40; Da 14:3-28).

BELIEF → BELIEVE
2Th 2:13 by the Spirit and **b** in truth.

BELIEVE → BELIEF, BELIEVED, BELIEVER, BELIEVES
Ex 4: 5 will take place so that they may **b**,"
Nu 14:11 How long will they refuse to **b**
Jer 12: 6 you. Do not **b** them, even if they are
Mt 18: 6 one of these little ones who **b** in me
24:23 Messiah!' or, 'There he is!' do not **b** it.
Mk 1:15 at hand. Repent, and **b** in the gospel."
9:24 cried out, "I do **b**, help my un-belief!"
Lk 24:25 of heart to **b** all that the prophets
Jn 1: 7 so that all might **b** through him.
3:18 but whoever does not **b** has al-ready
6:29 God, that you **b** in the one he sent."
10:38 them, even if you do not **b** me,
17:20 those who will **b** in me through their
20:29 to **b** because you have seen me?
Ac 16:31 "**B** in the Lord Jesus and you
28:24 he had said, while others did not **b**.
Ro 3:22 faith in Jesus Christ for all who **b**.
10: 9 **b** in your heart that God raised him

1Th 4:14 For if we **b** that Jesus died and rose,

Heb 11: 6 anyone who approaches God must **b**

Jas 2:19 You **b** that God is one. You do well.

2:19 do well. Even the demons **b**

1Pe 1: 8 you do not see him now yet **b**

Jude 1: 5 later destroyed those who did not **b**.

BELIEVED → BELIEVE

Ex 14:31 they feared the LORD and **b** in him

Jdt 14:10 of Israel had done, **b** firmly in him.

Jn 12:38 "Lord, who has **b** our preaching,

20: 8 at the tomb first, and he saw and **b**.

Ac 2:44 All who **b** were together and had all

Ro 4: 3 "Abraham **b** God, and it was credited

10:16 who has **b** what was heard from us?"

2Co 4:13 is written, "I **b**, therefore I spoke,"

Gal 3: 6 Thus Abraham "**b** God, and it was

1Ti 3:16 Gentiles, **b** in throughout the world,

Heb 4: 3 For we who **b** enter into [that] rest,

Jas 2:23 fulfilled that says, "Abraham **b** God,

BELIEVER → BELIEVE

2Co 6:15 Or what has a **b** in common

BELIEVES → BELIEVE

Pr 14:15 The simpleton **b** everything,

Jn 3:15 everyone who **b** in him may have

11:26 lives and **b** in me will never die.

Ro 9:33 whoever **b** in him shall not be put

10:10 For one **b** with the heart and so is

1Co 13: 7 It bears all things, **b** all things,

BELLY

Ge 3:14 On your **b** shall you crawl, and dirt

Lev 11:42 Whether it crawls on its **b**,

Mt 12:40 was in the **b** of the whale three days

BELONG → BELONGS

Jn 10:16 sheep that do not **b** to this fold.

15:19 because you do not **b** to the world,

1Co 12:15 "Because I am not a hand I do not **b**

12:15 it does not for this reason **b** any less

BELONGS → BELONG

Ps 22:29 For kingship **b** to the LORD, the ruler

62:12 I have heard: Power **b** to God;

BELOVED → LOVE

Mt 3:17 "This is my **b** Son, with whom I am

Mt 12:18 chosen, my **b** in whom I delight;

17: 5 "This is my **b** Son, with whom I am

Col 3:12 holy and **b**, heartfelt compassion,

Rev 20: 9 of the holy ones and the **b** city.

BELSHAZZAR

King of Babylon (Da 5; Bar 1:11-12).

BELT

1Sa 18: 4 and his sword, his bow and his **b**.

Isa 11: 5 and faithfulness a **b** upon his hips.

Mk 1: 6 with a leather **b** around his waist.

BELTESHAZZAR → See DANIEL

BEN-HADAD

1. King of Syria in time of Asa (1Ki 15:18-20; 2Ch 16:2-4).

2. King of Syria in time of Ahab (1Ki 20; 2Ki 6:24; 8:7-15).

3. King of Syria in time of Jehoahaz (2Ki 13:3, 24-25; Jer 49:27; Am 1:4).

BENAIAH

A commander of David's army (2Sa 8:18; 20:23; 23:20-30); loyal to Solomon (1Ki 1:8-2:46; 4:4).

BEND → BENT

Php 2:10 every knee should **b**, of those

BENEFICIAL → BENEFIT

1Co 6:12 for me," but not everything is **b**.

10:23 is lawful," but not everything is **b**.

BENEFIT

Gal 5: 2 Christ will be of no **b** to you.

BENJAMIN → BENJAMINITE

Twelfth son of Jacob by Rachel (Ge 35:16-24; 46:19-21; 1Ch 2:2). Jacob refused to send him to Egypt, but relented (Ge 42-45). Tribe of blessed (Ge 49:27; Dt 33:12), numbered (Nu 1:37; 26:41), allotted land (Jos 18:11-28; Eze 48:23), failed to fully possess (Jdg 1:21), nearly obliterated (Jdg 20-21), sided with Ish-Bosheth (2Sa 2), but turned to David (1Ch 12:2, 29), 12,000 from (Rev 7:8).

BENJAMINITE → BENJAMIN

Jdg 3:15 up for them a savior, the **B** Ehud,

1Sa 9:21 "Am I not a **B**, of one of the smallest

BENT → BEND

Jn 8: 6 Jesus **b** down and began to write

20: 5 he **b** down and saw the burial cloths

BEREAVES

La 1:20 In the streets the sword **b**, at home

BESIDES

Wis 12:13 is there any god **b** you who have

Isa 45:21 **b** whom there is no other God?

Da 14:41 Daniel, and there is no other **b** you!"

BEST → GOOD

Dt 33:21 He saw that the **b** should be his

BETHANY

Mt 26: 6 when Jesus was in **B** in the house

Jn 11: 1 Lazarus from **B**, the village of Mary

BETHEL

Ge 12: 8 on to the hill country east of **B**,

12: 8 pitching his tent with **B** to the west

28:19 He called that site **B**,

1Sa 7:16 passing through **B**,

BETHLEHEM

Ru 4:11 in Ephrathah and win fame in **B**.

1Sa 17:12 Jesse, who was from **B** in Judah.

Mt 2: 1 When Jesus was born in **B** of Judea,

Lk 2:15 to **B** to see this thing that has taken

BETRAY

Jn 13:11 For he knew who would **b** him;

BETTER → GOOD

1Sa 15:22 LORD? Obedience is **b** than sacrifice.

Tob 12: 8 but **b** than either is almsgiving

12: 8 righteousness is **b** than abundance

12: 8 It is **b** to give alms than to store

Ps 63: 4 For your love is **b** than life; my lips

Pr 15:16 **B** a little with fear of the LORD

27: 5 **B** is an open rebuke than a love

Ecc 2:24 There is nothing **b** for man than

9: 4 a live dog is **b** off than a dead lion.

Sir 40:26 but **b** than either, fear of God.

Da 1:20 found them ten times **b** than all

Mt 5:29 It is **b** for you to lose one of your

Mk 14:21 It would be **b** for that man if he had

Jn 11:50 do you consider that it is **b** for you

Php 1:23 be with Christ, [for] that is far **b**.

Heb 7:22 guarantee of an [even] **b** covenant.

9:23 by **b** sacrifices than these.

1Pe 3:17 For it is **b** to suffer for doing good,

BETWEEN

Ge 3:15 I will put enmity **b** you

3:15 and **b** your offspring and hers;

9:13 serve as a sign of the covenant **b** me

16: 5 May the LORD decide **b** you and me!"

Isa 2: 4 He shall judge **b** the nations,

Eze 34:17 GOD, I will judge **b** one sheep

34:17 and another, **b** rams and goats.

Ro 10:12 For there is no distinction **b** Jew

BETWEEN (cont.)

1Ti 2: 5 one mediator **b** God and the human

BEWARE

Ecc 12:12 As to more than these, my son, **b**.

Php 3: 2 **B** of the dogs!
3: 2 evil-workers! **B** of the mutilation!

BEYOND

Ps 147: 5 in power, with wisdom **b** measure.

2Co 4:17 weight of glory **b** all comparison,

BEZALEL

Judahite craftsman in charge of building the tabernacle (Ex 31:1-11; 35:30-39:31).

BILDAD

One of Job's friends (Job 2:11; 8; 18; 25; 42:9).

BILHAH

Servant of Rachel, mother of Jacob's sons Da and Naphtali (Ge 30:1-7; 35:25; 46:23-25).

BIND → BINDS

Dt 6: 8 **B** them at your wrist as a sign

Mt 16:19 Whatever you **b** on earth shall be

BINDS → BIND

Job 5:18 For he wounds, but he **b** up;

BIRD → BIRDS

Lev 20:25 the uncleanness of any beast or **b**

BIRDS → BIRD

Ge 1:21 teems, and all kinds of winged **b**,
1:22 and let the **b** multiply on the earth."
7: 3 and of all the unclean **b**, one pair,

Jer 7:33 will be food for the **b** of the sky

Mt 6:26 Look at the **b** in the sky; they do not

Rev 19:21 all the **b** gorged themselves on their

BIRTH → BEAR

Dt 32:18 forgot the God who gave you **b**.

Ps 22:11 the womb; since **b** you are my God.

Jas 1:18 He willed to give us **b** by the word

1Pe 1: 3 his great mercy gave us a new **b**

BIRTHRIGHT → BEAR, RIGHT

Ge 25:34 his way. Esau cared little for his **b**.

Heb 12:16 who sold his **b** for a single meal.

BISHOP

1Ti 3: 1 the office of **b** desires a noble task.

Tit 1: 7 For a **b** as God's steward must be

BIT → BITE, BITS

Ps 32: 9 with **b** and bridle their temper is

BITE → BIT

Sir 21: 2 that will **b** you if you go near it;

BITS → BIT

Jas 3: 3 If we put **b** into the mouths

BITTER → BITTERNESS

Ex 1:14 making life **b** for them with hard
12: 8 with unleavened bread and **b** herbs.
15:23 the water, because it was too **b**.

Ru 1:13 my lot is too **b** for you,

Rev 8:11 this water, because it was made **b**.

BITTERNESS → BITTER

Pr 14:10 The heart knows its own **b**,

Eph 4:31 All **b**, fury, anger, shouting,

BLACK

Zec 6: 2 horses, the second chariot **b** horses,

Mt 5:36 make a single hair white or **b**.

Rev 6: 5 and there was a **b** horse, and its

BLAMELESS

Ge 17: 1 Walk in my presence and be **b**.

1Ma 4:42 He chose **b** priests,

Job 1: 1 In the land of Uz there was a **b**

Ps 37:18 LORD watches over the days of the **b**;

Php 2:15 that you may be **b** and innocent,

1Th 5:23 be preserved **b** for the coming

Tit 1: 7 a bishop as God's steward must be **b**,

BLASPHEME → BLASPHEMED, BLASPHEMER, BLASPHEMES, BLASPHEMIES, BLASPHEMOUS

Ac 26:11 in an attempt to force them to **b**;

1Ti 1:20 over to Satan to be taught not to **b**.

BLASPHEMED → BLASPHEME

Eze 20:27 In this way also your fathers **b** me,

Mt 26:65 tore his robes and said, "He has **b**!

BLASPHEMER → BLASPHEME

Sir 3:16 A **b** is he who despises his father;

1Ti 1:13 I was once a **b** and a persecutor

BLASPHEMES → BLASPHEME

Lev 24:16 whoever **b** the name of the LORD

Lk 12:10 but the one who **b** against the holy

BLASPHEMIES → BLASPHEME

Mk 3:28 and all **b** that people utter will be

Rev 13: 6 its mouth to utter **b** against God,

BLASPHEMOUS → BLASPHEME

Ac 6:11 heard him speaking **b** words against

Rev 13: 1 and on its heads **b** name[s].

BLAZING

Heb 12:18 which could be touched and a **b** fire

BLEMISH

Ex 12: 5 be a year-old male and without **b**.

Eph 5:27 she might be holy and without **b**.

BLESS → BLESSED, BLESSING, BLESSINGS

Ge 12: 2 and I will **b** you; I will make your
17:16 I will **b** her, and I will give you
17:16 Him also will I **b**; he shall give rise
22:17 I will **b** you abundantly and make
26: 3 and I will be with you and **b** you;

Ex 20:24 name I will come to you and **b** you.

Nu 6:24 The LORD **b** you and keep you!

Dt 7:13 He will love and **b** and multiply
7:13 he will **b** the fruit of your womb
30:16 God, will **b** you in the land you are

1Ch 29:20 "Now **b** the LORD your God!"

Tob 4:19 At all times **b** the Lord God, and ask

Ps 5:13 For you, LORD, **b** the just;
29:11 may the LORD **b** his people
34: 2 I will **b** the LORD at all times;
103: 1 Of David. **B** the LORD, my soul;
103: 1 soul; all my being, **b** his holy name!
109:28 Though they curse, may you **b**;

Hag 2:19 yet borne. From this day, I will **b**!

Lk 6:28 **b** those who curse you,

Ro 12:14 **B** those who persecute [you],

1Co 4:12 hands. When ridiculed, we **b**;

Jas 3: 9 With it we **b** the Lord and Father,

BLESSED → BLESS

Ge 1:22 and God **b** them, saying, "Be fertile,
2: 3 So God **b** the seventh day and made
14:19 "**B** be Abram by God Most High,

Nu 24: 9 him? **B** is he who blesses you,

Tob 3:11 "**B** are you, O Lord, merciful God!
3:11 Forever **b** and honored is your holy

Jdt 13:17 saying with one accord, "**B** are you,

Job 1:21 away; **b** be the name of the LORD!"
42:12 Thus the LORD **b** the latter days

Ps 118:26 **B** is he who comes in the name

Isa 30:18 justice: **b** are all who wait for him!

Jer 17: 7 **B** is the man who trusts in the LORD,

Da 3:26 "**B** are you, and praiseworthy,

Mt 5: 3 "**B** are the poor in spirit, for theirs is

Mt 16:17 said to him in reply, "**B** are you,

Mk 10:16 Then he embraced them and **b** them,

Lk 1:42 said, "Most **b** are you among women,

1:42 and **b** is the fruit of your womb.

6:20 he said: "**B** are you who are poor,

Jn 12:13 **B** is he who comes in the name

20:29 **B** are those who have not seen

Ac 20:35 'It is more **b** to give than to receive.' "

Gal 3: 8 you shall all the nations be **b**."

Eph 1: 3 **B** be the God and Father of our Lord

1: 3 who has **b** us in Christ with every

1Pe 3:14 because of righteousness, **b** are you.

Rev 1: 3 **B** is the one who reads aloud and **b**

22: 7 soon." **B** is the one who keeps

BLESSING → BLESS

Ge 12: 2 name great, so that you will be a **b**.

22:18 all the nations of the earth shall find **b**—

27:36 and now he has taken away my **b**.

27:36 "Haven't you saved a **b** for me?"

Nu 23:20 It is a **b** I have been given

23:20 a **b** which I cannot restrain.

Dt 11:26 you here, this day, a **b** and a curse:

Ne 13: 2 our God turned the curse into a **b**.

Tob 8:15 O God, with every holy and pure **b**!

Eze 34:26 rains that shall be a **b** to them.

Mal 3:10 to pour down **b** upon you without

Mk 14:22 he took bread, said the **b**, broke it,

1Co 10:16 The cup of **b** that we bless, is it not

Gal 3:14 that the **b** of Abraham might be

Eph 1: 3 every spiritual **b** in the heavens,

Rev 5:12 and strength, honor and glory and **b**."

7:12 "Amen. **B** and glory,

BLESSINGS → BLESS

Dt 28: 2 all these **b** will come upon you

Jos 8:34 of the law, the **b** and the curses,

Ps 21: 7 make him the pattern of **b** forever,

Pr 10: 6 **B** are for the head of the just,

Ro 15:27 come to share in their spiritual **b**,

15:27 also to serve them in material **b**.

BLIND → BLINDED, BLINDNESS

Ex 4:11 sight to one and makes another **b**?

Dt 27:18 'Cursed be he who misleads a **b** man.'

Ps 146: 8 the LORD gives sight to the **b**.

Isa 35: 5 will the eyes of the **b** be opened,

42:19 Who is **b** but my servant, or deaf

Mt 11: 5 the **b** regain their sight, the lame

Lk 6:39 "Can a **b** person guide a **b** person?

Jn 9:25 One thing I do know is that I was **b**

Ro 2:19 that you are a guide for the **b**

2Pe 1: 9 Anyone who lacks them is **b**

BLINDED → BLIND

Jn 12:40 "He **b** their eyes and hardened their

2Co 4: 4 of this age has **b** the minds

BLINDNESS → BLIND

Dt 28:28 you with madness, **b** and panic,

BLOCK

Sir 31: 7 It is a stumbling **b** to those who are

Isa 44:19 of the rest, or worship a **b** of wood?"

Ro 11: 9 a stumbling **b** and a retribution

1Co 1:23 crucified, a stumbling **b** to Jews

BLOOD → BLOODSHED

Ge 4:10 Your brother's **b** cries out to me

9: 6 If anyone sheds the **b** of man,

9: 6 by man shall his **b** be shed;

Ex 7:17 hold, and it shall be changed into **b**.

12:13 the **b** will mark the houses where

12:13 Seeing the **b**, I will pass over you;

24: 8 he took the **b** and sprinkled it

24: 8 "This is the **b** of the covenant

Lev 1: 5 shall offer up its **b** by splashing it

3:17 shall not partake of any fat or any **b**."

17:11 the life of a living body is in its **b**,

17:11 because it is the **b**, as the seat

Nu 35:33 have no atonement for the **b** shed

35:33 it except through the **b** of him who

Ps 72:14 for precious is their **b** in his sight.

Isa 1:11 In the **b** of calves, lambs and goats

Mt 27: 8 even today is called the Field of **B**.

Mk 14:24 them, "This is my **b** of the covenant,

Lk 22:44 sweat became like drops of **b** falling

Jn 6:53 of the Son of Man and drink his **b**,

19:34 immediately **b** and water flowed

Ac 2:20 and the moon to **b**,

Ro 5: 9 since we are now justified by his **b**,

1Co 11:25 cup is the new covenant in my **b**.

Eph 1: 7 him we have redemption by his **b**,

6:12 our struggle is not with flesh and **b**

Heb 9:12 not with the **b** of goats and calves

9:12 goats and calves but with his own **b**,

9:22 almost everything is purified by **b**,

9:22 of **b** there is no forgiveness.

1Jn 5: 6 one who came through water and **b**,

5: 6 by water alone, but by water and **b**.

Rev 1: 5 has freed us from our sins by his **b**,

5: 9 with your **b** you purchased for God

6:12 and the whole moon became like **b**.

12:11 conquered him by the **b** of the Lamb

BLOODSHED → BLOOD, SHED

Isa 5: 7 He looked for judgment, but see, **b**!

BLOSSOMS

Ex 25:33 shaped like almond **b**, each with its

25:33 shaped like almond **b**, each with its

BLOT

Ps 51: 3 your abundant compassion **b** out my

BLOW → BLOWING

Joel 2: 1 **B** the trumpet in Zion.

Rev 8: 6 seven trumpets prepared to **b** them.

BOAST → BOASTING

Pr 27: 1 **B** not of tomorrow, for you know

Ro 2:23 You who **b** of the law, do you

1Co 1:31 boasts, should **b** in the Lord."

2Co 11:30 If I must **b**, I will **b** of the things

Gal 6:14 may I never **b** except in the cross

Eph 2: 9 is not from works, so no one may **b**.

BOASTING → BOAST

1Co 5: 6 Your **b** is not appropriate. Do you

BOAZ

Bethlehemite who showed favor to Ruth (Ru 2), married her (Ru 4). Ancestor of David (Ru 4:18-22; 1Ch 2:12-15), Jesus (Mt 1:5-16; Lk 3:23-32).

BODIES → BODY

Ro 12: 1 to offer your **b** as a living sacrifice,

1Co 6:15 not know that your **b** are members

Heb 10:22 and our **b** washed in pure water.

BODILY → BODY

Lk 3:22 upon him in **b** form like a dove.

BODILY → BODY (*cont.*)
Col   2: 9   the whole fullness of the deity b,

BODY → BODIES, BODILY
Mic   6: 7   the fruit of my b for the sin of my
Mt   6:22   "The lamp of the **b** is the eye. If your
         6:22   your whole **b** will be filled
Mk   14:22   them, and said, "Take it; this is my b."
Lk   12: 4   not be afraid of those who kill the **b**
Jn   2:21   speaking about the temple of his b.
Ro   7:24   will deliver me from this mortal b?
1Co   6:13   the other. The **b**, however, is not
         6:13   the Lord, and the Lord is for the b;
         10:17   are one **b**, for we all partake
         15:44   It is sown a natural b; it is raised
         15:44   a natural b; it is raised a spiritual **b**.
         15:44   If there is a natural b, there is
2Co   5: 8   we would rather leave the **b** and go
Eph   4: 4   one **b** and one Spirit, as you were
Col   2:19   from whom the whole b,

BOLDNESS
Eph   3:12   in whom we have **b** of speech

BONE → BONES
Ge   2:23   "This one, at last, is **b** of my bones
Eze   37: 7   bones came together, **b** joining b.

BONES → BONE
Ex   12:46   You shall not break any of its b.
Ps   34:21   God watches over all their b;

BOOK → BOOKS
Jos   1: 8   Keep this **b** of the law on your lips.
Ps   69:29   Strike them from the **b** of the living;
Rev   21:27   are written in the Lamb's **b** of life.

BOOKS → BOOK
Ecc   12:12   making of many **b** there is no end,
Da   7:10   convened, and the **b** were opened.
Jn   21:25   whole world would contain the **b**

BOOTHS
Lev   23:34   month is the LORD's feast of **B**,
Ezr   3: 4   kept the feast of **B** in the manner
Zec   14:16   and to celebrate the feast of **B**.

BORE → BEAR
Mt   8:17   our infirmities and **b** our diseases."
1Pe   2:24   He himself **b** our sins in his body

BORN → BEAR
Ecc   3: 2   A time to be b, and a time to die;
Isa   66: 8   or a nation be **b** in a single moment?
Lk   2:11   of David a savior has been **b** for you
Jn   3: 7   you, 'You must be **b** from above.'
1Co   15: 8   as to one **b** abnormally, he appeared
1Pe   1:23   You have been **b** anew,

BORROW → BORROWER
Dt   28:12   to many nations and **b** from none.
Ps   37:21   The wicked **b** but do not repay;
Mt   5:42   your back on one who wants to **b**.

BORROWER → BORROW
Pr   22: 7   and the **b** is the slave of the lender.

BOW → BOWED
Ge   9:13   I set my **b** in the clouds to serve as
Ex   20: 5   you shall not **b** down before them
Ps   95: 6   Enter, let us **b** down in worship;

BOWED → BOW
Ps   146: 8   raises up those who are **b** down;

BOWLS
Rev   16: 1   pour out the seven **b** of God's fury

BOY → BOYS
Lk   2:43   the **b** Jesus remained behind

BOYS → BOY
Ex   1:18   acted thus, allowing the **b** to live?"

BRANCH → BRANCHES
Isa   4: 2   The **b** of the LORD will be luster
Jn   15: 2   He takes away every **b** in me

BRANCHES → BRANCH
Jn   15: 5   I am the vine, you are the **b**.
Ro   11:21   if God did not spare the natural b,

BREAD
Ge   3:19   of your face shall you get **b** to eat,
Ex   12: 8   its roasted flesh with unleavened **b**
Dt   8: 3   that not by **b** alone does man live,
Ecc   11: 1   Cast your **b** upon the waters;
Wis   16:20   and furnished them **b** from heaven,
Sir   15: 3   him with the **b** of understanding,
Mt   6:11   Give us today our daily b;
Lk   4: 4   'One does not live by **b** alone.' "
Jn   6:35   said to them, "I am the **b** of life;
Ac   2:42   to the breaking of the **b**
1Co   10:17   Because the loaf of **b** is one, we,
         11:26   For as often as you eat this **b**

BREAK → BREAKING, BROKEN, BROKENHEARTED
Mt   6:19   destroys, and thieves **b** in and steal.
Jn   19:33   dead, they did not **b** his legs,

BREASTPIECE → BREASTPLATE
Ex   28:15   "The **b** of decision you shall

BREASTPLATE → BREASTPIECE
Wis   5:18   He shall don justice for a **b** and shall
Isa   59:17   He put on justice as his b, salvation,
Eph   6:14   clothed with righteousness as a b,

BREATH
Ge   2: 7   blew into his nostrils the **b** of life,
         6:17   in which there is the **b** of life;
Ecc   12: 7   the life **b** returns to God who gave
2Th   2: 8   will kill with the **b** of his mouth

BRIBE
Dt   16:19   You shall not take a b; for a **b** blinds

BRIDE → BRIDEGROOM
Isa   62: 5   as a bridegroom rejoices in his **b**
Rev   19: 7   come, his **b** has made herself ready.
         21: 9   I will show you the **b**, the wife

BRIDEGROOM → BRIDE
Mt   9:15   guests mourn as long as the **b** is
         9:15   will come when the **b** is taken away
Jn   3:29   The one who has the bride is the b;

BRIDLE
Ps   32: 9   bit and **b** their temper is curbed,
Jas   3: 2   man, able to **b** his whole body also.

BRIGHT → BRIGHTNESS
Mt   17: 5   a **b** cloud cast a shadow over them,
Rev   22:16   of David, the **b** morning star."

BRIGHTNESS → BRIGHT
Am   5:20   and not light, gloom without any b?

BRING → BRINGS, BROUGHT
Ge   6:19   living creatures you shall **b** two
Ecc   12:14   Because God will **b** to judgment
Jer   24: 6   and **b** them back to this land,
Mt   10:34   I have come to **b** peace
         10:34   I have come to **b** not peace
Ro   10:15   of those who **b** [the] good news!"

BRINGS → BRING
Jas   5:20   know that whoever **b** back a sinner

BROKE → BREAK
Ex   32:19   **b** them on the base of the mountain.

Jer 31:32 for they **b** my covenant and I had

Mt 14:19 he said the blessing, **b** the loaves,

1Co 11:24 he had given thanks, **b** it and said,

BROKEN → BREAK

Ps 51:19 My sacrifice, God, is a **b** spirit;
51:19 do not spurn a **b**, humbled heart.

Ro 11:20 is so. They were **b** off because

BROKENHEARTED → BREAK, HEART

Ps 147: 3 Heals the **b**, binds up their wounds,

Isa 61: 1 to heal the **b**, To proclaim liberty

BRONZE

Nu 21: 9 Moses accordingly made a **b** serpent
21: 9 by a serpent looked at the **b** serpent,

Dt 28:23 sky over your heads will be like **b**

Da 10: 6 and feet looked like bur-nished **b**,

BROOD

Mt 3: 7 he said to them, "You **b** of vipers!

Lk 13:34 a hen gathers her **b** under her wings,

BROTHER → BROTHER'S, BROTHER-IN-LAW, BROTHERS

Ge 4: 8 Cain said to his **b** Abel, "Let us go
4: 8 Cain attacked his **b** Abel and killed

Mt 5:24 first and be reconciled with your **b**,
10:21 **B** will hand over **b** to death,

BROTHER'S → BROTHER

Dt 25: 7 does not care to marry his **b** wife,
25: 7 to perpetuate his **b** name in Is-rael.'

Mk 6:18 lawful for you to have your **b** wife."

BROTHER-IN-LAW → BROTHER

Ge 38: 8 in fulfillment of your duty as **b**,

BROTHERS → BROTHER

Ge 9:25 lowest of slaves shall he be to his **b**.
37:11 So his **b** were wrought up against

Mk 3:33 "Who are my mother and [my] **b**?"

Lk 22:32 back, you must strengthen your **b**.

Heb 2:11 he is not ashamed to call them "**b**,"

BROUGHT → BRING

Ge 15: 7 "I am the LORD who **b** you from Ur

Jdg 2: 1 "It was I who **b** you up from Egypt

2Ch 36:18 princes, all these he **b** to Bab-ylon.

Ezr 6: 5 **b** to Babylon are to be sent back:

1Ti 6: 7 For we **b** nothing into the world,

BUILD → BUILDERS, BUILDING, BUILDS, BUILT, REBUILD

Ge 11: 4 let us **b** ourselves a city and a tower

Dt 6:10 fine, large cities that you did not **b**,

Ps 127: 1 Unless the LORD **b** the house,
127: 1 they labor in vain who **b**.

Isa 57:14 **B** up, **b** up, prepare the way,

Mt 16:18 upon this rock I will **b** my church.

BUILDERS → BUILD

Ps 118:22 The stone the **b** rejected has become

Mk 12:10 'The stone that the **b** rejected

1Pe 2: 7 "The stone which the **b** re-jected

BUILDING → BUILD

1Co 3: 9 you are God's field, God's **b**.

2Co 5: 1 destroyed, we have a **b** from God,

Eph 4:12 for **b** up the body of Christ,

BUILDS → BUILD

Pr 14: 1 Wisdom **b** her house, but Folly tears

1Co 3:10 each one must be careful how he **b**
8: 1 inflates with pride, but love **b** up.
10:23 is lawful," but not everything **b** up.

BUILT → BUILD

Tob 13:16 Jerusalem shall be **b** with sap-phire
13:16 of Jerusalem shall be **b** with gold,

1Ma 4:47 **b** a new altar like the former one.

Pr 9: 1 Wisdom has **b** her house, she has set

Eph 2:20 **b** upon the foundation

BULLS

1Ch 29:21 a thousand **b**, a thousand rams,

Ps 22:13 Many **b** surround me; fierce **b**

Heb 10: 4 it is impossible that the blood of **b**

BURDEN → BURDENS, BURDENSOME

Mt 11:30 For my yoke is easy, and my **b** light."

BURDENS → BURDEN

Lk 11:46 You impose on people **b** hard

Gal 6: 2 Bear one another's **b**, and so you will

BURDENSOME → BURDEN

1Jn 5: 3 And his commandments are not **b**,

BURIED → BURY

Ro 6: 4 We were indeed **b** with him through

1Co 15: 4 that he was **b**; that he was raised

BURN → BURNED, BURNING, BURNT

Ex 21:25 **b** for **b**, wound for wound,

Lk 3:17 his barn, but the chaff he will **b**

BURNED → BURN

Ex 3: 3 sight, and see why the bush is not **b**."

Jn 15: 6 them into a fire and they will be **b**.

1Co 3:15 But if someone's work is **b** up,

BURNING → BURN

Ps 79: 5 Will your rage keep **b** like fire?

Lk 24:32 not our hearts **b** [within us] while he

BURNT → BURN

Ps 51:18 a **b** offering you would not ac-cept.

Mk 12:33 is worth more than all **b** offer-ings

BURY → BURIED

Lk 9:60 him, "Let the dead **b** their dead.

BUSH

Ex 3: 2 to him in fire flaming out of a **b**.
3: 2 he was surprised to see that the **b**,

BUY → BUYS

Rev 3:18 I advise you to **b** from me gold
3:18 **b** ointment to smear on your eyes so

BUYS → BUY

Mt 13:44 sells all that he has and **b** that field.

BYWORD → WORD

Job 17: 6 and I am made a **b** of the people;

Ps 44:15 You make us a **b** among the nations;

C

CAESAREA

Mt 16:13 of C Philippi he asked his dis-ciples,

Ac 10: 1 Now in C there was a man named
25: 4 Paul was being held in custody in C

CAIAPHAS

High priest at trial of Jesus (Mt 26:3, 57; Lk 3:2; Jn 11:49; 18:13-28); at trial of disci-ples (Ac 4:6).

CAIN

Firstborn of Adam (Ge 4:1), murdered brother Abel (Ge 4:1-25; Heb 11:4; 1Jn 3:12; Jude 11).

CALAMITIES → CALAMITY

1Sa 10:19 you from all your evils and **c**,

CALAMITY → CALAMITIES

Da 9:13 of Moses, this **c** came full upon us.

CALEB

Judahite who spied out Canaan (Nu 3:6); allowed to enter land (Nu 13:30-14:38; Dt 1:36; Sir 46:7-9; 1Ma 2:56). Given Hebron (Jos 14:6-15:19).

CALF → CALVES
Ex 32: 4 a graving tool, made a molten **c**.
Lk 15:23 Take the fattened **c** and slaughter it.

CALL → CALLED, CALLING
Dt 4:26 I **c** heaven and earth this day
1Sa 3: 5 called me." "I did not **c** you," Eli said.
1Ki 18:24 You shall **c** on your gods, and I will
18:24 your gods, and I will **c** on the Lord.
Ps 61: 3 From the brink of Sheol I **c**;
Pr 8: 1 Does not Wisdom **c**,
Isa 65:24 Before they **c**, I will answer;
Mt 9:13 I did not come to **c** the righteous
Lk 6:46 "Why do you **c** me, 'Lord, Lord,'
Jn 15:15 I no longer **c** you slaves,
Ro 10:12 of all, enriching all who **c** upon him.
11:29 the gifts and the **c** of God are irrevocable.

CALLED → CALL
2Sa 22: 7 In my distress I **c** upon the Lord
Isa 43: 1 I have **c** you by name: you are mine.
Mt 23: 8 As for you, do not be **c** 'Rabbi.'
1Co 7:15 such cases; God has **c** you to peace.
1Jn 3: 1 we may be **c** the children of God.

CALLING → CALL
Php 3:14 goal, the prize of God's upward **c**,

CALVES → CALF
1Ki 12:28 the king made two **c** of gold

CAMEL
Mt 23:24 out the gnat and swallow the **c**!
Mk 10:25 for a **c** to pass through [the] eye

CANA
Jn 2: 1 third day there was a wedding in C

CANAAN → CANAANITE, CANAANITES
Ge 9:25 "Cursed be C! The lowest of slaves
Nu 13: 2 men to reconnoiter the land of C,
1Ch 16:18 "To you will I give the land of C

CANAANITE → CANAAN
Ge 28: 1 "You shall not marry a C woman!
Mt 15:22 a C woman of that district came

CANAANITES → CANAAN
Ex 33: 2 Driving out the C, Amorites,
Jdg 3: 5 Israelites were living among the C,

CAPERNAUM
Mt 4:13 and went to live in C by the sea,
Jn 6:59 teaching in the synagogue in C.

CAPTIVE → CAPTIVITY
2Ki 24:16 led **c** to Babylon all seven thousand
Ro 7:23 taking me **c** to the law of sin
Eph 4: 8 on high and took prisoners **c**;

CAPTIVITY → CAPTIVE
Dt 28:41 remain with you, but will go into **c**.
Ezr 8:35 those who had returned from the **c**,

CARE → CARELESS, CARES, CARING
Ps 8: 5 mere mortals that you **c** for them?
Heb 2: 6 the son of man that you **c** for him?
Jas 1:27 to **c** for orphans and widows in their

CARELESS → CARE
Mt 12:36 for every **c** word they speak.

CARES → CARE
1Pe 5: 7 upon him because he **c** for you.

CARMEL
1Ki 18:20 the prophets assemble on Mount C.

CARPENTER'S
Mt 13:55 Is he not the **c** son? Is not his

CARRY
Lk 14:27 Whoever does not **c** his own cross

CASE
Isa 41:21 Present your **c**, says the Lord;

CAST
Est 9:24 to destroy them and had **c** the pur,
Ps 22:19 them; for my clothing they **c** lots.
55:23 C your care upon the Lord, who will
Pr 16:33 When the lot is **c** into the lap,
Jn 19:24 **c** lots for it to see whose it will be,"
19:24 and for my vesture they **c** lots."
1Pe 5: 7 C all your worries upon him

CATTLE
Ge 1:25 all kinds of **c**, and all kinds

CAUGHT
2Co 12: 2 was **c** up to the third heaven.
1Th 4:17 will be **c** up together with them

CAUSE
Ps 9: 5 You upheld my right and my **c**,
Jn 15:25 fulfilled, 'They hated me without **c**.'

CAVE
Ge 23: 9 to sell me the **c** of Machpelah
1Sa 22: 1 and escaped to the **c** of Adullam.

CEASE
Ge 8:22 and day and night shall not **c**."
Jer 31:36 Then shall the race of Israel **c**

1Co 13: 8 to nothing; if tongues, they will **c**;

CEDAR
2Sa 7: 2 "Here I am living in a house of **c**,
Ps 92:13 tree, shall grow like a **c** of Lebanon.

CELEBRATE
1Co 5: 8 Therefore let us **c** the feast,

CENSER → CENSERS
Eze 8:11 each of them with his **c** in his hand,
Rev 8: 3 stood at the altar, holding a gold **c**.

CENSERS → CENSER
Lev 10: 1 Nadab and Abihu took their **c** and,

CENSUS
Nu 1: 2 "Take a **c** of the whole community

CENTURION
Mt 8: 5 a **c** approached him and appealed
Lk 23:47 The **c** who witnessed what had
Ac 10: 1 a **c** of the Cohort called the Italica,

CEPHAS → = PETER
Name given to the apostle Peter (Jn 1:42; 1Co 1:12; 3:22; 9:5; 15:5; Gal 1:18; 2:9, 11, 14).

CHAFF
Ps 1: 4 They are like **c** driven by the wind.
Lk 3:17 his barn, but the **c** he will burn

CHAINED → CHAINS
2Ti 2: 9 But the word of God is not **c**.

CHAINS → CHAINED
Eph 6:20 for which I am an ambassador in **c**,
Heb 11:36 even **c** and imprisonment.
2Pe 2: 4 them to the **c** of Tartarus

CHALDEANS
Ge 15: 7 of the C to give you this land as
Da 1: 4 the language and literature of the C;

CHANGE → CHANGED, CHANGERS
Nu 23:19 human, that he should **c** his mind.
Jas 1:17 no alteration or shadow caused by **c**.

CHANGED → CHANGE
1Co 15:51 all fall asleep, but we will all be **c**,
Heb 1:12 and like a garment they will be **c**.

CHANGERS → CHANGE
Mk 11:15 overturned the tables of the money **c**
Jn 2:15 and spilled the coins of the **m**

CHARACTER
Ro 5: 4 endurance, proven **c**, and proven **c**,

CHARGE
Mk 15:26 of the **c** against him read, "The King
Ro 8:33 will bring a **c** against God's chosen
1Co 9:18 I offer the gospel free of **c** so as not

CHARIOT → CHARIOTS
2Ki 2:11 a flaming **c** and flaming horses
Ps 104: 3 You make the clouds your **c**;

CHARIOTS → CHARIOT
Ex 14:28 it covered the **c** and the charioteers
Zec 6: 1 and saw four **c** coming

CHARM
Pr 31:30 **C** is deceptive and beauty fleeting;

CHEEK
Mt 5:39 strikes you on [your] right **c**,

CHEERFUL
2Co 9: 7 compulsion, for God loves a **c** giver.

CHEMOSH
1Ki 11: 7 then built a high place to **C**, the idol
Jer 48: 7 be captured. **C** shall go into exile,

CHERUB → CHERUBIM
Ps 18:11 Mounted on a **c** he flew,
Eze 28:14 With the **C** I placed you; you were

CHERUBIM → CHERUB
Ge 3:24 and he stationed the **c** and the fiery
Ex 25:18 Make two **c** of beaten gold
2Ch 3:11 wings of the **c** spanned twenty cubits:
Ps 80: 2 throne upon the **c** reveal yourself
Heb 9: 5 Above it were the **c** of glory

CHIEF
Mk 15: 3 The **c** priests accused him of many
1Pe 5: 4 when the **c** Shepherd is revealed,

CHILD → CHILDBEARING, CHILDISH, CHILDREN
Ge 17:17 "Can a **c** be born to a man who is
Isa 11: 6 with a little **c** to guide them.
49:15 tenderness for the **c** of her womb?
Hos 11: 1 When Israel was a **c** I loved him,
Mt 1:18 with **c** through the holy Spirit.
Mk 10:15 of God like a **c** will not enter it."
1Co 13:11 When I was a **c**, I used to talk as a **c**,
13:11 as a **c**, think as a **c**, reason as a **c**;
Gal 4: 7 So you are no longer a slave but a **c**,
4: 7 but a **c**, and if a **c** then also an heir,
Rev 12: 4 to devour her **c** when she gave birth.

CHILDBEARING → CHILD, BEAR
Ge 3:16 "I will intensify the pangs of your **c**;

CHILDISH → CHILD
1Co 13:11 I became a man, I put aside **c** things.

CHILDREN → CHILD
Ex 12:26 When your **c** ask you, 'What does
Dt 6: 7 Drill them into your **c**.
11:19 Teach them to your **c**,
Mt 3: 9 you, God can raise up **c** to Abraham
Lk 18:16 called the **c** to himself and said,
18:16 "Let the **c** come to me and do not
Jn 1:12 he gave power to become **c** of God,
Ro 8:14 by the Spirit of God are **c** of God.
Eph 6: 4 do not provoke your **c** to anger,
1Jn 3:10 the **c** of God and the **c** of the devil

CHOOSE → CHOOSES, CHOSE, CHOSEN
Dt 30:19 curse. **C** life, then, that you and your

CHOOSES → CHOOSE
Dt 12:14 the LORD **c** from among your tribes;

CHOSE → CHOOSE
Dt 4:37 your fathers he **c** their descendants
Ne 9: 7 are the God who **c** Abram,
Mk 13:20 for the sake of the elect whom he **c**,
1Co 1:27 God **c** the foolish of the world
1:27 and God **c** the weak of the world

CHOSEN → CHOOSE
Isa 42: 1 my **c** one with whom I am pleased,
Mt 22:14 Many are invited, but few are **c**."
Ro 11: 5 time there is a remnant, **c** by grace.
1Pe 2: 6 a cornerstone, **c** and precious,
2: 9 But you are "a **c** race, a royal

CHRIST → CHRISTIAN, CHRISTIANS, MESSIAH
Ro 5: 6 For **C**, while we were still helpless,
8:35 will separate us from the love of **C**?
10: 4 For **C** is the end of the law
1Co 1:23 but we proclaim **C** crucified,
3:11 one that is there, namely, Jesus **C**.
11: 1 Be imitators of me, as I am of **C**.
15: 3 received: that **C** died for our sins
Gal 5: 1 For freedom **C** set us free; so stand
Eph 4:15 way into him who is the head, **C**,
Php 1:21 For to me life is **C**, and death is

Php 2:11 tongue confess that Jesus **C** is Lord,
Col 1:27 it is **C** in you, the hope for glory.
Rev 20: 4 they reigned with **C** for a thousand

CHRISTIAN → CHRIST
Ac 26:28 will soon persuade me to play the **C**."
1Pe 4:16 suffer as a **C** should not be ashamed

CHRISTIANS → CHRIST
Ac 11:26 that the disciples were first called **C**.

CHURCH
Mt 16:18 and upon this rock I will build my **c**,
Ac 8: 1 persecution of the **c** in Jerusalem,
1Co 12:28 God has designated in the **c** to be,
14: 4 whoever prophesies builds up the **c**.
Col 1:18 He is the head of the body, the **c**.

CIRCUMCISE → CIRCUMCISED, CIRCUMCISION
Ge 17:11 **C** the flesh of your foreskin,
Dt 10:16 **C** your hearts, therefore, and be no
Lk 1:59 on the eighth day to **c** the child,
Jn 7:22 you **c** a man on the sabbath.

CIRCUMCISED → CIRCUMCISE
Ge 17:10 every male among you shall be **c**.
1Ma 1:60 had had their children **c** were put
Ac 15: 1 "Unless you are **c** according
Gal 6:13 having themselves **c** observe
6:13 they only want you to be **c** so
Col 2:11 were also **c** with a circumcision not

CIRCUMCISION → CIRCUMCISE
Ro 2:29 and **c** is of the heart, in the spirit,
Gal 5: 6 neither **c** nor uncircumcision counts

CISTERN
Pr 5:15 Drink water from your own **c**,
Jer 38: 6 him into the **c** of Prince Malchiah,
38: 6 There was no water in the **c**,

CITIES → CITY
Ge 19:25 He overthrew those **c** and the whole
19:25 with the inhabitants of the **c**
Jos 20: 2 the Israelites to designate the **c**
Rev 16:19 three parts, and the gentile **c** fell.

CITIZENSHIP
Php 3:20 But our **c** is in heaven, and from it

CITY → CITIES
1Ch 11: 7 thenceforth was called the **C**
Ps 127: 1 Unless the LORD guard the **c**, in vain

CITY → CITIES (*cont.*)

Pr 31:31 her works praise her at the **c** gates.
La 1: 1 the once crowded **c**! Widowed is
Da 9:24 for your people and for your holy **c**:
Mt 5:14 A **c** set on a mountain cannot be
Heb 12:22 Zion and the **c** of the living God,
Rev 21: 2 I also saw the holy **c**, a new

CLAP

Ps 47: 2 All you peoples, **c** your hands;
Isa 55:12 the countryside shall **c** their hands.

CLAY

Isa 45: 9 Dare the **c** say to its modeler,
Jer 18: 6 like **c** in the hand of the potter,
Ro 9:21 the potter have a right over the **c**,
2Ti 2:20 and silver but also of wood and **c**,

CLEAN → CLEANSE, CLEANSING

Ge 7: 2 Of every **c** animal, take with you
Lev 10:10 between what is **c** and what is
Mk 7:19 (Thus he declared all foods **c**.)
Jn 13:10 his feet washed, for he is **c** all over;
13:10 **c** all over; so you are **c**, but not all."
Ac 10:15 "What God has made **c**, you are not
Heb 10:22 our hearts sprinkled **c** from an evil

CLEANSE → CLEAN

Ps 51: 4 all my guilt; from my sin **c** me.
Sir 38:10 be just, **c** your heart of every sin;
1Jn 1: 9 and **c** us from every wrongdoing.

CLEANSING → CLEAN

Eph 5:26 **c** her by the bath of water
2Pe 1: 9 forgetful of the **c** of his past sins.

CLEAR

Ps 19: 9 The command of the LORD is **c**,
1Ti 3: 9 of the faith with a **c** conscience.
Rev 21:18 the city was pure gold, **c** as glass.

CLINGS

Ge 2:24 father and mother and **c** to his wife,
Heb 12: 1 of every burden and sin that **c** to us

CLOAK

Ex 22:26 this **c** of his is the only covering he
Heb 1:12 You will roll them up like a **c**,

CLOTHE → CLOTHED, CLOTHING

1Pe 5: 5 **c** yourselves with humility in your

CLOTHED → CLOTHE

2Co 5: 2 to be further **c** with our heavenly
Gal 3:27 into Christ have **c** yourselves
Rev 12: 1 in the sky, a woman **c** with the sun,

CLOTHING → CLOTHE

Ps 22:19 among them; for my **c** they cast lots.

CLOUD → CLOUDS

Ex 13:21 of a column of **c** to show them
1Ki 8:10 the **c** filled the temple of the LORD
18:44 "There is a **c** as small as a man's hand"
Eze 10: 4 the temple was filled with the **c**,
Mk 9: 7 Then a **c** came, casting a shadow
9: 7 then from the **c** came a voice,
Lk 21:27 of Man coming in a **c** with power
Heb 12: 1 by so great a **c** of witnesses, let us
Rev 14:14 I looked and there was a white **c**,
Rev 14:14 on the **c** one who looked like a son

CLOUDS → CLOUD

Ge 9:13 my bow in the **c** to serve as a sign
Da 7:13 on the **c** of heaven; When he
Mt 24:30 Man coming upon the **c** of heaven
1Th 4:17 them in the **c** to meet the Lord
Rev 1: 7 Behold, he is coming amid the **c**,

CLUSTER

Nu 13:23 a branch with a single **c** of grapes

COALS

Ps 11: 6 the wicked fiery **c** and brimstone,
Pr 25:22 For live **c** you will heap on his head,
Ro 12:20 by so doing you will heap burning **c**

COIN

Mt 17:27 you will find a **c** worth twice
22:19 Show me the **c** that pays the census
22:19 Then they handed him the Roman **c**.
Lk 15: 9 me because I have found the **c** that I

COLD

Zec 14: 6 that day there shall no longer be **c**
Mt 24:12 the love of many will grow **c**.
Rev 3:16 neither hot nor **c**, I will spit you

COLLECTOR → COLLECTORS

Mt 10: 3 Thomas and Matthew the tax **c**;
Lk 18:10 a Pharisee and the other was a tax **c**.
19: 2 who was a chief tax **c**

COLLECTORS → COLLECTOR

Mt 5:46 have? Do not the tax **c** do the same?
11:19 a friend of tax **c** and sinners.'

COLT

Zec 9: 9 on an ass, on a **c**, the foal of an ass.
Jn 12:15 king comes, seated upon an ass's **c**."

COME → COMES, COMING

Ps 144: 5 LORD, incline your heavens and **c**;
Isa 59:20 He shall **c** to Zion a redeemer
Zec 14: 5 shall **c**, and all his holy ones
Mt 6:10 your kingdom **c**, your will be done,
Lk 7:20 ask, 'Are you the one who is to **c**
Jn 6:37 the Father gives me will **c** to me,
Rev 1: 4 is and who was and who is to **c**,
22:20 coming soon." Amen! **C**, Lord Jesus!

COMES → COME

Ps 118:26 is he who **c** in the name of the LORD.
Lk 19:38 "Blessed is the king who **c**
Jn 14: 6 life. No one **c** to the Father except

COMFORT → COMFORTED, COMFORTERS, COMFORTS

Isa 40: 1 **C**, give **c** to my people, says your

COMFORTED → COMFORT

Mt 5: 4 they who mourn, for they will be **c**.

COMFORTERS → COMFORT

Job 16: 2 times. Wearisome **c** are you all!
Ps 69:21 was none, for **c**, but found none.

COMFORTS → COMFORT

Isa 66:13 As a mother **c** her son, so will I

COMING → COME

Mal 3: 2 who will endure the day of his **c**?
2Pe 3: 4 "Where is the promise of his **c**?
Rev 22:20 testimony says, "Yes, I am **c** soon."

COMMAND → COMMANDED, COMMANDMENT, COMMANDMENTS

Dt 1:26 and after defying the **c** of the LORD,

COMMANDED → COMMAND

Ge 7: 5 Noah did just as the LORD had **c** him.
Ex 40:32 the altar, as the LORD **c** Moses.
Jos 1:16 "We will do all you have **c** us,"
Mt 28:20 to observe all that I have **c** you.
Jn 14:31 that I do just as the Father has **c** me.

COMMANDMENT → COMMAND

Mt 22:38 This is the greatest and the first **c**.
Ro 7:12 and the **c** is holy and righteous

1Jn 3:23 And his **c** is this: we should believe

COMMANDMENTS → COMMAND
Ex 20: 6 those who love me and keep my **c**.
Dt 4:13 the ten **c**, which he wrote on two
6: 1 "These then are the **c**, the statutes
Ecc 12:13 Fear God and keep his **c**, for this is
Mt 19:17 wish to enter into life, keep the **c**."
22:40 the prophets depend on these two **c**."
Jn 14:15 "If you love me, you will keep my **c**.
1Co 7:19 what matters is keeping God's **c**.
1Jn 5: 3 of God is this, that we keep his **c**.
5: 3 his **c**. And his **c** are not burdensome,
Rev 14:12 the holy ones who keep God's **c**

COMMIT → COMMITS
Dt 5:18 'You shall not **c** adultery.
2Ki 17:21 LORD, causing them to **c** a great sin.
Mt 5:27 it was said, 'You shall not **c** adultery.'

COMMITS → COMMIT
Jn 8:34 everyone who **c** sin is a slave of sin.

COMMON
Ac 2:44 together and had all things in **c**;

COMPANY
1Co 15:33 astray: "Bad **c** corrupts good morals."

COMPARE
Pr 8:11 no choice possession can **c** with her.
Lk 7:31 to what shall I **c** the people of this

COMPASSION → COMPASSIONATE
Ps 103:13 As a father has **c** on his children,
103:13 so the LORD has **c** on the faithful.
Col 3:12 and beloved, heartfelt **c**, kindness,

COMPASSIONATE → COMPASSION
Sir 2:11 **C** and merciful is the LORD;
Jas 5:11 because "the Lord is **c** and merciful."

COMPETING
2Ti 2: 5 crown except by **c** according

COMPLAINING → COMPLAINT
1Pe 4: 9 hospitable to one another without **c**.

COMPLAINT → COMPLAINING
Job 10: 1 life. I will give myself up to **c**; I will
Ps 142: 3 Before God I pour out my **c**,
Hab 2: 1 what answer he will give to my **c**.

CONCEITED
Gal 5:26 Let us not be **c**, provoking one
1Ti 6: 4 is **c**, understanding nothing, and has
1Ti 3: 6 so that he may not become **c**

CONCEIVE
Lk 1:31 you will **c** in your womb and bear

CONDEMN → CONDEMNATION, CONDEMNED
Lk 11:31 this generation and she will **c** them,
Jn 3:17 Son into the world to **c** the world,
Ro 8:34 Who will **c**? It is Christ [Jesus] who
1Jn 3:21 if [our] hearts do not **c** us, we have

CONDEMNATION → CONDEMN
Mk 12:40 They will receive a very severe **c**."
Ro 5:18 as through one transgression **c** came
Jas 5:12 mean "No," that you may not incur **c**.

CONDEMNED → CONDEMN
Mt 12:37 and by your words you will be **c**."
Jn 3:18 believes in him will not be **c**,
3:18 does not believe has already been **c**,
16:11 the ruler of this world has been **c**.
1Co 11:32 that we may not be **c** along

CONDUCT
Tob 4:14 and discipline yourself in all your **c**.
Sir 37:17 The root of all **c** is the mind;
Eze 22:31 I have brought down their **c**
Ro 13: 3 are not a cause of fear to good **c**,
1Pe 1:15 in every aspect of your **c**,

CONFESS → CONFESSES, CONFESSION
Lev 5: 5 of these cases shall **c** the sin he has
16:21 he shall **c** over it all the sinful faults
Php 2:11 and every tongue **c** that Jesus Christ

CONFESSES → CONFESS
Ro 10:10 and one **c** with the mouth and so is
1Jn 2:23 whoever **c** the Son has the Father as

CONFESSION → CONFESS
1Ti 6:12 when you made the noble **c**
Heb 4:14 Son of God, let us hold fast to our **c**.

CONFIDENCE
Php 3: 3 Jesus and do not put our **c** in flesh,
Heb 10:19 of Jesus we have **c** of entrance

CONFIRM
2Sa 7:25 **c** for all time the prophecy you have

Ro 15: 8 to **c** the promises to the patriarchs,

CONFORMED
Ro 8:29 predestined to be **c** to the image

CONFUSE
Ge 11: 7 go down and there **c** their language,

CONQUER → CONQUERED, CONQUERS
Rev 17:14 but the Lamb will **c** them, for he is

CONQUERED → CONQUER
Jn 16:33 but take courage, I have **c** the world."
Heb 11:33 who by faith **c** kingdoms, did what
1Jn 2:13 because you have **c** the evil one.

CONQUERS → CONQUER
1Jn 5: 4 is begotten by God **c** the world.
5: 4 victory that **c** the world is our faith.

CONSCIENCE
Ro 2:15 while their **c** also bears witness
1Co 8: 7 to idols, their **c**, which is weak,
1Ti 1: 5 heart, a good **c**, and a sincere faith.
1Pe 3:21 but an appeal to God for a clear **c**.

CONSECRATE → CONSECRATED
Ex 13: 2 "**C** to me every first-born that opens

CONSECRATED → CONSECRATE
2Ch 7:16 **c** this house that my name may be

CONSIDER → CONSIDERED
Jas 1: 2 **C** it all joy, my brothers, when you

CONSIDERED → CONSIDER
Pr 17:28 a fool, if he keeps silent, is **c** wise;

CONSOLATION
Lk 2:25 and devout, awaiting the **c** of Israel,

CONSULT → CONSULTED
Isa 40:14 Whom did he **c** to gain knowledge?

CONSULTED → CONSULT
Eze 20: 3 not allow myself to be **c** by you,

CONSUME → CONSUMED, CONSUMING
Nu 16:21 this band, that I may **c** them at once."
Jn 2:17 "Zeal for your house will **c** me."

CONSUMED → CONSUME
Ex 3: 2 the bush, though on fire, was not **c**.
Ps 90: 7 Truly we are **c** by your anger,
Zep 3: 8 my jealousy shall all the earth be **c**.
Gal 5:15 that you are not **c** by one another.

CONSUMING → CONSUME
Heb 12:29 For our God is a **c** fire.

CONTAIN
Jn 21:25 the whole world would **c** the books

CONTEMPT
Mk 9:12 suffer greatly and be treated with **c**?
Heb 6: 6 themselves and holding him up to **c**.

CONTEND
Jude 1: 3 to encourage you to **c** for the faith

CONTENT → CONTENTMENT
Sir 29:23 or much, be **c** with what you have,
2Co 12:10 Therefore, I am **c** with weaknesses,
Heb 13: 5 money but be **c** with what you have,

CONTENTMENT → CONTENT
1Ti 6: 6 religion with **c** is a great gain.

CONTRIBUTE
Ro 12:13 **C** to the needs of the holy ones,

CONVERT
Mt 23:15 traverse sea and land to make one **c**,
1Ti 3: 6 He should not be a recent **c**,

CONVICT
Jude 1:15 and to **c** everyone for all the godless

CONVINCE → CONVINCED, CONVINCING
Ac 28:23 trying to **c** them about Jesus
2Ti 4: 2 **c**, reprimand, encourage through all

CONVINCED → CONVINCE
Ro 8:38 For I am **c** that neither death,

COPY
Dt 17:18 he shall have a **c** of this law made
Heb 9:24 made by hands, a **c** of the true one,

CORDS
2Sa 22: 6 The **c** of the nether world enmeshed
Hos 11: 4 I drew them with human **c**,

CORNELIUS
First Gentile Christian (Ac 10).

CORNERSTONE → STONE
Ps 118:22 builders rejected has become the **c**.
Isa 28:16 A precious **c** as a sure foundation;
Lk 20:17 builders rejected has become the **c**'?
1Pe 2: 6 in Zion, a **c**, chosen and precious,

CORRECTING → CORRECTION
2Ti 2:25 **c** opponents with kindness. It may

CORRECTION → CORRECTING
Jer 5: 3 laid them low, but they refused **c**;
2Ti 3:16 refutation, for **c**, and for training

CORRUPT → CORRUPTION
Ge 6:11 In the eyes of God the earth was **c**
Ac 2:40 yourselves from this **c** generation."

CORRUPTION → CORRUPT
Ac 2:31 netherworld nor did his flesh see **c**.
2Pe 1: 4 escaping from the **c** that is

COST
1Ch 21:24 up holocausts that **c** me nothing."
Lk 14:28 and calculate the **c** to see if there is

COUNCIL
Jer 23:18 who has stood in the **c** of the LORD,

COUNSEL → COUNSELOR, COUNSELORS
Isa 28:29 wonderful is his **c** and great his

COUNSELOR → COUNSEL
Ro 11:34 of the Lord or who has been his **c**?"

COUNSELORS → COUNSEL
Pr 11:14 people falls; security lies in many **c**.
24: 6 the victory is due to a wealth of **c**.

COUNT → COUNTED, COUNTS
Ps 90:12 Teach us to **c** our days aright,

COUNTED → COUNT
Ge 13:16 your descendants too might be **c**.
Mt 10:30 all the hairs of your head are **c**.

COURAGE → COURAGEOUS
Jn 16:33 but take **c**, I have conquered

COURAGEOUS → COURAGE
1Ma 2:64 be **c** and strong in keeping the law,
1Co 16:13 firm in the faith, be **c**, be strong.

COURT → COURTS
Ex 27: 9 also make a **c** for the Dwelling.
27: 9 south side the **c** shall have hangings
Da 7:10 The **c** was convened, and the books
Mt 5:25 while on the way to **c** with him.
1Co 6: 6 brother goes to **c** against brother,

COURTS → COURT
Ps 84:11 Better one day in your **c**
96: 8 name! Bring gifts and enter his **c**;

COVENANT → COVENANTS
Ge 6:18 But with you I will establish my **c**;

Ge 9: 9 I am now establishing my **c**
15:18 that the LORD made a **c** with Abram,
Ex 2:24 was mindful of his **c** with Abraham,
19: 5 hearken to my voice and keep my **c**,
24: 7 Taking the book of the **c**, he read it
Lev 26:42 I will remember my **c** with Jacob,
26:42 my **c** with Jacob, my **c** with Isaac,
26:42 with Isaac, and my **c** with Abraham,
Jdg 2: 1 I would never break my **c** with you,
1Ki 8:23 you keep your **c** of kindness
Ezr 10: 3 enter into a **c** before our God
Jdt 9:13 planned dire things against your **c**,
1Ma 1:15 and abandoned the holy **c**;
Ps 105: 8 He remembers forever his **c**,
Sir 28: 7 of the Most High's **c**, and overlook
Isa 61: 8 a lasting **c** I will make with them.
Jer 31:31 I will make a new **c** with the house
Eze 16:60 Yet I will remember the **c** I made
16:60 set up an everlasting **c** with you.
Mal 3: 1 of the **c** whom you desire. Yes, he is
Lk 22:20 "This cup is the new **c** in my blood,
1Co 11:25 "This cup is the new **c** in my blood.
2Co 3: 6 qualified us as ministers of a new **c**,
Heb 7:22 the guarantee of an [even] better **c**.
12:24 the mediator of a new **c**,
Rev 11:19 the ark of his **c** could be seen

COVENANTS → COVENANT
Ro 9: 4 glory, the **c**, the giving of the law,
Gal 4:24 These women represent two **c**.

COVER
Ex 33:22 will **c** you with my hand until I have
Jas 5:20 death and will **c** a multitude of sins.

COVET
Ex 20:17 "You shall not **c** your neighbor's
20:17 You shall not **c** your neighbor's
Ro 7: 7 I did not know what it is to **c** except
7: 7 that the law said, "You shall not **c**.
Jas 4: 2 You **c** but do not possess. You kill

CRAFTY
2Co 12:16 yet I was **c** and got the better of you

CREATE → CREATED, CREATION, CREATOR

Ps 51:12 A clean heart **c** for me, God;
Isa 65:17 Lo, I am about to **c** new heavens
Eph 2:15 that he might **c** in himself one new

CREATED → CREATE

Ge 1: 1 when God **c** the heavens
   1:27 God **c** man in his image;
   1:27 in the divine image he **c** him;
   1:27 **c** him; male and female he **c** them.
Dt 32: 6 Is he not your father who **c** you?
Sir 1: 4 all things else wisdom was **c**;
Mal 2:10 Has not the one God **c** us?
1Co 11: 9 nor was man **c** for woman,
Eph 2:10 **c** in Christ Jesus for the good works
Col 1:16 in him were **c** all things in heaven
   1:16 all things were **c** through him
1Ti 4: 4 For everything **c** by God is good,
Rev 4:11 for you **c** all things; because of your
   4:11 will they came to be and were **c**."

CREATION → CREATE

Ge 2: 3 from all the work he had done in **c**.
Mk 10: 6 But from the beginning of **c**,
Ro 8:19 For **c** awaits with eager expectation
2Co 5:17 So whoever is in Christ is a new **c**:
Gal 6:15 uncircumcision, but only a new **c**.
Col 1:15 invisible God, the firstborn of all **c**.
2Pe 3: 4 as it was from the beginning of **c**."

CREATOR → CREATE

Ecc 12: 1 Remember your **C** in the days
Ro 1:25 the creature rather than the **c**, who is
Col 3:10 for knowledge, in the image of its **c**.
1Pe 4:19 over to a faithful **c** as they do good.

CREATURE → CREATURES

Ro 1:25 and worshiped the **c** rather than

CREATURES → CREATURE

Ps 104:24 them all; the earth is full of your **c**.
Eze 1: 5 figures resembling four living **c**
Rev 4: 6 there were four living **c** covered
   19: 4 and the four living **c** fell down

CREDIT

Lk 6:33 good to you, what **c** is that to you?
1Pe 2:20 But what **c** is there if you are patient

CREEPING

Ge 1:24 cattle, **c** things, and wild animals

CRIED → CRY

Ex 2:23 and **c** out because of their slavery.
Nu 20:16 when we **c** to the LORD, he heard our
Jdg 3: 9 But when the Israelites **c**
Ps 22: 6 To you they **c** out and they escaped;
Mt 27:46 about three o'clock Jesus **c**

CRIMINAL → CRIMINALS

Jn 18:30 "If he were not a **c**, we would not
2Ti 2: 9 even to the point of chains, like a **c**.

CRIMINALS → CRIMINAL

Lk 23:32 both **c**, were led away with him

CROOKED

Dt 32: 5 children, a perverse and **c** race!
Ecc 1:15 What is **c** cannot be made straight,
Php 2:15 without blemish in the midst of a **c**

CROSS → CROSSROADS

Dt 31: 3 your God, who will **c** before you;
   31: 3 [It is Joshua who will **c** before you,
Mk 15:30 by coming down from the **c**."
Lk 14:27 Whoever does not carry his own **c**
1Co 1:18 The message of the **c** is foolishness
Gal 6:14 in the **c** of our Lord Jesus Christ,
Php 2: 8 obedient to death, even death on a **c**.
Col 1:20 making peace by the blood of his **c**
Heb 12: 2 lay before him he endured the **c**,

CROSSROADS → CROSS, ROAD

Pr 8: 2 road, at the **c** she takes her stand;

CROWD → CROWDS

Mk 8: 2 heart is moved with pity for the **c**,
   14:43 accompanied by a **c** with swords

CROWDS → CROWD

Mt 7:28 words, the **c** were astonished at his

CROWN → CROWNED, CROWNS

Pr 4: 9 a glorious **c** will she bestow on you."
Jn 19: 2 the soldiers wove a **c** out of thorns
Php 4: 1 my joy and **c**, in this way stand firm
2Ti 4: 8 on the **c** of righteousness awaits me,
1Pe 5: 4 you will receive the unfading **c**
Rev 6: 2 He was given a **c**, and he rode forth
   14:14 man, with a gold **c** on his head

CROWNED → CROWN

Ps 8: 6 a god, **c** them with glory and honor.

Heb 2: 9 but we do see Jesus "**c** with glory

CROWNS → CROWN

Rev 4:10 They throw down their **c** before

CRUCIFIED → CRUCIFY

Mt 27:22 They all said, "Let him be **c**!"
Lk 24: 7 be handed over to sinners and be **c**,
Ac 4:10 Christ the Nazorean whom you **c**,
Ro 6: 6 that our old self was **c** with him,
1Co 1:23 but we proclaim Christ **c**,
Gal 2:19 for God. I have been **c** with Christ;

CRUCIFY → CRUCIFIED

Lk 23:21 continued their shouting, "**C** him!
Jn 19:15 him away, take him away! **C** him!"
   19:15 said to them, "Shall I **c** your king?"

CRUSH → CRUSHED

Job 6: 9 that God would decide to **c** me,
Isa 53:10 was pleased to **c** him in infirmity.]
Ro 16:20 of peace will quickly **c** Satan under

CRUSHED → CRUSH

Ps 34:19 saves those whose spirit is **c**.

CRY → CRIED, CRYING

Ex 2:23 As their **c** for release went
Ps 5: 3 Hear my **c** for help, my king,
Hab 1: 2 How long, O LORD? I **c** for help
   1: 2 not listen! I **c** out to you, "Violence!"
Mk 15:37 Jesus gave a loud **c** and breathed his

CRYING → CRY

Mk 1: 3 A voice of one **c** out in the desert:

CRYSTAL

Eze 1:22 seeming like glittering **c**,
Rev 22: 1 sparkling like **c**,

CUP

Ps 23: 5 my head with oil; my **c** overflows.
Jer 25:15 Take this **c** of foaming wine
Mt 10:42 And whoever gives only a **c** of cold
   26:39 is possible, let this **c** pass from me;
Mk 10:38 Can you drink the **c** that I drink
Lk 22:17 Then he took a **c**, gave thanks,
1Co 11:25 In the same way also the **c**,
   11:25 "This **c** is the new covenant in my
Rev 14:10 full strength into the **c** of his wrath,

CURED

Mt 8:16 spirits by a word and **c** all the sick,
Ac 5:16 unclean spirits, and they were all **c**.

CURSE → ACCURSED, CURSED, CURSES

Ge 12: 3 you and **c** those who **c** you.
Nu 22:12 with them and do not **c** this people,
Dt 21:23 since God's **c** rests on him who
23: 5 Pethor in Aram Naharaim, to **c** you;
Job 2: 9 to your innocence? **C** God and die."
Ps 109:28 Though they **c**, may you bless;
Sir 4: 5 eyes, give no man reason to **c** you;
Mk 14:71 He began to **c** and to swear, "I do not
Lk 6:28 bless those who **c** you,
Ro 12:14 [you], bless and do not **c** them.
Gal 3:13 ransomed us from the **c** of the law
3:13 **c** of the law by becoming a **c** for us,

CURSED → CURSE

Ge 3:17 "**C** be the ground because of you!
9:25 he said: "**C** be Canaan! The lowest
27:29 to you. **C** be those who curse you,
Nu 23: 8 can I curse whom God has not **c**?
Job 3: 1 Job opened his mouth and **c** his day.
Mk 11:21 The fig tree that you **c** has withered."
Gal 3:10 "**C** be everyone who does not
Heb 6: 8 it will soon be **c** and finally burned.

CURSES → CURSE

Lev 24:15 Anyone who **c** his God shall bear
2Ch 34:24 all the **c** written in the book that has

CUSTOM → CUSTOMS

Jn 18:39 But you have a **c** that I release one

CUSTOMS → CUSTOM

1Ma 1:42 each abandoning his particular **c**.
Ac 16:21 are advocating **c** that are not lawful

CUT

Ps 37: 9 Those who do evil will be **c** off,
Isa 53: 8 When he was **c** off from the land
Mt 3:10 not bear good fruit will be **c** down
Mk 9:43 your hand causes you to sin, **c** it off.
Ro 11:22 otherwise you too will be **c** off.

CYMBAL → CYMBALS

1Co 13: 1 a resounding gong or a clashing **c**.

CYMBALS → CYMBAL

2Sa 6: 5 harps, tambourines, sistrums and **c**.
Ne 12:27 hymns and the music of **c**, harps,

Ps 150: 5 Give praise with crashing **c**,
150: 5 **c**, praise him with sounding **c**.

CYRUS
Persian king who allowed exiles to return (2Ch 36:22-Ezr 1:8), to rebuild temple (Ezr 5:13-6:14), as appointed by the LORD (Isa 44:28-45:13).

D

DAGON

Jdg 16:23 offer a great sacrifice to their god **D**
1Sa 5: 2 and brought it into the temple of **D**,
5: 2 the temple of **D**, placing it beside **D**.

DAILY → DAY

Mt 6:11 Give us today our **d** bread;
Lk 9:23 take up his cross **d** and follow me.

DAMASCUS

Ac 9: 3 as he was nearing **D**, a light

DAN
1. Son of Jacob by Bilhah (Ge 30:4-6; 35:25; 46:23). Tribe of blessed (Ge 49:16-17; Dt 33:22), numbered (Nu 1:39; 26:43), allotted land (Jos 19:40-48; Eze 48:1), failed to fully possess (Jdg 1:34-35), failed to support Deborah (Jdg 5:17), possessed Dan (Jdg 18).
2. Northernmost city in Israel (Ge 14:14; Jdg 18; 20:1).

DANCE

Ps 150: 4 Give praise with tambourines and **d**,
Ecc 3: 4 a time to mourn, and a time to **d**.
Lk 7:32 the flute for you, but you did not **d**.

DANIEL → = BELTESHAZZAR
1. Hebrew exile to Babylon, name changed to Belteshazzar (Da 1:6-7). Refused to eat unclean food (Da 1:8-21). Interpreted Nebuchadnezzar's dreams (Da 2; 4), writing on the wall (Da 5). Thrown into lion's den (Da 6; 14:31-42). Visions of (Da 7-12). Saves Susanna (Da 13). Destroys Bel and its priests (Da 14).
2. Son of David (1Ch 3:1).

DARE

Mt 22:46 did anyone **d** to ask him any more

DARIUS
1. King of Persia (Ezr 4:5), allowed rebuilding of temple (Ezr 5-6).
2. Mede who conquered Babylon (Da 5:31).

DARK → DARKNESS

Ps 139:12 Darkness is not **d** for you, and night
2Pe 1:19 it, as to a lamp shining in a **d** place,

DARKNESS → DARK

Ge 1: 2 and **d** covered the abyss,
Ex 10:22 there was dense **d** throughout
Dt 5:23 the voice from the midst of the **d**,

Zep 1:15 desolation, a day of **d** and gloom,
Mt 4:16 the people who sit in **d** have seen
6:23 bad, your whole body will be in **d**.
6:23 **d**. And if the light in you is **d**,
6:23 in you is **d**, how great will the **d** be.
Jn 1: 5 the light shines in the **d**, and the **d**
Eph 5: 8 For you were once **d**, but now you
Col 1:13 He delivered us from the power of **d**
1Jn 1: 5 light, and in him there is no **d** at all.

DATHAN
Involved in Korah's rebellion against Moses and Aaron (Nu 16:1-27; 26:9; Dt 11:6; Ps 106:17; Sir 45:18).

DAUGHTER → DAUGHTERS

Ex 2: 5 Pharaoh's **d** came down to the river
Jdt 10:12 "I am a **d** of the Hebrews, and I am
Est 2: 7 had taken her as his own **d**.
Ps 9:15 salvation in the gates of **d** Zion.
La 2: 1 has detested **d** Zion! He has cast
Mic 7: 6 the **d** rises up against her mother,
Zec 9: 9 Rejoice heartily, O **d** Zion,
9: 9 shout for joy, O **d** Jerusalem! See,
Mt 14: 6 the **d** of Herodias performed a dance
Lk 12:53 a mother against her **d** and a **d**

DAUGHTERS → DAUGHTER

Ge 6: 4 had intercourse with the **d** of man,
19:36 both of Lot's **d** became pregnant
Nu 27: 1 son of Joseph, had **d** named Mahlah,
Dt 12:31 their sons and **d** to their gods.
Job 42:15 women were as beautiful as the **d**
Ac 2:17 sons and your **d** shall prophesy,
2Co 6:18 and you shall be sons and **d** to me,

DAVID
Son of Jesse (Ru 4:17-22; 1Ch 2:13-15), ancestor of Jesus (Mt 1:1-17; Lk 3:31). Wives and children (1Sa 18; 25:39-44; 2Sa 3:2-5; 5:13-16; 11:27; 1Ch 3:1-9).
Anointed by Samuel (1Sa 16:1-13). Musician to Saul (1Sa 16:14-23; 18:10). Killed Goliath (1Sa 17). Relation with Jonathan (1Sa 18:1-4; 19-20; 23:16-18; 2Sa 1). Disfavor of Saul (1Sa 18:6-23:29). Spared Saul's life (1Sa 24; 26). Among Philistines (1Sa 21:10-14; 27-30). Lament for Saul and Jonathan (2Sa 1).
Anointed king of Judah (2Sa 2:1-11). Conflict with house of Saul (2Sa 2-4). Anointed king of Israel (2Sa 5:1-4; 1Ch 11:1-3). Conquered Jerusalem (2Sa 5:6-10; 1Ch 11;4-9). Brought ark to Jerusalem (2Sa

6; 1Ch 13; 15-16). The LORD promised eternal dynasty (2Sa 7; 1Ch 17; Ps 132). Showed kindness to Mephibosheth (2Sa 9). Adultery with Bathsheba, murder of Uriah (2Sa 11-12). Son Amnon raped daughter Tamar; killed by Absalom (2Sa 13). Absalom's revolt (2Sa 14-17); death (2Sa 18). Sheba's revolt (2Sa 20). Victories: Philistines (2Sa 5:17-25; 21:15-22; 1Ch 14:8-17; 20:4-8), Ammonites (2Sa 10; 1Ch 19), various (2Sa 8; 1Ch 18). Mighty men (2Sa 23:8-39; 1Ch 11-12). Punished for numbering army (2Sa 24; 1Ch 21). Appointed Solomon king (1Ki 1:28-2:9). Prepared for building of temple (1Ch 22-29). Last words (2Sa 23:1-7). Death (1Ki 2:10-12; 1Ch 29:28).

Psalmist (Mt 22:43-45), musician (Am 6:5), prophet (2Sa 23:2-7; Ac 1:16; 2:30).

Psalms of: 2 (Ac 4:25), 3-32, 34-41, 51-65, 68-70, 86, 95 (Heb 4:7), 101, 103, 108-110, 122, 124, 131, 133, 138-145.

DAWN → DAWNS
Isa   14:12   O morning star, son of the **d**!
Hos   6: 3   as certain as the **d** is his coming,

DAWNS → DAWN
Ps   97:11   Light **d** for the just; gladness,
2Pe   1:19   until day **d** and the morning star

DAY → DAILY, DAYS
Ge   1: 5   God called the light "**d**,"
      1: 5   and morning followed—the first **d**
      8:22   Summer and winter, and **d** and night
Ex   13:21   Thus they could travel both **d**
      20: 8   to keep holy the sabbath **d**.
Jos   1: 8   Recite it by **d** and by night, that you
Ps   1: 2   God's law they study **d** and night.
      118:24   This is the **d** the LORD has made;
Isa   66: 8   a country be brought forth in one **d**,
Joel 1:15   Alas, the **d**! for near is the **d**
Zec   14: 1   a **d** shall come for the LORD
Mal   3: 2   But who will endure the **d** of his
Mt   25:13   you know neither the **d** nor the hour.
Lk   11: 3   Give us each **d** our daily bread
      24:46   and rise from the dead on the third **d**
Jn   6:40   and I shall raise him [on] the last **d**."
Ro   14: 5   considers one **d** more important
2Co   6: 2   on the **d** of salvation I helped you."
      6: 2   behold, now is the **d** of salvation.
1Th   5: 2   the **d** of the Lord will come like
2Pe   3: 8   the Lord one **d** is like a thousand
      3: 8   and a thousand years like one **d**.
      3:10   the **d** of the Lord will come like

1Jn   4:17   the **d** of judgment because as he is,
Rev   1:10   caught up in spirit on the Lord's **d**
      16:14   on the great **d** of God the almighty.

DAYS → DAY
Ge   1:14   the fixed times, the **d** and the years,
      7: 4   Seven **d** from now I will bring rain
      7: 4   rain down on the earth for forty **d**
Ex   24:18   there he stayed for forty **d** and forty
1Ki   19: 8   he walked forty **d** and forty nights
1Ma   4:56   For eight **d** they celebrated
Mk   1:13   remained in the desert for forty **d**,
Eph   5:16   opportunity, because the **d** are evil.
2Ti   3: 1   will be terrifying times in the last **d**.
Heb   1: 2   in these last **d**, he spoke to us

DEACONS
1Ti   3: 8   Similarly, **d** must be dignified,

DEAD → DEATH, DIE, DIED, DYING
Dt   18:11   spirits or seeks oracles from the **d**.
Ps   115:17   The **d** do not praise the LORD,
Ecc   9: 4   a live dog is better off than a **d** lion.
Mt   8:22   me, and let the **d** bury their **d**."
Mk   12:27   He is not God of the **d**
Lk   24: 5   seek the living one among the **d**?
Ro   6:11   of yourselves as [being] **d** to sin
Eph   2: 1   You were **d** in your transgressions
Col   1:18   beginning, the firstborn from the **d**,
1Pe   4: 5   ready to judge the living and the **d**
Rev   1: 5   the firstborn of the **d** and ruler
      20:12   I saw the **d**, the great and the lowly,
      20:12   life. The **d** were judged according

DEAF
Ex   4:11   and makes another **d** and dumb?
Isa   29:18   On that day the **d** shall hear
Lk   7:22   lepers are cleansed, the **d** hear,

DEATH → DEAD
Dt   30:19   I have set before you life and **d**,
Ru   1:17   aught but **d** separates me from you!"
Ps   22:16   palate; you lay me in the dust of **d**.
Pr   18:21   **D** and life are in the power
SS   8: 6   For stern as **d** is love, relentless as
Sir   15:17   Before man are life and **d**,
Hos   13:14   shall I redeem them from **d**?
      13:14   Where are your plagues, O **d**!
Mt   16:28   who will not taste **d** until they see

Jn   5:24   but has passed from **d** to life.
Ro   6:23   For the wages of sin is **d**
1Co   15:55   Where, O **d**, is your victory? Where,
      15:55   victory? Where, O **d**, is your sting?"
2Co   2:16   to the latter an odor of **d** that leads
      2:16   latter an odor of **d** that leads to **d**,
Heb   2:14   through **d** he might destroy the one
      2:14   the one who has the power of **d**,
1Jn   3:14   that we have passed from **d** to life
      3:14   does not love remains in **d**.
Rev   1:18   ever. I hold the keys to **d**
      20:14   Then **D** and Hades were thrown
      20:14   (This pool of fire is the second **d**.)
      21: 4   and there shall be no more **d**

DEBAUCHERY
Eph   5:18   in which lies **d**, but be filled

DEBORAH
Prophetess; led victory over Canaanites (Jdg 4-5).

DEBTS
Dt   15: 1   you shall have a relaxation of **d**,
Mt   6:12   and forgive us our **d**, as we forgive

DECEIT → DECEITFUL, DECEIVE, DECEIVED, DECEIVERS
Dt   32: 4   A faithful God, without **d**, how just
1Pe   2:22   and no **d** was found in his mouth."

DECEITFUL → DECEIT
Ps   35:20   in the land they fashion **d** speech.
Zep   3:13   be found in their mouths a **d** tongue;
1Ti   4: 1   faith by paying attention to **d** spirits

DECEIVE → DECEIT
Eph   5: 6   Let no one **d** you with empty
1Jn   1: 8   "We are without sin," we **d** ourselves,
Rev   20: 8   to **d** the nations at the four corners

DECEIVED → DECEIT
1Ti   2:14   Adam was not **d**, but the woman
      2:14   the woman was **d** and transgressed.

DECEIVERS → DECEIT
Tit   1:10   idle talkers and **d**,
2Jn   1: 7   Many **d** have gone

DECISION
Pr   16:33   its **d** depends entirely on the LORD.

DECLARED
Mk   7:19   latrine?" (Thus he **d** all foods clean.)

DECREASE
Jn 3:30 He must increase; I must **d**."

DECREE → DECREED, DECREES
Ps 2: 7 I will proclaim the **d** of the LORD,
Lk 2: 1 In those days a **d** went

DECREED → DECREE
Da 9:24 "Seventy weeks are **d** for your people

DECREES → DECREE
Ps 119: 2 Happy those who observe God's **d,**

DEDICATED → DEDICATION
1Ki 8:63 all the Israelites **d** the temple

DEDICATION → DEDICATED
2Ch 7: 9 they had celebrated the **d** of the altar
Ezr 6:16 other returned exiles— celebrated the **d**
1Ma 4:56 eight days they celebrated the **d**

DEED → DEEDS
Jer 32:10 I had written and sealed the **d,**
Col 3:17 in word or in **d,** do everything

DEEDS → DEED
Dt 3:24 on earth can perform **d** as mighty as
Ps 9: 2 I will declare all your wondrous **d.**
Jer 50:29 Repay her for her **d;** as she has
Rev 19: 8 linen represents the righteous **d**

DEFEND
Ps 72: 4 he may **d** the oppressed among
Pr 31: 9 is just, **d** the needy and the poor!

DEFILE → DEFILED
Nu 35:34 Do not **d** the land in which you live
Mk 7:15 one from outside can **d** that person;
7:15 come out from within are what **d.**"

DEFILED → DEFILE
1Ma 1:37 the sanctuary; they **d** the sanctuary.
Ps 79: 1 they have **d** your holy temple,

DEFRAUD
Lev 19:13 "You shall not **d** or rob your
Mk 10:19 you shall not **d;** honor your father

DEITY
Col 2: 9 the whole fullness of the **d** bodily,

DELAY
Ps 70: 6 help and deliverer. LORD, do not **d!**
Heb 10:37 to come shall come; he shall not **d.**

DELIGHT → DELIGHTS
1Sa 15:22 "Does the LORD so **d** in holocausts
Ps 40: 9 To do your will is my **d;** my God,
Pr 8:30 and I was his **d** day by day,
Ro 7:22 For I take **d** in the law of God,

DELIGHTS → DELIGHT
Ps 5: 5 You are not a god who **d** in evil;

DELILAH
Philistine who betrayed Samson (Jdg 16:4-22).

DELIVER → DELIVERANCE, DELIVERER, DELIVERS
Mt 27:43 let him **d** him now if he wants him.

DELIVERANCE → DELIVER
Est 4:14 and **d** will come to the Jews
Php 1:19 this will result in **d** for me through

DELIVERER → DELIVER
Ro 11:26 "The **d** will come out of Zion, he will

DEMON → DEMONIACS, DEMONIC, DEMONS
Tob 3: 8 the wicked **d** Asmodeus killed them
6: 8 a woman who is afflicted by a **d**
Mt 11:18 they said, 'He is possessed by a **d.**'
17:18 him and the **d** came out of him,
Jn 10:21 surely a **d** cannot open the eyes

DEMONIACS → DEMON
Mt 8:28 two **d** who were coming

DEMONIC → DEMON
Rev 16:14 These were **d** spirits who performed

DEMONS → DEMON
Dt 32:17 They offered sacrifice to **d,**
Bar 4: 7 with sacrifices to **d,** to no-gods;
Lk 11:18 it is by Beelzebul that I drive out **d.**
1Co 10:20 [they sacrifice] to **d,** not to God,
10:20 you to become participants with **d.**
Jas 2:19 Even the **d** believe that and tremble.
Rev 9:20 to give up the worship of **d**

DEN
Jer 7:11 become in your eyes a **d** of thieves?
Mk 11:17 But you have made it a **d** of thieves."

DENARIUS
Mk 12:15 testing me? Bring me a **d** to look at."

DENIED → DENY
Mt 26:70 But he **d** it in front of everyone,
1Ti 5: 8 family members has **d** the faith
Rev 3: 8 my word and have not **d** my name.

DENIES → DENY
Lk 12: 9 whoever **d** me before others will be
1Jn 2:22 Whoever **d** that Jesus is the Christ.
2:22 Whoever **d** the Father and the Son,

DENY → DENIED, DENIES
Mt 16:24 to come after me must **d** himself,
2Ti 2:12 him. But if we **d** him he will **d** us.
2Pe 2: 1 even **d** the Master who ransomed

DEPART
Ge 49:10 The scepter shall never **d**
Php 1:23 two. I long to **d** this life and be

DEPRAVED
2Pe 2:10 follow the flesh with its **d** desire

DEPRIVE
1Co 7: 5 Do not **d** each other, except perhaps

DEPTH → DEPTHS
Ro 11:33 the **d** of the riches and wisdom
Eph 3:18 breadth and length and height and **d,**

DEPTHS → DEPTH
Ps 130: 1 Out of the **d** I call to you, LORD;
1Co 2:10 everything, even the **d** of God.

DESCENDANTS
Ge 15:18 "To your **d** I give this land,
Dt 4:37 love of your fathers he chose their **d**
Isa 44: 3 and my blessing upon your **d.**
Ro 9: 7 of Abraham because they are his **d;**
9: 7 Isaac that **d** shall bear your name."

DESCENDED → DESCENDING
Eph 4: 9 also **d** into the lower [regions]

DESCENDING → DESCENDED
Mk 1:10 the Spirit, like a dove, **d** upon him.
Jn 1:51 ascending and **d** on the Son of Man."

DESERT → DESERTED
Ps 106:14 In the **d** they gave way to their
Isa 40: 3 out: In the **d** prepare the way

DESERTED → DESERT
Mk 8: 4 to satisfy them here in this **d** place?"

DESERVE
Rev 2:23 give each of you what your works **d.**

DESIRE → DESIRED, DESIRES
Hos 6: 6 For it is love that I **d,** not sacrifice,
Mt 9:13 meaning of the words, 'I **d** mercy,
Jas 1:14 is lured and enticed by his own **d.**

DESIRED → DESIRE
Lk 22:15 "I have eagerly **d** to eat this Passover

DESIRES → DESIRE
Sir 18:30 your lusts, but keep your **d** in check.
2Ti 4: 3 following their own **d** and insatiable

DESOLATE → DESOLATING
Ex 23:29 else the land will become so **d**
1Ma 1:39 sanctuary was as **d** as a wilderness;
Mt 23:38 your house will be abandoned, **d**.

DESOLATING → DESOLATE
Mk 13:14 you see the **d** abomination standing

DESPAIR → DESPAIRED
2Co 4: 8 perplexed, but not driven to **d**;

DESPAIRED → DESPAIR
2Co 1: 8 strength, so that we **d** even of life.

DESPISE → DESPISED
Pr 1: 7 wisdom and instruction fools **d**.
Lk 16:13 be devoted to one and **d** the other.

DESPISED → DESPISE
1Co 1:28 chose the lowly and **d** of the world,

DESTINED
Eph 1: 5 he **d** us for adoption to himself
1Pe 1:11 to the sufferings **d** for Christ

DESTROY → DESTROYED, DESTROYER, DESTRUCTION
Ge 6:13 So I will **d** them and all life
Est 3: 6 he sought to **d** all the Jews,
Mt 10:28 of the one who can **d** both soul
Jn 10:10 only to steal and slaughter and **d**;
Jas 4:12 judge who is able to save or to **d**.
1Jn 3: 8 God was revealed to **d** the works

DESTROYED → DESTROY
1Co 15:26 The last enemy to be **d** is death,
2Co 5: 1 should be **d**, we have a building

DESTROYER → DESTROY
Ex 12:23 not let the **d** come into your houses
1Co 10:10 did, and suffered death by the **d**.

DESTRUCTION → DESTROY
Mt 7:13 and the road broad that leads to **d**,
Ro 9:22 the vessels of wrath made for **d**?
2Pe 3:16 and unstable distort to their own **d**,

DEVIL
Mt 4: 1 the desert to be tempted by the **d**.
Lk 8:12 but the **d** comes and takes away
Jn 8:44 You belong to your father the **d**
Eph 4:27 and do not leave room for the **d**.
    6:11 firm against the tactics of the **d**.
Heb 2:14 the power of death, that is, the **d**,
Jas 4: 7 Resist the **d**, and he will flee

1Pe 5: 8 Your opponent the **d** is prowling
1Jn 3: 8 Whoever sins belongs to the **d**,
    3: 8 **d**, because the **d** has sinned
    3: 8 to destroy the works of the **d**.
Jude 1: 9 with the **d** in a dispute over the body
Rev 12: 9 who is called the **D** and Satan,
    20: 2 serpent, which is the **D** or Satan,

DEVOTED → DEVOTION
Mt 6:24 or be **d** to one and despise the other.

DEVOTION → DEVOTED
Wis 10:12 that **d** to God is mightier than all else.
1Ti 4: 7 Train yourself for **d**,
2Pe 1: 3 everything that makes for life and **d**,

DEVOUR → DEVOURING
1Pe 5: 8 lion looking for [someone] to **d**.
Rev 12: 4 to **d** her child when she gave birth.

DEVOURING → DEVOUR
Gal 5:15 you go on biting and **d** one another,

DEW
Jdg 6:37 If **d** comes on the fleece alone,

DICTATED
Jer 36:18 "Jeremiah **d** all these words to me,"

DIE → DEAD
Ge 2:17 from it you are surely doomed to **d**."
    3: 4 woman: "You certainly will not **d**!
Ex 11: 5 Every first-born in this land shall **d**,
Ru 1:17 Wherever you **d** I will **d**, and there
Job 2: 9 your innocence? Curse God and **d**."
Pr 10:21 many, but fools **d** for want of sense.
Ecc 3: 2 A time to be born, and a time to **d**;
Isa 22:13 "Eat and drink, for tomorrow we **d**!"
Jer 31:30 his own fault only shall anyone **d**:
Mt 26:35 "Even though I should have to **d**
Jn 11:26 and believes in me will never **d**.
Ro 14: 8 and if we **d**, we **d** for the Lord;
    14: 8 whether we live or **d**, we are
1Co 15:32 eat and drink, for tomorrow we **d**."
Heb 9:27 that human beings **d** once,

DIED → DEAD
Ro 5: 6 yet **d** at the appointed time
1Co 15: 3 that Christ **d** for our sins
Gal 2:19 For through the law I **d** to the law,

DIFFERENT
2Co 11: 4 if you receive a **d** spirit from the one
    11: 4 or a **d** gospel from the one you
Gal 1: 6 [the] grace [of Christ] for a **d** gospel

DILIGENCE
Ro 12: 8 if one is over others, with **d**; if one

DINAH
    Only daughter of Jacob, by Leah (Ge 30:21; 46:15). Raped by Shechem; avenged by Simeon and Levi (Ge 34).

DIRECT → DIRECTS
2Th 3: 5 May the Lord **d** your hearts

DIRECTS → DIRECT
Pr 16: 9 his course, but the LORD **d** his steps.

DISAPPOINT
Ro 5: 5 and hope does not **d**.

DISASTER
Eze 7: 5 Thus says the Lord GOD **D** upon **d**!

DISCERNMENT
1Co 12:10 to another **d** of spirits; to another

DISCIPLE → DISCIPLES
Mt 10:24 No **d** is above his teacher, no slave
Lk 14:26 his own life, he cannot be my **d**.

DISCIPLES → DISCIPLE
Isa 8:16 sealed instruction kept among my **d**.
Mt 26:56 Then all the **d** left him and fled.
    28:19 and make **d** of all nations,
Lk 6:13 day came, he called his **d** to himself,
Jn 8:31 in my word, you will truly be my **d**,
Ac 11:26 the **d** were first called Christians.

DISCIPLINE → DISCIPLINED
Pr 5:23 He will die from lack of **d**,
Heb 12: 5 son, do not disdain the **d** of the Lord

DISCIPLINED → DISCIPLINE
1Co 11:32 we are being **d** so that we may not

DISEASE → DISEASES
Mt 4:23 curing every **d** and illness among
    9:35 and curing every **d** and illness.

DISEASES → DISEASE
Ex 15:26 any of the **d** with which I afflicted
Mt 8:17 away our infirmities and bore our **d**."

DISGRACE
1Ma 4:58 the **d** of the Gentiles was removed.
Pr 11: 2 When pride comes, **d** comes;

DISHONEST
Lk 16:10 the person who is **d** in very small
16:10 small matters is also **d** in great ones.

DISHONOR
Jn 8:49 I honor my Father, but you **d** me.
Ac 5:41 worthy to suffer **d** for the sake

DISMAYED
Jos 1: 9 Do not fear nor be **d**, for the LORD,

DISOBEDIENT → DISOBEYING
Ro 10:21 long I stretched out my hands to a **d**
Tit 3: 3 we ourselves were once foolish, **d**,

DISOBEYING → DISOBEDIENT
Lev 26:27 you still persist in **d** and defying me,
1Pe 2: 8 They stumble by **d** the word, as is

DISPERSION
Jn 7:35 not going to the **d** among the Greeks

DISQUALIFIED → DISQUALIFY
1Co 9:27 to others, I myself should be **d**.

DISQUALIFY → DISQUALIFIED
Col 2:18 Let no one **d** you,

DISSENSIONS
Gal 5:20 fury, acts of selfishness, **d**, factions,

DISTINCTION → DISTINCTIONS
Ro 3:22 all who believe. For there is no **d**;

DISTINCTIONS → DISTINCTION
Jas 2: 4 you not made **d** among yourselves

DISTRESS
Dt 4:30 In your **d**, when all these things
Jdg 2:15 would do, till they were in great **d**.
2Sa 22: 7 In my **d** I called upon the LORD
Ps 81: 8 In **d** you called and I rescued you;
Jer 30: 7 it! At time of **d** for Jacob, though he
Ro 8:35 Will anguish, or **d**, or persecution,

DISTRIBUTED
Ac 4:35 they were **d** to each according

DIVIDE → DIVIDED
Ps 22:19 they **d** my garments among them;

DIVIDED → DIVIDE
Lk 11:18 And if Satan is **d** against himself,

DIVINATION → DIVINE
1Sa 15:23 For a sin like **d** is rebellion,
2Ki 17:17 practiced fortune-telling and **d**,

DIVINE → DIVINATION
2Pe 1: 4 may come to share in the **d** nature,

DIVORCE → DIVORCED
Dt 24: 1 therefore he writes out a bill of **d**
Isa 50: 1 Where is the bill of **d** with which I
Jer 3: 8 her away and gave her a bill of **d**,
Mal 2:16 For I hate **d**, says the LORD, the God
Mt 5:31 his wife must give her a bill of **d**.'
19: 3 a man to **d** his wife for any cause
1Co 7:11 a husband should not **d** his wife.

DIVORCED → DIVORCE
Lev 21: 7 nor a woman who has been **d** by her
Mt 5:32 marries a **d** woman commits

DOCTRINE → DOCTRINES
2Ti 4: 3 people will not tolerate sound **d** but,
Tit 1: 9 be able both to exhort with sound **d**

DOCTRINES → DOCTRINE
Mk 7: 7 me, teaching as **d** human precepts.'
1Ti 1: 3 certain people not to teach false **d**

DOEG
Edomite; Saul's chief shepherd; murdered 85 priests at Nob (1Sa 21:7; 22:6-23; Ps 52).

DOERS → DOES, DONE
Jas 1:22 Be **d** of the word and not hearers

DOES → DOERS
Ps 135: 6 wishes he **d** in heaven and on earth,
Ecc 3:14 whatever God **d** will endure forever;
Mk 3:35 [For] whoever **d** the will of God is

DOG → DOGS
Jdg 7: 5 up the water as a **d** does with its
Pr 26:11 As the **d** returns to his vomit,
2Pe 2:22 "The **d** returns to its own vomit,"

DOGS → DOG
Mt 7: 6 "Do not give what is holy to **d**,
15:26 of the children and throw it to the **d**."
Php 3: 2 Beware of the **d**!
Rev 22:15 Outside are the **d**, the sorcerers,

DOMINION
Ge 1:26 Let them have **d** over the fish
Da 7:14 He received **d**, glory, and kingship;
7:14 serve him. His **d** is an everlasting **d**

DONE → DOERS
Mt 6:10 come, your will be **d**, on earth as
26:42 my drinking it, your will be **d**!"

Rev 16:17 from the throne, saying, "It is **d**."

DOOM → DOOMED
Dt 32:35 and their **d** is rushing upon them!
Ps 81:16 tremble, their **d** sealed forever.

DOOMED → DOOM
Ps 102:21 prisoners, to release those **d** to die."

DOOR → DOORPOSTS
Mt 7: 7 and the **d** will be opened to you.
Rev 3:20 " ' "Behold, I stand at the **d** and knock.
3:20 hears my voice and opens the **d**,

DOORPOSTS → DOOR
Ex 12: 7 apply it to the two **d** and the lintel

DORCAS
Disciple; raised from the dead (Ac 9:36-43).

DOUBLE
Dt 21:17 giving him a **d** share of whatever he
1Sa 1: 5 a **d** portion to Hannah because he
2Ki 2: 9 "May I receive a **d** portion of your
Rev 18: 6 others. Pay her back **d** for her deeds.
18: 6 her cup pour **d** what she poured.

DOUBT → DOUBTED, DOUBTING
Mt 14:31 "O you of little faith, why did you **d**?"

DOUBTED → DOUBT
Mt 28:17 him, they worshiped, but they **d**.

DOUBTING → DOUBT
Jas 1: 6 not **d**, for the one who doubts is like

DOUGH
Ex 12:39 Since the **d** they had brought
Gal 5: 9 yeast leavens the whole batch of **d**.

DOVE
Ge 8: 8 Then he sent out a **d**, to see
Mk 1:10 like a **d**, descending upon him.

DRAGON
Isa 27: 1 he will slay the **d** that is in the sea.
Da 14:23 There was a great **d**
Rev 12: 3 sky; it was a huge red **d**, with seven
20: 2 He seized the **d**, the ancient serpent,

DRANK → DRINK
Mk 14:23 it to them, and they all **d** from it.
1Co 10: 4 and all **d** the same spiritual drink,
10: 4 for they **d** from a spiritual rock

DRAW

Jn	12:32	earth, I will **d** everyone to my- self."
Jas	4: 8	**D** near to God, and he will **d** near

DREAM → DREAMER, DREAMS

1Ki	3: 5	appeared to Solomon in a **d** at night.
Da	7: 1	Daniel had a **d** as he lay in bed,
	7: 1	Then he wrote down the **d**;
Mt	1:20	of the Lord appeared to him in a **d**
Ac	2:17	your old men shall **d** dreams.

DREAMER → DREAM

Ge	37:19	another: "Here comes that master **d**!

DREAMS → DREAM

Nu	12: 6	to him, in **d** I will speak to him;
1Sa	28: 6	whether in **d** or by the Urim
Sir	34: 7	For **d** have led many astray,

DRIED → DRY

Jos	5: 1	that the LORD had **d** up the wa- ters
Isa	51:10	Was it not you who **d** up the sea,

DRINK → DRANK, DRUNK, DRUNKARD, DRUNKENNESS

Ex	32: 6	Then they sat down to eat and **d,**
Ecc	9: 7	and **d** your wine with a merry heart,
Isa	22:13	You eat meat and **d** wine: "Eat and **d,**
Mt	20:22	Can you **d** the cup that I am going
	20:22	you **d** the cup that I am going to **d**?"
Jn	18:11	Shall I not **d** the cup that the Father
Ro	14:17	of God is not a matter of food and **d,**
1Co	12:13	we were all given to **d** of one Spirit.
Rev	14:10	will also **d** the wine of God's fury,

DRIVE → DROVE

Ex	23:30	I will **d** them out little by little
Nu	33:52	**d** out all the inhabitants of the land
Mk	11:15	the temple area he began to **d**

DROSS

Ps	119:119	Like **d** you regard all the wicked
Isa	1:25	and refine your **d** in the fur- nace,
Eze	22:18	of Israel has become **d** for me.
	22:18	**d** from silver have they be- come.

DROVE → DRIVE

Jos	24:18	our approach the LORD **d** out [all
Mk	1:12	At once the Spirit **d** him

DRUNK → DRINK

Ge	9:21	he became **d** and lay naked inside
1Sa	1:13	not be heard. Eli, thinking her **d,**

Jn	2:10	and then when people have **d** freely,
Ac	2:15	These people are not **d,** as you
Eph	5:18	And do not get **d** on wine,

DRUNKARD → DRINK

Pr	23:21	For the **d** and the glutton come
Mt	11:19	he is a glutton and a **d,** a friend
1Co	5:11	a slanderer, a **d,** or a robber,
1Ti	3: 3	not a **d,** not aggressive, but gentle,

DRUNKENNESS → DRINK

Tob	4:15	nor let **d** accompany you on your

DRY → DRIED

Ge	1: 9	basin, so that the **d** land may appear."
	1: 9	its basin, and the **d** land ap- peared.
Ex	14:16	may pass through it on **d** land.
Jos	3:17	all Israel crossed over on **d** ground,
	3:17	remained motionless on **d** ground
Jdg	6:37	while all the ground is **d,** I shall
Eze	37: 4	**D** bones, hear the word of the LORD!

DUE

1Ch	16:29	to the LORD the glory **d** his name!
Mal	1: 6	father, where is the honor **d** to me?
	1: 6	where is the reverence **d** to me?—
Ro	13: 7	taxes to whom taxes are **d,**
	13: 7	**d,** toll to whom toll is **d,**
	13: 7	respect to whom respect is **d,**
	13: 7	is **d,** honor to whom honor is **d.**

DULL

Isa	6:10	to **d** their ears and close their eyes;
	59: 1	to save, nor his ear too **d** to hear.

DUST

Ge	13:16	make your descendants like the **d**
1Sa	2: 8	He raises the needy from the **d**;
Ps	103:14	formed, remembers that we are **d.**
Ecc	3:20	both were made from the **d,**
	3:20	the **d,** and to the **d** they both return.
Na	1: 3	and clouds are the **d** at his feet;
Mt	10:14	and shake the **d** from your feet.

DWELL → DWELLING, DWELLS

Ex	25: 8	for me, that I may **d** in their midst.
Ps	23: 6	life; I will **d** in the house of the LORD
Eph	3:17	Christ may **d** in your hearts through
Col	1:19	all the fullness was pleased to **d,**
Rev	21: 3	He will **d** with them and they will

DWELLING → DWELL

Lev	26:11	I will set my **D** among you, and will
Dt	12:11	chooses as the **d** place for his name
Jn	14: 2	house there are many **d** places.
Eph	2:22	being built together into a **d** place

DWELLS → DWELL

1Ki	8:27	it indeed be that God **d** among men
Jn	14:10	The Father who **d** in me is doing his
Ro	7:17	I who do it, but sin that **d** in me.
1Co	3:16	and that the Spirit of God **d** in you?
Col	2: 9	in him **d** the whole fullness

DYING → DEAD

2Co	6: 9	as **d** and behold we live.

E

EAGLE → EAGLES

Eze	1:10	finally each had the face of an **e.**
	17: 3	The great **e,** with great wings,
Rev	4: 7	the fourth looked like an **e** in flight.

EAGLES → EAGLE

Isa	40:31	they will soar as with **e**' wings;

EAR → EARS

Lk	22:51	he touched the servant's **e** and healed
1Co	2: 9	has not seen, and **e** has not heard,

EARLY

Dt	11:14	land, the **e** rain and the late rain,
Lk	24:22	were at the tomb **e** in the morning
Jas	5: 7	patient with it until it receives the **e**

EARS → EAR

Isa	35: 5	opened, the **e** of the deaf be cleared;
Mt	11:15	Whoever has **e** ought to hear.
Rev	2: 7	" ' "Whoever has **e** ought to hear what

EARTH → EARTHLY, EARTHQUAKE, EARTHQUAKES

Ge	1: 1	God created the heavens and the **e,**
	6:11	In the eyes of God the **e** was corrupt
Ex	19: 5	people, though all the **e** is mine.
Ps	47: 3	awe, the great king over all the **e,**
Sir	40:11	All that is of **e** returns to **e,** and what
Isa	6: 3	"All the **e** is filled with his glory!"
	65:17	and a new **e**; The things of the past
Jer	23:24	both heaven and **e**? says the LORD.
Mt	24:35	Heaven and **e** will pass away,
Lk	5:24	of Man has authority on **e** to forgive

EARTH → EARTHLY, EARTHQUAKE, EARTHQUAKES (*cont.*)

2Pe	3:13	and a new **e** in which right-eousness
Rev	21: 1	I saw a new heaven and a new **e**.
	21: 1	and the former **e** had passed away,

EARTHLY → EARTH

Jn	3:12	If I tell you about **e** things and you
2Co	5: 1	For we know that if our **e** dwelling,

EARTHQUAKE → EARTH, QUAKE

1Ki	19:11	the LORD was not in the **e**.
Mt	28: 2	And behold, there was a great **e**;
Ac	16:26	there was suddenly such a severe **e**
Rev	6:12	sixth seal, and there was a great **e**;

EARTHQUAKES → EARTH, QUAKE

Mt	24: 7	famines and **e** from place to place.

EASIER → EASY

Mt	9: 5	Which is **e**, to say, 'Your sins are
Lk	16:17	It is **e** for heaven and earth to pass
	18:25	For it is **e** for a camel to pass

EAST

Ge	2: 8	in the **e**, and he placed there
Ps	103:12	As far as the **e** is from the west,
Mt	2: 1	behold, magi from the **e** arrived

EASY → EASIER

Mt	11:30	For my yoke is **e**, and my burden

EAT → ATE, EATING, EATS

Ge	2:16	"You are free to **e** from any
Ex	12:11	"This is how you are to **e** it:
	12:11	you shall **e** like those who are
Lev	11: 4	you shall not **e** any of the fol-lowing
Ecc	2:24	is nothing better for man than to **e**
Mt	26:26	it to his disciples said, "Take and **e**;
Ac	10:13	him, "Get up, Peter. Slaughter and **e**."
1Co	10:31	So whether you **e** or drink,

EATING → EAT

Lk	7:34	The Son of Man came **e**
1Co	8: 4	So about the **e** of meat sacri-ficed

EATS → EAT

Jn	6:51	whoever **e** this bread will live
1Co	11:27	Therefore whoever **e** the bread

EDEN

Ge	2: 8	the LORD God planted a garden in **E**,
Isa	51: 3	Her deserts he shall make like **E**,
Eze	28:13	In **E**, the garden of God, you were,

EDOM → = ESAU

Ge	25:30	(That is why he was called **E**.)
Nu	20:18	But **E** answered him, "You shall not
Ob	1: 1	Of **E** we have heard a message
Mal	1: 4	If **E** says, "We have been crushed

EFFORT

2Pe	1: 5	make every **e** to supplement your

EGYPT

Ge	12:10	land; so Abram went down to **E**
	37:28	out of the cistern and took him to **E**.
	47:27	Thus Israel settled in the land of **E**,
Ex	1: 8	of Joseph, came to power in **E**.
	12:40	had stayed in **E** was four hun-dred
Jos	15:47	as far as the Wadi of **E** and the coast
Ne	9:18	God who brought you up out of **E**,'
Ps	78:51	He struck all the firstborn of **E**,
Hos	11: 1	loved him, out of **E** I called my son.
Mt	2:15	fulfilled, "Out of **E** I called my son."
Rev	11: 8	the symbolic names "Sodom" and "**E**,"

EHUD

Judge of Israel (Jdg 3:12-30).

ELAH

1. Son of Baasha; king of Israel (1Ki 16:6-14).

2. Valley in which David fought Goliath (1Sa 17:2, 19; 21:9).

ELDERS

Ex	24: 1	and seventy of the **e** of Israel.
Jdg	2: 7	of those **e** who outlived Joshua
Isa	3:14	with his people's **e** and princes: It is
Da	13:61	They rose up against the two **e**,
Mt	27:12	accused by the chief priests and **e**,
Mk	7: 3	hands, keeping the tradition of the **e**.
Rev	4: 4	thrones on which twenty-four **e** sat,

ELEAZAR

1. Third son of Aaron (Ex 6:23-25). Succeeded Aaron as high priest (Nu 20:26; Dt 10:6). Allotted land to tribes (Jos 14:1). Death (Jos 24:33).

2. Brother of Judas Maccabeus (1Ma 2:5; 6:43-46).

ELECT → ELECTION

Mt	24:22	sake of the **e** they will be short-ened.
Mk	13:22	mislead, if that were possible, the **e**.

ELECTION → ELECT

Ro	11:28	but in respect to **e**, they are beloved
2Pe	1:10	eager to make your call and **e** firm,

ELEMENTS

Heb	5:12	someone teach you again the basic **e**
2Pe	3:10	and the **e** will be dissolved by fire,

ELEVEN

Mt	28:16	The **e** disciples went to Galilee,
Ac	1:26	he was counted with the **e** apostles.

ELI

1. High priest in youth of Samuel (1Sa 1-4). Blessed Hannah (1Sa 1:12-18); raised Samuel (1Sa 2:11-26). Prophesied against because of wicked sons (1Sa 2:27-36). Death of Eli and sons (1Sa 4:11-22).

2. "Eli, Eli, lema sabachthani?" (Mt 27:46).

ELIAKIM → = JEHOIAKIM

1. Original name of Jehoiakim (2Ki 23:34; 2Ch 36:4).

2. Hezekiah's palace administrator (2Ki 18:17-37; 19:2; Isa 36:1-22; 37:2).

ELIEZER

1. Servant of Abraham (Ge 15:2).

2. Son of Moses (Ex 18:4; 1Ch 23:15-17).

ELIHU

A friend of Job (Job 32-37).

ELIJAH

Prophet; predicted famine in Israel (1Ki 17:1; Jas 5:17). Fed by ravens (1Ki 17:2-6). Raised Sidonian widow's son (1Ki 17:7-24). Defeated prophets of Baal at Carmel (1Ki 18:16-46). Ran from Jezebel (1Ki 19:1-9). Prophesied death of Azariah (2Ki 1). Succeeded by Elisha (1Ki 19:19-21; 2Ki 2:1-18). Taken to heaven in whirlwind (2Ki 2:11-12; Sir 48:1-12; 1Ma 2:58).

Return prophesied (Mal 4:5-6); equated with John the Baptist (Mt 17:9-13; Mk 9:9-13; Lk 1:17). Appeared with Moses in transfiguration of Jesus (Mt 17:1-8; Mk 9:1-8).

ELIMELECH

Ru	1: 3	**E**, the husband of Naomi, died,

ELIPHAZ

A friend of Job (Job 4-5; 15; 22; 42:7, 9).

ELISHA

Prophet; successor of Elijah (1Ki 19:16-21; Sir 48:12-14); inherited his mantle (2Ki 2:1-18). Purified bad water (2Ki 2:19-22). Cursed young men (2Ki 2:23-25). Provided widow with oil (2Ki 4:1-7). Raised Shunammite woman's son (2Ki 4:8-37). Purified food (2Ki 4:38-41). Fed 100 men (2Ki 4:42-44). Healed Naaman's leprosy (2Ki 5). Made axhead float (2Ki 6:1-7). Captured Arameans (2Ki 6:8-23). Political adviser to Israel (2Ki 6:24-8:6; 9:1-3; 13:14-19), Aram (2Ki 8:7-15). Death (2Ki 13:20).

ELIZABETH

Mother of John the Baptist (Lk 1:5-58).

ELKANAH

Husband of Hannah, father of Samuel (1Sa 1-2).

EMMANUEL → = IMMANUEL

Mt	1:23	and they shall name him **E**,"

EMMAUS
Lk 24:13 miles from Jerusalem called **E**,

EMPTIED → EMPTY
1Co 1:17 cross of Christ might not be **e** of its
Php 2: 7 Rather, he **e** himself,

EMPTY → EMPTIED, EMPTY-HANDED
Eph 5: 6 one deceive you with **e** arguments,

EMPTY-HANDED → EMPTY, HAND
Ex 23:15 No one shall appear before me **e**.
Ru 3:17 come back to my mother-in-law **e**!"

ENCOURAGEMENT
Ac 4:36 (which is translated "son of **e**"),
Ro 15: 5 and **e** grant you to think in harmony
Php 2: 1 If there is any **e** in Christ,

END → ENDS
Ge 6:13 decided to put an **e** to all mortals
Pr 14:12 a man, but the **e** of it leads to death!
Ecc 12:12 making of many books there is no **e**,
Mt 24:13 perseveres to the **e** will be saved.
28:20 you always, until the **e** of the age."
Jn 13: 1 world and he loved them to the **e**.
Ro 10: 4 For Christ is the **e** of the law
Rev 22:13 the last, the beginning and the **e**."

ENDOR
1Sa 28: 7 is a woman in **E** who is a medium."

ENDS → END
Ps 2: 8 your possession the **e** of the earth.
Isa 40:28 creator of the **e** of the earth. He does
Ro 10:18 their words to the **e** of the world."

ENDURANCE → ENDURE
Ro 5: 3 knowing that affliction produces **e**,
Heb 10:36 You need **e** to do the will of God
2Pe 1: 6 self-control with **e**, **e** with devotion,
Rev 1: 9 and the **e** we have in Jesus,

ENDURE → ENDURANCE, ENDURED, ENDURES
Mal 3: 2 who will **e** the day of his coming?

ENDURED → ENDURE
Heb 12: 2 that lay before him he **e** the cross,

ENDURES → ENDURE
1Ch 16:41 "because his kindness **e** forever,"
Sir 40:17 off, and justice **e** forever.
Bar 4: 1 the law that **e** forever; All who cling

Mt 10:22 whoever **e** to the end will be saved.
Jn 6:27 for the food that **e** for eternal life,
1Co 13: 7 things, hopes all things, **e** all things.

ENEMIES → ENEMY
Ex 23:22 I will be an enemy to your **e**
Jdt 8:35 you to take vengeance upon our **e**!"
Est 9: 5 The Jews struck down all their **e**
9: 5 they did to their **e** as they pleased.
1Ma 4:36 "Now that our **e** have been crushed,
Ps 110: 1 while I make your **e** your footstool."
Mt 5:44 love your **e**, and pray for those who
Lk 20:43 till I make your **e** your footstool."'
Ro 5:10 if, while we were **e**, we were

ENEMY → ENEMIES, ENMITY
Mt 13:39 the **e** who sows them is the devil.
1Co 15:26 The last **e** to be destroyed is death,
Jas 4: 4 of the world makes himself an **e**

ENJOY → ENJOYMENT
Ecc 9: 9 **E** life with the wife whom you love,

ENJOYMENT → ENJOY
1Ti 6:17 provides us with all things for our **e**.

ENLIGHTENED → LIGHT
Eph 1:18 May the eyes of [your] hearts be **e**,
Heb 6: 4 case of those who have once been **e**

ENLIGHTENS → LIGHT
Jn 1: 9 which **e** everyone, was coming

ENMITY → ENEMY
Ge 3:15 I will put **e** between you
Jas 4: 4 of the world means **e** with God?

ENOCH
Walked with God and taken by him (Ge 5:18-24; Heb 11:5; Sir 44:16). Prophet (Jude 14).

ENSLAVE → SLAVE
Gal 2: 4 in Christ Jesus, that they might **e** us—

ENTER → ENTRY
Ex 40:35 Moses could not **e** the meeting tent,
Nu 20:24 he shall not **e** the land I am giving
Ps 95:11 anger: "They shall never **e** my rest."
Mt 5:20 you will not **e** into the kingdom
7:13 "**E** through the narrow gate;
7:13 those who **e** through it are many.
Mk 10:15 of God like a child will not **e** it.

Jn 3: 5 no one can **e** the kingdom of God
Heb 3:11 "They shall not **e** into my rest." '
Rev 21:27 but nothing unclean will **e** it,
21:27 Only those will **e** whose names are

ENTHRONED → THRONE
1Ch 13: 6 the name "LORD **e** upon the cherubim."

ENTRUSTED → TRUST
Lk 12:48 required of the person **e** with much,
12:48 of the person **e** with more.
2Ti 1:12 to guard what has been **e** to me until

ENVY
Mk 7:22 deceit, licentiousness, **e**, blasphemy,
Ro 1:29 full of **e**, murder, rivalry treachery,

EPHOD
Ex 28: 6 "The **e** they shall make of gold
Jdg 8:27 Gideon made an **e** out of the gold

EPHRAIM
1. Second son of Joseph (Ge 41:52; 46:20). Blessed as firstborn by Jacob (Ge 48). Tribe of numbered (Nu 1:33; 26:37), blessed (Dt 33:17), allotted land (Jos 16:4-9; Eze 48:5), failed to fully possess (Jos 16:10; Jdg 1:29).
2. Term for the Northern Kingdom (Isa 7:17; Hos 5).

EQUAL → EQUALITY
Isa 40:25 To whom can you liken me as an **e**?
46: 5 you compare me with, as an **e**,
Jn 5:18 father, making himself **e** to God.

EQUALITY → EQUAL
Php 2: 6 of God, did not regard **e** with God

EQUIPPED
2Ti 3:17 competent, **e** for every good work.

ESAU → = EDOM
Firstborn of Isaac, twin of Jacob (Ge 25:21-26). Also called Edom (Ge 25:30). Sold Jacob his birthright (Ge 25:29-34); lost blessing (Ge 27). Married Hittites (Ge 26:34), Ishmaelites (Ge 28:6-9). Reconciled to Jacob (Ge 33). Genealogy (Ge 36). The LORD chose Jacob over Esau (Mal 1:2-3), but gave Esau land (Dt 2:2-12). Descendants eventually obliterated (Ob 1-21; Jer 49:7-22).

ESCAPE
Ps 68:21 **e** from death is in the LORD God's
Ro 2: 3 that you will **e** the judgment
1Th 5: 3 woman, and they will not **e**.
Heb 12:25 they did not **e** when they refused

ESTABLISH → ESTABLISHED
Ge 6:18 But with you I will **e** my covenant;

ESTABLISH → ESTABLISHED (*cont.*)

Dt 28: 9 he will **e** you as a people sacred

Ps 89: 5 and **e** your throne through all ages.”

Ro 10: 3 to **e** their own [righteousness],

ESTABLISHED → ESTABLISH

Ps 89: 3 For you said, “My love is **e** forever;

103:19 The LORD's throne is **e** in heaven;

Jer 10:12 power, **e** the world by his wisdom,

2Pe 1:12 and are **e** in the truth you have.

ESTHER

Jewess, originally named Hadassah, who lived in Persia; cousin of Mordecai (Est 2:7). Chosen queen of Xerxes (Est 2:8-18). Persuaded by Mordecai to foil Haman's plan to exterminate the Jews (Est 3-4). Revealed Haman's plans to Xerxes, resulting in Haman's death (Est 7), the Jews' preservation (Est 8-9), Mordecai's exaltation (Est 8:15; 9:4; 10). Decreed celebration of Purim (Est 9:18-32).

ETERNAL → ETERNITY

Mt 25:46 these will go off to **e** punishment,

25:46 but the righteous to **e** life.”

Mk 10:17 what must I do to inherit **e** life?”

Jn 3:16 not perish but might have **e** life.

4:14 spring of water welling up to **e** life.”

10:28 I give them **e** life, and they shall

Ro 5:21 **e** life through Jesus Christ our Lord.

2Co 4:17 us an **e** weight of glory beyond all

Heb 5: 9 he became the source of **e** salvation

1Jn 5:13 you may know that you have **e** life,

ETERNITY → ETERNAL

Sir 42:21 he is from all **e** one and the same,

2Pe 3:18 be glory now and to the day of **e**.

EUNUCH → EUNUCHS

Ac 8:27 Now there was an Ethiopian **e**,

EUNUCHS → EUNUCH

Isa 56: 4 To the **e** who observe my sabbaths

EUPHRATES

Ge 2:14 of Asshur. The fourth river is the **E**.

15:18 of Egypt to the Great River [the **E**],

Rev 16:12 his bowl on the great river **E**.

EUTYCHUS

Ac 20: 9 and a young man named **E** who was

EVANGELIST → EVANGELISTS

Ac 21: 8 we went to the house of Philip the **e**,

2Ti 4: 5 perform the work of an **e**;

EVANGELISTS → EVANGELIST

Eph 4:11 others as **e**, others as pastors

EVE

Ge 3:20 The man called his wife **E**,

4: 1 man had relations with his wife **E**,

Tob 8: 6 Adam and you gave him his wife **E**

2Co 11: 3 as the serpent deceived **E** by his

1Ti 2:13 For Adam was formed first, then **E**.

EVENING

Ge 1: 5 “night.” Thus **e** came, and morning

Ecc 11: 6 and at **e** let not your hand be idle:

Zec 14: 7 for in the **e** time there shall be light.

EVERLASTING → LAST

Ge 9:16 and recall the **e** covenant that I have

EVERY → EVERYTHING

Ge 7:23 The LORD wiped out **e** living thing

Ex 11: 5 **E** first-born in this land shall die,

Dt 8: 3 by **e** word that comes forth

Ecc 12:14 God will bring to judgment **e** work,

Isa 45:23 To me **e** knee shall bend; by me **e**

Mt 12:25 “**E** kingdom divided against itself

Ro 14:11 Lord, **e** knee shall bend before me,

14:11 **e** tongue shall give praise to God.”

Php 2:10 name of Jesus **e** knee should bend,

2Ti 3:17 equipped for **e** good work.

1Jn 4: 1 do not trust **e** spirit but test

Rev 21: 4 He will wipe **e** tear from their eyes,

EVERYTHING → EVERY

Ge 1:31 God looked at **e** he had made,

Ex 19: 8 together, “**E** the LORD has said,

Ecc 3: 1 There is an appointed time for **e**,

1Co 10:31 you do, do **e** for the glory of God.

1Ti 4: 4 For **e** created by God is good,

2Pe 1: 3 has bestowed on us **e** that makes

EVIL → EVILDOERS, EVILS

Ge 6: 5 conceived was ever anything but **e**,

Ex 32:22 how prone the people are to **e**.

Tob 12: 7 and **e** will not find its way to you.

Pr 8:13 [The fear of the LORD is to hate **e**;]

8:13 Pride, arrogance, the **e** way,

Sir 7: 1 Do no **e**, and **e** will not overtake

Isa 5:20 Woe to those who call **e** good,

5:20 those who call **e** good, and good **e**,

Mt 6:13 test, but deliver us from the **e** one.

12:35 an **e** person brings forth **e**

12:35 brings forth **e** out of a store of **e**.

Jn 17:15 that you keep them from the **e** one.

Ro 12:17 Do not repay anyone **e** for **e**;

Eph 5:16 opportunity, because the days are **e**.

1Pe 2:16 using freedom as a pretext for **e**,

1Jn 5:18 and the **e** one cannot touch him.

2Jn 1:11 greets him shares in his **e** works.

3Jn 1:11 do not imitate **e** but imitate good.

1:11 does what is **e** has never seen God.

EVILDOERS → EVIL

Ps 34:17 The LORD's face is against **e** to wipe

Lk 13:27 are from. Depart from me, all you **e**!’

1Pe 2:12 so that if they speak of you as **e**,

EVILS → EVIL

1Ti 6:10 love of money is the root of all **e**,

EXALT → EXALTED, EXALTS

Pr 4: 8 Extol her, and she will **e** you;

Jas 4:10 before the Lord and he will **e** you.

EXALTED → EXALT

Ps 97: 9 all the earth, **e** far above all gods.

Isa 2:11 and the LORD alone will be **e**.

Php 2: 9 Because of this, God greatly **e** him

EXALTS → EXALT

Pr 14:34 Virtue **e** a nation, but sin is

Sir 7:11 man; be mindful of him who **e**

Lk 14:11 For everyone who **e** himself will be

EXAMINE

1Co 11:28 A person should **e** himself, and so

2Co 13: 5 **E** yourselves to see whether you are

EXAMPLES

1Co 10: 6 These things happened as **e** for us,

1Pe 5: 3 to you, but be **e** to the flock.

EXCELLENCE → EXCELLENT

Php 4: 8 if there is any **e** and if there is

EXCELLENT → EXCELLENCE

1Co 12:31 I shall show you a still more **e** way.

Heb 1: 4 has inherited is more **e** than theirs.

EXCEPT

2Sa 22:32 “For who is God **e** the LORD? Who is

Mt 11:27 No one knows the Son **e** the Father,

Mt 11:27 no one knows the Father **e** the Son

Lk 11:29 will be given it, **e** the sign of Jonah.

Jn 14: 6 comes to the Father **e** through me.

EXCHANGED
Ps 106:20 They **e** their glorious God
Ro 1:23 **e** the glory of the immortal God

EXCUSE
Jn 15:22 as it is they have no **e** for their sin.
Ro 1:20 made. As a result, they have no **e**;

EXHORT
Tit 2:15 **E** and correct with all authority.

EXILE
2Ki 25:11 led into **e** the last of the people
Ezr 6:21 had returned from the **e** partook of it

EXIST → EXISTED, EXISTS
1Co 8: 6 all things are and for whom we **e**,
      8: 6 things are and through whom we **e**.
Heb 2:10 and through whom all things **e**,

EXISTED → EXIST
2Pe 3: 5 the fact that the heavens **e** of old

EXISTS → EXIST
Heb 11: 6 God must believe that he **e**

EXPECTING
Lk 6:35 to them, and lend **e** nothing back;

EXPLAIN → EXPLAINED
2Ch 9: 2 Solomon that he could not **e** to her.
Da 5:12 how to interpret dreams, **e** enigmas,

EXPLAINED → EXPLAIN
Mk 4:34 his own disciples he **e** everything

EXPOSE → EXPOSED
Mt 1:19 yet unwilling to **e** her to shame,
Eph 5:11 works of darkness; rather **e** them,

EXPOSED → EXPOSE
Jn 3:20 so that his works might not be **e**.
Eph 5:13 everything **e** by the light becomes
Heb 10:33 times you were publicly **e** to abuse

EYE → EYES, EYEWITNESSES
Ex 21:24 **e** for **e**, tooth for tooth,
Ps 17: 8 Keep me as the apple of your **e**;
Mt 5:29 If your right **e** causes you to sin,
      5:38 'An **e** for an **e** and a tooth for a tooth.'
      7: 3 the splinter in your brother's **e**,

Mt 7: 3 the wooden beam in your own **e**?
Mk 10:25 to pass through [the] **e** of [a] needle
1Co 15:52 in the blink of an **e**, at the last
Rev 1: 7 and every **e** will see him, even those

EYES → EYE
Ge 3: 7 the **e** of both of them were opened,
2Ch 16: 9 The **e** of the LORD roam over
Ps 121: 1 I raise my **e** toward the mountains.
Pr 3: 7 Be not wise in your own **e**,
   22:12 The **e** of the LORD safeguard
Eze 1:18 their rims were full of **e** all around.
Da 10: 6 his **e** were like fiery torches,
Zec 4:10 These seven facets are the **e**
Mt 9:30 And their **e** were opened.
  13:15 they have closed their **e**, lest they
  13:15 **e**, lest they see with their **e** and hear
Lk 24:31 With that their **e** were opened
Eph 1:18 May the **e** of [your] hearts be
1Pe 3:12 For the **e** of the Lord are
1Jn 2:16 lust, enticement for the **e**,
Rev 1:14 and his **e** were like a fiery flame.
    4: 6 four living creatures covered with **e**
  21: 4 He will wipe every tear from their **e**,

EYEWITNESSES → EYE, WITNESS
Lk 1: 2 just as those who were **e**
2Pe 1:16 but we had been **e** of his majesty.

EZEKIEL
    Priest called to be prophet to the exiles (Eze 1-3; Sir 49:8). Symbolically acted out destruction of Jerusalem (Eze 4-5; 12; 24).

EZRA
    Priest and teacher of the Law who led a return of exiles to Israel to reestablish temple and worship (Ezr 7-8). Corrected intermarriage of priests (Ezr 9-10). Read Law at celebration of Feast of Tabernacles (Ne 8). Participated in dedication of Jerusalem's walls (Ne 12).

F

FACE → FACES
Ex 3: 6 Moses hid his **f**, for he was afraid
  34:30 radiant the skin of his **f** had become,
Nu 6:25 The LORD let his **f** shine upon you,
  12: 8 **f** to **f** I speak to him, plainly and not
Ps 4: 7 LORD, show us the light of your **f**!"
Isa 54: 8 for a moment I hid my **f** from you;
Eze 39:29 No longer will I hide my **f**
Lk 9:29 While he was praying his **f** changed
2Co 3: 7 intently at the **f** of Moses because

Rev 1:16 and his **f** shone like the sun at its

FACES → FACE
Eze 1: 6 but each had four **f** and four wings,
Rev 9: 7 of gold; their **f** were like human **f**,

FACTIONS
1Co 11:19 there have to be **f** among you
Gal 5:20 acts of selfishness, dissensions, **f**,

FAIL → FAILED
Dt 31: 6 he will never **f** you or forsake you."
Eze 47:12 shall not fade, nor their fruit **f**.

FAILED → FAIL
Ro 9: 6 it is not that the word of God has **f**.

FAINT
Ps 142: 4 My spirit is **f** within me, but you
Isa 40:31 grow weary, walk and not grow **f**.

FAITH → FAITHFUL, FAITHFULNESS, FAITHLESS
Ps 146: 6 that is in them, Who keeps **f** forever,
Isa 7: 9 a nation. Unless your **f** is firm
Hab 2: 4 just man, because of his **f**, shall live.
Mt 17:20 to them, "Because of your little **f**.
  17:20 if you have **f** the size of a mustard
Mk 2: 5 When Jesus saw their **f**, he said
Lk 7:50 the woman, "Your **f** has saved you;
  18: 8 Man comes, will he find **f** on earth?"
Ac 3:16 And by **f** in his name, this man,
   3:16 the **f** that comes through it has given
Ro 1:17 the righteousness of God from **f** to **f**;
   1:17 one who is righteous by **f** will live."
   3:28 a person is justified by **f** apart
1Co 13:13 So **f**, hope, love remain, these three;
Gal 3:11 one who is righteous by **f** will live."
   5: 6 but only **f** working through love.
Eph 4: 5 one Lord, one **f**, one baptism;
Php 3: 9 which comes through **f** in Christ,
   3: 9 from God, depending on **f**
1Ti 6:11 righteousness, devotion, **f**, love,
2Ti 4: 7 finished the race; I have kept the **f**.
Heb 11: 1 **F** is the realization of what is hoped
  12: 2 Jesus, the leader and perfecter of **f**.
Jas 2:17 So also **f** of itself, if it does not have
   2:24 by works and not by **f** alone.

FAITH → FAITHFUL, FAITHFULNESS, FAITHLESS (*cont.*)

2Pe	1: 1	those who have received a **f** of equal
1Jn	5: 4	that conquers the world is our **f**.
Jude	1: 3	contend for the **f** that was once
Rev	2:13	and have not denied your **f** in me,

FAITHFUL → FAITH

Dt	32: 4	his way! A **f** God, without deceit,
Ps	4: 4	the LORD works wonders for the **f**;
	116:15	eyes of the LORD is the death of his **f**.
Wis	3: 9	the **f** shall abide with him in love:
Mic	7: 2	The **f** are gone from the earth,
Zec	8: 3	Jerusalem shall be called the **f** city,
Mt	24:45	then, is the **f** and prudent servant,
1Co	10:13	God is **f** and will not let you be tried
1Th	5:24	The one who calls you is **f**, and he
1Pe	4:19	over to a **f** creator as they do good.
1Jn	1: 9	he is **f** and just and will forgive our
Rev	1: 5	and from Jesus Christ, the **f** witness,
	19:11	its rider was [called] "**F** and True."

FAITHFULNESS → FAITH

Ps	26: 3	my eyes; I walk guided by your **f**.
Isa	11: 5	his waist, and **f** a belt upon his hips.
La	3:23	each morning, so great is his **f**.
Gal	5:22	patience, kindness, generosity, **f**,

FAITHLESS → FAITH

Mt	17:17	reply, "O **f** and perverse generation,

FALL → FALLEN, FALLING, FELL

Ps	91: 7	Though a thousand **f** at your side,
Pr	16:18	and a haughty spirit before a **f**.
Sir	28:23	who forsake the LORD will **f** victims
Lk	10:18	have observed Satan **f** like lightning
Ro	9:33	and a rock that will make them **f**,
1Co	10:12	secure should take care not to **f**.
Heb	10:31	It is a fearful thing to **f**

FALLEN → FALL

2Sa	1:19	how can the warriors have **f**!
Isa	14:12	How have you **f** from the heavens,
	21: 9	calls out and says, '**F**, **f** is Babylon,
Rev	9: 1	I saw a star that had **f** from the sky
	18: 2	voice: "**F**, **f** is Babylon the great.

FALLING → FALL

Lk	22:44	like drops of blood **f** on the ground.]

FALSE

Mt	7:15	"Beware of **f** prophets, who come
Mk	13:22	**F** messiahs and **f** prophets will arise
2Pe	2: 1	also **f** prophets among the people,
	2: 1	there will be **f** teachers among you,
Rev	16:13	and from the mouth of the **f** prophet.
	20:10	the beast and the **f** prophet were.

FAMILIES → FAMILY

Ac	3:25	your offspring all the **f** of the earth
Tit	1:11	as they are upsetting whole **f**

FAMILY → FAMILIES

Gal	6:10	who belong to the **f** of the faith.
Eph	3:15	from whom every **f** in heaven

FAMINE

Ge	12:10	There was **f** in the land; so Abram
	12:10	since the **f** in the land was severe.
	41:27	ears; they are seven years of **f**.
Ru	1: 1	the judges there was a **f** in the land;
Ps	37:19	in days of **f** they will have plenty.
Am	8:11	when I will send **f** upon the land:
	8:11	Not a **f** of bread, or thirst for water,
Ac	11:28	would be a severe **f** all over
Ro	8:35	or persecution, or **f**, or nakedness,

FAR

Isa	57:19	Peace, peace to the **f** and the near,
Jer	23:23	says the LORD, and not a God **f** off?
Mk	7: 6	lips, but their hearts are **f** from me;
	12:34	"You are not **f** from the kingdom

FAST → FASTED, FASTING

Isa	58: 5	ashes? Do you call this a **f**, a day
Mt	6:16	"When you **f**, do not look gloomy
Lk	18:12	I **f** twice a week, and I pay tithes

FASTED → FAST

Mt	4: 2	He **f** for forty days and forty nights,

FASTING → FAST

Mt	6:16	they may appear to others to be **f**.

FATHER → FATHER'S

Ge	2:24	That is why a man leaves his **f**
Ex	20:12	"Honor your **f** and your mother.

Ex	21:15	Whoever strikes his **f** or mother
2Sa	7:14	I will be a **f** to him, and he shall be
Ps	89:27	He shall cry to me, 'You are my **f**,
Pr	28:24	He who defrauds **f** or mother
Wis	2:16	the just and boasts that God is his **F**.
Sir	3: 3	He who honors his **f** atones for sins;
Isa	8: 4	the child knows how to call his **f**
Jer	3:19	would call me, "My **F**," I thought,
Mal	1: 6	A son honors his **f**, and a servant
	1: 6	If then I am a **f**, where is the honor
Mt	6: 9	you are to pray: Our **F** in heaven,
	28:19	baptizing them in the name of the **F**,
Lk	18:20	honor your **f** and your mother.' "
Jn	5:18	but he also called God his own **f**,
	8:44	You belong to your **f** the devil
	8:44	because he is a liar and the **f** of lies.
	14: 6	comes to the **F** except through me.
Ro	8:15	through which we cry, "Abba, **F**!"
Gal	4: 6	into our hearts, crying out, "Abba, **F**!"
Eph	6: 2	"Honor your **f** and mother." This is
Heb	1: 5	"I will be a **f** to him, and he shall be
	12: 9	all the more to the **F** of spirits
Jas	1:17	coming down from the **F** of lights,
Rev	3: 5	his name in the presence of my **F**

FATHER'S → FATHER

Lk	2:49	know that I must be in my **F** house?"
Jn	1:14	the glory as of the **F** only Son,
	2:16	here, and stop making my **F** house
	10:29	can take them out of the **F** hand.
	14: 2	In my **F** house there are many

FAULT

Sir	11: 7	Before investigating, find no **f**;
Ro	9:19	"Why [then] does he still find **f**?

FAVOR → FAVORED

Ge	6: 8	But Noah found **f** with the LORD.
Ex	33:12	and also, 'You have found **f** with me.'
Ps	30: 6	a moment; divine **f** lasts a lifetime.
Isa	49: 8	In a time of **f** I answer you,
Zec	11: 7	one of which I called "**F**,"

FAVORED → FAVOR

Lk	1:28	coming to her, he said, "Hail, **f** one!

FEAR → AFRAID, FEARED, FEARS
Dt   6:13 The LORD, your God, shall you f;
Ps 19:10 The f of the LORD is pure,
     23: 4 I f no harm for you are at my side;
     27: 1 whom do I f? The LORD is my life's
Pr   1: 7 The f of the LORD is the beginning
Ecc 12:13 all is heard: F God and keep his
Php 2:12 work out your salvation with f
1Pe 3:14 be afraid or terrified with f of them,
1Jn 4:18 There is no f in love, but perfect
     4:18 love drives out f because f has to do
Rev 14: 7 voice, "F God and give him glory,

FEARED → FEAR
Ex 14:31 they f the LORD and believed in him
Job 1: 1 Job, who f God and avoided evil.
Hag 1:12 the people f because of the LORD.

FEARS → FEAR
Jdt 16:16 one who f the LORD is forever great.
Ps 34: 5 me, delivered me from all my f.
Pr 31:30 the woman who f the LORD is to be
Sir 1:11 He who f the LORD will have
    15: 1 He who f the LORD will do this;

FED → FEED
Dt   8:16 and f you in the desert with manna,
Ps 80: 6 You have f them the bread of tears,

FEED → FED, FEEDS
Jn 21:15 He said to him, "F my lambs."
Ro 12:20 "if your enemy is hungry, f him; if he

FEEDS → FED
Isa 40:11 Like a shepherd he f his flock; in his

FEET → FOOT
Ps   8: 7 your hands, put all things at their f:
  119:105 Your word is a lamp for my f,
Da 2:33 iron, its f partly iron and partly tile.
Mt 22:44 I place your enemies under your f' '?
Lk 24:39 Look at my hands and my f, that it
Jn 12: 3 nard and anointed the f of Jesus
    13: 5 began to wash the disciples' f
Ro 16:20 quickly crush Satan under your f.
1Co 15:25 has put all his enemies under his f.
Rev 1:15 His f were like polished brass

FELLOWSHIP
2Co 6:14 Or what f does light have
1Jn 1: 3 so that you too may have f with us;
    1: 3 f with us; for our f is with the Father

FEMALE
Ge 1:27 him; male and f he created them.
Mk 10: 6 'God made them male and f.
Gal 3:28 free person, there is not male and f;

FESTIVALS
Lev 23: 2 The following are the f of the LORD,

FEVER
Dt 28:22 will strike you with wasting and f,
Mk 1:30 mother-in-law lay sick with a f.

FEW
Ps 105:12 When they were f in number,
Mt 22:14 Many are invited, but f are chosen."
Lk 13:23 "Lord, will only a f people be saved?"

FIELD → FIELDS
Pr 31:16 She picks out a f to purchase;
Mt 13:44 is like a treasure buried in a f,
    13:44 sells all that he has and buys that f.
    24:40 Two men will be out in the f;
1Co 3: 9 you are God's f, God's building.

FIELDS → FIELD
Lk 2: 8 in that region living in the f
Jn 4:35 up and see the f ripe for the harvest.

FIG → FIGS
Ge 3: 7 so they sewed f leaves together
Hab 3:17 For though the f tree blossom not
Mt 24:32 "Learn a lesson from the f tree.
Lk 13: 6 a person who had a f tree planted

FIGHT → FOUGHT
Ex 14:14 The LORD himself will f for you;
1Ti 1:18 Through them may you f a good f

FIGS → FIG
Jer 24: 1 of f placed before the temple
Lk 6:44 fruit. For people do not pick f

FILL → FILLED, FULL, FULLNESS
Ge 1:28 multiply; f the earth and subdue it.
    9: 1 fertile and multiply and f the earth.
Jer 23:24 Do I not f both heaven and earth?
Eph 4:10 heavens, that he might f all things.

FILLED → FILL
Ex 1: 7 strong that the land was f with them.
    40:34 the glory of the LORD f the Dwelling.

1Ki 8:11 the LORD's glory had f the temple
Ps 72:19 may all the earth be f with the LORD's
Eze 43: 5 that the temple was f with the glory
Lk 1:15 He will be f with the holy Spirit
Ac 2: 4 they were all f with the holy Spirit
Eph 5:18 debauchery, but be f with the Spirit,

FILTHY
Zec 3: 3 before the angel, clad in f garments.
Rev 22:11 still act wickedly, and the f still be f.

FIND → FINDS, FOUND
Dt 4:29 you shall indeed f him when you
Jer 29:13 you look for me, you will f me. Yes,
Mt 11:29 and you will f rest for yourselves.
    16:25 loses his life for my sake will f it.
Lk 11: 9 seek and you will f;

FINDS → FIND
Pr 8:35 For he who f me f life, and wins
    18:22 He who f a wife f happiness; it is

FINGER
Dt 9:10 by God's own f, with a copy of all
Mt 23: 4 they will not lift a f to move them.
Lk 11:20 if it is by the f of God that [I] drive

FINISHED
Ge 2: 2 the seventh day God was f
Ex 40:33 court. Thus Moses f all the work.
Jn 19:30 had taken the wine, he said, "It is f."

FIRE → FIERY
Ex 3: 2 appeared to him in f flaming
    3: 2 though on f, was not consumed.
    13:21 of a column of f to give them light.
Lev 9:24 F came forth from the LORD's
Nu 11: 1 that the f of the LORD burned among
Dt 4:24 is a consuming f, a jealous God.
1Ki 19:12 fire—but the LORD was not in the f.
1Ki 19:12 the f there was a tiny whispering
2Ch 7: 1 f came down from heaven
Isa 66:24 not die, nor their f be extinguished;
Da 3:92 walking in the f, and the fourth
Mal 3: 2 For he is like the refiner's f, or like
Mt 3:11 you with the holy Spirit and f.
Mk 9:43 Gehenna, into the unquenchable f.

FIRE → FIERY (*cont.*)

Ac	2: 3	appeared to them tongues as of **f**,
1Co	3:13	It will be revealed with **f**, and the **f**
Heb	12:29	For our God is a consuming **f**.
Jas	3: 6	The tongue is also a **f**. It exists
	3: 6	the entire course of our lives on **f**,
	3: 6	lives on **f**, itself set on **f** by Gehenna.
2Pe	3:10	the elements will be dissolved by **f**,
Rev	20:14	were thrown into the pool of **f**.
	20:14	(This pool of **f** is the second death.)

FIRM

Isa	7: 9	Unless your faith is **f** you shall not
	7: 9	your faith is **f** you shall not be **f**!
2Co	1:24	your joy, for you stand **f** in the faith.

FIRST → FIRSTBORN

Ge	1: 5	and morning followed—the **f** day.
Isa	41: 4	I, the LORD, am the **f**,
Mt	6:33	But seek **f** the kingdom [of God]
Mk	10:31	But many that are **f** will be last,
	10:31	**f** will be last, and [the] last will be **f**."
	16: 2	had risen, on the **f** day of the week,
Ac	11:26	disciples were **f** called Christians.
Ro	1:16	believes: for Jew **f**, and then Greek.
1Co	15:45	too, it is written, "The **f** man, Adam,
1Th	4:16	and the dead in Christ will rise **f**.
1Jn	4:19	We love because he **f** loved us.
Rev	1:17	not be afraid. I am the **f** and the last,
	20: 5	were over. This is the **f** resurrection.

FIRSTBORN, FIRST-BORN → BEAR, FIRST

Ex	4:22	Israel is my son, my **f**.
	12:29	At midnight the LORD slew every **f**
	13: 2	"Consecrate to me every **f** that opens
Ps	78:51	He struck all the **f** of Egypt,
Zec	12:10	over him as one grieves over a **f**.
Lk	2: 7	and she gave birth to her **f** son.
Col	1:15	invisible God, the **f** of all creation.
Rev	1: 5	the **f** of the dead and ruler

FISH

Ge	1:26	Let them have dominion over the **f**
Jnh	2: 1	But the LORD sent a large **f**,
	2: 1	in the belly of the **f** three days
Mt	7:10	or a snake when he asks for a **f**?
Jn	6: 9	has five barley loaves and two **f**;

FIVE

1Sa	17:40	David selected **f** smooth stones
Mt	14:19	Taking the **f** loaves and the two fish,
1Co	14:19	church I would rather speak **f** words

FLAME → FLAMES

| Isa | 10:17 | Israel's Holy One a **f**, That burns |
| Rev | 19:12 | His eyes were [like] a fiery **f**, |

FLAMES → FLAME

| Da | 3:49 | drove the fiery **f** out of the furnace, |

FLED → FLEE

Ex	2:15	But Moses **f** from him and stayed
Mk	14:50	And they all left him and **f**.
Rev	12: 6	The woman herself **f** into the desert
	20:11	and the sky **f** from his presence

FLEE → FLED

Ps	11: 1	me, "**F** like a bird to the mountains!
	139: 7	From your presence, where can I **f**?
Isa	30:17	one; if five threaten you, you shall **f**,
Jas	4: 7	the devil, and he will **f** from you.

FLESH

Ge	2:23	and **f** of my **f**; This one shall be
Job	19:26	And from my **f** I shall see God;
Mt	16:17	For **f** and blood has not revealed this
	26:41	spirit is willing, but the **f** is weak."
Jn	1:14	And the Word became **f** and made
	3: 6	What is born of **f** is **f** and what is
Ro	8: 4	who live not according to the **f**
	8:13	For if you live according to the **f**,
2Co	12: 7	a thorn in the **f** was given to me,
Gal	5:19	Now the works of the **f** are obvious:
Eph	6:12	For our struggle is not with **f**
1Pe	1:24	for: "All **f** is like grass, and all its
1Jn	4: 2	Jesus Christ come in the **f** belongs

FLOCK

Isa	40:11	Like a shepherd he feeds his **f**; in his
Mt	26:31	the sheep of the **f** will be dispersed";
Lk	12:32	little **f**, for your Father is pleased
Jn	10:16	voice, and there will be one **f**,
1Pe	5: 3	to you, but be examples to the **f**.

FLOGGED

| Ac | 5:40 | they had them **f**, ordered them |

FLOOD

| Ge | 7: 7 | ark because of the waters of the **f**. |

Ge	9:15	waters shall never again become a **f**
Ps	29:10	The LORD sits enthroned above the **f**!
2Pe	2: 5	he brought a **f** upon the godless

FLOW → FLOWING, FLOWS

| Zec | 14: 8 | living waters shall **f** from Jerusalem, |
| Jn | 7:38 | living water will **f** from within him.' " |

FLOWER

Isa	40: 7	The grass withers, the **f** wilts,
1Pe	1:24	all its glory like the **f** of the field;
	1:24	the grass withers, and the **f** wilts;

FLOWING → FLOW

Ex	3: 8	land, a land **f** with milk and honey,
Jos	5: 6	he would not let them see the land **f**
Eze	47: 1	I saw water **f** out from beneath
Rev	22: 1	**f** from the throne of God

FOE

| Ex | 23:22 | to your enemies and a **f** to your foes. |
| Ps | 60:13 | Give us aid against the **f**; |

FOLLOW → FOLLOWED

Ex	16: 4	see whether they **f** my instructions
Dt	6:14	You shall not **f** other gods, such as
1Ki	18:21	If the LORD is God, **f** him; if Baal,
Lk	9:23	and take up his cross daily and **f** me.
Jn	10:27	voice; I know them, and they **f** me.
Rev	14: 4	the ones who **f** the Lamb wherever

FOLLOWED → FOLLOW

Jdg	2:12	they **f** the other gods of the various
Mk	1:18	Then they left their nets and **f** him.
Rev	13: 3	the whole world **f** after the beast.

FOLLY → FOOL

Pr	13:16	prudence, but the fool peddles **f**.
	26: 4	not the fool according to his **f**,
Ecc	2:13	has the advantage over **f** as much as
Mk	7:22	envy, blasphemy, arrogance, **f**.

FOOD → FOODS

Ge	1:30	I give all the green plants for **f**."
1Ma	1:63	than to be defiled with unclean **f**
Ps	136:25	And gives **f** to all flesh, God's love
Mt	6:25	Is not life more than **f** and the body
Jn	6:55	For my flesh is true **f**, and my blood
1Co	8: 8	Now **f** will not bring us closer

FOODS → FOOD
Mk 7:19 (Thus he declared all **f** clean.)
1Ti 4: 3 require abstinence from **f** that God

FOOL → FOLLY, FOOLISH, FOOLISHNESS, FOOLS
Pr 15: 5 The **f** spurns his father's admonition,
  20: 3 strife, while every **f** starts a quarrel.
Mt 5:22 says, 'You **f**,' will be liable to fiery

FOOLISH → FOOL
Pr 17:25 A **f** son is vexation to his father,
Jer 5:21 to this, **f** and senseless people
Mt 25: 2 Five of them were **f** and five were
1Co 1:20 made the wisdom of the world **f**?
Tit 3: 3 For we ourselves were once **f**,

FOOLISHNESS → FOOL
1Co 1:18 of the cross is **f** to those who are
  3:19 wisdom of this world is **f** in the eyes

FOOLS → FOOL
Ps 14: 1 Of David. **F** say in their hearts,
Pr 1: 7 wisdom and instruction **f** despise.
  10:21 many, but **f** die for want of sense.
Ro 1:22 claiming to be wise, they became **f**
1Co 4:10 We are **f** on Christ's account, but you

FOOT → FEET, FOOTSTOOL
Ps 91:12 lest you strike your **f** against a stone.
Mt 18: 8 If your hand or **f** causes you to sin,
Lk 4:11 lest you dash your **f** against a stone.' "

FOOTSTOOL → FOOT
Ps 110: 1 while I make your enemies your **f**."
Isa 66: 1 the earth is my **f**. What kind
Heb 10:13 until his enemies are made his **f**.

FOREHEAD → FOREHEADS
Ex 13: 9 hand and as a reminder on your **f**;
1Sa 17:49 and struck the Philistine on the **f**.

FOREHEADS → FOREHEAD
Eze 9: 4 an X on the **f** of those who moan
Rev 7: 3 put the seal on the **f** of the servants
  13:16 image on their right hands or their **f**,
  20: 4 nor had accepted its mark on their **f**

FOREIGN → FOREIGNER, FOREIGNERS
Ps 81:10 There must be no **f** god among you;

FOREIGNER → FOREIGN
Ex 12:43 the Passover. No **f** may partake of it.
1Co 14:11 I shall be a **f** to one who speaks it,
  14:11 it, and one who speaks it a **f** to me.

FOREIGNERS → FOREIGN
1Co 14:21 and by the lips of **f** I will speak

FOREKNEW → KNOW
Ro 8:29 For those he **f** he also predestined
  11: 2 not rejected his people whom he **f**.

FORERUNNER → RUN
Heb 6:20 Jesus has entered on our behalf as **f**,

FORESKIN
Ge 17:14 flesh of his **f** has not been cut away,

FORETOLD → TELL
Isa 43: 9 this, or **f** to us the earlier things?

FOREVER
Ge 3:22 life also, and thus eat of it and live **f**."
  6: 3 "My spirit shall not remain in man **f**,
Ex 3:15 "This is my name **f**; this is my title
2Sa 7:13 I will make his royal throne firm **f**.
1Ch 16:15 He remembers **f** his covenant
Ps 19:10 enduring **f**. The statutes of the LORD
  110: 4 "Like Melchizedek you are a priest **f**."
  117: 2 the LORD is faithful **f**. Hallelujah!
Ecc 3:14 whatever God does will endure **f**;
Wis 5:15 But the just live **f**, and in the LORD is
Isa 40: 8 wilts, the word of our God stands **f**."
  51: 6 My salvation shall remain **f** and my
Jn 6:51 whoever eats this bread will live **f**;
Heb 5: 6 "You are a priest **f**
  13: 8 is the same yesterday, today, and **f**.
1Pe 1:25 but the word of the Lord remains **f**."
Rev 1:18 dead, but now I am alive **f** and ever.
  11:15 and he will reign **f** and ever.
  22: 5 and they shall reign **f** and ever.

FORFEIT
Mk 8:36 gain the whole world and **f** his life?

FORGAVE → FORGIVE
Ps 85: 3 You **f** the guilt of your people,

FORGET → FORGOT, FORGOTTEN
Dt 6:12 take care not to **f** the LORD,
Ps 137: 5 If I **f** you, Jerusalem, may my right
Pr 4: 5 Do not **f** or turn aside

FOREIGNER → FOREIGN
Isa 49:15 Can a mother **f** her infant,
  49:15 Even should she **f**, I will never **f**

FORGIVE → FORGAVE, FORGIVEN, FORGIVENESS, FORGIVING
Ex 32:32 If you would only **f** their sin! If you
Sir 5: 6 his mercy; my many sins he will **f**."
Mt 6:12 as we forgive our debts, as we **f** our
Lk 5:24 earth to **f** sins"—he said to the man who
1Jn 1: 9 just and will **f** our sins and cleanse

FORGIVEN → FORGIVE
Lev 4:20 for them, and they will be **f**.
Ps 32: 1 fault is removed, whose sin is **f**.
Mt 12:31 sin and blasphemy will be **f** people,
  12:31 against the Spirit will not be **f**.
Mk 2: 9 paralytic, 'Your sins are **f**.' or to say,
Ro 4: 7 are they whose iniquities are **f**
Eph 4:32 one another as God has **f** you

FORGIVENESS → FORGIVE
Mk 1: 4 of repentance for the **f** of sins.
  3:29 the holy Spirit will never have **f**,
Col 1:14 we have redemption, the **f** of sins.
Heb 9:22 the shedding of blood there is no **f**.

FORGIVING → FORGIVE
Ex 34: 7 and **f** wickedness and crime and sin;
Ps 86: 5 Lord, you are kind and **f**,
Eph 4:32 **f** one another as God has forgiven

FORGOT → FORGET
Dt 32:18 You **f** the God who gave you birth.
Jer 23:27 just as their fathers **f** my name

FORGOTTEN → FORGET
Ps 77:10 Has God **f** mercy, in anger withheld
Isa 49:14 has forsaken me; my Lord has **f** me.
Heb 12: 5 **f** the exhortation addressed to you as

FORM → FORMED, FORMLESS
Lk 3:22 upon him in bodily **f** like a dove.

FORMED → FORM
Ge 2: 7 the LORD God **f** man out of the clay
Ps 139:13 You **f** my inmost being; you knit me
Gal 4:19 in labor until Christ be **f** in you!

FORMLESS → FORM
Ge 1: 2 the earth was a **f** wasteland,
Wis 11:17 the universe from **f** matter, to send

FORSAKE → FORSAKEN
Dt 31: 6 you; he will never fail you or **f** you."

FORSAKE → FORSAKEN (*cont.*)
Jos 1: 5 I will not leave you nor **f** you.
Jer 17:13 all who **f** you shall be in dis-
grace;
Heb 13: 5 "I will never **f** you or abandon
you."

FORSAKEN → FORSAKE
Mt 27:46 God, my God, why have you
f me?"

FORTRESS
2Sa 22: 2 LORD, my rock, my **f**, my deliverer,
Ps 71: 3 for you are my rock and **f**.

FORTY
Ge 7: 4 rain down on the earth for **f**
days
7: 4 on the earth for **f** days and **f**
nights,
Nu 14:34 **F** days you spent in scouting
14:34 **f** years shall you suffer for
your
1Ki 19: 8 he walked **f** days and **f** nights
Jnh 3: 4 "**F** days more and Nineveh
shall be
Mt 4: 2 He fasted for **f** days and **f**
nights,
Heb 3:17 whom was he "provoked for **f**
years"?

FOUGHT → FIGHT
Jos 10:42 LORD, the God of Israel, **f** for
Israel.
Rev 12: 7 The dragon and its angels **f**
back,

FOUND → FIND
Isa 55: 6 Seek the LORD while he may
be **f**,
65: 1 to be **f** by those who sought me
not.
Lk 15:24 again; he was lost, and has
been **f**.'
Ro 10:20 "I was **f** [by] those who were
not
Rev 20:15 whose name was not **f** written

FOUNDATION → FOUNDATIONS
Ezr 3: 6 though the **f** of the temple
Isa 28:16 A precious cornerstone as a
sure **f**;
1Co 3:11 no one can lay a **f** other than
the one
Eph 2:20 built upon the **f** of the apostles
2Ti 2:19 God's solid **f** stands, bearing
this

FOUNDATIONS → FOUNDATION
1Ki 6:37 The **f** of the LORD's temple
were laid
Heb 11:10 looking forward to the city
with **f**,

FOUNTAIN
Ps 36:10 For with you is the **f** of life,
Pr 16:22 Good sense is a **f** of life to its
Zec 13: 1 Jerusalem, a **f** to purify from
sin

FOUR
Eze 1: 5 figures resembling **f** living
creatures
10:14 Each had **f** faces: the first face
was

Rev 4: 6 there were **f** living creatures
covered

FOXES
Jdg 15: 4 left and caught three hundred **f**.
Lk 9:58 "**F** have dens and birds of the
sky

FRAGRANT
Ex 25: 6 anointing oil and for the **f**
incense;
Eph 5: 2 offering to God for a **f** aroma.

FRANKINCENSE → INCENSE
Isa 60: 6 bearing gold and **f**, and pro-
claiming
Mt 2:11 and offered him gifts of gold, **f**,

FREE → FREED, FREEDOM
Ps 146: 7 hungry. The LORD sets prisoners **f**;
Sir 15:14 him subject to his own **f**
choice.
Jn 8:32 the truth, and the truth will set
you **f**."
Gal 3:28 there is neither slave nor **f**
person,
Eph 6: 8 he does, whether he is slave
or **f**.

FREED → FREE
Rev 1: 5 has **f** us from our sins by his
blood,

FREEDOM → FREE
2Co 3:17 the Spirit of the Lord is, there
is **f**.
Gal 5: 1 For **f** Christ set us free; so
stand
1Pe 2:16 yet without using **f** as a pretext

FRIEND → FRIENDS
Pr 17:17 He who is a **f** is always a **f**,
18:24 a true **f** is more loyal than a
brother.
Sir 7:18 Barter not a **f** for money, nor a
dear
Mt 11:19 a **f** of tax collectors and
sinners.'
Jas 2:23 and he was called "the **f** of
God."

FRIENDS → FRIEND
Job 2:11 when three of Job's **f** heard of
all
Jn 15:13 this, to lay down one's life for
one's **f**.
15:15 I have called you **f**, because I
have

**FRUIT → FRUITFUL, FRUITLESS,
FRUITS**
Ge 3: 6 So she took some of its **f** and
ate it;
Dt 28: 4 "Blessed be the **f** of your
womb,
Ps 1: 3 that yields its **f** in season; Its
leaves
Pr 8:19 My **f** is better than gold, yes,
Eze 47:12 **f** trees of every kind shall
grow;
47:12 leaves shall not fade, nor their
f fail.
47:12 Every month they shall bear
fresh **f**,
47:12 Their **f** shall serve for food,

Mt 3: 8 Produce good **f** as evidence of
your
Lk 1:42 and blessed is the **f** of your
womb.
6:44 every tree is known by its
own **f**.
Jn 15: 2 branch in me that does not
bear **f**,
15: 2 he prunes so that it bears
more **f**.
Gal 5:22 contrast, the **f** of the Spirit is
love,
Col 1:10 in every good work bearing **f**
Heb 13:15 the **f** of lips that confess his
name.
Rev 22: 2 that produces **f** twelve times a
year,

FRUITFUL → FRUIT
Ex 1: 7 the Israelites were **f** and prolific.

FRUITS → FRUIT
Pr 3: 9 with first **f** of all your produce;
Mt 7:16 By their **f** you will know them.

FULFILL → FULFILLED
Ecc 5: 4 a vow than make it and not
f it.
Mt 5:17 I have come not to abolish but
to **f**.
Gal 6: 2 and so you will **f** the law of
Christ.
Jas 2: 8 if you **f** the royal law according

FULFILLED → FULFILL
Lk 24:44 the prophets and psalms must
be **f**."
Ro 8: 4 decree of the law might be **f**
in us,

FULL → FILL
Eze 10:12 of the four wheels were **f** of
eyes all
Jn 1:14 only Son, **f** of grace and truth.

FULLNESS → FILL
Jn 1:16 From his **f** we have all received,
1Co 10:26 for "the earth and its **f** are the
Lord's."
Gal 4: 4 But when the **f** of time had
come,
Eph 1:10 as a plan for the **f** of times, to
sum
3:19 may be filled with all the **f** of
God.
Col 1:19 him all the **f** was pleased to
dwell,
2: 9 him dwells the whole **f** of the
deity

FURNACE
Isa 48:10 tested you in the **f** of affliction.
Da 3: 6 be instantly cast into a white-
hot **f**."
3:49 went down into the **f** with
Azariah
3:49 drove the fiery flames out of
the **f**,
Mt 13:42 will throw them into the
fiery **f**,

FURY
Ro 2: 8 **f** to those who selfishly disobey

Rev 16:19 the cup filled with the wine of his **f**

FUTURE
Pr 24:20 For the evil man has no **f**, the lamp
Jer 31:17 There is hope for your **f**,
1Co 3:22 life or death, or the present or the **f**:
1Ti 6:19 treasure a good foundation for the **f**,

G

GABRIEL
Angel who interpreted Daniel's visions (Da 8:16-26; 9:20-27); announced births of John (Lk 1:11-20), Jesus (Lk 1:26-38).

GAD
1. Son of Jacob by Zilpah (Ge 30:9-11; 35:26; 1Ch 2:2). Tribe of blessed (Ge 49:19; Dt 33:20-21), numbered (Nu 1:25; 26:18), allotted land east of the Jordan (Nu 32; 34:14; Jos 18:7; 22), west (Eze 48:27-28), 12,000 from (Rev 7:5).
2. Prophet; seer of David (1Sa 22:5; 2Sa 24:11-19; 1Ch 29:29).

GAIN
Lk 9:25 one to **g** the whole world yet lose
Php 1:21 to me life is Christ, and death is **g**.
3: 8 so much rubbish, that I may **g** Christ
1Ti 6: 5 religion to be a means of **g**.

GALILEAN → GALILEE
Mt 26:69 "You too were with Jesus the **G**."

GALILEANS → GALILEE
Ac 2: 7 these people who are speaking **G**?

GALILEE → GALILEAN, GALILEANS
Mt 4:15 the Jordan, **G** of the Gentiles,
Jn 7:41 "The Messiah will not come from **G**,

GAMALIEL
Pharisee (Ac 5:34-39), teacher of Paul (Ac 22:5).

GARDEN
Ge 2: 8 the Lord God planted a **g** in Eden,
Eze 28:13 In Eden, the **g** of God, you were,
Jn 19:41 he had been crucified there was a **g**,
19:41 **g**, and in the **g** a new tomb,

GARMENT → GARMENTS
Ps 102:27 they all wear out like a **g**;

GARMENTS → GARMENT
Ge 3:21 wife the Lord God made leather **g**,

GATE → GATES
Mt 7:13 "Enter through the narrow **g**;
7:13 for the **g** is wide and the road broad
Jn 10: 7 say to you, I am the **g** for the sheep.
Heb 13:12 Jesus also suffered outside the **g**,

GATES → GATE
Ge 24:60 possession of the **g** of their enemies!"
Dt 6: 9 of your houses and on your **g**.
Ps 100: 4 Enter the temple **g** with praise,
Mt 16:18 the **g** of the netherworld shall not
Rev 21:21 The twelve **g** were twelve pearls,
21:21 each of the **g** made from a single

GATH
1Sa 17: 4 champion named Goliath of **G** came
2Sa 1:20 "Tell it not in **G**, herald it not

GATHER → GATHERED
Ex 16: 4 to go out and **g** their daily portion;
Ru 2: 7 She asked leave to **g** the gleanings
Isa 11:12 and **g** the outcasts of Israel;
Mt 12:30 and whoever does not **g** with me
Lk 13:34 to **g** your children together as a hen

GATHERED → GATHER
Mt 18:20 or three are **g** together in my name,

GAVE → GIVE
Ge 28: 4 your descendants the blessing he **g**
Ex 31:18 he **g** him the two tablets
Ne 9:15 heaven you **g** them in their hunger,
Ecc 12: 7 life breath returns to God who **g** it.
Mt 25:35 I was hungry and you **g** me food,
25:35 I was thirsty and you **g** me drink,
Jn 1:12 who did accept him he **g** power
3:16 the world that he **g** his only Son,
Eph 4:11 And he **g** some as apostles, others as
1Ti 2: 6 who **g** himself as ransom for all.

GEDALIAH
Governor of Judah (2Ki 25:22-26; Jer 39-41).

GEHAZI
Servant of Elisha (2Ki 4:12-5:27; 8:4-5).

GENEALOGY
Mt 1: 1 The book of the **g** of Jesus Christ,

GENERATION → GENERATIONS
Ex 20: 6 mercy down to the thousandth **g**,
34: 7 third and fourth **g** for their fathers'
Mt 12:39 evil and unfaithful **g** seeks a sign,
Lk 21:32 this **g** will not pass away until all

GENERATIONS → GENERATION
Isa 51: 8 forever and my salvation, for all **g**.

GENEROSITY
Ro 12: 8 if one contributes, in **g**; if one is
Gal 5:22 patience, kindness, **g**, faithfulness,

GENTILE → GENTILES
1Ma 1:14 according to the **G** custom.
Mt 18:17 treat him as you would a **G** or a tax
Gal 2:14 are living like a **G** and not like

GENTILES → GENTILE
1Ma 1:11 an alliance with the **G** all around us;
Lk 21:24 be taken as captives to all the **G**;
21:24 underfoot by the **G** until the times
21:24 until the times of the **G** are fulfilled.
Ac 15:19 to stop troubling the **G** who turn
Ro 3:29 Does he not belong to **G**, too? Yes,
3:29 belong to **G**, too? Yes, also to **G**,
Gal 3: 8 God would justify the **G** by faith,
Eph 4:17 you must no longer live as the **G** do,

GENTLE → GENTLENESS
1Pe 3: 4 in the imperishable beauty of a **g**

GENTLENESS → GENTLE
Gal 5:23 **g**, self-control. Against such there is
1Ti 6:11 faith, love, patience, and **g**.

GETHSEMANE
Mk 14:32 Then they came to a place named **G**,

GHOST
Mt 14:26 "It is a **g**," they said, and they cried
Lk 24:39 because a **g** does not have flesh

GIANT
Sir 47: 4 As a youth he slew the **g** and wiped

GIBEON
Jos 10:12 Stand still, O sun, at **G**, O moon,
1Ki 3: 5 In **G** the Lord appeared to Solomon

GIDEON → = JERUBBAAL
Judge, also called Jerubbaal; freed Israel from Midianites (Jdg 6-8; Heb 11:32). The fleece (Jdg 8:36-40).

GIFT → GIFTS
Nu 18: 7 I give you the priesthood as a **g**.
Mt 5:23 if you bring your **g** to the altar,
Jn 4:10 "If you knew the **g** of God and who
Ac 2:38 you will receive the **g** of the holy
Ro 6:23 the **g** of God is eternal life in Christ
1Co 7: 7 each has a particular **g** from God,

GIFT → GIFTS (*cont.*)
Jas 1:17 and every perfect **g** is from above,
Rev 21: 6 the thirsty I will give a **g**

GIFTS → GIFT
Mt 2:11 treasures and offered him **g** of gold,
Lk 11:13 how to give good **g** to your children,
Ro 11:29 For the **g** and the call of God are
1Co 12: 1 Now in regard to spiritual **g**,
14: 1 but strive eagerly for the spiritual **g**,
Eph 4: 8 prisoners captive; he gave **g** to men."

GILGAL
Jos 5: 9 Therefore the place is called **G**
1Sa 7:16 **G** and Mizpah and judging Israel

GIRL
Ex 1:16 him; but if it is a **g**, she may live."
Mk 5:41 which means, "Little **g**, I say to you,

GIVE → GAVE, GIVEN, GIVER, GIVES
Ge 9: 3 I **g** them all to you as I did the green
12: 7 your descendants I will **g** this land."
1Ki 3: 5 of me and I will **g** it to you."
Tob 12: 9 Those who regularly **g** alms shall
Pr 25:21 enemy be hungry, **g** him food to eat,
25:21 eat, if he be thirsty, **g** him to drink;
30:15 two daughters of the leech are, "**G**,
30:15 daughters of the leech are, "**G, G.**"
Eze 36:26 I will **g** you a new heart and place
Mt 6:11 **G** us today our daily bread;
7: 6 "Do not **g** what is holy to dogs,
Mk 10:45 to **g** his life as a ransom for many."
Jn 10:28 I **g** them eternal life, and they shall
Ac 20:35 said, 'It is more blessed to **g** than

GIVEN → GIVE
Mt 7: 7 "Ask and it will be **g** to you;
Mk 4:25 To the one who has, more will be **g**;
Lk 22:19 is my body, which will be **g** for you;
Ro 5: 5 the holy Spirit that has been **g** to us.

GIVER → GIVE
2Co 9: 7 for God loves a cheerful **g**.

GIVES → GIVE
2Co 3: 6 brings death, but the Spirit **g** life.
Jas 4: 6 proud, but **g** grace to the humble."

GLAD → GLADNESS
Ps 16: 9 Therefore my heart is **g**, my soul
90:15 Make us **g** as many days as you
Pr 10: 1 A wise son makes his father **g**,
Mt 5:12 Rejoice and be **g**, for your reward
Ac 2:26 Therefore my heart has been **g**

GLADNESS → GLAD
Ps 100: 2 worship the LORD with cries of **g**;
Isa 16:10 joy and **g**, In the vineyards there is
Zep 3:17 He will rejoice over you with **g**,
Heb 1: 9 the oil of **g** above your companions";

GLASS
Rev 4: 6 resembled a sea of **g** like crystal.
21:18 the city was pure gold, clear as **g**.

GLEAN
Ru 2: 2 **g** ears of grain in the field of anyone

GLOOM
Isa 9: 1 those who dwelt in the land of **g**
Joel 2: 2 is near, a day of darkness and of **g**,

GLORIFIED → GLORY
Jn 13:31 "Now is the Son of Man **g**, and God
13:31 Son of Man **g**, and God is **g** in him.
17: 4 I **g** you on earth by accomplishing
Ac 3:13 has **g** his servant Jesus whom you
Ro 8:30 and those he justified he also **g**.

GLORIFY → GLORY
Ps 86:12 **g** your name forever, Lord my God.
Jn 17: 1 son, so that your son may **g** you,
1Co 6:20 Therefore **g** God in your body.
Rev 15: 4 or **g** your name? For you alone are

GLORIOUS → GLORY
Jdt 16:13 God. O LORD, great are you and **g**,
Da 3:26 fathers, and **g** forever is your name.
Jas 2: 1 the faith in our **g** Lord Jesus Christ.

GLORY → GLORIFIED, GLORIFY, GLORIOUS
Ex 24:16 The **g** of the LORD settled
33:18 Moses said, "Do let me see your **g**!"
40:34 tent, and the **g** of the LORD filled
1Sa 4:21 saying, "Gone is the **g** from Israel,"
1Ki 8:11 since the LORD's **g** had filled
1Ma 1:40 was as great as her **g** had been,

Ps 8: 6 crowned them with **g** and honor.
19: 2 The heavens declare the **g** of God;
24: 7 portals, that the king of **g** may enter.
Isa 6: 3 "All the earth is filled with his **g**!"
40: 5 the **g** of the LORD shall be revealed,
Bar 5: 4 of justice, the **g** of God's worship.
Eze 44: 4 I looked I saw the **g** of the LORD
Hos 4: 7 me, exchanging their **g** for shame.
Mt 25:31 the Son of Man comes in his **g**,
Lk 2:14 "**G** to God in the highest and on earth
Jn 1:14 us, and we saw his **g**, the **g** as
12:41 Isaiah said this because he saw his **g**
Ro 3:23 and are deprived of the **g** of God.
8:18 compared with the **g** to be revealed
9: 4 the adoption, the **g**, the covenants,
1Co 10:31 do, do everything for the **g** of God.
2Co 4:17 weight of **g** beyond all comparison,
Heb 1: 3 who is the refulgence of his **g**,
2Pe 1:17 **g** from God the Father
1:17 came to him from the majestic **g**,
Rev 4:11 to receive **g** and honor and power,
21:23 for the **g** of God gave it light, and its

GLUTTON
Pr 23:21 drunkard and the **g** come to poverty,
Mt 11:19 'Look, he is a **g** and a drunkard,

GNAT
Mt 23:24 who strain out the **g** and swallow

GO
Ex 5: 1 Let my people **g**, that they may
Jos 1: 9 God, is with you wherever you **g**."
Ru 1:16 you! for wherever you **g** I will **g**,
Mt 28:19 **G**, therefore, and make disciples
Jn 14: 3 if I **g** and prepare a place for you,

GOAT → GOATS
Lev 16: 9 The **g** that is determined by lot
Da 8:21 The **h** is the king of the Greeks,

GOATS → GOAT
Ps 50:13 of bulls or drink the blood of **g**?
Mt 25:32 separates the sheep from the **g**.
Heb 10: 4 blood of bulls and **g** take away sins.

GOD → GOD'S, GODDESS, GODLESS, GODLY, GODS

Ge 1: 1 when **G** created the heavens
1:27 **G** created man in his image;
3: 5 **G** knows well that the moment you
17: 1 him and said: "I am **G** the Almighty.
Ex 3: 4 **G** called out to him from the bush,
15: 2 my savior. He is my **G**, I praise him;
15: 2 him; the **G** of my father, I extol him.
20: 5 I, the LORD, your **G**, am a jealous **G**,
34: 6 a merciful and gracious **G**,
Nu 23:19 **G** is not man that he should speak
Dt 4: 7 our **G**, is to us whenever we call
6: 5 LORD, your **G**, with all your heart,
Jos 22:34 among them that the LORD is **G**.
1Sa 2: 2 LORD; there is no Rock like our **G**.
1Ki 8:27 indeed be that **G** dwells among men
18:24 The **G** who answers with fire is **G**."
2Ki 17: 7 their **G**, who had brought them
Ezr 6:16 of this house of **G** with joy.
Ne 8:18 book of the law of **G** day after day,
Tob 4:19 At all times bless the Lord **G**,
Ps 19: 2 The heavens declare the glory of **G**;
22: 2 My **G**, my **G**, why have you
46: 2 **G** is our refuge and our strength,
46:11 "Be still and confess that I am **G**!
47: 8 **G** is king over all the earth;
53: 2 "There is no **G**." Their deeds are
68:21 Our **G** is a **G** who saves;
90: 2 from eternity to eternity you are **G**.
136: 2 Praise the **G** of gods; God's love
145: 1 I will extol you, my **G** and king;
Ecc 12:13 all is heard: Fear **G** and keep his
Sir 32:14 He who would find **G** must accept
Isa 12: 2 **G** indeed is my savior; I am
40:28 The LORD is the eternal **G**,
44: 6 I am the last; there is no **G** but me.
Jer 10:10 The LORD is true **G**, he is the living
10:10 he is the living **G**, the eternal King,
Bar 4: 8 the Eternal **G** who nourished you,
Eze 28: 2 of Tyre: Thus says the Lord **G**:
28: 2 you say, "A **g** am I! I occupy a godly
28: 2 And yet you are a man, and not a **g**,

Eze 28: 2 you may think yourself like a **g**.
Da 14: 4 it; but Daniel adored only his **G**.
Hos 12: 6 The LORD, the **G** of hosts, the LORD
Am 4:12 prepare to meet your **G**, O Israel:
Mic 6: 8 and to walk humbly with your **G**.
Hab 3:18 the LORD and exult in my saving **G**.
Mal 2:10 Has not the one **G** created us?
Mt 1:23 which means "**G** is with us."
4: 4 comes forth from the mouth of **G**.' "
4: 7 put the Lord, your **G**, to the test.' "
4:10 Lord, your **G**, shall you worship
6:24 You cannot serve **G** and mammon.
27:40 if you are the Son of **G**, [and] come
Mk 1: 1 of Jesus Christ [the Son of **G**].
2: 7 Who but **G** alone can forgive sins?"
10: 9 Therefore what **G** has joined
12:30 You shall love the Lord your **G**
Lk 2:14 "Glory to **G** in the highest
18:19 good? No one is good but **G** alone.
22:70 asked, "Are you then the Son of **G**?"
Jn 1: 1 and the Word was with **G**,
1: 1 was with **G**, and the Word was **G**.
1:18 No one has ever seen **G**. The only
1:18 **G**. The only Son, **G**, who is
3:16 For **G** so loved the world that he
5:18 but he also called **G** his own father,
5:18 father, making himself equal to **G**.
20:28 said to him, "My Lord and my **G**!"
Ac 5:29 "We must obey **G** rather than men.
Ro 4: 3 "Abraham believed **G**, and it was
6:23 the gift of **G** is eternal life in Christ
8:31 If **G** is for us, who can be against
1Co 10:31 do, do everything for the glory of **G**.
2Co 4: 4 in whose case the **g** of this age has
4: 4 of Christ, who is the image of **G**.
6:16 agreement has the temple of **G**
6:16 we are the temple of the living **G**;
6:16 temple of the living **G**; as **G** said:
6:16 and I will be their **G** and they shall
Eph 4: 6 one **G** and Father of all, who is over

Php 2: 6 though he was in the form of **G**,
2: 6 regard equality with **G** something
Tit 2:13 of the glory of the great **G**
Heb 4:12 Indeed, the word of **G** is living
10:31 to fall into the hands of the living **G**.
12:29 For our **G** is a consuming fire.
Jas 2:23 "Abraham believed **G**, and it was
2:23 and he was called "the friend of **G**."
4: 8 Draw near to **G**, and he will draw
1Jn 1: 5 **G** is light, and in him there is no
4:16 to believe in the love **G** has for us.
4:16 **G** is love, and whoever remains
4:16 remains in love remains in **G** and **G**
5: 2 we love the children of **G** when we
5: 2 the children of **G** when we love **G**
Jude 1:21 Keep yourselves in the love of **G**
Rev 4: 8 holy, holy is the Lord **G** almighty,
19:13 his name was called the Word of **G**.
22: 5 for the Lord **G** shall give them light,

*GOD → *LORD

Ge 15: 2 "O Lord **G**, what good will your gifts
2Sa 7:18 I, Lord **G**, and who are the members
Isa 25: 8 forever. The Lord **G** will wipe away
61: 1 The spirit of the Lord **G** is upon me,

GOD'S → GOD

1Co 3: 9 For we are **G** co-workers; you are **G**
3: 9 you are **G** field, **G** building.
1Jn 3: 2 Beloved, we are **G** children now;

GODDESS → GOD

1Ki 11: 5 Astarte, the **g** of the Sidonians,
Ac 19:27 of the great **g** Artemis will be of no

GODLESS → GOD

Job 8:13 shall the hope of the **g** man perish.
1Ti 1: 9 lawless and unruly, the **g** and sinful,
2Pe 3: 7 and of destruction of the **g**.

GODLY → GOD

Mal 2:15 that one require but **g** offspring?
2Co 7:10 For **g** sorrow produces a salutary

GODS → GOD

Ex 12:12 judgment on all the **g** of Egypt—I,

GODS → GOD (*cont.*)

Ex 20: 3 shall not have other **g** besides me.
Jdg 2:17 to the worship of other **g**. They were
2Ki 17: 7 and because they venerated other **g**.
Jn 10:34 in your law, 'I said, "You are **g**" '?
1Co 8: 5 even though there are so-called **g**
    8: 5 to be sure, many "**g**" and many "lords"),

GOG

Eze 38:18 the day when **G** invades the land
Rev 20: 8 corners of the earth, **G** and Magog,

GOLD

Ex 20:23 silver nor gods of **g** shall you make
    25:17 then make a propitiatory of pure **g**.
    25:31 lampstand of pure beaten **g** — its shaft
    28: 6 ephod they shall make of **g** thread
    32:31 making a god of **g** for themselves!
1Ki 6:21 interior of the temple with pure **g**.
    6:21 overlaid it with **g**, and looped it
Tob 12: 8 to give alms than to store up **g**;
Job 28:15 Solid **g** cannot purchase it, nor can
Sir 31: 5 The lover of **g** will not be free
Isa 60:17 In place of bronze I will bring **g**,
Ac 3: 6 "I have neither silver nor **g**, but what
1Pe 1: 7 faith, more precious than **g** that is
Rev 21:21 the street of the city was of pure **g**,

GOLGOTHA

Mt 27:33 to a place called **G** (which means

GOLIATH

Giant killed by David (1Sa 17; 21:9; Sir 47:4).

GOMORRAH

Ge 19:24 **G** [from the LORD out of heaven].
Isa 1: 9 as Sodom, we should be like **G**.
Jude 1: 7 Sodom, **G**, and the surrounding

GOOD → BEST, BETTER, GOODNESS

Ge 1:31 he had made, and he found it very **g**.
    2: 9 delightful to look at and **g** for food,
    2: 9 the tree of the knowledge of **g**
    3:22 knowing what is **g** and what is bad!
    50:20 God meant it for **g**, to achieve
Dt 6:18 right and **g** in the sight of the LORD,

Dt 6:18 possess the **g** land which the LORD
2Ch 7: 3 "for he is **g**, for his mercy endures
Ps 34: 9 Learn to savor how **g** the LORD is;
    84:12 The LORD withholds no **g** thing
Ecc 12:14 hidden qualities, whether **g** or bad.
Isa 52: 7 Announcing peace, bearing **g** news,
Da 3:89 Give thanks to the Lord, for he is **g**,
Mt 5:45 his sun rise on the bad and the **g**,
    25:21 done, my **g** and faithful servant.
Mk 10:18 him, "Why do you call me **g**? No one
    10:18 me **g**? No one is **g** but God alone.
Lk 2:10 I proclaim to you **g** news of great
Lk 6:43 "A **g** tree does not bear rotten fruit,
    6:43 nor does a rotten tree bear **g** fruit.
Jn 10:11 I am the **g** shepherd. A **g** shepherd
Ro 7:16 not want, I concur that the law is **g**.
    12: 2 what is **g** and pleasing and perfect.
    12:21 by evil but conquer evil with **g**.
Eph 2:10 in Christ Jesus for the **g** works
1Ti 4: 4 For everything created by God is **g**,
Heb 10: 1 has only a shadow of the **g** things
1Pe 3:17 For it is better to suffer for doing **g**,

GOODNESS → GOOD

Ps 23: 6 Only **g** and love will pursue me

GOSHEN

Ge 45:10 You will settle in the region of **G**,

GOSPEL

Mk 8:35 sake and that of the **g** will save it.
Ro 1:16 For I am not ashamed of the **g**. It is
1Co 9:16 If I preach the **g**, this is no reason
2Co 4: 3 And even though our **g** is veiled,
Gal 1: 6 grace [of Christ] for a different **g**
Php 1:27 in a way worthy of the **g** of Christ,
    1:27 together for the faith of the **g**,

GOSSIP

2Co 12:20 selfishness, slander, **g**, conceit,

GRACE → GRACIOUS

Wis 3: 9 Because **g** and mercy are with his
Jn 1:14 Father's only Son, full of **g** and truth.
    1:16 have all received, **g** in place of **g**,
Ac 15:11 we are saved through the **g**

Ro 3:24 by his **g** through the redemption
    6: 1 we persist in sin that **g** may abound?
    6:14 are not under the law but under **g**.
    11: 6 But if by **g**, it is no longer because
    11: 6 otherwise **g** would no longer be **g**.
1Co 15:10 But by the **g** of God I am what I am,
    15:10 his **g** to me has not been ineffective.
    15:10 but the **g** of God [that is] with me.
2Co 12: 9 to me, "My **g** is sufficient for you,
Gal 5: 4 by law; you have fallen from **g**.
Eph 2: 5 Christ (by **g** you have been saved),
2Th 2:16 and good hope through his **g**,
Tit 2:11 For the **g** of God has appeared,
Heb 4:16 confidently approach the throne of **g**
    4:16 mercy and to find **g** for timely help.
Jas 4: 6 But he bestows a greater **g**;
    4: 6 proud, but gives **g** to the humble."
1Pe 5:10 The God of all **g** who called you
Jude 1: 4 who pervert the **g** of our God
Rev 22:21 The **g** of the Lord Jesus be with all.

GRACIOUS → GRACE

Ex 34: 6 a merciful and **g** God, slow to anger
Nu 6:25 shine upon you, and be **g** to you!
Ps 116: 5 **G** is the LORD and just; yes, our God
Col 4: 6 Let your speech always be **g**,

GRAFTED

Ro 11:17 were **g** in their place and have come

GRAIN

Dt 25: 4 an ox when it is treading out **g**.
Mk 2:23 he was passing through a field of **g**
    2:23 a path while picking the heads of **g**.

GRAPES

Nu 13:23 with a single cluster of **g** on it,
Isa 5: 2 Then he looked for the crop of **g**,
    5: 2 of **g**, but what it yielded was wild **g**.
Jer 31:29 "The fathers ate unripe **g**,
Mt 7:16 Do people pick **g** from thornbushes,
Rev 14:18 the earth's vines, for its **g** are ripe."

GRASS

Isa 40: 6 "All mankind is **g**, and all their glory
Mt 6:30 If God so clothes the **g** of the field,
1Pe 1:24 "All flesh is like **g**, and all its glory

1Pe 1:24 flower of the field; the **g** withers,

GRATIFY
Gal 5:16 you will certainly not **g** the desire

GRAVE → GRAVES
Ps 49:15 Straight to the **g** they descend,
Isa 53: 9 A **g** was assigned him among

GRAVES → GRAVE
Eze 37:12 I will open your **g** and have you rise
Lk 11:44 You are like unseen **g** over

GRAY
Pr 16:31 **G** hair is a crown of glory; it is

GREAT → GREATER, GREATEST
Ge 1:16 God made the two **g** lights,
12: 2 "I will make of you a **g** nation, and I
12: 2 I will make your name **g**,
Ex 32:11 the land of Egypt with such **g** power
Dt 10:17 the LORD of lords, the **g** God,
Ne 8: 6 Ezra blessed the LORD, the **g** God,
Jdt 16:13 O LORD, **g** are you and glorious,
Ps 95: 3 For the LORD is the **g** God, the **g**
Jer 10: 6 one is like you, O LORD, **g** are you,
La 3:23 morning, so **g** is his faithfulness.
Da 9: 4 Lord, **g** and awesome God, you who
Joel 2:11 For **g** is the day of the LORD,
Mt 4:16 have seen a **g** light, on those
13:46 When he finds a pearl of **g** price,
20:26 to be **g** among you shall be your
Eph 2: 4 because of the **g** love he had for us,
Tit 2:13 of the glory of the **g** God and of our
Heb 2: 3 if we ignore so **g** a salvation?
12: 1 we are surrounded by so **g** a cloud
13:20 the dead the **g** shepherd of the sheep
Rev 14: 8 "Fallen, fallen is Babylon the **g**,

GREATER → GREAT
Mt 12: 6 something **g** than the temple is here.
Mk 12:31 other commandment **g** than these."
Jn 14:12 I do, and will do **g** ones than these,
15:13 No one has **g** love than this, to lay
1Jn 4: 4 is in you is **g** than the one who is

GREATEST → GREAT
Mt 22:38 This is the **g** and the first
Lk 9:48 all of you is the one who is the **g**."
1Co 13:13 three; but the **g** of these is love.

GREECE → GREEK, GREEKS
1Ma 1: 1 in his place, having first ruled in G.

GREED → GREEDY
Lk 12:15 "Take care to guard against all **g**,
Col 3: 5 evil desire, and the **g** that is idolatry.

GREEDY → GREED
Pr 28:25 The **g** man stirs up disputes, but he
1Co 6:10 thieves nor the **g** nor drunkards nor
Tit 1: 7 aggressive, not **g** for sordid gain,

GREEK → GREECE
Jn 19:20 written in Hebrew, Latin, and **G**.
Ro 1:16 believes: for Jew first, and then **G**.
Gal 3:28 There is neither Jew nor **G**, there is

GREEKS → GREECE
1Co 1:22 signs and **G** look for wisdom,

GREEN
Ge 1:30 I give all the **g** plants for food."
Ps 23: 2 In **g** pastures you let me graze;

GREW → GROW
1Sa 2:21 while young Samuel **g**
Isa 53: 2 He **g** up like a sapling before him,
Lk 1:80 The child **g** and became strong
2:40 The child **g** and became strong,

GRIEVE → GRIEVED
Eph 4:30 And do not **g** the holy Spirit of God,
1Th 4:13 so that you may not **g** like the rest,

GRIEVED → GRIEVE
Isa 63:10 But they rebelled, and **g** his holy

GRINDING
Lk 17:35 will be two women **g** meal together;

GROAN → GROANING
Ro 8:23 **g** within ourselves as we wait
2Co 5: 2 For in this tent we **g**, longing to be

GROANING → GROAN
Ex 2:24 he heard their **g** and was mindful

GROUND
Ge 2: 7 formed man out of the clay of the **g**
3:17 eat, "Cursed be the **g** because of you!
Ex 3: 5 the place where you stand is holy **g**.
Mt 13: 5 Some fell on rocky **g**, where it had

GROW → GREW, GROWTH
Eze 47:12 fruit trees of every kind shall **g**;
2Pe 3:18 But **g** in grace and in the knowledge

GROWTH → GROW
1Co 3: 7 but only God, who causes the **g**.
Col 2:19 achieves the **g** that comes

GUARANTEE → GUARANTEED
Heb 7:22 become the **g** of an [even] better

GUARANTEED → GUARANTEE
Ro 4:16 and the promise may be **g** to all his

GUARD → GUARDIAN, GUARDS
Pr 2:11 over you, understanding will **g** you;
2Th 3: 3 you and **g** you from the evil one.
2Ti 1:12 is able to **g** what has been entrusted

GUARDIAN → GUARD
1Pe 2:25 to the shepherd and **g** of your souls.

GUARDS → GUARD
Mt 28: 4 The **g** were shaken with fear of him

GUIDANCE → GUIDE
Pr 11:14 For lack of **g** a people falls;

GUIDE → GUIDANCE
Isa 58:11 Then the LORD will **g** you always
Lk 6:39 a blind person **g** a blind person?
Jn 16:13 of truth, he will **g** you to all truth.

GUILT → GUILTY
Lev 5:15 to the LORD as his **g** offering
Ps 32: 5 my sin to you; my **g** I did not hide.
32: 5 and you took away the **g** of my sin.
Hos 14: 2 you have collapsed through your **g**.
Zec 3: 9 I will take away the **g** of the land

GUILTY → GUILT
Ex 23: 7 to death, nor shall you acquit the **g**.
Nu 14:18 yet not declaring the guiltless **g**,
Da 13:53 and freeing the **g**, although the Lord
Mk 3:29 but is **g** of an everlasting sin."

H

HABAKKUK
Prophet to Judah (Hab 1:1; 3:1; Da 14:33-39).

HADASSAH → See ESTHER

HADES
Rev 20:14 **H** were thrown into the pool of fire.

HAGAR
Servant of Sarah, wife of Abraham, mother of Ishmael (Ge 16:1-6; 25:12). Driven away by Sarah while pregnant (Ge 16:5-16); after birth of Isaac (Ge 21:9-21; Gal 4:21-31).

HAGGAI

Post-exilic prophet who encouraged rebuilding of the temple (Ezr 5:1; 6:14; Hag 1-2).

HAIL → HAILSTONES

| Ex | 9:19 | shelter shall die when the **h** comes |
| Rev | 8: 7 | there came **h** and fire mixed |

HAILSTONES → HAIL

| Jos | 10:11 | from these **h** than the Israelites slew |
| Rev | 16:21 | Large **h** like huge weights came |

HAIR → HAIRS

Jdg	16:22	the **h** of his head began to grow as
Lk	7:44	her tears and wiped them with her **h**.
Jn	12: 3	of Jesus and dried them with her **h**;
1Co	11: 6	she may as well have her **h** cut off.
	11: 6	for a woman to have her **h** cut off

HAIRS → HAIR

| Ps | 40:13 | see. They are more than the **h** of my |
| Mt | 10:30 | Even all the **h** of your head are |

HALF

Est	5: 3	Even if it is **h** of my kingdom,
Mk	6:23	of me, even to **h** of my kingdom."
Lk	19: 8	"Behold, **h** of my possessions, Lord,

HALLOWED

| Mt | 6: 9 | Father in heaven, **h** be your name, |

HAM

Son of Noah (Ge 5:32; 1Ch 1:4), father of Canaan (Ge 9:18; 10:6-20; 1Ch 1:8-16). Saw Noah's nakedness (Ge 9:20-27).

HAMAN

Agagite nobleman honored by Xerxes (Est 3:1-2). Plotted to exterminate the Jews because of Mordecai (Est 3:3-15). Forced to honor Mordecai (Est 5-6). Plot exposed by Esther (Est 5:1-8; 7:1-8). Hanged (Est 7:9-10).

HANANIAH → = SHADRACH

1. False prophet; adversary of Jeremiah (Jer 28).

2. Original name of Shadrach (Da 1:6-19; 2:17).

HAND → EMPTY-HANDED, HANDED, HANDS

Ex	15: 6	Your right **h**, O LORD,
	15: 6	your right **h**, O LORD, has shattered
Dt	19:21	tooth for tooth, **h** for **h**, and foot
1Ki	18:44	a cloud as small as a man's **h** rising
Jdt	9:10	their pride by the **h** of a woman.
Ps	110: 1	"Take your throne at my right **h**,

Pr	3:16	Long life is in her right **h**, in her left
Isa	5:25	he raises his **h** to strike them;
	5:25	back, and his **h** is still outstretched.
Da	5: 5	the fingers of a human **h** appeared,
	5: 5	king saw the wrist and **h** that wrote,
Hab	2:16	the cup from the LORD's right **h**,
Mt	3:12	His winnowing fan is in his **h**.
Mk	9:43	If your **h** causes you to sin, cut it
Lk	20:42	said to my lord, "Sit at my right **h**
Jn	10:28	No one can take them out of my **h**.
Ro	8:34	who also is at the right **h** of God,
1Co	12:15	I am not a **h** I do not belong
Heb	10:12	seat forever at the right **h** of God;
Rev	1:16	In his right **h** he held seven stars.
	5: 1	in the right **h** of the one who sat

HANDED → HAND

| Mt | 27:26 | he **h** him over to be crucified. |
| Ro | 4:25 | who was **h** over for our |

HANDS → HAND

Ps	115: 7	They have **h** but do not feel,
Isa	49:16	of my **h** I have written your name;
Lk	23:46	into your **h** I commend my spirit";
	24:40	he showed them his **h** and his feet.
Ac	8:18	by the laying on of the apostles' **h**,
Ro	10:21	I stretched out my **h** to a disobedient
Heb	6: 2	about baptisms and laying on of **h**,
	10:31	to fall into the **h** of the living God.

HANNAH

Wife of Elkanah, mother of Samuel (1Sa 1). Prayer at dedication of Samuel (1Sa 2:1-10). Blessed (1Sa 2:18-21).

HAPPY

Tob	13:14	**H** are those who love you, and **h**
	13:14	**H** are all the men who shall grieve
Ps	1: 1	**H** those who do not follow
	33:12	**H** the nation whose God is the LORD,
	84:13	hosts, **h** are those who trust in you!
Pr	3:13	**H** the man who finds wisdom,

HARD → HARDEN, HARDENED, HARDENING, HARDSHIPS

| Ex | 1:14 | for them with **h** work in mortar |
| Mt | 19:23 | it will be **h** for one who is rich |

HARDEN → HARD

| Ps | 95: 8 | Do not **h** your hearts as at Meribah, |

| Heb | 3: 8 | '**H** not your hearts as at the rebellion |

HARDENED → HARD

| Mk | 8:17 | or comprehend? Are your hearts **h**? |
| Ro | 11: 7 | the elect attained it; the rest were **h**, |

HARDENING → HARD

| Ro | 11:25 | a **h** has come upon Israel in part, |

HARDSHIPS → HARD

| 2Co | 12:10 | weaknesses, insults, **h**, persecutions, |

HARM

Ge	50:20	Even though you meant **h** to me,
Ne	6: 2	They were planning to do me **h**.
Pr	12:21	No **h** befalls the just, but the wicked
1Pe	3:13	Now who is going to **h** you if you

HARP → HARPS

| Ps | 150: 3 | the horn, praise him with **h** and lyre. |
| Rev | 5: 8 | Each of the elders held a **h** and gold |

HARPS → HARP

1Ch	15:16	to play on musical instruments, **h**,
Ne	12:27	hymns and the music of cymbals, **h**,
Ps	137: 2	of that land we hung up our **h**.

HARVEST

Ge	8:22	lasts, seedtime and **h**, cold and heat,
Ex	23:16	the feast of the grain **h** with the first
	23:16	the feast at the fruit **h** at the end
Mt	13:39	The **h** is the end of the age,
Mk	4:29	sickle at once, for the **h** has come."
Lk	10: 2	"The **h** is abundant but the laborers
	10: 2	so ask the master of the **h** to send
	10: 2	the **h** to send out laborers for his **h**.
Rev	14:15	"Use your sickle and reap the **h**,
	14:15	because the earth's **h** is fully ripe."

HASTENING

| 2Pe | 3:12 | and **h** the coming of the day of God, |

HATE → HATED, HATING

Ps	45: 8	You love justice and **h** wrongdoing;
	97:10	The LORD loves those who **h** evil,
Ecc	3: 8	A time to love, and a time to **h**;
Am	5:15	**H** evil and love good, and let justice
Mal	2:16	For I **h** divorce, says the LORD,
Mt	5:43	your neighbor and **h** your enemy.'

Lk 6:27 do good to those who **h** you,
Jn 7: 7 The world cannot **h** you, but it hates
Ro 7:15 do what I want, but I do what I **h**.

HATED → HATE
Jn 15:18 hates you, realize that it **h** me first.
Ro 9:13 is written: "I loved Jacob but **h** Esau."

HATES → HATE
Pr 6:16 There are six things the LORD **h**, yes,
Sir 15:13 Abominable wickedness the LORD **h**,
Jn 15:23 Whoever **h** me also **h** my Father.

HAUGHTY
Pr 6:17 **H** eyes, a lying tongue, and hands
16:18 disaster, and a **h** spirit before a fall.

HAY
1Co 3:12 precious stones, wood, **h**, or straw,

HEAD → BEHEADED, HEADS
Isa 59:17 salvation, as the helmet on his **h**;
Mt 8:20 of Man has nowhere to rest his **h**."
Mk 6:28 He brought in the **h** on a platter
1Co 11: 3 that Christ is the **h** of every man,
11: 3 and a husband the **h** of his wife,
11: 3 of his wife, and God the **h** of Christ.
Eph 1:22 gave him as **h** over all things

HEADS → HEAD
Eze 11:21 down their conduct upon their **h**,
Rev 12: 3 dragon, with seven **h** and ten horns,
12: 3 and on its **h** were seven diadems.

HEAL → HEALED, HEALING, HEALS, HEALTH
Dt 32:39 I who inflict wounds and **h** them,
Ecc 3: 3 A time to kill, and a time to **h**;
Isa 57:19 says the LORD; and I will **h** them.
Jn 12:40 be converted, and I would **h** them."

HEALED → HEAL
Isa 6:10 and they will turn and be **h**.
53: 5 us whole, by his stripes we were **h**.
Jas 5:16 for one another, that you may be **h**.
1Pe 2:24 By his wounds you have been **h**.

HEALING → HEAL
Pr 12:18 but the tongue of the wise is **h**.
1Co 12: 9 another gifts of **h** by the one Spirit;

HEALS → HEAL
Ps 103: 3 pardons all your sins, **h** all your ills,

HEALTH → HEAL
Sir 30:15 More precious than gold is **h**
3Jn 1: 2 in every respect and are in good **h**,

HEAR → HEARD, HEARERS, HEARING, HEARS
Dt 6: 4 "**H**, O Israel! The LORD is our God,
31:13 know it yet, must **h** it and learn it,
Isa 59: 1 to save, nor his ear too dull to **h**.
Jer 5:21 see not, who have ears and **h** not.
Eze 37: 4 Dry bones, **h** the word of the LORD!
Mt 13:17 and to **h** what you **h** but did not **h** it.
Mk 12:29 replied, "The first is this: '**H**, O Israel!
Lk 7:22 the deaf **h**, the dead are raised,
Heb 3: 7 that today you would **h** his voice,

HEARD → HEAR
Isa 40:21 Have you not **h**? Was it not foretold
Ro 10:17 Thus faith comes from what is **h**,
10:17 what is **h** comes through the word
1Co 2: 9 eye has not seen, and ear has not **h**,
1Jn 1: 3 what we have seen and **h**
Rev 22: 8 I, John, who **h** and saw these things,
22: 8 when I **h** and saw them I fell down

HEARERS → HEAR
Jas 1:22 doers of the word and not **h** only,

HEARING → HEAR
Am 8:11 but for **h** the word of the LORD.
1Co 12:17 were an eye, where would the **h** be?
12:17 be? If the whole body were **h**,

HEARS → HEAR
Ps 69:34 For the LORD **h** the poor, does not
Pr 15:29 but the prayer of the just he **h**.
Jn 5:24 whoever **h** my word and believes
1Jn 5:14 according to his will, he **h** us.
Rev 22:18 warn everyone who **h** the prophetic

HEART → BROKENHEARTED, HEART'S, HEARTLESS, HEARTS
Ge 6: 6 on the earth, and his **h** was grieved.
Dt 6: 5 with all your **h**, and with all your
Jos 22: 5 serve him with your whole **h**
1Sa 16: 7 but the LORD looks into the **h**."
Ps 19:15 the thoughts of my **h** before you,
51:12 A clean **h** create for me, God;

Pr 3: 5 Trust in the LORD with all your **h**,
7: 3 write them on the tablet of your **h**.
Eze 36:26 I will give you a new **h** and place
Da 3:39 with contrite **h** and humble spirit
Mt 5: 8 Blessed are the clean of **h**, for they
5:28 adultery with her in his **h**.
Mk 12:30 the Lord your God with all your **h**,
Lk 12:34 treasure is, there also will your **h** be.
Ro 2:29 and circumcision is of the **h**,
10: 9 in your **h** that God raised him
Heb 10:22 let us approach with a sincere **h**

HEART'S → HEART
Ro 10: 1 my **h** desire and prayer to God

HEARTLESS → HEART
Ro 1:31 are senseless, faithless, **h**, ruthless.

HEARTS → HEART
Dt 30:14 in your mouths and in your **h**;
Ps 95: 8 Do not harden your **h** as at Meribah,
Jer 31:33 them, and write it upon their **h**;
Mk 7: 6 lips, but their **h** are far from me;
Jn 14: 1 "Do not let your **h** be troubled.
Ro 2:15 of the law are written in their **h**,
5: 5 into our **h** through the holy Spirit
Eph 3:17 may dwell in your **h** through faith;
Col 3:15 the peace of Christ control your **h**,
Heb 3: 8 'Harden not your **h** as
10:16 "I will put my laws in their **h**, and I
2Pe 1:19 and the morning star rises in your **h**.
1Jn 3:20 in whatever our **h** condemn, for God
3:20 for God is greater than our **h**
Rev 2:23 to know that I am the searcher of **h**

HEAVEN → HEAVENLY, HEAVENS
Ge 14:19 High, the creator of **h** and earth;
Ex 16: 4 "I will now rain down bread from **h**
Dt 31:28 so may call **h** and earth to witness
Job 16:19 now, behold, my witness is in **h**,
Jer 23:24 Do I not fill both **h** and earth?
Mt 3: 2 for the kingdom of **h** is at hand!"
6: 9 Our Father in **h**, hallowed be your
24:35 **H** and earth will pass away, but my
26:64 and 'coming on the clouds of **h**.'"
Mk 10:21 and you will have treasure in **h**;

HEAVEN → HEAVENLY, HEAVENS
(cont.)

Lk 19:38 Peace in **h** and glory in the highest."

24:51 from them and was taken up to **h**.

Jn 3:13 to **h** except the one who has come

3:13 the one who has come down from **h**,

Ac 1:11 you into **h** will return in the same

1:11 as you have seen him going into **h**."

Ro 10: 6 your heart, 'Who will go up into **h**?"

2Co 12: 2 was caught up to the third **h**.

Php 3:20 But our citizenship is in **h**,

1Th 1:10 and to await his Son from **h**,

Heb 9:24 one, but **h** itself, that he might now

2Pe 1:18 voice come from **h** while we were

Rev 4: 1 I had a vision of an open door to **h**,

21: 1 Then I saw a new **h** and a new earth.

21: 1 The former **h** and the former earth

HEAVENLY → HEAVEN

Mt 5:48 just as your **h** Father is perfect.

2Co 5: 2 further clothed with our **h** habitation

Heb 3: 1 sharing in a **h** calling,

HEAVENS → HEAVEN

Ge 1: 1 when God created the **h**

28:12 with its top reaching to the **h**;

1Ki 8:27 If the **h** and the highest **h** cannot

Dt 10:14 The **h**, even the highest **h**,

Ps 57: 6 Show yourself over the **h**, God;

115:16 The **h** belong to the LORD,

Ecc 3: 1 a time for every affair under the **h**.

Isa 14:12 How have you fallen from the **h**,

65:17 Lo, I am about to create new **h**

Jer 10:11 the earth, and from beneath these **h**!

Eph 4:10 who ascended far above all the **h**,

Heb 4:14 priest who has passed through the **h**,

2Pe 3:10 the **h** will pass away with a mighty

HEAVY

Mt 23: 4 They tie up **h** burdens [hard

HEBREW → HEBREWS

Jnh 1: 9 "I am a **H**," Jonah answered them;

Jn 19:20 and it was written in **H**, Latin,

Php 3: 5 of Benjamin, a **H** of **H** parentage,

HEBREWS → HEBREW

Ex 3:18 the God of the **H**, has sent us word.

Jdt 10:12 "I am a daughter of the **H**, and I am

2Co 11:22 Are they **H**? So am I. Are they

HEBRON

Ge 13:18 terebinth of Mamre, which is at **H**.

2Sa 2:11 and six months in **H** as king

HEEL

Ge 3:15 your head, while you strike at his **h**."

25:26 came out next, gripping Esau's **h**;

Jn 13:18 my food has raised his **h** against me.'

HEIGHT → HIGH

Ro 8:39 nor **h**, nor depth, nor any other

Eph 3:18 breadth and length and **h** and depth,

HEIGHTS → HIGH

Ps 148: 1 the heavens; give praise in the **h**.

Hab 3:19 and enables me to go upon the **h**.

HEIR → HEIRS

Ge 15: 4 "No, that one shall not be your **h**;

15: 4 **h**; your own issue shall be your **h**."

Gal 4: 7 a child, and if a child then also an **h**,

Heb 1: 2 whom he made **h** of all things

HEIRS → HEIR

Ro 8:17 then **h**, **h** of God and joint **h**

Tit 3: 7 become **h** in hope of eternal life.

1Pe 3: 7 since we are joint **h** of the gift

HELMET

Isa 59:17 salvation, as the **h** on his head;

Eph 6:17 And take the **h** of salvation

HELP → HELPED, HELPER, HELPS

Jdt 6:21 called upon the God of Israel for **h**.

Ps 33:20 the LORD, who is our **h** and shield.

46: 2 an ever-present **h** in distress.

Sir 2: 6 Trust God and he will **h** you;

Mk 9:24 out, "I do believe, **h** my unbelief!"

Heb 2:18 able to **h** those who are being tested.

4:16 and to find grace for timely **h**.

HELPED → HELP

1Sa 7:12 "To this point has the LORD **h** us."

HELPER → HELP

Ps 30:11 have mercy on me; LORD, be my **h**."

Heb 13: 6 "The Lord is my **h**, [and] I will not

HELPS → HELP

Ps 37:40 The LORD **h** and rescues them,

HERBS

Ex 12: 8 with unleavened bread and bitter **h**.

HERMON

Dt 3: 8 from the Wadi Arnon to Mount **H**

Ps 133: 3 Like dew of **H** coming down

HEROD → HERODIANS

1. King of Judea; tried to kill Jesus (Mt 2; Lk 1:5).

2. Son of 1. Tetrarch of Galilee who arrested and beheaded John the Baptist (Mt 14:1-12; Mk 6:14-29; Lk 3:1, 19-20; 9:7-9); tried Jesus (Lk 23:6-15).

3. Grandson of 1. King of Judea who killed James (Ac 12:2); arrested Peter (Ac 12:3-19). Death (Ac 12:19-23).

HERODIANS → HEROD

Mk 3: 6 took counsel with the **H** against him

12:13 and **H** to him to ensnare him in his

HERODIAS

Wife of Herod the Tetrarch who persuaded her daughter to ask for John the Baptist's head (Mt 14:1-12; Mk 6:14-29; Lk 3:19).

HEWN

Mk 15:46 in a tomb that had been **h**

HEZEKIAH

King of Judah (Sir 48:17-25). Restored the temple and worship (2Ch 29-31). Sought the LORD for help against Assyria (2Ki 18-19; 2Ch 32:1-23; Isa 36-37). Illness healed (2Ki 20:1-11; 2Ch 32:24-26; Isa 38). Judged for showing Babylonians his treasures (2Ki 20:12-21; 2Ch 32:31; Isa 39).

HID → HIDE

Ge 3: 8 his wife **h** themselves from the LORD

Ex 2: 2 child, she **h** him for three months.

3: 6 Moses **h** his face, for he was afraid

Jos 6:17 because she **h** the messengers we

1Ki 18:13 of the LORD—that I **h** a hundred

Isa 49: 2 arrow, in his quiver he **h** me.

54: 8 for a moment I **h** my face from you;

HIDDEN → HIDE

Pr 2: 4 and like **h** treasures search her out:

Isa 40:27 Israel, "My way is **h** from the LORD,

Mk 4:22 there is nothing **h** except to be made

Col 3: 3 your life is **h** with Christ in God.

Rev 2:17 I shall give some of the **h** manna;

HIDE → HID, HIDDEN

Dt 31:17 them and **h** my face from them,

Ps 13: 1 How long will you **h** your face

17: 8 **h** me in the shadow of your wings

HIGH → HEIGHT, HEIGHTS, HIGHEST, HIGHLY

Ge 14:18 and being a priest of God Most **H**,

1Ki 3: 2 were sacrificing on the **h** places,

Ps 91: 1 dwell in the shelter of the Most **H**,

Mt	4: 8	took him up to a very **h** mountain,
	17: 1	and led them up a **h** mountain
Mk	5: 7	me, Jesus, Son of the Most **H** God?
Eph	4: 8	it says: "He ascended on **h** and took
Heb	2:17	and faithful **h** priest before God
	7:26	that we should have such a **h** priest:

HIGHEST → HIGH

1Ki	8:27	the **h** heavens cannot contain you,
Mt	21: 9	name of the Lord; hosanna in the **h**."
Lk	2:14	"Glory to God in the **h** and on earth

HIGHLY → HIGH

Ro	12: 3	of himself more **h** than one ought

HILL

Isa	40: 4	mountain and **h** shall be made low;
Lk	3: 5	mountain and **h** shall be made low.

HINDERED

1Pe	3: 7	so that your prayers may not be **h**.

HIRAM

King of Tyre; helped David build his palace (2Sa 5:11-12; 1Ch 14:1); helped Solomon build the temple (1Ki 5; 2Ch 2) and his navy (1Ki 9:10-27; 2Ch 8).

HITTITE → HITTITES

Ge	23:10	Hittites. So Ephron the **H** replied
2Sa	11: 3	[Joab's armor-bearer] Uriah the **H**."

HITTITES → HITTITE

Dt	20:17	You must doom them all—t he **H**,
Ezr	9: 1	their abominations [Canaanites, **H**,

HOLD → HOLDS

Ps	73:23	you; you take **h** of my right hand.
Col	1:17	and in him all things **h** together.

HOLDS → HOLD

Ps	37:24	never fall, for the LORD **h** their hand.
Rev	2: 1	" 'The one who **h** the seven stars

HOLES

Hag	1: 6	earned them for a bag with **h** in it.

HOLINESS → HOLY

Ex	15:11	is like to you, magnificent in **h**?
Ps	89:36	By my **h** I swore once for all: I will
Ro	1: 4	the spirit of **h** through resurrection
1Ti	2:15	persevere in faith and love and **h**,

Heb	12:14	that **h** without which no one will see

HOLOCAUST → HOLOCAUSTS

Lev	1: 3	"If his **h** offering is from the herd,

HOLOCAUSTS → HOLOCAUST

Ex	40: 6	Put the altar of **h** in front of the entrance
1Sa	15:22	"Does the LORD so delight in **h**
1Ma	1:45	to prohibit **h**, sacrifices, and libations
	4:56	and joyfully offered **h** and sacrifices
Hos	6: 6	and knowledge of God rather than **h**.
Mic	6: 6	Shall I come before him with **h**,

HOLOFERNES

Assyrian general (Jdt 2:4). Beguiled and beheaded by Judith (Jdt 10-13).

HOLY → HOLINESS

Ex	3: 5	place where you stand is **h** ground.
	20: 8	to keep **h** the sabbath day.
	26:33	which divides the **h** place from the **h**
Lev	11:44	shall make and keep yourselves **h**,
	11:44	keep yourselves **h**, because I am **h**.
Jos	5:15	on which you are standing is **h**."
1Sa	2: 2	There is no **H** One like the LORD;
1Ma	1:15	and abandoned the **h** covenant;
Ps	2: 6	my king on Zion, my **h** mountain."
	11: 4	The LORD is in his **h** temple;
Isa	6: 3	"**H**, **h**, **h** is the LORD of hosts!"
	40:25	me as an equal? says the **H** One.
Da	9:24	for your people and for your **h** city:
	9:24	and a most **h** will be anointed.
Mt	1:18	with child through the **h** Spirit.
	3:11	He will baptize you with the **h** Spirit
	24:15	in the **h** place (let the reader
Mk	1:24	I know who you are—the **H** One
	3:29	blasphemes against the **h** Spirit will
Lk	3:22	the **h** Spirit descended upon him
	11:13	in heaven give the **h** Spirit to those
Jn	14:26	the **h** Spirit that the Father will send
Ac	2: 4	they were all filled with the **h** Spirit
	2:27	nor will you suffer your **h** one to see
	5: 3	heart so that you lied to the **h** Spirit
Ro	12: 1	sacrifice, **h** and pleasing to God,
Eph	1: 4	to be **h** and without blemish before
	4:30	do not grieve the **h** Spirit of God,

Heb	6: 4	gift and shared in the **h** Spirit
1Pe	1:16	it is written, "Be **h** because I [am] **h**."
1Jn	2:20	that comes from the **h** one, and you
Jude	1:14	has come with his countless **h** ones
Rev	4: 8	"**H**, **h**, **h** is the Lord God almighty,
	21: 2	I also saw the **h** city, a new
	22:11	still do right, and the **h** still be **h**."

HOME → HOMELESS

Dt	6: 7	Speak of them at **h** and abroad,
Ps	68: 7	Who gives a **h** to the forsaken,
2Co	5: 8	leave the body and go **h** to the Lord.

HOMELESS → HOME

Isa	58: 7	sheltering the oppressed and the **h**;
1Co	4:11	roughly treated, we wander about **h**

HONEST

Lev	19:36	weights, an **h** ephah and an **h** hin. I,

HONEY

Ex	3: 8	a land flowing with milk and **h**,
Jdg	14: 8	of bees and **h** in the lion's carcass.
Ps	19:11	Sweeter also than **h** or drippings
Mt	3: 4	His food was locusts and wild **h**.

HONOR → HONORABLE, HONORED, HONORS

Dt	5:16	'**H** your father and your mother,
1Ch	29:12	"Riches and **h** are from you, and you
Tob	4: 3	**H** your mother, and do not abandon
Ps	8: 6	crowned them with glory and **h**.
Mal	1: 6	a father, where is the **h** due to me?
Mt	13:57	"A prophet is not without **h** except
	15: 4	said, '**H** your father and your mother,'
Jn	12:26	The Father will **h** whoever serves
Ro	13: 7	respect is due, **h** to whom **h** is due.
Eph	6: 2	"**H** your father and mother." This is
1Ti	5:17	who preside well deserve double **h**,
Heb	2: 7	you crowned him with glory and **h**,
Rev	4:11	to receive glory and **h** and power,

HONORABLE → HONOR

Php	4: 8	true, whatever is **h**, whatever is just,

HONORED → HONOR

1Co	12:26	if one part is **h**, all the parts share its

HONORS → HONOR
Mal 1: 6 A son h his father, and a servant
Mt 15: 8 'This people h me with their lips,

HOOFS
Lev 11: 3 any animal that has h you may eat,

HOOK → HOOKS
Mt 17:27 drop in a h, and take the first fish

HOOKS → HOOK
Isa 2: 4 and their spears into pruning h;

HOPE → HOPED, HOPES
Job 17:15 Where then is my h, and my
Ps 62: 6 alone, from whom comes my h.
146: 5 whose h is in the LORD, their God,
Pr 23:18 and your h will not be cut off.
Jer 14: 8 O H of Israel, O LORD, our savior
Da 13:60 blessing God who saves those that h
La 3:21 to mind, as my reason to have h:
Mt 12:21 And in his name the Gentiles will h."
Ro 5: 5 and h does not disappoint,
12:12 Rejoice in h, endure in affliction,
1Co 13:13 So faith, h, love remain, these three;
Col 1:27 it is Christ in you, the h for glory.
1Th 5: 8 the helmet that is h for salvation.
Heb 7:19 other hand, a better h is introduced,
1Pe 1: 3 a living h through the resurrection
1Jn 3: 3 Everyone who has this h based

HOPED → HOPE
Heb 11: 1 is the realization of what is h
1Pe 3: 5 how the holy women who h in God

HOPES → HOPE
1Co 13: 7 believes all things, h all things,

HOREB → = SINAI
Ex 3: 1 he came to H, the mountain of God.
Dt 5: 2 God, made a covenant with us at H;
1Ki 19: 8 nights to the mountain of God, H.

HORN → HORNS
Ps 18: 3 shield, my saving h, my stronghold!
Da 7: 8 a little h, sprang out of their midst,
7: 8 it. This h had eyes like a man,
8: 5 with a prominent h on its forehead

HORNS → HORN
Ge 22:13 a ram caught by its h in the thicket.
Ex 27: 2 At the four corners there are to be h,

Da 8: 3 by the river a ram with two great h,
Rev 5: 6 He had seven h and seven eyes;
9:13 the [four] h of the gold altar before
17: 3 names, with seven heads and ten h.

HORSE → HORSES
Ex 15: 1 h and chariot he has cast
Ps 33:17 Useless is the h for safety; its great
Zec 1: 8 There appeared the driver of a red h,
Rev 6: 2 and there was a white h, and its
19:11 opened, and there was a white h;

HORSES → HORSE
2Ki 2:11 and flaming h came between them,
Ps 20: 8 Some rely on chariots, others on h,
Joel 2: 4 Their appearance is that of h;
Rev 9: 7 was like that of h ready for battle.
19:14 mounted on white h and wearing

HOSANNA
Mk 11:10 that is to come! H in the highest!"
Jn 12:13 out to meet him, and cried out: "H!

HOSEA
Prophet whose wife and family pictured the unfaithfulness of Israel (Hos 1-3).

HOSHEA → = JOSHUA
1. Original name of Joshua (Nu 13:8, 16).
2. Last king of Israel (2Ki 15:30; 17:1-6).

HOSPITABLE → HOSPITALITY
1Ti 3: 2 decent, h, able to teach,
Tit 1: 8 but h, a lover of goodness,
1Pe 4: 9 Be h to one another without

HOSPITALITY → HOSPITABLE
Ro 12:13 needs of the holy ones, exercise h.
1Ti 5:10 practiced h, washed the feet
Heb 13: 2 Do not neglect h, for through it

HOST → HOSTS
2Ki 17:16 and worshiped all the h of heaven,
Lk 2:13 of the heavenly h with the angel,

HOSTILE
Col 1:21 and h in mind because of evil deeds

HOSTS → HOST
Dt 4:19 or any star among the heavenly h,
1Sa 1: 3 his city to worship the LORD of h
Ps 46: 8 The LORD of h is with us;
Isa 48: 2 Israel, whose name is the LORD of h.

HOT
Rev 3:15 that you are neither cold nor h.
3:15 h. I wish you were either cold or h.

HOUR
Mt 24:36 "But of that day and h no one knows,
Jn 2: 4 affect me? My h has not yet come."
17: 1 and said, "Father, the h has come.

HOUSE → HOUSEHOLD, HOUSES, HOUSETOP, HOUSETOPS, STOREHOUSE
Ex 20:17 shall not covet your neighbor's h.
2Sa 7:11 that he will establish a h for you.
Ezr 1: 5 to go up to build the h of the LORD
Ps 69:10 zeal for your h consumes me, I am
127: 1 Unless the LORD build the h,
Pr 9: 1 Wisdom has built her h, she has set
Isa 56: 7 and make joyful in my h of prayer;
56: 7 altar, For my h shall be called a h
Mt 7:24 be like a wise man who built his h
21:13 written: 'My h shall be a h of prayer,'
Mk 3:25 And if a h is divided against itself,
3:25 that h will not be able to stand.
Jn 2:17 "Zeal for your h will consume me."
14: 2 In my Father's h there are many
1Pe 2: 5 a spiritual h to be a holy priesthood

HOUSEHOLD → HOUSE
Jos 24:15 As for me and my h, we will serve
Mic 7: 6 a man's enemies are those of his h.
Mt 10:36 one's enemies will be those of his h.'
Eph 2:19 ones and members of the h of God,
1Ti 3: 4 He must manage his own h well,
3:15 how to behave in the h of God,
1Pe 4:17 to begin with the h of God; if it

HOUSES → HOUSE
Ex 12:27 LORD, who passed over the h
12:27 the Egyptians, he spared our h.' "
Mt 19:29 everyone who has given up h

HOUSETOP → HOUSE
Mt 24:17 a person on the h must not go down

HOUSETOPS → HOUSE
Mt 10:27 hear whispered, proclaim on the h.

HULDAH
Prophetess inquired by Hilkiah for Josiah (2Ki 22; 2Ch 34:14-28).

HUMAN → HUMANKIND, HUMANS
Jdt 8:16 nor h, that he may be given
Da 5: 5 the fingers of a h hand appeared,

Hos 11: 4 I drew them with **h** cords,
Mt   15: 9 teaching as doctrines **h** precepts.' "
1Co   2:13 not with words taught by **h** wisdom,
Php   2: 7 coming in **h** likeness; and found **h**
1Ti   2: 5 There is also one mediator between God and the **h** race, Christ Jesus, himself **h**,
Rev   4: 7 had a face like that of a **h** being,

HUMANS → HUMAN
Ps   8: 5 What are **h** that you are mindful

HUMBLE → HUMBLED, HUMBLY, HUMILITY
Ps   25: 9 Guides the **h** rightly, and teaches
     25: 9 **h** rightly, and teaches the **h** the way.
Zep   2: 3 the LORD, all you **h** of the earth,
Mt   11:29 me, for I am meek and **h** of heart;
Jas   4:10 **H** yourselves before the Lord and he
1Pe   5: 5 proud but bestows favor on the **h**."

HUMBLED → HUMBLE
Lk   14:11 who exalts himself will be **h**,
Php   2: 8 he **h** himself, becoming obedient

HUMBLY → HUMBLE
Mic   6: 8 and to walk **h** with your God.

HUMILITY → HUMBLE
Pr   15:33 wisdom, and **h** goes before honors.
Zep   2: 3 Seek justice, seek **h**; perhaps you
Col   3:12 kindness, **h**, gentleness,
1Pe   5: 5 clothe yourselves with **h** in your

HUNDRED
Ge   17:17 born to a man who is a **h** years old?
Isa 65:20 youth who reaches but a **h** years,
     65:20 of a **h** shall be thought accursed.
Ro   4:19 (for he was almost a **h** years old)

HUNG
Ps 137: 2 of that land we **h** up our harps.

HUNGER → HUNGRY
Dt   8: 3 therefore let you be afflicted with **h**,
Mt   5: 6 Blessed are they who **h** and thirst
Rev   7:16 They will not **h** or thirst anymore,

HUNGRY → HUNGER
Ps   50:12 Were I **h**, I would not tell you,
    146: 7 gives food to the **h**. The LORD sets
Pr   25:21 If your enemy be **h**, give him food

Mt   12: 1 His disciples were **h** and began
Ro   12:20 "if your enemy is **h**, feed him; if he is

HUSBAND → HUSBANDS
Ge   3: 6 it; and she also gave some to her **h**,
      3:16 Yet your urge shall be for your **h**,
Pr   31:28 praise her; her **h**, too, extols her:
Sir 26: 1 Happy the **h** of a good wife,
Isa 54: 5 has become your **h** is your Maker;
1Co   7:10 wife should not separate from her **h**
Eph   5:23 For the **h** is head of his wife just as
Rev 21: 2 as a bride adorned for her **h**.

HUSBANDS → HUSBAND
Jn   4:18 For you have had five **h**,
Eph   5:25 **H**, love your wives, even as Christ
Col   3:18 be subordinate to your **h**, as is
Tit   2: 4 train younger women to love their **h**
1Pe   3: 7 you **h** should live with your wives

HUSHAI
Wise man of David; foiled Absalom's revolt (2Sa 15:32-37; 16:15-17:16).

HYMN → HYMNS
Mt   26:30 after singing a **h**, they went

HYMNS → HYMN
Eph   5:19 one another [in] psalms and **h**
Col   3:16 singing psalms, **h**, and spiritual

HYPOCRISY → HYPOCRITE, HYPOCRITES
Mt   23:28 but inside you are filled with **h**
Mk   12:15 Knowing their **h** he said to them,

HYPOCRITE → HYPOCRISY
Lk   6:42 You **h**! Remove the wooden beam

HYPOCRITES → HYPOCRISY
Mt   6: 5 do not be like the **h**, who love
     23:13 to you, scribes and Pharisees, you **h**.
Mk   7: 6 did Isaiah prophesy about you **h**,

HYSSOP
Ex   12:22 Then take a bunch of **h**, and dipping
Nu   19: 6 **h** and scarlet yarn and throw them
Ps   51: 9 Cleanse me with **h**, that I may be
Jn   19:29 soaked in wine on a sprig of **h**

I

IDLE
Ecc 11: 6 at evening let not your hand be **i**:

IDOL → IDOLS
Isa 40:19 An **i**, cast by a craftsman,
1Co 10:19 anything? Or that an **i** is anything?

IDOLS → IDOL
Ex   20: 4 You shall not carve **i** for yourselves
1Ma   1:43 they sacrificed to **i** and profaned
Ps 115: 4 Their **i** are silver and gold, the work
1Co   8: 1 in regard to meat sacrificed to **i**:

IGNORANCE → IGNORANT
Ac   17:30 God has overlooked the times of **i**,
1Pe   2:15 doing good you may silence the **i**

IGNORANT → IGNORANCE
Heb   5: 2 is able to deal patiently with the **i**
2Pe   3:16 things hard to understand that the **i**

ILL
1Co 11:30 That is why many among you are **i**

ILLEGITIMATE
Jn   8:41 [So] they said to him, "We are not **i**.

IMAGE → IMAGES
Ge   1:26 "Let us make man in our **i**, after our
1Co 15:49 Just as we have borne the **i**
     15:49 also bear the **i** of the heavenly one.
Col   1:15 He is the **i** of the invisible God,
Rev 20: 4 or its **i** nor had accepted its mark

IMAGES → IMAGE
Nu   33:52 all their stone figures and molten **i**,

IMITATE → IMITATORS
Heb 13: 7 of their way of life and **i** their faith.
3Jn   1:11 Beloved, do not **i** evil but **i** good.

IMITATORS → IMITATE
1Co 11: 1 Be **i** of me, as I am of Christ.
Eph   5: 1 So be **i** of God, as beloved children,

IMMANUEL → = EMMANUEL
Isa   7:14 bear a son, and shall name him **I**.
      8: 8 wings the full width of your land, **I**!

IMMORAL → IMMORALITY
1Co   5: 9 letter not to associate with **i** people,
Heb 12:16 that no one be an **i** or profane

IMMORALITY → IMMORAL
2Co 12:21 have not repented of the impurity, **i**,

IMMORTAL → IMMORTALITY
Ro   1:23 exchanged the glory of the **i** God

IMMORTALITY → IMMORTAL
1Co 15:53 is mortal must clothe itself with **i**.
1Ti   6:16 who alone has **i**, who dwells

IMPERISHABLE
1Co 9:25 a perishable crown, but we an **i** one.
1Pe 1: 4 to an inheritance that is **i**, undefiled,

IMPORTANCE
1Co 15: 3 handed on to you as of first **i** what I

IMPOSSIBLE
Zec 8: 6 if this should seem **i** in the eyes
     8: 6 it in those days be **i** in my eyes also,
Mt 17:20 move. Nothing will be **i** for you."
Mk 10:27 "For human beings it is **i**, but not
Heb 11: 6 without faith it is **i** to please him,

IMPURE → IMPURITY
Eph 5: 5 this, that no immoral or **i** or greedy
1Th 2: 3 was not from delusion or **i** motives,

IMPURITY → IMPURE
Gal 5:19 immorality, **i**, licentiousness,
1Th 4: 7 For God did not call us to **i**

INCENSE → FRANKINCENSE
Ex 25: 6 anointing oil and for the fragrant **i**;

INCREASE → INCREASED
Lk 17: 5 apostles said to the Lord, "**I** our faith."
Jn 3:30 He must **i**; I must decrease."

INCREASED → INCREASE
Ro 5:20 where sin **i**, grace overflowed all

INDEPENDENT
1Co 11:11 Woman is not **i** of man or man

INFANTS
Ps 8: 3 Out of the mouths of babes and **i**
Mt 21:16 'Out of the mouths of **i** and nurslings
1Co 14:20 In respect to evil be like **i**,

INFIRMITIES
Isa 53: 4 Yet it was our **i** that he bore,
Mt 8:17 "He took away our **i** and bore our

INHERIT → INHERITANCE
Lk 10:25 what must I do to **i** eternal life?
1Co 6: 9 the unjust will not **i** the kingdom
Heb 1:14 sake of those who are to **i** salvation?

INHERITANCE → INHERIT
Col 1:12 to share in the **i** of the holy ones
Heb 9:15 may receive the promised eternal **i**.

INIQUITIES
Lev 16:22 is to carry off their **i** to an isolated
Ro 4: 7 are they whose **i** are forgiven

INJURY
Lev 24:20 The same **i** that a man gives another

INJUSTICE
Ro 9:14 to say? Is there **i** on the part of God?

INN
Lk 2: 7 there was no room for them in the **i**.
     10:34 took him to an **i** and cared for him.

INNER → INWARDLY
Mt 24:26 'He is in the **i** rooms,' do not believe
2Co 4:16 our **i** self is being renewed day

INNOCENCE → INNOCENT
Ps 26: 6 I will wash my hands in **i** and walk
Hos 8: 5 they be unable to attain **i** in Israel?

INNOCENT → INNOCENCE
Pr 6:17 tongue, and hands that shed **i** blood;
Mt 27:24 saying, "I am **i** of this man's blood.

INQUIRE
Dt 12:30 Do not **i** regarding their gods,

INSCRIBED → INSCRIPTION
Rev 19:12 He had a name **i** that no one knows

INSCRIPTION → INSCRIBED
Mk 15:26 The **i** of the charge against him
2Ti 2:19 bearing this **i**, "The Lord knows

INSIGHT
Eph 1: 8 upon us. In all wisdom and **i**,

INSPIRED
2Ti 3:16 All scripture is **i** by God and is

INSTITUTION
1Pe 2:13 to every human **i** for the Lord's sake,

INSTRUCT → INSTRUCTED, INSTRUCTION
1Co 14:19 mind, so as to **i** others also, than ten

INSTRUCTED → INSTRUCT
Isa 40:13 LORD, or has **i** him as his counselor?

INSTRUCTION → INSTRUCT
Pr 8:10 Receive my **i** in preference to silver,
Mic 4: 2 For from Zion shall go forth **i**,
Ro 15: 4 previously was written for our **i**,
1Ti 1: 5 The aim of this **i** is love from a pure

INSULTS
2Co 12:10 I am content with weaknesses, **i**,

INTEGRITY
Tit 2: 7 respect, with **i** in your teaching,

INTELLIGENT
Pr 11:12 no sense, but the **i** man keeps silent.

INTERCEDES → INTERCESSION
Ro 8:26 the Spirit itself **i** with inexpressible

INTERCESSION → INTERCEDES
Heb 7:25 he lives forever to make **i** for them.

INTERMARRY → MARRIAGE
Dt 7: 3 You shall not **i** with them,

INTERPRET → INTERPRETATION, INTERPRETATIONS
Ge 41:15 certain dreams that no one can **i**.
     41:15 you are told a dream you can **i** it."
1Co 12:30 Do all speak in tongues? Do all **i**?

INTERPRETATION → INTERPRET
1Co 12:10 of tongues; to another **i** of tongues.
2Pe 1:20 that is a matter of personal **i**,

INTERPRETATIONS → INTERPRET
Ge 40: 8 to them, "Surely, **i** come from God.

INVISIBLE
Col 1:15 He is the image of the **i** God,
1Ti 1:17 ages, incorruptible, **i**, the only God,

INVITE → INVITES
Lk 14:13 you hold a banquet, **i** the poor,

INVITES → INVITE
1Co 10:27 If an unbeliever **i** you and you want

INVOKE
1Pe 1:17 if you **i** as Father him who judges

INWARDLY → INNER
Ro 2:29 one is a Jew **i**, and circumcision is

IRON
Ps 2: 9 an **i** rod you shall shepherd them,
Pr 27:17 As **i** sharpens **i**, so man sharpens his
Da 2:33 the legs **i**, its feet partly **i** and partly
Rev 19:15 He will rule them with an **i** rod,

IRREVOCABLE
Ro 11:29 the gifts and the call of God are **i**.

ISAAC
Son of Abraham by Sarah (Ge 17:19; 21:1-7; 1Ch 1:28). Abrahamic covenant perpetuated with (Ge 17:21; 26:2-5). Offered up by Abraham (Ge 22; Heb 11:17-19). Rebekah taken as wife (Ge 24). Inherited Abraham's estate (Ge 25:5). Father of Esau and Jacob (Ge 25:19-26; 1Ch 1:34). Nearly lost Rebekah to Abimelech (Ge 26:1-11). Covenant with Abimelech (Ge 26:12-31). Tricked into blessing Jacob (Ge 27). Death (Ge 35:27-29). Father of Israel (Ex 3:6; Dt 29:13; Ro 9:10).

ISAIAH

Prophet to Judah (Isa 1:1). Called by the LORD (Isa 6). Announced judgment to Ahaz (Isa 7), deliverance from Assyria to Hezekiah (2Ki 19; Isa 36-37), deliverance from death to Hezekiah (2Ki 20:1-11; Isa 38). Chronicler of Judah's history (2Ch 26:22; 32:32).

ISCARIOT

| Mt | 10: 4 | and Judas **I** who betrayed him. |
| Lk | 22: 3 | Judas, the one surnamed **I**, who was |

ISHBAAL

Son of Saul; would-be king (2Sa 2:8-4:12).

ISHMAEL

Son of Abraham by Hagar (Ge 16; 1Ch 1:28). Blessed, but not son of covenant (Ge 17:18-21; Gal 4:21-31). Sent away by Sarah (Ge 21:8-21). Children (Ge 25:12-18; 1Ch 1:29-31). Death (Ge 25:17).

ISRAEL → ISRAELITE, ISRAELITES, = JACOB

1. Name given to Jacob (Ge 32:28; 35:10).
2. Corporate name of Jacob's descendants; often specifically Northern Kingdom.

Ge	49:28	All these are the twelve tribes of **I**,
Ex	28:11	with the names of the sons of **I**
Nu	24:17	and a staff shall rise from **I**,
Dt	6: 4	"Hear, O **I**! The LORD is our God,
Ps	125: 5	with the wicked. Peace upon **I**!
Jer	31:31	a new covenant with the house of **I**
Hos	11: 1	When **I** was a child I loved him,
Mt	2: 6	who is to shepherd my people **I**.' "
Mk	12:29	replied, "The first is this: 'Hear, O **I**!
Lk	22:30	judging the twelve tribes of **I**.
Ac	1: 6	going to restore the kingdom to **I**?"
Ro	9: 6	failed. For not all who are of **I** are **I**,
Heb	8: 8	house of **I** and the house of Judah.

ISRAELITE → ISRAEL

| Jn | 1:47 | and said of him, "Here is a true **I**. |
| Ro | 11: 1 | For I too am an **I**, a descendant |

ISRAELITES → ISRAEL

| Ex | 2:23 | Still the **I** groaned and cried |
| | 29:45 | I will dwell in the midst of the **I** |

ISSACHAR

Son of Jacob by Leah (Ge 30:18; 35:23; 1Ch 2:1). Tribe of blessed (Ge 49:14-15; Dt 33:18-19), numbered (Nu 1:29; 26:25), allotted land (Jos 19:17-23; Eze 48:25), assisted Deborah (Jdg 5:15), 12,000 from (Rev 7:7).

ITCHING

J

JACOB → = ISRAEL

1. Son of Isaac, younger twin of Esau (Ge 26:21-26; 1Ch 1:34). Bought Esau's birth-right (Ge 26:29-34); tricked Isaac into blessing him (Ge 27:1-37). Fled to Haran (Ge 28:1-5). Abrahamic covenant perpetuated through (Ge 28:13-15; Mal 1:2). Vision at Bethel (Ge 28:10-22). Served Laban for Rachel and Leah (Ge 29:1-30). Children (Ge 29:31-30:24; 35:16-26; 1Ch 2-9). Flocks increased (Ge 30:25-43). Returned to Canaan (Ge 31). Wrestled with God; name changed to Israel (Ge 32:22-32). Reconciled to Esau (Ge 33). Returned to Bethel (Ge 35:1-15). Favored Joseph (Ge 37:3). Sent sons to Egypt during famine (Ge 42-43). Settled in Egypt (Ge 46). Blessed Ephraim and Manasseh (Ge 48). Blessed sons (Ge 49:1-28; Heb 11:21). Death (Ge 49:29-33). Burial (Ge 50:1-14).

2. Corporate name of Jacob's descendants; often specifically Northern Kingdom.

1Ma	1:28	all the house of **J** was covered
Ps	135: 4	For the LORD has chosen **J**, Israel as
Mic	7:20	You will show faithfulness to **J**,
Ro	9:13	is written: "I loved **J** but hated Esau."

JAEL

Woman who killed the Canaanite general, Sisera (Jdg 4:17-22; 5:6, 24-27).

JAIRUS

Synagogue ruler whose daughter Jesus raised (Mk 5:22-43; Lk 8:41-56).

JAMES

1. Apostle; brother of John (Mt 4:21-22; 10:2; Mk 3:17; Lk 5:1-10). At transfiguration (Mt 17:1-13; Mk 9:1-13; Lk 9:28-36). Killed by Herod (Ac 12:2).

2. Apostle (Mt 10:3; Mk 3:18; Lk 6:15).

3. Brother of Jesus (Mt 13:55; Mk 6:3; Lk 24:10; Gal 1:19) and Judas (Jude 1). With believers before Pentecost (Ac 1:13). Leader of church at Jerusalem (Ac 12:17; 15; 21:18; Gal 2:9, 12). Author of epistle (Jas 1:1).

JAPHETH

Son of Noah (Ge 5:32; 1Ch 1:4-5). Blessed (Ge 9:18-28). Sons of (Ge 10:2-5).

JAR → JARS

1Ki	17:14	'The **j** of flour shall not go empty,
Mk	14: 3	with an alabaster **j** of perfumed oil,
	14: 3	She broke the alabaster **j** and poured
Lk	22:10	a man will meet you carrying a **j**

JARS → JAR

| Jn | 2: 6 | there were six stone water **j** there |

JEALOUS

Ex	34:14	other god, for the LORD is 'the **J** One';
	34:14	the LORD is 'the **J** One'; a **j** God is he.
Dt	4:24	God, is a consuming fire, a **j** God.
Eze	39:25	and I will be **j** for my holy name.
Ro	10:19	"I will make you **j** of those who are

JEBUSITES

Ex	3: 8	Amorites, Perizzites, Hivites and **J**.
Jos	15:63	the **J** who lived in Jerusalem
	15:63	so the **J** dwell in Jerusalem beside

JECONIAH → See JEHOIACHIN

JEHOAHAZ

1. Son of Jehu; king of Israel (2Ki 13:1-9).
2. Son of Josiah; king of Judah (2Ki 23:31-34; 2Ch 36:1-4).

JEHOASH → = JOASH

1. Son of Ahaziah, king of Judah (2Ki 12). See Joash, 1.
2. Son of Jehoahaz; king of Israel. Defeat of Aram prophesied by Elisha (2Ki 13:10-25). Defeated Amaziah in Jerusalem (2Ki 14:1-16). See Joash, 2.

JEHOIACHIN → = CONIAH, = JECONIAH

Son of Jehoiakim; king of Judah exiled by Nebuchadnezzar (2Ki 24:8-17; 2Ch 36:8-10; Eze 1:2). Status improved (2Ki 25:27-30; Jer 52:31-34).

JEHOIADA

Priest who sheltered Joash from Athaliah (2Ki 11-12; 2Ch 22:11-24:16).

JEHOIAKIM → = ELIAKIM

Son of Josiah; made king of Judah by Nebuchadnezzar (2Ki 23:34-24:6; 2Ch 36:4-8; Jer 22:18-23). Burned scroll of Jeremiah's prophecies (Jer 36).

JEHORAM → = JORAM

1. Son of Jehoshaphat; king of Judah. Prophesied against by Elijah; killed by the LORD (2Ch 21). See Joram, 1.
2. Son of Ahab; king of Israel (2Ch 22:5). Joined Jehoshaphat against Moab (2Ki 3). See Joram, 2.

JEHOSHAPHAT

1. Son of Asa; king of Judah. Strengthened his kingdom (2Ch 17). Joined with Ahab against Aram (2Ki 22; 2Ch 18). Established judges (2Ch 19). Joined Joram against Moab (2Ki 3; 2Ch 20).
2. Valley of judgment (Joel 3:2, 12).

JEHU

1. Prophet against Baasha (2Ki 16:1-7).
2. King of Israel. Anointed by Elijah to obliterate house of Ahab (1Ki 19:16-17); anointed by servant of Elisha (2Ki 9:1-13). Killed Joram and Ahaziah (2Ki 9:14-29; 2Ch 22:7-9), Jezebel (2Ki 9:30-37), relatives of Ahab (2Ki 10:1-17; Hos 1:4), ministers of Baal (2Ki 10:18-29). Death (2Ki 10:30-36).

JEPHTHAH

Judge from Gilead who delivered Israel from Ammon (Jdg 10:6-12:7). Made rash vow concerning his daughter (Jdg 11:30-40).

JEREMIAH

Prophet to Judah (Jer 1:1-3). Called by the LORD (Jer 1). Put in stocks (Jer 20:1-3). Threatened for prophesying (Jer 11:18-23; 26). Opposed by Hananiah (Jer 28). Scroll burned (Jer 36). Imprisoned (Jer 37). Thrown into cistern (Jer 38). Forced to Egypt with those fleeing Babylonians (Jer 43).

JERICHO

Jos 6: 2 "I have delivered **J** and its king
1Ki 16:34 his reign, Hiel from Bethel rebuilt **J**.
Lk 18:35 as he approached **J** a blind man was

JEROBOAM

1. Official of Solomon; rebelled to become first king of Israel (1Ki 11:26-40; 12:1-20; 2Ch 10). Idolatry (1Ki 12:25-33; Tob 1:5; Sir 47:23); judgment for (1Ki 13-14; 2Ch 13).
2. Son of Jehoash; king of Israel (1Ki 14:23-29).

JERUSALEM

2Sa 5: 5 thirty-three years in **J** over all Israel
15:29 took the ark of God back to **J**
2Ki 25:10 down the walls that surrounded **J**.
Ezr 2: 1 and who came back to **J** and Judah,
Ne 2:17 how **J** lies in ruins and its gates
2:17 let us rebuild the wall of **J**,
1Ma 1:29 he came to **J** with a strong force.
Isa 40: 2 Speak tenderly to **J**, and proclaim
La 1: 8 of which she is guilty, **J** is defiled;
Da 9:25 of the word that **J** was to be rebuilt
Mic 4: 2 and the word of the LORD from **J**.
Zec 1:14 I am deeply moved for the sake of **J**
Zec 14: 8 living waters shall flow from **J**,
Mt 23:37 "**J, J**, you who kill the prophets
Lk 4: 9 Then he led him to **J**, made him
Gal 4:25 it corresponds to the present **J**,
Heb 12:22 the heavenly **J**, and countless angels
Rev 21: 2 city, a new **J**, coming down

JESSE

Father of David (Ru 4:17-22; 1Sa 16; 1Ch 2:12-17).

JESUS

1. Jesus the Messiah.
LIFE: Genealogy (Mt 1:1-17; Lk 3:21-37). Birth announced (Mt 1:18-25; Lk 1:26-45). Birth (Mt 2:1-12; Lk 2:1-40). Escape to Egypt (Mt 2:13-23). As a boy in the temple (Lk 2:41-52). Baptism (Mt 3:13-17; Mk 1:9-11; Lk 3:21-22; Jn 1:32-34). Temptation (Mt 4:1-11; Mk 1:12-13; Lk 4:1-13). Ministry in Galilee (Mt 4:12-18:35; Mk 1:14-9:50; Lk 4:14-13:9; Jn 1:35-2:11; 4; 6), Transfiguration (Mt 17:1-8; Mk 9:2-8; Lk 9:28-36), on the way to Jerusalem (Mt 19-20; Mk 10; Lk 13:10-19:27), in Jerusalem (Mt 21-25; Mk 11-13; Lk 19:28-21:38; Jn 2:12-3:36; 5; 7-12). Last supper (Mt 26:17-35; Mk 14:12-31; Lk 22:1-38; Jn 13-17). Arrest and trial (Mt 26:36-27:31; Mk 14:43-15:20; Lk 22:39-23:25; Jn 18:1-19:16). Crucifixion (Mt 27:32-66; Mk 15:21-47; Lk 23:26-55; Jn 19:28-42). Resurrection and appearances (Mt 28; Mk 16; Lk 24; Jn 20-21; Ac 1:1-11; 7:56; 9:3-6; 1Co 15:1-8; Rev 1:1-20).

MIRACLES. *Healings:* official's son (Jn 4:43-54), demoniac in Capernaum (Mk 1:23-26; Lk 4:33-35), Peter's mother-in-law (Mt 8:14-17; Mk 1:29-31; Lk 4:38-39), leper (Mt 8:2-4; Mk 1:40-45; Lk 5:12-16), paralytic (Mt 9:1-8; Mk 2:1-12; Lk 5:17-26), cripple (Jn 5:1-9), shriveled hand (Mt 12:10-13; Mk 3:1-5; Lk 6:6-11), centurion's servant (Mt 8:5-13; Lk 7:1-10), widow's son raised (Lk 7:11-17), demoniac (Mt 12:22-23; Lk 11:14), Gadarene demoniacs (Mt 8:28-34; Mk 5:1-20; Lk 8:26-39), woman's bleeding and Jairus' daughter (Mt 9:18-26; Mk 5:21-43; Lk 8:40-56), blind man (Mt 9:27-31), mute man (Mt 9:32-33), Canaanite woman's daughter (Mt 15:21-28; Mk 7:24-30), deaf man (Mk 7:31-37), blind man (Mk 8:22-26), demoniac boy (Mt 17:14-18; Mk 9:14-29; Lk 9:37-43), ten lepers (Lk 17:11-19), man born blind (Jn 9:1-7), Lazarus raised (Jn 11), crippled woman (Lk 13:11-17), man with dropsy (Lk 14:1-6), two blind men (Mt 20:29-34; Mk 10:46-52; Lk 18:35-43), Malchus' ear (Lk 22:50-51). *Other Miracles:* water to wine (Jn 2:1-11), catch of fish (Lk 5:1-11), storm stilled (Mt 8:23-27; Mk 4:37-41; Lk 8:22-25), 5,000 fed (Mt 14:15-21; Mk 6:35-44; Lk 9:10-17; Jn 6:1-14), walking on water (Mt 14:25-33; Mk 6:48-52; Jn 6:15-21), 4,000 fed (Mt 15:32-39; Mk 8:1-9), money from fish (Mt 17:24-27), fig tree cursed (Mt 21:18-22; Mk 11:12-14), catch of fish (Jn 21:1-14).

MAJOR TEACHING: Sermon on the Mount (Mt 5-7; Lk 6:17-49), to Nicodemus (Jn 3), to Samaritan woman (Jn 4), Bread of Life (Jn 6:22-59), at Feast of Tabernacles (Jn 7-8), woes to Pharisees (Mt 23; Lk 11:37-54), Good Shepherd (Jn 10:1-18), Olivet Discourse (Mt 24-25; Mk 13; Lk 21:5-36), Upper Room Discourse (Jn 13-16).

PARABLES: Sower (Mt 13:3-23; Mk 4:3-25; Lk 8:5-18), seed's growth (Mk 4:26-29), wheat and weeds (Mt 13:24-30, 36-43), mustard seed (Mt 13:31-32; Mk 4:30-32), yeast (Mt 13:33; Lk 13:20-21), hidden treasure (Mt 13:44), valuable pearl (Mt 13:45-46), net (Mt 13:47-51), house owner (Mt 13:52), good Samaritan (Lk 10:25-37), unmerciful servant (Mt 18:15-35), lost sheep (Mt 18:10-14; Lk 15:4-7), lost coin (Lk 15:8-10), prodigal son (Lk 15:11-32), dishonest manager (Lk 16:1-13), rich man and Lazarus (Lk 16:19-31), persistent widow (Lk 18:1-8), Pharisee and tax collector (Lk 18:9-14), payment of workers (Mt 20:1-16), tenants in the vineyard (Mt 21:28-46; Mt 12:1-12; Lk 20:9-19), wedding banquet (Mt 22:1-14), faithful servant (Mt 24:45-51), ten virgins (Mt 25:1-13), talents (Mt 25:1-30; Lk 19:12-27).

DISCIPLES see APOSTLES. Call (Jn 1:35-51; Mt 4:18-22; 9:9; Mk 1:16-20; 2:13-14; Lk 5:1-11, 27-28). Named Apostles (Mk 3:13-19; Lk 6:12-16). Twelve sent out (Mt 10; Mk 6:7-11; Lk 9:1-5). Seventy sent out (Lk 10:1-24). Defection of (Jn 6:60-71; Mt 26:56; Mk 14:50-52). Final commission (Mt 28:16-20; Jn 21:15-23; Ac 1:3-8).

Ac 9: 5 "I am **J**, whom you are persecuting.
1Co 8: 6 and one Lord, **J** Christ,
Php 2:10 that at the name of **J** every knee
2Th 2: 1 to the coming of our Lord **J** Christ
1Ti 1:15 Christ **J** came into the world to save
Heb 12: 2 while keeping our eyes fixed on **J**,
13: 8 **J** Christ is the same yesterday,
1Jn 1: 7 the blood of his Son **J** cleanses us
Rev 1: 1 The revelation of **J** Christ,
22:20 coming soon." Amen! Come, Lord **J**!

2. Disciple, also called Justus (Col 4:11).
3. Writer of Sirach (Sir Pr:1; 50:27; 51:1).

JETHRO

Father-in-law and adviser of Moses (Ex 3:1; 4:18; 18). Also known as Reuel (Ex 2:18).

JEW → JEWS, JUDAISM

Est 10: 3 The **J** Mordecai was next in rank
Zec 8:23 take hold of every **J** by the edge
Ro 1:16 believes: for **J** first, and then Greek.
2:29 Rather, one is a **J** inwardly,
1Co 9:20 To the Jews I became like a **J** to win
Col 3:11 Here there is not Greek and **J**,

JEWS → JEW

Est 3:13 that all the **J**, young and old,
Mt 2: 2 "Where is the newborn king of the **J**?
27:11 him, "Are you the king of the **J**?"
Jn 4:22 because salvation is from the **J**.
Ro 3:29 Does God belong to **J** alone?

JEZEBEL

Sidonian wife of Ahab (1Ki 16:31). Promoted Baal worship (1Ki 16:32-33). Killed prophets of the LORD (1Ki 18:4, 13). Opposed Elijah (1Ki 19:1-2). Had Naboth killed (1Ki 21). Death (1Ki 21:17-24; 2Ki 9:30-37). Metaphor of immorality (Rev 2:20).

JEZREEL

2Ki 10: 7 baskets, and sent them to Jehu in **J**.
Hos 1: 4 Give him the name **J**, for in a little
1: 4 for the bloodshed at **J** And bring

JOAB

Nephew of David (1Ch 2:16). Commander of his army (2Sa 8:16). Victorious over Ammon (2Sa 10; 1Ch 19), Rabbah (2Sa 11; 1Ch 20), Jerusalem (1Ch 11:6), Absalom (2Sa 18), Sheba (2Sa 20). Killed Abner (2Sa 3:22-39), Amasa (2Sa 20:1-13). Numbered David's army (2Sa 24; 1Ch 21). Sided with Adonijah (1Ki 1:17, 19). Killed by Benaiah (1Ki 2:5-6, 28-35).

JOASH → = JEHOASH
1. Son of Ahaziah; king of Judah. Sheltered from Athaliah by Jehoiada (2Ki 11; 2Ch 22:10-23:21). Repaired temple (2Ch 24). See Jehoash, 1.
2. Son of Jehoahaz, king of Israel (2Ki 13; 2Ch 25:17-25). See Jehoash, 2.

JOB
Wealthy man from Uz; feared God (Job 1:1-5). Integrity tested by disaster (Job 1:6-22), personal affliction (Job 2). Maintained innocence in debate with three friends (Job 3-31), Elihu (Job 32-37). Rebuked by the LORD (Job 38-41). Vindicated and restored to greater stature by the LORD (Job 42). Example of righteousness (Eze 14:14, 20; Sir 49:9).

JOEL
1. Son of Samuel (1Sa 8:2; 1Ch 6:28).
2. Prophet (Joel 1:1; Ac 2:16).

JOHANAN
1. First high priest in the temple (1Ch 6:9-10).
2. Jewish leader who tried to save Gedaliah from assassination (Jer 40:13-14); took Jews, including Jeremiah, to Egypt (Jer 40-43).

JOHN
1. Son of Zechariah and Elizabeth (Lk 1). Called the Baptist (Mt 3:1-12; Mk 1:2-8). Witness to Jesus (Mt 3:11-12; Mk 1:7-8; Lk 3:15-18; Jn 1:6-35; 3:27-30; 5:33-36). Doubts about Jesus (Mt 11:2-6; Lk 7:18-23). Arrest (Mt 4:12; Mk 1:14). Execution (Mt 14:1-12; Mk 6:14-29; Lk 9:7-9). Ministry compared to Elijah (Mt 11:7-19; Mk 9:11-13; Lk 7:24-35).
2. Apostle; brother of James (Mt 4:21-22; 10:2; Mk 3:17; Lk 5:1-10). At transfiguration (Mt 17:1-13; Mk 9:1-13; Lk 9:28-36). Desire to be greatest (Mk 10:35-45). Leader of church at Jerusalem (Ac 4:1-3; Gal 2:9). Elder who wrote epistles (2Jn 1; 3Jn 1). Prophet who wrote Revelation (Rev 1:1; 22:8).
3. Cousin of Barnabas, co-worker with Paul, (Ac 12:12-13:13; 15:37; see Mark).
4. Son of Simon Maccabeus (1Ma 13:53; 16).

JOIN → JOINED
Eze 37:17 Then **j** the two sticks together,

JOINED → JOIN
Mt 19: 6 what God has **j** together, no human

JOINT → JOINTS
Ro 8:17 heirs of God and **j** heirs with Christ,

JOINTS → JOINT
Heb 4:12 soul and spirit, **j** and marrow,

JONAH
Prophet in days of Jeroboam II (2Ki 14:25). Called to Nineveh; fled to Tarshish (Jnh 1:1-3). Cause of storm; thrown into sea (Jnh 1:4-16). Swallowed by fish (Jnh 1:17). Prayer (Jnh 2). Preached to Nineveh (Jnh 3). Attitude reproved by the LORD (Jnh 4). Sign of (Mt 12:39-41; Lk 11:29-32).

JONATHAN
1. Son of Saul (1Sa 13:16; 1Ch 8:33). Valiant warrior (1Sa 13-14). Relation to David (1Sa 18:1-4; 19-20; 23:16-18). Killed at Gilboa (1Sa 31). Mourned by David (2Sa 1).
2. Brother and successor of Judas Maccabeus (1Ma 2:5; 9:28-31).

JOPPA
Jnh 1: 3 He went down to **J**, found a ship
Ac 9:43 And he stayed a long time in **J**

JORAM → = JEHORAM
1. Son of Jehoshaphat; king of Judah (2Ki 8:16-24). See Jehoram, 1.
2. Son of Ahab; king of Israel. Killed with Ahaziah by Jehu (2Ki 8:25-29; 9:14-26; 2Ch 22:5-9). See Jehoram, 2.

JORDAN
Ge 13:10 watered the whole **J** Plain was as far
Nu 34:12 boundary shall continue along the **J**
Jos 3:17 of the **J** until the whole nation had
Mt 3: 6 in the **J** River as they acknowledged

JOSEPH → = BARNABAS, = BARSABBAS
1. Son of Jacob by Rachel (Ge 30:24; 1Ch 2:2). Favored by Jacob, hated by brothers (Ge 37:3-4). Dreams (Ge 37:5-11). Sold by brothers (Ge 37:12-36). Served Potiphar; imprisoned by false accusation (Ge 39). Interpreted dreams of Pharaoh's servants (Ge 40), of Pharaoh (Ge 41:4-40). Made greatest in Egypt (Ge 41:41-57). Sold grain to brothers (Ge 42-45). Brought Jacob and sons to Egypt (Ge 46-47). Sons Ephraim and Manasseh blessed (Ge 48). Blessed (Ge 49:22-26; Dt 33:13-17). Death (Ge 50:22-26; Ex 13:19; Heb 11:22). 12,000 from (Rev 7:8).
2. Husband of Mary mother of Jesus (Mt 1:16-24; 2:13-19; Lk 1:27; 2; Jn 1:45).
3. Disciple from Arimathea; buried Jesus in his tomb (Mt 27:57-61; Mk 15:43-47; Lk 24:50-52).
4. Original name of Barnabas (Ac 4:36).

JOSHUA → = HOSHEA, = JESHUA
1. Son of Nun; name changed from Hoshea (Nu 13:8, 16; 1Ch 7:27). Fought Amalekites under Moses (Ex 17:9-14). Servant of Moses on Sinai (Ex 24:13; 32:17). Spied Canaan (Nu 13). With Caleb, allowed to enter land (Nu 14:6, 30). Succeeded Moses (Dt 1:38; 31:1-8; 34:9). Charged Israel to conquer Canaan (Jos 1). Crossed Jordan (Jos 3-4). Circumcised sons of wilderness wanderings (Jos 5). Conquered Jericho (Jos 6), Ai (Jos 7-8), five kings at Gibeon (Jos 10:1-28), southern Canaan (Jos 10:29-43), northern Canaan (Jos 11-12). Defeated at Ai (Jos 7). Deceived by Gibeonites (Jos 9). Renewed covenant (Jos 8:30-35; 24:1-27). Divided land among tribes (Jos 13-22). Last words (Jos 23). Death (Jos 24:28-31).
2. High priest during rebuilding of temple (Hag 1-2; Zec 3:1-9; 6:11). See Jeshua.

JOSIAH
Son of Amon; king of Judah (2Ki 21:26; 1Ch 3:14). Prophesied (1Ki 13:2). Book of the Law discovered during his reign (2Ki 22; 2Ch 34:14-31). Reforms (2Ki 23:1-25; 2Ch 34:1-13; 35:1-19; Sir 49:1-4). Killed in battle (2Ki 23:29-30; 2Ch 35:20-27).

JOTHAM
1. Son of Gideon (Jdg 9).
2. Son of Azariah (Uzziah); king of Judah (2Ki 15:32-38; 2Ch 26:21-27:9).

JOY
Job 20: 5 and the **j** of the impious
Ps 51:14 Restore my **j** in your salvation;
Pr 21:15 To practice justice is a **j** for the just,
Isa 12: 3 With **j** you will draw water
35:10 crowned with everlasting **j**;
35:10 They will meet with **j** and gladness,
La 2:15 city, the **j** of the whole earth?"
Bar 5: 9 For God is leading Israel in **j**
Mk 4:16 the word, receive it at once with **j**.
Lk 1:44 the infant in my womb leaped for **j**.
2:10 good news of great **j** that will be
Jn 16:22 no one will take your **j** away
Ro 14:17 peace, and **j** in the holy Spirit;
Gal 5:22 the fruit of the Spirit is love, **j**
Php 4: 1 I love and long for, my **j** and crown,
Heb 12: 2 the **j** that lay before him he endured
Jas 1: 2 Consider it all **j**, my brothers,

JUBILEE
Lev 25:10 It shall be a **j** for you, when every
Nu 36: 4 the Israelites celebrate the **j** year,

JUDAH → JUDEA
1. Son of Jacob by Leah (Ge 29:35; 35:23; 1Ch 2:1). Did not want to kill Joseph (Ge 37:26-27). Among Canaanites, fathered Perez by Tamar (Ge 38). Tribe of blessed as ruling tribe (Ge 49:8-12; Dt 33:7), numbered (Nu 1:27; 26:22), allotted land (Jos 15; Eze 48:7), failed to fully possess (Jos 15:63; Jdg 1:1-20).
2. Name used for Southern Kingdom.
2Sa 2: 4 Then the men of **J** came there
La 1: 3 **J** has fled into exile from oppression
Mt 2: 6 'And you, Bethlehem, land of **J**,
2: 6 means least among the rulers of **J**;
Heb 7:14 is clear that our Lord arose from **J**,
Rev 5: 5 The lion of the tribe of **J**, the root

JUDAISM → JEW
Ac 13:43 were converts to **J** followed Paul
Gal 1:13 heard of my former way of life in **J**,

JUDAS → = BARSABBAS, = JUDE, = THADDAEUS, MACCABEUS

1. Apostle; son of James (Lk 6:16; Jn 14:22; Ac 1:13). Probably also called Thaddaeus (Mt 10:3; Mk 3:18).

2. Brother of James and Jesus (Mt 13:55; Mk 6:3), also called Jude (Jude 1).

3. Christian prophet (Ac 15:22-32).

4. Apostle, also called Iscariot, who betrayed Jesus (Mt 10:4; 26:14-56; Mk 3:19; 14:10-50; Lk 6:16; 22:3-53; Jn 6:71; 12:4; 13:2-30; 18:2-11). Suicide of (Mt 27:3-5; Ac 1:16-25).

5. Leader of the Maccabean revolt (1Ma 2:4, 66). Recaptured Jerusalem and rededicated the temple and altar (1Ma 4:36-61). Death of (1Ma 9).

JUDE → See JUDAS, 2

JUDEA → JUDAH

Mt	2: 1	Jesus was born in Bethlehem of J,
Lk	3: 1	Pontius Pilate was governor of J,
Ac	1: 8	throughout J and Samaria,

JUDGE → JUDGED, JUDGES, JUDGMENT, JUDGMENTS

Ex	2:14	appointed you ruler and j over us?
Isa	11: 3	Not by appearance shall he j,
Eze	34:17	GOD, I will j between one sheep
Jn	7:24	judging by appearances, but j justly."
	18:31	and j him according to your law."
Ro	3: 6	For how else is God to j the world?
1Co	6: 2	that the holy ones will j the world?
2Ti	4: 1	who will j the living and the dead,
Heb	12:23	and God the j of all, and the spirits
Jas	5: 9	the J is standing before the gates.

JUDGED → JUDGE

Mt	7: 1	"Stop judging, that you may not be j.
Jas	3: 1	that we will be j more strictly,
Rev	20:12	The dead were j according to their

JUDGES → JUDGE

Jdg	2:16	the LORD raised up j to deliver them
1Sa	2:10	The LORD j the ends of the earth.
Sir	16:12	he j men, each according to his
Lk	11:19	out? Therefore they will be your j.
Ac	4:19	you rather than God, you be the j.
Jas	4:11	j his brother speaks evil of the law
	4:11	speaks evil of the law and j the law.
Rev	19:11	and True." He j and wages war

JUDGMENT → JUDGE

Ex	6: 6	arm and with mighty acts of j.
Ps	1: 5	the wicked will not survive j,

Ecc	12:14	God will bring to j every work,
Jer	25:31	he is to pass j upon all mankind:
Da	7:22	j was pronounced in favor
Mal	3: 5	I will draw near to you for j, and I
Mt	11:24	Sodom on the day of j than for you."
Ro	14:10	we shall all stand before the j seat
2Co	5:10	we must all appear before the j seat
Heb	9:27	beings die once, and after this the j,
	10:27	a fearful prospect of j and a flaming
Jas	2:13	For the j is merciless to one who has
	2:13	mercy; mercy triumphs over j.
1Pe	4:17	it is time for the j to begin
1Jn	4:17	on the day of j because as he is,
Rev	18:10	city. In one hour your j has come."

JUDGMENTS → JUDGE

Ro	11:33	How inscrutable are his j and how
Rev	19: 2	for true and just are his j. He has

JUDITH

Virtuous widow and heroine of the deuterocanonical book of Judith (Jdt 8-16).

JUST → JUSTICE, JUSTIFICATION, JUSTIFIED, JUSTIFY

Dt	32: 4	deceit, how j and upright he is!
Tob	3: 2	and all your deeds are j; All your
1Jn	1: 9	he is faithful and j and will forgive
Rev	15: 3	almighty. J and true are your ways,

JUSTICE → JUST

Job	37:23	his great j owes no one
Ps	33: 5	The LORD loves j and right and fills
Pr	21:15	To practice j is a joy for the just,
Isa	30:18	For the LORD is a God of j:
	42: 4	Until he establishes j on the earth;
Am	5:24	then let j surge like water,

JUSTIFICATION → JUST

Ro	4:25	and was raised for our j.
Gal	2:21	for if j comes through the law,

JUSTIFIED → JUST

Ro	3:24	They are j freely by his grace
	5: 1	since we have been j by faith,
	10:10	believes with the heart and so is j,
1Co	6:11	you were j in the name of the Lord
Gal	2:16	know that a person is not j by works
	2:16	Jesus that we may be j by faith
	2:16	works of the law no one will be j.
Jas	2:24	See how a person is j by works

JUSTIFY → JUST

Ro	3:30	will j the circumcised on the basis
Gal	3: 8	that God would j the Gentiles

K

KADESH → KADESH-BARNEA

Nu	20: 1	month, and the people settled at K.
Dt	1:46	had to stay as long as you did at K.

KADESH-BARNEA → KADESH

Nu	32: 8	I sent them from K to reconnoiter

KEEP → KEEPER, KEEPS, KEPT

Ge	17: 9	you must k my covenant throughout
Ex	19: 5	to my voice and k my covenant,
Nu	6:24	The LORD bless you and k you!
Dt	5:10	love me and k my commandments.
Ne	1: 5	you and k your commandments,
Pr	7: 2	K my commands and live,
Ecc	3: 6	a time to k, and a time to cast away.
	12:13	Fear God and k his commandments,
Sir	1:26	before men; over your lips k watch.
Jude	1:24	the one who is able to k you
Rev	22: 9	of those who k the message of this

KEEPER → KEEP

Ge	4: 9	"I do not know. Am I my brother's k?"

KEEPS → KEEP

Jas	2:10	For whoever k the whole law,

KEPT → KEEP

Jn	17: 6	to me, and they have k your word.
2Ti	4: 7	finished the race; I have k the faith.

KEY → KEYS

Isa	22:22	I will place the k of the House
Lk	11:52	law! You have taken away the k
Rev	3: 7	the true, who holds the k of David,

KEYS → KEY

Mt	16:19	I will give you the k to the kingdom
Rev	1:18	ever. I hold the k to death

KIDRON

2Sa	15:23	the king crossed the K Valley
Jn	18: 1	his disciples across the K valley

KILL

Ex	4:23	I warn you, I will k your son,
Ecc	3: 3	A time to k, and a time to heal;
Mt	10:28	be afraid of those who k the body
	10:28	k the body but cannot k the soul;

KIND → KINDNESS, KINDS
1Co 13: 4 Love is patient, love is **k**. It is not
Eph 4:32 [And] be **k** to one another,

KINDNESS → KIND
Ro 2: 4 Or do you hold his priceless **k**,
     2: 4 that the **k** of God would lead you
Gal 5:22 joy, peace, patience, **k**, generosity,

KINDS → KIND
Ge 6:20 Of all **k** of birds, of all **k** of beasts,
     6:20 and of all **k** of creeping things,
Lev 19:19 yours with two different **k** of seed;
     19:19 with two different **k** of thread.

KING → KINGDOM, KINGS
Ex 1: 8 Then a new **k**, who knew nothing
Dt 17:14 to have a **k** over you like all
1Sa 8: 7 they are rejecting me as their **k**.
2Sa 2: 4 anointed David **k** of the Judahites.
Jdt 9:12 waters, **K** of all you have created,
Ps 2: 6 "I myself have installed my **k**
     10:16 The Lord is **k** forever; the nations
Isa 6: 5 yet my eyes have seen the **K**,
Jer 10:10 he is the living God, the eternal **K**,
Mt 2: 2 "Where is the newborn **k**
     27:37 This is Jesus, the **K** of the Jews.
Lk 19:38 "Blessed is the **k** who comes
Jn 1:49 Son of God; you are the **K** of Israel."
1Ti 1:17 To the **k** of ages, incorruptible,
Rev 19:16 thigh, "**K** of kings and Lord of lords."

KINGDOM → KING
Ex 19: 6 You shall be to me a **k** of priests,
2Sa 7:12 loins, and I will make his **k** firm.
1Ki 11:31 says: 'I will tear away the **k**
Wis 10:10 ways, Showed him the **k** of God
Mt 4:17 for the **k** of heaven is at hand."
     5: 3 spirit, for theirs is the **k** of heaven.
     6:10 your **k** come, your will be done,
     13:24 "The **k** of heaven may be likened
Mk 1:15 fulfillment. The **k** of God is at hand.
     6:23 you ask of me, even to half of my **k**."
     10:24 how hard it is to enter the **k** of God!
     12:34 "You are not far from the **k** of God."
     13: 8 rise against nation and **k** against **k**.
Lk 17:21 behold, the **k** of God is among you.'

Lk 22:16 there is fulfillment in the **k** of God."
Jn 3: 5 you, no one can enter the **k** of God
     18:36 "My **k** does not belong to this world,
     18:36 If my **k** did belong to this world,
     18:36 Jews. But as it is, my **k** is not here."
Ac 1: 6 time going to restore the **k** to Israel?"
Ro 14:17 For the **k** of God is not a matter
1Co 6: 9 the unjust will not inherit the **k**
Eph 5: 5 any inheritance in the **k** of Christ
Col 1:13 us to the **k** of his beloved Son,
1Th 2:12 of the God who calls you into his **k**
Heb 12:28 the unshakable **k** should have
2Pe 1:11 entry into the eternal **k** of our Lord
Rev 11:15 "The **k** of the world now belongs

KINGS → KING
Ge 17: 6 of you; **k** shall stem from you.
Ps 2: 2 **K** on earth rise up and princes plot
     138: 4 All the **k** of earth will praise you,
Pr 8:15 By me **k** reign, and lawgivers
Isa 52:15 of him **k** shall stand speechless;
Da 7:24 The ten horns shall be ten **k**
     7:24 him, who shall lay low three **k**.
Ac 4:26 The **k** of the earth took their stand
1Ti 6:15 the King of **k** and Lord of lords,
Rev 19:16 thigh, "King of **k** and Lord of lords."

KISS
SS 1: 2 B Let him **k** me with kisses of his
Mt 26:48 saying, "The man I shall **k** is the one;
2Co 13:12 Greet one another with a holy **k**.

KNEE
Isa 45:23 To me every **k** shall bend; by me
Ro 14:11 Lord, every **k** shall bend before me,
Php 2:10 name of Jesus every **k** should bend,

KNEEL → KNELT
Ps 95: 6 let us **k** before the Lord who made

KNELT → KNEEL
2Ch 6:13 it, Solomon **k** in the presence

KNEW → KNOW
Dt 34:10 whom the Lord **k** face to face.
Jer 1: 5 I formed you in the womb I **k** you,
Mt 7:23 to them solemnly, 'I never **k** you.
Ro 1:21 for although they **k** God they did not

KNOCK
Lk 11: 9 **k** and the door will be opened

KNOW → FOREKNEW, KNEW, KNOWING, KNOWLEDGE, KNOWN, KNOWS
Ge 22:12 I **k** now how devoted you are
Ex 6: 7 You will **k** that I, the Lord, am your
1Ki 8:39 You who alone **k** the hearts of all
Job 19:25 for me, I **k** that my Vindicator lives,
Ecc 8:16 I applied my heart to **k** wisdom
Isa 1: 3 But Israel does not **k**, my people has
Jer 31:34 and kinsmen how to **k** the Lord. All,
     31:34 from least to greatest, shall **k** me,
Mt 6: 3 let your left hand **k** what your right
     24:42 For you do not **k** on which day your
Lk 11:13 **k** how to give good gifts to your
     22:34 will deny three times that you **k** me."
Jn 10:14 and I mine and mine **k** me,
     13:35 This is how all will **k** that you are
     21:24 and we **k** that his testimony is true.
Ac 1: 7 "It is not for you to **k** the times
Ro 8:28 We **k** that all things work for good
1Co 8: 2 he does not yet **k** as he ought to **k**.
     13:12 At present I **k** partially; then I shall
     13:12 I shall **k** fully as I am fully known.
Eph 3:19 to **k** the love of Christ that surpasses
Php 3:10 to **k** him and the power of his
Tit 1:16 They claim to **k** God, but by their
Heb 8:11 and kinsman, saying, "**K** the Lord,"
     8:11 for all shall **k** me, from least
1Jn 2: 4 Whoever says, "I **k** him," but does not
     3:16 The way we came to **k** love was
Rev 3: 3 you will never **k** at what hour I will

KNOWING → KNOW
Ge 3:22 us, **k** what is good and what is bad!
Jn 18: 4 **k** everything that was going
Php 3: 8 good of **k** Christ Jesus my Lord.

KNOWLEDGE → KNOW
Ge 2: 9 the tree of the **k** of good and bad.
Ps 94:10 who teaches humans not have **k**?
Pr 1: 7 of the Lord is the beginning of **k**;
     8:10 silver, and **k** rather than choice gold.

KNOWLEDGE → KNOW (*cont.*)
Ecc 1:18 he who stores up **k** stores up grief.
Isa 11: 2 a spirit of **k** and of fear of the LORD,
Hos 4: 6 My people perish for want of **k**!
      4: 6 **k**! Since you have rejected **k**, I will
Lk 11:52 You have taken away the key of **k**.
Ro 11:33 riches and wisdom and **k** of God!
1Co 8: 1 we realize that "all of us have **k**";
Eph 3:19 the love of Christ that surpasses **k**,
Col 2: 3 all the treasures of wisdom and **k**.
1Ti 6:20 and the absurdities of socalled **k**.
2Pe 1: 5 your faith with virtue, virtue with **k**,
1Jn 2:20 the holy one, and you all have **k**.

KNOWN → KNOW
Lk 6:44 For every tree is **k** by its own fruit.
1Co 2:16 For "who has **k** the mind of the Lord,
Eph 1: 9 he has made **k** to us the mystery

KNOWS → KNOW
Ps 103:14 For he **k** how we are formed,
Mt 6: 8 Your Father **k** what you need before
   24:36 "But of that day and hour no one **k**,
Ro 8:27 who searches hearts **k** what is
2Ti 2:19 "The Lord **k** those who are his"; and,
1Jn 4: 7 loves is begotten by God and **k** God.

KORAH → KORAHITES
Levite; led rebels against Moses (Nu 16; Jude 11).

KORAHITES → KORAH
Psalms of: Pss 42; 44-49; 84; 85; 87; 88.

L

LABAN
Brother of Rebekah (Ge 24:29), father of Rachel and Leah (Ge 29:16). Received Abraham's servant (Ge 24:29-51). Provided daughters as wives for Jacob in exchange for Jacob's service (Ge 29:1-30). Provided flocks for Jacob's service (Ge 30:25-43). Pursued and covenanted with Jacob (Ge 31).

LABOR → LABORER
Ex 1:11 to oppress them with forced **l**.
   20: 9 Six days you may **l** and do all your
1Co 15:58 that in the Lord your **l** is not in vain.

LABORER → LABOR
Lev 19:13 overnight the wages of your day **l**.
Lk 10: 7 you, for the **l** deserves his payment.

LACKING
Col 1:24 filling up what is **l** in the afflictions

LAID → LAY
Isa 53: 6 But the LORD **l** upon him the guilt
Mk 16: 6 Behold, the place where they **l** him.
1Jn 3:16 love was that he **l** down his life

LAMB → LAMBS
Isa 53: 7 mouth; Like a **l** led to the slaughter
Mk 14:12 when they sacrificed the Passover **l**,
Jn 1:29 "Behold, the **L** of God, who takes
1Co 5: 7 For our paschal **l**, Christ, has been
1Pe 1:19 as of a spotless unblemished **l**.
Rev 5:12 "Worthy is the **L** that was slain
   19: 7 the wedding day of the **L** has come,
   21:23 gave it light, and its lamp was the **L**.

LAMBS → LAMB
Ex 12:21 "Go and procure **l** for your families,
Isa 40:11 flock; in his arms he gathers the **l**,
Jn 21:15 love you." He said to him, "Feed my **l**."

LAME
Isa 35: 6 Then will the **l** leap like a stag,
Zep 3:19 I will save the **l**, and assemble
Mt 11: 5 blind regain their sight, the **l** walk,

LAMP → LAMPS, LAMPSTAND, LAMPSTANDS
1Ki 11:36 may always have a **l** before me
Ps 18:29 You, LORD, give light to my **l**;
  119:105 Your word is a **l** for my feet, a light
Mt 5:15 Nor do they light a **l** and then put it
   6:22 "The **l** of the body is the eye. If your
Rev 22: 5 nor will they need light from **l**

LAMPS → LAMP
Ex 25:37 You shall then make seven **l** for it
   25:37 set up the **l** that they shed their light
Mt 25: 1 be like ten virgins who took their **l**

LAMPSTAND → LAMP
Ex 25:31 "You shall make a **l** of pure beaten
1Ma 4:50 altar and lighted the lamps on the **l**,
Zec 4: 2 "I see a **l** all of gold, with a bowl

LAMPSTANDS → LAMP
Rev 1:20 right hand, and of the seven gold **l**,
Rev 1:20 the seven **l** are the seven churches.
   11: 4 the two **l** that stand before the Lord

LAND
Ge 1:10 God called the dry **l** "the earth,"
   12: 7 your descendants I will give this **l**."
Ex 3: 8 lead them out of that **l** into a good
   3: 8 of that **l** into a good and spacious **l**,
   3: 8 **l**, a **l** flowing with milk and honey,
   20: 2 brought you out of the **l** of Egypt,
Nu 13: 2 men to reconnoiter the **l** of Canaan.
Jos 11:23 the tribes. And the **l** enjoyed peace.
2Ki 17: 5 occupied the whole **l** and attacked
   25:21 death in Riblah, in the **l** of Hamath.
   25:21 Thus was Judah exiled from her **l**.
2Ch 7:14 pardon their sins and revive their **l**.
Ps 37:11 But the poor will possess the **l**,
Jer 22:29 O **l**, **l**, **l**, hear the word of the LORD—
Da 11:41 He shall enter the glorious **l**

LANGUAGE
Ac 2: 6 heard them speaking in his own **l**.

LAP
Pr 16:33 When the lot is cast into the **l**,

LASHES
2Co 11:24 Jews I received forty **l** minus one.

LAST → EVERLASTING
2Sa 23: 1 These are the **l** words of David;
Isa 44: 6 I am the first and I am the **l**; there is
Mt 19:30 But many who are first will be **l**,
   19:30 first will be **l**, and the **l** will be first.
Mk 9:35 first, he shall be the **l** of all
1Co 15:26 The **l** enemy to be destroyed is
   15:52 the blink of an eye, at the **l** trumpet.
2Ti 3: 1 will be terrifying times in the **l** days.
Heb 1: 2 in these **l** days, he spoke to us
1Jn 2:18 Children, it is the **l** hour; and just as
   2:18 Thus we know this is the **l** hour.
Rev 1:17 be afraid. I am the first and the **l**,

LAUGH → LAUGHINGSTOCK, LAUGHTER
Ge 18:13 "Why did Sarah **l** and say, 'Shall I
Ecc 3: 4 A time to weep, and a time to **l**;
Lk 6:21 are now weeping, for you will **l**.

LAUGHINGSTOCK → LAUGH
La 3:14 I have become a **l** for all nations,

LAUGHTER → LAUGH
Ps 126: 2 Our mouths were filled with l;
Jas   4: 9 Let your l be turned into
                mourning

LAW → LAWFUL, LAWLESSNESS
Dt   1: 5 began to explain the l in the
                land
      31: 9 Moses had written down this l,
Jos   1: 8 Keep this book of the l on your
                lips.
1Ma 2:48 They saved the l from the
                hands
Ps   1: 2 Rather, the l of the LORD is
                their joy;
      1: 2 God's l they study day and
                night.
Jer 31:33 I will place my l within them,
Mt   5:17 that I have come to abolish
                the l
      23:23 the weightier things of the l;
Lk 24:44 written about me in the l of
                Moses
Jn   1:17 because while the l was given
Ro   2:15 the demands of the l are
                written
      6:14 since you are not under the l
      10: 4 the end of the l for the justifi-
                cation
Gal   2:19 For through the l I died to the l,
Heb 10: 1 Since the l has only a shadow
Jas   2:10 For whoever keeps the whole l,

LAWFUL → LAW
Mt 12:12 So it is l to do good on the sab-
                bath."
1Co   6:12 "Everything is l for me," but
                not
      6:12 "Everything is l for me," but I
                will not
      10:23 "Everything is l," but not
                everything
      10:23 "Everything is l," but not
                everything

LAWLESSNESS → LAW
2Th   2: 7 the mystery of l is already at
                work.
1Jn   3: 4 who commits sin commits l,
                for sin
      3: 4 commits sin commits l, for sin
                is l.

LAY → LAID
Mt 28: 6 Come and see the place where
                he l.
Jn 10:15 I will l down my life for the
                sheep.
1Co   3:11 no one can l a foundation other
                than

LAZARUS
    1. Poor man in Jesus' parable (Lk 16:19-
31).
    2. Brother of Mary and Martha whom Je-
sus raised from the dead (Jn 11:1-12:19).

LAZY
Ex   5:17 "It is just because you are l that
                you

LEAD → LEADER, LEADERS, LEADS,
    LED
Ex 32:34 l the people whither I have told
                you.

Ro   2: 4 of God would l you to repen-
                tance?

LEADER → LEAD
1Ch 28: 4 For he chose Judah as l, then
                one

LEADERS → LEAD
Isa   3:12 O my people, your l mislead,
Lk 19:47 and the l of the people, mean-
                while,
Heb 13: 7 Remember your l who spoke

LEADS → LEAD
Ro   6:16 either of sin, which l to
                death,
      6:16 which l to righteousness?

LEAH
    Wife of Jacob (Ge 29:16-30); bore six
sons and one daughter (Ge 29:31-30:21;
34:1; 35:23; Ru 4:11).

LEAPED → LEAPING
Lk   1:41 greeting, the infant l in her
                womb,

LEAPING → LEAPED
1Ch 15:29 and when she saw King
                David l

LEARN → LEARNED, LEARNING
Dt   4:10 that they may l to fear me as
                long as
Isa   1:17 l to do good. Make justice your
                aim:

LEARNED → LEARN
Php   4:11 for I have l, in whatever situa-
                tion I

LEARNING → LEARN
Ac 26:24 Paul; much l is driving you
                mad."

LEAST → LESS
Mt   2: 6 are by no means l among the
                rulers
      5:19 one of the l of these command-
                ments
      5:19 do so will be called l in the
                kingdom
Lk   9:48 the one who is l among all of
                you is

LEAVE → LEFT
Nu 11:20 wailed, 'Why did we ever l
                Egypt?' "
Mk 10: 7 this reason a man shall l his
                father
Jn 14:18 I will not l you orphans; I will
                come

LEAVEN → LEAVENS
Ex 12:15 shall have your houses clear of
                all l.

LEAVENS → LEAVEN
Gal   5: 9 A little yeast l the whole
                batch

LEAVES
Ge   3: 7 so they sewed fig l together
Eze 47:12 their l shall not fade, nor their
                fruit
      47:12 for food, and their l for medi-
                cine."
Rev 22: 2 the l of the trees serve as medi-
                cine

LEBANON
Dt 11:24 from the desert and from L,
Isa 40:16 L would not suffice for fuel,
                nor its

LED → LEAD
Isa 53: 7 Like a lamb l to the slaughter
Mt   4: 1 Jesus was l by the Spirit
      27:31 and l him off to crucify him.
Ro   8:14 For those who are l by the
                Spirit

LEFT → LEAVE
Dt 28:14 the right or to the l from any
Mt   6: 3 do not let your l hand know
                what
      25:33 on his right and the goats on
                his l.
Lk 17:34 bed; one will be taken, the
                other l.

LEGION
Lk   8:30 name?" He replied, "L," be-
                cause many

LEGS
Jn 19:33 dead, they did not break his l,

LENDER
Pr 22: 7 the borrower is the slave of
                the l.

LEPER → LEPROUS
Mt   8: 2 And then a l approached, did
                him
      26: 6 Bethany in the house of Simon
                the l,

LEPERS → LEPROUS
Lk   7:22 the lame walk, l are cleansed,

LEPROUS → LEPER, LEPERS
Ex   4: 6 it, to his surprise his hand
                was l,

LESS → LEAST
Ex 30:15 nor shall the poor give l,
Ezr   9:13 have made l of our sinfulness
                than it

LETTER
Mt   5:18 not the smallest l or the
                smallest
      5:18 l or the smallest part of a l will
                pass
2Co   3: 6 new covenant, not of l but of
                spirit;
      3: 6 for the l brings death, but the
                Spirit

LEVI → LEVITES, LEVITICAL,
    = MATTHEW
    1. Son of Jacob by Leah (Ge 29:34; 46:11;
1Ch 2:1). With Simeon avenged rape of Dinah (Ge 34). Tribe of blessed (Ge 49:5-7; Dt
33:8-11), chosen as priests (Nu 3-4), numbered (Nu 3:39; 26:62), given cities, but not
land (Nu 18; 35; Dt 10:9; Jos 13:14; 21), land
(Eze 48:8-22), 12,000 from (Rev 7:7).
    2. See Matthew.

LEVIATHAN
Ps 74:14 You crushed the heads of L,

LEVITES → LEVI
Nu   1:53 the L shall camp around
      1:53 The L, then, shall have charge
Jos 14: 4 The L themselves received no
                share

LEVITES → LEVI *(cont.)*
Ne 8: 9 [and the **L** who were instructing

LEVITICAL → LEVI
Heb 7:11 came through the **l** priesthood,

LIAR → LIE
Pr 19:22 rather be a poor man than a **l**.
Jn 8:44 because he is a **l** and the father
Ro 3: 4 though every human being
is a **l**,
1Jn 2:22 Who is the **l**? Whoever denies

LIARS → LIE
1Ti 1:10 kidnapers, **l**, perjurers, and
whatever

LIBERTY
Lev 25:10 sacred by proclaiming **l** in the
land
Isa 61: 1 To proclaim **l** to the captives
1Co 8: 9 make sure that this **l** of yours
in no

LICENTIOUSNESS
Mk 7:22 malice, deceit, **l**, envy, blasphemy,
Gal 5:19 are obvious: immorality,
impurity, **l**,
Jude 1: 4 pervert the grace of our God
into **l**

LIE → LIAR, LIARS, LIES, LYING
Isa 11: 6 the leopard shall **l** down
1Jn 2:21 because every **l** is alien to the
truth.

LIES → LIE
Php 3:13 thing: forgetting what **l**
behind
3:13 straining forward to what **l**
ahead,

LIFE → LIVE
Ge 2: 7 blew into his nostrils the breath
of **l**,
2: 9 with the tree of **l** in the middle
9: 5 demand an accounting for human **l**.
Ex 21:23 injury ensues, you shall give **l**
for **l**,
Dt 12:23 for blood is **l**, and you shall not
12:23 you shall not consume this seat
of **l**
30:19 I have set before you **l** and
death,
30:19 Choose **l**, then, that you and
your
Ps 34:13 Who among you loves **l**,
Pr 18:21 and **l** are in the power of the
tongue;
Ecc 7:12 wisdom preserves the **l** of its
owner.
Sir 4:12 He who loves her loves **l**; those
who
Isa 53:10 If he gives his **l** as an offering
53:10 shall see his descendants in a
long **l**,
Mt 7:14 constricted the road that leads
to **l**.
10:39 Whoever finds his **l** will lose it,
10:39 whoever loses his **l** for my sake
will
20:28 to give his **l** as a ransom for
many."

Mk 10:30 and eternal **l** in the age to
come.
Jn 1: 4 through him was **l**, and this **l**
was
3:15 believes in him may have eternal **l**."
6:35 said to them, "I am the bread
of **l**;
11:25 her, "I am the resurrection and
the **l**;
14: 6 "I am the way and the truth
and the **l**.
Ac 3:15 The author of **l** you put to
death,
Ro 5:21 eternal **l** through Jesus Christ
our
8:11 the dead will give **l** to your
mortal
8:38 that neither death, nor **l**, nor
angels,
2Co 3: 6 brings death, but the Spirit
gives **l**.
Php 4: 3 whose names are in the book
of **l**.
1Jn 3:14 to **l** because we love our brothers.
5:20 He is the true God and
eternal **l**.
Rev 2: 8 who once died but came to **l**,
20: 4 They came to **l** and they
reigned
20:12 scroll was opened, the book
of **l**,
22: 2 of the river grew the tree of **l**

LIFTED
Jn 3:14 just as Moses **l** up the serpent
3:14 so must the Son of Man be
l up,

LIGHT → ENLIGHTENED,
ENLIGHTENS, LIGHTS
Ge 1: 3 said, "Let there be **l**," and there
was **l**.
Ex 13:21 of a column of fire to give
them **l**.
Ps 27: 1 The LORD is my **l** and my salvation;
Pr 4:18 the path of the just is like shining **l**,
Ecc 2:13 folly as much as **l** has the advantage
Isa 42: 6 of the people, a **l** for the nations,
Isa 60: 1 up in splendor! Your **l** has
come,
Mt 4:16 have seen a great **l**, on those
4:16 overshadowed by death **l** has
arisen."
5:14 You are the **l** of the world. A
city
11:30 my yoke is easy, and my burden **l**."
Jn 1: 9 The true **l**, which enlightens
8:12 saying, "I am the **l** of the
world.
8:12 darkness, but will have the **l** of
life."
Ro 13:12 [and] put on the armor of **l**;
2Co 11:14 Satan masquerades as an angel
of **l**.
1Pe 2: 9 out of darkness into his wonderful **l**.

1Jn 1: 7 if we walk in the **l** as he is in
the **l**,
Rev 22: 5 nor will they need **l** from lamp
22: 5 for the Lord God shall give
them **l**,

LIGHTNING
Ex 19:16 there were peals of thunder
and **l**,
Da 10: 6 his face shone like **l**, his eyes
were
Lk 10:18 "I have observed Satan fall
like **l**
Rev 4: 5 From the throne came flashes
of **l**,

LIGHTS → LIGHT
Ge 1:16 God made the two great **l**,
Jas 1:17 coming down from the Father
of **l**,

LIKE → LIKENESS
Ge 3: 5 you will be **l** gods who know
what
Ex 15:11 Who is **l** to you among the
gods,
15:11 Who is **l** to you,
2Sa 7:22 There is none **l** you and there
is no
Ps 113: 5 Who is **l** the LORD, our God
Isa 46: 9 other; I am God, there is none **l**
me.
Jer 10: 6 No one is **l** you, O LORD, great
are
Lk 13:18 said, "What is the kingdom of
God **l**?
Rev 1:13 the lampstands one **l** a son of
man,
10: 1 his face was **l** the sun and his
feet
10: 1 and his feet were **l** pillars of
fire.
16:15 ("Behold, I am coming **l** a
thief."

LIKENESS → LIKE
Ge 1:26 make man in our image, after
our **l**.
Ro 8: 3 his own Son in the **l** of sinful
flesh
Php 2: 7 coming in human **l**; and found

LINEN
Ex 26: 1 out of sheets woven of fine **l**
twined
Da 10: 5 I saw a man dressed in **l** with a
belt
Rev 19: 8 a bright, clean **l** garment."
(The **l**

LION → LION'S, LIONS
1Sa 17:34 whenever a **l** or bear came to
carry
Ecc 9: 4 a live dog is better off than a
dead **l**.
Isa 11: 7 rest; the **l** shall eat hay like the
ox.
Da 7: 4 The first was like a **l**,
Rev 4: 7 The first creature resembled
a **l**,
5: 5 The **l** of the tribe of Judah, the
root

LION'S → LION
2Ti 4:17 I was rescued from the **l**
mouth.

LIONS → LION
Da 6:20 morning and hastened to the l' den.

LIPS
Isa 6: 5 For I am a man of unclean l,
     6: 5 living among a people of unclean l;
Mt 15: 8 'This people honors me with their l,
Heb 13:15 the fruit of l that confess his name.

LISTEN → LISTENS
2Ki 17:40 They did not l, however,
Mk 9: 7 "This is my beloved Son. L to him."
Lk 16:31 'If they will not l to Moses
Ac 3:22 to him you shall l in all that he may

LISTENS → LISTEN
Jn 18:37 belongs to the truth l to my voice."
1Jn 4: 6 and anyone who knows God l to us,

LITTLE
Ex 16:18 a small amount did not have too l.
Ps 8: 6 you have made them l less than
Pr 15:16 Better a l with fear of the LORD
Sir 29:23 Be it l or much, be content
Mt 8:26 are you terrified, O you of l faith?"
2Co 8:15 and whoever had l did not have less."
Gal 5: 9 A l yeast leavens the whole batch

LIVE → ALIVE, LIFE, LIVES, LIVING
Ge 3:22 also, and thus eat of it and l forever."
Ex 1:16 kill him; but if it is a girl, she may l."
Dt 8: 3 that not by bread alone does man l,
Wis 5:15 But the just l forever,
Hab 2: 4 man, because of his faith, shall l.
Mt 4: 4 'One does not l by bread alone,
Jn 11:25 in me, even if he dies, will l,
Ro 1:17 one who is righteous by faith will l."
    14: 8 For if we l, we l for the Lord,
    14: 8 so then, whether we l or die, we are
2Co 5:15 that those who l might no longer l
Gal 3:12 "the one who does these things will l

LIVES → LIVE
Ex 33:20 for no man sees me and still l.
Tob 13: 1 Blessed be God who l forever,
Job 19:25 for me, I know that my Vindicator l,
Ps 18:47 The LORD l! Blessed be my rock!
Jn 11:26 everyone who l and believes in me
Ro 6:10 for all; as to his life, he l for God.
1Jn 3:16 to lay down our l for our brothers.

Rev 15: 7 fury of God, who l forever and ever.

LIVING → LIVE
Ge 2: 7 life, and so man became a l being.
    3:20 she became the mother of all the l.
    6:19 all other l creatures you shall bring
Dt 5:26 the voice of the l God speaking
Jer 2:13 forsaken me, the source of l waters;
Zec 14: 8 l waters shall flow from Jerusalem,
Mt 16:16 the Messiah, the Son of the l God."
Jn 4:10 he would have given you l water."
    6:51 I am the l bread that came down
Ro 12: 1 to offer your bodies as a l sacrifice,
2Co 6:16 For we are the temple of the l God;
Heb 4:12 the word of God is l and effective,
1Pe 2: 4 Come to him, a l stone,

LOAVES
Mk 6:41 taking the five l and the two fish
    6:41 broke the l, and gave them to [his]
    8: 6 taking the seven l he gave thanks,

LOCK
Mt 23:13 You l the kingdom of heaven before

LOCUST → LOCUSTS
Joel 2:25 the years which the l has eaten,

LOCUSTS → LOCUST
Ex 10: 4 tomorrow I will bring l into your
2Ch 6:28 or mildew, or l, or caterpillars;
Mt 3: 4 His food was l and wild honey.
Rev 9: 3 L came out of the smoke onto

LONELY → ALONE
La 1: 1 How l she is now, the once crowded

LONG → LONGING
Ex 20:12 you may have a l life in the land
Ps 13: 2 How l, LORD? Will you utterly
    13: 2 How l will you hide your face
Pr 3:16 L life is in her right hand, in her left
1Co 11:14 man wears his hair l it is a disgrace
1Pe 2: 2 l for pure spiritual milk so
Rev 6:10 out in a loud voice, "How l will it be,

LONGING → LONG
2Co 5: 2 l to be further clothed with our

LOOK → LOOKED, LOOKS
Ex 3: 6 face, for he was afraid to l at God.
Ps 80:15 hosts; l down from heaven and see;

Lk 24:39 L at my hands and my feet, that it is

LOOKED → LOOK
Ge 19:26 But Lot's wife l back, and she was

LOOKS → LOOK
1Sa 16: 7 but the LORD l into the heart."
Ps 14: 2 The LORD l down from heaven
Mt 5:28 everyone who l at a woman

LORD → LORD'S, LORDS
Ge 18:27 I am presuming to speak to my L,
Ex 4:10 said to the L, "If you please, L,
Dt 10:17 For the L, your God, is the God
    10:17 is the God of gods, the L of lords,
Jdt 6:19 "L, God of heaven, behold their
Ps 16: 2 I say to the L, you are my L, you are
    110: 1 of David. The L says to you, my l:
Wis 8: 3 God; even the L of all loved her.
Sir 1: 1 All wisdom comes from the L
Isa 6: 1 I saw the L seated on a high
Da 2:47 is the God of gods and L of kings
    3:57 Bless the L, all you works of the L,
Mic 1: 2 Let the L GOD be witness against
    1: 2 you, the L from his holy temple!
Mt 7:22 Many will say to me on that day, 'L,
    7:22 'L, L, did we not prophesy in your
    12: 8 the Son of Man is L of the sabbath."
Mk 1: 3 'Prepare the way of the L,
    12:29 O Israel! The L our God is L alone!
Lk 2:11 born for you who is Messiah and L.
    10:27 "You shall love the L, your God,
    19:38 in the name of the L.
Jn 20:28 and said to him, "My L and my God!"
Ac 2:34 he himself said: 'The L said to my L,
Ro 4:24 the one who raised Jesus our L
    10:12 the same L is L of all, enriching all
1Co 2:16 "who has known the mind of the L,
    8: 6 we exist, and one L, Jesus Christ,
    12: 3 "Jesus is L," except by the holy Spirit.
2Co 3:17 Now the L is the Spirit, and where
    3:17 and where the Spirit of the L is,
Eph 4: 5 one L, one faith, one baptism;
Php 2:11 that Jesus Christ is L, to the glory
    4: 5 be known to all. The L is near.

LORD → LORD'S, LORDS (cont.)
Col 3:13 as the **L** has forgiven you, so must
1Th 4:15 on the word of the **L**, that we who
  4:15 are left until the coming of the **L**,
1Ti 6:15 the King of kings and **L** of lords,
Heb 12:14 without which no one will see the **L**.
Jas 4:10 Humble yourselves before the **L**
1Pe 3:15 sanctify Christ as **L** in your hearts.
2Pe 3:9 The **L** does not delay his promise,
Jude 1:4 who deny our only Master and **L**,
Rev 4:8 holy, holy is the **L** God almighty,
Rev 19:16 thigh, "King of kings and **L** of lords."
  22:20 soon." Amen! Come, **L** Jesus!

*LORD → *GOD, *LORD'S
Ge 2:7 the **L** God formed man
  13:4 and there he invoked the **L** by name.
  18:14 too marvelous for the **L** to do?
  22:14 say, "On the mountain the **L** will see."
Ex 3:15 The **L**, the God of your fathers,
  5:2 "Who is the **L**, that I should heed his
  5:2 I do not know the **L**; even if I did,
  6:7 the **L**, am your God when I free you
  15:3 The **L** is a warrior, **L** is his name!
  34:6 Thus the **L** passed before him
  34:6 him and cried out, "The **L**, the **L**,
Lev 19:2 for I, the **L**, your God, am holy.
Nu 6:24 The **L** bless you and keep you!
  14:18 'The **L** is slow to anger and rich
Dt 6:4 The **L** is our God, the **L** alone!
Jos 24:15 does not please you to serve the **L**,
  24:15 my household, we will serve the **L**."
1Sa 2:2 There is no Holy One like the **L**;
1Ki 8:11 glory had filled the temple of the **L**.
  18:21 If the **L** is God, follow him; if Baal,
1Ch 16:11 Look to the **L** in his strength;
Ezr 7:10 practice of the law of the **L**
Ne 8:10 prepared; for today is holy to our **L**.
  8:10 in the **L** must be your strength!"
Job 1:21 The **L** gave and the **L** has taken
  1:21 away; blessed be the name of the **L**!"
  42:12 Thus the **L** blessed the latter days

Ps 1:2 Rather, the law of the **L** is their joy;
  10:16 The **L** is king forever; the nations
  18:2 He said: I love you, **L**, my strength,
  23:1 of David. The **L** is my shepherd;
  33:12 the nation whose God is the **L**,
  84:12 For a sun and shield is the **L** God,
  84:12 The **L** withholds no good thing
  110:1 David. The **L** says to you, my lord:
  113:5 Who is like the **L**, our God
  125:2 the **L** surrounds his people both now
  128:1 Happy are all who fear the **L**,
  145:18 You, **L**, are near to all who call
  150:6 give praise to the **L**! Hallelujah!
Pr 1:7 The fear of the **L** is the beginning
  3:5 Trust in the **L** with all your heart,
  19:23 The fear of the **L** is an aid to life;
  21:2 but it is the **L** who proves hearts.
Isa 2:11 and the **L** alone will be exalted,
  6:3 "Holy, holy, holy is the **L** of hosts!"
  33:22 Indeed the **L** will be there with us,
  33:22 yes, the **L** our judge, the **L** our
  33:22 the **L** our king, he it is who will
  53:6 But the **L** laid upon him the guilt
  64:8 Be not so very angry, **L**, keep not
Jer 4:4 For the sake of the **L**,
  31:34 and kinsmen how to know the **L**.
  31:34 says the **L**, for I will forgive their
  32:27 I am the **L**, the God of all mankind!
La 3:25 Good is the **L** to one who waits
Eze 3:23 I saw that the glory of the **L** was
  10:18 the glory of the **L** left the threshold
  37:4 Dry bones, hear the word of the **L**!
  44:4 of the **L** filling the LORD'S temple,
  48:35 shall henceforth be "The **L** is here."
Joel 1:15 for near is the day of the **L**, and it
Am 5:6 Seek the **L**, that you may live,
Ob 1:15 For near is the day of the **L** for all
Na 1:3 The **L** is slow to anger, yet great
  1:3 and the **L** never leaves the guilty
Zep 1:14 Near is the great day of the **L**,
  1:14 Hark, the day of the **L**! bitter, then,

Zec 14:9 The **L** shall become king over
  14:9 that day the **L** shall be the only one,
Mal 3:6 Surely I, the **L**, do not change,

LORD'S → LORD
Ro 14:8 whether we live or die, we are the **L**.
1Co 10:26 "the earth and its fullness are the **L**."

*LORD'S → *LORD
Nu 11:23 Moses, "Is this beyond the **L** reach?
Dt 32:9 While the **L** own portion was Jacob,
Ps 24:1 The earth is the **L** and all it holds,
Ob 1:21 and the kingship shall be the **L**.

LORDS → LORD
Dt 10:17 gods, the LORD of l, the great God,
Ps 136:3 Praise the Lord of l; God's love
1Co 8:5 to be sure, many "gods" and many "l",
Rev 19:16 thigh, "King of kings and Lord of l."

LOSE → LOSS, LOST
Mk 8:35 wishes to save his life will l it,
Heb 12:3 may not grow weary and l heart.
2Jn 1:8 that you do not l what we worked

LOSS → LOSE
1Co 3:15 is burned up, that one will suffer l;
Php 3:8 consider everything as a l because
  3:8 his sake I have accepted the l of all

LOST → LOSE
Ps 119:176 I have wandered like a l sheep;
Jer 50:6 L sheep were my people,
Eze 34:16 The l l will seek out, the strayed l
Mt 10:6 Go rather to the l sheep of the house
Lk 15:6 because I have found my l sheep.'
  19:10 to seek and to save what was l."

LOT → LOT'S, LOTS
 1. Nephew of Abraham (Ge 11:27; 12:5). Chose to live in Sodom (Ge 13). Rescued from four kings (Ge 14). Rescued from Sodom (Ge 19:1-29; 2Pe 2:7). Fathered Moab and Ammon (Ge 19:30-38).
 2. Object cast to make decisions.
Nu 33:54 the land among yourselves by l,
  33:54 Wherever anyone's l falls, there shall
Est 3:7 or l, was cast in Haman's presence,
  3:7 the l fell on the thirteenth day
Pr 16:33 When the l is cast into the lap,
Ac 1:26 and the l fell upon Matthias, and he

LOT'S → LOT, 1

Ge 19:26 But **L** wife looked back, and she

LOTS → LOT, 2

Ps 22:19 them; for my clothing they cast **l**.

Jnh 1: 7 let us cast **l** to find out on whose

1: 7 So they cast **l**, and thus singled

Mt 27:35 divided his garments by casting **l**;

LOVE → BELOVED, LOVED, LOVER, LOVERS, LOVES

Ex 20: 6 on the children of those who **l** me

Lev 19:18 You shall **l** your neighbor as

Dt 6: 5 Therefore, you shall **l** the Lord.

Ne 1: 5 of mercy toward those who **l** you

1Ma 4:33 by the sword of those who **l** you,

Ps 18: 2 He said: I **l** you, Lord, my strength;

Ps 116: 1 I **l** the Lord, who listened to my

119:97 How I **l** your teaching, Lord! I study

136: 1 is so good; God's **l** endures forever;

Pr 5:19 Her **l** will invigorate you always,

5:19 through her **l** you will flourish

8:17 "Those who **l** me I also **l**, and those

Ecc 3: 8 A time to **l**, and a time to hate;

SS 1: 2 More delightful is your **l** than wine!

8: 6 For stern as death is **l**, relentless as

Sir 2:15 those who **l** him keep his ways.

7:30 all your strength, **l** your Creator,

Isa 54: 8 with enduring **l** I take pity on you,

Da 9: 4 covenant toward those who **l** you

14:38 have not forsaken those who **l** you."

Hos 11: 4 with bands of **l**; I fostered them like

Mt 5:44 But I say to you, **l** your enemies,

6:24 will either hate one and **l** the other,

Mk 12:31 is this: 'You shall **l** your neighbor as

Lk 6:32 For if you **l** those who **l** you,

6:32 Even sinners **l** those who **l** them.

10:27 said in reply, "You shall **l** the Lord,

Jn 13:34 a new commandment: **l** one another.

13:34 so you also should **l** one another.

14:15 "If you **l** me, you will keep my

15:13 No one has greater **l** than this, to lay

Jn 21:16 "Simon, son of John, do you **l** me?"

21:16 "Yes, Lord, you know that I **l** you."

Ro 5: 5 because the **l** of God has been

5: 8 God proves his **l** for us in that while

12: 9 Let **l** be sincere; hate what is evil,

13: 8 to anyone, except to **l** one another;

1Co 8: 1 inflates with pride, but **l** builds up.

13: 4 **L** is patient, **l** is kind. It is not

13: 4 It is not jealous, [**l**] is not pompous,

13:13 So faith, hope, **l** remain, these three;

13:13 three; but the greatest of these is **l**.

Gal 5: 6 but only faith working through **l**.

5:22 the fruit of the Spirit is **l**, joy, peace,

Eph 2: 4 because of the great **l** he had for us,

3:19 and to know the **l** of Christ

5:25 Husbands, **l** your wives, even as

Col 3:14 And over all these put on **l**, that is,

1Th 5: 8 on the breastplate of faith and **l**

1Ti 6:10 For the **l** of money is the root of all

Tit 2: 2 sound in faith, **l**, and endurance.

Heb 10:24 how to rouse one another to **l**

13: 5 Let your life be free from **l**

Jas 2: 8 "You shall **l** your neighbor as

1Pe 1: 8 you have not seen him you **l** him;

2Pe 1: 7 affection, mutual affection with **l**.

1Jn 2:15 Do not **l** the world or the things

2:15 the **l** of the Father is not in him.

3: 1 See what **l** the Father has bestowed

3:16 The way we came to know **l** was

4: 7 Beloved, let us **l** one another,

4: 7 **l** one another, because **l** is of God;

4: 8 Whoever is without **l** does not know

4: 8 **l** does not know God, for God is **l**.

5: 3 For the **l** of God is this, that we keep

2Jn 1: 6 For this is **l**, that we walk according

Jude 1:21 Keep yourselves in the **l** of God

Rev 2: 4 you have lost the **l** you had at first.

LOVED → LOVE

Jer 31: 3 With age-old love I have **l** you; so I

Hos 11: 1 When Israel was a child I **l** him,

Mal 1: 2 I have **l** you, says the Lord; but you

1: 2 but you say, "How have you **l** us?"

Jn 3:16 For God so **l** the world that he gave

13: 1 He **l** his own in the world and he **l**

Gal 2:20 in the Son of God who has **l** me

Eph 5: 2 as Christ **l** us and handed himself

1Jn 4:19 We love because he first **l** us.

LOVER → LOVE

Ps 99: 4 O mighty king, **l** of justice,

1Ti 3: 3 not contentious, not a **l** of money.

LOVERS → LOVE

Jer 3: 1 But you have sinned with many **l**,

2Ti 3: 2 be self-centered and **l** of money,

LOVES → LOVE

Ps 33: 5 The Lord **l** justice and right and fills

Pr 3:12 For whom the Lord **l** he reproves,

Sir 4:12 He who **l** her **l** life; those who seek

Mt 10:37 "Whoever **l** father or mother more

10:37 and whoever **l** son or daughter more

Lk 7:47 to whom little is forgiven, **l** little."

Ro 13: 8 the one who **l** another has fulfilled

Eph 5:28 bodies. He who **l** his wife **l** himself.

Heb 12: 6 for whom the Lord **l**, he disciplines;

1Jn 4: 7 everyone who **l** is begotten by God

Rev 1: 5 To him who **l** us and has freed us

LOW → LOWER, LOWLY

Isa 40: 4 mountain and hill shall be made **l**;

Lk 3: 5 mountain and hill shall be made **l**.

LOWER → LOW

Heb 2: 7 for a little while **l** than the angels;

LOWLY → LOW

Jdt 9:11 but you are the God of the **l**,

Lk 1:52 from their thrones but lifted up the **l**.

Ro 12:16 be haughty but associate with the **l**;

LOYAL

Da 11:32 but those who remain **l** to their God

LUKE

Associate of Paul (Col 4:14; 2Ti 4:11; Phm 24).

LUKEWARM

Rev 3:16 because you are **l**, neither hot nor

LUST → LUSTS
Mt   5:28 l has already committed adultery

LUSTS → LUST
Ro   1:24 impurity through the l of their hearts

LYDIA
Ac   16:14 them, a woman named L, a dealer

LYING → LIE
1Ki 22:23 the LORD has put a l spirit
Pr   6:17 Haughty eyes, a l tongue, and hands
Wis   1:11 and a l mouth slays the soul.
Hos   4: 2 False swearing, l, murder,

LYRE
Ps   33: 2 on the ten-stringed l offer praise.

M

MACCABEUS → JUDAS
1Ma   2:66 And Judas M, a warrior from his

MACEDONIA
Ac   16: 9 words, "Come over to M and help us."

MADE → MAKE
Ge   1:31 God looked at everything he had m,
      3:21 the LORD God m leather garments,
Ge   6: 6 that he had m man on the earth,
     15:18 occasion that the LORD m a covenant
Ex   20:11 In six days the LORD m the heavens
     20:11 the sabbath day and m it holy.
     36: 8 m the Dwelling with its ten sheets
Ps   8: 6 Yet you have m them little less than
    118:24 This is the day the LORD has m;
    139:14 you, so wonderfully you m me;
Jer 27: 5 It was I who m the earth, and man
Mk   2:27 them, "The sabbath was m for man,
Ac   2:36 that God has m him both Lord
Rev 14: 7 Worship him who m heaven

MADNESS
Dt   28:28 the LORD will strike you with m,
Ecc   9: 3 and m is in their hearts during life;

MAGDALENE
Mt   27:56 Among them were Mary M

MAGICIANS
Ex   7:11 and they also, the m of Egypt,
Da   2: 2 So he ordered that the m,

MAGNIFY
Ps   34: 4 M the LORD with me; let us exalt his

MAJESTIC → MAJESTY
2Pe   1:17 came to him from the m glory,

MAJESTY → MAJESTIC
1Ch 29:11 and power, m, splendor, and glory.
Ps   93: 1 The LORD is king, robed with m;
Heb   1: 3 at the right hand of the M on high,
2Pe   1:16 we had been eyewitnesses of his m.

MAKE → MADE, MAKER
Ge   1:26 "Let us m man in our image,
      2:18 I will m a suitable partner for him."
     12: 2 "I will m of you a great nation, and I
     12: 2 bless you; I will m your name great,
Ex   32: 1 m us a god who will be our leader;
Isa 61: 8 a lasting covenant I will m
     66:22 which I will m Shall endure before
Jer 31:31 when I will m a new covenant
Mt   28:19 and m disciples of all nations,
Mk   1:17 me, and I will m you fishers of men."

MAKER → MAKE
Job   4:17 mortal be blameless against his M?
Isa 54: 5 become your husband is your M;

MALACHI
      Post-exilic prophet (Mal 1:1).

MALE
Ge   1:27 him; m and female he created them.
     17:10 keep: every m among you shall be
Lev 20:13 If a man lies with a m as
Mt   19: 4 beginning the Creator 'made them m
Rev 12: 5 She gave birth to a son, a m child,

MALICE
Ro   1:29 of wickedness, evil, greed, and m;
1Co   5: 8 the yeast of m and wickedness,

MAN → MEN
Ge   2: 7 the LORD God formed m
      2: 7 and so m became a living being.
      2:18 "It is not good for the m to be alone.
1Sa 13:14 sought out a m after his own heart
Mt   9: 6 the Son of M has authority on earth
Lk   6: 5 "The Son of M is lord of the sabbath."
Jn   9:35 "Do you believe in the Son of M?"
1Co 11: 3 that Christ is the head of every m,
Rev   1:13 the lampstands one like a son of m,
     14:14 one who looked like a son of m,

MANAGE
1Ti   3: 4 He must m his own household well,
      5:14 and m a home, so as to give

MANASSEH
      1. Firstborn of Joseph (Ge 41:51; 46:20). Blessed by Jacob but not as firstborn (Ge 48). Tribe of blessed (Dt 33:17), numbered (Nu 1:35; 26:34), half allotted land east of Jordan (Nu 32; Jos 13:8-33), half west (Jos 16; Eze 48:4), failed to fully possess (Jos 17:12-13; Jdg 1:27), 12,000 from (Rev 7:6).
      2. Son of Hezekiah; king of Judah (2Ki 21:1-18; 2Ch 33:1-20). Judah exiled for his detestable sins (2Ki 21:10-15). Repented (2Ch 33:12-19).

MANGER
Lk   2:12 swaddling clothes and lying in a m."

MANNA
Ex   16:31 The Israelites called this food m.
Jos   5:12 produce of the land, the m ceased.
      5:12 No longer was there m
Jn   6:49 Your ancestors ate the m
Rev   2:17 I shall give some of the hidden m;

MANTLE
2Ki   2: 8 Elijah took his m, rolled it

MANY
Isa 53:12 he shall take away the sins of m,
Mt   22:14 M are invited, but few are chosen."
Mk   10:45 to give his life as a ransom for m."
Jn   20:30 Now Jesus did m other signs
Ro   12: 5 though m, are one body in Christ

MARAH
Ex   15:23 they arrived at M, where they could
     15:23 Hence this place was called M.

MARK → MARKED, MARKS
      1. Cousin of Barnabas (Ac 12:12; 15:37-39; Col 4:10; 2Ti 4:11; Phm 24; 1Pe 5:13), see John.
      2. Brand or symbol:
Ge   4:15 So the LORD put a m on Cain,
Rev 14: 9 or accepts its m on forehead
     19:20 astray those who had accepted the m

MARKED → MARK
Eze   9: 6 But do not touch any m with the X;
Hab   1:12 LORD, you have m him for judgment,

MARKET → MARKETPLACE
1Co 10:25 Eat anything sold in the m,

MARKETPLACE → MARKET
Jn   2:16 stop making my Father's house a m."

MARKS → MARK
Gal   6:17 me; for I bear the m of Jesus on my

MARRIAGE → INTERMARRY, MARRIED, MARRIES

Mt 22:30 neither marry nor are given in **m**

Heb 13: 4 Let **m** be honored among all
13: 4 all and the **m** bed be kept undefiled,

MARRIED → MARRIAGE

Mal 2:11 and has **m** an idolatrous woman.

Mk 12:23 be? For all seven had been **m** to her."

1Ti 3: 2 be irreproachable, **m** only once,

Tit 1: 6 a man be blameless, **m** only once,

MARRIES → MARRIAGE

Mk 10:11 **m** another commits adultery against

1Co 7:28 an unmarried woman sin if she **m**;

MARTHA

Sister of Mary and Lazarus (Lk 10:38-42; Jn 11; 12:2).

MARVELOUS

Ps 98: 1 who has done **m** deeds, have won

MARY

1. Mother of Jesus (Mt 1:16-25; Lk 1:27-56; 2:1-40). With Jesus at temple (Lk 2:41-52), at the wedding in Cana (Jn 2:1-5), questioning his sanity (Mk 3:21), at the cross (Jn 19:25-27). Among disciples (Ac 1:14).
2. Magdalene; former demoniac (Lk 8:2). Helped support Jesus' ministry (Lk 8:1-3). At the cross (Mt 27:56; Mk 15:40; Jn 19:25), burial (Mt 27:61; Mk 15:47). Saw angel after resurrection (Mt 28:1-10; Mk 16:1-9; Lk 24:1-12); also Jesus (Jn 20:1-18).
3. Sister of Martha and Lazarus (Jn 11). Washed Jesus' feet (Jn 12:1-8).
4. Mother of James and Joses; witnessed crucifixion (Mt 27:56; Mk 15:40) and empty tomb (Mk 16:1; Lk 24:10).

MASTER → MASTERS, TASKMASTERS

Ge 4: 7 is toward you, yet you can be his **m**."

Mal 1: 6 and a servant fears his **m**; If then I
1: 6 to me? And if I am a **m**, where is

Mt 25:21 His **m** said to him, 'Well done,

Jn 15:20 you, 'No slave is greater than his **m**.'

2Pe 2: 1 and even deny the **M** who ransomed

MASTERS → MASTER

Mt 6:24 "No one can serve two **m**. He will

MATTANIAH → See ZEDEKIAH

MATTATHIAS

Priest who started the Maccabean revolt (1Ma 2).

MATTHEW → = LEVI

Apostle; former tax collector (Mt 9:9-13; 10:3; Mk 3:18; Lk 6:15; Ac 1:13). Also called Levi (Mk 2:14-17; Lk 5:27-32).

MATTHIAS

Disciple chosen to replace Judas (Ac 1:23-26).

MATURE

1Co 2: 6 speak a wisdom to those who are **m**,

Php 3:15 then, who are "perfectly **m**" adopt this

Heb 5:14 But solid food is for the **m**, for those

MEAN → MEANING

Ex 12:26 you, 'What does this rite of yours **m**?'

Jos 4: 6 ask you what these stones **m** to you,

MEANING → MEAN

Ge 40: 5 night, each dream with its own **m**.

MEASURE

Dt 25:15 and a true and just **m**, that you may

Mk 4:24 The **m** with which you **m** will be

Lk 6:38 a good **m**, packed together,
6:38 For the **m** with which you **m** will

MEAT

Ro 14:21 it is good not to eat **m** or drink wine

MEDIATOR

Gal 3:19 by angels at the hand of a **m**.

1Ti 2: 5 There is also one **m** between God

Heb 8: 6 more excellent a ministry as he is **m**

MEDIUM

Lev 20:27 man or a woman who acts as a **m**

MEEK

Mt 5: 5 Blessed are the **m**, for they will

MEET → MEETING

Ex 30:36 the meeting tent where I will **m** you.

Am 4:12 prepare to **m** your God, O Israel:

1Th 4:17 the clouds to **m** the Lord in the air.

MEETING → MEET

Ex 27:21 them before the LORD in the **m** tent,
40:34 Then the cloud covered the **m** tent,

MELCHIZEDEK

Ge 14:18 **M**, king of Salem, brought out bread

Ps 110: 4 "Like **M** you are a priest forever."

Heb 7: 1 This "**M**, king of Salem and priest

MELT

Ps 97: 5 The mountains **m** like wax before

MEMBERS

Ro 7:23 I see in my **m** another principle
7:23 the law of sin that dwells in my **m**.

1Co 6:15 that your bodies are **m** of Christ?
6:15 take Christ's **m** and make them the **m**

MEMORIAL

Jos 4: 7 are to serve as a perpetual **m**

MEN → MAN

Ge 18: 2 up, he saw three **m** standing nearby.

Sir 44: 1 Now will I praise those godly **m**,

Da 3:92 "I see four **m** unfettered and unhurt,

Lk 9:30 two **m** were conversing with him,

MENAHEM

King of Israel (2Ki 15:14-23).

MENE

Da 5:25 was inscribed: **M**, TEKEL, and PERES.

MEPHIBOSHETH

Son of Jonathan shown kindness by David (2Sa 4:4; 9; 21:7). Accused of siding with Absalom (2Sa 16:1-4; 19:24-30).

MERCIES → MERCY

La 3:22 not exhausted, his **m** are not spent;

MERCIFUL → MERCY

Dt 4:31 is a **m** God, he will not abandon

Ps 111: 4 deeds; gracious and **m** is the LORD.

Sir 2:11 Compassionate and **m** is the LORD;

Jer 3:12 with you; For I am **m**, says the LORD,

Mt 5: 7 Blessed are the **m**, for they will be

Lk 6:36 Be **m**, just as [also] your Father is
6:36 **m**, just as [also] your Father is **m**.

Heb 2:17 that he might be a **m** and faithful

MERCY → MERCIES, MERCIFUL

1Ch 21:13 of the LORD, whose **m** is very great,

Zec 1:12 how long will you be without **m**

Mt 9:13 the words, 'I desire **m**, not sacrifice.'
23:23 law: judgment and **m** and fidelity.

Ro 9:15 "I will show **m** to whom I will, I will

Eph 2: 4 who is rich in **m**,

Tit 3: 5 but because of his **m**, he saved us

Heb 4:16 the throne of grace to receive **m**

Jas 2:13 to one who has not shown **m**;

MERIBAH

Ex 17: 7 place was called Massah and **M**,

Ps 95: 8 Do not harden your hearts as at **M**,

MESHACH → = MISHAEL

Hebrew exiled to Babylon; name changed from Mishael (Da 1:6-7). Refused defilement by food (Da 1:8-20). Refused to worship idol (Da 3:1-18); saved from furnace (Da 3:19-30).

MESSAGE → MESSENGER

1Co	1:18	The **m** of the cross is foolishness
2Co	5:19	to us the **m** of reconciliation.

MESSENGER → MESSAGE

Isa	42:19	servant, or deaf like the **m** I send?
Mt	11:10	I am sending my **m** ahead of you;

MESSIAH → CHRIST, MESSIAHS

Mt	16:16	"You are the **M**, the Son of the living
Lk	2:11	has been born for you who is **M**
Ac	2:36	has made him both Lord and **M**,
Ro	9:5	according to the flesh, is t he **M**.

MESSIAHS → MESSIAH

Mk	13:22	False **m** and false prophets will arise

MICAH

1. Idolater from Ephraim (Jdg 17-18).
2. Prophet from Moresheth (Jer 26:18-19; Mic 1:1).

MICAIAH

Prophet of the LORD who spoke against Ahab (1Ki 22:1-28; 2Ch 18:1-27).

MICHAEL

Archangel (Jude 9); warrior in angelic realm, protector of Israel (Da 10:13, 21; 12:1; Rev 12:7).

MICHAL

Daughter of Saul, wife of David (1Sa 14:49; 18:20-28). Warned David of Saul's plot (1Sa 19). Saul gave her to Paltiel (1Sa 25:44); David retrieved her (2Sa 3:13-16). Criticized David for dancing before the ark (2Sa 6:16-23; 1Ch 15:29).

MIDDLE

Ge	3:3	the tree in the **m** of the garden
Rev	22:2	down the **m** of its street. On either

MIDIAN → MIDIANITES

Ex	18:1	the priest of **M**, heard of all

MIDIANITES → MIDIAN

Ge	37:36	The **M**, meanwhile, sold Joseph
Nu	31:2	"Avenge the Israelites on the **M**,

MIDWIVES

Ex	1:17	The **m**, however, feared God;

MIGHT → ALMIGHTY, MIGHTY

2Ch	20:6	In your hand is power and **m**,
Zec	4:6	an army, nor by **m**, but by my spirit,

MIGHTY → MIGHT

Ge	49:24	the power of the **M** One of Jacob,

Ex	6:1	Forced by my **m** hand, he will send
Ps	99:4	O **m** king, lover of justice,
Lk	1:49	The **M** One has done great things
Rev	18:8	**m** is the Lord God who judges her."

MILE

Mt	5:41	press you into service for one **m**,

MILK

Ex	3:8	a land flowing with **m** and honey,
Heb	5:12	You need **m**, [and] not solid food.
1Pe	2:2	pure spiritual **m** so that through it

MILLSTONE → STONE

Lk	17:2	him if a **m** were put around his neck

MIND → MINDFUL, MINDS

Nu	23:19	human, that he should change his **m**.
Sir	37:17	The root of all conduct is t he **m**;
Mt	22:37	all your soul, and with all your **m**.
Ro	1:28	their undiscerning **m** to do what is
1Co	2:16	"who has known the **m** of the Lord,
	2:16	him?" But we have the **m** of Christ.

MINDFUL → MIND

Ps	8:5	are humans that you are **m** of them,
	111:5	you, **m** of your covenant forever.
Heb	2:6	"What is man that you are **m** of him,

MINDS → MIND

2Co	4:4	of this age has blinded the **m**
Eph	4:23	be renewed in the spirit of your **m**,
Php	4:7	your hearts and **m** in Christ Jesus.

MINISTER → MINISTERS, MINISTRY

Ex	28:43	tent or approach the altar to **m**

MINISTERS → MINISTER

2Co	3:6	who has indeed qualified us as **m**
	11:15	So it is not strange that his **m**
	11:15	masquerade as **m** of righteousness.

MINISTRY → MINISTER

2Co	5:18	and given us the **m** of reconciliation,
Eph	4:12	the holy ones for the work of **m**,
Heb	8:6	so much more excellent a **m** as he is

MIRACLES → See also JESUS: MIRACLES

MIRIAM

Sister of Moses and Aaron (Nu 26:59). Led dancing at Red Sea (Ex 15:20-21).

Struck with leprosy for criticizing Moses (Nu 12). Death (Nu 20:1).

MIRROR

1Co	13:12	as in a **m**, but then face to face.
Jas	1:23	who looks at his own face in a **m**.

MISHAEL → See MESHACH

MOAB

Ge	19:37	birth to a son whom she named **M**,
Ru	1:1	sons to reside on the plateau of **M**.
Isa	15:1	Oracle on **M**: Laid waste in a night,
	15:1	Ar of **M** is destroyed; Laid waste
	15:1	in a night, Kir of **M** is destroyed.

MOCK → MOCKED

Ps	22:8	All who see me **m** me; they curl
Mk	10:34	who will **m** him, spit upon him,

MOCKED → MOCK

Gal	6:7	God is not **m**, for a person will reap

MOLECH

Lev	18:21	offspring to be immolated to **M**,

MOMENT → MOMENTARY

Ex	33:5	up in your company even f or a **m**,
Ps	30:6	For divine anger lasts but a **m**;
Isa	54:7	For a brief **m** I abandoned you,
	66:8	or a nation to be born in a single **m**?

MOMENTARY → MOMENT

2Co	4:17	this **m** light affliction is producing

MONEY

Ecc	10:19	glad, but **m** answers for everything.
Mk	11:15	the tables of the **m** changers
1Ti	3:3	not contentious, not a lover of **m**.
1Ti	6:10	the love of **m** is the root of all evils,
Heb	13:5	Let your life be free from love of **m**

MONTH

Ex	12:2	"This **m** shall stand at the head
	12:2	you shall reckon it the first **m**
Eze	47:12	Every **m** they shall bear fresh fruit,
Rev	22:2	twelve times a year, once each **m**;

MOON → MOONS

Ge	37:9	the **m** and eleven stars were bowing
Dt	17:3	the **m** or any of the host of the sky,
Jos	10:13	and the **m** stayed, while the nation
Ac	2:20	and the **m** to blood,
Rev	6:12	and the whole **m** became like blood.

Rev 21:23 no need of sun or **m** to shine on it,

MOONS → MOON
2Ch 8:13 at the new **m**, and on the fixed

MORALS
1Co 15:33 "Bad company corrupts good **m**."

MORDECAI
Benjamite exile who raised Esther (Est 2:5-15). Mordecai's dream (Est 11; 10:4-13). Exposed plot to kill Xerxes (Est 2:19-23; 12:1-6). Refused to honor Haman (Est 3:1-6; 5:9-14). Mordecai's prayer (Est 13). Charged Esther to foil Haman's plot against the Jews (Est 4). Xerxes forced Haman to honor Mordecai (Est 6). Mordecai exalted (Est 8-10). Established Purim (Est 9:18-32).

MORE → MOST
Ps 19:11 **M** desirable than gold, than a hoard
69:32 will please the LORD **m** than oxen,
Mk 4:25 the one who has, **m** will be given;
Lk 12:23 For life is **m** than food and the body
12:23 food and the body **m** than clothing.
1Co 12:31 show you a still **m** excellent way.
Rev 21:4 and there shall be no **m** death

MORIAH
Ge 22:2 you love, and go to the land of **M**.
2Ch 3:1 the LORD in Jerusalem on Mount **M**,

MORNING
Ge 1:5 came, and **m** followed—the first day.
La 3:23 They are renewed each **m**, so great
Lk 24:22 they were at the tomb early in the **m**
2Pe 1:19 and the **m** star rises in your hearts.
Rev 22:16 of David, the bright **m** star."

MORTAL
1Co 15:53 this which is **m** must clothe itself
2Co 5:4 so that what is **m** may be swallowed

MOSES
Levite; brother of Aaron (Ex 6:20; 1Ch 6:3). Put in basket into Nile; discovered and raised by Pharaoh's daughter (Ex 2:1-10). Fled to Midian after killing Egyptian (Ex 2:11-15). Married to Zipporah, fathered Gershom (Ex 2:16-22). Called by the LORD to deliver Israel (Ex 3-4). Pharaoh's resistance (Ex 5). Ten plagues (Ex 7-11). Passover and Exodus (Ex 12-13). Led Israel through Red Sea (Ex 14). Song of deliverance (Ex 15:1-21). Brought water from rock (Ex 17:1-7). Raised hands to defeat Amalekites (Ex 17:8-16). Delegated judges (Ex 18; Dt 1:9-18). Received Law at Sinai (Ex 19-23; 25-31; Jn 1:17). Announced Law to Israel (Ex 19:7-

8; 24; 35). Broke tablets because of golden calf (Ex 32; Dt 9). Saw glory of the LORD (Ex 33-34). Supervised building of tabernacle (Ex 36-40). Set apart Aaron and priests (Lev 8-9). Numbered tribes (Nu 1-4; 26). Opposed by Aaron and Miriam (Nu 12). Sent spies into Canaan (Nu 13). Announced forty years of wandering for failure to enter land (Nu 14). Opposed by Korah (Nu 16). Forbidden to enter land for striking rock (Nu 20:1-13; Dt 1:37). Lifted bronze snake for healing (Nu 21:4-9; Jn 3:14). Final address to Israel (Dt 1-33). Succeeded by Joshua (Nu 27:12-23; Dt 34). Death and burial by God (Dt 34:5-12). Praise of (Sir 45).
Law of (1Ki 2:3; Ezr 3:2; Mk 12:26; Lk 24:44). Book of (2Ch 25:12; Ne 13:1). Song of (Ex 15:1-21; Rev 15:3). Prayer of (Ps 90).

MOST → MORE
Ge 14:18 and being a priest of God **M** High,
Ps 91:1 dwell in the shelter of the **M** High,
Mk 5:7 me, Jesus, Son of the **M** High God?
Col 4:5 making the **m** of the opportunity.
Jude 1:20 yourselves up in your **m** holy faith;

MOTH
Mt 6:19 earth, where **m** and decay destroys,

MOTHER → MOTHER'S, MOTHERS
Ge 2:24 why a man leaves his father and **m**
3:20 because she became the **m** of all
Ex 20:12 "Honor your father and your **m**,
Jdg 5:7 rose, when I rose, a **m** in Israel,
Tob 4:3 Honor your **m**, and do not abandon
Pr 31:1 The advice which his **m** gave him:
Sir 3:6 LORD who brings comfort to his **m**.
Isa 66:13 As a **m** comforts her son, so will I
Mt 10:37 or **m** more than me is not worthy
Lk 14:26 me without hating his father and **m**,
Jn 2:3 ran short, the **m** of Jesus said to him,
19:27 said to the disciple, "Behold, your **m**."
Gal 4:26 above is freeborn, and she is our **m**.
Eph 5:31 shall leave [his] father and [his] **m**
Rev 17:5 the great, the **m** of harlots

MOTHER'S → MOTHER
Job 1:21 I came forth from my **m** womb,
Pr 1:8 and reject not your **m** teaching;
Jn 3:4 he cannot reenter his **m** womb

MOTHERS → MOTHER
Mk 10:30 and sisters and **m** and children

MOUNT → MOUNTAIN, MOUNTAINS
Ex 19:20 came down to the top of **M** Sinai,
Dt 11:29 the blessing on **M** Gerizim,
11:29 on **M** Gerizim, the curse on **M** Ebal.
Ps 78:68 of Judah, **M** Zion which he favored.
Mic 4:7 shall be king over them on **M** Zion,
Zec 14:4 feet shall rest upon the **M** of Olives,
14:4 The **M** of Olives shall be cleft
Mk 13:3 the **M** of Olives opposite the temple
Heb 12:22 you have approached **M** Zion
Rev 14:1 was the Lamb standing on **M** Zion,

MOUNTAIN → MOUNT
Ex 3:1 he came to Horeb, the **m** of God.
24:18 of the cloud as he went up on the **m**;
Isa 2:2 to come, The **m** of the LORD's house
2:2 shall be established as the highest **m**
Da 2:45 from the **m** without a hand being put
Mt 4:8 devil took him up to a very high **m**,
17:20 you will say to this **m**,
2Pe 1:18 we were with him on the holy **m**.

MOUNTAINS → MOUNT
Ge 7:20 cubits higher than the submerged **m**.
Ps 125:2 As **m** surround Jerusalem, the LORD
Isa 52:7 How beautiful upon the **m**
1Co 13:2 if I have all faith so as to move **m**,
Rev 16:20 island fled, and **m** disappeared.

MOURN → MOURNFUL, MOURNING
Ecc 3:4 a time to **m**, and a time to dance.
Sir 7:34 who weep, but **m** with those who **m**;
Zec 12:10 they shall **m** for him as one mourns
Mt 5:4 Blessed are they who **m**, for they

MOURNING → MOURN
Ps 30:12 You changed my **m** into dancing;
Isa 61:3 them oil of gladness in place of **m**,
Rev 21:4 there shall be no more death or **m**,

MOUTH → MOUTHS
Dt 8:3 comes forth from the **m** of the LORD.
Ps 19:15 Let the words of my **m** meet
Mt 4:4 comes forth from the **m** of God.' "
15:11 It is not what enters one's **m**
15:11 out of the **m** is what defiles one."
Jas 3:10 From the same **m** come blessing

MOUTH → MOUTHS (*cont.*)
Rev 19:15 Out of his **m** came a sharp sword

MOUTHS → MOUTH
Ps 115: 5 They have **m** but do not speak,

MUCH
Ecc 12:12 in **m** study there is weariness
Lk 12:48 **M** will be required of the person
12:48 of the person entrusted with **m**,
Jn 12:24 but if it dies, it produces **m** fruit.

MULTIPLY
Ge 1:28 "Be fertile and **m**; fill the earth
9: 7 Be fertile, then, and **m**;

MULTITUDE
Jas 5:20 death and will cover a **m** of sins.
1Pe 4: 8 because love covers a **m** of sins.

MURDER → MURDERER, MURDERERS
Hos 4: 2 lying, **m**, stealing and adultery!

MURDERER → MURDER
Nu 35:16 he is a **m** and shall be put to death.
Jn 8:44 He was a **m** from the beginning

MURDERERS → MURDER
Rev 21: 8 the depraved, **m**, the unchaste,

MUSTARD
Mt 17:20 you have faith the size of a **m** seed,
Mk 4:31 It is like a **m** seed that, when it is

MUTUAL
Ro 12:10 love one another with **m** affection;
Heb 13: 1 Let **m** love continue.

MYRRH
Mt 2:11 gifts of gold, frankincense, and **m**.
Mk 15:23 gave him wine drugged with **m**,

MYSTERY
Da 2:19 During the night the **m** was revealed
Ro 11:25 want you to be unaware of this **m**,
1Co 15:51 Behold, I tell you a **m**. We shall not
Eph 3: 4 my insight into the **m** of Christ,
1Ti 3: 9 holding fast to the **m** of the faith
Rev 17: 5 which is a **m**, "Babylon the great,

MYTHS
2Pe 1:16 did not follow cleverly devised **m**

N

NAAMAN
Aramean general whose leprosy was cleansed by Elisha (2Ki 5; Lk 4:27).

NABAL
Wealthy Carmelite the LORD killed for refusing to help David (1Sa 25). David married Abigail, his widow (1Sa 25:39-42).

NABOTH
Jezreelite killed for his vineyard (1Ki 21). Ahab's family punished (1Ki 21:17-24; 2Ki 9:21-37).

NADAB
1. Firstborn of Aaron (Ex 6:23); killed with Abihu for offering unauthorized fire (Lev 10; Nu 3:4).
2. Son of Jeroboam I; king of Israel (1Ki 15:25-32).

NAHUM
Prophet against Nineveh (Na 1:1; Tob 14:4).

NAILING → NAILS
Col 2:14 it from our midst, **n** it to the cross;

NAILS → NAILING
Jn 20:25 I see the mark of the **n** in his hands

NAKED → NAKEDNESS
Ge 2:25 The man and his wife were both **n**,
Job 1:21 "**N** I came forth from my mother's
1:21 and **n** I shall I go back again.
2Co 5: 3 taken it off, we shall not be found **n**.

NAKEDNESS → NAKED
Ro 8:35 or famine, or **n**, or peril,

NAME → NAMES
Ge 2:19 called each of them would be its **n**.
4:26 men began to invoke the LORD by **n**.
12: 2 I will make your **n** great, so that you
Ex 3:15 "This is my **n** forever; this is my title
20: 7 "You shall not take the **n** of the LORD,
20: 7 unpunished him who takes his **n**
34: 5 him there and proclaimed his **n**,
Dt 12:11 for his **n** you shall bring all
Ps 9:11 Those who honor your **n** trust
Pr 18:10 The **n** of the LORD is a strong tower;
Isa 42: 8 I am the LORD, this is my **n**;
Zec 14: 9 the only one, and his **n** the only one.
Mt 1:21 a son and you are to **n** him Jesus,
6: 9 in heaven, hallowed be your **n**,
28:19 them in the **n** of the Father,
Jn 1:12 God, to those who believe in his **n**,
20:31 belief you may have life in his **n**.
Ac 4:12 is there any other **n** under heaven
Php 2: 9 and bestowed on him the **n** that is

Php 2: 9 on him the **n** that is above every **n**,
Rev 13:17 the stamped image of the beast's **n**
13:17 **n** or the number that stood for its **n**.
19:13 his **n** was called the Word of God.
22: 4 and his **n** will be on their foreheads.

NAMES → NAME
Ge 2:20 The man gave **n** to all the cattle,
Ex 28: 9 engrave on them the **n** of the sons
Mt 10: 2 The **n** of the twelve apostles are
Rev 21:14 were inscribed the twelve **n**

NAOMI
Wife of Elimelech, mother-in-law of Ruth (Ru 1:2, 4). Left Bethlehem for Moab during famine (Ru 1:1). Returned a widow, with Ruth (Ru 1:6-22). Advised Ruth to seek marriage with Boaz (Ru 2:17-3:4). Cared for Ruth's son Obed (Ru 4:13-17).

NAPHTALI
Son of Jacob by Bilhah (Ge 30:8; 35:25; 1Ch 2:2). Tribe of blessed (Ge 49:21; Dt 33:23), numbered (Nu 1:43; 26:50), allotted land (Jos 19:32-39; Eze 48:3), failed to fully possess (Jdg 1:33), supported Deborah (Jdg 4:10; 5:18), David (1Ch 12:34), 12,000 from (Rev 7:6).

NARROW
Lk 13:24 "Strive to enter through the **n** gate,

NATHAN
Prophet and chronicler of Israel's history (1Ch 29:29; 2Ch 9:29). Announced the Davidic covenant (2Sa 7; 1Ch 17). Denounced David's sin with Bathsheba (2Sa 12). Supported Solomon (1Ki 1).

NATHANAEL → = BARTHOLOMEW?
Apostle (Jn 1:45-49; 21:2). Probably also called Bartholomew (Mt 10:3).

NATION → NATIONS
Ge 12: 2 "I will make of you a great **n**, and I
Ex 32:10 Then I will make of you a great **n**."
Ps 33:12 Happy the **n** whose God is the LORD,
Pr 14:34 Virtue exalts a **n**, but sin is
Isa 2: 4 One **n** shall not raise the sword
66: 8 or a **n** be born in a single moment?
Mt 24: 7 **N** will rise against **n**, and kingdom
1Pe 2: 9 a holy **n**, a people of his own,

NATIONS → NATION
Ge 18:18 and all the **n** of the earth are to find
2Ki 17:15 the surrounding **n** whom the LORD
Ps 47: 9 God rules over the **n**; God sits
Isa 2: 2 hills. All **n** shall stream toward it;

Isa 42: 1 he shall bring forth justice to the **n**,

Am 9:12 all the **n** that shall bear my name,

Mt 28:19 and make disciples of all **n**,

Ro 4:18 would become "the father of many **n**,

Rev 22: 2 the trees serve as medicine for the **n**.

NATURAL → NATURE

Ro 11:21 if God did not spare the **n** branches,

NATURE → NATURAL

2Pe 1: 4 may come to share in the divine **n**,

NAZARETH

Mt 2:23 went and dwelt in a town called **N**,

Jn 1:46 "Can anything good come from **N**?"

NAZIRITE

Nu 6: 2 a woman) solemnly takes the **n** vow

NEAR

Dt 30:14 No, it is something very **n** to you,

Isa 55: 6 be found, call him while he is **n**.

Zep 1:14 **N** is the great day of the LORD,

Jas 4: 8 Draw **n** to God, and he will draw **n**

Rev 22:10 book, for the appointed time is **n**.

NEBUCHADNEZZAR

Babylonian king, also spelled Nebuchadrezzar. Subdued and exiled Judah (2Ki 24-25; 2Ch 36; Jer 39). Dreams interpreted by Daniel (Da 2; 4). Worshiped God (Da 3:28-29; 4:34-37).

NECK → STIFF-NECKED

Pr 3:22 soul, and an adornment for your **n**.

Mt 18: 6 a great millstone hung around his **n**

NECO

Pharaoh who killed Josiah (2Ki 23:29-30; 2Ch 35:20-22), deposed Jehoahaz (2Ki 23:33-35; 2Ch 36:3-4).

NEED → NEEDY

Mt 6: 8 knows what you **n** before you ask

1Co 12:21 "I do not **n** you," nor again the head

12:21 the head to the feet, "I do not **n**

1Jn 2:27 you do not **n** anyone to teach you.

NEEDLE

Lk 18:25 pass through the eye of a **n** than

NEEDY → NEED

1Sa 2: 8 He raises the **n** from the dust;

Job 29:16 I was a father to the **n**; the rights

Ps 113: 7 The LORD raises the **n** from the dust,

NEGLECT

1Ti 4:14 Do not **n** the gift you have,

NEHEMIAH

Cupbearer of Artaxerxes (Ne 2:1); governor of Israel (Ne 8:9). Returned to Jerusalem to rebuild walls (Ne 2-6). With Ezra, reestablished worship (Ne 8). Prayer confessing nation's sin (Ne 9). Dedicated wall (Ne 12). Story of the miraculous fire (2Ma 1).

NEIGHBOR

Lev 19:18 You shall love your **n** as yourself.

Dt 5:20 dishonest witness against your **n**.

Mt 19:19 'you shall love your **n** as yourself.' "

Jas 2: 8 "You shall love your **n** as yourself,"

NESTS

Mt 8:20 dens and birds of the sky have **n**,

NEVER

Ps 15: 5 acts like this shall **n** be shaken.

Da 2:44 a kingdom that shall **n** be destroyed

Mt 7:23 to them solemnly, 'I **n** knew you.

Jn 10:28 eternal life, and they shall **n** perish.

1Co 13: 8 Love **n** fails. If there are prophecies,

Heb 13: 5 "I will **n** forsake you or abandon you."

NEW

Ex 1: 8 Then a **n** king, who knew nothing

Ps 33: 3 Sing to God a **n** song; skillfully play

Ecc 1: 9 be done. Nothing is **n** under the sun.

Isa 43:19 See, I am doing something **n**!

65:17 Lo, I am about to create **n** heavens

65:17 and a **n** earth; The things of the past

Jer 31:31 I will make a **n** covenant

Eze 36:26 I will give you a **n** heart and place

36:26 heart and place a **n** spirit within you,

Mt 9:17 People do not put **n** wine into old

9:17 Rather, they pour **n** wine into fresh

Mk 1:27 is this? A **n** teaching with authority.

Lk 22:20 "This cup is the **n** covenant in my

Jn 13:34 I give you a **n** commandment:

2Co 3: 6 us as ministers of a **n** covenant,

Col 3:10 and have put on the **n** self, which is

Heb 8: 8 I will conclude a **n** covenant

1Pe 1: 3 his great mercy gave us a **n** birth

2Pe 3:13 to his promise we await **n** heavens

3:13 and a **n** earth in which righteousness

1Jn 2: 7 I am writing no **n** commandment

Rev 21: 1 Then I saw a **n** heaven and a **n** earth.

21: 2 saw the holy city, a **n** Jerusalem,

21: 5 said, "Behold, I make all things **n**."

NEWS

Isa 52: 7 Announcing peace, bearing good **n**,

Mt 11: 5 poor have the good **n** proclaimed

NICODEMUS

Pharisee who visted Jesus at night (Jn 3). Argued for fair treatment of Jesus (Jn 7:50-52). With Joseph, prepared Jesus for burial (Jn 19:38-42).

NIGHT → NIGHTS

Ge 1: 5 "day," and the darkness he called "**n**."

Ex 13:21 at **n** by means of a column of fire

13:21 they could travel both day and **n**.

Jos 1: 8 Recite it by day and by **n**, that you

Mt 24:43 the house had known the hour of **n**

1Th 5: 2 the Lord will come like a thief at **n**.

Rev 22: 5 **N** will be no more, nor will they

NIGHTS → NIGHT

Ge 7:12 forty **n** heavy rain poured down

Ex 24:18 he stayed for forty days and forty **n**.

1Ki 19: 8 and forty **n** to the mountain of God,

Mt 4: 2 He fasted for forty days and forty **n**,

12:40 of the whale three days and three **n**,

12:40 of the earth three days and three **n**.

NINEVEH

Jnh 1: 2 "Set out for the great city of **N**,

Na 1: 1 Oracle about **N**. The book

Mt 12:41 the men of **N** will arise with this

NOAH

Righteous man (Eze 14:14, 20) called to build ark (Ge 6-8; Heb 11:7; 1Pe 3:20; 2Pe 2:5). God's covenant with (Ge 9:1-17). Drunkenness of (Ge 9:18-23). Blessed sons, cursed Canaan (Ge 9:24-27). Praised (Sir 44:17-18).

NOISE

Ex 32:17 Joshua heard the **n** of the people

NOON

Mk 15:33 At **n** darkness came over the whole

NORTH

Jer 4: 6 Evil I bring from the **n**, and great

NORTH (*cont.*)
Da   11: 6   to the king of the **n** in the interest

NOTHING
Ecc   1: 9   be done. **N** is new under the sun.
Sir   39:20   ages; to him there is **n** unexpected.
Jer   32:17   arm; **n** is impossible to you.
Mt   17:20   move. **N** will be impossible for you."
Jn   15: 5   because without me you can do **n**.
1Co   13: 2   but do not have love, I am **n**.

NULLIFY
Ro   3: 3   Will their infidelity **n** the fidelity
Gal   2:21   I do not **n** the grace of God;

NUMBER → NUMBERED, NUMEROUS
Nu   1:45   The total **n** of the Israelites
Ro   11:25   part, until the full **n** of the Gentiles
Rev   13:18   who understands can calculate the **n**
      13:18   for it is a **n** that stands for a person.
      13:18   His **n** is six hundred and sixty-six.

NUMBERED → NUMBER
2Sa   24:10   David regretted having **n** the people,

NUMEROUS → NUMBER
Ex   1: 9   "Look how **n** and powerful
Zec   10: 8   them they will be as **n** as before.

O

OATH
Dt   7: 8   his fidelity to the **o** he had sworn
Ps   132:11   The LORD swore an **o** to David,
Heb   7:20   others became priests without an **o**,

OBADIAH
  1. Believer who sheltered 100 prophets from Jezebel (1Ki 18:1-16).
  2. Prophet against Edom (Ob 1).

OBEDIENCE → OBEY
Ro   5:19   so through the **o** of the one the many
Heb   5: 8   he learned **o** from what he suffered;

OBEDIENT → OBEY
Php   2: 8   himself, becoming **o** to death,

OBEY → OBEDIENCE, OBEDIENT, OBEYED
Jos   24:24   the LORD, our God, and **o** his voice."
Ac   5:29   "We must **o** God rather than men.
Eph   6: 1   **o** your parents [in the Lord], for this

OBEYED → OBEY
Heb   11: 8   faith Abraham **o** when he was called

OBSERVE
Lev   20: 8   therefore, to **o** what I, the LORD,

OBSTACLE
1Co   9:12   so as not to place an **o** to the gospel

OBTAIN → OBTAINED
2Ti   2:10   they too may **o** the salvation that is

OBTAINED → OBTAIN
Heb   8: 6   Now he has **o** so much more

ODOR
Ge   8:21   When the LORD smelled the sweet **o**,

OFFENSE
Mk   6: 3   with us?" And they took **o** at him.

OFFER → OFFERING, OFFERINGS
Ps   4: 6   **O** fitting sacrifice and trust
Heb   9:25   that he might **o** himself repeatedly,

OFFERING → OFFER
Ge   4: 4   with favor on Abel and his **o**,
Ps   40: 7   Sacrifice and **o** you do not want;
Eph   5: 2   over for us as a sacrificial **o** to God
Heb   10:14   one **o** he has made perfect forever

OFFERINGS → OFFER
Mk   12:33   is worth more than all burnt **o**

OFFSPRING
Ge   3:15   and between your **o** and hers;

OHOLIAB
  Craftsman who worked on the tabernacle (Ex 31:6; 35:34; 36:1-2; 38:23).

OIL
Ex   25: 6   **o** for the light;
      25: 6   spices for the anointing **o**
Dt   14:23   wine and **o**, as well as the firstlings
Ps   23: 5   You anoint my head with **o**; my cup
Heb   1: 9   with the **o** of gladness above your
Jas   5:14   anoint [him] with **o** in the name

OLD
Ge   21: 7   I have borne him a son in his **o** age."
Ps   74:12   you, God, are my king from of **o**,
Mk   2:22   pours new wine into **o** wineskins.
Ro   4:19   he was almost a hundred years **o**)
Eph   4:22   you should put away the **o** self

OLIVE → OLIVES
Zec   4: 3   and beside it are two **o** trees,
Ro   11:17   a wild **o** shoot, were grafted in their
      11:17   to share in the rich root of the **o** tree,
Rev   11: 4   These are the two **o** trees

OLIVES → OLIVE
Zec   14: 4   feet shall rest upon the Mount of **O**,
      14: 4   The Mount of **O** shall be cleft
Mt   24: 3   he was sitting on the Mount of **O**,

OMEGA
Rev   1: 8   "I am the Alpha and the **O**,"

OMRI
  King of Israel (1Ki 16:21-26).

ONCE → ONE
Ex   30:10   **O** a year Aaron shall perform
      30:10   atonement is to be made **o** a year
Ro   6:10   death, he died to sin **o** and for all;
Heb   7:27   he did that **o** for all when he offered
      9:27   appointed that human beings die **o**,

ONE → FIRST, ONCE
Ge   2:24   and the two of them become **o** body.
Zec   14: 9   day the LORD shall be the only **o**,
      14: 9   the only **o**, and his name the only **o**.
Jn   10:30   The Father and I are **o**."
1Co   12:13   in **o** Spirit we were all baptized
      12:13   we were all baptized into **o** body,
      12:13   were all given to drink of **o** Spirit.
Gal   3:28   for you are all **o** in Christ Jesus.
Eph   4: 5   **o** Lord, **o** faith, **o** baptism;

ONLY
Ge   22: 2   "Take your son Isaac, your **o** one,
1Ki   18:22   "I am the **o** surviving prophet
Jn   1:14   the glory as of the Father's **o** Son,
      3:16   the world that he gave his **o** Son,
1Ti   1:17   invisible, the **o** God,
1Jn   4: 9   God sent his **o** Son into the world so

OPEN → OPENED, OPENS
Rev   5: 2   "Who is worthy to **o** the scroll

OPENED → OPEN
Ge   3: 7   the eyes of both of them were **o**,
Isa   53: 7   and not his mouth; Like a lamb
      53: 7   he was silent and **o** not his mouth.
Da   7:10   convened, and the books were **o**.
Lk   11: 9   knock and the door will be **o** to you.
Heb   10:20   living way he **o** for us through
Rev   20:12   the throne, and scrolls were **o**.
      20:12   Then another scroll was **o**, the

OPENS → OPEN
Rev   3: 7   who **o** and no one shall close,

OPPORTUNITY
Mt 26:16 he looked for an **o** to hand him over.
Gal 5:13 do not use this freedom as an **o**

OPPRESSED → OPPRESSION
Ge 15:13 and **o** for four hundred years.
Ex 1:12 Yet the more they were **o**, the more
Jdt 9:11 the helper of the **o**, the supporter
Ps 146: 7 secures justice for the **o**, gives food

OPPRESSION → OPPRESSED
Eze 45: 9 Put away violence and **o**, and do

ORDAIN
Ex 29: 9 thus shall you **o** Aaron and his sons.

ORDER
Heb 5:10 according to the **o** of Melchizedek.

ORIGIN
Mt 21:26 say, "Of human **o**," we fear the crowd,
Ac 5:38 or this activity is of human **o**, it will

ORNAMENTS
Ex 33: 6 the Israelites laid aside their **o**.

ORPHANS
Jas 1:27 to care for **o** and widows in their

OTHER → OTHERS
Ex 20: 3 shall not have **o** gods besides me.
Jdg 2:19 following **o** gods in service
2Ki 17: 7 and because they venerated **o** gods.
Isa 45: 5 I am the LORD and there is no **o**,
Mt 6:24 will either hate one and love the **o**,
6:24 be devoted to one and despise the **o**.

OTHERS → OTHER
Lk 6:31 Do to **o** as you would have them do
Php 2: 3 humbly regard **o** as more important

OTHNIEL
Nephew of Caleb (Jos 15:15-19; Jdg 1:12-15). Judge who freed Israel from Aram (Jdg 3:7-11).

OUTSIDE
Lk 11:39 Although you cleanse the **o**
Heb 13:12 Jesus also suffered **o** the gate,
Rev 22:15 **O** are the dogs, the sorcerers,

OUTSTRETCHED → STRETCH
Ex 6: 6 I will rescue you by my **o** arm
Ps 136:12 With mighty hand and **o** arm,
Jer 27: 5 by my great power, with my **o** arm;

OVERCOME
Jn 1: 5 and the darkness has not **o** it.

OVERSEERS
Ac 20:28 the holy Spirit has appointed you **o**,

OVERSHADOW
Lk 1:35 power of the Most High will **o** you.

OWE → OWES
Mt 18:28 demanding, 'Pay back what you **o**.'
Ro 13: 8 **O** nothing to anyone, except to love

OWN
Isa 53: 6 each following his **o** way;
Jer 31:30 but through his **o** fault only shall
Jn 1:11 He came to what was his **o**, but his
1:11 but his **o** people did not accept him.
10:18 from me, but I lay it down on my **o**.
1Co 6:19 God, and that you are not your **o**?

OX → OXEN
Dt 25: 4 "You shall not muzzle an **o** when it is
Isa 65:25 and the lion shall eat hay like the **o**
Eze 1:10 and on the left side the face of an **o**,
1Ti 5:18 "You shall not muzzle an **o** when it is

P

PAGANS
1Co 12: 2 how, when you were **p**, you were

PAIN → PAINS
Ge 3:16 in **p** shall you bring forth children.
1Pe 2:19 For whenever anyone bears the **p**
Rev 21: 4 wailing or **p**, [for] the old order has

PAINS → PAIN
Ro 8:22 groaning in labor **p** even until now;
1Th 5: 3 them, like labor **p** upon a pregnant

PALM → PALMS
Jn 12:13 they took **p** branches and
Rev 7: 9 holding **p** branches in their hands.

PALMS → PALM
Isa 49:16 the **p** of my hands I have written

PANGS
Ge 3:16 he said: "I will intensify the **p** of your

PARABLE → PARABLES
Mt 13:18 "Hear then the **p** of the sower.

PARABLES → PARABLE; See also JESUS: PARABLES
Mt 13:35 "I will open my mouth in **p**, I will

PARADISE
Lk 23:43 you, today you will be with me in **P**."
2Co 12: 4 was caught up into **P** and heard

PARALYTIC → PARALYZED
Mt 9: 2 to him a **p** lying on a stretcher.
9: 2 their faith, he said to the **p**, "Courage,

PARALYZED → PARALYTIC
Ac 8: 7 many **p** and crippled people were

PARCHMENTS
2Ti 4:13 papyrus rolls, and especially the **p**.

PARDON
Ex 34: 9 yet **p** our wickedness and sins,

PARENTS
Eph 6: 1 Children, obey your **p** [in the Lord],

PARTAKE
1Co 10:17 body, for we all **p** of the one loaf.

PARTIALITY
Pr 24:23 To show **p** in judgment is not good.
Ro 2:11 There is no **p** with God.

PARTNERSHIP
2Co 6:14 For what **p** do righteousness

PASHHUR
Priest; opponent of Jeremiah (Jer 20:1-6).

PASS → PASSED, PASSING
Ex 12:13 Seeing the blood, I will **p** over you;
33:19 make all my beauty **p** before you,
Am 5:17 when I **p** through your midst,
Mt 24:35 Heaven and earth will **p** away,
24:35 but my words will not **p** away.
2Pe 3:10 then the heavens will **p** away

PASSED → PASS
Ge 15:17 which **p** between those pieces.
Ex 12:27 LORD, who **p** over the houses
33:22 you with my hand until I have **p** by.
2Co 5:17 the old things have **p** away; behold,
1Jn 3:14 We know that we have **p** from death
Rev 21: 4 pain, [for] the old order has **p** away."

PASSING → PASS
1Co 7:31 world in its present form is **p** away.
1Jn 2:17 and its enticement are **p** away.

PASSIONS
Gal 5:24 have crucified their flesh with its **p**

PASSOVER
Ex 12:11 are in flight. It is the **P** of the LORD.
Dt 16: 1 Abib by keeping the **P** of the LORD.
Mk 14:12 when they sacrificed the **P** lamb,

PASSOVER (*cont.*)
Mk 14:12 go and prepare for you to eat the **P**?"

PASTORS
Eph 4:11 others as **p** and teachers,

PASTURES
Ps 23: 2 In green **p** you let me graze; to safe

PATH → PATHS
Ps 16:11 You will show me the **p** to life,
119:105 a lamp for my feet, a light for my **p**.
Mt 13: 4 some seed fell on the **p**, and birds

PATHS → PATH
Pr 3: 6 and he will make straight your **p**.
Mt 3: 3 of the Lord, make straight his **p**.' "
Heb 12:13 Make straight **p** for your feet,

PATIENCE → PATIENT
Mic 2: 7 "Is the LORD short of **p**, or are such
Ro 2: 4 and **p** in low esteem,
Gal 5:22 joy, peace, **p**, kindness, generosity,
2Pe 3:15 And consider the **p** of our Lord as

PATIENT → PATIENCE
1Co 13: 4 Love is **p**, love is kind. It is not
2Pe 3: 9 but he is **p** with you, not wishing

PATTERN
Ex 25:40 them according to the **p** shown you
Heb 8: 5 according to the **p** shown you

PAUL → = SAUL
Also called Saul (Ac 13:9). Pharisee from Tarsus (Ac 9:11; Php 3:5). Apostle (Gal 1). At stoning of Stephen (Ac 8:1). Persecuted Church (Ac 9:1-2; Gal 1:13). Vision of Jesus on road to Damascus (Ac 9:4-9; 26:12-18). In Arabia (Gal 1:17). Preached in Damascus; escaped death through the wall in a basket (Ac 9:19-25). In Jerusalem; back to Tarsus (Ac 9:26-30).
Brought to Antioch by Barnabas (Ac 11:22-26). First missionary journey to Cyprus and Galatia (Ac 13-14). Stoned at Lystra (Ac 14:19-20). At Jerusalem council (Ac 15). Split with Barnabas over Mark (Ac 15:36-41).
Second missionary journey with Silas (Ac 16-20). Called to Macedonia (Ac 16:6-10). Freed from prison in Philippi (Ac 16:16-40). In Thessalonica (Ac 17:1-9). Speech in Athens (Ac 17:16-33). In Corinth (Ac 18). In Ephesus (Ac 19). Return to Jerusalem (Ac 20). Farewell to Ephesian elders (Ac 20:13-38). Arrival in Jerusalem (Ac 21:1-26). Arrested (Ac 21:27-36). Addressed crowds (Ac 22), Sanhedrin (Ac 23:1-11). Sent to Caesarea (Ac 23:12-35). Trial before Felix (Ac 24), Festus (Ac 25:1-12). Before Agrippa (Ac 25:13-26:32). Voyage to Rome; shipwreck (Ac 27). Arrival in Rome (Ac 28).

PAVEMENT
Jn 19:13 bench in the place called Stone **P**,

PAY → REPAY
Dt 24:15 You shall **p** him each day's wages
Mt 22:17 Is it lawful to **p** the census tax
Ro 13: 7 **P** to all their dues, taxes to whom

PEACE → PEACEMAKERS
Lev 26: 6 I will establish **p** in the land,
Ps 122: 6 For the **p** of Jerusalem pray:
Isa 26: 3 of firm purpose you keep in **p**; in **p**,
57:19 life. **P, p** to the far and the near,
Isa 57:21 No **p** for the wicked! says my God.
Jer 6:14 the injury to my people: "**P, p!**"
6:14 "**P, p!**" they say, though there is no **p**.
Lk 2:14 and on earth **p** to those on whom his
Jn 14:27 **P** I leave with you; my **p** I give
Ro 16:20 of **p** will quickly crush Satan under
1Co 14:33 is not the God of disorder but of **p**.
Gal 5:22 of the Spirit is love, joy, **p**, patience,
Eph 4: 3 of the spirit through the bond of **p**:
Php 4: 7 Then the **p** of God that surpasses all
2Ti 2:22 and **p**, along with those who call

PEACEMAKERS → PEACE
Mt 5: 9 Blessed are the **p**, for they will be

PEARL → PEARLS
Mt 13:46 When he finds a **p** of great price,
Rev 21:21 of the gates made from a single **p**;

PEARLS → PEARL
Mt 7: 6 or throw your **p** before swine,

PEKAH
King of Israel (2Ki 15:25-31; 2Ch 28:6; Isa 7:1).

PEKAHIAH
Son of Menahem; king of Israel (2Ki 15:22-26).

PENALTY
Ro 1:27 their own persons the due **p** for their

PENTECOST
Ac 2: 1 When the time for **P** was fulfilled,

PEOPLE → PEOPLES
Ex 5: 1 Israel: Let my **p** go, that they may
33:13 this nation is, after all, your own **p**."
Dt 4:20 that you might be his very own **p**,

Ru 1:16 I will lodge, your **p** shall be my **p**,
2Sa 5: 2 'You shall shepherd my **p** Israel
Ps 29:11 May the LORD give might to his **p**;
29:11 his **p**; may the LORD bless his **p**
125: 2 the LORD surrounds his **p** both now
Isa 40: 1 Comfort, give comfort to my **p**,
42: 6 as a covenant of the **p**, a light
53: 8 and smitten for the sin of his **p**,
Jer 50: 6 Lost sheep were my **p**,
Da 9:24 for your **p** and for your holy city:
Zec 13: 9 I will say, "They are my **p**," and they
Mt 1:21 because he will save his **p**
Jn 11:50 one man should die instead of the **p**,
18:14 man should die rather than the **p**.
Ro 9:25 who were not my **p** I will call 'my **p**,"
Heb 8:10 their God, and they shall be my **p**.
1Pe 2: 9 a holy nation, a **p** of his own,

PEOPLES → PEOPLE
Ge 17:16 and rulers of **p** shall issue from him."
Ps 117: 1 you nations! Give glory, all you **p**!

PERFECT → PERFECTER
Ps 19: 8 The law of the LORD is **p**,
Mt 5:48 So be **p**, just as your heavenly
5:48 **p**, just as your heavenly Father is **p**.
Ro 12: 2 what is good and pleasing and **p**.
2Co 12: 9 for power is made **p** in weakness."
Heb 5: 9 and when he was made **p**,
1Jn 4:18 **p** love drives out fear because fear
4:18 and so one who fears is not yet **p**

PERFECTER → PERFECT
Heb 12: 2 on Jesus, the leader and **p** of faith.

PERISH → PERISHABLE
Jos 23:13 until you **p** from this good land
Est 4:16 king, contrary to the law. If I **p, I p!**"
Jn 3:16 who believes in him might not **p**
2Pe 3: 9 not wishing that any should **p**

PERISHABLE → PERISH
1Co 9:25 They do it to win a **p** crown, but we
1Pe 1:23 not from **p** but from imperishable

PERSECUTE → PERSECUTED, PERSECUTION
Mt 5:44 and pray for those who **p** you,
Ro 12:14 Bless those who **p** [you],

PERSECUTED → PERSECUTE
Jn 15:20 master.' If they **p** me, they will
2Co 4: 9 **p**, but not abandoned; struck down,
2Ti 3:12 religiously in Christ Jesus will be **p**.

PERSECUTION → PERSECUTE
Mt 13:21 or **p** comes because of the word,
Ro 8:35 or distress, or **p**, or famine,

PERSEVERE
Ro 12:12 endure in affliction, **p** in prayer.

PERSIA
Ezr 1: 1 king of **P**, in order to fulfill
1: 1 the LORD inspired King Cyrus of **P**

PESTILENCE
Dt 32:24 and bitter **p**, And the teeth of wild
Ps 91: 6 Nor the **p** that roams in darkness,

PETER → = CEPHAS, = SIMON
Apostle, brother of Andrew, also called Simon (Mt 10:2; Mk 3:16; Lk 6:14; Ac 1:13), and Cephas (Jn 1:42). Confession of Christ (Mt 16:13-20; Mk 8:27-30; Lk 9:18-27). At transfiguration (Mt 17:1-8; Mk 9:2-8; Lk 9:28-36; 2Pe 1:16-18). Caught fish with coin (Mt 17:24-27). Denial of Jesus predicted (Mt 26:31-35; Mk 14:27-31; Lk 22:31-34; Jn 13:31-38). Denied Jesus (Mt 26:69-75; Mk 14:66-72; Lk 22:54-62; Jn 18:15-27). Commissioned by Jesus to shepherd his flock (Jn 21:15-23).
Speech at Pentecost (Ac 2). Healed beggar (Ac 3:1-10). Speech at temple (Ac 3:11-26), before Sanhedrin (Ac 4:1-22). In Samaria (Ac 8:14-25). Sent by vision to Cornelius (Ac 10). Announced salvation of Gentiles in Jerusalem (Ac 11; 15). Freed from prison (Ac 12). Inconsistency at Antioch (Gal 2:11-21). At Jerusalem Council (Ac 15).

PHARAOH → PHARAOH'S
Ge 41:14 **P** therefore had Joseph summoned,
Ex 3:11 "Who am I that I should go to **P**
14:17 I will receive glory through **P**
Ro 9:17 For the scripture says to **P**, "This is

PHARAOH'S → PHARAOH
Heb 11:24 be known as the son of **P** daughter;

PHARISEE → PHARISEES
Lk 11:37 a **P** invited him to dine at his home.
Jn 3: 1 there was a **P** named Nicodemus,
Ac 5:34 But a **P** in the Sanhedrin named
Php 3: 5 in observance of the law a **P**,

PHARISEES → PHARISEE
Mt 5:20 surpasses that of the scribes and **P**,
16: 6 beware of the leaven of the **P**
23:13 you, scribes and **P**, you hypocrites.

PHILEMON
Phm 1: 1 brother, to **P**, our beloved and our

PHILIP
1. Apostle (Mt 10:3; Mk 3:18; Lk 6:14; Jn 1:43-48; 14:8; Ac 1:13).
2. Deacon (Ac 6:1-7); evangelist in Samaria (Ac 8:4-25), to Ethiopian (Ac 8:26-40).

PHILISTINE → PHILISTINES
1Sa 17:37 me safe from the clutches of this **P**."

PHILISTINES → PHILISTINE
Ge 26: 1 Abimelech, king of the **P** in Gerar.
1Sa 5: 1 The **P**, having captured the ark
17: 1 The **P** rallied their forces for battle
2Sa 8: 1 After this David attacked the **P**
8: 1 them, wresting . . . from the **P**.
Am 1: 8 and the last of the **P** shall perish.

PHILOSOPHERS → PHILOSOPHY
Ac 17:18 Stoic **p** engaged him in discussion.

PHILOSOPHY → PHILOSOPHERS
Col 2: 8 seductive **p** according to human

PHINEHAS
1. Grandson of Aaron (Ex 6:25; Jos 22:30-32). Zeal for the LORD (Nu 25:7-13; Ps 106:30).
2. A wicked priest (1Sa 1:3; 2:12-17; 4:1-19).

PHOEBE
Ro 16: 1 I commend to you **P** our sister,

PHYSICAL
1Ti 4: 8 while **p** training is of limited value,

PHYSICIAN
Mt 9:12 "Those who are well do not need a **p**,
Col 4:14 Luke the beloved **p** sends greetings,

PIECES
Ge 15:17 which passed between those **p**.
Lk 20:18 on that stone will be dashed to **p**;

PIERCED
Jn 19:37 look upon him whom they have **p**."
Rev 1: 7 him, even those who **p** him.

PIG
Dt 14: 8 and the **p**, which indeed has hoofs

PILATE
Governor of Judea. Questioned Jesus (Mt 27:1-26; Mk 15:15; Lk 22:66-23:25; Jn 18:28-19:16); sent him to Herod (Lk 23:6-12); consented to his crucifixion when crowds chose Barabbas (Mt 27:15-26; Mk 15:6-15; Lk 23:13-25; Jn 19:1-10).

PILLAR
Ge 19:26 and she was turned into a **p** of salt.

PIT
Ps 103: 4 Delivers your life from the **p**,

PITY
Dt 7:16 You are not to look on them with **p**,
Hos 1: 6 I no longer feel **p** for the house

PLACE → PLACES
Ex 26:33 divides the holy **p** from the holy
Ps 24: 3 LORD? Who can stand in his holy **p**?
Jn 14: 3 And if I go and prepare a **p** for you,

PLACES → PLACE
Lev 26:30 I will demolish your high **p**,
Ps 78:58 They enraged him with their high **p**;

PLAGUE → PLAGUES
Zec 14:12 this shall be the **p**
Rev 11: 6 with any **p** as often as they wish.

PLAGUES → PLAGUE
Hos 13:14 death? Where are your **p**, O death!
Rev 15: 1 seven angels with the seven last **p**,
22:18 to him the **p** described in this book,

PLAIN
Ge 13:12 settled among the cities of the **P**,
Isa 40: 4 The rugged land shall be made a **p**,

PLANNED
Isa 46:11 it; I have **p** it, and I will do it.

PLANT → PLANTED
Ge 1:29 you every seed-bearing **p** all over
Ecc 3: 2 a time to **p**, and a time to uproot
3: 2 time to **p**, and a time to uproot the **p**.

PLANTED → PLANT
Ge 2: 8 the LORD God **p** a garden in Eden.
Ps 1: 3 like a tree **p** near streams of water,
1Co 3: 6 I **p**, Apollos watered, but God

PLEASE → PLEASED, PLEASES, PLEASING, PLEASURE
Ps 69:32 My song will **p** the LORD more than
Sir 2:16 who fear the LORD seek to **p** him,
Ro 8: 8 who are in the flesh cannot **p** God.
15: 3 For Christ did not **p** himself; but,
1Co 10:33 just as I try to **p** everyone in every
1Th 4: 1 you should conduct yourselves to **p**
Heb 11: 6 faith it is impossible to **p** him,

PLEASED → PLEASE
Mic 6: 7 Will the LORD be **p** with thousands
Mt 3:17 Son, with whom I am well **p**."

PLEASED → PLEASE (*cont.*)
Col 1:19 him all the fullness was **p** to dwell,
2Pe 1:17 beloved, with whom I am well **p**."

PLEASES → PLEASE
1Jn 3:22 commandments and do what **p** him.

PLEASING → PLEASE
Ps 104:34 May my theme be **p** to God; I will
Eph 5:10 Try to learn what is **p** to the Lord.
Php 4:18 an acceptable sacrifice, **p** to God.

PLEASURE → PLEASE
Pr 21:17 He who loves **p** will suffer want;
Eze 18:32 For I have no **p** in the death
2Ti 3: 4 lovers of **p** rather than lovers

PLOWSHARES
Isa 2: 4 They shall beat their swords into **p**

PLUNDER
Eze 39:10 Thus they shall **p** those who

POISON
Jas 3: 8 It is a restless evil, full of deadly **p**.

POLE → POLES
Nu 21: 8 "Make a saraph and mount it on a **p**,
Dt 16:21 "You shall not plant a sacred **p**

POLES → POLE
2Ki 17:10 sacred **p** for themselves on every

POOR → POVERTY
1Sa 2: 8 from the ash heap he lifts up the **p**,
Ps 113: 7 dust, lifts the **p** from the ash heap,
Pr 19:22 shame; rather be a **p** man than a liar.
Mt 5: 3 "Blessed are the **p** in spirit, for theirs
Mk 10:21 give to [the] **p** and you will have
12:42 A **p** widow also came and put
Jn 12: 8 You always have the **p** with you,
2Co 6:10 rejoicing; as **p** yet enriching many;
2Co 8: 9 sake he became **p** although he was
Jas 2: 5 Did not God choose those who are **p**

PORTION
Dt 32: 9 While the LORD's own **p** was Jacob,
Ps 142: 6 my **p** in the land of the living.
La 3:24 My **p** is the LORD, says my soul;

POSSESS → POSSESSED, POSSESSION, POSSESSIONS
Isa 60:21 they shall always **p** the land, They,

POSSESSED → POSSESS
Mt 8:16 they brought him many who were **p**

POSSESSION → POSSESS
Ex 19: 5 you shall be my special **p**,
Jos 1:11 take **p** of the land which the LORD,
Ps 2: 8 nations, your **p** the ends of the earth.

POSSESSIONS → POSSESS
Lk 12:15 rich, one's life does not consist of **p**."

POSSIBLE
Mt 19:26 but for God all things are **p**."
26:39 if it is **p**, let this cup pass from me;

POTIPHAR
Egyptian who bought Joseph (Ge 37:36; 39:1-6), sent him to prison (Ge 39:7-30).

POTTER → POTTER'S
Sir 33:13 Like clay in the hands of a **p**, to be
Ro 9:21 does not the **p** have a right over

POTTER'S → POTTER
Jer 18: 2 Rise up, be off to the **p** house;
Mt 27: 7 it to buy the **p** field as a burial place

POUR → POURED
Dt 12:16 but must **p** it out on the ground like
Isa 44: 3 I will **p** out water upon the thirsty
44: 3 I will **p** out my spirit upon your
Ac 2:17 'that I will **p** out a portion of my
Rev 16: 1 **p** out the seven bowls of God's fury

POURED → POUR
Eze 39:29 for I have **p** out my spirit
Ac 2:33 Spirit from the Father and **p** it forth,
Ro 5: 5 the love of God has been **p**
Tit 3: 6 whom he richly **p** out on us

POVERTY → POOR
Pr 30: 8 me, give me neither **p** nor riches;
Sir 11:14 **p** and riches, are from the LORD.
Mk 12:44 from her **p**, has contributed all she
2Co 8: 9 by his **p** you might become rich.

POWER → POWERFUL, POWERS
Ex 9:16 to show you my **p** and to make my
15: 6 hand, O LORD, magnificent in **p**,
1Ch 29:11 "Yours, O LORD, are grandeur and **p**,
Jdt 9:14 clearly that you are the God of all **p**
Ps 68:35 Confess the **p** of God,
68:35 Israel, whose **p** is in the sky.
Pr 18:21 and life are in the **p** of the tongue;

Mt 22:29 know the scriptures or the **p** of God.
Mk 13:26 coming in the clouds' with great **p**
Ro 1:20 his invisible attributes of eternal **p**
1Co 15:24 and every authority and **p**.
Eph 1:19 of his **p** for us who believe,
Php 3:10 him and the **p** of his resurrection
2Ti 3: 5 a pretense of religion but deny its **p**.
2Pe 1: 3 His divine **p** has bestowed on us
1: 3 called us by his own glory and **p**.
Rev 20: 6 second death has no **p** over these;

POWERFUL → POWER
1Co 1:26 not many were **p**, not many were

POWERS → POWER
Ro 8:38 things, nor future things, nor **p**,
Eph 6:12 with the **p**, with the world rulers

PRACTICE → PRACTICES
Sir 50:29 If he puts them into **p**, he can cope
Mt 23: 3 For they preach but they do not **p**.

PRACTICES → PRACTICE
Col 3: 9 have taken off the old self with its **p**

PRAISE → PRAISED, PRAISES
Ex 15: 2 He is my God, I **p** him; the God
Tob 12: 6 God! Give him the **p** and the glory.
Ps 56: 5 God, I **p** your promise; in you I
150: 6 that has breath give **p** to the LORD!
Pr 27: 2 Let another **p** you—not your own
31:31 let her works **p** her at the city gates.
Mt 21:16 nurslings you have brought forth **p**'?"
1Co 14:15 I will sing **p** with the spirit, but I
14:15 but I will also sing **p** with the mind.
Rev 19: 5 "**P** our God, all you his servants,

PRAISED → PRAISE
Ps 48: 2 Great is the LORD and highly **p**

PRAISES → PRAISE
Sir 24: 1 Wisdom sings her own **p**, before her

PRAY → PRAYED, PRAYER, PRAYERS, PRAYING, PRAYS
1Sa 12:23 the LORD by ceasing to **p** for you
2Ch 7:14 humble themselves and **p**, and seek
Ps 5: 3 king, my God! To you I **p**, O LORD;
122: 6 For the peace of Jerusalem **p**:
Sir 37:15 Most important of all, **p** to God

Mt 5:44 and **p** for those who persecute you,
6: 5 "When you **p**, do not be like
6: 5 to stand and **p** in the synagogues
Lk 11: 1 to **p** just as John taught his disciples."
Ro 8:26 do not know how to **p** as we ought,
1Co 14:15 I will **p** with the spirit, but I will
14:15 but I will also **p** with the mind.
1Th 5:17 **P** without ceasing.
Jas 5:16 one another and **p** for one another,

PRAYED → PRAY
Mk 1:35 off to a deserted place, where he **p.**
14:35 **p** that if it were possible the hour

PRAYER → PRAY
Ps 6:10 The LORD has heard my **p**; the LORD
Pr 15:29 but the **p** of the just he hears.
Isa 56: 7 and make joyful in my house of **p**;
56: 7 called a house of **p** for all peoples.
Mt 21:13 'My house shall be a house of **p**,'
Mk 11:24 all that you ask for in **p**,
Ro 12:12 endure in affliction, persevere in **p**.
Jas 5:16 The fervent **p** of a righteous person

PRAYERS → PRAY
Mk 12:40 and, as a pretext, recite lengthy **p**.
Heb 5: 7 he offered **p** and supplications
Rev 5: 8 which are the **p** of the holy ones.

PRAYING → PRAY
2Ma 15:12 was **p** with outstretched arms

PRAYS → PRAY
2Ma 15:14 and fervently **p** for his people

PREACHING
1Ti 5:17 especially those who toil in **p**

PRECEPTS
Ps 19: 9 The **p** of the LORD are right,
119:15 I will ponder your **p** and consider
Mt 15: 9 me, teaching as doctrines human **p**.'"

PRECIOUS
Ps 72:14 for **p** is their blood in his sight.
Pr 3:15 She is more **p** than corals, and none
Isa 28:16 tested, A **p** cornerstone as a sure
1Pe 1:19 with the **p** blood of Christ as
2: 6 a cornerstone, chosen and **p**,

PREDESTINED
Ro 8:30 And those he **p** he also called;

PREPARE → PREPARED
Mal 3: 1 to **p** the way before me;
Mt 3: 3 in the desert, '**P** the way of the Lord,

Jn 14: 2 that I am going to **p** a place for you?

PREPARED → PREPARE
1Co 2: 9 what God has **p** for those who love

PRESENCE → PRESENT
Ps 51:13 Do not drive me from your **p**,
139: 7 From your **p**, where can I flee?

PRESENT → PRESENCE
Ro 6:13 do not **p** the parts of your bodies
6:13 **p** yourselves to God as raised
1Co 3:22 life or death, or the **p** or the future:
Eph 5:27 he might **p** to himself the church
2Ti 2:15 Be eager to **p** yourself as acceptable

PREVAIL
1Sa 2: 9 For not by strength does man **p**;

PRICE
Mt 27: 9 value of a man with a **p** on his head,
27: 9 a **p** set by some of the Israelites,
1Co 6:20 For you have been purchased at a **p**.

PRIDE → PROUD
Pr 16:18 **P** goes before disaster,
Sir 10:13 For **p** is the reservoir of sin,

PRIEST → PRIESTHOOD, PRIESTS
Ge 14:18 and being a **p** of God Most High,
Ex 2:16 daughters of a **p** of Midian came
Ps 110: 4 Melchizedek you are a **p** forever."
Mk 14:63 At that the high **p** tore his garments
Heb 3: 1 and high **p** of our confession,
5:10 God high **p** according to the order
7: 3 Son of God, he remains a **p** forever.
10:21 we have "a great **p** over the house

PRIESTHOOD → PRIEST
Ex 29: 9 them. Thus shall the **p** be theirs
Heb 7:24 has a **p** that does not pass away.
1Pe 2: 5 to be a holy **p** to offer spiritual

PRIESTS → PRIEST
Ex 28: 1 to you, that they may be my **p**.
Dt 31: 9 it to the livitical **p** who carry the ark
Mic 3:11 her **p** give decisions for a salary,
Mk 15: 3 The chief **p** accused him of many
Heb 7:27 as did the high **p**, to offer sacrifice
Rev 20: 6 they will be **p** of God and of Christ,

PRINCE → PRINCES
Eze 37:25 my servant David their **p** forever.

Da 10:21 all these except Michael, your **p**,

PRINCES → PRINCE
Da 8:25 he rises against the prince of **p**,

PRISCILLA
Wife of Aquila, also called Prisca; co-worker with Paul (Ac 18; Ro 16:3; 1Co 16:19; 2Ti 4:19); instructor of Apollos (Ac 18:24-28).

PRISON → PRISONER, PRISONERS
Ge 39:20 But even while he was in **p**,
Mt 14:10 and had John beheaded in the **p**.
Ac 12: 5 Peter thus was being kept in **p**,

PRISONER → PRISON
Mk 15: 6 to them one **p** whom they requested.
Eph 3: 1 I, Paul, a **p** of Christ [Jesus] for you

PRISONERS → PRISON
Ps 146: 7 to the hungry. The LORD sets **p** free;
Isa 61: 1 to the captives and release to the **p**,

PRIZE
1Co 9:24 in the race, but only one wins the **p**?
Php 3:14 goal, the **p** of God's upward calling,

PROCLAIM
Ps 97: 6 The heavens **p** God's justice;
Mt 10:27 hear whispered, **p** on the housetops.
Mk 16:15 and **p** the gospel to every creature.
Lk 4:19 to **p** a year acceptable to the Lord."

PRODUCE → PRODUCES
Jos 5:11 wealth of the **p** of the land
Pr 3: 9 wealth, with first fruits of all your **p**;

PRODUCES → PRODUCE
2Co 7:10 For godly sorrow **p** a salutary
7:10 regret, but worldly sorrow **p** death.
Jas 1: 3 testing of your faith **p** perseverance.

PROFANE
Lev 22:32 and do not **p** my holy name;
1Ma 1:45 to **p** the sabbaths and feast days,

PROFIT
Sir 29:11 that will **p** you more than the gold.
Mt 16:26 What **p** would there be for one

PROMISE → PROMISED, PROMISES
Ac 2:39 For the **p** is made to you and to your
Eph 2:12 and strangers to the covenants of **p**,
1Ti 4: 8 since it holds a **p** of life both
2Pe 3: 9 The Lord does not delay his **p**,

PROMISED → PROMISE
Dt 1:11 times over, and bless you as he **p**!

PROMISED → PROMISE (cont.)
Eph 1:13 were sealed with the **p** holy Spirit,

PROMISES → PROMISE
Ps 12: 7 The **p** of the LORD are sure,
2Co 1:20 For however many are the **p** of God,
Heb 8: 6 better covenant, enacted on better **p**.

PROOFS
Ac 1: 3 by many **p** after he had suffered,

PROPHECIES → PROPHESY
1Co 13: 8 If there are **p**, they will be brought

PROPHECY → PROPHESY
Ac 21: 9 four virgin daughters gifted with **p**.
1Co 12:10 to another **p**; to another discernment
2Pe 1:20 that there is no **p** of scripture that is

PROPHESY → PROPHECIES, PROPHECY, PROPHET, PROPHETS
Mt 7:22 Lord, did we not **p** in your name?
1Co 13: 9 know partially and we **p** partially,
Rev 11: 3 commission my two witnesses to **p**

PROPHET → PROPHESY
Ex 7: 1 your brother shall act as your **p**.
Dt 18:18 for them a **p** like you from among
1Ma 4:46 until a **p** should come and decide
Lk 4:24 no **p** is accepted in his own native
20: 6 are convinced that John was a **p**."
Rev 16:13 and from the mouth of the false **p**.
20:10 the beast and the false **p** were.

PROPHETS → PROPHESY
Nu 11:29 all the people of the LORD were **p**!
1Ki 18:40 said to them, "Seize the **p** of Baal.
1Ma 9:27 in Israel since the time **p** ceased
Ps 105:15 my anointed, to my **p** do no harm."
Mt 5:17 come to abolish the law or the **p**.
22:40 law and the **p** depend on these two
Lk 24:44 and in the **p** and psalms must be
1Co 12:28 apostles; second, **p**; third, teachers;
Eph 2:20 the foundation of the apostles and **p**,
4:11 others as **p**, others as evangelists,
Rev 11:10 because these two **p** tormented
18:20 you holy ones, apostles, and **p**.

PROSPERITY → PROSPERS
Dt 30:15 have today set before you life and **p**,
Ps 73: 3 when I saw the **p** of the wicked.
Isa 48:18 your **p** would be like a river,

PROSPERS → PROSPERITY
Ps 1: 3 never wither; whatever they do **p**.

PROSTITUTE → PROSTITUTES
1Co 6:15 and make them the members of a **p**?

PROSTITUTES → PROSTITUTE
Mt 21:31 **p** are entering the kingdom of God
1Co 6: 9 adulterers nor boy **p** nor practicing

PROTECTS
Jdt 9:14 there is no other who **p** the people
Ps 116: 6 The LORD **p** the simple; I was

PROUD → PRIDE
Ps 94: 2 earth; give the **p** what they deserve.
Pr 21: 4 Haughty eyes and a **p** heart—
Sir 10: 9 Why are dust and ashes **p**?
Jas 4: 6 "God resists the **p**, but gives grace

PROVERBS
Pr 1: 1 The **p** of Solomon, the son
Ecc 12: 9 scrutinized and arranged many **p**.

PROVIDE → PROVIDES
Ge 22: 8 "God himself will **p** the sheep
1Co 10:13 the trial he will also **p** a way out,

PROVIDES → PROVIDE
1Ti 6:17 who richly **p** us with all things

PROVOKE → PROVOKED
Dt 32:21 I will **p** them with a 'no-people';
Jer 25: 6 lest you **p** me with your handiwork,

PROVOKED → PROVOKE
Ps 78:41 God, **p** the Holy One of Israel.

PRUNES
Jn 15: 2 does he **p** so that it bears more fruit.

PSALMS
Lk 24:44 the prophets and **p** must be fulfilled."
Eph 5:19 addressing one another [in] **p**

PUBLIC
Col 2:15 he made a **p** spectacle of them,

PUNISH → PUNISHMENT
Ex 32:34 When it is time for me to **p**, I will **p**
Jer 21:14 I will **p** you, says the LORD, as your

PUNISHMENT → PUNISH
Ge 4:13 the LORD: "My **p** is too great to bear.
Mt 25:46 And these will go off to eternal **p**,

1Jn 4:18 fear because fear has to do with **p**,

PURE → PURIFICATION, PURIFIED, PURITY
Ps 19:10 The fear of the LORD is **p**,
Hab 1:13 Too **p** are your eyes to look tested,
Php 4: 8 whatever is **p**, whatever is lovely,
1Jn 3: 3 hope based on him makes himself **p**,
3: 3 on him makes himself **p**, as he is **p**.

PURIFICATION → PURE
Heb 1: 3 he had accomplished **p** from sins,

PURIFIED → PURE
Da 12:10 Many shall be refined, **p**, and
1Pe 1:22 Since you have **p** yourselves

PURIM
Est 9:26 so these days have been named **P**

PURITY → PURE
2Co 6: 6 by **p**, knowledge, patience,

PURPLE
Ex 25: 4 violet, **p** and scarlet yarn; fine linen
Mk 15:17 They clothed him in **p** and,

PURPOSE
Isa 46:10 stand, I accomplish my every **p**.
Ro 8:28 who are called according to his **p**.
Eph 3:11 the eternal **p** that he accomplished

PURSUE → PURSUED, PURSUES
Ps 34:15 and do good; seek peace and **p** it.
Ro 14:19 Let us then **p** what leads to peace
1Ti 6:11 Instead, **p** righteousness, devotion,

PURSUED → PURSUE
Ps 18:38 I **p** my enemies and overtook them;

PURSUES → PURSUE
Pr 21:21 He who **p** justice and kindness
Sir 31: 5 for he who **p** wealth is led astray

PUT
Isa 42: 1 Upon whom I have **p** my spirit;
Eze 36:27 will **p** my spirit within you
Eph 6:11 **P** on the armor of God so that you

Q

QUARRELED
Ex 17: 7 because the Israelites **q** there

QUEEN
1Ki 10: 1 The **q** of Sheba, having heard
Est 2:17 and made her **q** in place of Vashti.
Mt 12:42 the judgment the **q** of the south will
Rev 18: 7 'I sit enthroned as **q**; I am no widow,

QUESTIONS
2Ch 9: 1 Jerusalem to test him with subtle **q**,
Mt 22:46 anyone dare to ask him any more **q**.

QUICK → QUICKLY
Jas 1:19 everyone should be **q** to hear,

QUICKLY → QUICK
Jn 13:27 "What you are going to do, do **q**."
Ro 9:28 **q** will the Lord execute sentence
Gal 1: 6 you are so **q** forsaking the one who

QUIET
1Ti 2: 2 that we may lead a **q** and tranquil

QUIVER
Isa 49: 2 a polished arrow, in his **q** he hid me.

R

RABBI
Mt 23: 8 As for you, do not be called '**R**.'
Jn 1:38 to him, "**R**" (which translated means

RACE
Ecc 9:11 under the sun that the **r** is not won
1Co 9:24 in the stadium all run in the **r**,
Heb 12: 1 in running the **r** that lies before us
1Pe 2: 9 But you are "a chosen **r**, a royal

RACHEL
    Daughter of Laban (Ge 29:16); wife of Jacob (Ge 29:28); bore two sons (Ge 30:22-24; 35:16-24; 46:19). Stole Laban's gods (Ge 31:19, 32-35). Death (Ge 35:19-20).

RAHAB
    Prostitute who hid Israelite spies (Jos 2; 6:22-25; Heb 11:31; Jas 2:25). Mother of Boaz (Mt 1:5).

RAIN → RAINED, RAINS
Ge 7: 4 now I will bring **r** down on the earth
1Ki 17: 1 be no dew or **r** except at my word."
Isa 45: 8 like gentle **r** let the skies drop it
Mt 5:45 and causes **r** to fall on the just
Rev 11: 6 so that no **r** can fall during the time

RAINED → RAIN
Ge 19:24 time the LORD **r** down sulphurous
Ex 9:23 the LORD **r** down hail upon the land

RAINS → RAIN
Jas 5: 7 it receives the early and the late **r**.

RAISE → RISE
Dt 18:15 **r** up for you from among your own
2Ma 7: 9 the King of the world will **r** us

Jn 2:19 and in three days I will **r** it up."
2Co 4:14 who raised the Lord Jesus will **r** us

RAISED → RISE
Mt 17:23 and he will be **r** on the third day."
Ac 2:24 But God **r** him up, releasing him
Ro 4:25 and was **r** for our justification.
1Co 15: 4 that he was **r** on the third day

RAM → RAMS
Ge 22:13 he spied a **r** caught by its horns
    22:13 and took the **r** and offered it up as
Ex 29:22 from this **r** you shall take its fat:
    29:22 thigh, since this is the ordination **r**;
Da 8: 3 the river a **r** with two great horns,

RAMS → RAM
1Sa 15:22 and submission than the fat of **r**.

RANSOM → RANSOMED
Mt 20:28 and to give his life as a **r** for many."
1Ti 2: 6 who gave himself as **r** for all.

RANSOMED → RANSOM
Isa 35:10 whom the LORD has **r** will return

RAVENS
1Ki 17: 6 **R** brought him bread and meat
Lk 12:24 Notice the **r**: they do not sow

READ → READING
Ex 24: 7 he **r** it aloud to the people,
Jos 8:34 were **r** aloud all the words
Ne 8: 8 Ezra **r** plainly from the book
    8: 8 all could understand what was **r**.
Lk 4:16 on the sabbath day. He stood up to **r**
2Co 3:15 whenever Moses is **r**, a veil lies

READING → READ
Ac 8:30 and heard him **r** Isaiah the prophet
    8:30 "Do you understand what you are **r**?"

READY
Rev 19: 7 come, his bride has made herself **r**.

REAP
Gal 6: 7 a person will **r** only what he sows,
Rev 14:15 "Use your sickle and **r** the harvest,
    14:15 for the time to **r** has come,

REBEKAH
    Sister of Laban, secured as bride for Isaac (Ge 24). Mother of Esau and Jacob (Ge 25:19-26). Taken by Abimelech as sister of Isaac; returned (Ge 26:1-11). Encouraged Jacob to trick Isaac out of blessing (Ge 27:1-17).

REBEL → REBELLED, REBELLION
Ex 23:21 Do not **r** against him, for he will not
1Sa 12:14 him and do not **r** against the LORD'S

REBELLED → REBEL
Nu 20:24 because you both **r** against my

REBELLION → REBEL
1Sa 15:23 For a sin like divination is **r**,

REBUILD → BUILD
Ne 2:17 let us **r** the wall of Jerusalem,
Ac 15:16 and **r** the fallen hut of David;
    15:16 from its ruins I shall **r** it and raise it

REBUKE
Pr 27: 5 Better is an open **r** than a love
Zec 3: 2 Satan, "May the LORD **r** you, Satan;
    3: 2 who has chosen Jerusalem **r** you!
Mk 8:32 took him aside and began to **r** him.

RECEIVE → RECEIVED
Jn 3:27 "No one can **r** anything except what
    16:24 ask and you will **r**, so that your joy
    20:22 and said to them, "**R** the holy Spirit.
Ac 2:38 you will **r** the gift of the holy Spirit.
    20:35 'It is more blessed to give than to **r**.' "
1Co 4: 7 you boasting as if you did not **r** it?
Rev 4:11 to **r** glory and honor and power,

RECEIVED → RECEIVE
Mt 6: 2 say to you, they have **r** their reward.
1Co 11:23 For I **r** from the Lord what I

RECONCILE → RECONCILED, RECONCILIATION
Ac 7:26 and tried to **r** them peacefully,
Col 1:20 through him to **r** all things for him,

RECONCILED → RECONCILE
Mt 5:24 go first and be **r** with your brother,
1Co 7:11 remain single or become **r** to her

RECONCILIATION → RECONCILE
Ro 5:11 whom we have now received **r**.
2Co 5:18 and given us the ministry of **r**,

RED
Ex 15: 4 were submerged in the **R** Sea.
Mt 16: 3 for the sky is **r** and threatening.'
Rev 12: 3 it was a huge **r** dragon, with seven

REDEEMED → REDEMPTION
2Sa 7:23 which you **r** for yourself
Ps 107: 2 Let that be the prayer of the LORD's **r**,
    107: 2 **r**, those **r** from the hand of the foe,

REDEEMER → REDEMPTION
Ps 19:15 you, LORD, my rock and my **r**.
Isa 48:17 Thus says the LORD, your **r**, the Holy

REDEMPTION → REDEEMED, REDEEMER
Lk 21:28 raise your heads because your **r** is
Ro 3:24 by his grace through the **r** in Christ
Eph 1: 7 In him we have **r** by his blood,
Heb 9:12 own blood, thus obtaining eternal **r**.

REFINE → REFINED
Zec 13: 9 and I will **r** them as silver is refined,

REFINED → REFINE
Da 12:10 Many shall be **r**, purified,

REFUGE
Nu 35:11 unintentionally may take **r**.
Pr 30: 5 a shield to those who take **r** in him.
Jer 16:19 fortress, my **r** in the day of distress!

REGARD
Php 2: 6 of God, did not **r** equality with God

REGULATIONS
Col 2:20 why do you submit to **r** as if you
Heb 9:10 **r** concerning the flesh,

REHOBOAM
Son of Solomon (1Ki 11:43; 1Ch 3:10). Harsh treatment of subjects caused divided kingdom (1Ki 12:1-24; 14:21-31; 2Ch 10-12).

REIGN
Ex 15:18 The LORD shall **r** forever and ever.
Ps 146:10 The LORD shall **r** forever, your God,
1Co 15:25 For he must **r** until he has put all his
2Ti 2:12 we shall also **r** with him. But if we
Rev 11:15 and he will **r** forever and ever."
22: 5 and they shall **r** forever and ever.

REJECT → REJECTED
Isa 30:12 of Israel: Because you **r** this word,

REJECTED → REJECT
Ps 60: 3 O God, you **r** us, broke our
118:22 The stone the builders **r** has become
Mt 21:42 'The stone that the builders **r**
1Pe 2: 4 **r** by human beings but chosen

REJOICE → REJOICING
Ps 118:24 has made; let us **r** in it and be glad.
Isa 62: 5 his bride so shall your God **r** in you.
Zep 3:17 He will **r** over you with gladness,
Lk 6:23 **R** and leap for joy on that day!
Php 4: 4 **R** in the Lord always. I shall say it

Php 4: 4 Lord always. I shall say it again: **r**!

REJOICING → REJOICE
2Co 6:10 as sorrowful yet always **r**; as poor

RELEASE
Isa 61: 1 the captives and **r** to the prisoners,
Mt 27:15 the governor was accustomed to **r**

RELENT
Joel 2:14 Perhaps he will again **r** and leave
Jnh 3: 9 knows, God may **r** and forgive,

RELIGION
Jas 1:27 **R** that is pure and undefiled before

RELY
Pr 3: 5 on your own intelligence **r** not;
Sir 5: 1 **R** not on your wealth; say not:

REMAIN → REMAINS
1Co 7:20 Everyone should **r** in the state
Heb 1:11 They will perish, but you **r**;

REMAINS → REMAIN
Heb 7: 3 Son of God, he **r** a priest forever.
10:26 there no longer **r** sacrifice for sins

REMEMBER → REMEMBERED
Ex 20: 8 "**R** to keep holy the sabbath day.
Dt 8:18 **R** then, it is the LORD, your God,
Job 10: 9 **r** that you fashioned me from clay!
Ecc 12: 1 **R** your Creator in the days of your
Jer 31:34 evildoing and **r** their sin no more.
2Ti 2: 8 **R** Jesus Christ, raised from the dead,
Heb 8:12 evildoing and **r** their sins no more."

REMEMBERED → REMEMBER
Ps 78:35 They **r** that God was their rock,
106:45 For their sake he **r** his covenant
Rev 16:19 But God **r** great Babylon, giving it

REMNANT
Ge 45: 7 of you to ensure for you a **r** on earth
Isa 10:21 A **r** will return, the **r** of Jacob,
Jer 50:20 for I will forgive the **r** I preserve.
Ro 9:27 of the sea, only a **r** will be saved;

RENEW → RENEWED
Isa 40:31 in the LORD will **r** their strength,

RENEWED → RENEW
2Co 4:16 our inner self is being **r** day by day.
Eph 4:23 and be **r** in the spirit of your minds,

REPAY → PAY
Ps 28: 4 **R** them for their deeds, for the evil
28: 4 For the work of their hands **r** them;
Ro 12:17 Do not **r** anyone evil for evil;

REPENT → REPENTANCE
1Ki 8:47 may they **r** in the land of their
Job 42: 6 I have said, and **r** in dust and ashes.
Mt 3: 2 [and] saying, "**R**, for the kingdom
Ac 2:38 [said] to them, "**R** and be baptized,
Rev 16: 9 but they did not **r** or give him glory.

REPENTANCE → REPENT
Mk 1: 4 desert proclaiming a baptism of **r**
Lk 3: 8 good fruits as evidence of your **r**;
Ro 2: 4 of God would lead you to **r**?
2Co 7:10 produces a salutary **r** without regret,
2Pe 3: 9 perish but that all should come to **r**.

REPROVE
Rev 3:19 Those whom I love, I **r** and chastise.

RESCUE → RESCUES
Ps 22: 9 you; if he loves you, let him **r** you."
2Pe 2: 9 the Lord knows how to **r** the devout

RESCUES → RESCUE
Ps 37:40 The LORD helps and **r** them,

RESIST
Jas 4: 7 **R** the devil, and he will flee

RESPECT
Ro 13: 7 toll is due, **r** to whom **r** is due,

REST → RESTED
Ex 31:15 day is the sabbath of complete **r**,
2Sa 7:11 I will give you **r** from all your
Ps 95:11 anger: "They shall never enter my **r**."
Mt 11:28 are burdened, and I will give you **r**.
Heb 4:10 And whoever enters into God's **r**,

RESTED → REST
Ge 2: 2 he **r** on the seventh day from all
Ex 20:11 them; but on the seventh day he **r**.

RESTORE
Ps 51:14 **R** my joy in your salvation;
Mt 17:11 will indeed come and **r** all things;

RESURRECTION
Mt 22:30 At the **r** they neither marry nor are
Mk 12:18 who say there is no **r**, came to him
Jn 11:25 told her, "I am the **r** and the life;

1Co 15:12 some among you say there is no **r**

Php 3:10 the power of his **r** and [the] sharing

Rev 20: 5 years were over. This is the first **r**.

RETAIN

Jn 20:23 and whose sins you **r** are retained."

RETURN

Ge 3:19 to eat, Until you **r** to the ground,

3:19 you are dirt, and to dirt you shall **r**."

Dt 30: 2 you and your children **r** to the LORD,

Mal 3: 7 them. **R** to me, and I will **r** to you,

3: 7 hosts. Yet you say, "How must we **r**?"

REUBEN

Firstborn of Jacob by Leah (Ge 29:32; 46:8; 1Ch 2:1). Attempted to rescue Joseph (Ge 37:21-30). Lost birthright for sleeping with Bilhah (Ge 35:22; 49:4). Tribe of blessed (Ge 49:3-4; Dt 33:6), numbered (Nu 1:21; 26:7), allotted land east of Jordan (Nu 32; 34:14; Jos 13:15), west (Eze 48:6), failed to help Deborah (Jdg 5:15-16), supported David (1Ch 12:37), 12,000 from (Rev 7:5).

REVEAL → REVEALED, REVELATION, REVELATIONS

Mt 11:27 to whom the Son wishes to **r** him.

REVEALED → REVEAL

Isa 40: 5 the glory of the LORD shall be **r**,

Mt 16:17 and blood has not **r** this to you,

Lk 17:30 be on the day the Son of Man is **r**.

Ro 1:17 in it is **r** the righteousness of God

1Jn 3: 2 what we shall be has not yet been **r**.

3: 2 when it is **r** we shall be like him,

REVELATION → REVEAL

1Co 14: 6 if I do not speak to you by way of **r**,

Eph 3: 3 was made known to me by **r**, as I

Rev 1: 1 The **r** of Jesus Christ, which God

REVELATIONS → REVEAL

2Co 12: 1 go on to visions and **r** of the Lord.

REVERENCE

Eph 5:21 to one another out of **r** for Christ.

REWARD → REWARDED, REWARDS

Ps 19:12 obeying them brings much **r**.

Isa 40:10 strong arm; Here is his **r** with him,

Mt 6: 5 to you, they have received their **r**.

Lk 6:23 day! Behold, your **r** will be great

REWARDED → REWARD

2Sa 22:21 "The LORD **r** me according to my

REWARDS → REWARD

Heb 11: 6 and that he **r** those who seek him.

RIB

Ge 2:22 into a woman the **r** that he had taken

RICH → RICHES

Mt 19:23 one who is **r** to enter the kingdom

Lk 12:21 but is not **r** in what matters to God."

2Co 8: 9 he became poor although he was **r**,

8: 9 by his poverty you might become **r**.

Eph 2: 4 But God, who is **r** in mercy,

1Ti 6:18 good, to be **r** in good works, to be

Jas 1:10 and the **r** one in his lowliness, for he

RICHES → RICH

Pr 30: 8 me, give me neither poverty nor **r**;

Lk 8:14 are choked by the anxieties and **r**

Ro 11:33 the depth of the **r** and wisdom

RID

1Pe 2: 1 **R** yourselves of all malice and all

RIDER → RIDES, RIDING

Rev 19:11 its **r** was [called] "Faithful and True."

RIDES → RIDER

Dt 33:26 who **r** the heavens in his power,

33:26 and **r** the skies in his majesty;

RIDING → RIDER

Zec 9: 9 Meek, and **r** on an ass, on a colt,

RIGHT → BIRTHRIGHT

Ex 15: 6 Your **r** hand, O LORD,

15: 6 your **r** hand, O LORD, has shattered

Dt 6:18 Do what is **r** and good in the sight

Ps 110: 1 lord: "Take your throne at my **r** hand,

Pr 14:12 Sometimes a way seems **r** to a man,

Mt 25:33 He will place the sheep on his **r**

Ac 2:34 said to my Lord, "Sit at my **r** hand

Heb 1:13 "Sit at my **r** hand until I make your

RIGHTEOUS → RIGHTEOUSNESS

Job 4:17 "Can a man be **r** as against God?

Jer 23: 5 I will raise up a **r** shoot to David;

Mk 2:17 do. I did not come to call the **r**

Ro 1:17 "The one who is **r** by faith will live."

Ro 5:19 of one the many will be made **r**.

1Jn 2: 1 the Father, Jesus Christ the **r** one.

Rev 19: 8 (The linen represents the **r** deeds

RIGHTEOUSNESS → RIGHTEOUS

Ge 15: 6 who credited it to him as an act of **r**.

Mt 5: 6 are they who hunger and thirst for **r**,

Jn 16: 8 the world in regard to sin and **r**

Ro 3:22 the **r** of God through faith in Jesus

Gal 3: 6 God, and it was credited to him as **r**."

Eph 6:14 truth, clothed with **r** as a breastplate,

1Pe 2:24 free from sin, we might live for **r**.

2Pe 3:13 and a new earth in which **r** dwells.

Rev 19:11 True." He judges and wages war in **r**.

RIPE

Jn 4:35 and see the fields **r** for the harvest.

Rev 14:15 because the earth's harvest is fully **r**."

RISE → ARISE, RAISE, RAISED, ROSE

Nu 24:17 and a staff shall **r** from Israel,

2Ma 12:44 not expecting the fallen to **r** again;

Ps 94: 2 **R** up, judge of the earth;

Da 12:13 you shall **r** for your reward

1Th 4:16 and the dead in Christ will **r** first.

RIVER → RIVERS

Ps 46: 5 Streams of the **r** gladden the city

Isa 48:18 your prosperity would be like a **r**,

Eze 47:12 Along both banks of the **r**,

Mt 3: 6 the Jordan **R** as they acknowledged

Rev 22: 1 Then the angel showed me the **r**

RIVERS → RIVER

Ps 137: 1 By the **r** of Babylon we sat

Rev 8:10 It fell on a third of the **r**

ROAD → CROSSROADS

Mt 7:13 the **r** broad that leads to destruction,

ROARING → ROARS

1Pe 5: 8 around like a **r** lion looking

ROARS → ROARING

Hos 11:10 follow the LORD, who **r** like a lion;

11:10 lion; When he **r**, his sons shall come

Jer 25:30 The LORD **r** from on high,

25:30 Mightily he **r** over the range,

ROB → ROBBER

Mal 3: 8 Dare a man **r** God? Yet you are

3: 8 And you say, "How do we **r** you?"

ROBBER → ROB

1Co 5:11 or a **r**, not even to eat with such

ROBE → ROBED, ROBES

Ex 28: 4 an ephod, a **r**, a brocaded tunic,
Lk 15:22 'Quickly bring the finest **r** and put it
Rev 6:11 Each of them was given a white **r**,

ROBED → ROBE

Ps 93: 1 The LORD is king, **r** with majesty;
    93: 1 the LORD is **r**, girded with might.

ROBES → ROBE

Mk 12:38 who like to go around in long **r**
Rev 22:14 are they who wash their **r** so as

ROCK

Ex 17: 6 in front of you on the **r** in Horeb.
    17: 6 Strike the **r**, and the water will flow
Nu 20: 8 their presence order the **r** to yield its
    20: 8 the **r** you shall bring forth water
1Sa 2: 2 the LORD; there is no **R** like our God.
Ps 19:15 you, LORD, my **r** and my redeemer.
Isa 44: 8 Is there a God or any **R** besides me?
Mt 16:18 upon this **r** I will build my church.
Mk 15:46 that had been hewn out of the **r**.
1Pe 2: 8 and a **r** that will make them fall."

ROD

2Sa 7:14 I will correct him with the **r** of men
Ps 2: 9 an iron **r** you shall shepherd them,
    23: 4 your **r** and staff give me courage.
Pr 13:24 He who spares his **r** hates his son,
Rev 2:27 He will rule them with an iron **r**.

ROLL

Mk 16: 3 "Who will **r** back the stone for us

ROOF

Jos 2: 6 Now, she had led them to the **r**,
2Sa 11: 2 strolled about on the **r** of the palace.
    11: 2 the **r** he saw a woman bathing,
Mk 2: 4 they opened up the **r** above him.

ROOM

Mk 14:15 show you a large upper **r** furnished
Ro 12:19 revenge but leave **r** for the wrath;
Eph 4:27 and do not leave **r** for the devil.

ROOT → ROOTED

Isa 11:10 On that day, The **r** of Jesse,
Ro 11:16 and if the **r** is holy, so are
    15:12 says: "The **r** of Jesse shall come,
1Ti 6:10 love of money is the **r** of all evils,
Rev 5: 5 of the tribe of Judah, the **r** of David,

ROOTED → ROOT

Eph 3:17 that you, **r** and grounded in love,

ROSE → RISE

1Th 4:14 if we believe that Jesus died and **r**,

ROUGH

Isa 40: 4 plain, the **r** country, a broad valley.
Lk 3: 5 and the **r** ways made smooth,

ROYAL

Jas 2: 8 you fulfill the **r** law according
1Pe 2: 9 are "a chosen race, a **r** priesthood,

RUBBISH

1Co 4:13 We have become like the world's **r**,
Php 3: 8 and I consider them so much **r**,

RUINS

Ezr 9: 9 house of our God and restore its **r**,
Ne 2:17 how Jerusalem lies in **r** and its gates
Ac 15:16 from its **r** I shall rebuild it and raise

RULE → RULER, RULERS, RULES

Ps 110: 2 LORD says: "**R** over your enemies!
Rev 19:15 He will **r** them with an iron rod,

RULER → RULE

Ex 2:14 "Who has appointed you **r** and judge
Mt 2: 6 since from you shall come a **r**,
Rev 1: 5 dead and **r** of the kings of the earth.

RULERS → RULE

Isa 40:23 makes the **r** of the earth as nothing.
Eph 6:12 the world **r** of this present darkness,

RULES → RULE

Ps 66: 7 who **r** by might forever,
Isa 40:10 Lord GOD, who **r** by his strong arm;
2Ti 2: 5 by competing according to the **r**.

RUN → FORERUNNER, RUNNERS

Isa 40:31 They will **r** and not grow weary,
Gal 2: 2 not be running, or have **r**, in vain.

RUNNERS → RUN

1Co 9:24 that the **r** in the stadium all run

RUTH

Moabitess; widow who went to Bethlehem with mother-in-law Naomi (Ru 1).

Gleaned in field of Boaz; shown favor (Ru 2). Proposed marriage to Boaz (Ru 3). Married (Ru 4:1-12); bore Obed, ancestor of David (Ru 4:13-22), Jesus (Mt 1:5).

S

SABBATH

Ex 20: 8 "Remember to keep holy the **s** day.
1Ma 1:43 to idols and profaned the **s**.
Mt 12: 1 through a field of grain on the **s**.
Mk 2:28 the Son of Man is lord even of the **s**."

SACKCLOTH

Da 9: 3 prayer, with fasting, **s**, and ashes.
Mt 11:21 would long ago have repented in **s**

SACRED

Ex 28: 2 you shall have **s** vestments made.
    34:13 smash their **s** pillars, and cut down
Ex 34:13 **s** pillars, and cut down their **s** poles.

SACRIFICE → SACRIFICED, SACRIFICES

Ex 12:27 'This is the Passover **s** of the LORD,
1Sa 15:22 Obedience is better than **s**,
Ps 40: 7 **S** and offering you do not want;
Pr 15: 8 The **s** of the wicked is
Da 9:27 he shall abolish **s** and oblation;
Hos 6: 6 For it is love that I desire, not **s**,
Mt 9:13 of the words, 'I desire mercy, not **s**.'
Php 4:18 an acceptable **s**, pleasing to God.
Heb 13:15 let us continually offer God a **s**

SACRIFICED → SACRIFICE

1Co 5: 7 paschal lamb, Christ, has been **s**.
    8: 1 Now in regard to meat **s** to idols.

SACRIFICES → SACRIFICE

Mk 12:33 more than all burnt offerings and **s**."

SADDUCEES

Mt 16: 6 of the leaven of the Pharisees and **S**."
Mk 12:18 Some **S**, who say there is no

SAFE

Pr 18:10 the just man runs to it and is **s**.

SALT

Ge 19:26 and she was turned into a pillar of **s**.
Mt 5:13 "You are the **s** of the earth. But if **s**

SALVATION → SAVE

Ps 27: 1 The LORD is my light and my **s**;
    51:14 Restore my joy in your **s**;
Isa 12: 3 will draw water at the fountain of **s**,

Isa 52: 7 announcing s, and saying to Zion,

Lk 3: 6 and all flesh shall see the s of God.' "

Ac 4:12 There is no s through anyone else,

2Co 6: 2 and on the day of s I helped you."

6: 2 time; behold, now is the day of s.

Php 2:12 work out your s with fear

Heb 2: 3 we escape if we ignore so great a s?

2Pe 3:15 the patience of our Lord as s, as our

Rev 19: 1 S, glory, and might belong to our

SAMARIA → SAMARITAN

1Ki 16:24 bought the hill of S from Shemer

16:24 hill, naming the city he built S

2Ki 17: 6 the king of Assyria took S,

Jn 4: 4 He had to pass through S.

Ac 1: 8 throughout Judea and S,

SAMARITAN → SAMARIA

Lk 10:33 But a S traveler who came upon him

SAME

Ro 10:12 the s Lord is Lord of all,

1Co 12: 4 of spiritual gifts but the s Spirit;

Heb 13: 8 Jesus Christ is the s yesterday,

SAMSON

Danite judge. Birth promised (Jdg 13). Married a Philistine, but his wife given away (Jdg 14). Vengeance on the Philistines (Jdg 15). Betrayed by Delilah (Jdg 16:1-22). Death (Jdg 16:23-31). Feats of strength: killed lion (Jdg 14:6), 30 Philistines (Jdg 14:19), 1,000 Philistines with jawbone (Jdg 15:13-17), carried off gates of Gaza (Jdg 16:3), pushed down temple of Dagon (Jdg 16:25-30; Heb 11:32).

SAMUEL

Ephraimite judge and prophet (Heb 11:32). Birth prayed for (1Sa 1:10-18). Dedicated to temple by Hannah (1Sa 1:21-28). Raised by Eli (1Sa 2:11, 18-26). Called as prophet (1Sa 3). Led Israel to victory over Philistines (1Sa 7). Asked by Israel for a king (1Sa 8). Anointed Saul as king (1Sa 9-10). Farewell speech (1Sa 12). Rebuked Saul for sacrifice (1Sa 13). Announced rejection of Saul (1Sa 15). Anointed David as king (1Sa 16). Protected David from Saul (1Sa 19:18-24). Death (1Sa 25:1). Returned from dead to condemn Saul (1Sa 28).

SANCTIFICATION → SANCTIFIED

Ro 6:19 as slaves to righteousness for s.

SANCTIFIED → SANCTIFICATION

1Co 6:11 you were s, you were justified

SANCTUARY

Ex 25: 8 "They shall make a s for me, that I

1Ch 22:19 to build the s of the LORD God,

1Ma 1:21 He insolently invaded the s and took

4:36 let us go up to purify the s

Eze 37:26 and put my s among them forever.

Da 9:26 shall destroy the s. Then the end

Heb 9:24 Christ did not enter into a s made

SAND

Mt 7:26 like a fool who built his house on s.

SANDALS

Ex 3: 5 Remove the s from your feet,

Mt 3:11 I. I am not worthy to carry his s.

SARAH

1. Wife of Abraham, originally named Sarai; barren (Ge 11:29-31; 1Pe 3:6). Taken by Pharaoh as Abraham's sister; returned (Ge 12:10-20). Gave Hagar to Abraham; sent her away in pregnancy (Ge 16). Name changed; Isaac promised (Ge 17:15-21; 18:10-15; Heb 11:11). Taken by Abimelech as Abraham's sister; returned (Ge 20). Isaac born; Hagar and Ishmael sent away (Ge 21:1-21; Gal 4:21-31). Death (Ge 23).

2. Daughter of Raguel, wife of Tobias (Tob 3; 6-8; 10-12).

SATAN

1Ch 21: 1 A s rose up against Israel, and he

Job 1: 6 the LORD, S also came among them.

Zec 3: 2 And the angel of the LORD said to S,

3: 2 to S, "May the LORD rebuke you, S;

Mt 4:10 this, Jesus said to him, "Get away, S!

12:26 And if S drives out S, he is divided

16:23 and said to Peter, "Get behind me, S!

2Co 11:14 for even S masquerades as an angel

Rev 12: 9 who is called the Devil and S,

20: 7 S will be released from his prison.

SATISFY

Isa 55: 2 your wages for what fails to s?

SAUL → = PAUL

1. Benjamite; anointed by Samuel as first king of Israel (1Sa 9-10). Defeated Ammonites (1Sa 11). Rebuked for offering sacrifice (1Sa 13:1-15). Defeated Philistines (1Sa 14). Rejected as king for failing to annihilate Amalekites (1Sa 15). Soothed from evil spirit by David (1Sa 16:14-23). Sent David against Goliath (1Sa 17). Jealousy and attempted murder of David (1Sa 18:1-11). Gave David Michal as wife (1Sa 18:12-30). Second attempt to kill David (1Sa 19). Anger at Jonathan (1Sa 20:26-34). Pursued David: killed priests at Nob (1Sa 22), went to Keilah and Ziph (1Sa 23), life spared by David at En Gedi (1Sa 24) and in his tent (1Sa 26). Rebuked by Samuel's spirit for consulting witch at Endor (1Sa 28). Wounded by Philistines; took his own life (1Sa 31; 1Ch 10). Lamented by David (2Sa 1:17-27). Children (1Sa 14:49-51; 1Ch 8).

2. See Paul.

SAVE → SALVATION, SAVED, SAVIOR

Ps 54: 3 O God, by your name s me. By your

Isa 59: 1 of the LORD is not too short to s,

Mt 1:21 because he will s his people

16:25 wishes to s his life will lose it,

Lk 19:10 come to seek and to s what was lost."

Heb 7:25 s those who approach God through

SAVED → SAVE

Mt 10:22 endures to the end will be s.

Mk 15:31 themselves and said, "He s others;

Lk 13:23 "Lord, will only a few people be s?"

Ac 2:21 everyone shall be s who calls on

16:30 said, "Sirs, what must I do to be s?"

Ro 10:13 on the name of the Lord will be s."

Eph 2: 8 grace you have been s through faith,

SAVIOR → SAVE

Isa 49:26 that I, the LORD, am your s,

Hos 13: 4 me, and there is no s but me.

Lk 2:11 the city of David a s has been born

Ac 13:23 has brought to Israel a s, Jesus.

1Ti 4:10 the living God, who is the s of all,

Tit 2:13 great God and of our s Jesus Christ,

2Pe 3:18 of our Lord and s Jesus Christ.

SCARLET

Isa 1:18 Though your sins be like s,

Mt 27:28 threw a s military cloak about him.

SCATTER → SCATTERED

Dt 4:27 The LORD will s you among

SCATTERED → SCATTER

Dt 30: 3 all the nations wherein he has s you.

Jer 31:10 He who s Israel, now gathers them

SCEPTER

Ge 49:10 The s shall never depart from Judah,

Heb 1: 8 and a righteous s is the s of your

SCOFFERS

Ps 1: 1 sinners, nor sit in company with s.

2Pe 3: 3 the last days s will come [to] scoff,

SCRIBES

Mt 7:29 having authority, and not as their s.

23:13 "Woe to you, s and Pharisees,

SCRIPTURE → SCRIPTURES

Lk 4:21 "Today this s passage is fulfilled

Jn 10:35 came, and s cannot be set aside,

2Ti 3:16 All s is inspired by God and is

SCRIPTURES → SCRIPTURE
Mt 22:29 because you do not know the **s**
Lk 24:45 their minds to understand the **s.**
Jn 5:39 You search the **s**, because you think
1Co 15: 3 our sins in accordance with the **s**;

SCROLL
Lk 4:17 and was handed a **s** of the prophet
4:17 He unrolled the **s** and found
Rev 5: 2 "Who is worthy to open the **s**

SEA
Ge 1:26 dominion over the fish of the **s**,
Ex 15: 1 and chariot he has cast into the **s.**
Dt 30:13 Nor is it across the **s**, that you
Dt 30:13 'Who will cross the **s** to get it for us
Ps 95: 5 The **s** and dry land belong to God,
Mic 7:19 into the depths of the **s** all our sins;
Rev 4: 6 resembled a **s** of glass like crystal.
13: 1 come out of the **s** with ten horns
21: 1 away, and the **s** was no more.

SEAL → SEALS
2Co 1:22 he has also put his **s** upon us
Rev 7: 3 or the trees until we put the **s**
22:10 "Do not **s** up the prophetic words

SEALS → SEAL
Rev 5: 2 to open the scroll and break its **s**?"

SEARCH → SEARCHES
Dt 4:29 find him when you **s** after him

SEARCHES → SEARCH
Ro 8:27 the one who **s** hearts knows what is

SEASON → SEASONS
Ps 1: 3 that yields its fruit in **s**; Its leaves

SEASONS → SEASON
Gal 4:10 days, months, **s**, and years.
1Th 5: 1 Concerning times and **s**, brothers,

SEAT → SEATED
Ro 14:10 shall all stand before the judgment **s**
2Co 5:10 all appear before the judgment **s**

SEATED → SEAT
Lk 22:69 of Man will be **s** at the right hand

SECOND → TWO
Mt 22:39 The **s** is like it: You shall love your
Rev 20:14 (This pool of fire is the **s** death.)

SECURITY → SECURE
1Th 5: 3 "Peace and **s**," then sudden disaster

SEE → SEEN, SEES, SIGHT
Ex 33:20 But my face you cannot **s**, for no
Ps 115: 5 but do not speak, eyes but do not **s.**
Jn 9:25 is that I was blind and now I **s.**"
1Co 13:12 At present we **s** indistinctly,
1Jn 3: 2 like him, for we shall **s** him as he is.
Rev 1: 7 and every eye will **s** him, even those

SEED → SEEDS, SEEDTIME
Mt 17:20 have faith the size of a mustard **s,**
1Pe 1:23 perishable but from imperishable **s,**

SEEDS → SEED
Mk 4:31 the smallest of all the **s** on the earth.

SEEK
1Ch 28: 9 If you **s** him, he will let himself be
Ps 34:11 those who **s** the LORD lack no good
119:10 With all my heart I **s** you; do not let
Isa 55: 6 S the LORD while he may be found,
Sir 2:16 Those who fear the LORD **s** to please
Lk 19:10 For the Son of Man has come to **s**
Heb 11: 6 that he rewards those who **s** him.

SEEMS
Pr 16:25 Sometimes a way **s** right to a man,
Heb 12:11 all discipline **s** a cause not for joy

SEEN → SEE
Jn 1:18 No one has ever **s** God. The only
14: 9 Whoever has **s** me has **s** the Father.
20:29 to believe because you have **s** me?
20:29 Blessed are those who have not **s**
1Pe 1: 8 you have not **s** him you love him;

SELF-CONTROL → SELF-CONTROLLED
1Co 7: 5 tempt you through your lack of **s.**
2Pe 1: 6 knowledge with **s**, **s** with endurance,

SELF-CONTROLLED → SELF-CONTROL
Tit 1: 8 temperate, just, holy, and **s,**
2: 5 to be **s**, chaste, good homemakers,

SELFISH → SELFISHNESS
Php 1:17 proclaim Christ out of **s** ambition,
Jas 3:14 and **s** ambition in your hearts,

SELFISHNESS → SELFISH
2Co 12:20 jealousy, fury, **s**, slander, gossip,

SELL
Pr 23:23 Get the truth, and **s** it not—wisdom,
Mk 10:21 Go, **s** what you have, and give

SEND → SENT
Ex 33: 2 I will **s** an angel before you
Isa 6: 8 of the Lord saying, "Whom shall I **s**?
6: 8 go for us?" "Here I am;" I said; "**s** me!"
Jn 3:17 God did not **s** his Son into the world
14:26 the Father will **s** in my name—he will

SENNACHERIB
Assyrian king; siege of Jerusalem was overthrown by the LORD following prayer of Hezekiah and Isaiah (2Ki 18:13-19:37; 2Ch 32:1-21; Isa 36-37).

SENT → SEND
Ex 3:14 tell the Israelites: I AM **s** me to you."
Lk 10:16 rejects me rejects the one who **s** me."
Jn 17:18 As you **s** me into the world, so I **s**
20:21 As the Father has **s** me, so I send
1Jn 4:10 **s** his Son as expiation for our sins.

SEPARATE → SEPARATED
Mt 19: 6 together, no human being must **s.**"
Ro 8:35 What will **s** us from the love
1Co 7:10 Lord): A wife should not **s** from her

SEPARATED → SEPARATE
Heb 7:26 undefiled, **s** from sinners,

SERPENT → SERPENTS
Ge 3: 1 Now the **s** was the most cunning
3: 1 The **s** asked the woman, "Did God
Nu 21: 9 Moses accordingly made a bronze **s**
21: 9 who had been bitten by a **s** looked
21: 9 bitten by a **s** looked at the bronze **s,**
2Co 11: 3 that, as the **s** deceived Eve by his
Rev 20: 2 the ancient **s**, which is the Devil

SERPENTS → SERPENT
Mt 10:16 so be shrewd as **s** and simple as

SERVANT → SERVANTS
Ps 19:12 By them your **s** is instructed;
Isa 42: 1 Here is my **s** whom I uphold,
53:11 suffering, my **s** shall justify many,
Zec 3: 8 Yes, I will bring my **s** the Shoot.
Ac 3:13 has glorified his **s** Jesus whom you

Heb 3: 5 in all his house" as a "s" to testify

SERVANTS → SERVANT
2Ki 17:23 as he had foretold through all his s,
Rev 7: 3 the foreheads of the s of our God."

SERVE
Jos 24:15 it does not please you to s the LORD,
    24:15 decide today whom you will s,
    24:15 my household, we will s the LORD."
Mt 6:24 "No one can s two masters. He will
    6:24 You cannot s God and mammon.
Mk 10:45 to s and to give his life as a ransom
1Pe 4:10 it to s one another as good stewards

SETH
Ge 4:25 birth to a son whom she called S.

SETTLE
Nu 33:53 possession of the land and s in it,

SEVEN → SEVENTH
Ge 7: 2 take with you s pairs, a male and its
Ex 25:37 You shall then make s lamps for it
Jos 6: 4 s priests carrying ram's horns ahead
    6: 4 day march around the city s times,
Da 9:25 there shall be s weeks.
Mt 18:22 "I say to you, not s times but s times.
Rev 1:12 I turned, I saw s gold lamp-stands
    5: 1 sides and was sealed with s seals.
    8: 2 the s angels who stood before God
    8: 2 before God were given s trumpets.
   12: 3 dragon, with s heads and ten horns,
   12: 3 and on its heads were s diadems.
   15: 1 s angels with the s last plagues,

SEVENTH → SEVEN
Ge 2: 2 Since on the s day God was finished
    2: 2 he rested on the s day from all
Ex 20:10 the s day is the sabbath of the LORD,
   23:11 the s year you shall let the land lie
Heb 4: 4 spoken somewhere about the s day
    4: 4 God rested on the s day from all his

SEVENTY → SEVENTY-SEVEN
Ge 46:27 Egypt amounted to s persons in all.

2Ch 36:21 have rest while s years are ful-filled."
Jer 25:12 but when the s years have elapsed,
Da 9:24 "S weeks are decreed for your people

SEVENTY-SEVEN → SEVENTY
Mt 18:22 to you, not seven times but s times.

SHADOW
2Ki 20:11 who made the s retreat the ten steps
Ps 17: 8 eye; hide me in the s of your wings
   91: 1 who abide in the s of the Almighty,

SHADRACH → = HANANIAH
Hebrew exiled to Babylon; name changed from Hananiah (Da 1:6-7). Refused defilement by food (Da 1:8-20). Refused to worship idol (Da 3:1-18); saved from furnace (Da 3:19-30).

SHALLUM
King of Israel (2Ki 15:10-16).

SHALMANESER
King of Assyria; conquered and deported Israel (2Ki 17:3-4; 18:9; Tob 1:2).

SHAME → ASHAMED, SHAMEFUL
1Co 1:27 foolish of the world to s the wise,
    1:27 weak of the world to s the strong,
Heb 12: 2 despising its s, and has taken his
1Jn 2:28 not be put to s by him at his coming.

SHAMEFUL → SHAME
2Co 4: 2 we have renounced s, hidden things;
Eph 5:12 for it is s even to mention the things

SHAMGAR
Judge; killed 600 Philistines (Jdg 3:31; 5:6).

SHARE
Lk 3:11 "Whoever has two cloaks should s
Ro 15:27 the Gentiles have come to s in their
Col 1:12 who has made you fit to s
Heb 12:10 in order that we may s his holiness.

SHARP → SHARPENS, SHARPER
Pr 5: 4 as s as a two-edged sword.
Rev 19:15 his mouth came a s sword to strike

SHARPENS → SHARP
Pr 27:17 As iron s iron, so man s his fellow

SHARPER → SHARP
Heb 4:12 s than any two-edged sword,

SHEBA
1. Benjamite; rebelled against David (2Sa 20).
2. Queen of Sheba (1Ki 10; 2Ch 9; Mt 12:42; Lk 11:31).

SHECHEM
1. Raped Jacob's daughter Dinah; killed (Ge 34).
2. City where Joshua renewed the covenant (Jos 24). Abimelech as king (Jdg 9).

SHED → BLOODSHED, SHEDDING
Ge 9: 6 by man shall his blood be s;
Pr 6:17 and hands that s innocent blood;
Mt 23:35 you all the righteous blood s
Rev 16: 6 For they have s the blood

SHEDDING → SHED
Heb 9:22 without the s of blood there is no
   12: 4 yet resisted to the point of s blood.

SHEEP → SHEEPFOLD
1Ki 22:17 like s without a shepherd,
Isa 53: 6 We had all gone astray like s,
Eze 34:15 I myself will pasture my s; I myself
Zec 13: 7 that the s may be dispersed, and I
Mt 9:36 like s without a shepherd.
Lk 15: 4 man among you having a hundred s
Jn 10: 7 I say to you, I am the gate for the s.
   10:15 I will lay down my life for the s.
Heb 13:20 great shepherd of the s by the blood
1Pe 2:25 For you had gone astray like s,

SHEEPFOLD → SHEEP
Jn 10: 1 does not enter a s through the gate

SHELTER
Ps 91: 1 dwell in the s of the Most High,
Rev 7:15 who sits on the throne will s them.

SHEM
Son of Noah (Ge 5:32; 6:10). Blessed (Ge 9:26). Descendants (Ge 10:21-31; 11:10-32; Lk 3:36).

SHEOL
Ps 139: 8 if I lie down in S, you are there too.

SHEPHERD → SHEPHERDS
Ps 23: 1 The LORD is my s; there is nothing I
Isa 40:11 Like a s he feeds his flock; in his
Mt 2: 6 ruler, who is to s my people Israel.' "
   26:31 'I will strike the s, and the sheep
Jn 10:11 I am the good s. A good s lays down
Heb 13:20 the dead the great s of the sheep
1Pe 5: 4 And when the chief S is re-vealed,

SHEPHERDS → SHEPHERD
Eze 34: 2 prophesy against the s of Israel,
   34: 2 words prophesy to them [to the s]:

SHEPHERDS → SHEPHERD (*cont.*)

Eze 34: 2 to the s of Israel who have been

    34: 2 Should not s, rather, pasture sheep?

Lk 2: 8 Now there were s in that region

SHIELD

Ge 15: 1 I am your s; I will make your

Ps 7:11 A s before me is God who saves

Eph 6:16 hold faith as a s, to quench all

SHILOH

1Sa 1:24 him at the temple of the LORD in S.

SHIMEI

Cursed David (2Sa 16:5-14); spared (2Sa 19:16-23). Killed by Solomon (1Ki 2:8-9, 36-46).

SHINE → SHINES, SHINING

Nu 6:25 The LORD let his face s upon you,

Da 12: 3 But the wise shall s brightly

Mt 5:16 your light must s before others,

SHINES → SHINE

Jn 1: 5 the light s in the darkness,

Isa 60: 1 the glory of the Lord s upon you.

SHINING → SHINE

2Pe 1:19 as to a lamp s in a dark place,

1Jn 2: 8 away, and the true light is already s.

SHORT

Isa 59: 1 hand of the LORD is not too s to save,

SHOUT

Ps 47: 2 hands; s to God with joyful cries.

Zec 9: 9 s for joy, O daughter Jerusalem!

SHOW → SHOWED

Ge 12: 1 house to a land that I will s you.

Ps 85: 8 S us, LORD, your love; grant us your

Jn 14: 8 "Master, s us the Father, and that will

1Co 12:31 I shall s you a still more excellent

Rev 4: 1 and I will s you what must happen

SHOWED → SHOW

Dt 34: 1 the LORD s him all the land— Gilead,

Jn 20:20 he s them his hands and his side.

SHUT

Isa 22:22 when he opens, no one shall s,

SICK → SICKNESS

Mt 8:16 spirits by a word and cured all the s,

    9:12 not need a physician, but the s do.

Jas 5:14 Is anyone among you s? He should

SICKLE

Rev 14:14 his head and a sharp s in his hand.

SICKNESS → SICK

Ex 23:25 I will remove all s from your midst;

SIDE → ASIDE

Ps 91: 7 Though a thousand fall at your s,

Jn 19:34 soldier thrust his lance into his s,

SIFT

Lk 22:31 behold Satan has demanded to s all

SIGHT → SEE

Ps 72:14 for precious is their blood in his s,

Mt 11: 5 the blind regain their s, the lame

2Co 5: 7 for we walk by faith, not by s,

1Pe 3: 4 which is precious in the s of God.

SIGN → SIGNS

Ge 9:12 "This is the s that I am giving for all

Isa 7:14 Lord himself will give you this s:

Mt 24: 3 what s will there be of your coming,

Mk 8:12 "Why does this generation seek a s?

    8:12 no s will be given to this generation."

SIGNS → SIGN

Ex 7: 3 despite the many s and wonders

Mt 16: 3 you cannot judge the s of the times.]

Jn 20:30 Now Jesus did many other s

1Co 1:22 For Jews demand s and Greeks look

Rev 16:14 demonic spirits who performed s.

SILAS

Prophet (Ac 15:22-32); co-worker with Paul on second missionary journey (Ac 16-18; 2Co 1:19). Co-writer with Paul (1Th 1:1; 2Th 1:1); Peter (1Pe 5:12).

SILENT

Isa 53: 7 he was s and opened not his mouth.

Mk 14:61 But he was s and answered nothing.

1Co 14:34 women should keep s

SILVER

Ps 66:10 us, O God, tried us as s tried by fire.

Pr 8:10 my instruction in preference to s,

Isa 48:10 See, I have refined you like s,

Zec 13: 9 I will refine them as s is refined,

Mt 26:15 They paid him thirty pieces of s,

Ac 3: 6 "I have neither s nor gold, but what I

1Co 3:12 on this foundation with gold, s,

SIMEON → = SIMON

1. Son of Jacob by Leah (Ge 29:33; 35:23; 1Ch 2:1). With Levi killed Shechem for rape of Dinah (Ge 34:25-29). Held hostage by Joseph in Egypt (Ge 42:24-43:23). Tribe of blessed (Ge 49:5-7), numbered (Nu 1:23; 26:14), allotted land (Jos 19:1-9; Eze 48:24), 12,000 from (Rev 7:7).

2. Godly Jew who blessed the infant Jesus (2:25-35).

3. See Peter (Ac 15:14; 2Pe 1:1).

SIMON → = PETER, = SIMEON

1. See Peter.

2. Apostle; the Zealot (Mt 10:4; Mk 3:18; Lk 6:15; Ac 1:13).

3. Samaritan sorcerer (Ac 8:9-24).

SIMPLE

Ps 19: 8 trustworthy, giving wisdom to the s.

Pr 1:22 "How long, you s ones, will you love

SIN → SINFUL, SINNED, SINNER, SINNERS, SINS

Ge 4: 7 s is a demon lurking at the door:

Ex 32:32 If you would only forgive their s!

Nu 32:23 do this, you will s against the LORD,

    32:23 escape the consequences of your s.

1Ki 8:46 "When they s against you (for there

    8:46 there is no man who does not s),

Tob 12:10 of s are their own worst enemies.

Ps 119:11 that I may not s against you.

Wis 10:13 was sold, but delivered him from s.

Da 9:20 confessing my s and the s of my

Mt 5:29 If your right eye causes you to s,

Jn 1:29 who takes away the s of the world.

Ro 5:12 as through one person s entered

    5:12 the world, and through s, death,

    6:23 For the wages of s is death,

2Co 5:21 him to be s who did not know s,

Heb 4:15 tested in every way, yet without s.

1Jn 1: 7 his Son Jesus cleanses us from all s.

SINAI → = HOREB

Ex 19:20 came down to the top of Mount S,

Ps 68:18 S the Lord entered the holy place.

Gal 4:25 Hagar represents S, a mountain

SINFUL → SIN

1Ma 1:10 sprang from these a s offshoot,

Lk 5: 8 from me, Lord, for I am a s man."

Ro 8: 3 own Son in the likeness of s flesh

SING → SINGERS, SONG, SONGS, SUNG

Ex 15: 1 LORD: I will s to the LORD, for he is
Jdt 16:13 "A new hymn I will s to my God.
Ps 47: 7 S praise to God, s praise; s praise
    47: 7 praise; s praise to our king, s praise.
Isa 5: 1 Let me now s of my friend,
1Co 14:15 I will s praise with the spirit, but I
    14:15 I will also s praise with the mind.

SINGERS → SING

Ezr 2:70 but the s, the gatekeepers,

SINGLE

Mt 6:27 by worrying add a s moment to your
Rev 21:21 of the gates made from a s pearl;

SINNED → SIN

Ps 51: 6 Against you alone have I s; I have
La   5: 7 Our fathers, who s, are no more;
Da   9: 5 We have s, been wicked and done
Ro   3:23 all have s and are deprived
1Jn 1:10 "We have not s," we make him a liar,

SINNER → SIN

Lk 15: 7 heaven over one s who repents than
Jas 5:20 whoever brings back a s

SINNERS → SIN

Ps   1: 1 Nor go the way of s, nor sit
Pr 23:17 Let not your heart emulate s, but be
Lk   6:33 is that to you? Even s do the same.
Ro   5: 8 while we were still s Christ died
1Ti 1:15 Jesus came into the world to save s.

SINS → SIN

1Sa 2:25 If a man s against another man,
     2:25 but if a man s against the LORD,
2Ch 7:14 pardon their s and revive their land.
Ps 103:10 Has not dealt with us as our s merit,
Sir 2:11 he forgives s, he saves in time
Isa 1:18 LORD: Though your s be like scarlet,
    53:12 he shall take away the s of many,
Eze 18: 4 mine; only the one who s shall die.
Mic 7:19 into the depths of the sea all our s;
Mt   9: 6 has authority on earth to forgive s
Mk   1: 5 River as they acknowledged their s.
Lk 11: 4 and forgive us our s for we
Ac   3:19 that your s may be wiped away,

1Co 15: 3 Christ died for our s in accordance
Heb 9:28 once to take away the s of many,
1Jn 1: 9 If we acknowledge our s, he is
     1: 9 will forgive our s and cleanse us
Rev 1: 5 freed us from our s by his blood,

SISTER

Ge 12:13 that you are my s, so that it may go
    20: 2 said of his wife Sarah, "She is my s."
Pr   7: 4 Say to Wisdom, "You are my s!"
Mk   3:35 the will of God is my brother and s

SIT → SITS

Ps   1: 1 nor s in company with scoffers.
Mt 20:23 but to s at my right and at my left [,
Heb 1:13 has he ever said: "S at my right hand

SITS → SIT

Isa 28: 6 to him who s in judgment,

SIX

Ex 20: 9 S days you may labor and do all
Pr   6:16 There are s things the LORD hates,
Isa 6: 2 each of them had s wings: with two
Rev 4: 8 each of them with s wings,

SKILL

Ex 28: 3 whom I have endowed with s,
1Ki 7:14 from Tyre. He was endowed with s,

SKIN

Job 2: 4 answered the LORD and said, "S for s!
Jer 13:23 Can the Ethiopian change his s?

SKULL

2Ki 9:35 they found nothing of her but the s,
Mt 27:33 (which means Place of the S),

SKY

Dt 28:23 The s over your heads will be like
Mt 16: 3 for the s is red and threatening.'
    16: 3 to judge the appearance of the s,
Rev 6:14 the s was divided like a torn scroll

SLANDER → SLANDERED

Ps 15: 3 Who does not s a neighbor, does no
1Pe 2: 1 deceit, insincerity, envy, and all s;

SLANDERED → SLANDER

1Co 4:13 when s, we respond gently.

SLAUGHTER → SLAUGHTERED

Pr   7:22 like an ox that is led to s;
Isa 53: 7 Like a lamb led to the s or a sheep

Ac   8:32 "Like a sheep he was led to the s,

SLAUGHTERED → SLAUGHTER

Zec 11: 4 my God: Shepherd the flock to be s.
Rev 6: 9 those who had been s because

SLAVE → ENSLAVE, SLAVERY, SLAVES

Ge 21:10 "Drive out that s and her son! No son
    21:10 son of that s is going to share
Mk 10:44 be first among you will be the s
Jn   8:34 everyone who commits sin is a s
Gal 3:28 there is neither s nor free person,
Php 2: 7 taking the form of a s,
Phm 1:16 no longer as a s but more than a s,

SLAVERY → SLAVE

Ex 20: 2 of the land of Egypt, that place of s.
Ro   7:14 but I am carnal, sold into s to sin.
     8:15 you did not receive a spirit of s
Gal 5: 1 do not submit again to the yoke of s.

SLAVES → SLAVE

Ro   6:16 to someone as obedient s, you are s
     6:20 For when you were s of sin,
2Pe 2:19 though they themselves are s

SLEEP → ASLEEP, SLEEPER, SLEEPING, SLEEPS

Ge   2:21 So the LORD God cast a deep s
Da 12: 2 Many of those who s in the dust

SLEEPER → SLEEP

Eph 5:14 "Awake, O s, and arise

SLEEPING → SLEEP

Mt   9:24 The girl is not dead but s." And they

SLEEPS → SLEEP

Ps 121: 4 of Israel never slumbers nor s.

SLING

1Sa 17:50 overcame the Philistine with s

SLOW

Ex 34: 6 s to anger and rich in kindness
Nu 14:18 'The LORD is s to anger and rich
Ps 145: 8 s to anger and abounding in love.
Na   1: 3 The LORD is s to anger, yet great
Lk 24:25 How s of heart to believe all

SMALL → SMALLEST

Jas 3: 5 same way the tongue is a s member
     3: 5 Consider how s a fire can set a huge

SMALLEST → SMALL

Mk   4:31 is the s of all the seeds on the earth.

SMOKE → SMOKING
Ex 19:18 Mount Sinai was all wrapped in s,
19:18 The s rose from it as though
Isa 6: 4 and the house was filled with s.
Rev 15: 8 so filled with the s from God's glory

SMOKING → SMOKE
Ge 15:17 there appeared a s brazier
Ex 20:18 trumpet blast and the mountain s,

SNAKE
Lk 11:11 among you would hand his son a s

SNARE
Jdg 2: 3 their gods shall become a s for you."

SNOW
Ps 51: 9 wash me, make me whiter than s.
Isa 1:18 they may become white as s;
Da 7: 9 His clothing was s bright,
Rev 1:14 was as white as white wool or as s,

SOBER
1Th 5: 6 rest do, but let us stay alert and s.

SODOM
Ge 19:24 rained down sulphurous fire upon S
Isa 1: 9 We had become as S, we should be
Lk 10:12 it will be more tolerable for S
Rev 11: 8 which has the symbolic names "S"

SOLDIERS
Mt 28:12 gave a large sum of money to the s,
Jn 19:23 When the s had crucified Jesus,

SOLID
1Co 3: 2 I fed you milk, not s food,
Heb 5:14 But s food is for the mature,

SOLOMON
Son of David by Bathsheba; king of Judah (2Sa 12:24; 1Ch 3:5, 10). Appointed king by David (1Ki 1); adversaries Adonijah, Joab, Shimei killed by Benaiah (1Ki 2). Asked for wisdom (1Ki 3; 2Ch 1). Judged between two prostitutes (1Ki 3:16-28). Built temple (1Ki 5-7; 2Ch 2-5); prayer of dedication (1Ki 8; 2Ch 6). Visited by Queen of Sheba (1Ki 10; 2Ch 9). Wives turned his heart from God (1Ki 11:1-13). Jeroboam rebelled against (1Ki 11:26-40). Death (1Ki 11:41-43; 2Ch 9:29-31).
Proverbs of (1Ki 4:32; Pr 1:1; 10:1; 25:1); psalms of (Ps 72; 127); song of (SS 1:1).

SON → SONS
Ge 21: 2 bore Abraham a s in his old age,
Ex 4:23 Let my s go, that he may serve me.
4:23 I will kill your s, your first-born."
2Sa 7:14 to him, and he shall be a s to me.
Ps 2: 7 who said to me, "You are my s;

Sir 4:10 Thus will you be like a s
Isa 7:14 and bear a s, and shall name him
Mt 1:23 shall be with child and bear a s,
2:15 fulfilled, "Out of Egypt I called my s."
3:17 "This is my beloved S, with whom I
Mt 12: 8 For the S of Man is Lord
16:16 Messiah, the S of the living God."
Mk 10:45 For the S of Man did not come to be
Lk 1:35 will be called holy, the S of God.
20:44 calls him 'lord,' how can he be his s?"
Jn 1:34 and testified that he is the S of God."
3:16 the world that he gave his only S,
Ro 8:29 be conformed to the image of his S,
1Th 1:10 and to await his S from heaven,
Heb 1: 2 he spoke to us through a s, whom he
1: 5 say: "You are my s; this day I have
1: 5 to him, and he shall be a s to me"?
2Pe 1:17 glory, "This is my S, my beloved,
1Jn 4: 9 God sent his only S into the world
Rev 12: 5 She gave birth to a s, a male child,
14:14 the cloud one who looked like a s

SONG → SING
Ex 15: 1 the Israelites sang this s to the LORD:
Dt 31:21 this s, which their descendants will
Ps 40: 4 And put a new s in my mouth,
Rev 15: 3 and they sang the s of Moses,
15: 3 of God, and the s of the Lamb:

SONGS → SING
Col 3:16 and spiritual s with gratitude in your

SONS → SON
Ge 6: 2 the s of heaven saw how beautiful
35:22 The s of Jacob were now twelve.
Dt 7: 3 to their s nor taking their daughters
7: 3 taking their daughters for your s.
Ac 2:17 Your s and your daughters shall
2Co 6:18 you shall be s and daughters to me,

SOON
Rev 22:20 testimony says, "Yes, I am coming s."

SORCERERS → SORCERY
Rev 22:15 are the dogs, the s, the unchaste,

SORCERY → SORCERERS
Gal 5:20 idolatry, s, hatreds, rivalry,

SORROW → SORROWFUL
Est 9:22 was turned for them from s into joy,
Ecc 1:18 in much wisdom there is much s,
Isa 35:10 gladness, s and mourning will flee.

SORROWFUL → SORROW
2Co 6:10 as s yet always rejoicing; as poor

SOUL → SOULS
Dt 6: 5 and with all your s, and with all
Jos 22: 5 him with your whole heart and s."
Ps 16: 9 my heart is glad, my s rejoices;
25: 1 I wait for you, O LORD; I lift up my s
42: 2 so my s longs for you, O God.
Sir 7:29 With all your s, fear God, revere his
Mic 6: 7 fruit of my body for the sin of my s?
Mt 10:28 kill the body but cannot kill the s;
10:28 of the one who can destroy both s
Heb 4:12 penetrating even between s
Jas 5:20 his way will save his s from death
3Jn 1: 2 health, just as your s is prospering.

SOULS → SOUL
Jer 6:16 it; thus you will find rest for your s.
1Pe 2:25 the shepherd and guardian of your s.

SOUND
Eze 1:24 Then I heard the s of their wings,
1:24 the s of the tumult was like the din
1Co 15:52 For the trumpet will s, the dead will
2Ti 4: 3 will not tolerate s doctrine but,
Tit 1: 9 able both to exhort with s doctrine
Rev 1:15 his voice was like the s of rushing

SOW → SOWED, SOWER, SOWS
Ex 23:10 "For six years you may s your land
Ecc 11: 6 In the morning s your seed,
Hos 10:12 "S for yourselves justice,
Mt 13: 3 saying: "A sower went out to s.
1Co 15:36 What you s is not brought to life

SOWED → SOW
Mt 13:24 a man who s good seed in his field.

SOWER → SOW
Mk 4:14 The s sows the word.

SOWS → SOW
Jn 4:37 the saying is verified that 'One s

2Co 9: 6 whoever s sparingly will also reap
    9: 6 and whoever s bountifully will

SPAN
Isa 40:12 marked off the heavens with a s?
Mt 6:27 add a single moment to your l?

SPARE
Ro 11:21 God did not s the natural branches,
    11:21 [perhaps] he will not s you either.
2Pe 2: 4 God did not s the angels when they

SPARROWS
Lk 12: 7 You are worth more than many s.

SPEAK → SPEAKING, SPEECH, SPOKE
Ge 18:27 "See how I am presuming to s to my
Nu 12: 8 face to face I s to him,
    12: 8 fear to s against my servant Moses?"
Dt 18:20 a prophet presumes to s in my name
    18:20 that I have not commanded him to s,
Job 13: 3 But I would s with the Almighty;
Ecc 3: 7 a time to be silent, and a time to s.
Mt 13:13 This is why I s to them in parables,
Ac 2: 4 and began to s in different tongues,
1Co 12:30 of healing? Do all s in tongues?
Jas 1:19 to hear, slow to s, slow to wrath,

SPEAKING → SPEAK
1Co 14:39 and do not forbid s in tongues,

SPEAR → SPEARS
1Sa 19:10 to nail David to the wall with the s,
    19:10 so that the s struck only the wall,

SPEARS → SPEAR
Mic 4: 3 and their s into pruning hooks;

SPECTACLE
1Co 4: 9 since we have become a s

SPEECH → SPEAK
Ex 4:10 but I am slow of s and tongue."
Sir 4:29 Be not surly in your s, nor lazy
1Ti 4:12 for those who believe, in s, conduct,
1Jn 3:18 let us love not in word or s

SPICES
Ex 25: 6 s for the anointing oil
Jn 19:40 with burial cloths along with the s,

SPIES
Jos 2: 1 secretly sent out two s from Shittim,

SPIRIT → SPIRITS, SPIRITUAL
Ge 6: 3 said: "My s shall not remain in man

Nu 11:25 Taking some of the s that was
    11:25 and as the s came to rest on them,
2Ki 2: 9 I receive a double portion of your s."
Ne 9:20 "Your good s you bestowed on them,
Job 33: 4 For the s of God has made me,
Ps 31: 6 Into your hands I commend my s;
    51:19 My sacrifice, God, is a broken s;
Pr 16:18 and a haughty s before a fall.
Isa 42: 1 Upon whom I have put my s;
Eze 36:26 heart and place a new s within you,
Mt 1:18 found with child through the holy S.
    5: 3 "Blessed are the poor in s, for theirs
    12:31 blasphemy against the S will not be
    26:41 test. The s is willing, but the flesh is
Mk 1: 8 he will baptize you with the holy S."
Jn 3: 5 without being born of water and S.
    4:24 God is S, and those who worship
    4:24 who worship him must worship in S
    6:63 It is the s that gives life,
    6:63 words I have spoken to you are s
    14:26 the holy S that the Father will send
Ac 2: 4 they were all filled with the holy S
    2: 4 as the S enabled them to proclaim.
    2:38 will receive the gift of the holy S.
Ro 8: 9 you are in the s, if only the S of God
    8: 9 Whoever does not have the S
    8:26 the S too comes to the aid of our
    8:26 but the S itself intercedes
1Co 6:19 is a temple of the holy S within you,
    12: 4 of spiritual gifts but the same S;
2Co 3: 6 new covenant, not of letter but of s;
    3: 6 brings death, but the S gives life.
Gal 4: 6 God sent the s of his Son into our
    5:22 the fruit of the S is love, joy, peace,
Eph 1:13 sealed with the promised holy S,
    2:18 have access in one S to the Father.
    4:30 do not grieve the holy S of God,
    5:18 debauchery, but be filled with the S,
1Th 5:19 Do not quench the S.
Heb 4:12 even between soul and s,
1Jn 4: 1 do not trust every s but test

Rev 1:10 was caught up in s on the Lord's day

SPIRITS → SPIRIT
Nu 16:22 God of the s of all mankind,
Dt 18:11 nor one who consults ghosts and s
Lk 4:36 power he commands the unclean s,
1Co 12:10 to another discernment of s;
Rev 1: 4 from the seven s before his throne,

SPIRITUAL → SPIRIT
Ro 7:14 We know that the law is s; but I am
1Co 2:13 describing s realities in s terms.
    12: 1 Now in regard to s gifts, brothers,
    14: 1 but strive eagerly for the s gifts,
    15:46 But the s was not first;
    15:46 rather the natural and then the s.
Eph 1: 3 Christ with every s blessing
Col 1: 9 of his will through all s wisdom
1Pe 2: 2 long for pure s milk so that through
    2: 5 let yourselves be built into a s house
    2: 5 to offer s sacrifices acceptable

SPIT
Mk 14:65 Some began to s on him.
Rev 3:16 cold, I will s you out of my mouth.

SPLENDOR
Eph 5:27 present to himself the church in s,

SPOKE → SPEAK
Mk 4:33 many such parables he s the word
Heb 1: 1 God s in partial and various ways
2Pe 1:21 the holy Spirit s under the influence

SPOT
Eph 5:27 without s or wrinkle or any such
2Pe 3:14 be eager to be found without s

SPRING
Isa 45: 8 let justice also s up! I, the LORD,
Jn 4:14 become in him a s of water welling
Rev 21: 6 gift from the s of life-giving water.

SPRINKLE → SPRINKLED
Nu 8: 7 S them with the water of remission;
Eze 36:25 I will s clean water upon you

SPRINKLED → SPRINKLE
Lev 8:11 he s some of this oil seven times
Heb 10:22 with our hearts s clean from an evil

STAFF
Ex 4: 4 of it, and it became a s in his hand.

STAFF (*cont.*)

Ps	23: 4	your rod and s give me courage.
Zec	11:10	I took my s "Favor" and snapped it

STAND → STANDING

Ex	14:13	S your ground, and you will see
Job	19:25	he will at last s forth upon the dust;
Mt	12:25	house divided against itself will s.
Ro	14: 4	for the Lord is able to make him s.
	14:10	we shall all s before the judgment
Eph	6:11	be able to s firm against the tactics

STANDARDS

1Co	1:26	many of you were wise by human s,

STANDING → STAND

1Co	10:12	thinks he is s secure should take
Jas	5: 9	the Judge is s before the gates.

STAR → STARS

Nu	24:17	near: A s shall advance from Jacob,
Isa	14:12	O morning s, son of the dawn!
Mt	2: 2	We saw his s at its rising and have
2Pe	1:19	the morning s rises in your hearts.
Rev	9: 1	I saw a s that had fallen
	22:16	of David, the bright morning s."

STARS → STAR

Ge	1:16	govern the night; and he made the s.
Job	38: 7	While the morning s sang in chorus
Ps	148: 3	and moon; give praise, all shining s.
Da	12: 3	to justice shall be like the s forever.
Rev	1:16	In his right hand he held seven s.
	12: 4	away a third of the s in the sky

STATUE

Da	2:31	O king, you saw a s, very large

STATUTES

Dt	4: 1	hear the s and decrees which I am
Ne	9:13	laws, good s, and commandments;

STEADFAST

Ps	57: 8	My heart is s, God, my heart is s.
1Pe	5: 9	Resist him, s in faith,

STEAL

Ex	20:15	"You shall not s.
Mt	6:19	destroys, and thieves break in and s.
Jn	10:10	A thief comes only to s

STEPHEN

Early church leader (Ac 6:5). Arrested (Ac 6:8-15). Speech to Sanhedrin (Ac 7). Stoned (Ac 7:54-60; 8:2; 11:19; 22:20).

STEPS

Pr	16: 9	course, but the LORD directs his s.

STIFF-NECKED → NECK

Ex	32: 9	I see how s this people is,"
Ac	7:51	"You s people,

STILL

Ex	14:14	for you; you have only to keep s."
Jos	10:13	And the sun stood s, and the moon
Ps	46:11	"Be s and confess that I am God!
Mk	4:39	Be s!" The wind ceased and there
Ro	5: 8	while we were s sinners Christ died
Heb	11: 4	this, though dead, he s speaks.

STING

1Co	15:55	victory? Where, O death, is your s?"

STONE → CORNERSTONE, MILL-STONE, STONED, STONES

Ge	28:18	the next morning Jacob took the s
	28:18	head, set it up as a memorial s,
Ex	28:10	six of their names on one s,
	28:10	s, and the other six on the other s,
	31:18	the s tablets inscribed by God's own
1Sa	17:50	the Philistine with sling and s;
Ps	118:22	The s the builders rejected
Isa	28:16	See, I am laying a s in Zion, a s
Mt	4: 6	lest you dash your foot against a s.'"
Mk	12:10	'The s that the builders rejected
	16: 3	"Who will roll back the s for us
Ro	9:32	They stumbled over the s
2Co	3: 3	not on tablets of s but on tablets
1Pe	2: 4	a living s, rejected by human beings

STONED → STONE

2Ch	24:21	the king's order they s him to death
Ac	14:19	They s Paul and dragged him
Heb	11:37	They were s, sawed in two,

STONES → STONE

Jos	4: 3	to take up twelve s from this spot
1Sa	17:40	David selected five smooth s
Mt	3: 9	children to Abraham from these s.
Lk	19:40	they keep silent, the s will cry out!"
1Co	3:12	gold, silver, precious s, wood, hay,
1Pe	2: 5	like living s, let yourselves be built

STORE → SHOREHOUSE, STORING

Mt	6:19	"Do not s up for yourselves treasures

STOREHOUSE → HOUSE, STORE

Mal	3:10	into the s, That there may be food

STORING → STORE

Ro	2: 5	you are s up wrath for yourself

STRAIGHT

Pr	3: 6	him, and he will make s your paths.
Sir	2: 6	make s your ways and hope in him.
Isa	40: 3	Make s in the wasteland a highway
Mt	3: 3	way of the Lord, make s his paths.' "
Ac	9:11	go to the street called S and ask

STRANGE → STRANGER, STRANGERS

Dt	32:16	They provoked him with s gods
1Co	14:21	"By people speaking s tongues

STRANGER → STRANGE

Mt	25:35	drink, a s and you welcomed me,

STRANGERS → STRANGE

Eph	2:12	and s to the covenants of promise,
Heb	11:13	acknowledged themselves to be s

STRAW

Ex	5:10	I will not provide you with s.
1Co	3:12	precious stones, wood, hay, or s,

STRAY → ASTRAY

Ps	119:10	seek you; do not let me s from your

STREAM → STREAMS

Isa	2: 2	hills. All nations shall s toward it;
Am	5:24	and goodness like an unfailing s.

STREAMS → STREAM

Ps	1: 3	like a tree planted near s of water,
	42: 2	As the deer longs for s of water,

STREET

Pr	1:20	Wisdom cries aloud in the s,
Mt	6: 5	s corners so that others may see
Rev	21:21	the s of the city was of pure gold,

STRENGTH → STRONG

Ex	15: 2	My s and my courage is the LORD,
1Ch	16:11	Look to the LORD in his s;
Ne	8:10	in the LORD must be your s!"
Jdt	9:11	"Your s is not in numbers, nor does
1Ma	3:19	but on s that comes from Heaven.
Ps	46: 2	God is our refuge and our s,
Pr	31:25	She is clothed with s and dignity,
Isa	40:31	hope in the LORD will renew their s,
Mk	12:30	all your mind, and with all your s.'
1Co	1:25	of God is stronger than human s.

STRENGTHEN → STRONG
Jdg 16:28 S me, O God, this last time
Ps 119:28 in accord with your word to s me.
Lk 22:32 back, you must s your brothers."
Heb 12:12 So s your drooping hands and your

STRETCH → OUTSTRETCHED, STRETCHED
Mk 3: 5 he said to the man, "S out your hand."

STRETCHED → STRETCH
2Sa 24:16 the angel s forth his hand toward

STRIFE → STRIVE
Pr 23:29 Who have s? Who have anxiety?

STRIKE
Ge 3:15 and hers; He will s at your head,
3:15 at your head, while you s at his heel."
Ex 17: 6 S the rock, and the water will flow
Zec 13: 7 the LORD of hosts. S the shepherd
Mk 14:27 it is written: 'I will s the shepherd,
Rev 19:15 came a sharp sword to s the nations.

STRIVE → STRIFE
1Co 12:31 S eagerly for the greatest spiritual

STRONG → STRENGTH, STRENGTHEN, STRONGHOLD
Ps 140: 8 My revered LORD, my s helper,
Pr 18:10 The name of the LORD is a s tower;
Ro 15: 1 We who are s ought to put
1Co 1:27 weak of the world to shame the s,
2Co 12:10 for when I am weak, then I am s.

STRONGHOLD → STRONG
Ps 9:10 The LORD is a s for the oppressed,
9:10 oppressed, a s in times of trouble.

STRUGGLE
Eph 6:12 For our s is not with flesh and blood
Heb 12: 4 your s against sin you have not yet

STUBBORN
Hos 4:16 For Israel is as s as a heifer;

STUDY
Ezr 7:10 Ezra had set his heart on the s
Ecc 12:12 in much s there is weariness

STUMBLE → STUMBLING
Ps 37:24 May s, but they will never fall,
Pr 4:12 and should you run, you will not s.
Ro 9:33 that will make people s and a rock

1Pe 2: 8 "A stone that will make people s,
2: 8 They s by disobeying the word, as is

STUMBLING → STUMBLE
Ro 11: 9 a s block and a retribution for them;
1Co 8: 9 in no way becomes a s block

STUMP
Isa 11: 1 shall sprout from the s of Jesse,

SUBDUE
Ge 1:28 and multiply; fill the earth and s it.
1Ch 17:10 Israel. And I will s all your enemies.

SUBJECTED
Ro 8:20 but because of the one who s it,
1Co 15:28 When everything is s to him,
15:28 be s to the One who s everything

SUBMIT
Gal 5: 1 and do not s again to the yoke

SUCCEED
Pr 15:22 they s when counselors are many.

SUDDENLY
Mal 3: 1 And s there will come to the temple
Mk 13:36 May he not come s and find you

SUFFER → SUFFERED, SUFFERING, SUFFERINGS, SUFFERS
Lk 22:15 this Passover with you before I s,
24:46 is written that the Messiah would s
Ro 8:17 if only we s with him so that we
Heb 9:26 he would have had to s repeatedly
1Pe 3:17 For it is better to s for doing good,

SUFFERED → SUFFER
1Pe 2:21 because Christ also s for you,

SUFFERING → SUFFER
Job 2:13 for they saw how great was his s.
Isa 53: 3 a man of s, accustomed to infirmity,

SUFFERINGS → SUFFER
Ro 8:18 that the s of this present time are as
1Pe 4:13 that you share in the s of Christ,

SUFFERS → SUFFER
1Co 12:26 If [one] part s, all the parts suffer

SUFFICIENT
2Co 12: 9 he said to me, "My grace is s for you,

SULFUR
Rev 21: 8 is in the burning pool of fire and s,

SUMMED
Ro 13: 9 there may be, are s up in this saying,

SUN
Jos 10:13 And the s stood still, and the moon
10:13 The s halted in the middle
Ps 84:12 For a s and shield is the LORD God,
Ecc 1: 9 done. Nothing is new under the s.
Mt 5:45 for he makes his s rise on the bad
Ac 2:20 The s shall be turned to darkness,
Rev 1:16 and his face shone like the s at its
19:17 I saw an angel standing on the s.
Rev 22: 5 will they need light from lamp or s,

SUPERIOR
Heb 1: 4 as far s to the angels as the name he

SUPPLICATION → SUPPLICATIONS
Eph 6:18 With all prayer and s, pray at every
6:18 and s for all the holy ones

SUPPLICATIONS → SUPPLICATION
1Ti 2: 1 then, I ask that s, prayers, petitions,
Heb 5: 7 offered prayers and s with loud cries

SUPPORT
Ps 18:19 distress, but the LORD came to my s.
Ro 11:18 consider that you do not s the root;

SURE
Nu 32:23 and you can be s that you will not
Isa 28:16 cornerstone as a s foundation;
Heb 6:19 as an anchor of the soul, s and firm,

SURPASSES → SURPASSING
Sir 25:11 Fear of the LORD s all else,
Eph 3:19 the love of Christ that s knowledge,
Php 4: 7 s all understanding will guard your

SURPASSING → SURPASSES
2Co 9:14 because of the s grace of God

SURPRISED
1Pe 4:12 do not be s that a trial by fire is

SURROUNDED → SURROUNDS
Lk 21:20 you see Jerusalem s by armies,
Heb 12: 1 since we are s by so great a cloud
Rev 20: 9 and s the camp of the holy ones

SURROUNDS → SURROUNDED
Ps 125: 2 Jerusalem, the LORD s his people

SURVIVORS
Eze 14:22 still some s shall be left in it who

SUSA

Ne 1: 1 year, I was in the citadel of S
Est 1: 2 royal throne in the stronghold of S,

SUSANNA

Righteous woman wrongly accused of immorality (Da 13:1-44); vindicated by Daniel (Da 13:45-64).

SUSTAINS

Heb 1: 3 who s all things by his mighty word.

SWALLOW → SWALLOWED

Mt 23:24 strain out the gnat and s the camel!

SWALLOWED → SWALLOW

Ge 41: 7 the seven thin ears s up the seven
Nu 16:32 earth opened its mouth and s them
1Co 15:54 about: "Death is s up in victory.

SWEAR → SWORE, SWORN

Dt 10:20 hold fast to him and s by his name.
Mt 5:34 But I say to you, do not s at all;

SWEAT

Ge 3:19 By the s of your face shall you get
Lk 22:44 that his s became like drops

SWEET → SWEETER

Ps 119:103 How s to my tongue is your
Eze 3: 3 it was as s as honey in my mouth.
Rev 10:10 it. In my mouth it was like s honey,

SWEETER → SWEET

Jdg 14:18 said to him, "What is s than honey,
Ps 19:11 of purest gold, S also than honey

SWIFT

Ecc 9:11 sun that the race is not won by the s,
2Pe 2: 1 them, bringing s destruction

SWINE

1Ma 1:47 to sacrifice s and unclean animals,
Mt 7: 6 or throw your pearls before s,
Mk 5:12 with him, "Send us into the s. Let us

SWORD → SWORDS

Ge 3:24 cherubim and the fiery revolving s,
1Sa 17:47 shall learn that it is not by s or spear
1Ch 21:30 he was fearful of the s of the angel
Sir 21: 3 Every offense is a two-edged s;
Isa 2: 4 shall not raise the s against another,
49: 2 He made of me a sharp-edged s
Mt 10:34 come to bring not peace but the s.
Lk 2:35 you yourself a s will pierce) so
Eph 6:17 of salvation and the s of the Spirit,

Heb 4:12 sharper than any two-edged s,
Rev 1:16 A sharp two-edged s came
19:15 his mouth came a sharp s to strike

SWORDS → SWORD

Isa 2: 4 peoples. They shall beat their s

SWORE → SWEAR

Ex 6: 8 into the land which I s to give
32:13 and how you s to them by your own
Ps 132:11 The LORD s an oath to David,
Heb 6:13 by whom to swear, "he s by himself,"

SWORN → SWEAR

Ps 110: 4 The LORD has s and will not waver:
Heb 7:21 him: "The Lord has s, and he will not

SYMPATHIZE

Heb 4:15 have a high priest who is unable to s

SYNAGOGUE → SYNAGOGUES

Lk 4:16 into the s on the sabbath day.
8:41 an official of the s, came forward.
Ac 18:26 He began to speak boldly in the s;

SYNAGOGUES → SYNAGOGUE

Mt 4:23 teaching in their s,

T

TABITHA → See DORCAS

TABLE → TABLES

Ex 25:23 shall also make a t of acacia wood,
Ps 23: 5 You set a t before me as my

TABLES → TABLE

Mk 11:15 He overturned the t of the money

TABLETS

Ex 31:18 Sinai, he gave him the two t
31:18 the stone t inscribed by God's own
2Co 3: 3 not on t of stone but on t that are

TAKE → TAKEN, TAKES

Mt 11:29 T my yoke upon you and learn
Mk 8:34 must deny himself, t up his cross,

TAKEN → TAKE

Sir 44:16 walked with the LORD and was t up,
Heb 11: 5 By faith Enoch was t up so that he
11: 5 no more because God had t him."
11: 5 Before he was t up, he was attested

TAKES → TAKE

Jn 1:29 who t away the sin of the world.
10:18 No one t it from me, but I lay it
Rev 22:19 if anyone t away from the words

TALENT

Mt 25:25 off and buried your t in the ground.

TAMAR

1. Wife of Judah's sons Er and Onan (Ge 38:1-10). Children by Judah (Ge 38:11-30; Mt 1:3).
2. Daughter of David, raped by Amnon (2Sa 13).

TASTE → TASTED

Mt 16:28 here who will not t death until they
Col 2:21 not handle! Do not t! Do not touch!"

TASTED → TASTE

Heb 6: 4 enlightened and t the heavenly gift
1Pe 2: 3 for you have t that the Lord is good.

TAUGHT → TEACH

Isa 40:14 Who t him the path of judgment,
Jn 6:45 prophets: 'They shall all be t by God.'

TAX → TAXES

Mt 11:19 a friend of t collectors and sinners.'
Lk 18:10 and the other was a t collector.

TAXES → TAX

Ro 13: 7 all their dues, t to whom t are due,

TEACH → TAUGHT, TEACHER, TEACHERS, TEACHING

Ps 90:12 T us to count our days aright,
Jer 31:34 will they have need to t their friends
Jn 14:26 in my name—he will t you everything
Col 3:16 richly, as in all wisdom you t
1Ti 2:12 I do not permit a woman to t
1Jn 2:27 you do not need anyone to t you.

TEACHER → TEACH

Mt 10:24 No disciple is above his t, no slave
Jn 1:38 "Rabbi" (which translated means T),

TEACHERS → TEACH

Ps 119:99 more understanding than all my t,
1Co 12:28 third, t; then, mighty deeds;
Eph 4:11 evangelists, others as pastors and t,
Jas 3: 1 Not many of you should become t,

TEACHING → TEACH

Mk 1:27 is this? A new t with authority.
Tit 1:11 are upsetting whole families by t
2Jn 1: 9 in the t of the Christ does not have
1: 9 remains in the t has the Father

TEAR → TORN

Mk 2:21 from the old, and the t gets worse.
Rev 7:17 God will wipe away every t

TEETH → TOOTH
Mt 8:12 will be wailing and grinding of t."

TEKEL
Da 5:27 T, you have been weighed

TELL → FORETOLD
Ps 50:12 Were I hungry, I would not t you,
1Co 15:51 Behold, I t you a mystery. We shall

TEMPERATE
1Ti 3: 2 irreproachable, married only once, t,
Tit 2: 2 that older men should be t.

TEMPLE
1Sa 3: 3 in the t of the LORD where the ark
1Ma 4:48 the interior of the t and purified
Ps 11: 4 The LORD is in his holy t; the LORD's
Mt 4: 5 him stand on the parapet of the t,
Mt 12: 6 something greater than the t is here.
Jn 2:21 speaking about the t of his body.
1Co 3:16 not know that you are the t of God,
Eph 2:21 grows into a t sacred in the Lord;
Rev 21:22 I saw no t in the city, for its t is

TEMPTATION → TEMPTED, TEMPTER
1Ti 6: 9 who want to be rich are falling into t
Jas 1:12 is the man who perseveres in t,

TEMPTED → TEMPTATION
Mk 1:13 the desert for forty days, t by Satan.
Gal 6: 1 so that you also may not be t.

TEMPTER → TEMPTATION
Mt 4: 3 The t approached and said to him,
1Th 3: 5 fear that somehow the t had put you

TEN → TENTH
Ex 34:28 the covenant, the t command-ments.
Da 7:24 The t horns shall be t kings
Mt 25: 1 will be like t virgins who took their
Rev 17:12 The t horns that you saw represent t

TENDER
Lk 1:78 because of the t mercy of our God

TENT
Ex 27:21 before the LORD in the meet-ing t,
2Sa 7: 2 while the ark of God dwells in a t!"
2Co 5: 1 dwelling, a t, should be destroyed,

TENTH → TEN
Ge 14:20 Abram gave him a t of every-thing.
Isa 6:13 If there be still a t part in it,

TERROR
Ps 91: 5 You shall not fear the t of the night

TEST → TESTED, TESTING
Dt 6:16 God, to the t, as you did at Massah.
Lk 4:12 not put the Lord, your God, to the t.'"
10:25 of the law who stood up to t him
2Co 13: 5 you are living in faith. T your-selves.
13: 5 you?—unless, of course, you fail the t.
1Jn 4: 1 but t the spirits to see whether they

TESTED → TEST
Ps 78:41 Again and again they t God,
Heb 4:15 but one who has similarly been t

TESTIFIED → TESTIFY
Jn 1:15 John t to him and cried out, saying,
1Pe 1:11 them indicated when it t in advance

TESTIFIES → TESTIFY
1Jn 5: 6 The Spirit is the one that t,

TESTIFY → TESTIFIED, TESTIFIES, TESTIMONY
Jn 15:26 from the Father, he will t to me.
1Jn 5: 7 So there are three that t,

TESTIMONY → TESTIFY
Mk 14:59 Even so their t did not agree.
Rev 1: 9 God's word and gave t to Jesus.

TESTING → TEST
Jas 1: 3 that the t of your faith produces

THADDAEUS → = JUDAS
Apostle (Mt 10:3; Mk 3:18); probably also known as Judas son of James (Lk 6:16; Ac 1:13).

THANK → THANKS, THANKSGIVING
2Ch 29:31 t offerings for the house of the LORD."
29:31 the sacrifices and t offerings and all

THANKS → THANK
1Ch 16: 8 Give t to the LORD, invoke his name;
Ps 107: 1 "Give t to the LORD who is good,
Ro 1:21 him glory as God or give him t.
1Co 11:24 and after he had given t, broke it
2Co 9:15 T be to God for his indescrib-able
Rev 4: 9 t to the one who sits on the throne,

THANKSGIVING → THANK
Lev 7:12 anyone makes a peace offering in t,
7:12 with his t sacrifice he shall offer
Php 4: 6 with t, make your requests known
Rev 7:12 Blessing and glory, wisdom and t,

THEFT → THIEF
Mt 15:19 adultery, unchastity, t, false witness,

THIEF → THEFT, THIEVES
Ex 22: 1 "[If a t is caught in the act
Jn 10:10 A t comes only to steal
1Th 5: 2 the Lord will come like a t at night.
Rev 16:15 ("Behold, I am coming like a t."

THIEVES → THIEF
Mt 6:19 destroys, and t break in and steal.

THINK → THINKING, THOUGHT, THOUGHTS
Ro 12: 3 I tell everyone among you not to t
12: 3 more highly than one ought to t,
12: 3 t, but to t soberly, each accord-ing

THINKING → THINK
1Co 14:20 stop being childish in your t.
14:20 like infants, but in your t be mature.

THIRD → THREE
Hos 6: 2 on the t day he will raise us up,
Mt 26:44 withdrew again and prayed a t time,
Lk 18:33 him, but on the t day he will rise."
2Co 12: 2 was caught up to the t heaven.

THIRST → THIRSTY
Mt 5: 6 who hunger and t for right-eousness,
Rev 7:16 They will not hunger or t any-more,

THIRSTY → THIRST
Mt 25:35 I was t and you gave me drink,

THOMAS
Apostle (Mt 10:3; Mk 3:18; Lk 6:15; Jn 11:16; 14:5; 21:2; Ac 1:13). Doubted resur-rection (Jn 20:24-28).

THORN → THORNS
2Co 12: 7 a t in the flesh was given to me,

THORNS → THORN
Ge 3:18 T and thistles shall it bring forth
Mt 13: 7 Some seed fell among t, and the t
Jn 19: 2 the soldiers wove a crown out of t

THOUGHT → THINK
2Co 10: 5 take every t captive in obedi-ence

THOUGHTS → THINK
Isa 55: 8 For my t are not your t, nor are your
1Co 3:20 "The Lord knows the t of the wise,
Heb 4:12 reflections and t of the heart.

THOUSAND → THOUSANDS
Ps 90: 4 A t years in your eyes are merely
2Pe 3: 8 the Lord one day is like a t years
3: 8 a t years and a t years like one day.
Rev 20: 4 reigned with Christ for a t years.

THOUSANDS → THOUSAND
1Sa 18: 7 "Saul has slain his t, and David his
1Sa 18: 7 has slain his t, and David his ten t."
Da 7:10 T upon t were ministering to him,

THREE → THIRD
Ge 18: 2 up, he saw t men standing nearby.
Ex 23:14 "T times a year you shall celebrate
Mt 18:20 t are gathered together in my name,
26:34 crows, you will deny me t times."
Mk 8:31 and be killed, and rise after t days.
2Co 12: 8 T times I begged the Lord
1Jn 5: 7 So there are t that testify,

THRONE → THRONES
2Sa 7:13 I will make his royal t firm forever.
Ps 45: 7 Your t, O god, stands forever;
Isa 6: 1 Lord seated on a high and lofty t,
Jer 33:21 not have a son to be king upon his t,
Mt 19:28 of Man is seated on his t of glory,
Heb 4:16 So let us confidently approach the t
12: 2 his seat at the right of the t of God.
Rev 4:10 before the one who sits on the t
4:10 down their crowns before the t,
20:11 Next I saw a large white t

THRONES → THRONE
Da 7: 9 As I watched, T were set up
Rev 4: 4 the throne I saw twenty-four other t

THROW → THROWN
Ex 1:22 "T into the river every boy that is
Mt 7: 6 or t your pearls before swine,

THROWN → THROW
Rev 20:10 Devil who had led them astray was t

THUMMIM
Ex 28:30 you shall put the Urim and T,

THUNDER → THUNDERS
Ex 9:23 LORD sent forth hail and peals of t.

Rev 4: 5 lightning, rumblings, and peals of t.

THUNDERS → THUNDER
Rev 10: 3 out, the seven t raised their voices,

TIBNI
King of Israel (1Ki 16:21-22).

TIE
Mt 23: 4 They t up heavy burdens [hard

TIME → TIMES
Est 4:14 that it was for a t like this that you
Ecc 3: 1 There is an appointed t
3: 1 and a t for every affair under
Ro 5: 6 at the appointed t for the un-godly.
2Co 6: 2 "In an acceptable t I heard you,
6: 2 Behold, now is a very accept-able t;
Gal 4: 4 when the fullness of t had come,
Rev 22:10 book, for the appointed t is near.

TIMES → TIME
Jos 6: 4 day march around the city seven t,
Mt 16: 3 you cannot judge the signs of the t.]
18:22 you, not seven t but seventy-seven t.
Mk 14:30 twice you will deny me three t."

TIMOTHY
Believer from Lystra (Ac 16:1). Joined Paul on second missionary journey (Ac 16-20). Sent to settle problems at Corinth (1Co 4:17; 16:10). Led church at Ephesus (1Ti 1:3). Co-writer with Paul (1Th 1:1; 2Th 1:1; Phm 1).

TITHE
Dt 12:17 partake of your t of grain or wine
Mal 3:10 Bring the whole t

TITUS
Gentile co-worker of Paul (Gal 2:1-3; 2Ti 4:10); sent to Corinth (2Co 2:13; 7-8; 12:18), Crete (Tit 1:4-5).

TOBIAH
Enemy of Nehemiah (Ne 2:10-19; 4; 6; 13:4-9).

TOBIT
Tob 1: 1 This book tells the story of T,

TODAY
Dt 30:15 then, I have t set before you life
Ps 2: 7 "You are my son; t I am your father.
Lk 23:43 t you will be with me in Par-adise."
Heb 13: 8 Jesus Christ is the same yester-day, t,

TOGETHER
Mt 19: 6 what God has joined t, no human

TOLA
A judge of Israel (Jdg 10:1-2).

TOMB
Mk 15:46 laid him in a t that had been hewn
15:46 a stone against the entrance to the t.
Lk 24: 2 the stone rolled away from the t;

TOMORROW
Isa 22:13 wine: "Eat and drink, for t we die!"
Mt 6:34 Do not worry about t; t will take
Jas 4:14 no idea what your life will be like t.

TONGUE → TONGUES
Ex 4:10 but I am slow of speech and t."
Ps 139: 4 Even before a word is on my t,
Pr 18:21 and life are in the power of the t;
Isa 45:23 bend; by me every t shall swear,
1Co 14:19 also, than ten thousand words in a t.
Php 2:11 and every t confess that Jesus Christ
Jas 3: 8 but no human being can tame the t.

TONGUES → TONGUE
Ac 2: 3 there appeared to them t as of fire,
1Co 12:10 to another varieties of t; to an-other
12:10 of t; to another interpretation of t.
14: 5 I should like all of you to speak in t,
14: 5 is greater than one who speaks in t,

TOOTH → TEETH
Ex 21:24 eye for eye, t for t, hand for hand,
Mt 5:38 'An eye for an eye and a t for a t.'

TORCHES
Da 10: 6 his eyes were like fiery t, his arms
Rev 4: 5 Seven flaming t burned in front

TORMENTED
Rev 20:10 There they will be t day and night

TORN → TEAR
1Sa 28:17 me: he has t the kingdom from your
Lk 23:45 the temple was t down the middle.

TORTURED
Heb 11:35 Some were t and would not accept

TOUCH
Ge 3: 3 'You shall not eat it or even t it,
Mt 9:21 "If only I can t his cloak, I shall be
Lk 24:39 T me and see, because a ghost does
Col 2:21 not handle! Do not taste! Do not t!"

TOWER

Ge 11: 4 a city and a **t** with its top in the sky,

Pr 18:10 The name of the LORD is a strong **t**;

TRADITION

Mt 15: 2 "Why do your disciples break the **t**

Col 2: 8 philosophy according to human **t**,

TRAIN → TRAINING

Pr 22: 6 **T** a boy in the way he should go;

1Ti 4: 7 silly myths. **T** yourself for devotion,

TRAINING → TRAIN

1Ti 4: 8 while physical **t** is of limited value,

2Ti 3:16 and for **t** in righteousness,

TRAITOR

Lk 6:16 and Judas Iscariot, who became a **t**.

TRANSFIGURED

Mt 17: 2 And he was **t** before them; his face

TRANSFORMED

Ro 12: 2 be **t** by the renewal of your mind,

2Co 3:18 are being **t** into the same image

TRANSGRESSION

Da 9:24 Then **t** will stop and sin will end,

Gal 6: 1 even if a person is caught in some **t**,

TRAP

Lk 20:20 to be righteous who were to **t** him

Ro 11: 9 their table become a snare and a **t**,

TREAD → TREADING

Rev 19:15 and he himself will **t** out in the wine

TREADING → TREAD

Dt 25: 4 muzzle an ox when it is **t** out grain.

Mic 7:19 on us, **t** underfoot our guilt?

1Co 9: 9 shall not muzzle an ox while it is **t**

TREASURE → TREASURES

Ps 119:11 In my heart I **t** your promise, that I

Mt 6:21 For where your **t** is, there also will

2Co 4: 7 we hold this **t** in earthen vessels,

TREASURES → TREASURE

Col 2: 3 in whom are hidden all the **t**

TREE → TREES

Ge 3:24 to guard the way to the **t** of life.

Dt 21:23 shall not remain on the **t** overnight.

   21:23 curse rests on him who hangs on a **t**,

Mt 12:33 "Either declare the **t** good and its

Mt 12:33 or declare the **t** rotten and its fruit.

   12:33 rotten, for a **t** is known by its fruit.

Ac 5:30 him killed by hanging him on a **t**.

Ro 11:24 what is by nature a wild olive **t**,

   11:24 grafted back into their own olive **t**.

Rev 22: 2 side of the river grew the **t** of life

TREES → TREE

Ps 96:12 Then let all the **t** of the forest rejoice

Zec 4:11 "What are these two olive **t** at each

Rev 11: 4 These are the two olive **t**

TREMBLE → TREMBLED, TREMBLING

Ps 114: 7 **T**, earth, before the Lord,

Hab 3: 6 his look makes the nations **t**.

TREMBLED → TREMBLE

Ex 20:18 smoking, they all feared and **t**.

TREMBLING → TREMBLE

Ps 2:11 fear; with **t** bow down in homage,

Php 2:12 out your salvation with fear and **t**.

TRESPASSES

2Co 5:19 not counting their **t** against them

TRIAL → TRIALS

2Pe 2: 9 how to rescue the devout from **t**

Rev 3:10 safe in the time of **t** that is going

TRIALS → TRIAL

Jas 1: 2 when you encounter various **t**,

1Pe 1: 6 have to suffer through various **t**,

TRIBE → TRIBES

Nu 1: 4 there shall be a man from each **t**,

Ps 78:68 God chose the **t** of Judah,

Rev 5: 5 The lion of the **t** of Judah, the root

TRIBES → TRIBE

Ge 49:28 All these are the twelve **t** of Israel,

Ex 24: 4 pillars for the twelve **t** of Israel.

Mt 19:28 judging the twelve **t** of Israel.

Rev 21:12 of the twelve **t** of the Israelites.

TRIUMPHS

Jas 2:13 mercy; mercy **t** over judgment.

TROUBLE → TROUBLED

Job 14: 1 woman is short-lived and full of **t**,

Ps 9:10 a stronghold in times of **t**.

Pr 11: 8 The just man escapes **t**,

Sir 51:10 Do not abandon me in time of **t**,

Isa 33: 2 morning, our salvation in time of **t**!

TROUBLED → TROUBLE

Jn 14: 1 "Do not let your hearts be **t**.

TRUE → TRUTH

Jn 1: 9 The **t** light, which enlightens

   21:24 and we know that his testimony is **t**.

Ro 3: 4 God must be **t**, though every human

1Jn 5:20 to know the one who is **t**. And we

   5:20 **t**. And we are in the one who is **t**,

   5:20 He is the **t** God and eternal life.

Rev 3:14 the faithful and **t** witness, the source

   19:11 its rider was [called] "Faithful and **T**."

   22: 6 "These words are trustworthy and **t**,

TRUMPET → TRUMPETS

Ex 19:16 and a very loud **t** blast, so that all

Joel 2:15 Blow the **t** Zion! proclaim a fast,

1Co 15:52 in the blink of an eye, at the last **t**.

   15:52 **t**. For the **t** will sound, the dead will

1Th 4:16 an archangel and with the **t** of God,

TRUMPETS → TRUMPET

Nu 10: 2 "Make two **t** of beaten silver,

Rev 8: 2 before God were given seven **t**.

TRUST → ENTRUSTED, TRUSTED, TRUSTEES, TRUSTS, TRUSTWORTHY

Ps 9:11 Those who honor your name **t**

   37: 3 **T** in the LORD and do good that you

   119:42 with a word, for I **t** in your word.

Pr 3: 5 **T** in the LORD with all your heart,

Sir 2: 6 **T** God and he will help you;

Heb 2:13 and again: "I will put my **t** in him";

TRUSTED → TRUST

Ps 22: 5 In you our ancestors **t**; they **t**

Da 3:95 to deliver the servants that **t** in him;

   13:35 she **t** in the Lord wholeheartedly.

TRUSTS → TRUST

Ps 86: 2 save your servant who **t** in you.

Jer 17: 7 Blessed is the man who **t**

TRUSTWORTHY → TRUST

1Co 7:25 as one who by the Lord's mercy is **t**.

Rev 22: 6 to me, "These words are **t** and true,

TRUTH → TRUE

Tob 3: 2 All your ways are mercy and **t**;

Ps 25: 5 Guide me in your **t** and teach me,

Pr 23:23 Get the **t**, and sell it not— wisdom,

Jn 1:17 and **t** came through Jesus Christ.

TRUTH → TRUE (*cont.*)
Jn 4:23 worship the Father in Spirit and t;
8:32 and you will know the t, and the t
14: 6 "I am the way and the t and the life.
14:17 the Spirit of t, which the world
16:13 the Spirit of t, he will guide you
16:13 Spirit of t, he will guide you to all t.
Eph 4:15 Rather, living the t in love,
1Ti 3:15 God, the pillar and foundation of t.
2Ti 2:15 the word of t without deviation.

TUNIC
Lk 9: 3 and let no one take a second t.
Jn 19:23 They also took his t, but the t was

TURN
Isa 6:10 and they will t and be healed.
45:22 T to me and be safe, all you ends
Lk 1:17 of Elijah to t the hearts of fathers

TWELVE
Ge 49:28 All these are the t tribes of Israel,
Ex 24: 4 and t pillars for the t tribes of Israel.
Jos 4: 3 to take up t stones from this spot
Mt 10: 1 he summoned his t disciples
Lk 9:17 up, they filled t wicker baskets.
Rev 21:12 with t gates where t angels were
21:12 [the names] of the t tribes
22: 2 that produces fruit t times a year,

TWO → TWICE, TWO-EDGED
Ge 1:16 God made the t great lights,
6:19 living creatures you shall bring t
Ex 31:18 he gave him the t tablets
Dt 17: 6 The testimony of t or three
Mt 6:24 "No one can serve t masters. He will
19: 5 and the t shall become one flesh'?

TWO-EDGED → TWO
Heb 4:12 effective, sharper than any t sword,
Rev 1:16 A sharp t sword came out of his

TYRE
Eze 28:12 utter a lament over the king of T,
Mt 11:22 it will be more tolerable for T

U

UNBELIEF → UNBELIEVER, UNBELIEVERS
Mk 9:24 cried out, "I do believe, help my u!"
Ro 11:20 They were broken off because of u,

1Ti 1:13 I acted out of ignorance in my u.

UNBELIEVER → UNBELIEF
1Co 10:27 If an u invites you and you want
2Co 6:15 a believer in common with an u?

UNBELIEVERS → UNBELIEF
2Co 6:14 with those who are different, with u.

UNCIRCUMCISED →
     UNCIRCUMCISION
Ex 12:48 no man who is u may partake of it.
1Ma 1:48 to leave their sons u, and to let
Ac 7:51 people, u in heart and ears,
Ro 4:11 through faith while he was u.
4:11 the father of all the u who believe,

UNCIRCUMCISION →
     UNCIRCUMCISED
1Co 7:19 nothing, and u means nothing;
Gal 5: 6 neither circumcision nor u counts

UNCLEAN → UNCLEANNESS
Lev 5: 2 touches any u thing, as the carcass
5: 2 as the carcass of an u wild animal,
5: 2 or that of an u domestic animal,
5: 2 or that of an u swarming creature,
5: 2 and thus becomes u and guilty;
Isa 52:11 touch nothing u! Out from there!
Mk 3:11 whenever u spirits saw him they
Rev 21:27 but nothing u will enter it,

UNDER
Ac 4:12 any other name u heaven given
Ro 6:14 since you are not u the law but u

UNDERSTAND → UNDERSTANDING
Job 42: 3 with great things that I do not u;
Pr 2: 5 will you u the fear of the LORD;
Mt 13:15 ears and u with their heart and be
Lk 24:45 their minds to u the scriptures.
Ac 8:30 "Do you u what you are reading?"
Eph 5:17 try to u what is the will of the Lord.

UNDERSTANDING → UNDERSTAND
Ex 36: 1 u in knowing how to execute all
Pr 2: 6 his mouth come knowledge and u;
Isa 40:14 or showed him the way of u?
Lk 2:47 heard him were astounded at his u
Php 4: 7 that surpasses all u will guard your
2Ti 2: 7 for the Lord will give you u

UNFAITHFUL
Ro 3: 3 What if some were u? Will their

UNGODLY
Ro 5: 6 died at the appointed time for the u.

UNITY
Eph 4: 3 preserve the u of the spirit through

UNJUST
Ro 3: 5 say? Is God u, humanly speaking,
Heb 6:10 God is not u so as to overlook your

UNLEAVENED
Ex 12:17 then, this custom of the u bread.
Mt 26:17 first day of the Feast of U Bread,

UNPRODUCTIVE
1Co 14:14 spirit is at prayer but my mind is u.
Tit 3:14 needs, so that they may not be u.

UNRIGHTEOUS
2Pe 2: 9 to keep the u under punishment

UPHOLD
Isa 42: 1 Here is my servant whom I u,

UPRIGHT
Job 1: 1 a blameless and u man named Job,

UR
Ge 15: 7 the LORD who brought you from U

URIAH
Hittite husband of Bathsheba, killed (2Sa 11).

URIM
Ex 28:30 of decision you shall put the U

USE → USEFUL
Gal 5:13 But do not u this freedom as
2Ti 2:20 for lofty and others for humble u.

USEFUL → USE
2Ti 3:16 by God and is u for teaching,

UZZIAH → = AZARIAH
Son of Amaziah; king of Judah also known as Azariah (2Ki 15:1-7; 1Ch 6:24; 2Ch 26). Struck with leprosy because of pride (2Ch 26:16-23).

V

VAIN → VANITY
Lev 26:16 You will sow your seed in v,
Ps 2: 1 and the peoples grumble in v?
Mt 15: 9 in v do they worship me, teaching as
Php 2:16 Christ may be that I did not run in v
2:16 that I did not run in v or labor in v.

VALLEY
Ps 23: 4 Even when I walk through a dark v,

Isa 40: 4 Every **v** shall be filled in,
40: 4 plain, the rough country, a broad **v**.
Lk 3: 5 Every **v** shall be filled and every

VALUE
Ro 3: 1 Or what is the **v** of circumcision?
1Ti 4: 8 physical training is of limited **v**,

VANITY → VAIN
Ecc 1: 2 **V** of vanities, says Qoheleth,
1: 2 **v** of vanities! All things are **v**!
12: 8 **V** of vanities, says Qoheleth,
12: 8 says Qoheleth, all things are **v**!

VASHTI
Persian queen replaced by Esther (Est 1-2).

VEIL
Ex 34:33 with them, he put a **v** over his face.
2Co 3:15 is read, a **v** lies over their hearts,

VENGEANCE → AVENGE, AVENGER, AVENGES, AVENGING
Isa 34: 8 For the LORD has a day of **v**, a year
Na 1: 2 and angry; The LORD brings **v** on his

VICTORY
Pr 21:31 the day of battle, but **v** is the LORD's.
1Co 15:54 about: "Death is swallowed up in **v**.
1Jn 5: 4 the **v** that conquers the world is our

VINDICATED
Mt 11:19 But wisdom is **v** by her works."
1Ti 3:16 in the flesh, **v** in the spirit,

VINE → VINEYARD
Ps 80: 9 You brought a **v** out of Egypt;
Jer 2:21 I had planted you, a choice **v**
2:21 out obnoxious to me, a spurious **v**?
Jn 15: 1 "I am the true **v**, and my Father is
15: 1 **v**, and my Father is the **v** grower.

VINEYARD → VINE
1Ki 21: 1 as Naboth the Jezreelite had a **v**
Isa 5: 1 my friend's song concerning his **v**.
5: 1 his **v**. My friend had a **v** on a fertile
Mt 21:33 was a landowner who planted a **v**,

VIOLENCE
Hab 2:17 For the **v** done to Lebanon shall
2:17 and **v** done to the land, to the city

VIPERS
Mt 23:33 you brood of **v**, how can you flee

VIRGIN
Jer 31:21 Turn back, O **v** Israel, turn back
Mt 1:23 the **v** shall be with child and bear
2Co 11: 2 present you as a chaste **v** to Christ.

VISION → VISIONS
Isa 22: 1 Oracle of the Valley of **V**: What is
Da 8:26 The **v** of the evenings
8:26 however, keep this **v** undisclosed,
Ac 26:19 not disobedient to the heavenly **v**.

VISIONS → VISION
Nu 12: 6 you, in **v** will I reveal myself to him,
Eze 1: 1 heavens opened, and I saw divine **v**.
Da 1:17 to Daniel the understanding of all **v**
Ac 2:17 your young men shall see **v**,

VOICE
Isa 40: 3 A **v** cries out: In the desert prepare
Jn 1:23 "I am 'the **v** of one crying
10: 3 and the sheep hear his **v**, as he calls
Heb 3: 7 "Oh, that today you would hear his **v**,
Rev 3:20 If anyone hears my **v** and opens

VOW → VOWS
Ecc 5: 4 had better not make a **v** than make it
Sir 18:23 Before making a **v** have the means

VOWS → VOW
Ps 22:26 my **v** I will fulfill before those who

W

WAGES
Ro 6:23 For the **w** of sin is death, but the gift

WAIT
Ps 27:14 **W** for the LORD, take courage;
27:14 be stouthearted, **w** for the LORD!
Sir 2: 7 who fear the LORD, **w** for his mercy,
Hab 2: 3 If it delays, **w** for it, it will surely
Ro 8:23 groan within ourselves as we **w**

WALK → WALKED, WALKING
Ge 17: 1 **W** in my presence and be blameless.
Ps 23: 4 when I **w** through a dark valley,
Isa 2: 5 let us **w** in the light of the LORD!
40:31 grow weary, **w** and not grow faint.
Jer 6:16 Which is the way to good, and **w** it;
6:16 But they said, "We will not **w** it."

Jn 8:12 Whoever follows me will not **w**
2Co 5: 7 for we **w** by faith, not by sight.
Rev 21:24 The nations will **w** by its light,

WALKED → WALK
Ge 5:24 Then Enoch **w** with God, and he

WALKING → WALK
Mt 14:26 the disciples saw him **w** on the sea

WALL
Jos 6:20 The **w** collapsed, and the people
Ne 2:17 let us rebuild the **w** of Jerusalem,
Eph 2:14 and broke down the dividing **w**

WAR → WARRIOR, WARS
Ecc 3: 8 a time of **w**, and a time of peace.
Da 9:26 until the end there shall be **w**,
Ro 7:23 my members another principle at **w**
Rev 19:11 and wages **w** in righteousness.

WARRIOR → WAR
Ex 15: 3 The LORD is a **w**, LORD is his name!

WARS → WAR
Mt 24: 6 You will hear of **w** and reports of **w**;

WASH → WASHED
Ps 51: 9 **w** me, make me whiter than snow.
Jn 13: 5 began to **w** the disciples' feet and dry
Rev 22:14 are they who **w** their robes so as

WASHED → WASH
1Co 6:11 but now you have had yourselves **w**,

WATCH → WATCHES
Lk 2: 8 keeping the night **w** over their flock.
Heb 13:17 for they keep **w** over you and will

WATCHES → WATCH
Ps 1: 6 the LORD **w** over the way of the just,

WATER → WATERS
Ex 17: 1 Here there was no **w** for the people
Nu 20: 2 As the community had no **w**,
Jer 2:13 broken cisterns, that hold no **w**.
Eze 36:25 I will sprinkle clean **w** upon you
Mk 1: 8 I have baptized you with **w**; he will
Jn 2: 9 the headwaiter tasted the **w** that had
2: 9 who had drawn the **w** knew),
3: 5 of God without being born of **w**
4:10 he would have given you living **w**."
1Jn 5: 6 This is the one who came through **w**

WATER → WATERS (cont.)
1Jn 5: 6 not by w alone, but by w and blood.
Rev 22: 1 me the river of life-giving w,

WATERS → WATER
Ge 7: 7 ark because of the w of the flood.
Ecc 11: 1 Cast your bread upon the w;

WAY → WAYS
Ps 1: 6 The LORD watches over the w
1: 6 the w of the wicked leads to ruin.
86:11 Teach me, LORD, your w that I may
Pr 12:15 The w of the fool seems right in his
22: 6 Train a boy in the w he should go;
Isa 40: 3 the desert prepare the w of the LORD!
Mal 3: 1 to prepare the w before me;
Mt 3: 3 desert, 'Prepare the w of the Lord,
Jn 14: 6 "I am the w and the truth and the life.
Ac 9: 2 or women who belonged to the W,
1Co 12:31 show you a still more excellent w.
Heb 10:20 living w he opened for us through

WAYS → WAY
Dt 10:12 your and follow his w exactly,
Sir 2:15 those who love him keep his w.
Rev 15: 3 Just and true are your w, O king

WEAK → WEAKNESS, WEAKNESSES
Mt 26:41 spirit is willing, but the flesh is w."
Ro 14: 1 Welcome anyone who is w in faith,
1Co 1:27 and God chose the w of the world
2Co 12:10 for when I am w, then I am strong.

WEAKNESS → WEAK
Ro 8:26 Spirit too comes to the aid of our w;

WEAKNESSES → WEAK
2Co 12:10 I am content with w, insults,
Heb 4:15 is unable to sympathize with our w,

WEALTH
Ps 49: 7 Those who trust in their w and boast
Pr 19: 4 W adds many friends, but the friend
Sir 5: 1 Rely not on your w; say not: "I have

WEAPONS
2Co 6: 7 with w of righteousness at the right

WEAR
Mt 6:31 we to drink?' or 'What are we to w?'

WEARY
Isa 40:31 They will run and not grow w,
Heb 12: 3 in order that you may not grow w

WEDDING
Jn 2: 1 the third day there was a w in Cana

WEEKS
Ex 34:22 "You shall keep the feast of W
Lev 23:15 sheaf, you shall count seven full w,
Da 9:24 "Seventy w are decreed for your

WEEP → WEEPING
Ecc 3: 4 A time to w, and a time to laugh;
Ro 12:15 who rejoice, w with those who w.

WEEPING → WEEP
Ps 30: 6 At dusk w comes for the night;
Mt 2:18 Rachel w for her children, and she

WEIGHED
Da 5:27 you have been w on the scales

WELL
Mt 3:17 Son, with whom I am w pleased."
17: 5 Son, with whom I am w pleased;
2Pe 1:17 with whom I am w pleased."

WEST
Ps 103:12 As far as the east is from the w,
Isa 43: 5 from the w I will gather you.

WHEAT
Mt 13:25 and sowed weeds all through the w,
Lk 22:31 demanded to sift all of you like w,
Jn 12:24 you, unless a grain of w falls
12:24 dies, it remains just a grain of w;

WHIRLWIND → WIND
2Ki 2:11 and Elijah went up to heaven in a w.

WHITE → WHITER
Da 7: 9 the hair on his head as w as wool;
Mt 5:36 for you cannot make a single hair w
Rev 1:14 hair of his head was as w as w wool
20:11 Next I saw a large w throne

WHITER → WHITE
Ps 51: 9 wash me, make me w than snow.

WICKED → WICKEDNESS
Ge 13:13 Sodom were very w in the sins they
Ps 1: 5 Therefore the w will not survive
73: 3 when I saw the prosperity of the w.
Isa 48:22 [There is no peace for the w,
Eze 18:23 pleasure from the death of the w?

Da 12:10 and tested, but the w shall prove w;

WICKEDNESS → WICKED
Ge 6: 5 the LORD saw how great was man's w

WIDE
Mt 7:13 for the gate is w and the road broad

WIDOW → WIDOWS
Ps 146: 9 sustains the orphan and the w,
1Ti 5: 4 if a w has children or grandchildren,
Rev 18: 7 I am no w, and I will never know

WIDOWS → WIDOW
1Ti 5: 3 Honor w who are truly w.
Jas 1:27 for orphans and w in their affliction

WIFE → WIVES
Ge 2:24 and mother and clings to his w,
Ex 20:17 not covet your neighbor's w,
Tob 8: 6 Adam and you gave him his w Eve
Pr 18:22 He who finds a w finds happiness;
Sir 26: 3 A good w is a generous gift
Mt 5:32 whoever divorces his w (unless
19: 3 a man to divorce his w for any cause
Eph 5:28 He who loves his w loves himself.
Rev 21: 9 you the bride, the w of the Lamb."

WILD
Ex 32:25 Aaron had let the people run w,
Mk 1:13 He was among w beasts,
Ro 11:17 off, and you, a w olive shoot,

WILL → WILLING
Ps 40: 9 To do your w is my delight;
143:10 Teach me to do your w, for you are
Isa 53:10 life, and the w of the LORD shall be
Mt 6:10 kingdom come, your w be done,
Lk 22:42 still, not my w but yours be done."
Jn 4:34 to do the w of the one who sent me
Ro 9:19 You w say to me then,
9:19 fault? For who can oppose his w?"
Eph 6: 6 doing the w of God from the heart,
1Jn 5:14 we ask anything according to his w,

WILLING → WILL
Mt 26:41 test. The spirit is w, but the flesh is
Lk 22:42 if you are w, take this cup away

WIND → WHIRLWIND
1Ki 19:11 heavy w was rending the mountains
19:11 LORD—but the LORD was not in the w.

1Ki	19:11	in the **w**. After the **w** there was
Ps	1:4	They are like chaff driven by the **w**.
Ecc	1:14	all is vanity and a chase after **w**.
Jn	3:8	The **w** blows where it wills, and you
Ac	2:2	sky a noise like a strong driving **w**,

WINE

Dt	7:13	your soil, your grain and **w** and oil,
Ps	104:15	and **w** to gladden our hearts,
Pr	20:1	**W** is arrogant, strong drink is
SS	1:2	More delightful is your love than **w**!
Sir	40:20	**W** and music delight the soul,
Mt	9:17	People do not put new **w** into old
	9:17	the skins burst, the **w** spills out,
	9:17	Rather, they pour new **w** into fresh
Jn	2:9	tasted the water that had become **w**,
Eph	5:18	And do not get drunk on **w**,
Rev	18:3	the **w** of her licentious passion.

WINGS

Ex	19:4	how I bore you up on eagle **w**
Ps	17:8	hide me in the shadow of your **w**
Lk	13:34	a hen gathers her brood under her **w**,

WIPE → WIPED

Isa	25:8	The Lord GOD will **w** away the tears
Rev	21:4	He will **w** every tear from their

WIPED → WIPE

Ac	3:19	that your sins may be **w** away,

WISDOM → WISE

Dt	4:6	will you give evidence of your **w**
Job	11:6	And tell you that the secrets of **w**
Pr	1:20	**W** cries aloud in the street,
	9:10	The beginning of **w** is the fear
Ecc	1:13	investigate in **w** all things that are
Wis	6:12	Resplendent and unfading is **W**,
Sir	1:1	All **w** comes from the LORD
	24:1	**W** sings her own praises, before her
Mt	13:54	"Where did this man get such **w**
Lk	2:52	And Jesus advanced [in] **w** and age
Ro	11:33	the depth of the riches and **w**
1Co	1:19	"I will destroy the **w** of the wise,
Col	2:3	are hidden all the treasures of **w**
Jas	3:17	the **w** from above is first of all pure,
Rev	5:12	power and riches, **w** and strength,

WISE → WISDOM

Dt	4:6	'This great nation is truly a **w**
Pr	3:7	Be not **w** in your own eyes,

Pr	13:20	Walk with **w** men and you will
	13:20	with **w** men and you will become **w**,
Ecc	12:11	The sayings of the **w** are like goads;
Da	12:3	But the **w** shall shine brightly
Mt	25:2	them were foolish and five were **w**.
1Co	1:26	of you were **w** by human standards,
Eph	5:15	live, not as foolish persons but as **w**,

WITHER → WITHERED, WITHERS

Ps	1:3	Its leaves never **w**; whatever they do

WITHERED → WITHER

Mt	13:6	scorched, and it **w** for lack of roots.
	21:19	And immediately the fig tree **w**.

WITHERS → WITHER

1Pe	1:24	the grass **w**, and the flower wilts;

WITHOUT

2Ch	18:16	mountains, like sheep **w** a shepherd,
Pr	19:2	**W** knowledge even zeal is not good;
Mt	9:36	abandoned, like sheep **w** a shepherd.
Eph	2:12	were at that time **w** Christ,
	2:12	**w** hope and **w** God in the world.
Heb	4:15	been tested in every way, yet **w** sin.

WITNESS → EYEWITNESSES, WITNESSES

Dt	19:15	"One **w** alone shall not take the stand
Job	16:19	now, behold, my **w** is in heaven,
Ro	2:15	also bears **w** and their conflicting
Rev	1:5	the faithful **w**, the firstborn

WITNESSES → WITNESS

Mt	26:60	though many false **w** came forward.
Heb	12:1	surrounded by so great a cloud of **w**,
Rev	11:3	I will commission my two **w**

WIVES → WIFE

1Ki	11:3	He had seven hundred **w** of princely
	11:3	and his **w** turned his heart.
Eph	5:22	**W** should be subordinate to their
1Pe	3:1	you **w** should be subordinate to your
	3:1	without a word by their **w'** conduct

WOE

Mt	23:13	"**W** to you, scribes and Pharisees,
Rev	8:13	overhead cry out in a loud voice, "**W**!
	8:13	cry out in a loud voice, "**W**! **W**!

		WOLF → WOLVES
Isa	11:6	the **w** shall be a guest of the lamb,
Jn	10:12	sees a **w** coming and leaves
	10:12	and the **w** catches and scatters them.

WOLVES → WOLF

Mt	7:15	but underneath are ravenous **w**.

WOMAN → WOMEN

Ge	2:22	up into a **w** the rib that he had taken
	3:15	put enmity between you and the **w**,
Pr	11:16	A gracious **w** wins esteem, but she
	31:30	the **w** who fears the LORD is to be
Da	13:2	a very beautiful and God-fearing **w**,
Jn	19:26	he said to his mother, "**W**, behold,
Gal	4:4	born of a **w**, born under the law,
Rev	12:1	in the sky, a **w** clothed with the sun,

WOMB

Job	1:21	I came forth from my mother's **w**,
Ps	139:13	you knit me in my mother's **w**.
Jer	1:5	I formed you in the **w** I knew you,
Lk	1:42	and blessed is the fruit of your **w**,
	1:44	the infant in my **w** leaped for joy.

WOMEN → WOMAN

Ezr	10:2	by taking as wives foreign **w**
Mt	24:41	Two **w** will be grinding at the mill;
Lk	1:42	"Most blessed are you among **w**,
	23:55	The **w** who had come from Galilee
1Pe	3:5	how the holy **w** who hoped in God

WONDERS

Ps	136:4	Who alone has done great **w**,
Jn	4:48	"Unless you people see signs and **w**,
2Th	2:9	deed and in signs and **w** that lie,

WOOD

Dt	28:64	you will serve strange gods of **w**
1Co	3:12	silver, precious stones, **w**, hay,

WORD → BYWORD, WORDS

1Ki	8:56	Not a single **w** has gone unfulfilled
Ps	119:105	Your **w** is a lamp for my feet, a light
Pr	30:5	Every **w** of God is tested; he is
Isa	40:8	the **w** of our God stands forever."
	55:11	So shall my **w** be that goes forth
Mk	4:14	The sower sows the **w**.
Lk	1:38	be done to me according to your **w**."

WORD → BYWORD, WORDS (*cont.*)
Jn   1: 1   In the beginning was the **W**,
      1: 1   and the **W** was with God, and the **W**
      1:14   And the **W** became flesh and made
      14:23   "Whoever loves me will keep my **w**,
      17:17   them in the truth. Your **w** is truth.
Ro   9: 6   it is not that the **w** of God has failed.
2Ti   2:15   imparting the **w** of truth without
Jas   1:22   Be doers of the **w** and not hearers
1Jn   2: 5   But whoever keeps his **w**, the love
Rev 19:13   his name was called the **W** of God.

WORDS → WORD
Dt   11:18   take these **w** of mine into your heart
Ps   5: 2   Hear my **w**, O LORD; listen t o my
Pr   30: 6   Add nothing to his **w**, lest he
Hos   6: 5   I slew them by the **w** of my mouth;
Mt   24:35   away, but my **w** will not pass away.
Lk   6:47   listens to my **w**, and acts on them.
1Co   2:13   them not with **w** taught by human
      2:13   but with **w** taught by the Spirit,
Rev 22:19   from the **w** in this prophetic book,

WORK → WORKS
Ge   2: 2   with the **w** he had been doing,
      2: 2   from all the **w** he had undertaken.
Ex   20:10   No **w** may be done then either
Ps   8: 4   your heavens, the **w** of your fingers,
Jn   6:27   Do not **w** for food that perishes
Php   1: 6   the one who began a good **w** in you
      2:12   **w** out your salvation with fear
2Ti   3:17   equipped for every good **w**.
Heb   6:10   not unjust so as to overlook your **w**

WORKS → WORK
Ps   8: 7   have given them rule over the **w**
   92: 6   How great are your **w**, LORD!
Gal   2:16   a person is not justified by **w**
      2:16   in Christ and not by **w** of the law,
      2:16   because by **w** of the law no one will
      5:19   Now the **w** of the flesh are obvious:
Eph   2: 9   it is not from **w**, so no one may
1Ti   6:18   to be rich in good **w**, to be generous,
Jas   2:17   itself, if it does not have **w**, is dead.

WORLD
Ps   9: 9   It is God who governs the **w**
Mt   5:14   You are the light of the **w**. A city set
      16:26   there be for one to gain the whole **w**
Jn   1:10   He was in the **w**, and the **w** came
      1:10   him, but the **w** did not know him.
      3:16   God so loved the **w** that he gave his
      8:12   saying, "I am the light of the **w**.
      16:33   In the **w** you will have trouble,
      16:33   courage, I have conquered the **w**."
1Ti   6: 7   For we brought nothing into the **w**,
Jas   4: 4   to be a lover of the **w** means enmity
      4: 4   of the **w** makes himself an enemy
1Jn   2: 2   only but for those of the whole **w**.
      2:15   Do not love the **w** or the things
      2:15   not love the **w** or the things of the **w**.
      2:15   **w**. If anyone loves the **w**, the love
Rev 11:15   "The kingdom of the **w** now belongs

WORM
Ps   22: 7   But I am a **w**, hardly human,
Mk   9:48   where 'their **w** does not die,

WORRY
Mt   6:25   I tell you, do not **w** about your life,
      10:19   over, do not **w** about how you are

WORSHIP → WORSHIPED
Ex   20: 5   bow down before them or **w** them.
Ps 100: 2   **w** the LORD with cries of gladness;
Mt   4: 9   will prostrate yourself and **w** me."
Jn   4:24   those who **w** him must **w** in Spirit
Ro   12: 1   pleasing to God, your spiritual **w**.
Rev 22: 3   be in it, and his servants will **w** him.

WORSHIPED → WORSHIP
Rev   5:14   and the elders fell down and **w**.

WORTHY
Mt   10:38   and follow after me is not **w** of me.
Eph   4: 1   in a manner **w** of the call you have
Heb   3: 3   he is **w** of more "glory" than Moses,
Rev   4:11   "**W** are you, Lord our God, to receive
      5:12   voice: "**W** is the Lamb that was slain

WOUND → WOUNDS
Ex   21:25   burn for burn, **w** for **w**,
Rev   13: 3   but this mortal **w** was healed.

WOUNDS → WOUND
Ps 147: 3   the brokenhearted, binds up their **w**,
1Pe   2:24   By his **w** you have been healed.

WRAPPED
Mk 15:46   **w** him in the linen cloth and laid
Lk   2: 7   She **w** him in swaddling clothes

WRATH
Ps   2: 5   to them in anger, terrifies them in **w**:
      6: 2   LORD, nor punish me in your **w**.
Pr   15: 1   A mild answer calms **w**, but a harsh
Sir   16:11   though on the wicked alights his **w**.
La   4:11   poured out his blazing **w**; He has
Zep   1:15   A day of **w** is that day, a day
Mt   3: 7   you to flee from the coming **w**?
Ro   1:18   The **w** of God is indeed being
Eph   2: 3   we were by nature children of **w**,
1Th   1:10   who delivers us from the coming **w**.
Rev   6:17   the great day of their **w** has come

WRITE → WRITING, WRITTEN, WROTE
Ex   34:27   said to Moses, "**W** down these words,
Dt   6: 9   **W** them on the doorposts of your
Pr   7: 3   **w** them on the tablet of your heart.
Jer   31:33   them, and **w** it upon their hearts;
Heb   8:10   and I will **w** them upon their hearts.
Rev 21: 5   Then he said, "**W** these words down,

WRITING → WRITE
Da   5: 7   "Whoever reads this **w** and tells me

WRITTEN → WRITE
Jos   23: 6   all that is **w** in the book of the law
Da   12: 1   everyone who is found **w**
Lk   24:44   that everything **w** about me
Jn   21:25   contain the books that would be **w**.
Rev 21:27   those will enter whose names are **w**

WRONG → WRONGDOING
Nu   5: 7   he shall confess the **w** he has done,
Ac   23: 9   "We find nothing **w** with this man.

WRONGDOING → DO, WRONG
1Jn   5:17   All **w** is sin, but there is sin that is

WROTE → WRITE
Ex   24: 4   **w** down all the words of the LORD
   34:28   he **w** on the tablets the words
Jn   5:46   me, because he **w** about me.

Y

YEAR → YEARS
Ex 23:14 "Three times a **y** you shall celebrate
Heb 10: 1 that they offer continually each **y**.

YEARS → YEAR
Ge 1:14 the fixed times, the days and the **y**,
Ex 12:40 was four hundred and thirty **y**.
Nu 14:34 forty **y** shall you suffer for your
2Ch 36:21 rest while seventy **y** are fulfilled."
Ps 90: 4 A thousand **y** in your eyes
Jer 25:12 when the seventy **y** have elapsed,
Da 9: 2 Scriptures the counting of the **y**
9: 2 of Jerusalem seventy **y** must be
Gal 4:10 days, months, seasons, and **y**.
2Pe 3: 8 Lord one day is like a thousand **y**
3: 8 **y** and a thousand **y** like one day.
Rev 20: 2 and tied it up for a thousand **y**

YEAST
Gal 5: 9 A little **y** leavens the whole batch

YESTERDAY
Heb 13: 8 Jesus Christ is the same **y**, today,

YOKE
Mt 11:30 For my **y** is easy, and my burden
Gal 5: 1 not submit again to the **y** of slavery.

YOUNG → YOUTH
Ps 119: 9 How can the **y** walk without fault?
Ac 2:17 your **y** men shall see visions,

YOUTH → YOUNG
Ps 71: 5 Lord; my trust, GOD, from my **y**.
Ecc 12: 1 your Creator in the days of your **y**,

Z

ZACCHAEUS
Lk 19: 2 Now a man there named **Z**, who was

ZEAL → ZEALOUS
1Ma 2:26 Thus he showed his **z** for the law,
Ps 69:10 Because **z** for your house consumes
Isa 37:32 The **z** of the LORD of hosts shall do
Jn 2:17 "**Z** for your house will consume me."
Ro 10: 2 to them that they have **z** for God,
Php 3: 6 in **z** I persecuted the church,

ZEALOUS → ZEAL
Nu 25:13 because he was **z** on behalf of his
1Ki 19:10 "I have been most **z** for the LORD,

ZEBULUN
Son of Jacob by Leah (Ge 30:20; 35:23; 1Ch 2:1). Tribe of blessed (Ge 49:13; Dt 33:18-19), numbered (Nu 1:31; 26:27), allotted land (Jos 19:10-16; Eze 48:26), failed to fully possess (Jdg 1:30), supported Deborah (Jdg 4:6-10; 5:14, 18), David (1Ch 12:33), 12,000 from (Rev 7:8).

ZECHARIAH
1. Son of Jeroboam II; king of Israel (2Ki 15:8-12).
2. Post-exilic prophet who encouraged rebuilding of temple (Ezr 5:1; 6:14; Zec 1:1).

ZEDEKIAH → = MATTANIAH
1. False prophet (1Ki 22:11-24; 2Ch 18:10-23).

2. Mattaniah, son of Josiah (1Ch 3:15), made king of Judah by Nebuchadnezzar (2Ki 24:17-25:7; 2Ch 36:10-14; Jer 37-39; 52:1-11).

ZEPHANIAH
Prophet; descendant of Hezekiah (Zep 1:1).

ZERUBBABEL
Descendant of David (1Ch 3:19; Mt 1:3). Led return from exile (Ezr 2:2; Ne 7:7). Governor of Israel; helped rebuild temple (Ezr 3; Hag 1-2; Zec 4).

ZIMRI
King of Israel (1Ki 16:9-20).

ZION
2Sa 5: 7 David did take the stronghold of **Z**,
Ps 2: 6 my king on **Z**, my holy mountain."
48: 3 Mount **Z**, the heights of Zaphon,
78:68 Judah, Mount **Z** which he favored.
Isa 28:16 GOD: See, I am laying a stone in **Z**,
Mic 4: 2 from **Z** shall go forth instruction,
Zec 9: 9 Rejoice heartily, O daughter **Z**,
Mt 21: 5 "Say to daughter **Z**, 'Behold,
Ro 11:26 "The deliverer will come out of **Z**,
1Pe 2: 6 "Behold, I am laying a stone in **Z**,
Rev 14: 1 was the Lamb standing on Mount **Z**,

ZIPPORAH
Daughter of Reuel; wife of Moses (Ex 2:21-22; 4:20-26; 18:1-6).

ZOPHAR
One of Job's friends (Job 2:11; 11; 20; 42:9).

MAP 1

Jerusalem in New Testament times

- Medieval and Turkish Jerusalem
- Approximate lines of City Walls:
  - under Herod the Great
  - added by Agrippa I
- Wall of Aelia
- Modern roads

Original Rock Contours are shown.

☐ Tomb of Helena Princess of Adiabene

300 Metres
300 Yards

B = Bridge
C. of I. = Court of Israel.
C. of Priests = Court of Priests
C. of W. = Court of Women
G = Gate
G' = Gate of Coponius = Barclay's Gate
G" = Double (Huldah) Gate

© Oxford University Press

Mount of Olives
OUTWORK OF UNCERTAIN ORIGIN
Kidron Valley
Tyropoeon Valley
Hinnom Valley
TURKISH
Aqueduct
BEZETHA
CAVERNS
ROYAL
ANTONIA TOWER
TEMPLE
Court of Gentiles
Herodian Street
Pool of Siloam
Solomon's Pool
Gethsemane
Tombs
Pool of Bethzatha (Bethesda)
Fullers Tower
Demetrius Gate
Jewish Tombs
Golgotha
ROYAL PALACE
Gabbatha
Penthouse
Family Tomb of Herod
Bethlehem
Bethphage

Jerusalem in Old Testament times

- Medieval and Turkish Jerusalem
- Approximate lines of City Walls:
  - of original Zion (2 Sam 5:7)
  - extended under the Kings
  - extended after the Exile (by Maccabees, 2nd Cent. B.C.?)
  - Eastern wall of Nehemiah's city
- Modern roads

Original Rock Contours are shown.

☐ Post-exilic Jewish tombs

300 Metres
300 Yards

© Oxford University Press

Mount of Olives
Kidron Valley
Hinnom Valley (?Topheth)
Pre-exilic Judean tombs
SILOAM
CITY OF DAVID (LOWER CITY)
OPHEL
Central (Cheesemakers') Valley
MISHNAH (SECOND QUARTER)
UPPER CITY
Tombs
TEMPLE
ALTAR
PALACE
Solomon's
Tower of Hananel
Baris
Gihon Spring
En-rogel Spring
Wall of Hezekiah (Manasseh)
Wall of Zion

The lines of the southern walls of the city after the Exile are uncertain.

OUTER BORDER SHOWS 200 YARD SUBDIVISIONS

*Prepared by Oxford Cartographers
and based on the Oxford Bible Atlas*

MAP 2

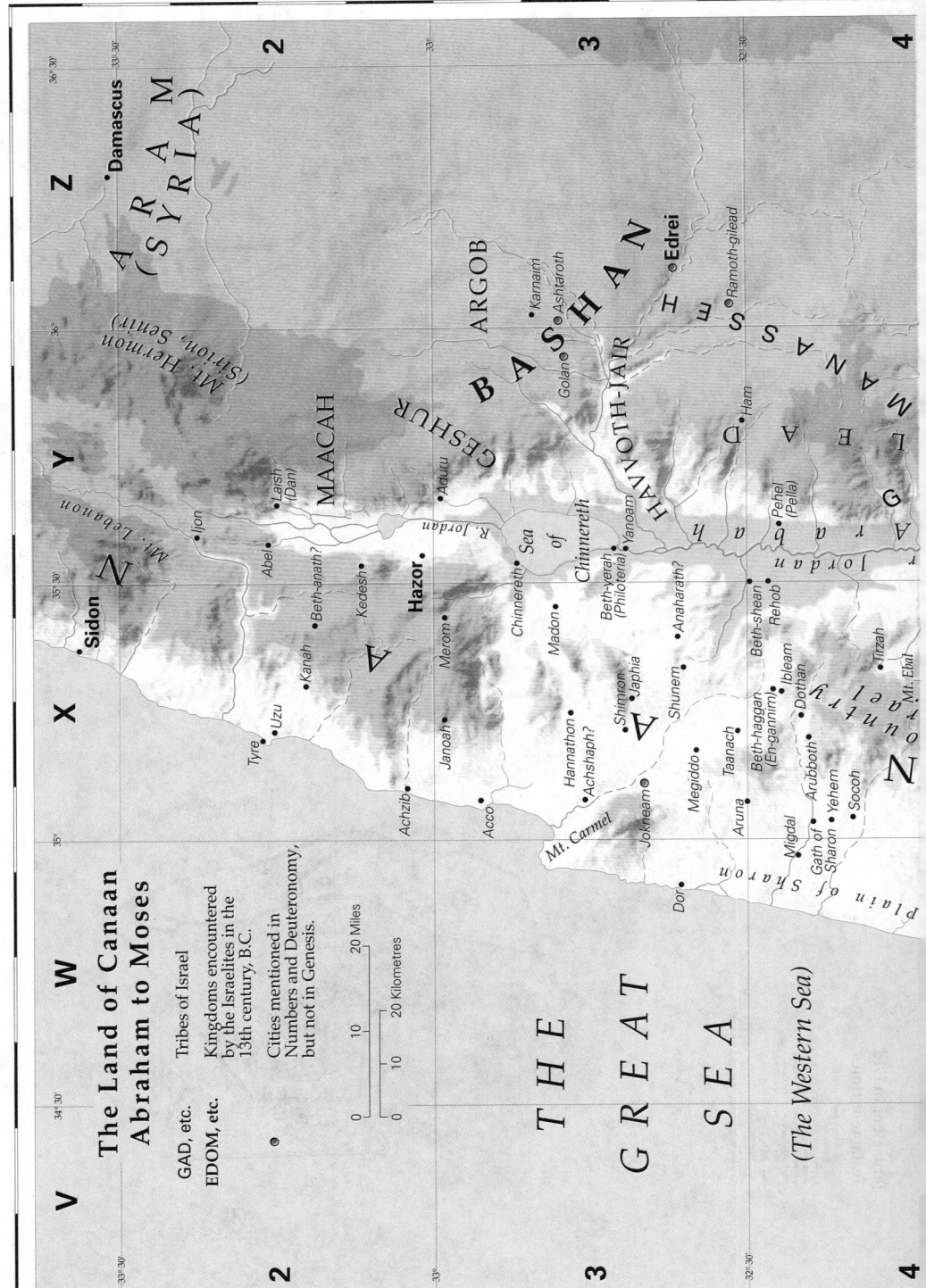

The Land of Canaan
Abraham to Moses

GAD, etc.   Tribes of Israel

EDOM, etc.   Kingdoms encountered
             by the Israelites in the
             13th century, B.C.

●   Cities mentioned in
     Numbers and Deuteronomy,
     but not in Genesis.

0   10   20 Miles
0   10   20 Kilometres

THE

GREAT

SEA

(The Western Sea)

ARAM
(SYRIA)

• Damascus

Mt. Hermon
(Sirion, Senir)

Mt. Lebanon

• Sidon

• Tyre
• Uzu

Achzib •

• Acco

Mt. Carmel

Dor •

Jokneam ◉

Megiddo •

Aruna •

Taanach •

Migdal •

Gath of
Sharon •

Yehem •

Socoh •

Arubboth •

Dothan •

Ibleam •

Beth-haggan
(En-gannim) •

Rehob •

Beth-shean •

Tirzah •

Mt. Ebal

Shunem •

Anaharath? •

Beth-verah
(Philoteria) •

Yanoam •

Yaphia •

Shimron •

Achshaph? •

Hannathon •

Janoah •

Madon •

Merom •

Chinnereth •

Sea
of
Chinnereth

Kanah •

Kedesh •

Beth-anath? •

Abel •

Ijon •

Laish
(Dan) •

Aduru •

MAACAH

GESHUR

ARGOB

BASHAN

• Karnaim
Ashtaroth ◉

Golan ◉

Edrei ⊞

Ham •

HAVVOTH-JAIR

Pehel
(Pella) •

Ramoth-gilead ⊞

R. Jordan

R. Jordan

Plain of Sharon

hill country of Israel

Arabah

GAD

MANASSEH

Hazor •

MAP 2

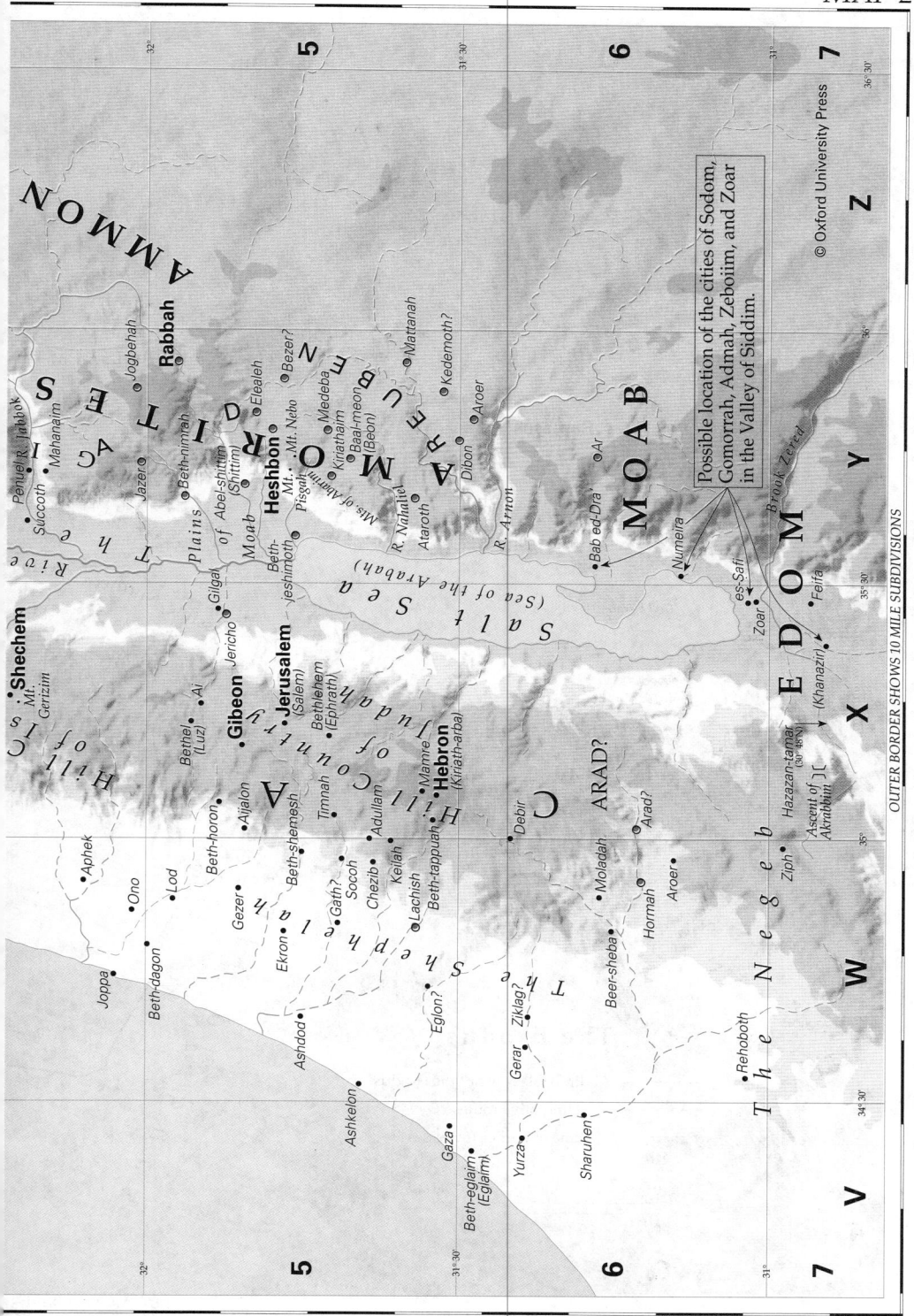

Possible location of the cities of Sodom, Gomorrah, Admah, Zeboiim, and Zoar in the Valley of Siddim.

© Oxford University Press

OUTER BORDER SHOWS 10 MILE SUBDIVISIONS

AMMON

Rabbah

Jogbehah

Penuel•R. Jabbok
Succoth•
Mahanaim•
Jazer•

Beth-nimrah•
Abel-shittim•
(Shittim)

Gilead

Elealeh•
Medeba•
Baal-meon•
(Beon)
Kiriathaim•

Bezer?•
Mattanah•
Kedemoth?•

Heshbon
Mt. Nebo•
Pisgah

Mts. of Abarim

Dibon•
Aroer•

Mt.:

REUBEN

AMORITES

Beth-
jeshimoth•

Beth-
Moab

Plains
of Moab

The

River

Ataroth•
R. Nahaliel
R. Arnon

Ar•

MOAB

Bab ed-Dra'•

Numeira•

es-Safi•

Zoar•
Felfa•

Brook Zered

EDOM

Shechem
•
Mt.
Gerizim

Hills of Israel

Bethel•
(Luz)
Ai•

Gibeon
Jericho•

Gilgal•

Jerusalem
(Salem)

Bethlehem•
(Ephrath)

Hill Country of Judah

Mamre•
Hebron
(Kiriath-arba)

Aphek•
Ono•
Lod•

Beth-horon•

Aijalon•
Beth-shemesh•
Timnah•

Adullam•
Keilah•
Beth-tappuah•

Socoh•
Chezib•
Lachish•

Debir•

ARAD?

Salt Sea
(Sea of the Arabah)

Joppa•

Beth-dagon•

Gezer•
Ekron•

Gath?•

Judah

Shephelah

The

Egion?•

Debir•

Moladah•
Arad?•

Hazazan-tamar
(30°48'N)

Ascent of
Akrabbim

(Khanazir)

Ashdod•

Gaza•

Ashkelon•

Beth-eglaim•
(Eglaim)
Yurza•

Gerar•
Ziklag?•

Sharuhen•

Rehoboth•

Beer-sheba•
Hormah•

Aroer•

Ziph•

The Negeb

32°

5

31°30'

6

31°

7

34°30'

35°

35°30'

36°

36°30'

MAP 3

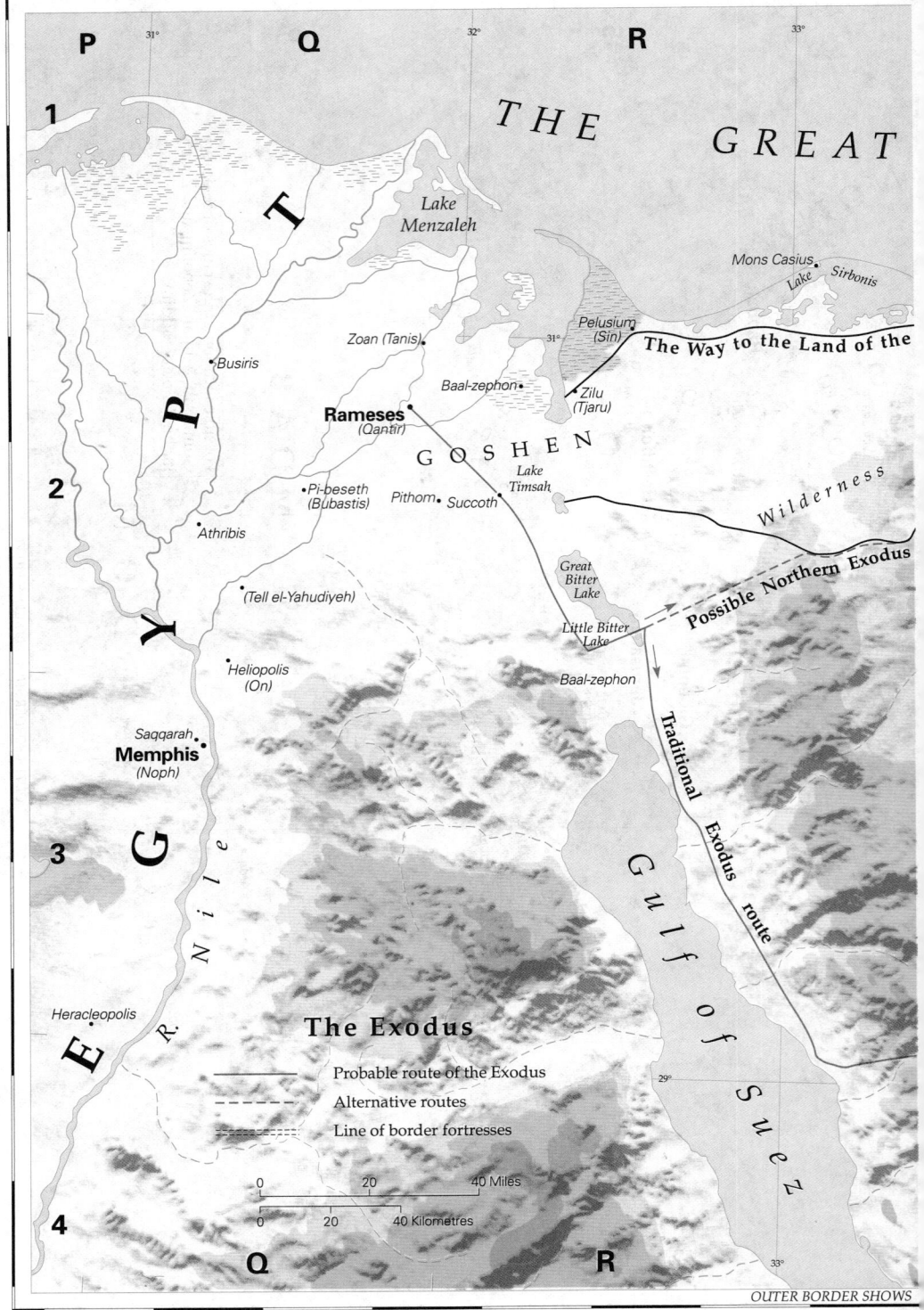

P · Q · R

31° · 32° · 33°

1

THE · *GREAT*

Lake Menzaleh

Mons Casius · *Lake Sirbonis*

Pelusium
(Sin)

Zoan (Tanis)

31°

The Way to the Land of the

Busiris · Baal-zephon · Zilu
(Tjaru)

Rameses
(Qantir) · G O S H E N

2 · Lake Timsah · *Wilderness*

· Pi-beseth
(Bubastis) · Pithom · Succoth

· Athribis

· (Tell el-Yahudiyeh) · Great
Bitter
Lake · **Possible Northern Exodus**

Little Bitter
Lake

· Heliopolis
(On) · Baal-zephon

Saqqarah · *Traditional*

Memphis
(Noph) · *Exodus*

route

3 · *G u l f*

Heracleopolis · *R. Nile* · *o f*

The Exodus · 29°

——————— Probable route of the Exodus · *S u e z*

– – – – – – Alternative routes

▦▦▦▦▦ Line of border fortresses

0 ———— 20 ———— 40 Miles

0 ———— 20 ———— 40 Kilometres

4 · Q · R · 33°

S

T

Bethel

U

Gezer

Rabbah

Ai

Ashdod

Shittim

Jericho

Heshbon

Jerusalem

Mt. Nebo

Plain of Philistia

Azekah

Medeba

Libnah?

Lachish

SEA

C A N A A N

Gaza

Hebron

Dibon

Salt

Gerar

R. Arnon

Sea

Raphia

Juttah

M O A B

1

Dabir

Philistines

ARAD?

E D O M

Beer-sheba

Kir-hareseth

Brook of Egypt

Hormah

Arad?

T h e N e g e b

of

Shur

Wilderness

The Way to Shur

of Zin

Hazazon-tamar

route

Sela

Bene-jaakan

Bozrah

(Beeroth)

Azmon

Punon

Mt. Sinai? (Horeb)

Hazar-addar

Oboth

2

(Jebel Helal)

Kadesh-barnea

(Meribah)

Paran

The Arabah

of

Wilderness

2

S I N A I

The King's Highway

Ezion-geber

Line of border fortresses

Alternative Exodus route

3

Red Sea (Gulf of Aqaba)

Wilderness

of Sin?

M I D I A N

4

© Oxford University Press

S

T

Mt. Sinai (Horeb)?

(Jebel Musa)

U

20 MILE SUBDIVISIONS

MAP 4

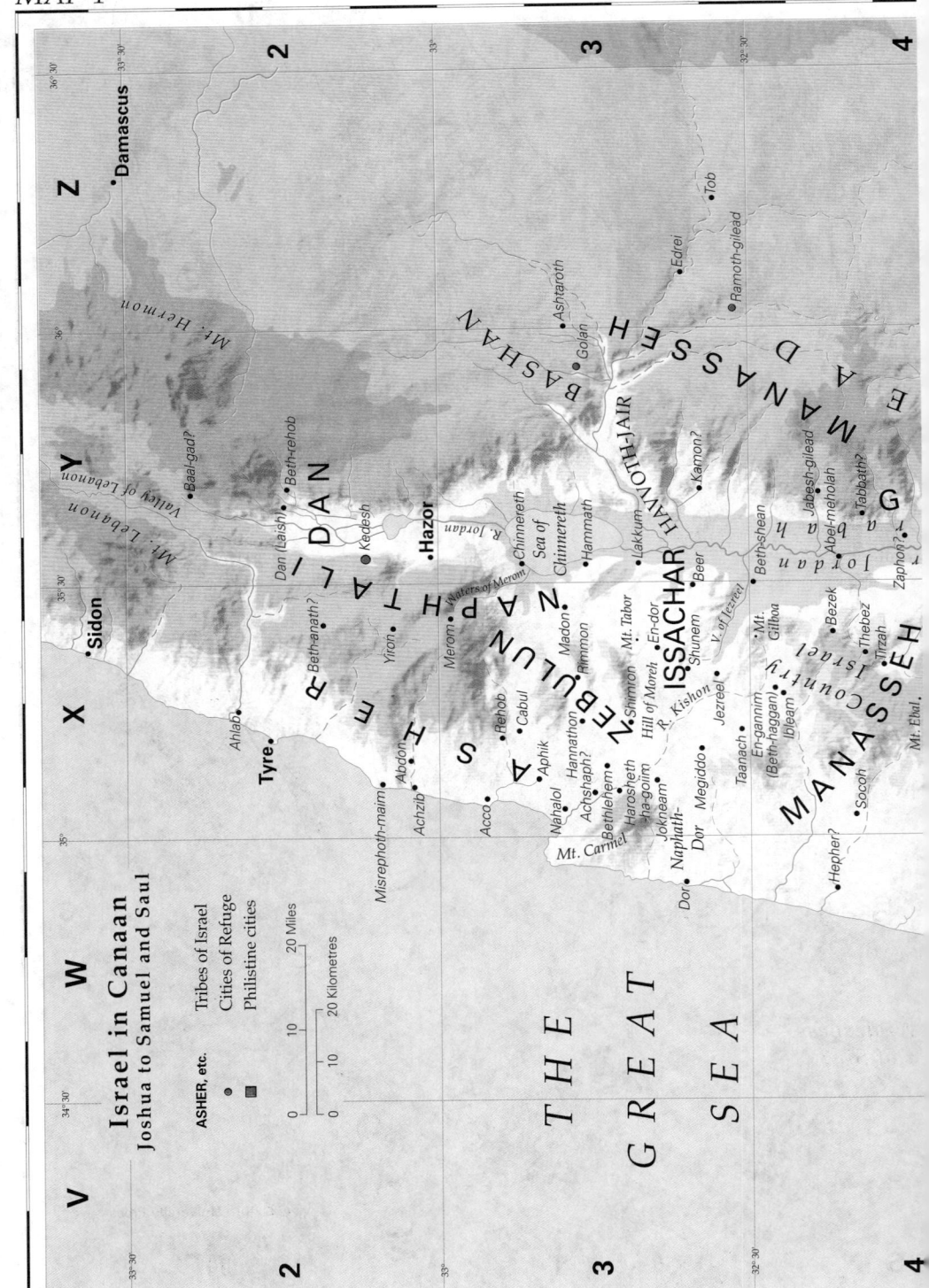

Israel in Canaan
Joshua to Samuel and Saul

ASHER, etc.   Tribes of Israel
●   Cities of Refuge
■   Philistine cities

0   10   20 Miles
0   10   20 Kilometres

MAP 4

OUTER BORDER SHOWS 10 MILE SUBDIVISIONS

MAP 5

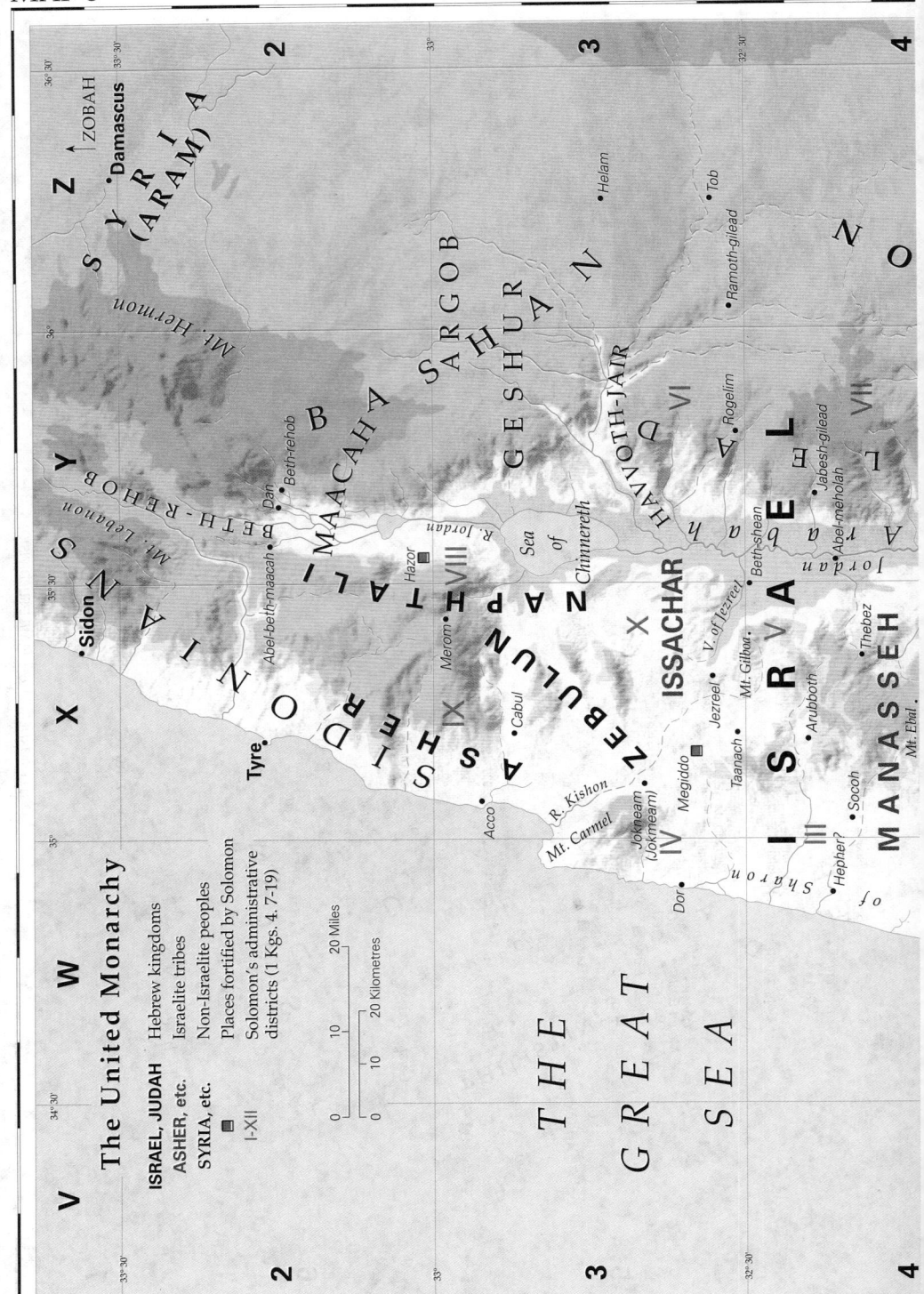

The United Monarchy

ISRAEL, JUDAH — Hebrew kingdoms
ASHER, etc. — Israelite tribes
SYRIA, etc. — Non-Israelite peoples
▪ — Places fortified by Solomon
I–XII — Solomon's administrative districts (1 Kgs. 4. 7-19)

0   10   20 Miles
0   10   20 Kilometres

MAP 5

OUTER BORDER SHOWS 10 MILE SUBDIVISIONS

Map labels (as printed):

AMMON · Rabbah (Rabbath-ammon) · Lo-debar? · R. Jabbok · Mahanaim · Succoth · Zarethan? · Jazer · Heshbon · Medeba · Dibon · Aroer · MOAB · R. Nahaliel · R. Arnon · Kir-hareseth · EDOM · Brook Zered

The River · GAD · XII · The Jordan · I · Z · Y

Mt. Gerizim · Shechem · Piraton · Shiloh · Baal-hazor · Ephraim · EPHRAIM · Bethel · Gilgal · Jericho · Upper Beth-horon · Gibeon · Geba · BENJAMIN · XI · Jerusalem · Anathoth · Gibeah · Beeroth · Elon · Beth-hanan · Lower Beth-horon · Zeredah · Gath-rimmon · Shaalbim · Gezer · Makaz · Sorek · Kiriath-jearim · Bethlehem · Netophah · Tekoa · Adullam · Giloh? · Hebron · Carmel · Arad · JUDAH · Wilderness of Judah · Salt Sea (Sea of the Arabah) · Debir · Kabzeel? · Valley of Salt · Libnah? · Beer-sheba · The Negeb · AMALEK · Tamar (30°48'N) · X · W

Joppa · Plain · Ashdod · Baalath? · Ekron · Gath? · Beth-shemesh · The Shephelah (Lowland) · PHILISTINES · Ashkelon · Gaza · Gerar · Ziklag? · Brook Besor · V

MAP 6

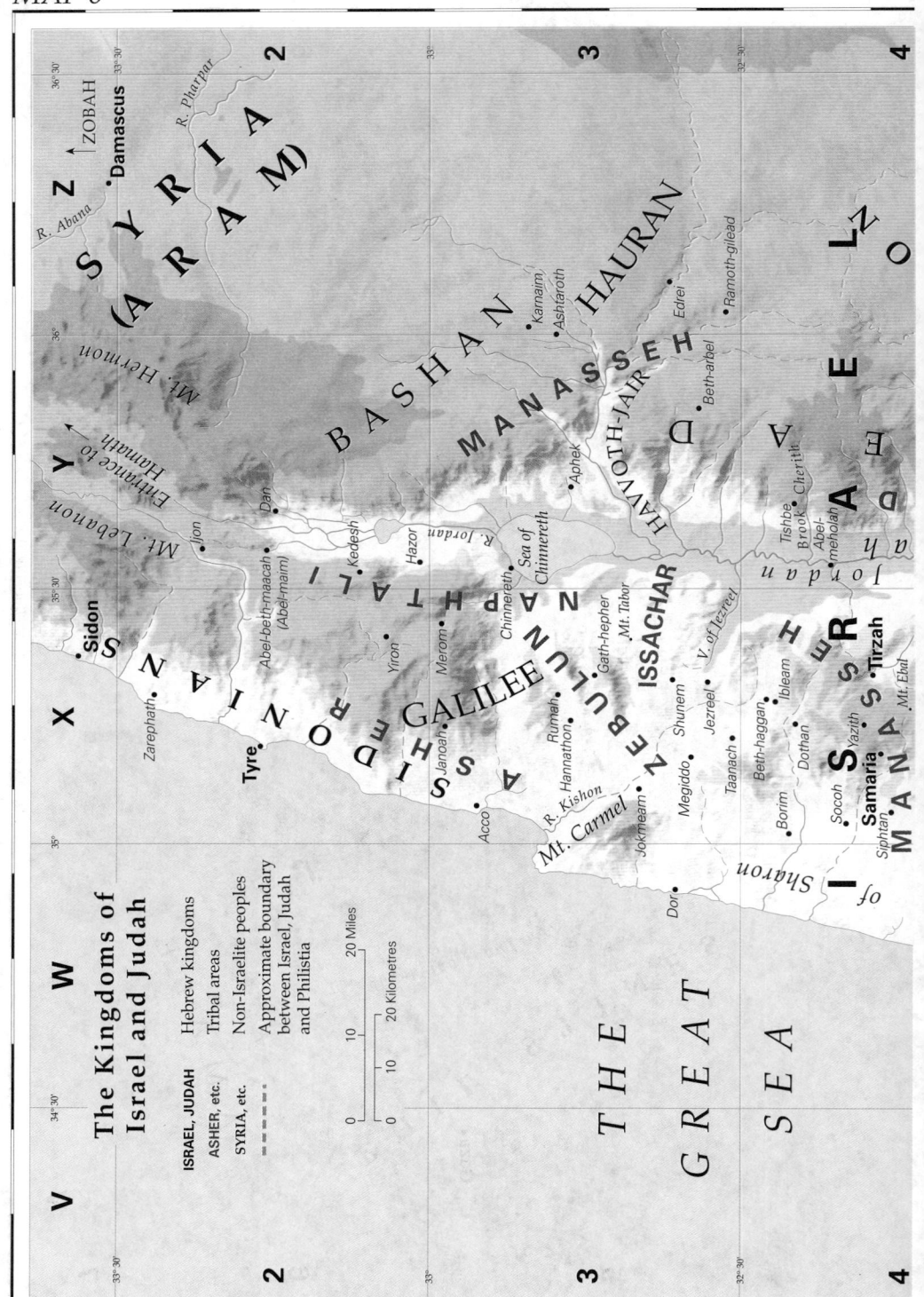

The Kingdoms of
Israel and Judah

ISRAEL, JUDAH   Hebrew kingdoms
ASHER, etc.   Tribal areas
SYRIA, etc.   Non-Israelite peoples
- - - -   Approximate boundary
                 between Israel, Judah
                 and Philistia

0   10   20 Miles

0   10   20 Kilometres

MAP 6

© Oxford University Press

OUTER BORDER SHOWS 10 MILE SUBDIVISIONS

AMMON

•Rabbah

GILEAD

Lo-debar? Panuel•
•Mahanaim
R. Jabbok

River Arnon

The

Heshbon•
Nebo•
Baal-peor•
Kinathaim•
Bezer? (Bozrah?)•
Medeba•
Beth-meon (Baal-meon)•
Beth-diblathaim•
Jahaz•

MOAB

R. Nahaliel•
Ataroth•
Dibon•
Aroer•

R. Arnon

Waters of Nimrim

Kir-hareseth•

EDOM

Brook Zered

Zoar•

Hazazon-tamar
(30° 48'N)

Mt. Gerizim. •Shechem

Pirathon•

EPHRAIM

Baal-shalishah•
Tappuah•
Zeredah•
•Shiloh
•Jeshanah
Baal-hazor•
Ephron•
Bethel•
Ai•
Zemaraim•
Mizpah•
•Gibbethon
Gimzo•

BENJAMIN

Gilgal•
Jericho•
City of Salt?
Secacah?
Nibshan?
Middin?
Jerusalem
Anathoth•
Ramah•
Geba•
Gibeah•
Aijalon•

Sea of
the
Arabah
(Salt Sea)

En-gedi•

Br. Kidron•
Ascent of Ziz•

Wilderness of Judah

Gath
(Gittaim)•
Beth-horon•
Shikkeron•
Ekron•
Gath?•

Timnah•
Zorah•
Beth-shemesh•
Azekah•
Socoh•
Adullam•
Libnah•
Mareshah•
Lachish•

JUDAH

Nibshan?
Etam•
Tekoa•
Beth-zur•
Zair•
Hebron•
Adoraim•
Ziph•
Carmel•

V. of Beracah

Great Arad•
Arad of Beth-yeroham?•

Joppa•

Plain

Jabneel (Jabneh)•
Mount Baalah•
Baalath?•

Ashdod•

Ashkelon•

PHILISTIA

V. of Zephathah•

Gaza•

Gerar•

Yurza•

Raphia
Sharuhen•

Brook Besor

The Shephelah (Lowland)

Beer-sheba•
Gurbaal•

Valley of Salt

SIMEON

The Negeb

5
31° 30'
6
7
32°
31°
31° 30'
36° 30'
35° 30'
35°
34° 30'
X
Y
Z
V
W

MAP 7

Black Sea

2

D   E   F   G

40° 30° 35°

R. Sangarius

PHRYGIA

Gordion •

Gomer
(Gimarrai)

LYDIA

R. Hermus

Meshech
(Mushki)

• *Usiana* *R. Halys*

Tubal
(Tabal) *Togarmah*

3

Sardis •
(Sepharad)

R. Maeander

J A V A N

COMMA-
KUMU

Musri

CILICIA
(KHILAKKU)

Kue

Amanus
Mts. • *Sam'al*
• *Carchemish*
Calno •
• *Arpad*
Aleppo •

Crete
(Caphtor)

Rhodes

R. Orontes

HATTINA

Hamath
• *Qarqar*
Riblah • *Kadesh*
Lebo-
Hamath
Helbon •

Cyprus
(Iadanna)

Arvad •

Gebal (Byblos) •
Berytus •

Sidon •

Tyre •

Acco • *Ushu*

Lebanon

SYRIA

Damascus

35°

The

4

25°

G r e a t

S e a

(The Upper Sea, the Western Sea)

Hauran

ISRAEL

Samaria

Jerusalem

JUDAH

AMMON

Saiecah

MOAB

L i b y a

Zoan
(Tanis) •
Sais • *Pelusium* •
Tahpanhes • *Migdol* •
Athribis •

Memphis •
(Noph) *Heliopolis*
• *(On)*

Raphia •
Gaza •

Sela •

EDOM

S i n a i

Ezion-geber
(Elath)

5

E G Y P T

Hermopolis •

Lycopolis
(Siut) •

R. Nile

Red Sea

6

Thebes •

Syene •

ETHIOPIA

E   F   G

30° 35° 25°

OUTER BORDER SHOWS

MAP 7

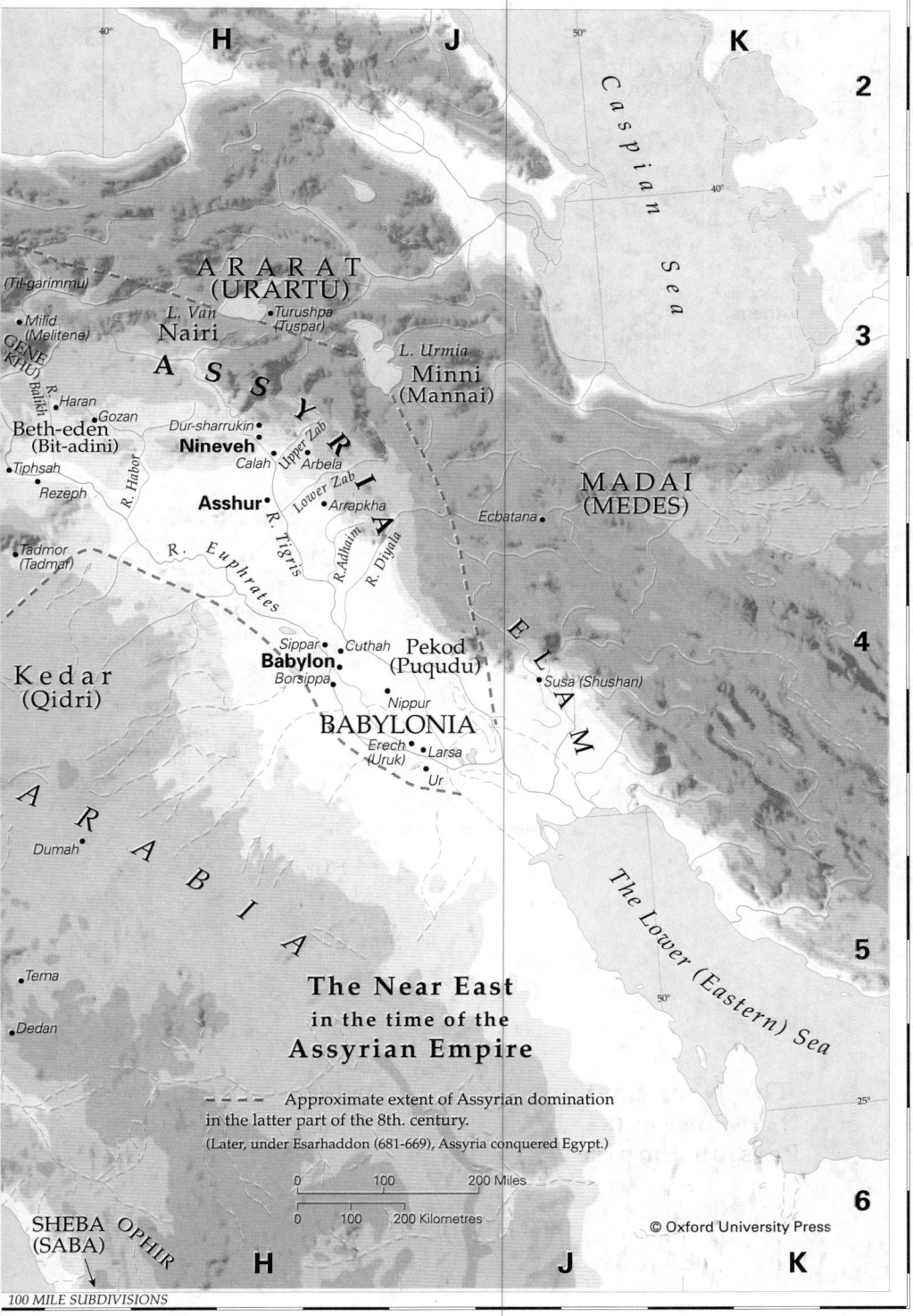

40°

H　　　**J**　　50°　　**K**

2

*C
a
s
p
i
a
n

S
e
a*

40°

3

(Til-garimmu)

**A R A R A T
(URARTU)**

• Milid
(Melitene)

L. Van　• Turushpa
　　　　　(Tuspar)

Nairi

L. Urmia

GENE
KHU

A　**S**　**S**

• Milid
(Melitene)

R. Haran
Balikh

• Gozan

• Dur-sharrukin

**Minni
(Mannai)**

**Beth-eden
(Bit-adini)**

Nineveh •

Calah •　• Arbela

Upper Zab

Y

R

A

**MADAI
(MEDES)**

• Tiphsah

R. Habor

Asshur •

R. Tigris

Lower Zab

• Arrapkha

R. Adhaim

R. Diyala

• Ecbatana

• Rezeph

• Tadmor
(Tadmar)

R.　Euphrates

4

**K e d a r
(Qidri)**

Sippar •　• Cuthah

Babylon •

Borsippa •

**Pekod
(Puqudu)**

• Susa (Shushan)

E

L

A

M

• Nippur

BABYLONIA

A

Erech • • Larsa
(Uruk)

• Ur

R

A

B

• Dumah

I

A

5

The Lower (Eastern) Sea

50°

• Tema

The Near East
in the time of the
Assyrian Empire

25°

• Dedan

– – – – Approximate extent of Assyrian domination
in the latter part of the 8th. century.

(Later, under Esarhaddon (681-669), Assyria conquered Egypt.)

0	100	200 Miles
0	100	200 Kilometres

© Oxford University Press

6

SHEBA
(SABA)　OPHIR

H　　　　　　　**J**　　　　**K**

100 MILE SUBDIVISIONS

MAP 8

THRACE (SKUDRA)

MACEDONIA

Doriscus

Byzantium

B l a c k   S e a

Sinope

PAPHLAGONIANS

R.Sangarius

CAPPADOCIA

MOSCHI

THESSALY

A e g e a n

40°

Hellespont

Mt. Ida

R. Granicus

D A S C Y L I U M

Gordion

CIMMERIANS

Pteria?

Thermopylae

Sea

Lesbos

Mytilene

P H R Y G I A

R. Halys

Delphi

LYDIA

COMMAGENE

Thebes

Marathon

Magnesia

Sardis

Melitene

Corinth

Ephesus

Salamis **Athens**

3

Samos

Magnesia on Maeander

Cilician

PELOPONNESUS

C. Mycale

Miletus

CARIA

Gates

Issus

Carchemish

Haran

Sparta

Tarsus

Aleppo

Arpad

LYCIA

PAMPHYLIA   CILICIA

Thapsacus

Rhodes

Xanthus

Crete

Kyrenia

Hamath

Arvad

Tadmor

35°

Gortyna

Soli

Salamis

Cyprus

Citium

Amathus

Gebal

Cyrene

Sidon

Tyre

Damascus

4

25°

U p p e r   S e a

(Mediterranean Sea)

PHOENICIA

BEYOND THE RIVER

K E D

Samaria

AMMON

Jerusalem

Ashdod

JUDAH

Gaza

MOAB

(Alexandria)

Sais

Zoan

Tahpanhes

Busiris

Pelusium

EDOMITES

Sela

Dumah

L I B Y A

30°

Memphis

Heliopolis

Sinai

A

5

R. Nile

Tema

Hermopolis

E G Y P T

Red

Dedan

The Near East
in the time of the
Persian Empire

Abydos

Coptos

Thebes

Sea

25°

Edfu

Yeb
(Elephantine)   Syene

35°

ETHIOPIA (CUSH)

E

F

G

MAP 8

MAP 9

Central
Palestine in
Old Testament
times

10 Miles

10 Kilometres

MAP 9

© Oxford University Press

A M M O N

Rabbah

•Jogbehah

•Jazer

•Gilead

•(Araq el-Emir)

Heshbon

•Elealeh

•Siloam

Bezer?
(Bozrah?)

•Beth-diblathaim
(Almon-diblathaim?)

•Jahaz?
•Mattanah

•Kedemoth?

M O A B

Betonim•

G I L E A D

•Abel-shittim
(Shittim)

•Beth-peor
(Baal-peor)

•Mt. Nebo
•Nebo

•Bamoth-baal
•Medeba

•Beth-meon
(Baal-meon)

Beth-baal-meon, Beon)

•Kiriathaim

•Dibon

•Ito-debar?
•Penuel
(Peniel)

Mahanaim•

•Zarethan?
(Zeredah, Zerah)

•Succoth

(Wadi Farah)

R. Jabbok

•Adam

T h e   R i v e r

•Beth-nimrah

Plains
of Moab

•Beth-haram

Mt. Pisgah•

Mts. of Abarim

•Beth-jeshimoth

•Ataroth

R. Nahaliel

•Ataroth

•Zereth-shahar

•Kerioth

•Dibon

R. Arnon

•Janoah

•Arumah

•Ataroth

Mt. Gerizim•

•Pirathon

Hill Country

•Baal-shalishah

of

•En-tappuah

•Tappuah

•Lebonah

Shiloh

•Gilgal?

•Jeshanah

•Baal-hazor

•Ephron,
(Ephraim, Ophrah)

•Rimmon

Naarah•

•Gilgal (Beth-gilgal)

•Jericho

•Beth-hoglah

•City of Salt?

S a l t   S e a

(Sea of
the Arabah)

•Middin?

•Secacah?

•Nibshan?

•En-gedi

E p h r a i m

•Zeredah

•Ramathaim-
zophim
(Ramah)

•Timnath-serah
(Timnath)

•Chephar-ammoni

•Ai

Bethel (Beth-aven)•

•Zemaraim

•Ataroth-addar

•Migron

•Geba

•Michmash

•Parah

•Taralah

•Hazor

•Anathoth

•Almon

Adummim•

•Laishah

•Debir

Asc ent of Ziz?

Br. Kidron

W i l d e r n e s s   o f   J u d a h

V. of Beracah

•Ephron

•Beeroth

Upper
•Beth-horon

•Beth-hanan

•Mizpah

•Ramah

Gibeon

•Chephirah

Gibeah

•Neptoah

•Nob •En-shemesh

•Ananiah

Jerusalem

•Rabbah

•Beth-haccherem

•Bethlehem

•Tekoa

•Etam

•Netophah

•Beth-zur

•Maarath

•Gedor

•Gloh

•Halhul

•Beth-anoth

Hebron (Kiriath-arba)

•Mamre

•Beth-tappuah

•Aphekah

•Kain

•Adoraim

J U D A H

X

W

•Eben-ezer

•Aphek

•Gath-rimmon?

•Bene-berak

•Ono

•Beth-dagon

•Aso r?

•Joppa

Brook of Kanah

•Neballat

•Hadid

•Gimzo

•Lod

•Gath (Gittaim)

•Shaalbim

•Gederah

•Gezer

•Makaz

Lower
•Beth-horon

•Aditaim

•Elon

•Ajalon

•Baalah
(Kiriath-jearim)

•Chesalon

•Eshtaol

•Lehi?

•Timnah

•Zanoah

•Enam

•Timnah

•Gloh

•Holon

•Nezib

•Keilah

•Nebo

•Zior (Zain)

•Eltekon?

•Eshtaol

P H I L I S T I A

•Jabneel?

Mount Baalah?

•Baalath?

•Shikkeron

•Ekron

•Zorah

•Beth-shemesh

•Sorek

•Makkedah?

•Azekah

•Jarmuth

•Socoh
(Soco)

•Harim

•Moresheth-gath?

•Ether

•Gath?

•Libnah?

•Mizpeh

•Achzib (Chezib)?

•Adullam

•Mareshah

•Lahmam

•Cabbon

•Bozkath

•Ashnah

•Iphtah

•Ashnah

Ashdod

5

P l a i n

•Eltekeh?

•Gibbethon

•Hadashah?

•Eglon?

•Lachish

•Chitlish?

•Dilean?

31°30′

MAP 10

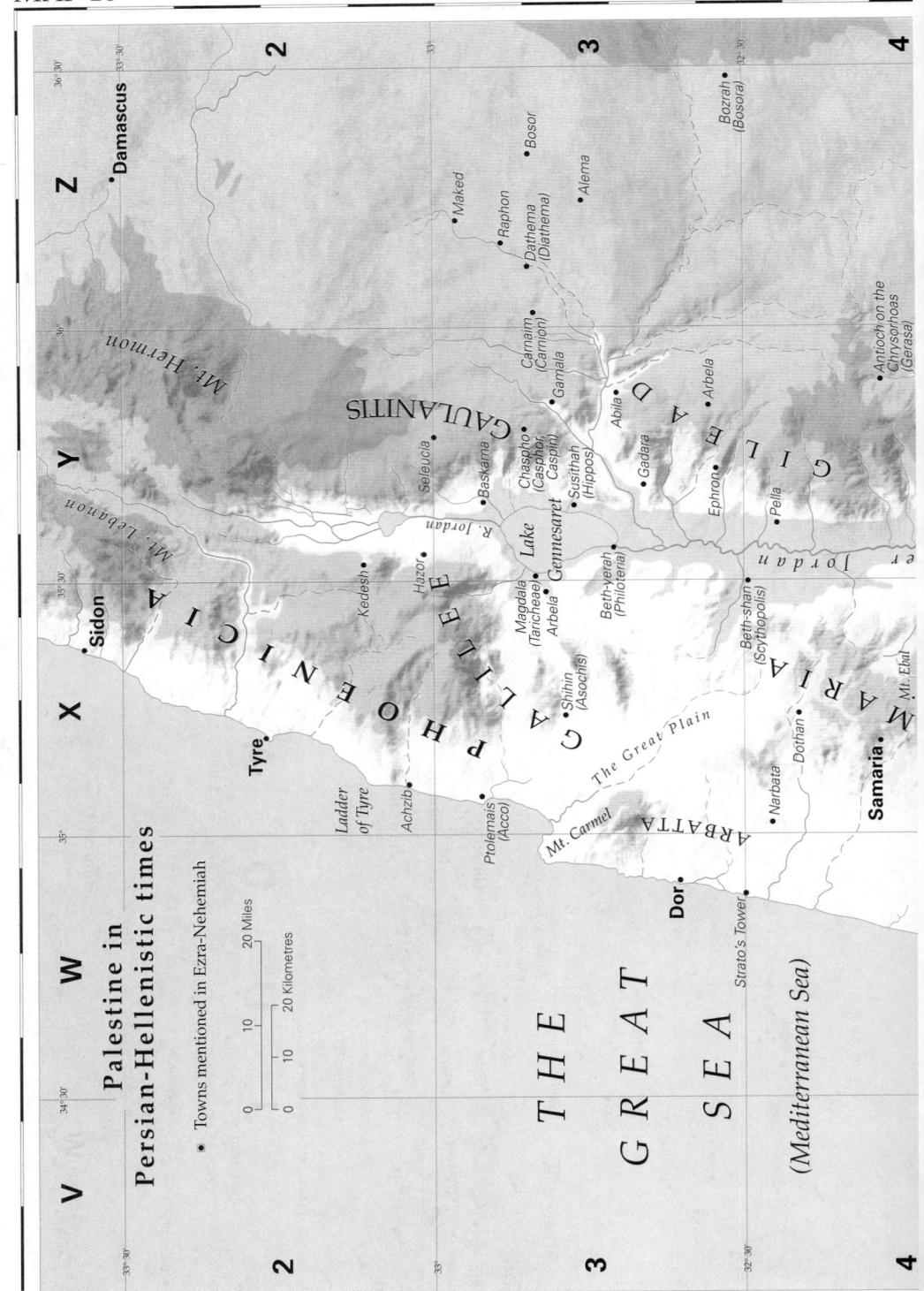

Palestine in Persian-Hellenistic times

• Towns mentioned in Ezra-Nehemiah

20 Miles

20 Kilometres

Damascus

Mt. Hermon

Mt. Lebanon

PHOENICIA

Sidon

Tyre

Ladder of Tyre

Achzib

Ptolemais (Acco)

Kedesh

Hazor

GALILEE

Magdala (Tarichea)

Arbela

Shihin (Asochis)

Mt. Carmel

The Great Plain

Dor

Strato's Tower

THE GREAT SEA

(Mediterranean Sea)

GAULANITIS

Seleucia

Baskama

Chaspho (Caspho, Caspin, Caspin)

Susithan (Hippos)

R. Jordan

Lake Gennesaret

Beth-yerah (Philoteria)

Abila

Gadara

Maked

Raphon

Dathema (Diathema)

Carnaim (Carnion)

Gamala

Bosor

Alema

Arbela

Ephron

Pella

GILEAD

Bozrah (Bosora)

Antioch on the Chrysorhoas (Gerasa)

River Jordan

Beth-shan (Scythopolis)

SAMARIA

Narbata

Dothan

Samaria

Mt. Ebal

ARBATTA

V   W   X   Y   Z

2   3   4

36° 30'   36°   35° 30'   35°   34° 30'   33° 30'

33° 30'   33°   32° 30'

MAP 10

5

Z

R. Jabbok

A M M O N

• Gadara
• Jazer
Alexandrium •
'Araq el-Emir) •
• Philadelphia
(Rabbah)

• Samaga

• Medeba
• Dabaloth?
• Libba
• Heshbon
• Machaerus

S A M A R I T A N S

B E R A I T A E N S

M O A B

N A B A T A E A N S

Y

R. Arnon

Akrabatta
(Akrabattene)
• Shechem
Mt. Gerizim

R i v e r

Shiloh •
Beth-gilgal/(Gilgal)
• Senaah
Dok •
• Jericho
• (Khirbet Qumran)
• Ain Feshkha

Lake
Asphalt
- itis
(Dead
Sea)

S A M A R I A S

Pharathon •
(Pirathon)
Tephon
(Tappuah)
• Rathamin (Ramathaim)
Timnath •
Beerzeth (Berzetho)
Gophna •
• Aphairema
Bethel •
Beth-haccherem •
Mizpah •
Geba •
Beth-basi •
Gibeon •
Anathoth •
Netophah •
Jerusalem
(JUDEA)
Beth-Tekoa •

X

• En-gedi

Beth-horon •
Emmaus •
Kiriath-jearim •
Beeroth •
Bethlehem •
Beth-zechariah •
Adullam •
Nebo- •
Beth-
Elam •
zaith •
Hebron
(Kiriath-arba) •

• Masada

Apollonia •

Aphek (Pegai) •
• Ono
Lod •
(Lydda)
• Neballat
• Hadid
Modein •
(Modin)
Gath •
(Gittaim)
Gazara •
(Gezer)
Zorah •
Zanoah •
Jarmuth •
Azekah •
Harim •
Keilah •
Adoraim •

J U D A H

Beth-zur •

I D U M E A

• En-rimmon
Jekabzeel? •
Moladah •
• Jeshua?

Joppa •

LAND OF THE PHILISTINES

Ekron •
Kedron •
Jamnia •
(Jabneel)
Marisa •
Lachish •
Eglon? •
Gerar •
Ziklag? •
Beer-sheba •
Hazar-shual •
Hormah •

W

Ashdod
(Azotus)

Ashkelon •
(Ascalon)
Anthedon •
Gaza •

• Raphia

V

6

7

MAP 11

D   **E**   **F**   **G**

THRACE

Black   Sea

MACEDONIA
Pella •
• *Philippi*
• Sinope

• *Thessalonica*
Thasos • *Lysimachia*
• *Byzantium* • *Calchedon*
• *Heraclea*
PAPHLAGONIA
PONTUS

EPIRUS

THESSALY
AETOLIA
Delphi •
Ilium
(Troy)
R.
Granicus
• *Nicaea*
Dascylium
R. *Sangarius*
R. *Halys*
• *Ancyra*
• *Pteria?*

ACHAEA
Corinth •
Athens •
Thebes •
Mytilene •
Pergamum •
GALATIA

Gordium
(Gordion)
CAPPADOCIA
• *Melitene*
COMMAGENE

Olympia •
3 *Magnesia* •
IONIA
Sardis •
PHRYGIA
• *Ipsus*
• *Sparta*
Samos •
Ephesus •
Apamea
(Calaenae)
S
Tyana
Cilician
Gates
L
Carchemish

Miletus •
R. *Maeander*
Didyma •
CARIA
E
Tarsus •
• *Issus*
• *Alexandria*

Delos
Halicarnassus •
PISIDIA
Perga •
CILICIA
Soli •
Aleppo •

Rhodes •
LYCIA
PAMPHYLIA
Antioch
SYRIA
Thapsacus •

Cydonia •
Xanthus •
Phaselis •

Knossos •
Cyprus
Laodicea •
Emesa •
Palmyra •

Gortyna •
Crete
Citium
Salamis •
Marathus •
Tripolis •
Byblos •

M e d i t e r r a n e a n
Paphos •
Berytus •
Coele-
Syria
Damascus

Cyrene •
Sidon •
Tyre •
Paneas •

4 CYRENAICA
S e a
Ptolemais •
Dora •

Samaria •
Antioch (Gerasa) •

Paraetonium •
Alexandria
• *Sais*
Azotus •
Gaza •
Jerusalem •
Philadelphia •

Raphia •
Pelusium •

P T O L E M A I C
Bubastis •
Heliopolis •
Petra •
NABATAEANS

E G Y P T
Memphis •
Arsinoe •

*Oasis of
Ammon
(Siwa)*
Crocodilopolis •

A

5

Hermopolis •

**The Near East
in the
Hellenistic Period**
Ptolemaic & Seleucid Empires
Lycopolis •
R. *Nile*

EMPIRE

Ptolemais •
Nag Hammadi •
• *Thebes*

Red

0   100   200 Miles
0   100   200 Kilometres

Syene •

Sea

6

E   **F**   **G**

OUTER BORDER SHOWS

MAP 11

100 MILE SUBDIVISIONS

MAP 12

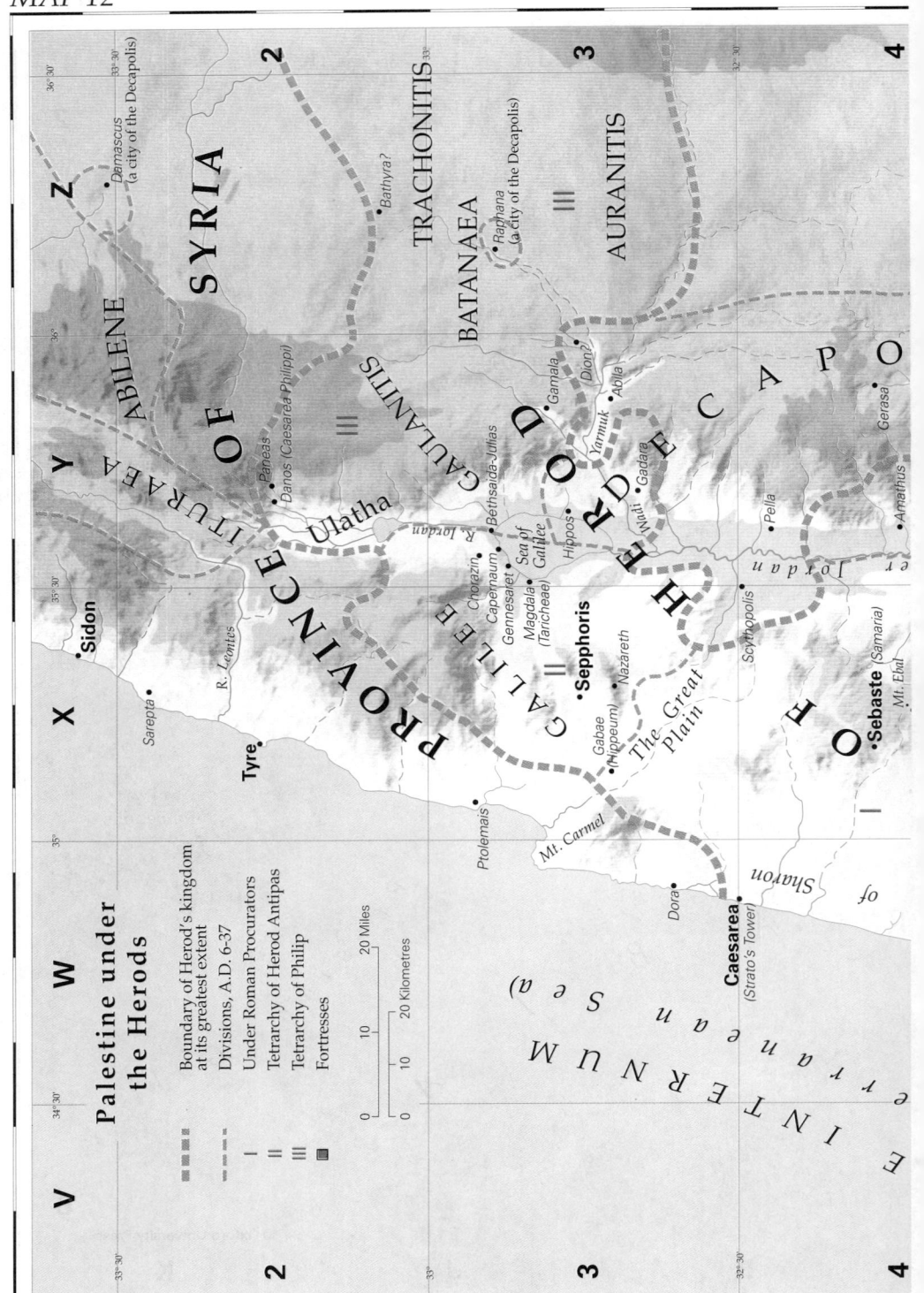

Palestine under the Herods

MAP 12

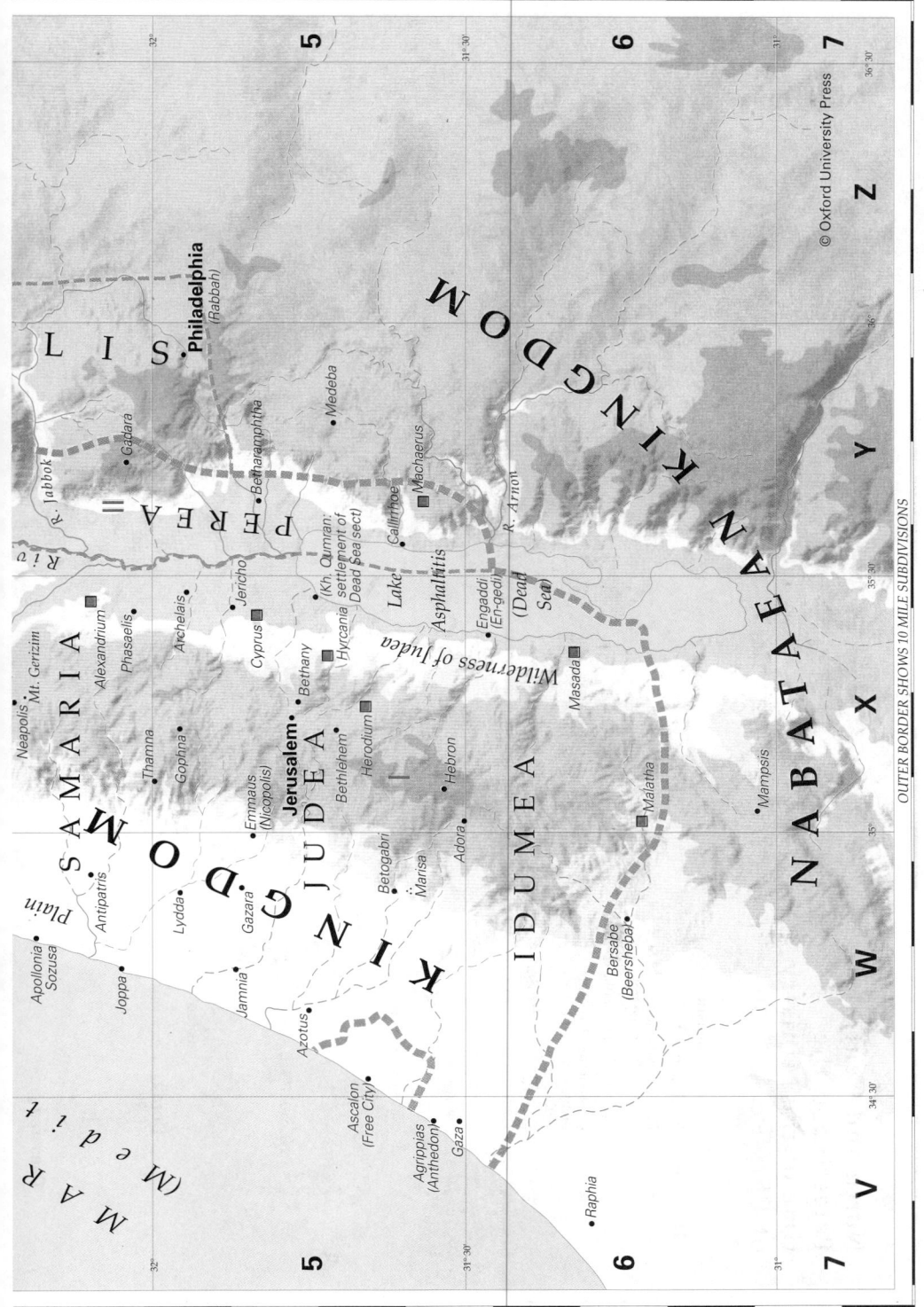

OUTER BORDER SHOWS 10 MILE SUBDIVISIONS

MAR
Medit
(Medit

Apollonia
Sozusa
Joppa

Jamnia

Azotus

Ascalon
(Free City)

Agrippias
(Anthedon)
Gaza

Raphia

Antipatris

Lydda

Gazara

Betogabri

Marisa

Adora

Bersabe
(Beersheba)

Mampsis

S A M A R I A

Neapolis
Mt. Gerizim

Alexandrium

Phasaelis

Thamna

Gophna

Emmaus
(Nicopolis)

Jerusalem

Bethlehem

Hebron

K I N G D O M

J U D E A

Herodium

Bethany

Cyprus

Hyrcania
(Kh. Qumran:
settlement of
Dead Sea sect)

Archelais

Jericho

R. Jabbok

Gadara

Betharamphtha

P E R E A

Philadelphia
(Rabbah)

L I S

Medeba

Machaerus

Callirrhoe

R. Arnon

Lake
Asphaltitis

Engaddi
(En-gedi)

(Dead
Sea)

Wilderness of Judea

Masada

Malatha

I D U M E A

N A B A T A E A N   K I N G D O M

Wilderness of Judea

R. Jo
R. Jor

MAP 13

North and Central Palestine at the time of the Ministry of Christ c.A.D. 30

JUDEA, etc.

- ───── Political boundaries
- Political units
- ◉ Places mentioned in the New Testament
- ▲ Cities of the Decapolis
- ▲ Cities of the Decapolis mentioned in the New Testament
- ▪ Fortresses

10 Miles

10 Kilometres

5

5

0

0

PROVINCE OF SYRIA

PHOENICIA

X

Tyre (33°16'N)

Ladder of Tyre

Ecdippa (Achzib)

Ptolemais

Caesarea Philippi (Paneas)

Daphne

Utatha

Lake Semechonitis (Lake Huleh)

TETRARCHY 2

Y

OF

PHILIP

GAULANITIS

SELEUCIS

Cadasa

Thella

Seleucia

Sogane

Bethsaida-Julias

R. Jordan

Gamala

Dion? 3

Abila

Capitolias

Arbela

DEC

Gadara

Wadi Yarmuk

Emmatha

Hippos (Susithab)

Gergesa?

Sea of Galilee

Capar Garaeoi

Gischala

Jamneith

Sepph

Acchabare

Chorazin

Capernaum

Ginnesar (Gennesaret)

Tiberias

Ammathus

Sennabris

Bethyerah (Philoteria)

Scythopolis

Meroth

Bersabe

Selame

Magdala (Taricheae)

Arbela

Bethmaus

Agrippina

Tetrarchy

GALILEE

G

Baca

Sogane

Cana

Rumah

Garis

Sigoph

Dabaritta (Dabira)

Itabyrium (Tabor)

V. of Jezreel

Mt.

Saab

Jotapata

Asochis

Nazareth

Japha

Exaloth

Nain

The Great Plain (Esdraelon)

Chabulon

Simonias

Sepphoris

Besara

R. Kishon

Gabae (Hippeum)

Mt. Carmel

Gabata

Sycaminum

Bucolon Polis

Dora (Dor)

Crocodilon Polis

Caesarea

3

35°

35°30'

33°

32°30'

3

MAP 13

© Oxford University Press

MAP 14

R. Po
B 45°
Pola
PANNONIA
C
Siscia
D
DACIA
E

Ravenna
Ariminum
Sirmium
Singidunum
Istros
Tomi

Ancona
Viminacium
MOESIA
Odessus

Perusia
ITALY
Salonae
ILLYRICUM
(DALMATIA)
R. Danube
Oescus
Novae
Mesembria

2
ROME
Ostia
Three Taverns
Forum of Appius
(Appii Forum)
Scodra
Sardica
Philippopolis
THRACE
Bosphorus

Antium
Tarracina
Capua
Beneventum
Canusium
Dyrrhachium
Scupi
Byzantium
Nicomedia

40°
Puteoli
Neapolis
Pompeii
Paestum
Apollonia
Egnatian Way
MACEDONIA
Beroea
Philippi
Thessalonica
Neapolis
Egnatian Way
Cyzicus
Nicaea
Prusa

Capreae
(Capri)
Tarentum
Brundisium
THESSALY
Larissa
Samothrace
Troas
(Alexandria)
Assos
Adramyttium

Sybaris
Corcyra
Nicopolis
Actium
Lesbos
Mitylene
Pergamum
ASIA
Thyatira

Panormus
Croton
Olympia
Corinth
Cenchreae
Athens
Chios
Smyrna
Sardis

SICILY
Messana
Rhegium
3
Catana
ACHAIA
Samos
Ephesus
Philadelphia
Laodicea

Syracuse
Sparta
(Lacedaemon)
Cos
Miletus
Colossae
Cnidus
LYCIA

Malta
(Melita)
35°
ROMAN EMP
Rhodes
Rhodes
Patara
Myra

Mediterranean
Paul's Journey to Rome
Phoenix
CRETE
Fair Havens
Lasea
Salmone
Cauda

15°
Lepcis Magna
4
(Mare Internum, Mare Nostrum)
Sea

Greater
Syrtis
20°
Cyrene

AFRICA
CYRENAICA
25°

LIBYA
Canopus
Alexandria
Naucratis
30°
EGYPT

Oxyrhynchus

Paul's 1st Journey

Paul's 2nd Journey

Paul's 3rd Journey

OUTER BORDER SHOWS

MAP 14

F **G** **H** **J**

S c y t h i a n s

★ Seven Churches of Asia
(Rev. 1-3)

Boundary of Roman
Empire (c.A.D. 65)

1

BOSPORAN
KINGDOM

Provincial boundaries
(c.A.D. 65)

ASIA, etc Roman Provinces

30°

45°

Chersonesus 35°

Selected Roman roads
(route between Rome
and the East)

E u x i n e   S e a

(*Pontus   Euxinus*)

40°

COLCHIS

0   100   200 Miles

0   100   200 Kilometres

2

Amastris *Sinope*

Heraclea

BITHYNIA and PONTUS

Amisus

Side *Trapezus*

Gangra *Amasea*

Ancyra *Tavium* *Comana*

Dorylaeum

Gordium

Pessinus

G A L A T I A

R. Halys

CAPPADOCIA

Lesser
Armenia

K I N G D O M

O F

A R M E N I A

Artaxata

R. Araxes

Tigranocerta

L. Van

MEDIA
ATROPATENE

L. Urmia

3

Antioch

PISIDIA

PAMPHYLIA

Iconium

Lystra

Derbe

Caesarea (Mazaca)

Archelais

Melitene

Commagene

Samosata

Zeugma

OSROENE

Edessa

Carrhae
(Haran)

Nisibis

GORDYENE

Ninus

ADIABENE

Arbela

M E D I A

Perga

Attalia

Cilicia
Trachea

Tarsus

CILICIA

Seleucia

Europus
(Carchemish)

Nicephorium

MESOPOTAMIA

R. Tigris

P A R T H I A N

I **R** **E**

CYPRUS

Salamis

Paphos

SYRIA

R. Orontes

and

Araca

Apamea

Epiphania

Emesa

35°

Tripolis

R. Euphrates

Palmyra

Dura-Europus

E M P I R E

ELAM

Berytus

Sidon

Abilene

Tyre

Damascus

Ptolemais

*Caesarea
Philippi*

Tiberias

A r a b i a n

Seleucia *Ctesiphon*

Babylon

4

Caesarea

Samaria

Joppa

Judaea

Jerusalem

Gaza

Nabataean Kingdom

D e s e r t

Sais

Pelusium

Heliopolis

Babylon
Memphis

R. Nile

Petra

Dumah

**The Background
of the
New Testament**

Rome and the East
(including St. Pauls's Journeys)

5

Aila (Aelana)

Mt.
Sinai

Red Sea

35°

Tema

© Oxford University Press

F **G** **H** **J**

INDEX TO MAPS